German–English

This headword belongs to the wordlist of *Zertifikat Deutsch*.

Indication of irregular verb forms in the 3rd person singular (present, preterite, perfect)

The intransitive senses take the auxiliary *sein*.

In the transitive form the verb may take either *haben* or *sein* as its auxiliary, depending on the sense.

② **lau·fen** ['laofn] <läuft, lief, ist/hat gelaufen>
[intr v] +*sein* **1.** run ◇ *Ich bin gelaufen, so schnell ich konnte.* ♦ *Die Tränen liefen ihm übers Gesicht.* ♦ *Sie ließ Wasser in den Eimer laufen.* ♦ *Die Straßenbahn läuft auf Schienen.* ♦ *Mein Vertrag läuft noch bis Januar.* ♦ *Bei Kälte läuft mir die Nase.* gegen etw./in etw. [acc] laufen run into sth **2.** walk ◇ *Ich laufe jeden Tag zur Arbeit.* ♦ *Kann der Kleine schon laufen?* **3.** work ◇ *Läuft dein Computer wieder?* **4.** *(television, in the cinema, on TV)* be on ◇ *Der Fernseher läuft den ganzen Tag.* ♦ *Der Film läuft im zweiten Programm.* **5.** go ◇ *Die Gespräche liefen gut.* ♦ *Das Auto läuft auf meinen Namen.* Die Geschäfte laufen schleppend. Business is sluggish. In meiner Ehe läuft gar nichts mehr. Nothing is going right in my marriage any more. **6.** be on-going ◇ *Gegen ihn läuft ein Verfahren wegen Steuerbetrugs.* Meine Bewerbung läuft noch. My application is still under consideration. **7.** sell ◇ *Die Zeitschrift läuft schlecht.* [tr v] +*haben/sein* **1.** +*haben/in South G, Austr, Swiss often* +*sein* run ◇ *Er hat noch nie einen Marathon gelaufen.* einen Rekord laufen run a record time **2.** +*sein* Rollschuh laufen roller-skate Schlittschuh laufen ice-skate Ski laufen ski [ref v] +*haben* **1.** sich warm laufen warm up sich müde laufen tire yourself out through walking sich wund laufen get sore feet through walking **2.** In den Schuhen läuft es sich bequem. The shoes are comfortable to walk in. Wenn es nicht so heiß ist, läuft es sich besser. It's easier to run when it's not so hot. **3.** sich [dat] Blasen laufen get blisters from walking sich [dat] die Füße wund laufen get sore feet through walking sich [dat] Löcher in die Schuhsohlen laufen wear holes in your shoes through walking
◉ **das ist gelaufen** *(fam)* it is too late now **wie läuft's** *(fam)* how is it going

Phonetic transcription for every German headword

This verb can be used with *haben* or *sein*.

Numerous examples to show the German usage

In the reflexive form the auxiliary is always *haben*.

Hueber
WÖRTERBUCH

Deutsch als Fremdsprache

Learner's Dictionary
German–English · English–German
Deutsch–Englisch · Englisch–Deutsch

Max Hueber Verlag, Ismaning

3. 2. 1. | Die letzten Ziffern
2010 09 08 07 06 | bezeichnen Zahl und Jahr des Druckes.
Alle Drucke dieser Auflage können, da unverändert,
nebeneinander benutzt werden.
1. Auflage
© 2006 Max Hueber Verlag, 85737 Ismaning, Deutschland
Redaktionelle Leitung: Dr. Juliane Forßmann
Umschlaggestaltung: Parzhuber & Partner, München
Layout: Holger Latzel, München
Sprachdatenverarbeitung: Andreas Lang, conTEXT AG, Zürich
Satz: Memminger Mediencentrum Druckerei und Verlags-AG, Memmingen
Druck und Bindung: Druckerei C. H. Beck, Nördlingen
Printed in Germany
ISBN 10: 3–19–001736–0
ISBN 13: 978–3–19–001736–2

Contents

Editorial Team

Managing Editor
Dr Juliane Forßmann

Senior Editors
Susanne Billes, Dr Catherine Minter, Veronika Schnorr, Eva Maria Vennebusch

Editors
Miriam Altmann, Monika Böhme-Garnweidner, Gudrun van den Boom,
Katrin Dorhmi, Dr Susanne Dyka, Stephen Hackett, Dr Michael Hönig, Olaf Knechten,
Alexandra Messer, Angelika Pfaller, Toby Skingsley, Beatrice Tauber-Graham

Phonetician
Dr Annaliese Benkwitz

Proofreaders
Hermann Josef Barth, Rolf Brüseke, Marion Kerner,
Maria Koettgen, Jutta Orth-Chambah, Dr Dörte Weers

Linguistic Data Processing
Andreas Lang, conTEXT AG, Zurich

Data base administrators and programmers:
Hendrik Schaal, Armin Schmidt

Consultants:
Werner Bönzli, Professor Ursula Hirschfeld, Dr Nora Tahy

Other contributors:
Maike Freudenberg, Isabel Krämer-Kienle, Thomas Stark,
Andreas Tomaszewski, Helga and Gerald Williams

ACKNOWLEDGEMENTS:
We would like to acknowledge the assistance of Macmillan Publishers Limited
who have kindly given permission to use the Macmillan English Dictionary,
© Bloomsbury Publishing Plc, 2002, as a reference source for inclusion of
idioms and, in some cases, additonal senses of main headwords.

Foreword

The primary aim of the specialist team for German Language Teaching at the Max Hueber Verlag in publishing this new dictionary is to help you to learn the German language successfully.

This completely new dictionary has been developed especially for learners of German and is the result of many years of experience in teaching *DaF* (German as a Foreign Language) in combination with the collective expertise of a team of specialized lexicographers.

Our innovative concept combines features of traditional monolingual dictionaries (German example sentences, synonyms and antonyms etc.) with pragmatic bilingual support: English translations of German headwords and vice versa. As a matter of principle, the dictionary provides only minimal information on the student's own language but a maximum on all German content.

Thus you will find valuable information not only on the German headwords in the German–English section of the dictionary, but also on the most important points relevant to the German translations of English headwords in the English–German section. This system removes the need to look up information in various different places.

Should you be unsuccessful in finding any particular German headword, try looking up its different elements separately. If, for example, you cannot find *Einkommenssteuer* (= income tax), you can look up *Einkommen* (= income) and *Steuer* (=tax) and work out the meaning of the compound accordingly. Try, too, to use your knowledge of your own language to guess the meaning of German words by association. There are more similarities than you may imagine.

The numerous German example sentences all stem from modern, current usage and have been, where necessary, slightly modified by our *DaF* experts to suit learners' needs. In the case of adjectives, for example, each entry contains, where relevant, examples of both predicative and attributive use *(Der Rock ist rot./der rote Rock)*. Job titles are listed both with the use of the article and without, and both male and female variants are included. *(Die Bäckerin holt das Brot aus dem Ofen./Er wurde Bäcker wie sein Vater)*.

These and many other advantages are yours to discover. In the introduction you will find detailed information on the content and composition of the dictionary. In the extensive middle section we have provided grammar tables and practice material to help you get used to working with the dictionary. These exercises can be downloaded from our website
`http://www.hueber.de/woerterbuch/`
and photocopied.

The whole team wishes you every success with our new German dictionary. We are sure you will find it not only a great help in your studies but also a pleasure to use.

Dr Juliane Forßmann
Managing Editor
Munich, February 2006

Using the dictionary

Spelling

The dictionary observes the rules laid down by the new German spelling reform throughout.

In the case of American headwords, a cross-reference is given to the British English variant. The British English entries include the American variants where relevant.

Entries – a brief overview

As a rule, an **entry** consists of the following:
- the headword,
- its phonetic transcription,
- the part of speech,
- its translation.

If necessary, **further information** may also be included, e.g.:
- constructions (typical speech patterns),
- details of valency with verbs,
- details of usage (e.g. style and register, regional variation or subject area),
- example sentences,
- synonyms and antonyms,
- idiomatic phrases,
- cross references,
- information boxes with notes on grammar and cultural background.

Example sentences demonstrate the typical usage of a word. Either complete sentences or parts of sentences are used. Established idioms (in most cases indicating the figurative use of the headword) are printed in bold type and placed together at the end of the entry after the symbol ⊙.

Headwords

Important vocabulary items required for the **Zertifikat Deutsch** (a recognized German language certificate) are marked with the symbol ⑦.

Syllabification is marked by dots (e.g. *Fri·sur*). In the case of separable verbs, a vertical line marks the division between prefix and verb (e.g. *an|pas·sen*).

NOUNS

All **nouns** include the following:
- the definite article,
- the genitive form,
- the plural (or alternatively, should the noun be uncountable or used only in the singular or plural, an appropriate note). Genitive und plural are placed in pointed brackets, regular forms indicating only the endings to be added to the headword.

If necessary, the following information is also included:
- the feminine form, indicated in the English–German section by the symbol ♀,
- additional notes should, for example, a noun only be used with the definite article (e.g. *die Schweiz*), or without the article, etc.

In the case of German nouns that are declined like adjectives, the headword is given the ending *-e* as it would appear in the nominative case after the definite article (e.g. *der/die Deutsche*). The definite article *der/die* indicates that the spelling of the masculine and feminine variants is identical.

ADJECTIVES AND ADVERBS

Adjectives and adverbs share the same entry when their meaning is identical. In the English–German section, adjective and adverb are dealt with separately whenever other entries come between them in the alphabetical order.

Adjectives entries indicate the following:
- whether an adjective has an invariable form (e.g. *lila*),
- whether an adjective is used only or predominantly either attributively or predicatively (e.g. *only* or *mostly before ns; not before ns* or *mostly after ns*),
- the comparative and superlative forms of irregular adjectives or those taking an *Umlaut*,
- whether comparative and superlative forms are in common use.

Adverb entries indicate:

- the comparative and superlative forms of irregular adverbs or those taking an *Umlaut,*
- whether comparative and superlative forms are in common use.

VERBS
The entries for **verbs** include:

- in the case of German headwords, whether a German verb is transitive (tr v), intransitive (intr v), reflexive (ref v), impersonal (imp v), modal (modal v) or an auxiliary verb (aux),
- the present, imperfect and perfect tense forms of irregular verbs and verbs whose past participle is not formed with *ge-* and, in the German–English section, for all separable verbs,
- which auxiliary verb is necessary.

DETERMINERS
Determiners are words that come directly before a noun and behave just like an article (e.g. *dieser* in *dieser Junge*). Here the following information is given:

- in the German–English section a table showing how the German word is declined,
- in the English–German section the German translation in the nominative.

PRONOUNS
Pronouns are usually defined in more detail: demonstrative pronouns, indefinite pronouns, interrogative pronouns, personal pronouns, possessive pronouns, reflexive pronouns, relative pronouns. In the middle section of the dictionary (page 554) under the heading *Grammatical Terminology* you will find a list of these for reference. Here, too, further useful information may be included

- a table with the declination of the German word. The nominative form of the personal pronouns is, as a rule, accompanied by a declination table.

PREPOSITIONS
Preposition entries include:

- what case a preposition takes.

PREFIXES
Prefixes are treated as separate entries and are followed by three dots: *he·raus/...*

How a word is used
Information on how a word is used is given either for a whole entry (i.e. for all meanings) or for one particular meaning of the headword or phrase. This is clearly indicated in each instance.

REGIONAL VARIANTS
In the German-English section information is given as to whether a word is used predominantly in Southern Germany *(SouthG)*, Northern Germany *(NorthG)*, Austria *(Austr)*, Switzerland *(Swiss)*, or only in specific regions *(reg)*.

STYLE AND REGISTER
Any German headwords or German translations that differ from normal, everyday use are indicated by the following : *fam, form, kidsp, lit, lofty, rude, slang, taboo* and *tech.* (See also *Symbols, Abbreviations and Short forms* on page 14)

ATTITUDE AND INTENTION
Depending on the position or attitude of the speaker a word or phrase may have a derogatory, ironic or figurative meaning. Such entries are indicated by the following: *emph, euph, fig, hum, iron* and *pej.* (See also *Symbols, Abbreviations and Short forms* on page 14)

SUBJECT AREA
A field of knowledge or subject area defines the place or circumstances in which the word is normally used. This does not necessarily mean that the word is an exclusively specialized term. Such subject or field labels are: ARCH, FIN, IT or PHILOS. (See also *Symbols, Abbreviations and Short forms* on page 14)

CONSTRUCTIONS
The headwords are accompanied by important speech patterns. For example: headword *stolz* (proud) followed by the construction *auf jdn/etw. stolz sein* (be proud of sb).

CASE

Information on case is given explicitly only where it cannot be inferred from the accompanying substitute for the subject or object (*jd* = nominative, *jdn* = accusative, *jdm* = dative, *jds* = genitive).

Prepositions that can be followed either by the accusative or by the dative object are always followed by a clear indication of the case required in the relevant context:

etw. mündet in etw. [acc].

If a noun needs to be followed by a genitive, it is indicated as follows:

die Fortsetzung ... [gen] = the continuation of sth.

The substitute *einer Sache* could stand for a dative or a genitive object; thus the required case is always clearly indicated: *einer Sache* [dat] *nachgehen* = follow sth up.

If the reflexive pronoun *sich* is in the dative, this is indicated accordingly. If no further information is given, it is in the accusative:

sich [dat] *die Haare kämmen*
sich anziehen.

Finding your way: Arrangement of headwords

Alphabetical Order

All headwords in the dictionary are arranged in alphabetical order. Hyphens are ignored. **Example:** *EC-Karte* appears between *echt* and *Ecke*.

In principle all vowels with an *Umlaut* are treated like vowels without. Headwords without Umlaute, however, appear before those with Umlaute: *sagen* before *sägen*.

ß is treated like *ss*. If both appear together, *ß* is treated first and then *ss:*

aß before *Ass*.

Numbers and numerals appear in the order they would have if they were written out in full: *Tempo-30-Zone* as *Tempo-Dreißig-Zone*.

Headwords beginning with small letters (lower case) appear before words beginning with capitals (upper case): *leben* before *Leben*

Homographs

Homographs are distinguished by superscription. They are words that have the same spelling but (for the purpose of this dictionary) differ in important grammatical points, such as part of speech

laugh as a noun = laugh[1],

laugh as a verb = laugh[2],

or a different article

der Kiefer (jaw) = Kiefer[1],

die Kiefer (pine tree) = Kiefer[2].

Idiomatic expressions and phrases

Phrases made up of several elements are listed in accordance with the first noun in the phrase, e.g. *ein Bad in der Menge nehmen* is listed under the headword *Bad*. If the phrase does not have a noun in it, the first adjective is taken, e.g. *sich grün und blau ärgern* is listed under *grün*. If the phrase just has a verb in it, it is listed under the verb (*wer zuletzt lacht, lacht am besten* is listed under *lachen*).

If an entry contains several expressions and phrases, they are listed alphabetically in order of the "most important" words, disregarding the headword. The priority is as follows: noun ▸ adjective ▸ adverb ▸ verb ▸ others.

Abbreviations

Abbreviations are shortened forms of words or groups of words. The phonetic transcription clarifies whether they are
- pronounced either in full
  usw. for **u**nd **s**o **w**eiter [ʊnt zoː'væte],
- or spelled out
  LKW for **L**ast**k**raft**w**agen ['ɛlkaːveː],
- or pronounced they way they are written
  TÜV for **T**echnischer **Ü**berwachungs**v**erein [tʏf].

Abbreviations form headwords in their own right. Each German abbreviation is followed by the expression in full. Headwords that may be abbreviated (e.g. chemical elements, weights and measures, etc.), also have the short form added.

Cross references

Cross references draw attention to other entries, e.g. to the form of the word, the infinitive or to a new or more usual form of spelling.

In many cases the reference is supplemented by a text explaining the relationship between the two (e.g. *fem of, pret of, pl of* etc.; See also *Symbols, Abbreviations and Short forms* on page 14).

Cross references may also refer to an information box or to examples contained within another entry.

Information boxes

Information boxes provide additional information on topics of grammar or explain the context and cultural background.

Symbols, Abbreviations and Short forms

@	go to
⊜	antonym
♀	feminine form of nouns
◊, ♦	example sentence
⊜	synonym
Ⓩ	signals that a headword is part of the vocabulary list of *Zertifikat Deutsch*
→	cross reference
abbr	abbreviation
acc	accusative
adj	adjective
adv	adverb
AGR	agriculture
ANAT	anatomy
ARCH	architecture
art	article
ARTS	drawing, painting, sculpture etc.
ASTROL	astrology
ASTRON	astronomy
Austr	Austrian
aux	auxiliary verb
AVIAT	aviation
BIO	biology
BOT	botany
CARDS	card game
CHEM	chemistry
CHESS	chess
comp	comparative
conjunc	conjunction
contract	contraction
dat	dative
demonstr pron	demonstrative pronoun
det	determiner
+direction	after verbs: an indication of direction (e.g. *irgendwohin tanzen*)
ECON	economics
emph	emphatically
esp	especially
etc.	etcetera
etw.	etwas
euph	euphemistic
f	feminine
fam	familiar
fem	feminine form
fig	figurative
FILM	film
FIN	finance
form	formal
FOTO	photography
GAME	game (for children or social)
gen	genitive
GEOG	geography
GEOL	geology
GOLF	golf
GRAM	grammar
+haben	takes auxiliary verb *haben*
+haben/sein	takes auxiliary verb *haben* or *sein*
HIST	history
indefinite	indefinite (e.g. in reference to words expressing quantities such as *viel* or *little*)
hum	humorous
indef pron	indefinite pronoun
+inf with 'zu'	this takes an infinitive construction with 'zu'
imp v	impersonal verb
interj	interjection
interrog pron	interrogative pronoun
intr v	intransitive verb
iron	ironic(al)
IT	information technology
jd	jemand (nominative)
jdm	jemandem (dative)
jdn	jemanden (accusative)
jds	jemandes (genitive)
kidsp	language of children (also used by parents when talking to children)
LAW	law, legal
LING	linguistic
lit	literary, poetic language
LIT	literature
lofty	elevated style or register
m	masculine
MATH	mathematics
MED	medicine
MEDIA	media; press
METEO	meteorology, weather
MIL	military
modal v	modal verb
most pl	mostly in the plural

most sing	mostly in the singular	*prov*	proverb
MUS	music	RADIO	radio
MYTH	mythology	*ref*	reflexive
nmrl	numeral	*ref v*	reflexive verb
no comp/superl	no comparative or superlative	*ref pron*	reflexive pronoun
		regional	regional
nom	nominative	REL	religion
no passive	no passive	*rel pron*	relative pronoun
no pl	no plural	*rude*	rude or vulgar language
NorthG	Northern German	sb	somebody
noun	noun	SCHOOL	school
ns	nouns	SHIP	shipping; nautical
nt	neuter	*+sein*	takes auxiliary verb *sein*
oldf	old-fashioned	*sing*	singular
only pl	only in the plural	*slang*	slang, jargon
outd	outdated	*SouthG*	Southern German
p	participle	SPORT	sport
part	particle	*sth*	something
past p	past participle	*subjunctive*	subjunctive
pej	pejorative	*suffix*	suffix
pers pron	personal pronoun	*superl*	superlative
PHILOS	philosophy	*Swiss*	Swiss
phras v	phrasal verb	*taboo*	taboo
PHYSICS	physics	*tech*	technical
pl	plural	TECHN	technology
+place	after verbs or pronouns: indication of place	THEAT	theater
		tr v	transitive verb
POL	politics	TRADE	trade
poss pron	possessive pronoun	TV	television
post positive	post positive (placed after)	UNI	university
prefix	prefix	*verb*	verb
prep	preposition	ZOO	zoology
pres	present		
pres perf	present perfect		
pret	imperfect		
pron	pronoun		

Phonetics: a short introduction

The characters used in phonetic transcription

VOWELS AND CONSONANTS

The following list can be found on the internet under:

http://www.hueber.de/woerterbuch/phonetik/

By clicking on to the appropriate symbol, you can listen to each sound (except for those marked with an *) and/or each example word.

Symbol	Example(s)
[a]	alle ['alə]
[aː]	haben ['haːbm̩], Zahl ['tsaːl], Staat [ʃtaːt], Etat [e'taː]
[ã]	Engagement [ãgaʒə'mãː]
[ãː]	Chance ['ʃãːs(ə)], Restaurant [rɛsto'rãː], Engagement [ãgaʒə'mãː]
[e]*	Verkäufer [fe'kɔøfe]
[g̊]*	Chor [koːg̊]
[ae]	drei [drae̯], Mai [mae̯], Bayern ['bae̯en]
[ao]	aus [ao̯s]
[b]	Bayern ['bae̯en], Hobby ['hɔbiː]
[ç]	richtig ['rɪçtɪç]
[d]	Dirndl ['dɪrˀndl̩], addieren [a'diːrən]
[dʒ]	Jeans [dʒiːns], Dschungel ['dʒʊŋl̩], Budget [by'dʒeː]
[e]	Etage [e'taːʒə]
[eː]	gegen ['geːgn̩], zehn [tseːn], Tee [teː], Budget [by'dʒeː]
[ɛ]	essen ['ɛsn̩], Männer ['mɛnɐ], Saison [zɛ'zõː]
[ɛː]	Qualität [kvali'tɛːt], zählen ['tsɛːlən]
[ɛ̃ː]	Timbre ['tɛ̃ːbrə], Satin [za'tɛ̃ː], Teint [tɛ̃ː]
[ə]*	bedanken [bə'daŋkn̩], Familie [fa'miːli̯ə], verwöhnen [fe'vøːnən]
[f]	fünf [fynf], Schiff [ʃɪf], Verkäufer [fe'kɔøfe], Motiv [mo'tiːf], Physik [fy'ziːk]
[g]	gegen ['geːgn̩], Flagge ['flagə]
[h]	haben ['haːbm̩]
[i]	Motivation [motiva'tsi̯oːn]
[iː]	Visum ['viːzʊm], addieren [a'diːrən], ihre ['iːrə], sieh [ziː], Jeans [dʒiːns]
[i̯]*	Familie [fa'miːli̯ə]
[ɪ]	richtig ['rɪçtɪç]
[j]	Jahr [jaːʳ]
[k]	kommen ['kɔmən], Akkusativ ['akuzatiːf], Zucker ['tsʊke], Chor [koːg̊], Computer [kɔm'pjuːte], Qualität [kvali'tɛːt], Tag [taːk]
[ks]	links [lɪŋks], sonntags ['zɔntaːks], sechs [zɛks], Knacks [knaks], Präfix ['prɛːfɪks]
[l]	links [lɪŋks], alle ['alə]
[l̩]*	Dschungel ['dʒʊŋl̩], Dirndl ['dɪrˀndl̩]
[m]	Mai [mae̯], kommen ['kɔmən]
[m̩]*	haben ['haːbm̩]
[n]	Nacht [naxt], können ['kœnən]
[n̩]*	essen ['ɛsn̩]
[ŋ]	bedanken [bə'daŋkn̩], Dschungel ['dʒʊŋl̩]
[n̩]*	bedanken [bə'daŋkn̩]
[o]	ökonomisch [øko'noːmɪʃ]
[oː]	ökonomisch [øko'noːmɪʃ], wohnen ['voːnən], Zoo [tsoː]
[o̯]*	Toilette [to̯a'lɛtə]
[õ]	Fondue [fõ'dyː]
[õː]	Saison [zɛ'zõː], Fond(s) [fõː]
[ɔ]	kommen ['kɔmən]
[ø]	ökonomisch [øko'noːmɪʃ]
[øː]	schön [ʃøːn], verwöhnen [fe'vøːnən]
[œ]	können ['kœnən]
[œ̃ː]	Parfum [paʳ'fœ̃ː]
[ɔø]	deutsch [dɔøtʃ], Verkäufer [fe'kɔøfe]
[p]	Papa ['papa(ː)], doppelt ['dɔpl̩t], ab [ap]
[pf]	pfui [pfʊi̯]
[r]	rechts [rɛçts], ihre ['iːrə], drei [drae̯], Rhythmus ['rʏtmʊs]
[ʳ]*	Dirndl ['dɪrˀndl̩], Herr [hɛrˀ], Jahr [jaːʳ]
[s]	aus [ao̯s], essen ['ɛsn̩], Straße ['ʃtraːsə]
[ʃ]	Schule ['ʃuːlə], sprühen ['ʃpryːən], Straße ['ʃtraːsə], Chance ['ʃãːs(ə)]

[t]	Toilette [to̯a'lɛtə], Theater [tel'a:tɐ], Rhythmus ['rʏtmʊs], Stadt [ʃtat], Geld [gɛlt]
[ts]	rechts [rɛçts], Satz [zats], zehn [tse:n], Pizza ['pɪtsa:], Motivation [motiva'tsi̯o:n]
[tʃ]	deutsch [dɔøtʃ], Cha-Cha-Cha [ˌtʃa,tʃa'tʃa]
[θ]	Thriller ['θrɪlɐ]
[u]	Akkusativ ['akuzati:f]
[u:]	Schule ['ʃu:lə], Stuhl [ʃtu:l]
[ʊ]	Zucker ['tsʊkɐ]
[ʊ̯i]	pfui [pfʊ̯i]
[v]	Visum ['vi:zʊm], wohnen ['vo:nən]
[x]	Nacht [naxt]
[y]	amüsieren [amy'zi:rən], Physik [fy'zi:k]
[y:]	über ['y:bɐ], sprühen ['ʃpry:ən], Typ [ty:p], Fondue [fõ'dy:]
[ỹ]*	Etui [e'tỹi:]
[ʏ]	fünf [fʏnf], Ypsilon ['ʏpsilɔn], Budget [bʏ'dʒe:]
[z]	Saison [zɛ'zõ:]
[ʒ]	Etage [e'ta:ʒə], Journal [ʒʊrˈna:l]

OTHER SYMBOLS AND SIGNS

|	marks syllable separation before a vowel within a word, e.g. Theater [tel'a:tɐ].
[:]	indicates a long vowel, follows immediately after it, e.g. Typ [ty:p].
[˜]	indicates a nasal vowel, placed immediately above it, e.g. engagieren [ãga'ʒi:rən].
[']	marks primary stress, placed immediately before the syllable, e.g. Programm [pro'gram].
[ˌ]	marks secondary stress, placed immediately before the syllable, e.g. TV–Programm [te:'faopro,gram].
[']/[ˌ]	indicates a syllabic consonant (consonant counted as a whole syllable), placed immediately under or above the consonant in question, e.g. essen ['ɛsn̩], danken ['daŋkn̩], Apfel ['apfl̩]. The endings -en, -em and -el can in cases like this be pronounced [ə] + [n], [m] or [l], e.g. ['ɛsən], ['daŋkən], ['apfəl].
[˘]/[_]	indicates a non-syllabic vowel (a vowel that is so short that it

cannot be counted as a syllable), placed immediately under or above the vowel, e.g. Familie [fa'mi:li̯ə], Etui [e'tỹi:].

[‿]	marks a diphthong (a sound made up from two vowels with the first vowel melting into the second to form one sound), placed immediately under both vowel symbols, e.g. Auto ['a‿oto:].

Transcription

The phonetic transcription is based on the pronunciation of the headwords as isolated and therefore stressed lexical items.

The transcription of constructions consisting of more than one word is based on the pronunciation of the words as a group taking stress into account. The stress patterns chosen for the dictionary are only one of many possibilities, since pronunciation can vary depending on the situation, context and intention of the speaker with words having secondary stress taking on the primary stress and vice versa – or losing their stress completely.

Substitutes like *jd, etw., einer Sache, sich* etc. occurring at the beginning or the end of constructions are not transcribed phonetically. Should they occur in the middle of a construction they are represented by "...".

Words in brackets are generally not transcribed phonetically.

If a vowel may be spoken long or short without loss of quality in either case, [:] is placed in round brackets, e.g. aha [a'ha(:)], Städte ['ʃtɛ(:)tə]. Should there be any change in vowel quality, two separate variants are given, e.g. Biskuit [bɪs'kvi:t] or [bɪs'kvɪt].

When it is possible to stress a word in various ways, these variants are given with a dash placed for each syllable, e.g. Analphabet ['anlalfabe:t], also [– – – '–].

In compounds, the second constituent or determining noun only bears a stress mark if it is of foreign origin or has four or more syllables, e.g. Agrarindustrie [a'gra:ˈrlɪndʊsˌtri:], Unfallversicherung ['ʊnfalfɛˌzɪçərʊŋ].

The following phenomena occurring regularly in German have for the purposes of this dictionary been ignored:

▸ the glottal stop [ʔ] for vowels at the beginning of words or syllables, e.g. eins [aɛns] (strictly [ʔaɛns]);

▸ aspiration of plosives at the beginning or at the end of a word or syllable, e.g. Papa ['papa] and Staat ['ʃtaːt] (strictly ['pʰapʰa], ['ʃtaːtʰ];

▸ [b, d, g, v, z, r] becoming unvoiced when following upon previous voiceless consonants, e.g. Abgabe ['apgaːbə] and Qualität [kvaliˈtɛːt] (strictly ['apɡaːbə], [kʋaliˈtɛːt]).

The syllable separation used in speech is not marked since it is often identical to that given orthographically, e.g. ei-ne ['aɛnə] (strictly ['aɛ.nə]).

The vowel sound [ɛː] is represented in some regions of Germany by [eː], e.g. Käse ['keːzə]. In the word list only the standard pronunciation is given ['kɛːzə].

Whenever two plosives occur in a word immediately following one another and the second forms the beginning of a new morpheme, they are spoken as one single unvoiced plosive. The phonetic transcription, however, follows phonological criteria so that both plosives are given one after the other, e.g. Abbau ['apbao] and mitteilen ['mɪtaɛlən] (strictly ['apb̯ao], ['mɪtaɛlən].

Words of foreign origin containing a nasal vowel are first given a German equivalent pronunciation without the nasal vowel, e.g. Restaurant [rɛstoˈraŋ], also [rɛstoˈrãː].

Words of foreign origin that end with a full vowel (i.e. not reduced), the final vowel is transcribed as being long even if it is not stressed, e.g. Baby ['beːbiː], Kino ['kiːnoː].

A few rules on German pronunciation

SOUNDS AND LETTERS

A vowel is pronounced long

▸ when written double, e.g. Staat, Tee, Zoo;

▸ when i is followed by e, e.g. sieben.

▸ when followed by an h, e.g. Zahl, zehn, zählen, ihr, sieh, wohnen;

A vowel is pronounced short

▸ when followed by a double consonant within the same morpheme, e.g. alle, essen, bitte, kommen;

▸ when followed by three or more consonants, e.g. sechs, Wurst. The vowel becomes long, however, if it can be made part of a separate syllable, e.g. (du) lebst – (ich) le-be.

The letters b, d, g, s, v are pronounced

▸ [b, d, g, z, v] at the beginning of words and syllables, e.g. bitte, danke, ge-ben, sein, Vi-sum;

▸ [p, t, k, s, f] at the end of words and syllables (final devoicing), e.g. abgeben, Geld, Tag, aus, Motiv.

The letter g in –ig is pronounced [ç] in standard German, but [g] in -ige, e.g. richtig, but richtige. In Southern German -ig at the end of a word is pronounced [ɪk]. (This variant is, however, not given.)

The letters ng are pronounced [ŋ], which means the g is not articulated whenever ng occurs at the end of a word or is followed by the endings -e, -el, -en, -em, -er or -(s)t, e.g. lang, (ich) singe, singen, Sänger, (du) singst, (er) singt.

The letters ch are pronounced

▸ [x] after a, o, u and au, e.g. machen, kochen, Buch, auch;

▸ [ç] after all other vowels, after l, n, r and in -chen, e.g. ich, sprechen, euch, Bücher, Milch, München, durch, Brötchen;

▸ [k] at the beginning of several foreign words, e.g. Chaos, Charakter, Chor, Christ and in the letter combination -chs, e.g. sechs.

The letters sp and st are pronounced [ʃp] and [ʃt] at the beginning of syllables in German words, e.g. spielen, gespielt, Straße.

The letter r is pronounced

▸ as a consonant [r, ʳ] at the beginning of words and syllables, after consonants, after short vowels and after a long a, e.g. Reise, ih–re, drei, Wurst, Herr, Jahr;

▸ as a vowel [ɐ, ɐ̯] in er-, ver-, zer- and -er and after long vowels (except after a long a), e.g. erfahren, einer, mehr, wir.

WORD STRESS

The root syllable is stressed
‣ in simple words and their derivatives with endings or suffixes, e.g. **Freund, Freund**e, **freund**lich, **Freund**lichkeit, **Ar**beit, **ar**beiten;
‣ in words with the prefix be-, ge-, er-, ver-, zer- and ent-, e.g. be**fah**ren, ge**fah**ren, er**fah**ren, ver**fah**ren, zer**geh**en, ent**geh**en;
‣ in inseparable verbs and their derivatives, e.g. über**setz**en (ich über**setz**e), Über**setz**ung, wieder**hol**en (ich wieder**hol**e), Wieder**hol**ung.

The prefix is stressed
‣ in separable verbs and their derivatives, e.g. **über**setzen (ich setze **über**), **wie**derholen (ich hole **wie**der), **ab**fahren (ich fahre **ab**), **Ab**fahrt;
‣ in words having the prefix un- and ur-, e.g. **un**wichtig, **un**modern, **un**bekannt, **Ur**laub, **Ur**großmutter.

The penultimate syllable is stressed
‣ in words of foreign origin ending with -e, -el, -ieren, -asmus/-ismus, -or, –oren, -orin and -um, e.g. Schoko**la**de, akzep**ta**bel, infor**mie**ren, Enthusi**as**mus, Journa**lis**mus, Di**rek**tor, Direk**to**ren, Direk**to**rin, **Vi**sum.

The last syllable is stressed
‣ in words with the suffix -ei, e.g. Bäcke**rei**, Par**tei**, Poli**zei**;
‣ in words of foreign origin ending with one or more consonants, e.g. internatio**nal**, hu**man**, popu**lär**, sepa**rat**, Pro**blem**, Inge**nieur**, Dia**log**, Reak**tion**, Speziali**tät**, Insti**tut**, Kon**takt**, Me**tall**, Pro**gramm**, Kon**trast**, Ten**denz**, infor**miert**, Pro**dukt**.

In compounds made up of a determinant word and a root word the former is stressed, e.g. **Fremd**sprache, **Sprach**unterricht.

A

a, A [aː] das <–(s), –(s)> **1.** a, A ◊ *Dieses Wort wird mit einem kleinen a/großen A geschrieben.* ♦ *A wie Anton* **2.** MUS A ◊ *Sie spielte ein A.* ⊙ wer A sagt, muss auch B sagen in for a penny, in for a pound das A und O ... [gen] the essential part of sth, the nuts and bolts of sth ◊ *Das Würzen ist das A und O des Kochens.* von A bis Z from A to Z, from start to finish, complete(ly), entire(ly)

ä, Ä [ɛː] das <–(s), –(s)> a umlaut, A umlaut ◊ *Dieses Wort wird mit einem kleinen ä/großen Ä geschrieben.* ♦ *Ä wie Ärger*

A [aː] die *(abbr of* Autobahn*) (on signs, street maps)* ⊜M ◊ *die A8 nach München* → Autobahn

Aa [aˈʔaː] das <–> *no pl (kidsp)* **1.** poo **2.** Aa machen (do a) poo

AA¹ [aˈʔaː] die *(abbr of* Anonyme Alkoholiker*)* AA box@ Anonyme Alkoholiker

AA² [aˈʔaː] das *(abbr of* Auswärtiges Amt*)* Foreign Office, State Department, Department/Ministry of Foreign Affairs

Aa·chen [ˈaːxn̩] das <–s> *article only in combination with attribute, no pl* Aachen der Frieden von Aachen the Treaty of Aix-la-Chapelle box@ Stadt

⑦ **ab¹** [ap] [adv] **1.** von ... ab from ..., from ..., onwards, from ... on ◊ *Von Oktober ab habe ich mehr Zeit.* ♦ *Von hier ab fahren Sie immer Richtung Bonn.* ⊜von ... an ⊜bis **2.** *(fam)* ab sein have come off ◊ *An ein paar Stellen ist die Farbe schon ab.* **3.** departing from ◊ *Fürth Hauptbahnhof ab 7.10 Uhr, Nürnberg Hauptbahnhof an 7.17 Uhr* ⊜an **4.** *(fam) (used when telling sb/an animal to go somewhere)* ab in/auf/unter etw. [acc] *(off)* into/to/under sth ◊ *Ab in die Badewanne mit dir!* ♦ *Rex, ab ins Körbchen!* ♦ *Ab unter die Dusche!* ab in den Urlaub off on holiday ab zum Skifahren off skiing **5.** THEAT exit ◊ *Hamlet (nach rechts ab).* ⊙ ab und zu now and then, from time to time ◊ *Ab und zu trinke ich ein Glas Rotwein.* ♦ *Es regnete viel, aber ab und zu war es auch sonnig.* ⊜manchmal, hin und wieder

⑦ **ab²** [ap] [prep] [+dat] **1.** from (... onwards) ◊ *Ab nächster Woche habe ich Urlaub.* ♦ *Ab 20 Uhr spielt hier eine Band.* ♦ *Ab hier sind es noch 25 Meter.* ♦ *ab Mitte Juli* Ab München ist es dann nur noch Autobahn. After Munich, it's all motorway. **2.** *(when giving age restrictions)* Kinder ab drei/ zwölf (Jahren) children aged three/twelve and over ◊ *Der Film ist freigegeben ab 12 Jahren.* ♦ *ein Buch für Kinder ab 8*

ab|... [ap] [prefix] +verb, *stressed and separable* **1.** ... off, ... away ◊ *Das Wasser fließt nicht ab.* ♦ *einen Brief abschicken* ⊜weg..., fort... **2.** ... off ◊ *eine Scheibe Wurst abschneiden* ♦ *einen Ast absägen* ♦ *ein Grundstück mit einem Zaun abtrennen* ♦ *die Heizung abdrehen/abschalten* ♦ *den Strom abstellen* **3.** *often not translated (cleaning off, removing sth)* ... (off) ◊ *den Tisch*

abwischen ♦ *sich die Schuhe abputzen* ♦ *den Staub (vom Tisch) abwischen;* ... (down) ◊ *die Jacke abbürsten* ♦ *eine Tür abschleifen* **4.** *often not translated directly* ein Motiv abmalen/ abpausen paint/trace an image ein Bild abfotografieren photograph a picture ein Gedicht abschreiben/abtippen write/type up a poem eine Zeitung abbestellen cancel your subscription to a newspaper sich von einem Kurs wieder abmelden cancel your registration for a course von etw. abraten advise against (doing) sth sich [dat] das Rauchen abgewöhnen quit smoking

ab|ar·bei·ten [ˈapˌʔarbaɪtn̩] <arbeitet ab, arbeitete ab, hat abgearbeitet> [tr v] **1.** work your way through, deal with ◊ *Diese Tagesordnungspunkte haben wir abgearbeitet.* ♦ *Bitte arbeiten Sie alle Aufgaben nacheinander ab.* **2.** *(a debt, fine)* work off ◊ *Schulden abarbeiten* ♦ *Die Strafe kann in Raten bezahlt oder abgearbeitet werden.* [ref v] sich abarbeiten wear yourself out, slave away, work yourself into the ground ◊ *Ich arbeite mich hier ab, und die anderen tun gar nichts.*

Ab·bau [ˈapbaʊ] der <–(e)s> *no pl* **1.** dismantling, taking down ◊ *der Abbau der Zelte* ♦ *der Abbau des Baugerüsts* **2.** CHEM, BIO breakdown ◊ *der Abbau von Zucker/Stärke* **3.** cutback, reduction ◊ *ein allmählicher Abbau der Staatsschulden* ♦ *der Abbau der Subventionen für die Landwirtschaft* **4.** reduction, elimination ◊ *Vorschläge zum Abbau der Arbeitslosigkeit* ♦ *der rasche/radikale Abbau des Schuldenbergs* **5.** mining, quarrying ◊ *der Abbau von Braunkohle*

ab|bau·en [ˈapbaʊən] <baut ab, baute ab, hat abgebaut> [tr v] **1.** dismantle, take down ◊ *ein Gerüst/Gestell/Zelt abbauen* **2.** *(mineral resources)* mine, quarry ◊ *Braunkohle abbauen* ⊜fördern **3.** *(unemployment, stock etc.)* reduce, cut back on, decrease ◊ *Personal/Stellen abbauen* ♦ *Maßnahmen, um die Arbeitslosigkeit abzubauen* ♦ *Vorräte abbauen* **4.** *(negative feelings)* break down, reduce ◊ *Der Schüleraustausch soll Vorurteile abbauen.* ♦ *Wie können Aggressionen abgebaut werden?* ♦ *ein Mittel, um Stress abzubauen* **5.** *(a debt)* reduce, cut ◊ *Schulden abbauen* **6.** CHEM break down ◊ *Mithilfe dieses Enzyms wird Stärke abgebaut.* ♦ *Bestimmte chemische Verbindungen können durch Bakterien abgebaut werden.* [intr v] jd baut ab sb declines, sb is in decline ◊ *Sie baut geistig/körperlich immer mehr ab.*

ab|be·kom·men [ˈapbəkɔmən] <bekommt ab, bekam ab, hat abbekommen> [tr v] **1.** etw. abbekommen (manage to) get sth ◊ *Sie hat keinen Nachtisch mehr abbekommen.* ♦ *rausgehen, um ein paar Sonnenstrahlen abzubekommen* etw. von etw. abbekommen get a share of sth ◊ *nichts vom Kuchen abbekommen* **2.** *(injuries, damage)* etw. abbekommen suffer sth, receive sth ◊ *ein paar*

Kratzer abbekommen ✦ *Der Polizist hatte einen Schulterschuss abbekommen.* **3.** *(stains, a sticker)* etw. abbekommen get sth off ◊ *Ich bekomme den Aufkleber/den Deckel nicht ab.*

ab|bie·gen ['apbiːɡn̩] <biegt ab, bog ab, hat/ist abgebogen> [intr v] +*sein* turn (off) ◊ *An der nächsten Kreuzung müssen Sie rechts/links abbiegen.* ✦ *Der Weg biegt nach 100 Metern nach rechts ab.* [tr v] +*haben* bend ◊ *Nach dem Sturz konnte ich das Knie nicht mehr abbiegen.*

ab|bil·den ['apbɪldn̩] <bildet ab, bildete ab, hat abgebildet> [tr v] depict, portray, show ◊ *Auf dem Foto war eine Frau abgebildet.* ⊖darstellen

Ab·bil·dung ['apbɪldʊŋ] die <-, -en> **1.** depiction, portrayal, representation ◊ *der Versuch einer Abbildung der Wirklichkeit durch die Kunst* **2.** picture, image, print ◊ *fotografische/realistische Abbildungen* ✦ *siehe nebenstehende Abbildung*

ab|bre·chen ['apbrɛçn̩] <bricht ab, brach ab, hat/ist abgebrochen> [tr v] +*haben* **1.** etw. (von etw.) abbrechen break sth off (sth) ◊ *Er brach einen Zweig (vom Baum) ab.* ✦ *Von seinem Auto wurde die Antenne abgebrochen.* **2.** break off, cut short ◊ *Er hat seine Ausbildung/seinen Urlaub abgebrochen.* ✦ *die diplomatischen Beziehungen abbrechen* ✦ *den Kontakt mit jdm abbrechen; (a match, game also)* call off ◊ *Wegen Regen musste das Rennen vorzeitig abgebrochen werden.; (a pregnancy)* terminate **3.** sein Studium abbrechen drop out (of university) ◊ *Er hat sein Studium nach fünf Semestern abgebrochen.* **4.** *(tents, a campsite)* take down ◊ *Am Freitag wurde das Zeltlager abgebrochen.* **5.** *(a building)* pull down, demolish ◊ *Das Gebäude wurde 1930 abgebrochen.* [intr v] **1.** +*sein* break (off) ◊ *Die Zweige brachen von selbst ab.* ✦ *Die Bleistiftmine ist abgebrochen.* **2.** +*sein* stop, break off ◊ *Der Kontakt zwischen den beiden ist abgebrochen.* **3.** +*haben* jd bricht ab sb stops, sb breaks off ◊ *Sie brach mitten im Satz/in ihrer Erzählung ab.*

ab|brin·gen ['apbrɪŋən] <bringt ab, brachte ab, hat abgebracht> [tr v] **1.** jdn von etw. abbringen stop sb (from) doing sth, dissuade sb from (doing) sth ◊ *Sie versuchte, ihn von seinem Entschluss abzubringen.* ✦ *Ich konnte ihn nicht davon abbringen, sie anzusprechen.* **2.** jdn vom Kurs/Weg abbringen make sb change course/direction ◊ *Der Kanzler ließ sich nicht von seinem politischen Kurs abbringen.*

Ab·bruch ['apbrʊx] der <-(e)s, Abbrüche> **1.** *no pl* demolition ◊ *Das Unternehmen wurde mit dem Abbruch der Brücke beauftragt.* ✦ *das vom Abbruch bedrohte Haus* ⊖Abriss ⊖Aufbau **2.** *often translated with a verb construction, no pl* taking down Nach dem Abbruch der Zelte wanderten sie weiter. After taking down the tents, they continued walking. **3.** *most sing* breaking off, termination ◊ *Der Streit führte zu einem Abbruch der Verhandlungen/diplomatischen Beziehungen.* ✦ *Ein Abbruch der Schwangerschaft kommt für mich nicht in Frage.* **4.** Abbruch des Studiums dropping out (of university) **5.** IT cancel(lation), abort(ing) ◊ *Bitte 0 für Abbruch eingeben, 1 für Fortfahren.*

◉ etw. tut einer Sache [dat] keinen Abbruch sth does not harm sth, sth does not diminish sth ◊ *Der Regen tat der guten Stimmung keinen*

Abbruch. ✦ *Der Vorfall tat dem Ansehen der Familie keinen Abbruch.*

ab|bu·chen ['apbuːxn̩] <bucht ab, buchte ab, hat abgebucht> [tr v] debit, collect by direct debit ◊ *Der Betrag wird automatisch von seinem Konto abgebucht.* etw. abbuchen lassen pay sth by direct debit ◊ *die Telefonrechnung abbuchen lassen*

Abc [aːbeː'tseː] das <-, -> *most sing* **1.** alphabet ◊ *Die Schüler lernen gerade das Abc.* ⊖Alphabet **2.** *(fig)* das ABC ... [gen] the ABC of sth ◊ *das Abc der Architektur/des Mietrechts*

ab|dan·ken ['apdaŋkn̩] <dankt ab, dankte ab, hat abgedankt> [intr v] resign ◊ *Der Präsident hat abgedankt.* ✦ *Er musste als Parteichef abdanken.; (monarch)* abdicate

ab|de·cken ['apdɛkn̩] <deckt ab, deckte ab, hat abgedeckt> [tr v] **1.** cover (up) ◊ *ein Loch mit einem Brett abdecken* **2.** *(a roof, tiles)* tear off ◊ *Beim gestrigen Sturm wurden viele Dächer abgedeckt.* **3.** den Tisch abdecken clear the table ◊ *Würdest du bitte den Tisch abdecken?* **4.** TRADE, FIN *(costs, a demand)* cover, meet ◊ *Die Einkünfte reichen nicht, um unsere Kosten abzudecken.* ✦ *die Nachfrage abdecken*

② **ab|dre·hen** ['apdreːən] <dreht ab, drehte ab, hat abgedreht> [tr v] **1.** turn off ◊ *Dreh das Wasser im Bad ab!* **2.** cut off ◊ *Uns wurde das Gas abgedreht.* [intr v] *(plane)* veer off, change course ◊ *Das Flugzeug musste ohne Landeerlaubnis abdrehen.*

Ab·druck ['apdrʊk] der <-(e)s, Abdrücke> **1.** mark, imprint, print ◊ *Das Bügeleisen hat einen Abdruck auf dem Stoff hinterlassen.* ✦ *Der Polizist nahm einen Abdruck des rechten Daumens.* **2.** *(model)* cast, impression ◊ *Er hat einen Abdruck seiner Hand gießen lassen.*

ab|dru·cken ['apdrʊkn̩] <druckt ab, druckte ab, hat abgedruckt> [tr v] print, publish ◊ *Seine Rede wurde abgedruckt.*

② **A·bend** ['aːbm̩t, 'aːbant] der <-s, -e> evening, night ◊ *gestern Abend* ✦ *am frühen Abend* ✦ *Gegen Abend kam es zu Gewittern.* ✦ *Er ist keinen Abend zu Hause.* ✦ *Am Abend stand er auf der Bühne.* ✦ *Nächste Woche findet dort ein literarischer Abend statt.* ✦ *Guten Abend!*

◉ ein bunter Abend a social evening ◊ *ein bunter Abend mit Gedichten und Musik* der Heilige Abend Christmas Eve ⊖Heiligabend zu Abend essen have dinner, have tea, have supper ◊ *Wir aßen in einem Restaurant zu Abend.*

A·bend·brot ['aːbm̩tbroːt, 'aːbəntbroːt] das <-s> *no pl* tea, supper ◊ *Um sechs Uhr gab es Abendbrot.* ✦ *Wir aßen gemeinsam Abendbrot.* ✦ *Zum Abendbrot gab es heiße Würstchen.* ⊖Abendessen box@ Abendessen

A·bend·es·sen ['aːbm̩tlɛsn̩, 'aːbəntlɛsn̩] das <-s, -> *most sing* dinner, tea, supper ◊ *Wann gibt es Abendessen?* ✦ *jdn zum Abendessen einladen* ✦ *Zum Abendessen gab es Pizza.; (in a hotel, guesthouse)* dinner, evening meal ◊ *Die Übernachtung mit Frühstück und Abendessen kostet 80 Euro.*

In Germany, the evening meal, which traditionally consisted of bread with cold meats or cheese and which is therefore sometimes called *Abendbrot*, is nowadays often the most important meal of the day, and can be a substantial hot meal.

A B C D E F G H I J K L M N O P Q R S T U V W X Y Z

A·bend·kas·se [ˈaːbm̩tkasə, ˈaːbəntkasə] die <–> most sing box office ◊ An der Abendkasse beträgt der Eintritt 10 Euro. ✦ Die Abendkasse öffnet eine Stunde vor Veranstaltungsbeginn/um 19 Uhr. ☺Vorverkauf

A·bend·mahl [ˈaːbm̩tmaːl, ˈaːbəntmaːl] das <–(e)s> no pl **1.** das (letzte) Abendmahl the Last Supper **2.** Communion ◊ Um 9.30 Uhr findet ein Gottesdienst mit Abendmahl statt. ✦ das Abendmahl empfangen

② **a·bends** [ˈaːbm̩ts, ˈaːbənts] adv in the evening ◊ Ich komme abends noch mal bei dir vorbei. ✦ In New York ist es jetzt 9 Uhr abends. ✦ Abends trinke ich gern ein Bier. dienstags abends on Tuesday evenings ☺morgens

A·ben·teu·er [ˈaːbm̩tɔɐ̯ɐ, ˈaːbəntɔɐ̯ɐ] das <–s, –> **1.** adventure ◊ Die Fahrt durch die Wüste war ein echtes Abenteuer. **2.** (sexual) fling, affair ◊ Sie hatte kein Interesse an einem kurzen Abenteuer.

② **a·ber¹** [ˈaːbɐ] conjunc but ◊ Alle saßen, aber er wollte unbedingt stehen. ✦ Es war sehr kalt, aber wir gingen dennoch nach draußen. ✦ Das ist sehr interessant, aber auch anstrengend. ✦ Gut, aber heute schaffe ich das nicht mehr. ✦ Aber wieso nur?

a·ber² [ˈaːbɐ] part (used to express surprise or to give emphasis) now, why ◊ Du bist aber mutig! ✦ Oh, das ist aber ein schönes Kleid!

A·ber·glau·be [ˈaːbɐɡlaʊ̯bə] der <–ns> no pl superstition, myth ◊ der Aberglaube, dass eine schwarze Katze Unglück bringt

ab|er·ken·nen [ˈapʔɛkɛnən] <erkennt ab, erkannte ab, hat aberkannt> tr v **1.** jdm etw. aberkennen strip sb of sth ◊ Man will ihr die Goldmedaille/den Weltmeistertitel aberkennen. ✦ Ihm wurde 1938 die deutsche Staatsangehörigkeit aberkannt. **2.** jdm ein Recht aberkennen deny sb a right ◊ Den Arbeitnehmern wurde das Recht aberkannt, Gewerkschaften zu gründen. jdm ein Tor aberkennen disallow sb's goal ◊ Der Mannschaft wurde das Tor aberkannt.

a·ber·mals [ˈaːbəmaːls] adv (once) again, once more ◊ Der Termin wurde abermals verschoben. ✦ Sie bewies abermals, dass sie die beste Spielerin war. ✦ Er spielte vor einer abermals ausverkauften Halle. ☺erneut

② **ab|fah·ren** [ˈapfaːrən] <fährt ab, fuhr ab, hat/ist abgefahren> intr v +sein **1.** leave, depart ◊ Übermorgen fährt die Familie wieder ab. ✦ Der Zug ist vor zehn Minuten abgefahren. Wo fährt die Buslinie 1 ab? Where does the number one bus leave from? **2.** go/drive/ride/ski down ◊ Von hier aus kann man ins Tal abfahren. **3.** (from a road) leave, turn off ◊ von der Autobahn abfahren ✦ Bei dieser Ausfahrt müssen wir abfahren. tr v **1.** +haben (rubbish, waste) take away, remove ◊ Heute wird der Müll/Schutt abgefahren. **2.** +sein/haben (a route) drive along, go along ◊ Ich bin diese Strecke heute schon einmal abgefahren. **3.** +haben (tyres) wear (out) ◊ In dieser kurzen Zeit hast du die Reifen aber stark abgefahren. ☻ (voll) auf jdn/etw. abfahren (slang) be mad about sb/sth, be (very much) into sb/sth ◊ Auf diesen Popstar fährt sie voll ab. ✦ Auf die Art von Witzen fahr ich nicht ab.

② **Ab·fahrt** [ˈapfaːɐ̯t] die <–, –en> **1.** departure ◊

Abfahrt um 9.05 Uhr auf Gleis 3. ✦ Die Abfahrt des Zuges/Busses verzögert sich um 15 Minuten. ☺Ankunft **2.** sport slope, run ◊ Er raste auf seinem Rennrad die steile Abfahrt hinunter. ✦ Die anspruchsvolle Abfahrt erfordert vollste Konzentration. **3.** sport (on skis) descent ◊ Wir genossen die Abfahrt durch den Tiefschnee. ✦ Das war eine schwierige Abfahrt! **4.** (of a motorway/freeway) exit ◊ Du musst die erste Abfahrt nach dem Tunnel rausfahren. ☺Ausfahrt

② **Ab·fall** [ˈapfal] der <–(e)s, Abfälle> **1.** rubbish, garbage, refuse, waste ◊ radioaktive/gefährliche/giftige Abfälle ✦ Abfall produzieren/entsorgen/vermeiden ✦ Viele wertvolle Rohstoffe landen im Abfall. etw. in den Abfall werfen throw sth away ☺Müll **2.** no pl (fig) drop, decline ◊ Schlafmangel führt zu einem Abfall der Leistung. ✦ ein deutlicher Abfall der Produktion **3.** no pl (of the ground) drop, slope ◊ Der Abfall des Geländes ist hier etwas steiler.

Ab·fall·ei·mer [ˈapfalʔaɛ̯mɐ] der <–s, –> (rubbish/litter) bin, trash can ◊ etw. in den Abfalleimer werfen ✦ Die Abfalleimer werden einmal pro Woche geleert. ☺Mülleimer

ab|fal·len [ˈapfalən] <fällt ab, fiel ab, ist abgefallen> intr v **1.** fall off ◊ Im Herbst fallen die Blätter ab. ✦ Das Rad ist einfach abgefallen. **2.** (ground) slope (downwards), drop ◊ eine Felswand, die von 50 auf 20 Meter abfällt ✦ Der Strand fällt flach ab. ☺ansteigen **3.** (in intensity) drop ◊ Der Blutzuckerspiegel fiel ab. ☺ansteigen **4.** bei/von etw. fällt etw. ab sth is left over from/after sth ◊ Dieses Material fällt bei der Produktion ab. bei/von etw. fällt etw. für jdn ab sb gets sth out of sth, sth is in sth for sb ◊ Was fällt bei dem Projekt für uns ab?

ab·fäl·lig [ˈapfɛlɪç] adj, adv disparaging(ly) ◊ abfällige Bemerkungen/Äußerungen/Kommentare ✦ Das meine ich nicht abfällig. ✦ Er hatte sich abfällig über ihn geäußert.

ab|fer·ti·gen [ˈapfɛɐ̯tɪɡŋ̩] <fertigt ab, fertigte ab, hat abgefertigt> tr v **1.** jdn abfertigen check sb in ◊ Die Passagiere sollen von nun an schneller abgefertigt werden. **2.** etw. abfertigen clear sth ◊ Sie müssen die Ware am Zoll abfertigen lassen. ✦ Der Lkw wurde an der Grenze abgefertigt. **3.** (pej) jdn abfertigen fob sb off ◊ Mit welchem Argument wurdest du abgefertigt? ✦ Der Kunde ist ziemlich unfreundlich abgefertigt worden.

ab|fin·den [ˈapfɪndn̩] <findet ab, fand ab, hat abgefunden> ref v sich mit etw. abfinden accept sth, resign yourself to sth, come to terms with sth ◊ Mit dieser Situation konnte/wollte sie sich nicht abfinden. ✦ Sie hat sich mit ihrem Schicksal abgefunden. tr v jdn (mit etw.) abfinden pay sb (sth in) compensation ◊ Sie wurde mit 10 000 Euro abgefunden. sich etw. abfinden lassen settle for sth ◊ Er ließ sich mit einer großzügigen Summe abfinden.

② **ab|flie·gen** [ˈapfliːɡŋ̩] <fliegt ab, flog ab, hat/ist abgeflogen> intr v +sein leave, take off ◊ Die Maschine nach London ist bereits abgeflogen. ✦ Wann fliegen wir endlich ab? Wir fliegen vom Flughafen Berlin Tegel ab. We're flying from Berlin Tegel. tr v +haben etw. abfliegen fly over sth, fly along sth ◊ Der Hubschrauber flog die Grenze ab.

ab|flie·ßen ['apfliːsn̩] <fließt ab, floss ab, ist abge-flossen> ⟨intr v⟩ drain away ◇ *Das Wasser im Waschbecken fließt schlecht ab.* ♦ *Das gestaute Blut konnte nicht abfließen.* ♦ *Die Gelder flossen nach Asien ab.*

Ab·flug ['apfluːk] der <–(e)s, Abflüge> departure ◇ *Bitte seien Sie eine Stunde vor Abflug am Flughafen.* ♦ *Der Abflug der Maschine verzögert sich um 30 Minuten.*

Ab·fluss ['apflʊs] der <–es, Abflüsse> **1.** drain, outlet ◇ *Der Abfluss des Spülbeckens war verstopft.* **2.** *no pl* drainage, draining ◇ *Das neue Rohr sorgt für einen besseren Abfluss des Wassers.*

Ab·fol·ge ['apfɔlgə] die <–> *no pl* order, sequence, succession ◇ *die zeitliche/chronologische Abfolge von Ereignissen* ♦ *die Abfolge der Nummern/ Stationen* ♦ *eine rasche Abfolge von Einzelbildern*

ab|fra·gen ['apfraːgn̩] <fragt ab, fragte ab, hat abgefragt> ⟨tr v⟩ **1.** (jdn) etw. abfragen test (sb on) sth ◇ *Ich fragte sie Vokabeln ab.* ♦ *Bei diesem Test wird Fachwissen abgefragt.* **2.** etw. abfragen access sth, find sth out ◇ *Diese Daten können tele-fonisch/per Telefon abgefragt werden.* ♦ *Informatio-nen im Internet abfragen* ♦ *den Kontostand am Geldautomaten abfragen*

Ab·fuhr ['apfuːɐ̯] die <–> *no pl* **1.** *(lofty)* removal ◇ *Die Abfuhr von Gartenabfällen erfolgt zweimal jährlich.* **2.** rebuff ◇ *jdm eine Abfuhr erteilen* ♦ *Er holte sich bei ihr eine Abfuhr.*

ab|füh·ren ['apfyːrən] <führt ab, führte ab, hat abgeführt> ⟨tr v⟩ **1.** jdn abführen take sb away ◇ *Man hatte ihn in Handschellen abgeführt.* **2.** etw. abführen pay sth ◇ *Sie mussten Steuern ans Finanzamt abführen.* ⟨intr v⟩ **1.** work as a laxative, have a laxative effect ◇ *Getrocknete Pflaumen führen ab.* **2.** branch off ◇ *Von der Hauptstraße führt rechts ein kleiner Weg ab.*

ab|fül·len ['apfʏlən] <füllt ab, füllte ab, hat abgefüllt> ⟨tr v⟩ bottle, fill ◇ *50 000 Flaschen werden jährlich abgefüllt.* ♦ *Das Öl war fertig abgefüllt und verpackt.* A in B ⟨acc⟩ abfüllen pour A into B, fill B with A ◇ *Er füllte das Öl in eine andere Flasche ab.*

Ab·ga·be ['apgaːbə] die <–, –n> **1.** *most pl* charge ◇ *die Erhöhung von Abgaben und Gebühren* ♦ *jährliche/kommunale Abgaben* **2.** *often translated with a verb construction, no pl* submission ◇ *Die Abgabe der Steuererklärung muss bis Ende Juni erfolgen. Wann ist der Termin für die Abgabe deiner Diplomarbeit?* When is your deadline for handing in your thesis? *Die Rebellen mussten sich zur Abgabe aller Waffen verpflichten.* The rebels had to agree to hand over all their weapons. **3.** dis-tribution ◇ *die Abgabe von Kleidung an Obdach-lose* **4.** *no pl (in a shop)* sale ◇ *Die Abgabe von Alkohol an Kinder ist untersagt.* ⓢVerkauf **5.** *no pl (of a statement, piece of advice)* giving, making ◇ *die Abgabe einer Erklärung der Bundesregierung* ♦ *Jeder Teilnehmer ist zur Abgabe eines Tipps berechtigt.* **6.** SPORT pass ◇ *Die Abgabe des Balls erfolgte zu spät.* ⓢAnnahme **7.** *no pl (of a shot)* firing ◇ *die gezielte Abgabe eines Schusses*

Ab·gang ['apgaŋ] der <–s, Abgänge> **1.** *no pl* exit ◇ *Nach dem Abgang der Band von der Bühne gab es Zugabe-Rufe.* **2.** *no pl* departure, resignation ◇ *Der Abgang des Präsidenten erfolgte überraschend.*

♦ *Abgänge des VfL Bochum zur Saison 2002/2003* **3.** *no pl (from school, university)* leaving ◇ *Die Schüler bekommen beim Abgang von der Schule ein Zeugnis ausgestellt.* **4.** SPORT *(in gymnastics)* dismount ◇ *Der Abgang vom Reck war fehlerfrei.* **5.** MED passing, discharge ◇ *ein plötzlicher Abgang von Urin* **6.** MED *(of a baby)* miscarriage ◇ *Ihre Schwangerschaft endete in einem Abgang.* einen Abgang haben have a miscarriage

② **Ab·gas** ['apgaːs] das <–es, –e> *most pl* Abgase emissions ◇ *Giftige Abgase verschmutzen die Luft.*; *(from a vehicle)* Abgas(e) (exhaust) fumes ◇ *Diese Fahrzeuge erzeugen weniger Abgase.*

② **ab|ge·ben** ['apgeːbm̩] <gibt ab, gab ab, hat abgegeben> ⟨tr v⟩ **1.** deliver, hand over ◇ *Der Postbote hat ein Paket abgegeben.* ♦ *Sie hat das Geschenk persönlich bei mir abgegeben.* ♦ *einen Stimmzettel abgeben* ♦ *den Führerschein abgeben*; hand in ◇ *Wann musst du die Diplomarbeit abgeben?* seinen Mantel an der Garderobe abgeben leave your coat in the cloakroom, check your coat. *(a shot)* fire ◇ *Der Polizist gab einen Warnschuss ab.* **3.** SPORT *(a ball)* pass ◇ *Er gab den Ball ab.* **4.** *(to another person)* give up, relin-quish ◇ *Sie musste den Vorsitz an ihren Rivalen abgeben.* ♦ *Erik Zabel musste die Führung abgeben.* **5.** PHYSICS emit, give off ◇ *Der Heizkörper gibt zu wenig Wärme ab.* ♦ *Bei der Verbrennung wird Kohlenmonoxid an die Atmosphäre abgegeben.* ⓢspeichern **6.** jdm etw. (von etw.) abgeben give sb sth (of sth), let sb have sth (of sth) ◇ *Sie gab ihm die Hälfte ihres Schokoriegels ab.* **7.** *(a comment, an opinion etc.)* make, give ◇ *einen Kommentar/Tipp abgeben* ♦ *Dazu kann ich kein Urteil abgeben.* ♦ *Sie müssen die Erklärung schriftlich abgeben.*; *(a vote)* cast ◇ *150 gültige Stimmen wurden abgegeben.* **8.** give out/away, hand out ◇ *Verhütungsmittel/Wanderkarten werden kostenlos abgegeben.* ♦ *Katze/Sofa abzugeben.* **9.** etw. abgeben make sth, prove to be sth ◇ *Sie wird sicher einmal eine gute Mutter abgeben.* ♦ *Das Museum gibt einen passenden Rahmen ab.* eine gute Figur abgeben look good ⟨refl v⟩ sich mit jdm abgeben spend time with sb ◇ *Er gibt sich viel mit den Nachbarskindern ab.* ♦ *Mit solchen Leuten gibt sie sich ab.*

ab|ge·hen ['apgeːən] <geht ab, ging ab, ist abge-gangen> ⟨intr v⟩ **1.** THEAT exit ◇ *Hamlet geht nach rechts ab.* **2.** SCHOOL *(von etw.)* abgehen leave (sth) ◇ *Sie ist nach der 10. Klasse vom Gymnasium abgegangen.* **3.** come off ◇ *Der Hebel ging plötzlich ab.* ♦ *Mein Knopf ist abgegangen.* **4.** *(sum)* be deducted ◇ *Von diesem Betrag geht noch die Mehrwertsteuer ab.* **5.** *(event)* go off ◇ *Die Diskussion ging nicht ohne Streit ab.*; *(project, scheme)* run ◇ *Ich hoffe, dass das Projekt diesmal ohne Probleme abgehen wird.* **6.** *(fam)* etw. geht ab sth is happening, sth is going on ◇ *Was geht denn hier ab?* ♦ *Ich verstehe nicht, was zwischen den beiden abgeht.*

ab·ge·le·gen ['apgəleːgn̩] ⟨adj⟩ remote, isolated, secluded ◇ *eine abgelegene Insel* ♦ *Der Bauernhof war ziemlich abgelegen.* ⟨adv⟩ in a remote/isolated/ secluded spot ◇ *Sie liegen recht abgelegen.*

ab·ge·neigt ['apgənaɪ̯kt] ⟨adj⟩ *no comp/superl, mostly after ns* einer Sache ⟨dat⟩ abgeneigt averse

to sth ◊ *Keiner von ihnen war dem Alkohol abgeneigt.* ♦ *Er stand dem neuen Projekt abgeneigt gegenüber.* ♦ *Dieser Lösung bin ich nicht abgeneigt.* jdm abgeneigt sein not be keen on sb ◊ *Der Personalchef war diesem Bewerber eher abgeneigt.* Wir sind diesem Kandidaten durchaus nicht abgeneigt. We have absolutely nothing against this candidate.

Ab·ge·ord·ne·te ['apgəlɔ'rdnətə] der/die <–n, die Abgeordneten> *but: ein Abgeordneter/eine Abgeordnete* **1.** POL Member of Parliament, MP, Representative ◊ *Sie ist Abgeordnete im Bundestag.* ♦ *die Abgeordneten des Europaparlaments* ♦ *Die Mehrheit der Abgeordneten stimmte zu.* ⊖Delegierte *box@* Substantivierung **2.** *(of an association, club etc.)* representative

ab·ge·ris·sen ['apgərɪsn̩] *past p of* abreißen [adj] *seldom comp/no superl* unkempt ◊ *Er sah völlig abgerissen aus.*; *(clothing)* ragged ◊ *abgerissene Kleidung*

Ab·ge·sand·te ['apgəzantə] der/die <–n, die Abgesandten> *but: ein Abgesandter/eine Abgesandte* emissary ◊ *der Abgesandte des Königs box@* Substantivierung

ab|ge·win·nen ['apgəvɪnən] <gewinnt ab, gewann ab, hat abgewonnen> [tr v] **1.** einer Sache [dat] etw. abgewinnen gain sth from sth, find sth appealing ◊ *Könnten Sie meinem Vorschlag etwas abgewinnen?* einer Sache [dat] Sinn abgewinnen make sense of sth ◊ *Ich kann dieser Regelung keinen Sinn abgewinnen.* **2.** *(a smile, promise)* jdm etw. abgewinnen extract sth from sb, coax sth from sb ◊ *Er hat mir das Versprechen abgewonnen, mit ihm in den Zoo zu gehen.*

ab|ge·wöh·nen ['apgəvøːnən] <gewöhnt ab, gewöhnte ab, hat abgewöhnt> [tr v] sich [dat] etw. abgewöhnen give sth up, stop sth, get out of the habit of sth ◊ *Ich muss mir das Rauchen abgewöhnen.* ♦ *Du solltest dir abgewöhnen, ständig andere zu kritisieren.* jdm etw. abgewöhnen stop sb from doing sth ◊ *Gewöhn deinem Hund das Betteln ab!* ⊚ zum Abgewöhnen sein *(fam)* be awful ◊ *Mein Mathelehrer ist wirklich zum Abgewöhnen.*

ab|gren·zen ['apgrɛntsn̩] <grenzt ab, grenzte ab, hat abgegrenzt> [tr v] **1.** *(a plot of land)* close off ◊ *ein Grundstück mit einer Hecke abgrenzen* **2.** *(fig)* etw. von etw. abgrenzen separate sth and sth, distinguish between sth and sth ◊ *zwei Begriffe voneinander abgrenzen* [ref v] **1.** sich von jdm abgrenzen keep yourself apart from sb ◊ *Sie versucht, sich von ihren Mitschülern abzugrenzen.* **2.** sich von etw. abgrenzen distance yourself from sth ◊ *Die Grünen wollen sich stärker von der Politik der Regierung abgrenzen.*

Ab·grund ['apgrʊnt] der <–(e)s, Abgründe> abyss ◊ *Sie ist in den Abgrund gestürzt.* ⊚ es tun sich Abgründe auf **1.** profound difficulties become apparent **2.** rifts are appearing ◊ *Zwischen Regierung und Opposition tun sich Abgründe auf.*

ab|ha·ben ['apha:bm̩] <hat ab, hatte ab, hat abgehabt> [tr v] *(fam)* etw. (von etw.) abhaben have some, have a piece (of sth) ◊ *Willst du auch etwas vom Kuchen abhaben?* ♦ *Kann ich ein Stück abhaben?*

ab|ha·ken ['apha:kŋ] <hakt ab, hakte ab, hat

abgehakt> [tr v] **1.** tick off, check off ◊ *alle Anwesenden auf der Liste abhaken* **2.** forget ◊ *Den Martin kannst du abhaken, der kommt heute nicht mehr.* ♦ *Dieses Thema ist längst abgehakt.*

ab|hal·ten ['aphaltŋ] <hält ab, hielt ab, hat abgehalten> [tr v] **1.** jdn (von etw.) abhalten stop sb (doing sth) ◊ *Wenn du gehen willst, lass dich von mir nicht abhalten.* ♦ *Ich will dich nicht von der Arbeit abhalten.* **2.** keep away ◊ *Ein Gitter hält die Fliegen ab.*; *(the rain, snow)* keep off ◊ *Das Dach hält den Regen ab.* **3.** *(an election, a meeting)* hold ◊ *Wahlen abhalten*; *(a course)* run ◊ *einen Kurs abhalten*; *(a trade fair)* organize ◊ *eine Messe abhalten*

ab|han·deln ['aphandl̩n] <handelt ab, handelte ab, hat abgehandelt> [tr v] **1.** deal with ◊ *Die Präpositionen werden in Lektion 12 abgehandelt.* **2.** jdm etw. abhandeln get sth off sb ◊ *Ich habe ihm den Teppich für 50 Euro abgehandelt.*

ab·han·den [ap'handn̩] [adv] *(always* abhanden kommen*)* be lost, go missing Mir ist mein Geldbeutel abhanden gekommen. I've lost my wallet.

Ab·hand·lung ['aphandlʊŋ] die <–, –en> treatise ◊ *eine philosophische Abhandlung* ⊖Schrift

Ab·hang ['aphaŋ] der <–(e)s, Abhänge> slope, incline ◊ *Der Ball rollte den Abhang hinunter.* ♦ *Sie haben ihr Haus an einem Abhang gebaut.*

⑦ **ab|hän·gen¹** ['aphɛŋən] <hängt ab, hing ab, hat abgehangen> [intr v] von jdm/etw. abhängen depend on sb/sth ◊ *Die Qualität des Weins hängt vom Wetter ab.* ♦ *Es hängt von meinen Eltern ab, ob ich mitkommen darf.*

⑦ **ab|hän·gen²** ['aphɛŋən] <hängt ab, hängte ab, hat abgehängt> [tr v] **1.** etw. abhängen take sth down ◊ *die Wäsche abhängen* ⊖aufhängen **2.** *(vehicles)* uncouple ◊ *einen Anhänger vom Auto abhängen* **3.** *(an opponent, a competitor)* jdn abhängen leave sb behind, shake sb off ◊ *Schumacher hat seine Gegner schon in der ersten Runde abgehängt.* ♦ *die Konkurrenz abhängen*

ab·hän·gig ['aphɛŋɪç] [adj] **1.** von jdm/etw. abhängig sein be dependent on sb/sth, depend on sb/sth ◊ *Sie ist finanziell von ihrem Mann abhängig.* ♦ *Die Ernte ist vom Wetter abhängig.* **2.** addicted ◊ *Wie kann man abhängigen Jugendlichen helfen?* von etw. abhängig sein/werden be/become addicted to sth ◊ *Von Heroin wird man leicht abhängig.*; *(a medicine)* be dependent on sth ◊ *Sie ist seit Jahren abhängig von Medikamenten.* ⊖süchtig **3.** etw. von etw. abhängig machen make sth conditional upon sth ◊ *Ich mache meinen Einsatz davon abhängig, wie gut ich bezahlt werde.*

ab|hau·en¹ ['aphaʊən] <haut ab, haute ab/hieb ab, hat abgehauen> [tr v] etw. abhauen chop sth off ◊ *Er haute den Ast mit der Axt ab.*

ab|hau·en² ['aphaʊən] <haut ab, haute ab, ist abgehauen> [intr v] *(fam)* **1.** run off ◊ *Als die Polizei kam, sind die Einbrecher abgehauen.* **2.** clear off ◊ *Hau bloß ab!* ⊖abschieben

⑦ **ab·he·ben** ['aphe:bm̩] <hebt ab, hob ab, hat abgehoben> [tr v] *(money)* withdraw ◊ *Er hat 100 Euro von seinem Konto abgehoben.* ⊖einzahlen [intr v] **1.** *(the phone)* answer, pick it up ◊ *Ich lasse es dreimal klingeln, bevor ich abhebe.* ⊖auflegen **2.** *(aircraft)* take off ⊖landen [ref v]

A
B
C
D
E
F
G
H
I
J
K
L
M
N
O
P
Q
R
S
T
U
V
W
X
Y
Z

sich von etw. **abheben** stand out against sth ◊ *Die hellen Sterne heben sich vom dunklen Himmel ab.*; *(person)* sich von jdm/etw. **abheben** stand out from sb/sth ◊ *Sie hebt sich von den anderen durch ihren Fleiß ab.*

Ab·hil·fe ['aphɪlfə] die <–, –n> remedy ◊ *Welche Abhilfe gibt es gegen die Arbeitslosigkeit?* Abhilfe schaffen remedy sth

② **ab|ho·len** ['apho:lən] <holt ab, holte ab, hat abgeholt> (tr v) **1.** etw. abholen collect sth ◊ *Die Müllarbeiter holen einmal in der Woche den Müll ab.* **2.** jdn abholen pick sb up ◊ *Ich hole dich von der Schule ab.*; *(by the police)* take sb away

ab|hö·ren ['aphø:rən] <hört ab, hörte ab, hat abgehört> (tr v) **1.** jdn abhören give sb an oral test ◊ *Heute hört unser Englischlehrer uns ab.* jdn (etw.) abhören test sb on sth ◊ *Meine Mutter hört mich immer die Vokabeln ab.* ♦ *Kanns du mich mal abhören?* **2.** *(a telephone)* bug ◊ *Mein Telefon wird abgehört.* **3.** MED listen to sb's chest ◊ *Der Arzt hat ihr die Lunge abgehört.* ♦ *Machen Sie sich bitte frei, ich möchte Sie abhören.*

A·bi ['abi:] das <–s, –s> *(fam)* *(abbr of* Abitur*)* ⊜*A levels* ◊ *das Abi machen*

② **A·bi·tur** [abi'tu:ɐ̯] das <–s, –e> *(abbr* Abi*)* ⊜*A levels* ◊ *Nur wer das Abitur hat, kann studieren.*

> The *Abitur* is the school-leaving examination of the *Gymnasium* and thus the highest qualification obtainable in German schools. It is also called *allgemeine Hochschulreife* and qualifies the student to study at university level. In addition, there is also a more practically-oriented *Fachabitur* which prepares the student to study at a *Fachhochschule* (comparable to the old concept of polytechnics in Britain), where the courses concentrate on vocational subjects.

A·bi·tu·ri·ent [abitu'ri̯ɛnt] der <–en, –en>, **A·bi·tu·ri·en·tin** [abitu'ri̯ɛntɪn] die <–, –nen> ⊜*A level student*

ab|kau·fen ['apkaofn] <kauft ab, kaufte ab, hat abgekauft> (tr v) jdm etw. abkaufen buy sth off sb ◊ *Ich habe ihm sein Auto günstig abgekauft.* ⊛ sich (dat) etw. teuer abkaufen lassen ask a lot in return for sth ◊ *Das Land ließ sich seine Zustimmung zum Krieg teuer abkaufen.*

Ab·kehr ['apke:ɐ̯] die <–> *no pl* (*always* eine/die Abkehr von) a/the rejection of ◊ *die völlige Abkehr von der Atomkraft*

ab|klä·ren ['apklɛ:rən] <klärt ab, klärte ab, hat abgeklärt> (tr v) clarify ◊ *Ich muss erst abklären, was wir machen sollen.* etw. mit jdm abklären clear sth with sb ◊ *Wir sollten das Problem mit dem Chef abklären.*

ab|ko·chen ['apkɔxn] <kocht ab, kochte ab, hat abgekocht> (tr v) sterilize ◊ *Milch abkochen, damit sie nicht sauer wird*; *(water)* boil

Ab·kom·men ['apkɔmən] das <–s, –> agreement ◊ *mit jdm ein Abkommen schließen*

ab|küh·len ['apky:lən] <kühlt ab, kühlte ab, hat abgekühlt> (tr v) cool (off) ◊ *Nach der Wanderung haben wir die Beine im Bach abgekühlt.* ⊝aufwärmen (intr v) *(in the fridge)* etw. abkühlen lassen chill sth ◊ *Die Creme vor Verzehr abkühlen lassen.* ⊝erwärmen (ref+intr v) cool down ◊ *Das Wetter hat (sich) merklich abgekühlt.* (ref v) sich abkühlen

cool down ◊ *Ich gehe jetzt schwimmen, um mich abzukühlen.*

ab|kür·zen ['apkʏrtsn̩] <kürzt ab, kürzte ab, hat abgekürzt> (tr v) shorten ◊ *eine Rede abkürzen*; *(word also)* abbreviate ◊ *In der Umgangssprache wird Abitur zu Abi abgekürzt.* Wir können die Strecke abkürzen, indem wir über die Felder gehen. We can take a short cut by going across the fields.

Ab·kür·zung ['apkʏrtsʊŋ] die <–, –en> **1.** shortening ◊ *die Abkürzung eines Verfahrens*; *(of a word)* abbreviation ◊ *In der EDV werden viele Abkürzungen benutzt.* **2.** *(of a route)* short cut, quick way ◊ *Wir sind die Abkürzung gefahren.*

> Abbreviations (*Abkürzungen —* short form *Abk.*) are very popular in German. They are used on the one hand to abbreviate common phrases in texts, such as *z. B.* (*zum Beispiel —* for example), *etc.* (*et cetera*), *bzw.* (*beziehungsweise —* respectively, and), *m. W.* (*meines Wissens —* to my knowledge), the above examples existing only in the written form. They are also used to shorten complex compound nouns, for example *OB* (*Oberbürgermeister —* mayor or Lord Mayor), *VHS* (*Volkshochschule —* adult education centre), *BMW* (*Bayerische Motorenwerke —* Bavarian Motor Works), these latter examples being both written and spoken. There are abbreviations in all areas of private and professional life.

ab|la·den ['apla:dn̩] <lädt ab, lud ab, hat abgeladen> (tr v) **1.** unload ◊ *Der Kies wurde vor dem Haus abgeladen.* ♦ *einen Lastwagen abladen* **2.** etw. auf jdn abladen offload sth onto sb ◊ *Er lädt die ganze Arbeit auf seine Kollegen ab.* **3.** etw. bei jdm abladen unload sth onto sth ◊ *seinen Kummer bei einer Freundin abladen*

Ab·la·ge ['apla:gə] die <–, –n> **1.** shelf ◊ *eine Ablage für Hüte* **2.** *(for files, post)* filing tray ◊ *die Briefe in der Ablage* **3.** *(of files)* filing ◊ *Freitags macht die Sekretärin die Ablage.*

ab|la·gern ['apla:gern] <lagert ab, lagerte ab, hat abgelagert> (tr+intr v) *(alcohol)* (allow to) mature ◊ *Wein in Fässern abgelagert* ♦ *Wie lange lagert der Whiskey schon ab?*; *(wood)* (allow to) season (tr v) deposit ◊ *Das Meer lagert Sand ab und es entsteht neues Land.* sich ablagern be deposited ◊ *Magma lagert sich ab*; *(limescale)* accumulate, build up ◊ *In den Gelenken lagert sich Kalk ab.*

ab|las·sen ['aplasn̩] <lässt ab, ließ ab, hat abgelassen> (tr v) **1.** *(a liquid)* let out ◊ *das Badewasser ablassen* **2.** *(a container)* empty ◊ *die Badewanne ablassen*; *(a lake, pond)* drain **3.** etw. an jdm ablassen take sth out on sb ◊ *seinen Frust an den Kindern ablassen* (intr v) *(lofty)* von etw. ablassen stop sth ◊ *Ich wünschte, sie würde von ihren ständigen Klagen ablassen!*; *(a plan, project)* abandon sth

Ab·lauf ['aplaof] der <–(e)s, Abläufe> **1.** order, sequence ◊ *den Ablauf des Geschehens* ♦ *Ablauf des Programms durchsprechen* **2.** *(progress)* course ◊ *den Ablauf des Programms stören* ♦ *der reibungslose Ablauf der Verhandlung* **3.** *(of a deadline, contract)* expiry ◊ *nach Ablauf der Frist* **4.** drain, outlet pipe ◊ *Der Ablauf ist verstopft.*

ab|lau·fen ['aplaofn̩] <läuft ab, lief ab, hat/ist abgelaufen> [intr v] +*sein* **1.** *(liquid)* drain, run out ◊ *Das Wasser aus der Badewanne läuft schlecht ab.* **2.** *(deadline, contract, membership etc.)* expire ◊ *den Pass verlängern lassen, bevor er abgelaufen ist* **3.** *(programme, course of events)* go ◊ *Wie soll der heutige Abend ablaufen?* [tr v] +*haben/sein* **1.** +*haben/sein (a route)* walk ◊ *Ich bin den ganzen Weg noch einmal abgelaufen.* **2.** +*haben (a carpet)* wear out ◊ *Der Teppich ist völlig abgelaufen.*

ab|le·gen ['aple:gn̩] <legt ab, legte ab, hat abgelegt> [tr v] **1.** *(clothing)* take off ◊ *Wollen Sie nicht Ihren Mantel ablegen?* **2.** *(a dossier, letter)* file ◊ *Wo haben Sie den Briefwechsel mit der Firma Hänsel abgelegt?* **3.** *(a bad habit, way of behaving)* get rid of ◊ *Mit der Zeit hat er seine Schüchternheit abgelegt.* **4.** *(an exam)* take ◊ *eine Prüfung ablegen; (a confession)* make ◊ *die Beichte ablegen* ♦ *ein Geständnis ablegen; (an oath)* swear [intr v] *(ship)* depart

② **ab|leh·nen** ['aple:nən] <lehnt ab, lehnte ab, hat abgelehnt> [tr v] **1.** refuse, turn down ◊ *Ich lehne es ab, mit Kindern zu diskutieren.* ♦ *Er hat das Amt des Vorsitzenden/meine Einladung abgelehnt.; (a proposal)* reject ◊ *einen Antrag ablehnen* ⊜annehmen **2.** etw./jdn ablehnen disapprove of sth/sb ◊ *Sie lehnt diese Art von Musik ab.* ♦ *Seine Familie lehnt mich ab.*

Ab·leh·nung ['aple:nʊŋ] die <-> *no pl* **1.** refusal ◊ *die Ablehnung eines Amtes* ♦ *seine Ablehnung des Geschenks* ⊜Annahme **2.** disapproval ◊ *Er stößt bei seinen Mitmenschen auf Ablehnung.* ♦ *die Ablehnung einer solchen Politik* ⊜Abwehr

ab|len·ken ['aplɛŋkn̩] <lenkt ab, lenkte ab, hat abgelenkt> [tr v] **1.** jdn ablenken distract sb ◊ *Lass dich nicht immer von der Arbeit ablenken!* **2.** etw. ablenken divert sth ◊ *Geschickt lenkte der Torwart den Schuss ab.* ♦ *einen Angriff ablenken*

ABM [a:be:|'ɛm] die *(abbr of* Arbeitsbeschaffungs-maßnahme(n)) *employment that is financed by the German state so that the unemployed or job starters can (re-)enter the working world*

② **ab|ma·chen** ['apmaxn̩] <macht ab, machte ab, hat abgemacht> [tr v] **1.** arrange ◊ *Hast du schon einen Termin mit ihm abgemacht?* **2.** *(fam)* remove, take off ◊ *An der Jacke kann man die Kapuze abmachen.* **3.** etw. untereinander abmachen sort sth out between yourselves ◊ *Macht untereinander ab, wer heute spült!* **4.** agree (on) ◊ *Wir hatten abgemacht, dass jeder eine Aufgabe übernimmt.*

② **ab|mel·den** ['apmɛldn̩] <meldet ab, meldete ab, hat abgemeldet> [tr v] **1.** jdn abmelden withdraw sb ◊ *Ich habe meine Tochter in der Realschule abgemeldet.* sich abmelden withdraw ◊ *Ich habe mich vom Kurs abgemeldet.* ⊜anmelden **2.** jdn/sich abmelden report sb's/your change of address ◊ *jdn/sich beim Einwohnermeldeamt abmelden* ⊜anmelden **3.** *(a vehicle)* take off the road ◊ *Im Winter meldet er sein Motorrad ab.; (the telephone)* have disconnected; *(the television)* cancel your licence ⊜anmelden

ab|mes·sen ['apmɛsn̩] <misst ab, maß ab, hat abgemessen> [tr v] measure ◊ *den Stoff für ein Kleid abmessen*

ab|neh·men ['apne:mən] <nimmt ab, nahm ab, hat abgenommen> [intr v] **1.** lose weight ◊ *Ich muss dringend abnehmen.* ⊜zunehmen **2.** *(the telephone)* answer ◊ *Es hat keiner abgenommen.* ⊜auflegen **3.** *(numbers)* decline, fall ◊ *Die Schülerzahlen nehmen ab.; (moon)* wane ⊜zunehmen [tr v] **1.** *(remove)* take off ◊ *den Hut abnehmen* ♦ *ein Bild von der Wand abnehmen; (the receiver)* pick up ◊ *den Telefonhörer abnehmen* **2.** *(goods)* buy ◊ *Wenn Sie 100 Stück abnehmen, bekommen Sie Rabatt.* **3.** zwei Kilo/Pfund etc. abnehmen lose two kilos/pounds etc. ◊ *Wie viel willst du abnehmen?* **4.** *(a task, responsibility)* jdm etw. abnehmen take sth over (from sb) ◊ *Ich nehme dir diese Aufgabe ab.* ♦ *jdm die Verantwortung für etw. abnehmen; (an object, children)* jdm etw./ jdn abnehmen take sth/sb off sb's hands ◊ *jdm einen schweren Gegenstand abnehmen* ♦ *jdm die Kinder nachmittags abnehmen* **5.** *(fam) (sth that was said)* jdm etw. abnehmen buy sth ◊ *Diese Geschichte nehme ich dir nicht ab.* **6.** etw. abnehmen take sth away from sb, confiscate sb's sth ◊ *Die Polizei hat ihm den Führerschein abgenommen.* **7.** *(money)* jdm etw. abnehmen get sth out of sb ◊ *Für die Eintrittskarte haben sie uns 20 Euro abgenommen.* **8.** eine Prüfung abnehmen conduct an exam ◊ *Wer wird die Prüfung abnehmen?*

Ab·nei·gung ['apnaegʊŋ] die <–, –en> aversion, antipathy ◊ *Er hat mich seine Abneigung spüren lassen.* ♦ *meine Abneigung gegen solche Literatur* ⊜Zuneigung

A·bon·ne·ment [abɔnə'mãŋ, abɔnə'mãː] das <-s, –s> *(abbr* Abo*)* subscription ◊ *ein Abonnement für eine Zeitung haben* ♦ *ein Abonnement abschließen*

a·bon·nie·ren [abo'niːrən] <abonniert, abonnierte, hat abonniert> [tr v] subscribe to ◊ *eine Zeitschrift abonnieren*

ab|ord·nen ['ap|ɔrdnən] <ordnet ab, ordnete ab, hat abgeordnet> [tr v] jdn irgendwohin abordnen send sb as a delegate somewhere ◊ *jdn in die Regierung abordnen*

ab|ra·ten ['apra:tn̩] <rät ab, riet ab, hat abgeraten> [intr v] advise against ◊ *Da kann ich nur abraten.* ♦ *Mein Arzt hat mir von einer Operation abgeraten.*

ab|räu·men ['aprɔɪmən] <räumt ab, räumte ab, hat abgeräumt> [tr v] clear ◊ *den Tisch abräumen* ♦ *das Geschirr vom Tisch abräumen*

② **ab|rech·nen** ['aprɛçnən] <rechnet ab, rechnete ab, hat abgerechnet> [intr v] **1.** total up, cash up ◊ *Die Bedienung wollte abrechnen.* **2.** mit jdm abrechnen get even with sb ◊ *Die Mafia hat mit ihm abgerechnet.* [tr v] etw. (von etw.) abrechnen deduct sth (from sth) ◊ *Wenn ich die Miete vom Gehalt abrechne, bleiben mir noch 500 Euro.*

Ab·rech·nung ['aprɛçnʊŋ] die <-, –en> **1.** *(statement of) account* ◊ *Einmal im Monat mache ich die Abrechnung der Heizkosten.* **2.** *(for payment)* invoice ◊ *Bitte schicken Sie uns die Abrechnung Ihrer Kosten.* **3.** reckoning ◊ *Der Tag der Abrechnung ist gekommen.*

Ab·rei·se ['apraeza] die <–, –n> departure

ab|rei·sen ['apraezn̩] <reist ab, reiste ab, ist abgereist> [intr v] leave, depart ◊ *Sie sind gestern*

A
B
C
D
E
F
G
H
I
J
K
L
M
N
O
P
Q
R
S
T
U
V
W
X
Y
Z

nach Australien abgereist. ⊝ankommen

ab|rei·ßen ['apraesn̩] <reißt ab, riss ab, hat/ist abgerissen> ⟨tr v⟩ +*haben* tear off ◊ *ein Kalenderblatt abreißen*; *(a building)* tear down ◊ *ein Gebäude abreißen* ⟨intr v⟩ +*sein* break off ◊ *Der Kontakt ist abgerissen.* nicht abreißen continue unabated ◊ *Der Flüchtlingsstrom wollte gar nicht mehr abreißen.*

Ab·riss ['aprɪs] der <-es, -e> **1.** *no pl (of a building)* demolition ◊ *Viele Häuser in der Altstadt sind vom Abriss bedroht.* ⊝Abbruch ⊝Aufbau **2.** *(of a topic)* summary, outline ◊ *ein Abriss der ägyptischen Kunst*

ab|ru·fen ['apru:fn̩] <ruft ab, rief ab, hat abgerufen> ⟨tr v⟩ **1.** request ◊ *Die bestellte Ware kann jederzeit abgerufen werden.* **2.** IT retrieve, call up ◊ *Daten abrufen*

ab|rut·schen ['aprʊtʃn̩] <rutscht ab, rutschte ab, ist abgerutscht> ⟨intr v⟩ **1.** slip ◊ *Als sie den Bach überqueren wollte, ist sie am Rand abgerutscht.* **2.** *(interest rates, shares)* fall ◊ *Die Kurse rutschen ab.* jd rutscht in etw. ⟨dat⟩ ab sb's sth deteriorates, sb's sth goes downhill ◊ *in seinen Leistungen abrutschen*

Ab·sa·ge ['apza:gə] die <-, -n> **1.** refusal, negative response ◊ *Sie haben vom Botschafter eine Absage bekommen.*; *(of a job application)* rejection ◊ *Er hat auf seine Bewerbungen lauter Absagen erhalten.* ⊝Zusage **2.** eine Absage an etw. ⟨acc⟩ a rejection of sth, a renunciation of sth ◊ *Eine solche Politik ist eine Absage an die Demokratie.* **3.** einer Sache/jdm eine Absage erteilen reject sth/sb, say no to sth/sb ◊ *Wir sollten jeder Form von Gewalt eine Absage erteilen.*

ab|sa·gen ['apza:gn̩] <sagt ab, sagte ab, hat abgesagt> ⟨tr+intr v⟩ cancel ◊ *eine Veranstaltung absagen* ✦ *Wie viele der Gäste haben abgesagt?* jdm absagen cancel sth with sb ◊ *Ich muss dir für morgen absagen, meine Tochter ist krank geworden.*; *(an applicant for a job)* reject sb ◊ *einem Bewerber absagen* ⊝zusagen

Ab·satz ['apzats] der <-es, Absätze> **1.** *(of a shoe)* heel ◊ *hohe Absätze* ✦ *Schuhe mit flachen Absätzen* **2.** *(in a text)* paragraph ◊ *Du solltest da einen Absatz machen.*; *(in a legal text)* clause ◊ *Paragraph 218, Absatz 2* **3.** TRADE sales ◊ *Der Absatz von Computern ist zurückgegangen.* reißenden Absatz finden sell like hot cakes **4.** *(of stairs)* landing ◊ *Sie ruhte sich auf dem Absatz der Kellertreppe aus.* ⊛ auf dem Absatz kehrtmachen turn on your heel

ab|schaf·fen ['apʃafn̩] <schafft ab, schaffte ab, hat abgeschafft> ⟨tr v⟩ **1.** abolish ◊ *ein Gesetz/eine Vorschrift abschaffen* ⊝einführen **2.** *(pets, equipment)* get rid of ◊ *Wegen einer Allergie musste sie ihre Katze abschaffen.* ✦ *Den Fernseher haben wir abgeschafft.* ⊝anschaffen

ab|schal·ten ['apʃaltn̩] <schaltet ab, schaltete ab, hat abgeschaltet> ⟨tr v⟩ turn off, switch off, shut down ◊ *Schaltet den Fernseher ab!* ✦ *Der Strom wird für zwei Stunden abgeschaltet.* ⊝ausschalten, abstellen ⊝einschalten ⟨intr v⟩ **1.** relax ◊ *Es fällt mir schwer, nach der Arbeit abzuschalten.* ⊝sich entspannen **2.** *(mentally)* switch off ◊ *während eines Vortrags abschalten*

ab|schät·zen ['apʃɛtsn̩] <schätzt ab, schätzte ab, hat abgeschätzt> ⟨tr v⟩ **1.** etw. abschätzen estimate sth, evaluate sth ◊ *die Kosten eines Produkts abschätzen* ✦ *das Gewicht von etw. abschätzen* ⊝schätzen **2.** jdn/etw. abschätzen size sb up/ assess sth ◊ *Ich versuchte, meinen Gegner abzuschätzen.* ⊝einschätzen

ab|schau·en ['apʃaʊən] *(SouthG)* <schaut ab, schaute ab, hat abgeschaut> ⟨tr+intr v⟩ *(in written exams)* (etw.) bei jdm abschauen copy (sth) off sb ⊝abschreiben ⟨ref+tr v⟩ *(gestures, behaviour)* (sich ⟨dat⟩) etw. (bei jdm) abschauen pick sth up (from sb) ◊ *Diese Geste hat er sich bei dir abgeschaut.*

ab·scheu·lich [ap'ʃɔɪlɪç] ⟨adj, adv⟩ *(lofty)* horrible(-ibly) ◊ *ein abscheulicher Mord* ✦ *Sie ist wirklich abscheulich!* ✦ *Er hat sich abscheulich benommen.* ⊝entsetzlich

ab|schi·cken ['apʃɪkn̩] <schickt ab, schickte ab, hat abgeschickt> ⟨tr v⟩ send (off), dispatch, post ◊ *einen Brief/ein Paket/eine E-Mail abschicken* ⊝verschicken, absenden, versenden

ab|schie·ben ['apʃi:bm̩] <schiebt ab, schob ab, hat/ist abgeschoben> ⟨tr v⟩ +*haben* **1.** POL *(a foreigner, refugee)* deport ◊ *Der Flüchtling wurde in seine Heimat abgeschoben.* ⊝ausweisen **2.** *(fig) (responsibility, blame)* etw. auf jdn abschieben shift sth onto sb ◊ *die Schuld auf jd anderen abschieben* **3.** dump ◊ *Viele ältere Menschen werden in Heime abgeschoben.* ⊛ Schieb ab! Get lost! ◊ *Schieb ab! Du hast hier nichts verloren!*

Ab·schied ['apʃi:t] der <-(e)s, -e> *most sing* parting ◊ *Er winkte zum Abschied.* ✦ *Der Abschied fiel ihr schwer.* ⊝Begrüßung ⊛ seinen Abschied einreichen/nehmen *(form)* resign, retire Abschied nehmen *(lofty)* say farewell, take your leave ◊ *Er nahm Abschied von seinem bisherigen Leben.*

Ab·schlag ['apʃla:k] der <-(e)s, Abschläge> **1.** reduction, discount ◊ *Auf diese Aktie gibt es 15% Abschlag für Kleinaktionäre.* ⊝Aufschlag **2.** FIN part payment ◊ *ein Abschlag auf die Gesamtsumme*; *(on salary)* advance ◊ *Könnten Sie mir auf mein Gehalt einen Abschlag geben?* **3.** GOLF tee(-off) ◊ *Es ist Zeit für den Abschlag.* ✦ *den Ball auf den Abschlag positionieren* **4.** SPORT goal kick ◊ *auf Abschlag entscheiden*

ab|schla·gen ['apʃla:gn̩] <schlägt ab, schlug ab, hat abgeschlagen> ⟨tr v⟩ **1.** (jdm) etw. abschlagen refuse (sb) sth ◊ *eine Einladung abschlagen* ✦ *jdm einen Wunsch abschlagen* **2.** (jdm/einem Tier/sich) etw. abschlagen cut (sb's/an animal's) sth off ◊ *einen Ast abschlagen* ✦ *einem Huhn den Kopf abschlagen* ✦ *Bei einem Unfall schlug er sich den Daumen ab.* **3.** GOLF tee off ◊ *den Ball auf dem Tee positionieren und abschlagen* ✦ *Um vier Uhr wurde beim Pro-Turnier abgeschlagen.* **4.** SPORT take a goal kick ◊ *Der Torwart schlug den Ball ab.* ⟨intr v⟩ **1.** GOLF tee off **2.** SPORT take a goal-kick ◊ *Der Torwart schlug ab.*

② **ab|schlie·ßen** ['apʃli:sn̩] <schließt ab, schloss ab, hat abgeschlossen> ⟨tr v⟩ **1.** lock (up) ◊ *die Wohnung/die Toilette/das Fahrrad/die Kasse abschließen* ⊝zusperren, absperren ⊝aufsperren **2.** finish, conclude, bring to an end ◊ *eine*

Lektion/die Schule/die Lehre abschließen
⊖beenden **3.** *(a piece of business, deal)* close, conclude, make; *(an agreement, a contract)* sign, enter into eine Versicherung abschließen take out an insurance ◊ *Viele Leute schließen eine Lebensversicherung ab.* (mit jdm) eine Wette abschließen make/have a bet (with sb), bet (sb) **4.** seal off, isolate ◊ *Der Ort ist vollkommen von der Außenwelt abgeschlossen.* [intr v] **1.** *(with a key)* lock up ◊ *Hast du abgeschlossen?* ⊖aufsperren **2.** *(container)* close, shut ◊ *Dieser Behälter schließt vollkommen luftdicht ab.* **3.** mit etw. abschließen end in/with sth ◊ *Der Rock schließt unten mit einem doppelten Saum ab.* ♦ *Der Film schließt mit einer Versöhnungsszene ab.* **4.** mit jdm/etw. abgeschlossen haben have finished with sb/sth ◊ *Sie hat mit ihrer Vergangenheit abgeschlossen.* mit dem Leben/der Welt abgeschlossen haben have given up on life/the world **5.** FIN close ◊ *Wie wird die Firma dieses Jahr abschließen?* mit Gewinn/Verlust abschließen close with a profit/loss

Ab·schluss ['apʃlʊs] der <–es, Abschlüsse> **1.** *no pl* conclusion ◊ *der Abschluss der Verhandlungen;* *(of a performance, festival)* finale ◊ *Zum Abschluss des Fests gab es ein Feuerwerk.* ⊖Ende ⊖Anfang **2.** *(of education, training)* qualification, diploma, degree ◊ *Ich habe einen Abschluss in Psychologie.* **3.** *no pl* TRADE *(of a contract, deal, piece of business, an agreement)* closing, signing, conclusion ◊ *der Abschluss eines Kaufvertrags* Abschluss einer Wette placing of a bet **4.** *no pl* FIN closing (the accounts), annual accounts ◊ *Nach dem Abschluss wiesen die Bücher einen Gewinn aus.*

ab|schnei·den ['apʃnaɛdn̩] <schneidet ab, schnitt ab, hat abgeschnitten> [tr v] **1.** cut (off) ◊ *Ich schneide das Fett vom Fleisch ab.* ♦ *Schneiden Sie mir bitte ein Stück Wurst ab!* **2.** *(a path, escape route)* cut off ◊ *Die Polizei schnitt dem Dieb den Fluchtweg ab.* **3.** *(a person's conversation)* cut short [intr v] bei etwas gut/schlecht etc. abschneiden do well/poorly etc. in sth ◊ *Bei der Prüfung schnitt sie nicht schlecht ab.* ♦ *Wie hast du beim Abi abgeschnitten?* als ... abschneiden come out/off ... ◊ *Beim Hochsprung schnitt sie als Beste ab.*

② **Ab·schnitt** ['apʃnɪt] der <–(e)s, –e> **1.** *(detachable piece)* stub, coupon, counterfoil, cut-off section ◊ *Schicken Sie den Abschnitt mit der Lösung an ...* **2.** *(of a document)* article, paragraph, section, chapter ◊ *der erste Abschnitt des Buches* ⊖Absatz **3.** *(of time)* phase, period ◊ *Das Studium ist ein sehr wichtiger Abschnitt im Leben.* **4.** *(also fig) (of an area)* sector, section, stretch ◊ *Dieser Abschnitt der Autobahn ist sehr stauanfällig.*

ab|schot·ten ['apʃɔtn̩] <schottet sich ab, schottete sich ab, hat sich abgeschottet> [ref v] *(fig)* sich (gegen jdn/etw.) abschotten, sich (von jdm/etw.) abschotten cut yourself off (from sb/sth), close yourself off (from sb/sth) ◊ *Er hat sich vollkommen von seiner Umwelt abgeschottet.* ♦ *Sie schottet sich ganz gegen seinen Einfluss ab.*

ab|schre·cken ['apʃrɛkn̩] <schreckt ab, schreckte ab, hat abgeschreckt> [tr v] **1.** etw. schreckt jdn ab sth deters sb, sth puts sb off ◊ *Ich lasse mich*

durch nichts abschrecken. ♦ *Der hohe Preis wird die Käufer abschrecken.* **2.** *shock vegetables etc. with cold water just after cooking* ◊ *Eier/Bohnen abschrecken*

ab|schrei·ben ['apʃraɛbm̩] <schreibt ab, schrieb ab, hat abgeschrieben> [tr v] **1.** etw. abschreiben copy sth (down/out) ◊ *Kann ich deine Mathehausaufgabe abschreiben?* **2.** *(in written exams)* etw. (bei jdm) abschreiben copy sth (off/from sb) ◊ *Diese Lösung hast du doch abgeschrieben!* ⊖abschauen **3.** FIN write off, amortize ◊ *Die Maschine ist vollständig abgeschrieben.* **4.** *(fam, fig)* jdn/etw. abschreiben write sb/sth off ◊ *Den kannst du abschreiben, den siehst du nie wieder!* ⊖mit jdm/etw. rechnen, auf jdn/etw. zählen [intr v] *cheat during exam/test by copying off sb* ◊ *Wer abschreibt, bekommt eine Sechs!* ⊖abschauen

Ab·schrift ['apʃrɪft] die <–, –en> *(form)* copy, transcript ◊ *eine beglaubigte Abschrift* eine Abschrift aus dem Geburtenbuch a copy/transcript from the register of births

ab|se·hen ['apze:ən] <sieht ab, sah ab, hat abgesehen> [imp v] **1.** *(be interested in)* es auf etw./jdn abgesehen haben be after sth/sb ◊ *Er hatte es schon seit Jahren auf sie abgesehen.* ♦ *Hat sie es nur auf das Geld abgesehen?* **2.** *(be against)* es auf jdn abgesehen haben have it in for sb **3.** von etw. absehen refrain from sth ◊ *Herzkranke sollten von der Ausübung dieses Sports absehen.* davon absehen, etw. zu tun refrain from doing sth [tr v] anticipate ◊ *Es ist abzusehen, dass unsere Mannschaft wieder verliert.* ♦ *die Folgen seines Handelns absehen* ⊖voraussehen, vorhersehen

ab·seits¹ ['apzaɛts] [adv] *(a little)* out of the way, remote ◊ *Der Ort liegt etwas abseits, lohnt aber einen Besuch.*

ab·seits² ['apzaɛts] [prep] [+gen] off, away from ◊ *Der Wasserfall liegt etwas abseits des Wegs.*

ab|sen·den ['apzɛndn̩] <sendet ab, sendete/sandte ab, hat abgesendet/abgesandt> [tr v] send (off), dispatch, post ◊ *einen Brief/ein Paket/eine E-Mail absenden* ⊖verschicken, abschicken, versenden

② **Ab·sen·der** ['apzɛndɐ] der <–s, –>, **Ab·sen·de·rin** ['apzɛndərɪn] die <–, –nen> *(abbr Abs.)* sender ⊖Empfänger

ab|set·zen ['apzɛtsn̩] <setzt ab, setzte ab, hat abgesetzt> [tr v] **1.** *(from office)* jdn absetzen depose sb, remove sb from office ◊ *Der Präsident wurde nach zahlreichen Protesten abgesetzt.* **2.** jdn absetzen drop sb off ◊ *Soll ich dich am Bahnhof absetzen?* **3.** *(a hat)* etw. absetzen take sth off ◊ *einen Hut absetzen; (a bag)* put sth down ◊ *Die Tasche ist schwer; ich muss sie absetzen.* **4.** *(a television programme)* etw. absetzen cancel sth; *(an election)* cancel sth, call sth off ◊ *Die geplante Wahl wurde abgesetzt.; (pills)* stop taking sth **5.** TRADE sell ◊ *Von dieser CD wurden 1200 Stück abgesetzt.* [ref v] sich (irgendwohin) absetzen clear off (to somewhere) ◊ *Der Diktator hat sich in ein anderes Land abgesetzt.*

ab|si·chern ['apzɪçɐn] <sichert ab, sicherte ab, hat abgesichert> [tr v] (gegen etw.) absichern protect sb/sth (from/against sth) ◊ *Du musst dich gegen diese Intrigen absichern.* ♦ *eine*

Baustelle mit einem Zaun absichern

② **Ab·sicht** [ˈapzɪçt] die <–, –en> intent, intention, purpose ◊ *Es war nie meine Absicht, Sie zu beleidigen.* ♦ *kriminelle Absichten* die Absicht haben, etw. zu tun intend to do sth ◊ *Der Vorstand hat die Absicht, einige Mitarbeiter zu entlassen.* mit Absicht on purpose, deliberately ◊ *Das hast du sicher mit Absicht gemacht!*

ab·sicht·lich [ˈapzɪçtlɪç] (adj, adv) no comp/superl; when used as an adj, mostly before ns intentional(ly), deliberate(ly) ◊ *ein absichtlicher Verstoß gegen die Spielregeln* ♦ *Ich habe es nicht absichtlich gemacht.* ⊖vorsätzlich, bewusst ⊕unabsichtlich

ab·so·lut [apzoˈluːt] (adj) no comp/superl; when used as an adj, only before ns absolute ◊ *Es gibt keine absolute Sicherheit.* (adv) (emph) totally, absolutely ◊ *Dieser PC ist absolut veraltet.* ♦ *Der Typ ist absolut cool!* ♦ *ein absolut seriöser Händler* ⊖total, völlig, vollkommen

Ab·sol·vent [apzolˈvɛnt] der <–en, –en>, **Ab·sol·ven·tin** [apzolˈvɛntɪn] die <–, –nen> sb who will sit an examination or has already passed it; (prospective) graduate ◊ *eine Absolventin der Realschule/Universität*

ab·sol·vie·ren [apzolˈviːrən] <absolviert, absolvierte, hat absolviert> (tr v) 1. (a test) pass ◊ *eine Prüfung absolvieren;* (university) graduate 2. complete ◊ *ein anstrengendes Trainingsprogramm absolvieren*

ab|spei·chern [ˈapʃpaeçɐn] <speichert ab, speicherte ab, hat abgespeichert> (tr+intr v) store, save ◊ *Daten abspeichern* ♦ *Zwischendurch sollten Sie immer wieder abspeichern.*

② **ab|sper·ren** [ˈapʃpɛrən] <sperrt ab, sperrte ab, hat abgesperrt> (intr v) (regional) (with a key) lock up ◊ *Vergessen Sie nicht abzusperren, wenn Sie das Gebäude verlassen.* ⊖abschließen, zusperren ⊕aufsperren (tr v) 1. lock ◊ *die Wohnungstür absperren* ⊖zusperren ⊕aufsperren 2. (a street, an accident site, a crime scene) close off, seal off, cordon off ◊ *Die Innenstadt wurde für zwei Tage abgesperrt.*

Ab·spra·che [ˈapʃpraːxə] die <–, –n> arrangement, agreement ◊ *sich an eine Absprache halten* ♦ *eine Absprache treffen* ♦ *In Absprache mit dem Chef wurde ihr eine Prämie ausgezahlt.*

ab|spre·chen [ˈapʃprɛçṇ] <spricht ab, sprach ab, hat abgesprochen> (tr v) 1. arrange, agree ◊ *Hast du schon einen Treffpunkt mit ihm abgesprochen?* 2. jdm etw. absprechen deny sb sth, refuse sb sth ◊ *Einen gewissen Charme kann man ihm nicht absprechen.*

Ab·stand [ˈapʃtant] der <–(e)s, Abstände> 1. (in space) distance, gap, space ◊ *der Abstand zwischen zwei Punkten;* (in time) gap, interval ◊ *Sie wurde mit einem Abstand von 1,3 Sekunden Zweite.* 2. (fig) (emotional) distance ◊ *Abstand von den Ereignissen gewinnen* ⊛ **von etw. Abstand nehmen** (lofty) 1. (from thoughts) distance yourself from sth ◊ *von einer Äußerung Abstand nehmen* (from daily routine) leave sth behind, get away from sth ◊ *Im Urlaub nahm sie Abstand vom Alltag.* 2. (not do) refrain from sth ◊ *von einer Anzeige Abstand nehmen* mit Abstand by far ◊ *Er ist mit Abstand der Beste in seiner Klasse.*

ab|stei·gen [ˈapʃtaeɡṇ] <steigt ab, stieg ab, ist abgestiegen> (intr v) 1. (from a bike, borse) von etw. absteigen get down from/off sth, dismount from sth ◊ *Jule stieg von ihrem Motorrad ab.* ⊛aufsteigen 2. (from mountains) descend, climb down ◊ *ins Tal absteigen* 3. sport be relegated ◊ *in die zweite Bundesliga absteigen* ⊛aufsteigen 4. (in a hotel, bed & breakfast) put up ◊ *in einem Hotel absteigen*

ab|stel·len [ˈapʃtɛlən] <stellt ab, stellte ab, hat abgestellt> (tr v) 1. (an appliance) turn off, switch off ◊ *Stellen Sie vor der Schranke den Motor ab!* ⊖ausmachen, abschalten, ausschalten ⊕anmachen 2. (an object) put down ◊ *das Tablett auf dem Tisch abstellen* ⊖hinstellen 3. (for storage) store, park ◊ *etw. im Keller/auf dem Dachboden abstellen*

ab|stim·men [ˈapʃtɪmən] <stimmt ab, stimmte ab, hat abgestimmt> (intr v) jd stimmt (über etw./jdn) ab sb votes (on sth/sb), sb casts a vote (on sth/sb) ◊ *Im Parlament wurde über den Gesetzentwurf abgestimmt.* ♦ *Wir stimmen ab, um eine Entscheidung zu treffen.* (tr v) 1. etw. mit jdm abstimmen agree sth with sb, reach an agreement about sth with sb ◊ *Die Strategie muss mit dem Vorstand abgestimmt werden.* 2. etw. auf jdn abstimmen adjust sth to sb, match sth to sb, customize sth for sb ◊ *ein Produkt auf seine Käufer abstimmen* ⊖etw. jdm anpassen

abs·trakt [apˈstrakt] (adj, adv) <abstrakter, am abstraktesten> abstract(ly) ◊ *abstrakt denken* ♦ *Diese Formulierung ist zu abstrakt.* ♦ *abstrakte Malerei*

Ab·stim·mung [ˈapʃtɪmʊŋ] die <–, –en> 1. vote ◊ *eine geheime Abstimmung über etw. abhalten* 2. no pl matching ◊ *die Abstimmung der Haarfarbe auf den eigenen Typ*

Ab·sturz [ˈapʃtʊrts] der <–es, Abstürze> fall ◊ *ein Absturz in die dritte Liga;* (of a plane, computer, currency, shares) crash ◊ *Die Fluggäste kamen beim Absturz ums Leben.* ♦ *ein Absturz an der Börse*

ab|stür·zen [ˈapʃtʏrtsṇ] <stürzt ab, stürzte ab, ist abgestürzt> (intr v) 1. fall ◊ *Er stürzte am Mount Everest ab.;* (plane, computer, currency, shares) crash ◊ *mit einem Flugzeug abstürzen* ♦ *Mir ist der PC abgestürzt.* ♦ *Der Dollar stürzte ab.* 2. (fam) get plastered; (in the UK also) get pissed ◊ *Gestern Abend sind wir in der Kneipe abgestürzt.*

Ab·teil [apˈtael] das <–s, –e> compartment

② **Ab·tei·lung** [apˈtaelʊŋ] die <–, –en> department, section ◊ *die Abteilung für Marketing und Vertrieb* ♦ *Das Kaufhaus hat eine Abteilung für Babykleidung.*

ab|tra·gen [ˈaptraːɡṇ] <trägt ab, trug ab, hat abgetragen> (tr v) 1. clear away, remove ◊ *eine Erdschicht/Farbschicht abtragen* 2. (debts) pay off ◊ *Schulden abtragen*

Ab·trei·bung [ˈaptraebʊŋ] die <–, –en> abortion ◊ *Sie hatte eine Abtreibung.* ⊖Schwangerschaftsabbruch

ab|tren·nen [ˈaptrɛnən] <trennt ab, trennte ab, hat abgetrennt> (tr v) 1. cut off ◊ *einen Knopf abtrennen;* (a limb) sever ◊ *Bei dem Unfall wurde ihr der Arm abgetrennt.* 2. (an area) partition off ◊ *das Zimmer mit einem Vorhang abtrennen*

② **ab|trock·nen** ['aptrɔknən] <trocknet ab, trocknete ab, hat abgetrocknet> [tr v] etw./jdn abtrocknen dry sth/sb ◊ *das Geschirr abtrocknen* sich die Hände abtrocknen dry your hands jdm den Rücken abtrocknen dry sb's back sich abtrocknen dry yourself ◊ *sich nach dem Duschen abtrocknen* [intr v] dry (the dishes) ◊ *Du hast abgespült. Ich trockne ab.*

② **Ab·wart** ['apvaˀt] der <-(e)s, -e or Abwärte>, **Ab·war·tin** ['apvaˀtɪn] die <-, -nen> *(Swiss)* caretaker, janitor ◊ *Er arbeitet als Abwart in einer Schule.* ✦ *Die Abwartin kümmert sich um die Repa-raturen.* ⊖Hausmeister

ab|war·ten ['apvaˀtn̩] <wartet ab, wartete ab, hat abgewartet> [tr v] etw. abwarten wait for sth ◊ *Ich warte die Pause ab, dann geh ich auf Toilette.* [intr v] wait a bit ◊ *Warte ab, er wird schon noch anrufen.*

② **ab·wärts** ['apvɛˀts] [adv] **1.** down, downwards, downhill ◊ *mit dem Aufzug abwärts fahren* ✦ *Wir nahmen den Wanderweg abwärts ins Tal.* ⊖aufwärts **2.** *(fig)* mit jdm/etw. geht es abwärts sb/sth is going downhill, sb/sth is on the decline ◊ *Es geht abwärts mit ihm.* ⊖aufwärts

② **ab|wa·schen** ['apvaʃn̩] <wäscht ab, wusch ab, hat abgewaschen> [tr v] wash (off/up) ◊ *Der Regen hat den Schmutz vom Auto abgewaschen.* ✦ *Wäschst du das Geschirr ab?* [intr v] wash up ◊ *Ich muss noch abwaschen, dann können wir los.* ⊖spülen

ab|wech·seln ['apvɛksl̩n] <wechselt sich ab, wechselte sich ab, hat sich abgewechselt> [ref v] sie wechseln sich ab they alternate with each other, they take it in turns ◊ *Wechseln wir uns beim Putzen ab?* ✦ *Sie wechseln sich mit dem Bereitschaftsdienst ab.*

Ab·wechs·lung ['apvɛkslʊŋ] die <-, -en> most sing change ◊ *Zur Abwechslung kannst du mal abspülen.* ✦ *Ein Urlaub an der See wäre eine schöne Abwechslung.*

Ab·wehr ['apveːɐ̯] die <-> *no pl* **1.** die Abwehr ... [gen] the defence against sth, repulsing sth ◊ *die Abwehr militärischer Gefahren* ✦ *Die Abwehr der Angreifer war erfolgreich.* eine Software zur Abwehr von Viren a software to combat viruses **2.** auf Abwehr stoßen meet with disapproval ◊ *Ihr Vorschlag stieß auf Abwehr.* eine innerliche Abwehr gegen etw. a dislike of sth ⊖Ablehnung **3.** SPORT defence, defense ◊ *Wer spielt in der Abwehr?* ⊖Ver-teidigung ⊖Angriff

② **ab·we·send** ['apveːznt, 'apveːzənt] [adj] *no comp/superl* absent ◊ *ein abwesender Schüler* ✦ *ohne Ent-schuldigung abwesend sein* ⊖anwesend [adj, adv] *(fig)* absent-minded(ly) ◊ *einen abwesenden Blick haben* ✦ *Sobald er vor dem PC sitzt, ist er geistig abwesend.* ✦ *Sie sah mich abwesend an.*

Ab·we·sen·heit ['apveːznhaet] die <-, -en> absence ◊ *In Abwesenheit des Direktors trifft sie die Entscheidungen.* ✦ *Schalten Sie bitte bei längerer Abwesenheit die Alarmanlage ein.* ⦿ **durch Abwesenheit glänzen** *(iron)* be con-spicuous by your absence

ab|wi·schen ['apvɪʃn̩] <wischt ab, wischte ab, hat abgewischt> [tr v] **1.** *(clean)* wipe ◊ *den Tisch abwischen* ✦ *Wisch dir den Mund ab!* **2.** *(remove)* wipe off, wipe away ◊ *Der Staub muss noch abge-wischt werden.*

ab|zah·len ['aptsaːlən] <zahlt ab, zahlte ab, hat abgezahlt> [tr v] pay off ◊ *Mein Auto ist noch nicht abgezahlt.* ✦ *Ich zahle jeden Monat 100 Euro ab.* ✦ *etw. in Raten abzahlen*

ab|zäh·len ['aptsɛːlən] <zählt ab, zählte ab, hat abgezählt> [tr v] count ◊ *Sie zählte im Bus die Schüler ab.*

ab|zeich·nen ['aptsaeçnən] <zeichnet ab, zeichnete ab, hat abgezeichnet> [tr v] copy ◊ *ein Motiv abzeichnen* [tr+intr v] initial, sign ◊ *Können Sie mir diese Rechnung abzeichnen?* ✦ *Der Chef muss noch abzeichnen.* [ref v] sich abzeichnen become apparent, manifest itself ◊ *Endlich zeichnet sich ein Aufschwung ab.*

ab|zie·hen ['aptsiːən] <zieht ab, zog ab, hat/ist abgezogen> [tr v] +*haben* **1.** *(from figures, a price, costs etc.)* etw. (von etw.) abziehen deduct sth (from sth), subtract sth (from sth) ◊ *Ziehen Sie zehn Prozent von der Rechnung ab.* ✦ *Können diese Kosten von den Steuern abgezogen werden?* ⊖subtrahieren ⊖addieren **2.** *(clothes, a ring)* take off, pull off, peel off ◊ *einen Ring abziehen* ✦ *einen Aufkleber abziehen*; *(a bed)* strip ◊ *das Bett abziehen* die Haut von etw. abziehen skin sth **3.** *(a photograph, document)* etw. abziehen copy sth, make a print of sth ◊ *Ziehst du mir dieses Foto noch mal ab?* ⊖fotokopieren **4.** *(troups)* withdraw ◊ *Der General ließ die Truppen aus dem Gebiet abziehen.* [intr v] +*sein* **1.** escape, move away ◊ *Die Gewitterwolken zogen nach Westen ab.* **2.** *(fam)* *(person)* go away, shove off ◊ *unverrichte-ter Dinge abziehen* Zieh ab! Shove off!, Get lost!

② **ach** [ax] [interj] **1.** *(expressing surprise)* ah, oh! ◊ *Ach, du warst das!* ✦ *Ach so! Jetzt verstehe ich das erst!* **2.** *(expressing desire, rejection)* oh ◊ *Ach, wie gerne wäre ich dabei gewesen!* ✦ *Ach, lass mich in Frieden!*

Ach·se ['aksə] die <-, -n> **1.** TECHN axle ◊ *die Achse der Hinterräder* **2.** *(line)* axis ◊ *Der Planet dreht sich um die eigene Achse.* ✦ *die Achse Berlin-Paris* ⦿ **auf Achse sein** *(fam, fig)* be on the road/move ◊ *Als Vertreterin ist sie ständig auf Achse.*

Ach·sel ['aksl̩] die <-, -n> **1.** armpit ◊ *unter der Achsel Fieber messen* **2.** shoulder ◊ *Er klopfte ihr besänftigend auf die Achsel.* mit der Achsel/den Achseln zucken shrug your shoulders

acht [axt] [nmrl] eight → vier

Acht¹ [axt] die <-, -en> **1.** eight → Vier 1. **2.** *(fam)* *(bus, tram etc.)* number eight → Vier 2.

Acht² [axt] Acht geben be careful, pay attention ◊ *Gebt Acht, wenn ihr über die Straße geht!* Habt Acht! Look out! außer Acht lassen ignore, disregard ◊ *Sie haben einen wichtigen Faktor außer Acht gelassen.* sich in Acht nehmen vor jdm/etw. be wary of sb/sth ◊ *Nimm dich vor fremden Leuten in Acht!*

ach·te ['axtə] [adj] <ein achter ..., eine achte ..., ein achtes ...> eighth → vierte

Ach·tel ['axtl̩] das <-s, -> eighth ◊ *Du bekommst ein Achtel der Summe.* ein Achtel (Wein) a (125 ml) glass of wine → Viertel

② **ach·ten** ['axtn̩] <achtet, achtete, hat geachtet> [tr v] jdn achten respect sb ◊ *Er wird aufgrund seiner Verdienste geachtet.* ⊖respektieren ⊖miss-achten [intr v] **1.** auf jdn/etw. achten pay attention

to sb/sth, listen to sb/sth ◊ *Er hörte, was sie sagte, aber er achtete nicht darauf.* ♦ *Achte nicht auf ihn, er redet Blödsinn.* ⊜beachten **2.** auf jdn/etw. achten keep an eye on sb/sth, look out for sb/sth, keep track of sb/sth ◊ *Sie hat nicht darauf geachtet und deswegen nichts bemerkt.* ⊜aufpassen **3.** *(lofty)* auf etw. [acc] achten pay attention to sth, look after sth ◊ *Achte bitte mehr auf dein Aussehen.*

ach·tens ['axtn̩s, 'axtəns] [adv] eighthly, in eighth place → viertens

acht·fach ['axtfax] [adj, adv] *when used as an adj, only before ns* eightfold, eight times ◊ *eine Abbildung in achtfacher Vergrößerung* ♦ *etw. achtfach kopieren* → vierfach

② **Ach·tung** ['axtʊŋ] die <–> *no pl* respect ◊ *Seine Verdienste um das Land verdienen hohe Achtung. Achtung vor jdm/etw. haben* respect sb/sth, have respect for sb/sth ⊜Respekt

☻ **Achtung** attention, watch out, beware ◊ *Achtung!* ♦ *„Achtung vor dem Hund!"* ♦ *Achtung, da kommt ein Auto!* ♦ *Achtung, Achtung! Hier spricht die Polizei.*

acht·zehn ['axtse:n] [nmrl] eighteen → vier

acht·zig ['axtsɪç] [nmrl] eighty → vier

ad·die·ren [a'di:rən] <addiert, addierte, hat addiert> [tr v] add (up) ◊ *Addieren Sie die zwei Zahlen.* ⊜zusammenzählen ⊜subtrahieren [ref v] sich zu etw. addieren add up to sth ◊ *Die kleinen Kosten addieren sich zu einer großen Summe.*

A·del ['a:dl̩] der <–s> *no pl* nobility, peerage, aristocracy ◊ *der deutsche/englische Adel*

☻ **Adel verpflichtet** noblesse oblige

A·der ['a:de] die <–, –n> **1.** ANAT blood vessel, vein ◊ *Eine Ader trat auf seiner Stirn hervor.* **2.** *no pl (inclination)* streak ◊ *eine künstlerische/mathematische Ader besitzen* ⊜Neigung **3.** GEOL vein ◊ *Die Goldsucher stießen auf eine reiche Ader.*

☻ **jdn zur Ader lassen 1.** MED bleed sb **2.** *(hum)* fleece sb

Ad·jek·tiv ['atjɛkti:f] das <–s, –e> adjective ⊜Eigenschaftswort

Adjectives are used to characterize objects, people and abstract nouns. There are two ways of doing this: *Mein Auto ist ganz schön* **schnell!** — Here the adjective comes after the noun at the end of the sentence. Or: *Ich habe ein ganz schön* **schnelles** *Auto!* — Now the adjective is placed before the noun and has an ending that depends on the noun. You can find out how to form these endings in the appendix in the middle of this dictionary. In Germany, your car can be not only *schnell* (fast) but also *schneller* (faster) and *am schnellsten* (fastest). Many German adjectives can also be used as adverbs, for example: *Mit meinem Auto bin ich ganz schnell verschwunden.*

Ad·ler ['a:dle] der <–s, –> eagle

a·dop·tie·ren [adɔp'ti:rən] <adoptiert, adoptierte, hat adoptiert> [tr v] adopt ◊ *ein Kind adoptieren*

② **A·dres·se** [a'drɛsə] die <–, –n> address ◊ *Schreibst du mir deine Adresse auf?* ♦ *Wie ist deine Adresse?*

a·dres·sie·ren [adrɛ'si:rən] <adressiert, adressierte, hat adressiert> [tr v] etw. adressieren

address sth ◊ *Das Paket ist falsch adressiert.* an jdn adressiert sein be addressed to sb ◊ *Das Schreiben ist an Sie adressiert.*

Ad·vent [at'vɛnt] der <–(e)s> *no pl* Advent

Advent is the four week period before Christmas including the last four Sundays. During this period in Germany, Christians celebrate the arrival of Christmas by lighting a candle on the Advent wreath every Sunday, singing Christmas carols, and enjoying biscuits and coffee or mulled wine.

Ad·verb [at'vɛrp] das <–s, Adverbien> GRAM adverb ⊜Umstandswort

An adverb indicates when, where and in what manner something takes place. It belongs to the verb, therefore it is called an adverb: *Ich glaube, das ist* **gestern** (when?) *passiert.* — *Ich bin noch nie* **dort** (where?) *gewesen.* — *Das habe ich* **langsam** (in what manner?) *verstanden.* In German adverbs can frequently be used as adjectives. In this case, they take endings that depend on the noun they describe if they come before it: *Das ist bei unserem* **gestrigen** *Treffen passiert.* — *Mit den* **dortigen** *Menschen habe ich nie gesprochen.* — *Manchmal habe ich einen* **langsamen** *Verstand.* Occasionally, adverbs consist of more than one word, for example *ab und zu, hin und wieder, drunter und drüber* etc.

Af·fä·re [a'fɛ:rə] die <–, –n> affair ◊ *Sie hat eine Affäre mit einem jüngeren Mann.* ♦ *Der ehemalige Kanzler war in dieser Affäre verwickelt.*

☻ **sich aus der Affäre ziehen** get/wriggle out of it

Af·fe ['afə] der <–n, –n> **1.** ZOO ape, monkey **2.** *(fam)* idiot, ponce ◊ *Du eingebildeterAffe!*

☻ **wie vom (wilden) Affen gebissen sein** (sein) *(fam)* (be) off your head/rocker **mich laust der Affe** *(fam)* I'll be damned

A·fri·ka ['a:frika:, 'afrika:] das <–s> *article only in combination with attribute, no pl* Africa box@ Land

A·fri·ka·ner [afri'ka:ne] der <–s, –>, **A·fri·ka·ne·rin** [afri'ka:nerɪn] die <–, –nen> African → Deutsche

a·fri·ka·nisch [afri'ka:nɪʃ] [adj] *mostly before ns* African ◊ *afrikanische Sprachen* ♦ *Die Musik dieser Band ist typisch afrikanisch.*

AG [a:'ge:] die *(abbr of* Aktiengesellschaft*)* ⊜PLC; ⊜Inc. ◊ *die Lufthansa AG*

A·gen·da [a'gɛnda] die <–, Agenden> agenda ◊ *Dieses Thema steht ganz oben auf der Agenda.* ♦ *etw. auf die Agenda setzen*

A·gent [a'gɛnt] der <–s, –en>, **A·gen·tin** [a'gɛnt ɪn] die <–, –nen> agent ◊ *eine Agentin des KGB* ♦ *Er ist als Agent für Tänzer tätig.*

A·gen·tur [agɛn'tu:ɐ] die <–, –en> agency ◊ *eine Agentur für Models*

Ag·gres·si·on [agrɛ'sjo:n] die <–, –en> aggression ◊ *Aggressionen gegen jdn haben* ♦ *Aggressionen abbauen*

ag·gres·siv [agrɛ'si:f] [adj, adv] aggressive(ly) ◊ *eine aggressive Politik betreiben* ♦ *Computerspiele können aggressiv machen.* ♦ *aggressiv reagieren* ♦ *eine aggressive Fahrweise*

a·gie·ren [aˈgiːrən] <agiert, agierte, hat agiert> intr v (*lofty*) act ◊ *In dieser schwierigen Situation agierte sie überlegt und souverän.* als etw./jd agieren act as sth/sb ◊ *Das Unternehmen agiert als Global Player.* ⊖handeln

A·grar... [aˈɡraːˀ] prefix farming, agricultural ◊ *Agrarwissenschaft* ♦ *Agrarpolitik* ⊖Landwirtschafts..., landwirtschaftlich

Ä·gyp·ten [ɛˈɡʏptn̩] das <–s> *article only in combination with attribute, no pl* Egypt → Deutschland

Ä·gyp·ter [ɛˈɡʏptɐ] der <–s, –>, **Ä·gyp·te·rin** [ɛˈɡʏptərɪn] die <–, —nen> Egyptian → Deutsche

ä·gyp·tisch [ɛˈɡʏptɪʃ] adj *mostly before ns* Egyptian ◊ *eine ägyptische Kunstsammlung*

a·ha [aˈha(ː), also aˈha] interj **1.** (*expressing sudden insight*) oh ◊ *Aha, du warst das also!* **2.** (*while listening*) I see, aha

äh·neln [ˈɛːnəln] intr v +*haben* jdm/einer Sache ähneln resemble sb/sth, be similar to sb/sth ◊ *Sie ähnelt ihrem Vater in Aussehen und Charakter.* ♦ *Die Symptome ähneln anfangs denen einer Erkältung.* sie ähneln sich they resemble each other, they are similar ◊ *Unsere Probleme ähneln sich.* ♦ *Obwohl sie Zwillinge sind, ähneln sie sich nicht sehr.*

ah·nen [ˈaːnən] tr v +*haben* have a premonition, suspect, guess ◊ *Sie ahnte, dass etwas passieren würde.* ♦ *Nichts Böses ahnend betrat er den Raum.*

② **ähn·lich¹** [ˈɛːnlɪç] adj, adv similar(ly) ◊ *ein ähnliches Beispiel* ♦ *Die Qualität dieses Produkts ist ähnlich schlecht wie die des anderen.* jdm ähnlich sein be like sb ◊ *Meine Nichte ist mir sehr ähnlich.* jdm ähnlich sehen look like sb ◊ *Er heißt Pfitzner oder so ähnlich.*
⊚ **ähnlich gelagert (sein)** (be) different/similar etw. sieht jdm ähnlich sth is typical of sb, sth is just like sb **oder so ähnlich** (*fam*) or something like that ◊ *Er heißt Pfitzner oder so ähnlich.*

ähn·lich² [ˈɛːnlɪç] prep +gen (*lofty*) like, similar to ◊ *Es ist geplant, eine Regelung ähnlich der britischen zu treffen.*

Ah·nung [ˈaːnʊŋ] die <–, –en> **1.** *no pl* (*fam*) (eine) Ahnung (von etw.) haben know something/anything (about sth), have an idea (about sth) ◊ *Hast du eine Ahnung, was das bedeuten soll?* Ahnung (von etw.) haben know a lot (about sth), be knowledgeable (about sth) ◊ *Er hat wirklich Ahnung auf diesem Gebiet.* keine/nicht die geringste Ahnung (von etw.) haben have no/not the slightest/faintest idea (about sth) ◊ *Ich habe nicht die geringste Ahnung von Trigonometrie.* **2.** (*feeling*) premonition, foreboding ◊ *Ich hatte so eine Ahnung, dass das passieren würde.* ♦ *Düstere Ahnungen quälten sie.*
⊚ **hast du eine Ahnung** (*fam*) you have no idea

② **Aids** [eːts, ɛɪts] das <–> *no pl* (*abbr of* Acquired Immune Deficiency Syndrome*) seldom with article* AIDS ◊ *Aids bricht oft erst nach einigen Jahren aus.*

A·ka·de·mie [akadeˈmiː] die <–, –n> academy, school, college ◊ *die Akademie der Wissenschaften* ♦ *Ich muss noch zur Akademie, ein Formular abholen.*

A·ka·de·mi·ker [akadeˈmiːkɐ] der <–s, –>, **A·ka·de·mi·ke·rin** [akadeˈmiːkərɪn] die

<–, –nen> graduate

a·ka·de·misch [akaˈdeːmɪʃ] adj, adv **1.** academic(ally) ◊ *ein akademischer Titel* ♦ *eine akademische Laufbahn* akademisch gebildet sein have a university education ◊ *akademisch gebildete Angestellte* **2.** (*style*) academic ◊ *akademischer Stil*

A·ka·de·mi·sche Aus·lands·amt [akaˌdeːmɪʃə ˈaʊslantsˌamt] das <Akademischen Auslandsamt(e)s, Akademischen Auslandsämter> international relations office ◊ *Das Akademische Auslandsamt kümmert sich um Studentenaustausch und Stipendien.*

Ak·kord [aˈkɔˀt] der <–(e)s, –e> **1.** MUS chord ◊ *einen Akkord spielen* **2.** ECON piecework, piece-rate ◊ *im Akkord arbeiten*

ak·ku·rat [akuˈraːt] adj, adv <akkurater, am akkuratesten> accurate(ly), precise(ly), exact(ly) ◊ *Die akkurate Ausführung des Auftrags ist sehr wichtig.* ♦ *Diese Beschreibung ist nicht akkurat.* ♦ *akkurat arbeiten* ⊖genau

Ak·ku·sa·tiv [ˈakuzatiːf] der <–s, –e> accusative

> Most verbs that are followed by an object require the noun or pronoun to take the accusative: *Ich schreibe* **einen Brief** (I'm writing a letter). A number of prepositions are also followed by the accusative, e.g. *durch, für, gegen*.

Akt [akt] der <–(e)s, –e> **1.** THEAT act ◊ *ein Drama in fünf Akten* ⊖Aufzug **2.** (*lofty*) (*deed*) action ◊ *ein Akt der Menschenliebe* ♦ *Das Vergehen war ein Akt der Verzweiflung.* ⊖Tat **3.** (*form*) ceremony ◊ *Die Medaille wurde in einem feierlichen Akt verliehen.* **4.** (*picture*) nude ◊ *ein Akt in Farbe/Schwarzweiß* **5.** (*slang*) effort ◊ *Der Umzug war ein echter Akt!*

Ak·te [ˈaktə] die <–, –n> file ◊ *Die Akten zu sämtlichen Vorgängen lagern im Keller.* ♦ *eine Akte anlegen*
⊚ **etw. zu den Akten legen** lay sth to rest ◊ *Dieses Thema sollte endlich zu den Akten gelegt werden.* Akten wälzen pore over files ◊ *Politiker müssen von Beruf viele Akten wälzen.*

Ak·teur [akˈtøːɐ̯] der <–s, –e>, **Ak·teu·rin** [akˈtøːrɪn] die <–, –nen> **1.** player ◊ *die wichtigsten Akteure im Entscheidungsprozess* ♦ *als Akteur in Erscheinung treten* **2.** FILM, THEAT actor Akteurin actress

Ak·tie [ˈaktsiə] die <–, –n> share, stock ◊ *Aktien ausgeben* ♦ *mit Aktien an der Börse handeln* ♦ *Die Aktien steigen/fallen.*
⊚ **wie stehen die Aktien 1.** (*fam*) how are things (going) ◊ *Wie stehen die Aktien? Kannst du bei ihr landen?* **2.** FIN how are the shares doing

Ak·ti·en·ge·sell·schaft [ˈaktsiənɡəzɛlʃaft] die <–, –en> (*abbr* AG) public limited company; (stock) corporation, joint stock company ◊ *die Siemens AG*

Ak·ti·o·när [aktsioˈnɛːɐ̯] der <–s, –e>, **Ak·ti·o·nä·rin** [aktsioˈnɛːrɪn] die <–, –nen> shareholder ◊ *der größte Aktionär dieser Bank*

② **ak·tiv** [akˈtiːf] adj, adv active(ly) ◊ *ein aktiver Vulkan* ♦ *Diese Firma ist auf dem Markt sehr aktiv.* ♦ *Ich möchte meine Freizeit aktiv gestalten.* ⊖passiv

ak·tu·a·li·sie·ren [aktualiˈziːrən] <aktualisiert,

aktualisierte, hat aktualisiert> [tr v] update ◊ *eine Webpage aktualisieren* ✦ *Daten/eine Datei aktualisieren* ✦ *Informationen aktualisieren*

② **ak·tu·ell** [aktu|'εl] [adj, adv] current(ly), topical(ly) ◊ *Zur Zeit sind Miniröcke wieder aktuell.* ✦ *eine aktuelle Meldung* ✦ *die aktuell gültigen Steuergesetze* die aktuelle Mode the latest fashion

a·kus·tisch [a'kʊstɪʃ] [adj, adv] *no comp/superl* acoustic(ally) ◊ *ein akustisches Signal* ✦ *Entschuldigung, ich habe Sie akustisch nicht verstanden.* ✦ *akustisch wahrnehmbar*

a·kut [a'ku:t] [adj, adv] <akuter, am akutesten> *seldom comp/superl* **1.** MED acute(ly) ◊ *Das ist eine akute Bronchitis.* ✦ *eine akut verlaufende Infektion* **2.** *(lofty) (problem, danger etc.)* immediate(ly), acute(ly), urgent(ly), pressing(ly) ◊ *in akuter Lebensgefahr schweben* ✦ *Die Geldnot ist akut.* ✦ *4000 Arbeitsplätze sind akut gefährdet.*

AKW [a:ka:'ve:] das *(abbr of Atomkraftwerk)* nuclear power station

ak·zep·tie·ren [aktsɛp'tiːran] <akzeptiert, akzeptierte, hat akzeptiert> [tr v] accept ◊ *Wir akzeptieren alle gängigen Kreditkarten.* ✦ *Sie akzeptiert ihn mit all seinen Schwächen.*

② **A·larm** [a'la'm] der <- (e)s, –e> **1.** alarm ◊ *Umweltschützer schlagen Alarm.* ✦ *Die Diebstahlsicherung löste am Ausgang Alarm aus.* ✦ *falscher Alarm* **2.** alert ◊ *Wegen des Fischsterbens herrscht Alarm.*

al·bern ['albɐn] [adj] silly ◊ *alberne Witze machen* ✦ *Musst du so albern sein?*

Alb·traum ['alptraom] der <–(e)s, Albträume> nightmare ◊ *Er hatte einen Albtraum.* ✦ *Bungeejumping ist ein Albtraum für mich.*

② **Al·ko·hol** ['alkoho:l] der <–s, tech –e> *most sing* alcohol ◊ *Er trinkt keinen Alkohol.* ✦ *Desinfizieren Sie die Hautstelle mit Alkohol.*

all [al] [indef pron] all ◊ *Wir werden ihn mit all unseren Kräften unterstützen.* ✦ *All die Menschen machen mir Angst.*

all-·... [al] [prefix] taking place at set intervals in time alljährlich every year alltäglich every day allabendlich every evening

All [al] das <–s> *no pl* space ◊ *durch das All fliegen* ⊖Weltraum

al·le¹ ['ala] [adj] not before ns *(fam)* all gone ◊ *Die Milch ist schon wieder alle!* etw. alle machen finish off ◊ *Du kannst den Pudding ruhig alle machen.*

⊚ **jdn alle machen** do sb in

al·le² ['ala] [det] all ◊ *Alle Kinder bitte aufstehen!*

al·le³ ['ala] [indef pron] everyone, everybody ◊ *Man kann es nie allen recht machen.* ✦ *Alle standen um mich herum.* ⊖niemand

⊚ **allen voran** led by

al·le·dem [ala'de:m] [pron] +prep all this/that ◊ *Ich habe von alledem nichts gewusst.* ✦ *Trotz alledem blickt er zuversichtlich in die Zukunft.*

Al·lee [a'le:] die <–, –n> avenue ◊ *eine von Eichen gesäumte Alle*

② **al·lein**¹ [a'laen] [adj] not before ns **1.** alone ◊ *Bist du allein zu Hause?* **2.** lonely ◊ *Ich fühle mich so allein.* ⊖einsam [adv] alone ◊ *Ich lebe allein.* ✦ *Bist du allein gekommen?; (without help)* on your own ◊ *Die Kleine kann sich schon allein anziehen.*

⊚ **allein erziehend** single, lone(-)parent ◊ *allein erziehende Mütter/Väter* allein stehend single ◊

Sind Sie verheiratet, geschieden oder allein stehend? ✦ *ein allein stehender älterer Herr*

al·lein² [a'laen] [part] alone ◊ *Du allein bist für diese Misere verantwortlich!* ✦ *Schon allein vom Geruch wird mir schlecht.*

Al·lein·er·zie·hen·de, al·lein Er·zie·hen·de [a'laen|e͵tsi:anda] der/die <–n, die Alleinerziehenden> *but: ein Alleinerziehender/eine Alleinerziehende* single parent ◊ *Seit der Scheidung ist sie Alleinerziehende.* box@ Substantivierung

al·len·falls ['alanfals] [adv] **1.** at most ◊ *Sie müssen nicht lange warten, allenfalls eine halbe Stunde.* **2.** if necessary, if need be ◊ *Das könnte man allenfalls versuchen.*

② **al·ler·...** ['ale] [prefix] *mostly spoken; reinforces a superlative* very, by far ◊ *in allerletzter Minute* ✦ *meine allerbeste Freundin* ✦ *meine allerbequemsten Schuhe*

② **al·ler·dings** ['ale'dɪŋs] [adv] **1.** indeed, certainly ◊ *„Kennst du ihn?" — „Allerdings!"* ✦ *„Ich habe meine Uhr verloren." — „Das ist allerdings schade."* **2.** though ◊ *Ich muss allerdings sagen, dass ich nicht viel Zeit habe.* ⊖aber

al·ler·ers·te ['ale'e:ɐsta] [adj] no comp/superl, only before ns <ein allererster ...>, eine allererste ..., ein allererstes ...> very first ◊ *Unser Kleiner hat heute seine allerersten Schritte gemacht.*

all·er·gisch [a'lɛ'gɪʃ] [adj] seldom comp/superl **1.** MED allergic ◊ *eine allergische Reaktion auf Katzenhaare* ✦ *Er ist gegen Hausstaub allergisch.* **2.** *(fig)* gegen etw./jdn allergisch sein get steamed up about sth/sb ◊ *Ich bin allergisch gegen schlechte Tischmanieren.* [adv] **1.** allergisch reagieren react allergically ◊ *auf Katzenhaare allergisch reagieren* **2.** *(fig)* allergisch reagieren react in a hostile manner ◊ *Sie reagierte allergisch auf seine Vorwürfe.*

al·ler·hand¹ ['ale'hant] [det] invariable *(fam)* all kinds of, all sorts of ◊ *allerhand Neues*

al·ler·hand² ['ale'hant] [indef pron] invariable *(fam)* all kinds of things, all sorts of things ◊ *Hier gibt es allerhand zu tun.*

⊚ **das ist doch/ja/wirklich allerhand** that's the absolute limit ◊ *Hat er das wirklich gesagt? Das ist ja allerhand!*

Al·ler·hei·li·gen ['ale'haelɪgn̩] seldom with definite article 'das' All Saints' Day ◊ *An Allerheiligen gehen wir auf den Friedhof.*

Allerheiligen is a Catholic bank holiday, celebrated on the first of November to commemorate all saints, martyrs, and the dead in general. The relatives decorate the graves of their dead with flowers and a burning candle, the *Seelenlicht* (light of the soul) — the symbol of eternal light. On the *Gräberumgang* (a procession from grave to grave) the priest blesses the graves.

al·ler·lei¹ ['ale'lae] [det] invariable all kinds of, all sorts of ◊ *Er hatte allerlei Ideen.*

al·ler·lei² ['ale'lae] [pron] invariable all kinds of things, all sorts of things ◊ *Wir hatten allerlei zu besprechen.*

Al·ler·see·len ['ale'ze:lan] seldom with definite article 'das' All Souls' Day ◊ *An Allerseelen besuchte er das Grab seiner Großmutter.* box@

Fest
al·les ['aləs] [indef pron] everything ◊ *Man kann nicht alles haben.* ♦ *Alles in Ordnung?*
⊙ **alles in allem** all in all ◊ *Alles in allem bin ich zufrieden mit deiner Arbeit.* **vor allem** above all, in particular ◊ *Man warf ihm vor allem seine Ungeduld vor.*
② **all·ge·mein** [algə'maen, '– – –] [adj, adv] *when used as an adj, mostly before ns* general(ly) ◊ *die allgemeine Öffentlichkeit* ♦ *allgemein bekannt/ gültig/anerkannt* ⊖generell, grundsätzlich
⊙ **im Allgemeinen** in general, generally ◊ *Im Allgemeinen interessiere ich mich nicht für Politik.*
All·ge·mein·heit [algə'maenhaet] die <-, –en> **1.** *no pl* general public ◊ *etw. für die Allgemeinheit tun* **2.** *no pl* generality ◊ *Der Mangel dieser Definition ist ihre zu große Allgemeinheit.* **3.** *only pl* generalities ◊ *In seiner Rede ging er über Allgemeinheiten nicht hinaus.*
② **all·mäh·lich¹** [al'mɛːlɪç] [adj, adv] *no comp/superl; when used as an adj, only before ns* gradual(ly) ◊ *ein allmählicher Ausstieg aus der Kernenergie* ♦ *Allmählich kam er wieder zu sich.* ⊖langsam
all·mäh·lich² [al'mɛːlɪç] [part] *translation varies (indicating a desire for change)* Es wird allmählich Zeit, nach Hause zu gehen. It is about time to go home. Das ist allmählich nicht mehr lustig. This is not funny any more.
② **All·tag** ['alta:k] der <-s, –e> *most sing* **1.** daily routine ◊ *Sie versuchten, dem grauen Alltag zu entfliehen.* ♦ *der berufliche Alltag* **2.** weekday ◊ *Morgen ist wieder ein ganz normaler Alltag.* ⊖Werktag ⊖Feiertag
all·täg·lich [al'tɛːklɪç] [adj] **1.** daily ◊ *Zähneputzen als alltägliche Routine* **2.** commonplace ◊ *Konflikte sind inzwischen alltäglich geworden.* **3.** mundane ◊ *Die Musik dieser Gruppe klingt ganz alltäglich.*
all·zu ['altsu:] [adv] all too ◊ *Er geht allzu großzügig mit Geld um.*
Al·pen ['alpm] die <-> *only pl (always* die Alpen*)* the Alps ◊ *ein Urlaub in den Alpen* ♦ *die Schweizer Alpen*
② **Al·pha·bet** [alfa'beːt] das <-(e)s, –e> alphabet ◊ *das hebräische Alphabet* ♦ *Der Index ist nach dem Alphabet geordnet.* ⊖Abc
al·pin [al'piːn] [adj] *only before ns* **1.** Alpine ◊ *die alpine Region* **2.** alpine ◊ *alpine Pflanzen* ♦ *alpiner Skisport*
② **als** [als] [conjunc] **1.** *(temporal)* when ◊ *Als wir anfingen zu essen, klingelte das Telefon.* ♦ *früher, als er noch einen Bart trug* **2.** *after comp (comparative)* than ◊ *Heute ist es kälter als gestern.* **3.** *introducing a subjunctive* as if ◊ *Sie sieht aus, als wäre sie krank.* ♦ *Als ob ich nicht schon genug Sorgen hätte!* **4.** *(explanatory)* as ◊ *Ich als der Ältere gebe dir den guten Rat, ...* **5.** *als dass* for me/you/them to ◊ *Das ist viel zu kompliziert, als dass ich es dir erklären könnte.* **6.** anders als unlike ◊ *Anders als du trinke ich keinen Alkohol.* **7.** nichts als nothing but ◊ *Er hat nichts als Fußball im Kopf.* ⊖nur
② **al·so¹** ['alzo:] [adv] **1.** *(expressing a consequence)* so, therefore ◊ *Sie ist 18, also kann sie wählen.* ⊖demnach, demzufolge **2.** *(explanatory)* that is ◊ *Alle meine Geschwister, also Anne, Lukas und Kerstin, kamen.*

al·so² ['alzo:] [part] well ◊ *Also, ich finde das nicht richtig!* ♦ *Also, was ist jetzt?*
⊙ **na also** there you are, you see
② **alt** [alt] [adj] <älter, am ältesten> old ◊ *Unser Haus ist zwei Jahre alt.* ♦ *Sie ist neun Jahre älter als er.* ♦ *eine alte Freundschaft* ♦ *So ein alter Gauner!*
⊙ **alt aussehen** *(fam)* look silly ◊ *Wenn das rauskommt, sehen wir alt aus.* **beim Alten bleiben** remain as it was ◊ *Trotz der Änderungsvorschläge blieb alles beim Alten.* **jdn alt machen** make sb look old ◊ *Diese Brille macht dich alt.*
Alt·bau ['altbao] der <-(e)s, –ten> old building ◊ *einen Altbau renovieren*
Al·te ['altə] der/die <-n, die Alten> *but: ein Alter/ eine Alte* **1.** *most pl* elderly (man/woman) ◊ *Hilfen für Alte und Behinderte* ⊖Senior **2.** *(fam, esp pej)* old man ◊ *He Alter, geh mir aus dem Weg!* ♦ *Ich habe Streit mit meinem Alten.; old woman* ◊ *He Alte, bring mir ein Bier!; (for a mother)* old girl ◊ *Meine Alte nervt ohne Ende!; (for superiors)* boss ◊ *Der Alte macht wieder mal Stress im Büro.* box@ Substantivierung
⊙ **wie ein Alter/eine Alte** like a grown-up, like a pro ◊ *Der Kleine spielt Poker wie ein Alter.*
② **Al·ten·heim** ['altnhaem] das <-(e)s, –e> old people's home ⊖Altersheim
äl·ter ['ɛltə] *comp of* alt [adj] *no comp/superl* **1.** getting on a bit ◊ *Mein Computer ist schon älter.* **2.** *(euph) (people)* elderly ◊ *ein bunter Nachmittag für ältere Bürger* die ältere Generation the older generation
② **Al·ter** ['altə] das <-s, –> **1.** old age ◊ *Sie war bis ins hohe Alter sehr rege.* ♦ *für das Alter vorsorgen* **2.** age ◊ *Er starb im Alter von 35 Jahren.* ♦ *Kinder im schulfähigen Alter* ♦ *Mit zunehmendem Alter verliert Whiskey an Alkoholgehalt.*
Äl·te·re ['ɛltərə] der/die <-n, die Älteren> *but: ein Älterer/eine Ältere* older person ◊ *Du als Ältere solltest vernünftig sein und nachgeben.; (with names)* Elder ◊ *Plinius der Ältere* box@ Substantivierung
al·tern ['alten] [intr v] +sein *(people, materials)* age ◊ *Carmen ist merklich gealtert, seit ich sie zuletzt gesehen habe.* ♦ *Plastik altert und bricht.; (wine, whisky)* mature
② **al·ter·na·tiv** [altena'tiːf] [adj, adv] alternative(ly) ◊ *alternative Medizin* ♦ *Alternativ können Sie dieses Formular verwenden.* ♦ *eine alternativ geprägte Veranstaltung*
Al·ter·na·ti·ve¹ [altena'tiːvə] die <-, die Alternativen> alternative ◊ *Er wurde vor die Alternative gestellt, mitzumachen oder zu gehen.* ♦ *Zu diesem Verfahren gibt es keine Alternative.*
Al·ter·na·ti·ve² [altena'tiːvə] der/die <-n, –n> *but: ein Alternativer/eine Alternative* person with alternative views box@ Substantivierung
② **Al·ters·heim** ['alteshaem] das <-(e)s, –e> old people's home ◊ *jdn in einem Altersheim unterbringen* ⊖Altenheim
alt·mo·disch ['altmo:dɪʃ] [adj] old-fashioned, outmoded ◊ *altmodische Kleider* ♦ *Deine Ansichten sind sehr altmodisch.*
Alt·pa·pier ['alt,papiːɐ] das <-s> *no pl* waste paper ◊ *Altpapier als Rohstoff zur Papierherstellung*
Alt·stadt ['altʃtat] die <-, Altstädte> old town, old

quarter ◊ *die historische Altstadt von Heidelberg*
Alt-Tas·te ['ʔalttastə] die <-, –n> Alt key ◊ *die Alt-Taste drücken*
Alt·wei·ber [alt'vaebə] *seldom with definite article 'das' last Thursday before Ash Wednesday when women call the tune* ◊ *an Altweiber ausgehen*
A·lu·... ['aːluː] (prefix) *(abbr of Aluminium)* aluminium ◊ *das Alurad* ♦ *in Alufolie einwickeln*
Alu·mi·ni·um [alu'miːnjʊm] das <–s> *no pl (abbr Al)* aluminium ◊ *eine Milchkanne aus Aluminium*
⑦ **am** [am] (contract) *an + dem* **1.** on (the), at the ◊ *am 15. Mai* ♦ *Düsseldorf am Rhein* ♦ *Wir treffen uns am Kino.* ♦ *am Anfang → an* **2.** *in the formation of the superlative* am schnellsten/schönsten/besten *the* quickest/most beautiful/best ◊ *Meine Mutter kocht am besten.* My mother is the best cook. **3.** *in certain idioms, not to be split: look up the relevant idiom* ◊ *am Ende sein*
am·bu·lant [ambu'lant] (adj) *only before ns* outpatient ◊ *eine ambulante Operation* ⊜stationär (adv) *as an outpatient* ◊ *ambulant behandelt/versorgt werden* ⊜stationär
A·mei·se ['aːmaezə] die <-, –n> ant
A·men ['aːmɛn, 'aːmən] das <–s, –> *most sing* amen ◊ *Der Pfarrer sprach das Amen.*
⊛ so sicher wie das Amen in der Kirche as sure as eggs are eggs
A·me·ri·ka [a'meːrikaː] das <–s> *article only in combination with attribute, no pl* America ◊ *die Indianer Amerikas* ♦ *der Präsident von Amerika* box@ Land
A·me·ri·ka·ner [ameriˈkaːnɐ] der <–s, –>,
A·me·ri·ka·ne·rin [ameriˈkaːnərɪn] die <-, –nen> American → Deutsche
a·me·ri·ka·nisch [ameriˈkaːnɪʃ] (adj) *mostly before ns* American → deutsch
A·me·ri·ka·nisch [ameriˈkaːnɪʃ] das <–(s)> *no pl* American English → Deutsch
⑦ **Am·mann** ['aman] der <–s, Ammänner>,
Am·män·nin ['amɛnɪn] die <-, –nen> *(Swiss)* mayor
⑦ **Am·pel** ['ampl] die <-, –n> traffic light ◊ *Die Ampel sprang auf Grün.* ♦ *Sie fuhr bei Rot über die Ampel.*
⑦ **Amt** [amt] das <–(e)s, Ämter> **1.** *(post)* office ◊ *politische Ämter* ♦ *Wird sie weiterhin im Amt bleiben?* ♦ *sein Amt niederlegen* **2.** *(part of the name of an authority)* Department, Office ◊ *Sie arbeitet beim Amt für Umweltschutz.* **3.** task, duty ◊ *Sie hatte das wichtige Amt, die Gäste zu begrüßen.* **4.** *the building in which an authority or government department is housed* ◊ *Wir treffen uns um 12 beim Amt.* ♦ *Ich muss heute aufs Amt.*
amt·lich ['amtlɪç] (adj, adv) official(ly), government ◊ *Die amtliche Nachrichtenagentur Anatolia meldete, dass ...* ♦ *Nun ist es amtlich, dass er ihr Nachfolger wird.* ♦ *ein amtlich anerkannter Experte* ⊜offiziell
Amts·arzt ['amts|aˈʔst] der <–es, Amtsärzte>,
Amts·ärz·tin ['amts|ɛˈʔstɪn] die <-, –nen> medical officer ◊ *eine Untersuchung durch einen Amtsarzt* ♦ *Sie ist als Amtsärztin tätig.*
Amts·deutsch ['amtsdɔøtʃ] das <–(s)> *no pl* **1.** *(pej)* officialese **2.** jargon used by the German authorities
Amts·ge·richt ['amtsgərɪçt] das <–(e)s, –e> *most*

sing **1.** local court, district court ◊ *Das Amtsgericht verurteilte ihn zu einer Geldstrafe.* **2.** local court building, district court building ◊ *Morgen muss er aufs Amtsgericht.*
Amts·rich·ter ['amtsrɪçtɐ] der <–s, –>,
Amts·rich·te·rin ['amtsrɪçtərɪn] die <-, –nen> local court judge, district court judge ◊ *die zuständige Amtsrichterin* ♦ *Er ist als Amtsrichter in Hamburg tätig.*
Amts·stun·den ['amtsʃtʊndn] die <-> *only pl (Austr)* public opening hours ◊ *während/außerhalb der Amtsstunden*
a·mü·sant [amy'zant] (adj, adv) <amüsanter, am amüsantesten> amusing(ly), entertaining(ly) ◊ *eine amüsante Anekdote* ♦ *Der Vorfall war recht amüsant.* ♦ *Das Buch ist amüsant zu lesen.* ⊜lustig
⑦ **a·mü·sie·ren** [amy'ziːrən] <amüsiert, amüsierte, hat amüsiert> (ref v) **1.** sich amüsieren enjoy yourself ◊ *Ich habe mich köstlich amüsiert.* **2.** sich über jdn/etw. amüsieren find sb/sth funny, laugh at sb/sth ◊ *Sie amüsierten sich über seine Aussprache.* (tr v) amuse ◊ *Dieser Gedanke amüsierte mich sehr.*
⑦ **an¹** [an] (adv) **1.** *(fam)* an sein be on ◊ *Ist der Computer noch an?* ♦ *Soll die Heizung über Nacht an sein?* ⊜aus **2.** arriving at ◊ *Regensburg ab: 7.32 Uhr. München an: 8.05 Uhr.* ⊜ab **3.** von ... an from ... onwards ◊ *Die neue Regelung gilt vom nächsten Monat an.* ♦ *Vom zehnten Stock an aufwärts gab es nur noch eine Treppe.* ⊜ab **4.** *(fam)* an die ... around ..., about ... ◊ *Es werden an die tausend Besucher erwartet.* ♦ *In die Wanne passen an die 150 Liter.* ⊜ungefähr, etwa ⊜genau
⑦ **an²** [an] (prep) **1.** *with acc when expressing motion towards a place, with dat when there is no or undirected motion on* ◊ *Das Bild hing an der Wand.* ♦ *Ich hängte den Kalender an die Wand.* ♦ *Regensburg liegt an der Donau.; to* ◊ *eine Verletzung an der Zehe* ♦ *Schicken Sie den Brief an folgende Adresse.; at* ◊ *Er studiert Informatik an der Universität München.* Er lehnte sein Fahrrad an den Zaun. He leaned his bike against the fence. Gewalt an Schulen violence in schools bis an ... up to ... ◊ *Wir fuhren bis an die Grenze, dann kehrten wir um.* ♦ *Das Wasser ging mir bis an die Hüfte.* an jdm/etw. vorbei past sb/sth ◊ *Führt der Weg am Bahnhof vorbei?* ♦ *Er ist an mir vorbeigelaufen, ohne mich zu erkennen.* **2.** *in response to the question 'when?'* (+dat) on ◊ *am 1. April* ♦ *am Montag* ♦ *an einem sonnigen Herbsttag* an Weihnachten/Pfingsten at Christmas/Whitsun **3.** (+dat) of ◊ *Sie ist an Krebs erkrankt.* ♦ *An was starb er?; (through, by way of)* by ◊ *Sie hat mich an der Stimme erkannt.* an etw. leiden suffer from sth **4.** (+dat) *(with figures, amounts)* of ◊ *ein Defizit an Informationen/an Magnesium; in* ◊ *Er ist noch jung an Jahren.* ♦ *Wir waren arm an der Zahl.; in the way of* ◊ *Was haben Sie an Tapeten vorrätig?* ♦ *Was haben wir denn noch an Geld?* **5.** (+dat) about ◊ *Was ist das Wichtigste an einem Wörterbuch?* ♦ *Das gefällt mir so an dir!* **6.** (+dat) an etw. bauen/lesen/nähen/schreiben build/read/sew/write sth ◊ *Er malt gerade an einem Bild für seine Mutter.* ♦ *Sie strickt an einem Pullover.* an etw. arbeiten

work on sth **7.** *in the continuous tense (fam)* am Arbeiten/Ausruhen/Lesen sein be working/resting/reading ◊ *Sie war schon am Aufräumen, als er endlich kam.* ⊖beim **8.** *+superl* am ältesten/besten/schönsten the oldest/best/most beautiful ◊ *am ältesten sein ♦ am besten singen ♦ am schönsten aussehen* **9.** *used to link two identical nouns* +dat ... an ...... to ... ◊ *Tür an Tür mit jdm wohnen ♦ Sie gingen Kopf an Kopf durchs Ziel.*

◉ **an (und für) sich** *(fam)* fundamentally, basically ◊ *Das ist an sich in Ordnung. ♦ Die Sache ist an und für sich sehr einfach.*

An·al·pha·bet [anˈalfaˈbeːt, ˈ– – – –] der <–en, –en>, **An·al·pha·be·tin** [anˈalfaˈbeːtɪn, ˈ– – – – –] die <–, –nen> illiterate person

⑦ **a·na·ly·sie·ren** [analyˈziːrən] <analysiert, analysierte, hat analysiert> tr v analyze ◊ *der Fall muss eingehend analysiert werden ♦ Bodenproben im Labor analysieren*

A·na·nas [ˈananas] die <–, – *or* –se> pineapple ◊ *drei Scheiben Ananas aus der Dose*

an|bah·nen [ˈanbaːnən] <bahnt an, bahnte an, hat angebahnt> tr v initiate, get on the way ◊ *Geschäfte/ein Projekt anbahnen* ref v sich anbahnen be developing, start to develop ◊ *Eine Katastrophe bahnte sich an. ♦ Zwischen den beiden scheint sich was anzubahnen!*

an|bau·en [ˈanbaʊən] <baut an, baute an, hat angebaut> tr v **1.** etw. (an etw. acc) anbauen build sth (on to sth) ◊ *Er möchte einen Balkon an die Südseite anbauen.* **2.** AGR grow, cultivate ◊ *Tomaten/Baumwolle/Tabak anbauen* intr v build an extension

an|be·hal·ten [ˈanbəhaltn̩] <behält an, behielt an, hat anbehalten> tr v keep on ◊ *Sie hat ihren Mantel anbehalten.*

an·bei [anˈbaɛ, ˈ– –] adv *(form)* enclosed, attached ◊ *Anbei die angeforderten Unterlagen.*

⑦ **an|bie·ten** [ˈanbiːtn̩] <bietet an, bot an, hat angeboten> tr v **1.** offer ◊ *Er bot ihr an, sie bis nach Bonn mitzunehmen. ♦ Sie bot ihm ihre Hilfe an. ♦ etw. zum Verkauf anbieten* **2.** suggest, propose ◊ *Ich bot ihm an, diese Arbeit zu übernehmen. ♦ Sie hat mir das Du angeboten.* ref v **1.** sich anbieten, etw. zu tun offer to do sth ◊ *Er bot sich an, das Paket zur Post zu bringen.* sich als etw. anbieten offer yourself as sth ◊ *Der Mann bot sich als Zeuge an.* **2.** etw. bietet sich an sth suggests itself, sth presents itself ◊ *Diese Lösung bietet sich hier geradezu an. ♦ Dieses Schloss bietet sich als Ziel für den Betriebsausflug an.*

an|bin·den [ˈanbɪndn̩] <bindet an, band an, hat angebunden> tr v **1.** jdn/etw. (an etw. acc) anbinden tie sb/sth (to sth) ◊ *Er band den Hund am Baum an.; (a boat)* moor ◊ *Sie hat das Boot am Steg angebunden.* **2.** *(fig)* etw. an etw. acc anbinden connect sth to sth ◊ *die südlichen Stadtteile ans Verkehrsnetz anbinden ♦ Der Großrechner ist an das Internet angebunden.*

◉ **kurz angebunden sein** be abrupt ◊ *Er war am Telefon sehr kurz angebunden.* **angebunden sein** be tied down ◊ *Mit einem Haustier ist man sehr angebunden.*

An·blick [ˈanblɪk] der <–(e)s, –e> sight ◊ *Ein gut*

gebauter Körper ist ein schöner Anblick. ♦ *Den Fußgängern bot sich ein ungewohnter Anblick. ♦ Bei seinem Anblick musste sie weinen.* beim bloßen Anblick ... gen, beim bloßen Anblick von etw. just looking at ..., the sheer sight of ... ◊ *Beim bloßen Anblick einer Spinne/von Spinnen gerate ich schon in Panik.*

an|bre·chen [ˈanbrɛçn̩] <bricht an, brach an, hat/ist angebrochen> tr v +haben **1.** crack ◊ *Er hat sich den Arm angebrochen.* **2.** open ◊ *eine neue Packung Cornflakes anbrechen* intr v +sein *(lofty)* begin, dawn ◊ *Für die Partei sind harte/schwere Zeiten angebrochen. ♦ Eine neue Ära ist angebrochen.* ⊖beginnen

an|bren·nen [ˈanbrɛnən] <brennt an, brannte an, ist angebrannt> intr v burn, get burned ◊ *Das Essen ist angebrannt. ♦ Lass das Gemüse nicht anbrennen!*

◉ **nichts anbrennen lassen** *(fam)* not miss a trick, not miss out on anything ◊ *Dieser Playboy lässt nichts anbrennen! ♦ Ein guter Journalist darf nichts anbrennen lassen.*

an|brin·gen [ˈanbrɪŋən] <bringt an, brachte an, hat angebracht> tr v **1.** fix ◊ *An der Tür wurde ein neues Namensschild angebracht.; (at a high level also)* put up ◊ *Er brachte ein Bild an der Wand an.; (by glueing)* stick ◊ *Sie brachte einen Aufkleber am Auto an.* **2.** display ◊ *Der Ausweis muss gut sichtbar im Auto angebracht sein.* **3.** make, voice ◊ *Verbesserungsvorschläge anbringen ♦ Konntest du deine Bitte anbringen?* **4.** *(corrections, improvements)* add ◊ *Sie brachte am Text wichtige Änderungen an.* **5.** sell, flog ◊ *Er konnte seine Waren nicht anbringen.* **6.** *(knowledge, expertise)* bring into, apply ◊ *Er konnte sein Wissen in der Prüfung gar nicht anbringen.* **7.** *(pej)* drag along ◊ *Er hat schon wieder eine neue Freundin angebracht. ♦ Mein Bruder brachte ein Meerschweinchen an.*

an·däch·tig [ˈandɛçtɪç] adj, adv reverent(ly), rapt(ly) ◊ *andächtige Stille ♦ Die Kinder waren ganz andächtig. ♦ andächtige lauschende Zuhörer; (in devotion)* devout(ly)

an|dau·ern [ˈandaʊɐn] <dauert an, dauerte an, hat angedauert> intr v continue, go on ◊ *Die Kämpfe dauern an. ♦ Wie lange wird dieser Zustand noch andauern?*

an·dau·ernd [ˈandaʊɐnt] pres p of andauern adj, adv no comp/superl; when used as an adj, only before ns constant(ly), continual(ly) ◊ *Seine andauernden Fragen nerven mich. ♦ Unterbrich mich nicht andauernd!* ⊖ständig

◉ **das passiert jdm andauernd** this/that happens to sb all the time ◊ *Ich habe schon wieder den Zug verpasst — das passiert mir andauernd!*

An·den·ken [ˈandɛŋkn̩] das <–s, –> **1.** memory, remembrance ◊ *dem Toten ein ehrendes Andenken bewahren* **2.** memento ◊ *Jeder erhielt als Andenken an den Wettbewerb eine Urkunde. ♦ Ich schenkte ihr zum Andenken ein Bild.* **3.** souvenir ◊ *ein Andenken aus Rom* ⊖Souvenir

an·de·re¹ [ˈandərə] adj *only before ns* <ein anderer ..., eine andere ..., ein anderes ...> other ◊ *Mit anderen Worten: ... ♦ die andere Hälfte ♦ Waren auf dem Fest noch andere Kinder?; (before sing n)* different ◊ *Er ging in eine andere Richtung*

davon. ♦ *Ich bin anderer Meinung.* die anderen ... the rest of ... ◊ *Wo sind die anderen Schüler?*

② **an·de·re²** ['andərə] indef pron **1.** ein anderer/eine andere/ein anderes another one ◊ *Das ist meine Tasse — nimm eine andere!* der/die/das andere the other one ◊ *Dieser Pulli ist zu klein — gib mir den anderen!* ♦ *Er trat von einem Fuß auf den anderen.* **2.** else ◊ *Alles andere war richtig.* ♦ *Fragen Sie doch jemand anderen.* ♦ *Ich war allein, kein anderer war gekommen.* ♦ *Kannst du nichts anderes tun?* etwas anderes something different ◊ *Ich bringe dir etwas anderes.* ein ganz anderer/eine ganz andere a completely different person ◊ *Sie ist eine ganz andere geworden.* ein ganz anderes a completely different one ◊ *Das Thema ist doch ein ganz anderes.* **3.** *pl* others ◊ *Warum kannst du das nicht? Andere können es doch auch!* ♦ *Ich esse nur diese Sorte Kekse, keine anderen.* die anderen the others, the rest ◊ *Die anderen kommen nach.*

☻ **alles andere als** anything but ◊ *Das ist alles andere als angenehm.* ♦ *Er ist alles andere als ein Held.*

an·de·ren·falls ['andərənfals] → andernfalls

an·de·rer·seits ['andərəzaɪ̯ts] adv however ◊ *Er war recht müde, andererseits wollte er aber noch ausgehen.*

☻ **einerseits ..., andererseits ...** on the one hand ..., on the other hand ... ⊖auf der einen Seite ..., auf der anderen Seite ...

an·der·mal ['andɐmaːl] *(always* ein andermal*)* another time ◊ *Schlafen kannst du ein andermal!* ♦ *Heute hab ich keine Zeit, ein andermal komme ich gerne mit.*

② **än·dern** ['ɛndɐn] tr v +haben change ◊ *die Spielregeln ändern* ♦ *Der Wind hat die Richtung geändert.* ♦ *Ich habe meine Meinung geändert.;* *(legislation)* amend sich ändern change ◊ *Meine Meinung dazu wird sich nicht ändern.* ♦ *Die Zeiten haben sich geändert.;* *(legislation)* be amended

an·dern·falls ['andɐnfals] adv otherwise ◊ *Kommen Sie rechtzeitig, andernfalls sind die Karten vielleicht schon verkauft.* ⊖sonst

② **an·ders** ['andɐs] adj, adv *when used as an adj, not before ns* **1.** different(ly) ◊ *Früher war alles anders.* ♦ *Alles kam ganz anders.* ♦ *anders denkende Menschen* nicht anders als no different than ◊ *Das Wetter ist heute nicht anders als gestern.* anders sein als differ from ◊ *Er ist anders als andere Männer.* anders geartet of a different nature ◊ *Dieser Virus ist anders geartet.* **2.** strange ◊ *Er benimmt sich heute so anders.* ♦ *Mir wird ganz anders, wenn ich an die Prüfung denke.* ⊖seltsam **3.** jemand/niemand/wer etc. anders somebody/nobody/who etc. else ◊ *Wollen wir irgendwo anders hingehen?* ♦ *Kann das jemand anders tun?*

☻ **anders gelagert (sein)** (be) different/similar **so und nicht anders** exactly like this/that, in this and no other way ◊ *Du machst das jetzt so und nicht anders!* ♦ *Warum haben Sie so und nicht anders reagiert?* **anders als** in contrast to, unlike ◊ *Anders als er, liebe ich die Oper über alles.*

an·ders·he·rum ['andɐsherʊm] adv the other way round ◊ *Er drehte den Stuhl andersherum.* ♦ *Ich versuchte es noch einmal andersherum.*

an·ders·rum ['andɐsrʊm] *(fam)* → andersherum

an·ders·wo ['andɛsvoː] adv *(fam)* elsewhere, somewhere else ◊ *anderswo hinziehen* ♦ *Sie arbeitet jetzt anderswo.*

an·dert·halb [andɛt'halp, '– – –] nmrl one and a half ◊ *in den letzten anderthalb Jahren* ♦ *eine anderthalb Meter breite Mauer* ⊖eineinhalb

Än·de·rung ['ɛndərʊŋ] die <–, –en> +gen change, alteration, modification ◊ *Er beschloss eine Änderung des Plans.* ♦ *Bitte nehmen Sie die nötigen Änderungen am Programm vor.;* *(to/of a law)* amendment

an·der·wei·tig ['andɐvaɪ̯tɪç] adj *only before ns* other ◊ *anderweitige Verpflichtungen haben* adv otherwise, in another way ◊ *anderweitig genutzte Räume*

an|deu·ten ['andɔɪ̯tn̩] <deutet an, deutete an, hat angedeutet> tr v **1.** intimate, hint at ◊ *Er deutete an, dass er ausziehen wolle.* **2.** outline, sketch ◊ *Der Maler hat die Schatten nur angedeutet.* ref v sich andeuten become visible/noticeable ◊ *Der Erfolg hatte sich bereits in den letzten Spielen angedeutet.*

An·drang ['andraŋ] der <–(e)s> *no pl* crowd, rush ◊ *Bei der Ausstellung war der Andrang groß.*

and·re ['andrə] → andere¹, andere²

an|dro·hen ['androːən] <droht an, drohte an, hat angedroht> tr v threaten ◊ *Man hatte angedroht, sie zu töten.* (jdm) etw. androhen threaten (sb) with sth ◊ *Seine Mutter drohte ihm Schläge an.*

an|eig·nen ['anʔaɪ̯gnən] <eignet sich an, eignete sich an, hat sich angeeignet> ref v *(always* sich dat*)* etw. aneignen) **1.** (mis)appropriate sth ◊ *Sie hatten sich das Land unrechtmäßig angeeignet.* **2.** *(knowledge, skills etc.)* learn sth, acquire sth ◊ *Er hat sich das nötige Wissen selbstständig angeeignet.*

an·ei·nan·der [anʔaɪ̯'nandɐ] adv to each other ◊ *Wir gewöhnten uns aneinander.* ♦ *nah aneinander* sich aneinander drängen crowd together, huddle together ◊ *Menschen drängten sich aneinander.* sich aneinander reihen follow one upon another

☻ **aneinander geraten** get into an argument aneinander vorbei... past each other ◊ *Sie gingen aneinander vorbei.* ♦ *aneinander vorbeireden*

an·er·kannt ['anʔɛkant] *past p of* anerkennen adj <anerkannter, am anerkanntesten> **1.** *seldom comp/ superl* respected, recognized ◊ *Diese Firma ist anerkannt für ihre Qualitätsprodukte.* **2.** *no comp/ superl* staatlich anerkannt accredited, state/government approved ◊ *eine staatlich anerkannte Schule*

an|er·ken·nen ['anʔɛkɛnən] <erkennt an, erkannte an, hat anerkannt> tr v **1.** accept, recognize ◊ *die Regeln anerkennen* ♦ *Die Krankenkasse erkennt diese Behandlung an.* **2.** respect, acknowledge ◊ *gesellschaftlich anerkannt* ♦ *Sie erkennt an, dass er sich bemüht hat.* **3.** *only passive* staatlich anerkannt state/government approved, accredited ◊ *Diese Heilquelle wurde 1912 staatlich anerkannt.*

an|fah·ren ['anfaːrən] <fährt an, fuhr an, hat/ist angefahren> tr v +haben **1.** hit, run into ◊ *Er wurde von einem Auto angefahren.* ♦ *Ich habe ein parkendes Auto angefahren.* **2.** stop at, call at ◊ *Der Bus fährt alle Dörfer an.* **3.** shout at ◊ *„Du Idiot!", anfahren* intr v +sein **1.** *(vehicle)* start ◊ *Der Zug fuhr langsam an.* **2.** angefahren kommen come driving/riding up ◊ *Ein Auto kam*

mit 100 km/h angefahren. ✦ *Er kam mit einem Motorrad angefahren.*

An·fahrt ['anfaːᵗt] die <–, –en> **1.** journey, drive ◊ *die Beschreibung zur Anfahrt des Theaters* ✦ *die Anfahrt mit eigenem Pkw* **2.** route ◊ *Die Anfahrt ist auf der Karte verzeichnet.*

An·fall ['anfal] der <–(e)s, Anfälle> **1.** MED attack, fit ◊ *Er bekam einen hysterischen Anfall.* ✦ *ein plötzlicher Anfall von Panik* **2.** *(lofty)* incurrence, production ◊ *ein hoher Anfall an/von Abfällen* ⊙ **einen Anfall bekommen/kriegen** lose your temper, have a fit

an|fal·len ['anfalən] <fällt an, fiel an, hat/ist angefallen> [tr v] +*haben* attack ◊ *Der Hund fiel einen Jogger im Park an.* ✦ *Der Arbeiter wurde von einem Bären angefallen.* [intr v] +*sein* be incurred, be produced ◊ *Hohe Kosten fielen an.* ✦ *Jährlich fallen Tonnen von Abfall an.*

an·fäl·lig ['anfɛlɪç] [adj] delicate ◊ *Computer sind anfällige Geräte.* anfällig für etw. susceptible to sth, prone to sth ◊ *für Krankheiten/Infektionen/ Drogen anfällig sein* ✦ *für Fehler anfällige Software*

② **An·fang** ['anfaŋ] der <–(e)s, Anfänge> **1.** beginning, start ◊ *Eine Medaille? Das ist ein vielversprechender Anfang.* ✦ *Das war der Anfang einer langen Erfolgsgeschichte.* Anfang Mai/Oktober etc. at the beginning of May/October etc. ◊ *Anfang Januar habe ich Geburtstag* Anfang ... [gen] early in ◊ *Anfang des 20. Jahrhunderts* ✦ *seit Anfang 2005* am Anfang in the beginning, initially ◊ *Am Anfang stand eine kleine Idee.* ✦ *Am Anfang war er nicht begeistert.* von Anfang an from the (very) beginning, right from the start ◊ *Das habe ich von Anfang an gesagt.* von Anfang bis Ende from the beginning to the end, from start to finish ◊ *Sie spielte die CD von Anfang bis Ende.* ✦ *Das Projekt war von Anfang bis Ende chaotisch.* ⊝Ende **2.** origin ◊ *Er machte sich Gedanken über den Anfang der Welt.* ⊝Ende ⊙ **den Anfang machen** make a start, make the first move ◊ *Möchten Sie den Anfang machen?* **Anfang zwanzig/dreißig etc. sein** be in your early twenties/thirties etc.

② **an|fan·gen** ['anfaŋən] <fängt an, fing an, hat angefangen> [tr+intr v] **1.** begin, start ◊ *Fangt schon mal an, das Essen wird kalt.* ✦ *Er fing zu weinen an.* ✦ *Wer hat mit dem Streit angefangen?* ✦ *Sie wollte ein neues Leben anfangen.* ✦ *Der Tag fing schon hektisch an.* ✦ *Hinter diesem Berg fängt die Schweiz an.* nochmal (ganz) von vorne anfangen start (all over) again ⊝beginnen **2.** (mit) etw. anfangen take sth up ◊ *Wann hast du angefangen, Fußball zu spielen?* ✦ *Wann hast du mit dem Rauchen angefangen?* ⊝aufhören [tr v] *(fam)* do ◊ *Was wollen wir jetzt mit dem Abend anfangen?* ✦ *Du bist ja ganz nass! Wie hast du das denn angefangen?* [intr v] *(fam)* mit/von etw. anfangen start about sth, bring sth up ◊ *Fängst du schon wieder damit an? Ich will nichts mehr davon hören!* ⊙ **(ganz) klein anfangen** start off small **bei null anfangen** start from scratch **mit etw./jdm nichts anfangen können** not be able to relate to sth/sb, not understand sth/sb ◊ *Mit moderner Kunst kann ich überhaupt nichts anfangen.* **mit jdm ist nichts anzufangen** sb is hopeless ◊ *Mit ihr war nichts anzufangen.*

An·fän·ger ['anfɛŋɐ] der <–s, –>, **An·fän·ge·rin** ['anfɛŋərɪn] die <–, –nen> beginner ◊ *Deutschkurse für Anfänger* ✦ *Im Segeln bin ich noch absolute Anfängerin.*

an·fäng·lich ['anfɛŋlɪç] [adj, adv] when used as an adj, only before ns initial(ly) ◊ *Ich war anfänglich sehr nervös.* nach anfänglichen Schwierigkeiten after an initial period of difficulties

② **an·fangs¹** ['anfaŋs] [adv] in the beginning, at first ◊ *Das war anfangs noch nicht erkennbar.* ⊝zunächst, zuerst

an·fangs² ['anfaŋs] [prep] +*gen* *(fam)* at the beginning of ◊ *anfangs des Jahres/des 19. Jahrhunderts*

② **an|fas·sen** ['anfasn] <fasst an, fasste an, hat angefasst> [tr v] **1.** touch ◊ *Fass mich nicht an!* **2.** handle ◊ *eine Vase vorsichtig anfassen* **3.** *(fig)* jdn hart/mit Samthandschuhen anfassen treat sb firmly/with kid gloves ◊ *Verbrecher sollen in Zukunft härter angefasst werden.* [intr v] *(fam)* (mit) anfassen lend a hand ◊ *Kannst du mal mit anfassen?*

an|fer·ti·gen ['anfɛ^rtɪgŋ] <fertigt an, fertigte an, hat angefertigt> [tr v] make, produce ◊ *Bastelarbeiten anfertigen* ✦ *individuell angefertigte Rahmen* ✦ *einen Ersatzschlüssel anfertigen lassen;* draw up ✦ *Fertigen Sie eine Skizze des Unfalls an.*

an|for·dern ['anfoⁿdɐn] <fordert an, forderte an, hat angefordert> [tr v] ask for, request ◊ *Infomaterial anfordern* ✦ *Der Polizist forderte einen Rettungswagen an.*

An·for·de·rung ['anfoⁿdərʊŋ] die <–, –en> **1.** most pl demand, requirement ◊ *Sie war den Anforderungen nicht gewachsen.* ✦ *Die Prüfung stellt hohe Anforderungen an die Teilnehmer.* ✦ *Diese Fenster entsprechen nicht mehr den heutigen Anforderungen.* **2.** order(ing), request(ing) ◊ *die Anforderung neuer Ware/von Technikern* ✦ *Die Genehmigung erfolgt nur auf schriftliche Anforderung.*

An·fra·ge ['anfraːgə] die <–, –n> request ◊ *eine Anfrage an jdn richten* auf Anfrage on request ◊ *Auf Anfrage senden wir Ihnen eine Preisliste.*

an|freun·den ['anfrɔøndn] <freundet sich an, hat sich angefreundet> [ref v] **1.** sich (mit jdm) anfreunden become friends (with sb) ◊ *Er hat sich mit seinen Nachbarn angefreundet.* ✦ *Die beiden haben sich angefreundet.* **2.** sich mit etw. anfreunden get to like sth, accept sth ◊ *Er konnte sich mit dieser Lösung so recht anfreunden.*

an|füh·len ['anfyːlən] <fühlt sich an, fühlte sich an, hat sich angefühlt> [ref v] sich rau/weich etc. anfühlen feel rough/soft etc. ◊ *Das Fell fühlte sich sehr weich an.* ✦ *Ihre Finger fühlten sich taub an.*

An·füh·rungs·zei·chen ['anfyːrʊŋstsaeçn] das <–s, –> most pl inverted comma, quotation mark ◊ *ein Wort in Anführungszeichen setzen* ✦ *„Pop" steht in Anführungszeichen.*

Quotation marks („ ... " in German) are used for emphasis, to mark a quotation or the name of a thing to which you are referring: *„Hamlet" ist ein Stück von Shakespeare.* They are also used to indicate direct speech: *Er sagte: „Lass uns nach Hause gehen." „Ich will aber noch bleiben!", antwortete sie.*

An·ga·be ['anga:bə] die <-, –n> 1. *most pl* information, statement ◊ *Die Partei hat nach eigenen Angaben 12 000 Mitglieder.* ✦ *Er konnte keine Angaben zum Ablauf des Unfalls machen.* 2. *most sing* SPORT service ◊ *Helga Böhm hatte Angabe.*

an|ge·ben ['ange:bm̩] <gibt an, gab an, hat angegeben> [tr v] 1. state, declare ◊ *Er hatte eine falsche Adresse angegeben.* ✦ *Der Betrag wird in Euro und Franken angegeben.* 2. set, decide ◊ *Gib du die Richtung an!* [intr v] (mit etw.) angeben brag (about sth), boast (about sth) ◊ *Gib nicht so an!* ✦ *Er gab mit seinem neuen Motorrad an.* ⊜aufschneiden

② **an·geb·lich** ['ange:plɪç] [adj, adv] *when used as an adj, only before ns* alleged(ly) ◊ *ein angeblicher Spion* ✦ *Sie war angeblich krank.*

an·ge·bo·ren ['angəbo:rən] [adj] innate, congenital ◊ *Seine Krankheit ist angeboren.* ✦ *ein angeborenes Talent*

② **An·ge·bot** ['angəbo:t] das <-(e)s, –e> 1. suggestion ◊ *Sie machte ihm ein faires Angebot.* 2. *no pl* offer, range, selection ◊ *Es gab ein reiches Angebot an Obst.* im Angebot sein be on (special) offer ◊ *Diese Woche sind Tomaten im Angebot.* 3. *no pl* ECON supply ◊ *Die Nachfrage überstieg das Angebot bei weitem.* ⊜Nachfrage

an·ge·bracht ['angəbraxt] *past p of* anbringen [adj] appropriate, advisable ◊ *Hier ist Vorsicht angebracht.* ✦ *angebrachte Kritik*

an·ge·bro·chen ['angəbrɔxən] *past p of* anbrechen [adj] *no comp/superl* new, open ◊ *eine angebrochene Packung Zigaretten* der angebrochene Abend the remainder of the evening ◊ *Wir nutzten den angebrochenen Abend für einen Spaziergang.* ⊜angefangen

an·ge·grif·fen ['angəgrɪfn̩] *past p of* angreifen [adj] 1. damaged, weakened ◊ *eine angegriffene Leber haben* ✦ *Das Herz ist angegriffen.* 2. *not before ns* exhausted ◊ *Er wirkt sehr angegriffen.*

② **an|ge·hen** ['ange:ən] <geht an, ging an, hat/ist angegangen> [tr v] +*haben/in South G, Austr, Swiss often* +*sein* 1. tackle, approach ◊ *Probleme gemeinsam angehen* ✦ *Er ging das Rennen locker an.* 2. jdn angehen corncern sb ◊ *Das geht dich überhaupt nichts an!* ✦ *Diese Probleme gehen uns alle an!* was jdn/etw. angeht as far as sb/sth is concerned ◊ *Was die Schule angeht, gibt es bei ihr keine Probleme.* ✦ *Was deinen Freund angeht, der darf auch bleiben.* 3. jdn um etw. angehen ask sb for sth ◊ *jdn um Geld/Hilfe angehen* [intr v] +*sein* 1. *(light)* go on ◊ *Plötzlich gingen uns die Scheinwerfer an.; (radio)* come on ◊ *Das Radio geht nicht mehr an.* 2. *(fam)* begin, start ✦ *Wann geht der Film endlich an?* ✦ *Das Wintersemester geht im Oktober an.* 3. gegen etw. angehen resist sth ◊ *Du musst gegen die Müdigkeit angehen!* 4. etw. langsam/ruhig/geruhsam angehen lassen start sth slowly, set about to do sth slowly ◊ *Heute lasse ich den Tag ruhig angehen.* ✦ *Lassen Sie das Training beim ersten Mal langsam angehen.*

⊙ **es geht nicht an, dass** it is unacceptable that ◊ *Es geht nicht an, dass er ständig zu spät kommt.*

an|ge·hö·ren ['angəhø:rən] <gehört an, gehörte an, hat angehört> [intr v] einer Sache [dat] angehören belong to sth, be member of sth ◊ *Sie*

gehört der Gewerkschaft an.

② **An·ge·hö·ri·ge** ['angəhø:rɪgə] der/die <-n, die Angehörigen> *but: ein Angehöriger/eine Angehörige* 1. *most pl* relative ◊ *Ist das eine Angehörige von Ihnen?* die Angehörigen the family, (close) relatives ◊ *die Angehörigen des Toten benachrichtigen* 2. [+gen] member ◊ *die Angehörigen einer Religion/Organisation etc.*

An·ge·klag·te ['angəkla:ktə] der/die <-n, die Angeklagten> *but: ein Angeklagter/eine Angeklagte* accused, defendant ◊ *Die Angeklagte wurde schuldig gesprochen.*

An·gel ['aŋl] die <-, –n> 1. fishing rod ◊ *die Angel auswerfen* ✦ *einen Fisch an der Angel haben* 2. hinge

⊙ etw./jdn an der Angel haben *(fig)* have netted sth/sb, have bagged sth/sb ◊ *Die Stadt hatte einen Investor an der Angel.* etw. aus den Angeln heben 1. turn sth upside down, shake sth up ◊ *Das Internet hat die Welt aus den Angeln gehoben.* 2. unhinge sth ◊ *eine Tür aus den Angeln heben*

An·ge·le·gen·heit ['angəle:gn̩haet] die <-, –en> matter, affair, business ◊ *Für diese Angelegenheit ist mein Kollege zuständig.* ✦ *Du solltest dich nicht in seine Angelegenheiten einmischen.*

an·ge·mes·sen ['angəmɛsn̩] [adj, adv] appropriate(ly), adequate(ly), reasonable(-ably) ◊ *eine angemessene Entschädigung zahlen* ✦ *Der Preis war durchaus angemessen.* ✦ *Wie kann man in solch einer Situation angemessen reagieren?* einer Sache [dat] angemessen sein be appropriate for sth, be adequate for sth ◊ *Diese Strafe wäre der Sache nicht angemessen gewesen.* ⊜unangemessen

② **an·ge·nehm** ['angəne:m] [adj, adv] pleasant(ly), enjoyable(-ably) ◊ *eine angenehme Atmosphäre* ✦ *Der Stoff ist sehr angenehm auf der Haut.* ✦ angenehm überrascht sein ✦ *Es ist angenehm warm/kühl.* ⊜unangenehm [adj] *(person)* nice, likeable ◊ *Sie ist eine wirklich nette, angenehme Frau.* ✦ *Seine Kinder sind sehr angenehm und freundlich.* ⊜unangenehm

⊙ (sehr) angenehm *(form)* how do you do, nice to meet you ◊ *„Das ist Thea Rieger." — „Sehr angenehm."*

an·ge·sagt ['angəza:kt] [adj] <angesagter, am angesagtesten> *(slang)* 1. fashionable, trendy, hip ◊ *angesagte Trends* ✦ *Welche Farben sind diesen Winter angesagt?* 2. etw. ist angesagt sth is due, sth is necessary, it is time for sth ◊ *Was ist als Nächstes angesagt?* ✦ *Jetzt ist erst mal ein Imbiss angesagt.*

an·ge·sichts ['angəzɪçts] [prep] [+gen] in the face of, in view of, considering ◊ *Was muss angesichts dieser Lage getan werden?* ✦ *Die Bürger sind angesichts der vielen Gewalttaten alarmiert.*

an·ge·spannt ['angəʃpant] [adj, adv] <angespannter, am angespanntesten> 1. *(person, atmosphere)* tense(ly), taut(ly) ◊ *angespannte Gesichtszüge* ✦ *Die Stimmung war leicht angespannt.* ✦ *Er studierte angespannt die Liste.* 2. *(situation)* tense(ly), tight(ly), strained(ly) ◊ *eine angespannte finanzielle Situation* ✦ *Die Beziehungen zwischen den Ländern waren angespannt.*

② **An·ge·stell·te** ['angəʃtɛltə] der/die <-n, die Angestellten> *but: ein Angestellter/eine*

Angestellte employee, white-collar worker ◊ *Ich bin Angestellter, aber meine Frau ist freiberuflich tätig.* ♦ *eine leitende Angestellte* box@ Substantivierung

an·ge·strengt [ˈangəʃtrɛŋt] *past p of* anstrengen [adj, adv] <angestrengter, am angestrengtesten> intense(ly), concentrated(ly), strained(ly) ◊ *Er hatte einen angestrengten Gesichtsausdruck.* ♦ *Sie wirkte äußerst angestrengt.* ♦ *Ich dachte angestrengt nach.*

an·ge·tan [ˈangətaːn] [adj] *no comp/superl, not before ns* von jdm/etw. angetan sein be taken with sb/sth ◊ *Er war von ihr/meinem Vorschlag recht angetan.*

an·ge·trun·ken [ˈangətrʊŋkn̩] [adj] tipsy ◊ *zwei angetrunkene Männer* ♦ *Er war ziemlich stark angetrunken.*

an·ge·wie·sen [ˈangəviːzn̩] [adj] auf jdn/etw. angewiesen sein (have to) rely (up)on sb/sth, depend (up)on sb/sth, need sb/sth ◊ *Ich bin auf niemanden angewiesen!* ♦ *Sie war auf das Geld angewiesen.* auf einen Rollstuhl angewiesen sein be wheelchair-bound

an|ge·wöh·nen [ˈangəvøːnən] <gewöhnt an, gewöhnte an, hat angewöhnt> [tr v] sich [dat] etw. angewöhnen get into the habit of sth, take sth up ◊ *Ich habe mir angewöhnt, viel Wasser zu trinken.* ♦ *Sie hatte sich das Rauchen wieder angewöhnt.* jdm etw. angewöhnen get sb used to sth, accustom sb to something ◊ *Man sollte dem Kind angewöhnen, länger zu schlafen.*

an|glei·chen [ˈanglaɛçn̩] <gleicht an, glich an, hat angeglichen> [tr v] etw. (einer Sache [dat]) angleichen, etw. (an etw. [acc]) angleichen bring sth in(to) line (with sth), adapt sth (to sth) ◊ *Die Preise sollen innerhalb der EU angeglichen werden.* ♦ *Die Gesetze sollen an die europäische Norm angeglichen werden.* sie gleichen sich an they are becoming alike, they are converging ◊ *Die Preise haben sich angeglichen.* ♦ *Man hat voneinander gelernt und sich angeglichen.* [ref v] sich jdm/an jdn angleichen adapt yourself, become like ◊ *Sie hat sich im Laufe der Ehe immer mehr an ihren Mann angeglichen.* ♦ *Er versucht, sich seinen Mitschülern anzugleichen.*

Ang·lis·tik [anˈglɪstɪk] die <–> *no pl* English (studies) ◊ *Sie studiert Anglistik.* ♦ *Das Studium der Anglistik umfasst folgende Bereiche: ...*

② **an|grei·fen** [ˈangraɛfn̩] <greift an, griff an, hat angegriffen> [tr+intr v] **1.** attack ◊ *Napoleon griff Russland 1812 an.* ♦ *Plötzlich griff die Armee an.* ♦ *Der Kritiker hat die Sängerin öffentlich angegriffen.* ♦ *Das Salz hat das Metall angegriffen.* **2.** *(a project, competitor)* tackle ◊ *Jetzt können wir das nächste Projekt angreifen.* ♦ *In der 13. Minute griff er den Libero an.* ♦ *Die Mannschaft griff bereits früh an.* [tr v] **1.** *mostly adjectival passive* weaken, exhaust* ◊ *Die Grippe hatte sie stark angegriffen* ♦ *Seine Gesundheit war angegriffen.* **2.** *(savings, provisions etc.)* touch, start to use ◊ *Sie mussten die Vorräte angreifen.*

An·griff [ˈangrɪf] der <–(e)s, –e> **1.** attack ◊ *ein gewaltsamer Angriff auf/gegen eine Person* ♦ *sich gegen einen Angriff verteidigen* ♦ *ein bewaffneter Angriff auf einen Staat*; *(verbal also)* criticism ◊ *Er hat erneut heftige/massive Angriffe gegen die*

Regierung gerichtet. ♦ *sich gegen unfaire Angriffe verteidigen* **2.** SPORT im Angriff in the attack line, in the forward line ◊ *Beckenham spielte im Angriff.* ⊝Abwehr, Verteidigung

◉ etw. in Angriff nehmen tackle sth ◊ *Welches Projekt nimmst du als Nächstes in Angriff?*

② **Angst** [aŋst] die <–, Ängste> **1.** fear Angst (vor etw./jdm) haben be afraid (of sth/sb), be frightened (of/by sth/sb) ◊ *Sie hat panische Angst vor Schlangen.* ⊝Furcht **2.** *(less intense but enduring)* Angst haben worry ◊ *Sie hatte Angst, dass ihm etwas passieren könnte.* ♦ *Er hatte Angst um seinen Arbeitsplatz.* ♦ *Sie haben Angst vor Datenmissbrauch.*

◉ Angst und Schrecken terror ◊ *Die Einbrecher versetzten die Stadt in Angst und Schrecken.*

② **ängst·lich** [ˈɛŋstlɪç] [adj, adv] **1.** *(by nature)* fearful(ly) ◊ *Er war von Natur aus ängstlich.* ♦ *Sie ist ein recht ängstliches Kind.* **2.** *(in a particular situation)* frightened(ly), scared(ly), anxious(ly) ◊ *nervöse und ängstliche Pferde* ♦ *Sie klammerte sich ängstlich an ihre Mutter.*

② **an|ha·ben** [ˈanhaːbm̩] <hat an, hatte an, hat angehabt> [tr v] **1.** *(fam)* etw. anhaben wear sth ◊ *Er hatte nichts an.* ♦ *Sie hatte einen blauen Pulli an.* ⊝tragen **2.** *mostly negated* jdm etwas/nichts anhaben können be able/unable to harm sb ◊ *Sei unbesorgt. Niemand kann dir etwas anhaben.* einer Sache [dat] etwas/nichts anhaben können be able/unable to damage sth ◊ *Der Sturm konnte den Bäumen nichts anhaben.*

an|hal·ten [ˈanhaltn̩] <hält an, hielt an, hat angehalten> [intr v] **1.** stop ◊ *Er bat den Taxifahrer, direkt vor dem Haus anzuhalten.* ♦ *Die Rolltreppe hielt plötzlich an.* **2.** etw. hält an sth goes on, sth continues ◊ *Der Regen hält weiter an.* ♦ *Die Nachfrage hält weiter an.* ♦ *ein seit zehn Jahren anhaltender Trend* [tr v] **1.** etw. anhalten stop sth ◊ *Die Polizei hielt verschiedene Autos an.* ♦ *Sie hielt den Videorekorder kurz an.* **2.** die Luft anhalten hold your breath **3.** *(lofty)* jdn zu etw. anhalten demand sth from sb ◊ *Sie hielt ihn zur Sorgfalt an.* jdn dazu anhalten, etw. zu tun urge sb to do sth ◊ *Er hielt den Fahrer dazu an, langsamer zu fahren.*

An·halts·punkt [ˈanhaltspʊŋkt] der <–(e)s, –e> clue, evidence, indication ◊ *Es gibt nicht den geringsten Anhaltspunkt dafür, dass er der Täter ist.* ♦ *Es gibt keinerlei Anhaltspunkte für die Richtigkeit der Theorie.*

an·hand [anˈhant] [prep] **1.** [+gen] with the help of, on the basis of ◊ *Anhand mehrerer Beispiele erklärt er die Grammatik.* **2.** *adverbial* [+dat] anhand von with, by means of ◊ *etw. anhand von Beispielen erklären*

An·hang [ˈanhaŋ] der <–(e)s, Anhänge> **1.** *most sing* appendix ◊ *Die Quellenangaben befinden sich im Anhang.* **2.** *no pl (fam)* family ◊ *Ich werde all meine Freunde mit Anhang einladen.* **3.** IT attachment ◊ *eine E-Mail mit Anhang*

an|hän·gen [ˈanhɛŋən] <hängt an, hängte an, hat angehängt> [tr v] **1.** *(an object)* etw. (an etw. [acc]) anhängen attach sth (to sth), hitch sth up (to sth), couple sth on/up (to sth) ◊ *An den Zug wurde noch ein Waggon angehängt.* ♦ *Kannst du diese Datei an die E-Mail anhängen?* **2.** *(fam) (time)* etw. (an etw. [acc]) anhängen add sth (to

A
B
C
D
E
F
G
H
I
J
K
L
M
N
O
P
Q
R
S
T
U
V
W
X
Y
Z

sth) ◊ *Der Spieler möchte gerne noch eine Saison anhängen.* **3.** *(fam, pej)* jdm etw. anhängen pin sth on sb ◊ *Ihm wurde dieser Mord angehängt.*
An·hän·ger¹ ['anhɛŋɐ] der <-s, -> **1.** *(on luggage)* tag ◊ *Entfernen Sie alte Anhänger von Ihrem Gepäck.* **2.** *(on keys)* fob, pendant ◊ *ein Schlüsselbund mit einem gelben Anhänger* **3.** *(jewellery)* pendant ◊ *ein Anhänger in Form eines Kreuzes* **4.** *(on a motor vehicle)* trailer ◊ *Der mit Stroh beladene Anhänger kippte um.*
An·hän·ger² ['anhɛŋɐ] der <-s, ->,
An·hän·ge·rin ['anhɛŋərɪn] die <-, -nen> fan, supporter ◊ *Der Autor hat treue Anhänger.* ♦ *Sie ist eine Anhängerin des VfB.*; *(of an ideology)* follower ◊ *die Anhänger der Partei*
an|he·ben ['anheːbm̩] <hebt an, hob an, hat angehoben> [tr v] **1.** *(an object)* lift (up) ◊ *Kannst du den Tisch kurz anheben?* **2.** *(prices, the minimum age etc.)* raise, put up ◊ *Die Preise wurden leicht/um 2% angehoben.* ♦ *Die Altersgrenze für den Waffenerwerb wurde angehoben.*
an|heu·ern ['anhɔøɐn] <heuert an, heuerte an, hat angeheuert> [tr v] **1.** *(tech) (sailors)* jdn anheuern sign sb up ◊ *Früher wurden Seeleute häufig in Kneipen angeheuert.* **2.** *(fam) (for a job)* jdn anheuern hire sb, book sb ◊ *In dieser Abteilung sollen 50 neue Mitarbeiter angeheuert werden.* ♦ *Sie hatte einen Killer angeheuert.* [intr v] **1.** *(tech) (on a ship etc.)* sign up ◊ *Er heuerte als Koch auf einem Schiff an.* **2.** *(fam, also pej)* start work, start jobbing ◊ *Er heuerte als Berater bei einer Telekommunikationsfirma an.*
An·hieb ['anhiːp] der <-s> no pl *(always* **auf Anhieb)** straight away, right away, at first go, at the first try ◊ *Er schaffte es auf Anhieb.* ♦ *Sie bestand die Prüfung auf Anhieb.*
An·hö·he ['anhøːə] die <-, -n> hill, elevation ◊ *Das Haus steht auf einer kleinen Anhöhe.*
an|hö·ren ['anhøːrən] <hört an, hörte an, hat angehört> [tr v] **1.** jdn anhören listen to sb ◊ *Nun hören Sie mich doch bitte erst an!* (sich [dat]) etw. anhören listen to sth ◊ *(sich) ein Tonband/eine CD anhören* ♦ *Ich hörte mir seinen Vortrag an.* ♦ *Er musste Tag für Tag ihre Streitereien anhören.* **2.** etw. (mit) anhören overhear sth, hear sth ◊ *Zufällig hat sie die Unterhaltung mit angehört.* **3.** jdm etw. anhören hear sth in sb's voice ◊ *Man hörte ihr die Aufregung an.* [ref v] *(fam)* etw./jd hört sich ... an sth/sb sounds ... ◊ *Seine Stimme hört sich komisch an.* ♦ *Dieser Vorschlag hört sich schon viel besser an.* ♦ *Er hört sich traurig/ängstlich/zufrieden an.*
a·ni·mie·ren [ani'miːrən] <animiert, animierte, hat animiert> [tr v] **1.** jdn zu etw. animieren; jdn dazu animieren, etw. zu tun encourage sb to do sth, inspire sb to do sth, prompt sb to do sth ◊ *Der Sänger animierte die Zuhörer zum Mitmachen.* ♦ *ein Film, der zum Nachdenken animiert* ♦ *Du solltest ihn nicht animieren, noch mehr zu trinken.* **2.** *(a film, graphics)* animate ◊ *eine Grafik animieren* ♦ *die Figuren eines Films am Computer animieren*
an|kämp·fen ['ankɛmpfn̩] <kämpft an, kämpfte an, hat angekämpft> [intr v] gegen etw./jdn ankämpfen fight (against) sth/sb, battle against sth/sb, struggle with/against sth/sb ◊ *Die Feuerwehr versuchte,*

gegen die Flammen anzukämpfen. ♦ *gegen die Angst/einen mächtigen Gegner ankämpfen*
an|kau·fen ['ankaofn̩] <kauft an, kaufte an, hat angekauft> [tr v] purchase, buy ◊ *Aktien/Immobilien ankaufen*
An·ker ['aŋkɐ] der <-s, -> anchor ◊ *Er warf den Anker aus.*
⊙ **vor Anker gehen** anchor, drop anchor ◊ *Das Schiff ging in Genua vor Anker.* **den Anker lichten** weigh anchor **vor Anker liegen** be anchored, be/lie at anchor ◊ *Das Schiff lag im Hafen von Genua vor Anker.*
An·kla·ge ['anklaːgə] die <-, -n> **1.** LAW charge, accusation ◊ *Die Anklage lautet auf Mord.* ♦ *In der Anklage heißt es, der Autofahrer habe die Ampel übersehen.* (gegen jdn) (wegen etw.) Anklage erheben charge sb (with sth), bring charges/a charge (of sth) (against sb) ◊ *Gegen ihn wurde Anklage wegen Steuerhinterziehung erhoben.* (wegen etw.) unter Anklage stehen be charged (with sth) ◊ *Er stand unter Anklage wegen Mordverdacht.* **2.** no pl LAW prosecution ◊ *Die Anklage hatte ihm vorgeworfen, die Behörden belogen zu haben.* ♦ *Die erste Zeugin der Anklage wurde vernommen.* ⊙Verteidigung **3.** *(fig)* Anklage (gegen etw.) indictment (of sth), condemnation (of sth) ◊ *Das Buch ist eine Anklage gegen die Zustände in Gefängnissen.*
An·klang ['anklaŋ] der <-(e)s, Anklänge> **1.** no pl (bei jdm) Anklang finden be well received (by sb), find favour/favor (with sb) ◊ *Die neue Lehrerin fand in der Schule großen Anklang.* ♦ *Das Theaterstück fand beim Publikum wenig Anklang.* **2.** most pl Anklänge/ein Anklang (an etw./jdn) an echo/echoes (of sth/sb) etw. enthält Anklänge an etw./jdn, in etw. [dat] findet man/finden sich/zeigen sich Anklänge an etw./jdn sth is reminiscent of sth/sb, sth echoes sth/sb ◊ *In diesem Roman findet man Anklänge an die Romantik.* ♦ *Dieses Theaterstück enthält Anklänge an Beckett.*
an|kle·ben ['anklɛːbm̩] <klebt an, klebte an, hat/ist angeklebt> [tr v] +haben etw. (an etw. [acc]) ankleben stick sth on (sth), paste sth on (sth) ◊ *Der Bart war nur angeklebt.* ♦ *Wo willst du die Plakate ankleben?*
an|klei·den ['anklaedn̩] <kleidet an, kleidete an, hat angekleidet> [tr v] sich ankleiden get dressed ◊ *Er kann sich nicht mehr alleine ankleiden.* jdn ankleiden dress sb ◊ *Er ist krank und braucht jemanden, der ihn ankleidet.*
an|klop·fen ['anklɔpfn̩] <klopft an, klopfte an, hat angeklopft> [intr v] knock ◊ *Bitte klopfen Sie immer zuerst an, bevor Sie einen Raum betreten.*
② **an|kom·men** ['ankɔmən] <kommt an, kam an, ist angekommen> [intr v] **1.** arrive ◊ *Wann kommt dein Zug an?* ♦ *Bist du gut/pünktlich in London angekommen?* ♦ *Der Brief ist nie bei ihm angekommen.* ⊙eintreffen **2.** go down (with sb) ◊ *Wie ist dein Vortrag beim Publikum angekommen?* (bei jdm) gut/schlecht ankommen go down well/not go down well (with sb), have success/no success (with sb) ◊ *Mein Geschenk kam schlecht an.* ♦ *Er kommt bei Frauen gut an.* **3.** *(fam, also pej)* mit etw. ankommen come bothering sb with sth ◊ *Ständig kommt er mit neuen Fragen an.* Mit was kommst du jetzt schon wieder an? What is it about

now? **4.** gegen jdn/etw. ankommen be able to compete with sb/sth, be able to fight sb/sth ◊ *Wie sollen wir bloß gegen die Konkurrenz ankommen?* [imp v] **1.** es kommt auf jdn/etw. an it depends on sb/sth ◊ *Es kommt ganz auf das Wetter an, ob wir morgen wandern gehen.* **2.** jdm kommt es auf etw. [acc] an sb is concerned about sth, sth is sb's concern ◊ *Bei Jungs kommt es ihr scheinbar nur auf das Aussehen an.* ♦ *Auf was kommt es dir am meisten an?* ◉ **es auf etw.** [acc] **ankommen lassen** risk sth ◊ *Ich werde es auf eine Gerichtsverhandlung ankommen lassen.* **es darauf ankommen lassen** take chances ◊ *Im Zweifel würde ich es nicht darauf ankommen lassen.* **wenn es drauf ankommt** *(fam)* when it (really) matters ◊ *Wenn es darauf ankommt, ist er immer pünktlich.*

an|kün·di·gen ['ankʏndɪgn̩] <kündigt an, kündigte an, hat angekündigt> [tr v] announce ◊ *Sie kündigte ihren Besuch für kommende Woche an.* ♦ *Der Film wurde bereits vor Monaten angekündigt.* **sich ankündigen** announce your visit ◊ *Er hat sich für 10 Uhr angekündigt.* **ein Gewitter/Sturm kündigt sich an** a thunderstorm/storm announces itself

② **An·kunft** ['ankʊnft] die <-, Ankünfte> arrival ◊ *Planmäßige Ankunft in Genf ist um 8.30 Uhr.* ♦ *Sie bereitete sich auf die Ankunft des Kindes gründlich vor.*

an|lä·cheln ['anlɛçl̩n] <lächelt an, lächelte an, hat angelächelt> [tr v] jdn anlächeln smile at sb ◊ *Sie lächelte ihn (freundlich/mitleidig) an.*

② **An·la·ge** ['anla:gə] die <-, -n> **1.** FIN investment ◊ *Er wollte sein Geld nur in sichere Anlagen investieren.* **2.** ground, park ◊ *Diese Anlage hat einen Rosengarten und Spielplätze.* ♦ *Die Fläche der Anlage beträgt 1250 m².* **3.** *(with buildings)* plant, compound, facility ◊ *Anlage für die Plutoniumproduktion* **4.** no pl creation, laying out, building ◊ *Was muss man bei der Anlage eines Teichs beachten?* **5.** TECHN installation, system, facility ◊ *sanitäre Anlagen* ♦ *technische Anlagen* ♦ *Die Wartung der Anlage ist sehr teuer.* **6.** *(fam)* stereo (system) ◊ *Mit dieser Anlage kann man noch Platten hören.* **7.** MED predisposition, tendency ◊ *eine genetische Anlage zu Diabetes* **8.** *(form) (in letters)* enclosure ◊ *In der Anlage schicke ich Ihnen meinen Lebenslauf.* **9.** IT attachment ◊ *Seine E-Mail enthielt eine Datei als Anlage.*

An·lass ['anlas] der <-es, Anlässe> **1.** reason, cause ◊ *Was war der Anlass zu diesem Streit?* ♦ *Die derzeitige Situation gibt Anlass zur Sorge.* **beim geringsten/kleinsten Anlass** for the slightest reason ◊ *Beim geringsten Anlass fängt das Kind an zu weinen.* **2.** occasion ◊ *die passende Kleidung zum festlichen Anlass* ♦ *Das ist wirklich ein Anlass zum Feiern.* **aus Anlass ...** [gen] on the occasion of ... ◊ *eine Feier aus Anlass des 250. Geburtstages von Johann Wolfgang von Goethe* **etw. zum Anlass nehmen(, etw. zu tun)** take sth as an opportunity (to do sth) ◊ *Die Firma hat diese Veränderungen zum Anlass genommen, ihre Website neu zu gestalten.* ⊜Gelegenheit ◉ **aus aktuellem Anlass** due to current events ◊ *Aus aktuellem Anlass senden wir eine Rede des Bundeskanzlers.*

an|las·sen ['anlasn̩] <lässt an, ließ an, hat angelassen> [tr v] **1.** *(clothes)* keep on ◊ *Du kannst deinen Mantel anlassen, wir gehen jetzt.* ♦ *Er ließ seine Socken an.* **2.** *(an engine)* start (up) ◊ *den Motor/das Auto anlassen* **3.** *(an appliance, a light)* leave on ◊ *Sie ließ die Heizung/das Licht über Nacht an.* [ref v] *(fam)* etw. lässt sich gut/ langsam an sth starts (off) well/slowly, sth develops well/slowly ◊ *2002 hat sich sehr gut angelassen.* ♦ *Das Geschäft hat sich langsamer als erwartet angelassen.*

an·läss·lich ['anlɛslɪç] [prep] [+gen] on the occasion of ◊ *eine Rede anlässlich des 70. Geburtstags der Königin*

an|las·ten ['anlastn̩] <lastet an, lastete an, hat angelastet> [tr v] *(lofty)* **1.** jdm etw. anlasten accuse sb of sth, blame sb for sth ◊ *Der Beklagten wird angelastet, ihren Vorgesetzten nicht darüber informiert zu haben.* ♦ *Man lastet ihr mangelnde Originalität an.* **2.** jdm werden die Kosten (für etw.) angelastet sb must bear the costs (of sth) ◊ *Die entstandenen Kosten werden dem Unfallverursacher anzulasten.*

An·lauf ['anlaof] der <-(e)s, Anläufe> **1.** SPORT run-up ◊ *Leo sprang mit Anlauf in den See.* ♦ *Sie nahm einen kurzen Anlauf und sprang.* **2.** *(fig)* attempt ◊ *Im zweiten Anlauf versuchte ich eine andere Technik.* ♦ *Beim dritten Anlauf funktionierte alles perfekt.* **einen neuen Anlauf (zu/für etw.) nehmen** make another attempt (at sth), have another go (at sth) ◊ *Der Konzern nimmt einen neuen Anlauf zur Eroberung des Marktes.* **3.** no pl *(of production)* start ◊ *Vor Anlauf der Produktion werden die Mitarbeiter geschult.*

an|le·gen ['anle:gn̩] <legt an, legte an, hat angelegt> [intr v] **1.** *(ship)* dock, moor ◊ *Das Schiff wird morgen im Hafen von Genua anlegen.* **2.** *(with a gun)* aim ◊ *Er legte an und schoss.* [tr v] **1.** lay out, start, create ◊ *Ich lege einen Gemüsegarten/neuen Ordner an.* **2.** *(money)* invest ◊ *Wie kann ich mein Geld am besten anlegen?* ♦ *Er legte 20 000 Euro in Aktien an.* **3.** *(lofty) (clothes, jewellery)* put on, don ◊ *Er legte seine Uniform an.* ♦ *Sie legte eine Perlenkette an.* **4.** einen Verband anlegen apply a bandage **jdm Handschellen anlegen** handcuff sb **einem Hund einen Maulkorb anlegen** muzzle a dog **5.** *(a tape measure, ruler, playing card)* place ◊ *ein Lineal genau anlegen* ♦ *eine Karte an eine andere anlegen* **6.** es auf etw. [acc] anlegen be prepared to risk sth, be determined to do sth ◊ *Du legst es wohl darauf an, entdeckt zu werden?* ♦ *Er legt es auf einen Streit an.* [ref v] sich mit jdm anlegen pick a fight/an argument with sb, provoke sb ◊ *Du willst dich wohl mit mir anlegen?*

an|leh·nen ['anle:nən] <lehnt an, lehnte an, hat angelehnt> [tr v] **1.** etw. an etw. [acc] anlehnen lean sth against sth, put sth against sth ◊ *Sie lehnte die Leiter an den Baum an.* **2.** leave ajar, open slightly ◊ *Er lehnte die Tür an.* ♦ *Das Fenster war nur angelehnt.* [ref v] **1.** sich an etw./jdn anlehnen follow sth/sb ◊ *ein Baustil, der sich an den Klassizismus anlehnt* ♦ *Der Film lehnt sich eng an den Roman an.* **2.** sich an jdn anlehnen lean on/against sb ◊ *Du kannst dich gern an mich anlehnen.* **sich an etw.** [acc] **anlehnen** lean against sth ◊ *Sie lehnte*

sich an die Wand an. **3.** sich bei jdm anlehnen lean on sb's shoulder ◊ *In Notsituationen kann ich mich immer bei dir anlehnen.*

An·lei·he ['anlaeə] die <–, –n> **1.** FIN borrowing, loan ◊ *öffentliche Anleihen* ♦ *eine Anleihe aufnehmen*; *(as an investment)* bond ◊ *in hochverzinsliche Anleihen investieren* **2.** *(fig)* reference, borrowing ◊ *ein Film mit deutlichen Anleihen bei Hitchcock* Anleihen bei jdm machen borrow from sb ◊ *Der Autor hat viele Anleihen bei Dostojewski gemacht.*

② **An·lei·tung** ['anlaetʊŋ] die <–, –en> **1.** instruction ◊ *Die Kinder legten unter erfahrener Anleitung ein Gemüsebeet an.* **2.** *(written)* instructions, (instruction) manual ◊ *eine genaue Anleitung zur Installation des Computerprogramms*

an|lie·gen ['anliːgŋ] <liegt an, lag an, hat angelegen> intr v **1.** *(fam)* etw. liegt an sth is on, sth is to be done ◊ *Was liegt diese Woche alles an?* ♦ *Liegt heute etwas Besonderes an?* **2.** *(clothes)* etw. liegt (eng) an sth fits tightly, sth hugs the body ◊ *Das Kleid liegt (eng) am Körper an.*

An·lie·gen ['anliːgŋ] das <–s, –> concern, matter ◊ *Sauberkeit ist ihm ein besonderes Anliegen.* ♦ *Es ist uns ein besonderes Anliegen, dass die Gäste zufrieden sind.*

An·lie·ger ['anliːgɐ] der <–s, –>, **An·lie·ge·rin** ['anliːgərɪn] die <–, –nen> *(form)* resident ◊ *die Anlieger der Schillerstraße* Anlieger frei residents only, access only

an|ma·chen ['anmaxn] <macht an, machte an, hat angemacht> tr v **1.** *(the light, heating, radio)* etw. anmachen turn sth on, switch sth on ◊ *Er machte den Fernseher/das Radio/die Heizung an.* ⊜einschalten ⊜ausmachen, abschalten, ausschalten **2.** *(a salad)* dress ◊ *Er machte den Salat mit einem Joghurtdressing an.* ♦ *Der Kartoffelsalat ist noch nicht angemacht.* **3.** *(fam, pej)* jdn anmachen try to chat sb up, flirt heavily with sb ◊ *Dieser Typ macht sie bereits den ganzen Abend an.* **4.** *(fam)* jdn anmachen provoke sb, pick a fight with sb ◊ *Er machte ihn blöd an.* **5.** *(fam)* etw. macht jdn an sth turns sb on, sb fancies sth ◊ *Die Tasche macht mich an — ich nehme sie.*

② **an|mel·den** ['anmɛldn] <meldet an, meldete an, hat angemeldet> tr v **1.** anmelden enrol ◊ *Er hat seine Mitarbeiter zur Fortbildung angemeldet.* sich anmelden enrol ◊ *sich telefonisch für einen Kurs anmelden* ⊜abmelden **2.** *(with an authority, organization)* register ◊ *Mein Motorrad ist nur sechs Monate im Jahr angemeldet.* sich anmelden register ◊ *Sie müssen sich beim Einwohnermeldeamt anmelden.* sich bei einem Arzt anmelden make an appointment with a doctor den Fernseher/das Radio anmelden get a TV/radio licence ein Patent (für/auf etw. acc) anmelden file a patent (for/on sth) Konkurs anmelden file for bankruptcy einen Telefonanschluss anmelden apply for a telephone line **3.** *(doubts, interest)* announce, express ◊ *Hat jemand bereits Interesse angemeldet?* ♦ *Ich meldete meine Bedenken an.*

② **An·mel·dung** ['anmɛldʊŋ] die <–, –en> **1.** *no pl* announcement ◊ *Zur Anmeldung des Besuchs wenden Sie sich bitte an das Büro.* ♦ *die Anmeldung eines wissenschaftlichen Beitrags zum*

Tübinger Symposium **2.** *(with an authority, organization)* registration, licencing, licensing ◊ *die Anmeldung eines Gewerbes/Patents/Neugeborenen* ♦ *Was kostet die Anmeldung eines Hundes?* **3.** *(for a course)* enrolment ◊ *Für diesen Kurs ist eine Anmeldung erforderlich.* ♦ *Anmeldungen nimmt ab sofort die Kursleiterin entgegen.* **4.** reception, register(ing) office ◊ *Die Anmeldung befindet sich im 2. Stock.*

an|mer·ken ['anmɛrkŋ] <merkt an, merkte an, hat angemerkt> tr v **1.** note, comment ◊ *Willst du dazu noch etwas anmerken?* ♦ *Hier sei noch anzumerken, dass …* **2.** *(in a text)* etw. anmerken mark sth ◊ *Das können Sie im Text anmerken.* ♦ *Diesen Tag werde ich rot im Kalender anmerken.* **3.** *translation varies* Man konnte ihr die Aufregung nicht anmerken. You couldn't see how excited she was. Ich konnte ihm die Angst sofort anmerken. I immediately noticed how frightened he was. Man merkte ihr an, dass sie von der Sache wusste. You could tell that she knew of the matter. sich dat etw. nicht anmerken lassen not let sth show ◊ *Sie hat sich ihre Enttäuschung nicht anmerken lassen.*

An·mer·kung ['anmɛrkʊŋ] die <–, –en> **1.** *(spoken)* remark, comment ◊ *eine Anmerkung machen* ♦ *Es gab auch ein paar kritische Anmerkungen.* **2.** *(written)* annotation ◊ *Er versah den Text mit ein paar Anmerkungen.*

An·mut ['anmuːt] die <–> *no pl (lofty)* grace, elegance, charm ◊ *Voll Anmut schwebte sie übers Eis.* ♦ *Er war von ihrer weiblichen Anmut schier überwältigt.*

an|nä·hern ['annɛːɐn] <nähert an, näherte an, hat angenähert> ref v sich einer Sache dat annähern come/get closer to sth ◊ *sich einer fremden Kultur annähern* ♦ *Hat sich Algerien diesem Ziel angenähert?* sie nähern sich (einander) an they converge/are converging ◊ *Die einzelnen Länder haben sich in den Zinsen sehr stark angenähert.* ♦ *Inwieweit haben sich die Standpunkte einander angenähert?* tr v etw. einer Sache dat annähern bring sth in line with sth, bring sth closer to sth ◊ *Der traditionelle Unterricht soll den neuen Konzepten angenähert werden.*

an·nä·hernd ['annɛːɐnt] adj, adv *when used as an adj, mostly before ns* approximate(ly), rough(ly) ◊ *Annähernd 400 Gäste waren auf der Hochzeit.* ♦ *Die Zahl ist sich in den letzten Jahren annähernd verdoppelt.* ♦ *Das hier sind nur annähernde Werte.*

An·nah·me ['annaːmə] die <–, –n> **1.** *no pl (of objects)* acceptance, receipt, receiving ◊ *die Annahme von Kleinanzeigen* ♦ *Die Annahme von Trinkgeld ist verboten.* **2.** *no pl* SPORT taking ◊ *eine Annahme eines gegnerischen Balls im Strafraum* ⊜Abgabe **3.** *no pl (of an offer, a proposal, plan)* acceptance, approval ◊ *eine Annahme des Beschlusses* ♦ *die Annahme eines Angebots* ⊜Ablehnung **4.** *(of a fact)* assumption ◊ *Es besteht kein Grund zur Annahme, dass …* ♦ *Sie gingen von falschen Annahmen aus.*

② **an|neh·men** ['anneːmən] <nimmt an, nahm an, hat angenommen> tr v **1.** accept ◊ *Ihr Nachbar nahm das Päckchen für sie an.* ♦ *So viel Geld kann ich nicht annehmen.* ♦ *Der Antrag wurde einstimmig angenommen.* ♦ *Kreditkarten/Schecks annehmen* ♦ *Er wurde von der Kunsthochschule angenommen.* ♦

eine Einladung annehmen ◆ *Er nahm die Herausforderung an.*; *(a job)* take up ◇ *eine neue Stelle annehmen* ⊖*ablehnen* **2.** *(a nationality, name)* adopt, take on ◇ *die deutsche Staatsangehörigkeit annehmen* ◆ *eine neue Identität annehmen* **3.** assume ◇ *Ist anzunehmen, dass es Ärger gibt?* ◆ *Ich habe angenommen, dass er noch hier wohnt.* ◆ *Nehmen wir mal an, du wirst krank ...* angenommen ... assuming ... ◇ *Angenommen, du wirst arbeitslos. Was ist dann?* ⊖*voraussetzen* **4.** *in combination with certain nouns* take, assume ◇ *Die Situation nimmt absurde Züge an.* ◆ *eine Krise, die bedrohliche Formen annimmt* ꇉ*ref v꒐ (lofty)* sich jds/einer Sache annehmen look after sb/sth, take care of sb/sth ◇ *Er ist neu hier. Würdest du dich seiner annehmen?* ◆ *Wer nimmt sich dieser Arbeit an?*

② **An·non·ce** [a'nɔ̃sə, a'nõːsə] die <–, –n> advertisement, ad ◇ *eine Annonce aufgeben/in eine Zeitschrift setzen* ◆ *Auf ihre Annonce meldete sich niemand.*

an|ord·nen ['an|ɔˀdnən] <ordnet an, ordnete an, hat angeordnet> ꇉtr v꒐ **1.** arrange, lay out, set out ◇ *Auf diesem Rechner sind die Tasten anders angeordnet.* **2.** order ◇ *Eine Untersuchung der Leiche wurde angeordnet.*

an|pas·sen ['anpasn̩] <passt an, passte an, hat angepasst> ꇉtr v꒐ adjust ◇ *Die Löhne wurden angepasst.* ◆ *Die Technik wurde angepasst.* etw. einer Sache ꇉdat꒐ anpassen adapt sth to sth, adjust sth to sth ◇ *Dieses Tier passt seine Farbe der Umgebung an.* ◆ *seine Kleidung der Jahreszeit anpassen*; *(to a concept, ideology also)* bring sth in line with sth ◇ *Er passte die Texte dem Zeitgeist an.* ꇉref v꒐ **1.** sich anpassen conform ◇ *Er muss endlich lernen, sich anzupassen.* **2.** sich an jdn/ etw. anpassen, sich jdm/einer Sache anpassen adapt to sb/sth, adjust to sb/sth ◇ *Die Tiere konnten sich an die veränderte Umwelt nicht anpassen.* ◆ *Das Angebot passte sich an die Nachfrage an.* ◆ *Er fand es schwierig, sich der Gruppe anzupassen.*

an|pro·bie·ren ['anprobiːrən] <probiert an, probierte an, hat anprobiert> ꇉtr v꒐ try on ◇ *Möchten Sie den Mantel anprobieren?*

an|re·gen ['anreːgŋ̍] <regt an, regte an, hat angeregt> ꇉtr v꒐ **1.** etw. anregen stimulate sth ◇ *Dieser Tee regt die Verdauung an.* **2.** jdn anregen, etw. zu tun inspire sb to do sth, stimulate sb to do sth ◇ *Seine unglückliche Liebe regte ihn an, den Roman zu schreiben.* etw. regt jdn zu etw. an sb gets the inspiration for sth from sth ◇ *Ihr Leben regte ihn zu dieser Kurzgeschichte an.* **3.** etw. anregen propose sth, suggest sth ◇ *Der Bürgermeister regte dieses Projekt an.* ◆ *Er regte an, eine neue Schule zu bauen.* etw. ꇉintr v꒐ **1.** have a stimulating effect ◇ *Kaffee und Tee regen an.* **2.** zu etw. anregen provoke sth, stimulate sth, engender sth, prompt sth ◇ *Diese Dekoration regt zum Kauf an.* ◆ *Die Geschichte regte zum Schmunzeln an.*

An·re·gung ['anreːgʊŋ] die <–, –en> **1.** *no pl (also fig)* stimulation ◇ *die Anregung von Reformen* ◆ *ein Mittel zur Anregung des Kreislaufs* **2.** suggestion ◇ *Die Ausstellung kam auf Anregung des Bürgermeisters zustande.* ⊖*Vorschlag* **3.** impulse ◇ *Anregungen für den Unterricht* ⊖*Impuls, Anstoß*

an|rich·ten ['anrɪçtn̩] <richtet an, richtete an, hat angerichtet> ꇉtr v꒐ **1.** *(on a plate etc.)* arrange ◇ *Er hat das Essen nett angerichtet.*; *(a salad)* prepare *Es ist angerichtet. Lunch/Dinner is served.* **2.** *(a bloodbath, confusion, disaster)* cause ◇ *Du hast ein großes Chaos angerichtet.*; *(damage)* do ◇ *Der Sturm hat große Schäden angerichtet. Was hat er da nur wieder angerichtet? What's he gone and done now?*

② **An·ruf** ['anruːf] der <–(e)s, –e> call ◇ *einen wichtigen Anruf bekommen/erwarten*

② **An·ruf·be·ant·wor·ter** ['anruːfbəˌantvɔˀtɐ] der <–s, –> answerphone ◇ *Er hinterließ eine Nachricht auf dem Anrufbeantworter.*

② **an|ru·fen** ['anruːfn̩] <ruft an, rief an, hat angerufen> ꇉtr+intr v꒐ phone, call, ring ◇ *Hat jemand für mich angerufen?* ◆ *Bitte rufen Sie mich morgen an.* ◆ *Ich muss mal kurz bei der Bank anrufen.*

ans [ans] ꇉcontract꒐ *an + das* **1.** *(fam)* to ◇ *ans Fenster gehen* ans Geld/Alter etc. denken think of the money/your old age etc. → an **2.** *with nominalized verbs, not to be split* ans Aufhören/Gehen etc. denken think about quitting/going home etc. sich ans Abspülen/Lernen etc. machen get down to wash the dishes/studying etc. **3.** *in certain idioms, not to be split:* look up the relevant idiom ◇ *sich* ꇉdat꒐ *etw. ans Bein binden lassen*

An·sa·ge ['anzaːgə] die <–, –n> announcement ◇ *eine Ansage machen* ◆ *Es kam eine Ansage, dass sich der Zug verspäten würde.*

an|sam·meln ['anzamↄ̩n] <sammelt an, sammelte an, hat angesammelt> ꇉtr v꒐ accumulate, amass ◇ *Überstunden/Daten ansammeln* ꇉref v꒐ sich ansammeln accumulate ◇ *Inzwischen sammelten sich Verluste von 5 Millionen Euro an.*; *(water also)* collect ◇ *In der Lunge hatte sich Wasser angesammelt.*; *(people)* gather; *(microbes)* be concentrated

an·säs·sig ['anzɛsɪç] ꇉadj꒐ resident ◇ *Die Familie ist in Berlin ansässig.*; *(company)* based ◇ *eine in Köln ansässige Firma*

An·satz ['anzats] der <–es, Ansätze> **1.** beginning(s) ◇ *Die Reform ist bereits im Ansatz gescheitert.* ◆ *Bei ihm ist ein leichter Ansatz von Bauch zu erkennen.* **2.** *(to a task)* approach ◇ *ein interdisziplinärer/theoretischer Ansatz* **3.** *(of the neck, nose etc.)* base ◇ *eine Rötung am Ansatz des Halses* **4.** *(of the hair)* roots ◇ *Am Ansatz sah man, dass er eigentlich blond war.*; *(on the forehead)* hairline

an·satz·wei·se ['anzatsvaɪzə] ꇉadv꒐ to some extent, to a limited extent ◇ *Er konnte seine Vorschläge nur ansatzweise durchsetzen.*

an|schaf·fen ['anʃafn̩] <schafft an, schaffte an, hat angeschafft> ꇉtr v꒐ (sich ꇉdat꒐) etw. anschaffen get (yourself) sth ◇ *Mit dem Geld will die Schule Computer anschaffen.* ◆ *Wir sollten uns ein neues Auto anschaffen.*

An·schaf·fung ['anʃafʊŋ] die <–, –en> acquisition, purchase ◇ *eine größere Anschaffung planen* ◆ *Der Drucker war eine gute Anschaffung.*

② **an|schau·en** ['anʃaʊən] *(SouthG, Austr, Swiss)* → ansehen

an·schau·lich ['anʃaʊlɪç] ꇉadj, adv꒐ vivid(ly), graphic(ally) ◇ *etw. auf anschauliche Weise*

A B C D E F G H I J K L M N O P Q R S T U V W X Y Z

A

B

C

D

E

F

G

H

I

J

K

L

M

N

O

P

Q

R

S

T

U

V

W

X

Y

Z

schildern ◆ *Der Vortrag war sehr anschaulich.* ⊖plastisch

An·schein ['anʃaen] der <-(e)s> *no pl* appearance, impression ◇ *Der Garten erweckte den Anschein liebevoller Pflege.* ◆ *Er gibt sich gern den Anschein, liberal zu sein.* allem/dem Anschein nach to all appearances es hat den Anschein, dass/als ob it appears that/as if ◇ *Es hat den Anschein, dass er ziemlich genau Bescheid weiß.* ◆ *Es hat den Anschein, als ob es bald regnen würde.*

② **an·schei·nend** ['anʃaenənt] [adv] apparently ◇ *Anscheinend hat er den Zug verpasst.* ⊖offenbar, scheinbar

An·schlag ['anʃlaːk] der <-(e)s, Anschläge> **1.** notice ◇ *ein Anschlag am schwarzen Brett* **2.** attack ◇ *Sie planten einen Anschlag auf den Flughafen.* ◆ *Bei dem Anschlag kamen 15 Menschen ums Leben.* **3.** *most pl* characters, keystrokes ◇ *100 Zeilen à 30 Anschläge* ◆ *Sie schreibt 180 Anschläge pro Minute.* **4.** *most sing* TECHN bis zum Anschlag as far as it will go, to its limit ◇ *Der Thermostat sollte nicht bis zum Anschlag aufgedreht werden.*

an|schlie·ßen ['anʃliːsn] <schließt an, schloss an, hat angeschlossen> [tr v] connect ◇ *Die Waschmaschine muss erst angeschlossen werden.* [intr v] *(temporal)* etw. schließt an etw. [acc] an sth is followed by sth ◇ *An die Vorlesung schließt ein Tutorium an.*; *(local)* sth is adjacent to sth ◇ *An das Haus schließt ein Park an.* [ref v] **1.** sich jdm. anschließen join sb ◇ *Ihr geht ins Kino? Da schließe ich mich euch an!* **2.** sich einer Sache [dat] anschließen endorse sth ◇ *Ich schließe mich Ihrer Meinung an.*

an·schlie·ßend ['anʃliːsnt, 'anʃliːsənt] *pres p of* anschließen [adv] afterwards ◇ *Erst gibt es einen Empfang. Anschließend findet die Sitzung statt.*

An·schluss ['anʃlʊs] der <-es, Anschlüsse> **1.** *(telephone)* connection, line ◇ *ein analoger/digitaler Anschluss* ◆ *Ihr Anschluss ist ständig besetzt.*; *(additional)* extension keinen Anschluss bekommen not get through kein Anschluss unter dieser Nummer number unobtainable **2.** *(to a train, plane, waste pipe etc.)* connection ◇ *In Nürnberg haben wir Anschluss an den ICE nach Köln.* ◆ *Das Haus hat keinen Anschluss an die Kanalisation.* **3.** POL annexation ◇ *In Linz verkündete Hitler den Anschluss Österreichs an Deutschland.* **4.** *no pl* contact, acquaintances ◇ *Er findet in der Klasse einfach keinen Anschluss.*

⊛ den Anschluss verlieren fall behind ◇ *Wir dürfen den Anschluss an die Konkurrenz nicht verlieren!* im Anschluss an etw. [acc] after sth ◇ *Im Anschluss an die Sitzung findet eine Pressekonferenz statt.* im Anschluss afterwards ◇ *Im Anschluss können Fragen gestellt werden.*

② **an|schnal·len** ['anʃnalən] <schnallt an, schnallte an, hat angeschnallt> [tr v] **1.** sich/jdn anschnallen fasten your/sb's seat belt ◇ *Wir landen bald. Bitte schnallen Sie sich an.* ◆ *Sie schnallte das Kind auf dem Rücksitz an.* angeschnallt sein be wearing a seat belt, be strapped in **2.** strap on ◇ *seine Ski anschnallen*

An·schrift ['anʃrɪft] die <-, -en> address ◇ *Bitte geben Sie Ihre Anschrift an.* ◆ *Seine Anschrift hat sich geändert.*

② **an·se·hen** ['anzeːən] <sieht an, sah an, hat angesehen> [tr v] **1.** look at ◇ *Er sah sie traurig an.* ◆ *Warum siehst du mich nicht an?* sich [dat] etw./jdn ansehen (have a) look at sth/sb ◇ *Sie sah sich die Urlaubsfotos an.* ◆ *Das musst du dir ansehen!* **2.** *(on TV)* watch ◇ *Ich wollte mir morgen das Fußballspiel ansehen.*; *(a film)* see ⊖gucken **3.** etw./jdn als etw./jdn ansehen regard sth/sb as sth/sb ◇ *Ich habe ihn als meinen Freund angesehen.* ◆ *Er sah es als seine Pflicht an, ihr zu helfen.* **4.** jdm etw. ansehen tell sth by looking at sb ◇ *Sieht man mir an, dass ich müde bin?* **5.** etw. mit ansehen stand by and watch sth ◇ *Er konnte nicht mit ansehen, wie sie sich quälte.*

An·se·hen ['anzeːən] das <-s> *no pl* reputation, standing ◇ *Mein Ansehen hat sehr gelitten.* ◆ *Sie hat in der Firma ein gutes Ansehen.* ⊖Prestige, Ruf

an|set·zen ['anzɛtsn] <setzt an, setzte an, hat angesetzt> [tr v] **1.** fix ◇ *Welchen Preis würdest du dafür ansetzen?*; schedule ◇ *Die Versammlung ist für morgen, 14 Uhr, angesetzt.* **2.** *(buds, fruit)* develop Rost/Schimmel ansetzen begin to rust/mo(u)ld Fett ansetzen begin to get fat Kalk ansetzen become furred up **3.** raise to your mouth/lips ◇ *Sie setzte das Glas/Saxofon an.* [intr v] zu etw. ansetzen prepare to do sth, get ready to do sth ◇ *Er wollte gerade zum Überholen/zum Sprung ansetzen.*

② **An·sicht** ['anzɪçt] die <-, -en> **1.** opinion, view ◇ *Was soll ich deiner Ansicht nach tun?* ◆ *Ich bin der Ansicht, du solltest den Job annehmen.* ◆ altmodische Ansichten haben **2.** *(of a building, landscape, on a computer)* view ◇ *Das Bild zeigt eine Ansicht von Windsor.* **3.** zur Ansicht for (your/our) inspection ◇ *Er bestellte das Buch zur Ansicht.*

⊛ geteilter Ansicht sein have different opinions ◇ *Sie waren geteilter Ansicht und konnten sich nicht einigen.*

an·sons·ten [an'zɔnstn] [adv] otherwise ◇ *Das Auto hat eine Schramme, aber ansonsten ist alles in Ordnung.* ◆ *Gibst du mir deine Nummer? Ansonsten kann ich dich nicht erreichen.* ⊖sonst

An·spie·lung ['anʃpiːlʊŋ] die <-, -en> allusion ◇ *eine versteckte Anspielung* in Anspielung auf/an etw. [acc], unter Anspielung auf etw. [acc] in allusion to sth ◇ *In Anspielung an das Topmodel nannte sie ihre Tochter Heidi.* eine Anspielung auf etw. [acc] machen allude to sth ◇ *Er machte eine Anspielung auf meine Frisur.*

an|spre·chen ['anʃprɛçn] <spricht an, sprach an, hat angesprochen> [tr v] **1.** speak to, talk to ◇ *Sie sprach ihn einfach auf der Straße an.* jdn auf etw. [acc] ansprechen speak to sb about sth ◇ *Er sprach sie auf ihre Doktorarbeit an.* **2.** jdn/sich irgendwie ansprechen address sb/each other in a certain manner ◇ *Er spricht sie ständig mit „Frau Doktor" an.* ◆ *Wir sollten uns ruhig mit dem Vornamen ansprechen.* **3.** appeal to ◇ *Spricht dich diese Vorstellung an?* **4.** mention, bring up ◇ *Ich finde, du solltest das Problem ansprechen!* ⊖vorbringen **5.** sich angesprochen fühlen feel as if sth is directed towards you, feel as if sth concerns you ◇ *Sie fühlte sich durch die Vorwürfe angesprochen.*

An·spruch ['anʃprʊx] der <-(e)s, Ansprüche> **1.** Anspruch auf etw. [acc] claim to sth ◇ *Anspruch*

auf Schadenersatz haben/erheben **2.** *most pl* Ansprüche (an etw./jdn) demands (on sth/sb), expectations (from sth/sb) ◊ *Er stellt hohe Ansprüche an die Qualität der Produkte.* ♦ *Welche Ansprüche hast du an das Leben?* große Ansprüche stellen be very demanding **3.** etw. in Anspruch nehmen take advantage of sth ◊ *ein Angebot/einen Vorteil in Anspruch nehmen; (on help, support)* call on sth ◊ *Ich nahm ihre Hilfe gerne in Anspruch.; (a credit, time)* take up sth **4.** etw. nimmt jdn in Anspruch sth takes up sb's time ◊ *Dieses Projekt nimmt ihn stark in Anspruch.*

an·spruchs·los ['anʃprʊxsloːs] [adj] <anspruchsloser, am anspruchslosesten> **1.** undemanding ◊ *Diese Pflanzen sind anspruchslos und pflegeleicht.* ♦ *Ein Hund ist kein anspruchsloses Tier.* ⊜anspruchsvoll **2.** *(literature, a play)* lowbrow, trivial ◊ *Der Film war uninteressant und anspruchslos.* ♦ *ein anspruchsloses Buch* ⊜anspruchsvoll

an·spruchs·voll ['anʃprʊxsfɔl] [adj] demanding ◊ *anspruchsvolle Kunden* ♦ *Was Qualität betrifft, bin ich sehr anspruchsvoll.* ♦ *eine anspruchsvolle Tätigkeit/Aufgabe* ⊜anspruchslos

An·stalt ['anʃtalt] die <-, -en> **1.** *(organization)* institution ◊ *die Anstalt für Arbeit* **2.** *(also pej) (particularly for psychiatric treatment)* institution ◊ *in eine Anstalt eingeliefert werden* ♦ *Sie hat drei Jahre in der geschlossenen Anstalt verbracht.* ⊚ Anstalt(en) machen, etw. zu tun be about to do sth ◊ *Einige Jungen machten Anstalten, sich auf den frechen Mitschüler zu stürzen.* ♦ *Es klingelte, aber er machte keine Anstalt aufzustehen.*

An·stand ['anʃtant] der <-(e)s> *no pl* decency, good manners ◊ *Du besitzt wohl gar keinen Anstand!* ♦ *eine Niederlage mit Anstand hinnehmen*

an·stän·dig ['anʃtɛndɪç] [adj, adv] decent(ly), respectable(-ably) ◊ *Es war sehr anständig von ihm, dass er sich entschuldigt hat.* ♦ *Machen Sie mir ein anständiges Angebot!* ♦ *sich anständig benehmen*

an·statt¹ [an'ʃtat] [prep] *sing nouns without article or attribute are not declined when following this prep, otherwise* [+gen] *or fam* [+dat] instead of ◊ *Anstatt ihres Mannes nahm sie ihre Freundin mit in den Urlaub.* ♦ *Anstatt Orangen hat sie Äpfel gekauft.* ⊜anstelle

an·statt² [an'ʃtat] [conjunc] instead of ◊ *Warum versöhnst sie sich nicht, anstatt ständig zu streiten?* ⊜statt

an|ste·cken ['anʃtɛkn] <steckt an, steckte an, hat angesteckt> [tr v] **1.** MED jdn (mit etw.) anstecken give sb sth, pass sth on to sb ◊ *Sie hat mich (mit Windpocken) angesteckt.* **2.** *(fig)* jdn mit etw. anstecken infect sb with sth; *(with panic, fear)* affect sb with sth ◊ *Willst du uns mit deiner Panik anstecken?* **3.** sich [dat] etw. anstecken pin sth on ◊ *Er steckte sich eine Nelke an. Er steckte ihr eine Brosche an.* He pinned a brooch to her dress/pullover etc. jdm einen Ring anstecken put a ring on sb's finger ◊ *Er steckte ihr einen Ring an.* [ref v] sich (bei jdm) anstecken catch something (from sb) ◊ *Er hat sich bei seinem Bruder angesteckt.* sich mit etw. anstecken catch sth (from sb) ◊ *Sie hat sich mit einer Erkältung angesteckt.*

an|ste·hen ['anʃteːən] <steht an, stand an, hat

angestanden> [intr v] *in South G, Austr, Swiss often* +sein **1.** queue up ◊ *Die Leute standen an der Kasse an.* ♦ *Wir mussten für die Eintrittskarten anstehen.* **2.** be due ◊ *Im März stehen Wahlen an.* **3.** be there to get through ◊ *Nächste Woche steht eine Menge Arbeit an.* ♦ *Was steht heute alles an?*

an|stei·gen ['anʃtaeɡn] <steigt an, stieg an, ist angestiegen> [intr v] **1.** rise ◊ *Die Temperaturen stiegen auf 27° C an.*; increase ◊ *Die Zahl der Internet-Nutzer ist angestiegen.* ⊜sinken **2.** *(road, path)* ascend ◊ *Hier steigt der Wanderweg bis zum Gipfel stark an.* ⊜abfallen

an·stel·le [an'ʃtɛlə] [prep] **1.** [+gen] instead of ◊ *Er erschien anstelle seiner Schwester zur Feier.* ⊜statt **2.** *adverbial* [+dat] anstelle von etw./jdm instead of sth ◊ *Sie kaufte Nektarinen anstelle von Pfirsichen.*

an|stel·len ['anʃtɛlən] <stellt an, stellte an, hat angestellt> [tr v] **1.** turn on, switch on ◊ *die Heizung anstellen* **2.** etw. (mit etw./jdm) anstellen do sth (with sth/sb) ◊ *Was kann man damit denn anstellen?* ♦ *Was hat die Katze mit dem Sofa angestellt?* ♦ *Blödsinn anstellen* **3.** *(fam)* get up to ◊ *Dass ihr mir ja nichts anstellt!* **4.** *(assumptions, comparisons, enquiries)* make ◊ *Für dieses Projekt stellte er eine Menge Recherchen an.; (experiments)* carry out **5.** employ ◊ *Nach dem Praktikum wurde er von der Firma angestellt.* ♦ *Sie ist bei einer Sprachschule angestellt.* [ref v] **1.** sich (irgendwo) anstellen queue up (somewhere) ◊ *Bitte stellen Sie sich hinten an!* ♦ *Wir mussten uns für die Karten anstellen.* **2.** sich geschickt/ungeschickt anstellen make a good/bad job of it **3.** *(fam, pej)* sich anstellen make a fuss ◊ *Stell dich nicht so an!* ⊚ es anstellen, dass make sure that ◊ *Wie stellen wir es an, dass sie uns anhören?*

An·stieg ['anʃtiːk] der <-(e)s, -e> *most sing* **1.** *no pl* der/ein Anstieg ... [gen], der/ein Anstieg von/bei etw. the/an increase of/in sth ◊ *ein Anstieg der Wassertemperatur* ♦ *Analysten rechnen mit einem Anstieg der Kosten um zwölf Prozent.* ♦ *ein Anstieg der Gebühren von 20,50 Euro auf 31,10 Euro* ♦ *ein starker Anstieg von Lungenkrebs bei Rauchern* ♦ *ein Anstieg bei psychischen Krankheiten* **2.** *(onto a mountain)* ascent ◊ *Wir haben den Anstieg gleich geschafft.* ♦ *die legendären Anstiege der Tour de France* ♦ *ein Anstieg von 500 Höhenmetern*

An·stoß ['anʃtoːs] der <-es, Anstöße> **1.** Anstoß erregen cause offence ◊ *Es erregte Anstoß, dass sie offen über Tabus sprach.* ♦ *Mit seinem Verhalten erregt er viel Anstoß.* Anstoß (an etw. [dat]) nehmen take offence (at sth) ◊ *Sie nahm Anstoß an seinen Ideen.* **2.** Anstoß zu etw. impetus for sth, initiative for sth ◊ *Woher kam der Anstoß zu diesem Film?* ⊜Anregung, Impuls **3.** *most sing* SPORT kick-off ◊ *Welcher Spieler führt den Anstoß aus?*

an|sto·ßen ['anʃtoːsn] <stößt an, stieß an, hat angestoßen> [tr v] **1.** jdn/etw. anstoßen give sb/sth a push ◊ *Er stieß mich mit dem Finger an.* ♦ *Ich habe das Tablett angestoßen und es fiel zu Boden.; (in a crowd)* push ◊ *Bei dem Gedränge wurde ich dauernd angestoßen.* **2.** *(fig)* etw. anstoßen set sth in motion ◊ *Grüne Politiker wollen Reformen anstoßen.* **3.** *(to make sth move)* etw.

A B C D E F G H I J K L M N O P Q R S T U V W X Y Z

A
B
C
D
E
F
G
H
I
J
K
L
M
N
O
P
Q
R
S
T
U
V
W
X
Y
Z

anstoßen kick sth, give sth a push ◊ *Er stieß den Stein an, um ihn ins Rollen zu bringen.* **4.** SPORT *(a football match)* etw. anstoßen kick sth off ◊ *Bayern stößt das Spiel an.* (intr v) **1.** (auf etw./jdn) anstoßen clink glasses (to celebrate sth/sb), drink to sb/sth ◊ *Ich möchte mit dir anstoßen!* ♦ *Worauf stoßen wir an?* ♦ *Wir stießen mit Champagner auf das neue Jahr an.* **2.** SPORT *(in billiards) perform the opening break* ◊ *Er nahm das Queue und stieß an.; (in football)* kick off ◊ *Die Kölner stießen an und verloren gleich den Ball.* (ref v) sich anstoßen bump into something ◊ *Mist, ich habe mich schon wieder angestoßen!* sich an etw. (dat) anstoßen bump into sth ◊ *Er stolperte und stieß sich an der Tischkante an.* sich (dat) etw. anstoßen hurt sth ◊ *Au, ich habe mir den großen Zeh angestoßen!* sich (dat) etw. an etw. (dat) anstoßen bump your sth on/against sth ◊ *Sie stößt sich immer wieder den Kopf am Küchenschrank an.*

an|strei·chen ['anʃtraeçn] <streicht an, strich an, hat angestrichen> (tr v) **1.** *(with a brush)* paint ◊ *Sie strich den Zaun mit wetterfester Farbe an.* etw. weiß/hell anstreichen paint sth white/in a light colo(u)r ◊ *Ich streiche die Wand weiß an.* **2.** *(with a pencil etc.)* mark ◊ *Im Diktat waren 13 Fehler angestrichen.* ♦ *Der Termin war mit Rot im Kalender angestrichen.*

② an|stren·gen ['anʃtrɛŋən] <strengt an, strengte an, hat angestrengt> (tr v) **1.** tire out ◊ *Diese Unterhaltung hat mich sehr angestrengt.; (the eyes)* strain **2.** LAW *(proceedings)* initiate, institute ◊ *Er strengt eine Klage gegen das Unternehmen an.* (ref v) sich anstrengen make an effort ◊ *Er sollte sich ein bisschen mehr anstrengen.* ♦ *Sie strengte sich an, um ihm die Aufgabe zu erklären.*

An·stren·gung ['anʃtrɛŋʊŋ] die <-, -en> **1.** effort ◊ *Die Regierung hat eine gewaltige Anstrengung unternommen.* **2.** strain, exertion ◊ *Bei körperlicher Anstrengung treten Schmerzen auf.* ♦ *Die Anstrengungen der Reise waren ihr zu viel.*

An·strich ['anʃtrɪç] der <-(e)s, -e> **1.** (coat of) paint ◊ *Unser Gartenzaun könnte einen neuen Anstrich vertragen!* ♦ *Der Anstrich muss dringend erneuert werden.* das Haus mit dem blauen Anstrich the house painted in blue einer Sache (dat) einen Anstrich geben paint sth ◊ *Geben Sie dem Holz einen Anstrich mit wetterfester Farbe.* **2.** *(fig)* feel ◊ *Durch die hellen Farben hat das Zimmer einen freundlichen Anstrich.* jdm/einer Sache einen wohnlichen/wissenschaftlichen Anstrich geben give a cosy/scientific feel to sb/sth ◊ *Der Anzug mit Krawatte gab ihm einen seriösen Anstrich.* ein Anstrich von etw. an air of sth ◊ *Die Firma gibt sich einen Anstrich von Professionalität.*

An·sturm ['anʃtʊrm] der <-(e)s, Anstürme> der/ein Ansturm (auf etw. (acc)) the/a run on sth ◊ *Der kleine Dorfladen war dem Ansturm der Kunden nicht gewachsen.* ♦ *Der erwartete Ansturm auf das neue Produkt blieb aus.*

An·teil ['antael] der <-(e)s, -e> share ◊ *Ihr Anteil an den Kosten beläuft sich auf 1500 Euro.* ♦ *Dieses Nahrungsmittel hat einen hohen Anteil an Fett.* ♦ *Er hat seine Anteile an der Firma verkauft.* ⓔ Anteil an etw. (dat) haben have contributed to sth ◊ *Die ganze Familie hat Anteil an ihrem Erfolg.* Anteil an etw. (dat) nehmen, Anteil für etw.

zeigen feel/show empathy for sth ◊ *Alle nahmen Anteil an ihrem Schicksal.* ♦ *Sie zeigte wenig Anteil für seine Probleme.*

An·teil·nah·me ['antaelna:mə] die <-> *no pl* sympathy ◊ *Unsere Anteilnahme gilt den Opfern und ihren Angehörigen.* ♦ *die Anteilnahme der Bevölkerung am Schicksal der Entführten* die/jds Anteilnahme an etw. (dat) sb's sympathy over sth ◊ *die Anteilnahme am Leid der Opfer* jds Anteilnahme an jds Tod, jds Anteilnahme am Tod ... (gen) sb's condolences over sb's death ◊ *In einem Brief teilte sie ihm ihre Anteilnahme am Tod seiner Frau mit.* Anteilnahme für jdn sympathy for sb ◊ *Der Präsident äußerte seine Anteilnahme für die Menschen im Katastrophengebiet.* unter Anteilnahme ... (gen) followed closely by sb ◊ *Er wurde unter Anteilnahme der ganzen Bevölkerung beerdigt.*

An·ten·ne [an'tɛnə] die <-, -n> aerial

an·tik [an'ti:k] (adj) *no comp/superl* **1.** *(from Roman times)* classical, ancient ◊ *ein antikes Drama* ♦ *Die Säulen des Tempels sind alle antik.* **2.** *(old)* antique ◊ *eine antike Uhr* ♦ *Der Schreibtisch ist echt antik.*

An·ti·qui·tät [antikvi'tɛ:t] die <-, -en> antique

An·to·nym [anto'ny:m] das <-s, -e> antonym
ⓢSynonym

> The German term for **antonym** is *Gegenteilwort*. This is a word opposite in meaning to another, such as quick – slow, comfortable – uncomfortable, come – go, trust – distrust, advantage – disadvantage, greeting – farewell, antonym – synonym.

② An·trag ['antra:k] der <-(e)s, Anträge> **1.** ein Antrag (auf etw. (acc)) application (for sth) ◊ *Ihr Antrag wurde genehmigt.* ♦ *Er stellte einen Antrag auf Kindergeld.* **2.** *(of marriage)* proposal jdm einen Antrag machen propose to sb **3.** *(in a parliament, meeting)* Antrag (auf etw. (acc)) motion (for sth) ◊ *über einen Antrag abstimmen* **4.** LAW Antrag (auf etw. (acc)) petition (for sth) ◊ *einen Antrag auf Bewährung stellen*

an|tre·ten [an'tre:tn] <tritt an, trat an, hat/ist angetreten> (tr v) +*haben* **1.** start, take up ◊ *Sie trat eine Stelle als Sekretärin an.* ♦ *eine Reise antreten* **2.** ein Erbe antreten accept an inheritance ◊ *Er wollte das Erbe seines Vaters nicht antreten.* jds Nachfolge antreten succeed sb, become sb's successor ◊ *Der Assistent des Professors trat seine Nachfolge an.* (intr v) +*sein* **1.** pünktlich zum Dienst antreten be there to start work on time Alle Studenten waren zur Klausur angetreten. All students had come to sit their exams. **2.** zu den/einer Wahl antreten compete as a candidate in the/a election ◊ *Sie wird zur Wahl antreten.* gegen jdn antreten compete against sb ◊ *Die Nationalmannschaft trat im Finale gegen Brasilien an.* **3.** MIL line up (in formation) ◊ *Alle Kompanien waren auf dem Platz angetreten.*

an|tun ['antu:n] <tut an, tat an, hat angetan> (tr v) jdm etw. antun do sth to sb ◊ *Wie konnten Sie mir das nur antun!* ♦ *Etwas Schlimmeres hätte sie mir gar nicht antun können.* (ref v) *(fam, pej)* **1.** sich (dat) etw./jdn antun wollen, sich (dat) etw./jdn antun müssen have to saddle yourself with sth/sb,

have to land yourself with sth/sb ◇ *Deine langweiligen Freunde wollen wir uns nicht schon wieder
antun.* ◆ *Diesen Berg Arbeit muss ich mir nicht
antun.* **2.** *(euph)* sich ⸤dat⸥ etwas antun do away
with yourself ◇ *Sie hat schon mehrmals versucht,
sich etwas anzutun.*

◉ **jd/etw. hat es jdm angetan** sb is taken with
sb/sth ◇ *Dieser Hut hatte es mir angetan.* ◆ *Meine
Freundin hatte es ihm offensichtlich angetan.*

② **Ant·wort** ['antvɔrt] die <-, –en> **1.** eine Antwort
(auf etw. ⸤acc⸥) answer (to sth), reply (to sth) ◇ *Er
gab ihr keine Antwort.* ◆ *Ich bekam eine positive
Antwort auf meine Anfrage.* **2.** *(nonverbal)*
response (to sth) ◇ *Zur Antwort deutete er auf das
Fenster.*

② **ant·wor·ten** ['antvɔrtn̩] <antwortet, antwortete, hat
geantwortet> ⸤tr+intr v⸥ **1.** (auf etw. ⸤acc⸥)
antworten answer (sth), reply (to sth) ◇ *Hat sie
dir überhaupt geantwortet?* ◆ *Was hat er auf deine
Frage geantwortet?* ◆ *auf einen Brief antworten* ◆
Willst du auf die Vorwürfe antworten? jdm
antworten answer sb, reply to sb ◇ *Sie wollte mir
nicht antworten.* **2.** *(non-verbal)* (auf etw. ⸤acc⸥)
antworten respond (to sth), react (to sth) ◇ *Er antwortete (auf die Frage) mit Kopfschütteln/lautem
Gelächter.*

an|ver·trau·en ['anfɛɐtraʊən] <vertraut an,
vertraute an, hat anvertraut> ⸤tr v⸥ jdm etw./jdn
anvertrauen entrust sth/sb to sb ◇ *jdm ein Amt/
eine Aufgabe anvertrauen* ◆ *Sie vertraute das Baby
einer Tagesmutter an.*; *(a secret, confidential
information)* confide sth to sb ◇ *Er hat ihr seine
Geheimnisse anvertraut.* ⸤ref v⸥ sich jdm anvertrauen confide in sb ◇ *Sie vertraute sich ihrem
Freund an.*

② **An·walt** ['anvalt] → Rechtsanwalt
An·wäl·tin ['anvɛltɪn] → Rechtsanwalt
An·wei·sung ['anvaɪzʊŋ] die <-, –en> instruction
◇ *auf Anweisung der Regierung* ◆ *Bitte befolgen
Sie die Anweisungen zur Benutzung des Geräts!*
an|wen·den ['anvɛndn̩] <wendet an, wendete/
wandte an, hat angewendet/angewandt> ⸤tr v⸥ use
◇ *Im Notfall würde er auch Gewalt anwenden.*; *(a
law, science)* apply ◇ *ein Verfahren anwenden*
An·wen·dung ['anvɛndʊŋ] die <-, –en> **1.** *no pl*
use ◇ *War die Anwendung von Schusswaffen
gerechtfertigt?* Anwendung finden be used ◇
*Dieses Medikament findet keine Anwendung in der
Humanmedizin.*; *(a law)* be applied **2.** ɪᴛ application ◇ *Bitte schließen Sie alle Anwendungen.*
② **an·we·send** ['anveːznt, 'anveːzant] ⸤adj⸥ present ◇
Sie war bei der Sitzung nicht anwesend. ◆ *Alle
anwesenden Mitglieder stimmten mit Ja.*
⊜abwesend
An·we·sen·heit ['anveːznhaɪt] die <-> *no pl*
presence ◇ *Deine Anwesenheit macht mich
glücklich.* ◆ *die Anwesenheit des Vaters bei der
Geburt*; *(at school etc.)* attendance ◇ *Anwesenheit
in den Sportstunden ist Pflicht.* in Anwesenheit …
⸤gen⸥, in Anwesenheit von jdm in sb's presence, in
the presence of sb ◇ *Die Übergabe der Preise fand
in Anwesenheit des Bürgermeisters statt.* ◆ *Die
Filmschule wurde in Anwesenheit von Wim Wenders
eröffnet.* ⊜Präsenz ⊜Abwesenheit
An·woh·ner ['anvoːnɐ] der <-s, ->,
An·woh·ne·rin ['anvoːnərɪn] die <-, –nen> local

resident
An·zahl ['antsaːl] die <-, –en> *most sing* number
◇ *Die Anzahl der Verletzten stieg ständig.* ◆ *eine
große Anzahl von Modellen* in großer Anzahl
vorhanden sein be there in large numbers
an|zah·len ['antsaːlən] <zahlt an, zahlte an, hat
angezahlt> ⸤tr+intr v⸥ make a down payment ◇ *Wie
viel muss ich anzahlen?* ◆ *Sie haben die Reise
schon angezahlt.*
An·zah·lung ['antsaːlʊŋ] die <-, –en> down
payment, deposit ◇ *Er verlangte eine Anzahlung in
Höhe von 30 Prozent der Gesamtsumme.* eine
Anzahlung auf/für etw. ⸤acc⸥ a down payment on/
for sth, a deposit on/for sth ◇ *eine Anzahlung auf
ein neues Auto machen*
An·zei·chen ['antsaɪçn̩] das <-s, -> sign ◇ *die
ersten Anzeichen einer Krankheit*
② **An·zei·ge** ['antsaɪgə] die <-, –n> **1.** charge(s) ◇ *Er
drohte ihr mit einer Anzeige.* Anzeige gegen jdn
erstatten report sb to the police ◇ *Er hatte Anzeige
gegen den Dieb erstattet.* **2.** *(in a newspaper)*
advertisement ◇ *Er meldete sich auf unsere Anzeige
hin.* ◆ *eine Anzeige aufgeben* **3.** ᴛᴇᴄʜɴ display ◇ *Das
Gerät besitzt eine digitale Anzeige.*
an|zei·gen ['antsaɪgn̩] <zeigt an, zeigte an, hat
angezeigt> ⸤tr v⸥ **1.** report ◇ *Sie hat ihn wegen
Brandstiftung angezeigt.* ◆ *Ich finde, du solltest
das bei der Polizei anzeigen.* **2.** ᴛᴇᴄʜɴ show,
indicate ◇ *Das Thermometer zeigt 39 Grad an.* ◆
Das Display zeigte drei Anrufe an.
② **an|zie·hen** ['antsiːən] <zieht an, zog an, hat
angezogen> ⸤tr v⸥ **1.** (sich ⸤dat⸥) etw. anziehen put
sth on ◇ *Sie zog (sich) ihren Mantel an.* jdm etw.
anziehen help sb put sth on ◇ *Er zog seinem Sohn
die Stiefel an.* sich anziehen get dressed ◇ *Zieh
dich bitte vor dem Frühstück an.* sich warm
anziehen put on warm clothes jdn anziehen dress
sb ◇ *Er zog das Baby an.* ⊜ausziehen **2.** *(insects,
visitors etc.)* attract ◇ *Er fühlte sich von ihr
angezogen.* **3.** *(the reins)* pull tight ◇ *Sie zog die
Zügel an.; (screws)* tighten ◇ *Du musst die
Schraube fester anziehen.; (a brake)* apply
4. *(knees, legs)* draw up
② **An·zug** ['antsuːk] der <-(e)s, Anzüge> suit ◇ *Er trug
einen dunklen Anzug.*
◉ **im Anzug sein** be approaching ◇ *Er spürte,
dass Gefahr im Anzug war.*
② **an|zün·den** ['antsʏndn̩] <zündet an, zündete an,
hat angezündet> ⸤tr v⸥ *(a candle, match, fire)*
light; *(a building)* set fire to sich eine Zigarette/
Zigarre anzünden light up a cigarette/cigar
AOK [aːoːˈkaː] die *(abbr of* Allgemeine Ortskranken-
kasse*)* ◇ *Sie ist bei der AOK versichert.*

> The *Allgemeine Ortskrankenkasse* is the largest
> statutory provider of medical insurance in
> Germany. In its capacity as a provider of compul-
> sory medical cover, the organization is obliged to
> cater for all employees as well as all those who
> are unemployed.

② **Ap·fel** ['apfl̩] der <-s, Äpfel> apple ◇ *einen Apfel
schälen*
◉ **in den sauren Apfel beißen** bite the bullet ◇
Sie biss in den sauren Apfel und zahlte die Strafe.
Ap·fel·saft ['apfl̩zaft] der <-(e)s, Apfelsäfte> apple
juice ◇ *„Was darf ich Ihnen bringen?" — „Zweimal*

A
B
C
D
E
F
G
H
I
J
K
L
M
N
O
P
Q
R
S
T
U
V
W
X
Y
Z

Apfelsaft, bitte."

② **Ap·fel·si·ne** [apf|'zi:nə] die <-, -n> orange ◊ *eine Apfelsine schälen* ⊝Orange

② **A·po·the·ke** [apo'te:kə] die <-, -n> pharmacy, chemist's (shop) ◊ *Dieses Medikament gibt es nur in der Apotheke.*

> Medicines requiring a prescription from a doctor can only be obtained at the *Apotheke* (chemist's). The prescription is processed there on payment of a fee (the remaining costs are billed to the patient's individual health insurance fund). Over-the-counter medicines are also obtainable at a chemist's, as are cosmetic products, but these are conceived to be more expensive than in other shops, hence the expression: *Das sind ja Preise wie in der Apotheke!* (Those are chemist shop prices!).

A·po·the·ker [apo'te:kə] der <-s, ->, **A·po·the·ke·rin** [apo'te:kərɪn] die <-, -nen> pharmacist, (dispensing) chemist ◊ *Sie ist Apothekerin.* ♦ *Ein Apotheker kann über dieses Medikament Auskunft geben.*

② **Ap·pa·rat** [apa'ra:t] der <-(e)s, -e> **1.** apparatus, appliance ◊ *einen Apparat ein-/ausschalten* ⊝Gerät **2.** telephone ◊ *Ich hole meine Mutter, bleiben Sie bitte am Apparat.*

ap·pel·lie·ren [apɛ'li:rən] <appelliert, appellierte, hat appelliert> [intr v] *(lofty)* an jdn appellieren, etw. zu tun appeal to sb to do sth ◊ *Man appellierte an die Bevölkerung, Ruhe zu bewahren.* an etw. [acc] appellieren appeal to sth ◊ *Der Außenminister appellierte an die Vernunft der Kriegsparteien.* ♦ *an das Gewissen/jds Verstand appellieren*

② **Ap·pe·tit** [ape'ti:t] der <-(e)s> *no pl* appetite ◊ *Zimt regt den Appetit an.* ♦ *Nach dieser Nachricht hatte er keinen Appetit mehr.* Appetit auf etw. [acc] haben feel like sth ◊ *Hast du Appetit auf Käsekuchen?*

⊛ **guten Appetit** enjoy your meal, bon appétit ⊝Mahlzeit

② **A·pri·ko·se** [apri'ko:zə] die <-, -n> apricot

② **A·pril** [a'prɪl] der <-(s), -e> *most sing* April → Januar

Ä·ra ['ɛːraː] die <-, -en> *most sing* era, epoch, age ◊ *Mit dem Fall der Berliner Mauer wurde eine neue Ära eingeleitet.* ♦ *während der kommunistischen Ära/eine Ära ...* [gen] the/an era of sth ◊ *Die Ära des digitalen Fernsehens hat begonnen.* ♦ *Das Land hoffte vergeblich auf eine Ära des Friedens.* ♦ *Südafrika in der Ära der Apartheid* die Ära Adenauer/Gorbatschow etc. the Adenauer era/Gorbachev era etc.

A·ra·ber ['arabɐ] der <-s, ->, **A·ra·be·rin** ['arabərɪn] die <-, -nen> Arab → Deutsche

a·ra·bisch [a'ra:bɪʃ] [adj] *mostly before ns* Arab(ic) arabische Zahlen/Ziffern Arabic numbers → deutsch

A·ra·bisch [a'ra:bɪʃ] das <-(s)> *no pl* Arabic → Deutsch

② **Ar·beit** ['arbaɛt] die <-, -en> **1.** work ◊ *seine Arbeit tun* ♦ *viel Arbeit haben* ♦ *Er ist auf dem Weg zur Arbeit.* ♦ *die Arbeiten eines Künstlers ausstellen* **2.** *no pl* job, employment ◊ *Sie hat ihre Arbeit verloren.* einer geregelten Arbeit nachgehen have a steady job **3.** UNI paper ◊ *eine Arbeit über*

Kafka **4.** SCHOOL test ◊ *Wir schreiben morgen in Chemie eine Arbeit.*

⊛ **etw. in Arbeit haben** be working on sth ◊ *Jule hat ein wichtiges Projekt in Arbeit.* **erst die Arbeit, dann das Vergnügen** business before pleasure

② **ar·bei·ten** ['arbaɛtn̩] [intr v] +*haben* work ◊ *Um das zu erreichen, hat er hart arbeiten müssen.* ♦ *Sie arbeitet als Lehrerin/beim Finanzamt/für den Tierschutz/mit Behinderten.* ♦ *Sein Herz arbeitet nicht mehr.* an etw. [dat] arbeiten work on sth ◊ *Sie arbeitet gerade an einem Aufsatz.* ♦ *Du musst an deinen Manieren arbeiten.* Die Zeit arbeitet für ihn. Time is on his side.

Ar·bei·ter ['arbaɛtɐ] der <-s, ->, **Ar·bei·te·rin** ['arbaɛtərɪn] die <-, -nen> worker ◊ *eine gewissenhafte Arbeiterin* ♦ *Er ist als Arbeiter in einer Autofabrik beschäftigt.* ♦ *Die Firma beschäftigt 200 Arbeiter und Angestellte.* die Arbeiter the working classes

② **Ar·beit·ge·ber** ['arbaɛtge:bɐ] der <-s, ->, **Ar·beit·ge·be·rin** ['arbaɛtge:bərɪn] die <-, -nen> employer ◊ *Als Arbeitgeber hat er viel Verantwortung.* ♦ *Seine Arbeitgeberin ist die Stadt Köln.* ⊝Arbeitnehmer

② **Ar·beit·neh·mer** ['arbaɛtne:mɐ] der <-s, ->, **Ar·beit·neh·me·rin** ['arbaɛtne:mərɪn] die <-, -nen> employee ◊ *Die Arbeitnehmerin hat Anspruch auf einen sicheren Arbeitsplatz.* ♦ *Die Arbeitnehmer protestierten gegen längere Arbeitszeiten.* ⊝Arbeitgeber

Ar·beits·amt ['arbaɛts|amt] das <-(e)s, Arbeitsämter> jobcentre ◊ *Arbeitssuchende sollen sich beim Arbeitsamt melden.* ♦ *beim Arbeitsamt einen Antrag auf Arbeitslosengeld stellen*

> Since the first of January 2004, the German job centre is officially called *Agentur für Arbeit*. However, in everyday use it is still referred to by its former name, *Arbeitsamt*.

Ar·beits·er·laub·nis ['arbaɛts|ɛlaɔpnɪs] die <-> *no pl* work permit ◊ *Er hat eine Arbeitserlaubnis beantragt.*

ar·beits·los ['arbaɛtslo:s] [adj] unemployed, out of work ◊ *Sie hatte Angst, arbeitslos zu werden.* ♦ *Kurse für arbeitslose Akademiker*

Ar·beits·lo·se ['arbaɛtslo:zə] der/die <-n, die Arbeitslosen> *but: ein Arbeitsloser/eine Arbeitslose* unemployed person die Arbeitslosen the unemployed ◊ *Es gibt im Augenblick über vier Millionen Arbeitslose.* box⊛ Substantivierung

Ar·beits·lo·sen·un·ter·stüt·zung ['arbaɛtslo:zn̩|ʊntɐʃtʏtsʊŋ] die <-> *no pl* unemployment benefit ◊ *Arbeitslosenunterstützung beantragen/bekommen* ♦ *Anspruch auf Arbeitslosenunterstützung haben*

Ar·beits·lo·sig·keit ['arbaɛtslo:zɪçkaɛt] die <-> *no pl* unemployment ◊ *von Arbeitslosigkeit bedroht/betroffen sein* ♦ *Die Arbeitslosigkeit ging leicht zurück.*

Ar·beits·platz ['arbaɛtsplats] der <-es, Arbeitsplätze> **1.** *(position)* job ◊ *seinen Arbeitsplatz verlieren* ♦ *einen Arbeitsplatz suchen* **2.** workplace ◊ *ein schlecht beleuchteter Arbeitsplatz* am Arbeitsplatz at work ◊ *sexuelle Belästi-*

gung am Arbeitsplatz; workstation ◊ eine EDV-Anlage mit fünf Arbeitsplätzen

Ar·beits·zeit ['aʳbaɛtsaɛt] die <–, –en> **1.** working hours ◊ Während der Arbeitszeit sind private Telefongespräche verboten. ✦ feste/flexible Arbeitszeiten **2.** hours/time spent working ◊ Die Arbeitszeit für dieses Projekt beträgt ca. 10 Stunden.

Ar·chä·o·lo·gie [aʳçɛolo'giː] die <–> no pl archaeology ◊ ein Student der Archäologie ✦ Sie studiert Klassische Archäologie. ✦ neue Publikationen zur Archäologie Europas

ARD [aːlɛʳdeː] die (abbr of Arbeitsgemeinschaft der öffentlich-rechtlichen Rundfunkanstalten Deutschlands) ◊ Dieser Film läuft heute Abend in der ARD. ✦ Die ARD zeigte eine Reportage über dieses Museum.

> The *ARD* is a public radio and television broadcasting authority controlled by the individual federal states. It is also referred to as *Erstes Programm* (Channel One). The regional version of this institution is known as *Drittes Programm* (Channel Three). Its remit is not only to entertain, but also to contribute to the public's general education. As it is only financed to a limited extent by advertising, it requires a licence fee from its viewers and listeners. In contrast to many independent broadcasting institutions it only shows advertising at certain times and ensures that feature films are not interrupted.

Ar·gen·ti·ni·en [aʳgɛn'tiːniən] das <–s> article only in combination with attribute, no pl Argentina → Deutschland

Ar·gen·ti·ni·er [aʳgɛn'tiːniɐ] der <–s, –>, **Ar·gen·ti·ni·e·rin** [aʳgɛn'tiːniərɪn] die <–, –nen> Argentinian → Deutsche

ar·gen·ti·nisch [aʳgɛn'tiːnɪʃ] adj mostly before ns Argentinian ◊ der argentinische Präsident

Är·ger ['ɛʳgɐ] der <–s> no pl **1.** Ärger (über jdn/etw.) anger (about sb/sth) ◊ Aus Ärger über seine Verspätung ließ sie ihn einfach stehen. ✦ Sein Ärger ist inzwischen verflogen. seinen Ärger an jdm auslassen vent your anger on sb ⊖Zorn **2.** Ärger (mit jdm/etw.) trouble ◊ Mit dir hat man nichts als Ärger.

② **är·ger·lich** ['ɛʳgɐlɪç] adj **1.** annoying ◊ Der Vorfall war sehr ärgerlich. ✦ ein paar ärgerliche Fehler **2.** annoyed, angry ◊ Ihr Vater wurde immer ärgerlicher. ✦ Sie warf ihm ärgerliche Blicke zu.

② **är·gern** ['ɛʳgɐn] tr v +haben **1.** annoy ◊ Ihr Benehmen ärgerte ihn. ✦ Ärgert es dich, wenn du Fehler machst? **2.** tease ◊ Hör auf, die Katze zu ärgern! ref v +haben sich (über jdn/etw.) ärgern be annoyed (about sb/sth), be angry (about sb/sth) ◊ Sie ärgerte sich furchtbar (über ihre Freundin). ✦ Er ärgerte sich (darüber), dass der Zug Verspätung hatte.

ar·gu·men·tie·ren [aʳgumɛn'tiːrən] <argumentiert, argumentierte, hat argumentiert> intr v argue ◊ Sie argumentierte (damit), dass das Haus ein Altbau sei.

A·rith·me·tik [arɪt'meːtɪk] die <–> no pl arithmetic(s) ◊ Er wurde in Schreiben und Arithmetik unterrichtet. ✦ eine Einführung in die Arithmetik

② **arm** [aʳm] adj <ärmer, am ärmsten> **1.** poor ◊ Die

Familie war ziemlich arm. ✦ Der arme Junge! Er hat keine Mutter mehr. ✦ Sie war wirklich arm dran ohne Freunde. um eine Hoffnung/Illusion etc. ärmer sein have one hope/illusion etc. less **2.** arm an etw. dat poor in sth ◊ Das Land ist arm an Rohstoffen.; lacking in sth ◊ ein an echten Höhepunkten armes Finale; low in sth ◊ Diese Kost ist arm an tierischem Fett. arm an Schadstoffen containing very few pollutants

② **Arm** [aʳm] der <–(e)s, –e> **1.** arm ◊ Sie stand mit hängenden Armen da. ✦ Er klemmte sich die Zeitung unter den Arm. ✦ Sie gingen Arm in Arm spazieren. jdm/sich in die Arme fallen fall into sb's/each other's arms sich/einander in den Armen liegen embrace one another jdn in den Arm nehmen take sb in your arms **2.** (of a river) branch ◊ der nördlichste Arm der Donau; (of a crane) jib; (of a candelabra) arm

◉ jdm unter die Arme greifen help sb out ◊ Sie wollte ihm finanziell unter die Arme greifen. jdn auf den Arm nehmen have sb on jdm in die Arme laufen run into sb ◊ Ich wollte gerade gehen, da lief ich meinem Chef in die Arme.

Arm·band ['aʳmbant] das <–(e)s, Armbänder> **1.** (jewellery) bracelet ◊ Er legte ihr ein goldenes Armband an. ✦ ein Armband tragen **2.** (not as an ornament) wristband ◊ Ein elektronisches Armband überwacht den Puls der Patienten.

Arm·band·uhr ['aʳmbant|uːɐ] die <–, –en> wristwatch ◊ Er trug eine goldene Armbanduhr.

Ar·mee [aʳmeː] die <–, –n> **1.** armed forces ◊ Er meldete sich freiwillig zur Armee. ⊖Militär **2.** army ◊ Eine Armee drang mit Panzern in die Stadt ein. ⊖Heer **3.** (fig) eine Armee von etw./jdm, eine Armee ... gen an army of... ◊ Eine Armee von Kindern tobte auf dem Spielplatz. ✦ eine Armee kleiner Spinnen ⊖Heer

Är·mel ['ɛʳml] der <–s, –> sleeve ◊ eine Bluse mit kurzen/langen Ärmeln.

◉ die Ärmel hochkrempeln roll your sleeves up

Ar·mut ['aʳmuːt] die <–> no pl **1.** poverty ◊ Sie lebten in Armut. ✦ In diesem Land herrscht große Armut. ⊖Not **2.** Armut an etw. dat lack of sth ◊ Armut an Bildung/Ideen ⊖Reichtum

A·ro·ma [a'roːma] das <–s, Aromen or –ta> **1.** flavour, flavor ◊ Diese Tomaten haben nur wenig Aroma. ✦ ein Wein mit fruchtigem Aroma **2.** flavouring, flavoring ◊ natürliche Aromen wie Vanille und Zimt ✦ ein Tee mit künstlichem Aroma **3.** aroma, smell ◊ ein Parfüm mit schwerem Aroma

ar·ran·gie·ren [araŋ'ʒiːrən, arãˈʒiːrən] (lofty) <arrangiert, arrangierte, hat arrangiert> tr v **1.** (jdm.) etw. arrangieren, etw. (für jdn) arrangieren arrange (sb) sth, arrange sth (for sb) ◊ Ihre Ehe wurde von den Eltern arrangiert. ✦ Ich werde Ihnen den Kredit bei der Großbank arrangieren. ✦ Können Sie einen Termin beim Chef für mich arrangieren? **2.** etw. (zu etw.) arrangieren arrange flowers (into sth) ◊ die Möbel anders arrangieren ✦ Soll ich Ihnen die Blumen zu einem Strauß arrangieren? ref v **1.** sich mit etw. arrangieren make the best of sth, come to terms with sth ◊ Er hat sich gut mit seiner Krankheit arrangiert. **2.** sich mit jdm arrangieren make a compromise with sb, come to terms with sb ◊ Versuchen Sie sich mit den Gläubigern zu arrangieren. sie arrangieren sich

they come to a compromise ◊ *Wir können uns sicher irgendwie arrangieren.*

Arsch [aɾʃ] der <-(e)s, Ärsche> *(rude, pej)* **1.** backside, arse, ass ◊ *Los, beweg deinen Arsch!* **2.** arsehole, asshole ◉ am Arsch der Welt miles from anywhere, at the back of beyond jdm in den Arsch kriechen suck up to sb jdn am Arsch lecken *(rude)* piss off, get stuffed am/im Arsch sein *(slang)* *(person)* be knackered *(object)* bust, kaputt kein Arsch *(slang)* fucking nobody

Arsch·loch [ˈaɾʃlɔx] das <-(e)s, Arschlöcher> *(rude, pej)* arsehole, asshole

② **Art** [aːrt] die <-, -en> **1.** *most sing* way ◊ *Er hat eine witzige Art.* ♦ *Die Art, wie sie sprach, erinnerte mich an meine Mutter.* ♦ *die einfachste Art, Daten zu erfassen* ♦ *Diese Frage lässt sich auf zwei Arten beantworten.* Art und Weise way ◊ *Das Buch verschwand auf geheimnisvolle Art und Weise.* ⊜Weise **2.** *no pl* nature, kind ◊ *ein Erlebnis besonderer Art* ♦ *Die Probleme waren von komplexer Art.* ♦ *Lügen ist nicht meine Art!* ⊜Natur **3.** *most sing* kind, sort ◊ *Ich mag jede Art von Nüssen.* ♦ *Kennst du noch mehr Gedichte dieser Art?* ♦ *Was für eine Art von Drucker brauchst du?* ⊜Sorte **4.** BIO species ◊ *die Rote Liste der gefährdeten Arten; (of a plant)* variety ◊ *Dieser Baum ist eine tropische Art.* ◉ eine Art ... a kind of ... ◊ *Ist das eine Art Umhang? (person)* ... of sorts ◊ *Er ist eine Art Künstler.*

ar·tig [ˈaːrtɪç] ⟨adj⟩ good, well-behaved ◊ *ein artiges Kind* ♦ *Warst du auch immer schön artig?* ⊜brav

② **Ar·ti·kel** [aˈrtɪkl̩, aˈrtiːkl̩] der <-s, -> article ◊ *Er schreibt regelmäßig Artikel für die Zeitung.* ♦ *Artikel 3 Absatz 2 des Grundgesetzes* ♦ *der Import indischer Artikel*

The *Artikel* accompanies the noun and indicates whether a certain thing in a text is new or already known. For example: *Es war einmal* ein *Wolf* (Once upon a time there was a wolf). Dieser *Wolf hatte ständig Hunger* (This wolf was always hungry). *Da dachte er sich, dass es doch sehr schön wäre, wieder mal* ein *Geißlein zu fressen* (So he thought to himself that it would be very nice to eat another little goat). The German language makes a distinction between definite articles (*der, die, das*) and indefinite articles (*ein, eine*).

ar·ti·ku·lie·ren [aˈrtikuˈliːrən] *(lofty)* <artikuliert, artikulierte, hat artikuliert> ⟨tr v⟩ etw. artikulieren articulate sth, express sth ◊ *Ich kann meine Gefühle nicht immer richtig artikulieren.* ♦ *Er hatte Schwierigkeiten, die arabischen Laute richtig zu artikulieren.* ⟨ref v⟩ **1.** sich artikulieren expresses yourself ◊ *Sie kann sich nicht einmal vernünftig artikulieren.* **2.** sich artikulieren manifest itself ◊ *Der öffentliche Widerstand artikuliert sich in Demonstrationen.* ♦ *Schon früh artikulierte sich sein unruhiges Temperament.*

Arz·nei [aˈrtsˈnae] die <-, -en> medicine ◊ *Sie hat vergessen, ihre Arznei einzunehmen.* ♦ *Der Arzt verschrieb ihr eine Arznei.* ⊜Medikament, Medizin

② **Arzt** [aɾtst] der <-es, Ärzte>, **Ärz·tin** [ˈɛɾtstɪn] die <-, -nen> doctor, physician ◊ *Sie ist Ärztin.* ♦ *zum*

Arzt gehen

ärzt·lich [ˈɛɾtstlɪç] ⟨adj, adv⟩ *when used as an adj, only before ns* medical(ly) ◊ *ein ärztliches Attest* ♦ *sich ärztlich untersuchen lassen*

② **Arzt·pra·xis** [ˈaɾtstpraksɪs] die <-, Arztpraxen> doctor's surgery ◊ *in der Arztpraxis behandelt werden* ♦ *eine Arztpraxis aufsuchen*

A·sche [ˈaʃə] die <-> *no pl* **1.** ash ◊ *zu Asche verbrennen* **2.** jds Asche sb's ashes ◊ *Friede sei ihrer Asche!*

A·scher·mitt·woch [aʃeˈrmɪtvɔx] der <-s> *no pl* Ash Wednesday ◊ *Am Aschermittwoch essen sie kein Fleisch.*

Ash Wednesday is the first day of the 40-day period of preparation (Lent) to mark the resurrection of Jesus at Easter. It signals the end of the German carnival season, a period of boisterous celebration.

A·si·at [aˈzjaːt] der <-en, -en>, **A·si·a·tin** [aˈzjaːtɪn] die <-, -nen> Asian → Deutsche

In the U.K. the expression **Asian** tends to be used to refer to the inhabitants and the culture of the Indian subcontinent. Other Asian cultures are usually referred to more specifically: Korean, Japanese, Chinese etc. Thus the translation for *Asiat* and *asiatisch* might vary considerably.

a·si·a·tisch [aˈzjaːtɪʃ] ⟨adj⟩ *mostly before ns* Asian ◊ *asiatische Sprachen*

A·si·en [ˈaːzjən] das <-s> *article only in combination with attribute, no pl* Asia box® Land

As·pi·rin® [aspiˈriːn] das <-s, -> aspirin ◊ *Sie nahm ein/zwei Aspirin.*

② **aß** [aːs] *pret of* essen

Ass [as] das <-es, -e> ace ◊ *Sie legte ein Ass ab.* ♦ *Sie beendete das Match mit einem Ass.* ♦ *Auf seinem Gebiet war er ein Ass.*

Ast [ast] der <-(e)s, Äste> branch, bough ◊ *Der Affe schwang sich von Ast zu Ast.* ◉ auf dem absteigenden Ast sein, sich auf dem absteigenden Ast befinden be going downhill

② **A·syl** [aˈzyːl] das <-s> *no pl* asylum ◊ *um Asyl bitten* ♦ *jdm Asyl gewähren* ♦ *Asyl beantragen*

A·sy·lant [azyˈlant] der <-en, -en>, **A·sy·lan·tin** [azyˈlantɪn] die <-, -nen> asylum seeker ◊ *als Asylant anerkannt werden*

A·syl·be·wer·ber [aˈzyːlbəvɛrbɐ] der <-s, ->, **A·syl·be·wer·be·rin** [aˈzyːlbəvɛrbərɪn] die <-, -nen> person applying for political asylum

A·tem [ˈaːtəm] der <-s> *no pl* **1.** breath ◊ *Er hat schlechten Atem.* ♦ *Sie holte tief Atem.* ♦ *Er war vom Laufen außer Atem.* **2.** *(respiration)* breathing ◊ *Sein Atem ging sehr schnell.* ◉ einen langen Atem brauchen/haben need/have a lot of stamina jdn in Atem halten keep sb busy

a·tem·los [ˈaːtəmloːs] ⟨adj, adv⟩ <atemloser, am atemlosesten> breathless(ly) ◊ *Es herrschte atemlose Stille.* ♦ *Das moderne Leben ist atemlos.* ♦ *Sie hörten ihm atemlos zu.*

② **at·men** [ˈaːtmən] <atmet, atmete, hat geatmet> ⟨tr+intr v⟩ breathe ◊ *Sie atmete ruhig.* ♦ *Er atmete durch die Nase.* ♦ *frische Landluft atmen*

② **At·mos·phä·re** [atmoˈsfɛːrə] die <-> *no pl* atmos-

phere ◊ *Schadstoffe in die Atmosphäre abgeben* ♦ *Auf der Party herrschte eine ungezwungene Atmosphäre.*

A·tom [aˈtoːm] *das* <-s, –e> atom

A·tom·kraft·werk [aˈtoːmkraftvɛʳk] *das* <-(e)s, –e> *(abbr* **AKW***)* nuclear power station

At·ten·tat [ˈatn̩taːt] *das* <-(e)s, –e> assassination (attempt) ◊ *Der Minister fiel einem Attentat zum Opfer.*

At·test [aˈtɛst] *das* <-(e)s *or* –e> medical certificate ◊ *beim Arbeitgeber ein ärztliches Attest vorlegen*

au [ao] ⟨interj⟩ *(expressing pain)* ouch ◊ *Au, du tust mir weh!*
● **au weia** oh dear ◊ *Au weia, da hast du dich ja auf etwas eingelassen!*

② **auch¹** [aox] ⟨adv⟩ **1.** also, too, as well ◊ *„Ich komme mit!"* — *„Ich auch."* ♦ *Es ist auch möglich, mit Karte zu zahlen.* ♦ *Er musste auch noch für die Busfahrt aufkommen.*; *(negated)* not/no … either, neither ◊ *„Ich will den Film nicht sehen."*—*„Ich auch nicht."* ♦ *Sie hat keine Zeit, und Lust hat sie auch keine.* sowohl … als auch … both … and …, … as well as … ◊ *Sowohl er als auch seine Frau sprechen Englisch.* ♦ *Diese Methode funktioniert sowohl theoretisch als auch praktisch.* **2.** even ◊ *Ich mache das jetzt so, auch wenn er meckert.* ♦ *Es wird schon besser, wenn auch nur langsam.*

auch² [aox] ⟨part⟩ **1.** *emphasizing your emotions, translation varies* Wieso trinkt er auch so viel? Why on earth does he drink so much? Sie muss aber auch immer einen Kommentar abgeben! She just has to make a comment, doesn't she! Er ist aber auch dickköpfig! He really is pig-headed! **2.** *reinforcing a statement* actually, in fact ◊ *Wir dachten, es sei ein Unfall passiert, und so war es dann auch.* ♦ *Er fühlte sich gut und man sah es ihm auch an.* Wenn er das gesagt hat, hält er sich auch daran. If he said that, then that's what he will do. **3.** *reinforcing an explanation* after all ◊ *Ich bin sehr müde, es ist ja auch schon spät.* ♦ *Er ist wütend, weil sie zu spät ist — er hat ja auch Recht!* **4.** *expressing doubt, translation varies* Ist das auch legal? Are you sure that's legal? Hat sie sich das auch gut überlegt? Did she consider it thoroughly, I wonder? Wird er denn auch kommen? Is he really going to come? **5.** *with interrogative pronouns* wie/was/wo auch immer however/whatever/wherever ◊ *Wie auch immer du vorgehst, sei vorsichtig!* ♦ *Was auch immer geschieht, ich werde zu ihm halten.* ♦ *Wo auch immer er auftaucht, gibt es Streit.*

② **auf¹** [aof] ⟨adv⟩ **1.** *(fam)* auf sein be open ◊ *Wieso ist das Fenster auf?* ♦ *Wie lange sind die Geschäfte heute auf?* ⊖geöffnet, offen ⊕zu, geschlossen **2.** auf sein be up ◊ *Sie war gestern Nacht bis 4 Uhr früh auf.* ♦ *Er war bereits seit sieben auf.* ⊖im Bett **3.** *in exclamations* (wide) open ◊ *Mund auf!* ♦ *Augen auf im Straßenverkehr!* ♦ *Fenster auf, hier stinkt's!* **4.** *in exclamations* jetzt aber auf, auf geht's let's go auf in etw. ⟨acc⟩ off to sth ◊ *Auf ins Kino!* **5.** *in exclamations* on ◊ *Helm auf!* ♦ *Brille auf beim Lesen!* ⊖ab
● **auf und ab 1.** up and down, up and fro ◊ *Sie ging auf dem Gang auf und ab.* ⊖hin und her

2. up and down ◊ *Sie sprangen auf und ab.* ⊖auf und nieder **auf und davon** *(fam)* away ◊ *Der Täter war längst auf und davon.* **auf und nieder** up and down ◊ *Die Türklinke bewegte sich auf und nieder.*

② **auf²** [aof] ⟨prep⟩ **1.** *with acc when expressing motion towards a place, with dat when there is no or undirected motion* on/on(to) ◊ *Das Buch lag auf dem Tisch.* ♦ *Sie legte das Buch auf den Tisch.*; in ◊ *Sie wohnt auf dem Land.* ♦ *Er ist bestimmt auf seinem Zimmer.*; at ◊ *Sie war gerade auf der Post/auf dem Rathaus.* **2.** *in response to the question 'to where?'* ⟨+acc⟩ to ◊ *Wir ziehen aufs Land.* ♦ *Geh auf dein Zimmer!* ♦ *Gehst du auf die Post?* ♦ *Auf welche Uni geht sie?* ♦ *Ich gehe nicht auf die Hochzeit/den Ball.* ♦ *Sie fuhren zusammen auf die Buchmesse.* auf jdn/etw. zu towards sb/sth mit Ziel auf etw. towards sth ◊ *Das Schiff segelte mit Ziel auf Afrika.* ein Ausflug aufs Land a trip into the countryside auf jdn schießen shoot at sb auf die Suche nach etw. gehen (start to) look for sth **3.** ⟨+dat⟩ at ◊ *Warst du auf ihrer Hochzeit?* ♦ *Wie viele Teilnehmer waren auf der Tagung?*; on ◊ *Auf der Rückfahrt wurde ihm plötzlich übel.* ♦ *Das Flugzeug wurde auf dem Weg von Rom nach Dubai entführt.* **4.** *in response to the question 'when?'* ⟨+acc⟩ after ◊ *Auf den Schnee folgte Straßenglätte.* ♦ *Es häufte sich Fehler auf Fehler.* in der Nacht von Dienstag auf Mittwoch on Tuesday night in der Nacht vom 12. auf den 13. September on the night of the twelfth of September **5.** *in response to the question 'how?'* ⟨+acc⟩ in ◊ *Die beiden Männer unterhielten sich auf Italienisch.* ♦ *Sie versuchte es zuerst auf die elegante Art.* ♦ *Sie empfing ihn auf das Herzlichste.* **6.** *in response to the question 'on what occasion?'* ⟨+acc⟩ upon ◊ *Auf Vorschlag/Initiative von Manuela fuhren wir nach Rom.* ♦ *Auch auf wiederholte Aufforderung hin zahlte der Kunde nicht.* auf etw. antworten reply to sth auf jds Wunsch according to sb's wishes ◊ *Er hat den Betrieb nur auf Wunsch seines Vaters übernommen.* **7.** *in response to the question 'how far?'* over ◊ *Der Fluss fließt auf weiten Strecken sehr schnell.* ♦ *Schon auf große Entfernung können Hunde das Wild riechen.* bis auf wenige Meter an jdn herankommen come within a few metres of sb **8.** *in response to the question 'for how long?'* for ◊ *Das Hotel ist auf Wochen (hin) ausgebucht.* ♦ *Wir wollen auf ein paar Tage ans Meer fahren.* **9.** *in combination with certain nouns/adjectives/verbs, translation varies* ⟨+dat⟩ or ⟨+acc⟩ das Recht auf etw. ⟨acc⟩ the right to sth böse auf jdn sein be angry with sb auf jdn/etw. aufpassen keep an eye on sb/sth auf etw. ⟨dat⟩ beruhen rest on sth sich auf jdn freuen look forward to seeing sb auf etw. ⟨acc⟩ hinweisen draw attention to sth

auf|... [aof] ⟨prefix⟩ **1.** up ◊ *Iss bitte alles auf.* ♦ *Reste aufbrauchen* ♦ *vom Stuhl aufspringen* ♦ *aufstehen* **2.** on ◊ *ein Etikett aufkleben* ♦ *Farbe auftragen* **3.** open ◊ *den Wasserhahn aufdrehen* ♦ *das Fenster auflassen* Die Tür ging auf. The door opened. **4.** *translation varies (suddenness, intensification)* sich aufregen get upset auflachen start laughing

auf|at·men [ˈaofˌaːtmən] <atmet auf, atmete auf, hat aufgeatmet> ⟨intr v⟩ heave a sigh of relief, breathe easily ◊ *Der Stress ist vorbei, wir können*

A B C D E F G H I J K L M N O P Q R S T U V W X Y Z

A

wieder aufatmen.

Auf·bau ['a͜ofba͜o] der <-s, -ten> **1.** *no pl* structure ◇ *der Aufbau von Sätzen* ◆ *der Aufbau eines Musikstücks* **2.** *no pl* construction ◇ *der Aufbau eines unabhängigen Staates* ◆ *Unser Onlineangebot befindet sich noch im Aufbau.*; *(of sth that existed before)* reconstruction ◇ *der Aufbau nach dem Krieg* **3.** superstructure ◇ *die Aufbauten für einen Kleinlaster*

auf|bau·en ['a͜ofba͜o͜ən] <baut auf, baute auf, hat aufgebaut> [trv] **1.** put up ◇ *ein Zelt aufbauen* ◆ *ein eingestürztes Haus wieder aufbauen* **2.** establish ◇ *sich eine Existenz aufbauen* ◆ *eine eigene Abteilung aufbauen* etw. auf etw. [dat] aufbauen base sth on sth ◇ *Er baute seine Verteidigung auf ihrer Aussage auf.* **3.** construct, structure ◇ *Die Argumentation ist überzeugend aufgebaut.* ◆ *Wie baue ich den Aufsatz am besten auf?* **4.** *mostly spoken* jdn aufbauen build sb up ◇ *Lobe ihn ab und zu. Das baut ihn auf.* [ref+intr v] (sich) auf etw. [acc] aufbauen be based on sth, be founded on sth ◇ *Information baut (sich) auf Zeichensysteme auf.* [ref v] **1.** *(weather)* sich aufbauen develop, build ◇ *Über Süddeutschland baut sich ein Hoch auf.* **2.** sich vor jdm aufbauen stand menacingly in front of sb

auf|be·wah·ren ['a͜ofbəva:rən] <bewahrt auf, bewahrte auf, hat aufbewahrt> [trv] keep ◇ *Milch muss kühl aufbewahrt werden.* ◆ *Sie hat die Münze als Andenken aufbewahrt.*

auf|de·cken ['a͜ofdɛkn̩] <deckt auf, deckte auf, hat aufgedeckt> [trv] **1.** uncover ◇ *Tatsachen/einen Betrug aufdecken* **2.** *(your cards)* turn up ◇ *Er deckte seine Karten auf.* **3.** *(the bed)* make (up) ◇ *die Betten aufdecken* ⊝machen **4.** *(the table)* set ◇ *Hilf mir, den Tisch aufzudecken!* ⊝decken ⊝abräumen

auf|drän·gen ['a͜ofdrɛŋən] <drängt auf, drängte auf, hat aufgedrängt> [trv] jdm etw. aufdrängen impose sth on sb, force sth on sb ◇ *Der Vertreter hat mir die Versicherung aufgedrängt.* jdm jdn aufdrängen impose sb on sb ◇ *Ich möchte dir meine Kinder nicht schon wieder aufdrängen.* [ref v] **1.** *(doubts, memories)* etw. drängt sich (jdm) auf sth occurs (to sb) ◇ *Angesichts der Ergebnisse drängten sich ihm Zweifel auf.* ◆ *Dutzende von Fragen drängen sich auf.* **2.** jd drängt sich (jdm) auf sb imposes themselves on sb ◇ *Musst du dich immer so aufdrängen?* ◆ *Dein Freund hat sich mir unangenehm aufgedrängt.*

auf·ei·nan·der [a͜ofa͜e'nandə] [adv] **1.** on top of each other, one on top of the other ◇ *Kartons aufeinander stapeln* **2.** each other ◇ *Die Hunde gingen aufeinander los.* ◆ *Zwei Weltanschauungen stoßen aufeinander.* sich aufeinander beziehen refer to each other sich aufeinander verlassen rely on each other aufeinander warten wait for each other ◇ *Nach dem Termin warteten sie aufeinander.*

⊙ aufeinander zugehen try to compromise ◇ *Statt zu streiten, solltet ihr aufeinander zugehen.*

ⓩ **Auf·ent·halt** ['a͜ofǝnthalt] der <-es, -e> **1.** stay ◇ *Wir wünschen Ihnen einen angenehmen Aufenthalt!* ◆ *mehrere Aufenthalte im Ausland* **2.** *(aircraft, train etc.)* stop ◇ *Der Zug hat in Nürnberg Aufenthalt.*

Auf·ent·halts·er·laub·nis ['a͜ofnthalts|ɛla͜opnɪs] die <-> *no pl* residence permit ◇ *eine Aufenthaltserlaubnis erteilen*

Auf·fahrt ['a͜offa:ʳt] die <-, -en> **1.** drive(way) ◇ *Der Kies in der Auffahrt knirschte unter den Reifen.* die Auffahrt zu etw. the drive of sth ◇ *Die Auffahrt zum Hotel ist links neben dem Dom.* **2.** die Auffahrt (zu etw.) approach road (to sth), slip road (to sth) ◇ *Nehmen Sie die Auffahrt Unterhaching!* ◆ *die Auffahrt zur B 6 in Richtung Neustadt* ⊝Ausfahrt **3.** bei der Auffahrt auf etw. [acc] when getting onto sth ◇ *Bei der Auffahrt auf die Autobahn kamen wir ins Schleudern.* **4.** die/eine Auffahrt (zu etw.) the/an ascent (to sth) ◇ *Nach vierstündiger Auffahrt erreichten wir den Pass.* ◆ *Mit der Bergbahn kostet die Auffahrt zur Zugspitze 32 Euro.* ⊝Abfahrt

auf|fal·len ['a͜offalən] <fällt auf, fiel auf, ist aufgefallen> [intr v] **1.** attract attention, stand out ◇ *Sie wollte nicht auffallen.* ◆ *Er fiel durch seine Kleidung auf.* **2.** jdm fällt etw. auf sb notices sth ◇ *Ist dir auf den Fotos gar nichts aufgefallen?* ◆ *Mir ist aufgefallen, dass er keinen Bart mehr trägt.*

auf·fäl·lig ['a͜offɛlɪç] [adj, adv] **1.** conspicuous(ly), noticeable(-ably) ◇ *Auffällig war, dass beide aus der gleichen Stadt stammten.* ◆ *sich auffällig benehmen* ⊝unauffällig **2.** striking(ly) ◇ *Sie trug ein auffälliges Kleid.* ⊝unauffällig

Auf·fas·sung ['a͜offasʊŋ] die <-, -en> **1.** view ◇ *jds Auffassung teilen* ◆ *eine orthodoxe Auffassung des Rechts* ◆ *eine strenge Auffassung von Ehre* **2.** ability to comprehend ◇ *Dolmetschen erfordert eine rasche Auffassung.*

ⓩ **auf|for·dern** ['a͜offoʳdɐn] <fordert auf, forderte auf, hat aufgefordert> [trv] jdn zu etw. auffordern ask sb to sth, request sb to do sth ◇ *Die Partei hat ihn aufgefordert zurückzutreten.* ◆ *jdn zur Zahlung auffordern* jdn (zum Tanz) auffordern ask sb for a dance

Auf·for·de·rung ['a͜offoʳdərʊŋ] die <-, -en> **1.** *most sing* request ◇ *Er kam der Aufforderung zurückzutreten nicht nach.* ◆ *Auf Aufforderung der Polizei machte er einen Alkoholtest.* eine Aufforderung an jdn call upon sb ◇ *eine Aufforderung an die Bürger, Blut zu spenden* **2.** *no pl* eine Aufforderung zu etw. an incitement to do sth ◇ *Das ist geradezu eine Aufforderung zur Nachlässigkeit.*

auf|füh·ren ['a͜offy:rən] <führt auf, führte auf, hat aufgeführt> [trv] **1.** perform, stage ◇ *Im Theater wurde „Romeo und Julia" aufgeführt.* **2.** list ◇ *Welche Gründe für ihre Entscheidung hat sie aufgeführt?* ◆ *Einige Produkte waren im Verzeichnis nicht aufgeführt.* [ref v] **1.** sich anständig/ unmöglich etc. aufführen behave well/badly etc. ◇ *Sie hat sich wie eine Irre aufgeführt.* **2.** *(fam, pej)* sich aufführen make a fuss ◇ *Führ dich nicht wegen jedem bisschen so auf!*

Auf·füh·rung ['a͜offy:rʊŋ] die <-, -en> performance ◇ *die Aufführung von „Hamlet"*

ⓩ **Auf·ga·be** ['a͜ofga:bə] die <-, -n> **1.** job, task ◇ *Die Übersetzerin hat ihre Aufgabe gut gelöst.* ◆ *Der Kühlschrank ist alt, erfüllt aber noch seine Aufgabe.* ◆ *Sie sah es als ihre Aufgabe, ihm zu helfen.* **2.** exercise ◇ *eine/eine Aufgabe stellen* ◇ *Was ist das Ergebnis bei der dritten Aufgabe?* Hast du deine Aufgaben gemacht? Have you done your

homework? **3.** *no pl* giving up ◇ *Sie sahen sich zur Aufgabe des Geschäfts gezwungen.*; abandonment ◇ *Sie wurde zur Aufgabe ihres Plans gezwungen.*

② **auf|ge·ben** ['aofgeːbm̩] <gibt auf, gab auf, hat aufgegeben> [tr+intr v] give up ◇ *ein Geschäft aufgeben* ♦ *Du darfst jetzt nicht aufgeben!* ♦ *Ich gebe die Hoffnung nicht auf, dass er doch noch kommt.* ♦ *Ich geb's auf, das wird nichts mehr!*; *(a habit)* stop, quit ◇ *das Rauchen/Trinken aufgeben* [tr v] **1.** (jdm) etw. aufgeben set (sb) sth ◇ *Diese Lehrerin gibt immer viele Hausaufgaben auf.* ♦ *Er hat uns einen Aufsatz aufgegeben.*; *(a riddle)* pose ◇ *Die Situation hat uns Rätsel aufgegeben.* **2.** *(a letter, parcel)* post ◇ *bei der Post ein Päckchen aufgeben* **3.** *(an advertisement, order)* place ◇ *Er hat eine Annonce in der Zeitung aufgegeben.* ♦ *eine Bestellung telefonisch aufgeben*

auf·ge·bracht ['aofgəbraxt] [adj] <aufgebrachter, am aufgebrachtesten> aufgebracht (über etw./jdn) angry (about sb/sth) ◇ *Ich war über die Verspätung sehr aufgebracht.* ♦ *Er konnte seine aufgebrachte Nachbarin beruhigen.*

auf|ge·hen ['aofgeːən] <geht auf, ging auf, ist aufgegangen> [intr v] **1.** *(sun, moon)* rise, go up ◇ *Der Mond ist aufgegangen.* ⊖untergehen **2.** *(fam)* open ◇ *Plötzlich ging die Tür auf und er trat ein.* ♦ *Der Schirm geht nicht auf.*; *(button, knot, zip)* come undone ◇ *Der Knoten geht nicht mehr auf.*; *(stage curtain)* go up ⊖sich öffnen **3.** *(seeds)* come up ◇ *Der Samen ging nicht auf.* **4.** *(pastry)* rise ◇ *warten, bis der Hefeteig aufgegangen ist* **5.** MATH work out, leave no remainder ◇ *Geht die Rechung auf?* ♦ *35 geteilt durch 3 geht nicht auf.* **6.** jdm aufgehen become clear to sb ◇ *Ist dir noch nicht aufgegangen, wie unsinnig das ist?* **7.** in etw. [dat] aufgehen be wrapped up in sth ◇ *Er geht in seinem Beruf voll und ganz auf.*

auf·ge·schlos·sen ['aofgəʃlɔsn̩] [adj] openminded, receptive ◇ *ein aufgeschlossener Mensch* ♦ *Neuen Ideen gegenüber war sie immer aufgeschlossen.*

auf·grund, auf Grund [aof'grʊnt] [prep] **1.** [+gen] because of, on the grounds/basis of ◇ *Diskriminierung aufgrund des Geschlechts* ♦ *Der Vorgang wird aufgrund eines Fehlers abgebrochen.* ♦ *Er wurde aufgrund seiner Unzuverlässigkeit entlassen.* ⊖wegen **2.** *adverbial* [+dat] aufgrund von on the strength/basis of ◇ *aufgrund von Fehlern* ♦ *eine Verurteilung aufgrund von Paragraph XY* ⊖wegen, infolge von

auf|ha·ben ['aofhaːbm̩] *(fam)* <hat auf, hatte auf, hat aufgehabt> [intr v] be open ◇ *Im Advent haben die Geschäfte samstags länger auf.* ♦ *Hat die Bank jetzt noch auf?* ♦ *Das Freibad hat schon seit letzter Woche auf.* [tr v] **1.** *(glasses, a hat)* have on ◇ *Er hat immer eine Baseballkappe auf.* **2.** SCHOOL have got for homework ◇ *Sie haben in Deutsch einen Aufsatz auf.* (et)was aufhaben have got homework (to do) ◇ *Wir haben heute nur in Mathe was auf.* **3.** *(your eyes, mouth, a window)* have open ◇ *Haben die Kätzchen schon die Augen auf?* ♦ *Sie hat die ganze Nacht das Fenster auf.* **4.** *(a lock, door)* get open ◇ *Als er die Tür endlich aufhatte, war es schon zu spät.*; *(a knot)* get undone

auf|hal·ten ['aofhaltn̩] <hält auf, hielt auf, hat aufgehalten> [ref v] **1.** sich irgendwo aufhalten be somewhere, stay somewhere ◇ *Sie hält sich derzeit im Ausland auf.* ♦ *Du solltest dich so kurz nach deiner Krankheit noch nicht so lange im Freien aufhalten.* ♦ *Er hält sich illegal im Land auf.* **2.** sich mit etw./jdm aufhalten spend time on sth/sb ◇ *Ich möchte mich nicht mit langen Reden aufhalten.* ♦ *Sie kann sich nicht mit jedem Patienten so lange aufhalten.* [tr v] **1.** hold up ◇ *Solche Probleme können mich nicht aufhalten.* ♦ *Geh ruhig, lass dich nicht aufhalten.* ♦ *Entschuldigen Sie meine Verspätung, ich bin aufgehalten worden.*; *(refugees)* detain ◇ *Reisende an der Grenze aufhalten* **2.** *(a process, development etc.)* check, delay ◇ *den Alterungsprozess mit Medikamenten aufhalten wollen* **3.** hold open ◇ *jdm die Tür aufhalten*; *(the eyes)* keep open ◇ *vor Müdigkeit kaum noch die Augen aufhalten können*; *(a band)* hold out ◇ *Halt mal die Hand auf, ich hab was für dich.*

auf|hän·gen ['aofhɛŋən] <hängt auf, hängte auf, hat aufgehängt> [tr v] **1.** *(an object)* hang up ◇ *nach dem Waschen die Gardinen wieder aufhängen* ♦ *seine Jacke an der Garderobe aufhängen*; *(the washing)* hang out ⊖abhängen **2.** *(a person)* hang ◇ *Sie hängten ihn an einem Baum auf.* ♦ *Wenn das so weitergeht, hänge ich mich noch auf!* [tr+intr v] *(the receiver)* hang up ◇ *Als sie seine Stimme hörte, hängte sie (den Hörer) sofort auf.* [ref v] *(fam)* IT sich aufhängen hang (up) ◇ *Was tun, wenn sich der PC aufhängt?*

auf|he·ben ['aofheːbm̩] <hebt auf, hob auf, hat aufgehoben> [tr v] **1.** *(a ruling, ban, decision)* repeal, rescind ◇ *ein Gesetz aufheben* **2.** *(a siege, meeting)* end; *(an embargo)* lift, raise; *(a roadblock)* remove ◇ *eine Straßensperre wieder aufheben* **3.** *(gravity, an effect)* offset ◇ *Die Verluste werden durch Gewinne in gleicher Höhe aufgehoben.* sie heben sich auf they cancel each other out ◇ *Die beiden Kräfte heben sich gegenseitig auf.* **4.** lift up, pick up ◇ *Heb das Papier, das du weggeworfen hast, bitte wieder auf!* ♦ *etw. vom Boden aufheben* **5.** keep ◇ *etw. zur Erinnerung aufheben* ♦ *Ich habe alle ihre Briefe aufgehoben.* ♦ *Den Rest heben wir fürs Abendessen auf.* sich [dat] etw. aufheben keep sth, hold onto sth ◇ *Heb dir die Quittung gut auf, du brauchst sie bestimmt noch.* Ich hebe mir das Beste immer bis zum Schluss auf. I always save the best until last.

Auf·he·bung ['aofheːbʊŋ] die <-, -en> *most sing* **1.** repeal ◇ *die Aufhebung des Gerichtsurteils* **2.** lifting, raising ◇ *die Aufhebung der Geschwindigkeitsbegrenzung nach dem Tunnel* ♦ *Die Aufhebung der Sanktionen verbesserte die wirtschaftliche Lage.*; *(of an effect)* neutralization ◇ *die Aufhebung der Wirkung eines Medikaments*

auf|ho·len ['aofhoːlən] <holt auf, holte auf, hat aufgeholt> [tr+intr v] make up ◇ *einen Rückstand/jds Vorsprung/eine Verspätung aufholen* ♦ *Er hat drei Minuten/Meter gegenüber dem Ersten aufgeholt.*; *(pursuers)* catch up ◇ *Beeil dich, die anderen holen auf!*

② **auf|hö·ren** ['aofhøːrən] <hört auf, hörte auf, hat aufgehört> [intr v] stop ◇ *Hier hört die Straße auf.* ♦ *Hört der Regen denn überhaupt nicht mehr auf?* ♦ *Das Faulenzen muss einfach aufhören!* ⊖enden

⊖anfangen $\boxed{\text{tr+intr v}}$ (mit etw.) aufhören stop (sth) ◊ *Jetzt hör schon auf (damit)!* ✦ *Sie versucht, mit dem Rauchen aufzuhören.*; *(work, study)* finish (sth) ◊ *Ich wollte eigentlich heute (mit dem Lernen) früher aufhören.* aufhören, etw. zu tun stop doing sth ◊ *Sie konnte nicht aufhören zu lachen/weinen.* ✦ *Es hat endlich aufgehört zu schneien/regnen.* bei einer Firma aufhören stop working at a company ◊ *Er hat bei Siemens aufgehört.* ⊖anfangen

◉ da hört (sich) doch alles auf *(fam)* that's the absolute limit

auf|kau·fen [ˈaʊfkaʊfn̩] <kauft auf, kaufte auf, hat aufgekauft> $\boxed{\text{tr v}}$ buy up ◊ *Die Firma wurde von der Konkurrenz aufgekauft.*

② **auf|klä·ren** [ˈaʊfklɛːrən] <klärt auf, klärte auf, hat aufgeklärt> $\boxed{\text{tr v}}$ 1. resolve ◊ *Die Hintergründe der Tat konnten nie aufgeklärt werden.*; *(a crime)* solve 2. jdn aufklären explain the facts of life to sb ◊ *Sie wurde erst spät aufgeklärt.* 3. jdn (über etw./jdn) aufklären enlighten sb (about sth/sb), inform sb (about sth/sb) ◊ *Patienten über die Risiken einer Behandlung aufklären* $\boxed{\text{ref v}}$ sich aufklären be resolved ◊ *Ihr Verschwinden/das Missverständnis hat sich aufgeklärt.*

Auf·klä·rung [ˈaʊfklɛːrʊŋ] die <-, -en> 1. *most sing* clearing up ◊ *die vollständige Aufklärung eines Skandals*; *(of a crime)* solving ◊ *zur Aufklärung eines Verbrechens beitragen* 2. *most sing* information, clarification ◊ *verstärkte gesundheitliche/politische Aufklärung* ✦ *um Aufklärung bitten* 3. *no pl* sex education, education on reproductive issues ◊ *Aufklärung im Biologieunterricht* 4. *no pl* HIST Enlightenment ◊ *Literatur/Kunst im Zeitalter der Aufklärung* 5. *(military)* reconnaissance ◊ *strategische/taktische Aufklärung*

Auf·kle·ber [ˈaʊfkleːbɐ] der <-s, -> sticker ◊ *einen Aufkleber am Auto anbringen*

Auf·kom·men [ˈaʊfkɔmən] das <-s, -> *most sing* 1. amount ◊ *Das Aufkommen an Spendengeldern ist gesunken.*; *(from taxes)* revenue 2. das Aufkommen ... $\boxed{\text{gen}}$, das Aufkommen von etw. $\boxed{\text{dat}}$ the advent of sth ◊ *Das Aufkommen des Internets ermöglichte weltweite Zusammenarbeit.* 3. *(of emotions)* das Aufkommen von etw. $\boxed{\text{dat}}$ the emergence of sth ◊ *das Aufkommen von Angst und Hass verhindern*

auf|kom·men [ˈaʊfkɔmən] <kommt auf, kam auf, ist aufgekommen> $\boxed{\text{intr v}}$ 1. spring up, emerge, appear ◊ *keine Langeweile aufkommen lassen* ✦ *Eine neue Mode kommt auf.* 2. für etw. aufkommen pay for sth ◊ *Wer kommt für den Schaden/die Kosten auf?* ✦ *für seinen Lebensunterhalt selbst aufkommen müssen* ⊖etw. tragen 3. *(on the ground)* land ◊ *Er kam nach dem Sprung unglücklich auf.* ⊖landen 4. get up (again) ◊ *Hilf mir hoch, ich komm nicht allein auf.*

auf|kün·di·gen [ˈaʊfkʏndɪɡŋ̍] <kündigt auf, kündigte auf, hat aufgekündigt> $\boxed{\text{tr v}}$ terminate ◊ *ein Bündnis/einen Vertrag aufkündigen* jdm die Freundschaft aufkündigen break off your friendship with sb jdm die Treue aufkündigen cease being loyal to sb

auf|la·den [ˈaʊflaːdn̩] <lädt auf, lud auf, hat aufgeladen> $\boxed{\text{tr v}}$ 1. charge ◊ *eine Batterie aufladen*; *(a telephone card etc.)* recharge ◊ *auf die Telefon-*karte einen Betrag von 50 Euro aufladen 2. etw. auf etw. $\boxed{\text{acc}}$ aufladen load sth onto sth ◊ *Kisten auf einen Lkw aufladen* ⊖abladen 3. sich $\boxed{\text{dat}}$/jdm etw. aufladen burden yourself/sb with sth ◊ *jdm die eigenen Probleme aufladen*; *(with a debt, responsibility also)* saddle yourself/sb with sth $\boxed{\text{ref v}}$ sich aufladen become charged ◊ *Ihre Haare hatten sich statisch aufgeladen.*

Auf·la·ge [ˈaʊflaːɡə] die <-, -n> 1. TRADE *(of print media)* print run ◊ *eine limitierte/hohe Auflage* ✦ *In erster Auflage wurden 20 000 Exemplare gedruckt.* ✦ *in einer Auflage von 2 Millionen erscheinen* 2. condition ◊ *jdm etw. zur Auflage machen* ✦ *mit einer Auflage verbunden sein* 3. *(for mattresses, chairs etc.)* cover ⊖Unterlage 4. *(of metal)* coating, plating ◊ *ein Löffel mit einer Auflage aus Silber/Gold*

auf|las·sen [ˈaʊflasn̩] <lässt auf, ließ auf, hat aufgelassen> $\boxed{\text{tr v}}$ *(fam)* 1. leave open ◊ *das Fenster auflassen* ✦ *Er ließ das Geschäft über Mittag auf.* den Mund/die Augen auflassen keep your mouth/eyes open ⊖zumachen 2. *(glasses, a hat)* keep on ◊ *Sie ließ die Sonnenbrille auch im Haus auf.* ⊖abnehmen

auf|lau·fen [ˈaʊflaʊfn̩] <läuft auf, lief auf, ist aufgelaufen> $\boxed{\text{intr v}}$ 1. *(fam)* zu etw. auflaufen attain sth ◊ *zur Hochform/Höchstform/Bestform auflaufen* 2. SPORT *(player, team)* turn out ◊ *Die Mannschaft lief in ihrer besten Besetzung auf.* 3. *(ships)* auf etw. $\boxed{\text{acc}}$ auflaufen run aground on sth ◊ *auf eine Sandbank/einen Felsen auflaufen* ◉ jdn auflaufen lassen *(fam)* give sb the brush-off ◊ *Ich wollte mich entschuldigen, aber sie hat mich voll auflaufen lassen.*

auf|le·gen [ˈaʊfleːɡŋ̍] <legt auf, legte auf, hat aufgelegt> $\boxed{\text{tr v}}$ 1. *(a record)* put on ◊ *Sie hat mein Lieblingslied aufgelegt.* 2. *(the receiver)* put down, replace ◊ *Sie legte wütend den Hörer auf.* 3. put on, lay on ◊ *ein neues Tischtuch/Gedeck auflegen* ✦ *jdm segnend die Hand auflegen* ✦ *Make-up/Lippenstift auflegen* 4. ECON issue ◊ *eine neue Briefmarke/Serie auflegen* ✦ *Das Buch soll wieder aufgelegt werden.*; *(a fund)* launch $\boxed{\text{intr v}}$ 1. put on (the) music ◊ *Welcher Discjockey legt heute auf?* 2. hang up ◊ *Sie legte auf, bevor er sich entschuldigen konnte.* ⊖abheben, abnehmen

auf|lö·sen [ˈaʊfløːzn̩] <löst auf, löste auf, hat aufgelöst> $\boxed{\text{tr v}}$ 1. dissolve ◊ *eine Ehe auflösen*; *(an engagement)* break off ◊ *eine Verlobung auflösen* 2. *(a group of people)* break up ◊ *Der Vorsitzende löste die Versammlung auf.* 3. *(a contract)* cancel 4. dissolve ◊ *einen Nierenstein auflösen* ⊖lösen 5. *(a puzzle, an equation)* solve; *(a contradiction)* resolve ◊ *Die Fragen werden am Schluss des Buches aufgelöst.* $\boxed{\text{ref v}}$ 1. sich auflösen break up ◊ *Die Menge löste sich nach dem Konzert langsam auf.* 2. sich auflösen come undone ◊ *Der Knoten/Zopf hat sich aufgelöst.* sich in seine Bestandteile auflösen fall to pieces, disintegrate ◊ *die Tablette löste sich im Wasser auf.* 4. *(puzzle)* sich auflösen be solved; *(contradiction)* be resolved ◉ sich in nichts auflösen vanish into thin air ◊ *Durch die Erbschaft haben sich ihre Probleme in nichts aufgelöst.*

Auf·lö·sung [ˈaofløːzʊŋ] die <-, –en> *most sing*
1. IT, TV resolution ◊ *eine hohe Auflösung* ♦ *eine Auflösung von 800 x 600 Pixeln wählen* **2.** *(of an organization)* dissolution ◊ *die Auflösung des Parlaments/der Partei beschließen; (of a contract)* cancellation ◊ *die Auflösung des Vertrages beschließen* **3.** *often translated with a verb construction (of a problem, task, equation)* solving Die Auflösung dieser Aufgabe war einfach. It was easy to solve this problem., Solving this problem was easy. ⊖Lösung **4.** *(to a crossword puzzle etc.)* solution ◊ *Die Auflösung des Rätsels finden Sie im nächsten Heft.* ⊖Lösung **5.** breaking up, disintegration ◊ *die Auflösung eines Tumors mit Lasern; (of fog)* dispersal ◊ *Das Wetter heute: nach Auflösung der Nebelfelder meist sonnig.*

⑦ **auf|ma·chen** [ˈaofmaxn] <macht auf, machte auf, hat aufgemacht> (tr+intr v) open ◊ *den Mund/die Augen aufmachen* ♦ *Hast du meine Post aufgemacht?* ♦ *eine neue Filiale aufmachen* ♦ *Die Bank macht um neun auf.* jdm aufmachen open the door to sb ◊ *Ich habe geklingelt, aber sie hat mir nicht aufgemacht.* ⊖öffnen ⊖zumachen (ref v) sich aufmachen(, (um) etw. zu tun) set off (to do sth) ◊ *Am nächsten Morgen machten sie sich nach Hause auf.* ♦ *Wir machten uns auf, die Burg zu besichtigen.*

Auf·marsch [ˈaofmaʁʃ] der <-(e)s, Aufmärsche> parade ◊ *der Aufmarsch von Truppen an der Grenze* ♦ *eine Demonstration gegen den Aufmarsch von Neonazis*

⑦ **auf·merk·sam** [ˈaofmɛʳkzaːm] (adj, adv) **1.** attentive(ly) ◊ *Dieser Schüler ist besonders aufmerksam.* ♦ *ein aufmerksamer Beobachter* ♦ *die Geschehnisse aufmerksam verfolgen* **2.** considerate(ly) ◊ *Ein aufmerksamer Herr half ihr über die Straße.* ♦ *Vielen Dank, das ist sehr aufmerksam von Ihnen!* ⊚ **jdn auf jdn/etw. aufmerksam machen** draw sb's attention to sb/sth ◊ *Sie machte ihn auf einen Fehler aufmerksam.* **auf jdn/etw. aufmerksam werden** begin to take an interest in sb/sth ◊ *Die Presse ist auf ihn/das Projekt aufmerksam geworden.*

Auf·merk·sam·keit [ˈaofmɛʳkzaːmkaet] die <-, –en> **1.** *no pl* attention ◊ *jds Aufmerksamkeit auf jdn/etw. lenken* ♦ *seine Aufmerksamkeit auf jdn/etw. richten* ♦ *Ihre Bemühungen verdienen unsere/mehr Aufmerksamkeit.* jds Aufmerksamkeit entgehen escape sb's attention, slip by sb ◊ *Der Fehler ist der Aufmerksamkeit der Lehrerin entgangen.* jds Aufmerksamkeit erregen/wecken attract sb's attention jdm/einer Sache Aufmerksamkeit schenken/zuteil werden lassen pay attention to sb/sth ⊖Beachtung **2.** sign/token of affection ◊ *jdn mit kleinen Aufmerksamkeiten verwöhnen*

Auf·nah·me [ˈaofnaːmə] die <-, –n> **1.** *most sing* start, commencement ◊ *die Aufnahme diplomatischer Beziehungen/der Verhandlungen/von Gesprächen* **2.** *most sing* admission ◊ *die Aufnahme von Flüchtlingen begrenzen wollen* ♦ *die stationäre Aufnahme von Patienten* die Aufnahme in etw. (acc) (the) admission (in)to sth ◊ *die Aufnahme weiterer Staaten in die EU beantragen* **3.** photograph, image ◊ *Die historische Aufnahme zeigt die Kirche um 1910.* ♦ *eine computertomographische*

Aufnahme **4.** recording ◊ *eine Aufnahme von jdm/etw. machen* ♦ *Das ist eine Aufnahme von ihrem letzten Konzert.* **5.** filming, shooting ◊ *die Aufnahme eines Programms* Achtung, Aufnahme! And action! **6.** *most sing* die Aufnahme (in etw. (acc)) (the) inclusion (in sth) ◊ *die Aufnahme eines Artikels ins Sortiment; (of pupils)* (the) admission (to sth) ◊ *die Aufnahme neuer Schüler* **7.** *most sing* reception ◊ *herzliche/freundliche Aufnahme bei jdm finden* ♦ *die begeisterte Aufnahme der Vorschläge durch die Kinder* **8.** *(at a hospital)* admissions ◊ *Bitte warten Sie in der Aufnahme.* **9.** *most sing* intake, absorption ◊ *die Aufnahme von Nahrung und Flüssigkeit im Körper* ⊚ **irgendwo Aufnahme finden** be included somewhere, be accepted somewhere ◊ *in einem Programm Aufnahme finden* ♦ *Die Flüchtlinge fanden in Deutschland Aufnahme.*

Auf·nah·me·prü·fung [ˈaofnaːməpryːfʊŋ] die <-, –en> entrance exam(ination) ◊ *bei der Aufnahmeprüfung für das Gymnasium durchfallen*

⑦ **auf|neh·men** [ˈaofneːmən] <nimmt auf, nahm auf, hat aufgenommen> (tr v) **1.** begin, start ◊ *Verhandlungen/Gespräche mit jdm aufnehmen; (a contact)* establish; *(a course)* embark on ◊ *ein Studium aufnehmen* etw. wieder aufnehmen resume sth ◊ *nach dem Streik die Arbeit/den Betrieb/die Produktion wieder aufnehmen* **2.** *(refugees, asylum-seekers, members)* take in, admit ◊ *Wir können keine weiteren Kursteilnehmer aufnehmen.* jdn/etw. in etw. (acc) aufnehmen admit sb/sth to sth ◊ *jdn in einen Verein aufnehmen* ♦ *in ein Krankenhaus aufgenommen werden* ♦ *neue Mitgliedsstaaten in die EU aufnehmen* **3.** *(on a list, in a product range, in the programme etc.)* jdn/etw. in etw. (acc) aufnehmen include sb/sth in/on sth ◊ *etw. in die Tagesordnung aufnehmen* ♦ *Er wurde in die Teilnehmerliste aufgenommen.* **4.** borrow ◊ *für den Kauf eines Autos 10.000 Euro aufnehmen müssen* für etw. einen Kredit aufnehmen take out a loan for sth **5.** *(music, a film etc.)* record ◊ *Sie haben ein neues Album aufgenommen.* ♦ *Hast du den Krimi im ersten Programm gestern aufgenommen?* **6.** *(orders, minutes, personal details)* take down, record ◊ *Die Polizei nahm den Unfall auf.* **7.** jdn/etw. irgendwie aufnehmen receive sb/sth in a certain way ◊ *Sie wurde (bei ihrer Ankunft) freundlich/herzlich aufgenommen.* ♦ *Er nahm die Nachricht mit Begeisterung auf.* **8.** *(energy, water, oxygen etc.)* absorb, take in ◊ *mit der Nahrung zahlreiche Schadstoffe aufnehmen* ♦ *Ich kann keine Informationen/nichts mehr aufnehmen.; (vehicle, ship)* hold ◊ *Das Schiff kann 200 Passagiere aufnehmen.* **9.** pick up ◊ *das weinende Kind aus der Wiege aufnehmen; (a liquid)* wipe up ◊ *das Wasser mit einem Schwamm aufnehmen* ⊚ **es mit jdm/etw. (in etw. (dat)) aufnehmen (können)** be a match for sb/sth (when it comes to sth) ◊ *Im Rechnen kann es niemand mit ihr aufnehmen.*

⑦ **auf|pas·sen** [ˈaofpasn̩] <passt auf, passte auf, hat aufgepasst> (intr v) **1.** look out, watch out ◊ *sehr aufpassen müssen, damit/dass nichts kaputtgeht* ♦ *He, pass doch mal auf! Jetzt hast du mich gestoßen.* **2.** auf jdn/etw. (acc) aufpassen keep an eye on sb/sth ◊ *Kannst du mal kurz auf deine*

A
B
C
D
E
F
G
H
I
J
K
L
M
N
O
P
Q
R
S
T
U
V
W
X
Y
Z

kleine Schwester/auf meine Tasche aufpassen? darauf aufpassen, dass make sure (that) ◊ *Pass bitte darauf auf, dass die Milch nicht überkocht.* ⊜achten **3.** pay attention ◊ *Was war das? Ich habe gerade nicht aufgepasst.* ✦ *Du musst schon aufpassen, wenn ich mit dir rede.* auf jdn/etw. aufpassen pay attention to sb/sth ◊ *auf jedes Wort aufpassen, das jd sagt* Pass mal auf, was jetzt gleich passiert. Wait for it.

Auf·prall ['aofpral] der <-(e)s, -e> *most sing* der Aufprall (auf etw. [acc]/[dat]) (the) impact (with/ against sth) ◊ *Das Glas zerbach beim Aufprall auf den/dem Boden.* ⊜Aufschlag

Auf·preis ['aofpraes] der <-es, -e> additional charge, surcharge ◊ *ein geringer/saftiger Aufpreis gegen Aufpreis* for an additional charge ◊ *Das Modell ist gegen Aufpreis auch mit Seitenairbags erhältlich.*

② **auf|räu·men** ['aofrɔɣmən] <räumt auf, räumte auf, hat aufgeräumt> [tr+intr v] tidy up, clear up ◊ *Ich muss mal (meinen Schreibtisch) aufräumen, ich finde schon gar nichts mehr.* ✦ *gründlich im ganzen Haus aufräumen* ✦ *Räum bitte deine Schulbücher auf.* ✦ *die Scherben/den Müll aufräumen* [intr v] **1.** *(idea, prejudice)* mit etw. aufräumen get rid of sth, dispense with sth, do away with sth ◊ *mit einem Vorurteil/Klischee aufräumen* ✦ *mit der Vorstellung aufräumen, die Frau gehöre an den Herd* **2.** unter jdm/etw. aufräumen clean sb/sth up ◊ *unter den Gegnern/Feinden ordentlich aufräumen*

auf·recht ['aofrɛçt] [adj] *(also fig)* upright ◊ *ein aufrechter Kämpfer für die Freiheit/gegen Korruption* sich aufrecht halten keep your body upright ◊ *jd kann sich kaum noch/nicht mehr aufrecht halten* sb can hardly keep upright etw. aufrecht lagern store sth in an upright position ◊ *Flaschen liegend, nicht aufrecht lagern*

auf·recht|er·hal·ten ['aofrɛçt|ɛhaltn̩] <erhält aufrecht, erhielt aufrecht, hat aufrechterhalten> [tr v] maintain, keep up ◊ *den Betrieb/den Kontakt/ die Ordnung aufrechterhalten* ✦ *Wird er unter diesen Umständen seine Behauptung/Forderung/ Vorwürfe aufrechterhalten?*

② **auf|re·gen** ['aofre:gŋ] <regt auf, regte auf, hat aufgeregt> [ref v] **1.** sich aufregen get excited/ upset ◊ *ein schwaches Herz haben und sich nicht aufregen dürfen* ✦ *Er hat sich völlig umsonst aufgeregt, es ist gar nichts passiert.* sich über jdn/etw. aufregen get agitated about sb/sth ◊ *sich über eine Beleidigung/einen Unfall aufregen* ✦ *sich über ein leichtsinniges Kind aufregen* **2.** *(fam)* sich (über jdn/etw.) aufregen get worked up (about sb/ sth) ◊ *Darüber kann er sich heute noch aufregen.* [tr v] annoy ◊ *So eine Frechheit regt mich einfach auf.* ✦ *Regen Sie sie bitte nicht mit solchen Geschichten auf.; (in a tense situation)* make nervous aufgeregt sein be nervous ◊ *vor einem Auftritt schrecklich aufgeregt sein*

auf·re·gend ['aofre:gŋt, 'aofre:gənt] *pres p of* aufregen [adj, adv] exciting(ly) ◊ *Das war ein aufregender Tag!* ✦ *Ein Abenteuerfilm kann mir gar nicht aufregend genug sein.* ✦ *aufregend schön/sexy* [adj] *(lingerie, music etc.)* erotic ◊ *Unterwäsche in aufregendem Design* ✦ *Diese Stimme finde ich sehr aufregend.*

Auf·re·gung ['aofre:gʊŋ] die <-, -en> excitement ◊

Vor lauter Aufregung/In der Aufregung habe ich meine Schlüssel vergessen. ✦ *Es herrschte allgemeine/beträchtliche Aufregung wegen seines Rücktritts.*; agitation ◊ *Ihr Verschwinden sorgte für große Aufregung.* Aufregung über/um jdn/etw. fuss about sb/sth, agitation about sb/sth ◊ *Ich kann die ganze Aufregung um/über diesen Fehler nicht verstehen.*

⊙ in heller Aufregung in total turmoil ◊ *Die ganze Schule war wegen des Einbruchs in heller Aufregung.*

auf|rei·ßen ['aofraesn̩] <reißt auf, riss auf, hat/ist aufgerissen> [tr v] +*haben* **1.** *(also fig)* open (up) ◊ *Jetzt hast du die Naht aufgerissen!* ✦ *eine tiefe Kluft aufreißen* **2.** tear open ◊ *eine Tüte Chips aufreißen* ✦ *Ich habe mir die Hose am Stacheldraht aufgerissen.; (a road, street)* dig up ◊ *die Straße aufreißen und neue Rohre verlegen* **3.** *(the eyes, mouth, a window, door etc.)* open wide ◊ *Die Vogeljungen rissen die Schnäbel weit auf und betteln um Futter.* **4.** *(slang)* pull ◊ *in der Disko Mädchen aufreißen* [intr v] +*sein* split, tear ◊ *Der Sack ist aufgerissen und Mehl rieselt heraus.; (clouds)* break up ◊ *Die Wolkendecke/Bewölkung reißt auf.* [imp v] +*haben* es reißt auf it's clearing up, it's brightening up

auf|rich·ten ['aofrɪçtn̩] <richtet auf, richtete auf, hat aufgerichtet> [ref v] sich aufrichten straighten up ◊ *sich bücken und wieder aufrichten; (animal)* rise up ◊ *Der Bär richtete sich auf seine Hinterbeine auf.* [tr v] **1.** *(a fence, post)* etw. aufrichten put sth upright ◊ *den umgefallenen Zaun wieder aufrichten* **2.** jd richtet jdn auf sb sits sb up ◊ *einen Kranken im Bett aufrichten* sich aufrichten sit up **3.** etw. richtet jdn auf sth gives sb a lift ◊ *Der Erfolg richtete sie wieder auf.*

auf·rich·tig ['aofrɪçtɪç] [adj, adv] sincere(ly) ◊ *Mein aufrichtiges Mitgefühl/Beileid zum Tod Ihrer Mutter!* ✦ *Ihre Entschuldigung/Bewunderung war aufrichtig.* ✦ *sich aufrichtig bemühen/entschuldigen* ✦ *Ich hoffe aufrichtig, dass wir uns wiedersehen.* [adj] honest ◊ *ein aufrichtiger Mensch* ✦ *Darf ich aufrichtig sein?* aufrichtig mit/zu jdm honest with sb ◊ *Ich war immer aufrichtig mit/zu dir.* ⊜ehrlich, offen

Auf·ruf ['aofru:f] der <-(e)s, -e> **1.** IT call, retrieval ◊ *Das Pop-up-Fenster erscheint beim Aufruf der Seite automatisch.* **2.** appeal ◊ *einen Aufruf veröffentlichen/unterzeichnen* ✦ *einem Aufruf folgen* ✦ *ein Aufruf zur Gewalt/zum Boykott* **3.** call ◊ *Letzter Aufruf für Flug LH 345 nach Amsterdam, Gate Nr. 20!*

auf|ru·fen ['aofru:fn̩] <ruft auf, rief auf, hat aufgerufen> [tr v] **1.** IT call up, retrieve ◊ *etw. mit einfachem Mausklick/mit Doppelklick aufrufen* **2.** *(in a waiting-room etc.)* call ◊ *meine Nummer/mein Flug ist aufgerufen worden; (in a lesson)* pick out ◊ *Er wurde in Deutsch aufgerufen und musste das Gedicht aufsagen.* **3.** jdn zu etw. aufrufen call upon sb to do sth ◊ *Die Bevölkerung wurde aufgerufen, Blut zu spenden.* [intr v] zu etw. aufrufen call for sth ◊ *zum Boykott/Streik aufrufen*

Auf·ruhr ['aofru:ɐ] der <-s, -e> *most sing* **1.** revolt ◊ *Im ganzen Volk herrschte offener Aufruhr gegen die Regierung.* ⊜Aufstand **2.** turmoil, pandemonium ◊ *die Herzen in Aufruhr*

A

versetzen ♦ *Die Enthüllungen sorgten für erheblichen Aufruhr in der Presse.*
Auf·rüs·tung [ˈa͜ofrʏstʊŋ] die <-, -en> **1.** upgrade, upgrading ◊ *die Aufrüstung eines Computers mit einem schnelleren Prozessor* **2.** *(military)* arming ◊ *die Aufrüstung mit chemischen Waffen/Atomwaffen*
aufs [a͜ofs] [contract] *auf + das* **1.** on the ◊ *Ich setzte mich aufs Bett.*; to the ◊ *Er geht aufs Postamt.* → **auf 2.** *in certain idioms, not to be split: look up the relevant idiom* ◊ *sich aufs Ohr legen/hauen*
Auf·satz [ˈa͜ofzats] der <-es, Aufsätze> **1.** article ◊ *einen Aufsatz schreiben/verfassen/veröffentlichen* ♦ *ein interessanter/kritischer Aufsatz über die Gentechnik* **2.** school essay ◊ *einen Aufsatz schreiben/aufhaben* **3.** *(for a cupboard)* detachable upper section ◊ *ein Schlafzimmerschrank mit Aufsatz*
auf|schie·ben [ˈa͜ofʃiːbm̩] <schiebt auf, schob auf, hat aufgeschoben> [tr v] put off, postpone ◊ *eine Entscheidung so lange aufschieben, bis es fast zu spät ist*
Auf·schlag [ˈa͜ofʃlaːk] der <-(e)s, Aufschläge> **1.** sport service, serve ◊ *jdm den Aufschlag abnehmen* ♦ *einen harten/schwachen Aufschlag haben* (den) Aufschlag haben be serving **2.** surcharge ◊ *ein Aufschlag von 20 Euro/15 Prozent (auf den alten Preis)* ⊜Abschlag **3.** impact ◊ *Der Teller zerbrach beim Aufschlag auf dem Boden.* ⊜Aufprall **4.** cuff ◊ *eine Jacke mit Aufschlägen*; *(on trousers)* turn-up
auf|schla·gen [ˈa͜ofʃlaːgn̩] <schlägt auf, schlug auf, hat/ist aufgeschlagen> [tr v] open ◊ *Schlag das Buch auf Seite 14 auf!* ♦ *Welche Seite soll ich aufschlagen?* [intr v] auf etw. [dat]/[acc] aufschlagen hit sth ◊ *Er schlug mit dem Kopf auf dem/den Boden auf.* ♦ *Der Stein ist auf dem/den Grund des Brunnens aufgeschlagen. Ich habe mir das Knie aufgeschlagen. I hurt my knee.*
Auf·schluss [ˈa͜ofʃlʊs] der <-es, Aufschlüsse> Aufschluss über etw. [acc] information about sth ◊ *Sein Verhalten gibt keinen Aufschluss darüber, was er wirklich denkt.* ⊜Aufklärung
auf|schnei·den [ˈa͜ofʃna͜edn̩] <schneidet auf, schnitt auf, hat aufgeschnitten> [tr v] **1.** cut open ◊ *einen Sack aufschneiden* ♦ *Ich habe mir an den Scherben den Fuß aufgeschnitten.* **2.** *(fam)* open up ◊ *jdm den Bauch aufschneiden* **3.** *(roast)* carve; *(bread)* slice [intr v] *(fam, pej)* boast ◊ *vor seinen Freunden mit dem neuen Auto/mit seinen Erfolgen aufschneiden* ⊜angeben
Auf·schrei [ˈa͜ofʃra͜e] der <-(e)s, -e> cry ◊ *sich mit einem Aufschrei auf jdn stürzen*; *(of protest, indignation)* outcry ◊ *Ein Aufschrei (der Empörung) ging durchs Land.*
ⓩ **auf|schrei·ben** [ˈa͜ofʃra͜ebm̩] <schreibt auf, schrieb auf, hat aufgeschrieben> [tr v] **1.** write down ◊ *eine Geschichte/seine Gedanken aufschreiben* sich [dat] etw. aufschreiben make a note of sth ◊ *sich jds Telefonnummer aufschreiben* ♦ *Hast du dir aufgeschrieben, was du einkaufen sollst?* ⊜notieren **2.** *(fam)* jdn aufschreiben book sb, give sb a ticket **3.** *(fam) (as a doctor)* prescribe ◊ *jdm zehn Massagen/ein Medikament aufschreiben*
Auf·schub [ˈa͜ofʃuːp] der <-(e)s, Aufschübe> delay, postponement ◊ *jdm Aufschub gewähren* ♦ *einen*

Aufschub der Entscheidung/Verhandlung erreichen *etw. duldet keinen Aufschub* sth admits no delay *um Aufschub bitten* ask for an extension
Auf·schwung [ˈa͜ofʃvʊŋ] der <-(e)s, Aufschwünge> boom, upswing, upturn ◊ *wirtschaftlicher/konjunktureller Aufschwung* ♦ *einen Aufschwung erleben* ♦ *für einen Aufschwung an der Börse sorgen*
Auf·se·hen [ˈa͜ofzeːən] das <-s> no pl stir, sensation Aufsehen erregen/verursachen, für Aufsehen sorgen create/cause a stir/sensation ◊ *großes/erhebliches/einiges Aufsehen erregen* ⊛ **Aufsehen erregend** sensational ◊ *Sie machten eine Aufsehen erregende Entdeckung.* ♦ *Die Ergebnisse der Studie waren Aufsehen erregend.*
auf|set·zen [ˈa͜ofzɛtsn̩] <setzt auf, setzte auf, hat aufgesetzt> [tr v] **1.** put on ◊ *Setz (dir) eine Mütze auf, wenn du nach draußen gehst.* ♦ *Kannst du Wasser für die Nudeln aufsetzen?* ♦ *Sie setzte eine freundliche Miene auf.* jdm einen Hut/eine Kappe etc. aufsetzen put a hat/a cap on sb ◊ *Sie setzte dem Kind einen Sonnenhut auf.* **2.** jdn aufsetzen sit sb up ◊ *Die Schwester setzte den Patienten zum Essen auf.* sich aufsetzen sit up ◊ *Schaffst du es, dich ohne Hilfe aufzusetzen?* **3.** put down ◊ *den verletzten Fuß vorsichtig aufsetzen* **4.** draft, draw up ◊ *einen Brief/Vertrag aufsetzen* [tr+intr v] land, set down ◊ *Der Pilot setzte das Flugzeug weich auf.* ♦ *Das Flugzeug setzte unsanft auf.*
Auf·sicht [ˈa͜ofzɪçt] die <-, -en> **1.** supervision, control ◊ *Die Therapie findet unter ärztlicher Aufsicht statt.*; *(in exams)* invigilation die Aufsicht (bei/über etw.) haben/führen supervise (sth), control (sth) ◊ *Wer hat bei der Prüfung die Aufsicht?* jdn/etw. ohne Aufsicht lassen leave sb/sth unattended ◊ *Lass das Feuer nie ohne Aufsicht!* **2.** supervisor ◊ *die Aufsicht um Auskunft bitten*; *(in exams)* invigilator
auf|sper·ren [ˈa͜ofʃpɛrən] <sperrt auf, sperrte auf, hat aufgesperrt> [tr v] **1.** *(SouthG)* unlock ◊ *eine Tür/ein Geschäft aufsperren* ⊜zusperren, absperren, abschließen **2.** *(fam)* open wide ◊ *Die jungen Vögel sperrten ihre Schnäbel auf.* ⊜aufmachen
auf|sprin·gen [ˈa͜ofʃprɪŋən] <springt auf, sprang auf, ist aufgesprungen> [intr v] **1.** burst (open) ◊ *Die Tür sprang plötzlich auf.* **2.** jump up, leap up ◊ *Als sie gehen wollte, sprang er auf, um ihr den Mantel zu holen.* **3.** auf etw. [acc] aufspringen jump on(to) sth ◊ *Sie sind auf den fahrenden Zug aufgesprungen.*
Auf·stand [ˈa͜ofʃtant] der <-(e)s, Aufstände> rebellion, revolt ◊ *Das Militär schlug den Aufstand nieder.* ⊜Aufruhr, Revolte ⊛ **es gibt einen Aufstand** *(fam, fig)* hell breaks loose ◊ *Wenn er uns weiter so behandelt, gibt es noch einen Aufstand.* einen Aufstand machen *(fam, fig)* make a fuss
ⓩ **auf|ste·hen** [ˈa͜ofʃteːən] <steht auf, stand auf, ist/hat aufgestanden> [intr v] **1.** +*sein* get up, stand up ◊ *Er stand auf, um der alten Dame Platz zu machen.*; *(from a bed)* get up ◊ *Ich bin heute schon um 5 Uhr aufgestanden.* **2.** +*haben/in South G, Austr, Swiss often +sein* be open, stand open ◊ *Die Tür stand einen Spalt auf.*
auf|stei·gen [ˈa͜ofʃta͜egn̩] <steigt auf, stieg auf, ist aufgestiegen> [intr v] **1.** rise ◊ *Vom Feuer stieg*

B
C
D
E
F
G
H
I
J
K
L
M
N
O
P
Q
R
S
T
U
V
W
X
Y
Z

kaum Rauch auf. ✦ *Er ist vom Tellerwäscher zum Chef der Firma aufgestiegen.* **2.** climb ◊ *Sie stiegen bis zum Gipfel auf.* ⊖absteigen **3.** *(emotions)* in jdm aufsteigen arise in sb, rise up in sb ◊ *in jdm steigt Ärger/Mitleid/Neid auf* **4.** *(team)* be promoted ◊ *in die Bundesliga aufsteigen* ⊖absteigen

auf|stel·len [ˈaʊfʃtɛlən] <stellt auf, stellte auf, hat aufgestellt> ⟨tr v⟩ **1.** put up, erect ◊ *ein Zelt/einen Sonnenschirm aufstellen* etw. (wieder) aufstellen stand sth up (again) ◊ *umgefallene Stühle wieder aufstellen* **2.** arrange, set up ◊ *Stühle im Kreis aufstellen; (in lines)* line up ◊ *Flaschen nebeneinander/hintereinander aufstellen* **3.** post, position ◊ *Wachen aufstellen* **4.** *(an invoice, a list, programme)* draw up, work out ◊ *eine Liste/Rechnung aufstellen* ✦ *Was für ein Programm habt ihr für morgen aufgestellt?* **5.** *(demands, rules)* make ◊ *Ich habe einige Regeln aufgestellt, an die sich alle halten müssen.; (a theory)* propose ◊ *Der Forscher hat eine neue Theorie zur Entstehung des Universums aufgestellt.* eine Behauptung aufstellen maintain sth **6.** *(a candidate)* nominate, put up ◊ *Sie wurde (als Kandidatin) für den Vorstand aufgestellt.; (a player)* pick, select ◊ *Ersatzspieler aufstellen; (a team)* put together sich aufstellen lassen run/stand as a candidate **7.** prick up ◊ *Der Hund stellte die Ohren auf.* ⊖aufrichten ⟨ref v⟩ **1.** sich aufstellen position yourself ◊ *Die Kinder stellten sich im Kreis um den Lehrer auf.; (in lines)* line up ◊ *Bitte stellt euch hintereinander in einer Reihe auf.* **2.** *(hair)* sich aufstellen bristle, rise ◊ *Der Hund begann zu knurren und sein Fell stellte sich auf.; (spikes)* sich aufstellen prick up ◊ *Die Stacheln des Igels stellten sich auf.* ⊖aufrichten

Auf·stieg [ˈaʊfʃtiːk] der <-(e)s, -e> **1.** ascent, climb ◊ *ein beschwerlicher Aufstieg* ✦ *Nach dreistündigem Aufstieg hatten sie den Gipfel erreicht.* **2.** rise, promotion, advancement ◊ *jds beruflicher/gesellschaftlicher Aufstieg* ✦ *der Aufstieg in die nächste Liga*

auf|sto·ßen [ˈaʊfʃtoːsn̩] <stößt auf, stieß auf, hat/ist aufgestoßen> ⟨tr v⟩ +*haben* **1.** push open ◊ *die Tür aufstoßen* **2.** *(injury)* sich ⟨dat⟩ etw. aufstoßen graze your sth ◊ *Sie ist gefallen und hat sich das Knie aufgestoßen.* ⟨intr v⟩ **1.** +*haben* belch, burp ◊ *Nach der Mahlzeit sollte das Baby aufstoßen.* **2.** +*sein* jdm (übel) aufstoßen annoy sb, haunt sb ◊ *Diese Bemerkung ist mir (übel) aufgestoßen.*

Auf·strich [ˈaʊfʃtrɪç] der <-(e)s, -e> spread ◊ *Haselnusscreme ist ein beliebter Aufstrich fürs Frühstücksbrot.*

auf|su·chen [ˈaʊfzuːxn̩] <sucht auf, suchte auf, hat aufgesucht> ⟨tr v⟩ *(lofty)* go to ◊ *die Toilette aufsuchen; (for advice also)* consult ◊ *Sie sollten einen Arzt aufsuchen.*

Auf·takt [ˈaʊftakt] der <-(e)s, -e> start, prelude ◊ *der Auftakt der Bundesligasaison* ✦ *Zum Auftakt des heutigen Abends spielen wir einen Walzer.*

auf|tan·ken [ˈaʊftaŋkn̩] <tankt auf, tankte auf, hat aufgetankt> ⟨tr+intr v⟩ fill up, refuel ◊ *ein Flugzeug auftanken* ✦ *Bevor wir losfuhren, haben wir aufgetankt.*

auf|tau·chen [ˈaʊftaʊxn̩] <taucht auf, tauchte auf,

---

ist aufgetaucht> ⟨intr v⟩ **1.** turn up ◊ *Rate mal, wer gestern bei uns aufgetaucht ist.* ✦ *Ist der Schlüssel wieder aufgetaucht?* **2.** appear, emerge ◊ *Ein dunkle Gestalt tauchte aus dem Nebel auf.* **3.** arise, crop up ◊ *Es ist da ein Problem aufgetaucht.* **4.** surface, emerge ◊ *Das U-Boot tauchte wieder auf.*

auf|tau·en [ˈaʊftaʊən] <taut auf, taute auf, hat/ist aufgetaut> ⟨tr v⟩ +*haben* **1.** defrost ◊ *Spinat in der Mikrowelle auftauen* **2.** melt, thaw ◊ *Um etwas zu trinken zu haben, haben sie Schnee aufgetaut.* ⟨intr v⟩ +*sein* **1.** defrost ◊ *Das Fleisch ist schon halb aufgetaut.* **2.** melt, thaw ◊ *Das Eis auf dem See taut langsam auf.* **3.** *(fig) (person)* thaw ◊ *Nach zwei Glas Wein ist er aufgetaut.*

auf|tei·len [ˈaʊftaɪlən] <teilt auf, teilte auf, hat aufgeteilt> ⟨tr v⟩ divide, split up, distribute ◊ *Nach dem Krieg wurde Deutschland in vier Zonen aufgeteilt.* ✦ *Wir haben den Gewinn unter uns aufgeteilt.* sich (in etw. ⟨acc⟩) aufteilen divide (into sth), split up (into sth) ◊ *Teilt euch jetzt bitte in drei Gruppen auf!* ✦ *Eure Gruppe ist zu groß — ihr müsst euch aufteilen!*

② **Auf·trag** [ˈaʊftraːk] der <-(e)s, Aufträge> **1.** directions, instructions ◊ *Der Chef hat mir den Auftrag gegeben, mich darum zu kümmern.* **2.** *(what is to be done)* task, job ◊ *ein unangenehmer Auftrag; (military, diplomatic)* mission **3.** TRADE *(for goods)* order ◊ *einer Firma einen Auftrag erteilen; (for doing sth)* commission ◊ *Sie haben den Auftrag zum Ausbau des Bahnhofs bekommen.* ⊚ im Auftrag … ⟨gen⟩, im Auftrag von jdm/etw. on behalf of sb/sth, on the instructions of sb/sth ◊ *Ich komme im Auftrag der Firma Hueber.* ✦ *Ich spreche im Auftrag von Herrn Hartl.*

auf|tra·gen [ˈaʊftraːgn̩] <trägt auf, trug auf, hat aufgetragen> ⟨tr v⟩ **1.** *(to a surface)* apply ◊ *Klebstoff/Lack auftragen* **2.** *(lofty)* serve ◊ *Speisen auftragen* **3.** *(clothing)* wear ◊ *Ich muss die Kleidung meines älteren Bruders auftragen.* **4.** *mostly passive* jdm etw. auftragen; jdm auftragen, etw. zu tun instruct sb to do sth ◊ *jdm die Beseitigung von Mängeln auftragen* ✦ *Dem Makler wurde aufgetragen, einen neuen Mieter zu suchen.* ⟨intr v⟩ *(fam)* **1.** be not (very) flattering ◊ *Der Rock trägt auf.* **2.** dick/ziemlich auftragen lay it on thick/a bit thick ◊ *Du darfst im Bewerbungsschreiben nicht zu dick auftragen.*

Auf·trags·la·ge [ˈaʊftraːkslaːgə] die <-, -n> business situation, number of orders ◊ *Eine Besserung der Auftragslage ist nicht in Sicht.*

auf|tre·ten [ˈaʊftreːtn̩] <tritt auf, trat auf, ist aufgetreten> ⟨intr v⟩ **1.** *(in front of an audience, as a witness)* appear ◊ *In diesem Film tritt er als brutaler Killer auf.* ✦ *als Zeuge vor Gericht auftreten* **2.** *(problems, mistakes)* arise, occur ◊ *Probleme traten auf.; (side-effects)* develop ◊ *Dabei können auch Nebenwirkungen auftreten.* ⊖sich einstellen, vorkommen **3.** selbstbewusst/aggressiv etc. auftreten make a confident/aggressive etc. impression, behave with confidence/aggressively etc. ◊ *Die Lehrerin trat den Schülern gegenüber entschieden auf.* **4.** tread ◊ *leise/vorsichtig auftreten* ⟨tr v⟩ kick open ◊ *Die Polizei musste die Tür auftreten.*

Auf·tritt [ˈaʊftrɪt] der <-(e)s, -e> **1.** performance

◊ *ein selbstbewusster Auftritt beim Vorstellungsgespräch* ♦ *Der Auftritt der Sängerin dauerte über drei Stunden.* **2.** *(on stage)* appearance ◊ *Ihren ersten öffentlichen Auftritt hatte sie schon mit zwölf.; (at a social event)* entrance

② **auf|wa·chen** ['aofvaxn̩] <wacht auf, wachte auf, ist aufgewacht> ⎡intr v⎤ *(aus etw.)* aufwachen wake up (from sth), awaken (from sth) ◊ *Ich wache jeden Morgen um 6 Uhr auf.* ♦ *aus einem Traum/seiner Lethargie aufwachen* aus der Narkose aufwachen come round from the anaesthetic ⊝einschlafen

auf|wach·sen ['aofvaksn̩] <wächst auf, wuchs auf, ist aufgewachsen> ⎡intr v⎤ grow up ◊ *zweisprachig aufwachsen* ♦ *bei den Großeltern/in bescheidenen Verhältnissen aufwachsen*

Auf·wand ['aofvant] der <-(e)s> *no pl* effort, trouble ◊ *Lohnt sich der Aufwand?* ♦ *unnötigen Aufwand treiben* finanzieller Aufwand expenditure

auf·wän·dig ['aofvɛndɪç] ⎡adj, adv⎤ elaborate(ly), lavish(ly) ◊ *ein aufwändiges Design* ♦ *ein aufwändig saniertes Gebäude*; *(time-consuming)* laborious(ly) ◊ *Diese Arbeit ist sehr aufwändig.*

auf|wär·men ['aofvɛrˈmən] <wärmt auf, wärmte auf, hat aufgewärmt> ⎡tr v⎤ **1.** heat up, warm up ◊ *Ich wärme dir das Essen von gestern auf.* **2.** *(fig)* dredge up, drag up, revive ◊ *eine alte Geschichte aufwärmen* ⎡ref v⎤ **1.** sich aufwärmen warm yourself (up) ◊ *sich an einem Ofen aufwärmen* ⊝sich abkühlen **2.** SPORT sich aufwärmen warm up ◊ *Vor dem Spiel wärmte die Mannschaft sich auf.*

② **auf·wärts** ['aofvɛrˈts] ⎡adv⎤ up, upwards ◊ *ein aufwärts fahrender Aufzug* ♦ *Die Kurse bewegten sich aufwärts.* ♦ *eine Dampferfahrt den Rhein aufwärts*; uphill ◊ *Der Weg ist sehr beschwerlich.* ⊝abwärts

⊛ **aufwärts gehen** *(fig)* improve, be picking up ◊ *Mit seiner Gesundheit geht es wieder aufwärts.*

ab/von etw. aufwärts from sth (upwards) ◊ *Ab 30 Euro aufwärts sind Bestellungen portofrei.* ♦ *Kinder von 12 Jahren aufwärts*

auf|we·cken ['aofvɛkn̩] <weckt auf, weckte auf, hat aufgeweckt> ⎡tr v⎤ wake up ◊ *Kannst du mich morgen um 6 Uhr aufwecken?*

auf·wen·dig ['aofvɛndɪç] → aufwändig

auf|wer·ten ['aofveːɐ̯tn̩] <wertet auf, wertete auf, hat aufgewertet> ⎡tr v⎤ **1.** revalue ◊ *Der Dollar wurde um fünf Prozent aufgewertet.* **2.** enhance, improve ◊ *Diese Kampagne soll das Image der Region aufwerten.*

Auf·wind ['aofvɪnt] der <-(e)s, -e> **1.** *no pl* *(fig)* impetus ◊ *Die Umweltschützer bekamen neuen Aufwind.* sich im Aufwind befinden be on the (way) up ◊ *Technologieaktien befinden sich im Aufwind.* **2.** METEO upwind ◊ *Aufwinde werden beim Segelflug genutzt.*

auf|zäh·len ['aofsɛːlən] <zählt auf, zählte auf, hat aufgezählt> ⎡tr v⎤ list, enumerate ◊ *seine Stärken aufzählen* ♦ *Sie zählte auf, was sie sich zu Weihnachten wünscht.*

auf|zeich·nen ['aofsaeçnən] <zeichnet auf, zeichnete auf, hat aufgezeichnet> ⎡tr v⎤ **1.** draw ◊ *Er hat mir die Route aufgezeichnet.* **2.** record ◊ *seine Gedanken in einem Tagebuch aufzeichnen* ♦ *Das Messgerät zeichnet die Schwankungen auf.* ♦ *Ihre Stimme ist auf Band aufgezeichnet.*

auf|zie·hen ['aofsiːən] <zieht auf, zog auf, hat/ist aufgezogen> ⎡tr v⎤ +*haben* **1.** *(a zip, blind etc.)* open ◊ *den Reißverschluss aufziehen; (a bow)* undo ◊ *jdm die Schnürsenkel aufziehen; (stitches)* unpick **2.** raise, rear ◊ *ein Kind allein aufziehen* ♦ *ein Kalb mit der Flasche aufziehen* **3.** wind (up) ◊ *eine Uhr aufziehen* **4.** *(a tyre)* put on, mount ◊ *neue Reifen aufziehen* **5.** MED *(a syringe)* fill ◊ *(Insulin in) eine Spritze aufziehen* **6.** *(fam) (a business, an organization etc.)* set up ◊ *ein Netzwerk für Frauen aufziehen; (an event)* put on **7.** *(fam, fig)* tease, make fun of ◊ *Ich wurde wegen meines Aussehens aufgezogen.* **8.** MUS neue Saiten (auf etw. ⎡acc⎤) aufziehen restring sth ◊ *neue Saiten auf eine Gitarre aufziehen* **9.** *(a sail, flag)* hoist ⎡intr v⎤ +*sein (also fig) (clouds, fog etc.)* be gathering ◊ *Dunkle Regenwolken zogen auf.* ♦ *Ein Gewitter zieht auf.*

② **Auf·zug** ['aofsuːk] der <-(e)s, Aufzüge> **1.** lift, elevator ◊ *mit dem Aufzug in den 10. Stock fahren; (for objects)* hoist ◊ *Das Restaurant hat einen Aufzug für Speisen.* **2.** *(pej) (clothes)* get-up ◊ *In diesem Aufzug kannst du doch nicht zu einer Beerdigung gehen!* **3.** *no pl* MIL deployment ◊ *der Aufzug von Truppen entlang der Grenze; (ceremonial)* parade, procession der Aufzug der Garde the mounting of the guard **4.** *no pl (of clouds, a storm)* gathering **5.** THEAT act ◊ *Er hat seinen Auftritt im dritten Aufzug.*

② **Au·ge** ['aogə] das <-s, -n> **1.** ANAT eye ◊ *Sie hat blaue/gute/scharfe Augen.* ♦ *Mein Opa ist auf einem Auge blind.* ♦ *Wenn er „Zirkus" hört, bekommt er leuchtende Augen.* **2.** *(of a rose, potato)* bud, eye **3.** *only pl* point, pip ◊ *Wie viele Augen zählt das Ass/hast du gewürfelt?*

⊛ **keine Augen im Kopf haben** be blind ◊ *Pass doch auf, wo du hintrittst, hast du denn keine Augen im Kopf?* **sich** ⎡dat⎤ **die Augen aus dem Kopf weinen** cry your eyes out **Augen wie ein Luchs haben** have eyes like a hawk **aus den Augen, aus dem Sinn** out of sight, out of mind **Auge um Auge, Zahn um Zahn** an eye for an eye, a tooth for a tooth **ein blaues Auge** a black eye **mit einem blauen Auge davonkommen** get off lightly ◊ *Er kam noch einmal mit einem blauen Auge davon und blieb straffrei.* **mit bloßem Auge** with the naked eye **große Augen machen** be wide-eyed, be flabbergasted ◊ *Beim Anblick der vielen Geschenke machte sie große Augen.* **mit offenen Augen schlafen** be daydreaming, be absent-minded **jdm schöne Augen machen** make eyes at sb **unter vier Augen** in private ◊ *Kann ich dich mal unter vier Augen sprechen?* **jdm wird schwarz vor Augen** everything goes black ◊ *Der Schmerz war so stark, dass ihr schwarz vor Augen wurde.* **bei etw. bleibt kein Auge trocken** *(fam)* sth makes you cry (with laughter/sadness) ◊ *Bei diesem Film bleibt bestimmt kein Auge trocken.* **so weit das Auge reicht** as far as the eye can see **jdm etw. von den Augen ablesen** read sth in/ from sb's eyes, anticipate sb's wish ◊ *Ihr Mann liest ihr jeden Wunsch von den Augen ab.* **etw./jdn im Auge behalten**, **ein Auge auf etw./jdn haben** keep an eye on sth/sb **jdm etw. aufs Auge drücken** saddle sb with sth ◊ *Wie konntest du dir das nur aufs Auge drücken lassen?* **ins Auge gehen** *(fam)* end in disaster ◊ *ein riskantes*

A B C D E F G H I J K L M N O P Q R S T U V W X Y Z

A

Manöver, das leicht ins Auge gehen kann **jdm aus den Augen gehen** stay away from sb ◊ *Auf dich bin ich echt sauer — geh mir bloß aus den Augen!* **jdn/etw. nicht aus den Augen lassen** not take your eyes off sb/sth ◊ *Sie hat ihren Koffer nicht aus den Augen gelassen.* **die/mit den Augen rollen** roll your eyes **seinen Augen nicht/kaum trauen** don't believe your eyes **aus den Augen verlieren 1.** lose sight of ◊ *Er ging schneller und ich verlor ihn aus den Augen.* **2.** lose touch/contact with ◊ *Nach dem Schulabschluss haben wir uns aus den Augen verloren.* **ein Auge zudrücken** turn a blind eye ◊ *Meinst du, du könntest ein Auge zudrücken und mich nicht verraten?* **kein Auge zutun** not sleep a wink ◊ *Ich habe die ganze Nacht kein Auge zugetan.* **Augen zu und durch** *(fam)* take a deep breath and go (for it), (keep your) head down and go ◊ *Wir müssen das heute noch fertig machen, also Augen zu und durch.* **unter/vor jds Augen** (right) in front of sb, before sb's (very) eyes ◊ *Er wurde vor meinen Augen überfahren.*

② **Au·gen·blick** [ˈaʊgn̩ˈblɪk, '– – –] der <-(e)s, -e> moment, instant ◊ *Einen Augenblick lang habe ich geglaubt, er fällt um.* ♦ *einen günstigen Augenblick abwarten* ♦ *die schönsten Augenblicke meines Lebens*

⊛ **im letzten Augenblick** in the last moment, in the nick of time **einen Augenblick** (just) a second/minute/moment ◊ *Einen Augenblick, bitte. Ich komme sofort.* **im Augenblick** at the moment, right now ◊ *Die Kollegin ist im Augenblick beschäftigt.*

② **au·gen·blick·lich** [ˈaʊgn̩ˈblɪklɪç, '– – – –] [adj, adv] *no comp/superl; when used as an adj, only before ns* current(ly), present(ly), momentary(-arily) ◊ *sein augenblicklicher Gesundheitszustand* ♦ *die augenblickliche Stärke des Dollar* ♦ *Die Gebühr liegt augenblicklich bei 100 Euro.* ♦ *Sie ist augenblicklich die Beste auf diesem Gebiet.* [adv] instantly, immediately ◊ *Wenn du nicht augenblicklich gehorchst, dann setzt es etwas!* ♦ *Ein Fehler stoppt das System augenblicklich.*

Au·gen·zeu·ge [ˈaʊgn̩ˈtsɔɪgə] der <-n, -n>, **Au·gen·zeu·gin** [ˈaʊgn̩ˈtsɔɪgɪn] die <-, -nen> eyewitness ◊ *Er war Augenzeuge eines Mordes geworden.* ♦ *die einzige Augenzeugin*

② **Au·gust** [aʊˈgʊst] der <-(e)s, -e> August → Januar

② **aus¹** [aʊs] [adv] **1.** *(fam)* aus sein be (turned/switched) off ◊ *Die Lampe/Der Computer ist aus.*; *(flames)* be out, be extinguished ◊ *Das Feuer ist noch nicht ganz aus.* ⊜an **2.** *(fam)* aus sein be over, have ended ◊ *Das Kino ist schon aus.* ♦ *Wann ist morgen die Schule aus?* **3.** out ◊ *Ich habe gestern angerufen, aber du warst wohl aus.* ♦ *Der Ball war aus!* ♦ *Licht aus und Augen zu!* **4.** *used as imperative* enough ◊ *Aus! Hört sofort auf damit!*

⊛ **auf etw.** [acc] **aus sein** be after sth, be interested in sth ◊ *Du bist wohl auf einen Streit aus?* ♦ *Sie ist darauf aus, die Beste in der Klasse zu werden.* **mit etw. ist es aus** sth is over ◊ *Ab heute ist es aus mit dem Faulenzen, jetzt wird gearbeitet!* **mit jdm ist es aus** sb has had it, sb is dead meat, sb is history ◊ *Wenn dein Vater*

dahinter kommt, dann ist es aus mit dir. **zwischen … ist es aus** it is (all) over between … ◊ *Zwischen Karin und Bernd ist es wohl endgültig aus.*

② **aus²** [aʊs] [prep] [+dat] **1.** *in response to the question 'from where?' (directional)* out of, from ◊ *Er sah aus dem Fenster.* ♦ *Er riss ein Blatt aus dem Heft.* ♦ *Sie nahm mir das Tablett aus der Hand.* ♦ *aus der Flasche trinken* **2.** *in response to the question 'from where?' (expressing origin, distance)* from ◊ *Er ist/kommt aus Italien.* ♦ *Und nun die Nachrichten aus aller Welt.* ♦ *aus guter Familie stammen* ♦ *Das kann man aus großer Entfernung erkennen.* ♦ *Aus der Ferne hörte man Donnergrollen.* **von … aus** from ◊ *Das kann ich von hier aus nicht erkennen.* **aus der Nähe** closely ◊ *Aus der Nähe betrachtet ist es noch schöner.* **3.** *in response to the question 'what from?'* (made) of, (made) from ◊ *eine Vase aus Glas* ♦ *Aus welchem Holz ist der Tisch?* ♦ *ein Herz aus Stein* haben etw. aus etw./jdm machen turn sth/sb into sth ◊ *einen anständigen Menschen aus jdm machen* etw. wird aus sb/ sth, sb/sth turns into sth ◊ *Was soll bloß mal aus dir werden?* ♦ *Aus der Raupe wird später ein Schmetterling.* ♦ *Aus dem Plan ist nichts geworden.* **4.** *(causal)* out of, for ◊ *Sie haben aus Liebe geheiratet.* ♦ *Aus Angst vor Bestrafung ist sie nicht nach Hause gegangen.* ♦ *Aus welchem Grund hat er wohl gelogen?* **aus Erfahrung** from experience **aus Prinzip** on principle **aus Versehen** by mistake **aus etw. heraus** out of, out of sth ◊ *Aus einer Laune heraus gingen wir noch etwas trinken.* **5.** *(temporal)* from ◊ *Geschichten aus meiner Jugend* ♦ *Fotos aus der Zeit vor dem Krieg* ♦ *Das stammt noch aus dem Mittelalter.*

Aus [aʊs] das <-> *no pl (always das Aus)* **1.** the end ◊ *Nach dem Skandal droht dem Kanzler das Aus.* ♦ *Diese Steuerreform bedeutet das Aus für kleine Unternehmen.* **2.** sport **im Aus sein** be out of play **den Ball ins Aus schießen** kick the ball out of play

aus|… [aʊs] [prefix] **1.** out ◊ *abends ausgehen* ♦ *aus einem Haus ausziehen* ♦ *sich ein Haar ausreißen* ♦ *Flecken aus einer Bluse auswaschen* **Zeitungen austragen** deliver the papers **2.** *translation varies (indicates that something is made longer, bigger etc., or lasts longer, gains momentum)* ◊ *einem Spaziergang ausdehnen* extend a walk **Die Grippe breitet sich aus.** The flu is spreading. **3.** *(ceasure, coming to an end)* off ◊ *das Radio ausdrehen* ♦ *das Handy ausschalten* eine ausgestorbene Tierart an extinct species **4.** *translation varies (selectivity)* etw. auswählen choose sth, select sth **sich etw. aussuchen** pick sth, choose sth ausgesucht freundlich sein be exceptionally friendly

aus|bau·en [ˈaʊsbaʊən] <baut aus, baute aus, hat ausgebaut> [tr v] **1.** *(a piece of machinery)* etw. (aus etw.) ausbauen remove sth (from sth) ◊ *den Motor aus dem Pkw ausbauen* **2.** *(also fig)* expand, develop ◊ *die Infrastruktur ausbauen* ♦ *seine Kontakte ausbauen; (a lead)* consolidate; *(a building)* extend; *(a loft, a cellar)* convert

aus|bes·sern [ˈaʊsbɛsɐn] <bessert aus, besserte aus, hat ausgebessert> [tr v] **1.** repair, mend ◊

Straßenschäden ausbessern ◆ einen Schaden im Lack ausbessern **2.** correct ◊ Der Lehrer besserte die Fehler im Diktat aus.

aus|beu·ten ['aosbɔɡtn̩] <beutet aus, beutete aus, hat ausgebeutet> ⟨tr v⟩ **1.** *(natural resources)* deplete, exhaust ◊ Ölquellen ausbeuten **2.** *(fig, pej)* jdn ausbeuten exploit sb ◊ Sie fühlten sich von ihrer Firma ausgebeutet.

aus|bil·den ['aosbɪldn̩] <bildet aus, bildete aus, hat ausgebildet> ⟨tr v⟩ **1.** train ◊ Lehrlinge/ Nachwuchs ausbilden ◆ sich zum Bäcker ausbilden lassen **2.** develop ◊ Blüten/Muskeln ausbilden

② **Aus·bil·dung** ['aosbɪldʊŋ] die <-, –en> training ◊ Ich bin noch in der Ausbildung. ◆ Die Ausbildung zum Bäcker dauert drei Jahre. ◆ eine Ausbildung als Bankkaufmann machen; education ◊ eine gute Ausbildung haben

> The traditional German 'dual system' vocational training course for school leavers consists of two to three years training within a company combined with a course of education at a vocational college. There are around 500 different jobs in technical and commercial fields and in the trades which demand formal vocational training. The situation is constantly reviewed and adapted to industry requirements by the Chambers of Crafts and the Chambers of Commerce and Industry.

aus|blei·ben ['aosblaebm̩] <bleibt aus, blieb aus, ist ausgeblieben> ⟨intr v⟩ **1.** not come ◊ Das Geschäft musste schließen, weil die Kunden ausblieben. ◆ Der dringend nötige Regen ist ausgeblieben.; not happen, not take place ◊ Die Besserung auf dem Arbeitsmarkt ist ausgeblieben. etw. konnte nicht ausbleiben sth was inevitable ☺eintreffen **2.** stay out ◊ Wie lange wirst du etwa ausbleiben?

Aus·blick ['aosblɪk] der <-(e)s, –e> **1.** view ◊ Vom Gipfel hatten wir einen wunderbaren Ausblick. ◆ ein Zimmer mit Ausblick aufs Meer ☺Aussicht **2.** outlook, prospect ◊ Das eröffnet uns einen positiven Ausblick in die Zukunft. ◆ ein Ausblick auf die künftigen Entwicklungen

② **aus|bor·gen** ['aosbɔʳgn̩] <borgt aus, borgte aus, hat ausgeborgt> ⟨tr v⟩ jdm etw. ausborgen lend sb sth ◊ Kannst du mir mal dein Fahrrad ausborgen? ☺leihen ⟨ref+tr v⟩ (sich ⟨dat⟩) etw. (von jdm) ausborgen borrow sth (from sb) ◊ Kann ich mir von euch morgen das Auto ausborgen?

aus|bre·chen ['aosbrɛçn̩] <bricht aus, brach aus, ist ausgebrochen> ⟨intr v⟩ **1.** (aus etw.) ausbrechen escape (from sth), break out (of sth) ◊ aus dem Gefängnis ausbrechen; break free/loose (from sth) ◊ Sie wollte aus ihrer Ehe ausbrechen. **2.** *(fire, war, epidemic, panic)* break out ◊ Das Feuer ist im dritten Stock ausgebrochen. ◆ Panik/Ein Krieg/ Eine Seuche brach aus.; *(volcano)* erupt ◊ Der Ätna ist erneut ausgebrochen. bei jdm bricht Fieber aus sb develops fever; *(sweat)* jdm bricht der Schweiß aus sb breaks out in sweat **3.** *(expressions of emotion)* etw. bricht bei/unter jdm aus, jd bricht in etw ⟨acc⟩ aus sb bursts out in sth ◊ Bei diesen Worten brach unter den Zuhörern Jubel aus. ◆ Sie brach in Tränen aus.

aus|brei·ten ['aosbraetn̩] <breitet aus, breitete

aus, hat ausgebreitet> ⟨tr v⟩ **1.** *(your arms, wings)* spread, extend ◊ Sie breitete die Arme aus, um mich zu drücken. ◆ Der Adler breitete seine Flügel aus und schwang sich in die Lüfte. **2.** spread (out) ◊ Sie breitete den Stadtplan auf dem Tisch aus.; *(for sb else to see or inspect)* lay out ◊ Jeden Morgen breitet die Marktfrau ihre Ware an ihrem Stand aus. ◆ Er breitete seine Gedanken vor den Zuhörern aus. ⟨ref v⟩ **1.** sich ausbreiten spread ◊ Der Waldbrand breitet sich weiter aus. ◆ Der Geruch hatte sich im ganzen Haus ausgebreitet. ◆ Angst breitete sich unter uns aus. **2.** *(fig, also pej)* sich über etw. ⟨acc⟩ ausbreiten go on about sth, expand on sth ◊ Er breitete sich seitenlang über die Zustände im Land aus.

Aus·brei·tung ['aosbraetʊŋ] die <-> *no pl* spread(ing) ◊ um eine Ausbreitung des Feuers zu verhindern ◆ die Ausbreitung des Christentums durch Missionare ◆ die Ausbreitung von Aids

Aus·bruch ['aosbrʊx] der <-(e)s, Ausbrüche> **1.** escape, breakout ◊ sein Ausbruch aus dem Gefängnis **2.** outbreak ◊ bei Ausbruch des Krieges ◆ Die Krankheit ist noch nicht zum Ausbruch gekommen. ◆ Hat er öfter solche Ausbrüche?; *(of a volcano)* eruption; *(of winter)* onset

Aus·dau·er ['aosdaoɐ] die <-> *no pl* endurance, stamina ◊ die Ausdauer eines Marathonläufers ◆ Er betreibt sein Hobby mit großer Ausdauer.

aus·dau·ernd ['aosdaoɐnt] ⟨adj, adv⟩ enduring(ly), persevering(ly) ◊ ein ausdauernder Sportler ◆ Du bist eben nicht ausdauernd genug. ◆ Du solltest etwas ausdauernder lernen!

aus|den·ken ['aosdɛŋkŋ̩] <denkt aus, dachte aus, hat ausgedacht> ⟨tr v⟩ sich ⟨dat⟩ etw. ausdenken think sth up, make sth up, come up with sth ◊ sich eine Überraschung für jdn ausdenken ◆ Da hast du dir eine gute Entschuldigung ausgedacht!

② **Aus·druck¹** ['aosdrʊk] der <-(e)s, Ausdrücke> **1.** expression ◊ Sein Gesicht hatte einen mürrischen Ausdruck. ◆ mit viel/ohne Ausdruck sprechen ◆ Sein nervöses Lachen ist Ausdruck seiner Unsicherheit.; *(in speech also)* term ◊ ein umgangssprachlicher Ausdruck ◆ Solche Ausdrücke möchte ich nicht mehr hören! **2.** token ◊ ein kleines Geschenk als Ausdruck meiner Dankbarkeit ⦿ etw. zum Ausdruck bringen express sth, voice sth ◊ Ich muss jetzt meine Unzufriedenheit zum Ausdruck bringen. zum Ausdruck kommen be expressed

Aus·druck² ['aosdrʊk] der <-(e)s, –e> printout ◊ Ich habe einen Ausdruck von der Liste gemacht.

aus|drü·cken ['aosdrʏkŋ̍] <drückt aus, drückte aus, hat ausgedrückt> ⟨tr v⟩ **1.** express ◊ Wie kann ich Ihnen nur mein Mitgefühl ausdrücken? **2.** squeeze (out), press ◊ einen Schwamm/eine Zitrone ausdrücken **3.** stub out ◊ die Zigarette auf dem Boden ausdrücken ⟨ref v⟩ **1.** sich ausdrücken express yourself ◊ Er drückte sich sehr unklar aus. **2.** sich in etw. ⟨dat⟩ ausdrücken express itself in sth ◊ In seinem ganzen Verhalten drückt sich seine Abneigung aus.

aus·drück·lich ['aosdrʏklɪç, – ' – –] ⟨adj, adv⟩ <ausdrücklicher, am ausdrücklichsten> *when used as an adj, only before no explicit* explicit(ly) ◊ etw. auf jds ausdrücklichen Wunsch tun ◆ etw. ausdrücklich verbieten

A B C D E F G H I J K L M N O P Q R S T U V W X Y Z

Aus·drucks·wei·se ['aosdruksvaezə] die <-, −n> language, style ◊ eine gepflegte/wissenschaftliche Ausdrucksweise

aus·ei·nan·der [aos|ae'nandɐ] [adv] apart ◊ Stehen die Stühle weit genug auseinander? ✦ Das Regal fällt schon auseinander. ✦ Der Mechaniker hat den Motor auseinander genommen. ✦ Wir haben uns auseinander gelebt.

◉ auseinander gehen 1. break up ◊ Nach dem Treffen gingen die Teilnehmer auseinander. ✦ Ihre Ehe ging nach wenigen Jahren auseinander. 2. differ ◊ Unsere Meinungen gehen da auseinander. etw./jdn auseinander halten tell sth/sb apart, distinguish between sth/sb ◊ Ich kann die Zwillinge einfach nicht auseinander halten. auseinander klaffen 1. be gaping ◊ Die Schnittwunde klaffte weit auseinander. 2. be worlds apart ◊ Wunsch und Wirklichkeit klaffen auseinander. auseinander sein have separated, have split up ◊ Jule und Joe sind schon seit Jahren auseinander. sich mit etw. auseinander setzen tackle sth, give sth serious thoughts ◊ Mit diesem Problem müssen wir uns auseinander setzen. sich mit jdm auseinander setzen argue with sb, confront sb auseinander treiben scatter ◊ Die Cowboys trieben die Rinder auseinander.

② **Aus·fahrt** ['aosfaːɐt] die <-, −en> 1. exit ◊ die Ein- und Ausfahrt der Baustelle ✦ Wir müssen bei der nächsten Ausfahrt von der Autobahn runter.; (of a private property) drive 2. no pl departure ◊ die Ausfahrt des Zuges aus dem Bahnhof ✦ die Ausfahrt aus dem Hafen ⊝Einfahrt 3. ride, trip ◊ Wir haben gestern eine kleine Ausfahrt mit dem Motorrad gemacht. ⊝Ausflug

Aus·fall ['aosfal] der <-(e)s, Ausfälle> 1. (of a machine etc.) failure, breakdown ◊ der Ausfall des Computersystems 2. (of a person) absence ◊ Wir hatten bei der letzten Grippewelle viele Ausfälle. ✦ bei Ausfall eines Mitarbeiters 3. (of an event) cancellation ◊ Wir bedauern den krankheitsbedingten Ausfall des Stücks. 4. no pl (of hair, teeth, feathers) loss ◊ Chemotherapie führt oft zum Ausfall der Haare.

aus|fal·len ['aosfalən] <fällt aus, fiel aus, ist ausgefallen> [intr v] 1. (machine, power) break down, fail ◊ Gestern ist der Strom/unser Großrechner ausgefallen. 2. (person) be absent ◊ Zwei Mitarbeiterinnen sind wegen Schwangerschaft ausgefallen. 3. be cancelled ◊ Heute fällt die letzte Stunde aus. ✦ Wegen des schlechten Wetters musste das Spiel ausfallen. ⊝stattfinden 4. gut/schlecht etc. ausfallen turn out well/badly etc. ◊ Dieses Jahr wird die Apfelernte reichlich ausfallen. ✦ Wie ist das Spiel ausgefallen? ✦ Sein Urteil fiel vernichtend aus. 5. (hair, hair, teeth, feathers) fall out ◊ Dem Vogel fallen die Federn aus. ⊝ausgehen

② **Aus·flug** ['aosfluːk] der <-(e)s, Ausflüge> excursion, (day) trip ◊ Morgen machen wir mit der Schule einen Ausflug in die Berge.

Aus·fuhr ['aosfuːɐ] die <-, −en> no pl export ◊ Die Ausfuhr von Devisen ist beschränkt. ✦ Alle Ausfuhren müssen verzollt werden. ⊝Export ⊝Einfuhr

aus|füh·ren ['aosfyːrən] <führt aus, führte aus, hat ausgeführt> [tr v] 1. export ◊ Autos nach Amerika/aus Deutschland ausführen ⊝einführen 2. carry out ◊ einen Befehl/Plan ausführen ✦ Die Reparatur ist zu unserer Zufriedenheit ausgeführt worden.; (an operation) perform 3. take out, take for a walk ◊ den Hund ausführen ✦ Ich führe dich heute Abend zum Essen aus. 4. explain, expand on ◊ Könnten Sie diese Theorie näher ausführen?

aus·führ·lich ['aosfyːɐlɪç, - '- -] [adj] detailed, explicit ◊ ein ausführlicher Bericht ✦ Die Gebrauchsanweisung war nicht ausführlich genug. [adv] in detail, explicitly ◊ Sie hat mir ausführlich beschrieben, was sie erlebt hat. ⊝eingehend

② **aus|fül·len** ['aosfʏlən] <füllt aus, füllte aus, hat ausgefüllt> [tr v] 1. fill in ◊ einen Antrag ausfüllen ✦ die Steuererklärung ausfüllen 2. fulfil ◊ ein Beruf, der einen ganz und gar ausfüllt ✦ Sie füllt ihre Führungsrolle bestens aus. 3. fill ◊ Die Hohlräume werden mit Gips ausgefüllt. ✦ Niemand wird die Lücke, die er hinterlassen hat, ausfüllen können.

Aus·ga·be ['aosgaːbə] die <-, −n> 1. most pl cost ◊ Die Ausgaben für Lebensmittel sind gestiegen. ✦ Wie hoch sind Ihre laufenden Ausgaben? 2. translated with a verb construction, no pl Die Ausgabe der Waren erfolgt gegen Barzahlung. The merchandise is handed over on cash payment. Wo erfolgt die Ausgabe von Gutscheinen? Where are the vouchers handed out? 3. (of a paper) issue ◊ Die nächste Ausgabe der Zeitung erscheint am Dienstag.; (of a book) edition 4. no pl FIN emission, issue ◊ die Ausgabe von Banknoten/Aktien

② **Aus·gang** ['aosgaŋ] der <-(e)s, Ausgänge> 1. exit ◊ Wo ist der Ausgang? ✦ Der Bahnhof hat fünf Ausgänge.; (of the intestines, stomach) outlet ◊ Der Patient hat einen künstlichen Ausgang bekommen.; (of a village, forest, tunnel) end ◊ Er wartete am Ausgang des Dorfes. ⊝Eingang 2. end(ing) ◊ der glückliche/tragische Ausgang einer Geschichte ✦ Dieses Ereignis markiert den Ausgang einer Ära.; outcome, result ◊ Der Ausgang des Prozesses/der Wahlen ist noch völlig ungewiss. eine Krankheit/ein Abenteuer etc. mit tödlichem Ausgang a fatal illness/adventure etc. ⊝Anfang 3. time off, leave ◊ Ich habe heute Ausgang; meine Schwester bleibt bei den Kindern. ◉ seinen Ausgang nehmen begin, originate ◊ Die Entwicklung der Schrift hat in China ihren Ausgang genommen.

② **aus|ge·ben** ['aosgeːbm̩] <gibt aus, gab aus, hat ausgegeben> [tr v] 1. spend ◊ Für die Miete geben wir im Monat 1000 Euro aus. ✦ Der Staat gibt mehr Geld aus, als er einnimmt. ⊝einnehmen 2. distribute, hand out ◊ Die Getränke werden dort drüben ausgegeben. ✦ Das Sozialamt gibt Essensgutscheine aus. 3. (shares, an order, coins) issue ◊ Er gab den Befehl zum Rückzug aus. ✦ Das Unternehmen hat neue Aktien ausgegeben. 4. (drinks, treats) buy ◊ Ich gebe die nächste Runde aus! jdm etw. ausgeben buy sb sth, treat sb to sth ◊ jdm ein Bier ausgeben einen ausgeben buy a round/drink ◊ Ich gebe heute nach der Arbeit einen aus. 5. jdn/etw. als jdn/etw. ausgeben pretend sth is sb/sth ◊ Sie hat ihren Freund als ihren Ehemann ausgegeben. ✦ Der Fälscher hatte das Bild als Original ausgegeben.

sich als etw. ausgeben pass yourself as sth, pretend to be sth ◊ *Er hatte sich als Arzt ausgegeben.* ♦ *Sie hat sich als seine Frau ausgegeben.*

aus·ge·fal·len ['a̠ʊsɡəfalən] *past p of* ausfallen [adj] extraordinary, unusual ◊ *ein ausgefallenes Design* ♦ *Diese Farbkombination ist ausgefallen.*

aus|ge·hen ['a̠ʊsɡeːən] <geht aus, ging aus, ist ausgegangen> [intr v] **1.** go out ◊ *Wollen wir am Samstag (zum Essen) ausgehen?* **2.** *(hair, teeth, feathers)* fall out ◊ *Mir gehen die Haare aus.* ⊝ausfallen **3.** end, turn out ◊ *Wie ist das Spiel/ der Film ausgegangen?* ♦ *Wenn das nur gut ausgeht!* ⊝enden **4.** dwindle, run out ◊ *Meine Vorräte/Kräfte gehen langsam aus.* jdm geht etw. aus sb runs out of sth ◊ *Mir geht allmählich die Geduld/das Geld aus.* **5.** go out, die (down/out) ◊ *Plötzlich ging das Licht aus.* ♦ *Ich warte, bis das Feuer ausgegangen ist.* **6.** start, go off ◊ *Von diesem Platz gehen alle Straßen sternförmig aus.* ♦ *Die Kreuzfahrt geht von Neapel aus und endet in Athen.* **7.** von etw. ausgehen assume sth ◊ *Ich gehe davon aus, dass ihr alle eure Vokabeln gelernt habt.* **8.** etw. geht von jdm aus sb gives sth off ◊ *Von ihr geht so eine wunderbare Ruhe aus.*

aus·ge·rech·net ['a̠ʊsɡərɛçnət, '– – ' – –] *past p of* ausrechnen [part] of all things ◊ *Ausgerechnet Schauspieler will er werden!* Ausgerechnet jetzt werde ich krank! Couldn't I have gotten sick some other time? ⊝gerade

② **aus·ge·spro·chen** ['a̠ʊsɡəʃprɔxn̩] *past p of* aussprechen [adj, adv] *no comp/superl; when used as an adj, only before ns* extreme(ly), marked(ly) ◊ *Sie ist eine ausgesprochene Schönheit.* ♦ *Das ist eine ausgesprochene Frechheit!* ♦ *Er ist ausgesprochen begabt.*

aus·ge·stor·ben ['a̠ʊsɡəʃtɔːʁbm̩] *past p of* aussterben [adj] *(always* wie ausgestorben wirken/sein*)* *(fig)* be/look deserted ◊ *Am Abend ist die Innenstadt wie ausgestorben.*

aus·ge·wi·chen ['a̠ʊsɡəvɪçn̩] *past p of* ausweichen

aus·ge·zeich·net ['a̠ʊsɡətsaeçnət, – – ' – –] *past p of* auszeichnen [adj, adv] *no comp/superl* excellent(ly), outstanding(ly) ◊ *Sie ist eine ausgezeichnete Schülerin.* ♦ *Das Essen dort ist ausgezeichnet.* ♦ *Unsere Mannschaft hat heute ausgezeichnet gespielt.* ⊝hervorragend, großartig

aus|glei·chen ['a̠ʊsɡlaeçn̩] <gleicht aus, glich aus, hat ausgeglichen> [tr v] **1.** balance out ◊ *Nachteile ausgleichen* **2.** make good ◊ *Der Verlust des Vorjahres ist wieder ausgeglichen.; (a conflict)* resolve **3.** FIN make up ◊ *Schulden ausgleichen* ♦ *ein Defizit ausgleichen* [intr v] SPORT draw ◊ *Mit diesem Tor glich der Spieler aus.* [ref v] sich ausgleichen even out ◊ *Die Unterschiede gleichen sich mit der Zeit aus.*

aus|hal·ten ['a̠ʊshaltn̩] <hält aus, hielt aus, hat ausgehalten> [tr v] **1.** *mostly negated with 'nicht'* bear, stand ◊ *Ich kann diese laute Musik nicht aushalten.* ♦ *Immer müsst ihr streiten. Das ist ja nicht auszuhalten!* es mit jdm aushalten be able to bear sb ◊ *Er hat es mit keinem Arbeitgeber lange ausgehalten.* **2.** jdn aushalten keep sb ◊ *Ich verdiene mein eigenes Geld und lasse mich nicht aushalten!* [intr v] hold out, last ◊ *Halten Sie aus — der Notarzt kommt sofort!*

⊙ **so lässt es sich (gut) aushalten** that's the way I like it ◊ *Ist das gemütlich hier! So lässt es sich aushalten!*

② **Aus·kunft** ['a̠ʊskʊnft] die <-, Auskünfte> **1.** information ◊ *Ich brauche eine Auskunft.* ♦ *Wo können wir diese Auskunft bekommen?* **2.** directory enquiries ◊ *Ruf doch mal die Auskunft an.* **3.** information desk, information office ◊ *An der Auskunft stand eine lange Schlange.* ⊝Information

② **Aus·land** ['a̠ʊslant] das <-(e)s> *no pl* foreign countries ◊ *Telefonvorwahlen für das Ausland* im/ ins Ausland abroad, overseas ◊ *Wir fahren ins Ausland.* ♦ *Wie wird das im Ausland beurteilt?* aus dem Ausland from abroad, from overseas ◊ *Güter, die aus dem Ausland kommen* ⊝Inland

② **Aus·län·der** ['a̠ʊslɛndɐ] der <-s, ->, **Aus·län·de·rin** ['a̠ʊslɛndərɪn] die <-, -nen> foreigner, alien ◊ *Er hat eine Ausländerin geheiratet.* ♦ *Als Ausländer ist man bei der Jobsuche oft im Nachteil.*

② **aus·län·disch** ['a̠ʊslɛndɪʃ] [adj] *mostly before ns* foreign, alien ◊ *unsere ausländischen Arbeitnehmer* ♦ *ausländische Erzeugnisse*

aus|lö·sen ['a̠ʊsløːzn̩] <löst aus, löste aus, hat ausgelöst> [tr v] cause ◊ *Diese Aussage hat die unterschiedlichsten Reaktionen ausgelöst.* ♦ *Wir wissen noch nicht, was den Brand ausgelöst hat.*; trigger (off) ◊ *Der Mord von Sarajewo hat den Ersten Weltkrieg ausgelöst.* ♦ *Mit einem Knopfdruck kann man den Alarm auslösen.*; set off ◊ *Das Feuer hat eine Panik ausgelöst.*; arouse ◊ *Ihr Versprecher hat allgemeine Heiterkeit ausgelöst.*

② **aus|ma·chen** ['a̠ʊsmaxn̩] <macht aus, machte aus, hat ausgemacht> [tr v] **1.** turn off, switch off ◊ *den Herd/Fernseher ausmachen*; put out ◊ *das Feuer/ die Zigarette ausmachen* ⊝anmachen **2.** agree, arrange ◊ *einen Termin beim Arzt ausmachen* ♦ *Ich habe mit ihm ausgemacht, dass wir uns um 14 Uhr treffen.* ⊝vereinbaren **3.** sort out ◊ *Das müsst ihr schon untereinander ausmachen!* **4.** etw. macht jdm etwas aus sb minds sth, sth upsets sb ◊ *Macht es dir etwas aus, wenn ich nicht mitkomme?* ♦ *Macht dir die Unordnung etwas aus?* etw. macht jdm nichts aus sb does not mind sth, sth does not bother sb ◊ *Die Hitze macht mir nichts aus.* ♦ *Und wenn er nicht kommt, dann macht mir das auch nichts aus!* **5.** make, amount to ◊ *Der Abstand macht zwei Meter aus.* ♦ *Was macht die gelungene Party aus?*; account for ◊ *Die Korrektur von Fehlern macht die Hälfte meiner Zeit aus.* **6.** make out, spot ◊ *Ich konnte ihn in der Menschenmenge leider nicht ausmachen.*

② **Aus·nah·me** ['a̠ʊsnaːmə] die <-, -n> exception ◊ *Ausnahmen bestätigen die Regel.* ♦ *Wir machen auch für Sie keine Ausnahme.* ♦ *Mit wenigen Ausnahmen ist alles richtig.*

② **aus|pa·cken** ['a̠ʊspakŋ̍] <packt aus, packte aus, hat ausgepackt> [tr v] unpack ◊ *den Koffer/die Einkäufe auspacken*; unwrap ◊ *ein Paket/die Geschenke auspacken* ⊝einpacken [intr v] *(fam)* talk, blow the whistle ◊ *Sie haben ihn umgebracht, damit er nicht bei der Polizei auspackt.*

② **aus|rech·nen** ['a̠ʊsrɛçnən] <rechnet aus, rechnete aus, hat ausgerechnet> [tr v] **1.** work out, figure out, calculate ◊ *die Summe/Entfernung ausrechnen* ♦ *Rechne mal aus, wie viel das kostet.* **2.** sich

dat etw. ausrechnen count on sth ◊ *Du hattest dir wohl eine Beförderung ausgerechnet. Er rechnet sich Chancen bei ihr aus.* He fancies he might get lucky with her.

Aus·re·de ['aͻsreːdə] die <–, –n> excuse ◊ *Ich will keine Ausreden hören!* ♦ *Das ist doch nur eine faule Ausrede.* ⊖Vorwand

aus|re·den ['aͻsreːdṇ] <redet aus, redete aus, hat ausgeredet> tr v jdm etw. ausreden talk sb out of sth, dissuade sb from sth ◊ *Wie kann ich ihr diesen verrückten Plan nur ausreden?* intr v finish ◊ *Lass mich doch bitte ausreden!*

⑦ **aus|rei·chen** ['aͻsraͻçṇ] <reicht aus, reichte aus, hat ausgereicht> intr v be enough, be sufficient ◊ *Die Stühle reichen nicht für alle Gäste aus.* ♦ *Seine Englischkenntnisse reichen aus, um sich halbwegs zu verständigen.* ⊖genügen, reichen

Aus·rei·se ['aͻsraͻezə] die <–, –n> *translated with a verb construction* jdm die Ausreise (in ein anderes Land) erlauben allow sb to leave the country ◊ *Ihm wurde die Ausreise nach Deutschland erlaubt.* bei der Ausreise on leaving the country

⑦ **aus|ru·hen** ['aͻsruːən] <ruht aus, ruhte aus, hat ausgeruht> ref+intr v (sich) ausruhen have a rest ◊ *Ich habe den ganzen Tag gearbeitet, jetzt will ich ausruhen.* ♦ *Wir haben uns im Urlaub gut ausgeruht.* tr v etw. ausruhen give sth a rest ◊ *Nach der Arbeit am PC muss ich meine Augen ausruhen.* ♦ *Wenn man den ganzen Tag steht, will man abends seine Beine ausruhen.*

Aus·rüs·tung ['aͻsrʏstʊŋ] die <–, –en> equipment, gear ◊ *eine Ausrüstung zum Motorradfahren* ♦ *die richtige Ausrüstung für etw.*

⑦ **aus|schal·ten** ['aͻsʃaltṇ] <schaltet aus, schaltete aus, hat ausgeschaltet> tr v **1.** turn off, switch off ◊ *das Licht/den Strom/den Motor ausschalten* ⊖abschalten, abstellen **2.** eliminate, get rid of ◊ *Wie können wir die Konkurrenz ausschalten?* ♦ *negative Einflüsse ausschalten* ref v sich ausschalten turn itself off, switch itself off ◊ *Das Gerät schaltet sich nach zwei Stunden selbst aus.*

⑦ **aus|schau·en** ['aͻsʃaͻən] <schaut aus, schaute aus, hat ausgeschaut> intr v **1.** nach jdm/etw. ausschauen look (out) for sb/sth ◊ *Wir sollten nach einer Tankstelle ausschauen.* **2.** *(SouthG, Austr)* look ◊ *In seinem Zimmer schaut es unordentlich aus.* ♦ *Du schaust müde aus.* für jdn schaut es schlecht aus things do not look good for sb ◊ *Für den Gegenkandidaten schaut es im Moment schlecht aus.*

⊛ **wie schaut's aus** how are things ◊ *Wie schaut's aus, kommst du mit?* ⊖wie steht's

aus|schla·fen ['aͻsʃlaːfṇ] <schläft aus, schlief aus, hat ausgeschlafen> ref+intr v (sich) ausschlafen have a lie-in, have/get enough sleep ◊ *Ich muss (mich) endlich mal wieder richtig ausschlafen.*

aus·schlag·ge·bend ['aͻsʃlaːkɡebṃt, 'aͻsʃlaːkɡebənt] adj *no comp/superl* crucial, decisive ◊ *von ausschlaggebender Bedeutung sein* ausschlaggebend (für etw.) sein be the crucial/decisive factor (in/for sth) ◊ *Das Tor war ausschlaggebend für den Sieg.*

⑦ **aus|schlie·ßen** ['aͻsʃliːsṇ] <schließt aus, schloss aus, hat ausgeschlossen> tr v **1.** jdn/etw. (aus/

von etw.) ausschließen exclude sb/sth (from sth) ◊ *Sie wurde von ihren Mitschülern ausgeschlossen.* ♦ *Mitarbeiter sind von der Teilnahme ausgeschlossen.* ♦ *Jeder macht mal einen Fehler, ich schließe mich da selbst nicht aus.;* *(from a school, party)* expel ◊ *Er wurde aus der Partei ausgeschlossen.;* *(from a contest)* disqualify **2.** rule out ◊ *Jeder Irrtum ist ausgeschlossen.* ♦ *Wir können diese Möglichkeit nicht ausschließen.* ♦ *Die Ärzte schließen eine Infektionsgefahr aus.* **3.** lock out ◊ *Ich habe mich aus Versehen selbst ausgeschlossen.*

aus·schließ·lich¹ ['aͻsʃliːslɪç, – '– –] adj, adv *no comp/superl; when used as an adj, only before ns* exclusive(ly), sole(ly) ◊ *Unterrichten ist zurzeit meine ausschließliche Beschäftigung.* ♦ *Diese Regelung trifft fast ausschließlich Beamte.*

aus·schließ·lich² ['aͻsʃliːslɪç, – '– –] prep *sing nouns without article or attribute are not declined when following this prep, otherwise* +gen *or fam* +dat exclusive of ◊ *excluding* ♦ *Unsere Preise verstehen sich ausschließlich Mehrwertsteuer.* ♦ *Die Arbeitszeit beträgt ausschließlich der Pausen 38 Stunden wöchentlich.* ⊖exklusive ⊖einschließlich

Aus·schnitt ['aͻsʃnɪt] der <–(e)s, –e> **1.** *most sing (of a piece of clothing)* neck, neckline jdm in den Ausschnitt gucken look down sb's top/dress etc. **2.** *(fig)* sample, example ◊ *Sie bot einen Ausschnitt ihres Könnens.;* *(from a film)* clip; *(from a text)* excerpt, extract

Aus·schuss ['aͻsʃʊs] der <–es, Ausschüsse> committee ◊ *in einem Ausschuss sitzen* ⊖Kommission

⑦ **aus|se·hen** ['aͻszeːən] <sieht aus, sah aus, hat ausgesehen> intr v **1.** look ◊ *Er sieht gut/krank aus.* ♦ *Wie sieht dein neues Auto aus?* ♦ *Die Lage am Arbeitsmarkt sieht nicht rosig aus.* aussehen wie look like, resemble ◊ *Er sieht genauso aus wie sein Vater.* ♦ *Das Auto sieht wie ein Panzer aus.* **2.** etw. sieht nach etw. aus sth looks like sth ◊ *Es sieht nach Regen aus.* ♦ *Die Sache sieht mir doch ganz nach Betrug aus.* imp v mit etw./für jdn sieht es gut/schlecht aus things look good/bad for sth/sb ◊ *Bei Krebs sieht es mit einer Heilung oft schlecht aus.* ♦ *Für unsere Mannschaft sieht es nicht gut aus.*

⊛ **so siehst du aus** *(fam)* that's what you think, I don't think so ◊ *Vor den Hausaufgaben fernsehen? So siehst du aus!*

⑦ **au·ßen** ['aͻsṇ] adv **1.** on the outside ◊ *Die Kiste ist außen rot und innen grün.;* outside ◊ *Kein Geräusch drang nach außen.* ♦ *Von außen sah das Haus ziemlich heruntergekommen aus.* ⊖innen **2.** *(fig)* outside, in public, publicly ◊ *Nach außen vertritt der Geschäftsführer eine ganz andere Politik.* nach außen dringen come out, become public

⊛ **nach außen hin** *(fig)* outwardly, on the outside ◊ *Nach außen hin wirkte sie immer fröhlich.*

Au·ßen·mi·nis·ter ['aͻsṇminɪste] der <–s, –>, **Au·ßen·mi·nis·te·rin** ['aͻsṇminɪstərɪn] die <–, –nen> Foreign Minister ◊ *Er ist in der Regierung als Außenminister tätig.* ♦ *die schwedische Außenministerin; (in the UK)* Foreign Secretary; *(in the US)* Secretary of State

Au·ßen·po·li·tik ['aͻsṇpoliˌtiːk] die <–, –en> *most*

sing foreign policy

Au·ßen·sei·ter ['aosn̩ˌzaete] der <-s, ->,
Au·ßen·sei·te·rin ['aosn̩zaetərɪn] die <-, –nen>
outsider ◊ *Sie gilt in der Schule als Außenseiterin.*
♦ *Im Derby gewann ein Außenseiter.*

② **au·ßer¹** ['aose] [prep] [+dat] **1.** apart from, except
(for) ◊ *Außer meiner Mutter waren alle Verwandten gekommen.* ♦ *Felix hat in allen Fächern außer
in Französisch gute Noten.* **2.** besides ◊ *Außer Ben
und Anna waren auch noch Andreas und Jule da.*
⊝neben **3.** out of, beyond ◊ *Der Patient ist außer
Lebensgefahr.* ♦ *Die Inflation ist außer Kontrolle
geraten.* ♦ *Herr Bönzli ist zurzeit außer Haus.* ♦
außer Sichtweite sein

⊛ **außer sich** [dat] **sein (vor etw.** [dat]) be beside
yourself (with sth) ◊ *Ich bin außer mir vor Wut/
Sorge/Glück.* ♦ *Ich war völlig außer mir, weil er
nicht heimkam.*

au·ßer² ['aose] [conjunc] **1.** unless, except ◊ *Wir
gehen jeden Tag spazieren, außer (wenn) es
regnet.* **2.** only ◊ *Ich benütze das Auto eigentlich
nicht, außer um einzukaufen.* ♦ *Der Roman ist
schon spannend, außer dass er zu lang ist.* ⊝nur

② **au·ßer·dem** ['aosedeːm, – – '–] [adv] **1.** besides, in
addition, as well ◊ *Sie spielt Geige und außerdem
Klavier und Flöte.* ♦ *Mit welchen Programmen sind
Sie außerdem noch vertraut?* ⊝weiterhin **2.** (and)
anyway ◊ *Es ist zu spät fürs Kino, und außerdem
bin ich müde.*

äu·ße·re ['aosərə] [adj] *only before ns* <ein äußerer
..., eine äußere ..., ein äußeres ...> **1.** outside,
exterior ◊ *äußere Umstände* ♦ *die äußeren
Planeten des Sonnensystems* ⊝innere **2.** (appearance, form) outer, outward ◊ *die äußere Erscheinung eines Menschen* ♦ *die äußere Form*
3. (security, injuries) external ◊ *die innere und
äußere Sicherheit des Staats* ♦ *eine äußere Verletzung* ⊝innere

au·ßer·ge·wöhn·lich ['aosegəvøːnlɪç] [adj, adv]
extraordinary(-arily), exceptional(ly), unusual(ly) ◊
eine außergewöhnliche Leistung ♦ *Seine Frau ist
außergewöhnlich.* ♦ *ein außergewöhnlich heißer
Sommer*

② **au·ßer·halb¹** ['aosehalp] [adv] out of town ◊ *Ich
wohne nicht direkt in München, sondern außerhalb.*
♦ *Sie kommt jeden Tag von weit außerhalb nach
Stuttgart zur Arbeit.*

② **au·ßer·halb²** ['aosehalp] [prep] [+gen] **1.** [+gen]
outside, beyond ◊ *Der Bauernhof liegt außerhalb
des Dorfes.* ♦ *Die Entscheidung liegt außerhalb
meiner Befugnisse.* ⊝innerhalb **2.** [+gen]
(temporal) outside, (out) of ◊ *außerhalb der
Geschäftszeiten/Saison* ⊝während **3.** adverbial
[+dat] außerhalb von outside ◊ *außerhalb von
Berlin/Deutschland* ⊝innerhalb von

äu·ßer·lich ['ɔøselɪç] [adj, adv] *when used as an
adj, mostly before ns* **1.** superficial(ly) ◊ *eine rein
äußerliche Ähnlichkeit* ♦ *Die Wunden/Schäden
waren nur äußerlich.*; outward(ly) ♦ *äußerliche
Ruhe* ♦ *äußerlich gelassen* ♦ *Das Haus macht
äußerlich einen stabilen Eindruck.*; on the outside/
surface ◊ *rein äußerlich betrachtet* ♦ *Das ist
äußerlich schwer zu erkennen.* **2.** external(ly) ◊
nur zur äußerlichen Anwendung ♦ *Kamillenöl
äußerlich anwenden*

äu·ßern ['ɔøsen] [tr v] +haben voice, express ◊

Kritik/Zweifel äußern ♦ *eine Bitte/seine Meinung
äußern* [ref v] +haben **1.** sich (zu etw.) äußern
comment (on sth) ◊ *Die Polizei äußerte sich nicht
zu möglichen Motiven der Tat.* ♦ *Hat er sich schon
zu dieser Frage geäußert?* sich (über jdn/etw.)
äußern express an opinion (on sb/sth) ◊ *Sie
äußert sich kritisch über ihren Mann.* ♦ *Über dieses
Thema möchte ich mich nicht äußern.* **2.** etw.
äußert sich in etw. [dat] sth manifests itself in sth ◊
*Die Unzufriedenheit der Bevölkerung äußerte sich
in Demonstrationen.*

au·ßer·or·dent·lich
['aoseˈɔˈdn̩tlɪç, 'aoseˈɔˈdn̩tlɪç] [adj] extraordinary,
exceptional ◊ *eine außerordentliche Kündigung* ♦
Ihre Leistung war außerordentlich. [adv] extremely
◊ *außerordentlich wichtig* ♦ *Das tut mir außerordentlich Leid.* ⊝ungeheuer, sehr

äu·ßerst ['ɔøsest] [adv] extremely ◊ *eine äußerst
umstrittene Frage* ⊝höchst

au·ßer·stan·de, au·ßer Stan·de ['aoseˈʃtandə]
[adj] no comp/superl, not before ns **1.** incapable ◊
*Sie ist außerstande, sich bei ihren Kindern durchzu-
setzen.* **2.** unable ◊ *Ich sehe mich außerstande,
Ihnen zu helfen.*

äu·ßers·te ['ɔøsestə] superl of äußere [adj] only
before ns **1.** extreme ◊ *Äußerste Vorsicht ist
geboten!* ♦ *im äußersten Notfall* **2.** final ◊ *Das ist
mein äußerstes Angebot.* ♦ *das äußerste Limit*

Äu·ße·rung ['ɔøsərʊŋ] die <-, –en> **1.** remark,
comment ◊ *eine unbedachte/verletzende Äußerung*
♦ *Die Zeitung zitierte eine Äußerung des Ministers.*
2. no pl expression ◊ *Er vermeidet die Äußerung
von Gefühlen.*

aus|set·zen ['aosɛtsn̩] <setzt aus, setzte aus, hat
ausgesetzt> [tr v] **1.** abandon ◊ *Zur Urlaubszeit
werden viele Tiere ausgesetzt.*; (a wild animal)
release **2.** (a reward, prize) etw. für etw.
aussetzen offer sth for sth ◊ *Für die Ergreifung des
Täters ist eine Belohnung ausgesetzt worden.*
3. etwas an etw./jdm auszusetzen haben find fault
with sth/sb ◊ *Immer hast du etwas an mir auszusetzen!* nichts an etw./jdm auszusetzen haben
can't find no fault with sth/sb ♦ jdn/sich/etw.
einer Sache [dat] aussetzen expose sb/yourself/sth
to sth ◊ *sich einem Risiko aussetzen* ♦ *Sein Körper
war einer hohen Strahlendosis ausgesetzt.* sich der
Konkurrenz aussetzen open yourself to competition
[intr v] **1.** stop, fail ◊ *Sein Herzschlag setzte
plötzlich aus.* **2.** take a break ◊ *Er musste mit
dem Training aussetzen.*; sit out, miss a turn ◊ *eine
Runde aussetzen müssen*

② **Aus·sicht** ['aoszɪçt] die <-, –en> **1.** view, outlook
◊ *ein Zimmer mit Aussicht aufs Meer* ◊ *Vom Schlafzimmer haben wir eine wunderbare Aussicht auf
die Berge.* ⊝Ausblick, Blick **2.** prospect, chance ◊
Er hat keine Aussichten bei ihr. ♦ *Wie sind meine
Aussichten, die Stelle zu bekommen?* ♦ *Wie stehen
die Aussichten auf einen Studienplatz?*

⊛ **etw. in Aussicht haben** have prospects/a
chance of sth ◊ *eine Beförderung in Aussicht
haben* **in Aussicht sein** be in prospect ◊ *Noch ist
keine Besserung am Arbeitsmarkt in Aussicht.* **jdm
etw. in Aussicht stellen** indicate to sb the
prospect/possibility of sth ◊ *Mein Chef hat mir eine
Beförderung in Aussicht gestellt.*

Aus·sied·ler ['aoziːdle] der <-s, ->,

Aus·sied·le·rin ['aoszi:dlərɪn] die <-, -nen> resettler ◊ *eine Aussiedlerin aus der Ukraine*

Aus·spra·che ['aosʃpraːxe] die <-, -n> **1.** *no pl* LING pronunciation ◊ *eine undeutliche Aussprache haben*; accent ◊ *Deine Aussprache (im Französischen) ist sehr gut.* **2.** discussion ◊ *eine Aussprache herbeiführen*

② **aus·spre·chen** ['aosʃprɛçn] <spricht aus, sprach aus, hat ausgesprochen> [tr v] **1.** pronounce ◊ *Ich weiß nicht, wie man das Wort ausspricht.* ✦ *ein stimmlos ausgesprochenes „s" nicht ausgesprochen werden* be silent/mute, remain unspoken ◊ *Dieses „e" wird nicht ausgesprochen.* **2.** express, utter ◊ *Kann ich meine Meinung hier offen aussprechen?* ✦ *Er hat (mir) sein Bedauern ausgesprochen.* ✦ *Kritik an etw.* [dat] *aussprechen* [ref v] **1.** sich aussprechen talk things out ◊ *Es wird Zeit, dass wir uns mal aussprechen.* sich bei jdm aussprechen confide in sb sich über etw. [acc] aussprechen get sth off your chest **2.** sich für jdn/etw. aussprechen favour sth/sb, declare yourself in favour/favor of sb/sth ◊ *Er hat sich für eine Änderung dieser Regelung ausgesprochen.* sich gegen jdn/etw. aussprechen side against sb/sth, declare yourself against sb/sth ◊ *Die Wähler haben sich gegen den Kandidaten ausgesprochen.*

Aus·stat·tung ['aosʃtatʊŋ] die <-, -en> *most sing* **1.** equipment ◊ *Zur Ausstattung des Autos gehören zwei Airbags.* eine behindertengerechte Ausstattung des Arbeitsplatzes equipment of the workplace for disabled staff **2.** decor, furnishings ◊ *die Ausstattung der Innenräume*

aus·ste·hen ['aosʃteːən] <steht aus, stand aus, hat ausgestanden> [intr v] be yet to come, be yet to be made ◊ *Die Antwort auf meine Frage steht noch aus.* [tr v] suffer, endure ◊ *Ich habe entsetzliche Qualen ausgestanden.* ✦ *Was man mit seinen Kindern alles ausstehen muss!*

⊛ jd kann jdn/etw. nicht ausstehen sb cannot stand sb/sth ◊ *Ich kann diese Musik nicht ausstehen.*

② **aus·stei·gen** ['aosʃtaegŋ] <steigt aus, stieg aus, ist ausgestiegen> [intr v] **1.** *(from a vehicle, lift)* get off/out ◊ *Er ist im dritten Stock aus dem Lift ausgestiegen.* ✦ *An der nächsten Haltestelle muss ich aussteigen.* ⊖einsteigen **2.** quit, opt out, drop out ◊ *Das wird mir zu gefährlich, ich steige aus.* ✦ *Einer der Partner will aus dem Geschäft aussteigen.* ⊖einsteigen

② **aus·stel·len** ['aosʃtɛlən] <stellt aus, stellte aus, hat ausgestellt> [tr v] **1.** exhibit, (put on) display ◊ *etw. auf einer Messe/im Schaufenster ausstellen* **2.** *(a passport, certificate, licence etc.)* issue ◊ *jdm einen Pass/Führerschein ausstellen; (an invoice, a cheque also)* write, make out ◊ *Er hat mir eine Rechnung über 500 Euro ausgestellt.* **3.** turn off ◊ *das Radio ausstellen* ⊖ausschalten, ausmachen

② **Aus·stel·lung** ['aosʃtɛlʊŋ] die <-, -en> **1.** exhibition, show, fair ◊ *eine Ausstellung moderner Kunst im Museum* ✦ *die Ausstellung über Handwerkerbedarf in der Messehalle* ✦ *eine Ausstellung von Rassekatzen* **2.** *no pl* issue, issuing ◊ *die Ausstellung eines Reisepasses beantragen* ✦ *Der Arzt verweigerte die Ausstellung eines Attestes.*

aus·ster·ben ['aosʃtɛʳbm̩] <stirbt aus, starb aus,

ist ausgestorben> [intr v] **1.** *(animal, species)* become extinct ◊ *Die Dinosaurier sind vor 65 Millionen Jahren ausgestorben.* **2.** *(fig)* die out ◊ *Ein Brauch/Dialekt muss gepflegt werden, sonst stirbt er aus.*

⊛ vom Aussterben bedroht sein be threatened with extinction ◊ *Der Tiger ist vom Aussterben bedroht.*

aus·strah·len ['aosʃtraːlən] <strahlt aus, strahlte aus, hat ausgestrahlt> [tr v] **1.** broadcast, transmit ◊ *Wann wird das Fußballspiel ausgestrahlt?* ✦ *einen Notruf ausstrahlen* **2.** emit, radiate ◊ *Radioaktivität/Wärme ausstrahlen* **3.** convey (a feeling of) ◊ *Hoffnung/Optimismus/Ruhe ausstrahlen* [intr v] *(pain)* spread, extend ◊ *Die Schmerzen strahlen vom Hals auf die Arme aus.*

② **aus·su·chen** ['aoszuːxn] <sucht aus, suchte aus, hat ausgesucht> [tr v] choose, pick, select ◊ *Unter allen Kandidaten haben sie mich ausgesucht.* ✦ *einen Mitarbeiter für eine Arbeit aussuchen* ✦ *Du kannst dir dein Geschenk selbst aussuchen.* ✦ *Er kann es sich aussuchen, was er tun will.* ⊖auswählen

⊛ man kann es sich nicht aussuchen you have no choice, you have to put up with it ◊ *Ich wünschte, ich wäre reich, aber man kann es sich eben nicht aussuchen.*

aus·tau·schen ['aostaoʃn] <tauscht aus, tauschte aus, hat ausgetauscht> [tr v] **1.** exchange ◊ *Gefangene/Informationen austauschen* ✦ *Sie tauschten heimlich Blicke miteinander aus.* ✦ *Die Geisel wurde gegen den Polizisten ausgetauscht.* **2.** replace ◊ *abgefahrene Reifen gegen neue austauschen* ✦ *Matratzen sollen alle 5 Jahre ausgetauscht werden.; (a battery, lightbulb)* change ◊ *eine Batterie/Glühbirne austauschen* [ref v] sich mit jdm austauschen exchange views wth sb ◊ *sich mit anderen Betroffenen/Eltern austauschen*

aus·tei·len ['aostaelən] <teilt aus, teilte aus, hat ausgeteilt> [tr v] **1.** distribute, hand out ◊ *Der Lehrer teilt die Klassenarbeit an die Schüler aus.; (playing cards)* deal **2.** *(fig) (blows, a punishment)* deal out; *(compliments)* give out [intr v] *(fig)* criticize others, judge others ◊ *Wer austeilt, muss auch einstecken können!*

aus·tra·gen ['aostraːgŋ] <trägt aus, trug aus, hat ausgetragen> [tr v] **1.** *(letters)* deliver ◊ *Briefe austragen* **2.** *(a conflict, controversy)* deal with ◊ *Der Streit wurde in aller Öffentlichkeit ausgetragen.* **3.** *(a child)* carry full term; *(a pregnancy)* carry out ◊ *ein Kind für jdn austragen* **4.** *(a match, competition)* hold ◊ *Wo werden die kommenden Olympischen Spiele ausgetragen?* ✦ *ein Match austragen*

Aus·tra·lien [aos'traːljən] das <-s> *article only in combination with attribute* Australia box@ Land

Aus·tra·li·er [aos'traːlje] der <-s, ->,

Aus·tra·li·e·rin [aos'traːljərɪn] die <-, -nen> Australian → Deutsche

aus·tra·lisch [aos'traːlɪʃ] [adj] *mostly before ns* Australian ◊ *Englisch mit australischem Akzent* ✦ *Was ist typisch australisch?*

Aus·tritt ['aostrɪt] der <-(e)s, -e> **1.** withdrawal ◊ *der Austritt aus der Kirche*; resignation ◊ *der Austritt aus der Partei* **2.** *most sing (of gas, oil etc.)* escape

aus·ü·ben ['aos|yːbm̩] <übt aus, übte aus, hat ausgeübt> (tr v) **1.** do, practise, practice ◊ *Welchen Beruf üben Sie aus?*; *(a sport)* play ◊ *Er übt eine gefährliche Sportart aus.* ⊖einer Sache nachgehen **2.** *(a right, power)* exercise ◊ *Ich habe bei der letzten Wahl mein Wahlrecht nicht ausgeübt.* **3.** etw. (auf jdn) ausüben exert sth (on sb) ◊ *Sie übt eine starke Wirkung auf Männer aus.* ◆ *Druck ausüben*

aus·ver·kauft ['aosfɛkaoft] (adj) *no comp/superl* sold out ◊ *Alle Wörterbücher sind ausverkauft.* ◆ *das ausverkaufte Stadion*

Aus·wahl ['aosvaːl] die <–> *no pl* **1.** choice ◊ *Sie haben die Auswahl unter zehn verschiedenen Modellen.* ◆ *Alle Artikel stehen zur freien Auswahl.*; *(of goods)* range, selection ◊ *Die Auswahl an günstigen Computern ist groß.* ◆ *nur in begrenzter Auswahl erhältlich* **2.** selection, samples ◊ *Die Ausstellung zeigt eine Auswahl der Künstler des 19. Jahrhunderts.*

⊚ **die engere Auswahl** the shortlist ◊ *in die engere Auswahl kommen*

aus|wäh·len ['aosvɛːlən] <wählt aus, wählte aus, hat ausgewählt> (tr+intr v) choose, select ◊ *Die Jury hat aus allen Beiträgen mein Bild ausgewählt.* ◆ *Welcher der Bewerber wurde ausgewählt?* ◆ *Die Zutaten wurden mit Sorgfalt ausgewählt.*; *(in a restaurant)* decide what you take (to drink/eat) ◊ *Da kommt der Kellner, hast du schon ausgewählt?* ⊖aussuchen

Aus·wan·de·rer ['aosvandərə] der <–s, –>, **Aus·wan·de·rin** ['aosvandərɪn] die <–, –nen> emigrant, émigré ◊ *deutsche Auswanderer in den USA*

aus|wan·dern ['aosvanden] <wandert aus, wanderte aus, ist ausgewandert> (intr v) emigrate ◊ *nach Australien/in die USA auswandern* ◆ *aus Indien auswandern* ⊖einwandern

aus·wärts ['aosvɛʁts] (adv) away ◊ *Besuch von auswärts* ◆ *Bayern München spielt heute auswärts.* auswärts essen gehen go out for a meal, go out to eat

aus|wech·seln ['aosvɛksl̩n] <wechselt aus, wechselte aus, hat ausgewechselt> (tr v) etw./jdn (gegen etw./jdn) auswechseln exchange sth/sb (for sth/sb), replace sth/sb (by sth/sb) ◊ *einen Reifen/ Spieler auswechseln*

Aus·weg ['aosveːk] der <–(e)s, –e> way out ◊ *einen Ausweg aus einer unangenehmen Lage finden* ◆ *Gibt es denn keinen anderen Ausweg, als die Firma zu verkaufen?* der letzte Ausweg the last resort

aus|wei·chen ['aosvaeçn̩] <weicht aus, wich aus, ist ausgewichen> (intr v) **1.** dodge ◊ *Er ist dem Schlag geschickt ausgewichen.*; swerve ◊ *nach links/rechts ausweichen* **2.** *(fig)* avoid ◊ *jdm im Gespräch ausweichen* ◆ *einer Gefahr/Frage ausweichen* **3.** auf etw. (acc) ausweichen switch to sth ◊ *auf ein anderes Verkehrsmittel ausweichen*

⑦ **Aus·weis** ['aosvaes] der <–es, –e> identity card ◊ *Der Polizist wollte meinen Ausweis sehen.*; student card; membership card ◊ *Wer sich ein Buch ausleihen möchte, braucht einen Ausweis.*

aus·wei·sen ['aosvaezn̩] <weist aus, wies aus, hat ausgewiesen> (tr v) **1.** *(from a country)* expel ◊ *Nachdem ihr Asylantrag abgelehnt worden war,*

wurde sie ausgewiesen. ⊖abschieben **2.** TRADE *(in accounts)* declare, report ◊ *Die Bilanz weist einen Verlust aus.* ◆ *Dieses Jahr können wir Gewinne ausweisen.* (ref v) sich ausweisen prove your identity, show your identity card/passport ◊ *„Können Sie sich ausweisen?", fragte der Polizist.*

Aus·wei·sung ['aosvaezʊŋ] die <–, –en> expulsion ◊ *Bei schweren Delikten muss mit der Ausweisung gerechnet werden.*

aus|wei·ten ['aosvaetn̩] <weitet aus, weitete aus, hat ausgeweitet> (tr v) **1.** extend, expand ◊ *Die Polizei weitet die Suche jetzt auf das ganze Land aus.* ◆ *seine Kontakte ausweiten*; *(figures, a share of sth)* increase ◊ *den Marktanteil ausweiten* **2.** stretch, widen ◊ *eine Hose ausweiten* (ref v) **1.** sich ausweiten spread ◊ *Der Konflikt weitet sich aus.* ◆ *Die Waldbrände weiten sich immer weiter aus.* **2.** sich ausweiten stretch, widen ◊ *Die Jeans hat sich so ausgeweitet, dass ich einen Gürtel tragen muss.*

aus·wen·dig ['aosvɛndɪç] (adv) by heart ◊ *ein Gedicht auswendig können/lernen* ◆ *Ich weiß deine Telefonnummer nicht auswendig.*

⊚ **etw. in- und auswendig kennen** know sth inside out ◊ *Sie kennt die Bibel/seine Entschuldigungen in- und auswendig.*

aus|wir·ken ['aosvɪʁkn̩] <wirkt sich aus, wirkte sich aus, hat sich ausgewirkt> (ref v) sich (auf etw. (acc) auswirken have an effect (on sth), have an influence (on sth) ◊ *Das Wetter wirkt sich positiv auf meine Stimmung aus.*

aus|zah·len ['aostsaːlən] <zahlt aus, zahlte aus, hat ausgezahlt> (tr v) **1.** (jdm) etw. auszahlen pay sth out (to sb) ◊ *Wann werden die Löhne ausgezahlt?* ◆ *Wie viel bekommst du netto ausgezahlt?* **2.** jdn auszahlen pay sb (off) ◊ *Der Verein ist pleite. Er kann seine Spieler nicht auszahlen.* (ref v) sich (für jdn) auszahlen be worth it (for sb) ◊ *Der Einsatz zahlt sich für mich nicht aus.*

aus|zeich·nen ['aostsaeçnən] <zeichnet aus, zeichnete aus, hat ausgezeichnet> (tr v) **1.** jdn/etw. (mit etw.) auszeichnen award sb/sth sth ◊ *jdn/ einen Film mit einem Preis auszeichnen* **2.** mark out ◊ *Das Symbol soll Ware von Biobauern auszeichnen.* **3.** etw. zeichnet jdn/etw. aus sb/sth is characterized by sth ◊ *Bodos Zuverlässigkeit zeichnet ihn aus.* **4.** price ◊ *Der Verkäufer zeichnet die Waren aus.* (ref v) sich durch etw. auszeichnen be distinguished by sth ◊ *Sie zeichnet sich durch Geduld aus.*

⑦ **aus|zie·hen** ['aostsiːən] <zieht aus, zog aus, hat/ ist ausgezogen> (tr v) +*haben* **1.** (sich (dat)) etw. ausziehen take your sth off, remove your sth ◊ *Zieh (dir) bitte die Schuhe aus!* jdm etw. ausziehen take sb's sth off, remove sb's sth ◊ *dem Kind die Hosen ausziehen* ⊖anziehen **2.** jdn ausziehen undress sb ◊ *Erst umarmte er sie, dann zog er sie aus.* sich ausziehen undress, get undressed ◊ *Er zog sich aus und legte sich schlafen.* ◆ *sich nackt ausziehen* ⊖anziehen **3.** extend, pull out ◊ *einen Tisch/die Antenne ausziehen* (intr v) +*sein* **1.** *(from a residence)* move out ◊ *Unsere Nachbarn sind ausgezogen.* ⊖einziehen **2.** aus etw. ausziehen leave sth ◊ *Die Sportler zogen aus dem Stadion aus.*

⑦ **Aus·zu·bil·den·de** ['aostsubɪldn̩də] der/die

<-n, die Auszubildenden> *but: ein Auszubildender/ eine Auszubildende (abbr* Azubi*)* trainee, apprentice ◇ *Er ist Auszubildender bei einer Bank.* ◆ *Die Auszubildende ist heute in der Berufsschule. box@* Substantivierung

② **Au·to** ['aoto:] *das <–s, –s>* car, automobile ◇ *Kann ich dich ein Stück im Auto mitnehmen?* ◆ *Sie holt die Kinder mit dem Auto von der Schule ab.* ◆ *Ich kann nicht Auto fahren.*

② **Au·to·bahn** ['aotoba:n] *die <–, –en>* motorway, freeway ◇ *Wir haben die Autobahn genommen.* ◆ *Auf der Autobahn München-Stuttgart gibt es oft Stau.*

> All large and medium-sized towns and cities in Germany are connected with each other by a network of motorways. On many routes there is no speed limit. On road maps, motorways are indicated by the letter **A** followed by a number (A1, A7 etc.). More information at *www.autobahn-online.de*

Au·to·fah·rer ['aotofa:re] *der <–s, –>*, **Au·to·fah·re·rin** ['aotofa:rərɪn] *die <–, –nen>* (car) driver, motorist

Au·to·gramm [aoto'gram] *das <–s, –e>* autograph ◇ *jdm ein Autogramm geben*

② **Au·to·mat** [aoto'ma:t] *der <–en, –en>* vending machine ◇ *sich am Automaten Zigaretten kaufen*; *(for money)* cash machine ◇ *Geld am Automaten abheben*

② **au·to·ma·tisch** [aoto'ma:tɪʃ] [adj, adv] *no comp/ superl; when used as an adj, mostly before ns* automatic(ally) ◇ *automatische Türen* ◆ *ein Vertrag, der sich automatisch verlängert*

au·to·nom [aoto'no:m] [adj] **1.** POL autonomous ◇ *ein autonomer Staat* ◆ *Diese Region ist autonom.* **2.** *only before ns* militant ◇ *Autonome Gruppen demonstrierten gegen das Atomkraftwerk.*

② **Au·tor** ['aoto:ɐ] *der <–s, –en>*, **Au·to·rin** [ao'to:rɪn] *die <–, –nen>* author ◇ *Sie arbeitet als Autorin für einen Schulbuchverlag.* ◆ *ein berühmter Autor*

Axt [akst] *die <–, Äxte>* axe

⊛ **wie die Axt im Walde** *(fam)* like a boor, like boors

A·zu·bi [a'tsu:bi] *der <–s, –s>*, **A·zu·bi** [a'tsu:bi:] *die <–, –s> (abbr of* Auszubildende*)* trainee ◇ *Tobias ist Azubi bei einer Bank.* ◆ *Unser Friseur sucht noch eine Azubi.* ⊖Lehrling

> An *Azubi* is a young person who is undergoing vocational training in a company.

B

b, B [be:] das <–(s), –(s)> **1.** b, B ◊ *Dieses Wort wird mit einem kleinen b/großen B geschrieben.* ♦ *B wie Berta* **2.** MUS flat b-Moll/B-Dur B flat minor/major

B [be:] die *(road classification)* ⊜A ◊ *Stau auf der B 417* → **Bundesstraße**

② **Ba·by** ['be:bi:] das <–s, –s> baby ◊ *ein Baby erwarten/bekommen*

Bach [bax] der <–(e)s, Bäche> stream ◊ *Der Bach fließt durch das Tal.* ♦ *Bäche von Schweiß liefen ihm den Rücken hinunter.*

⊛ **den Bach runtergehen** *(fam)* **1.** *(plans)* come to nothing ◊ *Ohne Hilfe geht unser Projekt den Bach runter.* **2.** *(morally, financially)* go downhill ◊ *Unsere Gesellschaft geht den Bach runter.*

Ba·cke ['bakə] die <–, –n> cheek ◊ *rote Backen* ♦ *eine dicke/geschwollene Backe*

⊛ **au Backe** oh dear

② **ba·cken** ['bakŋ] <backt/bäckt, backte/buk, hat gebacken> [tr+intr v] bake ◊ *Brot backen* ♦ *Ich backe jeden Samstag.* [intr v] be in the oven ◊ *Der Kuchen muss noch zehn Minuten backen.*

Bä·cker ['bɛkɐ] der <–s, –>, **Bä·cke·rin** ['bɛkərɪn] die <–, –nen> **1.** baker ◊ *Er wurde Bäcker wie sein Vater.* ♦ *Die Bäckerin holte das Brot aus dem Ofen.* **2.** *no fem* baker's ◊ *beim Bäcker frische Brötchen holen* ⊜**Bäckerei**

② **Bä·cke·rei** [bɛkə'raɛ] die <–, –en> baker's ◊ *Ich kaufe mein Brot in der Bäckerei.*

② **bäckt** [bɛkt] *pres of* backen

② **Bad** [ba:t] das <–(e)s, Bäder> **1.** bathroom ◊ *Ist das Bad frei?* **2.** *(bathing in a bathtub, water for bathing)* bath ◊ *ein heißes Bad nehmen* ♦ *Ich lasse mir ein Bad ein.* **3.** *no pl* swim ◊ *Nach einem Bad im Meer fühlte er sich frischer.* **4.** *(swimming)* pool, *(swimming)* bath(s) ◊ *Im Sommer gehen wir oft ins Bad.* ♦ *öffentliche Bäder in Berlin* **5.** spa ◊ *Der Arzt will mich in ein Bad zur Kur schicken.*

⊛ **ein Bad in der Menge nehmen** *(king, politician)* go on a walkabout *(star)* mingle with the fans

Ba·de·an·zug ['ba:dəʔantsu:k] der <–(e)s, Badeanzüge> swimming costume, swimsuit

Ba·de·ho·se ['ba:dəho:zə] die <–, –n> swimming trunks

Ba·de·meis·ter ['ba:dəmaɛstɐ] der <–s, –>, **Ba·de·meis·te·rin** ['ba:dəmaɛstərɪn] die <–, –nen> swimming pool attendant, lifeguard ◊ *die Bademeisterin des Freibads* ♦ *Er arbeitet als Bademeister im Hallenbad.*

② **ba·den** ['ba:dŋ] <badet, badete, hat gebadet> [intr v] **1.** have/take a bath ◊ *Sie badet jeden Abend.* **2.** swim ◊ *im Meer baden* [tr v] bath, bathe ◊ *Das Baby wird abends gebadet.* ♦ *einen entzündeten Fingernagel in Kamillenlösung baden*

⊛ **mit etw. baden gehen** *(fam)* come a cropper with sth ◊ *Mit seinem Konzept ist er baden gegangen.*

Ba·den-Würt·tem·berg [,ba:dn̩'vʏ'təmbɐ'k] das <–s> *article only in combination with attribute, no pl* Baden-Württemberg

Area: 35,752 km²; population: approx. 10.52 million; regional capital: Stuttgart. Baden-Württemberg's landscape is characterized by the Black Forest and viniculture. The state is the home of such successful companies as Daimler, Porsche and Bosch. The University of Heidelberg, Germany's oldest university, was founded in 1386.

② **Ba·de·wan·ne** ['ba:dəvanə] die <–, –n> bath(tub) ◊ *Wasser in die Badewanne einlaufen lassen*

BA·föG, Ba·fög ['ba:fœk] das *(abbr of* Bundesausbildungsförderungsgesetz*)* student grant

This law regulates the financial support of students from low income families. When students say *Ich bekomme Bafög* (I receive *Bafög*), they are referring to the amount of money they receive as financial support from the state. Part of the *Bafög* has to be repaid in instalments when they start working.

Bag·ger ['bagɐ] der <–s, –> digger, excavator ◊ *mit einem Bagger eine Grube graben*

Ba·guette [ba'gɛt] das <–s, –s> die <–, –n> baguette

② **Bahn** [ba:n] die <–, –en> **1.** *most sing* railway(s), railroad ◊ *Mein Vater arbeitet bei der Bahn.* **2.** train ◊ *mit der Bahn fahren* **3.** tram, streetcar ◊ *Welche Bahn fährt zum Rathaus?* **4.** *(building)* (train) station ◊ *Ich habe Heide zur Bahn gebracht.* **5.** lane ◊ *Der Fahrer kam auf die entgegengesetzte Bahn.* ♦ *Der deutsche Läufer läuft auf Bahn drei.*; *(in a swimming pool)* length ◊ *Ich bin heute 20 Bahnen geschwommen.* **6.** *(for races)* track, course ◊ *Die Pferde werden schon am Vortag zur Bahn gebracht.* ♦ *eine Bahn für Skater;* *(for ice skating)* rink **7.** flight path ◊ *die Bahn einer Rakete berechnen;* *(of a planet)* orbit ◊ *die Bahn des Mondes um die Erde* **8.** *(of fabric, paper)* strip, length ◊ *zwei Bahnen Seide* **9.** *(through snow, a jungle)* path, track ◊ *sich eine Bahn durch den Schnee schaufeln* **10.** *(way of life)* path ◊ *Jetzt bewegt sich mein Leben wieder in geregelten Bahnen.*

⊛ **Bahn frei** out of the way **auf die schiefe Bahn geraten/kommen** go astray ◊ *Sie verlor ihren Job und geriet auf die schiefe Bahn.* **jdn aus der Bahn werfen** throw sb off course ◊ *Der Tod seiner Mutter hat Torsten völlig aus der Bahn geworfen.*

bah·nen ['ba:nən] [tr v] +*haben* **1.** sich [dat] einen Weg bahnen make your way ◊ *Sie bahnte sich einen Weg durch die Menschenmenge.* ♦ *Das Wasser bahnt sich einen Weg durch das Tal.* jdm einen Weg irgendwohin bahnen cut/force sb a way somewhere ◊ *Unser Führer bahnte uns einen Weg*

durch den Dschungel. **2.** jdm/einer Sache den Weg bahnen/ebnen pave the way for sb/sth ◊ Sein Fleiß bahnte ihm den Weg zur Beförderung.

② **Bahn·hof** ['baːnhoːf] der <-(e)s, Bahnhöfe> (railway) station, railroad station ◊ Könnten Sie mich zum Bahnhof fahren? ⊛ großer Bahnhof big celebrations ◊ Großer Bahnhof zum 80. Geburtstag: ... nur Bahnhof verstehen (fam) not understand a single word

② **Bahn·steig** ['baːnʃtaɐ̯k] der <-(e)s, -e> platform ◊ Der Zug fährt vom Bahnsteig 13 ab.

② **bald** [balt] [adv] <eher, am ehesten> **1.** soon ◊ Wir sind bald wieder da. ♦ Ich komme so bald wie möglich. ♦ Er war eher fertig als ich. eher Schluss machen finish early ◊ Ich mache heute eher Schluss in der Arbeit. **2.** no comp/superl (fam) nearly ◊ Ich wäre bald gestorben vor Angst. **3.** no comp/superl (SouthG) (expressing impatience) just ◊ Hörst du jetzt bald auf damit! ⊛ wird's bald (pej) get a move on ◊ Wird's bald? Du kommst sonst zu spät! auf bald, bis bald see you soon

Bal·ken ['balkn̩] der <-s, -> **1.** beam, girder, joist ◊ die Decke mit Balken stützen **2.** SPORT (abbr of Schwebebalken) beam ◊ am Balken turnen **3.** (stripe) bar ◊ ein schwarzer Balken auf dem Bildschirm ⊛ lügen sich die Balken biegen lie through your teeth

② **Bal·kon** [bal'kɔŋ, bal'kõː, bal'koːn] der <-s, -s or -e> balcony ◊ Im Sommer frühstücken wir auf dem Balkon.

② **Ball** [bal] der <-(e)s, Bälle> **1.** (for playing) ball ◊ Als Kinder haben wir oft Ball gespielt. ♦ Der Ball ging ins Aus. **2.** (dance) ball ◊ Heute Abend gehe ich auf einen Ball. ⊛ am Ball bleiben **1.** keep at it, not give up ◊ Jetzt hast du eine gute Note geschrieben und solltest am Ball bleiben. **2.** (be well-informed) be on the ball ◊ In meinem Beruf gibt es ständig etwas Neues, da muss man am Ball bleiben.

bal·len ['balən] [tr v] +haben one. (zu etw.) ballen crumple sth (into sth) ◊ ein Stück Papier zu einer Kugel ballen die/seine Fäuste ballen clench your fist [ref v] +haben **1.** sich (zu etw.) ballen go lumpy ◊ Der Schnee hatte sich zu kleinen Klumpen geballt. **2.** sich ballen be concentrated ◊ In dieser Straße ballen sich die Supermärkte.

Bal·lungs·raum ['balʊŋsraɔm] der <-(e)s, Ballungsräume> conurbation

band [bant] pret of binden

Band¹ [bant] das <-(e)s, Bänder> **1.** ribbon ◊ sich die Haare mit einem Band zusammenbinden ♦ Zur Eröffnung der neuen Autobahnstrecke durchschnitt der Bürgermeister das Band. **2.** ANAT ligament ◊ Der Spieler hatte sich ein Band gezerrt. **3.** (for story, sound and images) tape ◊ einen Song auf Band aufnehmen **4.** assembly line ◊ Jeden Tag laufen 1000 Autos vom Band. **5.** conveyor belt; (for luggage at the airport) carousel ⊛ am laufenden Band non-stop, continuously ◊ Das Telefon klingelte am laufenden Band.

Band² [bant] der <-(e)s, -e> (book) volume ◊ Shakespeare in fünf Bänden

Band³ [bɛnt] die <-, -s> (group of musicians) band ◊ Er spielt Gitarre in einer Band.

Band⁴ [bant] das <-(e)s, -e> most pl (lofty, oldf) (close relationship) bonds, ties ◊ familiäre Bande ♦ die Bande der Freundschaft/Liebe ⊛ zarte Bande (mit jdm) knüpfen (also hum) begin a tender relationship (with sb)

Band·brei·te ['bantbraɛ̯tə] die <-> no pl **1.** range ◊ die gesamte Bandbreite klassischer Literatur **2.** IT bandwidth **3.** (of a currency) range of fluctuation

Ban·de ['bandə] die <-, -n> **1.** gang ◊ eine Bande von Verbrechern festnehmen ♦ eine übermütige Bande von Kindern **2.** SPORT (in billiards) cushion; (of a stadium) barrier ◊ Der Eishockeyspieler prallte gegen die Bande.; (with advertising) hoarding ◊ Bei Fußballspielen ist an der Bande Werbung zu sehen.; (of a bowling alley) edge

bän·di·gen ['bɛndɪɡn̩] [tr v] +haben tame, (bring under) control ◊ wilde Tiere bändigen ♦ Die Kinder sind kaum zu bändigen. ♦ seine Wut bändigen

bang [baŋ], **ban·ge** ['baŋə] [adj] <banger/bänger, am bangsten/bängsten> anxious ◊ banges Schweigen jdm ist bang sb is scared ◊ Mir ist ganz bang, wenn ich an die Prüfung denke. jdm wird bang sb becomes scared jdm wird bang ums Herz sb's heart sinks

ban·gen ['baŋən] [intr v] +haben (um jdn/etw.) bangen be worried (about sb/sth) ◊ Er bangt um seine kranke Frau. ♦ um seinen Arbeitsplatz bangen um jds Leben bangen fear for sb's life [imp v] +haben jdm bangt (es) vor etw. [dat] sb is afraid of sth ◊ Manchmal bangt mir vor der Zukunft.

② **Bank**¹ [baŋk] die <-, Bänke> (for sitting) bench ◊ Auf der Bank saß ein verliebtes Pärchen.; (in a church) pew; (in school) desk ◊ Paul und ich teilten in der Schule die gleiche Bank. ⊛ etw. auf die lange Bank schieben put sth off ◊ Unangenehme Arbeiten schiebt sie auf die lange Bank. durch die Bank (weg) without exception ◊ Die Bewerber sind durch die Bank sehr gut qualifiziert.

② **Bank**² [baŋk] die <-, -en> FIN bank ◊ All mein erspartes Geld ist auf der Bank. ♦ Ich muss noch auf die Bank.

Bank·leit·zahl ['baŋklaɛ̯tsaːl] die <-, -en> (abbr BLZ) sort code (number)

Bank·no·te ['baŋknoːtə] die <-, -n> banknote, bill ⊖Geldschein

Bank·rott [baŋ'krɔt] der <-(e)s, -e> most sing (also fig) bankruptcy ◊ Das Unternehmen steht kurz vor dem Bankrott. ♦ den Bankrott anmelden/erklären Bankrott gehen/machen go bankrupt ⊖Pleite

Bank·ver·bin·dung ['baŋkfɛbɪndʊŋ] die <-, -en> account details ◊ Wie lautet Ihre Bankverbindung?

Bann [ban] der <-(e)s> no pl **1.** spell ◊ etw. hält jdn in (seinem) Bann **2.** REL excommunication den Bann über jdn aussprechen/verhängen excommunicate sb ⊛ jdn in seinen Bann schlagen/ziehen captivate sb ◊ Die einzigartige Landschaft hatte ihn in ihren Bann geschlagen. ♦ Sie hat ihn völlig in ihren Bann gezogen.

ban·nen ['banən] [tr v] +haben **1.** mostly passive (wie) gebannt sein be spellbound, be fascinated ◊ Die Fans waren wie gebannt, als sie sang. jdn/etw.

bannen capture sb/sth ◇ *Der herrliche Anblick bannte die Zuschauer.* **2.** *(evil spirits)* ward off ◇ *einen bösen Geist bannen; (a danger)* avert ◇ *Die Gefahr ist noch nicht gebannt.*

② **bar¹** [baːʳ] ⎡adj, adv⎤ *no comp/superl; when used as an adj, only before ns* cash ◇ *Zahlen Sie bar oder mit Karte?* ✦ *Ich gebe dir dafür 100 Euro bar auf die Hand.* bares Geld cash ◇ *Diese Idee ist bares Geld wert.* gegen bar for cash ◇ *Wir liefern Ware nur gegen bar.* in bar cash ◇ *Früher wurden Arbeiter in bar ausbezahlt.*

bar² [baːʳ] ⎡adj⎤ *only before ns* utter, pure ◇ *Das ist doch barer Unsinn, was er da sagt.* ⊖pur

② **Bar** [baːʳ] die <-, –s> bar ◇ *Er trank in einer Bar in Soho ein Bier.* ✦ *Er stand an der Bar und unterhielt sich.*

Bär [bɛːɐ̯] der <-en, –en> bear

⊙ **jdm einen Bären aufbinden** have sb on **irgendwo ist der Bär los** *(fam)* there's really something going on ◇ *In dieser Kneipe ist echt der Bär los.*

Ba·ra·cke [baˈrakə] die <-, –n> shack, hut ◇ *Die Armen leben in Baracken.*

bar·fuß [ˈbaːʳfuːs] ⎡adj, adv⎤ *no comp/superl; when used as an adj, not before ns* barefoot ◇ *Bist du bei dieser Kälte barfuß?* ✦ *barfuß gehen/laufen*

Bar·geld [ˈbaːʳɡɛlt] das <-(e)s> *no pl* cash

Bä·rin [ˈbɛːrɪn] die <-, –nen> she-bear, female bear

barm·her·zig [baʳmˈhɛʳtsɪç] ⎡adj, adv⎤ compassionate(ly), merciful(ly) ◇ *der barmherzige Gott* ✦ *Sei barmherzig und hilf ihm!* ✦ *barmherzig (an jdm) handeln*

② **Bart** [baːʳt] der <-(e)s, Bärte> **1.** beard ◇ *einen Bart tragen* ✦ *Michel lässt sich einen Bart wachsen.; (over the mouth)* moustache, mustache ◇ *Er hatte einen Bart auf der Oberlippe.* **2.** *(of animals)* whiskers; *(of a goat)* beard **3.** *(of a key)* bit

⊙ **jdm um den Bart gehen** *(fam)* sweet-talk sb ◇ *Wenn er etwas will, geht er seinem Vater so lange um den Bart, bis er es bekommt.* **so einen Bart haben** *(fam)* be old hat ◇ *Der Witz hat doch so einen Bart.*

Ba·sar [baˈzaːʳ] der <-(e)s, –e> **1.** *(for charity)* bazaar, fête ◇ *etw. auf dem Basar kaufen* ✦ *einen Basar veranstalten* **2.** *(oriental market)* bazaar

ba·sie·ren [baˈziːrən] ⎡intr v⎤ *mostly written* etw. basiert auf etw. ⎡dat⎤ sth is based on sth ◇ *Diese Theorie basiert auf der Annahme, dass ...* ✦ *Der Film basiert auf einer wahren Begebenheit.* ⊖beruhen

Ba·si·li·kum [baˈziːlikʊm] das <-s> *no pl* basil

Ba·sis [ˈbaːzɪs] die <-, Basen> **1.** *mostly written, most sing (underlying element)* basis ◇ *eine gemeinsame Basis suchen* ✦ *Vertrauen bildet die Basis jeder Beziehung.* ⊖Grundlage, Fundament **2.** *(military, architectural, mathematical, for rockets)* base ◇ *eine Basis für militärische Aktionen* ✦ *die Basis eines Dreiecks* **3.** *most sing* ᴘᴏʟ grass roots ◇ *die Zustimmung der Basis einholen*

Bas·sin [baˈsɛn, baˈsɛ̃ː] das <-s, –s> pool ◇ *Die Delfine schwimmen in einem Bassin.*

bas·teln [ˈbastl̩n] ⎡tr v⎤ +*haben* make ◇ *Die Kinder basteln Weihnachtsgeschenke.* ⎡intr v⎤ +*haben* **1.** make things ◇ *Sie bastelt gerne.* **2.** *(also fig)* an etw. ⎡dat⎤ basteln work on sth, tinker with sth ◇ *Er bastelt schon wieder an dem alten Wagen.* ✦ *Sie bastelte an ihrem Referat.*

② **bat** [baːt] *pret of* bitten

② **Bau¹** [bao] der <-s, –ten> **1.** *no pl (of buildings, bridges)* building, construction ◇ *Die Brücke befindet sich noch im Bau.* **2.** *no pl (of products)* construction ◇ *Die Firma hat mit dem Bau eines Sportwagens begonnen.* **3.** *no pl* building site ◇ *Simon arbeitet auf dem Bau.* **4.** *(house etc.)* building ◇ *historische/moderne Bauten* **5.** *no pl* ᴀɴᴀᴛ build ◇ *Das Pferd hat einen kräftigen Bau.*

Bau² [bao] der <-(e)s, –e> *(of foxes)* den ◇ *Der Fuchs verschwand in seinem Bau.; (of badgers)* sett; *(of rabbits)* burrow, warren

Bau·ar·bei·ten [ˈbaoˌaʳbaetn̩] die <-> *only pl* roadworks

② **Bauch** [baox] der <-(e)s, Bäuche> **1.** *(of a person)* stomach, belly ◇ *Ich schlafe auf dem Bauch.* ✦ *Mir tut der Bauch weh.; (from too much food)* paunch ◇ *Mein Mann hat in letzter Zeit einen Bauch bekommen.* **2.** *(of an animal, a vase)* belly ◇ *eine Katze am Bauch kraulen* ✦ *eine Vase mit dickem Bauch* **3.** *(of a ship)* bowels ◇ *Die Güter wurden im Bauch des Schiffes transportiert.*

⊙ **aus dem hohlen Bauch (heraus)** *(fam)* off the cuff ◇ *Aus dem hohlen Bauch heraus kann ich nicht sagen, wie viel das kosten wird.* **mit etw. auf den Bauch fallen** *(fam)* have a disaster with sth ◇ *Sie sind mit ihrer Geschäftsidee auf den Bauch gefallen.*

Bauch·schmer·zen [ˈbaoxˌʃmɛʳtsn̩] die <-> *only pl; seldom with the article* stomach ache, belly ache ◇ *Bauchschmerzen bekommen/haben* ⊖Bauchweh

Bauch·weh [ˈbaoxveː] das <-s> *no pl (fam)* tummy ache ◇ *Von zu viel Kuchen bekommst du Bauchweh!* ⊖Bauchschmerzen

② **bau·en** [ˈbaoən] ⎡tr v⎤ +*haben* **1.** *(a building, bridge, nest)* build ◇ *ein Haus/eine Straße bauen* ✦ *Ein Vogel hat sein Nest im Apfelbaum gebaut.* **2.** *(machines etc.)* make, manufacture ◇ *Volkswagen werden in Wolfsburg gebaut.* **3.** *(fam)* einen Unfall bauen cause an accident ◇ *Er hat schon wieder einen Unfall gebaut.* Mist bauen mess things up ⎡intr v⎤ +*haben* **1.** a house, build ◇ *Meine Eltern wollen bauen.* **2.** *(also fig)* an etw. ⎡dat⎤ bauen be working on sth ◇ *Wie lange wurde am Kölner Dom gebaut?* **3.** *(fig)* auf jdn/etw. bauen rely on sb/sth ◇ *Ich baue auf dich/auf deine Unterstützung.*

② **Bau·er** [ˈbaoə] der <-n or –s, –n> **1.** ᴀɢʀ farmer ◇ *Er ist Bauer geworden wie sein Vater.* ✦ *Der Tag eines Bauern beginnt früh.* ⊖Landwirt **2.** *(fam, pej) (impolite person)* peasant ◇ *So ein Bauer, er hat sich nicht einmal bedankt!* **3.** ᴄʜᴇss pawn

Bäu·e·rin [ˈbɔøərɪn] die <-, –nen> **1.** farmer ◇ *Sie ist Bäuerin auf einem großen Hof.* ✦ *Die Bäuerin füttert die Hühner.* **2.** *farmer's wife*

bäu·er·lich [ˈbɔøəlɪç] ⎡adj, adv⎤ **1.** rustic(ally) ◇ *ein Haus im bäuerlichen Stil* ✦ *Die Küche der Region ist eher bäuerlich.* ✦ *bäuerlich rustikal* **2.** rural(ly) ◇ *eine bäuerliche Gegend* ✦ *Die Landschaft ist bäuerlich.* ◇ *Die Region ist bäuerlich strukturiert.*

Bau·ern·hof [ˈbaoənhoːf] der <-(e)s, Bauernhöfe> farm ◇ *auf einem Bauernhof arbeiten/leben*

Bau·jahr [ˈbaojaːʳ] das <-(e)s, –e> **1.** year of con-

struction ◊ *Dieses Haus ist Baujahr 1906.*; *(of a car)* year of manufacture **2.** *(bum)* *(year of birth)* vintage ◊ *Ich bin 1982 geboren — und welches Baujahr bist du?*

② **Baum** [baͅom] der <-(e)s, Bäume> tree ◊ *auf einen Baum klettern* ♦ *Die Bäume werden wieder grün.*

⦿ *jd könnte Bäume ausreißen* sb feels ready for anything ◊ *Ich habe mich im Urlaub so gut erholt, dass ich jetzt Bäume ausreißen könnte.*

Bau·markt ['baͅomarkt] der <-(e)s, Baumärkte> DIY store

bau·meln ['baͅomļn] [intr v] +*haben* dangle ◊ *Das Seil baumelt an einem Ast.* ♦ *Ich saß auf der Mauer und ließ die Beine baumeln.* ♦ *mit den Beinen baumeln*

Baum·wol·le ['baͅomvɔlə] die <-> *no pl* cotton ◊ *Baumwolle anbauen/pflücken* ♦ *eine Bluse aus reiner Baumwolle*

Bau·stel·le ['baͅoʃtɛlə] die <-, -n> building site; *(in a road)* road works ◊ *Wegen mehrerer Baustellen kam es zu einem Stau.*

② **Bau·ten** ['baͅotņ] *pl of* Bau¹

Bau·werk ['baͅovɛrk] das <-(e)s, -e> building, structure

bay·e·risch ['baͅɛərɪʃ] [adj] Bavarian → deutsch

Bay·ern ['baͅɛən] das <-s> *article only in combination with attribute* Bavaria box@ Land

Area: 70,553 km²; population: approx. 12.23 million; regional capital: Munich.
Situated on the northern edge of the Alps, Bavaria is the largest of the *Länder*, and attracts tourists from all over the world with its many sites of natural beauty. Many internationally successful companies, such as BMW, Siemens, and Audi, have their headquarters in Bavaria. Bavaria is also famous for the castles of Neuschwanstein, Hohenschwangau and Linderhof, built by King Ludwig II of Bavaria.

bay·risch ['baͅɛrɪʃ] [adj, adv] → bayerisch

be·ab·sich·ti·gen [bə|'apzɪçtɪɡņ] <beabsichtigt, beabsichtigte, hat beabsichtigt> [tr v] plan ◊ *Er beabsichtigt eine Reise nach Asien.* beabsichtigen, etw. zu tun intend to do sth ◊ *Wir beabsichtigen, noch dieses Jahr zu heiraten.* etw. ist beabsichtigt sth is intentional ⊜planen

② **be·ach·ten** [bə|'axtņ] <beachtet, beachtete, hat beachtet> [tr v] **1.** observe, follow ◊ *Gesetze/Konventionen beachten* ♦ *Er hatte die Vorfahrt nicht beachtet.* **2.** pay attention to, take notice of ◊ *Beachte ihn einfach nicht!* ⊜auf jdn/etw. achten **3.** take into account/consideration ◊ *Bei der Erstellung des Textes ist Folgendes zu beachten: ...* (man) beachte ... note ... ◊ *Beachte, dass nach einem langen Vokal ein β folgt.*

be·acht·lich [bə|'axtlɪç] [adj, adv] **1.** remarkable (-ably), considerable(-ably) ◊ *ein beachtlicher Anstieg der Produktivität* ♦ *Ihr Fortschritt war beachtlich.* ♦ *Er hat sich beachtlich verbessert.* **2.** significant(ly), substantial(ly) ◊ *beachtliche Verluste erleiden* ♦ *Die Strompreise sind beachtlich gestiegen.*

Be·ach·tung [bə|'axtʊŋ] die <-> *no pl* **1.** following, observance ◊ *die strenge Beachtung der Gesetze/Vorschriften* unter/mit Beachtung ... [gen] in accordance with ... ◊ *Ihre Daten werden* unter Beachtung des Datenschutzes gespeichert. ohne Beachtung ... [gen] ignoring ... ◊ *Er hat den Text ohne Beachtung des Copyrights übernommen.* **2.** attention Beachtung finden receive attention keine Beachtung finden be ignored jdm/etw. Beachtung schenken pay attention to sb/sth jdm/ einer Sache keine Beachtung schenken take no notice of sb/sth ⊜Aufmerksamkeit **3.** consideration ◊ *mangelnde Beachtung der Zielgruppe* mit/unter Beachtung ... [gen] considering ... ◊ *seine Entscheidung unter Beachtung der Umstände treffen* ohne Beachtung ... [gen] without consideration for sth, ignoring sth

⦿ **zur Beachtung** please note

② **Be·am·te** [bə|'amtə] der <-n, die Beamten>, **Be·am·tin** [bə|'amtɪn] die <-, -nen> *but: ein Beamter/pl without article:* Beamte ⊜civil servant ◊ *ein beim Finanzamt angestellter Beamter* ♦ *Frau Fuchs ist Beamtin.*; *(with the police)* ⊜officer box@ Substantivierung

In Germany, *Beamte* are public sector employees with certain privileges and duties which are set out in the Constitution. They must be loyal to the state, are not allowed to get involved in extreme political activity, and have no right to strike, but they enjoy a permanent position and excellent health and pension provisions paid for by the state. There are four different career paths for *Beamte* requiring different levels of education: (starting with the most junior level) *einfacher, mittlerer, gehobener, höherer Dienst.* Not everybody who works in the public sector is a *Beamter*, but they include police officers, many teaching professionals and people working for local, regional, and central government and many of those employed by formerly state-owned companies such as the railways, postal and telecommunication services.

be·ängs·ti·gend [bə|'ɛŋstɪɡņt, bə|'ɛŋstɪɡənt] [adj, adv] **1.** alarming(ly), frightening(ly) ◊ *eine beängstigende Entwicklung* ♦ *Der Anstieg der Arbeitslosigkeit ist beängstigend.* ♦ *Das Kind war beängstigend blass.* **2.** eerie(-ily), unsettling(ly) ◊ *Es war beängstigend still vor dem Sturm.* ♦ *Die politischen Entwicklungen sind beängstigend.* ♦ *ein beängstigendes Gefühl*

be·an·spru·chen [bə|'anʃprʊxņ] <beansprucht, beanspruchte, hat beansprucht> [tr v] **1.** claim ◊ *die Herrschaft über das Land beanspruchen* ♦ *Er beanspruchte die Hälfte des Gewinns für sich.* **2.** jdn beanspruchen demand a lot of sb, keep sb busy ◊ *Die Kinder beanspruchen ihn in seiner Freizeit sehr.* jdn (zeitlich) beanspruchen take up a lot of sb's time **3.** take (up), demand, require ◊ *Das Kind beansprucht ihre ganze Aufmerksamkeit.* **4.** put strain/stress on ◊ *Langes Sitzen beansprucht die Wirbelsäule.*

be·an·stan·den [bə|'anʃtandņ] <beanstandet, beanstandete, hat beanstandet> [tr v] **1.** object to ◊ *einen Beschluss beanstanden;* *(a bill etc.)* query ◊ *Beanstanden Sie die Rechnung schriftlich.* etw. ist nicht zu beanstanden there is nothing wrong with sth ◊ *Sein Verhalten ist nicht zu beanstanden.* **2.** complain about ◊ *Mängel an einer Ware beanstanden* beanstanden, dass complain that etwas/

nichts an etw./jdm zu beanstanden haben find fault/no fault with sth/sb ◊ *Ich hatte an ihrer Arbeit nichts zu beanstanden.* ⊜bemängeln, kritisieren
② **be·an·tra·gen** [bə|'antra:gn̩] <beantragt, beantragte, hat beantragt> ⟨tr v⟩ **1.** etw. *(bei jdm/etw.)* beantragen apply (to sb/sth) for sth ◊ *Sozialhilfe beantragen* ♦ *Er hat bei seiner Bank einen Kredit beantragt.* **2.** demand, call for ◊ *Der Staatsanwalt hat eine Freiheitsstrafe beantragt.* Konkurs beantragen file for bankruptcy **3.** propose ◊ *eine Unterbrechung der Sitzung beantragen; (a legislation)* move for ◊ *eine Gesetzesänderung beantragen*
be·ant·wor·ten [bə|'antvɔ‿tn̩] <beantwortet, beantwortete, hat beantwortet> ⟨tr v⟩ answer, reply to ◊ *einen Brief beantworten* eine Frage mit ja/nein beantworten answer yes/no to a question eine Frage mit einer Gegenfrage beantworten answer a question with another question
be·ar·bei·ten [bə|'a‿baetn̩] <bearbeitet, bearbeitete, hat bearbeitet> ⟨tr v⟩ **1.** deal with, handle, process ◊ *Kundenanfragen/Beschwerden bearbeiten* **2.** work (on), prepare ◊ *Holz/Metall bearbeiten; (with paint, a protective coat also)* treat **3.** *(land)* cultivate ◊ *Der Bauer bearbeitet seine Felder mit schweren Maschinen.* **4.** edit ◊ *Bearbeiten Sie als Hausaufgabe die ersten drei Fragen.* ♦ *einen Eintrag in einer Datenbank bearbeiten; (music)* arrange neu bearbeiten revise ◊ *Das Lernprogramm wurde völlig neu bearbeitet.; (literature)* adapt
be·auf·sich·ti·gen [bə|'aofzɪçtɪgn̩] <beaufsichtigt, beaufsichtigte, hat beaufsichtigt> ⟨tr v⟩ **1.** *(a person who cannot be left alone, an animal)* look after ◊ *Unser Hund muss ständig beaufsichtigt werden.; (a child also)* mind ◊ *Würdest du bitte kurz den Kleinen beaufsichtigen?* **2.** supervise ◊ *Er beaufsichtigte die Arbeiten.; (in an exam)* invigilate
be·auf·tra·gen [bə|'aoftra:gn̩] <beauftragt, beauftragte, hat beauftragt> ⟨tr v⟩ jdn beauftragen, etw. zu tun ask sb to do sth, instruct sb to do sth ◊ *Der Experte wurde beauftragt, ein Gutachten zu erstellen.* jdn mit etw. beauftragen entrust sb with sth, charge sb with sth ◊ *Ein Architekt wurde mit dem Entwurf beauftragt.*
be·ben ['be:bm̩] ⟨intr v⟩ +haben tremble ◊ *Ihre Lippen bebten vor Wut.* ♦ *Die Erde bebte.; (building, knees)* shake
Be·cher ['bɛçɐ] der <-s, -> **1.** *(for drinking, made of plastic)* beaker ◊ *aus dem Becher trinken; (of china)* mug; *(of metal)* goblet ein Becher Milch a cup of milk **2.** tub, pot ◊ *ein Becher Joghurt/Margarine*
Be·cken ['bɛkn̩] das <-s, -> **1.** *(in the bathroom, kitchen)* sink, basin ◊ *sich beim Zähneputzen über das Becken beugen* ♦ *Das Geschirr stapelt sich im Becken.; (for swimming)* pool ◊ *vom Sprungbrett ins Becken springen; (to keep animals, plants)* pond, tank; *(to store water)* reservoir **2.** ANAT pelvis Hosen für Frauen mit breitem Becken pants for women with broad hips **3.** GEOL basin ◊ *das Wiener Becken südlich der Donau*
② **be·dan·ken** [bə'daŋkn̩] <bedankt sich, bedankte sich, hat sich bedankt> ⟨ref v⟩ sich bedanken say thank you ◊ *Er hat sich nicht einmal bedankt.* sich bei jdm (für etw.) bedanken thank sb (for sth), say

thank you to sb (for sth) ◊ *Hast du dich bei Oma schon für die 50 Euro bedankt?*
② **Be·darf** [bə'da‿f] der <-(e)s> *no pl* need(s), requirement(s) ◊ *Offensichtlich ist bei den Kunden der Bedarf gedeckt.* (der/ein) Bedarf an jdm/etw. the/a need for sb/sth, the/a requirement for sb/sth ◊ *Es besteht ein großer Bedarf an Aufklärung.* ♦ *An IT-Spezialisten besteht noch immer Bedarf.* ⊚ **bei/(je) nach Bedarf** if/as required ◊ *Je nach Bedarf können wir Ihnen weitere Exemplare liefern.* jds Bedarf ist gedeckt *(esp iron)* sb has (had) enough ◊ *„Such dir doch einen Freund!" — „Nein danke, mein Bedarf ist gedeckt."*
be·dau·er·lich [bə'daoɐlɪç] ⟨adj⟩ regrettable, unfortunate, unpleasant ◊ *eine bedauerliche Niederlage* ♦ *Es ist bedauerlich, dass du so wenig liest.* ⊜erfreulich
be·dau·ern [bə'daoɐn] <bedauert, bedauerte, hat bedauert> ⟨tr v⟩ **1.** regret ◊ *Er bedauert seine unbedachten Äußerungen.* ♦ *Sie bedauert, dass sie keine Geschwister hat.* **2.** etw. bedauern be/feel sorry for sth, be sad about sth ◊ *Wir bedauern den Tod Ihres Bruders.* **3.** jdn bedauern feel sorry for sb, pity sb ◊ *Sie wollte nicht wegen ihrer Krankheit bedauert werden.* ⊚ **(ich) bedaure** (I'm) sorry ◊ *Bedaure, aber mehr kann ich nicht tun.* ♦ *Ich bedaure, die Chefin ist nicht zu sprechen.*
be·de·cken [bə'dɛkn̩] <bedeckt, bedeckte, hat bedeckt> ⟨tr v⟩ cover ◊ *Der erste Schnee bedeckt die Berge.* ♦ *Sie bedeckte ihr Gesicht und schluchzte.* mit Staub/Schmutz etc. bedeckt sein be covered in dust/dirt etc.
be·deckt [bə'dɛkt] *past p of* bedeckt ⟨adj⟩ <bedeckter, am bedecktesten> overcast, cloudy ◊ *Der Himmel ist heute bedeckt.* ♦ *ein bedeckter Tag* ⊚ **sich bedeckt halten** keep quiet, keep a low profile ◊ *Er hält sich noch bedeckt, was seine Pläne angeht.*
be·den·ken [bə'dɛŋkn̩] <bedenkt, bedachte, hat bedacht> ⟨tr v⟩ **1.** take into consideration, bear in mind, consider ◊ *die Folgen für die Gesundheit bedenken* zu bedenken geben ask to bear in mind/take into consideration ⊜berücksichtigen, beachten **2.** noch einmal bedenken reconsider, think over ◊ *eine Entscheidung noch einmal bedenken* wenn man es recht bedenkt, ... if you think about it properly ... ⊜überlegen
Be·den·ken [bə'dɛŋkn̩] die <-, -> *only pl* doubts, reservations, misgivings ◊ *Hast du keine Bedenken, ihn allein zur Schule gehen zu lassen?* Bedenken gegen etw. reservations/misgivings about sth ◊ *Hast du deine Bedenken gegen den Plan schon geäußert?* ohne Bedenken without hesitation ◊ *etw. kann ohne Bedenken getan werden* it is safe to do sth
be·denk·lich [bə'dɛŋklɪç] ⟨adj, adv⟩ alarming(ly), serious(ly) ◊ *eine bedenkliche Entwicklung* ♦ *Sein Zustand kommt mir bedenklich vor.* ♦ *eine bedenklich hohe Konzentration von Giften* etw. ist bedenklich sth gives cause for concern ◊ *Sein hoher Blutdruck ist bedenklich.* ⟨adj⟩ **1.** *not before ns* potentially dangerous/harmful ◊ *Schon fünf Zigaretten pro Tag sind bedenklich.* gesundheitlich/ökologisch bedenklich sein be a health/environmental

hazard **2.** dubious, questionable ◇ *juristisch bedenklich sein* ♦ *eine bedenkliche Messmethode* ⓔ *etw. stimmt jdn bedenklich* sth gives sb cause for concern

ⓩ **be·deu·ten** [bə'dɔøtn̩] <bedeutet, bedeutete, hat bedeutet> ⓣⓡⓥ mean ◇ *Was bedeutet dieses Wort?* ♦ *Sein Schweigen bedeutet nichts Gutes.* ♦ *Der Kauf großer Mengen bedeutet oft einen Preisvorteil.* *etw. zu bedeuten haben* mean sth ◇ *Was ihr starrer Blick wohl zu bedeuten hatte?* *etw./jd bedeutet etw. für jdn, etw./jd bedeutet jdm etw.* sb/sth means sth to sb ◇ *Er bedeutet mir sehr viel.* ♦ *Eine Prüfung bedeutet für die meisten Menschen Stress. Was soll das bedeuten?* What do you/they etc. mean? ⓔheißen

Be·deu·tung [bə'dɔøtʊŋ] die <–, –en> **1.** importance, significance ◇ *Der Flughafen hat eine große Bedeutung für die Insel.* ♦ *Diese Nachricht ist für uns ohne Bedeutung.* *einer Sache* ⓓⓐⓣ *große/keine Bedeutung beimessen* attach much/no importance to sth **2.** meaning ◇ *die Bedeutung eines Fremdworts kennen*

ⓩ **be·die·nen** [bə'diːnən] <bedient, bediente, hat bedient> ⓣⓡ+ⓘⓝⓣⓡⓥ **1.** *(customers)* serve, attend to ◇ *Tut mir Leid, aber ich bediene an diesem Tisch nicht. Werden Sie schon bedient?* Are you being served? Man wird gut/schlecht bedient. Service is good/bad. ◇ *In diesem Laden wird man sehr freundlich bedient.; (as if by a servant)* wait on ◇ *Er lässt sich gern von seiner Frau bedienen.* **2.** *(a machine)* operate ◇ *Meine Oma kann jeden Computer bedienen.* ⓡⓔⓥ **1.** *sich bedienen* help/serve yourself ◇ *Das Büffet ist eröffnet, bitte bedienen Sie sich.* **2.** *sich einer Sache/jds bedienen* use sth/sb ◇ *Zur Veranschaulichung bediene ich mich einer Grafik.* ⓔ *gut/schlecht bedient sein* **1.** be well-/ill-served ◇ *Mit diesem Rat war ich schlecht bedient.* **2.** get/not get value for money *bedient sein* have had enough, have had all you can take ◇ *War das langweilig, ich bin echt bedient!*

ⓩ **Be·die·nung** [bə'diːnʊŋ] die <–, –en> **1.** *no pl* service ◇ *Die Bedienung in diesem Restaurant ist schnell.* **2.** service charge ◇ *In den USA sind 15% Bedienung üblich.* **3.** *(of a machine, software, an appliance)* operation, operating ◇ *Die Bedienung dieser Waschmaschine ist nicht kompliziert.* **4.** waiter, waitress ◇ *Einen Moment, die Bedienung kommt gleich.; (in a shop)* (sales) assistant

be·dingt [bə'dɪŋt] ⓐⓓⓙ *no comp/superl* **1.** bedingt durch caused by, due to ◇ *eine durch Übergewicht bedingte Krankheit* erblich/psychologisch bedingt sein have hereditary/psychological causes **2.** *only before ns* conditional, limited ◇ *eine bedingte Aufenthaltserlaubnis* **3.** *(Austr, Swiss)* LAW conditional *bedingte Entlassung* release on parole ⓐⓓⓥ *nur bedingt* only to a certain extent, only partly ◇ *Das ist nur bedingt geeignet/vergleichbar.*

ⓩ **Be·din·gung** [bə'dɪŋʊŋ] die <–, –en> **1.** condition, term ◇ *Welche Bedingungen stellen die Streikenden?* ⓔForderung **2.** *only pl* conditions ◇ *An dieser Schule hat unser Kind ideale Bedingungen.* ♦ *eine Prüfung unter erschwerten Bedingungen ablegen* ⓔUmstände **3.** requirement, prerequisite ◇ *Gute Sprachkenntnisse sind eine Bedingung für diese Stelle.* ⓔVoraussetzung

ⓔ *unter der Bedingung, dass* on condition that ◇ *Ich helfe dir unter der Bedingung, dass du keinem etwas davon erzählst.*

be·dro·hen [bə'droːən] <bedroht, bedrohte, hat bedroht> ⓣⓡⓥ **1.** endanger, be a threat to ◇ *Die zunehmende Umweltverschmutzung bedroht die Erde.* die Gesundheit bedrohen be a health risk ◇ *Übergewicht bedroht die Gesundheit.* **2.** threaten ◇ *jdn mit einer Waffe bedrohen*

be·droh·lich [bə'droːlɪç] ⓐⓓⓙ, ⓐⓓⓥ **1.** alarming(ly) ◇ *Seine Wut nahm bedrohliche Züge an.* ♦ *Die Situation in Nahost ist bedrohlich.* ♦ *Die Kriminalität ist bedrohlich angestiegen.* **2.** threatening(ly) ◇ *Ein bedrohlicher Ausdruck lag in seinem Gesicht.* ♦ *Der Himmel sah bedrohlich aus.* ♦ *ein Hund, der sich bedrohlich verhält*

be·dür·fen [bə'dʏrfn̩] <bedarf, bedurfte, hat bedurft> ⓘⓝⓣⓡⓥ *(lofty) einer Sache* ⓖⓔⓝ bedürfen need sth, require sth ◇ *Seine Krankheit bedarf der Behandlung.* etw. bedarf der Schriftform sth must be in writing ◇ *Eine Kündigung bedarf der Schriftform.*

Be·dürf·nis [bə'dʏrfnɪs] das <–ses, –se> need ◇ *menschliche Bedürfnisse* ♦ *ein Bedürfnis befriedigen; (subjective)* desire, wish ◇ *Ich habe das Bedürfnis, mich zu entschuldigen.* ein Bedürfnis nach etw. a need/desire for sth ◇ *ein Bedürfnis nach Liebe/Ruhe haben*

ⓩ **be·ei·len** [bə'aelən] <beeilt sich, beeilte sich, hat sich beeilt> ⓡⓔⓥ hurry (up) ◇ *Nun beeil dich doch ein bisschen!* ♦ *Beeil dich mit deinen Hausaufgaben!* ⓔtrödeln

be·ein·dru·cken [bə'aendrʊkn̩] <beeindruckt, beeindruckte, hat beeindruckt> ⓣⓡⓥ impress, make an impression on ◇ *Dieses Buch hat mich sehr beeindruckt.* ♦ *Sie beeindruckte das Publikum mit ihrer schönen Stimme.* sich von etw. beeindrucken lassen be impressed by sth

ⓩ **be·ein·flus·sen** [bə'aenflʊsn̩] <beeinflusst, beeinflusste, hat beeinflusst> ⓣⓡⓥ influence ◇ *Du lässt dich zu leicht von ihm beeinflussen.* jdn/etw. günstig/nachhaltig beeinflussen have a favo(u)rable/lasting influence on sb/sth ⓔauf jdn/ etw. einwirken

be·ein·träch·ti·gen [bə'aentrɛçtɪgn̩] <beeinträchtigt, beeinträchtigte, hat beeinträchtigt> ⓣⓡⓥ diminish, impair, reduce ◇ *Lärm beeinträchtigt die Lebensqualität.; (traffic)* restrict ◇ *Schnee beeinträchtigt den Straßenverkehr.*

be·en·den [bə'ɛndn̩] <beendet, beendete, hat beendet> ⓣⓡⓥ **1.** finish, complete ◇ *ein Programm beenden* ♦ *Im Sommer beendet er sein Studium.* ⓔabschließen **2.** end, stop ◇ *ein Gespräch beenden* etw. vorzeitig beenden cut sth short ⓔfortsetzen

be·engt [bə'ɛŋt] ⓐⓓⓙ, ⓐⓓⓥ *seldom comp/superl* cramped ◇ *In der winzigen Küche ging es sehr beengt zu.* beengt/ in beengten Verhältnissen leben live in confined conditions Ich fühle mich in dieser Beziehung beengt. I feel stifled in this relationship.

be·er·di·gen [bə'eːɐdɪgn̩] <beerdigt, beerdigte, hat beerdigt> ⓣⓡⓥ bury ◇ *Meine Tante wird am Freitag beerdigt.* ♦ *Sie hat ihre Hoffnungen längst beerdigt.* ⓔbestatten, begraben

Bee·re ['beːrə] die <–, –n> berry ◇ *Beeren*

pflücken
be·fä·hi·gen [bəˈfɛːɪɡn̩] <befähigt, befähigte, hat befähigt> ⟨tr+intr v⟩ (jdn) zu etw. befähigen make sth possible (for sb) ◊ *Seine innere Distanz befähigte ihn zu einer nüchternen Einschätzung der Lage.*; *(officially)* jdn zu etw. befähigen qualify sb for sth ◊ *Diese Ausbildung befähigte ihn zur Leitung von Skikursen.* etw. befähigt zu etw. sth is the qualification needed for sth jdn/ein Tier befähigen, etw. zu tun enable sb/an animal to do sth ◊ *Seine breiten Flügel befähigen den Storch, weite Strecken zu fliegen.*
be·fahl [bəˈfaːl] *pret of* befehlen
be·fas·sen [bəˈfasn̩] <befasst sich, befasste sich, hat sich befasst> ⟨ref v⟩ sich mit etw. befassen deal with sth, look into sth ◊ *sich mit einer Frage befassen*; study sth ◊ *Er befasste sich intensiv mit der Geschichte Deutschlands.* ⊝sich beschäftigen
Be·fehl [bəˈfeːl] der <-(e)s, -e> 1. order, command ◊ *Auf Befehl des Königs wurden die Gefangenen freigelassen.* jdm den Befehl geben, etw. zu tun order sb to do sth (den) Befehl haben, etw. zu tun have orders/been ordered to do sth einen Befehl verweigern refuse to obey an order 2. den Befehl über jdn/etw. haben be in command of sb/sth jds Befehl unterstehen be under sb's command 3. IT command ◊ *Mit welchem Befehl kann man die Datei ausdrucken?* einen Befehl eingeben type a command
⊛ **zu Befehl** MIL yes, sir
be·feh·len [bəˈfeːlən] <befiehlt, befahl, hat befohlen> ⟨tr+intr v⟩ 1. order, command ◊ *„Ab ins Bett!", befahl seine Mutter.* ✦ *Er tat, was ihm befohlen wurde.* 2. MIL be in command
be·fes·ti·gen [bəˈfɛstɪɡn̩] <befestigt, befestigte, hat befestigt> ⟨tr v⟩ 1. etw. (an etw. ⟨dat⟩) befestigen fix sth (to sth), fasten sth (to sth), attach sth (to sth) ◊ *Das Regal wurde an der Wand befestigt.*; *(with screws)* screw sth on(to sth) 2. *(an embankment etc.)* reinforce, stabilize ◊ *Die Ufer der Teiche wurden künstlich befestigt.*; *(a road etc.)* make up 3. *(a town etc.)* fortify
be·fiehlt [bəˈfiːlt] *pres of* befehlen
be·fin·den [bəˈfɪndn̩] <befindet, befand, hat befunden> ⟨ref v⟩ 1. *(in a situation, phase etc.)* be ◊ *Der Kranke befindet sich in einem kritischen Zustand.* 2. *(in space)* sich irgendwo befinden be (situated) somewhere ◊ *Die Kanaren befinden sich westlich von Afrika.* ⟨tr v⟩ etw. für gut/rechtmäßig etc. befinden find sth (to be) good/lawful etc. jdn für (nicht) schuldig befinden find sb (not) guilty ⟨intr v⟩ über etw. ⟨acc⟩ befinden decide sth, make a decision on sth ◊ *Das Parlament befindet heute über die Sparmaßnahmen.*
Be·fin·den [bəˈfɪndn̩] das <-s> *no pl* 1. health, condition ◊ *Sie erkundigte sich nach dem Befinden des Kranken.* 2. *(lofty)* nach jds Befinden in sb's opinion ◊ *Nach meinem Befinden ist das die beste Lösung.*
be·foh·len [bəˈfoːlən] *past p of* befehlen
be·fol·gen [bəˈfɔlɡn̩] <befolgt, befolgte, hat befolgt> ⟨tr v⟩ follow, obey ◊ *einen Befehl/Rat befolgen* ⊝missachten
be·för·dern [bəˈfœrdɐn] <befördert, beförderte, hat befördert> ⟨tr v⟩ 1. transport, carry, convey ◊ *Güter (mit der Bahn) befördern* ✦ *In dem Bus*

können 40 Personen befördert werden. ✦ *einen Satelliten in die Umlaufbahn befördern* 2. *mostly passive* promote (zum Direktor etc.) befördert werden be promoted (to director etc.)
Be·för·de·rung [bəˈfœrdərʊŋ] die <-, -en> 1. transport, conveyance ◊ *die Beförderung gefährlicher Güter auf der Straße* 2. Beförderung (zu ...) promotion (to ...) ◊ *jdm zur Beförderung gratulieren* ✦ *eine Beförderung zur Geschäftsführerin*
be·fra·gen [bəˈfraːɡn̩] <befragt, befragte, hat befragt> ⟨tr v⟩ consult ◊ *ein Medium befragen*; *(a witness)* question, examine jdn (zu etw.) befragen ask sb (questions) (about sth), make inquiries/an inquiry (about sth) to sb ◊ *Die Zuschauer konnten einen Experten zum Thema Gentechnik befragen.* jdn nach seiner Meinung befragen ask sb for his/her opinion
be·frei·en [bəˈfraɛən] <befreit, befreite, hat befreit> ⟨tr v⟩ 1. *(a prisoner, an animal)* (set) free, release ◊ *jdn aus dem Gefängnis befreien* 2. *(a country, people)* liberate, free 3. *(of dirt, snow etc.)* von etw. befreien clear sth of sth ◊ *den Gehweg vom Schnee befreien; (of parasites etc.)* jdn/etw. von etw. befreien rid sb/sth of sth 4. jdn von jdm befreien rescue sb from sb ◊ *Befreie mich bitte von diesem Langweiler!* jdn von etw. befreien release sb from sth, free sb from sth ◊ *jdn von seinen Schmerzen/Sorgen befreien* 5. *(from tax, military service, duty)* von etw. befreit werden be exempted from sth, be released from sth; *(from tax etc.)* von etw. befreit sein be exempt from sth
be·freun·det [bəˈfrɔɪndət] ⟨adj⟩ *no comp/superl* 1. friendly ◊ *ein befreundetes Land* eine befreundete Familie etc. a family etc. we/they etc. are friends with ein befreundeter Kollege etc. a colleague etc. who is a friend of mine/his/hers/theirs etc. mit jdm befreundet sein be friends with sb Sie sind (miteinander) befreundet. They are friends. 2. *not before ns* mit jdm befreundet sein go out with sb, be in a relationship with sb ◊ *Sie ist mit einem Schauspieler befreundet.* Sie sind (miteinander) befreundet. They are a couple., They are in a relationship.
be·frie·di·gen [bəˈfriːdɪɡn̩] <befriedigt, befriedigte, hat befriedigt> ⟨tr v⟩ jdn befriedigen satisfy sb/sth ◊ *Seine Antwort hat sie befriedigt.* ✦ *die Neugier befriedigen; (a need, desire, wish also)* fulfil ◊ *ein Bedürfnis befriedigen*
② **be·frie·di·gend** [bəˈfriːdɪɡn̩t, bəˈfriːdɪɡənt] *pres p of* befriedigen ⟨adj⟩ 1. satisfactory, adequate ◊ *Das ist keine befriedigende Lösung.*; satisfying ◊ *Ich finde es wenig befriedigend, immer das Gleiche zu tun.* 2. SCHOOL *(mark, grade)* ⊕B- box⊕ Note
Be·fug·nis [bəˈfuːknɪs] die <-, -se> *(form)* authority ◊ *seine Befugnisse missbrauchen/überschreiten*; authorization ◊ *eine Befugnis erhalten/erteilen*
be·fugt [bəˈfuːkt] ⟨adj⟩ *no comp/superl (form)* authorized ◊ *Zutritt nur für befugte Mitarbeiter!* ✦ *Ich bin nicht befugt, Informationen zu geben.* zu etw. befugt sein have authorization for sth ◊ *Dieser Betrieb ist nur für Ausbildung von Handwerkern.*
Be·fund [bəˈfʊnt] der <-(e)s, -e> result(s), findings ◊ *ein ärztlicher Befund*
be·fürch·ten [bəˈfʏrçtn̩] <befürchtet, befürchtete,

A B C D E F G H I J K L M N O P Q R S T U V W X Y Z

hat befürchtet> [tr v] fear, be afraid of ◊ *Die Wis-senschaftler befürchteten eine Ausbreitung der Seuche.* ♦ *Er befürchtet, schwer krank zu sein.* ich befürchte, dass I'm afraid that

be·für·wor·ten [bəˈfyːɐ̯vɔʁtn̩] <befürwortet, befürwortete, hat befürwortet> [tr v] approve, support ◊ *ein Projekt/eine Idee befürworten* ⊖zustimmen ⊖ablehnen

be·gabt [bəˈgaːpt] [adj] <begabter, am begabtesten> talented, gifted ◊ *praktisch/mathematisch begabt sein* ♦ *Hoch begabte Schüler müssen besonders gefördert werden.* für etw. begabt sein have a gift/talent for sth ◊ *Das Kind ist sehr begabt für Musik.*

Be·ga·bung [bəˈgaːbʊŋ] die <-, -en> Begabung (für etw.) talent (for sth), gift (for sth) ◊ *Seine künstlerische Begabung ist beeindruckend.* ♦ *eine besondere Begabung für Mathematik/Musik haben*

② **be·gann** [bəˈgan] *pres p of* beginnen

be·ge·ben [bəˈgeːbm̩] <begibt sich, begab sich, hat sich begeben> [ref v] 1. *(lofty)* sich irgendwohin begeben go somewhere ◊ *Er musste sich zur Behandlung ins Krankenhaus begeben.* 2. sich an/auf etw. [acc] begeben commence sth ◊ *sich auf Jobsuche begeben* sich in Behandlung begeben undergo treatment sich auf eine Reise begeben undertake a journey sich auf einen Spaziergang begeben go for a walk 3. sich in Gefahr begeben put yourself in danger sich auf Erfolgskurs begeben take the road to success sich auf einen Irrweg begeben go off on the wrong track 4. *(lit)* etw. begibt sich sth happens, sth occurs, sth comes to pass ◊ *Es begab sich, dass die Tochter des Königs sehr krank wurde.*

Be·ge·ben·heit [bəˈgeːbm̩haɛ̯t] die <-, -en> event, occurrence ◊ *eine amüsante Begebenheit aus seinem Leben schildern*

② **be·geg·nen** [bəˈgeːgnən] <begegnet, begegnete, ist begegnet> [intr v] 1. jdm begegnen meet sb ◊ *Ich bin gestern deinem Lehrer begegnet.* sie begegnen sich they meet ◊ *Wir sind uns doch schon mal irgendwo begegnet?* 2. jdm freundlich/zurückhaltend begegnen be friendly/reserved towards sb ◊ *An manchen Orten ist man uns nicht sehr freundlich begegnet.* 3. einer Sache [dat] begegnen come across sth ◊ *Dieser Meinung begegnet man häufiger bei Jugendlichen.* 4. einer Sache [dat] begegnen respond to sth ◊ *Dieser gefährlichen Entwicklung müssen wir schnell und entschlossen begegnen.*

be·ge·hen [bəˈgeːən] <begeht, beging, hat begangen> [tr v] 1. commit ◊ *ein Verbrechen/einen Fehler begehen* 2. *(lofty)* celebrate ◊ *Das Jubiläum wurde mit einem großen Fest begangen.* ⊖feiern 3. *mostly passive* walk on ◊ *Im Winter kann dieser Weg kaum begangen werden.* ein viel begangener Weg a well-used path

be·geh·ren [bəˈgeːrən] <begehrt, begehrte, hat begehrt> [tr v] 1. desire, wish for, covet ◊ *Sie begehrt ihn seit ihrer ersten Begegnung.* alles, was dein/das Herz begehrt everything your heart desires begehrend longing ◊ *begehrende Blicke* 2. ask for, demand ◊ *Hunderte Fans stehen vor der Tür und begehren Einlass.* Schadensersatz/Unterhalt etc. begehren claim (for) damages/maintenance etc.

be·geis·tern [bəˈgaɛ̯stɐn] <begeistert, begeisterte, hat begeistert> [tr v] 1. etw./jd begeistert jdn sb is enthusiastic about sth/sb, sb is enthralled by sth/sb ◊ *Dieses Musical wird Sie begeistern!* 2. jdn für etw. begeistern fire sb's enthusiasm for sth ◊ *Der Lehrer konnte uns nicht für den Stoff begeistern.* das Publikum begeistern fire the audience [ref v] sich für etw. begeistern get/be enthusiastic about sth ◊ *sich für Sport/Technik begeistern*

Be·geis·te·rung [bəˈgaɛ̯stərʊŋ] die <-> *no pl* Begeisterung (über etw. [acc]) enthusiasm (about sth) ◊ *Er hörte voller Begeisterung zu.* ♦ *Die Begeisterung über den Sieg hielt lange an.* Begeisterung für etw. passion for sth, enthusiasm for sth ◊ *Begeisterung für das Lesen wecken* jdn in Begeisterung versetzen fire sb with enthusiasm in Begeisterung geraten become enthusiastic mit Begeisterung bei der Arbeit sein be enthusiastic/passionate about your work

② **be·gin·nen** [bəˈgɪnən] <beginnt, begann, hat begonnen> [tr+intr v] start, begin ◊ *Es beginnt zu regnen.* ♦ *Hier beginnt unser Grundstück.* ♦ *Wer hat den Streit begonnen?* ♦ *Ich habe mit der Arbeit noch nicht begonnen.; (a speech also)* open ◊ *Sie begann (ihre Rede) mit den Worten: „Liebe Freunde!"* ⊖anfangen

be·glau·bi·gen [bəˈglaʊ̯bɪɡn̩] <beglaubigt, beglaubigte, hat beglaubigt> [tr v] certify, authenticate ◊ *eine Kopie/Übersetzung beglaubigen lassen* notariell beglaubigen notarize eine Unterschrift beglaubigen attest/witness a signature

be·glei·chen [bəˈglaɛ̯çn̩] <begleicht, beglich, hat beglichen> [tr v] settle, pay ◊ *eine Rechnung begleichen*

be·glei·ten [bəˈglaɛ̯tn̩] <begleitet, begleitete, hat begleitet> [tr v] 1. accompany, go/come with ◊ *Ihre Freundin begleitete sie zum Arzt.; escort* ◊ *Die Transporte werden von der Polizei begleitet.* jdn zur Tür begleiten show sb to the door 2. *(fig)* accompany ◊ *Sie sang und er begleitete sie auf dem Klavier.* ♦ *Starke Proteste haben die Verhandlungen begleitet.; be with, follow* ◊ *Diese Erinnerungen begleiten mich mein ganzes Leben lang.; guide* ◊ *Der Tutor begleitet die Studenten während des Kurses.*

Be·glei·tung [bəˈglaɛ̯tʊŋ] die <-, -en> 1. companion(s), entourage ◊ *Der Minister und seine Begleitung wurden herzlich begrüßt.; (for protection)* escort, guard in jds Begleitung, in Begleitung von jdm accompanied by sb, in sb's company ◊ *Sie erschien in Begleitung eines unbekannten Mannes.* ohne Begleitung alone, unaccompanied 2. accompaniment ◊ *Er passte seine Begleitung dem Gesang an.; complement* ◊ *Das Seminar ist als Begleitung zur Vorlesung gedacht.*

be·glück·wün·schen [bəˈglʏkvʏnʃn̩] <beglückwünscht, beglückwünschte, hat beglückwünscht> [tr v] jdn (zu etw.) beglückwünschen congratulate sb (on sth) ◊ *jdn zu seinem Sieg/Preis beglückwünschen* jdn zu seinem Geburtstag beglückwünschen wish sb a happy birthday ⊖gratulieren

be·gna·det [bəˈgnaːdət] [adj, adv] *seldom comp/superl* divine(ly) ◊ *Als Regisseur ist er begnadet.* ♦ *eine begnadete Künstlerin* ♦ *begnadet Klavier spielen* mit etw. begnadet sein be blessed with sth ◊ *mit einem besonderen Talent begnadet sein*

be·gnü·gen [bəˈgnyːɡn̩] <begnügt sich, begnügte

sich, hat sich begnügt> [ref v] sich mit etw.
begnügen content yourself with sth, make do with
sth, be content with sth ◊ *Das Team musste sich
mit Platz drei begnügen.* ✦ *sich mit dem Nötigsten
begnügen* ⊖sich bescheiden

② **be·gon·nen** [bə'gɔnən] *past p of* beginnen

be·gra·ben [bə'gra:bm̩] <begräbt, begrub, hat
begraben> [tr v] **1.** bury ◊ *Sein Großvater wird am
Montag begraben.* ✦ *Die Schlammlawine begrub
ein ganzes Dorf unter sich.* **2.** *(fig)* give up ◊ *seine
Hoffnungen/einen Plan begraben* ⊖aufgeben

Be·gräb·nis [bə'grɛ:pnɪs] das <—ses, —se> burial,
funeral ◊ *Das Begräbnis fand im engsten Familien-
kreis statt.*

be·grei·fen [bə'graefn̩] <begreift, begriff, hat
begriffen> [tr v] understand, grasp, comprehend ◊
Begreifst du, was das für mich bedeutet? ✦ *Sie
begriff den Sinn seiner Worte nicht.* etw. als etw.
begreifen regard sth as sth, see sth as sth ◊ *Er
begreift die Fotografie als Kunst.*

be·gren·zen [bə'grɛntsn̩] <begrenzt, begrenzte, hat
begrenzt> [tr v] **1.** limit, restrict ◊ *Die Dauer wurde
auf zwei Jahre begrenzt.* ✦ *den Stromverbrauch
begrenzen* **2.** mark the boundary of ◊ *Ein hoher
Zaun begrenzt das Grundstück.*

Be·griff [bə'grɪf] der <—(e)s, —e> **1.** term ◊
„*Allergie*" *ist ein medizinischer Begriff.* **2.** concept,
idea, notion ◊ *der traditionelle Begriff der Ehe* ✦
Jeder Begriff von Wahrheit ist relativ. **3.** LAW legal
definition, (legal) notion ◊ *der Begriff des
Vermögens*
◉ **schwer von Begriff sein** be slow on the
uptake **etw. ist jdm ein/kein Begriff** sth means
sth/nothing to sb ◊ *Er hat von GPS gesprochen. Ist
dir das ein Begriff?* **im Begriff sein, etw. zu tun**
be about to do sth ◊ *Sie war im Begriff, das Haus
zu verlassen, als das Telefon klingelte.* **für jds
Begriffe, nach jds Begriff** in sb's opinion ◊ *Das
Essen war für seine Begriffe zu salzig.*

② **be·grün·den** [bə'grʏndn̩] <begründet, begründete,
hat begründet> [tr v] justify, give a reason/reasons
for ◊ *Kannst du diese Meinung denn begründen?*;
(a suspicion, claim) substantiate wie begründet jd
etw. how does sb account for sth, what reason(s)
does sb give for sth ◊ *Wie begründet er sein
langes Schweigen?*

② **be·grü·ßen** [bə'gry:sn̩] <begrüßt, begrüßte, hat
begrüßt> [tr v] **1.** *(also fig)* welcome ◊ *Ich freue
mich, Sie hier begrüßen zu dürfen.* ✦ *Er begrüßte
den Vorschlag.* **2.** greet ◊ *Sie begrüßten einander
mit einem Kopfnicken.*

Be·grü·ßung [bə'gry:sʊŋ] die <—, —en> welcome ◊
*Gegen Mittag ist eine offizielle Begrüßung der
Gäste geplant.* ✦ *jdm zur Begrüßung die Hand
geben* ⊖Abschied

be·güns·ti·gen [bə'gʏnstɪgn̩] <begünstigt, begünstigte, hat begünstigt> [tr v] **1.** encourage ◊ *Ein
lockerer Erdboden begünstigt die Entwicklung der
Wurzeln.*; *(accidents, diseases)* increase the risk
of ◊ *Stress und Müdigkeit begünstigen Arbeitsun-
fälle.* **2.** favour, favor ◊ *Die neue Regelung begünstigt Selbstständige.* steuerlich begünstigt werden
get a tax break **3.** jdn begünstigen benefit sb,
name sb as beneficiary ◊ *Sein Testament begünstigt seine beiden Kinder.*

be·gut·ach·ten [bə'gu:tʔaxtn̩] <begutachtet, begut-

achtete, hat begutachtet> [tr v] **1.** examine ◊ *ein
Fahrzeug begutachten*; *(a house, property)* survey
2. *(fam, also hum)* (have a) look at ◊ *Lass dich
begutachten — hübsch siehst du aus!*

be·hag·lich [bə'ha:klɪç] [adj, adv] comfortable(-
ably), cosy(-ily), cozy(-ily) ◊ *eine behagliche
Wohnung* ✦ *Das Zimmer war sehr behaglich.* ✦ *Wir
saßen behaglich am warmen Ofen.* behaglich
wohnen have a comfortable home

② **be·hal·ten** [bə'haltn̩] <behält, behielt, hat
behalten> [tr v] **1.** keep ◊ *Sie hat das Foto bis
heute behalten.* ✦ *jdn im Krankenhaus/in Haft
behalten* ✦ *seinen Humor behalten*; *(its value
also)* retain ◊ *Behält Gold seinen Wert?*; *(staff)*
keep on ◊ *Die Firma behält trotz der Krise alle Mitarbeiter.*; *(a dream, hope, illusions)* hang on to;
(a disability, scar) etw. (für immer) behalten be
left with sth (for ever) ◊ *Er hat von dem Unfall ein
steifes Bein behalten.* jdn als Freund behalten stay
friends with sb die Nerven behalten not lose your
nerve den Überblick (über etw.) [acc] behalten
keep track (of sth) ◊ *Wie soll man in diesem
Chaos den Überblick behalten?* immer seinen
Willen behalten always have your own way Platz
behalten stay seated, not get up ◊ *Behalten Sie
doch Platz!* den Hut auf dem Kopf behalten keep
the hat on wenn wir das Wetter behalten … if the
weather lasts … **2.** etw. für sich behalten keep
sth to yourself ◊ *Aber behalte das bitte für dich.*
ein Geheimnis behalten keep a secret
3. remember ◊ *Hast du seinen Namen behalten?*;
memorize ◊ *Ich kann nicht so viele Vokabeln auf
einmal behalten.* etw. im Gedächtnis behalten
keep sth in mind, remember sth eine Melodie im
Ohr behalten keep a tune in your head jdn in
guter Erinnerung behalten have fond memories of
sb **4.** *(food, drink)* etw. bei sich behalten keep
sth down ◊ *Der Patient kann nichts bei sich
behalten.*

Be·häl·ter [bə'hɛltɐ] der <—s, —> container, receptacle ◊ *einen Behälter mit Wasser füllen*; *(for
waste)* bin; *(for recycling)* bank ◊ *der Behälter
für Altpapier/Kunststoffe*

② **be·han·deln** [bə'handl̩n] <behandelt, behandelte,
hat behandelt> [tr v] **1.** *in combination with an
attribute* treat ◊ *jdn freundlich behandeln* ✦ *Bitte
behandeln Sie diese Information vertraulich.*; *(in
order to control sb/sth)* handle ◊ *Diese Maschine
muss sorgfältig behandelt werden.* **2.** *(a patient,
disease, an injury)* treat ◊ *Der Patient muss
sofort behandelt werden.* der behandelnde Arzt the
doctor/physician in attendance operativ behandeln
operate (on) **3.** deal with ◊ *Der Film behandelt
das Thema Todesstrafe.* **4.** *(to preserve or heal)*
etw. (mit etw.) behandeln treat sth (with sth) ◊ *Sie
sollten die Wunde mit Jod behandeln.* ✦ *Das Obst
wird mit radioaktiven Strahlen behandelt.*

Be·hand·lung [bə'handlʊŋ] die <—, —en>
1. treatment ◊ *ein internationales Abkommen über
die Behandlung Kriegsgefangener* ✦ *die chemische
Behandlung von Textilien* eine gute Behandlung
genießen be treated well, receive good treatment
2. MED care, treatment, therapy ◊ *eine ärztliche
Behandlung* ✦ *die Behandlung von Krebspatienten*
ambulante/stationäre Behandlung outpatient/
inpatient care/treatment **3.** *(of a topic, problem)*

discussion, treatment ◊ *Für die Behandlung dieser Frage brauchen wir einen ganzen Tag.*

be·har·ren [bəˈharən] <beharrt, beharrte, hat beharrt> [intr v] auf etw. [dat] beharren insist on sth, persist in sth ◊ *auf seinem Standpunkt beharren* ♦ *Sie beharrt darauf, alles richtig gemacht zu haben.*

be·harr·lich [bəˈharlɪç] [adj, adv] persistent(ly) ◊ *Beharrliche Kritik führte zum Erfolg.* ♦ *Sie ist beharrlich und gibt nicht auf.* ♦ *beharrlich schweigen*

② **be·haup·ten** [bəˈhaʊptn̩] <behauptet, behauptete, hat behauptet> [tr v] **1.** *(verbally)* claim, maintain ◊ *Wie kannst du so etwas behaupten?* ♦ *Er behauptet, er habe keinen Fehler gemacht.* **2.** *(successfully)* assert, maintain ◊ *Er konnte den ersten Platz behaupten.* [ref v] sich behaupten assert yourself/your authority ◊ *Sie kann sich bei den Schülern nicht behaupten.*; maintain your/its position ◊ *Wie können wir uns gegen die Konkurrenz behaupten?* ♦ *Das Produkt konnte sich auf dem Markt nicht behaupten.*; *(sports)* win (through)

Be·haup·tung [bəˈhaʊptʊŋ] die <-, -en> **1.** *(statement)* claim, assertion ◊ *eine Behauptung aufstellen/beweisen* **2.** MATH assumption **3.** *(proceedings)* defence, assertion ◊ *die Behauptung der Rechte der Arbeitgeber*

be·he·ben [bəˈheːbn̩] <behebt, behob, hat behoben> [tr v] **1.** remove, rectify, remedy ◊ *einen Fehler/Defekt beheben* einen Schaden beheben repair a damage eine Störung beheben clear a disturbance **2.** *(Austr)* withdraw ◊ *Geld beheben* ⊖abheben ⊖einzahlen

be·herr·schen [bəˈhɛrʃn̩] <beherrscht, beherrschte, hat beherrscht> [tr v] **1.** have mastered, be skilled at ◊ *eine Kunst beherrschen* ♦ *die wichtigsten Office-Programme beherrschen*; *(a language)* have a good command of **2.** dominate ◊ *Die Landwirtschaft beherrschte die Region.* den Markt beherrschen dominate/control the market **3.** *(a country, people)* rule ◊ *Avalon wird von Königin Elaine beherrscht.* **4.** control ◊ *seine Wut beherrschen* ♦ *Er musste sich beherrschen, um nicht zu lachen.*

be·hilf·lich [bəˈhɪlflɪç] [adj] seldom comp/superl, mostly after ns jdm (bei etw.) behilflich sein help sb (with sth) ◊ *jdm bei der Wohnungssuche behilflich sein* ♦ *Wie kann ich Ihnen behilflich sein?*

② **be·hin·dern** [bəˈhɪndɐn] <behindert, behinderte, hat behindert> [tr v] hinder, obstruct ◊ *Behindern dich die langen Fingernägel nicht beim Tippen?* ♦ *den Verkehr/die Sicht behindern*

be·hin·dert [bəˈhɪndɐt] *past p of* behindern [adj] disabled ◊ *Sie haben ein behindertes Kind.* ♦ *geistig/körperlich behindert sein*

Be·hin·der·te [bəˈhɪndɐtə] die <-n, die Behinderten> *but: ein Behinderter/eine Behinderte* disabled person; *(pl)* Behinderte the disabled, people with special needs ◊ *speziell für Behinderte eingerichtete Wohnungen* eine Schule für Behinderte a special needs school *box*@ Substantivierung

Be·hör·de [bəˈhøːɐdə] die <-, -n> authority, office, department ◊ *einen Antrag bei der zuständigen Behörde stellen*; *(as part of a name)* Department

◊ *die Behörde für Wissenschaft und Forschung* eine städtische Behörde a local/municipal authority eine staatliche Behörde a (central) government authority ⊖Amt

be·hut·sam [bəˈhuːtzaːm] [adj, adv] **1.** *when used as an adj, only before ns* careful(ly), cautious(ly) ◊ *eine behutsame Reform des Schulsystems* ♦ *Die Kirche wurde behutsam renoviert.* **2.** *when used as an adj, mostly before ns* gentle(-tly) ◊ *eine behutsame Geste* ♦ *Ihr Umgang mit dem Kind ist behutsam und zärtlich.* ♦ *mit jdm behutsam umgehen*

② **bei** [baɛ] [prep] [+dat] **1.** *(expressing closeness)* near, close to ◊ *Ludwigsburg liegt bei Stuttgart.* ♦ *Bleib bitte beim Gepäck.* ♦ *Er stand bei mir, als es passierte.*; next to ◊ *Ich wohne direkt bei der Kirche.*; at ◊ *Wir treffen uns beim Rathaus.* die Schlacht bei Hastings/Tannenberg the battle of Hastings/Tannenberg bei jdm with sb ◊ *Bleib bei mir!* ♦ *Karla saß bei Thomas im Auto.* **2.** *(in sb's pocket)* bei jdm on sb ◊ *Bei dem Toten wurden keine Papiere gefunden.* etw. bei sich haben have sth on you ◊ *Ich habe kein Geld bei mir.* eine Waffe bei sich tragen carry a weapon **3.** jdn/etw. bei etw. halten/nehmen/packen hold/take/grab sb/sth by sth ◊ *Er nahm mich bei der Hand.* ♦ *Er hielt das Kaninchen bei den Ohren.* **4.** *(in a place)* bei jdm übernachten stay/spend the night at sb's place bei jdm wohnen live with sb/at sb's home ◊ *Carolin wohnt noch bei ihren Eltern.* bei mir/uns zu Hause at home bei uns in Deutschland etc. (back home/here) in Germany etc. ◊ *Bei uns in Bayern sind Traditionen noch wichtig.* ◊ *Bei uns zu Hause in Deutschland/Hamburg* (back home) in Germany/Hamburg bei den Müllers/Smiths at the Müllers'/Smiths' (house); *(in correspondence)* bei ... care of ... ◊ *Tobias Dümmler, bei Veronika Schnorr* **5.** *(in a shop etc.)* beim Bäcker/Arzt etc. at the baker's/doctor's etc. ◊ *Sie ist gerade beim Friseur.* ♦ *Hast du das bei Karstadt gekauft?* bei uns in/at our shop ◊ *Bei uns bekommen Sie besonders günstige Computer.* ein Konto bei einer Bank haben have an account with a bank sich beim Rechtsanwalt/bei einer Kosmetikerin beraten lassen consult a lawyer/beautician; *(in a company, an institution etc.)* bei jdm/etw. arbeiten, bei jdm/etw. (angestellt/beschäftigt/ tätig) sein work for sb/sth ◊ *Er arbeitet bei der Post.* ♦ *Sie ist beim Fernsehen.* beim Militär etc. sein be in the army etc. bei jdm/etw. eine Ausbildung/Lehre machen train/serve your apprenticeship with sb/at sth bei jdm Unterricht/Nachhilfe haben be taught/coached by sb erscheinen bei be published by ◊ *Das Buch ist bei Hueber erschienen.* **6.** *(in literature)* bei Wittgenstein/Shakespeare etc. in Wittgenstein/Shakespeare etc. ◊ *Das habe ich bei Karl Marx gelesen.* bei Goethe/ Schiller etc. heißt es ... Goethe/Schiller etc. says/ writes ... **7.** among ◊ *Bei meinen Papieren befindet sich auch mein Testament.* **8.** *(amount)* der Wert/Preis ... [gen] liegt bei ... sth is worth/ costs about ... ◊ *Der Wert des Ringes liegt bei 500 Euro.* **9.** *(expressing attendance, assistance)* bei etw. sein be at sth ◊ *Ich war bei seiner Hochzeit.* bei etw. mitmachen join sth bei etw. mitarbeiten collaborate on sth bei etw. (mit)helfen help with

sth ◊ *Ich habe ihr bei der Übersetzung geholfen.*
bei etw. mitwirken be involved in sth; *(in a theatre play etc.)* appear in sth ◊ *Er hat bei der Vorstellung mitgewirkt.* **10.** *temporal* at ◊ *Sie stand das Sonnenaufgang auf.* ♦ *Bei Beginn der Veranstaltung waren wir noch nicht da.*; *(during, at the latest)* by ◊ *bei Tag/Nacht arbeiten* ♦ *Wir wollen bei Einbruch der Nacht wieder zurück sein.*; *(referring to a precise point of time)* on ◊ *Beim Glockenschlag ist es 12 Uhr.* **11.** *(referring to circumstances)* bei Regen/Nebel/Schnee in rain/fog/snow ◊ *Bei Regen sollte man vorsichtig fahren.* bei (einem) Unwetter in/during a storm bei Straßenglätte when the road is slippery bei fünf Grad unter null at five degrees below zero bei offenem Fenster with the window open bei Kerzenlicht/Mondschein by candlelight/moonlight bei Gefahr in case of emergency ◊ *Bei Gefahr Notbremse ziehen!* beim Essen sein be having lunch/dinner/supper etw. bei etw. tun do sth during sth/while/when doing sth ◊ *Bei der Überprüfung des Wagens haben wir folgende Schäden festgestellt.* ♦ *Er verliert beim Kartenspielen immer.* **12.** *(referring to a cause)* in ◊ *Er ist bei einem Unfall ums Leben gekommen.* ♦ *Bei diesem Vulkanausbruch wurden mehrere Dörfer zerstört.* **13.** *(referring to a precondition)* with ◊ *Bei meinem Einkommen kann ich mir so ein Auto nicht leisten.* ♦ *Bei ihrer Schönheit hat sie sicher viele Bewunderer.*; *(if sth happens)* in case of, in the event of ◊ *Bei schlechtem Wetter fällt das Spiel aus.* **14.** *(as regards sb/sth)* with ◊ *Er kommt bei Frauen gut an.* ♦ *Das ist bei ihr nicht der Fall.* ♦ *Man weiß bei ihr nie, ob sie es ernst meint.* ♦ *Bei meinem Computer funktioniert das nicht.* etw. ist bei etw./jdm verbreitet sth is common/frequent in sth/sb ◊ *Bei Hunden ist diese Krankheit sehr verbreitet.* bei mir ist Schluss für heute I call it a day Wie viel Uhr ist es bei dir? What time do you make it? **15.** in spite of, despite ◊ *Bei aller Vorsicht kann dennoch mal etwas passieren.* bei allem Verständnis, bei aller Liebe much as I sympathize ◊ *Bei aller Liebe, das kann ich nicht dulden.* beim besten Willen nicht not with the best will in the world **16.** *(in vows, incantations)* bei Gott by god ◊ *Ich schwöre bei Gott ...* bei meiner Ehre upon my hono(u)r ⊛ nicht ganz bei sich sein be out of your mind wieder bei sich sein have come round ◊ *Der Patient ist noch nicht wieder bei sich.*

bei|... ['baɛ] (prefix) *translation varies (often expresses addition)* einer Sache (dat) etw. (dat) beimischen add sth to sth Dem Brief war ein Formular beigelegt. A form was enclosed in the letter. einem Verein beitreten become a member in a club jdm etw. beibringen teach sb sth

bei|be·hal·ten ['baɛbəhaltn̩] <behält bei, behielt bei, hat beibehalten> (tr v) keep ◊ *eine Regelung beibehalten*

bei|brin·gen ['baɛbrɪŋən] <bringt bei, brachte bei, hat beigebracht> (tr v) **1.** jdm etw. beibringen teach sb sth ◊ *einem Kind Englisch beibringen* ♦ *Ich habe mir das Klavierspielen selbst beigebracht.* **2.** *(bad news)* jdm etw. beibringen break sth to sb ◊ *Er versuchte ihm behutsam beizubringen, dass seine Mutter krank war.* **3.** *(lofty)* *(an injury)* jdm/sich etw. beibringen inflict sth on sb/

yourself ◊ *sich eine Verletzung beibringen* **4.** *(form)* *(a proof, receipt)* provide, supply, produce ◊ *Beweismittel/Unterlagen beibringen*

Beich·te ['baɛçtə] die <–, –n> confession ◊ *zur Beichte gehen* ♦ *Der Richter hörte sich die Beichte des Angeklagten an.* vor/bei jdm die Beichte ablegen make your confession to sb jdm die Beichte abnehmen hear sb's confession

② **beid·...** [baɛt] (prefix) *(referring to both parts of a pair)* (on/with) both ... ◊ *beidseitig gelähmt* ♦ *ein Blatt Papier beidseitig beschreiben* beidhändig ambidextrous; *(tennis)* beidhändig spielen play with both hands

② **bei·de¹** ['baɛdə] (det) **1.** both ◊ *Beide Programme sind gleich gut.* ♦ *Ein Kind braucht beide Eltern.* ♦ *auf beiden Seiten des Flusses* **2.** *after the definite article or possessive determiner* two, both ◊ *ein Vergleich der beiden Abbildungen* ♦ *Die beiden Bücher, die du mir geliehen hast, sind langweilig.* Die beiden Männer sind gefasst worden. Both (the) men/the two men have been caught. meine beiden Brüder/Schwestern both my/my two brothers/sisters zwischen den beiden Weltkriegen between the (two) world wars alle beiden Teller/Kinder/Tage both (the) plates/children/days

② **bei·de²** ['baɛdə] (pron) **1.** *without the article* both, the two (of them) ◊ *Ich habe Elke und Tim eingeladen; beide sind gekommen.* ♦ *Da sind zwei Artikel — machen Sie bitte von beiden Kopien!* wir beide the two/both of us, we both ◊ *Wir beide(n) wollen heiraten.* ♦ *Wir arbeiten beide in der gleichen Firma.* ♦ *Das hat uns beiden gefallen.* Wer von uns beiden? Who of us (two)? ihr beide(n) you two ◊ *Habt ihr beide(n) euch entschieden?* ♦ *Ich habe speziell euch beide gemeint.* alle beide both of them ◊ *Ich habe alle beide gelesen.* keiner/keine/keines etc. von beiden neither (of them) ◊ *Ich möchte mit keinem von beiden in den Urlaub fahren.* **2.** *with the article* die/diese/jene beiden the/these/those two ◊ *Was unterscheidet die beiden?* ♦ *Ich nehme diese beiden.* ⊛ wie wär's mit uns beiden *(fam)* how about it ◊ *Er sprach mich in der Disko an: „Na, wie wär's mit uns beiden?"*

bei·des ['baɛdəs] (pron) *no gen* both ◊ *Beides ist schön.* ♦ *Du kannst nur eines von beiden haben.*

bei·ei·nan·der [baɛ|aɛ'nandə] (adv) **1.** together ◊ *beieinander sitzen und sich unterhalten* eng/dicht/nah beieinander sein/liegen be close together/to each other ◊ *Die beiden Städte liegen nah beieinander.* **2.** *(fam)* *(health)* gut/schlecht beieinander sein be in good/bad shape

Bei·fah·rer ['baɛfaːrɐ] der <–s, –>, **Bei·fah·re·rin** ['baɛfaːrərɪn] die <–, –nen> *(in a car)* (front-seat) passenger; *(as a job)* co-driver; *(on a motorbike)* pillion passenger; *(in a sidecar)* sidecar passenger

Bei·fall ['baɛfal] der <–(e)s> *no pl* applause, cheers, cheering ◊ *Es gab viel Beifall für seine Rede.* Beifall klatschen applaud, clap ⊛ Beifall ernten/finden meet with approval ◊ *Mit seiner Idee erntete er wenig Beifall.*

Bei·hil·fe ['baɛhɪlfə] die <–, –n> **1.** *(financial)* eine Beihilfe (zu etw.) an allowance (for sth), grant (for sth) ◊ *eine Beihilfe in Höhe von 10 000 Euro* **2.** *no pl* LAW Beihilfe (zu etw.) (being an)

accessory (to sth), aiding and abetting (sth) ◊ *Er wurde wegen Beihilfe zum Mord verurteilt.* zu einem Verbrechen Beihilfe leisten be an accessory to a crime, aid and abet a crime Beihilfe zum Freitod *assistance in suicide*

Bei·la·ge ['baela:gə] die <-, –n> **1.** supplement, insert ◊ *Als Beilage zum Buch gibt es einen Stadtplan.* **2.** side dish/order ◊ *Als Beilage gab es Kartoffeln.* ✦ *Sie hat ein Schnitzel mit Beilagen bestellt.* **3.** *(Austr, Swiss)* enclosure ◊ *Mehr Informationen sind in der Beilage angegeben.* ⊖Anlage

bei·läu·fig ['baelɔøfɪç] [adj, adv] *seldom comp/superl* casual(ly), (in) passing ◊ *eine beiläufige Bemerkung* ✦ *Die Frage war eher beiläufig.* ✦ *etw. beiläufig erwähnen* etw. interessiert jdn nur beiläufig sb has only a passing interest in sth

Bei·leid ['baelaet] das <-(e)s> *no pl* sympathy ◊ *Mein Beileid gilt den Betroffenen.* herzliches/aufrichtiges Beileid sincere condolences jdm sein Beileid aussprechen/ausdrücken offer sb your condolences

beim [baem] [contract] *bei + dem* **1.** near the, close to the ◊ *die Bushaltestelle beim Königsplatz* beim Arzt/Bäcker etc. at the doctor's/baker's etc. beim Militär in the army → bei **2.** *with nominalized verbs, not to be split* during, while, when ◊ *Beim Arbeiten mag sie keine Musik.* jdm beim Singen zuhören listen to sb singing Ich war gerade beim Aufräumen, als er kam. I was just tidying up when he arrived. **3.** *in certain idioms, not to be split:* look up the relevant idiom ◊ *beim Alten bleiben*

② **Bein** [baen] das <-(e)s, -e> leg ◊ *Er hat sich ein Bein gebrochen.* ✦ *Hosen mit weiten Beinen* ✦ *Der Hocker hat drei Beine.*

⊛ mit beiden Beinen auf der Erde stehen have both feet firmly on the ground mit einem Bein im Gefängnis stehen *be likely to end up in jail* mit einem Bein im Grab stehen have one foot in the grave gut auf den Beinen sein *be a good/fast walker* ◊ *Meine Oma war auch mit achtzig noch gut auf den Beinen.* mit dem linken Bein zuerst aufgestanden sein *(fam)* have got out of bed on the wrong side auf schwachen Beinen stehen rest on shaky foundations ◊ *Dein Vorwurf steht auf schwachen Beinen.* wackelig auf den Beinen sein be wobbly sich [dat] kein Bein ausreißen *(fam)* not overstrain/overexert yourself ◊ *Bei dem Aufsatz hast du dir aber kein Bein ausgerissen!* sich [dat] etw. ans Bein binden lassen, jdn/etw. am Bein haben *(fam)* be saddled with sth ◊ *viel Verantwortung am Bein haben* jd kann sich kaum noch auf den Beinen halten sb can hardly stand up jdm Beine machen *(fam)* **1.** chase sb away ich werde dir/euch Beine machen clear off (or else) **2.** put pressure on sb ich werde dir/euch Beine machen I'll make you work ◊ *Die Fünf in Englisch muss weg, ich werde dir schon Beine machen!* auf den Beinen sein be on your feet ◊ *Ich bin heute schon seit fünf Uhr auf den Beinen.* etw. auf die Beine stellen start sth, put sth together ◊ *Sie hat das Projekt ganz allein auf die Beine gestellt.* jdm ein Bein stellen trip sb up sich [dat] die Beine vertreten stretch your legs

bei·nah [bae'na:, '– –], **bei·na·he** [bae'na:ə] [adv] almost, nearly ◊ *Die Hausaufgaben sind beinahe*

fertig. ✦ *Beinah tausend Personen kamen.* ⊖fast, nahezu

be·in·hal·ten [bə'ɪnhaltn̩] <beinhaltet, beinhaltete, hat beinhaltet> [trv] **1.** include ◊ *Der Zimmerpreis beinhaltet das Frühstück.* **2.** contain ◊ *Viele Nahrungsmittel beinhalten künstliche Aromen.*

bei·sam·men [bae'zamən] [adv] **1.** together ◊ *Sie saßen in einer gemütlichen Runde beisammen.* **2.** next to each other ◊ *Sie lagen beisammen auf dem Sofa.* **3.** beisammen sein have been collected ◊ *1200 Unterschriften sind bisher beisammen.* **4.** *(money)* beisammen sein have been saved ◊ *Bald habe ich das Geld für ein neues Auto beisammen.* **5.** gut/schlecht beisammen sein be in good/bad shape ◊ *Der Patient ist heute schlecht beisammen.*

Bei·sein ['baezaen] das <-s> *no pl* in jds Beisein, im/unter Beisein von jdm in the presence of sb ◊ *Im Beisein zahlreicher Gäste wurde das Jubiläum gefeiert.* ohne jds Beisein in the absence of sb ◊ *Er wurde ohne Beisein seines Anwaltes vernommen.*

bei·sei·te [bae'zaetə] [adv] aside etw. beiseite legen/stellen/nehmen put sth aside ◊ *Kleine Knödel formen und beiseite legen.*

⊛ beiseite lassen **1.** ignore, disregard ◊ *einen Aspekt beiseite lassen* **2.** leave behind ◊ *den Alltagsstress beiseite lassen* jdn beiseite nehmen take sb aside ◊ *Sie nahm ihre Tochter beiseite und führte ein ernstes Gespräch mit ihr.* etw. beiseite räumen *(obstacles)* remove sth *(inhibitions, reservations)* dispel sth etw. beiseite schaffen hide sth (away) ◊ *Es heißt, er habe eine Million beiseite geschafft.* etw. beiseite schieben **1.** dismiss sth ◊ *Er schob meine Zweifel beseite.* **2.** push aside/to the side, move sth aside/to the side ◊ *Schieb dein Fahrrad beiseite!*

② **Bei·sel** ['baezl] das <-s, –n> *(Austr)* pub, bar ◊ *Nach der Arbeit gehen wir in ein Beisel auf ein Glas Wein.*

Bei·set·zung ['baezɛtsʊŋ] die <-, –en> burial, interment ◊ *die Beisetzung der sterblichen Überreste; (ceremony)* funeral

② **Bei·spiel** ['baeʃpi:l] das <-(e)s, -e> example ◊ *Sein Verhalten sollte uns allen ein Beispiel sein.* ✦ *„Ansehen" ist ein Beispiel für ein trennbares Verb.* mit gutem Beispiel vorangehen set an example sich ein Beispiel an jdm nehmen, jds Beispiel folgen follow sb's example ◊ *Du könntest dir ruhig an deinem Bruder ein Beispiel nehmen.*

⊛ (wie) zum Beispiel for example, for instance, such as ◊ *Säugetiere, wie zum Beispiel Wale, bringen lebende Junge zur Welt.*

bei·spiel·haft ['baeʃpi:lhaft] [adj] *seldom comp/superl* exemplary ◊ *ein beispielhafter Einsatz der Rettungsschwimmer* ✦ *Dieses Ergebnis ist beispielhaft für seine Leistungen.* [adv] in an exemplary way ◊ *Sie hat sich immer beispielhaft für Arme eingesetzt.*

bei·spiel·los ['baeʃpi:lo:s] [adj, adv] <beispielloser, am beispiellosesten> *seldom comp/superl* unique, unprecedented ◊ *eine beispiellose Karriere* ✦ *Diese Fusion ist bisher beispiellos in Deutschland.* eine beispiellos großzügige Geste a gesture of unprecedented generosity beispiellos heftig of unprecedented fierceness; *(negative also)* outrageous(ly) ◊ *mit beispielloser Brutalität* ✦ *Diese Frechheit war*

A B C D E F G H I J K L M N O P Q R S T U V W X Y Z

beispiellos. ♦ *beispiellos grausam*
bei·spiels·wei·se ['baɛʃpiːlsvaɛzə] [adv] for
example, for instance ◊ *Eine häufige Allergie ist bei-spielsweise die Pollenallergie.*
bei·ßen ['baɛsn̩] <beißt, biss, hat gebissen>
[tr+intr v] bite ◊ *Er wurde von einer Schlange gebissen.* ♦ *Komm doch näher, der Hund beißt nicht!* ein Stück aus etw. beißen take a bite from sth in etw. [acc] beißen bite into sth, take a bite from sth jdn/jdm in etw. [acc] beißen bite sb's sth, bite sb in sth ◊ *Sie hat dem/den Angreifer in die Hand gebissen.* auf etw. [acc] beißen bite on sth sich auf die Zunge/Lippe beißen bite your lip/tongue [intr v] **1.** *(fish)* bite ◊ *Heute beißen die Fische nicht gut.* **2.** *(smoke, acid)* sting ◊ *Der Rauch beißt ihm in den Augen.* [ref v] *(colo(u)rs)* sich mit etw. beißen clash with sth sie beißen sich they clash ◊ *Rosa und Orange beißen sich.*
bei|ste·hen ['baɛʃteːən] <steht bei, stand bei, hat beigestanden> [intr v] *in South G, Austr, Swiss often +sein (always jdm beistehen)* stand by sb ◊ *den Trauernden beistehen* ♦ *Seine Frau stand ihm in seiner Krankheit bei.*
② **Bei·trag** ['baɛtraːk] der <‑(e)s, Beiträge> **1.** ein Beitrag (zu etw.) a contribution (to sth) ◊ *ein Beitrag zum Umweltschutz* ♦ *Seine kritischen Hinweise waren ein wertvoller Beitrag.*; *(insurance also)* premium ◊ *der monatliche Beitrag zur Kran-kenversicherung; (for membership)* subscription (fee) ◊ *Der Beitrag für den Sportverein ist monatlich fällig.* einen Beitrag (zu etw.) leisten contribute (to sth), make a contribution (to sth) ◊ *Ich möchte einen Beitrag zum Energiesparen leisten.* **2.** *(in the media)* contribution, article, feature ◊ *Hast du seinen Beitrag in der Zeitung gelesen?*; *(broadcast)* programme, program ◊ *Im Fernsehen kommt ein Beitrag über Wale.*
bei|tra·gen ['baɛtraːgn̩] <trägt bei, trug bei, hat beigetragen> [tr+intr v] (etw. zu etw.) beitragen con-tribute (sth to sth) ◊ *Zu diesem Thema konnte er nichts beitragen.* ♦ *Zum Bau hat die Stiftung mit 12 500 Euro beigetragen.*
bei|tre·ten ['baɛtreːtn̩] <tritt bei, trat bei, ist beige-treten> [intr v] *(always einer Sache* [dat] *beitreten)* **1.** join sth ◊ *Bereits mit 7 Jahren trat er dem Schützenverein bei.* ♦ *einer Partei beitreten*
2. *(into an agreement, a pact)* enter into sth
be·ja·hen [bə'jaːən] <bejaht, bejahte, hat bejaht> [tr v] **1.** (etw.) bejahen say yes (to sth), answer (sth) in the affirmative, give an affirmative answer (to sth) ◊ *Als sie gefragt wurde, ob sie den Ver-dächtigen kenne, bejahte sie dies.* ⊖verneinen
2. *(a project, plan etc.)* etw. bejahen approve sth das Leben bejahen have a positive attitude towards life
② **be·kam** [bə'kaːm] *pret of* bekommen
be·kämp·fen [bə'kɛmpfn̩] <bekämpft, bekämpfte, hat bekämpft> [tr v] **1.** jdn bekämpfen fight sb sich bekämpfen have been fighting (each other) ◊ *Die beiden Stämme bekämpfen sich seit vielen Jahren.* **2.** *(a crime, disease)* etw. bekämpfen fight sth, combat sth ◊ *die Kriminalität bekämpfen; (pests)* control sth ◊ *Schädlinge/Ungeziefer bekämpfen*
② **be·kannt** [bə'kant] [adj] **1.** famous, well-known ◊ *Götz George ist ein bekannter deutscher Schauspie-*

ler. ♦ *Das Ulmer Münster ist weltweit bekannt.* für etw. bekannt sein be known for sth, be famous for sth ◊ *Van Gogh ist für seine Blumenbilder bekannt.* ♦ *Diese Autos sind dafür bekannt, dass sie sehr zuverlässig sind.* ⊖berühmt **2.** familiar ◊ *Auf der Party habe ich kaum bekannte Gesichter gesehen.* es ist bekannt, dass it is a well-known fact that ◊ *Es ist bekannt, dass es nicht so einfach ist,* *Werner zu überzeugen.* ⊖unbekannt **3.** etw. ist jdm bekannt sb knows (about) sth ◊ *Dieses Problem ist uns bekannt.* ♦ *Es war mir nicht bekannt, dass man das so nicht machen soll.* **4.** mit jdm bekannt sein know sb, be acquainted with sb ◊ *Meine Eltern sind mit dem Bürgermeister bekannt.* sie sind miteinander bekannt they know each other mit jdm bekannt werden get to know sb ◊ *Ich bin mit Isa über die Arbeit bekannt geworden.*
⊚ etw. bekannt geben announce sth ◊ *Die Ergeb-nisse werden heute Abend bekannt gegeben.* etw. bekannt machen announce sth, disclose sth ◊ *Der Minister machte gestern bekannt, dass eine Steuer-erhöhung vorgesehen sei.* ♦ *Genaue Details will die Polizei derzeit noch nicht bekannt machen.* jdn mit etw. bekannt machen familiarize sb with sth, tell sb about sth ◊ *Frau Pfaller wird Sie mit dem Projekt bekannt machen.* sie machen sich (mitei-nander) bekannt they introduce themselves ◊ *Ich sehe, Sie haben sich schon (miteinander) bekannt gemacht.* jdn mit jdm bekannt machen introduce sb to sb ◊ *Darf ich Sie mit meiner Frau bekannt machen?*
② **Be·kann·te** [bə'kantə] der/die <‑n, die Bekannten> *but: ein Bekannter/eine Bekannte* acquaintance ◊ *Sie hat viele Bekannte, aber wenig Freunde.*; friend ◊ *Michael ist ein guter Bekannter von mir.* box@ Substantivierung
be·kannt·lich [bə'kantlɪç] [adv] it is well known that ◊ *Bekanntlich fressen Pferde kein Fleisch.*
be·ken·nen [bə'kɛnən] <bekennt, bekannte, hat bekannt> [tr v] **1.** *(lofty)* admit (to), confess (to) ◊ *Er bekannte seine Schuld.* ♦ *Sie bekannte öffent-lich, dass sie sich falsch verhalten hatte.* ⊖einge-stehen **2.** REL seinen Glauben bekennen profess your faith (in sth) [ref v] sich zu jdm/etw. bekennen stand by sb/sth ◊ *sich zu seinen Taten bekennen; (for a scheme, an ideology)* sich zu etw. bekennen declare your support for sth
be·kla·gen [bə'klaːgn̩] <beklagt, beklagte, hat beklagt> [tr v] **1.** *(lofty)* mourn, lament ◊ *Er beklagte den Tod seiner Eltern sehr.* Menschenle-ben waren bei dem Unfall nicht zu beklagen. Nobody was killed in the accident. **2.** lament, bewail ◊ *Sie beklagte den Mangel an Verantwor-tungsgefühl.* [ref v] sich (bei jdm) (über etw. [acc]) beklagen complain (to sb) (about sth) ◊ *Sie beklagten sich beim Hoteldirektor über den Lärm.* ♦ *Dir geht es doch so gut — du brauchst dich wirklich nicht zu beklagen.* ⊖?sich beschweren
Be·klei·dung [bə'klaɛdʊŋ] die <‑, ‑en> *most sing* clothing, clothes ◊ *leichte/warme Bekleidung*
② **be·kom·men** [bə'kɔmən] <bekommt, bekam, hat/ ist bekommen> [tr v] +haben **1.** get ◊ *Ich habe einen Brief von Silke bekommen.* ♦ *Carolin hat in der Englischarbeit eine Zwei bekommen.* ♦ *Er hat dafür viel Lob bekommen.* ♦ *Das kannst du von*

mir schriftlich bekommen. ♦ den Nobelpreis bekommen ♦ Er hat für den Mord „lebenslänglich" bekommen. ♦ Ich habe noch zwei Karten für die Oper/einen Parkplatz bekommen. ♦ Hoffentlich bekommen wir bald besseres Wetter. ♦ Ich habe von meiner Mutter einige Ohrfeigen bekommen. ♦ Sozialhilfe bekommen ♦ Theo bekommt von Frau Schnorr Nachhilfe in Englisch. Glückwünsche bekommen receive congratulations Schwierigkeiten bekommen get into trouble Ärger mit jdm bekommen be in trouble with sb ◊ Wenn du das machst, bekommst du Ärger mit mir. Gäste bekommen have visitors eine Spritze bekommen have an injection jd bekommt Herzklopfen sb's heart races einen Stein an den Kopf bekommen be hit by a stone 2. *with past p* etw. verliehen/überreicht bekommen be given sth ◊ Er hat dafür eine Medaille verliehen bekommen. etw. geschenkt bekommen get sth as a present, be given sth (as a present); *(costs)* jd bekommt etw. erstattet sb's sth will be paid 3. would like ◊ Ich bekomme das Schnitzel und ein kleines Bier. ♦ Ich bekomme drei Kilo Tomaten.; have ◊ Kann ich die Speisekarte bekommen? ♦ Könnten wir noch einen Wein bekommen? 4. *(develop sth)* etw. bekommen get sth, be getting sth ◊ Ich bekomme langsam Hunger. ♦ Rudi hat einen Bauch bekommen. ♦ Das Kind bekommt Zähne. ♦ Die Wand bekommt Risse. ♦ Ich habe noch nie Heimweh bekommen. einen roten Kopf bekommen go red Angst bekommen become afraid Lust bekommen, etw. zu tun (begin to) feel like doing sth 5. get (back) ◊ Ich bekomme von dir noch 6,80 € Porto. 6. *(money)* get, earn, be paid ◊ Was bekommen Sie im Monat? 7. *(give birth or expect to give birth)* have ◊ Meine Schwester bekommt ein Kind. ♦ Mein Hund hat Junge bekommen. 8. achieve ◊ Ich habe bekommen, was ich beabsichtigt hatte. seinen Willen bekommen get your own way Recht bekommen be proved right ◊ Er hat mit seiner Voraussage Recht bekommen. 9. *(a bus, train etc.)* (manage to) catch 10. *(a connection)* get ◊ Ich bekomme leider keine Verbindung mit den USA. Anschluss bekommen make friends, make contacts ◊ Haben Sie in der neuen Stadt schnell Anschluss bekommen? Kontakt zu jdm bekommen be able to contact sb ◊ Wir haben noch keinen Kontakt zu ihm bekommen. 11. *+inf construction* etw. zu ... bekommen get to ... sth ◊ Wir haben auf der Safari viele wilde Tiere zu sehen bekommen. ♦ Wenn ich den zu fassen bekomme, dann kann er was erleben. etwas zu essen bekommen (manage to) get sth to eat (et)was (von jdm) zu hören bekommen get an earful (from sb) ◊ Wenn das dein Vater erfährt, wirst du etwas zu hören bekommen. jds ganze Wut zu spüren bekommen feel the full force of sb's anger/rage 12. etw./jdn irgendwohin bekommen get sth/sb somewhere ◊ Wie bekommen wir das Klavier in den dritten Stock? ♦ Ich habe den Fleck nicht mehr aus dem Pulli bekommen. ♦ Morgens ist er kaum aus dem Bett zu bekommen. 13. *+adj* get ◊ Hast du den Pulli wieder sauber bekommen? jdn satt bekommen feed sb ◊ Wie bekomme ich bloß so viele Leute satt? es satt bekommen, etw. zu tun have had enough of doing sth, be fed up of doing

sth ◊ Ich habe es ganz einfach satt bekommen, immer das Gleiche zu machen. 14. jdn dazu bekommen, etw. zu tun get sb to do sth ◊ Hast du deinen Chef dazu bekommen, dir mehr Geld zu zahlen? [intr v] +sein etw. bekommt jdm (gut) sth agrees with sb ◊ Der Urlaub ist ihr offensichtlich gut bekommen. etw. bekommt jdm nicht/schlecht sth doesn't agree with sb ◊ Das Essen ist mir nicht bekommen. ⊛ es nicht über sich [acc] bekommen, etw. zu tun not be able to bring yourself to do sth ◊ Ich bekomme es nicht über mich, ihm die Wahrheit zu sagen. bekommen Sie schon are you being served ◊ Bekommen Sie schon, oder wollen Sie bestellen?

be·kräf·ti·gen [bə'krɛftɪgn̩] <bekräftigt, bekräftigte, hat bekräftigt> [tr v] 1. confirm ◊ seine Absicht/Meinung bekräftigen etw. mit/durch etw. bekräftigen seal sth with sth, seal sth by doing sth ◊ Die beiden bekräftigten ihre Vereinbarung mit einem Händedruck. seine Aussage durch einen Eid bekräftigen give a sworn statement 2. etw. bekräftigt etw. supports sth, sth strengthens sth ◊ Dies bekräftigt den Verdacht/die Vermutung, dass ... etw. bekräftigt jdn in etw. [dat] sth confirms sb's sth, sth supports sb's sth, sth strengthens sb's sth ◊ Seine Aussage bekräftigte sie in ihrer Entscheidung.

be·küm·mern [bə'kʏmɐn] <bekümmert, bekümmerte, hat bekümmert> [tr v] worry, trouble ◊ Ihr schlechter Zustand bekümmerte ihn. ♦ Es bekümmert mich, ihn so leiden zu sehen.

be·lä·cheln [bə'lɛçl̩n] <belächelt, belächelte, hat belächelt> [tr v] mock, laugh at ◊ eine Antwort/eine Idee/einen Vorschlag belächeln ♦ Wir haben ihn wegen seiner hohen Stimme belächelt.

be·la·den [bə'la:dn̩] <belädt, belud, hat beladen> [tr v] 1. etw. (mit etw.) beladen load sth (with sth) ◊ einen Anhänger mit Kisten beladen ♦ Dieses Gestell darf man nicht zu schwer beladen. 2. jdn/sich (mit etw.) beladen load sb/yourself down (with sth) ◊ Er hatte sich mit Koffern und Taschen beladen.

Be·lag [bə'la:k] der <-(e)s, Beläge> 1. *(on a brake)* pad ◊ Die Bremsen brauchen neue Beläge.; *(on the floor)* covering ◊ Der Fußboden bekommt demnächst einen neuen Belag.; *(on the road)* surface ◊ Der Belag dieser Straße hat zahlreiche Risse. 2. *(of fungus, algae)* layer ◊ Der grüne Belag auf dem Brot ist Schimmel.; *(on copper)* coating; *(on your teeth)* plaque; *(on your tongue)* fur 3. no pl filling ◊ Biskuittorte mit einem Belag aus Aprikosen und Kirschen

be·la·gern [bə'la:gɐn] <belagert, belagerte, hat belagert> [tr v] *(also fig)* MIL besiege, lay siege to ◊ eine Burg belagern ♦ Tausende Fans belagerten den Bühnenausgang.

Be·lang [bə'laŋ] der <-(e)s, -e> 1. only pl concern ◊ Diese Organisation nimmt die Belange von behinderten Menschen wahr. 2. (für jdn) ohne Belang sein be not important (to sb), be unimportant (to sb) ◊ Euer Streit ist für mich ohne Belang. (für etw.) ohne Belang sein be not important (to/for sth) ◊ Das Einkommen des Ehepartners ist für diesen Zuschuss ohne Belang. (für jdn) von Belang sein

be important (to sb) (für etw.) von Belang sein be important (to/for sth)

be·lan·gen [bə'laŋən] <belangt, belangte, hat belangt> ⓣⓡⓥ jdn (für/wegen etw.) belangen prosecute sb (for sth) ◊ *Dafür kann man Sie wegen Betruges belangen!*

be·las·sen [bə'lasn̩] <belässt, beließ, hat belassen> ⓣⓡⓥ **1.** leave ◊ *Stühle/Tische in ihrer ursprünglichen Anordnung belassen* jdn in dem Glauben belassen, dass let sb go on thinking that ◊ *Wir wollen ihn in dem Glauben belassen, dass es seine Idee war.* es dabei belassen leave it at that ◊ *Wenn sie sich entschuldigt, wollen wir es dabei belassen.* **2.** *mostly written* etw. irgendwo belassen leave sth somewhere, not remove sth from somewhere ◊ *Bitte belassen Sie die Handtücher im Hotelzimmer.*

be·las·ten [bə'lastn̩] <belastet, belastete, hat belastet> ⓣⓡⓥ **1.** jdn (durch/mit etw.) belasten burden sb (with sth) ◊ *Ich will dich nicht mit meinen Problemen belasten.* Die Krankheit ihrer Tochter hat sie sehr belastet. Her daughter's illness put her under a great deal of pressure. ⊜entlasten **2.** weigh heavily on, burden ◊ *Eine schwere Schuld belastete ihr Gewissen.*; *(the digestion)* impede ◊ *Zu viel Fett im Essen belastet die Verdauung.*; *(nature, the environment)* pollute ◊ *die Gewässer/Luft/Umwelt mit Giftstoffen belasten* ⊜entlasten **3.** etw. (mit etw.) belasten load sth (with sth) ◊ *Mit wie viel Kilogramm kann man dieses Seil belasten?* **4.** FIN jdn/etw. (mit etw.) belasten charge sb/sth (sth) ◊ *die Bürger mit höheren Steuern belasten* ein Guthaben/Konto belasten debit an account ein Haus mit einer Hypothek belasten mortgage a house **5.** LAW jdn belasten incriminate sb ◊ *Die Aussage des Zeugen belastete ihn schwer.* ⊜entlasten

be·läs·ti·gen [bə'lɛstɪgn̩] <belästigt, belästigte, hat belästigt> ⓣⓡⓥ **1.** jdn (mit etw.) belästigen bother sb (with sth) ◊ *Bitte belästigen Sie mich nicht andauernd.* ◆ *Er wollte sie nicht mit seinen Problemen belästigen.* **2.** harass ◊ *Sie wurde an ihrem Arbeitsplatz sexuell belästigt.*

be·lau·fen [bə'laɔfn̩] <beläuft sich, belief sich, hat sich belaufen> ⓡⓔⓕⓥ sich auf etw. ⓐⓒⓒ belaufen amount to sth ◊ *Der Sachschaden beläuft sich auf 10 000 Euro.*

be·le·ben [bə'le:bm̩] <belebt, belebte, hat belebt> ⓣⓡⓥ **1.** etw. beleben liven sth up ◊ *Konkurrenz belebt das Geschäft.* ◆ *Die kühle Luft belebte mich.* ◆ *Ein wenig Farbe würde diesen Raum beleben.* **2.** jdn beleben refresh sb ◊ *Die kühle Luft belebte mich.* ⓡⓔⓕⓥ **1.** sich beleben be picking up ◊ *Die Konjunktur belebt sich.* **2.** *(face)* sich beleben brighten ◊ *Als sie seinen Namen hörte, belebte sich ihr Gesicht.* **3.** sich beleben get livelier ◊ *Erst am späten Vormittag belebten sich die Straßen.*

Be·leg [bə'le:k] der <-(e)s, -e> **1.** receipt ◊ *Für einen Umtausch benötigen wir den Beleg für den Kauf dieses Geräts.* **2.** evidence ◊ *Für diese Behauptung brauchen Sie Belege.*

be·le·gen [bə'le:gn̩] <belegt, belegte, hat belegt> ⓣⓡⓥ **1.** fill, cover ◊ *ein Brot mit Käse/Wurst belegen* **2.** prove ◊ *Ausgaben mit Quittungen belegen* Können Sie belegen, dass Sie das Kleid

bei uns gekauft haben? Do you have the receipt to prove that you bought the dress in this shop? **3.** occupy ◊ *Im Moment sind leider alle unsere Zimmer belegt.*; *(so that other people are annoyed: the telephone, computer, bathroom)* hog ◊ *Wer belegt denn da schon wieder seit Stunden das Telefon?* **4.** *(a course)* etw. belegen enrol for sth, enroll for sth ◊ *Welche Vorlesungen hast du letztes Semester belegt?* **5.** SPORT occupy ◊ *Rang 1 belegt die russische Läuferin.* den zweiten/dritten etc. Platz belegen come second/third etc. ◊ *Unsere Mannschaft hat den zweiten Platz belegt.* **6.** *(taxes, fines)* jdn/etw. mit etw. belegen impose sth on sb/sth ◊ *Exporte mit hohem Zoll belegen* ◆ *Der Fußballspieler wurde mit einer sechsmonatigen Sperre belegt.*

Be·leg·schaft [bə'le:kʃaft] die <-, -en> workforce ◊ *Von diesen Maßnahmen ist die gesamte Belegschaft betroffen.*

be·leh·ren [bə'le:rən] <belehrt, belehrte, hat belehrt> ⓣⓡⓥ **1.** educate ◊ *Dieser Film will seine Zuschauer unterhalten und zugleich belehren.* **2.** *(pej)* lecture ◊ *Ich lasse mich nicht gern ständig belehren.* **3.** jdn (über etw. ⓐⓒⓒ) belehren inform sb (of sth) ◊ *einen Verdächtigen über seine Rechte belehren;* tell sb (sth) ◊ *Versuch mich nicht zu belehren, was gut für mich ist.* **4.** teach ◊ *Die Großmutter belehrte ihn, dass auch Tiere Schmerzen empfinden können.* ⊙ **jd ist einfach nicht zu belehren** sb never learns ◊ *Manche Menschen sind einfach nicht zu belehren.*

⑦ **be·lei·di·gen** [bə'laedɪgn̩] <beleidigt, beleidigte, hat beleidigt> ⓣⓡⓥ **1.** jdn beleidigen offend sb, insult sb ◊ *Mit der Bemerkung hast du sie zutiefst beleidigt.* ◆ *Nun sei doch nicht gleich beleidigt.* **2.** das Auge beleidigen be an eyesore ◊ *Diese Betonbauten beleidigen das Auge.* jds Ohren beleidigen offend sb's ears

be·leucht·en [bə'lɔçtn̩] <beleuchtet, beleuchtete, hat beleuchtet> ⓣⓡⓥ **1.** illuminate, light (up) ◊ *Das Licht der Kerze beleuchtete ihr Gesicht.* ◆ *eine Bühne mit Scheinwerfern beleuchten* **2.** *(fig)* examine ◊ *Das Verhältnis zwischen Industrie und Politik sollte kritisch beleuchtet werden.*

Bel·gi·en ['bɛlgiən] das <-s> article only in combination with attribute Belgium → Deutschland

Bel·gi·er ['bɛlgiɐ] der <-s, ->, **Bel·gi·e·rin** ['bɛlgiərɪn] die <-, -nen> Belgian → Deutsche

bel·gisch ['bɛlgɪʃ] ⓐⓓⓙ mostly before ns Belgian ◊ *belgische Waffeln*

be·lie·big [bə'li:bɪç] ⓐⓓⓙ arbitrary, random ◊ *ein beliebiges Beispiel* ◆ *Die Reihenfolge der Zahlen ist beliebig.* jeder/jede/jedes beliebige ... any (old) ... ◊ *Ich würde jede beliebige Arbeit annehmen.* ⊜bestimmt ⓐⓓⓥ as you like, according to taste ◊ *ein Gericht, das man beliebig variieren kann* beliebig lang/groß etc. as long/big etc. as you like ◊ *eine beliebig große Anzahl*

⑦ **be·liebt** [bə'li:pt] ⓐⓓⓙ popular ◊ *beliebte Kinderlieder* ◆ *Dieser Lehrer ist bei den Schülern sehr beliebt.* sich (bei jdm) beliebt machen make yourself popular (with sb), endear yourself to sb ◊ *Warum sagst du das? Du willst dich doch nur (bei mir) beliebt machen.* ⊜unbeliebt

be·loh·nen [bə'lo:nən] <belohnt, belohnte, hat

belohnt> [tr v] **1.** jdn (für etw.) (mit etw.) belohnen reward sb (for sth) (with sth) ◊ *Belohnen Sie Ihren Hund, wenn er etwas richtig gemacht hat.*; *(for help, trouble)* repay sb (for sth) (with sth) ◊ *Womit kann ich Sie für Ihre Mühe belohnen?* **2.** etw. (durch/mit etw.) belohnen reward sth (with sth) ◊ *Der Einsatz des Sportlers wurde mit Gold belohnt.*

be·lü·gen [bə'ly:ɡn̩] <belügt, belog, hat belogen> [tr v] jdn belügen lie to sb ◊ *Warum hast du mich belogen?* sich selbst belügen delude yourself, kid yourself ◊ *Wenn du dir einredest, dass er zu dir zurückkommt, belügst du dich selbst.*

be·män·geln [bə'mɛŋəln] <bemängelt, bemängelte, hat bemängelt> [tr v] etw. (an/etw.) bemängeln criticize (sb's/sth's) sth ◊ *Meine Mutter bemängelt immer die Unordnung in meinem Zimmer.* an etw. [dat] gibt es nichts zu bemängeln I/you can't criticize sth ◊ *An dieser Arbeit gibt es wirklich nichts zu bemängeln.* ⊝beanstanden, kritisieren

ⓩ **be·mer·ken** [bə'mɛʳkn̩] <bemerkt, bemerkte, hat bemerkt> [tr v] **1.** notice ◊ *Hast du den merkwürdigen Geruch bemerkt?* ♦ *Ich habe an seiner Stimme bemerkt, dass es ihm nicht so gut geht.* **2.** notice, realize ◊ *Bemerkt er denn nicht, dass sie ihn belügt?* ⊝registrieren **3.** say ◊ *Dazu möchte ich bemerken, dass das so leicht nicht möglich sein wird.* nebenbei bemerkt by the way ◊ *Nebenbei bemerkt, ich glaube nicht, dass uns das gelingen wird.*

be·mer·kens·wert [bə'mɛʳkⁿsveːɐt, bə'mɛʳkənsveːɡt] [adj] remarkable ◊ *eine bemerkenswerte Leistung* ♦ *Sein Einsatz für dieses Projekt ist wirklich bemerkenswert.* [adv] remarkably, unusually ◊ *Für eine Anfängerin spielt sie bemerkenswert gut Klavier.*

Be·mer·kung [bə'mɛʳkʊŋ] die <-, -en> **1.** remark, comment, observation ◊ *eine treffende Bemerkung* eine Bemerkung (zu etw.) abgeben/machen comment (on sth) *Wenn ich mir eine Bemerkung erlauben darf: ... If I may be allowed to comment, ...* **2.** *(written)* comment ◊ *Er hatte einige Bemerkungen an den Rand geschrieben.*

be·mit·lei·den [bə'mɪtlae̯dn̩] <bemitleidete, bemitleidete, hat bemitleidet> [tr v] *(also pej)* pity ◊ *Als Behinderter man oft bemitleidet.* sich selbst bemitleiden feel sorry for yourself

ⓩ **be·mü·hen** [bə'my:ən] <bemühte, bemühte, hat bemüht> [ref v] **1.** sich bemühen try ◊ *In letzter Zeit bemüht er sich wirklich in der Schule.* bemühen Sie sich nicht please don't put yourself out ◊ *Bemühen Sie sich nicht, ich finde den Weg schon allein.* sich bemühen, etw. zu tun try to do sth ◊ *Er bemüht sich sehr, mich zu verstehen.* sich um etw. bemühen try to get sth ◊ *Sie bemüht sich um eine neue Stelle.* **2.** sich um jdn bemühen go through a lot of trouble for sb ◊ *Sie bemüht sich sehr um ihre Schüler.*; *(an injured or sick person)* take care of sb ◊ *Drei Sanitäter bemühten sich um den Verletzten.* **3.** sich um jdn bemühen court sb, woo sb ◊ *Er bemüht sich seit Jahren um sie, aber sie ist nicht an ihm interessiert.* [tr v] jdn bemühen call sb in ◊ *In dieser Angelegenheit sollten wir einen Spezialisten bemühen.*

be·nach·bart [bə'naxba:ʳt] [adj] *no comp/superl*

neighbouring, neighboring ◊ *eine benachbarte Familie* benachbart sein be neighbours, be neighbors ◊ *Wir sind seit Jahren benachbart und verstehen uns gut.*

be·nach·rich·ti·gen [bə'na:xrɪçtɪɡn̩] <benachrichtigt, benachrichtigte, hat benachrichtigt> [tr v] jdn (von etw.) benachrichtigen inform sb (of sth), notify sb (of sth) ◊ *Wen sollen wir im Falle eines Unglücks benachrichtigen?* ♦ *Er benachrichtigte die Polizei von dem Einbruch.*

be·nach·tei·li·gen [bə'na:xtae̯lɪɡn̩] <benachteiligt, benachteiligte, hat benachteiligt> [tr v] jdn benachteiligen discriminate against sb ◊ *Unsere Gesellschaft benachteiligt oft ältere Menschen.* jdn (gegenüber jdm) benachteiligen treat sb worse (than sb) ◊ *Sie fühlte sich gegenüber ihrer Schwester von den Eltern benachteiligt. She felt that her parents favoured/favored her sister.* ⊛bevorzugen

be·neh·men [bə'ne:mən] <benimmt, benahm, hat benommen> [ref v] **1.** sich anständig/gut/schlecht etc. benehmen behave properly/well/badly etc. ◊ *Die Kinder haben sich unmöglich benommen.* ♦ *Manchmal benimmst du dich wie ein kleines Kind!* **2.** sich benehmen behave (yourself) ◊ *Wenn er betrunken ist, kann er sich einfach nicht benehmen.*

be·nei·den [bə'nae̯dn̩] <beneidet, beneidete, hat beneidet> [tr v] jdn (um/wegen etw.) beneiden envy sb (their sth), be envious (of sb's sth) ◊ *Seine Kollegen beneiden ihn um seinen Erfolg.* ♦ *jdn wegen seiner besonderen Fähigkeiten beneiden* ⓔ nicht zu beneiden sein not be in an enviable position

be·no·ten [bə'no:tn̩] <benotet, benotete, hat benotet> [tr v] mark, grade, give a mark (to), a grade (to) ◊ *Wird das mündliche Referat in diesem Kurs auch benotet?* etw. mit etw. benoten give sth sth, award sth sth ◊ *Beim Wettkampf wurde die Turnerin mit zehn Punkten benotet.*

be·nö·ti·gen [bə'nø:tɪɡn̩] <benötigt, benötigte, hat benötigt> [tr v] need ◊ *Die Lebensmittel werden dringend benötigt.* ♦ *Für die Einreise in dieses Land benötigen Sie ein Visum.* ⊝brauchen

ⓩ **be·nut·zen** [bə'nʊtsn̩] <benutzt, benutzte, hat benutzt> [tr v] **1.** etw. (als etw.) benutzen use sth (as sth) ◊ *Zur Erstellung des Textes benutzen wir eine neue Software.* ♦ *Kann ich mal dein Faxgerät benutzen?* ♦ *Die Bahn wird immer seltener benutzt.* ♦ *Motorradfahrer benutzen diese Straße als Abkürzung.* ♦ *Welche Zahnpasta benutzt du?* ♦ *Zum Backen benutzt sie Margarine statt Butter.* ♦ *Ich habe für die Übersetzung ein Wörterbuch benutzt.* ♦ *Dürfte ich mal Ihre Toilette benutzen?* etw. zu etw. benutzen use sth to do sth, use sth for sth ◊ *Ich benutze das Auto hauptsächlich dazu, Leo in die Schule zu fahren.* **2.** *(esp pej)* jdn (als etw.) benutzen use sb (as sth) ◊ *Er benutzt dich nur als Babysitter.* jdn zu etw. benutzen use sb to do sth ◊ *Du benutzt mich dazu, dich finanziell abzusichern!* **3.** die Gelegenheit benutzen, etw. zu tun take the opportunity to do sth ◊ *Sie benutzte die Gelegenheit, um mal wieder gründlich zu putzen.* **4.** *(pej)* etw./jdn als Vorwand/Ausrede benutzen use sth/sb as an excuse ◊ *Sie benutzt ihre kranke Mutter als Ausrede, um keine Hausauf-*

gaben machen zu müssen.

② **Ben·zin** [bɛn'tsiːn] das <-s> *no pl* **1.** petrol, gasoline, gas ◇ *bleifreies Benzin tanken* ♦ *Fährt das Auto mit Benzin oder Diesel?* **2.** (lighter) fuel ◇ *In meinem Feuerzeug ist kein Benzin mehr.*

② **be·o·bach·ten** [bə|'oːbaxtn̩] <beobachtet, beobachtete, hat beobachtet> tr v **1.** watch, observe ◇ *Hast du beobachtet, wie er das gemacht hat?* ♦ *Sie beobachtete die Vögel mit dem Fernglas.* ♦ *Die Polizei lässt ihn beobachten.* ♦ *Irgendwie fühle ich mich beobachtet.* ♦ *Er soll ins Krankenhaus, wo ihn die Ärzte einige Zeit beobachten wollen.* **2.** observe, notice ◇ *Bei diesem Experiment kann man beobachten, wie sich Kohlendioxid auf Pflanzen auswirkt.* ♦ *Ich beobachte mit Sorge, dass deine Noten schlechter geworden sind.* ⊜sehen

② **be·quem** [bə'kveːm] adj **1.** comfortable ◇ *bequeme Kleidung* ♦ *Ein Anorak ist beim Wandern bequemer als ein Mantel.* ⊜unbequem **2.** convenient ◇ *Das wäre die bequemste Lösung.* **3.** (pej) lazy ♦ *Er war wieder mal zu bequem, das selber zu erledigen.* adv comfortably ◇ *Sie haben sich ihre Wohnung sehr bequem eingerichtet.; (chair, sofa)* auf etw. dat sitzt es sich bequem sth is comfortable ◇ *Auf diesem Stuhl sitzt es sich bequem.* sein Leben so bequem wie möglich gestalten make your life as comfortable as possible ⊛ **machen Sie es sich bequem** take a seat, make yourself comfortable

② **be·ra·ten** [bə'raːtn̩] <berät, beriet, hat beraten> tr v **1.** jdn beraten advise sb ◇ *Ich brauche einen neuen Kühlschrank. Kannst du mich beraten?* jdn gut beraten give sb (some) good advice ◇ *Die Verkäuferin hat mich sehr gut beraten.* sich von jdm beraten lassen consult sb, seek the advice of sb ◇ *Wir lassen uns von einem Rechtsanwalt beraten lassen.* **2.** etw. beraten discuss sth ◇ *Wir beraten noch, was wir machen sollen.* ♦ *Der Gesetzentwurf wird noch im Bundestag beraten.* ♦ *Das muss ich mit meinen Eltern beraten.* intr v discuss (sth) ◇ *Die Ärzte beraten noch.* über etw. acc beraten discuss sth ◇ *Die EU-Außenminister beraten über die Lage in Nahost.* ref v sich mit jdm beraten consult sb ◇ *In dieser Angelegenheit muss ich mich mit meinem Anwalt beraten.* ⊛ **gut/schlecht beraten sein** be well/ill-advised ◇ *Der Patient ist gut beraten, sich einen anderen Arzt zu suchen.* ♦ *Mit diesem Gerät war er schlecht beraten, es ist dauernd kaputt.*

Be·ra·tung [bə'raːtʊŋ] die <-, -en> **1.** advice ◇ *ärztliche Beratung* ♦ *Nach einer ausführlichen Beratung schlossen sie den Vertrag ab.* **2.** discussion ◇ *Die Richter ziehen sich zur Beratung zurück.* ♦ *Die Beratungen dauern noch an.* **3.** information centre, information center ◇ *Bevor Sie eine Abtreibung vornehmen lassen, müssen Sie eine Beratung aufsuchen.* ⊜Beratungsstelle

be·rau·ben [bə'raʊbm̩] <beraubt, beraubte, hat beraubt> tr v **1.** rob ◇ *Letzte Woche wurde hier ein älterer Mann überfallen und beraubt.* **2.** (lofty) jdn/ein Tier/etw. einer Sache gen berauben rob sb/an animal/sth of their sth ◇ *ein Tier seiner Freiheit berauben* ♦ *Diese Küste wurde durch die Wurstfabrik ihres besonderen Reizes beraubt.*

be·rech·nen [bə'rɛçnən] <berechnet, berechnete,

hat berechnet> tr v **1.** MATH calculate, work out ◇ *Berechnen Sie die Summe aus 14 und 65.* ♦ *die Kosten/den Preis von etw. berechnen* **2.** (jdm) etw. (für etw.) berechnen charge (sb) sth (for sth) ◇ *Für Porto und Verpackung berechnen wir pauschal 4,95 €.* ♦ *Leider muss ich Ihnen den Schaden berechnen.* **3.** etw. für etw. berechnen intend sth for sth ◇ *Dieses Büffet ist für 20 Personen berechnet.; (with expressions of time)* etw. auf etw. acc berechnen intend sth to last (for) sth ◇ *Die Bauzeit wurde auf etwa 8 Monate berechnet.*

be·rech·ti·gen [bə'rɛçtɪɡn̩] <berechtigt, berechtigte, hat berechtigt> tr v (form) jdn zu etw. berechtigen entitle sb to (do) sth ◇ *Diese Karte berechtigt Sie zum Eintritt ins Museum.* intr v **1.** (form) zu etw. berechtigen entitle sb to sth ◇ *Rückfahrkarten berechtigen zu einer Hin- und Rückfahrt.* **2.** zu etw. berechtigen give rise to sth ◇ *Seine gute Laune berechtigt zu der Annahme, dass er gewonnen hat.*

Be·reich [bə'raɛç] der <-(e)s, -e> **1.** area ◇ *Der Zeiger des Druckmessgeräts befindet sich bereits im roten Bereich.* ♦ *Im Bereich des Eingangs haben wir mehrere Lampen angebracht.; (geographical)* region ◇ *eine Pflanze aus den nördlichen Bereichen Europas* **2.** field, sphere ◇ *ein Thema aus dem Bereich der Medizin/Gentechnologie* ♦ *Diese Angelegenheit fällt nicht in den Bereich, für den ich zuständig bin.* ⊛ **im Bereich des Möglichen liegen** be within the bounds/realms of possibility

be·rei·chern [bə'raɛçən] <bereichert, bereicherte, hat bereichert> tr v **1.** etw. bereichern enrich sth ◇ *Kinder bereichern unser Leben.* etw. bereichert jdn sb profits from sth ◇ *Diese Erfahrung hat ihn sehr bereichert.* **2.** only written etw. (um etw.) bereichern add (sth) to sth ◇ *seine Sprachkenntnisse um eine weitere Fremdsprache bereichern* etw. mit etw. bereichern supplement sth with sth, enrich sth with sth ◇ *Bereichern Sie Ihre Ernährung mit Gemüse.* ♦ *Die Schüler bereichern den Unterricht mit eigenen Ideen.* intr v be very rewarding ◇ *Kulturelle Vielfalt kann bereichern.* ref v sich (an jdm/etw.) bereichern make a lot of money (out of sb/sth), profit (from sb/sth) ◇ *Der Betrüger bereicherte sich an seinen Opfern.* ♦ *Er wollte sich am Unglück anderer nicht bereichern.*

② **be·reit** [bə'raɛt] adj *not before ns* **1.** ready ◇ *Ich bin zur Abfahrt bereit.* ♦ *Ist das Essen bereit?* bereit sein, etw. zu tun; zu etw. bereit sein be ready to do sth ◇ *Sind Sie wirklich bereit, dieses Risiko einzugehen?* **2.** prepared, willing bereit sein, etw. zu tun; zu etw. bereit sein be prepared to do sth, be willing to do sth ◇ *Ich bin nicht bereit, unter diesen Bedingungen zu arbeiten.* ♦ *Er scheint zu allem bereit zu sein.* ⊛ **sich zu etw. bereit erklären/zeigen** say that you are prepared/willing to do sth, be prepared/willing to do sth ◇ *Er hat sich bereit erklärt, mir dabei zu helfen.* ♦ *Er zeigte sich zu einem Versuch bereit.* **sich bereit finden, etw. zu tun** be prepared/willing to do sth ◇ *Keiner hat sich bereit gefunden, dieses Projekt zu übernehmen.*

be·rei·ten [bə'raɛtn̩] <bereitet, bereitete, hat bereitet> tr v **1.** give ◇ *Dein Besuch hat mir viel Freude bereitet.* jdm Probleme bereiten cause

problems for sb **2.** *(lofty)* prepare ◊ *Sie ließ sich ein Bad bereiten.*

be·reit|hal·ten [bəˈraɛthaltn̩] <hält bereit, hielt bereit, hat bereitgehalten> [tr v] *etw.* bereithalten have sth ready ◊ *Halten Sie bitte Ihre Reisepässe bereit.* [ref v] sich (für etw.) bereithalten be ready (for sth) ◊ *Ich halte mich für den Einsatz bereit.*

be·reits [bəˈraɛts] [adv] **1.** as early as ◊ *Ich reise früher als geplant und fliege bereits in einer Stunde.*; already ◊ *Er ist erst 26 Jahre alt und hat bereits promoviert.* ⊜schon ⊜erst **2.** bereits ... sein be already ... ◊ *Als die letzten Gäste gingen, war es bereits hell.* ◆ *Sie ist bereits 45 und hat gerade erst ihr erstes Kind bekommen.* ⊜schon ⊜immer noch nicht **3.** already ◊ *Als wir am Bahnhof ankamen, war der Zug bereits abgefahren.* ◆ *Er war bereits dreimal auf der Buchmesse in Frankfurt.* ⊜schon ⊜noch nicht **4.** even ◊ *Bereits beim Gedanken an die Prüfung bekomme ich Bauchweh.* ⊜schon

Be·reit·schaft [bəˈraɛtʃaft] die <-, -en> **1.** *no pl* willingness, readiness ◊ *Vielen Menschen fehlt die Bereitschaft, sich für andere einzusetzen.* ◆ *ihre mangelnde Bereitschaft zur Mitarbeit* **2.** in Bereitschaft at the ready ◊ *Ein Rettungswagen steht in Bereitschaft.*; *(troops)* on standby ◊ *Die Feuerwehr steht das ganze Jahr über in Bereitschaft.* ◆ *Die Armee ist in Bereitschaft versetzt.* **3.** emergency service ◊ *die Bereitschaften des Roten Kreuzes* Bereitschaft haben be on call, be on duty ◊ *Welcher Arzt hat heute Nacht Bereitschaft?* ⊜Bereitschaftsdienst **4.** emergency team ◊ *Bereitschaften für den Katastrophenfall in Sachsen*

be·reit|ste·hen [bəˈraɛtʃteːən] <steht bereit, stand bereit, hat bereitgestanden> [intr v] *in South G, Austr, Swiss often +sein* be ready, be waiting ◊ *Der Bus stand zur Abfahrt bereit.*

be·reit|stel·len [bəˈraɛtʃtɛlən] <stellt bereit, stellte bereit, hat bereitgestellt> [tr v] **1.** make available, provide ◊ *Die Regierung stellt mehrere Millionen Euro für die Opfer bereit.* **2.** provide, supply ◊ *Auf Gleis 2 wird ein Ersatzzug bereitgestellt.* **3.** provide ◊ *Stellen Sie Informationen zum Thema Gesundheit bereit?* **4.** place ◊ *Stellen Sie den Abfall in gelben Säcken zur Abfuhr bereit.*

be·reit·wil·lig [bəˈraɛtvɪlɪç] [adj] eager, keen ◊ *ein bereitwilliger Zuhörer* ◆ *Die neue Schülerin ist bereitwillig und zuverlässig.* [adv] willingly ◊ *Die alte Dame gab bereitwillig Auskunft.* ◆ *Sie ging bereitwillig auf meine Forderungen ein.*

be·reu·en [bəˈrɔɣən] <bereut, bereute, hat bereut> [tr v] regret ◊ *Ich bereute niemals, dass ich ihn verlassen hatte.* ◆ *Es gibt Dinge in meiner Vergangenheit, die ich sehr bereue.* ◆ *Du wirst deine Tat noch bereuen!*

⊘ **Berg** [bɛrk] der <-(e)s, -e> GEOG **1.** *(also fig)* mountain ◊ *Der Mount Everest ist der höchste Berg der Welt.* ◆ *Er hat schon viele Berge bestiegen.* ◆ *der Gipfel des Berges* ◆ *Berge von Müll* **2.** *only pl* die Berge the mountains ◊ *Im Herbst fahren wir in die Berge.* ◆ *Sie liebt die Berge und das Meer.* ⊛ wenn der Berg nicht zum Propheten kommt, muss der Prophet zum Berg kommen if the mountain won't come to Mohammed, then Mohammed must go to the mountain über alle Berge sein *(fam)* be miles away ◊ *Als die Polizei*

kam, waren die Räuber längst über alle Berge. übern/über den Berg sein be over the worst ◊ *Der Patient ist noch nicht über den Berg.* Berge versetzen (können) (be able to) move mountains ◊ *Mit Wissen kann man Berge versetzen.* ◆ *Glaube kann Berge versetzen.*

Berg·bau [ˈbɛrkbaɔ] der <-(e)s> *no pl* mining im Bergbau arbeiten work in a/the mine

ber·gig [ˈbɛrɡɪç] [adj] mountainous ◊ *Mehr als zwei Drittel Griechenlands sind bergig.* ◆ *eine bergige Landschaft*

⊘ **Be·richt** [bəˈrɪçt] der <-(e)s, -e> report ◊ *Schreib einen Bericht über das Experiment.* ◆ *Laut mehreren Berichten kam es an den Grenzen zu Staus.* ◆ *jdm einen Bericht vorlegen* ◆ *Ein ausführlicher Bericht dazu folgt in der nächsten Ausgabe.* jdm Bericht erstatten report to sb ◊ *Ich muss meinem Chef einmal im Monat Bericht erstatten.*

⊘ **be·rich·ten** [bəˈrɪçtn̩] <berichtet, berichtete, hat berichtet> [tr v] report ◊ *Ich bin zurück und habe viel zu berichten.* ◆ *Gibt es etwas Neues zu berichten?* ◆ *Sie hat uns erstaunliche Dinge berichtet.* [intr v] **1.** (von etw.) berichten give a report (on sth), report ((on) sth) ◊ *Wenn ich zurück bin, berichte ich euch ausführlich.* ◆ *Berichten Sie mir von dem Ergebnis der Verhandlung.* **2.** (von/über etw.) berichten be reporting ((on) sth) ◊ *Unser Korrespondent berichtet aus Paris.* ◆ *Das Rote Kreuz berichtet von vielen Toten.*

be·rich·ti·gen [bəˈrɪçtɪɡn̩] <berichtigt, berichtigte, hat berichtigt> [tr v] jdn/etw. berichtigen correct sb/sth ◊ *einen Fehler berichtigen* ◆ *Ich muss mich berichtigen: ...* ◆ *Er berichtigte den Redner in Bezug auf die Höhe der Verluste.* ⊜korrigieren

be·rie·seln [bəˈriːzln̩] <berieselt, berieselte, hat berieselt> [tr v] **1.** *(esp pej)* jdn mit etw. berieseln expose sb to a constant stream of sth ◊ *Kunden mit Werbung berieseln* ◆ *Im Supermarkt wird man oft mit Musik berieselt.* sich von/mit etw. berieseln lassen allow sth to wash over you **2.** etw. (mit etw.) berieseln sprinkle sth (with sth) ◊ *Da es seit Wochen heiß und trocken ist, berieseln viele Bauern ihre Felder mit Wasser.*

Ber·lin [bɛrˈliːn] das <-s> *article only in combination with attribute* Berlin box@ Stadt

Size: 891 km²; population: approx. 3.38 million. Berlin is a regional capital, a state, and the national capital of Germany. It is the largest city in Germany, and was founded in 1237. From 1961 until 1989, the eastern and western sides of the city were separated by the Berlin Wall. East Berlin was the capital of the GDR. After Reunification, Berlin became the capital of the united Germany.

be·rüch·tigt [bəˈrʏçtɪçt] [adj] notorious ◊ *eine berüchtigte Gegend* ◆ *Er ist berüchtigt für seine Wutanfälle.*

⊘ **be·rück·sich·ti·gen** [bəˈrʏkzɪçtɪɡn̩] <berücksichtigt, berücksichtigte, hat berücksichtigt> [tr v] **1.** etw. berücksichtigen take sth into consideration, take sth into account ◊ *Ist sein Alter bei dem Test berücksichtigt worden?* ◆ *Wenn man berücksichtigt, dass sie keine Erfahrung hat: stellt sie sich sehr geschickt an.* ⊜bedenken **2.** jdn/etw. berücksichtigen consider sb/sth ◊ *Wir werden Ihre Bewerbung berücksichtigen.*

② **Be·ruf** [bə'ruːf] der <–(e)s, –e> job, career ◊ *Welchen Beruf möchtest du später einmal ergreifen?* ♦ *den Beruf des Arztes ausüben* ♦ *den Beruf wechseln* im Beruf in his/her etc. job/career ◊ *Im Beruf hat sie Erfolg.* freie/kirchliche Berufe independent/clerical professions etw. von Beruf sein work as sth ◊ *Sie ist Lehrerin von Beruf.*

be·ru·fen [bə'ruːfn̩] <beruft, berief, hat berufen> [tr v] jdn auf/in etw. [acc] berufen appoint sb to sth, call sb to sth ◊ *jdn in ein Amt berufen* ♦ *jdn auf den Posten des Außenministers berufen* jdn zu etw. berufen appoint sb sth ◊ *Sie wurde zur Vorsitzenden des Ausschusses berufen.* jdn (als etw.) irgendwohin berufen call sb somewhere (as sth) ◊ *Er wurde als Präsident der Europäischen Kommission nach Brüssel berufen.* [ref v] sich auf jdn/etw. berufen refer to sb/sth ◊ *Darf ich mich in der Bewerbung auf dich berufen?* ♦ *Die Verteidigung beruft sich auf ein Gutachten.*
⊛ **sich zu etw. berufen fühlen** feel a calling to be/do sth ◊ *Er fühlte sich schon als Kind dazu berufen, Priester zu werden.* ♦ *Sie fühlt sich zur Sängerin berufen.*

be·ruf·lich [bə'ruːflɪç] [adj, adv] no comp/superl professional(ly) ◊ *jds berufliche Laufbahn* ♦ *Mein Interesse an der Sache ist rein beruflich.* ♦ *Ich habe beruflich viel mit Menschen zu tun.* etw. beruflich machen work as sth, do sth for a living ⊖privat

Be·rufs·schu·le [bə'ruːfsʃuːlə] die <–, –n> ⊖technical college ◊ *eine Berufsschule besuchen* ♦ *auf die/zur Berufsschule gehen*

② **be·rufs·tä·tig** [bə'ruːfstɛːtɪç] [adj] no comp/superl working ◊ *berufstätige Mütter* berufstätig sein work ◊ *Mein Vater ist nicht mehr berufstätig.*

be·ru·hen [bə'ruːən] <beruht, beruhte, hat beruht> [intr v] auf etw. [dat] beruhen be based on sth ◊ *Dieser Film beruht auf einer wahren Begebenheit.* ⊖basieren
⊛ **etw. auf sich beruhen lassen** forget sth, let sth rest ◊ *Lassen wir dieses Versehen auf sich beruhen.*

② **be·ru·hi·gen** [bə'ruːɪgn̩] <beruhigt, beruhigte, hat beruhigt> [tr v] calm (down) ◊ *Er versuchte, das schreiende Kind zu beruhigen.* ♦ *Diese Spritze wird Sie beruhigen.* ♦ *Trink das, das beruhigt die Nerven.* jdn beruhigen reassure sb, put sb's mind at rest ◊ *Ich kann dich beruhigen, dass nichts geschehen.* ♦ *Na, dann bin ich ja beruhigt.* [ref v] sich beruhigen calm down ◊ *Langsam beruhigt er sich wieder.* ♦ *So beruhige dich doch!* ♦ *Die Lage am Arbeitsmarkt hat sich beruhigt.* ♦ *Die Fans wollten sich gar nicht wieder beruhigen.* jd kann sich nicht darüber beruhigen, dass sb cannot get over the fact that

② **be·rühmt** [bə'ryːmt] [adj] famous ◊ *Frankreich ist berühmt für seine Weine.* ♦ *Sting ist ein berühmter Musiker.* ♦ *Wenn ich groß bin, will ich berühmt werden.*

be·rüh·ren [bə'ryːrən] <berührt, berührte, hat berührt> [tr v] **1.** jdn/etw. berühren touch sb/sth ◊ *Ihr Kleid berührte fast den Boden.* ♦ *Seine Hand berührte sie kurz.* ♦ *An den alten Rüstungen im Museum stand: „Bitte nicht berühren."* sie berühren sich they touch ◊ *Ihre Lippen berührten sich sanft.* **2.** mention, touch on ◊ *Das Thema*

Geld wurde im Laufe ihres Gesprächs gar nicht berührt. ⊖ansprechen **3.** jdn berühren affect sb, touch sb ◊ *Die Nachricht vom Tode Ihres Mannes hat mich tief berührt.* **4.** etw. berühren irgendwie sth has a certain effect on sb ◊ *Er war von ihren Worten peinlich/unangenehm berührt.* [ref v] sie berühren sich they coincide, they converge ◊ *Ihre politischen Interessen berühren sich.*

be·sänf·ti·gen [bə'zɛnftɪgn̩] <besänftigt, besänftigte, hat besänftigt> [tr v] jdn besänftigen calm sb down ◊ *Ich konnte meinen aufgebrachten Mann gar nicht mehr besänftigen!* ⊖beruhigen

be·sann [bə'zan] pret of besinnen

Be·sat·zung [bə'zatsʊŋ] die <–, –en> **1.** crew ◊ *Bei dem Flugzeugabsturz kam die gesamte Besatzung ums Leben.* ⊖Mannschaft **2.** no pl MIL occupation army ◊ *Die Besatzung wird abgezogen.*; (period) occupation ◊ *die Besatzung Deutschlands nach dem Zweiten Weltkrieg*

② **be·schä·di·gen** [bə'ʃɛːdɪgn̩] <beschädigte, hat beschädigt> [tr v] damage ◊ *Wer hat mein Auto beschädigt?* ♦ *jds Ruf beschädigen*

be·schaf·fen[1] [bə'ʃafn̩] [adj] no comp/superl irgendwie beschaffen made in a certain way, constructed in a certain way ◊ *Das Gerät ist so beschaffen, dass es sich bei zu großer Hitze abschaltet.*

be·schaf·fen[2] [bə'ʃafn̩] <beschafft, beschaffte, hat beschafft> [tr v] obtain, get (hold of) ◊ *Wie soll ich bloß das Geld für die Miete beschaffen?* ♦ *Dieses Buch ist schwer zu beschaffen.* (jdm/sich) etw. beschaffen get (sb/yourself) sth ◊ *Kannst du mir eine Genehmigung beschaffen?* ♦ *sich Zugang zu etw. beschaffen* ⊖besorgen

② **be·schäf·ti·gen** [bə'ʃɛftɪgn̩] <beschäftigte, hat beschäftigt> [tr v] **1.** occupy ◊ *Kannst du bitte die Kinder beschäftigen?* ♦ *Kannst du dich nicht mal selbst beschäftigen?* **2.** jdn beschäftigen employ sb ◊ *Dieser Betrieb beschäftigt über 1000 Menschen.* **3.** (thoughts, problems) jdn beschäftigen (pre)occupy sb, be on sb's mind ◊ *Dieses Thema/Problem beschäftigt mich sehr.* [ref v] **1.** sich beschäftigen keep yourself busy ◊ *Ich kann mich allein beschäftigen, mir wird es nie langweilig.* ♦ *Sie beschäftigt sich am liebsten mit Gartenarbeit.* **2.** sich mit jdm/einem Tier beschäftigen look after sb/an animal ◊ *Und wer beschäftigt sich mit dem Gast?* ♦ *sich zwei Stunden täglich mit dem Hund beschäftigen* ⊖sich um jdn/ein Tier kümmern **3.** sich mit etw. beschäftigen deal with sth, be concerned with sth ◊ *Wir sind damit beschäftigt, die Ursachen des Unglücks herauszufinden.*; (inwardly) think about sth ◊ *Sie beschäftigt sich viel mit den Problemen anderer.*; (book, article etc.) be about sth ◊ *Der Artikel beschäftigt sich mit Albert Einsteins Theorien.* ⊖sich befassen

be·schäf·tigt [bə'ʃɛftɪçt] past p of beschäftigen [adj] **1.** busy ◊ *Einen Moment — ich bin gerade beschäftigt.* ♦ *ein viel beschäftigter Manager* **2.** irgendwo beschäftigt sein be employed somewhere, work somewhere ◊ *Sie ist bei einer großen Kosmetikfirma beschäftigt.* **3.** mit etw. beschäftigt sein be busy doing sth ◊ *mit der Lösung eines Problems beschäftigt sein* ♦ *Er ist gerade damit beschäftigt, die Koffer für seine*

A B C D E F G H I J K L M N O P Q R S T U V W X Y Z

Reise zu packen.

Be·schäf·ti·gung [bə'ʃɛftɪɡʊŋ] die <-, –en>
1. *most sing* activity, occupation ◊ *Wenn dir langweilig ist, such dir eine sinnvolle Beschäftigung.*
2. employment, job ◊ *einer Beschäftigung nachgehen* ♦ *Er ist seit einigen Monaten ohne Beschäftigung.* **3.** *no pl* die Beschäftigung mit etw. consideration of sth ◊ *Die Beschäftigung mit diesem Thema kostet viel Zeit.* **4.** *no pl* die Beschäftigung mit etw. (sb's) work with sth ◊ *Durch die intensive Beschäftigung mit dem Computer wurde sie bald zur Expertin.*

be·schä·men [bə'ʃɛːmən] <beschämt, beschämte, hat beschämt> [tr v] jdn beschämen put sb to shame ◊ *Seine Freundlichkeit und Hilfsbereitschaft beschämte sie.* ♦ *Du beschämst mich mit deiner Großzügigkeit.*

⑦ **Be·scheid** [bə'ʃaet] der <-(e)s, –e> **1.** notification ◊ *Ich warte noch immer auf einen Bescheid auf meine Anfrage.* ♦ *Wie lautet der Bescheid?* **2.** *no pl* Bescheid von jdm haben/bekommen hear from sb ◊ *Hast du schon Bescheid von ihr?* ♦ *Sie bekommen nächste Woche Bescheid von uns.* jdm Bescheid geben/sagen let sb know, tell sb ◊ *Gib mir Bescheid, wenn du fertig bist.* ♦ *Sag Bescheid, wann du ankommst.* Bescheid wissen know ◊ *Wenn er zwei Wochen lang nicht anruft, dann weiß ich Bescheid.*

⊙ jdm Bescheid sagen/stoßen tell sb what's what ◊ *Es wird Zeit, dass du deinem Chef mal kräftig Bescheid stößt.*

be·schei·den¹ [bə'ʃaedn̩] [adj, adv] **1.** modest(ly) ◊ *Trotz ihres Erfolges ist sie bescheiden geblieben.* ♦ *ein bescheidenes Auftreten* ♦ *„Diesen Erfolg habe ich auch euch zu verdanken", meinte sie bescheiden.* **2.** modest(ly), simple(-ply) ◊ *in bescheidenen Verhältnissen leben* ♦ *Meine Eltern lebten sehr bescheiden.* [adj] **1.** meagre ◊ *Die Bezahlung war eher bescheiden.* ♦ *eine bescheidene Leistung* **2.** *(fam, euph)* awful, dreadful ◊ *Seine Prüfungsergebnisse waren recht bescheiden.* ♦ *Mensch, das ist vielleicht heute ein bescheidenes Wetter!*

be·schei·den² [bə'ʃaedn̩] <bescheidet, beschied, hat beschieden> [tr v] **1.** *mostly adjectival passive and negated* grant ◊ *Seinen Plänen war kein Erfolg beschieden.* ♦ *Das Schicksal hat ihnen keine Kinder beschieden.* **2.** *mostly passive (form)* etw. abschlägig bescheiden turn sth down, reject sth ◊ *Ihr Antrag auf Sozialhilfe wurde abschlägig beschieden.* [ref v] *(lofty)* sich mit etw. bescheiden be content with sth ◊ *Seine Großeltern mussten sich nach dem Krieg mit wenigem begnügen.* ⊖sich begnügen

be·schei·ni·gen [bə'ʃaenɪɡn̩] <bescheinigt, bescheinigte, hat bescheinigt> [tr v] **1.** (jdm) etw. bescheinigen give (sb) written confirmation of sth ◊ *den Empfang eines Briefes/Erhalt des Geldes bescheinigen* **2.** jdm etw. bescheinigen attest sb's sth, certify sb's sth ◊ *Der Arzt hat ihm eine gute Gesundheit bescheinigt.* ♦ *jdm ausgezeichnete Sprachkenntnisse bescheinigen*

be·schei·ßen [bə'ʃaesn̩] *(fam)* <bescheißt, beschiss, hat beschissen> [tr v] jdn (um etw.) bescheißen con sb (out of sth) ◊ *Dieser Gauner hat mich um 100 Euro beschissen!* ♦ *Die haben*

uns ganz schön beschissen. [intr v] cheat ◊ *Ich glaube, er bescheißt beim Kartenspiel.*

be·sche·ren [bə'ʃeːrən] <beschert, bescherte, hat beschert> [tr v] **1.** jdm etw. bescheren give sb sth for Christmas ◊ *Was hat dir denn dieses Jahr der Weihnachtsmann beschert?* **2.** *only written* grant ◊ *Der Tag sollte ihnen noch allerhand Überraschungen bescheren.* [intr v] give sb the (Christmas) presents ◊ *Bei uns wird seit Jahren abends um 6 Uhr beschert.*

be·scheu·ert [bə'ʃɔøɐt] [adj, adv] *(fam)* **1.** stupid(ly) ◊ *Bist du völlig bescheuert?* ♦ *eine bescheuerte Idee* ♦ *Wie kann man sich nur so bescheuert anstellen!* **2.** bad(ly) ◊ *ein bescheuerter Unfall* ♦ *Es ist echt bescheuert, dass du jetzt schon nach Hause musst.* ♦ *Das Jahr hat bescheuert angefangen.*

be·schimp·fen [bə'ʃɪmpfn̩] <beschimpft, beschimpfte, hat beschimpft> [tr v] jdn (mit etw.) beschimpfen swear at sb, hurl abuse at sb ◊ *Die Nachbarn beschimpften ihn mit üblen Ausdrücken.* jdn als etw. beschimpfen call sb a sth ◊ *Sie beschimpften ihn als Verräter.*

be·schis·sen [bə'ʃɪsn̩] *past p of* bescheißen [adj, adv] *(fam)* lousy(-ily), awful(ly) ◊ *beschissene Umstände* ♦ *„Wie geht es dir?" — „Beschissen!"* ♦ *Das Essen schmeckt wirklich beschissen.* ♦ *ein beschissen geschriebener Aufsatz*

be·schlag·nah·men [bə'ʃla:kna:mən] <beschlagnahmt, beschlagnahmte, hat beschlagnahmt> [tr v] **1.** LAW confiscate, seize ◊ *gestohlene Waren beschlagnahmen* ⊖sicherstellen **2.** *(fam)* hog, nab ◊ *Sie hat die ganze Schokolade für sich beschlagnahmt.*

be·schleu·ni·gen [bə'ʃlɔønɪɡn̩] <beschleunigt, beschleunigte, hat beschleunigt> [tr v] speed up, accelerate ◊ *Viel Sonne beschleunigt das Reifen der Tomaten.* seine Schritte beschleunigen quicken your pace das Tempo beschleunigen increase the speed sich beschleunigen accelerate, be accelerated ◊ *Durch das Medikament beschleunigt sich die Heilung.; (sth negative also)* be precipitated ◊ *Die Zerstörung der Regenwälder beschleunigt sich.; (pulse, heart rate)* increase ◊ *Beim Sport beschleunigt sich der Puls/Herzschlag.* [intr v] accelerate ◊ *Das Motorrad beschleunigt in 10 Sekunden auf 0 auf 110 km/h.*

⑦ **be·schlie·ßen** [bə'ʃliːsn̩] <beschließt, beschloss, hat beschlossen> [tr v] **1.** decide (on) ◊ *Die Firma hat die Streichung von hundert Stellen beschlossen.; (a law)* pass ◊ *Das Gesetz muss erst noch vom Bundesrat beschlossen werden.* beschließen, etw. zu tun decide to do sth ◊ *Ich habe beschlossen, nicht mehr zu rauchen.* **2.** *(lofty)* close, end ◊ *Und damit beschließen wir das heutige Programm.* [intr v] make a decision ◊ *Die Regierung hat in dieser Sache noch nicht beschlossen.* über etw. [acc] beschließen decide on sth ◊ *Darüber muss mein Chef beschließen.*

Be·schluss [bə'ʃlʊs] der <-es, Beschlüsse> *(esp form)* decision, resolution ◊ *jdn durch einstimmigen Beschluss ernennen* ♦ *Die Bürger stimmten gegen den Beschluss, den Flughafen zu vergrößern.* ein Beschluss über etw. [acc] a decision on sth einen Beschluss fassen come to a decision mit Beschluss vom ... in accordance with the decision

of …

be·schnei·den [bəˈʃnaedn̩] <beschneidet, beschnitt, hat beschnitten> [tr v] **1.** etw. beschneiden curtail sth ◊ *Die Privilegien der Politiker wurden nicht beschnitten.* jdn in etw. [dat] beschneiden reduce sb's sth ◊ *Durch hohe Steuern werden viele Bürger in ihrem Einkommen beschnitten.*; *(freedom, rights)* restrict sb's sth ◊ *Gefangene in ihren Rechten beschneiden* **2.** *mostly passive* MED, REL jdn beschneiden circumcise sb **3.** BOT prune, trim ◊ *Hecken/Rosen/Sträucher beschneiden* **4.** *(photographs, paper etc.)* cut

be·schrän·ken [bəˈʃrɛŋkn̩] <beschränkt, beschränkte, hat beschränkt> [tr v] **1.** limit ◊ *die Ausfuhr/Einfuhr ausländischer Produkte beschränken* etw. auf etw. [acc] beschränken limit sth to sth ◊ *die Zahl der Teilnehmer auf 20 beschränken* **2.** *(freedom, rights)* restrict ◊ *die Pressefreiheit beschränken* jdn in etw. [dat] beschränken restrict sb's sth ◊ *Du darfst ihn nicht in seiner Freiheit beschränken.* ♦ *Der enge Rock beschränkte sie in ihrer Bewegungsfreiheit.* [ref v] sich auf etw. [acc] beschränken limit yourself to sth, confine yourself to sth, stick to sth ◊ *sich auf das Wesentliche/Notwendigste beschränken* ♦ *Ich beschränke mich auf ein Knäckebrot, denn ich bin auf Diät.*

be·schränkt [bəˈʃrɛŋkt] *past p of* beschränken [adj] <beschränkter, am beschränktesten> *(pej)* **1.** *(fam)* thick, dumb ◊ *Er ist ein bisschen beschränkt und kapiert nur langsam.* ⊜dumm ⊝klug **2.** narrow(-minded) ◊ *beschränkte Ansichten haben*

② **be·schrei·ben** [bəˈʃraebn̩] <beschreibt, beschrieb, hat beschrieben> [tr v] **1.** jdn/etw. beschreiben describe sb/sth ◊ *Können Sie den Täter beschreiben?* ♦ *Er hat mir den Weg ganz genau beschrieben.* **2.** etw. beschreiben write on sth 10 Blatt Papier beschreiben write 10 pages **3.** etw. beschreiben form sth ◊ *Beschreiben Sie mit den Armen einen Kreis.*

⊛ **nicht zu beschreiben sein** be indescribable ◊ *Es ist nicht zu beschreiben, welche Zustände dort herrschen.*

Be·schrei·bung [bəˈʃraebʊŋ] die <-, -en> **1.** description ◊ *Sie hat mir eine genaue Beschreibung von dir gegeben.* ♦ *Nach Miriams Beschreibung war die Party in voller Erfolg.* **2.** manual ◊ *In der Beschreibung steht, wie das Regal montiert wird.*

⊛ **etw. spottet jeder Beschreibung** *(pej)* sth defies description

be·schul·di·gen [bəˈʃʊldɪgŋ̍] <beschuldigt, beschuldigte, hat beschuldigt> [tr v] jdn beschuldigen accuse sb, blame sb jdn einer Sache [gen] beschuldigen, jdn wegen etw. beschuldigen accuse sb of sth ◊ *jdn eines Verbrechens beschuldigen* jdn als … beschuldigen accuse sb of being … ◊ *Er beschuldigte sie als Komplizin bei den Überfällen.* jdn beschuldigen, etw. getan zu haben accuse sb of doing sth

be·schüt·zen [bəˈʃʏtsn̩] <beschützt, beschützte, hat beschützt> [tr v] protect ◊ *Du musst deine kleine Schwester vor Gefahren beschützen.* jdn vor jdm/etw. beschützen protect sb from sb/sth ◊ *Die Mauer beschützte die Bürger der Stadt.*

Be·schwer·de [bəˈʃveːɐ̯də] die <-, -n> **1.** complaint ◊ *eine Beschwerde vorbringen* ♦

keinen Grund zur Beschwerde haben eine Beschwerde über etw. [acc] a complaint about sth **2.** LAW Beschwerde gegen etw. einreichen/einlegen appeal against sth **3.** *only pl* MED pain, trouble ◊ *akute/chronische Beschwerden* ♦ *Sein Zahn macht ihm Beschwerden.*

② **be·schwe·ren** [bəˈʃveːrən] <beschwert, beschwerte, hat beschwert> [ref v] sich (bei jdm) (über etw./jdn) beschweren complain (to sb) (about sth/sb) ◊ *Ich werde mich bei Ihrem Chef beschweren.* ♦ *Wir haben uns über die schlechte Bedienung beschwert.* ♦ *„Wie geht's?" — „Ach, ich kann mich nicht beschweren."* ⊜sich beklagen [tr v] weight down ◊ *Der Deckel der Kiste wird mit Steinen beschwert.*

be·schwer·lich [bəˈʃveːɐ̯lɪç] [adj] difficult, laborious ◊ *Der Weg aus der Armut ist beschwerlich.* ♦ *eine beschwerliche Reise* ⊜anstrengend

be·schwö·ren [bəˈʃvøːrən] <beschwört, beschwor, hat beschworen> [tr v] **1.** swear to ◊ *„Bist du dir sicher, dass er die Uhr gestohlen hat?" — „Ja, ich kann es beschwören!"* eine Aussage beschwören swear a statement under oath **2.** jdn beschwören, etw. zu tun entreat sb to do sth, implore sb to do sth ◊ *Ich beschwöre dich, nicht zu gehen!* **3.** *(also fig)* conjure up ◊ *Geister beschwören* ♦ *alte Zeiten/Erinnerungen beschwören* **4.** eine Schlange beschwören charm a snake

be·sei·ti·gen [bəˈzaetɪgŋ̍] <beseitigt, beseitigte, hat beseitigt> [tr v] **1.** fix, correct ◊ *einen Fehler/Mangel beseitigen* **2.** get rid of ◊ *ein Problem nicht beseitigen können* ♦ *Um einen Skandal zu verhindern, hat er die Akten heimlich beseitigt.* **3.** *(rubbish)* dispose of ◊ *In vielen Gemeinden wird der Müll getrennt beseitigt.* ⊜entsorgen **4.** *(stains, traces)* remove ◊ *Dieser Reiniger beseitigt Schmutz aller Art.* ♦ *alle Spuren beseitigen* **5.** *(fam, euph)* jdn beseitigen do away with sb ◊ *Sie hat ihren Mann beseitigt, um an sein Geld zu kommen.*

Be·sen [ˈbeːzn̩] der <-s, -> **1.** broom ◊ *den Boden mit einem Besen fegen* **2.** *(fam, pej)* dragon ◊ *Egons Frau ist ein richtiger Besen.*

⊛ **neue Besen kehren gut** a new broom sweeps clean **ich fress einen Besen, wenn …** *(fam)* I'll eat my hat if … ◊ *Ich fress einen Besen, wenn das stimmt.*

be·ses·sen [bəˈzɛsn̩] *past p of* besitzen [adj] **1.** von jdm/etw. besessen obsessed with/by sb/sth ◊ *von einem Wunsch/einer Idee besessen sein* **2.** (von jdm) besessen possessed (by sb) ◊ *vom Teufel besessen sein*

⊛ **wie besessen** like mad ◊ *Er schuftet wie besessen, um zum vereinbarten Termin fertig zu sein.*

be·set·zen [bəˈzɛtsn̩] <besetzt, besetzte, hat besetzt> [tr v] **1.** occupy ◊ *Aus Protest gegen die Bildungspolitik besetzten Studenten die Universität.* ♦ *Die Truppen besetzten das feindliche Gebiet.* ♦ *Das Telefon war besetzt.* ♦ *Das Klo/Der Platz ist besetzt.* **2.** squat ◊ *Sie besetzten das verlassene Haus, um es vor dem Abriss zu bewahren.* **3.** *mostly passive (a post)* fill ◊ *Das Amt des stellvertretenden Vorsitzenden ist im Moment nicht besetzt.* ♦ *Diese Stelle wird ab Oktober neu besetzt.*; *(a counter)* man ◊ *Die Schalter am*

Flughafen werden jeweils 90 Minuten vor Abflug besetzt. **4.** THEAT, TV, FILM eine Rolle/einen Film (mit jdm) besetzen cast (sb in) a role/film ◊ Die Rolle des Helden wird mit Leonardo Di Caprio besetzt. **5.** (fam, hum) hog ◊ Seit einer halben Stunde besetzt er jetzt schon das Telefon. **6.** etw. mit etw. besetzen trim sth with sth ◊ Die Bluse ist mit Glasperlen besetzt.

② **be·setzt** [bə'zɛtst] past p of besetzen

Be·set·zung [bə'zɛtsʊŋ] die <-, -en> most pl **1.** THEAT, FILM, TV, SPORT (of actors) casting ◊ Die Besetzung der Hauptrolle übernimmt der Regisseur.; (in sports) die Besetzung der Mannschaft putting the team together **2.** THEAT, FILM, TV, SPORT (of actors) cast ◊ eine großartige Besetzung mit vielen Oscar-Schauspielern in der Besetzung als tragischer Held/des tragischen Helden in the part of the tragic hero; (of a sports team) line-up ◊ Die Besetzung der Fußballmannschaft setzt sich zusammen aus: ... **3.** (of a post) filling ◊ die neue Besetzung des Postens in der Geschäftsführung **4.** occupation ◊ Das Volk muss unter feindlicher Besetzung leben.; (of a house) squatting in ◊ die illegale Besetzung eines zum Abriss bestimmten Hauses **5.** staff ◊ Die Besetzung der Filiale besteht aus einem vierköpfigen Team. **6.** staffing, equipping ◊ die Besetzung der Rettungswagen mit je drei Sanitätern

② **be·sich·ti·gen** [bə'zɪçtɪɡn̩] <besichtigt, besichtigte, hat besichtigt> tr v **1.** see, visit ◊ Wir haben in Paris den Eiffelturm und den Louvre besichtigt. ◆ Sie können das Haus am Samstag besichtigen. **2.** inspect ◊ Das Gesundheitsamt besichtigt alle Gaststätten regelmäßig.

be·sie·deln [bə'zi:dl̩n] <besiedelt, besiedelte, hat besiedelt> tr v **1.** inhabit ◊ Diese Pflanzen besiedeln feuchte Biotope.; (people, animals also) populate ◊ Unser Gartenteich ist von Fröschen besiedelt. ◆ Vor allem Bauern besiedeln das Hinterland der Insel. **2.** HIST (a region) settle in ◊ Wann wurde die Region besiedelt? **3.** (pej or hum) take over ◊ Im Sommer besiedeln Touristen die Innenstadt.

be·sie·gen [bə'zi:ɡn̩] <besiegt, besiegte, hat besiegt> tr v **1.** etw. besiegen overcome sth ◊ Ängste/Zweifel besiegen ◆ Sie hat den Krebs besiegt. **2.** jdn besiegen defeat sb, beat sb ◊ Das deutsche Volleyballteam besiegte Portugal mit 2:1. ◆ Napoleon wurde in der Schlacht von Waterloo besiegt. ⊖schlagen

be·sin·nen [bə'zɪnən] <besinnt sich, besann sich, hat sich besonnen> ref v **1.** sich besinnen remember ◊ Natürlich, jetzt besinne ich mich! Das war vor längerer Zeit. sich auf etw. acc besinnen remember sth ◊ Wir müssen uns auf unsere Stärken besinnen. **2.** sich besinnen calm down ◊ Besinn dich und schrei nicht so, die Kinder schlafen. ⊖sich fassen **3.** sich besinnen reflect, think ◊ Ich muss mich kurz besinnen, um die richtigen Worte zu finden. sich eines Besseren besinnen think better of it

Be·sin·nung [bə'zɪnʊŋ] die <-> no pl **1.** consciousness ◊ Er ist schwer gestürzt und hat die Besinnung verloren. wieder bei (voller) Besinnung sein have regained (full) consciousness **2.** bei Besinnung sein be in your right mind ◊ Vor Wut

war sie nicht mehr ganz bei Besinnung. jdn zur Besinnung bringen bring sb to their senses zur Besinnung kommen come to your senses **3.** reflection ◊ Der Wald ist für mich ein Ort der Besinnung.

Be·sitz [bə'zɪts] der <-es> no pl possession(s), property ◊ unerlaubter Besitz von Waffen ◆ Das Gebäude ist privater/staatlicher Besitz. in jds Besitz sein be owned by sb ◊ Das Schloss ist im Besitz eines reichen Schweizers. im Besitz ... gen sein own ... ◊ Wer ist im Besitz einer Videokamera? im vollen Besitz seiner geistigen Kräfte sein be in possession of your (mental) faculties in jds Besitz übergehen pass over to sb, become sb's property ◊ Nach der Scheidung ging das Haus in ihren Besitz über. in seinen Besitz bringen take possession of sth ◊ Er brachte die benachbarten Grundstücke in seinen Besitz. ⊖Eigentum

⊙ **von jdm Besitz ergreifen/nehmen** seize sb, take hold of sb ◊ Ein Gefühl der Furcht ergriff von ihm Besitz. ◆ Man sagte, der Teufel habe von ihr Besitz genommen.

② **be·sit·zen** [bə'zɪtsn̩] <besitzt, besaß, hat besessen> tr v have (got) ◊ Bettina besitzt viel Fantasie. ◆ Er besitzt nicht den Mut, ihr die Wahrheit zu sagen. ◆ Sie besitzt gute Sprachkenntnisse.; (a house, possessions also) own ◊ Wir besitzen ein eigenes Haus. ◆ Ich besitze gar nichts, was wertvoll wäre.

② **be·son·de·re** [bə'zɔndərə] adj only before ns <ein besonderer ..., eine besondere ..., ein besonderes ...> **1.** special, particular ◊ Sie hat ein ganz besonderes Hobby. ◆ Er ist ein ganz besonderer Freund. ◆ besondere Umstände ◆ Wir legen besonderen Wert auf Qualität. von besonderer Begabung/Schönheit of exceptional talent/beauty **2.** great ◊ Für dich gebe ich mir ganz besondere Mühe. ◆ Das war doch keine besondere Leistung. **3.** separate ◊ Sie will immer eine besondere Behandlung. ◆ Für Lieferanten gibt es einen besonderen Eingang.

Be·son·der·heit [bə'zɔndɐhaɪt] die <-, -en> peculiarity, special/unusual feature/quality ◊ Die Besonderheit liegt darin, dass der Kuchen ohne Mehl gemacht wird.

② **be·son·ders** [bə'zɔndɐs] adv **1.** particularly, especially ◊ Sie ist besonders begabt. ◆ Das war besonders teuer. ◆ Er hat sich nicht besonders bemüht. ◆ Das ist nicht besonders lustig. ◆ Er hat gestern besonders viel getrunken. ◆ Du solltest mehr für die Schule tun, besonders mehr Vokabeln lernen. Besonders du müsstest das wissen. You of all people should know that. **2.** exceptionally ◊ Cordula ist besonders hübsch. **3.** separately ◊ Diesen Eintrag werde ich besonders bearbeiten müssen.

⊙ **nicht besonders** nicht besonders sein be nothing special, be average ◊ Der Film war nicht besonders. jdm geht es nicht besonders sb doesn't feel too good

be·son·nen [bə'zɔnən] past p of besinnen adj, adv sensible(-ibly), calm(ly), level-headed(ly) ◊ eine besonnene Friedenspolitik ◆ Er gilt als ruhig und besonnen. ◆ Auf die schreckliche Nachricht reagierte sie besonnen. ◆ eine Arbeit ruhig und besonnen angehen ⊖umsichtig

② **be·sor·gen** [bə'zɔrɡn̩] <besorgt, besorgte, hat besorgt> tr v **1.** get, buy ◊ Ich muss noch Brot

besorgen. jdm etw. besorgen, für jdn etw. besorgen get sb sth, get sth for sb ◊ *Wir besorgen Ihnen ein Hotelzimmer.* ✦ *Wolfgang hat drei Theaterkarten für uns besorgt.* sich [dat] etw. besorgen get yourself sth ◊ *Ich habe mir ein Buch über Ägypten besorgt.* ⊖beschaffen **2.** etw. besorgen do sth, take care of sth ◊ *Die Übersetzung aus dem Englischen besorgte Herr Breitung.* jdm den Haushalt besorgen keep house for sb
● was du heute kannst besorgen, das verschiebe nicht auf morgen don't put off until tomorrow what you can do today es jdm besorgen **1.** *(fam)* give sb a piece of your mind ◊ *Dem hat er es aber besorgt!* **2.** *(rude)* give it to sb
Be·sorg·nis [bə'zɔrɡnɪs] die <-, -se> *most sing* anxiety, worry, concern ◊ *Mit Besorgnis nahm er sein schlechtes Prüfungsergebnis zur Kenntnis.* Besorgnis erregen raise concern wegen einer Sache in Besorgnis geraten/sein become/be worried/concerned about sth
be·sorgt [bə'zɔrkt] *past p of* besorgen [adj] **1.** worried, anxious ◊ *Die besorgten Eltern riefen die Polizei.* um/über etw. [acc] besorgt sein, wegen etw. besorgt sein be worried about sth ◊ *Der Arzt ist wegen seines Gesundheitszustands besorgt.* ✦ *Sie ist besorgt darüber, dass er immer noch nicht zu Hause ist.* um jdn besorgt sein be worried about sb **2.** concerned ◊ *eine besorgte Mutter* um jdn/etw. besorgt sein be concerned about sb/sth ◊ *Der Gastgeber war sehr um unsere Zufriedenheit besorgt.*
be·spre·chen [bə'ʃprɛçn] <bespricht, besprach, hat besprochen> [tr v] **1.** discuss ◊ *eine Angelegenheit/Sache näher besprechen* ✦ *Alles Weitere besprechen wir morgen.* etw. mit jdm besprechen talk sth over with sb, discuss sth with sb ◊ *Sie bespricht etwas Dienstliches mit einem Kollegen.* **2.** review ◊ *Der neue Roman wurde in der Zeitung besprochen.* **3.** etw. besprechen record on sth ◊ *eine Kassette mit einer Geschichte besprechen* [ref v] sich (über etw. [acc]) besprechen confer (about sth) ◊ *Wir haben uns besprochen und eine Entscheidung getroffen.* ✦ *Haben Sie sich mit ihm besprochen?*
bes·ser ['bɛsɐ] *comp of* gut [adj, adv] better ◊ *Er hat einen besseren Computer als ich.* ✦ *Ich hoffe, dass das Wetter bald besser wird.* ✦ *Dieser Bewerber ist besser qualifiziert als der andere.* ✦ *Du gehst jetzt besser.* jd kann etw. besser (als jd) sb is better at sth (than sb) ◊ *Er kann besser übersetzen als ich.* bessere Leute a better class of people ◊ *Er verkehrt nur mit besseren Leuten.* die besseren Kreise (the) better circles [adj] *only before ns (pej)* ein besserer/eine bessere/ein besseres ... a glorified ... ◊ *Dieses Lokal ist doch nur eine bessere Kneipe.*
● besser gesagt or rather ◊ *Er hat ein Auto, besser gesagt einen Sportwagen.* umso besser so much the better ◊ *„Karin kommt mit mit!" — „Umso besser, ich kann sie sowieso nicht leiden."*
bes·sern ['bɛsɐn] [ref v] +*haben* sich bessern improve, get better ◊ *Unser Verhältnis hat sich stark gebessert.* ✦ *Die Konjunktur bessert sich.* ✦ *Das Wetter bessert sich langsam wieder.* ⊖sich verschlechtern [tr v] +*haben* **1.** etw. bessern make sth better ◊ *Mit ständigem Kritisieren bessert man die*

Welt nicht.; *(a criminal)* jdn bessern reform sb sich bessern mend your ways ◊ *Wann wirst du dich endlich bessern?*; *(a criminal)* reform **2.** etw. bessern alleviate sth ◊ *ein Medikament, das den Husten bessert*
② **Bes·se·rung** ['bɛsərʊn] die <-, -en> **1.** improvement, recovery ◊ *Der Patient befindet sich auf dem Weg der Besserung.* ✦ *Eine Besserung auf dem Arbeitsmarkt ist nicht in Sicht.* **2.** *(of morals)* improvement, reforming ◊ *Ich bemerke eine Besserung in seinem Verhalten.* Besserung geloben promise to mend your ways
● gute Besserung get well soon
Be·stand [bə'ʃtant] der <-(e)s, Bestände> *most sing (of wild animals)* population ◊ *Das Füttern von Wildtieren kann deren Bestände verringern.; (of merchandise, cattle)* stock der Bestand an Mitgliedern the number of members
● zum eisernen Bestand gehören be part of the core um den Bestand ... [gen] bangen fear that sth might not last (keinen) Bestand haben (not) last, (not) survive ◊ *Wird eure Liebe Bestand haben?*
be·stän·dig [bə'ʃtɛndɪç] [adv] constantly, continuously ◊ *Er ist ein guter Schüler und lernt beständig Neues.* ✦ *Ein beständig auftretender Computerfehler macht uns zu schaffen.* ✦ *Es regnet beständig.* ⊖kontinuierlich [adj] **1.** constant ◊ *Er leidet unter der beständigen Angst, verfolgt zu werden.; (weather)* settled ◊ *Das Wetter ist beständig.* ⊖unbeständig **2.** stable, reliable ◊ *Das ist ein beständiges Unternehmen mit sicherem Umsatz.* ✦ *Meine Liebe zu dir ist beständig.* ⊖dauerhaft ⊖unbeständig **3.** *(material)* durable ◊ *Wie beständig ist dieses Material?* beständig gegen etw. resistant to sth ◊ *Das Material ist beständig gegen Chemikalien.* ⊖widerstandsfähig
Be·stand·teil [bə'ʃtanttael] der <-s, -e> part, ingredient, component ◊ *Hautcremes können schädliche Bestandteile enthalten.* ✦ *Wasser ist ein zentraler Bestandteil unserer Ernährung.* ✦ *Praktische Übungen sind ein fester Bestandteil des Sprachunterrichts.* etw. in seine Bestandteile zerlegen separate sth into its constituent parts
● sich in seine Bestandteile auflösen *(fam, hum)* **1.** vanish into thin air **2.** disintegrate
be·stär·ken [bə'ʃtɛrkn] <bestärkt, bestärkte, hat bestärkt> [tr v] jdn in etw. [dat] bestärken confirm sb in sth ◊ *jdn in seinem Plan/Vorsatz bestärken* ✦ *Er bestärkte mich in dem Glauben, dass ... jdn/sich gegenseitig bestärken, etw. zu tun encourage sb/each other to do sth ◊ *Seine Frau bestärkte ihn, weiter abzunehmen.* ✦ *Wir bestärken uns gegenseitig, bis zum Ende durchzuhalten.* ⊖unterstützen
② **be·stä·ti·gen** [bə'ʃtɛːtɪgn] <bestätigt, bestätigte, hat bestätigt> [tr v] **1.** confirm ◊ *Ich kann bestätigen, dass er das gesagt hat.* ✦ *Diese Meldung ist nicht offiziell bestätigt worden.* ✦ *Sein Verhalten hat meinen Verdacht bestätigt.* ✦ *Neue Forschungsergebnisse bestätigen diese Theorie.* ✦ *Bitte bestätigen Sie die Reservierung schriftlich.; (a verdict)* uphold ◊ *Das Urteil wurde in zweiter Instanz bestätigt.* sich bestätigen be confirmed, prove (to be) true ◊ *Der Verdacht auf Krebs hat sich bestätigt.* ✦ *Meine Vermutung hat sich bestätigt.* **2.** jdn in etw. [dat] bestätigen confirm sb in sth ◊

Nun bestätige ihn doch nicht auch noch in seinen Vorurteilen. **3.** jdn in etw. [dat] bestätigen endorse sb in sth ◊ *Die Wähler haben die Regierung im Amt bestätigt.*

Be·stä·ti·gung [bəˈʃtɛːtɪɡʊŋ] die <-, -en> **1.** Bestätigung (für/über etw. [acc]), Bestätigung (... [gen]) confirmation (of sth) ◊ *Laut Bestätigung der Prüfer habe ich das Examen bestanden.* ◆ *Wir benötigen eine Bestätigung ihrer Aussage vor Gericht.* Bestätigung finden be confirmed **2.** letter of confirmation ◊ *Bitte senden Sie uns eine Bestätigung der Kündigung zu.* Bestätigung über etw. [acc] certificate of sth ◊ *Der Arzt kann Ihnen eine Bestätigung über Ihre Krankheit ausstellen.*; *(of receipt)* acknowledgement of sth **3.** Bestätigung in etw. [dat] endorsement of sth ◊ *Der Bürgermeister hofft auf eine Bestätigung in seinem Amt.* **4.** recognition, appreciation ◊ *Er ist sehr unsicher und sucht immer die Bestätigung der anderen.*

be·stat·ten [bəˈʃtatn̩] <bestattet, bestattete, hat bestattet> [tr v] *only written (lofty)* bury ◊ *Er wurde auf dem Dorffriedhof feierlich bestattet.* ◆ *Sie wurde auf See bestattet.* ⊖beerdigen, begraben

be·stau·nen [bəˈʃtaʊnən] <bestaunt, bestaunte, hat bestaunt> [tr v] marvel at ◊ *Das Kunstwerk wurde von den Besuchern bestaunt.*

bes·te [ˈbɛstə] *superl of* gut [adj] <jds bester/beste/bestes ...> **1.** best ◊ *Mein bester Freund heißt Max.* ◆ *Meine Kenntnisse sind auf diesem Gebiet nicht die besten.* ◆ *ein Produkt von bester Qualität* in bester Gesundheit sein be in good health aus bester Familie/bestem Hause kommen come from a good background am besten the best ◊ *Welche Lösung ist am besten?* **2.** am besten better, best ◊ *„Ich sag jetzt nichts mehr."* — *„Das ist auch am besten so!"* [adv] am besten best, better ◊ *Wir nehmen am besten das Auto.* ◆ *Ich gehe jetzt am besten.* Sie arbeitet am besten. She's the best worker. Dieses Eis schmeckt mir am besten. This ice cream is my favourite. Dieses Parfüm riecht am besten. This is the nicest fragrance.

be·ste·chen [bəˈʃtɛçn̩] <besticht, bestach, hat bestochen> [tr v] jdn (mit etw.) bestechen bribe sb (with sth) ◊ *Die Mannschaft gewann, weil der Schiedsrichter bestochen worden war.* [intr v] durch etw. bestechen impress by sth ◊ *Die Bilder bestechen durch leuchtende, helle Farben.*

Be·ste·chung [bəˈʃtɛçʊŋ] die <-> *no pl* LAW **1.** bribery ◊ *ein eindeutiger Fall von Bestechung* ◆ *jdn wegen Bestechung verurteilen* **2.** bribing ◊ *Die Bestechung eines Zeugen ist strafbar.*

② **Be·steck** [bəˈʃtɛk] das <-(e)s, -e> **1.** cutlery **2.** MED instruments ◊ *Das Besteck muss sterilisiert werden.* **3.** *(of a drug user)* equipment ◊ *Er hat sich am Besteck eines anderen mit Aids infiziert.*

② **be·ste·hen** [bəˈʃteːən] <besteht, bestand, hat bestanden> [tr v] pass ◊ *Er hat das Abitur mit einer Drei bestanden.* ◆ *Sie hat die Prüfung erst beim zweiten Mal bestanden.* ◆ *Wenn Sie die Probezeit bestehen, werden Sie übernommen.*; *(a challenge)* get through, master ◊ *Unsere Mannschaft hat die Herausforderung bestanden.* [intr v] **1.** exist, be ◊ *Diese Regelung besteht auch weiterhin.* ◆ *Mein Büro besteht nun schon fünfzehn Jahre.* **2.** aus

etw. bestehen be made of sth, consist of sth ◊ *Die Türen bestehen aus massivem Holz.*; *(of several parts)* consist of sth, be made up of sth, be comprised of sth ◊ *Der Test besteht aus drei Teilen.* ◆ *Die Wohnung besteht aus drei Zimmern, Küche und Bad.* ◆ *Dieses Lexikon besteht aus zehn Bänden.* **3.** in etw. [dat] bestehen; darin bestehen, etw. zu tun consist of (doing) sth, consist in (doing) sth ◊ *Meine Aufgabe besteht darin, die Kinder zu beaufsichtigen.* Ich verstehe nicht, worin das Problem besteht. I don't understand what the problem is. **4.** *(an exam)* pass ◊ *Hast du bestanden?* **5.** in etw. [dat] bestehen prevail in sth, hold your ground in (the face of) sth ◊ *Wir haben im Kampf gegen den Feind bestanden.* vor jdm bestehen prevail with sb ◊ *vor Gott bestehen* ◆ *Mit diesem Roman bestand er nicht vor den Kritikern.* **6.** auf etw [dat] bestehen insist on sth ◊ *Er muss immer auf seiner Meinung bestehen.* ◆ *Ich bestehe darauf, dass das sofort gemacht wird.* [imp v] es besteht ... there is ... ◊ *Es besteht die Möglichkeit, den Test zu wiederholen.* ◆ *Es besteht noch Hoffnung.*

⊛ **bestehen bleiben** remain ◊ *Die Gefahr eines Brandes bleibt bestehen.* ◆ *Wir wollen, dass der Verein auch weiterhin bestehen bleibt.* etw. **bestehen lassen** leave sth as it is ◊ *Wir können diese Verhältnisse doch nicht bestehen lassen.*

② **be·stel·len** [bəˈʃtɛlən] <bestellt, bestellte, hat bestellt> [tr+intr v] order ◊ *Ich habe das Buch direkt beim Verlag bestellt.* ◆ *Sie können die Ware schriftlich, telefonisch oder per Fax bestellen.* ◆ *Ich habe das Schnitzel bestellt.* ◆ *Entschuldige bitte die Verspätung — hast du schon bestellt?* [tr v] **1.** *(a table, tickets etc.)* book, reserve ◊ *Meine Sekretärin hat für mich ein Zimmer bestellt.* **2.** call, send for ◊ *Er wurde zum Chef bestellt.* Kannst du bitte ein Taxi bestellen? **3.** jdm etw. bestellen tell sb sth ◊ *Bestellen Sie ihr, dass ich angerufen habe.* jd lässt bestellen, dass ... sb left a message/said that ... ◊ *Dein Mann lässt bestellen, dass es etwas später wird.* Soll ich ihr was bestellen? Can I take a message for her? jdm (schöne) Grüße von jdm bestellen give sb sb's (best) regards **4.** AGR cultivate, till ◊ *Das Feld wird schon lange nicht mehr bestellt.*

⊛ um jdn/etw. ist es gut/schlecht bestellt things are looking good/bad for sb/sth ◊ *Leider ist es um den Patienten nicht gut bestellt.* nichts zu bestellen haben have got nothing to say ◊ *Er hat bei seiner Frau nichts zu bestellen.*

Be·stel·lung [bəˈʃtɛlʊŋ] die <-, -en> **1.** order ◊ *Die Bestellung erfolgt auf Rechnung an die gewünschte Adresse.* ◆ *Kann ich Ihre Bestellung aufnehmen?* ◆ *Bitte geben Sie Ihre Bestellung auf.* ◆ *Möchten Sie Ihre Bestellung persönlich abholen?* eine/die Bestellung über etw. [acc] an/the order for sth ◊ *eine Bestellung über 25 Wörterbücher* **2.** *most sing* appointing ◊ *die Bestellung eines Betreuers für alte/behinderte Menschen* ⊖Berufung **3.** *no pl* AGR cultivation ◊ *die Bestellung der Felder durch Traktoren* **4.** *most sing* calling ◊ *die Bestellung von Handwerkern* **5.** booking, reservation ◊ *Die Bestellung der Theaterplätze ist telefonisch möglich.*

⊛ auf Bestellung *(fig)* **1.** on command ◊ *Der*

Kleine kann wirklich auf Bestellung heulen und bekommt so alles, was er will. **2.** TRADE to/on order ◊ *Auf Bestellung liefern wir auch große Mengen.*

bes·tens ['bɛstn̩s, 'bɛstəns] [adv] **1.** *(fam)* very well ◊ *Sie war bestens auf die Prüfung vorbereitet.* ✦ *Es verläuft alles bestens.* ✦ *„Wie geht's?"* — *„Bestens, vielen Dank!"* **2.** ich danke dir/Ihnen bestens, wir danken dir/Ihnen bestens thank you very much

be·steu·ern [bə'ʃtɔøɐn] <besteuert, besteuerte, hat besteuert> [tr v] POL, ECON tax, put tax on ◊ *In Zukunft sollen Renten stärker besteuert werden.* ✦ *Der Staat besteuert Benzin/Tabak.* jdn/etw. besteuern tax sb/sth ◊ *Besser Verdienende werden höher besteuert.*

Bes·tie ['bɛstjə] die <-, -n> beast ◊ *Eine wilde Bestie fiel die Schafe an.*; *(person also)* monster ◊ *Der Mörder ist eine richtige Bestie.*

② **be·stim·men** [bə'ʃtɪmən] <bestimmt, bestimmte, hat bestimmt> [tr v] **1.** determine ◊ *Wir sollten unsere Ziele neu bestimmen.* ✦ *Er bestimmt, wie es gemacht werden muss.* ✦ *Man kann das Alter von Pferden anhand ihrer Zähne bestimmen.* ✦ *In New York bestimmen Hochhäuser das Bild.*; *(a date)* fix ◊ *Wir sollten einen Zeitpunkt für unser nächstes Treffen bestimmen.* **2.** etw. für etw. bestimmen intend sth for sth ◊ *Das Geld ist für den Urlaub bestimmt.* jdn zu/für etw. bestimmen designate sb (as) sth ◊ *Frau Meyer hat mich zu ihrer Nachfolgerin bestimmt.* jdn dazu bestimmen, etw. zu tun designate sb to do sth ◊ *Ich wurde dazu bestimmt, den ganzen Text zu überprüfen.* zu Höherem/für Höheres bestimmt sein be destined for higher things [intr v] (über etw./jdn) bestimmen, (über etw./jdn) zu bestimmen haben be in charge (of sth/sb) ◊ *Du hast hier gar nicht zu bestimmen!* ✦ *Als Chef bestimmt er über 20 Mitarbeiter.* jd bestimmt (darüber), wie etw. getan wird sb decides how sth is to be done Über meine Zeit bestimme ich selbst. I decide how I spend my time. Du kannst doch nicht so einfach über mich bestimmen. You can't just tell me what to do.

be·stimmt [bə'ʃtɪmt] *past p of* bestimmen [adj] **1.** *only before ns* certain, particular, definite ◊ *Ich suche ein ganz bestimmtes Buch.* ✦ *Sie hat sehr bestimmte Vorstellungen von ihrem zukünftigen Mann.* ⊝beliebig **2.** decisive, determined, resolute ◊ *Sie sagte das in einem sehr bestimmten Ton.* [adv] **1.** certainly, definitely ◊ *Du findest deinen Ring bestimmt wieder.* ✦ *Das hat er bestimmt nicht gesagt.* ✦ *Weißt du das ganz bestimmt?* ⊝sicherlich **2.** firmly, resolutely ◊ *Sie tritt sehr bestimmt auf.*

Be·stim·mung [bə'ʃtɪmʊŋ] die <-, -en> **1.** LAW regulation, rule ◊ *Die Behörden haben neue Bestimmungen erlassen.* ⊝Vorschrift **2.** *no pl (of plants, animals)* classification ◊ *die Bestimmung von Pilzen* **3.** *no pl* definition ◊ *Der Chef ist für die Bestimmung der Ziele zuständig.* **4.** *no pl* determination ◊ *die Bestimmung des Alters eines Menschen* ⊝Einschätzung **5.** *no pl* fixing ◊ *Zur Bestimmung des Preises benötigen wir folgende Angaben: ...* ⊝Festlegung **6.** *no pl* jds Bestimmung sb's calling ◊ *Sie folgte ihrer inneren Bestimmung und wurde Nonne.* **7.** *no pl* destiny, fate ◊ *Es scheint meine Bestimmung, immer unglücklich*

verliebt zu sein.
⊙ adverbiale/nähere Bestimmung adverbial element etw. seiner Bestimmung übergeben *(form)* inaugurate sth ◊ *Der Bürgermeister übergab die neue Halle ihrer Bestimmung.*

② **be·stra·fen** [bə'ʃtraːfn̩] <bestraft, bestrafte, hat bestraft> [tr v] *often passive* jdn (für etw.) bestrafen punish sb (for sth) ◊ *Er wurde für den Einbruch mit fünf Jahren Haft bestraft.* ✦ *Schwarzarbeiter sollen härter bestraft werden.* ✦ *Jetzt werde ich für meine Dummheit bestraft.* etw. bestrafen punish sth ◊ *Mein Mathelehrer bestraft Zuspätkommen mit Nachsitzen.* jds etw. wird bestraft sb will (have to) pay dearly for sth ◊ *Jetzt wird deine Faulheit bestraft.*
⊙ mit jdm/etw. bestraft sein be cursed with sb/sth ◊ *Mit diesem Chef bist du wirklich bestraft.*

Be·stre·bung [bə'ʃtreːbʊŋ] die <-, -en> *most pl* effort ◊ *Mit der Umsetzung seiner Vorschläge hatte er das Ziel seiner Bestrebungen erreicht.* die Bestrebung, etw. zu tun the efforts to do sth

be·strei·ten [bə'ʃtraɛtn̩] <bestreitet, bestritt, hat bestritten> [tr v] **1.** deny ◊ *Sie bestreitet, das Geld gestohlen zu haben.* ✦ *Es lässt sich nicht bestreiten, dass er Recht hat.* **2.** finance, pay for ◊ *Sie muss den Unterhalt für die Familie allein bestreiten.* **3.** carry ◊ *Er musste das Spiel über vier Sätze bestreiten.* ✦ *Sie hat die ganze Diskussion alleine bestritten.*

be·stürzt [bə'ʃtʏɐ̯tst] [adj] distressed, shocked ◊ *Diese Politik löste im Ausland bestürzte Reaktionen aus.*; *(concerned)* worried ein bestürztes Gesicht machen look shocked; *(concerned)* look worried bestürzt (über etw. [acc]) sein be distressed (by/at sth), be shocked (by/at sth) ◊ *Er war tief bestürzt über den Tod seines Kameraden.* ⊝betroffen

② **Be·such** [bə'zuːx] der <-(e)s, -e> **1.** visit ◊ *Meine Mutter beklagt sich über meine seltenen Besuche.* ✦ *einen Besuch im Museum machen* ✦ *Ich würde Ihnen einen Besuch beim Arzt empfehlen.* jdm einen Besuch abstatten, einen Besuch bei jdm machen pay sb a visit, visit sb zu Besuch kommen come (a)round, visit ◊ *Komm doch mal wieder zu Besuch.* bei jdm zu Besuch sein be staying with sb, be visiting sb Besuche im Kino/Theater etc. visits to the cinema/theatre etc. **2.** attendance ◊ *Der Besuch dieses Sprachkurses hat ihr sehr geholfen.* nach dem Besuch der Universität after attending university **3.** visitor(s) ◊ *Ist euer Besuch noch da?*

② **be·su·chen** [bə'zuːxn̩] <besucht, besuchte, hat besucht> [tr v] **1.** visit, (come/go and) see ◊ *Besuch uns doch mal wieder!* ✦ *Ich besuche meine Eltern regelmäßig.* ✦ *Wir sollten sie im Krankenhaus besuchen.* ✦ *Habt ihr auch die Pyramiden besucht?* **2.** *(a school, course etc.)* attend ◊ *Sie besucht einen Kurs an der Volkshochschule.* ✦ *Ich habe neun Jahre das Gymnasium besucht.* **3.** *(the theatre, cinema etc.)* go to ◊ *Sylvia besucht regelmäßig das Theater.*

be·tagt [bə'taːkt] [adj] *(lofty)* elderly, well advanced in age ◊ *ein betagter Herr* ✦ *Meine Oma ist schon sehr betagt.*

be·tä·ti·gen [bə'tɛːtɪɡn̩] <betätigt, betätigte, hat betätigt> [tr v] *(lofty)* **1.** use, operate ◊ *einen Hebel/Schalter betätigen* ✦ *Nach der Eingabe betätigen Sie bitte die Enter-Taste.* **2.** *(muscles)*

use ◊ *Beim Tennis werden vor allem die Armmuskeln betätigt.* ⊜bewegen ⟨ref v⟩ *sich als etw.*
betätigen work as sth, act as sth ◊ *Ich betätige mich nebenher auch als Babysitterin.* *sich sportlich/künstlerisch etc.* betätigen do (some) sports/artwork etc.

be·täu·ben [bə'tɔɡbm̩] ⟨betäubt, betäubte, hat betäubt⟩ ⟨tr v⟩ **1.** MED anaesthetize, anesthetize, numb ◊ *Die Wunde wurde vor dem Nähen örtlich betäubt.* **2.** MED *(a person)* anaesthetize, anesthetize ◊ *Vor einer Operation wird der Patient mit einer Narkose betäubt.; (an animal)* stun ◊ *Der Löwe wurde betäubt und eingefangen.* **3.** stun, knock out ◊ *Der Sturz auf den Kopf hatte sie für kurze Zeit betäubt.* **4.** daze ◊ *Der Lärm dieser Baustelle betäubt mich.* ⟨ref v⟩ *sich mit etw.* **betäuben** seek consolation in sth ◊ *Um seine Probleme zu vergessen, betäubte er sich mit Alkohol.* *etw. durch Arbeit* betäuben escape sth by throwing yourself into your work

be·tei·li·gen [bə'taelɪɡn̩] ⟨beteiligt, beteiligte, hat beteiligt⟩ ⟨ref v⟩ **1.** *sich an etw.* ⟨dat⟩ beteiligen participate in sth, take part in sth ◊ *An dem Projekt beteiligen sich mehrere Unternehmen.* ♦ *sich an einer Diskussion beteiligen* **2.** FIN *sich (mit etw.) an etw.* ⟨dat⟩ beteiligen contribute (sth) to sth ◊ *sich an den Benzinkosten beteiligen* ♦ *Ich beteilige mich mit fünf Euro an dem Geschenk.* **3.** ECON *sich (mit ...) an etw.* ⟨dat⟩ beteiligen have a share (of ...) in sth ◊ *Das Unternehmen beteiligt sich (mit sechs Prozent) an Microsoft.* ⟨tr v⟩ **1.** *jdn an etw.* ⟨dat⟩ beteiligen let sb take part in sth ◊ *Die Schüler wurden an der Gestaltung des Unterrichts beteiligt.* **2.** *mostly passive (profits, sales)* jdn an etw. ⟨dat⟩ beteiligen give sb a share of sth ◊ *Die Kellner des Restaurants werden am Umsatz beteiligt.*

⑦ **be·ten** ['beːtn̩] ⟨betet, betete, hat gebetet⟩ ⟨tr v⟩ say (a prayer) ◊ *Sie betete drei Vaterunser.* ⟨intr v⟩ pray ◊ *Wir beten um Frieden in der Welt.*

Be·ton [be'tɔŋ, be'tõː] der ⟨-s⟩ *no pl* concrete ◊ *ein Pfeiler aus Beton*

be·to·nen [bə'toːnən] ⟨betont, betonte, hat betont⟩ ⟨tr v⟩ **1.** *(ausdrücklich)* betonen stress, emphasize ◊ *Er betonte ausdrücklich, dass er nicht kommen wird.* ♦ *Die Helfer betonten die Wichtigkeit medizinischer Einrichtungen.* **2.** emphasize, highlight, accentuate ◊ *ein enges Kleid betont ihre gute Figur.* ⊜hervorheben **3.** LING stress ◊ *ein Wort falsch oder richtig betonen* ♦ *Das Wort wird auf der zweiten Silbe betont.*

be·trach·ten [bə'traxtn̩] ⟨betrachtet, betrachtete, hat betrachtet⟩ ⟨tr v⟩ **1.** *jdn/sich/etw. als etw.* betrachten regard sb/yourself/sth as sth, consider sb/yourself/sth ◊ *Ich betrachte ihn als Freund.* ♦ *Er betrachtet es als seine Aufgabe, auf sie aufzupassen.* **2.** *etw. irgendwie* betrachten look at sth in a certain way ◊ *eine Angelegenheit kritisch betrachten* genau(er) betrachtet on closer examination **3.** *jdn/sich/etw.* betrachten look at sb/yourself/sth ◊ *Mit einem prüfenden Blick betrachtete er sich im Spiegel.* ♦ *Traurig betrachtete sie das Foto.* **4.** take a look at ◊ *ein Thema, das man näher betrachten sollte*

be·trächt·lich [bə'trɛçtlɪç] ⟨adj, adv⟩ considerable (-ably), significant(ly), substantial(ly) ◊ *Ein Handy bringt beträchtliche Vorteile.* ♦ *Der Sachschaden*

am Auto war beträchtlich. ♦ *Seit letztem Jahr ist sie beträchtlich gewachsen.*

Be·trag [bə'traːk] der ⟨-(e)s, Beträge⟩ amount, sum ◊ *Bitte überweisen Sie den fälligen Betrag auf mein Konto.* ♦ *ein hoher/niedriger Betrag* ⊜Summe

⑦ **be·tra·gen** [bə'traːɡn̩] ⟨beträgt, betrug, hat betragen⟩ ⟨tr v⟩ amount to, cost ◊ *Die Kosten haben über 500 Euro betragen.; (distance, measurement)* be ◊ *Die Entfernung beträgt 10 Kilometer.* ⟨ref v⟩ *sich gut/schlecht etc.* betragen behave well/badly etc. ◊ *Die Kinder haben sich heute beispielhaft betragen.* ⟨imp v⟩ *only pret (lit) (at the start of a story)* es betrug sich (so) happened ◊ *Im Jahre 1855 betrug es sich, dass ...*

Be·treff [bə'trɛf] der ⟨-s⟩ *only written, no pl (form) (abbr* **Betr.**⟩ reference

be·tref·fen [bə'trɛfn̩] ⟨betrifft, betraf, hat betroffen⟩ ⟨tr v⟩ **1.** concern ◊ *Alle Termine, die das Projekt betreffen, stehen im Kalender.* ♦ *Umweltschutz betrifft uns alle!* *was jdn/etw.* betrifft as far as sb/sth is concerned, as for sb/sth ◊ *Was mich betrifft, könnt ihr auf mich zählen.* ⊜in Bezug auf jdn/etw. **2.** affect ◊ *Lungenkrebs ist eine Krankheit, die vor allem Raucher betrifft.* ♦ *Die Inseln waren besonders vom Erdbeben betroffen.* **3.** *mostly pres perf or impersonal* upset, sadden ◊ *Sein Tod hat sie schwer betroffen.* ♦ *Es betrifft mich wirklich, dass sie so traurig ist.*

be·trei·ben [bə'traebm̩] ⟨betreibt, betrieb, hat betrieben⟩ ⟨intr v⟩ **1.** *etw.* betreiben pursue sth ◊ *wissenschaftliche Forschung betreiben* **2.** *(a business, farm etc.)* run, manage ◊ *Sie betreibt ein Schuhgeschäft.* **3.** *mostly passive* TECHN *etw. mit etw.* betreiben run sth by sth, operate sth by sth ◊ *Das Kraftwerk wird mit Turbinen betrieben.*

be·tre·ten¹ [bə'treːtn̩] ⟨adj⟩ *no comp/superl* embarrassed, ashamed ◊ *Mit betretener Miene sagte er ihr die Wahrheit.* ♦ *Er wirkte nach dem Streit ziemlich betreten.* ⟨adv⟩ ashamedly, awkwardly ◊ *Betreten blickte er zu Boden.*

be·tre·ten² [bə'treːtn̩] ⟨betritt, betrat, hat betreten⟩ ⟨tr v⟩ **1.** enter, go into ◊ *Verschlafen betrat er die Küche.* ♦ *Du kannst die Wohnung gern mit Schuhen betreten.* ♦ *Das Gelände der Bundeswehr darf nicht betreten werden.* **2.** *(platform, stage)* step onto ◊ *Der Redner betritt das Podium/ die Tribüne.* **3.** *(lawn, carpet)* walk on ◊ *Er darf den Teppich nur barfuß betreten.* Rasen nicht betreten! Keep off the grass!

⑦ **be·treu·en** [bə'trɔɡən] ⟨betreut, betreute, hat betreut⟩ ⟨tr v⟩ **1.** look after ◊ *Nachmittags werden die Kinder im Hort betreut.* ♦ *Herr Günzel wird die Besucher betreuen.* **2.** manage ◊ *Das Projekt wird von Frau Forßmann betreut.* ♦ *Das Gebiet wird von zwei Mitarbeitern der örtlichen Filiale betreut.; (team)* coach

⑦ **Be·treu·er** [bə'trɔɡɐ] der ⟨-s, ->⟩, **Be·treu·e·rin** [bə'trɔɡərɪn] die ⟨-, -nen⟩ supervisor, advisor ◊ *Herr Uhlmann ist Ihr Betreuer in Fragen der Produktentwicklung.; (of a team)* coach, manager ◊ *Robert ist der Betreuer unserer Tennismannschaft.; (of the sick, the old etc.)* carer

Be·treu·ung [bə'trɔɡʊŋ] die ⟨-⟩ *no pl* supervision, care ◊ *Wir legen großen Wert auf die Betreuung unserer Passagiere.* ♦ *Sie ist auf ärztliche Betreuung angewiesen.* ♦ *Er übernimmt die*

Betreuung unserer Fußballmannschaft.; (of a team) coaching

② **Be·trieb** [bə'triːp] der <-(e)s, -e> **1.** company, business ◊ *In unserem Betrieb arbeiten 150 Leute.* **2.** office, work(place) ◊ *Mein Mann ist noch im Betrieb.* **3.** operation ◊ *Während des Betriebes kam es immer wieder zu Störungen.* ♦ *Das neue Werk wird nächsten Monat den Betrieb aufnehmen.* außer Betrieb out of order ◊ *Der Fahrstuhl ist mal wieder außer Betrieb.* in Betrieb working ◊ *Ist der Lift wieder in Betrieb?* etw. in Betrieb nehmen put sth into operation/service ◊ *Die neue Anlage wird nächste Woche in Betrieb genommen.* den Betrieb einstellen close down **4.** bustle ◊ *Verglichen mit dem Betrieb auf dem Markt war es hier relativ ruhig.* in/auf/an etw. [dat] ist/herrscht viel/reger Betrieb sth is very busy ◊ *In der Stadt war heute viel Betrieb.* **5.** den ganzen Betrieb stören hold everybody up ◊ *Frag nicht so viel, du störst den ganzen Betrieb.* den ganzen Betrieb lahm legen bring everything to a standstill ◊ *Der Streik hat den ganzen Betrieb in der Stadt lahm gelegt.*

② **Be·triebs·rat¹** [bə'triːpsraːt] der <-(e)s, Betriebsräte> works council ◊ *Hans wurde in den Betriebsrat gewählt.*

② **Be·triebs·rat²** [bə'triːpsraːt] der <-(e)s, Betriebsräte>, **Be·triebs·rä·tin** [bə'triːpsrɛːtɪn] die <-, -nen> works council member ◊ *den Betriebsrat einschalten* ♦ *Sie war fünf Jahre lang Betriebsrätin.*

Be·triebs·sys·tem [bə'triːpszʏsteːm] das <-s, -e> IT operating system

Be·triebs·wirt [bə'triːpsvɪrt] der <-(e)s, -e>, **Be·triebs·wir·tin** [bə'triːpsvɪrtɪn] die <-, -nen> ECON business economist ◊ *Sie arbeitet als Betriebswirtin bei BMW.* ♦ *ein staatlich geprüfter Betriebswirt*

be·trin·ken [bə'trɪŋkn̩] <betrinkt sich, betrank sich, hat sich betrunken> [ref v] sich (mit etw.) betrinken get drunk (on sth) ◊ *sich aus Kummer betrinken* ♦ *Sie betranken sich mit Wein und Schnaps.* sich sinnlos betrinken get blind drunk

be·trof·fen [bə'trɔfn̩] *past p of* betreffen [adj] (über etw. [acc]) betroffen upset (by sth), shocked (by/at sth) ◊ *Im Raum herrschte betroffenes Schweigen.* ♦ *Die ganze Stadt war über das schwere Unglück zutiefst betroffen.* jdn betroffen machen upset sb, shock sb ◊ *Der Tod seines Kollegen machte ihn betroffen.* ⊝bestürzt

② **be·trog** [bə'troːk] *pret of* betrügen

② **be·tro·gen** [bə'troːgn̩] *past p of* betrügen

Be·trug [bə'truːk] der <-(e)s> *no pl* fraud, deception ◊ *Durch die Angabe falscher Personalien hat er sich des Betrugs schuldig gemacht.* ♦ *Urkundenfälschung ist Betrug.* Betrug (an jdm) begehen defraud (sb), cheat (sb)

② **be·trü·gen** [bə'tryːgn̩] <betrügt, betrog, hat betrogen> [tr v] **1.** jdn betrügen deceive sb ◊ *Die Politiker haben uns belogen und betrogen.* sich selbst betrügen deceive yourself **2.** defraud ◊ *Wer das Finanzamt betrügt, muss mit schweren Strafen rechnen.* jdn um etw. betrügen swindle sb out of sth ◊ *Er hat die alte Frau um all ihr erspartes Geld betrogen.* **3.** cheat on ◊ *Er hat seine Frau schon oft betrogen.*

be·trun·ken [bə'trʊŋkn̩] *past p of* betrinken [adj]

drunk ◊ *ein betrunkener Gast* ♦ *Ich bringe sie nach Hause, weil sie völlig betrunken ist.* betrunken Auto fahren drive drunk betrunken ein Verbrechen begehen commit a crime under the influence of alcohol ⊝nüchtern [adv] etw. betrunken tun do sth in a drunk state ◊ *betrunken einen Mord begehen* ♦ *betrunken Auto fahren* ⊝nüchtern

② **Bett** [bɛt] das <-(e)s, -en> bed das Bett (frisch) beziehen change the bed, put clean sheets on the bed

⊚ ans Bett gefesselt sein be bedridden ◊ *Nach dem Herzinfarkt war er lange ans Bett gefesselt.* sich ins gemachte Bett legen have things handed to you on a plate ◊ *Er hat die Tochter eines Millionärs geheiratet und sich damit ins gemachte Bett gelegt.* das Bett hüten müssen have to stay in bed ◊ *Du hast Fieber und wirst das Bett hüten müssen.*

bet·teln ['bɛtln̩] [intr v] +haben (also pej) (um etw.) betteln beg (for sth) ◊ *Der alte Mann bettelte auf der Straße um eine milde Gabe.* ♦ *Der Hund bettelte um eine Wurst.* ♦ *Er bettelte um Verzeihung, aber sie blieb stur.*

beu·gen ['bɔøgn̩] [ref v] +haben **1.** sich irgendwohin beugen bend somewhere ◊ *Wenn du dich nach vorne beugst, siehst du mehr.* sich über etw. [acc] beugen lean over sth ◊ *Er beugte sich über das Geländer.* sich aus dem Fenster beugen lean out of the window **2.** *mostly written* sich jdm/einer Sache beugen bow to sb/sth, submit to sb/sth ◊ *Der Präsident beugte sich dem internationalen Druck.* [tr v] +haben **1.** etw. beugen bend sth ◊ *Kannst du das Knie noch beugen?* **2.** GRAM decline, inflect ◊ *Adjektive/Substantive/Verben beugen* ⊝deklinieren

be·un·ru·hi·gen [bə'ʊnruːɪgn̩] <beunruhigt, beunruhigte, hat beunruhigt> [tr v] worry, alarm ◊ *Es beunruhigt mich etwas, dass sie so lange weg ist.* ♦ *Der Brief vom Finanzamt beunruhigte sie zutiefst.* [ref v] sich beunruhigen get worried ◊ *Ich beunruhige mich immer, wenn du so lange nichts von dir hören lässt.*

be·ur·lau·ben [bə'uːɐ̯laʊbn̩] <beurlaubt, beurlaubte, hat beurlaubt> [tr v] **1.** jdn beurlauben grant sb (sabbatical) leave ◊ *Sie wurde für den Auslandsaufenthalt vom Direktor beurlaubt.* sich beurlauben lassen take time off **2.** *(euph)* suspend ◊ *Der Mitarbeiter wurde bis zur Klärung des Vorfalls beurlaubt.*

be·ur·tei·len [bə'ʊɐ̯taelən] <beurteilt, beurteilte, hat beurteilt> [tr v] jdn/etw. (richtig/als gut) beurteilen judge sb/sth (correctly/positively), assess sb/sth (correctly/positively) ◊ *Soweit ich das beurteilen kann, bin ich morgen mit meiner Arbeit fertig.* ♦ *Er hat die Situation richtig beurteilt.* etw. falsch beurteilen misjudge sth jdn/etw. nach etw. beurteilen judge sb/sth by sth ◊ *Die Schüler werden nach ihrer Leistung im Unterricht beurteilt.* jd kann etw. nicht beurteilen sb is not in a position to judge sth

Beu·te ['bɔøtə] die <-> *no pl* **1.** loot, booty ◊ *Der Dieb wurde ertappt und flüchtete ohne Beute.* **2.** prey ◊ *auf Jagd nach Beute gehen; (in hunting)* bag; *(in fishing)* catch **3.** *mostly written (lofty, fig)* victim, sacrifice ◊ *Das Schiff wurde bei dem Unglück Beute der See.*

⊚ fette/reiche Beute rich pickings ◊ *Die Bank-*

räuber machten fette Beute. jdm/etw. **zur Beute fallen 1.** fall into the hands of sb/sth **2.** *(animal)* jdm/einem Tier zur Beute fallen become sb's/an animal's prey ◊ *Die Fliege fiel der Spinne zur Beute.*

Beu·tel [ˈbɔøtl̩] der <–s, –> **1.** bag ◊ *Er steckte seine Turnschuhe in den Beutel.* ✦ *ein Beutel Orangen/Äpfel*; *(for money)* purse **2.** ZOO pouch ◊ *Kängurus transportieren ihre Jungen in einem Beutel.*

◉ **tief in den Beutel greifen** *(fam, oldf)* dig deep into your pockets ◊ *An der Kasse musste sie tief in den Beutel greifen.*

be·völ·kern [bəˈfœlkɐn] <bevölkert, bevölkerte, hat bevölkert> [tr v] **1.** populate ◊ *Im Sommer bevölkern Touristen die sonst so ruhigen Strände.* **2.** inhabit ◊ *Etwa 300 000 Einwohner bevölkern die Stadt.*

② **Be·völ·ke·rung** [bəˈfœlkərʊŋ] die <–, –en> *most sing* population ◊ *Die gesamte Bevölkerung leidet unter dem Krieg.* ✦ *die französische/westdeutsche Bevölkerung* ⊜Einwohner

② **be·vor** [bəˈfoːɐ̯] [conjunc] before ◊ *Bevor ich mit der Arbeit anfange, muss ich noch schnell telefonieren.* ✦ *Das war, bevor ich ihn kennen lernte.* ⊜ehe ⊜nachdem

be·vor·ste·hen [bəˈfoːɐ̯ʃteːən] <steht bevor, stand bevor, hat/ist bevorgestanden> [intr v] *+haben, in South G, Austr, Swiss often +sein* **1.** lie ahead ◊ *Dem Wetterbericht zufolge steht ein Unwetter bevor.* kurz bevorstehen be imminent ◊ *Viele sind der Ansicht, dass ein Krieg kurz bevorsteht.* das Schlimmste steht uns noch bevor the worst is yet to come **2.** be coming, be on its way ◊ *Weihnachten/Ostern steht bevor.*

be·vor·zu·gen [bəˈfoːɐ̯tsuːɡŋ̍] <bevorzugt, bevorzugte, hat bevorzugt> [tr v] **1.** jdn/etw. (gegenüber/vor jdm) bevorzugen prefer sb/sth (to sb), favour sb/sth (over sb) ◊ *„Möchten Sie einen Kaffee?" — „Nein danke, ich bevorzuge Tee."* ✦ *Er bevorzugt rothaarige Frauen.* (es) bevorzugen, etw. zu tun prefer to do sth ◊ *Sie bevorzugt es, alleine zu wohnen.* ⊜vorziehen **2.** jdn (gegenüber/vor jdm) bevorzugen give sb preferential treatment (over sb) ◊ *Behinderte Kandidaten werden bei gleicher Qualifikation bevorzugt.* ⊜benachteiligen

be·wa·chen [bəˈvaxn̩] <bewacht, bewachte, hat bewacht> [tr v] **1.** guard, watch (over) ◊ *Der Parkplatz wird rund um die Uhr bewacht.* ✦ *Unser Hund bewacht das Baby.* **2.** SPORT mark

be·waff·nen [bəˈvafnən] <bewaffnet, bewaffnete, hat bewaffnet> [tr v] jdn/sich (mit etw.) bewaffnen arm sb/yourself (with sth) ◊ *Er bewaffnete sich mit einem Messer und überfiel eine Tankstelle.*

be·wah·ren [bəˈvaːrən] <bewahrt, bewahrte, hat bewahrt> [tr v] **1.** keep, maintain ◊ *Traditionen bewahren* ✦ *das Jagdgebiet des Adler bewahren* ein Geheimnis bewahren keep a secret **2.** etw. im Gedächtnis bewahren preserve the memory of sth jdm ein gutes Andenken bewahren preserve sb's memory **3.** jdn/etw. vor jdm/etw. bewahren preserve sb/sth from sb/sth, protect sb/sth from sb/sth ◊ *Sie konnte ihn nicht vor dem Unglück bewahren.* jdn davor bewahren, etw. zu tun prevent sb from doing sth, save sb from doing sth ◊ *Er hat mich davor bewahrt, einen Fehler zu*

begehen. jdn vor einer Enttäuschung bewahren spare sb a disappointment **4.** keep, retain ◊ *die Fassung/seinen Humor bewahren* seine Gelassenheit bewahren keep your cool **5.** keep, store ◊ *Er bewahrt ihr Foto in seinem Geldbeutel.*

be·wäh·ren [bəˈvɛːrən] <bewährt sich, bewährte sich, hat sich bewährt> [ref v] sich bewähren prove your worth ◊ *Er muss sich in seiner neuen Arbeit erst noch bewähren.* sich als Anwalt etc. bewähren prove to be a good lawyer etc. sich als gut bewähren prove to be good etw. bewährt sich (bestens) sth proves (very) successful ◊ *Dieses Medikament hat sich bestens bewährt.*

be·wäh·rung [bəˈvɛːrʊŋ] die <–, –en> **1.** LAW probation ◊ *Er bekam drei Jahre ohne Bewährung.* sechs Monate etc. mit Bewährung, eine Freiheitsstrafe von sechs Monaten etc. mit Bewährung a sixth months etc. suspended sentence eine Strafe (für die Dauer von drei Jahren) zur Bewährung aussetzen suspend a sentence (for three years) **2.** die Bewährung ... [gen] the successful use of sth ◊ *die Bewährung neuer Baustoffe in der Praxis* ✦ *die neuen Grundlagen des Scheidungsrechts und ihre praktische Bewährung* die Stunde der Bewährung the moment of truth

be·wäl·ti·gen [bəˈvɛltɪɡn̩] <bewältigt, bewältigte, hat bewältigt> [tr v] **1.** manage ◊ *Die Strecke ist auch für kleine Kinder zu bewältigen.* ✦ *Die Arbeit war leicht zu bewältigen.* ✦ *Es ist erstaunlich, wie sie mit fünf Kindern den Alltag bewältigt.* ⊜meistern **2.** get over, overcome ◊ *Ängste/Sorgen bewältigen* ✦ *Er hat die Trennung von seiner Frau bis heute nicht bewältigt.* ⊜überwinden

⑦ **be·we·gen¹** [bəˈveːɡn̩] <bewegt, bewegte, hat bewegt> [tr v] **1.** move ◊ *Ich kann meinen Arm nicht bewegen.* sich bewegen move ◊ *Die Fahnen bewegten sich im Wind.* **2.** TECHN drive, power ◊ *Das Wasser bewegt das Rad der Mühle.* **3.** *(emotionally)* move, touch ◊ *Das Schicksal dieser Kinder bewegt mich sehr.* ✦ *Der Film hatte sie zutiefst bewegt.* **4.** *(intellectually)* jdn bewegen occupy sb ◊ *Das ist eine Frage, die die Forscher seit langem bewegt.* [ref v] **1.** sich bewegen move ◊ *Er bewegt sich nicht mehr, ich glaube, er ist tot.* ✦ *Er bewegte sich schnell in Richtung Ausgang.* ✦ *Er bewegt sich nur in den besten Kreisen.* ✦ *Die Erde bewegt sich um die Sonne.* **2.** sich bewegen get exercise ◊ *Die Kinder sollten sich mehr bewegen.*

be·we·gen² [bəˈveːɡn̩] <bewegt, bewog, hat bewogen> [tr v] jdn zu etw. bewegen make sb do sth ◊ *Was hat ihn wohl zu dieser Tat bewogen?* Er ließ sich durch nichts bewegen, mir zu helfen. Nothing could have made him help me., Nothing could have persuaded him to help me.

be·weg·lich [bəˈveːklɪç] [adj] **1.** flexible, supple ◊ *Sie ist Tänzerin und hat einen sehr beweglichen Körper.* ✦ *Yoga macht beweglich.* ⊜unbeweglich **2.** movable ◊ *Die Puppe hat bewegliche Glieder.* ✦ *Die Stuhllehne ist beweglich.* ✦ *Einige Feiertage sind beweglich.* **3.** flexible ◊ *Der Chef hat sich beweglich gezeigt und das neue Konzept angenommen.* geistig beweglich nimble-minded ⊜unbeweglich **4.** *only before ns* mobile ◊ *Möbel sind bewegliche Güter.* ⊜unbeweglich

be·wegt [bəˈveːkt] *past p of* bewegen [adj]

1. moved, touched ◊ *Beim Abschied war er tief bewegt.* ♦ *Mit bewegten Worten dankte er allen Helfern.* 2. turbulent ◊ *Seine Vergangenheit war wohl ziemlich bewegt.* ♦ *Sie führt ein bewegtes Leben.* 3. *(sea)* rough, choppy ◊ *eine schwach/ leicht bewegte See mit kleinen Wellen*

② **Be·we·gung** [bə'veːɡʊn] die <–, –en> 1. movement ◊ *Jede Bewegung ist für sie schmerzhaft.* ♦ *Er ist Anhänger einer Bewegung, die für den Frieden kämpft.* ♦ *Sie studiert die Bewegung der Aktienkurse genau.* in Bewegung sein be moving ◊ *Die ganze Stadt war in Bewegung.* sich in Bewegung setzen start moving ◊ *Der Zug/Die Gruppe setzte sich langsam in Bewegung.* 2. motion ◊ *die Bewegung der Räder* ♦ *die Bewegung der Erde um die Sonne* 3. exercise ◊ *Du brauchst mehr Bewegung.* 4. emotion ◊ *Ihr Gesicht verriet keinerlei Bewegung.* ⊜Rührung

⊛ **Himmel und Hölle in Bewegung setzen** move heaven and earth in Bewegung bringen get underway ◊ *Er hat es geschafft, die Gespräche in Bewegung zu bringen.* in etw. ⌊acc⌋ Bewegung bringen push sth forward ◊ *Bewegung in eine Diskussion bringen* in Bewegung kommen pick up, move forward ◊ *Nach der Rezession kommt der Handel langsam wieder in Bewegung.* einiges in Bewegung setzen shake things up ◊ *Seit er im Amt ist, hat er schon einiges in Bewegung gesetzt.* den ganzen Tag in Bewegung sein be on your feet all day long keine Bewegung freeze ◊ *„Keine Bewegung!", rief der Räuber.*

② **Be·weis** [bə'vaɛs] der <–(e)s, –e> proof, evidence ◊ *Das ist der Beweis für seine Schuld.* ♦ *der Beweis des Satzes von Pythagoras* etw. unter Beweis stellen prove sth ◊ *Jetzt kannst du deine Fähigkeiten unter Beweis stellen.*

② **be·wei·sen** [bə'vaɛzn] <beweist, bewies, hat bewiesen> ⌊tr v⌋ 1. prove ◊ *Die Polizei konnte nicht beweisen, dass er der Täter war.* ♦ *Weißt du noch, wie man den Satz des Thales beweist?* 2. *(courage, love etc.)* show ◊ *Sie hat großen Mut bewiesen, als sie das tat.* ♦ *Damit hat er ihr seine Liebe bewiesen.*

② **be·wer·ben** [bə'vɛʳbm̩] <bewirbt sich, bewarb sich, hat sich beworben> ⌊ref v⌋ sich (um/für etw.) bewerben apply (for sth) ◊ *Keiner hat sich bislang um das Amt des Vorsitzenden beworben.* ♦ *Wer hat sich für die Rolle der Julia beworben?* sich als etw. bewerben apply for the post of sth ◊ *Sie hat sich als Sekretärin beworben.* sich irgendwo bewerben apply to somewhere ◊ *Ich habe mich in einem Verlag beworben.* ♦ *Er bewirbt sich bei Siemens.*

② **Be·wer·bung** [bə'vɛʳbʊn] die <–, –en> application ◊ *eine Bewerbung um/für eine Stelle schreiben* ♦ *unsere Bewerbung um diesen Auftrag* ♦ *die Bewerbung bei einer Firma* ♦ *ihre Bewerbung als Redakteurin*

be·werk·stel·li·gen [bə'vɛʳkʃtɛlɪɡn̩] <bewerkstelligt, bewerkstelligte, hat bewerkstelligt> ⌊tr v⌋ manage ◊ *Ich weiß nicht, wie ich es bewerkstelligen soll, in das Gebäude zu gelangen.*

be·wer·ten [bə'veːɐ̯tn̩] <bewertet, bewertete, hat bewertet> ⌊tr v⌋ 1. jdn/etw. bewerten judge sb/sth, assess sb/sth ◊ *etw. gerecht/gut/schlecht bewerten*; *(sb's performance at school, university)* etw. bewerten mark sth, assess sth, grade sth Sein

Aufsatz wurde mit der Note 3 bewertet. He got a 'C' for his essay. 2. *(lofty)* etw. als etw. bewerten consider sth (to be) sth ◊ *Der Vorstand bewertete das Angebot als fair.* 3. FIN etw. mit etw. bewerten value sth at sth ◊ *Mit 300 000 Euro ist dieses alte Haus viel zu hoch bewertet.*

Be·wer·tung [bə'veːɐ̯tʊn] die <–, –en> 1. *no pl* assessment, marking, grading ◊ *Die Bewertung der Klausur erfolgt durch zwei Prüfer.* 2. mark, grade ◊ *Viele Schüler waren mit ihrer Bewertung nicht einverstanden.* 3. reference, evaluation ◊ *Mein Professor schreibt mir eine Bewertung, wenn ich mich um das Stipendium bewerbe.* 4. *no pl* FIN valuation ◊ *Die Bewertung des Hauses ergab eine Summe von etwa 1 Million Euro.*

be·wil·li·gen [bə'vɪlɪɡn̩] <bewilligt, bewilligte, hat bewilligt> ⌊tr v⌋ *(form)* (jdm/etw.) etw. bewilligen grant (sb/sth) sth, award (sb/sth) sth ◊ *Ihm wurde ein Kredit bewilligt.* ⊜gewähren

be·wir·ken [bə'vɪʳkn̩] <bewirkt, bewirkte, hat bewirkt> ⌊tr v⌋ achieve, bring about, cause ◊ *Was soll denn das bewirken?* ♦ *das Gegenteil bewirken*

be·wo·gen [bə'voːɡn̩] *past p of* bewegen²

be·woh·nen [bə'voːnən] <bewohnt, bewohnte, hat bewohnt> ⌊tr v⌋ etw. bewohnen live in sth, occupy sth, inhabit sth ◊ *Sie bewohnen ein kleines Reihenhaus am Stadtrand.* ♦ *Ist diese Insel bewohnt?*

② **Be·woh·ner** [bə'voːnɐ] der <–s, –>, **Be·woh·ne·rin** [bə'voːnərɪn] die <–, –nen> resident ◊ *die Bewohner des ersten Stocks*; *(of a town or region)* inhabitant ◊ *Die Bewohner der Stadt Bonn haben einen neuen Bürgermeister.*

Be·wöl·kung [bə'vœlkʊn] die <–> *no pl* cloud(s) ◊ *dichte/leichte/starke Bewölkung* ♦ *Im Laufe des Vormittags zunehmende Bewölkung und vereinzelt Schauer möglich.*

be·wun·dern [bə'vʊndɐn] <bewundert, bewunderte, hat bewundert> ⌊tr v⌋ admire ◊ *Ich bewundere meine Mutter, weil sie immer so viel Geduld hat.* ♦ *Deine Ausdauer ist wirklich zu bewundern.* ♦ *kostbare Kunstwerke bewundern*

be·wusst [bə'vʊst] ⌊adj⌋ <bewusster, am bewusstesten> 1. only before sn deliberate, conscious ◊ *eine bewusste Lüge/Tat/Entscheidung* ⊜absichtlich ⊜unbewusst 2. aware, conscious ◊ *Die Verbraucher sind beim Kauf von Lebensmitteln bewusster geworden.* 3. sich ⌊dat⌋ einer Sache ⌊gen⌋ bewusst sein be aware of sth ◊ *Bist du dir der Folgen bewusst, die dein Handeln haben kann?* ♦ *Bist du dir eigentlich bewusst, was du da von mir verlangst?* sich ⌊dat⌋ bewusst sein, dass be aware that ◊ *Bist du dir bewusst, dass diese Entscheidung wichtige Konsequenzen hat?* etw. ist jdm bewusst sb is aware of sth ◊ *Mir war das Risiko nicht bewusst.* 4. sich ⌊dat⌋ einer Sache ⌊gen⌋ bewusst werden become aware of sth, realize sth ◊ *Mit einem Mal wurde sie sich des vollen Umfangs ihrer Verantwortung bewusst.* sich ⌊dat⌋ bewusst werden, dass become aware that, realize that ◊ *Erst später wurde sie sich bewusst, dass er Recht hatte.* etw. wird jdm bewusst sb becomes aware of sth, sb realizes sth ◊ *Erst viel zu spät wurde ihm bewusst, worauf er sich da eingelassen hatte.* jdm etw. bewusst machen make sb aware of sth ◊ *Sie will ihm seine Fehler bewusst machen.* sich ⌊dat⌋ etw. bewusst machen be aware of sth ◊ *Machen*

A B C D E F G H I J K L M N O P Q R S T U V W X Y Z

Sie sich bewusst, dass es immer mehrere Lösungen gibt. **5.** *only before ns* in question ◊ *Ist das die bewusste Stelle?* [adv] **1.** deliberately, consciously ◊ *Das hat er ganz bewusst getan.* ♦ *Du hast mich bewusst in die Irre geführt.* ⊖vorsätzlich ⊕unbewusst **2.** consciously ◊ *Wir alle sind bewusst oder unbewusst an der Umweltverschmutzung beteiligt.* ⊖unbewusst

be·wusst·los [bə'vʊstloːs] [adj] *no comp/superl* unconscious ◊ *Die Sanitäter beugten sich über den bewusstlosen Jungen.* ♦ *bewusstlos sein/zusammenbrechen* ♦ *Die Angreifer schlugen ihn fast bewusstlos.*

Be·wusst·sein [bə'vʊstzaɛn] das <–s> *no pl* **1.** consciousness ◊ *das Bewusstsein verlieren* ♦ *Manche Drogen erweitern das Bewusstsein.* **2.** knowledge, awareness, consciousness ◊ *In dem Bewusstsein, das Richtige getan zu haben, ging er nach Hause.* ♦ *sich etw. ins Bewusstsein rufen* **3.** convictions, consciousness ◊ *das geschichtliche/ nationale/politische Bewusstsein*

② **be·zah·len** [bə'tsaːlən] <bezahlt, bezahlte, hat bezahlt> [tr v] *etw./jdn bezahlen* pay sth/sb ◊ *Die Miete muss bis zum 5. des Monats bezahlt werden.* ♦ *Bist du dafür schon bezahlt worden?* ♦ *Viele Handwerker wollen bar bezahlt werden.* ♦ *Wie viel hast du für den Pulli bezahlt?*; *(finance)* (jdm) *etw. bezahlen* pay for (sb's) sth ◊ *Meine Mutter hat mir die Reise bezahlt.* ♦ *Sie hat ihr Auto in Raten bezahlt.* [intr v] pay ◊ *Lass mal, heute bezahle ich.* ♦ *Herr Ober, bezahlen bitte.* *für etw. bezahlen* pay for sth ◊ *Meine Eltern weigern sich, für mein Studium zu bezahlen.*

☺ **nicht zu bezahlen sein 1.** be too expensive ◊ *Wohnungen in der Innenstadt sind nicht zu bezahlen.* **2.** be invaluable ◊ *Gesundheit ist mit Geld nicht zu bezahlen.* ♦ *Ein Mitarbeiter, der so selbstständig wie er arbeitet, ist nicht zu bezahlen.*

Be·zah·lung [bə'tsaːlʊŋ] die <–, –en> *most sing* **1.** payment ◊ *Wir bitten Sie um Bezahlung der Rechnung bis zum 15. August. Bezahlung bitte an der Kasse.* Please pay at the checkout. **2.** *(sum)* pay, remuneration ◊ *Er arbeitet nur gegen Bezahlung.* ♦ *Wir bieten Ihnen gute Bezahlung für Ihre Dienste an.*

be·zeich·nen [bə'tsaɛçnən] <bezeichnete, hat bezeichnet> [tr v] **1.** *jdn/etw. (als etw.) bezeichnen* call sb/sth sth ◊ *Junge Hunde bezeichnet man als „Welpen".* Wie bezeichnet man im Deutschen/Englischen …? What is the German/ English word for …? **2.** *etw. bezeichnet etw.* sth signifies sth, sth denotes sth ◊ *Das Wort „Bäcker" bezeichnet jemanden, der Brot und Gebäck herstellt.* **3.** *jdn/etw. als etw. bezeichnen* describe sb/sth as sth ◊ *jdn als Dummkopf/Freund/Verräter bezeichnen* ♦ *Sie bezeichnet sich als intelligent.* **4.** *etw. mit etw. bezeichnen* mark sth with sth ◊ *Der Wanderweg ist mit einem roten Pfeil bezeichnet.* ⊖markieren

be·zeich·nend [bə'tsaɛçnənt] *pres p p of* bezeichnen [adj] typical, characteristic ◊ *ein bezeichnendes Merkmal* ♦ *Diese Reaktion ist bezeichnend für seine Eifersucht.*

Be·zeich·nung [bə'tsaɛçnʊŋ] die <–, –en> **1.** word, term ◊ *Für diese Erscheinung gibt es unterschiedliche Bezeichnungen.* **2.** *no pl* designa-

tion ◊ *eine Kiste ohne Bezeichnung des Inhalts* ♦ *Produkte ohne Bezeichnung des Herkunftlandes*

be·zeu·gen [bə'tsɔɪɡn̩] <bezeugt, bezeugte, hat bezeugt> [tr v] **1.** *etw. bezeugen* testify to sth ◊ *Würden Sie das vor Gericht bezeugen?* ♦ *Ich kann bezeugen, dass er an dem Tag mit mir zusammen war.* ♦ *etw. unter Eid bezeugen* **2.** *etw. bezeugt etw.* sth proves sth, sth shows sth ◊ *Dieses Dokument bezeugt, dass er der rechtmäßige Erbe ist.* ♦ *Seine Handlungen bezeugen, dass er es ehrlich meint. Die Existenz der Stadt ist schon im 13. Jahrhundert bezeugt.* The existence of the town is documented as far back as the 13th century. **3.** *jdm Dankbarkeit/Hochachtung bezeugen* show sb your gratefulness/respect

② **be·zie·hen** [bə'tsiːən] <bezieht, bezog, hat bezogen> [tr v] **1.** cover ◊ *Ich will mein Sofa neu beziehen.*; *(with bedlinen)* (frisch) beziehen change ◊ *Die Betten werden einmal im Monat frisch bezogen.* **2.** *(a house)* etw. beziehen move into sth ◊ *Die Villa kann in zwei Monaten bezogen werden.* **3.** get ◊ *Wir beziehen eine Tageszeitung.* ♦ *Er bezieht sein ganzes Wissen aus Büchern.* ♦ *Ersatzteile können Sie im Fachhandel beziehen.* **4.** *(money)* receive ◊ *Sie beziehen seit kurzem Sozialhilfe.* ♦ *Er bezieht ein Gehalt von 4000 Euro im Monat.*; *(a pension)* draw **5.** *(a post)* take up ◊ *Die Wache hat ihren Posten bezogen.* ♦ *Das Militär hat Stellungen entlang der Grenze bezogen.* **6.** *zu etw. Stellung beziehen* state your view on sth ◊ *Ich wollte dazu keine Stellung beziehen.* *einen klaren Standpunkt zu etw. beziehen* take a clear stance on sth **7.** *etw. auf etw.* [acc] *beziehen* compare sth to sth ◊ *Bezogen auf seinen Einsatz ist seine Bezahlung eher dürftig.* **8.** *etw. auf jdn/ etw. beziehen* apply sth to sb/sth ◊ *Sie hat die Kritik auf ihre Arbeit bezogen. Du musst nicht jede meiner Bemerkungen auf dich beziehen.* You mustn't take any of my remarks personally. [ref v] *sich auf jdn/etw. beziehen* refer to sb/sth ◊ *Ich beziehe mich hier auf die Aussagen von Frau Wenig.* ♦ *Ich sage dir das jetzt im Vertrauen, also beziehe dich bitte nicht darauf.* ♦ *Mein Artikel bezieht sich auf die Theorie von Marx. Dein Argument bezieht sich doch in keiner Weise auf das, was ich gesagt habe.* Your argument bears no reference to anything I said.

② **Be·zie·hung** [bə'tsiːʊŋ] die <–, –en> **1.** *(to a person)* relationship ◊ *Ich habe eine gute Beziehung zu meinen Eltern.* ♦ *Er will keine feste Beziehung.* **2.** *most pl (between countries, organizations)* relations ◊ *wirtschaftliche Beziehungen* ♦ *Er ist Professor für internationale Beziehungen.* ♦ *Wir unterhalten gute Beziehungen zu diesem Staat.* **3.** *only pl* Beziehungen contacts, connections ◊ *Ich habe die Stelle über Beziehungen bekommen.* ♦ *Da soll meine Tante mal ihre Beziehungen zum Bürgermeister spielen lassen.* **4.** *(between facts, events)* connection ◊ *Es besteht eine Beziehung zwischen den beiden Vorfällen.* ♦ *Aggressives Verhalten der Kinder steht oft in Beziehung zu ihrer Erziehung.* **5.** *(for literature, art)* jds/eine Beziehung zu etw. sb's/an appreciation of sth ◊ *Zu dieser Art von Musik habe ich keinerlei Beziehung.* **6.** respect ◊ *In dieser Beziehung versteht er keinen Spaß.* ♦ *In gewisser Beziehung muss ich dir da*

Recht geben.
ⓔ **zu jdm in Beziehung treten** *(form)* contact sb ◊ *Der Außenminister will zu seinem italienischen Kollegen deswegen in Beziehung treten.* miteinander in Beziehung treten interrelate ◊ *Wie treten Männer in unserer Gesellschaft miteinander in Beziehung?*

be·zie·hungs·wei·se [bəˈtsiːʊŋsvaɛzə] (adv) *(abbr bzw.)* **1.** or (rather) ◊ *Ich kann Ihnen den Wagen zu 6000,– bzw. 6500,– € anbieten.* ♦ *In England, beziehungsweise Großbritannien, ist der Euro bislang noch nicht eingeführt worden.* **2.** and, respectively ◊ *Ihre Kinder sind acht beziehungsweise elf Jahre alt.*

Be·zirk [bəˈtsɪrk] der <–(e)s, –e> district ◊ *Wir wohnen in einem ländlichen/städtischen Bezirk.* ♦ *Das Parlament eines Bezirks heißt Bezirkstag.*

Be·zug [bəˈtsuːk] der <–(e)s, Bezüge> **1.** *(of furniture)* cover ◊ *Der Bezug dieses Sessels hat kein schönes Muster.* **2.** *(of bedding)* duvet cover ◊ *Ich muss noch die Bezüge für das Kinderbett wechseln.; (for the pillow)* pillowcase, pillowslip **3.** *no pl (of goods, money)* receipt ◊ *zum Bezug von Arbeitslosengeld/Rente/Sozialhilfe berechtigt sein; (of a newspaper)* subscription **4.** *only pl* Bezüge income ◊ *Bitte teilen Sie uns die Höhe Ihrer monatlichen Bezüge mit.* **5.** *only written* Bezug auf jdn/etw. nehmen refer to sb/sth ◊ *In seiner Ansprache nahm er Bezug auf die Geschichte des Unternehmens.* ♦ *Bezug nehmend auf unser Telefongespräch vor drei Tagen ...* **6.** in Bezug auf jdn/etw. concerning sb/sth ◊ *Haben Sie unsere E-Mail in Bezug auf das Angebot erhalten?* in Bezug auf jdn/etw. regarding sb/sth, as regards sb/sth, with regard to sb/sth ◊ *In Bezug auf seine Gesundheit ist er sehr vorsichtig.* **7.** *only written (form)* mit/unter Bezug auf etw. (acc) with reference to sth ◊ *Unter Bezug auf Ihr Schreiben vom 15. Juli teilen wir Ihnen mit, dass ...* **8.** zu jdm/etw. keinen Bezug haben not be interested in sb/sth, not be into sb/sth ◊ *Sie hat keinen Bezug zu Tieren.*

be·züg·lich [bəˈtsyːklɪç] (prep) *sing nouns without article or attribute are not declined when following this prep, otherwise* (+gen) *or fam* (+dat) *with reference to* ◊ *Bezüglich Ihres Antrags möchten wir Ihnen mitteilen, dass ...* ⊜hinsichtlich

be·zwei·feln [bəˈtsvaɛfln̩] <bezweifelt, bezweifelte, hat bezweifelt> (tr v) etw. bezweifeln doubt sth, have your etc. doubts about sth ◊ *Ich bezweifle seine Aussage, da seine Geschichte sehr unglaubwürdig klingt.* bezweifeln, dass doubt whether, have your etc. doubts whether ◊ *Sie bezweifelte, dass dies eine gute Idee war.*

BH [beːˈhaː] der <–s, –s> *(fam) (abbr of* Büstenhalter*)* bra ◊ *einen BH tragen*

Bi·bel [ˈbiːbl̩] die <–, –n> **1.** die Bibel the Bible ◊ *Schon in der Bibel steht, dass ...* ⊜die Heilige Schrift **2.** bible ◊ *Die Werke Freuds sind die Bibel jedes Psychoanalytikers.*

ⓩ **Bib·li·o·thek** [biblioˈteːk] die <–, –en> library ◊ *die städtische Bibliothek* ♦ *Mein Onkel hat eine umfangreiche Bibliothek.* ⊜Bücherei

bie·der [ˈbiːdɐ] (adj, adv) **1.** conservative(ly), conventional(ly) ◊ *Sie sieht mit ihrer Frisur manchmal richtig bieder aus.* ♦ *ein biederes Kleid* ♦ *bieder*

gekleidet **2.** *(oldf)* upright, upstanding ◊ *ein biederer Bürger*

ⓩ **bie·gen** [ˈbiːɡn̩] <biegt, bog, hat/ist gebogen> (tr v) +*haben* bend ◊ *Er hat den Draht zu einer Schlinge gebogen.* ♦ *Und nun biegen Sie den Oberkörper nach vorn.* sich biegen bend ◊ *Die Bäume bogen sich im Wind.* ♦ *Die Äste biegen sich unter dem Gewicht der Äpfel.* (intr v) +*sein* turn ◊ *Biegen Sie nach der Kreuzung in die Goethestraße.* ♦ *Ich sah noch, wie er um die Ecke bog.*
ⓔ **auf Biegen und Brechen** at all costs ◊ *Sie will auf Biegen und Brechen Sängerin werden.*

Bie·ne [ˈbiːnə] die <–, –n> **1.** zoo bee ◊ *Mein Großvater züchtet Bienen.* ♦ *Bienen stechen nur, wenn sie sich bedroht fühlen.* **2.** *(fam, oldf)* eine flotte Biene a hot chick, a nice bit of stuff ◊ *Siehst du die flotte Biene, die da drüben an der Bar bedient?*

ⓩ **Bier** [biːɐ̯] das <–(e)s, –e> *pl 'Bier' when used with expressions of quantity* beer ◊ *In Deutschland gibt es ganz verschiedene Biere.* ♦ *Zwei Bier, bitte!* ♦ *Ich trinke selten Bier.*

German beers are famous for their quality. In Germany, beer production is regulated by the purity law of 1516. According to this law, beer should contain only barley malt, hops, yeast and water, and must be fermented. Since an EU ruling in 1987, drinks which do not conform to the purity law have been sold as beer; German brewers, however, continue to abide by the law. The most popular German beers are *Altbier, Pils, Weißbier* and *Hefeweizen. Altbier* or *Alt* (dark beer) is a dark-coloured, bitter and malty beer, which is produced in the area around Düsseldorf and Münster. *Pils* or *Pils(e)ner* is a light-coloured beer that is brewed using soft water. Its slightly bitter taste and creamy head are signs that it contains a lot of hops. *Weißbier* or *Weizenbier* (wheat beer) is made out of a mixture of barley malt and wheat malt and contains a lot of carbon dioxide. *Hefeweizen* is an unfiltered wheat beer which is very cloudy and contains yeast sediments.

ⓩ **Bier·gar·ten** [ˈbiːɐ̯ɡaˌtn̩] der <–s, Biergärten> beer garden ◊ *Wir gehen im Sommer oft in den Biergarten.*

Beer gardens are particularly popular in Bavaria. They offer a range of drinks other than beer.

ⓩ **bie·ten** [ˈbiːtn̩] <bietet, bot, hat geboten> (tr v) **1.** jdm etw. bieten give sb sth, offer sb sth ◊ *Sobald ihm die Chance geboten wird, wir er sich beruflich verändern.* ♦ *Das Rote Kreuz bietet den Flüchtlingen Unterkunft in Zelten.* ♦ *Diesen Kindern wird zu Hause wenig Liebe und Zuwendung geboten.* **2.** *(a film, an opera)* geboten werden/ sein be on ◊ *In der Oper wird momentan "Carmen" geboten.* ♦ *Abends ist hier nicht viel geboten.* **3.** *(a performance)* give ◊ *Die deutsche Mannschaft bot ein hervorragendes Spiel.* ♦ *Die Schauspieler haben uns eine großartige Vorstellung geboten.* **4.** *(certain features, a sum of money)* offer ◊ *Dieses Wörterbuch bietet dem Benutzer eine Vielzahl an Beispielen.* ♦ *Diese Wohnung bietet einen herrlichen Blick über die Stadt.* ♦ *Ich biete 100 Euro für die Vase.* ♦ *Wer bietet mehr?* (intr v)

A
B
C
D
E
F
G
H
I
J
K
L
M
N
O
P
Q
R
S
T
U
V
W
X
Y
Z

make a bid ◊ *Will noch jemand bieten?* [ref v] *(an opportunity, a possibility)* sich bieten arise ◊ *Sobald sich die Gelegenheit bietet, werde ich mit ihm sprechen.; (a prospect, view)* open up ◊ *Dir bieten sich doch so viele Chancen, ergreife sie!* ✦ *Vom Gipfel bot sich uns ein wunderschöner Ausblick.*

⊛ sich [dat] etw. bieten lassen tolerate sth, put up with sth ◊ *Dass du dir solche Frechheiten von deinen Schülern bieten lässt!* ✦ *Das lasse ich mir nicht länger bieten!*

Bi·lanz [bi'lants] die <-, -en> 1. ECON balance sheet, annual accounts ◊ *eine negative/positive Bilanz* ✦ *die Bilanz für 2005 veröffentlichen/vorlegen* 2. *no pl* result ◊ *Sieben Tote und über 100 Verletzte waren die traurige Bilanz des Erdbebens.*

⊛ (die) Bilanz (aus etw.) ziehen take stock (of sth) ◊ *Bilanz aus seinem Leben ziehen*

② **Bild** [bɪlt] das <-(e)s, -er> 1. painting, picture ◊ *Bilder von Rubens* ✦ *Da hast du aber ein schönes Bild gemalt.* 2. photo(graph), picture ◊ *Wann zeigst du uns mal deine Bilder von Hawaii?* ✦ *Er hat in der Brieftasche ein Bild seiner Frau.* ⊝Foto 3. illustration, picture ◊ *die Bilder in einem Kinderbuch ansehen* ✦ *Siehe dazu das Bild auf Seite 14.* 4. *(on TV, in the cinema)* picture ◊ *Bei meinem Fernseher war plötzlich das Bild weg.* ✦ *Bild und Ton: Wolfgang Schwarz.* 5. idea, notion ◊ *Du kannst dir gar kein Bild machen, wie schwierig das ist.* ✦ *Ich möchte mir selbst ein Bild von den dortigen Zuständen machen.* 6. *(fig)* image ◊ *Uns bot sich ein Bild des Schreckens.* ✦ *Ich werde diese Bilder nie vergessen. Dieser Schriftsteller bedient sich vieler Bilder. This author uses a lot of imagery.*

⊛ ein Bild für die Götter *(fam, hum)* a hilarious sight ■ im Bild(e) sein be in the picture ◊ *Aha, jetzt bin ich im Bilde.* ✦ *Bist du über die neuesten Entwicklungen im Bild?*

bil·den ['bɪldn̩] <bildet, bildete, hat gebildet> [tr v] 1. form etw. (aus etw.) bilden form sth (out of/from sth) ◊ *aus Wörtern Sätze bilden* ✦ *Die Kinder bildeten einen Kreis.* ✦ *eine Regierung bilden* ✦ *Dieser Fluss bildet die Grenze zwischen den beiden Staaten.* 2. *(a shape, figure)* etw. (aus etw.) bilden form sth (out of/from sth), shape sth (out of/from sth) ◊ *aus Ton eine Figur bilden* 3. *(plant)* develop ◊ *Die Pflanze hat neue Triebe gebildet.* 4. jdn bilden help sb to develop, educate sb ◊ *Reisen bildet den Menschen.* [intr v] broaden the mind ◊ *Reisen bildet ungemein.* ✦ *Niemand kann bezweifeln, dass Lesen bildet.* [ref v] 1. sich bilden form ◊ *Im Laufe des Tages bildeten sich Wolken.* ✦ *Auf seiner Stirn bildeten sich Schweißtropfen.* sich [dat] eine Meinung/ein Urteil (zu etw.) bilden form an opinion (about sth) ◊ *Er hat sich noch kein endgültiges Urteil zu dem Fall gebildet.* sich [dat] eine Meinung/ein Urteil (über jdn/etw.) bilden form an opinion (about sb/sth) ◊ *Darf ich mir darüber erst einmal eine Meinung bilden?* 2. sich bilden educate yourself ◊ *sich durch Reisen bilden*

Bild·hau·er ['bɪlthaoɐ] der <-s, ->,
Bild·hau·e·rin ['bɪlthaoərɪn] die <-, -nen> sculptor ◊ *Er arbeitet als Bildhauer.* ✦ *eine begnadete Bildhauerin*

bild·lich ['bɪltlɪç] [adj, adv] *no comp/superl* 1. *when used as an adj, only before ns* pictorial(ly), visual(ly) ◊ *eine bildliche Darstellung der Evolution des Menschen* ✦ *etw. bildlich darstellen* ✦ *sich etw. bildlich vorstellen* 2. figurative(ly), metaphorical(ly) ◊ *ein bildlicher Ausdruck* ✦ *Die Sprache in diesem Text ist bildlich und verständlich.* ✦ *Er hat, bildlich gesprochen, die Augen eines Adlers.*

② **Bild·schirm** ['bɪltʃɪrm] der <-(e)s, -e> 1. monitor, screen ◊ *Der Pilot hätte auf seinem Bildschirm die Gefahr erkennen müssen.* ✦ *Die Arbeit am Bildschirm ist schlecht für die Augen.* 2. TV screen ◊ *Wir saßen alle wie gebannt vor dem Bildschirm.*

Bil·dung ['bɪldʊŋ] die <-, -en> 1. *no pl* culture ◊ *Er hat keine Bildung.* ✦ *Wissen und Bildung vermitteln; (in school)* education ◊ *das Recht auf Bildung* ✦ *Frauen, die ein höhere Bildung haben* 2. *often translated with a verb construction, no pl* formation ◊ *Die Bildung von Rost ist eine chemische Reaktion.* ✦ *die Bildung einer Sonderkommission* ✦ *Wir haben heute die Bildung des Konjunktivs gelernt. Du musst ihm Zeit lassen für die Bildung seiner eigenen Meinung. You must give him time to form his own opinion. die Bildung einer Regierung forming of a government* 3. GRAM form ◊ *Alle Bildungen auf -or sind männlich.*

Bil·dungs·we·sen ['bɪldʊŋsveːzn̩] das <-s> education system ◊ *eine umfassende Reform des Bildungswesens*

② **Bil·lett** [bɪl'jet] das <-(e)s, -s> *(Swiss)* ticket ◊ *Das Billet muss vor Beginn der Fahrt gelöst werden.* ✦ *Ich habe für das Billet fürs Konzert 40 Franken bezahlt.*

② **bil·lig** ['bɪlɪç] [adj, adv] cheap(ly) ◊ *Wohnungen in München sind nicht gerade billig.* ✦ *billig einkaufen* ✦ *billig verarbeitete Kleidung* ✦ *Das ist doch eine ganz billige Ausrede.*

bil·li·gen ['bɪlɪgn̩] [tr v] +*haben; mostly written* approve ◊ *einen Plan/Vorschlag billigen* ✦ *Er kann es nicht billigen, dass sie so ein teures Auto kaufen will.* ✦ *ein Gesetz billigen* ⊝akzeptieren ⊝missbilligen

Bil·li·on [bɪ'ljoːn] die <-, -en> billion; *(in the USA)* trillion

Bin·de ['bɪndə] die <-, -n> 1. MED bandage ◊ *eine Binde abnehmen/anlegen* ✦ *Der Arzt wickelte eine Binde um das verletzte Knie.* ■ den Arm in einer Binde tragen have (got) your arm in a sling ⊝Verband 2. *(abbr of Damenbinde)* sanitary towel, sanitary napkin 3. *(over the eyes)* blindfold ◊ *Er trug eine dunkle Binde über den Augen.* 4. *(abbr of Armbinde)* armband ◊ *Viele Blinde tragen eine gelbe Binde mit schwarzen Punkten.*

⊛ sich [dat] einen hinter die Binde gießen/kippen *(fam, hum)* get a drink in you

bin·den ['bɪndn̩] <bindet, band, hat gebunden> [tr v] 1. jdn/etw. (mit etw.) an etw. [acc] binden tie sb/sth to sth (with sth) ◊ *den Hund mit der Leine an einen Baum binden* ✦ *das Boot an einen Pfahl binden* 2. etw. um etw. binden tie sth around sth, wind sth around sth ◊ *sich eine Krawatte um den Hals binden* 3. (jdm/sich) etw. binden tie (sb's/your) sth, fasten (sb's/your) sth ◊ *einem kleinen Kind die Schuhe binden* ✦ *einen Schal binden* ✦ *Er kann noch nicht alleine die Schnürsenkel binden.* 4. etw. (zu etw.) binden tie sth (into sth), fasten

sth (into sth) ◊ *einen Blumenstrauß binden* ♦ *Zweige zu einem Kranz binden* **5.** tie, bind ◊ *an Händen und Füßen gebunden sein* ♦ *Man band ihm die Hände auf den Rücken.* **6.** *(books)* bind *etw.* binden lassen have sth bound ◊ *ein Buch binden lassen* **7.** *etw.* (mit *etw.*) binden thicken sth (with sth) ◊ *Anschließend die Soße mit etwas Mehl binden.* **8.** *etw.* bindet *etw.* sth binds sth, sth absorbs sth ◊ *Der Regen bindet den Staub.* ♦ *Pflanzen binden Kohlendioxid.* **9.** jdn/sich an *etw.* ⸤acc⸥ binden bind sb/yourself to sth ◊ *sich an einen Vertrag binden* ♦ *Ich fühle mich durch dieses Abkommen nicht gebunden.* ⸤intr v⸥ **1.** *etw.* bindet sth sticks ◊ *Dieser Klebstoff bindet wirklich gut.* **2.** *etw.* bindet sth hardens ◊ *Der Zement bindet schnell.* ⸤ref v⸥ sich binden tie yourself down ◊ *Ich möchte mich noch nicht binden.*

Bin·de·strich ['bɪndəʃtrɪç] der <-(e)s, -e> hyphen ◊ *Straßennamen, die Eigennamen enthalten, schreibt man mit Bindestrich: Martin-Luther-Straße.*

Bin·dung ['bɪndʊŋ] die <-, -en> **1.** eine Bindung (an jdn/zu jdm) a tie (to sb), a bond (with sb) ◊ *eine Bindung auflösen* ♦ *eine starke Bindung an die Familie haben* ♦ *Sie hat eine besonders enge Bindung zu ihrer Schwester.* **2.** eine Bindung (an *etw.* ⸤acc⸥/zu *etw.*) a tie (to/with sth) ◊ *Ich spüre immer noch eine starke Bindung an meine Heimat.* **3.** eine Bindung (an *etw.* ⸤acc⸥) a commitment (to sth) ◊ *Sie hat alle persönlichen Bindungen gelöst.* ♦ *eine vertragliche Bindung eingehen* **4.** SPORT binding ◊ *Ich muss die Bindung der Skier einstellen lassen.* **5.** CHEM bond ◊ *eine schwache Bindung zwischen Molekülen*

bin·nen ['bɪnən] ⸤prep⸥ ⸤+gen⸥ or ⸤+dat⸥ *(form)* within ◊ *Binnen einer Frist von drei Monaten müssen sie ausgezogen sein.* ♦ *Ich möchte, dass das binnen drei Tagen erledigt ist.* ⊝innerhalb von, im Laufe von

Bi·o... ['bi:o:] ⸤prefix⸥ **1.** bio... ◊ *Biorhythmus* ♦ *Biotechnologie* ♦ *Biophysik* **2.** eco..., organic ... ◊ *Biogemüse* Bioladen health food shop

② **Bi·o·lo·gie** [biolo'gi:] die <-> *no pl* biology ◊ *In Biologie hat Max eine Zwei.* ♦ *eine Einführung in die Biologie*

Bi·o·ton·ne ['bi:otɔnə] die <-, -n> container for organic waste ◊ *Die Biotonne wird immer freitags geleert.*

Bi·o·top [bio'to:p] das or der <-s, -e> biotope ◊ *ein Biotop anlegen*

Bir·ke ['bɪrkə] die <-, -n> birch ◊ *ein Wald mit vielen Birken* ♦ *Möbel aus Birke*

② **Bir·ne** ['bɪrnə] die <-, -n> **1.** pear ◊ *eine Birne essen* ◊ *Die Birne im Garten blüht wunderschön.* **2.** (light) bulb ◊ *Die Birne meiner Schreibtischlampe ist kaputt.* **3.** *(fam, hum)* head ◊ *Warum will dir das nicht in die Birne, dass er nichts von dir wissen will?*

② **bis¹** [bɪs] ⸤prep⸥ ⸤+acc⸥ **1.** until, till ◊ *Er bleibt noch bis nächsten Freitag.* ♦ *Bis wann kann ich das behalten?* ♦ *Das Geschäft ist von 9 bis 20 Uhr geöffnet.* ♦ *Ich habe bis heute nicht verstanden, warum.* ♦ *Er hat bis zur letzten Minute damit gewartet.* **2.** by ◊ *Das Projekt müssen wir bis Ende Oktober abschließen.* ♦ *Bis Freitag sollte das fertig sein.* ♦ *Bis 18 Uhr bin ich längst zurück.* **3.** up

until ◊ *Bis 1995 war er ein völlig unbekannter Sänger.* **4.** not usually translated directly Also, dann bis bald! See you soon! Bis morgen! See you tomorrow! Bis später! See you later! **5.** spatial to, as far as ◊ *Bis hierher hat er mich begleitet.* ♦ *Bis Frankfurt fahre ich mit dem Zug, danach fliege ich.* bis an *etw.* ⸤acc⸥ up to ◊ *Unser Grundstück geht bis an den Fluss.* **6.** up to the age of ◊ *Bis 10 ist der Eintritt frei.* ♦ *Jugendliche bis 16 zahlen den halben Preis.*

⊙ bis auf den letzten/die letzte/das letzte ... down to the last ... ◊ *Das Kino war bis auf den letzten Platz belegt.* bis auf jdn/*etw.* apart from sb/sth ◊ *Bis auf Thomas waren alle meine Geschwister da.* bis in *etw.* ⸤acc⸥ **1.** *(temporal)* up until ◊ *Dieses Dorf hatte bis in die Fünfzigerjahre keinen Strom.* ♦ *Wir haben bis in den frühen Morgen gefeiert.* **2.** *(spatial)* to ◊ *Wie weit ist es bis ins Elsass?* ♦ *Es sind nur zwei Kilometer bis ins Zentrum.* bis nach **1.** *(spatial)* to ◊ *Wie weit ist es bis nach Frankfurt?* **2.** *(temporal)* until after ◊ *Er bleibt bis nach Weihnachten.* bis vor *etw.* ⸤dat⸥ *(temporal)* up until ◊ *Bis vor zwei Jahren war er noch gesund.* bis zu *(indicating upper limit)* up to ◊ *Heute wurden Werte von bis zu 35°C gemessen.* ♦ *Der Saal fasst bis zu 200 Leute.* ♦ *Bis zum Alter von 18 ist man unmündig.* bis zum/ zur ... **1.** *(spatial)* as far as ◊ *Er hat mich bis zur Haustür gebracht.* ♦ *Fährt dieser Bus bis zum Bahnhof? Das Wasser geht mir bis zu den Knien.* The water goes up to my knees. **2.** expresses the utmost limit to which one has done sth and can often be rendered with 'until' ◊ *Ich habe gestern bis zur Erschöpfung gearbeitet.*

bis² [bɪs] ⸤conjunc⸥ **1.** until ◊ *Wir bleiben heute am Strand, bis die Sonne untergeht.* ♦ *Er wiederholte es so oft, bis es er konnte.* ♦ *Du darfst nicht spielen, bis du deine Hausaufgaben gemacht hast. Bis ich das gelernt habe, vergehen ja Jahre!* It'll take me years to learn that! **2.** *(denoting range)* to ◊ *Die Reparatur kann 50 bis 100 Euro kosten.*

Bi·schof ['bɪʃɔf, 'bɪʃo:f] der <-s, Bischöfe>, **Bi·schö·fin** ['bɪʃø:fɪn] die <-, -nen> bishop ◊ *ein evangelischer/katholischer Bischof* ♦ *Frau Jespen war die erste Bischöfin Deutschlands.*

② **bis·her** [bɪs'he:ɐ] ⸤adv⸥ up to now, to date ◊ *Bisher haben wir das immer so gemacht.*; before ◊ *Das ist jetzt einfacher als bisher.* ♦ *Wir machen das wie bisher.* ⊝bislang

bis·he·rig [bɪs'he:rɪç] ⸤adj⸥ no comp/superl, only before ns previous ◊ *Der bisherige Wirtschaftsminister wird jetzt Außenminister.* jds bisheriges Leben sb's life up to now/then

bis·lang [bɪs'laŋ] ⸤adv⸥ up to now, to date ◊ *Ich habe bislang noch nichts von ihm gehört.* ♦ *Bislang war alles in Ordnung.* ⊝bisher

biss [bɪs] *pret of* beißen

biss·chen ['bɪsçən] ⸤indef pron⸥ invariable **1.** ein bisschen a bit ◊ *Ich habe ein bisschen gegessen.* ♦ *Ein bisschen Spaß muss der Mensch doch haben.* ♦ *Das hat aber ein bisschen lange gedauert.* **2.** kein bisschen not at all ◊ *„Hat er sich denn gefreut?" — „Nein, kein bisschen." ♦ sich kein bisschen* Mühe geben ⸤dat⸥ kein bisschen not make any effort at all **3.** das bisschen the little ◊ *Das bisschen Geld, das ich*

A B C D E F G H I J K L M N O P Q R S T U V W X Y Z

dafür bekomme, ist schnell ausgegeben.
⊛ **ach du liebes bisschen** *(fam)* gracious me ◊ *Ach du liebes bisschen, jetzt habe ich die Karten vergessen!*
bis·sig ['bɪsɪç] [adj] vicious ◊ *Mein Hund ist weder aggressiv noch bissig. Vorsicht, bissiger Hund!* Beware of the dog! [adj, adv] scathing(ly) ◊ *eine bissige Bemerkung machen* ♦ *Sie wird leicht bissig.* ♦ *„Du bist ja schon wieder zu spät", sagte er bissig.* ⊝sarkastisch
bis·wei·len [bɪsˈvaɪlən] [adv] mostly written from time to time, now and again ◊ *Bisweilen machte er einen Spaziergang, um auf andere Gedanken zu kommen.* ⊝mitunter, manchmal
② **bit·te** ['bɪtə] [part] **1.** ◊ *Könntest du bitte das Fenster zumachen?* ♦ *Bitte, darf ich jetzt gehen?* ♦ *Du bekommst den Ball, wenn du schön bitte sagst.* **2.** „Gibst du mir mal das Salz?" — „Hier bitte." "Could you pass me the salt?" — "Here you are." „Darf ich Platz nehmen?" — „Bitte." "May I sit down?" — "Please do." **3.** you're welcome ◊ *„Danke, dass du mir geholfen hast!"* — *„Bitte, ist doch gern geschehen."* **4.** sorry, (I beg your) pardon ◊ *Bitte, was hast du gesagt?*
⊛ **ja bitte** *(in response to a knock on the door)* come in ◊ *Ich klopfte, und von drinnen ertönte ein: „Ja bitte!"* **na bitte** see ◊ *Na bitte, du kannst es doch!* **wie bitte 1.** sorry, (I beg your) pardon ◊ *Wie bitte? Ich habe Sie nicht verstanden.* **2.** I beg your pardon ◊ *Wie bitte, ich soll das heute noch machen?* ♦ *„Ich will sofort mehr Taschengeld!"* — *„Wie bitte?"*
② **Bit·te** ['bɪtə] die <-, -n> request ◊ *Er hat meine Bitte erfüllt.* ♦ *Ich hätte da eine Bitte an dich.* ♦ *Mit Bitte um umgehende Benachrichtigung.* ♦ *Ich kann ihm diese Bitte schlecht abschlagen.*
② **bit·ten** ['bɪtn̩] <bittet, bat, hat gebeten> [tr v] **1.** jdn um etw. bitten ask sb for sth ◊ *Ich habe meinen Chef um eine Gehaltserhöhung gebeten.* ♦ *Kann ich dich um einen Gefallen bitten?* jdn bitten, etw. zu tun ask sb to do sth ◊ *Dürfte ich Sie bitten, kurz Platz zu nehmen?* **2.** jdn irgendwohin bitten ask sb (to go) somewhere ◊ *Der Herr Doktor bittet Sie jetzt zu sich.* ♦ *Ich habe alle Mitarbeiter ins Konferenzzimmer gebeten.* [intr v] ask, beg ◊ *Und wenn du noch so bittest, ich kann das nicht erlauben. Ich bitte um Aufmerksamkeit.* May I have your attention, please.
⊛ **Darf ich (um diesen Tanz) bitten?** May I have this dance? **bitten und betteln** beg and plead **ich bitte Sie/dich** I ask you ◊ *Ich bitte Sie, das können Sie doch nicht einfach behaupten!*
② **bit·ter** ['bɪtɐ] [adj, adv] bitter(ly) ◊ *Die Mandel war bitter.* ♦ *Das Medikament schmeckt sehr bitter.* ♦ *eine bittere Enttäuschung* ♦ *Sie hat sich sehr bitter über diese Zeit geäußert.* ♦ *Heute war es bitter kalt.* ♦ *Du hast mich bitter enttäuscht.*
⊛ **bitter ernst** deadly serious **etw. bitter nötig haben** be in desparate need of sth
Bla·ma·ge [blaˈmaːʒə] die <-, -n> embarrassment, disgrace ◊ *Was für eine schreckliche Blamage!*
bla·mie·ren [blaˈmiːrən] <blamiert, blamierte, hat blamiert> [tr v] embarrass, disgrace ◊ *Durch deinen peinlichen Auftritt auf der Party gestern hast du uns alle blamiert.* [ref v] sich (vor jdm) blamieren

make a fool of yourself (in front of sb) ◊ *Ich habe mich in dem altmodischen Kleid vor allen Leuten blamiert.*
blank [blaŋk] [adj] **1.** *(surface, floor)* shiny (clean), shiny (bright) ◊ *eine blanke Fensterscheibe* ♦ *Der Fußboden in der Küche ist blank.* ♦ *etw. blank reiben* **2.** *(fam) (clothes)* shiny ◊ *blanke Ärmel* ♦ *Die Treppenstufen waren ganz blank.* ♦ *Seine Hose war an den Knien blank gescheuert.* **3.** only before ns bare ◊ *auf dem blanken Boden schlafen* **4.** only before ns pure, sheer ◊ *Das ist doch blanker Unsinn.* ♦ *der blanke Neid*
⊛ **jd ist blank** *(fam)* sb is broke
Bla·se ['blaːzə] die <-, -n> **1.** bubble ◊ *Die Blase steigt auf und platzt.* **2.** MED blister ◊ *Ich habe mir in den neuen Schuhen Blasen gelaufen.* ♦ *Die verbrannte Haut bildet Blasen.* **3.** ANAT *(abbr of* Harnblase*)* bladder ◊ *eine empfindliche Blase haben*
bla·sen ['blaːzn̩] <bläst, blies, hat geblasen> [intr v] **1.** blow ◊ *auf die Suppe blasen, damit sie kühler wird* ♦ *Der Wind blies uns direkt ins Gesicht.* **2.** MIL zum Angriff/Rückzug blasen give the signal for the attack/to retreat [tr v] **1.** MUS play ◊ *Er bläst seit den Jahren im Orchester die Trompete.* ♦ *ein fröhliches Lied blasen* **2.** blow ◊ *die Krümel vom Tisch blasen*
⊛ **jdm einen blasen** *(rude)* give sb a blow job
② **blass** [blas] [adj] <blasser/blässer, am blassesten/blässesten> **1.** *(skin, person)* pale ◊ *eine blasse Haut* ♦ *Als sie das hörte, wurde sie blass.* ⊝bleich **2.** *(shade)* pale, light ◊ *Ich streiche mein Zimmer in einem blassen Rosa.* ⊝hell **3.** *(light)* pale, dim ◊ *Im blassen Licht des Mondes sah die Landschaft unheimlich aus.* ⊝grell **4.** *(notion)* vague ◊ *Die Erinnerung an ihren Vater war nur noch blass.* *Ich habe keinen blassen Schimmer, wo er sein könnte.* I haven't the faintest idea where he could be.
bläst [blɛːst] pres of blasen
② **Blatt** [blat] das <-(e)s, Blätter or -> **1.** pl 'Blätter' *(of a plant)* leaf ◊ *Im Herbst verlieren die Bäume ihre Blätter.* ♦ *Die Pflanze lässt die Blätter hängen.* **2.** pl 'Blatt' sheet (of paper) ◊ *Nehmt ein Blatt und schreibt euren Namen darauf.* ♦ *In dem Karton sind hundert Blatt Papier.* ⊝Bogen **3.** pl 'Blätter' (news)paper ◊ *Die Süddeutsche Zeitung ist ein seriöses Blatt.* **4.** no pl CARDS hand ◊ *Ich hatte ein gutes Blatt.* ♦ *Bei dem Blatt kann man ja nicht gewinnen.*
⊛ **kein Blatt vor den Mund nehmen** not mince your words **das steht auf einem anderen Blatt** that's a different matter, that's another matter **das Blatt wendet sich** the tables are turning, things are changing
blät·tern ['blɛtɐn] [intr v] +haben/sein **1.** +haben in etw. [dat] blättern leaf through sth, flick through sth ◊ *Sie blättert in ihrem neuen Buch.* **2.** +sein etw. blättert (von etw.) sth is peeling (off sth) ◊ *Die Farbe blättert vom Fensterrahmen.* [tr v] +haben etw. irgendwohin blättern spread sth somewhere, lay sth out somewhere ◊ *Geldscheine/Karten auf den Tisch blättern*
② **blau** [blaʊ] [adj] **1.** blue ◊ *Er hat blaue Augen.* ♦ *Ihre Lippen sind vor Kälte ganz blau.* **2.** not before ns *(fam)* drunk ◊ *Rudi war gestern mal wieder*

blau. **3.** *postpositive (trout)* blue ◊ *Es gab Forelle blau.* [adv] **1.** blue ◊ *Sie hat das Bad blau gestrichen.* **2.** in blue ◊ *Die Stichwörter sind blau gedruckt.* box@ Farbe

blau·äu·gig ['blaʊ|ɔʏɡɪç] [adj] **1.** no comp/superl blue-eyed ◊ *ein blauäugiges Kind* ♦ *Glaubst du wirklich, dass alle Schweden blond und blauäugig sind?* **2.** *(fig)* naive ◊ *Sei doch nicht so blauäugig — diese Leute wollen nur dein Geld!* ♦ *Das ist eine reichlich blauäugige Darstellung der Situation.* [adv] naively biauäugig fragen ask a naive question ⊖naiv

Blau·e ['blaʊə] das <-n> *no pl* **1.** blue ◊ *Die Farbe dieses Pullovers geht ins Blaue.* **2.** ins Blaue to nowhere in particular ◊ *ins Blaue fahren* einen Ausflug/eine Fahrt ins Blaue machen go on a mystery trip

◉ **das Blaue vom Himmel (herunter)lügen** *(fam)* tell a pack of lies ◊ *Glaub ihr kein Wort — sie lügt das Blaue vom Himmel herunter.* jdm das Blaue vom Himmel (herunter) versprechen *(fam)* promise sb the earth box@ Farbe

Blau·licht ['blaʊlɪçt] das <-(e)s, -er> flashing blue light ◊ *Schon von weitem sah er die Blaulichter an der Unfallstelle.* Sie wurde mit Blaulicht ins Krankenhaus gefahren. The ambulance rushed her to hospital.

blau|ma·chen ['blaʊmaxn̩] <macht blau, machte blau, hat blaugemacht> [intr v] skive off work ◊ *einen Tag blaumachen* ♦ *Am Freitag vor den Ferien machen viele Leute blau.*

Blech [blɛç] das <-(e)s, -e> **1.** tin ◊ *eine Dose aus Blech* **2.** *(abbr of* Backblech*)* (baking) tray ◊ *das Blech in den Ofen schieben* ♦ *Sie hat zwei Bleche Pizza gebacken.*

◉ **Blech reden** talk rubbish, talk hooey

Blei [blaɪ] das <-s> *seldom with the article, no pl* *(abbr* Pb*)* lead ◊ *mit Kugeln aus Blei schießen* ♦ *Meine Beine fühlen sich schwer wie Blei an.*

◉ **jdm wie Blei im Magen liegen 1.** lie heavily on sb's stomach, weigh heavily on sb's stomach **2.** *(fig)* weigh heavily on sb Blei gießen *New Year custom of pouring melted lead into water and reading the future from the shapes it forms*

Blei·be ['blaɪbə] die <-> *no pl* place to stay ◊ *keine Bleibe haben* ♦ *sich eine Bleibe für die Nacht suchen* ⊖Unterkunft

⑦ **blei·ben** ['blaɪbm̩] <bleibt, blieb, ist geblieben> [intr v] **1.** stay ◊ *Bleib doch noch ein bisschen.* ♦ *Du kannst gern zum Abendessen bleiben.* ♦ *Ich bleibe heute im Bett.*; *(in a certain state also)* remain ◊ *Die Wäsche bleibt draußen hängen.* ♦ *Er ist freundlich geblieben.* ♦ *Lass uns Freunde bleiben.* ♦ *Der Versuch blieb ohne Erfolg.* ♦ *Ich möchte anonym bleiben.* lieber stehen bleiben prefer to remain standing **2.** bei etw. bleiben stick to sth ◊ *Ich bleibe bei meiner Aussage.* ♦ *Du solltest bei der Wahrheit bleiben.* ♦ *beim Thema/ bei der Sache bleiben* Ich bleibe so lange bei dieser Arbeit, bis sie fertig ist. I'm going to carry on with this work until it is finished. **3.** be left, remain ◊ *Von meiner Rente ist nicht viel geblieben.* ♦ *Uns bleibt nicht mehr viel Zeit.* ♦ *Es bleiben noch drei Monate bis zur Eröffnung.* ♦ *Es bleibt abzuwarten, wie sich die Dinge entwickeln.* **4.** es bleibt bei … … *still stands* ◊ *Also, es bleibt bei Mittwoch.* ♦

Es bleibt bei unserer alten Vereinbarung.

◉ **das bleibt unter uns** that's just between ourselves ◊ *Das muss unter uns bleiben.* wo bleibt jd/etw. what's happened to …, where is … ◊ *Wo bleibt denn das Essen?* ♦ Keine Ahnung, wo er geblieben ist.

⑦ **bleich** [blaɪç] [adj] **1.** *(person, skin)* pale ◊ *Sie ist immer so bleich.* ♦ *Sie war/wurde bleich vor Schreck.* ⊖blass **2.** *(light)* pale, dim ◊ *das bleiche Licht des Monds* ⊖schwach

⑦ **Blei·stift** ['blaɪʃtɪft] der <-(e)s, -e> pencil ◊ *mit Bleistift schreiben*

blen·den ['blɛndn̩] <blendet, blendete, hat geblendet> [tr v] *(also fig)* dazzle, blind ◊ *Er blendete sie mit einer Taschenlampe.* ♦ *Du hast dich von dem vielen Geld blenden lassen.* [intr v] be dazzling ◊ *Die Sonne blendete stark.*

⑦ **Blick** [blɪk] der <-(e)s, -e> **1.** look, glance ◊ *Sie erkannte mit einem Blick, wo der Fehler lag.* auf einen Blick at a glance ◊ *Alle Vorteile auf einen Blick!* auf den ersten Blick at first glance ◊ *Auf den ersten Blick sah die Aufgabe gar nicht so schwierig aus.* einen Blick auf/in etw. [acc] werfen/tun have/take a look at sth ◊ *Sie warf einen Blick auf die Uhr.* ♦ *Kann ich mal einen Blick in deine Zeitung tun?* einen Blick aus dem Fenster werfen take a look out of the window Liebe auf den ersten Blick love at first sight jdn keines Blickes würdigen not deign to look at sb jdm einen bösen Blick zuwerfen look daggers at sb jdm einen fragenden Blick zuwerfen give sb a questioning look jdm einen nervösen Blick zuwerfen look at sb nervously ihre Blicke begegnen sich their eyes meet jdn mit Blicken verschlingen devour sb with your eyes **2.** expression, face, look ◊ *Er hat so einen freundlichen Blick.* ♦ *Mit erstauntem/fragendem/ vorwurfsvollem Blick sah er sie an.* ⊖Miene, Gesichtsausdruck **3.** *no pl* view ◊ *Von hier hat man einen herrlichen Blick auf die Berge.* ♦ *ein Zimmer mit Blick aufs Meer* ⊖Aussicht **4.** eye ◊ *der Blick des Experten* ♦ *Er hat einen Blick für das Wesentliche.*

◉ **wenn Blicke töten könnten** if looks could kill

bli·cken ['blɪkn̩] [intr v] +haben look ◊ *Sie blickte aus dem Fenster.* ♦ *Er blickte sehr traurig.*; *(briefly)* glance komisch blicken pull a face ◊ *Was blickst du so komisch?* ⊖schauen

◉ **tief blicken lassen** be very revealing sich blicken lassen show up, show your face ◊ *Lass dich hier bloß nicht mehr blicken!*

⑦ **blieb** [bliːp] *pret of* bleiben

⑦ **blies** [bliːs] *pret of* blasen

⑦ **blind** [blɪnt] [adj, adv] <blinder, am blindesten> blind(ly) ◊ *Sie ist von Geburt an blind.* ♦ *Er ist auf einem Auge blind.* ♦ *Im Alter ist er blind geworden.* ♦ *He, pass doch auf, oder bist du blind?* ♦ *In seiner blinden Wut hat er alles zerschlagen.* ♦ *Ihm kannst du blind vertrauen.* ♦ *blind Schach spielen* blindes Vertrauen zu jdm haben trust sb blindly für etw. blind sein be blind to sth ◊ *Sie ist blind für die Schönheiten der Natur.* blind vor etw. [dat] blinded by sth, blind with sth ◊ *Blind vor Tränen stürzte sie aus dem Haus.* ♦ *Er war blind vor Liebe.* [adj] clouded ◊ *Der Spiegel ist blind geworden.* ♦ *blinde Scheiben*

◉ **blind spielen** *(an instrument)* play without

A
B
C
D
E
F
G
H
I
J
K
L
M
N
O
P
Q
R
S
T
U
V
W
X
Y
Z

looking at the keyboard/music blind tippen touch-type

blin·ken ['blɪŋkn̩] [intr v] +haben **1.** *(car)* indicate ◊ *Sie hat vergessen, beim Abbiegen zu blinken.* ♦ *links/rechts blinken* **2.** *(light)* flash ◊ *Die Kontroll-lampe blinkte rot.; (stars)* twinkle, sparkle

② **Blitz** [blɪts] der <–es, –e> **1.** (flash of) lightning *vom Blitz getroffen werden* be struck by lightning *der Blitz hat (in etw.* [acc]*) eingeschlagen* lightning has struck (sth) **2.** FOTO flash ◊ *mit Blitz fotografie-ren*

◉ *wie ein Blitz aus heiterem Himmel* (like a bolt) from the blue *wie ein Blitz einschlagen* come as a bombshell

blit·zen ['blɪtsn̩] [intr v] +haben (vor etw. [dat]) blitzen flash (with sth) ◊ *Ihre Augen blitzten vor Zorn. vor Sauberkeit blitzen* be sparkling clean, be spick and span [tr v] +haben *(fam) (police)* flash *irgendwo geblitzt werden* be caught in a police speed trap somewhere ◊ *Sie wurde gestern auf der Landstraße geblitzt.* [imp v] +haben *es blitzt* there is lightning ◊ *Draußen blitzt und donnert es.*

Blitz·licht ['blɪtslɪçt] das <–(e)s, –er> flash(light) ◊ *Sie wurde von den Blitzlichtern der Reporter geblendet.*

② **Block** [blɔk] der <–(e)s, Blöcke or –s> **1.** pl 'Blöcke' *(of stone)* block ◊ *ein massiver Block Marmor* ♦ *Blöcke aus dem Eis schlagen* **2.** pl mostly 'Blocks' *(of houses)* block ◊ *Sie wohnt in einem Block mit vielen Sozialwohnungen.* ♦ *Ich gehe mal kurz mit dem Hund um den Block.* ⊖Häuserblock, Wohnblock **3.** pad ◊ *Die Sekretärin holte ihren Block heraus, um das Diktat aufzunehmen.* ♦ *Es gibt Blöcke zu 50 und zu 100 Blatt.* **4.** pl mostly 'Blöcke' POL bloc ◊ *der kommunistische Block*

blo·ckie·ren [blɔ'kiːrən] <blockiert, blockierte, hat blockiert> [tr v] *(also fig)* block ◊ *Der Kran blockierte die Straße.* ♦ *Der Politiker blockierte die Reformen.; (a country, port)* blockade ◊ *Alle Hauptstraßen im Land waren blockiert.* [intr v] lock ◊ *Die Schranke blockierte.; (wheels, brake)* jam ◊ *Der Wagen kam ins Schleudern, weil die Bremse blockierte.*

blöd [bløːt], **blö·de** ['bløːdə] [adj, adv] <blöder, am blödesten> *(fam)* stupid(ly), silly(-ily) ◊ *Sie ist eine blöde Kuh!* ♦ *Der blöde Computer ist schon wieder kaputt!* ♦ *Das war ganz schön blöd von ihm.* ♦ *Er hat sich dir gegenüber blöd verhalten.* *blöd fragen* ask stupid questions *blöd gucken/schauen* have a stupid expression, make a stupid face *sich blöd anstellen* be clumsy ⊖doof

◉ *blöd daherreden* talk gibberish *blöd dastehen* be in trouble *jdm wird es zu blöd* sb is getting annoyed *etw. ist zu blöd* sth is annoying ◊ *Dass das Fest nun doch nicht stattfin-det, ist wirklich zu blöd!*

Blöd·sinn ['bløːtzɪn] der <–(e)s> no pl *(words)* nonsense, rubbish ◊ *Er erzählt lauter Blödsinn!* ♦ *Ich hielt den Aufsatz für Blödsinn.; (act)* stupid tricks, nonsense ◊ *Wer hat mit diesem Blödsinn angefangen? Blödsinn machen* fool around ◊ *Wenn sie betrunken sind, machen sie gern Blödsinn.* ⊖Quatsch, Unsinn

② **blond** [blɔnt] [adj] fair(-haired), blond, blonde ◊ *Sie hatte blonde Haare.* ♦ *Mein Mann ist blond.*

② **bloß¹** [bloːs] [adj] no comp/superl **1.** bare, naked ◊

Frauen dürfen mit bloßen Armen und Beinen keine Moschee betreten. mit bloßem Oberkörper stripped to the waist ◊ *Die Männer arbeiteten mit bloßem Oberkörper.* ⊖nackt, unbedeckt **2.** only before ns mere ◊ *Das sind doch bloße Vermutungen!* ♦ *Der bloße Gedanke daran macht mir schon Angst.* ⊖rein [adv] **1.** only, just ◊ *Er hat bloß drei Fehler gemacht.* ♦ *Er ist nicht wirklich krank, er hat bloß keine Lust!* ♦ *Tu das nicht, sonst regt sie sich bloß wieder auf!* ⊖nur **2.** nicht bloß ... sondern auch ... *not only ... but also ...* ◊ *Das Haus ist nicht bloß alt, sondern auch verkommen.*

② **bloß²** [bloːs] [part] translation varies **1.** *(imploring, threatening)* Lass bloß die Finger davon! Don't you touch that! Mach das bloß nicht! Please don't do that! Sag bloß nicht, ich hätte dich nicht gewarnt! Don't (you dare) say I didn't warn you! Halt bloß den Mund! Just shut up! **2.** in questions and exclamations was/warum/wie etc. ... bloß ... what/why/how etc. ... on earth ... ◊ *Warum bist du bloß immer so gemein?* ♦ *Wie konnte das bloß passieren? wenn ... bloß ... if only ...* ◊ *Wenn ich das bloß früher gewusst hätte!*

◉ *sag bloß (fam)* don't say ◊ *Sag bloß, der hat schon wieder ein neues Auto!*

② **blü·hen** ['blyːən] [intr v] +haben **1.** *(plant)* be in) flower ◊ *Meine Rosen blühen gerade. rot/weiß/gelb blühend* red/white/yellow(-flowered) ◊ *Ich habe einen weiß blühenden Fliederbaum im Garten.* **2.** *(fig) (business, trade)* flourish, thrive ◊ *Der Handel blüht wie nie zuvor.* **3.** *jdm blüht etw.* sth is in store for sb ◊ *Da kann uns ja was blühen!* ♦ *Jetzt blüht ihm ein Jahr Knast!* [imp v] *es blüht* there are flowers in bloom ◊ *Überall blüht es, es ist wunderschön.*

② **Blu·me** ['bluːmə] die <–, –n> **1.** flower ◊ *Sollen wir der Gastgeberin Blumen mitbringen?* ♦ *einen Strauß Blumen* **2.** pot plant ◊ *Wenn ich in Urlaub bin, gießt Anne meine Blumen.* **3.** *(of beer)* head **4.** *(of wine)* bouquet

◉ *durch die Blume* in a roundabout way

Blu·men·kohl ['bluːmənkoːl] der <–(e)s> no pl BOT cauliflower

② **Blu·se** ['bluːzə] die <–, –n> blouse ◊ *Sie trägt eine weiße Bluse.* ♦ *eine Bluse mit langen Ärmeln*

② **Blut** [bluːt] das <–(e)s> no pl blood ◊ *Er spendet regelmäßig Blut. jdm Blut abnehmen* take blood from sb *bei etw. fließt Blut* sth is bloody ◊ *Floss bei dem Kampf Blut? Blut vergießen* shed blood

◉ *jdm gerinnt/gefriert/stockt das Blut in den Adern* sb's blood runs cold ◊ *Beim Anblick des Löwen stockte ihm das Blut in den Adern. an jds Händen klebt Blut (lofty)* sb has blood on their hands *Blut und Wasser schwitzen (fam)* sweat blood *böses Blut* bad blood ◊ *Diese Entscheidung hat für viel böses Blut gesorgt. frisches Blut* new/fresh blood *ruhig Blut (bewahren) (fam)* keep your cool ◊ *Nur ruhig Blut, es wird schon nicht so schlimm werden! Blut geleckt haben (fam)* have developed a taste for it *jdm im Blut liegen* be in sb's blood ◊ *Musik und Rhythmus liegen ihr im Blut. jdn bis aufs Blut peinigen* torment sb mercilessly *jdn bis aufs Blut reizen* make sb's blood boil

Blut·druck ['bluːtdrʊk] der <–(e)s> no pl MED blood pressure ◊ *einen hohen/niedrigen Blutdruck*

haben ♦ *Die Krankenschwester misst ihm den Blutdruck.*

Blü·te ['bly:tə] die <–, –n> **1.** flower, blossom, bloom ◊ *Der Baum hatte rosa Blüten.* ♦ *eine Schale mit getrockneten Blüten* **2.** *no pl* flowering, blossoming ◊ *Die Blüte der Kirschbäume war fast schon zu Ende.* in Blüte stehen be in flower/blossom ◊ *Die Rosen standen bereits in Blüte.* **3.** *no pl (lofty, fig)* heyday ◊ *Während ihrer Blüte hatte die Stadt 100 000 Einwohner.; (of life)* prime ◊ *Er war in der Blüte seiner Jugend.* seine Blüte erleben have its heyday eine wirtschaftliche Blüte erleben flourish economically ⊕Höhepunkt **4.** *(fam)* dud (note) ◊ *Die Polizei stellte Blüten im Wert von einer Million Euro sicher.*

② **blu·ten** ['blu:tn] <blutet, blutete, hat geblutet> [intr v] bleed ◊ *Die Wunde blutet immer noch.* ♦ *Er blutete stark.* ♦ *Sie blutete aus der Nase.*

blu·tig ['blu:tɪç] [adj] **1.** bloody ◊ *ein blutiger Verband* ♦ *blutige Knie haben* ganz blutig sein be covered in blood ◊ *Deine Hände sind ja ganz blutig!* **2.** violent ◊ *Es kam zu blutigen Unruhen.* ♦ *Das Ende des Aufstands war blutig.* **3.** *intensifying, only before ns (fig) (beginner)* absolute ◊ *Sie war eine blutige Anfängerin.* ⊕völlig, total **4.** *not before ns (meat)* rare ◊ *Ich mag mein Steak am liebsten blutig.* [adv] **1.** jdn blutig schlagen beat sb to a pulp sich blutig kratzen, sich [dat] etw. blutig kratzen scratch your sth until it bleeds ◊ *Der Hund kratzte sich die Ohren blutig.* **2.** violently ◊ *Der Kampf ist äußerst blutig verlaufen.* blutige Rache nehmen, sich blutig rächen take bloody revenge ⊕brutal

Blu·tung ['blu:tʊŋ] die <–, –en> **1.** bleeding, haemorrhage ◊ *eine schwache/starke Blutung* ♦ *eine Blutung stillen/stoppen* ♦ *Innere Blutungen sind gefährlich, weil sie oft unbemerkt bleiben.* **2.** (monatliche) Blutung period ◊ *Ihre Blutung kam diesen Monat sehr früh.* ♦ *Sie hat schwache/unregelmäßige Blutungen.* ⊕Regel, Periode

Blut·wurst ['blu:tvʊʁst] die <–, Blutwürste> black pudding ◊ *Es gab Blutwurst mit Sauerkraut und Kartoffeln.*

BLZ [be:ʔɛl'tsɛt] die *(abbr of* Bankleitzahl*)* sort code ◊ *Konto 27945 bei der Volksbank Bonn, BLZ 38060186* ♦ *Welche BLZ hat deine Bank?*

Bock [bɔk] der <–(e)s, Böcke> **1.** *(deer, rabbit)* buck ◊ *einen Bock schießen; (goat)* billy goat ♦ *eine Ziegenherde mit einem Bock; (sheep)* ram **2.** vaulting horse ◊ *Sie sprang über den Bock.* **3.** trestle ◊ *Er legte den Ast auf einen Bock, um ihn in Stücke zu sägen.* **4.** *(of a carriage)* box ◊ *Er saß auf dem Bock des Pferdewagens.* ⊙ **Bock haben** *(slang)* Bock auf etw. [acc] haben fancy (doing) sth ◊ *Hast du Bock auf Nudeln/Schwimmen?* keinen Bock auf etw. [acc] haben *not feel like sth* (jd hat) keinen Bock (sb) can't be bothered ♦ *„Willst du mitspielen?" — „Nein, keinen Bock!"*

Bock·wurst ['bɔkvʊʁst] die <–, Bockwürste> bockwurst ◊ *Am Imbiss gibt es Bockwürste mit Brötchen und Senf.*

② **Bo·den** ['bo:dn] der <–s, Böden> **1.** soil ◊ *Der Boden in dieser Gegend ist nicht besonders fruchtbar.* ♦ *sandige Böden* ♦ *Befinden wir uns hier noch auf deutschem Boden?* ⊕Erde **2.** *no pl (also*

fig) ground ◊ *Sie fiel auf den Boden/zu Boden.* ♦ *einen Pfahl in den Boden rammen* (an) Boden gewinnen/verlieren gain/lose ground ◊ *Die Truppen des Kaisers verloren immer mehr an Boden.* ♦ *Die Opposition konnte in den Wahlen an Boden gewinnen.* (verlorenen) Boden gutmachen/wettmachen make up for lost ground **3.** *no pl* floor ◊ *Er hob das Papier vom Boden auf.* ♦ *Sie putzte den Boden mit Schrubber und Lappen.* ⊕Fußboden ⊕Decke **4.** loft ◊ *Wir haben die alten Möbel auf den Boden gebracht.* ♦ *die Wäsche auf dem Boden aufhängen* ⊕Speicher, Dachboden ⊕Keller **5.** bottom ◊ *Sie stellt ihre Schuhe auf den Boden des Kleiderschranks.* ♦ *Das Schiff liegt jetzt auf dem Boden des Mittelmeers.; (for a flan)* base doppelter Boden false bottom ◊ *Der Koffer hatte einen doppelten Boden.; (in a pool, lake)* Boden unter den Füßen haben feel the bottom **6.** den Boden eines Gesetzes verlassen infringe a law ◊ *Wenn wir dies tun, verlassen wir den Boden des Grundgesetzes.* nicht mehr auf dem Boden der Demokratie sein leave democracy behind ⊙ **(wieder) festen Boden unter den Füßen haben 1.** be (back) on terra firma ◊ *Ich bin froh, wieder festen Boden unter den Füßen zu haben* **2.** be firmly on your feet (again) ◊ *Jetzt hat er wieder eine Arbeit und damit festen Boden unter den Füßen.* auf dem Boden der Tatsachen bleiben stick to the facts jd würde/möchte am liebsten im Boden versinken, jd könnte im Boden versinken sb wishes the ground would open up (and swallow them) ◊ *Sie wäre vor Verlegenheit am liebsten im Boden versunken.* ♦ *Ich hätte im Boden versinken können, so sehr schäme ich mich.* am Boden zerstört sein *(fam)* be shattered

Bo·den·schatz ['bo:dnʃats] der <–es, Bodenschätze> *most pl* mineral resource ◊ *Das Land verfügt über reiche Bodenschätze.* ♦ *Die großen Konzerne beuteten die Bodenschätze aus.*

Bo·dy ['bɔdi:] der <–s, –s> *(fam)* bodysuit, body stocking ◊ *Unter der Bluse trug sie einen schwarzen Body.* ♦ *Sie zieht dem Baby einen Body an.*

bog [bo:k] *pret of* biegen

Bo·gen ['bo:gn] der <–s, – *or regional* Bögen> **1.** curve, arc; *(road, path)* turn, bend einen Bogen machen curve in einem Bogen um etw. herumführen go round sth ◊ *Der Weg führt in einem Bogen um den Berg herum.; (aircraft)* einen Bogen fliegen make a turn ◊ *Das Flugzeug flog einen Bogen Richtung Osten.* etw. in hohem Bogen werfen lob sth ◊ *Sie warf die Flasche in hohem Bogen aus dem Fenster.* **2.** bow ◊ *Damals jagten sie Vögel noch mit Pfeil und Bogen.* ♦ *Sie klemmte die Geige unter das Kinn und setzte den Bogen an.* **3.** sheet ◊ *Wie viele Bogen hast du für den Aufsatz benötigt?* ein Bogen Papier/Geschenkpapier a sheet of paper/gift wrap ⊕Blatt **4.** ARCH arch ◊ *ein Bogen im romanischen Stil* ⊙ **einen großen Bogen um jdn/etw. machen** give sb/sth a wide berth, keep clear of sb/sth ◊ *Sie macht einen großen Bogen um Hunde/ihre Nachbarn.* ♦ *Um solche Internetseiten solltest du einen großen Bogen machen.* den Bogen (he)raushaben *(fam)* have the hang of it ◊ *Am*

A
B
C
D
E
F
G
H
I
J
K
L
M
N
O
P
Q
R
S
T
U
V
W
X
Y
Z

Anfang war sie noch ungeschickt, doch jetzt hat sie den Bogen raus. **den Bogen überspannen** go too far ◊ *Sie hat viel Geduld, aber pass auf, dass du den Bogen nicht überspannst!* **in hohem Bogen aus etw. (hinaus)fliegen/(hinaus)geworfen werden** *(fig)* be chucked out ◊ *Man hat ihn in hohem Bogen aus der Kneipe geworfen.* ◆ *Sie ist in hohem Bogen aus der Firma geflogen.*

② **Boh·ne** ['boːnə] die <–, –n> BOT bean ◊ *Die Bohnen ranken sich an den Stangen nach oben.* ◆ *Kaffee aus frisch gemahlenen Bohnen* grüne/weiße/dicke Bohnen green/haricot/broad beans ◊ *Heute gibt es dicke Bohnen mit Speck.* Bohnen in/mit Tomatensoße baked beans

⊕ **nicht die Bohne** *(fam)* not one little bit

boh·ren ['boːrən] [tr+intr v] +*haben* **1.** bore, drill ◊ *Er bohrte ein Loch in die Wand.* ◆ *Die Handwerker hämmerten und bohrten den ganzen Tag.* nach etw. bohren drill for sth ◊ *Sie bohren in der Nordsee nach Öl.* Der Zahnarzt musste bohren. The dentist had to drill the tooth. **2.** *(with a finger)* ein Loch in etw. [dat] bohren poke a hole in sth in etw. [dat] bohren pick at sth, poke in sth ◊ *Er bohrte in seinem Ohr/in der Wunde.* in der Nase bohren pick your nose mit dem Finger/den Zehen in etw. [dat] bohren poke your finger/toes in sth [tr v] +*haben (a well, pole etc.)* sink ◊ *einen Pfahl in die Erde bohren;* drive ◊ *Er bohrte ihm ein Messer ins Herz.* [ref v] +*haben* sich durch/in etw. [acc] bohren bore its way through/into sth ◊ *Der Pfeil bohrte sich in den Baumstamm.*

Boh·rer ['boːrɐ] der <–s, –> drill ◊ *Der Bohrer wird die Wand gleich durchbrechen.* ◆ *Der Zahnarzt griff zum Bohrer.*

Boi·ler ['bɔɪlɐ] der <–s, –> boiler ◊ *Sie stellte den Boiler im Bad an.* ◆ *Der Boiler fasst 200 Liter.*

bom·bar·die·ren [bɔmbarˈdiːrən] <bombardiert, bombardierte, hat bombardiert> [tr v] **1.** MIL bomb ◊ *Flugzeuge bombardierten die Stadt.* ◆ *Das Land wurde im Krieg schwer bombardiert.* **2.** *(fig)* bombard ◊ *Er hat sie mit Anrufen geradezu bombardiert.*

② **Bom·be** ['bɔmbə] die <–, –n> bomb ◊ *von Bomben zerstört* ◆ *aus dem Flugzeug Bomben auf eine Stadt abwerfen* eine Bombe legen plant a bomb

⊕ **wie eine Bombe einschlagen** *(news)* come as a bombshell **die Bombe ist geplatzt** the balloon has gone up ◊ *Gestern ist die Bombe geplatzt: 100 Mitarbeiter werden entlassen.*

Bon [bɔŋ] der <–s, –s> **1.** receipt, sales slip ◊ *Kein Umtausch ohne Bon!* ⊜Kassenzettel **2.** voucher, coupon ◊ *ein Bon im Wert von 10 Euro* ◆ *Den Bon kannst du in allen Geschäften einlösen.* ⊜Gutschein

② **Bon·bon** [bɔŋˈbɔŋ, bɔ̃ˈbɔ̃ː] das *or* der <–s, –s> sweet, candy ◊ *Bonbons lutschen*

② **Boot** [boːt] das <–(e)s, –e> boat ◊ *Wir sind mit dem Boot über den See gerudert.*

⊕ **im selben Boot sitzen** be in the same boat

Bord[1] [bɔrt] das <–(e)s, –e> shelf ◊ *Die Bücher stehen auf dem obersten Bord.*

Bord[2] [bɔrt] an Bord on board, aboard ◊ *Waren an Bord bringen/nehmen* an Bord gehen go on board, board (the ship/aircraft) von Bord gehen leave the ship/aircraft; *(with ships only)* über Bord

overboard ◊ *Hilfe! Mann über Bord!* ◆ *Bei den hohen Wellen ging er über Bord.*

⊕ **etw. über Bord werfen** *(fig)* jettison sth, throw sth overboard

Bor·dell [bɔrˈdɛl] das <–s, –e> brothel ◊ *ins Bordell gehen*

bor·gen ['bɔrgŋ] [tr v] +*haben* **1.** jdm etw. borgen lend sb sth ◊ *Kannst du mir einen Bleistift borgen?* ◆ *Ich borgte ihm mein Buch.* ⊜leihen **2.** sich [dat] (von jdm) etw. borgen borrow sth (from sb) ◊ *Ich habe mir von ihr 50 Euro geborgt.* ◆ *Das Kleid war nur geborgt.* ⊜leihen

Bör·se ['bœrzə] die <–, –n> **1.** ECON stock market ◊ *Das Unternehmen ging an die Börse.* ◆ *Sie hat an der Börse viel Geld verloren.* ◆ *die Londoner Börse* **2.** stock exchange ◊ *Die New Yorker Börse befindet sich in der Wall Street.* **3.** *(lofty, oldf)* purse ◊ *Sie öffnete ihre Börse und nahm ein paar Münzen heraus.* ⊜Geldbörse, Geldbeutel, Portmonee

bös·ar·tig ['bøːsˌʔaːrtɪç] [adj] **1.** *(person, remark, computer virus, nature etc.)* malicious ◊ *Ich finde ihn richtig bösartig.* ◆ *Das ist eine bösartige Behauptung!*; *(animal)* vicious ◊ *Der Hund wurde durch die schlechte Behandlung bösartig.* ⊜böse **2.** *(disease etc.)* serious ◊ *eine bösartige Krankheit; (tumor)* malignant ◊ *Ist die Geschwulst bösartig oder gutartig?* ⊜gutartig

② **bö·se** ['bøːzə] [adj] **1.** evil, wicked ◊ *Es geschah nicht in böser Absicht.* ◆ *Die Hexe war sehr böse.* Das ist nicht böse gemeint. I don't mean to be nasty. ⊜schlecht, gemein ⊜gut **2.** *(child, pet)* naughty, bad ◊ *Lukas war böse, deshalb habe ich ihn ins Bett geschickt.* ◆ *Pfui, böser Hund!* ⊜unartig ⊜brav [adj, adv] **1.** *when used as an adj, mostly after ns (fam)* cross(ly), angry(-ily) ◊ *Bist du immer noch böse?* ◆ *Hör endlich auf, oder muss ich erst böse werden?* böse auf jdn/mit jdm sein, jdm böse sein be mad at/cross with/angry with sb ◊ *Bist du mir noch böse?* ◆ *Sie ist böse mit mir/auf mich.* jdm einen bösen Blick/böse Blicke zuwerfen, jdn böse anschauen look daggers at sb ⊜wütend, sauer **2.** bad(ly), nasty(-ily) ◊ *Sie erlebten eine böse Überraschung.* ◆ *Die Wunde sieht böse aus.* ◆ *Der Finger hatte sich böse entzündet.* ein böses Ende nehmen come to a bad end, come to a sticky end ◊ *Mit ihm wird es noch ein böses Ende nehmen!* das Schicksal spielt jdm böse mit fate deals sb a severe blow jdn böse täuschen be badly disappointed by sb ⊜schlimm, unangenehm

Bö·se ['bøːzə] das <–n> *but: Böses, no pl* **1.** bad ◊ *Kannst du nicht zwischen Gut und Böse unterscheiden?* ◆ *Keine Angst, dir wird nichts Böses geschehen.* nichts Böses ahnen be unsuspecting nichts Böses ahnend unsuspectingly ◊ *Er öffnete, nichts Böses ahnend, den Brief.* jdm Böses tun/wollen do/mean sb harm ◊ *Du brauchst keine Angst haben, er will dir nichts Böses.* Böses im Sinn haben be up to no good **2.** *(lofty)* das Böse (the) evil ◊ *das Böse in der Welt* ◆ *die Herrschaft des Bösen*

② **bot** [boːt] *pret of* bieten

Bo·te ['boːtə] der <–n, –n>, **Botin** ['boːtɪn] die <–, –nen> **1.** messenger, courier ◊ *Der König schickte einen Boten ins Dorf.* ◆ *Der Bote brachte ein einen Brief.* **2.** *(fig)* herald ◊ *Weintrauben, die*

Boten des Herbstes
Bot·schaft ['bo:tʃaft] die <-, -en> **1.** message ◊
*Sie hat ihm eine Botschaft auf einem Zettel hinter-
lassen.* ♦ *Hat der Film eine Botschaft?* ♦ *Der
Boykott der Wahlen ist eine klare Botschaft an die
Politiker.* eine freudige/schlimme Botschaft good/
bad news **2.** POL embassy ◊ *Sie hat bei der
deutschen Botschaft um Asyl gebeten.*
◉ die Frohe Botschaft the Gospel
Bot·schaf·ter ['bo:tʃaftɐ] der <-s, ->,
Bot·schaf·te·rin ['bo:tʃaftərɪn] die <-, -nen> POL
ambassador ◊ *der ehemalige Schweizer Botschafter*
♦ *Sie war tschechische Botschafterin in Belgien.*
Box [bɔks] die <-, -en> **1.** box ◊ *Sie packte ihr
Brot für die Mittagspause in die Box.* ♦ *Sie brachte
das Pferd in seine Box.* **2.** *(for racing cars)* pit ◊
Der Rennwagen musste in die Box. **3.** speaker ◊
Aus den Boxen kam Popmusik.
bo·xen ['bɔksn̩] [intr v] +*haben* SPORT box ◊ *Er boxt
hervorragend.* gegen jdn boxen fight sb um etw.
boxen fight for sth ◊ *Sie boxte um die Weltmeisterschaft.* [tr v] +*haben* jdn/etw. irgendwohin boxen
punch sb/sth somewhere ◊ *Sie boxte ihn in den
Magen. Der Torwart boxte den Ball aus der linken
Ecke.* The goalkeeper fisted the ball away from the
left-hand corner.
boy·kot·tie·ren [bɔykɔ'ti:rən] <boykottiert, boykottierte, hat boykottiert> [tr v] boycott ◊ *die Wahlen/
Olympischen Spiele boykottieren*
brach [bra:x] *pret of* brechen
② **brach·te** ['braxtə] *pret of* bringen
Bran·che ['branʃə, 'brã:ʃə] die <-, -n> industry,
sector ◊ *In welcher Branche sind Sie tätig?* ♦ *Die
Branche der Telekommunikation erlebt wieder einen
Aufschwung.*
Brand [brant] der <-(e)s, Brände> **1.** fire ◊ *einen
Brand löschen* ♦ *Sollte ein Brand ausbrechen,
rufen Sie die Feuerwehr.* ♦ *Eine brennende Zigarette
hat den Brand verursacht.* in Brand geraten catch
fire ◊ *Der trockene Waldboden gerät leicht in
Brand.* einen Brand legen start a fire etw. in Brand
setzen/stecken set fire to sth, set sth alight ◊ *Unbekannte Täter haben einen Pkw in Brand gesetzt.*
2. *(fam)* raging thirst ◊ *Mann, hab ich einen
Brand!*
Bran·den·burg ['brandn̩bʊrk] das <-s> *article only
in combination with attribute* Brandenburg box⊕
Land

> Area: 29,476 km²; population: approx. 2.6
> million; regional capital: Potsdam.
> Brandenburg is the largest of the regional states
> in the former GDR in terms of area, and
> surrounds Berlin, the capital of Germany. It was
> only on 3rd October 1990 that this state was
> established in its current form. Brandenburg is
> home to many castles and cultural monuments,
> such as *Schloss Sanssouci* (Sans Souci Palace).

Brand·stif·tung ['brantʃtɪftʊŋ] die <-, -en> arson
◊ *Brandstiftung begehen* ♦ *Das Museum wurde
durch Brandstiftung zerstört.*
② **brann·te** ['brantə] *pret of* brennen
Bra·si·li·a·ner [brazi'lja:nɐ] der <-s, ->,
Bra·si·li·a·ne·rin [brazi'lja:nərɪn] die <- *or* –nen>
Brazilian → Deutsche
bra·si·li·a·nisch [brazi'lja:nɪʃ] [adj] *mostly before*

ns **1.** Brazilian **2.** Brazilian dialect → deutsch
Bra·si·li·a·nisch [brazi'lja:nɪʃ] das <-(s)> *no pl*
Brazilian Portuguese, Brazilian dialect → Deutsch
Bra·si·li·en [bra'zi:ljən] das <-s> *article only in
combination with attribute, no pl* Brazil →
Deutschland
② **brät** [brɛːt] *pres of* braten
② **bra·ten** ['bra:tn̩] <brät, briet, hat gebraten>
[tr+intr v] roast, bake ◊ *eine Gans im Ofen braten;
(in a frying pan)* fry ◊ *Kartoffeln in Öl braten* ♦
Der Speck brät in der Pfanne.
② **Bra·ten** ['bra:tn̩] der <-s, -> roast (meat), joint ◊
Am Sonntag gibt es bei uns immer Braten. ♦ *den
Braten in den Ofen schieben*
◉ den Braten riechen *(fam)* smell a rat
Brat·wurst ['bra:tvʊrst] die <-, Bratwürste> (fried/
grilled) sausage, bratwurst ◊ *eine Bratwurst mit
Sauerkraut* ♦ *eine Nürnberger/Thüringer Bratwurst*
Brauch [braox] der <-(e)s, Bräuche> custom,
tradition ◊ *einen Brauch pflegen* ♦ *ein christlicher
Brauch* ♦ *Touristen werfen nach altem Brauch
Münzen in den Brunnen.* ♦ *Es ist Brauch, an Ostern
Eier zu färben.* ⊖Sitte, Tradition
brauch·bar ['braoxba:r] [adj] **1.** usable, serviceable
◊ *Dieser Topf ist zwar alt, aber noch brauchbar.* ♦
eine brauchbare Methode **2.** *(fam)* useful ◊ *Er hat
mir brauchbare Tipps gegeben.* ♦ *Das Programm
ist für Anfänger brauchbar.* ⊖unbrauchbar
② **brau·chen**¹ ['braoxn̩] <braucht, brauchte, hat
gebraucht> [tr v] need ◊ *Ich brauche Ruhe/Urlaub/
mehr Geld.* ♦ *In schweren Zeiten braucht man
Freunde.* ♦ *Wenn Sie mich brauchen, sagen Sie
Bescheid.* ♦ *Was braucht man für das Rezept?* ♦
Ich brauche mindestens noch drei Tage. das
braucht seine Zeit it just takes time jd kann jdn/
etw. brauchen/nicht brauchen sb can/could do
with/without sb/sth ◊ *Gute Mitarbeiter können wir
immer brauchen.* ♦ *Diese Art von Sorgen kann ich
jetzt wirklich nicht brauchen.* jd kann jdn jetzt
nicht brauchen sb has no time for sb at the
moment
brau·chen² ['braoxn̩] <braucht, brauchte, hat
brauchen> [tr v] *only negated or restricting; fam
without 'zu' and quasi modal* jd braucht etw. nicht
zu tun sb doesn't need to do sth, there's no need
for sb to do sth ◊ *Sie brauchen mich wirklich nicht
zu begleiten.* ♦ *Du brauchst gar nicht lachen. Du
brauchst es nur zu sagen, dann helfe ich dir.* Just
let me know and I'll help you. Man braucht nicht
viel zu wissen. You don't have to know a lot.
Brau·e·rei [braoə'rae] die <-, -en> **1.** brewery ◊
Die Brauerei stellt verschiedene Biersorten her. ♦
eine Brauerei besichtigen **2.** *no pl* brewing ◊ *Er
versteht viel von der Brauerei.*
② **braun** [braon] [adj] *no comp/superl* **1.** brown ◊
braune Haare ♦ *Ihre Augen sind braun.* ♦ *Er hat
den Zaun braun gestrichen.* sich braun anziehen
dress in brown etw. braun unterstreichen
underline sth in brown **2.** (sun)tanned ◊ *Sie kam
ganz braun aus dem Urlaub zurück.* **3.** *(pej)* Nazi ◊
Deutschlands braune Vergangenheit
brau·sen ['braozn̩] [tr+intr v] +*haben (oldf)* (sich)
brausen take a shower ◊ *sich jeden Abend brausen*
♦ *heiß/kalt brausen* jdn brausen give sb a shower
◊ *Das Kind muss noch gebraust werden.* [intr v]
+*haben/sein* **1.** +*sein (fam)* irgendwohin brausen

speed off somewhere, race off somewhere ◊ *über die Autobahn brausen*; *(storm, hurricane)* rage somewhere ◊ *Ein Sturm ist über das Land gebraust.* ⊜rasen **2.** *+haben* roar ◊ *Hörst du das Meer/die Wogen/den Wind brausen?*

Braut [braʊt] die <-, Bräute> **1.** bride ◊ *Sie dürfen die Braut jetzt küssen.* **2.** *(slang)* bird ◊ *eine heiße Braut*

Bräu·ti·gam ['brɔʏtɪgam] der <-s, -e> (bride)groom ◊ *Braut und Bräutigam fuhren in einem Oldtimer zur Kirche.*

brav [braːf] adj **1.** *only before ns (also pej)* upright, worthy, honest ◊ *ein braver Bürger/ Ehemann/Polizist* **2.** *(child, pet)* good ◊ *ein braves Kind/Hund* ♦ *Seid brav, wenn ich weg bin!* ⊜artig ⊛böse **3.** *(clothes, hairstyle)* plain, conservative ◊ *ein braves Kleid* ♦ *Deine Frisur ist zu brav.* adv **1.** *(also pej)* like a good citizen/student etc. ◊ *brav Steuern zahlen* ♦ *Katrin besucht brav jede Vorlesung.* **2.** *(child)* like a good boy/girl ◊ *Wenn du brav deinen Salat isst, bekommst du ein Eis als Nachtisch.; (dog)* like a good dog ◊ *Der Hund hat brav vor dem Laden auf mich gewartet.* ⊜artig **3.** *(referring to clothes, a hairstyle)* plainly, conservatively ◊ *Du ziehst dich viel zu brav an!*

BRD [beːʔɛrˈdeː] *(always die BRD) (abbr of* Bundesrepublik Deutschland*)* the FRG, the Federal Republic of Germany

> The Federal Republic of Germany was founded on 23rd May 1949 following the enactment of the German constitution, the 'Basic Law', which provides for a constitutional, democratic form of government. Germany covers an area of 357,000 km², and has a population approaching 81 million, more than 6.5 million of whom are foreigners. It is therefore the most densely populated state in the European Union. Berlin with its population of 3.5 million has been the capital of Germany since reunification.

⑦ **bre·chen** ['brɛçn̩] <bricht, brach, hat/ist gebrochen> intr v **1.** *+sein* break ◊ *Die Achse war gebrochen.* **2.** *+haben* mit jdm/etw. brechen break with sb/sth ◊ *Er hat mit allen seinen alten Freunden gebrochen.* ♦ *mit einer Tradition brechen* **3.** *+sein (sun)* break ◊ *Endlich bricht die Sonne durch die Wolken.* Licht brach durch das Dunkel. Light penetrated the darkness. **4.** *+sein (waves)* break ◊ *Die Wellen brechen an den Felsen.; (sound)* rebound; *(light)* be refracted ◊ *Wenn Licht auf Glas trifft, bricht es.* **5.** *+haben* be sick, throw up ◊ *Ich glaube, ich muss brechen.* ⊜spucken, sich übergeben tr v *+haben* **1.** *(also fig)* break ◊ *Er brach den Stock in zwei Teile.* ♦ *Der Pfarrer bricht das Brot.* ♦ *einen Vertrag/ein Versprechen/sein Wort brechen* ♦ *den Weltrekord brechen* ♦ *den Widerstand/Willen eines Menschen brechen; (bones, leg)* sich/jdm etw. brechen break your/ sb's sth ◊ *Ich habe mir beim Skifahren den Arm gebrochen.* **2.** *(marble)* cut ◊ *In dieser Gegend wurde früher Marmor gebrochen.* **3.** vomit, bring up ◊ *Blut brechen* ⊜spucken ref v *(light)* sich brechen be refracted

Brei [braɪ] der <-(e)s, -e> **1.** mush, paste ◊ *Bananen zu einem Brei zerdrücken* ♦ *aus Gipspulver und Wasser einen zähen Brei anrühren* **2.** *(of*

oats*)* porridge ◊ *einen Brei aus Haferflocken und Milch kochen;* (semolina) pudding ⊛ **um den (heißen) Brei herumreden** *(fam)* beat about the bush ◊ *Sag endlich, was los ist, und red nicht immer um den (heißen) Brei herum!* **jdm Brei ums Maul schmieren** *(fam)* soft-soap sb

⑦ **breit** [braɪt] adj **1.** wide ◊ *ein breiter Fluss* ♦ *Die Brücke ist nicht sehr breit.* ♦ *Das Brett ist zwei Meter lang und einen Meter breit.* ♦ *eine drei Meter breite Straße; (shoulders)* broad ⊜schmal **2.** *only before ns* broad ◊ *Das wird in der Bevölkerung sicher auf breite Zustimmung stoßen.* die breite Öffentlichkeit the public at large, the general public *ein breites Publikum ansprechen* appeal to a wide audience ◊ *Diese Art von Film spricht ein breites Publikum an.* **3.** *(dialect, pronunciation)* broad ◊ *breiten Dialekt sprechen* ♦ *Die Aussprache der Texaner ist ziemlich breit.* adv **1.** in detail ◊ *Die Medien haben breit darüber berichtet.* **2.** *(of accent, pronunciation)* broadly, in a broad way ◊ *die Vokale breit aussprechen*

⑦ **Brei·te** ['braɪtə] die <-, -n> **1.** width ◊ *Das Zimmer hat eine Länge von vier und eine Breite von drei Metern.* ♦ *die Breite der Tür abmessen* ⊜Höhe **2.** latitude ◊ *auf dem 35. Grad nördlicher Breite liegen* lie 35 degrees north ⊜Länge **3.** *only pl* climes, parts ◊ *Diese Pflanze verträgt das Klima in unseren Breiten nicht.* ♦ *in südlicheren Breiten gehen* ⊛ **in epischer Breite** in great detail in die Breite *(fam)* put on weight ◊ *Seit er verheiratet ist, ist er ganz schön in die Breite gegangen.*

Bre·men ['breːmən] das <-s> *article only in combination with attribute* Bremen box⊛ Stadt

> Area: 404 km²; population: approx. 0.66 million. The free Hanseatic City of Bremen is Germany's smallest federal state in terms of area, and has the lowest population. It includes the cities of Bremen and Bremerhaven. Bremen was established in the year 787 and is the world's second oldest city state still in existence after San Marino. Both the port of Bremen and membership of the Hanseatic League secured wealth and prosperity for the city up until the 16th century. The port continues to be an important factor thanks to its location, but the city has also established itself in other branches of industry, such as aircraft manufacture and electrical engineering.

⑦ **Brem·se** ['brɛmzə] die <-, -n> brake ◊ *Die Bremsen haben versagt.* ⊛ **auf die Bremse treten 1.** brake **2.** *(fig)* put the brakes on

⑦ **brem·sen** ['brɛmzn̩] intr v *+haben* brake ◊ *Als er das Kind auf die Straße laufen sah, bremste er scharf.* tr v *+haben* **1.** *(a vehicle)* slow down, stop ◊ *Sie konnte den Wagen gerade noch bremsen.* **2.** *(the economy)* slow down ◊ *Die weltweite Rezession bremst die Wirtschaft.; (a negative development)* halt, put a stop to ◊ *Diese Entwicklung ist kaum mehr zu bremsen.* **3.** *(a person)* hold back, stop ◊ *Wenn sie erst mal loslegt, dann kann sie keiner bremsen.* jd ist nicht zu bremsen there is no stopping sb ◊ *Franz war nicht mehr zu bremsen; er erzählte einen Witz nach dem anderen.*

ⓩ **bren·nen** ['brɛnən] <brennt, brannte, hat gebrannt> [intr v] **1.** be on fire ◊ *Ruf die Feuerwehr, das Nachbarhaus brennt!* **2.** *(material, fire)* burn ◊ *Im Kamin brannte ein warmes Feuer.* ♦ *Auf dem Tisch brannte eine Kerze.; (match)* light ◊ *Das Streichholz brennt nicht.* **3.** *(light)* be on ◊ *In der ganzen Wohnung brannte das Licht.* ♦ *nachts eine Lampe brennen lassen* **4.** *(sun)* burn (down) ◊ *Die Sonne brannte auf meinen Kopf.* **5.** *(with pain)* sting ◊ *Das Jod brannte auf der Wunde.* ♦ *Meine Augen brennen.* **6.** vor etw. [dat] brennen burn with sth ◊ *vor Neugier/Leidenschaft brennen; (with impatience)* itch ◊ *vor Ungeduld brennen* darauf brennen, etw. zu tun be itching/dying to do sth ◊ *Sie brennt darauf, dich endlich mal kennen zu lernen.* [imp v] +*haben* es brennt there's a fire ◊ *Es brennt! Ruf die Feuerwehr!* ♦ *Bei dem Bauern hat es dieses Jahr schon zweimal gebrannt.* [tr v] +*haben* **1.** *(clay, tiles etc.)* fire ◊ *Porzellan/Ton/Ziegel brennen* **2.** distil ◊ *Er brennt seinen eigenen Schnaps.* **3.** *(cattle)* brand ◊ *Den Rindern wird das Zeichen in die Haut gebrannt.; (a hole into a material)* burn ◊ *Er hat ein Loch in meine Tischdecke gebrannt.*
⊙ **wo brennts denn** *(fam)* where's the fire, what's the panic
Brenn·punkt ['brɛnpʊŋkt] der <-(e)s, -e> **1.** focus, centre, center ◊ *Geld ist oft der Brennpunkt von Konflikten.* in den Brennpunkt des öffentlichen Interesses rücken become the focus of public attention im Brennpunkt des Weltgeschehens stehen be the focus of worldwide attention ein sozialer Brennpunkt a disadvantaged area **2.** PHYSICS focal point ◊ *Lichtstrahlen, die in einem Brennpunkt zusammentreffen*
Brenn·stoff ['brɛnʃtɔf] der <-(e)s, -e> **1.** fuel ◊ *ein fester/flüssiger Brennstoff* ♦ *Kohle und Erdöl sind Brennstoffe.* ♦ *zu viel Brennstoff verbrauchen* **2.** PHYSICS nuclear fuel ◊ *Plutonium als Brennstoff nutzen*
Brett [brɛt] das <-(e)s, -er> **1.** board, plank ◊ *ein dickes/dünnes Brett* ♦ *Gemüse auf einem Brett klein schneiden* **2.** *(fam)* SPORT board ◊ *Bei großen Wellen nehme ich das kleine Brett.* **3.** *only pl (fam, hum)* SPORT skis ◊ *Auf Bretter und den Berg runter!* **4.** *only pl (fam)* THEAT boards, stage ◊ *Ihr Traum ist es, einmal auf den Brettern zu stehen.* **5.** GAME board ◊ *die Schachfiguren auf dem Brett aufstellen*
⊙ **ein Brett vor dem Kopf haben** *(fam)* be slow on the uptake, not understand anything ◊ *In der Prüfung hatte sie ein Brett vor dem Kopf.* die Bretter, die die Welt bedeuten THEAT the stage das schwarze Brett the noticeboard ◊ *etw. am schwarzen Brett anschlagen*
ⓩ **bricht** [brɪçt] *pres of* brechen
ⓩ **Brief** [briːf] der <-(e)s, -e> letter ◊ *einen Brief (von jdm) bekommen* ♦ *jdm einen Brief schreiben* ♦ *Er hat nicht auf meinen Brief geantwortet.* ♦ *einen Brief per Einschreiben schicken*

A *blauer Brief* is either a letter giving notice of dismissal or, for German schoolchildren, a dreaded warning letter sent to their parents by the school advising that the pupil in question might have to repeat a year owing to unsatisfactory ▶

▶ grades. The letter does not necessarily have to be blue in colour; it merely got its name from the blue envelope that officers received in 19th-century Prussia when they were discharged from the army.
ⓩ **Brief·kas·ten** ['briːfkastn̩] der <-s, Briefkästen> **1.** postbox, letter box, mailbox ◊ *einen Brief in den Briefkasten werfen* ♦ *Der Briefkasten wird zweimal am Tag geleert.* **2.** letter box, mailbox ◊ *in den Briefkasten sehen, ob Post gekommen ist* ♦ *einen Brief aus dem Briefkasten holen*
ⓩ **Brief·mar·ke** ['briːfmaʳkə] die <-, -n> stamp ◊ *Briefmarken sammeln* ♦ *eine Briefmarke auf einen Umschlag kleben*
ⓩ **Brief·ta·sche** ['briːftaʃə] die <-, -n> wallet ◊ *seine Brieftasche verlieren* ♦ *Ich öffnete die Brieftasche und nahm einen Schein heraus.*
ⓩ **Brief·trä·ger** ['briːftrɛːɡɐ] der <-s, ->, **Brief·trä·ge·rin** ['briːftrɛːɡərɪn] die <-, -nen> postman, mailman ◊ *War der Briefträger heute schon da?* Briefträgerin postwoman, mailwoman ◊ *Sie ist seit drei Jahren Briefträgerin bei der Post.* ⊖Postbote
ⓩ **Brief·um·schlag** ['briːfʔʊmʃlaːk] der <-(e)s, Briefumschläge> envelope ◊ *einen Briefumschlag zukleben* ♦ *ein Briefumschlag mit/ohne Fenster*
Brief·wech·sel ['briːfvɛksl̩] der <-s, -> correspondence ◊ *der Briefwechsel zwischen den Brüdern Grimm* Briefwechsel (mit jdm) correspondence (with sb), exchange of letters (with sb) mit jdm einen Briefwechsel führen be in correspondence with sb mit jdm in Briefwechsel stehen correspond with sb
ⓩ **briet** [briːt] *pret of* braten
ⓩ **Bril·le** ['brɪlə] die <-, -n> **1.** glasses, spectacles, specs ◊ *Ohne Brille kann ich nichts lesen.* ♦ *eine Brille tragen* ♦ *Sie hat meist eine dunkle Brille auf.* **2.** *(toilet)* seat ◊ *eine alte Toilette ohne Brille und Deckel*
⊙ **etw. durch die rosarote Brille sehen** see sth through rose-tinted spectacles ◊ *Seit sie verliebt ist, sieht sie alles durch die rosarote Brille.*
ⓩ **brin·gen** ['brɪŋən] <bringt, brachte, hat gebracht> [tr v] **1.** jdm etw. bringen bring sb sth ◊ *Kannst du mir mal das Wörterbuch bringen?* jdm Blumen (ins Krankenhaus) bringen take flowers to sb (in hospital) jdn irgendwohin bringen take/bring sb somewhere ◊ *ein Kind jeden Morgen zur Schule bringen* ♦ *jdn zum Bahnhof bringen* sich [dat] eine Pizza bringen lassen have a pizza delivered ◊ *Ich habe mir eine Pizza bringen lassen.* **2.** broadcast Wir bringen jetzt Nachrichten. And now the news.; *(a film)* show ◊ *einen Spielfilm bringen; (newspaper)* publish, print ◊ *Die Zeitung hat heute einen interessanten Artikel dazu gebracht.* **3.** *(weather, trouble)* bring ◊ *Mach das nicht, das bringt bloß Ärger.* ♦ *Die dunklen Wolken bringen sicher Regen.; (interest etc.)* earn ◊ *eine Anlage, die wenig Zinsen bringt* ♦ *ein Feld, das kaum noch einen Ertrag bringt; (troubles, worries)* cause **4.** jdn zu etw. bringen get sb to do sth ◊ *seine Eltern dazu bringen, etw. zu erlauben* ◊ *jdn dazu bringen, bei einem Projekt mitzumachen* jdn zum Lachen/Weinen bringen make sb laugh/cry

5. *(fam) (a performance)* manage, achieve ◊ *Ich bring das einfach nicht!* ♦ *Torsten bringt in Englisch gute Leistungen.* **6.** jdn um den Schlaf bringen rob sb of their sleep jdn um seine Ersparnisse bringen do sb out of their savings **7.** etw. mit sich bringen entail sth ◊ *Dieser Job bringt viel Stress mit sich.* ♦ *Meine Arbeit bringt es mit sich, dass ich die Rechtschreibung gut beherrsche.* **8.** jdn auf andere Gedanken bringen take sb's mind off it/sth ein Zimmer in Ordnung bringen tidy a room jdn auf den neuesten Stand bringen bring sb up to date eine Angelegenheit wieder in Ordnung bringen set a matter straight etw. in Unordnung bringen mess sth up eine Sache ins Reine bringen clear a matter up, sort sth out [imp v] es auf etw. [acc] bringen manage sth, do sth ◊ *An guten Tagen verkaufe ich 100 Stück, an schlechten Tagen bringe ich es nur auf 50.* ♦ *Das Auto bringt es auf 300 Stundenkilometer.*

bri·sant [briˈzant] [adj] explosive ◊ *Die Lage in Nahost ist immer noch brisant.* ♦ *ein brisantes Thema*

Bri·te [ˈbriːtə, ˈbrɪtə] der <-n, -n>, **Bri·tin** [ˈbriːtɪn, ˈbrɪtɪn] die <-, -nen> Brit(on) → **Deutsche**

bri·tisch [ˈbriːtɪʃ, ˈbrɪtɪʃ] [adj] *mostly before ns* British ◊ *britisches Englisch sprechen* ♦ *Der Film ist typisch britisch.* → **deutsch**

brö·ckeln [ˈbrœkl̩n] [tr v] +haben crumble ◊ *Die Hefe aus das Mehl bröckeln und Milch hinzufügen.* [intr v] +sein *(also fig)* crumble (off/down) ◊ *Der Putz bröckelt von der Wand.* ♦ *Lansam bröckelte der unser Widerstand.*

Bro·cken [ˈbrɔkn̩] der <-s, -> **1.** lump (of stone) ◊ *einen Brocken vor eine Höhle wälzen; (of food)* piece, chunk ◊ *ein Brocken Fleisch* ♦ *einem Hund ein paar saftige Brocken geben* **2.** *(child)* lump; *(infant)* little bruiser ◊ *Ihr Baby ist ein richtiger Brocken.* **3.** scraps ◊ *Ich kann nur ein paar Brocken Spanisch.*
ⓔ **ein harter Brocken** hard going, a tough break ◊ *Dieser Roman ist wirklich ein harter Brocken.* ♦ *Dass er sie sitzen ließ, war für sie ein harter Brocken.*

ⓩ **Bro·schü·re** [brɔˈʃyːrə] die <-, -n> brochure, leaflet ◊ *eine Broschüre über das Museum*

ⓩ **Brot** [broːt] das <-(e)s, -e> **1.** bread ◊ *zum Essen Brot reichen* ♦ *Brot backen* **2.** loaf ◊ *Kannst du vom Bäcker bitte zwei Brote mitbringen?* ♦ *ein Brot aufschneiden* **3.** sandwich ◊ *sich ein Brot schmieren* ♦ *Was möchtest du auf dein Brot?*
ⓔ **ein hartes Brot** a hard way to make a living **sich** [dat] **sein Brot sauer verdienen** work hard for your living

---

Germany is famous for its bread. Over 200 different types of bread are sold ranging from choice white bread to strong brown rye bread, rich rye flour often being used in the baking process. Popular kinds of speciality bread include *Pumpernickel* (a very dark rye bread) from Westphalia and salt pretzels originally from Bavaria (which are cooked for a short time in caustic soda solution before being baked).

ⓩ **Bröt·chen** [ˈbrøːtçən] das <-s, -> roll ◊ *Samstags essen wir meist Brötchen zum Frühstück.* ♦ *beim*

Bäcker frische Brötchen holen ⊜Semmel

Bruch [brɔx] der <-(e)s, Brüche> **1.** break, fracture ◊ *mit schweren Brüchen ins Krankenhaus gebracht werden* einen offenen Bruch am Arm haben have a compound fracture of the arm **2.** hernia, rupture ◊ *am Bruch operiert werden* **3.** rupture ◊ *Die Straße war so schlecht, dass es zum Bruch der Achse kam.* ♦ *der Bruch eines Wasserrohrs* zu Bruch gehen break ◊ *Die Vase ist beim Transport zu Bruch gegangen.* **4.** *(of an agreement, a contract)* breach ◊ *der einseitige Bruch eines gültigen Vertrages* ♦ *Das ist ein klarer Bruch unserer Vereinbarung.* **5.** no pl *(of a relationship)* break-up, split ◊ *Sie hat den Bruch mit ihrem Bruder nie ganz verkraftet.* ♦ *Zwischen ihm und seiner Familie kam es wegen des Erbes zum Bruch.* **6.** MATH fraction ◊ *Null Komma fünf kann man auch als Bruch darstellen: ½* ♦ *das Rechnen mit Brüchen lernen* ♦ *einen Bruch kürzen*
ⓔ **in die Brüche gehen** break up ◊ *Ihre Ehe/Freundschaft ist in die Brüche gegangen.*

brü·chig [ˈbrʏçɪç] [adj] **1.** *(hair, nails)* brittle ◊ *brüchige Haare/Knochen/Nägel; (plaster)* crumbling; *(leather etc.)* cracked, split ◊ *Die Eisdecke/Das Leder ist mit der Zeit brüchig geworden.* **2.** *(voice)* weak, cracked ◊ *„Lasst mich in Frieden sterben", sagte sie mit brüchiger Stimme.* ♦ *Seine Stimme wurde immer brüchiger.* **3.** fragile ◊ *eine brüchige Koalition* ♦ *Der Frieden wird immer brüchiger.*

ⓩ **Brü·cke** [ˈbrʏkə] die <-, -n> **1.** bridge ◊ *über eine Brücke gehen/fahren* ♦ *eine Brücke bauen* ♦ *Der Zahnarzt hat ihr eine Brücke eingesetzt.* ♦ *Wir wollen Brücken zwischen den Kulturen bauen.* ♦ *Der Kapitän ist auf der Brücke.* **2.** rug ◊ *In seinem Wohnzimmer liegen ein paar wertvolle Brücken.*
ⓔ **jdm goldene Brücken bauen** smooth the way for sb ◊ *Der Prüfer hat mir goldene Brücken gebaut, aber ich kam trotzdem nicht auf die Antwort.* **alle Brücken hinter sich** [dat] **abbrechen** make a complete break with the past, make a completely new start

ⓩ **Bru·der** [ˈbruːdɐ] der <-s, Brüder> **1.** brother ◊ *Ich habe drei Brüder und eine Schwester.* ♦ *Das ist mein Bruder.* ♦ *Bruder Franziskus betete auch für die Tiere.* **2.** *(fam, pej)* bloke, character ◊ *Euch Brüdern traue ich nicht!*

brül·len [ˈbrʏlən] [tr v] +haben shout, yell ◊ *Er brüllte noch eine Warnung, aber es war zu spät.* [intr v] +haben **1.** shout, yell ◊ *Nun brüll doch nicht so, ich bin doch nicht taub!* vor Lachen brüllen roar with laughter vor Schmerz(en) brüllen scream/howl with pain ♦ cry ◊ *Das Baby hat die ganze Nacht gebrüllt.* **3.** *(monkey)* screech ◊ *Die Affen stürzten sich brüllend auf ihn.; (lion)* roar; *(cattle)* bellow, low
ⓔ **zum Brüllen sein** *(fam)* be hilarious, be a scream

brum·men [ˈbrʊmən] [tr v] +haben **1.** mumble, mutter ◊ *Sie brummte ein paar unverständliche Worte.* ♦ *„Lass mich in Ruhe!", brummte er.* **2.** hum ◊ *Er brummte ein Lied.* [intr v] +haben **1.** *(engine, aircraft etc.)* drone ◊ *Der Motor brummte laut.* ♦ *Über unseren Köpfen brummte ein Flugzeug.* **2.** *(bear)* growl ◊ *Der Bär brummt laut.; (fly, insect)* hum; *(person)* grunt ◊ *Sie brummte*

schlecht gelaunt. **3.** *(fam) (economy, trade)* boom ◇ *Die Wirtschaft brummt.* **4.** *(fam)* do time ◇ *Dafür muss er brummen.*

Brun·nen ['brʊnən] der <-s, —> **1.** well ◇ *einen Brunnen bohren* ♦ *Wasser aus dem Brunnen im Burghof* **2.** fountain ◇ *Die Fontana di Trevi ist der wohl bekannteste Brunnen Roms.*

ⓩ **Brust** [brʊst] die <-, Brüste> **1.** breast ◇ *dem Baby die Brust geben* ♦ *das Baby an die Brust legen* ♦ *Sie hat einen Knoten in der rechten Brust.* **2.** chest ◇ *eine behaarte Brust haben* ♦ *jdn an seine Brust drücken*
⦿ **es auf der Brust haben** *(fam)* have got chest trouble

brü·ten ['bryːtn̩] [intr v] +*haben* **1.** sit on its eggs, brood ◇ *Sieh mal, da sitzt ein Vogel im Nest und brütet.* **2.** *(a problem)* über etw. [dat] brüten ponder over sth ◇ *über einem Problem brüten* ♦ *Felix brütet über seinem Referat.*

brut·to ['brʊtoː] [adv] gross ◇ *Sie verdient 3000 Euro brutto.* ♦ *Das macht 100 Euro plus Mehrwertsteuer, also brutto 116 Euro.*

ⓩ **Bub** [buːp] der <-en, -en> *(Austr, SouthG, Swiss)* boy, lad ◇ *Sie hat einen Buben bekommen.*

ⓩ **Buch** [buːx] das <-(e)s, Bücher> book ◇ *ein spannendes Buch* ♦ *Welches Buch hast du zuletzt gelesen?* ♦ *Er schreibt ein Buch.* ♦ *Morgen kommt jemand vom Finanzamt, um die Bücher zu prüfen.* Buch führen do the books
⦿ **das Goldene Buch** the visitors' book ◇ *Der Kanzler hat sich ins Goldene Buch der Stadt Stuttgart eingetragen.*

ⓩ **bu·chen** ['buːxn̩] [tr v] +*haben* **1.** book ◇ *einen Flug/eine Reise/ein Hotel buchen* **2.** *(account)* credit ◇ *einen Geldbetrag auf ein Konto buchen* **3.** *(in accounts ledgers)* enter ◇ *Alle Ausgaben müssen gebucht werden.*

ⓩ **Bü·che·rei** [byːçəˈraɛ] die <-, -en> (public) library ◇ *sich ein Buch aus der Bücherei ausleihen* ⊖Bibliothek

Buch·hal·tung ['buːxhaltʊŋ] die <-, -en> **1.** bookkeeping ◇ *Mein Steuerberater macht jetzt für mich auch die Buchhaltung.* **2.** *(in a company)* accounts department ◇ *in der Buchhaltung einer Firma arbeiten*

Buch·hand·lung ['buːxhandlʊŋ] die <-, -en> bookshop ◇ *Ich habe das Buch in meiner Buchhandlung gekauft.*

ⓩ **Büch·se** ['bʏksə] die <-, -n> **1.** tin, can ◇ *eine Büchse Cola/Pfirsiche* ♦ *Wo ist die Büchse mit den Keksen?* ♦ *Fleisch in Büchsen* **2.** rifle, shotgun ◇ *mit der Büchse auf die Jagd gehen*

ⓩ **Buch·sta·be** ['buːxʃtaːbə] der <-ns, -n> letter ◇ *Das Alphabet hat 26 Buchstaben.* ♦ *große/kleine Buchstaben*

ⓩ **buch·sta·bie·ren** [buːxʃtaˈbiːrən] <buchstabiert, buchstabierte, hat buchstabiert> [tr v] spell ◇ *Können Sie das bitte buchstabieren?* ♦ *jdm seinen Namen buchstabieren*

buch·stäb·lich ['buːxʃtɛːplɪç] [adv] literally ◇ *Wegen des schlechten Wetters fiel das Gartenfest buchstäblich ins Wasser.* ♦ *Wir werden buchstäblich mit Werbung überschwemmt.* ⊖regelrecht

Bucht [bʊxt] die <-, -en> bay, cove ◇ *Der Strand liegt geschützt in einer kleinen Bucht.*

Bu·chung ['buːxʊŋ] die <-, -en> **1.** booking, res-

ervation ◇ *Wir bitten um rechtzeitige Buchung Ihrer Reise.* ♦ *Buchungen können telefonisch, per E-Mail oder Fax vorgenommen werden.* **2.** transaction ◇ *Auf Ihrem Kontoauszug sind alle Buchungen verzeichnet.* **3.** *(in an accounts ledger)* entry ◇ *Die Buchhaltung hat diese Buchung bereits berichtigt.*

bü·cken ['bʏkn̩] [ref v] +*haben* sich bücken bend (down), stoop ◇ *sich bücken, um etw. aufzuheben* ♦ *Ich bin so steif, dass ich mich nicht mehr bücken kann.*; *(as a sign of respect)* bow ◇ *sich tief bücken, um seinen Respekt auszudrücken* sich nach etw. bücken bend down to pick sth up ◇ *sich nach einem heruntergefallenen Stift bücken*

Bud·dhist [buˈdɪst] der <-en, -en>, **Bud·dhist·in** [buˈdɪstɪn] die <-, -nen> Buddhist ◇ *Er ist gläubiger Buddhist.*

bud·dhis·tisch [buˈdɪstɪʃ] [adj] buddhist ◇ *eine buddhistische Tradition* ♦ *Meine Familie ist buddhistisch.* [adv] jdn buddhistisch erziehen bring sb up in the buddhist tradition

ⓩ **Bud·dhis·mus** [buˈdɪsmʊs] der <-> *no pl* Buddhism ◇ *Meditation spielt im Buddhismus eine wichtige Rolle.*

Bu·de ['buːdə] die <-, -n> **1.** stall, stand ◇ *sich an der Bude ein Würstchen holen* **2.** *(fam)* place, pad ◇ *Wir können ja noch zu mir auf meine Bude gehen.*
⦿ **sturmfreie Bude haben** have got the place to yourself ◇ *Sobald ich mal wieder sturmfreie Bude habe, machen wir eine Party.* jdm die Bude einrennen *(fam)* descend on sb, beat a path to sb's door ◇ *Als ich mein Auto verkaufen wollte, haben mir die Leute fast die Bude eingerannt.*

Büf·fet [bʏˈfeː] das <-s, -s> **1.** sideboard ◇ *Die Weingläser stehen im Büffet.* **2.** buffet ◇ *ein (kaltes/warmes) Büffet bestellen*

Bü·gel ['byːgl̩] der <-s, -> **1.** (coat) hanger ◇ *Alle seine Hemden hängen auf Bügeln.* **2.** clip, (swing) stopper ◇ *Bierflaschen mit Bügeln sind wieder in Mode gekommen.* **3.** *(of a ski tow)* grip ◇ *Den Bügel bitte rechtzeitig loslassen.* **4.** *(of glasses)* earpiece, side ◇ *Ein Bügel meiner Brille zwickt hinter dem Ohr.* **5.** stirrup ◇ *Mein Reitlehrer half mir in die Bügel.*

Bü·gel·ei·sen ['byːgl̩|aezn̩] das <-s, -> iron ◇ *ein Bügeleisen, das mit Dampf bügelt*

bü·geln ['byːgl̩n] [tr+intr v] +*haben* iron ◇ *Hemden/ Wäsche bügeln* ♦ *Er sagt, er kann nicht bügeln.*

Büh·ne ['byːnə] die <-, -n> **1.** stage ◇ *Hamlet kommt auf die Bühne.* ♦ *Das Stuttgarter Theater hat eine drehbare Bühne.* **2.** theatre, theater ◇ *Sie sehen eine Aufführung der Ulmer Bühne.* ♦ *Sie wollte schon immer zur Bühne.*
⦿ **etw. über die Bühne bringen** complete sth ◇ *ein Projekt über die Bühne bringen*

Bul·ga·re [bʊlˈgaːrə] der <-n, -n>, **Bul·ga·rin** [bʊlˈgaːrɪn] die <-, -nen> Bulgarian → Deutsche

Bul·ga·ri·en [bʊlˈgaːrjən] das <-s> *article only in combination with attribute, no pl* Bulgaria → Deutschland

Bul·ga·rin [bʊlˈgaːrɪn] *fem of* Bulgare

bul·ga·risch [bʊlˈgaːrɪʃ] [adj] *mostly before ns* Bulgarian → deutsch

Bul·ga·risch [bʊlˈgaːrɪʃ] das <-(s)> *no pl* Bulgarian → Deutsch

A
B·
C
D
E
F
G
H
I
J
K
L
M
N
O
P
Q
R
S
T
U
V
W
X
Y
Z

Bul·le ['bʊlə] der <–n, –n> **1.** *(male cattle)* bull ◊ *Dieser Bulle ist nicht zur Zucht geeignet.* ⊖Stier **2.** *(male elephant, hippopotamus, rhinozeros, seal, whale)* bull; *(antelope, deer, moose)* buck **3.** *(slang, pej)* pig, cop(per) ◊ *Schnell weg! Die Bullen kommen!*

Bund¹ [bʊnt] der <–(e)s, Bünde> **1.** alliance ◊ *einen Bund schließen*; *(of states also)* federation, confederation ◊ *der Internationale Bund Freier Gewerkschaften*; *(in names)* association, society ◊ *der Bund der Steuerzahler* ♦ *der Bund für Umwelt und Naturschutz* **2.** *no pl* POL federal government ◊ *Bund und Länder werden je 50 % der Kosten tragen.* **3.** *no pl (fam)* MIL (federal) army ◊ *Mit 19 Jahren musste er zum Bund.* **4.** waistband ◊ *ein elastischer Bund*; waist ◊ *Die Hose ist am Bund zu eng.*
◉ *den Bund fürs Leben schließen* enter into the bond of marriage

Bund² [bʊnt] das <–(e)s, –e> bunch ◊ *ein Bund Radieschen/Petersilie*

Bün·del ['bʏndl̩] das <–s, –> *(also fig)* bundle ◊ *ein Bündel Briefe* ♦ *Das Baby war nur noch ein schreiendes Bündel.; (of bills also)* wad; *(of clothes, measures)* bunch ◊ *ein Bündel Wäsche* ♦ *ein ganzes Bündel von Maßnahmen*

bün·deln ['bʏndl̩n] [tr v] +*haben* **1.** bundle up ◊ *Zeitungen für die Altpapiersammlung bündeln; (straw, hay)* bale **2.** *(fig)* combine ◊ *Jetzt gilt es, alle Energien zu bündeln.* **3.** PHYSICS *(beams of light)* focus

⑦ **Bun·des·...** ['bʊndəs] [prefix] federal ◊ *die Bundeswehr* ◊ *der Bundesminister*

Bun·des·aus·bil·dungs·för·de·rungs·ge·setz [ˌbʊndəs'aʊsbɪldʊŋsˌfœrdərʊŋsɡəzɛts] das <–(e)s> *no pl* → BAföG

Bun·des·grenz·schutz [ˌbʊndəs'ɡrɛntsʃʊts] der <–es> *no pl (always der Bundesgrenzschutz) (abbr BGS) the Federal Border Guard*

Bun·des·kanz·ler ['bʊndəskantslɐ] der <–s, –>, **Bun·des·kanz·le·rin** ['bʊndəskantslərɪn] die <–, –nen> **1.** *(in Germany, Austria)* (federal) chancellor ◊ *ein Besuch des Bundeskanzlers* **2.** *(in Switzerland)* chancellor of the confederation ◊ *Annemarie Huber-Hotz wurde 1999 zur ersten Bundeskanzlerin gewählt.*

The Federal Chancellor holds the most important office in the Federal Republic of Germany and sets the political guidelines for the federal government. The chancellor's tenure of office (four years each term) and his/her duties are regulated by the Constitution. Because in the German political system power is concentrated in the federal chancellery, it is sometimes called a "chancellor democracy".

Bun·des·land ['bʊndəslant] das <–(e)s, Bundesländer> *(in Germany, Austria)* land, regional state ◊ *die neuen/alten Bundesländer* ♦ *das Bundesland Salzburg* ⊖Land

Today, Germany is a federation that consists of sixteen *Länder* (regional states): Baden-Württemberg, Bavaria, Berlin, Brandenburg, Bremen, Hamburg, Hesse, Mecklenburg-West Pomerania, Lower Saxony, North Rhine-Westphalia, Rhineland-Palatinate, Saarland, Saxony, Saxony-Anhalt, Schleswig-Holstein, and Thuringia.

Bun·des·li·ga ['bʊndəsˌliːgaː] die <–> *no pl (in Germany, Austria)* Bundesliga, national/federal division ◊ *Er spielt in der Bundesliga.* ♦ *Die Mannschaft stieg in die 1. Bundesliga auf.*

⑦ **Bun·des·mi·nis·ter** ['bʊndəsmiˌnɪstɐ] der <–s, –>, **Bun·des·mi·nis·te·rin** ['bʊndəsmiˌnɪstərɪn] die <–, –nen> Federal Minister, Federal Secretary ◊ *Er ist Bundesminister für Wirtschaft und Arbeit.* ♦ *die Bundesministerin für Gesundheit*

⑦ **Bun·des·mi·nis·te·ri·um** ['bʊndəsmiˌnɪsteːrjʊm] das <–, Bundesministerien> Federal Ministry ◊ *das Bundesministerium für Bildung und Forschung*

Bun·des·prä·si·dent ['bʊndəsprɛziˌdɛnt] der <–en, –en>, **Bun·des·prä·si·den·tin** ['bʊndəsprɛziˌdɛntɪn] die <–, –nen> **1.** *(in Germany, Austria)* president ◊ *Von 1949 bis 1959 war Theodor Heuss Bundespräsident.* ♦ *Der Bundespräsident hielt die Eröffnungsrede.* **2.** *(in Switzerland)* president of the confederation

Every five years, the German Federal Assembly elects the Federal President who has predominantly representational duties. He receives foreign diplomats, accredits German diplomats and represents the Federal Republic of Germany at social, cultural, and official events at home and abroad. As his country's representative under international law, he also ratifies treaties with other countries.

Bun·des·rat¹ ['bʊndəsraːt] der <–(e)s> *no pl* **1.** *(in Germany, Austria)* der Bundesrat the upper house of parliament, the Bundesrat ◊ *Das Gesetz muss noch durch den Bundesrat.* **2.** *(in Switzerland)* federal council

The German *Bundesrat* has 69 members, representing the governments of the *Länder* and their interests. Through the *Bundesrat* the *Länder* participate in federal legislation and administration processes. The larger the population of a *Land*, the more votes it has in the *Bundesrat*.

Bun·des·rat² ['bʊndəsraːt] der <–(e)s, Bundesräte>, **Bun·des·rä·tin** ['bʊndəsrɛːtɪn] die <–, –nen> **1.** *(in Switzerland)* federal councillor **2.** *(in Austria)* member of the upper house of parliament, member of the Bundesrat

Bun·des·re·gie·rung ['bʊndəsreˌgiːrʊŋ] die <–, –en> federal government

Bun·des·re·pu·blik ['bʊndəsrepuˌbliːk] die <–> *no pl* federal republic ◊ *die Bundesrepublik Deutschland/Österreich* ♦ *Überall in der Bundesrepublik fanden Demonstrationen statt.*

⑦ **Bun·des·staat** ['bʊndəsʃtaːt] der <–s, –en> federal state

Bun·des·stra·ße ['bʊndəsʃtraːsə] die <–, –n> federal highway, A-road ◊ *Die Bundesstraße 383 war blockiert.*

Federal highways are intended for long-distance traffic. Construction and maintenance costs are borne by the federal government. On roadmaps they are indicated by the letter **B** followed by a number. On the road they are indicated by yellow signs.

Bun·des·tag ['bʊndəstaːk] der <–(e)s> *no pl* POL *(always der Bundestag)* the lower house of parlia-

ment, the Bundestag ◊ *Das Gesetz wurde im Bundestag verabschiedet.* ✦ *Er sitzt seit 17 Jahren für die SPD im Bundestag.*

The *Bundestag* represents the people of the Federal Republic of Germany. Every four years the electorate vote for their representatives, the members of the *Bundestag*. The *Bundestag* has around 670 members. The duties of the *Bundestag* are determined by the Basic Law of the Federal Republic of Germany: formation of the government (election of the chancellor, legislation), control of government and administration, formulation of political demands and objectives, representation of the people and articulation of the people's concerns.

② **Bun·des·tags·prä·si·dent** ['bʊndəsta:ksprɛzi,dɛnt] der <-en, -en>, **Bun·des·tags·prä·si·den·tin** ['bʊndəsta:ksprɛzi,dɛntɪn] die <-, -nen> **1.** *Head of State of Germany or Austria* **2.** chairperson of the Swiss government

Bun·des·ver·fas·sungs·ge·richt [,bʊndəsfɛ'fasʊŋsɡərɪçt] das <-(e)s> *no pl (always das Bundesverfassungsgericht)* the Federal Constitutional Court ◊ *beim Bundesverfassungsgericht das Verbot einer Partei beantragen* ✦ *eine Beschwerde beim Bundesverfassungsgericht einreichen*

The Federal Constitutional Court was established in 1951 and has its seat in Karlsruhe. It watches over the observance of the Basic Law of the Federal Republic of Germany. Its verdicts are final and cannot be contested. It can influence legislation by declaring a law unconstitutional.

Bun·des·ver·samm·lung ['bʊndəsfɛzamlʊŋ] die <-> *no pl (always die Bundesversammlung) (in Germany, Switzerland)* the Federal Assembly

The Federal Assembly, the highest political organ of the Federal Republic of Germany, has the sole duty of electing the Federal President. The Federal Assembly is made up equally of members of the *Bundestag* and representatives of the regional state parliaments.

Bun·des·wehr ['bʊndəsve:ɐ] die <-> *no pl (always die Bundeswehr)* the German armed forces, the Bundeswehr ◊ *Auslandseinsätze der Bundeswehr* ✦ *Nach dem Abitur musste/ging er zur Bundeswehr.* ✦ *Er ist in/bei der Bundeswehr.*

The *Bundeswehr* (the armed forces of the Federal Republic of Germany) is subordinate to the ministry of defence. Its duties consist of the defence of the nation and its allies, UN missions, and emergency and humanitarian missions. The *Bundeswehr* is made up of professional soldiers and conscripts. Since January 1st 2001, women too have the opportunity to pursue a career in the German armed forces.

Bünd·nis ['bʏntnɪs] das <-ses, -se> alliance ◊ *das Bündnis für Politik- und Meinungsfreiheit* ✦ *ein Bündnis gegen Rassismus* ✦ *Sie gingen ein Bündnis mit Frankreich ein.*

Bun·ker ['bʊŋkɐ] der <-s, -> bunker ◊ *Sie flüchteten sich in den Bunker.* ✦ *ein Bunker aus dem 2.*

Weltkrieg

② **bunt** [bʊnt] ⟨adj, adv⟩ <bunter, am buntesten> **1.** colourful(ly), colorful(ly) ◊ *ein bunter Pulli* ✦ *Seine Welt ist bunt und fröhlich.* ✦ *bunt bemalte Eier* **2.** *(fig)* diverse(ly), mixed ◊ *eine bunte Mischung* ✦ *eine bunt zusammengewürfelte Truppe* bunt gemischt mixed, varied ein bunter Abend a social (evening) **3.** coloured, colored ◊ *Die Wand war nicht weiß, sondern bunt.* ✦ *buntes Glas etw.* bunt ausmalen/anmalen colo(u)r sth (in) ⊖farbig

Burg [bʊʳk] die <-, -en> **1.** castle ◊ *Schlösser und Burgen in Sachsen* ✦ *Die Feinde belagerten die Burg.* **2.** *(made of sand)* (sand) castle ◊ *Er baute am Strand eine Burg.*

② **Bür·ger** ['bʏʳɡə] der <-s, ->, **Bür·ge·rin** ['bʏʳɡərɪn] der <-, -nen> **1.** citizen, national ◊ *die Bürger Spaniens/der EU* ✦ *Die Bürger sind für mehr Datenschutz.* **2.** resident ◊ *„Liebe Bürgerinnen und Bürger, ..."* **3.** bourgeois(e) ◊ *Er war der Sohn eines reichen Bürgers.*

② **Bür·ger·i·ni·ti·a·ti·ve** ['bʏʳɡə|initsi̯a,ti:və] die <-, -n> citizens' (action) group, citizens' initiative ◊ *eine Bürgerinitiative für/gegen etw. gründen* **Bür·ger·krieg** ['bʏʳɡekri:k] der <-(e)s, -e> civil war ◊ *der Amerikanische Bürgerkrieg* ✦ *Ein Bürgerkrieg tobt in diesem Staat.*

② **Bür·ger·meis·ter** ['bʏʳɡemae̯stɐ] der <-s, ->, **Bür·ger·meis·te·rin** ['bʏʳɡemae̯stərɪn] die <-, -nen> mayor ◊ *Er ist zweiter Bürgermeister von Leipzig.* Bürgermeisterin mayoress ◊ *die Bürgermeisterin in Willich*

② **Bür·ger·steig** ['bʏʳɡeʃtae̯k] der <-(e)s, -e> pavement, sidewalk ◊ *Die Kinder spielten auf dem Bürgersteig.* ⊖Gehweg, Gehsteig

Bürg·schaft ['bʏʳkʃaft] die <-, -en> LAW guarantee, security ◊ *Die Bank hat den Kredit mit einer Bürgschaft abgesichert.* ✦ *für jdn eine Bürgschaft übernehmen*

② **Bü·ro** [by'ro:] das <-s, -s> office ◊ *Sie ist in ihrem Büro.* ✦ *Die restliche Arbeit erledigt unser Büro.* ✦ *Unser Büro in New York ist derzeit geschlossen.*

Bü·ro·kra·tie [byrokra'ti:] die <-, -n> **1.** *no pl (pej)* bureaucracy, red tape ◊ *Sie klagte über zu viel Bürokratie.* **2.** bureaucracy ◊ *die französische/Brüsseler Bürokratie* ⊖Verwaltung

Bur·sche ['bʊʳʃə] der <-n, -n> **1.** *(also oldf)* boy, lad ◊ *Die Burschen haben sich vorgedrängelt.* ⊖Junge **2.** fellow, chap, guy ◊ *ein toller/gerissener Bursche* ⊖Kerl **3.** *(pej)* matey ◊ *Na warte, Bursche!* ein übler Bursche a nasty piece of work ⊖Kerl

② **Bürs·te** ['bʏʳstə] die <-, -n> brush ◊ *Kamm und Bürste einpacken* ✦ *Zahnpasta auf die Bürste geben* ✦ *Er schrubbte seine Fingernägel mit der Bürste.*

② **Bus** [bʊs] der <-ses, -se> **1.** bus ◊ *Ich fuhr mit dem Bus in die Stadt.* ✦ *Willst du nicht lieber den Bus nehmen?;* *(for long journeys)* coach **2.** van ◊ *Nach dem dritten Kind kauften sie sich einen Bus.*

Busch [bʊʃ] der <-es, Büsche> **1.** bush, shrub ◊ *Bäume und Büsche säumen den Schulhof.* ✦ *Das Kind versteckte sich hinter einem Busch.* **2.** *no pl* GEOG jungle, bush ◊ *eine Safari durch den afrikanischen Busch*

⦿ (et)was ist im Busch sth is going on ◊ *Er grinst so komisch. Da ist doch was im Busch!*

Bu·sen ['buːzn̩] der <-s, -> *most sing* bust, bosom ◊ *Sie hat einen großen/kleinen Busen.*

Bus·hal·te·stel·le ['bʊshaltəʃtɛlə] die <-, -n> bus/coach stop ◊ *An der nächsten Bushaltestelle müssen wir aussteigen.* ♦ *Sie wartete an der Bushaltestelle.*

Bu·ße ['buːsə] die <-, -n> **1.** *no pl* REL penance ◊ *Wer gesündigt hat, muss Buße tun.* ♦ *zur Buße einen Rosenkranz beten* **2.** LAW fine ◊ *Gegen Zahlung einer Buße von 300 Euro wurde das Verfahren eingestellt.*

bü·ßen ['byːsn̩] tr+intr v +*haben* **1.** REL (für) etw. büßen atone for sth, do penance for sth ◊ *für seine Sünden büßen müssen* ♦ *Sind meine Sünden dadurch gebüßt?* **2.** (für) etw. büßen pay for sth, bear the consequences of sth ◊ *Ich lief am Anfang des Marathons zu schnell und musste später dafür büßen.* ♦ *Das wirst du mir büßen!* ♦ *Den Fehler musste er mit seinem Leben büßen.*

Buß·geld ['buːsɡɛlt] das <-(e)s, -er> LAW fine ◊ *Er musste ein Bußgeld zahlen.* ♦ *Wie hoch sind die Bußgelder in Österreich?*

Büs·ten·hal·ter ['byːstn̩haltɐ] der <-s, -> → BH

② **But·ter** ['bʊtɐ] die <-> *no pl* butter ◊ *ein Stück Butter in einem Topf schmelzen* ♦ *ein Brötchen mit Butter bestreichen*

⊛ **(es ist) alles in Butter** *(fam)* everything is fine

bzw. [bəˈtsiːʊŋsvaɛzə] → beziehungsweise

C

c, C [tse:] *das* <–(s), –(s)> **1.** c, C ◊ *Das Wort wird mit einem kleinen c/großen C geschrieben.* ♦ *C wie Cäsar* **2.** MUS C ◊ *Er spielte ein C.*

ca. [ˈtsɪ˞kaː] *(abbr of* circa*)* about, approximately ◊ *Wir kommen um ca. 20 Uhr in St. Moritz an.* ♦ *Die Datei hat ca. 23 KB.* ⊖etwa, ungefähr

② **Ca·fé** [kaˈfeː] *das* <–s, –s> café ◊ *Wir trafen uns in einem Café.*

② **Ca·mi·on** [kaˈmjõː] *der* <–s, –s> *(Swiss)* lorry, truck

② **Cam·ping** [ˈkɛmpɪŋ] *das* <–s> *no pl* camping ◊ *Wir fahren zum Camping nach Frankreich.* ♦ *Wir hatten viel Spaß beim Camping.*

② **CD** [tseːˈdeː] *die* <–, –s> *(abbr of* Compact Disc*)* CD ◊ *Sie hörten sich ein paar CDs an.* ♦ *Er wollte die Lieder auf eine CD brennen.*

② **CD-ROM** [tseːdeːˈrɔm] *die* <–, –s> CD-ROM ◊ *Er legte eine CD-ROM ein.* ♦ *Gibt es dieses Wörterbuch auf CD-ROM?*

CDU [tseːdeːˈʔuː] *die* *(abbr of* Christlich-Demokratische Union*)* German Christian Democrat party ◊ *Er gehört der CDU an.* ♦ *Sie wählt CDU.*

A German political party promoting free market economics and Christian values.

Cham·pig·non [ˈʃampɪnjɔn] *der* <–s, –s> (cap) mushroom ◊ *Champignons aus der Dose* ♦ *Es gab Schweinefilet mit Champignons.* brauner Champignon chestnut mushroom

② **Chan·ce** [ˈʃãs(ə), ˈʃãːs(ə)] *die* <–, –n> chance ◊ *Gegen diesen Gegner habe ich keine Chance.* ♦ *Er bekam eine zweite Chance.* die gleichen Chancen haben have the same chance Chancen auf den Sieg haben have a chance to win Chancen auf Erfolg haben have a chance of success gute Chancen haben, etw. zu tun have a good chance of doing sth die Chancen stehen gut the prospects are good, the odds are in your favour/favor bei jdm Chancen haben stand a chance with sb

② **Cha·rak·ter** [kaˈraktɐ] *der* <–s, –e> character ◊ *Er hat einen guten Charakter.* ♦ *Ein Mensch mit Charakter hätte sich entschuldigt!* ♦ *Die Mitgliedsbeiträge haben eher symbolischen Charakter.* ♦ *Fast alle Charaktere des Romans waren Männer.*

char·mant [ʃaˈrmant] [adj, adv] charming(ly) ◊ *Er war sehr charmant.* ♦ *ein charmantes Lächeln* ◊ *Sie lächelte charmant.*

② **Chauf·feur** [ʃɔˈføːɐ] *der* <–s, –e>, **Chauf·feu·rin** [ʃɔˈføːrɪn] *die* <–, –nen> chauffeur, driver ◊ *eine Limousine mit Chauffeur mieten* ♦ *Brauchen Sie einen Chauffeur?* ♦ *Sie arbeitet als Chauffeurin.*

② **Chef** [ʃɛf] *der* <–s, –s>, **Che·fin** [ˈʃɛfɪn] *die* <–, –nen> head, boss ◊ *Sie ist Uwes Chefin.* ♦ *Sie bekommen einen neuen Chef.* ⊖Vorgesetzte

② **Che·mie** [çeˈmiː] *die* <–> *no pl* **1.** chemistry ◊ *die anorganische/organische Chemie* ♦ *Chemie studieren* ♦ *Sie hat in Chemie eine Zwei.* **2.** chemicals ◊ *Chemie in Lebensmitteln* ♦ *Die*

Soße schmeckt nach Chemie und nicht nach Vanille.

Che·mi·ker [ˈçeːmɪkɐ] *der* <–s, –>, **Che·mi·ke·rin** [ˈçeːmɪkərɪn] *die* <–, –nen> chemist ◊ *Sie ist Chemikerin bei der BASF.* ♦ *der berühmte Chemiker Justus Liebig*

che·misch [ˈçeːmɪʃ] [adj, adv] *when used as an adj, mostly before ns* chemical(ly) ◊ *eine chemische Reaktion auslösen* ♦ *etw. chemisch untersuchen/analysieren* ♦ *Dieses Bonbon schmeckt chemisch.* chemische Reinigung dry-cleaner, dry-cleaning

② **chic** [ʃɪk] → schick

Chi·le [ˈtʃiːleː, ˈçiːleː] *das* <–s> *article only in combination with attribute, no pl* Chile → Deutschland

Chi·le·ne [tʃiˈleːnə, çiˈleːnə] *der* <–n, –n>, **Chi·le·nin** [tʃiˈleːnɪn, çiˈleːnɪn] *die* <–, –nen> Chilean → Deutsche

chi·le·nisch [tʃiˈleːnɪʃ, çiˈleːnɪʃ] [adj] *mostly before ns* Chilean ◊ *der chilenische Dichter Pablo Neruda*

Chi·na [ˈçiːnaː] *das* <–s> *article only in combination with attribute, no pl* China → Deutschland

Chi·ne·se [çiˈneːzə] *der* <–n, –n>, **Chi·ne·sin** [çiˈneːzɪn] *die* <–, –nen> Chinese → Deutsche

chi·ne·sisch [çiˈneːzɪʃ] [adj] *mostly before ns* Chinese → deutsch

Chi·ne·sisch [çiˈneːzɪʃ] *das* <–(s)> *no pl* Chinese → Deutsch

Chip [tʃɪp] *der* <–s, –s> **1.** *(for computers, gambling)* chip ◊ *die auf dem Chip gespeicherten Daten* ♦ *Er hat seine ganzen Chips beim Poker verspielt.* **2.** *only pl (food)* crisp, potato chip ◊ *Sie aßen Chips und tranken Cola.*

Chi·rurg [çiˈrʊ˞k] *der* <–en, –en>, **Chi·rur·gin** [çiˈrʊ˞gɪn] *die* <–, –nen> surgeon ◊ *Er ist ein erfolgreicher Chirurg.* ♦ *Sie ist Chirurgin am Amberger Krankenhaus.*

Chor [koːɐ̯] *der* <–(e)s, Chöre> **1.** MUS choir, chorus ◊ *Sie singt in einem gemischten Chor.* **2.** ARCH *(part of a church)* choir ◊ *1874 stieß man im Chor auf gotische Wandbilder.* **3.** THEAT chorus ◊ *der Chor im griechischen Drama* ⊙ im Chor in chorus

Christ [krɪst] *der* <–en, –en>, **Chris·tin** [ˈkrɪstɪn] *die* <–, –nen> Christian ◊ *Als Christ solltest du Nächstenliebe zeigen.* ♦ *Ich bin Christin und glaube an Jesus.*

Chris·ten·tum [ˈkrɪstn̩tuːm] *das* <–s> *no pl* Christianity ◊ *jdn zum Christentum bekehren*

Chris·tin [ˈkrɪstɪn] *fem of* Christ

christ·lich [ˈkrɪstlɪç] [adj] Christian(ly) ◊ *der christliche Glaube* ♦ *Das war nicht sehr christlich von dir!* ♦ *Er hat alles andere als christlich gehandelt.* jdn christlich erziehen bring sb up in the Christian faith streng christlich leben be a strict Christian

Chris·tus [ˈkrɪstus] *der* <Christi> *article only in combination with attribute, no pl* **1.** Christ ◊ *der Tod/die Auferstehung Christi* ♦ *das Motiv des*

leidenden Christus ♦ Christus ist von den Toten auferstanden. **2.** *(abbr v. Chr.)* vor Christus BC,
before Christ **3.** *(abbr n. Chr.)* nach Christus AD,
Anno Domini
cir·ca ['tsɪrkaː] [adv] *(abbr* ca.*)* about, approximately ◊ In der BRD leben circa 80 Millionen
Menschen. ♦ Circa 12 % der Schüler bekommen
die Note „gut". ⊖ungefähr, etwa
Cli·que ['klɪkə] die <–, –n> **1.** gang, crowd ◊ Ihre/
Die ganze Clique traf sich im Freibad. **2.** *(pej)*
clique ◊ Intrigen innerhalb der herrschenden
Clique
② **Club, Klub** [klʊp] der <–s, –s> club ◊ Der Club
organisiert Ausflüge für seine Mitglieder. ♦ der
Rotary Club Mannheim ♦ ein Club, wo man Salsa
tanzen kann
② **Coif·feur** [koa'føːʀ] der <–s, –e>, **Coif·feu·rin**
[koa'føːrɪn] die <–, –nen> *(Swiss)* hairdresser ◊ Er
arbeitet als Coiffeur. ♦ Wir suchen eine Coiffeurin
für Damen
② **Co·la** ['koːlaː] die <–, –s> *also* das <–s, –s> cola,
coke™ ◊ eine Dose Cola
② **Com·pu·ter** [kɔm'pjuːtɐ] der <–s, –> computer ◊
am Computer arbeiten/spielen ♦ Daten in den
Computer eingeben ♦ den Computer herunterfahren
⊖Rechner
② **Couch** [kaʊtʃ] die <–, –s *or* –en> couch, sofa ◊ Sie
saß auf der Couch. ⊖Sofa
② **Cou·sin** [ku'zɛŋ, ku'zɛ̃ː] der <–s, –s> cousin ◊ Mein
Cousin kommt morgen zu Besuch. ♦ Ich habe vier
Cousins und zwei Kusinen.

Cou·si·ne [ku'ziːnə] die <–, –n> → Kusine
② **Cou·vert** [ku'veːɐ̯] → Kuvert
② **Creme** [kreːm] die <–, –s *or Austr* –n *or Swiss* –n>
cream ◊ Die Creme zieht schnell in die Haut ein. ♦
Zum Nachtisch gab es eine Creme mit frischen
Erdbeeren. ♦ Die Windbeutel sind mit Creme
gefüllt.
CSU [tseːʔɛsˈʔuː] die *(abbr of* Christlich-Soziale
Union*)* Bavarian Christian social party ◊ Sie ist ein
Mitglied der CSU. ♦ Er wählt CSU.

The CSU is the Bavarian sister party of the *CDU*
with strong links to the two big Christian churches
in Germany, in particular the Roman Catholic
Church. Since 1949 the *CDU* and *CSU* have been
represented by a common *CDU/CSU* parliamentary
party in the *Bundestag* through which the party
has considerable political influence at national
level.

Cur·ry·wurst ['kœrivʊrst] die <–, Currywürste>
fried sausage, served with lots of tomato ketchup
and curry powder, a German take-away staple
CVP [tseːfaʊ'peː] die *(abbr of* Christlichdemokrati-
sche Volkspartei*)* Christian Democratic Party

The CVP was founded in 1912 under the name of
Konservativ-Christlichsoziale Volkspartei. It has
been known by its present name since 1970. As a
moderately conservative party it supports a federal-
istic, democratic Switzerland with a social market
economy.

D

d, D [de:] das <−(s), −(s)> **1.** d, D ◇ *Das Wort wird mit einem kleinen d/großen D geschrieben.* ♦ *D wie Dora* **2.** MUS D ◇ *Er spielte ein D.*

⑦ **da¹** [da:] [adv] **1.** *in response to the question 'where?'* there ◇ *Wohnt sie da denn noch?* ♦ *Da stehts doch: Öffnungszeiten von 18 Uhr bis 1 Uhr!* da draußen/drinnen out/in there ◇ *Die Wahrheit liegt irgendwo da draußen.* da drüben/vorne over there ◇ *Da drüben ist noch ein freier Sitzplatz.* da oben/unten up/down there ◇ *Schau, da oben fliegt ein Flugzeug!* da, wo ... where ◇ *Da, wo er herkommt, gibt es das nicht.* **2.** *in response to the question 'where?'* here ◇ *Da bin ich!* ♦ *Da kommt sie ja.* **3.** *often accompanied by a gesture (when handing sth over)* there ◇ *Da hast du das Geld!* ♦ *Da, nimm dir ein Stück Kuchen.* **4.** *in response to the question 'which?' (emphasizing a noun)* dieser/diese/dieses ... da that ... (over) there ◇ *Dieser Mann da folgt mir schon die ganze Zeit.* ♦ *Dieses Bild da gefällt mir ausgesprochen gut.* der/die/das da that one ◇ *„Welches Buch willst du kaufen?" — „Das da!"* **5.** *in response to the question 'when?'* then, (at) that moment ◇ *Da fing er plötzlich an zu weinen.* ♦ *Da bremste der Fahrer plötzlich.* von da an from then on ◇ *Von da an lief es wieder recht gut.* **6.** *(referring to circumstances)* in that case, then ◇ *Da kündige ich lieber gleich selbst.* ♦ *Da musste sogar ich lachen.* **7.** *(referring to something that was said previously)* there, in that respect ◇ *Da bin ich gar nicht deiner Meinung!* ♦ *Da kann ich Ihnen nur zustimmen.* **8.** *introducing a sentence (fam)* oh yes ◇ *Da kommt mir noch eine Idee ...* ♦ *Da fällt mir noch etwas ein: Wir wärs, wenn wir ...* ⊙ **da und dort, hier und da** here and there ◇ *Da und dort sind noch ein paar Fehler, aber ansonsten ist es gut.* **da sein 1.** be alive, live ◇ *Von ihren Freunden war keiner mehr da.* **2.** have arrived, have come ◇ *Ihr Flieger müsste doch schon längst da sein.* ♦ *Endlich war der Tag da, auf den sie gewartet hatte.* ♦ *Es war noch niemand von den anderen Gästen da.* **3.** be left ◇ *Ist noch Kaffee da?* ♦ *Es ist kein Brot mehr da.* **4.** *(not away)* be in ◇ *Ist dein Vater da?* wieder da sein be back ◇ *Einen Moment, ich bin gleich wieder da!* **5.** be mentally alert, be all there ◇ *Geistig ist sein Großvater noch voll da.* be conscious ◇ *Die Patientin ist nach der Narkose noch nicht wieder ganz da.*

⑦ **da²** [da:] [conjunc] **1.** *causal* since, as, because ◇ *Da er nur einige Meter entfernt wohnte, konnte er sofort kommen.* ♦ *Da er kein Geld hat, konnte er nicht in den Urlaub fahren.* **2.** *temporal (lofty)* jetzt/nun, da now that ◇ *Jetzt, da ich älter bin, sehe ich die Dinge anders.*

⑦ **da|...** [da:] [prefix] there ◇ *daliegen* ♦ *dasitzen* ♦ *dastehen*

DAAD [de:|a:|a:'de:] der *(abbr of* Deutscher Akade-

mischer Austauschdienst e.V.*) German Academic Exchange Service* ◇ *Der DAAD vergibt verschiedene Stipendien für die USA.*

da·bei [da'bae̯, 'da:bae̯] [adv] *relating to a previously specified noun or section of sentence* **1.** with it/them ◇ *Alle Kinder kamen aus der Schule, aber meine Tochter war nicht dabei.* Das Spielzeugauto war bei den Cornflakes dabei. The toy car was included with the cornflakes. **2.** *translation varies (expressing slight impatience)* Es ist doch gar nichts dabei, auch mal „nein" zu sagen. There is nothing wrong with saying 'no' once in a while. Was ist schon dabei, sich einen Zahn ziehen zu lassen? What is the problem with having a tooth out? Es ist doch nichts dabei, vor vielen Leuten eine Rede zu halten. There's nothing to giving a speech in front of a lot of people. **3.** there ◇ *Als er hörte, dass wir in die Kneipe gehen, war er sofort dabei.* ♦ *Die Familie war dabei, als er starb.* **4.** at the same time ◇ *Wenn ich bügle, höre ich dabei immer Radio.* **5.** and yet, although ◇ *Er fühlt sich alt; dabei sieht er doch so jung aus.* **6.** in the process of doing sth ◇ *Ich war gerade dabei, das Essen zu kochen, als das Telefon klingelte.* ⊙ **sich nichts dabei denken** think nothing of it

⑦ **da·bei|...** [da'bae̯] [prefix] ... with sth/sb ◇ *dabeisitzen* ♦ *dabeistehen*

da·bei|blei·ben [da'bae̯blae̯bm̩] <bleibt dabei, blieb dabei, ist dabeigeblieben> [intr v] stick with it ◇ *Ich habe damit begonnen, und jetzt bleibe ich auch dabei.* in der Bundesliga vorne dabeibleiben stay at the top of the bundesliga

da·bei|ha·ben [da'bae̯ha:bm̩] <hat dabei, hatte dabei, hat dabeigehabt> [tr v] **1.** have with you, have on you ◇ *kein Geld dabeihaben* ♦ *Sie hat immer ihre Kinder dabei.* **2.** have sb around ◇ *Geh weg, wir wollen dich nicht dabeihaben!*

⑦ **Dach** [dax] das <−(e)s, Dächer> roof ◇ *aufs Dach klettern* ♦ *Das Auto überschlug sich und landete auf dem Dach.* ⊙ **unter Dach und Fach** sorted (out) ◇ *Der Tarifvertrag ist unter Dach und Fach.* **unterm Dach** in the attic, right at the top ◇ *Unsere Wohnung ist unterm Dach.* **unter einem Dach** under one roof ◇ *Sie lebten jahrelang unter einem Dach.*

Dach·bo·den ['daxbo:dn̩] der <−s, Dachböden> loft, attic ◇ *Wir haben die alten Möbel auf den Dachboden gebracht.* ⊝Boden, Speicher

⑦ **dach·te** ['daxtə] *pret of* denken

da·durch [da'dʊrç, 'da:dʊrç] [adv] *relating to a previously specified noun or section of sentence* **1.** through this/that, in this/that way ◇ *Welche Vorteile habe ich dadurch?* ♦ *Denken Sie an schöne Dinge und motivieren Sie sich dadurch.* Probleme löst man nicht dadurch, dass man nicht darüber redet. You don't solve problems by not talking about them. **2.** as a result ◇ *Das Gerät ist*

klein und passt dadurch in jede Jackentasche.
da·für [da'fy:ɐ̯, 'da:fy:ɐ̯] ⎡adv⎤ *relating to a previously specified noun or section of sentence* **1.** *for that/it* ◊ *Was gibst du mir dafür?* ✦ *Bist du dafür oder dagegen?* jd kann etwas/nichts dafür it is/ isn't sb's fault ◊ *Man gab ihm die Schuld, obwohl er gar nichts dafürkonnte.* **2.** *considering that* ◊ *Dafür, dass sie erst sechs ist, drückt sie sich sehr gut aus.* **3.** *on the other hand, but then* ◊ *Die Arbeit ist schlecht bezahlt, dafür macht sie aber Spaß.* Ich bin aus dem Orchester ausgetreten, dafür singe ich in einem Chor. I left the orchestra, but I do sing in a choir now.
da·ge·gen [da'ge:gn̩, 'da:ge:gn̩] ⎡adv⎤ *relating to a previously specified noun or section of sentence* **1.** *against it* ◊ *sich gegen die Wand lehnen* ✦ *Bist du dafür oder dagegen?* Ich habe nichts dagegen einzuwenden, wenn du mein Auto nimmst. I've got nothing against you taking my car. Ich gehe mit Julian ins Kino. Hast du etwas dagegen? I'm going to the cinema with Julian. Do you object? **2.** *on the other hand, however* ◊ *Er ist von der Idee begeistert. Ich dagegen habe Bedenken.*
⊖hingegen
da·heim [da'haem] ⎡adv⎤ *at home* ◊ *Am liebsten bin ich daheim.* ✦ *Am Wochenende war ich daheim bei meinen Eltern.* ⊖zu Hause
② **da·her** [da'he:ɐ̯, 'da:he:ɐ̯] ⎡adv⎤ *often relating to a previously specified noun or section of sentence* **1.** *from (there)* ◊ *„Meine Frau stammt aus Italien." — „Oh, daher kommt auch mein Freund."* **2.** *that is why, therefore* ◊ *Ich habe Klavier gespielt und daher das Telefon nicht gehört. Das kommt ganz einfach daher, dass du nie zuhörst.* That is simply the result of your never listening. ⊖deshalb, deswegen
da·her|kom·men [da'he:ɐ̯kɔmən] <kommt daher, kam daher, ist dahergekommen> ⎡intr v⎤ *(pej)* **1.** *turn up* ✦ *appear* ✦ *Du kannst nicht einfach so daherkommen und Geld verlangen.* **2.** *(wearing certain clothes)* *go around* ◊ *Das ist eine Kirche! Mit einem Minirock kannst du nicht daherkommen!*
da·her|re·den [da'he:ɐ̯re:dn̩] <redet daher, redete daher, hat dahergeredet> ⎡tr v⎤ *(pej)* *talk away, rabbit on* ◊ *Wie kann man nur so dumm daherreden!*
da·hin [da'hɪn, 'da:hɪn] ⎡adv⎤ *relating to a previously specified noun or section of sentence* **1.** *(towards a destination)* *there* ◊ *Ich fahre nur dahin, weil du es möchtest.* **2.** *bis dahin* *by then, until then* ◊ *Morgen ist Bewerbungsschluss. Bis dahin brauchen wir Ihre Unterlagen.* ✦ *Bis dahin kannst du bei uns wohnen.*
⊛ **dahin gehend** *(form)* *to that effect* ◊ *ein dahin gehender Antrag* dahin gehend, dass to the effect that ◊ *Von den Befragten äußerten sich 84% dahin gehend, dass sie sich nie politisch engagieren.* dahin sein have gone, be over ◊ *Die Hoffnung ist dahin.*
da·hin·ge·gen [dahɪn'ge:gn̩, 'da:hɪnge:gn̩] ⎡adv⎤ *(lofty)* *on the other hand, however* ◊ *Sie liebt Beethoven. Wagner dahingegen verabscheut sie.*
da·hin·ten [da'hɪntn̩, 'da:hɪntn̩] ⎡adv⎤ *back there* ◊ *Was ist denn dahinten los?*
da·hin·ter [da'hɪntɐ, 'da:hɪntɐ] ⎡adv⎤ *relating to a previously specified noun or section of sentence*

1. *spatial* *behind it/that/them* ◊ *ein Schloss mit einem Park dahinter* **2.** *(in a sequence)* *behind it/ him/her etc.* ◊ *Maier wurde Erster, Schmitt belegte knapp dahinter den zweiten Platz.* **3.** *(fig)* *behind it* ◊ *Er vermutete dahinter politische Motive.*
⊛ **dahinter kommen** *find out, realize* ◊ *Ich bin dahinter gekommen, dass sie gelogen hat.* **dahinter stecken** *be behind it/that* ◊ *Das war eine großartige Idee. Dahinter steckt bestimmt die neue Chefin. Es steckt keine Absicht dahinter. It is not intentional.* **dahinter stehen** **1.** *be behind it/that, fully support it/that* ◊ *Das geht nur, wenn Ihre Familie dahinter steht.* **2.** *underlie it/that, be at the root of it/that* ◊ *Welche Überlegungen standen dahinter?*
da|las·sen ['da:lasn̩] <lässt da, ließ da, hat dagelassen> ⎡tr v⎤ *(fam)* *leave (here/there)* ◊ *Nimmst du den Schirm mit oder lässt du ihn da?*
da·ma·lig ['da:ma:lɪç] ⎡adj⎤ *no comp/superl; only before ns* *at the/that time, then* ◊ *seine damalige Frau*
② **da·mals** ['da:ma:ls] ⎡adv⎤ *at the/that time, then* ◊ *Damals kannte ich ihn noch nicht.*
② **Da·me** ['da:mə] die <-, -n> **1.** *lady* ◊ *Kennst du diese Dame?* ✦ *Sehr geehrte Damen und Herren!*; *(in sports)* *lady, woman* **2.** *(in card games, chess)* *queen* **3.** *no article, no pl* *draughts, checkers* ◊ *Dame spielen*
Da·men·to·i·let·te ['da:məntɔa,lɛta] die <-, -n> *Ladies, ladies' toilet* ◊ *Wo ist bitte die Damentoilette?*
② **da·mit¹** [da'mɪt, 'da:mɪt] ⎡adv⎤ *relating to a previously specified noun or section of sentence* **1.** *with it/them* ◊ *Damit will ich nichts zu tun haben!* ✦ *Hier sind die Eier, aber was willst du damit?* **2.** *because of that* ◊ *Er verlor die Dame und damit die Schachpartie.* **3.** *in this way, as a result* ◊ *Du hast mich angelogen und damit mein Vertrauen zerstört.*
da·mit² [da'mɪt] ⎡conjunc⎤ *so that* ◊ *Beeil dich, damit du nicht wieder zu spät kommst!*
däm·lich ['dɛ:mlɪç] ⎡adj, adv⎤ *(fam)* *stupid(ly)* ◊ *Lass deine dämlichen Bemerkungen!* ✦ *Der Vorschlag ist mir zu dämlich.* ✦ *Viel dämlicher hättest du dich kaum anstellen können!*
Damm [dam] der <-(e)s, Dämme> **1.** *dam* ◊ *Der Damm brach und das ganze Dorf wurde überschwemmt.*; *(to an island)* *causeway* **2.** ANAT *perineum*
⊛ **nicht auf dem Damm sein** *(fam)* *not feel yourself* ◊ *Obwohl er nicht ganz auf dem Damm war, ging er ins Büro.* **wieder auf dem Damm sein** *(fam)* *be fit again*
däm·mern ['dɛmɐn] ⎡intr v⎤ *+haben* **1.** *dawn* ◊ *Als der Morgen dämmerte, stand ich auf. es dämmert dawn is breaking, dawn breaks, it begins to get light* ◊ *Sobald es dämmert, beginnen die Vögel zu singen.* **2.** *get dark Der Abend dämmerte. Night was falling. es dämmert dusk is falling, the light is fading* **3.** *doze* ◊ *Er hat während der ganzen Zugfahrt vor sich hin gedämmert.* **4.** *(fam)* *(es) dämmert jdm it dawns on sb* ◊ *Da dämmerte (es) ihm, dass seine Kollegen dafür verantwortlich waren.*
Dampf [dampf] der <-(e)s, Dämpfe> *steam* ◊ *Diese Maschine wird mit Dampf betrieben.* ✦ *Das Bad*

war voller Dampf. giftige Dämpfe toxic vapours
⊛ **Dampf ablassen** *(fam)* let off steam **jdm
Dampf machen** *(fam)* **1.** hurry sb up **2.** put
pressure on sb ◇ *Die Opposition machte der
Regierung Dampf.*
dämp·fen ['dɛmpfn̩] [tr v] +*haben* **1.** steam ◇
Gemüse dämpfen **2.** steam iron ◇ *Dämpfen Sie
diese Seidenbluse mit einem feuchten Tuch.*
3. diminish ◇ *Die Prognosen dämpften die Erwartungen für das kommende Quartal.*; *(enthusiasm)*
put a dampener on; *(an impact)* absorb
gedämpfte Musik subdued music
Damp·fer ['dampfɐ] der <-s, -> steamer, steamship
da·nach [da'naːx, 'daːnaːx] [adv] *relating to a previously specified noun or section of sentence* **1.** after
it/that, afterwards ◇ *Zuerst regnete es, aber danach
schien die Sonne.* ⊖dann **2.** sich danach
umdrehen turn (a)round to (look at) it ◇ *Er
drehte sich noch nicht einmal danach um.* sich
danach umsehen look around for it ◇ *Ich habe
mich in der Stadt danach umgesehen, das Buch
aber nicht gefunden.* **3.** according to it/that ◇ *Du
solltest dich an das Rezept halten, und danach
müssen fünf Eier in den Teig.*
Dä·ne ['dɛːnə] der <-n, -n>, **Dä·nin** ['dɛːnɪn] die
<-, -nen> Dane → Deutsche
da·ne·ben [da'neːbn̩, 'daːneːbm̩] [adv] *relating to a
previously specified noun or section of sentence*
1. next to it/that ◇ *Hier ist das Museum und gleich
daneben befindet sich die Kapelle.* **2.** in addition
(to that), besides that ◇ *Sie arbeitet als Journalistin; daneben schreibt sie Kurzgeschichten.*
⊛ **(voll) daneben sein** *(fam)* **1.** be a (complete)
washout, be a (total) flop ◇ *Der Urlaub war voll
daneben.* **2.** be (completely) out of order ◇ *Diese
Bemerkung war voll daneben.*
Dä·ne·mark ['dɛːnəmaʳk] das <-s> *article only in
combination with attribute, no pl* Denmark →
Deutschland
Dä·nin ['dɛːnɪn] *fem of* Däne
dä·nisch ['dɛːnɪʃ] [adj] *mostly before ns* Danish →
deutsch
Dä·nisch ['dɛːnɪʃ] das <-(s)> *no pl* Danish →
Deutsch
dank [daŋk] [prep] *sing nouns without article or
attribute are not declined when following this prep,
otherwise* [+gen] *or fam* [+dat] thanks to ◇ *Dank
seines Einsatzes fand er schnell einen neuen Job.*
✦ *Das Fest wurde dank dem guten Wetter ein
Erfolg.*
② **Dank** [daŋk] der <-(e)s> *no pl* thanks ◇ *Zum Dank
überreichte er ihr einen Blumenstrauß.* ✦ *Vielen
Dank für die Einladung!*
② **dank·bar** ['daŋkbaːʳ] [adj, adv] grateful(ly) ◇ *Ich bin
ihr unendlich dankbar.* ✦ *dankbare Blicke* ✦ *Er
nahm ihre Hilfe dankbar an.* ⊖undankbar [adj]
rewarding ◇ *Diese Ruine ist ein dankbares Motiv
für Fotografen.* ✦ *Eine solche Aufgabe ist nicht
besonders dankbar.* ⊖undankbar
dan·ke ['daŋkə] [part] **1.** thank you, thanks ◇
Danke für die schönen Blumen! (für etw.) Danke
sagen say thank you (for sth), say thanks (for sth)
◇ *Ich möchte gern Danke sagen für Ihre Unterstützung.* **2.** (nein) danke no thank you, no thanks ◇
„Soll ich dir helfen?" — „Danke, ich kann das
alleine." ✦ *Atomkraft, nein danke!*

② **dan·ken** ['daŋkn̩] [tr+intr v] +*haben* thank ◇ *Sie
dankte ihm für die Blumen.* ✦ *Man hat ihr ihre
Großzügigkeit schlecht gedankt.* Er lehnte die
Einladung dankend ab. He declined the invitation
politely. Nichts zu danken! Don't mention it!

In German, there are several options available
when you want to thank somebody, and it is easy
to give the impression of being slightly rude or
over-polite. Which form is used very much
depends on the situation. *Danke!* is fairly neutral,
and is used, for example, when thanking
somebody for a piece of information. *Danke
schön!* or *Vielen Dank!* might be used when
accepting a small gift, and *Besten Dank!* is used
in a business context. All these forms can be inten-
sified. For example, *Oh, vielen Dank!* signifies
that a person is pleasantly surprised, and *Vielen
herzlichen Dank — das wäre aber nicht nötig
gewesen!* (Thank you very much indeed — you
really shouldn't have!) is a way of saying thank
you for a present when the person is almost too
embarrassed to receive it … or, at least, that is
the impression that is given.

Dan·ke·schön ['daŋkəʃøːn] das <-s> *no pl* thank
you ◇ *ein herzliches Dankeschön sagen*
② **dann** [dan] [adv] **1.** *temporal, spatial* then ◇ *Wir
gingen erst ins Kino und dann noch in die Kneipe.*
✦ *Gehen Sie hier geradeaus: Erst kommt die
Kirche, dann das Museum.* ⊖danach **2.** in that
case Wenn Ute mitkommt, dann bleibe ich zu
Hause. If Ute is going, I'm staying at home.
3. dann noch on top of that, into the bargain ◇ *Zu
Weihnachten wünsche ich mir eine Armbanduhr
und dann noch eine Halskette.*
⊛ **bis dann** *(fam)* see you then ◇ *Bis dann,
mach's gut!* **dann und wann** now and again ◇ *Wir
treffen uns dann und wann.*
da·ran [da'ran, 'daːran] [adv] *relating to a previously specified noun or section of sentence* on(to)
it/that ◇ *Man streicht den Kleister direkt auf die
Wand und klebt die Tapete daran.* Was interessiert
dich nur daran? What on earth do you find interesting about it? Kannst du mich daran erinnern? Can
you remind me? Er trägt die Schuld daran. He is
to blame for it. Es bestand kein Zweifel daran,
dass sie den Vorfall bedauert. There was no doubt
that she regretted the incident.
da·rauf [da'raof, 'daːraof] [adv] *relating to a previously specified noun or section of sentence*
1. *spatial* on it/that ◇ *ein Tisch mit einer Vase
darauf* **2.** *temporal* after that ◇ *Erst kam Eva, bald
darauf Max.* ✦ *Im darauf folgenden Jahr heirateten
sie.* **3.** *with certain verbs* darauf basieren be based
on it/that darauf zu sprechen kommen get to talk
about it/that darauf stürzen fall on it/that ◇ *Als
sie den Kuchen sahen, stürzten sie sich sofort
darauf.* würde darauf ganz wild! Darauf bin ich ganz wild!
Schokolade? Darauf bin ich ganz wild!
da·rauf·hin [daraof'hɪn, 'daːraofhɪn] [adv] *with
stress on the first syllable when seeking confirmation, relating to a previously specified noun or
section of sentence* **1.** after that ◇ *Sie verliebten
sich und heirateten daraufhin.* **2.** as to whether;
(with expressions of intention) with the purpose
of, with a view to ◇ *Das Experiment war daraufhin*

angelegt, seine Theorie zu überprüfen.
da·raus [da'raos, 'da:raos] [adv] *with stress on the first syllable when seeking confirmation, relating to a previously specified noun or section of sentence* out of it, from it ◊ *Du solltest daraus Konsequenzen ziehen.* ♦ *Machen wir das Beste daraus!* ♦ *Er nahm das Buch und las daraus vor.*
dar|bie·ten ['da:'bi:tn̩] <bietet dar, bot dar, hat dargeboten> [tr v] **1.** perform ◊ *Auf dem Schulfest wurde ein Theaterstück dargeboten.* **2.** *(food, commodities etc.)* offer ◊ *Es wurde edles Gebäck dargeboten.* [ref v] etw. bietet sich (jdm) dar sth presents itself (to sb) ◊ *Ein Bild des Schreckens bot sich uns dar.*
② **darf** [da:f] *pres of* dürfen
da·rin [da'rın, 'da:rın] [adv] *relating to a previously specified noun or section of sentence* **1.** *spatial* in it/that ◊ *eine Kiste mit Sand darin* **2.** *(concerning a certain matter)* in that respect ◊ *Wir müssen etwas tun. Darin sind wir uns einig.* **3.** *with certain verbs* darin bestehen consist of ◊ *Seine Aufgabe besteht darin, das Geschirr zu spülen.* darin liegen lie in the fact that ◊ *Seine Stärke liegt darin, dass er ein gutes Gedächtnis hat.*
Dar·le·hen ['da:'le:ən] das <-s, -> loan ◊ *Er hat zum Kauf eines Grundstücks ein Darlehen aufgenommen.*
Darm [da'm] der <-(e)s, Därme> **1.** ANAT intestine(s), bowel(s) ◊ *den Darm entleeren* **2.** *(for sausages)* skin
dar|stel·len ['da:'ʃtɛlən] <stellt dar, stellte dar, hat dargestellt> [tr v] **1.** depict, portray ◊ *Dieses Gemälde stellt die Schwester des Künstlers dar.* ♦ *etw. schematisch darstellen etw./jd lässt sich als etw.* [nom] darstellen sth/sb can be represented as sth, sth/sb can be portrayed as sth ◊ *Das lässt sich als Diagramm darstellen.* ⊜abbilden **2.** FILM, THEAT portray ◊ *Das Theaterstück stellt den Alltag von Jugendlichen dar.*; *(a role)* play ◊ *Sie würde gerne einmal die Mutter Courage darstellen.* die darstellenden Künste the performing arts **3.** *(in words)* describe ◊ *etw. anschaulich/verständlich darstellen* **4.** represent ◊ *Dieser Auftrag stellt eine besondere Herausforderung dar.* ⊜sein [ref v] **1.** etw. stellt sich dar sth appears ◊ *Die Angelegenheit stellte sich als äußerst komplex dar.* ♦ *Wie stellt sich das Problem dar?* **2.** sich darstellen present yourself ◊ *Sie weiß sich darzustellen.* ♦ *Er stellt sich gern als großer Menschenfreund dar.*
② **Dar·stel·lung** ['da:'ʃtɛlʊŋ] die <-, -en> **1.** representation ◊ *die grafische Darstellung von Daten*; *(of violence)* portrayal **2.** ARTS, FOTO *(photography etc.)* depiction, portrayal ◊ *die Darstellung des männlichen Körpers in der Kunst* ein Buch mit bildlichen Darstellungen a book with illustrations **3.** *(in words)* description, account ◊ *eine objektive Darstellung der Fakten* nach Darstellung ... [gen], nach ... Darstellung according to reports from ... ◊ *nach Darstellung der Regierung* ♦ *nach offizieller Darstellung* nach eigener Darstellung by sb's own account ◊ *Nach eigener Darstellung will das Unternehmen expandieren.* **4.** THEAT performance, interpretation ◊ *Die Kritiker lobten ihre Darstellung der Maria Stuart.*
da·rü·ber [da'ry:be, 'da:ry:be] [adv] *relating to a previously specified noun or section of sentence*

1. over it/that/them ◊ *ein Tisch mit einer Lampe darüber* ♦ *Sie rückte an ihrer Brille und schaute darüber hinweg.* **2.** *with certain verbs* sich darüber ärgern get annoyed about it ◊ *Er war frech. Darüber habe ich mich geärgert.* sich darüber ärgern, dass jd etw. tut get annoyed about sb doing sth darüber hinwegkommen get over it ◊ *Sie starb vor einem Jahr. Darüber kommt er nicht hinweg.* darüber hinwegsehen ignore it ◊ *Sie ist oft albern, aber darüber muss man hinwegsehen.* **3.** *(with figures)* above ◊ *Schiffe mit einer Länge von 60 Metern und darüber* **4.** while doing it, in doing so ◊ *Ich tröstete ihn und vergaß darüber meinen eigenen Kummer.*
◉ **darüber hinaus 1.** in addition (to that), apart from that ◊ *Sie ist freundlich und darüber hinaus äußerst großzügig.* ⊜außerdem **2.** beyond ◊ *Liefern Sie nur innerhalb Deutschlands oder auch darüber hinaus in andere Länder?*
② **da·rum** [da'rʊm, 'da:rʊm] [adv] *relating to a previously specified noun or section of sentence* **1.** *spatial* around it/that ◊ *ein See mit Bäumen darum* **2.** *with certain verbs* sich darum kümmern take care of it ◊ *Lassen Sie nur, darum kümmere ich mich.* **3.** *(giving a reason)* that's why, because of that ◊ *Ich bin müde, darum gehe ich jetzt schlafen.*
da·run·ter [da'rʊnte, 'da:rʊnte] [adv] *relating to a previously specified noun or section of sentence* **1.** *spatial* under it/that ◊ *Er trug einen Blazer und einen Pullover darunter.* **2.** *with figures* below (that), under that ◊ *Im August betrug die Besucherzahl 30 000. Im September lag sie weit darunter.* **3.** among them, including ◊ *Er besitzt viele Bücher, darunter auch einige Klassiker.*
◉ **Darunter kann ich mir nichts vorstellen. That doesn't mean anything to me.**
das¹ [das] [art] *definite* **1.** *with neut nouns in the nom and acc sing* the ◊ *Das Auto parkt da.* ♦ *Park das Auto woanders!* **2.** *(demonstrative)* that, this ◊ *Das Bild hier/da drüben finde ich am schönsten.* box@ Artikel, der¹
das² [das] [rel pron] *referring to neuter ns* who, that, which ◊ *Ein Kind, das zweisprachig aufwächst, hat viele Vorteile.* ♦ *Ich las ein Buch, das ich sehr spannend fand.* box@ Relativpronomen [demonstr pron] *that one* ◊ *Dieses Kleid ist schöner als das da drüben.*; this one ◊ *Das hier ist allerdings billiger.*; the one ◊ *Wolltest du das mit den gelben Punkten?* box@ Demonstrativpronomen, der²
Da·sein ['da:zaen] das <-s> *no pl (lofty)* existence ◊ *des Recht auf ein menschenwürdiges Dasein* ein kümmerliches Dasein fristen lead a miserable life
da|sit·zen ['da:zɪtsn̩] <sitzt da, saß da, hat/ist dagesessen> [intr v] *in South G, Austr, Swiss often +sein* **1.** sit there ◊ *Er saß da und starrte vor sich hin.* **2.** be left there ◊ *Alle gingen, und ich saß mit dem schmutzigen Geschirr da.*
das·je·ni·ge ['dasje:nɪgə] *neut of* derjenige¹, derjenige²
② **dass** [das] [conjunc] **1.** *introducing a subordinate clause* that ◊ *Es freut mich, dass du da bist.* ♦ *Wetten, dass es morgen regnet?* **2.** *translation varies* Die Geschichte ist zu unwahrscheinlich, als dass sie sie glauben könnte. The story is too

improbable for me to believe it. Er ist zu wenig durchtrainiert, als dass er gewinnen könnte. He is not fit enough to be able to win. Er verließ den Raum, ohne dass wir es bemerkten. He left the room without our noticing. Jetzt habe ich sie beleidigt, ohne dass ich es wollte. Now I have offended her without intending to. Kaum dass sie gesund ist, arbeitet sie schon wieder mit vollem Einsatz. Scarcely had she recovered then she was working flat out again. **3.** *(emph)* that ◊ *Dass das jetzt passieren musste!*

das·sel·be [das ˈzɛlbə] *neut of* derselbe

da|ste·hen [ˈdaːʃteːən] <steht da, stand da, hat/ist dagestanden> [intr v] *in South G, Austr, Swiss often +sein* **1.** stand there ◊ *Er stand geduldig da und wartete.* **2.** *(fig)* be in a certain position financially gut dastehen be doing well financially Nach dem Konkurs stand sie ohne Arbeit da. After the bankruptcy proceedings she was left without work. Am Ende stand die Mannschaft mit leeren Händen da. In the end the team were left empty-handed.

② **Da·tei** [daˈtae] die <-, -en> file ◊ *eine Datei öffnen/speichern*

② **Da·ten** [ˈdaːtn̩] *pl of* Datum die <-> *only pl* **1.** data, figures ◊ *die aktuellen Daten zum Aktienmarkt* **2.** IT data ◊ *Daten in den Computer eingeben* **3.** *(regarding a person)* details ◊ *Der Polizeibeamte nahm ihre Daten auf.*

Da·ten·bank [ˈdaːtn̩baŋk] die <-, -en> database ◊ *etw. in einer Datenbank erfassen*

Da·ten·schutz [ˈdaːtn̩ʃʊts] der <-(e)s> *no pl* data protection

Da·tiv [ˈdaːtiːf] der <-s, -e> dative

Relatively few verbs require the noun or pronoun to take the dative. For example, *Ich helfe* **dir** (I'll help you). In conjunction with the accusative, the dative is often used to indicate that a person is affected by an action: *Ich schreibe* **meiner Mutter** *einen Brief* (I'm writing a letter to my mother). A small number of prepositions are always followed by the dative: *ab, aus, bei, mit, nach, seit, von, zu.*

② **Da·tum** [ˈdaːtʊm] das <-s, Daten> date ◊ *ein bedeutendes historisches Datum* ✦ *Bitte legen Sie ein Foto jüngeren Datums bei.* ✦ *Das genaue Datum steht noch nicht fest.*

The Germans write the date in the following way: *Heute ist Montag, der 1. September 2012* (Today is Monday, 1st September 2012); *Wir treffen uns am Montag, den 1. September 2012* (We'll meet on Monday, 1st September 2012). The date is also often encountered in abbreviated form, e.g. *1. Sept. 2012* or *1.9.2012.*

Dau·er [ˈdaoe] die <-> *no pl* **1.** period ◊ *Er übernahm das Amt für die Dauer eines Jahres.* **2.** duration ◊ *Ein Projekt ist ein Vorhaben von begrenzter Dauer.*

● nicht von Dauer sein be short-lived ◊ *Seine Freude war nicht von Dauer.* von Dauer sein be long-lasting, endure auf Dauer permanently ◊ *auf Dauer angestelltes Personal* ✦ *Auf Dauer kann das nicht so weitergehen.* auf (die) Dauer in the long term ◊ *Auf die Dauer möchte ich hier nicht leben.*

Dau·er·auf·trag [ˈdaoeˌaoftraːk] der

<-(e)s, Daueraufträge> standing order ◊ *einen Dauerauftrag einrichten*

dau·er·haft [ˈdaoehaft] [adj] permanent ◊ *eine dauerhafte Lösung finden* ✦ *Wie dauerhaft wird der Frieden sein?* ⊖beständig [adv] on a permanent basis ◊ *Die Arbeitsplätze müssen dauerhaft gesichert werden.* ⊖vorübergehend

② **dau·ern** [ˈdaoen] [intr v] *+haben* **1.** last ◊ *Der Film dauert fast drei Stunden.* **2.** *(time)* take ◊ *Wie lange dauert die Fahrt dorthin?*

② **dau·ernd** [ˈdaoent] [adj, adv] *no comp/superl; when used as an adj, only before ns* constant(ly), perpetual(ly) ◊ *Hör auf mit dem dauernden Geschrei!* ✦ *Er ist dauernd erkältet.* ⊖ständig

Dau·men [ˈdaomən] der <-s, -> thumb ◊ *Sie hat sich den linken Daumen gebrochen.* ✦ *am Daumen lutschen*

● jdm die Daumen halten/drücken *(fam)* keep your fingers crossed for sb Däumchen drehen *(fam)* twiddle your thumbs

da·von [daˈfɔn, ˈdaːfɔn] [adv] *relating to a previously specified noun or section of sentence* **1.** from there, from it/that ◊ *Kennst du die Hirsch-Apotheke? Ich wohne nur hundert Meter davon entfernt.* **2.** of it/that ◊ *Hast du davon gehört?* ✦ *Der Eintopf ist prima. Kann ich mehr davon haben?* Nimm dir ruhig davon! Just help yourself! Das hast du jetzt davon! That's what comes of it!

da·von|kom·men [daˈfɔnkɔmən] <kommt davon, kam davon, ist davongekommen> [intr v] escape, get away ◊ *Er ist bei dem Unfall mit leichten Verletzungen davongekommen.*

da·von|ma·chen [daˈfɔnmaxn̩] <macht sich davon, machte sich davon, hat sich davongemacht> [ref v] sich davonmachen slip away, sneak off ◊ *sich heimlich davonmachen* ✦ *Wenn es ans Aufräumen geht, macht sie sich immer davon.*

da·vor [daˈfoːɐ, ˈdaːfoːɐ] [adv] *relating to a previously specified noun or section of sentence* **1.** *spatial* in front (of it/that/them) ◊ *Die Jungen standen in der zweiten Reihe, die Mädchen davor.* **2.** *temporal* before that, beforehand ◊ *Wir waren im Kino und davor waren wir einkaufen.* ⊖zuvor, vorher ⊖danach, nachher **3.** davor Angst haben be afraid of it/that ◊ *Davor habe ich keine Angst.*

da·zu [daˈtsuː, ˈdaːtsuː] [adv] *relating to a previously specified noun or section of sentence* **1.** with it/that ◊ *Wir essen heute Fisch. Was für einen Wein trinkt man dazu? Die Hochzeit ist morgen. Was zieht man dazu an?* The wedding is tomorrow. What should we wear (to it)? **2.** into the bargain, on top of everything, what is more ◊ *Es war eiskalt, und noch dazu hatte ich mein Schal vergessen.* **3.** etw./jdn dazu brauchen need sth/sb (for it/that) ◊ *Das Projekt ist komplex. Dazu brauchen wir viel Personal.* **4.** dazu meinen think (about it/that) ◊ *Geben wir ihm noch eine Chance — was meinst du dazu?* dazu sagen say (to it/that)

da·zu|ge·hö·ren [daˈtsuːgəhøːrən] <gehört dazu, gehörte dazu, hat dazugehört> [intr v] **1.** etw. gehört zu etw. dazu sth is part of sth ◊ *Liebeskummer gehört zum Erwachsenwerden dazu.* Golf und alles, was dazu gehört golf and everything about it **2.** *(person)* jd gehört irgendwo dazu sb belongs to somewhere ◊ *zu einer Gemeinschaft dazugehören* Als ich in die Gastfamilie kam, hatte ich gleich

das Gefühl dazuzugehören. When I met my host family, I immediately felt I belonged there. ⊕ **es gehört etw. dazu** it takes sth ◊ *Es gehört Mut dazu, dem Chef die Meinung zu sagen.*

da·zwi·schen [da'tsvɪʃn̩, 'da:tsvɪʃn̩] [adv] in between, between them ◊ *Auf dem Foto sind mein Vater, meine Mutter und dazwischen meine Geschwister.*

da·zwi·schen|kom·men [da'tsvɪʃn̩kɔmən] <kommt dazwischen, kam dazwischen, ist dazwischengekommen> [intr v] disrupt things, come up ◊ *Leider ist ein Problem dazwischengekommen.* etw. kommt jdm dazwischen sth holds sb up ◊ *Ich kann nicht kommen, mir ist leider etwas dazwischengekommen.*

da·zwi·schen|re·den [da'tsvɪʃn̩re:dn̩] <redet dazwischen, redete dazwischen, hat dazwischengeredet> [intr v] *(fam)* jd redet (jdm) dazwischen sb interrupts (sb) ◊ *Rede mir nicht immer dazwischen!*

DB [de:'be:] die → Deutsche Bahn

DDR [de:de:|'ɛr] POL *(always die DDR) (abbr of Deutsche Demokratische Republik)* the GDR

> On 7th October 1949 the German Democratic Republic was founded in the Soviet occupation zone as a separate state (independent from the Federal Republic of Germany) under one-party rule. It was the most industrially advanced country of the Eastern bloc. However, the authorities' constant spying on the citizens and the lack of individual freedom led to an uprising against the regime resulting in the fall of the Berlin Wall in 1989. Gorbachev's glasnost and perestroika finally paved the way for the reunification of Germany.

② **De·cke** ['dɛkə] die <–, –n> **1.** ceiling ◊ *Eine Glühbirne hing von der Decke herab.* ✦ *An der Decke sitzt eine Spinne.* ⊝Boden, Fußboden **2.** blanket, cover ◊ *Sie wickelte sich in die Decke.* ✦ *Komm zu mir unter die Decke!* **3.** (table)cloth ⊕ **an die Decke gehen** *(fam)* hit the roof ✦ *mir fällt die Decke auf den Kopf (fam)* I am going stir-crazy ◊ *Ich muss jetzt mal raus, mir fällt hier die Decke auf den Kopf.* **sich (finanziell) nach der Decke strecken müssen** tighten your belt ✦ **mit jdm unter einer Decke stecken** *(fam)* be in cahoots with sb

De·ckel ['dɛkl̩] der <–s, –> lid, top, cap, cover ◊ *der Deckel einer Schachtel/eines Marmeladenglases* ⊕ **jeder (Topf) hat/findet seinen Deckel** there's a lid for every pot, every Jack will find his Jill **eins auf den Deckel bekommen/kriegen** *(fam)* get a (good) dressing-down, get a (good) talking-to

de·cken ['dɛkn̩] [tr v] +*haben* **1.** cover (up) for ◊ *seine Komplizen decken* ✦ *Ich bin nicht bereit, deine Fehler weiterhin zu decken.* ⊝verraten **2.** *(a need, demand)* meet, satisfy ◊ *Das Angebot deckt bei weitem nicht die Nachfrage.* ✦ *den Vitaminbedarf decken; (costs, damages)* cover ◊ *Der Schaden wird von der Versicherung gedeckt.* **3.** ein/das Dach (eines Hauses) decken roof (a house) ◊ *Das Dach wurde mit roten Ziegeln gedeckt.* **4.** den Tisch decken lay the table, set the table ◊ *Deckst du bitte den Tisch?* [tr+intr v] +*haben* **1.** SPORT *(a player)* mark **2.** BIO *(stallion,*

bull etc.) cover, serve ◊ *Die Kuh wurde Ende Februar gedeckt.* [intr v] cover ◊ *Diese Farbe deckt sehr gut.* [ref v] etw. deckt sich mit etw. sth agrees with sth, sth tallies with sth ◊ *Seine Aussage deckt sich mit der des anderen Zeugen.* ⊝übereinstimmen

de·fi·nie·ren [defi'ni:rən] <definiert, definierte, hat definiert> [tr v] define ◊ *Ziele/Rahmenbedingungen definieren etw.* lässt sich als etw. definieren sth can be defined as sth

def·tig ['dɛftɪç] [adj, adv] **1.** *(cooking, food)* hearty(-ily) ◊ *ein deftiger Eintopf* ✦ *Die Küche Bayerns ist sehr deftig.* ✦ deftig gewürzt **2.** *(language)* coarse(ly), crude(ly) ◊ *eine deftige Ausdrucksweise* ✦ *Der Witz war ziemlich deftig.* ✦ *eine deftig geschriebene Geschichte* ⊝derb

dehn·bar ['de:nba:ʳ] [adj] **1.** elastic, stretchable ◊ *ein dehnbarer Bund* ✦ *Dieser Stoff ist dehnbar.* **2.** *(fig) (semantically)* loose ◊ *ein dehnbarer Begriff* ✦ *Der Paragraph ist dehnbar.*

deh·nen ['de:nən] [tr v] +*haben* stretch ◊ *die Muskeln dehnen; (person)* sich dehnen stretch (yourself) ◊ *Nach dem Aufwachen dehnte und streckte sie sich.; (rubber, clothes etc.)* stretch, expand ◊ *Die Hose dehnt sich noch.*

② **dein** [daen] [det] your ◊ *Wo ist dein Mann?* ✦ *Deine Freundin ist sehr attraktiv.* ✦ *Jemand hat dein Auto zerkratzt.* ✦ *Deine Eltern sind echt cool!* ✦ *Ich habe deinen Chef getroffen.*

	m	f	nt	pl
nom	dein	deine	dein	deine
acc	deinen	deine	dein	deine
dat	deinem	deiner	deinem	deinen
gen	deines	deiner	deines	deiner

dei·ne ['daenə] → deiner → dein

dei·ner ['daene] [poss pron] yours ◊ *Ich habe eine Geldbörse gefunden. Ist das vielleicht deine?* ✦ *Ich mag keine Hunde, aber deiner ist ganz nett.* ✦ *Mein Auto ist kaputt. Können wir deines nehmen?*

	m	f	nt	pl
nom	deiner	deine	dein(e)s	deine
acc	deinen	deine	dein(e)s	deine
dat	deinem	deiner	deinem	deinen
gen	-	-	-	-

dei·ner·seits ['daenezaets] [adv] on/for your part ◊ *Ich warte auf einen Kommentar deinerseits.* ✦ *Du könntest dich deinerseits auch etwas bemühen.*

dei·nes ['daenəs] → deiner

dei·net·we·gen ['daenət've:gn̩] [adv] because of you, for your sake ◊ *Sie ist nur deinetwegen gekommen.*

dei·ns [daens] → deiner

② **De·ka·gramm** ['de:kagram, 'dɛkagram] das <–s, –> *(Austr) (abbr* dag*) unit of mass equal to 10 grams* ◊ *15 Dekagramm Zucker in den Teig geben*

De·kli·na·ti·on [deklina'tsjo:n] die <–, –en> **1.** LING declension ◊ *die Deklination des Adjektivs* **2.** ASTRON declination

de·kli·nie·ren [dekli'ni:rən] <dekliniert, deklinierte, hat dekliniert> [tr+intr v] LING decline ◊ *Deklinieren Sie "Hund".* ⊝beugen

De·le·gier·te [dele'gi:gtə] der/die <–n, die Delegierten> *but: ein Delegierter/eine Delegierte* POL delegate, representative ⊝Abgeordnete

Del·fin [dɛl'fiːn] → Delphin

De·likt [de'lɪkt] das <-(e)s, -e> LAW offence ◊ das Delikt der Steuerhinterziehung

Del·phin [dɛl'fiːn] der <-s, -e> dolphin

dem [deːm] → der

dem·ent·spre·chend ['deːmlɛnt'ʃprɛçn̩t, 'deːmlɛnt'ʃprɛçənt] [adj] *no comp/superl* appropriate, fitting ◊ *Er hat mich blöd angeredet und eine dementsprechende Antwort bekommen.* ♦ *Die Absage war sehr unhöflich formuliert und ihre Reaktion dementsprechend.* [adv] correspondingly, therefore ◊ *Er muss Steuern nachzahlen und ist dementsprechend verärgert.*

dem·ge·gen·über ['deːmgeːgŋ̩'yːbɐ] [adv] *(form)* in contrast, on the other hand ◊ *2004 gab es weniger Unfälle. Demgegenüber stieg aber die Zahl der Verletzten.*

dem·nach ['deːmnaːx] [adv] *(form)* therefore, accordingly ◊ *Sie arbeitet schon lange hier und hat demnach viel Erfahrung.* ⊜somit, demzufolge

dem·nächst [dem'nɛːçst] [adv] soon, shortly ◊ *Demnächst eröffnet hier ein Café.* ⊜bald

② **De·mo·kra·tie** [demokra'tiː] die <-, -n> POL democracy

② **de·mo·kra·tisch** [demo'kraːtɪʃ] [adj, adv] democratic(ally) ◊ *demokratische Wahlen* ♦ *Dieses Regime ist alles andere als demokratisch.* ♦ *ein demokratisch gewählter Politiker* ⊜undemokratisch, totalitär

de·mo·lie·ren [demo'liːrən] <demoliert, demolierte, hat demoliert> [tr v] wreck, smash up ◊ *Die Telefonzelle wurde von Unbekannten demoliert.*

② **De·mons·tra·ti·on** [demɔnstra'tsi̯oːn] die <-, -en> demonstration ◊ *eine Demonstration gegen den Krieg/für den Frieden* ⊜Kundgebung

De·mons·tra·tiv·pro·no·men [demɔnstra'tiːfproˈnoːmən] das <-s, - or Demonstrativpronomina> demonstrative pronoun

> *Dieser, diese, dieses* are rarely used as pronouns; mostly they are used as articles. In the appendix you can look up how they are declined.

dem·zu·fol·ge ['deːmtsuˈfɔlgə] [adv] *(form)* therefore, consequently ◊ *Er ist der Projektleiter und trägt demzufolge die Verantwortung.* ⊜demnach, deshalb

den [deːn] → der

denk·bar ['dɛŋkbaːɐ̯] [adj] possible, conceivable ◊ *ein denkbarer Kompromiss* ♦ *Fortschritt ohne Risiko ist nicht denkbar.* ⊜möglich ⊜undenkbar, unmöglich [adv] very, extremely ◊ *Er hat sich denkbar dumm verhalten.* ♦ *ein denkbar einfaches Konzept* ⊜sehr

② **den·ken** ['dɛŋkŋ̩] <denkt, dachte, hat gedacht> [tr+intr v] think ◊ *„Das ist mir früher nie aufgefallen", dachte sie.* ♦ *nicht mehr klar denken können* ♦ *Ich dachte, ich hätte den Brief schon abgeschickt.* ♦ *Wer hätte das gedacht!* an sich/jdn/etw. denken think of yourself/sb/sth ◊ *Du denkst immer nur an dich!; (not forget)* an jdn/etw. denken remember sb/sth ◊ *Denk an deinen Termin morgen früh!* daran denken, etw. zu tun consider doing sth, think about doing sth, contemplate doing sth ◊ *Denkst du daran, mein Kleid aus der Reinigung zu holen?* ♦ *Er dachte daran, zu verreisen.* etw. über

jdn/etw. denken think sth about sb/sth ◊ *Was denkst du darüber?* ♦ *Es ist mir egal, was die Leute über uns denken.* etw. von jdm denken think sth of sb ◊ *Was denkst du nur von mir? Das würde ich nie tun!* [ref+tr v] jd kann sich [dat] etw. denken sb should know/expect sth ◊ *Du kannst dir doch denken, dass ich mir Sorgen mache. Ich habe mir gedacht, wir könnten heute auswärts essen. I thought we could go out for dinner tonight.* ⊛ **jd denkt sich nichts (weiter) bei etw.** sth does not strike sb as odd ◊ *Die Tür stand offen, aber ich habe mir nichts dabei gedacht.* jdm zu denken geben make sb wonder, make sb think, give sb something to think about ◊ *Gibt dir das nicht zu denken, wenn dich alle das Gleiche fragen?* seit jd denken kann for as long as sb can remember, all sb's life ◊ *Das war so, seit sie denken konnte.* nicht daran denken, etw. zu tun not dream of doing sth, have no intention of doing sth ◊ *denkste, das hast du dir so gedacht that's what you think* sich [dat] etw. bei etw. denken mean sth by sth, intend sth by sth ◊ *Was hat sich der Künstler dabei gedacht?* für jdn gedacht sein be meant for sb ◊ *Der Kuchen war nicht für dich gedacht!*

Denk·mal ['dɛŋkmaːl] das <-(e)s, Denkmäler> monument, memorial ◊ *ein Denkmal errichten/enthüllen* ♦ *Der Autor setzte seiner Geburtsstadt ein literarisches Denkmal.*

② **denn**[1] [dɛn] [conjunc] because, for ◊ *Ich schenkte mir ein Glas Wasser ein, denn ich hatte Durst.* ⊜weil

② **denn**[2] [dɛn] [part] 1. *in questions, seldom translated directly* Was ist denn? What (is it)? Was hat er denn? What's wrong with him? Was hast du denn vor? What are you planning, then?; So, what are you going to do? Wie geht es dir denn? How are you (then)? 2. *(emph)* Das geht denn doch zu weit! (But) that really is going too far! So einfach war die Lösung denn doch nicht. The solution wasn't so simple after all. So habe ich mir das denn doch nicht vorgestellt! That's not how I thought it would be at all! 3. *+comp (lofty)* reicher/teurer etc. denn je (zuvor) richer/more expensive etc. than ever ◊ *Heute liebt er sie mehr denn je (zuvor).*

den·noch ['dɛnɔx] [adv] *(lofty)* nevertheless, nonetheless ◊ *Wir sind sehr unterschiedlich, verstehen uns aber dennoch gut.* ♦ *Das ist gefährlich — wagen wir es dennoch!* ⊜trotzdem

De·o·do·rant [delodo'rant] das <-s, -s> *(abbr Deo)* deodorant ◊ *ein Deodorant auftragen*

De·po·nie [depo'niː] die <-, -n> tip, dump, landfill ◊ *Müll auf Deponien lagern*

de·po·nie·ren [depo'niːrən] <deponiert, deponierte, hat deponiert> [tr v] 1. *(valuables, luggage)* deposit ◊ *Gepäck in einem Schließfach deponieren* ♦ *Sie hat ihr Geld auf dem Sparbuch deponiert.* ⊜hinterlegen 2. *(waste, clothes, keys etc.)* put, keep, store ◊ *Den Schlüssel deponieren wir unter der Fußmatte.* ♦ *Wo soll der Atommüll deponiert werden?* ⊜aufbewahren

Depp [dɛp] der <-en, -en> *(fam, pej)* idiot, thicko

de·pri·mie·ren [depri'miːrən] <deprimiert, deprimierte, hat deprimiert> [tr v] depress ◊ *Das schlechte Wetter deprimiert mich richtig.* ♦ *Wir*

A
B
C
D
E
F
G
H
I
J
K
L
M
N
O
P
Q
R
S
T
U
V
W
X
Y
Z

haben sie mit der Nachricht vollkommen deprimiert. ⓩ **der¹** [deːɐ̯] [art] *definite* **1.** *with masc ns in the nom sing* the ◇ *der Nachbar* ♦ *der Kongress in Rom* **2.** *with fem ns in the gen and dat sing* of the ◇ *das Ende der Geschichte* ♦ *die Lieder der berühmten Sängerin Edith Piaf*; (to) the ◇ *Sag der Dame guten Tag.* **3.** *with all pl ns in the gen of the* ◇ *die Kinder der Frauen* ♦ *Die Fenster der Häuser waren offen.* ♦ *Gibt es eine Emanzipation der Männer?* **4.** *(demonstrative)* that, this ◇ *Der Tag passt mir gar nicht, geht es nicht an einem anderen?* ♦ *Der Kuchen hier schmeckt mir am besten.* box@ Artikel

	m	f	nt	pl
nom	der	die	das	die
acc	den	die	das	die
dat	dem	der	dem	den
gen	des	der	des	der

der² [deːɐ̯] [rel pron] *referring to masc ns* who, that, which ◇ *Er war ein Mann, der die Frauen liebte.* ♦ *ein Sturm, der alles zerstörte* box@ Relativpronomen [demonstr pron] that one ◇ *Dieser Mantel ist schöner als der da.*; this one ◇ *Den hier hätte ich gerne.*; the one ◇ *Kennst du den mit der Brille?* box@ Demonstrativpronomen **der·art** [ˈdeːɐ̯ˈʔaːɐ̯t] [adv] to such an extent, so much ◇ *Ich habe sie derart verärgert, dass sie nicht mehr mit mir spricht.*; *(before adj)* such ein derart teures Auto such an expensive car ⊜so **derb** [dɛrp] [adj, adv] crude(ly), coarse(ly) ◇ *ein derber Spaß* ♦ *Sein Humor ist recht derb.* ♦ *Er drückt sich sehr derb aus.* ⊜deftig [adj] **1.** *(shoes, material)* sturdy; *(material also)* rough, coarse **2.** *(person)* earthy, uncouth ⓩ **deren** [ˈdeːrən] *gen sing of* die *gen pl of* der, die, das [det] **1.** *referring to sing fem ns (relative)* whose, of whom, of which ◇ *eine Frau, deren Schönheit Legende war* ♦ *eine Aktie, deren Wert noch steigen wird*; *(demonstrative)* her ◇ *die Ministerin und deren Mitarbeiter*; its ◇ *die Truppe und deren Einsatz im Krisengebiet* **2.** *referring to pl ns (relative)* whose; *(demonstrative)* their ◇ *Sie luden die Müllers und deren Kinder ein.* → dessen **der·glei·chen¹** [deːɐ̯ˈglaeçn̩] [det] *invariable (lofty)* such ◇ *Dergleichen Vorkommnisse häuften sich.* ⊜derlei ⊜andere **der·glei·chen²** [deːɐ̯ˈglaeçn̩] [demonstr pron] *invariable (lofty)* such things, the like ◇ *Dergleichen fürchte ich nicht.* ⊜derlei ⊜andere **der·je·ni·ge¹** [ˈdeːɐ̯jeːnɪɡə] [det] the ◇ *Gewonnen hat derjenige Teilnehmer, der als erster ins Ziel kommt.* ♦ *Schadensersatz für diejenige Person, die einen Verlust erlitt* ⊜der

	m	f	nt	pl
nom	derjenige	diejenige	dasjenige	diejenigen
acc	denjenigen	diejenige	dasjenige	diejenigen
dat	demjenigen	derjenigen	demjenigen	denjenigen
gen	desjenigen	derjenigen	desjenigen	derjenigen

der·je·ni·ge² [ˈdeːɐ̯jeːnɪɡə] [demonstr pron] the one ◇ *Denjenigen, der hierfür verantwortlich ist, werde ich verklagen.* ♦ *Sie ist diejenige, die mich angerufen hat.* ♦ *Von allen Märchen war „Rotkäpp-*

chen" dasjenige, das ich als Kind am meisten liebte. diejenigen the ones ◇ *Wo sind diejenigen, die zu meiner Gruppe gehören?* **der·lei¹** [ˈdeːɐ̯lae] [det] *invariable (lofty)* such ◇ *Derlei Dinge gehen einem nicht mehr aus dem Kopf.* ⊜solche, dergleichen **der·lei²** [ˈdeːɐ̯lae] [pron] *invariable (lofty)* such things ◇ *Derlei kann ich mir gar nicht vorstellen.* ⊜dergleichen ⓩ **der·sel·be** [deːɐ̯ˈzɛlbə] [adj] the same ◇ *Wir haben denselben Vater, aber nicht dieselbe Mutter.* ♦ *Dieselbe Schülerin stört jeden Tag.* ♦ *Dort parkt immer dasselbe Auto.* ♦ *Es beschweren sich doch immer dieselben Leute.*

	m	f	nt	pl
nom	derselbe	dieselbe	dasselbe	dieselben
acc	denselben	dieselbe	dasselbe	dieselben
dat	demselben	derselben	demselben	denselben
gen	desselben	derselben	desselben	derselben

der·zeit [ˈdeːɐ̯tsaet] [adv] *(lofty)* currently, at present ◇ *Ich bin derzeit im Urlaub.* ⊜zurzeit, gegenwärtig, momentan **der·zei·tig** [ˈdeːɐ̯tsaetɪç] [adj, adv] *when used as an adj, only before ns* current(ly), present(ly) ◇ *der derzeitige Bundeskanzler* ♦ *Die Konjunktur ist derzeitig auf einem Tiefpunkt.* ♦ *der derzeitig beliebteste Star* ⓩ **des** [dɛs] *gen sing of* das, der¹ ⓩ **des·halb** [ˈdɛshalp] [adv] therefore, that is why, for that reason ◇ *Sie möchte Menschen helfen und will deshalb Ärztin werden.* ♦ *Ich habe Kopfweh. Deshalb lege ich mich jetzt hin.* ⊜deswegen, daher, also **des·sen** [ˈdɛsn̩] *gen sing of* der, das [det] *referring to masc or neut sing ns* **1.** whose, of whom, of which ◇ *Das Buch handelt von einem Mann, dessen Frau früh stirbt.* ♦ *Am Straßenrand stand ein Auto, dessen Tür aufgebrochen war.* **2.** *demonstrative* his ◇ *Wird er den Präsidenten nach dessen Rede auf das Thema ansprechen?*; its ◇ *Über das Unwetter und dessen Folgen wurde ausführlich berichtet.* → deren ⓩ **Des·sert** [dɛˈseːɐ̯] das ‹-s, -s› dessert, pudding ◇ *Was gibt es zum Dessert?* ⊜Nachtisch, Nachspeise ⓩ **des·to** [ˈdɛstoː] [conjunc] +comp *(always je ..., desto ...)* the ..., the ... ◇ *Je weniger Geld man ausgibt, desto mehr kann man sparen.* ♦ *Je früher (sie kommt), desto besser.* ⊜je ..., umso ... ⓩ **des·we·gen** [ˈdɛsveːgn̩] [adv] therefore, that is why, for that reason ◇ *Ich war krank; deswegen bin ich nicht gekommen.* ♦ *Sie will Pianistin werden und übt deswegen jeden Tag Klavier.* ⊜deshalb, daher **deu·ten** [ˈdɔɏtn̩] [tr v] +haben etw. (als etw.) deuten interpret sth (as sth), read sth (as sth), construe (as sth) ◇ *Er kann Träume deuten.* ♦ *Ich deute diese Aussage als Schuldeingeständnis.* [intr v] +haben **1.** (mit etw.) auf etw./jdn deuten point (sth/with sth) at sth/sb ◇ *mit dem Finger auf den Schuldigen deuten* ♦ *Sie deutete stumm auf die Tür.* ⊜zeigen **2.** etw. deutet auf etw. sth points to sth, sth indicates sth ◇ *Alles deutete auf Selbstmord.* etw. deutet auf jdn (als etw.) sth points to sb (as sth) ◇ *Ein Teil der Indizien deutete auf den Ehemann als Mörder.* ⊜verweisen ⓩ **deut·lich** [ˈdɔɏtlɪç] [adj, adv] clear(ly), distinct(ly)

◊ *Ihre Absicht war sehr deutlich.* ♦ *Es sind bereits deutliche Erfolge zu verzeichnen.* ♦ *deutlich sprechen* ♦ *Sein Gesicht war deutlich zu erkennen.* ♦ *Ich habe ihr das ganz deutlich gesagt.* ⊖klar ⊖undeutlich ⊛ **deutlich werden** be frank, put it plainly ◊ *Kapiert? Oder soll ich etwa noch deutlicher werden?*

deutsch [dɔøtʃ] ⌈adj, adv⌉ *when used as an adj, mostly before ns German* ◊ *die deutsche Nationalmannschaft/Nationalhymne* ♦ *ein Buch in deutscher Übersetzung* ♦ *die deutsch sprechende Bevölkerung* ♦ *Ordnung und Disziplin gelten als typisch deutsch.* ⊛ **mit jdm deutsch reden 1.** *(fig)* have a word with sb, speak plainly ◊ *Er kommt ständig zu spät. Ich muss wohl einmal deutsch mit ihm reden.* **2.** speak German with sb ◊ *Sie leben in Italien, aber zu Hause reden sie deutsch miteinander.*

Deutsch [dɔøtʃ] das <–s> *no pl* German ◊ *fließend Deutsch sprechen* ♦ *Sie spricht (ein) akzentfreies/ perfektes Deutsch.* ♦ *Er lernt seit zwei Jahren Deutsch.* ♦ *Mein Deutsch ist leider nicht so gut.* ♦ *Verstehen Sie Deutsch?* ♦ *Was heißt „reunion" auf Deutsch?* ♦ *Deutsch ist mein Lieblingsfach.* ♦ *Deutsch studieren* ♦ *In Deutsch nehmen wir gerade die Romantik durch.* ⊛ **auf (gut) Deutsch** in plain words ◊ *Meine Frau meinte, wir hätten uns auseinander gelebt. Auf gut Deutsch: Es war aus!*

Deut·sche [ˈdɔøtʃə] der/die <–n, die Deutschen> *but: ein Deutscher/eine Deutsche German* ◊ *Er ist mit einer Deutschen verheiratet.* ♦ *Die Deutschen sind Weltmeister im Reisen.* ♦ *Wie beliebt sind die Deutschen?* als Deutscher/Deutsche as a German *Er ist Deutscher./Sie ist Deutsche.* He/She is German.

Deut·sche Bahn [ˌdɔøtʃə ˈbaːn] <Deutschen Bahn> *no pl* (*always* die Deutsche Bahn) *the company that runs the German railway system*

Deutsch·land [ˈdɔøtʃlant] das <–s> *article only in combination with attribute* Germany ◊ *Deutschland liegt in Mitteleuropa.* ♦ *Das geteilte Deutschland wurde 1990 wieder vereinigt. box@ Land*

Deu·tung [ˈdɔøtʊŋ] die <–, –en> interpretation ◊ *die Deutung eines Gedichts/Traumes* ♦ *In diesem Fall gibt es mehrere mögliche Deutungen.*

De·vi·sen [deˈviːzn̩] *only pl* FIN foreign currency, foreign exchange ◊ *mit Devisen handeln* ♦ *in Devisen zahlen*

② **De·zem·ber** [deˈtsɛmbɐ] der <–s> *no pl* December → Januar

de·zent [deˈtsɛnt] ⌈adj, adv⌉ <dezenter, am dezentes­ten> discreet(ly), unobtrusive(ly) ◊ *Das Muster war sehr dezent.* ♦ *dezenter Service* ♦ *dezent geschminkt* ♦ *Als sie sich auszog, sah sie dezent zur Seite.*; *(colo(u)r, light, perfume, hint)* subtle(·ly) ◊ *eine Bluse in dezentem Gelb* ♦ *ein dezent beleuchteter Raum; (music, voice)* soft(ly)

② **De·zi·li·ter** [ˈdeˈtsiliːtɐ] der or das <–s, –> *(Austr) (abbr* dl*) unit of capacity equal to 100 ml* ◊ *Geben Sie einen Deziliter Milch in den Teig.*

DGB [deːgeːˈbeː] der *(abbr of* Deutscher Gewerkschaftsbund) *umbrella organization of the German trade unions*

d. h. [das ˈhaɛst] *(abbr of* das heißt) *i. e.* ◊ *ein Euro von hundert, d. h. ein Prozent*

② **Di·ät** [diˈɛːt] die <–, –en> **1.** diet ◊ *eine Diät machen/abbrechen* ♦ *Diät halten (müssen)* **2.** *only pl* POL *(of members of parliament)* Diäten parliamentary allowance, parliamentary salary ◊ *die Diäten erhöhen*

dich [dɪç] *acc of* du ⌈ref pron⌉ *not always translated* yourself ◊ *Geheimnisse solltest du besser für dich behalten. Bedank dich für das Geschenk!* Say thank you for the present.

② **dicht** [dɪçt] ⌈adj, adv⌉ <dichter, am dichtesten> **1.** thick(ly), dense(ly) ◊ *dichter Nebel/Verkehr* ♦ *Sein Haar ist sehr dicht.* ♦ *ein dicht besiedeltes Land* **2.** tight(ly) ◊ *Das Dach ist nicht mehr dicht.* ♦ *Die Fenster schließen dicht.* ⊖undicht **3.** *spatial or temporal* close(ly) ◊ *Keine Angst, ich bin dicht hinter dir.* ♦ *Der Wagen fuhr dicht an ihm vorbei.* dicht an dicht close together dicht davor sein, etw. zu tun be on the verge of doing sth, be about to do sth ◊ *Wir waren dicht davor zu verlieren.* **4.** *(fam)* be closed (off), be shut ◊ *Die Kneipe ist schon dicht.* ♦ *Die Grenzen sind dicht.* ⊛ **nicht ganz dicht sein** *(fam)* have a screw loose, be out of your mind

Dich·te [ˈdɪçtə] die <–> *no pl* **1.** density ◊ *Wasser hat eine höhere Dichte als Luft.* ♦ *ein Film von großer Dichte* **2.** *(of hair, a carpet)* thickness

② **Dich·ter** [ˈdɪçtɐ] der <–s, –>, **Dich·te·rin** [ˈdɪçtərɪn] die <–, –nen> poet, writer, author ◊ *Er ist Dichter und Schriftsteller.* ♦ *eine berühmte Dichterin*

Dich·tung [ˈdɪçtʊŋ] die <–, –en> **1.** literature ◊ *die deutsche Dichtung des 18. Jahrhunderts* ♦ *die Deutsche Akademie für Sprache und Dichtung; (prose also)* fiction; *(verse also)* poetry ◊ *die höfische Dichtung des Mittelalters* **2.** fiction, fantasy ◊ *Man fragt sich, was hier Dichtung und was Wahrheit ist.* **3.** TECHN washer, seal(ing), gasket ⊛ **Dichtung und Wahrheit** fact and fiction

② **dick** [dɪk] ⌈adj⌉ **1.** big, fat ◊ *einen dicken Bauch haben* ♦ *Er ist zu dick.; (cheeks)* chubby dick machen be fattening ⊖fett **2.** swollen, fat ◊ *Von der Hitze habe ich ganz dicke Finger bekommen.* ♦ *Mein Geldbeutel ist ganz dick vom Kleingeld.* **3.** *only before ns (fam, fig)* big, swanky ◊ *ein dickes Auto fahren; (salary)* fat ◊ *ein toller Job mit einem dicken Gehalt* ein dicker Kuss a big kiss ein dickes Lob bekommen be highly praised ⌈adj, adv⌉ thick(ly) ◊ *ein fünf Millimeter dickes Kabel* ♦ *Das Brett ist zehn Zentimeter dick.* ♦ *Eine dicke Schicht Eis liegt auf dem See.* ♦ *ein Brot dick mit Butter beschmieren* ⊛ **dick auftragen** *(fam)* lay it on thick jdn/etw. dick haben *(fam)* be fed up with sb/sth, have had enough of sb/sth **es dicke haben** *(fam)* be well-off ◊ *Das kann ich mir nicht leisten, so dicke habe ich es nicht.*

② **die¹** [diː] ⌈art⌉ *definite* **1.** *with fem ns in the nom and acc sing, and all pl ns in the nom and acc* the ◊ *die Nachbarin* ♦ *die Versammlung im Konferenzraum* ♦ *Ich habe die Frau in der Stadt getroffen.* ♦ *die Kinder* ♦ *Hast du die Fehler gezählt?* **2.** *demonstrative* that, this, those, these ◊ *Die Armbanduhr gefällt mir gar nicht; ich nehme die andere.* ♦ *Die Briefe hier sind für dich.*

box@ Artikel, der[1]

die[2] [di:] [rel pron] *referring to sing fem ns and all pl ns* who, that, which ◊ *Sie ist eine Frau, die viel Erfolg hat.* ♦ *Er erzählte eine Geschichte, die sehr spannend war.* ♦ *Vögel, die im Winter nach Süden fliegen, nennt man Zugvögel.* **box@** Relativpronomen [demonstr pron] **1.** *with sing fem ns* that one ◊ *Diese Bluse ist schöner als die da.*; this one ◊ *Die hier hätte ich gerne.*; the one ◊ *Kennst du die mit der Brille?* **box@** Demonstrativpronomen **2.** *with all pl ns* those ◊ *Willst du diese Stifte oder die?*; these ◊ *Die hier hätte ich gerne.*; the ones ◊ *Kennst du die da drüben?*

② **Dieb** [di:p] der <–(e)s, –e>, **Die·bin** ['di:bɪn] die <–, –nen> thief ◊ *Die Diebin wurde gefasst.* ♦ *Haltet den Dieb!*

Dieb·stahl ['di:pʃta:l] der <–(e)s, Diebstähle> theft ◊ *Er wurde wegen Diebstahls verurteilt.*

die·je·ni·ge ['di:je:nɪgə] → derjenige[1], derjenige[2]

Die·le ['di:lə] die <–, –n> **1.** hall (way) ◊ *Die Garderobe steht in der Diele.* ⊜Flur, Gang **2.** floorboard

② **die·nen** ['di:nən] [intr v] +*haben* **1.** einer Sache [dat] dienen, zu etw. dienen be for (the purpose of) sth ◊ *Das Geld dient einem guten Zweck.* ♦ *Dieser Knopf dient zum Ausschalten der Maschine.* jdm als etw. dienen serve sb as sth ◊ *Nelson Mandela dient ihr als Vorbild.* ♦ *Die Hecke dient uns als Sichtschutz.* **2.** jdm/irgendwo dienen serve sb ◊ *Er hat dem Grafen gedient.* ♦ *Sie diente auf dem Hof eines reichen Bauern.* **3.** MIL serve, do military service ◊ *Er dient im 4. Regiment.*

Dienst [di:nst] der <–(e)s, –e> **1.** work, duty ◊ *zum Dienst erscheinen* ♦ *Dieses Wochenende habe ich Dienst.* ♦ *Im September tritt er seinen Dienst als Lehrer an.* außer/im Dienst off/on duty vom Dienst duty ◊ *der Chef/Redakteur vom Dienst* jd ist der Witzbold/Idiot etc. vom Dienst sb is the resident joker/idiot etc. **2.** service ◊ *im diplomatischen/öffentlichen Dienst sein* ♦ *die Dienste eines Arztes in Anspruch nehmen* den Dienst quittieren resign außer Dienst retired ⦿ Dienst nach Vorschrift work-to-rule jdm einen Dienst erweisen do sb a service/favour/favor (jdm) gute Dienste leisten serve (sb) well ◊ *Der Toaster ist zwar alt, aber er leistet (uns) noch gute Dienste.* zu (jds) Diensten at sb's disposal, at sb's service ◊ *Zu (Ihren) Diensten, mein Herr!*

The *Öffentliche Dienst* (public service) is the most important employer in Germany. 14.8 million people are employed in public services, including soldiers. The biggest group among them are the 2.48 million manual and white-collar workers directly employed by local, state or federal governments. Salaries for the 1.66 million *Beamte* (career public servants, including judges) are prescribed by law. 490,000 people are indirectly employed by the government, working in areas such as social security. *Öffentlicher Dienst* also includes occupations in care, waste removal etc. Due to privatization, staff numbers are being reduced through the scrapping of posts when staff retire. But the *Öffentliche Dienst* cannot go bankrupt; and public service positions are ▶

▶ therefore generally considered secure, especially since *Beamte* cannot be dismissed and because other public service employees, from the age of 40 onwards, enjoy extensive protection against dismissal.

② **Diens·tag** ['di:nsta:k] der <–(e)s, –e> Tuesday → Montag

diens·tags ['di:nsta:ks] [adv] on Tuesdays → montags

Dienst·leis·tung ['di:nstlaestʊŋ] die <–, –en> ECON service ◊ *Welche Dienstleistungen bietet Ihre Firma an?*

dienst·lich ['di:nstlɪç] [adj] business ◊ *aus dienstlichen Gründen* ♦ *Das Treffen war rein dienstlich.* [adv] dienstlich unterwegs sein be away on business dienstlich verreist sein be on a business trip

Dienst·stel·le ['di:nstʃtɛlə] die <–, –n> *(form)* **1.** department, office, section ◊ *Wenden Sie sich an die zuständige Dienststelle.* **2.** branch (office)

dies [di:s] → dieser[1], dieser[2]

die·se ['di:zə] → dieser[1], dieser[2]

die·sel·be [di:'zɛlbə] → derselbe

② **die·ser**[1] ['di:ze] [det] this, that ◊ *Dieses Formular dürfen Sie behalten.* ♦ *Dieser Junge ist mein Sohn.* ♦ *Von diesem Vorfall habe ich nichts gewusst.* ♦ *Er hat ihr von dieser Sache erst gestern erzählt.* ♦ *Es ist nicht leicht, diese Frage zu beantworten.* ♦ *Das Treffen findet Anfang dieses Jahres statt.*; *(before pl nouns)* these ◊ *Diese Hosen passen mir nicht.*

	m	f	nt	pl
nom	dieser	diese	dieses	diese
acc	diesen	diese	dieses	diese
dat	diesem	dieser	diesem	diesen
gen	dieses	dieser	dieses	dieser

② **die·ser**[2] ['di:ze] [demonstr pron] **1.** this one ◊ *„Welcher Hut gefällt dir am besten?" — „Dieser."* ♦ *Die gelbe Bluse steht dir nicht, nimm lieber diese hier.* ♦ *„Ich nehme dieses hier", sagte er und zeigte auf das teuerste Handy.*; *(pl)* diese ◊ *Trinkwasser enthält geringe Mengen an Bakterien. Diese sind im Allgemeinen nicht schädlich.* **2.** dies(es) this, that ◊ *Er wollte nach München ziehen. Dies war wohl die beste Lösung.*

	m	f	nt	pl
nom	dieser	diese	dieses	diese
acc	diesen	diese	dieses	diese
dat	diesem	dieser	diesem	diesen
gen	-	-	-	-

dies·es ['di:zəs] → dieser[1], dieser[2]

② **dies·mal** ['di:sma:l] [adv] this time (around) ◊ *Mal abwarten, ob sie es diesmal schafft.* ♦ *Wer hält den Vortrag diesmal?* ♦ *Diesmal war er ohne Kinder im Urlaub.*

dies·seits ['di:szaets] [prep] [+gen] (on) this side of ◊ *Der Sänger ist diesseits des Atlantiks kaum bekannt.* ♦ *In Salzburg befindet sich der größte Barockbrunnen diesseits der Alpen.*

Dik·tat [dɪk'ta:t] das <–(e)s, –e> dictation ◊ *Welche Note hast du im Diktat?* ♦ *Sie rief die Sekretärin zum Diktat.*

Dik·ta·tur [dɪkta'tu:g] die <–, –en> dictatorship ◊

Deutschland unter der Diktatur Hitlers ✦ *Er hat über 30 Jahre in einer Diktatur gelebt.*

dik·tie·ren [dɪk'tiːrən] <diktiert, diktierte, hat diktiert> (tr+intr v) *(also lofty)* dictate ◊ *Du diktierst und ich tippe.* ✦ *Ich finde es nicht gut, dass ein einziger Konzern die Preise diktiert.* (jdm) etw. diktieren dictate sth (to sb) ◊ *Mein Chef diktierte mir einen Brief.* ✦ *Die Dozentin diktierte ein paar Sätze.* jdm diktieren dictate to sb ◊ *Diktier mir doch mal bitte.* ⊛ **sich** (dat) etw. (von jdm) diktieren lassen be told sth (by sb) ◊ *Ich will mir nicht diktieren lassen, was ich kaufen soll und was nicht.* ✦ *Sie wollten sich die Höhe der Beiträge nicht von den Gewerkschaften diktieren lassen.*

⑦ **Ding¹** [dɪŋ] das <-(e)s, -e> **1.** thing, object ◊ *Bitte lassen Sie alle wertvollen Dinge zuhause.* ✦ *Auf dem Dachboden fand sie viele alte/schöne Dinge.* **2.** *most pl* thing, matter ◊ *Den Lauf der Dinge kann man nicht ändern.* ✦ *Sie steht über den Dingen.* ✦ *Ich muss noch ein paar Dinge erledigen.* ⊛ **den Dingen ihren Lauf lassen** let things take their course **ein Ding der Unmöglichkeit sein** be impossible, be an impossibility **guter Dinge sein 1.** be optimistic, be full of hope **2.** be cheerful, be happy, be in good spirits **es geht nicht mit rechten Dingen zu** strange things are going on ◊ *In diesem Schloss ging es nicht mit rechten Dingen zu.* **das ist ja ein Ding 1.** well there you go, well fancy that **2.** that's outrageous, that's awful **vor allen Dingen** above all

Ding² [dɪŋ] das <-(e)s, -er> *(fam, also pej)* **1.** thing ◊ *Wo gibt es solche Dinger zu kaufen?* ✦ *Warum funktioniert dieses blöde Ding nicht?* ✦ *So ein Handy ist schon ein tolles Ding.* **2.** girl, lass ◊ *Er ist mit so einem jungen Ding durchgebrannt.*

Dip·lom [di'ploːm] das <-s, -e> **1.** certificate ◊ *Der Direktor überreichte ihm sein Diplom.* ✦ *Sie musste eine Kopie ihres Diploms beilegen.* **2.** diploma ◊ *Letztes Jahr hat sie ihr Diplom gemacht.* ✦ *Er hat/besitzt ein Diplom in Biologie.* ✦ *Für diese Stelle muss man über ein Diplom verfügen.*

In Germany, you can only call yourself a *Diplomingenieur, Diplompsychologin, Diplomchemiker* etc. if you have completed a course of study and have passed an examination in the relevant subject.

dir [diːɐ̯] *dat of* du (ref pron) *not translated* Was bildest du dir eigentlich ein? Who do you think you are? Hast du dir den Film schon angesehen? Have you watched this film yet?

⑦ **di·rekt** [di'rɛkt] (adj, adv) <direkter, am direktesten> **1.** direct(ly) ◊ *Sie nahm den direkten Weg.* ✦ *Diese Frage ist mir zu direkt.* ✦ *Er parkte direkt vorm Haus.* ✦ *ein Haus direkt am See* ✦ *Diese Sendung wird direkt übertragen.* ✦ *Von dieser Entscheidung bin ich direkt betroffen.* ✦ *Der Bürgermeister wird vom Volk direkt gewählt.* **2.** *when used as an adj, only before ns* immediate(ly) ◊ *dein direkter Vorgesetzer* ✦ *Er ist ihr direkt unterstellt.* (adv) straight ◊ *Der Ball ging direkt ins Tor.* ✦ *Dieser Weg führt direkt zum Strand.* direkt im Anschluss an etw. straight after sth

Di·rek·tor [di'rɛktoːɐ̯] der <-s, -en>, **Di·rek·to·rin** [dirɛk'toːrɪn] die <-, -nen> **1.** SCHOOL principal, head, headmaster ◊ *Er ist als Direktor eines Gymnasiums tätig.* Direktorin headmistress ◊ *Der Schüler musste zur Direktorin.* **2.** director ◊ *Der Direktor des Museums eröffnete die Ausstellung.* ✦ *Direktor für Forschung und Entwicklung; (of a research institute also)* head ◊ *Sie ist Direktorin des Instituts für Philosophie.; (of a police force)* chief

di·ri·gie·ren [diri'giːrən] <dirigiert, dirigierte, hat dirigiert> (tr+intr v) conduct ◊ *Er dirigierte mit beiden Händen.* jdn dirigieren conduct sb ◊ *Sie dirigierte das Orchester/die Musiker.; (a choir)* lead sb ◊ *Sie dirigierte den Chor.* etw. dirigieren conduct sth ◊ *Wer dirigiert das Konzert/die Oper?*

Dirndl ['dɪrndl̩] das <-s, -(n)> dirndl ◊ *Eine Kellnerin im Dirndl servierte uns Bier und Brezen.*

The dirndl (derived from *Dirndlgewand*) is the traditional Bavarian and Austrian costume for women. It consists of a skirt, apron and blouse, and the *Leibl*, a vest-like garment. Originally, this was the dress of the farm maid, also called *Dirn*, but towards the end of the 19th century it also became also popular with the higher classes of society.

Dis·co ['dɪskoː] → Disko

⑦ **Dis·ket·te** [dɪs'kɛtə] die <-, -n> IT (floppy) disk ◊ *Er legte eine leere/neue Diskette ein.* ✦ *etw. auf Diskette speichern*

Dis·ko ['dɪskoː] die <-, -s> *(abbr of* Diskothek*)* disco, club ◊ *Morgen Abend wollen sie in die Disko gehen.*

Dis·ko·thek [dɪsko'teːk] die <-, -en> *(abbr* Disko*)* discotheque ◊ *zum Tanzen in die Diskothek gehen*

dis·kret [dɪs'kreːt] (adj, adv) <diskreter, am diskretesten> **1.** discreet(ly), tactful(ly) ◊ *Sie war sehr diskret.* ✦ *ein diskreter Hinweis* ✦ *Er schweigt diskret.* **2.** confidential(ly) ◊ *Sie schätzen die diskrete Atmosphäre.* ✦ *Ihre Angaben werden diskret behandelt.*

⑦ **Dis·kus·si·on** [dɪsku'sjoːn] die <-, -en> discussion, debate ◊ *ein Vortrag mit anschließender Diskussion* ✦ *Es entwickelte sich eine lebhafte Diskussion über Gentechnologie.* ✦ *Er würde sich nie auf eine Diskussion darüber einlassen.* ✦ *Das Urteil hat heftige Diskussionen ausgelöst.* zur Diskussion stehen be under discussion

⑦ **dis·ku·tie·ren** [dɪsku'tiːrən] <diskutiert, diskutierte, hat diskutiert> (tr+intr v) **1.** talk ✦ *Wir diskutierten bis spät in die Nacht.* (mit jdm) etw./über etw. (acc) diskutieren talk (with sb) about sth, discuss sth (with sb) ◊ *Bitte fangt nicht wieder an (über Politik) zu diskutieren!* ✦ *Können wir darüber nicht ein andermal diskutieren?* ✦ *Sie diskutierten die verschiedenen Optionen/Varianten.* ✦ *Auf der Versammlung wurde diskutiert, ob dieser Plan sinnvoll sei.* ⊜erörtern **2.** mit jdm diskutieren discuss things with sb ◊ *Mit ihm kann man nicht diskutieren. Er akzeptiert keine andere Meinung.*

di·ver·se [di'vɛrzə] (adj) <diversere, am diversesten> *seldom comp/superl; +pl noun, only before ns* various ◊ *Zitate aus diversen Büchern.*

D-Mark ['deːmaʳk] die <-, -> *(abbr* DM*)* German

mark, Deutschmark ◊ *1948 trat die D-Mark an die Stelle der Reichsmark.* ♦ *Das Haus hat damals 200 000 D-Mark gekostet.*

doch¹ [dɔx] (adv) **1.** *after all* ◊ *Ich wollte diesen Film eigentlich nicht sehen, bin dann aber doch ins Kino gegangen.* ♦ *Er wollte mir helfen, hat es aber dann doch nicht getan.* ♦ *Sie ist eben doch anders als die anderen Frauen.* Hab ich's doch gewusst! I knew it! **2.** *used to contradict (emph)* „Das schaffst du nie!" —„Doch!" "You will never succeed with this!" — "Yes, I will!" „Dieser Film läuft noch nicht in den Kinos." — „Doch." "This film is not in the cinemas yet." — "Yes, it is." „Du bist hoffentlich nicht auf diese Party gegangen?" — „Doch, leider." "I hope you didn't go to this party?" — "Yes, unfortunately I did."

② **doch²** [dɔx] (conjunc) *but* ◊ *Sie wollte an der Kunsthochschule studieren, doch sie schaffte die Aufnahmeprüfung nicht.* ♦ *Ich versuchte ihn zu erreichen, doch sein Handy war nicht an.*

doch³ [dɔx] (part) **1.** *used in anticipation of agreement* ◊ *Ihr bleibt doch zum Essen?* ♦ *Das wirst du doch nicht wirklich tun?* **2.** *in questions when you are not quite sure about sth* ◊ *Wir haben uns doch schon einmal gesehen, oder?* ♦ *Wie hieß der Roman doch gleich?* **3.** *expressing a wish* ◊ *Wenn er doch nur kommen könnte!* ♦ *Hätte er doch nur auf mich gehört!* **4.** *expressing irritation, anger etc.* ◊ *Das gibt's doch nicht!* ♦ *Das darf doch nicht wahr sein!* **5.** *for emphasis* ◊ *Sei doch nicht so gemein zu ihr.* ♦ *Komm doch einfach mal bei uns vorbei!* **6.** *in response to accusations, questions etc. for emphasis* ◊ „Wieso?" — „Das habe ich dir doch bereits erklärt." ♦ „Mach bitte deine Hausaufgaben." — „Das habe ich doch längst getan." ♦ *Ich bin doch kein kleines Kind mehr!*

② **Dok·tor** ['dɔktoːɐ] der <–s, –en> *(abbr Dr.)* **1.** *no pl* doctorate ◊ *Sie macht gerade ihren Doktor.* Doktor der ... sein have a doctorate in ... ◊ *Sie ist Doktor der Linguistik.* **2.** doctor ◊ *ein Vortrag der Doktoren Schmidt und Schwarz* **3.** *(fam)* doctor ◊ *Der (Herr) Doktor sieht gleich nach Ihnen.* ♦ *Bei so einer schlimmen Grippe solltest du zum Doktor gehen.* ☺Arzt

A doctorate is the highest academic qualification. In Germany, you receive a doctorate either by completing a piece of written work (called a *Doktorarbeit* or *Dissertation*) and passing an oral examination in which you have to give a lecture and defend your dissertation (the *Disputation*), or by taking a series of examinations (the *Rigorosum*).

dol·met·schen ['dɔlmɛtʃn] (intr v) +*haben* interpret, act/work as an interpreter ◊ *Könnten Sie bitte für uns dolmetschen?* (tr v) +*haben* translate ◊ *Könnten Sie bitte dolmetschen, was er gesagt hat?* ♦ *Sein Freund dolmetschte die Rede.*

Dom [doːm] der <–(e)s, –e> cathedral ◊ *der Aachener/Kölner Dom*

do·mi·nie·ren [domi'niːrən] <dominiert, dominierte, hat dominiert> (intr v) etw. dominieren sth predominates, sth is predominant ◊ *In dieser Berufsgruppe dominieren Frauen.* ♦ *Auf dieser Website dominieren die Farben Weiß und Blau.* ☺überwiegen, vor-

herrschen (tr v) jdn/etw. dominieren dominate sb/sth, lead sb/sth ◊ *Diese Firma dominiert den Markt auch weiterhin.* ♦ *Die schwedische Mannschaft dominierte in der ersten Halbzeit das Spiel.* ♦ *Seit seiner Kindheit dominiert Gewalt sein Leben.*

Dö·ner ['døːnɐ] der <–s, –> *(abbr of* Dönerkebap*)* doner kebab ◊ *Möchten Sie Zwiebeln in den Döner?*

don·nern ['dɔnɐn] (imp v) +*haben* es donnert it is thundering ◊ *Draußen blitzte und donnerte es.* (intr v) +*haben/sein* **1.** +*haben (engines)* roar **2.** +*sein* irgendwohin donnern thunder somewhere ◊ *Die Lkws donnerten über die Brücke.*; *(vehicle)* gegen etw. donnern crash into sth; *(door)* ins Schloss donnern slam shut **3.** +*haben* gegen/auf etw. (acc) donnern hammer against/on sth ◊ *Er donnerte mit den Fäusten gegen die Tür/das Tor.* (tr v) +*haben (fam)* etw. irgendwohin donnern hurl sth somewhere ◊ *Er donnerte den Ball ins Tor/Netz.* ♦ *Sie donnerte ihre Schultasche in die Ecke.*

② **Don·ners·tag** ['dɔnɐstaːk] der <–(e)s, –e> Thursday → Montag

don·ners·tags ['dɔnɐstaːks] (adv) on Thursdays → montags

doof [doːf] (adj, adv) *(fam, pej)* stupid(ly) ◊ *ein doofer Witz* ♦ *Ist er wirklich doof.* ♦ *Stell dich nicht so doof an!* doof fragen ask a stupid question doof schauen/gucken make a stupid face

② **Dop·pel·...** ['dɔpl] (prefix) **1.** double... ◊ *eine Doppelhochzeit feiern* **2.** double ... ◊ *ein Doppelkinn haben* ♦ *ein Doppelleben führen*

② **Dop·pel·bett** ['dɔplbɛt] das <–(e)s, –en> double bed ◊ *im Doppelbett schlafen*

Dop·pel·punkt ['dɔplpʊŋkt] der <–(e)s, –e> colon ◊ *Auf den Doppelpunkt folgt eine Aufzählung.*

② **dop·pelt** ['dɔplt] (adj) *mostly before no* **1.** double ◊ *Sie bestellte einen doppelten Whisky.*; *(nationality)* dual die doppelte Menge twice as much **2.** twofold ◊ *Diese Umstände bergen ein doppeltes Risiko.* (adv) **1.** twice ◊ *Diese Gebühr haben wir Ihnen aus Versehen doppelt berechnet.* ♦ *Diese Klausur zählt doppelt.* doppelt so ... twice as ... ◊ *Diese Wohnung ist fast doppelt so groß wie unsere alte.* etw. doppelt haben have two copies of sth ◊ *Dieses Buch habe ich doppelt.* ☺zweifach **2.** doubly ◊ *Hier musst du doppelt aufpassen.* ♦ *Das ist doppelt ärgerlich.*

Dop·pel·zim·mer ['dɔpltsɪmɐ] das <–s, –> double room ◊ *Sie buchte ein Doppelzimmer.* ♦ *Die Patientin lag in einem Doppelzimmer.*

② **Dorf** [dɔʳf] das <–(e)s, Dörfer> village ◊ *Meine Kindheit habe ich auf dem Dorf verbracht.* ♦ *Wir fuhren durch verschiedene Dörfer.* ♦ *Das ganze Dorf war zur Hochzeit eingeladen.*

② **dort** [dɔʳt] (adv) **1.** there ◊ *Sie kommt auch von dort.* ♦ *Er ging ins Wohnzimmer und deckte dort den Tisch.* ♦ *Siehst du diesen Baum dort?* ♦ *Dort unten liegt Palermo.* ♦ *Er steht dort drüben vor der Kirche.* **2.** jdn/etw. dort behalten keep sb/sth (there) ◊ *Er ging ins Krankenhaus und wurde sofort dort behalten.*

In many sentences, *dort* is not translated directly: *Deine Jacke liegt dort, wo du sie hingeworfen hast.* (Your jacket is where you threw it down.)

dort·her ['dɔʳtheːɐ] (adv) (von) dorther from there

◊ *Von dorther kam der Schrei.* ✦ *Ihre Vorfahren stammen dorther.*
dort·hin ['dɔrˈthɪn] ⟨adv⟩ there ◊ *Wie gelangt man dorthin?* ✦ *Auf dem Weg dorthin traf ich zwei alte Freunde.* ✦ *Sie konnte nicht mehr dorthin zurückkehren.*

In many sentences *dorthin* is not translated directly: *Bitte stellen Sie das Buch dorthin, wo es hingehört.* (Please put the book where it belongs.)

② **Do·se** ['doːzə] die <–, –n> **1.** tin, can ✦ *eine Dose geschälte Tomaten* ✦ *zwei Dosen Bier* ✦ *Champignons aus der Dose* ⊖Konserve **2.** container, jar ◊ *Er füllte das Mehl in eine Dose um.* ✦ *eine eckige Dose aus Glas* ✦ *eine runde Dose aus Blech* → Dosis
Do·sen·öff·ner ['doːzn̩|œfnɐ] der <–s, –> tin/can opener ◊ *ein elektrischer Dosenöffner*
Do·sis ['doːzɪs] die <–, Dosen> dose, dosage ◊ *eine tödliche Dosis Zyanid*
Do·zent [do'tsɛnt] der <–en, –en>, **Do·zen·tin** [do'tsɛntɪn] die <–, –nen> **1.** lecturer, assistant professor ◊ *Er ist Dozent für Soziologie.* ✦ *die neue Dozentin für Linguistik* **2.** lecturer, tutor ◊ *Sie ist Dozentin für Italienisch.* ✦ *ein freiberuflicher Dozent*
Dr. ['dɔktoːɐ̯] der *(abbr of* Doktor*)* Dr ◊ *Frau Dr. Müller* → Doktor
Dra·chen ['draxn̩] der <–s, –> **1.** kite ◊ *Sie ließen ihre Drachen steigen.* **2.** hang-glider ◊ *Ein moderner Drachen kann bis zu 80 km/h schnell fliegen.*
Draht [draːt] der <–(e)s, Drähte> wire ◊ *etw. mit einem Stück Draht befestigen* ✦ *In der Glühbirne konnte man drei feine Drähte erkennen.*
 ⊛ **auf Draht sein** be on the ball, be on form
dran [dran] ⟨adv⟩ *(fam)* → daran
 ⊛ **gut/schlecht etc. dran sein** be in a good/bad etc. position ◊ *Sie war schlechter dran als die meisten ihrer Kollegen.* **an etw.** ⟨dat⟩ **ist etwas/ nichts dran** there's sth/nothing in sth ◊ *Ist an diesem Gerücht etwas dran?* ✦ *An dieser Geschichte ist nichts dran.* **jd ist dran 1.** it is sb's turn ◊ *Du bist mit dem Würfeln dran!* **2.** sb is on the phone ◊ „*Für dich. Deine Chefin ist dran.*" **3.** *(fam)* sb is in for it ◊ *Wenn ich ihn erwische, ist er dran!*
drang [draŋ] *pret of* dringen
drän·geln ['drɛŋl̩n] *(fam)* ⟨intr v⟩ +*haben* push and shove, jostle ◊ *Der Typ hinter mir drängelt schon die ganze Zeit.* ⟨ref v⟩ +*haben* sich irgendwohin drängeln push your way somewhere ◊ *Er drängelte sich an den Anfang der Schlange.*
drän·gen ['drɛŋən] ⟨intr v⟩ +*haben* **1.** push ◊ *Bitte drängen Sie nicht (so)!* **2.** irgendwohin drängen push your way somewhere ◊ *Die Menschen drängten zum Ausgang.* **3.** zu/auf etw. ⟨acc⟩ drängen insist on sth, press for sth ◊ *Sie drängte zur Eile.* ✦ *Er drängte auf Reformen.* ✦ *Sie drängten darauf, neue Gesetze einzuführen.* **4.** be pressing ◊ *Die Zeit drängt.* drängende Probleme pressing problems
⟨tr v⟩ +*haben* **1.** jdn/etw. irgendwohin drängen push sb/sth somewhere, force sb/sth somewhere ◊ *jdn zur Seite drängen* ✦ *Er drängt sich gern in den*

Vordergrund. ✦ *Sie ließ sich nicht in die typische Frauenrolle drängen.* **2.** jdn zu etw. drängen; jdn drängen, etw. zu tun urge sb to do sth, force sb to do sth ◊ *Sie drängten ihn, das Land zu verlassen.* ✦ *Ihre Eltern drängten sie zum Studium.; press sb to do sth* ◊ *Ich drängte ihn, endlich seine Schulden zu bezahlen.* ✦ *Sein Vater drängte uns zur Eile.* ⟨ref v⟩ +*haben* **1.** sich in/an ⟨dat⟩/um etc. etw. drängen crowd (in/at/round etc.) sth ◊ *Die Menge drängte sich im kleinen Saal.* ✦ *Die Kinder drängten sich um den Tisch.* **2.** sich irgendwohin drängen crowd somewhere ◊ *Die Kinder drängten sich nach vorn.* ✦ *Die Menschen drängten sich zum Ausgang.*
dran|kom·men ['drankɔmən] <kommt dran, kam dran, ist drangekommen> ⟨intr v⟩ *(fam)* **1.** jd kommt dran it is sb's turn ◊ *Es hat zwei Stunden gedauert, bis ich endlich drankam.* ✦ *Erst duscht Ute und nach ihr kommt Helga dran. etw.* kommt dran it is the turn of sth ◊ *Zuerst putze ich das Bad und dann kommt die Küche dran.* **2.** SCHOOL jd kommt dran *sb is called upon to answer questions in class* ◊ *Eva kam heute in Englisch dran.* **3.** SCHOOL *(in a test)* etw. kommt dran sth comes up ◊ *Ich habe so viel gelernt, aber nichts davon kam in der Prüfung dran.* **4.** an jdn/etw. drankommen get to sb/sth ◊ *An die Bücher ganz oben kam er trotz Leiter nicht dran.*
dras·tisch ['drastɪʃ] ⟨adj, adv⟩ drastic(ally) ◊ *drastische Maßnahmen* ✦ *Die Strafen für dieses Delikt sind drastisch.* ✦ *Die Zahl der Mitarbeiter wird drastisch reduziert.*
drauf [draof] *(fam)* → darauf
drauf|ge·hen ['draofgeːən] <geht drauf, ging drauf, ist draufgegangen> ⟨intr v⟩ *(fam)* **1.** bite the dust, die ◊ *Wir wären bei dem Unfall beinahe beide draufgegangen.* **2.** get ruined, go bust ◊ *Bei unserem Umzug sind ein paar Teller draufgegangen.* **3.** etw. geht für etw. drauf sth is spent on sth, sth goes on sth ◊ *Für diese Sucherei sind Stunden draufgegangen.* ✦ *All sein Taschengeld geht für Videospiele drauf.*
drauf|kom·men ['draofkɔmən] <kommt drauf, kam drauf, ist draufgekommen> ⟨intr v⟩ *(fam)* find out ◊ *Ich kam erst hinterher drauf, dass die Geschichte gar nicht wahr war.; (a solution)* get it ◊ *Ich grübele immer noch über die Lösung nach, doch ich komme einfach nicht drauf.* ⟨tr v⟩ jdm draufkommen get/an on to sb ◊ *Die Polizei/Die Versicherung ist ihr draufgekommen.*
② **drau·ßen** ['draosn̩] ⟨adv⟩ outside ◊ *Ich warte draußen auf dich.* ✦ *Er stand draußen vor der Haustür.* ✦ *Es drangen keinerlei Geräusche nach draußen.* ✦ *Hunde müssen (leider) draußen bleiben no dogs(, please)* ⊖drinnen
Dreck [drɛk] der <–(e)s> *no pl (fam)* **1.** dirt, muck ◊ *Ihr Schal fiel in den Dreck. Dreck machen make a mess* ◊ *Dieser Hund macht vielleicht einen Dreck!* ⊖Schmutz **2.** *(pej)* business ◊ *Kümmere dich gefälligst um deinen eigenen Dreck!* **3.** *(pej)* little thing, trifle ◊ *Wegen jedem Dreck geht er zum Arzt.* **4.** *(pej)* rubbish, crap ◊ *Du kennst/liest ja auch jeden Dreck.* ✦ *Dieser Film war ein Dreck dagegen!*
 ⊛ **seinen Dreck allein machen** do it yourself ◊ *Wenn du nicht freundlicher bist, kannst du deinen*

Dreck allein machen. jdn/etw. durch den Dreck ziehen drag sb/sth through the mud ◇ Ich will nicht, dass er meinen Namen durch den Dreck zieht. der letzte Dreck (rude, pej) the lowest of the low, scum ◇ Sie behandelte ihn wie den letzten Dreck. ♦ Er fühlte sich wie der letzte Dreck.

dre·ckig ['drɛkɪç] [adj] 1. (fam) dirty ◇ Sein Hemd war dreckig. ♦ dreckige Wäsche ♦ In dieser Küche war es ganz schön dreckig. sich dreckig machen get yourself dirty ☺sauber 2. (fam) vulgar, dirty ◇ Er erzählte einen dreckigen Witz. ♦ eine dreckige Bemerkung 3. (rude) filthy ◇ Er ist ganz ein dreckiger Lügner. ♦ Der Waffenhandel ist ein dreckiges Geschäft.

☻ jdm geht es dreckig (fam) things are really bad for sb, sb is in a bad way ◇ Seit ihn seine Frau verlassen hat, geht es ihm echt dreckig. ♦ Sie war da, als es ihrer Freundin so richtig dreckig ging.

Dreh·buch ['dreːbuːx] das <-(e)s, Drehbücher> script, screenplay ◇ Wer schrieb das Drehbuch?

② **dre·hen** ['dreːən] [tr v] +haben 1. turn ◇ Er drehte den Schlüssel zweimal im Schloss. ♦ Man muss den Knopf um 90 Grad nach links drehen. ♦ Er drehte den Kopf nach rechts. ♦ Kannst du die Lampe etwas drehen? Sie blendet. sich drehen turn round, spin round ◇ Kannst du dich einmal drehen? ♦ Das Windrad drehte sich. ♦ Die Kinder drehten sich im Kreis. 2. (fam) etw. lauter/höher drehen turn sth up ◇ Er drehte die Musik lauter. etw. leiser/niedriger drehen turn sth down ◇ Könntest du die Heizung ein bisschen niedriger drehen? 3. (cigarettes) roll ◇ Er drehte sich eine Zigarette. 4. (a film) make, shoot ◇ einen Kurzfilm/Werbespot drehen [intr v] +haben 1. turn round, change direction ◇ Der Autofahrer drehte und fuhr nochmal zurück. ♦ Der Wind hatte gedreht und kam jetzt aus Nordosten. 2. film ◇ Sie dreht gerade in New York. [ref v] +haben 1. sich um etw. drehen revolve (a)round sth; (planet, satellite) orbit sth ◇ Die Erde dreht sich um die Sonne. sich um die eigene Achse drehen rotate on its own axis 2. (fig) sich um etw./jdn drehen centre on sth/sb ◇ Die Diskussion drehte sich um Politik. ♦ Dauernd dreht sich alles nur um Eva.

drei [draɪ] [nmrl] three → vier
☻ nicht bis drei zählen können be as thick as two short planks

Drei [draɪ] die <-, -en> 1. three → Vier 1. 2. (fam) (bus, tram etc.) number three → Vier 2. 3. SCHOOL (grade) ☺B- ◇ In Mathe hatte er eine Drei. eine Drei schreiben get a B- ☺befriedigend box☺ Note

Drei·eck ['draɪ|ɛk] das <-s, -e> triangle ◇ ein gleichschenkliges/spitzwinkliges Dreieck
drei·fach ['draɪfax] [adj, adv] when used as an adj, only before ns triple, threefold ◇ ein dreifacher Mord; three times ◇ dreifache Weltmeisterin ♦ die dreifache Menge three times as much ◇ Er kaufte die dreifache Menge ein. [adv] trebly, threefold ◇ Frauen sind durch Beruf, Kinder und Haushalt oft dreifach belastet. ♦ ein dreifach erhöhtes Risiko
drei·ßig ['draɪsɪç] [nmrl] thirty → vier
dreist [draɪst] [adj] <dreister, am dreistesten> brazen, audacious ◇ Das war ganz schön dreist von ihm. ♦ dreiste Forderungen ♦ Die Autodiebe

werden immer dreister.
Drei·vier·tel·stun·de ['draɪfɪ'tl̩'ʃtʊndə] die <-, -n> three quarters of an hour ◇ Er braucht morgens eine Dreiviertelstunde zur Arbeit. ♦ Sie kam eine Dreiviertelstunde zu spät.
drei·zehn ['draɪtseːn] [nmrl] thirteen → vier
☻ jetzt schlägts (aber) dreizehn (fam) that's a bit much
drin [drɪn] (fam) → darin → drinnen
drin·gen ['drɪŋən] <dringt, drang, ist/hat gedrungen> [intr v] 1. +sein (also fig) durch/in etw. [acc] dringen get/come through/into sth ◇ Der Splitter drang ihm ins Auge. ♦ Nur wenig Licht drang durch den Vorhang. aus etw. [dat] dringen get/come out of sth ◇ Dichter Rauch drang aus der Küche.; (sounds) aus etw. dringen be coming from/out of sth ◇ Aus dem Proberaum drangen leise Töne. an die Öffentlichkeit dringen leak out, become public knowledge 2. +haben auf etw. [acc] dringen insist on sth ◇ Sie drangen auf umfassende Reformen.
② **drin·gend** ['drɪŋənt] pres p of dringen [adj, adv] urgent(ly) ◇ Ist diese Angelegenheit sehr dringend? ♦ Kann ich mit Ihnen sprechen? Es ist sehr dringend. ♦ In dringenden Fällen können Sie den Arzt auch nachts anrufen. ♦ Ein bisschen Ruhe ist dringend nötig. ♦ Die dringend notwendige Sanierung des Hauses beginnt nächste Woche. ♦ Ich hatte das dringende Bedürfnis nach Bewegung. ♦ Alle werden dringend gebeten mitzuhelfen. ♦ jdm dringend von etw. abraten; (suspicion) strong ◇ Sie steht unter dringendem Tatverdacht.
② **drin·nen** ['drɪnən] [adv] inside ◇ Das Tennisturnier wurde nach drinnen verlegt. ♦ Von drinnen drang kein Ton auf den Flur. ☺draußen
dritt [drɪt] (always zu dritt) three of us/them/you ◇ Wir fuhren zu dritt nach Rom. etw. zu dritt spielen play sth with three people Zu dritt ist alles einfacher. Everything is easier when there are three of you.
drit·te ['drɪtə] [adj] <ein dritter ..., eine dritte ..., ein drittes ...> 1. third ♦ vierte 2. (in proper names) Dritte Third ◇ das Dritte Reich ♦ die Länder der Dritten Welt
Drit·tel ['drɪtl̩] das <-s, -> third → Viertel
drit·tens ['drɪtn̩s] [adv] thirdly → viertens
② **Dro·ge** ['droːgə] die <-, -n> drug ◇ Er nimmt Drogen. ♦ Er handelt mit Drogen. ♦ harte/weiche Drogen ♦ Sie steht unter Drogen.
② **Dro·ge·rie** [drogə'riː] die <-, -n> chemist's (shop), drugstore

> In a Drogerie, you can buy toiletries, food supplements (such as vitamins) and cleaning products. In Germany, the large-scale version of this business, the Drogeriemarkt, is widespread.

dro·hen ['droːən] [intr v] +haben 1. threaten ◇ Sie drohte und weinte, doch es half alles nichts. jdm drohen threaten sb ◇ Willst du mir etwa drohen? ♦ Sie drohte ihm mit der Faust. mit etw. drohen; (damit) drohen, etw. zu tun threaten to do sth ◇ Er drohte mit Rücktritt. ♦ Sie drohten damit, die Geiseln zu ermorden. ♦ jdm mit einer Anzeige drohen threaten to inform/call sb ◇ Die Firma drohte mit dem Gerichtsvollzieher. jdm mit etw.

drohen threaten sb with sth, threaten to do sth to sb jdm mit jdm drohen threaten to get sb onto sb ◊ *Ich drohte ihm mit der Polizei.* **2.** etw. droht sth is looming, sth is threatening ◊ *Es drohte Gefahr.* ♦ *Ein Sturm/Gewitter drohte.* **3.** etw. droht jdm/etw. sb/sth faces sth ◊ *Ihr drohte eine Gefängnisstrafe.* **4.** +*inf with 'zu'* be about to ◊ *Sie drohte zu ersticken.* ♦ *Die Verhandlungen drohten zu scheitern.*

② **drü·ben** ['dry:bm̩] ⌷adv⌷ (dort/da) drüben over there ◊ *Setzen Sie sich doch dort drüben hin.* ♦ *Sollte man sein Auto nach Amerika mitnehmen oder drüben ein neues kaufen?* ♦ *Dort drüben beginnt bereits Polen.* drüben in over in ◊ *Gestern war er kurz drüben in Frankreich.*

drü·ber ['dry:bɐ] *(fam)* → darüber

Druck¹ [drʊk] der <–(e)s, Drücke> *most sing* **1.** pressure ◊ *der atmosphärische Druck* ♦ *Er hatte einen leichten Druck auf den Ohren.* ♦ *Unter Druck arbeitet sie am besten.* ♦ *jdn unter Druck setzen* ♦ *Die Regierung übte massiven Druck auf ihn aus.* unter Druck stehen be under pressure ◊ *Der Behälter steht unter Druck.*; *(in your body)* irgendwo einen Druck verspüren have a feeling of pressure somewhere **2.** *translated with a verb construction, no pl (of a button)* bei/mit Druck auf when/by pressing ◊ *Mit Druck auf die rechte Maustaste kannst du das Menü aufrufen.* ♦ *Beim Druck auf diesen Knopf öffnet sich ein neues Fenster.*

② **Druck²** [drʊk] der <–(e)s, –e> **1.** *no pl* printing etw. ist im Druck sth is being printed ◊ *Das Buch ist im Druck.* **2.** ARTS print ◊ *Er hat hübsche Drucke an der Wand hängen.*

② **dru·cken** ['drʊkn̩] ⌷tr+intr v⌷ +*haben* print ◊ *Die Überschrift war fett/kursiv gedruckt.* ♦ *etw. farbig drucken* ♦ *Wir werden ihr Inserat am Samstag drucken.* ♦ *Wir haben 400 Plakate drucken lassen.* ⓔ **lügen wie gedruckt** *(fam)* lie through your teeth

② **drü·cken** ['drʏkn̩] ⌷tr v⌷ +*haben* **1.** press ◊ *Sie drückte die rechte Maustaste.* jdm etw. in die Hand drücken press sth into sb's hand ◊ *Sie drückte ihm einen Geldschein in die Hand.* **2.** etw. irgendwohin drücken push sth somewhere, press sth somewhere ◊ *Er drückte die Klinke nach unten.* ♦ *Sie drückte eine Knoblauchzehe durch die Knoblauchpresse.* einen Kuss auf jds Wange drücken plant a kiss on sb's cheek **3.** etw. aus etw. drücken squeeze sth out of sth ◊ *Er drückte den Saft aus der Zitrone.* **4.** etw. drücken bring sth down ◊ *Das Überangebot an Arbeitskräften drückt die Löhne.*; *(sb's mood, spirits)* dampen ◊ *Die schlechte Nachricht drückte die Stimmung.* **5.** jdn irgendwohin drücken force sb somewhere ◊ *Sie drückte ihn an die Mauer.* ♦ *Er drückte ihn auf den Boden und würgte ihn.* **6.** jdn (an sich) drücken hug sb ◊ *Er drückte sie (ganz fest).* ♦ *Sie drückte ihn an sich.* **7.** etw. drückt jdn sb is weighed down/burdened by sth ◊ *Sorgen drückten sie.* ♦ *Ihn drückten finanzielle Probleme.* **8.** jdm die Hand drücken, jds Hand drücken shake sb's hand ◊ *Sie drückte ihm herzlich die Hand.* ⌷intr v⌷ +*haben* **1.** *(shoes)* pinch ◊ *Die Riemen der Tasche drückte sie an der Schulter.* ♦ *Diese Skistiefel drücken und scheuern.* **2.** auf etw. ⌷acc⌷ drücken press sth ◊ *Auf*

welchen Knopf muss ich drücken? ⌷ref v⌷ +*haben* sich vor etw. drücken try to get out of sth ◊ *Willst du dich vor dem Aufräumen drücken?* sich drücken try to get out of it ◊ *Sie hat sich mal wieder gedrückt.*

② **Dru·cker¹** ['drʊkɐ] der <–s, –> printer ◊ *In diesem Drucker ist ein Scanner integriert.*

Dru·cker² ['drʊkɐ] der <–s, –>, **Dru·cke·rin** ['drʊkərɪn] die <–, –nen> printer ◊ *Er ist gelernter Drucker.* ♦ *Sie macht eine Ausbildung zur Druckerin.*

Druck·schrift ['drʊkʃrɪft] die <–> *no pl* **1.** in Druckschrift schreiben print (clearly) etw. in Druckschrift ausfüllen fill sth out in block capitals/ letters ◊ *Bitte füllen Sie das Formular/den Antrag in Druckschrift aus.* **2.** pamphlet ◊ *Die Partei erwirkte das Verbot dieser Druckschrift.*

drum [drʊm] *(fam)* → darum

drun·ter ['drʊntɐ] *(fam)* → darunter

Drü·se ['dry:zə] die <–, –n> gland ◊ *geschwollene Drüsen* haben

Dschun·gel ['dʒʊŋl̩] der <–s, –> **1.** jungle ◊ *Diese Tiere leben versteckt im dichten Dschungel.* ♦ *eine Safari durch den afrikanischen Dschungel* **2.** *(fig)* maze ◊ *im Dschungel der Großstadt* ♦ *ein Weg durch den bürokratischen Dschungel*

② **du** [du:] ⌷pers pron⌷ **1.** you ◊ *Gehst du schon in die Schule?* ♦ *Du Blödmann!* ♦ *Ich habe einen Brief an dich geschrieben.* ♦ *Ich liebe dich, Andi.* ♦ *Wie geht es dir?*; *(to initiate a sentence)* du, ... listen, ...; excuse me, ... ◊ *Du, kannst du mir mal eben helfen?* ♦ *Du, hör mal, so geht das aber nicht.* **2.** *(in personifications)* Du liebe Güte!, Du liebe Zeit! Good grief!, My goodness! Du blöder Drucker, nun druck schon endlich! Stupid printer, start printing! **3.** *(fam)* you ◊ *Bei diesem Sport kommst du ganz schön ins Schwitzen.* ♦ *Da kannst du machen, was du willst, ändern wird sich hier nichts.* ⓔ **per du sein** address each other with the familiar form of '*du*' ◊ *Wir sind schon lange per du.* ♦ *Mit ihm bin ich per du.* auf du und du mit etw./jdm auf du und du mit etw. sein have a knack with sth ◊ *mit dem PC auf du und du sein* auf du und du mit jdm be rubbing shoulders with sb ◊ *mit Stars auf du und du* **wie du mir, so ich dir** you get as much as you give

nom	du
acc	dich
dat	dir
gen	deiner

Du [du:] das <–(s), –(s)> *familiar form of address* ◊ *Er redete mich einfach mit Du an.* jdm das Du anbieten ask sb to use the familiar form of address with you ◊ *Er hat mir gestern Abend das Du angeboten.* ♦ *Willst du ihr nicht endlich das Du anbieten?*

Duft [dʊft] der <–(e)s, Düfte> smell, fragrance, aroma ◊ *der Duft von Moschus/Glühwein* ♦ *der Duft von frisch gebackenem Kuchen* ♦ *ein angenehmer Duft* ♦ *der betörende Duft des Parfums* ♦ *Die Nelken verströmten einen wunderbaren Duft.*

duf·ten ['dʊftn̩] <duftet, duftete, hat geduftet> ⌷intr v⌷ smell, have a fragrance ◊ *Die Rosen duften ganz toll.* ♦ *Der Flieder duftete sehr intensiv.* nach

A
B
C
D
E
F
G
H
I
J
K
L
M
N
O
P
Q
R
S
T
U
V
W
X
Y
Z

etw. duften smell of sth ◊ *Das Badeöl duftete nach Orangen.* ♦ *Der ganze Raum duftete nach Gewürzen.* ⟨imp v⟩ es duftet (nach etw.) it smells (of sth), there is a pleasant fragrance (of sth) ◊ *Hier duftet es ja ganz wunderbar.* ♦ *In der Scheune duftete es nach frischem Heu.*

dul·den ['dʊldn̩] ⟨tr v⟩ +*haben* 1. tolerate, stand for ◊ *Ich dulde nicht, dass du ihn beleidigst.* ♦ *Ich dulde keinen Widerspruch!* 2. bear, suffer ◊ *Er duldete alles still.* 3. jdn dulden suffer sb, tolerate sb ◊ *Ich duldete ihn in meiner Nähe.* ♦ *Sie ist hier nur geduldet, aber keinesfalls erwünscht.*

② **dumm** [dʊm] ⟨adj⟩ <dümmer, am dümmsten> 1. stupid, dumb ◊ *Sie hielt mich für sehr dumm.* ♦ *Es war sehr dumm von dir, dieses Angebot zu akzeptieren.* ♦ *Ich hoffe, er kommt nicht auf dumme Gedanken.* ⊖intelligent, klug 2. silly, stupid, dumb ◊ *dummes Zeug reden* ♦ *Das ist bloß eine dumme Ausrede.* ♦ *Du dumme Gans!* 3. *(fam)* silly, ridiculous, dumb ◊ *Das war nur ein dummer Scherz.* ♦ *Diese Warterei war mir einfach zu dumm.* 4. *(fam)* annoying ◊ *Da ist mir eine sehr dumme Sache passiert.* ♦ *Das war ein sehr dummer Zufall.* ⟨adv⟩ 1. stupidly, foolishly ◊ *Sie stellten sich wirklich unglaublich dumm an.* ♦ *Er stand nur dumm rum und tat nichts.* ⊖klug, schlau 2. *(fam)* badly ◊ *Dieser Sturz hätte dumm ausgehen können.* ⊖schlimm ⊛ **dumm und dämlich** sich dumm und dämlich suchen search/hunt high and low sich dumm und dämlich verdienen earn vast amounts of money sich dumm und dämlich zahlen pay loads, pay silly amounts of money sich dumm stellen act stupid, act dumb ◊ *Er gab vor, nur Deutsch zu sprechen, und stellte sich dumm.* jdn für dumm verkaufen take sb for stupid ◊ *Die Regierung sollte das Volk nicht für dumm verkaufen.* sich nicht für dumm verkaufen lassen not let yourself be taken for stupid ◊ *Lasst euch bloß nicht für dumm verkaufen!* sich nicht von jdm für dumm verkaufen lassen not let sb take you for stupid ◊ *Von dir lass ich mich noch lang nicht für dumm verkaufen.*

Dumm·heit ['dʊmhaɪt] die <-, -en> 1. *no pl* stupidity ◊ *Das ist ja der Gipfel der Dummheit.* ♦ *Ihre Dummheit ist nicht zu ertragen.* ♦ *Dieses Verhalten grenzt schon fast an Dummheit.* 2. something stupid, stupid thing ◊ *Er hat eine große Dummheit begangen.* ♦ *Ich hoffe, du machst keine Dummheiten.*

Dumm·kopf ['dʊmkɔpf] der <-(e)s, Dummköpfe> *(pej)* idiot

dumpf [dʊmpf] ⟨adj⟩ 1. dull, muffled, low ◊ *ein dumpfes Grollen in der Ferne* ♦ *Der Aufprall war dumpf.* 2. *(pej)* mindless, ignorant ◊ *Sie grölten dumpfe Parolen.* 3. dull, vague ◊ *Ich spürte eine dumpfe Angst aufsteigen.* ♦ *Ist der Schmerz eher dumpf oder stechend?* ⟨adv⟩ dully ◊ *Seine Stimme tönte dumpf aus der Tiefe/aus dem Keller.* dumpf klingend dull-sounding eine dumpf klingende Aufnahme a muffled recording

Dü·ne ['dyːnə] die <-, -n> dune

② **dun·kel** ['dʊŋkl̩] ⟨adj, adv⟩ <dunkler, am dunkelsten> <der/die/das dunkle ...> 1. dark(ly) ◊ *Es bestellte ein dunkles Bier.* ♦ *dunkle Töne* ♦ *Es wird bereits um 17 Uhr dunkel.* ♦ *Er hatte eine dunklere Hautfarbe/dunkle Haare.* ♦ *dunkel gekleidet* dunkel

gefärbt dyed dark; *(glass)* dunkel getönt dark ◊ *eine dunkel klingende Stimme* a dark-sounding voice ⊖hell 2. vague(ly) ◊ *eine dunkle Vorstellung von etw. haben* ♦ *Er konnte sich nur dunkel an sie erinnern.* ⟨adj⟩ *(pej)* shady ◊ *Sie war in dunkle Geschäfte verwickelt.* ♦ *Er hat eine dunkle Vergangenheit.* ⊖finster

dun·kel·haa·rig ['dʊŋkl̩haːrɪç] ⟨adj⟩ dark, dark-haired, with dark hair ◊ *eine dunkelhaarige Frau* dunkelhaarig sein be dark, have dark hair

Dun·kel·heit ['dʊŋkl̩haɪt] die <-, -en> *most sing* dark(ness) ◊ *bei völliger Dunkelheit* ♦ *Ich habe das in der Dunkelheit nicht gesehen.* ⊖Helligkeit ⊛ **bei/nach Einbruch der Dunkelheit** at/after dusk, at/after nightfall

② **dünn** [dʏn] ⟨adj, adv⟩ thin(ly) ◊ *eine dünne Schicht* ♦ *ein dünner Bart* ♦ *Ihre Schwester ist zu dünn.* ♦ *Teig dünn ausrollen* dünn bekleidet sein be only scantily dressed ⟨adj⟩ 1. *(coffee, tea)* weak, watery ◊ *Der Kaffee ist mir zu dünn.* ⊖stark 2. *(voice)* thin, weak ◊ *Hinter mir ertönte ein dünnes Stimmchen.* ⊖kräftig ⊛ **dünn gesät** thin on the ground, few and far between

Dunst [dʊnst] der <-(e)s, Dünste> 1. *no pl* haze, mist ◊ *Über dem Fluss hing weißlicher Dunst.* ⊖Schleier 2. fumes, haze ◊ *In der Kneipe hing der Dunst von Zigaretten.* ⊛ **blauer Dunst** smoking

düns·ten ['dʏnstn̩] ⟨tr v⟩ +*haben (meat)* braise; *(fruit)* stew; *(fish, vegetables)* steam

durch¹ [dʊrç] ⟨adj⟩ *(fam)* 1. durch sein have gone through, have passed ◊ *Endlich sind wir hier durch!* ♦ *Ist die Straßenbahn schon durch?* 2. (well) done ◊ *Ist das Fleisch schon durch?* ♦ *Ich möchte mein Steak bitte durch.* 3. mit etw. durch sein have finished sth ◊ *Ich bin mit dem Buch durch.* 4. durch sein be through, be through ◊ *Ist der Antrag/das Gesetz durch?* 5. durch sein be worn through ◊ *Die Ellbogen an meiner Jacke sind durch.* 6. *temporal* durch sein ◊ *Er wollte um acht kommen und jetzt ist es schon neun Uhr durch.* ⊛ **durch und durch** thoroughly, completely ◊ *Diese Regierung ist durch und durch korrupt.*

② **durch²** [dʊrç] ⟨prep⟩ ⟨+acc⟩ 1. *directional* through ◊ *Gehen Sie durch die linke Tür.* ♦ *Der Einbrecher stieg durch ein Fenster ein.*; across ◊ *Wir mussten den Fluss schwimmen, weil es keine Brücke gab.* 2. all over ◊ *Das Baby krabbelt munter durch die Wohnung.* ♦ *Sie irrten durch die Stadt.* 3. by ◊ *Alte Programme werden durch neue ersetzt.* ♦ *Ich habe durch Zufall davon erfahren.* ♦ *Sechs geteilt durch drei ist zwei.* Ich habe ihn durch eine Freundin kennen gelernt. I met him through a friend. 4. because of, due to, as a result of ◊ *Durch die hohe Nachfrage steigen die Preise.* 5. *temporal, postpositive* throughout ◊ *Es geschahen die ganze Zeit durch merkwürdige Dinge.* ♦ *Das Restaurant ist die ganze Woche durch geöffnet.* ⊖hindurch, über ⊛ **unter/zwischen** ⟨dat⟩ durch under/between ... ◊ *„Wie bist du hier reingekommen?" — „Unter dem Zaun durch!"* ♦ *Er zwängte sich zwischen den Stäben durch.*

durch|... [dʊrç] ⟨prefix⟩ *stressed* through ◊ *Er will durch den Fluss durchschwimmen?* ♦ *Gehen Sie*

durch das Tor durch! ◆ durch etw. durchsehen ◆
Hast du Harry Potter schon ganz durchgelesen? Er
brach das Brett durch. He broke the plank in two.
[prefix] unstressed through ◊ Auf der Rallye durchqueren die Teilnehmer drei Länder. ◆ eine Absperrung durchbrechen ◆ eine Entwicklung durchlaufen
durch·aus [dʊˀçǀˈaos, '- -] [adv] **1.** quite, entirely ◊
Das ist durchaus möglich. durchaus nicht not at
all, by no means **2.** absolutely ◊ Na gut, wenn es
denn durchaus sein muss.
durch|bli·cken [ˈdʊˀçblɪkn̩] <blickt durch, blickte
durch, hat durchgeblickt> [intr v] **1.** (fam) get,
understand ◊ Blickst du da noch durch? ◆ In
Chemie habe ich noch nie durchgeblickt. **2.** look
through ◊ Das ist ein schönes Fernglas. Darf ich
auch mal durchblicken?
◉ **etw. durchblicken lassen** hint at sth, intimate
sth ◊ Er ließ durchblicken, dass er nicht kandidieren wolle.
durch·bre·chen¹ [dʊˀçˈbrɛçn̩] <durchbricht, durchbrach, hat durchbrochen> [tr v] break through,
burst through ◊ Die Demonstranten durchbrachen
die Absperrung.
durch|bre·chen² [ˈdʊˀçbrɛçn̩] <bricht durch, brach
durch, hat/ist durchgebrochen> [tr v] +*haben* break
in two ◊ Er brach den Bleistift einfach in der Mitte
durch. [intr v] +*sein* **1.** break (in two) ◊ Der Schau-
felstiel bricht gleich durch. **2.** fall through ◊ Er
brach durch den alten Holzboden durch. **3.** break
through ◊ Endlich brach die Sonne durch.
durch|brin·gen [ˈdʊˀçbrɪŋən] <bringt durch,
brachte durch, hat durchgebracht> [tr v] **1.** jdn
durchbringen support sb ◊ Als ihr Mann im
Gefängnis saß, musste sie die Familie allein durchbringen. **2.** get through ◊ Das Sofa bringt ihr nie
durch diese enge Tür durch! ◆ Habt ihr euren
Bauantrag durchgebracht? ◆ Er hat sein ganzes
Geld beim Pferderennen durchgebracht. **3.** save ◊
Die Ärzte konnten das Kind nicht durchbringen.
Durch·bruch [ˈdʊˀçbrʊx] der <-(e)s, Durchbrüche>
1. breakthrough ◊ Die Rolle des Hamlet hat ihm
zum Durchbruch verholfen. **2.** MED rupture, perforation, bursting ◊ Es kam zu einem Durchbruch des
Blinddarms. **3.** opening, breach ◊ ein Durchbruch
von der Küche zum Esszimmer
durch·den·ken [dʊˀçˈdɛŋkn̩] <durchdenkt, durchdachte, hat durchdacht> [tr v] think out/through ◊
die Folgen gut durchdenken ◆ Die Strategie war
nicht gut durchdacht.
durch·drin·gen¹ [dʊˀçˈdrɪŋən] <durchdringt, durchdrang, hat durchdrungen> [tr v] **1.** penetrate, come
through ◊ Das Prasseln des Regens durchdrang die
Stille. **2.** (sound, knife, bullet) pierce ◊ Die
Klinge durchdrang die Milz. ◆ Geräusche durchdringen die Stille. **3.** (emotion) overcome ◊ Von Liebe
durchdrungen schrieb er ihr ein Lied.
durch|drin·gen² [ˈdʊˀçdrɪŋən] <dringt durch,
drang durch, ist durchgedrungen> [intr v] **1.** mit
etw. durchdringen get sth accepted ◊ Bist du mit
deinem Vorschlag beim Lehrer durchgedrungen? ◆
mit einer Forderung durchdringen **2.** (zu jdm)
durchdringen reach (sb) ◊ Diese Neuigkeit ist
noch nicht zu ihnen durchgedrungen.
② **durch·ei·nan·der** [dʊˀçǀaɛˈnandɐ] [adj, adv] no
comp/superl; when used as an adj, not before ns
1. messy(-ily), (in) a mess ◊ Nach dem Einbruch

war alles durcheinander.; (figures, documents)
mixed up, muddled up ◊ Die Zahlen sind alle
durcheinander (geraten).; (loose sheets, leaves) all
over the place ◊ Die Blätter wurden durcheinander
gewirbelt. etw. durcheinander bringen muddle sth
up **2.** confused ◊ Ich bin ganz durcheinander von
dem Hin und Her. jdn durcheinander bringen
confuse sb
durch·fah·ren¹ [dʊˀçˈfaːrən] <durchfährt,
durchfuhr, hat durchfahren> [intr v] (lofty) **1.** travel
through, drive through, pass through ◊ Auf unserer
Reise nach Schweden durchfuhren wir Dänemark.
2. (emotion, thought) jdn durchfahren seize sb,
flash through sb's mind ◊ Ein eisiger Schreck
durchfuhr ihn. ◆ Ein schrecklicher Verdacht
durchfuhr sie.
durch|fah·ren² [ˈdʊˀçfaːrən] <fährt durch, fuhr
durch, ist durchgefahren> [intr v] **1.** drive through,
go through ◊ Das Tor ist gesperrt; niemand kann
durchfahren. **2.** travel/drive/go non-stop ◊ Dieser
Zug fährt bis Aachen durch.; (drive past without
stopping) pass (by) ◊ Der Bus ist einfach durchgefahren, ohne an der Haltestelle anzuhalten. die
Nacht durchfahren drive/travel through the night ◊
Wir sind die ganze Nacht durchgefahren.
Durch·fahrt [ˈdʊˀçfaːɐ̯t] die <-, -en> passage ◊ Die
Durchfahrt ist hier nicht erlaubt. ◆ Die Durchfahrt
ist gesperrt. Durchfahrt verboten no thoroughfare
◉ **auf der Durchfahrt sein** be passing through
Durch·fall [ˈdʊˀçfal] der <-(e)s, Durchfälle> seldom
with the article diarrhoea
durch|fal·len [ˈdʊˀçfalən] <fällt durch, fiel durch,
ist durchgefallen> [intr v] **1.** (an exam) (bei/in
etw. [dat]) durchfallen; (durch etw.) durchfallen fail
(sth) ◊ Er ist bei/in der Zwischenprüfung durchgefallen. ◆ durch das Abschlussexamen durchfallen ◆
Sie ist schon zum zweiten Mal durchgefallen.
2. flop ◊ Sein neues Stück ist beim Publikum
durchgefallen. **3.** fall through ◊ Sie sah die Falltür
nicht und fiel durch.
durch·führ·bar [ˈdʊˀçfyːɡbaːʳ] [adj] no comp/superl
feasible, practicable, workable ◊ Dieser Plan ist
praktisch nicht durchführbar. etw. ist durchführbar
sth can be done/carried out
durch|füh·ren [ˈdʊˀçfyːrən] <führt durch, führte
durch, hat durchgeführt> [tr v] **1.** carry out,
perform, complete ◊ Das Experiment wurde erfolgreich durchgeführt. **2.** (durch etw.) durchführen go/
pass through sth ◊ Die Wanderroute führt durch
den Wald. **3.** jdn (durch etw.) durchführen
lead sb through (sth), show sb around (sth) ◊ Soll
ich dich durch das Labyrinth durchführen? ◆ Jetzt
kommt die Tür. Augen zulassen — ich werde dich
durchführen.
Durch·gang [ˈdʊˀçgan] der <-(e)s, Durchgänge>
1. passage(way) ◊ Der Durchgang führte in einen
Innenhof. **2.** stage, run, round ◊ Die deutsche Ski-
fahrerin schied bereits im ersten Durchgang aus.
durch·ge·bra·ten [ˈdʊˀçgəbraːtn̩] [adj] well done,
completely cooked ◊ Das Steak war gut durchgebraten.
durch|ge·hen [ˈdʊˀçgeːən] <geht durch, ging
durch, ist durchgegangen> [intr v] **1.** go through ◊
Gehen Sie durch die Glastür durch! ◆ Das Öhr ist
winzig, da geht der Faden nicht durch. ◆ Die Straßenbahn geht bis zum Bahnhof durch.

2. *(temporal)* carry/go on (right) through ◊ *Die Sauferei ging die ganze Nacht durch.* **3.** *(bis)* zu ... durchgehen lead (up) to ... ◊ *Diese Passage geht zur Hauptstraße durch.* **4.** als etw. durchgehen pass as sth ◊ *Mit ihrer Aussprache geht sie glatt als Muttersprachlerin durch.* **5.** *(horse)* bolt ◊ *Das Pferd ging durch und die Reiterin stürzte.* etw. geht mit jdm durch sb gets carried away by sth, sth gets the better of sb ◊ *Da ist wohl deine Fantasie mit dir durchgegangen?* **6.** *(fam)* mit jdm/etw. durchgehen run off with sb/sth ◊ *Sie ist mit einem Liebhaber durchgegangen.* [tr v] go through ◊ *Bist du deine Hausaufgabe noch einmal durchgegangen?* ⊛ jdm etw. durchgehen lassen let sb get away with sth ◊ *Lehrer dürfen ihren Schülern nicht alles durchgehen lassen.*

durch·ge·hend ['dʊˣçgeːənt] *pres p of* durchgehen [adv] **1.** all the way, entirely, throughout ◊ *Die Straße ist wieder durchgehend befahrbar.* ◆ *Das Buch ist durchgehend farbig illustriert.* **2.** continuously, all day ◊ *Der Zoo ist täglich ab 9 Uhr durchgehend geöffnet.* ◆ *durchgehend warme Küche* durchgehend arbeiten work through

durch|hal·ten ['dʊˣçhaltn̩] <hält durch, hielt durch, hat durchgehalten> [tr v] etw. durchhalten keep sth up, stay with sth, keep to sth ◊ *Sie hielten ihre Strategie konsequent durch.* [intr v] hold out, persevere ◊ *Wenn du langsamer läufst, hältst du länger durch.*

durch|kom·men ['dʊˣçkɔmən] <kommt durch, kam durch, ist durchgekommen> [intr v] **1.** *(also fig)* get through ◊ *Das Loch ist ziemlich klein. Ich weiß nicht, ob ich da durchkomme.* ◆ *Sie ist im ersten Wahlgang durchgekommen.* ◆ *Ich wollte ihn anrufen, aber ich bin nicht durchgekommen.* ◆ *Da kommt kein Wasser durch.* **2.** *(trough a town or village)* come through ◊ *Auf dem Heimweg kommen wir durch Mannheim durch.* **3.** pull through ◊ *Die Ärzte wussten nicht, ob er durchkommen würde.* **4.** get by, manage ◊ *Wir hatten nie viel Geld, aber irgendwie sind wir immer durchgekommen.* **5.** mit etw. (bei jdm) durchkommen get sth accepted (by sb) ◊ *Bist du mit dem Vorschlag (bei der Chefin) durchgekommen?*

durch|las·sen ['dʊˣçlasn̩] <lässt durch, ließ durch, hat durchgelassen> [tr v] let through ◊ *Er wurde an der Grenze nicht durchgelassen.* ◆ *Das Zelt lässt Wasser durch.*

durch·läs·sig ['dʊˣçlɛsɪç] [adj] open, permeable ◊ *Der Arbeitsmarkt muss durchlässiger werden.* ◆ *Diese Pflanze braucht einen durchlässigen Boden.*

durch·lau·fen¹ ['dʊˣçlaʊfn̩] <durchläuft, durchlief, hat durchlaufen> [tr v] *(lofty)* **1.** pass (through), go through ◊ *Er durchlief seine Ausbildung sehr schnell.* **2.** run through ◊ *Ein Zucken durchlief seinen Körper. Er durchlief die Strecke in Rekordzeit.* He covered the distance in a record time.

durch·lau·fen² ['dʊˣçlaʊfn̩] <läuft durch, lief durch, ist/hat durchgelaufen> [intr v] +*sein* **1.** go through, pass (through) ◊ *Siehst du das Schild nicht? Da darf man nicht durchlaufen!* ◆ *Ich bin durch die Ausstellung nur durchgelaufen.* **2.** *(without stopping)* run through, walk through ◊ *Sie lief durch den ganzen Wald durch. Sie liefen zwei Stunden durch ohne anzuhalten.* They ran for

two hours without stopping. [tr v] +*haben (shoes, socks)* wear through

durch|le·sen ['dʊˣçleːzn̩] <liest durch, las durch, hat durchgelesen> [tr v] read through, finish ◊ *Ich habe das Buch an einem Tag durchgelesen.* ◆ *Lesen Sie sich den Vertrag genau durch.*

durch|ma·chen ['dʊˣçmaxn̩] <macht durch, machte durch, hat durchgemacht> [tr v] go through ◊ *einen Lernprozess/Wandel durchmachen* ◆ *Er hat in seinem Leben viel durchgemacht.* ⊛ *(die Nacht) durchmachen* go on/work/party all (through the) night

Durch·mes·ser ['dʊˣçmɛsɐ] der <-s, -> diameter ◊ *ein Durchmesser von 10cm* ◆ *Der Krater ist im Durchmesser12 Kilometer groß.*

Durch·rei·se ['dʊˣçraɛzə] die <-, -n> most sing passage, transit ◊ *An der Grenze wurde ihm die Durchreise verweigert.* auf der Durchreise on the way through, in transit

② **Durch·sa·ge** ['dʊˣçzaːgə] die <-, -n> announcement ◊ *Die Durchsage erfolgte auch auf französisch.*

durch|schla·gen¹ ['dʊˣçʃlaːgn̩] <schlägt durch, schlug durch, hat durchgeschlagen> [tr v] chop/break in two, split ◊ *Er kann ein Brett mit der Handkante durchschlagen.* [ref v] **1.** sich irgendwohin durchschlagen fight your way through to somewhere, make your way somewhere ◊ *Er hat sich illegal nach Großbritannien durchgeschlagen.* ◆ *Die deutsche Mannschaft schlug sich bis zum Endspiel durch.* **2.** sich mit etw./als etw. durchschlagen make ends meet with/as sth ◊ *Sie hat sich mit Gelegenheitsarbeiten/als Putzfrau durchgeschlagen.*

durch·schla·gen² ['dʊˣçʃlaːgn̩] <durchschlägt, durchschlug, hat durchschlagen> [tr v] smash ◊ *Ein Stein hat die Windschutzscheibe durchschlagen.*

durch|schnei·den ['dʊˣçʃnaɛdn̩] <schneidet durch, schnitt durch, hat durchgeschnitten> [tr v] cut through, cut in half/two ◊ *Sie schnitt das Blatt in der Mitte durch.*

Durch·schnitt ['dʊˣçʃnɪt] der <-(e)s, -e> most sing **1.** average, mean ◊ *Der Durchschnitt in der Klassenarbeit lag bei 2,5.* **2.** *(pej)* average ◊ *Das neue Album der Gruppe ist nur Durchschnitt.*

② **durch·schnitt·lich** ['dʊˣçʃnɪtlɪç] [adj, adv] seldom comp/superl (on) average ◊ *durchschnittliche Löhne* ◆ *Der Umsatz war durchschnittlich.* ◆ *Die Preise sind um durchschnittlich zehn Prozent gestiegen.* [adj] *(pej)* modest, ordinary ◊ *Seine Leistungen sind bestenfalls durchschnittlich.* ◆ *ein Fußballspiel auf nur durchschnittlichem Niveau* ☺mittelmäßig

durch|se·hen ['dʊˣçzeːən] <sieht durch, sah durch, hat durchgesehen> [tr v] **1.** see through ◊ *Kann man durch die Bluse durchsehen?* **2.** look over, check (over) ◊ *ein Schriftstück genau durchsehen* **3.** look through ◊ *Sieh bitte noch die Post durch* ◊ *ich erwarte eine Rechnung.*

durch|set·zen ['dʊˣçzɛtsn̩] <setzt durch, setzte durch, hat durchgesetzt> [tr v] enforce, get through, get accepted ◊ *Reformen durchsetzen* seinen Kopf/Willen durchsetzen have your way ◊ [ref v] **1.** sich (gegen jdn) durchsetzen assert yourself, prevail (over sb), get your way ◊ *Du musst lernen, dich durchzusetzen.* ◆ *Sie hat sich*

gegen die anderen Bewerber erfolgreich durchge-
setzt. **2.** *etw.* setzt sich durch sth becomes
accepted, sth catches on, sth takes hold ◊ *Nach*
und nach setzt sich die Erkenntnis durch, dass ...
durch·sich·tig ['dʊʳçzɪçtɪç] [adj, adv] *seldom comp/*
superl transparent(ly) ◊ *eine durchsichtige Folie* ♦
Seine Absichten sind ziemlich durchsichtig. ♦ *durch-*
sichtig bekleidet ⊖undurchsichtig
durch|strei·chen ['dʊʳçʃtraeçn̩] <streicht durch,
strich durch, hat durchgestrichen> [tr v] cross out,
delete ◊ *Unzutreffendes bitte durchstreichen.* ♦ *Sie*
strich das Wort durch und schrieb ein anderes
darüber.
durch·su·chen [dʊʳçˈzuːxn̩] <durchsucht, durchsuchte, hat durchsucht> [tr v] jdn/etw. (nach etw.)
durchsuchen search sb/sth (for sth) ◊ *Er durch-*
suchte seine Taschen nach Kleingeld. ♦ *jdn bei der*
Verhaftung durchsuchen
Durch·wahl ['dʊʳçvaːl] die <-, -en> direct line ◊
Nähere Informationen sind unter der folgenden
Durchwahl erhältlich: ...
durch·weg ['dʊʳçvɛk, - '-] [adv] without exception ◊
Die Resonanz beim Publikum war durchweg
positiv.; totally, in every respect ◊ *Die Vorwürfe*
waren durchweg unbegründet.
② **dür·fen¹** ['dʏʳfn̩] <darf, durfte, hat dürfen>
[modal v] *+inf* **1.** *(permission)* may, be allowed ◊
Darf ich hier rauchen? ♦ *Ich darf erst später mit*
dir spielen.; (probibition) jd darf etw. nicht tun
sb must not do sth, sb should not do sth, sb may
not do sth ◊ *Das hättest du nicht sagen dürfen!* ♦
Das darf aber niemand wissen! **2.** *(with good*
reason) jd darf etw. tun sb has reason to do sth,
sb can do sth ◊ *Das darfst du mir ruhig glauben!*
3. *subjunctive II (expressing an assumption)*
must ◊ *Diese Vase dürfte zweitausend Jahre alt*
sein. **4.** *in polite requests* may ◊ *Darf ich Ihnen*
nachschenken? ♦ *Darf ich mich vorstellen?*
② **dür·fen²** ['dʏʳfn̩] <darf, durfte, hat gedurft>
[tr+intr v] *(fam)* be permitted, be allowed, may ◊
Das hätte ich früher nicht gedurft. ♦ *Darfst du mit*
ins Kino? ♦ *Oh, Pralinen, darf ich?*
② **durf·te** ['dʊʳftə] *pret of* dürfen¹, dürfen²

dürf·tig ['dʏʳftɪç] [adj, adv] poor(ly), scanty(-ily),
feeble(-bly) ◊ *Die Auskunft, die wir bekamen, war*
dürftig. ♦ *eine dürftige Leistung* ♦ *dürftig bekleidet*
Dür·re ['dʏrə] die <-, -n> drought ◊ *In vielen*
Teilen der Erde herrscht Dürre.
② **Durst** [dʊʳst] der <-(e)s> *no pl* thirst ◊ *Im Festzelt*
können Sie Ihren Durst löschen. Durst haben be
thirsty
⊛ (einen) über den Durst trinken *(fam)* have
one too many
② **Du·sche** ['duːʃə, 'dʊʃə] die <-, -n> shower ◊ *In der*
Dusche war eine riesige Spinne. ♦ *eine (ausgie-*
bige) Dusche nehmen unter die Dusche gehen have
a shower
② **du·schen** ['duːʃn̩, 'dʊʃn̩] [intr v] *+baben* have/take a
shower ◊ *Er duscht täglich.* [tr v] *+baben* sich
duschen have/take a shower ◊ *Nachdem ich mich*
geduscht hatte, frühstückte ich. jdn duschen give
sb a shower
düs·ter ['dyːstɐ] [adj, adv] dark(ly), gloomy(-ily),
sombre(ly) ◊ *In der Kirche ist es düster.* ♦ *düstere*
Farben ♦ *düster dreinblicken* ♦ *Die Erfolgsaussich-*
ten sind eher düster. ⊖finster
Dut·zend ['dʊtsn̩t, 'dʊtsənt] das <-s, - *or* -e> *pl*
'Dutzend' when used with expressions of quantity
1. dozen ◊ *ein halbes Dutzend frische Austern* ♦
Ich kenne mindestens ein Dutzend solcher Fälle.
2. *only pl* ein paar/mehrere Dutzend a few dozen/
several dozen Dutzende (von) ... dozens of ... ◊
Dutzende (von) Fans scharten sich um den Popstar.
zu Dutzenden in their dozens
du·zen ['duːtsn̩] [tr v] *+baben* use the informal
address *'du'* instead of the formal *'Sie'* ◊ *Sie duzt*
alle ihre Studenten. ♦ *Wollen wir uns duzen?*
⊖siezen

The informal *du* is used among children and by
adults when addressing children, friends or family
members. Although today *du* is used more widely
in Germany, *Sie* still predominates in the
workplace, especially when addressing more
senior colleagues.

A B C D E F G H I J K L M N O P Q R S T U V W X Y Z

E

e, E [eː] das <–(s), –(s)> **1.** e, E ◊ *Dieses Wort wird mit einem kleinen e/großen E geschrieben.* ✦ *E wie Emil* **2.** MUS E ◊ *Spiel mal ein E.*

Eb·be ['ɛbə] die <–, –n> *most sing* low tide, ebb tide ◊ *Bei Ebbe suchen wir Muscheln.* ⊜Flut ◉ *irgendwo ist/herrscht Ebbe* sth is empty ◊ *In den öffentlichen Kassen ist Ebbe.*

② **e·ben¹** ['eːbm̩] [adj] level, flat, even ◊ *Die Fahrbahn ist nicht ganz eben.* ✦ *ein ebenes Gelände* [adv] **1.** *temporal* just ◊ *Sie geht eben aus dem Haus.* gerade eben, eben erst only just, just now ◊ *Ich bin eben erst fertig geworden.* **2.** eben noch, gerade so eben just (about), only just ◊ *Er hat die Prüfung gerade so eben bestanden.* ✦ *Er ist eben noch mal ohne Strafe davongekommen.* ⊜gerade noch

e·ben² ['eːbm̩] [part] **1.** *reinforcing a statement or request* just ◊ *Ich mache das so schnell es eben geht.* ✦ „*Ich bin schon wieder krank.*" — „*Dann leb eben gesünder!*" **2.** *reinforcing a conclusion* simply, just, after all ◊ *Mädchen sind eben anders als Jungen.* ⊜nun (ein)mal, halt **3.** *reinforcing an affirmative reply* exactly ◊ *Eben, das sage ich auch immer!* ✦ *Er ist nicht eben der Fleißigste/ Schnellste.* ✦ *Das war nicht eben klug von dir.*

E·be·ne ['eːbənə] die <–, –n> **1.** auf ... Ebene on a/at ... level ◊ *Politik auf nationaler Ebene* ✦ *Er sucht Akzeptanz auf breiter Ebene.* **2.** GEOG plain ◊ *eine karge, sandige Ebene* **3.** MATH plane ◊ *die Geometrie der Ebene*

② **e·ben·falls** ['eːbm̩fals] [adv] likewise, as well ◊ *Der zweite Versuch ist ebenfalls gescheitert.* ⊜auch, ebenso

② **e·ben·so** ['eːbm̩zoː] [adv] **1.** just as ◊ *Dieses Spiel mögen Kinder ebenso gern wie Erwachsene.* ✦ *Er ist ebenso groß wie seine Schwester.* ⊜genauso **2.** as well, just like ◊ *Der Vereinsvorsitzende war schon da, ebenso der Bürgermeister.* ✦ *Die Kinder sind müde, wir ebenso.* ⊜ebenfalls, auch, gleichfalls

eb·nen ['eːbnən] [tr v] +*haben* (make) level ◊ *Das Spielfeld wird mit einer Walze geebnet.*

EC [eːˈtseː] der *(abbr of Eurocity)* European intercity (train) ◊ *Ich nehme den EC, der ist schneller.*

echt [ɛçt] [adj, adv] **1.** genuine(ly) ◊ *ein echter Brillant* ✦ *Ihre Wut war echt.* ✦ *echt vergoldet* **2.** *when used as an adj, only before ns (fam)* real(ly) ◊ *ein echt cooler Typ* ✦ „*Ich habe 50 Euro gefunden.*" — „*Echt?*" **3.** *when used as an adj, only before ns (person)* typical(ly) ◊ *ein echter Bayer* ✦ *echt englisches Wetter* [adj] *only before ns, when the artist's name stands for the piece of art (signature, manuscript etc.)* authentic, genuine ◊ *Der Brief von Mary Shelley ist echt.* ✦ *Er besitzt einen echten Picasso.* ⊜falsch

EC-Kar·te [eːˈtseːkaʁtə] die <–, –n> Euro-Cheque debit card ◊ *mit EC-Karte bezahlen*

② **E·cke** ['ɛkə] die <–, –n> corner ◊ *Er stieß sich an*

der Ecke des Schreibtischs. ✦ *Der Hund verkroch sich winselnd in seine Ecke.* ✦ *Die Stadtbücherei ist an der Ecke Bachstraße/Mozartstraße.* ✦ *In dieser Ecke Frankreichs kenne ich mich gut aus.* ◉ *eine Ecke Schokolade/Käse* a piece/wedge of chocolate/cheese *eine ganze Ecke (fam)* **1.** quite a bit ◊ *So kann man eine ganze Ecke sparen.* **2.** quite a long way ◊ *Ich wohne eine ganze Ecke von hier.*

e·ckig ['ɛkɪç] [adj, adv] *seldom comp/superl* **1.** angular(ly), square(ly) ◊ *etwas in eckige Klammern setzen* ✦ *Seine Schultern sind ziemlich eckig.* ✦ *ein eckig geschnittenes Kinn* **2.** *(movement)* jerky(-ily) ◊ *Ihre Bewegungen wirken eckig.* ✦ *Er verbeugte sich eckig.*

e·del ['eːdl̩] [adj, adv] <edler, am edelsten> <der/ die/das edle ...> **1.** fine(ly), classy(-ily), luxurious(ly) ◊ *Dieses Brautkleid ist echt edel.* ✦ *Dieser Wein ist ein edler Tropfen.* ✦ *ein edel ausgestattetes Auto* **2.** *(character)* noble(-bly), honourable(-ably) ◊ *Es war sehr edel von ihm, ihr zu verzeihen.* ✦ *eine edle Geste* ✦ *edel handeln* ⊜nobel **3.** *(shape)* noble(-bly), fine(ly) ◊ *Seine Gesichtszüge sind edel.* ✦ *edles Design* ✦ *edel geformte Blüten*

E·del·stahl ['eːdl̩ʃtaːl] der <–(e)s, Edelstähle> stainless steel ◊ *Besteck aus Edelstahl*

E·del·stein ['eːdl̩ʃtaen] der <–(e)s, –e> gem(stone), precious stone ◊ *ein geschliffener Edelstein*

EDV [eːdeːˈfaʊ] die *(abbr of elektronische Datenverarbeitung)* IT ◊ *Kenntnisse in EDV* ✦ *die EDV umstellen*

ef·fek·tiv [ɛfɛkˈtiːf] [adj, adv] **1.** effective(ly) ◊ *Das Verfahren ist teuer, aber effektiv.* ✦ *effektive Maßnahmen* ✦ *ein Mittel, das Unkraut effektiv vernichtet* **2.** real(ly) ◊ *Was bedeutet das effektiv?* *effektive Kosten* actual costs

② **e·gal** [eˈgaːl] [adj] *no comp/superl, not before ns* ist (jdm) egal sth makes no difference (to sb), sth does not matter (to sb) ◊ *Es ist egal, ob du kommst oder nicht.* *es ist mir egal* I don't care *egal*, no matter what ◊ *Egal, was ich sage, er widerspricht immer.*

e·go·is·tisch [egoˈɪstɪʃ] [adj, adv] selfish(ly), egoistic(ally) ◊ *Sei nicht so egoistisch!* ✦ *eine Entscheidung aus egoistischen Motiven* ✦ *ein egoistisch denkender Mensch*

e·he ['eːə] [conjunc] before, until ◊ *Er musste lange warten, ehe Hilfe kam.* ✦ *Noch ehe alle Stimmen ausgezählt waren, feierte sie ihren Sieg.* ⊜bevor

② **E·he** ['eːə] die <–, –n> marriage ◊ *ihre Kinder aus erster Ehe* ✦ *Die Ehe wurde nach fünf Jahren geschieden.*

E·he·frau ['eːəfraʊ] die <–, –en> wife, married woman ⊜Ehemann

e·he·ma·lig ['eːəmaːlɪç] [adj, adv] *no comp/superl; when used as an adj, only before ns* former(ly)

der ehemalige Präsident ♦ die Altstadt der ehemalig römischen Garnisonsstadt

e·he·mals ['eːəmaːls] [adv] in former times, formerly ◊ Ihre ehemals beste Freundin hat geheiratet. ♦ Wo ehemals Felder waren, ist jetzt ein Einkaufszentrum.

E·he·mann ['eːəman] der <–(e)s, Ehemänner> husband, married man ⊜Ehefrau

E·he·paar ['eːəpaːʳ] das <–(e)s, –e> married couple

E·he·part·ner ['eːəpaʳtnɐ] der <–s, –>, **E·he·part·ne·rin** ['eːəpaʳtnərɪn] die <–, –nen> spouse

e·her ['eːɐ] comp of bald [adv] **1.** temporal earlier, sooner ◊ Kannst du nicht etwas eher kommen? ⊜früher **2.** comparative rather ◊ Ich finde das eher teuer. ♦ Ich würde eher nach Schottland als nach Portugal fahren.; more ◊ Er ist eher schlank als dick.; more likely ◊ „Bringst du jemanden mit?" — „Ich werde wohl eher alleine kommen."

E·he·ring ['eːərɪŋ] der <–es, –e> wedding ring ◊ einen Ehering tragen

Eh·re ['eːrə] die <–, –n> **1.** honour, honor ◊ Die Ehre des Vaterlandes ging ihm über alles. ♦ Ihr wurde eine besondere Ehre zuteil. es ist mir eine Ehre I have the honour, it is an honour (for me) **2.** (sense of) honour, self-respect ◊ Meine Ehre erlaubt mir das nicht.

⊛ jdm die letzte Ehre erweisen pay your last respects to sb

② **eh·ren** ['eːrən] [tr v] +haben honour, honor ◊ Er wurde für 25 Jahre Mitgliedschaft mit einer Medaille geehrt. ♦ „Ihre Einladung ehrt mich sehr," sagte er. ♦ Sie fühlte sich geehrt.

eh·ren·amt·lich ['eːrənamtlɪç] [adj] no comp/ superl voluntary, honorary ◊ Ihre Tätigkeit ist ehrenamtlich. ♦ ehrenamtliches Engagement [adv] ehrenamtlich tätig sein/arbeiten do voluntary work, work as a volunteer

Ehr·furcht ['eːɐfʊrçt] die <–> no pl reverence, awe ◊ jdm/einer Sache mit der gebotenen Ehrfurcht begegnen Ehrfurcht vor jdm/etw. haben have great respect for sb/sth ◊ Ehrfurcht vor der Natur/den Toten haben

⊛ Ehrfurcht einflößend/gebietend awe-inspiring

ehr·gei·zig ['eːɐgaetsɪç] [adj, adv] ambitious(ly) ◊ Sie ist ziemlich ehrgeizig. ♦ sich zielstrebig und ehrgeizig hocharbeiten ♦ ein ehrgeiziges Projekt

② **ehr·lich** ['eːɐlɪç] [adj, adv] **1.** honest(ly) ◊ Sei ehrlich, stimmt das wirklich? ♦ eine ehrliche Antwort ♦ Das muss ich offen und ehrlich zugeben.; (intentions) honourable, honorable; (competition) fair ehrlich zu jdm honest with sb ◊ Sie war immer ehrlich zu mir. ehrlich gesagt to be honest **2.** (feelings) sincere(ly) ◊ eine ehrlich gemeinte Entschuldigung ehrlich erschrocken truly shocked

⊛ ehrlich währt am längsten honesty is the best policy ehrlich verdient hard-earned ◊ ehrlich verdientes Geld

Eh·rung ['eːrʊŋ] die <–, –en> honour, honor ◊ Der Oscar ist die höchste Ehrung für Filmschaffende. ♦ jdm werden zahlreiche Ehrungen zuteil

② **Ei** [ae] das <–(e)s, –er> **1.** egg ◊ ein Brötchen mit Schinken und Ei ♦ Das Küken/Die Larve schlüpft aus dem Ei. ♦ Das befruchtete Ei nistet sich in der Gebärmutter ein. ein hartes/weiches Ei a hard-boiled/soft-boiled egg **2.** only pl (rude) Eier balls ◊ jdm in die Eier treten

⊛ das Ei des Kolumbus the perfect solution jdn/ etw. behandeln wie ein rohes Ei handle sb/sth with kid gloves ungelegte Eier things that haven't happened yet, future concerns sich um ungelegte Eier kümmern (fam) worry prematurely about sth, cross your bridges before you come to them sich gleichen wie ein Ei dem anderen be as alike as two peas in a pod (methods) be identical

Ei·che ['aeçə] die <–, –n> oak ◊ Die Eiche ist das germanische Symbol der Stärke. ♦ Der Tisch ist aus Eiche.

Eid [aet] der <–(e)s, –e> oath ◊ einen Eid schwören ♦ unter Eid einen Eid auf etw. [acc] leisten swear an oath on sth ◊ einen Eid darauf leisten, die Wahrheit zu sagen

Ei·er·be·cher ['aeɐbɛçɐ] der <–s, –> egg cup

Ei·fer ['aefɐ] der <–s> no pl enthusiasm, eagerness ◊ Sie machte sich mit großem Eifer an die Arbeit.

⊛ im Eifer des Gefechts in the heat of the moment missionarischer Eifer missionary zeal

Ei·fer·sucht ['aefezʊxt] die <–> no pl jealousy ◊ krankhafte/unbegründete Eifersucht Eifersucht auf jdn/etw. jealousy of/towards sb/sth ◊ Eifersucht auf die kleine Schwester

eif·rig ['aefrɪç] [adj, adv] eager(ly), keen(ly) ◊ ein eifriger Anhänger einer Theorie ♦ Dieser Schüler ist besonders eifrig. ♦ eifrig mitschreiben/lernen

Ei·gelb ['aegɛlp] das <–(e)s, –e> also pl 'Eigelb' when used with expressions of quantity (egg) yolk ◊ Er gab zwei Eigelb in den Teig.

② **ei·gen** ['aegn̩] [adj] no comp/superl **1.** only before ns own ◊ Ihr Sohn hat einen eigenen Fernseher. ♦ Das habe ich mit meinen eigenen Ohren gehört. **2.** jdm/einer Sache typical of sb/sth ◊ Sie ging die Aufgabe mit der ihr eigenen Begeisterung an. ⊜typisch

ei·gen·ar·tig ['aegn̩|aːʳtɪç] [adj, adv] strange(ly) ◊ ein eigenartiger Geruch ♦ Sein Benehmen ist schon sehr eigenartig. ♦ Die Musik hat mich eigenartig berührt. eigenartig aussehen/riechen/schmecken look/smell/taste strange ⊜merkwürdig, seltsam, komisch, sonderbar

ei·gen·hän·dig ['aegn̩hɛndɪç] [adj, adv] no comp/ superl; only before ns personal(ly) ◊ Der Ausweis ist nur mit eigenhändiger Unterschrift gültig. ♦ Die Bäume hier habe ich alle eigenhändig gepflanzt. ⊜selbst, persönlich

ei·gen·mäch·tig ['aegn̩mɛçtɪç] [adj] no comp/ superl, only before ns unauthorized ◊ eigenmächtiges Vorgehen/Handeln [adv] on your own authority ◊ eigenmächtig handeln

Ei·gen·na·me ['aegn̩naːmə] der <–ns, –n> proper name; (in linguistics) proper noun

ei·gens ['aegn̩s, 'aegəns] [adv] specially ◊ Ist er eigens zur Premiere angereist? ♦ eine eigens eingerichtete Hotline der Polizei eigens für diesen Zweck specifically for this purpose

Ei·gen·schaft ['aegn̩ʃaft] die <–, –en> characteristic, quality ◊ Zu ihren hervorstechendsten Eigenschaften gehört ihr Mut.; (of a substance) property ◊ die physikalischen/chemischen Eigenschaften eines Stoffes ⊜Merkmal

⊛ in amtlicher/offizieller Eigenschaft in an

A B C D E F G H I J K L M N O P Q R S T U V W X Y Z

official capacity in jds Eigenschaft als in sb's capacity as

Ei·gen·schafts·wort ['aeɡn̩ʃaftsvɔʳt] das <-(e)s, Eigenschaftswörter> adjective ⊖Adjektiv

ei·gen·sin·nig ['aeɡn̩zɪnɪç] [adj, adv] stubborn(ly), obstinate(ly) ◊ *ein eigensinniges Kind* ♦ *Leo blieb eigensinnig und wollte sich durchsetzen.* ♦ *eigensinnig auf etw.* [dat] bestehen ⊖stur

ei·gent·lich¹ ['aeɡn̩tlɪç, 'aeɡəntlɪç] [adj] *no comp/ superl, only before ns real* ◊ *Seine eigentliche Meinung/Seinen eigentlichen Namen hat er nie verraten.* [adv] *no comp/superl* **1.** really, originally ◊ *Bob Dylan heißt eigentlich Robert Zimmermann.* ♦ *Eigentlich wollten wir um vier Uhr dort sein, aber wir hatten eine Panne.* **2.** strictly speaking, actually ◊ *Wenn ich ehrlich bin, hat er ja eigentlich Recht.*

ei·gent·lich² ['aeɡn̩tlɪç, 'aeɡəntlɪç] [part] **1.** *(qualifying a negative response)* really ◊ *Ich habe eigentlich keine Lust mitzukommen, aber ich überlege es mir noch.; (qualifying a positive response)* actually yes ◊ *„Gefällt es dir in Bonn?" — „Eigentlich schon, nur ein bisschen wenig los ist hier."* **2.** *(on second thoughts)* actually ◊ *Eigentlich ist es doch ganz schön hier.* **3.** *+subjunctive II (certainly, or expressing disappointment)* really ◊ *Inzwischen sollte sie eigentlich schon angekommen sein.* ♦ *Eigentlich hätte ich mir denken können, dass das nicht klappt.* **4.** *in questions (introducing a subject)* tell me ◊ *Wie spät ist es eigentlich?* ♦ *Was gibt es heute eigentlich zum Essen?* **5.** *in questions (expressing anger)* exactly ◊ *Was hast du dir eigentlich dabei gedacht?* ♦ *Wofür halten Sie sich eigentlich?*

② **Ei·gen·tum** ['aeɡn̩tu:m] das <-s> *no pl* **1.** property ◊ *privates Eigentum* ♦ *mein rechtmäßiges Eigentum* geistiges Eigentum intellectual property ⊖Besitz **2.** LAW ownership ◊ *Das Haus ist in das Eigentum der Bank übergegangen.* **3.** real estate ◊ *Mietwohnungen in Eigentum umwandeln*

Ei·gen·tü·mer ['aeɡn̩ty:mɐ] der <-s, ->, **Ei·gen·tü·me·rin** ['aeɡn̩ty:mərɪn] die <-, -nen> owner, proprietor ⊖Inhaber

Ei·gen·tums·woh·nung ['aeɡn̩tu:msvo:nʊŋ] die <-, -en> owner-occupied flat

ei·gen·wil·lig ['aeɡn̩vɪlɪç] [adj, adv] wilful(ly) ◊ *ein eigenwilliges Kind* ♦ *Sein Stil ist höchst eigenwillig.* ♦ *eigenwillig interpretiert/geformt/gestaltet*

eig·nen ['aeɡnən] [ref v] *+haben* sich für/zu etw. eignen be suited to/suitable for sth ◊ *Dieses Programm eignet sich gut zum Erstellen von Tabellen.* ♦ *Ich eigne mich wenig dafür/dazu, komplizierte Zusammenhänge zu erklären.* sich für jdn eignen be suitable for sb ◊ *Die Methode eignet sich besonders für Anfänger.* sich als jd/etw. eignen be suitable as sb/sth ◊ *Diese Geschichte eignet sich als Stoff für einen Roman.* ♦ *Eignet er sich als Trainer?* für/zu etw. geeignet sein be suitable for sth ◊ *Ist dieses Öl zum Braten geeignet?* ♦ *Es wird sich zeigen, ob sie für den Job geeignet ist.* als etw. geeignet sein be suitable as sth ◊ *Holz ist als Baumaterial für Schiffe hervorragend geeignet.* als jd geeignet sein be cut out to be sb ◊ *Ich bin als Lehrer nicht geeignet.* für jdn geeignet sein be suitable for sb ◊ *Dieser Film ist für Kinder unter 12 Jahren nicht geeignet.*

Eil·brief ['aelbri:f] der <-(e)s, -e> express letter ◊

etw. per/als Eilbrief schicken

② **Ei·le** ['aelə] die <-> *no pl* hurry, rush ◊ *Er drängte zur Eile.* ♦ *In der Eile habe ich viele Fehler gemacht.* in aller Eile hurriedly ◊ *Er hat mir in aller Eile das Nötigste erklärt.* in Eile sein be in a hurry ◊ *Ich kann jetzt nicht mit ihm reden, ich bin zu sehr in Eile.* keine Eile haben not be urgent ◊ *Der Auftrag hat keine große Eile.* ⊖Hast

ei·len ['aelən] [intr v] *+sein/haben* **1.** *+sein* hurry, rush ◊ *jdm zu Hilfe eilen* ♦ *nach der Arbeit schnell nach Hause eilen von ... zu ...* eilen go from one ... to another ◊ *Die Mannschaft eilte von Sieg zu Sieg.* ♦ *Ich eilte von Amt zu Amt.* **2.** *+haben* be urgent ◊ *Lass dir Zeit, es eilt nicht.*

ei·lig ['aelɪç] [adj, adv] urgent(ly) ◊ *ein eiliger Auftrag* ♦ *Ist der Brief sehr eilig?* ♦ *sich eilig auf den Weg machen* [adj] **1.** *only before ns* hurried, in a hurry ◊ *eine Zusammenfassung für den eiligen Leser* **2.** *(marriage, retreat)* rapid, quick ◊ *Nach ihrer eiligen Heirat verreisten sie sofort.* ⊛ *es (mit etw.) eilig haben* be in a hurry (with sth) ◊ *Plötzlich hatte er es mit der Arbeit mächtig eilig.*

Ei·mer ['aemɐ] der <-s, -> **1.** bucket ◊ *einen Eimer voll Wasser laufen lassen* **2.** bucket(ful) ◊ *ein Eimer Wasser zum Putzen* ⊛ *im Eimer sein (fam)* be up the spout

ein¹ [aen] [adv] *(of a switch)* ein/aus on/off ⊛ *bei jdm/irgendwo ein und aus gehen* come and go from sb's place/somewhere ◊ *Berühmte Stars gingen in ihrem Haus ein und aus.* nicht mehr/weder ein noch aus wissen be at your wits' end ◊ *Sie wusste vor Angst eine Zeit lang weder ein noch aus.*

② **ein²** [aen] [art] indefinite a, an ◊ *Ein Mann stand auf der anderen Straßenseite und starrte herüber.* ♦ *der Brief eines Journalisten/meiner Freundin* ♦ *Rufen Sie einen Arzt!* ♦ *Eine Batterie muss immer richtig herum eingelegt werden.* ♦ *etw. in einem Brief mitteilen* ♦ *Ist das ein echter Renoir?* ♦ *Er ist ein neuer Einstein.* ♦ *Den Job hat jetzt eine Frau Müller.* → box@Artikel

	m	f	nt	pl
nom	ein	eine	ein	-
acc	einen	eine	ein	-
dat	einem	einer	einem	-
gen	eines	einer	eines	-

ein³ [aen] [nmrl] **1.** one ◊ *Ein Fehler ist schon zu viel.* ♦ *Die Beschwerde nur einer Kundin hat keine Wirkung.* ♦ *ein Kind macht noch viel Lärm, eine Mark ist heute die Post einer ganzen Woche erledigt.* ♦ *Ein Kind macht noch viel Lärm, eine Mark ist heute die Post einer ganzen Woche erledigt.* **2.** *referring to a previously mentioned noun* der/die/das Eine ... one ◊ *Ich habe zwei Mäntel, eine ist blau, eine der braun.* ♦ *Die eine Route ist schöner, die andere dafür kürzer.* ⊛ *jds und Alles sein* be sb's whole world, sb's everything ◊ *Mein Sohn Leo ist mein Ein und Alles.* der/das ein(e) *some (people)* ◊ *„So ein Quatsch!", wird so jetzt der eine oder andere denken.* der/die/das ein(e) oder andere ... one or two ... ◊ *Ich werde noch die eine oder andere Möglichkeit ausprobieren.* **dasselbe sein** be one and the same thing ein und derselbe/dieselbe/dasselbe one and the same,

the very same ◊ *Man kann nicht zwei Dateien unter ein und demselben Namen abspeichern.* **in einem fort** continuously, all the time ◊ *Er redet in einem fort, ich kann es nicht mehr hören!* **in einem** in one ◊ *Dieses Gerät ist Kamera und Handy in einem.* **ein oder/bis zwei** one or two, a couple of ◊ *Ich war nur ein oder zwei Stunden weg.* **ein, zwei** one or two ◊ *Kannst du noch ein, zwei Minuten warten?*

ein|... [a̲e̲n] prefix **1.** into ◊ *in ein Land einreisen* etw. **eingravieren** engrave sth **2.** in ◊ *eine neue Festplatte einbauen* ♦ *Sie atmete tief ein.* **3.** *translation varies (occurrence, start of an action)* einschlafen fall asleep Ein Unglück ist eingetreten. A disaster has happened. **4.** *translation varies (expresses that sth/sb is encircled)* jdn einkreisen surround sb ein Buch einbinden bind a book **5.** *(expresses that sth is damaged)* ein Haus einreißen tear down a house etw. einschneiden cut sth, make an incision into sth

② **ei·nan·der** [a̲e̲'nande] pron one another, each other ◊ *Sie sind einander nie begegnet.* ♦ *Die Methoden ähneln einander sehr.* ⊖sich

ein|ar·bei·ten ['a̲e̲n|ˈa̲ɐba̲etn̩] <arbeitet ein, arbeitete ein, hat eingearbeitet> ref v sich einarbeiten get used to things ◊ *Nun, haben Sie sich bei uns schon eingearbeitet?* sich in etw. acc einarbeiten get into sth ◊ *sich in ein Thema einarbeiten* tr v **1.** etw. (in etw. acc) einarbeiten incorporate sth (into sth), include sth (in sth) ◊ *Sind die neuesten Ergebnisse schon in den Bericht eingearbeitet?; (fertilizer)* work sth into sth ◊ *Dünger in den Boden einarbeiten* **2.** jdn einarbeiten train sb ◊ *Sie hat ihre Nachfolgerin noch selbst eingearbeitet.*

② **Ein·bahn·stra·ße** ['a̲e̲nba̲ːnʃtraːsə] die <-, -n> **1.** one-way street ◊ *verkehrt herum in eine Einbahnstraße fahren* **2.** *(fig)* eine Einbahnstraße sein be a one-way process ◊ *Erfolgreiche Kommunikation ist keine Einbahnstraße.*

ein|bau·en ['a̲e̲nba̲ʊən] <baut ein, baute ein, hat eingebaut> tr v **1.** install ◊ *Er hat neue Fenster einbauen lassen.* ♦ *Sie mussten einen neuen Motor ins Auto einbauen.* in etw. dat eingebaut built into sth ◊ *ein in der Wand eingebauter Schrank* **2.** *(fig)* etw. (in etw. acc) einbauen incorporate sth (into sth) ◊ *Software mit eingebautem Kopierschutz* ♦ *Die Szene ist erst nachträglich in den Film eingebaut worden.*

ein|be·ru·fen ['a̲e̲nbəruːfn̩] <beruft ein, berief ein, hat einberufen> tr v **1.** *(a meeting, conference etc.)* call, convene ◊ *Auf Wunsch der Leiterin wurde eine Besprechung einberufen.; (a committee, commission)* convene; *(a parliament)* summon **2.** MIL jdn (zu etw.) einberufen call sb up (to sth) ◊ *Er wurde sofort nach der Lehre zur Bundeswehr einberufen.*

ein|be·zie·hen ['a̲e̲nbətsiːən] <bezieht ein, bezog ein, hat einbezogen> tr v etw./jdn (in etw. acc) (mit) einbeziehen include sth/sb (in sth) ◊ *Die Bürger müssen in die Planung mit einbezogen werden.*

ein|bil·den ['a̲e̲nbɪldn̩] <bildet sich ein, bildete sich ein, hat sich eingebildet> ref v **1.** sich dat etw. einbilden imagine sth ◊ *Ist das wirklich geschehen oder habe ich es mir bloß eingebildet?*

Er bildet sich ein, ein großer Künstler zu sein. He thinks he's a great artist. **2.** *(pej)* sich dat nichts auf etw. acc einbilden not be proud of sth ◊ *Auf den Sieg brauchst du dir gar nichts einzubilden, das ist nicht dein Verdienst.* sich dat etwas/viel auf etw. acc einbilden be proud of sth ◊ *Sie bildet sich viel darauf ein, studiert zu haben.*

ein|bin·den ['a̲e̲nbɪndn̩] <bindet ein, band ein, hat eingebunden> tr v **1.** etw./jdn (in etw. acc) einbinden integrate sth/sb (into sth) ◊ *Grafiken in ein Dokument einbinden* ♦ *Mehrere Länder wurden in das Airbus-Projekt eingebunden.* **2.** jdm den Arm/die Hand etc. einbinden bandage sb's arm/hand etc. **3.** etw. (in etw. acc) einbinden cover sth (with sth), protect sth (with sth) ◊ *Schulbücher (in Plastikfolie) einbinden*

Ein·blick ['a̲e̲nblɪk] der <-(e)s, -e> **1.** ein Einblick in etw. acc an insight into sth ◊ *Der Roman gibt/vermittelt einen Einblick in das Leben zu jener Zeit.* ⊖ein Eindruck von etw. **2.** Einblick in etw. acc access to sth ◊ *jdm Einblick in Unterlagen gewähren* ♦ *Die Steuerfahndung wollte Einblick in die Geschäftsbücher nehmen.* ⊖Einsicht **3.** der Einblick in etw. acc (the) view of sth ◊ *Vom obersten Stock aus hat man Einblick in den Klostergarten.* ⊖Einsicht

ein|bre·chen ['a̲e̲nbrɛçn̩] <bricht ein, brach ein, hat/ist eingebrochen> intr v **1.** +*sein* in etw. acc einbrechen break into sth ◊ *Ein Unbekannter ist letzte Nacht in das Museum eingebrochen.; (into a computer)* hack into sth **2.** +*haben* in etw. dat einbrechen break into sth ◊ *Es ist noch unklar, wer in der Schule eingebrochen hat.* **3.** +*haben/sein* bei jdm einbrechen break into sb's home ◊ *Aus Rache hat/ist er bei ihr eingebrochen und hat das Haus verwüstet.* **4.** +*sein (exchange rate, price, turnover etc.)* fall ◊ *Die Gewinne sind im letzten Quartal dramatisch eingebrochen.; (sportsman, performer)* wilt ◊ *In der zweiten Spielhälfte brach er konditionsmäßig schwer ein.* **5.** +*sein (roof, surface)* cave in ◊ *Das Dach ist unter der Last des Schnees eingebrochen.* Sie ist im/ins Eis eingebrochen. She fell through the ice. **6.** +*sein (night)* fall; *(winter)* set in

Ein·bruch ['a̲e̲nbrʊx] der <-(e)s, Einbrüche> **1.** burglary, break-in ◊ *Bei einem Einbruch in ein Privathaus wurden 5000 Euro gestohlen.* **2.** *(of prices)* fall, slump ◊ *ein Einbruch an der Börse/im Aktienmarkt* ♦ *ein Einbruch um 15 %* **3.** *(of winter, darkness)* Einbruch ... gen onset of sth; *(of the night)* setting in, beginning

ein|bür·gern ['a̲e̲nbʏrɡɐn] <bürgert ein, bürgerte ein, hat eingebürgert> tr v **1.** *mostly passive (a person)* naturalize ◊ *vor Antrag einbürgern* **2.** *(a plant, an animal, a word etc.)* introduce ◊ *eine bedrohte Tierart wieder einbürgern* ref v sich einbürgern become established ◊ *Dieser Begriff hat sich im Deutschen eingebürgert.* ♦ *Bei uns hat es sich eingebürgert, dass wir samstags in die Sauna gehen.*

ein|bü·ßen ['a̲e̲nbyːsn̩] <büßt ein, büßte ein, hat eingebüßt> tr v lose ◊ *Diese Frage hat nichts von ihrer Wichtigkeit eingebüßt.* intr v an etw. dat einbüßen decline in sth ◊ *an Popularität/Glaubwürdigkeit/Bedeutung einbüßen*

ein|che·cken ['a̲e̲ntʃɛkn̩] <checkt ein, checkte ein,

hat eingecheckt> [tr+intr v] check in ◇ *Die Passa-giere/Fluggäste können an diesem Schalter einche-cken.* ♦ *Wir warten darauf, eingecheckt zu werden.*
ein·deu·tig ['aɛndɔøtɪç] [adj, adv] unam-biguous(ly) ◇ *eine eindeutige Antwort* ♦ *Die Rechts-lage ist in diesem Fall eindeutig.* ♦ *Sie konnte den Täter eindeutig indentifizieren.*
ein|drin·gen ['aɛndrɪŋən] <dringt ein, drang ein, ist eingedrungen> [intr v] **1.** (in etw. [acc]) eindrin-gen penetrate (into sth) ◇ *Die Viren dringen durch offene Wunden in den Körper ein.* **2.** (in etw. [acc]) eindringen enter (sth), force your way in(to sth) ◇ *Der Entführer versuchte, ins Cockpit einzudringen.* ♦ *Durch das undichte Fenster dringt kalte Luft ein.* **3.** auf jdn eindringen go for sb ◇ *Sie drangen mit Fäusten auf ihn ein.*; *(impressions, questions)* besiege sb ◇ *Eine Flut von Eindrücken drang auf sie ein.*
② **Ein·druck** ['aɛndrʊk] der <-(e)s, Eindrücke> impres-sion ◇ *Die Reifen haben tiefe Eindrücke in der Erde hinterlassen.* ♦ *Der erste Eindruck täuscht oft.* ♦ *Ich habe den Eindruck, dass sie lügt.* ♦ *von der Reise vielfältige Eindrücke mitbringen* einen guten/ schlechten etc. Eindruck hinterlassen/machen leave/make a good/bad etc. impression ◇ *Auf mich macht das keinen überzeugenden Eindruck.* Eindruck auf jdn machen make an impression on sb ⊚ Eindruck machen be impressive ◇ *Eine so perfekte Organisation macht Eindruck.* **(bei jdm)** Eindruck schinden *(fam)* try to make a good impression (on sb) ◇ *Er versuchte, mit teuren Geschenken bei ihr Eindruck zu schinden.*
ei·ne ['aɛnə] *fem of* ein², ein³, einer
ein·ein·halb ['aɛn|aɛn'halp] [nmrl] one and a half → vier
ei·ner ['aɛnɐ] [indef pron] **1.** one ◇ *Einer von uns sollte es tun.* ♦ *Gehört das einem von euch?* ♦ *Hast du zwei Töchter oder nur eine?* ♦ *Du hast so viele Bonbons, gibst du mir eines ab?* du bist mir einer/eine you're a one ◇ *Du bist mir vielleicht einer! Das kannst du doch nicht ernst meinen!* einen sitzen haben have had one too many einen trinken gehen go for a drink ◇ *Wir gehen nachher einen trinken — kommst du mit?* **2.** a person, somebody ◇ *Seltsam! Wie soll das einer verstehen?* ♦ *Das muss einem doch gesagt werden!* ♦ *So etwas kann einen ziemlich deprimieren.* **3.** *referring to an unknown person* someone, somebody ◇ *Das muss einer hier verloren haben.* ♦ *Wehe, du erzählst das einem/einer!* ⊖jemand **4.** *in phrases* eine/eins one ◇ *jdm eine/eins reinhauen/verpassen* ♦ *jdm eine kleben* ♦ *eine/eins auf die Nase kriegen*

	m	f	nt	pl
nom	einer	eine	eines	-
acc	einen	eine	eines	-
dat	einem	einer	einem	-
gen	-	-	-	-

ei·ner·seits ['aɛnɐzaɛts] [adv] einerseits ..., ande-rerseits ... on the one hand ..., on the other (hand) ... ◇ *Einerseits gefällt mir das Auto sehr gut, andererseits ist es zu teuer.*
ei·nes ['aɛnəs] *neut of* einer
② **ein·fach¹** ['aɛnfax] [adj, adv] **1.** easy(-ily), simple (-ply) ◇ *eine einfache Lösung* ♦ *Die Bedienung des*

CD-Spielers ist ganz einfach. ♦ *Die Aufgabe ist einfach zu lösen.* ♦ *Das ist nicht so einfach, wie es sich sagt.* ⊖leicht ⊖schwierig **2.** simple(-ply), modest(-ly) ◇ *ein einfaches Dasein führen* ♦ *einfach und bescheiden leben* [adj] **1.** *only before ns (ticket)* single ◇ *Eine einfache Fahrkarte nach Berlin, bitte.* **2.** *only before ns (worker, soldier, people)* ordinary ◇ *aus einfachen Verhältnissen kommen* ⊖normal **3.** *(clothes, meal)* plain ◇ *Der Schnitt des Kleides ist einfach und elegant.* ♦ *ein einfaches Abendessen aus Brot und Käse; (life, pleasures)* simple ◇ *die einfachen Dinge des Lebens* **4.** *(knot)* simple ◇ *ein einfacher Knoten; (bookkeeping)* single-entry eine einfache Mehrheit a simple majority ⊛ es einfach haben (mit jdm) have it easy (with sb), have an easy time (with sb) ◇ *Sie hat es nicht einfach (mit ihrem Bruder).*
② **ein·fach²** ['aɛnfax] [part] simply, just ◇ *Ich finde das einfach toll!* ♦ *Ich habe es schlicht und einfach vergessen.* ♦ *Probier es doch einfach mal aus!* ⊖wirklich
② **Ein·fahrt** ['aɛnfaːrt] die <-, -en> **1.** entrance, entry ◇ *Einfahrt freihalten!* ⊖Ausfahrt **2.** *no pl* Einfahrt (in etw. [acc]) entry (to sth) ◇ *Dem Tanker wurde die Einfahrt in den Hafen verwehrt.* ♦ *Einfahrt verboten!; (of a train)* arrival (at sth) ◇ *Vorsicht bei Einfahrt des Zuges!* ⊖Ausfahrt
Ein·fall ['aɛnfal] der <-(e)s, Einfälle> **1.** idea ◇ *einen Einfall haben* ♦ *Mir kam der Einfall, ihn mit einer Party zu überraschen.* ⊖Idee **2.** MIL der Einfall (in etw. [acc]) the invasion (of sth) ◇ *der Einfall der Mongolen in Ungarn*
② **ein|fal·len** ['aɛnfalən] <fällt ein, fiel ein, ist einge-fallen> [intr v] **1.** etw. fällt jdm (wieder) ein sb remembers sth ◇ *Ist dir eingefallen, wo du den Schlüssel hingelegt hast?* ♦ *Ihr Name will mir einfach nicht einfallen.* **2.** *(idea, plan)* etw. fällt jdm ein sth occurs to sb ◇ *Mir ist eingefallen, dass ich ihn mal besuchen könnte.* ♦ *Fällt dir nichts Besseres ein, als mich von der Arbeit abzuhalten?* sich [dat] etw. einfallen lassen think of sth ◇ *Wir müssen uns etwas einfallen lassen, wie wir ihn überlisten können.* **3.** (in etw. [acc]) einfallen invade (sth) ◇ *20 Bewaffnete fielen in das Dorf ein.* **4.** *(roof, building etc.)* collapse ◇ *Mein Kar-tenhaus ist eingefallen!* ⊖einstürzen → eingefal-len
ein|fan·gen ['aɛnfaŋən] <fängt ein, fing ein, hat eingefangen> [tr v] **1.** catch, capture ◇ *Straßenkat-zen einfangen und ins Tierheim bringen* **2.** *(fam) (an illness, sth unpleasant)* sich [dat] etw. einfangen catch sth ◇ *Mir geht's gar nicht gut, ich fürchte, ich hab mir eine Grippe eingefangen.; (a smack, punishment)* head for sth ◇ *Wenn du so weitermachst, fängst du dir eine saftige Ohrfeige ein.; (a goal)* concede sth ◇ *Leider fingen sie sich dann noch ein Gegentor ein.*
ein·far·big ['aɛnfaʁbɪç] [adj] *no comp/superl* (in) all one colo(u)r, (in) all one color ◇ *ein einfarbi-ges Kleid* ♦ *Sein Hemd ist einfarbig.* [adv] in one colo(u)r, (in) a uniform colo(u)r ◇ *einfarbig gestrichen* eine einfarbig weiße Bluse a plain white blouse
② **Ein·fluss** ['aɛnflʊs] der <-es, Einflüsse> *most sing* influence ◇ *an Einfluss gewinnen/verlieren* ♦ *Er*

A B C D E F G H I J K L M N O P Q R S T U V W X Y Z

steht unter Petras Einfluss. ♦ *unter dem Einfluss von Alkohol* ♦ *Das hat keinen Einfluss auf meine Entscheidung.* ♦ *Seine Freunde üben einen positiven Einfluss auf ihn aus.* Einfluss nehmen gain influence Einfluss auf jdn/etw. nehmen influence sb/sth

ein|frie·ren ['aɛnfriːrən] <friert ein, fror ein, hat/ist eingefroren> [tr v] +*haben (also fig)* freeze ◊ *Bohnen kochen und einfrieren* ♦ *ein Konto einfrieren; (relations)* suspend ◊ *Nach dem Putsch fror die EU sämtliche Kontakte zu dem Land ein.; (plans)* put on hold [intr v] +*sein* freeze ◊ *Die Leiche war in einem Eisblock eingefroren.; (ships)* become ice-bound

ein|fü·gen ['aɛnfyːgn̩] <fügt ein, fügte ein, hat eingefügt> [tr v] insert ◊ *eine Leerzeile einfügen etw. in etw.* [acc] einfügen insert sth into sth ◊ *eine Klausel in einen Vertrag einfügen* ⊖einsetzen [ref v] sich (in etw. [acc]) einfügen fit in (with sth), adapt (to sth) ◊ *Das neue Rathaus fügt sich harmonisch ins Stadtbild ein.* ♦ *Sie kann sich nur schwer (in die neue Umgebung) einfügen.*

Ein·fuhr ['aɛnfuːɐ] die <–, –en> import ◊ *die illegale Einfuhr raubkopierter Software* ♦ *Die Einfuhren aus Polen nach Deutschland haben zugenommen.* ⊖Import ⊖Ausfuhr

ein|füh·ren ['aɛnfyːrən] <führt ein, führte ein, hat eingeführt> [tr v] **1.** etw. (aus Deutschland/den USA/der Schweiz etc.) einführen import sth (from Germany/the USA/Switzerland etc.) ◊ *Das Gerät wurde aus Japan eingeführt.* etw. (nach Deutschland/in die USA/in die Schweiz etc.) einführen import sth (to Germany/the USA/Switzerland etc.) ◊ *Irland führt Butter nach Deutschland ein.* ⊖ausführen **2.** *(legislation, a procedure etc.)* introduce ◊ *die Todesstrafe/Studiengebühren/eine neue Steuer einführen* ⊖abschaffen **3.** *(shares)* float ◊ *Die Aktie wird nächsten Monat an der Börse eingeführt.* **4.** *(a catheter, probe etc.)* etw. (in etw. [acc]) einführen insert sth (into sth) ◊ *einen Schlauch durch die Speiseröhre in den Magen einführen* **5.** *(into a family, high society etc.)* jdn in etw. [acc] einführen introduce sb (in)to sth ◊ *auf dem Ball in die feine Gesellschaft eingeführt werden; (explain a new system or task)* familiarize sb with sth ◊ *Würden Sie mich in das System/meine neuen Pflichten einführen?* jdn ins Amt einführen inaugurate sb ◊ *Die neue Kanzlerin wurde gestern ins Amt eingeführt.* **6.** *(a company, goods)* etw. (irgendwo) gut/schlecht einführen establish/fail to establish sth (somewhere) ◊ *ein neues Produkt gut einführen* [ref v] sich (irgendwo) gut/schlecht einführen make a good/bad impression (somewhere) ◊ *Pass auf, dass du dich nicht gleich schlecht einführst.*

ein|fül·len ['aɛnfʏlən] <füllt ein, füllte ein, hat eingefüllt> [tr v] etw. in etw. [acc] einfüllen put sth into sth ◊ *Keine heiße Asche in den Mülleimer einfüllen!; (liquids)* pour sth into sth ◊ *Er füllte ihr Wasser ins Glas ein.*

Ein·ga·be ['aɛngaːbə] die <–, –n> POL petition ◊ *eine Eingabe beim Verfassungsgericht/an die Menschenrechtskommission* ⊖Antrag

② **Ein·gang** ['aɛngaŋ] der <–(e)s, Eingänge> **1.** entrance ◊ *eine Wohnung mit separatem Eingang* ♦ *getrennte Eingänge für Kunden und*

Personal ♦ *am Eingang der Speiseröhre/des Magens* ⊖Ausgang **2.** *no pl (of deliveries, post, payments, orders)* der Eingang (... [gen]/von etw.) (the) receipt (of sth) ◊ *Sie erhalten nach Eingang Ihrer Bestellung eine Bestätigung.* ♦ *Bei verspätetem Eingang der Zahlung wird eine Gebühr erhoben.* **3.** *most pl* incoming mail; *(of deliveries)* goods received; *(on a bank account)* amounts credited ◊ *Kontoauszüge geben einen Überblick über alle Eingänge und Abbuchungen.* **4.** *most pl* TECHN *(of an appliance)* input ◊ *analoge/digitale Eingänge; (of a computer)* port ⊖Ausgang ⊛ Eingang finden in etw. [acc] be included in sth ◊ *Ihre Ideen werden in die Projektplanung Eingang finden.*

ein|ge·ben ['aɛngeːbm̩] <gibt ein, gab ein, hat eingegeben> [tr v] **1.** etw. (in etw. [acc]) eingeben enter sth (into sth), key sth in(to sth) ◊ *seine PIN-Nummer ins Handy eingeben* ♦ *einen Suchbegriff in die Suchmaschine eingeben* **2.** *(lofty) (thoughts, feelings etc.)* jdm etw. eingeben put sth into sb's head ◊ *Er behauptete, diese Idee habe ihm der Teufel eingegeben.* **3.** MED *(medicine, drugs)* jdm etw. eingeben administer sth to sb, give sb sth ◊ *Geben Sie dem Kind 20 Tropfen von dem Mittel ein.*

ein·ge·bil·det ['aɛngəbɪldət] *past p of* einbilden [adj] **1.** *(illness)* imaginary; *(pregnancy)* false ◊ *ein eingebildeter Kranker* a hypochondriac **2.** *(pej)* conceited ◊ *ein eingebildeter Typ* ♦ *Warum ist sie bloß so furchtbar eingebildet?* ⊖bescheiden

Ein·ge·bo·re·ne ['aɛngəboːrənə] der/die <–n, die Eingeborenen> *but: ein Eingeborener/eine Eingeborene* native box@ Substantivierung

ein·ge·fal·len ['aɛngəfalən] *past p of* einfallen [adj] hollow, sunken ◊ *eingefallene Wangen haben*

ein|ge·hen ['aɛngeːən] <geht ein, ging ein, ist eingegangen> [tr v] **1.** *(risks, chances)* take ◊ *ein großes Wagnis eingehen; (a compromise, an obligation)* accept ◊ *Bei der Partnerwahl gehe ich keine Kompromisse ein.; (a bet)* have ◊ *Ich gehe jede Wette ein, dass das stimmt.* **2.** *(a coalition, partnership)* etw. (mit jdm/etw.) eingehen enter into sth (with sb/sth) ◊ *strategische Allianzen eingehen* eine Verbindung mit etw. eingehen come into contact with sth ◊ *Wenn Eisen mit Sauerstoff eine Verbindung eingeht, entsteht Rost.* [intr v] **1.** *(lofty) (into history, the annals etc.)* in etw. [acc] eingehen go down in sth ◊ *Der Fall ist in die Kriminalgeschichte eingegangen.* **2.** *(to needs, demands, views)* auf etw./jdn eingehen pay attention to sth/sb ◊ *In kleinen Klassen kann der Lehrer besser auf die einzelnen Kinder eingehen.; (to suggestions, wishes)* auf etw. [acc] eingehen be responsive to sth ◊ *Ist er auf deinen Vorschlag eingegangen?* auf alle Einzelheiten eingehen go into every minute detail **3.** *(calls, correspondence, deliveries etc.)* (bei jdm/etw.) eingehen be received (at sb's premises/at sth) ◊ *Es sind bereits Spenden in Höhe von einer Million Euro eingegangen.* ♦ *Bei der Polizei ist eine Bombendrohung eingegangen.* **4.** *(animal, plant, fig also: person)* die ◊ *Die Rosen sind eingegangen, weil sie keiner gegossen hat.* ♦ *Unser Hund hat etwas Giftiges gefressen und ist eingegangen.* ♦ *Ich geh noch ein vor Hitze/Langeweile.* ⊖umkommen **5.** *(fam) (business, firm)* fold, shut up shop ◊ *Die Kneipe*

an der Ecke ist eingegangen. **6.** *(clothes)* shrink ◊ *Der Pullover ist in der Wäsche ziemlich eingegangen.* ⊖*einlaufen* ● **etw. will jdm nicht eingehen** *(fam)* sb is not able to comprehend sth ◊ *Es will ihm nicht eingehen, wie das passieren konnte.*

ein·ge·hend ['aenge:ənt] *pres p of* eingehen [adj] *only before ns* detailed, in-depth ◊ *eine eingehende Analyse/Untersuchung* ⊖gründlich ⊖oberflächlich [adv] in detail, in depth ◊ *einen Vorschlag eingehend prüfen* ♦ *Ich habe mich mit dem Thema/Fall eingehend befasst.* ⊖gründlich, ausführlich ⊖oberflächlich

ein·ge·schrie·ben ['aengəʃri:bm̩] *past p of* einschreiben [adj] *no comp/superl, only before ns* registered ◊ *Die Kündigung wurde als eingeschriebener Brief geschickt.*

ein·ge·ste·hen ['aengəʃte:ən] <gesteht ein, gestand ein, hat eingestanden> [tr v] (jdm/sich) etw. eingestehen admit sth (to sb/yourself) ◊ *Er musste seine Niederlage eingestehen.* ♦ *Sie wollte sich nicht eingestehen, versagt zu haben.* ⊖etw. zugeben ⊖etw. leugnen

ein|gie·ßen ['aengi:sn̩] <gießt ein, goss ein, hat eingegossen> [tr+intr v] (jdm/sich) (etw.) eingießen pour (sb/yourself) (sth) ◊ *Ich goss mir ein Glas Bier ein.* ♦ *Kannst du bitte noch mal (Tee) eingießen?* ⊖einschenken

ein|glie·dern ['aengli:dɐn] <gliedert ein, gliederte ein, hat eingegliedert> [ref v] sich (in etw. [acc]) eingliedern fit into sth, integrate yourself (into sth) ◊ *Er gliederte sich nur schwer (in die Klassengemeinschaft) ein.* ⊖sich einordnen [tr v] jdn/etw. (in etw. [acc]) eingliedern integrate sb/sth (into sth) ◊ *Wir versuchen, das neue Verfahren in den Produktionsprozess einzugliedern.*

ein|grei·fen ['aengraefn̩] <greift ein, griff ein, hat eingegriffen> [intr v] (in etw. [acc]) eingreifen intervene (in sth) ◊ *Soll die UNO in die Kämpfe eingreifen?* ♦ *Man hätte früher eingreifen müssen, um das Unglück zu verhindern.; (upon rights, freedom)* in etw. [acc] eingreifen impinge on sth, intrude upon sth

Ein·griff ['aengrɪf] der <-(e)s, -e> **1.** MED operation ◊ *einen medizinischen Eingriff vornehmen* ein Eingriff an etw. [dat] an operation on sth ◊ *Sie musste sich einem Eingriff am Magen unterziehen.* ⊖Operation **2.** Eingriff (in etw. [acc]) intervention (in sth), interference (in sth); *(on sb's privacy)* intrusion (on/into sth) ◊ *Das ist ein schwerwiegender Eingriff in die Pressefreiheit/meine Privatsphäre!*

ein·hei·misch ['aenhaemɪʃ] [adj] *no comp/superl* **1.** indigenous ◊ *einheimische Tierarten* irgendwo einheimisch sein be indigenous to somewhere ◊ *eine Pflanze, die in den Hochalpen einheimisch ist* **2.** *(products, firms, businesses)* local ◊ *Er zieht die einheimische Küche exotischen Gerichten vor.* *Der Koch hier ist einheimisch.* The cook here is a local.

Ein·heit ['aenhaet] die <-, -en> **1.** *no pl* unity ◊ *die politische Einheit der EU-Länder* **2.** *no pl (of several things, people)* whole ◊ *Denken und Fühlen bilden eine Einheit.* ♦ *Der Elternbeirat trat der Schulleitung als geschlossene Einheit gegenüber.* **3.** *(part of a whole)* unit ◊ *militäri-*

sche Einheiten ♦ *Die Firma ist in organisatorische Einheiten gegliedert.* ♦ *In welcher Einheit sind die Entfernungen angegeben — in Kilometern oder Meilen?*

ein|ho·len ['aenho:lən] <holt ein, holte ein, hat eingeholt> [tr v] **1.** *(permission, advice)* obtain, get ◊ *bei jdm eine Erlaubnis/Genehmigung einholen* ♦ *Angebote/den Rat eines Fachmannes einholen* **2.** jdn/etw. einholen catch up with sb/sth ◊ *Die Polizei holte den fliehenden Einbrecher ein.* **3.** *(the net)* haul in ◊ *Sie holte die Leine ein und hatte einen Fisch am Haken.; (a flag, sail)* lower; *(the anchor)* weigh

ei·nig ['aenɪç] [adj] *no comp/superl, not before ns* **1.** sich einig sein be in agreement ◊ *Wir waren uns weitgehend einig.* ♦ *Sie waren sich völlig einig, dass es nicht so weitergehen kann.* sich über etw. [acc] einig sein agree on sth ◊ *Man ist sich über die Ziele der Aktion einig.* sich in etw. [dat] einig sein in agreement about sth ◊ *Die Regierung wird sich in diesem Punkt einig sein.* **2.** sich [dat] mit jdm (über etw. [acc]) einig sein agree with sb (on sth) ◊ *Ich bin mir ausnahmsweise mal einig mit ihr.* ♦ *Er ist sich mit der Opposition über die Notwendigkeit von Reformen einig.* sie sind sich (über etw. [acc]) einig they agree (on sth), they are in agreement (about sth) ◊ *Wir waren uns weitgehend (über die Ziele der Aktion) einig.* ♦ *Innerhalb der Regierung ist man sich in den meisten Punkten einig.* **3.** sich [dat] (mit jdm) (über etw. [acc])/in etw. [dat] einig werden reach an agreement (with sb) (on sth), agree (with sb) (on sth) ◊ *Seid ihr euch endlich einig geworden?* ♦ *Ich bin mir schnell mit ihr einig geworden, wer von uns schuld ist.* ♦ *Wir konnten uns über die Modalitäten nicht einig werden.* ♦ *Sie wurde sich mit ihm in den wichtigsten Punkten einig.*

⑦ **ei·ni·ge¹** ['aenɪgə] [det] indefinite **1.** some, a few ◊ *Ich habe einige Male, ihn anzurufen.* ⊖ein paar **2.** *before countable ns (esp emph)* many, a lot ◊ *Da sind aber nicht nur ein paar, sondern einige Fehler drin!* ⊖etliche **3.** *before uncountable ns (esp emph)* quite a bit of, a lot of ◊ *Das hat mich einige Mühe/Zeit gekostet.* ⊖ziemliche

⑦ **ei·ni·ge²** ['aenɪgə] [indef pron] some, a few ◊ *Einige wollen schon nach Hause.* ♦ *Einige der Spieler mussten ausgewechselt werden.*

ei·ni·gen ['aenɪgn̩] [ref v] +haben sich mit jdm (auf/über etw. [acc])einigen come to an agreement with sb (on sth) ◊ *Konntest du dich mit ihm einigen?* ♦ *Ich habe mich mit ihr darauf geeinigt, dass sie anfängt.* sie einigen sich they find an agreement ◊ *Nach langem Streit einigten sich die Kontrahenten* ♦ *Wir einigten uns auf einen Kompromiss.* ♦ *Habt ihr euch über den Preis geeinigt?; (in a court case, financial dispute)* settle ◊ *Die Kontrahenten konnten sich außergerichtlich einigen.* [tr v] +haben *(countries, people)* unite ◊ *Europa einigen* ♦ *Die Bedrohung von außen einigte die zerstrittenen Parteien.*

ei·ni·ger·ma·ßen ['aenɪgɐ'ma:sn̩] [adv] **1.** relatively ◊ *Mit dem Ergebnis können wir einigermaßen zufrieden sein.* ♦ *das Haus einigermaßen in Ordnung halten* ⊖ziemlich **2.** *used elliptically (as a reply to a question)* sort of, so-so ◊ *„Hast du*

das jetzt verstanden?" — „Na ja, so einigermaßen."
♦ *„Wie gehts ihm denn?" — „Wieder einigerma-*
ßen."

ei·ni·ges ['aɛnɪgɛs] [indef pron] *(esp emph)* a thing
or two, one or two things ◊ *Die Reise war toll, ich*
habe einiges zu erzählen! Das wird dich aber
einiges kosten! That'll cost you (a bit)!

Ein·kauf ['aɛnkaɔf] der <-(e)s, Einkäufe>
1. shopping ◊ *seine Einkäufe erledigen/machen* ♦
der Einkauf im Supermarkt/auf dem Markt; (goods
bought also) shopping, purchase ◊ *Hilfst du mir,*
die Einkäufe reinzutragen? **2.** TRADE buying department ◊ *im Einkauf tätig sein/arbeiten* ⊝Vertrieb

② **ein|kau·fen** ['aɛnkaɔfn̩] <kauft ein, kaufte ein, hat
eingekauft> [intr v] shop ◊ *Dort kann man gut/*
günstig einkaufen. einkaufen gehen/fahren go
shopping Warst du schon einkaufen? Have you
already been shopping? [tr v] **1.** buy ◊ *Hast du Brot*
eingekauft? ♦ *Weihnachtsgeschenke einkaufen*
⊝verkaufen **2.** TRADE *(for a company, state etc.)*
purchase ◊ *auf den Weltmärkten Rohstoffe*
einkaufen ♦ *Ägypten kauft große Mengen Weizen in*
den USA ein. ⊝verkaufen **3.** SPORT *(a sportsman,*
trainer) sign ◊ *Der Verein hat zwei brasilianische*
Spieler eingekauft. [ref v] sich in etw. [acc]
einkaufen buy your way into sth ◊ *Er hat sich in*
eine betreute Seniorenwohnanlage eingekauft.;
(into a company) buy into sth ◊ *Sie hat sich mit*
20 000 Euro in die Firma eingekauft.

② **Ein·kom·men** ['aɛnkɔmən] das <-s, -> *most sing*
income ◊ *ein gutes/schlechtes Einkommen haben*
♦ *Familien mit geringem Einkommen* ⊝Einkünfte

Ein·kunft ['aɛnkʊnft] die <-, Einkünfte> *most pl*
income ◊ *Einkünfte aus selbstständiger/nichtselbst-*
ständiger Tätigkeit

② **ein|la·den** ['aɛnlaːdn̩] <lädt ein, lud ein, hat einge-
laden> [tr v] **1.** *(to a party, an event)* jdn (zu etw.
[dat]) einladen invite sb (to sth) ◊ *Ich möchte dich*
zu meiner Geburtstagsparty einladen. ♦ *Wir sind*
zum Essen eingeladen. ♦ *Sie ist heute Abend einge-*
laden. **2.** *(for a drink)* jdn (auf etw. [acc])
einladen invite sb (for sth) ◊ *Darf ich Sie auf*
einen Kaffee einladen?; (to the cinema, theatre, a
café etc.) jdn (in etw. [acc]) einladen invite sb (to
sth) ◊ *Er hat mich ins Restaurant eingeladen.*
3. etw. (in etw. [acc]) einladen load sth (into sth)
◊ *Hast du alles (in den Kofferraum) eingeladen?*

Ein·la·dung ['aɛnla:dʊŋ] die <-, -en> invitation ♦
Ich habe heute eine Einladung zu einer Party
bekommen. ♦ *eine Einladung zum Vorstellungsge-*
spräch

Ein·la·ge ['aɛnla:gə] die <-, -n> *most sing*
1. *small pieces of meat, vegetable or dumplings in*
clear soup ◊ *Als Vorspeise gibt es klare Suppe mit*
Einlage. **2.** *most pl* FIN deposit ◊ *Die Einlagen auf*
dem Konto betragen 2000 Euro. ⊝Guthaben
3. *most pl* MED insole ◊ *Einlagen für ein Paar*
Schuhe anfertigen lassen **4.** interlude ◊ *eine akro-*
batische Einlage

ein|las·sen ['aɛnlasn̩] <lässt ein, ließ ein, hat ein-
gelassen> [tr v] **1.** Wasser (in etw. [acc]) einlassen
fill (sth) with water ◊ *Wasser in einen Eimer*
einlassen Badewasser/ein Bad einlassen run a
bath **2.** etw. (in etw. [acc]) einlassen set sth (into
sth) ◊ *Die Badewanne ist in den Boden eingelas-*
sen. **3.** jdn (in etw. [acc]) einlassen let sb in(to

somewhere), admit sb (to sth) ◊ *Sie können nicht*
hereinkommen. Ich soll niemanden einlassen.
[ref v] *(pej)* **1.** sich auf etw./jdn einlassen get
involved with sth/sb ◊ *Er hätte sich nie auf das*
Geschäft einlassen dürfen. **2.** *(sexually)* sich mit
jdm einlassen get involved with sb, get mixed up
with sb ◊ *Sie hat sich mit einem verheirateten*
Mann eingelassen!

ein|lau·fen ['aɛnlaɔfn̩] <läuft ein, lief ein, hat/ist
eingelaufen> [intr v] +*sein* **1.** etw. läuft in etw.
[acc] ein sth runs into sth ◊ *Das Wasser läuft in*
das Becken ein. etw. einlaufen lassen run sth ◊
Ich habe gerade Spülwasser einlaufen lassen.
Badewasser/ein Bad einlaufen lassen run a bath
2. *(clothes)* einlaufen shrink (in the wash) ◊ *Woll-*
pullover laufen in der Maschine oft ein. ⊝eingehen
3. im Hafen einlaufen come into/enter the harbour
◊ *Täglich laufen viele Schiffe im Hamburger Hafen*
ein. ⊝ankommen **4.** *(train)* come in ◊ *Der Regio-*
nalexpress nach Hannover läuft gerade ein.
⊝ankommen ⊝abfahren **5.** SPORT jd läuft (ins
Stadion/in die Arena etc.) ein sb comes in to(the
stadium/arena etc.) (ins Ziel) einlaufen finish ◊
Das Pferd, auf das ich gewettet hatte, ist an
zweiter Stelle eingelaufen. [tr v] +*haben* wear in ◊
Schuhe einlaufen [ref v] +*haben* SPORT jd läuft sich
ein sb warms up ◊ *Vor dem Wettkampf liefen sich*
die Athletinnen ein.

ein|le·ben ['aɛnle:bm̩] <lebt sich ein, lebte sich
ein, hat sich eingelebt> [ref v] sich einleben settle
down ◊ *Er hat sich hier immer noch nicht richtig*
eingelebt. sich in einem Haus/einer Wohnung
einleben settle in in a house/flat ◊ *Habt ihr euch in*
der neuen Wohnung schon eingelebt?

ein|lei·ten ['aɛnlaɛtn̩] <leitet ein, leitete ein, hat
eingeleitet> [tr v] **1.** *(a subject, talk, book)*
introduce ◊ *Ein kurzer Überblick über das Thema*
leitet den Vortrag ein. etw. in ein Gespräch einleiten start
a conversation **2.** *(lofty)* etw. (gegen jdn) einleiten
institute sth (against sb), initiate sth (against sb) ◊
Der Staatsanwalt hat das Verfahren gegen die
Firma eingeleitet. ♦ *eine Untersuchung gegen jdn*
einleiten ⊝veranlassen **3.** *(into rivers, lakes)* etw.
in etw. [acc] einleiten discharge sth into sth ◊ *ver-*
schmutztes Wasser in einen Fluss einleiten

ein|lö·sen ['aɛnløːzn̩] <löst ein, löste ein, hat
eingelöst> [tr v] **1.** etw. (gegen etw.) einlösen
redeem sth ◊ *einen Gutschein einlösen* ♦
Die Bonusmeilen können Sie gegen Flüge oder
Prämien einlösen.; (a coupon, voucher) cash in
sth (for sth) ◊ *einen Scheck einlösen* cash a cheque
2. keep ◊ *ein Versprechen einlösen; (an IOU,*
debts) pay ◊ *einen Schuldschein einlösen*

② **ein·mal¹** ['aɛnma:l] [adv] **1.** once ◊ *Das macht er nur*
einmal und dann nie wieder. ♦ *Ich war erst einmal*
in Spanien. noch einmal once again ⊝mehrmals
◉ **einmal ist keinmal** once doesn't count, once
won't hurt einmal und nie wieder *(fam, emph)*
never again **auf einmal 1.** suddenly ◊ *Auf einmal*
fing es an zu regnen. **2.** in one go ◊ *Hast du*
wirklich alles auf einmal aufgegessen?

ein·mal² ['aɛnma:l] [part] unstressed *(abbr* mal*)*
1. *(in the future)* some day ◊ *Ich möchte einmal*
(später) einmal Ärztin werden. **2.** *(in the past)*
once ◊ *Hier lebten einmal Römer. Warst du schon*
einmal in Portugal? Have you ever been to

A B C D E F G H I J K L M N O P Q R S T U V W X Y Z

Portugal? ⊛ **endlich einmal, jetzt einmal** finally ◊ *Würdest du mir endlich einmal erklären, was hier los ist?* **erst einmal** first ◊ *Jetzt lass uns erst einmal frühstücken.* **nicht einmal** not even ◊ *Er kann nicht einmal richtig lesen.*

ein·ma·lig [ˈaenmaːlɪç] [adj] **1.** *no comp/superl* unique, single ◊ *eine einmalige Gelegenheit* ♦ *Das Angebot ist einmalig!* **2.** fantastic ◊ *Der Film war wirklich einmalig!* ⊝toll [adv] **1.** once ◊ *Die Gebühr ist einmalig zu bezahlen.* **2.** *(fam)* extremely ◊ *Das schmeckt einmalig gut!* ⊝total

ein|mi·schen [ˈaenmɪʃn̩] <mischt sich ein, mischte sich ein, hat sich eingemischt> [ref v] sich (in etw. [acc]) einmischen interfere (in sth) ◊ *Misch dich nicht ein — das geht dich nichts an!* ♦ *sich in anderer Leute Angelegenheiten einmischen* sich in eine Schlägerei einmischen get involved in a brawl

ein|neh·men [ˈaenneːmən] <nimmt ein, nahm ein, hat eingenommen> [tr v] **1.** take, earn ◊ *Heute haben wir 2 000 Euro eingenommen.* ⊝ausgeben **2.** *(lofty)* jdn für sich einnehmen win sb over jdn für etw. einnehmen win sb over to sth ◊ *Sie konnte ihn für ihre Position zu diesem Thema einnehmen.* von etw. eingenommen sein be taken with sth ◊ *Er ist von dieser Theorie sehr eingenommen.* **3.** *(fig) (a point of view)* adopt ◊ *Er nimmt in dieser Diskussion einen sehr harten Standpunkt ein.* **4.** *(medication)* etw. (gegen etw.) einnehmen take sth (for sth) ◊ *eine Tablette gegen Kopfschmerzen einnehmen* ⊝nehmen **5.** eine Position einnehmen take a position seine Position einnehmen take your place/position ◊ *Haben alle Mitspieler ihre Position eingenommen?* **6.** MIL *(a town, country)* capture, occupy ◊ *Die Stadt ist vom Feind eingenommen worden.*

⊛ **(sehr) von sich eingenommen sein** *(pej)* be full of yourself

ein|ord·nen [ˈaenʔɔˀdnən] <ordnet ein, ordnete ein, hat eingeordnet> [tr v] **1.** file Bücher in ein Regal einordnen put books on a shelf (in the right order) **2.** etw./jdn einordnen classify sth/sb jd weiß nicht, wo er jdn einordnen soll sb can't place sb's face [ref v] **1.** *(in traffic)* sich (links/rechts etc.) einordnen get in(to the right-hand/left-hand) lane sich in eine Schlange einordnen join a queue **2.** *(a team, group)* sich in etw. [acc] einordnen integrate into sth ◊ *Der neue Angestellte hat sich gut in das Team eingeordnet.* ⊝sich eingliedern

② **ein|pa·cken** [ˈaenpakn̩] <packt ein, packte ein, hat eingepackt> [tr v] **1.** *(a present)* etw. (in etw. [acc]) einpacken wrap sth (in sth) ◊ *Ich habe das Geschenk schon eingepackt.; (goods)* pack sth (in sth) ◊ *Die Gläser werden in Kartons eingepackt.* **2.** jdn gut/warm (in etw. [acc]) einpacken wrap sb up well/warmly (in sth) sich einpacken wrap yourself up ◊ *Bei diesen Temperaturen muss man sich gut einpacken.*

⊛ **jd kann einpacken** *(fam)* sb has had it ◊ *Wenn er die Prüfung wieder nicht besteht, kann er einpacken.*

ein|par·ken [ˈaenpaˀkn̩] <parkt ein, parkte ein, hat eingeparkt> [intr v] park, get into a parking space rückwärts in eine Lücke einparken reverse into a (parking) space

ein|pla·nen [ˈaenplaːnən] <plant ein, plante ein,

hat eingeplant> [tr v] **1.** etw. in etw. [dat] einplanen include sth in (the plan for) sth etw. für etw. einplanen schedule sth for sth ◊ *Für die Arbeit habe ich zwei Monate eingeplant.; (in shift work)* jdn für etw. einplanen schedule sb for sth ◊ *Er ist für die Nachtschicht eingeplant.* **2.** allow for ◊ *Den Stau hatte ich natürlich nicht eingeplant.*

ein|prä·gen [ˈaenprɛːgn̩] <prägt ein, prägte ein, hat eingeprägt> [tr v] **1.** jdm etw. einprägen drum sth into sb ◊ *Meine Mutter hat mir eingeprägt, nicht mit fremden Leuten mitzugehen.* sich [dat] etw. einprägen memorize sth ◊ *Der Zeuge hatte sich das Gesicht des Täters genau eingeprägt.* **2.** etw. in etw. [acc] einprägen imprint sth on sth ◊ *ein Muster in Leder einprägen*

ein|räu·men [ˈaenrɔˀmən] <räumt ein, räumte ein, hat eingeräumt> [tr v] **1.** etw. in etw. [acc] einräumen put sth away in/on sth ◊ *die Einkäufe in den Kühlschrank einräumen* einen Schrank/ein Regal etc. einräumen put things into a cupboard/ on a shelf etc. **2.** *(lofty)* admit ◊ *Der Minister räumte ein, dass ...* ♦ *Der Angeklagte musste die Richtigkeit der Vorwürfe einräumen.* **3.** *(form)* jdm etw. einräumen grant sb sth ◊ *Die Bank räumte ihnen einen Kredit ein.*

ein|rei·chen [ˈaenraeçn̩] <reicht ein, reichte ein, hat eingereicht> [tr v] *(form)* hand in, submit ◊ *ein Formular bei einer Behörde einreichen* Klage gegen jdn einreichen file an action against sb

Ein·rei·se [ˈaenraezə] die <-, -n> *(form)* entry ◊ *Bestimmungen für die Einreise nach Deutschland* ♦ *die Einreise genehmigen/verweigern*

ein|rei·sen [ˈaenraezn̩] <reist ein, reiste ein, ist eingereist> [intr v] *(form)* enter (a/the country) ◊ *Wann sind Sie eingereist?* nach China einreisen enter China, travel to China

② **ein|rich·ten** [ˈaenrɪçtn̩] <richtet ein, richtete ein, hat eingerichtet> [tr v] **1.** furnish ◊ *Ihr Haus ist gemütlich eingerichtet.* ♦ *einen Raum als Kinderzimmer einrichten* **2.** *(form) (an account, office, a connection, position)* set up ◊ *einen Internetzugang einrichten* ♦ *Er hat ein Sparbuch für seinen Enkel eingerichtet* ♦ *eine Beratungsstelle einrichten* **3.** etw. einrichten arrange sth ◊ *Können Sie den Termin einrichten?* es so einrichten, dass see to it that ◊ *Kannst du es (dir) so einrichten, dass du um 17 Uhr zu Hause bist?* [ref v] sich auf etw. einrichten prepare for sth ◊ *Richten Sie sich auf eine längere Wartezeit ein.* ⊝sich einstellen

⊛ **sich häuslich einrichten** make yourself at home

Ein·rich·tung [ˈaenrɪçtʊŋ] die <-, -en> **1.** furnishing(s) ◊ *Das Wohnzimmer hat eine elegante Einrichtung.* **2.** *(form)* institution ◊ *staatliche/öffentliche Einrichtungen* ♦ *eine soziale Einrichtung*

eins¹ [aens] [nmrl] one → vier

⊛ **sich (über etw. [acc]) eins sein** be of the same opinion (about sth) mit jdm (über etw. [acc]) eins werden agree with sb (on sth) sich eins werden come to an agreement eins a ⊝A plus ◊ *In seinem Fachgebiet ist er wirklich eins a.* eins, zwei, drei before you know it ◊ *Mach die Abrechnung am Computer, dann ist sie eins, zwei, drei fertig.*

eins² [aens] *neut of* einer

Eins [aens] die <-, -en> **1.** one → Vier1 **2.** *(fam)*

(bus, tram etc.) number one → Vier2 **3.** school *(grade)* ⊛A ◊ *Ich habe eine Eins bekommen.* eine Eins schreiben get an A *box*@ Note ⊛ *wie eine Eins* **1.** perfectly ◊ *Seit der Reparatur läuft der Wagen wie eine Eins.* **2.** perfectly straight ◊ *„Steht der Weihnachtsbaum?" — „Ja, wie eine Eins".*

② **ein·sam** ['aɛnzaːm] [adj] **1.** lonely ◊ *Im Alter werden viele Leute einsam.* ♦ *ein einsamer Mensch* **2.** secluded ◊ *Sie leben in einer einsamen Gegend.* [adv] **1.** all by yourself ◊ *Er lebt einsam und zurückgezogen.* ⊖allein **2.** all alone ◊ *Die Hütte steht einsam am Fuß des Berges.*

Ein·satz ['aɛnzats] der <–(e)s, Einsätze> **1.** *(of police, military, fire brigade, paramedics etc.)* mission, operation ◊ *Er ist gerade bei einem Einsatz.* ♦ *ein Einsatz der Feuerwehr* im Einsatz on duty **2.** *no pl* use ◊ *Wir plädieren für den Einsatz stärkerer Medikamente.* im Einsatz sein be used, be deployed ◊ *Mehrere Fahrzeuge sind im Einsatz.* **3.** commitment ◊ *Sie zeigte vollen Einsatz.* **4.** game *(in poker, gambling etc.)* stake(s) ◊ *Der Croupier bat um die Einsätze für das Spiel.* ♦ *den Einsatz verdoppeln* **5.** mus cue ◊ *den Einsatz verpassen*

② **ein|schal·ten** ['aɛnʃaltn̩] <schaltet ein, schaltete ein, hat eingeschaltet> [tr v] **1.** switch on, turn on ◊ *den Fernseher/Computer einschalten* ⊖anmachen ⊖ausmachen, ausschalten, abschalten **2.** jdn einschalten notify sb ◊ *Der Kriminalinspektor schaltete den Staatsanwalt ein.* ⊖informieren [ref v] sich einschalten intervene ◊ *Der Passant schaltete sich in den Streit der beiden Männer ein.*

ein|schät·zen ['aɛnʃɛtsn̩] <schätzt ein, schätzte ein, hat eingeschätzt> [tr v] etw./jdn einschätzen assess sth/sb ◊ *eine Situation als gefährlich einschätzen* jdn/etw. falsch einschätzen misjudge sb/sth

ein|schen·ken ['aɛnʃɛŋkn̩] <schenkt ein, schenkte ein, hat eingeschenkt> [tr+intr v] jdm einschenken fill sb's glass/cup, top sb up jdm etw. einschenken pour sb a glass/cup of sth ◊ *Er schenkte ihr nochmals Kaffee ein.* etw. in etw. [acc] einschenken pour sth into sth ◊ *Sie hat das Bier tatsächlich in eine Tasse eingeschenkt! Oh, dein Glas ist leer. Darf ich dir einschenken? Oh,* your glass is empty. Would you like some more/a refill? ⊖eingießen

⊛ gut/schlecht einschenken fill a glass higher/ lower than the line ◊ *Das Glas ist aber gut eingeschenkt, es fließt ja fast über!*

② **ein|schla·fen** ['aɛnʃlaːfn̩] <schläft ein, schlief ein, ist eingeschlafen> [intr v] **1.** fall asleep, go to sleep jd kann nicht einschlafen sb can't get to sleep ⊖aufwachen **2.** *(limb)* etw. schläft (jdm) ein sb's sth goes to sleep ◊ *Mein Fuß ist (mir) eingeschlafen.* **3.** *(relationship, friendship)* peter out ◊ *Nach 11 Jahren war unsere Beziehung total eingeschlafen.* **4.** *(euph)* pass away ◊ *Nach langer, schwerer Krankheit war ihn sanft eingeschlafen.* ⊖sterben

ein|schlä·fern ['aɛnʃlɛːfɐn] <schläfert ein, schläferte ein, hat eingeschläfert> [tr v] *(an animal)* put to sleep, put down ◊ *Der Kater musste eingeschläfert werden.*

ein·schlä·fernd ['aɛnʃlɛːfɐnt] [adj] eine einschläfernde Wirkung auf jdn haben, auf jdn einschlä-

fernd wirken make somebody feel sleepy ◊ *Der Vortrag hatte eine einschläfernde Wirkung auf mich.* ♦ *Klassische Musik wirkt auf ihn einschläfernd.*

ein|schla·gen ['aɛnʃlaːgn̩] <schlägt ein, schlug ein, hat/ist eingeschlagen> [tr v] +haben **1.** smash ◊ *eine Scheibe/ein Fenster einschlagen* **2.** *(a path, direction, route etc.)* take ◊ *An der Kreuzung schlug er den Weg ins Dorf ein.* **3.** *(fig)* *(a career)* take up ◊ *Er hat die Beamtenlaufbahn eingeschlagen.* einen Kurs einschlagen follow a course **4.** etw. (in etw. [acc]) einschlagen drive sth in(to sth) ◊ *einen Nagel in die Wand einschlagen* [tr+intr v] +haben **1.** turn (the steering wheel) ◊ *Schlag mehr nach links ein, sonst kommst du nicht in die Lücke.* **2.** etw. (in etw. [acc]) einschlagen wrap sth up (in sth) ◊ *Können Sie mir die CD in Geschenkpapier einschlagen?* ⊖einwickeln [intr v] +haben/sein **1.** +haben/sein etw. schlägt (in etw. [acc]) ein sth strikes (sth), sth hits (sth) ◊ *Der Blitz schlug in unser Haus ein.* **2.** +haben auf jdn/ etw. einschlagen beat sb/sth ◊ *Der Junge schlug auf seinen Mitschüler ein.* **3.** +haben *(fig)* shake hands (on it) ◊ *Schlag ein! Die Wette gilt!*

ein·schlä·gig ['aɛnʃlɛːgɪç] [adj] *only before ns (form)* specialist ◊ *einschlägige Forschungsliteratur* ♦ *über einschlägige Erfahrungen verfügen* [adv] **1.** einschlägig vorbestraft sein have been previously convicted of a similar offence/offense **2.** appropriately ◊ *einschlägig ausgebildete Krankenpfleger*

ein|schlie·ßen ['aɛnʃliːsn̩] <schließt ein, hat eingeschlossen> [tr v] **1.** sich/jdn/ein Tier (in etw. [dat]/[acc]) einschließen lock yourself/sb/ an animal in (sth) ◊ *Sie haben den Hund im/ins Auto eingeschlossen.* ♦ *Sie hat sich eingeschlossen und will niemanden sehen.* ⊖einsperren **2.** etw. (in etw. [dat]/[acc]) einschließen lock sth away (in sth) ◊ *Schmuck im/in den Hotelsafe einschließen* **3.** *mostly passive* etw./jdn einschließen surround sth/sb ◊ *Sie wurden vom Feuer eingeschlossen.* **4.** etw./jdn einschließen include sth/sb ◊ *Die Preise auf der Karte schließen die Bedienung mit ein.* ♦ *Die Einladung schließt Ihren Partner mit ein.*

ein·schließ·lich¹ ['aɛnʃliːslɪç] [adv] einschließlich ... up to and including ... ◊ *Wir haben bis einschließlich 8. Januar Ferien.* ♦ *bis einschließlich Seite 12 lesen*

ein·schließ·lich² ['aɛnʃliːslɪç] [prep] *sing nouns without article or attribute are not declined in following this prep, otherwise* [+gen] *or fam* [+dat] including ◊ *Der Preis versteht sich einschließlich Mehrwertsteuer.* ♦ *Alle waren gekommen, einschließlich der kleinen Ida.* ⊖inklusive ⊖ausschließlich

ein|schnap·pen ['aɛnʃnapm̩] <schnappt ein, schnappte ein, hat eingeschnappt> [intr v] click shut, snap shut ◊ *Die Tür schnappte ins Schloss ein.*

⊛ eingeschnappt sein *(fam)* be in a huff

ein·schnei·dend ['aɛnʃnaɛdn̩t, 'aɛnʃnaɛdənt] [adj, adv] drastic(ally), radical(ly) ◊ *ein einschneidender Wandel* ◊ *Die Veränderungen sind einschneidend.* ♦ *Diese Technologie wird unser Leben einschneidend verändern.*

ein|schrän·ken ['aɛnʃrɛŋkn̩] <schränkt ein,

schränkte ein, hat eingeschränkt> (tr v) **1.** jdn einschränken restrict sb ◊ *Seine Krankheit schränkt ihn in seiner Beweglichkeit ein.* **2.** etw. einschränken reduce sth, cut down on sth ◊ *das Rauchen einschränken* ♦ *Das neue Gesetz schränkt die Rechte der Bürger ein.* (ref v) sich einschränken economize ◊ *Wir müssen uns, was das Essen angeht, etwas einschränken.*

ein|schrei·ben ['aenʃraebm̩] <schreibt ein, schrieb ein, hat eingeschrieben> (tr v) **1.** sich/jdn in etw. (acc) einschreiben put your/sb's name down on/in sth ◊ *Ich habe mich in die Teilnehmerliste eingeschrieben.* sich ins Goldene Buch etc. einschreiben sign the visitors' book etc. **2.** einen Brief einschreiben lassen send a letter by registered mail (ref v) sich an einer Universität einschreiben register at a university sich für einen Kurs einschreiben enrol on a course; *(a subject)* sich für etw. einschreiben sign up for sth, register for sth ◊ *Ich habe mich für Geografie eingeschrieben.* ⊖sich immatrikulieren

② **Ein·schrei·ben** ['aenʃraebm̩] das <-s, -> registered letter/parcel etw. per Einschreiben schicken send sth by registered mail

ein|schüch·tern ['aenʃʏçtɐn] <schüchtert ein, schüchterte ein, hat eingeschüchtert> (tr v) jdn einschüchtern intimidate sb ◊ *Er schüchterte sie mit Drohungen ein.* sich einschüchtern lassen be intimidated ◊ *Sie lässt sich leicht einschüchtern.*

ein|schu·len ['aenʃuːlən] <schult ein, schulte ein, hat eingeschult> (tr v) **1.** *mostly passive* eingeschult werden start school ◊ *In Deutschland wird man meist mit sechs Jahren eingeschult.* Kinder früher einschulen lower the school starting age **2.** train ◊ *neues Personal einschulen*

ein|se·hen ['aenzeːən] <sieht ein, sah ein, hat eingesehen> (tr v) **1.** see, understand ◊ *Hat er eingesehen, worum es dir geht?* ♦ *Ich sehe ein, dass man etwas tun muss.* **2.** *(a mistake, an error)* acknowledge, admit ◊ *Sie will ihren Fehler einfach nicht einsehen.* seinen Irrtum einsehen see where you were/went wrong **3.** *(files, documents)* inspect ◊ Akten einsehen **4.** *(a garden)* overlook ◊ *vom Balkon das benachbarte Grundstück einsehen*

ein·sei·tig ['aenzaetɪç] (adj, adv) **1.** one-sided(ly) ◊ *eine einseitige Berichterstattung* ♦ *Der Inhalt der Stellungnahme war einseitig.* ♦ *Der Artikel ist einseitig optimistisch.* einseitig argumentieren use one-sided arguments In den Medien wurde einseitig berichtet. Media reports were biased. **2.** unbalanced ◊ *Immer nur Pasta zum Abendessen ist zu einseitig.* einseitig essen, sich einseitig ernähren have an unbalanced diet ◊ *Dieses Kino hat ein sehr einseitiges Programm.* einseitig sein lack variety ◊ *Das Angebot an Sport ist hier sehr einseitig.* **4.** one page ◊ *ein einseitiges Dokument* Anschreiben in Bewerbungsmappen sollten einseitig sein. Covering letters for applications should be no longer than one page. **5.** down/on one side (only) ◊ *eine einseitige Verengung der Fahrbahn* ♦ *Er ist einseitig gelähmt.* einseitig taub sein be deaf in one ear **6.** *when used as an adj, only before ns* unilateral(ly) ◊ *eine einseitige Verpflichtung* ♦ *Der Vertrag ist einseitig gebrochen worden.* (adv) *(printing, writing)* (nur) einseitig on one side

(only) ◊ *Dieser Kopierer kann nur einseitig kopieren.* ♦ einseitig bedruckt

ein|sen·den ['aenzɛndn̩] <sendet ein, sandte/sendete ein, hat eingesandt/eingesendet> (tr v) send in ◊ *die Lösung einsenden* ♦ *seine Bewerbung einsenden*

② **ein|set·zen** ['aenzɛtsn̩] <setzt ein, setzte ein, hat eingesetzt> (tr v) **1.** *(lofty)* etw./jdn einsetzen use sth/sb ◊ *Diese Maschine wird bei der Ernte eingesetzt.* ♦ *Der Schlichter wird als neutraler Vermittler eingesetzt.* etw./jdn einsetzen, um etw. zu tun; etw./jdn dafür einsetzen, etw. zu tun employ sth/sb to do sth ◊ *Er hat alle seine Kräfte dafür eingesetzt, dieses Ziel zu erreichen.* **2.** insert, put in ◊ *eine Scheibe einsetzen* **3.** install, put in ◊ *einen Herzschrittmacher/Chip einsetzen* **4.** *(form)* jdn (als etw.) einsetzen appoint sb (as sth) ◊ *jdn als Erben einsetzen* ♦ *einen Ausschuss einsetzen* ⊖ernennen (intr v) start, come in ◊ *Die Musik setzte ein.*; *(rain)* set in (ref v) sich für etw./jdn einsetzen speak up for sth/sb, champion sth/sb ◊ *Sie hat sich beim Chef für mich eingesetzt.* ♦ *Diese Organisation setzt sich für den Naturschutz ein.* ⊖sich engagieren

Ein·sicht ['aenzɪçt] die <-, -en> **1.** *no pl* insight, reason, understanding ◊ *Er zeigte Einsicht und entschuldigte sich.* zu der Einsicht kommen, dass come to realize that ◊ *Wir sind zu der Einsicht gekommen, dass du Recht hattest.* **2.** *no pl* *(form) (files, documents)* Einsicht in etw. (acc) haben/nehmen examine sth ◊ *Einsicht in die Akten nehmen* jdm Einsicht in etw. (acc) gewähren allow sb access to sth ⊖Einblick **3.** Einsichten (in etw. (acc)) insight(s) (into sth) ◊ *interessante Einsichten in ein Gebiet vermitteln/geben* ♦ *ein Buch, dass mir neue Einsichten eröffnete* ⊖Einblick **4.** *no pl* Einsicht in etw. (acc) haben view ◊ *in den Garten der Nachbarn haben* ⊖Einblick

ein·sil·big ['aenzɪlbɪç] (adj, adv) *seldom comp/superl* monosyllabic(ally), laconic(ally) ◊ *eine einsilbige Antwort* ♦ *Er war den ganzen Abend über still und einsilbig.* ♦ *Sie hat ziemlich einsilbig reagiert.* (adj) LING monosyllabic ◊ *ein einsilbiges Wort* ♦ *Die meisten Präpositionen sind einsilbig.*

ein|spa·ren ['aenʃpaːrən] <spart ein, sparte ein, hat eingespart> (tr v) **1.** *(money, electricity)* save ◊ *Wer Geräte ohne Standby-Funktion hat, kann Strom einsparen.* Kosten einsparen cut costs **2.** cut (down on) ◊ *Wir werden einige Stellen im Unternehmen einsparen.* **3.** do without ◊ *Dieses Jahr sparen wir uns den Urlaub ein.*

ein|spei·sen ['aenʃpaezn̩] <speist ein, speiste ein, hat eingespeist> (tr v) **1.** IT *(data)* etw. in etw. (acc) einspeisen enter sth (into sth) ◊ *in eine Datenbank einspeisen* **2.** TECHN *(water, electricity)* supply etw. in etw. (acc) einspeisen feed sth into sth ◊ *Strom in ein Netz einspeisen*

② **ein|sper·ren** ['aenʃpɛrən] <sperrt ein, sperrte ein, hat eingesperrt> (tr v) **1.** jdn/sich/ein Tier (in etw. (dat)/(acc)) einsperren lock sb/yourself/an animal (in (sth)) ◊ *Vögel in einem/einen Käfig einsperren* ♦ *Er hat sich in seinem/sein Zimmer eingesperrt.* ⊖einschließen **2.** *(fam) (in prison)* jdn einsperren lock sb up ◊ *Er wurde zwei Monate eingesperrt.*

ein|spie·len ['aenʃpiːlən] <spielt ein, spielte ein, hat eingespielt> (tr v) **1.** *(money)* bring in ◊ *Das*

neue Album der Band spielte eine Rekordsumme ein. **2.** record ◊ *Herbert Grönemeyer hat ein neues Album eingespielt.* ⊖aufnehmen **3.** play ◊ *die Erkennungsmelodie einspielen* An dieser Stelle wird Werbung eingespielt. At this point there is an ad/a commercial break. ⎡ref v⎤ **1.** sich einspielen become second nature ◊ *Die Arbeitsabläufe spielten sich mit der Zeit ein.* sich aufeinander einspielen get used to one another **2.** *(athlete, musician)* sich einspielen warm up ◊ *Die Mannschaft spielt sich gerade ein.*

ein·spra·chig [ˈaɛnʃpraːxɪç] ⎡adj, adv⎤ *no comp/ superl* monolingual(ly) ◊ *ein einsprachiges Wörterbuch* ♦ *Die wenigsten Länder sind einsprachig.* ♦ *Die meisten Kinder in Deutschland wachsen einsprachig auf.*

ein|sprin·gen [ˈaɛnʃprɪŋən] <springt ein, sprang ein, ist eingesprungen> ⎡intr v⎤ für jdn einspringen fill in for sb ◊ *für jdn in der Nachtschicht einspringen*

Ein·spruch [ˈaɛnʃprʊx] der <-(e)s, Einsprüche> *(form)* LAW objection ◊ *Einspruch, Euer Ehren!* (gegen etw.) Einspruch einlegen/erheben raise an objection (to sth), lodge an appeal (against sth) ◊ *Binnen einer Woche kann Einspruch erhoben werden.* ♦ *gegen einen Bescheid Einspruch einlegen*

einst [aɛnst] ⎡adv⎤ *(lofty)* once, in the past ◊ *Einst lebten hier Dinosaurier.* von einst from the past, historic ◊ *Alltagsgegenstände von einst* ⊖früher

ein|ste·cken [ˈaɛnʃtɛkn̩] <steckt ein, steckte ein, hat eingesteckt> ⎡tr v⎤ **1.** take, pocket ◊ *Hast du die Autoschlüssel eingesteckt?*; *(fam)* etw. einstecken haben have sth on you ◊ *Du solltest immer etwas Kleingeld einstecken haben.* ⊖mitnehmen **2.** *(euph)* (sich ⎡dat⎤) etw. einstecken steal sth ◊ *Ich habe gesehen, wie derJunge sich eine Tafel Schokolade eingesteckt hat.* ⊖klauen, stehlen **3.** etw. (in etw. ⎡acc⎤) einstecken insert sth (in sth) ◊ *den Schlüssel (ins Schlüsselloch) einstecken* Briefe (in den Briefkasten) einstecken post letters; *(into a socket)* plug sth in ◊ *eine Lampe einstecken* ⎡tr+intr v⎤ *(fam) (negative situation)* etw. einstecken müssen deal with sth, take sth ◊ *Schläge/ eine Niederlage einstecken müssen* schlecht einstecken können find it difficult to accept criticism/ defeat etc.

② **ein|stei·gen** [ˈaɛnʃtaɛgŋ̍] <steigt ein, stieg ein, ist eingestiegen> ⎡intr v⎤ **1.** *(into a car, on a boat, train etc.)* get in/on in etw. ⎡acc⎤ einsteigen get into/on sth ◊ *Steig ins Auto ein, ich nehme dich mit.* Alles einsteigen! All aboard! ⊖aussteigen **2.** *(in a company, deal)* in etw. ⎡acc⎤ einsteigen get in on sth ◊ *in eine Firma einsteigen* bei jdm einsteigen go into business with sb ◊ *Er will bei uns einsteigen.* ⊖aussteigen **3.** in etw. ⎡acc⎤ einsteigen begin sth ◊ *ins Berufsleben einsteigen* ⊖aussteigen **4.** *(fam) (a remark, an argument)* auf etw. ⎡acc⎤ einsteigen respond to sth ◊ *Ich würde auf sein Gerede gar nicht erst einsteigen, das gibt nur Ärger.* **5.** (in etw. ⎡acc⎤) einsteigen climb in(to sth) ◊ *Die Einbrecher sind über den Balkon (in das Haus) eingestiegen.*

② **ein|stel·len** [ˈaɛnʃtɛlən] <stellt ein, stellte ein, hat eingestellt> ⎡tr v⎤ **1.** jdn (als etw.) einstellen employ sb (as sth), appoint sb (as sth) ◊ *Sie ist als Controllerin eingestellt worden.* ⊖engagieren

⊖entlassen **2.** etw. einstellen stop sth, discontinue sth ◊ *Die Produktion wird eingestellt.* **3.** *(an appliance)* etw. (auf etw. ⎡acc⎤) einstellen set sth (to sth) ◊ *den Backofen auf 200°C einstellen* ⎡ref v⎤ **1.** sich auf etw. ⎡acc⎤ einstellen prepare yourself for sth ◊ *sich auf Neues einstellen* ⊖sich einrichten **2.** *(lofty) (consequences)* sich einstellen set in ◊ *Einige Tage nach dem Unfall stellten sich Schmerzen ein.* ⊖auftreten

ein·stel·lig [ˈaɛnʃtɛlɪç] ⎡adj, adv⎤ *no comp/superl (number, percentage)* single-digit, single-figure ◊ *eine einstellige Zahl* Das Wahlergebnis der Partei war nur einstellig. The party only achieved a single-figure result in the election. einstellig wachsen/zunehmen grow/increase in the single-figure range einstellig prozentuales Wachstum single-figure percentage growth

Ein·stel·lung [ˈaɛnʃtɛlʊŋ] die <-, -en> **1.** Einstellung zu/gegenüber jdm/etw., Einstellung jdm/etw. gegenüber attitude towards sb/sth, opinion of sb/ sth ◊ *Sie hat ihn nach seiner Einstellung zu/ gegenüber Kindern gefragt.* ⊖Meinung **2.** *no pl* employment, appointment ◊ *Sie entschied sich für die Einstellung des Bewerbers.* **3.** TECHN setting ◊ *Die Einstellungen des Browsers müssen angepasst werden.*

Ein·stieg [ˈaɛnʃtiːk] der <-(e)s, -e> **1.** Einstieg (in etw. ⎡acc⎤) entry (into sth), start (to sth) ◊ *Zum Einstieg in das Thema wurde ein Film gezeigt.* ♦ *der Einstieg in den Beruf* **2.** boarding ◊ *Vor dem Einstieg ins Flugzeug erfolgt eine Sicherheitskontrolle.* **3.** *(into a building)* entry ◊ *Der Dieb wurde beim Einstieg in das Haus ertappt.* **4.** door(s) ◊ *Der hintere Einstieg des Busses war blockiert.*

eins·ti·ge [ˈaɛnstɪgə] ⎡adj⎤ *no comp/superl, only before ns* <eine einstige ..., eine einstige ..., ein einstiges ...> *(lofty)* former ◊ *Der einstige Spieler ist jetzt Trainer.* ⊖frühere ⊖zukünftige

ein|stim·men [ˈaɛnʃtɪmən] <stimmt ein, stimmte ein, hat eingestimmt> ⎡tr v⎤ sich/jdn (auf etw. ⎡acc⎤) einstimmen get yourself/sb in the mood (for sth) ◊ *sich mit einem Aperitif auf das Menü einstimmen* ⎡intr v⎤ *(also fig)* MUS (in etw. ⎡acc⎤) einstimmen join in (sth) ◊ *Alle stimmten in das Lied mit ein.* ♦ *Vater fing an zu schimpfen und Mutter stimmte mit ein.*

ein·stim·mig [ˈaɛnʃtɪmɪç] ⎡adj, adv⎤ *no comp/superl* **1.** unanimous(ly) ◊ *Das Ergebnis war einstimmig.* ♦ *ein einstimmiges Urteil* ♦ *etw. einstimmig beschließen* **2.** MUS monophonic(ally), for one voice ◊ *An dieser Stelle ist der Choral einstimmig.*

ein|stu·fen [ˈaɛnʃtuːfn̩] <stuft ein, stufte ein, hat eingestuft> ⎡tr v⎤ grade, classify jdn/etw. als etw. einstufen classify sb/sth as sth ◊ *ein Medikament als krebserregend einstufen* ♦ *Ich würde ihn als gefährlich einstufen.* jdn in eine Klasse/einen Kurs etc. einstufen put sb in a class/course etc.

ein·stün·dig [ˈaɛnʃtʏndɪç] ⎡adj⎤ *no comp/superl* one-hour ◊ *Der Zug hatte einen einstündigen Aufenthalt.* etw. ist einstündig sth takes/lasts one hour ◊ *Die Klausur ist einstündig.* ⎡adv⎤ for an hour ◊ *Der Unterricht in Musik wird einstündig erteilt.*

ein|stür·zen [ˈaɛnʃtʏʳtsn̩] <stürzt ein, stürzte ein, ist eingestürzt> ⎡intr v⎤ collapse ◊ *Bei dem Erdbeben stürzten einige Häuser ein.* ⊖einfallen

einst·wei·len ['aɛnstvaɛln̩] [adv] *(form)* in the meantime ◊ *Nehmen Sie doch einstweilen im Wartezimmer Platz.*

ein·tä·gig ['aɛntɛːgɪç] [adj] *no comp/superl* one-day ◊ *ein eintägiges Seminar etw.* ist eintägig *sth lasts/ takes one day* ◊ *Das Turnier ist eintägig.*

ein·tau·send ['aɛn'taɔzn̩t, 'aɛn'taɔzənt] [nmrl] a/ one thousand → vier

ein|tei·len ['aɛntaɛlən] <teilt ein, teilte ein, hat eingeteilt> [tr v] **1.** (sich [dat]) etw. einteilen ration sth ◊ *Du musst den Proviant so einteilen, dass er für eine Woche reicht.; (work)* plan sth, organize sth ◊ *Ich habe mir die Arbeit gut eingeteilt.* **2.** etw. einteilen classify sth, divide sth ◊ *Manche Menschen teilen die Welt in Gut und Böse ein.* ◆ *Tiere in Klassen, Arten und Rassen einteilen* **3.** jdn (für/als etw.) einteilen assign sb (to/as sth) ◊ *Er ist für die Nachtschicht eingeteilt.*

Ein·topf ['aɛntɔpf] der <-(e)s, Eintöpfe> stew ◊ *ein deftiger Eintopf mit Fleisch und Bohnen*

Ein·trag ['aɛntraːk] der <-(e)s, Einträge> entry ◊ *ein Eintrag im Kalender*

ein|tra·gen ['aɛntraːgn̩] <trägt ein, trug ein, hat eingetragen> [tr v] **1.** sich/jdn/etw. (in etw. [acc]) eintragen enter yourself/sb/sth (in sth) ◊ *seinen Namen in eine Liste eintragen* ◆ *einen Wert in ein Diagramm eintragen* **2.** register ◊ *Sie sind nicht als Mitglied eingetragen.* ◆ *Der Ort ist nicht auf der Karte eingetragen.* **3.** *(fig) (ridicule, criticism, recognition, admiration)* jdm etw. eintragen earn sb sth ◊ *Sein Vorschlag trug ihm große Anerkennung ein.* **4.** *(Gewinn)* eintragen be profitable ◊ *Das Geschäft trägt reichlich Gewinn ein.* ◆ *Das Amt trug nur wenig ein.*

ein|tref·fen ['aɛntrɛfn̩] <trifft ein, traf ein, ist eingetroffen> [intr v] *(lofty)* **1.** arrive ◊ *Die bestellte Ware ist eingetroffen.* ◆ *Die Gäste sind gestern in der Stadt eingetroffen.* ⊖ankommen **2.** happen ◊ *Jetzt ist das eingetroffen, was ich immer befürchtet hatte.* wenn der Fall eintrifft, dass in case wenn der Ernstfall eintrifft in case of emergency ⊖eintreten ⊖ausbleiben

ein|trei·ben ['aɛntraɛbm̩] <treibt ein, trieb ein, hat eingetrieben> [tr v] *(debts, taxes)* collect ◊ *Das Finanzamt treibt Steuern für den Staat ein.*

ein|tre·ten ['aɛntreːtn̩] <tritt ein, trat ein, hat/ist eingetreten> [intr v] *+sein/haben* **1.** +sein jd tritt (in etw. [acc]) ein sb enters (sth) ◊ *Treten Sie ein!* ◆ *in ein Haus eintreten* **2.** +sein *(an organization, a political party, club)* in etw. [acc] eintreten join sth ◊ *in die Kirche eintreten* **3.** +haben auf etw./ jdn/ein Tier eintreten kick sth/sb/an animal ◊ *Er trat brutal auf den Hund ein.* **4.** +sein happen, occur ◊ *Es ist eine ganz andere Situation eingetreten als erwartet.* jds schlimmste Befürchtungen sind eingetreten sb's worst fears have come true **5.** +sein für etw. eintreten stand up for sth, advocate sth ◊ *Er trat für die Rechte der Frauen ein.* ⊖sich engagieren **6.** +sein ASTRON *(an orbit)* in etw. [acc] eintreten (re-)enter sth ◊ *Der Satellit trat in die Umlaufbahn ein.* **7.** +sein *(lofty)* in etw. [acc] eintreten penetrate sth ◊ *Die Kugel ist direkt ins Herz eingetreten.; (water)* flood sth ◊ *Während der Flut ist Wasser in unseren Keller eingetreten.* ⊖eindringen **8.** +sein *(fig) (a project, discussion, negotiations)* in etw. [acc] eintreten enter into sth

◊ *Wir sind in Verhandlungen mit einem möglichen Käufer eingetreten.* in eine kritische Phase eintreten enter a critical phase [tr v] +haben etw. eintreten kick sth in ◊ *Die Polizei hat die Tür eingetreten.* [ref v] *(a nail, splinter)* sich etw. [dat] eintreten run sth into your foot ◊ *Ich habe mir einen Nagel eingetreten.*

② **Ein·tritt** ['aɛntrɪt] der <-(e)s, -e> **1.** admission ◊ *Die Ausstellung kostet fünf Euro Eintritt.* ◆ *Man muss den Eintritt an der Kasse zahlen.* **2.** joining ◊ *Bei seinem Eintritt in die Partei war er noch sehr unerfahren.* **3.** *no pl* entry, entering ◊ *Beim Eintritt in die Wohnung fällt sofort die Unordnung auf.* ◆ *der Eintritt eines Satelliten in die Erdumlaufbahn* ⊛ **bei Eintritt der Nacht** at nightfall **bei Eintritt eines Notfalls** in case of emergency

② **Ein·tritts·kar·te** ['aɛntrɪtskaˈtə] die <-, -n> ticket ◊ *Hast du die Eintrittskarten fürs Theater?*

② **ein·ver·stan·den** ['aɛnfɛʃtandn̩] [adj] *not before ns* (mit etw.) einverstanden sein agree (with sth), be in agreement (with sth) ◊ *Bist du damit einverstanden, dass wir das anders machen?* ◆ *Ich bin mit allem einverstanden.* sich (mit etw.) einverstanden erklären agree (to sth) ◊ *Er hat sich einverstanden erklärt, bei der Vorbereitung zu helfen.* ⊛ **einverstanden** okay, agreed ◊ *„Wollen wir ins Museum gehen?" — „Einverstanden!"*

Ein·ver·ständ·nis ['aɛnfɛʃtɛntnɪs] das <-ses, -se> *most sing* agreement, consent ◊ *Sie haben um unser Einverständnis gebeten.* ◆ *Dazu werde ich nie mein Einverständnis geben!* ⊖Einwilligung, Zustimmung

Ein·wand ['aɛnvant] der <-(e)s, Einwände> objection ◊ *Ich habe keine Einwände.* ◆ *Er hat den Vorschlag ohne Einwände akzeptiert.*

Ein·wan·de·rer ['aɛnvandərɐ] der <-s, ->, **Ein·wan·de·rin** ['aɛnvandərɪn] die <-, -nen> immigrant

ein|wan·dern ['aɛnvandɐn] <wandert ein, wanderte ein, ist eingewandert> [intr v] immigrate ◊ *Sie sind aus Korea in die USA eingewandert.* ⊖auswandern

ein·wand·frei ['aɛnvantfraɛ] [adj, adv] *(form)* flawless(ly), impeccable(-ably) ◊ *einwandfreie Ware* ◆ *Der Zustand des Wagens ist einwandfrei.* ◆ *Der neue Computer funktioniert einwandfrei.*

ein|wei·hen ['aɛnvaɛən] <weiht ein, weihte ein, hat eingeweiht> [tr v] **1.** *(hum)* etw. einweihen christen sth ◊ *Heute Abend weihen wir unser neues Sofa ein.* **2.** *(a building, shop etc.)* etw. einweihen inaugurate sth ◊ *Diese Kathedrale wurde 1493 eingeweiht.* **3.** jdn in etw. [acc] einweihen let sb in on sth ◊ *Wir haben sie ihn in dein Geheimnis einweihen.*

ein|wei·sen ['aɛnvaɛzn̩] <weist ein, wies ein, hat eingewiesen> [tr v] **1.** jdn einweisen brief sb, train sb ◊ *Er wurde fachgerecht eingewiesen.* jdn in etw. [acc] einweisen introduce sb to sth ◊ *Sie wurde von einer Kollegin in ihre Aufgaben eingewiesen.* **2.** *mostly passive (form) (to a hospital)* jdn in etw. [acc] einweisen admit sb (to sth) ◊ *Nach dem Anfall wurde er in die Klinik eingewiesen.* **3.** jdn in eine Parklücke einweisen direct sb into a parking space

ein|wen·den ['aɛnvɛndn̩] <wendet ein, wendete/ wandte ein, hat eingewendet/eingewandt> [tr v]

etwas gegen etw. einwenden (wollen) object to sth ◊ *Ich will nichts gegen diese Methode einwenden.* einwenden, dass object that ◊ *Er wandte ein, dass dies nicht seine Aufgabe sei.* nichts gegen etw. einzuwenden haben not mind sth ◊ *Gegen eine Nachspeise hätte ich nichts einzuwenden.* dagegen ist nichts einzuwenden there is nothing to be said against it
ein|wer·fen ['aɛnvɛ'fn̩] <wirft ein, warf ein, hat eingeworfen> [tr v] **1.** etw. (in etw. [acc]) einwerfen insert sth (in sth), put sth in(to sth) ◊ *Du musst einen Euro in den Getränkeautomaten einwerfen.* einen Brief (in den Briefkasten) einwerfen post a letter **2.** etw. (mit etw.) einwerfen smash sth (with sth) ◊ *Tom hat (mit einem Stein) eine Fensterscheibe eingeworfen.* **3.** *(lofty)* etw. einwerfen interject sth ◊ *Er warf ständig seine Kommentare ein.* **4.** *(fam) (a pill)* etw. einwerfen pop sth ◊ *Ich habe eine Tablette gegen die Kopfschmerzen eingeworfen.* [tr+intr v] SPORT *(a ball)* throw in ◊ *Der Spieler warf den Ball vom rechten Spielfeldrand ein.*

ein|wi·ckeln ['aɛnvɪkl̩n] <wickelt ein, wickelte ein, hat eingewickelt> [tr v] **1.** etw. (in etw. [acc]) einwickeln wrap sth (in sth) ◊ *Die Verkäuferin wickelte das Brot in Papier ein.* ⊝einschlagen **2.** *(in a blanket)* sich/jdn (in etw. [acc]) einwickeln wrap yourself/sb up (in sth) ◊ *sich in eine Decke einwickeln* **3.** *(fig)* jdn einwickeln take sb in ◊ *Ich lasse mich von niemandem so leicht einwickeln.*

ein|wil·li·gen ['aɛnvɪlɪgn̩] <willigt ein, willigte ein, hat eingewilligt> [intr v] LAW (in etw. [acc]) einwilligen agree (to sth), consent (to sth) ◊ *Ich habe in seinen Vorschlag eingewilligt.* ♦ *Schweren Herzens willigte er ein.* ⊝zustimmen

Ein·wil·li·gung ['aɛnvɪlɪgʊŋ] die <–, –en> LAW approval, consent ◊ *Er hat seine Einwilligung zu diesem Projekt gegeben.* ⊝Einverständnis, Zustimmung

ein|wir·ken ['aɛnvɪ'kn̩] <wirkt ein, wirkte ein, hat eingewirkt> [intr v] **1.** auf jdn/etw. einwirken have an effect on sb/sth, influence sb/sth ◊ *Sie wirkt sehr positiv auf ihn ein.* ♦ *Dieser Faktor kann auf das Ergebnis einwirken.* ⊝beeinflussen **2.** be absorbed ◊ *Die Salbe muss einwirken.* etw. einwirken lassen let sth be absorbed, allow sth to take effect ◊ *Die Haartönung muss man 30 Minuten einwirken lassen.*

ein·wö·chig ['aɛnvœçɪç] [adj] no comp/superl one-week ◊ *eine einwöchige Reise nach Madrid* ♦ *Derzeit müssen Sie mit einer einwöchigen Wartezeit rechnen.* etw. ist einwöchig sth lasts/takes one week ◊ *Die Veranstaltung ist einwöchig.*

② **Ein·woh·ner** ['aɛnvoːnɐ] der <–s, –>, **Ein·woh·ne·rin** ['aɛnvoːnərɪn] die <–, –nen> inhabitant ◊ *Hamburg hat 1,69 Millionen Einwohner.*

Ein·woh·ner·mel·de·amt [aɛnvoːneˈmɛldəˌamt] das <–(e)s, Einwohnermeldeämter> residents' registration office ◊ *sich beim Einwohnermeldeamt anmelden/ummelden/abmelden*

Ein·zahl ['aɛntsaːl] die <–, –en> most sing singular ⊝Singular ⊝Mehrzahl, Plural

② **ein|zah·len** ['aɛntsaːlən] <zahlt ein, zahlte ein, hat eingezahlt> [tr+intr v] pay in, deposit ◊ *Kann ich den Betrag am Schalter einzahlen?* ♦ *Es sind 300*

Euro auf das Sparbuch eingezahlt worden. ⊝abheben

② **Ein·zel·...** ['aɛntsl̩] [prefix] **1.** single ◊ *ein Einzelzimmer* ♦ *der Einzelunterricht* **2.** solitary ◊ *die Einzelhaft* **3.** individual ◊ *die Einzelleistung* ♦ *der Einzelunterricht das Einzelkind the only child ein Einzelkämpfer, eine Einzelkämpferin a lone wolf* **4.** separate, unique ◊ *der Einzelband* **5.** independent ◊ *eine Einzelaktion* **6.** detached ◊ *das Einzelhaus*

Ein·zel·fall ['aɛntsl̩fal] der <–(e)s, Einzelfälle> **1.** im Einzelfall on an individual basis ◊ *Das genaue Vorgehen muss dann im Einzelfall geklärt werden.* **2.** isolated case ◊ *Solche Vorkommnisse sind leider keine Einzelfälle.*

Ein·zel·gän·ger ['aɛntsl̩gɛŋɐ] der <–s, –>, **Ein·zel·gän·ge·rin** ['aɛntsl̩gɛŋərɪn] die <–, –nen> loner ◊ *Sie war schon immer eine Einzelgängerin.* ♦ *Katzen sind Einzelgänger.*

Ein·zel·han·del ['aɛntsl̩handl̩] der <–s> no pl ECON *(always der Einzelhandel)* the retail trade

⑦ **Ein·zel·heit** ['aɛntsl̩haɛt] die <–, –en> most pl detail ◊ *Nähere Einzelheiten sind noch nicht bekannt.*

② **ein·zeln** ['aɛntsl̩n] [adj, adv] when used as an adj, only before ns single(-gly) ◊ *Sie prüfte jedes einzelne Stück.* ♦ *ein einzelner Socken* ♦ *einzeln verkaufen; ((as) one among several)* individual(ly) ◊ *Er hatte das Auto in einzelne Teile zerlegt.* ♦ *Sie betraten den Raum einzeln.* ♦ *Die Gläser waren einzeln verpackt.; (building, tree)* solitary (-ily) ◊ *Auf der Wiese stand ein einzelnes Haus.* einzeln stehend solitary [adj] *with pl ns* einzelne ... some ..., a few ... ◊ *Es standen noch einzelne Gäste herum.;* isolated ..., scattered ... ◊ *Morgen kann es einzelne Regenschauer geben.*

Ein·zel·ne¹ ['aɛntsl̩nə] der/die <–n, die Einzelnen> *but: ein Einzelner/eine Einzelne* **1.** individual (person) ◊ *Jeder Einzelne kann etwas tun.* **2.** most pl Einzelne (only) a few people ◊ *Einzelne werden von diesem Plan profitieren.*

Ein·zel·ne² ['aɛntsl̩nə] das <–n> no pl Einzelne some/a few things ◊ *Einzelnes ist mir noch unklar.* im Einzelnen in detail ◊ *etw. im Einzelnen beschreiben bis ins Einzelne right down to the last detail etw. bis ins Einzelne ausarbeiten work out sth in great detail box@ Substantivierung*

Ein·zel·zim·mer ['aɛntsl̩tsɪmɐ] das <–s, –> single room ◊ *ein Einzelzimmer buchen; (in a hospital)* private room ⊝Doppelzimmer

② **ein|zie·hen** ['aɛntsiːən] <zieht ein, zog ein, hat/ist eingezogen> [intr v] ♦*sein* **1.** move in ◊ *Wann ziehen die neuen Mieter ein?* ♦ *Meine Kusine wird bei uns einziehen.* in eine Wohnung etc. einziehen move into a flat etc. ⊝ausziehen **2.** soak in ◊ *Das Öl muss eine Weile in das Holz einziehen.; (lotion, cream)* be absorbed ◊ *Die Creme zieht rasch (in die Haut) ein.* **3.** *(also fig) (a stadium, parliament)* enter ◊ *Die Sportler zogen ins Stadion ein.; (a political party)* be elected to ◊ *Die Partei zog erstmals in den Landtag ein.; (a cup round)* get through to ◊ *Die Mannschaft zog ins Halbfinale ein.* [tr v] ♦*haben* **1.** MIL einziehen werden be conscripted, be called up ◊ *Er wurde in die/zur Armee) eingezogen.* **2.** insert ◊ *einen neuen Gummi in die Hose einziehen; (a cable)* install **3.** build,

A B C **E** F G H I J K L M N O P Q R S T U V W X Y Z

add, put in ◊ *Sie zogen eine Trennwand ein.* **4.** *(a sail, some paper)* take in ◊ *Der Drucker will das Papier nicht einziehen.; (a fishing net)* pull in, haul in; *(a flag)* lower; *(the undercarriage)* retract **5.** *(feelers, claws etc.)* draw in ◊ *Die Katze zog ihre Krallen wieder ein.* ein Hund zieht den Schwanz ein a dog puts its tail between its legs den Kopf einziehen duck your head mit eingezogenem Kopf sitzen sit with your head bowed down **6.** *(bank notes, a driving licence etc.)* withdraw ◊ *Die alten Banknoten wurden eingezogen.* **7.** *(fees, taxes)* collect ◊ *Der Betrag wird vom Girokonto eingezogen.* **8.** *(enquiries)* make ◊ *Er zog Erkundigungen über sie ein.; (information)* obtain

② **ein·zig** ['aentsɪç] [adj, adv] *no comp/superl; when used as an adj, only before ns* only ◊ *Er war ihr einziges Kind.* ♦ *Das ist der einzig richtige Weg.* ♦ *Die Gebühr dient einzig zur Deckung der Kosten.* [adj] *only before ns* **1.** single ◊ *Der Mannschaft gelang kein einziger Treffer.* kein einziges Mal not once **2.** total ◊ *Sein Leben war ein einziges Chaos.*

⊛ einzig und allein entirely, solely ◊ *Ob der Ausflug stattfindet, hängt einzig und allein vom Wetter ab.* only ◊ *Beunruhigend ist einzig und allein, dass er sich nicht meldet.*

ein·zig·ar·tig ['aentsɪçla:'tɪç] [adj] **1.** unique ◊ *Diese Sammlung ist wohl einzigartig.* ♦ *einzigartige Fähigkeiten* **2.** breathtaking, incomparable ◊ *ein einzigartiger Blick auf die Berge* ♦ *Die Aussicht war einzigartig.*

Ein·zi·ge¹ ['aentsɪgə] der/die <–n, die Einzigen> *but: ein Einziger/eine Einzige only one* ◊ *Er war der Einzige, der sich dafür interessierte.* ♦ *Sie bekam als Einzige ein Geschenk.* kein Einziger not a/one single person *box@* Substantivierung

Ein·zi·ge² ['aentsɪgə] das <–n> *no pl (always das Einzige)* the only thing ◊ *Das ist das Einzige, was zählt. box@* Substantivierung

Ein·zug ['aentsu:k] der <–(e)s, Einzüge> *most sing* **1.** move ◊ *Vor dem Einzug muss noch tapeziert werden.* **2.** *(of money)* collection ◊ *der Einzug der Beiträge* **3.** *(also fig) (of troops, a sports team etc.)* entry ◊ *der Einzug der Mannschaften ins Stadion; (to a parliament)* election (to) ◊ *Die Grünen schafften den Einzug in den Landtag.; (to a cup round)* progression ◊ *Das Team hat den Einzug ins Finale geschafft.* **4.** IT indent, indentation ◊ *Er stellte den Einzug links auf 1,5 cm ein.*

⊛ Einzug halten arrive ◊ *Der Frühling hat Einzug gehalten. (an innovation)* become established ◊ *Mittlerweile hat der Computer überall Einzug gehalten.*

Ein·zugs·er·mäch·ti·gung ['aentsu:ks|eɐ̯ˌmɛçtɪgʊŋ] die <–, –en> direct debit mandate, collection authority ◊ *jdm eine Einzugsermächtigung erteilen*

② **Eis** [aes] das <–es, –> **1.** *no pl* ice ◊ *Er trank Cola mit viel Eis.* ♦ *Er ist ins Eis eingebrochen und ertrunken.* **2.** ice (cream) ◊ *Wollen wir Eis essen gehen?* ♦ *Zwei Eis mit je drei Kugeln, bitte!*

⊛ das Eis ist gebrochen the ice is broken ◊ *Nach fünf Minuten war das Eis gebrochen.* etw. auf Eis legen put sth on ice ◊ *Das Projekt wurde vorläufig auf Eis gelegt.* auf Eis liegen be on hold

Eis·be·cher ['aesbɛçɐ] der <–s, –> **1.** ice cream

(sundae) ◊ *ein Eisbecher mit Früchten und Sahne* **2.** ice cream dish

Ei·schnee ['aeʃne:] der <–s> *no pl* whipped egg white ◊ *Eiweiß zu Eischnee schlagen*

Eis·die·le ['aesdi:lə] die <–, –n> ice cream parlour, ice cream parlor ⊖Eiscafé

Ei·sen ['aezn] das <–s, –> **1.** *no pl* iron ◊ *eine Mauer aus Eisen und Beton* ♦ *Brokkoli enthält viel Eisen.* **2.** piece of iron ◊ *Er hatte sich an dem glühenden Eisen verbrannt.*

⊛ zum alten Eisen gehören/zählen belong/be on the scrapheap ein heißes Eisen a hot potato ein heißes Eisen anpacken/anfassen grasp the nettle

② **Ei·sen·bahn** ['aeznba:n] die <–, –en> **1.** *no pl* railway ◊ *Die Eisenbahn spielte bei der Industrialisierung eine wichtige Rolle.* **2.** train ◊ *Im Museum waren alte Eisenbahnen zu sehen.* ♦ *Die Eisenbahn fährt mehrmals täglich von Berlin nach Rostock.* mit der Eisenbahn fahren go by train/rail **3.** train set ◊ *Die Kinder spielten mit der Eisenbahn.*

⊛ es ist höchste Eisenbahn *(fam)* it's high time, it's about time

ei·sern ['aezn] [adj] *no comp/superl, only before ns (also fig)* iron ◊ *ein eisernes Tor* ♦ *Er regiert mit eiserner Hand.; (discipline)* rigid eine eiserne Regel a hard and fast rule die eiserne Reserve emergency reserves [adv] *(fig)* resolutely ◊ *Sie hielt eisern an ihren Prinzipien fest.*

⊛ eisern bleiben/sein remain/be resolute

Eis·fach ['aesfax] das <–s, Eisfächer> freezer compartment ◊ *etw. ins Eisfach legen*

ei·sig ['aezɪç] [adj] *(also fig)* icy ◊ *Der Wind war eisig.* ♦ *eisig kaltes Wasser* ♦ *Sie begrüßte mich mit eisiger Miene.* [adv] *(fig)* frostily ◊ *Sie lächelte eisig.*

Eis·sta·di·on ['aesˌʃta:djɔn] das <–s, Eisstadien> ice rink

ei·tel ['aetl] [adj] <eitler, am eitelsten> <der/die/das eitle...> vain ◊ *Er ist sehr eitel.* ♦ *eine eitle Frau*

Ei·ter ['aetɐ] das <–s> *no pl* pus

Ei·weiß ['aevaes] das <–es, – or –e> **1.** (egg) white ◊ *Trennen Sie vier Eiweiß vom Dotter.* **2.** *pl 'Eiweiße'* CHEM, BIO protein ◊ *Fleisch enthält viel Eiweiß.*

E·kel¹ ['e:kl] der <–s> *no pl* disgust, revulsion ◊ *Ekel vor Schnecken empfinden* Ekel erregend disgusting, revolting ◊ *ein Ekel erregender Geruch*

E·kel² ['e:kl] das <–s, –> *(fam, pej)* revolting character; *(child)* disgusting little beast ◊ *Er ist ein richtiges Ekel.*

E·lek·tri·ker [e'lɛktrɪkɐ] der <–s, –>,
E·lek·tri·ke·rin [e'lɛktrɪkərɪn] die <–, –en> electrician ◊ *Von Beruf war sie Elektrikerin.* ♦ *Ein Elektriker musste kommen, um die Leitung zu reparieren.*

② **e·lek·trisch** [e'lɛktrɪʃ] [adj, adv] *when used as an adj, mostly before ns* PHYSICS electric(ally), electrical(ly) ◊ *elektrischer Strom* ♦ *eine elektrische Gitarre* ♦ *ein elektrisch betriebenes Gerät*

E·lek·tri·zi·tät [elɛktritsi'tɛ:t] die <–> *no pl* electricity ◊ *Elektrizität erzeugen*

② **E·lek·tro-** [e'lɛktro-] [prefix] electric ... ◊ *Elektroherd* ♦ *Elektromotor*

e·lend ['e:lɛnt] [adj, adv] *when used as an adj, mostly before ns* wretched(ly), miserable(-ably)

Das Haus war in einem elenden Zustand. ◆ *Sein Leben war hart und elend.* ◆ *elend zugrunde gehen* [adj] **1.** *not before ns* awful, terrible ◊ *Du siehst so elend aus.* ◆ *Mir war nach dem Essen elend (zumute).* **2.** *only before ns (pej)* despicable ◊ *Du elender Lügner!*

E·lend ['eːlɛnt] *das* <–s> *no pl* **1.** poverty ◊ *Der Krieg hat das Land ins Elend gestürzt.* **2.** misery ◊ *Ihr Leben war voller Leid und Elend.*

elf [ɛlf] [nmrl] eleven → vier

Ell·bo·gen ['ɛlboːgn̩] *der* <–s, –> elbow ◊ *sich auf den Ellbogen stützen*

El·len·bo·gen ['ɛlənboːgn̩] → Ellbogen

El·tern ['ɛltɛn] *die* <–> *only pl* parents ◊ *Sind das seine leiblichen Eltern?*

② **E-Mail** ['iːmeːl, 'iːmɛɪl] *die* <–, –s> e-mail ◊ *jdm eine E-Mail schicken* ◆ *Informationen per E-Mail versenden*

② **emp·fahl** [ɛm'pfaːl] *pret of* empfehlen

Emp·fang [ɛm'pfaŋ] *der* <–(e)s, Empfänge> **1.** *no pl* reception ◊ *Mein Handy hat hier keinen Empfang.* ◆ *Sie bereiteten ihm einen herzlichen Empfang.* ◆ *ein offizieller Empfang* ◆ *Die Schlüssel liegen am Empfang.* **2.** *no pl* receipt ◊ *Würden Sie mir bitte den Empfang der Ware bestätigen?* etw. in Empfang nehmen receive sth, take delivery of sth ◊ *Glückwünsche/einen Scheck in Empfang nehmen*

Emp·fän·ger¹ [ɛm'pfɛŋɐ] *der* <–s, –> TECHN receiver

② **Emp·fän·ger²** [ɛm'pfɛŋɐ] *der* <–s, –>, **Emp·fän·ge·rin** [ɛm'pfɛŋərɪn] *die* <–, –nen> recipient ◊ *Das Porto zahlt der Empfänger.* ◆ *die Empfängerin des Spenderorgans*

Emp·fäng·nis·ver·hü·tung [ɛm'pfɛŋnɪsfɛhyːtʊŋ] *die* <–> *no pl* contraception ◊ *hormonelle/natürliche Empfängnisverhütung*

② **emp·feh·len** [ɛm'pfeːlən] <empfiehlt, empfahl, hat empfohlen> [tr v] (jdm) etw./jdn empfehlen recommend sth/sb (to sb) ◊ *Dieser Zahnarzt wurde mir empfohlen.* ◆ *Ich empfahl ihm, ein Taxi zu nehmen.* [ref v] etw. empfiehlt sich sth is advisable ◊ *Bei solchen Wanderungen empfiehlt sich festes Schuhwerk.* ◆ *Es empfiehlt sich, einen Regenschirm mitzunehmen.* **emp·feh·lens·wert** [ɛm'pfeːlənsveːɐt] [adj] recommended ◊ *empfehlenswerte Literatur zum Thema* ◆ *Wie viel Taschengeld ist empfehlenswert?*

② **emp·fiehlt** [ɛm'pfiːlt] *pres of* empfehlen

emp·fin·den [ɛm'pfɪndn̩] <empfindet, empfand, hat empfunden> [tr v] **1.** feel ◊ *Sie empfand große Angst.* **2.** etw. als etw. empfinden find sth sth ◊ *Sie empfand die laute Musik als störend.* **3.** etw. für jdn empfinden feel sth for sb ◊ *Für sie empfinde ich nur Abscheu.* **emp·find·lich** [ɛm'pfɪntlɪç] [adj, adv] **1.** *(also fig)* sensitive(ly) ◊ *empfindliche Haut/Messgeräte* ◆ *Seine Haut reagiert auf Sonne besonders empfindlich.* empfindlich gegen etw. sein be sensitive to sth ◊ *Diese Pflanze ist gegen Kälte sehr empfindlich.* **2.** *(defeat, loss etc.)* severe(ly) ◊ *eine empfindliche Geldstrafe* ◆ *Die Wirtschaft war dadurch empfindlich getroffen.* [adj] delicate ◊ *Sie hat einen empfindlichen Magen.* ◆ *Dieser Stoff ist sehr empfindlich.*

② **emp·foh·len** [ɛm'pfoːlən] *past p of* empfehlen

em·pört [ɛm'pøːɐt] [adj, adv] <empörter, am empör-

testen> indignant(ly) ◊ *Das Urteil löste empörte Reaktionen aus.* ◆ *Er war über ihr Verhalten sehr empört.* ◆ *Er schilderte empört, was ihm passiert war.*

Em·pö·rung [ɛm'pøːrʊŋ] *die* <–> *no pl* indignation, outrage ◊ *Die Nachricht löste Empörung aus.* ◆ *ein Sturm der Empörung*

② **En·de** ['ɛndə] *das* <–s, –n> *most sing* end ◊ *das Ende eines Romans* ◆ *am anderen Ende der Stadt* ◆ *Er fühlte sein Ende nahen.* Ende des Monats/Jahres etc. at the end of the month/year etc. ◊ *Ende des Jahres/Ende Oktober geht er in Ruhestand.* zu Ende gehen, ein Ende nehmen come to an end ◊ *Die Party nahm ein abruptes Ende.* ein gutes/glückliches Ende nehmen turn out well einer Sache [dat] ein Ende setzen put an end to sth ◊ *Er hat den Spekulationen ein Ende gesetzt.* ⊕Anfang

⊛ **am Ende sein 1.** be shattered ◊ *Nach dem Training bin ich immer total am Ende.* **2.** be at the end of your tether ◊ *Er war am Ende und wusste nicht mehr, was er tun sollte.* *(company, businessman etc.)* be finished **am Ende 1.** in the end ◊ *Ich hoffe, dass du die Entscheidung am Ende nicht bereust.* **2.** am Ende ist jd (noch) ... sb might be ... after all am Ende hat jd (noch) etw. getan sb might have done sth after all ◊ *Hat er das Feuer am Ende selbst gelegt?* **Ende zwanzig/dreißig etc. sein** be in your late twenties/thirties etc.

en·den ['ɛndn̩] [intr v] +haben **1.** end ◊ *Der Weg endete in einer Sackgasse.* ◆ *Das Spiel endet um 17 Uhr.* ◆ *Der Film endet tragisch.*; stop ◊ *Der Gesang endete abrupt.*; terminate ◊ *Die U-Bahn endet in Feldmoching.* tödlich enden have fatal consequences böse/schlimm enden come to a bad/sorry end **2.** LING auf etw. [acc] enden, mit etw. enden end in sth ◊ *Die Mehrheit der Verben endet auf „-en“.*

② **end·gül·tig** ['ɛntgʏltɪç] [adj, adv] *no comp/superl* final(ly), definitive(ly) ◊ *Ist diese Entscheidung endgültig?* ◆ *das endgültige Wahlergebnis* ◆ *Sie haben sich jetzt endgültig getrennt.*

② **end·lich** ['ɛntlɪç] [adv] finally, at last ◊ *Endlich ist hier auch einmal was los!* ◆ *Kommst du jetzt endlich?*

end·los ['ɛntloːs] [adj, adv] *no comp/superl* endless(ly) ◊ *eine schier endlose Liste* ◆ *Die Fahrt war endlos.* ◆ *endlos warten müssen*

En·dung ['ɛndʊŋ] *die* <–, –en> ending ◊ *Die Endung „-ung“ wird an den Verbstamm angehängt.* ◆ *eine Datei mit der Endung „.exe“*

② **E-ner·gie** [enɛɐ'giː] *die* <–, –n> *no pl* energy ◊ *Es hat mich viel Energie gekostet, ihr all das zu erklären.* ◆ *Energie sparen/verschwenden*

② **eng** [ɛŋ] [adj, adv] **1.** *when used as an adj, only before ns* close(ly) ◊ *eine enge Umarmung* ◆ *ein enger Freund* ◆ *Die Seiten waren eng bedruckt.* ◆ *Wir wollen künftig enger zusammenarbeiten.* ◆ *Wir sind eng (miteinander) befreundet/verwandt.* im engsten Familienkreis in the/your immediate family **2.** *(clothes, scoreline, finances etc.)* tight(ly) ◊ *Diese Schuhe sind zu eng.* ◆ *Uns wurden enge Grenzen gesetzt.* ◆ *ein eng anliegendes Kleid* ⊕weit [adj] narrow ◊ *enge Gassen* ◆ *Bei hellem Licht werden die Pupillen eng.*; *(space, living conditions)* confined, cramped ◊ *In dem Zimmer war*

es sehr eng. ✦ *Sie leben auf engem Raum zusammen.*
⊛ **es wird eng für jdn** sb is facing problems ◊ *Für diese Firma wird es eng auf dem Markt.*

en·ga·gie·ren [aŋgaˈʒiːrən, ãgaˈʒiːrən] <engagiert, engagierte, hat engagiert> (ref v) *sich für etw.* engagieren be active in sth ◊ *sich politisch engagieren* ✦ *Sie engagiert sich für den Naturschutz.* sich für jdn engagieren act on sb's behalf ⊜für etw./jdn eintreten (tr v) jdn engagieren hire sb, engage sb ◊ *Man hatte einen Pfleger für ihn engagiert.* ✦ *Sie wurde am Stadttheater engagiert.* ⊜einstellen ⊜entlassen

En·ge [ˈɛŋə] die <-> *no pl* **1.** narrowness, cramped conditions ◊ *die Enge der Gassen* ⊜Weite **2.** *(fig)* confinement ◊ *Er wollte der provinziellen Enge entfliehen.*
⊛ **jdn in die Enge treiben** drive sb into a corner ◊ *Er fühlte sich von den Fragen in die Enge getrieben.*

En·gel [ˈɛŋl] der <-s, -> angel ◊ *Der Engel Gabriel war ihm erschienen.* ✦ *Du bist ein wahrer Engel!*
⊛ **ein Engel in der Not** a friend in need jds rettender Engel sb's savio(u)r

Eng·land [ˈɛŋlant] das <-s> *article only in combination with attribute, no pl* England → Deutschland

Eng·län·der [ˈɛŋlɛndɐ] der <-s, ->, **Eng·län·de·rin** [ˈɛŋlɛndərɪn] die <-, -nen> Englishman, Englishwoman die Engländer the English → Deutsche

eng·lisch [ˈɛŋlɪʃ] (adj) *mostly before ns* English → deutsch

Eng·lisch [ˈɛŋlɪʃ] das <-(s)> *no pl* English → Deutsch

⑦ **En·kel** [ˈɛŋkl] der <-s, ->, **En·ke·lin** [ˈɛŋkəlɪn] die <-, -nen> grandchild

ent·beh·ren [ɛntˈbeːrən] <entbehrt, entbehrte, hat entbehrt> (tr v) *etw.* entbehren do without sth ◊ *Als Kind musste er vieles entbehren.* ✦ *Ich überließ ihr alles, was ich entbehren konnte.* (intr v) *(lofty)* *etw.* entbehrt einer Sache (dat) sth is devoid of sth, sth lacks sth ◊ *Die Vorwürfe entbehren jeder Grundlage.*

ent·bin·den [ɛntˈbɪndn] <entbindet, entband, hat entbunden> (intr v) give birth ◊ *Sie hat vorgestern entbunden.* (tr v) **1.** jdn (von einem Kind) entbinden deliver sb's baby ◊ *Welcher Arzt hat Sie entbunden?* von einem Mädchen entbunden werden give birth to a girl durch Kaiserschnitt von Zwillingen entbunden werden give birth to twins by Caesarean section **2.** *(a child)* jdn entbinden give birth to sb Hier wurde das Kind entbunden. The child was born here. **3.** jdn von etw. entbinden release sb from sth; relieve sb of sth ◊ *jdn von einer Pflicht entbinden*

Ent·bin·dung [ɛntˈbɪndʊŋ] die <-, -nen> **1.** birth ◊ *eine Entbindung durch/per Kaiserschnitt* ✦ *Sie steht kurz vor der Entbindung.* **2.** *no pl* release ◊ *Er bat um die Entbindung von seinem Mandat.* ✦ *eine Entbindung von der Schweigepflicht*

ent·blö·ßen [ɛntˈbløːsn] *(lofty)* <entblößt, entblößte, hat entblößt> (ref v) *sich entblößen* expose yourself ◊ *Sie entblößte sich völlig.* halb entblößt half naked (tr v) reveal ◊ *Beim Lachen entblößte sie die Zähne.*; *(your arm, skin etc.)*

bare, uncover ◊ *Er entblößte den rechten Arm.*

⑦ **ent·de·cken** [ɛntˈdɛkn] <entdeckt, entdeckte, hat entdeckt> (tr v) **1.** discover ◊ *Marie Curie entdeckte das Radium.* ✦ *Der Brand wurde rechtzeitig entdeckt.* ✦ *Bisher hat niemand sein Talent entdeckt.* **2.** *(a person, an error etc.)* find ◊ *Ich konnte meinen Bruder nirgendwo entdecken.*; *(a deception)* uncover ◊ *einen Betrug entdecken*

Ent·de·ckung [ɛntˈdɛkʊŋ] die <-, -en> discovery ◊ *die Entdeckung des Penicillins* ✦ *Sie machte eine überraschende Entdeckung.*

En·te [ˈɛntə] die <-, -n> **1.** duck ◊ *Im Teich schwamm eine Ente.* ✦ *Ente süßsauer* **2.** MEDIA newspaper talk ◊ *Ist das wahr oder nur eine Ente?*
⊛ **lahme Ente** *(pej or hum)* slowcoach ◊ *Beeil dich, du lahme Ente!*

ent·eig·nen [ɛntˈʔaɛɡnən] <enteignet, enteignete, hat enteignet> (tr v) **1.** dispossess ◊ *Sie wurden enteignet und vertrieben.* **2.** expropriate ◊ *Die Villa war von der Regierung enteignet worden.*

ent·fal·ten [ɛntˈfaltn] <entfaltet, entfaltete, hat entfaltet> (tr v) **1.** *(fig)* *(a flavo(u)r, capabilities)* develop ◊ *seine Fähigkeiten entfalten sich* entfalten develop, reach your/its full potential ◊ *Das Aroma entfaltet sich erst beim Garen.* ✦ *Ich kann mich in dieser Umgebung nicht richtig entfalten.*; *(splendo(u)r, magnificence etc.)* display ◊ *Die Rosen entfalteten ihre volle Pracht.* **2.** unfold ◊ *eine Zeitung entfalten*; *(a sail, flag)* unfurl (ref v) *sich entfalten* open (up)

ent·fer·nen [ɛntˈfɛrnən] <entfernt, entfernte, hat entfernt> (tr v) remove ◊ *Flecken entfernen* ✦ *Er entfernte seinen Namen von der Tür.* (ref v) *sich entfernen* leave ◊ *Er entfernte sich langsam.*; *(a noise)* move away

⑦ **ent·fernt** [ɛntˈfɛrnt] *past p of* entfernen (adj, adv) **1.** *when used as an adj, not before ns* away ◊ *Die Orte sind nicht weit voneinander/von der Küste entfernt.* ✦ *60 Kilometer entfernt liegt Bonn.* ⊜weg **2.** *when used as an adj, only before ns* (weit) entfernt remote(ly) ◊ *weit entfernte Galaxien* ✦ *Kommt das etwas entfernt bekannt vor?* **3.** *when used as an adj, only before ns* distant(ly) ◊ *ein entfernter Verwandter* ✦ *Ich bin entfernt mit ihm verwandt.* ⊜nah
⊛ **weit davon entfernt sein, etw. zu tun** not have the slightest intention of doing sth

⑦ **Ent·fer·nung** [ɛntˈfɛrnʊŋ] die <-, -en> **1.** distance ◊ *Die Entfernung beträgt zehn Zentimeter.* ✦ *Sie schoss aus kurzer Entfernung aufs Tor.* ✦ *Er hat das Ereignis aus sicherer Entfernung beobachtet.* **2.** *(form)* removal ◊ *die operative Entfernung eines Tumors* **3.** *(form)* departure ◊ *unerlaubte Entfernung vom Unfallort*

ent·frem·den [ɛntˈfrɛmdn] <entfremdet, entfremdete, hat entfremdet> (tr v) **1.** jdn jdm entfremden alienate sb from sb ◊ *Der Vorfall hat den Jungen seinen Eltern entfremdet.* **2.** etw. seinem Zweck entfremden use sth inappropriately, not use sth for its intended purpose ◊ *Das Kraftwerk wurde seinem Zweck entfremdet und dient nun als Museum.* (ref v) *sich von jdm entfremden* become alienated from sb, grow apart from sb ◊ *Sie entfremdeten sich zunehmend voneinander.*

ent·füh·ren [ɛntˈfyːrən] <entführt, entführte, hat

entführt> [tr v] **1.** abduct, kidnap ◊ *Sie wurde von einem Unbekannten entführt.* **2.** *(an aircraft)* hijack

ⓩ **ent·ge·gen¹** [ɛnt'geːgn̩] [adv] [+dat] towards ◊ *Sie lief zur Tür, ihrer Mutter entgegen.* entgegen dem Wind against the wind entgegen dem Uhrzeigersinn anti-clockwise

ent·ge·gen² [ɛnt'geːgn̩] [prep] [+dat] contrary to ◊ *Entgegen allen Behauptungen hatte sie keine Kenntnis von der Sache.*

ent·ge·gen|... [ɛnt'geːgn̩] [prefix] **1.** *(opposition)* against ◊ *Wir haben dem nichts entgegenzusetzen.* ♦ *jdm etw. entgegenhalten* **2.** jdm/etw. entgegen towards sb ◊ *Sie kam uns auf der Straße entgegen.*

ent·ge·gen·ge·setzt [ɛnt'geːgn̩ɡəzɛtst] *past p of* entgegensetzen [adj] opposite ◊ *in die entgegengesetzte Richtung fahren* ♦ *Seine Meinung war der meinen entgegengesetzt.*

ent·ge·gen|kom·men [ɛnt'geːgn̩kɔmən] <kommt entgegen, kam entgegen, ist entgegengekommen> [intr v] **1.** jdm/einer Sache entgegenkommen approach sb/sth, come towards sb/sth ◊ *Er kam mir schon auf dem Gang entgegen.; (encounter sb/sth on the street)* pass sb/sth **2.** jdm entgegenkommen make concessions ◊ *Die Firma kam uns finanziell entgegen.* jdm auf halbem Wege entgegenkommen meet sb halfway **3.** einer Sache [dat] entgegenkommen fit in well with sth, be consistent with sth ◊ *Ihr Angebot kommt meinen Interessen sehr entgegen.*

ent·ge·gen·kom·mend [ɛnt'geːgn̩kɔmənt] *pres p of* entgegenkommen [adj, adv] obliging(ly) ◊ *Der Prüfer war sehr entgegenkommend.* ♦ *Ich habe einen entgegenkommenden Chef.* ♦ *Sie wurde äußerst entgegenkommend behandelt.*

ent·ge·gen|neh·men [ɛnt'geːgn̩neːmən] <nimmt entgegen, nahm entgegen, hat entgegengenommen> [tr v] *(also fig)* receive, accept ◊ *Ich nahm für meinen Nachbarn ein Päckchen entgegen.* ♦ *einen Anruf entgegennehmen*

ent·ge·gen|set·zen [ɛnt'geːgn̩zɛtsn̩] <setzt entgegen, setzte entgegen, hat entgegengesetzt> [tr v] jdm/einer Sache etw. entgegensetzen counter sb/sth with sth ◊ *Welche Argumente kann man diesen Behauptungen entgegensetzen?* jdm Widerstand entgegensetzen offer resistance to sb

ent·ge·gen|wir·ken [ɛnt'geːgn̩vɪrˀkn̩] <wirkt entgegen, wirkte entgegen, hat entgegengewirkt> [tr v] einer Sache [dat] entgegenwirken counteract sth ◊ *Sie versuchten, dem negativen Trend entgegenzuwirken.* jdm entgegenwirken oppose sb

ent·geg·nen [ɛnt'geːgnən] <entgegnet, entgegnete, hat entgegnet> [tr v] reply, retort ◊ *Er entgegnete, dass er nicht daran denke, nachzugeben.*

ent·ge·hen [ɛnt'geːən] <entgeht, entging, ist entgangen> [intr v] **1.** jdm/einer Sache entgehen escape sb/sth, avoid sb/sth ◊ *Der Präsident entging nur knapp einem Attentat.* **2.** jdm entgeht etw. sb misses sth ◊ *Ein wichtiger Auftrag war ihm entgangen.* sich [dat] etw. entgehen lassen miss sth, miss out on sth ◊ *Diese Chance lasse ich mir nicht entgehen.* **3.** jdm entgeht etw. sb misses sth, sb fails to notice sth, sth escapes sb/sb's attention ◊ *Dieser Aspekt ist mir völlig entgangen.* ♦ *Ihr entgeht absolut nichts.*

ⓩ **ent·hal·ten** [ɛnt'haltn̩] <enthält, enthielt, hat enthalten> [tr v] contain, include ◊ *Das Buch enthält zahlreiche Abbildungen.* ♦ *Strom ist im Mietpreis enthalten.* [ref v] *(lofty)* sich einer Sache [dat] enthalten abstain from sth, refrain from sth ◊ *Sie enthielt sich jeder weiteren Äußerung.* sich der Stimme enthalten abstain (from voting)

Ent·hal·tung [ɛnt'haltʊŋ] die <-, -en> **1.** abstention ◊ *Der Beschluss wurde einstimmig bei zwei Enthaltungen angenommen.* **2.** *no pl* abstinence ◊ *eine zeitweilige Enthaltung von Fleischspeisen*

ent·hül·len [ɛnt'hʏlən] <enthüllt, enthüllte, hat enthüllt> [tr v] **1.** *(an object)* unveil, reveal ◊ *Die Bürgermeisterin enthüllte eine Gedenktafel.* **2.** *(fig) (facts)* reveal, expose, disclose ◊ *Die neue Napoleon-Biografie enthüllt Erstaunliches.*

ent·kof·fe·i·niert [ɛntkɔfeˀiˈniːɛt] [adj] *no comp/superl* decaffeinated ◊ *entkoffeinierter Kaffee* ♦ *Dieser Espresso ist entkoffeiniert.*

ent·kom·men [ɛnt'kɔmən] <entkommt, entkam, ist entkommen> [intr v] jdm/einer Sache entkommen escape (sb/sth), get away (from sb/sth) ◊ *Der Täter entkam unerkannt.* ♦ *dem Regenwetter entkommen*

ent·la·den [ɛnt'laːdn̩] <entlädt, entlud, hat entladen> [tr v] **1.** *(goods, a vehicle)* unload ◊ *einen Lkw entladen* ♦ *Die Hilfsgüter wurden entladen.* **2.** *(a weapon)* unload ◊ *kontrollieren, ob eine Waffe entladen ist.* **3.** *(a battery)* discharge ◊ *Der Akku ist vollständig entladen.* [ref v] sich entladen erupt, break, be released ◊ *Am Samstagabend entlud sich ein heftiges Gewitter.* ♦ *Seine Frustration entlädt sich oft in Gewalt.*

ⓩ **ent·lang¹** [ɛnt'laŋ] [adv] along ◊ *sich an der Wand entlang aufstellen* hier/da entlang this/that way ◊ *Hier entlang, bitte.* ♦ *"Wo geht es bitte zur Uni?" — "Da entlang!"*

ⓩ **ent·lang²** [ɛnt'laŋ] [prep] *with acc when postpositive, otherwise with gen or dat* along ◊ *immer die Straße entlang in Richtung Norden* ♦ *eine Reise entlang des Rheins/dem Rhein*

ⓩ **ent·las·sen** [ɛnt'lasn̩] <entlässt, entließ, hat entlassen> [tr v] **1.** make redundant; *(for misconduct)* dismiss; *(in football)* sack ◊ *Der Verein hat seinen Trainer entlassen.* ⊖kündigen ⊕einstellen, engagieren **2.** release, discharge ◊ *Ich wurde vorzeitig aus der Haft/dem Vertrag entlassen.* ♦ *Man hat die Patientin heute Morgen entlassen.*

ent·las·ten [ɛnt'lastn̩] <entlastet, entlastete, hat entlastet> [tr v] **1.** etw. entlasten relieve ◊ *Solarenergie kann die Umwelt entlasten.* jdn entlasten ease the strain on ◊ *Ganztagsschulen sollen die Eltern entlasten.* **2.** *(in court)* jdn entlasten exonerate sb ◊ *Der Zeuge entlastete den Angeklagten.* ⊖belasten

ent·lo·cken [ɛnt'lɔkn̩] <entlockt, entlockte, hat entlockt> [tr v] jdm/einer Sache etw. entlocken elicit sth from sb/sth, coax sth out of sb/sth ◊ *Ich ließ mir ein Lächeln entlocken.* ♦ *Es gelang ihr nicht, ihnen einen Kommentar zu entlocken.* ♦ *Er kann dem Akkordeon die unglaublichsten Töne entlocken.*

ent·loh·nen [ɛnt'loːnən] <entlohnt, entlohnte, hat entlohnt> [tr v] *(lofty)* pay, reward ◊ *Der Sieger wurde fürstlich für seine Leistung entlohnt.*

A B C D E F G H I J K L M N O P Q R S T U V W X Y Z

ent·mu·ti·gen [ɛnt'muːtɪɡn̩] <entmutigt, entmutigte, hat entmutigt> [tr v] discourage, dishearten ◊ *Sie war von dem Ergebnis enttäuscht, aber keineswegs entmutigt.* ♦ *Er lässt sich viel zu schnell entmutigen.*

ent·neh·men [ɛnt'neːmən] <entnimmt, entnahm, hat entnommen> [tr v] **1.** take, remove ◊ *eine Probe entnehmen* **2.** *(lofty, fig)* einer Sache [dat] etw. entnehmen gather sth from sth, infer sth from sth ◊ *einem Zeitungsartikel Information entnehmen* ♦ *Ich entnehme Ihrem Schreiben, dass …*

ent·rei·ßen [ɛnt'raɛsn̩] <entreißt, entriss, hat entrissen> [tr v] *(lofty)* **1.** jdm etw. entreißen snatch sth from sb ◊ *Der alten Dame wurde die Geldbörse entrissen.* **2.** rescue ◊ *einer Gefahr entrissen werden* **3.** *(fig)* transport away from, elicit ◊ *Dem Film gelingt es, die Zuschauer dem Alltag zu entreißen.*

ent·rüs·tet [ɛnt'rʏstət] [adj, adv] no comp/superl indignant(ly) ◊ *Mit seinem Vorschlag stieß er auf entrüstete Ablehnung.* ♦ *Er reagierte entrüstet auf die Vorwürfe.* über etw. [acc] entrüstet sein be indignant at sth, be outraged by/at sth ◊ *Die Kunden sind entrüstet über die Gebührenerhöhung.*

ent·schä·di·gen [ɛnt'ʃɛːdɪɡn̩] <entschädigt, entschädigte, hat entschädigt> [tr v] jdn (für etw.) entschädigen compensate sb (for sth), recompense sb (for sth), indemnify sb (for sth) ◊ *Das Opfer wurde finanziell entschädigt.* ♦ *Es gibt Erlebnisse, die einen für alle Mühen entschädigen.*

ent·schär·fen [ɛnt'ʃɛːɐ̯fn̩] <entschärft, entschärfte, hat entschärft> [tr v] defuse, mitigate, make safer ◊ *einen Konflikt/Streit entschärfen* ♦ *einen Sprengsatz entschärfen*

② **ent·schei·den** [ɛnt'ʃaɛdn̩] <entscheidet, entschied, hat entschieden> [tr+intr v] **1.** decide ◊ *Das Tor in der 89. Minute entschied das Fußballspiel.* über etw. [acc] entscheiden decide on sth ◊ *Sie haben noch nicht über den Antrag entschieden.* **2.** etw. für sich entscheiden win sth ◊ *Sie konnte die Wahl für sich entscheiden.* [ref v] **1.** sich entscheiden make up your mind ◊ *Ich kann mich einfach nicht entscheiden.* sich für/gegen etw./jdn entscheiden decide in favo(u)r of/against sth/sb ◊ *Du musst dich für einen der beiden entscheiden.* **2.** etw. entscheidet sich sth will be known, sth is decided ◊ *Gleich entscheidet sich, wer den Job bekommt.*

Ent·schei·dung [ɛnt'ʃaɛdʊŋ] die <-, –en> decision, ruling ◊ *Ich habe noch keine Entscheidung getroffen.* ♦ *Wie ist seine Entscheidung ausgefallen?* eine Entscheidung fällen make a decision; *(in court)* eine Entscheidung fällen make a decision; *(in court)*

ent·schie·den [ɛnt'ʃiːdn̩] *past p of* entscheiden [adj, adv] determined(ly), resolute(ly) ◊ *auf entschiedenen Widerstand stoßen* ♦ *Sein Tonfall war sehr entschieden.* ♦ *etw. entschieden anpacken* entschieden zu schwach/langsam/spät definitely too weak/slow/late

② **ent·schlie·ßen** [ɛnt'ʃliːsn̩] <entschließt sich, entschloss sich, hat sich entschlossen> [ref v] sich (zu/für/gegen etw.) entschließen decide (in favo(u)r of/against sth) ◊ *Wir haben uns gegen den Kauf des Hauses entschlossen.* ♦ *Er hat sich kurzfristig zur Teilnahme entschlossen.* sich entschließen, etw. zu tun decide to do sth ◊ *Sie haben sich spontan entschlossen, nach Mallorca*

zu fliegen.

ent·schlos·sen [ɛnt'ʃlɔsn̩] *past p of* entschließen [adj, adv] determined(ly), resolute(ly) ◊ *ein entschlossenes Vorgehen* ♦ *Ich bin fest entschlossen, nicht nachzugeben.* ♦ *jdm entschlossen entgegentreten*

Ent·schluss [ɛnt'ʃlʊs] der <-es, Entschlüsse> decision, resolution ◊ *Ich bin zu dem Entschluss gekommen, dass …* ♦ *Sie fasste einen spontanen Entschluss.*

② **ent·schul·di·gen** [ɛnt'ʃʊldɪɡn̩] <entschuldigt, entschuldigte, hat entschuldigt> [tr v] excuse ◊ *Sie entschuldigten sein Verhalten.* ♦ *Er entschuldigte sein Zuspätkommen mit einem Verkehrsstau.* ♦ *Dieser Umstand entschuldigt nichts.* [ref v] sich (bei jdm) (für etw.) entschuldigen apologize (to sb) (for sth) ◊ *Du musst dich bei deiner Tante für dein Benehmen entschuldigen.*

② **Ent·schul·di·gung** [ɛnt'ʃʊldɪɡʊŋ] die <-, –en> **1.** *(words)* apology ◊ *Sie nahm seine Entschuldigung an.* ♦ *Sie forderten eine offizielle Entschuldigung.* (jdn) um Entschuldigung bitten apologize (to sb) **2.** *(reason)* excuse ◊ *Zu seiner Entschuldigung sagte er, dass er verschlafen habe.* **3.** SCHOOL excuse note ◊ *Er schrieb seinem Sohn eine Entschuldigung für die Schule.* **4.** pardon ⑨ Entschuldigung sorry, excuse me ♦ *Entschuldigung, das wollte ich nicht!* ♦ *Entschuldigung, darf ich mal vorbei?* ⊜Verzeihung

> The way to apologize depends very much on the situation. It can range from an informal *'tschuldigung* or *sorry* when you collide with somebody to a very formal *Entschuldigen Sie bitte, das tut mir sehr Leid* when you accidentally hurt somebody. *Verzeihung* is a bit more formal and used when talking to strangers.

ent·setz·lich [ɛnt'zɛtslɪç] [adj, adv] **1.** horrible (-ibly), dreadful(ly) ◊ *ein entsetzlicher Unfall* ♦ *Sie war entsetzlich entstellt.* ⊜abscheulich **2.** *(fam)* terrible(-ibly) ◊ *Das Gedränge war entsetzlich.* ♦ *Das tut mir entsetzlich Leid!* ⊜schrecklich

ent·setzt [ɛnt'zɛtst] [adj, adv] seldom comp/no superl horrified ◊ *ein entsetzter Aufschrei* ♦ *Alle waren entsetzt über den Terroranschlag.* Sie stellten entsetzt fest, dass … They realized to their horror that …

ent·sor·gen [ɛnt'zɔʁɡn̩] <entsorgt, entsorgte, hat entsorgt> [tr v] dispose of, remove ◊ *Sondermüll fachgerecht entsorgen* ⊜beseitigen

ent·span·nen [ɛnt'ʃpanən] <entspannt, entspannte, hat entspannt> [tr v] **1.** *(muscles)* relax ◊ *Entspannen Sie die Rückenmuskulatur.* etw./jd entspannt sich sth/sb relaxes ◊ *Seine Muskeln entspannten sich.* ♦ *Im Urlaub habe ich mich richtig entspannt.* **2.** *(a situation)* ease ◊ *Die Maßnahmen haben die Lage entspannt.* sich entspannen ease ◊ *Die Situation auf dem Arbeitsmarkt hat sich deutlich entspannt.*

ent·spre·chen [ɛnt'ʃpʁɛçn̩] <entspricht, entsprach, hat entsprochen> [intr v] **1.** einer Sache [dat] entsprechen correspond to sth, live up to sth, be in accordance with sth ◊ *Die Ferienwohnung entsprach nicht unseren Vorstellungen.* **2.** *(lofty)* *(a wish, demand)* einer Sache [dat] entsprechen comply with sth ◊ *Nach anfänglichem Zögern ent-*

sprachen sie schließlich seinen Bedingungen.
ent·spre·chend¹ [ɛnt'ʃprɛçn̩t, ɛnt'ʃprɛçənt] *pres p of* entsprechen (adj, adv) appropriate(ly), relevant(ly), according(ly) ◊ *Er will eine Kneipe eröffnen und hat den entsprechenden Antrag gestellt.* ✦ *Seine Verdienste wurden von allen entsprechend gewürdigt.*
ent·spre·chend² [ɛnt'ʃprɛçn̩t, ɛnt'ʃprɛçənt] (prep) (+dat) in accordance with, according to ◊ *Seinem Wunsch entsprechend gab es keine Feier.* Nach der Operation ging es ihr den Umständen entsprechend gut. After the operation she was as well as could be expected.
② **ent·ste·hen** [ɛnt'ʃteːən] <entsteht, entstand, ist entstanden> (intr v) arise, develop, be created ◊ *Es entstand der Eindruck, dass alles in bester Ordnung sei.* ✦ *Über 2000 neue Arbeitsplätze sollen entstehen.* ✦ *Wie entstehen Erdbeben?* etw. entsteht aus/bei etw. sth is caused by sth, sth develops from sth, sth leads to sth ◊ *Daraus entstand eine große Freundschaft.* ✦ *Bei dem Brand entstand ein Sachschaden von 5000 €.* etw. entsteht durch etw. sth is caused as a result of sth
ent·stel·len [ɛnt'ʃtɛlən] <entstellt, entstellte, hat entstellt> (tr v) 1. (*a person, face*) disfigure ◊ *Ein Insektenstich hatte ihr Gesicht entstellt.* 2. (*facts*) distort ◊ *Deine Darstellung entstellt die Wirklichkeit.*
② **ent·täu·schen** [ɛnt'tɔʏʃn̩] <enttäuscht, enttäuschte, hat enttäuscht> (tr+intr v) disappoint ◊ *Er war von dem Ergebnis bitter enttäuscht.* ✦ *Sie enttäuschte unsere Erwartungen nicht.* ✦ *Er zeigte sich enttäuscht über die Absage.*
Ent·täu·schung [ɛnt'tɔʏʃʊŋ] die <-, -en> disappointment ◊ *Man konnte ihm seine Enttäuschung ansehen.* ✦ *Der Abstieg der Mannschaft war eine herbe Enttäuschung.*
② **ent·we·der** ['ɛntveːdɐ] (conjunc) entweder ... oder ... either ... or ... ◊ *Entweder du kommst mit, oder ich gehe alleine.* ✦ *Als Beilage gibt es entweder Reis oder Nudeln oder Pommes frites.*
ent·wer·fen [ɛnt'vɛrfn̩] <entwirft, entwarf, hat entworfen> (tr v) 1. (*draw*) design, sketch ◊ *Kostüme für eine Theateraufführung entwerfen* 2. (*a plan*) draft, draw (up), devise ◊ *ein Konzept entwerfen*
ent·wer·ten [ɛnt'veːɐtn̩] <entwertet, entwertete, hat entwertet> (tr v) 1. (*a ticket, credit card*) cancel ◊ *den Fahrschein entwerten* 2. (*money*) devalue, depreciate ◊ *Die Inflation entwertet das Geld.*
② **ent·wi·ckeln** [ɛnt'vɪkl̩n] <entwickelt, entwickelte, hat entwickelt> (tr v) 1. (*a product, method*) develop, evolve, produce, generate ◊ *einen neuen Impfstoff entwickeln* ✦ *Sie hat ihren eigenen Stil entwickelt.* ✦ *Ehrgeiz entwickeln* 2. etw. zu etw. entwickeln turn sth into sth, transform sth into sth ◊ *Ein neuer Koch hat das Gasthaus zum Feinschmeckerlokal entwickelt.* 3. FOTO develop, process ◊ *Kann man hier Fotos entwickeln lassen?* (refl v) sich entwickeln develop ◊ *Unser Baby entwickelt sich prächtig.* ✦ *Die Situation hat sich positiv entwickelt.* sich zu etw. entwickeln turn sth into sth ◊ *Er entwickelt sich zu einem richtigen Ekel.*
Ent·wick·lung [ɛnt'vɪklʊŋ] die <-, -en> 1. development ◊ *die Entwicklung eines Fötus* ✦ *die*

rasende Entwicklung von Computern ✦ *die Entwicklung einer neuen Theorie/von Formeln* 2. FOTO developing ◊ *die Entwicklung von Fotos im Labor*
Ent·wick·lungs·land [ɛnt'vɪklʊŋslant] das <-(e)s, Entwicklungsländer> 1. developing country 2. (*iron, fig*) underdeveloped country, backward country ◊ *Frauenpolitisch ist Deutschland ein Entwicklungsland.*
ent·wi·schen [ɛnt'vɪʃn̩] <entwischt, entwischte, ist entwischt> (intr v) (*fam*) escape, get away ◊ *Er konnte der Polizei entwischen.*
Ent·wurf [ɛnt'vʊrf] der <-(e)s, Entwürfe> 1. design, blueprint ◊ *Der Architekt zeichnete einen Entwurf für ein Mehrfamilienhaus.* 2. (*concept*) draft, outline; (*legislation*) bill ◊ *der Entwurf eines neuen Wahlgesetzes* im Entwurf sein be at the draft stage
ent·zie·hen [ɛnt'tsiːən] <entzieht, entzog, hat entzogen> (tr v) jdm etw. entziehen take sth away from sb, withdraw sth from sb, revoke sth from sb, deprive sb of sth ◊ *Man entzog ihm das Sorgerecht für seinen Sohn.* ✦ *Sie entzog ihm ihre Zuneigung.* (refl v) 1. (*person*) sich einer Sache (gen) entziehen evade sth, elude sth, escape from sth ◊ *Ich denke, dass er sich der Arbeit entziehen will.* ✦ *sich der Verantwortung für etw. entziehen* 2. (*pej*) (*action*) sich einer Sache (gen) entziehen be beyond sth ◊ *Seine Handlungsweise entzieht sich jeder vernünftigen Erklärung.* 3. sich einer Sache (gen) nicht entziehen können not be able to resist sth, succumb to sth ◊ *Sie konnte sich der Faszination nicht entziehen.* (intr v) (*fam*) undergo withdrawal treatment, cure your addiction, dry out ◊ *Er entzieht bereits zum dritten Mal.*
ent·zif·fern [ɛnt'tsɪfɐn] <entziffert, entzifferte, hat entziffert> (tr v) (*handwriting*) decipher ◊ *Ich kann deine Schrift kaum entziffern!*; (*a secret code also*) decode ◊ *Es gelang ihnen, die geheime Botschaft zu entziffern.*
Ent·zug [ɛnt'tsuːk] der <-(e)s, Entzüge> 1. withdrawal, deprivation, revocation ◊ *der Entzug einer Lizenz* ✦ *der Entzug von Nahrung* 2. (*fam*) (*from addiction*) withdrawal ◊ *Sie ist zurzeit auf Entzug.* ✦ *einen Entzug machen*
ent·zün·den [ɛnt'tsʏndn̩] <entzündet, entzündete, hat entzündet> (refl v) 1. MED sich entzünden become inflamed 2. sich entzünden catch fire ◊ *Eine Pfanne mit heißem Öl entzündete sich.* (tr v) 1. (*lofty*) light, set alight ◊ *ein Feuerwerk entzünden* 2. (*fig*) (*hatred*) inflame; (*argument, discussion*) start ◊ *eine Diskussion/Debatte entzünden*; (*enthusiasm*) kindle, fire
② **er** [eːɐ] (pers pron) 1. (*male person*) he, him ◊ *Das ist mein Bruder. Er heißt Hannes.* ✦ *Ich habe das für ihn gemacht.* ✦ *Ist dieser Brief an ihn?* ✦ *Hast du es ihm schon gesagt?* ✦ *ein Freund von ihm* Das ist eine Idee von ihm. That's his idea. 2. (*other nouns with masc article*) it ◊ *"Wo ist der Besen?" — "Er steht da drüben in der Ecke."* ✦ *Der Roman ist spannend. Hast du ihn schon gelesen?*; (*male animals also*) he ◊ *Der Vogel hat Hunger. Gib ihm was zu fressen.* ✦ *Der Hund bellt. Sieh mal nach, was er hat.*

A B C D E F G H I J K L M N O P Q R S T U V W X Y Z

A
B
C
D
E
F
G
H
I
J
K
L
M
N
O
P
Q
R
S
T
U
V
W
X
Y
Z

nom	er
acc	ihn
dat	ihm
gen	seiner

er·... [ɐ] (prefix) *translation varies* **1.** *(result)* etw. erforschen research sth Daraus können Probleme erwachsen. Problems may result from this. etw. erreichen achieve sth, reach sth **2.** *(setting in of a condition)* an Krebs erkranken fall ill with cancer vor Verlegenheit erröten go red with embarrassment jdn erstaunen astonish sb

er·ach·ten [ɐˈaxtn̩] <erachtet, erachtete, hat erachtet> (tr v) *(lofty)* etw. als ... erachten consider sth ..., deem sth ... ◊ etw. als sinnvoll erachten ♦ etw. als gute Lösung erachten

er·ar·bei·ten [ɐˈaʁbaetn̩] <erarbeitet, erarbeitete, hat erarbeitet> (tr v) **1.** *(a plan)* work out, devise ◊ eine Strategie/ein Programm erarbeiten **2.** *(knowledge)* study, work on, acquire ◊ ein Thema erarbeiten **3.** sich (dat) etw. erarbeiten work for sth ◊ Ich habe mir dieses Haus hart erarbeitet.

er·bärm·lich [ɐˈbɛʁmlɪç] (adj, adv) **1.** pitiful(ly), wretched(ly) ◊ in erbärmlichen Verhältnissen leben ♦ Der Hund jaulte erbärmlich. **2.** *(very bad)* pathetic(ally), miserable(-ably), appalling(ly) ◊ eine erbärmliche Vorstellung ♦ Die Luftqualität ist erbärmlich. **3.** *(morally)* mean(ly), wretched(ly) ◊ ein erbärmlicher Schuft ♦ Sein Verhalten gegenüber seiner Familie ist erbärmlich. **4.** *(intense)* terrible(-ibly), abominable(-ably) ◊ Die Hitze war erbärmlich. ♦ Hier stinkt es erbärmlich nach Fisch.

Er·be¹ [ˈɛʁbə] das <-s> *no pl* **1.** inheritance ◊ An ihrem 21. Geburtstag fiel ihr das großväterliche Erbe zu. **2.** heritage ◊ das kulturelle Erbe pflegen **3.** *(fig)* legacy ◊ Der neue Trainer trat ein schweres Erbe an.

Er·be² [ˈɛʁbə] der <-n, -n>, **Er·bin** [ˈɛʁbɪn] die <-, -nen> heir ◊ Er hat sie als alleinige Erbin eingesetzt.

er·ben [ˈɛʁbm̩] (tr v) +haben **1.** inherit ◊ Der älteste Sohn erbte den Bauernhof. ♦ Die musikalische Begabung hat er von dir geerbt. **2.** *(fam)* get, be given ◊ Als Kind habe ich die Kleider von meiner älteren Cousine geerbt. geerbte Kleidung hand-me-downs

Er·bin [ˈɛʁbɪn] *fem of* Erbe

er·bit·tert [ɐˈbɪtɐt] (adj, adv) **1.** *(fights, enemies)* bitter(ly), fierce(ly), violent(ly) ◊ erbitterte Feinde ♦ Die gestrigen Kämpfe waren besonders erbittert. ♦ erbittert kämpfen **2.** *(emotionally)* bitter(ly), angry(-ily) ◊ Sie war erbittert darüber, dass ihr Vorschlag abgelehnt wurde.

er·bli·cken [ɐˈblɪkn̩] <erblickt, erblickte, hat erblickt> (tr v) *(lofty)* spot, catch sight of, see ◊ Sie erblickte in der Ferne ein Licht. ♦ Er lächelte, als er sie erblickte.

er·bre·chen [ɐˈbʁɛçn̩] <erbricht, erbrach, hat erbrochen> (tr v) throw up, vomit ◊ Sie erbrach das Mittagessen. sich erbrechen throw up, vomit, be sick ◊ Er hat sich in der Nacht mehrmals erbrochen.

Erb·schaft [ˈɛʁpʃaft] die <-, -en> **1.** inheritance ◊ jdm eine Erbschaft hinterlassen ♦ eine Erbschaft

antreten ♦ Sie hat eine größere Erbschaft gemacht. **2.** *(fig)* legacy ◊ Unsere Vorfahren haben uns eine schwere Erbschaft hinterlassen.

Erb·se [ˈɛʁpsə] die <-, -n> *most pl* pea

② **Erd·ap·fel** [ˈeːɐ̯tapfl̩] der <-s, Erdäpfel> *(SouthG, Austr)* potato ⊖Kartoffel

Erd·be·ben [ˈeːɐ̯tbeːbm̩] das <-s, -> **1.** earthquake ◊ Ein schweres Erdbeben erschütterte die Türkei. **2.** *(fig)* upheaval ◊ Das Wahlergebnis löste ein politisches Erdbeben aus.

Erd·bee·re [ˈeːɐ̯tbeːʁə] die <-, -n> strawberry ◊ Erdbeeren pflücken

Erd·bo·den [ˈeːɐ̯tboːdn̩] der <-s, Erdböden> ground, earth ◊ etw. mit Stahlseilen im Erdboden verankern ♦ Er lag auf dem nackten Erdboden. ⊖Boden

ⓘ am liebsten im Erdboden versinken möchten wish the earth would swallow you (up) ◊ Ich möchte am liebsten im Erdboden versinken vor Scham. jd ist wie vom Erdboden verschluckt/ verschwunden it is as if the earth had swallowed sb up

② **Er·de** [ˈeːɐ̯də] die <-, -n> *most sing* **1.** *no pl* earth, world ◊ Die Astronauten umrundeten die Erde. ♦ jeder Mensch auf Gottes Erde **2.** soil, earth ◊ Erde aufschütten **3.** *no pl* ground ◊ auf der Erde sitzen ♦ Die Erde bebte. **4.** *no pl* spot ◊ ein romantisches Stückchen Erde

② **Erd·ge·schoss** [ˈeːɐ̯tgəʃɔs] das <-es, -e> ground floor; *(in the US)* first floor ◊ Das Büro befindet sich im Erdgeschoss.

Erd·kun·de [ˈeːɐ̯tkʊndə] die <-> *no pl* geography ◊ In der ersten Stunde haben wir Erdkunde.

Erd·nuss [ˈeːɐ̯tnʊs] die <-, Erdnüsse> peanut, groundnut ◊ geröstete Erdnüsse

Erd·öl [ˈeːɐ̯tøːl] das <-(e)s, -e> *most sing* petroleum, (mineral) oil ◊ Erdöl fördern

er·drü·cken [ɐˈdʁʏkn̩] <erdrückt, erdrückte, hat erdrückt> (tr v) **1.** crush (to death) ◊ Der Bauer wurde von einem Traktor erdrückt. **2.** *(fig)* *(a person)* overwhelm, suffocate ◊ Mich erdrücken die Schulden. ♦ eine Liebe, die beide Partner erdrückt **3.** *(fig)* *(an impression)* overpower, overshadow ◊ Der massive Rahmen erdrückt das Bild.

Erd·teil [ˈeːɐ̯ttael] der <-(e)s, -e> continent ◊ Künstler aus allen fünf Erdteilen ⊖Kontinent

② **er·eig·nen** [ɐˈaegnən] <ereignet sich, ereignete sich, hat sich ereignet> (ref v) sich ereignen happen, occur ◊ Auf der B9 ereignete sich gestern ein schwerer Unfall. ♦ Hat sich in der Besprechung noch etwas Wichtiges ereignet?

② **Er·eig·nis** [ɐˈaegnɪs] das <-ses, -se> event, occurrence, incident ◊ ein tragisches Ereignis ♦ Die Ereignisse überschlugen sich.

② **er·fah·ren** [ɐˈfaːʁən] <erfährt, erfuhr, hat erfahren> (tr+intr v) find out, learn, hear ◊ Ich habe das aus der Zeitung erfahren. ♦ Wenn Sie Näheres erfahren möchten, wenden Sie sich bitte an ... von uns. etw. erfahren learn of sth, hear about sth ◊ Warum erfahre ich erst jetzt davon? (tr v) *(lofty)* experience, undergo ◊ Die Umweltpolitik hat eine Aufwertung erfahren.

② **Er·fah·rung** [ɐˈfaːʁʊŋ] die <-, -en> experience ◊ Veronika hat viel Erfahrung auf dem Gebiet der Lexikographie. ♦ Das weiß ich aus persönlicher Erfahrung. ♦ Meine Erfahrungen mit diesem

Produkt sind schlechte.
⊙ **in Erfahrung bringen** find out ◊ *Hast du in Erfahrung gebracht, was das kostet?*

er·fas·sen [ɛˈfasn̩] <erfasst, erfasste, hat erfasst> ⟨tr v⟩ **1.** *(with your mind)* grasp, understand ◊ *Ich kann die künstlerische Aussage dieser Skulptur nicht erfassen.* **2.** *(data)* record, register ◊ *Daten elektronisch erfassen* **3.** *(in an accident)* catch ◊ *Ein Skifahrer wurde von einer Lawine erfasst und verschüttet.* **4.** *(by a feeling)* seize ◊ *Er wurde von großer Wehmut erfasst.*

② **er·fin·den** [ɛˈfɪndn̩] <erfindet, erfand, hat erfunden> ⟨tr v⟩ invent ◊ *Edison erfand die elektrische Glühlampe.* ✦ *Diese Geschichte hast du doch erfunden!*

Er·fin·dung [ɛˈfɪndʊŋ] die <–, –en> **1.** invention ◊ *die Erfindung neuer Produkte* ✦ *Er ließ sich seine Erfindung patentieren.* **2.** *(untrue story)* invention, fiction, fabrication ◊ *Das halte ich für eine pure Erfindung.*

② **er·folg** [ɛˈfɔlk] der <–(e)s, –e> success ◊ *Ihr neuester Roman ist ein voller Erfolg.* ✦ *Er absolvierte sein Studium mit großem Erfolg.* ✦ *Deine Bemühungen waren nicht von Erfolg gekrönt.*
⊖Misserfolg

er·fol·gen [ɛˈfɔlɡn̩] <erfolgt, erfolgte, ist erfolgt> ⟨intr v⟩ *(form)* **1.** follow, ensue ◊ *Wenige Tage nach der Bewerbung erfolgte ein Anruf.* ✦ *Ist schon eine Antwort erfolgt?* **2.** take place, occur ◊ *Die Eröffnung des Stadions erfolgte am 19. April.*

er·folg·reich [ɛˈfɔlkraɛç] ⟨adj, adv⟩ successful(ly) ◊ *ein erfolgreicher Abschluss* ✦ *Er ist als Schauspieler sehr erfolgreich.* ✦ *Sie hat ihre Lehre erfolgreich abgeschlossen.*

er·for·der·lich [ɛˈfɔˈdelɪç] ⟨adj⟩ *seldom comp/superl* required, necessary ◊ *eine Bewerbung mit den erforderlichen Unterlagen schicken* ✦ *Hier ist Abhilfe dringend erforderlich.*

er·for·schen [ɛˈfɔˈʃn] <erforscht, erforschte, hat erforscht> ⟨tr v⟩ explore, research, investigate ◊ *eine Krankheit wissenschaftlich erforschen*

er·freu·lich [ɛˈfrɔɡlɪç] ⟨adj, adv⟩ pleasant(ly), agreeable(-ably), gratifying(ly) ◊ *eine erfreuliche Entwicklung* ✦ *Er wertete das Ergebnis als besonders erfreulich.* ✦ *Es ist erfreulich, dass es ihm wieder besser geht.* ✦ *Die Aktion ist erfreulich verlaufen.* ⊖unerfreulich

er·frie·ren [ɛˈfriːrən] <erfriert, erfror, ist erfroren> ⟨intr v⟩ **1.** freeze to death, be killed by frost ◊ *In diesem Winter sind bereits mehrere Menschen erfroren.* ✦ *Bei dem späten Frost erfroren fast sämtliche Kirschblüten.* **2.** jdm erfriert etw. sb gets frostbite in sth ◊ *Bei einer Polarexpedition erfroren ihm beide Hände.*

Er·fri·schung [ɛˈfrɪʃʊŋ] die <–, –en> refreshment ◊ *Der Regenschauer war eine willkommene Erfrischung.* ✦ *Den Gästen wurden Erfrischungen serviert.*

② **er·fül·len** [ɛˈfʏlən] <erfüllt, erfüllte, hat erfüllt> ⟨tr v⟩ **1.** *(a dream, wish)* fulfil, grant, make come true ◊ *Mit dieser Reise erfüllte sie sich einen Lebenstraum.* **2.** *(a condition, prerequisite)* meet, fulfil, comply with, satisfy ◊ *die erforderlichen Voraussetzungen erfüllen* **3.** etw. erfüllt jdn sb is full of sth, sb is filled with sth ◊ *Ein Gefühl von Stolz erfüllte ihn. Die Mutterrolle erfüllt mich*

nicht. *The role of mother doesn't fulfil me.* **4.** etw. erfüllt etw. sth fills sth ◊ *Die Kirche war von feierlichen Klängen erfüllt.* ⟨ref v⟩ etw. erfüllt sich sth comes true, sth is fulfilled ◊ *Ihr Kinderwunsch erfüllte sich nicht.*

er·gän·zen [ɛˈɡɛntsn̩] <ergänzt, ergänzte, hat ergänzt> ⟨tr v⟩ complete, amend, replenish ◊ *Das Warenangebot soll sinnvoll ergänzt werden.* ✦ *Das Studium wurde durch ein Praktikum ergänzt.* ✦ *„Das Haus ist zu groß für uns", sagte sie. „Und viel zu teuer", ergänzte er.* ergänzend hinzufügen/ erläutern/bemerken add ◊ *Sie erläuterte ergänzend, dass ...* sie ergänzen sich they complement each other/one another ◊ *Gerd ist der Richtige für Eva, denn die beiden ergänzen sich gut.*

er·ge·ben [ɛˈɡeːbm̩] <ergibt, ergab, hat ergeben> ⟨tr v⟩ **1.** amount to, come to ◊ *Was ergibt 154 plus 217?* **2.** reveal ◊ *Wie die Ermittlungen ergaben, handelte es sich um Mord.* ⟨ref v⟩ etw. ergibt sich sth arises, sth turns up ◊ *Die Möglichkeit dazu ergab sich rein zufällig.* **2.** *(to a bad habit, an addiction)* sich einer Sache ⟨dat⟩ ergeben take to sth, devote yourself to sth ◊ *Er ergab sich dem Glücksspiel.* **3.** sich ergeben surrender ◊ *Nach zwölf Tagen Belagerung ergaben sie sich.* **4.** *(to a situation)* sich einer Sache ⟨dat⟩ ergeben submit to sth, resign yourself to sth ◊ *Sie ergab sich ihrem Schicksal/der ausweglosen Situation.*

② **Er·geb·nis** [ɛˈɡeːpnɪs] das <–es, –se> **1.** result, outcome ◊ *das Ergebnis eines Fußballspiels* ✦ *ein positives Ergebnis erzielen* ⊖Resultat **2.** conclusion ◊ *Nach gründlicher Prüfung kamen sie zu folgendem Ergebnis: ...* **3.** MATH result, sum ◊ *Was ist das Ergebnis von 132 geteilt durch 12?*

er·gie·big [ɛˈɡiːbɪç] ⟨adj⟩ **1.** *(product)* economical ◊ *ein ergiebiges Waschpulver* ✦ *Dieses Spülmittel ist sehr ergiebig.* **2.** extensive, informative ◊ *ein ergiebiger Text* ✦ *Sein Beitrag war wissenschaftlich ergiebig.* ⟨adj, adv⟩ abundant(ly) ◊ *Die Ernte war ergiebig.* ✦ *eine ergiebig sprudelnde Quelle an Informationen*

er·grei·fen [ɛˈɡraɛfn̩] <ergreift, ergriff, hat ergriffen> ⟨tr v⟩ **1.** *(lofty)* take hold of, grab (hold of) ◊ *Er ergriff sein Schwert und stellte sich dem Kampf. jds Arm/Hand ergreifen* seize sb's arm/ hand **2.** catch ◊ *Die Polizei konnte den Dieb ergreifen.* **3.** *(emotions)* etw. ergreift jdn sb is seized by sth ◊ *Mitleid ergriff mich, als ich das Leid der Kinder sah.* **4.** seize, take up ◊ *als das Militär die Macht ergriff das Wort ergreifen* (begin to) speak *die Initiative ergreifen* take the initiative **5.** move, affect ◊ *Ihre Musik/Rede hat mich sehr ergriffen.* **6.** affect, spread to ◊ *Die Krankheit ergriff weite Teile der Bevölkerung.*

② **er·hal·ten** [ɛˈhaltn̩] <erhält, erhielt, hat erhalten> ⟨tr v⟩ **1.** get, receive ◊ *Haben Sie unseren Brief erhalten? Für diese Arbeit erhalten Sie 25 Euro in der Stunde.* ✦ *Wir haben den Befehl erhalten, das Haus zu räumen.* ⊖bekommen **2.** preserve, keep ◊ *Gebäude unter Denkmalschutz müssen erhalten werden.* ✦ *Sie hat sich ihr jugendliches Aussehen erhalten.* ✦ *Maßnahmen, um den Frieden erhalten sollen* sich erhalten remain, be preserved ◊ *Dieser Brauch hat sich nur im Alpenraum erhalten.* sich jung etc. erhalten stay young etc.

A
B
C
D
E
F
G
H
I
J
K
L
M
N
O
P
Q
R
S
T
U
V
W
X
Y
Z

A

jdn am Leben erhalten keep sb alive Wir hoffen, dass du uns noch lange erhalten bleibst. We hope you'll be with us for a long time yet.

er·hält·lich [ɛˈhɛltlɪç] [adj] *no comp/superl* available ◊ *Die Zusatzteile sind nur im Fachhandel erhältlich.*

B

er·he·ben [ɛˈheːbm̩] <erhebt, erhob, hat erhoben> [tr v] **1.** *(lofty)* raise, lift ◊ *die Hand zum Gruß erheben* ♦ *Sie erhob den Blick zum Himmel.* **2.** *(fees)* charge, levy ◊ *Steuern/Gebühren erheben* **3.** *(demands)* make ◊ *Forderungen erheben* ♦ *Birma erhebt Anspruch auf dieses Gebiet.* gegen jdn Klage erheben bring a charge against sb (einen) Einwand gegen etw. erheben object to sth, raise an objection to sth Protest gegen etw. erheben protest against sth **4.** jdn/etw. in etw. [acc] erheben promote sb/raise sth to sth ◊ *eine Zahl in die dritte Potenz erheben* jdn in den Adelsstand erheben ennoble sb, bestow a title on sb jdn/etw. zu etw. erheben make sb/sth sth ◊ *Er wurde zum Kardinal erhoben.* ♦ *Das Gebäude wurde zum Weltkulturerbe erhoben.* [ref v] **1.** *(lofty)* *(person)* sich erheben rise, get up ◊ *Als sie das Zimmer betrat, erhoben sich alle.*; *(with effort)* raise yourself ◊ *Sie schaffte es kaum, sich vom Stuhl zu erheben.* **2.** *(lofty)* *(a bird, helicopter)* sich erheben rise ◊ *Der Adler erhob sich in die Lüfte.* **3.** *+place* sich irgendwo erheben rise up somewhere ◊ *Hinter dem Hotel erhoben sich die Berge.* **4.** *(lofty, fig)* *(laughter, cheering, indignation, a question)* sich erheben arise ◊ *Gelächter/ Jubel erhob sich.* ♦ *Ein Sturm der Entrüstung erhob sich.; (a scream)* ring out **5.** sich (gegen jdn/etw.) erheben rise up (against sb/sth), revolt (against sb/sth) ◊ *Das Volk erhob sich (gegen den Tyrannen).*

C

D

E

F

G

H

I

J

K

L

M

N

O

P

er·heb·lich [ɛˈheːplɪç] [adj, adv] considerable ◊ *Bei dem Unfall enstand erheblicher Sachschaden.* ♦ *Der Vorteil eines solchen Vorgehens ist erheblich.* ♦ *Er hat sich in der Schule erheblich verbessert.*

Q

er·hit·zen [ɛˈhɪtsn̩] <erhitzt, erhitzte, hat erhitzt> [tr v] **1.** heat (up) ◊ *Öl in einer Pfanne erhitzen* **2.** die Gemüter erhitzen make passions run high ◊ *Die Debatte um dieses Gesetz erhitzt die Gemüter.* [ref v] **1.** sich erhitzen get hot ◊ *Im Sommer erhitzt sich dieser Raum stark.* **2.** *(person)* sich (über/an etw. [acc]) erhitzen get heated (about sth) ◊ *sich an einer Frage erhitzen* ♦ *Kein Grund, sich zu erhitzen!* Die Gemüter erhitzen sich. Passions run high.

R

S

T

U

V

W

X

er·hof·fen [ɛˈhɔfn̩] <erhofft sich, erhoffte sich, hat sich erhofft> [ref v] expect ◊ *Man erhoffte sich von ihm eine Lösung des Problems.* ♦ *Wir erhoffen uns, damit neue Kunden zu gewinnen.* besser/früher/ schneller als erhofft better/earlier/faster than anticipated ◊ *Das Produkt verkaufte sich besser als erhofft.*

Y

Z

②**er·hö·hen** [ɛˈhøːən] <erhöht, erhöhte, hat erhöht> [tr v] **1.** put up, raise, increase ◊ *Die Produktion kann noch weiter erhöht werden.* ♦ *Rauchen erhöht das Risiko, an Krebs zu erkranken.* sich erhöhen go up, increase ◊ *Die Kosten haben sich um fünf Prozent erhöht.* ♦ *Durch die andauernde Trockenheit hat sich die Gefahr von Waldbränden erhöht.* ⊝senken **2.** make higher ◊ *Seit der letzten Überschwemmung sind alle Dämme erhöht worden.* ein

Gebäude um ein Stockwerk erhöhen add another storey to a building

②**er·ho·len** [ɛˈhoːlən] <erholt sich, erholte sich, hat sich erholt> [ref v] jd erholt sich sb has a rest, sb relaxes ◊ *Ich habe mich im Urlaub prima erholt.; (from a crisis, an illness etc.)* sich (von etw. [dat]) erholen recover (from sth) ◊ *Hast du dich inzwischen von dem Schock erholt?* ♦ So langsam erholen sich die Börsenkurse wieder. ⊝sich regenerieren

②**er·in·nern** [ɛˈɪnɐn] <erinnert, erinnerte, hat erinnert> [tr v] jdn an jdn/etw. erinnern remind sb of sb/sth ◊ *Sie erinnert mich sehr an meine Großmutter.* ♦ *Kannst du mich bitte daran erinnern, dass ich ihn anrufe?* [ref v] sich (an jdn/etw.) erinnern remember (sb/sth) ◊ *Ich erinnere mich gern an diese Zeit.* ♦ *Erinnern Sie sich noch an mich?*

②**Er·in·ne·rung** [ɛˈɪnərʊŋ] die <-, -en> **1.** memory ◊ *mit alten Freunden Erinnerungen austauschen* ♦ *Die Erinnerung an meine Kindheit ist verblasst.* Wenn mich meine Erinnerung nicht täuscht, ... If I remember rightly, ... sich [dat] etw. in Erinnerung rufen sth, remind yourself of sth **2.** memory, commemoration ◊ *ein Denkmal zur Erinnerung an die Kriegsopfer* **3.** souvenir ◊ *Sie hat mir einen Ring zur Erinnerung geschenkt.*

②**er·käl·ten** [ɛˈkɛltn̩] <erkältet sich, erkältete sich, hat sich erkältet> [ref v] sich erkälten catch/get a cold, catch a chill ◊ *Er hat sich erkältet und liegt jetzt mit Fieber im Bett.* sich [dat] etw. erkälten get a chill on sth ◊ *Sie hat sich die Blase erkältet.*

er·käl·tet [ɛˈkɛltət] [adj] *no comp/superl* erkältet sein have got a cold ◊ *Wenn du erkältet bist, solltest du im Bett bleiben.*

Er·käl·tung [ɛˈkɛltʊŋ] die <-, -en> cold, chill ◊ *Sie hat sich eine Erkältung geholt/zugezogen.*

er·kenn·bar [ɛˈkɛnbaːˀ] [adj, adv] recognizable (-ably), noticeable(-ably) ◊ *erkennbare Fortschritte* ♦ *Das Gemälde war leicht als Fälschung erkennbar.* ♦ *Seine Leistung hat sich erkennbar verbessert.*

②**er·ken·nen** [ɛˈkɛnən] [tr v] **1.** see, tell ◊ *Ich kann leider nicht erkennen, was auf dem Schild steht.* **2.** recognize ◊ *Ich hätte ihn fast nicht erkannt, so sehr war er gealtert.* ♦ *Diese Krankheit ist an den roten Flecken zu erkennen.* **3.** recognize, realize ◊ *Ich habe meinen Fehler erkannt und mich entschuldigt.* **4.** etw. erkennen lassen show sth ◊ *Der Patient lässt Zeichen der Besserung erkennen.* etw. lässt sich erkennen is apparent ◊ *Am Arbeitsmarkt ist ein leichter Aufwärtstrend erkennen.* [intr v] *(form)* auf etw. [acc] erkennen decide on sth ◊ *Im Fall Schmid hat das Gericht auf Freispruch erkannt.* ◉ jdm etw. zu erkennen geben indicate sth to sb, show sb sth ◊ *Sie hat mir ihr Interesse zu erkennen gegeben.* du bist erkannt got you, I know your game

Er·kennt·nis [ɛˈkɛntnɪs] die <-, -se> **1.** realization ◊ *Ich bin zu der Erkenntnis gekommen, dass mir dieser Beruf nicht liegt.* **2.** *most pl* knowledge ◊ *Die Untersuchung hat zu völlig neuen Erkenntnissen geführt.* **3.** *only pl (form)* information ◊ *Der Polizei liegen noch keine Erkenntnisse über den Täter.*

②**er·klä·ren** [ɛˈklɛːrən] <erklärt, erklärte, hat erklärt>

[tr v] **1.** explain ◊ *Kannst du mir erklären, wie das Handy funktioniert?* ✦ *Seine lange Krankheit erklärt die Lücken in seinem Wissen.* **2.** declare ◊ *Der Minister hat seinen Rücktritt erklärt.* ✦ *Franz hat ihr seine Liebe erklärt.* ✦ *den Krieg erklären* **3.** jdn zu etw. erklären name sb as sth ◊ *Die Jury hat ihn zum Sieger erklärt.* **4.** declare, pronounce ◊ *Nach ein paar Jahren wurde er für tot erklärt.* jdn als vermisst erklären report sb missing [ref v] **1.** sich solidarisch/einverstanden etc. erklären express your solidarity/consent etc. sich mit etw. zufrieden erklären express your satisfaction with sth sich bereit/willens erklären, etw. zu tun express your readiness/willingness to do sth **2.** sich etw. erklären können be able to understand sth ◊ *Ich kann mir nicht erklären, warum sie das getan hat.*

Er·klä·rung [eˈklɛːrʊŋ] die <-, -en> **1.** explanation ◊ *Die Erklärungen in diesem Wörterbuch sind leicht verständlich.* ✦ *Wir haben noch keine Erklärung für ihr Verschwinden.* **2.** statement ◊ *In einer Erklärung des Unternehmens heißt es, ...* ✦ *Der Minister gab keine Erklärung dazu ab.*

er·kran·ken [eˈkraŋkn̩] <erkrankt, erkrankte, ist erkrankt> [intr v] *(form)* become ill, be taken ill an etw. [dat] erkranken be ill with sth, suffer from sth ◊ *Sie ist an Krebs erkrankt.*

⑦ **er·kun·di·gen** [eˈkʊndɪgn̩] <erkundigt sich, hat sich erkundigt> [ref v] sich erkundigen ask, inquire ◊ *Frau Lerner hat sich nach dir erkundigt.* ✦ *Er hat sich bei mir erkundigt, wann du aus dem Urlaub zurückkommst.*

er·las·sen [eˈlasn̩] <erlässt, erließ, hat erlassen> [tr v] **1.** jdm etw. erlassen release sb from sth, relieve sb of sth ◊ *Diesen Ländern soll ein Teil ihrer Schulden erlassen werden.* Wegen guter Führung wurde ihm der Rest der Strafe erlassen. The rest of his sentence was remitted for good behavio(u)r. **2.** issue ◊ *einen Befehl/eine Verordnung erlassen; (a law)* pass; *(a ban)* impose ◊ *Für die gesamte Innenstadt wurde ein Fahrverbot erlassen.*

⑦ **er·lau·ben** [eˈlaʊbn̩] <erlaubt, erlaubte, hat erlaubt> [tr v] **1.** permit, allow ◊ *Meine Eltern erlauben mir nicht, so spät noch wegzugehen.* ✦ *Erlauben Sie, dass ich hier Platz nehme?* ⊖verbieten **2.** permit, make possible ◊ *Sein Gesundheitszustand erlaubt eine Verlegung nicht. Mein Geldbeutel erlaubt mir solche Reisen nicht.* I can't afford to go on trips like that. ⊖verbieten **3.** sich [dat] etw. erlauben; sich erlauben, etw. zu tun take the liberty of doing sth ◊ *Ich habe mir erlaubt, den Brief zu öffnen. Er erlaubt sich seinem Lehrer gegenüber so manche Frechheit.* He's very cheeky to his teacher. ☺ erlaube mal I ask you, really ◊ *Erlaube mal, du kannst doch nicht so einfach über mein Geld bestimmen!* erlauben Sie mal do you mind, if you don't mind ◊ *Erlauben Sie mal, ich bin zuerst dran!*

⑦ **Er·laub·nis** [eˈlaʊpnɪs] die <-, -se> **1.** permission ◊ *Hast du dafür die Erlaubnis deiner Eltern?* ✦ *Franz bat um die Erlaubnis, etwas früher gehen zu dürfen.* **2.** permit ◊ *Hier darf nur mit einer speziellen Erlaubnis geparkt werden.*

er·läu·tern [eˈlɔɪtɐn] <erläutert, erläuterte, hat erläutert> [tr v] *(form)* explain ◊ *Unser Physiklehrer hat uns die Formel erläutert.* ✦ *Er wollte seine Gründe nicht näher erläutern.* ⊖erklären

⑦ **er·le·ben** [eˈleːbm̩] <erlebt, erlebte, hat erlebt> [tr v] **1.** experience ◊ *Die Wirtschaft erlebt zurzeit einen Aufschwung.* ✦ *eine herbe Enttäuschung erleben* jd erlebt mit jdm immer wieder Überraschungen sb never ceases to surprise sb ◊ *Mit meinen Kindern erlebe ich immer wieder Überraschungen. Du hast ihn noch nicht erlebt, wenn er wirklich wütend ist.* You haven't seen him when he's really angry. **2.** live to see ◊ *Meine Oma hat die Geburt meiner Tochter leider nicht mehr erlebt.* ☺ man so was schon erlebt can you believe it dann kann jd was erleben then sb will be in for it ◊ *Wenn er das erfährt, kannst du was erleben!*

Er·leb·nis [eˈleːpnɪs] das <-ses, -se> **1.** experience ◊ *Sie hat uns ihre Erlebnisse in Japan erzählt.* ein an Erlebnissen reiches Leben an eventful life **2.** amazing experience, experience of a lifetime ◊ *Der Ballettabend war einfach ein Erlebnis!*

⑦ **er·le·di·gen** [eˈleːdɪgn̩] <erledigt, erledigte, hat erledigt> [tr v] **1.** do, take care of ◊ *Meine Sekretärin wird das für mich erledigen.* ✦ *Er hat die Einkäufe erledigt.* ✦ *Sobald ich diese Arbeit erledigt habe, schreibe ich ihr.* **2.** *(fam)* kill, finish off ◊ *Den hat die Mafia erledigt.* [ref v] sich erledigen sort itself out ◊ *Wart ab, vielleicht erledigt sich das Problem von selbst.* ☺ erledigt sein **1.** be finished ◊ *Wenn das rauskommt, dann ist mein Chef erledigt.* **2.** be shattered ◊ *Nach dem Training war ich völlig erledigt.*

er·leich·tern [eˈlaɪçtɐn] <erleichterte, hat erleichtert> [tr v] **1.** (jdm) etw. erleichtern make sth easier (for sb) ◊ *Das Programm erleichtert mir die Buchhaltung.* ⊖erschweren **2.** relieve ◊ *ein Medikament, um die Schmerzen zu erleichtern* ✦ *Die gute Nachricht hat uns alle erleichtert.* sein Herz erleichtern get it (all) off your chest sein Gewissen erleichtern unburden your conscience **3.** *(hum)* jdn um etw. erleichtern relieve sb of sth ◊ *Er hat mich beim Kartenspiel um 50 Euro erleichtert.*

er·lei·den [eˈlaɪdn̩] <erleidet, erlitt, hat erlitten> [tr v] suffer ◊ *einen Herzinfarkt erleiden* ✦ *Die Firma erlitt große Verluste.* ✦ *eine vernichtende Niederlage erleiden*

er·lischt [eˈlɪʃt] *pres* of erlöschen

Er·lös [eˈløːs] der <-es, -e> proceeds ◊ *Der Erlös der Veranstaltung wird für einen guten Zweck gespendet.*

er·losch [eˈlɔʃ] *pret* of erlöschen

er·lo·schen [eˈlɔʃn̩] *past p* of erlöschen

er·lö·schen [eˈlœʃn̩] <erlischt, erlosch, ist erloschen> [intr v] **1.** *(also fig)* go out ◊ *Das Feuer ist erloschen.* ✦ *Sein Lebenslicht ist erloschen.; (volcano)* become extinct **2.** expire, be annulled ◊ *Mit seinem Tod sind sämtliche Ansprüche an seine Familie erloschen.* **3.** diminish, disappear ◊ *Ihre Begeisterung war schnell erloschen.*

er·lö·sen [eˈløːzn̩] <erlöst, erlöste, hat erlöst> [tr v] jdn (von etw.) erlösen release sb (from sth) ◊ *Der Arzt hat ihn von seinen Schmerzen erlöst.; (biblical)* redeem sb (from sth) ◊ *Christus hat uns von unseren Sünden erlöst.* etw. erlösen release sb from sth, rescue sb from sth ◊ *jdn aus*

der Gefangenschaft erlösen; *(from a boring person or activity)* jdn von jdm/etw. erlösen *save sb from sb/sth, rescue sb from sb/sth* ◊ *Gott sei Dank hast du mich von diesem Langweiler erlöst!* ♦ *Ich halte es hier nicht mehr aus, komm und erlöse mich!*

er·mäch·ti·gen [ɛˈmɛçtɪɡŋ̩] <ermächtigt, ermächtigte, hat ermächtigt> [tr v] *authorize* ◊ *Ich habe ihn ermächtigt, über mein Konto zu verfügen.* ♦ *Ich bin nicht ermächtigt, darüber eine Entscheidung zu treffen.*

er·mah·nen [ɛˈmaːnən] <ermahnt, ermahnte, hat ermahnt> [tr v] *warn* ◊ *Der Polizist ermahnte die Kinder, besser auf die Verkehrsregeln zu achten.* jdn zu etw. ermahnen *tell sb to do sth, urge sb to do sth* ◊ *vom Arzt zur Einhaltung der Therapie ermahnt werden* jdn zur Vorsicht ermahnen *urge sb to be careful*

Er·mä·ßi·gung [ɛˈmɛːsɪɡʊŋ] die <-, -en> *reduction, discount* ◊ *Kinder, Rentner und Behinderte bekommen eine Ermäßigung.*

Er·mes·sen [ɛˈmɛsŋ̩] das <-s> *no pl (form) discretion* ◊ *Er kann nach eigenem Ermessen entscheiden.* ♦ *Das Strafmaß liegt im Ermessen des Gerichts.*
 ⊛ **nach menschlichem Ermessen** *as far as anyone can judge*

er·mit·teln [ɛˈmɪtl̩n] <ermittelt, ermittelte, hat ermittelt> [tr v] etw. ermitteln *find sth out, establish sth, identify sth* ◊ *Wie ermittelt man den Durchschnittswert?* ♦ *die Ursache einer Krankheit ermitteln* jdn ermitteln *identify sb, establish sb* ◊ *Die Polizei hat den Täter noch nicht ermitteln können.* [intr v] *investigate, carry out investigations* gegen jdn ermitteln *investigate sb* ◊ *In diesem Mordfall ermittelt die Staatsanwaltschaft gegen drei Personen.* in einem Fall ermitteln *investigate a case*

er·mög·li·chen [ɛˈmøːklɪçn̩] <ermöglicht, ermöglichte, hat ermöglicht> [tr v] *make possible, enable* ◊ *den Zugang zu Daten ermöglichen* jdm etw. ermöglichen; jdm ermöglichen, etw. zu tun *make it possible for sb to do sth, enable sb to do sth* ◊ *Meine Eltern haben mir ein Studium ermöglicht.* ♦ *Die Erbschaft ermöglicht es mir, eine Reise zu machen.*

er·mor·den [ɛˈmoˈdn̩] <ermordet, ermordete, hat ermordet> [tr v] *murder* ◊ *Der Diktator hat tausende Menschen ermorden lassen.*

er·mü·dend [ɛˈmyːdŋ̩t, ɛˈmyːdənt] [adj] *tiring, wearing* ◊ *Der Vortrag war sehr monoton und ermüdend.* ♦ *eine ermüdende Tätigkeit*

er·mun·tern [ɛˈmʊntɐn] <ermuntert, ermunterte, hat ermuntert> [tr v] *encourage* ◊ *Meine Freunde haben mich ermuntert, einen Roman zu schreiben.* ♦ *Der erste Erfolg hat sie zum Weitermachen ermuntert.*

er·mu·ti·gen [ɛˈmuːtɪɡŋ̩] <ermutigt, ermutigte, hat ermutigt> [tr v] *encourage* ◊ *Meine Eltern haben mich zu diesem Schritt ermutigt.* ♦ *Ihr Professor hat sie ermutigt, eine Doktorarbeit zu schreiben.*

② **er·näh·ren** [ɛˈnɛːrən] <ernährt, ernährte, hat ernährt> [tr v] jdn ernähren *provide sb with food, feed sb* ◊ *Von meinem Gehalt kann ich meine Familie nur knapp ernähren.* ♦ *Das Land kann die Bevölkerung nicht ernähren.* ein Tier ernähren *feed*

an animal [ref v] **1.** sich gesund/ungesund ernähren *have a healthy/poor diet* ◊ *Ich ernähre mich vegetarisch.* **2.** sich von etw. ernähren *live on sth* ◊ *Kühe ernähren sich von Gras.*

Er·näh·rung [ɛˈnɛːrʊŋ] die <-> *no pl* **1.** diet ◊ *Von zu fetter Ernährung bekommt man Gefäßkrankheiten.* **2.** feeding ◊ *Bei Ernährung mit Muttermilch ist das Baby resistenter gegen Krankheiten.* **3.** living, livelihood *Sein Gehalt reicht zur Ernährung seiner Familie nicht mehr aus. He no longer earns enough to feed his family.*

er·nen·nen [ɛˈnɛnən] <ernennt, ernannte, hat ernannt> [tr v] jdn zu etw. ernennen *appoint sb (as) sth, make sb sth* ◊ *Er wurde zum Bürgermeister/Klassensprecher ernannt.*

er·neu·ern [ɛˈnɔøɐn] <erneuert, erneuerte, hat erneuert> [tr v] **1.** replace ◊ *Unsere Büroeinrichtung wird alle fünf Jahre erneuert.* **2.** *(friendship, love)* revive ◊ *Wir wollen mit diesem Treffen unsere alte Freundschaft erneuern.; (written request, application)* resubmit, renew ◊ *Der Antrag auf Gebührenbefreiung muss jedes Jahr erneuert werden.* **3.** renovate ◊ *Die gesamte Kirche wurde erneuert.* [ref v] sich erneuern *recover* ◊ *Nach dem Waldbrand hat sich die Vegetation erstaunlich schnell erneuert.; (cells) renew themselves* ⊖sich regenerieren

er·neut [ɛˈnɔøt] [adj] *no comp/superl, only before ns* renewed ◊ *Ein erneuter Ausbruch der Krankheit ist nicht zu befürchten.* [adv] again ◊ *Wir haben erneut versucht, diese Frage zu klären.* ⊖abermals

⑦ **ernst** [ɛrnst] [adj, adv] <ernster, am ernstesten> serious(ly) ◊ *Sebastian ist ein sehr ernstes Kind.* ♦ *Die Lage ist äußerst ernst.* ♦ *eine ernste Gefahr* ♦ *Ich habe ernste Zweifel, ob wir das schaffen.* ♦ *Ich meine das ernst!* ♦ *In seiner Klasse nimmt ihn keiner ernst, weil er immer Witze macht. Es wird ernst. Things are getting serious.* ernst mit jdm reden *have a serious talk with sb* ⊛ **es steht ernst um jdn** *things are looking bad for sb*

Ernst [ɛrnst] der <-es> *no pl* seriousness ◊ *Du hast den Ernst der Lage offenbar nicht erkannt.* ⊛ **der Ernst des Lebens** *the real world* ◊ *Mit der Schule fängt der Ernst des Lebens an.* Ernst machen *be/get serious* mit einer Drohung Ernst machen *carry out a threat* etw. ist jds Ernst *sb is serious (about sth)* jdm ist (es) mit etw. Ernst *sb is serious about sth* ◊ *Es war ihm offensichtlich Ernst mit der Drohung.* aus etw. [dat] *wird Ernst sth gets serious* allen Ernstes *in all seriousness, seriously* ◊ *Du willst doch wohl nicht allen Ernstes kündigen?* im Ernst *seriously*

ernst·haft [ˈɛrnsthaft] [adj, adv] <ernsthafter, am ernsthaftesten> serious(ly) ◊ *Wir sollten ein ernsthaftes Gespräch darüber führen.* ♦ *Ist das ernsthaft deine Absicht?* ♦ *ernsthafte Mängel* ♦ *Er ist ernsthaft verletzt.*

② **Ern·te** [ˈɛrntə] die <-, -n> harvest ◊ *Wir hoffen auf eine gute Ernte.*

ern·ten [ˈɛrntn̩] <erntet, erntete, hat geerntet> [tr v] **1.** harvest, pick ◊ *Trauben werden im Herbst geerntet.* **2.** get, receive ◊ *Für seinen Vorschlag hat er nur Hohn und Spott geerntet.; (a reward)* reap ◊ *Jetzt kann ich den Lohn für meine Mühe ernten.*

er·o·bern [eǀ'oːbən] <erobert, eroberte, hat erobert> (tr v) **1.** conquer ◊ *Die Römer haben den ganzen Mittelmeerraum erobert.; (a town)* take, capture **2.** win ◊ *Wir hoffen, in diesem Turnier den ersten Platz zu erobern.* ♦ *Er setzte alles daran, ihr Herz zu erobern.*

② **er·öff·nen** [eǀ'œfnən] <eröffnet, eröffnete, hat eröffnet> (tr+intr v) open ◊ *Hiermit eröffne ich die heutige Sitzung.* ♦ *Im Mai eröffnet das neue Museum.* ein Verfahren eröffnen start proceedings ⊜schließen, beenden (tr v) **1.** jdm etw. eröffnen announce sth to sb, reveal sth to sb ◊ *Mein Sohn hat mir heute eröffnet, dass er Künstler werden will.* **2.** etw. eröffnet (jdm) etw. sth opens sth up (for sb) ◊ *Diese Technik eröffnet uns ganz neue Möglichkeiten.* sich (jdm) eröffnen open up (for sb) ◊ *Dadurch eröffnen sich uns neue Chancen.*

er·ör·tern [eǀ'œ'tɐn] <erörtert, erörterte, hat erörtert> (tr v) discuss ◊ *ein Problem/eine Frage erörtern* ⊜diskutieren

er·pres·sen [e'prɛsn̩] <erpresst, erpresste, hat erpresst> (tr v) jdn erpressen blackmail sb ◊ *Ich lasse mich von dir nicht erpressen!; (money)* etw. (von jdm) erpressen extort sth (from sb) ◊ *Er hat von ihm 2000 Euro erpresst.*

er·ra·ten [e'raːtn̩] <errät, erriet, hat erraten> (tr v) guess ◊ *Er hat mein Alter erraten.* ♦ *Ich habe die Antwort nicht gewusst; ich habe sie erraten.*

er·re·gen [e're:gn̩] <erregt, erregte, hat erregt> (tr v) **1.** upset, agitate ◊ *Der Streit erregte ihn sehr.* die Gemüter erregen make passions run high **2.** arouse ◊ *jdn sexuell erregen* **3.** cause ◊ *Aufsehen/Besorgnis erregen; (sympathy, anger)* arouse

Er·re·ger [e're:gɐ] der <-s, -> pathogen

② **er·rei·chen** [e'raeçn̩] <erreicht, erreichte, hat erreicht> (tr v) **1.** jdn erreichen reach sb, contact sb, get hold of sb ◊ *Sie können mich von 10 bis 18 Uhr im Büro erreichen.* **2.** reach, get to ◊ *Die Insel ist nur mit dem Schiff zu erreichen.* ♦ *In wenigen Minuten erreichen wir Bonn.* **3.** *(a train, bus)* catch ◊ *Wenn du den Zug noch erreichen möchtest, musst du jetzt losfahren.* **4.** achieve ◊ *Er will dieses Ziel auf alle Fälle erreichen.* ♦ *Was willst du damit erreichen?* ein hohes Alter erreichen live to a ripe old age

er·rich·ten [e'rɪçtn̩] <errichtet, errichtete, hat errichtet> (tr v) **1.** build ◊ *einen Palast/eine Mauer errichten* ⊜bauen **2.** erect, set up ◊ *Hindernisse/einen Zaun errichten* ⊜aufstellen **3.** found, set up ◊ *ein politisches System/eine Stiftung errichten* ⊜begründen

Er·satz [e'zats] der <-es> no pl **1.** replacement, substitute ◊ *Bernd ist als Ersatz für den verletzten Spieler eingesprungen.* **2.** compensation ◊ *Er forderte Ersatz für die zerbrochene Fensterscheibe.; (of costs)* reimbursement

Er·satz·dienst [e'zatsdiːnst] der <-es> no pl: community service as an alternative to the obligatory military service in Germany ◊ *Er leistet seinen Ersatzdienst in einem Altersheim.* ⊜Zivildienst

② **Er·satz·teil** [e'zatstael] das <-(e)s, -e> spare (part)

er·schaf·fen [e'ʃafn̩] <erschafft, erschuf, hat erschaffen> (tr v) create ◊ *Der Bibel zufolge hat Gott die Welt in sechs Tagen erschaffen.*

② **er·schei·nen** [e'ʃaenən] <erscheint, erschien, ist erschienen> (intr v) **1.** come, appear ◊ *Sie ist heute nicht zur Arbeit erschienen.* **2.** be published ◊ *Dieses Buch ist bei Hueber erschienen.* **3.** appear ◊ *Am Horizont erschien ein Schiff.* ♦ *Ihm erschien ein Gespenst.* **4.** seem ◊ *Du erscheinst mir in letzter Zeit so verändert.* in einem anderen Licht erscheinen appear in a different light

Er·schei·nen [e'ʃaenən] das <-s> no pl **1.** appearance ◊ *Bei Erscheinen dieser Anzeichen sollte man einen Arzt aufsuchen.* Um vollständiges und rechtzeitiges Erscheinen wird gebeten. You are all requested to turn up on time. **2.** publication ◊ *Schon vor dem Erscheinen hat dieses Buch für Furore gesorgt.*

Er·schei·nung [e'ʃaenʊŋ] die <-, -en> **1.** phenomenon, occurrence ◊ *eine seltene/alltägliche Erscheinung* **2.** appearance, looks ◊ *Er legt viel Wert auf seine äußere Erscheinung.* **3.** vision ◊ *Sie hatte eine Erscheinung der Jungfrau Maria.* **4.** publication ◊ *Kurz nach Erscheinung seines ersten Romans verstarb der Autor plötzlich.*

⊛ in Erscheinung treten appear

er·schie·ßen [e'ʃiːsn̩] <erschießt, erschoss, hat erschossen> (tr v) shoot (dead) ◊ *Der Täter hat eine Geisel erschossen.*

er·schla·gen [e'ʃlaːgn̩] <erschlägt, erschlug, hat erschlagen> (tr v) **1.** strike dead, kill ◊ *Er wurde von einem herabfallenden Ast erschlagen.* vom Blitz erschlagen werden be struck by lightning **2.** overwhelm ◊ *Von den vielen neuen Eindrücken war sie wie erschlagen.*

er·schöp·fen [e'ʃœpfn̩] <erschöpft, erschöpfte, hat erschöpft> (tr v) exhaust ◊ *Die lange Reise hatte sie erschöpft.* (ref v) sich in etw. (dat) erschöpfen be limited to sth ◊ *Seine Kritik erschöpft sich in vagen Andeutungen.*

Er·schöp·fung [e'ʃœpfʊŋ] die <-, -en> most sing exhaustion ◊ *Im Zug schlief sie vor Erschöpfung ein.* ♦ *die Erschöpfung der Erdölreserven* bis zur Erschöpfung to the point of exhaustion

er·schrak [e'ʃraːk] pret of erschrecken¹, erschrecken³

② **er·schre·cken¹** [e'ʃrɛkn̩] <erschrickt, erschrak, ist erschrocken> (intr v) be shocked, be horrified ◊ *Erschrick nicht, wenn du ihn siehst; er sieht sehr krank aus.*

② **er·schre·cken²** [e'ʃrɛkn̩] <erschreckt, erschreckte, hat erschreckt> (tr v) frighten, scare ◊ *Ich hoffe, ich habe dich nicht erschreckt.* Lass dich nicht von seinem Aussehen erschrecken. Don't be shocked by the way he looks.

er·schre·cken³ [e'ʃrɛkn̩] <erschrickt/erschreckt, erschrak sich/erschreckte sich, hat sich erschreckt/erschrocken> (ref v) *(fam)* sich erschrecken get a shock ◊ *Ich habe mich erschreckt, als ich den großen Hund sah.* sich über etw. (acc) erschrecken be shocked by sth ◊ *Ich habe mich über sein schlechtes Aussehen erschrocken.*

er·schre·ckend [e'ʃrɛkn̩t, e'ʃrɛkənt] (adj, adv) shocking(ly) ◊ *Seine Unkenntnis ist erschreckend.* ♦ *eine erschreckende Zahl von Drogentoten* ♦ *Erschreckend wenige Menschen kennen die Hintergründe.*

er·schrickt [e'ʃrɪkt] pres of erschrecken¹, erschrecken³

er·schro·cken [ɛ'ʃrɔkn̩] *past p of* erschrecken[1], erschrecken[3]

er·schüt·tern [ɛ'ʃʏtɐn] <erschüttert, erschütterte, hat erschüttert> [tr v] **1.** jdn erschüttern move sb deeply, upset sb (deeply) ◊ *Diese Nachricht hat mich erschüttert.* **2.** shake, send tremors through ◊ *Ein starkes Erdbeben hat gestern Teile des Landes erschüttert.* **3.** *(a belief, sb's confidence)* shake durch nichts zu erschüttern sein be unshakeable ◊ *Sein Glaube ist durch nichts zu erschüttern.*

er·schwe·ren [ɛ'ʃveːrən] <erschwert, erschwerte, hat erschwert> [tr v] etw. erschweren make sth difficult ◊ *Der Lärm im Raum erschwerte die Unterhaltung.* ⊜erleichtern

er·schwing·lich [ɛ'ʃvɪŋlɪç] [adj] affordable ◊ *Eine eigene Wohnung ist für mich nicht erschwinglich.* ♦ *Autos zu erschwinglichen Preisen*

er·set·zen [ɛ'zɛtsn̩] <ersetzt, ersetzte, hat ersetzt> [tr v] replace ◊ *Niemand kann Kindern die Mutter ersetzen.* ♦ *Ich werde diesen Computer durch einen neuen ersetzen.* (jdm) einen Schaden ersetzen pay compensation (to sb) for damages/any damage

er·spa·ren [ɛ'ʃpaːrən] <erspart, ersparte, hat erspart> [tr v] **1.** jdm etw. ersparen spare sb sth ◊ *Ich will dir diese Mühe gern ersparen.* **2.** sich [dat] etw. ersparen save (up) for sth ◊ *Sie hat sich ihr neues Auto mühsam erspart.*

② **erst**[1] [eːɐst] [adv] **1.** first ◊ *Erst mache ich eine Weltreise, dann kann ich immer noch studieren.* ♦ *Lass ihn doch erst mal ausreden.* **2.** only ◊ *Es ist erst 11 Uhr, und ihr wollt schon gehen?* ♦ *Ich habe erst die Hälfte des Buches gelesen.* gerade erst (only) just ◊ *Er ist gerade erst gekommen. Die nächste Straßenbahn geht erst in 12 Minuten.* The next tram doesn't go for another 12 minutes. ⊜bereits **3.** wenn ... erst once ... ◊ *Wenn du erst mal hier bist, regelt wir über alles.*

② **erst**[2] [eːɐst] [part] **1.** if only ◊ *Wären wir doch nur erst mit diesem Projekt fertig!* **2.** *expresses intensification, often not translated* erst recht really ◊ *Als ich das sagte, schrie er erst recht.* ♦ *Jetzt ist sie erst recht böse auf mich.* Sie ist hübsch und ihre Schwester erst recht. She is pretty and her sister even more so. etw. gar nicht erst tun müssen/zu tun brauchen not even have to do sth ◊ *Da muss ich gar nicht erst überlegen.* ♦ *Das brauchst du ihm gar nicht erst zu sagen.* etw. gar nicht erst tun not even bother doing sth ◊ *Damit fange ich gar nicht erst an.* ..., aber ... erst but ... even more so ◊ *Sie ist ja schon hübsch, aber ihre Schwester erst!*

er·stat·ten [ɛ'ʃtatn̩] <erstattet, erstattete, hat erstattet> [tr v] **1.** *(costs)* reimburse, refund ◊ *Die Fahrtkosten werden Ihnen erstattet.* **2.** *(form)* Bericht erstatten (give a) report ◊ *Er muss seinem Chef einmal im Monat Bericht erstatten.* gegen jdn Anzeige erstatten report sb to the police

Er·stau·nen [ɛ'ʃtaonən] das <-s> *no pl* amazement, astonishment ◊ *Zu meinem Erstaunen hat er sich gar nicht beklagt.* jdn immer wieder in Erstaunen versetzen never cease to amaze sb

er·staun·lich [ɛ'ʃtaonlɪç] [adj, adv] amazing(ly), astonishing(ly) ◊ *erstaunliche Leistungen vollbringen* ♦ *Seine Fähigkeit, andere zu überzeugen, ist erstaunlich.* ♦ *Er ist für sein Alter noch erstaunlich fit.*

er·staunt [ɛ'ʃtaont] [adj] amazed, surprised ◊ *ein erstaunter Blick* ♦ *Sie war über seine Geduld erstaunt.* [adv] in/with amazement ◊ *Er sah mich erstaunt an.*

ers·te ['eːɐstə] [adj] <ein erster ..., eine erste ..., ein erstes ...> first die erste Reihe the front row → vierte

Ers·te[1] ['eːɐstə] der <-n, die Ersten> *(always* der Erste) first ◊ *Die Miete ist jeweils am Ersten fällig.* box@ Substantivierung

Ers·te[2] ['eːɐstə] das <-n> *but:* ein Erstes, no pl first thing ◊ *Das Erste, was ich tue, ist zu duschen.* Sein Erstes war, seine Freundin anzurufen. The first thing he did was to phone his girlfriend. box@ Substantivierung

⊛ als Erstes first of all fürs Erste for the time being ◊ *Nach diesem Sturz habe ich fürs Erste genug vom Skaten.* ⊜vorerst zum Ersten in the first place ◊ *Zum Ersten habe ich keine Lust und zum Zweiten kein Geld. (at an auction)* going once

er·stel·len [ɛ'ʃtɛlən] <erstellt, erstellte, hat erstellt> [tr v] **1.** *(minutes of a meeting)* write ◊ *Wer erstellt das Protokoll?; (statistics)* compile; *(a homepage)* make ⊜verfassen **2.** *(form)* build ◊ *einen Anbau erstellen* ⊜errichten

ers·tens ['eːɐstn̩s, 'eːɐstəns] [adv] first(ly), in the first place ◊ *Ich habe keine Lust — erstens ist es schon spät, zweitens ist es kalt und drittens regnet es.*

er·sti·cken [ɛ'ʃtɪkn̩] <erstickt, erstickte, ist/hat erstickt> [intr v] +*sein* suffocate, die of suffocation ◊ *Die meisten Opfer des Brandes sind erstickt.; (on a bone etc.)* an etw. [dat] ersticken choke (to death) on sth ◊ *Er ist an einer Fischgräte erstickt.* [tr v] +*haben* **1.** suffocate, smother ◊ *Er hat sie mit einem Kissen erstickt.* **2.** smother ◊ *Es war ihnen gelungen, das Feuer mit Sand zu ersticken.* **3.** suppress ◊ *Unsere Lehrerin erstickt jeden Widerspruch sofort.*

Erst·kläss·ler ['eːɐstklɛslɐ] der <-s, ->, **Erst·kläss·le·rin** ['eːɐstklɛslərɪn] die <-, -nen> child in the first class of (primary school)

erst·mals ['eːɐstmaːls] [adv] for the first time ◊ *In diesem Match treffen beide Spieler erstmals aufeinander.*

er·stre·cken [ɛ'ʃtrɛkn̩] <erstreckt sich, erstreckte sich, hat sich erstreckt> [ref v] **1.** *spatial* sich über etw. [acc] erstrecken stretch over sth, extend over sth ◊ *Das Gebirge erstreckt sich über drei Länder.* Seine Ranch erstreckt sich über 1000 km². His ranch covers an area of 1000 km². sich entlang einer Sache [gen]/[dat] erstrecken run along sth ◊ *Die Grenze erstreckt sich entlang des Rheins/dem Rhein.* sich bis an etw. [acc] erstrecken extend as far as sth **2.** *temporal* sich über etw. [acc] erstrecken last for a period of, extend over a period of ◊ *Der Test erstreckte sich über zwei Stunden.* **3.** etw. erstreckt sich auf jdn/etw. sth includes sb, sth applies to sb/sth ◊ *Der Versicherungsschutz erstreckt sich auch auf den Ehepartner des Versicherten.*

er·tei·len [ɛ'taelən] <erteilt, erteilte, hat erteilt> [tr v] *(form)* give (out) ◊ *einen Befehl/Auftrag/eine Auskunft/Erlaubnis etc. erteilen* jdm ein Lob erteilen praise sb jdm eine Rüge erteilen

reprimand sb jdm das Wort erteilen give sb the floor

er·tö·nen [ɛ'tø:nən] <ertönt, ertönte, ist ertönt> [intr v] sound, ring out ◊ *Begeisterter Beifall ertönte, als er die Bühne betrat.* ◆ *Im Nebenzimmer ertönte laute Musik.*

Er·trag [ɛ'traːk] der <-(e)s, Erträge> **1.** harvest, yield ◊ *Die Bauern rechnen dieses Jahr mit guten Erträgen.* **2.** return, profit ◊ *Die Investitionen brachten einen Ertrag von sechs Prozent.*

er·tra·gen [ɛ'traːgŋ̩] <erträgt, ertrug, hat ertragen> [tr v] bear, stand, tolerate ◊ *Ich kann die Schmerzen kaum noch ertragen.* ◆ *Es ist nicht zu ertragen, dass du dich über alles beschwerst.* ◆ *Sie erträgt ihr Schicksal mit Gleichmut.*

er·trin·ken [ɛ'trɪŋkŋ̩] <ertrinkt, ertrank, ist ertrunken> [intr v] drown ◊ *Sie ist beim Baden im Meer ertrunken.*

er·wa·chen [ɛ'vaxn̩] <erwacht, erwachte, ist erwacht> [intr v] *(lofty)* **1.** awake ◊ *Er hat sich abends niedergelegt und ist nie wieder erwacht.* aus etw. erwachen awake from/out of sth ◊ *Es wird Zeit, dass du aus deinen Träumen erwachst.* aus der Narkose erwachen come round (from the anaesthetic) **2.** *(feelings, interest)* awaken, be aroused ◊ *Jetzt ist meine Neugier erwacht.*

er·wach·sen[1] [ɛ'vaksn̩] [adj] grown up ◊ *Meine Kinder sind schon alle erwachsen.* ◆ *Sie wohnt bei ihrem erwachsenen Sohn.* ⊖groß [adv] like an adult ◊ *Mit 25 sollte man sich erwachsen benehmen.*

er·wach·sen[2] [ɛ'vaksn̩] <erwächst, erwuchs, ist erwachsen> [intr v] arise, develop aus etw. erwachsen grow out of sth, develop out of sth ◊ *Aus dieser Situation erwuchsen zahlreiche Probleme.*

②**Er·wach·se·ne** [ɛ'vaksənə] der/die <-n, die Erwachsenen> *but: ein Erwachsener/eine Erwachsene* adult, grown-up ◊ *Der Film ist nur für Erwachsene freigegeben.* box@ Substantivierung

Er·wach·se·nen·bil·dung [ɛ'vaksənənbɪldʊŋ] die <-> *no pl* adult education ◊ *Meine Schwester ist in der Erwachsenenbildung tätig.*

er·wäh·nen [ɛ'vɛ:nən] <erwähnt, erwähnte, hat erwähnt> [tr v] mention ◊ *Dein Name wurde in diesem Zusammenhang auch erwähnt.* ◆ *Sie hat nur kurz erwähnt, dass sie verreist.*

er·wär·men [ɛ'vɛ:mən] <erwärmt, erwärmte, hat erwärmt> [tr v] **1.** heat up, warm up ◊ *Wasser auf 60 Grad erwärmen* etw. erwärmt sich sth warms up, sth gets warm ◊ *Langsam erwärmt sich der Raum.* ⊖abkühlen **2.** interest ◊ *Ich versuchte, ihn für dieses Projekt zu erwärmen.* sich (für etw.) erwärmen warm up enthusiasm (for sth) ◊ *Für diese Idee kann ich mich nicht so recht erwärmen.*

②**er·war·ten** [ɛ'va'tn̩] <erwartet, erwartete, hat erwartet> [tr v] **1.** expect ◊ *Erwartest du Gäste?* ◆ *Du erwartest zu viel von deinen Kindern.* ◆ *Wie zu erwarten war, hat er sich beklagt.* ein Kind erwarten be pregnant, be expecting (a child) **2.** sich [dat] etw. von etw. erwarten hope for sth from sth ◊ *Was erwartest du dir von diesem Posten?* ◆ *Sie erwartet sich nichts mehr vom Leben.*

Er·war·tung [ɛ'va'tʊŋ] die <-, -en> **1.** expectation ◊ *Die neue Mitarbeiterin hat unsere Erwartungen*

voll erfüllt. ◆ *In dich werden große Erwartungen gesetzt.* **2.** *(also form)* anticipation ◊ *Voller Erwartung rannte sie zum Briefkasten.*

er·wei·sen [ɛ'vaezn̩] <erweist, erwies, hat erwiesen> [tr v] **1.** erwiesen (sein) (be) proved/proven ◊ *Es ist erwiesen, dass Olivenöl sehr gesund ist.* ◆ *eine erwiesene Tatsache* **2.** *(a favo(u)r)* jdm etw. erweisen do sb sth ◊ *Damit hast du mir aber keinen Dienst erwiesen.* **3.** *(respect)* jdm etw. erweisen show sb sth ◊ *jdm seine Achtung erweisen* [ref v] sich als ... erweisen turn out to be ... ◊ *Es hat sich als schwierig erwiesen, ihn zu überzeugen.* ◆ *Er hat sich als völlig unfähig erwiesen.* ⊖sich herausstellen

er·wei·tern [ɛ'vaetɐn] <erweitert, erweiterte, hat erweitert> [tr v] expand, extend ◊ *Ich möchte meine PC-Kenntnisse erweitern.* ◆ *Der Flughafen soll erweitert werden.*; *(knowledge)* broaden sich erweitern grow, expand ◊ *Unser Absatzgebiet hat sich erweitert.*; *(pupils)* dilate

er·wer·ben [ɛ'vɛ'bm̩] <erwirbt, erwarb, hat erworben> [tr v] **1.** acquire ◊ *Grundkenntnisse des Deutschen erwerben* sich [dat] etw. erwerben acquire sth, gain sth ◊ *Mit diesen Forschungen hat er sich internationales Ansehen erworben.* ◆ *Mit dieser Prüfung erwerben Sie die Berechtigung, Leute auszubilden.* **2.** buy, purchase ◊ *Sie haben letztes Jahr ein Haus erworben.*

er·werbs·tä·tig [ɛ'vɛ'pstɛːtɪç] [adj] *no comp/superl* employed, in paid employment ◊ *Er ist nicht mehr erwerbstätig.* ◆ *ein Gesetz zum Schutz der erwerbstätigen Mütter*

er·wi·dern [ɛ'vi:dɐn] <erwidert, erwiderte, hat erwidert> [tr v] **1.** reply, respond ◊ *Ich wusste nicht, was ich ihr erwidern sollte.* jd kann auf eine Frage nichts erwidern sb cannot answer a question **2.** return ◊ *Sie hat meinen Gruß mit einem Nicken erwidert.*; *(love)* reciprocate ◊ *Ihre Liebe wurde nicht erwidert.* Gewalt mit Gewalt erwidern respond to violence with violence

er·wünscht [ɛ'vʏnʃt] [adj] *no comp/superl* **1.** desired ◊ *Meine Bemühungen hatten nicht den erwünschten Erfolg.* ◊ *Diese Wirkung war nicht erwünscht.* **2.** *mostly after* ns welcome ◊ *Du bist hier nicht erwünscht.*

er·wür·gen [ɛ'vʏ'gŋ̩] <erwürgt, erwürgte, hat erwürgt> [tr v] strangle ◊ *Sie wurde mit einem Schal erwürgt.*

②**er·zäh·len** [ɛ'tsɛːlən] <erzählt, erzählte, hat erzählt> [tr v] tell ◊ *Sie hat den Kindern ein Märchen erzählt.* ◆ *Er hat mir erzählt, wie es in Kanada war.* ◆ *Sie hat uns einen Unfall erzählt.* ◆ *Wie war's im Urlaub? Komm, erzähl mal!* [intr v] jdm von jdm/etw. erzählen tell sb about sb/sth ◊ *Erzähl aber keinem davon!* jd kann gut erzählen sb is a good story-teller ⊙ das kannst du einem anderen erzählen pull the other one dem/der werde ich was erzählen *(fam)* I'll give him/her a piece of my mind ◊ *Sie hat gesagt, ich sei zu faul? Na, der werde ich was erzählen!* mir kannst du viel erzählen *(fam)* don't give me that wem erzählen Sie das don't I know it

②**Er·zäh·lung** [ɛ'tsɛːlʊŋ] die <-, -en> story, narrative ◊ *Ich lese gerade Erzählungen von Siegfried Lenz.* ◆ *Die Kinder lauschten seinen Erzählungen.* ◆ *mit*

seiner Erzählung fortfahren

Erz·bi·schof ['ɛɾ'sbɪʃɔf, 'ɛɾ'sbɪʃoːf] der <–s, Erzbischöfe> archbishop

er·zeu·gen [ɐ'tsɔɡŋ] <erzeugt, erzeugte, hat erzeugt> ⟨tr v⟩ **1.** make, produce ◊ *Nahrungsmittel/Produkte erzeugen*; *(electricity, energy, warmth also)* generate ◊ *Strom/Wärme/Energie erzeugen* **2.** *(an emotional response)* create, generate ◊ *Damit wirst du die gegenteilige Reaktion erzeugen.* ♦ *Gewalt/Interesse erzeugen*

Er·zeug·nis [ɐ'tsɔɡknɪs] das <–ses, –se> product ◊ *landwirtschaftliche Erzeugnisse* ♦ *Das ist ein Erzeugnis seiner Fantasie.*

② **er·zie·hen** [ɐ'tsiːən] <erzieht, erzog, hat erzogen> ⟨tr v⟩ jdn (zu etw.) erziehen bring sb up (to be sth) ◊ *Wir wurden antiautoritär erzogen.* ♦ *jdn zur Höflichkeit erziehen* einen Hund erziehen train a dog

Er·zie·her [ɐ'tsiːɐ] der <–s, –>, **Er·zie·he·rin** [ɐ'tsiːərɪn] die <–, –nen> **1.** teacher ◊ *Sie haben einen privaten Erzieher für ihren Sohn engagiert.* **2.** nursery school teacher ◊ *Von Beruf ist sie Erzieherin.*

② **Er·zie·hung** [ɐ'tsiːʊŋ] die <–> no pl **1.** upbringing ◊ *Wir sind mit der Erziehung unserer Kinder überfordert.* schulische Erziehung education **2.** manners ◊ *Er vergaß seine gute Erziehung und beschimpfte mich übel.*

er·zie·hungs·be·rech·tigt [ɐ'tsiːʊŋsbərɛçtɪçt] ⟨adj⟩ no comp/superl *(form)* having parental authority die Unterschrift eines erziehungsberechtigten Erwachsenen the signature of a parent or (legal) guardian

er·zie·len [ɐ'tsiːlən] <erzielt, erzielte, hat erzielt> ⟨tr v⟩ achieve ◊ *einen Erfolg/Gewinn erzielen* ♦ *die gewünschte Wirkung erzielen*

② **es** [ɛs] ⟨pers pron⟩ *(referring to a neuter noun)* it ◊ *Ich sah das Schiff, wie es am Horizont verschwand.* ♦ *Wo ist dein Kaninchen? Hast du ihm schon sein Futter gegeben?* ♦ *Wir waren im Konzert. Es war sehr schön.* ♦ *Das ist ein tolles Buch; ich habe es schon zweimal gelesen.*; *(referring to a child or baby)* he, she ◊ *Sie haben ein Mädchen bekommen und ihm den Namen Lea gegeben.* ♦ *Das Kind hat Hunger; darum schreit es.* ⟨pron⟩ **1.** *impersonal* it ◊ *Es regnet.* ♦ *Es wird dunkel.* ♦ *Es hagelte Beschwerden.* ♦ *Es ist zwei Uhr.* ♦ *Es ist noch früh.* ♦ *Bald wird es Winter.* ♦ *Es sind vor allem die Kinder, die daran erkranken.* ♦ *„Was ist das für ein Film?" — „Es ist ein Krimi."* ♦ *Hier ist es gemütlich.* ♦ *Er hat es nicht ernst gemeint.* Mir ist es so kalt! I'm so cold! jd kann es kaum erwarten sb can hardly wait **2.** *mostly not translated (to avoid repetition of a predicative adj or noun)* ◊ *Mutter ist krank und ich werde es auch bald sein.* ♦ *Seine Eltern sind Musiker und er ist es auch.*; *(in negative phrases not translated)* Die anderen waren faul, er war es nicht. The others were lazy, he wasn't. Sie ist schön; ihre Mutter ist es nicht. She is beautiful, her mother isn't. **3.** there ◊ *Hat es gerade geklingelt?* ♦ *Schluss jetzt, sonst kracht's!* es hat sich ... there has been ... ◊ *Es hat sich ein Unfall ereignet.* es gibt ... there is/are ... ◊ *Hier gibt es kein Kino.* Es ist etwas Trauriges/Wunderbares etc. passiert. Something sad/wonderful etc. has happened. **4.** *translation varies (introductory)* Es

wird sich zeigen, ob er das kann. Time will tell whether he can do it. Es freut mich, Sie kennen zu lernen. It is a pleasure to meet you. Es dürfte doch nicht so schwer sein, das zu verstehen. This can't be so difficult to understand. **5.** *(indicating emotional or perceptional states, mostly not translated)* it ◊ *Hat es ihm in Frankreich gefallen?* ♦ *Mich hält es hier nicht länger!* jdn überläuft es kalt a cold shiver runs down sb's spine jdn juckt es sb has got an itch jdm geht es gut/schlecht etc. sb is well/poorly etc. **6.** *(as an object, mostly not translated)* es eilig haben be in a hurry es an der Leber/Blase etc. haben suffer from liver/ bladder etc. problems es weit bringen go far es gut mit jdm meinen mean sb well es auf jdn abgesehen haben have it in for sb **7.** *(with passive contructions, mostly not translated)* it ◊ *Es muss geklärt werden, ob sich das machen lässt.* Es darf gelacht/getanzt etc. werden Laughing/dancing etc. is welcome. Es soll hart gearbeitet werden. You are expected to work hard. **8.** *in impersonal constructions (expressing the manner in which sth can be done)* Hier lässt es sich gut Urlaub machen. Holidays are really enjoyable here. In den Schuhen läuft es sich wunderbar. These shoes are really comfortable to walk in. ⊖man

	nom	es
	acc	es
	dat	ihm
	gen	seiner

E·sel ['eːzl̩] der <–s, –> **1.** donkey ◊ *auf einem Esel reiten* **2.** *(fam, pej)* idiot ◊ *Wenn er das glaubt, dann ist er ein Esel.*

② **es·sen** ['ɛsn̩] <isst, aß, hat gegessen> ⟨tr+intr v⟩ eat ◊ *In Deutschland wird viel Brot gegessen.* ♦ *Die Patientin will nicht mehr essen.* ♦ *Du isst nicht besonders gesund.* zu Mittag/Abend essen have lunch/dinner warm essen have a hot meal ⟨ref v⟩ Wir haben uns satt gegessen. We ate until we were full. Du isst dich noch krank mit all den Hamburgern. You'll be ill if you eat all those burgers. ⊕ essen gehen go out for a meal gegessen sein *(fam)* be over and done with ◊ *Das Problem ist für mich gegessen.*

② **Es·sen** ['ɛsn̩] das <–s, –> most sing **1.** no pl food, eating ◊ *Meine Mutter legt Wert auf gesundes Essen.* Das Essen verweigern refuse to eat **2.** meal ◊ *Mittags gibt es bei uns zu Hause (ein) warmes Essen.* **3.** lunch, dinner ◊ *Das Essen ist fertig!* ♦ *jdn zum Essen einladen* ⊕ Essen auf Rädern meals on wheels

② **Es·sig** ['ɛsɪç] der <–s, –e> most sing vinegar ◊ *den Salat mit Essig und Öl anmachen*

Ess·löf·fel ['ɛslœfl̩] der <–s, –> dessertspoon etw. mit einem Esslöffel Sahne etc. abschmecken add a dessertspoonful of cream etc. to sth

Ess·zim·mer ['ɛstsɪmɐ] das <–s, –> dining room

Es·te ['eːstə] der <–n, –n>, **Es·tin** ['eːstɪn] die <–, –nen> Estonian → Deutsche

Est·land ['eːstlant] das <–s> *article only in combination with attribute* Estonia → Deutschland

Est·län·der ['eːstlɛndɐ] der <–s, –>, **Est·län·de·rin** ['eːstlɛndərɪn] die <–, –nen> Estonian → Deutsche

est·län·disch [ˈeːstlɛndɪʃ] [adj] *mostly before ns*
Estonian ◊ *die estländische Bevölkerung*
est·nisch [ˈeːstnɪʃ] [adj] *mostly before ns* Estonian
→ deutsch
Est·nisch [ˈeːstnɪʃ] *das <‑(s)> no pl* Estonian →
Deutsch
Es·zett [ɛsˈtsɛt] *das <‑, ‑> the letter 'ß' in the*
German alphabet ⊖scharfes S
E·ta·ge [eˈtaːʒə] *die <‑, ‑n>* floor, storey ◊ *Das*
Haus hat drei Etagen. ♦ *Ich wohne in der zweiten*
Etage. ⊖Stock, Stockwerk
E·tap·pe [eˈtapə] *die <‑, ‑n>* stage ◊ *Die erste*
Etappe unseres Projekts haben wir abgeschlossen.
♦ *eine Reise in mehreren Etappen*
E·tat [eˈtaː] *der <‑s, ‑s>* **1.** (state) budget ◊ *Der*
Finanzminister hat seinen Etat vorgelegt. ♦ *Dieses*
neue Gesetz reißt große Löcher in den Etat.
⊖Haushalt **2.** finances Ein Notebook ist in meinem
Etat derzeit nicht drin. I can't afford to buy a
notebook at the moment.
etc. [ɛt ˈtseːteraː] *(abbr of* et cetera*)* etc. ◊ *In*
diesem Laden kann man Postkarten, Andenken,
Stadtpläne etc. kaufen.
E·ti·kett [etiˈkɛt] *das <‑(e)s, ‑e(n)>* label ◊ *Waren*
mit einem Etikett versehen ⊖Schild
et·li·che¹ [ˈɛtlɪçə] [det] *(with pl ns)* (quite) a lot
of, many ◊ *Vor etlichen Wochen/Monaten/Jahren*
war ich in Rom. ♦ *etliche Freunde* ♦ *etliches*
Zubehör ⊖mehrere
et·li·che² [ˈɛtlɪçə] [indef pron] many ◊ *Etliche*
haben das immer noch nicht begriffen. ♦ *Ich habe*
die Rechnungen durchgesehen. Etliche fehlen.
et·li·ches [ˈɛtlɪçəs] [indef pron] a lot, quite a bit ◊
Etliches war ihr neu.
E·tui [ɛtˈviː, eˈtʏiː] *das <‑s, ‑s>* case ◊ *die Brille*
ins Etui legen
② **et·wa¹** [ˈɛtvaː] [adv] **1.** *(not exactly)* about,
around, approximately ◊ *Er ist etwa 35 Jahre alt.*
in etwa more or less ◊ *Das ist in etwa richtig.*
⊖ungefähr **2.** *(as an example)* for instance, for
example ◊ *Peter etwa hält überhaupt nichts von*
diesem Plan.
et·wa² [ˈɛtvaː] [part] *in questions (emph)* (expressing annoyance) *in English the emphasis that*
is conveyed by 'etwa' is obtained by intonation
Findest du das etwa okay, wenn man Kinder
schlägt? Do you think it's all right to smack
children? Willst du damit etwa sagen, dass du
pleite bist? Are you telling me that you're broke?
② **et·was¹** [ˈɛtvas] [det] *(small amount)* some, any, a
little ◊ *Da fehlt noch etwas Pfeffer.* ♦ *Ist noch*
etwas Tee da?
② **et·was²** [ˈɛtvas] [indef pron] **1.** *(indefinite)*
something, anything ◊ *Hier stimmt etwas nicht.* ♦
Ich würde gerne etwas Kaltes trinken. ♦ *Möchten*
Sie etwas sagen? **2.** *(small amount)* some, any, a
little ◊ *Die Suppe ist prima. Ist noch etwas da?*
3. *(temporal)* a bit, a little ◊ *Er kommt etwas*
später.
EU [eːˈʔuː] *die (abbr of* Europäische Union*)* EU
euch [ɔøç] *dat and acc of* ihr¹ [ref pron] **1.** *often*
not directly translated yourselves ◊ *Es gibt*
Kuchen — bitte bedient euch! ♦ *Habt ihr euch*
schon beim Chef vorgestellt? Wollt ihr euch frisch
machen? Would you like to freshen up? Haltet
euch da raus! Keep out of it! **2.** *reciprocal* each

---

other ◊ *Habt ihr euch wieder lieb?* ♦ *Hört auf, euch*
zu schlagen! ⊖einander
② **eu·er** [ˈɔøe] [det] your ◊ *Euer Vater ist wirklich*
cool! ♦ *Euer Auto ist zerkratzt.* ♦ *Eure Eltern*
gefallen mir! ♦ *Wie geht es eurer Schwester?* ♦ *Es*
geht um eure Zukunft.

	m	f	nt	pl
nom	euer	eure	euer	eure
acc	euren	eure	euer	eure
dat	eurem	eurer	eurem	euren
gen	eures	eurer	eures	eurer

eu·re [ˈɔørə] → eurer, euer
eu·rer [ˈɔøre] [poss pron] yours ◊ *Unser Sohn ist*
schon hier, wo bleibt denn eurer? ♦ *Diese Tasche*
gehört nicht uns — ist das vielleicht eure? ♦ *Ist*
das blaue Auto eures?

	m	f	nt	pl
nom	eurer	eure	eures	eure
acc	euren	eure	eures	eure
dat	eurem	eurer	eurem	euren
gen	-	-	-	-

eu·res [ˈɔørəs] → eurer
eu·ret·we·gen [ˈɔørətˈveːgn̩] [adv] because of you
◊ *Kommt rein, Leo ist euretwegen extra aufgeblie-*
ben.
Eu·ro [ˈɔøroː] *der <‑(s), ‑ or ‑s> pl 'Euro'* used
used with figures (abbr €) euro ◊ *Kann man hier*
mit Euros zahlen? ♦ *Das kostet 20 Euro.*
Eu·ro·pa [ɔøˈroːpaː] *das <‑s> article only in com-*
bination with attribute (continent) Europe ◊ *Die*
Popgruppe tourt derzeit durch Europa. box@ Land
Eu·ro·pä·er [ɔøroˈpɛːe] *der <‑s, ‑>,*
Eu·ro·pä·e·rin [ɔøroˈpɛːərɪn] *die <‑, ‑nen>*
1. *(citizen of a European country)* European →
Deutsche **2.** *(supporter of Europe)* pro-European
◊ *Er ist ein begeisterter Europäer.*
eu·ro·pä·isch [ɔøroˈpɛːɪʃ] [adj] European ◊ *ein*
europäisches Land ♦ *ein Gesetz auf europäischer*
Ebene ♦ *Unsere Zukunft ist europäisch.* ◊ *euro-*
päisch geprägt European ◊ *Diese amerikanische*
Stadt ist sehr europäisch geprägt. europäisch orientiert Europe-oriented
② **e·van·ge·lisch** [evaŋˈgeːlɪʃ] [adj] *no comp/superl*
Protestant ◊ *eine evangelische Kirchengemeinde*
evangelisch sein to be a Protestant ◊ *Sind Sie evange-*
lisch oder katholisch? ⊖protestantisch evangelisch getauft sein to be christened (a Protestant),
be baptized (a Protestant) ⊖protestantisch
E·van·ge·li·um [evaŋˈgeːli̯ʊm] *das*
<‑s, Evangelien> **1.** *no pl* Gospel ◊ *die Verkündi-*
gung des Evangeliums. **2.** *(during service)* reading
② **e·ven·tu·ell** [evɛntuˈɛl] [adj] *no comp/superl, only*
before ns possible, potential ◊ *Wer kommt für even-*
tuelle Schäden auf? [adv] possibly, perhaps ◊
Eventuell komme ich morgen. eventuell auftre-
tend... potential ◊ *eventuell auftretende Probleme*
⊖möglicherweise, womöglich
evtl. [evɛntuˈɛl] *abbr of* eventuell
② **e·wig** [ˈeːvɪç] [adj] *no comp/superl* **1.** eternal, everlasting ◊ *Er hat seine ewige Ruhe gefunden.* ♦ *Die*
Zeit ist ewig. für ewig for ever ◊ *Nichts ist für*
ewig. **2.** *only before ns (fam)* endless, never-ending
◊ *Deine ewige Nörgelei geht mir auf die Nerven.*
seit ewigen Zeiten for an eternity, for years [adv]

1. eternally, forever ◊ *ein ewig junger Schlagerstar*
2. *(fam)* always ◊ *Es ist doch ewig dasselbe mit dir!* ewig dauern take ages *ewig brauchen* take forever ◊ *Er braucht immer ewig für die Hausaufgaben.*

E·wig·keit ['eːvɪçkaᴇt] die <-, –en> **1.** *no pl* eternity ◊ *Er versprach, sie für alle Ewigkeit zu lieben.* **2.** *(fam)* eine Ewigkeit/Ewigkeiten ages ◊ *Das hat ja Ewigkeiten gedauert!*

ex [ɛks] adv *(fam)* ex gehen die ◊ *Die Batterien von meinem Walkman sind ex gegangen.* ⊙ etw. auf ex trinken down sth in one

Ex·..., **Ex·...** [ɛks] prefix ex- ◊ *meine Exfrau* ♦ *der Ex-Bundeskanzler*

② **e·xakt** [ɛ'ksakt] adj, adv exact(ly), precise(ly) ◊ *Exakte Zahlen liegen noch nicht vor.* ♦ *Ist diese Beschreibung exakt?* ♦ *Der Zeitplan wurde exakt eingehalten.* ⊖genau, präzise ⊕ungefähr, ungenau

E·xa·men [ɛ'ksaːmən] das <-s, – *or* Examina> exam, (final) examination, finals ◊ *Sie hat kürzlich ihr Examen als Krankenschwester abgelegt/ bestanden.* ♦ *durch das Examen fallen*

E·xem·plar [ɛksɛm'plaːᵎ] das <-s, –e> specimen ◊ *Diese Orchidee ist ein besonders schönes Exemplar.*; *(of a newspaper, book)* copy ◊ *ein Exemplar von Einsteins „Geometrie und Erfahrung"*

② **E·xis·tenz** [ɛksɪs'tɛnts] die <-, –en> **1.** *no pl* existence ◊ *Er glaubt an die Existenz von Ufos.* ♦ *Alle Menschen haben ein Recht auf eine würdige Existenz.* **2.** life, livelihood ◊ *In zwei Jahren hatte er sich eine neue Existenz aufgebaut.* **3.** *(pej) (person)* eine gescheiterte Existenz a failure ◊ *Er ist ein trauriges Beispiel für eine gescheiterte Existenz.*

② **e·xis·tie·ren** [ɛksɪs'tiːrən] <existiert, existierte, hat existiert> intr v **1.** exist ◊ *Die Firma existiert bereits seit 1954.* **2.** von etw. existieren live on sth, exist on sth

ex·klu·si·ve [ɛksklu'ziːvə] prep *sing nouns without article or attribute are not declined when following this prep, otherwise* +gen *or fam* +dat *exclusive of, excluding* ◊ *Die Reise kostet 750 Euro exklusive der Tagesausflüge.* ♦ *Der Preis versteht sich exklusive Mehrwertsteuer.* ⊖ausschließlich ⊕inklusive

Ex·ma·tri·ku·la·ti·on [ɛksmatrikula'tsjoːn] die <-, –en> deregistration

E·xot¹ [ɛ'ksoːt] der <-en, –en> exotic animal, exotic plant, exotic species ◊ *Die Orchidee ist ein belieber Exot.*

E·xot² [ɛ'ksoːt] der <-en, –en>, **E·xo·tin** [ɛ'ksoːtɪn] die <-, –nen> oddity ◊ *Unter den Eisläuferinnen ist die Kubanerin eine echte Exotin.* ♦ *Das Elektroauto wird noch heute als Exot bestaunt.*

② **Ex·plo·si·on** [ɛksplo'zjoːn] die <-, –en> **1.** *(of a bomb etc.)* explosion ◊ *die Explosion eines Sprengsatzes* **2.** *(rapid growth)* escalation, explosion ◊ *eine Explosion der Kosten*

② **Ex·port¹** [ɛks'pɔᵎt] der <-(e)s, –e> export ◊ *Der Export boomt.* ♦ *Die Exporte stiegen um 11%.* ⊖Ausfuhr ⊕Import

Ex·port² [ɛks'pɔᵎt] das <-(e)s, –> export beer ◊ *Ich trinke lieber Export als Pils.* ♦ *Sie bestellten drei Export.*

Ex·po·sé [ɛkspo'zeː] das <-s, –s> *(lofty)* plan, outline

ext·ra ['ɛkstraː] adj, adv *invariable; when used as an adj, only before ns (fam)* extra ◊ *Ich habe mir extra Mühe gegeben!* ♦ *eine extra große Portion* ♦ *Dafür muss extra gezahlt werden.* ♦ *Die Grundgebühr ist auf der Rechnung extra ausgewiesen.* **2.** *(fam)* on purpose, deliberately ◊ *Das hat er extra gemacht, um mich zu ärgern!* **3.** specially ◊ *Das muss wohl nicht extra erwähnt werden.*

F

f, F [ɛf] das <–(s), –(s)> **1.** F, f ◊ *Dieses Wort wird mit einem kleinen f/großen F geschrieben.* ♦ *F wie Friedrich* **2.** MUS F ◊ *Spiel mal ein F.*

fa·bel·haft ['faːblˌhaft] [adj, adv] <fabelhafter, am fabelhaftesten> fantastic(ally), fabulous(ly) ◊ *Der Film hat eine fabelhafte Besetzung.* ♦ *Die Akustik in diesem Saal ist fabelhaft.* ♦ *Das hast du fabelhaft gemacht!*

② **Fab·rik** [fa'briːk] die <–, –en> factory ◊ *eine pharmazeutische Fabrik* ♦ *In dieser Fabrik arbeiten 1500 Menschen.*

Fab·ri·kat [fabri'kaːt] das <–(e)s, –e> **1.** product ◊ *Diese Maschine ist ein deutsches Fabrikat.* **2.** make, brand ◊ *Welches Fabrikat ist dieser Fernseher?*

② **Fach** [fax] das <–(e)s, Fächer> **1.** compartment, shelf ◊ *Die Handtücher sind im obersten Fach links.* **2.** *(subject area)* field ◊ *Frag ihn, er ist in diesem Fach Experte.* **3.** SCHOOL, UNI subject ◊ *Welche Fächer studiert sie?*

Fach·a·bi·tur ['faxˌabiˌtuːɐ] das <–s> *no pl vocational qualification that enables you to study at a polytechnic* ◊ *Fachabitur machen*

Fach·be·griff ['faxbəgrɪf] der <–(e)s, –e> (technical) term ◊ *ein medizinischer Fachbegriff* ⊖Fachausdruck

Fach·be·reich ['faxbəraɛç] der <–(e)s, –e> **1.** field, discipline ◊ *Ärzte verschiedener Fachbereiche* **2.** *(of a university)* department, faculty ◊ *Studenten aus allen Fachbereichen* ♦ *die Forschung im Fachbereich Physik*

Fach·ge·biet ['faxgəbiːt] das <–(e)s, –e> field, discipline ◊ *sich auf ein Fachgebiet spezialisieren* ♦ *das Fachgebiet Religionswissenschaft*

Fach·han·del ['faxhandl̩] der <–s> *no pl* **1.** specialist stores, specialist shops ◊ *nur im Fachhandel erhältlich* **2.** specialist trade ◊ *der Fachhandel für Elektronik*

Fach·hoch·schu·le ['faxhoːxʃuːlə] die <–, –n> *(abbr FH)* ⊖polytechnic ◊ *ein Studium an einer Fachhochschule*

> The first German *Fachhochschulen* were founded in the 1970s. A course at a *Fachhochschule* is generally more vocational than a university course; it is also of limited duration. Whereas universities aim to educate students at a high intellectual level, *Fachhochschulen* prepare students in a more targeted way for their entry into certain jobs.

Fach·leu·te ['faxlɔ̯øtə] *pl of* Fachmann
Fach·mann ['faxman] der <–(e)s, Fachleute *or* Fachmänner>, **Fach·frau** ['faxfrɔ̯ø] die <–, –en> expert, specialist ◊ *ein anerkannter Fachmann* ♦ *Ein externer Fachmann wurde beigezogen.*

Fa·ckel ['fakl̩] die <–, –n> torch ◊ *die olympische Fackel*

fad [faːt], **fa·de** ['faːdə] [adj] **1.** *(food)* insipid, tasteless ◊ *fade Hausmannskost* ♦ *Ich finde die Soße etwas fade.* **2.** boring, uninspiring ◊ *eine fade Angelegenheit* ♦ *Die Party war fade.*

Fa·den ['faːdn̩] der <–s, Fäden> **1.** thread ◊ *Der Faden ist abgerissen.*; *(medical)* stitch **2.** trickle ◊ *ein dünner Faden Speichel*

⊚ **alle/die Fäden (fest) in der Hand haben/ halten** hold the reins an a einem (dünnen/ seidenen) **Faden hängen** hang by a thread **der rote Faden** the key theme, the recurrent theme **die Fäden ziehen 1.** *(fig)* pull the strings **2.** MED take the stitches out ◊ *Eine Woche nach der Operation bekam sie die Fäden gezogen.*

fä·hig ['fɛːɪç] [adj] **1.** capable, competent ◊ *ein fähiger Nachfolger* ♦ *Ich halte diesen Architekten für ausgesprochen fähig.* **2.** zu etw. fähig sein capable of sth, be able to do sth ◊ *Sie ist durchaus fähig, das Projekt zu leiten.* ♦ *Sie sind zu keiner Änderung fähig.*

⊚ **zu allem fähig sein** be capable of anything **Fä·hig·keit** ['fɛːɪçkaɛt] die <–, –en> **1.** *most pl* skill, capability ◊ *handwerkliche Fähigkeiten* ♦ *seine Fähigkeiten unter Beweis stellen* **2.** *no pl* ability ◊ *Sie besitzt die Fähigkeit, gut improvisieren zu können.*

fahn·den ['faːndn̩] <fahndet, fahndete, hat gefahndet> [intr v] search ◊ *Die Polizei fahndet fieberhaft nach dem Entführern.*

Fah·ne ['faːnə] die <–, –n> **1.** flag ◊ *die Fahne Österreichs* ♦ *die tschechische Fahne* ♦ *Die Fahnen sind auf halbmast gesetzt.* ⊖Flagge **2.** *(fam)* eine Fahne haben reek of alcohol

Fahr·bahn ['faːrˈbaːn] die <–, –en> carriageway ◊ *Er geriet auf der regennassen Fahrbahn ins Schleudern.*; *(single strip)* lane ◊ *die linke Fahrbahn*

Fäh·re ['fɛːrə] die <–, –n> ferry ◊ *Ich nehme die Fähre nach Dover.*

② **fah·ren** ['faːrən] <fährt, fuhr, hat/ist gefahren> [intr v] *+sein* **1.** *(vehicle)* go, leave ◊ *Der letzte Bus fährt um 23 Uhr.* **2.** *(person in a car)* go by car, come by car ◊ *Bist du zu Fuß hier oder bist du gefahren?*; *(driver)* drive ◊ *Ich fahre heute Abend, denn du hast zu viel getrunken.* **3.** *(travel)* go ◊ *Im Sommer fahren wir oft an die See.* **4.** mit etw. fahren go by sth, take sth ◊ *Ich fahre lieber mit dem Auto, da bin ich flexibler.* ⊖nehmen **5.** mit jdm fahren go in sb's car, go with sb, have a lift with sb ◊ *Kann ich mit Ihnen fahren? Mein Auto ist kaputt.* **6.** mit der Hand irgendwohin fahren stick your hand somewhere ◊ *Er fuhr mit der Hand in die Tasche, um seine Brieftasche herauszuholen.* (jdm/sich) über etw. [acc] fahren run your hand across sth, stroke sth ◊ *Sie fuhr ihm zärtlich übers Haar.* ♦ *Er fuhr sich über die Stirn aus dem Schlaf fahren* wake with a start **7.** *(fam)* mit etw. gut/ schlecht fahren fare well/badly with sth ◊ *Mit diesem Konzept sind sie bisher gut gefahren.* [tr v] *+haben/sein* **1.** *+haben* drive ◊ *Wer hat den Bus*

A

zur fraglichen Zeit gefahren? ◆ Fährst du mich
bitte zum Bahnhof? **2.** *+sein* take, go by ◊
Veronika fährt lieber Zug als Auto. **3.** *+sein* go on
◊ Bist du schon mal mit Jule Motorrad gefahren?
◆ Fährst du gern Geisterbahn?; *(a bike, as the
driver)* ride ◊ Kannst du Fahrrad/Motorrad
fahren? **4.** *+sein* take ◊ Welche Strecke fährt die
Linie 4? **5.** *+sein* drive (on) ◊ Er ist die 5000 km
ganz allein gefahren. ◆ Ich fahre am liebsten
Autobahn. **6.** *+sein* SPORT Snowboard fahren
snowboard Schlittschuh fahren skate Ski fahren
ski ⟨ref v⟩ *+haben (car)* sich gut/leicht etc. fahren
be good/easy etc. to drive
② **Fah·rer** ['faːrɐ] der <-s, ->, **Fah·re·rin** ['faːrərɪn]
die <-, -nen> driver ◊ Er arbeitet als Fahrer für
diese Spedition. ◆ Der Fahrer des Unfallwagens
wurde schwer verletzt.
Fahr·ge·mein·schaft ['faːɡəmaɛnʃaft] die
<-, -en> carpool ◊ eine Fahrgemeinschaft organi-
sieren/bilden
② **Fahr·kar·te** ['faːˈkaˀtə] die <-, -n> ticket ◊ Fahrkarten kaufen/lösen/entwerten
fahr·läs·sig ['faːˈlɛsɪç] ⟨adj, adv⟩ negligent(ly) ◊
fahrlässiges Verhalten ◆ Es war fahrlässig, dem
Verletzten nicht zu helfen. ◆ sich fahrlässig
verhalten fahrlässige Körperverletzung personal
injury resulting from negligence etw. fahrlässig verursachen cause sth by negligence
② **Fahr·plan** ['faːˈplaːn] der <-(e)s, Fahrpläne>
1. timetable, schedule ◊ Laut Fahrplan soll der Zug
in zehn Minuten ankommen. ◆ auf dem Fahrplan
nachsehen **2.** set of guidelines ◊ ein Fahrplan zur
Unternehmensgründung
Fahr·prü·fung ['faːˈpryːfʊŋ] die <-, -en> driving
test ◊ der praktische/theoretische Teil der Fahrprüfung ◊ die Fahrprüfung machen/bestehen ◆ bei der
Fahrprüfung durchfallen
② **Fahr·rad** ['faːˈraːt] das <-(e)s, Fahrräder> bicycle,
bike ◊ Er fuhr mit dem Fahrrad zur Schule. ◆ Sie
kann nicht Fahrrad fahren.
Fahr·schu·le ['faːˈʃuːlə] die <-, -n> driving school

> Driving schools are privately-run organizations
> which prepare their students for their driving
> tests. The test is made up of a theoretical part,
> which includes questions on traffic regulations,
> and a practical driving test.

Fahr·stuhl ['faːˈʃtuːl] der <-(e)s, Fahrstühle>
elevator, lift ◊ mit dem Fahrstuhl in den 6. Stock
fahren ⊜Lift, Aufzug
② **Fahrt** ['faːˈt] die <-, -en> **1.** journey ◊ während
der Fahrt ◆ die tägliche Fahrt zur Arbeit ◆ eine
Fahrt ans Meer; *(by car)* drive ◊ Die Fahrt nach
Köln dauerte vier Stunden. **2.** ride ◊ Die einfache
Fahrt kostet 25 Euro. freie Fahrt haben/erhalten
travel for free **3.** *no pl* speed ◊ Der Wagen hatte
einiges an Fahrt drauf.
⊙ **Fahrt ins Blaue** mystery tour, mystery trip in
Fahrt geraten/kommen 1. *(person)* liven up
2. get angry **3.** *(party, process, activity)* get going
② **fährt** [fɛːˈt] *pres of* fahren
Fahr·zeug ['faːˈtsɔɡk] das <-(e)s, -e> vehicle
Fahr·zeug·hal·ter ['faːˈtsɔɡkhaltɐ] der <-s, ->,
Fahr·zeug·hal·te·rin ['faːˈtsɔɡkhaltərɪn] die
<-, -nen> *(form)* vehicle owner
② **fair** [fɛːɐ] ⟨adj, adv⟩ fair(ly) ◊ ein fairer Preis/Handel

◆ Es wäre fair gewesen, mich vorher zu warnen. ◆
ein fairer Sportler ◆ jdn fair behandeln
Fa·kul·tät [fakʊlˈtɛːt] die <-, -en> faculty, department
② **Fall** [fal] der <-(e)s, Fälle> **1.** case, instance ◊ ein
typischer Fall von Selbstüberschätzung ◆ Was ist
in diesem Fall zu tun? ◆ Das ist von Fall zu Fall
verschieden. **2.** *(possibilty)* eventuality ◊ Für den
Fall, dass ich krank werde, gebe ich Ihnen rechtzeitig Bescheid. gesetzt den Fall, ... supposing that
... ◊ Gesetzt den Fall, wir würden gewinnen —
wie hoch wäre mein Anteil? **3.** *no pl (act of
falling)* fall ◊ ein Fall aus fünf Metern Höhe
4. GRAM case ◊ Der Dativ ist der 3. Fall. **5.** *(of an
empire)* fall, downfall ◊ der Fall des Inkareiches
6. LAW, MED case ◊ Der Fall kam vor Gericht. ◆ Die
leichten Fälle werden ambulant behandelt. **7.** FIN
drop ◊ der plötzliche Fall des Euro
⊙ **auf alle Fälle** definitely, at all costs **für alle
Fälle** just in case ◊ Ich habe für alle Fälle immer
einen Schirm dabei. **auf jeden Fall** in any case,
certainly ◊ Egal, was passiert, ich komme auf
jeden Fall. **auf keinen Fall** under no circumstances, certainly not ◊ Darauf solltest du dich auf
keinen Fall einlassen! **jds Fall sein** *(fam)* be sb's
thing ◊ Surfen ist absolut nicht mein Fall.
Fal·le ['falə] die <-, -n> **1.** trap ◊ eine Falle für
Mäuse ◊ Die Truhe wurde für das Kind zur
tödlichen Falle. ◆ Er hat uns in eine gemeine Falle
gelockt! **2.** *(fam)* bed ◊ Ab in die Falle!
fal·len ['falən] <fällt, fiel, ist gefallen> ⟨intr v⟩
1. *(to the ground)* fall ◊ Das Buch ist vom Regal
gefallen. ◆ In dieser Region ist seit Monaten kein
Regen gefallen. ◆ Gib Acht, dass du nicht fällst! ◆
Todmüde fiel er ins Bett. schwer fallen have a
serious fall etw. fallen lassen drop sth ◊ Lass den
Fotoapparat nicht fallen! etw. fällt jdm aus der
Hand sb drops sth **2.** *(decrease)* drop, go down ◊
Der Pegel des Flusses ist wieder gefallen. **3.** FIN
(shares) drop in value **4.** MIL fall, be killed ◊ Ihr
Großvater ist im Zweiten Weltkrieg gefallen.
5. *(happen)* take place, occur ◊ Der entscheidende Treffer fiel gegen Ende des Spiels.;
(decision) be made; *(date)* auf etw. ⟨acc⟩ fallen
fall on sth ◊ Auf welchen Wochentag fällt dieses
Jahr der 1. Mai? etw. fällt unter etw. ⟨acc⟩ sth
comes within/under sth ◊ Das fällt nicht in die Leis-
tungspflicht der Krankenkasse. **7.** das Wort ... fiel
there was talk of ... ◊ Auch das Wort „Entlassungen" fiel.
fäl·len ['fɛlən] ⟨tr v⟩ *+haben* **1.** *(a tree)* fell, cut
down ◊ Der Apfelbaum ist krank und muss gefällt
werden. **2.** *(a decision)* be made ◊ Entscheidungen über etw. ⟨acc⟩ fällen *(a judgement, sentence)* pass ◊ Es ist
oft schwierig, das richtige Urteil zu fällen.
fäl·lig ['fɛlɪç] ⟨adj⟩ **1.** FIN due ◊ fällige Zinsen ◆ Die
Zahlung ist am 15. Mai fällig. ◆ Ich fürchte, eine
Mieterhöhung ist fällig. **2.** *(action)* overdue,
needed ◊ Ein neuer Anstrich ist fällig. **3.** *(fam)* jd
ist fällig sb is in trouble ◊ Wenn er bis Montag
nicht zahlt, ist er fällig.
falls [fals] ⟨conjunc⟩ if ◊ Falls ich Zeit haben sollte,
schaue ich bei Oma vorbei. ⊜wenn
② **fällt** [fɛlt] *pres of* fallen
② **falsch** [falʃ] ⟨adj, adv⟩ <falscher, am falschesten>
1. wrong(ly) ◊ Er nahm die falsche Autobahnaus-

fahrt. ♦ *Die Vorwürfe sind völlig falsch.* falsch liegen be wrong ◊ *Mit dieser Einschätzung lag sie falsch.* falsch fahren take the wrong way *etw./jdn* falsch einschätzen misjudge sth/sb ⊖verkehrt ⊖richtig **2.** *(not genuine)* false(ly) ◊ *falsche Wimpern* ♦ *Mach dir keine falschen Hoffnungen!* ♦ *Sie machte eine falsche Aussage, um ihren Freund zu entlasten.* falsch aussagen make a false statement; *(money)* counterfeit ⊖echt

fäl·schen ['fɛlʃn] [tr v] +*haben* fake, forge ◊ *ein gefälschter Führerschein* ♦ *Er hat die Unterschrift gefälscht.*; *(money)* counterfeit

Fal·te ['faltə] die <-, –n> **1.** *(on your skin)* wrinkle, crease, line ◊ *tiefe Falten um den Mund* ♦ *Ihre Stirn hatte sich in Falten gelegt.* **2.** *(in material)* fold, pleat, crease ◊ *Dieser Vorhang wirft schöne Falten.* **3.** *(in a piece of clothing)* crease ◊ *Leg den Anzug vorsichtig in den Koffer, damit keine Falten entstehen.*

fal·ten ['faltn] <faltet, faltete, hat gefaltet> [tr v] fold ◊ *Er faltete den Brief und steckte ihn in den Umschlag.* ♦ *die Wäsche falten*

fa·mi·li·är [fami'liːɛːɐ] [adj] **1.** *only before ns (concerning the family)* family ◊ *familiäre Probleme haben* **2.** *(not stiff)* informal, relaxed ◊ *eine familiäre Atmosphäre* ♦ *Das Klima im Betrieb ist ausgesprochen familiär.* [adv] **1.** down to family affairs ◊ *familiär bedingte Probleme* **2.** MED familiär bedingt/gehäuft hereditary mit *etw./hinsichtlich einer Sache* [gen] familiär vorbelastet sein have sth in your family **3.** informally ◊ *ein familiär geführter Gasthof*

② **Fa·mi·lie** [fa'miːliə] die <-, –n> family ◊ *Ich bleibe heute Abend zu Hause bei meiner Familie.* ♦ *Im ersten Stock wohnt eine nette Familie .* ♦ *An Weihnachten trifft sich die ganze Familie bei Oma.* ♦ *Der Wellensittich gehört zu der Familie der Sittiche.*

Fa·mi·li·en·na·me [fa'miːliənnaːmə] der <-ns, –n> surname, family name ◊ *Wie heißen Sie mit Familiennamen?* ♦ *Ihr Familienname ist Poth, ihr Vorname Ursula.* ⊖Nachname ⊖Vorname

Fa·mi·li·en·pla·nung [fa'miːliənplaːnʊn] die <-> *no pl* family planning

Fa·mi·li·en·stand [fa'miːliənʃtant] der <-(e)s *no pl (form)* marital status

⑦ **fand** [fant] *pret of* finden

Fang [faŋ] der <-(e)s, Fänge> **1.** *no pl* der Fang von ... catching ..., hunting ... ◊ *eine Petition gegen den Fang von Walen* **2.** *(fish)* catch ◊ *Der Fang wird auf dem Fischmarkt verkauft.*; *(criminal)* haul ◊ *Den Drogenfahndern gelang ein großer Fang.* **3.** *(tooth)* fang ◊ *Die Löwin schlug ihre Fänge in die Beute.*
⊛ einen guten Fang machen/tun make a good catch

fan·gen ['faŋən] <fängt, fing, hat gefangen> [tr v] **1.** *(objects, animals, criminals)* catch ◊ *Mäuse kann man am besten mit Speck fangen.* ♦ *Die Polizei hat die Einbrecher gefangen.* ♦ *Fang den Ball!* **2.** *mostly passive (a person)* enchant ◊ *Ich war von ihrer Schönheit gefangen.* [ref v] **1.** *(not fall)* sich fangen steady yourself, keep your balance ◊ *Fast wäre ich gestürzt – ich konnte mich gerade noch fangen.* **2.** *(mentally)* sich fangen sort yourself out ◊ *Er war eine Zeit lang depressiv, aber jetzt hat er sich wieder gefangen.*

fängt [fɛŋt] *pres of* fangen

Fan·ta·sie [fanta'ziː] die <-, –n> **1.** *no pl (faculty)* imagination ◊ *Er dachte sich mit viel Fantasie Geschichten für seine Kinder aus.* ♦ *Dieses Buch regt die Fantasie an.* **2.** *(imagined thing)* fantasy ◊ *kindliche Fantasien*

fan·ta·sie·ren [fanta'ziːrən] <fantasiert, fantasierte, hat fantasiert> [intr v] **1.** dream, fantasize ◊ *Er fantasiert davon, ein berühmter Sänger zu werden.* **2.** be delirious ◊ *Sie bekam hohes Fieber und fantasierte.*

② **Far·be** ['farbə] die <-, –n> **1.** colour, color ◊ *die Farbe Rot* ♦ *Wolle in verschiedenen Farben* ♦ *Der Wind brachte frische Farbe in ihr Gesicht.* eine Broschüre in Farbe a colour/color brochure **2.** paint ◊ *rote Farbe* **3.** CARDS suit ◊ *Welche Farbe ist Trumpf?*
⊛ Farbe bekennen **1.** nail your colours to the mast ◊ *Nach der Wahl musste die Partei Farbe bekennen.* **2.** say what's what **3.** show everyone what you can do ◊ *Im der nächsten Runde muss die Mannschaft Farbe bekennen.*

Nouns deriving from adjectives that describe colours, e.g. *Rot* (red), *Blau* (blue), *Grün* (green), can be used with or without an article. No article is used when referring to the colour itself: *die Farbe Blau* (the colour blue) *–Blau ist eine schöne Farbe.* (Blue is a lovely colour.) But an article is needed when a specific hue of colour is being described: *Das Rot des Stoffes ist sehr hell.* (The red of this fabric is very bright.). Frequently, such nouns form part of an idiom: *ins Grüne fahren* (= go on an outing to the countryside). Nominal adjectives of colour ending in '-e' always take an article: *das Gelbe vom Ei — das Weiße in seinen Augen.*

---

fär·ben ['fɛʳbm] [tr v] +*haben* **1.** dye, colour, color ◊ *Ich möchte diese Bluse blau färben.* ♦ *Färbst du dir die Haare?* **2.** etw. rot/blau/dunkel färben give sth its red/blue/dark colour/color ◊ *Lycopin ist der Stoff, der die Tomate rot färbt.* **3.** run in the wash ◊ *Vorsicht beim Waschen – rote Sachen färben oft.* [ref v] sich blau/gelb färben turn blue/yellow ◊ *Der Inhalt des Reagenzglases färbte sich violett.*

⑦ **far·big** ['farbɪç] [adj] **1.** *(object)* colour, color ◊ *ein Buch mit farbigen Abbildungen* ♦ *Das ausgedruckte Bild ist farbig.* ⊖bunt **2.** *mostly before ns (person)* coloured, colored ◊ *eine farbige Amerikanerin* **3.** *(lively)* vibrant ◊ *eine farbige Instrumentation mit großem Orchester* [adv] farbig illustriert with colour/color illustrations

⑦ **Fa·schier·te** [fa'ʃiːɐtə] das <-n> *but: Faschiertes, no pl (Austr)* minced meat, mince ◊ *rohes Faschiertes* ♦ *Möchtest du etwas von dem Faschierten?* box@ Substantivierung

Fa·sching ['faʃɪŋ] der <-s, –e or –s> *most sing (SouthG, Austr)* Shrovetide; *a period prior to Lent characterised by a carnival* ◊ *Ich gehe dieses Jahr im Fasching als Clown.* ⊖Karneval box@ Fastnacht

Fa·ser ['faːzɐ] die <-, –n> fibre, fiber ♦ *Acryl ist eine synthetische Faser.*

Fass [fas] das <-es, Fässer> **1.** barrel ◊ *Whisky in Fässern lagern* ♦ *Das Bier wurde in Fässer*

abgefüllt. **2.** vom Fass on draught Bier vom Fass draught beer

ⓔ *etw.* ist (wie) ein Fass ohne Boden sth is (like) a bottomless pit

fas·sen ['fasn] ⟨tr v⟩ +*haben* **1.** take hold of, grab ◊ *Ich fasste ihn an der Hand.* ♦ *Sie fasste den Krug mit beiden Händen.* **2.** *(a culprit)* apprehend, catch ◊ *Der Einbrecher wurde kurz nach der Tat gefasst.* **3.** *etw.* in Worte/Verse etc. fassen put sth into words/verse etc.; *(in figures)* express sth in figures ◊ *Diese Vorteile lassen sich nicht in Zahlen fassen.* **4.** *mostly negated* etw. nicht/kaum etc. fassen können not/scarcely etc. be able to grasp sth ◊ *Er konnte sein Glück kaum fassen.* Das ist ja nicht zu fassen! That's absolutely unbelievable! **5.** keinen klaren Gedanken fassen können not be able to think straight **6.** *(a decision)* make, take ◊ *Er fasste den Entschluss, sein Studium abzubrechen.* **7.** *(courage)* summon up ◊ *Er fasste neuen Lebensmut.; (confidence, trust)* gain ◊ *Das Tier fasste Zutrauen zu ihr.* **8.** *no passive (container, can etc.)* hold ◊ *Der Heizöltank fasst 8000 Liter.* ♦ *Dieses Stadion fasst 60 000 Zuschauer.* ⟨intr v⟩ an etw. ⟨acc⟩ fassen touch sth ◊ *Pass auf, dass du nicht an die Herdplatte fasst!* in etw. ⟨acc⟩ fassen put your hand into sth ◊ *Ich fasste in die Hosentasche und holte meinen Geldbeutel hervor.* ins Wasser fassen dip your hand into the water ⟨ref v⟩ **1.** sich fassen compose yourself ◊ *Nur mühsam fasste er sich nach dem Schock wieder.* **2.** sich kurz fassen be brief, keep it short ◊ *Der Redner fasste sich kurz.*

Fas·sung ['fasʊŋ] die <-, -en> **1.** *(of texts, films)* version ◊ *Ich sah den Film in der englischen Fassung.* ♦ *eine gekürzte Fassung* **2.** TECHN mounting ◊ *Er schraubte das Objektiv wieder in die Fassung.; (for a lightbulb)* socket **3.** *(on a piece of jewellery)* setting ◊ *Der Diamant sitzt in einer goldenen Fassung.* **4.** composure ◊ *Ich bewahrte/ verlor die Fassung.* ♦ *Sie trug die Niederlage mit Fassung.*

fas·sungs·los ['fasʊŋsloːs] ⟨adj⟩ no comp/superl stunned ◊ *fassungsloses Staunen* ♦ *Ich war fassungslos, dass er so gemein sein konnte.* ⟨adv⟩ in disbelief, lost for words ◊ *Sie schüttelte fassungslos den Kopf.*

ⓩ **fast** [fast] ⟨adv⟩ almost, nearly ◊ *Ich bin fast fertig.* ♦ *Es ist schon fast fünf Uhr.* ♦ *Fast 100 Leute kamen.* ⓔbeinahe, nahezu

Fas·ten·zeit ['fastn̩saet] die <-, -en> **1.** period of fasting **2.** Lent

Fast·nacht ['fastnaxt] die <-> *no pl pre-Lent carnival period* ◊ *Fastnacht feiern*

Also referred to as *Karneval* or *Fasching*, the high season of Carnival in Germany covers a period of six days from the Thursday, known as *Altweiberfastnacht*, when the women roam the streets dressed as witches and get up to all sorts of mischief, to Carnival Tuesday. It is a period of audacious high spirits and indulgence. Children in particular love getting dressed up during the Carnival period and going to the Carnival Monday processions, which feature a series of colourful floats often with satirical themes inspired by the world of politics. Sweets are thrown to the ▶

▶children from the floats. All Carnival activities are over by Ash Wednesday, when a time of contemplation and fasting begins in preparation for the Easter celebrations.

fau·chen ['faoxn̩] ⟨intr v⟩ +*haben* hiss ◊ *Die Katze fauchte wild.* ♦ *„Lass mich in Ruhe!", fauchte sie.; (big cat)* snarl

ⓩ **faul** [faol] ⟨adj, adv⟩ lazy(-ily), idle/idly ◊ *Der Kater ist faul und träge.* ♦ *Wir lagen faul am Strand.* ♦ *Ich machte mir einen faulen Tag.* ♦ *Wir lagen faul am Strand.* ⓔfleißig ⟨adj⟩ **1.** rotten ◊ *Sie wurden mit faulen Eiern beworfen.* ♦ *faules Obst* ♦ *Das Holz des Fensterrahmens war faul.; (water)* stagnant, foul; *(smell)* putrid **2.** *(fam, fig)* dubious ◊ *eine faule Ausrede* ♦ *Er versuchte sie mit faulen Tricks hereinzulegen.* etwas ist faul something funny is going on

fau·len ['faolən] ⟨intr v⟩ +*haben/sein* be rotting, be decaying ◊ *Das Holz fault.* ♦ *Die Birnen faulten bereits am Baum.; (body)* be putrefying; *(water)* be stagnating

fau·len·zen ['faolɛntsn̩] ⟨intr v⟩ +*haben* loaf about, laze around ◊ *Er faulenzt den ganzen Tag.*

fau·lig ['faolɪç] ⟨adj, adv⟩ rotten, putrid, foul ◊ *Die Hälfte der Kartoffeln war schon faulig.* ♦ *fauliges Holz* ♦ *faulig riechendes Obst; (water)* stagnant

Faust [faost] die <-, Fäuste> fist ◊ *Sie ballte die Hand zu einer Faust.* ♦ *Er schlug ihm mit der Faust in den Magen.*

ⓔ auf eigene Faust on your own initiative ◊ *Er wollte die Umgebung auf eigene Faust erkunden.* sich ins Fäustchen lachen gloat, laugh up your sleeve

faust·dick ['faostdɪk] ⟨adj⟩ no comp/superl; only before ns huge, massive ◊ *Der Wettkampf sorgte für eine faustdicke Überraschung.* eine faustdicke Lüge a whopper (of a lie)

ⓩ **Fau·teuil** [fo'tøːj] der <-s, -s> *(Swiss, Austr)* armchair ◊ *im Fauteuil sitzen*

ⓩ **Fax** [faks] das <-, -e> **1.** fax ◊ *Können Sie mir das Dokument per Fax schicken?* ♦ *Gerade ist dieses Fax angekommen.* **2.** *(appliance)* fax machine

Fa·zit ['faːtsɪt] das <-s, -s or -e> result, conclusion ◊ *Was war das Fazit der Podiumsdiskussion?* ♦ *Er zog ein überraschend positives Fazit.* das Fazit aus etw. ziehen sum sth up

FDP [ɛfdeːˈpeː] die <-> **1.** *(abbr of* Freie Demokratische Partei)* **2.** *(Swiss) (abbr of* Freisinnig-Demokratische Partei)*

The German *FDP* is a liberal party with conservative inclinations. It has repeatedly been a coalition partner of the *CDU* and has thus formed part of the government. The Swiss *FDP* is also a liberal party. It supports a democratic state under the rule of law and a free and social market economy. With regard to national defence, it favours neutrality.

ⓩ **Fe·ber** ['feːbɐ] der <-s, -> *most sing (Austr)* February → Januar

ⓩ **Feb·ru·ar** ['feːbruaːɐ] der <-(s), -e> *most sing* February → Januar

fech·ten ['fɛçtn̩] <ficht, focht, hat gefochten> ⟨intr v⟩ fence

Fe·der ['feːdɐ] die <-, -n> **1.** feather ◊ *ein Vogel mit schwarzen Federn* **2.** *(fam)* aus den Federn

rise and shine, get up ◊ *Los, raus aus den Federn!*
in die Federn hit the sack, go to bed ◊ *Kinder, ab
in die Federn!* **3.** *(writing implement)* quill, pen ◊
Er tauchte die Feder ins Tintenfass. **4.** *(metal
spiral)* spring ◊ *Bei dem Sessel sind die Federn
kaputt.*

◉ **sich mit fremden Federn schmücken** take the
credit for someone else's efforts, bask in someone
else's glory **zur Feder greifen** take up your pen ◊
*Eines Tages griff sie zur Feder und schrieb einen
Roman.* **jd/etw. muss (bei etw.) Federn lassen**
sb/sth does not emerge (from sth) unscathed ◊
*Der deutsche Aktienmarkt musste ordentlich
Federn lassen.* **aus jds Feder stammen** come
from sb's pen ◊ *Aus wessen Feder stammt diese
Karikatur?*

Fe·der·ball ['feːdɐbal] *der* <-(e)s, Federbälle>
1. shuttlecock ◊ *Der Federball flog über den Zaun.*
2. *no pl* badminton ◊ *Sie spielten Federball.*

Fe·der·bett ['feːdɐbɛt] *das* <-(e)s, -en> continental quilt, duvet ◊ *Sie schüttelte das Federbett aus.*

Fe·der·mäpp·chen ['feːdɐmɛpçən] *das* <-s, ->
pencil case

Fe·der·wei·ße ['feːdɐvaɪ̯sə] *der* <-n> *but: ein Federweißer, no pl* new wine *box*@ Substantivierung

---

Federweißer is also referred to in Austria as
Sturm and in Switzerland as *Sauser*. It is a type of
cloudy must that ferments more slowly as time
goes by. It is particularly rich in vitamins and
contains very little yeast. Its alcohol content is just
under 10% and it is traditionally served with
onion tart.

---

fe·gen ['feːgn̩] [tr v] +*haben* sweep ◊ *Er fegte den
Boden.* ♦ *Sie hat mit dem Ärmel versehentlich das
Weinglas vom Tisch gefegt.* ♦ *Der Wind fegte die
Blätter von den Bäumen.* [intr v] +*sein* sweep ◊ *Ein
Orkan fegte über Nordeuropa.*

fehl [feːl] [adj] *(always* fehl am Platz(e)*)* out of
place ◊ *Übertriebener Ehrgeiz ist hier fehl am
Platz.* ♦ *Ich fühlte mich auf der Party völlig fehl
am Platz.;* in the wrong place ◊ *Wenn du das nicht
kannst, bist du hier fehl am Platz.*

Fehl·an·zei·ge ['feːlʔantsaɪ̯gə] *die* <-> *no pl*
(fam) not a hope, nothing doing ◊ *Ich hoffte auf
gutes Wetter. Aber Fehlanzeige!*

② **feh·len** ['feːlən] [intr v] +*haben* **1.** be missing ◊ *An
dem Schuh fehlte der Absatz.* ♦ *Seine Zustimmung
fehlt noch.* ♦ *Er hat in der Schule unentschuldigt
gefehlt.* **von jdm fehlt jede Spur** there is no trace
of sb **2.** etw. fehlt, es fehlt an etw. [dat] there is a
lack of sth ◊ *In diesen Bundesländern fehlt es an/
fehlen Lehrstellen.* **jdm fehlt etw.** [nom], jdm fehlt
es an etw. [dat] sb lacks sth, sb is lacking in sth ◊
Ihr fehlte das nötige Durchhaltevermögen.;
(money also) sb is short of sth ◊ *Mir fehlt es am
nötigen Geld für eine Reise.* Drei Punkte fehlten ihr
zur Medaille. She missed a medal by three points.
3. jdm fehlt jd/etw. sb misses sb/sth ◊ *Du fehlst
mir sehr!* ♦ *Deine liebevolle Betreuung fehlt mir.*
4. jdm fehlt (et)was something is wrong with sb,
something is the matter with sb **jdm fehlt nichts**
nothing is wrong with sb, nothing is the matter
with sb
◉ **jdm gerade noch gefehlt haben** *(iron)* be all
that sb needs ◊ *Diese Erkältung hat mir gerade*

noch gefehlt! **weit gefehlt** far from it ◊ *Du
glaubst, diese Meldung sei frei erfunden? Weit
gefehlt!*

② **Feh·ler** ['feːlɐ] *der* <-s, -> **1.** mistake, error ◊
Fehler korrigieren ♦ *ein grober/schwerer Fehler* ♦
Ich habe in meinem Leben viele Fehler gemacht.
2. defect, fault, flaw ◊ *Kann man den Fehler
beheben?* ♦ *Ein technischer Fehler war für den
Absturz verantwortlich.;* *(in software)* bug
3. *(trait)* failing, fault ◊ *Ihr größter Fehler ist ihr
Hang zum Perfektionismus.*

feh·ler·haft ['feːlɐhaft] [adj] *no comp/superl*
defective ◊ *Durch die fehlerhafte Software kam das
System zum Erliegen.* ♦ *Die Listen waren fehlerhaft
und unvollständig.* [adv] badly ◊ *Er arbeitet unkonzentriert und fehlerhaft.*

fehl|schla·gen ['feːlʃlaːgn̩] <schlägt fehl, schlug
fehl, ist fehlgeschlagen> [intr v] fail ◊ *Alle Rettungsversuche schlugen fehl.*

Fehl·start ['feːlʃtaʁt] *der* <-s, -s> **1.** false start ◊
Beim 100-Meter-Lauf kam es zu einem Fehlstart.
2. aborted launch ◊ *Ein Fehler im Triebwerk verursachte den Fehlstart der Rakete.*

② **Fei·er** ['faɪ̯ɐ] *die* <-, -n> party, celebration ◊ *Warst
du auf der Feier?* ♦ *eine Feier anlässlich des 50-
jährigen Bestehens des Vereins*
◉ **zur Feier des Tages** in honour of the occasion
◊ *Zur Feier des Tages gab es Champagner.*

Fei·er·a·bend ['faɪ̯ɐʔaːbm̩t, 'faɪ̯ɐʔaːbant] *der*
<-s, -e> **1.** *no pl* knocking-off time, end of work
◊ *Sie will sich nach Feierabend mit ihrer Freundin
treffen.* Feierabend machen finish work, knock off
(work) **2.** evening, time after work ◊ *Seinen Feierabend verbringt er meist vor dem Fernseher.*

fei·er·lich ['faɪ̯ɐlɪç] [adj, adv] ceremonial(ly), ceremonious(ly) ◊ *Sie bereiteten ihm einen feierlichen
Empfang.* ♦ *Die Veranstaltung war sehr feierlich.* ♦
Das Museum wurde gestern feierlich eröffnet.;
(church service, speech etc.) solemn(ly) ◊ *Im
Saal herrschte feierliche Stille.* ♦ *Er schüttelte ihr
feierlich die Hand.*

② **fei·ern** ['faɪ̯ɐn] [tr v] +*haben* **1.** celebrate ◊ *Wie
feiert ihr Weihnachten?* ♦ *Das muss gefeiert
werden!;* *(a party)* hold **2.** hail ◊ *Man feierte ihn
als neuen Star.* [intr v] party ◊ *Habt ihr gestern
Abend noch lange gefeiert?;* have a party ◊ *Er
hatte schon gestern Geburtstag, feiert aber erst
am Samstag.*

Fei·er·tag ['faɪ̯ɐtaːk] *der* <-(e)s, -e> (public)
holiday, statutory holiday ◊ *ein gesetzlicher/kirchlicher Feiertag* ♦ *An Sonn- und Feiertagen ist das
Museum geschlossen.* ⊕Werktag

feig [faɪ̯k], **fei·ge** ['faɪ̯gə] [adj] <feiger, am
feigsten> *(pej)* cowardly ◊ *Mein Bruder ist sehr
feige.* ♦ *Es war feige, ihr die Wahrheit zu verschweigen.* ♦ *ein feiger Mord*

Fei·ge ['faɪ̯gə] *die* <-, -n> fig ◊ *getrocknete/
frische Feigen* ♦ *Feigen blühen bis zu dreimal pro
Jahr.*

Feig·ling ['faɪ̯klɪŋ] *der* <-s, -e> *(pej)* coward ◊
Sie nannte ihn einen Feigling. ♦ *Sie wollte nicht
als Feigling dastehen.*

Fei·le ['faɪ̯lə] *die* <-, -n> file ◊ *Kanten mit
einer Feile abschleifen* **2.** nail file

feil·schen ['faɪ̯lʃn̩] [intr v] +*haben* haggle, barter ◊
Auf dem Basar wurde eifrig gefeilscht. ♦ *Er hat mit*

A
B
C
D
E
F
G
H
I
J
K
L
M
N
O
P
Q
R
S
T
U
V
W
X
Y
Z

dem Händler um jeden Cent gefeilscht.
② **fein** [faen] (adj, adv) fine(ly) ◊ *Er zog mit dem Pinsel feine Linien.* ✦ *Ihr Haar ist sehr fein.* ✦ *Zwischen diesen beiden Begriffen besteht ein feiner Unterschied.* ✦ *feines Gebäck* ✦ *fein gemahlener Kaffee; (bands, features also)* delicate(ly)*; (sandpaper)* fine grained; *(sugar)* finely granulated *eine fein abgestimmte Mischung* a fine blend (adj) **1.** *mostly before ns (instinct, bearing, nose)* keen ◊ *Er hat ein feines Gespür dafür, was seine Kunden wollen.* ✦ *Sie hat ein feines Gehör.* **2.** *(fam)* great ◊ *Fein, dass es doch noch geklappt hat!* ✦ *Er/Sie ist ein feiner Kerl.* **3.** *(also iron)* fine, refined ◊ *Sie mischten sich unter die feine Gesellschaft.* ✦ *eine feine Dame* sich (dat) für etw. zu fein sein think sth is beneath you ⊜vornehm
⊛ **fein säuberlich** carefully ◊ *Alles war fein säuberlich geordnet.* **sich fein machen** dress up, get dressed up
② **Feind** [faent] der <-(e)s, -e>, **Fein·din** ['faendɪn] die <-, -nen> **1.** enemy ◊ *Sie war meine größte Feindin.* ✦ *Die Maus hat viele natürliche Feinde.* ✦ *Die Zeit ist jetzt unser größter Feind.* sich (dat) Feinde machen make enemies sich (dat) jdn zum Feind machen antagonize sb, antagonise sb, make an enemy of sb **2.** *no pl* MIL der Feind the enemy ◊ *Der Feind ging zum Angriff über.* **3.** ein Feind von etw. sein be an opponent of sth ◊ *Sie ist ein ausgesprochener Feind von faulen Kompromissen.*
⊛ **ran an den Feind** get down to it/work *(referring to food)* tuck in
feind·lich ['faentlɪç] (adj) *mostly before ns* **1.** hostile ◊ *Die Klasse war in zwei feindliche Lager gespalten.* ✦ *Er nahm eine feindliche Haltung an.* **2.** MIL enemy ◊ *feindliche Soldaten* ✦ *ein feindlicher Angriff* (adv) (jdm/etw.) feindlich gesinnt/gesonnen hostile (towards sb/sth) ◊ *Er war dem Ganzen eher feindlich gesinnt.* feindlich gegen jdn/etw. eingestellt sein, jdm/etw. feindlich gegenüberstehen be opposed to sb/sth, be hostile towards sb/sth
Feind·schaft ['faentʃaft] die <-, -en> hostility, enmity ◊ *Zwischen den beiden besteht eine erbitterte Feindschaft.*
Fein·ge·fühl ['faengəfyːl] das <-s> *no pl* **1.** tact, tactfulness ◊ *Der Psychologe ging mit sehr viel Feingefühl vor.* ✦ *Ich schätze sein diplomatisches Feingefühl.* ⊜Takt **2.** sensitivity ◊ *Die Aquarellmalerei erfordert sehr viel Feingefühl.*
Fein·schme·cker ['faenʃmɛke] der <-s, ->, **Fein·schme·cke·rin** ['faenʃmɛkərɪn] die <-, -nen> gourmet ◊ *Sie ist eine echte Feinschmeckerin.* ✦ *Als Feinschmecker schwört er auf gutes Olivenöl.*
② **Feld** [fɛlt] das <-(e)s, -er> **1.** field ◊ *Die Felder wurden abgeerntet.* ✦ *Das Feld der Medizin ist unendlich weit.* ✦ *elektromagnetische Felder* ein Feld bestellen till a field **2.** *(of a board game)* square ◊ *Ein Schachbrett besteht aus 64 Feldern.; (on a document)* box ◊ *Bitte füllen Sie alle Felder vollständig aus.* **3.** SPORT court ⊜Platz **4.** *no pl (outd, euph)* MIL (battle)field ◊ *2000 Soldaten zogen ins Feld.*
⊛ **das Feld räumen** quit, call it a day ◊ *Ich räume lieber freiwillig das Feld.* **jdn aus dem Feld schlagen** defeat sb **jdm das Feld überlassen** make way for sb ◊ *Schließlich überließ er seinem*

jüngeren Kollegen das Feld.
Feld·sa·lat ['fɛltza'laːt] der <-(e)s> *no pl* lamb's lettuce
Fel·ge ['fɛlgə] die <-, -n> rim ◊ *Das Auto hatte verchromte Felgen.*
Fell [fɛl] das <-(e)s, -e> **1.** *most sing* fur ◊ *Die Katze hatte (ein) schwarzes Fell.* ✦ *Sie strich dem Hund übers Fell.; (of a horse)* coat **2.** *(from a large animal)* hide; *(from a small animal)* pelt einem Tier das Fell abziehen skin an animal ⊜Pelz **3.** *(of a drum)* skin
⊛ **ein dickes Fell** a thick skin ◊ *Für diesen Job braucht man ein dickes Fell.* **jdm schwimmen die/alle Felle davon** sb's hopes are fading fast
Fels¹ [fɛls] der <-en(s), -en> *(lofty)* rock ◊ *Das Auto war auf einen Fels geprallt.; (wall of rock)* cliff, rockface ◊ *ein steiler Fels*
⊛ **wie ein Fels in der Brandung** steady as a rock
Fels² [fɛls] der <-> *no pl* rock ◊ *Das Haus ist auf Fels gebaut.* ✦ *Die Stufen waren in den Fels gehauen.*
Fel·sen ['fɛlzn] der <-s, -> **1.** rock ◊ *der Felsen von Gibraltar* **2.** cliff, rockface ◊ *Das Auto prallte frontal gegen den Felsen.*
fe·mi·nin [femi'niːn, 'feːminiːn] (adj) feminine ◊ *Sie ist ein sehr femininer Typ.* ✦ *Das Wort „Katze" ist feminin.; (of a man)* effeminate ◊ *Er hatte ein sehr feminines Gesicht.* ⊜maskulin (adv) in a feminine way ◊ *Sie war auf dem Gemälde sehr feminin dargestellt.* ⊜maskulin
Fen·chel ['fɛnçl] der <-s> *no pl* fennel ◊ *Fenchel wird oft als Salat oder Gemüse gegessen.* ✦ *Was für ein Tee ist das? Kamille oder Fenchel?*
② **Fens·ter** ['fɛnste] das <-s, -> window ◊ *ein Fenster öffnen/kippen* ✦ *Sie schaute aus dem Fenster.* ✦ *Beim Surfen klicke ich Fenster mit Werbebannern sofort weg.*
Fens·ter·bank ['fɛnstebaŋk] die <-, Fensterbänke> window sill, window ledge ◊ *Auf der Fensterbank standen einige Pflanzen.* ⊜Fensterbrett
Fens·ter·brett ['fɛnstebrɛt] das <-(e)s, -er> → Fensterbank
Fens·ter·la·den ['fɛnstelaːdn] der <-s, Fensterläden> shutter ◊ *Sie schloss die Fensterläden.*
Fe·ri·en ['feːrjən] die <-> *only pl* holidays, vacation ◊ *Die Ferien an der Nordsee waren wirklich toll!* die großen Ferien the summer holidays, the summer vacation in die Ferien fahren go on holiday Ferien machen be on holiday, take a holiday ◊ *Unser Betrieb macht im August drei Wochen Ferien.* ✦ *Letztes Jahr haben wir Ferien auf Sylt gemacht.* zwei Wochen Ferien two weeks' holiday
Fer·kel ['fɛrkl] das <-s, -> **1.** piglet ◊ *Die Sau hat neun Ferkel geworfen.* **2.** *(bum or pej) (unkempt person)* dirty pig ◊ *Du Ferkel! Wasch dich mal.* **3.** *(pej)* dirty sod
② **fern¹** [fɛrn] (adj) distant, far-off ◊ *Sie reist gern in ferne Länder.* ✦ *ein Blick in die ferne Zukunft* fern von jdm/etw. far away from sb/sth ◊ *Das war ihr erstes Weihnachtsfest fern von zu Hause.* von fern from afar, from a distance ◊ *Er beobachtete den Streit von fern.* fern sein be far away/off ◊ *Der Urlaub ist nicht mehr fern.* in nicht allzu ferner Zukunft in the not-too-distant future ⊜nah
⊛ **jdn/etw. von jdm/etw. fern halten** keep sb/

sth away from sb/sth ◊ *schlimme Nachrichten von den Kindern fern halten* stay away from sb **etw. liegt jdm fern** sth is not sb's intention at all ◊ *Es liegt mir fern, Sie zu kritisieren.*

fern² [fɛˈn] (prep) (+dat) *(lofty)* far (away) from ◊ *Sie fühlte sich einsam, so fern der Heimat.*

fern·ab [fɛˈnˈʔap] (prep) (+gen) *(lofty)* far away from ◊ *Sie lebten fernab jeder Zivilisation.*

Fern·be·die·nung [ˈfɛˈnbədiːnʊŋ] die <-, -en> remote (control)

fern|blei·ben [ˈfɛˈnblaebm̩] <bleibt fern, blieb fern, ist ferngeblieben> (intr v) *(lofty)* etw. (dat) fernbleiben be absent from sth, stay away from sth ◊ *Sie blieb mehrere Tage dem Unterricht fern.*

Fer·ne [ˈfɛˈnə] die <-> *no pl* aus der Ferne from a distance ◊ *Sie beobachtete das Geschehen aus der Ferne.* in der Ferne in the distance ◊ *In der Ferne grollte der Donner.* in die Ferne into the distance ◊ *Sie blickte sehnsüchtig in die Ferne.* in weite(r) Ferne a long way off ◊ *Der Gipfel liegt noch in weiter Ferne.*; *(in the past)* in weiter Ferne a long time ago ◊ *Mein letzter Urlaub liegt bereits in weiter Ferne.* jds Gedanken schweifen in die Ferne sb lets their thoughts wander

fer·ner [ˈfɛˈnɐ] (conjunc) *(form)* in addition, additionally ◊ *Geplant ist ein Umbau, ferner die Anschaffung neuer Computer.*

Fern·glas [ˈfɛˈnɡlaːs] das <-es, Ferngläser> binoculars, field glasses ◊ *Vögel mit dem Fernglas beobachten*

Fern·licht [ˈfɛˈnlɪçt] das <-(e)s> *no pl* full beam, high beam ◊ *Bei Gegenverkehr muss man das Fernlicht ausschalten.*

Fern·rohr [ˈfɛˈnroːɐ] das <-(e)s, -e> telescope ◊ *Durch das Fernrohr beobachtete er die Sterne.*

② **fern|se·hen** [ˈfɛˈnzeːən] <sieht fern, sah fern, hat ferngesehen> (intr v) watch television, watch TV ◊ *Abends sieht er meist fern.*

② **Fern·se·hen** [ˈfɛˈnzeːən] das <-> *no pl* television, TV ◊ *Sie arbeitet fürs Fernsehen.* ◆ *Den Bericht habe ich im Fernsehen gesehen.*

② **Fern·se·her** [ˈfɛˈnzeːɐ] der <-s, -> television (set), TV ◊ *vor dem Fernseher sitzen* ◆ *Bei ihnen läuft dauernd der Fernseher.*

Fern·stu·di·um [ˈfɛˈnʃtuːdjʊm] das <-s> *no pl* distance learning course ◊ *ein Fernstudium absolvieren* ◆ *den Abschluss über ein Fernstudium erwerben*

Fern·uni·ver·si·tät [ˈfɛˈnˌunivɛˈzitɛːt] die <-, -en> university exclusively offering distance learning courses ◊ *Sie wollte an der Fernuniversität Hagen studieren.*

Fer·se [ˈfɛˈzə] die <-, -n> heel ◊ *Er hatte Blasen an den Fersen.* ◆ *Sie hatte ein Loch in der Ferse der linken Socke.*

⑨ **sich an jds Fersen heften** stick to sb's heels

② **fer·tig** [ˈfɛˈtɪç] (adj) *no comp/superl* **1.** finished ◊ *Das Dach war schon fertig.* ◆ *Kannst du die fertigen Briefe bitte abschicken?* mit etw. fertig sein have finished sth ◊ *Bist du mit den Hausaufgaben fertig?* etw. fertig machen/stellen finish sth, complete sth ◊ *Das Stadion wurde 1999 fertig gestellt.* etw. fertig bekommen/kriegen finish sth ◊ *Hast du den Aufsatz rechtzeitig fertig bekommen?* **2.** ready ◊ *Das Essen ist in zehn Minuten fertig.*

etw. fertig machen get sth ready ◊ *die Waren für den Abtransport fertig machen* sich (für etw.) fertig machen get ready (for sth) ◊ *Ich muss mich schnell noch fertig machen, dann können wir los.* **3.** *(fam)* shattered ◊ *Sie kam völlig fertig von der Arbeit heim. Diese Hitze macht mich ganz fertig.* This heat is really getting to me. ⊜platt, kaputt (adv) fertig lesen/schreiben etc. finish reading/writing etc. ◊ *Hast du bald fertig gegessen?* fertig angezogen/ausgebildet etc. fully dressed/trained etc. fertig abgepackt/geschnitten prepacked/precut

⑨ **etw. fertig bekommen/bringen/kriegen** *(fam)* manage sth, be able to do sth ◊ *Ich bringe es nicht fertig, ihr die Wahrheit zu sagen.* **jdn fertig machen 1.** give sb a hard/rough time ◊ *Meine Eltern haben mich wegen der schlechten Noten fertig gemacht.* **2.** ruin sb ◊ *Seine Konkurrenten wollen ihn fertig machen.* **3.** do sb in ◊ *Die Mafia hat ihn fertig gemacht.* **mit jdm fertig sein** be finished with sb ◊ *Wenn er sich nicht entschuldigt, bin ich fertig mit ihm!* **mit jdm/etw. fertig werden** cope with sb/sth ◊ *Sie wurde mit dem Stress in der Arbeit nicht fertig.*

fer·ti·gen [ˈfɛˈtɪɡn̩] (tr v) +haben *(lofty)* manufacture, make ◊ *Die Kacheln werden per/von Hand gefertigt.* ◆ *Die Figuren sind ganz aus Holz gefertigt.*

Fer·tig·ge·richt [ˈfɛˈtɪçɡərɪçt] das <-(e)s, -e> ready meal

Fes·sel [ˈfɛsl̩] die <-, -n> **1.** *most pl* bond ◊ *Sie bekamen Fesseln angelegt.*; *(metal)* shackle **2.** *(fig)* fetter ◊ *sich von den gesellschaftlichen Fesseln befreien* jdm Fesseln anlegen impose limits on sb ◊ *Der Presse wurden von Monat zu Monat engere Fesseln angelegt.* **3.** *(of a horse)* pastern ◊ *Das Pferd hatte weiße Fesseln.* **4.** *(lofty)* ankle ◊ *Sie hatte schlanke Fesseln.*

fes·seln [ˈfɛsl̩n] (tr v) +haben **1.** tie (up); *(with metal bonds)* shackle, chain ◊ *Sie fesselten die Geiseln.* ◆ *Er fesselte ihn an den Stuhl.* **2.** *(fig)* an etw. (acc) gefesselt sein be confined to sth ◊ *ans Bett/an den Rollstuhl gefesselt sein* **3.** *(fig)* captivate ◊ *Die Geschichte fesselte die Kinder.*

② **fest** [fɛst] (adj, adv) <fester, am festesten> **1.** firm(ly) ◊ *auf festem Boden stehen* ◆ *Er antwortete mit fester Stimme.* ◆ *eine feste Zusage erhalten* ◆ *Er glaubte fest an ihre Unschuld.*; *(bandage, embrace etc. also)* tight(ly) ◊ *Ist der Knoten fest genug?* ◆ *Sie drückte das Kind fest an sich. Ich drücke dir ganz fest die Daumen.* I shall keep my fingers crossed for you. **2.** *when used as an adj, only before ns (promise)* faithful(ly) ◊ *ein festes Versprechen* **3.** *when used as an adj, only before ns (rules, prices)* set, fixed ◊ *Gibt es schon einen festen Termin? Dieser Preis war fest vereinbart.* The price was set. ⊜fix **4.** *when used as an adj, only before ns (address, job)* permanent(ly) ◊ *Sie hatte ihren festen Wohnsitz in London.* ◊ *Sie war fest angestellt.*; *(relationship, gaze)* steady (-ily) ◊ *Hast du einen festen Freund?* ◆ *ein fester Blick* Die beiden sind fest zusammen. The two of them are going out on a steady basis. jdm fest in die Augen sehen look sb straight in the eye **5.** *(sleep)* sound(ly) ◊ *Er schlief tief und fest.* (adj) **1.** hard ◊ *ein Buch mit festem Einband*; *(food)*

solid ◊ *Er kann noch keine feste Nahrung zu sich nehmen.* **2.** robust, tough, strong ◊ *Das Seil muss fester sein.*; *(shoes)* sturdy **3.** *(opening hours, employment)* regular ◊ *Das Büro hat feste Öffnungszeiten.*
⊙ etw. **fest einplanen** plan sth definitely ◊ *Diesen Urlaub habe ich fest eingeplant.* **fest entschlossen sein** be absolutely determined **sich fest vornehmen, etw. zu tun** definitely want to do sth, pledge to do sth

② **Fest** [fɛst] das <-es, -e> **1.** party, celebration ◊ *Morgen Abend feiern wir ein Fest.* ✦ *Sie hatten das ganze Dorf zum Fest eingeladen.* **2.** REL festival ◊ *Ostern ist das Fest der Auferstehung.*

fest|... [fɛst] (prefix) *translation varies* **1.** *(restricted movement)* ◊ *Ich binde die Hundeleine an der Laterne fest.* I tie the dog lead to the lamppost. *Halte das Kind fest!* Hold on to the child. **2.** *(expresses that sth is binding)* die *Regeln festlegen* determine the rules *Steht das Datum schon fest?* Has a date been fixed?

② **fest|hal·ten** ['fɛsthaltn̩] <hält fest, hielt fest, hat festgehalten> (tr v) **1.** jdn/etw. **festhalten** hold (onto) sb/sth ◊ *Er hielt sie an der Schulter/am Arm fest.* ✦ *Sie hielt die Katze mit beiden Händen fest.* **2.** jdn **festhalten** hold sb, detain sb ◊ *Es werden immer noch 70 Geiseln festgehalten.* **3.** record ◊ *eine Vereinbarung schriftlich festhalten* ✦ *Alle Arbeitsschritte wurden auf Videofilm festgehalten.* **4.** make a (mental) note, record the fact ◊ *Zunächst einmal muss festgehalten werden, dass ...* (intr v) an etw. (dat) **festhalten** stick to sth ◊ *Die Partei hielt an ihren Plänen fest.* ✦ *Sie hielt unbeirrt an ihren Prinzipien fest.* (ref v) sich an etw./jdm **festhalten** hold onto sth/sb, cling to sth/sb ◊ *Er hielt sich am Tisch fest.*

fes·ti·gen ['fɛstɪɡn̩] (tr v) +*haben* (fig) strengthen, consolidate ◊ *Sie konnte ihre berufliche Position festigen.* ✦ *Würde das Baby ihre Beziehung festigen können?*

Fest·land ['fɛstlant] das <-(e)s, Festländer> mainland, continent ◊ *Die Insel liegt etwa 150 Kilometer vom Festland entfernt.* ⊖Insel

fest|le·gen ['fɛstleːɡn̩] <legt fest, legte fest, hat festgelegt> (tr v) fix, establish ◊ *Die Preise werden jedes Jahr neu festgelegt.* ✦ *Die Bedingungen sind vertraglich festgelegt.* ⊖festsetzen (ref v) sich (auf etw. (acc)) **festlegen** commit yourself (to sth) ◊ *Ich möchte mich auf keinen bestimmten Tag festlegen.*

fest·lich ['fɛstlɪç] (adj, adv) **1.** festive(ly) ◊ *festliche Kleidung* ✦ *Die Straßen waren festlich beleuchtet.* **2.** magnificent(ly) ◊ *ein festlich gedeckter Tisch*

fest|neh·men ['fɛstneːmən] <nimmt fest, nahm fest, hat festgenommen> (tr v) arrest, apprehend ◊ *Der Täter ließ sich widerstandslos festnehmen.* ✦ *jdn vorübergehend festnehmen* ⊖verhaften

Fest·netz ['fɛstnɛts] das <-es, -e> most sing fixed network, landline system ◊ *Das Telefonieren im Festnetz ist billiger geworden.*

Fest·plat·te ['fɛstplatə] die <-, -n> IT hard disk ◊ *Wie viel Platz ist auf der Festplatte bereits belegt?*

fest|set·zen ['fɛstzɛtsn̩] <setzt fest, setzte fest, hat festgesetzt> (tr v) fix, set ◊ *Der Eintrittspreis ist auf 12 Euro festgesetzt worden.* ⊖festlegen (ref v) *(dirt)* sich (irgendwo) **festsetzen** collect (somewhere) ◊ *In den Ritzen hat sich Schmutz festgesetzt.*

fest|ste·hen ['fɛstʃteːən] <steht fest, stand fest, hat festgestanden> (intr v) *in South G, Austr., Swiss often +sein* etw. **steht fest** sth is definite, sth is decided ◊ *Ein genauer Termin steht noch nicht fest. Morgen wird feststehen, wer sein Nachfolger wird.* Tomorrow it will be clear who his successor will be.

② **fest|stel·len** ['fɛstʃtɛlən] <stellt fest, stellte fest, hat festgestellt> (tr v) **1.** determine, establish ◊ *Am Gerät sind erhebliche Mängel festgestellt worden.* ✦ *Der Arzt konnte nur noch seinen Tod feststellen.* **2.** detect, note ◊ *Ich kann nichts Ungewöhnliches feststellen.* **3.** emphasise, emphasize, stress ◊ *Zusammenfassend kann festgestellt werden, dass ...*

Fe·te ['feːtə] die <-, -n> *(fam)* party ◊ *Ab 20 Uhr steigt bei ihm eine große Fete.*

② **fett** [fɛt] (adj) <fetter, am fettesten> **1.** fatty ◊ *Das Fleisch war sehr fett.* ✦ *Du solltest fette Speisen meiden. fette Soßen* sauces that contain a lot of fat ⊖mager **2.** *(skin)* oily; *(hair)* greasy ⊖fettig **3.** *(pej)* fat ◊ *ein fetter Kater* ✦ *Du bist ganz schön fett geworden.* etw. **macht fett** sth makes you fat *sich zu fett fühlen* feel overweight ⊖dick **4.** *(printed characters)* bold ◊ *In fetten Lettern stand das „ja" zu lesen.* **5.** *(fam, fig) (profit, pension etc.)* fat ◊ *Sie machen fette Gewinne.* *eine fette Beute* a rich haul *ein fettes Trinkgeld* a big tip *eine fette Prämie* a big bonus *eine fette Provision* a large commission (adv) *(of printed characters)* in bold ◊ *Der Titel war fett gedruckt.*

Fett [fɛt] das <-(e)s, -e> fat ◊ *Er briet das Fleisch in heißem Fett an.* ✦ *Jede Portion enthält fünf Gramm Fett.*
⊙ sein **Fett abkriegen/abbekommen** *(fam)* get what's coming to you ◊ *In diesem Zeitungsartikel hat jeder sein Fett abbekommen.*

fet·tig ['fɛtɪç] (adj) **1.** greasy ◊ *fettige Pommes* ✦ *Der Herd war ganz fettig.* ✦ *ein Shampoo für fettiges Haar* **2.** *(skin)* oily ◊ *eine Creme für fettige und unreine Haut*

Fet·zen ['fɛtsn̩] der <-s, -> **1.** *(also fig)* shred ◊ *Er zerriss den Zeitungsartikel in Fetzen.* ✦ *ein Fetzen Stoff; (paper)* scrap ◊ *Diese Aktien sind nur noch wertlose Fetzen Papier.* **2.** *(fig)* ein paar Fetzen des Gesprächs a few snatches of conversation *ein paar Fetzen Musik* a few strains of music **3.** *(fam, esp pej)* rag ◊ *Was für einen Fetzen trägt sie denn da?*
⊙ sich streiten, *dass die Fetzen fliegen* fight like mad

② **feucht** [fɔøçt] (adj) <feuchter, am feuchtesten> **1.** damp ◊ *Das Gras war immer noch feucht.* ✦ *Sie wischte den Tisch mit einem feuchten Tuch ab.* ⊖trocken **2.** *(air, weather)* humid ◊ *Die Luft war sehr feucht.* ✦ *feuchtes Wetter* ⊖trocken (adv) **1.** den Boden feucht wischen wipe the floor with a damp cloth *Ihre Augen schimmerten feucht.* Her eyes filled with tears. *Die Straße schimmerte feucht.* The road glistened. **2.** in a humid environment ◊ *Zigarren sollten nicht feucht gelagert werden.* ⊖trocken

② **Feu·er** ['fɔøɐ] das <-s, -> **1.** *no pl* fire ◊ *Er machte (ein) Feuer im Kamin.* ✦ *Das Feuer erlosch.*

♦ *In der Wohnung ist gestern Abend ein Feuer aus-gebrochen.* ♦ *Die Feuerwehr konnte das Feuer schnell löschen.* das olympische Feuer the Olympic Flame **2.** *(for cigarettes etc.)* a light ◊ *Haben Sie Feuer (für mich)?* **3.** *no pl (fig)* ardour, ardor ◊ *das Feuer der Leidenschaft* jugendliches Feuer youthful vigour/vigor Ⓔ **Feuer und Flamme sein** be full of enthusiasm **das Feuer eröffnen/einstellen** MIL open/cease fire jdn/etw. **unter Feuer nehmen** fire at sb/sth

Feu·er·lö·scher ['fɔɐløʃɐ] der <-s, -> fire extinguisher

Feu·er·mel·der ['fɔɐmɛldɐ] der <-s, -> fire alarm ◊ *Der automatische Feuermelder löste Alarm aus.*

feu·ern ['fɔɐn] [intr v] +*haben* **1.** fire ◊ *zur Warnung in die Luft feuern* auf jdn/etw. feuern fire at sb/sth ◊ *mit Raketen auf feindliche Stellungen feuern* **2.** mit etw. feuern use sth for heating ◊ *mit Holz/Gas/Kohle feuern* [tr v] +*haben (fam)* **1.** *(a person)* fire, sack ◊ *Nach der vierten Niederlage wurde der Trainer von Verein gefeuert.* **2.** *(an object)* sling, hurl; *(football)* fire, hit ◊ *den Ball ins Tor feuern*

② **Feu·er·wehr** ['fɔɐveːɐ] die <-, -en> fire brigade, fire department ◊ *Er ist bei der freiwilligen Feuerwehr.*

Feu·er·werk ['fɔɐvɛrk] das <-(e)s, -e> **1.** fireworks ◊ *das neue Jahr mit einem Feuerwerk begrüßen* ♦ *ein Feuerwerk abbrennen/zünden* **2.** *(fig)* ein Feuerwerk an etw. [dat] a cavalcade of sth

Feu·er·zeug ['fɔɐtsɔɪk] das <-(e)s, -e> (cigarette) lighter ◊ *Er zückte sein Feuerzeug und gab mir Feuer.*

FH [ɛfˈhaː] die *(abbr of* Fachhochschule*)* Ⓔpolytechnic ◊ *die FH für Gartenbau und Agrarwirtschaft* box@ Fachhochschule

Fi·a·ker [fiˈakɐ] der <-s, -> *(Austr)* horse-drawn carriage

Fich·te ['fɪçtə] die <-, -n> spruce ◊ *eine Fichte als Weihnachtsbaum nehmen* ♦ *Der Schrank ist (aus) Fichte.*

fi·cken ['fɪkŋ] [tr+intr v] +*haben (taboo)* fuck mit jdm ficken fuck sb

② **Fie·ber** ['fiːbɐ] das <-s> *no pl* **1.** MED fever, temperature ◊ *hohes/leichtes Fieber bekommen/haben* 38,5° Fieber haben have a temperature of 38.5° **2.** *(fig)* excitement, enthusiasm ◊ *Die ganze Stadt war im Fieber der Festspiele.*

② **fiel** [fiːl] *pret of* fallen

fies [fiːs] [adj] <fieser, am fiesesten> *(fam, pej)* **1.** *(person, trick)* mean ◊ *Das war ein ganz fieser Trick!* **2.** *(feeling, sound)* horrible, vile ◊ *Der Zahnarztbohrer macht ein absolut fieses Geräusch.*

② **Fi·gur** [fiˈɡuːɐ] die <-, -en> **1.** figure ◊ *eine gute/sportliche Figur haben* ♦ *auf seine Figur achten* ♦ *eine Weihnachtskrippe mit Figuren aus Holz* **2.** *(in a book, film)* figure, character ◊ *Er wurde als zentrale Figur des Skandals entlarvt.* **3.** MATH shape, figure ◊ *eine geometrische Figur* **4.** SPORT *(in ice skating, dance)* figure, move **5.** *(fam, pej)* character, individual ◊ *Er umgibt sich mit dubiosen Figuren.* ⒼGestalt Ⓔ **eine gute/glückliche etc. Figur abgeben/machen** make a good/favourable etc. impression ◊

In diesem Anzug gibst du eine lächerliche Figur ab.

Fi·li·a·le [fiˈljaːlə] die <-, -n> branch ◊ *eine Filiale eröffnen/schließen*

② **Film** [fɪlm] der <-(e)s, -e> **1.** film, movie ◊ *Der Film wurde in Neuseeland gedreht.* **2.** (roll of) film ◊ *einen neuen Film einlegen* **3.** films, movies, film business, movie business ◊ *Er ist Kameramann beim Film.* **4.** *(thin coating)* film ◊ *Das Öl bildet einen Film auf dem Wasser.*

fil·men ['fɪlmən] [tr+intr v] +*haben* film ◊ *Sie wollten Löwen in freier Wildbahn filmen.* ♦ *Im Gerichtssaal darf nicht gefilmt werden.*

Filz·stift ['fɪltsʃtɪft] der <-(e)s, -e> felt-tip (pen)

Fi·nanz·amt [fiˈnantsˌamt] das <-(e)s, Finanzämter> tax office ◊ *seine Steuererklärung beim Finanzamt abgeben*

② **fi·nan·zi·ell** [finanˈtsjɛl] [adj, adv] *no comp/superl*; *when used as an adj, only before ns* financial(ly) ◊ *Er sagte ihr finanzielle Unterstützung zu.* ♦ *Kann er sich das denn finanziell leisten?* finanzielle Mittel finances, financial resources jdn finanziell unterstützen give sb financial support

fi·nan·zie·ren [finanˈtsiːrən] <finanziert, finanzierte, hat finanziert> [tr v] finance, fund ◊ *Die Stiftung wird aus privaten Mitteln finanziert.* jdm etw. finanzieren finance sb's sth, fund sb's sth ◊ *Den Urlaub finanzieren mir meine Eltern.* [ref v] etw. finanziert sich sth pays for itself, sth finances itself ◊ *Die Zeitschrift finanziert sich durch Werbung selbst.*

② **fin·den** ['fɪndn] <findet, fand, hat gefunden> [tr v] **1.** find ◊ *Ich habe auf der Straße zwei Euro gefunden.* ♦ *Hat die Polizei schon eine Spur gefunden?* ♦ *eine Lösung finden* ♦ *Er fand die richtigen Worte, um sie zu trösten.* Ⓢsuchen **2.** bei jdm Anklang/Beifall finden meet with sb's approval (bei jdm) Beachtung/Anerkennung finden be well received (by sb) ◊ reißenden Absatz/zahlreiche Käufer finden sell very well in etw. [dat] Platz finden fit into sth ◊ *Hat die Schachtel noch in Kofferraum Platz gefunden?* **3.** etw. an etw./jdm finden see sth in sth/sb ◊ *Was findest du eigentlich an ihm?* Gefallen/Geschmack an etw. [dat] finden begin to enjoy sth [tr+intr v] think ◊ *Ich finde, er ist nett.* ♦ *Ich finde, dass er nett ist.* ♦ *Hast du den Film auch so langweilig gefunden?* „Ist das kalt hier!" — „Findest du? Ich nicht." [intr v] find your way ◊ *nicht mehr nach Hause finden* [ref v] etw. findet sich sth turns up ◊ *Es wird sich schon noch eine Lösung finden.* Ⓔ **das/es wird sich finden** it'll (all) be all right, it'll (all) sort itself out

fing [fɪŋ] *pret of* fangen

② **Fin·ger** ['fɪŋɐ] der <-s, -> finger ◊ *einen Ring am Finger tragen* ♦ *Kinderhandschuhe mit bunten Fingern* Finger weg! Hands off! Ⓔ **das kann man an den Fingern einer Hand abzählen**, das lässt sich an fünf Fingern abzählen *(fam, fig)* it's so obvious, it sticks out a mile die/seine Finger im Spiel haben *(fam, fig)* be involved den/seinen Finger auf die (offene) Wunde legen *(fig)* hit a sore point lange/krumme Finger machen *(fam, fig)* be lightfingered (bei) die Finger schmutzig machen [dat] **1.** dirty your hands **2.** *(through physical work)*

get your hands dirty *mit spitzen Fingern with your fingertips* ◊ *sich alle zehn/die Finger nach etw.* abschlecken/lecken *(fam)* be desperate for sth ◊ *Nach so einer Wohnung lecken die Leute sich hier die Finger.* jdn/etw. in die Finger bekommen/kriegen *(fam)* get your hands on sb/sth *es juckt/kribbelt jdm in den Fingern, etw. zu tun* sb feels very tempted to do sth, feel the urge to do sth *jdm auf die Finger klopfen (fam, fig)* give sb a rap over the knuckles *keinen Finger rühren/krumm machen (fam)* not lift a finger *die Finger von etw./jdm lassen (fam)* not touch sth/sb, not mess with sth/sb ◊ *Lass ja deine Finger von meinen Sachen!* sich [dat] etw. *aus den Fingern saugen* make sth up, invent sth *jdm auf die Finger schauen/sehen (fam)* keep a close eye on sb

Fin·ger·ab·druck ['fɪŋɐ|apdrʊk] *der* <-(e)s, Fingerabdrücke> fingerprint ◊ *am Tatort Fingerabdrücke hinterlassen* genetischer Fingerabdruck genetic fingerprint, genetic fingerprinting *jdm die/jds Fingerabdrücke abnehmen* take sb's fingerprints

Fin·ger·na·gel ['fɪŋena:gl] *der* <-s, Fingernägel> fingernail ◊ *kurz geschnittene/lange Fingernägel haben*

Fin·ne ['fɪnə] *der* <-n, -n>, **Fin·nin** ['fɪnɪn] *die* <-, -nen> Finn → **Deutsche**

fin·nisch ['fɪnɪʃ] [adj] *mostly before ns* Finnish → **deutsch**

Fin·nisch ['fɪnɪʃ] *das* <-(s)> *no pl* Finnish → **Deutsch**

Finn·land ['fɪnlant] *das* <-s> *article only in combination with attribute, no pl* Finland → **Deutschland**

fins·ter ['fɪnste] [adj] **1.** *(unpleasant)* dark, grim ◊ *Das ist eines der finstersten Kapitel der Geschichte.* ✦ *finstere Aussichten* ⊜düster **2.** *(wicked)* dark, shady ◊ *Da sind finstere Mächte am Werk.* ✦ *finstere Gestalten* ⊜böse **3.** *(miserable)* gloomy ◊ *eine finstere Miene machen* ✦ *Sie warf ihm finstere Blicke zu.* ⊜mürrisch **4.** *(with no light)* pitch black, dark ◊ *Sie verirrten sich im finsteren Wald.* ✦ *Bei Neumond ist es nachts besonders finster.* ⊜dunkel, düster ⊜hell [adv] gloomily, moodily ◊ *Er blickte finster drein. jdn finster anschauen* glare at sb ⊜fröhlich

⊛ **es wird finster** it's getting dark

Fins·ter·nis ['fɪnstenɪs] *die* <-, -se> **1.** ASTRON eclipse ◊ *eine totale/partielle Finsternis des Mondes* **2.** *no pl* darkness ◊ *Das Haus lag in völliger Finsternis.* ✦ *die Mächte/das Reich der Finsternis*

② **Fir·ma** ['fɪrma:] *die* <-, Firmen> company, firm ◊ *eine eigene Firma gründen* ✦ *eine mittelständische Firma mit 70 Angestellten* ⊜Unternehmen

Fir·mung ['fɪrmʊŋ] *die* <-, -en> Confirmation

② **Fisch** [fɪʃ] *der* <-(e)s, -e> **1.** *(animal, food)* fish ◊ *Fische fangen/angeln* ✦ *Am Freitag gibt es bei uns Fisch.* **2.** ASTROL, ASTRON Pisces

⊛ **ein großer/dicker Fisch** *(fam, esp hum)* a big fish ◊ *Mit dem Auftrag hat sie einen dicken Fisch an Land gezogen.* **kleine Fische** *(fam) (person)* small fry *(thing)* a doddle, no big deal **stumm wie ein Fisch** completely silent

② **Fi·so·le** [fi'zo:lə] *die* <-, -n> *most pl (Austr)* green bean, runner bean ⊜grüne Bohne

② **fit** [fɪt] [adj] <fitter, am fittesten> **1.** *(person)* fit ◊ *Er ist körperlich und geistig sehr fit.* ✦ *Sport macht/hält fit.* **sich für etw. fit machen** prepare yourself for sth **2.** *(object)* fit für etw. ready for sth ◊ *Machen Sie ihr Auto fit für den Winter.*

fix [fɪks] [adj] <fixer, am fixesten> **1.** *(salary, part)* fixed ◊ *ein fixer Bestandteil/Anteil* ⊜fest **2.** definite ◊ *eine fixe Zusage* ✦ *Seine Nominierung für den Wettkampf ist jetzt praktisch fix.* ⊜endgültig [adv] **1.** *(fam)* quickly ◊ *Keine Angst, das geht ganz fix.* ⊜rasch, schnell **2. etw. fix einplanen** plan sth in, make definite plans for sth **fix zusagen** give a definite yes ⊜fest

⊛ **fix und fertig** *(fam)* **1.** (all) ready ◊ *Alles war fix und fertig für den Umzug.* ✦ *So, jetzt ist alles fix und fertig, die Gäste können kommen.* **2.** exhausted, shattered, done in ◊ *Nach dem Joggen war sie fix und fertig.* **etw./jd macht jdn fix und fertig** *(fam)* sth/sb finishes sb off **fix und foxi** *(fam, hum)* done in, shattered

fi·xie·ren [fɪ'ksi:rən] <fixiert, fixierte, hat fixiert> [tr v] **1. etw. (schriftlich) fixieren** record sth (in writing) ◊ *Rechte und Pflichten in einem Vertrag fixieren* **2.** fix, set ◊ *ein gebrochenes Bein mit Gipsverband fixieren* **3.** jdn/etw. *(mit den Augen)* fixieren fix your eyes/gaze on sb/sth ◊ *Die Katze fixierte die erstarrte Maus (mit den Augen).* [ref v] **sich auf etw./jdn fixieren** become fixated on sth/sb, become obsessed by sth/sb *auf etw./jdn fixiert sein* be fixated on sth/sb, be obsessed by sth/sb ◊ *Ihre Eltern sind viel zu sehr auf gute Noten fixiert.*

② **flach** [flax] [adj, adv] **1.** flat ◊ *Das Land dort ist sehr flach.* ✦ *ein Unternehmen mit flachen Hierarchien* **sich flach auf den Boden legen** lie down flat on the floor **mit der flachen Hand** with the flat of your hand **2.** shallow(ly) ◊ *Bleibt bitte im flachen Wasser.* ✦ *Der Teller ist zu flach für Suppe.* ✦ *Die Kurve verläuft flach.* ✦ *flach atmen* **ein flach abfallendes Ufer** a gently sloping river bank [adj] **1.** low ◊ *flache Schuhe tragen* ✦ *Der Ball war zu flach.* ⊜niedrig ⊜hoch **2.** insipid, trivial ◊ *flache Unterhaltung* ✦ *Der Roman wirkt ziemlich geistlos und flach.* ⊜seicht, oberflächlich

② **Flä·che** ['flɛçə] *die* <-, -n> **1.** MATH area ◊ *ein Grundstück mit einer Fläche von zwei Hektar* **2.** area, space ◊ *weite Flächen Kanadas sind mit Wald bedeckt.* **3.** surface ◊ *Ein Würfel hat sechs quadratische Flächen.* ⊜Seite

flach|fal·len ['flaxfalən] <fällt flach, fiel flach, ist flachgefallen> [intr v] *(fam) (event)* be cancelled ◊ *Wegen dem schlechten Wetter fiel der Ausflug flach.; (benefit, payment)* cease to exist, come to an end ◊ *Diese Vergünstigung fällt in Zukunft flach.*

flach|le·gen ['flaxle:gŋ] *(fam)* <legt flach, legte flach, hat flachgelegt> [tr v] **1.** bring down ◊ *Er legte seinen Gegner schon in der ersten Runde flach.* ◊ *Der Sturm legte zahlreiche Bäume flach.* **2.** *(esp pej) (have sex with)* jdn flachlegen get sb into bed ◊ *Er hat sie gleich bei der ersten Verabredung flachgelegt.* [ref v] **sich flachlegen** lie down

flach|lie·gen ['flaxli:gn] <liegt flach, lag flach, hat/ist flachgelegen> [intr v] *in South G, Austr, Swiss often +sein* be laid up ◊ *Sie lag zwei*

Wochen mit einer Grippe flach.

fla·ckern ['flakɐn] [intr v] +*haben* flicker ◊ *Die Kerze flackerte und ging dann aus.* ♦ *Die Neonröhren flackern.* ♦ *Bunte Bilder flackern über den Bildschirm.* ♦ *Ihre Augen flackerten unruhig.*

Fla·den ['fla:dn̩] der <–s, –> **1.** pat ◊ *Die Kuh ließ einen Fladen fallen.* ♦ *Der Maisbrei wird zu einem Fladen geformt.* **2.** flatbread ◊ *Die Fladen werden aufgeschnitten und mit Fleisch gefüllt.* **3.** *flat cake that is cooked in a frying pan and eaten warm* ◊ *ein süßer Fladen*

Fla·den·brot ['fla:dn̩bro:t] das <–(e)s, –e> flatbread ◊ *In Griechenland aßen wir oft Fladenbrot mit Oliven und Schafskäse.*

Flag·ge ['flagə] die <–, –n> flag ◊ *eine Flagge hissen/einholen* ♦ *Das Schiff fährt unter deutscher Flagge.* ⊜Fahne

⊚ **Flagge zeigen** nail your colours/colors to the mast

Flam·me ['flamə] die <–, –n> flame ◊ *Die Flammen griffen auf das Nachbarhaus über.*

⊚ **auf kleiner Flamme** over a low heat ◊ *auf kleiner Flamme ziehen lassen* **in Flammen aufgehen** go up in flames **in Flammen stehen** be in flames

fla·nie·ren [fla'ni:rən] <flanierte, flanierte, hat/ist flaniert> [intr v] stroll, wander ◊ *durch die Stadt flanieren* ⊜spazieren

② **Fla·sche** ['flaʃə] die <–, –n> **1.** bottle ◊ *Sie trank das Bier direkt aus der Flasche.* ♦ *eine Flasche Wein* ♦ *Er gibt gerade dem Baby die/seine Flasche.* **2.** *(fam, pej)* loser ◊ *Schon wieder nicht getroffen — so eine Flasche!* ⊝Pfeife

Fla·schen·öff·ner ['flaʃn̩|œfnɐ] der <–s, –> bottle opener

Fla·schen·pfand ['flaʃn̩pfant] das <–(e)s> *no pl* deposit on a/the bottle

flat·tern ['flatɐn] [intr v] +*haben/sein* **1.** +*haben (flag, sail, washing)* flap ◊ *Die Fahne flatterte im Wind.; (hair)* stream **2.** +*sein (through the air)* fly, flutter ◊ *Als er die Tür öffnete, flatterten die Papiere zu Boden.* **3.** +*sein (fam) (letter)* jdm ins Haus flattern come through the letterbox ◊ *Letzte Woche flatterte uns plötzlich die Kündigung ins Haus.* jdm auf den Tisch flattern land on sb's desk **4.** +*sein (birds)* flutter ◊ *Der Schmetterling flatterte von Blüte zu Blüte.* **5.** +*haben (wings)* flap ◊ *mit den Flügeln flattern* **6.** +*haben (fig) (hands)* shake ◊ *Ihre Hände flatterten vor Angst, als sie den Brief öffnete.*

flau [flaʊ] [adj] **1.** ECON slack ◊ *eine flaue Konjunktur* **2.** flau (im Magen) queasy ◊ *Nach der Achterbahn war ihm ziemlich flau im Magen.* ♦ *Mir wird ganz flau (zumute), wenn ich an die Prüfung denke.*

flau·schig ['flaʊʃɪç] [adj] fluffy, fleecy, soft ◊ *ein flauschiger Bademantel* ♦ *Mit Weichspüler werden die Handtücher schön flauschig.*

Flau·te ['flaʊtə] die <–, –n> **1.** ECON lull ◊ *eine wirtschaftliche Flaute* ♦ *Auf dem Immobilienmarkt herrscht seit langem Flaute.* **2.** *(period of)* calm ◊ *Wir dümpelten stundenlang in einer Flaute.*

flech·ten ['flɛçtn̩] <flicht, flocht, hat geflochten> [tr v] weave ◊ *Kränze/Körbe flechten; (hair)* plait ◊ *Sie flochten sich die Haare zu Zöpfen.*

② **Fleck** [flɛk] der <–(e)s, –en or –e> **1.** spot ◊ *eine*

schwarze Katze mit einem weißen Fleck auf der Nase **2.** *(of dirt)* stain, spot ◊ *Die Flecken sind beim Waschen nicht rausgegangen.* **3.** *(location)* spot, place ◊ *Sie kennt die schönsten Flecken der Erde.* ◊ *Rühr dich nicht vom Fleck!* ⊝Stelle

⊚ **ein Fleck auf der (weißen) Weste** *(fig)* a blot in your copybook ◊ *Die Affäre ist der erste Fleck auf seiner weißen Weste.* **blauer Fleck** bruise ◊ *Nach dem Sturz war er mit/von blauen Flecken übersät.* **blinder Fleck** *(fig)* blind spot **ein weißer Fleck (auf der Landkarte)** uncharted territory **nicht/kaum vom Fleck kommen** not/hardly get anywhere, not/hardly make any headway **vom Fleck weg** on the spot, immediately

fle·ckig ['flɛkɪç] [adj] stained ◊ *Zieh ein frisches Hemd an, dieses ist schon ganz fleckig.; (face)* blotchy

Fle·gel ['fle:gl̩] der <–s, –> *(pej)* lout ◊ *ein unhöflicher/arroganter/unverschämter Flegel*

fle·hen ['fle:ən] [intr v] +*haben* implore, beg, plead ◊ *"Nein, bitte nicht!", flehte sie.* um etw. flehen beg for sth, plead for sth ◊ *um Gnade/sein Leben flehen*

② **Fleisch** [flaɪʃ] das <–(e)s> *no pl* **1.** *(for eating)* meat ◊ *rohes/gekochtes/gebratenes Fleisch* ♦ *Vegetarier essen kein Fleisch.* **2.** *(of a living being)* flesh ◊ *Das Halsband schneidet dem Hund ins Fleisch.*

⊚ **(jdm) in Fleisch und Blut übergehen** become second nature (to sb) **sich** [dat] **ins eigene Fleisch schneiden** *(fig)* cut off your nose to spite your face **Fleisch fressend** carnivorous ◊ *eine Fleisch fressende Pflanze* **vom Fleisch fallen** *(fam, also hum)* waste away

Flei·scher ['flaɪʃɐ] der <–s, –>, **Flei·sche·rin** ['flaɪʃərɪn] die <–, –nen> butcher ◊ *Er ist Fleischer von Beruf.* ♦ *Die Fleischerin schnitt zwei Steaks ab.*

Flei·sche·rei [flaɪʃə'raɪ] die <–, –en> butcher's (shop) ⊝Metzgerei, Fleischhauerei

Flei·sche·rin ['flaɪʃərɪn] *fem of* Fleischer

② **Fleisch·hau·e·rei** [flaɪʃhaʊə'raɪ] die <–, –en> *(Austr)* butcher's (shop) ⊝Metzgerei, Fleischerei

Fleisch·kä·se ['flaɪʃkɛ:zə] der <–s> *no pl* loaf baked from a mass of finely ground beef, bacon and onions ◊ *warmer Fleischkäse*

Fleisch·sa·lat ['flaɪʃza,la:t] der <–(e)s, –e> cold sausage meat salad with mayonnaise

Fleisch·wurst ['flaɪʃvo:rst] die <–, Fleischwürste> *most reg* ring bologna, Lyoner pork sausage *box*@ Wurst

Fleiß [flaɪs] der <–es> *no pl* diligence, conscientiousness, hard work ◊ *Durch unermüdlichen Fleiß hat sie sich enormes Wissen angeeignet.*

⊚ **ohne Fleiß kein Preis** *if you want to succeed, you have to work for it*

flei·ßig ['flaɪsɪç] [adj] industrious, diligent, hardworking ◊ *Er bedankte sich bei den fleißigen Helfern.* ♦ *fleißiges Üben/Trainieren* ⊝faul [adv] fleißig arbeiten/trainieren/üben etc. work/train/practise etc. hard

fli·cken ['flɪkn̩] [tr v] +*haben* mend, patch up ◊ *einen Reifen/ein Fahrrad/eine Hose flicken* ♦ *Die Löcher im Staatshaushalt sind nicht mehr zu flicken.; (a fabric)* darn

Flie·der ['fli:dɐ] der <–s, –> lilac (tree) ◊ *Der Flieder blüht im Mai.* ♦ *Die Handtücher gibt es in*

A B C D E F G H I J K L M N O P Q R S T U V W X Y Z

A
B
C
D
E
F
G
H
I
J
K
L
M
N
O
P
Q
R
S
T
U
V
W
X
Y
Z

Weiß und Flieder.
Flie·ge ['fliːɡə] die <-, -n> **1.** ZOO *fly* ◊ *Ein paar Fliegen schwirrten in der Küche herum.* **2.** *bow tie* ◊ *Er erschien im Frack mit schwarzer Fliege.*

Ⓔ **zwei Fliegen mit einer Klappe schlagen** *kill two birds with one stone* **die/eine Fliege machen** *(fam)* hop it **sterben/umfallen wie die Fliegen** *(fam)* drop like flies

② **flie·gen** ['fliːɡn̩] <fliegt, flog, hat/ist geflogen> [intr v] +*sein* **1.** *fly* ◊ *Der Vogel flog auf einen Baum.* ♦ *Die nächste Maschine nach Wien fliegt um elf Uhr.* ♦ *Der Ball flog ins Aus.* ♦ *Das Kind flog in die Arme seiner Mutter.* **2.** *(pollen)* be in the air ◊ *Wenn die Pollen der Birke fliegen, bekomme ich immer Heuschnupfen.* **3.** *(fam)* be thrown ◊ *Der Wagen flog aus der Kurve.* ♦ *Werbung fliegt bei uns gleich in den Müll.* **4.** *(fam)* fall ◊ *Pass auf, dass du nicht auf die Nase fliegst!* Ⓢfallen **5.** *(fam, fig)* be thrown out ◊ *Er ist aus der Firma/von der Schule geflogen.* ♦ *Noch ein Wort und du fliegst!* **6.** *(fam, fig) (exams)* durch etw. fliegen *fail sth* ◊ *Sie ist durch die Prüfung geflogen.* Ⓢdurchfallen **7.** *(fam)* auf jdn/etw. fliegen *go for sb/sth* ◊ *Sie fliegt auf blonde Jungs.* [tr v] +*haben/sein* **1.** +*haben fly* ◊ Hilfsgüter ins Krisengebiet fliegen **2.** +*haben (an aircraft)* pilot, fly ◊ *Er fliegt diese Maschine zum ersten Mal.* **3.** +*haben/sein* einen Angriff auf etw./jdn fliegen *launch an (air) attack on sth/sb* einen Umweg fliegen *make a detour* Warteschleifen fliegen *circle round* einen neuen Rekord fliegen *set a new (flying) record*

Flie·ger¹ ['fliːɡɐ] der <-s, -> *(fam)* plane ◊ *Sie sitzt schon im Flieger nach New York.* ⊖Flugzeug
Flie·ger² ['fliːɡɐ] der <-s, ->, **Flie·ge·rin** ['fliːɡərɪn] die <-, -nen> pilot ◊ *Er wurde Flieger bei der Luftwaffe.* ♦ *eine leidenschaftliche Fliegerin*
flie·hen ['fliːən] <flieht, floh, ist geflohen> [intr v] (vor jdm/etw.) fliehen *flee (from sb/sth)*, *escape (from sb/sth)* ◊ *Der Mörder ist vor der Polizei ins Ausland geflohen.* ♦ *Die Tiere flohen vor dem Feuer.* ⊖flüchten
Flie·se ['fliːzə] die <-, -n> tile *Fliesen legen tile* ⊖Kachel
Fließ·band ['fliːsbant] das <-(e)s, Fließbänder> assembly line, production line; *(in a supermarket)* conveyer belt ◊ *die Waren an der Kasse aufs Fließband legen* am Fließband arbeiten *work on the assembly line, work on the production line*
Ⓔ etw. wie am Fließband produzieren *churn sth out* wie am Fließband *automatically*
② **flie·ßen** ['fliːsn̩] <fließt, floss, ist geflossen> [intr v] **1.** *flow* ◊ *In seinen Adern fließt blaues Blut.* ♦ *Der Rhein fließt ins Meer.; (tap water, sweat)* run **2.** *(traffic, electricity)* flow ◊ *Nach dem Stau fließt der Verkehr nun wieder.* ♦ *Es fließt kein Strom, deswegen geht die Lampe nicht.; (news)* get through **3.** *(money, bribe)* change hands ◊ *Sind in dem Fall Bestechungsgelder geflossen?* an jdn/etw. fließen *go to sb/sth* ◊ *Es ist viel Geld an diese Firma geflossen.*
flie·ßend ['fliːsn̩t] pres p of fließen [adj, adv] **1.** fluent(ly) ◊ *ein Vortrag in fließendem Englisch* ♦ *Sein Deutsch ist fließend.* fließend Spanisch sprechen *be fluent in Spanish* ⊖flüssig ⊖gebrochen **2.** *(transition, border)* fluid(ly) ◊ *fließende*

Übergänge ♦ *Ist die Grenze zwischen Gut und Böse fließend?*
Flirt [flɪrt, flœːɐt] der <-s, -s> **1.** *(also fig)* flirtation ◊ *Er ist zu schüchtern für einen Flirt.* ♦ *der Flirt mit dem Beitritt zur NATO* **2.** bit of fun, affair ◊ *Ihr Flirt mit Leo war bald vorbei.*
flir·ten ['flɪrtn̩, 'flœːɐtn̩] <flirtet, flirtete, hat geflirtet> [intr v] flirt ◊ *Sie hat den ganzen Abend mit ihm geflirtet.*
flocht [flɔxt] pret of flechten
Flo·cke ['flɔkə] die <-, -n> flake ◊ *Flocken aus Hafer/Roggen/Gerste* ♦ *einige Flocken Seife in Wasser auflösen*
② **flog** [floːk] pret of fliegen
floh [floː] pret of fliehen
Floh [floː] der <-(e)s, Flöhe> flea ◊ *von einem Floh gebissen werden* ♦ *Unser Hund hat Flöhe.*
Floh·markt ['floːmaʁkt] der <-(e)s, Flohmärkte> flea market ◊ *auf den Flohmarkt gehen*
② **floss** [flɔs] pret of fließen
Flö·te ['fløːtə] die <-, -n> flute, recorder ◊ *ein Lied auf der Flöte spielen*
flott [flɔt] [adj, adv] <flotter, am flottesten> fast ◊ *ein flotter Fahrer* ♦ *Unser Tempo war ziemlich flott.* ♦ *Er arbeitet flott.* ⊖schnell, zügig ⊖langsam
Ⓔ etw. wieder flott machen/kriegen *(fam)* get sth working again, get sth running again
Flot·te ['flɔtə] die <-, -n> fleet
flu·chen ['fluːxn̩] [intr v] +*haben* swear, curse ◊ *Er fluchte laut.* über etw./jdn fluchen *curse sth/sb* ◊ *über die Steuern/Politiker fluchen*
② **Flucht** [flʊxt] die <-, -en> no pl *(also fig)* flight ◊ *Sie mussten bei ihrer überstürzten Flucht alles zurücklassen.; escape* ◊ *die Flucht aus dem Gefängnis* ♦ *die Flucht vor der Verantwortung* ♦ *die Flucht in eine Traumwelt* auf der Flucht (vor jdm) sein *be on the run (from sb)* ◊ *Er ist auf der Flucht vor der Polizei.* auf der Flucht vor etw. sein *be running away from sth*
Ⓔ die Flucht nach vorn antreten *take the bull by the horns* die Flucht ergreifen *flee, take flight* jdn in die Flucht schlagen *frighten sb off*
flüch·ten ['flʏçtn̩] [intr v] +*sein* (vor jdm) flüchten *flee (from sb)*, *escape (from sb)* ◊ *Die Täter sind geflüchtet.* ♦ *Sie mussten vor den Feinden flüchten.* ⊖fliehen [ref v] +*haben* **1.** sich (vor etw.) (irgendwohin) flüchten *run (somewhere) (to escape from etw.)*, *take refuge (from sth) (somewhere)* ◊ *Sie flüchteten sich vor dem Regen unter einen Baum.* sich ins Haus flüchten **2.** sich in etw. [acc] flüchten *seek/take refuge in sth*, *resort to sth* ◊ *sich in den Alkohol/in Drogen/in die Arbeit flüchten*
Flücht·ling ['flʏçtlɪŋ] der <-s, -e> refugee ◊ *Flüchtlinge aufnehmen*
② **Flug** [fluːk] der <-(e)s, Flüge> flight ◊ *Schwalben fangen ihre Beute im Flug.* ♦ *der Flug zum Mond* ♦ *Wir haben einen Flug nach Athen gebucht.*
Ⓔ wie im Flug vergehen *fly by, be over in a flash*
Flug·blatt ['fluːkblat] das <-(e)s, Flugblätter> flyer ◊ *Flugblätter drucken/verteilen*
Flü·gel ['flyːɡl̩] der <-s, -> **1.** wing ◊ *Vögel haben zwei Flügel, Libellen vier.* ♦ *Möchtest du eine Flügel vom Hähnchen?* ♦ *mit den Flügeln schlagen* ♦ *der linke Flügel der Partei* ♦ *Das Gebäude hat mehrere Flügel.* **2.** grand piano, concert piano ◊

Sie sitzt am Flügel. **3.** ein Flügel der Lunge one lung ein Flügel des Fensters/der Fensterläden/der Schranktür one of the windows/shutters/cupboard doors **4.** TECHN *(of a fan, propeller)* blade ◉ **die Flügel hängen lassen** lose heart, give up

⑦ **Flug·ha·fen** ['fluːkhaːfn̩] der <–s, Flughäfen> airport ◊ *Wir müssen zwei Stunden vor Abflug am Flughafen sein.*

Flug·steig ['fluːkʃtaɛk] der <–(e)s, –e> gate ◊ *Bitte begeben Sie sich zum Flugsteig acht.*

⑦ **Flug·zeug** ['fluːktsɔøk] das <–(e)s, –e> (aero)plane, airplane ◊ *Das Flugzeug landet/ startet gerade.* ⊜Flieger, Maschine

Flur¹ [fluːɐ̯] der <–(e)s, –e> corridor ◊ *Die Garderobe ist im Flur.; (in a house)* hall ⊜Gang, Diele, Korridor

Flur² [fluːɐ̯] die <–, –en> pasture ◊ *Streifzüge in Feld, Wald und Flur* ◉ **allein auf weiter Flur** out on your own

Fluss [flʊs] der <–es, Flüsse> **1.** river ◊ *Der Fluss mündet ins Meer.* ◆ *im Fluss schwimmen* ◆ *Auf dem Fluss fährt ein Boot.* **2.** no pl *(fig)* flow ◊ *Der Fluss des Verkehrs wird durch Baustellen behindert.* ◆ *der Fluss der Rede* **wieder in Fluss kommen** get going again

flüs·sig ['flʏsɪç] adj liquid ◊ *ein flüssiges Waschmittel; (honey)* runny nicht flüssig sein be solid etw. flüssig machen melt sth flüssig werden melt ◊ *Das Wachs ist flüssig geworden.* adj, adv fluent(ly) ◊ *flüssiges Französisch* ◆ *(eine Sprache) flüssig schreiben/sprechen; (traffic, movements)* flowing(ly) ◊ *Ihre Bewegungen waren sehr flüssig.* ⊜fließend ◉ **etw. flüssig machen** *(fam)* turn sth into cash **jd ist nicht flüssig** *(fam)* sb hasn't got any (ready) cash

Flüs·sig·keit ['flʏsɪçkaɛt] die <–, –en> liquid, fluid ◊ *große Mengen an Flüssigkeit zu sich nehmen*

flüs·tern ['flʏstɐn] tr+intr v +haben whisper ◊ *Die Schüler flüsterten miteinander.* ◆ *Flüstere es mir ins Ohr.* ◉ **jdm (et)was flüstern** *(fam)* **1.** tip sb off ◊ *Offensichtlich hat er der Polizei etwas geflüstert.* **2.** give sb an earful ◊ *Deine Eltern werden dir was flüstern, wenn du so spät kommst.* **das kann ich dir flüstern** *(fam)* let me tell you

Flut [fluːt] die <–, –en> **1.** no pl tide ◊ *Die Flut kommt/setzt ein.* Ebbe und Flut the tides, ebb and flow ⊜Ebbe **2.** *(also fig)* flood ◊ *Die Flut hat die Felder unter Wasser gesetzt.* ◆ *eine wahre Flut von Briefen/Beschwerden* **3.** *only pl (lit)* torrents ◊ *Aus den Wolken brachen wahre Fluten hervor.* die Fluten the water(s), the waves ◊ *sich in die Fluten stürzen*

flu·ten ['fluːtn̩] <flutet, flutete, hat geflutet> tr v flood ◊ *Die Schleuse/Der Stausee wurde geflutet.*

focht [fɔxt] pret of fechten

Foh·len ['foːlən] das <–s, –> foal

Föhn [føːn] der <–(e)s, –e> **1.** hairdryer ◊ *sich mit dem Föhn die Haare trocknen* ⊜Haartrockner **2.** most sing (the) Föhn ◊ *Bei Föhn bekomme ich immer Kopfschmerzen.*

föh·nen ['føːnən] tr v +haben blow-dry etw. trocken fönen blow-dry sth jdm/sich die Haare föhnen (blow-)dry sb's/your hair ◊ *Kannst du mir die Haare föhnen?*

Fol·ge ['fɔlɡə] die <–, –n> **1.** consequence, result ◊ *Die Folgen sind nicht abzusehen.* ◆ *Der Unfall hatte katastrophale Folgen.* etw. zur Folge haben result in sth an den Folgen einer Lungenentzündung etc. sterben die as a result of a chest infection etc. ⊜Ursache **2.** TV episode ◊ *Gleich kommt eine neue Folge der Lindenstraße.* **3.** sequence ◊ *die Folge der Speisen und Getränke* in Folge in a row ◊ *die dritte Niederlage in Folge für die Mannschaft* ◉ **einer Sache** dat **Folge leisten** *(lofty)* follow sth, obey sth ◊ *Sie haben den Anweisungen ihres Vorgesetzten Folge zu leisten.*

⑦ **fol·gen** ['fɔlɡn̩] intr v +haben/sein **1.** +sein follow ◊ *Folgen Sie mir — ich zeige Ihnen den Weg.* ◆ *Ich bin deinem Rat gefolgt und war beim Arzt.* ◆ *Ich hoffe, Sie konnten meinen Ausführungen folgen.; (a piece of advice, your intuition etc. also)* listen to etw. folgt auf etw. acc, etw. folgt einer Sache dat sth comes after sth, sth follows sth ◊ *Ein Unglück folgte dem anderen.* ◆ *Auf diesen Teil des Programms folgt dir die Pause.* jdm auf Schritt und Tritt folgen follow sb everywhere **2.** +haben *(fam)* obey ◊ *Er befahl ihnen aufzuräumen und sie folgten.; (child)* behave ◊ *Dieses Kind will einfach nicht folgen.; (animal)* (jdm) aufs Wort folgen do everything that it is told ◊ *Unser Hund folgt (mir) aufs Wort.* ⊜hören, gehorchen **3.** +sein jdm folgen, auf jdn folgen succeed sb ◊ *Gerhard Schröder folgte Helmut Kohl im Amt des Bundeskanzlers.* ◉ **und daraus folgt** and from this follows

fol·gern ['fɔlɡɐn] tr v +haben *(lofty)* conclude ◊ *„Wir brauchen eine neue Strategie“, folgerte sie.* etw. aus etw. folgern conclude sth from sth ⊜schließen

Fo·lie ['foːliə] die <–, –n> **1.** *(metal)* foil ◊ *Kartoffel in Folie garen; (plastic)* (cling) film, plastic wrap; *(for garden pond etc.)* plastic sheeting **2.** transparency ◊ *eine Folie auflegen*

Fol·ter ['fɔltɐ] die <–, –n> torture ◊ *etw. unter Folter gestehen* ◆ *Dieser Zustand ist die reinste Folter.* ◉ **jdn auf die Folter spannen** keep sb on tenterhooks

Fond [fɔn] der <–s, –s> most sing cooking juices ◊ *aus dem Fond eine Soße machen*

Fonds [fɔn, fɔ̃ː] der <–, –> **1.** unit trust ◊ *Er hat sein gesamtes Vermögen in Fonds investiert.* **2.** fund ◊ *Die Stadt hat einen Fonds für soziale Härtefälle.*

⑦ **for·dern** ['fɔɐ̯dɐn] tr v +haben **1.** etw. (von jdm/ etw.) fordern demand sth (from sb/sth) ◊ *Er hat eine Gehaltserhöhung/sein Recht gefordert.* ◆ *Rechenschaft (von jdm) fordern* ◆ *Sie fordert (von ihm), dass er sich entschuldigt.* lebenslänglich fordern call for a life sentence **2.** *(fig, emph)* *(victims)* claim ◊ *Das Unglück forderte fünf Todesopfer.* **3.** jdn/sich fordern stretch sb/yourself ◊ *Sie fühlt sich in ihrem Job nicht gefordert.*

för·dern ['fœɐ̯dɐn] tr v +haben **1.** fund, give financial support to ◊ *Die Stiftung fördert junge Musiker.* **2.** promote, support ◊ *Diese Vitamine fördern die Sehkraft.* **3.** *(tech)* *(coal, gold etc.)* mine ◊ *Im Ruhrgebiet wird Kohle gefördert.* ⊜abbauen

A
B
C
D
E
F
G
H
I
J
K
L
M
N
O
P
Q
R
S
T
U
V
W
X
Y
Z

For·de·rung ['fɔrdərʊŋ] die <-, -en> **1.** eine
Forderung (an jdn/etw.) a demand (on sb/sth) ◊
eine Forderung stellen **2.** *(tech)* FIN debt ◊ ausste-
hende Forderungen eintreiben; claim ◊ Ein
Gläubiger hat Forderungen an diese Firma.

För·de·rung ['fœrdərʊŋ] die <-, -en> **1.** FIN
funding ◊ die staatliche Förderung von Privatschulen **2.** *no pl* support, encouragement ◊ Die
Förderung ihres Kindes liegt ihr sehr am Herzen.
3. *(tech)* mining ◊ die Förderung von Kohle/
Eisenerz

Fo·rel·le [fo'rɛlə] die <-, -n> trout ◊ Die Forelle
ist ein Raubfisch. ♦ Am liebsten mag ich geräucherte Forelle ♦ Forelle blau

② **Form** [fɔrm] die <-, -en> **1.** shape ◊ Die Vase hat
eine schöne Form. ♦ Der Pullover hat seine Form
behalten/verloren.; form ◊ eine angenehme Form
der Freizeitgestaltung ♦ die Formen eines Verbs ♦
In welcher Form tritt dieses Problem auf? in Form
... gen, in Form von etw. in the form/shape of sth
◊ eine Entschuldigung in Form eines Briefs etw. in
jeder Form all forms of sth ◊ Ich lehne Gewalt in
jeder Form ab. in angemessener/höflicher etc.
Form appropriately/politely etc. **2.** *no pl* SPORT
condition in Form in shape, in/on form **3.** conven-
tion(s), etiquette ◊ Bitte wahren Sie die Form! gute
Formen good manners **4.** mould, mold ◊ Die
Bronze wird in eine Form gegossen. ♦ eine Form
aus Gips; *(in cooking)* (baking) tin, (baking) pan
◊ Den Kuchen noch 20 Minuten in der Form
abkühlen lassen.
● in aller Form formally ◊ jdm in aller Form
seinen Dank aussprechen **feste Formen**
annehmen take shape ◊ Ihr Plan, ein Buch zu
schreiben, nimmt feste Formen an. aus der Form
gehen put on weight der Form halber **1.** as a
matter of form **2.** for appearances' sake ◊ Er hat
sich nur der Form halber entschuldigt.

For·mat [fɔr'maːt] das <-(e)s, -e> **1.** size ◊ Fotos
im Format 10×15 **2.** standing, class ◊ Er ist ein
Mann von Format. ♦ Sie hat als Designerin internationales Format. **3.** TV, IT format ◊ ein neues Format
für eine Sendung entwickeln

Form·blatt ['fɔrmblat] das <-(e)s, Formblätter>
form ⊝Formular

For·mel ['fɔrmal] die <-, -n> **1.** formula ◊ HCl ist
die chemische Formel für Salzsäure. ♦ einen
komplexen Sachverhalt auf eine einfache Formel
bringen **2.** spell ◊ Diese Formel verwandelte den
Frosch in einen Prinzen.

for·mell [fɔr'mɛl] adj, adv *when used as an adj,
only before ns* formal(ly), official(ly) ◊ Nach dem
Empfang folgt ein formelles Abendessen. ♦ Der
Staatsgast wurde formell begrüßt. ♦ Rein formell
ist diese Baugenehmigung in Ordnung.

for·men ['fɔrmən] tr v +haben form, shape ◊ Ihre
Lippen formten ein „O". ♦ eine Brezel aus Teig
formen ♦ Der frühe Tod seines Vaters hat ihn
geformt.

② **For·mu·lar** [fɔrmu'laːr] das <-s, -e> form ◊ ein
Formular ausfüllen ⊝Formblatt

for·mu·lie·ren [fɔrmu'liːrən] <formuliert, formulierte, hat formuliert> tr v **1.** express, formulate ◊
Sie hat ihr Anliegen klar und deutlich formuliert.
⊝ausdrücken **2.** *(a letter, report etc.)* write,
compose ⊝schreiben intr v gut formulieren

können be good with words

for·schen ['fɔrʃn] intr v +haben **1.** do research ◊
Sie forscht im Bereich der Gentechnologie. über
etw. acc forschen research sth **2.** nach jdm/etw.
forschen look for sb/sth, search for sb/sth ◊ Sie
ließen nach dem Vermissten/der Unfallursache
forschen.

For·scher ['fɔrʃe] der <-s, ->, **For·sche·rin**
['fɔrʃərɪn] die <-, -nen> scientist ◊ Sie ist Forsche-
rin an der Uni. ♦ ein berühmter Forscher

② **For·schung** ['fɔrʃʊŋ] die <-, -en> research ◊ Nach
seinem Uni-Abschluss will er in die Forschung
gehen. ♦ die medizinische/chemische Forschung

Forst [fɔrst] der <-(e)s, -e or -en> forest ⊝Wald

Förs·ter ['fœrste] der <-s, ->, **Förs·te·rin**
['fœrstərɪn] die <- or -nen> forester ◊ Sie arbeitet
als Försterin. ♦ Der Förster ging in den Wald.

② **fort** [fɔrt] adv gone ◊ Sie ist fort. ♦ Das ganze
Geld ist fort. fort mit jdm/etw. off with sb/sth ◊
Fort mit dem ganzen Müll! ⊝weg
● in einem fort non-stop ◊ Sie redet in einem
fort nur über ihren neuen Freund. **(und so weiter)**
und so fort and so on

② **fort|...** [fɔrt] prefix **1.** away ◊ Er zog sie von der
Straße fort. ♦ fortbleiben ⊝weg... **2.** *translation
varies (continuation)* etw. fortsetzen continue sth
sich fortbilden continue your education fortschreiten progress

fort·an [fɔrt|'an] adv *(lit)* from then on ◊ Fortan
waren sie glücklich und zufrieden.

fort|be·we·gen ['fɔrtbəve:gn̩] <bewegt sich fort,
bewegte sich fort, hat sich fortbewegt> ref v sich
fortbewegen move, make progress ◊ Eine Schnecke
bewegt sich nur langsam fort.

Fort·bil·dung ['fɔrtbɪldʊŋ] die <-, -en> **1.** *no pl*
(further) training ◊ Wer ist hier in der Firma für
die Fortbildung zuständig? ⊝Weiterbildung
2. training course ◊ an einer Fortbildung teilnehmen

fort|fah·ren ['fɔrtfaːrən] <fährt fort, fuhr fort, ist/
hat fortgefahren> intr v +haben/sein **1.** +haben/
sein continue, go on ◊ Die Moderatorin fuhr mit
dem Interview fort. ♦ Entschuldigen Sie die Unterbrechung, bitte fahren Sie fort. ⊝fortsetzen ⊝un-
terbrechen **2.** +sein go away ◊ Fahrt ihr in den
Ferien fort?; *(for a short time)* go (off) ◊ Mein
Mann ist fortgefahren, um Wein zu kaufen. ⊝weg-
fahren tr v +haben take away ◊ den Schutt/
Sperrmüll fortfahren

fort·ge·schrit·ten ['fɔrtgəʃrɪtn̩] adj advanced ◊
ein fortgeschrittener Lerner ♦ Die Entwicklung ist
so weit fortgeschritten, dass ... ♦ Krebs im fortgeschrittenen Stadium zu fortgeschrittener Stunde at
a very late hour

fort|pflan·zen ['fɔrtpflantsn̩] <pflanzt sich fort,
pflanzte sich fort, hat sich fortgepflanzt> ref v
1. BIO sich fortpflanzen reproduce ◊ Vögel
pflanzen sich fort, indem sie Eier legen.; *(plant)*
propagate (itself) **2.** *(fig)* sich fortpflanzen be
carried over ◊ Die Fehlentwicklungen haben sich
bis heute fortgepflanzt. ⊝weitergehen ⊝aufhören

② **Fort·schritt** ['fɔrtʃrɪt] der <-(e)s, -e> *no pl* Fort-
schritt(e) progress ◊ erhebliche Fortschritte
machen ♦ Die Entwicklung der Software verzeichnet Fortschritte.

fort|set·zen ['fɔrtzɛtsn̩] <setzt fort, setzte fort, hat

fortgesetzt> [tr v] etw. fortsetzen continue (with) sth ◊ *die unterbrochenen Verhandlungen fortsetzen sich fortsetzen* continue ◊ *Dieser Fehler setzt sich durch das ganze Projekt hin fort.* seinen Weg fortsetzen continue on your way ⊜beenden

fort·wäh·rend ['fɔrtvɛːrənt] [adj, adv] *no comp/ superl; when used as an adj, only before ns (lofty)* constant(ly), continual(ly) ◊ *Das Material hielt der fortwährenden Belastung nicht stand.* ♦ *Die Lage verschlechtert sich fortwährend.* ⊜dauernd, ständig

② **Fo·to** ['foːto:] das <-s, -s> photo(graph) ◊ *Machst du mal ein Foto von mir?* ♦ *Er hat auf der Party viele Fotos geschossen.* ⊜Bild

Fo·to-... ['foːto:] [prefix] photo... ◊ *die Fotokopie* ♦ *die Fotografie*

Fo·to·graf [fotoˈɡraːf] der <-en, -en>,

Fo·to·gra·fin [fotoˈɡraːfɪn] die <-, -nen> photographer ◊ *Er ist Fotograf von Beruf.* ♦ *Die Fotografin hat schöne Hochzeitsfotos gemacht.*

② **fo·to·gra·fie·ren** [fotoɡraˈfiːrən] <fotografiert, foto­grafierte, hat fotografiert> [tr v] photograph, take a photo(graph) of ◊ *Fotografierst du uns bitte?* Sie wird nicht gern fotografiert. She doesn't like having her photo taken.

Fo·to·gra·fin [fotoˈɡraːfɪn] → Fotograf

fo·to·ko·pie·ren [fotokoˈpiːrən] <fotokopiert, foto­kopierte, hat fotokopiert> [tr v] photocopy ◊ *Ich muss diesen Artikel fotokopieren.* [intr v] do some photocopying ◊ *Ich gehe noch fotokopieren.*

FPÖ [ɛfpeːˈʔøː] die *(Austr) (abbr of* Freiheitliche Partei Österreichs) FPO

The FPO was founded in 1955 and occupies the conservative right wing of the political landscape in Austria. Among its main concerns are immigration and employment policies.

Fracht [fraxt] die <-, -en> **1.** freight, cargo ◊ *eine kostbare Fracht geladen/an Bord haben* per Fracht (by) freight; *(of a ship, an aircraft)* die Fracht löschen unload its cargo **2.** *(price)* carriage, freightage

Frack [frak] der <-(e)s, Fräcke *or* -s> tailcoat, tails ◊ *Der Bräutigam trug einen Frack.*

② **Fra·ge** ['fraːɡə] die <-, -n> question ◊ *eine Frage beantworten* ♦ *jdm eine Frage stellen* ♦ *Es stehen noch einige Fragen im Raum.* ♦ *Sein Verhalten wirft Fragen auf.* ⊜Antwort

⊛ **eine Frage der Ehre/des Geldes/der Zeit sein** be a question of honour/money/time die/eine Frage anschneiden raise the/a question in Frage kommen be possible ◊ *Welche Bewerber kommen für den Job in Frage?* nicht in Frage kommen be out of the question ohne Frage without doubt ◊ *Er ist ohne Frage sehr intelligent.* keine Frage sein go without saying etw./jdn in Frage stellen question sth/sb

Fra·ge·bo·gen ['fraːɡəboːɡn] der <-s, Fragebögen> questionnaire ◊ *einen Fragebogen ausfüllen*

② **fra·gen** ['fraːɡn] [tr+intr v] +*haben* ask ◊ *Ich wollte dich fragen, ob du mit ins Kino kommst.* ♦ *Er fragte nicht, warum.* ♦ *Wie viel verdienen Sie, wenn ich fragen darf?* ♦ *„Kommst du mit?" — „Ich muss erst einmal meine Eltern) fragen."* (jdn) um etw. fragen ask (sb) for sth ◊ *die Eltern um Erlaubnis fragen* ♦ *in einer Anwaltskanzlei um Rat fragen*

(jdn) nach jdm fragen ask after sb (jdn) nach etw. fragen ask (sb) about sth nach dem Weg fragen ask the way Da fragst du mich zu viel! Now you're asking! [ref v] +*haben* sich fragen, ob/warum/wie etc. wonder whether/why/how etc., ask yourself whether/why/how etc. ◊ *Ich frage mich, ob mir dieses Kleid wirklich steht.*

⊛ **nicht lange fragen** not mess around ◊ *Frag nicht lange, mach einfach!* gefragt sein be in demand nach etw./jdm fragen worry about sth/sb, care about sth/sb ◊ *Sie hat noch nie danach gefragt, was für sie dabei herausspringt.*

Fra·ge·zei·chen ['fraːɡətsaeçn] das <-s, -> question mark

Frak·ti·on [frakˈtsɪoːn] die <-, -en> **1.** POL (parliamentary) party ◊ *die Fraktion der SPD im Bundestag/im Bremer Senat etc.* ♦ *Die beiden Fraktionen wollen eine Koalition bilden.* **2.** *(fig)* contingent, faction ◊ *In unserer Familie gibt es eine starke Fraktion von Vegetariern.* ⊜Teil

Fran·ken ['fraŋkŋ] der <-s, -> FIN (Swiss) franc

fran·kie·ren [fraŋˈkiːrən] <frankiert, frankierte, hat frankiert> [tr v] put a stamp on ◊ *einen Brief/eine Postkarte/ein Paket/Päckchen frankieren etw. ist ausreichend frankiert* sth has got enough stamps on it ein frankierter Rückumschlag a stamped addressed envelope ⊜freimachen

Frank·reich ['fraŋkraeç] das <-s> *article only in combination with attribute, no pl* France → Deutschland

Fran·zo·se [franˈtsoːzə] der <-n, -n>, **Fran·zö·sin** [franˈtsøːzɪn] die <-, -nen> Frenchman Französin Frenchwoman die Franzosen the French → Deutsche

fran·zö·sisch [franˈtsøːzɪʃ] [adj] *mostly before ns* French → deutsch

Fran·zö·sisch [franˈtsøːzɪʃ] das <-(s)> *no pl* French → Deutsch

② **fraß** [fraːs] *pret of* fressen

② **Frau** [frao] die <-, -en> **1.** woman ◊ *eine verheiratete/geschiedene Frau* ♦ *Sie siegte beim Abfahrtslauf der Frauen.* ♦ *die Emanzipation der Frau* ⊜Mann **2.** wife ◊ *Darf ich Ihnen meine Frau vorstellen?* ♦ *Er fragte sie, ob sie seine Frau werden wollte.* ⊜Ehefrau ⊜Mann **3.** *(form of address)* Mrs, Ms ◊ *Frau Müller ist für die Finanzen zuständig.* ♦ *Das Seminar wird von Frau Dr. Schneider geleitet.* ⊜Herr

The official form of address is *Frau: Frau Wagner, dürfte ich Sie um einen Gefallen bitten? Fräulein* is obsolete and should be avoided.

② **Frau·en·arzt** ['fraoən|aˈtst] der <-es, Frauenärzte>, **Frau·en·ärz·tin** ['fraoən|ɛˈtstɪn] die <-, -nen> gynaecologist, gynecologist ◊ *Sie ist Frauenärztin.* ♦ *zum Frauenarzt gehen*

Fräu·lein ['frɔølaen] das <-s, - *or also fam* -s> *(oldf)* **1.** young lady **2.** Miss ◊ *Darf ich Ihnen Fräulein Maier vorstellen?* box@ Frau

② **frech** [frɛç] [adj, adv] **1.** cheeky(-ily), impudent(ly) ◊ *ein freches Grinsen/Kind* ♦ *Werd bloß nicht frech!* ♦ *Er streckte dem Nachbarn frech die Zunge raus.* **2.** saucy(-ily), provocative(ly) ◊ *Das Lied war ziemlich frech.* ♦ *eine freche Komödie/Satire*

Frech·heit ['frɛçhaet] die <-, -en> impudence,

(bit of) cheek, impertinence ◊ *Dazu braucht man Mut und eine gehörige Portion Frechheit.* ♦ *Diese Frechheiten höre ich mir nicht mehr länger an!* ♦ *Sein Artikel ist eine absolute Frechheit!*

② **frei** [fraɛ] [adj, adv] <freier, am frei(e)sten> **1.** *(also fig)* free(ly) ◊ *Sie fühlte sich herrlich frei und unbeschwert.* ♦ *Nach zwei Jahren Haft ist er wieder frei.* ♦ *Sie hatte freie Sicht auf die Berge.* ♦ *die freie Wirtschaft* ♦ *Die Gänse liefen frei herum.* ♦ *sich frei entscheiden können; (access)* open(ly) ◊ *frei zugänglich sein* frei laufend free-range ◊ *Eier von frei laufenden Hühnern* frei lebend wild ◊ *frei lebende Vögel* **2.** free (of charge) ◊ *Sonntags ist der Eintritt frei.* ♦ *Sie liefern frei Haus.* Lieferung frei Haus free delivery ⊖kostenlos [adj] **1.** *(flat, position, seat)* free, vacant, available ◊ *Sie bewarb sich auf die freie Stelle.* ♦ *In diesem Sprachkurs sind noch Plätze frei.* ♦ *Dieses Hotel hat noch Zimmer frei.; (road)* clear, empty; *(time, money)* spare ◊ *Wir hatten viel freie Zeit.* Ist dieser Stuhl/ Platz noch frei? Is this seat taken? **2.** *only before ns* open ◊ *etw. auf freiem Feld anbauen* unter freiem Himmel outdoors, in the open air **3.** *only before ns* freelance ◊ *Sie ist freie Journalistin.* freier Mitarbeiter freelance(r) **4.** der Film ist frei ab ... (Jahren) the film has a ... certificate **5.** bare ◊ *ein Kleid mit freien Schultern* sich frei machen strip, take your clothes off ◊ *Der Arzt sagte: „Bitte machen Sie sich frei."* den Oberkörper frei machen strip to the waist **6.** SPORT *(in football etc.)* unmarked frei stehen be unmarked ◊ *Der Mittelstürmer stand frei.* **7.** *(school, petrol station etc.)* independent ⊛ **frei erfunden** (entirely/completely) fictitious ◊ *Die Handlung des Films ist frei erfunden.* frei stehend **1.** solitary, isolated ◊ *ein frei stehender Baum* **2.** *(house)* detached ◊ *ein frei stehendes Einfamilienhaus* **3.** SPORT unmarked frei werden CHEM, PHYSICS be released frei nach etw. based (loosely) on ◊ *Othello — frei nach Shakespeare* frei von etw. free from sth, without sth ◊ *Dieser Saft ist frei von Zusätzen.* ♦ *Ist sie frei von Schuld?*

Frei·bad ['fraɛbaːt] das <-(e)s, Freibäder> outdoor (swimming) pool, open-air (swimming) pool, lido ◊ *Kommst du mit ins Freibad?*

frei·be·ruf·lich ['fraɛbəruːflɪç] [adj, adv] *when used as an adj, only before ns* freelance ◊ *freiberufliche Grafiker/Fotografen/Musiker* ♦ *Sie arbeitet freiberuflich für mehrere Zeitungen.* freiberuflich tätig sein work freelance, do freelance work

Frei·e ['fraɛə] das <-n> *no pl* **1.** im Freien in the open air, outdoors, alfresco ◊ *Bei schönem Wetter findet das Fest im Freien statt.* ⊖draußen **2.** ins Freie out, outdoors, outside ◊ *Führt diese Tür ins Freie?* ⊖nach draußen

frei|ha·ben ['fraɛhaːbm̩] <hat frei, hatte frei, hat freigehabt> [intr v] be off ◊ *Montags hat sie immer frei.*

frei|hal·ten ['fraɛhaltn̩] <hält frei, hielt frei, hat freigehalten> [tr v] **1.** (jdm) etw. freihalten keep sth (free) (for sb), save sth (for sb) ◊ *Kannst du mir einen Platz freihalten?* ♦ *Ich werde mir die erste Augustwoche freihalten.* **2.** keep clear ◊ *Auf dem Schild stand: „Ausfahrt freihalten!"* etw. von etw. freihalten keep sth clear/free of sth ◊ *die*

Beete von Unkraut freihalten

② **Frei·heit** ['fraɛhaɛt] die <-, -en> freedom, liberty ◊ *das Grundrecht auf persönliche Freiheit* ♦ *Sie hat dem Vogel die Freiheit geschenkt.; (animal)* in Freiheit in the wild in Freiheit lebend wild gewisse/viele etc. Freiheiten genießen have certain/many etc. privileges ⊛ **dichterische/künstlerische Freiheit** poetic/ artistic licence, freedom of artistic expression **Frei·heits·stra·fe** ['fraɛhaɛtsʃtraːfə] die <-, -n> prison sentence ◊ *Er wurde zu einer 3-jährigen Freiheitsstrafe verurteilt.* ♦ *eine Freiheitsstrafe verbüßen*

frei|las·sen ['fraɛlasn̩] <lässt frei, ließ frei, hat freigelassen> [tr v] release, (set) free ◊ *Man hat sie gegen Kaution freigelassen.* ♦ *den eingefangenen Vogel wieder freilassen*

frei|le·gen ['fraɛleːgn̩] <legt frei, legte frei, hat freigelegt> [tr v] uncover, expose ◊ *einen verschütteten Stollen freilegen*

frei·lich ['fraɛlɪç] [adv] **1.** admittedly, however ◊ *Geholfen hat das freilich nichts.* ♦ *Ihr Bruder sieht die Sache freilich ganz anders.* ⊖allerdings **2.** *(SouthG)* of course, sure ◊ *„Kommst du mit ins Kino?" — „Freilich!"*

frei|ma·chen ['fraɛmaxn̩] <macht frei, machte frei, hat freigemacht> [tr+intr v] *(fam)* take off ◊ *Er macht ein paar Tage frei.* [tr v] *(form) (a letter)* put a stamp on, frank ◊ *Bitte mit einer 56-Cent-Marke freimachen.* ⊖frankieren

frei|neh·men ['fraɛneːmən] <nimmt frei, nahm frei, hat freigenommen> [tr+intr v] *(fam)* (sich [dat]) freinehmen take time off ◊ *Nimm (dir) doch mal frei und ruh dich aus.* (sich [dat]) etw. freinehmen take sth off ◊ *Sie wollte (sich) ein paar Tage/ den Nachmittag frei nehmen.*

Frei·raum ['fraɛraɔm] der <-(e)s, Freiräume> freedom (for/of development) ◊ *Du solltest ihm mehr Freiraum gönnen/geben.*

frei·schaf·fend ['fraɛʃafnt, 'fraɛʃafənt] [adj, adv] freelance ◊ *ein freischaffender Künstler/Autor/ Grafiker etc.* ♦ *Seit 1990 ist sie freischaffend (tätig).*

frei|set·zen ['fraɛzɛtsn̩] <setzt frei, setzte frei, hat freigesetzt> [tr v] release, emit, give off ◊ *Bei einer Verbrennung wird Energie freigesetzt.*

Frei·spruch ['fraɛʃprʊx] der <-(e)s, Freisprüche> acquittal, (verdict of) not guilty ◊ *Das Urteil lautete auf Freispruch.* auf Freispruch plädieren plead not guilty

frei|ste·hen ['fraɛʃteːən] <steht frei, stand frei, hat freigestanden> [intr v] *in South G, Austr, Swiss often +sein* etw. steht jdm frei sth is up to sb ◊ *Diese Entscheidung steht dir natürlich frei.; (flat, house)* be vacant, be empty ◊ *Seit wann steht die Wohnung frei?* es steht jdm frei, etw. zu tun sb is free to do sth

Frei·staat ['fraɛʃtaːt] der <-(e)s, -en> der Freistaat Bayern/Thüringen/Sachsen the Free State of Bavaria/Thuringia/Saxony

② **Frei·tag** ['fraɛtaːk] der <-(e)s, -e> Friday → Montag

frei·tags ['fraɛtaːks] [adv] on Fridays → montags

frei·wil·lig ['fraɛvɪlɪç] [adj, adv] *no comp/superl* **1.** voluntary(-ily) ◊ *Sie suchen noch freiwillige Helfer.* ♦ *Der Test/Die Teilnahme ist freiwillig.* ♦ *Er*

gab sein Amt freiwillig auf. freiwillige Feuerwehr volunteer fire brigade/fighters **2.** freiwillig versichert sein *voluntarily take out statutory health insurance*

Frei·zei·chen ['fraɛ̯t͡saeçn̩] das <-s, -> dialling tone, dial tone

② **Frei·zeit** ['fraɛ̯t͡saet] die <-> *no pl* free time, spare time, time off ◊ *Er hat sehr viel Freizeit.* ♦ *In ihrer Freizeit lernt sie Italienisch.*

frei·zü·gig ['fraɛ̯t͡sy:gɪç] [adj, adv] **1.** liberal(ly), generous(ly) ◊ *Sein Umgang mit Regeln ist recht freizügig.* ♦ *eine freizügige Interpretation der Tatsachen* **2.** daring(ly) ◊ *freizügig gekleidete Personen*

② **fremd** [frɛmt] [adj] <fremder, am fremdesten> **1.** *only before ns* foreign ◊ *fremde Sprachen* **2.** sb else's, other people's ◊ *Sie ist auf fremde Hilfe nicht angewiesen.* ♦ *Wurde der Unfall durch fremdes Verschulden verursacht?* **3.** strange, unknown, alien ◊ *Sie fand eine fremde Person in ihrer Wohnung vor.* ♦ *Die Heimat war ihm fremd geworden.* ♦ *Ihre Stimme klang am Telefon ganz fremd.* irgendwo fremd sein be a stranger somewhere sich irgendwo fremd fühlen feel like a stranger somewhere **4.** jdm ist etw. fremd sth is unknown to sb, sth is alien to sb ◊ *Das Gesicht war ihr völlig fremd.* ♦ *Eitelkeit war ihm völlig fremd.*

Frem·de¹ ['frɛmdə] der/die <-n, die Fremden> *but: ein Fremder/eine Fremde* stranger ◊ *Ich darf nicht mit Fremden sprechen.* ♦ *Eine Fremde kam auf mich zu.* ♦ *Ich sah sie mit einem Fremden im Kino.*; *(on holiday)* visitor ◊ *Zimmer an Fremde vermieten* box@ Substantivierung

Frem·de² ['frɛmdə] die <-> *no pl (lofty)* foreign parts ◊ *Sie zogen in die Fremde.*

Frem·den·füh·rer ['frɛmdn̩fy:rɐ] der <-s, ->,
Frem·den·füh·re·rin ['frɛmdn̩fy:rərɪn] die <-, -nen> tourist guide ◊ *Ist Sie Fremdenführerin.* ♦ *Brauchen Sie einen Fremdenführer?*

Frem·den·ver·kehr ['frɛmdn̩fɛkeːɐ̯] der <-s> *no pl* tourism

Frem·den·zim·mer ['frɛmdn̩t͡sɪmɐ] das <-s, -> (guest) room ◊ *Vermieten Sie Fremdenzimmer?* ⊖Gästezimmer

fremd|ge·hen ['frɛmtgeːən] <geht fremd, ging fremd, ist fremdgegangen> [intr v] *(fam)* be unfaithful ◊ *Sie ging mit seinem besten Freund fremd.*

② **Fremd·spra·che** ['frɛmtʃpraːxə] die <-, -n> foreign language ◊ *Sie spricht/beherrscht drei Fremdsprachen.* ♦ *Sie unterrichtete Deutsch als Fremdsprache.*

Fremd·wort ['frɛmtvɔ'rt] das <-(e)s, Fremdwörter> foreign word ◊ *Er benutzt sehr viele Fremdwörter.* ⊚ etw. ist ein/kein Fremdwort sth is/is not unknown, sth is/is not unheard of ◊ *In dieser Stadt ist Kriminalität kein Fremdwort mehr.* etw. ist für jdn ein Fremdwort sb doesn't know the meaning of sth, sth is completely alien to sb ◊ *Freizeit ist für ihn ein Fremdwort.*

Fres·se ['frɛsə] die <-, -n> *(rude, pej)* gob ◊ *Ich hau dir gleich eins/eine in die Fresse!* ⊚ die Fresse halten *(taboo)* shut your gob

② **fres·sen** ['frɛsn̩] <frisst, fraß, hat gefressen> [tr+intr v] *(animal)* eat, feed (on) ◊ *Das Pony fraß ihr aus der Hand.* ♦ *Kühe fressen Gras.*

[tr v] *(holes)* etw. in etw. [acc] fressen eat sth in sth ◊ *Die Motten haben Löcher in den Pulli gefressen.* [ref v] *(fig)* etw. frisst sich durch/in etw. [acc] sth eats through/into sth ◊ *Die Säure fraß sich in das Plastik.* ♦ *Der Rost fraß sich durch das Blech.*

② **Freu·de** ['frɔɪ̯də] die <-, -n> joy, pleasure, delight ◊ *Er weinte/strahlte vor Freude.* ♦ *Auf dem Fest wollte keine rechte Freude aufkommen.* ♦ *Es ist mir eine große Freude, Sie hier begrüßen zu dürfen.* ♦ *die Freuden des Lebens/Urlaubs genießen* Freude über etw. [acc] joy at sth, delight at sth jdm (eine) Freude machen/bereiten make sb happy, bring sb pleasure ◊ *Seine Enkelkinder bereiten ihm viel Freude.* etw. macht/bereitet jdm Freude sb enjoys sth, sb takes (a) pleasure in sth ◊ *Laufen/Singen bereitet ihr viel Freude.* (seine) Freude an etw. [dat] haben enjoy sth, get pleasure from sth ◊ *An diesem Buch hatte sie viel Freude.*

② **freu·en** ['frɔɪ̯ən] [ref v] +*haben* **1.** sich (über etw. [acc]) freuen be pleased (with sth), be glad (about sth), be happy (about sth) ◊ *Freust du dich gar nicht?* ♦ *Er freute sich wahnsinnig (über das Geschenk).* ♦ *Ich freue mich, dass du kommen konntest.* **2.** sich auf etw. [acc] freuen look forward to sth ◊ *Sie freute sich auf die Ferien.* sich auf jdn freuen look forward to seeing sb, look forward to sb's arrival **3.** sich für jdn freuen be pleased for sb ◊ *Es freut mich für ihn, dass er endlich Arbeit hat.* [tr v] +*haben; no passive* etw. freut jdn sth makes sb happy, sb is pleased/ delighted with sth ◊ *Die Nachricht freute mich sehr.* es freut jdn, dass sb is pleased/glad/delighted that ◊ *Es freute ihn, dass sie Zeit hatte.* es würde mich freuen, wenn I would be delighted if Freut mich(, Sie kennen zu lernen)! Pleased to meet you!

② **Freund** [frɔɪ̯nt] der <-(e)s, -e>, **Freun·din** ['frɔɪ̯ndɪn] die <-, -nen> **1.** friend ◊ *Chris ist ein guter Freund von ihm.* ♦ *Ute ist ihre beste Freundin.* ♦ *Zuerst mochten wir uns nicht, doch im Urlaub wurden wir Freunde.*; *(political etc. also)* ally **2.** *(in a relationship)* boyfriend, partner ◊ *Sie hat sich von ihrem Freund getrennt.* Freundin girlfriend, partner ◊ *Er hat keine feste Freundin.* **3.** *seldom fem (fig)* ein Freund ... [gen], ein Freund von etw. a lover of ... ◊ *Er ist ein großer Freund von Jazz.* kein Freund von etw. sein not be one for sth ◊ *Sie ist kein Freund von vielen Worten.* ⊚ dicke Freunde sein be very good friends, be very close

Freun·des·kreis ['frɔɪ̯ndəskraes] der <-es, -e> circle of friends ◊ *Sie hat einen großen Freundeskreis.* Wir feierten ganz privat im Freundeskreis. We had a small celebration with close friends.

② **freund·lich** ['frɔɪ̯ntlɪç] [adj] **1.** friendly, amiable ◊ *ein freundliches Lächeln* ♦ *Sie war sehr freundlich zu ihm.* **2.** pleasant, cheerful ◊ *freundliches Wetter* ♦ *Der Raum wirkte hell und freundlich.* [adv] **1.** benevolently ◊ *Er nickte ihm freundlich zu.* jdn freundlich begrüßen/empfangen give sb a warm welcome **2.** pleasantly, cheerfully ◊ *ein freundlich eingerichtetes Zimmer*

② **Freund·schaft** ['frɔɪ̯ntʃaft] die <-, -en> friendship ◊ *Die beiden verbindet eine enge/langjährige Freundschaft.* ♦ *Sie schließt gern schnell neue Freundschaften.*

A B C D E F G H I J K L M N O P Q R S T U V W X Y Z

A
B
C
D
E
F
G
H
I
J
K
L
M
N
O
P
Q
R
S
T
U
V
W
X
Y
Z

② **Frie·den** ['friːdn̩] der <–s> no pl **1.** POL peace ◊ ein dauerhafter Frieden ♦ Wie kann der Frieden gesichert werden? ⊝Krieg **2.** POL peace treaty **3.** (fig) harmony, peace ◊ Der häusliche Frieden war gestört. mit jdm in Frieden leben live in harmony with sb jds innerer Frieden sb's peace of mind jdn/etw. in Frieden lassen leave sb/sth in peace, leave sb/sth alone ◊ Lass mich doch mit diesem Mist in Frieden! Ruhe in Frieden! (May you) rest in peace! Frieden stiften make peace ◊ Sie wollte zwischen den Kindern Frieden stiften. ⊛ Frieden geben (fam) leave it, stop (it) ◊ Gib endlich Frieden, du gehst mir auf die Nerven!

Fried·hof ['friːthoːf] der <–(e)s, Friedhöfe> cemetery, graveyard ◊ Auf welchem Friedhof liegt Franz Kafka? ♦ Er wird morgen auf dem Friedhof beigesetzt.

fried·lich ['friːtlɪç] adj, adv **1.** peaceful(ly) ◊ Sie kamen in friedlicher Absicht. ♦ Es ist so herrlich friedlich hier! ♦ Die Demonstration verlief weitgehend friedlich. **2.** (person) peaceable(-ably) ◊ Sie war ein sehr friedlicher Mensch. ♦ Die Stämme leben friedlich miteinander.; (animal) docile(ly) **3.** when used as an adj, only before ns civilian ◊ die friedliche Nutzung der Atomenergie Technologie friedlich nutzen use technology for civilian purposes ⊛ friedlich sein **1.** be quiet **2.** stop fighting

② **frie·ren** ['friːrən] <friert, fror, hat/ist gefroren> intr v **1.** +haben jd friert, jdn friert (es) sb is/feels cold, sb is freezing ◊ Die Kinder haben so gefroren. ♦ Mich fror es. jd/jdn friert an den Händen/Füßen sb has cold hands/feet ◊ Ich friere oft an den Füßen. ♦ Ihn fror (es) an den Händen. **2.** +sein, mostly present perf (ground, water) freeze ◊ Wasser friert bei 0° Celsius. ♦ Der Boden ist gefroren. ♦ Er taute die gefrorenen Erdbeeren auf. ⊝gefrieren imp v +haben es friert it is (below) freezing

Fri·ka·del·le [frika'dɛlə] die <–, –n> flat fried meatball

② **frisch** [frɪʃ] adj, adv **1.** fresh(ly) ◊ Du solltest mehr frisches Gemüse/Obst essen! ♦ Ist dieser Fisch frisch? ♦ frische Blumen/Brötchen/Eier/Milch ♦ Er war frisch rasiert. ♦ ein Glas frisch gepresster Orangensaft **2.** new(ly), recent(ly) ◊ Sie sind frisch verheiratet. adj **1.** mostly before ns fresh, clean ◊ Sie holte frische Unterwäsche aus dem Schrank. ♦ Die Bettwäsche ist frisch. ⊝neu **2.** cool, chilly ◊ Es wehte ein frischer Wind. ♦ Abends kann es hier frisch werden. **3.** only before ns renewed, new ◊ Er ging mit frischem Mut an die Arbeit. **4.** not before ns refreshed, lively ◊ Wir waren alle frisch und munter. **5.** healthy, rosy ◊ Er hatte eine frische Farbe im Gesicht. ♦ Ihr Teint wirkte frisch und rosig. ⊛ sich frisch machen freshen (yourself) up

Fri·sche ['frɪʃə] die <–> no pl **1.** freshness ◊ Das Gelingen des Gerichts hängt von der Frische der Zutaten ab. ♦ Rouge zaubert Frische ins Gesicht. **2.** (mental, physical) energy, vigour, vigor ◊ Sie strahlt jugendliche Frische aus. **3.** coolness ◊ die kühle Frische der Morgenluft

Frisch·hal·te·fo·lie ['frɪʃhaltəˌfoːljə] die <–> no pl cling film

Frisch·kä·se ['frɪʃkɛːzə] der <–s, –> most sing cream cheese ◊ Sie bestrich das Brot mit Frischkäse. ♦ Er kaufte zwei Becher Frischkäse.

② **Fri·seur** [fri'zøːɐ̯] der <–s, –e>, **Fri·seu·rin** [fri'zøːrɪn] die <–, –nen> **1.** hairdresser, barber ◊ Er ist Friseur. ♦ eine gelernte Friseurin **2.** hairdresser's, barber's ◊ Ich muss dringend zum Friseur (gehen)! → Friseursalon

Fri·seur·sa·lon [fri'zøːɐ̯zaˌlõ, fri'zøːɐ̯zaˌlɔ̃ː] der <–s, –s> (hairdressing) salon, hairdresser's

fri·sie·ren [fri'ziːrən] <frisiert, frisierte, hat frisiert> tr v **1.** jdn/sich frisieren do sb's/your hair ◊ Sie frisierte sich vor dem Spiegel. jdm/sich das Haar/die Haare frisieren, jds/sein(e) Haar(e) frisieren do sb's/your hair, comb sb's/your hair ◊ Sie frisierte mir die/meine Haare. **2.** (fam, fig) doctor, fiddle ◊ Die Statistiken waren frisiert. die Bilanzen frisieren cook the books **3.** (fam, fig) (an engine) soup up ◊ Er hat sein Mofa/den Motor frisiert.

② **frisst** [frɪst] pres of fressen

Frist [frɪst] die <–, –en> period, deadline ◊ Sie haben ihm eine Frist von zwei Monaten gesetzt. ◊ Die Frist für die Bewerbungen läuft Ende Mai ab. eine Frist einhalten/verlängern stick to/extend a deadline

frist·ge·recht ['frɪstɡəˌrɛçt] adj, adv no comp/superl within the period stipulated, on the due date ◊ die fristgerechte Erledigung der Aufgaben ♦ Die Kündigung war fristgerecht. ♦ die Steuererklärung fristgerecht einreichen jdm fristgerecht kündigen give sb proper notice

frist·los ['frɪstloːs] adj, adv when used as an adj, mostly before ns without notice, instant(ly) ◊ eine fristlose Kündigung ♦ Er wurde fristlos entlassen. ♦ einen Vertrag fristlos kündigen

Fri·sur [fri'zuːɐ̯] die <–, –en> hairstyle, hairdo ◊ Diese Frisur steht dir gut. ⊝Haarschnitt, Schnitt

Frit·te ['frɪtə] die <–, –n> most pl (NorthG, fam) chip, (French) fry ◊ Fritten mit Ketchup und Majonäse ⊝Pommes, Pommes frites

frit·tie·ren [frɪ'tiːrən] <frittiert, frittierte, hat frittiert> tr v deep-fry

② **froh** [froː] adj <froher, am froh(e)sten> **1.** happy, glad, pleased ◊ ein frohes Lachen ♦ Sie war froh, dass alles so gut geklappt hatte. ♦ Nach der guten Nachricht waren alle froh gestimmt. froh um/über etw. acc sein be thankful for sth, be pleased with sth, be happy/glad about sth ◊ Er war froh um jede Unterstützung. **2.** (event, time) happy, merry, joyful ◊ Ihre Geburt war ein frohes Ereignis. ♦ Auf der Karte stand „Frohe Weihnachten/Ostern". ♦ Ich wünsche Ihnen ein frohes Fest/neues Jahr!

② **fröh·lich** ['frøːlɪç] adj, adv **1.** happy(-ily), cheerful(ly), merry(-ily) ◊ Überall sah man fröhliche Gesichter. ♦ Das Fest wurde noch richtig fröhlich. ♦ Er lachte fröhlich. ⊝heiter ⊝traurig **2.** blithe(ly) ◊ Das Kind plapperte fröhlich vor sich hin.

fromm [frɔm] adj <frommer/frömmer, am frommsten/frömmsten> devout, religious, pious ◊ Sie ist sehr fromm. ♦ Sie stimmten ein frommes Lied an.

Fron·leich·nam [froːn'laɛçnaːm] seldom with definite article 'das' (the Feast of) Corpus Christi ◊ An Fronleichnam findet eine Prozession durch die

Innenstadt statt.

On this Catholic holiday, celebrated on the Thursday after Trinity Sunday, a monstrance with the Eucharist (the consecrated host representing the Body of Christ) is carried through the streets in a procession followed by the singing and praying congregation. The procession makes a stop at four altars which are placed around the parish according to the four points of the compass. There readings from the Gospel and intercessions take place. The benediction concludes the feast.

Front [frɔnt] die <–, –en> **1.** front ◇ *Die Front des Autos war eingedrückt.* ◆ *Es war Krieg und die meisten Männer waren an der Front.* **2.** *no pl* front line ◇ *ein Angriff auf die gegnerische Front* ◆ *Er kämpft an vorderster Front für diese Reformen.* hinter der Front behind the lines ⊙ **gegen jdn/etw. Front machen** openly oppose sb/sth ◇ *Die Bürger machten Front gegen die Steuererhöhung.* **die Fronten haben sich verhärtet** the positions have hardened

fron·tal [frɔnˈtaːl] [adj, adv] *when used as an adj, only before ns (also fig)* head-on, at/from the front ◇ *ein frontaler Angriff* ◆ *frontal zusammenstoßen* ◆ *Der Fußgänger wurde vom Auto frontal erfasst.*

② **fror** [froːɐ̯] *pret of* frieren

Frosch [frɔʃ] der <–(e)s, Frösche> frog ◇ *Man hörte Frösche quaken.*

fros·tig [ˈfrɔstɪç] [adj, adv] *(also fig)* frosty(-ily), icy(-ily) ◇ *Es war ein frostiger Morgen/Tag.* ◆ *Die Luft/Stimmung war frostig.* ◆ *Sie bereiteten ihm einen frostigen Empfang.*

Frot·tee [frɔˈteː, ˈ– –] das *or* der <–(s), –s> (terry) towelling ◇ *ein Waschlappen/Lätzchen/Bademantel aus Frottee*

Frucht [frʊxt] die <–, Früchte> **1.** fruit ◇ *kandierte/ tropische Früchte* ◆ *Die Frucht der Buche heißt Buchecker.* ◆ *Diese Politik hat Früchte getragen.* **2.** crops ◇ *die Frucht auf dem Feld*

frucht·bar [ˈfrʊxtbaːɐ̯] [adj] **1.** fertile ◇ *fruchtbare Böden/Gebiete/Pflanzen* ◆ *Dieses Ackerland ist sehr fruchtbar.* ⊝karg **2.** prolific ◇ *Ratten sind sehr fruchtbare Tiere.* **3.** fruchtbare Tage fertile days **4.** *(fig)* fruitful, productive ◇ *Die Zusammenarbeit erwies sich als besonders fruchtbar.* ◆ *ein fruchtbarer Gedankenaustausch*

fruch·tig [ˈfrʊxtɪç] [adj, adv] fruity ◇ *fruchtige Cocktails* ◆ *Dieser Wein ist besonders fruchtig.* **fruchtig schmecken/riechen** taste/smell fruity

Frucht·zu·cker [ˈfrʊxttsʊkɐ] der <–s> *no pl* fructose ◇ *Das Eis für Diabetiker wird mit Fruchtzucker hergestellt.*

② **früh** [fryː] [adj, adv] <früher, am früh(e)sten> **1.** early ◇ *in den frühen Morgenstunden/Achtzigerjahren* ◆ *Als sie aufwachte, war es noch sehr früh.* ◆ *Er steht immer sehr früh auf.* ◆ *Bitte reichen Sie Ihren Antrag möglichst früh ein.* ◆ *Schon in seiner frühen Jugend liebte er die Musik.* **zu früh** too early, too soon ◇ *Er war viel zu früh am verabredeten Treffpunkt.* **zu früh kommen** be early am frühen Abend/Morgen etc. early in the evening/ morning etc. ⊝spät **2.** premature(ly) ◇ *ein früher Wintereinbruch* [adv] in the morning, a.m. ◇ *Sie hat bis 8 Uhr früh Bereitschaftsdienst.* gestern/

heute/morgen früh yesterday/this/tomorrow morning ⊙ **früher oder später** sooner or later **von früh bis spät** from morning till night

Frü·he [ˈfryːə] die <–> *no pl (lofty)* in der Frühe in the morning ◇ *Wir feierten bis fünf Uhr in der Frühe.* **in aller Frühe** early in the morning, very early

② **frü·her** [ˈfryːɐ] *comp of* früh [adv] in the past, in the old days ◇ *War früher tatsächlich alles besser?* *Früher mochte sie Oliven.* She used to like olives. *Er war früher Gärtner.* He used to be a gardener. **von früher** from the past, from the old days, from some time ago ◇ *Die beiden kannten sich von früher (her).* **von früher sprechen/erzählen** talk about the past ⊝einst

frü·he·re [ˈfryːərə] [adj] *only before ns* <ein früherer ..., eine frühere ..., ein früheres ...> **1.** earlier ◇ *Frühere Ausgaben der Zeitschrift kann man im Internet bestellen.* **in früheren Jahren/Zeiten** in the past, formerly ⊝spätere **2.** previous ◇ *Ist das der frühere Besitzer des Ladens?* **3.** former ◇ *auf dem Gebiet der früheren Sowjetunion* ⊝ehemalige

frü·hes·tens [ˈfryːəstns, ˈfryːəstəns] [adv] at the earliest ◇ *Das Training beginnt frühestens Mitte Mai/in 14 Tagen.* ⊝spätestens

Früh·jahr [ˈfryːjaːɐ̯] das <–s, –e> spring ◇ *Das Gebäude soll im Frühjahr fertig sein.* ◆ *Das Frühjahr kommt bald!* ⊝Frühling

Früh·ling [ˈfryːlɪŋ] der <–s, –e> spring ◇ *Es war ein milder Frühling.* ◆ *Allmählich wird es Frühling.* ◆ *Tanja hat im Frühling Geburtstag.* ⊝Frühjahr ⊙ **einen/seinen zweiten Frühling erleben** live/ experience a second youth

Früh·lings·rol·le [ˈfryːlɪŋsrɔlə] die <–, –n> spring roll

Früh·lings·zwie·bel [ˈfryːlɪŋstsviːbl̩] die <–, –n> spring onion

früh·reif [ˈfryːraɛ̯f] [adj] precocious ◇ *Das Mädchen ist frühreif.* ◆ *ein frühreifes Kind*

Früh·ren·te [ˈfryːrɛntə] die <–> *no pl* early retirement (pension) in Frührente gehen take early retirement

Früh·schop·pen [ˈfryːʃɔpm̩] der <–s, –> *morning gathering of friends in a pub to have a drink together* ◇ *Sonntags treffen sie sich immer zum Frühschoppen.*

② **Früh·stück** [ˈfryːʃtʊk] das <–(e)s, –e> *most sing* breakfast ◇ *Eine Übernachtung mit Frühstück kostet 50 Euro.* ◆ *Er brachte ihr das Frühstück ans Bett.* zweites Frühstück elevenses, mid-morning snack

German breakfast habits are quite diverse. Many people just have a cup of coffee before work. Health conscious people might have muesli in the morning. A traditional German breakfast consists of bread (rolls) with jam, honey, cold meats, cheese and boiled eggs with coffee or tea.

② **früh·stü·cken** [ˈfryːʃtʏkn̩] [intr v] +*haben* have breakfast ◇ *Wir frühstücken meistens um acht Uhr.* ◆ *Hast du schon gefrühstückt?* [tr v] etw. frühstücken have sth for breakfast ◇ *Was hast du gefrühstückt?*

früh·zei·tig [ˈfryːtsaɛ̯tɪç] [adj, adv] **1.** early (on) ◇

Eine frühzeitige Operation ist empfehlenswert. ♦ *Er hatte das Problem bereits frühzeitig erkannt.* **2.** premature(ly) ◊ *ein frühzeitiger Wintereinbruch* ♦ *Die Spielerin ist frühzeitig ausgeschieden.*

Frust [frʊst] *der* <–(e)s> *no pl (fam)* frustration ◊ *aufgestauten Frust abreagieren* ♦ *Er isst nur aus Frust.*

Fuchs [fʊks] *der* <–es, Füchse> **1.** fox **2.** fox fur ◊ *Sie trug einen Fuchs.* **3.** chestnut (horse) ◊ *einen Fuchs reiten*

⊚ **ein (schlauer) Fuchs** a wily one

Füch·sin ['fʏksɪn] *die* <–, –nen> vixen

Fuch·tel ['fʊxt̩l] *die* <–, –n> *(fam, pej)* **1.** jdn unter seiner Fuchtel haben have sb under your thumb, dominate sb **2.** unter jds Fuchtel stehen be under sb's thumb, be dominated by sb

fü·gen ['fy:gn̩] [tr v] +*haben* **1.** etw. an etw. [acc] fügen place sth next to sth, put sth next to sth, add sth to sth ◊ *Sie fügte einen Ziegelstein an den anderen.* **2.** etw. in etw. [acc] fügen fit sth in(to) sth, place sth in(to) sth, put sth in(to) sth, add sth to sth ◊ *Sie fügte das fehlende Teil ins Puzzle.* **3.** etw. zu etw. fügen put sth together to make sth ◊ *Er versuchte, die Trümmer zu einem Ganzen zu fügen.* [ref v] +*haben* **1.** jd fügt sich (jdm/etw.) sb obeys (sb/sth) ◊ *Unser Hund fügt sich nur ungern.* ♦ *Er wollte sich ihren Anweisungen nicht fügen.* **2.** jd fügt sich in etw. [acc] sb accepts sth, sb resigns themself to sth ◊ *Sie fügte sich in ihr Schicksal/das Unvermeidliche.* **3.** etw. fügt sich zu etw. sth fits together to make sth ◊ *Die Teile fügten sich zu einem harmonischen Ganzen.* **4.** etw. fügt sich in etw. [acc] sth fits in(to) sth ◊ *Das fügt sich gut in das Gesamtkonzept.*

füg·sam ['fy:kza:m] [adj, adv] obedient(ly) ◊ *Sie ist weder brav noch fügsam.* ♦ *Sie war nicht mehr das fügsame Kind von einst.* ♦ *Der Hund blieb fügsam an der Seite seines Herrn.*

Fü·gung ['fy:gʊŋ] *die* <–, –en> **1.** providence, fate ◊ *War es Zufall oder Fügung?*; coincidence ◊ *Durch eine glückliche Fügung konnte er entkommen.* eine Fügung des Schicksals a stroke of fate eine Fügung Gottes divine providence **2.** LING construction ◊ *eine feste/idiomatische/präpositionale Fügung*

② **füh·len** ['fy:lən] [tr v] +*haben* **1.** feel ◊ *Ich fühlte die Kälte in meinem Gesicht.* ♦ *Sie wie sich ihre Augen mit Tränen füllten.* ♦ *Sie fühlte keinen Neid.* jdm den/jds Puls fühlen feel sb's pulse **2.** sense ◊ *Ich konnte die Gefahr fühlen.* ♦ *Sie fühlte, dass er ihr etwas verheimlichte.* [ref v] sich müde/einsam/zu jdm hingezogen fühlen feel tired/lonely/drawn to sb ◊ *Durch den Lärm fühle ich mich gestört.* sich wie jd fühlen feel like sb ◊ *Ich fühlte mich wie ein Star.* [intr v] nach etw. fühlen feel for sth ◊ *Er fühlte in seiner Tasche nach dem Brief.*

② **fuhr** [fu:ɐ] *pret of* fahren

② **füh·ren** ['fy:rən] [intr v] +*haben* **1.** zu etw. führen lead to sth ◊ *Das könnte zu Problemen führen.* zu keinem Ergebnis/Erfolg führen end inconclusively/unsuccessfully **2.** *(path, road etc.)* irgendwohin führen go somewhere, lead somewhere ◊ *Diese Straße führt direkt zum Zoo.* **3.** SPORT lead ◊ *„Wer führt?" — „Die Bochumer, mit 3:1."* **4.** *(programme/program)* present ◊ *Durch das*

Programm führt Michael Marwitz. [tr+intr v] +*haben* (jdn/etw.) irgendwohin führen lead (sb/sth) somewhere ◊ *Unsere Reise führte uns auch nach Lyon.* ♦ *Er führte das Land in den Krieg/zum Sieg.* [tr v] +*haben* **1.** *(a conversation, negotiations)* have, carry on ◊ *ein Telefongespräch führen* Krieg führen wage war die Krieg führenden Parteien the warring parties (bei/in einem Film) Regie führen direct (a film) einen Wahlkampf führen conduct an election campaign **2.** *(a country, political party)* lead; *(a class)* manage; *(a business, household etc.)* run ◊ *ein gut geführtes Restaurant* ⊖leiten **3.** jdn/ein Tier (irgendwohin) führen lead sb/an animal (somewhere) ◊ *Der Kellner führte uns zu einem freien Tisch.*; accompany sb (somewhere) ◊ *Könnten Sie mich bitte führen, allein finde ich den Weg nicht.* einen Hund an der Leine führen keep a dog on a lead **4.** jdn durch etw. führen show sb around sth ◊ *Besucher durch die Stadt/das Museum führen*; guide sb through sth ◊ *Der Benutzer wird automatisch durch das Menü geführt.* **5.** *(a list, accounts, minutes)* keep ◊ *Führst du ein Tagebuch?* ♦ *über alle Einnahmen und Ausgaben Buch führen* **6.** *(your life, existence etc.)* lead ◊ *ein interessantes/beneidenswertes Leben führen* **7.** TRADE *(goods)* stock, keep ◊ *Führen Sie auch Tapeten?* **8.** *(esp form)* etw. mit sich führen have got sth with you ◊ *Führen Sie Gepäck/zollpflichtige Waren mit sich?*; *(avalanche)* carry sth along with it **9.** *(lofty) (a designation, number)* have ◊ *Das Patent führt die Nummer 19838253.; (an academic title)* use ◊ *Sie darf jetzt den Doktortitel führen.*

⊚ **zu nichts führen** come to nothing **zu weit führen** take things too far

② **Füh·rer·aus·weis** ['fy:rɐʔaosvaes] *der* <–es, –e> *(Swiss)* → Führerschein

② **Füh·rer·schein** ['fy:rɐʃaen] *der* <–(e)s, –e> driving licence, driver's license den Führerschein machen take your driving test

You must have a driving licence in Germany for the following vehicles: private cars, motorbikes, lorries, buses, agricultural and forestry vehicles. To acquire a licence, practical and theoretical lessons are taken at a driving school that prepare the learner for the practical and theoretical driving tests. Every driver is obliged to carry their driving licence with them at all times.

② **Füh·rung** ['fy:rʊŋ] *die* <–, –en> **1.** leadership, leaders ◊ *die politische/militärische Führung* ♦ *in die Führung der Partei gewählt werden*; *(in business)* directors, management ⊖Leitung **2.** *no pl* die Führung *(einer Sache* [gen]*)* the leadership (of sth); *(in business)* the management (of sth); *(in sports)* the captaincy (of sth) unter jds Führung under sb's leadership; *(in the army)* under sb's command ⊖Leitung **3.** eine Führung *(durch etw.)* a guided tour (of sth) ◊ *an einer Führung durch die Burg/das Museum teilnehmen* **4.** *no pl* SPORT *(in sporting competitions)* lead in Führung gehen, die Führung übernehmen take the lead in Führung liegen be in the lead ◊ *Der Favorit liegt mit fünf Sekunden Vorsprung klar in Führung.*

⊚ **wegen guter Führung** for good behaviour/

behavior
fül·len ['fʏlən] [tr v] +*haben* **1.** etw. *(mit etw.)* füllen fill sth *(with sth)* ◊ *ein Glas randvoll (mit Milch) füllen* ♦ *die Badewanne mit Wasser füllen* ♦ *Wie/Womit können wir die entstandenen Lücken füllen?* sich *(mit etw.)* füllen fill *(up)* *(with sth)* ◊ *Die Blase hat sich mit Blut gefüllt.* etw. in etw. [acc] füllen put sth in(to) sth ◊ *Sie füllten Sand in Säcke.*; *(liquids)* pour sth into sth ⊜leeren **2.** fill, take up ◊ *Meine Bücher füllen mehrere Regale.*
Fül·ler ['fʏlɐ] der <-s, -> ◊ *Wir müssen in der Schule mit Füller schreiben.*
Fül·lung ['fʏlʊŋ] die <-, -en> filling; *(of petrol)* full tank ◊ *Mit einer Füllung kommen wir 600 km weit.*; *(of a roast joint, cushion etc.)* stuffing
fum·meln ['fʊmln] *(fam)* [tr+intr v] +*haben* fiddle around ◊ *stundenlang an einer Reparatur fummeln* [intr v] +*haben*; *only pl (sexually)* pet
Fund [fʊnt] der <-(e)s, -e> find ◊ *archäologische Funde* einen Fund machen make a find; *(of a corpse, something unpleasant)* make a discovery
Fun·da·ment [fʊnda'mɛnt] das <-(e)s, -e> **1.** *(fig)* foundation ◊ *ein Fundament für die eigene Karriere legen* ♦ *Ruht unsere Demokratie auf einem soliden Fundament?* ⊜Basis, Grundlage **2.** foundations ◊ *Jedes Haus braucht ein festes Fundament.*
⑦ **Fund·bü·ro** ['fʊntby,roː] das <-s, -s> lost property office, lost and found office
fünf [fʏnf] [nmrl] five → vier
⑥ **fünf gerade sein lassen** *(fam)* turn a blind eye, bend the rules a little
Fünf [fʏnf] die <-, -en> **1.** five → Vier **1. 2.** *(fam) (bus, tram etc.)* number five → Vier **2. 3.** SCHOOL ⊜D ◊ *Mit zwei Fünfen im Zeugnis bleibt man sitzen.* eine Fünf schreiben get a D *box@* Note
fünf·fach ['fʏnffax] [adj, adv] *when used as an adj, only before ns* fivefold, five times → vierfach
fünf·te ['fʏnftə] [adj] <ein fünfter ..., eine fünfte ..., ein fünftes ...> fifth → vierte
Fünf·tel ['fʏnftl̩] das <-s, -> ein Fünftel (einer Sache [gen]/von etw./jdm) a fifth (of sth/sb) → Viertel
fünf·tens ['fʏnftns, 'fʏnftəns] [adv] fifthly → viertens
fünf·zehn ['fʏnftseːn] [nmrl] fifteen → vier
fünf·zig ['fʏnftsɪç] [nmrl] fifty → vier
Funk [fʊŋk] der <-s> *no pl* radio ◊ *bekannt durch/aus Funk und Fernsehen* per/über Funk by radio, over the radio ◊ *Der Pilot gab per Funk seine Position.* etw. über Funk steuern operate sth by remote control
Fun·ke ['fʊŋkə] der <-ns, -n> spark ◊ *Funken sprühten, als die Lok scharf bremste.* ♦ *Beim Schmieden fliegen Funken.*
⑥ **der zündende Funke** the vital spark **der Funke springt von jdm auf jdn über** (the) enthusiasm spreads from sb to sb **ein/kein Funke ...** [nom] a/not a glimmer of ..., a/not a scrap of ..., a/not a touch of ... ◊ *ein kleiner Funke Hoffnung* ♦ *keinen Funken Anstand/Verstand haben*
fun·keln ['fʊŋkln] [intr v] +*haben* **1.** *(fig) (eyes)* sparkle ◊ *Ihre Augen funkelten vor Vergnügen/ Begeisterung.*; *(with anger)* flash ◊ *Er stürmte mit funkelnden Augen aus dem Zimmer.* **2.** *(stars)* twinkle ◊ *Der Diamant funkelte im Licht.*; *(stars)* twinkle
fun·ken ['fʊŋkn̩] [tr+intr v] +*haben* radio, transmit ◊

SOS/einen Hilferuf funken [imp v] +*haben* es funkt sparks fly ◊ *Es funkte, als sie die Steine aufeinander schlug.*
⑥ **es funkt** *(fam)* sth clicks, the chemistry is right **es funkt (bei jdm)** the penny drops (with sb)
Fun·ken ['fʊŋkn̩] der <-s, -> → Funke
Funk·strei·fe ['fʊŋkʃtraefə] die <-, -n> police radio patrol
⑦ **funk·ti·o·nie·ren** [fʊŋktsjo'niːrən] <funktioniert, funktionierte, hat funktioniert> [intr v] **1.** function, work ◊ *Jetzt funktioniert die Heizung wieder.* ⊜gehen **2.** work out ◊ *Beim Umzug hat alles reibungslos funktioniert.* ♦ *Ich wollte sie überraschen, aber es hat nicht funktioniert.* ⊜klappen
⑦ **für** [fyːɐ] [prep] [+acc] for ◊ *Er hat Käse für das Abendessen gekauft.* ♦ *Das ist zu schwer für mich.* ♦ *Sport ist gut für den Rücken/die Gesundheit.* ♦ *Sie arbeitet für einen Verlag.* ♦ *jdn für etw. belohnen/bestrafen/loben/tadeln* ♦ *eine Pizza für fünf Euro* ♦ *für zwei Wochen in Urlaub fahren* ♦ *Wir haben uns für morgen verabredet.* ♦ *für einen Anfänger machst du das schon sehr gut.* ♦ *bei einer Wahl für jdn/etw. stimmen* sich für jdn/etw. entscheiden decide in favo(u)r of sb/sth
⑥ **für sich** alone ◊ *gern für sich bleiben*
Furcht [fʊrçt] die <-> *no pl* Furcht (vor etw./jdm) fear (of sth/sb) ◊ *Sie flohen aus Furcht vor dem Feind/einer Hungersnot.* ♦ *Furcht und Schrecken verbreiten* ⊜Angst
⑥ **Furcht einflößend/erregend** terrifying(ly) ◊ *Er schrie Furcht erregend (laut).*
⑦ **furcht·bar** ['fʊrçtbaːr] [adj, adv] *(also fam)* terrible(-bly), dreadful(ly), awful(ly) ◊ *eine Tat mit furchtbaren Folgen* ♦ *Der Geschmack ist furchtbar.* ♦ *Es tut mir so furchtbar Leid!* ♦ *sich furchtbar aufregen/ärgern* ♦ *Pst, es ist gerade furchtbar spannend!* ⊜fürchterlich, schrecklich
⑦ **fürch·ten** ['fʏrçtn̩] <fürchtet, fürchtete, hat gefürchtet> [tr v] fürchten, (dass) ... be afraid (that) ..., fear (that) ... ◊ *Ich fürchte, dass ihm etwas passiert ist.* ♦ *Ich fürchte, er hat Recht.* jdn/etw. fürchten be afraid of sb/sth, fear sb/sth ◊ *Du brauchst keine Konkurrenz zu fürchten.* etw. fürchten müssen be afraid of sth ◊ *Muss ich fürchten, meinen Job zu verlieren?* Sie fürchtet zu versagen. She is afraid of being a failure. [ref v] sich (vor etw./jdm) fürchten be afraid (of sth/sb) ◊ *Das Kind fürchtet sich vor Hunden/im Dunkeln.* ◊ *Er fürchtet sich davor, ihr die Wahrheit zu sagen.* [intr v] um etw. fürchten fear for sth ◊ *um die Existenz/den Job fürchten müssen* ♦ *Sie fürchtete um die Gesundheit ihres Kindes.*
fürch·ter·lich ['fʏrçtɐlɪç] [adj, adv] terrible(-bly), dreadful(ly), awful(ly) ◊ *Die Schmerzen sind fürchterlich.* ♦ *fürchterlicher Gestank* ♦ *sich fürchterlich aufregen/blamieren* ⊜furchtbar, schrecklich
für·ei·nan·der [fyːɐ|ae'nandɐ] [adv] for each other, for one another ◊ *Wir haben nie genug Zeit füreinander.* ♦ *Sie empfanden auf Anhieb Sympathie füreinander.*
fürs [fyːɐs] [contract] für + *das* **1.** for (the) ◊ *eine Garage fürs Auto* → für **2.** *in certain idioms, not to be split: look up the relevant idiom* ◊ *der Mann fürs Leben* → Erste
Für·sor·ge ['fyːɐzɔrgə] die <-> *no pl* **1.** care ◊ *elterliche/medizinische Fürsorge* **2.** welfare ◊

öffentliche/staatliche Fürsorge

Fürst [fʏ'st] der <-en, -en>, **Fürs·tin** ['fʏ'stɪn] die <-, -nen> prince ◊ *Fürst Rainier von Monaco* Fürstin princess ◊ *Fürstin Gloria von Thurn und Taxis*
ⓔ der *Fürst der Unterwelt* the Prince of Darkness

Für·wort ['fyːɐ̯vɔ'rt] das <-(e)s, Fürwörter> GRAM pronoun ◊ *besitzanzeigendes/persönliches/unbestimmtes Fürwort* ⊖Pronomen

fur·zen ['fʊ'tsn̩] intr v +*haben (rude)* fart

Fu·si·on [fu'zjoːn] die <-, -en> 1. ECON merger ◊ *die Fusion von Daimler und/mit Chrysler* 2. PHYSICS fusion

② **Fuß** [fuːs] der <-es, Füße> 1. foot ◊ *eine Blase am linken Fuß haben* 2. *(of a piece of furniture etc.)* base, foot ◊ *eine Stehlampe mit einem Fuß aus Metall*
ⓔ *auf eigenen Füßen stehen* stand on your own two feet *auf freiem Fuß sein* be at large ◊ *Der Bankräuber ist immer noch auf freiem Fuß.* *jdn auf freien Fuß setzen* release sb, set sb free *gut/schlecht zu Fuß sein* 1. be steady/unsteady on your legs ◊ *Sie ist fast achtzig, aber noch recht gut zu Fuß.* 2. like/not like walking *trockenen Fußes* without getting wet *irgendwo Fuß fassen* gain a foothold somewhere, become established somewhere *(einer Sache* dat*) auf dem Fuß(e) folgen* follow (in the wake of sth), follow (sth) swiftly *jdm zu Füßen liegen (lofty)* be under sb's spell ◊ *Die ganze Stadt lag dem Star zu Füßen.* *jdm auf den Fuß/die Füße treten (fam)* 1. tread on sb's toes 2. *(a slowcoach)* chivvy sb along *etw./jdn mit Füßen treten* trample all over sth/sb ◊ *die Menschenrechte/sein Glück mit Füßen treten* *jdm etw. vor die Füße werfen* tell sb that they can keep/stuff sth *am Fuß(e)* ... gen *at the foot of sth* ◊ *am Fuße des Kilimandscharo/Empire State Buildings* *zu jds Füßen* at sb's feet *zu Fuß* on foot ◊ *zu Fuß gehen* *Wir sind zu Fuß gekommen.*

② **Fuß·ball** ['fuːsbal] der <-(e)s, Fußbälle> 1. *often without the article, no pl* football, soccer ◊ *Fußball spielen* *der europäische Fußball* 2. football, soccer ball ◊ *ein Fußball aus Leder*

Fuß·bo·den ['fuːsboːdn̩] der <-s, Fußböden> floor ◊ *etw. auf den Fußboden legen/stellen* *etw. vom Fußboden aufheben* ⊖Boden ⊖Decke

② **Fuß·gän·ger** ['fuːsgɛŋɐ] der <-s, ->, **Fuß·gän·ge·rin** ['fuːsgɛŋərɪn] die <-, -nen> pedestrian

② **Fuß·gän·ger·zo·ne** ['fuːsgɛŋɐtsoːnə] die <-, -n> pedestrian zone/precinct ◊ *Mein Laden liegt in der Fußgängerzone.*

Fuß·no·te ['fuːsnoːtə] die <-, -n> footnote ◊ *eine Fußnote machen/setzen* ⊖Anmerkung

Fut·ter ['fʊte] das <-s, -> 1. lining ◊ *ein Mantel mit einem Futter aus Seide* 2. *no pl* fodder, *(animal)* feed ◊ *Futter und Wasser bekommen* *das Futter für die Hühner*

fut·tern ['fʊtɐn] tr+intr v +*haben (fam)* scoff, polish off ◊ *Was gibt's denn heute zu futtern?*

füt·tern ['fʏtɐn] tr v +*haben* 1. ein Tier/jdn (mit etw.) füttern feed an animal/sb ((with) sth) ◊ *Enten füttern* *Pferde mit Heu füttern* *ein Baby mit Brei füttern* ein Baby mit der Flasche füttern bottle-feed a baby *(einem Tier) etw. füttern* give (an animal) sth as food 2. *(a computer, machine) etw. mit etw. füttern* put sth into sth, feed sth with sth ◊ *Er fütterte den Spielautomaten mit Kleingeld.* 3. *mostly passive* line ◊ *Die Stiefel sind mit Schaffell gefüttert.*

Fu·tur [fu'tuːɐ̯] das <-s, -e> *most sing* GRAM future tense

> The German future tense consists of the appropriate form of *werden* and the infinitive of the relevant verb: *Wir werden dich morgen besuchen.* However, it is very common to express the future simply by using the present tense and a temporal adverb: *Und am Abend gibt es dann noch eine Party.* The future tense is frequently used to state how one feels about a situation. Thus it might express hesitation *(Wir werden uns noch überlegen, ob wir da wirklich mitmachen wollen.)*, a threat *(Du wirst jetzt dein Zimmer sofort aufräumen!)*, a prophecy or forecast *(In circa drei Jahren wird es der Firma besser gehen.)* or reassurance *(Hab keine Angst, sie wird schon wiederkommen.).*

G

g, G [ge:] das <–(s), –(s)> **1.** g, G ◊ *Dieses Wort wird mit einem kleinen g/großen G geschrieben.* ♦ *G wie Gustav* **2.** MUS G ◊ *Spielen Sie ein G.*

② **gab** [ga:p] *pret of* geben

Ga·be ['ga:bə] die <–, –n> **1.** *(lofty)* gift, present ◊ *die Gaben unterm Weihnachtsbaum* ⊖Geschenk **2.** *(lofty)* gift ◊ *Er besitzt die Gabe, mit allen gut auszukommen.* ⊖Begabung **3.** *no pl (tech)* die Gabe von etw., die Gabe ... [gen] the use of sth; *(of medicines)* the administering of sth **4.** *(tech)* eine Gabe von etw., eine Gabe ... [gen] a dose of sth ◊ *Schon bald nach der ersten Gabe des Medikaments ging es ihm besser.* ⊖Dosis

◉ **milde Gabe(n)** alms

② **Ga·bel** ['ga:bl̩] die <–, –n> **1.** fork ◊ *mit Messer und Gabel essen* ♦ *die Kartoffeln mit der Gabel zerdrücken* ♦ *etw. mit der Gabel aufspießen* **2.** *(of an old-fashioned telephone)* cradle **3.** AGR (pitch)fork ◊ *mit der Gabel Mist auf dem Beet verteilen*

gäh·nen ['gɛ:nən] [intr v] +*haben* **1.** yawn ◊ *Das Publikum gähnte vor Langeweile.* **2.** *(lofty, fig)* yawn ◊ *Vor mir gähnte der Abgrund.* gähnende Löcher gaping holes

Gal·le ['galə] die <–, –n> **1.** ANAT gall bladder ◊ *jdn an der Galle operieren* **2.** *no pl* bile ◊ *Der Kranke erbricht Galle.*

② **galt** [galt] *pret of* gelten

② **Gang** [gaŋ] der <–(e)s, Gänge> **1.** TECHN gear ◊ *in den ersten/zweiten etc. Gang schalten* ♦ *den vierten Gang einlegen* ♦ *einen Gang zurückschalten* **2.** passageway, walkway ◊ *Über diesen Gang gelangt man ins Hauptgebäude.*; *(in a building)* hallway, corridor ◊ *An diesem Gang liegen vier Zimmer.*; *(subterranean)* tunnel, subway; *(in an aircraft, a cinema, theatre, train)* aisle ◊ *Willst du am Gang oder am Fenster sitzen?* **3.** *translation varies, no pl* der Gang zur Toilette (the) visit to the toilet der Gang zur Urne the way to the ballot box ein schwerer Gang sein be a difficult thing to do, be a struggle **4.** *no pl* gait ◊ *Sie hat einen federnden, leichten Gang.* **5.** *(of a meal)* course ◊ *ein Menü aus/mit fünf Gängen* **6.** course ◊ *den Gang der Ermittlungen behindern/stören* ♦ *Alles geht seinen gewohnten Gang.* ⊖Verlauf

◉ **der Gang zur/an die Börse** ECON (the) flotation on the stock market **etw. in Gang bringen/setzen** get sth going, start sth *(a development)* spark sth, trigger sth **etw. in Gang halten** keep sth going **in Gang kommen** get going **im Gang(e) sein, in Gang sein** be underway ◊ *Die Feier war schon im vollen Gang, als er kam.* **sich in Gang setzen** start to move *(person)* get moving

gän·gig ['gɛŋɪç] [adj] current, common, usual ◊ *Wir akzeptieren alle gängigen Kreditkarten.* ♦ *Welche Arbeitszeiten sind in diesem Beruf gängig?*

Gans [gans] die <–, Gänse> **1.** ZOO goose ◊ *Gänse halten/hüten/schlachten/rupfen* ♦ *Es gibt Gans süßsauer mit Ananas.* **2.** *(fam, pej)* cow ◊ *Du dumme Gans!*

Gän·se·haut ['gɛnzəhaʊt] die <–> *no pl* goose pimples, goose bumps ◊ *eine Gänsehaut bekommen/haben*

② **ganz** [gants] [adv] quite ◊ *Es ist ganz anders als du denkst.* ♦ *Keine Angst, das geht ganz einfach/leicht.* ♦ *Ich habe mir auch ganz viel Mühe gegeben.* ♦ *„Gefällt dir das Kleid?" — „Ja, ganz gut.";* *(indicating position)* right ◊ *Das steht ganz vorne im Buch.* [adj] <ein ganzer..., eine ganze..., ein ganzes ...> **1.** *only before ns* ganze whole ◊ *die ganze Welt/Familie;* *(when referring to a geographical area)* the whole of ◊ *Diese Regelung gilt in ganz Europa/Österreich/Berlin.* **2.** *only before ns (fam)* all ◊ *Ist das das ganze Geld, das du noch hast?* ♦ *Hast du die ganzen Bücher hier gelesen?* **3.** *before figures and quantities, only before ns (fam)* quite ◊ *Das ist eine ganze Menge/ein ganzer Haufen!;* *(when referring to a period of time)* a whole ◊ *Wir haben ganze zwei Stunden auf den Zug warten müssen.; just* ◊ *Es hat nur ganze zwei Minuten gedauert.* **4.** *(fam)* intact ◊ *Der Teller ist runtergefallen, aber ganz geblieben.* etw. ganz machen mend sth ⊖heil

◉ **ganz schön** *(fam)* quite ◊ *Das hat ganz schön viel Geld gekostet.* ♦ *Das hat mich ganz schön geärgert.* **ganz und gar** totally, absolutely ⊖völlig **ganz und gar nicht** not at all Das finde ich ganz und gar nicht lustig! I don't find that at all funny! **ganz zu schweigen von etw./jdm** to say nothing of sth/sb ◊ *Der Unfall hat mich viel Geld gekostet, vom Ärger ganz zu schweigen.*

Gan·ze ['gantsə] das <–n> *no pl* **1.** whole ◊ *Der Stadtkern bildet ein geschlossenes Ganzes. im (großen) Ganzen* on the whole; *(with figures, quantities)* in all, in total ◊ *Im Ganzen hat der Urlaub 2000 Euro gekostet.* **2.** das Ganze the thing, it ◊ *Wie soll das Ganze eigentlich funktionieren?*

◉ **aufs Ganze gehen** *(fam)* go all out, go for broke **es geht ums Ganze** everything is at stake **aufs Ganze gesehen** all in all

ganz·tä·gig ['gantstɛ:gɪç] [adj] all-day ◊ *eine ganztägige Veranstaltung/Betreuung* [adv] all day ◊ *werktags ganztägig geöffnet*

gar¹ [ga:ʳ] [adj] cooked, done ◊ *Die Kartoffeln sind noch nicht gar. etw. bei schwacher Hitze gar kochen* cook sth on a low heat (until it is done)

② **gar²** [ga:ʳ] [adv] at all ◊ *Das hat von gar nichts damit zu tun.* ♦ *Ich habe heute gar keine Lust zum Arbeiten.* ♦ *Das hab ich doch gar nicht gesagt!* ⊖überhaupt

gar³ [ga:ʳ] [part] **1.** gar so/zu really, so ◊ *Das würde ich gar zu gerne machen.* ♦ *Warum hast du es denn gar so eilig?* **2.** *(intensifying sth negative)* even ◊ *Ist er verletzt oder gar tot?* wenn nicht gar if not ⊖sogar **3.** *(iron, emph)*

actually ◊ *Er glaubte gar, man würde ihn dafür befördern!* ⊜tatsächlich

② **Ga·ra·ge** [ga'raːʒə] die <-, -n> garage ◊ *das Auto in der Garage abstellen/in die Garage fahren*

② **Ga·ran·tie** [garan'tiː] die <-, -n> **1.** TRADE guarantee, warranty ◊ *Das Gerät hat eine Garantie von zwei Jahren.* ♦ *Diese Schäden fallen nicht unter die Garantie.* ♦ „*Geht die Reparatur noch auf Garantie?*" — „*Nein, die Garantie ist leider schon abgelaufen.*" eine Garantie auf etw. [dat] a guarantee on sth, a warranty on sth ◊ *Auf dem Gerät ist eine Garantie von zwei Jahren.* **2.** eine Garantie (für etw./einer Sache [gen]) a guarantee (of sth) ◊ *Reichtum ist keine Garantie für Glück.* keine Garantie für die Richtigkeit der Angaben übernehmen accept no responsibility for the accuracy of the data/information **3.** FIN security, surety ◊ *Was erkennt die Bank als Garantie für einen Kredit an?*

ga·ran·tie·ren [garan'tiːrən] <garantiert, garantierte, hat garantiert> [tr+intr v] (jdm) etw. garantieren guarantee (sb) sth ◊ *Das neue Verfahren garantiert bessere Qualität.* ♦ *die Menschen- und Bürgerrechte garantieren* (jdm) garantieren, dass guarantee that, swear to it that ◊ *Garantierst du mir, dass ich die CD heil zurückbekomme?* für etw. garantieren guarantee sth, swear to sth ◊ „*Wird es klappen?*" — „*Ich garantiere für nichts!*" dafür garantieren, dass swear that

② **Gar·de·ro·be** [gaʁdə'roːbə] die <-, -n> **1.** (*in a theatre, museum*) cloakroom ◊ *seinen Mantel an der Garderobe abgeben/in der Garderobe lassen* **2.** hatstand ◊ *seinen Hut/Mantel an die Garderobe hängen* **3.** (*for an actor*) dressing room **4.** wardrobe, clothing ◊ *Sie schneidert ihre Garderobe selbst.* **5.** coat(s) and hat(s) ◊ *Wo kann ich meine Garderobe abgeben/ablegen?*

Gar·di·ne [gaʁ'diːnə] die <-, -n> net curtain ◉ hinter schwedische(n) Gardinen behind bars

ga·ren ['gaːrən] [tr+intr v] +haben cook ◊ *den Spargel fünfzehn Minuten in Salzwasser garen* ♦ *Der Braten gart seit zwei Stunden im Ofen.*; (*on a low heat*) simmer

Garn [gaʁn] das <-(e)s, -e> thread ◊ *zu Garn versponnene Wolle* ♦ *ein Knäuel/eine Rolle Garn*

gar·nie·ren [gaʁ'niːrən] <garniert, garnierte, hat garniert> [tr v] (*also fig*) etw. (mit etw.) garnieren garnish sth (with sth) ◊ *Er garnierte die Soße mit Basilikumblättern.* ♦ *Sie garnierte ihre Rede mit witzigen Anekdoten.*

② **Gar·ten** ['gaʁtn̩] der <-s, Gärten> garden ◊ *Blumen/Gemüse/Obst aus dem eigenen Garten* ♦ *Er fand sie im Garten hinter dem Haus.* der botanische Garten the botanical gardens der zoologische Garten the zoo

Gärt·ner ['gɛʁtnɐ] der <-s, ->, **Gärt·ne·rin** ['gɛʁtnərɪn] die <-, -nen> gardener ◊ *Er arbeitet als Gärtner bei der Stadt.* ♦ *Die Gärtnerin schneidet die Rosen.*

Gärt·ne·rei [gɛʁtnə'raɪ] die <-, -en> nursery

② **Gas** [gaːs] das <-es, -e> **1.** CHEM gas ◊ *Bei dem Unfall wurden giftige Gase frei.* ♦ *Heizt ihr mit Gas oder Öl?* **2.** (*fam*) (*of a vehicle*) accelerator ◊ *aufs Gas treten* ♦ *den Fuß vom Gas nehmen* ♦ *vom Gas gehen* Gas geben put your foot down (das) Gas wegnehmen take your foot off the accel-

erator

Gas·pe·dal ['gaːspeˌdaːl] das <-s, -e> most sing accelerator (pedal) ◊ *aufs Gaspedal drücken/treten*

Gas·se ['gasə] die <-, -n> alley(way) ◊ *durch eine enge/schmale Gasse fahren* ♦ *in den verwinkelten Gassen der Altstadt*

② **Gast** [gast] der <-(e)s, Gäste> **1.** guest ◊ *ein geladener/ungebetener Gast* ♦ *Gäste erwarten/haben* ♦ *Als Gäste in meiner Talkshow darf ich heute begrüßen: ... zu Gast sein* be a guest **2.** (*in a hotel, restaurant*) guest, customer, patron **3.** only pl SPORT Gäste visitors, visiting team ⊜Gastgeber

Gast·ar·bei·ter ['gast|aɐ̯baɪtɐ] der <-s, ->, **Gast·ar·bei·te·rin** ['gast|aɐ̯ˌbaɪtərɪn] die <-, -nen> (*oldf*) immigrant worker, foreign worker ◊ *Gastarbeiter anwerben* ♦ *osteuropäische Gastarbeiter*

Gäs·te·zim·mer ['gɛstətsɪmɐ] das <-s, -> **1.** guest/spare room ◊ *Du kannst bei uns im Gästezimmer übernachten.* **2.** (hotel) room ◊ *In der Stadt gibt es 200 Gästezimmer.* ⊜Fremdenzimmer

② **Gast·freund·schaft** ['gastfrɔ͜yntʃaft] die <-> no pl hospitality

Gast·ge·ber ['gastgeːbɐ] der <-s, ->, **Gast·ge·be·rin** ['gastgeːbərɪn] die <-, -nen> **1.** host, hostess ⊜Gast **2.** most pl SPORT home team/side ◊ *Das Spiel endete drei zu eins für die Gastgeber.* ⊜Gäste

② **Gast·haus** ['gasthaʊs] das <-es, Gasthäuser> inn ◊ *in einem Gasthaus übernachten*

Gast·hof ['gasthoːf] der <-(e)s, Gasthöfe> ⊜Gasthaus

Gas·tro·no·mie [gastrono'miː] die <-> no pl (*tech*) catering (trade) ◊ *Sie ist seit zehn Jahren in der Gastronomie tätig.*

② **Gast·stät·te** ['gastʃtɛtə] die <-, -n> pub, restaurant ◊ *Er betreibt eine Gaststätte.*

Gast·wirt ['gastvɪʁt] der <-(e)s, -e>, **Gast·wir·tin** ['gastvɪʁtɪn] die <-, -nen> pub landlord, restaurant owner, pub landlady ◊ *ein beliebter Gastwirt aus der Region* Gastwirt sein own a pub/restaurant ◊ *Seine Mutter ist Gastwirtin.*

Gat·te ['gatə] der <-n, -n>, **Gat·tin** ['gatɪn] die <-, -nen> (*lofty, also oldf or hum*) spouse

Gat·tung ['gatʊŋ] die <-, -en> **1.** ARTS genre, form ◊ *Welche literarische Gattungen bevorzugt dieser Autor?* **2.** BIO genus ◊ *Die Weiden gehören zur Gattung Salix.* ◉ eine aussterbende Gattung a dying breed

Gau·men ['gaʊmən] der <-s, -> **1.** roof of the/sb's mouth ◊ *Die Erdnussbutter blieb am Gaumen kleben.* **2.** (*fig*) palate ◊ *Das Essen war ein Fest für Auge und Gaumen.*

Gau·ner ['gaʊnɐ] der <-s, ->, **Gau·ne·rin** ['gaʊnərɪn] die <-, -nen> **1.** (*also fig*) crook ◊ *Die Gauner erbeuteten über zwei Millionen Euro.* **2.** (*fam, hum*) rascal ◊ *Unser Hund ist ein richtiger Gauner!*

ge·ach·tet [gə'axtət] past p of achten [adj] respected ◊ *Er ist ein allseits geachteter Mann.*

② **Ge·bäck** [gə'bɛk] das <-(e)s> no pl biscuits, cookies ◊ *Sie servierte ihnen Kaffee und Gebäck.* salziges/süßes Gebäck savo(u)ry/sweet pastries

② **ge·ba·cken** [gə'bakŋ̍] past p of backen

ge·ballt [gə'balt] *past p of* ballen ⸢adj⸣ concentrated ◊ *ein Roman mit einer geballten Ladung Erotik* mit geballter Kraft with all your might
ge·bannt [gə'bant] *past p of* bannen ⸢adj⸣ fascinated, spellbound ◊ *Das Publikum war gebannt von seiner Geschichte.* ♦ *Im Saal herrschte gebannte Stille.* ⸢adv⸣ (wie) gebannt (as if) transfixed ◊ *Wie gebannt blickte er auf den Monitor.*
② **ge·bar** [gə'baːɐ] *pret of* gebären
Ge·bär·de [gə'bɛːɐdə] die <–, –n> gesture ◊ *ausholende Gebärden* ♦ *Er machte drohende Gebärden.*
② **ge·bä·ren** [gə'bɛːrən] <gebiert, gebar, hat geboren> ⸢intr v⸣ give birth ◊ *Immer mehr Frauen gebären ambulant im Krankenhaus.* ⸢tr v⸣ **1.** give birth to ◊ *ein Kind gebären* ♦ *Sie hat eine gesunde Tochter geboren.* **2.** geboren werden be born ◊ *1970 wurde ihr erster Sohn geboren.* ♦ *Diese Idee wurde bereits vor zehn Jahren geboren.* Er ist am 25. Mai 1986 geboren. He was born on 25th May in 1986.
② **Ge·bäu·de** [gə'bɔɣdə] das <–s, –> building ◊ *ein riesiges/leer stehendes Gebäude* ♦ *Sie hat ihr Büro im 1. Stock des Gebäudes.*
② **ge·ben** ['geːbm̩] <gibt, gab, hat gegeben> ⸢tr v⸣ **1.** give ◊ *Du solltest dir eine Quittung geben lassen.* ♦ *Er gab ihr 20 Euro als Belohnung.* ♦ *Du solltest mir noch eine Chance/etwas Zeit geben.* ♦ *Der Verkäufer gab mir 5% Rabatt.* ♦ *Die Nachricht gab ihm Hoffnung/neuen Mut.* ♦ *Ich gebe dir mein Wort darauf.* **2.** +*inf* jdm etw. zu ... geben give sb sth to ... ◊ *Er gab dem Kind etwas zu trinken/ essen.* ♦ *Er gab uns einen Text zum Übersetzen.* **3.** jdn/etw. irgendwohin geben take sb/sth somewhere, leave sb/sth somewhere ◊ *Ich gebe den Mantel in die/zur Reinigung.* ♦ *Sie gaben den Hund ins Tierheim.*; *(manuscript)* in Druck gegeben werden go to press, be printed **4.** jdm Bescheid geben let sb know jdm das Versprechen geben, etw. zu tun promise sb that you will do sth **5.** *(fam)* teach ◊ *Sie gibt Chemie und Biologie.* **6.** *(on the telephone)* jdm jdn/etw. geben put sb through to sb/sth ◊ *Er ließ sich den zuständigen Mitarbeiter geben.* **7.** *(a concert etc.)* give ◊ *ein Konzert geben; (a party)* throw ◊ *ein großes Essen/eine Party geben* **8.** *(a goal, free kick etc.)* allow ◊ *Der Schiedsrichter gab einen Elfmeter.* **9.** produce ◊ *Die Ziege gibt Milch.* ♦ *Feuer gibt Wärme und Licht.* **10.** *(fam) (have as a result)* make ◊ *Fünf mal zehn gibt fünfzig.* **11.** auf etw. ⸢acc⸣ nichts geben pay no attention to sth, not think much of sth ◊ *Er gibt nichts auf die Meinung anderer.* auf etw. ⸢acc⸣ viel geben pay a lot of attention to sth, set great store by sth ⸢imp v⸣ **1.** es gibt there is/are ◊ *In dieser Stadt gibt es viele Sehenswürdigkeiten.* ♦ *Es gibt Spaghetti mit Soße.* ♦ *Es gibt viele Neuigkeiten.* ♦ *Wird es Krieg geben?* **2.** *(be for sale)* be available ◊ *Die Karten gibt es nur an der Abendkasse.* ⸢ref v⸣ **1.** sich ... geben behave in a ... way, act in a ... way ◊ *Er gab sich recht freundlich/selbstbewusst.* **2.** sich geben go away, disappear ◊ *Diese Probleme werden sich mit der Zeit geben.* ⸢intr v⸣ CARDS do the dealing, deal ◊ *Wer gibt?* ♦ *Du gibst.*
⊙ das gibt's (doch) nicht I don't believe it was gibt's Neues? what's new?, any news? es jdm geben *(fam)* **1.** *(beat sb)* give it to sb **2.** tell sb what you think, tell it to sb straight was gibt's?

what's up?
Ge·bet [gə'beːt] das <–(e)s, –e> prayer ◊ *ein Gebet sprechen* jdn zum Gebet aufrufen urge sb to pray
② **ge·be·ten** [gə'beːtn̩] *past p of* bitten
② **Ge·biet** [gə'biːt] das <–(e)s, –e> **1.** area ◊ *die ländlichen Gebiete Chinas*; *(geographical)* region ◊ *ein geologisch interessantes Gebiet* **2.** *(scientific etc.)* field ◊ *Auf welchem Gebiet forscht sie/ist er tätig?*
Ge·bil·de [gə'bɪldə] das <–s, –> *(also fig)* structure ◊ *Afghanistan ist politisch immer noch ein fragiles Gebilde.*; *(shaped form)* creation ◊ *kunstvolle Gebilde aus Marzipan*
ge·bil·det [gə'bɪldət] *past p of* bilden ⸢adj⸣ educated ◊ *ein vielseitig gebildeter Mann* juristisch/medizinisch gebildet with legal/medical training ⊖ungebildet
② **Ge·bir·ge** [gə'bɪrgə] das <–s, –> mountains ◊ *ins Gebirge fahren* ♦ *Sie waren im Gebirge wandern/ klettern.*
Ge·biss [gə'bɪs] das <–es, –e> **1.** ANAT (set of) teeth ◊ *ein völlig gesundes Gebiss* **2.** ein (künstliches/falsches) Gebiss (a set of) false teeth, (a set of) dentures ◊ *Sie trägt ein falsches Gebiss.* **3.** *(part of a bridle)* bit ◊ *Er schob dem Pferd das Gebiss ins Maul.*
ge·bis·sen [gə'bɪsn̩] *past p of* beißen
ge·bla·sen [gə'blaːzn̩] *past p of* blasen
② **ge·blie·ben** [gə'bliːbm̩] *past p of* bleiben
ge·blümt [gə'blyːmt] ⸢adj⸣ *no comp/superl* flowered, flowery ◊ *ein geblümtes Kleid rot/weiß/blau* geblümt with red/white/blue flowers
ge·bo·gen [gə'boːgn̩] *past p of* biegen ⸢adj⸣ *no comp/superl* bent, curved ◊ *ein leicht gebogenes Dach*
② **ge·bo·ren** [gə'boːrən] *past p of* gebären ⸢adj⸣ *only before ns* **1.** *(with maiden names)* geborene ... née ◊ *Cornelia Jaekel, geborene Baum* Sie ist eine geborene Beck. Her maiden name was Beck. **2.** *only before ns* born ◊ *ein in München geborener Künstler* ein geborener Hamburger sein be born in Hamburg **3.** *(used to describe a talent or gift)* born ◊ *Sie ist die/eine geborene Schauspielerin.*
② **ge·bo·ren wer·den** [gə'boːrən ˌveːɐdn̩] → gebären
ge·bor·gen [gə'bɔrgn̩] ⸢adj⸣ safe ◊ *Er fühlte sich bei ihr geborgen.* ♦ *in einer geborgenen Umgebung aufwachsen*
Ge·bot [gə'boːt] das <–(e)s, –e> **1.** principle, precept ◊ *Freundliches Grüßen ist ein Gebot der Höflichkeit.* **2.** REL Commandment ◊ *Das fünfte Gebot heißt „Du sollst nicht töten".* **3.** das oberste Gebot sein, das Gebot der Stunde sein be top priority ◊ *Es ist das Gebot der Stunde, die Steuern zu senken.* ♦ *Sicherheit für alle ist oberstes Gebot.* **4.** *(at auctions etc.)* bid ◊ *Das letzte Gebot lautet 125 Euro.*
② **ge·bo·ten** [gə'boːtn̩] *past p of* bieten
② **ge·bracht** [gə'braxt] *past p of* bringen
② **ge·brannt** [gə'brant] *past p of* brennen ⸢adj⸣ *no comp/superl, only before ns* caramelised, caramelized ◊ *gebrannte Mandeln*
② **ge·bra·ten** [gə'braːtn̩] *past p of* braten
Ge·brauch [gə'braɔx] der <–(e)s, Gebräuche> **1.** *no pl* use ◊ *Gegenstände des täglichen Gebrauchs* etw. in Gebrauch nehmen use sth ◊

1968 wurde der Aufzug zum ersten Mal in Gebrauch genommen.; (an object) von etw. Gebrauch machen use sth ◊ *Er machte von der Schusswaffe Gebrauch.* **2.** *(of a possibility, right)* von etw. Gebrauch machen make use of sth, take sth up ◊ *Sie machte von ihrem Wahlrecht keinen Gebrauch.* **3.** *most pl* custom ◊ *fremde/religiöse Gebräuche*

② **ge·brau·chen** [gəˈbraoxn̩] <gebraucht, gebrauchte, hat gebraucht> [tr v] **1.** use ◊ *Du gebrauchst viele Fremdwörter.* ◆ *Wie gebraucht man einen Kompass?* **2.** jdn/etw. gebrauchen können can use sb/sth; *(find sb/sth helpful)* jdn/etw. gebrauchen können can do with sb/sth ◊ *Ein bisschen Unterstützung könnte ich gut gebrauchen.* jd/etw. ist zu nichts zu gebrauchen sb/sth is useless, sb/sth is good for nothing

ge·bräuch·lich [gəˈbrɔøçlɪç] [adj] usual, recognized ◊ *ein heute noch gebräuchliche Redewendung/ Bezeichnung* ◆ *eine alte Methode, die immer noch gebräuchlich ist* ◆ *Was ist die gebräuchlichere Methode/Bezeichnung?*

Ge·brauchs·an·lei·tung [gəˈbraoxs|anlaetʊŋ] die <-, -en> → Gebrauchsanweisung

② **Ge·brauchs·an·wei·sung** [gəˈbraoxs|anvaezʊŋ] die <-, -en> instructions, instruction manual ◊ *Lesen Sie bitte die Gebrauchsanweisung genau durch.*

ge·braucht [gəˈbraoxt] *past p of* brauchen, gebrauchen [adj] *no comp/superl* used ◊ *gebrauchte Spielsachen* etw. gebraucht kaufen buy sth secondhand

ge·brech·lich [gəˈbrɛçlɪç] [adj] frail, infirm ◊ *alte und gebrechliche Menschen* ◆ *Mutter Theresa sah zierlich und gebrechlich aus.*

ge·bro·chen [gəˈbrɔxn̩] *past p of* brechen [adj, adv] *when used as an adj, mostly before ns* broken ◊ *eine gebrochene Linie* ◆ *Sie starb 1920 als gebrochene Frau.* gebrochen Deutsch/Italienisch sprechen speak broken German, Italian

② **Ge·bühr** [gəˈbyːɐ̯] die <-, -en> fee ◊ *Ab Mai müssen Studierende höhere Gebühren zahlen.* ◆ *Die Gebühr für die Entsorgung von Sperrmüll beträgt zurzeit 20 Euro.*

ge·büh·ren·pflich·tig [gəˈbyːrənpflɪçtɪç] [adj] *(form)* liable to a fee ◊ *ein gebührenpflichtiger Parkplatz* gebührenpflichtige Autobahn toll road, turnpike gebührenpflichtige Verwarnung fine

ge·bun·den [gəˈbʊndn̩] *past p of* binden

② **Ge·burt** [gəˈbuːɐ̯t] die <-, -en> birth ◊ *Bei der Geburt ihres zweiten Kindes war sie 36 Jahre alt.* ◆ *Die Geburt wurde künstlich eingeleitet.* ◆ *Sie ist seit ihrer Geburt/von Geburt an blind.* ◆ *Er war Schwede von Geburt.*

ge·bür·tig [gəˈbʏrtɪç] [adj] *Sie ist gebürtige Engländerin. She was born in England.*

Ge·burts·da·tum [gəˈbuːɐ̯tsdaːtʊm] das <-s, Geburtsdaten> date of birth

② **Ge·burts·ort** [gəˈbuːɐ̯ts|ɔˈt] der <-(e)s, -e> place of birth

② **Ge·burts·tag** [gəˈbuːɐ̯tstaːk] der <-(e)s, -e> **1.** birthday ◊ *Er feiert heute seinen 80. Geburtstag.* ◆ *Sie hat morgen Geburtstag.* ◆ *jdm zum Geburtstag gratulieren* **2.** *(form) (on official documents etc.)* date of birth

Ge·burts·ur·kun·de [gəˈbuːɐ̯ts|u:ɐ̯kʊndə] die <-, -n> birth certificate

Ge·büsch [gəˈbʏʃ] das <-(e)s, -e> bushes ◊ *Die Beute hatte er im Gebüsch versteckt.*

ge·dacht [gəˈdaxt] *past p of* denken, gedenken

Ge·dächt·nis [gəˈdɛçtnɪs] das <-ses, -se> *no pl* memory ◊ *Nach dem Unfall hatte er sein Gedächtnis verloren.* ◆ *ein ausgezeichnetes Gedächtnis haben* ◆ sich etw. ins Gedächtnis rufen ◆ *ein Denkmal zum Gedächtnis an die Opfer des Krieges*

② **Ge·dan·ke** [gəˈdaŋkə] der <-ns, -n> **1.** thought ◊ *Sie spielt mit dem Gedanken zu kündigen.* ◆ *Ihre Gedanken kreisten um ihren nächsten Urlaub.* der Gedanke (an etw./jdn) the (very) thought (of sth/ sb) ◊ *Schon beim Gedanken an Oliven wurde ihr übel.* ◆ *Der bloße Gedanke löste in ihm Panik aus.* keinen Gedanken an etw./jdn verschwenden not waste any time thinking about sth/of sb in Gedanken versunken lost in thought **2.** sich [dat] (über jdn/etw.) Gedanken machen worry (about sb/sth) ◊ *Ich machte mir Gedanken über meine Zukunft.* ◆ *Ich habe mir schon Gedanken gemacht, wo er wohl bleibt.* **3.** *only pl* thought, opinion ◊ *Die beiden tauschten ihren Gedanken über den Film aus.* **4.** idea ◊ *auf dumme Gedanken kommen*

ge·dan·ken·los [gəˈdaŋkl̩o:s] [adj] thoughtless, inconsiderate ◊ *der gedankenlose Umgang mit Trinkwasser* ◆ *Wie kann man nur so gedankenlos sein!* ⊖unbedacht [adv] **1.** unthinkingly ◊ *Medikamente werden oft gedankenlos eingenommen.* ⊖unüberlegt **2.** absent-mindedly ◊ *Sie blickte gedankenlos aus dem Fenster.*

Ge·dan·ken·strich [gəˈdaŋkŋ̍ʃtrɪç] der <-(e)s, -e> dash ◊ *Er setzte einen Gedankenstrich.*

Ge·deck [gəˈdɛk] das <-(e)s, -e> *(lofty) (at a meal)* place ◊ *Pro Tisch wurden vier Gedecke aufgelegt.*

ge·den·ken [gəˈdɛŋkŋ̍] <gedenkt, gedachte, hat gedacht> [tr v] *no passive (lofty)* gedenken, etw. zu tun think of doing sth ◊ *Er gedenkt, ein Haus zu kaufen.* [intr v] jds/einer Sache gedenken remember sb/sth, commemorate sb/sth ◊ *Sie gedachten der Verstorbenen.*

Ge·denk·stät·te [gəˈdɛŋkʃtɛtə] die <-, -n> memorial site

Ge·dicht [gəˈdɪçt] das <-(e)s, -e> poem ◊ *Sie schreibt Gedichte.* ◆ *ein Gedicht von Trakl/Shakespeare* ⦿ etw. ist ein Gedicht sth is delightful

Ge·drän·ge [gəˈdrɛŋə] das <-s> *no pl* **1.** pushing (and shoving), crush ◊ *Im Saal herrschte dichtes Gedränge.* **2.** crowd, mass of people ◊ *Er verschwand blitzschnell im Gedränge.*

Ge·drän·gel [gəˈdrɛŋl̩] das <-s> *no pl (fam)* pushing (and shoving) ◊ *Es gab ein großes Gedrängel um die besten Plätze.*

ge·drängt [gəˈdrɛŋt] *past p of* drängen [adj] terse ◊ *Der Kurs gibt eine gedrängte Übersicht über die literarischen Epochen.; (programme of events, diary)* der gedrängt gefüllte Terminkalender

ge·drückt [gəˈdrʏkt] *past p of* drücken [adj] depressed, dejected ◊ *Es herrschte gedrückte Stimmung.*

ge·drun·gen [gəˈdrʊŋən] *past p of* dringen

Ge·duld [gəˈdʊlt] die <-> *no pl* patience ◊ *Sie ertragt ihre Krankheit mit viel Geduld.* ◆ *Allmählich verlor er die Geduld.* Geduld mit jdm haben be patient with sb

ge·dul·den [gə'dʊldn̩] <geduldet sich, geduldete sich, hat sich geduldet> [ref v] *(lofty)* sich gedulden wait, be patient

② **ge·durft** [gə'dʊft] *past p of* dürfen²

ge·ehrt [gə|'e:ɐt] *past p of* ehren

◉ **Sehr geehrter Herr Bönzli, Sehr geehrte Frau Dr. Tahy** Dear Mr Bönzli, Dear Dr. Tahy **Sehr geehrte Damen und Herren** Ladies and gentlemen **Sehr geehrte Gäste, sehr geehrter Herr Bürgermeister** (My) Honoured guests, honorable mayor

② **ge·eig·net** [gə|'aegnət] *past p of* eignen [adj] suitable ◊ *Ist sie für diesen Job/als Programmiererin geeignet?* ♦ *Er war auf der Suche nach einer geeigneten Wohnung.* ⊖ungeeignet

② **Ge·fahr** [gə'fa:ʳ] die <-, -en> danger ◊ *Der Patient ist nun außer Gefahr.* ♦ *Es besteht die Gefahr, dass der Behälter explodiert.* ♦ *Gefahren im Straßenverkehr*

◉ **auf eigene Gefahr** at your own risk

ge·fähr·den [gə'fɛːɐdn̩] <gefährdet, gefährdete, hat gefährdet> [tr v] *(also fig)* jdn/etw. gefährden endanger sb/sth, put sb/sth at risk ◊ *andere Verkehrsteilnehmer durch zu schnelles Fahren gefährden* ♦ *die Friedensverhandlungen gefährden*

② **ge·fah·ren** [gə'fa:rən] *past p of* fahren

② **ge·fähr·lich** [gə'fɛːɐlɪç] [adj, adv] dangerous(ly) ◊ *Radioaktive Strahlung ist sehr gefährlich.* ♦ *Das ist eine gefährliche Straßenkreuzung/Kurve.* ♦ *Der Tiger kam ihm gefährlich nah.*

Ge·fäl·le [gə'fɛlə] das <-s, -> *most sing* **1.** *(of land)* incline; *(of a road, river)* gradient ◊ *Diese Straße hat ein Gefälle von 14%.* **2.** *(fig)* gap, divide ◊ *Wächst das soziale Gefälle?*

② **ge·fal·len** [gə'falən] *past p of* fallen <gefällt, gefiel, hat gefallen> [intr v] etw./jd gefällt jdm sb likes sth/sb ◊ *Dieser Pulli gefällt mir.* ♦ *Sie gefiel ihm sehr gut.* ♦ *Wie gefällt es dir in dieser Stadt?*

◉ **sich** [dat] **etw. gefallen lassen** take sth (lying down)

Ge·fal·len¹ [gə'falən] der <-s, -> favour, favour ◊ *Tu mir den Gefallen und hör auf zu schreien.* ♦ *Sie bat ihn um einen kleinen Gefallen.*

Ge·fal·len² [gə'falən] das <-s> *no pl* jd/etw. findet bei jdm Gefallen sb/sth finds favour with sb, sb/sth finds favor with sb ◊ *Sein Beitrag fand bei der Jury Gefallen.* **Gefallen an etw.** [dat] **finden** like sth, enjoy sth ◊ *Schnell fand er Gefallen am Rudern.*

ge·fäl·ligst [gə'fɛlɪçst] [part] *(fam)* kindly ◊ *Lass mich gefälligst in Ruhe!*

ge·fan·gen [gə'faŋən] *past p of* fangen

Ge·fan·ge·ne [gə'faŋənə] der/die <-n, die Gefangenen> *but: ein Gefangener/eine Gefangene* prisoner, prisoner of war ◊ *Der Gefangene wurde gestern entlassen.* box@ Substantivierung

Ge·fäng·nis [gə'fɛŋnɪs] das <-ses, -se> **1.** *(place)* prison ◊ *Er wurde gestern aus dem Gefängnis entlassen.* ♦ *Sie sitzt im Gefängnis.* **2.** *(punishment)* imprisonment ◊ *Sie wurde zu acht Jahren Gefängnis verurteilt.*

Ge·fäß [gə'fɛːs] das <-es, -e> **1.** vessel ◊ *Das Öl wurde in ein verschließbares Gefäß gefüllt.* **2.** BIO, MED blood vessel ◊ *Erhöhte Cholesterinwerte schädigen die Gefäße.*; lymph vessel

ge·fasst [gə'fast] *past p of* fassen [adj] <gefasster, am gefasstesten> **1.** composed ◊ *Er machte einen gefassten Eindruck.* ♦ *Sie war erstaunlich gefasst.* **2.** auf etw. [acc] gefasst sein be ready for sth, be prepared for sth ◊ *Ich bin auf alles gefasst.* **3.** sich auf etw. [acc] gefasst machen prepare yourself for sth ◊ *Mach dich bitte auf das Schlimmste gefasst.* [adv] with composure ◊ *Er nahm die Nachricht sehr gefasst auf.*

ge·floch·ten [gə'flɔxtn̩] *past p of* flechten

② **ge·flo·gen** [gə'flo:gn̩] *past p of* fliegen

ge·flo·hen [gə'flo:ən] *past p of* fliehen

② **ge·flos·sen** [gə'flɔsn̩] *past p of* fließen

Ge·flü·gel [gə'fly:gl̩] das <-s> *no pl* poultry ◊ *Sie isst nur Geflügel und Fisch.*

ge·foch·ten [gə'fɔxtn̩] *past p of* fechten

② **ge·fragt** [gə'fra:kt] *past p of* fragen [adj] <gefragter, am gefragtesten> popular, sought after ◊ *ein gefragtes Fotomodell* ♦ *Dieses Buch ist im Augenblick sehr gefragt.*

② **ge·fres·sen** [gə'frɛsn̩] *past p of* fressen

② **ge·frie·ren** [gə'fri:rən] <gefriert, gefror, ist gefroren> [intr v] freeze ◊ *Das Wasser gefror zu Eis.* ♦ *Der Boden war gefroren.* ⊖frieren

Ge·frier·fach [gə'fri:ɐfax] das <-(e)s, Gefrierfächer> freezer compartment, ice compartment ◊ *ein Kühlschrank mit Gefrierfach*

Ge·frier·tru·he [gə'fri:ɐtru:ə] die <-, -n> deep freeze, freeze box

ge·fro·ren [gə'fro:rən] *past p of* frieren, gefrieren

② **Ge·fühl** [gə'fy:l] das <-(e)s, -e> **1.** *(physical)* feeling, sensation ◊ *Er hatte kein Gefühl mehr in den Zehen.* ♦ *ein prickelndes Gefühl auf der Haut spüren* **2.** *(psychological)* feeling, emotion ◊ *Sie tut sich schwer, ihre Gefühle zu zeigen.* ♦ *Ich verfolgte die Entwicklung mit gemischten Gefühlen.* **3.** sentiment ◊ *moralische/religiöse Gefühle* **4.** *no pl (impression)* feeling ◊ *Ich habe ein gutes Gefühl, was diese neue Stelle betrifft.* ♦ *Der Gurt vermittelte ihr ein Gefühl der Sicherheit.*

◉ **mit Gefühl** with care, with skill

② **ge·fun·den** [gə'fʊndn̩] *past p of* finden

② **ge·gan·gen** [gə'gaŋən] *past p of* gehen

ge·ge·ben [gə'ge:bm̩] *past p of* geben [adj] *no comp/superl (lofty)* **1.** given aus gegebenem Anlass for given reasons unter den gegebenen Umständen in the circumstances, given the circumstances **2.** *only before ns* zu (einem) gegebenen Zeitpunkt in due course

ge·ge·be·nen·falls [gə'ge:bənən'fals] [adv] *(lofty) (abbr* ggf.) in that case, if necessary, if appropriate ◊ *Er wird gegebenenfalls rechtliche Schritte einleiten.*

Ge·ge·ben·heit [gə'ge:bm̩haęt] die <-, -en> condition ◊ *Sie ist mit den örtlichen Gegebenheiten bestens vertraut.*

② **ge·gen¹** ['ge:gn̩] [adv] *+figure* around, about ◊ *Am Schluss waren es gegen 300 Leute.* ⊖ungefähr, etwa

② **ge·gen²** ['ge:gn̩] [prep] [+acc] **1.** against ◊ *Das Auto prallte gegen einen Baum.* ♦ *Sie schwamm gegen die Strömung.* ♦ *Er wehrte sich gegen diese Entscheidung.* ♦ *Sie setzte Anzeige gegen ihn.* ♦ *Ich wurde gegen Kinderlähmung geimpft.* ♦ *Morgen spielen sie gegen Bayern München.* gegen jdn/etw. verlieren lose to sb/sth gegen ein/das

A
B
C
D
E
F
G
H
I
J
K
L
M
N
O
P
Q
R
S
T
U
V
W
X
Y
Z

Gesetz verstoßen break a/the law der Kampf gegen den Terror the war on terror **2.** (in exchange) for ◊ *Die alten Reifen wurden gegen neue ausgetauscht.* ♦ *Die Gärtnerei liefert nur gegen Barzahlung.* **3.** around, towards ◊ *Gegen 20 Uhr wollen wir in Wien sein.* ♦ *Gegen Morgen kam ein Sturm auf.* **4.** in comparisons *(fam)* compared to/with ◊ *Gegen sie bist du ein Zwerg.*

② **Ge·gend** ['geːɡn̩t, 'geːɡənt] die <-, -en> **1.** area, region ◊ *Er kommt auch aus dieser Gegend.* ♦ *eine abgelegene Gegend* in der Gegend von ... wohnen live near ... **2.** *(in a city)* district ◊ *Er wohnt in einer vornehmen Gegend von München.*

ge·gen·ei·nan·der [geːɡn̩|aeˈnandɐ] [adv] against each other, against one another ◊ *Es treten jeweils zwei Mannschaften gegeneinander an.* ♦ *Vor- und Nachteile gegeneinander abwiegen* ... gegeneinander austauschen exchange ... for each other, exchange ... for one another

② **Ge·gen·satz** ['geːɡn̩zats] der <-es, Gegensätze> **1.** opposition, contrast ◊ *Gegensätze ziehen sich an.* etw. steht im Gegensatz zu etw. sth is in contrast/opposition to sth ◊ *Der Rückgang steht im krassen Gegensatz zu den Prognosen.* **2.** im Gegensatz zu jdm/etw. unlike sb/sth, in contrast to sb/sth ◊ *Im Gegensatz zu ihrer Mutter ist sie sehr schlank.* **3.** only pl difference ◊ *ideologische Gegensätze überwinden*

ge·gen·sei·tig ['geːɡn̩zaetɪç] [adj] no comp/superl, mostly before ns mutual ◊ *gegenseitiges Vertrauen* ♦ *Der Vertrag wurde im gegenseitigen Einvernehmen aufgelöst.* ♦ *Die Sympathie war gegenseitig.* [adv] each other ◊ *Sie halfen sich gegenseitig.*

② **Ge·gen·stand** ['geːɡn̩ʃtant] der <-(e)s, Gegenstände> **1.** object ◊ *Mit einem spitzen Gegenstand zerkratzte er das Auto.* ♦ *Gegenstände des täglichen Gebrauchs* **2.** *(focus of attention)* subject ◊ *Das ist doch nicht Gegenstand der heutigen Diskussion.*

② **Ge·gen·teil** ['geːɡn̩tael] das <-(e)s, -e> most sing opposite ◊ *Dein Bruder behauptet das Gegenteil.* ♦ *Das Gegenteil von „hell" ist „dunkel".* ganz im Gegenteil quite the reverse

② **ge·gen·ü·ber**[1] [geːɡn̩ˈyːbɐ] [adv] das Haus gegenüber the house opposite, the house across the road die Leute von gegenüber the people from across the road gegenüber von etw. on the opposite side, on the other side ◊ *Cambridge, direkt gegenüber von Boston am Charles River* ⊖vis-à-vis

② **ge·gen·ü·ber**[2] [geːɡn̩ˈyːbɐ] [prep] [+dat] **1.** spatial opposite ◊ *Gegenüber der Bank ist ein Brunnen.* ♦ *Das Museum befindet sich gegenüber der Post.* **2.** compared with ◊ *Gegenüber dem Vorjahr ist der Umsatz leicht gestiegen.* **3.** to ◊ *Ihm gegenüber ist sie stets freundlich.* ♦ *Gegenüber der Zeitung/ einem Journalisten erklärte er, ...*

ge·gen·über|... [geːɡn̩ˈyːbɐ] [prefix] facing each other ◊ *Sie standen sich schweigend gegenüber.* ♦ *Wir haben uns schweigend gegenübergesessen. Das Geschäft liegt gleich gegenüber.* The shop is right on the other side., The shop is just across the road. die Vor- und Nachteile gegenüberstellen compare advantages and disadvantages

Ge·gen·ver·kehr ['geːɡn̩fɛkeːɐ] der <-s> no pl oncoming traffic ◊ *Er wurde vom Gegenverkehr*

geblendet. ♦ *Auf dieser Straße herrscht reger Gegenverkehr.*

② **Ge·gen·wart** ['geːɡn̩vaˈt] die <-> no pl **1.** present ◊ *Seine Kunstsammlung reicht bis zur Gegenwart.* ... der Gegenwart contemporary ..., ... alive today ◊ *Er ist einer der erfolgreichsten Autoren der Gegenwart.* **2.** LING present (tense) ◊ *Das Verb stand in der Gegenwart.* ⊖Präsens **3.** in jds Gegenwart in sb's presence, when sb is/was there ◊ *Sie hat ihn in meiner Gegenwart beleidigt.*

ge·gen·wär·tig ['geːɡn̩vɛˈtɪç] [adj] no comp/superl; only before ns present, current ◊ *die gegenwärtige Situation* [adv] at the moment, currently, at present ◊ *Ich sehe gegenwärtig keine Gefahr.* ⊖zurzeit, derzeit, momentan

② **ge·ges·sen** [gəˈɡɛsn̩] past p of essen
ge·gli·chen [gəˈɡlɪçn̩] past p of gleichen
ge·glit·ten [gəˈɡlɪtn̩] past p of gleiten
Geg·ner ['geːɡnɐ] der <-s, ->, **Geg·ne·rin** ['geːɡnərɪn] die <-, -nen> **1.** opponent ◊ *Wer wird sein Gegner im Halbfinale sein?* ♦ *Bist du ein Gegner von Atomenergie?* **2.** MIL enemy ◊ *Sie griffen den Gegner an.*

② **ge·gol·ten** [gəˈɡɔltn̩] past p of gelten
ge·gos·sen [gəˈɡɔsn̩] past p of gießen
ge·gra·ben [gəˈɡraːbm̩] past p of graben
ge·grif·fen [gəˈɡrɪfn̩] past p of greifen
② **ge·habt** [gəˈhaːpt] past p of haben
② **Ge·halt**[1] [gəˈhalt] das <-(e)s, Gehälter> salary ◊ *Sie bezieht ein Gehalt von rund 50 000 Euro im Jahr.* ♦ *Die Löhne und Gehälter sollen erhöht werden.*
Ge·halt[2] [gəˈhalt] der <-(e)s, -e> most sing content ◊ *der Gehalt an Alkohol im Wein* ♦ *der künstlerische Gehalt des Werkes*
② **ge·hal·ten** [gəˈhaltn̩] past p of halten
② **ge·han·gen** [gəˈhaŋən] past p of hängen[1]
ge·häuft [gəˈhɔøft] past p of häufen [adj, adv] no comp/superl repeated(ly), frequent(ly) ◊ *gehäuftes Vorkommen* ♦ *Dieser Virus tritt in letzter Zeit gehäuft auf.* [adj] *(spoonful)* heaped ◊ *zwei gehäufte Esslöffel Zucker* ⊖gestrichen
Ge·häu·se [gəˈhɔøzə] das <-s, -> **1.** *(of a snail)* shell **2.** *(of an appliance, a watch)* cover, case ◊ *eine Uhr mit wasserdichtem Gehäuse.*
② **ge·heim** [gəˈhaem] [adj, adv] secret ◊ *in geheimer Mission unterwegs sein* ♦ *Das soll aber geheim bleiben!* streng geheim top secret geheim abstimmen/tagen hold a secret ballot/meeting etw. geheim halten keep sth secret; *(only before ns)* geheimste innermost, most private ◊ *jds geheimste Wünsche/Sehnsüchte*
Ge·heim·nis [gəˈhaemnɪs] die <-ses, -se> **1.** secret ◊ *Soll ich dir ein Geheimnis verraten/ anvertrauen?* ♦ *kein Geheimnis aus etw. machen* keine Geheimnisse vor jdm haben have no secrets from sb **2.** das Geheimnis/die Geheimnisse (einer Sache [gen]) the secret(s) (of sth) ◊ *Können Sie mir das Geheimnis Ihres Erfolges verraten?* das Geheimnis um jdn/etw. the mystery of sb/sth ⊛ ein Geheimnis lüften reveal a secret, solve a mystery
② **ge·hei·ßen** [gəˈhaesn̩] past p of heißen
② **ge·hemmt** [gəˈhɛmt] past p of hemmen [adj] inhibited, self-conscious ◊ *In fremder Gesellschaft ist das Kind sehr gehemmt.* ♦ *ein gehemmtes*

Verhalten ⊖schüchtern

② **ge·hen** ['geːən] <geht, ging, ist gegangen> [intr v]
1. *(on foot)* walk ◊ *Ich möchte zu Fuß gehen.* ✦ *barfuß gehen* auf Zehenspitzen gehen *(walk on)* tiptoe spazieren gehen go for a walk über die Straße gehen cross the street **2.** irgendwohin/ irgendwie gehen go somewhere/in a certain way ◊ *zur Schule/nach Hause/ins Bett gehen* ✦ *Der Weg geht am Rathaus vorbei zum Fluss.* ✦ *Geht der Zug bis Nürnberg?* ✦ *Ist in der Küche gehen?* ✦ *Ist in der Prüfung alles gut gegangen?* Ski fahren/ schwimmen gehen go skiing/swimming zum Arzt gehen go to/see a doctor **3.** leave, go ◊ *Wann geht der nächste Bus/Zug nach Köln?* aus dem Haus gehen go out ⊖weggehen ⊖bleiben **4.** *(attend regularly)* zur/in die Schule etc. gehen go to/ attend school etc. ◊ *Gehst du schon in den Kinder- garten?* zur/auf die Universität gehen be at univer- sity **5.** *(start attending)* in/an/auf etw. [acc] gehen enter sth ◊ *Er soll nächstes Jahr ans/aufs Gymnasium gehen.* ✦ *in den Staatsdienst gehen* ✦ *Ab September geht er aufs Gymnasium.* in Rente/ in den Ruhestand/in Pension gehen retire **6.** *(window)* irgendwohin gehen face somewhere ◊ *Die Fenster gehen nach Süden/auf die Straße.* **7.** *(letter, parcel)* etw. gehen ◊ *Der Brief ging irrtümlich an mich.* **8.** nach Plan/ jds Wünschen gehen go according to plan/sb's wishes nach Vorschrift/nach dem Gesetz gehen comply with the rules/law **9.** über etw. [acc] gehen be beyond sth ◊ *Das geht über meine Kräfte/finan- ziellen Möglichkeiten.* **10.** nichts geht über etw./ jdn there's nothing like sth/sb ◊ *Es geht nichts über eine schöne Tasse Tee!* **11.** irgendwohin gehen fit somewhere ◊ *Wie viele Leute gehen in den Bus?* ⊖passen **12.** work ◊ *Ich kann mir nicht vorstellen, wie das gehen soll.* ✦ *Das Telefon geht nicht.* die Uhr geht falsch/richtig the clock is wrong/right ⊖funktionieren **13.** be possible ◊ *Geht das, dass ich morgen später komme?* **14.** etw. geht sth will do, sth is (just about) all right ◊ *Das Essen ging ja noch, aber der Service war schlecht!* **15.** vor sich gehen happen, go on ◊ *Dort gehen seltsame Dinge vor sich.* **16.** *(fam) (without per- mission)* an etw. [acc] gehen be at sth ◊ *Die Kinder sind heimlich an den Computer gegangen!* **17.** *(fam)* mit jdm gehen go out with sb, date sb ◊ *Sie gehen schon zwei Jahre miteinander.* [imp v]
1. *(physically, emotionally)* jdm geht es gut/ schlecht etc. sb is well/unwell etc. ◊ *Geht es dir wieder besser?* Wie geht es Ihnen/dir? How are you? **2.** *(financially)* jdm geht es gut/schlecht etc. sb does well/badly (for themselves) ◊ *Finanzi- ell geht es ihr ziemlich schlecht.* **3.** bei/in etw. [dat] geht es um etw. sth is about sth ◊ *Worum ging es bei dem Streit/in dem Film?* bei jdm geht es um etw. sb's concern/problem etc. is (about) sth **4.** jdm geht es um etw. sb wants (to achieve) sth, sth is important to sb ◊ *Ihr geht es um die Wahrheit.* **5.** wenn es nach jdm ginge, ... if sb had a say in it/the matter ...
⊛ geh mir doch mit jdm/etw. *(fam, emph)* don't talk to me about sb/sth zu weit gehen go too far sich gehen lassen let yourself go, lose control (of yourself) wie geht's(, wie steht's)? how are you?, how are things going? (ach,) geh *(fam)*

(oh,) come on ◊ *Ach, geh, das glaubst du doch selbst nicht!* wo jd geht und steht everywhere, all over the place, constantly, all the time von uns gehen *(euph)* pass on ◊ *Gestern ist Schwester Maria von uns gegangen.*

ge·hetzt [gə'hɛtst] *past p of* hetzen [adj] harassed, stressed, hunted ◊ *gehetzt aussehen/wirken* ✦ *Er sah sich mit gehetztem Blick um.*

Ge·hirn [gə'hɪrn] das <-(e)s, -e> **1.** ANAT brain ◊ *eine Schädigung des Gehirns* ⊖Hirn **2.** *(intellec- tual capacity)* brains ◊ *Er ist zwar nett, hat aber leider nicht viel Gehirn.* sein Gehirn anstrengen rack your brains ⊖Hirn

Ge·hirn·er·schüt·te·rung [gə'hɪrnʔɛɐ̯ʃʏtərʊŋ] die <-, -en> MED concussion ◊ *Sie erlitt/hatte eine schwere Gehirnerschütterung.*

ge·ho·ben [gə'hoːbm̩] *past p of* heben [adj] **1.** *only before ns (in a hierarchy)* higher, senior, upper ◊ *der gehobene Mittelstand* ein Beamter des gehobenen Dienstes a senior official/civil servant **2.** upmarket, refined, sophisticated, lofty ◊ *für gehobene Ansprüche*

② **ge·hol·fen** [gə'hɔlfn̩] *past p of* helfen

Ge·hör [gə'høːɐ̯] das <-(e)s> *no pl* hearing ◊ *ein ausgezeichnetes/feines Gehör haben*
⊛ das absolute Gehör MUS perfect pitch etw. zu Gehör bringen *(lofty)* perform sth, recite sth ◊ *Sie brachte mehrere Chansons von Edith Piaf zu Gehör.* (bei jdm) Gehör finden meet with a positive response (from sb) jdm/einer Sache (sein) Gehör schenken be prepared to listen to sb/sth ◊ *Er wollte mir/meinem Rat kein Gehör schenken.* sich (bei jdm/etw.) Gehör verschaffen gain (sb's/sth's) attention ◊ *Wie kann man sich bei der Öffentlichkeit Gehör verschaffen?*

ge·hor·chen [gə'hɔrçn̩] <gehorchte, gehorcht, hat gehorcht> [intr v] jdm/einer Sache gehorchen obey sb/sth ◊ *Der Hund gehorchte einfach nicht.* ✦ einem Befehl gehorchen; *(a natural law also)* follow ◊ *Das Glas gehorchte dem Gesetz der Schwerkraft und fiel zu Boden.; (body parts, senses)* etw. gehorcht jdm nicht mehr sb has lost control of sth

② **ge·hö·ren** [gə'høːrən] <gehört, gehörte, hat gehört> [intr v] **1.** zu etw./jdm gehören be one of sth/sb, belong to sth/sb ◊ *Dieser Moment gehörte zu den Höhepunkten seines Lebens.* **2.** *(possessions)* jdm gehören belong to sb ◊ *„Wem gehört diese Jacke?" — „Die gehört mir".* **3.** *(necessity)* zu etw. gehört etw. sth takes sth, sth requires sth ◊ *Es gehört viel Mut dazu, als Dompteur zu arbeiten.* **4.** etw./jd gehört irgendwohin sth/sb should be somewhere, sth/sb belongs somewhere ◊ *Mit so einer Grippe gehörst du ins Bett!* [ref v] sich gehören be good manners, be proper ◊ *Bohr nicht in der Nase, das gehört sich nicht!* nicht wissen, was sich gehört have no manners ⊖sich schicken

Ge·hör·lo·se [gə'høːɐ̯loːzə] die/der <-n, -n> (ein Gehörloser/eine Gehörlose) deaf person Untertitel/Fernsehsendun- gen für Gehörlose subtitles/TV programmes for deaf viewers ⊖Taube *box@* Substantivierung

ge·hor·sam [gə'hoːɐ̯zaːm] [adj, adv] obedient(ly) ◊ *ein gehorsamer Hund* ✦ *Die Kinder wuschen sich gehorsam die Hände.* jdm gehorsam sein obey sb ⊖brav

② **Geh·steig** ['geːʃtaek] der <-(e)s, -e> pavement,

A B C D E F **G** H I J K L M N O P Q R S T U V W X Y Z

sidewalk ◊ *Kleine Kinder dürfen mit dem Rad auf dem Gehsteig fahren.* ⊖Bürgersteig, Gehweg

Geh·weg ['ge:ve:k] der <-(e)s, -e> → Gehsteig

Gei·ge ['gaegə] die <-, -n> MUS violin ◊ *Geige spielen*

● **die erste Geige spielen** *(fig)* be the leader/leading the field **die zweite Geige spielen** play second fiddle

geil [gael] [adj] **1.** *(slang)* wicked, fab, cool ◊ *Das sieht echt geil aus!* ♦ *'ne geile CD* ⊖super **2.** *(rude, pej)* horny, randy ◊ *jdn geil machen* ⊖scharf **3.** *(rude)* hot, sexy ◊ *Lara hat eine geile Figur.* ♦ *Der Typ ist geil.* **4.** *(slang)* geil auf etw. [acc] sein crave sth, be keen on sth ◊ *geil auf eine Zigarette/auf Geld/auf dem Kuchen* geil auf jdn sein have the hots for sb [adv] *(slang)* wickedly ◊ *Der Film war wirklich geil gemacht.* ⊖super

Gei·sel ['gaezl] die <-, -n> hostage ◊ *jdn als Geisel nehmen* ♦ *eine Geisel nehmen*

Geist [gaest] der <-(e)s, -er> **1.** *no pl* mind, wit ◊ *Das ist gesund für Geist und Körper.* ⊖Verstand **2.** *no pl* spirit ◊ *Der olympische Geist war bei allen Wettkämpfen spürbar.* **3.** ghost, spirit ◊ *Geister beschwören* ♦ *In der Burg geht ein Geist um/spuken Geister.* ⊖Gespenst

● **von allen guten Geistern verlassen sein** *(fam)* have taken leave of your senses, be out of your mind **jdm auf den Geist gehen** *(fam)* get on sb's nerves **an etw.** [dat] **scheiden sich die Geister** opinions differ about sth, sth is controversial **im Geiste** in your thoughts ◊ *Sie sah sich im Geiste schon am Strand liegen.*

geis·tes·krank ['gaestəskraŋk] [adj] *no comp/superl* mentally ill, deranged ◊ *unheilbar geisteskrank sein* ♦ *ein geisteskranker Mörder* ⊖geistesgestört

Geis·tes·wis·sen·schaft ['gaestəsvɪsnʃaft] die <-, -en> *most pl (pl)* (die) Geisteswissenschaften the arts, the humanities ◊ *Geisteswissenschaften studieren/lehren* Ist dieses Fach eine Geisteswissenschaft? Does this subject belong to the humanities/the arts?

geist·lich ['gaestlɪç] [adj] *only before ns* spiritual ◊ *geistliche und weltliche Dichtung* ♦ *jdm geistlichen Beistand leisten*; *(of the Church)* clerical ◊ *ein geistlicher Beruf* ⊖kirchlich ⊖weltlich

gei·zig ['gaetsɪç] [adj] mean, tight, stingy, miserly ◊ *Du bist zu geizig, um anderen ein Geschenk zu kaufen!* ♦ *geizige Leute*

② **ge·kannt** [gə'kant] *past p of* kennen

ge·kenn·zeich·net [gə'kɛntsaeçnət] [adj] *no comp/superl* **1.** *(for identification)* marked, labelled, signposted ◊ *Wir folgten dem blau gekennzeichneten Weg.* ♦ *Wie sind die Bioweine gekennzeichnet?* **2.** *(by a characteristic)* durch/von etw. gekennzeichnet characterized by sth, marked by sth ◊ *eine von Widersprüchen gekennzeichnete Zeit*

ge·klei·det [gə'klaedət] [adj] *no comp/superl* dressed ◊ *schwarz/ganz in Schwarz gekleidet* ♦ *in Jeans/Anzug und Krawatte gekleidet*

ge·klun·gen [gə'kloŋən] *past p of* klingen

ge·knif·fen [gə'knɪfn] *past p of* kneifen

② **ge·kom·men** [gə'kɔmən] *past p of* kommen

② **ge·konnt** [gə'kɔnt] *past p of* können² [adj, adv] <gekonnter, am gekonntesten> competent(ly) ◊ *eine gekonnte Darbietung* ♦ *Sein Auftritt war*

wirklich gekonnt. ♦ *Die Vorlage wurde gekonnt umgesetzt.*

ge·kro·chen [gə'krɔxn] *past p of* kriechen

Ge·läch·ter [gə'lɛçtɐ] das <-s, -> *most sing* laughter ◊ *brüllendes/schadenfrohes/schallendes Gelächter* ♦ *Unter allgemeinem Gelächter verließen sie den Saal.*

ge·lähmt [gə'lɛ:mt] *past p of* lähmen [adj] paralysed, paralyzed; *(limbs also)* stiff ◊ *ein gelähmtes Bein haben* halbseitig gelähmt paralysed on one side, hemiplegic

Ge·län·de [gə'lɛndə] das <-s, -> **1.** site, area, grounds ◊ *Wir befinden uns hier auf dem Gelände des Krankenhauses.* ⊖Grundstück **2.** terrain, area ◊ *ein steiles/felsiges Gelände* ⊖Gebiet, Gegend, Terrain

Ge·län·der [gə'lɛndɐ] das <-s, -> banister(s), railing(s) ◊ *sich an/über das Geländer lehnen*

② **ge·lang** [gə'laŋ] *pret of* gelingen

ge·lan·gen [gə'laŋən] <gelangt, gelangte, ist gelangt> [intr v] **1.** arrive at, reach ◊ *Bald gelangte er zum Theater.* in die Umwelt gelangen get into the environment an die Öffentlichkeit gelangen be leaked (to the public) ins Freie gelangen get out ⊖kommen **2.** *(an objective)* zu etw./an etw. [acc] gelangen attain sth zum/ans Ziel gelangen reach your goal zu Ruhm gelangen become famous an die/zur Macht gelangen come (in)to power zu der Einsicht/Erkenntnis gelangen, dass ... come to the realization that, realize that ⊖kommen

ge·lang·weilt [gə'laŋvaelt] *past p of* langweilen [adj, adv] <gelangweilter, am gelangweiltesten> *seldom comp/superl* bored ◊ *Sie hörten mit gelangweilter Miene zu.* ♦ *Das Publikum wirkte von der langen Rede gelangweilt.* ♦ *Gelangweilt blätterte sie in einer Zeitschrift.*

ge·las·sen [gə'lasn] *past p of* lassen² [adj, adv] calm(ly) ◊ *Er blieb völlig gelassen.* ♦ *Ihre gelassene Reaktion überraschte ihn.* ♦ *Ich sehe der Prüfung gelassen entgegen.* ⊖ruhig

② **ge·lau·fen** [gə'laofn] *past p of* laufen

ge·läu·fig [gə'lɔøfɪç] [adj] **1.** common, familiar ◊ *Markus ist ein sehr geläufiger Vorname.* ♦ *Der Begriff „Hotline" ist in Deutschland schon lange geläufig.* **2.** jdm ist etw. geläufig sb is familiar with sth ⊖jd ist mit etw. vertraut

ge·launt [gə'laont] [adj, adv] gut gelaunt in a good mood, cheerful(ly) schlecht/übel gelaunt in a bad mood, bad-tempered(ly)

② **gelb** [gɛlp] [adj] yellow ◊ *Tulpen mit leuchtend gelben Blüten* ♦ *Deine Zähne sind ganz gelb.*

② **Geld** [gɛlt] das <-(e)s, -er> **1.** *no pl* money ◊ *viel/wenig Geld haben* ♦ *Geld sparen/verdienen* ♦ *ein Geld ausgeben* ♦ *Die Neuerung kostet den Staat viel Geld.* **2.** *most pl* fund, money ◊ *öffentliche Gelder*

● **Geld zum Fenster hinauswerfen** pour money down the drain **jdm rinnt das Geld durch die Finger** money slips through sb's fingers **Geld haben wie Heu, im Geld schwimmen** *(fam)* be rolling in it, be loaded, be filthy/stinking rich **jdm Geld in den Rachen werfen** *(fam)* give up your money to sb **bares Geld** hard cash **großes/das große Geld** a fortune **kleines Geld** small) change **teures Geld** a lot of money ◊ *Sie haben sich für teures Geld*

eine Jacht gekauft. **ins Geld gehen** cost you dearly ◊ *Die vielen Strafzettel gehen ganz schön ins Geld.* **(mit etw.) Geld machen** *(fam)* make money (with sth) etw. **zu Geld machen** sell sth off, turn sth into money/cash, cash in on sth ◊ *Ich hab meine alte Schallplattensammlung zu Geld gemacht.* **bei jdm sitzt das Geld locker** money burns a hole in sb's pocket **Geld waschen** launder money

Geld·au·to·mat [ˈɡɛltlaˌo̯to,maːt] der <–en, –en> cash point, ATM ◊ *Ich habe mir am Geldautomaten 300 Euro geholt/gezogen.*

Geld·beu·tel [ˈɡɛltbɔɪ̯tl̩] der <–s, –> → Geldbörse

② **Geld·bör·se** [ˈɡɛltbœrzə] die <–, –n> purse, wallet ◊ *die Geldbörse verlieren* ♦ *Ich öffnete die Geldbörse und nahm ein paar Münzen heraus.*
⊜Börse, Geldbeutel, Portmonee

Geld·schein [ˈɡɛltʃaɛ̯n] der <–(e)s, –e> banknote, bill ◊ *ein Bündel Geldscheine* ♦ *ein gefälschter Geldschein* ⊜Banknote

Geld·stra·fe [ˈɡɛltʃtraːfə] die <–, –n> fine **eine Geldstrafe über/gegen jdn verhängen, jdn zu einer Geldstrafe verurteilen** fine sb

Geld·stück [ˈɡɛltʃtʏk] das <–(e)s, –e> coin
⊜Münze ⊜Geldschein

Ge·lee [ʒeˈleː] das *or* der <–s, –s> jelly ◊ *ein Brötchen mit Gelee bestreichen* ♦ *Hering in Gelee*

ge·le·gen [ɡəˈleːɡn̩] *past p of* liegen [adj]
1. situated, located **günstig gelegen** conveniently located *idyllisch gelegen* in an idyllic location/spot **2.** jdm ist an etw./jdm gelegen sth/sb matters to sb ◊ *Mir ist sehr daran gelegen, dass du pünktlich kommst.* [adv] **etw. kommt (jdm) gelegen** sth is convenient (for sb), sth comes at a convenient time (for sb)

② **Ge·le·gen·heit** [ɡəˈleːɡn̩haɛ̯t] die <–, –en> **1.** Gelegenheit (zu etw./etw. zu tun) opportunity (for sth/ to do sth) ◊ *eine Gelegenheit nutzen* ♦ *Gelegenheit haben, etw. zu tun* ⊜Möglichkeit, Chance **2.** occasion ◊ *Bei welcher Gelegenheit habt ihr euch kennen gelernt?* ⊜Anlass

ge·le·gent·lich [ɡəˈleːɡn̩tlɪç, ɡəˈleːɡn̩tlɪç] [adj, adv] *when used as an adj, only before ns* occasional(ly) ◊ *gelegentliche Zwischenrufe* ♦ *Sie besucht mich gelegentlich.*

ge·lehrt [ɡəˈleːɐ̯t] *past p of* lehren [adj] learned, erudite, scholarly ◊ *einen gelehrten Vortrag halten* ♦ *Unser Professor war sehr gelehrt.* ⊜gebildet

Ge·lenk [ɡəˈlɛŋk] das <–(e)s, –e> **1.** ANAT joint ◊ *geschwollene/entzündete Gelenke* **2.** TECHN joint, hinge ◊ *eine Schreibtischlampe mit Schwenkarm und zwei Gelenken*

ge·lernt [ɡəˈlɛɐ̯nt] *past p of* lernen [adj] *only before ns* qualified, trained ◊ *Sie ist gelernte Krankenschwester.*

② **ge·le·sen** [ɡəˈleːzn̩] *past p of* lesen

Ge·lieb·te [ɡəˈliːptə] der/die <–n, die Geliebten> *but: ein Geliebter/eine Geliebte* lover ◊ *Sie hat einen heimlichen Geliebten.; (woman also)* mistress

② **ge·lie·hen** [ɡəˈliːən] *past p of* leihen

② **ge·lin·gen** [ɡəˈlɪŋən] <gelingt, gelang, ist gelungen> [intr v] succeed, be successful ◊ *Hoffentlich gelingt das Experiment.* **jdm gelingt etw.** sb accomplishes sth ◊ *Uns gelang ein guter Start. Das Projekt ist dir gelungen.* Your project is a success.

Der Kuchen ist dir gut gelungen. Your cake turned out well. ⊜misslingen [imp v] **es gelingt jdm, etw. zu tun** sb manages to do sth, sb succeeds in doing sth ◊ *Es ist mir nicht gelungen, ihn zu überzeugen.*

② **ge·lit·ten** [ɡəˈlɪtn̩] *past p of* leiden

ge·lockt [ɡəˈlɔkt] *past p of* locken [adj] curly (-haired) ◊ *gelocktes Haar* blond/braun etc. **gelockt** with blonde/brown etc. curls

② **ge·lo·gen** [ɡəˈloːɡn̩] *past p of* lügen

② **gel·ten** [ˈɡɛltn̩] <gilt, galt, hat gegolten> [intr v] **1.** *(ticket)* be valid; *(rule, law)* be in force ◊ *Diese Bestimmungen gelten seit erstem Januar.; (price)* be effective ◊ *Der Preis gilt für ein Jahr.* **2. für jdn/etw. gelten** apply to sb/sth ◊ *Ich habe gesagt, ihr sollt still sein, das gilt auch für dich!; (price)* für Kinder gilt der halbe Preis etc. children pay half price etc. **3. als jd/etw. gelten** be regarded as sb/sth, be considered (to be) sb/ sth ◊ *Er gilt als Favorit im ersten Rennen.* ♦ *Die Stadt gilt als Brennpunkt der Kriminalität.* **4.** *(mistake, goal)* count ◊ *Der Ball gilt nicht, der war im Aus!* ⊜zählen **5.** be allowed, be permitted ◊ *Schummeln gilt nicht!* ⊜erlaubt sein **6. etw. gelten lassen** accept sth ◊ *Diesen Einwand/Vorwurf kann ich nicht gelten lassen.* **7.** jdm/etw. [dat] **gelten** be aimed at sb/sth, be directed at sb/sth, focus on sb/sth ◊ *Die Kritik gilt nicht Ihnen persönlich, sondern Ihrer ganzen Partei.* [imp v] **es gilt, etw. zu tun** it is essential/important/crucial to do sth ◊ *Jetzt gilt es nur noch, bis zum Schluss durchzuhalten.*

Gel·tung [ˈɡɛltʊŋ] die <–> *no pl* **1. etw. zur Geltung bringen** draw attention to sth etw. **gut/vorteilhaft etc. zur Geltung bringen** show sth to its best advantage **2. zur Geltung kommen** be set off, show to advantage **3.** recognition, prestige, importance ◊ *Mit diesem Produkt hat das Unternehmen internationale Geltung erlangt.* **4. Geltung haben/besitzen** be valid, be in force, be effective

ge·lun·gen [ɡəˈlʊŋən] *past p of* gelingen [adj] **1.** successful ◊ *ein gelungener Abend* ♦ *Das Fest war gelungen.* **2.** *(fam) (joke)* priceless ◊ *ein gelungener Scherz*

ge·mah·len [ɡəˈmaːlən] *past p of* mahlen

Ge·mäl·de [ɡəˈmɛːldə] das <–s, –> painting

ge·mäß [ɡəˈmɛːs] [prep] *sing nouns without article or attribute are not declined when following this prep, otherwise* [+dat] *(form)* in accordance with, under ◊ *gemäß Artikel 81 der Verfassung* ⊜entsprechend, nach

ge·mein [ɡəˈmaɛ̯n] [adj] **1.** mean, nasty, vicious ◊ *Ich finde es gemein, wie ihr euch über ihn lustig macht!* **ein gemeiner Lügner/Trick** a dirty liar/trick ⊜mies **2.** *only before ns (oldf)* common, ordinary ◊ *das gemeine Volk* ⊜gewöhnlich, einfach **3.** *only before ns* BOT, ZOO common

Ge·mein·de [ɡəˈmaɛ̯ndə] die <–, –n> **1.** POL community, municipality **2.** REL community, parish, congregation ◊ *die jüdische Gemeinde Frankfurts* **3.** community ◊ *Die Gemeinde ihrer Fans/von Internetnutzern wächst täglich.* ⊜Gemeinschaft **4.** *(government, administration)* local authority, (local) council, municipality ◊ *bei der Gemeinde arbeiten* ⊜Gemeindeverwaltung

ge·mein·nüt·zig [ɡəˈmaɛ̯nnʏtsɪç] [adj] LAW nonprofit, (for) charity **gemeinnützige Organisationen/**

A B C D E F **G** H I J K L M N O P Q R S T U V W X Y Z

Stiftungen/Vereine charities, non-profit organizations/foundations/associations Fonds für gemeinnützige Zwecke charity fund; *(as a punishment)* gemeinnützige Arbeit community service

② **ge·mein·sam** [gə'maɛnzaːm] (adj) **1.** common, shared, joint ◊ *eine gemeinsame Sprache sprechen* ♦ *Dieses Merkmal ist allen ihren Produkten gemeinsam.* etw. (mit jdm/etw.) gemeinsam haben have sth in common (with sb/sth), share sth (with sb/sth) **2.** *only before ns* joint, concerted ◊ *das gemeinsame Sorgerecht für die Kinder haben* **3.** *only before ns* joint, common ◊ *ein gemeinsames Konto* (adv) together, jointly ◊ *Wir nutzen den Computer gemeinsam.*

② **Ge·mein·schaft** [gə'maɛnʃaft] die <-, -en> **1.** community ◊ *Es gelang ihm nicht, sich in die Gemeinschaft der Klasse zu integrieren.* **2.** *no pl* company, group ◊ *Herdentiere fühlen sich nur in der Gemeinschaft mit anderen wohl.* **3.** POL community, alliance
◉ **eheliche Gemeinschaft** matrimony in **häuslicher Gemeinschaft leben** cohabit in **Gemeinschaft mit etw. auftreten** occur together with sth **in Gemeinschaft mit etw./jdm** in cooperation with sth/sb

② **ge·mes·sen** [gə'mɛsn̩] *past p of* messen
ge·mie·den [gə'miːdn̩] *past p of* meiden
ge·mischt [gə'mɪʃt] *past p of* mischen (adj) mixed ◊ *ein gemischter Salat* ♦ *gemischte Gefühle haben* ♦ *Das Publikum war altersmäßig gemischt.* ♦ *ein bunt gemischtes Programm* ♦ *Die Sauna ist heute gemischt.* ethnisch/konfessionell gemischte Gruppen/Ehen groups/married couples from different ethnic/religious backgrounds

② **ge·mocht** [gə'mɔxt] *past p of* mögen¹
② **Ge·mü·se** [gə'myːzə] das <-s, -> *most sing* vegetables ◊ *Es gab Kotelett mit Kartoffeln und gemischtem Gemüse.* ♦ *Gemüse dünsten/kochen* ein Gemüse a vegetable
◉ **junges Gemüse** *(fam, oldf, hum)* youngsters

② **ge·musst** [gə'mʊst] *past p of* müssen²
② **ge·müt·lich** [gə'myːtlɪç] (adj, adv) **1.** *(atmosphere, pub, house)* cosy(-ily), cozy(-ily), snug(ly), comfortable(-ably) ◊ *ein gemütliches Lokal* ♦ *Dein neues Sofa ist sehr gemütlich.* ♦ *Wir saßen gemütlich vor dem Kamin.* es sich gemütlich machen make yourself comfortable, relax, snuggle down ◊ *Komm, machen wir es uns bei einer Tasse Kaffee gemütlich.* **2.** leisurely ◊ *ein gemütlicher Spaziergang* ♦ *Die Fahrt nach Hause war gemütlich.* ♦ *Am Nachmittag radelten wir ganz gemütlich wieder zurück.* (adj) *(personality)* relaxed, easy-going ◊ *ein gemütlicher Mensch* ♦ *Sie ist gemütlich und gutmütig.*

Gen ['geːn] das <-s, -e> gene ◊ *Unsere Eigenschaften liegen in den Genen.*

② **ge·nannt** [gə'nant] *past p of* nennen
② **ge·nau** [gə'nao] (adj, adv) *when used as an adj, only before ns* **1.** precise(ly), exact(ly), accurate(ly) ◊ *genauere Informationen* ♦ *Der Wettbewerb findet in Irland, genauer gesagt in Dublin, statt.* ♦ *Das ist genau das Richtige für mich!* ♦ *auf den Tag genau heute vor 100 Jahren* genau genommen strictly speaking etw. genau wissen know sth exactly ⊖exakt, präzise ⊕ungefähr **2.** careful(ly),

precise(ly), meticulous(ly) ◊ *jdn/etw. genau beobachten* ♦ *Hast du dir das auch wirklich genau überlegt?* es mit etw. genau nehmen be particular about sth ◊ *es mit der Sauberkeit sehr genau nehmen* ⊖sorgfältig ⊕oberflächlich
◉ **(stimmt) genau** *(fam)* absolutely, exactly

② **ge·nau·so** [gə'naozoː] (adv) *+adj* etw. genauso tun wie jd do sth just the same as sb, do sth exactly the same way as sb genauso ... wie just as ... as ◊ *Sie läuft genauso schnell wie du.* ⊖ebenso

② **ge·neh·mi·gen** [gə'neːmɪɡn̩] <genehmigt, genehmigte, hat genehmigt> (tr v) **1.** approve, grant, authorize ◊ *Die Behörde hat den Antrag/Etat genehmigt.* ⊖gestatten ⊕verbieten **2.** *(fam, hum)* sich (dat) etw. genehmigen treat yourself to sth ◊ *Ich genehmige mir jetzt mal eine Pause/ein Glas Bier.*

② **Ge·neh·mi·gung** [gə'neːmɪɡʊŋ] die <-, -en> authorization, permit, licence, license ◊ *ohne ausdrückliche/schriftliche Genehmigung* ♦ *Haben Sie eine Genehmigung dafür?*

ge·neigt [gə'naekt] *past p of* neigen (adj) **1.** geneigt sein/sich geneigt zeigen, etw. zu tun be inclined to sth, be ready to do sth, be willing to do sth ◊ *Ich bin fast geneigt, dir zuzustimmen.* **2.** *only before ns (lofty)* willing, kind, gentle ◊ *Der geneigte Leser/Zuschauer wird mir wohl darin zustimmen, dass ...*

ge·ne·rell [genə'rɛl] (adj, adv) *when used as an adj, only before ns* general(ly), in general, on principle ◊ *Ich lehne Gewalt generell ab.* ♦ *die generelle Einführung von Studiengebühren* ⊖allgemein, grundsätzlich, prinzipiell

ge·ni·al [ge'njaːl] (adj) brilliant, inspired, ingenious ◊ *Deine Erfindung/Idee/Lösung ist einfach genial!* ein genialer Künstler/Wissenschaftler etc. an artistic/a scientific etc. genius

Ge·nick [gə'nɪk] das <-(e)s, -e> *most sing* ANAT nape, (back of the) neck
◉ **jdm/etw. das Genick brechen** *(fam, fig)* be sb's/sth's undoing ◊ *Die sinkenden Absatzzahlen brachen der Firma das Genick.*

Ge·nie [ʒe'niː] das <-s, -s> genius ◊ *Mozart, das musikalische Genie*

ge·nie·ßen [gə'niːsn̩] <genießt, genoss, hat genossen> (tr v) enjoy ◊ *Er genießt bei uns hohes Ansehen.* ♦ *jds Vertrauen genießen* ♦ *sein Leben/ein Glas Wein genießen*
◉ **nicht/kaum zu genießen sein 1.** *(food)* be inedible/scarcely edible *(drink)* be undrinkable/scarcely drinkable **2.** *(person)* be in a foul mood (nur) mit Vorsicht zu genießen sein be taken with a grain/pinch of salt, be treated with caution

Ge·ni·tiv ['geːnitiːf] der <-s, -e> GRAM genitive (case)

The genitive is used to indicate that sth/sb belongs to sth/sb: *die Schönheit des Bayerischen Waldes/meiner Frau/eines Landes.* Proper names just take an 's' ending in the genitive: *Leos Geburtstag.* A number of prepositions also require the noun to take the genitive, e.g. *anhand, anlässlich, bezüglich, mithilfe.*

---

② **ge·nom·men** [gə'nɔmən] *past p of* nehmen
ge·noss [gə'nɔs] *pret of* genießen
ge·nos·sen [gə'nɔsn̩] *past p of* genießen

② **ge·nug¹** [gə'nuːk] [adv] enough ◊ *alt genug für den Führerschein sein* nicht genug, dass not only ... ◊ *Nicht genug, dass es regnet, jetzt hagelt es sogar!* schlimm genug bad enough schlimm/traurig etc. genug, dass as if it wasn't bad/sad etc. enough that

⊙ **nicht/nie genug (von etw.)** bekommen not be able to get enough (of sth) (von jdm/etw.) genug haben have had enough (of sb/sth)

② **ge·nug²** [gə'nuːk] [det] *invariable* enough ◊ *Hast du genug Geld dabei?*

ge·nü·gen [gə'nyːɡn] <genügt, genügte, hat genügt> [intr v] **1.** (für/zu etw.) genügen be enough (for sth), be sufficient (for sth) ◊ *Das Heizöl sollte für diesen Winter genügen.* etw. genügt (jdm) sth will do (for sb), sth is enough (for sb) ◊ *Genügen dir zehn Euro für die Disko?* ⊜reichen, ausreichen **2.** (*lofty*) etw. [dat] genügen satisfy sth, meet sth, fulfil sth ◊ *den Anforderungen/Kriterien/Standards genügen*

Ge·nus ['geːnʊs, 'ɡɛnʊs] das <–, Genera> GRAM gender ◊ *Im Deutschen gibt es drei Genera: männlich, weiblich und sächlich.*

The grammatical gender is neither simple nor logical in German. Therefore it is important to always memorize the article when learning a new noun. Only a few word endings indicate the gender of a noun. Nouns ending in **-keit**, **-heit** and **-ung** are feminine, those ending in **-ling** and **-er** are mostly masculine while nouns ending in **-nis** and **-ment** and those nouns borrowed from English which end in '-ing' such as *das Camping* are neuter.

Ge·nuss [gə'nʊs] der <–es, Genüsse> **1.** in den Genuss von etw./einer Sache [gen] kommen receive sth, enjoy sth ◊ *in den Genuss von Privilegien kommen* **2.** consumption ◊ *regelmäßiger Genuss von Alkohol*; (*of tobacco*) smoking **3.** pleasure, treat ◊ *ein ästhetischer/kulinarischer/sinnlicher Genuss* etw. bereitet jdm Genuss sb enjoys sth ◊ *Das Streicheln bereitete der Katze sichtlich Genuss.* etw. mit Genuss essen/verspeisen/verzehren eat/consume sth with relish

ge·öff·net [gə'œfnət] *past p of* öffnen [adj] **1.** geöffnet sein/haben be open ◊ *Die Ausstellung/Messe ist täglich von 10 bis 18 Uhr geöffnet.* ⊜auf ⊜geschlossen **2.** open ◊ *bei geöffnetem Fenster schlafen* einen Spaltbreit geöffnet ajar ⊜offen ⊜geschlossen

② **Ge·päck** [gə'pɛk] das <–(e)s> *no pl* luggage, baggage ◊ *mit leichtem/kleinem/wenig Gepäck reisen* etw. im Gepäck haben have packed sth; (*ideas etc.*) im Gepäck in tow ◊ *Er reiste mit neuen Ideen im Gepäck an.*

Ge·päck·trä·ger¹ [gə'pɛktrɛːɡɐ] der <–s, –> carrier, rack ◊ *Das Fahrrad hatte keinen Gepäckträger.*

Ge·päck·trä·ger² [gə'pɛktrɛːɡɐ] der <–s, –>, **Ge·päck·trä·ge·rin** [gə'pɛktrɛːɡərɪn] die <–, –nen> porter ◊ *Er arbeitet als Gepäckträger.* ◆ *Sie rief einen Gepäckträger herbei.*

ge·pfif·fen [gə'pfɪfn] *past p of* pfeifen

ge·pflegt [gə'pfleːkt] *past p of* pflegen [adj] **1.** well(-)cared for ◊ *Der Rasen war sehr gepflegt.* ◆ *ein gepflegtes Haus* **2.** (*outward appearance*)

well(-)groomed ◊ *ein gepflegtes Äußeres* sehr gepflegt immaculate ◊ *Ihre Fingernägel waren sehr gepflegt.* sehr gepflegt aussehen/wirken look immaculate **3.** civilized, cultivated, refined ◊ *gepflegte Atmosphäre* ◆ *Das Ambiente des Cafés ist sehr gepflegt.*; (*language, conversation*) cultured ◊ *Er sprach gepflegtes Hochdeutsch.*

② **ge·ra·de¹** [gə'raːdə] [adj] **1.** straight ◊ *Der Zug entgleiste auf einer geraden Strecke.* ◆ *Die Linie ist nicht gerade.* ⊜schief **2.** MATH (*number*) even ◊ *20 ist eine gerade Zahl, 21 eine ungerade.* [adv] **1.** straight ◊ *Sitz bitte gerade!*; (*picture*) gerade hängen be straight etw. gerade biegen/stellen straighten sth gerade verlaufen run in a straight line **2.** at the moment, just now ◊ *Er duscht gerade.* ◆ *Ich habe leider gerade keine Zeit.* **3.** just ◊ *Der Film hat gerade begonnen.* ◆ *Was hat er gerade gesagt?* ⊜eben **4.** gerade noch (only) just ◊ *Der Wagen konnte gerade noch ausweichen.* gerade rechtzeitig just in time gerade mal just ◊ *Er war gerade mal zwei Jahre jünger als ich.*

ge·ra·de² [gə'raːdə] [part] **1.** (*emph*) in particular, particularly ◊ *Gerade das wollte ich eigentlich vermeiden.* gerade jetzt right now **2.** gerade jetzt, wo just now when; now, of all times, when ◊ *Gerade jetzt, wo es so stressig ist, taucht sie auf.* gerade jd sb of all people ◊ *Wieso hat sie gerade ihn geheiratet?* ⊜ausgerechnet **3.** (*fam*) nicht gerade not exactly ◊ *Das war nicht gerade klug von ihm.* ◆ *20 Euro ist ja nicht gerade viel.*

② **ge·ra·de·aus** [ɡəraːdə'|aʊs] [adv] straight on/ahead ◊ *Fahren Sie geradeaus bis zur Ampel.* ◆ *Er blickte starr geradeaus.*

ge·ra·de·zu [gə'raːdətsuː:, – – – '–] [adv] **1.** really, absolutely ◊ *Diese Lage ist geradezu ideal für ein Restaurant.* **2.** virtually ◊ *Sie hat mir den Job geradezu aufgedrängt.*

② **ge·rannt** [gə'rant] *past p of* rennen

② **Ge·rät** [gə'rɛːt] das <–(e)s, –e> **1.** appliance ◊ *Auf dem Gerät sind noch drei Monate Garantie.* ⊜Apparat **2.** *most pl* Geräte equipment ◊ *optische und elektronische Geräte* **3.** (*in gymnastics*) (piece of) apparatus ◊ *Geräte in der Turnhalle aufbauen*

ge·ra·ten [gə'raːtn] *past p of* raten <gerät, geriet, ist geraten> [intr v] **1.** land, end up ◊ *Wie sind diese Blätter in die Wohnung geraten?* **2.** in etw. [acc] geraten get into sth ◊ *Kurz vor München gerieten wir in einen Stau.* ◆ *Er gerät leicht in Wut.* in Brand geraten catch fire in die Kritik geraten come under criticism; (*car etc.*) ins Schleudern geraten go into a skid ins Schwärmen geraten go into raptures jd gerät ins Stocken sb's words falter ins Stottern/Schwitzen geraten start stammering/sweating in Verdacht geraten come under suspicion in Vergessenheit geraten be forgotten **3.** an etw. [acc] geraten come across sth ◊ *Neulich bin ich an einige alte Fotos von meiner Mutter geraten.* **4.** an jdn geraten find sb, meet sb ◊ *Wie sind Sie damals an diesen Arzt geraten?* an den Falschen/die Falsche geraten come to the wrong person; (*in a relationship*) end up with the wrong person **5.** (vor Zorn) außer sich geraten go mad, flip (vor Freude) außer sich geraten go wild (with joy) **6.** nach jdm geraten become just like sb ◊ *Er*

gerät nach seinem Großvater. **7.** gut/schlecht etc. geraten turn out well/badly etc. ◊ Der Braten ist sehr gut geraten.

ge·räu·mig [gə'rɔømɪç] [adj] spacious, roomy ◊ Der Raum war hell und geräumig. ✦ ein geräumiges Badezimmer

Ge·räusch [gə'rɔøʃ] das <-(e)s, -e> noise ◊ Der Drucker gab seltsame Geräusche von sich. ✦ ein leises/lautes Geräusch

ge·recht [gə'rɛçt] [adj] <gerechter, am gerechtesten> **1.** fair ◊ eine gerechte Lösung ✦ Als Chef ist er streng, aber gerecht.; (punishment) just ⊙ungerecht **2.** einer Sache [dat] gerecht adequate for sth ◊ Wir werden Sie mit der Ihrem Bedarf gerechten Technik ausstatten. **3.** einer Sache [dat] gerecht werden satisfy sth, fulfil sth ◊ jds Erwartungen/Anforderungen/Wünschen gerecht werden jd/ etw. wird seinem Ruf mehr als gerecht sb/sth surpasses themselves/itself **4.** jdm gerecht werden do justice to sb ◊ Dieses Bild/Diese Beurteilung wird ihm nicht gerecht. [adv] fairly ◊ Sie wollten das Geld gerecht aufteilen. ⊙ungerecht

Ge·rech·tig·keit [gə'rɛçtɪçkaet] die <-> no pl **1.** justice ◊ Er demonstrierte für Frieden und Gerechtigkeit. ausgleichende Gerechtigkeit poetic justice **2.** fairness ◊ Beurteilen Sie die Gerechtigkeit dieser Regeln.

Ge·re·de [gə're:də] das <-s> no pl (pej) **1.** talk ◊ leeres Gerede **2.** gossip das Gerede der Leute (the) gossip, what people say ⊙ jd/etw. kommt/gerät ins Gerede sb/sth gets a bad reputation

ge·re·gelt [gə're:gl̩t] past p of regeln [adj] regular ◊ Sein Tagesablauf ist sehr geregelt. ✦ einer geregelten Arbeit nachgehen; (life) orderly

ge·reizt [gə'raetst] past p of reizen [adj] <gereizter, am gereiztesten> irritated ◊ eine gereizte Stimmung ✦ Sie wirkte sehr gereizt.; irritable ◊ Er ist heute sehr gereizt. [adv] in irritation ◊ Die Katze fauchte gereizt.

② **Ge·richt** [gə'rɪçt] das <-(e)s, -e> **1.** dish ◊ ein kaltes/scharfes Gericht **2.** court (of law) ◊ Sie arbeitet auf dem/am Gericht. vor Gericht stehen stand trial vor Gericht erscheinen appear in court **3.** court building, law courts, courthouse ◊ Ich muss morgen früh aufs/ins/zum Gericht. **4.** court, judges ◊ Das Gericht zog sich für 15 Minuten zurück.
⊙ mit jdm (hart) ins Gericht gehen be harsh on sb jdn vor Gericht zerren (pej) drag sb before the court das Jüngste Gericht REL the Day of Judgement, the Last Judgement

ge·richt·lich [gə'rɪçtlɪç] [adj] only before ns **1.** legal, court ◊ ein gerichtliches Verfahren ✦ Sie drohte, gerichtliche Schritte einzuleiten. **2.** forensic ◊ ein Institut für gerichtlichen Psychologie eine gerichtliche Obduktion a postmortem examination [adv] legally, by a court ◊ eine gerichtlich angeordnete Hausdurchsuchung gegen jdn gerichtlich vorgehen take legal action against sb jdn gerichtlich belangen sue sb, prosecute sb gerichtlich beeidet sworn ◊ ein gerichtlich beeideter Sachverständiger

ge·rie·ben [gə'ri:bm̩] past p of reiben

② **ge·ring** [gə'rɪŋ] [adj] small, minimal ◊ eine geringe Wahlbeteiligung ✦ Der Aufwand war relativ gering.

die Kosten gering halten keep the costs down ⊙ verschwindend gering minute, tiny ⊚winzig etw./jdn gering achten disregard sth/sb jd sollte etw. nicht so gering achten sb should take sth more seriously etw./jdn gering schätzen think little of sth/sb, not care for sth/sb

ge·ring·fü·gig [gə'rɪŋfyːgɪç] [adj] minor ◊ geringfügige Änderungen vornehmen ✦ Die Unterschiede sind geringfügig. geringfügig Beschäftigte parttime employees with earnings below a certain limit [adv] slightly ◊ Die Zahl der Arbeitslosen stieg geringfügig. ⊚leicht

ge·ris·sen [gə'rɪsn̩] past p of reißen [adj] (fam) crafty ◊ ein gerissener Geschäftsmann ✦ Du bist ganz schön gerissen!

ge·rit·ten [gə'rɪtn̩] past p of reiten

② **gern** [gɛrn], **ger·ne** [gɛ'rnə] [adv] <lieber, am liebsten> **1.** (affection, willingness, delight) gladly ◊ Ich beantworte gern Ihre Fragen. etw. (sehr) gern mögen like sth (very much), be (very) fond of sth jdn gern haben/mögen like sb, be fond of sb etw. gern tun like doing sth ◊ Sie kocht sehr gern. etw. gern essen like sth **2.** (approval) jd kann gern etw. tun sb is welcome to do sth ◊ Du kannst gern bei uns mitfahren. jd glaubt jdm etw. gern sb fully believes sb when they say sth ◊ Dass Japan teuer ist, glaube ich ihm gern. **3.** (in polite requests) jd hätte gern etw. sb would like sth ◊ Ich hätte gern ein Eis. jd würde gern etw. tun sb would like to do sth ◊ Sie würde heute Abend gern ins Kino gehen. **4.** (preferment) jd würde etw. lieber/am liebsten tun sb would prefer to do sth ◊ Am liebsten würde er sofort ins Bett gehen jd hätte etw. lieber/am liebsten sb would prefer (to have) sth ◊ Am liebsten hätte ich ein paar Stunden meine Ruhe. jdm wäre etw. lieber/am liebsten sb would prefer sth ◊ Weißwein wäre mir am liebsten. **5.** (fam) easily ◊ An dieser Kreuzung ereignen sich gern Unfälle.
⊙ (liebend) gern, (sehr) gern very much ◊ „Kommst du mit ins Kino?" — „Sehr gern!" gern geschehen my pleasure, you're welcome gern gesehen welcome ◊ gern gesehene Gäste ✦ Du bist bei uns immer gern gesehen! er/sie etc. kann mich mal gern haben (fam, iron) I can't be bothered with him/her etc.

② **ge·ro·chen** [gə'rɔxn̩] past p of riechen

ge·ron·nen [gə'rɔnən] past p of rinnen

Gers·te ['gɛrstə] die <-> no pl barley ◊ Gerste anbauen

Ge·ruch [gə'rʊx] der <-(e)s, Gerüche> smell, odour, odor ◊ Das Essen verströmte einen köstlichen Geruch.

Ge·rücht [gə'rʏçt] das <-(e)s, -e> rumour ◊ In der Firma kursieren Gerüchte, dass er kündigen will.

② **ge·ru·fen** [gə'ru:fn̩] past p of rufen

Ge·rüst [gə'rʏst] das <-(e)s, -e> **1.** scaffolding ◊ ein Gerüst aufbauen/abbauen **2.** (fig) framework ◊ Diese Vorlage kann als Gerüst für einen Brief dienen.

ge·sal·zen [gə'zaltsn̩] past p of salzen [adj] (fam) **1.** (prices) high, steep ◊ gesalzene Preise **2.** severe ◊ Die Strafe war gesalzen!

② **Ge·samt-...** [gə'zamt] [prefix] total ..., whole ... ◊ Gesamtauflage ✦ Gesamtdeutschland ✦ Gesamtein-

druck

② **ge·sam·te** [gə'zamtə] [adj] <ein gesamter ..., eine gesamte ..., ein gesamtes ...> whole, entire ◊ *Sie ist im gesamten Bundesgebiet tätig.* ♦ *Die gesamte Mannschaft kam zur Party. Die Autobahn war gestern für den gesamten Verkehr gesperrt.* The motorway was closed to all traffic yesterday.

Ge·samt·hoch·schu·le [gə'zamtho:xʃu:lə] die <-, -n> ◊ *Sie studiert an der Gesamthochschule Paderborn.*

At this type of German higher education institution, courses normally taught in universities, polytechnics and sometimes even art colleges are combined in order to bridge the gap between scientific/theoretical knowledge and practical/vocational know-how. Typically, all students take the same foundation course and then go on to take different types of exam after three or four years. Just like at a university, a student can study for a doctoral degree or *Habilitation* at a *Gesamthochschule.*

Ge·samt·schu·le [gə'zamtʃu:lə] die <-, -n> ◊ *Er besucht die Gesamtschule.*

Gesamtschulen came into being only after the more traditional types of school — *Hauptschule, Realschule, Gymnasium.* Their aim is social integration. A *Gesamtschule* is a type of secondary school in which the three traditional school types are united and at which pupils can gain a wide range of qualifications. A pupil of a *Gesamtschule* does not have to leave after his or her fourth/sixth year in order to pursue a more specialized course of study at a further education institution, but can carry on studying at the *Gesamtschule.*

② **ge·sandt** [gə'zant] *past p of* senden[1]

Ge·sang [gə'zaŋ] der <-(e)s, Gesänge> 1. singing ◊ *Sie studiert Gesang.* 2. song ◊ *der Gesang der Vögel* gregorianische Gesänge Gregorian chants

② **ge·schaf·fen** [gə'ʃafn] *past p of* schaffen

② **Ge·schäft** [gə'ʃɛft] das <-(e)s, -e> 1. shop, store ◊ *Morgen haben die Geschäfte bis 20 Uhr geöffnet.* 2. firm, business ◊ *Er leitet das Geschäft.* 3. Geschäft(e) business ◊ *Mit ihm mache ich keine Geschäfte.* ♦ *Morgen wollen wir das Geschäft abwickeln.* ♦ *Das Geschäft läuft gut.* mit jdm ins Geschäft kommen do business with sb 4. *no pl* deal ◊ *Er hat bei diesem Deal ein gutes Geschäft gemacht.* mit etw. ist kein Geschäft zu machen sth is not profitable 5. *only pl* job ◊ *Ich muss in der Stadt noch ein paar Geschäfte erledigen.*
ⓔ **sein Geschäft erledigen/machen/verrichten** *(euph)* do your business ◊ *Der Hund hat sein Geschäft gemacht.*

ge·schäft·lich [gə'ʃɛftlɪç] [adj] business ◊ *geschäftliche Beziehungen ins Ausland unterhalten* Das ist geschäftlich. This is a business matter. *Unsere Beziehung ist rein geschäftlich.* We only have a business relationship. [adv] geschäftlich verreisen go away on business geschäftlich irgendwo sein be away on business somewhere

Ge·schäfts·frau [gə'ʃɛftsfrao] *fem of* Geschäftsmann

Ge·schäfts·füh·rer [gə'ʃɛftsfy:rɐ] der <-s, ->,

Ge·schäfts·füh·re·rin [gə'ʃɛftsfy:rərɪn] die <-, -nen> 1. managing director ◊ *Sie ist Geschäftsführerin einer großen Firma.* 2. *(of a club, an association)* secretary ◊ *der Geschäftsführer des Tischtennisvereins*

Ge·schäfts·mann [gə'ʃɛftsman] der <-(e)s, Geschäftsleute or seldom Geschäftsmänner>,

Ge·schäfts·frau [gə'ʃɛftsfrao] die <-, Geschäftsleute or seldom -en> businessman, businesswoman ◊ *Er ist ein erfolgreicher Geschäftsmann.* ♦ *Ich bin Geschäftsfrau.*

Ge·schäfts·stel·le [gə'ʃɛftsʃtɛlə] die <-, -n> office(s)

Ge·schäfts·zei·ten [gə'ʃɛftstsaetn] die <-> *only pl* hours of business ◊ *Unsere Geschäftszeiten sind werktags von 8-18 Uhr.*

② **ge·schah** [gə'ʃa:] *pret of* geschehen

② **ge·sche·hen** [gə'ʃe:ən] <geschieht, geschah, ist geschehen> [intr v] happen ◊ *Der Überfall geschah am helllichten Tag.* jd weiß nicht, wie ihm geschieht sb doesn't know what is going on, sb doesn't know what is happening to them etw. geschieht jdm sth happens to sb ◊ *Keine Angst, dir kann nichts geschehen.* geschehen lassen, dass jd etw. tut let sb do sth
ⓔ **es ist um jdn geschehen** sb is smitten ◊ *Als ich dich das erste Mal sah, war es um mich geschehen.* **es ist um etw. geschehen** sth is over, sth is at an end ◊ *Als die Presse davon erfuhr, war es um unseren Frieden geschehen.*

Ge·sche·hen [gə'ʃe:ən] das <-s> *no pl (lofty)* events ◊ *Am Ort des Geschehens drängte sich eine Menschenmenge.* ♦ *im Mittelpunkt des Geschehens stehen* ♦ *Sie verfolgte aufmerksam das Geschehen auf der Bühne.*

② **Ge·schenk** [gə'ʃɛŋk] das <-s, -e> present, gift jdm ein Geschenk machen give sb a present/gift

② **Ge·schich·te** [gə'ʃɪçtə] die <-, -n> 1. *no pl* history ◊ *die deutsche/irische Geschichte* ♦ *die Geschichte Italiens/Amerikas* ♦ *die Geschichte des Judentums/der Astronomie* ♦ *Sie studiert Geschichte.* 2. story ◊ *Er erzählte den Kindern eine Geschichte.* 3. *(fam)* business ◊ *Die ganze Geschichte dauerte etwa drei Stunden.* eine dumme Geschichte something stupid
ⓔ **in die Geschichte eingehen** go down in history

Ge·schick [gə'ʃɪk] das <-(e)s, -e> 1. *no pl* skill ◊ *Er besitzt großes politisches Geschick.* 2. *no pl* skill, dexterity ◊ *Mit sehr viel Geschick schnitzte sie eine Figur.* 3. *most pl* Geschick(e) future ◊ *die Geschicke der Weltpolitik*

ge·schickt [gə'ʃɪkt] *past p of* schicken [adj, adv] <geschickter, am geschicktesten> 1. skilful(ly), dexterous(ly) ◊ *Er ist sehr geschickt im Umgang mit Holz.* ♦ *eine geschickte Handwerkerin* ♦ *Geschickt balancierte er das Tablett in die Küche.* handwerklich geschickt sein, geschickte Hände haben be good with your hands ⊖ungeschickt
2. clever(ly) ◊ *eine geschickte Taktik* ♦ *Sie war diplomatisch sehr geschickt.* ♦ *sich nicht sehr geschickt verhalten* ⊖schlau ⊖ungeschickt

② **ge·schie·den** [gə'ʃi:dn] *past p of* scheiden

Ge·schie·de·ne [gə'ʃi:dənə] der/die <-n, die Geschiedenen> *but: ein Geschiedener/eine Geschiedene* divorcee *box@* Substantivierung

A B C D E F G H I J K L M N O P Q R S T U V W X Y Z

Ⓩ **ge·schieht** [gə'ʃiːt] *pres of* geschehen

Ⓩ **ge·schie·nen** [gə'ʃiːnən] *past p of* scheinen

Ⓩ **Ge·schirr** [gə'ʃɪʳ] das <–(e)s, –e> **1.** *no pl* crockery, china, dishes ◊ *weißes Geschirr* **2.** *no pl* dishes ◊ *Sie spülte das Geschirr.* **3.** harness ◊ *einem Pferd das Geschirr anlegen*

Ge·schirr·spü·ler [gə'ʃɪʳʃpyːlɐ] der <–s, –> *(fam)* dishwasher ◊ *Sie räumte den Geschirrspüler ein/ aus.* ⊜Spülmaschine

ge·schis·sen [gə'ʃɪsn̩] *past p of* scheißen

Ⓩ **ge·schla·fen** [gə'ʃlaːfn̩] *past p of* schlafen

Ⓩ **ge·schla·gen** [gə'ʃlaːgn̩] *past p of* schlagen

Ge·schlecht [gə'ʃlɛçt] das <–(e)s, –er> **1.** sex ◊ *der Kampf der Geschlechter* männlichen/weiblichen Geschlechts male/female **2.** *(lofty)* family ◊ *Die Familie Vergy war ein altes und vornehmes Geschlecht.*; dynasty ◊ *ein Herzog aus dem Geschlecht der Karolinger* **3.** LING gender ◊ *Der Artikel zeigt das Geschlecht eines Nomens an.*

⦿ *das schwache/zarte Geschlecht (fam, hum)* the weaker/fair sex *das starke Geschlecht (fam, hum)* the stronger sex *das menschliche Geschlecht* the human race

Ge·schlechts·ver·kehr [gə'ʃlɛçtsfɛkeːɐ̯] der <–(e)s> *no pl* sex(ual intercourse) ◊ *Geschlechtsverkehr mit jdm haben* ⊜Sex

ge·schli·chen [gə'ʃlɪçn̩] *past p of* schleichen

ge·schlif·fen [gə'ʃlɪfn̩] *past p of* schleifen² [adj] polished ◊ *die geschliffene Sprache des Autors*

Ⓩ **ge·schlos·sen** [gə'ʃlɔsn̩] *past p of* schließen [adj] **1.** united ◊ *Sie forderten ein geschlossenes Vorgehen der Partei.* **2.** private ◊ *Hier findet heute eine geschlossene Veranstaltung statt.* **3.** *(area of a town etc.)* built-up ◊ *innerhalb geschlossener Ortschaften* **4.** LING *(vowel, syllable)* closed ⊜offen [adv] unanimously, as one ◊ *Sie stimmten geschlossen gegen den Antrag.*

Ⓩ **Ge·schmack** [gə'ʃmak] der <–(e)s, Geschmäcker or Geschmäcke> **1.** flavour, flavor ◊ *Beim Trocknen verliert Petersilie stark an Geschmack.* ◆ *ein milder/schaler/komischer Geschmack* **2.** taste ◊ *Sie hat einen guten Geschmack, was Kleidung betrifft.* ◆ *Die Geschmäcker sind verschieden.* ◆ *die Grenzen des guten Geschmacks*

⦿ *auf den Geschmack (von etw.) kommen* acquire a taste (for sth)

ge·schmis·sen [gə'ʃmɪsn̩] *past p of* schmeißen

ge·schmol·zen [gə'ʃmɔltsn̩] *past p of* schmelzen

Ⓩ **ge·schnit·ten** [gə'ʃnɪtn̩] *past p of* schneiden

Ⓩ **ge·scho·ben** [gə'ʃoːbm̩] *past p of* schieben

Ⓩ **ge·scho·ren** [gə'ʃoːrən] *past p of* scheren

ge·schos·sen [gə'ʃɔsn̩] *past p of* schießen

Ge·schrei [gə'ʃraɛ] das <–s> *no pl* **1.** shouting, screaming ◊ *Das Geschrei des Kindes/Babys nervte ihn.* **2.** fuss ◊ *Deswegen brauchst du doch kein solches Geschrei machen!*

Ⓩ **ge·schrie·ben** [gə'ʃriːbm̩] *past p of* schreiben

Ⓩ **ge·schrien** [gə'ʃriːən] *past p of* schreien

ge·schrit·ten [gə'ʃrɪtn̩] *past p of* schreiten

ge·schwei·ge [gə'ʃvaɛgə] [conjunc] geschweige (denn) let alone ◊ *Mich hat niemand informiert, geschweige denn gefragt.*

Ⓩ **ge·schwie·gen** [gə'ʃviːgn̩] *past p of* schweigen

Ⓩ **Ge·schwin·dig·keit** [gə'ʃvɪndɪçkaɛt] die <–, –en> speed ◊ *eine Geschwindigkeit von 130 km/h* ◆ *der*

Benzinverbrauch bei einer Geschwindigkeit von 100 km/h ◆ *Die Viren vermehrten sich mit rasender Geschwindigkeit.*

Ⓩ **Ge·schwin·dig·keits·be·schrän·kung** [gə'ʃvɪndɪçkaɛtsbəʃrɛŋkʊŋ] die <–, –en> speed limit ◊ *Hier gilt eine Geschwindigkeitsbeschränkung von 30 km/h.*

Ge·schwis·ter [gə'ʃvɪstɐ] die <–> *only pl* brothers and/or sisters, siblings ◊ *Ich habe vier Geschwister.*

ge·schwol·len [gə'ʃvɔlən] *past p of* schwellen [adj, adv] pompous(ly) ◊ *Sie hat einen geschwollenen Schreibstil.* ◆ *Sie drückte sich sehr geschwollen aus.*

Ⓩ **ge·schwom·men** [gə'ʃvɔmən] *past p of* schwimmen

ge·schwo·ren [gə'ʃvoːrən] *past p of* schwören

Ge·schwulst [gə'ʃvʊlst] die <–, Geschwülste> tumour ◊ *eine bösartige/gutartige Geschwulst*

ge·schwun·gen [gə'ʃvʊŋən] *past p of* schwingen

Ge·schwür [gə'ʃvyːɐ̯] das <–(e)s, –e> ulcer ◊ *ein eitriges Geschwür*

Ⓩ **ge·se·hen** [gə'zeːən] *past p of* sehen

Ge·sel·le [gə'zɛlə] der <–n, –n>, **Ge·sel·lin** [gə'zɛlɪn] die <–, –nen> trained craftsman/technician Gesellin trained craftswoman/technician

Ⓩ **Ge·sell·schaft** [gə'zɛlʃaft] die <–, –en> **1.** most *sing* society ◊ *Wir leben in einer multikulturellen Gesellschaft.* **2.** company ◊ *Er befindet sich in schlechter Gesellschaft.* ◆ *Sie sucht verstärkt seine Gesellschaft.* **3.** geschlossene Gesellschaft private function **4.** ECON society, association, company ◊ *Die Gesellschaft erzielte einen Gewinn von 0,5 Mio. Euro.*

⦿ *jdm Gesellschaft leisten* keep sb company

Ⓩ **ge·ses·sen** [gə'zɛsn̩] *past p of* sitzen

Ⓩ **Ge·setz** [gə'zɛts] das <–es, –e> **1.** law ◊ *Der Bundestag hat ein neues Gesetz verabschiedet.* ◆ *gegen das Gesetz verstoßen;* *(in parliament)* bill **2.** rule ◊ *Das Wohl des Kranken ist oberstes Gesetz.* **3.** law, principle ◊ *physikalische/ chemische Gesetze* ◆ *das Gesetz von Angebot und Nachfrage*

⦿ *mit dem Gesetz in Konflikt geraten/kommen* have a brush with the law

Ge·setz·ge·ber [gə'zɛtsgeːbɐ] der <–s> *no pl* legislator, legislative body

Ⓩ **Ge·sicht** [gə'zɪçt] das <–(e)s, –er> **1.** face ◊ *Sie hatte ein hübsches Gesicht.* ◆ *Ein Lächeln huschte über sein Gesicht.* ◆ *Auf der Party sah man viele unbekannte Gesichter. das Gesicht verziehen* pull a face *ein ängstliches/ernstes etc. Gesicht machen* look anxious/serious etc. **2.** *(fig)* look, appearance ◊ *Die Internetseite der Firma hat ein neues Gesicht bekommen.*

⦿ *über das ganze Gesicht strahlen* grin from ear to ear, grin like a Cheshire cat *etw./jd zeigt sein wahres Gesicht* sth/sb shows its/their true colo(u)rs *das zweite Gesicht* (the) second sight *jdn/etw. zu Gesicht bekommen* catch a glimpse of sb/sth, see sb/sth *jdm etw. ins Gesicht sagen* tell sb sth to their face *jdm steht/ist etw. ins Gesicht geschrieben* sth is written all over sb's face *das Gesicht wahren* save face

Ge·sichts·punkt [gə'zɪçtspʊŋkt] der <–(e)s, –e> perspective, point of view ◊ *Nach welchen Gesichtspunkten wird das Konzept beurteilt?*

Ge·sin·nung [gəˈzɪnʊŋ] die <-, -en> *most sing*
attitude, conviction ◊ *ein Mann mit christlicher/
liberaler Gesinnung*
ge·sof·fen [gəˈzɔfn̩] *past p of* saufen
ge·so·gen [gəˈzoːgn̩] *past p of* saugen
ge·son·dert [gəˈzɔndɐt] [adj, adv] *no comp/superl;
when used as an adj, only before ns* separate(ly) ◊
eine gesonderte Vereinbarung treffen ♦ *Dieser
Betrag muss gesondert abgerechnet werden.*
ge·spannt [gəˈʃpant] *past p of* spannen [adj] tense
◊ *Ihr Verhältnis war sehr gespannt.* ♦ *eine
gespannte Atmosphäre* [adj, adv] expectant(ly),
eager(ly) ◊ *Gespannt blickten die Kinder zur Tür.* jd
ist gespannt sb can't wait Ich bin gespannt, wer
die Wahl gewinnt. I can't wait to see who'll win
the election.
Ge·spenst [gəˈʃpɛnst] das <-(e)s, -er> **1.** ghost ◊
Angeblich geht dort ein Gespenst um. In diesem
Schloss spukt ein Gespenst. This castle is haunted.
⊖Geist **2.** *(fig)* spectre, specter ◊ *Das Gespenst
des Terrorismus geistert durch die Köpfe.*
◉ **Gespenster sehen** be imagining things
ge·spon·nen [gəˈʃpɔnən] *past p of* spinnen
② **Ge·spräch** [gəˈʃprɛːç] das <-(e)s, -e> **1.** conversation ◊ *Er hat sie in ein Gespräch verwickelt.* ♦ *Wir
führten ein langes Gespräch über Kunst.* **2.** talk ◊
Ihr neuer Freund war das Gespräch des Tages. →
Telefongespräch
◉ **im Gespräch sein** be under consideration ◊
Sie ist als seine Nachfolgerin im Gespräch.
ge·sprä·chig [gəˈʃprɛːçɪç] [adj] talkative ◊ *Er war
heute nicht besonders gesprächig.* ♦ *ein gesprächiger junger Mann* ⊖schweigsam
② **ge·spro·chen** [gəˈʃprɔxn̩] *past p of* sprechen
② **ge·sprun·gen** [gəˈʃprʊŋən] *past p of* springen
Ge·stalt [gəˈʃtalt] die <-, -en> **1.** *most sing* figure
◊ *Eine gedrungene Gestalt stach ihr sofort ins
Auge.* ♦ *Am Bahnhof trieben sich dunkle Gestalten
herum.* von kräftiger/zierlicher etc. Gestalt sein be
of powerful/delicate etc. build **2.** character ◊ *Ist er
eine historische oder fiktive Gestalt?* ⊖Figur
3. *most sing* form ◊ *Die Sparbüchse hatte die
Gestalt eines Schweins.* in Gestalt ... [gen]/von
etw. in the shape of sth ◊ *Der Heilige Geist kam in
der Gestalt einer Taube herab.*
◉ **Gestalt annehmen** take shape
ge·stal·ten [gəˈʃtaltn̩] <gestaltet, gestaltete, hat
gestaltet> [tr v] **1.** design ◊ *Der Park soll neu
gestaltet werden.* **2.** *(fig)* organize ◊ *Wie gestalten
Sie Ihre Freizeit/Wochenenden?* [ref v] etw.
gestaltet sich (als) schwierig/einfach etc. sth turns
out to be difficult/easy etc. etw. gestaltet sich
positiv sth is taking a positive turn
ge·stan·den [gəˈʃtandn̩] *past p of* stehen,
gestehen [adj] *only before ns* well-established, successful ◊ *Sie ist eine gestandene Frau.* ♦ *ein
gestandenes Unternehmen*
Ge·ständ·nis [gəˈʃtɛntnɪs] das <-ses, -se> confession ein Geständnis ablegen make a confession
(jdm) ein Geständnis machen make a confession
(to sb)
Ge·stank [gəˈʃtaŋk] der <-(e)s> *no pl* stench ◊
einen bestialischen Gestank verbreiten
ge·stat·ten [gəˈʃtatn̩] <gestattet, gestattete, hat
gestattet> [tr v] *(lofty)* permit, allow ◊ *Rauchen ist
hier nicht gestattet.* ♦ *Gestatten Sie eine Frage?*

sich [dat] etw. gestatten permit yourself sth, allow
yourself sth ◊ *Er gestattete sich erst einmal eine
Pause.* ⊖erlauben, genehmigen
Ges·te [ˈgeːstə, ˈgɛstə] die <-, -n> gesture ◊ *Er
machte mit dem Arm eine einladende Geste.* ♦ *Sein
Geschenk war eine nette Geste.*
ge·ste·hen [gəˈʃteːən] <gesteht, gestand, hat
gestanden> [tr+intr v] (etw.) gestehen confess (to
sth) ◊ *Glaubst du, der Angeklagte wird gestehen?*
♦ *Er hat den Mord gestanden.* jdm etw. gestehen
confess sth to sb ◊ *Sie gestand ihm ihren Fehler.* ♦
Er gestand ihr seine Liebe.
Ge·stell [gəˈʃtɛl] das <-(e)s, -e> **1.** stand ◊ *ein
Gestell für die Lagerung von Weinflaschen*
2. frame ◊ *Das Gerät kann auf ein fahrbares
Gestell montiert werden.*; *(of glasses)* frames
② **ges·tern** [ˈgɛstɐn] [adv] yesterday ◊ *Gestern waren
wir schwimmen.* ♦ *Wir haben bis gestern Mittag
die Wohnung geputzt.* von gestern ancient ◊ *Der
Witz ist doch von gestern!*
② **ge·stie·gen** [gəˈʃtiːgn̩] *past p of* steigen
② **ge·sto·chen** [gəˈʃtɔxn̩] *past p of* stechen
② **ge·stoh·len** [gəˈʃtoːlən] *past p of* stehlen
② **ge·stor·ben** [gəˈʃtɔrbm̩] *past p of* sterben
ge·sto·ßen [gəˈʃtoːsn̩] *past p of* stoßen
ge·streift [gəˈʃtraeft] *past p of* streifen [adj]
striped ◊ *Er trug ein gestreiftes T-Shirt.* Der Stoff
war weißrot gestreift. The material was red and
white striped.
② **ge·stri·chen** [gəˈʃtrɪçn̩] *past p of* streichen [adj]
only before ns level ◊ *ein gestrichener Esslöffel
Zucker/Salz* ⊖gehäuft
② **ges·trige** [ˈgɛstrɪgə] [adj] *only before ns* <ein
gestriger ..., eine gestrige ..., ein gestriges ...>
yesterday's ◊ *Die gestrigen Demonstrationen
verliefen friedlich.* der gestrige Tag yesterday Ich
rufe wegen unserer gestrigen Unterhaltung an. I'm
calling with regard to the conversation we had
yesterday.
② **ge·strit·ten** [gəˈʃtrɪtn̩] *past p of* streiten
② **ge·stun·ken** [gəˈʃtʊŋkn̩] *past p of* stinken
② **ge·sund** [gəˈzʊnt] [adj, adv] <gesünder/gesunder, am
gesündesten/gesundesten> healthy(-ily) ◊ *ein
gesundes Baby* ♦ *Der Arzt sagt, sie sei völlig
gesund.* ♦ *ein gesunder Baum* ♦ *Er isst sehr
gesund.* jdn gesund pflegen nurse sb back to
health etw. ist gesund sth is good for you gesund
leben have a healthy lifestyle der gesunde Menschenverstand common sense
② **Ge·sund·heit** [gəˈzʊnthaet] die <-> *no pl* health ◊
sich guter geistiger und körperlicher Gesundheit ♦
Rauchen gefährdet die Gesundheit. ♦ *Trinken wir
auf seine Gesundheit!*
◉ **Gesundheit!** *(after a sneeze)* Bless you!
② **ge·sun·gen** [gəˈzʊŋən] *past p of* singen
② **ge·sun·ken** [gəˈzʊŋkn̩] *past p of* sinken
② **ge·tan** [gəˈtaːn] *past p of* tun
② **ge·tra·gen** [gəˈtraːgn̩] *past p of* tragen
② **Ge·tränk** [gəˈtrɛŋk] das <-(e)s, -e> drink, beverage
◊ *alkoholfreie/kalte/heiße Getränke*
② **Ge·trei·de** [gəˈtraedə] das <-s> *no pl* grain, corn,
cereal(s) ◊ *Getreide anbauen* ♦ *Erzeugnisse aus
Getreide*
② **ge·tre·ten** [gəˈtreːtn̩] *past p of* treten
② **ge·trie·ben** [gəˈtriːbm̩] *past p of* treiben
② **ge·trof·fen** [gəˈtrɔfn̩] *past p of* treffen

② **ge·trun·ken** [gə'trʊŋkŋ] *past p of* trinken

ge·wach·sen [gə'vaksn̩] *past p of* wachsen
- ⊙ jdm **gewachsen sein** be sb's equal ◊ *Er ist seinem Bruder in jeder Hinsicht gewachsen.* einer Sache [dat] **gewachsen sein** be up to sth ◊ *Ich weiß nicht, ob ich diesem Job gewachsen bin.*

ge·wagt [gə'va:kt] *past p of* wagen [adj] <gewagter, am gewagtesten> **1.** bold, daring ◊ *ein gewagtes Experiment* ♦ *Seine Thesen sind sehr gewagt.* ⊝riskant **2.** risqué ◊ *Der Rock war ganz schön gewagt!*

ge·wäh·ren [gə'vɛ:rən] <gewährt, gewährte, hat gewährt> [tr v] *(lofty)* **1.** grant ◊ *Das Land gewährte den Flüchtlingen Asyl.* ♦ *Die Bank gewährte ihm ein Darlehen über 100 000 Euro.* ♦ *Der Papst gewährte ihm eine Audienz.* ⊝bewilligen **2.** give ◊ *Das Erbe gewährte ihr finanzielle Sicherheit.* [intr v] jdn **gewähren lassen** not stop sb ◊ *Er berührte ihre Schulter und sie ließ ihn gewähren.*

ge·währ·leis·ten [gə'vɛ:ɐ̯laɛstn̩] <gewährleistet, gewährleistete, hat gewährleistet> [tr v] (jdm) etw. **gewährleisten** guarantee (sb) sth ◊ *Ein Zugang zu den Daten muss gewährleistet sein.* ⊝etw. sicherstellen

② **Ge·walt** [gə'valt] die <-, -en> **1.** *no pl* violence ◊ *eine Studie über Gewalt in der Familie/in Schulen* ♦ *Mit Gewalt erreichst du gar nichts.* **2.** *no pl* mit Gewalt forcibly ◊ *Das Fenster ließ sich nur mit Gewalt öffnen.* **3.** *(also fig)* power ◊ *die drei Gewalten Legislative, Exekutive und Judikative* die Gewalt über etw. [acc] **verlieren** lose control of sth
- ⊙ **mit aller Gewalt** at all costs **höhere Gewalt** an act of God

ge·wal·tig [gə'valtɪç] [adj] violent, powerful ◊ *eine gewaltige Explosion; (interest)* tremendous ◊ *Das Interesse daran ist gewaltig.* [adv] *(fam)* really ◊ *Du gehst mir gewaltig auf die Nerven!*

ge·walt·sam [gə'valtza:m] [adj] *mostly before ns* violent ◊ *eines gewaltsamen Todes sterben* ♦ *Seine Methoden sind sehr gewaltsam.* [adv] by force ◊ *Der Dieb drang gewaltsam in das Haus ein.*

ge·wandt [gə'vant] *past p of* wenden

② **ge·wann** [gə'van] *pret of* gewinnen

② **ge·wa·schen** [gə'vaʃn̩] *past p of* waschen

Ge·wäs·ser [gə'vɛsɐ] das <-s, -> stretch of water, body of water, waters ◊ *fließende/stehende Gewässer*

Ge·we·be [gə'veːbə] das <-s, -> **1.** fabric, material ◊ *eine Hose aus weichem Gewebe* **2.** tissue ◊ *aus einem Organ Gewebe entnehmen*

Ge·wehr [gə'veːɐ̯] das <-(e)s, -e> rifle, shotgun ◊ *ein Gewehr abfeuern*

Ge·wer·be [gə'vɛʳbə] das <-s, -> **1.** occupation, trade ◊ *In diesem Gewerbe wird man nicht reich.* das verarbeitende Gewerbe the manufacturing sector **2.** *no pl* business ◊ *ein Gewerbe anmelden*

Ge·wer·be·ge·biet [gə'vɛʳbəɡəbiːt] das <-(e)s, -e> business park, industrial estate ◊ *Diese Firma hat ihren Sitz im Gewerbegebiet.*

② **Ge·werk·schaft** [gə'vɛʳkʃaft] die <-, -en> trade union ◊ *die Gewerkschaft der Polizei* ♦ *einer Gewerkschaft angehören*

② **ge·we·sen** [gə'veːzn̩] *past p of* sein

② **Ge·wicht** [gə'vɪçt] das <-(e)s, -e> *(also fig)* weight ◊ *Geben Sie bitte das Gewicht in Kilogramm an.* ♦ *Gewichte auf die Waage legen; (prestige)*

influence, importance, clout ◊ *Er hat in der Partei an politischem Gewicht verloren.* ♦ *Sie müssen Ihrem Anliegen mehr Gewicht verleihen.*
- ⊙ **ins Gewicht fallen** be of consequence auf etw. [acc] **Gewicht legen** attach importance to sth, lay stress on sth

ge·wie·sen [gə'viːzn̩] *past p of* weisen

② **Ge·winn** [gə'vɪn] der <-(e)s, -e> **1.** prize ◊ *Bei der Tombola gibt es schöne Gewinne.* **2.** profit ◊ *hohe Gewinne bringen* ⊝Profit **3.** *no pl* gain, valuable addition ◊ *Die neue Schauspielerin ist ein echter Gewinn für das Ensemble.*

② **ge·win·nen** [gə'vɪnən] <gewinnt, gewann, hat gewonnen> [tr+intr v] **1.** win ◊ *eine Schachpartie/den ersten Preis gewinnen* ♦ *Welche Mannschaft hat gewonnen?* ♦ *Sie hat im Lotto gewonnen.* jdn für etw. **gewinnen** win sb over to sth ◊ *Es gelang uns, ihn für unsere Ziele zu gewinnen.* **2.** gain ◊ *Erkenntnisse gewinnen* an etw. [dat] **gewinnen** gain in sth ◊ *Sie gewann mehr und mehr an Selbstvertrauen.* [tr v] *(natural resources)* extract ◊ *Erdöl gewinnen* aus etw. gewinnen produce sth from sth ◊ *Benzin wird aus Erdöl gewonnen.; improve* ◊ *Dieser Wein gewinnt durch Lagern.*

ge·wiss [gə'vɪs] [adj, adv] <gewisser, am gewissesten> *seldom comp/superl* certain(ly) ◊ *Voraussetzungen müssen erfüllt werden.* ♦ *Ein gewisser Jochen hat angerufen.* ♦ *Diese Kritik ist gewiss berechtigt.* etw. für gewiss halten Der Erfolg ist ihm gewiss. He is certain to succeed.

Ge·wis·sen [gə'vɪsn̩] das <-s, -> *most sing* conscience ◊ *ein schlechtes Gewissen haben* ♦ *etw. mit gutem Gewissen tun* ♦ *Kannst du das mit deinem Gewissen vereinbaren?*
- ⊙ jdn/etw. **auf dem Gewissen haben** have sb/sth on your conscience ◊ *Er hat vier unschuldige Menschen auf dem Gewissen.* jdm **ins Gewissen reden** appeal to sb's conscience

Ge·wis·sen·haft [gə'vɪsn̩haft] [adj, adv] <gewissenhafter, am gewissenhaftesten> conscientious(ly) ◊ *die gewissenhafte Arbeit engagierter Mitarbeiter* ♦ *Sie ist in allem, was sie tut, äußerst gewissenhaft.* ♦ *Ich habe mich gewissenhaft auf die Prüfung vorbereitet.*

② **Ge·wit·ter** [gə'vɪtɐ] das <-s, -> (thunder)storm ◊ *Ein Gewitter zog auf.*

ge·wo·gen [gə'voːɡŋ] *past p of* wiegen¹ [adj] *(lofty)* well-meaning ◊ *ein gewogenes Publikum* Das Schicksal war ihm gewogen. Fate was kind to him.

② **ge·wöh·nen** [gə'vøːnən] <gewöhnt, gewöhnte, hat gewöhnt> [tr v] **1.** jdn/etw. an etw./jdn **gewöhnen** get sb/sth used to sth/sb, accustom sb/sth to sth/sb ◊ *Wir müssen die Kinder an die neue Umgebung gewöhnen.* **2.** sich an jdn/etw. **gewöhnen** get used to sb/sth ◊ *An das neue Auto muss ich mich erst noch gewöhnen.*

② **Ge·wohn·heit** [gə'voːnhaɛt] die <-, -en> habit ◊ *zur Gewohnheit werden* ♦ *eine Gewohnheit annehmen/ablegen* ♦ *Er geht aus Gewohnheit jeden Abend in die Kneipe.*

② **ge·wöhn·lich** [gə'vøːnlɪç] [adj, adv] **1.** ordinary(-ily) ◊ *ein gewöhnlicher Tag* **2.** usual(ly) ◊ *Was ist sein gewöhnlicher Aufenthaltsort?* ♦ *Es ist durchaus gewöhnlich, dass so etwas geschieht.* ♦ *Gewöhnlich gehe ich einmal im Monat ins Theater.* für

gewöhnlich usually, normally **3.** *(outd)* common(ly) ◊ *eine gewöhnliche Ausdrucksweise* ✦ *Ich halte sie für gewöhnlich.* ✦ *sich gewöhnlich ausdrücken*

ge·wohnt [gə'voːnt] adj <gewohnter, gewohnteste> *only before ns* usual ◊ *Mir fehlt die gewohnte Umgebung.* adv as usual ◊ *Er machte seine Sache gewohnt souverän.*

⊛ etw. gewohnt sein be used to sth ◊ *Sie ist dieses Klima nicht gewohnt.*

ge·wollt [gə'vɔlt] *past p of* wollen² adj *no comp/ superl* **1.** deliberate, forced ◊ *Seine Aussage war eine gewollte Provokation.* ☺ungewollt **2.** desirable ◊ *Lebhafte Diskussionen über aktuelle Probleme sind gewollt.* adv deliberately ◊ *Er gebärdete sich gewollt originell.*

⑦ **ge·won·nen** [gə'vɔnən] *past p of* gewinnen

⑦ **ge·wor·den** [gə'vɔˈdn] *past p of* werden¹

⑦ **ge·wor·fen** [gə'vɔˈfn̩] *past p of* werfen

⑦ **Ge·würz** [gə'vvˈʦ] das <-es, -e> spice ◊ *orientali- sche/scharfe Gewürze*

ge·würzt [gə'vvˈʦt] *past p of* würzen adj *no comp/superl* *(fig)* seasoned ◊ *eine mit feiner Ironie gewürzte Geschichte*

⑦ **ge·wusst** [gə'vʊst] *past p of* wissen

Ge·zei·ten [gə'ʦaetn̩] die <-> *only pl* tides

ge·zielt [gə'ʦiːlt] *past p of* zielen adj <gezielter, am gezieltesten> targeted ◊ *die gezielte Förderung Hochbegabter* ✦ *Ihre Fragen waren sehr gezielt.* adv in a targeted way ◊ *etw. gezielt fördern*

⑦ **ge·zo·gen** [gə'ʦoːɡn̩] *past p of* ziehen

ge·zwun·gen [gə'ʦvʊŋən] *past p of* zwingen adj forced ◊ *gezwungene Heiterkeit* ✦ *Sein Humor wirkte gezwungen.* adv in a forced manner ◊ *Sie lächelte gezwungen.*

Gib·ral·tar [gi'braltaˈ, gibral'taːˈ] das <-s> *article only in combination with attribute, no pl* Gibraltar → Deutschland

⑦ **gibt** [giːpt] *pres of* geben

gie·rig ['giːrɪç] adj, adv greedy(-ily) ◊ *Mit gierigen Blicken starrte er auf das Geld.* ✦ *Sie stürzten sich gierig auf das Büffet.*

gie·ßen ['giːsn̩] <gießt, goss, hat gegossen> tr v **1.** pour ◊ *Die Soße durch ein feines Sieb gießen.*; *(by accident)* spill **2.** *(plants)* water ◊ *die Zimmer- pflanzen gießen* **3.** *(a sculpture)* cast ◊ *eine Skulptur aus Bronze gießen* imp v *(fam)* es gießt it's pouring (with rain)

⑦ **Gift** [gɪft] das <-(e)s, -e> poison, toxin ◊ *tödliches Gift*

⊛ Gift für jdn/etw. sein be extremely bad for sb/sth ◊ *Die Steuererhöhungen sind Gift für die Kon- junktur.*

gif·tig ['gɪftɪç] adj poisonous, toxic ◊ *giftige Gase/Beeren* ✦ *Diese Substanz wird als leicht giftig eingestuft.* adj, adv **1.** *(fam)* venomous(ly) ◊ *giftige Kommentare abgeben* ✦ *Sei doch nicht so giftig!* **2.** *(of colours)* garish(ly) ◊ *ein giftig grünes Stofftier*

⑦ **gilt** [gɪlt] *pres of* gelten

⑦ **ging** [gɪŋ] *pret of* gehen

Gip·fel ['gɪpfl̩] der <-s, -> **1.** peak, summit ◊ *der Gipfel des Matterhorns* ✦ *einen Gipfel erklimmen* **2.** *(fig)* height ◊ *der Gipfel der Dummheit* **3.** summit (conference/meeting) ◊ *einen Gipfel ein- berufen*

⊛ das ist (doch) der Gipfel that's the limit, that has to be the limit

Gips [gɪps] der <-es, -e> **1.** gypsum ◊ *Gips abbauen* **2.** plaster (of Paris) ◊ *eine Plastik aus Gips* **3.** MED plaster cast ◊ *jdm einen Gips anlegen* den Arm in Gips haben have got your arm in plaster

Gi·ro·kon·to ['ʒiːroːˌkɔntoː] das <-s, Girokonten *or* -s> current account, Giro account ◊ *ein Girokonto eröffnen* ✦ *Der Betrag wurde vom Girokonto abgebucht.*

⑦ **Gi·tar·re** [gi'tarə] die <-, -n> guitar ◊ *eine akusti- sche/elektrische Gitarre* ✦ *Sie spielt gut Gitarre.*

Git·ter ['gɪtɐ] das <-s, -> railings, bars ◊ *ein eisernes Gitter; (metal netting)* wire mesh ◊ *ein engmaschiges Gitter*

⊛ hinter Gitter(n) *(fam)* behind bars

⑦ **Glace** [glaːs] die <-, -s *or* -n> *(Swiss)* ice cream ◊ *Wir bekamen eine Glace spendiert.*

Glanz [glants] der <-es> *no pl* **1.** brilliance, bright- ness ◊ *der strahlende Glanz der Sonne* **2.** radiance ◊ *Das renovierte Schloss erstrahlt in neuem Glanz.*

⊛ mit Glanz und Gloria *(fam)* **1.** with flying colours/colors **2.** *(iron)* *(when describing a failure, disappointment)* big time ◊ *Der Plan scheiterte mit Glanz und Gloria.* mit Glanz *(fam)* with flying colours/colors ◊ *ein mit Glanz bestande- nes Examen*

glän·zen ['glɛntsn̩] intr v +*haben* **1.** shine, sparkle ◊ *Der Sand glänzt golden in der Sonne.* ☺schim- mern **2.** *(a person)* shine, excel ◊ *Er glänzte mit hervorragenden Leistungen.*

⑦ **Glas** [glaːs] das <-es, Gläser> **1.** *no pl* glass ◊ *Glas kann recycelt werden.* ✦ *Stell bitte noch die Gläser auf den Tisch.* ✦ *Möchten Sie ein Glas Wein?; (food container)* (glass) jar ◊ *ein Glas Honig* **2.** lens ◊ *Aus meiner Brille ist ein Glas gefallen.*

⑦ **glatt** [glat] adj <glatter/glätter, am glattesten/glät- testen> **1.** smooth, even ◊ *eine glatte Oberfläche* **2.** slippery ◊ *Achtung, die Fahrbahn ist glatt!* **3.** *(hair)* straight ◊ *Ihr Haar ist ganz glatt.* **4.** *(without problems)* smooth ◊ *Er trug zu dem glatten Verlauf der Veranstaltung bei.* **5.** *only before ns (fam) (defeat)* outright ◊ *eine glatte Nie- derlage; (failure)* downright ◊ *Als Gretchen ist sie eine glatte Fehlbesetzung.* **6.** *(of a person)* smooth, slick ◊ *Er wirkt glatt und arrogant.* adv **1.** smoothly ◊ *ein glatt rasierter Mann* ✦ *Alles verlief glatt und ohne Zwischenfälle.* **2.** *(fam)* com- pletely ◊ *Das hatte ich glatt vergessen.* **3.** *transla- tion varies* etw. glatt streichen/bügeln press/iron sth flat etw. glatt rühren beat/whisk sth until it is smooth MED glatt schleifen sand sth down die Haare glatt föhnen dry your hair straight

Glät·te ['glɛtə] die <-> *no pl* **1.** smoothness ◊ *die Glätte des Papiers* **2.** slipperiness; *(on roads)* icy conditions ◊ *Bei Glätte müssen Radfahrer besonders vorsichtig sein.*

Glatt·eis ['glatˌaes] das <-es> *no pl* black ice ◊ *auf den Straßen ist Glatteis.* ✦ *bei Glatteis ins Schleudern kommen*

Glat·ze ['glatsə] die <-, -n> **1.** bald patch, bald head ◊ *Er bekommt langsam eine Glatze.* sich dat eine Glatze scheren lassen have your head shaved

A B C D E F G H I J K L M N O P Q R S T U V W X Y Z

2. *(slang)* skinhead ◊ *Zwei Glatzen schlugen ihn krankenhausreif.*

Glau·be ['glaobə] der <–ns> *no pl* **1.** belief ◊ *Wir ließen sie in dem Glauben, dass er mitkommen würde.* Glaube an jdn/etw. belief in sb/sth ◊ *der Glaube an die Gleichheit aller Menschen* jdm keinen Glauben schenken können not be able to believe sb **2.** *(religious)* faith ◊ *Welchem Glauben gehören Sie an?* Glaube an Gott faith in God ⊚ in gutem Glauben in good faith

② **glau·ben** ['glaobm̩] [intr v] +*haben* **1.** *(in God)* be a believer **2.** an etw./jdn glauben believe in sth/sb ◊ *Glaubst du an ein Leben nach dem Tod?* [tr v] +*haben* **1.** think ◊ *Ich glaube, dass Hanna morgen Geburtstag hat.* ◆ *Ich glaube, du gehst jetzt besser.* ⊝meinen **2.** believe ◊ *Du darfst nicht alles glauben, was er dir erzählt.*

⊚ jdn etw. glauben machen lead sb to believe sth dran glauben müssen *(fam)* **1.** snuff it, peg it **2.** have to face it ◊ *Wenn er mir nicht hilft, musst du halt dran glauben.*

Gläu·bi·ger ['glɔybɪge] der <–s, –>, **Gläu·bi·ge·rin** ['glɔybɪgərɪn] die <–, –nen> creditor

glaub·wür·dig ['glaopvʏ'dɪç] [adj] credible ◊ *eine glaubwürdige Erklärung liefern* ◆ *Seine Aussage war glaubwürdig.*

② **gleich¹** [glaeç] [adj] *no comp/superl* (the) same ◊ *Sie sind in der gleichen Stadt geboren.* ◆ *Unsere Nöte und Probleme sind gleich.* ◆ *Unser Umsatz ist im Vergleich zum Vorjahr gleich geblieben.* Sieben plus drei ist gleich zehn. Seven plus three make ten. [adv] **1.** the same, equally ◊ *Wir sind gleich groß.* ◆ *Sie bemüht sich, alle Schüler gleich zu behandeln.* ⊝unterschiedlich **2.** *temporal* almost, in a moment ◊ *Ich bin gleich fertig. Ach, das hätte ich mir ja gleich denken können. I might have known it!* **3.** +*prep* just ◊ *Ich wohne hier gleich um die Ecke.*

⊚ (es ist) gleich it makes no difference ◊ *Ganz gleich, was der Pullover kostet, ich kaufe ihn.* jdm gleich sein be all the same to sb ◊ *Es ist mir gleich, ob du mitkommst oder nicht.*

gleich² [glaeç] [part] **1.** *in surprising statements, not translated directly* sich [dat] einen Film gleich dreimal sehen see a film three times Die Fans fielen gleich reihenweise in Ohnmacht. The fans were fainting rows at a time. **2.** now ◊ *Wo wohnt er doch gleich?* Was wollte ich gleich sagen? Now what was it I was going to say? **3.** *(to express disapproval)* just ◊ *Wenn du nichts Vernünftiges zu sagen hast, dann sei doch gleich ruhig.*

② **gleich·be·rech·tigt** ['glaeçbərɛçtɪçt] [adj, adv] *no comp/superl* equal(ly) ◊ *gleichberechtigte Mitglieder* ◆ *Die beiden Geschäftsführer sind gleichberechtigt.* ◆ *Sie entscheiden in allen Angelegenheiten gleichberechtigt mit.*

glei·chen ['glaeçn̩] <gleicht, glich, hat geglichen> [intr v] be like, resemble ◊ *Der Garten glich einer Müllhalde.* sie gleichen sich they are alike, they resemble each other ◊ *Sie gleichen sich in Aussehen und Charakter.*

② **gleich·falls** ['glaeçfals] [adv] **1.** (the) same to you ◊ *„Guten Appetit!"* — *„Danke, gleichfalls."* **2.** also, likewise ◊ *Ich bedankte mich gleichfalls.* ⊝ebenfalls, ebenso

Gleich·ge·wicht ['glaeçgəvɪçt] das <–(e)s> *no pl* **1.** balance ◊ *Sie verlor das Gleichgewicht und stürzte.* ◆ *Pestizide schaden dem ökologischen Gleichgewicht.* **2.** *(psychological)* equilibrium ◊ *Die schlechte Nachricht brachte mich völlig aus dem Gleichgewicht.*

gleich·gül·tig ['glaeçgʏltɪç] [adj] **1.** indifferent ◊ *ein gleichgültiges Achselzucken* jdn gleichgültig lassen leave sb cold, fail to touch sb **2.** immaterial ◊ *Es ist gleichgültig, was er sagt.* jdm gleichgültig (sein) be unimportant to sb ◊ *Es ist mir gleichgültig, wohin wir in Urlaub fahren.* ◆ *Ich weiß, dass meine Schwester dir nicht gleichgültig ist.* [adv] indifferently, with indifference ◊ *Solchem Vandalismus darf man nicht gleichgültig gegenüberstehen.*

gleich|kom·men ['glaeçkɔmən] <kommt gleich, kam gleich, ist gleichgekommen> [intr v] **1.** einer Sache [dat] gleichkommen amount to sth, be equivalent to sth ◊ *Der Verlust dieser Arbeitsplätze kommt einer Katastrophe gleich.* **2.** jdm bei/an/in etw. [dat] gleichkommen match sb (for/in sth), equal sb (in sth) ◊ *Niemand kommt ihr an Schönheit gleich.* **3.** einer Sache [dat] gleichkommen compare with sth ◊ *Nichts kommt den Kochkünsten meiner Mutter gleich.*

② **gleich·mä·ßig** ['glaeçmɛːsɪç] [adj, adv] **1.** regular(ly) ◊ *in gleichmäßigen Abständen* ◆ *Der Puls des Verletzten ist gleichmäßig.* ◆ *Er atmet gleichmäßig.* ⊝regelmäßig **2.** even(ly) ◊ *eine gleichmäßige Verteilung der Ressourcen* ◆ *eine Creme gleichmäßig auftragen*

Glei·chung ['glaeçʊŋ] die <–, –en> equation ◊ *eine lineare Gleichung* ◆ *Weniger Waffen gleich weniger Kriminalität — geht diese simple Gleichung auf?*

② **gleich·zei·tig** ['glaeçtsaetɪç] [adj, adv] *no comp/superl* simultaneous(ly) ◊ *Diese beiden Vorlesungen finden gleichzeitig statt. Er ist gleichzeitig Schauspieler und Regisseur.*

② **Gleis** [glaes] das <–es, –e> **1.** *most pl* track, rail **2.** *(train stop)* platform ◊ *Der Intercity nach Hamburg fährt auf Gleis 4 ein.*

⊚ aus dem Gleis geraten go off the rails, lose the plot

glei·ten ['glaetn̩] <gleitet, glitt, ist geglitten> [intr v] **1.** glide ◊ *Das Segelflugzeug gleitet durch die Luft.* seine Augen über etw. [acc] gleiten lassen cast your eyes over sth ◊ *Er ließ seine Augen über sein Spiegelbild gleiten.* **2.** *(to the ground)* slide ◊ *Das Tischtuch war zu Boden geglitten.* ◆ *Er glitt elegant vom Sattel.*

Glet·scher ['glɛtʃe] der <–s, –> glacier

glich [glɪç] *pret of* gleichen

Glied [gliːt] das <–(e)s, –er> **1.** limb ◊ *Ich fror und alle meine Glieder schmerzten.* **2.** *(of finger, toe)* joint ◊ *das obere/mittlere Glied des Mittelfingers* **3.** penis ◊ *ein eregiertes Glied* **4.** *(also fig) (of a chain)* link ◊ *das schwächste Glied einer Kette* **5.** *(of a whole)* section, part ◊ *die Glieder eines Satzes*

Glie·de·rung ['gliːdərʊŋ] die <–, –en> structuring, organization ◊ *eine übersichtlich strukturierte Gliederung aller Informationen*

glitt [glɪt] *pret of* gleiten

② **Glo·cke** ['glɔkə] die <–, –n> **1.** bell ◊ *Eine Glocke läutete den Weihnachtsmarkt ein.* **2.** bell, cover

Käse behält unter einer Glocke sein Aroma.
⊙ etw. **an die große Glocke hängen** broadcast sth, make sth general knowledge
glot·zen ['glɔtsn̩] *(fam)* ⌊intr v⌋ +*haben* **1.** stare, gawp ◊ *Er glotzte auf die Uhr und wartete.* **2.** watch TV ◊ *Manchmal glotze ich die ganze Nacht.* ⌊tr v⌋ +*haben (on TV)* watch ◊ *Sport/Musikvideos glotzen*
② **Glück** [glʏk] *das* <–(e)s> *no pl* **1.** luck, good fortune ◊ *Da hast du aber Glück gehabt!* ⊖Unglück **2.** happiness ◊ *Sie weinte vor Glück.* ⊖Unglück
⊙ **jd hat Glück im Unglück gehabt** it could have been worse **auf gut Glück** on the off chance **von Glück reden können** be able to count yourself lucky **zum Glück** fortunately, as luck would have it
② **glück·lich** ['glʏklɪç] ⌊adj⌋ **1.** lucky ◊ *glückliche Umstände* ♦ *ein glücklicher Zufall* ⊖unglücklich **2.** happy ◊ *eine glückliche Ehe/Kindheit* ♦ *Wir sind sehr glücklich miteinander.* ⊖unglücklich ⌊adv⌋ **1.** happily ◊ *Glücklich lächelnd schauten sie ihr Baby an.* ⊖unglücklich **2.** safely ◊ *Gegen Mitternacht kam er glücklich nach Hause.*
② **Glück·wunsch** ['glʏkvʊnʃ] *der* <–(e)s, Glückwünsche> congratulations ◊ *Herzliche Glückwünsche zum bestandenen Examen!*

> In German, there are special forms of congratulation for every occasion. On New Year's Eve: *Guten Rutsch!*. For the New Year: *Frobes neues Jahr!*. For someone's birthday: *Herzlichen Glückwunsch zum Geburtstag!*. At Christmas: *Fröhliche Weihnachten!*. During the *Karneval* period: *Helau!*. When someone is ill: *Gute Besserung!*. Before exams and other stressful situations: *Hals- und Beinbruch!*. Finally, at Easter people say: *Frohe Ostern!* and at the start of a holiday it is customary to wish someone *Einen schönen Urlaub!*.

Glüh·bir·ne ['glyːbɪrnə] *die* <–, –n> light bulb
glü·hen ['glyːən] ⌊intr v⌋ +*haben* **1.** glow ◊ *Das Feuer glühte rot.; (head, face)* turn red ◊ *Unsere Köpfe glühten vor Anstrengung.* glühende Hitze blazing heat **ein glühend heißer Tag** a boiling hot day **2.** *(with passion)* burn ◊ *Sein Herz glühte vor Liebe.* **ein glühender Patriot** an ardent patriot **jdn glühend verehren** worship sb with all your heart
Glüh·wein ['glyːvaen] *der* <–(e)s, –e> *pl 'Glühwein' when used with expressions of quantity* glühwein, mulled wine

> A drink for the winter months consisting of warm red wine flavoured with cloves, cinnamon, slices of orange or lemon, and orange or lemon peel mixed with sugar, *Glühwein* is especially popular at Christmas markets.

Glut [gluːt] *die* <–, –en> **1.** embers ◊ *die Glut des Feuers neu entfachen* **2.** heat ◊ *die Glut der Savanne* **3.** *(lofty) (of a passion)* ardour ◊ *eine Affäre voller Glut und Leidenschaft*
GmbH [geːʔɛmbeːʹhaː] *die (abbr of* Gesellschaft mit beschränkter Haftung*)* limited company, Ltd ◊ *eine GmbH gründen*
Gna·de ['gnaːdə] *die* <–, –n> mercy ◊ *Die Behörden kennen keine Gnade.* ♦ *Der zum Tode Verurteilte flehte um Gnade.*

Golf¹ [gɔlf] *das* <–s> *often without the article, no pl* golf ◊ *Spielen Sie Golf?*
Golf² [gɔlf] *der* <–(e)s, –e> GEOG gulf ◊ *der Golf von Mexiko*
gön·nen ['gœnən] ⌊tr v⌋ +*haben* **1.** jdm etw. gönnen not begrudge sb sth ◊ *Ich gönne ihr, dass sie die Stelle bekommen hat.* **2.** jdm/sich etw. gönnen allow sb/yourself sth ◊ *Diesen Luxus gönne ich mir.*
goss [gɔs] *pret of* gießen
② **Gott¹** [gɔt] *der* <–es> *no pl; article only in combination with attribute* God ◊ *Gott schütze dich!* ♦ *ein barmherziger Gott*
⊙ **Gott sei Dank** thank God **leider Gottes** unfortunately, I'm afraid ◊ *Ich bin momentan leider Gottes arbeitslos.* **grüß Gott** *(SouthG)* hello, good morning/afternoon/evening **weiß Gott** God knows ◊ *Das hat er weiß Gott nicht verdient.* **um Gottes willen** for God's sake
Gott² [gɔt] *der* <–es, Götter>, **Göt·tin** ['gœtɪn] *die* <–, –nen> god ◊ *die römischen Götter Jupiter und Minerva* Göttin goddess ◊ *die Göttin der Liebe*
Got·tes·dienst ['gɔtəsdiːnst] *der* <–(e)s, –e> service
Grab [graːp] *das* <–(e)s, Gräber> grave ◊ *ein Grab ausheben* ♦ *Er besuchte das Grab seiner Großeltern.* jdn zu Grabe tragen bury sb
⊙ **etw. zu Grabe tragen** abandon sth ◊ *eine Idee zu Grabe tragen*
gra·ben ['graːbm̩] <gräbt, grub, hat gegraben> ⌊tr+intr v⌋ **1.** dig ◊ *einen Tunnel graben* **2.** nach etw. graben ◊ *Sie gruben in den Trümmern nach Verwundeten.* ⌊ref v⌋ sich in/unter etc. etw. ⌊acc⌋ graben burrow into/under etc. sth ◊ *Der Regenwurm gräbt sich in die Erde.; (river)* sich durch etw. graben carve a course through sth
Gra·ben ['graːbm̩] *der* <–s, Gräben> **1.** *(for drainage)* drain ◊ *einen Graben ausheben; (on the side of the road)* ditch ◊ *Der Lkw rutschte bei Glatteis in den Graben.; (of a castle)* moat; *(for soldiers)* trench **2.** *(fig)* gulf ◊ *Der Graben zwischen den beiden Ländern wird tiefer.*
gräbt [grɛːpt] *pres of* graben
Grad [graːt] *der* <–(e)s, –e *or* –> *pl 'Grad' when used with expressions of quantity* degree ◊ *Es herrschen Temperaturen um 20 Grad plus.* ♦ *ein Winkel von 90 Grad.* ♦ *Er ist nur bis zu einem bestimmten Grad belastbar.* ♦ *einen akademischen Grad erwerben; (military)* rank
Graf [graːf] *der* <–en, –en>, **Grä·fin** ['grɛːfɪn] *die* <–, –nen> count ◊ *der Graf von Montechristo* Gräfin countess
Gra·fik ['graːfɪk] *die* <–, –en> **1.** diagram, illustration ◊ *Die Grafik zeigt alle Ergebnisse im Überblick.* **2.** IT graphics **3.** IT icon, picture ◊ *Zum Download bitte auf die entsprechende Grafik klicken.* **4.** ARTS print ◊ *Grafiken von Andy Warhol* **5.** *no pl (subject, trade)* graphics, graphic design ◊ *Grafik und Design studieren* ♦ *Unser Angebot umfasst Layout, Grafik und Satz.*
Gramm [gram] *das* <–s, –> *(abbr* g*)* gram ◊ *zweihundert Gramm Schinken kaufen*
Gram·ma·tik [graʹmatɪk] *die* <–, –en> **1.** grammar ◊ *die deutsche Grammatik beherrschen* **2.** grammar (book) ◊ *Können Sie mir eine gute englische Grammatik empfehlen?*
② **Gras** [graːs] *das* <–es, Gräser> grass ◊ *das Gras*

A B C D E F **G** H I J K L M N O P Q R S T U V W X Y Z

mähen ♦ *Diese Pflanze gehört zur Familie der Gräser.* ♦ *Gras rauchen* ⊛ **ins Gras beißen** *(fam)* bite the dust **über etw.** [acc] **wächst Gras** *(fam)* the dust settles on sth **das Gras wachsen hören** *(fam, iron)* read too much into things

gräss·lich ['grɛslɪç] [adj, adv] horrible(-ibly), terrible(-ibly), dreadful(ly), awful(ly) ◊ *ein grässliches Verbrechen* ♦ *Das Wetter ist heute grässlich.* ♦ *Es war grässlich kalt.* ⊜schrecklich, furchtbar

Grä·te ['grɛːtə] die <-, -n> (fish) bone ◊ *Fischfilet ohne Gräten*

⑦ **gra·tis** ['graːtɪs] [adj, adv] *when used as an adj, not before ns* free (of charge) ◊ *Die Broschüren sind gratis.* ♦ *etw. gratis bekommen* ⊜kostenlos, umsonst

⑦ **Gra·tu·la·ti·on** [gratula'tsjoːn] die <-, -en> eine Gratulation (zu etw.) congratulations (on sth) ◊ *Meine Gratulation zum 20. Firmenjubiläum!*

⑦ **gra·tu·lie·ren** [gratu'liːrən] <gratuliert, gratulierte, hat gratuliert> [intr v] (jdm) (zu etw.) gratulieren congratulate (sb) (on sth) ◊ *Hast du (ihm) schon gratuliert?* ♦ *Sie hat mir zum bestandenen Examen gratuliert.* ⊜beglückwünschen

⑦ **grau** [graʊ] [adj] **1.** grey, gray ◊ *Der Himmel ist ganz grau.* ♦ *der graue Markt; (hair)* grau werden/sein go/be grey, go/be gray **2.** dull, dreary ◊ *Ohne sie erschien ihm das Leben grau und leer.* ⊜langweilig **3.** *only before ns* in grauer Vorzeit, vor grauen Zeiten in the (dim and) distant past ⊛ **grau meliert** *(hair)* greying *(fabric)* mottled grey

Grau·en ['graʊən] das <-s, -> *most sing* horror ◊ *die Grauen des Krieges* Grauen erregend terrible, atrocious jdn packt/überkommt das (kalte) Grauen sb shudders with horror

grau·sam ['graʊzaːm] [adj, adv] **1.** cruel(ly) ◊ *ein grausamer Mord* ♦ *jdn grausam foltern* **2.** terrible(-ibly), horrible(-ibly) ◊ *Sein Schicksal war grausam.* ♦ *Das ist die grausame Wahrheit.* ⊜schrecklich, grässlich

grei·fen ['graɛfn] <greift, griff, hat gegriffen> [tr v] grasp, (take) hold (of) ◊ *Er griff das Lenkrad fester.* sich [dat] etw. greifen grasp sth, grab sth ◊ *Er griff sich das Geld und verschwand damit.* [intr v] **1.** +*direction* in/unter/hinter etw. [acc] greifen reach into/under/behind sth ◊ *Er griff unter den Sitz und holte den Autoatlas hervor.* zu etw. greifen reach for sth ◊ *zum Telefonhörer greifen* zu den Waffen greifen take up arms nach etw./jdm greifen reach for sth/sb **2.** *(fig)* zu etw. greifen resort to sth ◊ *zu drastischen Mitteln greifen* zur Flasche/Zigarette/zu Drogen etc. greifen turn to alcohol/cigarettes/drugs etc. **3.** *(fig)* tief in die Tasche/den Geldbeutel/die Kasse etc. greifen dig deep into your pocket/wallet/coffers etc. **4.** *(fig)* take effect, be effective ◊ *Wir hoffen, dass die Reformen bald greifen.* zu kurz greifen be insufficient **5.** ineinander greifen mesh **6.** um sich greifen spread ◊ *Panik griff um sich.* ⊜sich ausbreiten ⊛ **zu hoch/niedrig gegriffen** too high/low

grell [grɛl] [adj] **1.** glaring ◊ *Die Sonne ist grell.* ♦ *grelles Licht; (colour)* garish ◊ *Ich finde das Rot zu grell.* ⊜blass **2.** shrill, piercing ◊ *ein greller Ton/Schrei*

Gre·mi·um ['greːmjʊm] das <-s, Gremien> body,

committee

⑦ **Gren·ze** ['grɛntsə] die <-, -n> **1.** border ◊ *Waffen über die Grenze schmuggeln* die Grenze nach/zu etw. the border with sth ◊ *ein Dorf unweit der Grenze zu/nach Polen* **2.** *(also fig)* boundary ◊ *Die Grenze von „psychisch gesund" zu „krank" ist fließend.* **3.** limit ◊ *Eine Verlängerung über diese Grenze hinaus ist nicht möglich.* die obere Grenze the upper limit die untere Grenze the lower limit die Grenze des Machbaren the bounds of possibility/the possible die Grenze erreichen/überschreiten reach/exceed the limit(s) jdm/einer Sache Grenzen setzen set limits for sb/sth **4.** *only pl* jds Grenzen sb's limitations, sb's limits ◊ *seine Grenzen kennen (lernen)* ⊛ **die grüne Grenze** stretch of border where there are no/few controls **sich in Grenzen halten** be limited ◊ *Sein Arbeitseifer hält sich in Grenzen.*

gren·zen ['grɛntsn̩] [intr v] +*haben* **1.** *(in space)* an etw. [acc] grenzen border (on) sth ◊ *Spanien grenzt an Frankreich und Portugal.* **2.** *(fig)* an etw. [acc] grenzen verge on sth, be almost sth ◊ *Was er da tut, grenzt schon an Betrug!*

Grie·che ['griːçə] der <-n, -n>, **Grie·chin** ['griːçɪn] die <-, -nen> Greek → Deutsche

Grie·chen·land ['griːçn̩lant] das <-s> *article only in combination with attribute, no pl* Greece → Deutschland

Grie·chin ['griːçɪn] *fem of* Grieche

grie·chisch ['griːçɪʃ] [adj] *mostly before ns* Greek → deutsch

Grie·chisch ['griːçɪʃ] das <-(s)> *no pl; seldom with the article* Greek → Deutsch

Grieß [griːs] der <-es> *no pl* semolina

griff [grɪf] *pret of* greifen

⑦ **Griff** [grɪf] der <-(e)s, -e> **1.** grip ◊ *seinen Griff lockern; (in sports)* hold **2.** mit einem Griff, mit wenigen Griffen with little effort **3.** der Griff zu etw. resorting to sth ◊ *Der Griff zum Alkohol verschaffte ihm nur kurze Erleichterung.* **4.** handle ◊ *Halt dich am Griff fest.* ⊛ **etw. in den Griff bekommen/kriegen 1.** get sth under control **2.** get the hang of sth **etw./jdn im Griff haben** have sth/sb under control **mit geübtem Griff** expertly

Grill [grɪl] der <-s, -s> grill; *(outside)* barbecue ◊ *Würstchen auf dem Grill braten* vom Grill barbecued

gril·len ['grɪlən] [tr+intr v] +*haben* ◊ *Forellen grillen; (outside)* barbecue; *(as a special/social event)* have a barbecue

grin·sen ['grɪnzn̩] [intr v] +*haben* grin ◊ *verlegen grinsen*

⑦ **Grip·pe** ['grɪpə] die <-> *no pl* **1.** *(fam)* cold, flu ⊜Erkältung **2.** MED influenza, flu ◊ *sich gegen Grippe impfen lassen*

grob [groːp] [adj, adv] <gröber, am gröbsten> **1.** coarse(ly) ◊ *grober Sand* ♦ *grob gemahlenes Mehl* grob gewebt/gestrickt loose woven/knit ⊜fein **2.** rough(ly) ◊ *eine grobe Schätzung* ♦ *Au, sei doch nicht so grob!* ♦ *Grob gerechnet wird das 12 Millionen kosten.* **3.** *when used as an adj, only before ns* gross(ly) ◊ *ein grober Fehler* ♦ *grob fahrlässig handeln* **4.** rude(ly) ◊ *Sie war zu ihm zurückwies, wurde er grob.* ♦ *„Du Idiot!", fuhr sie ihn grob an.*

⑦ **groß** [groːs] [adj] <größer, am größten> **1.** large, big ◊ *ein großes Haus* ♦ *Die Schuhe sind mir zu groß.*

⊜klein **2.** *(height of a person)* tall ◊ *Ich bin größer als du.* gleich groß sein be the same height *Das Baby war bei der Geburt nur 45 cm groß. The baby was only 45 cm long at birth.* ⊜klein **3.** *(measurement of a room or object etc.)* etw. ist ... groß sth measures/is ... ◊ *Das Zimmer ist nur fünf Quadratmeter groß.* **4.** *(significant)* great, big ◊ *Die Überraschung war groß.* ♦ *Ich bin ein großer Fan von ihr.* ♦ *Er ist kein großer Tänzer.* in etw. ⌊dat⌋ (ganz) groß sein be great at sth ⊜gering **5.** *temporal* long ◊ *über große Zeiträume hinweg* in großer Ferne far-off ⊜kurz **6.** *(intensive)* bad, great ◊ *Hast du sehr große Schmerzen?* großen Durst/Hunger haben be very thirsty/hungry ⊜gering **7.** *(fam)* grown-up ◊ *Wenn er groß ist, will er Pilot werden.* groß werden grow up ⊜erwachsen ⊜klein **8.** *(fam)* (siblings) older, big ⊜älter **9.** (letter) capital, upper case ◊ *Schreibt man „deutsch" mit großem oder kleinem d?* ⊜klein ⌊adv⌋ groß feiern have a big party groß geraten turn out big groß dimensioniert with large dimensions groß angelegt large-scale ◊ *ein groß angelegter Plan* in etw. ⌊acc⌋ ganz groß einsteigen get into sth in a big way groß gewachsen tall ⊛ etw. groß ankündigen announce sth with a lot of fanfare groß ausgehen go out somewhere expensive etw. groß schreiben attach great importance to sth ◊ *Pünktlichkeit wird bei uns groß geschrieben.* was ist schon groß dabei what's the big deal

> If *groß* in combination with a verb cannot be compared or expanded, the combination is written as one word: *Nomen werden im Deutschen immer großgeschrieben.* (In German, nouns are always written with a capital letter.) But: *Ehrlichkeit wird bei den meisten Eltern groß geschrieben.* (Most parents attach great importance to honesty.)

⑦ **Groß·...** [gro:s] ⌊prefix⌋ **1.** grand... ◊ *die Großeltern*; great-... ◊ *die Großtante* **2.** *(indicating a large scale)* eine Großfamilie an extended family der Großhandel the wholesale trade eine Großstadt a big city

groß·ar·tig ['gro:s|aːˈtɪç] ⌊adj, adv⌋ **1.** brilliant(ly), great ◊ *Ich finde ihn einfach großartig!* ♦ *eine großartige Schauspielerin* ♦ *Das hast du großartig gemacht!* ⊜wunderbar, ausgezeichnet, hervorragend **2.** *(fam, esp pej)* big, great ◊ *Auf großartige Entschuldigungen kann ich verzichten.* etw. großartig ankündigen announce sth with a lot of fanfare ⊜groß ⌊adv⌋ at (great) length, long ◊ *Ich will das jetzt nicht alles großartig erklären.* ⊜groß, lange

Groß·bri·tan·ni·en [gro:sbri'tanjən] das <–s> article only in combination with attribute, no pl Great Britain → Deutschland

Groß·buch·sta·be ['gro:sbuːʃtaːbə] der <–n(s), –n> capital (letter), upper case (letter) ◊ *Schreiben Sie Ihren Namen in Großbuchstaben.*

Gro·ße¹ ['gro:sə] der/die <–n, die Großen> *but: ein Großer/eine Große* **1.** der Große, unser Großer our oldest/eldest (son), our older/ elder son die Große, unsere Große our oldest/eldest (daughter), our older/elder daughter ◊ *Unsere Große macht schon bald ihr Abitur.* **2.** the Great ◊ *Katharina die Große* ♦ *Friedrich der Große box@* Substantivierung ⊛ **die Großen** *(kidsp)* **1.** the grown-ups ◊ *Warum dürfen die Großen immer alles bestimmen?* **2.** the

older children ◊ *In Ordnung, du darfst mit den Großen ins Kino gehen.*

Gro·ße² ['gro:sə] das <–n> *but: Großes, no pl* das Große the big things ◊ *Im Leben kommt es nicht nur auf das Große, sondern auch auf die kleinen Dinge an.* Großes great things ◊ *Großes leisten* ⊛ im Großen und Ganzen by and large, on the whole *box@* Substantivierung

⑦ **Grö·ße** ['grø:sə] die <–, –n> **1.** size ◊ *ein Kleid in Größe 40* Von der Größe her ist das Auto genau richtig für mich. The car is exactly the right size for me. eine Größe von hundert Quadratmetern etc. haben be a hundred square metres etc. **2.** height **3.** *most sing* extent, scale ◊ *Sie war sich der Größe der Gefahr bewusst.* **4.** *(also fig)* MATH quantity ◊ *eine physikalische Größe* an essential/indispenable part **5.** *most sing* magnanimity ◊ *Sie bewies wahre Größe und vergab ihm.* **6.** outstanding/important figure ◊ *Einstein und andere Größen der Wissenschaft;* celebrity ◊ *Er kennt viele Größen des Showgeschäfts.*

Groß·el·tern ['gro:s|ɛltɐn] die <–> *only pl* grandparents ◊ *die Großeltern mütterlicherseits/väterlicherseits*

Groß·mut·ter ['gro:smʊtɐ] die <–, Großmütter> grandmother

groß|schrei·ben ['gro:sʃraebm̩] <schreibt groß, schrieb groß, hat großgeschrieben> ⌊tr v⌋ write with a capital (letter), capitalise, capitalize ◊ *Im Deutschen schreibt man alle Substantive groß. box@* groß

Groß·stadt ['gro:sʃtat] die <–, Großstädte> city

Groß·teil ['gro:staɛl] der <–s> *no pl* **1.** major part ◊ *Den Großteil ihrer Freizeit verbringt sie beim Sport.* **2.** majority ◊ *Ein Großteil der Messebesucher war aus der Region.*

größ·ten·teils ['grø:stn̩taɛls] ⌊adv⌋ largely, for the larger part ◊ *Die Umstellung erfolgte größtenteils reibungslos.*

Groß·va·ter ['gro:sfa:tɐ] der <–s, Großväter> grandfather

groß·zü·gig ['gro:stsy:gɪç] ⌊adj, adv⌋ **1.** generous(ly) ◊ *ein großzügiger Gastgeber* ♦ *Sie war so großzügig, ihm zu verzeihen.* ♦ *Er hat sie überaus großzügig unterstützt.* großzügig bemessen generous **2.** spacious(ly) ◊ *eine großzügige Wohnanlage* ♦ *großzügig angelegt* großzügig geschnitten spacious

grub [gru:p] *pret of* graben

Gru·be ['gru:bə] die <–, –n> **1.** mine, pit ◊ *In dieser Grube wird Eisenerz abgebaut.* **2.** hole, pit ◊ *eine Grube ausheben/graben* ⊛ wer andern eine Grube gräbt (, fällt selbst hinein) *you can easily fall into your own trap*

Gruft [grʊft] die <–, Grüfte> *most sing* crypt, vault

⑦ **grün** [gry:n] ⌊adj⌋ **1.** green ◊ *Die Ampel ist grün.* ♦ *sich ins grüne Gras legen* ♦ *Die Tomaten sind noch grün.* grün werden (turn) green **2.** POL Green, green ◊ *ein grüner Abgeordneter* ⊛ grün hinter den Ohren sein be wet behind the ears grün und blau *(fam)* black and blue ◊ *jdn grün und blau schlagen* sich grün und blau ärgern go mad sich nicht grün sein not like each other

Grün [gry:n] das <–s, –> **1.** green ◊ *ein leuchten-*

A
B
C
D
E
F

G

H
I
J
K
L
M
N
O
P
Q
R
S
T
U
V
W
X
Y
Z

des Grün ♦ ein Kleid in Grün Die Ampel steht auf/ zeigt Grün. the traffic lights are green bei Grün die Straße überqueren cross at green (lights) box@ Farbe **2.** greenery ◊ das erste Grün des Frühlings ⊛ etw. ist dasselbe in Grün (fam) sth is (basically) the same, sth does not make a (real) difference

② **Grund** [grɔnt] der <-(e)s, Gründe> **1.** reason ◊ ohne Angabe von Gründen ♦ Nenne mir nur einen guten Grund dafür. ... Gründen for ... reasons (ein) Grund zu etw. a reason for sth ◊ Er hat Grund zum Feiern. **2.** land ◊ Sie befinden sich hier auf privatem Grund. Grund und Boden land **3.** bottom ◊ Im Grunde meines Herzens bin ich Optimist. auf Grund laufen run aground **4.** background ◊ Die Schrift ist blau auf weißem Grund. ⊖Hintergrund **5.** ground ◊ Das Haus steht auf felsigem Grund. ⊖Untergrund, Boden ⊛ in Grund und Boden bomben bomb into oblivion jdn in Grund und Boden reden **1.** not let sb get a word in edgeways **2.** shoot sb's arguments to pieces sich in Grund und Boden schämen be utterly ashamed jdn in Grund und Boden spielen (in sports) thrash sb in Grund und Boden wirtschaften ruin (completely) einer Sache [dat] auf den Grund gehen get to the bottom of sth im Grund(e) (genommen) really, basically ◊ Das ist im Grunde gar kein Problem. von Grund auf/aus complete(ly), entire(ly) ◊ eine Erneuerung von Grund auf

grund·... [grɔnt] [prefix] totally, completely ◊ grundverkehrt ♦ grundverschieden; thoroughly ◊ grundanständig

② **Grund·...** [grɔnt] [prefix] **1.** basic ◊ die Grundgebühr ♦ Grundkenntnisse **2.** land ◊ der Grundbesitzer

② **grün·den** ['grʏndn] <gründet, gründete, hat gegründet> [tr v] found ◊ Augsburg wurde von den Römern gegründet. eine Familie gründen start a family [ref v] sich auf etw. [acc] gründen be based on sth ◊ Worauf gründet sich der Verdacht?

Grund·ge·setz ['grɔntgəzɛts] das <-es> no pl POL Basic Law (of the Federal Republic of Germany) ◊ gegen das Grundgesetz verstoßen

The Basic Law, the constitution of the Federal Republic of Germany, was passed in 1949. Amendments to the Basic Law have to be agreed by a minimum of two thirds of the members of both houses (Bundestag and Bundesrat). Amendments that would affect Germany's federal structure or change the nature of constitutional rights are not permitted.

Grund·kurs ['grɔntkʊˀs] der <-es, -e> **1.** beginners' course ◊ Er besuchte einen Grundkurs in Deutsch. **2.** foundation subject during the sixth form/senior high school

In a Grundkurs a student acquires elementary knowledge of a subject. In the Kollegstufe or Oberstufe (the sixth form of a grammar or comprehensive school) a student studies a number of subjects in Grundkursen (two or three lessons of 45 minutes a week) and two subjects in Leistungskursen (main courses, usually five lessons a week).

② **Grund·la·ge** ['grɔntlaːgə] die <-, -n> basis, foun-

dation ◊ eine gesetzliche Grundlage für etw. schaffen ♦ Die Behauptung entbehrt jeder Grundlage. ⊖Basis, Fundament

gründ·lich ['grʏntlɪç] [adj, adv] thorough(ly) ◊ eine gründliche Untersuchung ♦ Die Arbeit ist sehr gründlich. ♦ Hast du dir das auch gründlich überlegt? ⊖sorgfältig [adv] completely ◊ Das ging gründlich daneben!

② **grund·sätz·lich** ['grɔntzɛtslɪç] [adv] **1.** absolutely ◊ Ich lehne Kriege grundsätzlich ab. ⊖prinzipiell, generell **2.** in principle ◊ Ich stimme Ihnen grundsätzlich zu, aber ... ⊖im Prinzip, eigentlich [adj] fundamental ◊ ein grundsätzliches Problem ♦ Sind die Unterschiede grundsätzlich?

Grund·schu·le ['grɔntʃuːlə] die <-, -n> primary school, elementary school ◊ Sie geht noch in die Grundschule.

In Germany, children start school at the age of six. During the first four years they go to a Grundschule where they acquire basic skills, literacy, numeracy etc., are taught arts and technical subjects and have PE. At this stage, equal importance is attached to acquiring social skills, learning how to study, playing with others and learning how to accept rules. The Grundschule prepares pupils for education in secondary schools. A teacher evaluates the pupil's needs and abilities and suggests which type of secondary school — Gymnasium, Gesamtschule, Realschule, Hauptschule — is most appropriate.

Grund·stück ['grɔntʃtʏk] das <-(e)s, -e> plot (of land), site ◊ ein 500 Quadratmeter großes Grundstück erwerben; (built on) property

Grün·dung ['grʏndʊŋ] die <-, -en> founding ◊ die Gründung eines Unternehmens; (of a family) starting

Grü·ne¹ ['gryːnə] das <-n> but: Grünes, no pl leaves, greenery ◊ Radieschen waschen und das Grüne entfernen ⊛ ins Grüne to the country ◊ ins Grüne fahren im Grünen in the country ◊ im Grünen wohnen box@ Farbe

Grü·ne² ['gryːnə] der/die <-n, die Grünen> but: ein Grüner/eine Grüne POL Green

The German Greens started out as a very mixed alliance of conservative farmers, respectable citizens, committed Christians, former Social Democrats, feminists, and left-wing extremists. Their calls for a better environment, a more inclusive society, equal opportunities, solidarity, and a more democratic party structure appealed to many voters. Now they are established as one of the major political parties in Germany with a strong environmental agenda.
The Austrian Greens have been represented in parliament since 1990. Like their German namesakes, they are slightly left of centre and promote sustainable environmental policies.

② **Grup·pe** ['grʊpə] die <-, -n> group eine/die Gruppe ... [gen], eine/die Gruppe von etw./jdm a/ the group of sth/sb ◊ eine Gruppe Jugendlicher

② **Gruß** [gruːs] der <-es, Grüße> **1.** regards ◊ Herzliche Grüße an Ihren Mann! Bitte richten Sie ihm Grüße von mir aus. Please give him my

regards. **die besten Grüße** best wishes **mit besten Grüßen** with compliments, with best wishes; *(in letters to friends etc.)* herzliche/viele/liebe Grüße (lots of) love; *(in business letters)* Mit freundlichen Grüßen, ... Yours sincerely, ...; Yours faithfully, ...; *(in letters to friends etc.)* Gruß und Kuss love and kisses **2.** greeting ◊ *jds Gruß erwidern* Zum Gruß nickte sie mit dem Kopf. She nodded a greeting. Er streckte mir die Hand zum Gruß hin. He held out his hand in greeting. **ein letzter Gruß** a last farewell

ⓔ **Gruß und Kuss** *(in letters)* love and kisses

In German, there are many different forms of greeting. Before noon you say *Guten Morgen!*. During the whole day you can say *Guten Tag!* or just an informal *Hallo!*. When it gets dark or from about 6pm onwards you say *Guten Abend!*. To say goodbye late at night you might say *Gute Nacht!*. Otherwise you say *Auf Wiedersehen!* or an informal *Tschüss!*. There are also regional differences, for example in Bavaria people often say *Grüß Gott!* as a greeting and *Auf Wiederschauen!* as a goodbye.

② **grü·ßen** ['gry:sn] [tr+intr v] +*haben* **1.** (jdn) grüßen say hello (to sb), greet sb ◊ *Er grüßte sie mit einem Lächeln.* ✦ *Sie grüßte freundlich, als sie das Zimmer betrat.* **2.** (jdn) grüßen lassen send (sb) your regards ◊ *Tim lässt (dich) herzlich grüßen.* [tr v] +*haben* **1.** jdn von jdm grüßen give sb's regards to sb ◊ *Grüßen Sie Ihre Mutter von mir.* **2.** *only spoken (fam)* Grüß dich! Hello!, Hi!

② **gu·cken** ['gʊkn̩] *(fam)* [intr v] +*haben* look ◊ *Guck mal, was ich hier habe!* ✦ *aus dem Fenster gucken* ⊜schauen [tr v] +*haben* watch ◊ *Fernsehen/DVDs gucken*

Gu·lasch ['gu:laʃ] *das or also der* <-(e)s> *no pl* goulash

② **gül·tig** ['gʏltɪç] [adj] **1.** valid ◊ *Die neue Regelung ist ab Januar gültig.* ✦ *eine gültige Arbeitserlaubnis* **2.** accepted ◊ *allgemein gültige Werte wie Toleranz und Gerechtigkeit* ⊜anerkannt

Gum·mi¹ ['gʊmi:] *der or das* <-s, -s> **1.** *seldom with the article* rubber ◊ *Schuhsohlen aus Gummi* **2.** rubber band, elastic band ◊ *die Haare mit einem Gummi zusammenbinden*

Gum·mi² ['gʊmi:] *der* <-s, -s> *(fam) (condom, for erasing pencil)* rubber ◊ *einen Gummi benutzen* ✦ *Dieser Gummi radiert schlecht.*

② **güns·tig** ['gʏnstɪç] [adj, adv] **1.** günstig favourable (-ably), favorable(-ably) ◊ *Die Aussichten sind günstig.* ✦ *günstig urteilen* **eine günstige Gelegenheit** a good opportunity **im günstigsten Fall** at best ⊜ungünstig **2.** cheap(ly) ◊ *Der Kredit ist wirklich günstig.* ✦ *das günstigste Angebot* ✦ *günstig einkaufen* ⊜billig **3.** convenient(ly) ◊ *Sie wählten das Haus wegen seiner günstigen Lage.* ⊜ungünstig

gur·geln ['gʊrɡl̩n] [intr v] +*haben* **1.** gargle ◊ *mit Kamillentee gurgeln* **2.** gurgle ◊ *ein gurgelnder Bach*

Gur·ke ['gʊrkə] *die* <-, -n> **1.** cucumber ◊ *eine Gurke in Scheiben schneiden; (pickled)* gherkin, pickle **saure Gurke** (pickled) gherkin **2.** *(fam, pej)* hooter, conk

Gurt [gʊrt] *der* <-(e)s, -e> strap ◊ *Die Fracht war mit Gurten gesichert.; (at a seat)* seat belt, safety belt

Gür·tel ['ɡʏrtl̩] *der* <-s, -> belt ◊ *einen Gürtel tragen* ✦ *ein grüner Gürtel aus Bäumen und Sträuchern*

ⓔ **den Gürtel enger schnallen** *(fam)* tighten your belt

⑦ **gut** [gu:t] [adj] <besser, am besten> **1.** good ◊ *Sie hat gute Gewinnchancen.* ✦ *Du hast bessere Augen als ich.* ✦ *Er hat seinen besten Anzug an.* ✦ *Guten Morgen!* ✦ *Zum Spielen ist die Hose noch gut genug.* ✦ *Der Fisch wog ein gutes Pfund.* ✦ *Der Urlaub hat mir gut getan.* **Gute Fahrt/Reise!** Have a good trip/journey! **jdn/etw. gut finden** like sb/sth **gut in etw.** [dat] **sein** be good at sth **gut zu etw. sein** be good for sth **Guten Appetit!** Enjoy your meal! **Gute Besserung!** Get well soon! **Ein gutes neues Jahr!** Happy New Year! **na/nun/also gut** all right, fair enough **schon gut** (that's) all right **gut gegen etw. sein** be good for sth ◊ *Gurgeln mit Salzwasser ist gut gegen Halsweh.* **für jdn gut sein** be good for sb **2.** *(mark)* ⊜B ◊ *In Mathe hatte sie die Note „gut".* **sehr gut** ⊜A **box@** Note **3.** *(healthwise)* jdm geht es gut sb is fine/well, sb feels fine/well **jdm geht es besser** sb is better, sb feels better; *(financially)* jdm geht es gut sb is doing well [adv] **1.** well ◊ *gut vorbereitet sein* **Das ist noch einmal gut gegangen!** That was a lucky escape! **es sich** [dat] **gut gehen lassen** pamper yourself **2.** *with expressions of quantity* just over ◊ *Das dauert gut zwei Stunden.*

ⓔ **gut und gern(e)** as much as **so gut wie** *(fam)* almost ◊ *Das kostet so gut wie nichts.* ⊜praktisch

Gut [gu:t] *das* <-(e)s, Güter> **1.** property ◊ *gestohlenes Gut* **(un)bewegliche Güter** (im)movable property **Hab und Gut** possessions, belongings **2.** *(fig)* good ◊ *Das Leben ist unser höchstes Gut.* **3.** *most pl* Güter goods ◊ *der Transport gefährlicher Güter* ⊜Waren **4.** *(agricultural)* estate

Gut·ach·ten ['gu:tʔaxtn̩] *das* <-s, -> ein Gutachten (über etw./jdn), ein Gutachten (zu etw.) a(n expert) report (on sth/sb) ◊ *ein medizinisches Gutachten* ✦ *ein Gutachten zu den Brandursachen* **ein Gutachten erstellen** draw up a(n expert) report **ein Gutachten vorlegen** submit a(n expert) report **ein Gutachten einholen** ask for a(n expert) report

gut·ar·tig ['gu:tʔaːrtɪç] [adj] **1.** MED benign ◊ *ein gutartiger Tumor* ✦ *Der Knoten in ihrer Brust war gutartig.* ⊜ungefährlich ⊜bösartig **2.** good-natured ◊ *ein gutartiger Hund* ⊜brav ⊜aggressiv

Gu·te¹ ['gu:tə] *das* <-n> *no pl:* (ein) Gutes, no pl good, good thing(s) ◊ *Er hat viel Gutes getan.* ✦ *Das Gute ist, dass ...* **Was gibt's heute Gutes zu essen?** What is there to eat today? **Alles Gute!** All the best! **des Guten zu viel** too much **des Guten zu viel tun** overdo it **auch sein Gutes haben** be no bad thing **das bedeutet nichts Gutes** that's not a good sign/omen **box@** Substantivierung

ⓔ **im Guten wie im Bösen** the nice way and the not so nice way

Gu·te² ['gu:tə] *der/die* <-n, die Guten> *but: ein Guter/eine Gute* **1.** der/die Gute the good soul **meine Gute** my dear **mein Guter** my dear friend **2.** goody ◊ *die Guten gegen die Bösen* **box@** Substantivierung

Gut·ha·ben ['guːthaːbm̩] das <-s, -> FIN balance ◊ *ein Guthaben von 100 Euro auf dem Konto haben*

gü·tig ['gyːtɪç] [adj, adv] kind(ly) ◊ *ein gütiger Mensch* ♦ *Der König war weise und gütig.* ♦ *Der Nikolaus lächelte uns gütig an.*

ⓔ **du gütiger Himmel** *(oldf)* good heavens

gut|ma·chen ['guːtmaxn̩] <macht gut, machte gut, hat gutgemacht> [tr v] **1.** etw. (wieder) gutmachen make up for sth ◊ *Wie kann ich den Fehler wieder gutmachen?* **2.** gain ◊ *Er konnte noch zwei Sekunden auf den Führenden gutmachen.*

⊝aufholen

gut·mü·tig ['guːtmyːtɪç] [adj, adv] good-natured(ly) ◊ *ein gutmütiger Mensch* ♦ *Sie ist sehr gutmütig.* ♦ *Er lächelte gutmütig.*

Gut·schein ['guːtʃaen] der <-(e)s, -e> ein Gutschein (für/über etw. [acc]) a voucher (for/of sth), a token (for/of sth), a coupon (for/of sth) ◊ *ein Gutschein über 50 Euro; (for returned goods)* credit note ⊝Bon

Gut·schrift ['guːtʃrɪft] die <-, -en> **1.** credit ◊ *eine Gutschrift in Höhe von 1000 Euro* **2.** crediting ◊ *Sie hob das Geld sofort nach der Gutschrift ab.*

Gym·na·si·um [gʏmˈnaːziʊm] das <-s, Gymnasien> grammar school ◊ *Sie kommt nächstes Jahr ans/ aufs Gymnasium.*

The German *Gymnasium* is a secondary school that helps pupils acquire an extensive general education and prepares them for university. The education takes eight or nine years to complete. Those years are divided into three sections: *Unterstufe, Mittelstufe, Oberstufe/Kollegstufe*. In the latter, pupils can choose from a range of *Grundkurse* (basic courses) and select two *Leistungskurse* (main courses). In order to obtain the *Abitur* (the certificate necessary for university entry) pupils must sit exams in four subjects studied in the *Leistungskurse* and two studied in the *Grundkurse*.

H

h, H [haː] das <-(s), -(s)> **1.** h, H ◊ *Dieses Wort wird mit einem kleinen h/großen H geschrieben.* ♦ *ein stummes h* ♦ *H wie Heinrich* **2.** MUS B natural ◊ *Sie spielte ein H.*

② **Haar** [haːʳ] das <-(e)s, -e> hair ◊ *blonde/lockige Haare haben* ♦ *blondes/lockiges Haar haben* ♦ *die Haare/das Haar kurz tragen* ♦ *jdn an den Haaren ziehen* ⊙ **jdm stehen die Haare zu Berge** *(fam)* sb's hair stands on end **jdm die Haare vom Kopf fressen** eat sb out of house and home **ein Haar in der Suppe finden** *(fam, esp pej)* find sth to quibble about **jd hat Haare auf den Zähnen** sb is a battleaxe **sich über etw.** [acc]/**wegen etw. keine grauen Haare wachsen lassen** not lose any sleep about sth **kein gutes Haar an jdm/etw. lassen** *(fam)* not have a good word to say about sb/sth **sich** [dat] **(mit jdm) in die Haare geraten/kriegen** *(fam)* argue (with sb), quarrel (with sb) **jdm aufs Haar gleichen** *(fam)* be the spitting image of sb **etw. ist an den Haaren herbeigezogen** *(fam, pej)* sth is far-fetched **sich in den Haaren liegen** *(fam)* quarrel, squabble, be at loggerheads **um ein Haar** *(fam)* almost, (very) nearly ◊ *Er wäre um ein Haar überfahren worden.*
haa·rig [ˈhaːrɪç] [adj] **1.** hairy ◊ *haarige Arme und Beine haben* **2.** *(fig)* tricky, nasty ◊ *eine haarige Angelegenheit* ⊖heikel
haar·scharf [ˈhaːrˈʃaʳf] [adv] *no comp/superl* by a hair's breadth ◊ *Der Schuss ging haarscharf daneben.* ⊖knapp
Haar·schnitt [ˈhaːrˈʃnɪt] der <-(e)s, -e> haircut, hairstyle ⊖Frisur, Schnitt
Haar·trock·ner [ˈhaːrˈtrɔknɐ] der <-s, -> hairdryer ⊖Föhn
② **ha·ben** [ˈhaːbm̩] <hat, hatte, hat gehabt> [tr v] *no passive* **1.** have, have got ◊ *ein eigenes Haus haben* ♦ *Erfahrung/Zeit haben* ♦ *Grippe/Kopfweh haben* ♦ *So gut wie du möchte ich es auch mal haben!* ♦ *Ich habe den Job!* ♦ *Was hast du eigentlich gegen ihn? Hast du den Koffer?* Have you brought the suitcase? **es an der Leber/am Magen haben** have liver/stomach trouble/problems **etw. hinter sich** [dat] **haben** have finished with sth **nichts/(et)was mit jdm haben** not have/have it off with sb ◊ *Glaubst du, sie haben es miteinander?* **etw./jd hat es an sich** [dat] **, etw. zu tun/sein** sth/sb has the habit of doing/being sth ◊ *Glas hat es nun mal an sich, durchsichtig zu sein.* **2.** Wir haben zwei Uhr/halb drei. It is two o'clock/half past two. Wir haben den 5. Oktober. Today is October 5th. Den Wievielten haben wir heute? What is the date today? [tr+intr v] *no passive, +inf with 'zu'* **etw. zu tun haben** have to do sth ◊ *Wir haben noch einen Berg Wäsche zu waschen.* **(viel) zu tun haben** be (very) busy **etwas/nichts zu sagen haben** have a/ no say **jdm nichts zu verbieten haben** have no right to forbid sb sth **etwas zu meckern/jammern**

haben have anything/something to grumble/moan about [aux] *+past p; no pres perf* geküsst/gelacht/ finanziert haben have kissed/laughed/financed ◊ *Ich habe gesungen.* ♦ *Du hattest geschlafen.* ♦ *Er wird schon gegessen haben, wenn du zurückkommst.* ♦ *Sie sagte, sie habe den Film schon gesehen.* ♦ *Wir hätten uns gerne noch ein bisschen ausgeruht.* ⊙ **wie hätte jd etw. denn gern** how would sb like sth **wenig von jdm haben** not see much of sb **etw. hat etwas/viel für sich** there is something/a lot to be said for sth **jd wird schon sehen, was er davon hat** sb will live to regret this **(immer) für etw. zu haben sein** (always) be up for sth, never turn sth down **zu haben sein 1.** *(object)* be available, be for sale **2.** *(fam)* *(person)* be single, be available **etwas/nichts von etw. haben** be able/not be able to enjoy sth, be able/not be able to benefit from sth **es in sich** [dat] **haben** be deceptive, be surprisingly strong ◊ *Der Wein hat es ganz schön in sich.* **jd hätte nichts gegen etw.** sb could do with sth **hat jd was** is sb all right, is there something the matter with sb ◊ *Hat er was? Er ist so still.* **das haben wir gleich/werden wir gleich haben** it won't take a second **was hat es mit etw. auf sich** what is sth about **jd hat es ja** *said about sb who is spending a lot of money when they really cannot afford it* **das hast du (jetzt) davon** now see what's happened **ich hab's** I've got it **wie gehabt** as usual **es nicht (so) mit etw. haben** not care (very much) for sth
Hab·gier [ˈhaːpɡiːɐ] die <-> *no pl (pej)* greed ◊ *jdn aus Habgier ermorden*
Ha·cke [ˈhakə] die <-, -n> **1.** hoe ◊ *die Erde mit einer Hacke auflockern* **2.** *(regional)* heel ◊ *Mir tun die Hacken weh.* ⊖Ferse **3.** *(regional)* (hohe) Hacken (high) heels ⊙ **sich (nach etw.) die Hacken ablaufen/abrennen** go to the ends of the earth (to get sth) **jdm auf den Hacken bleiben/sein** stay/be on sb's heels **auf den Hacken kehrtmachen, sich auf den Hacken umdrehen** do an about-turn, turn on your heels
② **Hack·fleisch** [ˈhakflaɪʃ] das <-(e)s> *no pl* mince, ground meat ◊ *Hackfleisch vom Rind/Schwein*
② **Ha·fen** [ˈhaːfn̩] der <-s, Häfen> harbour, harbor; *(for trade)* port ◊ *Ein Schiff ist in den Hafen eingelaufen.* ⊙ **der Hafen der Ehe** *(hum)* the state of matrimony
Ha·fer [ˈhaːfɐ] der <-s> *no pl* oats
Haft [haft] die <-> *no pl* **1.** imprisonment; *(of political prisoners, young people)* detention **aus der Haft entlassen werden** be released from prison **in Haft (sitzen/sein)** (be) in custody **in Haft genommen werden** be taken into custody **2.** *(prison)* sentence ◊ *23 Monate Haft* **zu lebenslanger Haft verurteilt werden** be given a

life sentence, be sentenced to lifelong imprisonment

haf·ten ['haftn̩] <haftet, haftete, hat gehaftet> intr v +haben **1.** stay on ◊ *Dieser Nagellack haftet nicht gut.* ♦ *Farbe haftet schlecht auf Aluminium.* **2.** be stuck ◊ *Unter der Tischplatte haftete ein Kaugummi.* **3.** *(fig)* stick ◊ *Dieses Ereignis haftete ihm im Gedächtnis.* ♦ *Ist von der letzten Lektion etwas haften geblieben?* **4.** LAW be legally responsible ◊ *Eltern haften für ihre Kinder.*

Häft·ling ['hɛftlɪŋ] der <-s, -e> prisoner ◊ *ein entflohener Häftling; (political)* detainee

Haft·pflicht ['haftpflɪçt] die <-> no pl **1.** liability ◊ *die gesetzliche Haftpflicht für etw.* **2.** *(fam) (abbr of* Haftpflichtversicherung) (personal) liability insurance

Haf·tung ['haftʊŋ] die <-, -en> most sing liability, (legal) responsibility ◊ *Dafür übernehmen wir keine Haftung.*; *(form)* in Haftung genommen werden be held liable

ha·geln ['haːgln̩] imp v +haben **1.** es hagelt it's hailing. *(fig)* es hagelt etw. sth rains down ◊ *Es hagelte Kritik.*

Hahn [haːn] der <-(e)s, Hähne> **1.** cock, cockerel, rooster ◊ *Der Hahn kräht.* **2.** TECHN tap, faucet ◊ *ein tropfender Hahn*
 ☻ **der Hahn im Korb** the only man **nach jdm/ etw. kräht kein Hahn** nobody gives a damn about sb/sth

⑦ **Hähn·chen** ['hɛːnçən] das <-s, -> chicken

⑦ **Ha·ken** ['haːkn̩] der <-s, -> **1.** hook ◊ *Sie zog ihre Jacke aus und hängte sie an den Haken.* ♦ *Nach einem mächtigen rechten Haken ging er zu Boden.* **2.** tick, check ◊ *erledigte Aufgaben mit einem Haken versehen* **3.** *(fam)* snag ◊ *Der einzige Haken an der Sache sind die Kosten.*
 ☻ **einen Haken schlagen** dart sideways

halb [halp] adv **1.** half(-) ◊ *Du hast wieder nur halb zugehört!* ♦ *ein halb betrunkener Gast* **2.** half past ◊ *Ich warte um halb am Eingang auf dich.* halb drei/neun etc. half past two/eight etc., two/eight etc. thirty
 ☻ **halb ..., halb ...** half ..., half ...; part(ly) ..., part(ly) ... ◊ *Er ist halb Engländer, halb Deutscher.* **halb und halb 1.** more or less ◊ *Er hat mich halb und halb überzeugt.* **2.** in (two) equal portions, half ... (and) half ...

halb-... [halp] prefix half-... ◊ *halbblind* ♦ *halbrund* ♦ *halbstündig* halbhoch medium-high

Halb-... [halp] prefix **1.** semi(-)... ◊ *das Halbmetall* **2.** half-... ◊ *das Halbjahr* ♦ *die Halbschwester*

hal·be ['halbə] adj no comp/superl, only before ns <ein halber ..., eine halbe ..., ein halbes ...> **1.** half ◊ *Ich komme in einer halben Stunde.* ♦ *ein halber Meter* die halbe Klasse half of the class ☻ganze **2.** partial Das ist doch nur die halbe Wahrheit! That's not the whole truth! Sie hörte nur mit halber Aufmerksamkeit zu. She wasn't paying full attention. ☻ganze

hal·bie·ren [hal'biːrən] <halbiert, halbierte, hat halbiert> tr v **1.** halve, cut into two; *(a number)* divide by two **2.** sich halbieren halve ◊ *Der Umsatz hat sich in den letzten fünf Jahren halbiert.* etw. halbieren halve sth, reduce sth by half ◊ *Die Regierung will die Arbeitslosigkeit halbieren.* ☻verdoppeln

Halb·jahr ['halpjaːɐ̯] das <-(e)s, -e> **1.** half-year, half of a/the year ◊ *der Geschäftsbericht für das erste Halbjahr 2003* **2.** SCHOOL first/second term

Halb·pen·si·on ['halppaŋˌzi̯oːn, 'halppãˌzi̯oːn] die <-> no pl half board ◊ *eine Woche Halbpension* eine Unterkunft mit Halbpension half-board accommodation

halb·tags ['halptaːks] adv **1.** in the mornings/afternoons ◊ *Sara wird halbtags von einer Tagesmutter betreut.* **2.** *(employment)* part-time ◊ *eine halbtags arbeitende Sekretärin*

halb·wegs ['halpveːks] adv halfway ◊ *Jeder halbwegs gebildete Mensch weiß das.*; partially ◊ *Er versuchte, wenigstens halbwegs den Überblick zu behalten.*

Halb·zeit ['halptsae̯t] die <-, -en> **1.** half ◊ *In der zweiten Halbzeit wurde der Spieler ausgewechselt.* **2.** half time ◊ *Zur Halbzeit stand es 4:2.*

⑦ **half** [half] pret of helfen

⑦ **Hälf·te** ['hɛlftə] die <-, -n> **1.** half ◊ *Die Hälfte von vier ist eine Vier.* ♦ *Fast die Hälfte der Schüler hatte eine Vier.* ♦ *In der zweiten Hälfte war Köln die bessere Mannschaft.* zur Hälfte half ◊ *Der Bus ist nur zur Hälfte besetzt.* **2.** *(fam)* half, part ◊ *Die größere Hälfte der Insel ist von Wald bedeckt.*

⑦ **Hal·le** ['halə] die <-, -n> **1.** hall ◊ *Besuchen Sie unseren Stand in Halle 9.* **2.** lobby, vestibule ◊ *die Halle des Museums* **3.** sports hall Wegen des Regens trainieren wir heute in der Halle. We're training indoors today because of the rain.

Hal·len·bad ['halənbaːt] das <-(e)s, Hallenbäder> indoor (swimming) pool

⑦ **hal·lo** ['haloː, - '—] interj *(fam)* hello ◊ *Hallo, Peter!* ♦ *Hallo, Sie haben Ihre Tasche liegen lassen!* ♦ *Hallo, ist da jemand?* ♦ *Hallo? Sind Sie noch am Apparat?*

⑦ **Hals** [hals] der <-es, Hälse> **1.** neck ◊ *eine Creme für Hals und Gesicht* ♦ *eine Flasche mit engem Hals* ♦ *Der Hals des Cellos ist aus Ahornholz.* **2.** throat ◊ *Sie wachte mit Schmerzen im Hals auf.*
 ☻ **Hals über Kopf** in a rush ◊ *Sie reisten Hals über Kopf ab.* head over heels **seinen Hals aus der Schlinge ziehen** save your neck **jd bekommt etw. in den falschen Hals** *(fam)* **1.** sb gets the wrong end of the stick **2.** *(when swallowing)* sth goes down the wrong way **aus vollem Hals** at the top of your voice **jdn/etw. am Hals haben** *(fam, pej)* be saddled with sb/sth ◊ *Ich habe jede Menge Probleme am Hals.* **sich jdm an den Hals werfen** *(fam)* throw yourself at sb **bis zum/über den Hals** *(fam)* up to your ears ◊ *Sie sind bis über den Hals verschuldet.*

⑦ **halt¹** [halt] part *(SouthG, Austr, Swiss)* just, simply ◊ *„Opa hat mir nicht gratuliert!" — „Er ist halt vergesslich."* ♦ *Sag ihm halt, was du von ihm denkst!* ☻eben

halt² [halt] interj stop ◊ *Halt! Keinen Schritt weiter!*

Halt [halt] der <-(e)s, -e> **1.** no pl hold ◊ *Dieses Gel verleiht dem Haar besseren Halt.*; grip, something to hold onto ◊ *Er taumelte und suchte verzweifelt nach Halt.* Halt finden (get a) grip **2.** no pl *(fig)* support ◊ *Meine Freunde sind mir ein großer Halt.* den Halt verlieren become (emotionally) unstable **3.** most sing stop ◊ *Nächster*

Halt: *Rathaus.* ohne Halt without stopping, non-stop Halt machen stop ⊙ vor jdm/etw. nicht Halt machen not spare sb/sth ◊ *Anorexie macht auch vor Jungen nicht Halt.* vor nichts Halt machen stop at nothing

② **hält** [hɛlt] *pres of* halten

② **halt·bar** ['haltbaːʳ] adj **1.** long-life, non-perishable ◊ *haltbare Nahrungsmittel* Medikamente sind nicht unbegrenzt haltbar. Medicines won't keep forever. **2.** durable, hardwearing ◊ *eine haltbare Beschichtung* **3.** tenable ◊ *juristisch haltbare Argumente* ♦ *Diese Empfehlung ist nicht länger haltbar.*

② **hal·ten** ['haltn̩] <hält, hielt, hat gehalten> tr v **1.** hold ◊ *ein Buch in der Hand halten* ♦ *Sie saßen Händchen haltend auf einer Parkbank.* ♦ *Er hielt schützend den Arm vor das Gesicht.* ♦ *Dieser Schwimmring hält die Luft nicht mehr.* **2.** hold (in place) ◊ *Das Kleid wird von Spaghettiträgern gehalten.* **3.** jdn halten stop sb ◊ *Geh doch, ich halte dich nicht!* **4.** die Stellung halten hold your position einen Rekord halten hold a record das/sein Gewicht halten keep your weight down; *(a promise)* keep ◊ *Ich halte meine Versprechen.* **5.** keep ◊ *Wir können das Haus nicht länger halten.* **6.** maintain, keep up ◊ *Diese Theorie ist nach heutigen Erkenntnissen nicht mehr zu halten.* **7.** *(pets, farm animals)* keep, have ◊ *eine Katze als Haustier halten* **8.** jdn/etw. für jdn/etw. halten think that sb/sth is sb/sth ◊ *Ich halte sie für sehr begabt.*; *(mistakenly)* take sb/sth for sb/sth ◊ *Aus der Ferne hielt ich ihn für meinen Bruder.* **9.** *(a speech)* give ◊ *eine Abschiedsrede halten;* *(a church service)* hold **10.** etw. geheim/warm etc. halten keep sth secret/warm etc. **11.** SPORT save ◊ *einen Ball halten* intr v **1.** stop ◊ *Wo hält der Bus zum Bahnhof?* **2.** keep, last ◊ *Schnittblumen halten oft nicht lange.* **3.** last ◊ *Unsere Waschmaschine hat nur zwei Jahre gehalten.*; hold up ◊ *Meinst du, die Leiter hält bei deinem Gewicht?* **4.** SPORT make a save Der Torwart hält prima. The goal keeper does a great job. **5.** auf etw. acc halten set store by sth, attach importance to sth ◊ *Sie hält sehr auf Manieren.* **6.** etw./viel/wenig etc. von jdm/etw. halten think sth/a lot/little etc. of sb/sth ◊ *Was halten Sie von dem Essen in der Kantine?* nichts von jdm/etw. halten not think much of sb/sth **7.** zu jdm halten stick by sb, support sb ♦ *Sie hielt immer zu ihrem Bruder.* **8.** *often adjectival passive* etw. kurz/klassisch etc. halten keep sth short/classic etc. ◊ *Das Design war klassisch gehalten.* ref v **1.** jd kann sich halten sb can keep their balance; *(posture)* sich aufrecht/gerade halten hold yourself straight ◊ *„Halt dich gerade",* ermahnte ihn die Mutter. sich kaum (noch) auf den Beinen halten können hardly be able to stand **2.** sich halten last ◊ *Hier hält sich kein Geschäft sehr lange.* **3.** sich ausgezeichnet/hervorragend halten do extremely well ◊ *Beim Marathon hielt sie sich hervorragend.* sich schlecht halten do poorly **4.** sich gut/einigermaßen halten age well/fairly well ◊ *Für sein hohes Alter hat er sich gut gehalten.* **5.** sich an etw. acc halten stick to sth, follow sth ◊ *Du musst dich an die Regeln halten.* **6.** sich an jdn halten turn to sb, go to sb ◊ *Halten Sie sich mit Beschwerden bitte an meinen Chef.* **7.** sich irgendwo halten stay

somewhere ◊ *Das Lied hielt sich wochenlang in den Charts.* **8.** sich links/rechts halten keep left/right sich geradeaus halten keep going straight on ⊙ nicht zu halten sein **1.** be untenable ◊ *Nach der Beweislage ist diese Aussage ist nicht zu halten.* **2.** be unstoppable ◊ *Kaum läuft die Musik, ist Maike nicht mehr zu halten.* an sich acc halten control yourself etwas auf sich acc halten be self-respecting

Hal·ter¹ ['haltɐ] der <-s, -> holder ◊ *ein Halter für Räucherstäbchen*

Hal·ter² ['haltɐ] der <-s, ->, **Hal·te·rin** ['haltərɪn] die <-, -nen> *(form)* owner ◊ *der Halter eines Pferdes/Wagens*

② **Hal·te·stel·le** ['haltəʃtɛlə] die <-, -n> stop ◊ *An welcher Haltestelle muss ich aussteigen?*

Hal·tung ['haltʊŋ] die <-, -en> **1.** *(abbr of* Körperhaltung*)* posture ◊ *eine gebeugte Haltung* **2.** attitude ◊ *die Haltung der Regierung gegenüber dem Irak-Krieg* **3.** no pl dignity, composure ◊ *Sie konnte nur mühsam die Haltung bewahren.* **4.** *(abbr of* Tierhaltung*)* keeping ◊ *Die Haltung von Haustieren ist verboten.*; husbandry ◊ *Milch aus artgerecht ökologischer Haltung*

Ham·burg ['hambʊʳk] das <-s> *article only in combination with attribute, no pl* Hamburg box@ Stadt

> Area: 755 km²; population: approx. 1.72 million. In the Middle Ages, the free town Hamburg was one of the first towns to profit from joining the Hanseatic League. The city established itself as Germany's largest and most important port. Many foreign companies have branches in Hamburg. It is famous as a media capital thanks to the presence of the German Press Agency (*Deutsche Presse-Agentur* or *dpa*) and large publishing houses such as *Springer, Gruner und Jahr,* and *Jahreszeiten.*

Ham·mel ['haml̩] der <-s, -> **1.** wether **2.** no pl *(abbr of* Hammelfleisch*)* mutton ◊ *Es gibt Hammel mit Bohnen.*

② **Ham·mer** ['hamɐ] der <-s, Hämmer> **1.** hammer ◊ *mit dem Hammer Nägel in die Wand schlagen* **2.** *(fam)* howler ◊ *sich einen richtigen Hammer leisten* ⊙ unter den Hammer kommen come under the hammer ◊ *Das Gemälde ist für 140 000 Euro unter den Hammer gekommen.* ein/der Hammer sein *(fam)* **1.** be fantastic ◊ *Das Auto ist echt der Hammer.* **2.** be outrageous ◊ *Die Preise hier sind ein Hammer.*

häm·mern ['hɛmɐn] tr v *+haben* **1.** hammer ◊ *Er hämmerte einen Nagel in die Wand.* **2.** *(fam)* hammer out ◊ *Er hämmerte eine Melodie auf dem Klavier.* **3.** slam ◊ *Der Mittelstürmer hämmerte den Ball ins Tor.* intr v *+haben* **1.** hammer ◊ *Er hämmerte mit den Fäusten gegen die Tür.* ♦ *Der Regen hämmerte auf das Zeltdach.* ♦ *Sie saß am Computer und hämmerte in die Tasten.* **2.** *(with pain etc.)* be pounding, be thumping ◊ *Mein Kopf hämmerte, als wolle er gleich zerspringen.*

② **Hand** [hant] die <-, Hände> **1.** hand ◊ *Er kam mit ausgestreckter Hand auf mich zu.* ♦ *Was hast du denn da in der Hand?* ♦ *Ein Fullhouse ist eine gute*

A
B
C
D
E
F
G
H
I
J
K
L
M
N
O
P
Q
R
S
T
U
V
W
X
Y
Z

Hand im Poker. jdm die Hand geben give sb your hand, shake sb's hand **2.** *(fam)* SPORT *(abbr of* Handspiel*)* a handball ◊ *Das war eindeutig Hand.* ⊙ **Hand aufs Herz** hand on heart, honestly **die Hände überm Kopf zusammenschlagen** *(fam)* throw up your hands in despair/horror **die Hände in den Schoß legen** be idle (bei etw.) **die Hand im Spiel haben,** (bei etw.) **seine Hände im Spiel haben** be involved (in sth) **seine Hände in Unschuld waschen** deny all responsibility **alle/ beide Hände voll zu tun haben** have your hands full **aus erster Hand** etw. aus erster Hand wissen have first-hand knowledge of sth aus erster Hand informieren give first-hand advice **eine Hand frei haben** have got a free hand **keine Hand frei haben** have got your hands full **eine gute Hand** eine gute Hand bei etw./jdm an instinct for sth/sb, a feel for sth/sb **eine gute Hand für etw. haben** have a feel for sth, be good at sth **eine gute Hand für jdn haben** be good with sb **mit der linken Hand** with no trouble at all **zwei linke Hände haben** be all fingers and thumbs **linker/rechter Hand** on the left/right-hand side ◊ *Rechter Hand sehen Sie das Schloss.* **die öffentliche Hand** public funds ◊ *Zuwendungen aus öffentlicher Hand* **jds rechte Hand** sb's right-hand man/woman **hinter vorgehaltener Hand** off the record **unter der Hand** off the record ◊ *Wir erhielten diesen Tipp unter der Hand.* under the counter ◊ *In dieser Firma fließen die Informationen unter der Hand.* **eine Hand voll 1.** a handful of **2.** *(fig)* a little ◊ *ein Hand voll Zärtlichkeit* **ein Händchen für etw. haben** have the knack of sth **Händchen halten** hold hands **auf der Hand liegen** *(fam)* be quite clear, be obvious **etw. in die Hand nehmen** take charge of sth **etw. von der Hand weisen** dismiss sth **zu Händen** *(form)* for the attention of

Hand·ar·beit ['hant|ar͜baet] die <-, -en> **1.** *without the article, no pl* craftsmanship etw. ist in Handarbeit erstellt sth is handmade **2.** handmade article ◊ *Dieser Teppich ist eine Handarbeit aus Persien.* **3.** needlework ◊ *Sie beschäftigt sich gerne mit Handarbeiten.*

Hän·de·druck ['hɛndədrʊk] der <-(e)s> *no pl* handshake, squeeze of the hand ◊ *Er verabschiedete ihn mit einem festen Händedruck.*

In Germany, you shake hands when you are introduced to a person and when you say goodbye to them. Business colleagues often shake hands when greeting and leaving each other; this is less common among friends.

② **Han·del** ['handl] der <-s> *no pl* **1.** trade; *(illegal also)* traffic der Handel mit etw. the trade/traffic in sth ◊ *der illegale Handel mit Raubkopien* **2.** commerce ◊ *Die CD-Preise werden vom Handel gemacht.* **3.** im Handel in the shops ◊ *Das Buch zur Serie ist ab sofort im Handel erhältlich.* **4.** deal ◊ *Der Handel gilt!*

② **han·deln** ['handln] [intr v] *+haben* **1.** mit etw. handeln deal in sth **2.** haggle ◊ *Beim Kauf eines Autos sollte man immer handeln.* **3.** act ◊ *Er hat vollkommen unverantwortlich gehandelt.*; do something ◊ *Angesichts dieser Lage müssen wir handeln.* **4.** von jdm/etw. handeln be about sb/sth ◊ *Die Geschichte handelt von einem Mädchen*

namens Rita. [imp v] *+haben* **1.** es handelt sich (hier) um etw./jdn this/it is sth/sb ◊ *Es handelt sich hier um eine Notsituation.* es handelt sich bei jdm/etw. um jdn/etw. sb/sth is sb/sth **2.** es handelt sich darum, etw. zu tun it is a question of doing sth [tr v] *+haben*; *mostly passive* sell, trade ◊ *Die Gemälde werden zu hohen Preisen gehandelt.*

Han·dels·kam·mer ['handl͜skamɐ] die <-, -n> chamber of commerce

Han·dels·schu·le ['handl͜sʃuːlə] die <-, -n> ◊ *Sie geht zur/auf die Handelsschule.*

In Germany, after successfully completing your secondary schooling, you can attend a *Handelsschule* where courses last two years. This type of school gives you the training you need to take up a career in retail or administration. In Austria and Switzerland, courses last three years. The training includes courses which extend and deepen your general education, courses in foreign languages, and in particular courses in aspects of economics and industry. If you have a qualification from a *Handelsschule*, it is possible that the length of any training contract you subsequently secure in the field of business or administration may be reduced by one year, subject to the agreement of your employer.

hand·fest ['hantfɛst] [adj] <handfester, am handfesten> *seldom comp/superl* **1.** solid, sound ◊ *handfeste Gründe* ♦ *Diese Aussage ist handfest und bedarf keiner Erklärung.* **2.** *only before ns (food etc.)* substantial ◊ *handfeste Nahrung zu sich nehmen* [adv] seriously ◊ *Sie haben in letzter Zeit oft handfest gestritten.*

Hand·ge·lenk ['hantɡəlɛŋk] das <-(e)s, -e> wrist ⊙ **etw. aus dem Handgelenk schütteln** produce sth out of thin air **aus dem Handgelenk (heraus) 1.** off the cuff **2.** from the wrist

Hand·ge·päck ['hantɡəpɛk] das <-(e)s> *no pl* hand luggage/baggage

hand·greif·lich ['hantɡraeflɪç] [adj] **1.** violent ◊ *Es kam zu handgreiflichen Tumulten.* ♦ *Er wird gelegentlich handgreiflich gegen seine Frau.* **2.** clear ◊ *Wir haben handgreifliche Fortschritte gemacht.* ♦ *Der Nutzen dieses Vorgehens ist handgreiflich.* etw. handgreiflich machen explain sth, illustrate sth

Hand·griff ['hantɡrɪf] der <-(e)s, -e> **1.** (hand) movement ◊ *Sie bereitete mit raschen Handgriffen das Frühstück zu.* **2.** handle ◊ *eine Kamera mit Handgriff* ⊙ **nur ein Handgriff** quick and easy

hand·ha·ben ['hanthaːbm̩] [tr v] *+haben* **1.** use, operate ◊ *Weißt du, wie man diesen Rasenmäher handhabt?* **2.** handle, manage ◊ *Wie sollen wir das Problem handhaben?*

Händ·ler ['hɛndlɐ] der <-s, ->, **Händ·le·rin** ['hɛndlərɪn] die <-, -nen> trader ◊ *Die Händler sind vom Weihnachtsgeschäft enttäuscht.*; dealer ◊ *eine Liste der nächstgelegenen Händler*

hand·lich ['hantlɪç] [adj] handy, convenient ◊ *ein handlicher Reiseführer* ♦ *Dieser Camcorder ist klein und handlich.* [adv] conveniently ◊ *Das Regal ist handlich verpackt.*

Hand·lung ['handlʊŋ] die <-, -en> **1.** action; act, deed ◊ *eine kriminelle Handlung begehen* ⊖Tat **2.** plot, action ◊ *Der Film enthält keine durchge-*

hende Handlung.

Hand·schel·le ['hantʃɛlə] die <–, –en> *most pl* handcuff ◊ *Der Angeklagte wurde in Handschellen vorgeführt.*

Hand·schrift ['hantʃrɪft] die <–, –en> **1.** handwriting ◊ *eine schöne Handschrift haben* ⊖Schrift **2.** *(fig)* trademark, signature ◊ *Die Attacke trägt die Handschrift des gesuchten Mannes.* **3.** manuscript ◊ *eine mittelalterliche Handschrift*

Hand·schuh ['hantʃuː] der <–(e)s, –e> glove, mitten

Ⓩ **Hand·ta·sche** ['hanttaʃə] die <–, –n> handbag, purse

Ⓩ **Hand·tuch** ['hanttuːx] das <–(e)s, Handtücher> towel

Hand·werk ['hantvɛʳk] das <–(e)s, –e> **1.** craft ◊ *das Handwerk der Teppichknüpferei;* trade ◊ *Sie versteht ihr Handwerk.* **2.** das Handwerk the craft industry

Ⓩ **Hand·wer·ker** ['hantvɛʳkɐ] der <–s, –>, **Hand·wer·ke·rin** ['hantvɛʳkarɪn] die <–, –nen> craftsman/woman, tradesman/woman ◊ *ein selbstständiger Handwerker* ♦ *Sie ist Handwerkerin.*

Ⓩ **Han·dy** ['hɛndiː] das <–s, –s> mobile (phone), cellphone ◊ *per/mit dem Handy telefonieren*

Hang [haŋ] der <–(e)s, Hänge> **1.** slope ◊ *Sie fuhren auf Skiern die Hänge hinunter.* ♦ *ein Haus am Hang* **2.** *no pl* ein Hang zu etw. a tendency towards sth ◊ *Er hat einen ausgeprägten Hang zum Perfektionismus.* einen Hang dazu haben, nachtragend zu sein have a tendency to bear grudges

Hän·ge·mat·te ['hɛŋəmatə] die <–, –n> hammock ◊ *in der Hängematte liegen*

Ⓩ **hän·gen¹** ['hɛŋən] <hängt, hing, hat gehangen> ⓘⓝⓣⓡⓥ *in South G, Austr, Swiss often +sein* **1.** hang ◊ *Die Lampe hängt an der Decke.* ♦ *Der Junge hing am Klettergerüst.* ♦ *Seine Freundin hing an seinem Arm.* **2.** cling ◊ *Seine Haare hingen ihm wirr ins Gesicht.* **3.** be stuck ◊ *In ihren Haaren hing Stroh.* **4.** an etw. ⓓⓐⓣ hängen depend on sth ◊ *An dieser Entscheidung hängen viele Konsequenzen.* **5.** an etw./jdm hängen be attached to sb/sth ◊ *Sie hängt sehr an ihren Geschwistern.* ⊙ **mit Hängen und Würgen** by the skin of your teeth ◊ *Er hat mit Hängen und Würgen sein Abitur bestanden.* **hängen bleiben 1.** *(fam)* stick von etw. ist bei jdm nichts hängen geblieben sb doesn't remember any of sth **2.** get caught ◊ *mit dem Pulli an einem Nagel hängen bleiben* **3.** *(fam)* stay ◊ *Wir sind bis nach Mitternacht in der Kneipe hängen geblieben.* **4.** *(fam)* etw. bleibt an jdm hängen sb ends up with sth, sb gets lumbered with sth **hängen lassen 1.** etw. hängen lassen leave sth behind **2.** jdn hängen lassen let sb down **3.** sich hängen lassen give in to depression, let yourself go

hän·gen² ['hɛŋən] <hängt, hängte, hat gehängt> ⓣⓡⓥ **1.** etw. irgendwohin hängen hang sth somewhere ◊ *Wohin sollen wir das Bild hängen?* ♦ *die Jacke an die Garderobe/über den Stuhl hängen* **2.** hang ◊ *Lassen Sie die Arme locker hängen.* **3.** jdn hängen hang sb ⓡⓔⓕⓥ **1.** sich an etw. ⓐⓒⓒ hängen hold onto sth **2.** sich an jdn hängen cling to sb ◊ *Die Kinder hängen sich an ihre Mutter.*

Han·se·stadt ['hanzəʃtat] die <–, Hansestädte> Hanseatic/Hanse/Hansa town ◊ *die Hansestadt Rostock*

> The *Hanse* or 'Hanseatic League' began in the Middle Ages as a confederation of North German merchants united by the wish to protect their own economic interests. In the 14th century, this confederation was replaced by a league of towns. The core of the league was formed by 70 towns in present-day North Germany, Denmark and Holland. Some of these towns still call themselves Hanseatic towns, for example Bremen and Hamburg (as is shown by the letters HH and HB on their respective car number plates).

han·tie·ren [han'tiːrən] <hantiert, hantierte, hat hantiert> ⓘⓝⓣⓡⓥ **1.** fiddle (about) ◊ *Sara hantierte eifrig hinter der Theke.* **2.** mit etw. hantieren handle sth; operate sth ◊ *Der Lokführer hantierte mit schweren Hebeln.*; play around with sth ◊ *Das Kind hantierte mit dem Besteck.*

Ⓩ **Har·ass** ['haras] der <–es, –e> *(Swiss)* crate ◊ *ein Harass Bier*

Har·fe ['haʳfə] die <–, –n> harp ◊ *Sie spielt Harfe.* ♦ *Er spielte ein Lied auf der Harfe.*

Har·ke ['haʳkə] die <–, –n> *(NorthG)* rake ⊚ **jdm zeigen, was eine Harke ist** *(fam)* show sb what you can do

harm·los ['haʳmloːs] ⓐⓓⓙ <harmloser, am harmlosesten> **1.** harmless ◊ *Die Schwebfliege ist ein harmloses Insekt.* ♦ *Der Ausschlag ist zwar lästig, aber harmlos.* **2.** innocent ◊ *ein harmloser Spaß* ♦ *Es hörte sich alles ganz harmlos an.*

Harn [ha'n] der <–(e)s, –e> *most sing* urine Harn lassen urinate ⊖Urin

har·ren ['harən] ⓘⓝⓣⓡⓥ +*haben (lofty)* wait ◊ *Wir harrten gespannt vor dem Fernseher.* einer Person/Sache ⓖⓔⓝ harren, auf jdn/etw.harren wait for sb/sth, await sb/sth ◊ *Sie harrten der Dinge, die auf sie zukommen sollten.* ♦ *Sie harrte ihres Freundes.* ♦ *Er warf die Angel aus und harrte auf einen Fang.*

Ⓩ **hart** [ha't] ⓐⓓⓙ <härter, am härtesten> **1.** hard, tough, strong ◊ *Kristallglas ist besonders hart.* ♦ *harte Muskeln* ⊖weich **2.** hard, difficult ◊ *Sie haben harte Zeiten hinter sich.* ♦ *Die Ausbildung war hart.* **3.** harsh, severe ◊ *eine harte Strafe* ♦ *Der Urteilsspruch war hart aber gerecht.* ♦ *ein hartes Klima;* *(person)* hart bleiben be unyielding **4.** *(accent)* strong; *(pronunciation)* hard **5.** strong ◊ *Das ist nur etwas für harte Männer.* ♦ *Rum ist mir zu hart.* ♦ *Wie hart ist der Euro?* **6.** *(water)* hard ◊ *hartes Trinkwasser* ⓐⓓⓥ **1.** harshly ◊ *Die Polizei ging hart gegen die Randalierer vor.* ♦ *jdn hart bestrafen* **2.** hard ◊ *Ich arbeite hart für mein Geld.* ♦ *hart trainieren* **3.** +*prep* right ◊ *Der Film ist hart an der Grenze zum Kitsch.*

Här·te ['hɛʳtə] die <–, –n> *most sing* **1.** strength, hardness ◊ *die Härte von Stahl* **2.** toughness ◊ *Hat er die nötige Härte, diese Firma zu leiten?* **3.** *(of a law etc.)* Härte(n) severity, severe consequences ◊ *ein Reformpaket mit sozialen Härten* **4.** tough measures/action ◊ *Es wurde mehr Härte gegen Schwerverbrecher gefordert.* mit Härte gegen etw./jdn vorgehen take tough action against sth/sb **5.** hardship(s) ◊ *Sie wurde nicht von der Härte des Lebens verschont.* **6.** coldness ◊ *Die Härte seines Blicks machte ihr Angst.* **7.** *(of climate)*

harshness ◊ *die unerbittliche Härte des Klimas*
8. FIN strength ◊ *die Härte des Euros* **9.** *(of water)* hardness
◉ *es/das ist die Härte (fam)* it's outrageous
hart·nä·ckig ['haʳtnɛkɪç] [adj, adv] **1.** persistent(ly) ◊ *Sie kann sehr hartnäckig sein.* ♦ *eine hartnäckige Erkältung* ♦ *Die Behörde verweigerte hartnäckig jegliche Auskunft.* sich hartnäckig halten be persistent ◊ *Der Husten hält sich hartnäckig.* **2.** obstinate(ly), stubborn(ly) ◊ *hartnäckig schweigen/leugnen*
Harz¹ [haːʳts] der <-es> *no pl (always der Harz)* the Harz Mountains
Harz² [haːʳts] das <-es, -e> resin
Ha·se ['haːzə] der <-n, -n> **1.** ZOO hare **2.** *(fam)* rabbit ⊝Kaninchen ◉ **da liegt der Hase im Pfeffer** *(fam)* that's the real problem **ein alter Hase** *(fam)* an old hand ◊ *Er ist ein alter Hase beim Segeln.* **wie der Hase läuft** *(fam)* which way the wind blows
Ha·sel·nuss ['haːzlnʊs] die <-, Haselnüsse> hazelnut
Hass [has] der <-es> *no pl* **1.** hatred, hate ◊ *Sie sah ihn voller Hass an.* ⊝Liebe **2.** *(fam)* einen Hass (auf jdn/etw.) haben/schieben be furious (with sb) einen Hass (auf jdn/etw.) kriegen get furious ⊝Wut
② **has·sen** ['hasn̩] [tr+intr v] +*haben* hate ◊ *Die beiden hassen einander.* ♦ *Sie hasst Knoblauch wie die Pest.* ♦ *Er hasst es, zu spät zu kommen.* ⊝lieben
häss·lich ['hɛslɪç] [adj] **1.** ugly ◊ *eine hässliche Fratze* ♦ *Er findet sich hässlich.* ⊝schön, hübsch **2.** nasty ◊ *Bei dem Streit sagte er viele hässliche Dinge.* ♦ *Ich finde es hässlich von dir, wie du ihn behandelst.*
Hast [hast] die <-> *no pl* haste ◊ *In großer/fliegender Hast packte sie ihre Sachen.* ohne Hast und Eile without hurrying or rushing ⊝Eile ⊝Ruhe
② **hat** [hat] *pres of* haben
② **hat·te** ['hatə] *pret of* haben
Hauch [haox] der <-(e)s, -e> *most sing* **1.** hint, touch ◊ *ein Hauch (von) Luxus* ein Hauch von etw./...* [gen] a trace of sth ◊ *ein Hauch von Schnee* ♦ *Hast du nicht den leisesten Hauch eines Zweifels?* nicht den Hauch einer Chance haben not have the ghost of a chance ⊝Spur **2.** breath of air ◊ *Ein eiskalter Hauch wehte mir in das Gesicht.* **3.** *(fragrance)* waft **4.** der Hauch von jds Atem/ jds Atems sb's breath **5.** *(atmosphere)* aura, air ◊ *ein Hauch von Nostalgie*
hau·en ['haoən] *(fam)* <haut, haute/hieb, hat gehauen> [intr v] *pret only 'haute'* irgendwohin hauen hit (down on) sth ◊ *Er haute wild in die Tasten des Klaviers.* auf etw. [acc] hauen slap (on) sth ◊ *Sie haute auf den Tisch.* nach jdm/etw. hauen take a swipe at sb/sth [tr v] **1.** *pret only 'haute'* jdn hauen beat sb sie hauen sich they are fighting, they are having a punch-up ⊝prügeln **2.** *pret only 'haute'* jdn irgendwohin hauen hit sb somewhere ◊ *Martin hat mich ins Gesicht gehauen!* jdm etw. irgendwohin hauen hit sb somewhere with sth ◊ *Er hat mir das Buch auf den Kopf gehauen!* ⊝schlagen **3.** *pret also 'bieb'* cut, open up ◊ *mit dem Pickel ein Loch ins Eis hauen; (a statue)* carve ◊ *Die Statue wurde in Marmor gehauen.* etw. in Stücke/kurz und klein hauen

smash sth to pieces etw. irgendwohin hauen belt sth somewhere ◊ *den Ball (mit dem Schläger) übers Netz hauen* etw. in etw. [acc] hauen bang sth into somewhere ◊ *einen Nagel in die Wand hauen* [ref v] *pret only 'haute'* **1.** sich irgendwohin hauen fling yourself somewhere **2.** sich aufs Ohr hauen hit the sack
Hau·fen ['haofn̩] der <-s, -> **1.** ein Haufen (... [gen]/[acc]) a pile (of sth), a heap (of sth) ◊ *ein Haufen heißer/heiße Asche* **2.** *(fam)* ein Haufen Geld/Probleme/Ärger a load of money/problems/ trouble ◊ *Das kostet einen Haufen Geld.* ⊝eine Menge **3.** *(fam) (of people)* ein Haufen (... [gen]/ [acc]) a bunch (of ...) ◊ *Unsere Kinder sind ein ziemlich wilder Haufen.*
◉ jdn über den Haufen fahren *(fam)* run sb over jdn über den Haufen rennen *(fam)* knock sb down jdn über den Haufen schießen *(fam)* shoot sb down, gun sb down jdn über den Haufen schmeißen/werfen *(fam)* knock sb over etw. über den Haufen schmeißen/werfen *(fam)* **1.** chuck sth in ◊ *Er hat seine Terminplanung über den Haufen geworfen.* **2.** mess sth up ◊ *Das wirft meine schöne Theorie über den Haufen!* auf einem Haufen *(fam)* **1.** *(simultaneously)* all at once **2.** in one place
häu·fen ['hɔøfn̩] [ref v] +*haben* **1.** etw. häuft sich sth increases, sth is on the increase ◊ *In letzter Zeit häufen sich die Diebstähle.* **2.** etw. häuft sich sth piles up ◊ *Auf der Straße häuft sich der Müll.* [tr v] +*haben* (sich [dat]) etw. irgendwohin häufen heap sth somewhere, pile sth somewhere ◊ *Sie häufte sich Reis und Gemüse auf den Teller.*
② **häu·fig** ['hɔøfɪç] [adv] often, frequently ◊ *ein häufig vorkommender Fehler* ♦ *Tritt dieses Problem häufig auf?* ⊝oft ⊝selten [adj] frequent ◊ *häufige Wiederholungen* ♦ *Tornados sind in Europa nicht so häufig wie in Amerika.; (widespread)* common ◊ *eine häufige Krankheit* ⊝selten
② **Haupt-...** [haopt] [prefix] main ◊ *der Hauptfehler* ♦ *die Hauptrolle*
Haupt·bahn·hof ['haoptbaːnhoːf] der <-(e)s, Hauptbahnhöfe> main station
② **Haupt·ge·richt** ['haoptgərɪçt] das <-(e)s, -e> main course ◊ *Als Hauptgericht gab es Schweinebraten.*
② **Haupt·rol·le** ['haoptrɔlə] die <-, -n> leading part ◊ *Die Hauptrolle wurde mit Tom Hanks besetzt.* ◉ jd/etw. spielt die Hauptrolle (für jdn) sb/sth is the most important thing (for sb)
Haupt·sa·che ['haoptzaxə] die <-, -n> *most sing* **1.** main thing ◊ *Für mich ist die Hauptsache, dass die Arbeit Spaß macht.* ⊝Nebensache **2.** in der Hauptsache in the main, mainly ⊝hauptsächlich
haupt·säch·lich ['haoptzɛçlɪç] [adj, adv] *no comp/ superl; when used as an adj, only before ns* main(ly) ◊ *Die hauptsächliche Arbeit ist geschafft.* ♦ *Der menschliche Körper besteht hauptsächlich aus Wasser.*
Haupt·schu·le ['haoptʃuːlə] die <-, -n>

Broadly equivalent to the British post-war secondary modern school, the *Hauptschule* generally incorporates years 5 to 9 and, in certain cases, year 10 as well. It is intended for pupils who wish to embark on an apprenticeship after ▶

▶ having completed their school leaving certificate. The aim of the *Hauptschule* is to prepare pupils for working life by imparting in particular practical knowledge and skills, but also theoretical knowledge. On completion of their studies the pupils are awarded a *Hauptschulabschluss* (leaving certificate).

Haupt·stadt [ˈhaɔptʃtat] die <–, Hauptstädte> capital (city)

Haupt·stra·ße [ˈhaɔptʃtraːsə] die <–, –n> **1.** high street ◊ *Rathaus und Theater liegen an der Hauptstraße.* **2.** main road ◊ *gut ausgebaute Hauptstraßen*

Haupt·wort [ˈhaɔptvɔˀt] das <–(e)s, Hauptwörter> **1.** noun ◊ *Hauptwörter werden im Deutschen großgeschrieben.* ⊜Substantiv, Nomen **2.** operative word

② **Haus** [haɔs] das <–es, Häuser> **1.** house ◊ *die Häuser in unserer Straße* ♦ *Sie geht kaum noch aus dem Haus.* ♦ *Ich habe in Haus und Garten einiges zu tun.* ♦ *Er war so laut, dass er das ganze Haus wach gemacht hat.* das erste Haus am Platz(e) the best hotel/restaurant etc. in town volles Haus haben have a full house hohes Haus House ◊ *Die SPD ist die älteste Partei in diesem hohen Haus.* **2.** nach Hause home ◊ *nach Hause gehen/fahren/kommen* ⊜heim **3.** zu Hause at home ◊ *zu Hause sein/bleiben* von zu Hause (aus) arbeiten work from home ⊜daheim **4.** außer Haus away from home, out of the office außer Haus essen eat out **5.** dynasty ◊ *die Tragödien im Haus Kennedy*; House ◊ *das Haus Habsburg* aus gutem Haus sein come from a good family **6.** firm, company ◊ *Das in Lübeck ansässige Haus ist berühmt für sein Marzipan.*; (*in the fashion industry*) House **7.** (*fam, hum*) altes Haus old chap
⦿ **Haus und Hof** house and home (mit etw.) Haus halten be prudent (with sth) (jdm) ins Haus stehen be upon sb von Haus aus **1.** from the outset ◊ *Er lehnt von Haus aus alles ab, was er nicht kennt.* **2.** really, actually ◊ *Ich bin von Haus aus Optimist.*

Haus·arzt [ˈhaɔs|aˀtst] der <–es, Hausärzte>, **Haus·ärz·tin** [ˈhaɔs|ɛˀtstɪn] die <–, –nen> jds Hausarzt sb's family doctor, sb's GP

Haus·auf·ga·be [ˈhaɔs|aɔfgaːbə] die <–, –n> homework ◊ *Was habt ihr in Deutsch als Hausaufgabe aufbekommen?* ♦ *Hast du deine Hausaufgaben schon gemacht?*

② **Haus·frau** [ˈhaɔsfraɔ] die <–, –en> housewife ◊ *Sie ist Hausfrau und Mutter.* ♦ *eine perfekte Hausfrau*

② **Haus·halt** [ˈhaɔshalt] der <–(e)s, –e> **1.** POL budget ◊ *den Haushalt beraten/beschließen/verabschieden* ⊜Etat **2.** *most sing* housework ◊ *Wer macht bei euch den Haushalt?* ♦ *Er hilft seinen Eltern im Haushalt.* **3.** household ◊ *Wie viele Personen leben in ihrem Haushalt?* (jdm) den Haushalt führen keep house (for sb)

② **Haus·meis·ter** [ˈhaɔsmaɛstɐ] der <–s, –>, **Haus·meis·te·rin** [ˈhaɔsmaɛstərɪn] die <–, –nen> caretaker, janitor ◊ *Er arbeitet als Hausmeister.* ♦ *Die Hausmeisterin wird das reparieren.* ⊜Abwart

Haus·tier [ˈhaɔstiːɐ] das <–(e)s, –e> domesticated animal; pet ◊ *Haustiere halten*

② **Haut** [haɔt] die <–, Häute> **1.** *most sing* skin ◊ *trockene/fettige/faltige Haut haben* ♦ *Isst du bei*

den Pfirsichen die Haut mit? ♦ *die Haut auf der Milch*; (*of large mammals*) hide etw. auf der nackten Haut tragen wear sth next to your skin nass/durchnässt bis auf die Haut wet through, soaked to the skin **2.** *most pl* pelt ◊ *rohe/gegerbte Häute*
⦿ **mit Haut und Haar(en)** (*fam*) completely, totally sich mit Haut und Haaren verlieben fall head over heels in love eine dicke/dünne Haut haben (*fam*) be thick-skinned/thin-skinned die eigene/nackte/seine Haut retten (*fam*) save your own skin auf der faulen Haut liegen/sich auf die faule Haut legen (*fam*) sit back and do nothing, laze around mit heiler Haut davonkommen (*fam*) escape unscathed jdm ist nicht wohl in seiner Haut, jd fühlt sich nicht wohl in seiner Haut (*fam*) sb doesn't feel at ease (with sth) wie eine zweite Haut (*fam*) be skin tight ◊ *Die Hose passt/sitzt wie eine zweite Haut.* sich seiner Haut ⟨gen⟩ (er)wehren (*fam*) defend yourself vigorously aus der Haut fahren (*fam*) hit the roof, go bananas (jdm) unter die Haut gehen (*fam*) get under sb's skin nicht aus seiner Haut (heraus)können (*fam*) not be able to change the way you are in jds Haut stecken (*fam*) be in sb's shoes

Heb·am·me [ˈheːp|amə, ˈheːbamə] die <–, –n> midwife ◊ *Meine Mutter ist Hebamme.* ♦ *Welchen Rat hat dir die Hebamme gegeben?*

He·bel [ˈheːbl̩] der <–s, –> lever ◊ *einen Hebel betätigen/umlegen*
⦿ **alle Hebel in Bewegung setzen** (*fam*) pull out all the stops am längeren/kürzeren Hebel sitzen (*fam*) have/not have the whip hand, have more/less clout den Hebel ansetzen (*fig*) start making changes

② **he·ben** [ˈheːbn̩] <hebt, hob, hat gehoben> ⟨tr v⟩ **1.** lift, raise ◊ *den Arm/die Hand heben* ♦ *Lasten mit einem Gabelstapler/Kran heben* **2.** (*fig*) improve ◊ *Das Niveau der Zeitschrift soll gehoben werden.* ⊜senken **3.** (*a treasure, wreck etc.*) raise **4.** (*fam*) einen heben have a drink ⟨ref v⟩ **1.** heben go up, rise ◊ *Der Vorhang hob sich und die Vorstellung begann.*; (*fog*) lift ⊜sich senken **2.** (*fig*) sich heben improve ◊ *Ihre trübe Laune/Stimmung hob sich, als wir sie besuchten.*

heb·rä·isch [heˈbrɛːɪʃ] ⟨adj⟩ *mostly before ns* Hebrew → deutsch

Heb·rä·isch [heˈbrɛːɪʃ] das <–(s)> *no pl* Hebrew → Deutsch

Hecht [hɛçt] der <–(e)s, –e> **1.** ZOO pike **2.** (*fam, hum*) ein toller Hecht quite a guy

Heck [hɛk] das <–(e)s, –s or –e> (*of a ship*) stern; (*of a car*) rear, back; (*of an aircraft*) tail

He·cke [ˈhɛkə] die <–, –n> hedge, hedgerow

Heer [heːɐ] das <–(e)s, –e> **1.** MIL army ⊜Armee **2.** +*pl noun* (*fig*) ein Heer ... ⟨gen⟩, ein Heer von ... an army of ... ◊ *das wachsende Heer der Arbeitslosen* ♦ *Ein Heer von Fotografen umlagerte die Stars.* ⊜Armee

He·fe [ˈheːfə] die <–> *no pl* yeast

② **Heft** [hɛft] das <–(e)s, –e> **1.** exercise book, notebook ◊ *die Hefte einsammeln/austeilen* **2.** magazine ◊ *Leihst du mir das Heft, wenn du es gelesen hast?*; comic; (*specific edition*) number, issue ◊ *Fortsetzung im nächsten Heft* **3.** booklet ◊ *Zum Lehrbuch gehört ein Heft mit Übungen.*

A B C D E F G **H** I J K L M N O P Q R S T U V W X Y Z

hef·ten ['hɛftn̩] ⟨ref v⟩ +*haben (fig)* sich auf etw./ jdn. ⟨acc⟩ heften fix onto sth/sb ◊ *Seine Augen hefteten sich auf einen Punkt am Horizont.* sich an jds Fersen heften stick to sb's heels sich an jds Spur heften follow sb's trail ⟨tr v⟩ +*haben* **1.** *(a seam)* tack ◊ *Der Saum wurde per Hand geheftet.* etw. an etw. ⟨acc⟩ heften pin sth to sth ◊ *einen Zettel an die Pinnwand heften* **2.** staple ◊ *Sie ließ die Kopien zu einer Mappe heften.*

hef·tig ['hɛftɪç] ⟨adj, adv⟩ fierce(ly) ◊ *heftige Kämpfe* ♦ *Der Streit war ziemlich heftig.* ♦ *Er protestierte heftig.; (criticism, illness etc.)* severe(ly) ◊ *Mein Rücken schmerzt heftig.; (reaction, storm etc.)* violent(ly) ◊ *Sie haben sich heftig gestritten.* ⊜stark

Hei·de¹ ['haɛdə] die ⟨-, -n⟩ **1.** GEOG heath, heathland ◊ *die Lüneburger Heide; (moist)* moor, moorland **2.** BOT heather ◊ *Die Heide blüht.*

Hei·de² ['haɛdə] der ⟨-n, -n⟩, **Hei·din** ['haɛdɪn] die ⟨-, -nen⟩ *(outd or iron)* REL heathen, pagan ◊ *War er Heide oder Christ?*

Hei·del·bee·re ['haɛdl̩ˌbeːrə] die ⟨-, -n⟩ bilberry, blueberry

hei·kel ['haɛkl̩] ⟨adj⟩ <der/die/das heikle ...> **1.** delicate, tricky ◊ *Das ist eine heikle Frage.* ⊜schwierig, haarig **2.** particular ◊ *Er ist sehr heikel und isst vieles nicht.*

heil [haɛl] ⟨adj⟩ *no comp/superl* **1.** unhurt, uninjured ◊ *heile Glieder* ♦ *einen Unfall heil überstehen; (arm, leg etc.)* unbroken ein Bein wieder heil machen mend a leg eine Person wieder heil machen make a person better again **2.** undamaged ◊ *Mir ist ein Glas runtergefallen, es ist aber heil geblieben.; (clothing)* without holes etw. heil machen mend sth ⊜ganz ⊜kaputt **3.** *(esp iron)* ideal ◊ *Seine Welt ist noch heil.* ♦ *Sie versuchten, uns eine heile Familie vorzuspielen.*

Heil [haɛl] das ⟨-(e)s⟩ *no pl* **1.** salvation ◊ *Jeder versucht, sein persönliches Heil zu finden.* sein Heil in der Flucht suchen flee for your life Heil bringend beneficial ◊ *die Heil bringende Wirkung eines Medikaments* **2.** hail ◊ *Heil dir, Helvetia!* Petri Heil! Good fishing! Ski Heil! Good skiing!

hei·len ['haɛlən] ⟨tr v⟩ +*haben* cure ◊ *von einer Sucht/Krankheit geheilt werden* ⟨intr v⟩ +*sein* heal ◊ *Die Verbrennungen heilten schnell.*

hei·lig ['haɛlɪç] ⟨adj⟩ **1.** REL holy ◊ *die heilige Messe* ♦ *Diese Stätte ist heilig.; (+name)* der/die heilige ... Saint ... ◊ *der heilige Nikolaus* die heilige Jungfrau Maria the Blessed Virgin Mary jdn heilig sprechen canonize sb **2.** solemn ◊ *Er sieht das als seine heilige Pflicht an.; (indignation)* righteous; *(anger, enthusiasm)* tremendous Das ist mein heiliger Ernst. I am being deadly serious. jdm heilig sein be sacred to sb ◊ *Ich schwöre bei allem, was mir heilig ist!*

Hei·lig·a·bend [haɛlɪçˈʔabm̩t, haɛlɪçˈʔabant] der ⟨-s, -e⟩ *most sing* Christmas Eve ⊜der Heilige Abend

The birth of Jesus is celebrated on 25th December, but in Germany people exchange presents on Christmas Eve. Shortly before this happens the Christmas tree is decorated and people may go to church for the Christmas Service. Typical meals eaten on Christmas Eve ▶

▶ vary from region to region, but for the most part they are very simple and modest. In Bavaria, for example, people traditionally eat potato salad with sausages, whereas in the north the tendency is to eat fish. The traditional Christmas goose is usually eaten on Christmas Day, but nowadays this custom is beginning to die out and the range of dishes varies.

Hei·li·ge ['haɛlɪgə] der/die ⟨-n, die Heiligen⟩ *but:* ein Heiliger/eine Heilige **1.** saint ◊ *als Heiliger/ Heilige verehrt werden* **2.** *(fam, iron)* ein komischer/seltsamer Heiliger a funny/weird customer

heil·los ['haɛloːs] ⟨adj, adv⟩ *when used as an adj, only before ns (pej)* hopeless(ly), terrible(-ibly) ◊ *Er stiftete ein heilloses Durcheinander.* ♦ *Sie haben sich heillos zerstritten.* ⊜schrecklich, furchtbar

Hei·lung ['haɛlʊŋ] die ⟨-, -en⟩ healing ◊ *Diese Salbe fördert die Heilung von Hautverletzungen.; (restoring to health)* curing, cure

heim... [haɛm] ⟨prefix⟩ home ◊ *Ich will heim.* ♦ *Komm bitte heim.* ⊜nach Hause

⑦ **Heim** [haɛm] das ⟨-(e)s, -e⟩ **1.** home ◊ *sich ein gemütliches Heim schaffen* ♦ *in ein Heim eingewiesen werden* ein geschlossenes Heim a secure home **2.** clubhouse

ⓔ trautes Heim, Glück allein home sweet home

⑦ **Hei·mat** ['haɛmaːt] die ⟨-⟩ *no pl* home ◊ *in die (alte) Heimat zurückkehren* ♦ *Die Heimat der Eisbären ist die Arktis.*

hei·misch ['haɛmɪʃ] ⟨adj⟩ **1.** domestic ◊ *die heimische Wirtschaft; (plants, animals etc.)* native, indigenous ◊ *Holz aus heimischen Wäldern* ♦ *Dieses Tier ist nur hier heimisch.* **2.** *only before ns* own ◊ *am heimischen PC arbeiten* **3.** sich irgendwo heimisch fühlen feel at home somewhere heimisch werden settle; *(plants etc.)* become established

Heim·kehr ['haɛmkeːɐ] die ⟨-⟩ *no pl* return ◊ *die Heimkehr aus dem Exil* ♦ *Wir freuen uns auf seine Heimkehr nach Deutschland.*

heim·lich ['haɛmlɪç] ⟨adj, adv⟩ *when used as an adj, only before ns* secret(ly), clandestine(ly) ◊ *Niemand erfuhr von ihrem heimlichen Treffen.* ♦ *jdn heimlich beobachten*

ⓔ heimlich, still und leise on the quiet

heim·su·chen ['haɛmzuːxn̩] <sucht heim, suchte heim, hat heimgesucht> ⟨tr v⟩ strike ◊ *Ein Unglück hat die Familie heimgesucht.; (repeatedly)* plague ◊ *Vor der Prüfung wurde ich oft von Alpträumen heimgesucht.*

heim·tü·ckisch ['haɛmtʏkɪʃ] ⟨adj, adv⟩ insidious(ly) ◊ *einem heimtückischen Anschlag zum Opfer fallen* ♦ *Darmkrebs gilt als besonders heimtückisch.* ♦ *Er hat heimtückisch gehandelt.*

⑦ **Heim·weh** ['haɛmveː] das ⟨-s⟩ *no pl* homesickness ◊ *Sie war krank vor Heimweh.* Heimweh bekommen get homesick Heimweh (nach jdm/etw.) haben be homesick (for sb/sth)

Hei·rat ['haɛraːt] die ⟨-, -en⟩ *most sing* marriage ◊ *eine Heirat aus Liebe* ⊜Hochzeit

⑦ **hei·ra·ten** ['haɛraːtn̩] <heiratet, heiratete, hat geheiratet> ⟨tr+intr v⟩ marry ◊ *standesamtlich/kirchlich heiraten* ◊ *Willst du mich heiraten?* ♦ *Sie hat in eine reiche Familie geheiratet.*

hei·ser ['haɛzɐ] [adj] **1.** hoarse sich heiser schreien shout yourself hoarse **2.** *(type of voice)* husky ◊ *Sein Markenzeichen ist seine heisere Stimme.; (of birds)* croaky ◊ *das heisere Kreischen der Möwen*

② **heiß** [haɛs] [adj] **1.** hot ◊ *heiße Suppe essen* ♦ *ein heißer Tipp* ♦ *Das Wasser war kochend heiß.* glühend heiß burning hot jdm ist heiß sb is hot eine heiße Spur a firm lead ◊ *Hat die Polizei schon eine heiße Spur?* ⊖kalt **2.** *only before ns* heated, hot ◊ *eine heiße Diskussion über etw.* führen ♦ *Der Wahlkampf ging in seine heißeste Phase.; (fight, battle etc.)* fierce ⊖heftig **3.** *only before ns* passionate, hot ◊ *Sie hatten eine heiße Affäre miteinander.; ardent,* fervent ◊ *Ein Porsche ist ein heißer Wunsch von mir.* **4.** *(fam, emph)* fantastic, terrific, cool ◊ *Ist das ein heißes Auto!* ♦ *Du siehst wirklich heiß aus in dem Outfit.* ⊖scharf, geil [adv] heiß begehrt much sought after heiß diskutiert/ umstritten etc. hotly debated/disputed heiß ersehnt much longed for heiß geliebt dearly loved, beloved jdn/etw. heiß und innig lieben love sb/sth madly heiß umkämpft bitterly fought over

② **hei·ßen** ['haɛsn̩] <heißt, hieß, hat geheißen> [intr v] **1.** be called ◊ *Sie heißt Maria nach ihrer Großmutter.* ♦ *Weißt du, wie dieser Fluss heißt?* **2.** mean ◊ *Soll das heißen, du bist müde?* ♦ *Was heißt denn das auf Deutsch?* das heißt ... that is (to say) ... ◊ *Wir, das heißt alle Beteiligten, sind sehr motiviert.* ⊖bedeuten [imp v] **1.** es heißt, (dass) ... the word is (that) ..., they say (that) ... ◊ *Es heißt, die Firma soll verkauft werden.* **2.** in der Reportage etc. hieß es, ... the report said ... wie es schon bei Shakespeare/in der Bibel heißt: ... as Shakespeare/the Bible says: ... **3.** *(lofty)* Jetzt/ Morgen/Bald heißt es ... Now/Tomorrow/Soon is the time ... ◊ *Morgen heißt es früh aufstehen.* In so einer Situation heißt es ... In such a situation the thing is to ... Zunächst einmal heißt es Ruhe (zu) bewahren I/We/You need to remain calm for the time being. ⊛ **nichts heißen wollen** not mean anything

hei·ter ['haɛtɐ] [adj] **1.** cheerful ◊ *jdn heiter stimmen* ♦ *ein heiteres Lachen* ⊖fröhlich ⊖traurig **2.** *(weather)* bright, fine ⊖trüb ⊛ **Das kann ja heiter werden!** *(fam, iron)* That should be good fun!

② **hei·zen** ['haɛtsn̩] [tr+intr v] +*haben* ◊ *Womit heizt ihr?* noch im Mai heizen not turn the heating off before the end of May [tr v] +*haben* light ◊ *den Ofen mit Holz/Kohle heizen*

Heiz·kör·per ['haɛtskœrpɐ] der <-s, -> radiator ◊ *die Heizkörper andrehen/ausdrehen/zurückdrehen; (appliance)* heater

Hei·zung ['haɛtsʊŋ] die <-, -en> **1.** heating ◊ *die Heizung anstellen/abstellen/aufdrehen/abdrehen* **2.** *(fam)* radiator ◊ *Handtücher zum Trocknen über die Heizung hängen; (individual appliance)* heater ⊖Heizkörper

Held [hɛlt] der <-en, -en>, **Hel·din** ['hɛldɪn] die <-, -nen> hero, heroine ◊ *als Held gefeiert werden* ♦ *den Helden spielen* ♦ *Er ist ein wahrer Held.*

② **hel·fen** ['hɛlfn̩] <hilft, half, hat geholfen> [intr v] **1.** (jdm) (bei etw.) helfen help (sb) (with sth) ◊ *Sie hat mir schon oft geholfen.* ♦ *Hilfst du mir*

bitte beim Abwasch? ♦ *jdm über die Straße/aus dem Bett/in den Rollstuhl helfen* ♦ *jdm in den/aus dem Mantel helfen* jdm ist nicht zu helfen sb is beyond help **2.** *(medicine, therapy etc.)* (jdm) (bei/gegen etw.) helfen be good (for sth) ◊ *Bewegung hilft gegen Rückenschmerzen.* ⊛ **sich** [dat] **nicht anders zu helfen wissen** see no other way out **sich** [dat] **nicht (mehr) zu helfen wissen** be at your wits' end

② **hell** [hɛl] [adj, adv] bright(ly) ◊ *Durch die großen Fenster sind die Räume sehr hell.* ♦ *hell leuchten/strahlen* ⊖dunkel [adj] **1.** *(colo(u)rs)* light ◊ *Die Möbel sind hell und schlicht.; (hair, skin)* fair helles Bier lager ⊖dunkel **2.** *only before ns* great ◊ *Daran wirst du deine helle Freude haben!* in heller Aufregung in uproar heller Wahnsinn utter madness **3.** intelligent, bright ◊ *Er ist ein heller Junge.* **4.** high-pitched ◊ *eine helle Knabenstimme* helles Lachen ringing laughter

hell·... [hɛl] [prefix] light ◊ *hellblau* ♦ *hellrot*

Hel·lig·keit ['hɛlɪçkaɛt] die <-> *no pl* brightness ◊ *Die Helligkeit der Sonne schadet den Augen.; light ◊ *Helligkeit zieht Insekten an.*

hell·wach ['hɛl'vax] [adj] *no comp/superl* **1.** wide awake ◊ *Nach der kalten Dusche war ich hellwach.* **2.** alert, bright ◊ *Ihre hellwachen Augen blitzten.*

Helm [hɛlm] der <-(e)s, -e> **1.** *(for motorcycle, bicycle, inline skates etc., of a knight)* helmet ◊ *einen Helm tragen/aufsetzen/abnehmen* **2.** *(for construction workers)* hard hat, (safety) helmet

② **Hemd** [hɛmt] das <-(e)s, -en> **1.** shirt ◊ *Er trug ein weißes Hemd mit Krawatte.* **2.** vest, undershirt ⊛ **jdm/für jdn sein letztes Hemd geben** give (for) sb the shirt off your back **nass bis aufs Hemd** soaked to the skin **sich ins Hemd machen** *(slang)* be a coward

hem·men ['hɛmən] [tr v] +*haben (also fig)* hinder, hamper, slow down, inhibit, check, stem, suppress, impede ◊ *Die Sträucher hemmten den Lauf des Flusses.* ♦ *den Handel/Fortschritt/das Wirtschaftswachstum hemmen*

Hem·mung ['hɛmʊŋ] die <-, -en> **1.** inhibition, hindering, slowing down ◊ *ein Medikament zur Hemmung des Tumorwachstums* **2.** inhibition, scruple ◊ *alle Hemmungen verlieren* **3.** *only pl* inhibition ◊ *Als Kind war sie unsicher und voller Hemmungen.*

② **Hen·del, Hendl** ['hɛndl̩] das <-s, -(n)> *(Austr, SouthG)* chicken

Hen·kel ['hɛŋkl̩] der <-s, -> handle ◊ *Bei dieser Tasse ist der Henkel abgebrochen.*

Hen·ne ['hɛnə] die <-, -n> hen ◊ *Wieso legt diese Henne keine Eier?* ⊛ **die Henne im Korb** the only woman

② **her** [heːɐ̯] [adv] **1.** *expressing movement towards sb/ sth* von/vom ... her from ◊ *Die Truppen griffen das Land vom Meer her an.* von überall her from everywhere **2.** *temporal* etw. ist lange/eine Ewigkeit her sth was/has been a long time/ages (ago) Das ist zwei/drei Jahre her. That was two/three years ago. **3.** *temporal* von/vom ... her from, since ◊ *Ich kenne sie noch von früher her.* **4.** von etw. her by sth, through sth, in respect of sth, as far as sth is concerned ◊ *Diese exotische Frucht erinnert vom Geschmack her an eine Birne.* ⊛ **her mit ...** give me ... ◊ *Los, her mit der*

Waffe! **hinter jdm/etw. her sein** be after sb/sth ◊ *Die Polizei ist hinter ihr her.*

her|... [heːɐ̯] (prefix) **1.** here ◊ *Komm doch mal her!* ♦ *Sieh mal her!* Holst du bitte noch ein Glas her? Would you get another glass, please? *Gib das Buch her!* Give me the book! **2.** *(origin)* from ◊ *Wo hast du das Buch her?* ♦ *Ich möchte wissen, wo sie herkommt.* **3.** *translation varies (expressing relatedness and simultaneity)* Er lief neben ihr her. He was running at her side. *Sie rief etw. hinter ihm her.* She was shouting sth after him.

he·rab [hɛˈrap] (adv) *(lofty)* down ◊ *Vom Big Ben herab könnte sie die Themse sehen.* von oben herab from above ⊜hinunter ⊜herauf

⊛ **von oben herab 1.** *(pej)* condescending(ly) ◊ *Ihr Ton war sehr von oben herab.* **2.** from above ◊ *Von oben herab sehen die Wolken wie Watte aus.*

he·rab|... [hɛˈrap] (prefix) *expressing downward movement* down ◊ *Er wurde durch einen herabfallenden Ast verletzt.* ♦ *Die Eiszapfen hingen vom Dach herab.* ♦ *Blut rann an seinem Bein herab.*

he·rab|las·sen [hɛˈraplasn̩] <lässt herab, ließ herab, hat herabgelassen> (tr v) *(lofty)* let down, lower ◊ *Ich ließ mich an einem Seil herab.* (ref v) *(iron)* sich herablassen, etw. zu tun; sich zu etw. herablassen condescend to (do) sth, deign to (do) sth ◊ *Sie ließ sich dazu herab, ihn zu begrüßen.*

he·rab|se·hen [hɛˈrapzeːən] <sieht herab, sah herab, hat herabgesehen> (intr v) **1.** look down ◊ *Vom Aussichtsturm kann man auf die Stadt herabsehen.* **2.** auf jdn herabsehen look down on sb

he·rab|set·zen [hɛˈrapzɛtsn̩] <setzt herab, setzte herab, hat herabgesetzt> (tr v) **1.** reduce, lower, cut ◊ *den Preis für ein Produkt herabsetzen* ⊜senken ⊜heraufsetzen **2.** *(achievements etc.)* belittle, disparage ◊ *Er setzte die Verdienste seiner Kollegin herab.*

he·ran [hɛˈran] (adv) *expressing movement towards sb/sth* an etw. (acc) heran (close) to sth, towards sth

he·ran|... [hɛˈran] (prefix) *expressing movement towards sb/sth (close) to, towards* ◊ *Sie ließ ihn nicht an sich heran.* ♦ *Lkws donnerten heran.* ♦ *Seine Mutter kam herangeeilt.*

he·ran|ge·hen [hɛˈrangeːən] <geht heran, ging heran, ist herangegangen> (intr v) **1.** *(also fig)* an etw./jdn herangehen go up to sth/sb, approach sth/sb ◊ *Er ging sehr nah an die Schlange heran.* ♦ *Er ging sehr sachlich an das Thema heran.* **2.** an etw. (acc) herangehen tackle sth ◊ *Er ging euphorisch/skeptisch an die neue Aufgabe heran.*

he·ran|kom·men [hɛˈrankɔmən] <kommt heran, kam heran, ist herangekommen> (intr v) **1.** come close, approach ◊ *Der Zug kam immer näher heran.* **2.** (an etw. (acc)) herankommen be able to reach (sth) ◊ *Ich komme nicht an die Lampe heran.* **3.** an etw. (acc) herankommen get hold of sth ◊ *Wie seid ihr an das Geld herangekommen?*

he·ran|zie·hen [hɛˈrantsiːən] <zieht heran, zog heran, hat/ist herangezogen> (tr v) +*haben* **1.** etw. heranziehen refer to sth, consult sth, use sth ◊ *Welche Quellen zog er für seine Untersuchung heran?* **2.** jdn heranziehen consult sb, call sb in, bring sb in ◊ *Fachleute zur Beratung heranziehen* **3.** *(a plant, an animal)* rear, raise, grow ◊ *einen Setzling heranziehen* ♦ *Auf dem Hof werden Kälber*

herangezogen. (intr v) +*sein* approach ◊ *Ein Unwetter/Gewitter zog heran.*

he·rauf [hɛˈraɔ̯f] (adv) up ◊ *Hier herauf!* von unten herauf (up) from below ⊜hinauf ⊜herab

he·rauf|... [hɛˈraɔ̯f] (prefix) up ◊ *Die Taucher holten die Wrackteile herauf.* ♦ *Weitere Wanderer kamen den Berg herauf.*

he·rauf|be·schwö·ren [hɛˈraɔ̯fbəʃvøːrən] <beschwört herauf, beschwor herauf, hat heraufbeschworen> (tr v) **1.** provoke, cause, bring about ◊ *einen Skandal/Krieg heraufbeschwören* **2.** evoke ◊ *Sein Duft beschwor Erinnerungen herauf.*

he·rauf|set·zen [hɛˈraɔ̯fzɛtsn̩] <setzt herauf, setzte herauf, hat heraufgesetzt> (tr v) raise, increase, put up ◊ *Die Bahngesellschaft will die Preise heraufsetzen.* ⊜herabsetzen, senken

he·raus [hɛˈraɔ̯s] (adv) *outward movement* **1.** Heraus (mit dir)! Get out! ⊜hinein **2.** *emphasizing 'aus'* aus etw. heraus out of sth ◊ *Er fragte sie aus einer Laune heraus.* ♦ *Aus der Krise ist das Land noch lange nicht heraus.* **3.** aus etw. heraus sein have left sth, have come out of sth ◊ *Der Fuchs war nur kurz aus seinem Bau heraus.* **4.** *(product etc.)* heraus sein be out, be released, be on sale ◊ *Ist sein neues Buch schon heraus?* **5.** *(news etc.)* etw. ist heraus sth has come out ◊ *Es ist noch nicht heraus, wer sein Nachfolger wird.* **6.** *(an age, a phase etc.)* aus etw. heraus sein be past sth, be over sth ◊ *Aus diesem Alter bin ich heraus!* ♦ *Meine Kinder sind aus dem Gröbsten heraus.*

he·raus|... [hɛˈraɔ̯s] (prefix) *expressing outward movement* out ◊ *Sie ließ den Vogel aus dem Käfig heraus.* ♦ *Er streckte ihr die Zunge heraus.* ⊜hinein...

he·raus|be·kom·men [hɛˈraɔ̯sbəkɔmən] <bekommt heraus, bekam heraus, hat herausbekommen> (tr v) **1.** *(money)* get (back) ◊ *Sie bekommt monatlich 1200 Euro netto heraus.* **2.** *(information)* find out ◊ *Die Polizei hat herausbekommen, wer der Mörder war.* etw. aus jdm herausbekommen get sth out of sb **3.** *(an object)* get out ◊ *einen Fleck aus der Bluse herausbekommen* ♦ *Ich bekomme den Korken nicht heraus.* **4.** *(fam) (a result, solution)* work out, find (out) ◊ *Was hast du bei Aufgabe 3 herausbekommen?* **5.** *(a sound, word)* (be able to) say/utter ◊ *Er war so heiser, dass er keinen Ton herausbekam.*

he·raus|brin·gen [hɛˈraɔ̯sbrɪŋən] <bringt heraus, brachte heraus, hat herausgebracht> (tr v) **1.** *(out of the house)* bring out ◊ *Kannst du mal ein paar Gläser herausbringen?* **2.** *(a book etc.)* publish, bring out ◊ *Der Autor hat seinen vierten Roman herausgebracht.* **3.** *(a product etc.)* launch, bring out ◊ *Die Post hat neue Sondermarken herausgebracht.* **4.** *(a sound, word)* (be able to) say/utter ◊ *Sie war so heiser, dass sie keinen Ton herausbrachte.* **5.** *(information)* find out

he·raus|fin·den [hɛˈraɔ̯sfɪndn̩] <findet heraus, fand heraus, hat herausgefunden> (tr v) find out ◊ *Forscher haben herausgefunden, dass ...* (intr v) aus etw. herausfinden find your way out of sth ◊ *Wir fanden nicht mehr aus dem Wald/Park heraus.*

he·raus|for·dern [hɛˈraɔ̯sfɔrdɐn] <fordert heraus, forderte heraus, hat herausgefordert> (tr v) **1.** jdn herausfordern challenge sb ◊ *Er forderte ihn zum*

Duell heraus. **2.** etw. herausfordern provoke sth, invite sth ◊ Durch seine Experimente fordert er das Schicksal heraus. ✦ Ihre Strenge fordert den Trotz der Kinder geradezu heraus.

He·raus·ge·ber [hɛˈraʊsgeːbɐ] der <–s, –>, **He·raus·ge·be·rin** [hɛˈraʊsgeːbərɪn] die <–, –nen> publisher, editor ◊ die Herausgeberin einer Zeitung

he·raus|hel·fen [hɛˈraʊshɛlfn̩] <hilft heraus, half heraus, hat herausgeholfen> intr v jdm aus etw. heraushelfen help sb out of/off sth ◊ Er half ihr aus dem Boot heraus. ✦ Sie war es, die ihm aus dieser Krise heraushalf.

he·raus|ho·len [hɛˈraʊshoːlən] <holt heraus, holte heraus, hat herausgeholt> tr v **1.** (out of the house) get out, bring out ◊ Sie holte den Grill heraus und stellte ihn in den Garten. **2.** (fam) (a performance) get out ◊ Der Sportler holte beim Wettkampf alles aus sich heraus. **3.** squeeze out ◊ die letzten Reste aus der Tube herausholen **4.** (fam) (by asking) get out ◊ Aus der Zeugin konnte man nicht viel herausholen. **5.** gain, win ◊ einen Vorteil/Vorsprung herausholen

⑦ **he·raus|kom·men** [hɛˈraʊskɔmən] <kommt heraus, kam heraus, ist herausgekommen> intr v **1.** come out ◊ Er kam mit einem Tablett auf die Terrasse heraus. ✦ Komm doch endlich aus deinem Zimmer heraus! ✦ Wann kommt dieser Film heraus? ✦ Ist inzwischen herausgekommen, wer es war? **2.** (as a result) etw. kommt bei etw. heraus sth is the result of sth, sth emerges from sth ◊ Was kommt bei der zweiten Aufgabe heraus? ✦ Bei unserem Gespräch kam nicht viel heraus.

he·raus|neh·men [hɛˈraʊsneːmən] <nimmt heraus, nahm heraus, hat herausgenommen> tr v **1.** etw. aus etw. herausnehmen take sth out of sth ◊ den Hamster aus dem Käfig herausnehmen **2.** (an organ etc.) remove ◊ Sie ließ sich die Polypen herausnehmen. ref v (fam) sich dat zu viel herausnehmen go too far sich dat Freiheiten herausnehmen take liberties sich dat alles herausnehmen können get away with anything

he·raus|stel·len [hɛˈraʊsʃtɛlən] <stellt heraus, stellte heraus, hat herausgestellt> tr v put outside ◊ Stellen Sie die Pflanzen nur an milden Tagen heraus. ref v sich (als etw.) herausstellen turn out (to be sth), emerge (to be sth) ◊ Die Aktion stellte sich als Fehler heraus. etw. wird/muss sich (erst) noch herausstellen sth remains to be seen

herb [hɛʳp] adj, adv **1.** (taste, smell) tangy, bitter ◊ Sie trug ein herbes Parfüm. ✦ Dieses Bier schmeckt sehr herb und würzig. ✦ Aloe Vera riecht herb und frisch. **2.** (fig) (experience) bitter(ly), severe(ly) ◊ Das war eine herbe Enttäuschung für sie. ✦ ein herber Verlust/Rückschlag ✦ Sie wurde herb enttäuscht. **3.** (fig) (criticism, words) harsh(ly) ◊ Er musste herbe Kritik einstecken. ✦ Er hatte den Minister herb kritisiert. adj (fig) (visual impression) severe, austere ◊ Sie besaß einen herben Charme. ✦ die herbe Schönheit der Alpen ✦ Er wirkte männlich und herb.

her·bei [hɛʳˈbaɛ] adv expressing movement towards sb/sth Herbei (zu mir)! Come here!

her·bei|... [hɛʳˈbaɛ] prefix expressing movement towards sb/sth: up to (the person speaking) ◊ Er eilte herbei. ✦ Die Leute kamen herbeigeströmt.

her·bei|füh·ren [hɛʳˈbaɛfyːrən] <führt herbei, führte herbei, hat herbeigeführt> tr v bring about, cause, achieve, reach ◊ Er wollte einen wirtschaftlichen Aufschwung herbeiführen.

Herbst [hɛʳpst] der <–(e)s, –e> most sing autumn, fall ◊ Im Herbst 1998 zog sie nach Berlin. ✦ Es war ein kalter/regnerischer Herbst. ✦ Man merkt, dass es allmählich Herbst wird.

Herd [heːʳt] der <–(e)s, –e> **1.** (in the kitchen) cooker, stove ◊ Er stand am Herd und bereitete eine Soße zu. ✦ Sie nahm die Suppe vom Herd. **2.** MED focus, seat ◊ Der Herd der Entzündung muss gefunden werden. **3.** (fig) focus, centre, center, origin ◊ Dort liegt also der Herd des Übels!

Her·de [ˈheːʳdə] die <–, –n> **1.** herd, flock ◊ ein Schäfer mit seiner Herde **2.** (fig, pej) crowd, herd ◊ Er wollte nicht mit der Herde laufen.

he·rein [hɛˈraɛn] adv expressing inward movement right in, right inside ◊ Immer herein mit euch!; (after a knock on the door) Herein! Come in!

he·rein|... [hɛˈraɛn] prefix expressing inward movement, inside ◊ Sie bat ihn herein. ✦ Sie holte den Hund herein. ✦ Es regnet durchs Dach herein.

he·rein|fal·len [hɛˈraɛnfalən] <fällt herein, fiel herein, ist hereingefallen> intr v **1.** (light) shine in ◊ Von draußen fiel Licht herein. **2.** auf jdn hereinfallen be taken for a ride by sb ◊ Sie fiel auf den Gauner herein. auf etw. acc hereinfallen fall for sth ◊ Ist sie tatsächlich auf diesen Trick hereingefallen?

he·rein|kom·men [hɛˈraɛnkɔmən] <kommt herein, kam herein, ist hereingekommen> intr v **1.** come in(side), get in ◊ Er kam ins Zimmer/zur Tür herein. ✦ Sie kam aus dem Garten ins Haus herein. **2.** (money etc.) come in, be made ◊ Wir müssen zusehen, dass mehr Geld hereinkommt.

he·rein|le·gen [hɛˈraɛnleːgn̩] <legt herein, legte herein, hat hereingelegt> tr v **1.** (fam) trick, fool ◊ Er wollte uns mit einem Trick hereinlegen. **2.** take inside, bring in ◊ Können Sie mir die Akte hereinlegen?

her|ge·ben [ˈheːʳgeːbm̩] <gibt her, gab her, hat hergegeben> tr v **1.** hand over ◊ Gib das Geld her, das ist nicht deins! **2.** lend ◊ Sie gibt ihre Bücher/ ihr Fahrrad nicht gern her. **3.** sich für etw. hergeben be involved in sth ◊ Er gibt sich für solche Jobs nicht her. seinen Namen für etw. hergeben lend your name to sth **4.** etw. gibt viel her there is a lot to/in something etw. gibt nichts/ wenig her sth is no/not much use ◊ Dieses Thema gibt rein gar nichts her.

her|hal·ten [ˈheːʳhaltn̩] <hält her, hielt her, hat hergehalten> tr v hold out ◊ Kannst du bitte mal deine Tasse herhalten? intr v jd muss für etw. herhalten sb must suffer sth, sb is made responsible for sth ◊ Wegen seiner Statur muss er oft für Witze herhalten. jd muss als etw. herhalten sb has to stand in as sth ◊ als Sündenbock herhalten müssen etw. muss herhalten sth must do ◊ Meine Auto war kaputt, und so musste seines herhalten. etw. muss als/für etw. herhalten sth must serve as/for sth ◊ Mein Handy muss auch als Terminkalender herhalten.

He·ring [ˈheːrɪŋ] der <–s, –e> **1.** (fish) herring ◊ Es gab gebratenen Hering. geräucherter Hering

kipper 2. *(for tents)* peg

her|kom·men ['heːɡkɔmən] <kommt her, kam her, ist hergekommen> ⟨intr v⟩ 1. come (here) ◊ *Komm doch bitte mal her und sieh dir das an.* 2. *(von)* irgendwo herkommen come from somewhere, be from somewhere

her·kömm·lich ['heːɡkœmlɪç] ⟨adj⟩ *only before ns* conventional, usual ◊ *Die herkömmlichen Methoden haben einige Nachteile.*

Her·kunft ['heːɡkʊnft] die <-, Herkünfte> *most sing* 1. *(of a person)* origin(s), background, descent, extraction ◊ *Sie war jüdischer/türkischer/bürgerlicher Herkunft.* 2. *(of things)* origin ◊ *Dieser Wirkstoff ist rein pflanzlicher Herkunft.*

her|lei·ten ['heːɡlaɛtn] <leitet her, leitete her, hat hergeleitet> ⟨tr v⟩ derive ◊ *eine mathematische Formel herleiten etw. aus etw.* herleiten derive sth from sth, base sth on sth ◊ *Er konnte aus dem Vertrag keine Rechte herleiten.* ⟨ref v⟩ sich von/aus etw. herleiten derive from sth ◊ *Dieses Wort leitet sich aus dem Griechischen her.*

her|ma·chen ['heːɡmaxn] <macht her, machte her, hat hergemacht> ⟨intr v⟩ etwas/viel hermachen, etw. macht etwas/viel her look impressive/great ◊ *Er wollte, dass der Laden etwas hermachte.* wenig/nicht viel hermachen not look very impressive nichts hermachen not look like much ⟨ref v⟩ *mostly spoken* 1. sich über etw. ⟨acc⟩ hermachen tackle sth, get stuck into sth ◊ *Er kaufte sich einen Roman und machte sich sofort darüber her.* 2. *(eat)* sich über etw. ⟨acc⟩ hermachen fall upon sth, get stuck into sth ◊ *Sie machten sich über das Büffet her.*

② **Herr¹** [hɛʳ] der <-n, -en> 1. *(man)* gentleman ◊ *Wer war der Herr neben ihr?* 2. *(address)* Mr, Sir ◊ *Guten Morgen, Herr Fritze!* ✦ *Entschuldigen Sie, Herr Kollege, aber ...* ✦ *Was wünscht der Herr?* (die) Herren gentlemen 3. REL (der) Herr (the) Lord ◊ *Herr, erhöre uns.* 4. *only pl* SPORT (die) Herren (the) men('s team) ◊ *Bei den Herren siegte der Österreicher Hermann Meier.*
⊙ Herr der Lage/Situation sein/bleiben be/remain master of the situation sein eigener Herr sein be your own master/boss

Herr² [hɛʳ] der <-n, -en>, **Her·rin** ['hɛrɪn] die <-, -nen> *(lofty, oldf)* master, lord, ruler ◊ *Wer ist der Herr des Hauses?* ✦ *Der König war ein gerechter Herr.* Herrin mistress, lady, ruler ◊ *Wer ist die Herrin des Hauses/Gutes?*

her|rich·ten ['heːɡrɪçtn] <richtet her, richtete her, hat hergerichtet> ⟨tr v⟩ 1. get ready ◊ *das Gästezimmer herrichten* 2. repair, renovate, do up ◊ *Er hat das alte Fahrrad für sie hergerichtet.* ⊖richten ⟨ref v⟩ *(fam)* get ready, smarten yourself up, make up ◊ *sich für die Oper herrichten*

Her·rin ['hɛrɪn] *fem of* Herr²

② **herr·lich** ['hɛrlɪç] ⟨adj, adv⟩ magnificent(ly), glorious(ly), wonderful(ly) ◊ *Das Wetter war herrlich.* ✦ *Wir hatten eine herrliche Sicht auf das Meer.* ✦ *Die Blumen dufteten herrlich.* ✦ *Sie war herrlich unverkrampft.* ⊖wunderbar, wundervoll

Herr·schaft ['hɛrʃaft] die <-, -en> 1. *no pl* rule, control ◊ *Macao stand lange Zeit unter portugiesischer Herrschaft.* 2. *only pl* ladies and gentlemen ◊ *Die älteren Herrschaften gingen schon früher heim.*

② **herr·schen** ['hɛrʃn] ⟨intr v⟩ +haben 1. *(also fig)* rule, reign ◊ *Dieser Fürst herrschte über zwei Staaten.* 2. *(condition, atmosphere, weather, view etc.)* be, prevail ◊ *Im Büro herrscht gedämpfte Stimmung.* ✦ *Damals herrschte Krieg in Polen.* ⟨imp v⟩ *(a condition, atmosphere, weather, view etc.)* es herrscht ... there is ... ◊ *Es herrscht Ruhe und Ordnung.* ✦ *Es herrschte strömender Regen.*

② **her|stel·len** ['heːɡʃtɛlən] <stellt her, stellte her, hat hergestellt> ⟨tr v⟩ 1. *(goods)* produce, make, manufacture ◊ *Diese Autoteile werden im Ausland hergestellt.* ✦ *Die Tische sind aus Tropenholz hergestellt.* 2. *(bring about)* establish, make ◊ *eine Verbindung mit dem Internet herstellen* 3. *(to original state)* restore 4. etw. zu jdm herstellen put sth (down) close/next to sb ⟨ref v⟩ sich zu jdm herstellen come over to sb

he·rü·ber [hɛˈryːbɐ] ⟨adv⟩ *expressing movement toward the speaker* over (here/to me/to us) ◊ *„Hier herüber!", riefen sie ihm zu.*

he·rü·ber|... [hɛˈryːbɐ] ⟨prefix⟩ *expressing movement toward the speaker* over (here/to me/to us) ◊ *Sie blickte zu uns herüber.* ✦ *Sie kamen herübergerudert.*

he·rü·ber|kom·men [hɛˈryːbɐkɔmən] <kommt herüber, kam herüber, ist herübergekommen> ⟨intr v⟩ 1. come over ◊ *Sie kam zu unserer Gruppe herüber.* ✦ *Kannst du mal ins Wohnzimmer herüberkommen?* 2. *(for a visit)* pop round ◊ *auf einen Kaffee herüberkommen*

he·rum [hɛˈrʊm] ⟨adv⟩ 1. *(expressing circular movement, expressing change of direction)* round, around ◊ *links herum* ✦ *immer im Kreis herum* ◊ *um jdn/etw. herum* around sb/sth ◊ *Um das Haus herum wachsen viele Büsche.* ✦ *Die Menschen um sie herum litten mit ihr mit.* 3. verkehrt/falsch herum inside out ◊ *Er hatte die Jacke verkehrt herum an.* 4. verkehrt/falsch herum back to front ◊ *Er hatte das T-Shirt falsch herum an. Das Etikett war vorne.* 5. verkehrt/falsch herum upside down ◊ *Ich glaube, dieses Bild hängt verkehrt herum.* 6. *(fam)* herum sein be over ◊ *In fünf Minuten ist die Pause herum.* 7. oben/unten herum around/round the top/bottom, above/below the waist ◊ *Oben herum war er warm angezogen, doch an den Füßen trug er nur Sandalen.* ◊ *Unten herum hatte die Pflanze keine Blätter mehr.* sich oben herum freimachen strip to the waist

he·rum|... [hɛˈrʊm] ⟨prefix⟩ 1. *(expressing circular movement, expressing circular order)* round, around ◊ *Die Kinder drehten sich im Kreis herum.* ✦ *Sie reichte ein paar Häppchen herum.* 2. *(expressing change of direction)* round, around ◊ *Er drehte den Schlüssel herum.* ✦ *Sie riss das Steuer herum, als sie das Reh sah.* 3. *(expressing aimlessness, uncertainty, indecision, hesitation etc.)* round, around, about ◊ *Sie irrten stundenlang im Wald herum.* ✦ *Der Hund biss auf einem Knochen herum.* ✦ *Sie albern die ganze Zeit herum.* ✦ *Steh nicht so herum! Hilf mir lieber.* 4. translation varies *(referring to unpleasant actions that might go on over a certain time)* Nörgel bitte nicht dauernd an mir herum! Stop nagging me! Ständig muss ich mich mit dem

Computer herumärgern! This PC is forever causing trouble.

he·rum|hän·gen [hɛˈʀʊmhɛŋən] <hängt herum, hing herum, hat herumgehangen> (intr v) **1.** *(objects)* hang around, hang all over the place ◊ *Auf dem Gang hängen viele Poster herum.* **2.** *(person)* hang around/about/out ◊ *Er hängt den ganzen Tag nur auf dem Sofa herum.* ♦ *Wieso hängt sie die ganze Zeit nur daheim/in Diskos herum?*

he·rum|kom·men [hɛˈʀʊmkɔmən] <kommt herum, kam herum, ist herumgekommen> (intr v) **1.** get round ◊ *Mit dem Regal kommen wir nicht um die Ecke herum.* **2.** viel (in der Welt)/weit herumkommen get around a lot, see a lot of the world **3.** um etw. nicht herumkommen not be able to avoid sth, not get out of sth ◊ *Um ein Treffen wirst du nicht herumkommen.*

he·rum|lie·gen [hɛˈʀʊmliːɡn̩] <liegt herum, lag herum, hat herumgelegen> (intr v) *in South G, Austr, Swiss often +sein (object, person)* lie around/about ◊ *Wieso liegen deine Klamotten überall herum?* ♦ *Er liegt daheim nur herum und tut nichts.*

he·run·ter [hɛˈʀʊntɐ] (adv) *expressing downward movement* down ◊ *Wir hatten einen hübschen Blick vom Aussichtsturm herunter.* ⊜hinunter ⊜herauf

he·runter|... [hɛˈʀʊntɐ] (prefix) **1.** *(expressing downward movement)* down, off ◊ *Er beugte sich zu mir herunter.* ♦ *Sie stieg langsam die Leiter herunter.* **2.** *(expressing reduction)* down ◊ *Die Löhne wurden heruntergestuft.*

he·run·ter·ge·kom·men [hɛˈʀʊntɐɡəkɔmən] *past p of* herunterkommen (adj) *(area, town etc.)* run-down ◊ *Die Straßen waren heruntergekommen.; (house etc. also)* dilapidated; *(person)* down-and-out

he·run·ter|kom·men [hɛˈʀʊntɐkɔmən] <kommt herunter, kam herunter, ist heruntergekommen> (tr+intr v) come down, get down/off ◊ *Er kam die Treppe herunter.*

he·run·ter|la·den [hɛˈʀʊntɐlaːdn̩] <lädt herunter, lud herunter, hat heruntergeladen> (tr v) download ◊ *neue Software aus dem Internet herunterladen* ♦ *Diese Klingeltöne lassen sich aus dem Internet herunterladen.*

her·vor [hɛˈfoːɐ̯] (adv) Hervor mit dir/euch! Come out! Hervor mit ihm/ihr! Get him/her out!

her·vor|... [hɛˈfoːɐ̯] (prefix) out ◊ *Er holte ein Bonbon aus seiner Tasche hervor.* ♦ *Ab und zu blickte die Sonne hervor.*

her·vor|brin·gen [hɛˈfoːɐ̯bʀɪŋən] <bringt hervor, brachte hervor, hat hervorgebracht> (tr v) **1.** produce, yield ◊ *Dieses Land hat viele Komponisten hervorgebracht.* **2.** *(a performance, an achievement etc.)* create, make, produce ◊ *Die Mannschaft brachte beachtliche Erfolge hervor.*

her·vor|ge·hen [hɛˈfoːɐ̯ɡeːən] <geht hervor, ging hervor, ist hervorgegangen> (intr v) **1.** jd/etw. geht aus etw. hervor sth produces sb/sth, sb/sth comes from sth, sb/sth stems from sth ◊ *Aus ihrer Ehe gingen drei Kinder hervor.* **2.** aus etw. (als) ... hervorgehen emerge from sth (as) ... ◊ *Er ging aus dem Boxkampf als Sieger hervor.* **3.** aus etw. geht hervor ... it follows from sth ... ◊ *Aus dieser E-Mail geht hervor, dass er Bescheid wusste.*

her·vor|he·ben [hɛˈfoːɐ̯heːbm̩] <hebt hervor, hob hervor, hat hervorgehoben> (tr v) emphasize, stress, mark ◊ *Begriffe im Text farblich hervorheben* ⊜betonen

her·vor·ra·gend [hɛˈfoːɐ̯ʀaːɡn̩t, hɛˈfoːɐ̯ʀaːɡənt] (adj, adv) outstanding(ly), excellent(ly), very well ◊ *hervorragende Ergebnisse erzielen* ♦ *Das letzte Geschäftsjahr war hervorragend.* ♦ *Die Vorhänge passen hervorragend zum Sofa.* ⊜großartig, ausgezeichnet

her·vor|ru·fen [hɛˈfoːɐ̯ʀuːfn̩] <ruft hervor, rief hervor, hat hervorgerufen> (tr v) cause, provoke, arouse, elicit ◊ *Das Ergebnis rief großen Unmut hervor.* ♦ *Konservierungsmittel können Allergien hervorrufen.*

⑦ **Herz** [hɛʁts] das <-ens, -en or –> **1.** *pl 'Herzen'* heart ◊ *Sie hat ein schwaches Herz.* ♦ *Er isst gern Herz.* ♦ *An der Kette war ein Herz befestigt.* ♦ *Sie malte ein rotes Herz auf den Brief.* ♦ *Im Grunde ihres Herzens mochte sie ihn.* **2.** *no pl (fig)* heart, centre, center ◊ *Paraguay liegt im Herzen Südamerikas.* **3.** *no article, no pl* CARDS hearts ◊ *Herz war Trumpf.* **4.** *pl 'Herz' with expressions of quantity (playing card)* heart ◊ *Er stach mit einem Herz.* ⊛ jdn/etw. auf Herz und Nieren prüfen/testen examine sb/sth thoroughly ein Herz und eine Seele sein be the best of friends seinem Herzen einen Stoß geben have a heart von ganzem/aus tiefstem Herzen with all your heart, wholeheartedly etw. lässt jds Herz höher schlagen sth makes sb's heart beat with joy jdm wird das Herz schwer sb's heart grieves ◊ *Bei diesem Gedanken/Anblick wurde ihr Herz schwer.* schweren Herzens with a heavy heart jdm sein Herz ausschütten pour out your heart to sb jd/etw. bricht jdm das Herz sb/sth breaks sb's heart sich (dat) ein Herz fassen pluck up your courage nicht das Herz haben, etw. zu tun not have the heart to do sth sich (dat) etw. zu Herzen nehmen **1.** take sth to heart **2.** be upset by sth

herz·haft [ˈhɛʁtshaft] (adj, adv) <herzhafter, am herzhaftesten> *when used as an adj, mostly before ns* hearty(-ily) ◊ *ein herzhaftes Lachen* ♦ *Er biss herzhaft in das Brötchen.* (adj) *(food, drink etc.)* (tasty and) substantial ◊ *ein herzhaftes Frühstück* ♦ *Das Steak war herzhaft.; (not sweet)* spicy ⊜pikant

herz|zie·hen [ˈhɛʁtsiːən] <zieht her, zog her, hat/ist hergezogen> (tr v) *+haben* etw./jdn hinter sich (dat) herziehen pull sth/sb (along) behind you ◊ *Das Kind zog eine Holzente hinter sich her.* (intr v) *+sein* **1.** vor/hinter/neben jdm/etw. herziehen walk/march along in front of/behind/beside sb/sth ◊ *Sie zogen neben der Prozession her.* **2.** *(move house)* move here ◊ *Sie sind gerade aus Bonn hergezogen.* **3.** *(fam)* über jdn herziehen slag sb off

Herz·in·farkt [ˈhɛʁtsˌɪnfaʁkt] der <-(e)s, -e> heart attack, myocardial infarction ◊ *Sie hatte einen Herzinfarkt.* ⊜Infarkt

⑦ **herz·lich** [ˈhɛʁtslɪç] (adj, adv) **1.** kind(ly), sincere(ly) ◊ *Der Empfang war herzlich.* ♦ *Sie ist ein herzlicher Mensch.* ♦ *Ich möchte mich herzlich bei Ihnen bedanken.* ♦ *Bitte grüße dem Mutter ganz herzlich von mir.* ♦ *Herzlichen Dank für alles.* **2.** *(laughter)* hearty(-ily) ⊛ herzlich wenig precious little ◊ *Deine Entschul-*

A B C D E F G **H** I J K L M N O P Q R S T U V W X Y Z

digungen interessieren mich herzlich wenig.
Her·zog ['hɛʳtsoːk] der <–s, Herzöge>, **Her·zo·gin** ['hɛʳtsoːgɪn] die <–, –nen> duke, duchess ◊ Herzog Max Joseph war sein Vater. ♦ die Herzogin von Kent

Hes·sen ['hɛsn̩] das <–s> article only in combination with attribute Hesse box@ Land

Area: 21,114 km²; population: approx. 6.07 million; regional capital: Wiesbaden. Hesse was established by the American military government in 1945. Its largest city, Frankfurt, home of the Frankfurt stock exchange, is Germany's most important financial centre with the country's largest airport. The Rhine-Main region is one of the most important economic areas in Germany.

het·zen ['hɛtsn̩] (pej) [tr v] +haben 1. harass, hound ◊ Jagdhunde hetzten das Wild vor sich her. jdn auf jdn hetzen get sb on(to) sb ◊ die Polizei auf jdn hetzen ein Tier auf jdn hetzen set an animal on(to) sb 2. rush, hurry ◊ Hetz mich nicht so — ich komme ja schon! [intr v] +haben/sein 1. +haben Hör auf so zu hetzen! Don't be in such a rush! 2. +sein rush, hurry ◊ Er hetzte die Treppe hinauf. 3. +haben stir up hatred, say malicious things ◊ gegen Andersdenkende hetzen

Heu [hɔɡ] das <–(e)s> no pl hay
⊛ Geld wie Heu haben (fam) have loads of money

heu·cheln ['hɔɡçl̩n] [tr+intr v] +haben feign, pretend ♦ Er heuchelte Betroffenheit. ♦ Du brauchst nicht zu heucheln, ich weiß, was los ist.

② **heu·er** ['hɔɡe] [adv] (SouthG, Austr, Swiss) this year ◊ Der Verein feiert heuer sein 50-jähriges Jubiläum.

heu·len ['hɔɡlən] [intr v] +haben 1. howl ◊ Im Camp heulten die Huskys. 2. wail ◊ Ein Martinshorn heulte durch die Straßen.; (storm) howl 3. (fam) weep ◊ Sie warf sich auf ihr Bett und heulte.

Heu·ri·ge ['hɔɡrɪgə] der <–n, die Heurigen> but: ein Heuriger (Austr) 1. new wine ◊ Ich trank einen Heurigen. 2. establishment selling new wine ◊ Der Besuch eines Heurigen ist ein besonderes Vergnügen.

Both the wine from the most recent harvest and the establishment in which it is sold are referred to in German as Heuriger. Genuine Heurige wine taverns can be recognized by branches of evergreen (which is why they are also known as Buschenschänke — bush taverns) or wreaths above the entrance. This indicates that the owner of the Heuriger has grown the grapes and pressed the wine himself. After Martinmas on 11th November, the wine from last year's crop becomes 'old wine'.

Heu·schnup·fen ['hɔɡʃnupfn̩] der <–s> no pl; seldom with the article hay fever ◊ Heuschnupfen haben ♦ an Heuschnupfen leiden

② **heu·te** ['hɔɡtə] [adv] today ◊ Was machst du heute Nachmittag? ♦ Ich habe heute in einer Woche Geburtstag.
⊛ lieber heute als morgen the sooner, the better; today rather than tomorrow von heute auf

morgen 1. overnight ◊ Das Problem lässt sich nicht von heute auf morgen lösen. 2. suddenly ◊ Er verließ sie von heute auf morgen.

heu·tig ['hɔɡtɪç] [adj] seldom comp/superl, only before ns 1. today's ◊ die heutige Ausgabe der Tageszeitung am heutigen Dienstag this Tuesday 2. today's, present-day, contemporary ◊ nach heutigen Erkenntnissen ♦ in der heutigen Zeit

heut·zu·ta·ge ['hɔɡttsutaːgə] [adv] nowadays, these days ◊ Schreibmaschinen gelten heutzutage als überholt.

He·xe ['hɛksə] die <–, –n> 1. witch ◊ die böse Hexe aus „Hänsel und Gretel". 2. (fam, pej) (alte) Hexe old hag, old bag

hieb [hiːp] pret of hauen

Hieb [hiːp] der <–(e)s, –e> 1. blow ◊ ein Hieb mit der Faust; (with a dagger etc.) slash, cut 2. only pl (fam) hiding, thrashing ◊ Tu das bloß nicht, ansonsten gibt's Hiebe! 3. most pl (fig) cutting remark ◊ In seiner Rede teilte er Hiebe nach allen Seiten aus.

hieb ab [hiːp 'ap] pret of abhauen

② **hielt** [hiːlt] pret of halten

② **hier** [hiːɐ] [adv] here ◊ Hier können wir nicht bleiben. ♦ Das hier ist mein Auto. ♦ Hier unten liegt dein Schlüssel. ♦ hier draußen/drinnen ♦ Ist der Kanzler schon hier? ♦ Das wollen wir hier nicht diskutieren. hier entlang this way
⊛ ... hier, ... da yes …, no …, anything you say ... Er will sich beim Lehrer einschmeicheln: Herr Lehrer hier, Herr Lehrer da! He wants to ingratiate himself with the teacher: yes sir, no sir, anything you say, sir. hier und da/dort 1. here and there ◊ Hier und da kann es zu Gewittern kommen. 2. now and then, every so often ◊ Auch Freunde streiten hier und da. hier und jetzt/heute here and now

hier|... [hiːɐ] [prefix] 1. pointing to a specific location here ◊ Komm sofort hierher! ♦ Stell dich hierhin. Dann kannst du besser sehen. 2. temporal sequence hierauf, hiernach then, afterwards 3. relating to previously specified facts, translation varies hierzu about this, in this connection Es handelte sich hierbei um Betrug. Deceit was involved here.

hie·rauf ['hiːˈraʊf] [adv] stress first syllable only when used demonstratively 1. on here/this ◊ Klicken Sie hierauf, um das Menü aufzurufen. 2. to this, on this/that ◊ Hierauf antwortete er nicht. 3. after that, whereupon ◊ Er klopfte. Hierauf öffnete sich die Tür einen Spalt weit.

hier·bei ['hiːˈbaɪ] [adv] stress first syllable only when used demonstratively in/while so doing ◊ Er fuhr auf ein Auto auf und richtete hierbei großen Sachschaden an.; in this connection/regard Können Sie mir hierbei helfen? Can you help me with this? Hierbei handelt es sich um einen angemessenen Preis. This is an appropriate price.

hier·durch ['hiːˈdʊʳç] [adv] stress first syllable only when used demonstratively 1. through this, as a result ◊ Wer trägt die hierdurch entstehenden Kosten? 2. thereby, hereby ◊ Hierdurch bestätige ich meine Teilnahme am Kurs.

hier·für ['hiːˈfyːɐ] [adv] stress first syllable only when used demonstratively for this ◊ Hierfür gibt es keine Entschuldigung.

hier·her ['hiːɐ'heːɐ] [adv] stress first syllable only

when used demonstratively **1.** here ◊ *Bring das Buch bitte hierher.* ✦ *Hätte ich das gewusst, wäre ich nicht hierher gekommen.* **2.** *Was du sagst, gehört wirklich nicht hierher.* What you are saying is really irrelevant. *Das Argument passt nicht hierher.* The argument has no relevance here.

hier·hin ['hiːɐ̯'hɪn] [adv] *stress first syllable only when used demonstratively* here ◊ *Legen Sie die Unterlagen hierhin.* ⊛ **bis hierhin und nicht weiter 1.** that's far enough **2.** up to here and no further

hie·rin [hiˈrɪn] [adv] *stress first syllable only when used demonstratively* in this ◊ *Hierin bewahrt sie ihren Schmuck auf.* Hierin täuschte er sich he was mistaken about this

hier·mit ['hiːɐ̯'mɪt] [adv] *stress first syllable only when used demonstratively* **1.** with this ◊ *Hiermit kannst du das Geschirr abtrocknen.* ✦ *Hiermit möchte ich nichts zu tun haben.* **2.** *(form)* herewith ◊ *Ich erkläre hiermit die Diskussion für eröffnet.*

hie·rü·ber ['hiː'ry:bɐ] [adv] *stress first syllable only when used demonstratively* **1.** over this ◊ *„Ich würde das Bild hierüber hängen", meinte sie und zeigte auf das Sofa.* **2.** about this ◊ *Hierüber möchte ich nicht sprechen.* **3.** over here ◊ *Komm hierüber, da kannst du besser sehen.* **4.** while doing so ◊ *Sie arbeitete im Garten. Hierüber vergaß sie ihre Verabredung.*

hie·rum ['hiː'rʊm] [adv] *stress first syllable only when used demonstratively* **1.** around this/here ◊ *Lass uns hierum gehen.* **2.** about this ◊ *Hierum will ich nicht mit dir streiten. Wir könnten hierum pokern.* We could play poker for this.

hier·von ['hiːɐ̯'fɔn] [adv] *stress first syllable only when used demonstratively* **1.** in der unmittelbaren Nähe hiervon in the immediate vicinity Finger weg hiervon! hands off! **2.** about this ◊ *Hiervon habe ich keine Ahnung.* **3.** of this/these ◊ *Hiervon nehme ich drei Kilo. Gefällt Ihnen hiervon etwas?* Do you like anything amongst these?

hier·zu ['hiːɐ̯'tsu:] [adv] *stress first syllable only when used demonstratively* **1.** about/on this ◊ *Hierzu habe ich keine Meinung.* **2.** with this ◊ *Hierzu trinkt man am besten Rotwein.* **3.** this includes, these include, included ◊ *Rom hat viele Attraktionen. Hierzu zählt das Kolosseum.*

hier·zu·lan·de ['hiːtsu'landə] [adv] *stress first syllable only when used demonstratively* in this country, in these parts ◊ *Biergärten gibt es hierzulande reichlich.*

hie·sig ['hiːzɪç] [adj] *no comp/superl, only before ns* local ◊ *die hiesigen Firmen*

② **hieß** [hiːs] *pret of* heißen

② **Hil·fe** ['hɪlfə] die <-, -n> **1.** help ◊ *Er bat sie um Hilfe.* ✦ *Hilfe! Ich ertrinke!* ✦ *Ich brauche eine Hilfe für den Haushalt.* ✦ *Ist dieses Buch eine Hilfe bei den Hausaufgaben?* ✦ *Hilfen für den Unterricht auf* (jds) Hilfe angewiesen sein to be dependent/reliant on (sb's) help jdm zu Hilfe eilen rush to sb's aid **2.** aid, help ◊ *Die Bevölkerung benötigt humanitäre Hilfe.* ⊛ **erste Hilfe first aid** ◊ *Ein Passant leistete erste Hilfe.*

hilf·los ['hɪlflo:s] [adj, adv] <hilfloser, am hilflosesten> **1.** helpless(ly) ◊ *ein hilfloses Opfer der*

Skinheads ✦ *Die Regierung ist der steigenden Arbeitslosigkeit gegenüber hilflos.* **2.** clumsy(-ily), ineffective(ly) ◊ *hilflose Versuche* ✦ *hilflos reagieren*

hilf·reich ['hɪlfraɛç] [adj] **1.** helpful ◊ *hilfreiche Nachbarn* ✦ *Entspannungsübungen können bei Stress hilfreich sein.* **2.** useful ◊ *hilfreiche Informationen* [adv] helpfully, in a helpful way ◊ *Er stand ihr hilfreich zur Seite.*

hilfs·be·reit ['hɪlfsbəraɛt] [adj] helpful, willing to help ✦ *hilfsbereite Freunde* ✦ *Sie ist ihren Kollegen gegenüber immer hilfsbereit.* [adv] helpfully, in a helpful way ◊ *Er verhielt sich hilfsbereit.*

Hilfs·verb ['hɪlfsvɛʁp] das <-s, -en> auxiliary verb

② **hilft** [hɪlft] *pres of* helfen

② **Him·bee·re** ['hɪmbeːrə] die <-, -n> raspberry

② **Him·mel** ['hɪml̩] der <-s, -> *most sing* **1.** sky ◊ *ein wolkenloser Himmel* ✦ *Der Mond stand hoch am Himmel.* **2.** heaven ◊ *Er betete zu Gott im Himmel.* ②Hölle ⊛ **der Himmel auf Erden heaven on earth Himmel und Hölle in Bewegung setzen** move heaven and earth **aus heiterem Himmel** out of the blue **(ach) du lieber Himmel** good Heavens **der siebte Himmel** seventh heaven **Himmel noch mal** for goodness sake **weiß der Himmel** God knows, Heaven only knows **um Himmels willen** for Heaven's sake

Him·mel·fahrt ['hɪml̩faːʳt] die <-, -en> *most sing* **1.** ascent ◊ *die Himmelfahrt Jesu* Christi Himmelfahrt the Ascension of Christ **2.** *no article, no pl* Ascension Day

Him·mels·rich·tung ['hɪml̩srɪçtʊŋ] die <-, -en> direction in alle Himmelsrichtungen to all four corners of the earth ◊ *Meine Familie ist in alle Himmelsrichtungen verstreut.*

himm·lisch ['hɪmlɪʃ] [adj] heavenly, devine ◊ *eine himmlische Eingebung* ✦ *Das Essen schmeckte einfach himmlisch.* [adv] *(fam)* marvellously, wonderfully ◊ *Das Publikum hat sich himmlisch amüsiert.*

② **hin** [hɪn] [adv] **1.** *spatial* zu etw. hin leading to sth ◊ *Die Tür zum Garten hin stand offen.* **zum Westen/Osten hin** towards the west/east **2.** *temporal* über die Jahre hin over the years Es ist nicht mehr lange hin, dann kommt er in die Schule. It is not long to go now before he starts going to school as well. es ist noch lange hin bis ... it is a long time until ... ⊛ **... hin, ... her** *(fam)* ..., or no ... ◊ *Arbeit hin, Arbeit her, ich fahre übers Wochenende ans Meer.* **hin sein** *(fam)* **1.** be off there ◊ *Als sie hörte, dass es dort billige Kleider gibt, ist sie sofort hin.* **2.** be dead ◊ *Meine Kakteen sind hin.* **3.** be exhausted, be all in ◊ *Ich bin vollkommen hin, ich lege mich erst mal aufs Ohr.* **4.** have had it ◊ *Unser Fernseher ist hin.* **5.** *(reputation, happiness etc.)* be ruined, be gone **6.** be mad, be in raptures ◊ *Sie war ganz hin von der neuen Wohnung.* **auf etw.** [acc] **hin 1.** for sth ◊ *Ich sehe diesen Kurs als die Vorbereitung auf die Prüfung hin.* **2.** on the basis of sth ◊ *Auf ihren Rat hin bewarb er sich.* **3.** ◊ *Sie suchten das Dach auf lose Ziegel hin ab.* **4.** *(temporal)* in the run up to sth, towards sth ◊ *auf das Ende des Monats hin* hin und her to and fro, up and down ◊ *Sie*

A B C D E F G **H** I J K L M N O P Q R S T U V W X Y Z

gingen im Park **hin und her**. *(talking sth over)* at length ◊ *Wir haben lange hin und her diskutiert.* **hin und wieder** now and again, now and then **hin und zurück** there and back, return

② **hin|...** [hɪn] `prefix` **1.** *translation varies* Möchtest du nicht hingehen? Don't you like to go there? Sag mir, wie man am schnellsten zum Kino hinkommt! Tell me the quickest way to the cinema. Zu ihm wage ich mich kaum dem Streit mehr hin. I don't dare go anywhere near him after our argument. Wo soll ich die Bücher hintragen? Where should I take the books to? ◉weg... **2.** to ◊ *Wo soll das noch hinführen?* ♦ *refer to sth* auf etw. hinarbeiten work towards sth **3.** hin- und her... ♦ *hin- und herfahren* ♦ *Sie pendelt zwischen Berlin und Dresden hin und her.*

hi·nab [hɪˈnap] `adv` *(lofty)* down ◊ *Der Weg hinab zur Mosel ist teilweise sehr steil.* ◉herab ◉hinauf

hi·nab|... [hɪˈnap] `prefix` *(lofty)* down ◊ *Der Weg hinab ins Tal.* ♦ *Er ist den Hang hinabgestürzt.*

hi·nauf [hɪˈnaɔf] `adv` up ◊ *Wie weit ist es, da ganz hinauf?* ♦ *Erst verlief der Pfad eben, aber dann ziemlich steil hinauf.* ◉herauf ◉hinauf

hi·nauf|... [hɪˈnaɔf] `prefix` up ◊ *Sie stiegen den Berg hinauf.* ♦ *Gehen Sie einfach die Straße hinauf.* ♦ *Soll ich dir aufs Pony hinaufhelfen?*

hi·naus [hɪˈnaɔs] `adv` **1.** *spatial* out ◊ *Lass uns alleine! Hinaus mit dir!* ♦ *Ich will raus hier, hinaus an die frische Luft.* ♦ *eine Tür zum Garten hinaus* **2.** über etw. `dat` hinaus beyond sth ◊ *Darüber hinaus weiß ich nichts.* **3.** +time auf/über Monate/Stunden etc. hinaus for months/hours etc. ◊ *Das Hotel ist auf Monate hinaus ausgebucht.*

◉ **über etw.** `acc` **hinaus sein** be past sth, be beyond sth

hi·naus|... [hɪˈnaɔs] `prefix` out ◊ *Soll ich dich noch hinausbringen?* ♦ *Wir schlichen uns zur Hintertür hinaus.*

hi·naus|ge·hen [hɪˈnaɔsgeːən] <geht hinaus, ging hinaus, ist hinausgegangen> `intr v` **1.** jd geht hinaus sb goes out ◊ *Nimm einen Regenschirm mit, wenn du hinausgehst.* **2.** etw. geht zu etw. hinaus sth faces sth, sth looks out on sth ◊ *Unser Hotelzimmer ging zum See hinaus.* **3.** etw. geht über etw. `acc` hinaus sth goes/gets beyond sth ◊ *Das geht weit über meine Kompetenzen hinaus.* **4.** etw. geht hinaus sth goes out ◊ *Die Einladungen zu unserem Treffen sind bereits hinausgegangen.*

hi·naus|lau·fen [hɪˈnaɔslaɔfn] <läuft hinaus, lief hinaus, ist hinausgelaufen> `intr v` **1.** (aus etw.) hinauslaufen run out (of sth) ◊ *Die Kinder liefen aus der Schule hinaus.* **2.** *(fig)* auf etw. `acc` hinauslaufen amount to sth ◊ *Die Reformpläne laufen auf einen Stellenabbau hinaus.*

hi·naus|zie·hen [hɪˈnaɔstsiːən] <zieht hinaus, zog hinaus, hat/ist hinausgezogen> `tr v` +haben **1.** *spatial* pull out (of) ◊ *Der Schwimmer wurde aufs Meer hinausgezogen.* **2.** *(fig)* entice out ◊ *Das schöne Wetter zog sie hinaus ins Freie. Es zog sie hinaus in die Welt.* She had an urge to see the world. **3.** +time drag out ◊ *Der Chef zog die Besprechung über Stunden hinaus. Die Dauer des Verfahrens kann jahrelang hinausgezogen werden.* The proceedings can drag on for years. sich

hinausziehen be protracted **4.** +time delay, put off ◊ *den Beginn des Kurses (um) eine Stunde hinausziehen* sich hinausziehen take longer than expected `intr v` +sein *(esp lit)* in etw. `acc` hinausziehen go out into sth ◊ *Er zog in die Welt hinaus.*

hin|brin·gen [ˈhɪnbrɪŋən] <bringt hin, brachte hin, hat hingebracht> `tr v` **1.** take there, drive there ◊ *Du musst zur Post? Ich bringe dich schnell hin.* **2.** *(fam)* manage ◊ *Ich bringe das einfach nicht hin. Hilf mir doch!*

② **hin·dern** [ˈhɪndɐn] `tr v` +haben jdn an etw. `dat` hindern; jdn (daran) hindern, etw. zu tun prevent sb from doing sth ◊ *Der Lärm hinderte ihn am Einschlafen.* ♦ *Sie wurden an der Ausreise gehindert.* `intr v` +haben; seldom an etw. `dat` hindern be a hindrance/an obstacle to sth ◊ *Lärm hindert am Einschlafen.*

Hin·der·nis [ˈhɪndɐnɪs] das <-ses, -se> **1.** obstacle, hindrance **2.** obstacle ◊ *ein unüberwindbares Hindernis*; *(in horse-racing)* fence

hin|deu·ten [ˈhɪndɔøtn] <deutet hin, deutete hin, hat hingedeutet> `intr v` **1.** auf etw./jdn hindeuten point to sth/sb, indicate sth/sb ◊ *Nichts deutete auf etwas Ungewöhnliches hin.* ♦ *Die Indizien deuten auf sie als die Täterin hin.* **2.** (zu jdm) hindeuten point (at sb) ◊ *Er deutete mit dem Finger zu ihr hin.*

Hin·di [ˈhɪndiː] das <-> *no pl* Hindi → Deutsch

Hin·du [ˈhɪnduː] der <-(s), -(s)>, **Hin·du** [ˈhɪnduː] die <-, -(s)> Hindu ◊ *Meine Frau ist Hindu.*

Hin·du·is·mus [hɪnduˈɪsmʊs] der <-> *no pl* Hinduism ◊ *jdn zum Hinduismus bekehren*

hin·durch [hɪnˈdʊrç] `adv` **1.** *temporal* (durch) etw. hindurch through(out) sth ◊ *Den Sommer hindurch hat die Eisbahn geschlossen.* ♦ *Durch den ganzen Roman hindurch erzählt die Hauptfigur.* **2.** *spatial* durch etw. hindurch through sth ◊ *Der kürzeste Weg ist der durch den Park hindurch.*

hin·durch|... [hɪnˈdʊrç] `prefix` through ◊ *unter einer Brücke hindurchfahren* ♦ *durch ein Loch im Zaun hindurchkriechen* ♦ *durch ein Teleskop hindurchsehen*

hi·nein [hɪˈnaen] `adv` **1.** hinein mit dir in you go immer hinein (in etw. `acc`) go right in(to) sth ◉heraus **2.** bis in etw. `acc` hinein until sth ◊ *Sie arbeiteten bis in den Morgen hinein. Noch bis ins 15. Jahrhundert hinein hatte der Ort einen Hafen.* The town had a harbo(u)r up until the early part of the 15th century. Der Film ist bis in die Nebenrollen hinein gut besetzt. The film is well cast right down to the minor roles.

hi·nein|... [hɪˈnaen] `prefix` in(to) ◊ *Ich bar ihn, die Wäsche hineinzubringen.* ♦ *Er fuhr das Auto in die Garage hinein.* ♦ *etw. in eine Kiste hineinlegen* ◉heraus...

hi·nein|den·ken [hɪˈnaendɛŋkn] <denkt sich hinein, dachte sich hinein, hat sich hineingedacht> `ref v` sich in jdn hineindenken put yourself in sb's position sich in etw. `acc` hineindenken become attuned to sth ◊ *Der Schauspieler hatte sich perfekt in die Rolle hineingedacht.*

hi·nein|stei·gern [hɪˈnaenʃtaegɐn] <steigert sich hinein, steigerte sich hinein, hat sich hineingesteigert> `ref v` sich in etw. `acc` hineinsteigern work yourself up into a state of sth sich in die Vorstellung hineinsteigern, (dass) ... manage to convince

yourself that ...

hin|fah·ren ['hɪnfaːrən] <fährt hin, fuhr hin, hat/ist hingefahren> ⟨intr v⟩ +*sein* go there, drive there ◇ *Wir können gleich mit dem Fahrrad hinfahren.* ⊕zurückfahren ⟨tr v⟩ +*haben* drive there ◇ *Du musst zum Bahnhof? Da kann ich dich hinfahren.* ⊕zurückfahren

hin|fal·len ['hɪnfalən] <fällt hin, fiel hin, ist hingefallen> ⟨intr v⟩ **1.** (*person*) fall (down) ◇ *Er stolperte und fiel hin.* **2.** (*object*) fall over/down ◇ *Ist (dir) der Fotoapparat mal hingefallen?*

hin·fäl·lig ['hɪnfɛlɪç] ⟨adj⟩ **1.** invalid ◇ *ein hinfälliges Versprechen* ♦ *Bei einer Verspätung wird die Reservierung hinfällig.* **2.** frail ◇ *Sie macht einen gesundheitlich hinfälligen Eindruck.*

⑦ **hing** [hɪŋ] *pret of* hängen[1]

Hin·ga·be ['hɪngaːbə] die <—> *no pl* dedication, devotion ◇ *Seine Aufgaben erfüllt er mit Hingabe.*

hin|ge·ben ['hɪngeːbm̩] <gibt hin, gab hin, hat hingegeben> ⟨tr v⟩ (*lofty*) give up, sacrifice ◇ *Er gab sein Leben für das Vaterland hin.* ⟨ref v⟩ **1.** sich einer Sache ⟨dat⟩ hingeben devote yourself to sth ◇ *Er gab sich seiner Leidenschaft für Motorräder hin.* **2.** sich Illusionen/Täuschungen hingeben entertain illusions/delusions **3.** (*sexually*) sich jdm hingeben give yourself to sb

hin·ge·gen [hɪn'geːgn̩] ⟨conjunc⟩ however, on the other hand ◇ *Ralf freut sich darüber. Alex hingegen ist verärgert.* ♦ *Der Dienstleistungssektor floriert, die Industrie hingegen nicht.* ⊕dagegen

hin|ge·hen ['hɪngeːən] <geht hin, ging hin, ist hingegangen> ⟨intr v⟩ **1.** go (there) ◇ *Karin gibt eine Party. Gehst du mit mir hin?* ⊕zurückgehen **2.** +*time* pass, go by ◇ *Jahre gingen hin und es änderte sich nichts.* **3.** (*fig*) just about do ◇ *Diesmal mag das noch hingehen, aber in Zukunft musst du dir mehr Mühe geben.*

hin|ge·hö·ren ['hɪngəhøːrən] <gehört hin, hat hingehört> ⟨intr v⟩ (*fam*) belong, go ◇ *Dieser Stuhl gehört in die Küche.*

hin|hö·ren ['hɪnhøːrən] <hört hin, hörte hin, hat hingehört> ⟨intr v⟩ listen ◇ *Die Politiker sollten genauer hinhören, was die Wähler wollen.*

hin·ken ['hɪŋkn̩] ⟨intr v⟩ +*haben/sein* **1.** +*haben* limp auf/mit dem rechten Bein hinken have a limp in your right leg **2.** +*sein* irgendwohin hinken limp somewhere ◇ *Sie hinkte zum Auto.* **3.** +*haben* (*comparison etc.*) be inappropriate, be inapt ◇ *Dieser Vergleich hinkt gewaltig.*

hin|kom·men ['hɪnkɔmən] <kommt hin, kam hin, ist hingekommen> ⟨intr v⟩ **1.** get there ◇ *Als ich hingekommen bin, war Eva schon fort.* **2.** irgendwo hinkommen go somewhere ◇ *Wo kommen die Tassen hin?* Wo ist der Brief hingekommen? Where has the letter got to? **3.** wo ist jemand hingekommen wherever has sb got to **4.** (*fam*) mit etw. hinkommen manage with sth ◇ *Ich komme mit meinem Geld ganz gut hin.* **5.** (*fam*) go near ◇ *Komm da bloß nicht hin. Da ist frisch gestrichen.* **6.** (*fam*) be about right ◇ *„Wie weit ist das von hier? 20 km?" — „Ja, das kommt ungefähr hin."* ⊚ **wo käme jemand (da) hin, wenn ...** (*fam*) where would sb be if ...

hin|krie·gen ['hɪnkriːgn̩] <kriegt hin, kriegte hin, hat hingekriegt> ⟨tr v⟩ (*fam*) **1.** manage, do ◇ *Bis jetzt haben wir immer alles irgendwie hingekriegt.*

2. mend, fix ◇ *Fabian hat den kaputten Wecker wieder hingekriegt.* **3.** cure, make better ◇ *Dein Knie sieht ja schlimm aus, aber das kriegen wir wieder in.*

hin|le·gen ['hɪnleːgn̩] <legt hin, legte hin, hat hingelegt> ⟨tr v⟩ **1.** put down ◇ *Sie können die Post da drüben hinlegen.* ♦ *Das Baby schreit jedes Mal, wenn man es hinlegt.* **2.** (*fam*) fork out, shell out ◇ *Wie viel hast du für den PC hingelegt?* **3.** (*fam*) perform, do ◇ *Er legte eine Notbremsung hin.* ⟨ref v⟩ (*fam*) sich hinlegen lie down ◇ *Er legt sich nachmittags immer ein wenig hin.*

hin|neh·men ['hɪnneːmən] <nimmt hin, nahm hin, hat hingenommen> ⟨tr v⟩ **1.** accept ◇ *Die Mannschaft hat die Niederlage gelassen hingenommen. Verluste hinnehmen (müssen)* suffer losses **2.** take (along) ◇ *Die Kamera ist sehr klein und kann überall mit hingenommen werden.*

hin·rei·chend ['hɪnraɛçn̩t, 'hɪnraɛçənt] ⟨adj, adv⟩ seldom *comp/superl* adequate(ly), sufficient(ly) ◇ *Es lag ein hinreichender Tatverdacht vor.* ♦ *Der Proviant war hinreichend.* ♦ *Das ist noch nicht hinreichend bewiesen.* ⊕ausreichend

hin|rei·ßen ['hɪnraɛsn̩] <reißt hin, riss hin, hat hingerissen> ⟨tr v⟩ jdn zu etw. hinreißen drive sb to do sth ◇ *Die Premiere riss die Kritiker zu Begeisterungsstürmen hin.* sich zu etw. hinreißen lassen allow yourself to get carried away and do sth

hin|se·hen ['hɪnzeːən] <sieht hin, sah hin, hat hingesehen> ⟨intr v⟩ look ◇ *Man bemerkt den Fleck nur, wenn man genau hinsieht.*

⑦ **hin|set·zen** ['hɪnzɛtsn̩] <setzt hin, setzte hin, hat hingesetzt> ⟨ref v⟩ sich hinsetzen sit down ⟨tr v⟩ put down ◇ *Wo soll ich die Puppe hinsetzen?*

Hin·sicht ['hɪnzɪçt] die <—, —en> *most sing* in vielerlei Hinsicht in many respects in wissenschaftlicher Hinsicht scientifically in Hinsicht auf etw. ⟨acc⟩ with regard to sth

hin·sicht·lich ['hɪnzɪçtlɪç] ⟨prep⟩ *sing nouns without article or attribute are not declined when following this prep, otherwise* +gen (*form*) with regard to, in view of ◇ *Es wurden Bedenken hinsichtlich der Durchführbarkeit des Plans geäußert.* ⊕bezüglich

hin|stel·len ['hɪnʃtɛlən] <stellt hin, stellte hin, hat hingestellt> ⟨tr v⟩ **1.** put down ◇ *Stell die Vase dort drüben hin.* **2.** jd/etw./sich als etw. hinstellen make sb/sth/yourself out to be sth ◇ *Er stellte sie als dumm hin.* ♦ *Sie stellt sich gerne als weltoffen hin.* ⟨ref v⟩ sich irgendwo hinstellen stand somewhere ◇ *Er stellte sich vor mich hin.*

⑦ **hin·ten** ['hɪntn̩] ⟨adv⟩ **1.** behind ◇ *Ich habe sie nur von hinten gesehen. Das Haus ist hinten grün gestrichen.* The rear of the house is painted green.; at/on the back ◇ *auf dem Motorrad hinten mitfahren* ♦ *Schreiben Sie Ihren Namen hinten auf das Foto.* ⊕vorn **2.** da/dort hinten back there ⊕da/dort vorn

⊙ **hinten und vorne nicht** (*fam*) Das (Geld) reicht hinten und vorne nicht. That's nowhere near enough (money). Das hat hinten und vorne nicht funktioniert. This didn't work in any way. **nicht (mehr) wissen, wo hinten und vorne ist** (*fam*) not/no longer know whether you are coming or going

⑦ **hin·ter** ['hɪntɐ] ⟨prep⟩ **1.** *with acc when expressing*

motion towards a place, with dat when there is no or undirected motion behind ◊ *Der Parkplatz ist hinter dem Gebäude.* ◆ *Er stellte sich hinter seine Tochter.* ◆ *Die Schulzeit liegt schon lange hinter mir.* etw. hinter sich (dat) herziehen pull sth along behind you etw. hinter sich (acc) bringen get sth done, get sth over (and done) with ⊖vor **2.** +dat after ◊ *Er kam knapp hinter dem Ersten ins Ziel.* ◆ *Kurz hinter der Grenze streikte der Motor.* hinter jdm/etw. hergehen/herlaufen etc. go/run etc. after sb/sth ⊖vor

② **hin·te·re** ['hɪntərə] adj only before ns <ein hinterer …, eine hintere …, ein hinteres …> back, rear ◊ *die hintere Stoßstange* der hinterste Backenzahn the last molar in der hintersten Ecke der Schublade at the very back of the drawer ⊖vordere

Hin·ter·blie·be·ne [hɪntɐ'bliːbənə] der/die <-n, die Hinterbliebenen> *but: ein Hinterbliebener/ eine Hinterbliebene* surviving relatives/dependants box@ Substantivierung

hin·ter·ei·nan·der [hɪntɐ|ae'nandɐ] adv **1.** one behind/after the other ◊ *hintereinander aufgereihte Stühle* **2.** running, in a row ◊ *Sie sah sich den Film zweimal hintereinander an.*

hin·ter·fra·gen [hɪntɐ'fraːgn̩] <hinterfragst, hinterfragte, hat hinterfragt> tr v analyse, question ◊ *Dieser Reformvorschlag sollte hinterfragt werden.*

hin·ter·ge·hen [hɪntɐ'geːən] <hinterging, hat hintergangen> tr v jdn hintergehen deceive sb

Hin·ter·grund ['hɪntɐgrʊnt] der <-(e)s, Hintergründe> background ◊ *ein Muster mit schwarzem Hintergrund* ◆ *Sie fühlte sich in den Hintergrund gedrängt.* ◆ *Im Hintergrund hörte sie Kinderstimmen.* ◆ *der Hintergrund seines Handelns*; (pl) Hintergründe background ◊ *Die Tat hatte rassistische Hintergründe.*

hin·ter·häl·tig ['hɪntɐhɛltɪç] adj underhand ◊ *Er ist ein ganz hinterhältiger Kerl.* ◆ *Das war sehr hinterhältig von ihr.* adv in an underhand manner ◊ *Du hast mich hinterhältig betrogen.*

② **hin·ter·her** [hɪntɐ'heːɐ, '– – –] adv afterwards ◊ *Hinterher tat es ihm furchtbar Leid.*
◉ mit/in etw. (dat) hinterher sein be behind with sth

hin·ter·her|lau·fen [hɪntɐ'heːɐ|laofn̩] <läuft hinterher, lief hinterher, ist hinterhergelaufen> intr v (also fig) jdm/etw. hinterherlaufen run after sb/sth ◊ *Der Ladenbesitzer lief dem Dieb hinterher.*
◆ *ein Mann, dem die Frauen hinterherlaufen*

Hin·ter·land ['hɪntɐlant] das <-(e)s> no pl hinterland, surroundings ◊ *Das Dorf liegt im Hinterland von Cannes.*

hin·ter·las·sen [hɪntɐ'lasn̩] <hinterlässt, hinterließ, hat hinterlassen> tr v **1.** leave ◊ *eine Nachricht hinterlassen* ◆ *Er hinterließ viele Schulden.* ◆ *Die schlechten Erfahrungen haben bei ihr Spuren hinterlassen.*; (a person) leave behind ◊ *Sie hinterlässt einen Mann und zwei Kinder.* **2.** jdm etw. hinterlassen leave sb sth, bequeath sth to sb ◊ *Er hinterließ ihr sein Vermögen.* ⊖vererben

hin·ter·le·gen [hɪntɐ'leːgn̩] <hinterlegst, hinterlegte, hat hinterlegt> tr v deposit, leave (for collection) ◊ *Er hat die Schlüssel an der Rezeption hinterlegt.* ⊖deponieren

hin·term ['hɪntɐm] contract hinter + dem (fam) **1.** behind (the) ◊ *hinterm Haus* → hinter **2.** in certain idioms: look up the relevant idiom ◊ *hinterm Mond leben*

Hin·tern ['hɪntɐn] der <-s, -> (fam) behind, bottom, bum, backside ◊ *Nach der Fahrradtour tat mir der Hintern weh.* ⊖Po
◉ ich könnte mir/mich in den Hintern beißen I could kick myself sich auf den Hintern setzen (fam) sit down on your backside jdn/jdm in den Hintern treten (fam) **1.** (fig) tell sb off and make him/her work/perform (better) **2.** kick sb in/up the backside

hin·ters ['hɪntɐs] contract hinter + das (fam) **1.** behind (the) ◊ *hinters Haus gehen* → hinter **2.** in certain idioms: look up the relevant idiom ◊ *jdn hinters Licht führen*

hin·ter·zie·hen [hɪntɐ'tsiːən] <hinterzieht, hinterzog, hat hinterzogen> tr v misappropriate ◊ *Er hinterzog rund drei Millionen Euro aus Spendengeldern.*; (tax) evade ◊ *Steuern hinterziehen*

hi·nü·ber [hɪ'nyːbɐ] adv über etw. (acc) hinüber over sth, across sth da/dort hinüber over there (nach) links/rechts hinüber over to the left/right bis hinüber as far as ◊ *Die Musik war bis hinüber in den anderen Stadtteil zu hören.* adj not before ns (fam) (object) hinüber sein have had it, be ruined ◊ *Das Auto ist hinüber.*; (food, wine etc.) have gone off; (person) be plastered; (person, animal) be knackered

hi·nun·ter [hɪ'nʊntɐ] adv down ◊ *Sie nahm die kurvenreiche Straße hinunter nach Padola.* ⊖herunter ⊖herauf

hi·nun·ter|... [hɪ'nʊntɐ] prefix down ◊ *Sie blickten ins Tal hinunter.* ◆ *eine Treppe hinuntersteigen* ⊖herauf...

hin·weg [hɪn'vɛk] adv **1.** (also fig) (in space) über etw. (acc) hinweg over sth, across sth ◊ *Über die Straße hinweg rief er ihr etwas zu.* **2.** (temporal) über Wochen/Jahre/Jahrzehnte etc. hinweg for weeks/years/decades etc. ◊ *Er hatte sie über Jahre hinweg belogen.* **3.** (fam) jd ist über etw./jdn hinweg sb got over sth/sb
◉ über jdn hinweg entscheiden decide over sb's head

hin·weg|... [hɪn'vɛk] prefix **1.** away ◊ *Das kleine Boot wurde von den Wellen hinweggetragen.* **2.** in combination with 'über'+acc over ◊ *Der Sturm fegte über die Stadt hinweg.* ◆ *Der Ball sprang über ihn hinweg.*

hin·weg|ge·hen [hɪn'vɛkgeːən] <geht hinweg, ging hinweg, ist hinweggegangen> intr v über etw. (acc) hinweggehen disregard sth, pass over sth ◊ *Er ging über ihre Einwände hinweg.*

hin·weg|kom·men [hɪn'vɛkkɔmən] <kommt hinweg, kam hinweg, ist hinweggekommen> intr v über etw./jdn hinwegkommen get over sth/sb ◊ *Er brauchte Jahre, um über ihren Tod hinwegzukommen.* ◆ *Du wirst schon über ihn hinwegkommen.*

hin·weg|se·hen [hɪn'vɛkzeːən] <sieht hinweg, sah hinweg, hat hinweggesehen> intr v **1.** über jdn/ etw. hinwegsehen see over sb's head/sth ◊ *Er konnte über die Köpfe der Zuschauer hinwegsehen.* **2.** über jdn/etw. hinwegsehen ignore sb/sth, overlook sb/sth ◊ *Er sah einfach über mich hinweg.*

hin·weg|set·zen [hɪn'vɛkzɛtsn̩] <setzt hinweg,

setzte hinweg, hat hinweggesetzt> [intr v] über etw.
[acc] hinwegsetzen jump over sth ◇ *Das Reh setzte
über die Büsche hinweg und verschwand.* [ref v]
sich über etw. [acc] hinwegsetzen ignore sth,
disregard sth ◇ *Er hat sich über alle Regeln hinweg-
gesetzt.*

② **Hin·weis** ['hɪnvaes] der <–es, –e> **1.** hint, tip ◇ *Er
gab ihr ein paar nützliche Hinweise.* ⊖Tipp, Rat
2. note, notice ◇ *Hinweise für den Benutzer* **3.** indication, clue ◇ *Gibt es Hinweise dafür, dass sich die
Lage verbessern wird?*; *(for the police)* lead
◉ **unter Hinweis auf etw.** [acc] *(form)* with
reference to sth

hin|wei·sen ['hɪnvaezn] <weist hin, wies hin, hat
hingewiesen> [tr v] (jdn) auf etw. [acc] hinweisen
point sth out (to sb), draw (sb's) attention to sth
◇ *Auf diese Probleme wurde mehrmals hingewie-
sen.* [intr v] auf etw. [acc] hinweisen indicate sth ◇
Die Indizien weisen klar auf Brandstiftung hin.

hin·zu|... [hɪn'tsu:] [prefix] *expressing that sth is
added to sth/sb joins sb* ◇ *Du musst noch das Mehl
hinzugeben.* ♦ *Sie müssen diesen Betrag hinzuad-
dieren.*

hin·zu|fü·gen [hɪn'tsu:fy:gn̩] <fügt hinzu, fügte
hinzu, hat hinzugefügt> [tr v] etw. ((zu) einer Sache
[dat]) hinzufügen add sth (to sth) ◇ *Zucker hinzufügen* ♦ *Ich habe dem nichts mehr hinzuzufügen.*

Hirn [hɪrn] das <–(e)s, –e> **1.** brain ⊖Gehirn
2. *(food)* brains **3.** *(fam, fig)* brains ◇ *Er sollte
mal sein Hirn anstrengen!*

② **Hit** [hɪt] der <–s, –s> *(fam)* hit ◇ *Das Lied wurde
ein Hit.* ein/der Hit sein be a success, be a hit
Hit·pa·ra·de ['hɪtpaˌraːdə] die <–, –n> charts ◇
Das Lied war auf Platz zehn der Hitparade.

② **Hit·ze** ['hɪtsə] die <–> *no pl* heat ◇ *Es herrschte
eine unerträgliche Hitze.* bei mäßiger/mittlerer/
starker Hitze backen bake in a moderate/medium/
hot oven ⊖Kälte
◉ **in der Hitze des Gefechts** in the heat of the
moment

hit·zig ['hɪtsɪç] [adj] **1.** hot-headed, quick-tempered
◇ *ein hitziger Mensch* ♦ *Sie ist sehr hitzig und
gerät leicht in Wut.* **2.** *(debate, discussion etc.)*
heated ◇ *Sie lieferten sich hitzige Debatten.*

H-Milch ['haːmɪlç] die <–> *no pl* UHT/long-life
milk

② **hob** [hoːp] *pret of* heben

② **Hob·by** ['hɔbiː] das <–s, –s> hobby ◇ *Was sind
deine Hobbys?* ♦ *Sie betreibt das Schreiben nur als
Hobby.*

② **hoch¹** [hoːx] [adj, adv] <höher, am höchsten> <der/
die/das hohe ...> **1.** *(from bottom to top)* high,
tall ◇ *Wie hoch ist dieser Berg?* ♦ *Stiefel mit hohen
Absätzen* ♦ *Das Regal ist 1,80 m hoch.*; *(ladder
etc.)* long hoch aufgeschossen lanky hoch
aufragend soaring, towering hoch gewachsen tall
2. *(above ground etc.)* high (up) ◇ *hohe Zimmer-
decken* ♦ *Er warf den Ball hoch in die Luft.* hoch
gelegen high-lying **3.** *(amount, quantity,
hierarchy, standard)* high(ly) ◇ *Das Buch hat eine
hohe Auflage.* ♦ *Ihre Erwartungen sind sehr hoch.*
♦ hoch begabt/qualifiziert sein jdm etw. hoch
anrechnen think highly of sb for sth; *(fine)*
heavy(-ily) ◇ *eine hohe Strafe zahlen* hoch verschuldet sein; *(sum etc.)* large; *(age, speed etc.)*
great(ly) ◇ *Er ist in hohem Maße unzuverlässig.* ♦

jdn hoch achten ♦ hoch gelobt werden; *(profit,
loss etc. also)* big; *(penalty also)* severe eine
hohe Auszeichnung a great hono(u)r, an important
award ein hoher/höherer Beamter a high-ranking
official ein hohes Alter erreichen live to (a ripe)
old age 90 ist ein hohes Alter 90 is (quite) old
eine hoch entwickelte Kultur an advanced culture/
civilisation **4.** *(sound, voice)* high(-pitched) ◇ *Ihre
Stimme ist sehr hoch.* das hohe C top C zu hoch
singen/spielen sing/play sharp ⊖tief [adv] very ◇
Er war hoch zufrieden.
◉ **etw. hoch und heilig versprechen** promise
sth faithfully **etw. ist jdm/für jdn zu hoch** sth is
beyond sb, sth goes over sb's head **wenn es hoch
kommt** at most

> When *hoch* is inflected, the *ch* becomes *h* to
> which the usual adjective endings are added: *der
> Turm ist hoch,* but *ein hoher Turm.*

hoch² [hoːx] [prep] ᴍᴀᴛʜ the power of ◇ *fünf hoch
drei*

Hoch [hoːx] das <–s, –s> **1.** high, high-pressure
area ◇ *Ein Hoch lag über Nordeuropa.* ⊖Tief **2.** ein
Hoch auf jdn ausbringen give cheers for sb ein
dreifaches Hoch auf jdn three cheers for sb

hoch|... [hoːx] [prefix] up ◇ *Er blickte von seinem
Buch hoch.*

hoch·ach·tungs·voll ['hoːxˌaxtʊŋsfɔl] [adv] *(form,
oldf)* yours faithfully

hoch|brin·gen ['hoːxbrɪŋən] <bringt hoch, brachte
hoch, hat hochgebracht> [tr v] etw./jdn (zu jdm)
hochbringen take sth/sb up (to sb) ◇ *das Gepäck
in den ersten Stock hochbringen* ♦ *Ich bringe Sie
zum Chef hoch.* jdm etw. hochbringen bring sb sth
up

hoch·deutsch ['hoːxdɔøtʃ] [adj] *only before ns*
standard/High German → deutsch

Hoch·deutsch ['hoːxdɔøtʃ] das <–(s)> *no pl*;
seldom with the article standard/High German →
Deutsch

hoch|ge·hen ['hoːxgeːən] <geht hoch, ging hoch,
ist hochgegangen> [intr v] **1.** *(object)* go up, rise ◇
Die Schranke ging nicht hoch. **2.** *(fam) (person)*
go up(stairs) ◇ *die Treppe hochgehen* **3.** *(fam)*
(bomb, explosives etc.) go off ◇ *Die Mine ging
hoch.* **4.** *(fam)* blow your top ◇ *Er geht immer
gleich hoch!*
◉ **jdn/etw. hochgehen lassen** bust sb/sth

Hoch·haus ['hoːxhaos] das <–es, Hochhäuser>
high-rise building

hoch|kom·men ['hoːxkɔmən] <kommt hoch, kam
hoch, ist hochgekommen> [intr v] *(fam)* **1.** come
up ◇ *Er kam langsam die Treppe hoch.* **2.** emerge
◇ *Anja tauchte unter und kam nicht mehr hoch.*
3. jd kommt nicht (mehr/wieder) hoch sb can't get
up (again) ◇ *Sie fiel hin und kam nicht wieder
hoch.* **4.** etw. kommt jdm hoch sb throws sth up,
sb brings sth up ◇ *Beim Gedanken daran kommt
mir das Essen wieder hoch.* **5.** *(fig) (anger etc.)*
rise ◇ *Zorn kam in ihr hoch.*; *(thought, memory
etc.)* come back

hoch·mü·tig ['hoːxmyːtɪç] [adj, adv] arrogant(ly) ◇
Sie sieht ihn für hochmütig. ♦ *Seine hochmütige Art
ärgerte mich.* ♦ *Hochmütig sah sie auf ihn herab.*

hoch|rech·nen ['hoːxrɛçnən] <rechnet hoch,
rechnete hoch, hat hochgerechnet> [tr v] project,

A B C D E F G **H** I J K L M N O P Q R S T U V W X Y Z

make a projection of ◊ *das Wahlergebnis hochrechnen*

Hoch·sai·son ['ho:xzɛ,zɔŋ, 'ho:xzɛ,zõ:] *die* <–> *no pl* high season ◊ *Während der Hochsaison kommen viele Touristen ins Schloss.*
◉ *etw.* **hat Hochsaison** it's the high season for sth

Hoch·schul·ab·schluss ['ho:xʃu:l|apʃlʊs] *der* <–es, Hochschulabschlüsse> degree ◊ *Hat sie einen Hochschulabschluss?*

② **Hoch·schu·le** ['ho:xʃu:lə] *die* <–, –n> university, college ◊ *An welcher Hochschule haben Sie studiert?* *Hochschule für Musik/Kunst* school of music/art

Hoch·som·mer ['ho:xzɔmɐ] *der* <–s, –> *most sing* midsummer ◊ *Wir machen meistens im Hochsommer Urlaub.*

Hoch·span·nung ['ho:xʃpanʊŋ] *die* <–, –en> **1.** high voltage/tension **2.** *no pl* (*fig*) tension *unter Hochspannung stehen* be very tense *etw.* **mit Hochspannung erwarten**, *einer Sache* [dat] *mit Hochspannung entgegensehen* wait for/expect sth with tense anticipation

hoch|spie·len ['ho:xʃpi:lən] <spielt hoch, spielte hoch, hat hochgespielt> [tr v] (*fam*) *etw.* hochspielen play sth up, blow sth out of (all) proportion ◊ *Die Sache wurde ziemlich hochgespielt.*

höchst [hø:çst] [adv] highly, most ◊ *Es ist höchst unwahrscheinlich, dass er noch kommt.*; (*annoyed, appreciated*) greatly ◊ *Er ist höchst verärgert.*
◉äußerst

höchs·te [hø:çstə] *superl of* hoch

② **höchs·tens** ['hø:çstns, 'hø:çstəns] [adv] **1.** at most, not more than ◊ *Sie ist höchstens 1,50 m groß.* ♦ *Das Baby war höchstens vier Monate alt. bei höchstens 30/60 Grad waschen* wash at 30/60 degrees maximum *Es ist höchstens acht Uhr.* It can't be later than eight. ◉mindestens **2.** except (for), only ◊ *Sie verlässt das Haus nicht, höchstens zum Einkaufen. Du könntest es höchstens mit einem anderen Arzt versuchen.* You might try a different doctor.

Höchst·ge·schwin·dig·keit ['hø:çstɡə,ʃvɪndɪçkaet] *die* <–, –en> *most sing* **1.** top/maximum speed **2.** speed limit ◊ *die zulässige Höchstgeschwindigkeit überschreiten*

Hoch·was·ser ['ho:xvasɐ] *das* <–s, –> *most sing* flood *Hochwasser haben* be in flood

② **Hoch·zeit** ['hɔxtsaet] *die* <–, –en> wedding ◊ *die standesamtliche/kirchliche Hochzeit* ♦ *Ihre Hochzeit fand am 6. Mai statt.* ◉Heirat
◉ **silberne/goldene etc. Hochzeit** silver/golden etc. wedding (anniversary)

ho·cken ['hɔkŋ] [intr v] +haben/sein **1.** +haben, *in South G, Austr, Swiss often* +sein squat, crouch ◊ *Ich hockte mich auf die Treppe.* **2.** +sein (*SouthG, Austr, fam*) sit ◊ *Er hockte auf dem Sofa.* **3.** +haben, *in South G, Austr, Swiss often* +sein (*fam, esp pej*) sit around ◊ *Er hockt jeden Abend in der Kneipe.*

② **Ho·cker** ['hɔkɐ] *der* <–s, –> stool ◊ *Sie stellte sich auf einen Hocker.*
◉ *etw.* **haut jdn vom Hocker/nicht vom Hocker** (*fam*) sth bowls/doesn't bowl sb over

② **Hof** [ho:f] *der* <–(e)s, Höfe> **1.** courtyard ◊ *Sie stellte ihr Fahrrad im Hof ab.* **2.** farm ◊ *Der Bauer*

will seinen Hof verkaufen. **3.** court ◊ *Er lebte am Hof Jakobs I.*
◉ **jdm den Hof machen** (*oldf*) court sb, pay court to sb

② **hof·fen** ['hɔfŋ] [tr+intr v] +haben hope ◊ *Ich hoffe, er lügt mich nicht an.* ♦ *Jetzt können wir nur noch hoffen.* *auf etw.* [acc] hoffen hope for sth ◊ *Er hatte auf ein Wunder gehofft.*

② **hof·fent·lich** ['hɔfņtlɪç, 'hɔfəntlɪç] [adv] hopefully, I hope ◊ *Hoffentlich gewinnt sie! Hoffentlich!* I hope so!

② **Hoff·nung** ['hɔfnʊŋ] *die* <–, –en> Hoffnung (*auf etw.* [acc]) hope (for sth) ◊ *Es besteht noch Hoffnung auf Heilung.* *jdm Hoffnung auf etw.* [acc] machen raise sb's hopes for sth, lead sb to expect sth *sich (falsche) Hoffnungen machen* have (false) hopes *die Hoffnung aufgeben/verlieren* give up/lose (all) hope *in der (stillen/heimlichen) Hoffnung (quietly/secretly)* hoping *voller Hoffnung sein* be full of hope, be (very) confident
◉ **jd/etw. ist jds große Hoffnung** (all) sb's hopes are pinned on sb/sth **Hoffnung in jdn setzen** put your trust in sb

② **höf·lich** ['hø:flɪç] [adj, adv] polite(ly), courteous(ly) ◊ *Ich wollte nur höflich sein.* ♦ *eine höfliche Frage* ♦ *Sie grüßte ihn höflich.* ◉unhöflich

ho·he ['ho:ə] → hoch

② **Hö·he** ['hø:ə] *die* <–, –n> **1.** (*from bottom to top*) height ◊ *Der Monitor hat eine Höhe von 42 Zentimetern.* ◉Breite **2.** (*above sea level/the ground*) height, altitude ◊ *Das Flugzeug gewann an Höhe.* ♦ *Das Gebiet liegt in 4000 Metern Höhe.* *aus der Höhe* from above *in die Höhe* up(wards) ◉Tiefe **3.** level, size, amount ◊ *Die Steuern richten sich nach der Höhe des Einkommens. ein Betrag/Umsatz/eine Gebühr etc. in Höhe von ... an* amount/turnover/charge etc. of ... *in die Höhe gehen* go up, increase *in die Höhe treiben* force up **4.** (*fig*) height, peak ◊ *Sie befand sich auf der Höhe ihrer Laufbahn.* ◉Höhepunkt **5.** (*of a sound, voice*) pitch; (*die Höhen*) treble
◉ **die Höhe sein** be outrageous

Ho·heit ['ho:haet] *die* <–, –en> (Seine/Ihre/Eure) Hoheit (His/Her/Your) Highness *die Hoheiten their Highnesses*

Hö·he·punkt ['hø:əpʊŋkt] *der* <–(e)s, –e> **1.** climax ◊ *Die Veranstaltung erreichte ihren Höhepunkt.*; (*sexual also*) orgasm *zum Höhepunkt kommen* reach the climax; (*of a career*) peak, height; (*of a crisis etc.*) critical/turning point, critical stage **2.** (*of a party etc.*) highlight

ho·her ['ho:ɐ] → hoch

hö·her ['hø:ɐ] *comp of* hoch

ho·hes ['ho:əs] → hoch

hohl [ho:l] [adj] **1.** hollow ◊ *Der alte Baum war hohl.* ♦ *ein hohler Zahn* ♦ *Seine Stimme klang hohl.* **2.** (*hand*) cupped *in/mit der hohlen Hand* in/with the hollow of your hand **3.** (*fig, pej*) empty, shallow ◊ *hohles Gerede* **4.** (*fam*) dumb, stupid ◊ *Der Typ ist so hohl!*

Höh·le ['hø:lə] *die* <–, –n> **1.** cave, cavern ◊ *als die Menschen noch in Höhlen lebten* **2.** (*of animals*) lair, nest, den
◉ **sich in die Höhle des Löwen wagen** enter the lion's den

Hohn [ho:n] *der* <–(e)s> *no pl* **1.** scorn, derision ◊

Sie lachte voller Hohn. nur Hohn und Spott ernten meet with nothing but scorn and derision **2.** mockery ◊ *Dieses Gerichtsurteil ist blanker Hohn!*

höh·nisch ['høːnɪʃ] adj, adv scornful(ly), mocking(ly) ◊ *Seine höhnischen Worte verletzten mich.* ♦ *Sein Lachen war höhnisch.* ♦ *Sie grinste höhnisch.*

Ⓩ **ho·len** ['hoːlən] tr v +*haben* **1.** (go to) get, fetch ◊ *Hilfe holen* ♦ *Würdest du mir ein Glas Wasser holen?* ♦ *Ich gehe schnell zum Bäcker, ein Brot holen.* **2.** pick up ◊ *Kleidung aus der Reinigung holen* **3.** etw. aus etw. holen take sth from sth ◊ *Sie holte ihr Handy aus der Handtasche.* **4.** jdn holen call sb ◊ *einen Arzt holen* ♦ *Sie holte ihre Kollegin ans Telefon.* **5.** *(fam)* win, get ◊ *Sie holte eine Goldmedaille.* **6.** *(fam) (a disease etc.)* sich dat etw. holen catch sth ◊ *Bei dem Wetter kannst du dir leicht eine Erkältung holen.* sich den Tod holen catch your death **7.** (tief) Luft holen take a (deep) breath Atem holen get your breath back

Hol·land ['hɔlant] das <-s> *article only in combination with attribute, no pl* Holland → Deutschland

Hol·län·der ['hɔlɛndɐ] der <-s, ->, **Hol·län·de·rin** ['hɔlɛndərɪn] die <-, -nen> Dutchman, Dutchwoman die Holländer the Dutch → Deutsche

hol·län·disch ['hɔlɛndɪʃ] adj *mostly before ns* Dutch holländische Soße (sauce) hollandaise → deutsch

Hol·län·disch ['hɔlɛndɪʃ] das <-(s)> *no pl; seldom with article* Dutch → Deutsch

Höl·le ['hœlə] die <-> *no pl* hell ◊ *Seine Ehe war die (reinste) Hölle.* ♦ *durch die Hölle gehen* in die Hölle kommen, zur Hölle fahren go to hell jdm das Leben zur Hölle machen makes sb's life hell Ⓔ Himmel

Ⓔ die Hölle ist los all hell has broken loose jdm die Hölle heiß machen give sb hell

Ⓩ **Holz** [hɔlts] das <-es, Hölzer> wood ◊ *Er sammelte Holz fürs Lagerfeuer.* ♦ *Der Schrank war aus massivem Holz.*; *(for construction)* timber, lumber

Ⓔ viel Holz vor der Hütte haben *(fam)* have big boobs aus dem gleichen Holz geschnitzt sein be cast in the same mould

Ⓩ **Ho·nig** ['hoːnɪç] der <-s, -e> honey ◊ *eine Scheibe Brot mit Honig*

Ⓔ jdm Honig um den Bart/ums Maul schmieren/streichen *(fam)* butter sb up

Ho·no·rar [honoˈraːɐ̯] das <-s, -e> fee ◊ *ein höheres Honorar für etw. verlangen*

Hop·fen ['hɔpfn̩] der <-s> *no pl* hops

Ⓔ (bei jdm/etw.) ist Hopfen und Malz verloren *(fam)* sb/sth is a hopeless case

hor·chen ['hɔrçn̩] intr v +*haben* **1.** eavesdrop ◊ *Hör auf zu horchen — das Gespräch geht dich nichts an!* an etw. dat horchen listen at sth ◊ *an der Tür/Wand horchen* **2.** listen ◊ *Horch mal, wie schnell mein Herz klopft.* **3.** *(SouthG, Austr, Swiss)* auf jdn/etw. horchen listen to sb/sth ◊ *Er wollte einfach nicht auf mich horchen.*

Ⓩ **hö·ren** ['høːrən] tr+intr v +*haben* **1.** hear ◊ *Er kann dich nicht hören, er ist taub.* ♦ *Über sie hört man nur Gutes.* ♦ *Die Zeugen sind noch nicht*

gehört worden. etw. an etw. dat hören (be able to) tell sth from sth ◊ *Man konnte an seiner Stimme hören, dass er zufrieden war.* jd hört gut/ schlecht sb's hearing is good/bad von etw. hören hear about sth ◊ *Hast du von dem Erdbeben gehört?* von jdm hören hear from sb Lass mal wieder von dir hören. Keep in touch. **2.** (etw.) hören listen (to sth) ◊ *Bastian hört am liebsten Popmusik.* ♦ *Hör mal, da klopft doch jemand!* auf jdn/etw. hören listen to sb/sth ◊ *Ein Kind sollte auf seine Eltern hören.*

Ⓔ sich gern reden hören *(pej)* like the sound of your own voice (von jdm) etwas zu hören bekommen be in trouble (with sb) wer nicht hören will, muss fühlen what did I tell you/ him etc. sich hören lassen können sound good, look good ◊ *Dieses Angebot kann sich hören lassen.* etwas von sich hören lassen get in touch (with sb), contact sb man höre und staune would you believe it hör/hören Sie mal listen na hör/hören Sie mal listen

Hö·rer¹ ['høːrɐ] der <-s, -> receiver der Hörer auflegen/abnehmen put down/pick up the phone

Hö·rer² ['høːrɐ] der <-s, ->, **Hö·re·rin** ['høːrərɪn] die <-, -nen> listener ◊ *Guten Abend, liebe Hörerinnen und Hörer.*

Hör·ge·rät ['høːɐ̯ɡərɛːt] das <-(e)s, -e> hearing aid ◊ *Er trägt ein Hörgerät.*

Ho·ri·zont [horiˈtsɔnt] der <-(e)s, -e> **1.** *no pl* horizon ◊ *Die Sonne versank am Horizont.* ♦ *Am Horizont zeichnet sich eine positive Entwicklung ab.* **2.** outlook ◊ *Man sollte versuchen, den eigenen Horizont zu erweitern.* etw. geht über meinen Horizont sth is beyond me

Horn [hɔrn] das <-(e)s, Hörner> horn ◊ *ein Stier mit spitzen Hörnern* ♦ *ein Schuhlöffel aus Horn* ♦ *Wer spielt in eurem Orchester das Horn?*

Ⓔ jdm Hörner aufsetzen *(fam)* cheat on sb ins gleiche Horn blasen/stoßen say the same thing, tell sb the same thing jdn/etw. auf die Hörner nehmen **1.** tackle sb/sth **2.** catch sb/sth on its horns

Ⓩ **Hörn·chen** ['hœrnçən] das <-s, -> **1.** crescent-shaped pastry ◊ *Hörnchen mit Nussfüllung* **2.** cone ◊ *Zwei Kugeln Vanilleeis im Hörnchen, bitte!*

Hör·saal ['høːɐ̯zaːl] der <-(e)s, Hörsäle> lecture theatre, lecture theater, auditorium ◊ *Die Vorlesung findet in Hörsaal 127 statt.*

Hort [hɔrt] der <-(e)s, -e> **1.** after-school nursery, after-school club ◊ *Seit ich berufstätig bin, geht mein Sohn in den Hort.* **2.** *(lofty)* bastion ◊ *Die Akademie ist der Hort der Sprache.*

> Until about the age of 12, children whose parents are at work can go to a *Hort* (after-school club). *Horte* are sometimes open during the school holidays. In Germany, where lessons normally finish at lunchtime, places in after-school clubs are in great demand. There are not always enough nursery places.

Ⓩ **Ho·se** ['hoːzə] die <-, -n> *both sing and pl describe the individual piece of clothing* **1.** trousers, pants ◊ *Er trug eine graue Hose.* ♦ *Sie hatte lange Hosen an.* **2.** (under)pants ◊ *Das Kind hatte die Hosen voll.*

Ⓔ tote Hose *(slang)* dead boring die Hosen voll

haben *(fam)* be dead scared in die Hose gehen *(fam)* be a flop sich ⸤dat⸥ in die Hose machen *(fam)* wet yourself

⓶ **Ho·tel** [ho'tɛl] das <–s, –s> hotel ◊ in einem Hotel übernachten

⓶ **hübsch** [hʏpʃ] ⸤adj⸥ pretty ◊ ein hübsches Gesicht ♦ All ihre Kinder sind hübsch. ♦ eine hübsche Stange Geld kosten ⊖schön ⸤adv⸥ **1.** attractively ◊ eine hübsch eingerichtete Wohnung sich hübsch machen dress up, make yourself up ⊖schön **2.** nicely ◊ Sie spielt schon ganz hübsch Klavier. **3.** *(fam, emph)* pretty ◊ Heute ist es hübsch kalt draußen.; *(to a child)* Jetzt sei hübsch artig und geh ins Bett. Be a good boy/girl and go to bed now. Iss mal hübsch deinen Teller leer. Be a good boy/girl and eat up now. ⊖schön

Hub·schrau·ber ['hu:pʃraobɐ] der <–s, –> helicopter ◊ mit/in einem Hubschrauber fliegen

Huf [hu:f] der <–(e)s, –e> hoof ◊ die Hufe eines Pferdes

Hüf·te ['hʏftə] die <–, –n> **1.** hip ◊ chronische Schmerzen an/in der Hüfte **2.** *sing or pl* hips ◊ breite Hüften haben ♦ Das Kleid ist zu eng um die Hüfte.

Hü·gel ['hy:gl̩] der <–s, –> **1.** hill ◊ Das Haus steht auf einem Hügel. **2.** heap, mound ◊ Er hatte die Erde zu einem Hügel aufgeschüttet.

⓶ **Huhn** [hu:n] das <–(e)s, Hühner> **1.** chicken ◊ Hühner halten (Fleisch vom) Huhn chicken ◊ (Fleisch vom) Huhn schmeckt mir besser als Schweinefleisch. **2.** hen ◊ Eier von frei laufenden Hühnern
● mit den Hühnern aufstehen get up at the crack of dawn, get up with the lark da lachen ja die Hühner that's a laugh

Hühn·chen ['hy:nçən] das <–s, –> **1.** chicken ◊ Hühnchen in Rotweinsoße **2.** chick ◊ Im Hof rennen zwei Hühnchen herum.
● mit jdm ein Hühnchen zu rupfen haben *(fam)* have got a bone to pick with sb

Hül·le ['hʏlə] die <–, –n> cover ◊ etw. in eine Hülle stecken; case ◊ eine Hülle für die Lesebrille; *(for records)* sleeve
● in Hülle und Fülle in abundance jds sterbliche Hülle *(lit)* sb's mortal remains die Hüllen fallen lassen *(fam)* strip (down to nothing)

hu·man [hu'ma:n] ⸤adj, adv⸥ humane(ly) ◊ Es gibt keinen humanen Krieg. ♦ Unsere Medizin ist immer human. ♦ jdn human behandeln

⓶ **Hu·mor** [hu'mo:ɐ] der <–s> *no pl* sense of humour, sense of humor ◊ (keinen) Humor haben ♦ einen trockenen Humor haben den Humor verlieren lose your good humour, lose your good spirits

hum·peln ['hʊmpl̩n] ⸤intr v⸥ +haben/with indication of direction +sein limp ◊ Nach dem Unfall ist sie wochenlang gehumpelt. ♦ Sie humpelte ans Fenster.

⓶ **Hund** [hʊnt] der <–(e)s, –e> **1.** dog ein scharfer Hund a tracker dog **2.** *(fam, pej)* swine ◊ Du fauler Hund!
● armer Hund *(fam)* poor devil bekannt sein wie ein bunter Hund *(fam)* be very well-known ein dicker Hund *(fam)* a whopper keine schlafenden Hunde wecken let sleeping dogs lie ◊ Wir sollten keine schlafenden Hunde wecken und ihn lieber nicht auf diese Sache ansprechen. Hunde,

die bellen, beißen nicht empty vessels make the most noise ◊ Lass ihn ruhig drohen — Hunde, die bellen, beißen nicht. vor die Hunde gehen *(fam)* go to the dogs

hun·dert ['hʊndɐt] ⸤nmrl⸥ (a/one) hundred → vier
⑨ hundert(e) und aberhundert(e) hundreds and hundreds (of) ◊ Er hat hundert und aberhundert Euro gespart.

> **Hundert** and **hunderte** can also be written with a capital **H** when used with indefinite expressions of quantity: *Sie hat ein paar hundert/Hundert CDs. — hunderte/Hunderte von Malen.*

Hun·dert¹ ['hʊndɐt] die <–, –en> (a/one) hundred ◊ Die Zahl der Besucher hatte die Hundert schnell überschritten. → Vier

Hun·dert² ['hʊndɐt] das <–, –> (one) hundred ◊ Mit dieser Kiste ist jetzt das zweite Hundert voll.

Hun·der·ter ['hʊndɐtɐ] der <–s, –> **1.** hundred ◊ die Einer, Zehner und Hunderter addieren **2.** *(fam)* hundred (euro/pound/dollar note) ◊ Er blätterte ein paar Hunderter vor mich hin.

⓶ **Hun·ger** ['hʊŋɐ] der <–s> *no pl* **1.** hunger ◊ seinen Hunger stillen Hunger haben be hungry **2.** starvation ◊ vom Hunger bedroht sein ♦ der Kampf gegen den Hunger Hunger leiden starve
⑨ Hunger nach etw. desire for sth, hunger for sth ◊ Sein Hunger nach Wissen wurde gestillt.

hun·gern ['hʊŋɐn] ⸤intr v⸥ +haben starve, go hungry; *(voluntarily)* starve yourself ◊ Sie hungert, um zuzunehmen.

⓶ **hung·rig** ['hʊŋrɪç] ⸤adj⸥ hungrig (nach/auf etw. ⸤acc⸥) hungry (for sth) ◊ hungrige Menschen ♦ Sport macht hungrig. ♦ Das Kind ist hungrig nach Zuwendung.

Hu·pe ['hu:pə] die <–, –n> horn ◊ Sie drückte auf die Hupe.

⓶ **hu·pen** ['hu:pm̩] ⸤intr v⸥ +haben sound the/your horn, hoot the/your horn

hüp·fen ['hʏpfn̩] ⸤intr v⸥ +sein jump ◊ Die Kinder hüpften vor Freude. ♦ über einen Bach hüpfen; hop ◊ auf einem Bein hüpfen

Hür·de ['hʏɐdə] die <–, –n> hurdle ◊ finanzielle Hürden nehmen/überwinden ♦ Der Läufer hat eine Hürde gerissen.; *(in showjumping)* fence

⓶ **hus·ten** ['hu:stn̩] <hustet, hustete, hat gehustet> ⸤intr v⸥ **1.** cough **2.** *(fam)* auf etw. ⸤acc⸥ husten not give a damn about sth ◊ Ich huste auf deine guten Ratschläge. ⸤tr v⸥ cough up ◊ Der Patient hustet Blut.
● jdm etwas husten *(fam)* tell sb where to get off

⓶ **Hus·ten** ['hu:stn̩] der <–s> *no pl* cough ◊ ein trockener Husten ♦ Sie hat (einen) Husten bekommen.

Hut [hu:t] der <–(e)s, Hüte> **1.** hat ◊ einen Hut tragen **2.** ʙᴏᴛ cap
● ein alter Hut old hat etw./jdn unter einen Hut bringen reconcile sth/sb mit jdm/etw. nichts am Hut haben *(fam)* not be interested in sb/sth ◊ Mit Sprachen hat er nichts am Hut. jd kann sich ⸤dat⸥ etw. an den Hut stecken *(fam)* sb can stick sth etw. aus dem Hut zaubern *(fam)* pull sth out of a hat Hut ab! I take my hat off to …!

hü·ten ['hy:tn̩] ⸤tr v⸥ +haben **1.** look after ◊ Kannst

du morgen die Kinder hüten? **2.** *das Bett hüten*
stay in bed *das Haus hüten* stay at home, stay
indoors ⟨ref v⟩ +*haben* **1.** *sich vor jdm/etw. hüten*
watch out for sb/sth *Er soll sich bloß hüten, dass
ich ihn nicht dabei erwische! He* should make sure
that I don't catch him doing it! **2.** *sich hüten, etw.
zu tun* take care not to do sth ◊ *Er wird sich*

schwer hüten, ihr das zu sagen. jd wird sich hüten
sb will do nothing of the kind ◊ *„Erzähle ihm bloß
nichts davon!" — „Ich werde mich hüten."*
Hüt·te ['hʏtə] die <–, –n> hut
Hy·po·thek [hypo'teːk] die <–, –en> **1.** mortgage ◊
Er hat auf sein Haus eine Hypothek aufgenommen.
♦ *eine Hypothek tilgen* **2.** *(fig)* burden

I

i, I [iː] das <–(s), –(s)> i, I ◊ *Dieses Wort wird mit einem kleinen i/großen I geschrieben.* ♦ *I wie Ida*

IC™ [iːˈtseː] der *(abbr of* Intercityzug*)* Intercity ◊ *der IC nach München*

ICE™ [iːtseːˈˈeː] der *(abbr of* Intercityexpresszug*)* Intercity Express ◊ *Ich nehme den ICE nach Berlin.*

> *Intercity Express* trains travel at speeds of up to 330 km/h and have been used in Germany since 1991 to cover the stretches between the big German cities and to Vienna and Zurich. The very high speeds and few stops mean that travel by *Intercity Express* is fast, if not exactly cheap. *Intercity Express* trains are recognizable by their aerodynamic design and their colours: white with a red stripe.

② **ich** [ɪç] pers pron I, me ◊ *Ich bin traurig.* ♦ *Immer ich!* ♦ *„Wer ist da?" — „Ich bin's!"* ♦ *Rufst du mich an?* ♦ *Was hast du gegen mich?* ♦ *Gib mir mal das Messer!* ♦ *Er ist mit mir zum Zahnarzt gegangen.*

nom	ich
acc	mich
dat	mir
gen	meiner

i·de·al [ideˈaːl] adj no comp/superl ideal, perfect ◊ *die ideale Mitarbeiterin* ♦ *Diese Lösung ist natürlich ideal.*

② **I·dee** [iˈdeː] die <–, –n> **1.** idea ◊ *Ich habe eine Idee, was wir ihm schenken könnten.* ♦ *Wie kommst du denn auf die Idee?* ♦ *Die Idee zu dem Roman kam ihm auf einer Reise.* ⊜Einfall **2.** eine Idee ... a bit (of) ... ◊ *Der Rock könnte eine Idee kürzer sein.* ⊜ein bisschen ...

IG [iːˈgeː] die *(abbr of* Industriegewerkschaft*)* industrial union

I·gel [ˈiːgl̩] der <–s, –> hedgehog

IHK [iːhaːˈkaː] die *(abbr of* Industrie- und Handelskammer*)* Chamber of Industry and Commerce

> There are over 80 regional Chambers of Industry and Commerce in Germany, all of which belong to an umbrella organization, the Association of German Chambers of Industry and Commerce (*DIHT*). Except for agricultural businesses, the independent professions (lawyers and doctors), and craft businesses, all German businesses are legal members of a Chamber of Industry and Commerce. The Chambers give advice to businesses and represent them publicly, for instance to local governments and local authorities. They also hold technical, business and foreign-language exams, and advise people doing training and those businesses that offer training.

ihm [iːm] dat of er dat of es
ihn [iːn] acc of er
ih·nen [ˈiːnən] dat of sie²

Ih·nen [ˈiːnən] dat of Sie

② **ihr¹** [iːɐ] dat of sie¹ pers pron you ◊ *Geht ihr schon in die Schule?* ♦ *Wie geht es euch?* ♦ *Was ist denn mit euch los?* ♦ *Ich heiße euch willkommen!*

nom	ihr
acc	euch
dat	euch
gen	eurer

② **ihr²** [iːɐ] det **1.** her ◊ *Ihr Mann arbeitet an der Uni.* ♦ *Ihre Brille ist kaputt.* ♦ *Das ist ihr Buch.* ♦ *Während ihrer Krankheit konnte sie nicht arbeiten.* ♦ *Die Maus ist kaputt. Ihre Tasten klemmen.* **2.** their ◊ *Kinder und ihre Mutter* ♦ *Da sind Lou und Tom in ihrem neuen Auto.*

	m	f	nt	pl
nom	ihr	ihre	ihr	ihre
acc	ihren	ihre	ihr	ihre
dat	ihrem	ihrer	ihrem	ihren
gen	ihres	ihrer	ihres	ihrer

② **Ihr** [iːɐ] det your ◊ *Ihre Frau ist gut angekommen.* ♦ *Ihr Auto muss repariert werden.* ♦ *das Büro Ihres Kollegen* ♦ *Ich habe heute Ihre Mutter getroffen, Frau Tahy.* ♦ *Geht es Ihrer Freundin wieder besser?* ♦ *Liebe Gäste, Ihr Frühstück ist fertig.* ♦ *die Anforderungen Ihrer Prüfungen*

	m	f	nt	pl
nom	Ihr	Ihre	Ihr	Ihre
acc	Ihren	Ihre	Ihr	Ihre
dat	Ihrem	Ihrer	Ihrem	Ihren
gen	Ihres	Ihrer	Ihres	Ihrer

ih·re [ˈiːrə] → ihrer, ihr²
Ih·re [ˈiːrə] → Ihrer, Ihr
ih·rer [ˈiːrə] poss pron **1.** hers ◊ *„Ist das deine Lesebrille?" — „Nein, ihre."* ♦ *Ich mag keine Hunde, und ihren schon gar nicht.* **2.** theirs ◊ *„Ist das nicht das Auto der Meiers?" — „Ja, das könnte ihres sein."* ♦ *„Hier, die Mäntel deiner Kinder." — „Oh, das sind aber nicht ihre."*

	m	f	nt	pl
nom	ihrer	ihre	ihr(e)s	ihre
acc	ihren	ihre	ihr(e)s	ihre
dat	ihrem	ihrer	ihrem	ihren
gen	-	-	-	-

Ih·rer [ˈiːrə] poss pron yours ◊ *Das Buch auf dem Tisch, ist das Ihr(e)s?* ♦ *Von allen Vorschlägen finde ich nur Ihren gut.*

	m	f	nt	pl
nom	Ihrer	Ihre	Ihr(e)s	Ihre
acc	Ihren	Ihre	Ihr(e)s	Ihre
dat	Ihrem	Ihrer	Ihrem	Ihren
gen	-	-	-	-

Ih·res [ˈiːrəs] → Ihrer

ih·ret·we·gen ['iːrətveːgn̩] [adv] **1.** *sing* because of her ◊ *Ich mache mir ihretwegen Sorgen — sie ist schwer krank.* **2.** *pl* because of them ◊ *Die Kinder wollten nicht aufstehen — ihretwegen bin ich zu spät dran.*
Ih·ret·we·gen ['iːrətveːgn̩] [adv] because of you ◊ *Sie kommen zu spät! Ihretwegen verpassen wir nun den Bus.*
Ihrs [iːɐ̯s] → Ihrer
② **Il·lus·trier·te** [ɪlʊs'triːgtə] die <–n, die Illustrierten> *but: zwei Illustrierte* (glossy) magazine
im [ɪm] [contract] *in + dem* **1.** in the ◊ *im Schrank* ♦ *im Theater* im März in March → in **2.** *with nominalized verbs, not to be split* in ◊ *Im Joggen ist er unschlagbar.*; *while* ◊ *Noch im Gehen telefonierte sie auf dem Handy.*
Im·biss ['ɪmbɪs] der <–es, –e> **1.** snack ◊ *einen kleinen Imbiss einnehmen* ♦ *In der Pause wurde ein kalter Imbiss gereicht.* **2.** (food) stand, snack bar, diner ◊ *ein Döner vom türkischen Imbiss*
im·ma·tri·ku·lie·ren [ɪmatriku'liːrən] [tr v] +*haben* sich (irgendwo) immatrikulieren register (somewhere), enrol (somewhere) ◊ *Sie hat sich an der Universität Augsburg immatrikuliert.* jdn (irgendwo) immatrikulieren register sb (somewhere), enrol sb (somewhere) ◊ *Derzeit sind im Fach Maschinenbau 2000 Studenten immatrikuliert.* ⊖einschreiben ⊖exmatrikulieren
② **im·mer¹** ['ɪmɐ] [adv] **1.** always ◊ *Das haben wir schon immer so gemacht.* ♦ *Er war immer sehr nett zu mir.* für immer for good immer während eternal, everlasting ◊ *immer während e Freundschaft* auf immer (und ewig) for ever (and ever) immer wenn whenever ◊ *Immer wenn die Sonne scheint, gehe ich zu Fuß zur Arbeit.* **2.** immer wieder time and again, over and over **3.** +*comp* immer häufiger/öfter more and more frequently immer weniger less and less immer schwieriger/häufiger etc. more and more difficult/often etc. **4.** noch immer, immer noch still ◊ *Sie ist noch immer krank.*
im·mer² ['ɪmɐ] [part] **1.** *not usually translated* (fam) Immer mit der Ruhe! One after the other!, One by one! Immer hübsch vorsichtig sein, hörst du? Now just be careful, do you hear? Immer mal langsam jetzt, was ist denn passiert? Now just slow down and tell me what happened. **2.** wann/was/wer (auch) immer whenever/whatever/whoever ◊ *Was immer du tust, sei bitte vorsichtig!* wie (auch) immer no matter how, no matter what
im·mer·hin ['ɪmɐhɪn] [part] **1.** still ◊ *Das macht immerhin zehn Prozent des Umsatzes aus.* **2.** at least ◊ *Es hat nicht geklappt, aber wir haben es immerhin versucht!* ⊖wenigstens, zumindest **3.** after all ◊ *Du solltest ihm vertrauen, er ist immerhin dein Bruder!* ⊖schließlich, doch
im·mer·zu ['ɪmɐ'tsuː] [adv] (fam) constantly, always ◊ *Ich denke immerzu daran.* ⊖andauernd, ständig
Im·mo·bi·lie [ɪmo'biːljə] die <–, –n> most *pl* (piece of) property ◊ *eine vermietete/selbst genutzte Immobilie* Immobilien property, real estate ⊖Objekt
imp·fen ['ɪmpfn̩] [tr v] +*haben* jdn/ein Tier (gegen etw.) impfen vaccinate sb/an animal (against sth) ◊ *Ich habe meine Kinder gegen Windpocken impfen*

lassen. Bist du gegen Grippe geimpft? Have you had a flu jab?
Impf·pass ['ɪmpfpas] der <–es, Impfpässe> vaccination card ◊ *Haben Sie Ihren Impfpass dabei?*
② **Imp·fung** ['ɪmpfʊŋ] die <–, –en> MED vaccination ◊ *eine Impfung gegen Grippe*
im·po·nie·ren [ɪmpo'niːrən] <imponiert, imponierte, hat imponiert> [intr v] jdm imponieren impress sb ◊ *Sein Mut imponiert mir.* ⊖jdn beeindrucken
② **Im·port** [ɪm'pɔɐ̯t] der <–(e)s, –e> import ◊ *der Import von Rohstoffen* ♦ *Dieser Wein ist ein Import aus Südafrika.* ⊖Einfuhr ⊖Export
Im·puls [ɪm'pʊls] der <–es, –e> **1.** stimulus ◊ *der entscheidende Impuls zum Aufschwung* ⊖Anstoß, Anregung **2.** impulse ◊ *Sie unterdrückte den Impuls, einfach wegzurennen.* ♦ *ein elektrischer/ elektromagnetischer Impuls*
im·stan·de, im Stan·de [ɪm'ʃtandə] [adj] no comp/superl, not before ns **1.** capable, able ◊ *Ich bin nicht imstande, dieses Gerät zu bedienen.* **2.** in a position ◊ *Wir sind nicht imstande, Ihnen in dieser Sache zu helfen.* Er ist imstande und erzählt ihr alles. I wouldn't put it past him to tell her everything.
in¹ [ɪn] [adj] not before ns (fam) (always in sein) be in fashion ◊ *Sind solche Frisuren jetzt noch in?*
② **in²** [ɪn] [prep] **1.** *in response to the question 'where/when/how?'* +dat in ◊ *Er wohnt in Köln.* ♦ *Das ist in der Armee so üblich.* ♦ *Im Winter wird es hier ziemlich kalt.* ♦ *Kannst du das in zwei Stunden schaffen?* ♦ *Das Gesetz ist in Kraft.* ♦ *100 Dollar, wie viel ist das in Euro?* ♦ *Sie hat eine Eins in Erdkunde.* Bist du schon in der Schule? Are you already at school? in der letzten Nacht last night in großer Eile in great haste, hurriedly in aller Ruhe quietly **2.** *in response to the question 'to where?'* +acc in(to) ◊ *Sie legte die Wäsche in den Koffer.* ♦ *in die Schweiz einreisen* ♦ *Schreib das bitte auch in den Brief.* ♦ *Sie haben sich in Widersprüche verstrickt.* Sie kommt bald in die Schule. She's starting school soon. in eine Partei eintreten join a political party **3.** +acc bis in ..., (bis) in ... hinein right (on) into ... ◊ *Er blieb bis in die frühen Morgenstunden weg.* **4.** +acc into ◊ *Die Hexe verzauberte ihn in einen Wolf.* ♦ *das Essen in Portionen aufteilen* eine Sache in Ordnung bringen sort sth out
in-... [ɪn] [prefix] (lofty) un..., in... ◊ *ein inakzeptabler Vorschlag* ♦ *die inhumane Behandlung von Gefangenen*
in·be·grif·fen ['ɪnbəgrɪfn̩] [adj] (in etw. [dat]) inbegriffen included (in sth) ◊ *Ist die Mehrwertsteuer im Preis inbegriffen?*
In·de·fi·nit·pro·no·men [ɪndefi'niːtpronoːmən, '– – – – –,– –] das <–s, –> indefinite pronoun

An indefinite pronoun refers to a person or thing that is unknown or little known. Examples include *irgendein* (some), *jemand* (someone), *keiner* (nobody, none'). In the middle part of this dictionary you can find information on the declension of indefinite pronouns.

in·dem [ɪn'deːm] [conjunc] by ◊ *Er beruhigte das Baby, indem er es auf den Arm nahm.*

In·der ['ɪndɐ] der <-s, ->, **In·de·rin** ['ɪndərɪn] die <-, –nen> *(person from India)* Indian; *(UK also)* Asian → Deutsche

in·des [ɪn'dɛs], **in·des·sen** [ɪn'dɛsn] [adv] **1.** but, however ◊ *Das muss indessen nicht immer ein Nachteil sein.* ⊜jedoch, aber **2.** meanwhile ◊ *Du hättest indessen schon anfangen können!* ⊜inzwischen, unterdessen

In·di·a·ner [ɪn'dja:nɐ] der <-s, ->, **In·di·a·ne·rin** [ɪn'dja:nərɪn] die <-, –nen> (American) Indian ◊ *Geschichten über Indianer und Cowboys*

In·di·en ['ɪndjən] das <-s> *article only in combination with attribute, no pl* India → Deutschland

In·di·ka·tiv ['ɪndikati:f] der <-s, -e> *most sing (abbr Ind.)* indicative ◊ *Bei der indirekten Rede wird oft der Indikativ statt des Konjunktivs verwendet.*

in·disch ['ɪndɪʃ] [adj] *mostly before ns* Indian → deutsch

In·disch ['ɪndɪʃ] das <-(s)> *seldom with article, no pl* Hindi, an Indian language → Deutsch

In·diz [ɪn'di:ts] das <-es, –ien> **1.** *(lofty)* ein Indiz (für etw.) indication (of sth), sign (of sth) ◊ *ein sicheres/wichtiges Indiz* ♦ *ein Indiz für eine Klimaveränderung* **2.** *most pl* LAW Indizien circumstantial evidence ◊ *Die Indizien weisen darauf hin, dass er der Täter ist.*

in·do·ne·sisch [ɪndo'ne:zɪʃ] [adj] *mostly before ns* Indonesian → deutsch

② **In·dus·trie** [ɪndʊs'tri:] die <-, –n> *most sing* industry ◊ *Er will später in die Industrie gehen.* ♦ *die Papier verarbeitende Industrie*

In·dus·trie·ge·werk·schaft [ɪndʊs'tri:gəvɛˈkʃaft] die <-, –en> *(abbr IG)* industrial union ◊ *die Industriegewerkschaft Metall*

In·dus·trie- und Han·dels·kam·mer [ɪndʊsˌtri: ʊnt 'handlˌskamɐ] die <-, –n> *(abbr IHK)* chamber of industry and commerce box@ IHK

in·ei·nan·der [ɪn|ae'nandɐ] [adv] into each other, into one another ◊ *Die Zahnräder greifen ineinander* sich ineinander verlieben fall in love (with each other)

In·farkt [ɪn'faˈkt] der <-(e)s, -e> **1.** MED heart attack, infarct(ion) ◊ *einen Infarkt erleiden* ♦ *an einem Infarkt sterben* ⊜Herzinfarkt **2.** *(fig)* collapse ◊ *Dem Gesundheitswesen droht der Infarkt.*

In·fi·ni·tiv ['ɪnfiniti:f] der <-s, -e> infinitive ◊ *der Infinitiv mit „zu"* ⊜Grundform

② **In·fla·ti·on** [ɪnfla'tsjo:n] die <-, –en> *most sing* inflation ◊ *Im Jahr 2000 lag die Inflation in Deutschland bei 1,4%.*

In·fo¹ ['ɪnfo:] die <-, –s> *(fam) (abbr of* Information*)* info, information ◊ *Weitere Infos erhalten Sie unter der Nummer …*

In·fo² ['ɪnfo:] das <-s, –s> *(fam) (abbr of* Informationsblatt*)* information guide ◊ *Die Infos über Diabetes liegen im Wartezimmer aus.*

in·fol·ge [ɪn'fɔlgə] [prep] [+gen] or [+dat] as a result of, due to ◊ *Sie ist infolge eines Unfalls gelähmt.*; *(adverbial)* infolge von as a result of, due to ◊ *Er fehlte an 20 Arbeitstagen infolge von Krankheit.* ⊜aufgrund

in·fol·ge·des·sen [ɪnfɔlgə'dɛsn] [adv] therefore, consequently ◊ *Er ist krank und kann infolgedessen*

nicht arbeiten. ⊜deshalb

In·for·ma·tik [ɪnfɔˈ'ma:tɪk] die <-> *no pl* information technology, computer science ◊ *Informatik studieren*

② **In·for·ma·ti·on** [ɪnfɔˈma'tsjo:n] die <-, –en> **1.** *most pl* information ◊ *Informationen aus erster Hand* Informationen über etw./jdn information on/about sth/sb ◊ *Informationen über das Projekt einholen* Informationen zu etw. information on/about sth ◊ *Wo bekomme ich Informationen zum Studium?* **2.** *no pl* der/jds Information dienen as for information purposes zu jds Information for sb's information **3.** *no pl* information desk ◊ *Fragen Sie an der Information im Erdgeschoss.* ⊜Auskunft

② **in·for·mie·ren** [ɪnfɔˈ'mi:rən] <informiert, informierte, hat informiert> [tr v] inform ◊ *Habt ihr die Polizei informiert?* jdn über etw./jdn informieren inform sb of/about sth/sb ◊ *Wir wurden nicht über den Vorfall informiert.* jdn von etw. informieren inform sb of/about sth [ref v] sich über etw./jdn informieren find out about sth/sb ◊ *Ich habe mich darüber informiert, was die Flüge kosten.*; *(for an exam)* read up on sth/sb

in·fra·ge, in Fra·ge [ɪn'fra:gə] **1.** etw. infrage stellen threaten sth, put sth under threat ◊ *Der Skandal hat seine Glaubwürdigkeit infrage gestellt.* ⊜etw. gefährden **2.** etw. infrage stellen call sth into question ◊ *Niemand will deine Leistungen infrage stellen.* **3.** (für/als etw.) infrage kommen come under consideration (for/as sth) ◊ *Kommt diese Wohnung für euch infrage? Kommt (gar) nicht infrage! That's out of the question!*

② **In·ge·ni·eur** [ɪnʒe'njø:ɐ] der <-s, -e>, **In·ge·ni·eu·rin** [ɪnʒe'njø:rɪn] die <-, –nen> *(abbr* Ing*)* (qualified) engineer ◊ *die Ausbildung zum Ingenieur* ♦ *Sie ist Ingenieurin.*

In·ha·ber ['ɪnha:bɐ] der <-s, ->, **In·ha·be·rin** ['ɪnha:bərɪn] die <-, –nen> **1.** owner ◊ *Er ist Inhaber eines Softwareunternehmens.* ♦ *die alleinige Inhaberin eines Lokals*; *(of shares etc.)* holder ◊ *Inhaber eines gültigen Passes sein* ⊜Eigentümer **2.** holder, possessor ◊ *die Inhaber hoher Ämter*

in·haf·tie·ren [ɪnhaf'ti:rən] <inhaftiert, inhaftierte, hat inhaftiert> [tr v] *mostly passive (form)* jdn inhaftieren arrest sb, take sb into custody ◊ *Ein Verdächtiger wurde inhaftiert.*

in·ha·lie·ren [ɪnha'li:rən] <inhaliert, inhalierte, hat inhaliert> [tr+intr v] inhale, breathe in ◊ *den Rauch einer Zigarette inhalieren*; *(for medical reasons)* inhale ◊ *mehrmals täglich (Kamillendämpfe) inhalieren*

② **In·halt** ['ɪnhalt] der <-(e)s, -e> **1.** contents ◊ *Sie leerte den Inhalt ihrer Tasche auf den Tisch.* **2.** capacity, volume ◊ *Unsere Mülltonne hat 120 Liter Inhalt.* **3.** content ◊ *ein Artikel mit brisantem Inhalt*

in·klu·si·ve [ɪnklu'zi:və] [prep] *sing nouns without article or attribute are not declined when following this prep, otherwise* [+gen] or *fam* [+dat] inclusive of, including ◊ *Der Flug kostete 620 Euro inklusive (der) Flughafensteuer.* ♦ *Übernachtung inklusive Frühstück/Halbpension* ⊜einschließlich ⊜exklusive

In·land ['ɪnlant] das <-(e)s> *no pl* home ◊ *Der Umsatz im Inland stieg um 5%. Die Studie ergab,*

dass drei von zehn Urlaubern im Inland bleiben wollen. The study showed that three out of every ten holidaymakers intend to stay in their own countries. ⊖Ausland

in·mit·ten [ɪn'mɪtn̩] (prep) (+gen) in the middle of, amid(st) ◊ *Das Dorf liegt inmitten grüner Wiesen.* ♦ *eine Oase der Ruhe inmitten des Trubels*

in·ne·ha·ben ['ɪnəhaːbm̩] <hat inne, hatte inne, hat innegehabt> (tr v) *(lofty)* hold ◊ *das Amt des Vorsitzenden innehaben*

in·ne·hal·ten ['ɪnəhaltn̩] <hält inne, hielt inne, hat innegehalten> (intr v) *(lofty)* pause ◊ *Lasst uns für einen Moment innehalten und der Toten gedenken.*

② **in·nen** ['ɪnən] (adv) inside ◊ *Der Baum war innen ganz hohl.* nach innen inwards ⊖außen

In·nen·hof ['ɪnənhoːf] der <-(e)s, Innenhöfe> courtyard ◊ *Das Fenster ging zum Innenhof hinaus.*; *(of a building)* quad(rangle)

② **In·nen·stadt** ['ɪnənʃtat] die <-, Innenstädte> city centre, city center, downtown ◊ *die Fußgängerzone in der Münchner Innenstadt* ⊖Stadtzentrum

② **in·ner·...** ['ɪnɐ] (prefix) within ... ◊ *der innereuropäische Handel* innerparteiliche Machtkämpfe party-internal struggles for power

in·ne·re ['ɪnərə] (adj) *only before ns* <ein innerer ..., eine innere ..., ein inneres ...> **1.** POL, MED internal ◊ *die inneren Angelegenheiten eines Staates* ♦ *innere Blutungen/Verletzungen haben* ⊖äußere **2.** inner ◊ *die innere Struktur eines Textes* ♦ *jds inneres Gleichgewicht* **3.** interior ◊ *die innere Gestaltung eines Hauses* ⊖äußere

In·ne·re ['ɪnərə] das <-n or Innern> *but: mein Inneres, no pl* **1.** POL Inneres interior ◊ *der Minister für Inneres* **2.** das Innere ... (gen) the inside of sth ◊ *einen Blick ins Innere eines Hauses werfen* **3.** das Innere ... (gen) the centre of sth, the center of sth, the middle of sth ◊ *eine Reise ins Innere der Mongolei* ⊖Zentrum, Mitte **4.** jds/das Innere sb's/the heart ◊ *In dem Brief hat er ihr sein Inneres offenbart.* ♦ *Im tiefsten Inner(e)n kann ich nicht daran glauben.*

② **in·ner·halb** ['ɪnəhalp] (prep) (+gen) or (+dat) **1.** (+gen) (with)in ◊ *Das Problem muss innerhalb der nächsten Wochen gelöst werden.* ⊖während, binnen **2.** (+gen) (with)in, inside ◊ *innerhalb vorgegebener Grenzen* ♦ *Auseinandersetzungen innerhalb der Partei* ⊖außerhalb **3.** *adverbial* (+dat) innerhalb von within sth ◊ *innerhalb von Tagen* ♦ *innerhalb von Städten*

in·ner·orts ['ɪnɐʔɔrts] (adv) in built-up areas ◊ *Sie wollen innerorts Tempo 30 durchsetzen.*

ins [ɪns] (contract) *in + das* **1.** into (the) ◊ *ins Haus laufen* ♦ *sich ins Bett legen* ♦ *in* **2.** *in certain idioms, not to be split:* look up the relevant idiom ◊ *ins Auge gehen*

In·sas·se ['ɪnzasə] der <-n, -n>, **In·sas·sin** ['ɪnzasɪn] die <-, -nen> *most pl (form)* **1.** passenger ◊ *Bei dem Absturz kamen sämtliche Insassen ums Leben.* **2.** occupant, resident ◊ *die Insassen psychiatrischer Anstalten; (of a prison)* inmate

ins·be·son·de·re [ɪnsbə'zɔndərə] (adv) in particular, particularly, especially ◊ *Das ist wichtig, insbesondere für dich.* ⊖vor allem, besonders, namentlich

In·schrift ['ɪnʃrɪft] die <-, -en> inscription ◊ *Wie lautet die Inschrift auf dem Denkmal?*

② **In·sel** ['ɪnzl̩] die <-, -n> island ◊ *Rügen ist die größte Insel Deutschlands.* ⊖Festland

in·se·rie·ren [ɪnze'riːrən] <inseriert, inserierte, hat inseriert> (tr+intr v) advertise ◊ *in der Zeitung inserieren* ♦ *eine Wohnung inserieren*

ins·ge·heim [ɪnsgə'haɛm, '‒ ‒ ‒] (adv) secretly, in secret ◊ *etw. insgeheim planen/vorhaben*

② **ins·ge·samt** [ɪnsgə'zamt, '‒ ‒ ‒] (adv) altogether, in total ◊ *Insgesamt beschäftigt der Konzern 69 000 Mitarbeiter.*

in·so·fern [ɪn'zoːfɛrn] (adv) in that (respect) ◊ *Die Situation ist ziemlich hoffnungslos, insofern gebe ich Ihnen Recht.* insofern ..., als ..., in that; ..., in so far as; ..., inasmuch as ◊ *Dies ist insofern bemerkenswert, als es doch recht ungewöhnlich ist.*

In·stal·la·teur [ɪnstala'tøːɐ] der <-s, -e>, **In·stal·la·teu·rin** [ɪnstala'tøːrɪn] die <-, -nen> plumber ◊ *Sie ist von Beruf Installateurin.* ♦ *einen Installateur rufen* ⊖Klempner

in·stand, in Stand [ɪn'ʃtant] (adv) **1.** etw. instand setzen repair sth; *(buildings)* renovate sth ⊖etw. reparieren, etw. sanieren **2.** etw. instand halten maintain sth ◊ *Es kostet viel Geld, die Maschinen instand zu halten.* ⊖etw. erhalten

Ins·tanz [ɪn'stants] die <-, -en> **1.** authority ◊ *Diese Instanz ist für Ihren Antrag nicht zuständig.* **2.** court ◊ *Sein Fall wurde an die nächsthöhere Instanz verwiesen.*; hearing ◊ *Er wurde in erster Instanz verurteilt.*

② **Ins·ti·tut** [ɪnsti'tuːt] das <-(e)s, -e> **1.** institute ◊ *das Institut für Kunstgeschichte* **2.** *(abbr of* Geldinstitut*)* (financial) institution

② **Ins·tru·ment** [ɪnstru'mɛnt] das <-(e)s, -e> instrument ◊ *Spielst du ein Instrument?* ♦ *Die Instrumente eines Chirurgen müssen steril sein.* ♦ *Geld — das Instrument der Macht.*

in·sze·nie·ren [ɪnstse'niːrən] <inszeniert, inszenierte, hat inszeniert> (tr v) **1.** direct ◊ *Spielfilme inszenieren*; put on, stage **2.** *(lofty, pej)* stage, orchestrate ◊ *Sie haben ein regelrechtes Medienspektakel inszeniert.*

② **in·tel·li·gent** [ɪntɛli'gɛnt] (adj, adv) intelligent(ly), clever(ly) ◊ *Sie ist nicht besonders intelligent.* ♦ *eine intelligente Frage* ♦ *Er hat das Problem sehr intelligent gelöst.* ⊖schlau ⊖dumm

In·ten·siv·sta·ti·on [ɪntɛn'ziːfʃta͜tsioːn] die <-, -en> intensive care unit ◊ *Nach dem Infarkt kam er auf die Intensivstation.* auf der Intensivstation liegen be in intensive care

② **in·te·res·sant** [ɪntərɛ'sant] (adj) **1.** interesting ◊ *ein interessantes Leben führen* ♦ *Ich halte Ihr Projekt für sehr interessant.* ⊖uninteressant **2.** TRADE attractive ◊ *Die Bank hat mir interessante Konditionen geboten.* ⊖uninteressant (adv) in an interesting way ◊ *Das Buch ist interessant geschrieben.* etw. interessant gestalten make sth interesting

② **In·te·res·se** [ɪntə'rɛsə] das <-s, -n> **1.** *no pl* Interesse an jdm/etw.) interest (in sb/sth) ◊ *Ich verfolge diese Entwicklung mit großem Interesse.* ♦ *jds Interesse wecken* ♦ *Derzeit steigt das Interesse an Aktien wieder.* Interesse an jdm/etw. haben be interested in sb/sth **2.** *only pl* interest, inclination ◊ *Dieser Beruf entspricht genau meinen Interessen.*

(nicht) viele gemeinsame Interessen haben (not) have a lot in common ⊖Neigungen **3.** interest, concern ◊ *Die Gewerkschaften vertreten die Interessen der Arbeitnehmer.* in jds Interesse sein be in sb's interest(s), be of benefit to sb

⑦ **in·te·res·sie·ren** [ɪntərɛˈsiːrən] <interessiert, interessierte, hat interessiert> [tr v] **1.** jdn interessieren interest sb, be of interest to sb ◊ *Das Leben dieses Mannes interessiert uns.* etw. hat jdn nicht zu interessieren sth is none of sb's business **2.** jdn für etw. interessieren interest sb in sth ◊ *Ich konnte ihn leider nicht für das Projekt interessieren.* [ref v] sich für etw./jdn interessieren be interested in sth/sb ◊ *Interessierst du dich für Kunst?* ◆ *Tom scheint sich sehr für Lisa zu interessieren.*

⑦ **in·te·res·siert** [ɪntərɛˈsiːɐt] [adj] <interessierter, am interessiertesten> interested ◊ *ein interessierter Kunde* an etw. [dat] interessiert sein be interested in sth politisch interessiert sein be interested in politics

In·ter·jek·ti·on [ɪntɛjɛkˈtsjoːn] die <–, –en> interjection

> An interjection is a short word that can be used to express the speaker's emotions: **Ach,** *jetzt hab ich mich schon wieder bekleckert!* (unpleasant surprise); **Pfui,** *kannst du nicht aufpassen!* (strong criticism); **Oh,** *die schöne neue Hose!* (regret or disappointment).

In·ter·nat [ɪntɐˈnaːt] das <–(e)s, –e> boarding school ◊ *Sie ging auf ein teures Internat in der Schweiz.*

in·ter·na·ti·o·nal [ɪntɐnatsjoˈnaːl] [adj] *mostly before ns* international ◊ *internationaler Protest* [adv] internationally, on an international level ◊ *Diese Firma operiert international.*

⑦ **In·ter·net** [ˈɪntɐnɛt] das <–s> *no pl* Internet, (World Wide) Web ◊ *im Internet surfen* ⊖Netz

In·ter·punk·ti·on [ɪntɐpʊŋkˈtsjoːn] die <–> *no pl* punctuation ⊖Zeichensetzung

⑦ **In·ter·view** [ˈɪntɐvjuː, – – '–] das <–s, –s> interview ◊ *Sie gibt keine Interviews.*

in·tran·si·tiv [ˈɪntranzitiːf] [adj, adv] *no comp/superl; when used as an adj, only before ns* intransitive(ly) ◊ *ein intransitives Verb* ◆ *Der intransitive Gebrauch dieses Verbs ist selten.* ◆ *Dieses Verb wird nur intransitiv gebraucht.* ⊖transitiv

In·ven·tar [ɪnvɛnˈtaːɐ] das <–s, –e> *(tech)* **1.** furniture, fittings, house contents ◊ *Wir sollten das gesamte Inventar erneuern.* **2.** lebendes Inventar livestock **3.** inventory ◊ *ein Inventar erstellen*

In·ven·tur [ɪnvɛnˈtuːɐ] die <–, –en> stocktaking ◊ *Inventur machen* ◆ *eine Inventur durchführen*

in·wie·weit [ɪnviˈvaet] [adv] to what extent ◊ *Inwieweit stimmen Sie seinen Prognosen zu?*

⑦ **in·zwi·schen** [ɪnˈtsvɪʃn] [adv] in the meantime ◊ *Koch du bitte das Essen, ich spüle inzwischen.* ◆ unterdessen; (by) now ◊ *Inzwischen habe ich gelernt, mit Computern umzugehen.*

I·re [ˈiːrə] der <–n, –n>, **I·rin** [ˈiːrɪn] die <–, –nen> Irishman Iren Irishwoman die Iren the Irish → Deutsche

⑦ **ir·gend...** [ˈɪrɡn̩t, ˈɪrɡənt] [prefix] **1.** some... ◊ *Sie muss das Ticket doch irgendwohin getan haben!; (in questions, negative and conditional*

sentences) any... ◊ *Hast du mir irgendwas zu sagen?* **2.** just any ... ◊ *Sie wollte nicht irgendeinen, sondern genau diesen Mann.* irgendwas (just) anything ◊ *„Was möchtest du zu essen?" — „Egal, irgendwas."*

ir·gend·ein [ˈɪrɡn̩tˈaen, ˈɪrɡəntˈaen] [det] **1.** some ◊ *die Mutter irgendeines Schülers* ◆ *Irgendeine Frau hat vorhin für dich angerufen.* ◆ *Irgendeine Lösung wird sich schon finden lassen.; (in questions, negative and conditional sentences)* any ◊ *Hast du noch irgendeinen Wunsch?* **2.** (just) any (old) ◊ *Das war nicht irgendein Kind, sondern Ihr Sohn!*

ir·gend·ei·ner [ˈɪrɡn̩tˈaene, ˈɪrɡəntˈaene] [indef pron] **1.** somebody, someone ◊ *Irgendeiner hat mir gesagt, dass er das machen will.; (in questions, negative and conditional sentences)* (just) anybody, (just) anyone **2.** one ◊ *Ich suche eine Vase, hast du irgendeine?; (in questions, negative and conditional sentences)* any (old) one

ir·gend·et·was [ˈɪrɡn̩tˈɛtvas, ˈɪrɡəntˈɛtvas] [indef pron] something ◊ *Irgendetwas stimmt nicht mit meinem Computer.; (in questions, negative and conditional sentences)* anything ◊ *Hast du ihm irgendetwas darüber erzählt?*

ir·gend·je·mand [ˈɪrɡn̩tˈjeːmant, ˈɪrɡəntˈjeːmant] [indef pron] **1.** somebody, someone ◊ *Irgendjemand hat mir gesagt, du seist verreist.; (in questions, negative and conditional sentences)* anybody, anyone ◊ *Hast du das irgendjemandem erzählt?* **2.** just anybody, just anyone ◊ *Ich möchte nicht mit irgendjemandem sprechen, sondern mit Frau Dr. Witt!*

ir·gend·wann [ˈɪrɡn̩tˈvan, ˈɪrɡəntˈvan] [adv] irgendwann (einmal/mal) sometime, some day ◊ *Ich möchte irgendwann mal nach Indien.; at some point* ◊ *Wenn du irgendwann mal Zeit hast, dann schreib mir doch.* (schon) irgendwann (einmal) ever ◊ *Hast du so etwas schon irgendwann einmal gesehen?*

ir·gend·wel·che [ˈɪrɡn̩tˈvɛlçə, ˈɪrɡəntˈvɛlçə] [det] **1.** some, any ◊ *Er hat wieder irgendwelchen Blödsinn angestellt!* ◆ *Falls irgendwelche Probleme auftauchen, ruf mich an.* **2.** any (old) ... ◊ *Ich werde mich nicht mit irgendwelchen Ausreden zufrieden geben!* irgendwelche Leute just anybody

ir·gend·wer [ˈɪrɡn̩tˈveːɐ, ˈɪrɡəntˈveːɐ] [indef pron] **1.** somebody, someone, anybody, anyone ◊ *Irgendwer hat mir gesagt, dass er im Ausland ist.* ◆ *War irgendwer da, solange ich weg war?* **2.** just anybody, just anyone ◊ *Sie will nicht irgendwen heiraten, sondern nur Alex.* declined like wer

ir·gend·wie [ˈɪrɡn̩tˈviː, ˈɪrɡəntˈviː] [adv] somehow, in some way ◊ *Irgendwie werden wir das schon schaffen.* ◆ *Er hat sich irgendwie verändert.*

ir·gend·wo [ˈɪrɡn̩tˈvoː, ˈɪrɡəntˈvoː] [adv] **1.** somewhere, someplace ◊ *Das liegt irgendwo bei Bonn.* ◆ *Irgendwo muss mein Pass doch sein.; (in questions, negative and conditional sentences)* anywhere ◊ *Gibt es hier irgendwo eine Apotheke?* **2.** *(fam)* somehow ◊ *Irgendwo ist das schon verrückt.*

ir·gend·wo·hin [ˈɪrɡəntvoˈhɪn] [adv] somewhere, someplace ◊ *Sie hat den Brief irgendwohin gelegt und ist wieder gegangen.; anywhere, any place* ◊

Wo fahrt ihr hin? — Irgendwohin, Hauptsache weg.

I·rin [ˈiːrɪn] *fem of* Ire

i·risch [ˈiːrɪʃ] [adj] *mostly before ns* Irish → deutsch

I·risch [ˈiːrɪʃ] das <–(s)> *no pl* Irish → Deutsch

Ir·land [ˈɪrlant] das <–s> *article only in combination with attribute, no pl* Ireland → Deutschland

irr [ɪr] → irre

② **ir·re** [ˈɪrə] [adj] <irrer, am irrsten> **1.** mad, crazy, insane ◊ *ein irrer Blick* ♦ *Du bist wohl irre?* **2.** *no comp/superl (fam)* great, cool ◊ *Das war eine irre Party.* **3.** *no comp/superl, mostly before ns (fam)* huge, tremendous ◊ *Er gibt sich irre Mühe.* [adv] **1.** in a confused manner ◊ *sich wie irre verhalten* Sie sah mich irre an. She gave me a mad look. **2.** *(fam)* really ◊ *Sie hat sich irre gefreut.*

Ir·re¹ [ˈɪrə] die <–> *(always* in die Irre*)* jdn in die Irre führen/leiten lead sb astray, mislead sb in die Irre gehen be mistaken, be on the wrong track

Ir·re² [ˈɪrə] der/die <–n, die Irren> *but: ein Irrer/ eine Irre (fam, pej)* maniac, madman, madwoman ◊ *Diesem Irren glaube ich kein Wort.;* *(fem)* madwoman, maniac *box@* Substantivierung

◉ **armer Irrer** *(fam)* poor fool

② **ir·ren** [ˈɪrən] [ref v] *+haben* sich irren be wrong, be mistaken ◊ *Wenn du denkst, dann irrst du dich aber gewaltig.* sich in jdm irren be wrong/mistaken about sb sich in der Richtung irren lose your way ⊖sich täuschen [intr v] *+sein, +place* wander, roam ◊ *Sie irrte durch die leeren Gassen.*

◉ **Irren ist menschlich** to err is human

ISDN [iːɛsdeːˈɛn] das *(abbr of* integrated services digital network) ISDN

Is·lam [ɪsˈlaːm, ˈɪslam] der <–(s)> *no pl* Islam ◊ *Der Islam ist eine der großen Weltreligionen.*

Is·land [ˈiːslant] das <–s> *article only in combination with attribute, no pl* Iceland → Deutschland

Is·län·der [ˈiːslɛndɐ] der <–s, –>, **Is·län·de·rin** [ˈiːslɛndərɪn] die <–, –nen> Icelander → Deutsche

is·län·disch [ˈiːslɛndɪʃ] [adj] *mostly before ns* Icelandic → deutsch

Is·län·disch [ˈiːslɛndɪʃ] das <–(s)> *no pl* Icelandic → Deutsch

i·so·lie·ren [izoˈliːrən] <isoliert, isolierte, hat isoliert> [tr v] **1.** insulate ◊ *Das Kabel ist schlecht isoliert.;* soundproof ◊ *Die Wände hier sind schlecht isoliert — man hört jedes Wort von nebenan.* **2.** isolate ◊ *Die Politik des Diktators hatte das Land vom Westen isoliert.* sich isolieren isolate yourself ◊ *Seit dem Tod ihres Mannes hat sie sich immer mehr isoliert.;* *(a sick person)* jdn isolieren quarantine sb, put sb in quarantine, isolate sb; *(a prisoner)* put sb in solitary confinement

Is·ra·el [ˈɪsraeːl] das <–s> *article only in combination with attribute* Israel → Deutschland

Is·ra·e·li [ɪsraˈʔeːliː] der <–(s), –s>, **Is·ra·e·li** [ɪsraˈʔeːliː] die <–, –s> Israeli → Deutsche

is·ra·e·lisch [ɪsraˈʔeːlɪʃ] [adj] *mostly before ns* Israeli ◊ *die israelische Politik*

② **ist** [ɪst] *pres of* sein

② **isst** [ɪst] *pres of* essen

I·ta·li·en [iˈtaːljən] das <–s> *article only in combination with attribute, no pl* Italy → Deutschland

I·ta·li·e·ner [itaˈljeːne] der <–s, –>, **I·ta·li·e·ne·rin** [itaˈljeːnərɪn] die <–, –nen> Italian → Deutsche

i·ta·li·e·nisch [itaˈljeːnɪʃ] [adj] *mostly before ns* Italian → deutsch

I·ta·li·e·nisch [itaˈljeːnɪʃ] das <–(s)> *no pl* Italian → Deutsch

A
B
C
D
E
F
G
H
I
J
K
L
M
N
O
P
Q
R
S
T
U
V
W
X
Y
Z

J

j, J [jɔt] das <–(s), –(s)> j, J ◊ *Dieses Wort wird mit einem kleinen j/großen J geschrieben.* ♦ *J wie Julius*

② **ja** [jaː] (part) **1.** yes ◊ *„Kommst du mit ins Kino?" — „Ja."* ja doch yes Ja bitte? Yes? **2.** yes, OK ◊ *Ja, ich verstehe.* **3.** *(to add emphasis)* really, just ◊ *Du bist ja wohl nicht mehr ganz bei Trost!* ♦ *Das ist ja furchtbar!* **4.** *(to express surprise)* Ja? Really? ◊ *„Du darfst nun doch mitkommen." — „Ja?"* **5.** ja (sogar) in fact, even ◊ *Er liebt Bücher, ja, er verschlingt sie regelrecht.* **6.** *(anticipating agreement)* Ja? *the translation depends on the preceding clause* Du kommst doch auch, ja? You're coming too, aren't you? Ich kann jetzt gehen, ja? I can go now, can't I? **7.** *(emph)* (auch) ja *used when urging/warning sb* ◊ *Komm ja rechtzeitig nach Hause!* sich auch ja (gut) benehmen behave (well) jdm (auch) ja nichts sagen not tell sb etw./jdn auch ja nicht vergessen not forget sth/sb Mach das ja nicht! Don't do that! **8.** *to start a sentence* Ja, das muss ich mir noch überlegen. *Well, I have to think about it.* Ja, mal sehen, vielleicht komme ich doch mit. Let's see, maybe I'll come along after all. **9.** *pointing sth (obvious) out* Du weißt ja, wie das ist mit kleinen Kindern. You know how it is with little children. Keine Aufregung, noch haben wir ja genügend Zeit. Don't panic, we've still got plenty of time. **10.** *expressing amazement* Er hat sich ja heute noch gar nicht beschwert! He hasn't complained yet today! **11.** *expressing (qualified) consent* Das ist ja richtig, aber ... That's right but ... Ich kann es ja mal versuchen, aber versprechen kann ich nichts. I can give it a go but I can't promise anything. **12.** *exasperated* Du hast ja keine Ahnung, wie schwer das ist! You have no idea how difficult it is. Ja musst du mich denn immer beim Mittagessen stören? Do you always have to disturb me when I'm having my lunch? ◉ **aber ja** (but) of course ◊ *„Darf ich hereinkommen?" — „Aber ja!"* ich glaube ja I think so **wenn ja** if so

② **Ja·cke** [ˈjakə] die <–, –n> jacket ◊ *Er trug eine graue Jacke.*; *(thick)* coat; *(knitted)* cardigan

Jagd [jaːkt] die <–, –en> **1.** hunt bei der Jagd *(while)* hunting ◊ *Er wurde bei der Jagd von einem Bären angegriffen.* die Jagd auf ... ... hunting ◊ *die Jagd auf Großwild/Füchse* auf (die) Jagd gehen, zur Jagd ausreiten go hunting auf der Jagd sein be hunting **2.** preserve ◊ *Er hat eine Jagd in der Eiffel.* **3.** chase ◊ *die Jagd auf Verbrecher* auf jdn Jagd machen hunt sb down **4.** *(fig)* search, quest, pursuit ◊ *die Jagd nach dem Glück* auf der Jagd nach etw. sein be on the hunt for sth, be in pursuit of sth

ja·gen [ˈjaːɡn̩] (tr v) +*haben* **1.** hunt ◊ *Die Löwen jagten eine Gazelle.* **2.** hunt, pursue ◊ *Der Terrorist wird vom FBI gejagt.* **3.** jdn/ein Tier ... jagen chase sb/an animal ..., drive sb/an animal ... ◊ *Chris jagt jede Katze aus seinem Garten.* jdn aus dem Haus jagen throw sb out of your house **4.** *(fam)* jdm/sich etw. ... jagen drive sth into sb's/your ..., stick sth in(to) sb's/your ... ◊ *Der Arzt hat mir eine Spritze in den Po gejagt.* (intr v) +*sein* race ◊ *Er jagte mit dem verletzten Kind ins Krankenhaus.* ◉ **ein ... jagt das andere** it's one ... after another, one ... comes hot on the heels of another ◊ *ein toller Krimi, in dem ein Höhepunkt den anderen jagt* man kann jdn mit etw. jagen sb can't stand sth ◊ *Mit Spinat kannst du mich jagen.*

Jä·ger [ˈjɛːɡɐ] der <–s, –>, **Jä·ge·rin** [ˈjɛːɡərɪn] die <–, –nen> hunter ◊ *ein begeisterter Jäger* ♦ *Sie ist Jägerin von Beruf.*

jäh [jɛː] (adj, adv) *when used as an adj, only before ns* sudden(ly), abrupt(ly) ◊ *ein jähes Ende nehmen* ♦ *Unser Gespräch wurde jäh unterbrochen.* (adv) steeply ◊ *Der Fels fällt jäh ab.*

Jahr [jaːɐ̯] das <–(e)s, –e> year ◊ *Sie hat acht Jahre in Schottland gelebt.* ♦ *Das wird erst in zwei Jahren fertig sein.* ♦ *Ich arbeite schon seit Jahren hier.* ♦ *nächstes/letztes Jahr* ♦ *Max ist jetzt fünf Jahre alt.* ♦ *In welchem Jahr bist du geboren?* mit den Jahren as years go by es wird Jahre dauern, bis ... it will be years before ... mit 50 Jahren, in jds fünfzigsten Jahr at the age of 50, aged 50; *(film)* ab 18 etc. certificate im Jahre 1914 in (the year) 1914 aus dem Jahre 1945 from (the year) 1945 ◉ **in den besten Jahren** in the prime of your life ein gutes neues Jahr Happy New Year lange Jahre for many years in die Jahre gekommen sein be getting on Jahr für Jahr year in, year out

jah·re·lang [ˈjaːrəlaŋ] (adj) *no comp/superl; only before ns* die jahrelangen Bemühungen (the) years of effort nach jahrelangem Bau etc. after years of building etc. etw. entsteht in jahrelanger Arbeit sth takes years (of work) (adv) for years ◊ *Wir haben uns jahrelang nicht gesehen.*

② **Jah·res·zeit** [ˈjaːrəstsaɛ̯t] die <–, –en> season ◊ *Ich mag Italien zu jeder Jahreszeit.*

Jahr·gang [ˈjaːɐ̯ɡaŋ] der <–(e)s, Jahrgänge> **1.** year ◊ *Mein Jahrgang trifft sich alle fünf Jahre in unserer alten Schule.* ♦ *Ich brauche die Ausgabe 30 dieses Jahrgangs.* Jahrgang 1980 etc. sein be born in 1980 etc. der Jahrgang 1990 etc. those born in 1990 etc. **2.** *(of wine)* vintage, year ◊ *2002 war ein guter Jahrgang.*

Jahr·hun·dert [jaːɐ̯ˈhʊndɐt] das <–s, –e> century ◊ *Kunstwerke aus dem 18. Jahrhundert*

jähr·lich [ˈjɛːɐ̯lɪç] (adj) *only before ns* annual, yearly ◊ *das jährliche Einkommen* ♦ *unser jährliches Treffen* (adv) annually, yearly ◊ *Sie können den Beitrag jährlich oder monatlich zahlen.*; every year ◊ *Wir treffen uns jährlich, immer im April.*

Jahr·markt [ˈjaːɐ̯markt] der <–(e)s, Jahrmärkte>

fair ◊ *auf den Jahrmarkt gehen* ⊜Rummel

Jahr·zehnt [ja:"tse:nt] *das* <-(e)s, -e> decade ◊ *seit einem Jahrzehnt* ✦ *im vergangenen Jahrzehnt*

jam·mern ['jamen] [intr v] +*haben (esp pej)*
1. complain ◊ *Die Lehrer jammern über die schlechten Schüler.* ✦ *Es hat keinen Sinn zu jammern, so ist es nun eben.* **2.** wail, whine ◊ *Das Kind saß auf dem Boden und jammerte.*

ⓩ **Jän·ner** ['jɛnɐ] *der* <-s, -> *most sing (Austr)* January → *Januar*

ⓩ **Ja·nu·ar** ['janua:ɐ] *der* <-s, -e> *most sing* January ◊ *Sie ist im Januar geboren.* ✦ *Heute ist der 10. Januar.* ✦ *Das war am 15. Januar 1999.* ✦ *Köln, den 4. Januar 2005* ✦ *Er ist am Mittwoch, dem/ den 4. Januar abgereist.* ✦ *Die Januare verbringt sie immer auf Hawaii.* ✦ *Nächsten Januar ziehen wir um.* ✦ *Letzten Januar waren wir in Indien.* ✦ *Ich mache Anfang/Mitte/Ende Januar ein paar Tage Urlaub.* ✦ *im Laufe des Januars*

Ja·pan ['ja:pan] *das* <-s> *article only in combination with attribute, no pl* Japan → *Deutschland*

Ja·pa·ner [ja'pa:nɐ] *der* <-s, ->, **Ja·pa·ne·rin** [ja'pa:nərɪn] *die* <-, -nen> Japanese → *Deutsche*

ja·pa·nisch [ja'pa:nɪʃ] [adj] *mostly before ns* Japanese → *deutsch*

Ja·pa·nisch [ja'pa:nɪʃ] *das* <-(s)> *no pl* Japanese → *Deutsch*

ⓩ **Jazz** [dʒɛs, jats] *der* <-> *no pl* jazz ◊ *Er spielt Jazz und Klassik.*

ⓩ **je¹** [je:] [adv] ever ◊ *Warst du je in Amerika?* ✦ *Hat er dir je gesagt, dass er dich liebt?* ✦ *Ihr Zustand ist schlimmer denn je.*
◉ **je nach, je nachdem** depending on, according to ◊ *Je nach Größe kosten die Äpfel 50 bis 80 Cent.* ✦ *Das mache ich je nach Lust und Laune.*

ⓩ **je²** [je:] [prep] each ◊ *Wir haben zwei Brötchen je Person gerechnet.* Gruppen zu je fünf etc. groups of five etc.

ⓩ **je³** [je:] [conjunc] je ..., desto/umso ... the ..., the ... ◊ *Je früher wir anfangen, desto/umso eher sind wir fertig.*

Jeans [dʒi:ns] *die* <-, -> (pair of) jeans ◊ *Ich brauche eine neue Jeans.* ✦ *Sie trug Jeans und T-Shirt.*

ⓩ **je·de** ['je:də] → *jeder¹, jeder²*

ⓩ **je·der¹** ['je:də] [det] every (single) ◊ *Jeder Tag bringt etwas Neues.* ✦ *Jede Frau kennt dieses Problem.* ✦ *Ich habe von jedem Auto ein Foto gemacht.* ✦ *Er hat jedes Wort verstanden.* ✦ *Ich gehe jeden Tag ins Büro.* jede Verantwortung ablehnen refuse to accept any responsibility

	m	f	nt	pl
nom	jeder	jede	jedes	-
acc	jeden	jede	jedes	-
dat	jedem	jeder	jedem	-
gen	jedes	jeder	jedes	-

ⓩ **je·der²** ['je:də] [indef pron] *jeder/jede/jedes*
1. everyone ◊ *Jeder sollte das wissen.* ✦ *Sie hat jedem erzählt, dass sie schwanger ist.* ⊜niemand **2.** every one ◊ *Jede meiner Freundinnen hat mir geschrieben.* ✦ *Er hat jeder eine rote Rose geschenkt.* ✦ *Alle Autos waren toll, ich habe jedes fotografiert.* ⊜keiner

je·des ['je:dəs] → *jeder¹, jeder²*

ⓩ **je·den·falls** ['je:dn̩'fals] [part] at least, at any rate ◊ *Das sind ganz neue Erkenntnisse, jedenfalls für mich.* ✦ *Wir jedenfalls sind damit zufrieden.*

je·der·zeit ['je:de'tsaet] [adv] **1.** at any time, always ◊ *Du kannst mich jederzeit anrufen.* **2.** at any moment ◊ *Die Bombe kann jederzeit losgehen.*

ⓩ **je·doch** [je'dɔx] [conjunc] *(lofty)* but ◊ *Ich habe überall danach gesucht, jedoch nichts gefunden.* ✦ *Wir kommen gern, jedoch ohne die Kinder.*

je·mals ['je:ma:ls] [adv] ever ◊ *Hat man jemals so einen Unsinn gehört?*

ⓩ **je·mand** ['je:mant] [indef pron] somebody, someone ◊ *Du solltest mit jemandem darüber reden.* ✦ *Könnte das nicht jemand anders übernehmen?; (in questions and negative sentences)* anybody, anyone ◊ *Hat jemand meinen Kuli gesehen?* ⊜niemand

je·ne ['je:nə] *fem of* jener¹, jener²

ⓩ **je·ner¹** ['je:nə] [det] *(lofty)* that, those ◊ *Genau an jenem Tag hat er ihr einen Antrag gemacht.* ✦ *Nein, ich meine nicht dieses, sondern jenes Bild.*

ⓩ **je·ner²** ['je:nə] [demonstr pron] *jener/jene/jenes (lofty)* the latter ◊ *Er studierte Religion und Philosophie, aber weder diese noch jene sagte ihm ganz zu.*

je·nes ['je:nəs] *neut of* jener¹, jener²

jen·seits¹ ['je:nzaets, 'jɛnzaets] [adv] *(always jenseits von)* beyond, on the other side of ◊ *die Gegend jenseits von Oder und Neiße* ✦ *jenseits von Zeit und Raum; (with sums of money)* (well) over ◊ *Gute Karten sind jenseits von 50 Euro angesiedelt.*

jen·seits² ['je:nzaets, 'jɛnzaets] [prep] +*gen*
1. jenseits (des/der) on the other side of ◊ *Jenseits der Alpen herrscht schönes Wetter.; (rivers, seas etc. also)* across **2.** jenseits (des/ der) outside of ◊ *Manche Organisationen operieren jenseits der Legalität.* jenseits des guten Geschmacks beyond the boundaries of good taste

Jen·seits ['je:nzaets, 'jɛnzaets] *das* <-> *no pl* afterlife, hereafter ◊ *Wir werden uns im Jenseits wiedersehen.*
◉ **jdn ins Jenseits befördern** *(fam)* bump sb off

ⓩ **jetzt¹** [jɛtst] [adv] **1.** now ◊ *Wir müssen jetzt handeln.* ✦ *Muss das jetzt sein?* ⊜nun **2.** nowadays ◊ *Das ist jetzt große Mode.*

jetzt² [jɛtst] [part] *(fam)* used for emphasis; not translated directly Hast du das jetzt endlich begriffen? Have you got it? Jetzt sag bloß nicht, dass du nicht mitkommst. Don't you're not coming.

je·wei·li·ge ['je:vaelɪɡə] [adj] *no comp/superl, only before ns* <ein jeweiliger ..., eine jeweilige ..., ein jeweiliges ...> **1.** particular ◊ *Welche Maßnahmen sind im jeweiligen Fall zu ergreifen?* **2.** current ◊ *Sie folgt immer dem jeweiligen Modetrend.*

ⓩ **je·weils** ['je:vaels] [adv] each, in each case ◊ *Die Gläser kosten jeweils drei Euro.* Das Paket enthält jeweils ... Each package contains ... jeweils am Jahresanfang at the beginning of every year jeweils zu zweit in pairs

ⓩ **Job** [dʒɔp] *der* <-s, -s> **1.** job ◊ *Er hat einen Job für die Ferien gefunden.* **2.** job, task ◊ *Es ist nicht mein Job, mich darum zu kümmern.*

job·ben ['dʒɔbm̩] [intr v] +*haben* have got a job, work (casually/temporarily) ◊ *als Kellnerin jobben*

Jod [joːt] das <-s> *no pl* iodine ◊ *eine Wunde mit Jod desinfizieren* ✦ *Seefisch enthält viel Jod.*

② **Jog·ging** ['dʒɔgɪn] das <-s> *no pl* jogging

Jo·han·nis·bee·re [jo'hanɪsbeːrə] die <-, –n> currant rote Johannisbeere redcurrant schwarze Johannisbeere blackcurrant

② **Jour·na·list** [ʒʊ'na'lɪst] der <-en, –en>, **Jour·na·lis·tin** [ʒʊ'na'lɪstɪn] die <-, –nen> journalist ◊ *Er arbeitet als Journalist.* ✦ *eine freie Journalistin*

ju·beln ['juːbl̩n] ⟨intr v⟩ +*haben* cheer ◊ *Die Zuschauer jubelten auf der Tribüne.* über etw. ⟨acc⟩ jubeln rejoice over sth ⟨tr v⟩ +*haben* shout with joy ◊ *„Wir sind Weltmeister!", jubelten sie.*

Ju·bi·lä·um [jubi'lɛːʊm] das <-s, Jubiläen> anniversary, jubilee

ju·cken ['jʊkn̩] ⟨intr v⟩ +*haben* itch, cause itching ◊ *Ich trage keine Wollpullis, die jucken so.* ⟨tr v⟩ +*haben (fam)* sich/jdn jucken scratch yourself/sb jdn am Rücken etc. jucken scratch sb's back etc. ⊝kratzen ⟨imp v⟩ +*haben* es juckt jdn am Rücken etc. sb's back etc. itches es juckt jdn an der Kopfhaut etc. sb has an itchy scalp etc.

⊛ etw. juckt jdn nicht *(fam)* sth doesn't bother sb, sb doesn't care about sth

Ju·de ['juːdə] der <-n, –n>, **Jü·din** ['jyːdɪn] die <-, –nen> Jew Er ist Jude. He is Jewish.

Ju·den·tum ['juːdn̩tuːm] das <-s> *no pl* Judaism ◊ *Im Judentum ist der Samstag heilig.*

② **Ju·gend** ['juːgn̩t, 'juːgənt] die <-> *no pl* **1.** youth ◊ *eine schöne/schwierige Jugend gehabt haben* in/ seit früher Jugend at/from an early age **2.** die Jugend the youth, young people

Ju·gend·her·ber·ge ['juːgn̩thɛɐ̯bɛɐ̯gə, 'juːgənthɛɐ̯bɛɐ̯gə] die <-, –n> youth hostel ◊ *in der Jugendherberge übernachten*

② **Ju·gend·li·che** ['juːgn̩tlɪçə, 'juːgəntlɪçə] der/die <-n, die Jugendlichen> *but: ein Jugendlicher/eine Jugendliche* **1.** young person, youth ◊ *ein Jugendlicher von 16 Jahren* die Jugendlichen (the) young people **2.** LAW juvenile *box@* Substantivierung

② **Ju·li** ['juːli] der <-(s), –s> July → Januar

② **jung** [jʊn] ⟨adj, adv⟩ <jünger, am jüngsten> **1.** young ◊ *eine junge Frau* ✦ *Leo ist zwei Jahre jünger als du.* ✦ *In Jeans sieht er aus sehr jung aus.* sich jung fühlen feel young sich jung kleiden/aufmachen dress young ⊝alt **2.** young, at an early age ◊ *Sie heiratete jung.* ✦ *Er war jung gestorben.* ⊝früh **3.** *(nation, company)* young ◊ *Israel ist ein junger Staat mit alter Tradition.; (project)* new jung vermählt newly-wed

⊛ auf jung machen *(pej)* try to look young, pretend to be young

② **Jun·ge¹** ['jʊnə] der <-n, –n> **1.** boy ◊ *Ist das Baby ein Junge oder ein Mädchen?* ⊝Mädchen **2.** *(form of address)* mate, pal ◊ *He, Junge, wie geht's?* (mein) alter Junge (my) old pal

⊛ jdn wie einen dummen Jungen behandeln *(fam)* treat sb like a child Junge, Junge *(fam)* boy oh boy

Jun·ge² ['jʊnə] das <-n, die Jungen> *but: ein Junges (young animal)* baby; *(cat)* kitten; *(dog)* pup; *(bird)* nestling *box@* Substantivierung

jüngst [jʏnst] ⟨adv⟩ recently ◊ *eine jüngst eröffnete Firma* ⊝neulich

jüngs·te ['jʏnstə] *superl of* jung ⟨adj⟩ *only before ns* most recent ◊ *Nach jüngsten Erkenntnissen soll Rotwein gut fürs Herz sein.*

Jung·frau ['jʊnfraʊ] die <-, –en> **1.** virgin ◊ *noch Jungfrau sein* ✦ *keine Jungfrau mehr sein* **2.** ASTROL, ASTRON Virgo

⊛ jd kommt zu etw. wie die Jungfrau zum Kinde sb gets sth by sheer coincidence die Jungfrau Maria the Virgin Mary die Heilige Jungfrau REL the Holy Virgin

Jung·ge·sel·le ['jʊnɡəzɛlə] der <-n, –n>, **Jung·ge·sel·lin** ['jʊnɡəzɛlɪn] die <-, –nen> Junggeselle bachelor ein überzeugter Junggeselle a confirmed bachelor Junggesellin single/unmarried woman

② **Ju·ni** ['juːni] der <-(s), –s> June → Januar

② **Jupe** [ʒyːp] der *or* das <-s, –s> *(Swiss)* skirt ◊ *Sie trägt einen kurzen Jupe.*

Ju·ra¹ ['juːraː] das *no pl* law ◊ *Sie studiert Jura in Tübingen.*

Ju·ra² ['juːraː] der <-(s)> *no pl* Jura mountains ◊ *der Schweizer Jura*

Ju·rist [ju'rɪst] der <-en, –en>, **Ju·ris·tin** [ju'rɪstɪn] die <-, –nen> lawyer ◊ *Er arbeitet als Jurist.*

Jus·tiz [jʊs'tiːts] die <-> *no pl* justice system, court(s) ◊ *sich in einer Sache an die Justiz wenden* Irreführung der Justiz misleading the court jdn der Justiz übergeben bring sb to justice einen Fall der Justiz übergeben bring a case to court

Jus·tiz·voll·zugs·an·stalt [jʊs,tiːtsfol'tsuːksˌanʃtalt] die <-, –en> *(tech) (abbr* JVA*)* prison, penal institution ◊ *eine Strafe in der Justizvollzugsanstalt abbüßen*

Ju·we·lier [juve'liːɐ̯] der <-s, –e>, **Ju·we·lie·rin** [juve'liːrɪn] die <-, –nen> **1.** jeweller ◊ *Sie ist Juwelierin von Beruf.* ✦ *Der Juwelier prüfte das Schmuckstück.* **2.** jeweller's (shop) ◊ *Ich muss noch zum Juwelier, den Ring abholen.*

K

A
B
C
D
E
F
G
H
I
J
K
L
M
N
O
P
Q
R
S
T
U
V
W
X
Y
Z

k, K [ka:] das <–(s), –(s)> k, K ◊ *Dieses Wort wird mit einem kleinen k/großen K geschrieben.* ✦ *K wie Kaufmann*

Ka·ba·rett [kaba'rɛt, kaba're:, '– – –] das <–s, –s> **1.** (satirical) revue ◊ *politisches Kabarett* **2.** *a theatre/theater where satirical revues are staged*

Ka·bel ['ka:bl̩] das <–s, –> **1.** cable, wire, flex ◊ *ein Kabel verlegen* **2.** *(metal rope)* cable ◊ *Die Kabine der Seilbahn hängt an einem dicken Kabel.*

② **Ka·bi·ne** [ka'bi:nə] die <–, –n> **1.** cabin ◊ *In der Kabine gibt es zwei Kojen.* **2.** *(for changing your clothes in)* cubicle ◊ *sich in der Kabine umziehen* **3.** (cable) car ◊ *Er zwängte sich in die enge Kabine der Seilbahn.*

Ka·bi·nett [kabi'nɛt] das <–s, –e> **1.** POL Cabinet **2.** *(exhibition room)* gallery ◊ *Im Kabinett wurden Raritäten ausgestellt.* **3.** *(Austr)* small room ◊ *Er verwahrte seine Akten im Kabinett.*

Ka·chel ['kaxl̩] die <–, –n> tile ◊ *Kacheln verlegen*

ka·cken ['kakn̩] [intr v] +*haben (rude)* (have/take a) shit, (have/take a) crap ◊ *Der Hunde kackt auf den Bürgersteig.*

Kä·fer ['kɛ:fɐ] der <–s, –> beetle ◊ *Auf dem Weg krabbelten viele Käfer.*

◉ VW Käfer Volkswagen Beetle, Volkswagen Bug

② **Kaf·fee** ['kafe:] der <–s, –s> *pl 'Kaffee' when used with expressions of quantity* **1.** coffee ◊ *Ich trinke jeden Morgen eine Tasse Kaffee.* ✦ *ein Päckchen Kaffee* ✦ *Kaffee anpflanzen* Kaffee kochen make some coffee **2.** ⊖*afternoon coffee (with cakes)* ◊ *Ich bin morgen zum Kaffee eingeladen.*

◉ etw. ist kalter Kaffee *(fam, fig)* sth is old hat, sth is of no importance

> For many people in the German-speaking world, coffee is a breakfast staple. It is also a very popular afternoon drink. *Kaffee und Kuchen* is a social event where friends chat over coffee and cake.

Kaf·fee·klatsch ['kafe:klatʃ] der <–(e)s, –e> *(fam, hum) a social gathering at which a group of friends meet for a chat over coffee and a piece of cake* ◊ *Sie lädt ihre Freundinnen zu einem Kaffeeklatsch ein.*

Kä·fig ['kɛ:fɪç] der <–s, –e> cage ◊ *Der Papagei sitzt im Käfig.*

◉ im goldenen Käfig sitzen be (a bird) in a gilded cage

kahl [ka:l] [adj] **1.** bald ◊ *ein kahles Haupt* ✦ *Er ist fast kahl geworden.* kahl geschoren close-cropped; *(animal)* (completely) shorn **2.** *(landscape, tree)* bare ◊ *Die Landschaft war kahl und karg.* ✦ *kahle Bäume im Winter* etw. kahl fressen/schlagen strip sth bare

Kai [kaɛ] der <–s, –s> quay ◊ *Sie ging am Kai spazieren.*

Kai·ser ['kaɛzɐ] der <–s, –>, **Kai·se·rin** ['kaɛzərɪn] die <–, –nen> emperor ◊ *der römische Kaiser Augustus; (in Germany, Austria also)*

Kaiser ◊ *Kaiser Wilhelm* Kaiserin empress

◉ um des Kaisers Bart streiten *(fig)* be engaged in a pointless argument

Kai·ser·schmar·ren ['kaɛzɐʃmarən] der <–s> *no pl (SouthG, Austr)* pancake with raisins, torn up and sprinkled with icing sugar

Ka·kao [ka'kao] der <–s, –s> *pl 'Kakao' when used with expressions of quantity, most sing* **1.** cocoa ◊ *eine Tasse Kakao* ✦ *Kakao anpflanzen* **2.** cocoa powder ◊ *ein Päckchen Kakao*

◉ jdn durch den Kakao ziehen *(fam, fig)* take the mickey out of sb

Kalb [kalp] das <–(e)s, Kälber> **1.** calf **2.** *no pl (meat)* veal ◊ *Ich esse lieber Kalb als Rind.*

◉ das goldene Kalb anbeten *(lofty)* worship the golden calf

② **Ka·len·der** [ka'lɛndɐ] der <–s, –> **1.** calendar, diary ◊ *etw. in den Kalender eintragen* ✦ *auf/in den Kalender schauen* **2.** der julianische Kalender the Julian calendar der gregorianische Kalender the Gregorian calendar

◉ sich [dat] etw. im Kalender rot anstreichen mark sth as a red-letter day

② **kalt** [kalt] [adj, adv] <kälter, am kältesten> **1.** cold ◊ *Das Wetter ist kalt.* ✦ *Das Essen wird kalt.* ✦ *die kälteste Zeit des Jahres* jdm ist (es) kalt sb is (feeling) cold kalt duschen have/take a cold shower kalt schlafen sleep in an unheated room etw. kalt stellen chill sth ⊖heiß, warm **2.** *(fig)* cold(ly), frosty(-ily) ◊ *Ein kalter Blick streifte mich.* ✦ *Sie wies meine Hilfe kalt ab.* jdn kalt lassen leave sb unmoved/cold kalt bleiben remain unmoved jdn kalt anblicken/ansehen give sb a frosty look

◉ jdn überläuft es kalt cold shivers run down sb's spine

② **Käl·te** ['kɛltə] die <–> *no pl* **1.** cold es herrscht eisige Kälte it is freezing cold vor Kälte zittern shiver with cold ⊖Wärme, Hitze **2.** *(fig)* coldness ◊ *In ihrer Stimme lag Kälte.* die Kälte des Herzens (the) cold-heartedness ⊖Wärme **3.** +*temperature below zero, below freezing, frost* ◊ *15 Grad Kälte* ⊖Wärme

käl·ter ['kɛltə] *comp of* kalt

② **kam** [ka:m] *pret of* kommen

Ka·mel [ka'me:l] das <–s, –e> **1.** ZOO camel ◊ *Wir sind auf Kamelen durch die Wüste geritten.* **2.** *(fam, pej)* idiot, fool ◊ *Und ich Kamel habe ihm geglaubt!*

② **Ka·me·ra** ['kaməra:] die <–, –s> camera ◊ *Er macht mit seiner Kamera wunderschöne Fotos.* ✦ *Der Reporter sah in die Kamera.*

Ka·me·rad [kamə'ra:t] der <–en, –en>, **Ka·me·ra·din** [kamə'ra:dɪn] die <–, –nen> *(oldf)* friend ◊ *Er ist ein guter Kamerad.; (soldier)* comrade

Ka·mil·le [ka'mɪlə] die <–, –n> camomile

Ka·mil·len·tee [ka'mɪlənte:] der <–s, –s> camomile tea ◊ *eine Tasse Kamillentee trinken*

Ka·min [ka'miːn] der <–s, –e> 1. fireplace, hearth ◊ *Im Kamin brannte ein gemütliches Feuer.* 2. *(SouthG, Austr, Swiss)* chimney ◊ *Fabriken mit hohen Kaminen* ⊜Schornstein

Kamm [kam] der <–(e)s, Kämme> 1. comb ◊ *mit dem Kamm einen Scheitel ziehen* ♦ *Der Hahn hat einen roten Kamm.* 2. ridge, crest ◊ *Wir sind den Kamm entlanggewandert.*
⊙ **über einen Kamm scheren** lump together ◊ *Man darf nicht alle Politiker über einen Kamm scheren.*

käm·men ['kɛmən] tr v +*haben* jdn/sich kämmen comb sb's/your hair jdm/sich etw. kämmen comb sb's/your sth ◊ *Er kämmte sich die Haare.*; *(hair)* sich gut kämmen lassen be manageable

Kam·mer ['kamɐ] die <–, –n> 1. (little) room, boxroom ◊ *Ich schlafe in einer Kammer unterm Dach.*; larder 2. POL chamber, house 3. professional association ◊ *eine gemeinsame Kammer für Ärzte und Zahnärzte* 4. LAW court division ◊ *die Kammer für zivile Strafsachen* 5. ANAT ventricle ◊ *Das menschliche Herz hat zwei Kammern.* 6. TECHN chamber ◊ *die Kammer eines Motors*

Kam·mer·chor ['kameːoːɐ̯] der <–(e)s, Kammerchöre> chamber choir

Kam·pag·ne [kam'panjə] die <–, –n> campaign ◊ *An den Schulen läuft eine Kampagne gegen Drogen.*

Kampf [kampf] der <–(e)s, Kämpfe> 1. battle ◊ *der Kampf der Geschlechter* der Kampf um etw. the battle for sth ◊ *der Kampf um Stalingrad* im Kampf fallen die in action jdm einen Kampf liefern fight a battle with sb ◊ *Die Rebellen lieferten den Truppen einen blutigen Kampf.* 2. fight ◊ *Er hat seinen Rivalen zum Kampf herausgefordert.* ein Kampf auf Leben und Tod a fight to the death Kämpfe fighting ◊ *Es kam zu schweren Kämpfen.* 3. SPORT contest ◊ *der Kampf um die Goldmedaille*; *(boxing also)* fight 4. *(fig)* der Kampf für etw. the fight for sth, struggle for sth ◊ *der Kampf für den Frieden* der Kampf gegen etw. the war on sth ◊ *der Kampf gegen das organisierte Verbrechen* der Kampf um etw. the struggle for sth ◊ *der Kampf ums Überleben*
⊙ **jdm/einer Sache den Kampf ansagen** declare war on sb/sth ◊ *Die Polizei hat dem organisierten Verbrechen den Kampf angesagt.*

ⓩ **kämp·fen** ['kɛmpfn̩] intr v +*haben* 1. fight ◊ *Die Soldaten haben tapfer gekämpft.* ♦ *Ich habe lange mit mir gekämpft, ob ich das machen soll.* ♦ *Klitschko kämpft nächste Woche gegen Lewis.* ♦ *für bessere Arbeitsbedingungen kämpfen* um etw./ jdn kämpfen fight for sth/sb ◊ *um den Sieg kämpfen* ♦ *Ich werde um dich kämpfen, weil ich dich liebe.* mit dem Tod kämpfen fight for your life mit den Tränen kämpfen fight back the tears 2. mit etw. zu kämpfen haben have to contend with sth ◊ *Ich habe momentan mit ziemlichen Problemen zu kämpfen.*

Ka·na·da ['kanada:] das <–s> *article only in combination with attribute* Canada → Deutschland

Ka·na·di·er [ka'naːdiɐ] der <–s, –>,
Ka·na·di·e·rin [ka'naːdiərɪn] die <–, –nen> Canadian → Deutsche

ka·na·disch [ka'naːdɪʃ] adj *mostly before ns* Canadian ◊ *Vancouver ist eine kanadische Stadt.* ♦ *typisch kanadisch sein*

Ka·nal [ka'naːl] der <–s, Kanäle> 1. SHIP canal ◊ *Main und Donau sind durch einen Kanal verbunden.* 2. sewer ◊ *Wasser in den Kanal ableiten* 3. channel, ditch ◊ *Das Wasser wurde über Kanäle auf die Felder geleitet.* 4. RADIO, TV channel ◊ *Auf welchem Kanal sendet Antenne 1?* 5. *only pl (fig)* channel ◊ *Wir müssen diese Informationen durch die richtigen Kanäle weiterleiten.* dunkle Kanäle dubious channels
⊙ **den Kanal voll haben** *(fam)* 1. be drunk, have had one too many 2. have had enough, have had it up to here ◊ *Ich lasse mich nicht länger belügen, ich habe den Kanal voll!*

Ka·na·ren [ka'naːrən] die <–> *only pl (always die Kanaren)* the Canaries ◊ *Den Winter verbringt sie immer auf den Kanaren.*

Ka·na·ri·sche In·sel [ka,naːrɪʃə 'ɪnzl̩] die <Kanarischen Insel, –n> *most pl* Canary Island ◊ *Auf den Kanarischen Inseln herrscht trocken-heißes Klima.*

Kan·di·dat [kandi'daːt] der <–en, –en>,
Kan·di·da·tin [kandi'daːtɪn] die <–, –nen> candidate ◊ *ein Kandidat für die Schulleitung* ♦ *Die Liberale Partei hat einen eigenen Kandidaten aufgestellt.*; *(on a quiz show)* contestant

kan·di·die·ren [kandi'diːrən] <kandidiert, kandidierte, hat kandidiert> intr v stand ◊ *als Bürgermeister kandidieren* ♦ *Wer kandidiert für die SPD?*

Kän·gu·ru ['kɛŋguruː] das <–s, –s> kangaroo

Ka·nin·chen [ka'niːnçən] das <–s, –> rabbit ◊ *Wir haben drei Kaninchen zu Hause.* ♦ *Es gibt Kaninchen zum Mittagessen.*
⊙ **sich wie die Kaninchen vermehren** *(pej)* breed like rabbits

Ka·nis·ter [ka'nɪstɐ] der <–s, –> can, canister, jerrycan ◊ *ein Kanister mit Benzin*

ⓩ **kann** [kan] *pres of* können[1], können[2]

Kan·ne ['kanə] die <–, –n> 1. pot ◊ *eine Kanne Kaffee/Tee*; jug ◊ *Sie stellte eine Kanne (mit) Saft auf den Tisch.* 2. watering can ◊ *Sie füllte die Kanne mit Regenwasser.* 3. churn

ⓩ **kann·te** ['kantə] *pret of* kennen

Ka·non ['kaːnɔn] der <–s, –s> MUS, ARTS canon ◊ *einen Kanon singen* ♦ *Zum Kanon der englischen Tugenden gehört die Höflichkeit.*

Ka·no·ne [ka'noːnə] die <–, –n> 1. cannon ◊ *eine Kanone laden/zünden* 2. *(fam, oldf)* shooter 3. *(fam)* ace, star ◊ *In Sport ist er eine Kanone.*
⊙ **mit Kanonen auf Spatzen schießen** take a sledgehammer to crack a nut unter aller Kanone *(fam)* terrible(-ibly), dreadful(ly)

Kan·te ['kantə] die <–, –n> edge ◊ *Sie setzte sich auf die Kante meines Betts.* ♦ *Die Kanten ihres Mantels waren abgestoßen.*
⊙ **etw. auf der hohen Kante haben** have got sth put by etw. auf die hohe Kante legen put sth by ◊ *Er hat ein Vermögen auf die hohe Kante gelegt.*

ⓩ **Kan·ti·ne** [kan'tiːnə] die <–, –n> canteen ◊ *Mittags isst er in der Kantine.*

Kan·ton [kan'toːn] der <–s, –e> canton ◊ *Andreas lebt im Kanton Zürich.*

For political purposes, Switzerland is divided into 26 cantons, each of which enjoys a high degree of autonomy. Each canton has its own constitution, parliament, laws and courts, as well as its own police force.

Kanz·lei [kantsˈlaɪ] die <-, -en> *(SouthG, Austr, Swiss)* office; *(of a lawyer, notary)* chambers

Kanz·ler [ˈkantslɐ] der <-s, ->, **Kanz·le·rin** [ˈkantslərɪn] die <-, -nen> 1. (Federal) Chancellor ◊ *Helmut Kohl war 16 Jahre lang Kanzler.* ♦ *die deutsche Kanzlerin* 2. HIST (Imperial) Chancellor ◊ *Bismarck wurde der Eiserne Kanzler genannt.* 3. UNI registrar

Kap [kap] das <-s, -s> cape, Cape ◊ *Sie umsegelten das Kap.* ♦ *das Kap der Guten Hoffnung*

Ka·pa·zi·tät [kapatsiˈtɛːt] die <-, -en> 1. capacity ◊ *freie Kapazität haben* ♦ *Das Stadion hat eine Kapazität von 60 000 Zuschauern.* ♦ *die Kapazität eines Rechners* 2. expert ◊ *Er ist eine Kapazität auf dem Gebiet der Genforschung.*

Ka·pel·le [kaˈpɛlə] die <-, -n> 1. chapel 2. MUS band, orchestra ◊ *Die Kapelle spielte Tanzmusik.*

ka·pie·ren [kaˈpiːrən] *(fam)* <kapiert, kapierte, hat kapiert> tr v understand, get ◊ *In Mathe habe ich heute gar nichts kapiert.* intr v get it, understand ◊ *So langsam kapiere ich.* ♦ *Du darfst nicht gehen, kapiert?*

Ka·pi·tal [kapiˈtaːl] das <-s, -e or Austr –ien> 1. capital ◊ *Die Gesellschaft will ihr Kapital erhöhen.* ♦ *verfügbares Kapital* ♦ *Kapital Gewinn bringend anlegen* 2. asset ◊ *Die Bildung der Jugend ist das Kapital des Staates.*

ⓔ **totes Kapital** dead capital **aus etw. Kapital schlagen** *(esp pej)* capitalize on sth

Ka·pi·ta·lis·mus [kapitaˈlɪsmʊs] der <-> *no pl* capitalism

Ka·pi·tän [kapiˈtɛːn] der <-s, -e>, **Ka·pi·tä·nin** [kapiˈtɛːnɪn] die <-, -nen> SHIP, AVIAT, SPORT captain ◊ *der neue Kapitän des Dampfers* ♦ *Er ist Kapitän bei der Lufthansa.* ♦ *Sie ist Kapitänin der Volleyballdamen.*

Ka·pi·tel [kaˈpɪtl] das <-s, -> *(also fig)* chapter ◊ *Der Roman hat 25 Kapitel.* ♦ *Das ist ein dunkles Kapitel in seinem Leben.*

ⓔ **ein anderes Kapitel sein** be another matter **ein Kapitel für sich sein** be a complex issue

ka·pi·tu·lie·ren [kapituˈliːrən] <kapituliert, kapitulierte, hat kapituliert> intr v 1. MIL surrender, capitulate 2. *(fig)* (vor etw.) kapitulieren surrender (in the face of sth), give up (in the face of sth) ◊ *Sie hat vor all den Problemen kapituliert.*

Kap·pe [ˈkapə] die <-, -n> 1. cap ◊ *Setz eine Kappe auf, draußen ist es windig.* ♦ *Am rechten Hinterrad habe ich die Kappe verloren.* 2. *(of a pen)* top 3. toe ◊ *Schuhe mit metallverstärkten Kappen*

ⓔ **etw. auf seine Kappe nehmen** *(fam)* take the responsibility for sth

Kap·sel [ˈkapsl] die <-, -n> 1. capsule ◊ *Das Medikament wird in Form von Kapseln verabreicht.* ♦ *die Kapsel des Schultergelenks* 2. space capsule ◊ *eine unbemannte Kapsel* 3. BOT seed pod

ⓩ **ka·putt** [kaˈpʊt] adj <kaputter, am kaputtesten> *seldom comp/superl* 1. *no comp/superl* broken ◊ *Die Fensterscheibe ist kaputt.* ♦ *ein kaputtes Radio* ⊖heil 2. *not before ns (fam)* exhausted, worn out ◊ *Ich bin total kaputt von der Arbeit.* ⊖platt, fertig 3. *(relationship)* ruined; *(marriage)* on the rocks ◊ *Ihre Ehe ist schon lange kaputt.* 4. *(fam)* damaged ◊ *psychisch kaputte Kinder*

ka·putt|ge·hen [kaˈpʊtɡeːən] <geht kaputt, ging kaputt, ist kaputtgegangen> intr v *(fam)* 1. break ◊ *Die Fensterscheibe ging dabei kaputt.* 2. (an etw. dat) kaputtgehen be destroyed (by sth), be ruined (by sth) ◊ *An seinen Lügen ist unsere Beziehung kaputtgegangen.; (business etc.)* go bankrupt (because of sth) 3. jd geht an etw. dat kaputt sb has a nervous breakdown because of sth, sth gives sb a nervous breakdown ◊ *Viele Lehrer gehen an dem Stress in der Schule kaputt.*

ka·putt|ma·chen [kaˈpʊtmaxn̩] <macht kaputt, machte kaputt, hat kaputtgemacht> tr v *(fam)* 1. break, destroy ◊ *Max hat sein Spielzeugauto kaputtgemacht.* 2. *(a relationship etc.)* ruin, destroy ◊ *Mit deiner Eifersucht machst du alles kaputt.* ♦ *Diese Frau hat meine Ehe kaputtgemacht.* 3. jdn/sich kaputtmachen wear sb/ yourself out ◊ *Diese Sorgen machen mich ganz kaputt.* ♦ *Ich mach mich doch für euch nicht kaputt!*

Ka·pu·ze [kaˈpuːtsə] die <-, -n> hood ◊ *die Kapuze aufsetzen*

Ka·ra·te [kaˈraːtə] das <-(s)> *no pl* karate ◊ *Sie macht seit Jahren Karate.*

Kar·di·nal [kardiˈnaːl] der <-s, Kardinäle> cardinal ◊ *Er ist jetzt Kardinal.* ♦ *Der Papst machte ihn zum Kardinal.* ♦ *Die Kardinäle wählen den Papst.*

Kar·frei·tag [kaːrˈfraɛtaːk] der <-, -e> Good Friday

karg [kaⁱk] adj <karger/kärger, am kargsten/ kärgsten> 1. meagre, meager, sparse ◊ *ein karges Mahl* ♦ *Die Nachrichtenlage ist eher karg.* ein karges Dasein fristen eke out a wretched existence 2. *(soil, landscape etc.)* barren ⊖fruchtbar adv sparsely ◊ *karg ausgestattete Räume; (payment)* karg bemessen meagre, meager; *(funds etc.)* karg bemessen limited, sparse

Ka·ri·bik [kaˈriːbɪk] die <-> *no pl* Caribbean ◊ *Urlaub in der Karibik machen*

ka·ri·bisch [kaˈriːbɪʃ] adj *mostly before ns* Caribbean ◊ *karibische Musik* ♦ *Dieses Fischgericht ist typisch karibisch.*

ka·riert [kaˈriːɐt] adj 1. squared ◊ *kariertes Papier* ◊ *Ist dieser Block kariert?* 2. check(ed) ◊ *ein kariertes Hemd* ♦ *Der Stoff ist kariert, nicht gestreift.* adv *(fam)* kariert reden talk rubbish/ nonsense Frag doch nicht so kariert! Don't ask such stupid questions! kariert gucken look puzzled

Ka·ri·es [ˈkaːrjɛs] die <-> *no pl; seldom with the article* (tooth) decay ◊ *Tägliches Zähneputzen beugt Karies vor.*

Ka·ri·ka·tur [karikaˈtuːɐ] die <-, -en> caricature ◊ *(in newspapers etc.)* cartoon

Kar·ne·val [ˈkarnəval] der <-s, -e or -s> carnival (season) ⊖Fasching

The heathen origins of the carnival season lie in the spring festivals of the Teutons, which celebrated the end of the long and often harsh winter. In ancient times, people tried to banish the evil spirits associated with winter by wearing frightening masks and disguises. The church took over these festivals; and by the Middle Ages, people in Germany were celebrating carnival season. At the beginning of the nineteenth century, a change in the nature of the celebrations was introduced in Cologne, where the first official carnival procession took place in 1823. Separate 'carnival ▶

▶ associations' were now established; and traditions began which still persist today. The newly structured, less anarchic way of celebrating the carnival season was quickly taken over by other towns on the River Rhine. Eventually, the carnival came to be celebrated even in Protestant parts of Germany.

Ka·ro ['kaːroː] *das* <–s, –s> **1.** diamond **2.** check, checked pattern ◊ *ein Hemd mit großem Karo* **3.** CARDS diamonds ◊ *Er spielte Karo.*; *(individual card)* diamond

Ka·ros·se·rie [karəsəˈriː] *die* <–, –n> bodywork

Ka·rot·te [kaˈrɔtə] *die* <–, –n> carrot ⊖Möhre

Karp·fen ['karpfn̩] *der* <–s, –> carp

Kar·re ['karə] *die* <–, –n> **1.** wheelbarrow ◊ *Er lud Sand auf die Karre.* **2.** *(fam, pej)* (old) junkheap ◊ *Mit der Karre willst du in Urlaub fahren?*

Kar·ri·e·re [kaˈrjeːrə] *die* <–, –n> career Karriere machen make a career (for yourself) ◊ *Er hat in der Politik Karriere gemacht.* eine steile Karriere a meteoric career

② **Kar·te** ['kaɐtə] *die* <–, –n> **1.** postcard ◊ *Schreib mir eine Karte aus Rom!* **2.** (greetings) card ◊ *Ich schicke ihr eine Karte zum Geburtstag.* **3.** index card ◊ *Der Name des Patienten steht auf der Karte.* **4.** ticket ◊ *Ich hab Karten fürs Kino.* **5.** membership card **6.** map ◊ *Welchen Maßstab hat die Karte?* **7.** card ◊ *Ich spiele gern Karten.* ♦ *Der Vertreter hat mir seine Karte gegeben.* jdm die Karten legen read sb's fortune from the cards **8.** coupon ◊ *Nach dem Krieg gab es Lebensmittel nur auf Karten.* **9.** menu ◊ *Herr Ober, könnten wir bitte die Karte haben?* **10.** debit card, credit card ◊ *Zahlen Sie bar oder mit Karte?*

⊛ die Karten auf den Tisch legen put your cards on the table mit offenen Karten spielen be quite honest sich [dat] nicht in die Karten sehen lassen play your cards close to your chest, not give anything away alles auf eine Karte setzen put all your eggs in one basket

Kar·tei [kaɐˈtaɪ̯] *die* <–, –en> card index, card catalog ◊ *Die Namen aller Kunden stehen in der Kartei.*

Kar·tell [kaɐˈtɛl] *das* <–s, –e> cartel ◊ *Die Firmen schlossen sich zu einem Kartell zusammen.*

② **Kar·tof·fel** [kaɐˈtɔfl̩] *die* <–, –n> **1.** potato ◊ *Kannst du bitte die Kartoffeln schälen?* **2.** potato (plant)

⊛ jdn fallen lassen wie eine heiße Kartoffel *(fam)* drop sb like a hot potato rein in die Kartoffeln, raus aus den Kartoffeln *(fam)* first it's one thing, then it's another

Potatoes came to Europe from South America via Spain and England. They quickly became a staple food, not only in Germany. From time to time, their popularity has suffered: occasionally, they have been described as poor man's food, and sometimes, people have said that they cause weight gain. However, experts now confirm their nutritional value; and every German consumes approx. 75 kg of potatoes a year, partly in the form of chips or crisps, but also in more traditional forms in meals such as potato salad with sausage.

Kar·tof·fel·gra·tin [kaɐˈtɔflɡraˌtɛ̃ː] *das* <–s, –s> *most sing* potato gratin/bake

Kar·tof·fel·puf·fer [kaɐˈtɔflpʊfɐ] *der* <–s, –> potato fritter/pancake

Kar·ton [kaɐˈtɔŋ, kaɐˈtɔ̃ː] *der* <–s, –s *or seldom* –e> **1.** cardboard ◊ *Verpackungen aus Karton* **2.** cardboard box, carton ◊ *etw. in einem Karton verpacken*

Kar·wo·che ['kaːˌvɔxə] *die* <–, –n> Holy Week

② **Kä·se** ['kɛːzə] *der* <–s, –> **1.** cheese ◊ *Sie belegt ihr Brötchen mit Käse.* **2.** *(fam, pej)* rubbish, garbage ◊ *Sie redet nur Käse.*

⊛ so ein Käse *(fam)* **1.** *(venting frustration)* blast, sugar **2.** *(expressing that you regard sth as nonsense)* what a lot of rubbish/garbage

Kä·se·ku·chen ['kɛːzəkuːxn̩] *der* <–s, –> cheesecake ◊ *ein Stück Käsekuchen*

Ka·ser·ne [kaˈzɛɐnə] *die* <–, –n> barracks

② **Kas·sa** ['kasaː] *die* <–, Kassen> *(Austr)* → Kasse

② **Kas·se** ['kasə] *die* <–, –n> **1.** till ◊ *Die Kassiererin nimmt das Wechselgeld aus der Kasse.* **2.** cashdesk ◊ *die Ware an der Kasse bezahlen* **3.** cashier's office ◊ *Bitte zahlen Sie die Gebühr an der Kasse.* **4.** *(at a cinema, theatre)* box office ◊ *die reservierten Karten an der Kasse abholen* **5.** health insurance (fund) ◊ *Bei welcher Kasse bist du versichert?*

⊛ einen Griff in die Kasse tun dip into the till gemeinsame Kasse machen go halves getrennte Kasse machen pay separately gut bei Kasse sein be well off knapp/schlecht bei Kasse sein be short of cash, be badly off Kasse machen cash up

Kas·sen·zet·tel ['kasn̩tsɛtl̩] *der* <–s, –> (till) receipt ◊ *Umtausch nur gegen Vorlage des Kassenzettels* ⊖Bon

② **Kas·set·te** [kaˈsɛtə] *die* <–, –n> **1.** cassette ◊ *eine Kassette einlegen/anhören* etw. auf Kassette aufnehmen record sth on a cassette **2.** (video) cassette **3.** *(for books, CDs etc.)* box, slip case ◊ *fünf Bände in einer Kassette* **4.** cash box ◊ *Er bewahrt sein Geld in der Kassette auf.*; jewellery box ◊ *Sie legt ihren Schmuck in die Kassette.*

② **Kas·set·ten·re·kor·der** [kaˈsɛtn̩reˌkɔɐdɐ] *der* <–s, –> cassette recorder ◊ *Sie spielt die Kassette auf dem Kassettenrecorder ab.*

kas·sie·ren [kaˈsiːrən] <kassiert, kassierte, hat kassiert> [tr v] **1.** collect ◊ *Die Gebühr wird monatlich kassiert.* **2.** *(fam)* make ◊ *Bei dem Verkauf von Autos kassiert er ganz schön Geld.* **3.** *(fam)* get, earn ◊ *Sie hat für ihr Verhalten eine Menge Ärger kassiert.* **4.** *(fam)* confiscate ◊ *Die Polizei hat seinen Führerschein kassiert.* [intr v] *(bei jdm)* kassieren collect money (from sb) ◊ *Die Kellnerin kassiert bei den Gästen. Darf ich kassieren, bitte?* Could I ask you to settle up, please?

Kass·ler ['kaslɐ] *das* <–s, –> cured rib of pork, cured pork loin

② **Kas·ten** ['kastn̩] *der* <–s, Kästen> **1.** case ◊ *ein hölzerner Kasten mit Deckel*; *(for bottles)* crate ◊ *ein Kasten Bier* **2.** *(fam, pej)* (TV) der Kasten the box ◊ *Jetzt sitzt du schon seit drei Stunden vor dem Kasten!* **3.** *(fam)* FILM der Kasten the camera ◊ *Hast du die Szene im Kasten?* **4.** *(fam, pej)* alter Kasten old banger, old crate ◊ *Mein alter Kasten springt wieder nicht an.* **5.** showcase, display case

◊ *in einem Kasten ausgestellte Funde* **6.** *(for text, pictures)* box ◊ *Das Wörterbuch hat Kästen mit Informationen zur Landeskunde.* **7.** *(SouthG, Austr, Swiss)* cupboard ◊ *Sie stellte die Teller in den Kasten.*

⊚ **etwas auf dem Kasten haben** *(fam)* be brainy, have something upstairs **im Kasten** in the can

Ka·sus ['kaːzʊs] *der* <–, –> *(tech)* case ◊ *Welchen Kasus zieht diese Präposition nach sich?*

Ka·ta·ly·sa·tor [kataly'zaːtoːɐ̯] *der* <–s, –en> **1.** CHEM catalyst ◊ *organische Katalysatoren* **2.** TECHN catalytic converter ◊ *ein Auto mit Katalysator*

② **Ka·tas·tro·phe** [katas'troːfə] *die* <–, –n> **1.** catastrophe, disaster ◊ *Meine Mathearbeit ist eine Katastrophe: Null Punkte!* **2.** catastrophe ◊ *Der vierte Akt des Dramas endet mit einer Katastrophe.* **3.** *(fam)* disaster ◊ *Die neue Mitarbeiterin ist eine absolute Katastrophe!*

Ka·ter ['kaːtɐ] *der* <–s, –> **1.** (tom)cat **2.** *(fam)* hangover ◊ *ein Mittel gegen Kater*

⊚ **der gestiefelte Kater** Puss-in-Boots

② **ka·tho·lisch** [ka'toːlɪʃ] *(adj)* *no comp/superl* Catholic ◊ *Seine ganze Familie ist katholisch.* ♦ *die katholische Kirche* *(adv)* jdn katholisch erziehen bring sb up in the Catholic faith streng katholisch leben be a strict Catholic

② **Kat·ze** ['katsə] *die* <–, –n> cat

⊚ **wie die Katze um den heißen Brei schleichen** *(fam)* beat about the bush **wenn die Katze aus dem Haus ist, tanzen die Mäuse (auf dem Tisch)** when the cat's away the mice will play **die Katze lässt das Mausen nicht** the leopard cannot change its spots **die Katze im Sack kaufen** *(fam)* buy a pig in a poke

kau·en ['kaʊ̯ən] *(tr+intr v)* *+haben* chew ◊ *Kaugummi kauen* ♦ *Du solltest gründlicher kauen.* an etw. *(dat)* kauen chew (on) sth ◊ *Er kaute an seinem Butterbrot.* an den Nägeln/Fingernägeln kauen, Nägel/Fingernägel kauen bite your nails *(intr v)* *+haben* *(fig)* an etw. *(dat)* kauen struggle with sth ◊ *Die Schulen werden noch lange an diesem Problem kauen.* an etw. noch lange zu kauen haben take a long time to get over sth

Kauf [kaʊ̯f] *der* <–(e)s, Käufe> purchase, buy ◊ *Mit diesem Auto hast du einen schlechten Kauf gemacht.* jdm etw. zum Kauf anbieten offer sth for sale **beim Kauf ...** *(gen)*, **beim Kauf von etw.** when buying/purchasing sth ⊜Verkauf

⊚ **etw. in Kauf nehmen** accept sth **jdn in Kauf nehmen** put up with sb

② **kau·fen** ['kaʊ̯fn̩] *(tr+intr v)* *+haben* buy ◊ *Er kauft ein neues Auto.* sich/jdm etw. kaufen buy yourself/sb sth ◊ *Ich habe dir einen Pulli gekauft.* etw. auf Raten kaufen buy sth in instalments *(tr v)* *+haben* *(pej)* jdn kaufen bribe sb, buy sb off ◊ *Die Mafia kaufte die Zeugen.*

⊚ **dafür kann sich jd nichts kaufen** *(fam)* that's not a lot of use to sb

Käu·fer ['kɔɪ̯fɐ] *der* <–s, –>, **Käu·fe·rin** ['kɔɪ̯fərɪn] *die* <–, –nen> buyer, purchaser ⊜Verkäufer

② **Kauf·haus** ['kaʊ̯fhaʊ̯s] *das* <–es, Kaufhäuser> department store ⊜Warenhaus

Kauf·mann ['kaʊ̯fman] *der* <–(e)s, Kaufleute>, **Kauf·frau** ['kaʊ̯fraʊ̯] *die* <–, –en> **1.** trader,

dealer, businessman ◊ *Er ist Kaufmann von Beruf.* **Kauffrau** trader, dealer, businesswoman ◊ *eine erfolgreiche Kauffrau* **2.** *no fem (fam)* beim Kaufmann at the grocer's zum Kaufmann gehen go to the grocer's

Kau·gum·mi ['kaʊ̯gʊmiː] *der or also das* <–s, –s> chewing gum ◊ *Kaugummi kauen*

② **kaum** [kaʊ̯m] *(adv)* hardly, scarcely ◊ *Sie kann es kaum erwarten, in Urlaub zu fahren.* ♦ *Kaum jemand interessiert sich dafür.* ♦ *Ihre Stimme war kaum zu hören.*

⊚ **kaum auszudenken** it hardly bears thinking about ◊ *„Was ist, wenn er es erfährt?" — „Kaum auszudenken!"*

Kau·ti·on [kaʊ̯'tsi̯oːn] *die* <–, –en> **1.** deposit ◊ *eine Kaution für etw. hinterlegen* ♦ *eine Kaution an den Vermieter zahlen* **2.** LAW bail ◊ *Sie kam auf Kaution frei.*

ke·geln ['keːgl̩n] *(intr v)* *+haben* play skittles, go (ten-pin) bowling *(tr v)* *+haben* bowl, score ◊ *Er hat eine Fünf gekegelt.*

Keh·le ['keːlə] *die* <–, –n> throat ◊ *eine trockene/wunde Kehle haben* ♦ *jdm die Kehle durchschneiden*

⊚ **sich** *(dat)* **die Kehle aus dem Hals schreien** shout your head off **aus voller Kehle** at the top of your voice ◊ *Sie schrie aus voller Kehle.* **etw. bleibt jdm in der Kehle stecken** sth sticks in sb's throat **an die Kehle springen 1.** jdm/einem Tier an die Kehle springen go for sb's/an animal's throat **2.** jdm an die Kehle springen go for sb

keh·ren ['keːrən] *(tr v)* *+haben* **1.** sweep ◊ *die Treppe kehren* **2.** turn ◊ *Sie kehrte ihm den Rücken zu.* etw. nach außen kehren turn sth inside out *(intr v)* *+haben/sein* **1.** *+haben* sweep (up), do the sweeping ◊ *Ich muss noch kehren, bin dich im fertig.* **2.** *in adjectival passive constructions* in sich gekehrt lost in thought *(ref v)* *+haben* **1.** sich nicht an etw. *(acc)* kehren not care about sth, pay no attention to sth ◊ *Er kehrt sich nicht an das Verbot.* ♦ *Sie kennt die Regeln, aber sie kehrt sich nicht daran.* **2.** sich gegen jdn/etw. kehren turn against sb/sth ◊ *Die Gruppe kehrte sich gegen ihn.*

⊚ **kehrt** MIL about turn ◊ *Abteilung kehrt!*

Kehr·sei·te ['keːɐ̯zaɪ̯tə] *die* <–, –n> **1.** drawback, downside ◊ *Hautkrebs ist die Kehrseite der Solarienbräune.* **2.** jds Kehrseite sb's behind

⊚ **die Kehrseite der Medaille** the other side of the coin

kehrt|ma·chen ['keːɐ̯tmaxn̩] <macht kehrt, machte kehrt, hat kehrtgemacht> *(intr v)* *(fam)* turn round ◊ *Er machte kehrt und ging nach Hause.;* *(military)* do an about-turn

Keil [kaɪ̯l] *der* <–(e)s, –e> **1.** wedge ◊ *Er treibt einen Keil ins Holz.* **2.** (door) wedge ◊ *einen Keil unter die Tür klemmen* **3.** (wedge-type) gusset

Keim [kaɪ̯m] *der* <–(e)s, –e> **1.** BOT shoot, sprout ◊ *Die Samen treiben Keime.* **2.** BIO embryo, fertilized cell **3.** BIO, MED germ ◊ *ein Wundverband zum Schutz vor Keimen* **4.** *(fig)* seeds ◊ *der Keim der Erneuerung* ♦ *den Keim für Konflikte legen*

⊚ **etw. im Keim ersticken** nip sth in the bud

kein [kaɪ̯n] *(det)* **1.** no ◊ *Kein Auto ist ihm schnell genug.* ♦ *Ich habe leider keine Ideen. Ich brauche keinen neuen Reifen.* I don't need a new tyre. Er

hat keine Lust zu arbeiten. *He doesn't feel like working.* **2.** *before a negative adj to express the opposite* not a ◊ *Das ist keine schlechte Lösung.* **3.** *(fam)* less than, under ◊ *Es dauert keine fünf Minuten, bis sie da war.* ♦ *Seit meiner Scheidung ist noch kein Jahr vergangen.*

	m	f	nt	pl
nom	kein	keine	kein	keine
acc	keinen	keine	kein	keine
dat	keinem	keiner	keinem	keinen
gen	keines	keiner	keines	keiner

kei·ne ['kaenə] *fem of* kein *fem of* keiner
kei·ner ['kaenɐ] (indef pron) *keiner/keine/kein(e)s*
1. nobody, no one ◊ *Keiner will das übernehmen.* ♦ *Ich lasse mich von keinem auf den Arm nehmen.* ♦ *Das kann man keinem zumuten. You can't expect that of anyone.* **2.** *relating to a previously specified noun* none, not any „*Ich habe den Schirm in den Ständer gestellt.*" — „*Aber da ist keiner!*" *I placed the umbrella in the umbrella stand.*" — *"But there aren't any there!"* Zivildienst, Berufsarmee oder kein(e)s von beiden? *Community service, the military or neither of the two?* „*Die Suppe ist fertig!*" — „*Ich will keine.*" *"The soup is ready!"* — *"I don't want any."* Bei leeren Kassen ist geliehenes Geld besser als gar keines. *When you're out of funds borrowed money is better than none at all.*

	m	f	nt	pl
nom	keiner	keine	keines	keine
acc	keinen	keine	keines	keine
dat	keinem	keiner	keinem	keinen
gen	-	-	-	-

kei·ner·lei ['kaenɐ'lae] (det) *invariable* no ... what(so)ever, no ... at all ◊ *Wir übernehmen keinerlei Verantwortung.* ♦ *Es gibt keinerlei Einwände.*
kei·nes ['kaenəs] *neut of* keiner
kei·nes·falls ['kaenəs'fals] (adv) under no circumstances, on no account ◊ *Sie dürfen die Dosis keinesfalls erhöhen.*
kei·nes·wegs ['kaenəs've:ks] (adv) not at all, by no means ◊ *Er nimmt die Kritik keineswegs übel.* ♦ *Die Gefahr sollte keineswegs unterschätzt werden.*
keins [kaens] *neut of* keiner
Keks [ke:ks] *der* <-es, -e> *esp Austr das* <-, -(e)> biscuit ◊ *Nimm doch einen Keks!* ♦ *Kekse backen*
ⓔ *etw./jd geht jdm auf den Keks (fam)* sth/sb is getting on sb's nerves
Kel·le ['kɛlə] *die* <-, -n> **1.** ladle ◊ *Suppe mit der Kelle austeilen* **2.** trowel **3.** signal disk ◊ *Der Polizist winkt mit der Kelle.*
ⓩ **Kel·ler** ['kɛlɐ] *der* <-s, -> cellar ◊ *Kartoffeln im Keller lagern* ⊖Dachboden, Boden, Speicher
ⓔ *zum Lachen in den Keller gehen* have no sense of humour *in den Keller fallen* FIN go through the floor
ⓩ **Kell·ner** ['kɛlnɐ] *der* <-s, ->, **Kell·ne·rin** ['kɛlnərɪn] *die* <-, -nen> waiter ◊ *Ruf doch mal den Kellner. Kellnerin* waitress ◊ *Sie ist Kellnerin in einem Bistro.*
Ke·nia ['ke:nja] *das* <-s> *no pl* Kenya → Deutschland
Ke·nia·ner [ke'nja:nɐ] *der* <-s, ->, **Ke·nia·ne·rin**

[ke'nja:nərɪn] *die* <-, -nen> Kenyan → Deutsche
ke·ni·a·nisch [ke'nja:nɪʃ] (adj) *mostly before ns* Kenyan ◊ *Die Landschaft hier ist typisch kenianisch.* ♦ *das kenianische Hinterland*
ⓩ **ken·nen** ['kɛnən] <kennt, kannte, hat gekannt> (tr v) **1.** know ◊ *Kennst du dieses Buch?* ♦ *Wir kennen das Risiko noch nicht.* ♦ *Wie ich ihn kenne, wird er das schaffen.* ♦ *Kennst du meine Freundin schon?* ♦ *Sie kennt keine Schmerzen.* ♦ *Der Täter kannte keine Gnade.* sich kennen know yourself sie kennen sich *they know each other* Sie kennen sich noch nicht. *They haven't met yet.* etw. (noch/nicht mehr) kennen (still/no longer) know sth ◊ *Sie kennt die Märchen ihrer Kindheit noch heute.* ♦ *Ich kenne diese Gegend wie meine Westentasche.* **2.** jdn/etw. kennen recognize sb/sth, still know sb/sth ◊ *Ich würde sie jederzeit an ihrem Gang kennen.* ♦ *Kennst du mich überhaupt noch?*
⊖erkennen
ⓔ *etw./jdn kennen lernen* get to know sth/sb ◊ *Ich würde dich gern besser kennen lernen.* da kennt jd nichts *sb has no scruples whatsoever*
Kennt·nis ['kɛntnɪs] *die* <-, -se> *no pl* knowledge ◊ *Die Kenntnis von zwei Fremdsprachen wird vorausgesetzt.* Kenntnisse (in etw. (dat)) knowledge (of sth) ◊ *seine Kenntnisse auffrischen/vertiefen* ♦ *Er verfügt über gute Kenntnisse in Medizin.* etw. entzieht sich jds Kenntnis *sb has no knowledge of sth* ohne Kenntnis ... (gen) *without knowing sth* Kenntnis von etw. bekommen *learn about sth* Kenntnis davon erhalten, dass ... *learn that, hear that* Kenntnis davon haben, dass *know that* ◊ *Haben Sie von Kenntnis davon, dass wir die Gebühren erhöhen werden?* etw. zur Kenntnis nehmen *take note of sth* jdn (nicht) zur Kenntnis nehmen *take (no) notice of sb* Kenntnis nehmen *take notice of sb/sth* jdn in Kenntnis setzen *inform sb* ◊ *Die Angehörigen wurden von seinem Tod in Kenntnis gesetzt.*
Kenn·wort ['kɛnvɔrt] *das* <-(e)s, Kennwörter> **1.** password ◊ *das Kennwort eingeben* ♦ *Das heutige Kennwort heißt/lautet: „...".* **2.** reference ◊ *Geben Sie bei allen Zusendungen das Kennwort „..." an.* etw. mit dem Kennwort „..." versehen *mark sth "..."*
Kenn·zei·chen ['kɛntsaeçn] *das* <-s, -> **1.** registration (number), number, license (plate) number ◊ *das Fahrzeug mit dem Kennzeichen S-MJ 1414* ♦ *Wie lautet das amtliche Kennzeichen Ihres Wagens?* ⊖Nummer **2.** feature, characteristic ◊ *Das Atomium ist ein berühmtes Kennzeichen der Stadt Brüssel.* ♦ *Zu seinen bemerkenswerten Kennzeichen gehört sein Humor.* ♦ *ein auffälliges/typisches Kennzeichen; (outstanding physical attribute)* jds Kennzeichen *sb's trademark* **3.** badge, insignia
Kerl [kɛrl] *der* <-s, -e> *(fam)* bloke, guy ♦ *So ein blöder Kerl!* ♦ *Hat der Kerl Probleme?* ♦ *Dein Sohn ist ein hübscher Kerl.* ⊖Bursche
ⓔ *ein feiner Kerl* a good sort *ein ganzer Kerl* a real man *ein netter Kerl* a nice guy/girl
Kern [kɛrn] *der* <-(e)s, -e> **1.** pip ◊ *Isst du bei Äpfeln die Kerne mit?; (in stone fruit)* stone, pit **2.** kernel ◊ *Sie knackte die Nuss und holte den Kern heraus.* **3.** centre, core ◊ *Der Kern der Erde besteht aus Magma.* **4.** PHYSICS nucleus **5.** essence,

core ◊ *Das ist der Kern des Problems.*
◉ **ein guter Kern** a good heart **der harte Kern** the hard core

ⓩ **Kern·...** [kɛʳn] prefix **1.** core ... ◊ *die Kernaussage einer Rede* ♦ *Die Finanzierung war natürlich die Kernfrage.* ♦ *Wie viele Kernfächer muss man fürs Abitur belegen?* **2.** nuclear ... ◊ *Kernforschung* ♦ *Kernreaktor*

Kern·e·ner·gie [ˈkɛʳnʔenɛʳˌgiː] die <-> *no pl* nuclear energy

Kern·kraft·werk [ˈkɛʳnkraftvɛʳk] das <-(e)s, -e> nuclear power station

Ker·ze [ˈkɛʳtsə] die <-, -n> **1.** candle ◊ *die Kerzen am Weihnachtsbaum* ♦ *Die Kerze ist heruntergebrannt.* ♦ *die Kerzen der Kastanie* **2.** candle bulb ◊ *Kerzen zu 30 und zu 40 Watt* **3.** (spark) plug ◊ *Bei der Inspektion wurden die Kerzen ausgewechselt.* **4.** shoulder stand ◊ *Kannst du eine Kerze machen?*

Kes·sel [ˈkɛsl̩] der <-s, -> **1.** kettle ◊ *Er setzte den Kessel mit dem Teewasser auf.* **2.** cauldron, pot ◊ *einen Kessel Eintopf vorbereiten* **3.** tank ◊ *Das Warmwasser wird im Kessel des Boilers erhitzt.* **4.** basin ◊ *Die Stadt liegt in einem Kessel.* **5.** MIL encirclement

ⓩ **Ket·te** [ˈkɛtə] die <-, -n> **1.** necklace, chain ◊ *Sie trug eine goldene Kette mit Anhänger.* **2.** chain ◊ *Der Hofhund zerrte an seiner Kette.* ♦ *Die Kette meines Fahrrads ist gerissen.* ♦ *Dieses Restaurant gehört zu einer amerikanischen Kette.* ♦ *Die Menschen bildeten bei der Demonstration eine Kette.* **3.** *eine Kette ...* gen, eine Kette von etw. a series of sth, a chain of sth ◊ *Die Kette der Enttäuschungen wollte nicht abreißen.*
◉ **jdn an die Kette legen** (*fig*) keep sb on a short leash

KFZ-Kenn·zei·chen [kaːʔɛfˈtsɛtkɛnsˌtsaeçn̩] das <-s, -> (*abbr of* Kraftfahrzeug-Kennzeichen) number plate, license plate

By law, every vehicle must have a number plate. German number plates are white with black lettering. The first one to three letters are an abbreviation of the name of the place where the vehicle was licensed. Single letters usually stand for big cities, e.g. **B** for Berlin, **M** for Munich.

kg [ˈkiːlogram] (*abbr of* Kilogramm) kg

Kie·fer¹ [ˈkiːfɐ] der <-s, -> jaw

Kie·fer² [ˈkiːfɐ] die <-, -n> pine ◊ *Vor dem Haus steht eine Kiefer.* ♦ *Möbel aus Kiefer*

Kies [kiːs] der <-es> *no pl* gravel ◊ *Der Gartenweg war mit Kies bestreut.*

Ki·lo [ˈkiːlo] das <-s, -s> *pl Kilo when used with expressions of quantity* (*abbr of* Kilogramm) kilo ◊ *zwei Kilo Tomaten* ♦ *Der Kampf gegen die Kilos.*

Ki·lo·gramm [kiloˈgram, ˈkiːlogram] das <-s, -e> *pl Kilogramm when used with expressions of quantity* (*abbr* kg) kilogram ◊ *fünf Kilogramm Kartoffeln*

Ki·lo·me·ter [kiloˈmeːte] der <-s, -> (*abbr* km) kilometre, kilometer ◊ *Wir sind im Urlaub 5000 Kilometer gefahren.* ♦ *Das Auto bringt es auf 200 Kilometer in der Stunde.*

ⓩ **Kind** [kɪnt] das <-(e)s, -er> **1.** child ◊ *Du benimmst dich wie ein kleines Kind.* ♦ *Karl ist ihr einziges Kind.* **ein Kind ...** gen a child of sth ◊ *Sein Biograf beschreibt ihn als Kind seiner Zeit.*

2. baby ◊ *Sie erwartet ein Kind.* ♦ *Sie hat gestern ein Kind bekommen.*
◉ **das Kind mit dem Bade ausschütten** throw out the baby with the bathwater **mit Kind und Kegel** with the whole family **aus Kindern werden Leute** children grow up quickly/fast, don't they **das Kind beim Namen nennen** call a spade a spade **kein Kind von Traurigkeit sein** know how to enjoy yourself **ein gebranntes Kind sein** have had bad experiences **jds liebstes Kind** sb's prized possession, sb's most treasured possession **von Kind an/auf** since I/he/she was a child, since we/you/they were children **wir werden das Kind schon schaukeln** we'll manage it

ⓩ **Kin·der·gar·ten** [ˈkɪndegaʳtn̩] der <-s, Kindergärten> nursery (school) ◊ *in den Kindergarten gehen/kommen*

Nursery schools are designed for children from the age of three up to primary school age. Special attention is paid to developing the child's personality and improving his or her social integration through play. Nurseries are intended to help parents with their children's upbringing and, as far as possible, to give special help to children who have learning difficulties.

Kin·der·krip·pe [ˈkɪndekrɪpə] die <-, -n> creche, crèche ◊ *Vor der Arbeit bringt sie ihr Baby in die Kinderkrippe.*

Creches are designed for children up to the age of three, or until they go to nursery school. In Germany, there are very few creches; and demand for places always exceeds supply. Creches are intended to support parents and guardians in bringing up their children. A particular aim is to help children develop their physical and intellectual abilities in equal measure.

Kin·der·ta·ges·stät·te [ˈkɪndeˌtaːgəsʃtɛtə] die <-, -n> (day) nursery ◊ *in die Kindertagesstätte gehen*

Day nurseries are virtually identical to nursery schools (*Kindergärten*) in terms of what they offer. In some cases, children of primary school age attend day nurseries in the afternoons.

Kind·heit [ˈkɪnthaet] die <-, -en> *most sing* childhood ◊ *Sie hatte eine glückliche/unbeschwerte Kindheit.* ♦ *Er hat seine Kindheit auf dem Land verbracht.*

Kinn [kɪn] das <-s, -e> chin

ⓩ **Ki·no** [ˈkiːno] das <-s, -s> **1.** cinema, the movies ◊ *Sie geht jeden Sonntag ins Kino.* ♦ *Er ist ein Star des deutschen Kinos.* **2.** cinema, movie theater ◊ *Wir treffen uns um acht vor dem Kino.*

ⓩ **Ki·osk** [ˈkiːɔsk] der <-(e)s, -e> kiosk ◊ *Sie betreibt einen Kiosk am Bahnhof.* ♦ *eine Zeitung am Kiosk kaufen*

ⓩ **Kip·fel** [ˈkɪpfl̩], **Kip·ferl** [ˈkɪpfel] das <-s, -(n)> (*SouthG, Austr*) *crescent-shaped pastry with or without filling* ◊ *Zum Frühstück gab es Kipferl mit Marmelade.*

kip·pen [ˈkɪpm̩] tr v +*haben* **1.** tilt ◊ *Kippen Sie jetzt den Oberkörper nach vorn.* ♦ *Die Fenster lassen sich kippen.* etw. nach oben/unten kippen flip sth up/down **2.** etw. irgendwohin kippen tip

A B C D E F G H I J K L M N O P Q R S T U V W X Y Z

sth somewhere, empty sth somewhere ◊ *Er kippte den vollen Aschenbecher einfach auf die Straße.*; *(rubbish)* dump sth somewhere; *(liquids)* pour sth somewhere **3.** *(fam)* down ◊ *Er kippte einen Schnaps nach dem anderen.* einen kippen gehen go for a drink **4.** *(a sentence, law)* overturn ◊ *Die nächste Instanz hat das Urteil gekippt.* **5.** *(a government, politician)* topple, oust ◊ *Der umstrittene Minister ist endlich gekippt worden.* [intr v] +*sein* **1.** fall over ◊ *Die Leiter kippte, und er fiel runter.*; *(chair)* tip; *(boat)* capsize, overturn **2.** suddenly change (to the worse) ◊ *Die Stimmung an der Börse ist gekippt.*

⑦ **Kir·che** ['kɪrçə] die <–, –n> **1.** church ◊ *eine gotische Kirche* ♦ *Wir gehen jeden Sonntag in die Kirche.* **2.** Church ◊ *Sie ist aus der Kirche ausgetreten.* ♦ *Der Papst ist das Oberhaupt der katholischen Kirche.*

Kirch·weih ['kɪrçvaɛ] die <–, –en>

The anniversary of the consecration of a church is celebrated annually. The custom of consecrating churches began in the 4th century. Then, in the seventh century, altars were consecrated, and holy relics placed beside them. In Germany, the anniversary of the consecration of the church is often linked with the parish fair called *Kirtag, Kirbe* or *Kirmes.* In earlier times, this fair, which took place at the end of the harvest, was one of the favourite fairs of the rural population, with celebrations (dancing and eating) usually lasting for three days. Many of today's big festivals (e.g. the Munich Beer Festival) have their roots in this tradition.

Kir·sche ['kɪrʃə] die <–, –n> cherry ◊ *ein Kuchen mit Kirschen* ♦ *In ihrem Garten steht eine Kirsche.* ♦ *Möbel aus Kirsche*

◉ **mit jdm ist nicht gut Kirschen essen** sb is difficult to get along with

⑦ **Kis·sen** ['kɪsn̩] das <–s, –> pillow ◊ *Sie schläft immer mit zwei Kissen.*; cushion ◊ *Auf ihrem Sofa liegen viele bunte Kissen.*

⑦ **Kis·te** ['kɪstə] die <–, –n> **1.** box ◊ *Das Kind räumte seine Spielsachen in die Kiste.*; *(without a lid)* crate; *(for bottles of wine)* case **2.** *(fam)* banger, beater ◊ *Dein Auto ist so eine alte Kiste, verkauf es doch.*

kit·zeln ['kɪtsl̩n] [tr+intr v] +*haben* tickle ◊ *Er hat mich an den Füßen gekitzelt.* ♦ *Nicht da anfassen, das kitzelt!* etw. kitzelt in der Nase sth tickles your nose [tr v] +*haben* tempt es kitzelt jdn, etw. zu tun sb is (very) tempted to do sth, sb is itching to do sth

klaf·fen ['klafn̩] [intr v] +*haben* gape ◊ *An seiner Stirn klaffte eine Wunde.*

Kla·ge ['kla:gə] die <–, –n> **1.** complaint ◊ *Wir haben keinen Anlass zur Klage.* ♦ *Und dass mir keine Klagen kommen!*; *(more general)* complaining ◊ *Ich bin deine Klagen leid, denk doch mal positiv.* **2.** suit, action ◊ *Ich werde Klage gegen Sie einreichen.* Klage auf etw. [acc] suit for sth, action for sth ◊ *Klage auf Schadensersatz erheben* **3.** lament, lamentation ◊ *Sie brach in laute Klagen aus.*

⑦ **kla·gen** ['kla:gn̩] [intr v] +*haben* **1.** complain ◊ *"Wie geht es Ihnen?" — "Ach, ich kann nicht klagen."* ♦

Er klagt dauernd, dass er keine Zeit hat. über jdn/etw. klagen complain about sb/sth; *(when you are in pain)* über etw. [acc] klagen complain of sth ◊ *Sie klagt über Schmerzen im rechten Arm.* **2.** sue, take (legal) action gegen jdn/etw. klagen sue sb/sth, take (legal) action against sb/sth ◊ *Ich werde gegen Sie klagen.* auf etw. [acc] klagen sue for sth ◊ *Er klagte auf Schadensersatz.* **3.** *(lofty)* moan, wail, lament ◊ *Sie weinte und klagte.* [tr v] +*haben* complain, moan ◊ *"Ich kann nicht mehr", klagte das Kind auf dem Spaziergang.* jdm sein Leid klagen tell sb your woes, tell sb your troubles

Klä·ger ['klɛːɡɐ] der <–s, –>, **Klä·ge·rin** ['klɛːɡərɪn] die <–, –nen> plaintiff ◊ *Klägerin in dieser Sache ist die Stadt Speyer.*

kläg·lich ['klɛːklɪç] [adj, adv] **1.** sorrowful(ly) ◊ *Aus dem Nebenzimmer drangen klägliche Laute.* ♦ *"Keiner liebt mich", sagte er kläglich.* **2.** miserable(-ably), wretched(ly) ◊ *ein klägliches Bild abgegeben* ♦ *Das Ende war kläglich.* ♦ *Sie sind kläglich gescheitert.*

Klam·mer ['klame] die <–, –n> **1.** (clothes) peg, clothespin ◊ *Sie befestigte die Wäsche mit Klammern an der Leine.* **2.** bracket, parenthesis ◊ *Die Phonetik steht in eckigen Klammern.* ♦ *Klammer auf/zu* **3.** paper clip; *(from a stapler)* staple **4.** MED (wound) clip **5.** *(for teeth)* brace(s)

klam·mern ['klamɐn] [tr v] +*haben* **1.** etw. an etw. [acc] klammern attach sth to sth, clip sth to sth ◊ *Er klammerte ein Passfoto an die Bewerbung.*; *(washing on a line)* peg sth to sth **2.** *(a wound)* etw. klammern close sth (with clips) ◊ *Die Platzwunde musste geklammert werden.* **3.** etw. klammern put sth in brackets, put sth in parentheses, put sth in a parenthesis ◊ *Einschübe werden oft geklammert.* [intr v] +*haben* be clingy ◊ *Ich bin nicht der Typ, der klammert.* [ref v] +*haben* *(also fig)* sich an jdn/etw. klammern cling to sb/sth ◊ *Das Kind klammerte sich an seine Mutter.* ♦ *Er klammerte sich an meine Hand.*

Kla·mot·ten [kla'mɔtn̩] die <–> *only pl (fam)* clothes, togs ◊ *Ich brauche neue Klamotten.* ⊖Kleider

klang [klaŋ] *pret of* klingen

Klang [klaŋ] der <–(e)s, Klänge> **1.** tone ◊ *Diese Geige hat einen sehr schönen Klang.* **2.** sound; *(of bells, glasses)* ringing ◊ *Das Brautpaar betrat zum Klang der Glocken die Kirche.* **3.** etw. hat einen guten, angenehmen etc. Klang sth has a good, pleasant etc. ring to it **4.** *only pl* Klänge tunes ◊ *Ich freute mich, als ich heimatliche Klänge hörte.*; *(sounds of music)* strains

Klap·pe ['klapə] die <–, –n> **1.** flap ◊ *Er öffnete die Klappe des Briefkastens.* ♦ *Die Katze schlüpfte durch die Klappe.* **2.** *(fam, pej)* mouth, trap, gob ◊ *Halt die Klappe!* ♦ *Der Egon hat eine große Klappe.* **3.** clapperboard

◉ **Klappe die dritte** take three **und Klappe** action

⑦ **klap·pen** ['klapm̩] [intr v] +*haben/sein (fam)* **1.** +*sein* nach vorne/hinten/oben/unten etc. klappen fold forward/backward/up/down etc., flip forward/backward/up/down etc. Sein Unterkiefer klappte nach unten. His lower jaws dropped. **2.** +*haben* go all right, go well ◊ *Ich hoffe, es klappt alles.*; *(plan, trick etc.)* work ⊖funktionie-

ren ⸢tr v⸣ +*haben* etw. nach vorne/hinten/oben/ unten etc. klappen fold sth forward/backward/up/ down etc., flip sth forward/backward/up/down etc. ◊ *Er klappte den Mantelkragen nach oben.*

klap·pern ['klapɐn] ⸢intr v⸣ +*haben* rattle ◊ *Dein Schutzblech klappert.*; *(pots and pans)* clatter

② **klar** [klaːɐ̯] ⸢adj, adv⸣ clear(ly) ◊ *eine klare Winternacht* ♦ *ein klares Nein* ♦ *eine klare Niederlage* ♦ *klare Suppe* ♦ *Das Wasser des Sees ist klar.* ♦ *Sie hat sich sehr klar ausgedrückt.*; *(not dirty)* clean ◊ *Die Gläser mit klarem Wasser abspülen.* jdm ist etw. klar sth is clear to sb jdm wird etw. klar sth becomes clear to sb, sb realizes sth klar siegen be the clear winner(s) klar geschlagen werden be the clear loser(s) sich ⸢dat⸣ etw. klar machen realize sth
◉ **klipp und klar** perfectly clear(ly) **klar sehen** *(fam)* understand sich ⸢dat⸣ **über etw.** ⸢acc⸣ **im Klaren sein** be aware of sth **(na) klar** of course, naturally

klä·ren ['klɛːrən] ⸢tr v⸣ +*haben* **1.** solve ◊ *Die Polizei hat diesen Fall nie geklärt.* **2.** establish, find out ◊ *Hast du inzwischen klären können, ob sie uns helfen?* **3.** clarify ◊ *Ich muss diese Frage mit meinem Chef klären.* **4.** treat ◊ *In dieser Anlage wird das Abwasser geklärt.* ⸢ref v⸣ +*haben* **1.** sich klären be resolved ◊ *Hat es sich denn nun geklärt, wer das bezahlt?*; *(problem, misunderstanding etc.)* sort itself out; *(question)* solve itself, be solved **2.** *(river, lake etc.)* sich klären clear itself

klar|ge·hen ['klaːɐ̯ˌɡeːən] <geht klar, ging klar, ist klargegangen> ⸢intr v⸣ *(fam)* be OK, be all right ◊ *Mutti, ich möchte am Samstag eine Party feiern, geht das klar?*; go OK, go okay, go all right ◊ *Ist in der Prüfung alles klargegangen?*

klar|kom·men ['klaːɐ̯ˌkɔmən] <kommt klar, kam klar, ist klargekommen> ⸢intr v⸣ *(fam)* manage, cope ◊ *Kommst du klar oder soll ich dir helfen?*

klar|stel·len ['klaːɐ̯ˌʃtɛlən] <stellt klar, stellte klar, hat klargestellt> ⸢tr v⸣ make clear ◊ *Eines möchte ich doch klarstellen: Ich habe das nie gesagt.*

Klar·text ['klaːɐ̯ˌtɛkst] der <-es> *no pl* Klartext reden give sb a piece of your mind im Klartext in plain language

② **klas·se** ['klasə] *(fam)* ⸢adj⸣ *invariable* great, brilliant ◊ *Die Band war einfach klasse.* ♦ *Er hat ein klasse Auto.* ⊜super, prima, toll ⸢adv⸣ really well, brilliantly ◊ *Sie kann klasse singen.* sich klasse amüsieren have a brilliant time klasse aussehen be really good-looking ⊜super, prima, toll

② **Klas·se** ['klasə] die <-, -n> **1.** class ◊ *Bernd ist in derselben Klasse wie Daniel.* ♦ *die unteren sozialen Klassen* ♦ *Ein Fahrschein zweiter Klasse kostet 35 Euro.* ♦ *Der Mensch gehört zu der Klasse der Säugetiere.*; *(in sport)* league **2.** year, grade ◊ *Er ist in der neunten Klasse.*
◉ **große Klasse sein** *(fam)* be brilliant, be excellent

② **Klas·sen·ar·beit** ['klasn̩ʔaˌbaɛ̯t] die <-, -en> test ◊ *Wir schreiben morgen in Englisch eine Klassenarbeit.* ⊜Probe

Klas·sik ['klasɪk] die <-> *no pl* **1.** classicism, classical period ◊ *ein Vertreter der deutschen Klassik* **2.** classical antiquity ◊ *die Götterwelt der Klassik* **3.** classical music ◊ *Klassik hören*

② **klas·sisch** ['klasɪʃ] ⸢adj⸣ *seldom comp/superl* **1.** *only before ns* classical ◊ *Sagen des klassischen Altertums* ♦ *Sie hört gerne klassische Musik.* **2.** classic ◊ *Bauwerke von klassischer Schönheit* ♦ *Dieser Übersetzungsfehler ist klassisch.* ♦ *Das ist ein klassischer Fall von Betrug.*

Klatsch [klatʃ] der <-es> *no pl* gossip

klat·schen ['klatʃn̩] ⸢intr v⸣ +*haben* **1.** clap, applaud ◊ *Das Publikum hat begeistert geklatscht.* in die Hände klatschen clap you hands **2.** lash ◊ *Der Regen klatschte gegen die Scheiben.* **3.** gossip, talk ◊ *Die Leute klatschen schon über uns.* es wird viel geklatscht there's a lot of gossiping ⸢tr v⸣ +*haben* **1.** Beifall klatschen applaud, clap **2.** *(fam)* slap ◊ *Der Maurer klatschte den Mörtel an die Wand.*

klau·en ['klaʊ̯ən] ⸢tr+intr v⸣ +*haben* *(fam)* ((jdm) etw.) klauen nick (sth (from sb)), pinch (sth (from sb)) ◊ *Er hat ihr den Geldbeutel geklaut.* ♦ *Wer hat meinen Kugelschreiber geklaut?* ⊜stehlen

Klau·sur [klaʊ̯ˈzuːɐ̯] die <-, -en> *(at university)* exam; *(in the sixth form)* test
◉ **in Klausur tagen** have a closed session

② **Kla·vier** [klaˈviːɐ̯] das <-s, -e> piano ◊ *Carolin spielt Klavier.*

② **kle·ben** ['kleːbm̩] ⸢tr v⸣ +*haben* **1.** stick ◊ *Sie klebte eine Briefmarke auf den Brief.* ♦ *Sie hat die Fotos ins Album geklebt.* **2.** glue ◊ *Die Tasse kann man wieder kleben.* ⸢intr v⸣ +*haben* **1.** be stuck ◊ *Unter dem Tisch klebte ein Kaugummi.* **2.** stick, stay stuck ◊ *Die Tapete wollte nicht kleben.* **3.** *(fam, esp pej)* an jdm/etw. kleben cling to sb/sth
◉ **jdm eine kleben** *(fam)* give sb a clip around the ear

kleb·rig ['kleːbrɪç] ⸢adj⸣ sticky ◊ *Ich habe ganz klebrige Finger.* ♦ *Der Teig ist furchtbar klebrig.*

Kleb·stoff ['kleːpʃtɔf] der <-(e)s, -e> glue, adhesive

kle·ckern ['klɛkɐn] +*haben/sein* **1.** +*haben* make a mess ◊ *Sie hat beim Essen gekleckert.* **2.** +*sein* splash ◊ *Igitt, jetzt ist die ganze Soße auf die Tischdecke gekleckert.* ⸢tr v⸣ +*haben* spill, splash ◊ *Pass auf, dass du die Soße nicht auf dein T-Shirt kleckerst.*
◉ **nicht kleckern, sondern klotzen** *(fam)* do things in a big way

② **Kleid** [klaɛ̯t] das <-(e)s, -er> **1.** dress ◊ *Sie trug ein geblümtes Kleid.* **2.** *only pl* Kleider clothes ◊ *Seine Kleider lagen im ganzen Zimmer verstreut.* ⊜Klamotten

Klei·der·bü·gel ['klaɛ̯dɐbyːɡl̩] der <-s, -> coat hanger, clothes hanger, hanger ◊ *Sie hängt all ihre Blusen auf Kleiderbügel.*

② **Klei·dung** ['klaɛ̯dʊŋ] die <-> *no pl* clothes, clothing ◊ *Sie trägt gern sportliche Kleidung.*

② **klein** [klaɛ̯n] ⸢adj⸣ **1.** small ◊ *Der Pulli ist mir zu klein.* ♦ *Ich will mir ein kleineres Auto kaufen.* ◊ *Das ist die kleinste Größe, die wir haben.* ♦ *Wiltrud ist kleiner als Silke.* etw. klein hacken chop sth up ⊜groß **2.** little ◊ *Er ist noch zu klein, um das zu verstehen.* ♦ *Darf ich meinen kleinen Bruder mitbringen?* ⊜groß **3.** short ◊ *Ich mache jetzt eine kleine Pause.* **4.** minor ◊ *Er ist nur ein kleiner Angestellter.* aus kleinen Verhältnissen kommen/ stammen be of humble beginnings ⸢adv⸣ klein gemustert with a small print klein geblümt with a

A
B
C
D
E
F
G
H
I
J
K
L
M
N
O
P
Q
R
S
T
U
V
W
X
Y
Z

small flower print klein kariert with small check klein gedruckt in small print ⊕ ein kleines bisschen a little bit ◊ Kannst du vielleicht ein kleines bisschen schneller machen? a little while ◊ Ich wollte nur ein kleines bisschen bleiben. klein und hässlich insignificant ein klein wenig a little bit klein beigeben give in es klein haben *(fam)* have got the change Haben Sie es nicht kleiner? Haven't you got any smaller change? klein machen *(fam)* pee klein müssen *(fam)* need a pee etw. klein schreiben not attach very much importance to sth ◊ Pünktlichkeit scheint bei dir klein geschrieben zu werden. auf klein on(to) a low heat etw. auf klein drehen turn sth down bis ins Kleinste down to the last detail von klein auf from an early age

Klein-geld ['klaɪngɛlt] das <-(e)s> *no pl* change ◊ Ich habe leider kein Kleingeld.

Klei-nig-keit ['klaɪnɪçkaɪt] die <-, -en> little thing ◊ Er regt sich über jede Kleinigkeit auf. ♦ Ich muss noch ein paar Kleinigkeiten besorgen.; *(present)* little something eine Kleinigkeit essen have a bite to eat für jdn eine Kleinigkeit sein be no trouble for sb, be no big deal for sb für jdn keine Kleinigkeit sein be quite a lot of money for sb, be quite difficult for sb

Klein-kind ['klaɪnkɪnt] das <-(e)s, -er> toddler

klein|krie-gen ['klaɪnkriːgn̩] <kriegt klein, kriegte klein, hat kleingekriegt> [tr v] *(fam)* **1.** jdn kleinkriegen get sb down ◊ Mein Chef wird mich diesmal nicht kleinkriegen. **2.** etw. kleinkriegen manage to destroy ◊ Mein Sohn kriegt alle seine Spielsachen klein. nicht kleinzukriegen sein be indestructible

klein-laut ['klaɪnlaʊt] [adj, adv] sheepish(ly) ◊ eine kleinlaute Antwort ♦ Er war ziemlich kleinlaut. ♦ Der Verlierer zog kleinlaut ab.

klein-lich ['klaɪnlɪç] [adj] **1.** petty, narrow-minded, pedantic ◊ Musst du immer so kleinlich sein? ♦ ein kleinlicher Mensch **2.** stingy ◊ Beim Trinkgeld bin ich nicht kleinlich.

Kleis-ter ['klaɪste] der <-s> *no pl* paste ◊ Sie rührte in einem Eimer Kleister an.

klem-men ['klɛmən] [tr v] +*haben* **1.** tuck, stick ◊ etw. unter den Arm klemmen ♦ Er klemmte ein Stück Holz unter die Tür. **2.** sich [dat] den Finger/die Hand etc. (in etw. [acc]) klemmen catch your finger/hand (in sth), get your finger/hand caught (in sth) [intr v] jam, stick ◊ Der Reißverschluss klemmt.

Klemp-ner ['klɛmpne] der <-s, ->, **Klemp-ne-rin** ['klɛmpnərɪn] die <-, -nen> plumber, tinsmith ◊ Sie ist Klempnerin. ♦ Der Klempner reparierte die Leitung. ⊖Installateur

② **klet-tern** ['klɛtɐn] [intr v] +*sein* climb, clamber ◊ Die Katze kletterte auf den Baum. ♦ über einen Zaun klettern ♦ Wir wollen in die Berge klettern gehen.

② **kli-cken** ['klɪkn̩] [intr v] +*haben* click ◊ mit der Maus auf ein Icon klicken ♦ Man hörte die Fotoapparate klicken.

② **Kli-ma** ['kliːma] das <-s, -ta or seldom -s> most sing climate ◊ Dort herrscht ein tropisches/mildes Klima.; *(figurative also)* atmosphere ◊ Das Klima in der Firma war vergiftet.

② **Kli-ma-an-la-ge** ['kliːmaʔanlaːgə] die <-, -n> air conditioning (system)

Klin-ge ['klɪŋə] die <-, -n> blade ◊ Das Messer hatte eine stumpfe Klinge.

② **Klin-gel** ['klɪŋl̩] die <-, -n> bell ◊ Welcher Name steht an der Klingel? ♦ Das Fahrrad hatte keine Klingel.

② **klin-geln** ['klɪŋl̩n] [intr v] +*haben* ring ◊ Das Telefon klingelt! ♦ Er klingelte an der Haustür/bei den Nachbarn.; *(alarm also)* go off nach jdm klingeln ring for sb ⊖läuten [imp v] es klingelt (an der Tür) there is a ring at the door, there is sb at the door; *(in school)* es klingelt the bell goes ⊖es läutet

klin-gen ['klɪŋən] <klingt, klang, hat geklungen> [intr v] **1.** sound ◊ Dieses Lied klingt nach Bob Dylan. ◊ Sein Vorschlag klingt nicht schlecht. ♦ Ihr Anruf klang dringend. **2.** *(bells)* ring die Gläser klingen lassen clink glasses

Kli-nik ['kliːnɪk] die <-, -en> hospital, clinic ◊ Sie brachten ihn in die Klinik. ⊖Krankenhaus

Klin-ke ['klɪŋkə] die <-, -n> (door) handle ◊ Er drückte auf die Klinke. ⊕ sie geben sich die Klinke in die Hand they are (continuously) coming and going (bei jdm) Klinken putzen canvass (sb), go from door to door

Klip-pe ['klɪpə] die <-, -n> **1.** cliff, rock ◊ Er stürzte sich von einer Klippe ins Meer. **2.** *(fig)* hurdle, obstacle eine Klippe umschiffen negotiate an obstacle

Kli-schee [kliˈʃeː] das <-s, -s> *(lofty, esp pej)* cliché, stereotype ◊ ein Horrorfilm, der alle Klischees erfüllt

② **Klo** [kloː] das <-s, -s> *(fam)* *(abbr of* Klosett*)* loo, toilet ◊ Sie ging/musste aufs Klo. ♦ Er ist/sitzt auf dem Klo. ⊖Toilette, WC

② **Klo-pa-pier** ['kloːpapiːɐ] das <-s> *no pl* *(fam)* loo paper, toilet paper ◊ eine Rolle Klopapier ⊖Toilettenpapier

② **klop-fen** ['klɔpfn̩] [tr+intr v] +*haben* **1.** knock ◊ Er klopfte an die Tür. ♦ einen Nagel in die Wand klopfen jdm auf etw. [acc] klopfen pat sb on sth, slap sb on sth ◊ Sie klopfte ihm anerkennend auf die Schulter. **2.** beat ◊ Das Herz klopfte ihm vor Aufregung bis zum Hals. ♦ Schnitzel/Teppiche klopfen ♦ Sie klopfte sich den Staub von der Jacke. [imp v] es klopft (an etw. [dat]) there is sb (knocking) (at sth) ◊ Es klopfte an der Tür.

Klops [klɔps] der <-es, -e> **1.** *(NorthG)* meatball ◊ Königsberger Klopse ⊖Kloß **2.** *(fam)* howler, clanger

Kloß [kloːs] der <-es, Klöße> dumpling, ball ◊ Sie formte das Hackfleisch zu kleinen Klößen. ♦ Es gab Schweinebraten mit Klößen. ⊖Knödel ⊕ einen Kloß im Hals haben have a lump in your throat

Klos-ter ['kloːste] das <-s, Klöster> monastery, convent, nunnery ◊ Sie ging für ein Jahr ins Kloster.

Klotz [klɔts] der <-es, Klötze> **1.** block (of wood), log **2.** GAME *(for children)* (building) block ◊ Das Kind baute mit den Klötzen einen Turm. **3.** *(pej)* *(building)* block ◊ Die neue Schule war ein hässlicher Klotz. ⊕ jdm/für jdn ein Klotz am Bein sein be a millstone round sb's neck

Klub [klʊp] der <–s, –s> club ◊ einem Klub
beitreten

Kluft¹ [klʊft] die <–, Klüfte> (esp fig) cleft, gap,
golf, chasm ◊ Spalten und Klüfte im Fels ♦ Es tat
sich eine große Kluft zwischen Theorie und Praxis
auf.

Kluft² [klʊft] die <–, –en> most sing (fam) gear,
get-up ◊ Er schmiss sich in seine beste Kluft.

② **klug** [kluːk] adj, adv <klüger, am klügsten>
1. clever(ly), intelligent(ly) ◊ Sie war sehr klug. ♦
eine kluge Frage/Antwort ♦ Er hat das Problem
klug gelöst. ⊜schlau ⊝dumm **2.** wise(ly),
astute(ly) ◊ eine kluge Entscheidung ♦ Sie
handelte äußerst klug. ⊝weise
⊛ hinterher ist man immer klüger it is easy to
be wise after the event aus etw./jdm nicht klug
werden not be able to make head or tail of sth/sb
◊ Ich werde aus dieser Anleitung einfach nicht
klug. ⊝aus etw. nicht schlau werden

Klum·pen ['klʊmpm̩] der <–s, –> lump, clod ◊ aus
einem Klumpen Ton eine Vase formen ♦ Die Masse
bildete kleine Klumpen. ein Klumpen Gold a gold
nugget

km [kilo'meːtɐ] (abbr of Kilometer) km

km/h [kaːlɛmˈhaː] (abbr of Kilometer pro Stunde)
kph ◊ Sie bog mit 30 km/h um die Ecke. ♦ Er fuhr
53 km/h.

knab·bern ['knabɐn] tr+intr v +haben nibble,
gnaw ◊ Das Kaninchen knabberte an einer Karotte.
♦ Erdnüsse knabbern
⊛ an etw. dat zu knabbern haben get to grips
with sth

Knä·cke·brot ['knɛkəbroːt] das <–(e)s, –e> most
sing crispbread ◊ drei Scheiben Knäckebrot

kna·cken ['knakn̩] intr v +haben creak, crack,
crackle ◊ Die Zweige/Seine Fingergelenke
knackten. tr v +haben **1.** crack (open) ◊ Nüsse/
einen Safe knacken; (a lock) break ◊ Sie knackten
das Schloss.; (a car) break into **2.** (fig) crack ◊
einen Code/Jackpot/ein Rätsel knacken imp v
+haben es knackt there is a crackling/creaking
noise

Knacks ['knaks] der <–es, –e> **1.** (fam, fig) blow,
knock ◊ ein Knacks für das Selbstbewusstsein;
(relationship etc.) einen Knacks haben be
marred, be crumbling, be cracking (up)
2. (sound, in glass) crack ◊ Ich hörte einen
Knacks. ♦ Vorsicht, dieses Glas hat einen Knacks.

Knall [knal] der <–(e)s, –e> most sing **1.** bang ◊
Mit einem lauten Knall fiel das Brett zu Boden.
2. (fig) shock, trouble, row
⊛ Knall auf Fall (fam) all of a sudden einen
Knall haben (fam) be bonkers, be raving mad, be
off your rocker

knal·len ['knalən] intr v +haben/sein **1.** +haben
bang, slam, explode, pop, crack ◊ Die Sektkorken
knallten. ♦ Er ließ die Peitsche knallen. **2.** +sein
gegen etw. knallen crash into sth ◊ Sie knallte mit
dem Fahrrad gegen ein Auto. tr v +haben (fam)
1. etw. irgendwohin knallen slam sth down/
somewhere ◊ Er knallte die Haustür ins Schloss.
2. jdm eine/ein paar knallen slap sb (in the face),
clout sb round the ear

knall·hart ['knal'haʳt] adj, adv <knallhärter, am
knallhärtesten> seldom comp/superl fierce(ly),
ruthless(ly), brutal(ly) ◊ Der Wettbewerb war

knallhart. ♦ ein knallharter Bursche ♦ Knallhart
sagte sie ihm die Meinung.

② **knapp** [knap] adj, adv **1.** scarce(ly), meagre(ly) ◊
knappe Rohstoffe ♦ Die Zeit wird zu knapp. ♦ Die
Nudeln waren zu knapp bemessen. jdn/etw. knapp
halten keep sb/sth short (of money); (win, result)
narrow(ly) ◊ ein knappes Ergebnis ♦ Die Mannschaft verlor nur knapp. **2.** when used as an adj,
only before ns just under ◊ Sie zahlten eine knappe
Million Dollar. ♦ Es dauerte knapp fünf Minuten.
3. (clothes) tight(-fitting), short, scanty ◊ eine
knappe Jeans ♦ Dieses T-Shirt ist zu knapp. knapp
sitzend tight(-fitting) **4.** brief(ly), terse(ly),
concise(ly) ◊ mit knappen Worten ♦ Dein Aufsatz
ist etwas zu knapp. ♦ ein knapper Überblick ♦ etw.
knapp beschreiben/zusammenfassen adv
1. closely ◊ Die Kugel verfehlte ihn knapp.
2. (only) just, barely ◊ Als er starb, war er knapp
dreißig. ♦ Der Schuss ging knapp daneben/am Tor
vorbei.

knei·fen ['knaefn̩] <kneift, kniff, hat gekniffen>
tr v pinch ◊ Er kniff sich selbst in den Arm. ♦ Au,
er hat mich gekniffen! ⊝zwicken intr v (fam)
chicken out, back out ◊ Sie hat vor der Klausur
gekniffen.

② **Knei·pe** ['knaepə] die <–, –n> pub, bar ◊ Nach
dem Kino gingen wir noch in die Kneipe.

In Germany, the Kneipe is an important institution. People meet there after the gym, the theatre
or cinema, or just for a social drink. If service is
satisfactory a tip of about 10% is appropriate
(and expected).

kni·cken ['knɪkn̩] tr v +haben snap, bend ◊ Der
Sturm hat die Bäume geknickt. ♦ Der Umschlag
darf nicht geknickt werden. intr v +sein snap ◊
Viele Bäume knickten im Sturm.

② **Knie** [kniː] das <–s, –> knee ◊ Ich habe mir das
Knie angeschlagen. ♦ Sie fiel vor ihr auf die Knie.
♦ Bei seiner Jeans waren die Knie durchgescheuert.
⊛ weiche Knie trembling knees, knees like jelly
in die Knie gehen **1.** sink to your knees, bend
your knees **2.** (fig) be brought to your knees jdn/
etw. in die Knie zwingen (fig) bring sb/sth to
his/her/its knees

knien [kniːn, 'kniːən] <kniet, kniete, hat gekniet>
intr v in South G, Austr, Swiss often +sein kneel ◊
Er kniete auf dem Boden. ♦ Sie kniete vor dem
Altar. ref v sich irgendwohin knien kneel down ◊
Er kniete sich neben den Verletzten/auf den Boden.

kniff [knɪf] pret of kneifen

knis·tern ['knɪstɐn] intr v +haben (fire) crackle;
(paper etc.) rustle mit etw. knistern rustle sth ◊
Er knisterte mit der Alufolie.

Knob·lauch ['knoːplaʊx] der <–(e)s> no pl garlic

Knö·chel ['knœçl̩] der <–s, –> **1.** ankle ◊ Er hat
sich den Knöchel gebrochen. **2.** knuckle ◊ Er
klopfte mit dem Knöchel gegen das Holz.

Kno·chen ['knɔxn̩] der <–s, –> bone ◊ Sie gab
dem Hund einen Knochen. jdm tun alle Knochen
weh every bone in sb's body aches
⊛ bis auf die Knochen abgemagert sein be just
a bag of bones nass bis auf die Knochen soaked
to the skin jdn/sich bis auf die Knochen
blamieren make a proper fool of sb/yourself

A
B
C
D
E
F
G
H
I
J
K
L
M
N
O
P
Q
R
S
T
U
V
W
X
Y
Z

Knö·del ['knøːdl] der <–s, –> dumpling ◊ *Schweinebraten mit Knödeln* ⊖Kloß

ⓩ **Knopf** [knɔpf] der <–(e)s, Knöpfe> button ◊ *einen Knopf annähen* ♦ *Sie drückte auf den Knopf.; (on a door)* knob

Kno·ten ['knoːtn] der <–s, –> **1.** knot ◊ *In der Schnur/ihrem Haar waren Knoten.* ♦ *Sie machte einen doppelten Knoten.* ♦ *Das Schiff fährt über 30 Knoten.* **2.** *(hairstyle)* bun ◊ *Sie hatte ihr Haar zu einem Knoten gebunden.* **3.** MED lump ◊ *ein Knoten in der Brust*

Knül·ler ['knʏlɐ] der <–s, –> *(fam)* sensation, hit ◊ *Der Film ist ein echter Knüller!*

knüp·fen ['knʏpfn] tr v +*haben* **1.** tie ◊ *einen Knoten knüpfen* **2.** *(a carpet)* knot; *(a net)* mesh **3.** *(fig) (hope, conditions etc.)* etw. an etw. acc knüpfen attach sth to sth, pin sth on sth ◊ *Sie knüpfte hohe Erwartungen an die Verhandlungen.* **4.** *(fig) (contacts etc.)* establish ◊ *Es gelang ihm, schnell neue Kontakte zu knüpfen.*

knur·ren ['knʊrən] intr v +*haben* **1.** growl, snarl ◊ *Der Hund knurrte laut.* **2.** *(also fig) (stomach)* rumble ◊ *Ihm knurrte der Magen.*

knusp·rig ['knʊspriç] adj crisp, crusty, crunchy ◊ *knusprige Waffeln* ♦ *Die Ente war sehr knusprig.*

knut·schen ['knuːtʃn] tr+intr v +*haben (fam)* snog, smooch jdn/mit jdm knutschen snog sb, smooch sb ◊ *Mit wem knutscht sie da?*

Koch [kɔx] der <–(e)s, Köche>, **Kö·chin** ['kœçɪn] die <–, –nen> cook ◊ *Sie ist eine begeisterte/ schlechte Köchin.; (in a restaurant etc. also)* chef

ⓩ **ko·chen** ['kɔxn] tr+intr v +*haben* **1.** cook ◊ *Er kann nicht kochen.* ♦ *Wie lange müssen die Kartoffeln noch kochen?* ♦ *Wie kocht man Spargel?; (coffee, tea etc.)* make; *(a meal also)* prepare gut kochen (können) be a good cook Soll ich kochen? Shall I do the cooking? **2.** boil ◊ *Kocht das Wasser schon?* ♦ *Soll ich die Eier kochen oder braten?* etw. zum Kochen bringen bring sth to the boil tr v +*haben* wash at 95°C ◊ *Die Handtücher darf man kochen.*

ⓩ **Kof·fer** ['kɔfɐ] der <–s, –> *(suit)*case, trunk ◊ *den Koffer packen/auspacken*

ⓩ **Kof·fer·raum** ['kɔfɐraʊm] der <–(e)s, Kofferräume> *(car)* boot, trunk ◊ *Sie verstaute die Einkäufe im Kofferraum.*

Kohl [koːl] der <–(e)s> *no pl* cabbage, kale, greens ◊ *ein kräftiger Eintopf mit Kohl*

ⓩ **Koh·le** ['koːlə] die <–, –n> **1.** coal ◊ *Hier wird Kohle abgebaut.* ♦ *Sie legte noch ein paar Kohlen nach.* **2.** *no pl* ARTS charcoal ◊ *Sie zeichnete mit Kohle.* **3.** *no pl (slang)* dosh, dough ◊ *Ich hab' keine Kohle mehr!*

Koh·len·di·o·xid [ˌkoːlənˈdiːˌɔksiːt], **Koh·len·di·o·xyd** [ˌkoːlənˈdiːˌɔksyːt] das <–(e)s> *seldom with the article, no pl (abbr CO₂)* carbon dioxide

Koh·len·hyd·rat ['koːlənhyˌdraːt] das <–(e)s, –e> *seldom with the article* carbohydrate

ⓩ **Kol·le·ge** [kɔˈleːgə] der <–n, –n>, **Kol·le·gin** [kɔˈleːgɪn] die <–, –nen> colleague ◊ *Er ist ein Kollege von mir.* ♦ *Frau Kollegin, ich darf doch sehr bitten!*

Kol·leg·stu·fe [kɔˈleːkʃtuːfə] die <–, –n> 6th form, upper school ◊ *Sie kommt nächstes Jahr in die Kollegstufe.*

The *Kollegstufe*, or *gymnasiale Oberstufe*, consists of grades 11 to 13 of a *Gymnasium* (grammar school) or *Gesamtschule* (comprehensive school). At this level pupils can choose, within certain restrictions, a number of basic courses and two intensive courses in preparation for their *Abitur* exams. Performance in grade 12 and 13 assessed by a point system (together with the final *Abitur* exam results) counts towards the *Abitur* certificate that is required by those who intend to go on to higher education.

Köln [kœln] das <–s> *article only in combination with attribute, no pl* Cologne ◊ *Er lebt in Köln.* box@ Stadt

kom·bi·nie·ren [kɔmbiˈniːrən] <kombiniert, kombinierte, hat kombiniert> intr v deduce, reason, draw a conclusion richtig kombinieren draw the right conclusion tr v combine ◊ *Sie kombinierte das rote Kostüm mit den schwarzen Schuhen.*

ⓩ **ko·misch** ['koːmɪʃ] adj funny, comic(al) ◊ *eine komische Geschichte* ♦ *Ich finde deine Scherze gar nicht komisch!* ⊖lustig, amüsant adj, adv strange(ly), odd(ly), funny(-ily) ◊ *Gestern ist mir eine komische Sache passiert.* ♦ *Dieser Zufall ist wirklich komisch.* ♦ *Warum verhält er sich so komisch?* jdm ist/wird komisch sb feels/starts to feel strange/funny ⊖eigenartig, seltsam, merkwürdig, sonderbar

Kom·ma ['kɔmaː] das <–s, –s *or* –ta> **1.** comma ◊ *Kommt hier ein Komma hin?* ♦ *ein Komma setzen* ♦ *Ein Relativsatz wird durch ein Komma abgetrennt.* **2.** MATH (decimal) point ◊ *auf eine Stelle hinter dem Komma runden*

ⓩ **kom·men** ['kɔmən] <kommt, kam, ist gekommen> intr v **1.** come ◊ *Wir kamen relativ früh nach Hause.* ♦ *Sie kam gestern nicht zur Arbeit.* ♦ *Kommst du jetzt endlich?* ♦ *Der Wind kommt aus östlicher Richtung.* ♦ *Am Wochenende kommen meine Eltern.* ♦ *Kommst du auch auf die Party/mit ins Theater?* ♦ *Woher kommt das Geld?* ♦ *Der Lottogewinn kommt zur rechten Zeit.* als Erster/ Letzter etc. kommen come first/last etc. an etw. acc kommen come (in)to sth ◊ *Wann kam er an die Macht/Regierung?* etw. kommt überraschend sth comes as a surprise etw. kommt ungelegen/ nicht gelegen sth is inconvenient etw. kommt daher, dass the reason for sth is **2.** get ◊ *Weißt du, wie man zum Museum kommt?* ♦ *in Gefahr/ Schwierigkeiten kommen* **3.** arrive ◊ *Wann kommt der nächste Zug?* ♦ *Sie ist gerade aus Rom gekommen.* ♦ *Ist noch mehr Post gekommen?* ♦ *Im März kommen die ersten Blüten.* zu früh/spät kommen be early/late **4.** jdn kommen lassen send for sb ◊ *Er ließ einen Arzt kommen.* etw. kommen lassen order sth ◊ *Sie ließ ein kaltes Büffet kommen.* **5.** aus München/Italien etc. kommen be from Munich/Italy etc. ◊ *Sie kommt aus München/ Italien.* ♦ *Woher kommst du?* **6.** *(fam)* irgendwohin kommen go somewhere ◊ *Wohin kommen diese Töpfe?* **7.** in/auf etw. acc kommen go to sth, be admitted to sth ◊ *Sie kommt im September in die Schule/aufs Gymnasium.* **8.** turn out ◊ *Alles kam so, wie ich es gehofft hatte. Das musste ja so kommen!* It was bound to happen. **9.** jdm kommt etw. sth springs to sb's mind jdm kommt eine

Idee/ein Einfall sb has an idea **10.** *(a solution)* auf etw. acc kommen come to sth, figure sth out ◊ *Wie bist du so rasch auf diese Zahl gekommen?*; *(information)* recall sth, remember sth ◊ *Er kam einfach nicht auf seinen Namen.* wie kommst du auf ...? what makes you think of ...? **11.** etw./jd kommt auf jdn/etw. there is sth/sb for sb/sth ◊ *Auf zwei Einwohner kommt im Schnitt ein Pkw.* etw. kommt auf etw. acc sth (is added) to ◊ *Auf 10 Teile Mehl kommt 1 Teil Butter.* **12.** *(fam)* hinter etw. acc kommen find sth out, figure sth out, suss sth ◊ *Er kam zufällig hinter ihr Geheimnis.* **13.** etw. kommt im Fernsehen/Kino etc. sth is on television/ on at the cinema etc. **14.** ins Stottern/Wanken etc. kommen begin to stutter/totter etc. ◊ *Die Ladung kam ins Rutschen.* **15.** zu etw. kommen gain sth, obtain sth ◊ *Durch ihre Heirat kam sie zu großem Reichtum.* ♦ allmählich wieder zu Kräften kommen **16.** zu etw. kommen get round to sth ◊ *Ich komme gerade nicht dazu, ihn anzurufen.* imp v es kam zu etw. there was sth, sth occurred ◊ *Beim Abendessen kam es zum Streit.* ◉ das kommt davon, wenn that's what happens if wie kommst du etc. dazu how dare you etc. wieder zu sich kommen come round jd lässt auf jdn nichts kommen sb won't hear anything said against sb

Kom·men·tar [kɔmɛn'taːʳ] der <-s, -e> comment, commentary ◊ *einen Kommentar abfassen/ schreiben* ♦ *Auf deinen Kommentar kann ich verzichten.* einen Kommentar zu etw. abgeben comment on sth

② **kom·mer·zi·ell** [kɔmɛr'tsi̯ɛl] adj, adv *seldom comp/ superl* commercial(ly) ◊ *Diese Datenbank nutzen auch kommerzielle Anbieter.* ♦ *kommerziell erfolgreich* ♦ *Diese Art von Musik ist ihm zu kommerziell.*

Kom·mi·li·to·ne [kɔmili'toːnə] der <-n, -n>,
Kom·mi·li·to·nin [kɔmili'toːnɪn] die <-, –nen> fellow student ◊ *Sie ist eine ehemalige Kommilitonin von mir.*

② **Kom·mis·si·on** [kɔmɪ'si̯oːn] die <-, -en> **1.** commission **2.** *(of experts)* committee ◉ (jdm) etw. in Kommission geben give sth (to a dealer) for sale on commission

Kom·mo·de [kɔ'moːdə] die <-, -n> chest (of drawers) ◊ *Sie verstaute die Handtücher in der Kommode.*

kom·mu·nal [kɔmu'naːl] adj, adv local(ly), municipal(ly), by the (local) council, by local government ◊ *Die kommunalen Abgaben wurden erhöht.* ♦ *Die Energieversorgung wird kommunal verwaltet.*

② **Kom·mu·ni·ka·ti·on** [kɔmunika'tsi̯oːn] die <-, -en> *most sing* communication ◊ *Die Kommunikation erfolgte über E-Mail und Telefon.* ♦ *die Kommunikation von Daten*

Ko·mö·die [ko'møːdi̯ə] die <-, –n> comedy ◊ *Tragödie und Komödie sind Gattungen des Dramas.* ♦ *Der Film war eine Komödie.*

Kom·pa·ra·tiv ['kɔmparatiːf] der <-s, -e> comparative ◊ *„Besser" ist der Komparativ von „gut".*

kom·pen·sie·ren [kɔmpɛn'ziːrən] <kompensiert, kompensierte, hat kompensiert> tr v compensate for, make up for ◊ *Die Mannschaft kompensierte den Ausfall eines Spielers.* etw. durch etw. acc kompensieren make up for sth by sth

kom·plett [kɔm'plɛt] adj, adv **1.** complete(ly), entire(ly), (as a) whole ◊ *Ist die Gruppe komplett?* ♦ *Die komplette Namensliste hing aus.* ♦ *Sie konnte die Anforderungen nicht komplett erfüllen.* ♦ *Sie verkauft das Tafelservice nur komplett.* ⊖vollständig **2.** *(fam)* utter(ly), complete(ly), absolute(ly) ◊ *Dieser Plan war kompletter/der komplette Wahnsinn.* ⊖absolut, völlig

Kom·pli·ze [kɔm'pliːtsə] der <-n, -n>,
Kom·pli·zin [kɔm'pliːtsɪn] die <-, –nen> accomplice ◊ *seine/die mutmaßlichen Komplizen* jdn zu seinem/zum Komplizen machen make sb your/an accomplice

② **kom·pli·ziert** [kɔmpli'tsiːɐt] adj complicated, intricate ◊ *Er ist ein komplizierter Mensch.* ♦ *Die Rechenaufgabe war kompliziert.* adv etw. kompliziert ausdrücken say/express sth in a complicated way/manner

Kom·po·nist [kɔmpo'nɪst] der <-en, -en>,
Kom·po·nis·tin [kɔmpo'nɪstɪn] die <-, –nen> composer ◊ *Sein Vater war Komponist.* ♦ *eine bekannte Komponistin*

Kom·po·si·tum [kɔm'poːzitʊm] das <-s, Komposita> compound ⊖Zusammensetzung

Kon·di·tor [kɔn'diːtoːɐ̯] der <-s, -en>,
Kon·di·to·rin [kɔndi'toːrɪn] die <-, –nen> confectioner, pastry cook ◊ *Er ist Konditor.* ♦ *eine gelernte Konditorin*

② **Kon·dom** [kɔn'doːm] das *or* der <-s, -e> condom ◊ *ein Kondom benutzen* ⊖Präservativ

Kon·duk·teur [kɔndʊk'tøːɐ̯] der <-s, -e>,
Kon·duk·teu·rin [kɔndʊk'tøːrɪn] die <-, –nen> *(Swiss, also outd)* conductor, ticket collector ◊ *Der Kondukteur kam ins Abteil.* ♦ *Sie arbeitet als Kondukteurin.*

② **Kon·fe·renz** [kɔnfe'rɛnts] die <-, -en> conference, meeting, committee ◊ *an einer Konferenz teilnehmen* ♦ *Sie hielt einen Vortrag auf der Konferenz.*

② **Kon·fes·si·on** [kɔnfɛ'si̯oːn] die <-, -en> denomination ◊ *Welcher Konfession gehören Sie an?*

② **Kon·fi·tü·re** [kɔnfi'tyːrə] die <-, –n> jam ◊ *ein Glas Konfitüre*

② **Kö·nig** ['køːnɪç] der <-s, -e> king ◊ *Welcher König herrschte damals?* ♦ *Georg IV war König von England.* ♦ *Der König steht im Schach.* ◉ die Heiligen Drei Könige the Three Kings

Kö·ni·gin ['køːnɪgɪn] die <-, –nen> queen ◊ *Königin Elisabeth II* ♦ *Sie wurde zur Königin gekrönt.*

kon·ju·gie·ren [kɔnju'giːrən] <konjugiert, konjugierte, hat konjugiert> tr v conjugate, inflect ◊ *lateinische Verben konjugieren* ⊖beugen

Kon·junk·ti·on [kɔnjʊŋk'tsi̯oːn] die <-, -en> conjunction ◊ *Die Teilsätze sind durch eine Konjunktion verbunden.* ♦ *Jupiter steht in Konjunktion mit der Sonne.*

Kon·junk·tiv ['kɔnjʊŋktiːf] der <-s, -e> subjunctive ◊ *Indirekte Rede steht immer im Konjunktiv.*

> The subjunctive is used to express a wish, an assumption, uncertainty or politeness: *Könnten Sie mir bitte helfen? — Wenn ich das gewusst hätte, wäre ich daheim geblieben! — Wenn es nur nicht so kalt wäre! — Ich würde sagen, hier stimmt etwas nicht. — Ich würde hier nicht baden.* ▶

A
B
C
D
E
F
G
H
I
J
K
L
M
N
O
P
Q
R
S
T
U
V
W
X
Y
Z

▶The simple form of *Konjunktiv II*, e.g. *flösse* (of *fließen*), *fröre* (of *frieren*), *stände* and *stünde* (of *stehen*), is becoming obsolete for most verbs but is generally used for auxiliaries and modal verbs, e.g.: *wäre, hätte, würde, müsste, könnte, möchte, dürfte, sollte, wollte.* For other verbs *Konjunktiv II* is usually constructed with *würde* + infinitive. To indicate the past, *Konjunktiv II* is constructed with *hätte/wäre* + past participle: *Wenn ich meinen Schlüssel nicht* **verloren hätte**, *dann* **wäre** *ich in meine Wohnung* **gegangen** *und* **hätte** *nicht bei Ihnen* **geklingelt**, *Herr Maier!* *Konjunktiv I* is used predominantly in written language to indicate reported speech: *Und dann, so der Minister,* **seien** *die Rahmenbedingungen zu prüfen. Seine Partei* **habe** *diesbezüglich die ersten Schritte eingeleitet und* **wolle** *rasch eine Lösung herbeiführen.* In spoken language the indicative is generally used to indicate reported speech: *Du hast doch gesagt, dass du mich liebst.*

Kon·junk·tur [kɔnjʊŋk'tuːɐ̯] die <-, –en> economy, economic situation, economic activity ◊ *Maßnahmen, um die Konjunktur anzukurbeln*

Kon·kur·renz [kɔnkʊ'rɛnts, kɔŋkʊ'rɛnts] die <–> no pl **1.** competition ◊ *Unser Buch steht nicht in Konkurrenz zu Fachbüchern.* ♦ *Er ist keine Konkurrenz für mich.*; *(more intense)* rivalry jdm/etw. Konkurrenz machen compete with sb/sth in Konkurrenz mit jdm/etw. treten enter into competition with sb/sth **2.** die/jds Konkurrenz sb's competitor(s), sb's rivals ◊ *Die Firma muss gegen die Konkurrenz bestehen.*

◉ außer Konkurrenz outside the (main) competition

Kon·kurs [kɔn'kʊrs, kɔŋ'kʊrs] der <–es, –e> bankruptcy, insolvency ◊ *Die Firma steht kurz vor dem Konkurs.* Konkurs anmelden file for bankruptcy Konkurs machen, in Konkurs gehen go bankrupt, go into receivership

② **kön·nen¹** ['kœnən] <kann, konnte, hat können> [modal v] +*inf* **1.** *(ability, possibility)* jd kann laufen/sprechen etc. sb can walk/speak etc., sb is able to walk/speak etc. ◊ *Kann das Kind schon lesen?* ♦ *Kann ich bei dir schlafen?* jd kann gut kochen/tanzen etc. sb can cook/dance etc. well, sb is a good cook/dancer etc. **2.** *(permission, prohibition)* jd kann etw. tun sb can do sth, sb may do sth ◊ *Du kannst nicht gehen, bevor du fertig bist.* ♦ *Kann ich mir ein Glas Wein einschenken?* **3.** *(with good reason)* jd kann etw. tun sb can do sth ◊ *Das kannst du mir ruhig glauben!* **4.** *(probability)* jd/etw. kann etw. tun sb/sth may do sth, sb/sth might do sth ◊ *Sie kann jederzeit auftauchen.* ♦ *Da könntest du Recht haben.* es kann sein, dass maybe, it is possible that Kann sein! Maybe!, Perhaps!

② **kön·nen²** ['kœnən] <kann, konnte, hat gekonnt> [tr v] **1.** know ◊ *Kannst du Karate/Yoga?* ♦ *Sie kann das Gedicht schon auswendig.* Deutsch/Englisch etc. können speak German/English etc. Bridge/Schach etc. können (know how to) play bridge/chess etc. ich etc. kann es (gut) I etc. can do it (well) **2.** für etw. etwas/nichts können be/

not be responsible for sth Ich kann nichts dafür! It's not my fault., I'm not to blame., I can't help it. Was kann ich (denn) dafür? Why are you/is he etc. blaming me? [intr v] *(fam)* **1.** irgendwohin können be allowed to go somewhere ◊ *Mit dem Ausschlag kann er nicht ins Schwimmbad.* kann ich ...? can I go ...?, may I go ...? ◊ *Kann ich mit Uli ins Kino?* **2.** be able to go on ◊ *Kannst du noch? Mir geht allmählich die Puste aus.* jd kann nicht mehr sb cannot go on

◉ du kannst/er kann etc. mich mal *(taboo)* you/he etc. can stuff it

② **konn·te** ['kɔntə] *pret of* können¹, können²

kon·se·quent [kɔnze'kvɛnt] [adj, adv] **1.** consistent(ly) ◊ *eine konsequente Umsetzung des Konzepts* ♦ *Sie führten den Ausbau der Firma konsequent fort.* ♦ *Er ist in dieser Hinsicht nicht konsequent genug.* **2.** strict(ly), resolute(ly), rigorous(ly) ◊ *Sie waren konsequente Gegner der Abtreibung.* ♦ *Diese Regeln müssen konsequent eingehalten werden.*

② **Kon·se·quenz** [kɔnze'kvɛnts] die <-, –en> **1.** consequence, repercussion, effect, result ◊ *Du solltest aus diesem Vorfall Konsequenzen ziehen.* ♦ *Das wird Konsequenzen haben!* **2.** resolution, determination ◊ *Sie setzte sich mit Konsequenz durch.*

② **kon·ser·va·tiv** [kɔnzɛr'vaːtiːf, '– – – –] [adj, adv] conservative(ly) ◊ *eine konservative Partei* ♦ *Seine Ansichten sind ziemlich konservativ.* ♦ *Sie kleidet sich konservativ.*

Kon·ser·ve [kɔn'zɛrvə] die <-, –n> **1.** tin, can ◊ *Bohnen aus der Konserve* ⊝Dose **2.** Konserven tinned/canned/preserved food ◊ *Sie ernähren sich hauptsächlich von Konserven.*

Kon·su·lat [kɔnzu'laːt] das <-(e)s, –e> consulate ◊ *zum Konsulat gehen*

② **Kon·takt** [kɔn'takt] der <-(e)s, –e> *most sing* contact ◊ *Sie hat den Kontakt zu mir abgebrochen.* ♦ *einen elektrischen Kontakt herstellen* in Kontakt mit jdm stehen, Kontakt mit/zu jdm haben be in contact/touch with sb mit jdm Kontakt aufnehmen, mit jdm in Kontakt treten contact sb, get in(to) contact with sb, get in touch with sb Kontakte zu jdm/etw. haben have dealings with sb/sth; *(a dangerous animal, substance etc.)* mit etw. in Kontakt kommen, in Kontakt mit etw. sein come into contact with sth

② **Kon·ti·nent** [kɔnti'nɛnt] der <-(e)s, –e> continent ◊ *der europäische Kontinent*

◉ der Schwarze Kontinent the Dark Continent

kon·ti·nu·ier·lich [kɔntinu'iːɐ̯lɪç] [adj, adv] *when used as an adj, mostly before ns (lofty)* steady(-ily), continuous(ly) ◊ *eine kontinuierliche Verbesserung der Situation* ♦ *kontinuierlich verlaufen* ⊝beständig

② **Kon·to** ['kɔntoː] das <-s, Konten> account ◊ *ein Konto eröffnen* ♦ *Ich möchte 500 Euro von meinem Konto abheben.*

◉ etw. geht auf jds Konto, etw. geht auf das Konto von jdm *(fam)* sb is responsible for sth

Kon·to·aus·zug ['kɔntoˌaʊ̯stsuːk] der <-(e)s, Kontoauszüge> (bank) statement

Kon·to·stand ['kɔntoˌʃtant] der <-(e)s, Kontostände> bank balance ◊ *den Kontostand abfragen*

kon·tra [kɔn'traː] [prep] against ◊ *eine Entscheidung pro oder kontra Atomenergie* ⊝gegen ⊛pro

② Kon·trol·le [kɔn'trɔlə] die <–, –n> **1.** supervision ◊ *unter ärztlicher Kontrolle abnehmen* **2.** control ◊ *außer Kontrolle geraten* ♦ *die Kontrolle über etw.* [acc] *haben*

kon·trol·lie·ren [kɔntrɔ'liːrən] <kontrolliert, kontrollierte, hat kontrolliert> [tr v] **1.** check ◊ *Lassen Sie regelmäßig Ihren Blutdruck kontrollieren.*; *(more formal)* monitor, supervise ◊ *Der Waffenhandel muss stärker kontrolliert werden.* **2.** control ◊ *Er konnte seine Emotionen nicht kontrollieren.*

kon·ven·ti·o·nell [kɔnvɛntsjo'nɛl] [adj, adv] conventional(ly), conservative(ly) ◊ *konventionelle Umgangsformen* ♦ *Er ist mir zu konventionell.* ♦ *Sie kleidet sich sehr konventionell.*; *(methods also)* traditional(ly) ◊ *konventionelle Medizin* ♦ *Patienten konventionell behandeln* konventionell bewirtschaften farm in the traditional way

② kon·zen·trie·ren [kɔntsɛn'triːrən] <konzentriert, konzentrierte, hat konzentriert> [tr v] focus, concentrate ◊ *Konzentrieren Sie alle Ressourcen auf dieses Projekt.* [ref v] **1.** sich (auf etw. [acc]) konzentrieren concentrate (on sth) ◊ *Ich kann mich einfach nicht konzentrieren.* **2.** sich irgendwo konzentrieren be concentrated somewhere ◊ *Der Tourismus konzentriert sich an der Küste.*

Kon·zept [kɔn'tsɛpt] das <–(e)s, –e> **1.** plan ◊ *ein detailliertes Konzept vorlegen* **2.** draft etw. im Konzept ausarbeiten write/make a draft of sth ⊛ *jdn aus dem Konzept bringen* put sb off aus dem Konzept geraten/kommen lose the/your thread etw. passt jdm nicht ins Konzept sth doesn't suit sb, sth doesn't fit in with sb's plans

Kon·zern [kɔn'tsɛʳn] der <–(e)s, –e> group (of companies)

② Kon·zert [kɔn'tsɛʳt] das <–(e)s, –e> **1.** concert ◊ *Heute gehe ich ins Konzert.* **2.** concerto ◊ *ein Konzert für Cello und Orchester*

ko·o·pe·rie·ren [koʔope'riːrən] <kooperiert, kooperierte, hat kooperiert> [intr v] *(lofty)* (mit jdm) kooperieren collaborate (with sb), work together (with sb)

② Kopf [kɔpf] der <–(e)s, Köpfe> **1.** *(also fig)* head ◊ *Auf meine Frage schüttelte er nur den Kopf.* ♦ *Die Kosten betragen pro Kopf 250 Euro.* ♦ *der Kopf eines Dokuments* **2.** mind ◊ *Er ist ein schlauer Kopf.* **3.** leader, head ◊ *der Kopf einer Organisation* **4.** ein Kopf Salat a (head of) lettuce ein Kopf Rotkohl a (head of) red cabbage; *(of asparagus)* tip **5.** *(of a bottle)* top ⊛ Kopf und Kragen riskieren risk everything, take a big/huge risk den/seinen Kopf aus der Schlinge ziehen save your bacon Kopf hoch chin up einen kühlen Kopf bewahren stay calm einen roten Kopf bekommen go red über jds Kopf hinweg without consulting sb den Kopf voll haben have got a lot of things on your mind den Kopf mit etw. voll haben have got sth on your mind da kann man sich nur an den Kopf fassen/greifen *(fam)* you can only laugh (really) etw. geht jdm nicht (mehr) aus dem Kopf, etw. will jdm nicht aus dem Kopf gehen sb can't get sth out of their head sich [dat] etw. durch den Kopf gehen lassen have a think about sth den Kopf hängen lassen be despondent etw. auf den Kopf hauen *(fam) (money)* blow sth den Kopf hinhalten (müssen) *(fam)* (have to) take the

blame sich keinen Kopf machen not worry seinen Kopf riskieren risk your neck, take a risk Köpfe rollen *(fig)* heads roll sich [dat] etw. aus dem Kopf schlagen forget about sth jdm schwirrt der Kopf sb's head is spinning sich [dat] etw. in den Kopf setzen get sth into your head Kopf stehen *(fam)* go mad nicht wissen, wo einem der Kopf steht not know whether you're coming or going jdm zu Kopf steigen go to sb's head etw. auf den Kopf stellen *(fam)* turn sth upside down jdn vor den Kopf stoßen *(fam)* offend sb jdm den Kopf verdrehen *(fam)* turn sb's head den Kopf verlieren panic jdm über den Kopf wachsen get too much for sb jdm etw. an den Kopf werfen hurl sth at sb sich den Kopf zerbrechen *(fam)* rack your brains jdm den Kopf zurechtrücken/zurechtsetzen *(fam)* set sb straight

Kopf·schmerz ['kɔpfʃmɛʳts] der <–es, –en> *most pl* Kopfschmerz(en) headache ◊ *Von dem Lärm bekomme ich Kopfschmerzen.* ⊛ *etw. bereitet/macht jdm Kopfschmerzen (fam)* sth is a headache for sb

② Ko·pie [ko'piː] die <–, –n> copy ◊ *von einer Urkunde/Datei eine Kopie anfertigen* ♦ *die Kopie eines Rubensgemäldes*

② ko·pie·ren [ko'piːrən] <kopiert, kopierte, hat kopiert> [tr v] **1.** copy ◊ *CDs kopieren* ♦ *Der Inhalt dieser Website darf kopiert werden.*; *(documents, papers etc.)* (photo)copy **2.** copy, imitate ◊ *Diese Band kopiert die Beatles.* ♦ *ein Verfahren kopieren*

② Ko·pie·rer [ko'piːrɐ] der <–s, –> (photo)copier

② Ko·ran [ko'raːn] der <–s> *no pl (always* der Koran*)* the Koran

Korb [kɔʳp] der <–(e)s, Körbe> basket ◊ *Sie legte ihre Einkäufe in einen Korb.* ♦ *ein Korb (voller) Kirschen* ♦ *einen Korb werfen* ⊛ *einen Korb bekommen* get turned down jdm einen Korb geben turn sb down

Kor·ken ['kɔʳkŋ] der <–s, –> cork ◊ *den Korken einer Flasche ziehen*

Kor·ken·zie·her ['kɔʳkŋtsiːɐ] der <–s, –> corkscrew

② Korn¹ [kɔʳn] das <–(e)s, Körner> **1.** grain ◊ *Die Hühner pickten die Körner auf.* ♦ *einige Körner Reis* **2.** corn, grain ◊ *Die Ernte kann beginnen, sobald das Korn reif ist.*

Korn² [kɔʳn] der <–(e)s, –> *(fam)* a strong clear spirit distilled from various types of grain ◊ *Er bestellte zwei Bier und zwei Korn.*

② Kör·per ['kœʳpɐ] der <–s, –> **1.** body ◊ *ein athletischer Körper* ♦ *das Zeichnen geometrischer Körper* **2.** torso ◊ *Der Ausschlag ist nur am Körper, nicht an den Armen und Beinen.*

Kor·rek·tur [kɔrɛk'tuːɐ] die <–, –en> *(lofty)* correction ◊ *Korrekturen vornehmen*; amendment ◊ *Der politische Kurs bedarf einer Korrektur.*

Kor·ri·dor ['kɔridoːɐ] der <–s, –e> corridor ◊ *Vom Korridor aus führt eine Tür ins Wohnzimmer.*

② kor·ri·gie·ren [kɔri'giːrən] <korrigiert, korrigierte, hat korrigiert> [tr v] **1.** mark, correct ◊ *eine Klassenarbeit korrigieren* **2.** correct ◊ *einen Sehfehler korrigieren*; amend ◊ *Einige Firmen mussten nach dem ersten Quartal ihre Zahlen deutlich korrigieren.* ⊜berichtigen

Ko·se·na·me ['koːzənaːmə] der <–ns, –en> pet

A B C D E F G H I J K L M N O P Q R S T U V W X Y Z

name
Kos·me·tik [kɔs'meːtɪk] die <–, –a> **1.** cosmetics ◊ *allergiegetestete Kosmetika* **2.** *no pl (pej)* etw. ist reine Kosmetik sth is purely cosmetic

Kost [kɔst] die <–> *no pl* food ◊ *ballaststoffreiche Kost* Kost und Logis board and lodging

kost·bar ['kɔstbaːʳ] [adj] valuable, precious ◊ *ein kostbares Schmuckstück* ◆ *Meine Zeit ist kostbar.* [adv] exquisitely ◊ *eine kostbar verzierte Handschrift aus dem Mittelalter*

② **kos·ten** ['kɔstn̩] [tr v] +haben **1.** cost ◊ *Diese Reise kostet Unsummen von Geld.* etw. kostet jdn ... sb pays ... for sth ◊ *Dieses Kleid hat mich 300 Euro gekostet.* Wie viel/Was kostet/kosten ...? How much is/are ...? **2.** etw. kostet jdn etw. sth costs sb sth ◊ *Dieser Fehler kostet mich meinen Job.* **3.** take ◊ *Eine Sprache zu lernen, kostet viel Zeit und Energie.* [tr+intr v] (etw./von etw.) kosten try (sth), taste (sth) ◊ *Koste mal von der Soße.* ◆ *Hast du die Suppe schon gekostet?* ⊜versuchen, probieren

⊛ **sich** [dat] etw. etwas/viel kosten lassen *(fam)* spend a lot (of money) on sth koste es, was es wolle whatever the cost

Kos·ten ['kɔstn̩] die <–> *only pl* costs ◊ *Es fallen hohe Kosten an.* ◆ *nur geringe Kosten verursachen* Kosten sparend money-saving, cost-saving

⊛ **auf seine Kosten kommen** *(fam)* get what you want/need **auf jds Kosten** at sb's expense **auf Kosten** ... [gen] at the expense of sth ◊ *Das Essen ging auf seine Kosten.* ◆ *Straßenplanung auf Kosten der Natur*

kos·ten·los ['kɔstn̩loːs] [adj, adv] no comp/superl free (of charge) ◊ *kostenlose Beratung* ◆ *Diese Broschüre gibt es kostenlos.* ◆ *etw. kostenlos verteilen* ⊜gratis, unentgeltlich

köst·lich ['kœstlɪç] [adj, adv] **1.** delicious(ly) ◊ *ein köstliches Rezept* ◆ *Der Nachtisch war einfach köstlich.* **2.** marvellous(ly), priceless(ly) ◊ *eine köstliche Satire* ◆ *Ich fand die Komödie köstlich.* sich köstlich unterhalten have a marvellous time

kost·spie·lig ['kɔstʃpiːlɪç] [adj] expensive ◊ *ein kostspieliges Hobby* ◆ *Ein eigenes Auto ist mir zu kostspielig.*

② **Kos·tüm** [kɔs'tyːm] das <–s, –> **1.** *(for ladies)* suit ◊ *Sie trug ein elegantes dunkelblaues Kostüm.* **2.** costume

> Strictly speaking, the word *Kostüm* is used to describe the clothing worn on particular occasions (e.g. during the carnival season or at other festivals) or for particular pursuits (such as hunting, dancing, swimming). Nowadays, the term *Kostüm* is mostly used in connection with fancy dress or to describe ladies' formal suits that are made up of a jacket and skirt.

Ko·te·lett [kɔt'lɛt] das <–s, –s> chop, cutlet

kot·zen ['kɔtsn̩] [intr v] +haben *(rude)* puke, throw up

krab·beln ['krabl̩n] [intr v] +sein crawl ◊ *Kann die Kleine schon krabbeln?* ◆ *Da krabbelt ein Käfer.*

Krach [krax] der <–(e)s, Kräche> **1.** *no pl* noise, row, din ◊ *Die Kinder machten ohrenbetäubenden Krach.* **2.** crash ◊ *Die Teekanne fiel mit lautem Krach zu Boden.* **3.** *(fam)* row ◊ *Meine Eltern haben Krach.*

⊛ **Krach machen/schlagen** *(fam)* kick up/make a fuss

kra·chen ['kraxn̩] [intr v] +haben/sein **1.** +haben *(timber, ice)* creak ◊ *Das Eis krachte gefährlich unter meinen Füßen.* Ein Schuss krachte laut. ◊ *(fireworks)* go off **2.** +sein break (with a crash) ◊ *Vorsicht, wenn der Ast kracht, fällst du tief!* **3.** +sein gegen etw. krachen crash into sth [imp v] +haben **1.** es kracht there is a loud noise **2.** *(fam)* es kracht there's a crash ◊ *An dieser Kreuzung kracht es oft.*

⊛ **es krachen lassen** *(fam)* really let rip **es kracht bei jdm** *(fam)* sb has a row ◊ *Bei uns hat es gestern heftig gekracht.*

② **Kraft** [kraft] die <–, Kräfte> **1.** strength ◊ *Ich habe nicht genug Kraft, um diesen Koffer zu tragen.* ◆ *Der Marathon kostete ihn viel Kraft.* über jds Kräfte gehen be too much for sb etw. aus eigener Kraft schaffen manage (to do) sth on your own, do sth single-handedly **2.** power ◊ *die Kraft der Magie* **3.** employee, worker ◊ *gelernte Kräfte* **4.** force ◊ *Diese Partei ist die stärkste Kraft im Parlament.* ◆ *elektromagnetische Kraft*

⊛ **die treibende Kraft sein** be the driving force **außer Kraft sein** be no longer in force **in Kraft sein** be in force etw. **außer Kraft setzen** cancel sth, annul sth etw. **in Kraft setzen** enforce sth

Kraft·fahr·zeug ['kraftfaːʳtsɔɪk] das <–(e)s, –e> *(form) (abbr* Kfz*)* motor vehicle

② **kräf·tig** ['krɛftɪç] [adj] **1.** strong ◊ *ein kräftiger Bursche* ◆ *kräftige Kursgewinne* ◆ *Dieser Käse ist sehr kräftig im Geschmack.*; *(blow etc.)* powerful **2.** *only before ns* hearty ◊ *eine kräftige Brühe* [adv] **1.** strongly, powerfully ◊ *ein kräftig gebauter Mann* kräftig zupacken get down to work **2.** a lot ◊ *Die Mieten sind kräftig gestiegen.* jdn kräftig auslachen have a good laugh at sb **3.** sich kräftig ausdrücken use (some) strong language/words

Kraft·stoff ['kraftʃtɔf] der <–(e)s, –e> fuel ⊜Treibstoff

② **Kraft·werk** ['kraftvɛʳk] das <–(e)s, –e> power station

Kra·gen ['kraːgn̩] der <–s, – *or* Krägen> collar ◊ *ein Hemd mit weißem Kragen*

⊛ **jdm geht es an den Kragen** *(fam)* sb is/will be in for it **jdm platzt der Kragen** *(fam)* sb explodes jdm/einem Tier den Kragen umdrehen *(fam)* wring sb's/an animal's neck

Kram [kraːm] der <–(e)s> *no pl (fam, pej)* **1.** stuff ◊ *Lass deinen Kram nicht überall rumliegen!* **2.** business ◊ *Lass mich doch mit diesem Kram zufrieden!*

⊛ **jdm in den Kram passen** suit sb

Krampf [krampf] der <–(e)s, Krämpfe> **1.** cramp ◊ *einen Krampf im rechten Oberschenkel bekommen/haben* **2.** *(fam, pej)* rubbish ◊ *Was soll der Krampf?*

Kran [kraːn] der <–(e)s, Kräne> crane

② **krank** [kraŋk] [adj] <kränker, am kränksten> ill, sick ◊ *unheilbar krank* ◆ *Er ist vor jedem Auftritt krank vor Aufregung.* ◆ *Eure Streitereien machen mich ganz krank.* ⊜gesund

② **Kran·ke** ['kraŋkə] der/die <–n, die Kranken> *but: ein Kranker/eine Kranke* ill person; *(in a hospital etc.)* patient psychisch Kranke the mentally ill box⊛ Substantivierung

krän·ken [ˈkrɛŋkŋ̩] [tr v] +*haben* wound, hurt ◊ *Seine Worte haben mich tief gekränkt.* jdn in seiner Ehre kränken wound sb's honour

② **Kran·ken·haus** [ˈkraŋkŋ̩haʊs] das <–es, Krankenhäuser> hospital ◊ *jdn ins Krankenhaus einliefern* ◆ *aus dem Krankenhaus entlassen werden* im Krankenhaus liegen be in hospital ⊖Klinik

② **Kran·ken·kas·sa** [ˈkraŋkŋ̩kasaː] die <–, Krankenkassen> *(Austr)* → Krankenkasse

② **Kran·ken·kas·se** [ˈkraŋkŋ̩kasə] die <–, –n> health insurance (company) ◊ *die gesetzliche/private Krankenkasse*

> In Germany, health insurance is a compulsory form of insurance, which pays for medical treatment should you become ill. In order to visit a doctor or dentist, you need an insurance document, which includes the following information: the name of the relevant health insurance company; the surname and Christian name of the person insured; his or her date of birth, address, health insurance number and insurance status; and the date from which medical cover is to be provided.

② **Kran·ken·pfle·ger** [ˈkraŋkŋ̩pfleːgɐ] der <–s, –>, **Kran·ken·pfle·ge·rin** [ˈkraŋkŋ̩pfleːgərɪn] die <–, –nen> nurse ◊ *Er ist Krankenpfleger.* ◆ *eine erfahrene Krankenpflegerin*

② **Kran·ken·schein** [ˈkraŋkŋ̩ʃaɛn] der <–(e)s, –e> health insurance certificate ◊ *eine Behandlung auf Krankenschein*

② **Kran·ken·schwes·ter** [ˈkraŋkŋ̩ʃvɛstɐ] die <–, –n> nurse ◊ *Sie ist Krankenschwester von Beruf.* ◆ *die erfahrenste Krankenschwester der Station*

② **Kran·ken·wa·gen** [ˈkraŋkŋ̩vaːgŋ̩] der <–s, –> ambulance ◊ *Rufen Sie einen Krankenwagen!*

krank·haft [ˈkraŋkhaft] [adj, adv] <krankhafter, am krankhaftesten> *seldom comp/superl* **1.** *mostly before ns* abnormal(ly) ◊ *eine krankhafte Störung des Essverhaltens* krankhaft verändert sein be abnormal **2.** pathological(ly) ◊ *krankhafte Selbstüberschätzung* ◆ *Sie ist krankhaft eifersüchtig.*

② **Krank·heit** [ˈkraŋkhaɛt] die <–, –en> disease, illness, sickness ◊ *Er leidet an einer ansteckenden Krankheit.* ◆ *Sie musste wegen Krankheit absagen.*

krank|schrei·ben [ˈkraŋkʃraɛbm̩] <schreibt krank, schrieb krank, hat krankgeschrieben> [tr v] jdn krankschreiben sign sb off (sick) sich krankschreiben lassen be signed off (sick)

Kranz [krants] der <–es, Kränze> **1.** wreath ◊ *Er legte an Grab einen Kranz nieder.* **2.** ring ◊ *Der Park war von einem Kranz von Bäumen umgeben.*

Krap·fen [ˈkrapfn̩] der <–s, –> *(SouthG, Austr)* doughnut

krass [kras] [adj] <krasser, am krassesten> **1.** stark, marked, glaring, blatant ◊ *ein krasser Widerspruch* ◆ *Hier ist der Unterschied besonders krass.* **2.** *(slang)* wicked, ace ◊ *ein krasses Tattoo* ◆ *Die CD ist echt krass.* **3.** *(slang)* tough ◊ *Um sechs Uhr aufzustehen war krass!* [adv] **1.** markedly ◊ *Sie unterscheiden sich krass voneinander.* **2.** *(slang)* really ◊ *Er hat mich krass genervt.*

krat·zen [ˈkratsn̩] [tr v] +*haben* **1.** scratch ◊ *Ihr kleiner Bruder hat sie gekratzt.* ◆ *Der Hund kratzte sich.* ◆ *Er kratzte seinen Namen in die Bank.* sich

an etw. [dat] kratzen scratch your sth ◊ *Er kratzte sich am Fuß.* sich/jdm etw. kratzen scratch your/sb's sth **2.** etw. kratzt jdn sth is itching sb etw. kratzt jdn an etw. [dat] sth is itching sb's sth ◊ *Der Wollpulli kratzt mich am Hals.* **3.** etw. aus etw. kratzen scrape sth out of sth ◊ *Er kratzte die Reste aus der Schüssel.* [intr v] +*haben* **1.** be scratchy, be itchy ◊ *Dieser Stoff kratzt.* **2.** irgendwo kratzen scratch about somewhere ◊ *Die Hühner kratzten im Dreck.* **3.** grate ◊ *Die Schaufel kratzte über den Boden.*; *(voice)* rasp **4.** *(fam)* an etw. [dat] kratzen impinge on sth; *(confidence)* dent sth ⦿ etw. kratzt jdn *(fam)* sth bothers sb, sb is bothered by sth ◊ *Der Strafzettel kratzt mich nicht. Was kratzt dich das?* What do you care?

krau·len [ˈkraʊlən] [tr v] +*haben* stroke ◊ *einer Katze den Nacken kraulen* [intr v] +*haben/sein* **1.** +*haben/sein* do the crawl zehn Bahnen/100 m kraulen do a ten lengths/100 m crawl **2.** +*sein* irgendwohin kraulen swim (the crawl) somewhere

Kraut [kraʊt] das <–(e)s, Kräuter> **1.** *most pl* herb ◊ *eine Suppe mit Kräutern verfeinern* **2.** *no pl (SouthG, Austr)* sauerkraut ◊ *Würstchen mit Kraut* **3.** *no pl (SouthG, Austr)* cabbage ◊ *Kraut anbauen* ◆ *Die äußeren Blätter entfernen und das Kraut in feine Streifen schneiden.* ⦿ wie Kraut und Rüben *(fam)* irgendwo sieht es wie Kraut und Rüben aus a place is a real mess etw. ist wie Kraut und Rüben sth is a real mess

Kra·wall [kra·val] der <–s, –> **1.** riot ◊ *Die Kundgebung war von Krawallen begleitet.* **2.** *no pl (fam)* row, din ◊ *Die Hunde machten einen riesigen Krawall.* ⊖Spektakel

Kra·wat·te [kra·vatə] die <–, –n> tie ◊ *eine Krawatte binden/tragen*

Krebs [kreːps] der <–es, –e> **1.** BIO crab **2.** *seldom with the article, no pl* MED cancer ◊ *an Krebs erkranken* Krebs erregend carcinogenic **3.** ASTROL, ASTRON Cancer

② **Kre·dit** [kreˈdiːt] der <–(e)s, –e> loan ◊ *Er nahm einen Kredit über 5000 Euro auf.* jdm einen Kredit gewähren/einräumen give/grant sb a loan, give sb credit etw. auf Kredit kaufen buy sth on credit

② **Kre·dit·kar·te** [kreˈdiːtˈkaʳtə] die <–, –n> credit card ◊ *mit Kreditkarte bezahlen*

Krei·de [ˈkraɛdə] die <–, –n> chalk ◊ *Der Lehrer schrieb mit Kreide an die Tafel.* ◆ *Kreide ist ein lockeres Gestein.*

② **Kreis** [kraɛs] der <–es, –e> **1.** MATH circle ◊ *ein Punkt auf einem Kreis* ◆ *die Stühle im Kreis anordnen*; *(bird etc.)* Kreise ziehen circle (a)round **2.** circle, group ◊ *Er wurde im engsten Kreis beigesetzt.* ◆ *Dies verlautete aus gut informierten Kreisen.* **3.** sphere ◊ *der Kreis der behandelten Themen* **4.** *(abbr of* Landkreis) district ◊ *die Schulen im Kreis Eichstätt* ⦿ (weite) Kreise ziehen have (serious/wide) repercussions

krei·sen [ˈkraɛzn̩] [intr v] +*haben/sein* **1.** +*haben/sein* circle ◊ *Am Himmel kreisten die Geier.* um etw. kreisen circle sth ◊ *Mücken kreisten um das Licht.*; *(planet, satellite)* orbit sth **2.** +*haben (a body part)* mit etw. kreisen, etw. kreisen lassen rotate sth ◊ *Sie kreiste mit den Hüften.* **3.** +*haben* etw. kreisen lassen pass sth round ◊ *eine Flasche kreisen lassen* **4.** +*sein* um etw. kreisen centre on

sth, revolve around sth ◊ *Die Diskussion kreiste um das Thema Politik.*

Kreis·lauf ['kraeslaof] der <-(e)s, Kreisläufe>
1. cycle ◊ *der Kreislauf des Wassers* ein verhängnisvoller Kreislauf a vicious circle **2.** *(abbr of* Blutkreislauf) circulation ◊ *den Kreislauf in Schwung bringen* ♦ *Sein Kreislauf war zusammengebrochen.*

kre·mig ['kre:mɪç] → cremig

kreuz [krɔøts] *(always* kreuz und quer) all over (the place) ◊ *kreuz und quer durchs Land reisen*

Kreuz [krɔøts] das <-es, -e> **1.** cross ◊ *etw. mit einem Kreuz markieren* **2.** REL cross, crucifix ◊ *eine Halskette mit einem Kreuz aus Silber* **3.** ANAT lower back ◊ *das Kreuz durchdrücken* **4.** CARDS club(s) **5.** *(abbr of* Autobahnkreuz) intersection ◊ *Stau auf der Autobahn am Mannheimer Kreuz*
◉ **das Rote Kreuz** the Red Cross **es ist ein Kreuz mit jdm/etw.** sb/sth is a nuisance **jdn aufs Kreuz legen** take sb for a ride, con sb

⓶ **Kreu·zung** ['krɔøtsʊŋ] die <-, -en> **1.** crossroads, intersection, junction ◊ *an der Kreuzung links/rechts abbiegen* **2.** cross-breed, hybrid ◊ *eine Kreuzung aus verschiedenen Rebsorten*

krie·chen ['kri:çn] <kriecht, kroch, ist gekrochen> intr v **1.** (irgendwo/irgendwohin) kriechen crawl (somewhere), creep (somewhere) ◊ *Er kroch durch den Schlamm.* ♦ *Die Fahrzeuge krochen im Schneckentempo dahin.* ♦ *Sie kroch in ihren Schlafsack.* **2.** *(pej)* (vor jdm) kriechen crawl (to sb), grovel (to sb) ◊ *Es ist richtig peinlich, wie er vor dem Chef kriecht!*

⓶ **Krieg** [kri:k] der <-(e)s, -e> war ◊ *In diesem Land herrscht Krieg.* jdm den Krieg erklären declare war on sb ⊖Frieden
◉ **der kalte Krieg** the Cold War

⓶ **krie·gen** ['kri:gn] tr v +haben *(fam)* get ◊ *Was hast du zu Weihnachten gekriegt?* ♦ *eine Ohrfeige kriegen* ⊖bekommen
◉ **jd kriegt (noch) zu viel** sb will go mad

⓶ **Kri·mi** ['krɪmi:] der <-s, -s> *(also fig) (abbr of* Kriminalfilm/-roman) thriller ◊ *Er liest gern Krimis.* etw. ist der reinste Krimi sth is a real thriller

⓶ **Kri·mi·nal-...** [krɪmi'na:l] prefix detective ..., crime ... ◊ *ein Kriminalbeamter* ♦ *eine Kriminalgeschichte*

Kri·mi·nal·film [krɪmi'na:lfɪlm] der <-(e)s, -e> *(abbr* Krimi) thriller, crime film, crime movie

Kri·mi·na·li·tät [krɪminali'tɛːt] die <-> *no pl* **1.** crime, criminality ◊ *Er ist in die Kriminalität abgerutscht.* **2.** crime (rate) ◊ *Die grenzüberschreitende Kriminalität nimmt zu.*

Kri·mi·nal·po·li·zei [krɪmi'na:lpoli,tsae] die <-, -en> *most sing (abbr* Kripo) criminal investigation department ◊ *In diesem Fall ermittelt die Kriminalpolizei.*

Kri·mi·nal·ro·man [krɪmi'na:lro,ma:n] der <-s, -e> *(abbr* Krimi) thriller, detective/crime novel

Kri·po ['kri:po:] die <-, -s> → Kriminalpolizei

Krip·pe ['krɪpə] die <-, -n> **1.** manger ◊ *Rehe an der Krippe* **2.** crib, nativity ◊ *Unter dem Weihnachtsbaum war eine Krippe aufgebaut.* **3.** crèche ◊ *Während ich arbeite, ist mein Kind in der Krippe.*

⓶ **Kri·se** ['kri:zə] die <-, -n> crisis ◊ *in eine Krise geraten* ♦ *Die Branche steckt in einer tiefen Krise.* ♦ *Der Kranke hat die Krise überwunden.*
◉ **jd kriegt (noch) die Krise** sb is going mad, sb

will go mad

Kri·te·ri·um [kri'te:rjʊm] das <-s, Kriterien> criterion ◊ *ein bestimmtes Kriterium erfüllen*

⓶ **Kri·tik** [kri'ti:k] die <-, -en> **1.** *no pl* criticism ◊ *in die Kritik geraten* ♦ *Ihr Vorschlag stieß auf Kritik.* an etw./jdm Kritik üben criticize sth/sb **2.** review ◊ *Das Buch bekam gute Kritiken.* **3.** *no pl* critics ◊ *Die Kritik lobte die Inszenierung.*

⓶ **kri·tisch** ['kri:tɪʃ] adj, adv critical(ly) ◊ *Es wurden kritische Stimmen laut.* ♦ *Der Zustand der Verletzten war kritisch.* ♦ *sich kritisch mit etw. auseinander setzen* sich kritisch zu etw. äußern be critical of sth

kri·ti·sie·ren [kriti'zi:rən] <kritisiert, kritisierte, hat kritisiert> tr v **1.** criticize ◊ *etw. offen kritisieren* ⊖bemängeln **2.** review ◊ *Sein Roman wurde wohlwollend kritisiert.*

kroch [krɔx] pret of kriechen

Kro·ne ['kro:nə] die <-, -n> **1.** crown ◊ *Der König trug eine Krone.* ♦ *Der Zahnarzt passte die Krone an.* **2.** monarchy ◊ *die schwedische Krone* **3.** BOT treetop **4.** *no pl (fig)* pinnacle ◊ *Dieses Bier ist die Krone der Braukunst.* die Krone der Schöpfung the pride of creation
◉ **einen in der Krone haben** *(fam)* be a bit drunk

Krü·cke ['krʏkə] die <-, -n> **1.** crutch ◊ *sich auf eine Krücke stützen* **2.** *(fam, pej)* jd ist eine Krücke sb is hopeless

Krü·mel ['kry:ml] der <-s, -> crumb

krumm [krʊm] adj, adv <krummer/krümmer, am krummsten/krümmsten> crooked(ly) ◊ *eine krumme Wirbelsäule* ♦ *Sie findet ihre Nase zu krumm.* Sitz nicht so krumm! Sit up straight! adj dodgy ◊ *krumme Geschäfte machen*
◉ **etw. krumm nehmen** *(fam)* take sth the wrong way

⓶ **Kü·che** ['kʏçə] die <-, -n> **1.** kitchen ◊ *Er ist in der Küche.* **2.** fitted kitchen ◊ *eine Wohnung mit kompletter Küche* **3.** food, cooking, cuisine ◊ *die italienische Küche*
◉ **kalte Küche** cold food/meals **warme Küche** hot food/meals

⓶ **Ku·chen** ['ku:xn] der <-s, -> cake ◊ *Möchten Sie noch ein Stück Kuchen?* ♦ *Am Nachmittag gab es Kaffee und Kuchen.*

Ku·gel ['ku:gl] die <-, -n> **1.** sphere, ball ◊ *Der Christbaum war mit goldenen Kugeln geschmückt.* ♦ *Die Welt ist eine Kugel.*; *(at shot-putting)* shot **2.** bullet ◊ *Er wurde von einer Kugel getroffen.*
◉ **eine ruhige Kugel schieben** *(fam)* take it easy

⓶ **Ku·gel·schrei·ber** ['ku:gl,ʃraebe] der <-s, -> (ballpoint) pen, biro™ ◊ *mit Kugelschreiber schreiben*

Kuh [ku:] die <-, Kühe> **1.** *(also fam, also pej)* cow ◊ *die Kühe melken* ♦ *Du blöde Kuh!* **2.** ZOO cow ◊ *Die Elefantenherde besteht aus 11 Kühen.*; *(deer)* doe

⓶ **kühl** [ky:l] adj, adv **1.** cool(ly) ◊ *kühle Getränke* ♦ *Seine Mutter war zu ihr sehr kühl.* ♦ „*Das geht Sie nichts an*", *erwiderte sie kühl.*; *(air etc.)* chilly Ist dir kühl? Are you feeling chilly? kühl lagern/aufbewahren keep in a cool place kühl halten keep cool, keep chilled **2.** cold(ly) ◊ *Sie wirkt immer sehr kühl und besonnen.* ♦ *In dieser gefährlichen Situation reagierte sie kühl.* ein kühler Rechner a

cold, calculating person

küh·len ['ky:lən] [tr v] +*haben* chill ◊ *ein paar Dosen Bier im Kühlschrank kühlen* [intr v] +*haben* be cooling ◊ *Dieses Gel kühlt angenehm.*

② **Kühl·schrank** ['ky:lʃraŋk] der <–(e)s, Kühlschränke> fridge, refrigerator ◊ *etw. im Kühlschrank aufbewahren*

② **Kul·tur** [kʊl'tu:ɐ̯] die <–, –en> 1. *no pl* culture ◊ *Wenn du Kultur suchst, solltest du nach Paris fahren.* ♦ *Die beiden Ehepartner gehören verschiedenen Kulturen an.* 2. *no pl* AGR, MED cultivation

Kum·mer ['kʊmɐ] der <–> *no pl* 1. distress, sadness ◊ *Zum Kummer ihrer Eltern gab sie ihr Studium auf.* ♦ *Seine Krankheit bereitet mir viel Kummer.* ⊜Leid 2. problems, trouble ◊ *Sie hat Kummer mit ihrer Figur.*

② **küm·mern** ['kʏmɐn] [ref v] +*haben* 1. *sich um jdn/ etw. kümmern* look after sb/sth, care for sb/sth ◊ *Er kümmert sich um seine jüngeren Geschwister.* ♦ *Um den Garten kümmert sich mein Mann.* 2. *sich um etw. kümmern* worry about sth ◊ *Um solche Kleinigkeiten kümmere ich mich nicht.* [tr v] +*haben etw. kümmert jdn* sb is bothered about sth *Was kümmert jdn ...?* What does sb care ...?, What is it to sb ...?

Kum·pel ['kʊmpl̩] der <–s, –(s)> *(fam)* mate, buddy ◊ *Er ging mit seinen Kumpeln einen trinken.*

② **Kun·de** ['kʊndə] der <–n, –n>, **Kun·din** ['kʊndɪn] die <–, –nen> customer ◊ *einen Kunden bedienen* ⓞ *der Kunde ist König* the customer is always right

Kun·den·dienst ['kʊndn̩di:nst] der <–(e)s, –e> customer/after-sales service (department) ◊ *eine Beschwerde an den Kundendienst richten* ♦ *Sie hat den Wagen zum Kundendienst gebracht.*

Kund·ge·bung ['kʊntge:bʊŋ] die <–, –en> 1. rally, demonstration ◊ *Ich war auf einer Kundgebung.* ⊜Demonstration 2. *(lofty)* declaration ◊ *In ihrer Kundgebung betonte sie, dass ...*

② **kün·di·gen** ['kʏndɪgn̩] [tr+intr v] +*haben* (seine Stelle) kündigen hand in your notice *(seine Wohnung) kündigen* give the landlord notice, terminate your tenancy *jdm (die Stellung) kündigen* give sb (their) notice, dismiss sb *jdm (die Wohnung) kündigen* give sb notice to quit; *(a tenant also)* terminate sb's tenancy [tr v] *(a subscription, contract)* cancel, terminate, discontinue; *(a loan)* call in

Kund·schaft ['kʊntʃaft] die <–, –en> customers, clientele

künf·tig ['kʏnftɪç] [adj, adv] *no comp/superl; when used as an adj, only before noun* 1. *(in)* future ◊ *Seine künftige Ehefrau ist aus gutem Hause.* ♦ *Der Reisekonzern will künftig Billigreisen anbieten.*

② **Kunst** [kʊnst] die <–, Künste> 1. art ◊ *das Institut für moderne Kunst* ♦ *Nach der Pause haben wir Kunst.* bildende Kunst fine/visual art(s) die schönen Künste fine art(s) 2. *(fig)* art, skill ◊ *Kochen/Das Faulenzen ist eine Kunst.* ♦ *die Kunst des Redens beherrschen* ⓞ *mit seiner Kunst am Ende sein (fam)* be at your wits' end *etw. ist eine brotlose Kunst* sth doesn't pay the bills, you can't live off sth *das ist die ganze Kunst (fam)* it's that easy, that's all there is to it *die schwarze Kunst* black magic *keine Kunst sein (also pej)* not be difficult, be a

piece of cake

② **Künst·ler** ['kʏnstlɐ] der <–s, –>, **Künst·le·rin** ['kʏnstlərɪn] die <–, –nen> 1. artist ◊ *Sie ist Künstlerin.* ♦ *ein berühmter Künstler* bildender Künstler/ bildende Künstlerin visual artist 2. acrobat, artiste ◊ *Im Zirkus traten sensationelle Künstler auf.* 3. *(fig)* genius

② **künst·lich** ['kʏnstlɪç] [adj, adv] 1. artificial(ly), synthetic(ally) ◊ *ein künstliches Herz* ♦ *Das Erdbeereis schmeckt künstlich.* ♦ *künstliche Vitamine* ♦ *Die Patientin wird künstlich ernährt.* künstlicher Schmuck imitation jewellery/jewelry, fake jewellery/ jewelry; *(teeth)* false; *(fibre)* synthetic, man-made 2. unnatural(ly) ◊ *Ihr Lachen ist künstlich.* künstliche Heiterkeit forced cheerfulness *sich künstlich aufregen* get worked up (about nothing)

② **Kunst·stoff** ['kʊnstʃtɔf] der <–(e)s, –e> plastic, synthetic material ◊ *Die Tragetaschen sind aus Kunststoff.; (fibre also)* synthetics

Kunst·werk ['kʊnstvɛ:ɐ̯k] das <–(e)s, –e> work (of art) ◊ *die Kunstwerke Picassos*

Kup·fer ['kʊpfɐ] das <–s> *no pl* CHEM copper ◊ *ein Dach aus Kupfer* etw. in Kupfer stechen etch sth in copper

Kupp·lung ['kʊplʊŋ] die <–, –en> 1. clutch ◊ *die Kupplung treten/kommen lassen* 2. coupling ◊ *Er löste den Anhänger von der Kupplung.*

Kur [ku:ɐ̯] die <–, –en> (course of) treatment (in a spa/health resort) ◊ *eine Kur machen* in/auf Kur gehen go to a spa/health resort for treatment

Kür·bis ['kʏrbɪs] der <–ses, –se> pumpkin, marrow

ku·ri·os [ku'rjo:s] [adj] <kurioser, am kuriosesten> strange, odd, curious ◊ *Seine Geschichte ist kurios.* ♦ *eine kuriose Idee*

② **Kurs** [kʊrs] der <–es, –e> 1. FIN (exchange) rate, price ◊ *Der Kurs des Euro ist gestiegen/gefallen.* zum Kurs von at a rate of 2. *(also fig) (of an aircraft, ships)* course ◊ *den Kurs ändern/halten* ♦ *vom Kurs abweichen; (figurative also)* direction, line ◊ *der liberale Kurs der Regierung* Kurs auf etw. [acc] haben be heading for sth Kurs auf etw. [acc] nehmen set course for sth, head for sth einen neuen Kurs einschlagen go in a new direction, follow a new course einen harten Kurs einschlagen follow a hard line/policy/strategy 3. *(for learners)* course, classes ◊ *Sie nimmt an einem Kurs für Fortgeschrittene teil.* ♦ *einen Kurs machen/besuchen* Der ganze Kurs macht mit. Everybody on the course is taking part. ⊜Lehrgang ⓞ *bei jdm hoch im Kurs stehen (fig)* be popular with sb, be highly appreciated by sb

② **Kurs·buch** ['kʊrsbu:x] das <–(e)s, Kursbücher> 1. timetable ◊ *das Kursbuch der Deutschen Bahn* 2. coursebook

② **Kurs·lei·ter** ['kʊrslaetɐ] der <–s, –>, **Kurs·lei·te·rin** ['kʊrslaetərɪn] die <–, –nen> course leader ◊ *eine erfahrene Kursleiterin* ♦ *Er arbeitet als Kursleiter in/an der Volkshochschule.*

② **Kur·ve** ['kʊrvə] die <–, –n> 1. *(of a road)* bend, curve ◊ *in der Kurve ins Schleudern geraten* ♦ *eine scharfe Kurve* eine Kurve machen bend; *(on a motorbike)* sich in die Kurve legen lean into the curve eine Kurve schneiden cut a corner 2. curve ◊ *eine Kurve zeichnen/berechnen; (in statistics also)* graph; *(in ballistics)* trajectory

A B C D E F G H I J **K** L M N O P Q R S T U V W X Y Z

⊚ die Kurve kratzen *(fam)* make yourself scarce, hit the road die Kurve kriegen/bekommen make it

② **kurz** [kʊɐ̯ts] [adj, adv] <kürzer, am kürzesten>
1. *spatial* short(ly) ◊ Sie trägt einen kurzen Rock. ♦ Der Weg erschien mir kurz. eine kurze Hose shorts kurz geschnitten short etw. kürzer machen shorten sth kurz hinter/nach just past kurz vor just before **2.** *temporal* short(ly), brief(ly) ◊ ein kurzer Aufenthalt in Bath ♦ Das Leben ist kurz. ♦ Ich muss kurz in die Stadt zum Einkaufen, nach kurzer Zeit after a little while Kannst du mal kurz kommen/zuhören? Could you come/listen for a moment/minute? kurz nach just/shortly after kurz vor just/shortly before **3.** *(texts, reports)* brief(ly), concise(ly), succinct(ly) ◊ eine kurze Zusammenfassung ♦ Sein Aufsatz war zu kurz. ♦ Sie schilderte kurz, was geschehen war. in kurzen Worten in a few words, briefly, tersely kurz gesagt in brief, in a word
⊚ kurz und bündig tersely etw. kurz und klein schlagen *(fam)* smash sth up über kurz oder lang sooner or later jdn kurz halten keep sb short (of money), keep sb on a tight reign zu kurz kommen **1.** not get your fair share **2.** be neglected jd muss kürzer treten **1.** sb must take it easy **2.** sb must be (more) frugal den Kürzeren ziehen *(fam)* draw the short straw, come off worse binnen kurzem shortly, before long seit kurzem for a short time/while vor kurzem recently

kür·zen [ˈkʏɐ̯tsn̩] [tr+intr v] +haben **1.** shorten ◊ eine Hose kürzen ♦ Die Rede ist zu lang; wir werden kürzen müssen.; *(a book also)* abridge; *(a film)* cut **2.** MATH *(a fraction)* reduce, break/cancel down; *(factors)* cancel (off) [tr v] *(an amount)* cut, reduce ◊ Die Regierung will die Renten kürzen. jdm das Gehalt kürzen cut/reduce sb's salary

kurz·fris·tig [ˈkʊɐ̯tsfrɪstɪç] [adj] *only before ns* **1.** at short notice, last-minute ◊ eine kurzfristige Kündigung **2.** short-term ◊ eine kurzfristige Gefängnisstrafe [adv] **1.** at short notice, at the last minute ◊ Sie entschlossen sich kurzfristig, die Reise zu buchen. ♦ etw. kurzfristig entscheiden **2.** for a short period/time ◊ Das Unternehmen wird kurzfristig stillgelegt.

② **kürz·lich** [ˈkʏɐ̯tslɪç] [adv] recently, lately ◊ eine kürzlich erschienene Studie ♦ Ich habe ihn erst kürzlich getroffen. ⊖unlängst

kurz·sich·tig [ˈkʊɐ̯tszɪçtɪç] [adj, adv] shortsighted(ly) ◊ Der Junge ist kurzsichtig und benötigt eine Brille. ♦ Sein kurzsichtiges Handeln bringt ihm viel Ärger. ♦ Sie haben äußerst kurzsichtig entschieden. ⊖weitsichtig

ku·scheln [ˈkʊʃl̩n] [ref v] +haben sich an jdn kuscheln snuggle up to sb, cuddle up to sb sich in etw. [acc] kuscheln snuggle up in sth [intr v] +haben cuddle ◊ Mein Sohn kuschelt gern.

Ku·si·ne [kuˈziːnə] die <-, -n> *(female)* cousin

② **Kuss** [kʊs] der <-es, Küsse> kiss ◊ Sie gab ihm zum Abschied einen Kuss.

② **küs·sen** [ˈkʏsn̩] [tr+intr v] +haben kiss ◊ Er küsste sie zum Abschied. ♦ Er küsst leidenschaftlich gerne. jdm/jdn auf etw. [acc] küssen kiss sb on sth, kiss sb's sth ◊ Sie küssen sich zum Abschied auf die Wangen. jdm die Hand küssen kiss sb's hand sie küssen sich they kiss

② **Küs·te** [ˈkʏstə] die <-, -n> coast ◊ Makarska liegt direkt an der Küste.

② **Ku·vert** [kuˈveːɐ̯, kuˈveɐ̯t] das <-s, -s> envelope ◊ Sie steckte den Brief in ein Kuvert. ⊖Umschlag

L

l, L [ɛl] das <–(s), –(s)> l, L ◇ *Dieses Wort wird mit einem kleinen l/großen L geschrieben.* ♦ *L wie Ludwig*

L [ɛl] *(abbr of* large) *(clothing size)* large ◇ *ein T-Shirt in (der) Größe L*

la·bil [laˈbiːl] ⟨adj⟩ unstable, weak ◇ *Er ist psychisch labil.* ♦ *ein labiles Gleichgewicht* labile Gesundheit delicate/frail health, weak constitution

La·bor [laˈboːɐ̯] das <–s, –s *or* –e> *(abbr of* Laboratorium) lab(oratory) ◇ *Der Fund wird im Labor untersucht.*

ⓐ **lä·cheln** [ˈlɛçl̩n] ⟨intr v⟩ +*haben* smile jd lächelt über etw./jdn sth/sb makes sb smile ◇ *Die Chefin lächelte über seinen Eifer.*

ⓐ **la·chen** [ˈlaxn̩] ⟨tr+intr v⟩ +*haben* **1.** laugh ◇ *Die Kinder lachten vor Freude.* Tränen lachen cry with laughter **2.** *(fig) (sun)* shine (brightly) ◇ *Die Sonne lachte vom Himmel.*
ⓔ wer zuletzt lacht, lacht am besten he who laughs last laughs longest das wäre doch gelacht *(fam)* it would be incredible, it would be ridiculous nichts zu lachen haben *(fam)* have a hard time

lä·cher·lich [ˈlɛçɐlɪç] ⟨adj, adv⟩ *(pej)* ridiculous(ly), ludicrous(ly) ◇ *Sie trug einen lächerlichen Hut.* ♦ *Die Situation war einfach lächerlich.* ♦ *Er verdient lächerlich wenig.* sich/jdn (vor jdm) lächerlich machen make a fool of yourself/sb (in front of sb) etw. lächerlich machen deride sth

Lachs [laks] der <–es, –e> salmon ◇ *Es gibt heute geräucherten Lachs.* gebeizter Lachs gravadlax

Lack [lak] der <–(e)s, –e> paint ◇ *Hier ist der Lack abgeblättert.*; *(transparent)* lacquer, varnish; *(for nails)* varnish
ⓔ bei etw./jdm ist der Lack ab *(fam, pej)* the novelty of sth/sb has worn off, sb/sth shows signs of wear

la·den [ˈlaːdn̩] <lädt, lud, hat geladen> ⟨tr v⟩ **1.** load ◇ *Er lud sein Gewehr.* ♦ *ein Programm aus dem Internet auf die Festplatte laden* etw. geladen haben be loaded with sth etw. in/auf etw. ⟨acc⟩ laden load sth into/onto sth etw. von etw./aus etw. laden unload sth from sth ◇ *Sie luden die Kartons aus dem Transporter.* **2.** *(with power)* charge ◇ *Ist der Akku geladen?* **3.** *(fig)* etw. auf sich ⟨acc⟩ laden burden yourself with sth, take on the heavy burden of sth (schwere) Schuld auf sich laden commit a (serious) crime, be involved in (serious) wrongdoing

ⓐ **La·den** [ˈlaːdn̩] der <–s, Läden> shop, store ◇ *Der Kunde schaute sich im Laden um.* ♦ *Der Laden hat zu/auf.*
ⓔ den Laden dichtmachen close down (the business/shop) den Laden schmeißen *(fam)* run/manage everything/the business

lädt [lɛːt] *pres of* laden

ⓐ **lag** [laːk] *pret of* liegen

ⓐ **La·ge** [ˈlaːɡə] die <–, –n> **1.** *most sing* situation, position ◇ *in einer unangenehmen Lage sein* ♦ *Nach dem Bankrott war seine Lage schwierig.* jdn in eine dumme Lage bringen put sb in an awkward position nach Lage der Dinge as things stand/stood Na, wie ist die Lage? How are things?, How is it going? ⊜Situation **2.** in der Lage sein, etw. zu tun be able to do sth, be in a position to do sth **3.** *most sing* location ◇ *Das Hotel befindet sich in ruhiger Lage.* **4.** *most sing (way of lying)* position ⊜Position, Stellung **5.** layer ◇ *Der Kuchen besteht aus drei Lagen.* **6.** MUS register

La·ger [ˈlaːɡɐ] das <–s, –> **1.** *(also fig)* camp ◇ *das Lager der Soldaten* ♦ *Ich halte es mit den Umweltschützern. Zu welchem Lager gehören Sie?* sein Lager aufschlagen set up camp, pitch camp **2.** storeroom, warehouse ◇ *Nachschub aus dem Lager holen* **3.** stock, store(s) ◇ *Das Lager wurde um weitere Produkte ergänzt.*; *(secret)* cache **4.** TECHN bearing
ⓔ etw. auf Lager haben *(also fig)* have sth in store

la·gern [ˈlaːɡɐn] ⟨tr v⟩ +*haben* **1.** store, keep ◇ *Der Winzer lagert den Wein an einem kühlen Ort.* etw. kühl/trocken lagern keep/store sth in a cool/dry place **2.** lay (down) ◇ *einen Patienten auf dem/den Rücken lagern* die Beine hoch lagern put your/sb's legs up **3.** TECHN support, mount drehbar gelagert mounted on a pivot ⟨intr v⟩ +*haben* **1.** camp down, make up camp ◇ *Wir lagerten am Fluss/unter den Bäumen.* **2.** be stored, be kept ◇ *Die Kartoffeln lagern im Keller.* **3.** GEOL etw. lagert irgendwo there are deposits of sth somewhere ◇ *Vor der Küste lagert Erdöl.*

lahm [laːm] ⟨adj⟩ **1.** lame ◇ *Sie hat ein lahmes Bein.* ♦ *Das Pferd ist lahm.* **2.** stiff ◇ *Er spielte Geige, bis ihm der Arm und die Finger lahm wurden.* **3.** *(fam, pej) (attempt, excuse)* lame, feeble; *(person, speed)* slow, sluggish; *(not interesting)* dull ◇ *Das Fest war ziemlich lahm.*
ⓔ jdn/etw. lahm legen bring sb/sth to a halt/standstill, paralyze sb/sth

läh·men [ˈlɛːmən] ⟨tr v⟩ +*haben* **1.** *mostly passive* paralyze ◇ *Seit dem Unfall ist sie gelähmt.* **2.** *(fig)* paralyze, bring to halt/standstill ◇ *Die Straßenarbeiten lähmten den Verkehr.* vor Angst wie gelähmt sein be paralyzed with fear

Laie [ˈlaɛ̯ə] der <–n, –n> layman, laywoman die Laien the laity jd ist (ein) Laie sb is not an expert

La·ken [ˈlaːkn̩] das <–s, –> sheet ◇ *Das Bett ist mit einem frischen Laken überzogen.*

Lak·rit·ze [laˈkrɪtsə] die <–, –n> *most sing* liquorice

Lamm [lam] das <–(e)s, Lämmer> **1.** lamb **2.** ein Lamm sein be guileless, be naive
ⓔ das Lamm Gottes REL the Lamb of God

ⓐ **Lam·pe** [ˈlampə] die <–, –n> light, lamp ◇ *die Lampe einschalten/ausschalten* ♦ *Im Cockpit leuchtete eine rote Lampe auf.*

ⓩ **Land¹** [lant] das <-es, Länder> **1.** *no pl* land ◊ *Das Meer begrenzt das Land.*; *(for farming also)* soil ein Stück Land a plot (of land) an Land ashore, on dry land ◊ *Wir ankerten und gingen an Land.* ♦ *Die meisten Säugetiere leben an Land.* **2.** *no pl* country(side) auf dem Land in the country ◊ *Unsere Familie wohnt auf dem Land.* aufs Land ziehen move to the country ⊜Stadt **3.** POL country ◊ *In welchem Land sind Sie geboren?* außer Landes abroad, out of the country **4.** POL *(federal)* Land, *(regional)* state das Land Hessen/Niedersachsen the Land of Hesse/Lower Saxony; *(in Austria)* province das Land Oberösterreich/Kärnten the Province of Upper Austria/ Carinthia ⊜Bundesland

ⓘ **Land und Leute kennen lernen** get to know the country and its people **andere Länder, andere Sitten** different strokes for different folks, every country has its own customs **kein Land mehr sehen** *(fig)* be lost, be overworked/overburdened, be in the mire **(wieder) Land sehen** see the light at the end of the tunnel **ins Land gehen/ziehen** pass **etw. an Land ziehen** *(fam)* land sth, get your hands on sth

> Generally the names of countries do not take an article in German unless they are accompanied by an attribute:: *Ich lebe in Deutschland. — Er kommt aus England*, but: *das China der Jahrhundertwende — das südliche Frankreich.* There are, however, a few exceptions which always take an article, including *die Schweiz, die Türkei, die Ukraine, der Senegal.*

Land² [lant] das <-es, Lande> region, area, country ◊ *Das Land dort ist hügelig/flach/gebirgig.* ♦ *Aus deutschen Landen frisch auf den Tisch!* durch das Land/die Lande ziehen travel around ⊜Gegend

ⓘ **wieder im Lande sein** be back

ⓩ **lan·den** ['landn̩] <landet, landete, hat/ist gelandet> ⟨intr v⟩ +*sein* **1.** AVIAT *(aircraft)* land ◊ *Das Flugzeug landete sanft.* ♦ *Sie müssten jetzt schon in London gelandet sein.* ⊜abheben **2.** *(fam, fig)* end up ◊ *in einer Sackgasse landen* ♦ *Er wird noch im Gefängnis landen!* ⟨tr v⟩ +*haben* land ◊ *Der Pilot hat das Flugzeug sicher gelandet.*

ⓘ **bei jdm landen (können)** get anywhere with sb
Lan·des·kun·de ['landəskʊndə] die <-> *no pl; seldom with article* regional studies
lan·des·weit ['landəsvaet] ⟨adj, adv⟩ *no comp/ superl; when used as an adj, only before ns* countrywide, nationwide, all over the country/state, in the whole country/state ◊ *eine landesweite Kampagne* ♦ *Die Partei errang landesweit über fünfzig Prozent.*
Land·kar·te ['lantkaːtə] die <-, -n> map ◊ *Sie suchte die Stadt auf der Landkarte.*
Land·kreis ['lantkraes] der <-es, -e> district ◊ *aus dem Landkreis Goslar kommen*
länd·lich ['lɛntlɪç] ⟨adj, adv⟩ rural(ly) ◊ *ein ländliches Gebiet* ♦ *Die Gegend ist sehr ländlich.* ♦ *ländlich leben* idyllisch eingerichtet furnished in country style ⊜städtisch
ⓩ **Land·schaft** ['lantʃaft] die <-, -en> *(also fig)* landscape ◊ *Der Ackerbau veränderte die Landschaft.* ♦ *die politische Landschaft Deutschlands;*

(view) scenery
Land·stra·ße ['lantʃtraːsə] die <-, -n> country road, secondary road
Land·tag ['lanttaːk] der <-(e)s, -e> Landtag ◊ *eine Anhörung im Landtag* ♦ *der sächsische Landtag;* *(in Germany also)* regional state parliament, provincial parliament
ⓩ **Land·wirt·schaft** ['lantvɪrtʃaft] die <-> *most sing* agriculture, farming
ⓩ **lang¹** [laŋ] ⟨adj⟩ <länger, am längsten> long ◊ *Sie hat lange Fingernägel.* ♦ *Der Rock ist mir zu lang.* ♦ *für eine lange Zeit; (person)* tall ... Meter lang ... metres/meters long ... Stunden/Wochen lang ... hour/week, lasting ... hours/weeks ◊ *ein drei Stunden langer Vortrag* ⟨adv⟩ **1.** lang anhaltend prolonged, long-lasting lang ersehnt long-awaited lang gehegt long-cherished ◊ *ein lang gehegter Wunsch* → lange **2.** ... Sekunden/Jahre lang for ... seconds/years etw. dauert ... Sekunden/Jahre lang sth lasts ... seconds/years, sth goes on for ... seconds/years, sth takes ... seconds/years

ⓘ **lang und breit** *(pej)* at great length, in great detail **seit langem** for a long time
lang² [laŋ] *(fam)* → entlang
lang·at·mig ['laŋʔaːtmɪç] ⟨adj, adv⟩ long-winded(ly), tedious(ly), wordy(-ily) ◊ *eine langatmige Erklärung* ♦ *Ihr Bericht war sehr langatmig.* ♦ *Er hat die Geschichte zu langatmig erzählt.*
ⓩ **lan·ge** ['laŋə] → lang ⟨adv⟩ **1.** long, (for) a long time ◊ *Das ist noch gar nicht lange her.* schon lange (for) a long time, long (ago) (abends) lange arbeiten work late (morgens) lange schlafen get up late (in the morning), have a lie-in Ich komme gleich wieder, wartest du so lange? I'll be back in a minute, would you mind waiting? Ich fange so lange schon mal an, o.k.? I'll get started in the meantime, ok? so lange bis until, till **2.** noch lange nicht not by any means, not by a long chalk (noch) lange nicht so gut/schön etc. not nearly as well/ beautifully etc.

ⓘ **da kann jd (noch) lange warten** sb will wait forever, sb is in for a long wait
ⓩ **Län·ge** ['lɛŋə] die <-, -n> **1.** length ◊ *Die Länge der Mauer beträgt fünf Meter.* ♦ *Wie viele Längen Vorsprung hat er?* eine Länge von ... Metern haben be ... metres/meters in length auf einer Länge von ... for/over a distance of ... nach lengthwise, lengthways ◊ *Sie faltete das Papier der Länge nach.* der Länge nach hinfallen fall flat on your face der Länge nach sortieren sort by length/size **2.** GEOG longitude ⊜Breite

ⓘ **in voller Länge** in its entirety **Längen haben** be tedious at times **sich in die Länge ziehen** go on and on
lan·gen ['laŋən] *(fam)* ⟨intr v⟩ +*haben* **1.** be enough ◊ *Das Geld langt nicht für ein neues Auto.* ⊜ausreichen **2.** nach etw. langen reach for sth ◊ *Er langt nach der Flasche, um zu trinken.* nach unten/oben langen reach up/down in/unter/hinter etw. ⟨acc⟩ langen reach into/under/behind sth ⊜greifen **3.** extend ◊ *Der Wald langt von hier bis zum Stadtrand.*; *(history)* stretch back; go back ⊜reichen ⟨ref v⟩ sich ⟨dat⟩ etw. langen take sth ⊜nehmen

ⓘ **jdm eine langen** slap sb (in the face), give sb a clout **jdm langt es** sb has had enough

Lan·ge·wei·le [laŋə'vaelə, '– – – –] die <–> *no pl*
boredom Langeweile haben be bored aus (lauter)
Langeweile out of (sheer) boredom sich (dat) die
Langeweile vertreiben pass the time, kill time jdm
die Langeweile vertreiben entertain sb

lang·fris·tig ['laŋfrɪstɪç] (adj) *only before ns* long-
term ◊ *eine langfristige Strategie* (adv) in the long
term ◊ *Diese Maßnahme wird langfristig Kosten
sparen.*

längs¹ [lɛŋs] (adv) lengthways, lengthwise ◊ *Soll ich
die Melone längs aufschneiden?* längs gestreift
with vertical stripes

längs² [lɛŋs] (prep) (+gen) along ◊ *Sie bauten
Dutzende von Villen längs des Flusses.*

ⓩ **lang·sam** ['laŋzaːm] (adj, adv) **1.** slow(ly) ◊ *Seine
Bewegungen sind sehr langsam.* ♦ *Die Kassiererin arbeitet sehr langsam.*;
(intellectually) slow(-minded), slow on the uptake
⊜schnell **2.** gradual(ly) ◊ *eine langsame Steigerung des Tempos* es wird (aber auch) langsam Zeit
it's about time Bist du langsam fertig? Are you
ready yet? langsam sollte er wissen ... he should
know by now ... ⊜allmählich

längst [lɛŋst] (adv) **1.** long (ago), for a long time
◊ *Ihre Anfrage hatte sich längst erledigt.* ♦ *Sie
haben ihre langst fälligen Schulden endlich
beglichen.* **2.** längst (noch) nicht nowhere near,
not nearly ◊ *Sie ist längst noch nicht fertig mit der
Arbeit.*

lang·wei·len ['laŋvaelən] (tr v) +*haben* jdn langweilen bore sb ◊ *Der Film hat die Zuschauer gelangweilt.* ♦ *Er langweilt mich mit seinem Gejammer.*
(ref v) +*haben* sich langweilen be bored ◊ *sich zu
Tode langweilen*

ⓩ **lang·wei·lig** ['laŋvaelɪç] (adj, adv) boring(ly),
tedious(ly) ◊ *eine langweilige Geschichte* ♦ *Alleine
joggen zu gehen ist mir zu langweilig.* ♦ *Die
Geschichte ist ein wenig langweilig geschrieben.*
⊜öde ⊜spannend

Lang·zeit·... ['laŋtsaet] (prefix) long-term ... ◊
Langzeitarbeitslose ♦ *die Langzeitwirkung eines
Medikaments* Langzeitkranke chronically ill
persons/patients

Lap·pen ['lapm̩] der <–s, –> **1.** cloth, flannel ◊
*etw. mit einem Lappen abputzen/abwischen/
säubern* ♦ *ein Lappen zum Staubwischen; (for
grease)* rag **2.** zoo dewlap, wattle **3.** anat lobe
⊛ jdm durch die Lappen gehen *(fam)* slip
through sb's fingers sich (dat) etw. durch die
Lappen gehen lassen *(fam)* miss (out on) sth,
let sth slip through your fingers

ⓩ **Lärm** [lɛ'm] der <–(e)s> *no pl* noise, row ◊ *Der
Lärm, den die Kinder machten, war nicht auszuhalten.* ♦ *Die Maschine verursacht sehr viel Lärm.*
⊜Stille
⊛ viel Lärm um nichts/jdn/etw. machen *(fam)*
make a big fuss about nothing/sb/sth

ⓩ **las** [laːs] *pret of* lesen

ⓩ **las·sen**¹ ['lasn̩] <lässt, ließ, hat lassen> (modal v)
+*inf* **1.** jdn/etw. etw. tun lassen let sb/sth do sth
◊ *Lass mich jetzt bitte arbeiten.* ♦ *Ich habe das
Telefon klingeln lassen.* jdn warten lassen keep sb
waiting etw. sehen/blicken lassen show your face sich
einen Bart/die Haare etc. wachsen lassen grow a
beard/your hair etc. Sie lässt sich nicht dazu
zwingen. She won't be coerced into it. Lass dich

von ihm nicht so ärgern! Don't allow him to annoy
you like that! Lassen Sie sich das gesagt sein! Let
me tell you this! Du hast schon wieder das Licht
brennen lassen. You have left the light on again.
2. jdn etw. tun lassen make sb do sth, get sb to
do sth ◊ *Der Lehrer ließ uns den ganzen Text
zweimal abschreiben.* etw. tun lassen have sth
done ◊ *Sie hat sich die Haare schneiden lassen.*
Wir sollten einen Arzt holen lassen. We ought to
fetch a doctor. Wir haben uns eine Pizza kommen
lassen. We sent for a pizza. Der Lehrer hat uns
nachsitzen lassen The teacher gave us a detention.
Wir haben Drachen steigen lassen. We flew kites.
3. +*adv and reflexive infinitive construction* sich
gut/schwer etc. ... lassen be easy/difficult etc. to
... ◊ *Die Tür lässt sich schwer öffnen.* etw. lässt
sich irgendwie/sicher machen etc. sth can be done
etc. somehow/certainly ◊ *Jedes Problem lässt sich
irgendwie lösen.* etw. lässt sich nicht tun sth
cannot be done Hier lässt es sich gut leben. This
is a nice place to live. **4.** etw. irgendwo stehen/
liegen/hängen lassen leave sth somewhere
⊛ lasset uns beten let us pray es nicht lassen
können not to be able to stop (doing) it etw. mit
sich (dat) machen lassen put up with sth lassen
Sie mal, lass mal don't, leave it

ⓩ **las·sen**² ['lasn̩] <lässt, ließ, hat gelassen> (tr v)
1. stop ◊ *Sie kann das Rauchen einfach nicht
lassen.* ♦ *Lass endlich das ewige Jammern!* Ich
wollte es zuerst machen, habe es aber dann doch
gelassen. At first I wanted to do it, but in the end
I didn't. Wenn du keine Lust hast, dann lass es. If
you don't feel like it then don't do it. **2.** leave ◊
Ich habe den Schirm im Büro gelassen. ♦ *Lass
mich in Ruhe!* ♦ *Sie haben nichts unversucht
gelassen.* ♦ *Lass den Kindern bitte noch etwas von
dem Kuchen.* jdn etw. lassen sb (alone), let sb be
3. let (out) ◊ *die Luft aus dem Reifen lassen* (das)
Wasser in die Wanne lassen run a bath **4.** let ◊
*Lass die Katze nicht ins Schlafzimmer. Lass mich,
sonst trete ich dich.* Let me go or I'll kick you.
⊛ das muss man jdm lassen you have to give it
to sb

läs·sig ['lɛsɪç] (adj) **1.** laid back ◊ *eine lässige Art
haben* ♦ *Der Typ ist echt lässig.* **2.** *(fam)* simple,
easy ◊ *Die Englischarbeit war ganz lässig.* ♦ *eine
lässige Prüfung* (adv) **1.** casually ◊ *Sie kleidet sich
sehr lässig.* **2.** *(fam)* easily ◊ *Unser Team hat ganz
lässig gewonnen.*

ⓩ **lässt** [lɛst] *pres of* lassen¹, lassen²

Last [last] die <–, –en> **1.** load ◊ *Lasten bis zu
200 Kilo* **2.** *most sing (fig)* burden ◊ *die Last der
Verantwortung* Das nimmt mir eine Last von der
Seele. That's a load off my mind. **3.** fin costs,
charges die Umverteilung der Lasten the redistribu-
tion of the financial burden
⊛ jdm zur Last fallen be a burden on sb zu jds
Lasten gehen **1.** *(invoice etc.)* be charged to sb
◊ *Die Reparatur geht zu Lasten des Mieters.* **2.** be
to the detriment of sb ◊ *Wenn Eltern sich streiten,
geht das immer zu Lasten der Kinder.* jdm etw.
zur Last legen *(form)* accuse sb of sth

Las·ter¹ ['laste] das <–s, –> vice ◊ *Er ist dem
Laster des Spielens verfallen.* ⊜Tugend

Las·ter² ['laste] der <–s, –> *(fam)* lorry, truck
⊜Lastwagen

läs·tern ['lɛstɐn] [intr v] +*haben* (über jdn/etw.) lästern make nasty remarks (about sb/sth)

läs·tig ['lɛstɪç] [adj] annoying, bothersome, troublesome ◊ *Immer diese lästigen Fragen!* ♦ *Diese Arbeit ist wirklich lästig.* ♦ *Der Verband wird mir langsam lästig.*

② **Last·kraft·wa·gen** ['lastkraftvaːgn̩] der <-s, –> *(form) (abbr* Lkw) heavy goods vehicle

② **Last·wa·gen** ['lastvaːgn̩] der <-s, –> lorry, truck ⊝Lkw

La·tein·a·me·ri·ka [laˈtaɛn|aˌmeːrikaː] das <-s> *no pl* Latin America box@ Land

La·ter·ne [laˈtɛrnə] die <-, –n> 1. street light/lamp 2. lamp ◊ *Sie suchten das Grundstück mit Laternen ab.* 3. Chinese lantern

Lat·te ['latə] die <-, –n> 1. slat ◊ *Die Tür war mit Latten vernagelt.* 2. SPORT bar ◊ *Sie legte die Latte auf 1,80 m.* 3. SPORT *(football)* crossbar ◊ *Der Ball ging gegen die Latte.*

◉ **eine ganze Latte** *(fam)* a whole load of things **eine lange Latte** *(fam)* a beanpole **eine lange Latte von etw.** *(fam)* a whole string of, a long list of **eine Latte haben** *(slang)* have a hard-on

Latz [lats] der <-es, Lätze> bib ◊ *Sie band dem Kind den Latz um.* ♦ **eine Hose mit Latz**

◉ **jdm eins vor den Latz knallen** *(fam)* thump sb

lau [laʊ] [adj] <lauer, am lau(e)sten> mild ◊ *laue Maiabende; (water)* tepid, lukewarm ◊ *Das Wasser war nur lau.*

Laub [laʊp] das <-(e)s> *no pl* leaves, foliage

Lau·be ['laʊbə] die <-, –n> arbour ◊ *Sie saßen unter der Laube im Schatten.*

Lauch [laʊx] der <-(e)s> *no pl* leek

lau·ern ['laʊɐn] [intr v] +*haben* 1. lurk ◊ *Überall lauern Gefahren.* auf jdn/etw. lauern lie in wait for sb/sth ◊ *Die Katze lauert vor dem Loch auf die Maus.* 2. auf etw. [acc] lauern wait for sth ◊ *Er lauert nur darauf, dass ich einen Fehler mache.*

Lauf [laʊf] der <-(e)s, Läufe> 1. *no pl* run(ning) ◊ *Er wurde dem langen Lauf erschöpft.* 2. SPORT race ◊ *ein Lauf über 1000 Meter* 3. *no pl* course ◊ *der Lauf der Dinge* ♦ *der gewundene Lauf des Flusses* 4. barrel ◊ *Die Kugel war im Lauf stecken geblieben.* 5. *(of an animal)* leg

◉ **einer Sache** [dat] **freien Lauf lassen** give vent to sth, give free rein to sth **seinen Lauf nehmen** take its course **im Lauf(e) …** [gen] during the course of … ◊ *Wir werden uns im Laufe der nächsten Woche melden.* ⊝binnen

Lauf·bahn ['laʊfbaːn] die <-, –en> 1. *most sing* career ◊ *eine künstlerische Laufbahn einschlagen* 2. SPORT running track

② **lau·fen** ['laʊfn̩] <läuft, lief, ist/hat gelaufen> [intr v] +*sein* 1. run ◊ *Ich bin gelaufen, so schnell ich konnte.* ♦ *Die Tränen liefen ihm übers Gesicht.* ♦ *Sie ließ Wasser in den Eimer laufen.* ♦ *Die Straßenbahn läuft auf Schienen.* ♦ *Mein Vertrag läuft noch bis Januar.* ♦ *Bei Kälte läuft mir die Nase.* gegen etw./in etw. [acc] laufen run into sth 2. walk ◊ *Ich laufe jeden Tag zur Arbeit.* ♦ *Kann der Kleine schon laufen?* 3. work ◊ *Läuft dein Computer wieder?* 4. *(television, in the cinema, on TV)* be on ◊ *Der Fernseher läuft den ganzen Tag.* ♦ *Der Film läuft im zweiten Programm.* 5. go ◊ *Die Gespräche liefen gut.* ♦ *Das Auto läuft auf meinen Namen.*

Die Geschäfte laufen schleppend. Business is sluggish. *In meiner Ehe läuft gar nichts mehr.* Nothing is going right in my marriage any more. 6. be on-going ◊ *Gegen ihn läuft ein Verfahren wegen Steuerbetrugs.* *Meine Bewerbung läuft noch.* My application is still under consideration. 7. sell ◊ *Die Zeitschrift läuft schlecht.* [tr v] +*haben/sein* 1. +*haben/in South G, Austr, Swiss often* +*sein* run ◊ *Er hat noch nie einen Marathon gelaufen.* einen Rekord laufen run a record time 2. +*sein* Rollschuh laufen roller-skate Schlittschuh laufen ice-skate Ski laufen ski [ref v] +*haben* 1. sich warm laufen warm up sich müde laufen tire yourself out through walking sich wund laufen get sore feet through walking 2. In den Schuhen läuft es sich bequem. The shoes are comfortable to walk in. Wenn es nicht so heiß ist, läuft es sich besser. It's easier to run when it's not so hot. 3. sich [dat] Blasen laufen get blisters from walking sich [dat] die Füße wund laufen get sore feet through walking sich [dat] Löcher in die Schuhsohlen laufen wear holes in your shoes through walking

◉ **das ist gelaufen** *(fam)* it is too late now **wie läuft's** *(fam)* how is it going

lau·fend ['laʊfn̩t, 'laʊfənt] *pres p of* laufen [adj, adv] *no comp/superl; when used as an adj, only before ns* constant(ly), continual(ly) ◊ *laufende Unterbrechungen* ♦ *Stör mich doch nicht laufend.* [adj] *no comp/superl, only before ns (week, month, year)* current ◊ *in der laufenden Woche; (costs also)* running

◉ **auf dem Laufenden bleiben** keep up-to-date, keep abreast of things **jdn auf dem Laufenden halten** keep sb informed, keep sb up-to-date **auf dem Laufenden sein** be up-to-date on sth, be au fait with sth

Läu·fer¹ ['lɔɪfɐ] der <-s, –> 1. bishop ◊ *Sie hat meinen Läufer geschlagen.* 2. rug ◊ *Auf dem Parkettboden lag ein Läufer.*

Läu·fer² ['lɔɪfɐ] der <-s, –>, **Läu·fe·rin** ['lɔɪfərɪn] die <-, –nen> runner

② **läuft** [lɔɪft] *pres of* laufen

② **Lauf·werk** ['laʊfvɛrk] das <-(e)s, -e> drive ◊ *Diskette in Laufwerk A einschieben*

② **Lau·ne** ['laʊnə] die <-, –n> mood ◊ *Er war bester Laune.* ♦ *jdm die Laune verderben* ♦ *Er hat sehr unter ihren Launen zu leiden.* gute/schlechte Laune haben be in a good/bad mood ⊝Stimmung

◉ **jdn bei Laune halten** keep sb happy **aus einer Laune heraus** on a whim

Laus [laʊs] die <-, Läuse> 1. louse 2. greenfly, blackfly, aphid ◊ *Margariten haben oft Läuse.*

◉ **jdm ist eine Laus über die Leber gelaufen** *(fam)* sth is eating sb

lau·schen ['laʊʃn̩] [intr v] +*haben* 1. (jdm/einer Sache) lauschen listen (to sb/sth) ◊ *Andächtig lauschte sie dem Pfarrer.* 2. eavesdrop ◊ *Jetzt lauscht er wieder an der Tür.*

lau·sig ['laʊzɪç] [adj, adv] *(fam, pej)* lousy(-ily) ◊ *ein lausiger Schüler* ♦ *Das Wetter ist lausig.* ♦ *Wir werden lausig bezahlt.*

◉ **lausig kalt** perishing cold

② **laut¹** [laʊt] [adj, adv] <lauter, am lautesten> loud(ly) ◊ *Sie hat eine laute Stimme.* ♦ *Die Musik war schrecklich laut.* ♦ *Schrei doch nicht so laut.*

(stereo etc.) etw. lauter stellen turn sth up lauter sprechen speak up ⊖leise [adj] noisy ◊ *Sie wohnt an einer lauten Straße.* ◆ *Diese Gegend ist besonders laut.* ⊖ruhig

⊚ laut denken think aloud laut werden become known, be made known

laut² [laʊt] [prep] *sing nouns without article or attribute are not declined when following this prep, otherwise* [+gen] *or fam* [+dat] *according to* ◊ *laut Paragraph 118*

Laut [laʊt] der <-(e)s, -e> sound ◊ *Das Kind gab klägliche Laute von sich.* ◆ *ein schriller Laut*

lau·ten ['laʊtn̩] <lautet, lautete, hat gelautet> [intr v] **1.** etw. lautet ... sth is ... ◊ *Wie lautet das fünfte Gebot?* ◆ *Die Antwort lautet nein.* **2.** etw. lautet auf etw. [acc] sth is sth ◊ *Das Urteil lautete auf Freispruch.*

② **läu·ten** ['lɔʏtn̩] <läutete, läutete, hat geläutet> [tr+intr v] ring ◊ *Der Wecker/Das Telefon hat geläutet.* ◆ *Wer läutet eigentlich die Kirchenglocken?* [imp v] es läutet there is a ring ⊖es klingelt

⊚ etw. läuten hören hear sth rumoured

lau·ter ['laʊtɐ] [indef pron] *(fam)* nothing but, lots of ◊ *Der Text wies lauter Fehler auf.* ◆ *Er hat lauter Blödsinn geredet.* vor lauter Wut because of all the work vor lauter Wut in pure rage

Laut·schrift ['laʊtʃrɪft] die <-> *no pl* phonetic alphabet

② **Laut·spre·cher** ['laʊtʃprɛçɐ] der <-s, -> loudspeaker ◊ *Es ertönte eine Stimme aus dem Lautsprecher.; (of a stereo system)* speaker

Laut·stär·ke ['laʊtʃtɛrkə] die <-, -n> loudness, volume ◊ *die Lautstärke regeln*

lau·warm ['laʊvaʳm] [adj] *no comp/superl* barely warm ◊ *Das Essen war lauwarm.; (liquid)* lukewarm ◊ *lauwarmes Wasser*

La·wi·ne [la'viːnə] die <-, -n> avalanche ◊ *von einer Lawine verschüttet* ◆ *eine Lawine von Bewerbungen*

② **le·ben** ['leːbm̩] [intr v] +haben live, be alive ◊ *Lebt er noch?* ◆ *Wann hat Goethe gelebt?* [tr+intr v] +haben live ◊ *Sie lebt jetzt in Frankreich.* ◆ *Das Kind lebt bei seinem Vater.* ◆ *Wir leben ein ruhiges Leben.* irgendwie leben live in a certain way ◊ *Sie leben zurückgezogen.* ◆ *ärmlich leben* ◆ *Ameisen leben in Staaten.* von etw. leben live on sth ◊ *Sie lebt von ihren Ersparnissen.* für jdn/etw. leben live for sb/sth

⊚ leben und leben lassen live and let live es lebe ... long live ...

② **Le·ben** ['leːbm̩] das <-s, -> *most sing* life ◊ *Er hat sein ganzes Leben hier verbracht.* ◆ *ein gesundes Leben führen* ◆ *Auf dem Marktplatz herrschte ein reges Leben.* ◆ *das gesellschaftliche Leben* am Leben sein be alive jdm das Leben retten save sb's life sein Leben lang throughout your life

⊚ jdm das Leben zur Hölle machen make sb's life hell, make sb's life a misery wie das blühende Leben the very picture of health seines Lebens nicht mehr froh werden not enjoy life any more etw. für sein Leben gern tun love doing sth jdn ums Leben bringen take sb's life ums Leben kommen die, lose your life sich [dat] das Leben nehmen take your (own) life etw. ins Leben rufen bring sth into being, set up sth jdm

das Leben schenken give birth to sb jds Leben sein be sb's whole life nie im Leben not on my life

② **le·ben·dig** [le'bɛndɪç] [adj] **1.** lively ◊ *Frau Orth macht einen sehr lebendigen Unterricht.* ◆ *Das Kind ist sehr lebendig.* **2.** living, alive ◊ *ein lebendiger Frosch* ◆ *lebendig gerettet werden* bei lebendigem Leib alive ⊖tot [adv] in a lively manner ◊ *Sie schreibt sehr lebendig.*

② **Le·bens·ge·fahr** ['leːbm̩sɡəfaːʳ, 'leːbənsɡəfaːʳ] die <-> *no pl* mortal danger ◊ *Es besteht Lebensgefahr.* in Lebensgefahr schweben be hovering between life and death außer Lebensgefahr sein be no longer in danger of dying Vorsicht Lebensgefahr! Beware, danger of death!

Le·bens·ge·fähr·te ['leːbm̩sɡəfɛːɐ̯tə, 'leːbənsɡəfɛːɐ̯tə] der <-n, -n>, **Le·bens·ge·fähr·tin** ['leːbm̩sɡəfɛːɐ̯tɪn, 'leːbənsɡəfɛːɐ̯tɪn] die <-, -nen> partner (in life)

Le·bens·hal·tungs·kos·ten ['leːbm̩shaltʊŋskɔstn̩, 'leːbənshaltʊŋskɔstn̩] die <-> *only pl* cost of living ◊ *Die Lebenshaltungskosten sind gestiegen.*

le·bens·läng·lich ['leːbm̩slɛŋlɪç, 'leːbənslɛŋlɪç] [adj] *no comp/superl* (for) life ◊ *eine lebenslängliche Haftstrafe*

⊚ lebenslänglich bekommen get life zu lebenslänglich verurteilt werden be sentenced to life imprisonment

Le·bens·lauf ['leːbm̩slaʊf, 'leːbənslaʊf] der <-(e)s, Lebensläufe> curriculum vitae, C.V., résumé ◊ *ein tabellarischer Lebenslauf*

② **Le·bens·mit·tel** ['leːbm̩smɪtl̩, 'leːbənsmɪtl̩] die <-> *only pl* food ⊖Nahrungsmittel

Le·bens·un·ter·halt ['leːbm̩sʊntɐhalt, 'leːbənsʊntɐhalt] der <-(e)s> *no pl* living, livelihood ◊ *sich den Lebensunterhalt selbst verdienen* für jds Lebensunterhalt aufkommen support sb

Le·ber ['leːbɐ] die <-, -n> liver ◊ *Alkohol schadet der Leber.* ◆ *Heute gibt es gebratene Leber mit Karoffelbrei.*

⊚ frei von der Leber weg *(fam)* frei von der Leber weg sprechen make impromptu remarks etw. frei von der Leber weg äußern/sagen blurt out sth

Le·ber·kä·se ['leːbɛɐ̯kɛːzə] der <-s> *no pl* loaf baked from a mass of finely ground beef, bacon and onions ◊ *warmer Leberkäse mit Kartoffelsalat*

Le·ber·wurst ['leːbɐvʊʳst] die <-> *no pl* liver sausage

⊚ die beleidigte Leberwurst spielen *(fam)* be in a huff

Le·be·we·sen ['leːbəveːzn̩] das <-s, -> creature, being, living thing ◊ *ein menschliches Lebewesen*

Le·be·wohl [leːbə'voːl] das <-(e)s, -e or -s> *(lofty)* farewell

⊚ jdm Lebewohl sagen bid sb farewell

leb·haft ['leːphaft] [adj] <lebhafter, am lebhaftesten> **1.** lively ◊ *Saskia ist ein sehr lebhaftes Kind.* ◆ *eine lebhafte Diskussion* ◆ *Deine Fantasie ist sehr lebhaft.* **2.** *(memory etc.)* vivid ⊖vage [adv] **1.** in a lively manner ◊ *Sie haben lebhaft über diesen Punkt debattiert.* es geht lebhaft zu things are lively **2.** vividly sich [dat] etw. lebhaft vorstel-

len können have a vivid picture of sth ⊖vage **3.** lebhaft an etw. [dat] interessiert sein take a keen interest in sth
Leb·ku·chen ['le:pku:xn̩] der <–s, –> gingerbread

> Gingerbread was originally made from honey and flour and then refined with spices, candied lemon and orange peel and nuts. The centre of gingerbread-making in Germany is Nuremberg, where there have been gingerbread bakers since the year 1395. Later, in 1643, a gingerbread bakers' guild was founded in the city. The art of making gingerbread can probably be traced back to the Franconian monks. Since the Middle Ages, gingerbread has been baked on wafers to stop it sticking to the baking tray. Today, approximately 4,000 people are employed in Nuremberg's gingerbread industry with *Elisen* gingerbread being the speciality of the gingerbread bakers' guild. Named after the daughter of a Nuremberg gingerbread baker, *Elisen* gingerbread has been made since 1808, and is baked using ground nuts instead of wheat flour.

leb·los ['le:plo:s] [adj] <lebloser, am leblosesten> lifeless ◊ *ein lebloser Gesichtsausdruck* ♦ *Die Umgebung war still und leblos.* [adv] lifelessly, showing no signs of life ◊ *Die Katze trieb leblos auf der Wasseroberfläche.*
le·cken ['lɛkn̩] [tr+intr v] +haben lick ◊ *Das Kind leckte ein Eis.* ♦ *Der Tiger leckte die Wunde.*; lap up ◊ *Die Katze leckte die Milch.* jdm/sich etw. von etw. lecken lick sth off sb's/your sth ◊ *Sie leckte sich den Honig von den Fingern.* an etw. [dat] lecken lick sth; *(animal)* sich lecken lick itself [intr v] +haben etw. leckt is leaking ⊚ *etw. sieht aus/ist wie geleckt* sth looks spotless, sth looks spick and span
le·cker ['lɛkɐ] [adj] delicious, tasty ◊ *Der Kuchen war lecker.* ♦ *eine leckere Nachspeise* [adv] in an appetizing way ◊ *Das Essen war lecker zubereitet.*
② **Le·der** ['le:dɐ] das <–s> no pl **1.** leather ◊ *eine Tasche aus Leder* **2.** chammy/chamois (leather) ◊ *Nimm zum Fensterputzen dieses Leder hier.* **3.** *(fam)* SPORT *(football)* das Leder the ball ⊚ *zäh wie Leder* as tough as old boots jdm ans Leder wollen *(fam)* want to get your hands on sb vom Leder ziehen *(fam)* let rip, let fly ◊ *Jetzt zieht er wieder über die Regierung vom Leder.*
Le·der·ho·se ['le:dɐho:zə] die <–, –n> **1.** leather trousers ◊ *Motorradfahrer tragen meist Lederhosen.* **2.** *(regional dress)* lederhosen

> *Lederhosen*, the traditional dress of Bavarian men, are shorts or knee-length trousers made of brown or grey suede. Nowadays they are worn in rural areas and only occasionally as an everyday form of attire. They can frequently be seen at festivals where the men put them on as a sign of local solidarity. The female equivalent is a dress known as a *Dirndl*.

② **le·dig** ['le:dɪç] [adj] no comp/superl **1.** single ◊ *Ich habe drei ledige Brüder.* ◊ *Damals war sie noch ledig.* ⊖verheiratet **2.** *(lofty)* einer Sache [gen] ledig sein be free of sth
le·dig·lich ['le:dɪklɪç] [adv] merely, simply ◊ *Lediglich mein Bruder ist erschienen — niemand*

sonst. ⊖nur, bloß
② **leer** [le:ɐ] [adj] **1.** empty ◊ *Der Tank ist leer.* ♦ *leere Versprechungen sein Glas leer trinken* empty your glass **2.** empty, deserted ◊ *Der Pfarrer predigte vor fast leeren Bänken.* ♦ *Am Sonntag ist die Innenstadt ganz leer.* ⊖voll **3.** blank ◊ *Er hat den Fragebogen leer gelassen.* ♦ *ein leeres Blatt Papier* ⊚ *wie leer gefegt* deserted leer stehend empty, unoccupied leer ausgehen come away empty-handed sich leer fühlen feel empty leer laufen **1.** *(engine)* idle **2.** *(container)* empty, drain etw. leer laufen lassen empty sth, drain sth
lee·ren ['le:rən] [tr v] +haben empty ◊ *Er leerte sein Glas mit einem Zug.* ♦ *Wann wird der Briefkasten geleert?* sich leeren empty ◊ *Nach dem Spiel leerte sich das Stadion.* ⊖füllen
Leer·lauf ['le:ɐlaof] der <–(e)s, Leerläufe> **1.** *(engine)* neutral ◊ *Er ließ das Auto im Leerlauf den Berg hinunterrollen.* **2.** slack period ◊ *Wir müssen unbedingt Leerläufe im Betrieb vermeiden.*
Leer·tas·te ['le:ɐtastə] die <–, –n> space bar ◊ *Sie drückte auf die Leertaste.*
② **le·gen** ['le:gn̩] [tr v] +haben **1.** lay, place ◊ *Er legte die Hemden in den Schrank.* ♦ *Er legte mir die Hand auf die Schulter.* jdn irgendwohin legen put sb down somewhere sich irgendwohin lie down somewhere ◊ *Wir legten uns an den Strand in die Sonne.* sich ins Bett legen go to bed **2.** lay on its side ◊ *Weinflaschen sollte man legen, nicht stellen.* **3.** lay ◊ *Fliesen legen* ♦ *Rohre legen* **4.** put, place ◊ *Legen Sie den Teig eine Stunde lang in den Kühlschrank.* **5.** *(hair)* [tr+intr v] +haben *(eggs)* lay ◊ *Im Winter legen die Hühner nicht.* ♦ *Diese Henne legt viele Eier.* [ref v] +haben **1.** sich auf etw. [acc] legen settle on sth ◊ *Dicker Staub hatte sich auf die Regale gelegt.* **2.** *(wind)* sich legen die down, abate; *(mist, fog etc.)* clear; *(anger, indignation)* subside sich Enttäuschung hat sich gelegt sb got over their disappointment
le·gen·där [legɛn'dɛ:ɐ] [adj] legendary ◊ *der legendäre König Midas* ♦ *Der Fall Schneider ist inzwischen legendär geworden.*
le·ger [le'ʒe:ɐ, le'ʒɛ:ɐ] [adj, adv] casual(ly) ◊ *legere Freizeitkleidung* ♦ *Die Atmosphäre im Klub ist leger.* ♦ *eine legere Haltung* ♦ *Sie hat eine schwierige Situation leger gehandhabt.*
Leh·ne ['le:nə] die <–, –n> back(rest) ◊ *die Lehne des Aut sitzes verstellen*; arm(rest) ◊ *die Arme auf die Lehnen stützen*
leh·nen ['le:nən] [tr+intr v] +haben lean ◊ *das Fahrrad gegen eine Hauswand lehnen* ♦ *Er lehnte seinen Kopf an sie.* ♦ *Die Leiter lehnt am Apfelbaum.* sich lehnen ◊ *Lehn dich nicht zu weit aus dem Fenster!*
Lehr·buch ['le:ɐbu:x] das <–(e)s, Lehrbücher> textbook ◊ *ein mathematisches Lehrbuch* ♦ *ein Lehrbuch der/über Biologie* ein Fall wie aus dem Lehrbuch a textbook case
② **Leh·re** ['le:rə] die <–, –n> **1.** doctrine, teaching ◊ *die christliche Lehre* ♦ *die Lehren Luthers* **2.** die Lehre von etw. the science of sth ⊖Wissenschaft **3.** teaching ◊ *Lehre und Forschung an der Universität* ⊖Unterricht **4.** apprenticeship, training ◊ *eine dreijährige/kaufmännische Lehre* ♦ *Er hat eine Lehre als Bäcker gemacht.* bei jdm/etw. in die Lehre gehen, bei jdm/etw. eine Lehre machen

serve your apprenticeship with sb/sth, train with sb/sth/at sth *box@* Ausbildung **5.** lesson ◊ *Der Unfall war eine heilsame Lehre für sie.* jdm eine Lehre erteilen teach sb a lesson eine Lehre aus etw. ziehen learn a lesson from sth ⊜Erfahrung

leh·ren ['leːrən] [tr+intr v] +*haben* **1.** (jdn etw. [acc]) lehren teach (sb sth) ◊ *Wer hat dich so gut Klavier spielen gelehrt?* das wird dich lehren that will teach you jdn das Fürchten lehren scare sb ◊ *Ihr Erfolg lehrte die Konkurrenz das Fürchten* die Erfahrung lehrt (uns) ... experience tells us ... ◊ *Die Erfahrung lehrt (uns), dass diese Methode nicht ungefährlich ist.* ⊜beibringen ⊜lernen **2.** (etw.) lehren teach (sth), lecture (in sth) ◊ *Er lehrt (Theologie) an der Universität Augsburg.* ♦ *Sie lehrt die erste Klasse Deutsch.* ⊜unterrichten

② **Leh·rer** ['leːrɐ] der <-s, ->, **Leh·re·rin** ['leːrərɪn] die <-, -nen> teacher ◊ *Er ist Lehrer von Beruf.* ♦ *Die Lehrerin hat uns keine Hausaufgaben aufgegeben.*; *(private)* tutor; *(driving)* instructor

Lehr·gang ['leːɡɡan] der <-(e)s, Lehrgänge> course ◊ *ein Lehrgang zum zertifizierten Projektmanager* einen Lehrgang machen, an einem Lehrgang teilnehmen take a course ⊜Kurs

② **Lehr·ling** ['leːɡlɪŋ] der <-s, -e> apprentice, trainee ◊ *Lehrlinge ausbilden* ⊜Azubi

Lehr·stel·le ['leːɡʃtɛlə] die <-, -n> apprenticeship, traineeship ◊ *eine Lehrstelle als Friseur* ⊜Ausbildungsplatz

Leib [laɛp] der <-(e)s, -er> body; *(uterus)* womb ◊ *die Entwicklung des Kindes im Leib der Mutter* am ganzen Leib all over Leib und Leben life and limb bei lebendigem Leib, lebendigen Leibes alive ◊ *Sie verbrannten ihn bei lebendigem Leib.* kein trockenes Kleidungsstück mehr am Leib haben be soaked to the skin jdm die Kleider vom Leib reißen tear sb's clothes off

◉ mit Leib und Seele with all your heart and soul etw. am eigenen Leib erfahren/zu spüren bekommen experience sth for yourself jdm (mit etw.) vom Leib(e) bleiben/gehen *(fam)* leave sb alone (with sth) jdm (wie) auf den Leib geschrieben/geschneidert/geschnitten sein be tailor-made for sb sich [dat] jdn/etw. vom Leib(e) halten *(fam)* keep sb/sth at bay jdm etw. vom Leib(e) halten *(fam)* spare sb sth jdm jdn vom Leib(e) halten *(fam)* keep sb away from sb einer Sache [dat] zu Leibe/auf den Leib rücken tackle sth

leib·lich ['laɛplɪç] [adj] *no comp/superl* **1.** *only before ns* biological ◊ *die leiblichen Eltern* **2.** physical, bodily ◊ *das leibliche Wohl*

Lei·che ['laɛçə] die <-, -n> (dead) body, corpse ◉ (noch) eine Leiche im Keller haben have a skeleton in the cupboard/closet jds Weg ist mit Leichen gepflastert **1.** *sb is unscrupulous and has stopped at nothing in order to be successful* **2.** sb's path is strewn with corpses über Leichen gehen *(pej)* stop at nothing

② **leicht** [laɛçt] [adj] <leichter, am leichtesten> light ◊ *leichte Kleidung tragen* ♦ *leichte Lektüre* ♦ *Der Koffer ist ganz leicht.* [adj, adv] **1.** slight(ly), light(ly) ◊ *leichter Regen* ♦ *eine leichte Besserung/Verschlechterung* ♦ *Die Schmerzen waren zunächst leicht, wurden aber immer stärker.* ♦ *Er war nur leicht verletzt.* leicht erkältet sein have a slight

cold ⊜geringfügig **2.** easy(-ily) ◊ *kein leichtes Leben haben* ♦ *Diese Aufgabe ist nicht leicht.* ♦ *Dieser Effekt ist relativ leicht zu erreichen.* ♦ *So etwas kann leicht schief gehen!* etw. fällt jdm leicht sth is easy for sb es leicht haben (mit jdm/etw.) have it easy (with sb/sth) (jdm) etw. leicht machen make sth easy (for sb) es jdm nicht leicht machen give sb a hard time es sich [dat] leicht machen take the easy option, take an easy way out etw. leicht nehmen take sth easy sich leicht tun (mit etw.) manage (sth) easily ◊ *Er tut sich leicht mit dem Lernen/in der Schule.* leicht verderblich/entflammbar highly perishable/inflammable

◉ leicht möglich quite possible du hast leicht reden/lachen it's all right for you to talk/laugh nichts leichter als das there's nothing to it, it's a piece of cake

Leicht·ath·le·tik ['laɛçtlat,leːtɪk] die <-> *no pl* SPORT athletics, track and field

leicht·fer·tig ['laɛçtfɛˀtɪç] [adj, adv] careless(ly) ◊ *eine leichtfertige Art haben* ♦ *Sie ist leichtfertig und verantwortungslos.* ♦ *Er hat seine letzte Chance leichtfertig vertan.* ♦ *etw. leichtfertig aufs Spiel setzen* ⊜leichtsinnig

leicht·sin·nig ['laɛçtzɪnɪç] [adj, adv] careless(ly), irresponsible(-ibly) ◊ *ein leichtsinniger Umgang mit Feuer* ♦ *Als nichts passierte, wurde sie leichtsinnig.* ♦ *leichtsinnig mit Geld umgehen* ⊜leichtfertig ⊜umsichtig

leid [laɛt] [adj] *invariable* jdn/etw. leid sein be fed up with sb/sth, be tired of sb/sth ◊ *Ich bin diesen frechen Schüler leid!* etw. leid werden get fed up with sth, get tired of sth es leid sein, etw. zu tun be fed up with doing sth, be tired of doing sth

Leid [laɛt] das <-(e)s> *no pl* **1.** suffering ◊ *jdm großes Leid zufügen/antun* ♦ *Sie versuchten, das Leid der Kranken zu lindern.* jdm sein Leid klagen tell sb your troubles ⊜Kummer **2.** jd tut jdm Leid sb feels sorry for sb etw. tut jdm Leid sb feels sorry for/about sth, sb regrets sth ◊ *Das wird ihm noch einmal Leid tun!* es/das tut jdm Leid sb is sorry ◊ *Es tut mir Leid, dass es nicht geklappt hat.*

◉ geteiltes Leid ist halbes Leid a sorrow shared is a sorrow halved, a trouble shared is a trouble halved jdm etw. zu Leid(e) tun → zuleide

② **lei·den** ['laɛdn] <leidet, litt, hat gelitten> [tr+intr v] suffer ◊ *Sie hat sehr gelitten, als ihre Ehe zerbrach.* ♦ *Hunger und Durst leiden müssen* unter jdm/etw. leiden suffer because of sb/sth ◊ *Die Kinder litten unter dem strengen Lehrer.* an/unter etw. [dat] leiden suffer from sth Schaden leiden be damaged [tr v] jdn/etw. (gut) leiden können/mögen like sb/sth jd kann etw./jdn nicht leiden sb cannot stand sth/sb

Lei·den·schaft ['laɛdnʃaft] die <-, -en> passion ◊ *Seine große Leidenschaft gilt der Kunst.* mit/voller Leidenschaft passionately ein Verbrechen aus Leidenschaft a crime of passion Lehrer/Tänzer etc. aus Leidenschaft sein be a passionate teacher/dancer etc.

② **lei·der** ['laɛdɐ] [adv] unfortunately ◊ *Ich muss dich leider enttäuschen.* ♦ *Er konnte leider nicht kommen.* leider ja/nein I'm afraid so/not

Ⓩ **lei·hen** ['laɐən] <leiht, lieh, hat geliehen> ⟨tr v⟩
1. jdm etw. leihen lend sb sth, lend sth to sb ◊ *Er hat mir für den Umzug sein Auto geliehen.* **2.** (sich ⟨dat⟩) etw. (von/bei jdm/etw.) leihen borrow sth (from sb/sth) ◊ *Ich musste mir Geld bei der Bank leihen.* ⊖borgen

Leim [laɛm] der <-(e)s> *no pl* glue ◊ *etw. mit Leim bestreichen*
● *jdm auf den Leim gehen (fam, hum)* be taken in by sb, fall for sb's tricks

Lei·ne ['laɛnə] die <-, –n> **1.** *(for dogs)* lead, leash ◊ *einen Hund an die Leine legen/nehmen* ♦ *einen Hund an der Leine führen/von der Leine lassen* **2.** *(fig)* jdn an die Leine legen bridle sb jdn an die kurze Leine nehmen keep sb on a short leash jdn an der langen Leine lassen allow sb leeway **3.** *(clothes)* line ◊ *die Wäsche an/auf die Leine hängen* ♦ *Wäsche von der Leine nehmen* **4.** SHIP rope Leinen los! Cast off! **5.** *(fishing)* line **6.** string ◊ *die Leine eines Drachens*
● **Leine ziehen** *(fam, emph)* push off ◊ *Zieh Leine, du störst!*

Lei·nen ['laɛnən] das <-s> *no pl* linen ◊ *feinstes Leinen* ♦ *ein Hemd aus Leinen; (of a book cover)* cloth; *(for painting)* canvas

Lein·wand ['laɛnvant] die <-, Leinwände> **1.** *(also fig)* screen ◊ *Die Dias werden auf eine Leinwand projiziert.* ♦ *Stars der Leinwand* **2.** ARTS canvas ◊ *Diese Gemälde sind Öl auf Leinwand.*

Ⓩ **lei·se** ['laɛzə] ⟨adj, adv⟩ <leiser, am leisesten>
1. quiet(ly) ◊ *Seid bitte leise, das Baby schläft!* ♦ *leise lachen* mit leiser Stimme in a low voice sei(d) ein bisschen leiser! don't make so much noise! etw. leiser stellen/drehen turn sth down ⊖laut **2.** faint(ly), slight(ly) ◊ *Er wacht schon vom leisesten Geräusch auf.* ♦ *Allmählich regten sich in ihr leise Zweifel.* ♦ *Die Seide raschelte leise.* **3.** *(wind, touch etc.)* light(ly), gentle(-tly) ◊ *einen leisen Luftzug spüren*

Leis·te ['laɛstə] die <-, –n> **1.** strip ◊ *eine schmale Leiste aus Holz*; skirting board, baseboard ◊ *Der Teppich ist verlegt, jetzt fehlen nur noch die Leisten.*; trim ◊ *Die Leisten an den Kotflügeln dienen nur der Zierde.* **2.** IT bar ◊ *ein Symbol auf der Leiste anklicken* **3.** ANAT groin ◊ *an der Leiste operiert werden*

Ⓩ **leis·ten** ['laɛstn̩] <leistet, leistete, hat geleistet> ⟨tr v⟩ **1.** achieve, do ◊ *Er hat das Gefühl, nicht genug zu leisten.* Großes leisten achieve sth great; *(engine, machine etc.)* produce Weißt du, wie viel dieser Motor leistet? Do you know how powerful this engine is? **2.** *empty verb* gute/ganze Arbeit leisten do a good/thorough job jdm einen Dienst leisten render sb a service seinen Militärdienst leisten do your military/national service (jdm) (als etw.) gute Dienste leisten serve (sb) well (as sth) Überstunden leisten do overtime (viel) Überzeugungsarbeit leisten do a lot of convincing einen Beitrag (zu etw.) leisten make a contribution (to sth) (jdm) für etw. Ersatz leisten compensate (sb) for sth eine Zahlung leisten make a payment (jdm) Hilfe leisten help (sb) jdm Beistand leisten give/lend sb your support Geburtshilfe leisten assist at a birth einen Eid leisten swear/take an oath Widerstand (gegen jdn/etw.) leisten resist (sb/sth), put up resistance (against sb/sth)

einer Sache Vorschub leisten promote sth ⟨ref v⟩
1. sich ⟨dat⟩ etw. leisten treat yourself to sth ◊ *Sie haben sich ein neues Auto geleistet.* sich ⟨dat⟩ eine Dummheit leisten do sth stupid sich ⟨dat⟩ eine Frechheit leisten be cheeky Was hast du dir da wieder geleistet? What have you been up to again? **2.** jd kann sich ⟨dat⟩ etw. leisten sb can afford sth

Ⓩ **Leis·tung** ['laɛstʊŋ] die <-, –en> **1.** performance ◊ *Sie hätten eine bessere Leistung bringen können.* ♦ *eine schwache Leistung zeigen* ♦ *Seine schulischen Leistungen haben nachgelassen.* ♦ *jdn nach Leistung bezahlen* **2.** achievement ◊ *Dieser Aufsatz ist eine hervorragende/schwache Leistung.* **3.** TECHN capacity, power ◊ *die Leistung eines Rechners* ♦ *ein Motor mit 80 PS Leistung* **4.** *most pl* benefit ◊ *staatliche Leistungen für Familien* vermögenswirksame Leistung *employer's contribution to employees' saving schemes* **5.** *most pl* service ◊ *die Leistungen eines Rechtsanwalts in Anspruch nehmen*
● **eine reife Leistung** *(fam)* **1.** well done, a great job **2.** *(iron)* just great

Leis·tungs·kurs ['laɛstʊŋskʊɐs] der <-es, –e> SCHOOL main subject during the sixth form/senior high school ◊ *einen Leistungskurs belegen* box@ Grundkurs, Kollegstufe

In the *Kollegstufe*, or *gymnasiale Oberstufe*, pupils can generally choose two main subjects from among a number of subjects. These should reflect their talents and inclinations. They have more classes in their main subjects than in other subjects and these main subjects play an essential part in their final *Abitur* exams. However, this system is under review in some of the German states.

Ⓩ **lei·ten** ['laɛtn̩] ⟨tr v⟩ +haben **1.** run, manage ◊ *ein Unternehmen/Projekt leiten*; *(a team)* lead; *(a discussion, meeting etc.)* head, chair; *(a school)* be head of; *(an orchestra)* conduct; *(a sports match)* referee etw. kommissarisch leiten be the interim manager of sth ⊖führen **2.** *(through a pipe)* pipe ◊ *Abwässer in einen Fluss leiten*; *(traffic)* route sich von etw. leiten lassen follow sth ⟨tr+intr v⟩ +haben PHYSICS, TECHN conduct, carry gut/schlecht leiten be a good/bad conductor

Lei·ter¹ ['laɛtɐ] die <-, –n> ladder ◊ *auf eine Leiter steigen*

Lei·ter² ['laɛtɐ] der <-s, –> PHYSICS, TECHN conductor

Lei·ter³ ['laɛtɐ] der <-s, –>, **Lei·te·rin** ['laɛtərɪn] die <-, –nen> *(of a company etc.)* manager, director; *(of a group)* leader; *(of a meeting, discussion etc.)* chair; *(of a school)* head(teacher), principal; *(of an orchestra)* conductor; *(of a band)* leader

Leit·plan·ke ['laɛtplaŋkə] die <-, –n> crash barrier, guard rail

Ⓩ **Lei·tung** ['laɛtʊŋ] die <-, –en> **1.** *no pl (of a task)* management ◊ *Das Projekt steht unter ihrer Leitung.* künstlerische Leitung artistic direction ◊ *die künstlerische Leitung eines Theaters* die Leitung (... ⟨gen⟩) haben be in charge (of sth) die Leitung (... ⟨gen⟩) übernehmen take over the management (of sth), become head/director/manager (of sth); *(instruction)* unter der Leitung von jdm/unter jds Leitung under sb's direction/guidance;

(of an orchestra) conducted by sb ⊖Führung
2. chair(s) ◊ *die Leitung der Kommission; (of a company)* management ⊖Führung, Spitze **3.** *(of a telephone)* line ◊ *Die Leitung ist frei/besetzt/unterbrochen/gestört/tot.* Hold (the line). **4.** TECHN *(for electricity)* cable, lead, wire; *(for water, gas)* pipe *Wasser aus der Leitung tap water; (leading to the house)* main(s)
⊛ **eine lange Leitung haben** *(fam)* be slow on the uptake **auf der Leitung stehen** *(fam)* not really be with it

Lek·ti·on [lɛkˈtsjoːn] die <–, –en> *(also fig)* lesson ◊ *Wir sind bei Lektion 12.* ♦ *Die Niederlage war eine bittere Lektion für sie.* jdm eine Lektion erteilen teach sb a lesson eine Lektion in Sachen ... a lesson in ...

Lek·tü·re [lɛkˈtyːrə] die <–, –n> **1.** reading matter *Lektüre für den Urlaub* books/a book for the holidays *keine Lektüre für Kinder* unsuitable for children to read *etw.* als Lektüre *(im Unterricht)* haben study/read sth as a set book **2.** *no pl* reading ◊ *Bei der Lektüre des Artikels bin ich auf Widersprüche gestoßen.*

Len·de [ˈlɛndə] die <–, –n> loin ◊ *ein Stück Lende vom Schwein* ♦ *Er hatte ein Handtuch um die Lenden gewunden.*

len·ken [ˈlɛŋkn̩] [tr+intr v] +*haben* **1.** steer ◊ *Sie lenkte (uns) sicher durch den Verkehr.* ♦ *Lenk den Schlitten nach rechts!* ♦ *Lass mich auch mal lenken!* ⊖steuern **2.** drive ◊ *Wer lenkte den Bus zum Zeitpunkt des Unfalls?; (as a pilote)* be in control ⊖steuern [tr v] +*haben* **1.** *etw.* in die richtigen Bahnen lenken put sth on the right track jds Aufmerksamkeit auf sich lenken attract sb's attention jds Aufmerksamkeit auf etw./jdn lenken draw sb's attention to sb/sth den Verdacht auf jdn lenken throw suspicion on sb das Gespräch auf etw. [acc]/in eine andere Richtung lenken steer the conversation onto sth/ into another direction **2.** seine Aufmerksamkeit auf etw./jdn lenken turn your attention to/towards sth/sb seinen Blick auf etw./jdn lenken turn your gaze on sth/sb seine Gedanken auf etw. [acc] lenken focus your thoughts on sth ⊖richten **3.** govern, rule ◊ *Wer wird nach der Wahl das Land lenken?* ⊖führen **4.** *(also pej)* control ◊ *Die Industrie in diesem Land wird staatlich gelenkt.*

Len·ker¹ [ˈlɛŋkɐ] der <–s, –> **1.** handlebars **2.** *(fam)* steering wheel ◊ *Er sitzt täglich am/ hinter dem Lenker seines Lkw.* ⊖Lenkrad

Len·ker² [ˈlɛŋkɐ] der <–s, –>, **Len·ke·rin** [ˈlɛŋkərɪn] die <–, –nen> **1.** driver ◊ *Der Lenker des Unfallwagens flüchtete.* ⊖Fahrer **2.** *(lofty)* leader ◊ *Im Spiel ist er der Denker und Lenker der Mannschaft.*

Lenk·rad [ˈlɛŋkraːt] das <–(e)s, Lenkräder> steering wheel ◊ *am/hinterm Lenkrad sitzen* ♦ *das Lenkrad einschlagen* das Lenkrad verreißen swerve ⊖Steuer, Lenker
⊛ **sich hinters Lenkrad klemmen** *(fam, hum)* get behind the wheel

② **ler·nen** [ˈlɛrnən] [tr+intr v] +*haben* **1.** learn ◊ *Vokabeln lernen* ♦ *Sie muss noch lernen, höflicher zu sein.* Ordnung/Geduld lernen learn to be tidy/ patient; *(+inf)* ... lernen learn (how) to do sth ◊

Ich möchte gerne Gitarre spielen lernen. (etw.) aus etw. lernen learn (sth) from sth ◊ *aus seinen Fehlern lernen* **2.** revise ◊ *Für die Schulaufgabe hat er fleißig gelernt.* **3.** *(etw.)* lernen train (as sth) ◊ *Er will Schlosser lernen.*

Ler·ner [ˈlɛrnɐ] der <–s, –>, **Ler·ne·rin** [ˈlɛrnərɪn] die <–, –nen> learner ◊ *Lerner des Deutschen*

les·bisch [ˈlɛsbɪʃ] [adj] *no comp/superl* lesbian ◊ *lesbische Paare* sie ist lesbisch she is a lesbian

② **le·sen** [ˈleːzn̩] <liest, las, hat gelesen> [tr+intr v] **1.** read ◊ *Hast du das Buch schon gelesen?* ♦ *Kannst du Noten lesen?* ♦ *Er saß am Frühstückstisch und las (die) Zeitung.* über etw./jdn lesen, von etw./jdm lesen read about sth/sb **2.** UNI lecture ◊ *Er liest (Physik) an der Technischen Universität.* über etw./jdn lesen lecture on sth/sb ◊ *Professor Buhr liest dieses Semester über Goethe.* [tr v] REL eine/die Messe lesen say mass [ref v] *etw.* liest sich gut/schlecht sth is easy/hard to read sich lesen wie ein Krimi read like a detective story

Le·ser [ˈleːzɐ] der <–s, –>, **Le·se·rin** [ˈleːzərɪn] die <–, –nen> reader geneigter Leser gentle reader ♦

le·ser·lich [ˈleːzɐlɪç] [adj, adv] legible(-ibly) ◊ *leserliche Buchstaben* ♦ *Seine Schrift wird allmählich leserlicher.* ♦ *leserlich schreiben* kaum leserlich almost illegible jd schreibt kaum leserlich sb's (hand)writing is hard to read

Let·te [ˈlɛtə] der <–n, –n>, **Let·tin** [ˈlɛtɪn] die <–, –nen> Latvian → Deutsche

Let·tin [ˈlɛtɪn] *fem of* Lette

let·tisch [ˈlɛtɪʃ] [adj] *mostly before ns* Latvian → deutsch

Let·tisch [ˈlɛtɪʃ] das <–(s)> *seldom with article, no pl* Latvian → Deutsch

Lett·land [ˈlɛtlant] das <–s> *article only in combination with attribute* Latvia → Deutschland

letz·te [ˈlɛtstə] [adj] *no comp/superl, only before ns* <ein letzter ..., eine letzte ..., ein letztes ...> last ◊ *im letzten Augenblick* an letzter Stelle liegen be last letztes Mal, beim letzten Mal last time in den letzten Tagen/Jahren in the last few days/years in letzter Zeit, in der letzten Zeit recently

② **Letz·te¹** [ˈlɛtstə] der/die <–n, die Letzten> *but: ein Letzter/eine Letzte* der/die Letzte the last person, the last one ◊ *Er wäre der Letzte, dem ich vertrauen würde.* als Letzte(r) ins Ziel kommen, Letzte(r) werden come last
⊛ **der Letzte (des Monats)** the last day of the month

Letz·te² [ˈlɛtstə] das <–n> *but: ein Letztes, no pl* **1.** das Letzte the last thing ◊ *Das war das Letzte, was sie gesagt hat.* als Letztes finally, in the end **2.** bis zum Letzten with all your might ◊ *Er hat sich bis zum Letzten dagegen gewehrt.* sein Letztes geben give your all jdm das Letzte an etw. [dat] abverlangen demand the utmost/maximum sth from/of sb bis zum Letzten gehen go to the limit(s); *(fam)* das Letzte sein be the pits

letz·te·re [ˈlɛtstərə] [adj] *no comp/superl, only before ns* latter ◊ *Ich ziehe (die) letztere Möglichkeit vor.*

letzt·lich [ˈlɛtstlɪç] [adv] **1.** finally ◊ *Seine Suche war letzlich erfolgreich.* **2.** ultimately, in the end (of the day) ◊ *Der Streit beruht letzlich auf einem Missverständnis.*

leuch·ten [ˈlɔɥçtn̩] <leuchtet, leuchtete, hat

geleuchtet> [intr v] **1.** shine, glow ◇ *Das Zifferblatt leuchtet in der Dunkelheit.* ♦ *Die Augen der Kinder leuchteten.* **2.** *(colo(u)rs)* be bright, glow ◇ *leuchtend rot/gelb/orange* bright red/yellow/orange **3.** mit etw. irgendwohin leuchten shine sth somewhere [tr v] jdm den Weg leuchten light the way for sb

leug·nen ['lɔɡnən] <leugnet, leugnete, hat geleugnet> [tr v] deny ◇ *Er leugnete seine Schuld.* ♦ *Sie leugnete, davon gewusst zu haben.* es ist nicht zu leugnen, dass ... it is undeniable that ... ⊜zugeben, gestehen, eingestehen

Leu·te ['lɔɡtə] die <–> *only pl* **1.** people ◇ *Manche Leute wollen das nicht glauben.* ♦ *Solche Musik gefällt den (jungen) Leuten.* ♦ *Auf der Party waren etwa 50 Leute.* ♦ *Was werden bloß die Leute sagen?* vor den/allen Leuten in front of everybody **2.** *(fam)* family, folks ◇ *Schnell heim, das muss ich meinen Leuten erzählen!*; *(employees etc.)* people, staff ◇ *Er bezahlt seine Leute gut.*; *(address)* guys ◇ *Was sollen wir jetzt machen, Leute?*

⊚ **wir sind geschiedene Leute 1.** our ways have parted **2.** I will have no more to do with you etw. **unter die Leute bringen** *(fam)* **1.** spread sth ◇ *Wer hat dieses Gerücht unter die Leute gebracht?* **2.** sell sth ◇ *Wie bringen wir dieses Produkt unter die Leute?* **unter (die) Leute gehen/kommen** go/get out

Le·xi·kon ['lɛksikɔn] das <–s, Lexika> encyclopaedia ◇ *ein medizinisches Lexikon* ♦ *ein Lexikon der Literatur* ♦ *etw. im Lexikon nachschlagen*

⊚ **ein wandelndes Lexikon** *(fam, hum)* a walking encyclopaedia

② **li·be·ral** [libeˈraːl] [adj] **1.** POL Liberal ◇ *ein liberaler Poltiker* ♦ *Ist er eher konservativ oder liberal?* ⊜konservativ **2.** liberal ◇ *gegenüber etw. eine liberale Haltung einnehmen* ♦ *Ihre Erziehungsmethoden waren sehr liberal.*

licht [lɪçt] [adj] <lichter, am lichtesten> **1.** *(lofty, also fig)* light ◇ *Die Kirche war ein wunderbar lichter Bau.* ⊜hell ⊖dunkel **2.** sparse ◇ *ein lichter Wald* ♦ *Sein Haar war schon etwas licht.* ⊖dicht **3.** lucid ◇ *Manchmal hat er auch lichte Momente.* **4.** *only before ns* TECHN internal; *(of a bridge)* lichte Höhe headroom lichte Weite span

② **Licht** [lɪçt] das <–(e)s, –er> light **1.** *Setz dich ans Fenster, da hast du mehr Licht.* ♦ *Geh mir bitte aus dem Licht.* ♦ *das Licht anmachen/anschalten* ♦ *das Licht ausmachen/löschen* ♦ *Im Wohnzimmer ist Licht an.* etw. gegen das Licht halten hold sth up to the light etw. das Licht machen turn the light on

⊚ **Licht in die Sache/Angelegenheit bringen** shed some light on the matter das Licht der Welt erblicken *(lofty)* come into the world, be born das ewige Licht REL the Sanctuary Lamp (jdm) (für etw.) grünes Licht geben give (sb) the green light (for sth) in einem guten/schlechten/ungünstigen etc. Licht erscheinen appear in a good/bad/an unfavourable etc. light jdn/etw. ins rechte Licht rücken/setzen put sb/sth in a favourable light ein schlechtes etc. Licht auf jdn/etw. werfen throw/cast a bad etc. light on sb/sth bei Licht(e) besehen/betrachten upon closer consideration etw. ans Licht bringen bring sth out into the open jdn hinters Licht führen pull

the wool over sb's eyes jdm geht ein Licht auf *(fam)* it dawns on sb ans Licht kommen be revealed, come to light

Licht·bild ['lɪçtbɪlt] das <–(e)s, –er> *(form)* (passport) photograph ◇ *Bitte legen Sie dem Antrag zwei Lichtbilder bei.*

Lid [liːt] das <–(e)s, –er> eyelid

Lid·schat·ten ['liːtʃatn] der <–s, –> eyeshadow ◇ *Lidschatten auftragen*

② **lieb** [liːp] [adj] **1.** kind, nice ◇ *Andi ist ein lieber Kerl.* ♦ *Das war aber lieb von dir.* ♦ *Sei so lieb und mach das Fenster zu!* ♦ *Du bist viel zu lieb zu ihm.* ⊜nett **2.** good, nice ◇ *Heute haben wir sehr liebe Kinder.* ⊜brav **3.** welcome, pleasant ◇ *ein lieber Gast* ♦ *Dein Besuch ist mir sehr lieb.* es wäre jdm lieb, wenn ... sb would like it if ... es wäre jdm lieber/am liebsten, wenn ... sb would prefer it if ... ◇ *Es wäre mir am liebsten, wenn du jetzt gingst.* ♦ *Morgen wäre mir lieber.* **4.** *only before ns* dear (old) ◇ *meine lieben Eltern* die lieben Kleinen the little darlings/angels das liebe Geld the wretched money jds liebster/liebste/liebstes ... sb's favourite ..., sb's favorite ... ◇ *Der Sessel ist mein liebster Platz zum Lesen.* **5.** *(address)* dear ◇ *Liebe Frau Lerch, ...* ♦ *Mein lieber Schatz, ...* Lieber Gott (Good) Lord [adv] **1.** ◇ *Er geht mit seinem Sohn sehr lieb um.* ♦ *Sie hat sich lieb bedankt. Er hat mir ganz lieb geholfen.* He was very kind and helped me. jdn liebe Grüße ausrichten/bestellen, jdn lieb grüßen send sb your love ◇ *Max lässt dich lieb grüßen.* **2.** well, nicely ◇ *sich lieb benehmen* ⊜unartig

⊚ **jdn lieb behalten** love sb, go on loving sb jdn **lieb gewinnen** grow fond of sb **lieb geworden** much loved ◇ *liebe gewordene Traditionen zur Weihnachtszeit* etw. ist jdm lieb geworden sb has grown very fond of sth jdn **lieb haben** love sb ◇ *Andi, ich hab dich lieb.*

② **Lie·be** ['liːbə] die <–> *no pl* **1.** love ◇ *Die beiden verbindet eine große Liebe.* ♦ *aus Liebe heiraten* ♦ *Die erste Liebe vergisst man nie.* **2.** Liebe (zu etw.) love (for sth) ◇ *seine Liebe zur Musik*

⊚ **Liebe auf den ersten Blick** love at first sight **Liebe geht durch den Magen** the way to a man's heart is through his stomach **bei aller Liebe** *(fam)* much as I sympathize **käufliche Liebe** prostitution **mit Liebe** lovingly, with loving care ◇ *Das Essen war mit Liebe gekocht.*

② **lie·ben** ['liːbm̩] [tr v] +haben **1.** love ◇ *Ich liebe dich, Andi.* ♦ *Er liebt seine Heimat.* sie lieben sich they love one another ◇ *Wir lieben uns nicht mehr.* ⊜hassen **2.** love, like, be fond of ◇ *Sie liebt Kuchen.* es lieben, etw. zu tun enjoy doing sth ⊜mögen ⊖hassen **3.** *(sexual)* sie lieben sich they make love ◇ *Sie haben sich im Heu geliebt.*

⊚ **was sich liebt, das neckt sich** *those in love will tease each other*

lie·ber ['liːbɐ] *comp of* gern, lieb

lie·bens·wür·dig ['liːbm̩svʏrˌdɪç, 'liːbənsvʏrˈdɪç] [adj] kind, charming ◇ *Wären Sie so liebenswürdig, mir die Tür aufzuhalten?* ♦ *ein liebenswürdiger junger Mann* ⊜freundlich

Lie·bes·kum·mer ['liːbəskʊmɐ] der <–s> *no pl* lovesickness Liebeskummer haben be lovesick

lie·be·voll ['liːbəfɔl] [adj, adv] **1.** loving(ly), with loving care ◇ *Katze in liebevolle Hände abzugeben.*

♦ *jdn liebevoll umsorgen* ⊖*lieblos* **2.** affectionate(ly) ◊ *Sie warf ihm einen liebevollen Blick zu.*
♦ *Seine Umarmung war so liebevoll.* ♦ *Sie sah ihn liebevoll an.* ⊖*zärtlich*

Lieb·ha·ber ['liːphaːbɐ] der <-s, ->,
Lieb·ha·be·rin ['liːphaːbərɪn] die <-, -nen>
1. lover **2.** *(of things)* enthusiast, lover, aficionado ◊ *Diese Sammlung ist etwas für Liebhaber.* ein Liebhaber guten Essens etc. sein love good food etc.

⑦ **Lieb·ling** ['liːplɪŋ] der <-s, -e> **1.** *(address)* darling ◊ *Liebling, würdest du mal bitte kommen?* ⊖*Schatz* **2.** favourite, favorite, darling ◊ *Felix ist mein Liebling.* ♦ *Er ist der Liebling aller Frauen.* der Liebling des Lehrers/der Lehrerin the teacher's pet

⑦ **Lieb·lings·...** ['liːplɪŋs] [prefix] favourite ..., favorite ... ◊ *Das ist unser Lieblingslied.* ♦ *Latein ist Ullas Lieblingsfach.*

Lieb·lings·ge·richt ['liːplɪŋsɡərɪçt] das <-(e)s, -e> favourite dish, favorite dish ◊ *Heute koche ich dein Lieblingsgericht.*

lieb·los ['liːploːs] [adj, adv] <liebloser, am lieblosesten> **1.** unfeeling(ly), unkind(ly) ◊ *eine lieblose Kindheit* ♦ *Mein Mann ist so lieblos.* ♦ *Wir sind ziemlich lieblos erzogen worden.* ⊖*liebevoll*
2. *when used as an adj, only before ns* careless(ly) ◊ *die lieblose Behandlung von etw.* ♦ *lieblos mit etw. umgehen* Essen lieblos zubereiten prepare food without care

⑦ **liebs·ten** ['liːpstn̩] *superl of* gern, lieb

⑦ **Lied** [liːt] das <-(e)s, -er> **1.** song ◊ *ein Lied singen/trällern* ♦ *das Lied der Lerche*; *(in church)* hymn; *(at Christmas)* carol **2.** lied ◊ *Lieder von Franz Schubert*
⊙ *es ist immer dasselbe Lied* it's always the same old story *davon kann ich ein Lied singen* I could tell you a thing or two about that

⑦ **lief** [liːf] *pret of* laufen

Lie·fe·rant [lifə'rant] der <-en, -en>,
Lie·fe·ran·tin [lifə'rantɪn] die <-, -nen> supplier ◊ *unser Lieferant für Obst* ♦ *eine verlässliche Lieferantin*; *(person also)* deliveryman Lieferantin deliverywoman der Eingang für Lieferanten the delivery entrance

lie·fer·bar ['liːfebaːɐ] [adj] *no comp/superl* available, in stock ◊ *ein lieferbarer Artikel* ♦ *Das Buch ist zurzeit nicht lieferbar.* etw. ist sofort/kurzfristig lieferbar sth can be supplied/delivered immediately/at short notice

⑦ **lie·fern** ['liːfen] [tr v] +*haben* **1.** deliver, supply ◊ *Wir liefern Ihre Möbel frei Haus.* jdm etw. liefern supply sb with sth, deliver sth to sb ◊ *Wer hat Ihnen bislang das Öl geliefert?* **2.** provide, produce ◊ *Ich kann Beweise für seine Unschuld liefern.* ♦ *Das tägliche Leben liefert den Stoff für viele Bücher.*; *(in sports, a performance etc.)* put on ◊ *Unsere Mannschaft hat ein gutes Spiel geliefert.* sie liefern sich eine Schlacht/einen guten Wettkampf etc. they put on a battle/a good contest etc. [intr v] +*haben* deliver ◊ *Wir liefern innerhalb von 24 Stunden.* frei Haus liefern deliver free of charge

Lie·ge ['liːɡə] die <-, -n> **1.** folding bed ◊ *Ich schlafe auf der Liege.* **2.** (sun)lounger ◊ *sich auf der Liege sonnen*

⑦ **lie·gen** ['liːɡn̩] <liegt, lag, hat gelegen> [intr v] *in South G, Austr, Swiss often* +*sein* **1.** *(person, animal)* lie ◊ *Er liegt im Bett.* ♦ *Der Patient muss liegen.* **2.** be, lie ◊ *Auf dem Tisch lag ein Zettel für mich.* ♦ *Die Betonung liegt auf der ersten Silbe.* ♦ *In den Alpen liegt viel Schnee.*; *(fog etc.)* hang somewhere ◊ *Dichter Nebel lag über der Stadt.* vor Anker liegen be anchored, lie at anchor im Hafen liegen be in port **3.** be (situated) ◊ *Ulm liegt an der Donau.* ♦ *Das Hotel liegt in günstiger Verkehrslage.* **4.** *(room, window)* zu etw. liegen face sth, look out on/over sth ◊ *Das Schlafzimmer liegt zum Innenhof.* nach Süden/Norden etc. liegen face south/north etc. **5.** *(sequential)* be ◊ *Wir liegen auf Platz zwei in der Tabelle.* (weit) vor/hinter jdm liegen be (far) ahead of/behind sb in Führung liegen be in the lead an der Spitze (... [gen]) liegen be (at the) top (of sth) **6.** etw. liegt jdm sth suits sb, sb has a talent/an aptitude for sth, sb likes sth ◊ *Die Rolle des Machos liegt ihm.* ♦ *Naturwissenschaften liegen ihm nun mal nicht.* **7.** etw. liegt an jdm/etw. sth is caused by sb/sth, sb/sth is responsible for sth, sth is sb's/sth's fault ◊ *Der Fehler liegt an der Software.* ♦ *„Ich bin ständig müde."* — *„Das liegt am Wetter."* es liegt daran, dass it is because **8.** bei jdm liegen be up to sb ◊ *Die Entscheidung liegt bei dir.*
⊚ jdm liegt an etw. [dat] sth is of importance to sb jdm liegt viel/wenig/nichts an etw. [dat] sth is very/not (very) important to sb, sth means a lot/little/nothing to sb ◊ *Meinem Vater liegt wenig an uns.* liegen bleiben **1.** *(on the ground etc.)* not get up again *(in bed)* stay in bed, have a lie-in **2.** *(snow)* stay **3.** be left behind ◊ *Bei dem Konzert sind einige Schirme liegen geblieben.* **4.** be left undone ◊ *Während meines Urlaubs ist viel liegen geblieben.* **5.** *(car)* break down ◊ *Wir sind auf der Autobahn liegen geblieben.* etw. liegen lassen **1.** leave sth ◊ *Lass den Zettel bitte da liegen.* **2.** forget sth ◊ *das Handy liegen lassen* **3.** leave sth (undone) ◊ *Lass das doch bis morgen liegen.* an mir solls nicht liegen I'm all for it, I have nothing against it

⑦ **lieh** [liː] *pret of* leihen

⑦ **ließ** [liːs] *pret of* lassen¹, lassen²

⑦ **liest** [liːst] *pres of* lesen

⑦ **Lift** [lɪft] der <-(e)s, -e> **1.** lift, elevator ◊ *Ich fahre nicht gern mit dem Lift.* ⊖*Aufzug, Fahrstuhl* **2.** (ski) lift

Li·ga ['liːɡaː] die <-, Ligen> **1.** SPORT league, division ◊ *Der FC Bayern ist in eine höhere Liga aufgestiegen.* **2.** POL league ◊ *die Liga der Arabischen Staaten* **3.** POL *(party)* league ◊ *In Pakistan gibt es eine Moslem-Liga.*

Li·kör [li'køːɐ] der <-s, -e> liqueur ◊ *einen Likör trinken*

li·la ['liːlaː] [adj] *invariable* lilac, mauve, purple ◊ *Sie trug einen lila Pullover.* etw. blüht lila sth has lilac/mauve/purple flowers

Li·mo ['lɪmoː, 'liːmoː] die <-, -s> *also pl 'Limo'* *when used with expressions of quantity (fam)* *(abbr of* Limonade) lemonade ◊ *Ich nehme eine Limo.*

⑦ **Li·mo·na·de** [limo'naːdə] die <-, -n> *(abbr* Limo) lemonade

Lin·de ['lɪndə] die <-, -n> lime ◊ *die Linde vor dem Haus* ♦ *ein Regal aus Linde*

lin·dern ['lɪndən] ⟨tr v⟩ +*haben* relieve, ease, alleviate ◊ *Die Salbe lindert die Schmerzen.* ✦ *Das hat meinen Kummer gelindert.*

Li·ne·al [line'a:l] das ⟨-s, -e⟩ ruler mit dem Lineal einen Strich ziehen rule a line, draw a line with a ruler

② **Li·nie** ['li:njə] die ⟨-, -n⟩ **1.** line ◊ *eine durchgezogene Linie auf der Straße; (paper)* mit Linien ruled **2.** row, line ◊ *Die Bäume sind in einer Linie gepflanzt.* **3.** route, line ◊ *Der Kapitän ist diese Linie schon oft gefahren.* **4.** number ◊ *Welche Linie fährt zum Bahnhof?* **5.** line, policy, direction ◊ *Unser Chef versucht, immer nur seine Linie durchzusetzen.* eine klare Linie erkennen lassen reveal a clear line/policy **6.** line (of the hand) **7.** sport line, boundary ◊ *Sein Aufschlag traf genau auf die Linie.*

◉ in erster Linie most/first of all ◊ *In erster Linie sollten wir auf den Inhalt achten.* auf ganzer/der ganzen Linie complete(ly), all along the line ◊ *In Englisch hat Max auf ganzer Linie versagt.* (schlanke) Linie figure ◊ *Sie achtet sehr auf ihre (schlanke) Linie.* jdn/etw. auf Linie bringen bring sb/sth into line ◊ *Die Basis muss auf Linie gebracht werden.*

Li·ni·en·bus ['li:njənbʊs] der ⟨-ses, -se⟩ (regular) bus ◊ *Zwischen Stadion und Bahnhof verkehrt ein Linienbus.*

Li·ni·en·flug ['li:njənflu:k] der ⟨-(e)s, Linienflüge⟩ scheduled flight

② **lin·ke** ['lɪŋkə] ⟨adj⟩ ⟨linker, linkeste⟩ ⟨ein linker ..., eine linke ..., ein linkes ...⟩ **1.** left(-hand) ◊ *Mein linker Arm ist geschwollen.* ✦ die linke Hälfte des Gehirns auf der linken Seite on the left(-hand side) ⊖rechte **2.** pol left(wing), leftist ◊ *Er gehört zum linken Flügel der Partei.* ⊖rechte

② **links¹** [lɪŋks] ⟨adv⟩ **1.** left ◊ *links abbiegen* links fahren drive on the left ◊ *In England fährt man links.* nach links to the left von links from the left; on the left(-hand side) ◊ *Links siehst du dann die Tankstelle.* ⊖rechts **2.** pol links stehen be leftwing, be on the left links wählen vote for the left ⊖rechts **3.** auf links inside out, on the reverse ◊ *Du hast das T-Shirt auf links an.* ✦ *Sie trägt die Bluse auf links.*

◉ jdn/etw. links liegen lassen ignore sb/sth, snub sb/sth links stricken purl ◊ *Der Schal ist zwei links, zwei rechts gestrickt.* mit links **1.** with the left hand ◊ *Ich kann mit links nicht schreiben.* **2.** easily, without any trouble ◊ *Das macht der mit links.*

② **links²** [lɪŋks] ⟨prep⟩ ⟨+gen⟩ or ⟨+dat⟩ **1.** +gen on the left side of ◊ *Frankreich liegt links des Rheins.* **2.** *adverbial* ⟨+dat⟩ links von jdm to sb's left ◊ *Sie saß links von mir.* links von etw. to the left of sth

Links·hän·der ['lɪŋkshɛndɐ] der ⟨-s, -⟩, **Links·hän·de·rin** ['lɪŋkshɛndərɪn] die ⟨-, -nen⟩ left-hander ◊ *eine Gitarre für Linkshänder* Linkshänder(in) sein be left-handed ◊ *Anja ist Linkshänderin.*

Links·par·tei ['lɪŋkspa'taɪ] die ⟨-⟩ *no pl* → PDS

Lin·se ['lɪnzə] die ⟨-, -n⟩ **1.** *(glass, plastic)* lens ◊ *Die Linse meiner Kamera ist verschmutzt.* **2.** anat lens ◊ *Im Alter hatten sich seine Linsen getrübt.* **3.** *most pl* bot lentil ◊ *Heute gibt es Linsen mit Speck.*

Lip·pe ['lɪpə] die ⟨-, -n⟩ lip ◊ *Sie hatte sich die Lippen geschminkt.*

◉ eine freche Lippe riskieren *(fam)* be brazen, get fresh eine große Lippe riskieren *(fam)* shoot your mouth off etw. nicht über die Lippen bringen not bring yourself to say sth an jds Lippen hängen **1.** hang on sb's every word **2.** give sb a (long and) lingering kiss

Lip·pen·stift ['lɪpm̩ʃtɪft] der ⟨-(e)s, -e⟩ lipstick ◊ *Sie trägt Lippenstift.* ✦ *Lippenstift auftragen*

List [lɪst] die ⟨-, -en⟩ (cunning) trick, ruse ◊ *eine List anwenden*

◉ mit List und Tücke *(fam, hum)* by cunning

② **Lis·te** ['lɪstə] die ⟨-, -n⟩ **1.** list (sich ⟨dat⟩ eine Liste machen draw up/make a list jdn/etw. von einer Liste streichen cross sb/sth off a list etw./ sich in eine Liste eintragen put sth/yourself (down) on a list **2.** pol *(of candidates)* (party) list ◊ *Sie kandidiert auf der Liste der Grünen.*

◉ (bei jdm) auf der schwarzen Liste stehen **1.** be blacklisted (by sb) **2.** *(fig)* be unpopular (with sb), be crossed off the/sb's Christmas card list

Li·tau·en [litaʊən ˌlɪtaʊən] das ⟨-s⟩ *article only in combination with attribute* Lithuania → Deutschland

Li·tau·er [litaʊɐ ˌlɪtaʊɐ] der ⟨-s, -⟩, **Li·tau·e·rin** [litaʊərɪn ˌlɪtaʊərɪn] die ⟨-, -nen⟩ Lithuanian → Deutsche

li·tau·isch [litaʊɪʃ ˌlɪtaʊɪʃ] ⟨adj⟩ *mostly before ns* Lithuanian → deutsch

Li·tau·isch [litaʊɪʃ ˌlɪtaʊɪʃ] das ⟨-(s)⟩ *seldom with article, no pl* Lithuanian → Deutsch

Li·ter ['li:tɐ] der ⟨-s, -⟩ litre, liter ◊ *fünf Liter Wein* ✦ *ein halber Liter Milch*

li·te·ra·risch [lɪtə'ra:rɪʃ] ⟨adj, adv⟩ literary ◊ *Er hat eine ausgesprochene literarische Begabung.* literarisch interessiert interested in literature etw. literarisch verwerten use sth in your writing ein literarisch anspruchsvoller Schriftsteller an author of quality literature

Li·te·ra·tur [lɪtəra'tu:ɐ] die ⟨-, -en⟩ literature ◊ *die Literatur des 19. Jahrhunderts* ✦ *romanische Sprachen und Literaturen* ✦ *Literatur zum Thema Gentechnik* ✦ *Literatur studieren*

② **litt** [lɪt] *pret of* leiden

live [laɪf] ⟨adv⟩ live ◊ *Das Spiel wird live übertragen.*

Li·zenz [li'tsɛnts] die ⟨-, -en⟩ **1.** licence, license ◊ *Wir haben eine Lizenz zur Produktion dieser Maschinen.* **2.** licence, license, registration, accreditation ◊ *Dem Trainer wurde die Lizenz entzogen.*

② **Lkw** ['ɛlka:ve:, - - '-] der *(abbr of* Lastkraftwagen*)* lorry, truck ◊ *einen Lkw fahren* ⊖Lastwagen

Lob [lo:p] das ⟨-(e)s⟩ *no pl* praise ◊ *Er verlor kein Wort des Lobes.* jdm ein Lob aussprechen praise sb voll des Lobes für jdn sein be full of praise for sb ein Lob auf jdn/etw., ein Lob ... ⟨dat⟩ (my/our) compliments to sb ◊ *Ein Lob der Köchin/auf die Technik!* ⊖Tadel

② **lo·ben** ['lo:bm̩] ⟨tr v⟩ +*haben* jdn/etw. (für/wegen etw.) loben praise sb/sth (for sth) ◊ *Ein Lehrer sollte seine Schüler auch loben.* ✦ *Sie hat mich für diese Arbeit gelobt.* (hoch) gelobt werden be acclaimed

② **Loch** [lɔx] das ⟨-(e)s, Löcher⟩ **1.** hole ◊ *ein Loch*

graben **2.** *(in clothes)* hole ◊ *Du hast ein Loch in
der Hose.; (in the head also)* gash; *(tooth also)*
cavity; *(road)* pothole ◊ *Die Straße war voller
Löcher.; (tyre)* puncture **3.** sport *(golf)* hole ◊ *ein
Platz mit 18 Löchern; (pool)* pocket **4.** *(fig)* gap,
hole ◊ *Der Staatshaushalt weist ein Loch von einer
Billiarde auf.* ein großes Loch in jds Geldbeutel
reißen make a big hole in sb's pocket **5.** *(fam,
pej)* dump, hole ◊ *Er haust in einem dunklen,
feuchten Loch.*

◉ jdm Löcher in den Bauch fragen *(fam)* pester
sb with questions Löcher in die Luft starren
(fam) stare into space

Lo·cke ['lɔkə] die <-, -n> curl Locken haben have
curly hair sich [dat] Locken machen lassen have
your hair curled

lo·cken ['lɔkɳ] [tr v] +*haben* **1.** ein Tier irgendwohin locken lure an animal somewhere jdn irgendwohin locken lure/bring sb somewhere ◊ *Die Aktion
soll mehr Kunden in den Laden locken.* **2.** *(an
animal)* call **3.** etw. lockt jdn sb is tempted by sth
ein lockendes Angebot a tempting offer [intr v]
+*haben* have great appeal ◊ *Im Sommer locken die
Freibäder.*

lo·cker ['lɔkɐ] [adj] **1.** loose ◊ *Die Schraube ist
locker.* ✦ *ein lockerer Zahn* ⊖los ⊕fest **2.** light,
loose ◊ *Pulverschnee liegt schön locker.* ✦ *ein
lockerer Kuchenteig* **3.** slack, loose ◊ *ein lockeres
Brett* ✦ *Der Knoten ist zu locker.* **4.** relaxed, not
strict ◊ *Die Disziplin ist dort ziemlich locker.* ✦ *eine
lockere Handhabung der Regeln* **5.** *(fam)* easygoing, cool ◊ *Nun bleib mal ganz locker!* ⊖steif
6. *(remark etc.)* casual, frivolous ◊ *ein lockerer
Spruch* [adv] **1.** slackly, loosely ◊ *Das Seil hing
locker durch.* ✦ *Er hielt die Zügel locker in der
Hand.* **2.** not strictly ◊ *die Vorschriften locker
handhaben* **3.** *(fam) (remark etc.)* casually ◊
locker daherreden sich locker unterhalten have an
easy-going conversation ◊ *Wir haben uns ganz
locker unterhalten.* etw. locker sehen not take sth
too seriously ⊖steif **4.** *(fam)* easily, with ease ◊
*Die Firma zahlt eine solche Summe doch ganz
locker.* **5.** ein locker fallendes Kleid a loose-fitting
dress ⊖los ⊕fest

◉ locker flockig *(fam)* cool as you like locker
sitzen **1.** be loose ◊ *Die Schraube/Der Zahn sitzt
locker.* **2.** *(clothes)* fit loosely, be slack ◊ *Die Hose
saß auch mal lockerer.*

lo·cker|las·sen ['lɔkɐlasṇ] <lässt locker, ließ
locker, hat lockergelassen> [intr v] *(always* nicht
lockerlassen) not give up, not let up ◊ *Nur nicht
lockerlassen, du schaffst das schon!*

lo·ckern ['lɔkɐn] [tr v] +*haben* **1.** *(the soil)* break
up ◊ *Würmer lockern den Boden.* **2.** loosen,
slacken ◊ *Er lockerte seine Krawatte.* **3.** *(muscles)*
relax, loosen up **4.** *(controls, rules etc.)* relax ◊
*An den Grenzen sind die Kontrollen gelockert
worden.* [ref v] +*haben* **1.** *(screw, tooth etc.)* come
loose **2.** *(athlete)* loosen up, limber up ◊ *Vor dem
Turnen wollen wir uns lockern.* **3.** *(relationship
etc.)* get more relaxed die Fronten lockern sich
positions soften

⑦ **Löf·fel** ['lœfl] der <-s, -> **1.** *(cutlery)* spoon ◊ *Sie
rührte mit dem Löffel in der Tasse.* **2.** spoonful ◊
ein gehäufter Löffel Zucker

⑦ **log** [lo:k] *pret of* lügen

Lo·ge ['lo:ʒə] die <-, -n> box ◊ *Plätze in der Loge*

lo·gisch ['lo:gɪʃ] [adj, adv] **1.** logical(ly) ◊ *das
logische Denken fördern* ✦ *Diese Folgerung ist
nicht logisch.* ✦ *logisch denken können* **2.** *(fam)*
logisch (,dass ...) sure (...) ◊ *„Kommst du auch
mit?“ — „Logisch!“*

⑦ **Lohn** [lo:n] der <-(e)s, Löhne> **1.** wages, pay ◊
einen höheren Lohn fordern **2.** reward ◊ *Als Lohn
für das gute Zeugnis bekam er ein Rad.*

⑦ **loh·nen** ['lo:nən] [ref v] +*haben* sich lohnen be
worth it, be worthwhile ◊ *Es lohnt sich nicht, den
alten Computer aufzurüsten.* die Mühe lohnt sich it
is worth the effort der/ein Besuch ... [gen] lohnt
sich sth is worth a visit ◊ *Ein Besuch des
Deutschen Museums lohnt sich wirklich.* Der Film
lohnt sich. The film is worth seeing/watching.

⊖sich rentieren

Lohn·steu·er ['lo:nʃtɔøɐ] die <-, -n> income tax ◊
Lohnsteuer zahlen

Lohn·steu·er·kar·te ['lo:nʃtɔøɐkaʁtə] die <-, -n>
card showing tax payments and social security contributions made by an employee during a tax year

Lok [lɔk] die <-, -s> *(abbr of* Lokomotive) locomotive, engine

⑦ **Lo·kal** [lo'ka:l] das <-s, -e> bar, pub, restaurant ◊
Wir gehen in einem netten Lokal.

Lol·li ['lɔli] der <-s, -s> *(fam)* lollipop ◊ *einen/an
einem Lolli lutschen*

⑦ **los¹** [lo:s] [adj] *no comp/superl, not before ns* loose
◊ *Vorsicht, das Brett ist los.* ⊖locker ⊕fest

◉ jdn/etw. los sein *(fam)* **1.** be rid of sb/sth
2. have lost sb/sth mit jdm ist nichts los *(fam)*
sb is a waste of time, sb is a dead loss es ist viel/
wenig/nichts/etwas los there is a lot/not much/
nothing/something going on Wo ist denn hier was
los? Where is the action around here? was ist
(denn) los *(fam)* what is the matter, what's up
was ist mit jdm los *(fam)* what's wrong with sb,
what's the matter with sb, what's up with sb

los² [lo:s] [interj] come on, get going ◊ *Los, beeil
dich, wir verpassen sonst den Zug!* Los, hau
endlich ab! Clear off quick!

Los [lo:s] das <-es, -e> **1.** *(lottery)* ticket; *(raffle)*
ticket ◊ *ein Los kaufen/ziehen; (for making
decisions)* lot ◊ *Das Los soll entscheiden.*
2. *(lofty) (fate)* lot ◊ *ein schweres Los haben*

◉ mit jdm/etw. das große Los ziehen hit the
jackpot with sb/sth

⑦ **los|...** [lo:s] [prefix] **1.** off ◊ losfahren ✦ *Wann
fliegt ihr los?* ✦ *Er lief los.* **2.** start doing sth ◊ losschlagen ✦ losweinen **3.** losschrauben unscrew
etw. nicht losbekommen not be able to get sth off
loskoppeln unhitch

lö·schen ['lœʃn] [tr v] +*haben* **1.** extinguish, put
out ◊ *einen Brand löschen* **2.** *(the light)* switch
off, turn off ⊖ausmachen ⊖anmachen **3.** delete ◊
Daten löschen; (an account) close **4.** erase, wipe
◊ *Ich habe das Tonband gelöscht.* **5.** seinen Durst
löschen quench your thirst **6.** *(a ship etc.)* unload
⊖entladen

lo·se ['lo:zə] [adj] **1.** loose ◊ *An deinem Mantel ist
ein Knopf lose.* ✦ *lose Blätter* ✦ *Hier kann man
Schrauben lose kaufen.* **2.** cheeky ◊ *Sie hat ein
loses Mundwerk.* ✦ *lose Sprüche*

⑦ **lö·sen** ['lø:zən] [tr v] +*haben* **1.** dissolve ◊ *Lösen Sie
die Tablette in einem Glas Wasser.* sich lösen

dissolve ◊ *Fett löst sich nicht in Wasser.*
⊖auflösen **2.** remove ◊ *Er versuchte, die Brief-marke vom Umschlag zu lösen.*; *(wallpaper also)* peel off *sich lösen come off* ⊖befestigen **3.** undo; *(the handbrake)* release, let off *sich lösen come undone* ◊ *Der Knoten löste sich.*; detach itself, come off ◊ *Das Hinterrad hatte sich gelöst.* **4.** ease ◊ *Eine Massage löst die Verspannungen.*; *(a cough, phlegm)* loosen *sich lösen* ease, loosen ◊ *Der Husten löst sich.* **5.** *(form)* buy ◊ *den Fahr-schein im Zug lösen* **6.** solve ◊ *Dieser Fall wurde nie gelöst.*; *(a maths problem, crossword puzzle)* do *sich lösen* be solved ◊ *Das Rätsel hat sich gelöst.* ⌈ref v⌉ +haben **1.** *(shot)* go off ◊ *Plötzlich löste sich ein Schuss.* **2.** sich von jdm/etw. lösen break away from sb/sth ◊ *sich von der Vergangen-heit lösen*

los|fah·ren ['loːsfaːrən] <fährt los, fuhr los, ist los-gefahren> ⌈intr v⌉ set off

los|ge·hen ['loːsgeːən] <geht los, ging los, ist los-gegangen> ⌈intr v⌉ **1.** set off ◊ *Wir sollten losgehen, sonst verpassen wir den Zug.* **2.** *(fam)* start ◊ *Wann geht das Kino los?* gleich geht's los it's starting *auf „los" geht's los* they're off on the word "go" **3.** go off ◊ *Plötzlich ging der Alarm los.* **4.** *(fam)* (mit etw.) auf jdn losgehen go for sb (with sth)

los|kom·men ['loːskɔmən] <kommt los, kam los, ist losgekommen> ⌈intr v⌉ **1.** *(fam)* von jdm/etw. loskommen get away from sb/sth ◊ *Er kommt von dieser Frau einfach nicht los.*; *(drugs etc.)* come off sth **2.** von etw. loskommen free yourself from sth

los|krie·gen ['loːskriːgn̩] <kriegt los, kriegte los, hat losgekriegt> ⌈tr v⌉ *(fam)* **1.** get off ◊ *Der Knoten war so fest, dass ich die Schnur nicht los-gekriegt habe.*; get undone ◊ *Ich kann die Schraube nicht loskriegen.* **2.** get rid of ◊ *Das alte Auto kriegen wir sicher nicht mehr los.*

los|las·sen ['loːslasn̩] <lässt los, ließ los, hat los-gelassen> ⌈tr+intr v⌉ let go ◊ *He, lass (mich) los!* ⌈tr v⌉ **1.** *(also fig)* ein Tier/jdn (auf jdn) loslassen let an animal/sb loose (on sb) ◊ *Die Polizei ließ die Hunde auf den Flüchtigen los.* **2.** jdn nicht loslassen haunt sb ◊ *Der Gedanke an die armen Kinder lässt mich nicht los.*

los|le·gen ['loːsleːgn̩] <legt los, legte los, hat losgelegt> ⌈intr v⌉ *(fam)* get going, get started ◊ *Sie bekam den Auftrag und legte gleich los.*

lös·lich ['løːslɪç] ⌈adj⌉ soluble ◊ *löslicher Kaffee* ◆ *Zucker ist in Wasser löslich.*

los|rei·ßen ['loːsraɪsn̩] <reißt los, riss los, hat los-gerissen> ⌈tr v⌉ tear off ◊ *Der Sturm hat das Boot losgerissen.* ⌈ref v⌉ **1.** sich losreißen break free, break loose ◊ *Der Hund hat sich von der Leine los-gerissen.* **2.** sich von etw. losreißen tear yourself away from sth ◊ *Kannst du dich mal vom Computer losreißen und mir helfen?*

② **Lö·sung** ['løːzʊŋ] die <-, -en> **1.** solution ◊ *eine elegante Lösung finden* ◆ *eine hochprozentige Lösung* **2.** answer, solution ◊ *Die Lösungen der Aufgaben stehen hinten im Buch.* ⊖Auflösung

los|wer·den ['loːsveːɐdn̩] <wird los, wurde los, ist losgeworden> ⌈tr v⌉ **1.** get rid of ◊ *Ich werde meine Erkältung einfach nicht los.* **2.** lose ◊ *beim Glücks-spiel sein Geld loswerden*

Lot·to ['lɔto] das <-s> *no pl* lottery ◊ *Sie hat im Lotto gewonnen.*

Lö·we ['løːvə] der <-n, -n> **1.** lion **2.** ASTROL, ASTRON Leo

Lö·win ['løːvɪn] die <-, -nen> lioness

lt. [laʊt] *(abbr of* laut*)* according to ◊ *lt. § 12 der Straßenverkehrsordnung*

Lü·cke ['lʏkə] die <-, -n> gap ◊ *Da ist eine Lücke im Zaun.* ◆ *Grammatikkenntnisse mit großen Lücken* ◆ *Sein Tod hinterlässt eine schmerzliche Lücke.*; *(in legislation)* loophole

lud [luːt] *pret of* laden

② **Luft** [lʊft] die <-, Lüfte> **1.** air ◊ *frische Luft herein-lassen* ◆ *Sie warf den Ball in die Luft.* ◆ *Er wollte etwas frische Luft schnappen.* etw. in die Luft sprengen blow sth up in die Luft gehen explode **2.** *no pl* breath, air ◊ *nach Luft ringen* ◆ *die Luft anhalten* Luft holen take a breath

⊙ **von Luft und Liebe leben** live on love and air **dicke Luft** *(fam)* a tense atmosphere **die Luft anhalten** *(fam)* be quiet **2.** keep things in pro-portion **sich in Luft auflösen** *(fam)* vanish into thin air **jdn wie Luft behandeln** *(fam)* totally ignore sb **in die Luft gehen** *(fam)* blow your top, hit the roof **in der Luft liegen** be in the air **einer Sache** ⌈dat⌉ **Luft machen** *(fam)* give vent to sth ◊ *Jetzt muss ich meinem Ärger mal Luft machen.* **aus der Luft gegriffen sein** be plucked out of thin air

Luft·bal·lon ['lʊftbaˌlɔŋ, ˈlʊftbaˌloːŋ] der <-s, -s *or* -e> balloon ◊ *Luftballons steigen lassen*

lüf·ten ['lʏftn̩] <lüftet, lüftete, hat gelüftet> ⌈tr v⌉ **1.** air ◊ *die Wohnung/Betten lüften* **2.** reveal, disclose ◊ *ein Geheimnis lüften* ⌈intr v⌉ let some air in ◊ *Wird hier eigentlich nie gelüftet?*

Luft·mat·rat·ze ['lʊftmaˌtratsə] die <-, -n> air mattress, Lilo™

② **Luft·post** ['lʊftpɔst] die <-> *no pl* airmail ◊ *einen Brief per Luftpost verschicken*

Luft·zug ['lʊftsuːk] der <-(e)s, Luftzüge> *most sing* current (of air) ◊ *Ein Luftzug ließ die Tür zufallen.*; *(unpleasant)* draught, draft ◊ *ein kalter Luftzug*

② **Lü·ge** ['lyːgə] die <-, -n> lie ◊ *Erzähl mir keine Lügen.* ⊖Wahrheit

⊙ **Lügen haben kurze Beine** the truth will out **jdn Lügen strafen** prove sb a liar

② **lü·gen** ['lyːgn̩] <lügt, log, hat gelogen> ⌈intr v⌉ lie **wie gedruckt lügen** lie through your teeth

Lun·ge ['lʊŋə] die <-, -n> ANAT lung(s) ◊ *Rauchen schadet der Lunge.*

⊙ **sich** ⌈dat⌉ **die Lunge aus dem Hals schreien** *(fam)* scream your head off, shout at the top of your voice **die eiserne Lunge** the iron lung **die grüne Lunge** the green lungs **auf Lunge rauchen** inhale

Lu·pe ['luːpə] die <-, -n> magnifying glass ◊ *etw. unter die Lupe betrachten*

⊙ **jdn/etw. unter die Lupe nehmen** take a close look at sb/sth

② **Lust** [lʊst] die <-, Lüste> **1.** *no pl* pleasure, joy **Lust haben, etw. zu tun** feel like doing sth **Lust auf etw.** ⌈acc⌉ **haben** feel like sth ◊ *Lust zu etw.* **haben** feel like sth ◊ *Ich habe selten Lust zum Arbeiten. Mir ist die Lust vergangen.* I've lost all

enthusiasm. sich mit Lust an die Arbeit machen set
to work enthusiastically Lust verlieren lose interest
etw. aus purer Lust machen do sth for the love of
it **2.** lust, desire ◊ *seine Lust befriedigen*
⦿ nach Lust und Laune *as you like* ◊ *Du kannst
hier nicht einfach nach Lust und Laune kommen
und gehen.* as much as you like

② **lus·tig** ['lʊstɪç] [adj] **1.** funny, amusing ◊ *eine
lustige Geschichte* ♦ *Ich finde seine Witze
überhaupt nicht lustig.* ⊝komisch **2.** merry, jolly ◊
Ich mag ihre lustige Art. ♦ *An dem Abend waren
wir alle lustig.* ⊝heiter ⊕mürrisch
⦿ das kann ja (noch) lustig werden *(fam)*
that's going to be fun sich über jdn/etw. lustig
machen make fun of sb/sth so lange/wie jd
lustig ist *(fam)* (for) as long as you like

lut·schen ['lʊtʃn] [tr+intr v] *+haben* suck ◊
Bonbons lutschen an etw. [dat] lutschen suck sth ◊
am Daumen lutschen

Lu·xem·burg ['lʊksm̩bʊʳk] das <–s> *article only in
combination with attribute, no pl* Luxembourg →
Deutschland

Lu·xem·bur·ger[1] ['lʊksm̩bʊʳgɐ] [adj] *invariable,
only before ns* Luxembourg, Luxembourg

Lu·xem·bur·ger[2] ['lʊksm̩bʊʳgɐ] der <–s, –>,
Lu·xem·bur·ge·rin ['lʊksm̩bʊʳgərɪn] die
<–, –nen> Luxembourger → Deutsche

lu·xem·bur·gisch ['lʊksm̩bʊʳgɪʃ] [adj] *mostly before
ns* Luxemburgish → deutsch

Lu·xem·bur·gisch ['lʊksm̩bʊʳgɪʃ] das <–(s)> *no pl*
Luxemburgish → Deutsch

Lu·xus ['lʊksʊs] der <–> *no pl* luxury ◊ *im Luxus
leben* ♦ *Das ist der reinste Luxus.*

Ly·rik ['lyːrɪk] die <–> *no pl* (lyric) poetry
⊝Poesie

M

m, M [ɛm] das <-(s), -(s)> m, M ◊ *Dieses Wort wird mit einem kleinen m/großen M geschrieben.* ♦ *M wie Martha*

M [ɛm] *(abbr of* medium*) (clothing size)* medium ◊ *ein T-Shirt in (der) Größe M*

ⓩ **ma·chen** [ˈmaxn̩] [tr v] *+haben* **1.** do ◊ *Was macht er beruflich?* ♦ *Hast du deine Hausaufgaben!* ♦ *Das lässt sich machen.* ♦ *Das hast du gut gemacht.* **2.** make ◊ *Den Tisch hat mein Mann selbst gemacht.* ♦ *Wein wird aus Trauben gemacht.* ♦ *Lärm/Fehler machen* ♦ *Gewinn machen* ♦ *jdn glücklich machen* etw. aus jdm machen make sb into sth ◊ *Er hat einen großen Star aus ihr gemacht.* jdn zu jdm machen make sb sth ◊ *Sie haben ihn zum Direktor gemacht.* **3.** *(sorrow, anxiety, problems)* cause ◊ *Du machst mir Sorgen.* ♦ *Leo macht oft Schwierigkeiten.; (a headache, courage, pleasure, a fright, hope)* give **4.** *(fam)* repair, fix ◊ *Ich habe den kaputten Stuhl machen lassen.* etw. wieder ganz machen mend sth **5.** have ◊ *Er macht am Samstag eine Party.* **6.** *(an examination, a test, break)* take ◊ *das Abitur machen* ♦ *den Führerschein machen* ♦ *eine Pause machen* **7.** *(with prices, figures)* be ◊ *Das macht zusammen 25 Euro.* **8.** *(animal)* go ◊ *Die Katze macht miau.* **9.** *(regional, fam)* put ◊ *Sie macht immer drei Löffel Zucker in den Kaffee.* **10.** *(fam)* play the part of, be ◊ *Wer macht den Hamlet?* **11.** etw. aus etw. machen turn sth into sth ◊ *Aus der Kirche wurde eine Galerie gemacht.* [intr v] *+haben* **1.** do ◊ *Lass mich mal machen.* **2.** *(fam)* hurry (up) ◊ *Nun mach schon! Mach, dass du verschwindest!* Clear off quick! **3.** *(fam)* wet ◊ *Hat er ins Bett gemacht.; (faeces)* soil **4.** etw. macht müde/hungrig/schlank etc. sth makes you tired/hungry/(look) slim **5.** *(pej)* auf Chef/Diva etc., machen act the boss/diva etc. auf beleidigt/dumm/schlau machen act offended/stupid/clever, pretend to be offended/stupid/clever [ref v] *+haben* **1.** sich (gut) machen come on/along (well) ◊ *Er macht sich gut in der Schule.* **2.** sich gut/schön/nicht gut machen look good/beautiful/not so good ◊ *Das Bild macht sich gut an dieser Wand.* **3.** sich an die Arbeit/ans Kochen/an die Schulaufgaben [acc] machen get down to work/cooking/doing your homework

◉ mach, dass du wegkommst get out of here etw. macht etwas sth matters (to sb) etw. macht jdm etwas sb minds etw. macht nichts sth doesn't matter ◊ *„Oje, das habe ich vergessen!" — „Das macht nichts!"* etw. macht jdm nichts sb doesn't mind ◊ *Es macht mir nichts, wenn er nicht kommt.* sich [dat] nichts/viel/wenig aus etw. machen not care at all for/care a lot about/not to care much about sth

ⓩ **Macht** [maxt] die <-, Mächte> **1.** power ◊ *Er hat keine Macht über mich.* ♦ *an der Macht sein* ♦ *die Macht ergreifen* ♦ *eine feindliche Macht* in jds Macht stehen be (with)in sb's power **2.** force ◊ *die Macht der Gewohnheit* mit (aller) Macht with all your might **3.** *most pl (supernatural being)* power, force ◊ *von bösen Mächten besessen sein*

mäch·tig [ˈmɛçtɪç] [adj] **1.** powerful ◊ *China ist ein mächtiges Land.* **2.** *only before ns* massive ◊ *eine mächtige Eiche* Ich habe mächtigen Hunger. I am terribly hungry. Da hast du aber mächtiges Glück gehabt. You were mightily lucky there. Das wird mächtigen Ärger geben. That will cause a tremendous amount of trouble. **3.** *(lofty)* einer Sache [gen] mächtig sein be in control of sth; *(a language)* speak ◊ *Ich bin des Chinesischen leider nicht mächtig.* [adv] *(fam)* mightily ◊ *Ich bin mächtig stolz auf dich.* sich mächtig anstrengen make a tremendous effort sich mächtig beeilen get a real move on sich mächtig ins Zeug legen work flat out mächtig frieren be frozen to the bone

Ma·cke [ˈmakə] die <-, -n> *(fam)* **1.** quirk ◊ *Wir haben alle unsere Macken.* **2.** defect, blemish ◊ *Möbel mit kleinen Macken*

ⓩ **Mäd·chen** [ˈmɛːtçən] das <-s, -> girl ◎ Junge ◉ Mädchen für alles *(fam)* dogsbody ◊ *Er ist in der Firma das Mädchen für alles.*

Mäd·chen·na·me [ˈmɛːtçənnaːmə] der <-ns, -n> **1.** maiden name ◊ *Sie hat ihren Mädchennamen behalten.* **2.** girl's name

ⓩ **mag** [maːk] *pres of* mögen¹, mögen²

Ma·ga·zin [magaˈtsiːn] das <-s, -e> **1.** *(for reading, of a gun)* magazine ◊ *Er liest ein Magazin für Politik und Kultur.* ♦ *Er hat das ganze Magazin leer geschossen.* **2.** magazine programme, magazine program ◊ *ein Magazin im Fernsehen* **3.** storeroom ◊ *im Magazin der Bibliothek*

ⓩ **Ma·gen** [ˈmaːgn̩] der <-s, Mägen> stomach ◊ *Ich habe mir den Magen verdorben.* ♦ *Mein Magen knurrt.*

◉ jdm (schwer) im Magen liegen *(fam)* **1.** prey on sb's mind ◊ *Die Prüfung liegt mir ziemlich im Magen.* **2.** lie heavily on sb's stomach ◊ *Das fette Essen lag ihm im Magen.* jdm dreht sich der Magen um *(fam)* sth turns sb's stomach jdm auf den Magen schlagen **1.** upset sb **2.** upset sb's stomach

ⓩ **ma·ger** [ˈmaːgɐ] [adj] **1.** thin, skinny ◊ *Sie ist furchtbar mager geworden.* ◎ dick **2.** *(meat)* lean; *(dairy products, sausage)* low-fat ◎ fett **3.** *(pej)* poor, meagre ◊ *ein mageres Ergebnis* ♦ *Die Ernte war in diesem Jahr sehr mager.*

Ma·gis·ter [maˈgɪstɐ] der <-s, -> **1.** MA, Master of Arts ◊ *Sie hat ihren Magister in Politologie gemacht.* **2.** person with a Master's degree Er ist Magister. He has got an MA.

Ma·gis·trat¹ [magɪsˈtraːt] der <-(e)s, -e> town/city council

Ma·gis·trat² [magɪsˈtraːt] der <-(e)s, -e>, **Ma·gis·tra·tin** [magɪsˈtraːtɪn] die <-, -nen> *(Swiss)* councillor

mä·hen ['mɛːən] tr v +*haben* cut, mow ◊ *den Rasen mähen*

Mahl [maːl] das <-(e)s, -e *or* Mähler> *most sing (lofty)* **1.** meal ◊ *ein bescheidenes Mahl* **2.** banquet ◊ *Wir waren zu einem festlichen Mahl geladen.*

mah·len ['maːlən] <mahlt, mahlte, hat gemahlen> tr v grind ◊ *Kaffee/Getreide mahlen*

Ⓩ **Mahl·zeit** ['maːltsaet] die <-, -en> meal ◊ *eine Mahlzeit zu sich nehmen*
     ⊛ **Mahlzeit 1.** enjoy your meal **2.** *(fam) (around midday)* hello na **Mahlzeit** *(fam)* how super

mah·nen ['maːnən] tr+intr v +*haben* **1.** urge ◊ *Sie mahnten, das Abkommen zu respektieren.* ◆ *Er hat sie gemahnt, nicht so stur zu sein.* jdn davor mahnen, etw. zu tun urge sb not to do sth jdn zur Eile/Vorsicht etc. mahnen urge sb to hurry/be careful etc. zu etw. mahnen call for sth ◊ *Er mahnte zur Vorsicht.* davor mahnen, etw. zu tun warn against doing sth ◊ *Sie mahnte davor, sich in den Streit einzumischen.* **2.** (jdn) mahnen send (sb) a reminder/demand for payment ◊ *Die Firma hat ihn am dritten Mai gemahnt.* ◆ *Wir haben zweimal gemahnt, jetzt reicht es.*

Ⓩ **Mai** [mae] der <-(e)s, -s> *most sing* May → Januar

Mail [meːl, mɛɪl] → E-Mail

mai·len ['meːlən, 'mɛɪlən] tr v +*haben* e-mail ◊ *Ich mailte ihr die Übersetzung.* intr v +*haben* e-mail, send an e-mail ◊ *Er mailt mir fast täglich.* ◆ *Ich maile privat nicht gern.*

Mais [maes] der <-es> *no pl* **1.** maize, corn **2.** *no pl (food)* sweetcorn, corn

Ma·jo·nä·se [majo'nɛːzə] die <-, -n> *(abbr* Majo*)* mayonnaise

Ma·kel ['maːkl] der <-s, -> stigma ◊ *Ihm haftete der Makel der Korruption an.*; ashamed of ◊ *Gilt Altsein hier als Makel?*; flaw ◊ *ein Gesicht ohne (jeden) Makel* flawless, perfect ◊ *ein Gesicht ohne jeden Makel*

Ⓩ **Mak·ler** ['maːklɐ] der <-s, ->, **Mak·le·rin** ['maːklərɪn] die <-, -nen> **1.** (real) estate agent, realtor ◊ *Die Maklerin zeigte ihnen die Wohnung.* ◆ *Er ist Makler von Beruf.* **2.** broker

Ⓩ **mal¹** [maːl] adv **1.** MATH times ◊ *Wie viel ist zehn mal fünf?* ◆ *Dieses Spiel ist bereits eine halbe Million mal verkauft worden.* **2.** *translation varies (fam)* Wir sollten uns mal wieder treffen. We should get together again (some time). Er will mal Rechtsanwalt werden. He wants to be a lawyer. irgendwann (...) mal some day, one day ◊ *Irgendwann will ich mal nach Südamerika.* ⊖einmal **3.** *(fam)* War sie nicht mal Lehrerin? She used to be a teacher, didn't she? Er war mal ganz gut in Mathe. He used to be quite good at maths. Warst du schon mal in Indien? Have you ever been to India? ⊖einmal
     ⊛ **(auch) mal** *(fam)* for once ◊ *Notfalls kann ich auch mal ohne Abendessen auskommen.*

mal² [maːl] part *(fam) not translated* Hör/Sieh etc. mal! Listen/Look etc.! Dann wollen wir mal sehen, wie das funktioniert. Now let's see how it works. Reich mir doch bitte mal das Handtuch. Can you hand me the towel?

Ⓩ **Mal** [maːl] das <-(e)s, -e> *einige/mehrere/wenige/viele Male* **1.** *pl 'Mal' when used with numerals* time ◊ *das erste/zweite/nächste/letzte etc. Mal* ◆ *ein paar Mal* ◆ *Dieses Mal waren die Fragen einfacher als beim letzten Mal.* ◆ *Jedes Mal das Gleiche!* ◆ *Das sagst du jetzt schon zum tausendsten Mal.* ein einziges Mal just once **2.** birthmark ◊ *Er hat ein Mal hinter dem Ohr.*
     ⊛ **ein für alle Mal** once and for all ◊ *Ich hoffe, das ist jetzt ein für alle Mal klar!* **das eine oder andere Mal** now and then/again **ein ums andere Mal** time after time **mit einem Mal** suddenly, all at once ◊ *Mit einem Mal wurde ihm vieles klar.* **von Mal zu Mal, Mal für Mal** every time, all the time ◊ *Das ist von Mal zu Mal verschieden.* ◆ *Es wird Mal für Mal besser.*

Ⓩ **ma·len** ['maːlən] tr+intr v +*haben* *(also fig)* paint ◊ *Sie malt mit Ölfarben.* ◆ *Wer hat diese Bilder gemalt?* ◆ *Er hat die Fürstin in Lebensgröße gemalt.* ◆ *Er malte ein weißes Kreuz auf den Baumstamm.* ◆ *Der Minister malte die Zukunft in rosigen Farben.*; *(with a pencil etc.)* draw

mal|neh·men ['maːlneːmən] <nimmt mal, nahm mal, hat malgenommen> tr+intr v multiply ◊ *Die Zahl wird mit 18 malgenommen.* ◆ *Muss ich da malnehmen oder teilen?* ⊜multiplizieren ⊕teilen

Mal·ta ['malta] das <-s> *article only in combination with attribute* Malta ◊ *auf Malta Urlaub machen*

Mal·te·ser [malteːzɐ] der <-s, ->, **Mal·te·se·rin** [maltezərɪn] die <-, -nen> Maltese → Deutsche

mal·te·sisch [maltezɪʃ] adj *mostly before ns* Maltese → deutsch

Mal·te·sisch [maltezɪʃ] das <-(s)> *seldom with article, no pl* Maltese → Deutsch

Ma·ma ['mamaː] die <-, -s> *(fam) mostly spoken* mum(my), mom(my) ◊ *„Ich will zu meiner Mama!", rief das Kind.* ◆ *Mama, kommst du mal?*

Ⓩ **man** [man] indef pron you, one ◊ *Man muss seine Eltern so nehmen, wie sie sind.* ◆ *Hier kann man Tennis spielen.* ◆ *Man spricht nicht mit vollem Mund!*; they ◊ *Vor fünf Jahren hat man die Schule renoviert.*; people ◊ *Man ist in diesen Sachen heutzutage toleranter.*; I, we ◊ *Es war so dunkel, dass man gar nichts sehen konnte.* ◆ *Es war so laut, dass man nichts mehr verstand.* Man trägt die Haare wieder kurz. Short hair is in fashion again. man befürchtet/vermutet, dass it is feared/suspected that man munkelt, dass rumour has it that, there is a rumour that ◊ *Man munkelt, dass er der Vater des Kindes ist.* Er war der Meinung, dass man sie anzeigen sollte. He thought that she should be reported to the police. Wie sagt man dazu auf Englisch? What's the English word for it?

Ⓩ **manch** [manç] indef pron *(lofty)* many (a) ◊ *Sie besaß manch gute Eigenschaft.* ◆ *Manch ein Kritiker spottete über diesen Autor.* ◆ *Manch anderer hätte das nicht getan.* manch eine/einer many people, many a person ◊ *Manch einer träumt davon, berühmt zu werden.*

Ⓩ **man·che¹** [mançə] det *indefinite* some ◊ *Manche Fremdwörter kannte selbst sie nicht.* ◆ *In mancher Beziehung ist sie ihm überlegen.*; a number of, many (a) ◊ *Manches Mal war ich schon frustriert.* ◆ *So manche Fehler hätten sich vermeiden lassen.*

Ⓩ **man·che²** [mançə] indef pron *mancher/manche/manches* **1.** some (people), quite a few (people), a number of people ◊ *Mancher hat sich hier schon*

verirrt. ♦ *Manche glaubten ihm.* **2.** manches some things, (quite) a few things, a number of things ◊ *Manches gelang, manches nicht.* ♦ *In manchem stimme ich mit ihr überein.* ♦ *Früher war manches besser.*

② **manch·mal** ['mançmaːl] [adv] sometimes, occasionally ◊ *Seine Sprache wirkt manchmal gekünstelt.* ♦ *Es regnete meistens. Nur manchmal schien die Sonne.* ♦ *Manchmal kann das gerechtfertigt sein.* ⊜bisweilen, mitunter, gelegentlich

Man·del ['mandl̩] die <–, –n> **1.** almond ◊ *ein Päckchen gemahlene Mandeln* ♦ *eine Tüte gebrannte Mandeln* **2.** *most pl* MED tonsil ◊ *Sie ließ sich die Mandeln herausnehmen.* ♦ *eitrige Mandeln*

Man·gel¹ ['maŋl̩] der <–s, Mängel> **1.** *no pl* lack ◊ *der Mangel an qualifiziertem Personal* ♦ *Er wurde aus Mangel an Beweisen freigesprochen.* ♦ *Über Mangel an Beifall konnte sie sich nicht beklagen.*; shortcoming ◊ *etw. als Mangel empfinden* **2.** *most pl* fault, defect ◊ *Das Auto hatte einige Mängel.* ♦ *Die Reform wies in einigen Punkten Mängel auf.*

Man·gel² ['maŋl̩] die <–, –n> mangle ⓔ **jdn in die Mangel nehmen** give sb a hard time

man·geln ['maŋl̩n] [imp v] +*haben* **1.** jdm mangelt es an etw. [dat] sb lacks sth, sb is lacking in sth ◊ *Ihr mangelt es an Selbstwertgefühl.* ♦ *Dem Kind mangelt es bei uns an nichts.* **2.** es mangelt an etw. [dat] there is a lack/shortage of sth ◊ *In der Innenstadt mangelt es an Parkplätzen.*

Ma·nie·ren [ma'niːrən] die <–> *only pl* manners ◊ *gute/schlechte/keine Manieren haben*

② **Mann** [man] der <–(e)s, Männer> *pl 'Mann' when used in the sense of 'person'* **1.** man ◊ *Er ist ein gut aussehender Mann.* ♦ *Er ist für unsere Firma nicht der richtige Mann.*; *(in sport)* player ⊜Frau **2.** husband ◊ *Ihr Mann heißt Christian.* ♦ *Seit gestern sind sie Mann und Frau.* ♦ *Er ist bereits ihr dritter Mann.* ⊜Ehemann ⊜Frau **3.** person ◊ *Sie brauchen noch einen dritten Mann zum Skat.* ♦ *eine Teilnahmegebühr von 18 € pro Mann; (plural)* people ◊ *Auf der Party waren ungefähr 50 Mann.* alle Mann everybody ◊ *Alle Mann zu mir!* alle Mann an Deck all hands on deck ⓔ **der Mann fürs Leben** Mr. Right etw. an den Mann bringen **1.** sell sth, get rid of sth ◊ *Konntest du die Ware an den Mann bringen?* **2.** *(knowledge etc.)* show sth *(questions)* ask sth **seinen Mann stehen** prove yourself ◊ *Er musste bereits früh seinen Mann stehen.* Mann hey ◊ *Mann! Was soll das?* (oh) Mann (oh) God, (oh) boy ◊ *Oh Mann! Das darf doch nicht wahr sein!*

② **männ·lich** ['mɛnlɪç] [adj] **1.** male ◊ *War der Täter männlich oder weiblich?* ♦ *die männliche Hauptrolle in einem Film* ♦ *Eine männliche Gans heißt Ganter.* ⊜weiblich **2.** masculine ◊ *Seine Stimme ist sehr männlich.* ♦ *der männliche Artikel* ♦ *Ist das Wort „Mond" männlich oder weiblich?* ⊜weiblich **3.** manly, masculine ◊ *Er fühlte sich längst nicht so männlich und stark, wie sie dachte.* ♦ *männliche Tugenden* ⊜weiblich

② **Mann·schaft** ['manʃaft] die <–, –en> team ◊ *Im Fußball besteht eine Mannschaft aus elf Spielern.* ♦ *unsere Mannschaft für den Wahlkampf* ⓔ **vor versammelter Mannschaft** *(fam)* in front of everybody ◊ *Er hat sie vor versammelter Mann-*

schaft kritisiert.

Ma·nö·ver [ma'nøːve] das <–s, –> **1.** MIL manoeuvres, maneuvers ◊ *Soldaten beim Manöver* **2.** manoeuvre, maneuver, move ◊ *Er wendete mit einem halsbrecherischen Manöver.* ♦ *ein taktisches Manöver*

② **Man·tel** ['mantl̩] der <–s, Mäntel> **1.** coat ◊ *Sie trug einen warmen Mantel.* ♦ *Er zog seinen Mantel an/aus.* ♦ *jdm in den Mantel helfen* **2.** outer tyre, outer tire, rubber, casing

Map·pe ['mapə] die <–, –n> **1.** folder, file ◊ *etw. in eine Mappe legen/heften/tun* ♦ *eine Mappe mit Arbeitsproben* **2.** briefcase

② **Mär·chen** ['mɛːɐçən] das <–s, –> **1.** LIT fairy tale ◊ *jdm ein Märchen erzählen/vorlesen* ♦ *die Märchen der Gebrüder Grimm* **2.** *(fig, pej)* story ◊ *Erzähl mir bloß keine Märchen!* ⓔ **wie im Märchen klingen/sein** be/sound like a fairy tale

② **Mar·ga·ri·ne** [maʳga'riːnə] die <–> *no pl* margarine ◊ *sich* [dat] *Margarine aufs Brot schmieren/streichen*

② **Ma·ril·le** [ma'rɪlə] die <–, –n> *(Austr)* apricot ⊜Aprikose

Ma·ri·na·de [mari'naːdə] die <–, –n> marinade ◊ *etw. in Marinade einlegen*

Mark¹ [maʳk] die <–> *– (abbr* DM*)* mark ◊ *Ein Euro entspricht 1,95583 Mark.*

Mark² [maʳk] das <–(e)s> *no pl* **1.** bone marrow **2.** *(of a fruit)* flesh ⓔ **jdm geht etw. durch Mark und Bein** sth goes right through sb ◊ *Sein Schrei ging mir durch Mark und Bein.* **bis ins Mark** to the core ◊ *Er war bis ins Mark erschüttert.*

② **Mar·ke** ['maʳkə] die <–, –n> **1.** stamp ◊ *Er klebte eine Marke auf den Brief.* ⊜Briefmarke **2.** brand ◊ *Ich möchte diese Marke Sekt probieren.*; *(of a car)* make ◊ *ein Pkw der Marke Mercedes* **3.** *(of a police officer etc.)* badge, ID ◊ *Der Polizist zeigte seine Marke.*; *(for a dog etc.)* tag; *(in a theatre etc.)* cloakroom ticket **4.** record ◊ *Der Hochspringer verbesserte seine eigene Marke um einen Zentimeter.*

② **mar·kie·ren** [maʳ'kiːrən] <markiert, markierte, hat markiert> [tr v] **1.** mark ◊ *Sind die Wanderwege markiert?*; *(in a computer file also)* highlight ◊ *wichtige Textpassagen markieren* etw. mit etw./durch etw. markieren mark sth with sth ◊ *Er markierte mit einem roten Stift die Namen, die er sich merken wollte.* ♦ *Die Grundstücksgrenze war durch einen Zaun markiert.* **2.** *(fig)* mark, signify ◊ *Der Roman markierte den Beginn der Moderne.* ♦ *Diese Entdeckung markierte einen Höhepunkt seiner Forschung.* **3.** *(fam)* be pretending ◊ *Ich glaube nicht, dass er krank ist. Er markiert doch nur.* den Unwissenden markieren play dumb

② **Markt** [maʳkt] der <–(e)s, Märkte> **1.** market ◊ *Mittwochs ist Markt.* ♦ *auf den Markt gehen* ♦ *Im Herbst kommt ein neuer PC auf den Markt.* ♦ *neue Märkte erschließen* ♦ *Für dieses Produkt gibt es keinen Markt.* etw. auf den Markt bringen bring sth out ◊ *Das Unternehmen brachte ein neues Handy auf den Markt.* auf dem Markt gut ankommen sell well ◊ *Der Artikel kam auf dem Markt gut an.* **2.** marketplace, market square ◊ *Sie wohnt direkt am Markt.*

Markt·platz ['maʳktplats] der <–es, Marktplätze>

(also fig) marketplace, market square ◊ *Das Fest findet auf dem Marktplatz statt.*

② **Mar·me·la·de** [maʳməˈlaːdə] die <–, –n> jam ◊ *sich* dat *Marmelade aufs Brot streichen* ♦ *Marmelade kochen; (made out of citrus fruit)* marmalade

Mar·mor ['maʳmoːɐ̯] der <–s> *no pl* marble ◊ *Säulen/ein Fußboden aus Marmor*

Marsch [maʳʃ] der <–(e)s, Märsche> **1.** march ◊ *ein Marsch durch die Wüste* ♦ *Die Soldaten kehrten vom Marsch zurück.* ♦ *einen Marsch spielen/komponieren* **2.** walk, hike ◊ *ein zweistündiger Marsch* ♦ *ein Marsch von zehn Kilometern*

mar·schie·ren [maʳˈʃiːrən] <marschiert, marschierte, ist marschiert> intr v march ◊ *Soldaten marschierten durch die Straßen.* ♦ *Sie marschierte sofort aufs Revier und erstattete Anzeige.*

② **März** [mɛʳts] der <–(es), –e> *most sing* March → **Januar**

Ma·sche ['maʃə] die <–, –n> **1.** stitch ◊ *eine Masche fallen lassen; (of a net)* mesh ◊ *die Maschen (eines/des Netzes)* the mesh (of a/the net) *rechte/linke Maschen stricken* knit/purl **2.** *(fig, pej)* trick ◊ *Mit dieser Masche hat er immer wieder Erfolg.* ♦ *Ist das ihre neueste Masche?* ⊖Trick

② **Ma·schi·ne** [maˈʃiːnə] die <–, –n> **1.** machine ◊ *eine Maschine anstellen/bedienen/abstellen* **2.** AVIAT plane ◊ *Die Passagiere stiegen in die Maschine.* ⊖Flugzeug **3.** *(fam)* (motor)bike ◊ *Jule fährt eine schwere Maschine.* ⊖Motorrad **4.** typewriter ◊ *einen Bogen in die Maschine einspannen (mit der) Maschine schreiben* type ◊ *Er kann gut Maschine schreiben.* ♦ *Der Brief war mit der Maschine geschrieben.* **5.** sewing machine *mit der Maschine genäht* machine-sewed **6.** (washing) machine ◊ *Die Maschine schleudert gerade.* ⊖Waschmaschine

Mas·ke ['maskə] die <–, –n> **1.** (face) mask ◊ *Er trug eine Furcht erregende Maske.* ♦ *Wegen dem Rauch trugen die Feuerwehrleute Masken.* ♦ *eine pflegende Maske auftragen* **2.** THEAT die Maske make-up ◊ *Die Schauspielerin musste in die Maske.*

mas·ku·lin [masku'liːn, '– – –] adj masculine ◊ *Ihre Gesichtszüge waren hart, fast maskulin.* ♦ *ein maskuliner Duft* ♦ *Das Wort „Frühling" ist maskulin.* ♦ *der maskuline Artikel* ⊖feminin

② **maß** [maːs] *pret of* messen

② **Maß**[1] [maːs] das <–es, –e> **1.** unit of measurement, measure ◊ *Auf Golfplätzen wird oft das englische Maß ‚inch' gebraucht.* ♦ *Maße und Gewichte* **2.** gauge, gage ◊ *Das Maß muss man regelmäßig eichen lassen.* **3.** *most pl* measurement ◊ *Die Maße des Schranks stimmen nicht.* ♦ *Welche Maße hat dieses Fotomodell?* **4.** *no pl* degree, extent, measure ◊ *Er zeichnet sich durch ein hohes Maß an Zuverlässigkeit aus.* ♦ *Das trifft in geringem/hohem Maße zu.* ♦ *Dazu gehört ein beträchtliches Maß Mut.*

⊙ **ohne Maß und Ziel** excessive(ly) *das Maß ist voll* enough is enough ◊ *Das Maß war voll. Ich packte meine Sachen und ging. Nach dieser Lüge war das Maß voll und sie verließ ihn.* After this lie she had enough and left him. *mit zweierlei Maß messen* apply double standards *Maß halten* not overdo it ◊ *Beim Trinken hält er Maß.* *(bei jdm) Maß nehmen* take (sb's) measurements ◊ *Die*

Schneiderin nahm bei ihm Maß für einen Anzug. *in Maßen* in moderation ◊ *Er darf Nüsse nur in Maßen essen.* *nach Maß* made to measure/fit, custom-made ◊ *Kleidung nach Maß* etw. *nach Maß anfertigen lassen* have sth custom-made/-built

Maß[2] [maːs], **Mass** [regional mas] die <–, –> *(SouthG, Austr)* litre of beer, liter of beer ◊ *eine/zwei etc. Maß Bier bestellen*

Mas·se ['masə] die <–, –n> mass ◊ *Teer ist eine klebrige schwarze Masse.* ♦ *Der Stein hat eine Masse von 714 g.* ♦ *Sie erhielt eine ganze Masse Leserbriefe.* ♦ *Wir fanden sie in der Masse von Zuschauern nicht mehr.* ♦ *Er hob sich von der Masse der Studenten ab.* ♦ *Die Masse der Bevölkerung war dafür; (of people also)* crowd *die Massen, die breite Masse* the masses ◊ *Die Partei wurde von den Massen/der breiten Masse unterstützt.* ... *in Massen* masses of ... ◊ *Im Augenblick gibt es Marienkäfer in Massen.*

mas·sen·haft ['masn̩haft] adj *no comp/superl; only before n:* widespread, large-scale ◊ *der massenhafte Abbau von Arbeitsplätzen* ♦ *Es kam zu massenhaften Protesten gegen die Reform.* adv on a large/huge scale; in huge/large numbers ◊ *Diese Schädlinge vermehren sich massenhaft. massenhaft Geld//Briefe etc.* loads of money/letters etc. ◊ *Er hat massenhaft Geld.* ♦ *Sie verschickt massenhaft E-Mails.*

maß·geb·lich ['maːsgeːplɪç] adj, adv significant(ly), decisive(ly) ◊ *eine maßgebliche Rolle spielen* ♦ *Welches Kriterium war bei dieser Auswahl maßgeblich?* ♦ *Von welchem Künstler wurde er maßgeblich beeinflusst? Er war maßgeblich am Anschlag beteiligt.* He played a significant role in the attack.

mas·sie·ren [maˈsiːrən] <massiert, massierte, hat massiert> trv massage ◊ *Er massierte ihren Nacken.* *jdn massieren* give sb a massage *sich massieren lassen* have a massage, go for a massage

mä·ßig ['mɛːsɪç] adj, adv *seldom comp/superl* **1.** moderate(ly) ◊ *Der Erfolg des Films war mäßig.* ♦ *Der Vorschlag stieß nur auf mäßige Zustimmung.* ♦ *Sie trinkt nur mäßig.* ♦ *Das Match war nur mäßig spannend.* **2.** mediocre ◊ *Seine Leistungen sind mäßig.* ♦ *Sie erzielte nur mäßige Ergebnisse.* *(nur/ziemlich) mäßig abschneiden/laufen etc.* not do/go etc. very well ◊ *Die Geschäfte laufen im Augenblick nur mäßig.*

mä·ßi·gen ['mɛːsɪɡn̩] ref v +*haben* sich mäßigen control yourself, exercise (more) restraint ◊ *Ihr solltet euch etwas mäßigen und vor den Kindern nicht streiten.* ♦ *Auf dieser Tagung mäßigten sich alle Parteien. sich in seiner Kritik mäßigen* tone down/moderate your criticism *Meine Freude mäßigte sich, als ich das Endergebnis sah.* My joy was dampened when I saw the final result. trv +*haben* moderate ◊ *Du solltest deinen Ton ihm gegenüber mäßigen.; (speed)* reduce

mas·siv [maˈsiːf] adj, adv **1.** solid(ly) ◊ *ein Ring aus massivem Gold* ♦ *Das Holz ist massiv, nicht furniert.* ♦ *massiv gebaut* **2.** strong(ly) ◊ *ein massives Kinn* ♦ *Der Bernhardiner ist ein massiv gebauter Hund.* **3.** extensive(ly), significant(ly) ◊ *massiver Stellenabbau* ♦ *die Preise massiv erhöhen; (pressure)* enormous ◊ *Der Druck, den*

sie auf mich ausübt, ist massiv. jdn massiv unter Druck setzen put enormous pressure on sb ⊜stark

Maß·nah·me ['maːsnaːmə] die <-, -n> measure, step ◊ Wer ist von diesen Maßnahmen betroffen? ◆ Maßnahmen ergreifen ◆ Welche Maßnahmen gegen Spam sind vorgesehen?

Maß·stab ['maːsʃtaːp] der <-(e)s, Maßstäbe> **1.** scale ein Stadtplan im Maßstab 1:15 000 a street map on a scale of 1:15 000 **2.** standard, criterion ◊ Nach welchen Maßstäben erfolgt die Bewertung der Kandidaten? ◆ Die Verkaufszahlen sind ein Maßstab für den Erfolg unseres Konzepts. strenge Maßstäbe anlegen apply strict standards

② **Ma·te·ri·al** [mateˈri̯aːl] das <-s, Materialien> material ◊ ein robustes/temperaturbeständiges Material ◆ Türen aus Kunststoff und anderen Materialien ◆ die Materialien für den Kunstunterricht kaufen ◆ Material für einen Aufsatz sammeln

Ma·te·rie [maˈteːri̯ə] die <-, -n> **1.** no pl matter ◊ feste/flüssige/gasförmige Materie **2.** (lofty) subject (matter) ◊ Ich muss mich erst in die Materie einlesen. ◆ eine schwierige Materie verständlich darstellen

ma·te·ri·ell [mateˈri̯ɛl] adj, adv seldom comp/superl **1.** financial(ly), material(ly) ◊ materielle Sorgen ◆ Nicht jede Not ist materiell. materiell benachteiligt financially disadvantaged materiell von jdm abhängig sein depend financially on sb jdn materiell unterstützen support sb financially, provide financial assistance for sb ⊜finanziell **2.** when used as an adj, only before ns material ◊ materielle Schäden **3.** (esp pej) materialistic(ally) ◊ materiell eingestellt sein **4.** when used as an adj, only before ns die materielle Ausstattung the equipment die materielle Beschaffenheit/Zusammensetzung the (material) composition materiell gut ausgestattet well equipped

Ma·the ['matə] die <-> mostly used without an article, no pl (fam) (abbr of Mathematik) math(s) ◊ Was haben wir in Mathe auf?

② **Ma·the·ma·tik** [matemaˈtiːk] die <-> no pl; used without an article when referring to school/uni subject (abbr Mathe) mathematics ◊ die höhere Mathematik ◆ Mathematik studieren eine Klausur in Mathematik a mathematics exam(ination)

Mat·rat·ze [maˈtratsə] die <-, -n> mattress ◊ auf einer harten/weichen Matratze schlafen
◉ an der Matratze horchen (fam) have a kip

Matsch [matʃ] der <-(e)s> no pl (fam) **1.** (soil) mud, sludge ◊ Kinder spielen gerne im Matsch. ⊜Schlamm **2.** (snow) slush **3.** (food etc.) mush ◊ Das Obst ist in der Tasche zu Matsch geworden.

matt [mat] adj, adv <matter, am mattesten> seldom comp/superl **1.** (surface) matt ◊ Die Oberfläche des Materials ist matt.; (glass) frosted; (light bulb) pearl eine matte Oberfläche/Politur a matt finish matt poliert with a matt (polish) finish matte (Foto-)Abzüge matt (finish) prints **2.** (colour, light) soft(ly), pale, subdued ◊ ein mattes Grün ◆ ein mattes Licht matt leuchten glow/shine softly/in a pale light **3.** (person, animal, sound, voice etc.) weak(ly) ◊ Nach dem Streit war er matt. ◆ Mit matter Stimme antwortete sie. ◆ matt lächeln ⊜schwach ⊜kräftig
◉ (Schach und) matt checkmate jdn matt setzen **1.** CHESS checkmate sb **2.** (fig) put sb out of action ◊

Die Grippe hat gleich fünf Spieler der Mannschaft matt gesetzt. **3.** (an opponent) defeat sb

Mat·te ['matə] die <-, -n> mat ◊ auf einer Matte turnen/schlafen ⊜Unterlage
◉ bei jdm auf der Matte stehen turn up/be at sb's place (on time)

② **Ma·tu·ra** [maˈtuːra] die <-> no pl (Austr, Swiss) school-leaving exam required for higher education ◊ die Matura erwerben

② **Mau·er** ['maoɐ] die <-, -n> (also fig) wall ◊ Die Mauern des Hauses stehen schon. eine Mauer des Schweigens/der Ablehnung a wall of silence/opposition
◉ die Mauer the Berlin Wall nach der Mauer after the fall of the Berlin Wall

> The Berlin Wall was built in 1961 by the East German government in order to separate the eastern part of the city from the west. It was the ultimate symbol of the Cold War. Many people were killed in attempts to flee over the wall into the west. On November 9th 1989, after months of peaceful protests, the border was opened and the wall subsequently demolished. Today only small parts of it remain and attract many visitors.

Maul [maol] das <-(e)s, Mäuler> **1.** (of animals) mouth ◊ Dem Hund hängt die Zunge aus dem Maul. **2.** (rude) (of a person) gob ⊜Fresse **3.** no pl (rude) tongue ◊ ein böses/lockeres Maul haben ein großes Maul haben be a loudmouth dem Volk aufs Maul schauen listen to the way people speak
◉ das/sein Maul halten (rude) shut up jdm das Maul stopfen (rude) shut sb up sich dat das Maul (über jdn/etw.) zerreißen wag your tongue (at sb/about sth)

Mau·rer ['maoɐ] der <-s, ->, **Mau·re·rin** ['maoɐrɪn] die <-, -nen> bricklayer ◊ Er ist Maurer von Beruf. ◆ Sie ist die einzige Maurerin auf der Baustelle.
◉ pünktlich wie die Maurer bang on time

② **Maus** [maos] die <-, Mäuse> **1.** ZOO mouse ◊ Die Katze ist eine Maus gefangen. **2.** IT mouse ◊ mit der Maus auf etw. klicken **3.** only pl (fam) dosh ◊ Ich hab keine Mäuse mehr. ein paar Mäuse a few quid/bucks **4.** (fam) (girl or woman) darling, sweetheart ◊ Du bist aber eine süße Maus!
◉ da beißt die Maus keinen Faden ab (fam) there's nothing you can do about it eine graue Maus a mousy type, a plain Jane weiße Mäuse sehen (fam) see pink elephants

Maut [maot] die <-, -en> toll, road charge ◊ (eine) Maut erheben levy a toll

Ma·yon·nai·se [majoˈnɛːzə] = Majonäse

MC [ɛmˈtseː] die (abbr of Musikkassette) AC, audio cassette ◊ Der Titel ist auf CD und MC erhältlich.

② **Me·cha·ni·ker** [meˈçaːnɪkɐ] der <-s, ->, **Me·cha·ni·ke·rin** [meˈçaːnɪkərɪn] die <-, -nen> mechanic ◊ Sie ist Mechanikerin. ◆ ein arbeitsloser Mechaniker

me·ckern ['mɛkɐn] intr v +haben **1.** (fam, pej) (über etw. acc) meckern moan (about sth), bleat (about sth) ◊ Hör auf zu meckern! ◆ Er meckert immer über das Essen. **2.** ZOO (goat) bleat

Meck·len·burg-Vor·pom·mern [ˌmeːklənbʊɐkˈfoːɐpɔmɐn, ˌmɛklənbʊɐkˈfoːɐpɔmɐn] das <-s> article only in combination with

attribute, no pl GEOG Mecklenburg-West Pomerania
box@ Land

> Area: 23,559 km²; population: approx. 1.8
> million; regional capital: Schwerin.
> Mecklenburg-West Pomerania, the *Land* with the
> lowest population density, is characterized by agri-
> culture. The Baltic coast as well as numerous
> lakes, conservation areas, and nature reserves
> make it an area of outstanding natural beauty.

Me·dail·le [me'daljə] die <–, –n> medal ◊ *eine
Medaille bei der Olympiade gewinnen* jdm eine
Medaille (für etw.) verleihen, jdn mit einer
Medaille (für etw.) auszeichnen award sb a medal
(for sth), decorate sb with a medal (for sth)
Me·di·en ['me:djən] *pl of* Medium
② **Me·di·ka·ment** [medika'mɛnt] das <–(e)s, –e>
medicine, medication, drug ◊ *ein Medikament verschreiben* Medikamente (ein)nehmen take (your)
medication/medicine ⊖Arznei, Präparat
Me·di·um ['me:djʊm] das
<–s, Medien *or seldom* Media> **1.** *most pl* medium
◊ *in den Medien über etwas berichten* ◆ *das
Medium Internet* sich an die Medien wenden turn
to the media **2.** (electronic) storage medium
② **Me·di·zin** [medi'tsi:n] die <–, –en> **1.** *no pl*
medicine ◊ *die moderne Medizin* ◆ *Medizin
studieren* Fakultät für Medizin school of medicine,
medical school **2.** *most sing* medicine, medication,
drug ◊ *Nimm deine Medizin ein.* ◆ *(eine) wirksame
Medizin gegen Malaria* ⊖Arznei
◉ *etw. ist die beste Medizin* sth is the best cure
② **Meer** [me:ɐ] das <–(e)s, –e> *(also fig)* sea ◊ *ans
Meer fahren* ◆ *am Meer liegen* ◆ *mit dem Schiff
aufs offene Meer fahren* ein Meer von/aus etw.,
ein Meer ... [gen] a sea of sth ◊ *ein Meer von
Menschen* ◆ *ein Meer roter Tulpen*
Meer·schwein·chen ['me:ɐʃvaɛnçən] das <–s, –>
guinea pig
② **Mehl** [me:l] das <–(e)s, –e> *most sing* flour ◊ *die
Soße mit Mehl binden*
mehr[1] [me:ɐ] [adv] **1.** mehr als more than ◊ *Ich
war mit dem Service mehr als zufrieden.* **2.** nicht
mehr not anymore ◊ *Er arbeitet nicht mehr bei
uns.* etw. nicht mehr haben have run out of sth,
have no more sth ◊ *Ich habe jetzt keine Geduld
mehr.* kein/keine ... mehr sein not be a ...
anymore ◊ *Das ist kein Spaß mehr!* kein/keine/
keinen ... mehr haben have run out of ..., have no
more ... **3.** more (often) ◊ *Sie gehen jetzt mehr
ins Theater als früher.*
◉ *etw. ist nicht mehr das, was es einmal war*
sth is not what it used to be nicht mehr sein
(euph) have passed away ◊ *Ihr Großvater ist leider
nicht mehr.* ich werd nicht mehr *(fam)* I don't
believe it mehr oder weniger/minder more or
less mehr und mehr ever more, increasingly
mehr[2] [me:ɐ] *comp of* viel[2] [det] *indefinite and
invariable* more ◊ *Ich brauche mehr Geld und
Unterstützung.* ◆ *Mehr junge Paare entscheiden
sich zur Heirat.*
mehr[3] [me:ɐ] *comp of* viel[3] [indef pron] more ◊
Das ist mehr, als ich erwartet habe.
◉ *nicht mehr und nicht weniger* no more and
no less
mehr·deu·tig ['me:ɐdɔøtɪç] [adj, adv] *seldom comp/
superl* ambiguous(ly) ◊ *ein mehrdeutiger Titel* ◆
Die Bilder des Künstlers sind mehrdeutig. ◆ *mehrdeutig gemeint sein* ⊖vieldeutig ⊖eindeutig
② **meh·re·re** ['me:rərə] [det] *indefinite* several, a
number of ◊ *Er hat mehreren Leuten Bescheid
gesagt.* ◆ *Sie war mehrere Jahre im Ausland.*
⊖einige
mehr·fach ['me:ɐfax] [adj] *no comp/superl, only
before ns* multiple ◊ *die mehrfache Gewinnerin* in
mehrfacher Hinsicht in more than one respect
[adv] repeatedly, several times ◊ *Ich habe dir
mehrfach gesagt, dass ...* ◆ *ein mehrfach ausgezeichneter Film* ⊖vielfach, mehrmals
② **Mehr·heit** ['me:ɐhaɛt] die <–, –en> majority ◊
Die Mehrheit der Bürger ist für Reformen. ◆ *Ein
Vorschlag findet eine Mehrheit.* die schweigende
Mehrheit the silent majority eine absolute/
einfache Mehrheit an absolute/a simple majority
eine Mehrheit erzielen win a majority ⊖Minder-
heit
mehr·mals ['me:ɐma:ls] [adv] several times,
repeatedly ◊ *etw. mehrmals versuchen* ◆ *etw.
schon mehrmals gemacht haben* ⊖wiederholt
⊖einmal
Mehr·wert·steu·er ['me:ɐve:ɐtʃtɔøɐ] die <–> *no
pl (abbr* MwSt.) value added tax, VAT ◊ *Im Preis
sind 16% Mehrwertsteuer enthalten.*
Mehr·zahl ['me:ɐtsa:l] die <–> *no pl* **1.** majority ◊
die Mehrzahl der Bürger ◆ *Die Mehrzahl ist dafür/
dagegen.* ⊖Mehrheit ⊖Minderheit **2.** LING plural ◊
„Bäume" ist die Mehrzahl von „Baum". ⊖Plural
⊖Einzahl, Singular
mei·den ['maɛdn] <meidet, mied, hat gemieden>
[tr v] etw./jdn meiden avoid sth/sb ◊ *Ich meide
Massenveranstaltungen.* ◆ *Sie meidet ihn.*
Mei·le ['maɛlə] die <–, –n> **1.** mile ◊ *Das Haus
liegt zwei Meilen von hier entfernt.* **2.** *most pl* air
mile
◉ *etw. riecht drei Meilen gegen den Wind*
nach etw. sth reeks of sth jd riecht etw. drei/
zehn/hundert Meilen gegen den Wind *(fig)* sb
has a nose for sth man riecht etw. drei Meilen
gegen den Wind you can smell sth a mile off
② **mein** [maɛn] [det] my ◊ *Mein Mann arbeitet an der
Uni.* ◆ *Meine Brille ist kaputt.* ◆ *Gib mir mein Buch
zurück.* ◆ *Das sind meine zwei Schwestern.* ◆
*Während meiner Krankheit konnte ich nicht
arbeiten.*

	m	f	nt	pl
nom	mein	meine	mein	meine
acc	meinen	meine	mein	meine
dat	meinem	meiner	meinem	meinen
gen	meines	meiner	meines	meiner

mei·ne ['maɛnə] → mein, meiner
② **mei·nen** ['maɛnən] [tr+intr v] +*haben* think ◊ *Ich
meine, dass sie Recht hat.* ◆ *Was meinst du
dazu?* ◆ *„Soll ich mir einen neuen Job
suchen?" — „Ich meine ja."* meinst du?,
meinen Sie? do you think so? man könnte/sollte
meinen, ... you'd think ... ⊖glauben [tr v]
+*haben* **1.** etw./jdn meinen mean sth/sb ◊ *He,
du! Ja, dich meine ich.* **2.** es nicht so meinen
not mean it that way es gut mit jdm meinen have good
intentions es gut mit jdm meinen mean well by
sb es nicht böse meinen mean no harm wie

meinst du/meint er etc. das?, was meinst du/meint er etc. damit? what do you/does he etc. mean (by that)? **3.** etw. (zu jdm) meinen say sth (to sb) ◊ *Was hat sie da eben zu dir gemeint?*

◉ **ich meine ja nur** it was just a thought, I just meant **wie Sie meinen** as you wish **das will ich (auch) meinen** absolutely

mei·ner ['maɛnɐ] [poss pron] mine ◊ *Das hier ist dein Mantel, aber wo ist meiner? ◊ Da steht sein Auto. Wo hab ich nur meins geparkt? ♦ Deine Mutter ist schon da, nur meine kommt zu spät.*

	m	f	nt	pl
nom	meiner	meine	mein(e)s	meine
acc	meinen	meine	mein(e)s	meine
dat	meinem	meiner	meinem	meinen
gen	-	-	-	-

mei·nes ['maɛnəs] → meiner

② **mei·net·we·gen** ['maɛnət've:gn̩] [adv] **1.** because of me, on my behalf, for my sake ◊ *Sie ist extra meinetwegen gekommen.* **2.** if you like ◊ *„Gehen wir ins Kino?" — „Meinetwegen."* meinetwegen ... as far as I'm concerned ... ◊ *Du kannst meinetwegen machen, was du willst.*

meins [maɛns] → meiner

② **Mei·nung** ['maɛnʊŋ] die <-, -en> opinion ◊ *Sie hat keine eigene Meinung.* jds Meinung nach in sb's opinion anderer Meinung sein disagree sich [dat] eine Meinung bilden form an opinion jds Meinung teilen share sb's opinion die Meinungen gehen auseinander opinions differ seine Meinung vertreten speak out die Meinung vertreten, dass be of the opinion that

◉ **jdm die Meinung sagen** give sb a piece of your mind

② **meist** [maɛst] [adv] *(lofty)* mostly, usually ◊ *Wenn es drauf ankommt, ist meist kein Verlass auf sie.* ⊖meistens ⊖selten

meis·te ['maɛstə] → viel² [det] *indefinite before uncountable ns, pl before countable ns* most ◊ *Sie verdient das meiste Geld von uns. ◊ der Ort mit dem meisten Regen ♦ Die meisten Menschen glauben nicht an Wunder. ♦ In den meisten Fällen hat er Recht.*

meis·ten¹ ['maɛstn̩] → viel¹ [superl] *(always am meisten)* the most ◊ *Er hat am meisten von uns gearbeitet. ♦ Am meisten ärgern mich deine Lügen.*

meis·ten² ['maɛstn̩] [indef pron] *(always die meisten)* most (people) ◊ *Die meisten ekeln sich vor Spinnen.*

② **meis·tens** ['maɛstn̩s, 'maɛstəns] [adv] mostly, usually ◊ *Meistens esse ich Müsli zum Frühstück.* ⊖meist ⊖selten

② **Meis·ter** ['maɛstɐ] der <-s, ->, **Meis·te·rin** ['maɛstərɪn] die <-, -nen> **1.** sport champion ◊ *Sie ist deutsche Meisterin im Eiskunstlauf.* **2.** master craftsman ◊ *Ein Meister darf Lehrlinge ausbilden.* Meisterin master craftswoman **3.** *(also iron)* Meister einer Sache [gen]/in etw. [dat] master of (the art of) sth ◊ *ein Meister der Sprache ♦ Er ist Meister im Verdrängen.*

meis·tern ['maɛstɐn] [tr v] +*haben (a problem etc.)* overcome, master ◊ *Wir haben die Krise gemeistert.; (an exam)* pass; *(a mountain)* conquer ⊖schaffen, bewältigen

Meis·ter·schaft ['maɛstɐʃaft] die <-, -en> championship ◊ *die deutschen Meisterschaften im Kunstturnen ♦ die Meisterschaft gewinnen* bei einer Meisterschaft antreten compete in a championship

② **mel·den** ['mɛldn̩] <meldet, meldete, hat gemeldet> [tr v] (jdm jdn/etw.) melden report (sb/sth to sb) ◊ *Die Medien melden einen neuen Skandal. ♦ Der Polizei wurde ein Diebstahl gemeldet.* [ref v] **1.** school sich melden put your hand up ◊ *Der Schüler meldet sich zu wenig im Unterricht.* **2.** jd meldet sich, wenn ... sb lets sb know if ... ◊ *Du meldest dich, wenn du Hilfe brauchst?* sich (bei jdm) melden get in touch (with sb), contact (sb) ◊ *Melde dich, wenn du zurück bist. ♦ Er meldete sich bei der Polizei.* **3.** sich (freiwillig) zu/für etw. melden volunteer for sth ◊ *Er hat sich freiwillig für den Einsatz gemeldet.*

◉ **bei jdm nichts zu melden haben** be under sb's thumb in einer Sache [dat] nichts zu melden haben have no say in sth

Me·lo·ne [me'lo:nə] die <-, -n> **1.** *(fruit)* melon ◊ *Parmaschinken mit Melone* **2.** *(hat)* bowler (hat) ◊ *eine Melone tragen*

② **Men·ge** ['mɛŋə] die <-, -n> **1.** eine Menge lots/a lot (of) ◊ *Eine Menge Leute sagen, dass ... ♦ Heute habe ich eine Menge erledigt.* **2.** eine/die Menge (von) etw. a/the amount/quantity of sth ◊ *die doppelte Menge der Zutaten* **3.** *(of people)* crowd ◊ *Die Menge drängte aus dem Stadium. ♦ Der Mann verschwand in der Menge.* **4.** math set ◊ *eine leere Menge*

◉ **etw. in rauen Mengen, jede Menge etw.** *(fam)* loads of sth, galore ◊ *Auf der Party gab es Bier in rauen Mengen.*

Men·sa ['mɛnza:] die <-, Mensen *or fam* –s> refectory, cafeteria ◊ *Die Studenten essen in der Mensa.*

② **Mensch** [mɛnʃ] der <-en, -en> **1.** human, man ◊ *Menschen können grausam sein.* **2.** person ◊ *Er ist ein netter Mensch.* Menschen people ◊ *junge/alte Menschen* kein Mensch nobody ◊ *Weit und breit war kein Mensch zu sehen.* ⊖Person, Leute

◉ **der Mensch lebt nicht vom Brot allein** man shall not live by bread alone **Mensch Meier** *(fam)* boy oh boy des Menschen Wille ist sein Himmelreich whatever makes sb happy sich wieder als Mensch fühlen feel human again von Mensch zu Mensch **1.** in private, person-to-person ◊ *eine Beratung von Mensch zu Mensch* **2.** from person to person ◊ *Jedes Medikament wirkt von Mensch zu Mensch anders.* **Mensch** *(fam, emph)* **1.** *(surprised)* boy ◊ *Mensch! Dass es dich noch gibt!* **2.** *(annoyed)* for God's sake ◊ *Mensch, pass doch auf!*

Mensch·heit ['mɛnʃhaɛt] die <-> *no pl* humanity, mankind ◊ *die Geschichte der Menschheit*

② **mensch·lich** ['mɛnʃlɪç] [adj] human ◊ *das menschliche Dasein ♦ Schwach zu sein ist menschlich.* [adj, adv] humane(ly), in a humane manner ◊ *Die Chefin ist sehr menschlich. ♦ Er hat sich sehr menschlich verhalten.*

② **Me·nü** [me'ny:] das <-s, -s> **1.** *(food)* (set) menu ◊ *ein besonders feines Menü zu Weihnachten* **2.** it menu ◊ *Klicken Sie im Menü auf Datei und Öffnen.*

② **mer·ken** ['mɛʳkn̩] [tr v] +*haben* notice, feel ◊ *Sie merkt nicht, wenn sie stört. ♦ Er hat nichts*

gemerkt. [ref v] +*haben* sich [dat] etw. merken remember sth ◊ *Ich kann mir seinen Namen einfach nicht merken.*

merk·lich ['mɛʳklɪç] [adj, adv] *no comp/superl; when used as an adj, only before ns* noticeable(-ably) ◊ *eine merkliche Zu-/Abnahme* ♦ *Unsere Situation ist merklich besser als vor einem Jahr.* ⊖spürbar

Merk·mal ['mɛʳkmaːl] das <-(e)s, –e> feature, characteristic ◊ *ein besonderes/typisches Merkmal eines Autos; (in passport etc.)* besondere Merkmale distinguishing marks ⊖Eigenschaft

② **merk·wür·dig** ['mɛʳkvʏʳdɪç] [adj, adv] strange(ly), odd(ly) ◊ *ein merkwürdiger Typ* ♦ *Ich finde solche Zufälle reichlich merkwürdig.* ♦ *Er verhält sich sehr merkwürdig.* ⊖seltsam, eigenartig, komisch, sonderbar

Mes·se ['mɛsə] die <-, –n> **1.** REL, MUS mass ◊ *eine Messe lesen* ♦ *zur Messe gehen* ♦ *Mozarts Messe in c-Moll* **2.** ECON (trade) fair, exhibition ◊ *Diese Woche fahren wir auf die Messe nach Frankfurt.*

Germany hosts many trade fairs of international importance. Every year, German industry invests large sums in trade exhibitions. Berlin, Cologne, Düsseldorf, Essen, Frankfurt, Hamburg, Hanover, Leipzig, Munich, Nuremberg and Stuttgart are the cities where most German fairs take place, e.g. the Hanover Fair, the largest industrial fair worldwide, and CeBIT (office and information technology), also held in Hanover. The Frankfurt fairs, such as the International Motor Show (IAA) and the Book Fair, are among the most popular in the world.

② **mes·sen** ['mɛsn̩] <misst, maß, hat gemessen> [tr v] measure ◊ *etw. mit dem Lineal messen* ♦ *den Abstand messen* ♦ *die Höhe eines Schranks messen* jds Fieber/Blutdruck/Puls messen take sb's temperature/blood pressure/pulse [intr v] etw. misst zwei Meter etc. (in der Höhe/Länge) sth is two meters etc. high/long jd misst zwei Meter etc. sb is two meters etc. tall [ref v] *(lofty)* sich mit jdm messen compete with sb

② **Mes·ser** ['mɛsɐ] das <-s, –> knife ◊ *etw. mit dem Messer klein schneiden* ♦ *mit Messer und Gabel essen*
◉ auf Messers Schneide stehen hang in the balance jdm ins offene Messer laufen *(fam)* fall into sb's trap jdn ans Messer liefern *(fam)* inform on sb jd muss unters Messer *(fam)* sb must go under the knife

② **Me·tall** [me'tal] das <-s, –e> metal ◊ *eine Skulptur aus Metall* die Metall verarbeitende Industrie metalworking industries

Me·ter ['meːtɐ] der *or* das <-s, –> *(abbr* m) metre, meter ◊ *Das Zimmer ist fünf mal zehn Meter groß.* ♦ *Ein Kilometer hat 1000 Meter.*

② **Me·tho·de** [me'toːdə] die <-, –n> method
◉ etw. hat Methode there is (a) method behind sth

Mett·wurst ['mɛtvʊʳst] die <-, Mettwürste> *most sing* smoked pork *or* beef sausage

Metz·ger ['mɛtsgɐ] der <-s, –>, **Metz·ge·rin** ['mɛtsgərɪn] die <-, –nen> *(SouthG)* **1.** butcher ◊ *ein gelernter Metzger* ♦ *Sie arbeitet als Metzgerin.* **2.** *no fem* butcher's (shop) ◊ *Ich gehe mal schnell zum Metzger.*

② **Metz·ge·rei** [mɛtsgə'raɛ] die <-, –en> *(SouthG)* butcher's (shop) ◊ *Ich kaufe mein Fleisch in der Metzgerei.* ⊖Fleischerei, Fleischhauerei

Metz·ge·rin ['mɛtsgərɪn] *fem of* Metzger

MEZ [ɛmleː'tsɛt] die *(abbr of* mitteleuropäische Zeit) CET ◊ *Es geschah um 15 Uhr MEZ.*

mich [mɪç] [pers pron] *acc of* ich [ref pron] myself ◊ *Ich frage mich, ob ich das machen soll.* Ich wasche/dusche mich. I wash/have a shower. Ich habe mich erkältet. I cought a cold. Ich kann mich daran nicht erinnern. I don't remember that.

mied [miːt] *pret of* meiden

Mie·ne ['miːnə] die <-, –n> expression, face ◊ *Er setzte eine ernste Miene auf.* ⊖Blick, Gesichtsausdruck
◉ gute Miene zum bösen Spiel machen grin and bear it, put a good face on it/things keine Miene verziehen not turn a hair

mies [miːs] [adj, adv] <mieser, am miesesten> *(fam)* **1.** lousy(-ily), very bad(ly) ◊ *Das Wetter war mies.* ♦ *miese Laune haben* ♦ *Wir werden mies bezahlt.* ♦ *Meiner Schwester geht es zurzeit mies.* ⊖schlecht **2.** *(pej)* nasty(-ily) ◊ *Dieser Trick war mies.* ♦ *ein mieser kleiner Gauner* ♦ *sich mies verhalten* ⊖gemein

② **Mie·te** ['miːtə] die <-, –n> **1.** rent zur Miete wohnen live in rented accommodation **2.** rental, charge
◉ das ist schon die halbe Miete *(fam)* that's half the battle kalte Miete rent exclusive of heating/utility etc. bills

② **mie·ten** ['miːtn̩] <miete, mietete, hat gemietet> [tr v] **1.** rent ◊ *ein Büro in der Innenstadt mieten* **2.** hire, rent ◊ *ein Auto mieten*

Mie·ter ['miːtɐ] der <-s, –>, **Mie·te·rin** ['miːtərɪn] die <-, –nen> tenant

Miet·ver·trag ['miːtfɛʳtraːk] der <-(e)s, Mietverträge> tenancy agreement ◊ *einen Mietvertrag unterschreiben*

Mik·ro·wel·le ['miːkrovɛlə] die <-, –n> **1.** microwave **2.** microwave (oven) ◊ *Essen in der Mikrowelle aufwärmen*

② **Milch** [mɪlç] die <-> *no pl* **1.** milk ◊ *ein Glas Milch* **2.** *(of a plant)* juice; *(of a coconut)* milk **3.** lotion ◊ *Dieses Sonnenschutzmittel gibt es als Creme oder als Milch.*

mild [mɪlt] [adj, adv] **1.** mild(ly) ◊ *Es war ein milder Maiabend.* ♦ *Der letzte Winter war mild.* ♦ *Der Wind wehte mild aus Süden.* ♦ *ein milder Käse* ♦ *eine milde Seife* **2.** gentle(-ly) ◊ *Das rötliche Licht ist besonders mild.* ♦ *Sie hat mich mit milden Worten ermahnt.* ⊖sanft **3.** lenient(ly) ◊ *Das Urteil war mild.* ♦ *eine milde Strafe* ♦ *Der Richter hat sehr mild geurteilt.* ⊖streng

mil·dern ['mɪldɐn] [tr v] +*haben* **1.** alleviate ◊ *Schmerzen mildern* **2.** mitigate ◊ *eine Strafe mildern* [ref v] +*haben* sich mildern abate ◊ *Als sie in Tränen ausbrach, milderte sich sein Zorn.*

Mi·li·eu [mi'ljøː] das <-s, –s> **1.** background ◊ *aus einem ärmlichen Milieu stammen* **2.** environment ◊ *Diese Arten fühlen sich in feuchtem Milieu am wohlsten.* **3.** world of prostitution ◊ *Er ist ein Kenner des Züricher Milieus.; (criminal)* underworld das Milieu der Drogenabhängigen the drug scene

Mi·li·tär¹ [mili'tɛːɐ] das <-s> *no pl* armed forces,

military, army ◊ *Daniel ist zurzeit beim Militär.* zum Militär müssen have to join up ⊕Armee

Mi·li·tär² [mili'tɛːɐ̯] der <-s, -s> most pl (high-ranking) army officer

Mil·li·ar·de [mɪr'lja'də] die <-, -n> (abbr Mrd.) thousand million, billion ◊ *Milliarden von Menschen*

Mil·li·gramm ['mɪlɪgram] das <-s, -e> pl 'Milligramm' when used with expressions of quantity (abbr mg) milligram

Mil·li·li·ter ['mɪlili:te] der <-s, -> (abbr ml) millilitre, milliliter ◊ *250 Milliliter Milch*

Mil·li·me·ter ['mɪlime:te] der or das <-s, -> (abbr mm) millimetre, millimeter ◊ *eine Öffnung von zehn Millimeter Durchmesser*

Mil·li·on [mɪ'ljoːn] die <-, -en> (abbr Mio.) (eine) Million (a/one) million ◊ *eine Million Menschen ♦ Millionen von Fliegen schwirrten umher.* in die Millionen gehen amount to millions

Mi·mik ['miːmɪk] die <-> no pl facial expression ◊ *Seine Mimik verriet, dass er entsetzt war.*

② **Min·der·heit** ['mɪndehaet] die <-, -en> minority ◊ *in der Minderheit sein* ⊕Mehrheit

min·der·jäh·rig ['mɪndejɛːrɪç] [adj] no comp/superl under(-)age ◊ *Er ist noch minderjährig. ♦ Minderjährige Teilnehmer brauchen das Einverständnis der Eltern.* minderjährige Jugendliche minors ⊕volljährig, mündig

min·dern ['mɪnden] [tr v] +haben diminish, reduce ◊ *Ein Unfall mindert den Wert eines Autos.* ⊕reduzieren [ref v] +haben sich mindern lessen, abate ◊ *Die Zahl der Straftaten hat sich im letzten Jahr gemindert.* ⊕sich reduzieren

min·der·wer·tig ['mɪndeveːɐ̯tɪç] [adj] inferior ◊ *minderwertige Qualität ♦ Neben meiner Schwester fühle ich mich oft minderwertig.*

min·des·te ['mɪndəstə] [superl] only before ns slightest, least ◊ *Er zeigte nicht das mindeste Interesse.* nicht die mindeste Lust haben, etw. zu tun not feel at all like doing sth ⊕geringste

Min·des·te ['mɪndəstə] das <no gen> no pl das Mindeste, ein Mindestes the (very) least ◊ *Ein Dankeschön ist das Mindeste, was man erwarten kann.* etw. auf ein Mindestes reduzieren reduce sth to a minimum nicht im Mindesten not in the least zum Mindesten at least ◊ *Du solltest dich zum Mindesten bedanken.*

② **min·des·tens** ['mɪndəstn̩s, 'mɪndəstəns] [adv] at least ◊ *Das kostet mindestens 200 Euro.* ⊕höchstens

Mi·ne ['miːnə] die <-, -n> 1. (of a pencil) lead ◊ *ein Bleistift mit weicher Mine; (of a biro) refill 2. mine ◊ Der Panzer fuhr auf eine Mine. ♦ eine Mine stilllegen*

② **Mi·ne·ral·was·ser** [minə'raːlvase] das <-s, Mineralwässer> pl 'Mineralwasser' when used with expressions of quantity mineral water

② **Mi·nis·ter** [mi'nɪstɐ] der <-s, ->, **Mi·nis·te·rin** [mi'nɪstərɪn] die <-, -nen> (cabinet) minister, Secretary of State, secretary ◊ *Er war Minister unter Helmut Schmidt. ♦ Sie wurde zur Ministerin ernannt. ♦ Er ist (der) Minister für Wirtschaft und Arbeit.*

Mi·nis·te·ri·um [minɪs'teːrjom] das <-s, Ministerien> ministry, department ◊ *das Ministerium für Umwelt und Naturschutz*

mi·nus¹ ['miːnʊs] [adv] 1. minus ◊ *zehn Grad minus ♦ Der Strom fließt von minus nach plus.* ⊕plus 2. SCHOOL indicates the bottom end of a grade or mark ◊ *Er hat eine Eins minus im Test.* ⊕plus box@ Note

mi·nus² ['miːnʊs] [prep] [+gen] less, minus ◊ *Sie bekommen die Summe minus der Anmeldegebühr zurück.* ⊕plus

mi·nus³ ['miːnʊs] [conjunc] MATH minus ◊ *Fünf minus drei ist gleich zwei.* ⊕weniger, weg ⊕plus

Mi·nus ['miːnʊs] das <-> no pl deficit ◊ *ein Minus von 2 Millionen Euro; (on bank account) overdraft* ⊕Plus ⊙ im Minus sein 1. be overdrawn ◊ *Ihr Konto ist im Minus. 2. have an overdraft ◊ Du bist ständig im Minus!*

Mi·nu·te [mi'nuːtə] die <-, -n> minute ◊ *Die Straßenbahn fährt alle 10 Minuten. ♦ Es ist zehn Minuten vor/nach drei. ♦ Hättest du mal eine Minute Zeit für mich? ♦ Das Spiel war bis zur letzten Minute spannend.* in letzter Minute at the last minute ⊙ es ist fünf Minuten vor zwölf it is high time, time is running out auf die Minute (fam) right on the dot

Mio. [mɪ'ljoːn(ən)] die (abbr of Million(en)) m. ◊ *2 Mio. Menschen*

mir [miːɐ̯] [pers pron] dat of ich [ref pron] not translated directly *Ich bitte mir Ruhe aus! I must insist on silence! Ich mache mir Sorgen über ihn. I worry about him. Ich mache mir nichts aus Opern. I don't really like the opera.*

② **mi·schen** ['mɪʃn̩] [tr+intr v] +haben mix ◊ *Apfelsaft mit Mineralwasser mischen; (playing cards) shuffle ◊ Wer mischt die Karten?; (a salad) toss* sie mischen sich they mix ◊ *Öl und Wasser mischen sich nicht.* [tr v] 1. etw. unter/in etw. [acc] mischen add sth to sth ◊ *Rosinen unter den Teig mischen ♦ Er hat ihr Gift ins Essen gemischt. 2. (fig) etw. mischen mingle sth ◊ In diesem Roman mischt er Wahres und Erfundenes.* sie mischen sich they intermingle ◊ *Hier mischen sich Dichtung und Wahrheit.* sich mit etw. mischen intermingle with sth ◊ *Die Erinnerung mischt sich mit Wunschvorstellungen.* [ref v] +haben 1. sich unter jdn/etw. [acc] mischen mingle with sb/sth 2. sich in etw. [acc] mischen interfere in sth, meddle in sth

Mi·schung ['mɪʃʊŋ] die <-, -en> (also fig) mixture ◊ *fertige Mischungen für Kuchen ♦ Die Musik ist eine Mischung aus Jazz und Hip-Hop.; (of tobacco, tea, coffee) blend*

mi·se·ra·bel [miza'raːbl̩] [adj] <miserabler, am miserabelsten> <der/die/das miserable ...> dreadful ◊ *Seine schulischen Leistungen sind miserabel. ♦ miserables Essen ♦ Mir geht's miserabel.* [adv] very badly ◊ *Der Roman ist miserabel übersetzt. ♦ Er hat sie ganz miserabel hintergangen.*

miss-... [mɪs] [prefix] (negation) dis... ◊ *jdm misstrauen ♦ jdn missachten ♦ Er missbilligte mein Verhalten. Die Prüfung ist mir missglückt. I wasn't successful in the exam. Da hast du mich missverstanden. You didn't understand me properly. Rechte missbrauchen abuse rights*

miss·ach·ten [mɪs'axtn̩] <missachtet, missachtete, hat missachtet> [tr v] 1. disregard ◊ *Gesetze*

missachten die Vorfahrt missachten fail to give way ⊜befolgen **2.** despise ◇ *Sie missachtet ihn für sein Verhalten.* ⊜achten

miss·bil·li·gen [mɪsˈbɪlɪɡŋ] <missbilligt, missbilligte, hat missbilligt> ⟨tr v⟩ etw. missbilligen disapprove of sth ◇ *Ich kann deinen Entschluss nur missbilligen.* ✦ *Ich missbillige es, wenn Jugendliche rauchen.* ⊜billigen, akzeptieren

miss·brau·chen [mɪsˈbʀaɔxn] <missbraucht, missbrauchte, hat missbraucht> ⟨tr v⟩ **1.** abuse ◇ *Jugendliche, die Drogen missbrauchen; (for a wrong purpose)* misuse ◇ *Er hat sein Amt dazu missbraucht, sich persönlich zu bereichern.* **2.** jdn missbrauchen rape sb, abuse sb ◇ *Er hat schon mehrmals Frauen missbraucht.* ⊜vergewaltigen

② **Miss·er·folg** [ˈmɪsˌʔɛfɔlk] der <-(e)s, -e> failure ◇ *Sein erster Roman war ein Misserfolg.* ⊜Erfolg

miss·han·deln [mɪsˈhandl̩n] <misshandelt, misshandelte, hat misshandelt> ⟨tr v⟩ ill-treat, mistreat ◇ *Wer Tiere misshandelt, macht sich strafbar.*

miss·lang [mɪsˈlaŋ] *pret of* misslingen

miss·lin·gen [mɪsˈlɪŋən] <misslingt, misslang, ist misslungen> ⟨intr v⟩ fail, be unsuccessful ◇ *Der Versuch ist misslungen.* Die Überraschung ist uns misslungen. Our surprise failed. Der Kuchen ist misslungen. The cake went wrong. ⊜gelingen

miss·lun·gen [mɪsˈlʊŋən] *past p of* misslingen

② **misst** [mɪst] *pres of* messen

Miss·trau·en [ˈmɪstʀaɔən] das <-s> *no pl* Misstrauen (gegenüber jdm/etw.), Misstrauen (gegen jdn./etw.) mistrust (of sb/sth), distrust (of sb/sth) jds Misstrauen erregen make sb suspicious

② **Miss·ver·ständ·nis** [ˈmɪsfɛʃtɛntnɪs] das <-ses, -se> misunderstanding ◇ *Das muss ein Missverständnis sein.* ✦ *Zwischen den beiden kommt es häufig zu Missverständnissen.*

② **miss·ver·ste·hen** [ˈmɪsfɛʃteːən] <missversteht, missverstand, hat missverstanden> ⟨tr v⟩ misunderstand ◇ *Missversteh mich bitte nicht, aber ich habe dazu wirklich keine Lust.* ✦ *Ach entschuldigen Sie, da habe ich Sie wohl missverstanden.*

Mist [mɪst] der <-(e)s> *no pl* **1.** manure, dung **2.** *(fam)* rubbish, trash, nonsense ◇ *Wer hat dir denn diesen Mist erzählt?* ✦ *Der Film war der reinste Mist.*

⊛ *(verdammter) Mist (fam)* damn ◇ *Mist, jetzt habe ich meinen Geldbeutel vergessen.* Mist bauen/machen *(fam)* mess things up ◇ *In der Prüfung hat sie Mist gebaut.* Bau/Mach keinen Mist! Don't do anything stupid! etw. ist nicht auf jds Mist gewachsen sb didn't think sth up himself/herself ◇ *Diese Lösung ist sicher nicht auf seinem Mist gewachsen.* Mist verzapfen *(fam)* talk rubbish ◇ *Was verzapfst du da für einen Mist?*

② **Mist·kü·bel** [ˈmɪstkyːbl̩] der <-s, -> *(Austr, Swiss)* (rubbish/litter) bin, trash/garbage can ◇ *Mistkübel leeren*

mit¹ [mɪt] ⟨adv⟩ *(fam)* too, as well, also ◇ *Warst du bei der Party mit dabei?* ✦ *Es gehört mit zu meinen Aufgaben, für Ordnung zu sorgen.* mit der/die/das beste/wichtigste etc. ... one of the best/most important etc. ... ◇ *Das ist mit der beste Film, den ich je gesehen habe.* ✦ *Er ist mit der bekannteste Schriftsteller unserer Zeit.*

② **mit²** [mɪt] ⟨prep⟩ +dat **1.** with ◇ *Würstchen mit Senf* ✦ *mit Messer und Gabel essen* ✦ *Er kam mit*

seinem Freund. ✦ *Mit Mehrwertsteuer kostet das 150 Euro.* ✦ *Der Fahrschein mit Zuschlag kommt auf 25 Euro.* ✦ *Sie eilte ihm mit schnellen Schritten entgegen.* ✦ *Das ist mit viel Sorgfalt gemacht.* Zimmer mit Frühstück bed and breakfast mit Absicht on purpose, deliberately **2.** *(means of transport)* by ◇ *mit dem Taxi fahren* ✦ *Wir fahren mit dem Zug in Urlaub.* **3.** *(point of time, age)* at ◇ *Mit dem Gongschlag wird es 11 Uhr.* ✦ *Sie hat mit 21 geheiratet.* **4.** *(along)* with ◇ *Wir sind mit dem Strom geschwommen.* ✦ *Wir sind mit dem Wind gesegelt.* ⊜gegen

② **mit|...** [mɪt] ⟨prefix⟩ **1.** *(expressing that sb/sth joins sb/sth (in doing sth))* too, with sb ◇ *Willst du mitsingen?* ✦ *Er hat im Krieg mitgekämpft.* ✦ *Du kannst gern mitessen.* ✦ *Du kannst meinen Computer mitbenutzen.* **2.** *(expressing that sb/sth is carrying sth along)* along, with you ◇ *Hast du genügend Geld mit?* ✦ *Er schleppt seine Kuscheldecke überall mit.*

mit|ar·bei·ten [ˈmɪtʔaˌbaɛtn̩] <arbeitet mit, arbeitete mit, hat mitgearbeitet> ⟨intr v⟩ **1.** bei/an etw. ⟨dat⟩ mitarbeiten work on sth ◇ *Wie viele haben an diesem Projekt mitgearbeitet?* **2.** participate, take part ◇ *Max arbeitet im Unterricht gut mit.*

② **Mit·ar·bei·ter** [ˈmɪtʔaˌbaɛtɐ] der <-s, ->, **Mit·ar·bei·te·rin** [ˈmɪtʔaˌbaɛtərɪn] die <-, -nen> **1.** collaborator ein freier Mitarbeiter/eine freie Mitarbeiterin a freelance(r) ◇ *Sie ist freie Mitarbeiterin bei einer Zeitung.* **2.** employee ◇ *Die Firma entlässt Mitarbeiter.* ✦ *ein Unternehmen mit 45 Mitarbeitern*

② **Mit·be·stim·mung** [ˈmɪtbəˌʃtɪmʊŋ] die <-> *no pl* co-determination ◇ *Der Betriebsrat fordert Mitbestimmung in Fragen der Kurzarbeit.*

Mit·be·woh·ner [ˈmɪtbəˌvoːnɐ] der <-s, ->, **Mit·be·woh·ne·rin** [ˈmɪtbəˌvoːnərɪn] die <-, -nen> **1.** housemate; flatmate **2.** resident

mit|brin·gen [ˈmɪtbʀɪŋən] <bringt mit, brachte mit, hat mitgebracht> ⟨tr v⟩ **1.** bring along ◇ *Kann ich eine Freundin mitbringen?* **2.** (jdm) etw. mitbringen bring (sb) sth ◇ *Ich habe dir Blumen mitgebracht.* **3.** have, possess ◇ *Mein Traumpartner sollte viel Humor mitbringen.*

mit·ei·nan·der [mɪtʔaeˈnandɐ] ⟨adv⟩ **1.** with each other ◇ *Wir reden nicht mehr miteinander.* ✦ *Diese Dinge kann man nicht miteinander vergleichen.* miteinander streiten argue with each other again miteinander vertragen/versöhnen make it up **2.** together ◇ *Wir fahren immer miteinander in den Urlaub.*

mit|fah·ren [ˈmɪtfaːʀən] <fährt mit, fuhr mit, ist mitgefahren> ⟨intr v⟩ go (too), come (too) ◇ *Fährst du mit nach Österreich?* mit jdm mitfahren go with sb, come with sb ◇ *Ich bin mit meinen Eltern mitgefahren.* Willst du zum Bahnhof mitfahren? Do you want a lift to the station?

Mit·ge·fühl [ˈmɪtɡəˌfyːl] das <-s> *no pl* Mitgefühl mit jdm sympathy for sb ◇ *Er zeigt wenig Mitgefühl mit anderen.* sein Mitgefühl aussprechen express your sympathy

mit|ge·hen [ˈmɪtɡeːən] <geht mit, ging mit, ist mitgegangen> ⟨intr v⟩ **1.** come (too) ◇ *Gehst du mit zu der Party?* mit jdm mitgehen go/walk with sb, accompany sb ◇ *Ich gehe noch ein Stück mit dir mit.* **2.** respond ◇ *Sie geht mit der Musik mit.*

ⓔ **etw. mitgehen lassen** *(fam)* nick sth, pinch sth

② **Mit·glied** ['mɪtgliːt] das <-(e)s, -er> member ◇ *Bist du Mitglied in einem Sportverein?* ♦ *ein langjähriges Mitglied* ♦ *ein Mitglied des Parlaments*

Mit·glied·schaft ['mɪtgliːtʃaft] die <-, -en> membership ◇ *Die Mitgliedschaft im Sportverein kostet monatlich 40 Euro.*

mit|hal·ten ['mɪthaltn] <hält mit, hielt mit, hat mitgehalten> [intr v] **1.** mithalten können be able to compete mit jdm/etw. mithalten können be able to keep up with sb/sth ◇ *Er konnte mit den anderen Läufern nicht mithalten.*

mit|hel·fen ['mɪthɛlfn] <hilft mit, half mit, hat mitgeholfen> [intr v] help ◇ *Mein Mann hilft im Haushalt mit.* bei etw. mithelfen help with sth ◇ *Er half beim Schmücken des Weihnachtsbaums mit.*

mit·hil·fe, mit Hil·fe [mɪt'hɪlfə] [prep] **1.** +gen with, with the help of ◇ *Kranke mithilfe neuer Therapien heilen* ♦ *Mithilfe meiner Eltern konnte ich das Geld aufbringen.* **2.** *adverbial* +dat mithilfe von with, by means of ◇ *eine Homepage mithilfe von HTML erstellen*

mit|kom·men ['mɪtkɔmən] <kommt mit, kam mit, ist mitgekommen> [intr v] **1.** come (too) ◇ *Darf meine Freundin zur Party mitkommen?* **2.** be able to keep up ◇ *Nun renn doch nicht so, bei deinem Tempo komme ich nicht mit.* **3.** *(fam) (understand)* be able to follow ◇ *Obwohl die Vorlesung auf Englisch war, bin ich gut mitgekommen.; (in school etc.)* gut mitkommen get on well nicht mitkommen be lost ◇ *Er kommt im Unterricht oft nicht mit.* da komme ich nicht mit that's beyond me, you've lost me there

Mit·leid ['mɪtlaet] das <-(e)s> *no pl* sympathy, pity ◇ *Er empfand Mitleid mit dem armen Wesen.*

mit|ma·chen ['mɪtmaxn] <macht mit, machte mit, hat mitgemacht> [tr+intr v] etw. mitmachen, bei/in etw. [dat] mitmachen participate in sth ◇ *Ich werde das Rennen mitmachen.* ♦ *Bastian macht im Unterricht selten mit.* ♦ *Wer hat bei dem Projekt alles mitgemacht?* [tr v] **1.** do as well/too ◇ *Da die Kollegin krank ist, muss ich ihre Arbeit mitmachen.* **2.** etw. mitmachen go through sth ◇ *Sie hat im Leben schon viel Leid mitgemacht.* [intr v] **1.** join in ◇ *Wir wollen für sie eine Überraschung vorbereiten, machst du mit?* **2.** etw. macht nicht mehr mit sth is giving up (on sb), (sb's) sth can't take it anymore ◇ *Mein altes Auto macht sicher nicht mehr lang mit.*

ⓔ **das kann ich nicht mitmachen** I can't go along with that **das mache ich nicht länger mit** I won't take it anymore, I won't put up with this anymore ◇ *Ich mache das nicht länger mit! Ich kündige.*

mit|neh·men ['mɪtneːmən] <nimmt mit, nahm mit, hat mitgenommen> [tr v] **1.** take (with you/along) ◇ *Ich hatte nicht genügend Geld mitgenommen.* **2.** upset, affect badly ◇ *Die Scheidung der Eltern hat den Jungen mitgenommen.; (physically)* weaken **3.** *(fam)* visit, do ◇ *Er hat im Urlaub alles mitgenommen, was sich so bot.* **4.** *(fam)* bump into ◇ *Als er aus der Garage fuhr, hat er den Mülleimer mitgenommen.*

Mit·neh·men ['mɪtneːmən] *(always* zum Mitnehmen) to take away, to go ◇ *eine Pizza zum*

Mitnehmen

mit|rei·ßen ['mɪtraesn] <reißt mit, riss mit, hat mitgerissen> [tr v] **1.** sweep away, carry away ◇ *Die Lawine hat mehrere Bäume mitgerissen.* **2.** carry away ◇ *Mit seiner Ansprache hat er alle Zuhörer mitgerissen.*

mit·rei·ßend ['mɪtraesnt] *pres p of* mitreißen [adj] infectious ◇ *ein mitreißender Rhythmus* ♦ *Ihre Begeisterung war mitreißend.*

Mit·schü·ler ['mɪtʃyːle] <-s, ->, **Mit·schü·le·rin** ['mɪtʃyːlərɪn] die <-, -nen> **1.** classmate **2.** schoolmate

mit|spie·len ['mɪtʃpiːlən] <spielt mit, spielte mit, hat mitgespielt> [intr v] **1.** *(a game)* play ◇ *Willst du mitspielen?* ♦ *bei einer Mannschaft mitspielen* in einem Film/Stück mitspielen be in a film/play **2.** bei etw. mitspielen go along with sth das Wetter spielt mit the weather is favourable/favorable wenn das Wetter mitspielt weather permitting **3.** bei etw. mitspielen play a part in sth

ⓔ **jdm übel/hart/schlimm mitspielen** treat sb badly

② **Mit·tag** ['mɪtaːk] der <-(e)s, -e> **1.** *no pl* midday, noon ◇ *Vor Mittag steht sie nie auf.* ♦ *Ich komme gegen Mittag an.* **2.** lunchtime am/über Mittag at lunchtime ◇ *Über Mittag sind viele Geschäfte geschlossen.* heute/morgen/gestern Mittag at lunchtime today/tomorrow/yesterday, today/tomorrow/yesterday lunchtime **3.** *no pl* lunch hour, lunch break Mittag machen have your lunch break ⊖Mittagspause

ⓔ **zu Mittag essen** have lunch

Mit·tag·es·sen ['mɪtaːkʔɛsn] das <-s, -> lunch ◇ *Wann gibt es Mittagessen?* ♦ *Willst du nicht zum Mittagessen bleiben?*

> In Germany, lunch, which was traditionally the main meal of the day, usually consists of a substantial hot meal. However, when people are in a hurry they very often just have a sandwich and a drink at lunchtime.

mit·tags ['mɪtaːks] [adv] at lunchtime ◇ *Mittags esse ich in der Kantine.* um 12 Uhr mittags at midday

② **Mit·te** ['mɪtə] die <-, -n> *most sing* **1.** middle, centre, center ◇ *Wir wohnen in der Mitte der Stadt.* **2.** *(temporal)* middle Mitte Januar/des Monats/Jahres in the middle of January/ the month/year bis Mitte ... by the middle ... ◇ *Das Projekt muss bis Mitte des Jahres fertig sein.* **3.** Mitte vierzig etc. in your mid-forties etc. **4.** POL centre, center ein Politiker/eine Partei/Koalition etc. der Mitte a centrist politician/party/coalition etc.

ⓔ **die goldene Mitte** the golden mean jdn in die Mitte nehmen take sb between you ab durch die Mitte *(fam)* (let's) beat it aus unserer Mitte *(lofty)* from our midst in unserer Mitte *(lofty)* in our midst, among us

② **mit|tei·len** ['mɪttaelən] <teilt mit, teilte mit, hat mitgeteilt> [tr v] etw. mitteilen announce sth ◇ *Der Konzern hat mitgeteilt, dass die Umsätze gestiegen sind.* jdm etw. mitteilen inform sb of/about sth jd lässt jdm etw. mitteilen sb wishes to inform sb [refl v] sich mitteilen express oneself ◇ *Er ist ein Mensch, der sich nur schlecht mitteilen kann.* sich jdm mitteilen confide in sb

Mit·tei·lung ['mɪttaɐ̯lʊŋ] die <-, -en> information ◊ *eine schriftliche/vertrauliche Mitteilung; (by a correspondent etc.)* report

② **Mit·tel** ['mɪtl̩] das <-s, -> **1.** means, method ◊ *Das Auto ist für mich ein Mittel, um von A nach B zu kommen.* zum Mittel der Gewalt greifen resort to violence **2.** *(chemical agent)* Mittel gegen Flecke stain remover; *(for the washing)* detergent Mit welchem Mittel behandelst du dein Silber? What do you use to clean your silver? **3.** drug, medicine ein Mittel gegen etw. remedy for sth ◊ *Das beste Mittel gegen Erkältung ist ein heißes Bad.* **4.** *only pl* funds ◊ *öffentliche Mittel* **5.** average ◊ *das Mittel errechnen*
◉ **(ein) Mittel zum Zweck** a means to an end **jdm ist jedes Mittel recht** sb would do anything **mit allen Mitteln versuchen(, etw. zu tun); kein Mittel unversucht lassen(, um etw. zu tun)** try everything/your utmost (to do sth)

② **Mit·tel·...** ['mɪtl̩] prefix **1.** middle, centre ◊ *am Mittelgang sitzen* ◆ *ein Mittelklassewagen* **2.** medium(-sized) ◊ *Mittelbetrieb*

Mit·tel·al·ter ['mɪtl̩ʔaltɐ] das <-s> *no pl* Middle Ages ◊ *Die Kreuzzüge fanden im Mittelalter statt.* ◆ *das frühe/späte Mittelalter*
◉ **wie im tiefsten/finstersten Mittelalter** like (in) the Dark Ages

Mit·tel·a·me·ri·ka ['mɪtl̩ʔa,me:rika:] das <-s> *article only in combination with attribute, no pl* Central America box@ Land

Mit·tel·eu·ro·pa ['mɪtl̩ʔɔy,ro:pa:] das <-s> *article only in combination with attribute, no pl* Central Europe box@ Land

Mit·tel·fin·ger ['mɪtl̩fɪŋɐ] der <-s, -> middle finger ◊ *Sie trägt einen Ring am Mittelfinger.*

mit·tel·fris·tig ['mɪtl̩frɪstɪç] adj *no comp/superl* medium-term ◊ *eine mittelfristige Maßnahme/ Regelung* ◆ *Der Kredit ist mittelfristig.* adv in/for the medium term ◊ *mittelfristig planen*

mit·tel·mä·ßig ['mɪtl̩mɛ:sɪç] adj, adv mediocre, indifferent(ly) ◊ *Er ist ein mittelmäßiger Schüler.* ◆ *Die Qualität war mittelmäßig.* mittelmäßig ausfallen turn out (to be) mediocre ⊖durchschnittlich

Mit·tel·meer ['mɪtl̩me:ɐ̯] das <-s> *no pl* Mediterranean ◊ *ans Mittelmeer fahren*

② **Mit·tel·punkt** ['mɪtl̩pʊŋkt] der <-(e)s, -e>
1. centre, center ◊ *der Mittelpunkt eines Kreises* **2.** focal point, centre ◊ *Das Kind ist Mittelpunkt der Familie.*
◉ **im Mittelpunkt stehen** be the centre of attention ◊ *Sie will immer im Mittelpunkt stehen. (in a discussion etc.)* be the main focus

mit·tels ['mɪtl̩s] prep *sing nouns without article or attribute are declined when following this prep, otherwise* ɪgen *or fam* +dat *by means of* ◊ *etw. mittels Schraubenzieher öffnen*

Mit·tel·weg ['mɪtl̩ve:k] der <-(e)s, -e> middle way
◉ **der goldene Mittelweg** the happy medium, the golden mean

② **mit·ten** ['mɪtn̩] adv mitten in/auf/an etw. acc (right) into the middle of sth, right into sth ◊ *Er ist mitten in die Pfütze getreten.* mitten in/auf/an dat etw. (right) in the middle of sth ◊ *Mitten auf dem Tisch stand eine Vase.* ◆ *mitten in der Nacht*

mitten aus etw. from the middle of sth, right from sth mitten aus dem Leben (from) real life mitten durch etw. right through (the middle/centre) of sth mitten durchbrechen break right in the middle

② **Mit·ter·nacht** ['mɪtɐnaxt] die <-> *no pl* midnight ◊ *Um Mitternacht ging das Feuerwerk los.*

② **mitt·le·re** ['mɪtlərə] adj *only before ns* <ein mittlerer ..., eine mittlere ..., ein mittleres ...>
1. der/die/das mittlere the middle (one) ◊ *Ich bin das mittlere der drei Kinder.* ◆ *Der mittlere Teil des Buches ist ziemlich langweilig.* **2.** intermediate ◊ *ein mittlerer Schwierigkeitsgrad* **3.** medium(-sized) ◊ *Ich hätte gern die mittlere Packung.* ◆ *ein mittleres Unternehmen* **4.** mittleren Alters middle-aged in mittleren Jahren, in mittlerem Alter in middle age **5.** average box@ Reife

mitt·ler·wei·le ['mɪtlɐˌvaɐ̯lə] adv **1.** in the meantime ◊ *Mach du schon mal den Salat, ich decke mittlerweile den Tisch.* **2.** by now, by then ◊ *Mittlerweile wussten alle Bescheid.* ⊖nunmehr

② **Mitt·woch** ['mɪtvɔx] der <-(e)s, -e> Wednesday → Montag

mitt·wochs ['mɪtvɔxs] adv on Wednesdays → montags

mit·un·ter [mɪtl̩'ʔʊntɐ] adv *(form)* sometimes, occasionally ◊ *Mitunter führt das Medikament zu allergischen Reaktionen.* ◆ *ein mitunter schwieriger Geschäftspartner* ⊖bisweilen, manchmal

Mit·wir·kung ['mɪtvɪrˀkʊŋ] die <-> *no pl* Mitwirkung (an etw. dat) collaboration (on sth), cooperation (in sth); involvement (in sth) ◊ *die Mitwirkung an einem Forschungsprojekt;* participation (in) ◊ *die Mitwirkung an einer Veranstaltung; (by an actor)* appearance; *(by a dancer, musician)* performance unter jds Mitwirkung, unter Mitwirkung von jdm together with

② **Mö·bel** ['mø:bl̩] das <-s, -> *most pl* furniture

Mo·bi·li·ar [mobi'lja:ˀ] das <-s, -e> *most sing* furniture, furnishings

mo·bi·li·sie·ren [mobili'zi:rən] <mobilisiert, mobilisierte, hat mobilisiert> tr v **1.** MIL mobilize ◊ *Truppen mobilisieren* **2.** activate ◊ *die letzten Energiereserven mobilisieren*

② **möb·liert** [mø'bli:ɐ̯t] adj *no comp/superl* furnished ◊ *Alle Zimmer sind komplett möbliert.* ◆ *in eine möblierte Wohnung ziehen*

② **moch·te** ['mɔxtə] *pret of* mögen¹, mögen²

② **möch·te** ['mœçtə] *subjunctive II of* mögen¹, mögen²

Mo·dal·verb [mo'da:lvɛrˀp] das <-s, -en> modal verb

② **Mo·de** ['mo:də] die <-, -n> fashion ◊ *sich nach der neuesten Mode kleiden* ◆ *Lederkleidung ist wieder groß in Mode.* aus der Mode kommen go out of fashion in Mode kommen come into fashion

Mo·dell [mo'dɛl] das <-s, -e> **1.** model ◊ *mit einem Projekt ein Modell für alle anderen schaffen* **2.** cast (model) ◊ *ein Modell aus der Gießform lösen* **3.** ARTS subject; model ◊ *das bevorzugte Modell eines Künstlers* jdm Modell stehen sit for sb

Mo·de·ra·tor [mode'ra:to:ɐ̯] der <-s, -en>, **Mo·de·ra·to·rin** [modera'to:rɪn] die <-, -nen> RADIO, TV presenter, announcer ◊ *Der Moderator dieser Sendung ist Georg Schneider.* ◆ *Sie ist Moderatorin beim Fernsehen.*

mo·dern¹ ['mo:dɐn] [intr v] +*haben* rot ◊ *Im Feuchten modert das Holz.*

② **mo·dern²** [mo'dɛrn] [adj] **1.** *(clothes etc.)* fashionable ◊ *Die Schuhe sind sehr modern.* ◆ *ein modernes Kleid* **2.** modern ◊ *die Möglichkeiten der modernen Medizin* ◆ *Der neue Flughafen ist sehr modern.* [adv] **1.** fashionably ◊ *sich modern kleiden* **2.** in a modern way/style modern denken be open-minded

mo·disch ['mo:dɪʃ] [adj, adv] fashionable(-ably) ◊ *Die Hose ist modisch.* ◆ *eine modische Frisur* ◆ *modisch gekleidet sein*

Mo·dul [mo'du:l] das <-s, -e> *(tech)* module

Mo·fa ['mo:fa:] das <-s, -s> *(abbr of Motorfahrrad)* (small) moped ◊ *mit dem Mofa zur Arbeit fahren*

mo·geln ['mo:gln] *(fam)* [intr v] +*haben* cheat ◊ *beim Kartenspiel mogeln* [tr v] +*haben* etw. irgendwohin mogeln smuggle sth somewhere, slip sth somewhere ◊ *sich irgendwohin mogeln* slip somewhere ◊ *Einige Tippfehler haben sich in den Text gemogelt.*

② **mö·gen¹** ['mø:gn̩] <mag, mochte, hat gemocht> [tr v] **1.** *(expressing likes and dislikes)* etw./jdn. mögen like sth/sb ◊ *Er mag seine Kollegin sehr.* ◆ *Sie mag keine Schokolade.* ◆ *Horrorfilme mag ich gar nicht.* **2.** indicative or subjunctive *(expressing a wish)* jd mag/möchte (gern) etw. sb would like sth ◊ *Mögen/möchten Sie eine Tasse Kaffee?* [intr v] **1.** indicative or subjunctive irgendwohin mögen/möchten want to go somewhere ◊ *Er mag/möchte noch nicht nach Hause.* **2.** want to ◊ *Sie möchte schon, aber traut sich nicht so recht.*

mö·gen² ['mø:gn̩] <mag, mochte, hat mögen> [modal v] +*inf* **1.** subjunctive II, in polite requests jd möchte (gern) etw. tun sb would like to do sth ◊ *Ich möchte mich herzlich bedanken. Ich möchte Sie nicht stören.* I don't want to bother you. **2.** *(possibility, probability)* might, would ◊ *Sie mag 12 Jahre alt sein.* Wie viel mag das kosten? How much would that be likely to cost? **3.** es mag sein, dass it may be that, it might be that ◊ *Es mag sein, dass wir vieles nicht verstehen.* wie auch immer etw. sein mag whatever sth will be like ◊ *Wie auch immer das Wetter sein mag, ich gehe spazieren.* **4.** subjunctive I, requests and wishes; translation varies *(lofty)* Richten Sie ihm aus, dass er sich schämen möge. Tell him that he should be ashamed. Sag Lisa, sie möge bitte die Türe schließen. Please tell Lisa to kindly close the door. **5.** *(lofty)* *(in various idioms)* may ◊ *Möge sie gewinnen!* Er möge uns verzeihen. Let's hope he forgives us.

② **mög·lich** ['mø:klɪç] [adj] no comp/superl **1.** possible ◊ *Es ist möglich, dass sie heute noch kommt.* ◆ *mögliche Gründe für das Scheitern des Projekts* jdm ist etw. möglich; jdm ist (es) möglich, etw. zu tun sth is possible for sb, sb is able to do sth (jdm) etw. möglich machen make sth possible (for sb), enable (sb to do) sth **2.** das ist doch nicht möglich I don't believe it es ist doch nicht möglich, dass I can't believe that man sollte es nicht für möglich halten you wouldn't believe it man sollte (es) nicht für möglich halten, ... you wouldn't believe ...
◉ alles Mögliche all sorts of things, all manner

of things ◊ *alles Mögliche zu verschenken haben*

mög·li·cher·wei·se ['mø:klɪçɐ'vaɛzə] [adv] possibly ◊ *Der Prozess wird möglicherweise eingestellt.* ⊖womöglich, eventuell

② **Mög·lich·keit** ['mø:klɪçkaɛt] die <-, -en> **1.** possibility ◊ *eine Möglichkeit, Geld zu verdienen* ◆ *Gibt es noch eine andere Möglichkeit?* nach Möglichkeit if possible ◊ *Ihre Wünsche werden nach Möglichkeit berücksichtigt.* Er versucht nach Möglichkeit, alle Fragen zu beantworten. He tries to answer all questions if he can. **2.** opportunity, chance ◊ *gute berufliche Möglichkeiten haben* ◆ *die Möglichkeit nutzen, etw. zu tun* ⊖Gelegenheit **3.** only pl means ◊ *begrenzte finanzielle Möglichkeiten*

② **mög·lichst** ['mø:klɪçst] [adv] **1.** möglichst schnell/oft etc. as quickly/often etc. as possible ◊ *eine möglichst genaue Beschreibung* ◆ *Er sollte möglichst oft trainieren.* **2.** if possible ◊ *Fehler möglichst verbessern*
◉ sein Möglichstes tun do all you can, do your best, do your utmost

Möh·re ['mø:rə] die <-, -n> carrot ⊖Karotte

② **Mo·ment¹** [mo'mɛnt] der <-(e)s, -e> **1.** moment, minute ◊ *Einen Moment bitte!* ◆ *Sie sahen sich einen Moment lang an.* **2.** moment, point in time ◊ *den geeigneten Moment abwarten* im Moment at the moment
◉ jeden Moment any minute

Mo·ment² [mo'mɛnt] das <-(e)s, -e> **1.** element ◊ *ein Moment der Überraschung in die Geschichte einbringen* das auslösende Moment the trigger **2.** PHYSICS moment

② **mo·men·tan** [momɛn'ta:n] [adj, adv] no comp/superl; when used as an adj, only before ns **1.** current(ly), at the moment ◊ *Die momentane Lage ist gut.* ◆ *Ich habe momentan keine Zeit.* ⊖gegenwärtig **2.** current(ly), temporary(-ily) ◊ *momentane Lieferschwierigkeiten* ◆ *Das Produkt ist momentan nicht verfügbar.*

② **Mo·nat** ['mo:nat] der <-(e)s, -e> month ◊ *Veranstaltungen des kommenden Monats* im Monat a/per month, monthly ◊ *400 Euro Miete im Monat bezahlen* im Monat Dezember in the month of December in diesem Monat, diesen Monat this month Ihr Schreiben vom 15. dieses Monats your letter of the 15th (inst.)

mo·nat·lich ['mo:natlɪç] [adj] no comp/superl; only before ns monthly ◊ *Der monatliche Beitrag beträgt 20 Euro.* [adv] every month ◊ *Das Gehalt wird monatlich auf Ihr Konto überwiesen.*

Mönch [mœnç] der <-(e)s, -e> monk

② **Mond** [mo:nt] der <-(e)s, -e> ASTRON moon ◊ *eine Landung auf den Mond* ◆ *abnehmender/zunehmender Mond*
◉ nach dem Mond gehen *(fam)* *(clock)* not work properly hinter dem/hinterm Mond leben *(fam)* be out of touch with reality jd würde jdn am liebsten auf den Mond schießen, jd könnte jdn auf den Mond schießen *(fam)* sb could kill sb

② **Mo·ni·tor** ['mo:nito:ɐ] der <-s, -en or -e> screen, monitor ◊ *Dieser Computer hat einen besonders guten Monitor.*

② **Mon·tag** ['mo:nta:k] der <-(e)s, -e> Monday ◊ *Die Ware wird am Montag geliefert.* ◆ *von Montag bis Freitag arbeiten* ◆ *ein regnerischer Montag* ◆

Nächsten Montag ist Feiertag. ◆ *Heute ist Montag, der 12. April.*
ⓔ **einen blauen Montag machen** do a sicky on a Monday

Mon·ta·ge [mɔn'taːʒə] die <-, –n> 1. *(of a machine etc.)* installation, assembly ◊ *Unsere Firma übernimmt auch die Montage der Geräte.* 2. *(fam)* auf Montage away on a construction job ◊ *Am Mittwoch ist er auf Montage.* 3. ARTS, FOTO, TV montage ◊ *eine filmische Montage*

mon·tags ['moːntaːks] adv on Mondays ◊ *Der Arzt hat montags keine Sprechstunde.* ◆ *Wir haben montags bis freitags von 9 bis 20 Uhr geöffnet.* montags vormittags/nachmittags/abends on Monday mornings/afternoons/evenings

mon·tie·ren [mɔn'tiːrən, mɔn'tiːrən] <montiert, montierte, hat montiert> tr v 1. install, fit ◊ *Maschinen montieren* 2. etw. irgendwo(hin) montieren install sth somewhere, fit sth somewhere ◊ *eine Kamera an die/die Wand montieren* 3. ARTS, FOTO, TV *(texts, images etc.)* put together

Moor [moːɐ] das <-(e)s, –e> bog ◊ *im Moor versinken; (drier)* moor ◊ *eine Wanderung durchs Moor machen*

Moos [moːs] das <-es, –e> moss ◊ *Am Baumstumpf wächst Moos.* Moose types of moss
ⓔ **ohne Moos nichts los** *(slang)* no dough, no go

② **Mord** [mɔrt] der <-(e)s, –e> murder, homicide ◊ *wegen Mordes verurteilt werden* ◆ *ein politischer Mord* einen Mord begehen commit a murder einen Mord an jdm begehen murder sb
ⓔ **es gibt Mord und Totschlag** *(fam, fig)* all hell will be let loose, there'll be chaos

Mör·der ['mœrdɐ] der <-s, ->, **Mör·de·rin** ['mœrdərɪn] die <-, –nen> murderer, killer

② **mor·gen** ['mɔrgn] adv tomorrow ◊ *Wir gehen morgen ins Kino.* morgen in einer Woche a week tomorrow bis morgen see you tomorrow morgen früh/Mittag/Abend tomorrow morning/afternoon/evening
ⓔ **guten Morgen** good morning

② **Mor·gen** ['mɔrgn] der <-s, –> morning heute Morgen this morning am Morgen in the morning am nächsten Morgen the next morning eines Morgens one morning bis in den Morgen (hinein) until the early hours
ⓔ **guten Morgen** good morning

② **Mor·gen·es·sen** ['mɔrgn|ɛsn] das <-s, –> *(Swiss)* breakfast ◊ *Wir nehmen das Morgenessen um halb acht ein.*

② **mor·gens** ['mɔrgns, 'mɔrgəns] adv in the morning ◊ *Ich muss morgens um sechs Uhr aufstehen.* dienstags morgens on Tuesday mornings ⓔabends
ⓔ **von morgens bis abends** all day long, constantly

mor·gig ['mɔrgɪç] adj no comp/superl, only before ns tomorrow's ◊ *das morgige Spiel* der morgige Tag tomorrow

Mo·schee [mɔ'ʃeː] die <-, –n> mosque

Mo·sel ['moːzl] <-> no pl *(always* die Mosel) the Moselle ◊ *ein Weinort an der Mosel*

Mos·lem ['mɔsləm] der <-s, –s>, **Mos·le·min** [mɔs'leːmɪn] die <-, –nen> Muslim ◊ *Sie ist Moslemin.*

Most [mɔst] der <-(e)s, –e> *most sing* 1. must ◊

Most machen/trinken 2. *(SouthG, Austr, Swiss)* fruit wine

Mo·tiv [mo'tiːf] das <-s, –e> 1. motive ◊ *ein politisches Motiv* das Motiv einer Tat the motive for a deed/action 2. *(in art, literature etc.)* motif

② **Mo·tor** ['moːtoːɐ, mo'toːɐ] der <-s, –en> 1. TECHN motor ◊ *den Motor anlassen/abstellen; (of a vehicle)* engine ◊ *Der Motor springt nicht an.* 2. *(fig)* driving force ◊ *der Motor des geschäftlichen Erfolgs*

② **Mo·tor·rad** ['moːtoːɐraːt, mo'toːɐraːt] das <-(e)s, Motorräder> motorcycle, motorbike ◊ *Motorrad fahren*

Mot·to ['mɔtoː] das <-s, –s> theme ◊ *Die Tagung stand unter dem Motto der Globalisierung.; motto*

Mö·we ['møːvə] die <-, –n> (sea)gull

Mrd. [mɪ'l̩jaːrdə(n)] die *(abbr of Milliarde(n))* 1000 m.; *(in the US)* bn ◊ *Der Umsatz betrug 2,8 Mrd. Euro.*

Mü·cke ['mʏkə] die <-, –n> midge, gnat, mosquito ◊ *von einer Mücke gestochen werden*
ⓔ **aus einer Mücke einen Elefanten machen** *(fam)* make a mountain out of a molehill **die/eine Mücke machen** *(slang)* do a runner, take off

② **mü·de** ['myːdə] adj, adv <müder, am müdesten> 1. tired(ly) ◊ *Ich bin müde.* ◆ *ein müder Gang* ◆ *müde dahinschlendern* zum Umfallen/Sterben müde sein be tired to death jds/einer Sache müde sein be tired of sb/sth ◊ *des Wartens müde sein* 2. *(lofty)* nicht müde werden, etw. zu tun never tire of doing sth

Mü·dig·keit ['myːdɪçkaet] die <-> no pl 1. fatigue ◊ *Sie trinkt Kaffee, um ihre Müdigkeit zu überwinden.* 2. *(fam)* vor Müdigkeit umfallen collapse with/in exhaustion
ⓔ **(nur) keine Müdigkeit vorschützen** *(fam)* tiredness is no excuse

② **Mü·he** ['myːə] die <-, –n> effort, trouble ◊ *Es kostete sie viel Mühe, ihn zu überreden.* seine Mühe mit jdm/etw. haben have got a lot on your hands with sb/sth
ⓔ **mit Müh(e) und Not** with great difficulty **der Mühe** gen **(nicht) wert sein** (not) be worth the trouble **sich** dat **(viel) Mühe geben, sich** dat **viel Mühe machen** go to a lot of trouble ◊ *Er gibt/macht sich viel Mühe bei der Arbeit.* **sich** dat **die Mühe machen** go to the trouble **jdm keine Mühe machen** be no trouble to sb Kannst du mich mit dem Auto mitnehmen? Aber nur, wenn es dir keine Mühe macht. Could you give me a lift, if it isn't too much trouble? **jd kann sich** dat **die Mühe sparen** sb can save themselves the trouble

Müh·le ['myːlə] die <-, –n> 1. *(for grain)* mill; *(for coffee)* grinder 2. mill ◊ *Am Bach steht eine alte Mühle.* 3. *without the article, no pl* GAME nine men's morris ◊ *Mühle spielen*

② **Müll** [mʏl] der <-s> no pl rubbish, refuse, garbage, trash ◊ *etw. in den Müll werfen* ◆ *den Müll trennen/wegbringen* ⓔAbfall

Müll·ab·fuhr ['mʏl|apfuːɐ] die <-, –en> refuse collection, garbage collection; *(people)* dustmen, refuse collectors, garbage collectors ◊ *Am Montag kommt die Müllabfuhr.*

② **Müll·ei·mer** ['mʏl|aeme] der <-s, –> *(rubbish)* bin, trash can ◊ *etw. in den Mülleimer werfen* ⓔAbfalleimer

Müll·ton·ne ['mʏltɔnə] die <–, –n> dustbin, garbage can, trash can ◊ *Die Mülltonne wird jede Woche geleert.*

mul·mig ['mʊlmɪç] [adj] *(fam)* **1.** *(feeling)* queasy ◊ *ein mulmiges Gefühl haben* **2.** *(affair, situation)* dubious, dodgy ◊ *Die Sache ist mir etwas zu mulmig.*

mul·ti·pli·zie·ren [mʊltipli'tsiːrən] <multipliziert, multiplizierte, hat multipliziert> [tr v] *etw. mit etw.* multiplizieren multiply sth by sth

Mün·chen ['mʏnçn] das <–s> *no pl; article only in combination with attribute* Munich das Oktoberfest in München the Munich Beer Festival box@ Stadt

② **Mund** [mʊnt] der <–(e)s, Münder> mouth ◊ *mit vollem Mund sprechen* ♦ *jdn auf den Mund küssen*

◉ **sich den Mund fransig/fusselig reden** *(fam)* talk until you're blue in the face **einen großen Mund haben, den Mund voll nehmen** *(fam)* talk big, be all talk, be full of talk **jdm den Mund wässrig machen** *(also fig)* make sb's mouth water, wet sb's appetite ◊ *Der Bratenduft machte mir den Mund wässrig.* **den Mund nicht aufbekommen** *(fam)* not be able to get a word out **nicht auf den Mund gefallen sein** *(fam)* never be at a loss for words **den Mund halten** *(fam)* **1.** shut up, shut your mouth **2.** keep your mouth shut **jdm den Mund verbieten** shut sb up, silence sb ◊ *sich den Mund nicht verbieten lassen*

Mund·art ['mʊntlaːɐ̯t] die <–, –en> dialect ◊ *Texte und Lieder in Mundart*

mün·den ['mʏndn] <mündet, mündete, hat/ist gemündet> [intr v] *etw. mündet in etw.* [acc] sth flows into sth ◊ *Der Fluss mündet ins Meer.; (road etc.)* sth leads to sth

mün·dig ['mʏndɪç] [adj] *no comp/superl* **1.** of age **ein mündiger Schüler** a pupil who is of age, a student who is of age **mündig werden** come of age ⊖volljährig ⊖unmündig, minderjährig **2.** responsible, self-determined ◊ *der mündige Bürger* [adv] responsibly ◊ *mündig handeln*

② **münd·lich** ['mʏntlɪç] [adj, adv] *no comp/superl; when used as an adj, mostly before ns* oral(ly), verbal(ly) ◊ *eine mündliche Überlieferung* ♦ *etw. mündlich vereinbaren* ⊖schriftlich

Mün·dung ['mʏndʊŋ] die <–, –en> *(of a river)* mouth; *(of a street)* end; *(of a weapon)* muzzle ◊ *die Mündung einer Pistole*

mun·ter ['mʊntɐ] [adj] **1.** lively, cheerful ◊ *eine muntere Komödie* **2.** awake ◊ *um fünf Uhr morgens schon munter sein* **munter werden** wake up **jdn munter machen** wake sb up [adv] happily ◊ *munter drauflosreden*

Mün·ze ['mʏntsə] die <–, –n> coin ◊ *eine Münze einwerfen* ⊖Geldstück

◉ **etw. für bare Münze nehmen** take sth as gospel **jdm etw. in/mit gleicher Münze heimzahlen** pay sb back for sth in their own coin **etw. in klingende Münze umsetzen** *(lofty)* turn sth into money/cash, cash in on sth

mür·risch ['mʏrɪʃ] [adj, adv] sulky(-ily), sullen(ly) ◊ *ein mürrisches Gesicht* ♦ *Die Bedienung in diesem Restaurant ist ziemlich mürrisch.* ♦ *Mürrisch folgte das Kind seinen Eltern.* ⊖gut gelaunt

Mus [muːs] das <–es, –e> *most sing* purée

Mu·schel ['mʊʃl] die <–, –n> **1.** mussel ◊ *Heute frische Muscheln!* **2.** bivalve **3.** shell ◊ *Muscheln am Strand sammeln*

② **Mu·se·um** [mu'zeːʊm] das <–s, Museen> museum ◊ *ins Museum gehen* ♦ *ein Museum für moderne Kunst*

② **Mu·sik** [mu'ziːk] die <–> *no pl* music ◊ *klassische Musik*

◉ **Musik im Blut haben** have got music in your blood **Musik in jds Ohren sein** *(fam)* be music to sb's ears

Mus·kel ['mʊskl] der <–s, –n> muscle ◊ *die Muskeln anspannen*

② **muss** [mʊs] *pres of* müssen¹, müssen²

② **müs·sen¹** ['mʏsn] <muss, musste, hat müssen> [modal v] *+inf* **1.** have to ◊ *eine schwere Entscheidung treffen müssen* ♦ *Er muss jeden Tag um sechs Uhr aufstehen.* ♦ *lachen/weinen müssen* Muss das sein? Is that really necessary? wir müssen Ihnen leider mitteilen, dass we regret to inform you that **2.** wann/wo/wie muss jd etw. tun when/where/how should sb do sth ◊ *Wann musst du den Aufsatz abgeben?* ♦ *Wo und wie muss man sich für diesen Studiengang bewerben?* **3.** *no participle (assumption)* must ◊ *Die Straße ist nass, es muss geregnet haben.* **4.** *subjunctive II (wish)* Geld müsste man haben. If only I/we were rich. Man müsste noch mal jung sein! Oh, to be young again!

② **müs·sen²** ['mʏsn] <muss, musste, hat gemusst> [intr v] **1.** *(expressing obligation)* have to ◊ *Sie wollte nicht, sie musste.* jd muss irgendwohin sb has to go somewhere Der Brief muss heute noch zur Post. The letter must be posted today. **2.** *seldom in the perfect tense (fam)* need the toilet/loo ◊ *Ich muss mal.*

② **muss·te** ['mʊstə] *pret of* müssen¹, müssen²

Mus·ter ['mʊstɐ] das <–s, –> **1.** model ◊ *Dieser Vertrag gilt als Muster.* **2.** ein Muster an etw. [dat] a model of sth; *(person also)* a paragon of sth ◊ *Sie ist ein Muster an Zuverlässigkeit.* **3.** design, pattern ◊ *ein Muster für einen Teppich entwerfen* **4.** sample ◊ *ein Muster, das nicht zum Verkauf steht*

mus·tern ['mʊstɐn] [tr v] *+haben* **1.** scrutinize ◊ *jdn neugierig mustern* **2.** MIL jdn mustern give sb a medical

② **Mut** [muːt] der <–(e)s> *no pl* courage ◊ *in einer Situation viel Mut beweisen* jdm Mut zusprechen/machen encourage sb neuen Mut fassen take heart all seinen Mut zusammennehmen summon all your courage, pluck up all your courage sich [dat] Mut antrinken get some Dutch courage

◉ **frohen Mutes** *(outd)* in high spirits **den Mut nicht verlieren** not give up

mu·tig ['muːtɪç] [adj, adv] brave(ly), courageous(ly) ◊ *Der Soldat galt als mutig und furchtlos.* ♦ *eine mutige Passantin* ♦ *mutig handeln*

mut·maß·lich ['muːtmaːslɪç] [adj] *no comp/superl, only before ns* presumed, probable ◊ *der mutmaßliche Mörder*

② **Mut·ter¹** ['mʊtɐ] die <–, Mütter> mother ◊ *Sie ist jetzt Mutter.* ♦ *Sie ruft täglich ihre Mutter an.* eine werdende Mutter a mother-to-be

◉ **Mutter Erde** *(lit)* Mother Earth **die Mutter**

Gottes the Mother of God, the Madonna

Mut·ter² ['mʊtɐ] die <-, –n> nut ◊ *Schrauben und Muttern*

Mut·ter·spra·che ['mʊtɐʃpraːxə] die <-, –n> native/first language, mother tongue ◊ *Meine Muttersprache ist Russisch.*

mut·wil·lig ['muːtvɪlɪç] [adj, adv] *no comp/superl* deliberate(ly) ◊ *Diese Aktion war mutwillig und* unverantwortlich. ♦ *ein mutwilliges Vorgehen; (damage also)* wilful(ly) ◊ *etw. mutwillig zerstören*

Müt·ze ['mʏtsə] die <-, –n> cap; *(of wool, fur)* hat ◊ *im Winter eine Mütze tragen*
🅜 **eine Mütze voll Schlaf** *(fam)* a nap **eins auf die Mütze kriegen** *(fam)* **1.** get a telling-off **2.** get thrashed

A
B
C
D
E
F
G
H
I
J
K
L
M
N
O
P
Q
R
S
T
U
V
W
X
Y
Z

N

n, N [ɛn] das <-(s), -(s)> n, N ◊ *Dieses Wort wird mit einem kleinen n/großen N geschrieben.* ♦ *N wie Nordpol*

na [na(:)] ⟨interj⟩ **1.** well ◊ *Na, kommst du mit?* na ja well na schön/gut all right then **2.** *often not translated directly (encouragement)* na also there you are ◊ *Na also, es ist alles wieder gut!; (expressing threat)* Na warte! Just you wait!; *(doubt)* Na, wenn das mal gut geht! Let's just hope that all goes well.; *(confirmation)* Na und ob ich heute Abend kommen werde! You bet I'm coming this evening! **3.** *(comforting)* na, na(, na) come, come; come on ◊ *Na, na, na, wer wird denn da gleich weinen!*

Na·bel ['naːbļ] der <-s, -> belly button, navel ◊ *sich den Nabel piercen lassen*

◉ **der Nabel der Welt** *(lofty, esp iron)* the centre of the world

nach¹ [naːx] ⟨adv⟩ mir/ihm/ihr etc. nach after me/him/her etc.

◉ **nach und nach** gradually ◊ *Die Gäste trafen nach und nach ein.* ⊜allmählich **nach wie vor** still ◊ *Der Bau der Autobahn ist nach wie vor umstritten.* ⊜immer noch

② **nach²** [naːx] ⟨prep⟩ ⟨+dat⟩ **1.** *in response to the question 'when/where?'* after ◊ *Sie hat gleich nach Erhalt der Rechnung bezahlt.* ♦ *die vierte Straße nach der Kreuzung* Nach einer Stunde kam sie vom Einkaufen zurück. She came back from the shops an hour later. Was wird man nach zehn Jahren über ihn denken? What will people think of him in ten years' time? ⊜vor **2.** *in response to the question 'to where?'* to ◊ *Wir fliegen nach Athen.* nach Hause gehen go home nach links/rechts left/right ◊ *An der Kreuzung bog sie nach links ab.* nach außen/innen outside/inside eine nach außen aufgehende Tür a door that opens outwards sich nach vorn/hinten beugen lean forwards/backwards nach allen Richtungen in all directions **3.** *in response to the question 'how?'* according to ◊ *Sie werden nach Leistung bezahlt.; (smell, taste)* of ◊ *Hier stinkt es nach Abgasen!* jds Meinung nach in sb's opinion nach rheinischer Art in the Rhenish style

nach|ah·men ['naːxʔaːmən] <ahmt nach, ahmte nach, hat nachgeahmt> ⟨tr v⟩ copy, imitate ◊ *Die Kinder ahmen ihre Mutter nach.* ⊜nachmachen

② **Nach·bar** ['naxbaːɐ̯] der <-n or seldom -s, -n>, **Nach·ba·rin** ['naxbaːrɪn] die <-, -nen> neighbour, neighbor

Nach·bar·schaft ['naxbaːɐ̯ʃaft] die <-, -en> **1.** neighbours, neighbors ◊ *Die ganze Nachbarschaft weiß darüber Bescheid.* **2.** (neighbourly/neighborly) relations ◊ *eine gute Nachbarschaft pflegen* **3.** neighbourhood, neighborhood ◊ *in der Nachbarschaft wohnen* ♦ *ein Junge aus der Nachbarschaft; (more general)* vicinity

② **nach·dem** [naːxˈdeːm] ⟨conjunc⟩ **1.** *(temporal)* after

◊ *Nachdem sie den Tisch gedeckt hatte, aß sie zu Abend.* **2.** *(regional, fam) (consecutive)* since, because ◊ *Nachdem er ja ohnehin nicht kommt, habe ich für ihn auch nicht gekocht.*

◉ **je nachdem** depending on

② **nach|den·ken** ['naːxdɛŋkņ] <denkt nach, dachte nach, hat nachgedacht> ⟨intr v⟩ *(über etw.* ⟨acc⟩*)* nachdenken think (about sth) ◊ *über seine Karriere nachdenken* ♦ *Sie redet manchmal, ohne nachzudenken.*

Nach·druck ['naːxdrʊk] der <-(e)s, -e> **1.** *no pl* mit Nachdruck emphatically ◊ *mit Nachdruck gegen etw.* protestieren seinen Worten Nachdruck verleihen give/lend emphasis to your words besonderen Nachdruck auf etw. ⟨acc⟩ legen place special emphasis on sth **2.** *(of a book)* reprint ◊ *Der Nachdruck erschien im selben Verlag.;* reprinting ◊ *Der Nachdruck ist ausgeschlossen.*

nach·ei·nan·der [naːxʔae̯ˈnandɐ] ⟨adv⟩ **1.** one after the other/another ◊ *nacheinander das Zimmer betreten* zwei/drei etc. Tage nacheinander for two/three etc. consecutive days, for two/three etc. days in a row **2.** *translation varies* sich nacheinander umsehen look around for each other sich nacheinander umdrehen turn around and look at each other

Nach·fol·ger ['naːxfɔlɡɐ] der <-s, ->, **Nach·fol·ge·rin** ['naːxfɔlɡərɪn] die <-, -nen> successor ◊ *jds designierter Nachfolger* ♦ *einen würdigen Nachfolger für jdn suchen* ⊜Vorgänger

② **Nach·fra·ge** ['naːxfraːɡə] die <-, -n> **1.** *no pl* ECON die Nachfrage (nach etw.) the demand (for sth) ⊜Angebot **2.** *most pl* enquiry ◊ *Auf Nachfragen gab er ausweichende Antworten.*

nach|ge·ben ['naːxɡeːbm̩] <gibt nach, gab nach, hat nachgegeben> ⟨intr v⟩ **1.** ⟨+dat⟩ *(person)* give in ◊ *jds Bitten/Drängen/Forderungen nachgeben* ♦ *Schließlich gab sie der Versuchung nach.* **2.** ECON *(exchange rate, price etc.)* drop, fall ◊ *Die Immobilienpreise haben etwas nachgegeben.* ⊜fallen **3.** *(material, construction)* give way ◊ *Plötzlich gab der Boden unter ihnen nach.*

nach|ge·hen ['naːxɡeːən] <geht nach, ging nach, ist nachgegangen> ⟨intr v⟩ **1.** ⟨+dat⟩ *(a profession)* practise, practice ◊ *Geht sie einer geregelten Arbeit nach?; (a hobby etc.)* pursue seinen Geschäften nachgehen go about your business ⊜ausüben **2.** ⟨+dat⟩ *(a supposition, suspicion)* investigate, look into ◊ *Die Polizei geht den zahlreichen Hinweisen nach.* ♦ *Er versprach, der Sache nachzugehen.* ⊜untersuchen **3.** ⟨+dat⟩ *(a person, trail)* follow ◊ *Er ging ihr heimlich nach.* ⊜folgen **4.** *(watches, clocks)* be slow ◊ *Meine Uhr geht fünf Minuten nach.* ⊜vorgehen **5.** ⟨+dat⟩ *(positive experience)* jdm nachgehen stay with sb; *(negative experience)* haunt sb

nach|ha·ken ['naːxhaːkņ] <hakt nach, hakte nach, hat nachgehakt> ⟨intr v⟩ *(fam)* probe further ◊

noch einmal nachhaken, ob nicht doch Interesse besteht

nach|hel·fen ['naːxhɛlfn̩] <hilft nach, half nach, hat nachgeholfen> [intr v] help things along, give sb a hand ◊ *Gehst du jetzt freiwillig oder muss ich erst nachhelfen?* einer Sache nachhelfen boost sth/give sth a helping hand dem Glück/Zufall nachhelfen help your luck along a bit/give chance a helping hand jds Gedächtnis nachhelfen prompt sb's memory

② **nach·her** [naːxˈheːɐ̯, '– –] [adv] **1.** afterwards ◊ *Wir gingen spazieren und nachher noch ins Kino.* ⊖danach ⊕vorher **2.** later ◊ *„Machst du das bitte?" — „Jetzt nicht, vielleicht nachher."* ⊖später ⊕früher ♦ bis nachher see you later

Nach·hil·fe ['naːxhɪlfə] die <–> *no pl* Nachhilfe (in etw. [dat]) private tuition (in sth) ◊ *Nachhilfe in Mathe brauchen/bekommen*

Nach·hi·nein ['naːxhɪnaɛn] *(always* im **Nachhinein)* **1.** afterwards ◊ *Das lässt sich erst im Nachhinein feststellen.* ⊖nachträglich, später **2.** with hindsight, in retrospect ◊ *Im Nachhinein betrachtet/gesehen war das ein großer Fehler.*

nach|ho·len ['naːxhoːlən] <holt nach, holte nach, hat nachgeholt> [tr v] **1.** *(lost time etc.)* make up for, catch up on ◊ *den Stoff der letzten Woche nachholen müssen* **2.** *(family members)* jdn (irgendwohin/irgendwoher) nachholen bring sb over (to/from somewhere) ◊ *Frau und Kinder in die neue Heimat nachholen*

Nach·kom·me ['naːxkɔmə] der <–n, –n> descendant ◊ *keine direkten Nachkommen hinterlassen* ⊖Vorfahr

nach|kom·men ['naːxkɔmən] <kommt nach, kam nach, ist nachgekommen> [intr v] **1.** follow on, come later ◊ *Geht schon mal los, ich komme später nach.* **2.** *(lofty)* einer Sache [dat] nachkommen fulfil sth, carry sth out ◊ *seinen Verpflichtungen/Pflichten/Aufgaben nachkommen; (a request)* comply with

nach|las·sen ['naːxlasn̩] <lässt nach, ließ nach, hat nachgelassen> [intr v] **1.** decrease, diminish ◊ *Der Umsatz hat gegenüber dem Vorjahr nachgelassen.* ♦ *Der Druck auf die Regierung lässt nicht nach.; (heat, rain)* abate, ease off ◊ *Der Regen ließ nach und der Himmel wurde wieder klar.; (pain, temperature etc.)* subside; *(ailment)* clear up; *(effect)* wear off ◊ *Die Wirkung des Medikaments lässt schon nach 2 Stunden nach.* ⊖sich verringern, sich vermindern **2.** *(health, sight, memory, performance etc.)* deteriorate ◊ *Ab 0,5 Promille lässt das Sehvermögen nach.* ⊖sich verschlechtern **3.** *often negated (person)* ease up, give up (in etw. [dat]) nachlassen give up (on sth) ◊ *Wir dürfen jetzt nicht in unseren Anstrengungen nachlassen!* [tr v] (jdm) den Preis nachlassen, (jdm) etw. vom Preis nachlassen allow (sb) a discount on the price, allow (sb) a reduction on the price

nach·läs·sig ['naːxlɛsɪç] [adj] careless, slipshod ◊ *Bei der nachlässigen Kontrolle wurde der Fehler übersehen.* ♦ *Das zu übersehen war ziemlich nachlässig von ihr.* ⊖schlampig ⊕sorgfältig [adv] carelessly, in a slipshod manner ◊ *Diese Regelung wird ziemlich nachlässig gehandhabt.* nachlässig

gekleidet sein be dressed untidily

nach|ma·chen ['naːxmaxn̩] <macht nach, machte nach, hat nachgemacht> [tr v] **1.** (jdm) etw. nachmachen copy sth (sb does) *Das soll mir erst mal jemand nachmachen!* I'd like to see someone else do that! *Das macht mir/dir etc. so schnell keiner nach!* Nobody else is going to do that in a hurry! **2.** *(a typical behaviour etc.)* jdn/etw. nachmachen mimic sb/sth, imitate sb/sth ◊ *Kannst du einen Hund/Zug nachmachen?* ⊖nachahmen **3.** *(an original)* etw. nachmachen copy sth, duplicate sth ◊ *einen Schlüssel nachmachen lassen; (illegally)* forge sth, counterfeit sth ◊ *Banknoten/jds Unterschrift nachmachen* **4.** *(fam) (missed work)* make up ◊ *Gestern war ich krank, muss ich die Hausaufgaben nachmachen?* ⊖nachholen

Nach·mit·tag ['naːxmɪtaːk] der <–(e)s, –e> afternoon ◊ *Ich habe heute Nachmittag frei.* ♦ *Am Nachmittag macht er gern ein Nickerchen.*

nach·mit·tags ['naːxmɪtaːks] [adv] in the afternoon ◊ *Wir machen nachmittags immer eine Kaffeepause.*

Nach·na·me ['naːxnaːmə] der <–ns, –n> surname ◊ *Wie heißt er mit Nachnamen?* ⊖Familienname ⊕Vorname

nach|prü·fen ['naːxpryːfn̩] <prüft nach, prüfte nach, hat nachgeprüft> [tr v] verify, check ◊ *Hast du nachgeprüft, ob alle Fenster zu sind?*

nach|rei·chen ['naːxraɛçn̩] <reicht nach, reichte nach, hat nachgereicht> [tr v] hand in later ◊ *Bitte reichen Sie Ihre Zeugnisse baldmöglichst nach.*

② **Nach·richt** ['naːxrɪçt] die <–, –en> **1.** *(item/piece of)* news ◊ *Er überraschte sie mit der Nachricht, dass er gekündigt habe.; (personal specific information)* message ◊ *eine Nachricht auf dem Anrufbeantworter hinterlassen* eine Nachricht von jdm/etw., eine Nachricht über jdn/etw. news about sb/sth eine Nachricht (von jdm) an/für jdn a message (from sb) for sb, news (from sb) for sb ◊ *Ich habe eine gute/schlechte Nachricht für Sie.* **2.** *only pl* RADIO, TV news ◊ *Hast du heute die Nachrichten gesehen/angehört?*

Nach·ruf ['naːxruːf] der <–(e)s, –e> obituary ein Nachruf (auf jdn) an obituary (of sb)

nach|sa·gen ['naːxzaːgn̩] <sagt nach, sagte nach, hat nachgesagt> [tr v] **1.** *(fam)* (jdm) etw. nachsagen repeat sth (after sb) ◊ *Meine Kleine sagt mir immer alles nach.* ⊖wiederholen **2.** jdm etw. nachsagen accuse sb of sth ◊ *Ihm wird Eitelkeit nachgesagt.* ⊖behaupten

Nach·schlag ['naːxʃlaːk] der <–(e)s, Nachschläge> *(also fig)* second helping

② **nach|schla·gen** ['naːxʃlaːgn̩] <schlägt nach, schlug nach, hat nachgeschlagen> [tr v] etw. (in etw. [dat]) nachschlagen look sth up (in sth) ◊ *im Wörterbuch nachschlagen, wie man ein Wort schreibt* [intr v] jdm nachschlagen take after sb ◊ *Sie schlägt ganz ihrer Großmutter nach.*

Nach·schub ['naːxʃuːp] der <–(e)s, Nachschübe> *most sing* new supply ◊ *Wenn euch die Arbeit ausgeht, kann ich jederzeit für Nachschub sorgen.; (military)* supplies

nach·se·hen ['naːxzeːən] <sieht nach, sah nach, hat nachgesehen> [tr+intr v] *(examine)* check ◊ *Sieh mal nach, ob das Wasser schon kocht.* ♦ *Der*

Schlüssel muss doch irgendwo sein. Sieh bitte noch einmal nach.; (school work) mark `tr v` jdm etw. nachsehen forgive sb for sth, overlook sb's sth ◊ *Diesen Fehler werde ich dir kein zweites Mal nachsehen.* `intr v` `+dat` follow with your eyes ◊ *Er sah dem Schiff noch lange sehnsüchtig nach.*

Nach·se·hen ['naːxzeːən] *das <–s> no pl (always* **das Nachsehen haben)** das Nachsehen haben be left empty-handed

nach|sit·zen ['naːxzɪtsn̩] *<sitzt nach, saß nach, hat nachgesessen>* `intr v` SCHOOL get/have a detention, stay behind

② **Nach·spei·se** ['naːxʃpaɛzə] *die <–, –n>* dessert ◊ *Möchtest du Eis als Nachspeise?* ⊖Nachtisch, Dessert ⊖Vorspeise

② **nächst** [nɛːçst] `prep` `+dat` *(lofty)* apart from, next to ◊ *Nächst der Arbeitslosigkeit ist die Rentensicherung das dringendste Problem.*

② **nächst·...** [nɛːçst] `prefix` **1.** *+adj or pres p* next ◊ *Wann wäre denn der nächstmögliche Termin?* der nächstgelegene Flughafen the nearest airport die nächstliegende Lösung the most obvious solution **2.** *+comp* next ◊ *Wenn die Hose nicht passt, probier mal die nächstgrößere.* in den nächsthöheren Gang schalten change up a gear **3.** *+superl* next ◊ *Er ist nach mir der nächstgrößte Schüler in der Klasse.*

nächst·bes·te ['nɛːçst'bɛstə] `superl` *only before ns* nearest ◊ *Er griff sich einfach die nächstbeste Zeitschrift.* die nächstbeste CD nehmen take the first CD you come across jdn bei der nächstbesten Gelegenheit absetzen drop sb off at the first opportunity

nächs·te ['nɛːçstə] *superl of* nah `adj` **1.** *sequential, temporal* next ◊ *Nächstes Mal gewinne ich!* ◆ *Die Möbel werden nächste Woche geliefert.* als Nächstes next ◊ *Was sollen wir als Nächstes tun?* ⊖vorige, letzte **2.** *spatial* nearest, next ◊ *Bis zur nächsten Tankstelle sind es etwa 10 km.* **3.** ein nächster, eine nächste, ein nächstes another ◊ *Er hofft auf eine nächste Chance.* ◆ *Ein nächstes Mal wird es nicht geben.*

Nächs·te ['nɛːçstə] *der/die <–n, die Nächsten> but: dein Nächster/deine Nächste* **1.** next (one) ◊ *„Kommst du bald dran?" — „Ja, ich bin der Nächste/ich bin als Nächster dran."* **2.** *(lofty)* neighbour, neighbor ◊ *Du sollst deinen Nächsten lieben wie dich selbst.*
◉ **jeder ist sich selbst der Nächste** everyone looks after number one

nach|ste·hen ['naːxʃteːən] *<steht nach, stand nach, hat nachgestanden>* `intr v` take second place ◊ *Er war so großzügig, da wollten wir natürlich nicht nachstehen.* jdm/etw. (an/in etw. `dat`) nicht nachstehen be no way inferior to sb/sth (in sth/in terms of sth) ◊ *Sie steht ihm an Selbstbewusstsein nicht nach.* jdm/etw. in nichts nachstehen be sb's/sth's equal in every way ◊ *Preisgünstige Produkte stehen teuren Markenartikeln meist in nichts nach.*

Nacht [naxt] *die <–, Nächte>* **1.** night ◊ *Im Juni sind die Nächte kurz und die Tage lang.* ◆ *Sie feierten die ganze Nacht.* ◆ *bis tief/weit in die Nacht hinein* ◆ *eine unruhige/schlaflose/schlechte Nacht haben* bei Nacht at night eines Nachts one night über Nacht overnight ◊ *Kann ich über Nacht*

hier bleiben? zur Nacht at night **2.** gestern/letzte/ vergangene Nacht yesterday/last night heute Nacht tonight morgen/kommende Nacht tomorrow night **3.** gute Nacht! good night!
◉ **bei Nacht und Nebel** under cover of darkness **die Nacht zum Tag(e) machen** stay up all night **(na,) dann gute Nacht** *(fam)* (then) that'll be that **die Heilige Nacht** Christmas Eve

② **Nach·teil** ['naːxtaɛl] *der <–(e)s, –e>* disadvantage ◊ *Die Sache hat einen entscheidenden/großen Nachteil: ...* ◆ *Der einzige Nachteil an diesem Hobby ist, dass es sehr teuer ist.* (jdm/etw. gegenüber) im Nachteil be at a disadvantage (compared with sb/sth) jdm/etw. zum Nachteil gereichen be to sb's/sth's detriment ⊖Vorteil

② **Nach·tisch** ['naːxtɪʃ] *der <–(e)s>* no pl dessert ◊ *Zum Nachtisch gab es Erdbeeren mit Schlagsahne.* ⊖Nachspeise, Dessert ⊖Vorspeise

Nach·trag ['naːxtraːk] *der <–(e)s, Nachträge>* ein Nachtrag (zu etw.) postscript (to sth), appendix (to sth) ◊ *einen Nachtrag zum Haushalt vorlegen/ verabschieden; (to a will)* codicil; *(book)* supplement

nach|tra·gen ['naːxtraːgŋ̩] *<trägt nach, trug nach, hat nachgetragen>* `tr v` **1.** *(an error, insult etc.)* jdm etw. nachtragen hold sth against sb ⊖verzeihen **2.** *(missing information)* etw. (zu etw.) nachtragen add sth (to sth) ◊ *die fehlenden Angaben im Formular nachtragen* ⊖hinzufügen, ergänzen **3.** *(heavy objects etc.)* jdm etw. nachtragen follow sb with sth ◊ *Ein Hoteldiener trug ihnen die Koffer aufs Zimmer nach.; (forgotten items)* go after sb with sth

nach·träg·lich ['naːxtrɛːklɪç] `adj, adv` *when used as an adj, only before ns* subsequent(ly) ◊ *Eine nachträgliche Änderung ist nicht möglich.* ◆ *Er wurde nachträglich wegen Dopings disqualifiziert.* ⊖im Nachhinein

nachts [naxts] `adv` at night ◊ *Die Tankstelle hat auch nachts geöffnet.* ◆ *Ich bin heute um drei Uhr nachts aufgewacht.*

Nacht·tisch ['naxttɪʃ] *der <–(e)s, –e>* bedside table

nach|voll·zie·hen ['naːxfɔltsiːən] *<vollzieht nach, vollzog nach, hat nachvollzogen>* `tr v` *mostly inf or past p* understand, comprehend ◊ *Ich kann deine Argumente durchaus nachvollziehen.*

Nach·weis ['naːxvaɛs] *der <–es, –e>* ein Nachweis für/von etw., ein Nachweis ... `gen` proof of sth ◊ *Die Polizei verlangte von ihm den Nachweis seiner Identität.* der Nachweis, dass (the) proof that den Nachweis führen/erbringen furnish proof ⊖Beweis

nach|wei·sen ['naːxvaɛzn̩] *<weist nach, wies nach, hat nachgewiesen>* `tr v` **1.** prove ◊ *Die Schuld des Angeklagten ist zweifelsfrei nachgewiesen.; (organisms etc.)* detect **2.** jdm etw. nachweisen prove sb did sth ◊ *Der Mord ist ihm nie nachgewiesen worden.*

Nach·wuchs ['naːxvuːks] *der <–es>* no pl **1.** *(children, young animals)* offspring bei jdm hat sich Nachwuchs angekündigt/ist Nachwuchs unterwegs sb is expecting (a happy event) **2.** *(in a profession)* new blood, new recruits, up-and-coming personnel ◊ *der wissenschaftliche Nachwuchs*

Nach·züg·ler ['naːxtsyːglɐ] *der <–s, –>* *(also hum)*

latecomer, late arrival ◊ *Wir müssen noch auf ein paar Nachzügler warten.*

Na·cken ['nakn̩] der <-s, -> ANAT neck ◊ *einen steifen/verspannten Nacken haben* die Haare im/ am Nacken kurz tragen wear your hair short at the back den Kopf in den Nacken legen throw your head right back den Hut in den Nacken schieben push your hat right back

◉ jdn/etw. im Nacken dogged by jd sitzt jdm im Nacken sb breathes down sb's neck ◊ *Bei der Arbeit sitzt mir der Chef ständig im Nacken.* etw. sitzt jdm im Nacken *(fear etc.)* sb feels sth in the pit of their stomach ◊ *Die Angst vor der Prüfung saß ihr im Nacken.*

nackt [nakt] adj 1. naked, nude nackt sein be naked sich nackt ausziehen get completely undressed, strip down; *(arms, legs, skin etc.)* naked, bare ◊ *Sie spürte den Wind auf ihrer nackten Haut.* mit nacktem Oberkörper bare from the waist up mit nackten Füßen with bare feet jdn nackt malen/fotografieren paint/photograph sb in the nude 2. *mostly before ns (fig) (ground, wall, facts)* bare ◊ *auf dem nackten Boden schlafen* bei etw. geht es ums nackte Überleben sth is about sheer survival; *(truth)* plain ⊜bloß 3. *only before ns (fig) (fear, poverty etc.)* sheer ◊ *Dort herrscht die nackte Gewalt/nacktes Elend.* adv naked ◊ *An dem See kann man auch nackt baden.*

② **Na·del** ['naːdl̩] die <-, -n> 1. needle ◊ *eine Nadel einfädeln* ♦ *Die Nadel am Kompass zeigt stets nach Norden.; (for securing)* pin; *(for decoration)* brooch; *(of a record player)* needle, stylus 2. *most pl* BOT needle ◊ *Die Lärche wirft ihre Nadeln im Winter ab.*

◉ mit heißer Nadel gestrickt *(fam)* put together hurriedly an der Nadel hängen *(fam)* be hooked on drugs

② **Na·gel** ['naːgl̩] der <-s, Nägel> nail ◊ *einen Nagel in die Wand schlagen* ♦ *jdm/sich die Nägel schneiden/lackieren*

◉ Nägel mit Köpfen machen *(fam)* do the job properly, make a good job of sth jdm auf/unter den Nägeln brennen *(fam)* be urgent to sb etw. an den Nagel hängen *(fam)* give sth up, chuck sth in sich dat etw. unter den Nagel reißen *(fam)* pinch sth, make off with sth

na·gen ['naːgn̩] intr v +*haben* 1. an etw. dat nagen gnaw on sth an der Unterlippe nagen chew your lower lip etw. von etw. nagen gnaw sth off sth ◊ *das Fleisch vom Knochen nagen* 2. *(fig)* an jdm/etw. nagen take its toll on sb/sth ◊ *Die Krankheit/Das schlechte Gewissen nagte an mir.* tr v +*haben (animal)* ein Loch in etw. acc nagen gnaw a hole in sth

② **nah¹** [naː], **na·he** ['naːə] adj <näher, am nächsten> 1. near ◊ *Das Problem sollte in naher Zukunft gelöst werden.* ♦ *Das Ende ist nah!* ♦ *Die beiden Punkte sind sehr nahe beieinander.* sich im nahen Wald verlaufen go astray in the nearby woods nah an/bei etw./jdm near to sth/sb, close to sth/sb ◊ *Sie wohnen ziemlich nah am Meer.* 2. *only before ns (relative, relationship, departure)* close, immediate ◊ *die nächsten Angehörigen verständigen* ♦ *Seine Abreise ist nahe.* adv 1. nearby ◊ *nahe stationierte Soldaten* ⊜weit entfernt 2. close jdm nahe kommen get on close terms with sb jdm

nahe stehen be close to sb 3. closely ◊ *nahe befreundet sein*

◉ von nah und fern from near and far, from far and wide jdm etw. nahe legen suggest sth to sb nahe liegen suggest itself, stand to reason ◊ *Der Verdacht liegt nahe, dass er gelogen hat.* nahe liegend obvious, natural jdm zu nahe treten give offence to sb von nahem close up, at close quarters

② **nah²** [naː], **na·he** ['naːə] prep *(lofty)* +*dat* near, close to ◊ *Die Stadt liegt nahe der Grenze.* ⊜fern

② **Nä·he** ['nɛːə] die <-> *no pl* 1. *(spatial)* vicinity, closeness, proximity ◊ *Die Schule befindet sich in nächster/erreichbarer Nähe.* Nähe zu etw./jdm closeness to sth/sb, proximity to sth/sb in der Nähe in the vicinity, nearby in der Nähe von/zu jdm/etw. in the vicinity of sb/sth, near sb/sth in der Nähe ... gen in the vicinity of sth, near sth ◊ *Das Hotel liegt in der Nähe des Flughafens.* in jds Nähe close to sb ◊ *Bleib in meiner Nähe, damit wir uns nicht verlieren.* aus der Nähe from close up, at close quarters aus der Nähe betrachtet viewed more closely 2. *(temporal)* closeness in greifbare Nähe rücken be close at hand 3. *(contact, relationship etc.)* closeness ◊ *ein Bedürfnis nach körperlicher/ emotionaler Nähe empfinden* Nähe zu jdm/etw. closeness to sb/sth ◊ *die Nähe zum Bürger/ Kunden/Publikum etc. suchen*

② **nä·hen** ['nɛːən] tr+intr v +*haben* 1. *(clothes etc.)* sew ◊ *Sie näht ihre Kleider selbst.* ♦ *Ich kann nicht gut nähen.*; *(a hole, tear etc.)* sew up, mend etw. an/auf etw. acc nähen sew sth to/on sth 2. MED *(a wound, cut)* stitch; *(a person)* jdn nähen stitch sb up ◊ *Sie hatte eine Platzwunde und musste genäht werden.* Müssen Sie nähen? Do I/Does he etc. need stitches?

nä·her ['nɛːɐ] *comp of* nah adv 1. in more detail ◊ *Er konnte den Täter nicht näher beschreiben.* 2. jdm etw. näher bringen give sb an understanding of sth 3. jdn näher kennen know sb well 4. näher rücken approach 5. näher treten come closer, get closer

nä·here ['nɛːɐ] adj 1. *(information etc.)* further, more detailed ◊ *Wo bekomme ich nähere Informationen dazu?* ♦ *Nähere Einzelheiten sind nicht bekannt.* 2. *(surroundings, future etc.)* immediate ◊ *Wir haben in der näheren Umgebung alles abgesucht.*; *(contact)* closer ◊ *Ich habe keinen näheren Kontakt zu ihnen.*

Nä·he·re ['nɛːərə] das <-n> *no pl* further details ◊ *Weiß man schon Näheres über das Unglück?*

② **nä·hern** ['nɛːɐn] ref v +*haben* sich jdm/etw. nähern approach sb/sth ◊ *Er näherte sich ihr/der Tür auf Zehenspitzen.* sich dem Ende nähern draw to a close

na·he·zu ['naːə'tsuː] adv virtually, nearly, almost ◊ *Eine Lösung des Konfliktes erscheint nahezu unmöglich.* ⊜fast, beinahe

② **nahm** [naːm] *pret of* nehmen

Nah·ost [naː'ɔst] POL Middle East ◊ *der Krisenherd Nahost* ♦ *Flüchtlinge aus Nahost*

Nähr·stoff ['nɛːɐʃtɔf] der <-(e)s, -e> *most pl* nutrient ◊ *Sandiger Boden enthält wenig Nährstoffe.*

Nah·rung ['naːrʊŋ] die <-> *no pl* food ◊ *keine*

feste Nahrung zu sich nehmen können flüssige
Nahrung liquids

ⓢ einer Sache (dat) Nahrung geben *(fig)* help
nourish sth, help nurture sth (neue) Nahrung
erhalten *(fig)* receive fresh impetus

② **Nah·rungs·mit·tel** ['naːrʊŋsmɪtl̩] das <-s, ->
food(stuff) ⊖Lebensmittel

Naht [naːt] die <-, Nähte> **1.** seam ◊ *Die Naht ist
aufgegangen.* **2.** MED suture ◊ *Die Naht ist noch
leicht geschwollen.* **3.** TECHN seam, weld ◊ *eine
Naht schweißen*

ⓢ aus allen/den/sämtlichen Nähten platzen
(fam) be bursting at the seams

② **Na·me** ['naːmə] der <-ns, –n> name ◊ *Bitte geben
Sie Ihren vollständigen Namen an.* ♦ *Wie ist Ihr
Name bitte?* (nur) dem Namen nach (only) by
name

ⓢ mein Name ist Hase (ich weiß von nichts)
(fam, hum) I know nothing at all, it's nothing to
do with me sich (dat) einen Namen machen
make a name for yourself etw. beim Namen
nennen call a spade a spade im Namen von jdm/
in jds Namen on behalf of sb, in the name of sb

> Proper names are not only used to designate
> people, but also rivers, cities, countries etc. As a
> rule, they do not require an accompanying article
> (e. g. when mentioning people's names without an
> attribute — *Alex liest gerne* (Alex likes reading),
> or with a title — *Professor Schmidt*). This is also
> the case with forms of address *(Herr/Frau
> Schulz)*. An article is required, however, when
> there is an attribute in front of the person's name
> *(die kleine Lisa* — little Lisa), or as an indicator
> of case *(Das erzähle ich gleich der Katrin.* —
> I'll tell Katrin straight away). An article is also
> used in colloquial language in some parts of
> Germany *(Wo ist denn heute die Martina?* —
> Where has Martina got to today?).

na·mens ['naːməns] (adv) +*name* called, by the
name of ◊ *Dort traf sie einen Mann namens Otto.*
na·ment·lich ['naːməntlɪç] (adv) **1.** by name ◊ *Die
Autoren sind nicht namentlich bekannt.* **2.** particularly, especially ◊ *Die Europäer, namentlich
Franzosen und Deutsche, sind davon betroffen.*
⊖besonders, insbesondere (adj) only before ns by
name ◊ *Eine namentliche Nennung des Übersetzers
ist nicht üblich.*
nam·haft ['naːmhaft] (adj) *mostly before ns*
1. famous, renowned ◊ *ein namhaftes Unternehmen der Baubranche* ⊖bedeutend **2.** *(form)* jdn/
etw. namhaft machen identify sb/sth
② **näm·lich** ['nɛːmlɪç] (adv) **1.** *(being specific)*
namely, to be precise ◊ *Sie liebten beide dasselbe
Mädchen, nämlich Marie.* **2.** *(giving a reason)* you
see ◊ *Ich mag jetzt nicht ausgehen, ich bin
nämlich ziemlich müde.*
② **nann·te** ['nantə] *pret of* nennen
na·nu [na'nuː] (interj) well now, well I never ◊
Nanu, was machst du denn hier?
Nar·be ['naʳbə] die <-, –n> scar ◊ *Das Ereignis
hat Narben auf seiner Seele hinterlassen.*
Nar·ko·se [naʳ'koːzə] die <-, –n> MED **1.** *(physical
state)* anaesthesia ◊ *jdn in Narkose versetzen* ⊖Be-
täubung **2.** *(substance)* anaesthetic ◊ *Die Wirkung
der Narkose setzte sehr schnell ein.*

na·schen ['naʃn̩] (intr v) +*haben* have a nibble, eat
a few sweets ◊ *Wer hat von den Bonbons/am
Kuchen genascht?* (tr v) +*haben* eat, nibble ◊ *ein
paar Kekse naschen*
② **Na·se** ['naːzə] die <-, –n> **1.** *(also fig)* nose ◊ *Sie
hielt sich* (dat) *die Nase zu und sprang ins Wasser.*
♦ *Mir läuft schon den ganzen Tag die Nase.* ♦ *sich*
(dat) *die Nase putzen* ♦ *Er hat eine (gute) Nase für
einträgliche Geschäfte.* in der Nase bohren pick
your nose **2.** *(fam)* pro Nase per head ⊖pro
Person, pro Kopf **3.** *(fam)* (immer) der Nase nach
straight ahead ⊖geradeaus

ⓢ sich an die eigene Nase fassen *(fam)* look
to your own failings die Nase (gestrichen) voll
haben *(fam)* be fed up, have had a bellyful die
Nase vorn haben *(fam)* be leading, have the edge
(mit etw.) auf die Nase fallen *(fam)* fall flat on
your face (with sth) nach jds Nase gehen *(fam)*
fall in with sb's plans jdn an der Nase herumführen *(fam)* lead sb up the garden path jdm auf
der Nase herumtanzen *(fam)* walk all over sb
jdm etw. unter die Nase reiben *(fam)* rub sb's
nose in sth die Nase (über etw.) (acc) rümpfen
turn your nose up (at sth) jdm etw. aus der
Nase ziehen *(fam)* drag sth out of sb vor die/
der/jds Nase *(spatially)* right in front of sb's
nose, right in sb's face ◊ jdm die Tür vor der Nase
zuschlagen *(temporally)* right under sb's nose ◊
*Sie hat mir die Wohnung vor der Nase wegge-
schnappt.*
② **nass** [nas] (adj) <nasser/nässer, am nassesten/
nässesten> wet ◊ *Sie hängte die nassen Sachen
zum Trocknen auf.* jdn/etw. nass machen/spritzen
soak sb/wet sth ◊ *Der Mai war ungewöhnlich kühl
und nass.* ⊖trocken
Näs·se ['nɛsə] die <-> *no pl* wetness, dampness,
moisture ◊ *Bei Nässe darf man hier nur 80 km/h
fahren.* überfrierende Nässe black ice
näs·ser ['nɛsɐ] *comp of* nass
② **Na·ti·o·nal·rat¹** [natsjoˈnaːlraːt] der <-(e)s> *(Austr,
Swiss)* National Council ◊ *eine Abstimmung im
Nationalrat*
② **Na·ti·o·nal·rat²** [natsjoˈnaːlraːt] der
<-(es), Nationalräte>, **Na·ti·o·nal·rä·tin**
[natsjoˈnaːlrɛːtɪn] die <-, –nen> *(Austr, Swiss)*
National Councillor ◊ *Sie wurde zur Nationalrätin
gewählt.*
② **Na·tur** [naˈtuːɐ] die <-, –en> **1.** *no pl* nature ◊ *die
Wunder der Natur* ♦ *ungestört die Natur genießen*
Natur sein be natural **2.** character ◊ *Die beiden
Schwestern haben völlig verschiedene Naturen.* von
Natur aus naturally, by nature ◊ *Sie ist von Natur
aus eher schüchtern.* etw. ist nicht jds Natur sth is
not in sb's nature ⊖Wesen, Art **3.** *no pl* kind, type
◊ *Fragen spezieller Natur* eine Verletzung leichter
Natur a slight injury ⊖Art

ⓢ in der Natur der Dinge liegen be in the
nature of things
② **na·tür·lich** [naˈtyːɐlɪç] (adj, adv) natural(ly) ◊ *Ihre
Locken sind natürlich.* ♦ *eine natürliche Begabung
für Sprachen* ♦ *Er ist eines natürlichen Todes
gestorben.* ♦ *Gib dich ganz natürlich.* (adv) **1.** of
course, naturally ◊ *"Kommst du mit?"* —
"Natürlich!" ♦ *Karin ist natürlich wieder zu spät
gekommen.* **2.** *(qualifying)* of course ◊ *Natürlich
kannst du das tun, aber es könnte auch schief*

gehen.
Na·tur·schutz [na'tu:ɡʃʊts] der <–(e)s> no pl conservation unter Naturschutz stehen be a protected
species; *(area)* be a conservation area/nature
reserve unter Naturschutz stellen classify an
animal/a plant as a protected species; *(an area)*
designate as a conservation area/nature reserve
Na·tur·wis·sen·schaft [na'tu:ɡvɪsnʃaft] die
<–, –en> science
NC [ɛn'tse:] der *(abbr of* Numerus clausus) entry
quota ◊ *In diesem Fach gibt es noch keinen NC.*
② **Ne·bel** ['ne:bl̩] der <–s, –> fog ◊ *Heute ist/herrscht
hier dichter Nebel.*
② **ne·ben** ['ne:bm̩] prep **1.** *with acc when expressing
motion towards a place, with dat when there is no
or undirected motion* next to ◊ *Sie stand neben
mir.* ♦ *Er stellte sich neben mich.* ♦ *Unser Haus ist
neben der Kirche.* **2.** +dat alongside, in addition to
◊ *Neben ihm habe ich noch zwei weitere Mitarbeiter.* ⊝außer **3.** compared to/with ◊ *Neben ihr
komme ich mir immer so dumm vor.*
② **ne·ben·an** [ne:bm̩'an] adv *(nach)* nebenan next
door ◊ *Das Büro von Herrn Schulze ist nebenan.* ♦
Ich gehe nach nebenan zum Nachbarn. von
nebenan *(from)* next door ◊ *die Leute von
nebenan*
② **ne·ben·bei** [ne:bm̩'baɛ̯] adv **1.** in passing ◊ *Sie
hat ganz nebenbei erwähnt, dass sie geheiratet
hat.* nebenbei bemerkt/gesagt incidentally, by the
way ⊝beiläufig **2.** on the side ◊ *Er macht nebenbei
Gartenarbeiten für eine alte Dame.* ⊝zusätzlich,
nebenher
ne·ben·ei·nan·der [ne:bm̩|aɛ̯'nandɐ] adv
1. *(spatial)* side by side, next to each other ◊
Stühle nebeneinander stellen ♦ *Sie saßen im
Konzert nebeneinander.* **2.** *(temporal)* side by side,
together ◊ *Beruf und Familie, geht das nebeneinander?* nebeneinander existieren coexist ⊝miteinan-
der
Ne·ben·fach ['ne:bm̩fax] das <–(e)s, Nebenfächer>
subsidiary subject, minor subject ◊ *Welche Nebenfä-
cher hast du belegt?* ♦ *Sie studiert Germanistik im
Nebenfach.*
ne·ben·her [ne:bm̩'he:ɐ̯] adv **1.** alongside ◊ *Er
ging spazieren und sein Hund lief nebenher.* **2.** at
the same time, on the side ◊ *Ich bügle und höre
nebenher Musik.* ⊝nebenbei
Ne·ben·kos·ten ['ne:bm̩kɔstn̩] die <–> only pl
additional costs; *(of rent)* costs of heating, water,
waste disposal etc. ◊ *Die Miete beträgt ohne Nebenkosten 1500 Euro.*
Ne·ben·sa·che ['ne:bm̩zaxə] die <–, –n> trifle,
triviality ◊ *Sex ist die schönste Nebensache der
Welt.* etw. ist (für jdn) Nebensache sth is irrelevant
(as far as sb is concerned) ⊝Hauptsache
Ne·ben·satz ['ne:bm̩zats] der <–es, Nebensätze>
subordinate clause ◊ *Die Konjunktion „weil" leitet
einen Nebensatz ein.*
Ne·ben·wir·kung ['ne:bm̩vɪr'kʊŋ] die <–, –en> side
effect ◊ *Nebenwirkungen dieses Medikaments sind
nicht bekannt.*
② **neb·lig** ['ne:blɪç] adj foggy ◊ *ein nebliger Novembertag* ♦ *Heute ist es neblig.*
nebst [ne:pst] prep +dat *(oldf)* (along) with ◊ *Er
war nebst seinem Sohn erschienen.* ♦ *ein Haus
nebst Swimmingpool*

ne·cken ['nɛkn̩] tr v +haben tease ◊ *Sie wurde
wegen ihrer roten Haare schon viel geneckt.* sie
necken sich they tease each other
② **Nef·fe** ['nɛfə] der <–n, –n> nephew
② **ne·ga·tiv** ['ne:gati:f] adj negative ◊ *Ich habe einen
negativen Bescheid bekommen.* ♦ *Sie hat eine
negative Einstellung zum Leben.* ♦ *Sein Urteil war
negativer als befürchtet.* ♦ *der negative Pol* ♦ *Der
Test fiel negativ aus.* ⊝positiv adv negatively, in
the negative ◊ *auf eine Frage negativ antworten* ♦
sich negativ über jdn äußern etw. negativ beurtei-
len/einschätzen judge/assess sth unfavourably sich
negativ auf etw. acc auswirken be detrimental to
sth
② **neh·men** ['ne:mən] <nimmt, nahm, hat genommen>
tr v **1.** take ◊ *Er nahm das Kind bei der Hand.* ♦
Der Vater nahm seinen Sohn auf den Schoß. ♦
Nimm den Schirm; es regnet. ♦ *eine Wohnung
nehmen* ♦ *Ich nehme Schnitzel mit Pommes.* ♦ *Sie
haben den jüngeren Bewerber genommen.* ♦ *Was
nehmen Sie für Medikamente?* ♦ *Wann nimmst du
Urlaub?* ♦ *Sie nimmt jetzt Fahrstunden.* ♦ *Woher
nimmst du das Recht, so etwas zu tun?* ♦ *ein Bad
nehmen* ♦ *Ich nahm die Dokumente an mich.* ♦ *Ich
nehme nie das Auto, um in die Stadt zu fahren.* ♦
Man nehme drei Eier, 200 g Mehl und 100 g Butter.
etw. auf sich acc nehmen take sth on ◊ *Sie haben
erhebliche Kosten auf sich genommen.* jdn/etw. mit
sich nehmen take sb/sth along ◊ *Sie nimmt ihren
Hund immer mit sich.* jdn zu sich nehmen take sb
in ◊ *Sie hat ihre alten Eltern zu sich genommen.*
etw. zu sich nehmen have sth (to eat) **2.** (sich
dat) etw. nehmen help yourself to sth, take sth,
have sth ◊ *Nimm ruhig noch ein Stück Kuchen.*
3. etw. (für etw.) nehmen charge sth (for sth) ◊
Meine Putzfrau nimmt 15 Euro die Stunde. ⊝verlan-
gen **4.** jdm etw. nehmen take sth away from sb,
deprive sb of sth ◊ *Der Baum nimmt uns die
Sicht.; (an emotion, a pain)* etw. von jdm
nehmen relieve sb of sth ◊ *Das hat eine Sorge von
mir genommen.* ⊝geben **5.** sich dat jdn nehmen
hire sb, take sb on ◊ *Du solltest dir einen Anwalt
nehmen.* **6.** etw. als etw. nehmen take sth as sth,
interpret sth as sth ◊ *Nimm das als Beweis für
seine Liebe.* jdn/etw. ernst/wichtig nehmen take
sb/sth seriously etw. leicht nehmen take sth easy
etw. wörtlich nehmen take sth literally
⊛ sich dat etw. nicht nehmen lassen insist on
sth woher nehmen und nicht stehlen *(fam)*
where on Earth will I/you etc. find the money jdn
zu nehmen wissen know how to handle sb wie
man's nimmt *(fam)* that depends
Neid [naɛ̯t] der <–(e)s> no pl envy, jealousy ◊ *Nur
keinen Neid, gönn ihm doch den Erfolg.*
⊛ grün/blass vor Neid green with envy vor Neid
erblassen turn pale with envy das muss jdm der
Neid lassen you have to give that to sb
nei·disch ['naɛ̯dɪʃ] adj envious, jealous ◊ *Er warf
neidische Blicke auf unser neues Auto.* ♦ *Er ist
neidisch auf meinen Erfolg.*
nei·gen ['naɛ̯gn̩] tr v +haben tilt, tip ◊ *die Flasche
etwas neigen; (your head, torso)* (nach vorn)
neigen incline den Kopf zur Seite neigen cock
your head intr v +haben zu etw. neigen have a
tendency to (do) sth ◊ *Sie neigt zu Übertreibungen.; (to disease, parasites etc.)* zu Depressio-

A
B
C
D
E
F
G
H
I
J
K
L
M
N
O
P
Q
R
S
T
U
V
W
X
Y
Z

nen/Blattläusen etc. neigen be susceptible to depression/greenfly etc. ref v +*haben* **1.** sich über etw. acc neigen lean over sth sich aus dem Fenster neigen lean out of the window **2.** sich neigen bend sich zur Seite neigen tilt to one side
Nei·gung ['naɪgʊŋ] die <–, –en> **1.** *no pl* eine Neigung zu etw. a tendency to (do) sth, a susceptibility to sth ◊ *Sie hat eine Neigung zum Dickwerden.* ⊜Tendenz **2.** inclination ◊ *Dieser Beruf entspricht seinen Neigungen.* ⊜Interesse **3.** *no pl* inclination, slope ◊ *Die Straße hat hier eine steile Neigung.*

② **nein** [naɪn] *part* **1.** *(negating, refusing)* no ◊ *„Möchtest du noch ein Stück Kuchen?" — „Nein danke."* ♦ *Nein, ich will das nicht!* ♦ *Antworten Sie mit ja oder nein.* ♦ *Das wird Hunderte, nein Tausende kosten.* zu etw. nein sagen say no to sth ⊜ja **2.** *(expression of surprise)* my (goodness) ◊ *Nein, bist du aber groß geworden!*
Nein [naɪn] das <–(s)> *no pl* no ◊ *Das war ein klares Nein.* bei seinem Nein bleiben stick to your refusal
Nel·ke ['nɛlkə] die <–, –n> **1.** BOT carnation **2.** clove ◊ *den Schweinebraten mit Nelken spicken*
② **nen·nen** ['nɛnən] <nennt, nannte, hat genannt> trv **1.** name, call ◊ *Wie wollt ihr euer Kind nennen?* ♦ *Wie nennt man diese Methode?* **2.** call ◊ *Sie heißt Veronika, aber alle nennen sie Vroni.* ♦ *Sie hat ihn einen Idioten genannt.* ♦ *Das nenne ich Liebe!* **3.** address as ◊ *Er will Herr Doktor genannt werden.* **4.** name, give the name of ◊ *Der Zeuge konnte den Täter nennen.* ♦ *Nennt mir drei deutsche Großstädte.* **5.** mention ◊ *Er wollte den Grund seines Anrufs nicht nennen.* ref v **1.** jd nennt sich etw. sb is supposed to be sth ◊ *Wer sich heutzutage alles Künstler nennt!* **2.** etw. nennt sich etw. sth is called sth ◊ *Das Verfahren nennt sich Kernspintomographie.*
Nen·ner ['nɛnɐ] der <–s, –> denominator ⊛ etw. auf einen gemeinsamen Nenner bringen find common ground on sth einen gemeinsamen Nenner finden find a common denominator
Nerv [nɛrf] der <–s, –en> nerve ◊ *Als Lehrer braucht man starke Nerven.* ♦ *Meine Nerven sind etwas angespannt.* ♦ *Verlier bloß nicht die Nerven!* ♦ *Er ist mit seinen/den Nerven am Ende.* ♦ *Der Zahnarzt hat den Nerv betäubt.* ⊛ jdm auf die Nerven gehen get on sb's nerves Nerven haben *(fam)* have a nerve den Nerv haben, etw. zu tun have the nerve to do sth jdm den (letzten) Nerv töten *(fam)* drive sb round the bend Nerven zeigen get nervy
ner·ven ['nɛrfn̩] *(fam)* trv +*haben* jdn nerven get on sb's nerves, wind sb up ◊ *Lass dich doch von dem nicht nerven!* ⊜aufregen intr v +*haben* be annoying ◊ *Jürgen, du nervst!*
② **ner·vös** [nɛr'vøːs] adj, adv nervous(ly) ◊ *Du machst mich ganz nervös.* ♦ *Er hat ein nervöses Zucken im Augenlid.* ♦ *Er lief nervös auf und ab.*
Ner·vo·si·tät [nɛrvozi'tɛːt] die <–> *no pl* nervousness, tension ◊ *Vor lauter Nervosität konnte sie nicht schlafen.*
Nest [nɛst] das <–(e)s, –er> **1.** nest ◊ *Wie viele Eier liegen im Nest?* **2.** *(fam, pej)* dump, hole ◊ *Sie wohnt in irgendeinem Nest in der Eifel.*

⊛ jd hat sich ins gemachte Nest gesetzt sb has got it made
② **nett** [nɛt] adj, adv <netter, am nettesten> nice(ly) ◊ *Er sagte mir ein paar nette Worte.* ♦ *Unsere Englischlehrerin ist nett.* ♦ *Es war nicht nett von dir, mich anzulügen.* ♦ *Wärst du so nett und würdest das Fenster öffnen?* ♦ *Nett habt ihr's hier!* ♦ *Sie hat sich nett bedankt.* adj *mostly before ns (iron)* fine ◊ *Du bist mir ein netter Freund, fällst mir einfach in den Rücken.*
net·to ['nɛto] adv net ◊ *Netto kostet das 100 Euro, also inklusive Mehrwertsteuer 116.*
② **Netz** [nɛts] das <–es, –e> **1.** net ◊ *Die Fischer werfen ihre Netze aus.* ♦ *Sie hatten am Strand ein Netz gespannt und spielten Volleyball.; (in sports)* ins Netz gehen go into/hit the net **2.** safety net ◊ *Diese Artisten arbeiten ganz ohne Netz.* **3.** *(a spider's)* web ins Netz gehen be caught in the web **4.** *(for electricity, water, gas)* mains, grid; *(for telephone, traffic, computers etc.)* network **5.** IT das Netz the Net, the Web ◊ *Er surft schon seit Stunden im Netz.* ⊜Internet **6.** string bag ◊ *die Einkäufe in ein Netz packen* **7.** *(for luggage)* rack ⊛ das soziale Netz the social security net jdm ins Netz gehen walk into sb's trap ein Netz von ... a web of ... ◊ *Sie hat ein Netz von Lügen gesponnen.*
Netz·werk ['nɛtsvɛrk] das <–(e)s, –e> network ◊ *ein weltweites Netzwerk* ♦ *Der Computer ist ans Netzwerk angeschlossen.* ⊜Netz
② **neu** [nɔʏ] adj <neuer, am neu(e)sten> **1.** new ◊ *neuer Schüler* ♦ *in eine neue Wohnung ziehen* ♦ *Morgen fange ich ein neues Leben an.* ♦ *Ich bin neu hier.* ♦ *Jetzt sieht das Auto aus wie neu.* jdm neu sein be news to sb ⊜alt **2.** fresh, clean ◊ *Zieh bitte ein neues Hemd an.* ⊜frisch **3.** *only before ns* recent, new ◊ *die neuere Literatur* modern languages adv **1.** re...; *(a book)* neu bearbeiten revise neu einrichten refurnish neu formulieren rephrase **2.** newly ◊ *Der Laden ist neu eröffnet.* ♦ *neu geschaffene Stellen* **3.** again ◊ *Die Datei ist abgestürzt, jetzt kann ich alles neu schreiben.* ♦ *noch einmal neu anfangen* ⊛ seit neuestem recently
neu·ar·tig ['nɔʏaːɐ̯tɪç] adj novel ◊ *eine neuartige Methode* ♦ *Dieses Verfahren ist völlig neuartig.*
neu·er·dings ['nɔʏɐdɪŋs] adv recently, lately ◊ *Du bist neuerdings immer so mürrisch.* ♦ *Diese Frage ist neuerdings wieder ganz aktuell.*
Neu·e·rung ['nɔʏərʊŋ] die <–, –en> innovation ◊ *Der Chef hat lauter Neuerungen eingeführt.*
Neu·gier ['nɔʏgiːɐ̯], **Neu·gier·de** ['nɔʏgiːɐ̯də] die <–> *no pl* curiosity ◊ *die natürliche Neugier eines Kindes* ♦ *Ich platze vor Neugier, deinen Freund endlich kennen zu lernen.* Neugier(de) auf etw./jdn curiosity about sth/sb
② **neu·gie·rig** ['nɔʏgiːrɪç] adj, adv curious(ly) ◊ *Ich bin neugierig, ob er das schafft.; nosy(-ily), inquisitive(ly)* ♦ *Meine Mutter ist schrecklich neugierig.* ♦ *Die Kinder schauten neugierig durchs Schlüsselloch.* neugierig auf etw./jdn curious about sth/sb
Neu·heit ['nɔʏhaɪt] die <–, –en> **1.** novelty ◊ *die Neuheit einer Idee* **2.** new product ◊ *Auf der Messe wurden alle möglichen Neuheiten vorgestellt.*
Neu·ig·keit ['nɔʏɪçkaɪt] die <–, –en> Neuigkeit(en) news ◊ *Und jetzt die Neuigkeiten des Tages: ...* ♦

Diese Neuigkeit muss ich sofort weitergeben.
Neu·jahr ['nɔ̯ɡja:'] *seldom with definite article 'das'*
New Year('s Day) ◊ *Die Chinesen feiern Neujahr
erst am 22. Januar.*
   ⊛ prost/prosit Neujahr happy New Year
② **neu·lich** ['nɔ̯ɡlɪç] adv recently ◊ *Ich habe ihn erst
neulich kennen gelernt.* ♦ *Neulich ist mir etwas
Seltsames passiert.* ⊝jüngst
Neu·ling ['nɔ̯ɡlɪŋ] der <-s, –e> newcomer, new
man/woman/boy/girl ◊ *Die Klasse hat den Neuling
gut aufgenommen.* ♦ *Ich bin ein Neuling auf
diesem Gebiet.*
neun [nɔ̯ɡn] nmrl nine → vier
neun·zehn ['nɔ̯ɡntse:n] nmrl nineteen → vier
neun·zig ['nɔ̯ɡntsɪç] nmrl ninety → vier
Neut·rum ['nɔ̯ɡtrʊm] das <-s, Neutren> GRAM
neuter ◊ *Das Neutrum hat den bestimmten Artikel
,das'.*
neu·wer·tig ['nɔ̯ɡveːɐ̯tɪç] adj (good) as new ◊ *für
neuwertigen Ersatz sorgen* ♦ *Der Computer ist
neuwertig.*
② **nicht**[1] [nɪçt] adv not ◊ *Er hat sich nicht gefreut.* ♦
„Meinst du, er kommt?" — „Ich glaube nicht." ♦
Gehst du jetzt hin oder nicht? ♦ *„Will noch jemand
Sahne?" — „Ich nicht."* ♦ *Ist das nicht schön?* ♦
Willst du nicht auch mitkommen? nicht ein/eine/
eines not one ◊ *Nicht einer hat sich auf die
Anzeige gemeldet.*
   ⊛ **nicht dass** it's not that ◊ *Nicht dass ich keine
Lust hätte, aber ich habe keine Zeit.*
② **nicht**[2] [nɪçt] part 1. (as a question tag) Du
kommst doch mit, nicht, Karin? You're coming too,
aren't you, Karin? Das gefällt dir doch auch, nicht
wahr? You like that too, don't you? Das ist doch
eine Frechheit, oder etwa nicht? That's a cheek,
isn't it? 2. (emph) (expressing surprise) Was er
nicht alles weiß! It's unbelievable how much he
knows! Was es dort nicht alles zu sehen gibt! You
wouldn't believe how much there is to see! Was
einem im Leben nicht alles so passiert! All the
things life has in store for you. Was du nicht
sagst! You don't say!
② **Nich·te** ['nɪçtə] die <-, –n> niece
Nicht·rau·cher[1] ['nɪçtraͅɔxɐ] das <-s, –> (in a
restaurant etc.) non-smoking section; (on a
train) non-smoking carriage ◊ *ein Platz im Nichtraucher* ⊝Raucher
② **Nicht·rau·cher**[2] ['nɪçtraͅɔxɐ] der <-s, –>,
Nicht·rau·che·rin ['nɪçtraͅɔxərɪn] die <-, –nen>
non-smoker jd ist Nichtraucher/in sb doesn't
smoke ⊝Raucher
② **nichts** [nɪçts] indef pron nothing, not … anything ◊
Ich habe noch nichts gegessen. ♦ *Hast du denn gar
nichts zu tun?* ♦ *Sie schreckt vor nichts zurück.* Der
Film ist nichts für kleine Kinder. The film is not/no
good for small children. etw. nützt (jdm) nichts sth
is no use (to sb) nichts ahnend unsuspectingly
nichts als nothing but ◊ *Mit dir habe ich nichts als
Ärger.* nichts sagend meaningless
   ⊛ **nichts da** (fam) no way **für nichts** (fam) for
nothing ⊝umsonst **für nichts und wieder nichts**
(fam, emph) for nothing at all **mir nichts, dir
nichts** (fam) just like that **wie nichts** (fam) in a
flash **nichts wie …** (fam) nichts wie weg let's
scram nichts wie hin what are you/we waiting for
nichts wie ins Bett right to bed now

② **ni·cken** ['nɪkŋ̩] intr v +haben nod zustimmend
nicken nod your agreement mit dem Kopf nicken
nod (your head)
Ni·cker·chen ['nɪkeçən] das <-s, –> (fam) nap ◊
Nach dem Essen macht er ein Nickerchen.
② **nie** [niː] adv never ◊ *Er darf das nie erfahren.* ♦
Das werde ich nie vergessen. ♦ *Er lügt nie.* ♦ *Ob
das wohl stimmt?" — „Nie!"* nie und nimmer
never ever nie im Leben not in a million years
(noch) nie never (before) ◊ *Das habe ich ja noch nie gesehen.* Ich war sauer
wie noch nie. I'd never been so cross. nie wieder/
mehr never (again) ◊ *Dir erzähle ich nie wieder
etwas!* ♦ *Nach Neuseeland werde ich wohl nie
mehr kommen.* ⊝niemals
nie·der ['niːdɐ] adj 1. only before ns (in a
hierarchy) low(er) ◊ *Er ist ein niederer Beamter.;
(origin etc.) lowly* ◊ *von niederer Geburt/Herkunft*
niedere Dienste menial work 2. only before ns
base ◊ *niedere Instinkte* ⊝edel 3. (SouthG, Austr,
Swiss) (spatial) low ◊ *ein Bauernhaus mit einer
niederen Decke* ⊝niedrig ⊝hoch
   ⊛ **nieder mit jdm/etw.** down with sb/sth
nie·der·ge·schla·gen ['niːdɐɡəʃlaːɡŋ̩] past p of
niederschlagen adj depressed, dejected ◊ *eine nie-
dergeschlagene Stimmung* ♦ *Völlig niedergeschlagen kamen die Verlierer nach Hause.*
Nie·der·la·ge ['niːdɐlaːɡə] die <-, –n> defeat ◊
eine schwere Niederlage erleiden ⊝Sieg
Nie·der·lan·de ['niːdɐlandə] die <-> only pl
(always die Niederlande) the Netherlands ◊ *Sie
lebt in den Niederlanden.* box➔ Land
Nie·der·län·der ['niːdɐlɛndɐ] der <-s, –>,
Nie·der·län·de·rin ['niːdɐlɛndərɪn] die <-, –nen>
Dutchman, Dutchwoman die Niederländer the
Dutch → Deutsche
nie·der·län·disch ['niːdɐlɛndɪʃ] adj mostly before
ns Dutch → deutsch
Nie·der·län·disch ['niːdɐlɛndɪʃ] das <-(s)> seldom
with article, no pl Dutch → Deutsch
Nie·der·las·sung ['niːdɐlasʊŋ] die <-, –en>
branch
nie·der|le·gen ['niːdɐleːɡŋ̩] <legt nieder, legte
nieder, hat niedergelegt> tr v 1. lay down, put
down ◊ *Sie legten den Toten auf die Bahre nieder.*
die Waffen niederlegen lay down your arms die
Arbeit niederlegen go on strike 2. (an office, a
post etc.) resign (from) ◊ *Sein Anwalt hat das
Mandat niedergelegt.* ⊝aufgeben 3. (lofty) put
down in writing, set down ◊ *Vereinbarungen schriftlich niederlegen*
nie·der|ma·chen ['niːdɐmaxŋ̩] <macht nieder,
machte nieder, hat niedergemacht> tr v (fam)
1. (with criticism) pan ◊ *Sie macht immer meine
Arbeit nieder.* 2. (with weapons) massacre ◊ *Die
Gefangenen machten die Wachen nieder.*
Nie·der·sach·sen ['niːdɐzaksŋ̩] das <-s> article
only in combination with attribute Lower Saxony
box@ Land

Area: 47,616 km²; population: approx. 7.93
million; regional capital: Hanover.
Lower Saxony is home to a variety of landscapes,
ranging from the coastal region with its mud flats
and islands to the heath and the Weser
mountains. More than 20 percent of the area ▶

▶ is a protected nature reserve. Agriculture is an important economic factor, but Lower Saxony is also home to Volkswagen – one of the most important employers in the region. Its capital Hanover is known around the world for its trade fairs.

Nie·der·schlag ['niːdɐʃlaːk] der <-(e)s, Niederschläge> *most pl* METEO precipitation ◊ *Heftige Niederschläge haben zu Hochwasser geführt.; (amount)* rain ◊ *Bei dem Gewitter fiel gestern 70 Millimeter Niederschlag.* radioaktiver Niederschlag nuclear fallout
● **seinen Niederschlag in etw.** [dat] **finden** be reflected in sth
nie·der|schla·gen ['niːdɐʃlaːɡn̩] <schlägt nieder, schlug nieder, hat niedergeschlagen> [tr v] **1.** knock down ◊ *Bei der Prügelei wurde er niedergeschlagen.* **2.** put down, suppress ◊ *Die Armee hat den Aufstand blutig niedergeschlagen.* [ref v] **1.** sich in etw. [dat] be reflected in sth **2.** sich niederschlagen condensate ◊ *Der Wasserdampf schlug sich auf dem Spiegel nieder.; (chemical)* precipitate
nied·lich ['niːtlɪç] [adj] cute, sweet ◊ *Sieh mal, die niedlichen Kätzchen.* ◆ *Ich finde ihn sehr niedlich.* ⊝reizend, süß [adv] in a cute manner niedlich lächeln have/smile a sweet smile
② **nied·rig** ['niːdrɪç] [adj] **1.** low ◊ *Die Brücke ist zu niedrig.* ◆ *eine niedrige Mauer* ◆ *niedrige Löhne/ Mieten/Preise/Temperaturen* ◆ *Wir müssen die Kosten niedrig halten.* ⊝hoch **2.** base ◊ *niedrige Motive haben* (eine) niedrige Gesinnung low-mindedness ⊝edel **3.** *(oldf)* lowly, humble ◊ *Er schämt sich seiner niedrigen Herkunft.* [adv] low ◊ *Heute fliegen die Vögel niedrig.* ◆ *Du hast die Kosten zu niedrig veranschlagt.* niedrig verzinst low(-)interest etw. niedrig dosieren use a small amount of sth; *(a drug)* administer/use a low dose of sth
nie·mals ['niːmaːls] [adv] never ◊ *Das wird er dir niemals verzeihen.* ◆ *Man sollte Fremden niemals Geld leihen.* ⊝nie ⊝immer
② **nie·mand** ['niːmant] [indef pron] nobody, no one ◊ *Das darf niemand wissen.* ◆ *Am Telefon hat sich niemand gemeldet.; (in negative statements and questions)* not anybody, not anyone ◊ *Das darfst du niemandem erzählen.* ⊝jeder, jemand
Nie·re ['niːrə] die <-, -n> **1.** kidney ◊ *Ihre Nieren arbeiten nicht richtig.* ◆ *saure Nieren mit Bratkartoffeln* **2.** künstliche Niere dialysis machine
● **jdm an die Nieren gehen** *(fam)* get sb down
nie·seln ['niːzl̩n] [imp v] +*haben* es nieselt it's drizzling
nie·sen ['niːzn̩] [intr v] +*haben* sneeze ◊ *Wer Schnupfen hat, muss meist auch niesen.*
Nie·te ['niːtə] die <-, -n> **1.** *(in a raffle)* blank ◊ *Ich habe nur Nieten gezogen.* **2.** *(fam, pej)* loser ◊ *Ich bin eine echte Niete, aus mir wird nie was!* eine Niete in etw. [acc] sein be useless at sth ⊝Null **3.** rivet ◊ *Jeans/ein Hundehalsband mit Nieten*
Ni·ko·laus ['nɪkolaʊ̯s] der <-es, Nikoläuse> **1.** Saint Nicholas ◊ *Was hat dir denn der Nikolaus gebracht?* **2.** chocolate Father Christmas, chocolate Santa Claus **3.** *(festival)* Saint Nicholas' Day ◊ *Heute ist Nikolaus.*

Every 6th of December, people in Germany commemorate Saint Nicholas, a charitable bishop who lived in Myra (Turkey) in the 4th century and who, according to legend, helped the poor. He is also known as the children's friend. On the eve of Saint Nicholas's Day, German children put their shoes outside the door to be filled with fruit, nuts, sweets and small presents during the night.

② **nimmt** [nɪmt] *pres of* nehmen
② **nir·gends** ['nɪrɡn̩ts, 'nɪrɡants] [adv] nowhere ◊ *Nirgends ist es schöner als zu Hause.; (in negative statements and questions)* not anywhere ◊ *Ich habe den Schlüssel nirgends gesehen.* ◆ *Du findest nirgends billigere Computer.* ⊝überall
Ni·sche ['niːʃə] die <-, -n> **1.** *(in a room)* niche, recess ◊ *Sie saß in der hintersten Nische des Cafés.* in allen Winkeln und Nischen in every nook and cranny **2.** niche ◊ *eine ökologische Nische* ◆ *Unser Marketing ist immer auf der Suche nach Nischen.*
Ni·veau [ni'voː] das <-s, -s> **1.** level, standard ◊ *Das Niveau an unseren Schulen muss sich bessern.; (person)* kein Niveau haben be uncultured **2.** *(spatial)* level ◊ *Alle Fenster liegen auf gleichem Niveau.*
nix [nɪks] [indef pron] *(fam)* nothing ◊ *Du kapierst aber auch gar nix!* ◆ *„Was hat er gesagt?" — „Nix!"* ⊝nichts
no·bel ['noːbl̩] [adj] <der/die/das noble ...> **1.** elegant, posh, classy ◊ *eine noble Gegend* ◆ *Die Einrichtung des Hotels ist sehr nobel.* ⊝vornehm **2.** generous ◊ *Du hast sie sich aber nobel gezeigt.* ⊝großzügig **3.** *(lofty)* noble ◊ *Sie übte noble Zurückhaltung.* (eine) noble Gesinnung noble-mindedness ⊝edel [adv] in grand style ◊ *Gestern haben wir ganz nobel gespeist.* nobel wohnen live in posh surroundings ⊝vornehm
② **noch¹** [nɔx] [adv] **1.** still ◊ *Wir haben noch etwas Zeit.* ◆ *Noch können wir das ändern.* ◆ *Es gibt noch Suppe.* ◆ *Kann ich das auch morgen noch machen?* ◆ *Konnten Sie sie noch erreichen?* ◆ *Machst du das noch, bevor wir gehen?* immer noch, immer noch still ◊ *Ich habe das noch immer nicht verstanden.* noch nicht not yet ◊ *„Bist du fertig?" —„Nein, noch nicht!"* noch nie never before ◊ *Sie war noch nie in Indien.* nur noch only ◊ *Ich habe nur noch zehn Euro.* Das waren noch Zeiten. Those were the days. **2.** *usually not translated (promise or confirmation that sth will be done or explained soon)* Das werden wir noch sehen. We'll see about that. Ich komme später noch darauf zurück. I'll come back to that later. Ich mache das noch heute. I'll do this today. **3.** *(warning)* one day ◊ *Du bringst mich noch zum Wahnsinn.* ◆ *Das wird dir noch Leid tun!* Du wirst noch an mich denken! You'll remember my words! **4.** noch einen Wein/ein Bier etc. another wine/beer etc. etw. noch (ein)mal sein/tun be/do sth once more, be/do sth once again ◊ *Du solltest den Brief noch mal schreiben.* **5.** noch vor einer Stunde/ gestern/letzte Woche only an hour ago/yesterday/ last week **6.** +*comp* noch lauter/schlimmer/schöner even louder/worse/more beautiful **7.** comparatively ◊ *Im Gegensatz zu mir wirst du ja noch gut bezahlt.* ⊝relativ
● **auch noch** also, on top ⊝obendrein **auch das noch** *(fam, emph)* just what I needed **auch noch so** ▶

auch wenn jd sich noch so ... no matter how sb ...
auch wenn etw. noch so ..., wenn etw. auch noch so
... no matter how ... sth ... ◊ *Auch wenn das noch
so teuer ist, ich muss es haben.* ⊖*egal wie* **noch
und noch** *(fam)* **1.** loads of ◊ *Er hat Geld noch und
noch.* **2.** loads of times **noch und nöcher 1.** *(fam,
hum)* lots and lots **2.** lots and lots of times ◊ *Ich
muss das noch und nöcher wiederholen.*

② **noch²** [nɔx] ⦋part⦌ noch (mal/gleich) again ◊ *Wie
hieß sie noch (mal)?* ✦ *Was macht er noch (gleich)
beruflich?*

noch·mals [ˈnɔxmaːls] ⦋adv⦌ once more ◊ *Du
solltest es nochmals versuchen.* ✦ *Können Sie das
nochmals sagen?* ⊖*noch (ein)mal*

No·men [ˈnoːmən] das <–s, – or Nomina> noun
⊖Substantiv, Hauptwort

No·mi·na·li·sie·rung [noːminaliˈziːrʊŋ] → Substantivierung

No·mi·na·tiv [ˈnoːminatiːf] der <–s, –e> nominative

> The subject of a sentence usually takes the nom-
> inative case: **Ich** *begrüße meine Freunde.* – **Der
> Zug** *hielt im Bahnhof.* All German nouns have
> one of three possible genders: masculine *(der)*,
> feminine *(die)* or neuter *(das)*. The plural is
> always *die.* These gender forms – *der, die, das* –
> are the nominative forms. In dictionaries nouns
> are always listed in the nominative case.

Non·ne [ˈnɔnə] die <–, –n> nun

② **Nord** [nɔrt] <–> *without the article, invariable*
1. +*prep* aus/von Nord from the north nach Nord
to the north, northwards ⊖Norden ⊖Süd, Süden
2. North ◊ *das Autobahnkreuz Köln Nord* ⊖Süd

② **Nord·...** [nɔrt] ⦋prefix⦌ north ..., northern ... ◊ *die
Nordhalbkugel der Erde* ✦ *das Nordfenster* die
Nordländerin, der Nordländer the northerner; *(in
names)* North ..., Northern ... ◊ *Nordamerika* ✦
Nordeuropa ⊖Süd...

② **Nor·den** [ˈnɔrdn̩] der <–s> *no pl* north ◊ *im Norden
des Landes* ✦ *Der Wind kommt von Norden.* nach
Norden to the north, northwards Züge in Richtung
Norden northbound trains ⊖Süden
◉ **der hohe Norden** far north

nor·disch [ˈnɔrdɪʃ] ⦋adj⦌ *only before ns* Nordic ◊
nordische Länder/Sprachen

nörd·lich¹ [ˈnœrtlɪç] ⦋adj⦌ *only before ns*
1. northern ◊ *der nördliche Teil Europas* ⊖südlich
2. *(wind, direction)* northerly aus nördlicher
Richtung from the north ◊ *Der Wind weht aus nördlicher Richtung.* ⊖südlich

nörd·lich² [ˈnœrtlɪç] ⦋prep⦌ ⦋+gen⦌ or ⦋+dat⦌ **1.** ⦋+gen⦌
(to the) north of ◊ *die Wohngebiete nördlich der
Stadt* ⊖südlich **2.** *adverbial* ⦋+dat⦌ nördlich von
north of ◊ *Welches Land liegt nördlich von
Deutschland?* ⊖südlich

Nord·rhein-West·fa·len [ˌnɔrtraɛnvɛstˈfaːlən] das
<–s> *article only in combination with attribute, no
pl* North Rhine-Westphalia box@ Land

> Area/size: 34,081 km²; population: approx. 18.01
> million; regional capital: Düsseldorf.
> North Rhine-Westphalia is Germany's most
> populous *Bundesland.* The Ruhr region is one of
> Europe's biggest conurbations. Traditional indus-
> tries include steel production, engineering and
> coal mining.

Nord·see [ˈnɔrtzeː] die <–> *no pl (always* die
Nordsee*)* the North Sea

nör·geln [ˈnœrgl̩n] ⦋intr v⦌ +*haben (pej)* nag ◊
Meine Frau nörgelt immerzu. über etw. ⦋acc⦌
nörgeln moan about sth ◊ *über das schlechte
Essen in der Kantine nörgeln*

Norm [nɔrm] die <–, –en> **1.** TECHN standard ◊ *Die
Papiergröße DIN A 4 ist eine technische Norm.*
2. norm, rule ◊ *sich an die gesellschaftlichen
Normen halten* ✦ *der Norm entsprechen* **3.** quota,
target ◊ *die Norm erfüllen* **4.** SPORT qualifying
standard die Norm (für etw.) erfüllen/schaffen/
meistern qualify (for sth)

② **nor·mal** [nɔrˈmaːl] ⦋adj, adv⦌ normal(ly) ◊ *Ist es
normal, dass sie so ruhig ist?* ✦ *ein ganz normaler
Tag* ✦ *ein normal begabter Schüler* Bist du noch
normal? Have you lost your mind?

② **nor·ma·ler·wei·se** [nɔrˈmaːleˈvaɛzə] ⦋adv⦌ normally,
usually, under normal circumstances ◊ *Normalerweise geht sie um elf Uhr ins Bett.* ✦ *Wo ist sie
bloß? Normalerweise müsste sie schon da sein.*

Nor·we·gen [ˈnɔrveːgn̩] das <–s> *article only in
combination with attribute, no pl* Norway →
Deutschland

Nor·we·ger [ˈnɔrveːge] der <–s, –>,
Nor·we·ge·rin [ˈnɔrveːgərɪn] die <–, –nen>
Norwegian → Deutsche

nor·we·gisch [ˈnɔrveːgɪʃ] ⦋adj⦌ *mostly before ns*
Norwegian → deutsch

Nor·we·gisch [ˈnɔrveːgɪʃ] das <–(s)> *seldom with
article, no pl* Norwegian → Deutsch

② **Not** [noːt] die <–, Nöte> **1.** *no pl* want, need,
poverty ◊ *Nach der Dürre herrscht dort große Not.*
in Not in need aus Not because of want ◊ *Er gab
zu, das Geld aus Not gestohlen zu haben.* Not
leiden be needy/impoverished Not leidend needy,
impoverished ⊖Armut ⊖Reichtum **2.** *most sing*
distress ◊ *Er lebt in finanzieller Not.* seelische/
innere Not emotional distress in Not geraten get
into difficulties jdm seine Not/seine Nöte klagen
pour out your troubles to sb Rettung in/aus
höchster Not rescue from extreme difficulties, help
in the nick of time in der Stunde der Not at a/the
time of distress, in times of distress
◉ **wenn Not am Mann ist** when/if the need
arises in der Not frisst der Teufel Fliegen *(fam)*
beggars can't be choosers aus der Not eine
Tugend machen make a virtue of necessity mit
knapper Not only just, by the skin of your teeth
seine (liebe) Not mit jdm/etw. haben have a lot
of problems with sb/sth Not macht erfinderisch
necessity is the mother of invention Not tun be
necessary ohne Not without good cause zur Not if
necessary

No·tar [noˈtaːr] der <–s, –e>, **No·ta·rin** [noˈtaːrɪn]
die <–, –nen> notary ◊ *Sie ist Notarin.* ✦ *ein Notar
mit gutem Ruf*

Not·arzt [ˈnoːtlaːrt͡st] der <–es, Notärzte>,
Not·ärz·tin [ˈnoːtlɛrt͡stɪn] die <–, –nen>
emergency doctor ◊ *Sie arbeitet als Notärztin.* ✦
Sie mussten den Notarzt kommen lassen.

② **Not·auf·nah·me** [ˈnoːtlaɔfnaːmə] die <–, –n>
accident and casualties department, casualty department ◊ *jdn in die Notaufnahme einliefern*

② **Not·aus·gang** [ˈnoːtlaɔsgaŋ] der
<–(e)s, Notausgänge> emergency exit

Not·brem·se ['noːtbrɛmzə] die <-, -n> emergency brake ◊ *bei Gefahr die Notbremse ziehen* ◉ **die Notbremse ziehen** *(fam, fig)* put the brakes on

not·dürf·tig ['noːtdʏʳftɪç] [adj, adv] *when used as an adj, only before ns* makeshift, emergency, provisional(ly), temporary(-ily) ◊ *Kerzen als notdürftige Beleuchtung* ♦ *etw. notdürftig reparieren* notdürftig bekleidet scantily dressed ⊖provisorisch

② **No·te** ['noːtə] die <-, -n> **1.** *(in school)* mark, grade ◊ *Sie hat auf den Aufsatz eine gute Note bekommen.; (in sports)* score, mark **2.** mus note ◊ *eine halbe/ganze Note* **3.** *only pl* mus (sheet) music Noten lesen read music nach Noten singen/spielen sing/play from (sheet) music **4.** *no pl* eine elegante/besondere etc. Note an elegant/special etc. touch jds persönliche Note sb's trademark **5.** pol *(diplomatic)* note

> The German school marking system consists of six different marks: 1 *(sehr gut)*, 2 *(gut)*, 3 *(befriedigend)*, 4 *(ausreichend)*, 5 *(mangelhaft)*, 6 *(ungenügend)*. 1 is the best and 4 is a pass. Each mark can be graded more precisely with a + (plus) or a − (minus). A pupil with two marks of 5 or one 6 in the school report at the end of a year has failed and must repeat that year. In Austria there are only five marks, with 5 *(nicht genügend)* being a fail. In Switzerland marks are on a scale from 6 to 1, with 6 *(sehr gut)* being the best and 1 *(unbrauchbar)* the worst.

Not·fall ['noːtfal] der <-(e)s, Notfälle> emergency ◊ *ein medizinischer Notfall bei/in einem Notfall* in an emergency *für den Notfall* for emergencies ◉ **(sich** [dat]**) für den Notfall Geld zurücklegen** put away money for a rainy day **für den Notfall** just in case **im Notfall 1.** if necessary **2.** in an emergency

not·ge·drun·gen ['noːtgədrʊŋən] [adv] notgedrungen etw. tun (müssen) be forced to do sth, have no choice but to do sth ◊ *Nachdem sie den letzten Bus verpasst hatte, nahm sie notgedrungen ein Taxi.*

no·tie·ren [noˈtiːrən] <notiert, notierte, hat notiert> [tr v] (sich [dat]) etw. notieren note sth down, make a note of sth ⊖aufschreiben [tr+intr v] econ (mit/bei ...) notiert werden, (mit/bei ...) notieren be quoted (at ...) ◊ *Die Aktie wird derzeit bei 78,5 Euro notiert.*

② **nö·tig** ['nøːtɪç] [adj] necessary ◊ *Wir halten es für nötig, weitere Maßnahmen zu ergreifen.* ♦ *Wenn nötig, helfe ich gern.* etw. ist bitter/dringend nötig sth is desperately needed der nötige Respekt (the) due respect ⊖notwendig, erforderlich ⊖unnötig [adv] *(fam)* urgently ◊ *Er braucht das Geld wirklich nötig.* nötig (aufs Klo) müssen be dying to go (to the toilet) ⊖dringend ◉ **etw. nötig haben 1.** need to do sth **2.** need sth es nicht nötig haben, etw. zu tun be above doing sth es nicht für nötig halten, etw. zu tun think you are above doing sth das ist doch nicht nötig you don't have to das wäre doch nicht nötig gewesen you shouldn't have

nö·ti·gen ['nøːtɪɡn̩] [tr v] +haben **1.** law jdn zu etw. nötigen coerce sb into (doing) sth ◊ *Frauen zu sexuellen Handlungen nötigen* **2.** jdn (zu etw.)

nötigen force sb (to do sth) ◊ *Die Panne nötigte uns zu einer Übernachtung im Motel.* ⊖zwingen **3.** jdn (zu etw.) nötigen urge sb (to do sth) ◊ *Obwohl er keinen Hunger hatte, nötigte Oma ihn zum Essen.* ⊖drängen

② **No·tiz** [noˈtiːts] die <-, -en> **1.** *most pl* note sich [dat] Notizen machen make/take notes **2.** *(in a newspaper)* eine Notiz (über jdn/etw.) an item (about sb/sth) ◉ **keine Notiz von jdm/etw. nehmen** take no notice of sb/sth

② **Not·ruf** ['noːtruːf] der <-(e)s, -e> **1.** emergency number ◊ *die Polizei/Feuerwehr über Notruf alarmieren* **2.** emergency call ◊ *Bei der Feuerwehr gingen an Silvester hunderte Notrufe ein.*

Not·wehr ['noːtveːɐ̯] die <-> no pl (aus/in) Notwehr (in) self-defence ◊ *Er handelte aus/in Notwehr und wurde deshalb nicht bestraft.*

② **not·wen·dig** ['noːtvɛndɪç] [adj] **1.** necessary ◊ *über die notwendigen Kenntnisse für etw. verfügen* ♦ *War das wirklich notwendig?* ⊖nötig, erforderlich ⊖unnötig **2.** *only before ns* inevitable ◊ *Kopfschmerzen sind häufig die notwendige Folge von Überanstrengung.* ⊖zwangsläufig [adv] urgently ◊ *Er braucht das Geld ganz notwendig.* notwendig (aufs Klo) müssen be dying to go (to the toilet) ⊖dringend ◉ **das wäre doch nicht notwendig gewesen** you shouldn't have etw. notwendig haben need sth es nicht notwendig haben, etw. zu tun be above doing sth das ist doch nicht notwendig you don't have to

② **No·vem·ber** [noˈvɛmbɐ] der <-s, -> *most sing (abbr* Nov.) November → Januar

NRW [ɛn|ɛʳˈveː, ˌnoːˈtraɛnvɛstˈfaːlən] *(abbr of* Nordrhein-Westfalen) box@ Nordrhein-Westfalen

Nr. [ˈnʊmɐ] die *(abbr of* Nummer) No. ◊ *Wir sitzen in Reihe Nr. 9.*

Nu [nuː] *(fam) (always* im Nu*)* in no time ◊ *Ich bin im Nu wieder da.* ♦ *Das neue Waschmittel entfernt Flecken im Nu.* ⊖rasch

Nu·an·ce [ˈnyãsə, ˈnyãːsə] die <-, -n> **1.** nuance, touch ◊ *kleinste/feinste Nuancen erkennen* ♦ *Das Parfüm enthält eine Nuance Vanille.* **2.** shade ◊ *Der Ring schimmert in verschiedenen Nuancen.* ♦ *Das Make-up ist in fünf Nuancen erhältlich.*

nüch·tern ['nʏçtɐn] [adj] **1.** sober ◊ *Sie war nicht mehr ganz nüchtern.* ♦ *in nüchternem Zustand* nüchtern werden sober up ⊖betrunken **2.** with an empty stomach ◊ *nüchtern zur Untersuchung kommen* nüchtern bleiben don't eat and drink ◊ *vor einer Operation nüchtern bleiben* auf nüchternen Magen on an empty stomach **3.** down-to-earth ◊ *Seine Denkweise ist eher nüchtern.* ♦ *Sie ist eine nüchterne Karrierefrau.* ⊖objektiv, sachlich ⊖subjektiv **4.** bare, plain ◊ *Die Wand wirkt ohne Bilder kahl und nüchtern.* [adv] objectively, soberly ◊ *Sie versuchte, ihr Problem möglichst nüchtern zu schildern.* ♦ *Nüchtern betrachtet/gesehen, habe ich vielleicht doch übertrieben reagiert.* ⊖objektiv, sachlich ⊖subjektiv

Nu·del ['nuːdl̩] die <-, -n> **1.** *most pl* noodle ◊ *Hühnerbrühe mit Nudeln*; *(European style)* Nudeln pasta ◊ *Heute gibt es Nudeln mit Tomatensoße.* **2.** *mostly in combination with attribute, most sing (fam)* dumme/freche Nudel silly/cheeky cow

ulkige/lustige Nudel joker

null¹ [nʊl] `adj` *invariable, only before ns (slang)* null ... no ... whatsoever ◊ *Sie hat null Interesse an ihm.* von etw. null Ahnung haben not know the first thing about sth ◊ `acc` null Bock haben; null Bock haben, etw. zu tun not feel at all like (doing) sth ⊖keinerlei

② **null²** [nʊl] `nmrl` *invariable* **1.** zero, nought ◊ *null Komma drei Sekunden* ♦ *Drei minus null bleibt drei.* ♦ *Nachts bleiben die Temperaturen über/unter null.* null Grad zero degrees auf null stehen be at zero etw. auf null drehen/stellen/schalten turn sth off null Fehler no mistakes **2.** nil ◊ *Sie hat in der Prüfung null Punkte bekommen.* drei etc. zu null three etc. - nil ◊ *Das Finale endete (mit) eins zu null für Frankreich.*

◉ gleich null sein be nil/zero wieder bei null anfangen start all over again, start from scratch again gegen null gehen/tendieren be virtually non-existant

② **Null** [nʊl] die <-, -en> **1.** nought, zero ◊ *Wie viele Nullen hat eine Million?* **2.** *most sing (fam, pej)* loser, dead loss ◊ *Er ist eine totale Null.* eine Null in etw. `dat` sein be hopeless/useless at sth ⊖Niete

Nu·me·rus clau·sus [ˌnuːmerʊs ˈklaͦozʊs, ˌnomerʊs ˈklaͦozʊs] der <-> *no pl (abbr NC)* numerus clausus ◊ *Der Numerus clausus für Medizin ist ziemlich hoch/liegt dieses Jahr bei 1,2.* ♦ *Gibt es einen Numerus clausus/NC auf Informatik?* ♦ *Die Kunsthochschule hat keinen Numerus clausus.*

> The *Numerus clausus* restricts the number of students for the most popular university courses by only admitting students who obtained a minimum average mark in their *Abitur* (school leaving exam). However, students who don't have the required minimum mark can get onto the course at a later date by waiting for a place (without enrolling on another university course in the meantime) or by drawing lots.

② **Num·mer** [ˈnʊmɐ] die <-, -n> *(abbr Nr.)* **1.** number ◊ *Das Los mit der Nummer 68 hat gewonnen.* ♦ *eine Nummer wählen* ♦ *Wegen des Fouls erhielt die Nummer 8 die gelbe Karte.*; *(magazine also)* issue ◊ *Das Interview erscheint in der nächsten Nummer.*; *(music also)* track ◊ *eine Nummer aus der aktuellen CD*; *(secret)* PIN eine Nummer ziehen take a ticket **2.** *(performance)* act, routine ◊ *eine Nummer einstudieren/ vorführen* **3.** *(of clothes, shoes)* size ◊ *Der Rock ist zu eng! — Können Sie mir eine Nummer größer bringen?* **4.** registration (number) ◊ *Konnten Sie sich die Nummer des Wagens merken?* ⊖Kennzeichen **5.** *(fam, hum) (person)* character ◊ *Der kleine Nils ist schon so eine Nummer für sich.* **6.** *(slang)* eine Nummer schieben/machen have it off

◉ eine Nummer/ein paar Nummern zu groß für jdn sein *(fam)* be out of sb's league auf Nummer sicher gehen *(fam)* not take any chances

num·me·rie·ren [nʊmeˈriːrən] <nummeriert, nummerierte, hat nummeriert> `tr v` number ◊ *die Seiten eines Dokuments nummerieren*

Num·mern·schild [ˈnʊmɐnʃɪlt] das <-(e)s, -er>

number/license plate *box*@ KFZ-Kennzeichen

② **nun¹** [nuːn] `adv` now ◊ *Ich gehe nun ins Bett.* ♦ *Nun ist sie an der Reihe.* ♦ *Nun, wo ich sie besser kenne, finde ich sie ganz nett.* ♦ *Ich bin mit allem fertig. Was nun?*; *(in the past tense)* then ◊ *Nun erst konnten sie ausruhen.*; by now/then ◊ *Wir kennen/kannten uns nun schon zehn Jahre.* von nun an/ab from now/then on ◊ *Ich werde mich von nun an bessern!* ♦ *Von nun ab ging es nur noch bergauf.* ⊖jetzt

② **nun²** [nuːn] `part` **1.** *(expressing irritation, bewilderment)* now ◊ *Kommst du nun oder nicht?* ♦ *Wer ist denn das nun schon wieder?* **2.** *(introductory)* well ◊ *Nun, ich persönlich finde, sie hat Recht.* ♦ *Nun? Kommst du jetzt oder nicht?* **3.** adding emphasis to a rhetorical question ◊ *Hat sich dieser Aufwand nun wirklich gelohnt?* ♦ *Und das soll nun fair sein?* ⊖etwa **4.** *(qualifying)* however ◊ *Nun muss ich dazusagen, dass sie sich wirklich geändert hat.* ⊖allerdings, aber

◉ nun denn, ...; nun gut, ...; nun schön, ... all right then ... ◊ *Nun denn, lass uns mal anfangen.* ♦ *Nun gut, dann nehme ich dich halt mit.* ♦ *Nun schön, ich lade dich ein.* nun (ein)mal *(fam)* just, simply ◊ *Ich kann nun mal nicht überall gleichzeitig sein. Das ist nun einmal so.* That's just the way things are. nun ja, ... *(hesitating)* well, ...

nun·mehr [ˈnuːnmeːɐ] `adv` *(lofty)* now, in the meantime ◊ *Drei Jahre waren nunmehr vergangen.* ♦ *Die Sachlage wird nunmehr anders beurteilt.* ⊖mittlerweile

② **nur¹** [nuːɐ] `adv` only, just ◊ *Sie hatte nur fünf Euro dabei.* ♦ *Ich habe leider nur wenig Zeit.* ♦ *Er trinkt nur morgens Kaffee, abends nie.* ♦ *Er wollte nur sagen, dass ...* ⊖lediglich, bloß

② **nur²** [nuːɐ] `part` **1.** *(expressing bewilderment in questions)* wer/was/warum/wie etc. ... nur who/ what/why/how etc. on earth ... ◊ *Wo habe ich nur meine Tasche?* ♦ *Warum hat er das nur getan?* ♦ *Wie konntest du nur so gemein sein?* ⊖bloß **2.** *(adding emphasis to a rhetorical question or exclamation)* Wie kannst du es nur wagen? How dare you? Was bin ich nur für ein toller Typ! Aren't I a clever guy? **3.** *(encouraging, warning, threatening)* just ◊ *Geh nur zu dem Hund, er tut dir nichts!* ♦ *Werd jetzt nur nicht unverschämt!* **4.** *(in wishes)* only ◊ *Hätte er doch nur auf meinen Rat gehört!* ♦ *Wäre doch nur schon Sommer!* wenn ... nur ... if only ... ◊ *Wenn er doch nur da wäre!*

◉ (einfach) nur so *(fam)* just like that nur so ... just ... ◊ *Sie war so durchnässt, dass ihre Kleidung nur so triefte.* nur zu go on nur zu ... only too ◊ *Ich bin nur zu gespannt, wie der Film endet.*

② **nur³** [nuːɐ] `conjunc` only, but ◊ *Die Party war toll, nur gab es wenig zu trinken.* nur dass only (that), except (that) ◊ *Die Kette gefällt mir, nur dass sie zu teuer ist.* nicht nur ..., sondern auch ... not only ... but also ... ◊ *Er sieht nicht nur gut aus, sondern ist auch nett.*

Nuss [nʊs] die <-, Nüsse> nut ◊ *Nüsse knacken* ♦ *eine Schokolade mit Nüssen*

◉ eine blöde/dumme/hohle/taube Nuss *(fam, pej)* a stupid twit eine harte Nuss *(fam)* a tough nut (to crack) eins auf die Nuss bekommen *(fam)* be belted over the head jdm eins auf die

Nuss geben *(fam)* belt sb over the head
② **nut·zen** ['nʊtsn̩] [tr+intr v] *+haben; no passive* be of use/help, be useful/helpful ◊ *Hat dir meine Hilfe genutzt?* ♦ *Nutzt das denn was?* ♦ *Das nutzt mir wenig, wenn du dich jetzt entschuldigst.* Was nutzt das (schon)? What's the use? [tr v] *+haben* use ◊ *Ich nutze jede freie Minute (dazu), mich in die Sonne zu legen.* etw. landwirtschaftlich nutzen cultivate sth, use sth for agricultural purposes zur Wiederverwertung nutzen recycle; *(an opportunity etc.)* take advantage of ◊ *Wir haben den Schnee zum Skifahren genutzt.*

◉ **es nutzt (alles) nichts** it can't be helped
Nut·zen ['nʊtsn̩] der <-s> *no pl* benefit ◊ *Die Kosten für das Auto sind höher als der Nutzen.* jdm wenig/keinen Nutzen bringen be of little/no benefit to sb jd hat keinen Nutzen von etw. sth is (of) no use to sb einen Nutzen aus etw. ziehen benefit from sth (jdm) von Nutzen sein be useful (to sb) ◊ *Es wäre von Nutzen, wenn du mithelfen würdest.* zu jds. Nutzen for sb's benefit ◊ *Ich sage das doch nur zu deinem eigenen Nutzen!* jdm zum Nutzen gereichen redound to sb's benefit
② **nüt·zen** ['nʏtsn̩] *(SouthG)* → nutzen
② **nütz·lich** ['nʏtslɪç] [adj] useful, helpful ◊ *Danke für den nützlichen Tipp!* ♦ *Der Ventilator hat als sehr nützlich erwiesen.* jdm nützlich sein be useful to sb sich nützlich machen make yourself useful

O

o, O [oː] das <-(s), -(s)> o, O ◊ *Dieses Wort wird mit einem kleinen o/großen O geschrieben.* ♦ *O wie Otto*

ö, Ö [øː] das <-(s), -(s)> o umlaut, O umlaut ◊ *Dieses Wort wird mit einem kleinen ö/großen Ö geschrieben.* ♦ *Ö wie Ökonom*

② **ob¹** [ɔp] ⸤conjunc⸥ whether ◊ *Er wollte wissen, ob ich heute Abend Zeit habe.* ♦ *Ich frage mich, ob etwas passiert ist.* ♦ *Sag mir endlich, ob das wahr ist!* ob ..., ob wether ... or ◊ *Ob Groß, ob Klein, der Park ist für jeden ein Erlebnis.*
◉ **und ob** *(fam)* you bet ◊ *„Mögt ihr ein Eis?"* — *„Und ob!"*

ob² [ɔp] ⸤prep⸥ +gen, +place upon ◊ *Sie wohnt in Rothenburg ob der Tauber.* ⊝oberhalb

ob·dach·los [ˈɔpdaxloːs] ⸤adj⸥ no comp/superl homeless ◊ *ein obdachloser Bettler* ♦ *Er ist obdachlos geworden.*

② **o·ben** [ˈoːbm̩] ⸤adv⸥ **1.** oben (an/auf/in etw. ⸤dat⸥) at the top (of sth) ◊ *Sie band den Müllsack oben zu.* ♦ *Die Adresse steht oben links.* ♦ *Die Tassen stehen oben im Schrank.*; *(on a surface)* on (the) top (of sth) ◊ *Mein Heft lag oben (auf dem Stapel).* oben am Tisch at the top end of the table, at the head of the table ab Seite 3 etc. oben from the top of page 3 etc. onwards (ganz) nach oben to the top ◊ *Sie will als Sängerin mal ganz nach oben.* von (ganz) oben (right) from the top ◊ *Die Entscheidung kommt von ganz oben.* **2.** up ◊ *Siehst du das Flugzeug da oben?* ♦ *Es ist kalt hier oben in den Bergen.* ♦ *Von hier oben sieht alles so klein aus.* hoch oben up high von oben from above ◊ *Das Bild zeigt die Erde von oben.* nach oben up(wards) ◊ *Alle schauen mit etw. (nach) oben* sth facing up(wards) ⊝unten **3.** *(in a building)* (nach) oben upstairs ◊ *Der Lärm kommt von oben.* ♦ *Nimmst du gleich die Taschen mit nach oben?* eine Etage weiter oben one floor up ⊝unten **4.** *(in a text)* oben (stehend) above ◊ *siehe oben* ♦ *Genauere Informationen finden Sie oben.* oben genannt mentioned above das oben Stehende/Genannte/Erwähnte the above(-mentioned) ⊝unten **5.** *(fam)* up north ◊ *Wir haben oben an der Nordsee Urlaub gemacht.* ♦ *Hoch oben in Norwegen schneit es viel.* ⊝unten
◉ **von oben bis unten** from top to bottom *(person)* from head to toe **nicht mehr wissen, wo oben und unten ist** have lost it **oben ohne** *(fam, hum)* topless ◊ *sich oben ohne sonnen*

② **O·ber** [ˈoːbɐ] der <-s, -> waiter ◊ *Er arbeitet als Ober in einem Restaurant.* ♦ *Der Ober nahm ihre Bestellung auf.* ♦ *(Herr) Ober! Die Rechnung bitte!* ⊝Kellner

② **o·ber·...** [ˈoːbɐ] ⸤prefix⸥ *(fam)* utterly ... ◊ *Das ist oberwichtig!* ♦ *Du hältst dich wohl für oberschlau!*

② **O·ber·...** [ˈoːbɐ] ⸤prefix⸥ **1.** chief ..., senior ... ◊ *ein Oberförster/Oberkellner/Oberschulrat*; overall ..., supreme ... ◊ *die Oberaufsicht führen* **2.** GEOG

Upper ... ◊ *Oberitalien/Oberfranken/Oberbayern* ♦ *das Oberrheintal* **3.** upper ... ◊ *die Oberlippe* ♦ *der Oberarm/Oberkiefer/Oberschenkel* ♦ *ein Obergeschoss* ♦ *die Oberschicht* **4.** outer ... ◊ *ein Oberhemd* ♦ *Oberbekleidung* **5.** higher ... ◊ *das Oberlandesgericht/Oberverwaltungsgericht* **6.** *(fam, pej)* utter ... ◊ *Sie ist total unspontan und eine Oberlangweilerin.* ♦ *Er ist einfach ein Obertrottel.*

o·be·re [ˈoːbərə] ⸤adj⸥ no comp, only before ns <ein oberer ..., eine obere ..., ein oberes ...> **1.** upper, top ◊ *Sie wohnt in einem der oberen Stockwerke.* ♦ *die obere Hälfte des Brötchens* ⊝untere **2.** outer ◊ *Die Creme versorgt die oberen Hautschichten mit Feuchtigkeit.* **3.** no superl GEOG Upper ◊ *der obere Lech* **4.** *(hierarchically)* higher, upper ◊ *die obere Schicht der Gesellschaft* ♦ *Die oberen Klassen müssen sich auf das Abitur vorbereiten.* → oberste

O·ber·flä·che [ˈoːbɐflɛçə] die <-, -n> surface ◊ *die glatte Oberfläche des Spiegels* ♦ *Der Wal kam an die Oberfläche, um Luft zu holen.*

o·ber·fläch·lich [ˈoːbɐflɛçlɪç] ⸤adj, adv⸥ superficial(ly) ◊ *Die Verletzung war nur oberflächlich.* ♦ *Sie führten ein oberflächliches Gespräch über das Wetter.* ♦ *jdn/etw. oberflächlich untersuchen* jdn nur oberflächlich kennen know sb only slightly oberflächlich atmen take shallow breaths oberflächlich betrachtet after a quick/fleeting glance ⸤adj⸥ *(pej)* shallow ◊ *ein oberflächlicher Mensch*

o·ber·halb [ˈoːbɐhalp] ⸤prep⸥ +gen or +dat **1.** +gen above ◊ *Sie hat einen Stich oberhalb des Knies.* ⊝unterhalb **2.** *adverbial* +dat oberhalb von above ◊ *Sie wohnen in einem Hotel oberhalb von Meran.* ⊝unterhalb von

O·ber·haupt [ˈoːbɐhaʊpt] das <-(e)s, Oberhäupter> head, leader ◊ *das Oberhaupt der Familie* ♦ *Der Papst ist das Oberhaupt der katholischen Kirche.*

O·ber·kör·per [ˈoːbɐkœrpɐ] der <-s, -> upper body, torso ◊ *Er hat einen muskulösen Oberkörper.* den Oberkörper frei machen strip to the waist

O·ber·schen·kel [ˈoːbɐʃɛŋkl̩] der <-s, -> ANAT thigh ◊ *Muskelkater in den Oberschenkeln haben* ♦ *Sie hat sich den Oberschenkel gebrochen.*

o·bers·te [ˈoːbəstə] ⸤superl⸥ **1.** top, uppermost ◊ *Die Stifte sind in der obersten Schublade.* ♦ *Der oberste Knopf an meiner Bluse fehlt.* **2.** *(in a hierarchy)* highest ◊ *die obersten Verwaltungsorgane* ♦ *Beim Fliegen hat Sicherheit oberste Priorität.*; *(court)* supreme; most important, first ◊ *Bei Feuer ist das oberste Gebot: Ruhe bewahren.* → obere

O·ber·stu·fe [ˈoːbɐʃtuːfə] die <-, -n> most sing upper school, sixth form ◊ *die Oberstufe besuchen*

O·ber·teil [ˈoːbɐtaɪl] das <-(e)s, -e> or seldom der <-(e)s, -e> top ◊ *Sie kaufte sich ein kurzes rotes Oberteil.* ♦ *eine Box mit transparentem Oberteil*

ob·gleich [ɔpˈglaɪç] ⸤conjunc⸥ (al)though ◊ *Sie hat*

keine Jacke angezogen, obgleich es draußen kalt ist. ♦ Obgleich er schon alt ist, ist er immer noch topfit. ⊖obwohl

Ob·hut [ˈɔphuːt] die <-> no pl (lofty) in/unter jds Obhut in sb's care, in sb's custody ◊ Der Kleine befindet sich in Obhut seiner Tante.; (of an instructor etc.) under sb's guidance unter jds Obhut stehen be in sb's care (bei jdm) in guter Obhut sein be well looked after (by sb), be safe (with sb) jdn/etw. in seine Obhut nehmen take care/charge of sb/sth, look after sb/sth

Ob·jekt [ɔpˈjɛkt, '– –] das <-(e)s, -e> **1.** most sing object ◊ Da lag ein kleines, rundes Objekt. ♦ Das Objekt seiner Forschungen sind derzeit Spinnen. ♦ Subjekt, Prädikat und Objekt sind Satzglieder. ein lebendes Objekt an animate object jdn/etw. zum Objekt einer Sache machen make sb/sth the subject (matter) of sth **2.** ECON property ◊ Der Makler zeigte uns mehrere Objekte. ⊖Immobilie **3.** ARTS work of art, art object ◊ Wir bewundern die ausgestellten Objekte.; (ornamental) objet d'art

ob·jek·tiv [ɔpjɛkˈtiːf, '– – –] adj, adv **1.** objective(ly) ◊ Sie versuchte, objektiv und nüchtern zu bleiben. ♦ etw. objektiv beurteilen/darstellen/schildern; factual(ly) ◊ ein objektiver Bericht ♦ Das ist objektiv richtig/falsch. ⊖sachlich ⊖subjektiv **2.** (lofty) real, actual ◊ Der Glaube kann sich nicht auf objektive Tatsachen stützen. ⊖tatsächlich

② **Obst** [oːpst] das <-(e)s> no pl fruit ◊ Du solltest mehr Obst essen. ♦ einen Tortenboden mit Obst belegen

obs·zön [ɔpsˈtsøːn] adj, adv obscene(ly) ◊ Der Witz war obszön. ♦ Sie erhielt obszöne Anrufe. ♦ Rede nicht so obszön daher! ⊖unanständig

② **ob·wohl** [ɔpˈvoːl] conjunc al(though) ◊ Obwohl sie krank ist, geht sie in die Arbeit. ♦ Er friert, obwohl er einen Pulli anhat. ⊖obgleich

Och·se [ˈɔksə] der <-n, -n> **1.** ZOO ox ◊ Der Bauer spannte Ochsen vor den Pflug. junger Ochse bullock ○ a. (fam, pej) ass ◊ So ein blöder Ochse! ⊖Dummkopf

ö·de [ˈøːdə] adj <öder, am ödesten> **1.** tedious, dull, dreary ◊ In der Schule ist es immer so öde. ♦ Er führt ein ödes Leben ohne Abwechslung. ⊖langweilig **2.** deserted ◊ Im Winter ist es in dem Urlaubsort öde und leer. **3.** barren ◊ ein öder Landstrich **4.** dreary, dismal ◊ Ohne seine Frau ist die Welt für ihn öde.

② **o·der** [ˈoːdɐ] conjunc **1.** (abbr od.) or ◊ Kommst du mit oder bleibst du da? ♦ Willst du Kaffee oder Tee? ♦ Du musst mir helfen, egal, ob du willst oder nicht. ♦ Sie kommt in einer Stunde oder zwei. ♦ die Europäische Zentralbank oder kurz EZB **2.** (fam) otherwise, or (else) ◊ Wir müssen uns beeilen oder wir verpassen den Zug. ♦ Er muss sich entschuldigen oder er bekommt großen Ärger. ⊖andernfalls, sonst **3.** (fam) (inquiring) Du kommst (doch) heute Abend, oder? You will come tonight, won't you? Das ist (doch) dein Bruder, oder? That's your brother, isn't it? Du wirst (doch) jetzt nicht kneifen, oder? You won't chicken out now, will you? Du glaubst mir doch, oder etwa nicht? You do believe me, don't you? ... oder was ... or what ◊ Hat er jetzt einfach aufgelegt, oder

was?

⊙ oder so (was/ähnlich) (fam) or something ◊ Er macht eine Studienreise oder so was. um fünf Uhr oder so around five o'clock

② **O·fen** [ˈoːfn̩] der <-s, Öfen> **1.** oven ◊ den Braten/Kuchen in den Ofen schieben ♦ den Ofen auf 180 Grad vorheizen **2.** stove, heater ◊ Ein Feuer knistert im Ofen. ♦ den Ofen anzünden/anmachen

⊙ jdn hinter dem Ofen hervorlocken (fam) tempt sb, lure sb out of the house hinter dem Ofen hocken, sich hinter dem Ofen verkriechen (fam) stay in der Ofen ist aus (fam) that's it

② **of·fen** [ˈɔfn̩] adj seldom comp/superl **1.** (also fig) open ◊ Lass bitte die Tür offen. ♦ Manche Geschäfte sind abends bis 20 Uhr offen. ♦ eine offene Beziehung führen ♦ Das Schiff fährt auf das offene Meer hinaus. ♦ eine offene Wunde ♦ offener Widerstand offen haben be open bei offenem Fenster with the window open offen für/gegenüber etw. sein be open to sth offen für jdn/gegenüber jdm sein be open-minded towards sb mit offenem Verdeck fahren drive with the top/hood down **2.** unlocked ◊ Komm rein, die Tür ist offen. ♦ Ich habe das Auto offen gelassen.; (lock) open, released ⊖auf ⊖zu **3.** uncertain, not decided/settled ◊ Bisher ist noch alles offen. ♦ offen bleiben be left open sich (dat) etw. offen halten leave sth open offen lassen, ob/wann etc. ... leave it open whether/when etc. ... **4.** honest, frank ◊ ein offenes Wesen haben ♦ Sie ist sehr offen und ehrlich gewesen. ♦ ein offenes Gespräch führen gegenüber/zu jdm offen sein be honest/frank with sb ⊖aufrichtig **5.** no comp/superl outstanding ◊ Ich muss noch eine offene Rechnung bezahlen. **6.** no comp/superl vacant ◊ Es gibt zu wenig offene Stellen. ⊖frei ⊖besetzt **7.** no comp/superl MED sore ◊ Vom ständigen Spülen hat er schon ganz offene Hände.; ulcerated ◊ offene Beine adv **1.** (also fig) offen stehen be open; (bill) be unsettled, be outstanding einen Spaltbreit offen stehen be ajar jdm offen stehen, für jdn offen sein be open to sb es steht jdm offen, etw. zu tun sb is free to do sth **2.** jdm offen seine Meinung sagen be honest/frank with sb offen gestanden/gesagt frankly, to be honest offen und ehrlich open and frank etw. offen und ehrlich zugeben own up to sth ⊖aufrichtig **3.** no comp/superl loose ◊ Nägel/Wurst etc. offen kaufen/verkaufen ⊖lose **4.** no comp/superl die/seine Haare offen tragen wear your hair loose

⊙ etw. offen legen (lofty) disclose sth ◊ Rechnungen/seine Absichten offen legen

② **of·fen·bar** [ˈɔfn̩baːɐ̯, – – '–] adv apparently ◊ Sie liegt schon im Bett — offenbar ist sie müde. ♦ Er ist offenbar gut gelaunt, so wie er strahlt. ⊖anscheinend adj (lofty) obvious, evident ◊ Das ist eine offenbare Lüge! ♦ Er ist in sie verliebt, das ist doch offenbar! ⊖offensichtlich, offenkundig

of·fen·kun·dig [ˈɔfn̩kʊndɪç] adv obviously ⊖offenbar, offensichtlich adj, adv obvious(ly), evident(ly), manifest(ly) ◊ ein offenkundiger Betrug/Fehler ♦ Es ist offenkundig, dass sie schwanger ist. ♦ Es ist offenkundig nicht an ihm interessiert.; (proof) clear ⊖offensichtlich, offenbar

of·fen·sicht·lich [ˈɔfn̩zɪçtlɪç, – – '– –] adj, adv

obvious(ly), clear(ly) ◊ *Er hat offensichlich keine Lust, mitzukommen.* ♦ *Es ist doch ganz offensichtlich, dass er lügt.* ♦ *ein offensichtlicher Fall von Betrug* ⊖offenbar, offenkundig

of·fen·siv [ɔfɛnˈziːv] [adj, adv] offensive(ly), aggressive(ly) ◊ *ein offensiver Kampf* ♦ *Sein Fußballspiel war offensiv.* ♦ *offensiv auftreten*

② **öf·fent·lich** [ˈœfn̩tlɪç, ˈœfəntlɪç] [adj, adv] *seldom comp/superl* public(ly) ◊ *ein öffentlicher Auftritt/ Vortrag* ♦ *Die Veranstaltung ist öffentlich und der Eintritt frei.* ♦ *die öffentliche Meinung/Sicherheit* ♦ *Sie wollen ihre Verlobung öffentlich machen.* ♦ *Das Hilfsprojekt wird öffentlich unterstützt.* etw. öffentlich bekannt geben announce sth in public ein öffentliches Geheimnis an open secret öffentlich zugänglich open to the public etw. öffentlich ausschreiben put sth out to (public) tender

② **Öf·fent·lich·keit** [ˈœfn̩tlɪçkaɪt, ˈœfəntlɪçkaɪt] die <–> *no pl* **1.** public ◊ *sich an die Öffentlichkeit wenden* unter Ausschluss der Öffentlichkeit in private, behind closed doors im Licht der Öffentlichkeit (stehen) (be) in the public eye der breiten/für die breite Öffentlichkeit zugänglich open to the general public an die Öffentlichkeit dringen/gelangen become public mit etw. an die Öffentlichkeit treten make sth public **2.** die Öffentlichkeit einer Sache [gen] *the fact that sth is public* ◊ *die Öffentlichkeit einer Sitzung/eines Verfahrens* in der/aller Öffentlichkeit in public

⊛ etw. an die Öffentlichkeit zerren *(pej)* drag sth into the public eye

② **of·fi·zi·ell** [ɔfiˈtsi̯ɛl] [adj, adv] *seldom comp/superl* **1.** official(ly) ◊ *die offizielle Genehmigung einer Behörde* ♦ *Raubkopien sind offiziell verboten.* von offizieller Seite officially ⊖amtlich **2.** formal(ly) ◊ *Bei offiziellen Anlässen trägt sie immer einen Anzug.* ♦ *Der Minister hat sich für seinen Fehltritt offiziell entschuldigt.* **3.** *(fam)* certain ◊ *Wir wollen heiraten, aber das ist noch nicht offiziell.* [adv] *(fam)* supposedly ◊ *Offiziell ist sie bei einer Freundin, aber in Wirklichkeit ist sie bei ihm.*

② **öff·nen** [ˈœfnən] <öffnet, öffnete, hat geöffnet> [tr+intr v] open ◊ *ein Buch/ein Fenster/den Mund/ einen Schirm öffnen* ♦ *eine Dose mit dem Dosenöffner öffnen* ♦ *Das Land hat seine Grenzen geöffnet.* ♦ *Die Bank öffnet nur vormittags.*; *(a knot)* untie (jdm) öffnen open the door (for/to sb) ◊ *Er klingelte fünfmal, aber sie öffnete (ihm) nicht.* seine Praxis samstags etc. öffnen hold a surgery on Saturdays etc. etw. lässt sich nicht öffnen sth doesn't open ⊖aufmachen ⊜schließen [ref v] **1.** sich öffnen open ◊ *Das Garagentor öffnet sich automatisch.* ⊖aufgehen ⊜sich schließen **2.** sich einer Sache [dat] öffnen open up to sth ◊ *Europa öffnet sich dem Osten.* **3.** *(lofty)* sich jdm öffnen be/become more open with sb, trust sb

Öff·nung [ˈœfnʊŋ] die <–, –en> *no pl* opening ◊ *eine wieder verschließbare Öffnung* ♦ *die Öffnung der Grenzen innerhalb der EU*

Öff·nungs·zeit [ˈœfnʊŋstsaɪt] die <–, –en> *most pl* opening hours ◊ *einen Termin außerhalb der normalen Öffnungszeiten vereinbaren*

② **oft** [ɔft] [adv] <öfter, am öftesten> *seldom superl* often ◊ *Ich denke oft an ihn.* ♦ *Er besucht seinen Opa oft.* ♦ *Sie ist abends oft unterwegs.* ♦ *Die Züge verkehren vormittags öfter als abends.* immer

öfter ever more often Das ist schon oft passiert. That has happened many times. ⊖häufig ⊜selten

öf·ter [ˈœftɐ] *comp of* oft [adv] **1.** (schon) öfter often, quite a few times ◊ *Wir haben uns schon öfter getroffen.* **2.** öfter (einmal/mal) now and then, every once in a while ◊ *Sie probiert gerne öfter mal was Neues.* ⊖ab und zu

② **oh·ne¹** [ˈoːnə] [prep] [+acc] without ◊ *ein Saft ohne Zucker* ♦ *Sie ist gerade ohne Arbeit.* ♦ *Eine Übernachtung ohne Frühstück kostet 30 Euro.* ♦ *Das habe ich ohne fremde Hilfe geschafft!*

⊛ (gar) nicht (so) ohne sein *(fam)* *(task etc.)* be quite a challenge *(idea etc.)* not be so bad (after all) *(person)* be somebody to be reckoned with ohne mich *(fam)* count me out, I'm not standing for it

oh·ne² [ˈoːnə] [conjunc] *(always ohne zu/dass)* without ◊ *Er half uns, ohne zu zögern.* ♦ *Sie hat ihn gekränkt, ohne dass sie es wollte.*

oh·ne·hin [oːnəˈhɪn] [adv] anyway ◊ *Ich kann dich abholen, deine Wohnung liegt ohnehin auf dem Weg.* ⊖sowieso

Ohn·macht [ˈoːnmaxt] die <–, –en> **1.** *no pl* powerlessness ◊ *In seiner Ohnmacht rannte er einfach davon.* Ohnmacht gegenüber jdm/etw. powerlessness against sb/sth **2.** MED faint sich einer Ohnmacht nahe fühlen feel faint in Ohnmacht fallen faint aus der Ohnmacht erwachen come to

② **Ohr** [oːɐ] das <–(e)s, –en> ANAT ear ◊ *jdm etw. ins Ohr flüstern/sagen* ♦ *Er ist auf dem rechten Ohr taub.* ♦ *Sie hielt den Telefonhörer ans Ohr.* abstehende Ohren ears that stick out gute/schlechte Ohren haben have good/bad hearing sich [dat] die Ohren zuhalten put your hands over your ears ein Tier legt die Ohren an an animal lays its ears back jd bekommt rote Ohren sb's ears turn red

⊛ es faustdick hinter den Ohren haben *(fam)* be really crafty noch feucht/grün/nicht trocken hinter den Ohren sein *(fam)* be still wet behind the ears (nur) mit halbem/einem Ohr hinhören, (nur) mit halbem/einem Ohr zuhören (only) listen with half an ear lange Ohren bekommen/machen *(fam)* prick up your ears jdm die Ohren lang ziehen *(fam, hum)* take sb by the ears and give them a good talking to ein offenes Ohr (für etw. bei jdm) finden find a sympathetic listener (to sth in sb) ein offenes Ohr für jdn/etw. haben be ready to listen to sb/sth die Ohren steif halten *(fam)* keep your pecker up auf dem Ohr taub sein be deaf to that sort of thing tauben Ohren predigen cry in the wilderness bis über beide Ohren verliebt sein *(fam)* be head over heels in love etw. ist nichts für zarte Ohren *(fam)* sth is not for the easily offended auf dem/ diesem Ohr hört jd schlecht, auf dem/diesem Ohr ist jd taub *(fam)* sb won't hear of it viel um die Ohren haben have a lot on (your plate) jd heult/jammert jdm die Ohren voll *(fam)* sb keeps complaining to sb ein paar/eins/eine hinter die Ohren bekommen *(fam)* get a clip round the ear die Ohren hängen lassen *(fam)* lose heart jd hat etw. (noch) im Ohr sth (still) goes through sb's head jd übers Ohr hauen *(fam)* take sb for a ride jdm eins aufs Ohr hauen/ legen *(fam)* have a kip bei jdm zum einen Ohr hinein- und zum anderen hinausgehen *(fam)* go

in one ear and out the other **jdm klingen die Ohren** sb's ears are ringing **jdm mit etw. in den Ohren liegen** *(fam)* badger sb about sth **mit den Ohren schlackern** *(fam)* be staggered/speechless **schreib dir das hinter die Ohren** just remember that **auf den/seinen Ohren sitzen** *(fam)* be deaf **die Ohren spitzen** prick up your ears **bis über beide Ohren in etw.** ⟨dat⟩ **stecken** *(fam)* be up to the eyeballs in sth **sich bis über beide Ohren verlieben** *(fam)* fall head over heels in love **die/ seine Ohren vor etw.** ⟨dat⟩ **verschließen** turn a deaf ear to sth

Ohr·fei·ge ['oːgfaɪɡə] die <-, -n> slap (round the ear/in the face) ◊ *eine Ohrfeige bekommen* jdm eine Ohrfeige geben/versetzen/verpassen slap sb

ö·ko·lo·gisch [øko'loːɡɪʃ] ⟨adj, adv⟩ **1.** eco-friendly ◊ *ein ökologisches Verfahren* ✦ *Pappbecher sind ökologischer als Kunststoffbecher.* ökologisch denken be concerned about the environment ökologisch sinnvoll sein make environmental sense ökologisch verpackt wrapped/packed in eco-friendly material ökologisch verträglich sustainable **2.** organic ◊ *ökologisches Gemüse* aus ökologischem Anbau organic(ally farmed/cultivated) ökologisch abbaubar biodegradable ⟨adj⟩ *no comp/superl, only before ns* ecological ◊ *das ökologische Gleichgewicht*

② **Ok·to·ber** [ɔk'toːbɐ] der <-s, -> *most sing (abbr Okt.)* October → Januar

Ok·to·ber·fest [ɔk'toːbɐfɛst] das <-(e)s> *no pl* Munich beer festival ◊ *aufs Oktoberfest gehen*

> On 12 October 1810 the future King Ludwig I invited the aristocracy and the citizens of Munich to celebrate his marriage to Therese, Princess of Saxe-Hildburghausen, in a field which thus was named *Theresienwiese*. Since that date, a 16-day festival — later named *Oktoberfest* — has been held here every year from late September until mid-October. It is now the greatest festival worldwide, attracting 6 million visitors from around the globe who consume 5 million litres of beer every year.

② **Öl** [øːl] das <-(e)s, -e> oil ◊ *eine Salatsoße aus Essig und Öl* ✦ *beim Auto das Öl wechseln* ✦ *eine Massage mit ätherischen Ölen* ✦ *nach Öl bohren* ✦ *mit Öl heizen* ✦ *ein Gemälde in Öl*
  ⊛ **Öl auf die Wogen gießen** pour oil on troubled waters **etw. geht jdm runter wie Öl** sb is flattered by sth

O·lym·pi·a·de [olʏm'pjaːdə] die <-, -n> Olympic Games, Olympics ◊ *an der Olympiade teilnehmen*

O·ma ['oːma(ː)] die <-, -s> **1.** *(kidsp)* granny, grandma, nan **2.** *(fam, pej)* old woman, grandma, old granny ◊ *Was will denn die Oma da?*
  ⊛ **wie zu Omas Zeiten** *(fam)* like in the old days

② **On·kel** ['ɔŋkl] der <-s, -> uncle
  ⊛ **der große Onkel** *(kidsp)* the/your big toe

OP [oːˈpeː] der *(abbr of Operationssaal)* operating theatre, operating room

O·pa ['oːpa(ː)] der <-s, -s> **1.** *(kidsp)* grandad **2.** *(fam, pej)* old man, grandad ◊ *Mensch, Opa, das ist nichts für dich.*

O·per ['oːpɐ] die <-, -n> **1.** opera ◊ *Gehst du gerne in die Oper?* **2.** opera house ◊ *Die Oper wird zurzeit renoviert.* **3.** *no pl* opera company ◊ *Die*

Leipziger Oper präsentiert eine neue Inszenierung von „Fidelio".

② **O·pe·ra·ti·on** [opəra'tsɪoːn] die <-, -en> **1.** MED, MIL, MATH operation ◊ *eine Operation am offenen Herz vornehmen* ✦ *eine groß angelegte militärische Operation* **2.** *(lofty)* operation, procedure ◊ *Die Übernahme eines Unternehmens ist eine komplexe Operation.*

② **o·pe·rie·ren** [opə'riːrən] <operiert, operierte, hat operiert> ⟨tr+intr v⟩ MED operate (on) ◊ *einen Bruch operieren* ✦ *jdn am Gehirn operieren* ✦ *Ich fürchte, wir müssen operieren.* operiert werden have an operation ⟨intr v⟩ **1.** MIL be operating ◊ *Die Flotte operierte vor der Ostküste.* **2.** *(lofty)* operate ◊ *Dieses Unternehmen operiert bundesweit.*

② **Op·fer** ['ɔpfɐ] das <-s, -> **1.** victim ◊ *das Opfer eines Verbrechens werden* ✦ *Das Unwetter forderte viele Opfer.* ⊜Täter. **2.** REL sacrifice Sie brachten den Göttern eine Ziege zum Opfer. They sacrificed a goat to the gods. **3.** *(fig)* sacrifice ◊ *Dem Bürger werden immer mehr finanzielle Opfer abverlangt.* jd würde für jdn/etw. jedes Opfer bringen sb would sacrifice everything for sb/sth
  ⊛ **jdm/einer Sache zum Opfer fallen** fall victim to sb/sth, be the victim of sb/sth

op·fern ['ɔpfɐn] ⟨intr v⟩ +haben make a sacrifice ◊ *Bevor sie in den Krieg zogen, opferten sie den Göttern.* ⟨tr v⟩ +haben **1.** sacrifice ◊ *Sie opferten ihrem Gott ein Schaf.* **2.** *(fig)* sacrifice, give up ◊ *Er opfert viel Zeit für sein Ehrenamt.* ⟨ref v⟩ +haben **1.** sich opfern sacrifice yourself ◊ *Er opferte sich, damit seine Kameraden fliehen konnten.* **2.** *(iron)* sich opfern be a martyr ◊ *Wer opfert sich und isst das letzte Stück Kuchen?*

② **Op·po·si·ti·on** [ɔpozi'tsɪoːn] die <-, -en> *most sing* **1.** POL Opposition **2.** *(lofty)* opposition ◊ *Ihre Pläne stießen auf starke Opposition.*

Op·ti·ker ['ɔptɪkɐ] der <-s, ->, **Op·ti·ke·rin** ['ɔptɪkərɪn] die <-, -nen> optician ◊ *Er arbeitet als Optiker.* ✦ *Die Optikerin hat mir Kontaktlinsen empfohlen.*

op·ti·mal [ɔpti'maːl] ⟨adj⟩ *no comp/superl* perfect, ideal ◊ *optimale Bedingungen zum Skifahren* ✦ *Dieses Hotel ist optimal für Kongresse.* ⟨adv⟩ perfectly, as well as possible ◊ *Der Sportler hatte sich optimal vorbereitet.*

op·tisch ['ɔptɪʃ] ⟨adj⟩ *no comp/superl, only before ns* optical ◊ *eine optische Täuschung* ⟨adj, adv⟩ visual(ly) ◊ *der erste optische Eindruck* ✦ *Die beiden sind rein optisch ein Traumpaar.* etw. optisch hervorheben highlight sth Er hat sich aus optischen Gründen die Nase operieren lassen. He has had a nose-job for cosmetic reasons.

o·ran·ge [o'ranʃ, o'rãːʒə] ⟨adj⟩ orange ◊ *Die Küche ist orange.* ✦ *ein oranges Hemd*

O·ran·ge¹ [o'ranʃ, o'rãːʒə] das <-> *no pl* orange ◊ *Orange ist meine Lieblingsfarbe.* ✦ *Der Stuhl ist in einem knalligen Orange lackiert.* box@ Farbe

O·ran·ge² [o'ranʒə, o'rãːʒə] die <-, -n> orange ◊ *eine Orange schälen* ⊜Apfelsine.

② **or·dent·lich** ['ɔrdntlɪç, 'ɔrdəntlɪç] ⟨adj⟩ **1.** tidy ◊ *Julia ist ein sehr ordentliches Kind.* **2.** *(place)* orderly, tidy ◊ *Die Wohnung war sauber und ordentlich.* **3.** *only before ns (conforming to rules)* proper, official ◊ *eine ordentliche Bürgerversammlung* **4.** decent, good ◊ *Die Bezahlung ist hier*

ordentlich. ♦ *Sie bekam eine ordentliche Abreibung.* **5.** *(fam)* large ◇ *eine ordentliche Portion essen* [adv] **1.** neatly ◇ *die Wäsche ordentlich zusammenlegen* **2.** officially ◇ *Das Arbeitsverhältnis wurde ordentlich gekündigt.* **3.** *(fam)* well, properly ◇ *Er hat seine Sache ganz ordentlich gemacht.* ♦ *sich ordentlich auf eine Prüfung vorbereiten* **4.** *(fam)* really ◇ *ordentlich auf den Tisch hauen* ♦ *Das Baby hält mich ordentlich auf Trab.*

② **Or·di·na·ti·on** [ɔrdinaˈtsjoːn] die <-, -en> *(Austr)* surgery ♦ *Montag keine Ordination* ♦ *Grippeimpfstoff ist in der Ordination vorrätig.*

② **ord·nen** [ˈɔrdnən] [tr v] +*haben* **1.** put in order, tidy up ◇ *Ich muss dringend meine Finanzen/mein Leben ordnen.* **2.** organize ◇ *Du musst deine Papiere besser ordnen.* neu ordnen restructure, rearrange alphabetisch/chronologisch geordnet sein be in alphabetical/chronological order etw. nach etw. ordnen put sth in order of sth ◇ *Die Aufträge werden nach Priorität geordnet.*

Ord·ner [ˈɔrdnɐ] der <-s, -> folder ◇ *einen neuen Ordner anlegen* ♦ *eine Datei in einen anderen Ordner verschieben*

② **Ord·nung** [ˈɔrdnʊŋ] die <-, -en> **1.** *no pl* order, tidiness Auf meinem Schreibtisch herrscht Ordnung. My desk is tidy. Halten Sie besonders in der Küche Ordnung. Please keep the kitchen particularly tidy. in Ordnung in order seine Krawatte in Ordnung bringen straighten your tie ⊚Unordnung **2.** in Ordnung right nicht in Ordnung wrong (wieder) in Ordnung sein be all right (now) **3.** LAW rules, regulations ◇ *gegen die verfassungsmäßige Ordnung verstoßen* **4.** order ◇ *die hierarchische Ordnung einer Firma* **5.** *no pl* ordering, sorting ◇ *Sie befasste sich mit der Ordnung ihrer Papiere. Die Ordnung der Erbangelegenheiten wird lange dauern.* It will take a long time to sort out the details of the inheritance. **6.** *most sing* BIO order ◇ *Die Geckos gehören zur Ordnung der Echsen.* ⊛ Ordnung ist das halbe Leben order is the key to success erster/zweiter/dritter Ordnung of the first/second/third degree in Ordnung gehen *(fam)* be OK, be all right jd ist in Ordnung sb is OK, sb is all right

Or·gan [ɔrˈgaːn] das <-(e)s, -e> **1.** ANAT organ ◇ *Die Leber ist ein lebenswichtiges Organ.* **2.** *(lofty)* *(publication)* organ, mouthpiece ◇ *das offizielle Organ des Verbandes* **3.** *(lofty)* representative ◇ *Der Europäische Rat ist das höchste Organ der Europäischen Union.* **4.** *(fam, pej)* voice ◇ *Unsere Nachbarin hat ein sehr lautes Organ.*

② **Or·ga·ni·sa·ti·on** [ɔrganizaˈtsjoːn] die <-, -en> **1.** organization, association ◇ *sich einer Organisation anschließen* **2.** *no pl* *(planning)* organization ◇ *mit der Organisation einer Hochzeit beschäftigt sein* **3.** *no pl* organization, structure ◇ *die Organisation eines Unternehmens* **4.** *no pl* *(of people)* coordination, cohesion

② **or·ga·ni·sie·ren** [ɔrganiˈziːrən] [tr v] **1.** organize ◇ *eine Reise/einen Kongress organisieren* **2.** *(fam)* sort out ◇ *Organisierst du noch ein paar Gläser?* [ref v] **1.** sich organisieren unite ◇ *Die Arbeiter organisierten sich und streikten.* **2.** sich in etw. organisieren form sth ◇ *Wir organisieren uns in einer Bürgerinitiative.* sich neu organisieren re-form

Or·gel [ˈɔrgl̩] die <-, -n> organ ◇ *(an/auf der) Orgel spielen*

o·ri·en·tie·ren [ɔrjɛnˈtiːrən] <orientiert, orientierte, hat orientiert> [ref v] **1.** *(also fig)* sich orientieren find your bearings sich an/nach etw. orientieren use sth to get your bearings ◇ *Orientieren Sie sich an der unten abgedruckten Karte.* ♦ *sich nach Norden/dem Polarstern orientieren* **2.** *(lofty)* sich an jdm./etw. orientieren be governed by sb/sth, follow sb/sth ◇ *sich an bestimmten Grundsätzen orientieren* [tr v] jdn über etw. [acc] orientieren tell sb about sth, give sb information about/on sth sich über etw. [acc] orientieren inform yourself about sth

O·ri·en·tie·rungs·stu·fe [ɔrjɛnˈtiːrʊŋsʃtuːfə] die <-, -n>

> In some German *Länder*, the *Orientierungsstufe* (the fifth and sixth school years) gives pupils the opportunity to choose what type of secondary school they would like to attend. The 'orientation stage' offers pupils a further two years after primary school in which to decide on their future schooling. During these two years, main subjects such as maths and German are taught on three levels (A, B and C). Pupils are given as much encouragement as possible. After the sixth year, a pupil can then make a decision based on his or her talents and interests about which school he or she will go on to attend.

o·ri·gi·nal [origiˈnaːl] [adj] *no comp/superl* original ◇ *originale Werke berühmter Künstler* ♦ *Die Orgel in dieser Kirche ist noch original.* [adv] **1.** etw. original wieder aufbauen/errichten restore sth to its original condition **2.** genuine ◇ *original russischer Wodka* **3.** live ◇ *Das Konzert wurde original übertragen.* ⊛ original signiert signed by the artist etw. ist original verpackt sth is in its original packaging

② **O·ri·gi·nal** [origiˈnaːl] das <-s, -e> **1.** original ◇ *Dieses Gemälde ist ein Original.* ♦ *Bitte legen Sie nur Originale, keine Kopien, bei.* **2.** *(person)* character ◇ *Mein Opa war ein richtiges Original.*

o·ri·gi·nell [origiˈnɛl] [adj] **1.** novel ◇ *eine originelle Mischung aus beidem* ♦ *Dieser Gedanke ist weder originell noch revolutionär.* **2.** amusing ◇ *Die Lehrerin fand den Streich nicht besonders originell.* [adv] in a novel way, imaginatively ◇ *Das Geschenk war originell verpackt.*

Or·kan [ɔrˈkaːn] der <-(e)s, -e> hurricane

② **Ort** [ɔrt] der <-(e)s, -e> **1.** place, location ◇ *erste Eindrücke vom Ort des Geschehens* ♦ *Sie hält sich an einem geheimen Ort auf.* ♦ *etw. an einem sicheren Ort aufbewahren* **2.** village, (small) town ◇ *ein kleiner Ort in den Bergen* hier vom Ort sein be a local ⊛ an Ort und Stelle **1.** on the spot ◇ *Ich habe mich an Ort und Stelle beschwert.* **2.** in place ◇ *Es dauerte ewig, bis alles an Ort und Stelle war.* vor Ort on the spot ◇ *Die Kriminalpolizei ermittelte vor Ort.*>

ört·lich [ˈœrtlɪç] [adj] *no comp/superl, only before ns* **1.** patchy ◇ *örtliche Nebelbildung* **2.** local ◇ *die örtliche Bevölkerung* [adv] locally ◇ *örtlich zuständig/begrenzt/durchgeführt etc.* örtlich betäubt werden be given a local anaesthetic/anesthetic

Ort·schaft ['ɔrtʃaft] die <-, -en> village, (small) town

Os·si ['ɔsiː] der <-s, -s> *(fam)* ⊕Wessi

Ossi is a (frequently pejorative) term for a person from one of the East German *Länder*. This term and its counterpart *Wessi*, someone from the former West Germany , became established after reunification; they illustrate the difficulties posed by the reunification process.

⊘ **Ost** [ɔst] <-> *without the article, invariable* **1.** +*prep* aus/von Ost from the east nach Ost to the east, eastwards ⊖Osten ⊕West, Westen **2.** East ◇ das Autobahnkreuz München Ost ⊕West **3.** East Germany, the East ◇ Wer finanzierte den Aufbau Ost? ⊖Ostdeutschland ⊕Westdeutschland

⊘ **Ost·...** [ɔst] prefix east ..., eastern ... ◇ die Ostseite des Hauses ♦ der Ostwind; *(in names)* East ..., Eastern ... ◇ Ostdeutschland ♦ Osteuropa ⊕West...

ost·deutsch ['ɔstdɔɥtʃ] adj *mostly before ns* POL East German ⊖westdeutsch → deutsch

Ost·deut·sche ['ɔstdɔɥtʃə] der/die <-n, die Ostdeutschen> *but:* ein Ostdeutscher/eine Ostdeutsche East German ⊖Westdeutsche → Deutsche, Ossi

Ost·deutsch·land ['ɔstdɔɥtʃlant] das <-s> *article only in combination with attribute, no pl (political)* East Germany ◇ der schwierige Arbeitsmarkt in Ostdeutschland; *(geographical)* Eastern Germany ◇ durch Nord- und Ostdeutschland reisen → Deutschland

⊘ **Os·ten** ['ɔstn̩] der <-s> *no pl* **1.** East, east ◇ Im Osten geht die Sonne auf. nach Osten to the East, eastwards Züge Richtung Osten eastbound trains ⊖Westen **2.** POL, HIST der Osten the East ◇ Über Jahrzehnte hat der Osten den Westen geeint. ⊖Westen

⊛ der Nahe Osten the Middle East

Os·tern ['oːstən] *seldom with definite article 'das'* Easter ◇ Er wünschte uns frohe Ostern. ♦ Über Ostern waren wir bei meinen Eltern.

Easter is the most important Christian festival. In Germany, it is particularly popular with children because they are given presents and chocolate rabbits and eggs. They also go on a hunt in the garden for sweets and brightly-coloured eggs that have been hidden by the 'Easter bunny'. Often, cakes are baked in the shape of lambs. To celebrate Easter, the Germans decorate their homes with Easter bouquets made of branches covered with blown or artificial eggs, and sometimes hang eggs from trees in their gardens.

Ös·ter·reich ['øːstəraɛç] das <-s> *article only in combination with attribute, no pl* Austria → Deutschland

Ös·ter·rei·cher ['øːstəraɛçɐ] der <-s, ->, **Ös·ter·rei·che·rin** ['øːstəraɛçərɪn] die <-, -nen> Austrian → Deutsche

ös·ter·rei·chisch ['øːstəraɛçɪʃ] adj *mostly before ns* Austrian ◇ der österreichische Dialekt ♦ Diese Nachspeise ist typisch österreichisch.

⊛ österreichisch gefärbtes Deutsch German with a hint of Austrian

öst·lich¹ ['œstlɪç] adj **1.** *only before ns* eastern ◇ das östliche Mittelmeer ⊖westlich **2.** *only before ns* (wind, direction) easterly ◇ stürmische Böen aus östlicher Richtung ⊖westlich **3.** Eastern ◇ eine östliche Religion ⊖westlich **4.** HIST Eastern-bloc, East-bloc ◇ ein östlicher Geheimdienst ⊖westlich

öst·lich² ['œstlɪç] prep +gen or +dat **1.** +gen (to the) east ◇ Östlich der Stadt ist eine Fabrik. ⊖westlich **2.** *adverbial* +dat östlich von east of ◇ östlich von Kassel wohnen ⊖westlich

Ost·see ['ɔstzeː] die <-> *no pl (always* die Ostsee) the Baltic (Sea) ◇ Ferien an der Ostsee machen

ÖVP [øːfaʊ'peː] die *(Austr) (abbr of* Österreichische Volkspartei) ÖVP, People's Party

The ÖVP was founded in Austria in 1945 and is a Christian-Democratic party. It supports a liberal constitutional state and an ecosocial market economy.

P

p, P [pe:] das <–(s), –(s)> p, P ◊ *Dieses Wort wird mit einem kleinen p/großen P geschrieben.* ✦ *P wie Paula*

②**paar** [pa:'] ⟨det⟩ *invariable and indefinite* ein paar … a few …, a couple of … ◊ *Wir fahren ein paar Tage in Urlaub.* ✦ *Ich war mit ein paar Freunden im Kino.* ✦ *ein paar Tausend Meter* alle paar … every few … ◊ *Wir fahren alle paar Jahre nach London.*

②**Paar** [pa:'] das <–(e)s, –e> **1.** pair, couple ◊ *ein verliebtes Paar* ✦ *Das Spiel wird in Paaren gespielt.* **2.** *pl* 'Paar' *when used with numerals* ein Paar … a pair of … ◊ *ein Paar Hosen* zwei/drei etc. Paar … two/three etc. pairs of … ◊ *Ich brauche zwei Paar neue Socken.*

paa·ren ['pa:rən] ⟨ref v⟩ +*haben* BIO sich paaren mate ◊ *Füchse paaren sich im Februar.*
Ⓟ mit etw. gepaart sein *(lofty)* be united with sth ◊ *In diesem Produkt ist Nützliches mit Schönem gepaart.*

pach·ten ['paxtn̩] <pachtet, pachtete, hat gepachtet> ⟨tr v⟩ etw. pachten lease sth, take (out) a lease on sth, rent sth ◊ *ein Grundstück pachten*
Ⓟ etw. für sich gepachtet haben have a monopoly on sth ◊ *Er scheint das Glück für sich gepachtet zu haben.*

Päch·ter ['pɛçtɐ] der <–s, –>, **Päch·te·rin** ['pɛçtərɪn] die <–, –nen> leaseholder, tenant

Pack¹ [pak] der *or* das <–(e)s, –e *or* Päcke> *pl 'Pack' when used with expressions of quantity* **1.** packet, pack ◊ *zwei Pack Papiertaschentücher* **2.** bundle ◊ *ein zusammengeschnürtes Pack Briefe*
Ⓟ mit Sack und Pack → Sack

Pack² [pak] das <–(e)s> *no pl (pej)* bunch ◊ *So ein faules Pack!*

②**Päck·chen** ['pɛkçən] das <–s, –> **1.** packet ◊ *ein Päckchen Zigaretten* **2.** *(to be sent by post)* parcel ◊ *ein Päckchen aufgeben* **3.** bundle ◊ *ein Päckchen Banknoten*

②**pa·cken** ['pakn̩] ⟨tr v⟩ +*haben* **1.** pack (up) ◊ *die Schultasche packen* ✦ *Umzugskartons packen* **2.** grab ◊ *Er packte sie an den Schultern und schüttelte sie.* **3.** *(fam)* manage ◊ *Er hat die Fahrprüfung erst beim dritten Mal gepackt.* **4.** etw. packt jdn be seized with/by sth ◊ *Ihn packte die Neugier.* **5.** *(fam)* jdn/etw. irgendwohin packen put sb/sth somewhere ◊ *Sie packt ihre Kinder immer schon früh ins Bett.* sich irgendwohin packen place yourself somewhere **6.** jdn packen grip sb ◊ *Das Buch packte ihn derart, dass er es nicht mehr weglegen konnte.* ⟨intr v⟩ +*haben* pack ◊ *Wir fahren morgen in Urlaub, und ich habe noch nicht gepackt.*
Ⓟ pack dich/packt euch *(pej)* clear off

②**Pa·ckerl** [pakɐl] das <–s, –n> *(Austr)* → Päckchen

Pä·da·go·ge [pɛda'go:gə] der <–n, –n>, **Pä·da·go·gin** [pɛda'go:gɪn] die <–, –nen> *(lofty)* **1.** teacher ◊ *Sie ist Pädagogin von Beruf.* ✦ *Das*

sollte ein Pädagoge aber wissen! **2.** educationalist

②**Pa·ket** [pa'ke:t] das <–(e)s, –e> **1.** bundle ◊ *Zeitschriften zu einem Paket schnüren* **2.** packet ◊ *ein Paket Nudeln öffnen* **3.** *(to be sent by post)* parcel, package ◊ *ein Paket bei der Post aufgeben* **4.** *(fig)* package ◊ *Dem Paket an Sparmaßnahmen wurde zugestimmt.*

Pa·last [pa'last] der <–(e)s, Paläste> palace

②**Pa·lat·schin·ke** [palat'ʃɪŋkə] die <–, –n> *most pl (Austr)* pancake

Pa·let·te [pa'lɛtə] die <–, –n> **1.** range, spectrum ◊ *Wir bieten eine breite Palette von Videos an.* **2.** ARTS palette ◊ *Farben auf die Palette auftragen*

Pal·me ['palmə] die <–, –n> palm (tree) ◊ *ein Strand mit Palmen*
Ⓟ jdn auf die Palme bringen *(fam)* drive sb mad

pa·nie·ren [pa'ni:rən] <paniert, panierte, hat paniert> ⟨tr v⟩ *coat sth with a mixture of egg and breadcrumbs (or similar) before frying it* ◊ *Die Schnitzel mit Mehl, Eiern und Semmelbröseln panieren.*

pa·nisch ['pa:nɪʃ] ⟨adj⟩ panic-stricken ◊ *panische Furcht* ✦ *Sie war panisch vor Angst.* ⟨adv⟩ in panic, panic-stricken ◊ *Sie flüchteten panisch.*

②**Pan·ne** ['panə] die <–, –n> **1.** breakdown ◊ *Der Bus hatte eine Panne.* ✦ *mit einer Panne liegen bleiben* **2.** *(mistake)* slip(-up) ◊ *Es ist uns eine peinliche Panne unterlaufen.; (setback)* hitch

Pan·tof·fel [pan'tɔfl̩] der <–s, –n> mule, slipper ◊ *Pantoffeln tragen/anziehen*

Pan·zer ['pantsɐ] der <–s, –> **1.** shell ◊ *der Panzer der Schildkröte* **2.** MIL tank ◊ *Panzer rollten in die Stadt ein.* **3.** armour, armor ◊ *der eiserne Panzer des Ritters*

Pa·pa ['papa(:)] der <–s, –s> *(kidsp)* daddy, dad

Pa·pa·gei [papa'gaɛ] der <–en *or* –s, –en> parrot

②**Pa·pier** [pa'pi:ɐ] das <–s, –e> **1.** *no pl* paper ◊ *ein Stück Papier* ✦ *Weihnachtssterne aus Papier* **2.** paper, document ◊ *einen Stapel Papiere durchsehen* Papiere papers ◊ *Kann ich bitte Ihre Papiere sehen?* **3.** FIN security
Ⓟ etw. zu Papier bringen put sth down on paper, write sth (down) nur auf dem Papier only in theory

Pa·pier·korb [pa'pi:ɐkɔrp] der <–(e)s, Papierkörbe> **1.** waste-paper basket, wastebasket **2.** IT wastebasket ◊ *Dateien in den Papierkorb verschieben*

Pap·pe ['papə] die <–, –n> card(board) ◊ *ein Bilderbuch mit dicken Seiten aus Pappe*
Ⓟ nicht von Pappe sein *(fam)* be considerable, be substantial

Pap·ri·ka¹ ['paprika:] der <–s> *no pl* paprika ◊ *einen Teelöffel Paprika zugeben*

Pap·ri·ka² ['paprika:] die <–, –(s)> **1.** pepper(s), bell pepper(s) ◊ *die Paprika in Streifen schneiden* **2.** BOT pepper plant ◊ *Paprikas pflanzen*

Papst [pa:pst] der <–(e)s, Päpste> Pope

Pa·ra·dei·ser [para'daeze] der <-s, -> *(Austr)* tomato ◊ *eine Dose geschälte Paradeiser*

par·al·lel [para'leːl] adj *no comp/superl* **1.** parallel ◊ *parallele Linien* parallel sein run parallel to each other parallel zu etw. sein run parallel to sth **2.** *only before ns* simultaneous ◊ *parallele Prozesse* adv **1.** parallel verlaufende Gleise parallel tracks Die Stühle sind parallel zur Wand angeordnet. The chairs are lined up against the wall. **2.** at the same time ◊ *zwei parallel stattfindende Veranstaltungen*

pa·rat [pa'raːt] adj *no comp/superl, not before ns* etw. parat haben/halten have sth ready ◊ *Er hatte auf Anhieb eine Lösung parat.*

Pär·chen ['pɛːçən] das <-s, -> **1.** (romantic) couple ◊ *Auf der Bank saß eng umschlungen ein Pärchen.* **2.** BIO pair ◊ *Ich habe zwei Meerschweinchen, ein Pärchen.*

Par·fum [paʁˈfœː] → Parfüm

Par·füm [paʁˈfyːm] das <-s, -e or -s> perfume, fragrance ◊ *ein Parfüm mit herbem Duft*

Pa·ri·ser¹ [pa'riːze] der <-s, -> *(fam)* condom ◊ *einen Pariser verwenden/überziehen* ⊜Kondom, Präservativ

Pa·ri·ser² [pa'riːze] der <-s, ->, **Pa·ri·se·rin** [pa'riːzərɪn] die <-, -nen> Parisian → Deutsche

② **Park** [paʁk] der <-s, -s> park ◊ *im Park spazieren gehen*

② **par·ken** ['paʁkn] tr+intr v +*haben* park ◊ *Wo hast du (das Auto) geparkt?* intr v +*haben* be parked ◊ *Das Auto parkt vor dem Haus.*

Par·kett [paʁˈkɛt] das <-(e)s, -e or -s> **1.** parquet (flooring) ◊ *spiegelblankes Parkett* **2.** *no pl* THEAT stalls, orchestra, parquet ◊ *Plätze im Parkett* **3.** *no pl* dance floor ◊ *übers Parkett schweben* **4.** *no pl* (fig) sphere ◊ *Erfahrungen auf dem diplomatischen Parkett*

② **Park·haus** ['paʁkhaos] das <-es, Parkhäuser> multi-storey car park, parking garage ◊ *Das Auto steht im Parkhaus.*

② **Park·platz** ['paʁkplats] der <-es, Parkplätze> **1.** car park, parking lot ◊ *ein bewachter Parkplatz* **2.** (for one car) space ◊ *eine Tiefgarage mit 100 Parkplätzen*

Park·schei·be ['paʁkʃaebə] die <-, -n> parking disc, parking disk

In many German car parks, you are only allowed to park for a limited period. For this reason, you should state your time of arrival (always rounded off to the next half hour) on your parking disc and leave it in a visible place in the car so that the traffic wardens can check it if necessary.

② **Park·uhr** ['paʁkuːɐ] die <-, -en> (parking) meter ◊ *Münzen in die Parkuhr werfen*

② **Par·la·ment** [paʁla'mɛnt] das <-(e)s, -e> **1.** parliament, Parliament ◊ *Sie wurde ins Parlament gewählt.* ♦ *Das Parlament wurde aufgelöst.* **2.** parliament building ◊ *Das Parlament brannte.; (in England)* Houses of Parliament

② **Par·tei** [paʁˈtae] die <-, -en> **1.** POL (political) party ◊ *die stärkste Partei im Bundestag* ♦ *einer konservative Partei* ◊ *einer Partei angehören* **2.** party, side ◊ *die Parteien in der Diskussion um die Atomenergie* **3.** LAW party ◊ *Bei der Scheidung konnten sich beide Parteien schnell einigen.* **4.** tenant ◊ *Wir wohnen mit sechs Parteien im*

Haus.

⊛ **für jdn/etw. Partei ergreifen/nehmen** take sb's/sth's side, take the side of sb/sth, support sb/sth **Partei ergreifen/nehmen** take sides

② **Par·ter·re** [paʁˈtɛrə, paʁˈtɛrˠ] das <-s, -s> *most sing* ground floor, first floor ◊ *eine Wohnung im Parterre*

Par·tie [paʁˈtiː] die <-, -n> **1.** part, section ◊ *ein Kleid, das die mittlere Partie des Rückens frei lässt* **2.** game, round ◊ *eine Partie Bridge/Schach spielen* **3.** part ◊ *Sie singt die Partie der Königin der Nacht in Mozarts „Zauberflöte".*

⊛ **ein gute Partie** a good match (bei etw.) **mit von der Partie sein** *(fam)* be in (on sth)

Par·ti·kel¹ [paʁˈtiːkl̩, paʁˈtɪkl̩] die <-, -n> LING particle

Par·ti·kel² [paʁˈtiːkl̩, paʁˈtɪkl̩] das <-s, -> particle ◊ *energiereiche Partikel*

Par·ti·zip [paʁtiˈtsiːp] das <-s, -ien> participle

In the following sentence, the past participle of *zubereiten — zubereitet —* is used with the perfect tense: *Ich habe das Essen zubereitet.* And in the following sentence, it is used to express the passive: *Dieses Essen wurde lecker* **zubereitet.** Past participles can also be used as adjectives *(dieses lecker zubereitete Essen)* and adverbs *(Das Essen kam fertig zubereitet aus der Küche.).* With regular verbs, the past participle is formed using the prefix *ge-* and the suffix *-t.* With verbs that have a non-separable prefix (such as **be-, ent-, er-, ver-** and **zer-**), the past participle is formed without *ge-: verstehen — verstanden.* In verbs with separable prefixes (such as **ab-, an-, auf-, aus-, ein-**), the past participle is formed by inserting *-ge-* between the prefix and the stem of the verb: *anfangen — angefangen.* Verbs ending in **-ieren** do not begin their past participles with the prefix *ge-: finanzieren — finanziert.*

The present participle is less common in German than the past participle. It can be used as an adjective *(Das war aber ein Ekel* **erregendes** *Essen.),* and less frequently as an adverb *(Die Suppe kam* **dampfend** *auf den Tisch.).*

② **Part·ner** ['paʁtne] der <-s, ->, **Part·ne·rin** ['paʁtnərɪn] die <-, -nen> partner ◊ *Ich suche eine Partnerin zum Tennisspielen.* ♦ *eine Ehe, in der beide Partner erwerbstätig sind* ♦ *Ein Partner ist aus dem Geschäft ausgestiegen.*

Part·ner·schaft ['paʁtneʃaft] die <-, -en> **1.** relationship ◊ *eine neue Partnerschaft eingehen* **2.** ECON partnership ◊ *Die Verlage gingen eine Partnerschaft ein.*

② **Par·ty** ['paʁti] die <-, -s> party ◊ *eine Party feiern/geben* ♦ *Am Samstag gehe ich auf eine Party.*

② **Pass** [pas] der <-es, Pässe> **1.** passport ◊ *einen Pass verlängern lassen* **2.** (in the mountains) pass ◊ *Der Pass ist für Lkw gesperrt.* **3.** SPORT pass ◊ *Bei einem Pass von Scholl stand Elber im Abseits.*

Pas·sa·ge [pa'saːʒə] die <-, -n> **1.** passage ◊ *Durch eine Passage gelangt man in den Innenhof.* ♦ *Sie buchte eine Passage nach New York.* ♦ *Er zitierte die entsprechende Passage.* **2.** TRADE arcade ◊ *ein Geschäft in einer lichtdurchfluteten Passage*

Ⓩ **Pas·sa·gier** [pasa'ʒiːɐ̯] der <-s, -e>,
Pas·sa·gie·rin [pasa'ʒiːrɪn] die <-, -nen>
passenger
◉ blinder Passagier stowaway
Pas·sant [pa'sant] der <-en, -en>, **Pas·san·tin**
[pa'santɪn] die <-, -nen> passer-by
Ⓩ **pas·sen** ['pasn̩] ⟨intr v⟩ +*haben* **1.** jdm passen fit sb
◊ Diese Schuhe passen mir nicht. **2.** irgendwohin
passen fit somewhere ◊ Der Stecker passt nicht in
die Steckdose. **3.** zu etw. passen go with sth gut
zueinander passen go well together **4.** *(fam)* pass
◊ Die Hauptstadt von Mali? Da muss ich passen.
5. jdm passen suit sb ◊ Samstag passt mir gut.
⟨tr v⟩ +*haben* SPORT pass ◊ Er passte den Ball quer
über den Strafraum zu Klose.
Ⓩ **pas·sie·ren** [pa'siːrən] <passiert, passierte, hat/ist
passiert> ⟨intr v⟩ +*sein* **1.** happen ◊ Was ist denn
hier passiert? ♦ Hoffentlich ist ihm nichts passiert.
Mir ist ein Unglück passiert. Something awful has
happened to me. ⊖geschehen **2.** be done ◊ So
geht das nicht weiter. Es muss endlich etwas
passieren! ⟨tr v⟩ +*haben* **1.** go through ◊ Diesen
Tunnel passieren täglich etwa 10 000 Fahrzeuge.
2. pass (by) ◊ Auf dem Weg passierten wir einen
kleinen See. **3.** cross ◊ eine Ampelanlage
passieren **4.** strain ◊ Passieren Sie die Suppe
durch ein feines Sieb.
Ⓩ **pas·siv** ['pasiːf] ⟨adj, adv⟩ passive(ly) ◊ zum
passiven Widerstand aufrufen ♦ Sie ist eher
schüchtern und passiv. ♦ passiv herumstehen und
nichts tun das passive Wahlrecht the right to stand
as a candidate sich bei etw. passiv verhalten take
no active part in sth ⊖aktiv ⟨adj⟩ ECON eine passive
Handelsbilanz an adverse trade balance ⊖aktiv
Pas·siv ['pasiːf] das <-s, -e> *most sing* passive im
Passiv stehen be in the passive
Pass·wort ['pasvɔrt] das <-(e)s, Passwörter> IT
password ◊ ein Passwort eingeben
Pas·te·te [pas'teːtə] die <-, -n> **1.** pie ◊ Die
Pastete im Ofen ca. 40 Minuten backen. **2.** pâté ◊
ein Brötchen mit Pastete bestreichen
Pa·te ['paːtə] der <-n, -n>, **Pa·tin** ['paːtɪn] die
<-, -nen> REL Pate godparent, godfather Patin
godparent, godmother
Pa·ter ['paːtɐ] der <-s, -> REL Father ◊ Pater
Benedikt ist schon seit 40 Jahren im Kloster.
Ⓩ **Pa·ti·ent** [pa'tsi̯ɛnt] der <-en, -en>, **Pa·ti·en·tin**
[pa'tsi̯ɛntɪn] die <-, -nen> patient ◊ Der Patient
wurde gestern aus dem Krankenhaus entlassen.
Pat·ro·ne [pa'troːnə] die <-, -n> cartridge
pau·ken ['paokn̩] ⟨tr+intr v⟩ +*haben (fam)* SCHOOL
swot ◊ für einen Test pauken Englischvokabeln
pauken swot up on English vocabulary
pau·schal [pao'ʃaːl] ⟨adj⟩ *seldom comp/superl* **1.** FIN
(price, amount, reimbursement etc.) all-inclusive
ein pauschaler Betrag a lump sum **2.** *(statement,
assertion etc.)* sweeping; *(criticism, judgement)*
wholesale ◊ ein pauschales Urteil ⟨adv⟩ **1.** on an
all-inclusive basis, as a package ◊ Sie können ihren
Urlaub pauschal buchen. pauschal zahlen pay a
flat rate **2.** in general terms ◊ Dieses Thema lässt
sich nicht pauschal abhandeln. pauschal
behaupten, dass make the sweeping claim that
Pau·scha·le [pao'ʃaːlə] die <-, -n> **1.** flat rate ◊
eine wöchentliche Pauschale von 20 Euro zahlen
2. lump sum ◊ eine Pauschale für Porto und Verpa-

ckung erheben
Ⓩ **Pau·se** ['paozə] die <-, -n> **1.** break ◊ Eben hat
es zur Pause geklingelt.; *(in a play)* interval eine
Pause einlegen take/have a break Das Theater
macht im Sommer eine Pause. The theatre is
closed in summer. **2.** *(when talking)* pause,
pregnant pause ◊ Nach ihrer Rede trat eine Pause
des Schweigens ein. **3.** MUS rest **4.** *(tech)* tracing ◊
die Pause eines darunter liegenden Originals
5. photostat, photocopy
pau·sie·ren [pao'ziːrən] <pausiert, pausierte, hat
pausiert> ⟨intr v⟩ **1.** pause ◊ Ich bin außer Atem
und muss kurz pausieren. **2.** *(in sports)* be out of
action, sit out; *(artist)* take a break ◊ Die
Sängerin wollte zwei Jahre pausieren.
PDS [peːdeː|'ɛs] die *(abbr of* Partei des Demokrati-
schen Sozialismus*)* PDS

> Founded in the December of 1989, the *PDS* (Party
> of Democratic Socialism) was a product of the
> former East German *SED* Party (*Sozialistische Ein-
> heitspartei Deutschlands* — German Socialist
> Unity Party). In 2005 the PDS was renamed to
> „die Linkspartei". Situated towards the left of the
> political spectrum, the party makes a point of
> championing the cause of the former regions of
> the GDR that are lagging behind the rest of
> Germany in economic terms. The Party is also a
> member of the Forum of the New European Left.

Ⓩ **Pech** [pɛç] das <-(e)s, -e> **1.** *no pl* bad luck ◊
das Pech, sich in den Falschen zu verlieben
(großes) Pech haben be (very) unlucky ◊ Er hat
großes Pech bei der Prüfung gehabt. Pech gehabt!
tough!, unlucky! vom Pech verfolgt sein be dogged
by bad luck Pech für jdn that's just too bad for sb
2. *most sing* pitch ◊ Fugen mit Pech abdichten
◉ zusammenhalten wie Pech und Schwefel be
inseparable, stick together
Pe·dal [pe'daːl] das <-s, -e> pedal (fest/kräftig)
in die Pedale treten pedal (hard)
Pe·gel ['peːgl̩] der <-s, -> **1.** level ◊ Der Lärm hat
einen nicht mehr akzeptablen Pegel erreicht.
2. water level indicator ◊ den Wasserstand am
Pegel abrufen
pein·lich ['paenlɪç] ⟨adj⟩ **1.** embarrassing ◊ Seine
Antwort war eher peinlich als witzig. ♦ Wir sind
schockiert über ihr peinliches Benehmen. jdm ist
etw. peinlich sb finds sth embarrassing, sb is
embarrassed by sth **2.** meticulous ◊ In ihrem
Zimmer herrscht peinlichste Ordnung. ⟨adv⟩ **1.** jdn
peinlich berühren profoundly embarrass sb
2. peinlich genau meticulously ◊ die Anweisungen
des Arztes peinlich genau befolgen
◉ etw. peinlichst vermeiden take the utmost
pains to avoid sth
Peit·sche ['paetʃə] die <-, -n> whip ◊ Der
Dompteur knallte mit der Peitsche.
◉ mit Zuckerbrot und Peitsche *(fam)* with a
carrot and a stick
Pel·le ['pɛlə] die <-, -n> *(NorthG) (of sausages)*
skin; *(of potatoes)* jacket, peel ◊ Kartoffeln mit
Pelle essen; *(of eggs)* shell
◉ sich/jdm auf der Pelle hocken/sitzen *(fam)*
be on each other's backs/sb's back jdm auf die
Pelle rücken *(slang)* **1.** move in on sb **2.** crowd
sb ◊ Rück mir nicht so auf die Pelle — da ist doch

A B C D E F G H I J K L M N O P Q R S T U V W X Y Z

A
B
C
D
E
F
G
H
I
J
K
L
M
N
O

P

Q
R
S
T
U
V
W
X
Y
Z

Platz genug!

Pelz [pɛlts] der <–es, –e> **1.** pelt; *(of a large animal)* hide ⊝Fell **2.** fur ◊ *Er hat ihr einen Pelz gekauft.*
◉ **jdm eins auf den Pelz brennen** *(fam)* snipe at sb

Pen·del ['pɛndl̩] das <–s, –> PHYSICS pendulum

pen·deln ['pɛndl̩n] [intr v] +haben/sein **1.** +haben swing to and fro ◊ *die Arme locker pendeln lassen* an etw. [dat] pendeln swing on sth, dangle on sth ◊ *Die Ringe pendeln an den Seilen.* **2.** +sein *(person)* commute ◊ *zur Arbeit pendeln;* *(bus, train etc.)* run ◊ *Die Züge pendeln zwischen den beiden Städten.*

Pend·ler ['pɛndlɐ] der <–s, –>, **Pend·le·rin** ['pɛndlərɪn] die <–, –nen> commuter

Pen·ner ['pɛnɐ] der <–s, –>, **Pen·ne·rin** ['pɛnərɪn] die <–, –nen> *(fam, pej)* tramp, dosser

② **Pen·si·on** [paŋ'zi̯oːn, pã'zi̯oːn] die <–, –en> **1.** guest-house, boarding-house ◊ *eine Pension für Skitouristen* **2.** in Pension gehen retire in Pension sein be retired, be in retirement **3.** pension eine Pension beziehen draw a pension

② **pen·si·o·nie·ren** [paŋzi̯o'niːrən, pãzi̯o'niːrən] <wird pensioniert, wurde pensioniert, ist pensioniert worden> [tr v] *mostly passive* pensioniert werden retire ◊ *Er wurde schon mit 62 pensioniert.* jdn pensionieren pension sb off sich (vorzeitig) pensionieren lassen take (early) retirement

Pen·sum ['pɛnzʊm] das <–s, –sen or Pensa> **1.** quota (of work), stint ◊ *sein tägliches Pensum erledigen* **2.** *(oldf)* SCHOOL curriculum, syllabus

per [pɛr] [prep] [+acc] **1.** by ◊ *Ich sag dir per SMS Bescheid.* etw. per Nachnahme bestellen order sth cash-on-delivery per Anhalter fahren hitchhike, thumb a lift **2.** per Pfund/Kilo/Stück etc. per pound/kilo/unit etc. ◊ *Das Rindfleisch kostet 6,90 Euro per Kilo.* ⊝pro, je **3.** by the ... ◊ *Die Äpfel werden per Pfund und nicht einzeln verkauft.*
◉ **per sofort** immediately, as of now

② **per·fekt** [pɛr'fɛkt] [adj, adv] <perfekter, am perfektesten> perfect(ly) ◊ *Den perfekten Partner gibt es nicht.* ♦ *Dieser Wein ist perfekt als Dessertwein.* ♦ *Sie spricht perfekt Englisch.* [adj] **1.** *not before ns (fam)* complete ◊ *Der Umbau soll bis 2004 perfekt sein.;* *(sporting victory etc.)* sealed ◊ *Mit diesem Sieg war sein Einzug ins Finale perfekt.* **2.** *not before ns* TRADE finalized, a done deal ◊ *Nach kurzer Diskussion war der Kaufvertrag perfekt.* perfekt machen finalize

Per·fekt ['pɛrfɛkt] das <–s, –e> *most sing* perfect ◊ *ein Verb im Perfekt*

German speakers describe events that have happened in the past in everyday language by using the perfect tense. For example: *Erst sind wir ins Kino gegangen, und dann haben wir noch ein Bier getrunken.* The preterite, which also expresses past events, is only used in spoken German with auxiliary and modal verbs. In the written language, the perfect is becoming ever more frequent. In certain cases, it is also used to express future events. For example: *Ich denke, wir haben bald alle Zweifel beseitigt.* In this instance, the speaker suggests that there will soon no longer be any doubt.

Pe·ri·ode [pe'ri̯oːdə] die <–, –n> period ◊ *die gallo-römische Periode* ♦ *Sie hat ihre Periode.* ♦ *die Periode einer Sinusschwingung*

Per·le ['pɛrlə] die <–, –n> **1.** bead ◊ *Die Perlen meiner Kette sind aus Glas.* **2.** pearl ◊ *ein Ring mit einer echten Perle* **3.** *(fig)* gem, jewel ◊ *Dalmatien ist eine Perle an der Adria.* **4.** *(in wine)* bubble
◉ **Perlen vor die Säue werfen** *(fam, fig)* cast pearls before swine

② **Per·ron** [pɛ'rõː] der or das <–s, –s> *(Swiss, Austr)* platform ◊ *auf dem/am Perron auf den Zug warten*

Per·ser¹ ['pɛrzɐ] die <–, –> ZOO Persian cat

Per·ser² ['pɛrzɐ] der <–s, –> Persian carpet/rug

Per·ser³ ['pɛrzɐ] der <–s, –>, **Per·se·rin** ['pɛrzərɪn] die <–, –nen> Persian → Deutsche

② **Per·son** [pɛr'zoːn] die <–, –en> **1.** person ◊ *Der Bus fasst 40 Personen.* ♦ *Die erste Person Singular ist ,ich'.* **2.** ... in einer Person sein be ... rolled into one ◊ *Er war Hausmeister und Gärtner in einer Person.* **3.** LAW jdn zur Person vernehmen/befragen question sb concerning their identity **4.** THEAT Personen der Handlung characters, dramatis personae **5.** *(fam, pej)* woman
◉ **die eigene Person** *(lofty)* yourself ◊ *Angaben zur eigenen Person machen* in eigener Person *(form)* in person, personally in Person personified ◊ *Sie ist die Güte in Person.* der Teufel in Person the devil incarnate jd für seine Person *(lofty)* ich für meine Person I for my part er für seine Person as far as he was concerned he

Per·so·nal [pɛrzo'naːl] das <–s> *no pl* staff, personnel ◊ *Der Betrieb will weniger Personal beschäftigen.;* servants ◊ *Die Herrschaft ist aus und das Personal hat frei.* das fliegende Personal the flight personnel, the aircrew(s)

Per·so·nal·aus·weis [pɛrzo'naːlˌlaʊsvaɪs] der <–es, –e> identity card ◊ *den Personalausweis vorzeigen*

Per·so·na·li·e [pɛrzo'naːli̯ə] die <–, –n> **1.** item of personal information Personalien particulars ◊ *seine Personalien angeben* **2.** staff change

Per·so·nal·pro·no·men [pɛrzo'naːlˌpro,noːmən] das <–s, –> personal pronoun

Personal pronouns can refer to both people and objects. As a rule, these have appeared previously in the text, or are known as a result of the context: *Die Tat war so grausam, dass* sie *alle schockiert waren.* (The crime was so cruel that they were all shocked.); *Der Mörder wurde festgenommen;* er *gestand sofort.* (The murderer was apprehended; he confessed immediately.); *Das Opfer war sofort tot.* Es *ist noch nicht identifiziert worden.* (The victim died at once. It has still not been possible to identify him/her.)

per·so·nell [pɛrzo'nɛl] *(form)* [adj] *no comp/superl* staff, personnel ◊ *Im Unternehmen gibt es personelle Veränderungen.* [adv] in terms of staff/personnel personell aufstocken take on more staff etw. personell verstärken increase staff numbers at/of sth

Per·so·nen·kraft·wa·gen [pɛr'zoːnənkraftvaːgn̩] der <–s, –> *(form) (abbr Pkw)* (private) car

② **per·sön·lich** [pɛr'zøːnlɪç] [adj] **1.** personal ◊ *Der Pfarrer findet für jeden ein persönliches Wort.* ♦ *Diese Bemerkung war mir zu persönlich.* **2.** GRAM

persönliches Fürwort personal pronoun [adv] personally ◊ *Sie setzt sich persönlich für mich ein.* ♦ *Er haftet persönlich für Schäden.* ♦ *Die Einladungskarten waren sehr persönlich gestaltet.*

Per·sön·lich·keit [pɛrˈzøːnlɪçkaet] die <-, -en> **1.** personality *eine (echte/schwache/starke) Persönlichkeit* a (real/weak/strong) personality **2.** person(ality) ◊ *eine berühmte Persönlichkeit* eine Persönlichkeit des öffentlichen Lebens a public figure

Pers·pek·ti·ve [pɛrˈspɛktiːvə] die <-, -n> **1.** (also fig) perspective *aus einer Perspektive* from a perspective **2.** prospect ◊ *berufliche Perspektiven im Ausland* neue Perspektiven new prospects; *(in scientific research)* new horizons

Pe·rü·cke [peˈrʏkə] die <-, -n> wig

per·vers [pɛrˈvɛrs] [adj] <perverser, am perversesten> **1.** MED perverted ◊ *eine perverse Sexualität* ♦ *Ich bin doch nicht pervers!* **2.** (fam, pej) scandalous ◊ *Es ist pervers, wie viel Geld für Rüstung ausgegeben wird!* [adv] MED pervers veranlagt sein be of a perverted disposition, have a perversion

Pest [pɛst] die <-> *no pl; mostly with the article* plague ◊ *Die Pest raffte viele Menschen dahin.*
⊛ jdn/etw. wie die Pest hassen *(fam)* loathe sb/sth, detest sb/sth **wie die Pest stinken** *(slang)* stink to high heaven

Pe·ter·si·lie [peteˈziːljə] die <-, -n> parsley

pet·zen [ˈpɛtsn̩] (kidsp, pej) [intr v] +haben tell tales ◊ *Meist petzt sie nur über ihre Mitschülerinnen.* [tr v] +haben (jdm) etw. petzen go and tell (sb) sth ◊ *Wehe, du petzt das Mama!*

Pfad [pfaːt] der <-(e)s, -e> **1.** path ◊ *Ein enger Pfad führte durch das Gebüsch.* **2.** (fig) direction *neue Pfade betreten* take a new direction
⊛ vom Pfad der Tugend abkommen/abweichen *(lofty, fig)* wander from the straight and narrow

Pfahl [pfaːl] der <-(e)s, Pfähle> **1.** post ◊ *einen Pfahl in den Boden treiben* **2.** pillar ◊ *Das Dach wurde durch Pfähle gestützt.*; *(of a bridge)* pier

Pfand [pfant] das <-(e)s, Pfänder> **1.** (a) deposit ◊ *ein Pfand auf Bierflaschen* ♦ *für etw. Pfand hinterlegen* Pfand für etw. bezahlen pay a deposit on sth **2.** security *etw. in Pfand nehmen* take sth as security

pfän·den [ˈpfɛndn̩] <pfändet, pfändete, hat gepfändet> [tr v] **1.** etw. pfänden seize sth (under distress) ◊ *Man hat ihr die Möbel gepfändet.* jds Lohn pfänden levy attachment of earnings on sb **2.** jdn pfänden get the bailiffs onto sb

ⓩ **Pfan·ne** [ˈpfanə] die <-, -n> (frying) pan ◊ *ein Steak in der Pfanne braten*
⊛ jdn in die Pfanne hauen do sb down

ⓩ **Pfann·ku·chen** [ˈpfankuːxn̩] der <-s, -> pancake

Pfar·rer [ˈpfarɐ] der <-s, ->, **Pfar·re·rin** [ˈpfarərɪn] die <-, -nen> **1.** priest, vicar ◊ *Er wollte Pfarrer werden.* ♦ *eine protestantische Pfarrerin* **2.** (title) Herr/Frau Pfarrer … the Reverend …

ⓩ **Pfef·fer** [ˈpfɛfɐ] der <-s> *no pl* pepper ◊ *den Eintopf mit Pfeffer und Salz abschmecken*
⊛ **Pfeffer im Arsch** *(rude)* gusto, pizazz **bleiben/ hingehen, wo der Pfeffer wächst** *(fam)* go to hell **jdn dorthin schicken, wo der Pfeffer wächst** *(fam)* tell sb to get lost

Pfei·fe [ˈpfaefə] die <-, -n> **1.** pipe ◊ *sich eine Pfeife anzünden* Pfeife rauchen be a pipe smoker

2. (slang) useless prat, loser ⊖Flasche
⊛ jdn/etw. in der Pfeife rauchen können *(fam)* forget about sb/sth **nach jds Pfeife tanzen** dance to sb's tune

pfei·fen [ˈpfaefn̩] <pfeift, pfiff, hat/ist gepfiffen> [tr+intr v] +haben whistle ◊ *Er pfeift nach seinem Hund.* ♦ *eine Melodie pfeifen; (bird)* sing [intr v] +haben/sein **1.** +haben (lungs etc.) wheeze **2.** +sein (projectile) whistle, whizz ◊ *Plötzlich pfiff ihm eine Kugel um die Ohren.*
⊛ etw./jd pfeift aus dem letzten Loch → Loch **auf jdn/etw. pfeifen** *(fam)* not give a damn about sb/sth **jdm eins pfeifen** *(fam)* give sb a piece of your mind

Pfeil [pfael] der <-(e)s, -e> arrow ◊ *Der Pfeil traf ihn im Rücken.* ♦ *den roten Pfeilen folgen*
⊛ grüner Pfeil *(at traffic lights)* filter, green filter arrow **so schnell wie ein Pfeil** as quick as lightning

Pfei·ler [ˈpfaelɐ] der <-s, -> *(also fig)* pillar ◊ *Vier Pfeiler stützen die Decke.* ♦ *die Informationsfreiheit als Pfeiler der Demokratie; (of a bridge)* pier

Pfen·nig [ˈpfɛnɪç] der <-s, -e> *pl 'Pfennig' when used with figures* pfennig ◊ *Früher kostete eine Kugel Eis 50 Pfennig.*
⊛ wer den Pfennig nicht ehrt, ist des Talers nicht wert **1.** who needs not a penny will never have many **2.** take care of the pennies and the pounds will look after themselves **auf den Pfennig genau** correct to the last penny **keinen Pfennig mehr haben** be penniless **jeden Pfennig umdrehen** think twice about every penny you spend

Pferd [pfeːɐt] das <-(e)s, -e> horse ◊ *auf einem Pferd reiten* zu Pferde on horseback
⊛ das beste/unser bestes Pferd im Stall sein *(fam)* be the/our number one (man) *(car etc.)* be the/our number one seller **die Pferde scheu machen 1.** frighten the horses **2.** *(fam)* unsettle people **wie ein Pferd arbeiten** work like a Trojan **keine zehn Pferde bringen jdn dazu, etw. zu tun** *(fam)* wild horses wouldn't make sb do sth **mit jdm kann man Pferde stehlen** *(fam)* sb is game for anything **ich glaub, mich tritt ein Pferd** *(fam)* well, I'm damned; stone me

Pfer·de·schwanz [ˈpfeːɐdəʃvants] der <-es, Pferdeschwänze> **1.** horse's tail **2.** ponytail ◊ *Ihr Haar ist zu einem Pferdeschwanz gebunden.*

Pfer·de·stär·ke [ˈpfeːɐdəʃtɛrkə] die <-, -n> TECHN *(abbr PS)* horsepower

pfiff [pfɪf] pret of pfeifen

Pfiff [pfɪf] der <-(e)s, -e> **1.** whistle ◊ *der Pfiff des Schiedsrichters* **2.** *(fam)* style, flair ◊ *Du solltest dich mit mehr Pfiff kleiden.* einer Sache [dat] fehlt der (letzte) Pfiff sth lacks that little something

Pfif·fer·ling [ˈpfɪfɐlɪŋ] der <-s, -e> chanterelle
⊛ keinen Pfifferling *(fam)* not/nothing at all ◊ *Sie kümmert sich keinen Pfifferling um Modetrends.*

pfif·fig [ˈpfɪfɪç] [adj, adv] **1.** smart(ly) ◊ *pfiffige Ideen* ♦ *Der Junge ist kreativ und pfiffig.* ♦ *pfiffig gestaltete Software; (laugh etc.)* knowing(ly) ◊ *ein pfiffiges Lachen* **2.** smart(ly), neat(ly) ◊ *eine pfiffige Frisur* ♦ *ein pfiffig gebundener Schal*

Pfings·ten [ˈpfɪŋstn̩] *seldom with definite article*

'das' (zu/an) Pfingsten (at) Whitsun

Pfir·sich ['pfɪrˈzɪç] der <-s, -e> peach

② **Pflan·ze** ['pflantsə] die <-, -n> plant ◇ eine Pflanze gießen

pflan·zen ['pflantsn̩] ⓣⓥ +haben **1.** plant ◇ einen Baum pflanzen **2.** implant ◇ Dem Tier wurde ein Chip unter die Haut gepflanzt. ⓡⓔⓕⓥ +haben (fam) sich irgendwohin pflanzen plonk yourself down somewhere

② **Pflas·ter** ['pflastɐ] das <-s, -> **1.** plaster ◇ ein Pflaster auf eine Wunde kleben **2.** (road) surface ◇ Pflaster verlegen

ⓔ **ein gefährliches/heißes/teures Pflaster** (fam) a dangerous/an exciting/expensive place

② **Pflau·me** ['pflaʊmə] die <-, -n> **1.** plum getrocknete Pflaume prune **2.** (fam, fig, pej) pillock ◇ Dieser Pflaume solltest du keine Träne nachweinen! **3.** (rude) fanny, pussy

Pfle·ge ['pfleːgə] die <-> no pl **1.** (of patients, old people, animals) care ◇ die Pflege von Schwerkranken jdn/ein Tier in Pflege/zur Pflege geben ask sb to look after sb/an animal jdn/ein Tier in Pflege/zur Pflege nehmen/haben look after sb/an animal; (for a longer period) ein Kind in Pflege nehmen/haben foster a child **2.** (of machines) maintenance, upkeep ◇ Die Lebensdauer eines Autos steigt bei guter Pflege. **3.** (of languages, art, relationships) fostering ◇ die Pflege von Minderheitssprachen **4.** (animal, plant) viel/wenig Pflege brauchen need a lot of/ little attention

② **pfle·gen** ['pfleːgn̩] ⓣⓥ +haben **1.** look after, care for ◇ Sie pflegt ihre kranke Mutter. **2.** jdn/ ein Tier gesund pflegen nurse sb/an animal back to health **3.** (your skin, teeth) look after; (a vehicle) maintain ◇ das Auto mit Wachs pflegen **4.** (plants, the garden) tend **5.** (interests, relationships, contacts, a cooperation, sciences) maintain ◇ Der Vater pflegt eine liebevolle Beziehung zu seinen Kindern. ✦ Kontakte pflegen **6.** (lofty) etw. zu tun pflegen be accustomed to do ◇ Samstags pflegte sie in die Oper zu gehen. ⓡⓔⓕⓥ +haben sich pflegen take care of yourself, pamper yourself

Pfle·ger ['pfleːgɐ] der <-s, ->, **Pfle·ge·rin** ['pfleːgərɪn] die <-, -nen> **1.** (male) nurse, carer ◇ Er ist Pfleger von Beruf. ✦ von einer Pflegerin betreut werden **2.** (for animals) carer, keeper

② **Pflicht** [pflɪçt] die <-, -en> **1.** duty ◇ Es ist ihre Pflicht, die Kinder zur Schule zu bringen. **2.** no pl Pflicht sein be compulsory etw. zur Pflicht machen make sth compulsory sich zur Pflicht machen, etw. zu tun take it upon yourself to do sth etw. ist jds Pflicht und Schuldigkeit sth is sb's bounden duty to do **3.** SPORT compulsory exercises

ⓔ **die Pflicht ruft** duty calls

pflü·cken ['pflʏkn̩] ⓣⓥ +haben pick ◇ Unterwegs hatte er ihr Blumen gepflückt. sich (dat) etw. pflücken pick sth (for yourself), pick your own sth

Pfor·te ['pfɔrtə] die <-, -n> gate ◇ Ein eiserne Pforte führte in das Kloster.; (of a theatre etc.) door

ⓔ **seine Pforten öffnen/schließen** (lofty, fig) open/close your gates/doors (business, enterprise) start trading/shut up shop

Pfört·ner ['pfœrtnɐ] der <-s, ->, **Pfört·ne·rin** ['pfœrtnərɪn] die <-, -nen> doorman ◇ Ein Paket wurde beim Pförtner abgegeben. ✦ Sie ist Pförtnerin im Krankenhaus.

Pfo·te ['pfoːtə] die <-, -n> **1.** paw ◇ Der Hund leckte seine Pfoten sauber. Pfote geben offer its paw „Gib Pfote!" "Give me your paw!" **2.** (fam, pej) mitt ◇ Wasch dir die Pfoten!

ⓔ **sich** (dat) **die Pfoten verbrennen** (fam) **1.** burn your hand **2.** burn your fingers **Pfoten weg** (fam) hands off

pfui [pfʊi] ⓘⓝⓣⓔⓡⓙ (fam) **1.** pfui (Teufel) ugh, yuck **2.** tut, tut ◇ Du hast wieder gelogen. Pfui, schäm dich!

ⓔ **außen hui und innen pfui** good on the outside, bad on the inside

Pfund [pfʊnt] das <-(e)s, -e> pl 'Pfund' when used with figures **1.** pound ◇ ein Pfund Mehl abwiegen **2.** no pl (abbr £) pound ◇ Das kostet vier Pfund.

ⓔ **mit seinen Pfunden wuchern** (lofty) make the most of your capabilities, show yourself to advantage

pfu·schen ['pfʊʃn̩] ⓘⓝⓣⓡⓥ +haben (fam, pej) **1.** do a botched job ◇ Der Arzt pfuschte bei der Operation. **2.** cheat ◇ Bei der gestrigen Deutsch-Klausur haben die Schüler gepfuscht. **3.** (Austr) do work on the sly ◇ nebenbei am Wochenende pfuschen

Pfüt·ze ['pfʏtsə] die <-, -n> puddle

Phan·tom [fanˈtoːm] das <-s, -e> **1.** phantom ◇ Ein Phantom geht um. **2.** invention, figment of the imagination ◇ das Phantom der Freiheit

ⓔ **einem Phantom nachjagen** chase after shadows

Phan·tom·bild [fanˈtoːmbɪlt] das <-(e)s, -er> Identikit (picture) ◇ ein Phantombild zeichnen/veröffentlichen

Pho·to·... ['foːtoː] → Foto...

Phra·se ['fraːzə] die <-, -n> **1.** (pej) cliché ◇ zur Phrase verkommen eine hohle/leere Phrase an empty phrase, empty words ◇ Das ist keine leere Phrase, sondern ehrlich gemeint. **2.** LING phrase

ⓔ **Phrasen dreschen** (pej) come out with clichés

② **Phy·sik** [fyˈziːk] die <-> no pl physics ◇ die experimentelle Physik ✦ Sie studiert im 7. Semester Physik.

Phy·si·ker ['fyːzɪkɐ] der <-s, ->, **Phy·si·ke·rin** ['fyːzɪkərɪn] die <-, -nen> physicist ◇ Er ist Physiker von Beruf. ✦ eine berühmte Physikerin Sie ist promovierte Physikerin. She's got a PhD in physics.

phy·sisch ['fyːzɪʃ] ⓐⓓⓙ, ⓐⓓⓥ no comp/superl; when used as an adj, only before ns physical(ly) ◇ verbale und physische Attacken ✦ Die physische Kondition des Sportlers war schlecht. ✦ Sie war physisch sehr angeschlagen. ⓔpsychisch

Pi·ckel ['pɪkl̩] der <-s, -> **1.** MED spot, zit ◇ Er hat viele Pickel im Gesicht. **2.** pickaxe, pickax ◇ Mit Seil und Pickel machten sich die Bergsteiger auf den Weg.; ice axe, ice-ax ◇ mit dem Pickel ein Loch ins Eis schlagen

② **Pick·nick** ['pɪknɪk] das <-s, -s> picnic ◇ Wir machten ein Picknick auf der Wiese.

piep·sen ['piːpsn̩] ⓘⓝⓣⓡⓥ +haben (mouse) squeak;

(bird) cheep; *(watch, mobile phone etc.)* beep
[tr v] +*haben* squeak ◊ „Nein", piepste das Kind.
Pik [piːk] das <-s, -> **1.** *no pl* spades ◊ *Pik war
Trumpf.* **2.** *(individual card)* spade ◊ *Er spielte
ein kleines Pik aus.*
pi·kant [pi'kant] [adj] <pikanter, am pikantesten>
1. savoury, savory ◊ *Pfannkuchen mit pikanter
Füllung*; spicy ◊ *Die Soße ist sehr pikant.* ⊖herzhaft
2. *(fig) (situation)* risqué ◊ *Der Minister war in eine
pikante Affäre verwickelt.; (details)* juicy [adv] with/
in spices pikant gewürzt spicy
pil·gern ['pɪlgen] [intr v] +*sein (also fig)* irgendwohin pilgern go on/make a pilgrimage somewhere ◊
Sie pilgerten nach Rom.
② **Pil·le** ['pɪlə] die <-, –n> **1.** pill, tablet ◊ *Pillen
schlucken* ♦ *eine Pille gegen Haarausfall* **2.** *no pl*
die Pille the pill ◊ *Nimmt sie die Pille?*
Pils [pɪls] das <-, -> pils(ner) ◊ *Er hatte vier Pils
getrunken.*
② **Pilz** [pɪlts] der <-es, –e> **1.** mushroom, fungus ◊
Ist dieser Pilz essbar/giftig? **2.** BIO mould, mold ◊
Hefe ist ein einzelliger Pilz. **3.** *no pl (fam)* MED
fungal infection ◊ *Für den Juckreiz ist ein Pilz verantwortlich.*
◉ **wie Pilze aus dem Boden/der Erde schießen**
spring up like mushrooms
pink [pɪŋk] [adj, adv] *invariable; when used as an
adj, not before ns* (bright/shocking) pink ◊ *Das
Kleid war pink.* ♦ *ein pink gestrichener Container*
Pin·sel ['pɪnzl] der <-s, -> brush
pin·seln ['pɪnzln] [tr+intr v] +*haben (fam)* paint ◊
Sie pinselte weiße Farbe auf die Wand. ♦ *Pinselst
du immer noch?*
Pin·zet·te [pɪn'tsɛtə] die <-, –n> tweezers ◊ *Er
entfernte den Stachel mit einer Pinzette.*
Pi·o·nier [pio'niːɐ] der <-s, –e>, **Pi·o·nie·rin**
[pio'niːrɪn] die <-, –nen> **1.** pioneer ◊ *Er war ein
Pionier der modernen Physik.* **2.** MIL sapper,
engineer **3.** HIST *member of a Communist youth
organization for children aged between 6 and 14 in
the GDR* ◊ *In seiner Jugend war er Pionier.*
pis·sen ['pɪsn] *(rude)* [intr v] +*haben* piss ◊ *pissen
müssen* [imp v] +*haben* es pisst it's pissing down ◊
Es pisst schon den ganzen Tag. ⊖regnen
Pis·ta·zie [pɪs'taːtsjə] die <-, –n> pistachio ◊
gesalzene/geröstete Pistazien
Pis·te ['pɪstə] die <-, –n> **1.** piste ◊ *eine vereiste
Piste* **2.** racetrack ◊ *Der Fahrer kam von der Piste
ab.* **3.** runway ◊ *Das Flugzeug hob von der Piste
ab.*
Pkw ['peːkaːveː, – – '–] der *(abbr of* Personenkraftwagen*)* car
plä·die·ren [plɛ'diːrən] <plädiert, plädierte, hat
plädiert> [intr v] **1.** *(lofty)* für etw. plädieren argue
for sth, speak in favour of sth, speak in favor of
sth ◊ *Sie plädierte für eine einvernehmliche
Lösung.* **2.** LAW (für/auf) etw. [acc] plädieren plead
sth ◊ *Er plädierte (auf) nicht schuldig. Der Anwalt
plädierte für/auf Freispruch.* The lawyer asked the
court to find the defendant not guilty.
Plä·do·yer [plɛdoaˈjeː] das <-s, –s> **1.** LAW
summing up, final speech ◊ *Der Anwalt hielt ein
beeindruckendes Plädoyer.* **2.** *(lofty, fig)* ein
Plädoyer für etw. a speech in favour of sth, a
speech in favor of sth
Pla·ge ['plaːgə] die <-, –n> nuisance ◊ *Zur Zeit

sind die Wespen eine echte Plage.; chore ◊ Früher
war das Wäschewaschen eine rechte Plage.* eine/
seine Plage mit etw./jdm haben struggle with sth/
sb, have problems with sth/sb
pla·gen ['plaːgn] [tr v] +*haben* torment ◊ *Schreckliche Kopfschmerzen plagten sie.* ♦ *Er wurde von
Zweifeln geplagt. Plagt dich etwa schon der
Hunger?* Are you hungry yet? ⊖quälen [ref v]
+*haben* sich (mit etw./jdm) plagen struggle (with
sth/sb) ◊ *Sie plagte sich mit einer Grippe.*
Pla·kat [plaˈkaːt] das <-(e)s, –e> poster, bill ◊ *ein
Plakat aufhängen*
pla·ka·tiv [plakaˈtiːf] [adj, adv] *(lofty)* striking(ly) ◊
ein plakatives Beispiel ♦ *Die Aussage war sehr
plakativ.* ♦ *Die Missstände wurden im Film plakativ
dargestellt.*
Pla·ket·te [plaˈkɛtə] die <-, –n> **1.** sticker, badge
◊ *eine Plakette an/auf etw.* [dat] anbringen
2. plaque ◊ *Eine Plakette erinnert an den Besuch
des Präsidenten.*
② **Plan** [plaːn] der <-(e)s, Pläne> **1.** plan ◊ *ein raffinierter Plan* ♦ *Es lief alles genau nach Plan.* ♦ *Er
legte die Pläne zum Umbau des Gebäudes vor.*
einen Plan fassen make a plan Pläne schmieden
make plans **2.** auf dem Plan stehen be on the
agenda **3.** map ◊ *Die Haltestellen sind im Plan eingezeichnet.*
Pla·ne ['plaːnə] die <-, –n> tarpaulin ◊ *Er breitete
eine Plane auf dem Boden aus.*
② **pla·nen** ['plaːnən] [tr v] +*haben* plan ◊ *Die beiden
Banken planten eine Fusion.* ♦ *alles bis ins letzte
Detail planen* ♦ *Er hat, wie geplant, im Mai seine
Prüfungen abgelegt.*
plan·mä·ßig ['plaːnmɛːsɪç] [adj] *only before ns*
scheduled ◊ *Wann wird die planmäßige Übergabe
erfolgen?; as planned ◊ die planmäßige Durchführung der Aktion* [adv] according to plan, as planned
◊ *Alles verlief planmäßig.*; on schedule ◊ *Das
Flugzeug landete planmäßig um 13 Uhr.*
Plan·stel·le ['plaːnʃtɛlə] die <-, –n> established
post ◊ *neue Planstellen schaffen*
Pla·nung ['plaːnʊŋ] die <-, –en> planning ◊
*Welche Faktoren müssen bei der Planung berück-
sichtigt werden?; plan ◊ Die Planungen für die
Olympiade laufen auf Hochtouren.*
plap·pern ['plapen] [intr v] +*haben (fam)*
1. chatter away ◊ *Das Kind plapperte fröhlich vor
sich hin.* **2.** *(pej)* babble ◊ *Was plappert er da die
ganze Zeit ins Mikrofon?* Unsinn plappern talk
nonsense
plär·ren ['plɛrən] [tr+intr v] +*haben (pej)* shout,
bawl ◊ *Alle plärrten durcheinander.* ♦ *Hör auf zu
plärren, so schlimm war das nicht!; (baby)* bawl,
scream; *(radio, loudspeaker)* blare
② **Plas·tik**[1] ['plastɪk] das <-s> *no pl* plastic ◊ *Cam-
pinggeschirr aus Plastik.* ♦ *in Plastik verpackte
Waren*
Plas·tik[2] ['plastɪk] die <-, –en> sculpture ◊
Plastiken von Rodin ♦ *Kunstwerke aus den
Bereichen Malerei und Plastik*
Plas·tik·tü·te ['plastɪktyːtə] die <-, –n> plastic
bag, carrier bag
plas·tisch ['plastɪʃ] [adj] **1.** *only before ns* plastic
◊ *Er ist Experte für plastische Chirurgie.* plasti-
sches Gestalten sculpture das plastische Werk
eines Künstlers an artist's sculptures **2.** three-

dimensional ◊ *eine starke plastische Wirkung erzielen* ⊖räumlich **3.** *(fig)* vivid, graphic ◊ *plastische Beispiele/Erklärungen* ⊖anschaulich [adv] **1.** in 3-D ◊ *etw. plastisch darstellen* ⊖räumlich **2.** *(fig)* vividly, graphically ◊ *Er schilderte das Geschehen sehr plastisch.* ⊖anschaulich

plät·schern ['plɛtʃen] [intr v] +*haben/sein* **1.** +*haben* splash ◊ *Man hörte die Wellen leise plätschern.* **2.** +*sein* irgendwohin plätschern splash somewhere, flow somewhere ◊ *Das Wasser plätscherte in die Wanne.* **3.** +*haben* splash about ◊ *Die Kinder plätscherten am Brunnen.* **4.** +*sein* *(fig)* etw. plätschert vor sich [acc] hin sth flows by

platt [plat] [adj] <*platter, am plattesten*> **1.** flat ◊ *Um das Haus herum war nur plattes Land.* ♦ *Sein linkes Vorderrad war platt.* etw. platt drücken/ walzen etc. flatten sth, squash sth (flat) **2.** *(pej, fig)* *(jokes, comments)* stupid, banal ◊ *platte Sprüche/Witze* **3.** platt sein be amazed ◊ *Du bist schwanger? Da bin ich aber platt!* **4.** platt sein be exhausted, be done in ◊ *Abends bin ich meistens total platt.* ⊖fertig, kaputt [adv] (in) Low German ◊ *platt sprechen*

platt·deutsch ['platdɔɣtʃ] [adj] *mostly before ns* Low German → deutsch

Platt·deutsch ['platdɔɣtʃ] das <-(s)> *no pl* Low German → Deutsch

② **Plat·te** ['platə] die <-, -n> **1.** board ◊ *eine Platte aus Holz; (of a table)* top **2.** hotplate ◊ *ein Herd mit vier Platten* **3.** record **4.** platter ◊ *eine Platte mit Häppchen*

⊛ eine kalte Platte a cold platter

Plat·ten·bau ['platn̩baʊ] der <-(e)s, -ten> *building made of precast concrete slabs*

Plat·ten·spie·ler ['platn̩ʃpiːlɐ] der <-s, -> record player

② **Platz** [plats] der <-es, Plätze> **1.** *no pl* Platz (für etw./jdn) room (for sth/sb), space (for sth/sb) ◊ *Im Koffer war kein Platz mehr.* ♦ *Die Wohnung bot genug Platz für zwei Personen.* ♦ *Die Autos machten für den Krankenwagen Platz.* ⊖Raum **2.** place ◊ *Seiner Meinung nach war ihr Platz am Herd.* ♦ *ein Platz im Kindergarten* An welchen Platz wollt ihr das neue Sofa stellen? Where are you going to put the new sofa? **3.** seat ◊ *Ist dieser Platz noch frei?* ♦ *Alle erhoben sich von ihren Plätzen.* Platz nehmen sit down **4.** *(in a race, competition)* place ◊ *Er gewann den dritten Platz.* **5.** square ◊ *Vor dem Theater ist ein großer Platz mit einem Brunnen.* **6.** SPORT field ◊ *Nach dem Regen war der Platz recht matschig.; (for football also)* pitch jdn vom Platz verweisen send sb off the field/pitch ⊖Feld **7.** auf die Plätze, fertig, los on your marks, get set, go **8.** Platz! Sit! **9.** Platz da! Make way!, Stand aside!

⊛ fehl am Platz(e) **1.** inappropriate **2.** out of place jdn vom Platz fegen SPORT thrash sb, wipe the floor with sb

Plätz·chen ['plɛtsçən] das <-s, -> biscuit, cookie

plat·zen ['platsn̩] [intr v] +*sein* **1.** burst ◊ *Der Luftballon platzte mit einem lauten Knall.* **2.** *(fig)* vor etw. [dat] platzen be bursting with sth ◊ *Ich platze gleich vor Neid.* **3.** *(fam, fig)* fall through ◊ *Die Verhandlungen sind leider geplatzt.; (engagement)* be off ◊ *Ihre Verlobung ist geplatzt.; (appointment, event)* be cancelled; *(dreams, hopes)* be shattered

etw. platzen lassen cancel sth; *(cheque)* bounce sth **4.** *(fam)* in etw. [acc] platzen burst into sth ◊ *Ohne zu klopfen platzte er in mein Zimmer.*

plat·zie·ren [pla'tsiːrən] <platziert, platzierte, hat platziert> [tr v] **1.** put, place, position ◊ *Sollten wir das Bild nicht weiter links platzieren?* **2.** SPORT *(a ball, shot)* aim ein platzierter Schuss a well-aimed shot [ref v] SPORT sich irgendwo platzieren be placed somewhere sich nicht platzieren können be unplaced die an letzter Stelle platzierte Mannschaft the bottom team

Platz·kar·te ['platskaɐtə] die <-, -n> ticket, seat ◊ *Alle Platzkarten waren ausverkauft, es gab nur noch Stehplätze.*

Platz·wun·de ['platsvʊndə] die <-, -n> abrasion, cut ◊ *Er hatte eine Platzwunde am Kopf.*

plau·dern ['plaʊdɐn] [intr v] +*haben* talk, chat ◊ *Wir plauderten über das Wetter.* (mit jdm) plaudern have a chat (with sb)

plei·te ['plaɪtə] [adj] pleite sein be broke; *(business, company)* be bankrupt

Plei·te ['plaɪtə] die <-, -n> *(fam)* **1.** bankruptcy ◊ *Der Firma drohte die Pleite.* Pleite gehen/machen go bankrupt, go bust ⊖Bankrott **2.** *(fig)* flop, letdown ◊ *Die Reform stellte sich als Pleite heraus.* ♦ *Was sagt der Torwart zu der Pleite gegen Bayern München?* ⊖Reinfall

Ple·nar·saal [ple'naːɐzaːl] der <-(e)s, Plenarsäle> plenary chamber ◊ *der Plenarsaal des Deutschen Bundestags*

Plom·be ['plɔmbə] die <-, -n> **1.** (lead) seal **2.** MED *(in a tooth)* filling

② **plötz·lich** ['plœtslɪç] [adj, adv] *when used as an adj, mostly before ns* sudden(ly) ◊ *Sein plötzlicher Tod überraschte uns.* ♦ *Sein Entschluss war sehr plötzlich.* ♦ *Plötzlich fing es zu regnen an.* ♦ *Sie starb sehr plötzlich.*

plump [plʊmp] *(pej)* [adj, adv] <plumper, am plumpesten> crude(ly) ◊ *Die Fälschung war ziemlich plump.* ♦ *eine plump gestrickte Geschichte*; heavy-handed(ly) ◊ *eine plumpe Anmache* ♦ *Ich finde, er verhielt sich zu plump.* [adj] **1.** heavy ◊ *Sein Körper wirkte ziemlich plump.* ♦ *Sie trug plumpe Schuhe.* **2.** awkward, ungainly ◊ *Sie hatte einen plumpen Gang.*

plump·sen ['plʊmpsn̩] [intr v] +*sein* fall ◊ *Der Stein plumpste ins Wasser.* Er ließ sich auf das Sofa plumpsen. He threw himself onto the sofa.

plün·dern ['plʏndɐn] [tr+intr v] +*haben* plunder, loot ◊ *Die Soldaten plünderten die eroberte Stadt.* [tr v] +*haben* (bum, fig) raid ◊ *Die Gäste plünderten das Büffet.*

Plu·ral ['pluːraːl] der <-s, -e> plural ◊ *Was ist der Plural von „Kaktus?"* ⊖Mehrzahl ⊖Singular, Einzahl

The plural endings in German are: **-e** *(das Bein, die Beine)*, **-er** *(das Bild, die Bilder)*, **-n** *(die Fackel, die Fackeln)*, **-en** *(die Frau, die Frauen)* and **-s** *(das Radio, die Radios)*. Sometimes, though, there is no plural ending at all *(der Bewohner, die Bewohner)*, or an umlaut *(der Mann, die Männer)*, or some other irregular form *(der Bau, die Bauten)*. For this reason, it is best to learn the plural forms of nouns at the same time as you learn the nouns.

plus[1] [plʊs] [adv] **1.** plus ◊ *eine Zahl zwischen minus drei und plus drei* ♦ *zwei Grad plus* ⊜minus **2.** SCHOOL *indicates the top end of a grade or mark* ◊ *Er hat eine Drei plus im Test.* ⊜minus *box@* Note

plus[2] [plʊs] [conjunc] MATH plus ◊ *Fünf plus drei ist gleich acht.* ⊜und ⊜minus

Plus [plʊs] das <-> *no pl* **1.** profit ◊ *Sie hat bei diesem Geschäft ein Plus gemacht.*; *(bank account)* im Plus sein to be in the black **2.** plus, advantage ◊ *Sein Plus ist seine Auslandserfahrung.* ⊜Vorteil

Plus·quam·per·fekt ['plʊskvampɛ'fɛkt] das <-s, -e> pluperfect, past perfect

The pluperfect or past perfect is the form of a verb that expresses all actions, processes and states that were completed before a particular point in the past. Generally, it refers to a point in the past which precedes that referred to by the perfect or imperfect tenses: *Nachdem das Gebäude gebaut worden war, stand es noch ein Jahr leer* (After the building had been built, it stood empty for a year).

PLZ [pe:ʔɛl'tsɛt, 'pɔstlaɛttsa:l] die *(abbr of* Postleitzahl*)* postcode, Zip code ◊ *Wohnort: Burghausen; PLZ: 84489*

⑦ **Pneu** [pnɔʏ] der <-s, -s> *(Swiss)* tyre ◊ *Haben die Pneus genügend Profil?*

Po [po:] der <-s, -s> *(fam)* backside, bum ◊ *Sie stürzte und landete auf dem Po.* ⊜Hintern

po·chen ['pɔxn] [intr v] +*haben* **1.** pound, throb ◊ *Sein Herz pochte heftig.* **2.** an etw. [acc] pochen knock on sth ◊ *Sie pochte ans Fenster/an die Tür.* ⊜klopfen **3.** *(fig)* auf etw. [acc] pochen insist on sth ◊ *Er pochte auf seinen Vertrag.* [imp v] +*haben* es pocht there is a knock

Po·cken ['pɔkṇ] die <-> *only pl* smallpox ◊ *an Pocken erkranken*

Po·dest [po'dɛst] das *or seldom* der <-(e)s, -e> podium, platform, pedestal ◊ *Der Redner stand auf einem Podest.*

Po·di·um ['po:diʊm] das <-s, Podien> podium, platform ◊ *Die Diskussionsteilnehmer saßen auf dem Podium.*

Po·e·sie [poe'zi:] die <-, -> *no pl* poetry ◊ *romantische/japanische Poesie* ⊜Lyrik ⊜Prosa

Poin·te ['pɔɛ̃tə, po'ɛ̃:tə] die <-, -n> punchline ◊ *Er hat die Pointe des Witzes nicht verstanden.*

Po·kal [po'ka:l] der <-s, -e> **1.** *(trophy)* cup ◊ *Der Sportpräsident übergab ihr den Pokal.* **2.** *(competition)* Cup ◊ *Die Mannschaft hat den Pokal gewonnen.* **3.** goblet ◊ *ein vergoldeter Pokal*

po·kern ['po:kɐn] [intr v] +*haben* **1.** play poker ◊ *Sie pokerten um viel Geld.* **2.** *(fig)* haggle hoch pokern play for high stakes

Pol [po:l] der <-s, -e> GEOG, TECHN, PHYSICS pole ◊ *die geographischen/magnetischen Pole*
⊚ ruhender Pol calming influence

Po·le ['po:lə] der <-n, -n>, **Po·lin** ['po:lɪn] die <-, -nen> Pole → Deutsche

po·le·misch [po'le:mɪʃ] [adj, adv] *(lofty)* polemical(ly) ◊ *polemische Schriften* ♦ *Er ist mir in Diskussionen zu polemisch.* ♦ *eine polemisch geführte Debatte*

Po·len ['po:lən] das <-s> *article only in combination with attribute, no pl* Poland → Deutschland

po·lie·ren [po'li:rən] <poliert, polierte, hat poliert> [tr v] polish ◊ *Sie polierte ihre Schuhe.*
⊚ jdm die Fresse polieren *(rude)* smash sb's face in

Po·lin ['po:lɪn] *fem of* Pole

⑦ **Po·li·tik** [poli'ti:k] die <-> *no pl* **1.** politics ◊ *Sie will in die Politik gehen.* ♦ *eine konservative/ liberale Politik* **2.** tactics, policy ◊ *Welche Politik verfolgt er?*

⑦ **Po·li·ti·ker** [po'li:tɪkɐ] der <-s, ->, **Po·li·ti·ke·rin** [po'li:tɪkərɪn] die <-, -nen> politician ◊ *Er will Politiker werden.* ♦ *eine einflussreiche Politikerin*

⑦ **po·li·tisch** [po'li:tɪʃ] [adj, adv] *when used as an adj, only before ns* political(ly) ◊ *jdn wegen seiner politischen Überzeugung verfolgen* ♦ *Er war politisch sehr engagiert.* eine politische Laufbahn a career in politics jds politische Freunde sb's friends in politics *box@* System

⑦ **Po·li·zei** [poli'tsaɛ] die <-, -n> *most sing* **1.** police ◊ *Er arbeitet bei der Polizei.* ♦ *Sie rief die Polizei.* **2.** *(police)* station ⊜Polizeirevier

Po·li·zei·prä·si·di·um [poli'tsaɛprɛ,zi:diʊm] das <-s, Polizeipräsidien> police headquarters

Po·li·zei·re·vier [poli'tsaɛre,vi:ɐ] das <-s, -e> *(police)* station ◊ *Sie musste sich auf dem Polizeirevier melden.* ⊜Polizei

Po·li·zei·schutz [poli'tsaɛʃʊts] der <-es> *no pl* police protection ◊ *Er steht unter Polizeischutz.*

Po·li·zei·strei·fe [poli'tsaɛʃtraɛfə] die <-, -n> police patrol ◊ *Er wurde von einer Polizeistreife gestoppt.*

⑦ **Po·li·zist** [poli'tsɪst] der <-en, -en>, **Po·li·zis·tin** [poli'tsɪstɪn] die <-, -nen> police officer/constable, policeman ◊ *Er wurde von dem Polizisten abgeführt.* Polizistin (woman) police officer/ constable, policewoman ◊ *Meine Mutter ist Polizistin.*

Pol·len ['pɔlən] der <-s, -> (type of) pollen ◊ *Sie ist gegen verschiedene Pollen allergisch.*

pol·nisch ['pɔlnɪʃ] [adj] *mostly before ns* Polish → deutsch

Pol·nisch ['pɔlnɪʃ] das <-(s)> *no pl* Polish → Deutsch

⑦ **Pols·ter** ['pɔlstɐ] das <-s, – *or also Austr* Pölster> **1.** cushion ◊ *Sie legte Polster auf die Gartenstühle.*; upholstery ◊ *Flecken aus Polstern entfernen* **2.** *(fig)* (finanzielles) Polster nest egg

Pol·ter·a·bend ['pɔltɐ|a:bṃt, 'pɔltɐ|a:bənt] der <-s, -e>

On the eve of a wedding in Germany, it is traditional to hold a party at which pottery, porcelain and glass are smashed. This custom was originally intended to banish evil spirits. Additionally, according to a German proverb *(Scherben bringen Glück)*, pieces of broken pottery, porcelain or glass are lucky. *Polterabend* parties are usually much more informal and less exclusive than wedding receptions.

pol·tern ['pɔltɐn] [intr v] +*haben/sein* **1.** +*sein* clatter, crash (about) ◊ *Die Kisten polterten vom Lkw auf die Fahrbahn.* ♦ *Poltert nicht so laut auf der Treppe!* **2.** +*haben* rant ◊ *Er polterte und schimpfte.* [imp v] +*haben* es poltert there is a crash/clatter

Pom·mes ['pɔməs] die <-> *only pl (fam)* chips,

A B C D E F G H I J K L M N O **P** Q R S T U V W X Y Z

fries ◊ *Pommes mit Ketchup/Majonäse*
Pommes frites [pɔmˈfrɪt(s)] die <-> *only pl*
chips, (French) fries ◊ *eine Portion Pommes frites*
pom·pös [pɔmˈpøːs] adj <pompöser, am pompöses-
ten> very grand, lavish ◊ *ein pompöses Schloss* ◆
Der Empfang war pompös. adv in a very grand
way, lavishly ◊ *ein pompös eingerichtetes Haus*
Po·ny¹ [ˈpɔniː] das <-s, -s> pony ◊ *Das Kind ritt
auf einem Pony.*
Po·ny² [ˈpɔniː] der <-s, -s> fringe, bangs ◊ *Sie
trug einen Pony.*
po·pu·lär [popuˈlɛːɐ̯] adj popular ◊ *eine populäre
Bürgermeisterin* ◆ *Die Reform ist bei den Wählern
nicht sehr populär.*
Po·re [ˈpoːrə] die <-, -n> most pl pore ◊ *Schweiß
brach ihm aus allen Poren.*
⊘ **Porte·mon·naie** [pɔrtmoˈneː] → Portmonee
⊘ **Port·mo·nee** [pɔrtmoˈneː] das <-s, -s> purse ◊
Geld im Portmonee haben ⊖Börse, Geldbörse,
Geldbeutel
⊚ **tief ins Portmonee greifen müssen** have to
shell out (a lot of money)
Por·ti [ˈpɔrti] *pl of* Porto
Por·tier [pɔrˈtie:] der <-s, -s> porter, doorman ◊
Er arbeitet als Portier in einem Hotel. ◆ *Sie gaben
den Zimmerschlüssel beim Portier ab.*
⊘ **Por·ti·on** [pɔrˈtsjoːn] die <-, -en> 1. eine gehörige/
ordentliche/gute etc. Portion … a large/decent/good
portion of … ◊ *eine gesunde Portion Skepsis* 2. *(of
food)* portion, helping 3. *(of coffee, tea)* pot
Por·to [ˈpɔrto] das <-s, -s *or* Porti> postage ◊ *Wie
viel Porto kostet ein Brief nach Irland?*
Por·trät [pɔrˈtrɛː] das <-s, -s> portrait ◊ *jds
Porträt malen* ◆ *ein literarisches Porträt Londons*
Por·tu·gal [ˈpɔrtugal] das <-s> *article only in com-
bination with attribute, no pl* Portugal → Deutsch-
land
Por·tu·gie·se [pɔrtuˈgiːzə] der <-n, -n>,
Por·tu·gie·sin [pɔrtuˈgiːzɪn] die <-, -nen> Portu-
guese → Deutsche
por·tu·gie·sisch [pɔrtuˈgiːzɪʃ] adj *mostly before ns*
Portuguese → deutsch
Por·tu·gie·sisch [pɔrtuˈgiːzɪʃ] das <-(s)> *no pl*
Portuguese → Deutsch
Por·zel·lan [pɔrtsɛˈlaːn] das <-s, -e> china,
porcelain ◊ *Geschirr aus Porzellan* eine Zahnfül-
lung aus Porzellan a porcelain filling
⊚ **Porzellan zerschlagen** *(fam)* cause a lot of
trouble
Po·si·ti·on [poziˈtsjoːn] die <-, -en> position ◊
Angestellte in leitender Position ◆ *Die Läufer
gingen zum Start in Position.* jds Position
gegenüber/zu etw./jdm sb's position on sth/as far
as sb is concerned eine Position beziehen/
einnehmen take a position Position beziehen take
a stance
⊘ **po·si·tiv** [ˈpoːzitiːf] adj, adv positive(ly) ◊ *eine
positive Entwicklung/Zahl* ◆ *Die Reaktionen waren
durchweg positiv.* ◆ *Der Film wurde vom Publikum
positiv aufgenommen.; (answer)* affirmative(ly) Ihr
Test auf Alkohol im Blut ist positiv ausgefallen.
You tested positive for alcohol. ein positiv
denkender Mensch a positive person sich (auf jdn/
etw.) positiv auswirken have a positive effect (on
sb/sth) einer Sache/jdm positiv gegenüberstehen
be in favour/favor of sth/sb ⊖negativ

Pos·ses·siv·pro·no·men
[pɔsɛˈsiːfpro,noːmən, '– – – – ,– –] das
<-s, – *or* Possessivpronomina> GRAM possessive
pronoun ⊖besitzanzeigendes Fürwort

Mein, dein, sein in German are often used like
an article and are only infrequently encountered
as genuine pronouns. For example, in *He, gib
den Ball her! Das ist* **mein** *Ball!* (Hey, give me
the ball! That's my ball!), *mein* is a possessive
adjective. In contrast, in *Nein, ist er nicht! Das
ist* **meiner.** (No it's not! It's mine.), *meiner* is a
possessive pronoun. The possessive pronouns take
the same forms as the definite article; you can
find them at their relevant entries in this dictionary.

⊘ **Post** [pɔst] die <-> *no pl* 1. post office ◊ *Sie
arbeitet bei der Post.* ◆ *einen Brief zur Post
bringen* etw. mit der Post/per Post schicken send
sth by post 2. die Post™ *the German post office*
3. post, mail ◊ *Hast du deine Post schon gelesen?*
◆ *Die Rechnung war gestern in der Post.* elektronische Post electronic mail, e-mail
⊚ **irgendwann/irgendwo geht die Post ab**
(fam) things really get going ◊ *Bei seinen Partys
geht echt die Post ab!* things really get heated ◊
*Wenn die beiden sich streiten, geht ganz schön die
Post ab.* ab (geht) die Post *(fam)* off we go,
they're away
Post·bo·te [ˈpɔstboːtə] der <-n, -n>, **Post·bo·tin**
[ˈpɔstboːtɪn] die <-, -nen> postman ◊ *War der
Postbote heute schon da?* Postbotin postwoman ◊
Sie arbeitet als Postbotin. ⊖Briefträger
Pos·ten [ˈpɔstn̩] der <-s, -> 1. *(on a list, invoice
etc.)* item 2. *(job)* post, position ◊ *Er hat seinen
Posten als Hausmeister verloren.* 3. sentry ◊ *einen
Posten ablösen; (police, intelligence service)* sur-
veillance officer ◊ *Posten zur Bewachung des
Lagers austellen* ⊖Wache 4. *(position)* post ◊ *Der
Soldat hat unerlaubt seinen Posten verlassen.*
5. Posten stehen/schieben stand guard, stand
sentry ⊖Wache 6. TRADE quantity, batch ◊ *Soeben
ist ein größerer Posten Pelze eingetroffen.*
⊚ **auf verlorenem Posten** auf verlorenem Posten
sein/stehen be in a no-win situation auf verlorenem Posten kämpfen fight a losing battle **auf dem
Posten** *(fam)* (top) fit, one hundred percent
Post·fach [ˈpɔstfax] das <-(e)s, Postfächer> 1. PO
box 2. IT inbox, mailbox ◊ *Mein Postfach quillt
über von E-Mails.* 3. pigeonhole
⊘ **Post·kar·te** [ˈpɔstkaʁtə] die <-, -n> postcard ◊
Schreibst du mir eine Postkarte?
⊘ **Post·leit·zahl** [ˈpɔstlaɛtsaːl] die <-, -en>
postcode, zip code
⊘ **Post·ler** [ˈpɔstlɐ] der <-s, ->, **Post·le·rin**
[ˈpɔstlərɪn] die <-, -nen> *(fam)* postal worker ◊
Die Postler wollen streiken. ◆ *Sie ist Postlerin.*
⊘ **Pöst·ler** [ˈpœstlɐ] der <-s, ->, **Pöst·le·rin**
[ˈpœstlərɪn] die <-, -nen> *(SouthG, Austr, fam)*
postal worker ◊ *Er ist Pöstler.* ◆ *eine gewissenhafte Pöstlerin.* → Postler
post·wen·dend [ˈpɔstvɛndn̩t, ˈpɔstvɛndənt] adv
by return of post, immediately ◊ *Er schickte die
Lieferung postwendend zurück.* ◆ *Die Quittung für
den Fehler kam postwendend.* ⊖prompt,
umgehend

po·tent [po'tɛnt] [adj] <potenter, am potentesten>
1. potent ◊ *ein potenter Liebhaber* ♦ *Sie wünscht sich ihren Mann stark, maskulin, potent.* **2.** *(lofty)* financially sound ◊ *Wir suchen noch potente Investoren.* **3.** *(lofty)* powerful, impressive ◊ *ein potenter Gegenspieler* ♦ *Das Land war damals militärisch sehr potent.* ⊜mächtig **4.** *(lofty) (appliance, drugs etc.)* powerful ◊ *ein potentes Schmerzmittel*

Po·tenz [po'tɛnts] die <–, –en> **1.** *no pl* potency ◊ *Viagra steigert die Potenz.* **2.** *most sing (lofty)* power ◊ *die wirtschaftliche Potenz eines Staates;* *(of substances)* potency **3.** MATH power ◊ *das Rechnen mit Potenzen und Wurzeln* **4.** *most sing (lofty)* (finanzielle) Potenz financial strength ◊ *ein Unternehmen mit großer finanzieller Potenz* ⊕ in (höchster) Potenz to the highest degree

Po·ten·zi·al [potɛn'tsia:l] das <–s, –e> *(lofty)* potential ◊ *Er schöpft sein geistiges Potenzial nicht aus.* ♦ *Die Aktie besitzt noch viel/ein großes Potenzial.*

po·ten·zi·ell [potɛn'tsiɛl] [adj, adv] *no comp/superl; when used as an adj, only before ns (lofty)* potential(ly) ◊ *potenzielle Kunden ansprechen* ♦ *eine potenziell lebensgefährliche Erkrankung*

② **Pou·let** [pu'le:] das <–s, –s> *(Swiss)* chicken → Hähnchen

Pracht [praxt] die <–> *no pl* splendour, splendor, magnificence ◊ *Nach der Restaurierung erstrahlt der Palast wieder in alter Pracht.* etw. ist eine (wahre) Pracht sth is (really) marvellous

präch·tig ['prɛçtɪç] [adj, adv] magnificent(ly), splendid(ly) ◊ *eine prächtige Villa* ♦ *Wir haben uns ganz prächtig amüsiert.; (weather, idea etc.)* fantastic, marvellous ◊ *Seine Idee war wirklich prächtig.*

prä·di·ka·tiv [prɛdika'ti:f] [adj, adv] *no comp/superl* GRAM predicative(ly) ◊ *ein prädikativ verwendetes Adjektiv*

Prä·fix ['prɛ:fɪks] das <–es, –e> LING prefix ⊜Vorsilbe ⊜Suffix

prä·gen ['prɛ:gn̩] [tr v] +*haben* **1.** shape, characterize ◊ *Zahlreiche Kanäle prägen das Stadtbild Amsterdams.; (a person)* form, shape, mould, mold ◊ *Diese frühen Erfahrungen haben ihn geprägt.* **2.** emboss ◊ *Braille in Papier prägen; (coins)* mint

prag·ma·tisch [prag'ma:tɪʃ] [adj, adv] *(lofty)* pragmatic(ally) ◊ *eine pragmatische Lösung* ♦ *Das muss man pragmatisch sehen.* ⊜rational

präg·nant [prɛg'nant] [adj, adv] <prägnanter, am prägnantesten> *(lofty)* concise(ly), succinct(ly) ◊ *eine prägnante Schilderung der Sachlage* ♦ *Sein Stil ist sachlich und prägnant.* ♦ *Das war prägnant formuliert.*

② **Prak·ti·kant** [prakti'kant] der <–en, –en>, **Prak·ti·kan·tin** [prakti'kantɪn] die <–, –nen> trainee, intern ◊ *Sie ist Praktikantin in einem Verlag.*

② **Prak·ti·kum** ['praktikʊm] das <–s, Praktika> work experience (placement), internship ◊ *Damals war er noch Arzt im Praktikum.* ♦ *mehrere Praktika absolvieren/machen*

② **prak·tisch** ['praktɪʃ] [adj, adv] practical(ly) ◊ *der praktische Teil der Ausbildung* ♦ *Ich finde es praktisch, so nah am Bahnhof zu wohnen.* ♦ *Vollkommene Gerechtigkeit ist praktisch unmöglich.* ♦

Das kommt praktisch nie vor. Sie ist praktisch veranlagt. She's very practical.

prak·ti·zie·ren [prakti'tsi:rən] <praktiziert, praktizierte, hat praktiziert> [tr+intr v] practise, practice ◊ *In dieser Klinik praktizieren 90 Ärzte.* ♦ *Die Behörden wollen mehr Bürgernähe praktizieren.* praktizierender Christ/Jude/Moslem sein be a practising/practicing Christian/Jew/Moslem

Pra·li·ne [pra'li:nə] die <–, –n> chocolate ◊ *eine Schachtel Pralinen*

prall [pral] [adj] **1.** *(fruit, thigh)* firm; *(breast also)* full; *(ball, balloon etc.)* fully inflated ◊ *einen Wasserball prall aufblasen; (sail)* billowing, full ◊ *Mit prallen Segeln machten sie gute Fahrt.; (bag, pocket etc.)* (crammed) full, bulging ◊ *prall gefüllte Taschen* **2.** *(fam) (very intense: sun)* blazing ◊ *Leg dich nicht in die pralle Sonne.; (life)* full, dynamic ◊ *das pralle Leben genießen*

pral·len ['pralən] [intr v] +*sein* gegen/auf/an etw. [acc] prallen collide with sth, crash into sth ◊ *Sie ist mit dem Auto gegen die Leitplanke geprallt.; (ball)* hit sth, bounce off sth

Prä·mie ['prɛ:mjə] die <–, –n> **1.** bonus ◊ *eine Prämie ausloben/ausschütten* ♦ *eine Prämie für besondere Leistungen erhalten* **2.** *(insurance)* premium ◊ *Die Prämie richtet sich nach der Versicherungssumme.* ⊜Beitrag **3.** *(for savers)* premium ⊜Zulage

Prä·pa·rat [prɛpa'ra:t] das <–(e)s, –e> **1.** medicine, drug, preparation ◊ *ein neues Präparat zulassen* ⊜Medikament **2.** BIO, MED specimen ◊ *Präparate von Wildtieren*

Prä·po·si·ti·on [prɛpozi'tsio:n] die <–, –en> LING preposition ⊜Verhältniswort

Prepositions are used to express spatial, temporal, causal and modal relationships in noun phrases. Time/place: *Wir haben uns* **zum ersten Mal in** *Hamburg getroffen.* (We met for the first time in Hamburg.) Time: *Das war kurz* **nach** *meinem Geburtstag.* (That was shortly after my birthday.) Reason/circumstance/place: **Wegen** *einer Erkältung lag ich eine Woche* **mit** *Fieber* **im** *Bett.* (As a result of a cold I spent a week in bed with a temperature.)
Prepositions determine the case. This is mostly the accusative, but the dative often occurs too, and sometimes both are possible. For example, *Gehst du mit mir* **ins** *Theater?* (Are you coming to the theatre with me?) (movement from A to B: accusative) — *Ach, weißt du,* **im** *Theater gefällt's mir nicht so gut!* (You know, I don't like the theatre that much.) (place, answering the question, where?: dative). It is best to make a note of the small group of prepositions that always take the dative. These are: *aus, bei, mit, nach, seit, von, zu.* The remainder take the accusative, the case governed by the 'movement/place rule'. Prepositions taking the genitive, such as *seitens, aufgrund, anstelle, bezüglich, mithilfe* etc. usually only occur in the written language. The prepositions *wegen, trotz* and *während* are often used with the genitive when written, but tend to be used with the dative in the spoken language.

Prä·sens ['prɛ:zɛns] das <–> *no pl* present (tense) ◊ *Der Roman ist im Präsens geschrieben.* ⊜Gegen-

wart

When using the present tense, the Germans are able to express actions both in the present and the future. For example, *Ich warte auf den Bus.* (I am waiting for the bus.) (now: present) — *In fünf Minuten stehe ich auf und mache mir einen Kaffee.* (In five minutes I'm going to get up and make myself a coffee.) (in five minutes: future). The forms of the present tense are quite simple: *ich steh**e**, du steh**st**, er/sie/es steh**t**, wir steh**en**, ihr steh**t**, sie/Sie steh**en**. In the case of irregular verbs, there is sometimes a vowel change, e. g. *fahren — sie fährt.* For irregular verb forms look up the relevant verb entries.

prä·sen·tie·ren [prɛzɛn'tiːrən] <präsentiert, präsentierte, hat präsentiert> [tr v] present ◇ *Sie präsentierten ihre neuesten Modelle auf der Messe.* jdm etw. präsentieren present sb with sth ◇ *jdm die Rechnung präsentieren* sich/jdn jdm/etw. präsentieren present yourself/sb to sb/sth
Prä·ser·va·tiv [prɛzɛr'vaːtiːf] das <–s, –e> condom ⊜Kondom
② **Prä·si·dent** [prɛzi'dɛnt] der <–en, –en>, **Prä·si·den·tin** [prɛzi'dɛntɪn] die <–, –nen> president ◇ *der französische Präsident* ♦ *der Präsident der Bundesagentur für Arbeit*
Prä·si·di·um [prɛ'ziːdjʊm] das <–s, Präsidien> **1.** committee ◇ *Er wurde ins Präsidium des Vereins gewählt.*; (of a political party) executive ⊜Vorstand **2.** (police) headquarters ◇ *Ich muss Sie bitten, mit aufs Präsidium zu kommen.*
Prä·te·ri·tum [prɛ'teːritʊm] das <–s, Präterita> imperfect (tense), preterite ⊜Imperfekt, erste Vergangenheit

In German, the imperfect is only infrequently used in everyday language to express past events, the perfect being preferred. For example, *Sie* **lachten** *minutenlang über ihren gelungenen Witz.* (preterite) — *Sie* **haben** *minutenlang über ihren gelungenen Witz* **gelacht**. (perfect). Only in the case of modal and auxiliary verbs is there a marked tendency to use the imperfect: *sein/war, haben/hatte, werden/wurde, wollen/wollte, mögen/mochte, sollen/sollte, dürfen/durfte, können/konnte.* The imperfect tense is, however, also favoured in factual media reporting and in literary texts.

② **Pra·xis¹** ['praksɪs] die <–> no pl practice ◇ *einen Plan in die Praxis umsetzen* ♦ *eine gängige Praxis*
Pra·xis² ['praksɪs] die <–, Praxen> practice ◇ *eine Praxis für Krankengymnastik/Physiotherapie etc.*; (of a doctor also) surgery
prä·zi·se [prɛ'tsiːzə] [adj, adv] <präziser, am präzisesten> (lofty) precise(ly) ◇ *präzise Angaben machen* ♦ *Sind die Zahlen präzise?* ♦ *den Tathergang präzise beschreiben* ⊜exakt, genau ⊜ungefähr, ungenau
pre·di·gen ['preːdɪɡn̩] [tr+intr v] +haben **1.** REL preach, give a sermon ◇ *Der Pfarrer predigt über die Auferstehung.* **2.** (fam, also pej) lecture ◇ *Ja, ja, schon gut. Hör auf zu predigen!* (jdm) etw. predigen sermonize about sth, lecture sb on sth ◇ *jdm Moral predigen*
Pre·digt ['preːdɪçt] die <–, –en> **1.** REL sermon ◇

Wer hält die Predigt im heutigen Gottesdienst? **2.** (fam, also pej) lecture ◇ *Ich kann deine ewigen Predigten nicht mehr hören!*
② **Preis** [praɛs] der <–es, –e> **1.** (also fig) price ◇ *überhöhte Preise* ♦ *Er hat einen hohen Preis für seine Unabhängigkeit gezahlt.* jdm einen guten/günstigen Preis machen give sb a good price unter Preis cut-price, below the going rate um jeden Preis at all costs um keinen Preis on no account **2.** (in a competition, game) prize ◇ *den zweiten Preis gewinnen*; (for an achievement) award ◇ *Sie erhielt den Preis für die beste weibliche Hauptrolle.* **3.** (for assistance, information etc.) reward ◇ *Auf seinen Kopf ist ein hoher Preis ausgesetzt.*
preis|ge·ben ['praɛsɡeːbm̩] <gibt preis, gab preis, hat preisgegeben> [tr v] (lofty) **1.** reveal, divulge ◇ *Sie wollte ihre Identität nicht preisgeben.* ⊜verraten **2.** jdn/etw. einer Sache [dat] preisgeben expose sb/sth to sth ◇ *jdn/etw. der Lächerlichkeit preisgeben* etw. dem Verfall preisgeben leave sth to decay ⊜aussetzen **3.** (a stronghold, military base etc.) (jdm) etw. preisgeben abandon sth (to sb), surrender sth (to sb) ⊜aufgeben
② **preis·wert** ['praɛsveːɐt] [adj, adv] <preiswerter, am preiswertesten> inexpensive(ly) ◇ *Das Angebot war sehr preiswert.* ♦ *ein preiswertes Hotel* ♦ *preiswert einkaufen*
prel·len ['prɛlən] [tr v] +haben **1.** jdn (um etw.) prellen swindle sb (out of sth) ◇ *Sie haben den Staat um Millionen geprellt.* die Zeche/das Fahrgeld prellen avoid paying the bill/fare ⊜betrügen **2.** MED jdm/sich etw. prellen bruise sb's/your sth ◇ *sich beim Training das Knie prellen*
Prel·lung ['prɛlʊŋ] die <–, –en> MED bruise ◇ *sich bei einem Sturz mehrere Prellungen zuziehen*
② **Pres·se** ['prɛsə] die <–, –n> **1.** no pl press ◇ *Wie die internationale/lokale Presse berichtete, hat ...* gute/schlechte Presse good/bad press **2.** TECHN press ◇ *eine mechanische Presse*
pres·sen ['prɛsn̩] [tr v] +haben **1.** press ◇ *Äpfel zu Saft pressen* ♦ *die Lippen fest aufeinander pressen* ♦ *ein Tuch auf eine Wunde pressen* **2.** (with your hands or body) squeeze ◇ *die Zahnpasta aus der Tube pressen* ♦ *Sie pressten sich in die überfüllte U-Bahn.* ⊜quetschen **3.** (through a sieve) strain ⊜drücken **4.** (a record) cut **5.** etw. aus jdm pressen press sth out of sb, force sth out of sb ◇ *ein Geständnis aus jdm pressen*
② **pres·sie·ren** [prɛ'siːrən] (SouthG, Austr, Swiss) <pressiert, pressierte, hat pressiert> [imp v] jdm pressiert es sb is in a hurry [intr v] be urgent ◇ *Es pressiert nicht so, lassen Sie sich ruhig Zeit.*
Pres·ti·ge [prɛs'tiːʃ] das <–s> no pl (lofty) prestige, reputation, standing ◇ *Der Konzern hat an Prestige gewonnen.* ⊜Ansehen, Ruf
pri·ckeln ['prɪkl̩n] [intr v] +haben **1.** (in the glass) sparkle, bubble ◇ *Sekt prickelt in den Gläsern.*; (in your mouth, on your skin) tingle ◇ *Der Badeschaum prickelt angenehm auf der Haut.* **2.** tingle, have pins and needles ◇ *Nach dem Kälteschock prickelt die Haut.* **3.** es prickelt there is a thrill, there is a spark ◇ *Zwischen ihnen prickelte es.*
pri·ckelnd ['prɪkl̩nt] pres p of prickeln [adj] **1.** mostly negated (fam) nicht/wenig prickelnd not/not particularly great ◇ *Das Ergebnis war wenig prickelnd.* **2.** exciting, thrilling ◇ *ein prickelndes*

Abenteuer ⊜spannend, aufregend

Pries·ter ['priːstə] der <-s, ->, **Pries·te·rin** ['priːstərɪn] die <-, -nen> REL priest ◊ *Er wollte Priester werden.* ♦ *eine anglikanische Priesterin*

② **pri·ma** ['priːmaː] *(fam)* [adj] *invariable* great, brilliant ◊ *Das ist eine prima Idee.* ♦ *Das Wetter war prima.* ⊜super, klasse [adv] really well, brilliantly ◊ *Das hat ganz prima geklappt.* ⊜super, klasse

② **Pri·mar·schu·le** [priˈmaːˌʃuːlə] die <-, -n> *(Swiss)* primary school, elementary school ◊ *in der Primarschule sein*

pri·mi·tiv [primiˈtiːf] [adj] **1.** *(also pej)* primitive ◊ *primitive Kulturen* ♦ *unter primitivsten Bedingungen leben* **2.** *(pej) (person, behaviour)* crude ◊ *Was er gesagt hat, war dumm und primitiv.*

Prinz [prɪnts] der <-en, -en>, **Prin·zes·sin** [prɪnˈtsɛsɪn] die <-, -nen> prince ◊ *Der Frosch war ein verzauberter Prinz.* Prinzessin princess ◊ *Prinzessin Margaret starb am 9.2.2002.*

Prin·zip [prɪnˈtsiːp] das <-s, -ien> principle ◊ *seinen Prinzipien treu bleiben/untreu werden* ♦ *Qualität ist unser oberstes Prinzip!* im Prinzip in principle ◊ *Das ist ja auch im Prinzip dasselbe.* aus Prinzip on principle, as a matter of principle ◊ *Er verkauft seine Bilder aus Prinzip nicht.* ⊛ es geht (jdm) ums Prinzip it is a matter of principle (as far as sb is concerned)

prin·zi·pi·ell [prɪntsiˈpi̯ɛl] [adj, adv] *no comp/superl* **1.** in principle ◊ *Ich bin prinzipiell bereit, ihm zu helfen.* ♦ *Die prinzipielle Möglichkeit besteht, aber ...* ⊜grundsätzlich, generell **2.** unreserved(ly) ◊ *Ich lehne Gewalt prinzipiell ab.* ⊜grundsätzlich, generell [adj] fundamental ◊ *Ich habe keine prinzipiellen Bedenken.* ⊜wesentlich, grundsätzlich

Pri·se ['priːzə] die <-, -n> pinch ♦ *eine Prise Pfeffer zugeben; (of humour)* touch ◊ *Sein Vortrag war mit einer Prise Ironie gewürzt.*

② **pri·vat** [priˈvaːt] [adj, adv] <privater, am privatesten> private(ly) ◊ *ein privates Telefongespräche führen* ♦ *Diese Angelegenheit ist rein privat.* ♦ *etw. privat finanzieren* Er ist privat versichert/krankenversichert. He has got private health insurance. Das habe ich mir/für mich privat gekauft. I bought it for my own personal use. [adv] *(not connected with work)* in a private capacity ◊ *Können wir uns vielleicht einmal privat treffen?* jdn privat kennen know sb outside work ⊜beruflich, dienstlich ⊛ an privat to private individuals von privat for private sale

Pri·vi·leg [priviˈleːk] das <-(e)s, -ien> privilege ◊ *Privilegien gegenüber anderen besitzen*

② **pro** [proː] [prep] [+acc] **1.** per, a ◊ *Das wiederholt sich fünf- bis zehnmal pro Tag.* ♦ *Der Eintritt kostet zehn Euro pro Person.* ⊜je, per **2.** for ◊ *eine Entscheidung pro oder kontra den Ausbau der Straße treffen* ⊜für ⊝kontra

Pro·be ['proːbə] die <-, -n> **1.** test ◊ *sich einer Probe unterziehen* eine Probe auf etw. [acc] a test for sth zur/auf Probe on a trial basis; *(person)* auf Probe on probation (etw.) Probe fahren test drive (sth) **2.** jdn/etw. auf eine harte/die Probe stellen put sb/sth to the test **3.** THEAT rehearsal **4.** sample ◊ *Proben nehmen/untersuchen* ♦ *eine Probe seines Könnens geben* **5.** SCHOOL test ◊ *eine Probe in Deutsch/Mathe schreiben* ⊜Klassenarbeit

⊛ **die Probe aufs Exempel machen** put it to the test

pro·ben ['proːbm̩] [tr+intr v] *+haben* rehearse, practise, practice ◊ *Das Orchester probt täglich.*

Pro·be·zeit ['proːbəˌtsaet] die <-, -en> probationary period, trial period ◊ *Ihm wurde während der Probezeit gekündigt.*

② **pro·bie·ren** [proˈbiːrən] <probiert, probierte, hat probiert> [tr+intr v] **1.** try ◊ *Wenn der Bäcker kein Brot mehr hat, probier's doch mal im Supermarkt.* ⊜versuchen **2.** *(food, drink)* try, have a taste ◊ *Hmm, riecht das gut! Darf ich mal probieren?* ⊜versuchen, kosten [tr v] *(clothes)* try on ⊛ **Probieren geht über Studieren** the proof of the pudding is in the eating

② **Prob·lem** [proˈbleːm] das <-s, -e> problem ◊ *ein ernstes Problem* ♦ *Das Problem besteht darin, dass ...* ♦ *Wir haben Probleme mit unseren Nachbarn.* ⊛ **Probleme wälzen** *(fam)* wrestle with problems

prob·le·ma·tisch [probleˈmaːtɪʃ] [adj] problematic ◊ *Das ist eine höchst problematische Situation.* ♦ *Ist das für dich problematisch?*

② **Pro·dukt** [proˈdʊkt] das <-(e)s, -e> product ◊ *ein neues Produkt entwickeln* ♦ *Konsumsucht ist ein typisches Produkt unserer Zeit.*

② **Pro·duk·ti·on** [prodʊkˈtsi̯oːn] die <-, -en> production ◊ *die Produktion von Insulin im Körper* ♦ *In der Produktion sind 100 Mitarbeiter beschäftigt.* in Produktion gehen go into production

pro·duk·tiv [prodʊkˈtiːf] [adj, adv] productive(ly) ◊ *produktive Arbeit leisten* ♦ *Morgens bin ich am produktivsten.* ♦ *Er ist ein äußerst produktiver Autor.* ♦ *produktiv arbeiten*

Pro·du·zent [produˈtsɛnt] der <-en, -en>, **Pro·du·zen·tin** [produˈtsɛntɪn] die <-, -nen> **1.** producer, manufacturer ◊ *Deutschland ist einer der größten Produzenten von Gerste.* **2.** MEDIA producer ◊ *George Lucas, der Produzent von „Star Wars"*

② **pro·du·zie·ren** [produˈtsiːrən] <produziert, produzierte, hat produziert> [tr+intr v] produce ◊ *Das Kraftwerk produziert günstigen Strom.* ♦ *Musikstücke produzieren* ♦ *Um Gewinne zu machen, müssten wir billiger produzieren.* [ref v] *(fam)* sich irgendwo produzieren show off somewhere ◊ *Er produziert sich gern vor seinen Freunden.*

Prof. [proˈfɛsoːɐ̯] *(abbr of Professor) only written* Prof. ◊ *Frau Prof. Dr. Berger*

pro·fes·sio·nell [profɛsi̯oˈnɛl] [adj, adv] professional(ly) ◊ *Du solltest dir professionelle Hilfe suchen.* ♦ *So ein Verhalten ist wenig professionell.* ♦ *sehr professionell arbeiten*

Pro·fes·sor [proˈfɛsoːɐ̯] der <-s, -en>, **Pro·fes·so·rin** [profɛˈsoːrɪn] die <-, -nen> UNI *(abbr Prof.)* **1.** professor ◊ *die Professoren der Uni Augsburg* ♦ *Sie ist seit zwei Jahren Professorin.* Professor für etw. professor of sth **2.** *(Austr, also oldf)* SCHOOL grammar school teacher

② **Pro·fi** ['proːfiː] der <-s, -s> *(fam)* professional ◊ *die hoch bezahlten Profis der Bundesliga* ♦ *Die Betrüger waren echte Profis.*

Pro·fil [proˈfiːl] das <-s, -e> **1.** profile ◊ *das politische Profil eines Landes* ♦ *Auf dem Foto ist sie im Profil zu sehen.* **2.** *(of a tyre/tire)* tread ◊ *Das Profil dieser Reifen ist ziemlich abgefahren.*

Pro·fit [pro'fiːt, pro'fɪt] der <-(e)s, -e> profit ◊ *Der Konzern macht zu wenig Profit.* ⊖Gewinn

pro·fi·tie·ren [profi'tiːrən] <profitiert, profitierte, hat profitiert> [intr v] von/bei etw. profitieren profit from sth, benefit from sth ◊ *Von/Bei einem Kompromiss profitieren beide Seiten.*

② **Pro·gramm** [pro'gram] das <-(e)s, -e> **1.** IT program ◊ *ein Programm installieren/starten* **2.** programme, program ◊ *ein Programm zur Bekämpfung der Arbeitslosigkeit* ♦ *im Theater ein Programm kaufen* **3.** RADIO, TV channel ◊ *Auf/In welchem Programm kommt der Krimi?* ⊖Sender **4.** TRADE *(of goods, services)* range, programme, program ◊ *neue Produkte ins Programm aufnehmen* **5.** agenda, schedule ◊ *Morgen haben wir ein volles Programm.* auf dem/jds Programm stehen be on the/sb's agenda nach Programm as planned ◊ *Alles verläuft ganz nach Programm.*

pro·gram·mie·ren [progra'miːrən] <programmiert, programmierte, hat programmiert> [tr+intr v] IT **1.** program ◊ *Software programmieren* **2.** programme, program ◊ *einen Videorekorder programmieren*

② **Pro·jekt** [pro'jɛkt] das <-(e)s, -e> project ◊ *Das Projekt ließ sich leider nicht realisieren.*

Pro·jek·tor [pro'jɛktoːɐ] der <-s, -en> projector ◊ *Dias mit dem Projektor an die Wand werfen*

Pro·mil·le [pro'mɪlə] das <-s, -> thousandth (part); *(when measuring how much sb has been drinking)* alcohol level

pro·mi·nent [promi'nɛnt] [adj] <prominenter, am prominentesten> prominent ◊ *eine Talkshow mit prominenten Gästen* ♦ *Der Chirurg ist hier sehr prominent.* ⊖bekannt, berühmt

Pro·mi·nenz [promi'nɛnts] die <-, -en> **1.** *no pl* celebrities, prominent people ◊ *Bei der Veranstaltung war viel Prominenz zugegen.* **2.** *most pl (individual person)* celebrity ◊ *Prominenzen aus Film und Fernsehen* **3.** *no pl* celebrity status ◊ *Ihre Prominenz verdankt sie vor allem diesem Film.*

Pro·mo·ti·on [promo'tsjoːn] die <-, -en> UNI PhD, doctorate ◊ *Für die Promotion brauchte er drei Jahre.*

pro·mo·vie·ren [promo'viːrən] <promoviert, promovierte, hat promoviert> [intr v] **1.** do a PhD, do a doctorate ein promovierter .../eine promovierte ... a ... with a PhD/doctorate ◊ *ein promovierter Biologe/Jurist* **2.** über etw./jdn promovieren do a PhD on sth/sb, do a doctorate on sth/sb

prompt [prɔmpt] [adj, adv] <prompter, am promptesten> prompt(ly) ◊ *Er erhielt eine prompte Reaktion.* ♦ *Die Antwort war prompt.* ♦ *Er reagierte prompt.* ⊖umgehend, postwendend [adv] *(fam, iron)* duly, naturally, as expected ◊ *Er war auch prompt beleidigt.* ⊖gleich

Pro·no·men [pro'noːmən] das <-s, - or Pronomina> LING pronoun ◊ *die unbestimmten Pronomen „man" und „es"* ⊖Fürwort

Pro·phe·zei·ung [profe'tsaeʊŋ] die <-, -en> prophecy ◊ *Seine Prophezeiung hat sich nicht erfüllt.*

Pro·sa ['proːza] die <-> *no pl* prose ◊ *schlichte/ einfache Prosa* ⊖Poesie

pro·sit ['proːzɪt] [interj] *(fam)* **1.** cheers ◊ *Prosit allerseits! Prosit Neujahr! Here's to the New Year!* ⊖prost, zum Wohl(e) **2.** *(oldf) (used when sb*

sneezes) bless you ⊖Gesundheit

② **Pros·pekt** [pro'spɛkt, prɔs'pɛkt] der <-(e)s, -e> brochure ◊ *Laut Prospekt ist das Hotel direkt am Meer.* ♦ *einen ausführlichen Prospekt anfordern*

② **prost** [proːst] [interj] *(fam)* cheers ⊖prosit, zum Wohl(e)

Pros·ti·tu·ier·te [prɔstitu'iːɐtə] der/die <-n, die Prostituierten> *but: ein Prostituierter/eine Prostituierte* prostitute ◊ *Sie arbeitet als Prostituierte.* ♦ *zu einer Prostituierten gehen*

Pros·ti·tu·ti·on [prɔstitu'tsjoːn] die <-> *no pl* prostitution

② **Pro·test** [pro'tɛst] der <-(e)s, -e> protest ◊ *heftiger/schwacher Protest gegen etw.* ♦ *etw. unter lautem Protest tun*

Pro·tes·tant [protɛs'tant] der <-en, -en>, **Pro·tes·tan·tin** [protɛs'tantɪn] die <-, -nen> Protestant ◊ *Ich bin Protestant.* ♦ *eine gläubige Protestantin*

pro·tes·tan·tisch [protɛs'tantɪʃ] [adj] *no comp/ superl* Protestant ◊ *die protestantische Kirche* ♦ *Die Mehrheit der Bevölkerung ist protestantisch.* ⊖evangelisch [adv] jdn protestantisch erziehen bring sb up in the Protestant faith streng protestantisch leben be a strict Protestant ⊖evangelisch

② **pro·tes·tie·ren** [protɛs'tiːrən] <protestiert, protestierte, hat protestiert> [intr v] (gegen jdn/etw.) protestieren protest (against/about sb/sth) ◊ *Also das geht nun wirklich nicht — ich protestiere!* ♦ *gegen den Krieg protestieren*

Pro·the·se [pro'teːzə] die <-, -n> prosthesis, artificial limb ◊ *eine Prothese tragen; (teeth)* set of dentures, false teeth ◊ *Zum Schlafen nimmt sie ihre Prothese heraus.*

Pro·to·koll [proto'kɔl] das <-s, -e> **1.** *(of a meeting)* minutes ◊ *Nehmen Sie das bitte ins Protokoll auf.; (in a court of law)* record of the proceedings; *(at the police)* statement **2.** *(of an experiment)* record ◊ *über ein Experiment genau Protokoll führen* **3.** *(conventions)* protocol ◊ *Das Protokoll verlangt, dass der Gast mit militärischen Ehren begrüßt wird.*

⊚ etw. zu Protokoll geben have sth put on record *(at the police)* say sth in your statement

Pro·vi·ant [pro'vjant] der <-s, -e> *most sing* provisions, supplies ◊ *Habt ihr genug Proviant für die Reise dabei?*

Pro·vinz [pro'vɪnts] die <-, -en> **1.** *(administrative)* province ◊ *eine ehemalige römische Provinz* **2.** *no pl (pej) (rural area)* provinces, country ◊ *Er kam aus der tiefsten Provinz nach New York.*

Pro·vi·si·on [provi'zjoːn] die <-, -en> commission ◊ *eine Provision von 15 % erhalten*

pro·vi·so·risch [provi'zoːrɪʃ] [adj, adv] provisional(ly), temporary(-ily) ◊ *ein provisorischer Verband* ♦ *Diese Aufstellung ist nur provisorisch.* ♦ *etw. provisorisch reparieren* ⊖vorläufig, notdürftig ⊖endgültig

Pro·vo·ka·ti·on [provoka'tsjoːn] die <-, -en> provocation ◊ *etw. als Provokation auffassen*

pro·vo·zie·ren [provo'tsiːrən] <provoziert, provozierte, hat provoziert> [tr v] **1.** jdn (zu etw.) provozieren provoke sb (into doing sth) ◊ *Du hast mich zu dieser Bemerkung provoziert.* ♦ *Sie lässt sich nicht provozieren.* **2.** etw. provozieren provoke sth ◊ *eine Schlägerei provozieren*

Pro·ze·dur [protse'duːɐ̯] die <-, -en> 1. *(also pej) (mode of operation)* procedure ◊ *eine umständliche Prozedur* 2. *(pej) (action)* palaver, carry-on ◊ *eine schmerzhafte Prozedur über sich ergehen lassen*

Pro·zent [pro'tsɛnt] das <-(e)s, -e or -> *pl 'Prozent' when used with figures* 1. MATH per cent ◊ *20 Prozent von 100 sind 20.* 2. *only pl (fam) (of profits)* Prozente bekommen get a percentage 3. *only pl (fam) (off the price)* discount ◊ *Gibt es Prozente, wenn man größere Mengen kauft?*

Pro·zent·satz [pro'tsɛntsats] der <-es, Prozentsätze> percentage ◊ *ein geringer/ hoher/niedriger Prozentsatz an/von ...*

Pro·zess [pro'tsɛs] der <-es, -e> 1. process ◊ *ein chemischer Prozess* 2. LAW *(court proceedings)* trial; *(law suit)* (legal) action einen Prozess gegen jdn führen/anstrengen instigate/institute legal proceedings against sb einen Prozess gewinnen/verlieren win/lose a court case ⊛ **kurzen Prozess mit jdm machen** *(fam)* deal swiftly with sb

prü·de ['pryːdə] adj <prüder, am prüdesten> prudish ◊ *Er ist ziemlich prüde.* ♦ *eine prüde Einstellung*

② **prü·fen** ['pryːfn̩] tr v +haben 1. *(a bill, invoice, brakes etc.)* check ◊ *prüfen, ob etw. richtig eingestellt ist* jdn/etw. auf etw. acc (hin) prüfen check sb/sth for sth ◊ *einen Computer auf Viren prüfen* ♦ *jdn auf seine Eignung für etw. prüfen* 2. *(an offer etc.)* consider ◊ *Wie werden Sie Ihre Unterlagen eingehend prüfen.* 3. *(knowledge)* test ◊ *Ein Student wird in mehreren Fächern geprüft.* ♦ *jdn mündlich/schriftlich prüfen* intr v +haben examine ◊ *Welcher Professor prüft diese Woche?*

② **Prü·fung** ['pryːfʊŋ] die <-, -en> 1. examination ◊ *eine Prüfung ablegen/bestehen* ♦ *durch die Prüfung fallen* 2. *(encumbrance)* test, trial ◊ *Das Leben stellte ihn vor harte Prüfungen.* 3. *no pl (of a thesis, documents etc.)* inspection ◊ *etw. einer Prüfung* dat *unterziehen* ♦ *Bei der Prüfung Ihrer Unterlagen wurde festgestellt, ...*

Prü·gel ['pryːgl̩] die <-> *only pl* beating, thrashing ◊ *jdm Prügel verpassen* ⊝Schläge

prü·geln ['pryːgl̩n] tr v +haben beat, thrash ◊ *Er prügelte seine Kinder.* ⊝schlagen ref v +haben sich (mit jdm) prügeln fight (sb) ⊛ **sich um etw. prügeln** *(fam)* fight over/for sth

PS¹ [peːʔˈɛs] das *(abbr of Pferdestärke)* hp ◊ *Wie viel PS hat dein neuer Wagen?*

PS² [peːʔˈɛs] das *(abbr of Postskript(um))* PS ◊ *PS: Bitte antworte so schnell wie möglich!*

pst [pst] interj shush ◊ *Pst! Ich glaube, ich habe ein Geräusch gehört.*

Psy·che ['psyːçə] die <-, -n> psyche ◊ *Körper und Psyche als Einheit* (sich) auf die Psyche schlagen have an emotional impact

Psy·chi·a·ter [psyˈçiaːtɐ] der <-s, ->,
Psy·chi·a·te·rin [psyˈçiaːtərɪn] die <-, -nen> psychiatrist ◊ *Sie ist Psychiaterin.* ♦ *zum Psychiater gehen*

psy·chisch ['psyːçɪʃ] adj, adv *no comp/superl* emotional(ly), psychological(ly) ◊ *Diese Krankheit hat psychische Ursachen.* ♦ *Seine Abhängigkeit ist rein psychisch.* ♦ *ein psychisch bedingtes Leiden* ⊝seelisch ⊝physisch

Psy·cho·lo·ge [psyço'loːgə] der <-n, -n>,
Psy·cho·lo·gin [psyço'loːgɪn] die <-, -nen> psychologist ◊ *einen Psychologen aufsuchen* ♦ *Sie ist Psychologin von Beruf.*

② **Psy·cho·lo·gie** [psyçolo'giː] die <-> *no pl* psychology ◊ *Er hat Psychologie studiert.* ♦ *Mit ein wenig Psychologie kannst du bei ihr viel erreichen.*

psy·cho·lo·gisch [psyço'loːgɪʃ] adj, adv *no comp/ superl* psychological(ly) ◊ *ein psychologisches Gutachten* ♦ *jdn psychologisch behandeln*

Pu·ber·tät [pubɛr'tɛːt] die <-> *no pl* puberty ◊ *Mein Sohn ist in der Pubertät.* ♦ *in die Pubertät kommen*

pub·lik [pu'bliːk] adj *no comp/superl, not before ns* public ◊ *etw. ist/wird publik* ♦ *Machen Sie das bitte nicht publik.*

Pub·li·ka·ti·on [publika'tsi̯oːn] die <-, -en> publication ◊ *Wann ist der Termin für die Publikation ihres neuen Romans?* ♦ *als Publikation erscheinen* ⊝Veröffentlichung

② **Pub·li·kum** ['puːblikʊm] das <-s> *no pl* 1. *(in theatre etc.)* audience ◊ *Diese Show ist beim Publikum sehr beliebt.*; *(at a sporting event)* crowd 2. *(people at large)* public ◊ *Wir möchten mit dieser Zeitschrift ein breites Publikum erreichen.* 3. *(patrons)* customers ◊ *Hier verkehrt überwiegend gehobenes Publikum.*

pub·li·zie·ren [publi'tsiːrən] <publiziert, publizierte, hat publiziert> tr+intr v publish ◊ *einen Roman publizieren* ♦ *Der Autor durfte fortan nicht mehr publizieren.* ⊝veröffentlichen tr v make public ◊ *Der Name des Spenders darf nicht publiziert werden.* ⊝publik machen

② **Pud·ding** ['pʊdɪŋ] der <-s, -s or -e> *(cooked sweet dish)* pudding ◊ *Soll ich dir einen Pudding kochen?*

Pu·der ['puːdɐ] der or fam das <-s, -> powder ◊ *sich mit Puder schminken* ♦ *Dieser Puder hilft gegen deinen Juckreiz.*

Pul·li ['pʊli] der <-s, -s> *(fam) (abbr of Pullover)* pullover, jumper

② **Pul·lo·ver** [pʊ'loːvɐ] der <-s, -> pullover, jumper ◊ *einen Pullover anziehen/überziehen*

Puls [pʊls] der <-es> *no pl* pulse ◊ *jdm den Puls fühlen/messen* ♦ *Wie hoch ist sein Puls?*

② **Pult** [pʊlt] das <-(e)s, -e> 1. *(for a speaker)* lectern ◊ *Er trat ans Pult und bat um Ruhe.*; *(in an orchestra)* rostrum 2. SCHOOL desk ◊ *sich ans Pult setzen* ♦ *Komm bitte mal hier vor ans Pult.*

Pul·ver ['pʊlfɐ, 'pʊlvɐ] das <-s, -> 1. powder ◊ *etw. zu Pulver zermahlen/zerreiben* 2. *(for firearms)* powder, gunpowder ◊ *eine Waffe mit Pulver und Blei laden* 3. *(fam)* dough ◊ *Für so einen Luxusschlitten brauchst du erst mal das nötige Pulver.* ⊛ **das Pulver (auch) nicht (gerade) erfunden haben** *(fam)* not to be very bright

Pum·pe ['pʊmpə] die <-, -n> 1. TECHN pump ◊ *Mein Fahrrad hat einen Platten — leihst du mir mal deine Pumpe?* 2. *(fam, fig, hum)* ticker ◊ *Die alte Pumpe mag nicht mehr so recht.*

pum·pen ['pʊmpm̩] tr v +haben 1. etw. irgendwohin/irgendwoher pumpen pump sth out of/into sth ◊ *Luft in einen Reifen pumpen* ♦ *Wasser aus einem Becken pumpen* 2. *(fam)* jdm etw. pumpen lend sb sth sich dat etw. (von jdm) pumpen borrow sth

(from sb) ⊝leihen, borgen [intr v] +*haben* pump ◊ *Du musst kräftig pumpen, bis das Wasser läuft.*

Pum·per·ni·ckel ['pʊmpɛnɪkl] der <–s, –> *most sing* pumpernickel ◊ *eine Scheibe Pumpernickel mit Käse*

② **Punkt** [pʊŋkt] der <–(e)s, –e> **1.** (*of colour, light*) spot ◊ *ein blaues Kleid mit weißen Punkten* **2.** (*location*) spot ◊ *Wir treffen uns genau an diesem Punkt.* **3.** GRAM full stop, period ◊ *einen Punkt machen/setzen* **4.** MATH point ◊ *Die Gerade schneidet den Kreis im Punkt S.* **5.** (*moment etc.*) point ◊ *einen kritischen Punkt erreichen/überschreiten* **6.** (*in games, sports etc., at the stock exchange*) point ◊ *einen Punkt erzielen/gewinnen/machen/verlieren* ♦ *Der DAX verlor fast 20 Punkte.* **7.** (*topic, aspect*) point ◊ *ein strittiger/wichtiger Punkt* ♦ *Sie waren sich in allen Punkten einig.; (of a list etc.)* item ◊ *der nächste Punkt auf der Tagesordnung* **8.** (*at a precise time*) Punkt ... ... on the dot, dot on ... ◊ *Es ist jetzt Punkt acht (Uhr).* ⊝Schlag

ⓔ **ohne Punkt und Komma reden** (*fam*) talk nonstop, rabbit on incessantly **der springende Punkt** the crucial point, the essential factor **ein toter Punkt** a low point ◊ *an einem toten Punkt angelangt sein (in negotiations)* an impasse *(in the catering trade)* slack period **etw. auf den Punkt bringen** sum sth up, put sth in a nutshell **auf den Punkt kommen** get to the point **nun mach (aber) mal einen Punkt** (*fam*) come off it **Punkt für Punkt** point by point

The *Grüne Punkt* adorns all retail packaging capable of being recycled. Based in Bonn, *Duales System Deutschland*, a company responsible for the avoidance of refuse and the recovery of secondary materials, has been issuing licences under a private-sector initiative since 1991 that permit the use of the 'Green Dot' logo in exchange for payment of a fee. Packaging labelled in this way can be disposed of in prescribed containers and can thus be made available for recycling. This system has, in the meantime, proved successful far beyond the borders of Germany.

② **pünkt·lich** ['pʏŋktlɪç] (*adj*) punctual ◊ *Er ist immer sehr pünktlich.* ♦ *eine pünktliche Mitarbeiterin* (*adv*) punctually, on time ◊ *Der Zug ist pünktlich angekommen.*

Pu·pil·le [pu'pɪlə] die <–, –n> pupil ◊ *Die Pupillen erweitern/verengen sich.*

② **Pup·pe** ['pʊpə] die <–, –n> **1.** (*toy*) doll ◊ *Spielt sie noch mit Puppen?* **2.** THEAT puppet ◊ *Die Puppen wirkten sehr lebensecht.* **3.** BIO pupa ◊ *Aus der Puppe schlüpfte ein Schmetterling.*

ⓔ **die Puppen tanzen lassen** (*fam*) paint the town red **bis in die Puppen** (*fam*) till all hours

pur [puːɐ̯] (*adj*) **1.** pure ◊ *pures Gold* ♦ *Am besten trinkt man pures Wasser.* ♦ *Der Geschmack ist pur und unverfälscht. ... pur* pure ... ◊ *Trinkst du den Saft pur?; (alcohol)* neat ... **2.** (*fam*) pure ◊ *etw. aus purer Bosheit/Dummheit tun* ♦ *Das ist doch der pure Neid!* ⊝rein, bloß

Pü·ree [py'reː] das <–s, –s> purée ◊ *ein Püree aus Kartoffeln und Erbsen*

Pus·te ['puːstə] die <–> *no pl* (*fam*) **1.** **aus der Puste kommen/sein** be puffed out **jdm geht die Puste aus** sb is getting short of breath **2.** (*fig*) **jdm geht die Puste aus** sb is running out of steam; (*concerning funds etc.*) sb is going broke

pus·ten ['puːstn̩] (*fam*) <pustet, pustete, hat gepustet> [tr v] +*haben* **1.** blow ◊ *Staub von einem Buch pusten* **2.** etw. aus etw. pusten blow sth out of sth; (*pollutants*) emit sth from sth ◊ *Aus den Auspüffen werden weiterhin Abgase gepustet.* [intr v] +*haben* **1.** blow ◊ *pusten, damit das Essen kühler wird* **2.** (*at a training session*) puff ◊ *ganz schön ins Pusten kommen*

Pu·te ['puːtə] die <–, –n> turkey ◊ *Im Gehege waren Puten und Hühner.* ♦ *Zu Weihnachten gibt es bei uns Pute.*

Putz [pʊts] der <–es> *no pl* plaster ◊ *Leitungen über/unter Putz verlegen* ♦ *Der Putz bröckelt.*

ⓔ **auf den Putz hauen** (*fam*) **1.** have a rave-up, really party ◊ *An meinem 50. Geburtstag hauen wir mal anständig auf den Putz!* **2.** kick up a fuss ◊ *Ich glaube, ich muss hier mal wieder ordentlich auf den Putz hauen!* **3.** show off ◊ *Mit seinem neuen Sportwagen haut er ganz schön auf den Putz!*

② **put·zen** ['pʊtsn̩] [tr v] +*haben* **1.** clean ◊ *Ich muss mal wieder die Fenster putzen.* (sich [dat]) die Zähne putzen brush your teeth, clean your teeth ⊝reinigen **2.** (*food*) wash ◊ *Lauch/Pilze/Spinat putzen* **3.** (sich/jdm) die Nase putzen wipe your/sb's nose (sich/jdm) die Fingernägel putzen clean your/sb's nails [intr v] +*haben* clean ◊ *Hier muss man mal wieder putzen.; (job)* putzen gehen go cleaning [ref v] +*haben* (*animal*) sich putzen wash itself, clean itself; (*bird*) preen itself

Putz·frau ['pʊtsfʁaʊ] die <–, –en> cleaner, (char)woman ◊ *als Putzfrau arbeiten* ♦ *eine gewissenhafte Putzfrau*

Puz·zle ['pʊzl̩, 'pazl̩] das <–s, –s> jigsaw (puzzle) ◊ *ein Puzzle zusammensetzen*

Py·ra·mi·de [pyra'miːdə] die <–, –n> pyramid ◊ *Berechnen Sie das Volumen der Pyramide.* ♦ *die berühmten Pyramiden von Gizeh* ♦ *eine Pyramide aus Tomatendosen*

Q

q, Q [kuː] das <–(s), –(s)> q, Q ◊ *Dieses Wort wird mit einem kleinen q/großen Q geschrieben.* ♦ *Q wie Quelle*

Quad·rat [kvaˈdraːt] das <–(e)s, –e> square ◊ *ein Quadrat zeichnen* ♦ *Das Quadrat von 4 ist 16.* zwei zum Quadrat two squared

quad·ra·tisch [kvaˈdraːtɪʃ] adj *no comp/superl* square ◊ *ein quadratischer Grundriss* ♦ *Dieses Zimmer ist nahezu quadratisch.* eine quadratische Gleichung a quadratic equation adv in the form of a square ◊ *Der Garten ist quadratisch angelegt.*

Quad·rat·me·ter [kvaˈdraːtmeːtɐ] der <–s, –> *(abbr* m²) square metre, square meter ◊ *Unsere Wohnung hat 75 Quadratmeter.*

Qual [kvaːl] die <–, –en> 1. *most pl* pain, agony ◊ *große Qualen erleiden/erdulden* ♦ *unter Qualen sterben* 2. *most sing (fig)* agony etw. ist eine Qual für jdn sth is agony for sb jdm das Leben zur Qual machen make sb's life a misery
◉ die Qual der Wahl haben have the dilemma of choosing

quä·len [ˈkvɛːlən] tr v *+haben* 1. *(an animal, a person)* torture ◊ *Sie hat ihren Sohn fast zu Tode gequält.* ♦ *Seit Jahren quälen ihn heftige Kopfschmerzen* 2. *(thought, emotion)* torment ◊ *Der Gedanke an seine Krankheit quälte ihn.* ⊜plagen 3. *(with incessant questions)* pester ◊ *jdn mit bohrenden Fragen quälen; (with reproaches)* plague ref v *+haben* 1. *(mentally)* sich (mit etw.) quälen torture yourself (with sth) ◊ *Viele Eltern quälen sich mit Schuldgefühlen.* 2. *(physically)* sich (mit etw.) quälen struggle (with sth) ◊ *Er quält sich mit den schweren Kisten — willst du ihm nicht helfen?* 3. sich irgendwohin quälen labour/labor to get somewhere ◊ *sich durch den Dschungel/Schnee quälen*

Qua·li·fi·ka·ti·on [kvalifikaˈʦjoːn] die <–, –en> 1. *(for a job etc.)* qualification ◊ *Sie verlangen als Qualifikation die mittlere Reife.* ♦ *Mit ihren Qualifikationen kann sie fast jeden Job haben.* 2. *(competence)* ability ◊ *Ihre Qualifikation als Abteilungsleiterin steht außer Frage.* 3. sport qualification ◊ *das Rennen um die Qualifikation*

qua·li·fi·zie·ren [kvalifiˈʦiːrən] <qualifiziert, qualifizierte, hat qualifiziert> tr v *(lofty)* etw. als ... qualifizieren describe sth as ..., designate sth as ... ◊ *Die Mieterhöhung wurde vom Gericht als unzulässig qualifiziert.* ref v sich (für etw.) qualifizieren qualify (for sth) ◊ *sich für die Weltmeisterschaft qualifizieren*

qua·li·fi·ziert [kvalifiˈʦiːɐt] *past p of* qualifizieren adj <qualifizierter, am qualifiziertesten> 1. *(job, grade etc.)* qualified ◊ *jd ist für einen Posten qualifiziert* 2. *(requiring specific knowledge)* professional, skilled ◊ *eine qualifizierte Tätigkeit ausüben* 3. expert ◊ *Kann jemand ein qualifiziertes Urteil dazu abgeben?*

ⓩ **Qua·li·tät** [kvaliˈtɛːt] die <–, –en> quality ◊ *Wir*

legen großen Wert auf Qualität. ♦ *ein Produkt von erstklassiger/schlechter Qualität* ♦ *über zahlreiche Qualitäten verfügen*

Qualm [kvalm] der <–(e)s> *no pl* (dense) smoke ◊ *der Qualm einer Zigarre*

qual·men [ˈkvalmən] intr v *+haben* give off smoke ◊ *Der Schornstein qualmte.* tr+intr v *+haben (fam)* smoke ◊ *Er qualmte eine Zigarette nach der anderen.* ♦ *Sie standen im Hof und qualmten.*

Quan·ti·tät [kvantiˈtɛːt] die <–, –en> *(lofty)* quantity ◊ *Qualität der Arbeit geht vor Quantität.*

Qua·ran·tä·ne [karanˈtɛːnə] die <–> *no pl* quarantine ◊ *jdn/etw. unter Quarantäne stellen* ♦ *unter Quarantäne stehen/sein*

ⓩ **Quark** [kvaːrk] der <–s> *no pl* 1. quark, sour curd cheese ◊ *Zum Nachtisch gibt es Quark mit Früchten.* 2. *(fam)* rubbish, nonsense ◊ *Red keinen Quark!*

Quar·tal [kvarˈtaːl] das <–s, –e> quarter ◊ *Im ersten Quartal hat die Firma 25% Gewinn gemacht.*

Quar·tett [kvarˈtɛt] das <–(e)s, –e> 1. quartet ◊ *Sie singen aus dem berühmte Quartett aus „Rigoletto".* ♦ *letzter Auftritt des Golden Gate Quartetts* 2. *(card game)* Happy Families ◊ *Wollen wir Quartett spielen?* 3. set of four cards ◊ *Hast du schon ein Quartett?*

Quar·tier [kvarˈtiːɐ] das <–, –e> 1. accommodation ◊ *Wir suchen für unseren Italienurlaub noch ein Quartier.* 2. mil quarters, billet ◊ *Wo ist das Quartier dieser Truppe?*

Quatsch [kvatʃ] der <–(e)s> *no pl (fam)* rubbish ◊ *So ein Quatsch!* ♦ *Was soll der Quatsch?* ⊜Blödsinn, Unsinn
◉ Quatsch mit Soße utter rubbish

quat·schen [ˈkvatʃn] *(fam)* tr v *+haben (esp pej)* blather ◊ *Quatsch keinen Unsinn!* intr v *+haben* 1. *(esp pej)* prattle on ◊ *Quatsch nicht — mach dich an die Arbeit!* 2. *(pej) (tell a secret)* squeal ◊ *Wer von euch hat gequatscht?* 3. *(mit jdm)* quatschen natter (to sb), chat (to sb) ◊ *Wir haben die ganze Nacht gequatscht.*

Quel·le [ˈkvɛlə] die <–, –n> 1. source ◊ *einen Fluss von der Quelle bis zur Mündung verfolgen* ♦ *verschiedene Quellen zitieren* ♦ *eine Quelle der Angst/Freude sein* ♦ *etw. aus sicherer/zuverlässiger Quelle haben/wissen* 2. spring ◊ *an einer Quelle trinken* ♦ *eine heiße Quelle*
◉ etw. aus erster Quelle haben have sth first hand an der Quelle sitzen have access to inside information

quen·geln [ˈkvɛŋln] intr v *+haben (pej)* 1. *(baby)* grizzle 2. *(child)* whine ◊ *Hör jetzt auf zu quengeln — du bekommst kein Eis mehr!* 3. *(adult)* whinge ◊ *Sie quengelt dauernd, dass sie umziehen will.*

ⓩ **quer** [kveːɐ] adv *no comp/superl* 1. quer durch/ über etw. acc straight through/across sth ◊ *Er rannte quer über den Rasen.* ♦ *quer durch das*

Land/die Stadt fahren **2.** quer zu etw. at right angles to sth ◊ *quer zur Straße parken* ⊖längs ⊙ **quer gestreift** with horizontal stripes ◊ *ein quer gestreifter Pulli* **sich quer legen** *(fam)* make things difficult ◊ *Wenn sich der Abteilungsleiter wieder quer legt, gehen wir zum Chef.*

Que·re ['kve:rə] *(always* jdm in die Quere kommen*)* get in sb's way

Quer·schnitt ['kve:ɡʃnɪt] der <–(e)s, –e> cross-section ◊ *ein Querschnitt durch einen Baumstamm* ♦ *ein Querschnitt durch die Geschichte der Fotografie*

Quer·stra·ße ['kve:ɡʃtra:sə] die <–, –n> side-street ◊ *Biegen Sie in die dritte Querstraße rechts ein.*

quet·schen ['kvɛtʃn] [tr v] +*haben* **1.** *(a person, car etc.)* jdn/etw. irgendwohin quetschen crush sb/sth somewhere ◊ *Der Bus quetschte das Auto regelrecht gegen die Mauer.; (into a bag)* squeeze sth somewhere ⊖pressen **2.** jdm/sich den Daumen etc. in der Tür quetschen catch sb's/your thumb etc. in the door **3.** *(potatoes)* mash [ref v] +*haben* sich irgendwohin quetschen squeeze into/through sth ◊ *Die Menschen quetschten sich in den überfüllten Zug.* ♦ *sich durch eine enge Öffnung/Tür quetschen*

quiet·schen ['kvi:tʃn] [intr v] +*haben* **1.** *(door)* creak ◊ *Die Tür zum Wohnzimmer quietscht.; (tyres, brakes)* squeal ◊ *In der Kurve quietschten die Reifen.* **2.** *(children)* squeal ◊ *Die Kinder quietschten vor Freude/Vergnügen.*

Quirl [kvɪrl] der <–(e)s, –e> whisk ◊ *Butter und Zucker mit dem Quirl schaumig rühren*

quir·lig ['kvɪrlɪç] [adj] *(person, drama)* lively ◊ *eine quirlige Komödie* ♦ *Sie ist quirlig und sehr neugierig.; (daily life)* animated, bustling ◊ *In den Gassen der Altstadt herrscht quirliges Leben.*

quitt [kvɪt] [adj] *no comp/superl, not before ns (fam) (always* (mit jdm) quitt sein*)* be quits (with sb) ◊ *Wenn ich dir noch fünf Euro gebe, sind wir quitt, oder?*

② **Quit·tung** ['kvɪtʊŋ] die <–, –en> **1.** receipt ◊ *jdm eine Quittung (über 100 Euro) ausstellen* **2.** *(fam, fig)* comeuppance ◊ *Das Wahlergebnis ist die Quittung für seine halbherzige Politik.*

Quiz [kvɪs] das <–, –> quiz ◊ *an einem Quiz teilnehmen*

Quo·te ['kvo:tə] die <–, –n> proportion, number, rate ◊ *Die Quote an Motorradunfällen ist gestiegen.* ♦ *eine Quote berechnen/ermitteln; (in the commercial world)* quota

R

r, R [ɛrʲ] das <–(s), –(s)> r, R ◊ *Dieses Wort wird mit einem kleinen r/großen R geschrieben.* ◆ *R wie Richard*

Ra·batt [raˈbat] der <–(e)s, –e> discount ◊ *Beim Kauf von 10 Stühlen erhalten Sie 10% Rabatt.* Rabatt auf etw. ⌊acc⌋ discount on sth

ra·bi·at [raˈbiaːt] ⌊adj⌋ <rabiater, am rabiatesten> violent, aggressive ◊ *ein rabiater Autofahrer* ◆ *Wenn er trinkt, wird er rabiat.*

Ra·che [ˈraxə] die <–> *no pl* revenge, vengeance ◊ *Rache war das Motiv für den Brandanschlag.* Rache (an jdm) nehmen take revenge (on sb) aus Rache in revenge

rä·chen [ˈrɛçn̩] ⌊tr v⌋ +*haben* avenge ◊ *Er rächte den Tod seines Vaters.* ⌊ref v⌋ +*haben* **1.** *(person)* sich rächen take revenge ◊ *Die betrogene Ehefrau rächte sich.* sich an jdm für etw. rächen take (your) revenge on sb for sth ⊖sich revanchieren **2.** etw. rächt sich sth takes its toll ◊ *Chronischer Schlafmangel rächt sich.* jds ... wird sich rächen sb will pay for their ...

② **Rad** [raːt] das <–(e)s, Räder> **1.** wheel ◊ *die Räder eines Uhrwerks* die Räder stehen still the wheels/machines are idle **2.** *(abbr of Fahrrad)* bicycle ◊ *Er schwang sich aufs Rad und fuhr los.* Rad fahren cycle ◊ *Fährst du gern Rad?*

◉ das Rad der Geschichte/Zeit zurückdrehen halt the march of time, turn the clock back **das fünfte Rad am Wagen sein** *(fam, fig)* be in the way **unter die Räder kommen 1.** *(in an accident)* be run over **2.** *(fam, fig)* go to the dogs **ein Rad schlagen 1.** *(person)* do a cartwheel **2.** *(peacock)* spread his tail

Ra·dar [raˈdaːr, ˈraːdaːr] der *or* das <–s, –e> radar ◊ *Ein unbekanntes Flugobjekt wurde vom Radar erfasst.*

ra·deln [ˈraːdl̩n] ⌊intr v⌋ +*sein (SouthG, Austr, fam)* cycle ◊ *Wir sind auf verkehrsarmen Nebenstraßen geradelt.*

② **Rad·fah·ren** [ˈraːtfaːrən] das <–s> *no pl* **1.** cycling beim Radfahren stürzen come off your bicycle, have a bicycle accident **2.** *(fam, fig, pej)* grovelling

Rad·fah·rer [ˈraːtfaːrɐ] der <–s, –>, **Rad·fah·re·rin** [ˈraːtfaːrərɪn] die <–, –nen> **1.** cyclist ◊ *Radfahrer sollten einen Helm tragen.* ⊖Radler **2.** *(fam, fig, pej)* groveller

ra·die·ren [raˈdiːrən] <radiert, radierte, hat radiert> ⌊intr v⌋ *(also fig)* erase ◊ *Zeichne sorgfältiger, dann musst du nicht so viel radieren.* ◆ *Die Stadt wurde im Krieg von der Landkarte radiert.* ⌊tr v⌋ ARTS etch ◊ *eine Platte/ein Motiv radieren*

Ra·dier·gum·mi [raˈdiːɐɡʊmiː] der <–s, –s> rubber, eraser ◊ *ein Bleistift mit Radiergummi*

Ra·dies·chen [raˈdiːsçən] das <–s, –> (small red) radish

◉ **die Radieschen von unten betrachten** *(slang, hum)* be pushing up daisies

ra·di·kal [radiˈkaːl] ⌊adj, adv⌋ radical(ly) ◊ *Er forderte eine radikale Umkehr in der Wirtschaftspolitik.* ◆ *Ihre Position in der Ausländerfrage ist radikal.* ◆ *Der Text muss radikal gekürzt werden.* radikale Linke/Rechte left/right-wing extremist(s) radikal denken have radical views radikal denkend with radical views radikal gegen jdn vorgehen take radical action against sb ⌊adv⌋ categorically ◊ *Er sagt radikal „nein" zu allem.*

② **Ra·dio** [ˈraːdioː] das <–s, –s> radio ◊ *ein tragbares Radio* ◆ *Sie schaltete das Radio ein/aus.* ◆ *Die Sendung wird im Radio übertragen.* ◆ *Radio Bremen* Radio hören listen to the radio beim Radio sein/arbeiten work for (the) radio

ra·di·o·ak·tiv [radioʔakˈtiːf] ⌊adj, adv⌋ radioactive(ly) ◊ *Das Wasser, das den Reaktorkern verlässt, ist radioaktiv.* ◆ *eine radioaktive Substanz* radioaktiv verseucht/verunreinigt radioactively contaminated

Rad·ler[1] [ˈraːdlɐ] das <–s, –> *(SouthG)* shandy ◊ *ein Radler bestellen*

Rad·ler[2] [ˈraːdlɐ] der <–s, –>, **Rad·le·rin** [ˈraːdlərɪn] die <–, –nen> cyclist ◊ *Bei dem schönen Wetter waren viele Radler unterwegs.* ⊖Radfahrer

Rad·weg [ˈraːtveːk] der <–(e)s, –e> cycle path/lane ◊ *den Radweg benutzen*

raf·fen [ˈrafn̩] ⌊tr v⌋ +*haben* **1.** *(pej)* heap, pile ◊ *Sie raffte so viel Geld in ihre Tasche, wie sie nur konnte.* etw. an sich raffen grab sth **2.** *(a curtain, clothing)* gather ◊ *Die Bluse ist am Bund gerafft.* **3.** *(a text etc.)* shorten, condense ⊖kürzen

raf·fi·niert [rafiˈniːɐt] ⌊adj, adv⌋ <raffinierter, am raffiniertesten> **1.** *(plan, trick, gadget)* clever(ly), cunning(ly) ◊ *Ihr Plan war sehr raffiniert.* ◆ *ein raffinierter Trick* ◆ *Der Einbruch war so raffiniert geplant, dass die Täter nie gefasst wurden.* **2.** *(person)* crafty(-ily), artful(ly) ◊ *Der Täter war sehr raffiniert.* ◆ *Die Einbrecher sind beim Einbruch sehr raffiniert vorgegangen.* ⊖geschickt, schlau ⌊adj⌋ *(sugar)* refined

Ra·ge [ˈraːʒə] die <–> *no pl (fam)* fury, rage in Rage geraten/sein become/be furious jdn in Rage bringen infuriate sb ⊖Wut

ra·gen [ˈraːɡn̩] ⌊intr v⌋ +*haben* aus etw. ragen protrude from sth ◊ *Der Löffel ragt aus dem Glas.; (island, cliff)* aus dem Meer ragen rise out of the sea in etw. ⌊acc⌋ ragen stick out into sth ◊ *Ein Baum ragt in die Straße.*

② **Rahm** [raːm] der <–(e)s> *no pl (SouthG, Austr)* cream ◊ *den Rahm steif schlagen* ⊖Sahne

Rah·men [ˈraːmən] der <–s, –> **1.** *(of an object)* frame ◊ *Die Rahmen der Fenster müssen neu gestrichen werden.* ◆ *Der Dieb hat das Gemälde aus dem Rahmen geschnitten.* ◆ *Der Rahmen des Fahrrads ist aus Aluminium.; (of a car)* chassis **2.** *(fig)* framework, basis ◊ *Der Haushalt soll den Rahmen für neue Arbeitsplätze und Stabilität schaffen.*

 im großen **Rahmen** on a large scale im **Rahmen bleiben** be reasonable, be/stay within reasonable limits aus dem **Rahmen fallen** be beyond the ordinary *(costs)* make a spectacle of yourself im **Rahmen** ... gen **1.** within the bounds of sth ◊ *im Rahmen der Bestimmungen* **2.** in the context of sth ◊ *Vorträge im Rahmen des Programms* **3.** within the framework of sth, on the basis of sth ◊ *Friedenssicherung im Rahmen der OSZE*

Ra·ke·te [ra'keːtə] die <–, –n> **1.** *(aircraft)* rocket ◊ *mit einer Rakete zum Mond fliegen* **2.** *(weapon)* missile ◊ *Der Panzer wurde von einer Rakete getroffen.* **3.** firework ◊ *Raketen für Silvester kaufen*

ram·men ['ramən] tr v +*haben* **1.** etw. in etw. acc rammen ram/jam sth into sth ◊ *Er rammte den Spaten in den Boden.* **2.** *(in an accident)* hit ◊ *Der Bus rammte ein entgegenkommendes Auto.*

Ram·pe ['rampə] die <–, –n> **1.** *(for access)* ramp ◊ *Neben dem Eingang befindet sich eine Rampe für Behinderte.* **2.** *(for loading)* loading platform ◊ *Die Lagerhalle hat eine Rampe zum Be- und Entladen.* **3.** *(of a stage)* apron, forestage ◊ *Der Sänger trat bis an die Rampe vor.*

Ram·pen·licht ['rampm̩lɪçt] das <–(e)s, –er> footlights ◊ *Vom Rampenlicht geblendet, konnte er das Publikum nicht erkennen.*

 im **Rampenlicht** (der Öffentlichkeit) stehen be in the limelight

ran [ran] adv *(fam)* (always ran an etw. acc) ran an die Arbeit/ans Werk get going, get down to it/ work ran an den Mann go at him

Rand [rant] der <–(e)s, Ränder> **1.** brim, edge, brink, fringe ◊ *Der Weg auf dem Rand des Kraters ist brüchig.* ♦ *Das Glas war voll bis zum Rand.*; *(of a town/city)* outskirts; *(of a document)* margin ◊ *einen drei Zentimeter breiten Rand frei lassen* **2.** *(of paper)* border ◊ *ein Trauerbrief mit schwarzem Rand;* *(of fabric)* edging ◊ *eine Tischdecke mit einem Rand aus Spitzen;* *(of spectacles, china, glass)* rim ◊ *Das Glas hatte einen goldenen Rand.;* *(of dirt)* (tide)mark ◊ *Ein Rand von Schmutz blieb in der Badewanne zurück.;* *(of the eyes)* rote Ränder red rims

 außer **Rand** und Band sein *(fam)* be wild jdn/etw. an den **Rand** einer Sache gen bringen *(fig)* bring sb/sth to the brink of sth den/seinen **Rand halten** *(slang, emph)* shut your face am **Rande** *(fig)* in passing ◊ *Ich möchte dazu nur ein Detail am Rande erwähnen.* ⊝nebenbei

ran·da·lie·ren [randa'liːrən] <randaliert, randalierte, hat randaliert> intr v create an uproar ◊ *Der betrunkene Gast randalierte im Wirtshaus.*

rand·voll ['rantfɔl] adj, adv no comp/superl **1.** randvoll (gefüllt) brimful, full to the brim ◊ *Sie reichte ihm vorsichtig die randvolle Tasse.* ♦ *Das Gefäß war randvoll mit Wein gefüllt.* etw. randvoll gießen/schenken/laufen lassen fill sth to the brim **2.** *(fam)* packed, crammed ◊ *Das Kino/Der Koffer war randvoll.* ♦ *Wir hatten ein randvolles Programm vor uns.*

rang [raŋ] pret of ringen

Rang [raŋ] der <–(e)s, Ränge> **1.** *(within a hierarchy)* rank, position ◊ *einen hohen Rang in der Regierung/Armee einnehmen/bekleiden* ♦ *Die*

deutschen Teilnehmer belegten die Ränge 10 und 12. im Rang ... gen with the rank of ... von Rang eminent ◊ *Er ist ein Dichter von Rang.* ersten Ranges top, of the highest order ◊ *Das Erdbeben war eine Katastrophe ersten Ranges.* **2.** *(row of seats)* circle ◊ *Ein Sitzplatz im Rang kostet 64 Euro.* vor überfüllten/leeren Rängen spielen play to a packed/an empty house die Zuschauer auf den Rängen the audience in the circle seats der erste Rang the dress/upper circle

 alles, was **Rang** und Namen hat everybody who is anybody jdm/einer Sache den **Rang ablaufen** outstrip sb/sth

ran·gie·ren [raŋ'ʒiːrən, rã'ʒiːrən] <rangiert, rangierte, hat rangiert> tr+intr v shunt ◊ *Der Fahrer musste den Lkw rückwärts durch das Tor rangieren.* ♦ *Er musste lange rangieren, bis er aus der engen Parklücke heraus war.* intr v an erster/ zweiter Stelle rangieren come first/second hinter jdm rangieren rank behind sb

ran·ken ['raŋkŋ̍] ref+intr v +*haben* an etw. dat ranken climb/grow up sth ◊ *Efeu rankt an der Hauswand.* sich um etw. ranken entwine itself around sth ref v +*haben* *(lofty, fig)* sich um jdn/ etw. ranken have grown up around sb/sth ◊ *Legenden ranken sich um das alte Schloss/um König Arthur.*

rann [ran] pret of rinnen

② **rann·te** ['rantə] pret of rennen

Rap·pen ['rapm̩] der <–s, –> (Swiss) centime ◊ *100 Rappen sind ein Franken.*

rar [raːɐ̯] adj scarce ◊ *Gutes Personal ist rar.* ♦ *In der Wüste ist Wasser ein rares Gut.*

 sich **rar** machen *(fam)* stay away

Ra·ri·tät [rari'tɛːt] die <–, –en> rarity, rare good/ item ◊ *Er verkauft kostbare Raritäten.* ♦ *Friedliche Tage sind bei uns eine Rarität.*

ra·sant [ra'zant] *(fam)* adj <rasanter, am rasantesten> **1.** *(car, driver, development etc.)* very fast ◊ *Der Aktienkurs erlebte eine rasante Talfahrt.;* *(speed)* tremendous, lightning ◊ *Unser Tempo war sehr rasant.* **2.** *(performance)* dynamic, lively ◊ *Die Darbietung des Zauberkünstlers war sehr rasant.;* *(person)* vivacious ◊ *Der Star umgibt sich gern mit rasanten Frauen.* adv rasant fahren race rasant steigen/wachsen/zunehmen rise/grow/ increase dramatically/very fast

rasch [raʃ] adj, adv <rascher, am raschesten> quick(ly), swift(ly), fast ◊ *Ihr Tempo beim Arbeiten ist rasch.* ♦ *Die Geschichte nahm ein rasches Ende.* ♦ *Die Geschichte ist rasch erzählt.* rasch im Urteil sein make rash judgements zu rasch rash, hasty ◊ *Er hat seine zu rasche Entscheidung bereits bereut.* ⊝schnell, fix

ra·scheln ['raʃl̩n] intr v +*haben* rustle ◊ *Das trockene Laub raschelte unter unseren Füßen.* mit etw. rascheln rustle sth ◊ *Er raschelte mit dem Papier.*

ra·sen ['raːzn̩] intr v +*sein/haben (fam)* **1.** +*sein (move quickly)* dash ◊ *Die Kinder sind zur Schule gerast.;* *(in a vehicle, on a (motor)bike)* race ◊ *Eine Motorradgruppe raste durch die Straßen.* gegen etw. rasen crash into sth Ras nicht so! Not so fast! **2.** +*haben (also fig) (heart, pulse)* race ◊ *Sein Herz/Puls raste.* jds Atem rast sb is breathing very fast **3.** +*haben (person, audience)* rave ◊ *Sie*

hat gerast wie eine Wahnsinnige. vor Wut rasen be mad with rage vor Begeisterung rasen go wild with excitement ⊖toben

Ra·sen ['raːzn̩] der <–s, –> *most sing* lawn, turf, grass ◊ *(den) Rasen mähen* ♦ *Die Kinder spielen auf dem Rasen. Rasen betreten verboten!* Keep off the grass!

⊛ **den Rasen verlassen** *(fam)* sport **1.** leave the field/pitch **2.** den Rasen verlassen müssen be sent off

Ra·sen·mä·her ['raːzn̩mɛːɐ] der <–s, –> lawnmower

Ra·sier·ap·pa·rat [ra'ziːɐ|apaˌraːt] der <–(e)s, –e> electric shaver/razor ◊ *Sie rasiert sich mit dem Rasierapparat die Achseln.*

② **ra·sie·ren** [ra'ziːrən] <rasiert, rasierte, hat rasiert> ⟨tr v⟩ shave ◊ *Er ließ sich vom Barbier rasieren.* sich (nass) rasieren have a (wet) shave sich trocken rasieren use an electric shaver jdm/sich etw. rasieren shave sb's/your sth ◊ *Sie rasiert sich die Beine.* jdm/sich den Bart rasieren shave off sb's/ your beard

Ras·pel ['raspl̩] die <–, –n> **1.** *(for food)* grater ◊ *Sie zerkleinert die Karotten mit der Raspel.* **2.** *(for wood, metal)* rasp ◊ *Holz mit einer Raspel glätten*

Ras·se ['rasə] die <–, –n> *(of an animal)* breed, pedigree ◊ *Was für eine Rasse ist/hat der Hund?*; *(of a human)* race ◊ *ein Angehöriger der weißen Rasse*

⊛ **Rasse haben** *(fam)* be vivacious/spirited

ras·sis·tisch [ra'sɪstɪʃ] ⟨adj, adv⟩ racist ◊ *Ihre Anspielung auf seine Hautfarbe war rassistisch.* ♦ *rassistische Propaganda* rassistisch gesinnt sein be racist rassistisch motiviert **racially motivated**

Rast·platz ['rastplats] der <–es, Rastplätze> **1.** place to rest ◊ *Sie fanden einen Rastplatz im Schatten.* **2.** *(along the motorway)* picnic area ◊ *Am nächsten Rastplatz machen wir eine Pause.*

Rat¹ [raːt] der <–(e)s, Räte> **1.** *no pl* advice ◊ *Der Patient hörte nicht auf den Rat des Arztes.* bei jdm Rat suchen seek sb's advice jdm den Rat geben, etw. zu tun advise sb to do sth sich ⟨dat⟩ bei jdm (einen) Rat holen get/take advice from sb **2.** *(assembly)* council ◊ *der Rat der Europäischen Union*

⊛ **jdm mit Rat und Tat zur Seite stehen** advise and assist sb **guter Rat ist teuer** it is hard to know what to do **(sich ⟨dat⟩) keinen Rat mehr wissen** be at your wits' end

② **Rat²** [raːt] der <–(e)s, Räte>, **Rä·tin** ['rɛːtɪn] die <–, –nen> councillor, council member ◊ *Wie viele Räte gehören dem Kirchenrat an?*

② **rät** [rɛːt] *pres of* raten

Ra·te ['raːtə] die <–, –n> **1.** fin instal(l)ment ◊ *Die erste Rate wird sofort nach Kauf fällig.* ♦ *Die Rückzahlung erfolgt in Raten.* etw. auf Raten kaufen buy sth in instal(l)ments/on hire-purchase **2.** *(number)* rate ◊ *In den Wintermonaten steigt die Rate der Unfälle.*

② **ra·ten** ['raːtn̩] <rät, riet, hat geraten> ⟨tr+intr v⟩ **1.** jdm raten(, etw. zu tun) advise sb (to do sth) ◊ *Sie riet ihnen, mit dem Papier sparsam umzugehen.* ♦ *Was raten Sie mir?* (jdm) zu etw. raten recommend sth (to sb) ◊ *In diesem Fall rate ich zur Vorsicht.* **2.** (etw.) raten guess (sth) ◊ *Rate*

mal, wer morgen kommt? ♦ *Ich habe sein Alter richtig geraten.* richtig/falsch raten guess right/ wrong

⊛ **dreimal darfst du raten** *(fam, iron)* I'll give you three guesses **das möchte ich dir auch geraten haben** you better had

② **Rat·ge·ber** ['raːtgeːbɐ] der <–s, –> guide ◊ *ein Ratgeber mit Tipps für den Hauskauf*

② **Rat·haus** ['raːthaʊs] das <–es, Rathäuser> town hall ◊ *Das Rathaus ist der Sitz von Bürgermeister und Verwaltung.*

② **Rä·tin** ['rɛːtɪn] *fem of* Rat

ra·ti·o·nal [ratsi̯oˈnaːl] ⟨adj, adv⟩ rational(ly) ◊ *Es fiel ihr schwer, rational zu bleiben.* ♦ *ein rationales Vorgehen* ♦ *rational denken/handeln*

rat·los ['raːtloːs] ⟨adj, adv⟩ <ratloser, am ratlosesten> helpless(ly), baffled, at a loss ◊ *Die Ärzte sind in seinem Fall völlig ratlos.* ♦ *Er warf mir einen ratlosen Blick zu.* ♦ *Der Schüler saß ratlos vor seinen Mathematikaufgaben.* einer Sache ⟨dat⟩ ratlos gegenüberstehen be at a loss (when) faced with/facing sth

Rat·schlag ['raːtʃlaːk] der <–(e)s, Ratschläge> piece of advice ◊ *jds Ratschlag befolgen* Ratschläge advice

⊛ **auf deine/solche (klugen) Ratschläge kann ich verzichten, spar dir deine klugen Ratschläge** *(iron)* keep your advice to yourself

Rät·sel ['rɛːtsl̩] das <–s, –> **1.** mystery des Rätsels Lösung the answer, the explanation jdm Rätsel aufgeben, jdn vor ein Rätsel stellen, jdm ein Rätsel sein baffle sb, puzzle sb ◊ *Es ist mir ein Rätsel, wo mein Schlüssel ist.* ♦ *Sein Verschwinden gab der Polizei Rätsel auf.* vor einem Rätsel stehen be faced with a mystery, be puzzled **2.** riddle, puzzle ◊ *ein Rätsel lösen* jdm ein Rätsel aufgeben ask/give sb a riddle

rät·sel·haft ['rɛːtsl̩haft] ⟨adj⟩ <rätselhafter, am rätselhaftesten> mysterious ◊ *Der Unfallverlauf ist rätselhaft.* ♦ *Sie litt an einer rätselhaften Krankheit.* rätselhaft bleiben remain a mystery etw. ist jdm rätselhaft sth baffles sb ◊ *Es ist mir völlig rätselhaft, wo er so lange bleibt.*

Rat·te ['ratə] die <–, –n> **1.** *(animal)* rat **2.** *(fig, pej) (person)* weasel ◊ *Diese Ratte hat mich hereingelegt!*

rau [raʊ] ⟨adj⟩ <rauer, am rauesten> **1.** *(not smooth)* rough ◊ *Ihre Haut ist rau.* ♦ *Er glättet die raue Wand.* **2.** *(not mild)* harsh, raw ◊ *Die Winter sind dort sehr rau.* **3.** *(region)* inhospitable der raue Norden the rugged North **4.** *(throat)* sore ◊ *Ich habe vom vielen Reden einen rauen Hals bekommen.* ⟨adj, adv⟩ **1.** *(voice)* husky(-ily), hoarse(ly) ◊ *Mit vor Rührung rauer Stimme dankte er ihr.* ♦ *rau lachen* **2.** *(person)* tough; *(manners, behavio(u)r, treatment, tone)* harsh(ly), rough(ly) ◊ *Dort herrschen raue Sitten.* ♦ *Sie sind rau mit ihm umgegangen.* rau aber herzlich rough but jovial ⊖hart, grob

Raub [raʊp] der <–(e)s, –e> **1.** *(theft)* robbery ◊ *einen Raub begehen* **2.** *no pl (animal)* auf Raub ausgehen/aus sein go/be out hunting **3.** *no pl (stolen goods)* loot, booty ◊ *Sie versteckten ihren Raub in einer Höhle.* ⊖Beute. **4.** *(of a person)* abduction ◊ *Er hat den Raub des Mädchens geplant.* der Raub der Sabinerinnen the rape of

the Sabine women

⊚ **ein Raub der Flammen werden** be consumed by the flames

rau·ben ['raʊbm̩] ⟨tr+intr v⟩ +*haben (also fig)* rob ◊ *Die Bande zog raubend und mordend durchs Land.* etw. rauben steal sth; *(children)* kidnap, carry off ◊ *Die Soldaten raubten ihnen die Kinder.* jdm etw. rauben rob sb of sth ◊ *Er raubte ihr die Handtasche.* jdm den Verstand/Schlaf/die Sinne rauben rob sb of their reason/sleep/senses jdm den Atem/die Freiheit rauben take sb's breath/freedom away jdm den letzten Nerv rauben drive sb crazy (jdm) Zeit rauben cost (sb) time jdm das Leben rauben take sb's life

Räu·ber ['rɔʏbɐ] der <-s, ->, **Räu·be·rin** ['rɔʏbərɪn] die <-, -nen> **1.** *(person)* robber ◊ *Ein Räuber hat ihr die Handtasche gestohlen.* **2.** GAME Räuber und Gendarm cops and robbers **3.** ZOO predator ◊ *Löwen und Hyänen sind Räuber.* ⊜Raubtier

⊚ **(kleiner) Räuber** *(fig, hum)* (little) rascal

Raub·tier ['raʊptiːɐ] das <-(e)s, -e> predator, beast of prey ⊜Räuber

Rauch [raʊx] der <-(e)s> *no pl* smoke ◊ *Der Waldbrand hatte enormen Rauch erzeugt.* in Rauch und Flammen aufgehen go up in smoke/flames

⊚ **kein Rauch ohne Feuer** there's no smoke without fire sich in Rauch auflösen *(fig)* go up in smoke ◊ *Seine Ersparnisse haben sich in Rauch aufgelöst.*

② **rau·chen** ['raʊxn̩] ⟨tr+intr v⟩ +*haben* smoke ◊ *Sie raucht wie ein Schlot.* ◆ *Der Schornstein in der Fabrik raucht.* ◆ *Zigarren rauchen* Rauchen verboten no smoking

Rau·cher¹ ['raʊxɐ] <-s, -> smoking compartment ◊ *Wo möchten Sie sitzen: Raucher oder Nichtraucher?* ⊜Nichtraucher

② **Rau·cher²** ['raʊxɐ] der <-s, ->, **Rau·che·rin** ['raʊxərɪn] die <-, -nen> smoker ◊ *Sie ist eine starke Raucherin.* ⊜Nichtraucher

rauf [raʊf] ⟨adv⟩ *(fam)* (get) up ◊ *Rauf aufs Rad, wir wollen endlich fahren!* rauf mit euch up you go ⊜herauf ⊜runter

rau·fen ['raʊfn̩] ⟨ref+intr v⟩ +*haben* (sich) (mit jdm) raufen fight (with sb), scrap (with sb) ◊ *Er raufte sich mit seinem Bruder.* (sich) um etw. raufen fight over sth ◊ *Die beiden Jungen rauften (sich) um den Ball.* ⟨tr v⟩ +*haben* sich ⟨dat⟩ die Haare/den Bart raufen tear your hair/beard

② **Raum** [raʊm] der <-(e)s, Räume> **1.** room ◊ *Sie richtete sich ihr Büro im kleinsten Raum ein.* ◆ *Feuerwerkskörper nicht in geschlossenen Räumen abbrennen!* ⊜Zimmer **2.** *no pl (also fig)* space ◊ *Der Erweiterungsbau soll mehr Raum schaffen.* Raum sparend space saving auf engstem Raum leben live in very cramped conditions ein luftleerer Raum a vacuum; *(topic)* viel Raum einnehmen be much discussed ⊜Platz **3.** der Raum Ulm/Köln etc. the Ulm/Cologne etc. area der süddeutsche/norddeutsche Raum South/North Germany ⊜Gebiet, Gegend **4.** *no pl* (outer) space ◊ *Die Erde bewegt sich durch den Raum.* ⊜Weltraum, All

⊚ **im Raum stehen** be (hanging) in the air etw. in den Raum stellen *(a question, problem)* pose sth

räu·men ['rɔʏmən] ⟨tr v⟩ +*haben* **1.** clear ◊ *Wir räumen unser Teppichlager.* ◆ *Die Mieter müssen selbst Schnee räumen.* etw. von etw. räumen clear sth from/off sth ◊ *Räumst du bitte deine Bücher vom Tisch?* etw. aus etw. räumen take/clear sth out of sth **2.** etw. irgendwohin räumen put sth (away) somewhere ◊ *Räum bitte deine Sachen in die Schultasche.* **3.** *(leave a place)* vacate ◊ *eine Wohnung räumen* ◆ *Die Zimmer müssen bis 10 Uhr geräumt sein/werden.; (the road)* clear, move off **4.** *(force to leave a place)* evacuate, clear ◊ *Ruhe, oder ich lasse den Saal räumen!*

Raum·fahrt ['raʊmfaːɐt] die <-> *no pl* space travel/exploration ◊ *die bemannte/unbemannte Raumfahrt*

räum·lich ['rɔʏmlɪç] ⟨adj, adv⟩ *no comp/superl; when used as an adj, mostly before ns* **1.** in space, spatial(ly) ◊ *Sie wurden zeitlich und räumlich voneinander getrennt.* der räumliche Abstand the (physical) distance, the spacing the räumliche Aufteilung the layout räumlich aufgeteilt sein be laid out ◊ *Wie ist das Haus räumlich aufgeteilt?* räumliche Enge/Beengtheit crampedness räumlich beengt wohnen live in cramped condition räumlich begrenzt in a confined space, cramped for space große räumliche Nähe very close (proximity) **2.** three-dimensional ◊ *Zum räumlichen Sehen braucht man zwei Augen.* ◆ *Die Darstellung war räumlich.* etw. räumlich darstellen show/display/depict sth in three dimensions nicht räumlich sehen können have no three-dimensional vision ⊜plastisch

Rau·pe ['raʊpə] die <-, -n> **1.** *(animal, vehicle)* caterpillar ◊ *Die Raupen des Zitronenfalters sind grün.* ◆ *Erdreich mit schweren Raupen zur Seite schieben* **2.** TECHN caterpillar track

Rausch [raʊʃ] der <-(e)s, Räusche> **1.** *(from alcohol)* intoxication im Rausch under the influence (of alcohol) einen Rausch haben be drunk sich ⟨dat⟩ einen Rausch antrinken get drunk seinen Rausch ausschlafen sleep it off **2.** der Rausch der Begeisterung/Leidenschaft ecstatic enthusiasm/passion der Rausch des Sieges the exhilaration of victory der Rausch der Geschwindigkeit the thrill of speed

rau·schen ['raʊʃn̩] ⟨intr v⟩ +*haben/sein* **1.** +*haben* *(gently)* murmur ◊ *Der Wind rauschte in den Bäumen.; (noisily)* rush ◊ *Hörst du den Bach rauschen?; (leaves)* rustle; *(sea)* roar; *(radio, telephone)* hiss rauschender Beifall resounding applause **2.** +*sein (vehicle)* whoosh ◊ *Raketen rauschten durch die Luft.; (water)* irgendwohin rauschen rush somewhere ◊ *Das Wasser rauscht in Strömen zu Tal.* **3.** +*sein (fam) (person)* (irgendwohin/aus etw.) rauschen sweep (somewhere/out of sth) ◊ *Sie rauschte wutentbrannt aus dem Zimmer.*

Rausch·gift ['raʊʃɡɪft] das <-(e)s, -e> narcotic, drug ◊ *Sie nimmt Rauschgift, um der Realität zu entfliehen.*

Raz·zia ['ratsia] die <-, Razzien *or seldom* -s> raid in etw. ⟨dat⟩ eine Razzia durchführen raid sth

② **re·a·gie·ren** [rea'giːrən] <reagiert, reagierte, hat reagiert> ⟨intr v⟩ **1.** (auf etw. ⟨acc⟩) reagieren react (to sth), respond (to sth) ◊ *Er reagierte gereizt.* ◆

Sie sprach ihn an, aber er reagierte nicht.
ablehnend auf etw. ⟨acc⟩ reagieren decline sth ausweichend/mit Befremden auf eine Frage reagieren answer a question evasively/disconcertedly **2.** CHEM mit etw. (zu etw.) reagieren react with sth (to produce sth) ◇ *Schwefel reagiert mit Sauerstoff zu Schwefeldioxid.* miteinander reagieren react (together)

② **Re·ak·ti·on** [reak'tsi̯oːn] die ⟨-, -en⟩ reaction ◇ *Wie war Ihre erste Reaktion, als Sie davon hörten?* ◆ *eine allergische Reaktion* Reaktion auf etw. ⟨acc⟩ reaction to sth

re·al [re|'aːl] ⟨adj, adv⟩ **1.** real ◇ *Sind die Gefahren, vor denen er warnt, real?* ◆ *Im realen Leben ist er ziemlich ängstlich.* real vorhanden sein/existieren be real (and present) real verfügbares Einkommen real (available) income real zurückgehen/steigen etc. decrease/increase etc. in real terms ⊖wirklich **2.** *(sensible)* realistic ◇ *Bei realer Einschätzung sind die Erfolgschancen eher gering.* ⊖realistisch, reell

② **re·a·li·sie·ren** [reali'ziːrən] ⟨realisiert, realisierte, hat realisiert⟩ ⟨tr v⟩ **1.** *(lofty) (make come true)* carry out, implement ◇ *Das Projekt hat sich nicht realisieren lassen.* ⊖verwirklichen **2.** *(understand, earn)* realize ◇ *Er hat immer noch nicht realisiert, was gemeint war.*

② **re·a·lis·tisch** [rea'lɪstɪʃ] ⟨adj, adv⟩ realistic(ally) ◇ *sich realistische Ziele setzen* ◆ *Alle anderen Alternativen sind wenig realistisch.* ◆ *eine Situation realistisch einschätzen* realistisch betrachtet (viewed/seen) realistically

Re·a·li·tät [reali'tɛːt] die ⟨-, -en⟩ *(lofty)* **1.** *no pl* reality ◇ *Diese Theorie widerspricht der Realität.* etw. ist Realität sth is true/a reality an der Realität vorbeigehen miss the truth sich in der Realität beweisen prove yourself/itself in the real world ⊖Wirklichkeit **2.** fact ◇ *Du musst dich den Realitäten des Alltags stellen.* ⊖Tatsache

Re·al·schu·le [re|'aːlʃuːlə] die ⟨-, -n⟩ ◇ *die sechsstufige/vierstufige Realschule* ◆ *Er geht auf die Realschule.* box@ Gesamtschule, Gymnasium, Hauptschule

The *Realschule* is an intermediate school, positioned between the *Hauptschule* and the *Gymnasium.* It imparts a more comprehensive general education than the *Hauptschule* and places strong emphasis on independent learning, but is more vocationally oriented than the *Gymnasium.* It encompasses six years of schooling, grades 5 to 10 (approx. from age 10 to 16), and culminates in the *mittlere Reife* (intermediate school certificate).

Re·al·schü·ler [re|'aːlʃyːlɐ] der ⟨-s, -⟩, **Re·al·schü·le·rin** [re|'aːlʃyːlərɪn] die ⟨-, -nen⟩ *pupil at a 'Realschule'* ◇ *Die Ausbildung dauert für Realschüler drei, für Abiturienten zwei Jahre.*

Re·be ['reːbə] die ⟨-, -n⟩ **1.** *(branch)* (vine) shoot/tendril ◇ *Die Rebe rankt sich um das Spalier.* **2.** *(plant)* (grape)vine ◇ *Reben anpflanzen/beschneiden* **3.** *(type)* grape (variety) ◇ *Der Silvaner ist die klassische fränkische Rebe.*

Re·bell [re'bɛl] der ⟨-en, -en⟩, **Re·bel·lin** [re'bɛlɪn] die ⟨-, -nen⟩ rebel

Re·chen·schaft ['rɛçnʃaft] die ⟨-⟩ *no pl* account

von jdm Rechenschaft (über etw. ⟨acc⟩) verlangen/fordern demand an explanation/account from sb (for sth) Rechenschaft über etw. ⟨acc⟩ ablegen/geben account for sth jdm Rechenschaft (über etw. ⟨acc⟩) schulden owe sb an explanation (for/of sth) jdn (für etw.) zur Rechenschaft ziehen call sb to account (for sth)

② **Re·cher·che** [re'ʃɛrʃə] die ⟨-, -n⟩ research, investigation, enquiry ◇ *eine Recherche im Internet* eine Recherche anstellen research, make an investigation

re·cher·chie·ren [reʃɛr'ʃiːrən] ⟨recherchiert, recherchierte, hat recherchiert⟩ ⟨tr+intr v⟩ *(lofty)* investigate, research ◇ *Er recherchiert die Hintergründe zu aktuellen Themen.* ◆ *Sie hat gründlich für das Buch recherchiert.* ◆ *ein gut recherchierter Artikel*

② **rech·nen** ['rɛçnən] ⟨rechnet, rechnete, hat gerechnet⟩ ⟨tr v⟩ **1.** *(do sums)* work out ◇ *Kannst du das im Kopf rechnen?* **2.** estimate, reckon on ◇ *Sie müssen zehn Stunden für die Fahrt rechnen.* **3.** jdn/etw. (zu etw.) rechnen include sb/sth (in sth) ◇ *Wir werden etwa 50 Personen sein, Kinder nicht gerechnet.* **4.** jdn/etw. zu jdm/etw. rechnen count sb/sth among sb/sth ◇ *Rechnest du ihn noch zu deinen Freunden?* ⊖zählen ⟨intr v⟩ **1.** *(work out figures)* make calculations/a calculation richtig rechnen calculate correctly falsch rechnen make a mistake (in your calculation) gut/schlecht rechnen können be good/bad at sums/arithmetic **2.** grob/großzügig gerechnet roughly/generously estimated ⊖schätzen **3.** mit etw./jdm rechnen count on sth/sb, expect sb/sth, reckon with sb/sth ◇ *Sie muss mit einer Absage rechnen.* ◆ *Ich rechne damit, demnächst befördert zu werden.* mit dem Schlimmsten rechnen be prepared for the worst **4.** auf jdn/etw. rechnen count on sb/sth ◇ *Wir rechnen auf Ihre Mithilfe/Mitarbeit.* ⊖zählen ⟨ref v⟩ *(fam)* sich rechnen pay off, be worthwhile ◇ *Ökologisch zu denken rechnet sich für alle.* ⊖sich rentieren

⊚ mit jedem Cent/Euro etc. rechnen watch/count every cent/Euro etc.

Rech·nen ['rɛçnən] das ⟨-s⟩ *no pl* arithmetic ◇ *Heute haben wir in der ersten Stunde Rechnen.*

Rech·ner[1] ['rɛçnɐ] der ⟨-s, -⟩ **1.** IT computer ◇ *Die Daten werden auf dem zentralen Rechner gespeichert.* ⊖Computer **2.** *(fam)* calculator ◇ *Dürft ihr bei den Mathearbeiten Rechner benutzen?*

Rech·ner[2] ['rɛçnɐ] der ⟨-s, -⟩, **Rech·ne·rin** ['rɛçnərɪn] die ⟨-, -nen⟩ **1.** ein guter Rechner sein be good at sums/arithmetic **2.** ein sparsamer Rechner sein be thrifty kühle Rechner people who know their sums

② **Rech·nung** ['rɛçnʊŋ] die ⟨-, -en⟩ **1.** calculation, sum ◇ *etw. durch eine simple Rechnung ermitteln* eine Rechnung lösen work out/solve a calculation/sum nach meiner Rechnung according to my calculations **2.** *(for services, goods)* bill, invoice ◇ *Lass mich die Rechnung zahlen/übernehmen/begleichen.* ◆ *eine Rechnung über 100 Euro.* (jdm) eine Rechnung (aus)stellen/schreiben issue an invoice (to sb) jdm etw. in Rechnung stellen charge (sb) for sth ◇ *Er stellte für die Reparatur 200 Euro in Rechnung.* auf jds Rechnung at sb's expense ◇ *Lassen Sie das auf meine Rechnung reparieren.*

etw. geht auf jds Rechnung sb is paying for sth ⊛ jd hat die Rechnung ohne den Wirt gemacht *(fig)* there was something sb hadn't reckoned with eine (alte) Rechnung (mit jdm) begleichen *(fig)* settle a(n old) score (with sb) (mit jdm) noch eine Rechnung offen haben have a score to settle (with sb) die Rechnung geht nicht auf *(fig)* the plan doesn't work out etw. geht auf jds Rechung *(fig)* sb is responsible/to blame for sth jdm wird die Rechnung (für etw.) präsentiert *(fig)* sb has to pay (for sth) einer Sache [dat] Rechnung tragen *(fig)* take sth into account

② **recht** [rɛçt] [adj, adv] *no comp/superl* **1.** *when used as an adj, mostly before ns (appropriate)* right ◊ *Sie suchen noch den rechten Standort für die Filiale.* das Rechte tun do the right thing gerade recht kommen be just in time wenn man es sich recht überlegt ... when you stop and think about it ... *Ich höre wohl nicht recht., Höre ich recht? Am I hearing things? Gehe ich recht in der Annahme ...? Am I right in assuming ...?* ⊜richtig **2.** so ist es recht, recht so that's fine nichts Rechtes lernen not learn a proper trade nichts Rechtes mit sich/ seiner Zeit anzufangen wissen not know what to do with yourself/your time **3.** etw. ist jdm recht sth is all right with sb, sb approves of sth ◊ *Wenn es euch recht ist, gehen wir ins Kino.* ♦ *Ihm ist jedes Mittel recht, zum Ziel zu kommen.* es jdm recht machen please sb ◊ *Sie will es immer allen recht machen.* **4.** *negated; when used as an adj, only before ns* real, proper ◊ *Sie scheint keinen rechten Appetit zu haben.* nicht recht not really/quite ◊ *Sie konnte sich nicht so recht entschließen.* ⊜richtig **5.** *when used as an adj, only before ns* quite ◊ *Er ist ein rechter Langweiler.* ♦ *Um diese Zeit bin ich immer schon recht müde.* ◊ *Das sieht recht nett aus.* ⊜ziemlich, relativ, verhältnismäßig ⊛ recht und billig right and proper alles, was recht ist fair is fair, there is a limit

② **Recht** [rɛçt] das <–(e)s, –e> **1.** *no pl (legal)* law ◊ *das Recht brechen/verletzen/mit Füßen treten* ♦ *Er studiert Recht und Volkswirtschaft in Paris.* Recht sprechen administer justice gegen geltendes Recht verstoßen contravene the law in force das Studium des Rechts law study/studies **2.** *(moral)* right ◊ *Du hast das Recht, angehört zu werden.* ♦ *Der Erfolg gibt ihm das Recht, optimistisch zu sein.* jds gutes Recht sein be sb's right das Recht auf etw. [acc] the right to sth ◊ *Ich habe ein Recht darauf, die Prüfung zu wiederholen.* alle Rechte vorbehalten all rights reserved auf seine Rechte pochen insist on your rights **3.** *no pl (what is correct)* right Recht behalten be (proved) right immer Recht behalten wollen always want to be right jdm Recht geben admit sb is right ich gebe dir Recht you are right Recht haben be right im Recht sein be in the right mit/zu Recht rightly ◊ *Er hat diesen Preis (völlig) zu Recht bekommen.* ♦ *Sie war mit (vollem) Recht verärgert.* mit welchem Recht by what right zwischen Recht und Unrecht unterscheiden können know right from wrong ⊛ das Recht beugen bend the law, pervert the course of justice von Rechts wegen by law

rech·te [ˈrɛçtə] [adj] *only before ns* <ein rechter ..., eine rechte ..., ein rechtes ...> **1.** right ◊ *Auf dem rechten Ohr ist er taub.* ♦ *Er schoss den Ball in die*

rechte Ecke. ⊜linke **2.** POL right wing ◊ *Skinheads und andere rechte Gewalttäter* der rechte Flügel the right wing die rechte Szene the far right (scene) ⊜linke **3.** MATH ein rechter Winkel a right angle

recht·fer·ti·gen [ˈrɛçtfɛˈtɪgn̩] [tr v] *+haben* (sich/ etw.) rechtfertigen (vor jdm) justify (yourself/sth) (to sb) ◊ *Ich halte den hohen Preis durchaus für gerechtfertigt.* ♦ *Er rechtfertige seine Verspätung mit einer Autopanne.* ♦ *Du musst dich für deine Taten vor mir nicht rechtfertigen.* etw. ist durch nichts zu rechtfertigen nothing can justify sth

recht·lich [ˈrɛçtlɪç] [adj, adv] *no comp/superl; when used as an adj, only before ns* legal(ly) ◊ *Wir haben keine rechtliche Handhabe gegen ihn.* ♦ *Der Vertrag ist rechtlich verbindlich.* rechtlich nicht zulässig not permissable in law

recht·mä·ßig [ˈrɛçtmɛːsɪç] [adj, adv] *no comp/ superl* legitimate(ly), lawful(ly), rightful(ly), legal(ly) ◊ *Die Verordnung ist rechtmäßig.* ♦ *eine rechtmäßige Kündigung* ♦ *rechtmäßig hergestellte Kopien* etw. steht jdm rechtmäßig zu sb is legally entitled to sth

② **rechts¹** [rɛçts] [adv] **1.** on the right rechts oben/ unten/hinten in the top/bottom/far right-hand corner ◊ *Du musst noch rechts unten unterschreiben.* (nach) rechts to the right ◊ *Du musst hier (nach) rechts abbiegen.* rechts ranfahren pull up on the right sich rechts einordnen move to/take the right-hand lane von rechts from the right ◊ *Das von rechts kommende Fahrzeug hat Vorfahrt.* ⊜links **2.** POL rechts stehen be right-wing, be on the right rechts wählen vote for the right ⊜links **3.** SPORT rechts außen outside right

rechts² [rɛçts] [prep] [+gen] or [+dat] **1.** [+gen] on the right side of ◊ *Rechts des Flusses sieht man einen Wanderweg.* **2.** *adverbial* [+dat] rechts von jdm to sb's right ◊ *Er saß rechts von mir.* rechts von etw. to the right of sth ◊ *Rechts vom Schreibtisch steht sein Aktenkoffer.*

Rechts·an·walt [ˈrɛçtsʔanvalt] der <–(e)s, Rechtsanwälte>, **Rechts·an·wäl·tin** [ˈrɛçtsʔanvɛltɪn] die <–, –nen> lawyer, solicitor, attorney, barrister ◊ *Sie ist Rechtsanwältin.* ♦ *sich einen Rechtsanwalt nehmen*

Recht·schrei·bung [ˈrɛçtʃraɛbʊŋ] die <–> *no pl* spelling ◊ *In der Schule hat er Probleme mit der Rechtschreibung.*

rechts·kräf·tig [ˈrɛçtskrɛftɪç] [adj, adv] *no comp/ superl (verdict)* final ◊ *Das Urteil ist rechtskräftig.; (contract)* legally binding ◊ *Sie haben einen rechtskräftigen Vertrag geschlossen.* rechtskräftig verurteilt werden be issued with a final sentence einen Vertrag rechtskräftig abschließen make a contract legally binding

rechts·ra·di·kal [ˈrɛçtsradiˌkaːl] [adj, adv] *no comp/ superl* rechtsradikal (orientiert) extremely/radically right-wing, far-right ◊ *Die gewaltbereite Gruppe ist rechtsradikal.* ♦ *Rechtsradikal orientierte Jugendliche bedrohten Asylbewerber.* ♦ *rechtsradikale Übergriffe*

Rechts·ver·kehr [ˈrɛçtsfɛkeːɐ̯] der <–s> *no pl* **1.** right-hand traffic In den Ländern auf dem europäischen Kontinent herrscht Rechtsverkehr. They drive on the right on the Continent. **2.** legal

relations ◊ *elektronischer Rechtsverkehr*
rechts·wid·rig ['rɛçtsviːdrɪç] [adj, adv] *seldom comp/superl* unlawful(ly), illegal(ly) ◊ *eine rechtswidrige Kündigung* ◆ *Das Gericht hat dieses Vorgehen für rechtswidrig erklärt.* ◆ *rechtswidrig handeln*

recht·zei·tig ['rɛçtsaetɪç] [adj] *seldom comp/superl* prompt, punctual ◊ *Wir bitten um rechtzeitige Anmeldung. Das war gerade noch rechtzeitig!* That was close! [adv] in (good) time ◊ *Es ist wichtig, dass das Problem rechtzeitig erkannt wird.*

Reck [rɛk] das <-(e)s, –e *or* –s> horizontal bar ◊ *ein Unterschwung am Reck*

re·cken ['rɛkṇ] [tr v] +haben stretch ◊ *Sie reckte die Arme und gähnte.; (your neck)* crane

Re·dak·teur [redak'tøːɐ̯] der <-s, –e>, **Re·dak·teu·rin** [redak'tøːrɪn] die <-, –nen> editor ◊ *der leitende Redakteur einer Zeitung* ◆ *Sie ist Redakteurin beim Rundfunk.*

Re·dak·ti·on [redak'tsi̯oːn] die <-, –en> **1.** editing ◊ *Für die Redaktion des Heftes war Julia Schmidt verantwortlich.* **2.** editorial staff, editors ◊ *Die gesamte Redaktion steht hinter dieser Stellungnahme.* **3.** editorial department ◊ *Die Redaktion ist im zweiten Stock.*

ⓩ **Re·de** ['reːdə] die <-, –n> **1.** speech ◊ *Anlässlich des Jubiläums hielt er eine Rede.* **2.** conversation ◊ *Die Rede kam auf klassische Musik.* Davon war nicht die Rede. There was no mention of that. **3.** GRAM direkte/wörtliche Rede direct speech indirekte Rede reported/indirect speech ⊛ jdm Rede und Antwort stehen answer sb's questions, face sb ◊ *Die Bürgermeisterin stand den Bürgern Rede und Antwort.* lange Rede, kurzer Sinn to put it briefly, in short von etw. kann keine/nicht die Rede sein there is no question of sth nicht der Rede wert sein be not worth mentioning eine Rede schwingen *(fam)* give a speech jdn zur Rede stellen confront sb

ⓩ **re·den** ['reːdṇ] [tr+intr v] +haben talk, speak ◊ *Er redet nur Blödsinn.* ◆ *Möchtest du darüber reden?* ◆ *Mit Marco rede ich nicht mehr.* [intr v] give a speech ◊ *Sie redete vor dem Bundestag.* ⊜sprechen ⊛ mit sich reden lassen be persuadable von sich reden machen cause a stir

Re·de·wen·dung ['reːdəvɛndʊŋ] die <-, –en> saying, expression, idiom ◊ *eine gebräuchliche/ gängige Redewendung*

Red·ner ['reːdnɐ] der <-s, –>, **Red·ne·rin** ['reːdnərɪn] die <-, –nen> **1.** speaker ◊ *Wir erwarten folgende Redner zu der Konferenz: ...* **2.** (public) speaker ◊ *Sie ist eine brillante Rednerin.*

re·du·zie·ren [redu'tsiːrən] <reduziert, reduzierte, hat reduziert> [tr v] **1.** reduce ◊ *die Zahl der Arbeitslosen reduzieren* ⊜senken, mindern **2.** etw. auf etw. [acc] reduzieren reduce sth to sth ◊ *ein Thema auf das Wesentliche reduzieren* [ref v] sich reduzieren go down, decrease, drop ◊ *Der Umsatz hat sich um acht Prozent reduziert.* ⊜sich verringern

re·ell [re'ɛl] [adj] **1.** respectable ◊ *Dieses Geschäft ist eine reelle Sache.* ◆ *Das Angebot ist reell und fair.* ⊜fair, anständig **2.** real ◊ *Für ihn ist die Gefahr ganz reell.* ◆ *reelle Zahlen* ⊜real, echt

Re·fe·rat [refe'raːt, rɛfə'raːt] das <-(e)s, –e> **1.** (seminar) paper; *(oral)* presentation ◊ *ein Referat halten* **2.** department ◊ *das Referat für Presse und Information*

Re·fe·ren·dar [referɛn'daːɐ̯, refərɛn'daːɐ̯] der <-s, –e>, **Re·fe·ren·da·rin** [referɛn'daːrɪn, refərɛn'daːrɪn] die <-, –nen> **1.** civil service trainee ◊ *als Referendar im Vermessungsamt tätig sein* **2.** trainee lawyer ◊ *Er ist Referendar am Landgericht Kassel.* **3.** trainee/student teacher ◊ *In Mathe haben wir dieses Jahr einen Referendar als Lehrer.*

If you want to be a teacher in Germany, you have to do two years of practical training after you have finished your studies. During these two years, the trainee teachers observe lessons and also do some supervised teaching themselves. At the end of this training period, each trainee must pass an exam and practical tests before they can go on to take the second *Staatsexamen* (state examination).

Re·fe·rent [refe'rɛnt, rɛfə'rɛnt] der <-en, –en>, **Re·fe·ren·tin** [refe'rɛntɪn, rɛfə'rɛntɪn] die <-, –nen> **1.** speaker ◊ *Unser heutiger Referent ist Dr. Julian Bausch.* ⊜Sprecher **2.** adviser ◊ *die zuständige Referentin für Umweltpolitik*

re·flek·tie·ren [reflɛk'tiːrən] <reflektiert, reflektierte, hat reflektiert> [tr+intr v] **1.** PHYSICS reflect ◊ *Der weiße Sand reflektiert das Sonnenlicht.* ◆ *Eine Fläche reflektiert besser als eine Kugel.* ⊜widerspiegeln **2.** *(lofty)* etw./über etw. [acc] reflektieren reflect on sth ◊ *(über) verschiedene Aspekte eines Problems reflektieren* ⊜über etw. nachdenken

Re·flex [re'flɛks] der <-es, –e> **1.** MED reflex (action) ◊ *Der Arzt prüft die Reflexe des Verletzten.* **2.** PHYSICS reflection ◊ *die Reflexe des Sonnenlichts auf der Meeresoberfläche*

Re·fle·xiv·pro·no·men [reflɛ'ksiːfpro,noːmən] das <-s, – *or* Reflexivpronomina> reflexive pronoun

ⓩ **Re·form** [re'fɔrm] die <-, –en> reform ◊ *nötige Reformen durchsetzen*

Re·form·haus [re'fɔrmhaos] das <-es, Reformhäuser> health food shop, health food store

Towards the end of the nineteenth century, a movement began in Germany to reduce excessive alcohol consumption, industrialized food production, and other potential threats to human health. Homeopathy and vegetarianism played an important role in this movement. In 1900, the first German health food shop opened in Wuppertal, offering alternatives to normal products and representing the values of the health reform movement. The idea caught on; and today there are many health food stores all over Germany, which sell organic food and natural cosmetics and medicines.

re·for·mie·ren [refɔr'miːrən] <reformiert, reformierte, hat reformiert> [tr v] reform ◊ *das Gesundheitswesen reformieren* ◆ *Luther reformierte die Kirche.*

ⓩ **re·for·miert** [refɔr'miːɐ̯t] past p of reformieren [adj] *mostly before ns* reformed ◊ *die reformierte Oberstufe/Rechtschreibung*

ⓩ **Re·gal** [re'gaːl] das <–s, –e> shelf, shelves ◊ *Die Bücher stehen im/auf dem Regal.*

re·ge ['reːgə] [adj] <reger, am regsten> **1.** busy, active ◊ *Unsere Spendensammler waren sehr rege.* ♦ *ein reger Austausch in der Wissenschaft* geistig rege alert ⊖aktiv **2.** *(interest, demand, imagination)* lively ◊ *Der Vorschlag stieß auf reges Interesse.* ♦ *Die Nachfrage ist rege.* ⊖groß [adv] *translation varies* Es wurde rege diskutiert. There was a lively discussion about it. Von dem Angebot wurde rege Gebrauch gemacht. A lot of people made use of the offer. sich rege über etw. [acc] austauschen have a lively exchange about sth

ⓩ **Re·gel** ['reːgl] die <–, –n> **1.** *(also fig)* rule ◊ *die Regeln der deutschen Grammatik* ♦ *klare Regeln aufstellen* ♦ *Gute Beratung ist hier leider nicht die Regel.* sich [dat] etw. zur Regel machen make a habit of (doing) sth **2.** *no pl* (menstrual) period ◊ *Wann hatten Sie Ihre letzte Regel?* ⊖Periode, Blutung

⊙ nach allen Regeln der Kunst *(fam)* perfectly, immaculately ⊖perfekt, fachmännisch in der/aller Regel as a rule ⊖gewöhnlich, normalerweise ⊖ausnahmsweise

ⓩ **re·gel·mä·ßig** ['reːglmɛːsɪç] [adj, adv] **1.** regular(ly) ◊ *regelmäßige Kontrollen* ♦ *Dieses Verb ist regelmäßig.* ♦ *Ich gehe regelmäßig joggen.* **2.** *(teeth, handwriting etc.)* even(ly) ◊ *regelmäßige Zähne* ♦ *Seine Schrift ist klein und regelmäßig.* ♦ *regelmäßig geformte Objekte* ⊖gleichmäßig **3.** *when used as an adj, only before ns* frequent(ly) ◊ *ein regelmäßiger Gast* ♦ *regelmäßig ins Theater gehen* ⊖häufig [adv] *(fam)* constantly ◊ *Das vergesse ich regelmäßig!* ⊖dauernd

ⓩ **re·geln** ['reːgln] [tr v] +haben **1.** *often in adjectival constructions* work out, arrange ◊ *etw. gesetzlich/ neu regeln* ♦ *Wie sind die Zuzahlungen bei chronischen Erkrankungen geregelt?* ⊖festlegen **2.** regulate, control ◊ *ein Thermostat, der die Wärme regelt* ⊖regulieren **3.** sort out ◊ *Die Formalitäten sind schon geregelt.* etw. regelt sich sth sorts itself out ⊖erledigen

re·gel·recht ['reːglrɛçt] *(fam)* [adj] no comp/superl, only before ns real, genuine ◊ *Vor Prüfungen habe ich jedes Mal regelrechte Panik.* ⊖ausgesprochen, richtig [adv] literally ◊ *Wir werden mit Werbung regelrecht überschwemmt.* ⊖buchstäblich

Re·ge·lung ['reːgəlʊŋ] die <–, –en> **1.** *no pl* regulation, control ◊ *ein Gesetz zur Regelung der Miethöhe* **2.** rules ◊ *die geltende Regelung* ♦ *die amtliche Regelung der deutschen Rechtschreibung*

re·gen ['reːgŋ] [ref v] +haben **1.** sich regen move, stir ◊ *Alle standen still, niemand regte sich.* ♦ *Kein Lufthauch regte sich.* **2.** *(lofty, fig)* sich regen stir ◊ *Regt sich da nicht dein Gewissen?* [tr v] +haben *(lofty)* move ◊ *Vor Schreck konnte er kein Glied regen.* ⊖rühren

ⓩ **Re·gen** ['reːgŋ] der <–s> no pl **1.** rain ◊ *Wir gingen im Regen spazieren.* ♦ *saurer Regen* **2.** *(fig)* ein Regen von etw. a shower of sth ◊ *Ein Regen von Blütenblättern ging auf das Brautpaar nieder.*

⊙ vom Regen in die Traufe kommen go from the frying pan into the fire ein warmer Regen a windfall jdn im Regen stehen lassen leave sb in the lurch

Re·gen·bo·gen ['reːgŋboːgŋ] der <–s, – or Regenbögen> rainbow

re·ge·ne·rie·ren [regene'riːrən] *(lofty)* <regeneriert, regenerierte, hat regeneriert> [tr v] revitalize, regenerate ◊ *Diese Creme regeneriert die Haut.* etw. regeneriert sich sth regenerates ◊ *Diese Zellen regenerieren sich nach einiger Zeit.* ⊖erneuern [ref v] jd regeneriert sich sb recharges their batteries ◊ *sich im Urlaub regenerieren* ⊖erholen

Re·gen·schirm ['reːgŋʃɪrm] der <–(e)s, –e> umbrella ◊ *den Regenschirm öffnen/schließen*

⊙ gespannt wie ein Regenschirm sein *(fam, hum)* be dying to know/see

Re·gen·wald ['reːgŋvalt] der <–(e)s, Regenwälder> rainforest

Re·gie [re'ʒiː] die <–> no pl **1.** *(of a film, play etc.)* direction ◊ *Er hat oft unter der Regie von Peter Zadek gespielt.* Regie führen direct **2.** *(lofty, fig)* leadership ◊ *Unter seiner Regie expandierte das Unternehmen.*

⊙ in eigener Regie yourself Sie haben ihr Haus in eigener Regie umgebaut. They converted the house themselves.

ⓩ **re·gie·ren** [re'giːrən] <regiert, regierte, hat regiert> [tr+intr v] *(also fig)* rule ◊ *Er regierte das Land viele Jahre lang.* ♦ *Salomo regierte über Israel.* ♦ *Geld regiert die Welt.; (monarch also)* reign [tr v] GRAM take, govern ◊ *„Bei" regiert den Dativ.*

ⓩ **Re·gie·rung** [re'giːrʊŋ] die <–, –en> government ◊ *eine Regierung bilden* ♦ *die Regierung Adenauer* ♦ *die Regierung übernehmen* die Regierung ausüben be in power

Re·gime [re'ʒiːm] das <–s, –s> *(pej)* regime ◊ *ein totalitäres/korruptes Regime*

ⓩ **Re·gi·on** [re'gioːn] die <–, –en> region, area ◊ *Besucher aus der gesamten Region kamen zum Fest.* ♦ *die Region Berlin-Brandenburg*

re·gi·o·nal [regio'naːl] [adj, adv] no comp/superl; when used as an adj, only before ns local(ly), regional(ly) ◊ *eine regionale Tageszeitung* ♦ *ein regional tätiger Verband* Die Ernte ist dieses Jahr regional sehr unterschiedlich ausgefallen. The harvest has differed greatly from region to region this year.

Re·gis·seur [reʒɪ'søːɐ̯] der <–s, –e>, **Re·gis·seu·rin** [reʒɪ'søːrɪn] die <–, –nen> director ◊ *Sie ist Regisseurin von Beruf.* ♦ *ein bekannter Regisseur*

Re·gis·ter [re'gɪstɐ] das <–s, –> **1.** index ◊ *ein alphabetisches Register* **2.** register ◊ *Die Eheschließung wurde in das Register des Standesamtes eingetragen.* ⊖Verzeichnis **3.** stop ◊ *Die Orgel in dieser Kirche hat 53 Register.* **4.** LING register

⊙ alle Register ziehen pull out all the stops

re·gis·trie·ren [regɪs'triːrən] <registriert, registrierte, hat registriert> [tr v] **1.** register ◊ *Das Standesamt registrierte letztes Jahr 289 Geburten.* ♦ *ein Sensor, der auch reine Temperaturschwankungen registriert* **2.** jd registriert etw. sb notices sth, sth registers with sb ◊ *Hast du überhaupt registriert, dass ich aufgeräumt habe?* ⊖bemerken, wahrnehmen

Reg·ler ['reːglɐ] der <–s, –> control ◊ *Die Temperatur wird von einem automatischen Regler gesteuert.*

reg·nen ['reːgnən] <regnet, regnete, hat geregnet>

[imp v] **1.** es regnet it rains, it's raining ◊ *Es regnete in Strömen.* **2.** es regnet etw. it's raining sth ◊ *Vor dem Standesamt regnete es Blumen.* **3.** *(fig)* es regnet etw. sth floods in ◊ *Es regnete Lob von allen Seiten.*

re·gu·lär [regu'lɛːɐ] [adj, adv] *no comp/superl* **1.** proper(ly), according to the rules ◊ *ein regulärer Streik* ♦ *Die Bedingungen waren nicht ganz regulär.* ♦ *Einkünfte regulär versteuern* **2.** normal(ly) ◊ *Das gehört zu unseren regulären Leistungen.* ♦ *auf den regulären Preis zehn Prozent Rabatt gewähren* ♦ *Wir haben ab Montag wieder regulär geöffnet.* regulär ... kosten cost ... at the normal price ◊ *Das hat regulär das Doppelte gekostet.* ⊜normal

re·gu·lie·ren [regu'liːrən] <reguliert, regulierte, hat reguliert> [tr v] regulate ◊ *ein Medikament, das den Blutdruck reguliert* sich regulieren regulate itself ◊ *Der Markt reguliert sich von selbst.* ⊜regeln

Reh [reː] das <–(e)s, –e> roe deer

rei·ben ['raɛbm̩] <reibt, rieb, hat gerieben> [tr+intr v] **1.** rub ◊ *Das Pferd rieb seinen Kopf an Inas Schulter.* ♦ *Die neuen Schuhe reiben an der Ferse.* sich [dat] den Arm/das Knie reiben rub your arm/knee sich [dat] die Hände wund reiben rub your hands raw **2.** *(cheese, vegetables etc.)* grate [ref v] **1.** sich an jdm reiben not get along with sb jd reibt sich an etw. sth gives sb something to think about ◊ *An diesem Thema reiben sich die Experten.* **2.** sich mit jdm/etw. reiben clash with sb/sth ◊ *Die neuen Strukturen reiben sich mit den alten Gewohnheiten.*

Rei·bung ['raɛbʊŋ] die <–> *no pl* friction ◊ *durch Reibung erzeugte Wärme*

rei·bungs·los ['raɛbʊŋsloːs] [adj, adv] *no superl*; *when used as an adj, mostly before ns* smooth(ly) ◊ *Er ist für den reibungslosen Ablauf des Projekts verantwortlich.* ♦ *Alles funktionierte reibungslos.*

② **reich** [raɛç] [adj, adv] **1.** rich(ly) ◊ *eine reiche Erbin* ♦ *Er wurde über Nacht reich.* ♦ *ein Schloss mit reich ausgestatteten Zimmern* reich heiraten marry money **2.** rich(ly), abundant(ly) ◊ *reiche Beute machen* ♦ *Die Flora hier ist reich und vielseitig.* ♦ *Sie wurden reich beschenkt.* reich an etw. [dat] rich in sth **3.** *when used as an adj, mostly before ns* lavish(ly) ◊ *eine Fassade mit reichen Verzierungen* ♦ *Der Weihnachtsbaum war reich geschmückt.* ⊜aufwändig [adj] *mostly before ns* (selection, collection) extensive ◊ *eine reiche Auswahl*

Reich [raɛç] das <–(e)s, –e> **1.** kingdom, realm ◊ *Im ganzen Reich herrschte Friede.*; *(of one ruler)* empire ◊ *das Reich Alexanders des Großen* **2.** *(fig)* realm ◊ *Solche Pläne gehören ins Reich der Fantasie!*

⊛ **das Deutsche Reich** the German Empire **das Dritte Reich** the Third Reich

rei·chen ['raɛçn̩] [intr v] +*haben* **1.** bis irgendwohin reichen go somewhere, stretch somewhere ◊ *Die Chronik reicht bis ins Jahr 1608.* ♦ *Unser Grundstück reicht bis an den Bach.* jdm bis irgendwohin reichen go down to sb's sth ◊ *Der Rock reicht ihr bis zum Knöchel.*; come up to sb's sth ◊ *Das Wasser reicht ihm bis zum Knie.* **2.** be enough ◊ *Reicht deine Kraft, um diese Kiste zu heben?* Wie lange reichen die Vorräte noch? How much longer will stocks last for? ⊜genügen, ausreichen [tr v]

+*haben (lofty)* **1.** jdm etw. reichen give sb sth, offer sb sth ◊ *Sie reichte ihm die Hand zur Versöhnung.* ⊜anbieten **2.** jdm etw. reichen give sb sth, hand sb sth ◊ *Reichen Sie mir bitte das Brot?* ⊜geben **3.** *(food, drink)* serve ◊ *Vor dem Essen wurde ein Aperitif gereicht.* ⊜servieren

⊛ **es/das reicht** that's enough, that's it jdm reicht es *(fam)* sb has had enough

reich·lich ['raɛçlɪç] [adj] **1.** abundant, generous ◊ *Das Büffet bot eine reichliche Auswahl an Salaten.* ♦ *Die Mahlzeit war reichlich.* **2.** *only before ns* good ◊ *Wir waren eine reichliche halbe Stunde unterwegs.* ⊜gut [adv] **1.** generously ◊ *Wir wurden reichlich beschenkt. Zu essen gab es reichlich.* There was more than enough to eat. Wir hatten reichlich Gesprächsstoff. We had a lot to talk about. **2.** more than ◊ *Das war vor reichlich hundert Jahren.* ⊜gut, über **3.** *(fam, iron)* rather ◊ *Die Geschichte ist reichlich konfus.* Von einer Krise zu reden, halte ich für reichlich übertrieben. I think it's a considerable exaggeration to speak of a crisis. ⊜ziemlich

Reichs·tag ['raɛçstaːk] der <–(e)s> *no pl* **1.** Reichstag ◊ *den Reichstag besichtigen* ♦ *die im Reichstag vertretenen Parteien* **2.** parliament ◊ *der schwedische Reichstag*

> The present Reichstag building in Berlin has been the seat of the German parliament since 1999. The original building was built by Paul Wallot between 1884 and 1894 to serve as a parliament building. On the ninth of November 1918, the Weimar Republic was declared from one of its windows. The fire at the Reichstag in 1933 gave the National Socialist Party an excuse to persecute its opponents. The Reichstag was rebuilt without a dome between 1961 and 1971. Between 1994 and 1999, it was then redesigned by Sir Norman Foster. Its initially controversial glass dome has now become one of Berlin's landmarks.

Reich·tum ['raɛçtuːm] der <–s, Reichtümer> **1.** wealth, riches ◊ *Er ist zu plötzlichem Reichtum gelangt.* ♦ *unermessliche Reichtümer* ⊜Armut **2.** *no pl (fig)* Reichtum an etw. [dat] wealth of sth ◊ *der Reichtum eines Landes an Bodenschätzen* ♦ *Er erstaunt durch seinen Reichtum an Ideen.* ⊜Mangel

Reich·wei·te ['raɛçvaɛta] die <–, –n> reach ◊ *Bewahren Sie Medikamente außer Reichweite von Kindern auf.* ♦ *in (jds) Reichweite sein*; *(of a missile, transmitter)* range ◊ *eine Rakete mit einer Reichweite von 1300 Kilometern*; *(of a newspaper)* circulation

Reif[1] [raɛf] der <–(e)s> *no pl* (hoar) frost ◊ *Reif bedeckte die Wiesen.*

Reif[2] [raɛf] der <–(e)s, –e> *(lit)* band ◊ *Sie trug einen goldenen Reif um den Arm.*

② **reif** [raɛf] [adj] <reifer, am reif(e)sten> **1.** ripe ◊ *reife Tomaten* ♦ *Die Himbeeren sind bald reif.* ⊜unreif, grün **2.** *(also fig)* mature ◊ *Sie ist sehr reif für ihr Alter.* ♦ *eine Creme für die reife Haut* **3.** BIO, MED *(egg cell, tumour)* fully developed **4.** reif für etw. ready for sth ◊ *Die Zeit ist noch nicht reif für diese Maßnahmen.* ♦ *Ich bin reif für eine Pause!*

⊛ **eine reife Leistung** *(fam, also iron)* what an

A
B
C
D
E
F
G
H
I
J
K
L
M
N
O
P
Q

R

S
T
U
V
W
X
Y
Z

achievement

Rei·fe ['raefə] die <–> no pl ripeness ◊ die Reife einer Melone prüfen; maturity ◊ Ihm fehlt die nötige geistige Reife.
⊚ mittlere Reife ◊ Sie hat die mittlere Reife.

> The mittlere Reife is a qualification you obtain at the end of your tenth year at school in Germany. You can get this qualification either at a Real-schule (a secondary school which specializes in business and technical subjects), at a Gesamt-schule (the equivalent of a comprehensive school), at the Gymnasium (which leads to uni-versity studies), or by taking evening classes.

rei·fen ['raefn̩] intr v +sein 1. (also fig) ripen, mature ◊ Die Trauben reifen gut. ♦ Sie war zu einer Persönlichkeit gereift. 2. (fig) in jdm reifen grow within sb, take shape within sb ◊ Eine bittere Erkenntnis reifte in ihm.
② **Rei·fen** ['raefn̩] der <–s, –> 1. tyre, tire ◊ Das Taxi kam mit quietschenden Reifen um die Ecke. ♦ Kannst du Reifen wechseln? 2. hoop ◊ Er jong-lierte mit fünf Reifen. ⊖Ring
Rei·fe·zeug·nis ['raefətsɔɡknɪs] das <–ses, –se> (form) qualification awarded to German students when they finish grammar school and which entitles them to go on to university, equivalent to English A levels and the high school graduation certificate in the US ⊖Abiturzeugnis
② **Rei·he** ['raeə] die <–, –n> 1. row ◊ in der letzten Reihe sitzen ♦ Die Kinder stellten sich in einer Reihe auf. 2. der Reihe nach one after the other, one after another jd kommt an die Reihe/ist an der Reihe it is sb's turn, sb has their turn 3. no pl host ◊ Er hatte eine ganze Reihe von Fragen. 4. series ◊ Die Reihe umfasst 14 Bände. ♦ Die Reihe der Gespräche wird fortgeführt. ⊖Serie 5. most pl ranks ◊ Sie nahmen sie in ihre Reihen auf. ♦ Der Optimismus in den Reihen der Partei ist ungebrochen. ⊖Kreis
⊚ etw. auf die Reihe bringen/kriegen (fam) 1. manage sth, get sth sorted out ◊ Das bringen wir schon auf die Reihe! 2. get it ◊ Wann kriegst du es endlich auf die Reihe? Ich will das nicht! ⊖kapieren aus der Reihe tanzen (fam) be different außer der Reihe special, exceptional ◊ Geld für Dinge außer der Reihe specially, exception-ally
② **Rei·hen·fol·ge** ['raeənfɔlɡə] die <–, –n> order ◊ etw. in chronologischer/beliebiger Reihenfolge auflisten
Rei·hen·haus ['raeənhaos] das <–es, Reihenhäuser> terraced house, row house, town house
reih·um ['rae'ʊm] adv (all) around ◊ Die Pralinen-schachtel wurde reihum gereicht. ♦ Strahlende Gesichter reihum! ⊖rundum
Reim [raem] der <–(e)s, –e> 1. rhyme Er versuchte, einen Reim auf ‚Birne' zu finden. He tried to find something to rhyme with 'Birne'. ein Gedicht ohne Reim an unrhyming poem 2. rhyme, (rhyming) poem ◊ Die Kinder sagten ein paar Reime auf.
⊚ sich dat einen Reim auf etw. machen (fam) get your head around sth, make sense of sth
rei·men ['raemən] intr v +haben write (little)

poems ◊ Sie reimt gerne. tr v +haben (poems, verse) compose ◊ Er reimte ein paar Zeilen für den Geburtstag seines Vaters. ref v +haben sich reimen (auf etw.) rhyme (with sth) ◊ Diese Wörter reimen sich nicht. ♦ Was reimt sich auf „Liebe"?
rein¹ [raen] adv (fam) in ◊ Was nun, raus oder rein? Rein damit! In it goes!, Put it in! Immer rein in die gute Stube! Come on in! Er ist gerade zur Hintertür rein. He just went in through the back door.
② **rein²** [raen] adj 1. mostly before ns pure ◊ reiner Bienenhonig ♦ Das Wasser des Baches ist ganz rein. 2. only before ns sheer, pure ◊ eine reine Vor-sichtsmaßnahme der reinste Schwachsinn utter nonsense die reinste Frechheit pure cheek, the height of impertinence ⊖pur, bloß 3. clean ◊ Er zog ein reines Hemd an. ⊖sauber 4. innocent, pure ◊ alle, die reinen Herzens sind; (conscience) clear adv 1. purely …, on a purely … basis ◊ Rein äußerlich sind sich die Geschwister sehr ähnlich. 2. rein zufällig by pure coincidence/chance rein spekulativ sein be pure speculation rein gar nichts begreifen not understand a thing ⊖absolut
Rei·ne [raenə] (always ins Reine) 1. etw. ins Reine bringen clarify sth mit jdm/etw. ins Reine kommen become reconciled with sb/sth 2. etw. ins Reine schreiben copy sth out neatly
Rein·fall ['raenfal] der <–(e)s, Reinfälle> disap-pointment ◊ Obwohl er viele Reinfälle erlebt hat, lässt er sich nicht entmutigen.; (record, film etc. also) flop ◊ Ihr neues Album erwies sich als totaler Reinfall. ⊖Pleite
rein|hau·en ['raenhaoən] (fam) <haut rein, haute rein, hat reingehauen> tr v 1. jdm eine/ein paar reinhauen sock sb one 2. sport (a ball into the net) etw. reinhauen hammer sth in intr v 1. stuff your face ◊ Heute haue ich noch mal richtig rein, ab morgen mache ich Diät. 2. pack a punch ◊ Der Titelsong haut voll rein. ♦ Ein Glas Sekt auf nüch-ternen Magen haut ziemlich rein. 3. go for it ◊ Wenn wir das schaffen wollen, müssen wir aber reinhauen.
② **rei·ni·gen** ['raenɪɡn̩] tr v +haben clean ◊ etw. mit einem feuchten Schwamm reinigen chemisch gereinigt werden be dry-cleaned die Zähne mit Zahnseide reinigen floss your teeth
Rei·ni·ger ['raenɪɡɐ] der <–s, –> cleaner, cleaning agent ◊ Welchen Reiniger benutzt du für die Toilette?
Rei·ni·gung ['raenɪɡʊŋ] die <–, –en> 1. most sing cleansing ◊ eine Lotion zur Reinigung trockener Haut ♦ die Reinigung von Industrieabwässern 2. dry cleaner's ◊ Ich habe deinen Anzug in die Reinigung gebracht.
② **Reis** [raes] der <–es> no pl rice ◊ Als Beilage gab es Reis. ♦ Reis anbauen
② **Rei·se** ['raezə] die <–, –n> 1. (also fig) journey ◊ eine Reise durch Skandinavien ♦ Auf der Reise wurde sie krank. ♦ eine musikalische Reise durch die Fünfzigerjahre ⊖Fahrt 2. holiday, trip ◊ Der erste Preis ist eine Reise nach Paris. ⊖Urlaub
② **Rei·se·bü·ro** ['raezəby,roː] das <–s, –s> travel agent's, travel agency ◊ Sie arbeitet in einem Reisebüro.
Rei·se·bus ['raezəbʊs] der <–ses, –se> coach

Rei·se·füh·rer¹ ['raezafy:re] der <-s, -> guide(book), travel guide ◊ *ein Reiseführer über die Philippinen*

Rei·se·füh·rer² ['raezafy:re] der <-s, ->, **Rei·se·füh·re·rin** ['raezafy:rərɪn] die <-, –nen> tour guide ◊ *Er arbeitet als Reiseführer in Bolivien.* ♦ *eine qualifizierte Reiseführerin* ⊜Reiseleiter

② **rei·sen** ['raezn̩] ⟨intr v⟩ +*sein* travel ◊ *mit dem Flugzeug reisen* ♦ *Kinder reisen zum halben Preis.* ♦ *Sie reiste nach Hamburg.*

Rei·se·pass ['raezəpas] der <-es, Reisepässe> passport ◊ *ein gültiger Reisepass* ♦ *einen Reisepass beantragen*

rei·ßen ['raesn̩] ⟨reißt, riss, hat/ist gerissen⟩ ⟨tr v⟩ +*haben* **1.** tear ◊ *Der Sturm riss Dächer von den Häusern.* ♦ *eine Seite aus einem Buch reißen* etw. in Fetzen reißen tear sth to shreds etw. in Stücke reißen tear sth apart etw. in etw. ⟨acc⟩ reißen tear sth in sth ◊ *Ich habe mir ein Loch ins Hemd gerissen.* jdm etw. aus der Hand reißen snatch sth from sb's hand **2.** *(also fig)* etw./jdn an sich reißen seize sb/sth ◊ *Sie riss das Kind an sich.* ♦ *Er hat die Macht an sich gerissen.* jdn/etw. irgendwohin reißen sweep sb/sth away somewhere ◊ *Die Lawine riss eine Scheune mit sich ins Tal. Die Flutwelle riss viele Menschen in den Tod.* The tidal wave claimed many lives. **3.** jdn aus etw. reißen shake sb out of sth ◊ *Das Telefon riss sie aus ihrem Tagtraum. Sie wurden unsanft von der Sirene aus dem Schlaf gerissen.* They were rudely awakened by the sound of the siren. **4.** *(an animal)* kill ◊ *Die Wölfe haben ein Lamm gerissen.* ⟨intr v⟩ +*haben/sein* **1.** +*sein* tear ◊ *Der Faden ist gerissen.* **2.** +*haben* an etw. ⟨dat⟩ reißen pull at sth, tug at sth ◊ *Der Hund reißt an der Leine.* ⟨ref v⟩ +*haben (fam)* sich um jdn/etw. reißen fall over yourself to get sb/sth ◊ *Die Fans rissen sich um ein Autogramm ihres Idols.*

rei·ßend ['raesn̩t, 'raesənt] *pres p of* reißen ⟨adj⟩ **1.** raging, torrential ◊ *ein reißender Gebirgsbach* ♦ *Nach dem Gewitter war der Fluß reißend.* **2.** wild, raging ◊ *eine reißende Bestie* **3.** *(demand, turnover)* massive ◊ *reißende Nachfrage finden* **4.** reißenden Absatz finden sell like hot cakes ⟨adv⟩ in a torrent ◊ *Das Wasser schoss reißend zu Tal.*

Reiß·ver·schluss ['raesfɛʃlʊs] der <-es, Reißverschlüsse> zip(per) ◊ *(sich) den Reißverschluss zumachen*

rei·ten ['raetn̩] ⟨reitet, ritt, hat/ist geritten⟩ ⟨intr v⟩ +*sein* (auf etw. ⟨dat⟩) reiten ride (sth) ◊ *auf einem Schimmel reiten* im Galopp/Trab/Schritt reiten ride at a gallop/trot/walk ⟨tr v⟩ +*haben/sein* **1.** +*haben* ride ◊ *ein Pony reiten* **2.** +*haben/sein* ride in ◊ *Er reitet Rodeos.* ♦ *einen Bogen reiten* Galopp/Trab/Schritt ride at a gallop/trot/walk **3.** *only inf* Wellen reiten ride the waves ⊜surfen

Rei·ter ['raete] der <-s, ->, **Rei·te·rin** ['raetərɪn] die <-, –nen> rider ◊ *Sie ist eine gute Reiterin.*

Reiz [raets] der <-(e)s, –e> **1.** attraction, charm ◊ *Was ist der besondere Reiz am Segelfliegen?* der Reiz des Verbotenen the lure of the forbidden **2.** stimulus ◊ *Das Gehirn reagiert auf optische und akustische Reize. Dieser Hustensaft lindert den Reiz.* This cough syrup will soothe the irritation.

reiz·bar ['raetsba:ʳ] ⟨adj⟩ irritable ◊ *Wenn er*

schlecht geschlafen hat, ist er sehr reizbar. ♦ *eine Creme für leicht reizbare Haut*

rei·zen ['raetsn̩] ⟨tr+intr v⟩ +*haben* **1.** etw. reizt jdn sth appeals to sb, sb finds sth appealing ◊ *Die Aufgabe reizte sie.* (jdn) zu etw. reizen encourage (sb to do) sth, invite (sb to do) sth ◊ *Gezielte Werbung soll (die Kunden) zum Kauf reizen.* **2.** irritate ◊ *Trockene Luft reizt die Atemwege.* ⟨tr v⟩ +*haben* jdn/ein Tier reizen provoke sb/an animal

rei·zend ['raetsn̩t, 'raetsənt] *pres p of* reizen ⟨adj, adv⟩ *(also iron)* charming(ly) ◊ *Sie hat eine reizende Wohnung.* ♦ *Ich finde deine Schwester reizend.* ♦ *Du überlässt mir den Abwasch? Wie reizend von dir!* ♦ *Sie war ganz reizend gekleidet.*

Re·kla·ma·tion [reklama'tsjo:n] die <-, –en> complaint

② **Re·kla·me** [re'kla:ma] die <-, –n> *(fam)* advert(s), advertisement(s) ◊ *Bitte keine Reklame einwerfen.* ♦ *Der Vorfall ist keine gute Reklame für die Schule.* ⊜Werbung

⊛ für etw./jdn Reklame machen advertise sth/sb

re·kla·mie·ren [rekla'mi:rən] ⟨reklamiert, reklamierte, hat reklamiert⟩ ⟨tr+intr v⟩ complain (about), make a complaint (about) ◊ *Er reklamierte das defekte Fernsehgerät.* ♦ *Sie reklamierte, weil ihr Essen kalt war.* ⟨tr v⟩ etw. für sich reklamieren lay claim to sth ◊ *Die Partei reklamierte den Wahlsieg für sich für sich.* ♦ *Mehrere Länder reklamierten diese Region für sich.*

re·kons·tru·ie·ren [rekɔnstru'i:rən] ⟨rekonstruiert, rekonstruierte, hat rekonstruiert⟩ ⟨tr v⟩ reconstruct ◊ *Die römische Villa wurde teilweise rekonstruiert.* ♦ *den genauen Unfallhergang rekonstruieren; (a building also)* restore

② **Re·kord** [re'kɔʳt] der <-(e)s, –e> record ◊ *einen Rekord aufstellen/brechen* ♦ *Die Arbeitslosenzahlen haben einen Rekord erreicht.*

Rek·tor ['rɛkto:ʳ] der <-s, –en>, **Rek·to·rin** [rɛk'to:rɪn] die <-, –nen> **1.** *(of a school)* head, principal ◊ *Er soll demnächst Rektor werden.* ♦ *die neue Rektorin der Grundschule* **2.** *(of a university)* vice chancellor, president ◊ *Er wurde zum Rektor der TU gewählt.*

Re·la·ti·on [rela'tsjo:n] die <-, –en> relation ◊ *Daten in Relation zueinander stellen* ♦ *die Relation zwischen Arbeitskosten und Löhnen* in keiner Relation zu etw. stehen bear no relation to sth

re·la·tiv [rela'ti:f, 're:lati:f] ⟨adj, adv⟩ *no comp/superl* relative(ly) ◊ *die relative Mehrheit haben* ♦ *Im Moment herrscht noch relative Ruhe.* ♦ *Glück ist relativ.* ♦ *Die Gefahr ist relativ gering.*

Re·la·tiv·pro·no·men [rela'ti:fpro,no:mən] das <-s, – or Relativpronomina> relative pronoun

In German, a relative pronoun *(der, die, das, welcher, welche, welches)* has the same gender and number as the noun to which it relates: *der Spion, **der** mich liebte.* The case taken by the relative pronoun depends on the structure of the relative clause, and for this reason does not necessarily agree with the case of the noun to which it refers: *das Haus, in **dem** ich wohne.*

Re·la·tiv·satz [rela'ti:fzats] der <-es, Relativsätze> relative clause

re·le·vant [rele'vant] ⟨adj⟩ <relevanter, am relevantesten> *(lofty)* relevant, significant ◊ *relevante*

Informationen ♦ Ich halte diesen Gesichtspunkt für relevant.

② **Re·li·gi·on** [reli'gio:n] die <–, –en> **1.** religion ◊ Er gehört keiner Religion an. **2.** no pl religious studies ◊ Die Klasse hat zwei Stunden Religion in der Woche.

re·li·gi·ös [reli'giø:s] <adj, adv> <religiöser, am religiösesten> religious(ly) ◊ eine religiöse Gemeinschaft ♦ Sie ist tief religiös. ♦ religiös motivierte Gewalt

Re·likt [re'lɪkt] das <–(e)s, –e> (also fig) relic ◊ ein Relikt aus der Steinzeit ♦ Für ihn ist Religion ein überholtes Relikt.

Re·ling ['re:lɪŋ] die <–, –s or –e> most sing (ship's) rail, railing ◊ Sie stand an der Reling und winkte. ♦ über die Reling beugen

② **ren·nen** ['rɛnən] <rennt, rannte, ist gerannt> [intr v] **1.** run ◊ Er rannte über die Straße. ♦ mit jdm um die Wette rennen **2.** (fam, pej, fig) irgendwohin rennen run somewhere ◊ Sie rennt immer zum Lehrer und petzt. ⊝laufen **3.** (fam) gegen/an jdn/ etw. rennen walk into sb/sth ◊ Er ist gegen einen Laternenpfahl gerannt. ⊝stoßen **4.** (fig) in etw. [acc] rennen run headlong into sth ◊ Er rannte sehenden Auges in sein Unglück.

Ren·nen ['rɛnən] das <–s, –> race ◊ Schumacher ist ein hervorragendes Rennen gefahren. ♦ Die beiden lieferten sich ein spannendes Rennen.

◉ gut im Rennen liegen (fam) have a good chance, be a front runner das Rennen ist gelaufen (fam) it's all over das Rennen (um etw.) machen (fam) win (sth) ◊ Sie machte das Rennen um den Posten.

Renn·fah·rer ['rɛnfa:rɐ] der <–s, –>, **Renn·fah·re·rin** ['rɛnfa:rərɪn] die <–, –nen> racing driver ◊ ein berühmter Rennfahrer ♦ Sie möchte Rennfahrerin werden.

re·nom·miert [reno'mi:ɐt] <adj> (lofty) renowned, famous ◊ ein renommierter Wissenschaftler ♦ Diese Universität ist sehr renommiert.

re·no·vie·ren [reno'vi:rən] <renoviert, renovierte, hat renoviert> [tr+intr v] renovate, redecorate ◊ Wir mussten (die Wohnung) von Grund auf renovieren lassen.

ren·ta·bel [rɛn'ta:bl] <adj> <rentabler, am rentabelsten> <der/die/das rentable ...> lucrative, profitable ◊ eine rentable Kapitalanlage ♦ Ist diese Investition wirklich rentabel? <adv> profitably, at a profit ◊ Das Unternehmen arbeitet rentabel.

② **Ren·te** ['rɛntə] die <–, –n> **1.** pension ◊ die gesetzliche Rente ♦ Rente beziehen **2.** no pl retirement vorzeitig in Rente gehen take early retirement Sie ist seit drei Jahren in Rente. She has been retired for three years. **3.** annuity ◊ Die Unfallversicherung bezahlt bei Arbeitsunfähigkeit eine Rente.

Ren·ten·ver·si·che·rung ['rɛntn̩fɛɐˌzɪçərʊŋ] die <–, –en> pension scheme ◊ in die gesetzliche Rentenversicherung einzahlen

The German pension scheme is a branch of social security which provides insurance cover for elderly people, those who are unable to work, and the dependents of people who have died. People with a pension scheme receive financial help when they are ill or convalescent, payments towards their health insurance, and an old age pension.

ren·tie·ren [rɛn'ti:rən] <rentiert sich, rentierte sich, hat sich rentiert> [ref v] sich rentieren be worthwhile ◊ Die Investition hat sich rentiert. ⊝sich lohnen, sich rechnen

Rent·ner ['rɛntnɐ] der <–s, –>, **Rent·ne·rin** ['rɛntnərɪn] die <–, –nen> pensioner, senior citizen ◊ eine rüstige Rentnerin ♦ Er ist seit drei Jahren Rentner.

② **Re·pa·ra·tur** [repara'tu:ɐ] die <–, –en> repair ◊ Bei unserem Auto sind größere Reparaturen notwendig. in (der) Reparatur sein be being repaired etw. in (die)/zur Reparatur geben take sth in to be repaired, take sth in for repair

② **re·pa·rie·ren** [repa'ri:rən] <repariert, reparierte, hat repariert> [tr v] repair, mend ◊ Ich muss diese Schuhe reparieren lassen.

Re·por·ta·ge [repɔr'ta:ʒə] die <–, –n> report ◊ Sie schrieb eine Reportage über Großfamilien.

Re·por·ter [re'pɔrtɐ] der <–s, –>, **Re·por·te·rin** [re'pɔrtərɪn] die <–, –nen> reporter ◊ Sie arbeitet als freiberufliche Reporterin. ♦ ein Reporter vom Fernsehen

re·prä·sen·ta·tiv [reprɛzɛnta'ti:f] <adj> (lofty) typical ◊ Cranach gilt als repräsentativer Maler der Reformation. ♦ Diese Erzählung ist repräsentativ für den Stil des Autors. ⊝typisch <adj, adv> **1.** representative(ly) ◊ eine repräsentative Untersuchung ♦ Die Studie ist repräsentativ für Österreich. ♦ repräsentativ ausgewählte Bürger **2.** impressive(ly) ◊ repräsentative Räume ♦ Der Eingangsbereich des Hotels ist repräsentativ. ♦ eine repräsentativ gestaltete Fassade

re·prä·sen·tie·ren [reprɛzɛn'ti:rən] (lofty) <repräsentiert, repräsentierte, hat repräsentiert> [tr v] represent ◊ Er hat seine Firma glänzend repräsentiert. ♦ Was repräsentiert Deutschland für Sie? [intr v] perform official duties

Rep·til [rɛp'ti:l] das <–s, –ien> reptile

Re·pub·lik [repu'bli:k] die <–, –en> republic ◊ die Weimarer Republik

Re·pub·li·ka·ner¹ [republi'ka:nɐ] der <–s, –>, **Re·pub·li·ka·ne·rin** [republi'ka:nərɪn] die <–, –nen> **1.** (in the US) Republican **2.** republican ◊ Im Norden Irlands wurden drei Republikaner verhaftet. **3.** member of the radical right-wing party (REP) founded in Germany in 1983

Re·ser·ve [re'zɛrvə] die <–, –n> **1.** most pl reserve ◊ auf seine finanziellen Reserven zurückgreifen ♦ Die Reserven an fossilen Brennstoffen werden knapp. jdn/etw. in Reserve haben/halten have sb/ sth in reserve ⊝Vorrat **2.** ECON stille Reserven undisclosed reserves **3.** only pl Reserven energy ◊ Der Läufer verfügte über ungeahnte Reserven. **4.** most sing MIL, SPORT reserves ◊ Er spielt immer nur in der Reserve. Offizier der Reserve reserve officer **5.** no pl jdn aus der Reserve locken break down sb's reserve

Re·ser·ve·rad [re'zɛrvəˌra:t] das <–(e)s, Reserveräder> spare wheel

② **re·ser·vie·ren** [rezɛr'vi:rən] <reserviert, reservierte, hat reserviert> [tr+intr v] reserve ◊ Ich habe einen Tisch für zwei Personen reserviert. ♦ Haben Sie reserviert? ♦ Kinokarten reservieren

re·ser·viert [rezɛr'vi:ɐt] past p of reservieren <adj, adv> <reservierter, am reserviertesten> reserved(ly) ◊ Sie gab ihre reservierte Haltung ihm

gegenüber auf. ✦ *Er blieb den ganzen Abend lang reserviert.* ✦ *Sie reagierte reserviert auf seinen Vorschlag.*

Re·ser·vie·rung [rezɛʳ'viːrʊŋ] die <-, –en> reservation(s) ◊ *Eine frühzeitige Reservierung ist ratsam.*

Re·si·denz [rezi'dɛnts] die <-, –en> **1.** residence ◊ *die Residenz des Schweizer Botschafters in Berlin* **2.** capital ◊ *Heinrich der Löwe wählte Braunschweig zu seiner Residenz.*

re·sis·tent [rezɪs'tɛnt] adj <resistenter, am resistentesten> resistent (gegen/gegenüber etw.) resistant (to sth) ◊ *resistente Keime* ✦ *Immer mehr Bakterien sind resistent gegen Antibiotika.*

Re·so·nanz [rezo'nants] die <-, –en> **1.** *(lofty)* reaction, response ◊ *Die Resonanz auf die Änderungen war durchweg positiv.* ✦ *Das Konzept ist nur auf schwache Resonanz gestoßen.* **2.** PHYSICS resonance ◊ *magnetische Resonanz*

Res·pekt [rɛs'pɛkt, re'spɛkt] der <-(e)s> *no pl* Respekt (vor jdm/etw.), Respekt (für jdm/etw.) respect (for sb/sth) ◊ *Ich habe großen Respekt vor ihr.* ✦ *Er muss sich bei den Schülern erst Respekt verschaffen.* Respekt einflößend formidable bei allem Respekt with all due respect ⊛ Respekt!; Respekt, Respekt! very impressive

res·pek·tie·ren [rɛspɛk'tiːrən, respɛk'tiːrən] <respektiert, respektierte, hat respektiert> tr v respect ◊ *Ich respektiere ihn sehr.* ✦ *Seine Wünsche wurden respektiert.* ⊜achten

② **Rest** [rɛst] der <-(e)s, –e> **1.** der Rest rest ◊ *Den Rest seines Lebens verbrachte er in Wien.* ein Rest a bit left (over) ◊ *Vom Büffet ist noch ein kleiner Rest übrig.* Reste remains ◊ *An den Brettern hafteten Reste von Zement.*; *(of food)* leftovers ◊ *Reste essen* **2.** *(less than usually present)* vestige ◊ *Er hatte noch einen Rest Vernunft bewahrt.* **3.** MATH remainder ◊ *20 geteilt durch 3 ist 6, Rest 2.* ⊛ etw. gibt jdm den Rest sth finishes sb off

② **Res·tau·rant** [rɛsto'rãː, rɛsto'rãː] das <-s, –s> restaurant ◊ *Sonntags isst er gern im Restaurant.*

rest·li·che ['rɛstlɪçə] adj *no comp/superl; only after the definite article* remaining ◊ *Wo ist das restliche Geld?* ⊜übrige

rest·los ['rɛstloːs] adj, adv *no comp/superl; when used as an adj, only before ns* complete(ly), total(ly) ◊ *Er forderte die restlose Aufklärung des Verbrechens.* ✦ *Das Stadion war restlos ausverkauft.* ⊜völlig

② **Re·sul·tat** [rezʊl'taːt] das <-(e)s, –e> *(lofty)* result ◊ *das Resultat einer Umfrage/Multiplikation* ✦ *ein schwaches/starkes Resultat erzielen* ⊜Ergebnis

re·sul·tie·ren [rezʊl'tiːrən] <resultiert, resultierte, hat resultiert> intr v *(lofty)* **1.** etw. resultiert in etw. dat sth results in sth **2.** etw. resultiert aus etw. sth results from sth, sth is the result of sth ◊ *Das Break resultierte aus einem Doppelfehler des Gegners.*

Re·sü·mee [rezy'meː] das <-s, –s> *(lofty)* summary, conclusion ◊ *Wie lautet das Resümee der Teilnehmer?* ein Resümee (aus etw.) ziehen draw a conclusion (from sth)

② **ret·ten** ['rɛtn] tr v +haben jdn/etw. (vor etw.) retten save sb/sth (from sth) ◊ *Seine Lüge rettete ihn.* ✦ *Sie rettete das Kind vor dem Ertrinken.* sich vor etw./jdm retten escape sth/sb ◊ *sich vor seinen*

Verfolgern retten jdn/etw. aus etw. retten save sb/sth from sth ◊ *Er rettete den Hund aus dem brennenden Auto.* sich (aus etw.) retten escape (from sth) ◊ *Ich rettete mich aus der Gefahrenzone.* jdm das Leben retten save sb's life ref v +haben sich irgendwohin retten manage to get somewhere ◊ *Er konnte sich ins Freie retten.* ⊛ sich vor jdm/etw. kaum/nicht retten können be inundated with sb/sth, be swamped with sb/sth bist du noch zu retten have you gone completely mad rette sich, wer kann save yourselves

Ret·ter ['rɛtɐ] der <-s, –>, **Ret·te·rin** ['rɛtərɪn] die <-, –nen> saviour, savior ◊ *Sie dankten ihrer Retterin.* Retter in der Not knight in shining armour

Ret·tich ['rɛtɪç] der <-s, –e> radish

② **Ret·tung** ['rɛtʊŋ] die <-, –en> **1.** rescue ◊ *Die Verschütteten hofften auf Rettung.* **2.** salvation ◊ *Rettung nahte in Gestalt meines Bruders.* jds letzte Rettung sein be sb's last hope **3.** *(Austr) (ambulance)* rescue service ◊ *Die Rettung traf am Unfallort ein.* ⊜Rettungswagen

Ret·tungs·schwim·mer ['rɛtʊŋsʃvɪmɐ] der <-s, –>, **Ret·tungs·schwim·me·rin** ['rɛtʊŋsʃvɪmərɪn] die <-, –nen> lifeguard ◊ *Er ist ausgebildeter Rettungsschwimmer.*

German lifeguards supervise not only swimmers at lakes and in indoor and outdoor pools, but also sailing and pedal boats out on the water. In an emergency they carry out rescue procedures, in which they have been trained to the level of the DRSA (*Deutsches Rettungsschwimm-Abzeichen* — German lifeguard badge) bronze badge.

Ret·tungs·wa·gen ['rɛtʊŋsvaːgn̩] der <-s, –> ambulance

Reue ['rɔɣə] die <-> *no pl* remorse ◊ *Der Täter zeigte keine Reue.*

re·van·chie·ren [revãˈʃiːrən, revãˈfiːrən] <revanchiert, revanchierte, hat revanchiert> ref v *(fam)* **1.** sich (für etw.) revanchieren return the favour/favor (of sth) ◊ *Sie wollte sich für den Gefallen revanchieren.* **2.** sich (für etw.) revanchieren take revenge (for sth), get your own back (for sth) ◊ *Sie revanchierte sich mit einer Ohrfeige.* ⊜sich rächen

Re·vier [re'viːɐ̯] das <-s, –e> **1.** *(also fig, hum)* territory ◊ *Die Wölfe verteidigten ihr Revier.* ✦ *Die Küche ist sein Revier.*; *(of a forester)* (bit of) forest **2.** *(of the police)* district, precinct; *(office)* police station ◊ *Der Polizist nahm den Betrunkenen mit aufs Revier.*

Re·vol·te [re'vɔltə] die <-, –n> revolt ◊ *Es kam zur Revolte gegen den König.* ⊜Aufruhr, Aufstand

Re·vo·lu·ti·on [revolu'tsi̯oːn] die <-, –en> revolution ◊ *die Revolution von 1848/49* ✦ *Diese Theorie war damals eine Revolution.*

Re·vol·ver [re'vɔlvɐ] der <-s, –> revolver ◊ *Sie hielt ihm einen Revolver an den Kopf.*

② **Re·zept** [re'tsɛpt] das <-(e)s, –e> **1.** recipe ◊ *Sie kocht nur nach Rezept.* ✦ *Gibt es ein Rezept für einen Erfolgsroman?* ein bewährtes Rezept gegen Nervosität a proven cure for nervousness **2.** MED prescription ◊ *Diese Tabletten gibt es nur auf (ärztliches) Rezept.*

re·zept·frei [re'tsɛptfraɛ] [adj] *no comp/superl* over the counter, available without a prescription ◊ *rezeptfreie Medikamente* ♦ *Diese Tabletten sind rezeptfrei.* [adv] over the counter ◊ *Das Medikament ist rezeptfrei erhältlich.*

② **Re·zep·ti·on** [retsɛp'tsjoːn] die <-, -en> reception ◊ *den Schlüssel an der Rezeption abgeben*

Re·zes·si·on [retsɛ'sjoːn] die <-, -en> ECON recession ◊ *Das Land steckte in einer Rezession.*

Rhein [raɛn] der <-s> *no pl (always* der Rhein*)* the Rhine ◊ *Köln liegt am Rhein.*

Rhein·land-Pfalz [,raɛnlant'pfalts] das <-> *article only in combination with attribute, no pl* Rhineland-Palatinate *box*@ Land

> Area: 19,847 km²; population: approx. 4.04 million; regional capital: Mainz.
> Characteristic features of the landscape are the Rhine and Moselle rivers, with vineyards and numerous castles along their banks of Rhineland-Palatinate. Tourism, wine growing, forestry and the chemical industry are the most important economic factors in the region.

Rhe·to·rik [re'toːrɪk] die <-, -en> *most sing* rhetoric ◊ *Sie unterrichtet Rhetorik.* ♦ *Seine Versprechungen erwiesen sich als bloße Rhetorik.*

rhe·to·risch [re'toːrɪʃ] [adj, adv] *no comp/superl* rhetorical(ly) ◊ *Seine Frage war rein rhetorisch.* ♦ *Er besitzt beachtliche rhetorische Fähigkeiten.* ♦ *ein rhetorisch ausgefeilter Artikel*

Rheu·ma ['rɔɥmaː] das <-s> *no pl (abbr of* Rheumatismus*) seldom with the article* rheumatism

rhyth·misch ['rʏtmɪʃ] [adj] rhythmic(al) ◊ *rhythmische Sportgymnastik* ♦ *Deine Bewegungen sind nicht rhythmisch genug.* [adv] rhythmically ◊ *Sie bewegten sich rhythmisch zur Musik.*

Rhyth·mus ['rʏtmʊs] der <-, Rhythmen> rhythm ◊ *Sie klatschten zum/im Rhythmus der Trommeln.* ♦ *Beim Lernen konnte sie bisher ihren Rhythmus noch nicht finden.*

rich·ten ['rɪçtn] <richtet, richtete, hat gerichtet> [tr v] +*haben* 1. *(also fig)* etw. auf jdn/etw. richten point sth at sb/sth ◊ *Er richtete die Pistole auf sie.* ♦ *Sie richtete ihre Aufmerksamkeit auf den Film.* etw. an jdn richten direct sth to sb/sth ◊ *An wen war der Brief gerichtet?* 2. *(esp SouthG, Austr, Swiss)* fix ◊ *Er ließ sich seine Zähne richten.* 3. *(esp SouthG, Austr, Swiss)* make ◊ *Sie richtete das Mittagessen.* ⊜herrichten [intr v] +*haben* über jdn/etw. richten judge sb/sth ◊ *Du solltest nicht so streng über andere richten.* [ref v] +*haben* 1. sich (mit etw.) an jdn/etw. richten address (sth) to sb/ sth ◊ *Du musst dich mit der Beschwerde an deinen Vorgesetzten richten.* 2. sich gegen jdn/etw. richten be directed against sb/sth ◊ *Diese Kritik richtet sich nicht gegen dich.* 3. sich auf jdn/etw. richten be focussed on sb/sth ◊ *Alle Blicke richteten sich auf den Sänger.* 4. sich nach jdm richten fit in with what sb wants ◊ *Was den Zeitpunkt betrifft, richte ich mich völlig nach dir.* 5. *(person)* sich nach etw. richten act in accordance with sth ◊ *Du solltest dich auch nach seinen Wünschen richten.* 6. *(thing)* sich nach etw. richten depend on sth ◊ *Das Porto richtet sich nach dem Gewicht des Pakets.*

Rich·ter ['rɪçtɐ] der <-s, ->, **Rich·te·rin**

['rɪçtərɪn] die <-, -nen> judge ◊ *Wie hat der Richter entschieden?* ♦ *Sie war Richterin am Europäischen Gerichtshof.*

② **rich·tig** ['rɪçtɪç] [adj] 1. right, correct ◊ *eine richtige Antwort* ♦ *Ist die Lösung richtig?* ⊜falsch 2. appropriate, proper, right ◊ *Wäre es nicht richtiger, ihr die Entscheidung zu überlassen?* ♦ *Sie hatte die richtigen Argumente.* ⊜verkehrt 3. real ◊ *Das war eine richtige Gemeinheit!* 4. *(moral)* right ◊ *Es war nicht richtig von dir, sie anzulügen.* ⊜falsch, verkehrt [adv] 1. correctly, (in) the right way ◊ *Er hat ihren Namen nicht richtig ausgesprochen. Geht deine Uhr richtig? Is your watch right?* (mit etw.) richtig liegen be right (about sth) ⊜falsch 2. properly ◊ *Das kann ich nicht richtig beurteilen.* ⊜verkehrt 3. really ◊ *Er hat sich am Samstag richtig betrunken.* ◉ etw. richtig stellen put sth right ◊ *Diese Vorwürfe musst du richtig stellen.*

Rich·ti·ge¹ ['rɪçtɪgə] das <-n> *but: Richtiges, no pl;* das Richtige the right one, the right thing ◊ *Ist dieses Studium für dich das Richtige?* etwas/ nichts Richtiges something/nothing proper, anything/not anything proper ◊ *Gibt es hier nichts Richtiges zu essen?* nichts Richtiges lernen/sagen not really learn/say anything *box*@ Substantivierung

Rich·ti·ge² ['rɪçtɪgə] der/die <-n, die Richtigen> *but: ein Richtiger/eine Richtige* der/die Richtige the right person ◊ *Ist er der Richtige für mich?* ♦ *Er glaubt, die Richtige gefunden zu haben.* ◉ sechs Richtige im Lotto six right numbers in the lottery *box*@ Substantivierung

② **Rich·tung** ['rɪçtʊŋ] die <-, -en> 1. direction ◊ *Der Wind kam aus nordwestlicher Richtung.* ♦ *Die Reform ist ein Schritt in die richtige Richtung.* Richtung ... towards ... ◊ *Er war Richtung Ulm unterwegs.* 2. *(stylistic, political etc.)* movement, school (of thought) ◊ *Welcher politischen/literarischen Richtung ist sie zuzuordnen?*

rieb [riːp] *pret of* reiben

② **rie·chen** ['riːçn] <riecht, roch, hat gerochen> [tr v] 1. smell ◊ *Ich roch, dass etwas angebrannt war.* 2. *(fam, fig)* guess ◊ *Sie muss die Gefahr gerochen haben.* etw. nicht riechen können not be able to know sth [intr v] 1. (irgendwie) riechen smell (somehow) ◊ *Seine Füße riechen.* nach etw. riechen smell of sth ◊ *Im Auto roch es nach Alkohol.* 2. (an etw. [dat]) riechen sniff (at) sth, smell sth ◊ *Sie roch an der Parfümflasche.* 3. *(fam, fig)* irgendwie/nach etw. riechen smack of sth ◊ *Die Sache riecht nach Betrug.* ◉ jdn nicht riechen können *(fam)* not be able to stand sb

② **rief** [riːf] *pret of* rufen

Rie·gel ['riːgl] der <-s, -> 1. bolt ◊ *Sie schob den Riegel zurück und öffnete das Tor.* 2. *(to eat)* bar ◊ *ein Riegel Schokolade* ◉ einer Sache einen Riegel vorschieben put a stop to sth

Rie·men ['riːmən] der <-s, -> strap ◉ sich am Riemen reißen pull yourself together

Rie·se ['riːzə] der <-n, -n> giant ◊ *In diesem Märchen kommt ein Riese vor.* ♦ *ein Riese im Bereich der Elektronik* ⊜Zwerg

rie·seln ['riːzln] [intr v] +*sein* trickle ◊ *Aus dem*

Brief rieselte ein weißes Pulver.; (snow) fall softly
Rie·sen·rad ['riːznraːt] das <–(e)s, Riesenräder>
big wheel, Ferris wheel ◊ *Sie fuhren mit dem
Riesenrad.*

rie·sig ['riːzɪç] adj **1.** huge, enormous ◊ *riesige
Wellen* ♦ *Seine Freude war riesig.* **2.** *(fam)*
fantastic, super ◊ *Der Urlaub war einfach riesig!*
⊖großartig adv *(fam)* extremely, tremendously,
terribly ◊ *Sie ärgerte sich riesig darüber.*
⊖überaus, sehr

② **riet** [riːt] *pret of* raten

Ril·le ['rɪlə] die <–, –n> groove

Rind [rɪnt] das <–(e)s, –er> **1.** *(male)* bull;
(female) cow Rinder cattle ◊ *Rinder züchten* **2.** no
pl *(fam)* beef ◊ *Isst du lieber Rind oder Schwein?*
⊖Rindfleisch

Rin·de ['rɪndə] die <–, –n> **1.** bark ◊ *Birken haben
eine weiße Rinde.* **2.** crust ◊ *Sie schnitt die Rinde
vom Toastbrot weg.; (of cheese)* rind

Rind·fleisch ['rɪntflaɪʃ] das <–(e)s> *no pl* beef ◊
ein Kilo Rindfleisch ⊖Rind

② **Ring** [rɪŋ] der <–(e)s, –e> **1.** ring ◊ *jdm/sich einen
Ring an den Finger stecken* ♦ *die olympischen
Ringe* ♦ *Sie hatte dunkle Ringe unter den Augen.* ♦
Er turnte an den Ringen. ♦ *Der Boxer stieg in den
Ring.* ♦ *ein internationaler Ring von Schmugglern*
2. *(fam)* ring road ◊ *Es gab einen Stau auf dem
Ring.*

Ring·buch ['rɪŋbuːx] das <–(e)s, Ringbücher> ring
binder

rin·geln ['rɪŋln] ref v +haben sich (um etw.)
ringeln curl (around sth) ◊ *Bei nassem Wetter
ringeln sich ihre Haare.* ♦ *Die Schlange ringelte
sich um den Holzpflock.*

rin·gen ['rɪŋən] <ringt, rang, hat gerungen> intr v
wrestle ◊ *Sie rangen miteinander.* ♦ *Mit diesem
Problem ringt sie schon länger.* mit sich ringen
wrestle with your conscience nach etw. ringen
struggle for sth ◊ *Er rang nach Luft.* um etw.
ringen struggle for sth ◊ *Sie rangen um ihre Unabhängigkeit.*

rings·he·rum ['rɪŋshɛ'rʊm] adv all around ◊
Ringsherum herrschte große Hektik. ⊖rundum

Rin·ne ['rɪnə] die <–, –n> **1.** channel ◊ *Durch den
Regen waren Rinnen im Boden entstanden.*
2. gutter ◊ *Das Wasser floß über eine Rinne ab.*

rin·nen ['rɪnən] <rinnt, rann, ist geronnen> intr v
run ◊ *Sie ließ den Sand durch die Finger rinnen.* ♦
Schweiß rann ihm von der Stirn.

Rip·pe ['rɪpə] die <–, –n> **1.** rib ◊ *Sie brach sich
bei dem Unfall mehrere Rippen.* **2.** *(of a radiator)*
fin; *(of chocolate)* row

② **Ri·si·ko** ['riːziko] das <–s, Risiken> risk ◊ *Er wollte
kein Risiko eingehen.* ♦ *Damit ist ein hohes/
geringes Risiko verbunden.*

ris·kant [rɪs'kant] adj, adv <riskanter, am riskantes-
ten> risky(-ily) ◊ *eine riskante Entscheidung* ♦ *Die
Flucht erschien ihm zu riskant.* ♦ *Er hat viel zu
riskant gespielt.* riskant überholen overtake danger-
ously ⊖gewagt

ris·kie·ren [rɪs'kiːrən] <riskiert, riskierte, hat
riskiert> tr v risk ◊ *Sie riskierte ihr Leben für ihn.*
♦ *Er riskiert damit, dass ihm gekündigt wird.*
⊖wagen

riss [rɪs] *pret of* reißen

Riss [rɪs] der <–es, –e> **1.** crack ◊ *In der Mauer*

war ein Riss.; tear ◊ *In meiner Jacke ist ein Riss.*
2. *(fig)* split ◊ *Zwischen ihnen war ein tiefer Riss
entstanden.*

ris·sig ['rɪsɪç] adj cracked ◊ *Das Holz war rissig.*
♦ *eine rissige alte Mauer; (skin etc.)* chapped ◊
Sie hatte rissige Hände.

ritt [rɪt] *pret of* reiten

Rit·ze ['rɪtsə] die <–, –n> crack

Ri·va·le [ri'vaːlə] der <–n, –n>, **Ri·va·lin** [ri'vaːlɪn]
die <–, –nen> rival ◊ *Sie sah in ihr ihre größte
Rivalin.*

Ro·be ['roːbə] die <–, –n> **1.** evening gown ◊ *Die
Damen erschienen in langen Roben.* **2.** *(official
vestment)* robe

Ro·bo·ter ['rɔbɔtɐ] der <–s, –> robot ◊ *Roboter
einsetzen*

ro·bust [ro'bʊst] adj <robuster, am robustesten>
robust ◊ *Dieses Material ist sehr robust.* ♦ *Er hatte
eine robuste Gesundheit.*

② **roch** [rɔx] *pret of* riechen

rö·cheln ['rœçln] intr v +haben breathe with a
rattling sound ◊ *Der Kranke röchelte. Wieso röchelt
das Kind so? Why does the child's breath rattle
like that?*

② **Rock¹** [rɔk] der <–(e)s, Röcke> skirt ◊ *Der Rock
reicht bis zum Knie.*

Rock² [rɔk] der <–(s)> *no pl (fam)* mus rock

Ro·del ['roːdl] der <–s, –(n)> *(SouthG, Austr)*
toboggan, sledge, luge ⊖Schlitten

ro·deln ['roːdln] intr v +sein/haben (SouthG, Austr)
1. +sein/haben toboggan ◊ *Im Winter rodeln die
Kinder immer auf diesem Hügel.* ♦ *Komm, wir
wollen rodeln gehen.* ⊖Schlitten fahren **2.** +sein
sport luge

ro·den ['roːdn] <rodet, rodete, hat gerodet> tr v
+haben etw. roden clear sth, grub sth up ◊
Bäume/Waldflächen roden intr v clear the land ◊
Wann werden sie roden?

② **roh** [roː] adj <roher, am roh(e)sten> **1.** raw,
uncooked ◊ *rohes Gemüse* ♦ *Kann man das auch
roh essen? Das Fleisch war innen noch ganz roh.
The meat wasn't cooked through.* **2.** *only before ns*
untreated, rough ◊ *rohe Häute* einer roher Entwurf a
rought draft ein roher Diamant an uncut diamond
adj, adv *(pej)* rough(ly) ◊ *ein roher Kerl* ♦ *Sei
doch nicht so roh zu ihr!* ♦ *Er fasste sie roh am
Arm.* rohe Gewalt brute force

Rohr [roːɐ] das <–(e)s, –e> **1.** pipe ◊ *Der Klempner
verlegte neue Rohre.* **2.** *(SouthG, Austr) (for
baking/roasting)* oven ◊ *Sie schob den Braten ins
Rohr.* ⊖Ofen **3.** reed; cane ein aus Rohr geflochtener Korb a wicker basket

Röh·re ['røːrə] die <–, –n> **1.** tube, pipe ◊ *eine
Röhre mit einem Durchmesser von 60 cm; (electronics, tunnel)* tube **2.** *(for baking, roasting)*
oven ◊ *Er schob den Kuchen in die Röhre.* ⊖Ofen
◉ in die Röhre schauen/gucken etc. *(fam)* end
up with nothing

Roh·stoff ['roːʃtɔf] der <–(e)s, –e> raw material

② **Rol·le** ['rɔlə] die <–, –n> **1.** *(of an actor)* part,
role ◊ *Sie spielt die Rolle der Ophelia.* **2.** *(in
society etc.)* role ◊ *die Rolle der Frau im Mittelalter* ♦ *eine aktive Rolle spielen/übernehmen* **3.** roll,
reel ◊ *Er hat das Poster in einer Rolle verschickt.;
reel* ◊ *eine Rolle Nähfaden* **4.** pulley; castor ◊ *ein
Nachttisch auf Rollen; runner* ◊ *Die Schublade*

gleitet auf Rollen. **5.** SPORT roll ◊ *eine Rolle vorwärts/rückwärts*
ⓔ *etw.* **spielt keine Rolle** sth doesn't matter ◊ *Geld spielt bei ihm keine Rolle.* **eine (wichtige) Rolle spielen** be important **bei/in** *etw.* dat **eine Rolle spielen** play a part in sth

ⓩ **rol·len** ['rɔlən] intr v +*sein* roll ◊ *Der Zug rollte in den Bahnhof.* tr v +*haben* **1.** roll ◊ *Er rollte das Fass zur Seite.* ◆ *Die Bayern rollen das „R".* **etw. zu etw. rollen** roll sth into sth ◊ *Teig zu einer Kugel rollen* **2.** wheel ◊ *Sie rollte den Servierwagen ins Zimmer.*

Rol·len·spiel ['rɔlənʃpiːl] das <-(e)s, -e> role play
Rol·ler ['rɔlɐ] der <-s, -> scooter ◊ *Das Kind bekam einen Roller geschenkt.* ◆ *Der Roller fährt maximal 60 km/h.*
Roll·kra·gen ['rɔlkraːɡn̩] der <-s, Rollkrägen> polo neck, turtleneck ◊ *ein Pullover mit Rollkragen*
ⓩ **Roll·stuhl** ['rɔlʃtuːl] der <-(e)s, Rollstühle> wheelchair **im Rollstuhl sitzen** be in a wheelchair **an den Rollstuhl gefesselt sein** be confined to a wheelchair
Roll·trep·pe ['rɔltrɛpə] die <-, -n> escalator ◊ *Sie nahm die Rolltreppe in den ersten Stock.* **(mit der) Rolltreppe fahren** take the escalator
Rom [roːm] das <-s> *article only in combination with attribute, no pl* Rome box@ Stadt
Ro·man [ro'maːn] der <-s, -e> novel ◊ *Sie schreibt Romane.*
ro·ma·nisch [ro'maːnɪʃ] adj **1.** Romance ◊ *romanische Sprachen* **2.** Romanesque ◊ *eine romanische Kirche* ◆ *Der Stil ist romanisch.*
ro·man·tisch [ro'mantɪʃ] adj, adv romantic(ally) ◊ *Ich fand seinen Heiratsantrag sehr romantisch.* ◆ *romantische Musik* ◆ *Sie ist sehr romantisch veranlagt.* ◆ *Die* Romantic ◊ *ein bedeutender romantischer Dichter*
rönt·gen ['rœntɡən] tr v +*haben* X-ray ◊ *Gepäck röntgen* **zum Röntgen ins Krankenhaus gehen** go to the hospital to have an X-ray **Sie muss geröntgt werden.** She needs an X-ray.
ro·sa ['roːzaː] adj *invariable* pink ◊ *ein rosa Lippenstift* ◆ *Das T-Shirt ist rosa.* ◆ *Die Wände waren rosa gestrichen.*
Ro·se ['roːzə] die <-, -n> rose ◊ *ein Strauß roter Rosen*
Ro·sen·kohl ['roːznkoːl] der <-s> *no pl* Brussels sprouts ◊ *Er mag keinen Rosenkohl.*
Ro·sen·mon·tag [roːzn̩'moːntaːk] der <-(e)s> *no pl* Shrove Monday ◊ *Am Rosenmontag gehen wir auf einen Ball.*

> Shrove Monday (48 days before Easter, between 2nd February and 8th March) represents the highlight of the carnival festivities in Germany — street celebrations, fancy dress parties and balls take place everywhere. The most famous are the carnival processions and parties in the Rhine area. People dress up and line the streets to watch the processions. Children catch the sweets thrown to them from the carnival floats.

ro·sig ['roːzɪç] adj, adv rosy ◊ *Die Haut des Babys war rosig.* ◆ *rosige Aussichten* ◆ *Ihre Wangen glänzten rosig.*
Ro·si·ne [ro'ziːnə] die <-, -n> raisin
ⓔ **sich** dat **die Rosinen herauspicken/aus**

dem Kuchen picken take the pick of the bunch
Rost [rɔst] der <-es, -e> **1.** *no pl* rust ◊ *Der Deckel hatte Rost angesetzt.* **2.** grill, grate ◊ *Er legte die Steaks auf den Rost.*
ros·ten ['rɔstn̩] <rostet, rostete, hat/ist gerostet> intr v rust, go rusty ◊ *Dieses Material rostet nicht.*
rös·ten ['rœstn̩] tr v +*haben* roast ◊ *Würstchen über dem offenen Feuer rösten*; *(bread)* toast
ros·tig ['rɔstɪç] adj rusty ◊ *ein rostiges altes Fahrrad* ◆ *Mein Englisch ist etwas rostig.*
ⓩ **rot** [roːt] adj <röter/roter, am rötesten/rotesten> red ◊ *rote Kleidung/Haare* ◆ *Seine Ohren waren ganz rot.* ◆ *Rot vor Wut rannte er aus dem Zimmer.* ◆ *rot geschminkte Lippen* **rot werden, einen roten Kopf bekommen** blush **ein rot angehauchter Politiker** a leftish politician
ⓔ **rot angehaucht** *(politician)* leftish
rö·ten ['røːtn̩] ref v +*haben* **sich röten** turn red ◊ *Der Himmel rötete sich.* ◆ *Sein Gesicht rötete sich vor Aufregung.* tr v +*haben* *(lofty)* redden ◊ *Die Kälte rötete ihr Gesicht.*
rot·haa·rig ['roːthaːrɪç] adj *no comp/superl* red-haired ◊ *Sie war rothaarig.* ◆ *ein rothaariges Kind*
ro·tie·ren [ro'tiːrən] <rotiert, rotierte, hat rotiert> intr v **1.** rotate ◊ *Das Objekt rotierte um die eigene Achse.* ◆ *Der Vorsitz rotiert jährlich zwischen den Mitgliedern.* **2.** *(fam)* be in a flap ◊ *Unser Trainer rotiert vor jedem Spiel.* **anfangen zu rotieren** get into a flap
Rot·kraut ['roːtkraʊt] das <-s> *no pl (SouthG, Austr)* red cabbage
Rot·stift ['roːtʃtɪft] der <-(e)s, -e> red pen ◊ *einen Text mit Rotstift korrigieren*
ⓔ **dem Rotstift zum Opfer fallen** be cut, be axed **den Rotstift ansetzen** make cuts, make cutbacks, cut back
Rot·wein ['roːtvaɪn] der <-(e)s, -e> *pl 'Rotwein' when used with expressions of quantity* red wine ◊ *ein Glas Rotwein zum Essen trinken*
Rouge [ruːʃ] das <-s, -s> *most sing* rouge, blusher ◊ *Rouge mit einem Pinsel auftragen*
Rou·lett [ru'lɛt] das <-(e)s, -s> → Roulette
Rou·lette [ru'lɛt(ə)] das <-s, -s> roulette ◊ *beim Roulette Geld gewinnen*
Rou·te ['ruːtə] die <-, -n> route ◊ *Welche Route sollen wir nehmen?*
Rou·ti·ne [ru'tiːnə] die <-> *no pl* **1.** experience ◊ *durch jahrelange Erfahrung Routine in etw.* dat *bekommen/haben* **2.** routine ◊ *Ihr Eheleben ist zur Routine geworden.*
rou·ti·niert [ruti'niːɐt] adj <routinierter, am routiniertesten> experienced ◊ *Die Bedienung ist in diesem Restaurant sehr routiniert.* ◆ *routinierter Umgang mit etw.* adv expertly ◊ *routiniert mit Kunden umgehen*
Rü·be ['ryːbə] die <-, -n> **1.** BOT turnip **2.** *(fam)* head, nut ◊ *jdm eins auf die Rübe geben*
ⓔ **Gelbe Rübe** carrot ⊖Karotte **Rote Rübe** beetroot ⊖Rote Bete
Ru·bin [ru'biːn] der <-s, -e> ruby ◊ *ein mit Rubinen besetzter Ring*
Ru·brik [ru'briːk] die <-, -en> column, section ◊ *Anzeigen in der Rubrik „Sonstiges"* **unter der Rubrik** under the heading; *(in a newspaper)* in the column/section
Ruck [rʊk] der <-(e)s, -e> **1.** jolt, jerk ◊ *Es gab*

einen Ruck, und der Wagen blieb stecken. Der Zug machte einen Ruck. The train jolted. *mit einem Ruck* suddenly **2.** POL *ein Ruck nach rechts/links* a swing to the right/left

⊛ *sich* [dat] *einen Ruck geben* force yourself, make an effort, give yourself a kick up the backside

② **Rück·...** [rʏk] [prefix] **1.** back ... ◊ *die Rückansicht des Hauses* ♦ *die Rückbank eines Autos* **2.** *translation varies* um Rückantwort bitten request a reply *eine Rückfahrkarte kaufen* buy a return ticket, buy a round-trip ticket *einen Rückblick mit Fotos vom letzten Treffen zusammenstellen* put together a retrospective of photos from the last gathering

rü·cken ['rʏkn̩] [tr v] *+haben* move ◊ *das Bett an die Wand rücken* [intr v] *+haben/sein* **1.** *+sein* move beiseite/zur Seite rücken move over, move aside **2.** *+sein* etw. *rückt in weite Ferne* sth is becoming more distant **3.** *+haben* an seiner Brille rücken push your glasses up, tug at your glasses

② **Rü·cken** ['rʏkŋ] der <-s, -> back ◊ *auf dem Rücken liegen* ♦ *jdm den Rücken zuwenden*; *(of a book)* spine; *(of a mountain)* ridge

⊛ *jdm läuft es (heiß und) kalt den Rücken herunter (fam)* a chill goes down sb's spine *jdm in den Rücken fallen* stab sb in the back *jdm den Rücken freihalten/stärken* protect sb, support sb *jdm./etw. den Rücken kehren* turn your back on sb/sth *im Rücken* behind sb

② **Rück·fahr·kar·te** ['rʏkfaːˈkaˑrtə] die <-, -n> return (ticket), round-trip ticket ◊ *am Fahrkartenschalter eine Rückfahrkarte lösen*

Rück·fahrt ['rʏkfaːˑt] die <-, -en> return journey, journey back, way back ◊ *die Rückfahrt antreten* ♦ *Auf der Rückfahrt ereignete sich ein Unfall.*

Rück·flug ['rʏkfluːk] der <-(e)s, Rückflüge> return flight ◊ *Auf dem Rückflug gab es Turbulenzen.*

Rück·ga·be ['rʏkgaːbə] die <-, -n> return ◊ *die Rückgabe der Bücher in der Bibliothek*

rück·gän·gig ['rʏkgɛŋɪç] [adj] no comp/superl **1.** falling ◊ *Die Einwohnerzahl ist rückgängig.* ♦ *eine rückgängige Tendenz* **2.** *etw. rückgängig machen* cancel sth

Rück·grat ['rʏkgraːt] das <-(e)s, -e> most sing spine, backbone ◊ *sich das Rückgrat brechen* ⊝Wirbelsäule]

⊛ *jdm das Rückgrat brechen* ruin sb *Rückgrat haben* have got backbone

Rück·halt ['rʏkhalt] der <-(e)s> no pl support, backing ◊ *Ihm fehlt der Rückhalt seiner Kollegen.* ♦ *Jugendlichen einen Rückhalt geben* ⊝Unterstützung

Rück·kehr ['rʏkkeːɐ̯] die <-> no pl return ◊ *die Rückkehr in die Heimat* ♦ *die Angst vor einer Rückkehr der Seuche*

② **Rück·licht** ['rʏklɪçt] das <-(e)s, Rücklichter> tail light ◊ *Jedes Auto ist mit einem Rücklicht ausgestattet.*; *(on a bicycle also)* back light

Rück·rei·se ['rʏkraɛ̯zə] die <-, -n> return journey, journey back, way back ◊ *Auf der Rückreise war es im Bus sehr heiß.*

Rück·ruf ['rʏkruːf] der <-(e)s, -e> **1.** auf jds Rückruf warten wait for sb to call (you) back *Der Kunde bittet um Rückruf.* The customer would like you to call them back. **2.** recall ◊ *den Rückruf eines Arzneimittels anordnen*

Ruck·sack ['rʊkzak] der <-(e)s, Rucksäcke> rucksack, backpack

Rück·schlag ['rʏkʃlaːk] der <-(e)s, Rückschläge> **1.** setback ◊ *einen Rückschlag erleiden* ♦ *einen herben Rückschlag einstecken müssen* **2.** SPORT return

② **Rück·sei·te** ['rʏkzaɛ̯tə] die <-, -n> back ◊ *die Rückseite eines Gebäudes* ♦ *auf der Rückseite des Fragebogens unterschreiben*; *(of a coin also)* reverse

② **Rück·sicht** ['rʏkzɪçt] die <-, -en> **1.** consideration ◊ *finanzielle Rücksichten* keine Rücksicht kennen have no consideration *auf jdn/etw. Rücksicht nehmen* consider sb/sth, take sb/sth into consideration ◊ *im Verkehr auf Kinder Rücksicht nehmen* mit Rücksicht auf jdn/etw. for sb's/sth's sake, for the sake of sb/sth ◊ *Hier gilt mit Rücksicht auf die Anwohner Tempo 30.* **2.** no pl rear view

⊛ *ohne Rücksicht auf Verluste (fam)* regardless

rück·sichts·los ['rʏkzɪçtsloːs] [adj, adv] <rücksichtsloser, am rücksichtslosesten> **1.** thoughtless(ly), inconsiderate(ly), reckless(ly) ◊ *Das war ziemlich rücksichtslos von dir!* ♦ *die rücksichtslose Rodung der Wälder* ♦ *rücksichtslos rasen* **2.** ruthless(ly) ◊ *die rücksichtslose Ausbeutung der Sklaven* ♦ *rücksichtslos seine Interessen verfolgen*

Rück·sitz ['rʏkzɪts] der <-es, -e> back seat ◊ *Kinder gehören auf den Rücksitz.*

Rück·spie·gel ['rʏkʃpiːɡl̩] der <-s, -> rear-view mirror ◊ *vor dem Überholen in den Rückspiegel sehen*

Rück·spiel ['rʏkʃpiːl] das <-(e)s, -e> return match, return game

Rück·spra·che ['rʏkʃpraːxə] die <-, -n> most sing consultation ◊ *Das kann ich nicht ohne Rücksprache mit dem Chef entscheiden.* mit jdm Rücksprache halten consult sb, speak to sb

Rück·stand ['rʏkʃtant] der <-(e)s, Rückstände> **1.** residue ◊ *im Wasser Rückstände von Pestiziden finden* **2.** most pl Rückstände arrears, debts ◊ *seine Rückstände bei einer Firma bezahlen* **3.** mit etw. im Rückstand sein be behind with sth; *(payments also)* be in arrears with sth ◊ *mit der Miete im Rückstand sein* **4.** SPORT im Rückstand behind ◊ *Unsere Mannschaft liegt mit 0:3 im Rückstand.* einen Rückstand aufholen catch up ⊝Vorsprung

Rück·tritt ['rʏktrɪt] der <-(e)s, -e> **1.** resignation ◊ *einen Minister zum Rücktritt auffordern* seinen Rücktritt erklären hand in your resignation **2.** LAW rescission ◊ *das Recht zum Rücktritt vom Vertrag*

② **rück·wärts** ['rʏkvɛˑts] [adv] backwards ◊ *rückwärts gehen* ♦ *eine Rolle rückwärts machen* das Auto rückwärts in die Garage fahren back/reverse the car into the garage einen Film rückwärts laufen lassen rewind a film *eine rückwärts gewandte Politik* a backward-looking policy ⊝vorwärts

Rück·weg ['rʏkveːk] der <-(e)s, -e> way back, journey back, way home ◊ *Der Rückweg führt durch die Heide.* ♦ *auf dem Rückweg eine kurze Rast machen* sich auf den Rückweg machen head back

Rück·zug ['rʏktsuːk] der <-(e)s, Rückzüge> **1.** resignation, retirement ◊ *Sie kündigte ihren Rückzug aus der Politik an.* **2.** retreat, withdrawal ◊ *der Rückzug der Truppen* den Rückzug antreten start to

retreat
Ru·der ['ruːdɐ] das <-s, -> 1. oar ◊ *die Ruder ein-tauchen* 2. rudder ◊ *das Ruder führen/herumrei-ßen*
◉ *das Ruder fest in der Hand haben* have (got) everything under control *ans Ruder kommen* take the helm
ru·dern ['ruːdɐn] (intr v) +haben/sein 1. +haben/ with direction +sein ◊ *Wir sind über den See gerudert.* ♦ *Du musst schneller rudern.* 2. +haben *(fam) (with your arms, legs)* flap ◊ *beim Laufen mit den Armen rudern* (tr v) +haben jdn/etw. (irgendwohin) rudern row sb/sth (somewhere) ◊ *Er ruderte sie über den Fluss.*
Ruf [ruːf] der <-(e)s, -e> 1. cry ◊ *der Ruf der Mutter nach ihrem Kind* 2. zoo cry, call 3. *(fig)* call *der Ruf nach etw.* the call for sth *der Ruf zu den Waffen* the call to arms *dem Ruf des Herzens folgen* follow your heart *einen Ruf an die Universi-tät … bekommen* be called to a chair at the Univer-sity of … 4. *no pl* reputation ◊ *einen guten Ruf genießen/haben* ♦ *etw. schadet jds Ruf* von Ruf of high repute, of standing ◊ *eine Universität von Ruf* den Ruf haben, etw. zu sein/tun be reputed to be/ do sth ◊ *Er hat den Ruf, feige/ein Experte zu sein.*
◉ *jd/etw. ist besser als sein Ruf* sb/sth isn't as bad as everyone says they are/it is
ⓩ **ru·fen** ['ruːfn] <ruft, rief, hat gerufen> (tr+intr v) 1. shout, cry ◊ *Sie riefen: „Bravo!"* ♦ *Er rief: „Hallo!/Hilfe!"* ♦ *mit lauter Stimme rufen* 2. *(also fig)* call ♦ *die Polizei rufen* ♦ *Ruf mich, wenn das Essen fertig ist.* nach jdm/etw. rufen call for sb/sth *um Hilfe rufen* call for help *(zu etw.) rufen* call (sb to sth) ◊ *Die Klingel ruft zum Unterricht.* ♦ *Die Arbeit ruft!* (tr v) jdm/sich etw. ins Gedächtnis rufen remind sb/yourself of sth
◉ *jdm wie gerufen kommen (fam)* come at exactly the right time (for sb)
Rü·ge ['ryːgə] die <-, -n> reprimand für/wegen etw. *eine Rüge bekommen* be reprimanded for sth *jdm eine Rüge erteilen* reprimand sb ⊖Tadel ⊕Lob
ⓩ **Ru·he** ['ruːə] die <-> *no pl* 1. silence, quiet ◊ *Im Zimmer herrschte absolute Ruhe.* *Darf ich kurz um Ruhe bitten?* Could I have your attention for a minute? ⊖Stille ⊕Lärm 2. peace (and quiet) ◊ *Beim Lernen braucht er viel Ruhe.* jdn (mit etw.) in Ruhe lassen stop bothering sb (with sth) *Schauen Sie sich in Ruhe um.* Please have a look round. *Ruhe vor jdm haben* get away from sb 3. rest ◊ *jdm eine angenehme Ruhe wünschen* ♦ *Die Kugel kommt zur Ruhe.* 4. equilibrium ◊ *sich durch gar nichts aus der Ruhe bringen lassen* auch in schwie-rigen Situationen die Ruhe bewahren keep calm even in difficult situations *in aller Ruhe* calmly ⊖Unruhe
◉ *jdn zur letzten Ruhe betten (lofty, euph)* bury sb *sich zur Ruhe setzen* retire *die Ruhe weghaben (fam)* be keeping calm *immer mit der Ruhe* slow down, calm down
ru·hen ['ruːən] (intr v) +haben 1. *(also fig)* rest ◊ *Ich werde nicht ruhen, bevor das geklärt ist.* ♦ *Die Toten ruhen in Frieden.* ♦ *jds Blick ruht auf jdm/ etw.* etw. ruhen lassen let sth rest, leave sth aside, forget (about) sth 2. *(lofty)* sleep, (get a) rest ◊ *Haben Sie wohl geruht?* 3. *(work, production*

etc.) stop, cease ◊ *Die Produktion ruht.*
Ru·he·stand ['ruːəʃtant] der <-(e)s> *no pl* retire-ment *in den Ruhestand gehen/treten* retire *in den Ruhestand versetzt werden* be retired *seit einem Jahr im Ruhestand sein* have been retired for a year
Ru·he·tag ['ruːətaːk] der <-(e)s, -e> 1. *(restaur-ant, cafe)* Ruhetag haben be closed, be shut ◊ *Wir haben montags Ruhetag.* Montag Ruhetag closed on Mondays 2. day of rest ◊ *sich einen Ruhetag gönnen*
ⓩ **ru·hig**[1] ['ruːɪç] (adj, adv) 1. quiet(ly), peaceful(ly), in peace (and quiet) ◊ *Die Mutter bat ihre Kinder, ruhig zu sein.* ♦ *ein ruhiges Leben auf dem Land* ♦ *ruhig wohnen* ruhig schlafen sleep soundly *sich ruhig verhalten* keep quiet, hold your peace 2. calm(ly), still ◊ *während eines Gespräches ruhig bleiben* ♦ *ruhig auf dem Boden liegen* Ganz ruhig! Take it easy! *etw. ruhigen Gewissens tun können* be able to do sth with an easy conscience *ruhig zusehen* stand (by) and watch ⊕unruhig 3. steady(-ily) ◊ *eine ruhige Hand haben* ♦ *ruhig atmen;* smooth(ly), uneventful ◊ *eine ruhige Überfahrt* ♦ *Der Flug war/verlief ruhig.* ⊕unruhig
ru·hig[2] ['ruːɪç] (part) *(fam) not translated directly* Sie soll sich ruhig darüber aufregen, es ist mir egal. Let her get upset about it, I don't care. Mach du ruhig, was du willst. You can do what you like. Kommen Sie ruhig herein! Come on in. Fang ruhig mit dem Essen an. Go ahead and start (eating). Er kann sich ruhig mal um seine kranke Mutter kümmern. Let him look after his sick mother. Sie könnte ruhig mal mehr Verantwortung überneh-men. She could take on more responsibility.
Ruhm [ruːm] der <-(e)s> *no pl* fame ◊ *unsterb-lichen Ruhm erlangen*
Ruhr [ruːɐ] die <-> *no pl (always* die Ruhr*)* the (River) Ruhr ◊ *Mülheim an der Ruhr*
rüh·ren ['ryːrən] (tr v) +haben 1. stir ◊ *Zucker in den Kaffee rühren* 2. move ◊ *nach einem Unfall seine Beine nicht mehr rühren können* sich rühren move, stir ◊ *Rühr dich nicht vom Fleck!* ⊖regen 3. *(emotionally)* touch, move ◊ *Seine Offenheit rührte sie.* (intr v) +haben 1. stir ◊ *mit dem Löffel in der Suppe rühren* 2. *(lofty)* etw. rührt daher/ davon, dass sth stems from the fact that ◊ *Sein Erfolg rührt daher, dass er dauernd trainiert.* 3. *(lofty, fig)* an etw. (acc) rühren touch on sth ◊ *mit einem Buch an Tabuthemen rühren* (ref v) +haben sich rühren say sth ◊ *Warum hast du dich nicht gerührt? Ich hätte dir geholfen.* sich (bei jdm) rühren keep in touch, let sb know ◊ *Wenn du mich brauchst, dann rühr dich (bei mir).*
◉ *rührt euch* MIL at ease
Ruhr·ge·biet ['ruːɐgəbiːt] das <-(e)s> *no pl (always* das Ruhrgebiet*)* the Ruhr ◊ *die Industrie im Ruhr-gebiet*
Rüh·rung ['ryːrʊŋ] die <-> *no pl* emotion ◊ *Ihr kamen vor Rührung die Tränen.*
Ru·in [ru'iːn] der <-s> *no pl* ruin, downfall ◊ *Der Alkohol war sein Ruin.* ♦ *finanziell am Rande des Ruins sein*
Ru·i·ne [ru'iːnə] die <-, -n> ruin ◊ *Von der Burg ist nur noch eine Ruine übrig.*
ru·i·nie·ren [rui'niːrən] <ruiniert, ruinierte, hat ruiniert> (tr v) ruin ◊ *Er hat meinen Ruf ruiniert.*

jdn finanziell ruinieren
Ru·mä·ne [ruˈmɛːnə] der <–n, –n>, **Ru·mä·nin** [ruˈmɛːnɪn] die <–, –nen> Romanian → Deutsche
Ru·mä·ni·en [ruˈmɛːnjən] das <–s> no pl; article only in combination with attribute Romania → Deutschland
Ru·mä·nin [ruˈmɛːnɪn] fem of Rumäne
ru·mä·nisch [ruˈmɛːnɪʃ] [adj] mostly before ns Romanian → deutsch
Ru·mä·nisch [ruˈmɛːnɪʃ] das <–(s)> no pl Romanian → Deutsch
Rum·mel [ˈrʊml̩] der <–s> no pl (fam) **1.** Rummel (um jdn/etw.) fuss (about sb/sth) ◊ der ganze Rummel um den Popstar **2.** (esp NorthG) (fun)fair ◊ auf den Rummel gehen ⊜Jahrmarkt
rum·peln [ˈrʊmpl̩n] [intr v] +haben/with direction +sein (fam) rumble ◊ Es rumpelte, als wir über die Brücke fuhren. ◆ Der Wagen rumpelte durch einen Wald.
Rumpf [rʊmpf] der <–(e)s, Rümpfe> **1.** ANAT torso, trunk ◊ den Rumpf beugen **2.** SHIP hull ◊ der Maschinenraum im Rumpf des Schiffes **3.** AVIAT fuselage, body ◊ Im Rumpf des Flugzeugs ist Platz für 136 Passagiere.
② **rund** [rʊnt] [adj] <runder, am rundesten> **1.** round ◊ Die Erde ist rund. ◆ runde Wangen haben ◊ eine runde Summe ein runder Geburtstag special birthday such as the 20th, 30th, 40th etc. **2.** plump ◊ Er ist etwas rund geworden. ◆ ein runder Bauch ⊜dick **3.** (taste, sound) full ◊ ein Likör mit rundem Geschmack eine runde Sache sein be great [adv] **1.** about, around ◊ Das Auto hat rund 20 000 Euro gekostet. ⊜etwa, ungefähr **2.** rund um (a)round ◊ Wir wanderten rund um die Zugspitze. **3.** rund um all about ◊ Tipps rund um den PC
Run·de [ˈrʊndə] die <–, –n> **1.** round ◊ Die Verhandlungen gehen in die nächste Runde. ◆ eine Runde Golf spielen ◆ in der Kneipe eine Runde ausgeben **2.** lap, circuit ◊ fünf Runden laufen mit dem Auto eine Runde drehen take the car for a spin; (leisurely on foot) walk, stroll ◊ eine Runde durch den Park drehen; (of a policeman) beat **3.** group, gathering ◊ ein Spieleabend in geselliger Runde
⊛ über die Runden kommen (fam) get by die Runde machen (bottle) be passed around (news, rumo(u)r) do/go/make the rounds (doctor) do your rounds
run·den [ˈrʊndn̩] <rundet, rundete, hat gerundet> [tr v] round ◊ die Kanten/eine Zahl runden [ref v] (also fig) (moon) sich runden wax ◊ Wenn der Mond sich rundet, ...; (picture) be rounded off ◊ Mit jeder Information rundet sich das Bild und die Zusammenhänge werden klar.
② **Rund·funk** [ˈrʊntfʊŋk] der <–s> no pl radio ◊ sich die Nachrichten im Rundfunk anhören ◆ Sie

arbeitet beim Norddeutschen Rundfunk.
Rund·gang [ˈrʊntgaŋ] der <–(e)s, Rundgänge> **1.** walkabout, tour ◊ einen Rundgang durch die Stadt machen **2.** ARCH gallery
rund·he·rum [ˈrʊnthɛˈrʊm] → rundum
Rund·schrei·ben [ˈrʊntʃraebm̩] das <–s, –> circular ◊ vierteljährlich ein Rundschreiben erhalten
rund·um [rʊnt|ˈʊm] [adv] **1.** all around, on all sides ◊ Inseln sind rundum von Wasser umgeben. ⊜ringsherum **2.** thoroughly, absolutely ◊ mit dem Ergebnis rundum zufrieden sein ⊜völlig
run·ter [ˈrʊntɐ] [adv] (fam) down ◊ Runter mit den Klamotten! ⊜herunter ⊜rauf
Ruß [ruːs] der <–es, –e> most sing soot ◊ Wände und Decken waren nach dem Brand voller Ruß.
Rus·se [ˈrʊsə] der <–n, –n>, **Rus·sin** [ˈrʊsɪn] die <–, –nen> Russian → Deutsche
Rüs·sel [ˈrʏsl̩] der <–s, –> (of a pig) snout; (of an elephant) trunk; (of an insect) proboscis
Rus·sin [ˈrʊsɪn] fem of Russe
rus·sisch [ˈrʊsɪʃ] [adj] mostly before ns Russian → deutsch
Rus·sisch [ˈrʊsɪʃ] das <–(s)> no pl Russian → Deutsch
Russ·land [ˈrʊslant] das <–s> no pl; article only in combination with attribute Russia → Deutschland
rüs·ten [ˈrʏstn̩] <rüstet, rüstete, hat gerüstet> [intr v] MIL arm ◊ Das Land rüstet zum Krieg. [ref v] (lofty) sich (für etw.) rüsten prepare yourself (for sth) ◊ sich für die lange Reise gut rüsten
rüs·tig [ˈrʏstɪç] [adj] sprightly ◊ Der alte Mann ist noch sehr rüstig. ◆ eine rüstige Rentnerin
rus·ti·kal [rʊstiˈkaːl] [adj, adv] rustic(ally) ◊ rustikale Möbel ◆ Das Lokal war recht rustikal (eingerichtet).
Rüs·tung [ˈrʏstʊŋ] die <–, –en> **1.** most sing MIL armament ◊ viel Geld für Rüstung und Militär ausgeben **2.** (suit of) armour ◊ ein Ritter in Rüstung
Rutsch·bahn [ˈrʊtʃbaːn] die <–, –en> slide ◊ die Rutschbahn hinunterrutschen
rut·schen [ˈrʊtʃn̩] [intr v] +sein **1.** (smoothly) slide ◊ Auf dem Spielplatz kann man rutschen und schaukeln.; (uncontrolled) skid ◊ auf dem Eis ins Rutschen kommen; (accidentally) slip ◊ Die Hose rutscht. ◆ Das Glas ist ihm aus der Hand gerutscht. **2.** (fam) move over ◊ Rutsch mal, bitte! auf dem Stuhl hin und her rutschen fidget in your seat
rüt·teln [ˈrʏtl̩n] [tr v] +haben shake ◊ jdn an der Schulter rütteln [intr v] +haben rattle ◊ Der kleine Wagen rüttelte über den Feldweg. an etw. [dat] rütteln rattle (at) sth
⊛ daran gibt es nichts zu rütteln that's that, there's no changing it

A
B
C
D
E
F
G
H
I
J
K
L
M
N
O
P
Q
R
S
T
U
V
W
X
Y
Z

S

s, S [ɛs] *das* <-, -> s, S ◇ *Dieses Wort wird mit einem kleinen s/großen S geschrieben.* ♦ *S wie Siegfried*
Ⓢ **scharfes S** *the letter 'ß' in the German alphabet* ◇ *„Fuß" schreibt man mit scharfem S.* ⊖Eszett
S [ɛs] (*abbr of* small) (*clothing size*) small ◇ *ein T-Shirt in (der) Größe S*
Saal [zaːl] *der* <-(e)s, Säle> room, hall ◇ *ein festlich geschmückter Saal*
Saar·land ['zaːˈlant] <-(e)s> *no pl* (*always* das Saarland*) the Saarland ◇ *Er wohnt im Saarland.* box@ Land

Area: 2567 km²; inhabitants: approx. 1.07 million; regional capital: Saarbrücken.
The Saarland is the region around the River Saar. Important industries are car and steel manufacture, and coal mining. Saarbrücken has made itself a name as an important centre for trade fairs and conferences.

Saat [zaːt] *die* <-, -en> **1.** sowing ◇ *vor der Saat den Boden lockern* **2.** seedlings ◇ *Die junge Saat ist erfroren.* **3.** seeds ◇ *die Saat mit Erde bedecken*
Sach·be·ar·bei·ter ['zaxbə,aˈbaɛte] *der* <-s, ->, **Sach·be·ar·bei·te·rin** ['zaxbə,aˈbaɛtərɪn] *die* <-, -nen> administrator ◇ *die zuständige Sachbearbeiterin* ♦ *als Sachbearbeiter bei einer Krankenkasse arbeiten*
Ⓩ **Sa·che** ['zaxə] *die* <-, -n> **1.** *most pl* thing ◇ *seine Sachen in den Koffer packen* **2.** matter, affair ◇ *Die Politik ist eine Sache für sich.* ♦ *Ich habe in dieser Sache noch eine Frage. Das lass mal ruhig meine Sache sein!* That's my business! **3.** LAW case ◇ *in einer Sache als Zeuge aussagen* **4.** *no pl* cause ◇ *für eine gerechte Sache kämpfen* **5.** (*fam*) ... Sachen ... kilometres an/per hour, ... kilometers an/per hour ◇ *mit 80 Sachen durch die Stadt rasen*
Ⓢ **bewegliche/unbewegliche Sachen** LAW movables/immovables **mit jdm gemeinsame Sache machen** collaborate with sb, be in collaboration with sb **sich** [dat] **seiner Sache sicher sein** be sure of your ground **zur Sache kommen** come/get to the point **bei der Sache sein** have got your mind on the job **in Sachen** in matters of
sach·lich ['zaxlɪç] [adj, adv] **1.** objective(ly) ◇ *Seine Kritik war sachlich und nüchtern.* ♦ *ein sachlicher Erzählstil* ♦ *sachlich urteilen* ⊖objektiv, nüchtern ⊖unsachlich **2.** *when used as an adj, only before ns* factual(ly) ◇ *ein sachlicher Unterschied* ♦ *eine sachlich falsche Darstellung*
Sach·scha·den ['zaxʃaːdn̩] *der* <-s, Sachschäden> damage ◇ *Bei dem Brand entstand ein Sachschaden von 10 000 Euro.*
Sach·sen ['zaksn̩] *das* <-s> *article only in combination with attribute, no pl* Saxony box@ Land

Area: 18,413 km²; population: approx. 4.43 million; regional capital: Dresden.
Saxony was reestablished as a German *Bundesland* after reunification. For centuries, it has been famous for its industry and crafts, e.g. the world-famous Plauen Lace and Meissen Porcelain. The 'Saxon Switzerland' (the Elbe sandstone mountains) south of Dresden are a popular walking and leisure destination. Another tourist centre is Dresden itself, with its Baroque-style buildings (many of which have been restored since the Second World War) and its museums.

Sach·sen-An·halt [,zaksn̩|ˈanhalt] *das* <-s> *article only in combination with attribute, no pl* Saxony-Anhalt box@ Land

Area: 20,447 km²; inhabitants: approx. 2.62 million; regional capital: Magdeburg.
Saxony-Anhalt was reestablished as a German *Bundesland* after reunification. The most important industries are food and chemicals. The mountainous and wooded part of the region (the Harz) includes the Brocken, the mountain on which, according to legend, witches gather to celebrate Walpurgis Night (30 April). In historical terms, the towns of Wittenberg and Eisleben are particularly important for their links with Luther and the Reformation.

Sach·ver·stän·di·ge ['zaxfɛʃtɛndɪgə] *der/die* <-n, die Sachverständigen> *but: ein Sachverständiger/eine Sachverständige* expert ◇ *Sie wurde als Sachverständige vorgeladen.* ◇ *die Prüfung durch einen Sachverständigen* box@ Substantivierung
Sack [zak] *der* <-(e)s, Säcke> **1.** sack ◇ *ein Sack Kartoffeln* ♦ *drei Säcke mit/voll Gold* **2.** (*rude*) balls **3.** (*fam, pej*) sod, git ◇ *Ihr faulen Säcke!*
Ⓢ **mit Sack und Pack** with all your worldly possessions **etw. im Sack haben** (*fam*) have got sth in the bag

In Germany, the 'yellow sack' is a special kind of rubbish bag in which recyclable packaging is collected. This waste is then sorted at special depots and sent on to recycling plants.

Ⓩ **Sa·ckerl** ['zakɐl] *das* <-s, -(n)> (*Austr, SouthG*) bag ◇ *ein Sackerl Mehl*
Sack·gas·se ['zakgasə] *die* <-, -n> (*also fig*) dead end ◇ *in eine Sackgasse abbiegen* ♦ *Die Verhandlungen gerieten in eine Sackgasse.*
sa·dis·tisch [za'dɪstɪʃ] [adj, adv] sadistic(ally) ◇ *sadistische Neigungen haben* ♦ *Er ist sadistisch.* ♦ *seine Opfer sadistisch quälen* sadistisch veranlagt sein have sadistic tendencies
sä·en ['zɛːən] [tr v] +*haben* **1.** sow ◇ *Getreide/Salat säen* **2.** (*fig*) sow the seeds of ◇ *Hass säen* [intr v] +*haben* sow (the) seeds
Ⓩ **Saft** [zaft] *der* <-(e)s, Säfte> **1.** (*from fruit*) juice

◊ *der Saft von frisch gepressten Orangen* ♦ *Möchtest du Saft oder Wasser?* **2.** *(from meat or poultry)* juice(s) ◊ *Fleisch im eigenen Saft garen* **3.** sap ◊ *Der Saft der Aloe Vera enthält heilsame Substanzen.* **4.** *(fam) (of a battery)* juice ◊ *Die Batterie hat keinen Saft mehr.*
◉ **ohne Saft und Kraft** weak and feeble
saf·tig ['zaftɪç] [adj] **1.** juicy ◊ *Das Fruchtfleisch der Aprikose ist sehr saftig.* ♦ *ein saftiges Steak* ⊖trocken **2.** lush ◊ *saftige Weiden/Wiesen* **3.** *(fam) (bill, fine)* hefty ◊ *eine saftige Rechnung bekommen; (prices)* high [adv] **1.** juicily ◊ *ein saftig gebratenes Steak* **2.** *(fam)* jdn saftig bestrafen give sb a hefty fine ◊ *die Preise saftig erhöhen* raise your prices a lot
Sa·ge ['za:gə] die <-, -n> legend ◊ *die Sage von König Artus*
Sä·ge ['zɛ:gə] die <-, -n> saw
⊘ **sa·gen** ['za:gn̩] [tr v] +*haben* **1.** say ◊ *Kannst du das auch auf Englisch sagen?* ♦ *Er sagt, er wolle das nicht.* ♦ *Sag, dass das nicht wahr ist!* man sagt, ... it is said that ...; *(a piece of information)* jdm etw. sagen tell sb sth ◊ *Er wollte mir sein Alter nicht sagen.* ♦ *Können Sie mir sagen, wie spät es ist?* jdm einen schönen Gruß von jdm sagen give sb sb's regards **2.** etw. (zu jdm/etw.) sagen call (sb/sth) sth ◊ *Sag nicht immer Schatzi zu mir!* **3.** *(an opinion)* was sagt jd zu ... what does sb think about ... ◊ *Was sagst du zu meiner neuen Frisur? Dazu will ich lieber nichts sagen.* I had better say nothing. **4.** jdm sagen, er soll etw. tun tell sb to do sth Tu, was man dir sagt! Do as you are told! sich [dat] von jdm nichts sagen lassen not take any orders from sb ⊖befehlen **5.** decide, say ◊ *Das muss meine Frau sagen, das kann ich nicht entscheiden.* ♦ *Wer kann schon sagen, ob das auch stimmt?* etwas/nichts zu sagen haben have a/no say ⊖entscheiden **6.** das sagt uns, dass ... this means (that) ... etw. hat wenig/nichts zu sagen sth doesn't mean much/anything mit etw. ist ... sth doesn't mean that ... jdm (etwas)/nichts sagen mean something /nothing to sb ◊ *Sagt Ihnen der Name Worsch etwas?; (allowing a conclusion)* etw. (über jdn/etw.) sagen say sth (about sb/sth) ◊ *Das Aussehen sagt noch gar nichts über den Charakter.*
◉ **um nicht zu sagen** not to say ◊ *Die Übersetzung ist ungenau, um nicht zu sagen völlig falsch.* **unter uns gesagt** between you and me **gesagt, getan** no sooner said than done **sich nichts mehr zu sagen haben** have stopped talking to each other **sich** [dat] **etw. nicht zweimal sagen lassen** not need to be told sth twice **sage und schreibe** *(fam)* believe it or not **jd will nichts gegen etw./jdn gesagt haben** *(fam)* sb has got nothing against sth/sb **du sagst es, Sie sagen es** *(fam)* very true **sag mal, sagen Sie mal** *(fam)* tell me, listen **sagen wir (mal)** *(fam)* (let's) say **was du nicht sagst, was Sie nicht sagen** *(fam)* you don't say **wem sagst du das, wem sagen Sie das** *(fam)* you don't need to tell me, I know that only too well **wer sagt's denn** *(fam)* there you are **wie gesagt** as I have said/mentioned
sä·gen ['zɛ:gn̩] [tr+intr v] +*haben* saw ◊ *Er hat das Brett in kurze Stücke gesägt.* ♦ *Heute Nachmittag*

wird es laut, weil ich sägen muss. [intr v] +*haben* *(fam, hum)* snore (loudly) ◊ *Er hat die ganze Nacht neben mir gesägt.* ⊖schnarchen
sa·gen·haft ['za:gn̩haft] [adj] <sagenhafter, am sagenhaftesten> **1.** *(fam)* fabulous ◊ *Der Urlaub war sagenhaft.* ♦ *Er hat es in Amerika zu sagenhaftem Reichtum gebracht.* **2.** only before ns *(fam)* incredible ◊ *Das war aber sagenhaftes Pech.* **3.** no comp/superl, only before ns legendary ◊ *der sagenhafte König Artus* [adv] *(fam)* incredibly ◊ *Sie ist sagenhaft begabt.* ♦ *Die Mannschaft hat sagenhaft schlecht gespielt.*
⊘ **sah** [za:] pret of sehen
⊘ **Sah·ne** ['za:nə] die <-> no pl **1.** cream süße Sahne (whipping) cream saure Sahne soured cream ⊖Rahm **2.** whipped cream ◊ *Möchten Sie Sahne zum Kuchen?* ⊖Schlagsahne
◉ **erste Sahne** *(fam)* absolutely great ◊ *Dein Notebook ist erste Sahne.*
⊘ **Sai·son** [zɛ'zɔ̃, zɛ'zɔ̃:] die <-, -s> season ◊ *Ich verreise immer außerhalb der Saison.* ♦ *die Modelle der nächsten Saison* ♦ *Jetzt haben Trauben gerade Saison.*
Sai·te ['zaɛtə] die <-, -n> string ◊ *die Saiten einer Geige* ♦ *An meinem Tennisschläger ist eine Saite gerissen.*
◉ **andere Saiten aufziehen** *(fam)* get tough
⊘ **Sa·lat** [za'la:t] der <-(e)s, -e> **1.** *(dish)* salad ◊ *Schnitzel mit gemischtem Salat* **2.** *(plant)* lettuce ◊ *Es gab Braten, Spätzle und (grünen) Salat.* ♦ *Salat anpflanzen/säen*
◉ **jetzt haben wir den Salat** *(fam)* now we're in a right mess
⊘ **Sal·be** ['zalbə] die <-, -n> ointment ◊ *eine Salbe gegen Rheumaschmerzen*
Sal·do ['zaldo:] der <-s, -s or Saldi or Salden> balance per Saldo on balance
Sa·lon [za'lɔŋ, za'lõ:] der <-s, -s> salon ◊ *Meine Friseurin hat jetzt ihren eigenen Salon eröffnet.; (for massage also)* parlour, parlor
sa·lon·fä·hig [za'lɔŋfɛ:ɪç, za'lõ:fɛ:ɪç] [adj] socially acceptable ◊ *salonfähiges Benehmen; (joke)* nicht salonfähig rude salonfähig gekleidet sein be presentable
Sal·to ['zalto:] der <-s, -s or Salti> somersault ◊ *einen Salto vorwärts/rückwärts machen*
⊘ **Salz** [zalts] das <-es, -e> salt ◊ *eine Prise Salz* ♦ *Salze lösen sich in wässrigen Lösungen.*
sal·zen ['zaltsn̩] <salzt, salzte, hat gesalzen> [tr v] salt ◊ *Die Suppe war zu wenig gesalzen.*
sal·zig ['zaltsɪç] [adj] salty ◊ *Die Suppe war zu salzig.* ♦ *salziges Meerwasser*
Salz·kar·tof·fel ['zaltskartɔfl̩] die <-, -n> most pl boiled potato ◊ *Zum Fisch gibt es Salzkartoffeln.*
Salz·streu·er ['zaltsʃtrɔɛ] der <-s, -> salt cellar
Salz·was·ser ['zaltsvasɐ] das <-s> no pl **1.** salted water ◊ *Die Nudeln in kochendes Salzwasser geben und etwa zehn Minuten kochen.* **2.** saltwater ◊ *Dieser Fisch kommt nur in Salzwasser vor.* ⊖Meerwasser
Sa·men ['za:mən] der <-s, -> **1.** seed ◊ *Ich ziehe mein Basilikum immer aus Samen.* **2.** sperm, semen
⊘ **sam·meln** ['zamln̩] [tr v] +*haben* **1.** collect, gather ◊ *Die Polizei sammelt Beweise.* ♦ *den Müll getrennt sammeln* ♦ *Thomas sammelt Briefmarken.*

A
B
C
D
E
F
G
H
I
J
K
L
M
N
O
P
Q
R
S
T
U
V
W
X
Y
Z

2. pick ◊ *Wir waren im Wald, Pilze sammeln.*
3. gather ◊ *Lass sie ihre eigenen Erfahrungen sammeln.* **4.** *(a group of people)* jdn um sich sammeln gather sb round yourself (tr+intr v) +*haben (for charities)* collect ◊ *Wir sammeln (Geld) für den Tierschutzverein.* (ref v) +*haben* **1.** *(people, animals)* sich sammeln gather, assemble ◊ *Wo sie auch auftritt, sammeln sich Scharen von Menschen um sie.* **2.** *(things, tasks)* sich sammeln gather, accumulate ◊ *Es ist erstaunlich, was sich an unerledigter Post bei mir sammelt.* **3.** sich sammeln collect yourself, gather yourself together ◊ *Vor dem Auftritt braucht er etwas Zeit, um sich zu sammeln.* ⊖sich konzentrieren

Samm·lung ['zamlʊŋ] die <–, –en> **1.** collection ◊ *Die Sammlung brachte zwei Millionen Euro ein.* ♦ *Er hat eine Sammlung antiker Münzen.* **2.** composure ◊ *Vor dem Vortrag brauche ich ein paar Minuten Ruhe zur Sammlung.*

② **Sams·tag** ['zamsta:k] der <–(e)s, –e> Saturday ⊖Sonnabend → Montag

sams·tags ['zamsta:ks] (adv) on Saturdays ⊖sonnabends → montags

samt [zamt] (prep) (+dat) **1.** together with ◊ *Er kam samt Frau und Hund.* **2.** including ◊ *Ein Notebook samt Zubehör kostet um die 1500 Euro.* ⊖mit

sämt·li·che ['zɛmtlɪçə] (adj) *no comp/superl, only before ns* all (the) ◊ *Er hat seinen sämtlichen Besitz verloren.* ♦ *Sämtliche Angaben waren falsch.* Schillers sämtliche Werke the complete works of Schiller (adv) all ◊ *Die Vorstellungen waren sämtlich überfüllt.* ⊖alle

Sand [zant] der <–(e)s> *no pl* sand
◉ jdm Sand in die Augen streuen pull the wool over sb's eyes Sand im Getriebe sein be gumming up the works etw./jdn gibt es wie Sand am Meer there are loads of sth/sb, there is no shortage of sth/sb etw. in den Sand setzen *(fam)* make a mess of sth im Sande verlaufen come to nothing

San·da·le [zan'da:lə] die <–, –n> sandal

san·dig ['zandɪç] (adj) sandy ◊ *Der Boden ist hier sehr sandig.* ♦ *Ich habe sandige Hände.*

Sand·kas·ten ['zantkastn̩] der <–s, Sandkästen> sandpit, sandbox ◊ *Die Kinder spielen im Sandkasten.*

② **sand·te** ['zantə] *pret of* senden[1]

sanft [zanft] (adj, adv) <sanfter, am sanftesten>
1. *(also fig) (person, look, eyes)* gentle(-tly), soft(ly) ◊ *Sie sprach mit sanfter Stimme.* ♦ *Diese Creme ist besonders sanft zu ihrer Haut.* ♦ *Er streichelte sie sanft.* mit sanfter Gewalt gently but firmly Im Alter ist er sanfter geworden. He has mellowed in his old age. ⊖aggressiv **2.** *(light, colo(u)rs, sound)* soft(ly) ◊ *die sanften Töne einer Harfe* ♦ *Das Zimmer war in sanften Farben gehalten.* ♦ *Der Wind wehte sanft. Das ist noch sanft ausgedrückt. That's putting it mildly.* ⊖mild **3.** *(hill, climb)* gentle(-tly) ◊ *eine sanfte Steigung* ♦ *Das Gelände fällt sanft zum Meer hin ab.* ⊖steil **4.** *(sleep, death)* peaceful(ly) ◊ *Das Kind hat einen sanften Schlaf.* ♦ *Der alte Mann ist sanft eingeschlafen.* ⊖friedlich

② **sang** [zaŋ] *pret of* singen

② **Sän·ger** ['zɛŋɐ] der <–s, –>, **Sän·ge·rin** ['zɛŋərɪn]

die <–, –nen> singer ◊ *Er will Sänger werden.* ♦ *eine bekannte Sängerin*

sa·nie·ren [za'ni:rən] <saniert, sanierte, hat saniert> (tr v) **1.** *(an area)* redevelop ◊ *Die Ulmer Altstadt wurde saniert.; (a building)* renovate ◊ *Der Altbau muss grundlegend saniert werden.* ⊖instand setzen **2.** *(a company etc.)* put back on its feet, rehabilitate; *(financially)* return to the black (ref v) *(pej)* sich sanieren line your pockets

sa·ni·tär [zani'tɛːɐ̯] (adj) *no comp/superl, only before ns* sanitary ◊ *sanitäre Anlagen*

Sa·ni·tä·ter [zani'tɛːtɐ] der <–s, –>,
Sa·ni·tä·te·rin [zani'tɛːtərɪn] die <–, –nen> first-aid attendant, paramedic ◊ *Sie macht eine Ausbildung als Sanitäterin.* ♦ *ein Sanitäter des Roten Kreuzes*

② **sank** [zaŋk] *pret of* sinken

Sankt [zaŋkt] <–> *only in combination with names* REL *(abbr St.)* Saint ◊ *Sankt Nikolaus*

Sank·ti·on [zaŋk'tsi̯oːn] die <–, –en> **1.** *only pl* sanction ◊ *Die Regierung hat diesem Betrieb mit Sanktionen gedroht.* **2.** *(lofty)* approval, sanction ◊ *Wenn der Direktor dafür seine Sanktion erteilt, können wir anfangen.*

Sa·phir [za'fiːɐ̯, 'zaːfiːɐ̯] der <–(e)s, –e> sapphire

Sar·di·ne [zar'diːnə] die <–, –n> sardine ◊ *eine Dose Sardinen*

Sarg [zark] der <–(e)s, Särge> coffin ◊ *Sie wurde in einem Sarg aus Eiche bestattet.*

sar·kas·tisch [zar'kastɪʃ] (adj, adv) *(lofty)* sarcastic(ally) ◊ *sarkastische Bemerkungen* ♦ *Du bist immer so sarkastisch.* ♦ *Er hat die Debatte sarkastisch kommentiert.* ⊖bissig

② **saß** [zaːs] *pret of* sitzen

Sa·tel·lit [zatɛ'liːt] der <–en, –en> *(also fig)* satellite ◊ *Die Sendung wird über Satellit übertragen.* ♦ *Der Mond ist der einzige Satellit der Erde.* ◊ *Dieses Land war früher ein Satellit Moskaus.*

Sa·tel·li·ten·schüs·sel [zatɛ'liːtn̩ʃʏsl̩] die <–, –n> *(fam)* satellite dish

② **satt** [zat] (adj) <satter, am sattesten> **1.** full (up) ◊ *Danke, ich bin satt.* satt machen be filling satt werden have enough (to eat) sich satt essen eat as much as you want, eat your fill eine Familie satt kriegen/bekommen feed a family ⊖hungrig **2.** *only before ns (fam, emph)* fat ◊ *eine satte Prämie/Summe* eine satte Mehrheit a comfortable majority ein Anstieg von satten 45% an impressive increase of 45%. **3.** *only before ns (colo(u)rs)* rich, deep ◊ *ein sattes Rot* ⊖kräftig **4.** *only before ns (fig, pej) (person)* smug, self-satisfied ◊ *die satten Konsumenten, die keine Wünsche mehr haben* (adv) *(fam)* more than enough ◊ *Es gab Champagner/Sonne satt.*
◉ sich an etw. (dat) satt gesehen haben have enough of sth jdn/etw. satt haben/sein *(fam)* be fed up with sb/sth ⊖jdn/etw. über haben sich an etw. (dat) nicht satt sehen können not be able to take your eyes off sth

Sat·tel ['zatl̩] der <–s, Sättel> saddle ◊ *Sie legte dem Pferd den Sattel über.* ♦ *Der Sattel meines Fahrrads ist zu hart.* ♦ *den Sattel eines Berges überqueren*
◉ fest im Sattel sitzen be firmly in the saddle

② **Satz** [zats] der <–es, Sätze> **1.** sentence ◊ *etw. mit/in wenigen Sätzen schildern* mitten im Satz in

mid-sentence **2.** rate ◊ *Die Krankenkassen erhöhen ihre Sätze.* **3.** *(before printing)* setting *etw.* geht in den Satz *sth is being set* **4.** set ◊ *ein Satz Winterreifen* ♦ *Er gewann das Tennismatch in drei Sätzen.; (table tennis, badminton)* game **5.** MUS movement, period ◊ *das Tempo im zweiten Satz von Ravel* **6.** MATH theorem *der Satz des Pythagoras* Pythagoras' theorem **7.** *(wine)* sediment; *(coffee)* grounds **8.** leap, jump, bound ◊ *Er nahm die Hürde mit einem Satz.* ♦ *Er machte einen Satz über den Graben.*

Sat·zung ['zatsʊŋ] die <-, -en> articles of association, statutes ◊ *So steht es in der Satzung unseres Vereins.*

Satz·zei·chen ['zatsˌtsaeçn̩] das <-s, -> punctuation mark ◊ *Die Satzzeichen werden im Diktat mitdiktiert.*

Sau [zao] die <-, -en or Säue> **1.** sow ◊ *Die Sau hat zehn Ferkel bekommen.* **2.** *(rude, pej)* dirty pig ◊ *Welche Sau hat den Dreck ins Haus geschleppt?* ◉ *jdn zur Sau machen (fam)* tear a strip off sb ◊ *die Sau rauslassen (slang)* let your hair down ◊ *keine Sau (fam)* not a (bloody/damn) soul ◊ *unter aller Sau (fam, pej)* (bloody) awful(ly), lousy(-ily) ◊ *Seine Noten sind unter aller Sau.*

② **sau·ber** ['zaobɐ] [adj] **1.** clean ◊ *Zieh ein sauberes Hemd an.* ♦ *Jetzt ist die Wohnung wieder sauber.* ⊖schmutzig, dreckig **2.** neat ◊ *Er führt ein sehr sauberes Heft.* ♦ *Ihre Arbeitsweise ist sauber und ordentlich.* ⊖ordentlich ⊖schlampig **3.** *(iron)* fine, nice ◊ *Das war eine saubere Überraschung.* **4.** *(business etc.)* honest *An der Sache ist doch etwas nicht ganz sauber.* There's something fishy about this. **5.** house-trained ◊ *Zum Glück ist unser Hund endlich sauber.* **6.** toilet-trained ◊ *Es wird Zeit, dass der Kleine endlich sauber wird.* [adv] **1.** etw. sauber putzen clean *sth* etw. sauber schrubben scrub *sth* clean **2.** neatly ◊ *Schreib bitte etwas sauberer.* ♦ *Sie arbeitet sauber und gewissenhaft.* ⊖schlampig **3.** perfectly, faultlessly ◊ *Der Sopran hat nicht immer sauber gesungen.* ◉ sauber machen clean (up) ◊ *Am Samstag macht er seine Wohnung sauber.*

Sau·ber·keit ['zaobɐkaet] die <-> *no pl* **1.** cleanliness ◊ *Wir legen sehr großen Wert auf Sauberkeit.; (of environment)* cleanness ◊ *die Sauberkeit unserer Straßen vor Sauberkeit strahlen* be spick and span **2.** *(fig)* honesty ◊ *In die Politik muss wieder mehr Sauberkeit einziehen.; (in sports)* die Sauberkeit (des Fußballs etc.) fair play (in football etc.)

säu·bern ['zɔybɐn] [tr v] +*haben* clean, cleanse ◊ *Womit säuberst du deine Teppiche?* ♦ *Der Arzt säuberte die Wunde.*

Sau·ce ['zoːsə] → Soße

② **sau·er** ['zaoɐ] [adj, adv] <saurer, am sauersten> <der/die/das saure ...> **1.** sour ◊ *saure Bonbons* ♦ *Die Äpfel sind sauer.; (milk etc.)* sauer sein/ werden be/turn sour; *(wine)* acidic ◊ *Der Wein schmeckt sauer.* sauer aufstoßen belch with acidic taste ⊖süß **2.** *(fam)* annoyed, cross ◊ *Bist du jetzt sauer auf mich?* ♦ *Sie machte ein saures Gesicht.* ⊖böse ◉ etw. stößt jdm sauer auf *sth* really annoys sb ◊ *Dieser abfällige Satz ist mir sauer aufgestoßen.* **sauer reagieren** get annoyed

Sau·e·rei [zaoə'rae] die <-, -en> *(fam, pej)* **1.** mess ◊ *Sieh mal, was du da für eine Sauerei gemacht hast.* **2.** scandal ◊ *Es ist eine Sauerei, wie viel Steuern ich zahlen muss!* **3.** filth ◊ *Was man im Internet alles für Sauereien findet!* Sauereien erzählen tell filthy stories

Sau·er·kraut ['zaoɐkraot] das <-(e)s> *no pl* sauerkraut ◊ *Bratwürste mit Sauerkraut*

> This German speciality consists of finely chopped and salted white cabbage which is fermented without any additional ingredients. Lactic acid develops through the mixture of common salt with cabbage juice. You can eat sauerkraut both cooked and raw. It is very healthy because it is high in vitamin B1 and C, has a high mineral content, and stimulates digestion.

Sau·er·stoff ['zaoɐʃtɔf] der <-(e)s> *seldom with the article, no pl (abbr* O) oxygen ◊ *Luft enthält Sauerstoff.*

sau·fen ['zaofn̩] <säuft, soff, hat gesoffen> [tr v] **1.** drink ◊ *Die Katze hat die ganze Milch gesoffen.* **2.** *(fam)* drink, knock back, swig ◊ *Er säuft literweise Cola.* [intr v] *(also fam)* drink ◊ *Seit dem Tod seiner Frau säuft er.* saufen wie ein Loch drink like a fish

Säu·fer ['zɔyfɐ] der <-s, ->, **Säu·fe·rin** ['zɔyfərɪn] die <-, -nen> *(rude, pej)* boozer, drunkard ◊ *Du wirst noch zum Säufer werden.* ♦ *eine notorische Säuferin*

säuft [zɔyft] *pres of* saufen

sau·gen ['zaogn̩] <saugt, saugte/sog, hat gesaugt/ gesogen> [tr+intr v] +*haben* **1.** suck ◊ *Er sog die frische Luft in seine Lungen.; (baby also)* suckle; *(butterfly, bee)* extract ◊ *Die Schmetterlinge saugen den Nektar der Blumen.* an etw. [dat] saugen suck on *sth* ◊ *Sie saugte an ihrem Strohhalm.; (a pipe, cigarette)* draw on *sth* **2.** *pret 'saugte' and perf 'hat gesaugt'* hoover, vacuum ◊ *den Teppich/das Wohnzimmer saugen* ⊖staubsaugen

Säu·ge·tier ['zɔygəˌtiːɐ] das <-(e)s, -e> mammal

Säug·ling ['zɔyklɪŋ] der <-s, -e> baby, infant ◊ *ein neugeborener Säugling* ⊖Baby

Säu·le ['zɔylə] die <-, -n> **1.** ARCH column, pillar ◊ *eine korinthische Säule* **2.** *(also fig)* pillar ◊ *Er gehört zu den Säulen unserer Gesellschaft.*

Saum [zaom] der <-(e)s, Säume> **1.** hem ◊ *Sie hat den Saum ihres Rockes von Hand genäht.* **2.** *(lofty, fig)* edge ◊ *Am Saum des Waldes stand eine Hütte.*

Sau·na ['zaona:] die <-, Saunen> sauna ◊ *Sie geht einmal in der Woche in die Sauna.*

Säu·re ['zɔyrə] die <-, -n> **1.** acid ◊ *Der Wein hat mir zu viel Säure.* **2.** *no pl* acidity ◊ *die angenehme Säure der Limone*

sau·sen ['zaozn̩] [intr v] +*haben/sein (fam)* **1.** +*sein* irgendwohin sausen rush somewhere, race somewhere ◊ *Ich sause mal eben zum Bäcker.* ♦ *Er sauste mit 200 über die Autobahn.* **2.** +*haben (wind)* whistle; *(storm)* roar **3.** +*sein* durch etw. sausen fail *sth* ◊ *Er ist schon zweimal durch die Fahrprüfung gesaust.*

S-Bahn ['ɛsbaːn] die <-, -en> *commuter train (network)* ◊ *Ich nehme die S-Bahn ins Stadtzentrum.*

schä·big ['ʃɛːbɪç] [adj, adv] **1.** shabby(-ily) ◊ *ein*

alter, schäbiger Mantel ♦ Der Teppich sieht allmählich sehr schäbig aus. ♦ schäbig gekleidet
2. (fam) stingy(-ily) ◊ Das war aber schäbig von ihm, dass er dir gar nichts geschenkt hat. ♦ schäbig entlohnt werden; (pay) poor(ly) ◊ Mit dem schäbigen Gehalt kommst du aber nicht weit.
3. mean(ly), nasty(-ily) ◊ ein schäbiger Trick ♦ Ich kam mir richtig schäbig vor, als ich seine Enttäuschung sah. ♦ Er hat sich ihr gegenüber ziemlich schäbig verhalten.; (excuse) pathetic(ally)

Schach [ʃax] das <-s> no pl **1.** chess ◊ Ich kann nicht Schach spielen. **2.** (position) check ◊ Sein König befindet sich im Schach. jdm Schach bieten check sb Schach (dem König) check (the king) Schach und matt checkmate

ⓔ **jdn in Schach halten** keep sb in check

Schach·brett [ˈʃaxbrɛt] das <-(e)s, –er> chessboard ◊ die Figuren auf dem Schachbrett aufstellen

Schacht [ʃaxt] der <-(e)s, Schächte> shaft ◊ der Schacht eines Aufzugs ♦ Morgens fahren die Kumpels in den Schacht ein.; (of a staircase) (stair)well; (of sewers) manhole

ⓩ **Schach·tel** [ˈʃaxtl̩] die <-, –n> box ◊ Meinen Hut bewahre ich immer in seiner Schachtel auf. ♦ eine Schachtel Pralinen/Streichhölzer eine Schachtel Zigaretten a packet of cigarettes

ⓩ **scha·de** [ˈʃaːdə] adj not before ns **1.** pity, shame ◊ Es ist schade, dass du nicht dabei warst! ♦ „Ich kann leider nicht kommen." — „Schade!" schade um jdn/etw. pity/shame about sb/sth ◊ Es ist schade um ihn, aus ihm hätte etwas werden können. **2.** für jdn/etw. zu schade sein be too good for sb/sth ◊ Das Kleid ist mir für die Arbeit zu schade. jd ist sich dat für etw. zu schade sth is below sb, sth is beneath sb ◊ Fürs Putzen bist du dir wohl zu schade?

Schä·del [ˈʃɛːdl̩] der <-s, –> **1.** skull jdm den Schädel einschlagen smash sb's skull/head (in) **2.** (fam) head ◊ Am Morgen nach der Party tat mein Schädel weh. seinen Schädel anstrengen tax your brains

ⓔ **jdm brummt der Schädel** (fam) **1.** sb's head is going round and round ◊ Nach dem Vortrag hat mir der Schädel gebrummt. **2.** sb's head is throbbing ◊ Da war vielleicht ein Krach, mir brummt jetzt noch der Schädel!

ⓩ **scha·den** [ˈʃaːdn̩] <schadet, schadete, hat geschadet> intr v jdm/einer Sache schaden damage sb/sth, harm sb/sth, do harm to sb/sth ◊ Dein Verhalten schadet unserer Firma. Rauchen schadet der Gesundheit. Smoking damages your health.

ⓔ **etw. kann (jdm) nicht schaden** sth won't do (sb) any harm **etw. würde jdm/einer Sache nicht schaden** sth would do sb/sth no harm

ⓩ **Scha·den** [ˈʃaːdn̩] der <-s, Schäden> **1.** damage ◊ Der Hurrikan hat enorme Schäden angerichtet. ♦ finanzielle Schäden Schaden an etw. dat damage to sth ◊ Die Schäden an der Leitung sind wieder behoben. gesundheitliche Schäden damage to your health; (physically) zu Schaden kommen be injured bleibende Schäden davontragen suffer permanent damage; (insurance) einen Schaden regeln settle a damage claim **2.** disadvantage ◊ Wenn Sie mitmachen, soll das nicht zu Ihrem

Schaden sein. jds eigener Schaden sein be to sb's own disadvantage ⊖Nachteil ⊕Vorteil

ⓔ **wer den Schaden hat, braucht für den Spott nicht zu sorgen** the laugh is always on the loser **aus Schaden wird man klug** once bitten, twice shy

Scha·den·er·satz [ˈʃaːdn̩|ɛzats] der <-es> no pl damages ◊ eine Klage auf Schadenersatz Schadenersatz leisten pay damages

Scha·den·freu·de [ˈʃaːdn̩frɔɪdə] die <-> no pl pleasure taken in the failures and bad luck of others ◊ Schadenfreude empfinden

Scha·dens·er·satz [ˈʃaːdn̩s|ɛzats] → Schadenersatz

schä·di·gen [ˈʃɛːdɪɡn̩] tr v +haben damage, harm ◊ Die Leber ist bereits vom Alkohol geschädigt. ♦ Das hat seinen Ruf geschädigt. jdn/etw. um etw. schädigen cause losses of sth to sb/sth

schäd·lich [ˈʃɛːtlɪç] adj harmful, damaging ◊ schädliche Substanzen schädlich für etw. sein be damaging to sth ◊ Rauchen ist schädlich für die Gesundheit.

Schaf [ʃaːf] das <-(e)s, –e> **1.** sheep ◊ eine Herde Schafe ♦ Schafe hüten **2.** (fam) fool ◊ Komm, sei kein Schaf! ein geduldiges Schaf sein be as meek as a lamb

ⓔ **das schwarze Schaf** the black sheep

ⓩ **schaf·fen¹** [ˈʃafn̩] <schafft, schaffte, hat geschafft> tr v **1.** (be able to) manage, (be able to) do ◊ Die Arbeit schaffe ich nicht allein. ♦ Sie schaffte es nicht, ihn zu überzeugen.; (an exam) pass ◊ Hat er die Prüfung geschafft? ♦ Sie haben es nicht geschafft. Das wäre geschafft! That's done then! **2.** bring yourself to (do/be sth) ◊ Er schafft es nicht, die Wahrheit zu sagen. **3.** (fam) (a train, plane) catch ◊ Wenn du dich beeilst, dann schaffen wir den Zug noch.; (an appointment) make (it for) ◊ Ich schaffe den Termin um 15.00 Uhr leider nicht. ⊕versäumen, verpassen **4.** (fam) jdn/etw. irgendwohin schaffen take sb/sth somewhere ◊ das Gepäck zum Flughafen schaffen **5.** (fam) wear sb out ◊ Der Umzug hat sie völlig geschafft. geschafft sein be worn out/knackered intr v (SouthG) work ◊ Tim kann nicht kommen, er muss schaffen.

ⓔ **mit jdm/etw. etwas/nichts zu schaffen haben** have something/nothing to do with sb/sth **jdm zu schaffen machen** cause sb trouble/work ◊ Mein Rücken macht mir mal wieder zu schaffen. **sich** dat **an etw.** dat **zu schaffen machen** fiddle around with sth

schaf·fen² [ˈʃafn̩] <schafft, schuf, hat geschaffen> tr v (lofty) create ◊ ein Kunstwerk/neueArbeitsplätze schaffen ♦ die Voraussetzungen für etw. schaffen Klarheit schaffen clear things up Platz/Raum schaffen make room Ordnung schaffen sort things out

ⓔ **sich** dat **Feinde/Freunde schaffen** make enemies/friends **für jdn/etw. wie geschaffen sein** be perfect for sb/sth

Schaff·ner [ˈʃafnɐ] der <-s, –>, **Schaff·ne·rin** [ˈʃafnərɪn] die <-, –nen> conductor, ticket collector/inspector ◊ Der Schaffner in dem Zug zeigen ♦ Marco ist Schaffner bei der Deutschen Bahn.

schal [ʃaːl] adj, adv stale, flat ◊ schales Bier ♦ Der

Champagner ist/schmeckt schal.

Schal [ʃaːl] der <–s, –s or –e> scarf, shawl ◊ *sich einen Schal umbinden*

Scha·le ['ʃaːlə] die <–, –n> **1.** *(of fruit, vegetables)* skin; *(of a potato also)* jacket; *(removed)* peel, zest **2.** shell ◊ *die Schale knacken* ♦ *Eier mit brauner Schale* **3.** bowl, dish ◊ *eine Schale mit Obst auf den Tisch stellen* **4.** *(Austr)* *(shallow)* cup ◊ *eine Schale Kaffee*

◉ **in einer rauen Schale steckt oft ein weicher Kern; raue Schale, weicher Kern** under a/that rugged exterior beats a heart of gold **sich in Schale schmeißen/werfen** *(fam)* dress up

schä·len ['ʃɛːlən] [tr v] +*haben* peel ◊ *Kartoffeln/ eine Orange schälen*; *(tomatoes, almonds)* skin; *(eggs, nuts, shellfish, peas)* shell **sich schälen** peel ◊ *Nach dem Sonnenbrand schälte sich ihre Haut.* **sich aus etw. schälen** peel sth off ◊ *Sie schälte sich aus ihrem Mantel.*

Schall [ʃal] der <–(e)s, –e or Schälle> *most sing* sound ◊ *der Schall der Trommeln* ♦ *Licht ist viel schneller als Schall.*

◉ **Schall und Rauch sein** *(lofty)* be meaningless/ irrelevant, be hot air

⑦ **schal·ten** ['ʃaltn̩] [tr+intr v] +*haben* turn, switch ◊ *Schalt doch mal ins dritte Programm!* die Heizung wärmer/kälter schalten turn the heating up/down; *(traffic lights)* auf rot/gelb/grün schalten turn red/orange/green, change to red/orange/green [intr v] +*haben* **1.** change/shift gear ◊ *vor der Kurve schalten* in den dritten Gang schalten change into third gear **2.** *(live)* irgendwohin schalten go *(live)* somewhere ◊ *Wir schalten jetzt live ins Stadion nach München.* **3.** *(fam)* latch on, react

◉ **jd kann schalten und walten, wie er will; jd kann frei schalten und walten** sb can do as they please

⑦ **Schal·ter** ['ʃalte] der <–s, –> **1.** switch ◊ *Wo ist denn der Schalter zum Abstellen?* einen Schalter betätigen turn a switch **2.** counter, desk ◊ *Der Schalter ist nicht besetzt.*

Schal·tung ['ʃaltʊŋ] die <–, –en> **1.** gear lever, gears ◊ *Bei meinem Wagen ist die Schaltung kaputt.* **2.** circuit, wiring *(system)* ◊ *eine einfache Schaltung für die Stromversorgung*

schä·men ['ʃɛːmən] [ref v] +*haben* **1.** sich schämen be ashamed ◊ *Ich schämte mich, weil ich die Antwort nicht wusste.* **sich wegen jdm/etw. schämen, sich jds/einer Sache schämen** be ashamed of sb/sth ◊ *Sie schämt sich wegen ihrer schiefen Zähne.* ♦ *Er schämt sich seines Vaters, der Alkoholiker ist.* **sich für jdn/etw. schämen** be ashamed for sb/of sth ◊ *Er schämte sich für seinen Zorn.* Schäm dich! Shame on you! **2.** sich (vor jdm) schämen be/feel ashamed (in front of sb) ◊ *Ich schäme mich in der Sauna.* ♦ *Vor mir brauchst du dich doch nicht zu schämen!*

Schan·de ['ʃandə] die <–> *no pl* disgrace, shame ◊ *Es ist eine Schande, dass er sie mit den Kindern sitzen gelassen hat.* ♦ *Zu meiner Schande muss ich gestehen, dass ...* **Schande über jdn/etw. bringen**, jdm/einer Sache Schande machen bring shame upon sb/sth Mach mir keine Schande! Don't show me up! Schande über dich! Shame on you!

Schar [ʃaːr] die <–, –en> eine Schar ... [gen], eine Schar von ... a crowd/horde of ... ◊ *eine Schar fröhlicher Kinder* ♦ *Scharen von Pilgern kommen jedes Jahr an diesen Ort.*; *(of birds)* a flock of ... ◊ *eine Schar von Hühnern* in Scharen in droves ◊ *Die Fans kamen in Scharen zum Konzert.*

⑦ **scharf** [ʃarf] [adj] <schärfer, am schärfsten> **1.** *(blade, pointed object, pitcure, outline, road bend)* sharp ◊ *Achtung, das Messer ist sehr scharf.* ♦ *Dieses Foto ist nicht scharf.* ♦ *eine scharfe Kurve* **2.** *(spice, food)* hot ◊ *ein scharfes Gewürz* ♦ *Die Chilisauce ist sehr scharf!* ⊜mild **3.** *(perception)* keen, sharp ◊ *Die Augen des Adlers sind scharf.* ♦ *Sie hat einen scharfen Verstand.* einen scharfen Blick für etw. haben have a keen eye for sth **4.** *(smell)* pungent, acrid ◊ *ein scharfer Geruch nach Desinfektionsmitteln* **5.** *(wind, frost)* biting, cutting ◊ *Der Wind ist so scharf, er pfeift durch alle Ritzen.* ♦ *scharfer Frost* **6.** *(chemical substance)* caustic ◊ *scharfe Putzmittel* **7.** *(facial feature, profile)* clear-cut, distinctive ◊ *ein scharfes Profil* **8.** *mostly before ns (criticism, judgement)* harsh, severe ◊ *scharfe Kritik* ⊜mild **9.** *(protest, opposition, dog)* fierce ◊ *scharfer Protest* ♦ *Pass auf, dieser Wachhund ist scharf!* ⊜zahm **10.** *only before ns (speed)* fast ◊ *Er gab ein scharfes Tempo vor.* ♦ *In dem Kleid siehst du scharf aus!* ⊜geil **13.** *(fam)* *(expressing admiration)* cool, great ◊ *Scharfes Auto!* ♦ *Das ist ja scharf!* ⊜toll, super [adv] **1.** scharf schneiden cut well **2.** ein Gericht scharf würzen make a dish hot/spicy ⊜mild **3.** scharf sehen (können) have sharp/keen eyes nicht scharf sehen (können) have blurred vision etw./jdn scharf beobachten watch sth/sb closely jdn scharf ansehen look sharply at sb die Kamera scharf stellen focus the camera (accurately) **4.** pungently, acridly ◊ *Hier riecht es so scharf nach Essig.* **5.** der Wind bläst/weht scharf (durch etw.) a cutting/biting wind blows (through sth) **6.** scharf geschnitten clearly defined, distinctive ◊ *scharf geschnittene Gesichtszüge* **7.** harshly, severely ◊ *jdn scharf kritisieren* ♦ *scharf widersprechen*; hard ♦ *scharf bremsen/nachdenken müssen* scharf durchgreifen take drastic measures; *(in football)* ein scharf geschossener Ball a well-hit ball **8.** closely ◊ *Der Wagen fuhr scharf an mir vorbei.*

◉ **gestochen scharf** crystal clear ◊ *Das Foto ist gestochen scharf.* **jdn scharf machen** *(fam)* **1.** turn sb on **2.** stir up sb's feelings/hatred **scharf schießen 1.** fire live ammunition **2.** shoot to kill/ disable **scharf auf etw.** [acc] **sein** *(fam)* fancy sth, be keen on sth ◊ *Sie ist ganz scharf auf Vanilleeis.* **scharf auf jdn sein** *(fam)* fancy sb, have the hots for sb **auf das/aufs schärfste, auf das/aufs Schärfste** in the strongest possible terms ◊ *Ich verurteile dieses Vorgehen auf das Schärfste!*

Schär·fe ['ʃɛrfə] die <–> *no pl* **1.** sharpness ◊ *Das Gefährliche an scharfen Messern ist seine Schärfe.* **2.** spiciness ◊ *Mexikanisches Essen ist für seine Schärfe bekannt.* **3.** keenness ◊ *Hier fehlt Ihrem Blick noch die nötige Schärfe.* **4.** pungency ◊ *Den*

Geruch von Essig erkennt man an seiner Schärfe. **5.** focus, definition, sharpness ◊ *Du musst beim Fotografieren immer auf die Schärfe achten.* einer Sache [dat] fehlt die Schärfe *sth is blurred* **6.** harshness, severity ◊ *ein Urteil von unerwarteter Schärfe*

Schar·nier [ʃaˈniːɐ] das <–s, –e> hinge ◊ *Die Scharniere quietschen beim Öffnen.*

Schasch·lik [ˈʃaʃlɪk] der *or* das <–s, –s> shashlik, shish kebab

② **Schat·ten** [ˈʃatn̩] der <–s, –> **1.** *no pl* shade ◊ *Ich liege lieber im Schatten als in der Sonne.* ✦ *Wir haben 30 Grad im Schatten.* Schatten spenden *give shade* **2.** shadow ◊ *Als sein Schatten auf ihr Gesicht fiel, wachte sie auf.* ✦ *jdm wie ein Schatten folgen* mit/durch etw. fällt ein Schatten auf etw. *a shadow is cast on sth as a result of sth* ⊚ die Schatten der Vergangenheit holen jdn ein *sb's past catches up with them* nur noch ein Schatten seiner selbst sein *be a shadow of your former self* über seinen Schatten springen *pluck up your courage* man kann nicht über seinen eigenen Schatten springen *a leopard cannot change its spots* in jds Schatten stehen *be in sb's shadow* jdn/etw. in den Schatten stellen *eclipse sb/sth* seine Schatten vorauswerfen *be foreshadowed/anticipated*

Schat·ten·sei·te [ˈʃatn̩zaetə] die <–, –n> **1.** *most pl (fig)* drawback, disadvantage ◊ *die Schattenseiten des Ruhms*; *(of life)* dark side ◊ *Das Leben hat auch seine Schattenseiten.* **2.** shady side ◊ *Es ist so heiß; gehen wir lieber auf die Schattenseite.*

schat·tig [ˈʃatɪç] [adj] shady ◊ *ein schattiges Plätzchen* ✦ *Im Wald war es angenehm schattig.* ⊝sonnig

Schatz [ʃats] der <–es, Schätze> **1.** *(also fig)* treasure ◊ *einen Schatz vergraben/suchen* ✦ *Kinder sind unser kostbarster Schatz.* ein Schatz ... [gen], ein Schatz von/an etw. [dat] *a wealth of sth* ◊ *ein Schatz an Wissen* ✦ *Das Buch enthält einen Schatz von Zitaten.*; *(of things also)* a precious collection of sth ◊ *ein Schatz an seltenen Briefmarken* **2.** *(fam)* darling ◊ *(Mein) Schatz, kommst du mal bitte?* ⊝Liebling **3.** *(fam)* angel ◊ *Vielen Dank für Ihre Hilfe — Sie sind wirklich ein Schatz!*

schät·zen [ˈʃɛtsn̩] [tr v] +haben **1.** estimate ◊ *das Gewicht/die Höhe von etw. schätzen* jdn/etw. auf etw. [acc] schätzen *reckon/estimate that sb/sth is sth* ◊ *Ich schätze ihn auf Ende 30.* ✦ *Er schätzte den Abstand auf 20 Meter.* **2.** value, appraise ◊ *ein Schmuckstück schätzen lassen* etw. auf etw. [acc] schätzen *value sth at sth* ◊ *Der Händler schätzte den gebrauchten VW auf 2000 Euro.* **3.** appreciate ◊ *Sie schätzt guten Wein zum Essen.* ✦ *Ich schätze Ihre Hilfsbereitschaft sehr.* jdn als ... schätzen *appreciate/value sb as ...* ◊ *Ich schätze ihn als guten Freund und Ratgeber.* etw. zu schätzen wissen *appreciate sth* ◊ *Er weiß ihre Großzügigkeit nicht zu schätzen.* **4.** *(fam)* reckon ◊ *Ich schätze, er kommt wieder mal zu spät.*

Schät·zung [ˈʃɛtsʊŋ] die <–, –en> **1.** estimate ◊ *Einer Schätzung zufolge waren 10 000 Demonstranten auf der Straße.* **2.** valuation ◊ *Eine Schätzung ergab, dass das Gemälde eine Million Euro wert ist.*

schät·zungs·wei·se [ˈʃɛtsʊŋsvaezə] [adv] **1.** roughly, approximately ◊ *Der Film dauert schätzungsweise zwei Stunden.* ⊝ungefähr **2.** *(fam)* I reckon ◊ *Das Problem liegt schätzungsweise bei der Software.* ⊝wahrscheinlich

Schau [ʃao] die <–, –en> **1.** exhibition, show ◊ *etw. auf einer Schau ausstellen/präsentieren/zeigen* etw. zur Schau stellen *exhibit sth, display sth* **2.** *(fam, pej)* show ◊ *Dieses Theater ist doch nur Schau.* eine Schau machen/abziehen *put on a show, make a fuss* **3.** TV show ◊ *eine Schau mit Thomas Gottschalk* ⊚ eine Schau sein *(fam)* be great/fantastic jdm die Schau stehlen *steal the show from sb* etw./sich zur Schau stellen *(fam, pej)* show off sth/show off

② **schau·en** [ˈʃaoən] [intr v] +haben **1.** look ◊ *jdm in die Augen schauen* ✦ *Ich will auch mal durchs Fernglas schauen.* ✦ *„Wo ist nur der Schlüssel?" — „Schau doch mal in deine Tasche."* Schau nicht so böse. *Don't give me that evil look.* **2.** nach etw. schauen *check sth* ◊ *Schaust du bitte nach dem Braten?* schauen, ob *check whether* ◊ *Ich schau mal, ob die Post schon da war.* ⊝nachsehen **3.** *(SouthG)* nach jdm/etw. schauen *look after sb/sth* ◊ *Könnten Sie ab und zu nach unserem Hund schauen?* **4.** *(fam)* auf etw. [acc] schauen *set great store by sth* ◊ *Sie schaut sehr auf ihr Äußeres.* **5.** *(SouthG, fam)* schauen, dass *make sure that* ◊ *Schau bitte, dass du pünktlich bist.* selbst schauen, ob *try something* without help ◊ *Schau selbst, wie du zurechtkommst.* *You'll have to manage by yourself.* ⊚ schau, schau *(fam)* well, well; how about that

Schau·er [ˈʃaoɐ] der <–s, –> **1.** METEO shower ◊ *von einem Schauer überrascht werden* **2.** ein Schauer überläuft jdn *sb shudders* ◊ *Ein Schauer überlief ihn, als er den Toten sah.*

Schau·fel [ˈʃaofl̩] die <–, –n> shovel ◊ *Sie grub mit der Schaufel ein Loch.* ✦ *ein paar Schaufeln Erde*

schau·feln [ˈʃaofl̩n] [tr v] +haben **1.** shovel ◊ *Kohlen schaufeln* ✦ *Er schaufelte Erde in die Grube.* Schnee schaufeln *shovel (away) the snow* **2.** dig ◊ *ein Loch schaufeln*

② **Schau·fens·ter** [ˈʃaofɛnstɐ] das <–s, –> shop window ◊ *Der Anzug war im Schaufenster ausgestellt.*

Schau·kel [ˈʃaokl̩] die <–, –n> swing ◊ *auf der Schaukel sitzen*

schau·keln [ˈʃaokl̩n] [tr v] +haben **1.** rock ◊ *Sie schaukelte das Baby sanft in ihren Armen.* Lass mich auch mal schaukeln! *Let me have a go on the swing!*; *(ship)* pitch and toss ◊ *Mir wird schlecht, wenn das Schiff so stark schaukelt.* [intr v] +haben **1.** swing Lass mich auch mal schaukeln! *Let me have a go on the swing!* **2.** *(ship)* pitch and toss ◊ *Mir wird schlecht, wenn das Schiff so stark schaukelt.*

Schaum [ʃaom] der <–(e)s, Schäume> *most sing* foam, froth, lather ◊ *ein Bier mit viel Schaum* ✦ *Auf dem Wasser hat sich Schaum gebildet.* Eiweiß zu Schaum schlagen *whisk egg white* Schaum vor dem Mund haben *foam/froth at the mouth*

② **Schau·spie·ler** [ˈʃaoʃpiːlɐ] der <–s, –>, **Schau·spie·le·rin** [ˈʃaoʃpiːlərɪn] die <–, –nen>

actor, acress ◊ *Will Smith ist ein guter Schauspieler.* ♦ *Sie möchte Schauspielerin werden.*
ⓔ *jd ist ein guter/schlechter Schauspieler (fig)* sb's act is convincing/unconvincing

ⓩ **Scheck** [ʃɛk] der <–s, –s> cheque, check ◊ *Zahlen Sie bar oder mit Scheck?* ein gedeckter Scheck a valid cheque ein ungedeckter Scheck a dud cheque, a bounced cheque einen Scheck ausstellen/einlösen issue/cash a cheque ein Scheck über 150 Euro a cheque for 150 euros

ⓩ **Scheck·kar·te** [ˈʃɛkkaˈtə] die <–, –n> debit card ◊ *mit der Scheckkarte bezahlen*

Schei·be [ˈʃaebə] die <–, –n> **1.** disc ◊ *Früher dachten die Menschen, die Erde sei eine Scheibe.* **2.** (window) pane ♦ *Wer hat die Scheibe zerbrochen?; (of a car)* window **3.** slice ◊ *Er schnitt sich eine dicke Scheibe Brot ab.* etw. in Scheiben schneiden slice sth
ⓔ *jd kann sich von jdm eine Scheibe abschneiden* sb can learn a thing or two from sb

Schei·ben·wi·scher [ˈʃaebṃvɪʃə] der <–s, –> windscreen wiper, windshield wiper ◊ *die Scheibenwischer einschalten*

Schei·de [ˈʃaedə] die <–, –n> **1.** ANAT vagina **2.** sheath ◊ *Er zog das Schwert aus der Scheide.*

ⓩ **schei·den** [ˈʃaedn̩] <scheidet, schied, ist/hat geschieden> tr v +*haben; mostly passive* eine Ehe wird geschieden a marriage is dissolved jd wird geschieden sb is getting divorced sich scheiden lassen get divorced sich von jdm scheiden lassen divorce sb ◊ *Mein Bruder lässt sich von seiner Frau scheiden.* jd ist geschieden sb is divorced ◊ *Ich bin seit zwei Jahren geschieden.* intr v +*sein* **1.** *(lofty) (from a post)* aus etw. scheiden retire from sth ◊ *vorzeitig aus dem Amt scheiden* **2.** *(euph)* aus dem Leben scheiden depart from this life

Schei·dung [ˈʃaedʊŋ] die <–, –en> divorce ◊ *Er hat bereits mehrere Scheidungen hinter sich.* die Scheidung einreichen file for divorce
ⓔ *in Scheidung leben* be in the process of getting a divorce

ⓩ **Schein** [ʃaen] der <–(e)s, –e> **1.** note, bill ◊ *Der Automat nimmt Münzen und Scheine.* ⊖Geldschein, Banknote **2.** *no pl* light, glow ◊ *Sie saßen im Schein des Feuers zusammen.* ♦ *der Schein des Mondes* **3.** appearance(s) ◊ *Er wirkt glücklich, aber der Schein trügt.* den Schein wahren keep up appearances dem Schein nach (zu schließen) to all appearances **4.** pretence ◊ *Seine Begeisterung ist nur Schein.* etw. zum Schein tun pretend to do sth ◊ *Zum Schein ging er auf das Angebot ein.* **5.** UNI certificate ◊ *Ich habe dieses Semester die letzten Scheine gemacht.* **6.** licence, license ◊ *Wo darf man noch ohne Schein angeln?*
ⓔ *etw. ist mehr Schein als Sein* sth is just on the surface

schein·bar [ˈʃaenbaː] adj *no comp/superl, mostly before ns* apparent, seeming ◊ *Dieser scheinbare Widerspruch lässt sich schnell erklären.* etw. ist nur scheinbar sth is only an illusion adv **1.** etw. scheinbar tun pretend/feign to do sth ◊ *Sie reagierte scheinbar gelassen, obwohl sie am liebsten geschrien hätte.* **2.** *(fam)* apparently ◊ *Er ist scheinbar krank, denn sonst wäre er schon lange im Büro.* ⊖anscheinend, offenbar

ⓔ **schei·nen** [ˈʃaenən] <scheint, schien, hat geschienen> intr v **1.** shine ◊ *Die Sonne scheint.* ♦ *Der Scheinwerfer schien ihm ins Gesicht.* **2.** seem, appear ◊ *Diese Erklärung scheint mir plausibel.* ♦ *Das Baby scheint zu schlafen.* ♦ *Es scheint, dass das Wetter besser wird.* wie es scheint apparently imp v +*subjunctive II* jdm scheint, als … it seems to sb as if … ◊ *Ihm schien, als würde sie seinen Blick vermeiden.*

Schein·wer·fer [ˈʃaenvɛ'fə] der <–s, –> floodlight ◊ *Der Kirchturm wird nachts von Scheinwerfern beleuchtet.; (of a car)* (head)light; *(in a theatre)* spotlight ◊ *im Licht der Scheinwerfer*

Schei·ße [ˈʃaesə] die <–> *no pl (rude)* shit, crap ◊ *Hier stinkt es nach Scheiße.* ♦ *Red keine Scheiße!* etw. ist große Scheiße sth is a load of crap/shit (so eine) Scheiße oh shit, bloody hell
ⓔ *jd sitzt/steckt in der Scheiße,* jdm steht die Scheiße bis zum Hals sb is in deep shit jdn aus der Scheiße ziehen get sb out of the shit

schei·ßen [ˈʃaesn̩] <scheißt, schiss, hat geschissen> intr v *(rude)* (take a) shit, (have a) crap
ⓔ auf etw. acc scheißen not give a shit about sth scheiß drauf to hell with that jdm (et)was scheißen tell sb to piss/bugger off

Schei·tel [ˈʃaetl̩] der <–s, –> **1.** parting ◊ *den Scheitel auf der rechten Seite haben* einen Scheitel ziehen make a parting **2.** vertex ◊ *im Scheitel der Kurve leicht beschleunigen*
ⓔ vom Scheitel bis zur Sohle from head to toe ⊖von Kopf bis Fuß

schei·tern [ˈʃaeten] intr v +*sein* (an etw./jdm) scheitern fail (because of sth/sb) ◊ *Er scheiterte an ihrem hartnäckigen Widerstand.* ♦ *Der Gesetzentwurf scheiterte.* jd scheitert mit etw. sb's thing fails ◊ *Sie ist mit ihren Plänen gescheitert.*

Schen·kel [ˈʃɛŋkl̩] der <–s, –> **1.** ANAT thigh sich auf die Schenkel schlagen slap your thigh ⊖Oberschenkel **2.** leg ◊ *Möchtest du vom Hähnchen einen Flügel oder einen Schenkel?* **3.** MATH *(one of a triangle's two sides that have identical length)* side ◊ *Die beiden Schenkel bilden einen Winkel von 60°.*

ⓩ **schen·ken** [ˈʃɛŋkŋ̩] tr v +*haben* **1.** jdm etw. schenken give sb sth, give sth to sb ◊ *Was schenkst du deiner Frau zu Weihnachten?* etw. geschenkt bekommen be given sth, get sth as a present **2.** *translation varies* jdm/einer Sache Beachtung schenken pay attention to sb/sth jdm/einer Sache keine Beachtung schenken take no notice of sb/sth einem Tier/jdm die Freiheit schenken set an animal/sb free jdm/einer Sache Gehör schenken listen to sb/sth einem Kind das Leben schenken give birth (to a child) jdm Vertrauen schenken put your trust in sb **3.** *(fam)* sich dat etw. schenken give sth a miss ◊ *Den Besuch hättest du dir schenken können.* sich dat seine Entschuldigungen/Ausreden schenken können save your excuses ⊖sich etw. sparen intr v give presents ◊ *Sie schenkt gerne.*
ⓔ *etw. ist fast geschenkt (fam)* sth is practically a giveaway es wird einem nichts geschenkt, man bekommt nichts geschenkt there's no such thing as a free lunch jd wollte etw. nicht (einmal) geschenkt haben *(fam)* sb wouldn't (even) take sth for free

A B C D E F G H I J K L M N O P Q R **S** T U V W X Y Z

Scher·be ['ʃɛʳbə] die <-, -n> (broken) piece ◊ *sich an einer Scherbe schneiden* ♦ *Die Schüssel zersprang in tausend Scherben.*; *(in archeology)* (pot)sherd *in Scherben gehen* break, shatter ◊ *Bei der Schlägerei gingen etliche Gläser in Scherben.*

> If somebody breaks a piece of crockery, Germans may say *Scherben bringen Glück* (broken crockery is lucky), which is meant to comfort the person who broke it.

② **Sche·re** ['ʃeːrə] die <-, -n> **1.** scissors ◊ *eine spitze Schere* ♦ *sich* dat *die Nägel mit der Schere schneiden; (for the garden)* shears **2.** *most pl* zoo claw ◊ *Der Krebs packte seine Beute mit den Scheren.* **3.** *(fig)* divide ◊ *Die Schere zwischen Arm und Reich klafft immer weiter auseinander.*

sche·ren¹ ['ʃeːrən] <schert, schor, hat geschoren> tr v **1.** shear ◊ *Die Schafe sind frisch geschoren.* *jdn kahl scheren* shave sb's head *jdm die Haare/ den Kopf scheren* crop sb's hair **2.** trim, clip ◊ *die Hecke scheren*

sche·ren² ['ʃeːrən] *(fam)* <schert, scherte, hat geschert> tr+intr v *jdn schert etw. nicht* sb doesn't care about sth ◊ *Das Gerede schert mich nicht.* *es schert jdn nicht, ...* sb doesn't care ... ◊ *Es schert mich nicht, warum er das getan hat.* *was schert es jdn, ...* what does sb care ... ◊ *Was schert es dich, wohin ich gehe?* ⊖kümmern ref v **1.** *sich um etw. nicht scheren* not care about sth ◊ *Er schert sich nicht um ihre Bedürfnisse.* *sich um seinen eigenen Kram scheren* mind your own business ⊖kümmern **2.** *sich nach Hause scheren* go home (right away) *Scher dich fort!* Bugger off!, Beat it! *Scher dich zum Teufel!* Go to hell!

Scherz [ʃɛʳts] der <-es, -e> joke ◊ *ein harmloser/ schlechter Scherz* ♦ *Da hat sich wohl jemand einen Scherz erlaubt.* *aus/im/zum Scherz* as a joke ⊛ *... und ähnliche/solche Scherze (fam, iron)* ... and what have you, ... and whatnot *machen Sie/mach keine Scherze, das ist doch wohl ein Scherz (fam)* you must be joking *(ganz) ohne Scherz (fam)* seriously, no kidding

scher·zen ['ʃɛʳtsn̩] intr v +*haben* **1.** *über jdn/etw. scherzen* joke about sb/sth ◊ *Über so etwas soll man nicht scherzen.* **2.** *mit jdm scherzen* banter with sb ◊ *Er scherzte mit einer Kollegin.* ⊛ *mit etw. ist nicht zu scherzen* sth is not to be trifled with, sth is not to be taken lightly ◊ *Mit Asthma ist nicht zu scherzen.*

scheu [ʃɔɪ] adj, adv <scheuer, am scheu(e)sten> **1.** shy(ly) ◊ *ein scheues Kind* ♦ *Sie lächelte scheu.*; *(animals)* timid(ly) ◊ *Das Wild hier ist sehr scheu.* *scheu werden* become frightened *die Pferde scheu machen* frighten the horses **2.** tentative ◊ *ein scheuer Kuss*

scheu·ern ['ʃɔɪɐn] tr v +*haben* scrub, scour ◊ *Töpfe und Pfannen scheuern* ♦ *Der Boden muss gescheuert werden* ⊖schrubben tr+intr v +*haben* chafe ◊ *Ich mag dieses Hemd nicht; der Kragen scheuert. an etw.* dat *scheuern* rub against sth *etw. wund scheuern* chafe sth *sich* dat *etw. wund scheuern* chafe your sth ◊ *Er hat sich die Fersen wund gescheuert.* ⊛ *eine gescheuert kriegen (fam)* get a clip round the ear *jdm eine scheuern (fam)* give sb a clip round the ear

scheuß·lich ['ʃɔʏslɪç] adj, adv horrible(-ibly), dreadful(ly), terrible(-ibly) ◊ *Das Wetter ist wirklich scheußlich.* ♦ *ein scheußlicher Gestank* ♦ *Das tut scheußlich weh! scheußlich schmecken* taste awful

Schi [ʃiː] → Ski

② **Schicht** [ʃɪçt] die <-, -en> **1.** layer ◊ *Auf dem Schrank liegt eine dicke Schicht Staub.*; *(of paint)* coat **2.** *(social)* stratum ◊ *Sie gehört einer anderen sozialen Schicht an* *die obere/ untere Schicht* the upper/lower classes **3.** *(at work)* shift ◊ *Die erste Schicht dauert von 6.30 bis 14.00 Uhr.*

② **schick** [ʃɪk] adj **1.** stylish, chic, smart ◊ *ein schickes Kleid* ♦ *Deine Wohnung ist aber schick!* **2.** trendy ◊ *Im Augenblick gilt es als schick, in teuren Lokalen zu verkehren.* adv stylishly, smartly ◊ *sich schick anziehen* *schick wohnen* live in a smart house *schick essen gehen* go to a fancy restaurant

② **schi·cken** ['ʃɪkn̩] tr+intr v +*haben* *(jdm) etw. schicken, etw. (an jdn) schicken* send (sb) sth, send sth (to sb) ◊ *Ich schicke ihm eine Postkarte aus dem Urlaub.* ♦ *Die Rechnung wird an Ihren Mann geschickt.* *jdn/etw. irgendwohin schicken* send sb/sth somewhere ◊ *Wenn er kommt, schicken wir ihn zu dir.* ♦ *ein Kind auf sein Zimmer schicken* nach jdm/etw. schicken send for sb/sth ◊ *nach einem Arzt/Krankenwagen schicken* ref v +*haben* **1.** *etw. schickt sich nicht* sth is not proper ◊ *Es schickt sich nicht, mit vollem Mund zu sprechen.* ⊖sich gehören **2.** *(lofty)* *sich in etw.* acc *schicken* resign yourself to sth ◊ *sich in sein Los schicken*

Schick·sal ['ʃɪkzaːl] das <-s, -e> fate, destiny ◊ *Das Schicksal nahm seinen Lauf.* *schlimme/ tragische Schicksale* tragic cases *jd hat ein schweres/tragisches Schicksal gehabt* fate has been unkind/cruel to sb *eine Laune des Schicksals* a twist of fate *das Schicksal herausfordern* tempt fate *das Schicksal meint es gut mit jdm* fortune smiles on sb *sich dem/in sein Schicksal fügen* accept your fate *jds Schicksal sein* be sb's destiny *jdn seinem Schicksal überlassen* leave sb to their fate

② **schie·ben** ['ʃiːbm̩] <schiebt, schob, hat geschoben> tr+intr v push, shove ◊ *das Fahrrad schieben* ♦ *Als der Tank leer war, mussten wir schieben.* ♦ *die Möbel beiseite schieben* *die Ärmel nach oben schieben* roll your sleeves up *jdn von sich schieben* push sb away *sich durch etw. schieben* push your way through sth *sich vor etw. schieben* move in front of sth tr v **1.** *etw. irgend-wohin schieben* put/slip/slide sth somewhere ◊ *den Braten in den Ofen schieben* **2.** *etw. auf jdn/etw. schieben* blame sb/sth for sth ◊ *Sie versuchte, die Verspätung auf ihre Kollegin zu schieben.* *die Schuld auf jdn schieben* put the blame on sb *die Verantwortung auf jdn schieben* lay the responsibility at sb's door/feet ⊖wälzen

② **schied** [ʃiːt] *pret of* scheiden

Schieds·rich·ter ['ʃiːtsrɪçtɐ] der <-s, ->, **Schieds·rich·te·rin** ['ʃiːtsrɪçtərɪn] die <-, -nen> **1.** sport referee ◊ *Der Schiedsrichter zeigte ihm die rote Karte.* ♦ *Sie wurde als Schiedsrichterin eingesetzt.; (in table) tennis, cricket, hockey,*

badminton) umpire **2.** arbitrator

② **schief** [ʃiːf] [adj] **1.** crooked, lopsided, inclined ◊ *eine schiefe Ebene* ♦ *Ist das schief oder gerade?* der schiefe Turm von Pisa the Leaning Tower of Pisa ⊜gerade **2.** *(fig)* distorted ◊ *sich* [dat] *ein schiefes Bild von der Realität machen* ein schiefer Vergleich a false comparison [adv] **1.** crookedly, lopsidedly, at an angle ◊ *Deine Krawatte sitzt schief.* schief hängen be crooked ◊ *Das Bild hängt schief.; (tree)* schief gewachsen sein be leaning **2.** *(fig)* etw. schief sehen look at sth the wrong way

◉ jdn schief ansehen look at sb askance **schief liegen/gewickelt sein** *(fam)* be wrong/on the wrong track mit etw. schief liegen have sth wrong ◊ *Mit dieser Vermutung liegst du schief.* da/dann bist du aber schief gewickelt you have another think coming

schie·len [ˈʃiːlən] [intr v] +*haben* **1.** squint, be cross-eyed ◊ *Er schielt auf dem rechten Auge.* **2.** durch etw. schielen peep through sth ◊ *durchs Schlüsselloch schielen* zu jdm schielen look at sb out of the corner of your eye **3.** auf etw. [acc]/ nach etw. schielen have your eye on sth ◊ *Sie schielt doch nur aufs Geld/nach seinem Geld!*

② **schien** [ʃiːn] *pret of* scheinen

Schie·ne [ˈʃiːnə] die <–, –n> **1.** Schienen rails, track ◊ *Ein Zug ist aus den Schienen gesprungen.* **2.** slide bar, guide rail ◊ *Wir brauchen eine neue Schiene für die Vorhänge.* **3.** MED splint ◊ *eine Schiene für das gebrochene Bein* **4.** *(fig)* dieselbe Schiene fahren follow the same track/path ◊ *Beide Musiker fahren dieselbe Schiene.*

schier [ʃiːɐ] [adj] *no comp/superl, only before ns* **1.** pure ◊ *schieres Gold* ⊜rein **2.** sheer ◊ *Er hat das aus schierer Bosheit getan.* das schiere Gegenteil the exact opposite [adv] almost, virtually ◊ *Das ist schier unmöglich.* ⊜nahezu, beinahe, fast

schie·ßen [ˈʃiːsn̩] <schießt, schoss, hat/ist geschossen> [tr+intr v] **1.** +*haben* (auf jdn/etw.) schießen shoot (at sb/sth), fire (at sb/sth) ◊ *Jemand hat auf die Demonstranten geschossen.* ♦ *Hände hoch oder ich schieße!* ♦ *Der Indianer schoss ihm einen Pfeil in die Brust.* ein Tier schießen shoot (and kill) an animal eine Rakete ins All schießen launch a rocket into space **2.** +*haben* kick, shoot ◊ *Warum schießt er nicht — das Tor ist frei!* ♦ *einen Ball ins Tor schießen* ein Tor schießen score (a goal) [tr v] *(fam)* +*haben* ein Bild/Foto (von jdm/etw.) schießen shoot a picture (of sb/sth), take a shot (of sb/sth) [intr v] +*sein* **1.** *(person)* rush ◊ *Sie schoss wütend aus dem Haus.; (vehicle)* race ◊ *Plötzlich schoss sein Wagen um die Ecke.* **2.** *(water, blood)* aus etw. schießen spurt out of sth ◊ *Blut schoss aus der Wunde.; (flames)* shoot out of sth die Röte schießt jdm ins Gesicht blood rushes to sb's face **3.** *(fam)* (plant, child) shoot up; (prices) in die Höhe schießen rocket ◉ etw. schießt jdm durch den Kopf sth suddenly occurs to sb

② **Schiff** [ʃɪf] das <–(e)s, –e> **1.** ship ◊ *Das Schiff lag im Hafen vor Anker.* ♦ *Das Schiff legte am Ufer an.* ♦ *an Bord eines Schiffes gehen* **2.** ARCH nave ◉ klar Schiff machen *(fam)* **1.** sort things out

2. make a clean sweep

② **Schild**[1] [ʃɪlt] das <–(e)s, –er> **1.** sign(post), plate ◊ *ein Schild aufstellen* **2.** label ◊ *das Schild von einem neuen Pullover entfernen* ⊜Etikett

Schild[2] [ʃɪlt] der <–(e)s, –e> shield ◊ *Die Ritter hoben ihre Schilde.*

◉ etw. im Schilde führen be up to sth

schil·dern [ˈʃɪldɐn] [tr v] +*haben* (jdm) etw./jdn schildern describe sth/sb (to sb) ◊ *etw. anschaulich/lebhaft/minutiös schildern* etw. in den rosigsten Farben schildern paint sth in the most glowing colours/colors ⊜beschreiben

Schild·krö·te [ˈʃɪltkrøːtə] die <–, –n> *(on land)* tortoise; *(in water)* turtle; *(in freshwater also)* terrapin

Schilf [ʃɪlf] das <–(e)s, –e> *most sing* reed(s); *(roof)* thatch ◊ *Die Dächer der Hütten waren aus Schilf.*

② **Schil·ling** [ˈʃɪlɪŋ] der <–s, –e> *pl 'Schilling' when used with figures (Austr, outd)* schilling ◊ *Wie viel Schilling hat das Auto damals gekostet?*

Schim·mel [ˈʃɪml̩] der <–s, –> **1.** *no pl* BIO mould ◊ *Die Marmelade hat schon Schimmel angesetzt/ bekommen/gebildet* ♦ *von Schimmel befallene Lebensmittel* ♦ *Schimmel an den Wänden* **2.** ZOO white horse, grey ◊ *Der Prinz kam auf einem prächtigen Schimmel geritten.*

schim·mern [ˈʃɪmɐn] [intr v] +*haben* glimmer, gleam ◊ *Die Augen der Katze schimmerten golden.; (tears, water etc.)* shimmer ◊ *In ihren Augen schimmerten Tränen.* ♦ *Das Wasser schimmerte im Sonnenlicht.* ⊜glänzen

② **schimp·fen** [ˈʃɪmpfn̩] [tr v] +*haben* **1.** jdn schimpfen tell sb off, get angry with sb **2.** *(lofty)* jdn etw. schimpfen call sb sth ◊ *jdn einen Halsabschneider schimpfen* [intr v] +*haben* grumble, moan ◊ *„So ein Mist!", schimpfte er.; (foul language)* swear ◊ *Bitte nicht schimpfen!* mit jdm schimpfen tell sb off über/auf etw./jdn schimpfen grumble about sth/sb ◊ *über das schlechte Wetter schimpfen* ♦ *Er schimpfte auf den Nachbarn, der ihm das Leben schwer machte.* [ref v] +*haben* *(fam, iron)* sich etw. schimpfen call yourself sth ◊ *Und so was schimpft sich Arzt — Pfuscher wäre passender!*

Schimpf·wort [ˈʃɪmpfvɔʳt] das <–(e)s, Schimpfwörter> swear-word

② **Schin·ken** [ˈʃɪŋkn̩] der <–s, –> **1.** *most sing* ham ◊ *eine Scheibe/hundert Gramm Schinken* ♦ *Spargel mit Schinken* gekochter/roher Schinken cooked/ uncooked ham **2.** *(fam, hum or pej)* tome ◊ *Sie liest gern dicke Schinken wie 'Vom Winde verweht'.* ♦ *ein alter Schinken; (large-format)* painting ◊ *Im Museum hängen riesige barocke Schinken in Öl.; (film)* epic

② **Schirm** [ʃɪʳm] der <–(e)s, –e> **1.** umbrella ◊ *seinen Schirm aufspannen;* sunshade, parasol **2.** *(of a television, computer, X-ray equipment)* screen ◊ *Gerade flimmerten die Nachrichten über den Schirm.* ♦ *sich zum Schutz vor Röntgenstrahlung hinter einen Schirm stellen* **3.** *(of a lamp)* shade **4.** *(of a cap)* peak ◊ *die Baseballkappe mit dem Schirm im Nacken tragen* **5.** *(for skydiving)* parachute ◊ *Sein Schirm öffnete sich nicht und er stürzte in den Tod.*

schiss [ʃɪs] *pret of* scheißen

schi·zo·phren [ʃitso'freːn] [adj] *no comp/superl*
1. MED schizophrenic ◊ *eine schizophrene Psychose*
♦ *Er ist schizophren.* **2.** *(lofty, fig)* contradictory,
inconsistent, absurd ◊ *Das ist doch eine schizophrene Argumentation!* ♦ *Die rechtliche Situation
ist schizophren.* ⊜widersprüchlich

Schlacht [ʃlaxt] die <–, –en> *(also fig)* MIL battle ◊
*die Schlacht um Stalingrad/von Waterloo/am Little
Big Horn* ♦ *eine entscheidende Schlacht gewinnen/
verlieren* ♦ *in die Schlacht ziehen* ♦ *Die Diskussionsteilnehmer lieferten sich eine heiße Schlacht.; (for
seats, food etc.)* mad scramble ◊ *die Schlacht am
kalten Büffet*

schlach·ten [ʃlaxtn] <schlachtet, schlachtete, hat
geschlachtet> [tr v] slaughter ◊ *ein Huhn/Rind/
Schwein schlachten* [intr v] do the slaughtering ◊
Mittwochs wird geschlachtet.

Schlaf [ʃlaːf] der <–(e)s> *no pl* sleep ◊ *in einen
tiefen/traumlosen/unruhigen Schlaf sinken* keinen
Schlaf finden be unable to sleep jdm den Schlaf
rauben rob sb of their sleep jdn um den Schlaf
bringen keep sb awake einen leichten/gesunden
Schlaf haben be a light/sound sleeper unsanft aus
dem Schlaf gerissen werden be rudely awakened
◉ den Schlaf des Gerechten schlafen *(hum)*
sleep the sleep of the just im Schlaf in your sleep
◊ *ein Gedicht im Schlaf beherrschen*

Schlaf·an·zug [ʃlaːfʔantsuːk] der
<–(e)s, Schlafanzüge> pyjamas

Schlä·fe [ʃlɛːfə] die <–, –n> ANAT temple graue
Schläfen greying temples jdm eine Pistole an die
Schläfe halten hold a gun to sb's head

ⓩ **schla·fen** [ʃlaːfn] <schläft, schlief, hat geschlafen>
[intr v] **1.** sleep, be asleep ◊ *tief und fest schlafen*
♦ *schlecht/unruhig schlafen* ♦ *Schlaf gut, gute
Nacht!* ♦ *Er schläft schon/noch halb und hört die
gar nicht richtig zu.* ♦ *Er schläft heute bei uns/im
Hotel.* ♦ *Willst du das wirklich? Schlaf erst noch
mal eine Nacht drüber!* schlafen gehen go to bed
sich schlafen legen lie down (for a sleep), go to
bed ein Kind schlafen legen put a child to bed
2. *(fam)* not be quite there, be absent-minded ◊
*„Du hättest eben abbiegen müssen." — „Entschul-
digung, da habe ich wohl geschlafen.";* be caught
napping ◊ *Da hat der Gesetzgeber geschlafen und
nicht auf die Entwicklung reagiert.* mit offenen
Augen schlafen be daydreaming [ref v] sich gesund
schlafen get your strength back through sleep
◉ jdn schlafen legen put sb to bed sich
schlafen legen go to bed mit jdm schlafen sleep
with sb, have sex with sb

schlaff [ʃlaf] [adj] **1.** *(rope, sail etc.)* slack ◊ *die
schlaffe Wäscheleine nachspannen* ♦ *Das Seil ist
schlaff.* ⊜straff **2.** *(skin, muscle etc.)* flabby ◊
einen schlaffen Bauch/schlaffe Wangen haben
⊜prall, straff [adj, adv] **1.** limp(ly) ◊ *ein schlaffer
Händedruck* ♦ *Seine Arme hingen schlaff herunter.*
2. listless(ly) ◊ *Ich fühle mich heute entsetzlich
schlaff.* ♦ *schlaff vorm Fernseher herumhängen*

Schlaf·sack [ʃlaːfzak] der <–(e)s, Schlafsäcke>
sleeping bag

ⓩ **schläft** [ʃlɛːft] *pres of* schlafen

Schlaf·zim·mer [ʃlaːftsɪmɐ] das <–s, –> (master)
bedroom ◊ *Die Wohnung besteht aus Küche, Bad,
Schlafzimmer und zwei Kinderzimmern.*

ⓩ **Schlag** [ʃlaːk] der <–(e)s, Schläge> **1.** slap, smack;

(with the fist) punch ◊ *Schläge und Tritte
austeilen/einstecken* ♦ *jdm einen Schlag auf die
Nase versetzen; (with a stick etc.)* blow ◊ *mit
dem Stock zum Schlag ausholen; (to fit sth to a
wall)* tap ◊ *mit wenigen Schlägen ein Bild an die
Wand nageln; (in golf etc.)* stroke ◊ *fünf Schläge
benötigen, um einzulochen* **2.** *only pl* a hiding ◊
von jdm Schläge bekommen/beziehen/kriegen ♦
jdm Schläge androhen/verabreichen ⊜Prügel
3. bang ◊ *Mit einem lauten Schlag durchbrach das
Flugzeug die Schallmauer.; (of lightning)* crack;
thud ◊ *Sie hörte nur einen dumpfen Schlag, als er
zu Boden fiel.; (of a clock)* chime **4.** *(fig)* blow ◊
*Die Scheidung war ein harter/herber/schwerer
Schlag für ihn.* ♦ *Der Polizei gelang ein entschei-
dender/vernichtender Schlag gegen die Drogenmafia.;* strike ◊ *ein militärischer Schlag gegen ein
Land* **5.** *(fam, also fig)* MED stroke ◊ *einen Schlag
erleiden* ♦ *an einem Schlag sterben* wie vom
Schlag gerührt/getroffen sein be gobsmacked, be
thunderstruck Mich trifft der Schlag! I don't
believe it! Der Schlag soll mich treffen, wenn ich
lüge! May God strike me down if I am lying!
6. *(electric)* shock ◊ *einen (elektrischen) Schlag
bekommen* **7.** *(of the heart, pulse etc.)* beat ◊ *ein
Puls von 70 Schlägen in der Minute* ♦ *die Schläge
des Herzens* **8.** *no pl* von deinem/seinem/jenem
etc. Schlag, deines/seines/jenes etc. Schlages of
your/his/that etc. ilk vom alten Schlag, alten
Schlages of the old school vom gleichen Schlag of
the same ilk **9.** +*time* (auf den) Schlag ... on the
stroke of ... ♦ *Schlag Mitternacht/zwölf fing der
Spuk an. Er kam auf den Schlag um neun Uhr. He
arrived at nine o' clock on the dot. Es ist jetzt
(auf den) Schlag acht Uhr. It is now exactly eight
o' clock.* ⊜Punkt
◉ ein Schlag ins Gesicht a slap in the face ein
Schlag ins Wasser a washout keinen Schlag tun
(fam) not do a stroke Schlag auf Schlag in quick
succession, thick and fast auf einen/mit einem
Schlag *(fam)* in one go mit einem Schlag *(fam)*
at a stroke

schlag·ar·tig [ʃlaːkʔaːɐtɪç] [adj, adv] *when used as
an adj, only before ns; no comp/superl* sudden(ly)
◊ *die schlagartige Veränderung der Situation* ♦
durch ein Lied schlagartig berühmt werden ♦ *Mir
wurde schlagartig klar, dass ich etwas tun musste.*
⊜plötzlich

ⓩ **schla·gen** [ʃlaːgn] <schlägt, schlug, hat/ist
geschlagen> [tr v] +*haben* **1.** *(once with the
hand)* hit ◊ *Bitte schlag mich nicht!* ♦ *jdn ins
Gesicht/auf den Kopf/auf die Finger schlagen;
(with the fist)* punch ⊜hauen **2.** *(repeatedly)*
beat ◊ *Sie nahm sich vor, ihre Kinder nie zu
schlagen.* jdn zu Boden schlagen knock sb down
jdn bewusstlos schlagen beat sb unconscious jdn
blutig schlagen beat sb to a pulp jdn grün und
blau schlagen beat sb black and blue jdn krankenhausreif schlagen put sb in hospital **3.** etw. kurz
und klein/in Stücke schlagen smash sth to pieces
4. ein paar Bälle übers Netz schlagen hit a few
balls over the net jdm etw. aus der Hand schlagen
knock sth out of sb's hand die Hände vors Gesicht
schlagen cover your face einen Nagel in die Wand
schlagen knock a nail into the wall eine Tür
schlagen slam a door die Zähne /Krallen etc. in

etw. [acc] schlagen sink its teeth/claws etc. into sth
5. *(in a fight, game etc.)* beat ◊ *Sie schlug die anderen Läuferinnen um Längen.* ♦ *Der diesjährige Umsatz schlägt alle Rekorde!* Napoleon wurde in Waterloo vernichtend geschlagen. Napoleon was wiped out at Waterloo. sich geschlagen geben admit defeat, give up ⊜besiegen, übertreffen **6.** *(a hole)* knock ◊ *ein Loch ins Eis schlagen; (a path, gap)* clear ◊ *eine Bresche/Schneise in den Wald schlagen* **7.** *(eggs etc.)* (schaumig) schlagen beat (until frothy), whisk (until frothy); *(cream)* whip **8.** *(a tree)* fell; *(wood)* chop **9.** *(clock)* chime, strike ◊ *Die Uhr schlägt zwölf (Uhr)/Mitternacht.* **10.** Profit/Gewinn aus etw. schlagen make a profit out of sth, profit from sth **11.** etw. auf etw. [acc] schlagen add sth to sth ◊ *die Mehrwertsteuer auf den Preis schlagen* [intr v] +*haben/sein* **1.** +*haben* hit ◊ *Bitte nicht schlagen!* ♦ *jdm ins Gesicht/auf den Kopf/auf die Finger etc. schlagen* mit der Faust an den Tisch schlagen thump the table with your fist **2.** +*haben (clock)* strike, chime ◊ *Hörst du die Kirchenuhr schlagen?* **3.** +*sein (fall somewhere)* der Länge nach auf den Boden schlagen fall flat on your face mit dem Kopf an die Tür schlagen bang your head on the door **4.** +*haben* nach jdm/etw. schlagen lash out at sb/ sth, hit out at sb/sth ◊ *mit der Zeitung nach einer Fliege schlagen* um sich schlagen lash out **5.** +*haben/sein (shutters, rain etc.)* beat ◊ *Die Fensterläden schlugen im Wind.* ♦ *Der Regen schlug ans Fenster.; (sails)* flap; *(waves)* pound **6.** +*haben (heart, pulse)* beat ◊ *Wenn ich sie sehe, schlägt mein Herz höher/schneller.; (more vehemently)* pound Mir schlug vor Aufregung das Herz im Halse. My heart was in my mouth with all the excitement. **7.** +*haben* mit den Flügeln schlagen beat its wings **8.** +*sein (flames, sparks)* aus etw. schlagen come out of sth ◊ *Flammen schlugen aus dem Dach.* **9.** +*sein* (jdm) auf etw. [acc] schlagen affect (sb's) sth ◊ *Der ewige Regen schlug ihnen auf die Stimmung.* jdm auf den Magen schlagen upset sb's stomach [ref v] +*haben* **1.** sich (mit jdm) (um etw.) schlagen fight (sb) (for/over sth) ◊ *sich um die besten Plätze schlagen* **2.** sich tapfer/wacker/nicht schlecht schlagen put up a brave/good performance, do rather well sich allein durchs Leben schlagen go through life alone sich mehr schlecht als recht durchs Leben schlagen muddle through sich mühsam durchs Leben schlagen struggle through life **3.** sich auf jds Seite schlagen side with sb ⊙ mit jdm/etw. geschlagen sein be saddled with sb/sth *(a disease, disability)* be afflicted with sth, be ridden with sth

Schla·ger ['ʃlaːɡɐ] der <–s, –> **1.** MUS (pop) song ◊ *ein populärer/seichter Schlager* ♦ *der deutsche Schlager; (successful)* hit **2.** best-seller ◊ *Dieses Modell wird bestimmt ein Schlager!* ⊜Knüller

Schlä·ger[1] ['ʃlɛːɡɐ] der <–s, –> *(for tennis, badminton)* racket; *(golf)* club; *(baseball, cricket, table tennis)* bat; *(hockey)* stick

Schlä·ger[2] ['ʃlɛːɡɐ] der <–s, –>, **Schlä·ge·rin** ['ʃlɛːɡərɪn] die <–, –nen> **1.** *(pej)* thug, heavy ◊ *Er ist ein richtiger Schläger.* **2.** SPORT batter, striker ◊ *Er ist ein besserer Schläger als Fänger oder Werfer.*

Schlä·ge·rei [ʃlɛːɡəˈraɛ] die <–, –en> fight, brawl,

punch-up ◊ *eine Schlägerei anzetteln* ♦ *Die Fußball-fans lieferten sich handfeste/wüste Schlägereien.*

schlag·fer·tig ['ʃlaːkfɛɐtɪç] [adj, adv] quick-witted(ly) ◊ *eine schlagfertige Antwort geben* ♦ *Sie ist schlagfertig und charmant.* ♦ *schlagfertig antworten/reagieren*

⑦ **Schlag·o·bers** ['ʃlaːkɔbes] das <–> *no pl (Austr)* **1.** (whipping) cream ⊜süße Sahne, Schlagsahne **2.** whipped cream ◊ *Eis mit Schlagobers* ⊜Sahne, Schlagsahne

Schlag·sah·ne ['ʃlaːkzaːnə] die <–> *no pl* **1.** (whipping) cream ⊜süße Sahne **2.** whipped cream ◊ *Erdbeerkuchen mit Schlagsahne* ⊜Sahne

⑦ **schlägt** [ʃlɛːkt] *pres of* schlagen

⑦ **Schlag·zei·le** ['ʃlaːktsaɛlə] die <–, –n> headline in die Schlagzeilen geraten make the headlines Schlagzeilen machen, für Schlagzeilen sorgen make headlines

Schlamm [ʃlam] der <–(e)s, –e or Schlämme> mud ◊ *im Schlamm stecken bleiben/versinken* giftiger Schlamm toxic sludge ⊜Matsch

schlam·pig ['ʃlampɪç] *(fam)* [adj] **1.** *(performance, work)* sloppy, slipshod ◊ *Die Kontrollen waren sehr schlampig.* ♦ *schlampige Arbeit* ⊜nachlässig ⊜sorgfältig **2.** *(person)* slovenly, untidy ◊ *Er ist schrecklich schlampig.* ♦ *ein schlampiger Mensch* ⊜unordentlich ⊜ordentlich [adv] **1.** *(activity etc.)* sloppily, in a slipshod fashion ◊ *schlampig arbeiten* ♦ *eine schlampig recherchierte Reportage* ⊜sauber **2.** *(clothes etc.)* scruffily ◊ *schlampig gekleidet sein* ⊜unordentlich ⊜ordentlich

Schlan·ge ['ʃlaŋə] die <–, –n> **1.** ZOO snake **2.** *(of people, cars)* queue ◊ *Am Eingang bildete sich eine lange Schlange.* (irgendwo) Schlange stehen queue (up) (somewhere) **3.** *(pej) (woman, girl)* viper, snake in the grass

⑦ **schlank** [ʃlaŋk] [adj] **1.** slim ◊ *ein langbeiniges, schlankes Model* ♦ *Früher war er sehr schlank.* ♦ *eine Diät machen, um schlank zu werden; (fingers)* slender ◊ *Sport macht schlank!; (clothes etc.)* make you look slim ⊜dick **2.** *(fig) (administration etc.)* lean ◊ *eine schlanke Verwaltung* ♦ *Der Staat soll schlanker werden.*

schlau [ʃlaʊ] [adj] <schlauer, am schlau(e)sten> **1.** shrewd, cunning, wily ◊ *Sie ist schlau wie ein Fuchs.* ♦ *ein schlauer Bursche* ⊜raffiniert ⊜dumm **2.** smart ◊ *Das hat sich mal ein schlauer Kopf ausgedacht. Jetzt bin ich genauso schlau wie vorher!* I am no further forward in understanding this! sich (irgendwo) (über etw./jdn) schlau machen get clued up (on sth/sb) (somewhere) ⊜klug, intelligent **3.** *(idea, answer etc.)* clever ◊ *viele schlaue Sprüche auf Lager haben* ♦ *Diese Antwort war ziemlich schlau.* ⊜geschickt, raffiniert ⊜dumm [adv] cleverly, cunningly ◊ *Der Plan war schlau ausgedacht/eingefädelt.* ⊜raffiniert

Schlauch [ʃlaʊx] der <–(e)s, Schläuche> *(of a tyre)* inner tube ◊ *den Schlauch eines Rads flicken; (for petrol)* tube ◊ *Benzin durch einen Schlauch absaugen; (for water)* hose(pipe) ◊ *den Rasen mit dem Schlauch sprengen*

⑦ **schlecht** [ʃlɛçt] [adj] <schlechter, am schlechtesten> **1.** bad ◊ *schlechte Nachrichten für jdn haben* ♦ *Das Wetter/Die Lage ist schlecht.* ♦ *mit etw.*

A
B
C
D
E
F
G
H
I
J
K
L
M
N
O
P
Q
R
S
T
U
V
W
X
Y
Z

schlechte Erfahrungen machen ♦ Das ist gar keine so schlechte Idee! ♦ Der Film war entsetzlich schlecht. ♦ schlechte Augen/Nerven haben ♦ ein schlechter Schwimmer sein ♦ Übelkeit durch schlechtes Essen ♦ Er ist durch und durch schlecht. etw. ist schlecht für die Gesundheit sth is bad for your health Die Milch ist schlecht (geworden). The milk has gone off. Sie hatte es nicht schlecht bei den Pflegeeltern. Her foster parents took care of her fairly well. (mit etw.) schlecht dran sein be in a bad way (with sth); (financially) jdm geht es schlecht sb is doing badly jdn (bei jdm) schlecht machen run sb down (in the presence of sb) ◊ Er macht die anderen Kinder immer in seinem Lehrer schlecht. **2.** jdm geht es schlecht sb is ill; (mentally) sb is in a bad way ⊜gut **3.** jdm ist/wird schlecht sb feels sick [adv] **1.** badly ◊ jdn schlecht behandeln ♦ schlecht informiert/vorbereitet sein ♦ ein schlecht bezahlter Job ♦ Ich habe schlecht geschlafen. schlecht hören/sehen have bad hearing/eyesight „Wo ist es denn?" — „Siehst du schlecht? Direkt vor deiner Nase!" "Where is it then?" — "Are you blind? Right in front of your nose!" schlecht gelaunt in a bad mood **2.** sich etw. [dat] schlecht merken können have a bad memory for sth schlecht nein sagen können find it difficult to say no Sprich bitte lauter, ich verstehe dich so schlecht. Please speak up, I can't hear you very well. ⊜schwer ⊜gut, leicht **3.** Das kann ich schlecht sagen. I can't really say. Ich kann ihn jetzt ja schlecht wieder ausladen, das wäre unhöflich. I can't really tell him now not to come, that would be rude. Er kann sich weitere Fehler schlecht erlauben/leisten. He can't really afford to make any more mistakes. ⊛ mehr schlecht als recht after a fashion **schlecht und recht** somehow or other **nicht schlecht** (fam) **1.** not bad **2.** Er wird nicht schlecht staunen, wenn er dein Geschenk sieht. He won't half be surprised when he sees your present. Ich hab mich nicht schlecht darüber geärgert. I was rather annoyed about it.

schlecht·hin [ʃlɛçtˈhɪn, '– –] [adv] **1.** Dieses Buch ist der Klassiker schlechthin. This book is the quintessential classic. Das war für ihn das Böse schlechthin. For him that was the epitome of evil. Die Venus gilt schlechthin als Inbegriff der Schönheit. Venus is considered to be the very personification of beauty. **2.** absolutely ◊ Das ist schlechthin unzulässig/unmöglich/unhaltbar/unbegreiflich. ⊜völlig, ganz und gar

schlei·chen [ˈʃlaeçn̩] <schleicht, schlich, hat/ist geschlichen> [intr v] +sein **1.** (softly) creep, sneak ◊ heimlich in die Speisekammer schleichen ♦ auf Zehenspitzen durchs Haus schleichen **2.** (fam) (slowly) creep (about) ◊ Jetzt schleich nicht so, beeil dich ein bisschen. [ref v] +haben (also fig) (softly) sich irgendwohin schleichen creep somewhere, sneak somewhere ◊ sich unbemerkt ins Haus schleichen ♦ Hier haben sich ein paar Fehler in die Geschichte geschlichen.
⊛ schleich dich, schleicht euch (fam) get lost, buzz off

Schlei·er [ˈʃlaeɐ] der <-s, –> **1.** (also fig) veil ◊ einen Schleier tragen ♦ den Schleier des Geheimnisses lüften **2.** haze, mist ◊ Die Berge waren in einen

feinen Schleier gehüllt. ⊜Dunst

Schlei·fe [ˈʃlaefə] die <-, –n> **1.** bow ◊ eine Schleife binden ♦ eine Schleife im Haar tragen **2.** loop; (of a road etc.) horseshoe bend ◊ Die Straße macht dort eine Schleife zurück in Richtung Süden.

schlei·fen¹ [ˈʃlaefn̩] <schleift, schleifte, hat geschleift> [tr v] +haben drag ◊ Der Zug schleifte das Auto mehrere hundert Meter mit sich. ♦ Gestern ist sie mich sogar in die Oper geschleift! ⊜schleppen [intr v] +haben/sein trail, drag ◊ Das Kleid war so lang, dass es auf dem/über den Boden schleifte.; (brake etc.) scrape ◊ Die Bremse schleift beim Fahren an der Felge.
⊛ etw. schleifen lassen (fam) let sth slide

schlei·fen² [ˈʃlaefn̩] <schleift, schliff, hat geschliffen> [tr v] **1.** (a knife, shears etc.) sharpen ◊ ein Messer schleifen lassen **2.** (a workpiece) grind; (a diamond, precious stone etc.) cut **3.** (the floor etc.) polish ◊ das Parkett schleifen lassen; (a workpiece) smooth ◊ Unebenheiten von den Schienen schleifen **4.** (fam) MIL drill hard ◊ Der Offizier hat die Rekruten ziemlich geschliffen.

Schleim [ʃlaem] der <-(e)s, -e> mucus ◊ den Schleim in der Nase/Lunge mit Medikamenten lösen; (in the throat) phlegm; (of a snail) slime ◊ Schnecken sondern während des Kriechens Schleim ab.

schlen·dern [ˈʃlɛndɐn] [intr v] +sein stroll ◊ über den Marktplatz/durch die Fußgängerzone schlendern

schlep·pen [ˈʃlɛpm̩] [tr v] +haben **1.** (a suitcase, crate etc.) lug ◊ Eimer/Kisten/Koffer schleppen **2.** +indication of direction (a person, an object) drag ◊ Er schleppte den großen Sandsack mühsam hinter sich her. ♦ ein Netz durchs Wasser schleppen; (a ship, car etc.) tow ◊ einen Frachter in den Hafen schleppen **3.** +indication of direction (fam) (an object) take ◊ Er schleppt mir ständig neue Geräte ins Haus!; (an unwilling person) drag ◊ Ich muss dich wohl zum Arzt schleppen? Sie schleppten ihn vors Gericht. He was hauled before the judge. sich irgendwohin schleppen drag yourself somewhere ⊜schleifen

Schles·wig-Hol·stein [ˌʃleːsvɪçˈhɔlʃtaen] das <-s> article only in combination with attribute Schleswig-Holstein box@ Land

Area: 15,763 km²; population: approx. 2.79 million; regional capital: Kiel.
For long periods, Schleswig-Holstein was part of Denmark, and even today the Danish minority there elects a representative to the regional parliament in Kiel. There are hardly any expanses of forest in this most northerly regional state, the North Sea and the Baltic being the main features. Apart from five main islands, Schleswig-Holstein is famous for a series of tiny islets known as the 'Halligen' that can only be reached on foot at low tide. Tourism is an important economic factor in the area.

schleu·dern [ˈʃlɔødɐn] [tr v] +haben **1.** hurl ◊ Die Insassen wurden bei dem Unfall aus dem Fahrzeug geschleudert. ♦ voller Wut eine Flasche an/gegen die Wand schleudern jdm Beleidigungen ins Gesicht schleudern hurl insults at sb **2.** spin-dry ◊

Die Gardinen dürfen nicht geschleudert werden.
[intr v] +*haben/sein* **1.** +*sein* skid ◊ *mit dem Auto gegen die Leitplanke schleudern* ins Schleudern geraten/kommen go into a skid **2.** +*haben* (*washing*) spin ◊ *Die Wäsche ist gleich fertig, die Maschine schleudert schon.*
⊙ *jdn ins Schleudern bringen* (*fam*) throw sb *ins Schleudern geraten/kommen* (*fam*) run into trouble, lose the plot
Schleu·se ['ʃlɔɪzə] die <–, –n> **1.** (*also fig*) lock ◊ *Das Schiff fuhr in die Schleuse ein/passierte die Schleuse. Der Himmel öffnete seine Schleusen.* The heavens opened. **2.** (*to a sterile area etc.*) transfer port ◊ *durch eine elektronisch gesicherte Schleuse gehen;* (*in a refrigerated area*) cold trap; (*in a space station*) airlock
schlich [ʃlɪç] *pret of* schleichen
schlicht [ʃlɪçt] [adj] <schlichter, am schlichtesten> **1.** plain, simple ◊ *Der Baustil ist schlicht, aber elegant.* ◆ *ein Grab nur mit einem schlichten Holzkreuz schmücken* ◆ *Die schlichte Wahrheit ist: Ich habe es vergessen.* ◆ *etw. auf eine schlichte Formel bringen* **2.** (*intellect*) simple ◊ *ein schlichtes Gemüt* ◆ *Er ist ein wenig schlicht.* [adv] schlicht (*und einfach/ergreifend*) quite simply ◊ *Das ist schlicht und einfach falsch/unmöglich/ Unsinn!* ◆ *Er hat schlicht vergessen, uns zu benachrichtigen.*
schlich·ten ['ʃlɪçtn̩] <schlichtet, schlichtete, hat geschlichtet> [tr v] settle (by mediation) ◊ *einen Konflikt/Streit schlichten* [intr v] mediate, arbitrate ◊ *Er versuchte, zwischen den streitenden Parteien zu schlichten.*
② **schlief** [ʃliːf] *pret of* schlafen
② **schlie·ßen** ['ʃliːsn̩] <schließt, schloss, hat geschlossen> [tr v] **1.** close, shut ◊ *ein Fenster/eine Tür schließen* ◆ *die Augen schließen* ◆ *das Buch schließen, in dem man gerade gelesen hat* ◆ *die Praxis von 12 bis 14 Uhr schließen;* (*a suitcase, gap etc.*) close ◊ *eine Grenze/einen Koffer/eine Lücke schließen;* (*a tap*) turn off; (*a bottle*) put the top on sich schließen close ◊ *Die Tür schloss sich leise.* ◆ *Dann schlossen sich seine Augen für immer.* ⊖öffnen **2.** (*a software application, speech*) close ◊ *vor der Installation eines Programms alle anderen Anwendungen schließen* ◆ *Der Vorsitzende schließt die Verhandlung.* ◆ *Sie schloss ihren Vortrag mit einem Gedicht.* ⊖beenden **3.** (*an ailing enterprise etc.*) close down, shut down ◊ *Das Museum wurde aus Kostengründen geschlossen.* ⊖zumachen ⊖eröffnen **4.** *etw./jdn irgendwohin schließen* lock sth/sb (up) somewhere ◊ *Geld/Wertsachen in einen Safe schließen* sich in ein Zimmer schließen shut yourself in a room ⊖sperren **5.** (*a contract, an agreement etc.*) etw. (*mit jdm*) schließen conclude sth (*with sb*) ◊ *Beide Staaten schlossen ein Bündnis/einen Pakt/ein Abkommen (miteinander).* einen Kompromiss schließen reach a compromise Frieden/Freundschaft (*mit jdm*) schließen make peace/friends (*with sb*) **6.** etw. aus etw. schließen conclude sth from sth ◊ *Er schloss aus ihrer Ähnlichkeit, dass sie miteinander verwandt sind.* ⊖folgern [intr v] **1.** close ◊ *Wir/Die Wahllokale schließen um 20 Uhr;* (*ailing enterprise etc.*) close down, shut down ◊ *Mehrere Filialen mussten*

schließen.; (*lid*) go on; (*key*) fit ◊ *Der Schlüssel schließt schlecht.;* (*door*) automatisch/selbsttätig schließen close automatically, shut automatically *Die Dose schließt schlecht.* The lid doesn't fit the tin very well. **2.** (*von etw.*) auf etw. schließen judge sth (*from sth*) ◊ *von einem Fall auf einen anderen schließen* (*von jdm*) auf jdn schließen judge sb (*by sb*) *Sein Verhalten lässt darauf schließen, dass er sich schämt.* His behavio(u)r suggests that he is ashamed of himself. **3.** (*speech, event etc.*) close, conclude ◊ *Sie schloss mit den Worten/folgendermaßen: ...* ◆ *Die Veranstaltung schloss mit einem Feuerwerk.* ⊖enden ⊖beginnen
Schließ·fach ['ʃliːsfax] das <–(e)s, Schließfächer> (left-luggage) locker ◊ *das Gepäck in ein Schließfach tun*
② **schließ·lich** ['ʃliːslɪç] [adv] **1.** finally ◊ *Der Täter konnte schließlich doch noch gefasst werden.* ◆ *Es gab Suppe, Hauptspeise, Nachspeise und schließlich noch einen Kaffee.* **2.** after all ◊ *Ich kann mich schließlich nicht um alles kümmern.* ◆ *Das traue ich ihr schon zu, schließlich ist sie ja fast erwachsen.* ⊖immerhin
⊙ **schließlich und endlich** when all is said and done
schliff [ʃlɪf] *pret of* schleifen²
② **schlimm** [ʃlɪm] [adj, adv] bad(ly) ◊ *ein schlimmer Fehler* ◆ *Das ist schlimm für sie.* ◆ *Die Schmerzen wurden immer schlimmer.* ◆ *Die Wunde hat schlimm geblutet.* jdn hat es schlimm erwischt sb is in a bad way *Bei dem Unfall hat es ihn ziemlich schlimm erwischt.* He was injured quite badly in the accident. *Das ist doch nicht so/nur halb so schlimm!* It's not as bad as all that!
Schlin·ge ['ʃlɪŋə] die <–, –n> **1.** (*also fig*) loop ◊ *die Schlinge eines Lassos/Seils;* noose ◊ *Die Schlinge um den Hals des Diktators wird immer enger.;* sling ◊ *den Arm in einer Schlinge tragen* **2.** snare ◊ *Die Vögel werden in/mit Schlingen und Netzen gefangen.* **3.** (*of a net etc.*) mesh ◊ *sich in den Schlingen eines Netzes verfangen* ⊖Masche
⊙ **seinen Hals/Kopf aus der Schlinge ziehen** → Hals, Kopf
Schlit·ten ['ʃlɪtn̩] der <–s, –> **1.** (*for children*) sledge, sled ◊ *auf dem Schlitten den Berg hinuntersausen* Schlitten fahren go tobogganing; (*with horses etc.*) sleigh ◊ *im zweispännigen Schlitten fahren* **2.** (*fam*) motor ◊ *Er fährt einen amerikanischen/teuren/tollen Schlitten.*
⊙ **mit jdm Schlitten fahren** (*fam*) have sb on the carpet
Schlitt·schuh ['ʃlɪtʃuː] der <–(e)s, –e> (ice) skate ◊ *im Eisstadion Schlittschuhe ausleihen* Schlittschuh laufen (ice-)skate ◊ *Sie sind heute Schlittschuh gelaufen.*
Schlitz [ʃlɪts] der <–es, –e> slit ◊ *der Schlitz des Briefkastens/des Sparschweins* ◆ *Seine Augen waren nur einen winzigen Schlitz geschlossen.* ◆ *ein Rock mit seitlichem Schlitz;* (*of a machine*) slot ◊ *Sie warf die Münze in den Schlitz am Automaten.* ◆ *Stecken Sie die Karte in den Schlitz am Geldautomaten.*
② **schloss** [ʃlɔs] *pret of* schließen
Schloss [ʃlɔs] das <–es, Schlösser> **1.** palace, castle ◊ *Schloss Neuschwanstein* ◆ *Der Königssohn*

führte die Prinzessin heim auf sein Schloss.
2. lock ◊ *Der Schlüssel dreht sich im Schloss.* ♦ *eine Tür mit mehreren Schlössern sichern*
ⓔ **hinter Schloss und Riegel** (put) behind bars ◊ *hinter Schloss und Riegel kommen/sitzen*

Schlos·ser ['ʃlɔsɐ] der <-s, ->, **Schlos·se·rin** ['ʃlɔsərɪn] die <-, -nen> fitter, metalworker ◊ *Er ist Schlosser von Beruf.* ♦ *Tina ist eine geschickte Schlosserin.*; (*for doorlocks*) locksmith ◊ *einen Schlosser kommen lassen*

Schlucht [ʃlʊxt] die <-, -en> gorge, ravine ◊ *in eine tiefe Schlucht stürzen*

schluch·zen ['ʃlʊxtsn̩] (tr+intr v) +*haben* sob ♦ *herzzerreißend/laut schluchzen* ♦ *„Bitte nicht!", schluchzte er.*

Schluck [ʃlʊk] der <-(e)s, -e> swig, sip, mouthful ◊ *in kleinen Schlucken trinken* ♦ *einen kräftigen Schluck aus der Flasche nehmen*

schlu·cken ['ʃlʊkn̩] (tr v) +*haben* **1.** swallow ◊ *Du solltest nicht so viele Pillen schlucken.* ♦ *Hat er die Ausrede/Geschichte geschluckt?* **2.** (*fam, pej*) swallow (up) ◊ *Der Konzern hat wieder ein paar Konkurrenten geschluckt.* **3.** (*fam*) (*sound, light etc.*) absorb ◊ *Schwarze Farbe schluckt Licht.* **4.** (*fam*) (*alcohol*) (gulp) down ◊ *auf einer Party ordentlich Bier und Schnaps schlucken*.; (*petrol*) guzzle ◊ *Dieser Riesenschlitten schluckt jede Menge Sprit.*; (*money*) swallow (intr v) +*haben* **1.** swallow ◊ *vor Halsschmerzen kaum schlucken können* (schwer) schlucken müssen have to swallow hard ◊ *Als er mir den Preis nannte, musste ich erst einmal schlucken.* **2.** (*fam*) booze ◊ *Sie haben auf der Party ordentlich geschluckt.*

ⓐ **schlug** [ʃluːk] *pret of* schlagen

ⓐ **Schluss** [ʃlʊs] der <-es, Schlüsse> **1.** *no pl* end ◊ *Am/Zum Schluss wurde das Buch noch richtig spannend.* ♦ *Er hat nicht bis zum Schluss durchgehalten.* ♦ *sich am Schluss der Schlange anstellen* ♦ *Das Buch hat einen absolut verblüffenden/überraschenden Schluss.* am/zum Schluss finally, in the end ◊ *ganz zum Schluss an die Reihe kommen* mit etw. ist Schluss that's the end of sth, sth is over **2.** conclusion ◊ *Ich habe aus ihrem Verhalten meine Schlüsse gezogen.* ♦ *zu dem richtigen/logischen/voreiligen Schluss gelangen/kommen, dass …* **3.** (*with an activity*) (mit etw.) Schluss machen finish (with sth) ◊ *Macht endlich Schluss mit eurer Streiterei!* Just stop arguing, will you! Machen wir Schluss für heute. Let's call it a day.; (*a habit*) mit etw. Schluss machen stop sth, pack sth in/up ◊ *mit dem Rauchen/Trinken Schluss machen*; (*commit suicide*) Schluss machen end it all; (*finish a relationship*) mit jdm Schluss machen finish with sb ◊ *Er hat mit seiner Freundin Schluss gemacht.* (miteinander) Schluss machen split up

ⓔ **Schluss mit lustig** (*fam*) the serious stuff begins, things start to get serious

ⓐ **Schlüs·sel** ['ʃlʏsl̩] der <-s, -> **1.** (*also fig*) key ◊ *den Schlüssel abziehen/(im Schloss/in der Tür) stecken lassen* ♦ *den Schlüssel zum/für den Keller verlieren* ein Schlüssel (zu etw.) a key (to sth) ◊ *Beharrlichkeit ist hier der Schlüssel zum Erfolg.* **2.** distribution formula ◊ *etw. nach einem bestimmten Schlüssel berechnen* **3.** cipher ◊ *der Schlüssel zu einem Code*

schmack·haft ['ʃmakhaft] (adj) <schmackhafter, am schmackhaftesten> tasty ◊ *schmackhafte Gerichte/Speisen* ♦ *Die Suppe war wirklich schmackhaft.*
ⓔ **jdm etw. schmackhaft machen** make sth palatable to sb

ⓐ **schmal** [ʃmaːl] (adj) <schmaler/schmäler, am schmalsten/schmälsten> **1.** narrow ◊ *Papier in schmale Streifen schneiden* ♦ *Der Gang/Spalt war sehr lang und schmal.*; (*figure*) slim, slender ◊ *eine schmale Taille bekommen*; (*person*) schmal werden lose (a lot of) weight ⊖breit **2.** (*lofty*) (*income, cost etc.*) low ◊ *mit einem schmalen Budget auskommen müssen* ♦ *Ihre Rente ist sehr schmal.*

Schmalz¹ [ʃmalts] das <-es> *no pl* lard ◊ *ein Brot mit Schmalz bestreichen*

Schmalz² [ʃmalts] der <-es> *no pl* (*fam, pej*) soppy sentimentality, schmaltz ◊ *ein Buch/Film/Lied voller Schmalz*

ⓐ **schme·cken** ['ʃmɛkn̩] (intr v) +*haben* **1.** irgendwie schmecken taste a certain way ◊ *gut/schlecht schmecken* ♦ *bitter/süß schmecken* nach etw. schmecken taste of sth ◊ *Der Kuchen schmeckt nach Mandeln. Melonen schmecken nach Sommer.* The taste of melons reminds you of summer. **2.** taste good ◊ *Das schmeckt aber!* ♦ *Schmeckt das denn?* Das schmeckt nicht! That doesn't taste nice! jdm schmeckt etw. (gut) sb likes sth ◊ *Kaffee schmeckt mir nicht.* ♦ *Hat es/das Essen euch (gut) geschmeckt?* **3.** sich (dat) etw. schmecken lassen enjoy sth (tr+intr v) +*haben* taste ◊ *Schmeckst du den Wein in der Soße?* ♦ *Schmeckst du mal, ob an der Suppe noch etwas fehlt?*
ⓔ **nach mehr schmecken** (*fam*) taste so good that you want more, taste moreish **jdm nicht schmecken** (*fig*) not to be to sb's liking

schmei·cheln ['ʃmaeçln̩] (tr+intr v) +*haben* (jdm) schmeicheln flatter (sb) Sie schmeichelte (ihm), dass er der klügste Mensch sei, den sie je getroffen habe. She flattered him by saying he was the cleverest person she had ever met. „Du siehst fantastisch aus", schmeichelte er ihr. "You look fantastic", he flattered her. etw. schmeichelt jdm/etw. sth flatters sb/sth ◊ *Sein Interesse schmeichelte ihrer Eitelkeit/ihr.* ♦ *sich von etw. geschmeichelt fühlen* ♦ *Das Kleid schmeichelt der Figur.*

schmei·ßen ['ʃmaesn̩] <schmeißt, schmiss, hat geschmissen> (tr v) (*fam*) **1.** jdn/etw./sich irgendwohin schmeißen throw sb/sth/yourself somewhere, fling sb/sth/yourself somewhere ◊ *Steine nach etw. schmeißen* ♦ *Er schmiss sich mit Schwung aufs Sofa.* ♦ *jdn/etw. ins Wasser schmeißen* Schmeiß mal den Ball zu mir. Chuck me the ball. Er stolperte und schmiss dabei das Glas vom Tisch/zu Boden. He stumbled and knocked the glass off the table/to the floor. ⊖werfen **2.** (*a training, your studies*) chuck in ◊ *die Lehre/Schule schmeißen* ⊖abbrechen **3.** jdn (aus etw.) schmeißen chuck sb out (of sth) ◊ *jdn aus/von der Schule/aus dem Verein schmeißen* ♦ *jdn aus dem Haus schmeißen* **4.** (*a party*) throw; (*a business, shop etc.*) run ◊ *den Laden mal eine Weile allein schmeißen* **5.** (*a recording, presentation etc.*) mess up ◊ *Er musste lachen und schmiss die ganze Szene.* ⊖ruinieren (intr v) **1.** throw, chuck ◊ *Schmeiß mal zu mir!* mit etw.

schmeißen throw sth ◊ *mit Steinen (nach einer Katze) schmeißen* ⊜*werfen* **2.** mit etw. um sich schmeißen chuck sth around, throw sth around ◊ *mit Geld um sich schmeißen* mit Beleidigungen/ Schimpfwörtern um sich schmeißen hurl insults/ abuse in all directions ⌊ref v⌋ sich in etw. ⌊acc⌋ schmeißen get (all) dressed up in sth ◊ *sich zur Feier des Tages in seinen besten Anzug schmeißen*

schmel·zen [ˈʃmɛltsn̩] <schmilzt, schmolz, hat/ist geschmolzen> ⌊intr v⌋ *+sein* **1.** melt ◊ *Das Eis/Der Schnee schmilzt in der Sonne.* ♦ *Gold schmilzt bei 1063° Celsius.* **2.** *(fig) (money, supplies etc.)* melt away ◊ *Der strenge Winter ließ unsere Ölreserven schmelzen.* ⌊tr v⌋ *+haben* melt ◊ *Die Sonne schmilzt den Schnee/das Eis.; (ore)* smelt ◊ *Erz im Hochofen schmelzen*

② **Schmerz** [ʃmɛʳts] der <-es, -en> pain ◊ *vor Schmerz schreien/vergehen/weinen* ♦ *ein brennender/dumpfer/heftiger/stechender Schmerz* ♦ *jdm Schmerzen zufügen* ♦ *bei jds Tod tiefen Schmerz empfinden; (mental also)* anguish

schmer·zen [ˈʃmɛʳtsn̩] ⌊tr+intr v⌋ *+haben* etw. schmerzt (jdn) sth hurts (sb) ◊ *Mein Kopf/Die Wunde schmerzt sehr.* ♦ *Es schmerzt immer noch, wenn ich daran denke.; (mentally also)* sth causes (sb) anguish ◊ *Es schmerzte sie, ihn so reden zu hören.* ⊜*wehtun*

Schmet·ter·ling [ˈʃmɛtɐlɪŋ] der <-s, -e> ZOO, SPORT butterfly ◊ *ein bunter Schmetterling* ♦ *die 100 m Schmetterling in neuer Rekordzeit schwimmen*

schmie·ren [ˈʃmiːrən] ⌊tr v⌋ *+haben* **1.** *(butter, jam etc.)* (jdm/sich) etw. auf ein Brot etc. schmieren spread sth on a slice of bread etc. (for sb/ yourself) (jdm/sich) Brote/Stullen schmieren make sandwiches (for sb/yourself) jdm/sich ein Brötchen mit Frischkäse schmieren spread some cream cheese on a roll for sb/yourself **2.** *+direction* Schmier die Marmelade nicht an dein Hemd/in das Handtuch. Don't get jam on your shirt/the towel. Gips in ein Loch schmieren fill a hole with plaster jdm/sich Sonnencreme ins Gesicht schmieren rub suntan cream on sb's/your face **3.** lubricate ◊ *die Fahrradkette reinigen und mit Öl schmieren* **4.** *(pej) (obscene language etc.)* scrawl ◊ *obszöne Zeichnungen an die Wände der Toilette schmieren* **5.** *(pej)* scribble ◊ *die Hausaufgaben ins Heft schmieren* **6.** *(fam, pej)* jdm schmieren bribe sb, grease sb's palm ◊ *Die Firma soll jahrelang Mitarbeiter der Baubehörde geschmiert haben.* ⊜*bestechen* **7.** *(fam, pej)* jdm eine/ein paar schmieren give sb a clout/a couple of clips round the ear ⌊intr v⌋ *+haben (fam) (person)* scribble ◊ *Schmier doch nicht so!; (pen etc.)* smear ◊ *Der Stift schmiert, nimm einen anderen.* ⊚ **wie geschmiert** *(fam)* like clockwork ◊ *„Hat es geklappt?" — „Ja, es ging/lief alles wie geschmiert."*

schmilzt [ʃmɪltst] *pres of* schmelzen

Schmin·ke [ˈʃmɪŋkə] die <-, -n> make-up ◊ *Sie legte ein bisschen Schminke auf.*

schmin·ken [ˈʃmɪŋkn̩] ⌊tr v⌋ *+haben* sich/jdn schminken put on your/sb's make-up, make yourself/sb up Sie schminkt sich nie. She never wears make-up. Sie war zu stark geschminkt. She was wearing too much make-up. Sie schminkte sich die Augen. She put on some eye make-up.

schmiss [ʃmɪs] *pret of* schmeißen

schmolz [ʃmɔlts] *pret of* schmelzen

② **Schmuck** [ʃmʊk] der <-(e)s> *no pl* **1.** jewellery, jewelry ◊ *Der Einbrecher nahm den ganzen Schmuck mit.* ♦ *Er kaufte ihr kostbaren Schmuck.* **2.** decoration ◊ *Der einzige Schmuck des Gebäudes besteht aus den farbigen Kacheln.*

schmü·cken [ˈʃmʏkn̩] ⌊tr v⌋ *+haben* **1.** decorate ◊ *Sie schmückte den Weihnachtsbaum.* ♦ *ein festlich geschmückter Saal* **2.** *Ringe schmückten ihre Finger/Hände.* ♦ *Viele Gemälde schmückten die Wände.*

schmuck·los [ˈʃmʊkloːs] ⌊adj⌋ *no comp/superl; mostly before ns* bare, plain, simple ◊ *ein schmuckloser Sarg* ♦ *Der Saal war schmucklos.*

② **Schmug·gel** [ˈʃmʊgl̩] der <-s> *no pl* smuggling ◊ *Er wurde beim Schmuggel von Drogen/Zigaretten erwischt.* ♦ *Der Schmuggel zwischen den beiden Ländern blüht.*

schmug·geln [ˈʃmʊgl̩n] ⌊tr+intr v⌋ *+haben* smuggle ◊ *Zigaretten/Alkohol schmuggeln* ♦ *Waffen/Flüchtlinge ins Land/über die Grenze schmuggeln* ♦ *An dieser Grenze wird viel geschmuggelt.* ⌊tr v⌋ *+haben (fig)* etw./jdn irgendwohin schmuggeln sneak sth/ sb into somewhere ◊ *Sie schmuggelte heimlich ihren Freund in ihr Zimmer.* jdm etw. irgendwohin schmuggeln sneak sth into sb's sth ◊ *Sie schmuggelte ihm 20 Euro in die Tasche. Er schmuggelte ihr eine Nachricht ins Gefängnis.* He sneaked a message for her into prison.

schmu·sen [ˈʃmuːzn̩] ⌊intr v⌋ *+haben (mit jdm)* schmusen (kiss and) cuddle (sb) ◊ *Sie schmusten miteinander.* ♦ *Sie schmuste mit dem Baby.; (couple) also)* canoodle (with sb) ◊ *Das Paar schmuste in der Öffentlichkeit.*

Schmutz [ʃmʊts] der <-es> *no pl* dirt, muck ◊ *Ihre Schuhe waren voller Schmutz.* ♦ *Das Kind hat anscheinend draußen im Schmutz gespielt.* ♦ *ein Waschmittel für besonders hartnäckigen Schmutz* Schmutz abweisend dirt-repellent

② **schmut·zig** [ˈʃmʊtsɪç] ⌊adj⌋ **1.** dirty ◊ *Sie stellte das schmutzige Geschirr in den Geschirrspüler.* ♦ *Deine Hände sind schmutzig.* ♦ *Das ist eine schmutzige Arbeit.* ♦ *ein schmutziges Weiß/Gelb* etw./sich schmutzig machen get sth/yourself dirty ◊ *Er macht sich* ⌊dat⌋ *bei der Arbeit nicht gern die Hände schmutzig.* ⊜*sauber* **2.** *(fig)* dirty, filthy ◊ *eine schmutzige Fantasie haben* ♦ *einen schmutzigen Witz erzählen*

Schna·bel [ˈʃnaːbl̩] der <-s, Schnäbel> beak ◊ *Der Vogel hatte einen Wurm im Schnabel.* ♦ *Die Jungen sperrten ihre Schnäbel auf und bettelten um Futter.* ⊚ **sprechen/reden, wie einem der Schnabel gewachsen ist** **1.** talk (quite) naturally **2.** speak your mind

Schnal·le [ˈʃnalə] die <-, -n> buckle ◊ *An ihrer linken Sandale war die Schnalle abgegangen.* ♦ *Er kaufte einen schwarzen Gürtel mit silberner Schnalle.*

schnap·pen [ˈʃnapm̩] ⌊intr v⌋ *+haben/sein* **1.** *+haben (animal)* nach jdm/etw. schnappen go for sb/sth ◊ *Sie hielt dem Hund eine Wurst hin und er schnappte danach.* ♦ *Das Krokodil schnappte nach ihrem Bein.* **2.** *+haben* nach Luft schnappen gasp for air ◊ *Er tauchte aus dem Wasser auf und*

schnappte nach Luft. **3.** +*sein* ins Schloss
schnappen snap shut [tr v] +*haben* **1.** (sich [dat])
etw./jdn schnappen grab sth/sb ◊ *Jedes Kind
schnappte sich einen Ball.* ♦ *Sie schnappte sich
das Kind und verließ das Haus.* **2.** *(fam)* catch ◊
Die Kontrolleure schnappten einen Schwarzfahrer. ♦
Die Polizei hat den Täter geschnappt. **3.** (frische)
Luft schnappen get a breath of (fresh) air, go out
for a breath of (fresh) air
Schnaps [ʃnaps] der <-es, Schnäpse> *also pl
'Schnaps' when used with expressions of quantity*
schnapps ◊ *Er schenkte sich einen Schnaps ein.* ♦
Wie viele Schnäpse hast du schon getrunken?
schnar·chen [ˈʃnaʁçn̩] [intr v] +*haben* snore ◊
Schnarchst du? ♦ *Er schnarcht ganz furchtbar.* ♦
Sie schnarchte laut.
Schnau·ze [ˈʃnaʊtsə] die <-, -n> **1.** muzzle, nose
◊ *Der Hund legte seine Schnauze auf ihr Bein.* ♦
Das Tier hatte eine lange schmale Schnauze.
2. *(rude)* mouth, gob ◊ *Sei ruhig, sonst bekommst
du eins auf die Schnauze!* (Halt die) Schnauze!
Shut your trap!, Shut up!
⊛ auf die Schnauze fallen *(fam)* come a
cropper die Schnauze (gestrichen) voll haben
(fam) have had it up to here, have had enough
schnäu·zen [ˈʃnɔʏtsn̩] [ref+intr v] +*haben* (sich)
schnäuzen blow your nose ◊ *Sie schnäuzte sich.* ♦
Er schnäuzte geräuschvoll in sein Taschentuch.
Schne·cke [ˈʃnɛkə] die <-, -n> **1.** snail ◊ *Habt ihr
auch so viele Schnecken im Garten?*; slug ◊ *Sie
fand eine Schnecke im Salat.* **2.** snail, escargot ◊
*Als Vorspeise wurden Schnecken in Knoblauchbut-
ter serviert.*
⊛ jdn zur Schnecke machen *(fam)* lay into sb
② **Schnee** [ʃneː] der <-s> *no pl* **1.** snow ◊ *In der
Nacht fiel eine Menge Schnee.* ♦ *Sie schippten eine
Stunde lang Schnee.* ♦ *In den Alpen liegt bereits
Schnee.* **2.** *(of an egg)* white ◊ *das Eiweiß zu
Schnee schlagen*
⊛ Schnee von gestern/vom letzten Jahr etc.
old hat *(problem, difficulty etc. that is now
forgotten)* water under the bridge
Schnee·ball [ˈʃneːbal] der <-(e)s, Schneebälle>
snowball
Schnee·flo·cke [ˈʃneːflɔkə] die <-, -n> snowflake
◊ *Es fielen große/dicke Schneeflocken.*
Schnee·glät·te [ˈʃneːglɛtə] die <-> *no pl* hard-
packed snow ◊ *Schneeglätte führte gestern zu
vielen Unfällen.*
Schnee·ket·te [ˈʃneːkɛtə] die <-, -n> *most pl*
snow chain ◊ *Schneeketten sind auf dieser Straße
Pflicht.* ♦ *Er hielt an und legte die Schneeketten
an.*
Schnee·mann [ˈʃneːman] der
<-(e)s, Schneemänner> snowman ◊ *Die Kinder
bauten einen Schneemann.*
② **schnei·den** [ˈʃnaɪdn̩] <schneidet, schnitt, hat
geschnitten> [tr v] **1.** cut ◊ *einen Apfel in zwei
Hälften schneiden* ♦ *Sie schnitt den Artikel aus der
Zeitschrift.* ♦ *ein Loch ins Tischtuch schneiden* ♦
Auf den Feldern wird gerade das Korn geschnitten.
♦ *Sie schnitt dem Kind/sich die Fingernägel.* ♦ *Er
hat sich beim Rasieren/an einer Glasscherbe
geschnitten.* ♦ *Er hatte die Kurve geschnitten und
war ins Schleudern geraten.* ♦ *Der Wind schnitt
ihm ins Gesicht.* ♦ *Wer hat den Film geschnitten?*;

(a hedge, trees) cut down, clip, trim ◊ *Die Hecke
muss dringend geschnitten werden.*; *(bread,
salami etc.)* etw. (in Scheiben) schneiden slice sth
◊ *Kannst du bitte das Brot/den Braten schneiden?*
♦ *Sie schnitt die Wurst in Scheiben.* He cut himself
eine Scheibe vom Brot. He cut himself a slice of
bread. sich [dat] die Haare (kurz) schneiden lassen
have your hair cut (short) sich [dat] die Haare
selbst schneiden cut your own hair **2.** *(when overtaking sb in a vehicle)* jdn/etw. schneiden cut in
front of sb/sth ◊ *Der Lastwagen hatte ihn geschnitten.* **3.** *(lines, routes)* intersect (with), cross ◊
Strecke A schneidet Strecke B in Punkt C. sich
schneiden intersect, cross (each other) ◊ *Diese
beiden Linien schneiden sich.* **4.** jdn schneiden cut
sb dead, ignore sb, snub sb ◊ *Seine Kollegen
schnitten ihn.* **5.** (jdm) eine Grimasse/Fratze
schneiden pull a face (at sb) [intr v] **1.** *(scissors,
knives)* cut ◊ *Diese Messer schneiden gut/
schlecht.* **2.** in etw. [acc] schneiden make a cut in
sth ◊ *Sie hat versehentlich in die Tischdecke
geschnitten.* ♦ *Ich hab mir in den Finger geschnitten.* **3.** *(hairdresser)* cut hair ◊ *Dieser Friseur
schneidet sehr gut.*
Schnei·der [ˈʃnaɪdɐ] der <-s, ->, **Schnei·de·rin**
[ˈʃnaɪdərɪn] die <-, -nen> tailor, dressmaker ◊ *Er
war Schneider von Beruf.* ♦ *Sie ließ das Kleid von
einer Schneiderin anfertigen.* ein Anzug vom
Schneider a tailored suit
② **schnei·en** [ˈʃnaɪən] [imp v] +*haben* es schneit it
snows ◊ *Gestern hat es heftig geschneit.* ♦ *In
Tunesien schneit es nie.* Es schneit schon seit
Stunden. It's been snowing for hours. Draußen
schneit es große weiße Flocken. It's snowing big
white flakes outside. Gestern Nacht schneite es
einen halben Meter. Half a metre/meter of snow
fell last night.
② **schnell** [ʃnɛl] [adj] **1.** quick, fast ◊ *Er kam mit
schnellen Schritten auf mich zu.* ♦ *Seine Bewegungen waren schnell und präzise.* ♦ *einen schnellen
Imbiss zu sich nehmen* ♦ *Ich helfe dir. Zu zweit
geht es schneller.* eine schnelle Auffassungsgabe
haben be (very) quick (on the uptake) ⊖rasch
⊕langsam **2.** *(vehicle, machine)* fast ◊ *Er fährt
ein schnelles Motorrad.* ♦ *Sein neuer Computer ist
sehr schnell.* zu schnelles Fahren speeding ◊ *Er
bekam ein Bußgeld für zu schnelles Fahren.*
schneller werden speed up, gain speed ⊕langsam
[adv] **1.** fast, quickly ◊ *Sie spricht relativ schnell.* ♦
Sie rannte so schnell sie konnte. ♦ *Das ging mir zu
schnell. Ich kapiere gar nichts.* ♦ *Ich muss ganz
schnell zum Arzt.* schnell kapieren/lernen be a fast
learner Dieses Gericht lässt sich schnell zubereiten. This meal is very quick to prepare. Sie lebten
sich schnell in Berlin ein. They soon found their
feet in Berlin. **2.** *(fam)* for a minute ◊ *Kannst du
mir mal schnell helfen?* ♦ *Ich geh schnell mal zum
Nachbarn.* Warte mal schnell, ich bin gleich fertig.
Wait a minute, I'm almost ready. ⊖kurz **3.** *(fam)*
schnell machen hurry up, get a move on
② **schnitt** [ʃnɪt] *pret of* schneiden
Schnitt [ʃnɪt] der <-(e)s, -e> **1.** cut ◊ *Aus dem
Schnitt in ihrer Hand quoll Blut.* ♦ *Der Arzt durchtrennte mit zwei Schnitten den Nerv.* ♦ *Der Schnitt
dieses Sakkos gefällt mir nicht.*; *(of a hedge)* clip
2. (hair) cut ◊ *Deine Haare bräuchten dringend*

mal einen Schnitt. **3.** hairstyle ◊ *Sie wollte einen moderneren Schnitt.* ♦ *Du siehst so verändert aus. Hat dein Haar einen anderen Schnitt?* ⊖Haarschnitt, Frisur **4.** *(for a piece of clothing)* pattern ◊ *Sie kaufte einen Schnitt für ein Kleid.* **5.** *(of a flat, house)* layout ◊ *Größe und Schnitt der Wohnung waren perfekt.* **6.** *(of a film)* editing ◊ *Dieses Problem kann später beim Schnitt gelöst werden.* **7.** average ◊ *Wir fuhren einen Schnitt von 60 km/h.* ♦ *Beim Abitur erreichte sie einen Schnitt von 1,8.* im Schnitt on average ◊ *In diesem Land liegt der Verdienst im Schnitt bei 800 Euro.* ♦ *Die Kosten verringern sich im Schnitt um 50%.* ♦ *Die Sportler sind im Schnitt 23 Jahre alt.*
◉ *einen guten Schnitt machen* make a decent profit **seinen Schnitt machen** make a profit

Schnit·te ['ʃnɪtə] die <–, –n> *(regional)* **1.** *(of bread)* slice ◊ *Er griff in den Brotkorb und nahm sich zwei Schnitten.* ♦ *„Willst du noch Brot?"* — *„Ja, gib mir bitte noch eine Schnitte."* ⊖Scheibe **2.** ⊖*sandwich* ◊ *Ich mache dir eine Schnitte mit Salami.*

Schnitt·kä·se ['ʃnɪtkɛ:zə] der <–s, –> most sing sliced cheese, cheese slices ◊ *Sie kaufte 200 Gramm Schnittkäse.* ♦ *Das Brötchen war mit Schnittkäse belegt.*

Schnitt·lauch ['ʃnɪtlaox] der <–(e)s> no pl chives ◊ *Sie aß ein Butterbrot mit Schnittlauch.* ♦ *Er kaufte ein Bund Schnittlauch.*

Schnitt·stel·le ['ʃnɪtʃtɛlə] die <–, –n> **1.** IT interface ◊ *Über welche Schnittstellen kann ich auf andere Datenbanken zugreifen?* **2.** *(fig)* point of contact ◊ *Die Stadt ist eine historische Schnittstelle zwischen Ost und West.*

ⓩ **Schnit·zel** ['ʃnɪtsl̩] das <–s, –> **1.** schnitzel ◊ *Die Schnitzel klopfen, in Ei wenden und panieren.* ♦ *Sie bestellten (Wiener) Schnitzel mit Pommes.* **2.** scrap ◊ *Auf dem Boden lagen viele Schnitzel herum.*; *(of wood)* splinter

schnit·zen ['ʃnɪtsn̩] [tr+intr v] +haben carve ◊ *Er schnitzt Holzfiguren.* ♦ *Sie schnitzten ein Herz in den Baum. Sie kann gut schnitzen.* She's good at carving.

schnor·ren ['ʃnɔrən] [tr+intr v] +haben *(pej)* scrounge ◊ *Er schnorrt ständig bei anderen.* ♦ *Sie schnorrte eine Zigarette von ihm.*

schnüf·feln ['ʃnʏfl̩n] [intr v] +haben **1.** (an etw. [dat]) schnüffeln sniff ((at) sth) ◊ *Der Hund schnüffelte an meinem Bein.* **2.** *(pej)* (in etw. [dat]) schnüffeln snoop around (in sth) ◊ *Der Journalist schnüffelte in ihrem Privatleben.* ♦ *Was hast du in meinen Sachen zu schnüffeln?* [tr+intr v] +haben sniff (glue) ◊ *Klebstoff schnüffeln* ♦ *Wie viele Jugendliche schnüffeln?*

Schnul·ler ['ʃnʊlɐ] der <–s, –> dummy, pacifier ◊ *Sie steckte dem Baby einen Schnuller in den Mund.*

ⓩ **Schnup·fen** ['ʃnʊpfn̩] der <–s, –> most sing cold, chill ◊ *Sie hatte einen (leichten) Schnupfen.* ♦ *Er hat sich beim Bootsausflug einen Schnupfen geholt.* ♦ *Sie lag mit Husten und Schnupfen im Bett.*

schnup·pern ['ʃnʊpɐn] [intr v] +haben (an etw. [dat]) schnuppern sniff ((at) sth) ◊ *Er schnupperte kurz und sagte: „Rieche ich hier Kaffee?"* ♦ *Sie schnupperte an der Parfümflasche.*

Schnur [ʃnu:ɐ] die <–, Schnüre> **1.** piece of string, cord ◊ *Sie wickelte eine Schnur um das Päckchen.*

♦ *Sie fädelte die Perlen auf eine Schnur.* **2.** *(fam)* cable, lead, flex, cord ◊ *Vorsicht, dass du nicht über die Schnur stolperst.* ♦ *Die Schnur des Telefons ist verheddert.* ⊖Kabel

Schnür·sen·kel ['ʃny:ɐʦɛŋkl̩] der <–s, –> (shoe)lace ◊ *Sie band sich die Schnürsenkel zu.*

ⓩ **schob** [ʃo:p] *pret of* schieben

Schock [ʃɔk] der <–(e)s, –s> shock ◊ *Der Fahrer des Wagens erlitt einen leichten Schock.* ♦ *Er hatte sich von dem Schock noch nicht erholt.* ♦ *Die Nachricht war für sie ein Schock.* unter Schock stehen be in shock

scho·ckie·ren [ʃɔ'ki:rən] <schockiert, schockierte, hat schockiert> [tr+intr v] shock ◊ *Seine Bemerkung schockierte sie.* ♦ *Er war von diesem brutalen Verhalten schockiert. Der Film wollte schockieren.* The film was meant to shock people.

ⓩ **Scho·ko·la·de** [ʃoko'la:də] die <–, –n> **1.** chocolate ◊ *eine Tafel/ein Riegel Schokolade* ♦ *ein mit Schokolade überzogener Kuchen* **2.** *(as a drink)* (hot) chocolate ◊ *Sie schenkte dem Kind einen Becher Schokolade ein.* ♦ *heiße Schokolade mit Sahne* ⊖Kakao

ⓩ **schon¹** [ʃo:n] [adv] **1.** already ◊ *Ich kam spät und er war schon weg.* ♦ *Was? Es ist schon 23 Uhr?* ♦ *Die Party wurde schon zweimal verschoben.* ♦ *Ich warte schon seit Stunden.* ♦ *Schon mit 14 war sie ein Star.* Kaum war ich losgefahren, da hatte ich schon einen Unfall. No sooner had a driven off than I had an accident.; *(in questions)* yet ◊ *Bist du schon fertig?* ♦ *Hast du es schon erledigt?* ⊖bereits **2.** as early as ◊ *Er steht schon um vier Uhr auf.* ♦ *Wir hatten schon 1950 ein Auto.* ♦ *Mir ging es gestern schon schlecht.* ⊖bereits **3.** if only ◊ *Du solltest hier bleiben, schon weil es spät ist.* schon aus diesem Grund/diesen Gründen for this reason/these reasons alone **4.** *translation varies* In zwei Wochen fängt die Schule schon an. School starts in only two weeks. Eine Tablette genügt schon. Just one tablet is enough. Karten gibt es schon für 15 Euro. Tickets are available for as little as 15 euros. Das reicht schon, um dich zu ärgern? This is enough to make you angry? Schon beim Anblick von Blut wird ihm schlecht. The very sight of blood makes him feel ill.
◉ **schon immer** always ◊ *Das haben wir schon immer so gemacht.* **schon mal** before ◊ *Ich hab das schon mal gemacht.* *(in questions also)* ever ◊ *Warst du schon mal in Wales?* **schon oft** often, many times ◊ *Du hast dich schon so oft geirrt!* **schon wieder** yet again

ⓩ **schon²** [ʃo:n] [part] **1.** *translation varies (emph)* Du wirst schon noch sehen, dass ich Recht habe! You'll soon see that I'm right! Sogar sie war zufrieden und das heißt schon was. Even she was pleased, which is really saying something. „Du kannst das sicher nicht." — „Doch, kann ich schon!" "You can't do that." — "Oh yes I can!" Das ist schon ein ziemliches Pech. Now that is bad luck. **2.** *translation varies (fam) (used to express impatience or irritation)* Los, mach schon! Go on, get on with it! Jetzt hör schon auf! Stop that right now! Was ist denn nun schon wieder? What's wrong now? Was weißt du schon von Autos? What do you know about cars? Was hilft das schon? What good is that? **3.** *translation varies (used to*

give encouragement or reassurance) Ach, komm schon, sei wieder lieb. Come on, be nice again. Nun geh schon, ich komme gleich nach. You go ahead. I'll be right behind you. Keine Sorge, das wird schon klappen! Don't worry, it'll be fine. Ihm wird schon nichts passieren. He'll be fine. Schon gut, reg dich nicht auf. All right now, don't get upset. Na, das klingt doch schon besser! Now that sounds better! **4.** *translation varies (used to express (reluctant) agreement)* Das stimmt schon, ich dachte nur, ... Yes, that's quite right, but I just thought … Ja, ja, du hast schon Recht. Yes, yes, you're quite right. **5.** *not directly translated (used when one statement is qualified by another)* Lust auf Urlaub hätte sie schon, aber leider kein Geld. She'd very much like to go on holiday, but she hasn't got any money. Ihm gefiel es in Rom gar nicht, mir aber schon. He didn't like Rome at all, but I did. Kapern mag sie gar nicht, Oliven schon eher. She doesn't like capers at all, but she doesn't mind olives. **6.** wenn schon ..., dann ... if …, then … ◊ *Wenn ich schon mal in Italien bin, dann möchte ich auch nach Rom.*

② **schön**[1] [ʃøːn] [adj] **1.** beautiful, attractive ◊ *eine schöne Frau/Landschaft* ♦ *Ich finde seine Augen so schön.* sich schön machen dress up, make yourself up ⊖hübsch **2.** lovely, pleasant, nice ◊ *Sie hatte eine schöne Kindheit.* ♦ *Das Wetter soll morgen sehr schön werden.* ♦ *Schön, dass du kommen konntest.* ♦ *Das war nicht sehr schön von ihm!* **3.** *only before ns (in polite expressions)* Ich wünsche Ihnen noch einen schönen Tag/ein schönes Wochenende! Have a nice day/weekend! Richte ihr doch schöne Grüße aus. Send her my best wishes. Einen schönen Gruß an deine Mutter. Best wishes to your mother. **4.** *only before ns (fam) (considerable)* fair ◊ *Das ist ja eine schöne Summe/Stange Geld.* ♦ *Das wird noch ein schönes Stück Arbeit.* ⊖beträchtlich, hübsch **5.** *mostly before ns (iron)* nice ◊ *Du hast mir einen schönen Schrecken eingejagt.* ♦ *Das sind ja schöne Aussichten!* **6.** all right, okay ◊ *Schön, dann fangen wir an.* ♦ *Na schön, wenn du darauf bestehst.* [adv] **1.** beautifully ◊ *ein schön gestalteter Katalog* ♦ *Sie hat sehr schön gesungen.* ♦ *Das Wasser war schön sauber/klar/blau.; (with adj also)* nice and … ◊ *Der Test war schön einfach.* ♦ *Der Tee schmeckte schön süß.* **2.** very well ◊ *Die Mannschaft hat heute schön gespielt.* ♦ *Du kannst aber schön malen!* ⊖gut **3.** *(fam)* (ganz) schön really ◊ *Schön blöd, wenn du ihm das glaubst!* ♦ *50 Euro ist ganz schön teuer.* ♦ *Sie ist ganz schön schlau!* ⊖sehr **4.** *(iron)* Wie heißt es doch so schön? How does the saying go? wie man so schön sagt, wie es so schön heißt as the saying goes, as they say ⊛ bitte schön **1.** here you are/go, there you are/ go ◊ *„Kann ich mal das Salz haben?" — „Hier, bitte schön."* **2.** that's all right, don't mention it ◊ *„Vielen Dank!" — „Bitte schön, gern geschehen."* **3.** please ◊ *Wo geht es denn hier zum Bahnhof, bitte schön? (when you have not heard sth properly)* I beg your pardon, sorry ◊ *Bitte schön?* Ich habe Sie nicht verstanden. danke schön thank you very much, many thanks

② **schön**[2] [ʃøːn] [part] *reinforcing, not translated directly (fam)* Bleib schön sitzen! Sit still! Sei

schön brav! Be good! Immer schön der Reihe nach! One after another!

scho·nen [ˈʃoːnən] [tr v] +*haben* **1.** treat with care, protect ◊ *Er wollte die Schuhe ein bisschen schonen.* ♦ *Das Sofa muss geschont werden.* ⊖strapazieren **2.** spare, be/go easy on ◊ *jds Gefühle schonen* ♦ *Er wollte sie schonen und hat ihr daher seine Entlassung verschwiegen.* ♦ *Sie ist heiser und sollte ihre Stimme schonen.; (yourself, your heart, health etc.)* look after, take care of ◊ *Du musst dein schwaches Herz schonen.; (yourself also)* take it easy ◊ *Du solltest dich mehr schonen.* ⊖belasten

Schön·heit [ˈʃøːnhaɪt] die <–, –en> no pl beauty ◊ *Ihre Schönheit hat unter der Operation nicht gelitten.* ♦ *eine Landschaft von außergewöhnlicher/ atemberaubender Schönheit* ♦ *Sie war eine echte/ große Schönheit.* landschaftliche Schönheit (a) beautiful landscape

Scho·nung [ˈʃoːnʊŋ] die <–, –en> **1.** no pl preservation, protection ◊ *Zur Schonung der Grünflächen wurde der Park eingezäunt.* Seine Nerven bedurften der Schonung. He needed to spare his nerves. um Schonung bitten ask for mercy **2.** young plantation, fenced-in plantation ◊ *eine Schonung mit jungen Tannen*

schöp·fen [ˈʃœpfn̩] [tr v] +*haben* **1.** scoop ◊ *Er schöpfte sich mit den Händen Wasser ins Gesicht.; (soup also)* ladle ◊ *Sie schöpfte Suppe aus dem Topf in die Teller.; (water from a well)* draw ◊ *am Brunnen Wasser schöpfen* **2.** draw ◊ *Woher schöpft er all diese Kraft?* Hoffnung schöpfen gain hope Verdacht schöpfen become suspicious **3.** Atem schöpfen take a breath frische Luft schöpfen take a breath of fresh air

Schöp·fer [ˈʃœpfɐ] der <–s, –>, **Schöp·fe·rin** [ˈʃœpfərɪn] die <–, –nen> creator ◊ *Der Schöpfer dieses Begriffs war Karl Marx.* ♦ *die Schöpferin von Pippi Langstrumpf*

Schop·pen [ˈʃɔpn̩] der <–s, –> *(SouthG, Austr)* (250 ml) glass of wine ◊ *Sie bestellte einen Schoppen Wein.* ♦ *Wollen wir einen Schoppen trinken?*

schor [ʃoːɐ] *pret of* scheren

Schorf [ʃɔrf] der <–(e)s> no pl scab ◊ *Auf der Wunde hatte sich Schorf gebildet.* ♦ *Nach zwei Wochen fiel der Schorf ab.*

Schor·le [ˈʃɔrlə] die <–, –n> (saure) Schorle *wine or fruit juice with sparkling water* (süße) Schorle *wine or fruit juice with lemonade*

Schorn·stein [ˈʃɔrnʃtaɪn] der <–(e)s, –e> chimney ◊ *Aus dem Schornstein stieg Rauch auf.; (on a boat)* funnel ⊖Kamin

Schorn·stein·fe·ger [ˈʃɔrnʃtaɪnfeːgɐ] der <–s, –>, **Schorn·stein·fe·ge·rin** [ˈʃɔrnʃtaɪnfeːgərɪn] die <–, –nen> *(NorthG)* chimney sweep ◊ *Sie arbeitete als Schornsteinfegerin.* ♦ *Der Schornsteinfeger kommt zweimal im Jahr.*

schoss [ʃɔs] *pret of* schießen

Schoß [ʃoːs] der <–es, Schöße> **1.** lap ◊ *Sie nahm das Kind auf ihren Schoß.* ♦ *Sie setzte sich auf seinen Schoß.* ♦ *Sie hatte die Hände in ihrem Schoß gefaltet.* **2.** *(lofty, also fig)* womb ◊ *Sie trug ein Kind in ihrem Schoß.* ♦ *Er kehrte enttäuscht in den Schoß seiner Familie zurück.* ⊛ jdm in den Schoß fallen fall into sb's lap

Schot·te ['ʃɔtə] der <–n, –n>, **Schot·tin** ['ʃɔtɪn] die <–, –nen> Scot → **Deutsche**

schot·tisch ['ʃɔtɪʃ] [adj] *mostly before ns* Scottish, Scots ◊ *eine schottische Tradition* ♦ *Diese Musik ist typisch schottisch.*

Schott·land ['ʃɔtlant] das <–s> *article only in combination with attribute, no pl* Scotland → **Deutschland**

schräg [ʃrɛːk] [adj] **1.** sloping, slanting ◊ *Einige Wände in der Mansardenwohnung waren schräg.* ♦ *ein extrem schräges Dach; ((part of a) road)* steep ◊ *Die Einfahrt ist so schräg, dass man beim Parken die Handbremse ziehen muss.* **2.** unusual ◊ *Er ist echt ein schräger Typ.* ♦ *Seine Klamotten waren total schräg.* [adv] diagonally ◊ *Sie ging schräg über die Straße.* ♦ *Er schlug den Pfahl schräg in die Erde.* ♦ *Sie streckte ihren Arm schräg nach oben.* jdm/etw. schräg gegenüber diagonally across from sb/sth Das Bild hängt schräg. The picture isn't straight.

schrak [ʃraːk] *pret of* schrecken¹

Schram·me ['ʃramə] die <–, –n> scratch ◊ *Das Kind hatte eine blutige Schramme am Knie.* ♦ *Das Auto hatte nur eine Schramme am Kotflügel abbekommen.*

② **Schrank** [ʃraŋk] der <–(e)s, Schränke> cupboard ◊ *Holst du mal das Geschirr aus dem Schrank?*; wardrobe, closet ◊ *Sie verstaute ihre Kleidung im Schrank.*

Schran·ke ['ʃraŋkə] die <–, –n> **1.** limit, boundary ◊ *Deiner Kreativität sind keine Schranken gesetzt.* ♦ *kulturelle/soziale Schranken überwinden* jdn in seine/die Schranken (ver)weisen put sb in their place **2.** barrier ◊ *Die Schranke öffnete/schloss sich.* ♦ *Sie passierten die Schranke.* ♦ *ein Bahnübergang mit/ohne Schranke*

Schrau·be ['ʃraʊbə] die <–, –n> **1.** screw ◊ *Er befestigte das Brett mit Schrauben an der Wand.* ♦ *Du musst die Schraube fester anziehen!* ♦ *Die Schraube sitzt sehr fest.* **2.** SPORT twist ◊ *ein gestreckter Doppelsalto mit Schraube*
ⓔ **bei jdm ist eine Schraube locker** *(fam)* sb has got a screw loose

schrau·ben ['ʃraʊbm̩] [tr v] +*haben* **1.** screw ◊ *Sie schraubte ein Namensschild an die Tür.* ♦ *Sie schraubte die Glühbirne in die Lampe.* ♦ *Sie schraubte den Deckel wieder aufs Glas.* Sie schraubte den Klavierstuhl höher/niedriger. She raised/lowered the piano stool. **2.** *(fig)* seine Erwartungen zu hoch schrauben get your expectations up too high seine Preise in die Höhe schrauben raise your prices

Schrau·ben·zie·her ['ʃraʊbm̩tsiːɐ] der <–s, –> screwdriver

Schreck [ʃrɛk] der <–(e)s, –e> fright, shock ◊ *Vor Schreck ließ er das Glas fallen.* ♦ *Der Schreck steckte/saß ihr immer noch in den Gliedern.* ♦ *Sie bekam einen furchtbaren Schreck, als sie das sah.* ein freudiger Schreck a pleasant shock ⊝Schrecken
ⓔ **Schreck, lass nach** *(fam)* oh no ach du **Schreck** *(fam)* oh no

② **schre·cken**¹ ['ʃrɛkn̩] <schrickt, schreckte/schrak, ist geschreckt> [intr v] start ◊ *Sie schreckte aus dem Schlaf.* ♦ *Er schreckte aus dem Sessel.*

② **schre·cken**² ['ʃrɛkn̩] <schreckt, schreckte, hat geschreckt> [tr v] *(lofty)* scare, frighten ◊ *Die Gefahr schreckt mich nicht!* ♦ *Seine Drohungen können mich nicht schrecken.*

Schre·cken ['ʃrɛkŋ̩] der <–s, –> **1.** shock ◊ *Du hast mir einen richtigen Schrecken eingejagt!* ♦ *Die Entführer versetzten die Touristen in Angst und Schrecken.* ♦ *Er hatte mit Schrecken festgestellt, dass er kein Geld dabeihatte.* Schrecken erregend terrifying, horrifying **2.** horror ◊ *die Schrecken des Krieges* ♦ *Chemotherapie hat inzwischen viel von ihrem Schrecken verloren.* **3.** *(person)* terror ◊ *Das Kind war der Schrecken der Straße/des Internats.*

schreck·haft ['ʃrɛkhaft] [adj] <schreckhafter, am schreckhaftesten> nervous, easily frightened ◊ *Sie ist sehr schreckhaft.* ♦ *eine schreckhafte Katze*

② **schreck·lich** ['ʃrɛklɪç] [adj, adv] *(also fam, fig)* terrible(-ibly), awful(ly), dreadful(ly), horrible(-ibly) ◊ *schreckliche Angst/Schmerzen* ♦ *Was für ein schrecklicher Mensch!* ♦ *Das ist ja schrecklich!* ♦ *Er hat einen schrecklichen Geschmack.* ♦ *Sie ist schrecklich schüchtern/nett/dumm.* ♦ *Ich würde schrecklich gern mitkommen.* ♦ *sich schrecklich ärgern/freuen/schämen etc.* ♦ *Er hat sich auf der Party ganz schrecklich benommen.* ⊝furchtbar, entsetzlich

Schrei [ʃraɛ] der <–, –e> cry, yell, shout ◊ *Man konnte laute Schreie hören.* ♦ *Sie stieß einen empörten Schrei aus.* ♦ *Ein Schrei der Entrüstung ging durch die Menge.; (of horror, terror also)* scream ein stummer Schrei a silent cry
ⓔ **der letzte Schrei** the latest craze, the latest thing

② **schrei·ben** ['ʃraɛbm̩] <schreibt, schrieb, hat geschrieben> [tr+intr v] **1.** write ◊ *Sie schrieb ihre Telefonnummer auf einen Zettel.* ♦ *lesen und schreiben lernen* ♦ *Er schreibt sehr unleserlich/schön.* ♦ *In der Prüfung darf man nicht mit Bleistift schreiben.* ♦ *Er schreibt Gedichte.* ♦ *Der Roman war spannend geschrieben.* ♦ *Sie schreibt gerade an einem Buch.* ♦ *Er hat den Soundtrack geschrieben.* ♦ *Der Kuli schreibt nicht mehr.; (words also)* spell ◊ *Wie schreibt man Ihren Namen?* etw. falsch schreiben misspell sth **2.** (jdm) (etw.) schreiben write (to sb) (about sth), write (sb) (about sth) ◊ *Hat er schon geschrieben?* ♦ *Sie schreibt ihm regelmäßig.* ♦ *Von ihrer Verlobung hat sie (mir) nichts geschrieben.* ♦ *In dem Brief schreibt er, dass es ihm gut geht.* Schreibst du mir aus dem Urlaub eine Karte? Are you going to send me a postcard when you're on holiday? [ref v] sich irgendwie schreiben be spelt in a certain way ◊ *Wie schreibt sich Ihr Name?* ♦ *Sie schreibt sich mit „y", nicht mit „i".*

② **Schrei·ben** ['ʃraɛbm̩] das <–s, –> **1.** letter, communication ◊ *Er verfasste ein Schreiben an das Finanzamt.* ♦ *An wen war das Schreiben gerichtet/adressiert?* ♦ *Betreff: Ihr Schreiben vom 03.05.* **2.** *no pl* writing, composition ◊ *Das Schreiben des Briefes nahm über eine Stunde in Anspruch.*

② **Schreib·tisch** ['ʃraɛptɪʃ] der <–(e)s, –e> desk ◊ *Sie setzte sich an den Schreibtisch.* ♦ *Die Akten befinden sich auf seinem Schreibtisch.*

② **schrei·en** ['ʃraɛən] <schreit, schrie, hat geschrien> [tr+intr v] **1.** cry, yell, shout ◊ *Ich habe ein Kind schreien hören.* ♦ *Sie schrie vor Schmerzen.* ♦

A B C D E F G H I J K L M N O P Q R S T U V W X Y Z

„Ruhe!", schrie sie. ♦ Er schrie ihren Namen.; *(in horror, terror also)* scream **2.** um Hilfe schreien cry for help nach jdm/etw. schreien cry out for sb/sth

Schrei·ner ['ʃraɛnɐ] der <-s, ->, **Schrei·ne·rin** ['ʃraɛnərɪn] die <-, -nen> carpenter ◊ *Er ist ein guter Schreiner.* ♦ *Von Beruf war sie Schreinerin.*; *(maker of window frames and doors)* joiner ⊜Tischler

schrei·ten ['ʃraɛtn̩] <schreitet, schritt, ist geschritten> [intr v] *(lofty)* **1.** step, walk ◊ *Er schritt durchs Eingangstor.* ♦ *Sie schritt ans Fenster und blickte hinaus.* **2.** *(fig)* zu etw. schreiten get down to sth, get on with sth Schreiten wir zur Tat/ans Werk! Let's get on with it! zur Abstimmung/Wahl schreiten proceed to a vote

schrickt [ʃrɪkt] *pres of* schrecken[1]

② **schrie** [ʃriː] *pret of* schreien

② **schrieb** [ʃriːp] *pret of* schreiben

② **Schrift** [ʃrɪft] die <-, -en> **1.** script ◊ *Die Schilder waren in lateinischer Schrift.* die kyrillische/griechische Schrift the Cyrillic/Greek alphabet **2.** lettering, letters, writing ◊ *Das Auto hatte ein gelbes Nummernschild mit schwarzer Schrift.* ♦ *Die Schrift auf der Tafel war kaum mehr zu lesen.* ♦ *Die Schrift war ganz verblasst.* **3.** typeface ◊ *Er wählte eine größere Schrift.* gothische Schrift Gothic script **4.** (hand)writing ◊ *Ich kann seine Schrift nicht lesen/entziffern.* ♦ *Ihre Schrift war vollkommen unleserlich.* ⊜Handschrift **5.** *(text)* work, writing ◊ *eine Schrift Platons* ♦ *Der Band enthält Kants gesammelte Schriften.* ⊜Abhandlung

⊛ die Heilige Schrift the Holy Scriptures ⊜die Bibel

② **schrift·lich** ['ʃrɪftlɪç] [adj] no comp/superl; mostly before vb written ◊ *Der Minister gab eine schriftliche Erklärung ab.* ♦ *Sie musste drei schriftliche Prüfungen ablegen.* ⊜mündlich [adv] in writing ◊ *Sie wurde schriftlich benachrichtigt/dazu aufgefordert.* ♦ *Die Beschlüsse der Sitzung wurden schriftlich fixiert.* jdm etw. schriftlich geben give sb sth in writing etw. schriftlich haben have (got) sth in writing ◊ *Ich hätte das gern schriftlich von Ihnen.* ⊜mündlich

Schrift·stel·ler ['ʃrɪftʃtɛlɐ] der <-s, ->, **Schrift·stel·le·rin** ['ʃrɪftʃtɛlərɪn] die <-, -nen> writer ◊ *eine bekannte Schriftstellerin* ♦ *Er lebt heute als freier Schriftsteller in Berlin.* ⊜Autor

schritt [ʃrɪt] *pret of* schreiten

② **Schritt** [ʃrɪt] der <-(e)s, -e> **1.** *(also fig)* step ◊ *Würden Sie bitte einen Schritt/ein paar Schritte zurücktreten?* ♦ *Das war ein sehr mutiger Schritt von dir.* ♦ *Deine Entschuldigung war ein Schritt in die richtige Richtung.* ♦ *Sie hat mit juristischen Schritten gedroht.; (larger)* stride ◊ *Mit wenigen Schritten war er am Telefon.* seine Schritte/seinen Schritt beschleunigen walk faster, speed up Ich habe heute noch keinen Schritt vor die Tür getan. I haven't been out of the house yet today. **2.** at (a) walking pace ◊ *In der Fußgängerzone darf man nur Schritt fahren.* ♦ *ein Pferd im Schritt gehen lassen* **3.** crotch, crutch ◊ *Diese Hose spannt/ zwickt im Schritt.* ♦ *Er kratzte sich am/im Schritt.* ⊛ auf Schritt und Tritt everywhere, all over the place ◊ *Er verfolgte sie auf Schritt und Tritt.* mit etw./jdm Schritt halten keep up with sth/sb ◊

Die Firma musste mit der Konkurrenz Schritt halten. ♦ *Ich konnte mit ihm nicht Schritt halten. Er ging viel zu schnell.* Schritt für Schritt step by step

Schrott [ʃrɔt] der <-(e)s> *no pl* **1.** scrap metal ◊ *Der Schrott wird auf dem Schrottplatz sortiert.* **2.** *(fam, pej)* rubbish, crap ◊ *Im Fernsehen kommt unglaublich viel Schrott.* ♦ *Das ist doch Schrott, was er da erzählt!* ⊜Müll, Quatsch

⊛ etw. zu Schrott fahren write sth off

schrub·ben ['ʃrʊbm̩] [tr v] +haben **1.** scrub ◊ *sich* [dat] *die Fingernägel schrubben* **2.** etw. von etw. schrubben rub sth off sth, scrub sth off sth ◊ *Sie schrubbten die Farbspritzer von den Fliesen.* ⊜scheuern

Schrub·ber ['ʃrʊbɐ] der <-s, -> scrubbing brush ◊ *Er holte Schrubber und Eimer.*

Schub·la·de ['ʃuːplaːdə] die <-, -n> drawer ◊ *eine Kommode mit drei Schubladen* ♦ *Sie holte Unterwäsche aus der Schublade.*

schub·sen ['ʃʊpsn̩] [tr v] +haben push, shove ◊ *Er hat ihn vom Stuhl geschubst.* ♦ *Sie schubste ihn zur Tür.* ♦ *Die Fans drängelten und schubsten.*

schüch·tern ['ʃʏçtɐn] [adj, adv] shy(ly) ◊ *Er ist sehr schüchtern.* ♦ *Er warf ihr einen schüchternen Blick zu.* ♦ *Sie lächelte schüchtern.*

② **schuf** [ʃuːf] *pret of* schaffen

schuf·ten ['ʃʊftn̩] <schuftet, schuftete, hat geschuftet> [intr v] +haben work hard, labour, labor ◊ *Sie schuftet Tag und Nacht, doch das Geld reicht nie.* ♦ *Selbst Kinder mussten damals in Bergwerken schuften.*

② **Schuh** [ʃuː] der <-(e)s, -e> shoe ◊ *Sie fand ihren rechten/linken Schuh nicht.* ♦ *Sie kaufte ein neues Paar Schuhe.* ♦ *hochhackige/bequeme/feste Schuhe* ♦ *Er zog seine Schuhe aus.*

⊛ jdm etw. in die Schuhe schieben blame sb for sth, lay the blame for sth on sb

Schuh·ma·cher ['ʃuːmaxɐ] der <-s, ->, **Schuh·ma·che·rin** ['ʃuːmaxərɪn] die <-, -nen> shoemaker ◊ *Herr Franz ist Schuhmacher.* ♦ *Hat die Schuhmacherin die Stiefel bald fertig?*

② **Schul·ar·beit** ['ʃuːlʔarbaɛt] die <-, -en> **1.** homework ◊ *Heute habe ich nur in Englisch eine Schularbeit auf.* ♦ *Hast du deine Schularbeiten schon gemacht?* **2.** *(Austr)* test ◊ *Unsere Französischlehrerin hat für morgen eine Schularbeit angesagt.*

Schul·buch ['ʃuːlbuːx] das <-(e)s, Schulbücher> textbook

② **Schuld** [ʃʊlt] die <-, -en> **1.** *no pl* jdm die Schuld geben blame sb etw. ist/liegt jds Schuld sth is (not) sb's fault Schuld an etw. [dat] haben be responsible/to blame for sth die Schuld auf sich [acc] nehmen take the blame die Schuld auf jdn schieben put the blame on sb **2.** *no pl* guilt ◊ *Sie kommt mit dieser Schuld nicht zurecht.* sich [dat] keiner Schuld bewusst sein not be aware of any wrongdoing (on your part) jds Schuld beweisen prove sb guilty **3.** *only pl* FIN Schulden debt(s) ◊ *Wir mussten Schulden machen, um das Auto zu kaufen.*

⊛ tief in jds Schuld stehen be greatly indebted to sb

schul·den ['ʃʊldn̩] <schuldet, schuldete, hat geschuldet> [tr v] +haben owe ◊ *Du schuldest mir*

noch Geld. ♦ *Du schuldest mir noch eine Antwort auf meine Frage.*

② **schul·dig** ['ʃʊldɪç] adj *no comp/superl* **1.** guilty *sich einer Sache* gen *schuldig machen* be guilty of sth *jdn (einer Sache* gen*) schuldig sprechen/befinden* find sb guilty (of sth) ◊ *Sie wurde des Mordes schuldig befunden.* ⊕unschuldig **2.** schuldig (an etw. dat) responsible (for sth) *sich schuldig fühlen/vorkommen* feel guilty **3.** jdm etw. schuldig sein/bleiben owe sb sth ◊ *Ich bin ihr noch 15 Euro schuldig.* ♦ *Ich bin dir doch keine Rechenschaft schuldig.* ♦ *Er ist mir die Antwort schuldig geblieben.*

Schuld·ner ['ʃʊldnɐ] der <-s, ->, **Schuld·ne·rin** ['ʃʊldnərɪn] die <-, -nen> debtor ◊ *säumige Schuldner mahnen*

② **Schu·le** ['ʃuːlə] die <-, -n> school ◊ *in die Schule/ zur Schule gehen* ♦ *In Deutschland kommt man mit sechs in die Schule.* ♦ *Nicht für die Schule, fürs Leben lernen wir.* ♦ *Wann fängt bei euch morgens die Schule an?* ♦ *die verschiedenen Schulen der Philosophie*
  ⊚ *der alten Schule* (of the) old school ◊ *ein Kavalier der alten Schule* *Schule machen* become common practice

schu·len ['ʃuːlən] tr v +*haben* **1.** train ◊ *Man sagt, Latein schult das logische Denken.* ♦ *sein Gedächtnis schulen* **2.** school, train ◊ *Wir werden in der Anwendung des neuen Programms geschult.*

② **Schü·ler** ['ʃyːlɐ] der <-s, ->, **Schü·le·rin** ['ʃyːlərɪn] die <-, -nen> **1.** school pupil, student ◊ *eine gute/schlechte Schülerin*; *(masc)* Schüler schoolboy Schülerin schoolgirl **2.** *(of a school of thought)* pupil ◊ *eine bekannte Schülerin des Psychoanalytikers Freud*

Schü·ler·aus·weis ['ʃyːlɐ|aosvaes] der <-es, -e> school identity card, student card ◊ *Ermäßigung gibt es nur bei Vorlage des Schülerausweises.*

Schul·fe·ri·en ['ʃuːlfeːrjən] die <-> *only pl* school holidays

> The dates for school holidays are different in every *Bundesland* and change each year. The best way to find out is by searching for *Schulferien in Deutschland* on the Internet. There are several web pages with up-to-date information on this topic.

Schul·jahr ['ʃuːljaːɐ] das <-(e)s, -e> (school) year ◊ *Bernd kommt jetzt ins neunte Schuljahr.* ♦ *Was steht für dieses Schuljahr auf dem Lehrplan?*

Schul·sys·tem ['ʃuːlzʏsteːm] das <-s, -e> school system

Schul·ter ['ʃʊltɐ] die <-, -n> shoulder ◊ *Er hat breite Schultern.* ♦ *Sie trug ihren Sohn auf den Schultern.* ♦ *Er klopfte mir auf die Schulter.* ♦ *Wattierte Schultern sind wieder außer Mode gekommen.*
  ⊚ *jdm die kalte Schulter zeigen* give sb the cold shoulder *etw. auf die leichte Schulter nehmen* make light of sth *mit den Schultern zucken* shrug your shoulders *Schulter an Schulter* shoulder to shoulder

Schu·lung ['ʃuːlʊŋ] die <-, -en> **1.** training course ◊ *Alle Mitarbeiter müssen an dieser Schulung teilnehmen.* **2.** training ◊ *Zur Schulung des Gehörs hört sie sich Tonleitern an.*

Schup·pe ['ʃʊpə] die <-, -n> **1.** scale ◊ *Schleierfische haben rote Schuppen.* **2.** *only pl* Schuppen dandruff ◊ *ein Shampoo gegen Schuppen*

Schup·pen ['ʃʊpn̩] der <-s, -> shed ◊ *Die Gartengeräte sind draußen im Schuppen.*

Schür·ze ['ʃʏʁtsə] die <-, -n> apron ◊ *Er trägt beim Kochen immer eine Schürze.* ♦ *Der Fleischer band sich die Schürze um.*

② **Schuss** [ʃʊs] der <-es, Schüsse> shot ◊ *Der Jäger erlegte das Reh mit einem gezielten Schuss.* ♦ *Der Schuss verfehlte das Tor.*

Schüs·sel ['ʃʏsl̩] die <-, -n> **1.** bowl, dish ◊ *Welche Schüssel soll ich für die Nudeln nehmen?* **2.** dish ◊ *In unserem Viertel ist auf fast jedem Dach eine Schüssel.*

Schutt [ʃʊt] der <-(e)s> *no pl* rubble Schutt abladen verboten no tipping
  ⊚ *in Schutt und Asche* in ruins

schüt·teln ['ʃʏtl̩n] tr v +*haben* shake ◊ *Er schüttelte den Bewusstlosen.* ♦ *Du musst die Flasche vor Gebrauch schütteln.* ♦ *Sie schüttelte den Kopf, um mir zu bedeuten, dass sie das nicht wollte.* *jdm die Hand schütteln* shake sb's hand *etw. von etw. schütteln* shake sth off sth ◊ *Er schüttelte den Schnee von seinem Mantel.* *sich schütteln* shake yourself ◊ *Als der Hund aus dem Wasser kam, schüttelte er sich.* *sich vor Lachen schütteln* shake with laughter *sich vor Ekel schütteln* shudder in disgust *mit dem Kopf schütteln* shake your head

schüt·ten ['ʃʏtn̩] <schüttet, schüttete, hat geschüttet> tr v pour ◊ *Er hat den Kaffee auf die Tischdecke geschüttet.* ♦ *Schütte den Zucker in diese Dose.* imp v *(fam)* es schüttet it's pouring

② **Schutz** [ʃʊts] der <-es> *no pl* protection ◊ *eine Sonnencreme zum Schutz gegen Sonnenbrand* ♦ *Die Wand dient als Schutz gegen Lärm.* ♦ *Kein Land wollte ihnen Schutz gewähren.*; shelter, cover ◊ *Als es anfing zu regnen, haben wir Schutz in einer Hütte gesucht.*
  ⊚ *jdn in Schutz nehmen* come to sb's defence

Schüt·ze[1] ['ʃʏtsə] der <-n, -n> **1.** *no pl* ASTROL, ASTRON Sagittarius **2.** ASTROL *(person)* Sagittarian, Sagittarius **3.** MIL private ◊ *Der Schütze wurde zum Gefreiten befördert.*

Schüt·ze[2] ['ʃʏtsə] der <-n, -n>, **Schüt·zin** ['ʃʏtsɪn] die <-, -nen> **1.** marksman ◊ *Rund um das Gebäude waren Schützen postiert.* Schützin markswoman *jd ist ein guter Schütze* sb is a good shot **2.** gunman Schützin gunwoman **3.** archer Schützin archeress **4.** goal scorer **5.** *member of one of the many traditional rifle clubs ('Schützenvereine')* in Germany

② **schüt·zen** ['ʃʏtsn̩] tr v +*haben* protect ◊ *Tierarten, die vom Aussterben bedroht sind, werden geschützt.* ♦ *Der Text ist urheberrechtlich geschützt.* (jdn/etw./sich) (vor jdm/etw./gegen jdn/etw.) schützen protect (sb/sth/yourself) (from/ against sb/sth) ◊ *Die Creme schützt (die Haut) vor Sonnenbrand.* ♦ *Das Material ist gegen Nässe schützen!* ♦ *Die Armee schützt uns vor feindlichen Angriffen.* ♦ *Er schützte sie mit seinem Körper.*

② **schwach** [ʃvax] adj <schwächer, am schwächsten> **1.** weak ◊ *Der Patient ist noch sehr schwach.* ♦ *ein schwaches Herz ◊ Das Auto hat einen schwachen Motor.* ♦ *Sie ist zu schwach, um gegen die Sucht anzukämpfen.* ♦ *Er hat einen schwachen*

Willen. ♦ *ein schwacher Charakter;* frail ◊ *Sie wird älter und schwächer.* sich schwach fühlen feel faint schwache Augen poor eyesight schwache Nerven bad nerves schwach werden give in, waver **2.** *(drink)* weak ◊ *schwacher Kaffee; (in chemistry)* dilute ◊ *eine schwache Säure* [adj, adv] **1.** faint(ly) ◊ *schwacher Beifall* ♦ *eine schwache Hoffnung* ♦ *ein schwacher Duft von Lavendel* ♦ *Es regte sich schwacher Widerspruch.* ♦ *Der Wind wehte schwach.*; poor(ly) ◊ *eine schwache Wahlbeteiligung* ♦ *Frauen sind in diesem Beruf sehr schwach vertreten.* schwach besiedelt sparsely populated etw. ist ein schwacher Trost sth is not much consolation **2.** *(achievement, performance etc.)* poor(ly), bad(ly) ◊ *schwache schulische Leistungen* ♦ *In Mathematik war ich schon immer schwach.* ♦ *Der Sopran hat schwach gesungen.* ⊜schlecht **3.** GRAM weak ◊ *schwache Verben* ein Wort wird schwach konjugiert/dekliniert a word is weak ⊜stark

Schwä·che ['ʃvɛçə] die <−, −n> **1.** *no pl* weakness, faintness ◊ *die Schwäche des Patienten* ♦ *Sie konnte sich vor Schwäche kaum mehr auf den Beinen halten.* **2.** weakness ◊ *die Schwäche seines Herzens* ♦ *Ich kenne seine Schwäche.* ♦ *Ja, ich gebe zu, das ist meine persönliche Schwäche.* die zunehmende Schwäche ihrer Augen her increasingly poor eyesight ⊜Stärke **3.** lack of ability ◊ *Sie hat ausgesprochene Schwächen in den Naturwissenschaften.* **4.** flaw, weak point ◊ *Abgesehen von ein paar Schwächen war der Film ganz unterhaltsam.* ♦ *Ich habe in der Übersetzung einige Schwächen bemerkt.*

⊛ **eine Schwäche für jdn/etw. haben** have a soft spot for sb/sth ⊜eine Vorliebe für jdn/etw. haben

Schwach·sinn ['ʃvaxzɪn] der <−s> *no pl* **1.** mental deficiency ◊ *Bei einem IQ von 50 spricht man von Schwachsinn.* **2.** *(fam, pej)* rubbish, nonsense ◊ *Er hat nur Schwachsinn erzählt.*

Schwa·ger ['ʃva:gɐ] der <−s, Schwäger> brother-in-law

Schwä·ge·rin ['ʃvɛːgərɪn] die <−, −nen> sister-in-law

② **schwamm** [ʃvam] *pret of* schwimmen

Schwamm [ʃvam] der <−(e)s, Schwämme> sponge ◊ *Sie wischte die Tafel mit einem nassen Schwamm.* ♦ *sich mit einem Schwamm einseifen*

② **Schwam·merl** ['ʃvamɐl] das <−s, −(n)> *(SouthG, Austr)* mushroom

Schwan [ʃva:n] der <−(e)s, Schwäne> swan

schwang [ʃvaŋ] *pret of* schwingen

② **schwan·ger** ['ʃvaŋɐ] [adj] *no comp/superl* pregnant ◊ *Mach der schwangeren Frau mal Platz.* ♦ *Sie ist schwanger geworden.* im fünften Monat schwanger sein be in your fifth month (of pregnancy)

Schwan·ger·schaft ['ʃvaŋɐʃaft] die <−, −en> pregnancy

schwan·ken ['ʃvaŋkn̩] [intr v] +haben/sein **1.** +*haben* sway ◊ *Der Bambus schwankte im Wind.* ♦ *Die Brücke schwankte unter der Last des schweren Fahrzeugs.* ♦ *Du bist ja betrunken, du merkst ja gar nicht, dass du schwankst.*; *(ship, boat)* rock ◊ *Je mehr das Schiff schwankte, desto übler wurde mir.* **2.** +*sein* stagger, totter ◊ *Der Betrunkene ist nach Hause geschwankt.* **3.** +*haben*

fluctuate, vary ◊ *Die Preise schwanken zwischen 10 und 15 Euro.* ♦ *Im Herbst schwanken die Temperaturen zwischen 5 und 15 Grad.*; *(mood)* change **4.** +*haben* be undecided ◊ *Ich schwanke noch zwischen Urlaub in Indien und Urlaub in China.*

Schwanz [ʃvants] der <−es, Schwänze> **1.** tail; *(dog)* mit dem Schwanz wedeln wag its tail **2.** *(rude)* dick, cock

Schwarm [ʃvaʳm] der <−(e)s, Schwärme> **1.** swarm ◊ *ein Schwarm Bienen* ♦ *Im Sommer kommen Schwärme von Japanern nach Heidelberg.*; *(of birds also)* flock; *(of fish)* shoal **2.** heart-throb jd ist jds Schwarm sb has a crush on sb ◊ *Unser Mathelehrer ist Inas Schwarm.*

schwär·men ['ʃvɛʳmən] [intr v] +haben/sein **1.** +*sein* swarm ◊ *Am Samstag schwärmen die Menschen in die Stadt, um einzukaufen.* ♦ *Bienen schwärmten um die Blüten.* **2.** +*haben* (von etw./ jdm) schwärmen rave (about sth/sb), enthuse (about sth/sb) ◊ *Sie schwärmt bei jeder Gelegenheit von ihrem Urlaub auf Hawaii.* **3.** +*haben* für jdn schwärmen have a crush on sb ◊ *Tanja schwärmt für unseren Deutschlehrer.*

schwarz [ʃvaʳts] [adj] <schwärzer, am schwärzesten> black ◊ *Er hat schwarze Haare.* ♦ *Deine Fingernägel sind ja ganz schwarz.* ♦ *die schwarze Bevölkerung der USA* ♦ *Das war der schwärzeste Tag in meinem Leben.* ♦ *schwarzer Humor* ♦ *Sie hat ihr Zimmer schwarz gestrichen.* ♦ *Sie hat schwarz gefärbte Haare.* schwarz gekleidet/möbliert sein be dressed/furnished in black [adj, adv] *when used as an adj, only before ns* illegal(ly), illicit(ly) ◊ *Das Geld hat er mit schwarzen Geschäften verdient.* ♦ *Das Geld hat er schwarz verdient.* der schwarze Markt the black market

⊛ **schwarz auf weiß** in writing ◊ *Das kann ich dir schwarz auf weiß geben.* **schwarz in schwarz** gloomily ◊ *Sie sieht alles schwarz in schwarz.* **schwarz malen** paint a gloomy picture *(für etw.)* **schwarz sehen** be pessimistic *(about sth)* etw. **schwarz trinken** drink sth black ◊ *den Kaffee/Tee schwarz trinken*

Schwarz [ʃvaʳts] das <−(e)s, −> *most sing* black

Schwarz·ar·beit ['ʃvaʳtsˌaʳbaɛt] die <−> *no pl* illicit work, moonlighting

Schwarz·brot ['ʃvaʳtsbro:t] das <−(e)s, −e> whole grain rye bread

schwarz|fah·ren ['ʃvaʳtsfa:rən] <fährt schwarz, fuhr schwarz, ist schwarzgefahren> [intr v] dodge fares/the fare ◊ *Wer schwarzfährt, muss mit einer Geldstrafe rechnen.*

Schwarz·wald ['ʃvaʳtsvalt] der <−(e)s> *no pl (always* der Schwarzwald*)* Black Forest

schwe·ben ['ʃveːbm̩] [intr v] +haben/sein **1.** +*sein* glide ◊ *Das Flugzeug schwebte langsam zu Boden.* ♦ *Die Tänzer schwebten über die Tanzfläche.*; float ◊ *Seifenblasen schwebten durch die Luft.* **2.** +*haben (bird)* hover ◊ *Hoch oben schwebte ein Adler.*; *(balloon, cloud)* hang ◊ *Am Himmel schwebten Ballons.*

Schwe·de ['ʃveːdə] der <−n, −n>, **Schwe·din** ['ʃveːdɪn] die <−, −nen> Swede → Deutsche

Schwe·den ['ʃveːdn̩] das <−s> *article only in combination with attribute, no pl* Sweden → Deutschland

Schwe·din [ˈʃveːdɪn] *fem of* Schwede
schwe·disch [ˈʃveːdɪʃ] [adj] *mostly before ns*
Swedish → deutsch
Schwe·disch [ˈʃveːdɪʃ] das <-(s)> *no pl* Swedish
→ Deutsch
② **schwei·gen** [ˈʃvaɛgn̩] <schweigt, schwieg, hat
geschwiegen> [intr v] be/remain silent, say nothing,
keep quiet ◊ *Wenn ich nichts zu sagen haben,
dann schweige ich.* zu etw. schweigen say nothing
in reply to sth ◊ *Er schwieg zu den Vorwürfen.*
Schweig! Be quiet! Kannst du schweigen? Can you
keep a secret?
schweig·sam [ˈʃvaɛkzaːm] [adj] quiet, taciturn ◊ *Er
ist ein schweigsamer Mensch.* ◆ *Du bist ja heute
so schweigsam.* ⊖gesprächig
Schwein [ʃvaen] das <-(e)s, -e> 1. pig ◊ *Er
züchtet Schweine.* 2. pork ◊ *Magst du lieber Rind
oder Schwein?* 3. *(fam)* (dirty) pig ◊ *Er frisst wie
ein Schwein.* 4. *(fam)* bastard, swine ◊ *Und dann
hat das Schwein sie einfach sitzen lassen.*
⊛ Schwein haben *(fam)* be lucky
Schweiß [ʃvaes] der <-es> *no pl* sweat ◊ *Er war
in Schweiß gebadet.* ◆ *Mir lief der Schweiß
herunter.*
Schweiz [ʃvaets] die <-> *no pl (always* die
Schweiz*)* Switzerland ◊ *Er wohnt in der Schweiz.*
box@ Land
Schwei·zer¹ [ˈʃvaetse] [adj] *invariable, only before
ns* Swiss ◊ *Urlaub in den Schweizer Bergen* ◆
Schweizer Käse
Schwei·zer² [ˈʃvaetse] der <-s, ->,
Schwei·ze·rin [ˈʃvaetsərɪn] die <-, -nen> Swiss →
Deutsche
schwei·zer·deutsch [ˈʃvaetsedɔɛ̯tʃ] [adj] *mostly
before ns* Swiss German → deutsch
Schwei·zer·deutsch [ˈʃvaetsedɔɛ̯tʃ] das <-(s)> *no
pl* Swiss German → Deutsch
Schwei·ze·rin [ˈʃvaetsərɪn] *fem of* Schweizer
② **schwei·ze·risch** [ˈʃvaetsərɪʃ] [adj] *mostly before ns*
Swiss ◊ *das schweizerische Parlament* ◆ *Dieses
Käsegericht gilt als typisch schweizerisch.*
Schwel·le [ˈʃvɛlə] die <-, -n> 1. threshold ◊ *Er
trug seine Braut über die Schwelle.* 2. *(railroad)*
sleeper ◊ *Die Schienen sind auf den Schwellen
befestigt.*
schwel·le [ˈʃvɛlən] <schwillt, schwoll, ist
geschwollen> [intr v] swell (up) ◊ *In der Hitze
schwellen die Beine.* zu etw. schwellen swell to sth
◊ *Nach dem Regen schwillt der Bach zu einem
Strom. Der Sturm schwoll zum Orkan.* The storm
rose to a hurricane.
Schwel·lung [ˈʃvɛlʊŋ] die <-, -en> swelling ◊ *Der
Insektenstich führte zu einer schmerzhaften Schwellung.* ◆ *eine Salbe für Schwellungen*
schwen·ken [ˈʃvɛŋkn̩] [tr v] +*haben* 1. *(a flag
etc.)* wave ◊ *Die Kinder schwenkten Fähnchen zur
Begrüßung des Präsidenten.* 2. swing, swivel ◊ *eine
Lampe, die man schwenken kann; (a camera)* pan
② **schwer** [ʃveːɐ̯] [adj] 1. *(also fig)* heavy ◊ *Mein
Koffer ist schwer.* ◆ *Das ist ein schwerer Wein.* ◆
schwere Speisen ◆ *schwere Literatur* ⊖leicht 2. ...
schwer sein weigh ... ◊ *Der Koffer ist 15 Kilo
schwer.* ◆ *Wie schwer bist du?* ◆ *Du bist zu schwer
für diesen Stuhl.* ◊ *ein 20 Gramm schwerer Brief*
3. *mostly before ns* severe, heavy ◊ *Wir haben
schwere Verluste gemacht.* ◆ *ein schweres Gewitter*

◆ *schwere Schneefälle* ⊖stark 4. *only before ns
(mistake, crime, disease, injury, accident)*
serious, grave ◊ *ein schwerer Fehler/Vorwurf* ◆ *ein
schweres Verbrechen* eine schwere Erkältung a bad
cold ⊖ernst 5. hard, difficult ◊ *Diese Aufgabe ist
zu schwer.* ◆ *Sie hat ein schweres Leben.* ⊖schwie-
rig 6. hard, physically demanding ◊ *Gartenarbeit
ist schwere Arbeit.* ◆ *Seine Arbeit ist sehr schwer.*
[adv] 1. *(also fig)* heavily ◊ *ein schwer beladenes
Auto* ◆ schwer bewaffnet schwer zu tragen haben
have a heavy load to carry schwer auf jdm/etw.
lasten weigh heavily on sb/sth ⊖leicht 2. really ◊
*Unser Chef ist schwer in Ordnung.; (disappointed,
hurt, impressed also)* deeply ◊ *Du hast mich
schwer enttäuscht.* jdm schwer zu schaffen
machen cause sb a lot of trouble ⊖wirklich, sehr
3. *(ill, injured)* seriously ◊ *Er ist schwer verletzt/
krank.* schwer erkältet sein have a bad cold
⊖ernsthaft 4. schwer hören be hard of hearing
schwer verdaulich hard to digest etw. ist schwer
zu verstehen sth is hard/difficult to understand bei
etw. schwer nein sagen können find it hard to
resist sth, find it difficult to say no to sth ein
schwer erziehbares Kind a difficult child ein
schwer verträgliches Medikament a drug with
severe side effects
⊛ schwer geladen haben 1. be heavily loaded
2. *(fam, bum)* be plastered *(UK also)* be pissed
etw. fällt jdm schwer sb finds sth difficult sich
schwer hüten, etw. zu tun take good care not to
do sth sich schwer täuschen be very much
mistaken
Schwer·be·hin·der·te [ˈʃveːɐ̯gbahɪndetɐ] der/die
<-n, die Schwerbehinderten> *but: ein Schwerbehind-
erter/eine Schwerbehinderte* severely disabled
person; *(pl)* Schwerbehinderte the severely
disabled
schwer·hö·rig [ˈʃveːɐ̯høːrɪç] [adj] *no comp/superl*
hard of hearing ◊ *Meine Sekretärin ist schwerhörig.*
schwerhörige Menschen the hard of hearing
Schwer·kraft [ˈʃveːɐ̯kraft] die <-> *no pl* gravity
Schwer·punkt [ˈʃveːɐ̯pʊŋkt] der <-(e)s, -e> focus,
emphasis ◊ *Ich bestimme jeden Tag den Schwerpunkt meiner Arbeit neu.* ◆ *Die Schwerpunkte in
der Schule haben sich verlagert.* den Schwerpunkt
auf etw. [acc] legen focus on sth
Schwert [ʃveːɐ̯t] das <-(e)s, -er> sword ◊ *mit
dem Schwert kämpfen* ◊ *das Schwert ziehen*
⊛ ein zweischneidiges Schwert a mixed
blessing
② **Schwes·ter** [ˈʃvɛstɐ] die <-, -n> 1. sister ◊ *meine
ältere Schwester* 2. nurse ◊ *Schwester, ich habe
Schmerzen.* ◆ *Er hat nach der Schwester geklingelt.* 3. Sister ◊ *Schwester Maria betet für uns.*
② **schwieg** [ʃviːk] *pret of* schweigen
② **Schwie·ger·...** [ˈʃviːgɐ] [prefix] ...-in-law ◊ *die
Schwiegermama*
Schwie·ger·el·tern [ˈʃviːgɐ|ɛltɐn] die <-> *only pl*
parents-in-law
Schwie·ger·mut·ter [ˈʃviːgɐmʊtɐ] die
<-, Schwiegermütter> mother-in-law
Schwie·ger·sohn [ˈʃviːgɐzoːn] der
<-(e)s, Schwiegersöhne> son-in-law
Schwie·ger·toch·ter [ˈʃviːgɐtɔxtɐ] der
<-, Schwiegertöchter> daughter-in-law
Schwie·ger·va·ter [ˈʃviːgɐfaːtɐ] der

<—s, Schwiegerväter> father-in-law

② **schwie·rig** ['ʃviːrɪç] [adj] **1.** difficult, hard ◊ *Das ist eine schwierige Frage.* ♦ *Die Klassenarbeit war sehr schwierig.* ⊖schwer ⊖einfach **2.** difficult ◊ *ein schwieriger Mensch* ♦ *Er hat einen schwierigen Charakter.* ⊖umgänglich

② **Schwie·rig·keit** ['ʃviːrɪçkaet] die <—, —en> **1.** difficulty ◊ *Dieses Projekt hat uns vor einige Schwierigkeiten gestellt.* ♦ *Ich bin mir der Schwierigkeit dieser Situation sehr wohl bewusst.* **2.** *only pl* trouble, problems ◊ *finanzielle Schwierigkeiten* ♦ *Er ist in Schwierigkeiten.* ♦ *Wir rechnen mit Schwierigkeiten.* ♦ *Machen Sie keine Schwierigkeiten und kommen Sie mit!* das Herz/der Kreislauf macht jdm Schwierigkeiten sb has heart/circulation problems

schwillt [ʃvɪlt] *pres of* schwellen

② **Schwimm·bad** ['ʃvɪmbaːt] das <—(e)s, Schwimmbäder> swimming pool/baths ◊ *ins Schwimmbad gehen*

② **schwim·men** ['ʃvɪmən] <schwimmt, schwamm, hat/ist geschwommen> [intr v] **1.** +*haben/with indication of direction only* +*sein* swim ◊ *Kannst du schwimmen?* ♦ *Ich schwimme ans andere Ufer.* ♦ *Mein Goldfisch schwimmt im Aquarium hin und her.* **2.** +*haben; in South G, Austr, Swiss often* +*sein* float ◊ *Sieh mal, da schwimmt ein Brett im Fluss.* ♦ *Auf der Suppe schwammen Fettaugen.* **3.** +*haben* (fam) in etw. [dat] schwimmen have heaps of sth im/in Geld schwimmen be rolling in it [tr v] +*haben/sein* swim ◊ *Ich habe heute einen Kilometer geschwommen.* ♦ *Er ist die 200 Meter in einer Rekordzeit geschwommen.*

Schwimm·wes·te ['ʃvɪmvɛstə] die <—, —n> life jacket

Schwin·del ['ʃvɪndl̩] der <—s> *no pl* **1.** (fam, pej) swindle, fraud ◊ *Er hat jahrelang Geld abgezweigt, aber jetzt ist der Schwindel herausgekommen.* ♦ *Du wirst doch auf diesen Schwindel nicht reinfallen.* **2.** vertigo, dizziness, giddiness ◊ *Wenn ich auf einem hohen Turm stehe, überkommt mich der Schwindel.* Schwindel erregende Höhen dizzy heights

schwin·de·lig ['ʃvɪndəlɪç] [adj] *not before ns* jdm ist schwindelig sb feels dizzy, sb feels giddy jdm wird schwindelig sb gets dizzy, sb gets giddy

Schwind·ler ['ʃvɪndlɐ] der <—s, —>,

Schwind·le·rin ['ʃvɪndlərɪn] die <—, —nen> (fam, pej) **1.** swindler, con artist ◊ *Sie ist auf den Schwindler hereingefallen.* **2.** liar ◊ *Du Schwindlerin, du warst heute gar nicht bei Oma!*

schwin·gen ['ʃvɪŋən] <schwingt, schwang, hat geschwungen> [tr v] swing ◊ *Er schwang die Axt und zerteilte den Baumstamm.* ♦ *Und jetzt bitte die Arme schwingen.; (a flag)* wave ◊ *Der Fahnenträger schwang seine Fahne.* [intr v] swing ◊ *Der Turner schwingt an den Ringen.* ♦ *Er versetzte dem Pendel einen Stoß, damit es wieder schwang.; (string, bridge)* vibrate ◊ *Die Brücke fing an zu schwingen.* ♦ *Wenn die Saite zu schwingen anfängt, erklingen Töne.* [ref v] sich irgendwohin schwingen leap somewhere ◊ *Tarzan schwang sich von Ast zu Ast.* sich auf etw. [acc] schwingen leap on(to) sth ◊ *Er schwang sich aufs Motorrad und brauste davon.* ♦ *Sie schwang sich in den Sattel.; (bird)* sich in die Luft/Lüfte schwingen soar into

the air

Schwips [ʃvɪps] der <—es, —e> (fam) *translated with a verb construction* being tipsy einen Schwips haben/bekommen be/get tipsy

② **schwit·zen** ['ʃvɪtsn̩] [tr+intr v] +*haben* sweat ◊ *Blut und Wasser schwitzen* ♦ *Er schwitzte stark.* ♦ *Ich fing vor Angst an zu schwitzen.* an den Händen/unter den Armen schwitzen have sweaty hands/armpits etw. nass schwitzen soak sth with sweat ◊ *Ich habe die Bluse nass geschwitzt.*

schwoll [ʃvɔl] *pret of* schwellen

schwor [ʃvoːɐ̯] *pret of* schwören

schwö·ren ['ʃvøːrən] <schwört, schwor, hat geschworen> [tr+intr v] swear ◊ *Der Zeuge musste auf die Bibel schwören.* ♦ *Ich schwöre jeden Eid, dass ich das nicht gewusst habe.* ♦ *Der Zeuge hat geschworen, den Täter am Tatort gesehen zu haben.* ♦ *Ich schwöre, dass das wahr ist.* ♦ *Er hat Rache geschworen.* einen Meineid schwören commit perjury sich [dat] etw. schwören swear sth to yourself

② **schwul** [ʃvuːl] [adj] (fam) gay ◊ *Wusstest du, dass Uli schwul ist?* ♦ *ein schwules Pärchen*

schwül [ʃvyːl] [adj] humid, muggy ◊ *Heute ist es unerträglich schwül.* ♦ *Das schwüle Wetter macht ihr sehr zu schaffen.*

Schwu·le ['ʃvuːlə] der <—n, die Schwulen> *but: ein Schwuler* (fam) gay man/boy

Schwung [ʃvʊŋ] der <—(e)s, Schwünge> **1.** *no pl* enthusiasm, verve ◊ *Nach dem Urlaub ging sie mit frischem Schwung an die Arbeit.* ♦ *Die Rede war ohne Schwung.* **2.** swing ◊ *Schwünge ums Reck Schwung holen* swing back Er warf das Fenster mit Schwung zu. He slammed the window shut. Er schwenkte die Fahne mit kräftigen Schwüngen. He waved the flag vigorously. **3.** (fam) ein Schwung ... [nom] a stack of ... ◊ *Ich habe noch einen ganzen Schwung Hefte zu korrigieren.*

⊛ in Schwung kommen **1.** get going ◊ *Die Party kommt so langsam in Schwung.* **2.** gain momentum ◊ *Die Kampagne kam in Schwung.*

Schwur [ʃvuːɐ̯] der <—(e)s, Schwüre> vow ◊ *Sie glaubte seinen Schwüren und heiratete ihn.; (official)* oath einen Schwur auf die Bibel ablegen swear on the Bible

sechs [zɛks] [nmrl] six → vier

Sechs [zɛks] die <—, —en> **1.** six → Vier 1. **2.** (fam) (bus, tram etc.) number six → Vier 2. **3.** SCHOOL (grade) ⊖E eine Sechs schreiben get an E ⊖ungenügend box@ Note

sechs·fach ['zɛksfax] [adj, adv] *when used as an adj, only before ns* sixfold; six times → vierfach

sechs·te ['zɛkstə] [adj] +*ein* sechster ..., eine sechste ..., ein sechstes ...> sixth → vierte

Sechs·tel ['zɛkstl̩] das <—s, —> sixth → Viertel

sechs·tens ['zɛkstn̩s, 'zɛkstəns] [adv] sixthly → viertens

sech·zehn ['zɛçtseːn] [nmrl] sixteen → vier

sech·zig ['zɛçtsɪç] [nmrl] sixty → vier

② **See¹** [zeː] der <—s, —n> lake ◊ *Der Bodensee ist Deutschlands größter See.*

See² [zeː] die <—> *no pl* sea auf See sein be (away) at sea an die See fahren go to the seaside ⊖Meer

see·krank ['zeːkraŋk] [adj] *no comp/superl* seasick ◊ *Sie wird leicht seekrank.* ♦ *Die seekranken Passa-*

giere hingen über die Reling.
See·le ['zeːlə] die <–, –n> **1.** soul ◊ *Die Seele kommt nach dem Tod in den Himmel oder die Hölle.* ♦ *Das Dorf hat zweihundert Seelen.* ♦ *Keine Seele war zu sehen.* ♦ *Sie ist eine treue Seele.* **2.** heart, soul ◊ *Hast du denn keine Seele, wie kannst du sie nur so verletzen?* es tut mir in der Seele weh it hurts me deeply
◉ **eine Seele von Mensch** a good soul **aus tiefster Seele** with all your heart
see·lisch ['zeːlɪʃ] [adj] no comp/superl mental ◊ *seelische Krankheiten* ♦ *das seelische Gleichgewicht;* emotional ◊ *Er hat mir all seine seelischen Nöte geschildert.* ♦ *Ich habe große seelische Qualen ausgestanden.* ♦ *Ihr Leid war mehr seelisch als körperlich.* ⊜psychisch ⊜körperlich, physisch [adv] mentally ◊ *Seelisch kranke Menschen.* seelisch bedingt sein have psychological causes
See·not ['zeːnoːt] die <–> no pl distress (at sea) ◊ *Das Schiff geriet in Seenot und funkte SOS.*
Se·gel ['zeːɡl̩] das <–s, –> sail ◊ *die Segel hissen/ streichen* ♦ *Der Wind blähte die Segel.*
se·geln ['zeːɡl̩n] [intr v] +haben/sein **1.** +haben/ with indication of direction +sein sail ◊ *Wir sind am Wochenende zum Friedrichshafen gesegelt.* ♦ *Das Schiff segelt übers Meer.* ♦ *Am Wochenende gehen wir segeln.* **2.** +sein glide ◊ *Er segelte mit seinem Flugzeug hoch über den Wäldern.; (bird)* sail ◊ *Hoch oben am Himmel segelte ein Adler.* **3.** +sein *(fam)* fall, go flying ◊ *Er ist zu schnell gefahren und aus der Kurve gesegelt.* ♦ *Er sprang und segelte direkt in die Pfütze.* **4.** +sein *(fam)* durch etw. segeln flunk sth ◊ *Er ist schon zweimal durch die Führerscheinprüfung gesegelt.*
② **se·hen** ['zeːən] <sieht, sah, hat gesehen> [tr v] see ◊ *Kannst du sie irgendwo sehen?* ♦ *Ich habe das Auto nicht gesehen.* ♦ *Ich habe es mit meinen eigenen Augen gesehen.* ♦ *Hast du die neueste Ausstellung im Kunsthaus schon gesehen?* ♦ *Hast du Ingrid mal wieder gesehen?* ♦ *Du siehst das völlig falsch.* ♦ *Wir sollten das Problem in einem größeren Zusammenhang sehen.* etw. in jdm sehen see sb as sth ◊ *Sie sieht in ihm den großen Helden.* Seit dem Unfall sieht er nichts mehr. The accident left him blind. sie sehen sich they see each other, they meet [intr v] **1.** scharf/gut/schlecht sehen have keen/good/bad eyesight nur auf einem Auge sehen be blind in one eye Seit der Operation kann er wieder sehen. The operation restored his eyesight. **2.** *(in a certain direction)* look ◊ *Sieh mal aus dem Fenster!* ♦ *Alle Schüler sahen zur Lehrerin.* ♦ *Ich will auch mal durchs Fernglas sehen.* ♦ *Er sah auf die Uhr.* **3.** nach jdm/etw. sehen look after sb/sth ◊ *Sie sieht nach meinen Pflanzen, wenn ich im Urlaub bin.* ♦ *Die Nachbarn sehen nach meiner Mutter.* **4.** nach etw. [dat] sehen check sth ◊ *Sieh mal nach den Nudeln, ob die schon fertig sind.* mal sehen, ob check whether ◊ *Ich sehe mal, ob die Post schon da war.* nach dem Rechten sehen see that everything is all right [ref v] sich gezwungen sehen, etw. zu tun feel compelled to do sth sich außerstande sehen, etw. zu tun; sich nicht in der Lage sehen, etw. zu tun feel unable to do sth sich imstande sehen, etw. zu tun; sich in der Lage sehen, etw. zu tun feel up to

doing sth, be able to do sth
◉ **es nicht gern sehen, wenn jd etw. tut** not like it when sb does sth **jd kann jdn/etw. nicht mehr sehen** sb can't stand the sight of sb/sth (any more) **etw. kommen sehen** see sth coming **sich sehen lassen 1.** pop round, come by and visit **2.** Lass dich nie wieder hier sehen! Don't show your face here again! **sich sehen lassen können 1.** be something to be proud of ◊ *Dieses Ergebnis kann sich sehen lassen.* not be half bad ◊ *Dein Zeugnis kann sich sehen lassen.* **2.** man kann sich mit jdm sehen lassen sb is nothing to be ashamed of **und siehe da** would you believe it **mal sehen** maybe ◊ *„Kommst du auch zu Marions Party?" — „Mal sehen."* **sehen, ob …** see whether … ◊ *Jetzt will ich doch mal sehen, ob das nicht doch möglich ist.* **mal sehen, ob …** let's see whether … ◊ *Mal sehen, ob ich das nicht doch kann.*
② **Se·hens·wür·dig·keit** ['zeːənsvʏʁdɪçkaɛt] die <–, –en> sight ◊ *Wir haben in London fast alle Sehenswürdigkeiten angesehen.* etw. ist eine Sehenswürdigkeit sth is worth seeing
Seh·ne ['zeːnə] die <–, –n> **1.** ANAT tendon, sinew ◊ *Er hat sich beim Fußballspiel eine Sehne gezerrt.* ♦ *Eine Sehne ist gerissen.* ♦ *ein Stück Fleisch voller Sehnen* **2.** *(of a bow)* string ◊ *Er legte den Pfeil auf die Sehne und spannte den Bogen.* **3.** MATH chord ◊ *die Länge der Sehne berechnen*
seh·nen ['zeːnən] [ref v] +haben sich nach jdm/ etw. sehnen long for sb/sth, yearn for sb/sth ◊ *Er sehnte sich nach seiner Familie.* ♦ *Sie sehnt sich nach Geborgenheit.* ♦ *Er sehnte sich danach, sie bald wiederzusehen.*
sehn·süch·tig ['zeːnzʏçtɪç] [adj, adv] when used as an adj, only before ns longing(ly), wistful(ly) ◊ *sehnsüchtige Blicke* ♦ *Sie wartete sehnsüchtig auf seine Rückkehr.*
② **sehr** [zeːɐ] [adv] very ◊ *Sie war sehr enttäuscht.* ♦ *Es kamen sehr viele Leute.* ♦ *Es tut mir sehr Leid, dass ich zu spät komme.; (before verbs)* much ◊ *Er schämte sich sehr.* ♦ *Das stört mich nicht allzu sehr.*
◉ **sehr wohl** perfectly well ◊ *„Ich kann das nicht!" — „Doch, das kannst du sehr wohl!"*
Seh·test ['zeːtɛst] der <–(e)s, –s or –e> eye test ◊ *für den Führerschein einen Sehtest machen*
seicht [zaɛçt] [adj] <seichter, am seichtesten> *(waters)* shallow ◊ *das seichte Wasser am Ufer* ♦ *Die Bucht ist für Schiffe zu seicht.* ⊜flach ⊜tief [adj, adv] *(pej, fig) (as regards content)* shallow(ly), superficial(ly) ◊ *eine seichte Unterhaltung* ♦ *Dieses Buch ist mir zu seicht (geschrieben).* ⊜flach, oberflächlich ⊜anspruchsvoll
② **seid** [zaɛt] pres of sein¹
② **Sei·de** ['zaɛdə] die <–, –n> silk ◊ *eine Bluse aus reiner Seide*
② **Sei·fe** ['zaɛfə] die <–, –n> soap ◊ *ein Stück Seife* ♦ *sich mit Seife waschen*
Seil [zaɛl] das <–(e)s, –e> rope ◊ *Zwischen zwei Pfosten war ein langes Seil gespannt.; (made out of wire)* cable
◉ **in den Seilen hängen** *(fig)* be knackered, be shattered
Seil·bahn ['zaɛlbaːn] die <–, –en> cable railway ◊ *Das Skigebiet ist vom Tal aus mit der Seilbahn erreichbar.*

A
B
C
D
E
F
G
H
I
J
K
L
M
N
O
P
Q
R
S
T
U
V
W
X
Y
Z

② **sein**¹ [zaen] <ist, war, ist gewesen> [intr v] **1.** be ◊ *Ich bin nicht von hier.* ♦ *Bist du hungrig?* ♦ *Er ist Lehrer.* ♦ *Wir sind Deutsche.* ♦ *Wo seid ihr denn alle?* ♦ *Sind das deine Kinder?* ♦ *Sein Geburtstag war gestern.* ♦ *Bist du schon mal in Italien gewesen?* ♦ *Dieses T-Shirt ist ein Souvenir aus Mallorca.* ♦ *Was ist? Du guckst so traurig.* ♦ *Sie hat den zweiten Platz belegt, das ist schon was!* ♦ *Das kann nicht sein!* ♦ *Muss das denn sein?* ♦ *Heute ist der 31. August.* ♦ *Sind in dem Buch auch Bilder?* ♦ *Wie viel Uhr ist es?* **2.** MATH equal, be ◊ *Vier plus vier ist acht.* ♦ *Drei mal drei ist neun.* ⊖geben **3.** +*inf (indicating a necessity or possibility)* ist/sind etc. zu ... is/are etc. to be ... ◊ *Was ist zu tun?* ♦ *Alle Fragen sind zu beantworten.* ♦ *Dieses Grundstück ist zu kaufen.* ♦ *Das muss doch zu schaffen sein!* **4.** +*nominalized verb (expressing simultaneity)* beim/am Schlafen/Lesen/Arbeiten etc. sein be sleeping/jogging/working etc. ◊ *Wir waren beim Joggen, als uns das Gewitter überraschte.* ♦ *Ich war gerade am Einschlafen, da klingelte das Telefon.* **5.** *(current activity)* etw. sein lassen stop (doing) sth ◊ *Das solltest du lieber sein lassen oder ich werde böse!* ♦ *Lass das Lachen sein, das ist nicht lustig!* ♦ *Komm, lass das jetzt sein und mach eine Pause!*; *(plan)* don't do, drop the idea (of), forget (about) ◊ *Ich wollte ins Kino, aber ich glaube, ich lasse das doch sein. Lass sein!* Don't bother. **6.** *negated (fam)* ... ist/war nicht there is/was no ..., is/was not allowed to ... ◊ *Los, mach weiter! Faulenzen ist nicht!* [imp v] **1.** *(indicating a feeling)* jdm ist ... sb feels (like/as if) ..., sb is ... ◊ *Mir ist nicht gut.* ♦ *Ist dir zu warm?* ♦ *Es war ihm zum Heulen.* ♦ *Ihr war, als ob ihr Herz gleich stehen bliebe.* **2.** mit etw. ist (es) nichts there is no sth, sth is not taking place ◊ *Da es regnete, war es nichts mit dem Ausflug.* ♦ *Mit der Beförderung ist dieses Jahr wieder nichts.* ♦ *Mit Einkaufen ist nichts; ich habe kein Geld mehr!* [aux] +*past p* **1.** no pres perf *(in the German perfect tense)* gelaufen/gefahren/geflogen etc. sein have run/driven/flown etc., ran/drove/flew etc. ◊ *Ich bin zu Fuß gekommen.* ♦ *Das Schiff ist gesunken.* ♦ *Gestern sind wir mit der Straßenbahn gefahren.* ♦ *Er war schon gegangen, als wir ankamen.* ♦ *Ich wäre gerne gekommen.* **2.** *(forming the adjectival passive)* be ◊ *Das Geschäft ist geschlossen.* ♦ *Wenn du zurückkommst, wird das Problem gelöst sein.*

⊙ **das war's/wär's** *(fam)* that's it, that's all ◊ *Das war's für heute. Morgen mehr!* ♦ *"Sonst noch etwas?" — "Nein, das wär's."* dem ist nicht so that/this is not true **es sei denn(, dass)** unless ◊ *Genug für heute, es sei denn, dass es noch Fragen gibt.* ♦ *Ich komme zu spät zur Schule, es sei denn, du bringst mich mit dem Auto hin.* sei es ..., sei es ...; sei es ... oder ... *(lofty)* whether ... or ... ◊ *Sei es abends oder morgens, ich bin immer müde.* ♦ *Ich liebe Bücher, seien es ernste, seien es heitere.* **nicht so sein** *(fam)* make no fuss, not be fussy ◊ *Sei doch nicht so und gib deiner Schwester etwas ab!* **wie dem auch sei** be that as it may ② **sein²** [zaen] [det] **1.** *before masculine ns* his ◊ *Da kommt Leo. Sein Bruder ist auch dabei.* ♦ *Er hat wieder seine Brille vergessen.* ♦ *Gib ihm sein Buch*

zurück. ♦ *Das sind seine Schwestern.* ♦ *Während seiner Krankheit konnte er nicht arbeiten.* **2.** *before neuter ns* its ◊ *ein Werk und sein Schöpfer* ♦ *Das Unternehmen hat seine Bilanz vorgelegt.* ♦ *Das Leben hat seine Tücken.*; *(before neuter ns that refer to a male baby or child)* his ◊ *Das Baby schreit. Seine Windel ist voll.*; *(before neuter ns that refer to a female person)* her ◊ *ein Mädchen und sein kleiner Hund*

	m	f	nt	pl
nom	sein	seine	sein	seine
acc	seinen	seine	sein	seine
dat	seinem	seiner	seinem	seinen
gen	seines	seiner	seines	seiner

sei·ne ['zaenə] → sein², seiner
sei·ner ['zaenə] [poss pron] **1.** *before masculine ns* his ◊ *Mein Stift ist kaputt, ich nehme seinen zum Schreiben.* ♦ *"Ist das Richards Frau?" — "Nein, die Rothaarige ist seine."* ♦ *Das ist nicht mein Buch, das ist seins.* ♦ *Die fünf Kinder sind alle seine.* **2.** *(before German neuter ns referring to a male baby or child)* his ◊ *Das Baby schreit nach dem Schnuller. Ist dieser blaue hier seiner?* ♦ *"Gehören die Spielzeugautos deinem Kind?" — "Ja, das sind seine."*; *(before neuter ns referring to a female baby or child)* hers ◊ *Da liegt eine Tasche. Das Mädchen behauptet, es sei seine.*; *(before neuter ns referring to animals and objects)* its ◊ *Das Meerschweinchen hat Hunger. Welches Futter ist seins?*

	m	f	nt	pl
nom	seiner	seine	sein(e)s	seine
acc	seinen	seine	sein(e)s	seine
dat	seinem	seiner	seinem	seinen
gen	-	-	-	-

sei·ner·seits ['zaenɐzaets, '– – '–] [adv] for his part ◊ *Seinerseits wurden keine Vorwürfe laut.* ♦ *Er verwies seinerseits auf andere Möglichkeiten.*
sei·ner·zeit ['zaenɐtsaet] [adv] in those days, at that time ◊ *Seinerzeit hatten wir kein Telefon.*
sei·nes ['zaenəs] → seiner
sei·net·we·gen ['zaenətveːɡn̩, '– – '– –] [adv] because of him, for his sake ◊ *Sie ist nur seinetwegen gekommen.*
seins [zaens] → seiner
② **seit**¹ [zaet] [prep] [+dat] since, for ◊ *Sie sind seit 1985 verheiratet.* ♦ *Wir wohnen seit einem Jahr in diesem Haus.* ♦ *Seit wann seid ihr schon hier?*
② **seit**² [zaet] [conjunc] since ◊ *Seit sie in Frankreich war, schwört sie auf Paris.*
seit·dem¹ [zaet'deːm] [adv] since then ◊ *Ich habe das Buch zu Weihnachten bekommen. Seitdem habe ich es schon dreimal gelesen.*
seit·dem² [zaet'deːm] [conjunc] since ◊ *Seitdem wir zusammenziehen, streiten wir dauernd.*
② **Sei·te** ['zaetə] die <–, –n> **1.** page ◊ *Dieses Buch hat fast 500 Seiten.* ♦ *Schlagen Sie bitte Seite 23 auf.* **2.** *(fig)* side ◊ *die vier Seiten eines Quadrats* ♦ *Sie wohnen auf der anderen Seite der Straße.* ♦ *Dreh dich mal auf die andere Seite.* ♦ *Ich kann der Sache keine positiven Seiten abgewinnen.* ♦ *Er kämpfte auf der Seite der Aufrührer.* **3.** *(distance or proximity to sb/sth)* an die/zur Seite aside, out of the way ◊ *Er trat zur/ging an die Seite, um sie*

vorbeizulassen. an jds Seite by sb's side ◊ *Bleib bitte in dem Gedränge an meiner Seite.* Seite an Seite side by side ◊ *Die tapferen Krieger kämpften Seite an Seite.* **4.** direction ◊ *Sie redeten von allen Seiten auf ihn ein.* ♦ *Von welcher Seite kommt der Wind?* ⊖*Richtung* **5.** *(fig)* jds beste/schwache/ starke Seite sb's best/weak/strong point ◊ *Geduld ist nicht gerade ihre stärkste Seite.* ♦ *In der Schule war Physik immer meine schwache Seite.* sich von der/seiner besten Seite zeigen show yourself at your best **6.** *no pl (fig)* sources ◊ *Förderung von staatlicher/privater Seite*
◉ etw. auf die Seite schaffen/bringen *(fam)* help yourself to sth ◊ *Er soll Geld auf die Seite geschafft haben.* jdm nicht von der Seite weichen/gehen not move from sb's side, not leave sb's side jdm zur Seite stehen stand by sb auf der einen Seite ..., auf der anderen Seite ... on the one hand ... on the other hand ... ⊖*einerseits ..., andererseits ...* zwei Seiten einer/ derselben Medaille two sides of a coin

sei·tens ['zaɛtn̩s, 'zaɪtəns] [prep] [+gen] *(form)* on the part of ◊ *Es gab Interesse seitens einiger Personen.* ♦ *Man erwartet finanzielle Unterstützung seitens der EU.*

Sei·ten·sprung ['zaɪtn̩ʃprʊŋ] der <–(e)s, Seitensprünge> affair, infidelity ◊ *jdm einen Seitensprung gestehen/verzeihen*

Sei·ten·strei·fen ['zaɪtn̩ʃtraɛfn̩] der <–s, –> verge, hard shoulder ◊ *Das Auto geriet auf den unbefestigten Seitenstreifen und kam ins Schleudern.* ♦ *Seitenstreifen nicht befahrbar!*

seit·her [zaɛt'heːɐ] [adv] since then, ever since ◊ *Sie ist letztes Jahr weggezogen. Seither habe ich nicht mehr von ihr gehört.*

Se·kre·tär¹ [zekre'tɛːɐ] der <–s, –e> bureau, secretaire ◊ *ein antiker Sekretär*

Se·kre·tär² [zekre'tɛːɐ] der <–s, –e>, **Se·kre·tä·rin** [zekre'tɛːrɪn] die <–, –nen> secretary ◊ *Sie ist als Sekretärin tätig.* ♦ *der persönliche Sekretär des Direktors*

Sekt [zɛkt] der <–(e)s, –e> *pl 'Sekt' when used with expressions of quantity* sparkling wine ◊ *Sie stießen mit einem Glas Sekt auf ihren Erfolg an.*

Sek·te ['zɛktə] die <–, –n> sect ◊ *Er gehört einer obskuren Sekte an.*

se·kun·där [zekʊn'dɛːɐ] [adj, adv] *no comp/superl (lofty)* secondary(-ily) ◊ *Das spielt nur eine sekundäre Rolle.* ♦ *Die Kostenfrage ist sekundär.* ♦ *Unsere Firma ist nur sekundär an dem Projekt beteiligt.* ♦ *ein sekundär auftretendes Problem*

Se·kun·dar·stu·fe [zekʊn'daːɐʃtuːfə] die <–, –n> most sing secondary stage

In German secondary schools there are secondary stage I (class 7 to 10) and secondary stage II (class 11 to 13), although the latter only exists at grammar or comprehensive schools.

Se·kun·de [ze'kʊndə] die <–, –n> second ◊ *Datenverkehr mit 54 Megabit pro Sekunde* ♦ *Das Erdbeben dauerte 45 Sekunden.* ♦ *Warte eine Sekunde, ich bin gleich fertig.*

② **sel·be** ['zɛlbə] [adj] *demonstrative*; *+contraction of prep and article* same ◊ *Alle Verletzten wurden ins selbe Krankenhaus eingeliefert.* ♦ *Sie wurden am selben Tag geboren.* ♦ *jeden Tag zur selben Zeit*

selbst¹ [zɛlpst] [adv] even ◊ *Selbst der sonst so kritische Peter war zufrieden.* ♦ *Selbst wenn ich wollte, könnte ich nicht mitkommen.* ⊖*sogar, auch*

② **selbst²** [zɛlpst] [demonstr pron] *invariable* **1.** myself/yourself/himself etc. ◊ *Das kann ich selbst.* ♦ *Sehen Sie selbst!* ♦ *Er selbst war nicht betroffen.* ♦ *Daran bist du aber selbst schuld!* ♦ *Das hab ich für mich selbst gekauft, nicht für dich.* **2.** *+past p* selbst gebacken/gekocht/gemacht etc. home-made, self-made ◊ *selbst gekochte Marmelade* ♦ *selbst gemachtes Eis* selbst ... self... ◊ *ein selbst gebautes Haus* ♦ *ein selbst gemaltes Bild* selbst ernannt self-styled **3.** von selbst by myself/yourself/itself etc. ◊ *Die Tür fiel von selbst zu.* ♦ *Kannst du nicht von selbst aufräumen, ohne dass ich es erst sagen muss?* wie von selbst as if by magic, without effort
◉ für sich selbst entscheiden decide for yourself

selb·stän·dig ['zɛlpʃtɛndɪç] → selbstständig

Selbst·be·die·nung ['zɛlpstbədiːnʊŋ] die <–> *no pl* self-service ◊ *Die Tankstelle wurde auf Selbstbedienung umgestellt.*

selbst·be·wusst ['zɛlpstbəvʊst] [adj, adv] <selbst­bewusster, am selbstbewusstesten> selfassured(ly), confident(ly) ◊ *ein selbstbewusster junger Mann* ♦ *Sie wirkt äußerst selbstbewusst.* ♦ *selbstbewusst auftreten* ⊖*selbstsicher*

Selbst·mord ['zɛlpstmɔɐ̯t] der <–(e)s, –e> *(also fig)* suicide ◊ *Er beging/verübte Selbstmord, indem er vor einen Zug sprang.* ♦ *An dieser Stelle zu surfen, wäre glatter Selbstmord.*

selbst·si·cher ['zɛlpstzɪçɐ] [adj, adv] confident(ly), self-assured(ly) ◊ *ein selbstsicherer Mensch* ♦ *Sie ist in letzter Zeit selbstsicherer geworden.* ♦ *ein selbstsicher auftretender Mann* ⊖*selbstbewusst*

② **selbst·stän·dig** ['zɛlpstʃtɛndɪç] [adj, adv] **1.** independent(ly) ◊ *selbstständiges Lernen* ♦ *Meine neunjährige Tochter ist schon sehr selbstständig.* ♦ *Kinder müssen lernen, ihre Hausaufgaben selbstständig zu machen.* ♦ *Das Land wurde 1991 selbstständig.* **2.** self-employed ◊ *ein selbstständiger Architekt* ♦ *Sie ist selbstständig tätig.* sich selbstständig machen set up on your own ◊ *Er hat sich als Steuerberater selbstständig gemacht.*
◉ etw. macht sich selbstständig *(fam)* sth takes off on its own, sth grows legs ◊ *Schau mal, da macht sich gerade dein Boot selbstständig!*

② **selbst·ver·ständ·lich** ['zɛlpstfɛʃtɛntlɪç] [adj, adv] natural(ly) ◊ *eine selbstverständliche Pflicht* ♦ *Die Angelegenheit wird selbstverständlich vertraulich behandelt.* selbstverständlich sein be a matter of course Das ist doch selbstverständlich! That goes without saying. etw. als selbstverständlich behandeln/betrachten take sth for granted

Selbst·ver·trau·en ['zɛlpstfɛtraʊən] das <–s> *no pl* self-confidence, self-reliance ◊ *Ihm fehlt das nötige Selbstvertrauen.* ♦ *Der Sieg hat der Mannschaft neues Selbstvertrauen gegeben.* ♦ *voller Selbstvertrauen*

② **sel·ten** ['zɛltn̩] [adj, adv] rare(ly) ◊ *eine seltene Gelegenheit* ♦ *Diese Krankheit ist äußerst selten.* ♦ *Diesen Vogel sieht man nur selten. Das passiert nur/höchst/äußerst selten. It hardly ever happens.* ⊖*häufig* [adv] *+adj* exceptionally ◊ *Er stellte sich selten dämlich an.* ♦ *Das war ein selten komischer*

Anblick. ⊖ausgesprochen

Sel·ten·heit ['zɛltn̩haet] die <-, -en> **1.** no pl rarity ◊ Aufgrund seiner Seltenheit ist der Stein sehr wertvoll. **2.** eine/keine Seltenheit sein be rare/frequent ◊ Temperaturen unter 0°C sind hier eine große Seltenheit. ♦ Lange Wartezeiten sind hier keine Seltenheit.

② **selt·sam** ['zɛltzaːm] [adj, adv] strange(ly), peculiar(ly), odd(ly) ◊ Er ist ein seltsamer Typ. ♦ Ich finde ihr Benehmen seltsam. ♦ ein seltsam geformter Baum ⊖eigenartig, komisch, merkwürdig, sonderbar

② **Se·mes·ter** [ze'mɛstɐ] das <-s, -> semester ◊ Sie studiert im zweiten Semester Medizin. ♦ Ich bin im siebten Semester.

Se·mes·ter·fe·ri·en [ze'mɛstɐˌfeːrjən] die <-> only pl university vacation ◊ In den Semesterferien arbeitet sie in einem Altersheim.

Se·mi·nar [zemi'naːɐ̯] das <-s, -e> **1.** seminar ◊ ein zweisemestriges Seminar zur Softwareentwicklung ♦ ein berufsbegleitendes Seminar **2.** department ◊ das Anglistische Seminar der Universität Heidelberg **3.** seminary ◊ das Seminar für Waldorfpädagogik in Hamburg

② **Sem·mel** ['zɛml̩] die <-, -n> (SouthG, Austr) bread roll ◊ Semmeln zum Frühstück essen ♦ eine Semmel mit Schinken ⊖Brötchen

⊕ weggehen wie warme Semmeln sell like hot cakes

Se·nat [ze'naːt] der <-(e)s, -e> **1.** senate ◊ der Hamburger Senat ♦ Cäsar wurde vom Senat zur Rechenschaft gezogen. **2.** LAW (higher court) panel of judges

② **sen·den**[1] ['zɛndn̩] <sendet, sandte/sendete, hat gesandt/gesendet> [tr v] (lofty) send ◊ eine Ansichtskarte aus dem Urlaub senden ♦ Er sandte ihr einen Blumenstrauß. ⊖schicken

sen·den[2] ['zɛndn̩] <sendet, sendete, hat gesendet> [tr+intr v] broadcast, transmit, air ◊ stündlich Nachrichten senden ♦ Die Show wird live gesendet.

Sen·der ['zɛndɐ] der <-s, -> **1.** broadcasting station ◊ ein kommerzieller Sender ♦ der Sender Freies Berlin **2.** transmitter ◊ Das Babyphon besteht aus einem Sender und einem Empfänger.

② **Sen·dung** ['zɛnduŋ] die <-, -en> **1.** broadcast ◊ die Sendung mit der Maus ♦ Diese Sendung kommt jeden Montag um 20 Uhr. **2.** auf Sendung sein be on the air Das Programm geht nächste Woche auf Sendung. The programme is due to air next week. **3.** TRADE consignment ◊ Der Wert der Sendung beträgt 1000 Euro. ♦ Die Sendung konnte nicht zugestellt werden. **4.** delivery ◊ Vielen Dank für die schnelle Sendung der Waren. ⊖Versand **5.** no pl (lofty) mission ◊ die göttliche Sendung eines Propheten

Senf [zɛnf] der <-(e)s, -e> mustard ◊ Bockwurst mit Senf ♦ ein Klacks Senf ♦ Weißwürste mit süßem Senf

⊕ seinen Senf dazugeben (fam, pej) get one's word in, have your say

se·nil [ze'niːl] [adj] (lofty, esp pej) senile ◊ Opa wird langsam senil. ♦ senile Osteoporose

Se·ni·or[1] ['zeːnjoːɐ̯] der <-s> no pl **1.** (as regards the older superior) senior partner, boss ◊ Die Firma wurde 1970 von dem heutigen Senior

gegründet. **2.** (as regards the father) senior ◊ Vater und Sohn feierten beide runde Geburtstage: Der Senior wurde 90, der Junior 60 Jahre alt.

Se·ni·or[2] ['zeːnjoːɐ̯] der <-s, -en>, **Se·ni·o·rin** [zeːnjoːrɪn] die <-, -nen> **1.** most pl senior citizen ◊ eine rüstige Seniorin ♦ ein Treffpunkt für Senioren ⊖Alte **2.** oldest member ◊ Franz ist der Senior in unserer Skatrunde. **3.** SPORT senior (player) ◊ Die Senioren trainieren dienstags und donnerstags.

sen·ken ['zɛŋkn̩] [tr v] +haben **1.** (spatial) lower ◊ Verlegen senkte er den Kopf/den Blick. ♦ Der Zauberer senkte seinen Stab. ♦ den Wasserspiegel senken ⊖heben **2.** (quantitative) reduce, lower ◊ die Kosten/Preise drastisch senken ♦ die Zinsen/Steuern senken ♦ Das Medikament konnte das Fieber/den Blutdruck senken. ⊖reduzieren
⊖erhöhen [ref v] +haben sich senken go down, sink ◊ Die Sonne senkte sich und warf lange Schatten. ♦ Der Dollarkurs senkte sich leicht.; (temperature, water level etc.) drop, fall; (floor, ground) subside, give way

② **senk·recht** ['zɛŋkrɛçt] [adj, adv] no comp/superl **1.** vertical(ly) ◊ eine Tapete mit senkrechten Streifen ♦ Die Felswand ist nahezu senkrecht. ♦ ein senkrecht aufragender Felsen ⊖waagerecht **2.** MATH perpendicular, at right angles ◊ Die Gerade L ist senkrecht zur Geraden H. ♦ Der Vektor steht senkrecht zur Fläche. ⊖parallel

Sen·kung ['zɛŋkuŋ] die <-, -en> **1.** reduction, lowering ◊ Er sprach sich für eine Senkung der Erbschaftssteuer aus. ♦ ein Programm zur Senkung der Kriminalität **2.** subsiding, sinking ◊ Am Gipfelkrater hatte eine starke Senkung stattgefunden. **3.** MED prolapse ◊ eine Senkung der Gebärmutter

Sen·sa·ti·on [zɛnzaˈtsjoːn] die <-, -en> sensation ◊ Der Fund ist eine archäologische Sensation.

sen·si·bel [zɛnˈziːbl̩] [adj, adv] <sensibler, am sensibelsten> <ein sensibler ..., eine sensible ..., ein sensibles ...> sensitive(ly) ◊ Sie ist für ihre sensible Berichterstattung bekannt. ♦ Er ist sehr sensibel für Veränderungen. ♦ einen sensiblen Magen haben ♦ auf eine Substanz sensibel reagieren ♦ Es handelt sich hierbei um sensible Daten.

sen·ti·men·tal [zɛntimɛnˈtaːl] [adj, adv] sentimental(ly) ◊ ein sentimentaler Liebesroman ♦ Wenn ich diese Melodie höre, werde ich ganz sentimental. ♦ Das Publikum war sentimental gestimmt.

② **Sep·tem·ber** [zɛpˈtɛmbɐ] der <-(s), -> September → Januar

Se·rie ['zeːrjə] die <-, -n> **1.** series ◊ Das ZDF zeigte eine fünfteilige Serie über Indianer. ♦ Eine Serie von Explosionen erschütterte die Stadt. ♦ Die Serie der Zwischenfälle reißt nicht ab. ♦ Diese Möbel werden in Serie hergestellt. In Serie gehen go into series/full-scale production ◊ Dieses Auto soll noch vor Jahresende in Serie gehen. **2.** set ◊ Er besitzt die komplette Serie dieser Sondermarken.

se·ri·en·mä·ßig ['zeːrjənmɛːsɪç] [adj] no comp/superl standard ◊ Das gehört zur serienmäßigen Ausstattung. ♦ Bei diesem Modell sind elektrische Fensterheber serienmäßig. [adv] **1.** as standard ◊ Dieses Modell ist serienmäßig mit Servolenkung ausgestattet. **2.** in series ◊ etw. serienmäßig produzieren

Se·ri·en·num·mer ['ze:rɪənnʊmɐ] die <-, -n> series number ◇ *Jedes Modell ist mit einer Seriennummer versehen.*

se·ri·ös [ze'rjø:s] [adj, adv] <seriöser, am seriöse­sten> respectable(-ably) ◇ *eine seriöse Zeitung/ Geschäftsfrau* ♦ *Er beurteilt die Firma als absolut seriös.* ♦ *ein seriös gekleideter Geschäftsmann*

Se·rum ['ze:rʊm] das <-s, Seren> serum ◇ *jdm ein Serum gegen etw. spritzen* ♦ *Der Erreger wurde im Serum von Tieren nachgewiesen.*

Ser·vice ['sœ'vɪs] der <-, -s> **1.** service ◇ *Der Service in diesem Restaurant ist rasch und freundlich.* ♦ *Die Bibliothek bietet jetzt einen besseren Service.* **2.** SPORT serve

ser·vie·ren [zɛ'vi:rən] <serviert, servierte, hat serviert> [tr+intr v] serve ◇ *Servieren Sie dazu Rotwein.* ♦ *Als Nachtisch wurden Erdbeeren serviert.* ♦ *Sie können jetzt servieren.*

Ser·vi·et·te [zɛr'vjɛtə] die <-, -n> napkin, serviette

Ser·vus ['zɛ'vʊs, 'sɛ'vʊs] (SouthG, Austr, fam) **1.** hello ◇ *Servus Bernd, wie geht's?* **2.** goodbye, so long ◇ *Servus, ich geh jetzt!*

② **Ses·sel** ['zɛsl̩] der <-s, -> armchair ◇ *ein bequemer Sessel* ♦ *im Sessel vor dem Fernseher sitzen* ♦ *eine Garnitur aus Sofa und zwei Sesseln*

Ses·sel·lift ['zɛsl̩lɪft] der <-(e)s, -e or -s> chairlift ◇ *Wir fuhren mit dem Sessellift zur Mittelstation.*

sess·haft ['zɛshaft] [adj] <sesshafter, am sesshaf­testen> seldom comp/superl settled (down) ◇ *Aus den Nomaden wurden sesshafte Bauern.* ♦ *Dieses Wüstenvolk ist heute überwiegend sesshaft.* sesshaft werden, sich sesshaft machen settle down ◇ *Hier sind mehr als 40 Firmen sesshaft geworden.*

② **set·zen** ['zɛtsn̩] [ref v] +haben **1.** sich setzen sit down ◇ *Setzen Sie sich doch bitte.* ♦ *Der Hund setzte sich auf die Hinterpfoten.* ♦ *Setzt du dich ein bisschen zu mir und erzählst mir was?* **2.** sich setzen settle, sink ◇ *Der Schnee hat sich gesetzt und ist jetzt ideal zum Skifahren.* ♦ *Warten Sie, bis die Teeblätter sich gesetzt haben.* **3.** sich an etw. [acc] setzen get down to sth ◇ *Setz dich endlich an deine Hausaufgaben!* ♦ *Sie setzte sich an die Arbeit.* [tr v] +haben **1.** etw./jdn irgendwo hinsetzen place sth/sb somewhere ◇ *Sie setzte ihre Kinder vor den Fernseher, um ein paar Minuten Ruhe zu haben.* ♦ *einen Wasserkessel auf den Herd setzen* ♦ *eine Anzeige in die Zeitung setzen* ♦ *seine Unterschrift unter einen Vertrag setzen* ♦ *Vergiss nicht, am Satzende einen Punkt zu setzen.* **2.** set ◇ *einen Schwerpunkt setzen* ♦ *sich* [dat] *neue Ziele setzen* ♦ *einem Kind Grenzen setzen* ♦ *Mit dieser Aktion will die Initiative Zeichen für bessere Integration setzen.* **3.** etw. an etw. [acc] setzen summon up sth for sth ◇ *Sie setzte ihren ganzen Ehrgeiz daran, Japanisch zu lernen.* **4.** empty verb etw. in Betrieb setzen start sth up, put sth into operation etw. außer Betrieb setzen stop sth, take sth out of service jdn unter Druck setzen put pressure on sb etw. in Gang setzen get sth going einer Sache [gen] ein Ende setzen set an end to sth [tr+intr v] +haben etw. (auf etw./jdn) setzen put sth (on sth) ◇ *Er setzte sein Roulette sein ganzes Geld auf Rot.* ♦ *100 Euro auf die Startnummer 5 setzen.* (auf etw./ jdn) setzen make a bet (on sth/sb) ◇ *Du hast*

noch nicht gesetzt. [intr v] +haben/sein **1.** +sein *(across water)* über etw. [acc] setzen cross sth ◇ *über einen Fluss setzen; (by jumping)* jump over sth, leap over sth ◇ *Der Hirsch setzte über die Büsche.* **2.** +haben auf etw. [acc] setzen rely on sth ◇ *Sie setzte auf gutes Wetter und lud zu einer Gartenparty ein.* ♦ *Er setzte darauf, dass die anderen ihn unterstützen würden.* [imp v] +haben es setzt was, es setzt eine Tracht Prügel sb will get a hiding, sb will get a thrashing

Seu·che ['zɔyçə] die <-, -n> **1.** epidemic ◇ *Die Seuche breitet sich aus.* ♦ *Eine gefährliche Seuche ist ausgebrochen.* **2.** *(fam, pej)* scourge ◇ *Das Telefonieren mit Handys hat sich zu einer wahren Seuche entwickelt.*

seuf·zen ['zɔyftsn̩] [intr v] +haben sigh ◇ *Als sie die Urlaubsfotos betrachtete, seufzte sie sehnsüchtig.*

Seuf·zer ['zɔyftsɐ] der <-s, -> sigh ◇ *Er stieß einen tiefen Seufzer aus.*

Sex [sɛks] der <-(es)> no pl **1.** sex ◇ *ungeschützten Sex haben* ♦ *eine Geschichte voller Sex und Erotik* **2.** sex appeal ◇ *Sie strahlt Sex aus.* ♦ *Dieser Sänger hat Sex in der Stimme.*

se·xis·tisch [zɛ'ksɪstɪʃ] [adj] sexist ◇ *sexistische Bemerkungen* ♦ *Diese Werbung ist extrem sexistisch.*

Se·xu·a·li·tät [zɛksuali'tɛːt] die <-> no pl sexuality ◇ *seine Sexualität ausleben*

se·xu·ell [zɛksu'ɛl] [adj, adv] seldom comp/superl sexual(ly) ◇ *sexuelle Handlungen* ♦ *Ihre Beziehung ist rein sexuell.* ♦ *Das Kind wurde sexuell missbraucht.* ♦ *Er soll mehrere Frauen sexuell belästigt haben.*

Shorts [ʃɔ'ts] die <-> only pl shorts ◇ *Sie trug (ein Paar) weiße Shorts.*

Show [ʃo:] die <-, -s> show ◇ *eine Show mit vielen bekannten Künstlern*
  Ⓡ **eine Show abziehen** *(fam, esp pej)* put on a show

② **sich** [zɪç] [ref pron] **1.** yourself, oneself; *(often not translated)* sich [dat] die Hände/Füße etc. waschen wash your hands/feet etc. sich ausbreiten spread sich beeilen hurry sich verändern change; *(sing nouns or pronouns describing a male)* himself ◇ *Frank trocknete sich ab.* ♦ *Er hatte sich unbeliebt gemacht.; (sing nouns or pronouns describing a female)* herself ◇ *Die Frau hatte sich* [dat] *selbst die Haare geschnitten.* ♦ *Sie bereitete sich gründlich auf den Test vor.; (most other sing nouns or pronouns)* itself ◇ *Das Konzept ist in sich schlüssig.* ♦ *Das Baby zappelte. Es wollte sich umdrehen.; (referring to pl nouns or pronouns)* themselves ◇ *Sie verletzten sich, als sie über den Zaun kletterten.; (referring to the polite address)* yourself, yourselves ◇ *Hätten Sie sich nicht besser vorbereiten können?* ♦ *Haben Sie sich* [dat] *den Film selber ausgesucht?; (reciprocal)* each other ◇ *Sie lieben/mögen/hassen sich.* ♦ *Die beiden Brüder schenken sich* [dat] *zu Weihnachten nie etwas.* sich [dat] etw./jdn wünschen wish for sth/sb ◇ *Sie wünschen sich ein Kind. box@ es, er, sie[1], sie[2], Sie* **2.** impersonal, not directly translated *In diesem Bett schläft es sich echt gut.* In this bed you sleep really well. *Chinesisch lernt sich nicht so leicht.* It is not so easy to learn Chinese. *Der Wagen fährt sich gut.* This car offers a comfortable

drive.

ⓢ **an sich** itself ◊ *Das Haus an sich ist schön, aber die Lage ist nicht besonders gut.* **von sich** `dat` aus *on his/her/their/your own free will* ◊ *Er ist von sich aus zur Polizei gegangen.*

ⓩ **si·cher** ['zɪçɐ] `adj, adv` **1.** safe(ly), secure(ly) ◊ *eine sichere Geldanlage* ◆ *ein sicherer Schulweg* ◆ *Dieser Hubschrauber gilt als besonders sicher.* ◆ *Atommüll muss sicher endgelagert werden.* ⓢungefährlich ⓢunsicher **2.** reliable(-ably), secure(ly) ◊ *eine sichere Einnahmequelle* ◆ *ein sicherer Tipp* ◆ *Wie sicher ist diese Prognose?* ◆ *Die Ursachen sind noch nicht sicher bewiesen.* ⓢverlässlich ⓢunsicher **3.** confident(ly) ◊ *ein sicherer Pilot* ◆ *Er fühlt sich sehr sicher im Umgang mit dieser Software.* ◆ *Sie ist in der letzten Zeit im Auftreten viel sicherer geworden.* ⓢunsicher **4.** sure(ly), certain(ly) ◊ *Sie fühlte sich als sichere Siegerin.* ◆ *Der Erfolg ist ihm sicher.* ◆ *Dazu hat er sicher keine Zeit.* ◆ *Sicher regnet es morgen wieder!* ◆ *„Rufst du mich an, sobald du zu Hause bist?" — „Sicher."* (sich `dat`) **sicher sein** be sure ◊ *Bist du (dir) ganz sicher, dass du die Rechnung bezahlt hast?*

ⓩ **Si·cher·heit** ['zɪçɐhaɛt] die <-, –en> **1.** *most sing* security, safety ◊ *die innere Sicherheit eines Landes* ◆ *ein Programm für mehr Sicherheit im Straßenverkehr* ◆ *Die Bank verlangt Sicherheiten für den Kredit.* **in Sicherheit bringen** bring to safety, rescue; *(yourself)* escape ◊ *Er brachte sich vor dem Feuer/den Verfolgern in Sicherheit.* **in Sicherheit sein** be safe **2.** *no pl* certainty ◊ *Das kann ich noch nicht mit Sicherheit sagen.* **mit Sicherheit** certainly, for certain, definitely ◊ *Er kommt mit Sicherheit wieder zu spät.* **mit an Sicherheit grenzender Wahrscheinlichkeit** most certainly **3.** *no pl* confidence ◊ *Sie spielte die Sonate mit traumwandlerischer Sicherheit.* ◆ *mehr Sicherheit im Umgang mit etw. gewinnen*

Si·cher·heits·na·del ['zɪçɐhaɛtsnaːdl] die <-, –n> safety pin

si·cher·lich ['zɪçɐlɪç] `adv` certainly ◊ *Dieses Buch hat sie sicherlich schon gelesen.* ⓢbestimmt

ⓩ **si·chern** ['zɪçɐn] `tr v` +*haben* **1.** make secure, make safe ◊ *Die Unfallstelle wurde gesichert.* ◆ *ein Fenster mit einem Schloss sichern* ◆ *Die Soldaten sicherten das Krankenhaus.* **2.** protect, safeguard ◊ *durch internationale Zusammenarbeit den Frieden sichern* ◆ *das Überleben einer Tierart zu sichern versuchen* **3.** secure ◊ *Wir sicherten uns die besten Plätze.* ◆ *Die Polizei sicherte die Fingerabdrücke am Tatort.* **4.** IT save ◊ *Sichern Sie ihre Daten in regelmäßigen Abständen.* ⓢspeichern ⓢlöschen

si·cher|stel·len ['zɪçɐʃtɛlən] <stellt sicher, stellte sicher, hat sichergestellt> `tr v` **1.** guarantee ◊ *die Finanzierung der Renten sicherstellen* ⓢgewährleisten **2.** impound, seize ◊ *Die Polizei hat mehrere Kilogramm Heroin sichergestellt.* ⓢbeschlagnahmen

Si·che·rung ['zɪçərʊŋ] die <-, –en> **1.** TECHN safety catch **2.** fuse ◊ *eine Sicherung auswechseln* **3.** *no pl* safeguarding, protection ◊ *die langfristige Sicherung von Arbeitsplätzen* ◆ *die Sicherung des Friedens* **4.** securing ◊ *die Sicherung von zukünftigen Marktanteilen* **5.** IT saving ◊ *die automatische Sicherung von Daten*

ⓢ **(bei) jdm brennt die/eine Sicherung durch** sb fuses, sb goes berserk

Sicht [zɪçt] die <-> *no pl* **1.** visibility ◊ *Die Sicht verschlechterte sich.* ◆ *Wir hatten gute/klare/schlechte Sicht.* ◆ *Der Nebel war so dicht, dass die Sicht unter 50 Meter betrug.* **in Sicht** in sight ◊ *Am Horizont kam ein Flugzeug in Sicht.* ◆ *Land in Sicht!* ◆ *Noch ist kein Erfolg in Sicht.* **außer Sicht** out of sight ◊ *Wir winkten dem Zug hinterher, bis er außer Sicht war.* **2.** Sicht (auf etw. `acc`) view (of sth) ◊ *Eine Hecke versperrte mir die Sicht.* ◆ *Von meinem Platz aus hatte ich gute Sicht auf die Bühne.* ⓢBlick **3.** *(fig)* aus … Sicht from … point of view, in … view ◊ *Aus meiner Sicht ist das völlig falsch.* ◆ *Aus heutiger Sicht ist das nur schwer zu verstehen.*

ⓢ **auf lange/kurze Sicht** in the long/short term, in the long/short run

sicht·bar ['zɪçtbaːʳ] `adj, adv` visible(-ibly) ◊ *ein sichtbarer Erfolg* ◆ *Der Sturm hinterließ sichtbare Schäden.* ◆ *Die Kühltürme sind von weitem sichtbar.* ◆ *Das Namensschild muss gut sichtbar getragen werden.* ◆ *Sie war sichtbar erleichtert.*

Sicht·wei·te ['zɪçtvaɛtə] die <-, –n> **1.** visibility ◊ *Aufgrund von Nebel beträgt die Sichtweite weniger als 50 Meter.* ⓢSicht **2.** außer/in Sichtweite out of/in sight ◊ *Eine Einigung in dem Tarifkonflikt ist in Sichtweite.* ◆ *Er verschwand außer Sichtweite.* ◆ *Das Hotel ist in Sichtweite des Vesuvs.*

ⓩ **sie¹** [ziː] `pers pron` **1.** *referring to a female person (in the nominative case)* she ◊ *Ich habe gestern Susi getroffen. Sie lässt dich grüßen.*; *(in the accusative case)* her ◊ *Britta ist krank. Ich rufe sie morgen an.* **2.** *referring to a fem noun that does not designate a person or animal* it ◊ *„Hast du meine Tasche gesehen?" — „Sie liegt auf dem Tisch."*

nom	sie
acc	sie
dat	ihr
gen	ihrer

sie² [ziː] `pers pron` *3. pers pl* **1.** *(in the nominative case)* they ◊ *Jule und Andi haben eine Karte geschrieben. Sie sind auf Gomera.*; *(in the accusative case)* them ◊ *Karl und Lea sind aus dem Urlaub zurück. Ich rufe sie morgen an.* ◆ *„Sind das neue Schuhe?" — „Ja, ich habe sie erst gestern gekauft."* **2.** *(fam)* they ◊ *Sie haben ihn beim Fahren ohne Gurt erwischt.*

nom	sie
acc	sie
dat	ihnen
gen	ihrer

Sie¹ [ziː] die <-, –s> her ◊ *Mode für Sie und Ihn.* **eine Sie** a she ◊ *Ist das Meerschweinchen ein Er oder eine Sie?*

ⓩ **Sie²** [ziː] `pers pron` you ◊ *Setzen Sie sich bitte, Herr Sommer.* ◆ *Frau Schnorr! Ich habe Sie gar nicht erkannt!* ◆ *Meine Damen und Herren, ich heiße Sie recht herzlich willkommen.* ◆ *Darf ich Sie zu Ihren Plätzen bringen?*

ⓢ **jdn mit „Sie" anreden, zu jdm „Sie" sagen** address sb as „Sie", use the polite form of address for sb **per Sie sein** use „Sie" as the form of

address ◇ *Obwohl sie schon seit Jahren zusammen-arbeiten, sind sie noch per Sie.*

nom	Sie
acc	Sie
dat	Ihnen
gen	Ihrer

Sieb [ziːp] das <–(e)s, –e> sieve, riddle ◇ *Sieben Sie die Erde mit einem groben/feinen Sieb.* ♦ *eine Soße durch ein Sieb passieren*
sie·ben ['ziːbm̩] [nmrl] seven → vier
Sie·ben ['ziːbm̩] die <–, –(en)> **1.** seven → Vier 1. **2.** *(fam) (bus, tram etc.)* number seven → Vier 2.
sie·ben·fach ['ziːbm̩fax] [adj, adv] *when used as an adj, only before ns* sevenfold, seven times → vierfach
sieb·te ['ziːptə] [adj] <ein siebter ..., eine siebte ..., ein siebtes ...> seventh → vierte
Sieb·tel ['ziːptl̩] das <–s, –> seventh → Viertel
sieb·tens ['ziːptn̩s, 'ziːptəns] [adv] seventhly → viertens
sieb·zehn ['ziːptseːn] [nmrl] seventeen → vier
sieb·zig ['ziːptsɪç] [nmrl] seventy → vier
sie·deln ['ziːdl̩n] [intr v] +haben settle (down) ◇ *In früheren Zeiten siedelten hier indogermanische Stämme.*
Sied·lung ['ziːdlʊŋ] die <–, –en> **1.** settlement ◇ *Hier befand sich eine bronzezeitliche Siedlung.* **2.** estate ◇ *Die Siedlung wurde in die Gemeinde Maxdorf eingegliedert.* ♦ *Die ganze Siedlung ist gegen das Bauvorhaben.*
Sieg [ziːk] der <–(e)s, –e> victory ◇ *einen klaren Sieg erringen* ♦ *den Sieg davontragen* ♦ *der Sieg über einen Gegner* ⊖Niederlage
sie·gen ['ziːɡn̩] [intr v] +haben (also fig) win ◇ *Die schwedische Mannschaft hat 1:0 gesiegt.* ♦ *Am Ende siegte die Vernunft.* über jdn/etw. siegen beat sb/sth ◇ *Kaiserslautern siegte über Bayern München.* ⊖verlieren
Sie·ger ['ziːɡɐ] der <–s, –>, **Sie·ge·rin** ['ziːɡərɪn] die <–, –nen> *(of a competition)* winner ◇ *Er ging als Sieger aus der Wahl hervor.* ♦ *Er wurde zum Sieger erklärt.* ♦ *die eindeutige/strahlende Siegerin* ♦ *Sieger nach Punkten; (in war etc.)* victor ◇ *die Sieger des Zweiten Weltkriegs* ⊖Verlierer
⊚ **zweiter Sieger** *(iron)* runner-up
sie·he ['ziːə] → sehen
⊘ **sieht** [ziːt] *pres of* sehen
sie·zen ['ziːtsn̩] [tr v] +haben jdn siezen address sb with 'Sie' sie siezen sich they adress each other with 'Sie' ⊖duzen
Sig·nal [zɪɡ'naːl] das <–s, –e> **1.** sign, signal ◇ *Nicht jeder abweichende Blutwert ist ein Signal für eine Krankheit.* ♦ *Sie gab das Signal zum Aufbruch.* ♦ *ein digitales Signal aussenden* ♦ *Das Signal stand auf „Stopp!"* ein Signal setzen set a new direction ◇ *Er wollte mit seiner Aktion Signale für mehr Toleranz setzen.* ⊖Zeichen **2.** *(Swiss)* traffic sign
sig·na·li·sie·ren [zɪɡnali'ziːrən] [tr v] <signalisiert, signalisierte, hat signalisiert> signal, indicate ◇ *Er signalisierte Bereitschaft zur Zusammenarbeit.* ♦ *Das Umfrageergebnis signalisiert einen Trend zum Online-Einkauf.*

Sil·be ['zɪlbə] die <–, –n> **1.** GRAM syllable ◇ *ein Wort mit vier Silben* **2.** *(fig)* word ◇ *Er erwähnte sie mit keiner Silbe.* ⊖Wort
Sil·ber ['zɪlbɐ] das <–s> *no pl (also fam)* silver ◇ *ein Armreif aus massivem Silber* ♦ *Das Silber muss poliert werden.* ♦ *olympisches Silber*
⊘ **Sil·ves·ter** [zɪl'vɛstɐ] *seldom with definite article 'das'* New Year's Eve

> On the last day of the year, German people hold New Year's Eve parties where there is lots to drink, dancing and food. At midnight, the New Year is seen in with fireworks and gun salutes. In accordance with an old custom, as much noise as possible is made to drive away evil spirits. It is also common to try to forecast the future, for example by pouring lead into cold water to tell one's fortune for the coming year. Often, people give away lucky charms such as marzipan pigs containing a lucky penny.

Sims [zɪms] der <–es, –e> ledge, sill ◇ *Auf dem Sims steht ein Blumentopf.*
si·mu·lie·ren [zimu'liːrən] <simuliert, simulierte, hat simuliert> [tr+intr v] feign, fake ◇ *Sie simulierte Kopfschmerzen.* ♦ *Dir ist überhaupt nicht schlecht. Du simulierst nur!* [tr v] *(tech)* simulate ◇ *einen Flugzeugabsturz am PC simulieren*
si·mul·tan [zimʊl'taːn] [adj, adv] *no comp/superl; when used as an adj, only before ns (lofty)* simultaneous(ly) ◇ *Die Veranstaltungen sind simultan/finden simultan statt.* ♦ *Der Vortrag wird in zehn Sprachen simultan gedolmetscht.* ⊖gleichzeitig
⊘ **sind** [zɪnt] *pres of* sein¹
⊘ **sin·gen** ['zɪŋən] <singt, sang, hat gesungen> [tr+intr v] sing ◇ *Sie sang ein Liebeslied.* ♦ *Im Garten singen die Vögel.* ♦ *Sie sang ihr Kind in den Schlaf.*
Sin·gu·lar ['zɪŋɡulaːɐ] der <–s, –e> *no pl* singular ◇ *Das Verb steht im Singular.* ♦ *Das Wort „Leute" hat keinen Singular.* ⊖Einzahl ⊖Plural, Mehrzahl
⊘ **sin·ken** ['zɪŋkŋ̍] <sinkt, sank, ist gesunken> [intr v] **1.** *(slowly)* sink, go down ◇ *Die Sonne sank unter den Horizont.* ♦ *Der Ring sank auf den Grund des Teichs.* ♦ *Hilfe, wir sinken!* ♦ *Unsere Stimmung sank beträchtlich.* jdm in die Arme sinken fall/sink into sb's arms **2.** *(quickly)* drop, fall ◇ *Sie sank bewusstlos zu Boden.* ♦ *Sie sank vor ihr auf die Knie.* ♦ *Sie sank völlig erschöpft aufs Sofa.* ♦ *Die Zinsen/Preise/Temperaturen sind gesunken.* ⊖fallen **3.** *(chances)* dwindle ◇ *Die Chancen, ihn lebend zu finden, sinken mit jeder Stunde.* ⊖steigen
⊘ **Sinn** [zɪn] der <–(e)s, –e> **1.** *(perception)* sense ◇ *ein Erlebnis für alle Sinne* ♦ *Das Sehen ist unser stärkster Sinn.* ♦ *Für Gefahren habe ich einen sechsten Sinn.* Sinn für etw. sense for sth ◇ *Er hat Sinn/keinen Sinn für Humor.* ♦ *Ihr Sinn für Gerechtigkeit ist stark ausgebildet.* im engeren Sinne in the strict sense **2.** *no pl* point, sense ◇ *Das war nicht Sinn der Sache!* ♦ *im wahrsten Sinne des Wortes* ♦ *Hat es Sinn, Kalorien zu zählen?* ♦ *Freiheit im engeren Sinn* ♦ *Die Geschichte ergibt überhaupt keinen Sinn!* der Sinn des Lebens the meaning of life es hat keinen Sinn, etw. zu tun there is no point in doing sth jds Leben macht keinen Sinn there is no purpose to sb's life

A B C D E F G H I J K L M N O P Q R **S** T U V W X Y Z

Ⓔ ohne Sinn und Verstand for no apparent reason, without rhyme or reason im wahrsten Sinne des Wortes *(emph)* in the true sense of the word, literally seine fünf Sinne beisammen haben *(fam)* be quite right in the head wieder zu Sinnen kommen come to your senses etw. geht jdm nicht aus dem Sinn sb cannot get sth out of their mind, sb cannot forget sth jdm durch den Sinn gehen be on sb's mind etw. im Sinn haben have sth in mind mit jdm/etw. nichts im Sinn haben have nothing to do with sb/sth, have no interest in sb/sth jdm in den Sinn kommen come to sb's mind bei Sinnen sein be in your right mind in jds Sinn sein be to sb's liking, be to sb's way of thinking ◊ Ist das in deinem Sinn oder sollen wir es ändern? jdm steht der Sinn nach etw. sb feels like sth ◊ Mir steht der Sinn nach einem Glas Wein. (wie) von Sinnen out of your mind ◊ Er stach wie von Sinnen auf sein Opfer ein.

sinn·lich ['zɪnlɪç] [adj] **1.** sensual ◊ *sinnliche Freuden* ♦ *Ihre Lippen waren sehr sinnlich.* **2.** *(perception)* sense ◊ *sinnliche Wahrnehmung*

sinn·los ['zɪnloːs] [adj, adv] <sinnloser, am sinnlosesten> pointless(ly) ◊ *sinnlose Gewalt* ♦ *Sie hatte das Gefühl, dass ihr Leben sinnlos geworden war.* ♦ *Du solltest aufhören, sinnlos Geld auszugeben.* ♦ *Sie standen sinnlos herum und wussten nicht, was sie tun sollten.* ⊝sinnvoll

sinn·voll ['zɪnfɔl] [adj, adv] useful(ly), sensible (-ibly) ◊ *eine sinnvolle Beschäftigung* ♦ *Es wäre sinnvoll, das Ganze noch einmal zu überdenken.* ♦ *seine Zeit sinnvoll nutzen* ⊝sinnlos, unsinnig

Si·re·ne [ziˈreːnə] die <-, -n> siren ◊ *Die Feuerwehr fuhr mit Blaulicht und Sirene zum Einsatz.*

Si·rup [ˈziːrʊp] der <-s, -e> *most sing* **1.** syrup, sirup **2.** cordial, high juice ◊ *Sirup mit Wasser verdünnen*

Sit·te [ˈzɪtə] die <-, -n> **1.** custom Sitten und Bräuche/Gebräuche customs and traditions Sitte sein be the custom, be customary ⊝Brauch, Tradition **2.** common decency gegen die guten Sitten verstoßen offend common decency **3.** *no pl (fam) (police)* vice squad

Ⓩ **Si·tu·a·ti·on** [zituaˈtsjoːn] die <-, -en> situation ◊ *Was kann ich in dieser Situation tun?* ♦ *jds finanzielle Situation* ⊝Lage

Ⓩ **Sitz** [zɪts] der <-es, -e> **1.** seat ◊ *Das Publikum erhob sich von den Sitzen.* ♦ *ein Stuhl mit gepolstertem Sitz* ♦ *Bei den Landtagswahlen hat die FDP zwei Sitze erobert.* **2.** *(of an institution, a company)* head office, headquarters ◊ *ein internationales Unternehmen mit Sitz in Chicago*

Ⓩ **sit·zen** [ˈzɪtsn̩] <sitzt, saß, hat/ist gesessen> [intr v] **1.** +*haben; in South G, Austr, Swiss often* +*sein* sit ◊ *Der Vogel sitzt auf einem Ast.* ♦ *vor dem Fernseher sitzen* ♦ *am Computer/Schreibtisch sitzen* beim Essen sitzen be eating, be having a meal an seiner Doktorarbeit sitzen be working on your doctoral thesis **2.** +*haben (clothes)* fit ◊ *Der Anzug sitzt nicht.* etw. sitzt wie angegossen sth fits like a glove **3.** +*haben (fam) (in prison)* do (time) ◊ *Dafür muss er mindestens fünf Jahre sitzen.* **4.** +*haben (as a member)* irgendwo sitzen sit somewhere, be somewhere ◊ *im Gemeinderat sitzen* **5.** +*haben (fam) (vocabulary, lines etc.)*

sink in ◊ *Vokabeln so lange wiederholen, bis sie sitzen* **6.** +*haben (emotion etc.)* hit home ◊ *Das war eine Beleidigung, die saß.; (hatred, shame)* be deep seated ◊ *Der Hass gegen seinen Rivalen sitzt tief.* Mir sitzt noch der Schreck in den Gliedern. I am still in shock.

Ⓔ sitzen bleiben **1.** ꜱᴄʜᴏᴏʟ *(in school)* repeat a year ◊ *Sie ist schon wieder sitzen geblieben.* **2.** remain seated ◊ *Bleiben Sie doch sitzen; ich stehe lieber.* **3.** auf etw. [dat] sitzen bleiben be left with sth ◊ *Die Marktfrau ist auf ihrem Gemüse sitzen geblieben.* einen sitzen haben *(fam)* have had one too many etw. nicht auf sich [dat] sitzen lassen not stand for sth jdn sitzen lassen **1.** *(a partner)* leave sb in the lurch, walk out on sb **2.** *(an infant)* leave sb sitting **3.** ꜱᴄʜᴏᴏʟ *(in school)* keep sb down a year

If pupils at German schools fail to achieve the necessary grades they have to repeat the academic year they have just completed, instead of progressing to the next class. This gives them another opportunity to catch up on their studies and improve their grades.

Sitz·platz [ˈzɪtsplats] der <-es, Sitzplätze> seat ◊ *Ich habe im Zug keinen Sitzplatz mehr bekommen.*

Ⓩ **Sit·zung** [ˈzɪtsʊŋ] die <-, -en> meeting ◊ *die Sitzung des Gemeinderats* einen Fall in einer nicht öffentlichen Sitzung verhandeln hear a case behind closed doors

Ska·la [ˈskaːla] die <-, Skalen> **1.** *(for measuring)* scale ◊ *einen Wert auf der Skala zwischen eins und zehn angeben* **2.** *(of goods, services)* range ◊ *Die Skala der Rottöne reicht von Rosa bis zu Tiefrot.*

Ⓩ **Skan·dal** [skanˈdaːl] der <-s, -e> scandal ◊ *Es ist ein Skandal, wie hier Gelder verschwendet werden.*

Skan·di·na·vi·en [skandiˈnaːvjən] das <-s> *article only in combination with attribute* Scandinavia box@ Land

Skan·di·na·vi·er [skandiˈnaːvjɐ] der <-s, ->, **Skan·di·na·vi·e·rin** [skandiˈnaːvjərɪn] die <-, -nen> Scandinavian → Deutsche

skan·di·na·visch [skandiˈnaːvɪʃ] [adj] *mostly before ns* Scandinavian ◊ *ein skandinavisches Land* ♦ *Der Baustil dieser Häuser ist typisch skandinavisch.*

Skat [skaːt] der <-(e)s> *no pl* skat ◊ *Skat spielen*

Skat is a popular card game played by three people. The pack consists of 32 playing cards (7, 8, 9, 10, Jack, Queen, King, and Ace). After the cards have been shuffled and dealt, a decision is made as to which two players will form a team and who will play against them on their own. The person playing on their own has to tell the other two which colour is trumps, and then the game can begin. The winner is the one who collects the highest number of points.

Ske·lett [skeˈlɛt] das <-(e)s, -e> ᴀɴᴀᴛ skeleton

Skep·sis [ˈskɛpsɪs] die <-> *no pl* scepticism, skepticism ◊ *etw. voller Skepsis betrachten*

Ⓩ **Ski** [ʃiː] der <-s, -er *or* -> ski ◊ *Ich habe mir ein Paar neue Skier gekauft.* Ski fahren/laufen ski

Ski·fah·ren [ˈʃiːfaːrən] das <-s> *no pl* skiing ◊ *Sein Hobby ist Skifahren.*

Skiz·ze [ˈskɪtsə] die <-, -n> **1.** sketch ◊ *eine*

Skizze von etw. anfertigen **2.** outline, brief account ◊ *die Skizze eines Vortrags* ein paar Skizzen zu den Tagesordnungspunkten notieren jot down a few comments regarding the items on the agenda
Skla·ve [ˈsklaːvə] der <–n, –n>, **Skla·vin** [ˈsklaːvɪn] die <–, –nen> slave ◊ *seine Frau wie eine Sklavin behandeln* ♦ *Sklave seiner Gewohnheiten sein*
Skor·pi·on [skɔrˈpjoːn] der <–s, –e> **1.** ZOO scorpion **2.** ASTROL, ASTRON Scorpio
skru·pel·los [ˈskruːpl̩oːs] adj, adv <skrupelloser, am skrupellosesten> unscrupulous(ly) ◊ *ein skrupelloser Geschäftsmann* ♦ *Seine Methoden sind skrupellos.* ♦ *skrupellos gegen seine Konkurrenten vorgehen*
② **Slip** [slɪp] der <–s, –s> *(for men)* (pair of) briefs ◊ *Tobias trägt lieber Boxershorts als Slips.; (for women)* (pair of) panties ⊜Unterhose
Slo·wa·ke [sloˈvaːkə] der <–n, –n>, **Slo·wa·kin** [sloˈvaːkɪn] die <–, –nen> Slovak → Deutsche
Slo·wa·kei [slovaˈkaɪ̯] <–> *no pl (always die Slowakei)* Slovakia ◊ *Sie lebt in der Slowakei. box@* Land
Slo·wa·kin [sloˈvaːkɪn] *fem of* Slowake
slo·wa·kisch [sloˈvaːkɪʃ] adj *mostly before ns* Slovak(ian) → deutsch
Slo·wa·kisch [sloˈvaːkɪʃ] das <–(s)> *no pl* Slovak(ian) → Deutsch
Slo·we·ne [sloˈveːnə] der <–n, –n>, **Slo·we·nin** [sloˈveːnɪn] die <–, –nen> Slovene → Deutsche
Slo·we·ni·en [sloˈveːnjən] das <–> *article only in combination with attribute, no pl* Slovenia → Deutschland
Slo·we·nin [sloˈveːnɪn] *fem of* Slowene
slo·we·nisch [sloˈveːnɪʃ] adj *mostly before ns* Slovenian → deutsch
Slo·we·nisch [sloˈveːnɪʃ] das <–(s)> *no pl* Slovenian → Deutsch
② **Smog** [smɔk] der <–s> *no pl* smog
② **so**¹ [zoː] adv **1.** like this/that ◊ *So habe ich mir meinen Urlaub nicht vorgestellt.* ♦ *Das machst du gut so.* ♦ *So kannst du unmöglich zu einer Hochzeit gehen!* So, wie du das machst, ist es falsch. The way you are doing it is wrong. *etw. so erklären, dass auch Kinder es verstehen* explain sth in such a way that even children can understand it *so etwas something like that* ◊ *Mit so etwas kann man ihr immer eine Freude machen.* So etwas habe ich ja noch nie gehört. I've never heard anything like it. *so jemand someone like that/her etc.* ◊ *Wie kann man nur mit so jemandem in Urlaub fahren?* oder so or so, or something (like that) ◊ *Er heißt Karl Jens oder so.* **2.** so ◊ *Es ist so schön hier!* ♦ *Ich habe mich so sehr bemüht.* ♦ *Sie war so nett, mir das abzunehmen.* ♦ *Sie war so müde, dass sie sofort einschlief.* So lange kann ich nicht bleiben. I can't stay that long. Ich bin schon so groß. I'm big enough already. So viel kann ich nicht essen. I can't eat that much. So weit kann ich aber nicht gehen. I really can't go that far. So schlecht war der Film nun auch wieder nicht. The film certainly wasn't that bad. *so viel so much* ◊ *Er arbeitet so viel.*; however much ◊ *So viel er auch arbeitet, er schafft sein Pensum nie.* Was — so viel hast du dafür bezahlt? What — you paid that much for it? So viel Geld habe ich

nicht. I haven't got that much money. Er hat nicht so viel wie ich. He hasn't got as much as I have. *so viele so many* ◊ *Ich habe so viele Bücher, dass ich schon keinen Platz auf dem Regal mehr habe.* So viele wie du habe ich nicht. I don't have as many as you. **3.** *so ein/eine such* ◊ *Sie war so eine kluge Frau.* So ein Idiot! What an idiot! **4.** according to ◊ *Das Projekt soll noch dieses Jahr fertig sein, so unser Chef.* **5.** *(fam)* about, around ◊ *Das wird so 100 Euro kosten.* **6.** *(fam)* for nothing ◊ „Was hast du dafür bezahlt?“ — „Gar nichts, das habe ich so bekommen.“ ⊜umsonst **7.** as I am/you are/it is etc. ◊ „Brauchen Sie eine Tüte?“ — „Nein danke, ich nehme das Brot so.“
⊛ **so genannt** so-called, as it is/they are referred to **so oder so** *(fam)* **1.** anyway **2.** one way or another **3.** like this or like that **so und so** either way ◊ *Dieses Problem kann man so und so angehen.* **so was** *(fam)* well, I never ◊ *So was, sagt er mir doch, ich solle es selbst machen.* **so … wie** as … as ◊ *Du musst so schnell wie möglich kommen.* ♦ *Gestern war das Wetter nicht so schön wie heute.* **und so** *(fam)* and things like that ◊ *Am Wochenende muss ich den Haushalt und so machen.*
② **so**² [zoː] conjunc **1.** *(comparison)* so …, so … as … as ◊ *So schön Motorradfahren ist, so gefährlich ist es auch.* **2.** *(concessive)* as much as ◊ *So sehr er sich auch bemüht, er begreift es einfach nicht.* → sodass
② **so**³ [zoː] part **1.** *(requesting)* just ◊ *So lass ihn doch, wenn er nicht will.* **2.** *(enquiring)* really ◊ „Wir fahren in Urlaub.“ —„So, wohin geht's denn?“ **3.** *(appreciating)* ach so oh, I see **4.** *(sarcastic)* So? Is that so? **5.** *(interjection)* well, right ◊ *So, nun hast du die Uhr endgültig kaputt gemacht!*
② **so·bald** [zoˈbalt] conjunc as soon as ◊ *Sobald wir zu Hause sind, rufe ich dich an.* ⊜sowie
② **So·cke** [ˈzɔkə] die <–, –n> sock
So·ckel [ˈzɔkl̩] der <–s, –> pedestal; *(for a statue)* plinth ◊ *Die Statue steht auf einem Sockel aus Marmor.*
so·dass, so dass [zoˈdas] conjunc so that ◊ *Ich erkläre es noch einmal, sodass es alle verstehen.*
so·e·ben [zoˈʔeːbm̩] adv just (now) ◊ *Er ist soeben weggegangen.*
② **So·fa** [ˈzoːfaː] das <–s, –s> sofa, settee ⊜Couch
so·fern [zoˈfɛrn] conjunc provided (that) ◊ *Sofern du nichts dagegen hast, würde ich auch gern Juliane einladen.* ⊜wenn
soff [zɔf] *pret of* saufen
② **so·fort** [zoˈfɔrt] adv immediately, straight/right away ◊ *Komm sofort nach Hause!* ♦ *Sie hat sofort begriffen, worum es ging.*
sog [zoːk] *pret of* saugen
Sog [zoːk] der <–(e)s, –e> suction ◊ *in den Sog von etw. geraten; (of a river)* current ◊ *gegen den Sog des Flusses anschwimmen; (of a hurricane, tornado etc.)* vortex
② **so·gar** [zoˈgaːr] adv even ◊ *Das macht Spaß und wird sogar noch gut bezahlt.* ♦ *Sie arbeitet sogar am Wochenende.*
Soh·le [ˈzoːlə] die <–, –n> **1.** sole ◊ *Diese Schuhe haben Sohlen aus Leder.* ♦ *Sie kitzelte ihr Baby an*

A
B
C
D
E
F
G
H
I
J
K
L
M
N
O
P
Q
R
S
T
U
V
W
X
Y
Z

A
B
C
D
E
F
G
H
I
J
K
L
M
N
O
P
Q
R
S
T
U
V
W
X
Y
Z

den Sohlen. **2.** *(insert)* insole **3.** *(of a valley, pit etc.)* bottom ◇ *Vom Rand bis zur Sohle des Grabens sind es gut drei Meter.*

② **Sohn** [zo:n] der <-(e)s, Söhne> son ⊖Tochter

② **so·lang¹** [zo'laŋ], **so·lan·ge** [zo'laŋə] [adv] in the meantime ◇ *Mach du deine Aufgaben, ich koche solange.*

② **so·lang²** [zo'laŋ], **so·lan·ge** [zo'laŋə] [conjunc] **1.** as long as ◇ *Solange ich nicht weiß, was das kostet, unterschreibe ich auch keinen Vertrag.* **2.** *(fam)* so long as ◇ *Ich gehe gern mit zu der Ausstellung, solange sie keinen Eintritt kostet.*

So·lar·e·ner·gie [zo'la:ʳ|enɛʳˌgi:] die <-> *no pl* solar energy/power ◇ *eine mit Solarenergie betriebene Heizung*

② **solch** [zɔlç] [demonstr pron] *invariable (lofty)* such ◇ *Er ist solch ein lieber Mensch.* ♦ *Solch eine Frechheit lasse ich mir nicht gefallen.*

② **sol·che** ['zɔlçə] [adj] *no comp/superl, only before ns* <ein solcher ..., eine solche ..., ein solches ...> such ◇ *Solche Fragen beantworte ich nicht.* ♦ *Ein solches Problem hatte ich bis jetzt noch nicht. Ich habe einen solchen Hass auf ihn!* I hate him so much! *Das war eine solche Frechheit!* What impudence that was! ⊖derlei

② **Sol·dat** [zɔl'da:t] der <-en, -en>, **Sol·da·tin** [zɔl'da:tɪn] die <-, -nen> soldier ◇ *Er will Soldat werden.* ♦ *eine amerikanische Soldatin*

so·li·de [zo'li:də] [adj, adv] <solider, am solidesten> *(foundations etc.)* solid(ly), sturdy(-ily) ◇ *ein solides Fundament* ♦ *Büromöbel sollten solide sein.* ♦ *Das Gebäude ist solide gebaut.* ⊖stabil [adj] **1.** *(knowledge etc.)* sound ◇ *Seine Grammatikkenntnisse sind solide.* ♦ *eine solide Ausbildung* **2.** financially sound ◇ *Dieses Familienunternehmen ist solide.* ♦ *eine solide Geldanlage* **3.** respectable ◇ *ein solider junger Mann* ♦ *Sie ist solider geworden.* ⊖anständig

So·list [zo'lɪst] der <-en, -en>, **So·lis·tin** [zo'lɪstɪn] die <-, -nen> soloist

② **sol·len¹** ['zɔlən] <soll, sollte, hat sollen> [modal v] +inf **1.** *(order)* should ◇ *Der Arzt sagte, ich solle mich ausruhen.; (stronger)* be to ◇ *Du sollst sofort nach Hause kommen.* ♦ *Was soll ich tun? Du sollst nicht töten.* Thou shalt not kill. *Soll ich dir mal sagen, was ich davon halte?* Shall I tell you what I think of it? *Soll ich lieber gehen?* Would it be better if I went? *Ich soll dir schöne Grüße von ihr bestellen.* She sends you her best wishes. **2.** *subjunctive II (obligation, recommendation)* ought to, should ◇ *Du solltest dich schämen.* ♦ *Du solltest den Rat deines Arztes befolgen.* ♦ *Du hättest hingehen sollen.* **3.** *translation varies (helplessness, doubt)* Was soll ich ihm nur sagen? Whatever am I going to tell him? *Sollte ich mich in ihm getäuscht haben?* Was I wrong about him? *Wozu soll das gut sein?* What's the use of that? **4.** *(intention)* let *Du sollst dich hier wie zu Hause fühlen.* I want you to feel at home here. *Das soll mich an den Termin erinnern.* That is to remind me of the appointment. *Ich verspreche dir, das soll nicht wieder vorkommen.* I promise you it won't happen again. *Sollen wir jetzt Schluss machen?* Shall we call it a day? **5.** *translation varies (fam) (in rhetorical questions)* Wie oft

soll ich das denn noch sagen? How many more times have I got to say it? *Soll ich mich denn um alles kümmern?* Am I supposed to take care of everything then? **6.** *translation varies (fam) (challenge)* „Er sagt, er kündigt!" — „Soll er doch!" "He says he is handing his notice in!" — "Let him!" *Dann soll er es doch allein versuchen!* Then let him do it on his own! **7.** *translation varies (indifference)* Mir soll's recht sein, wenn er nicht kommt. It's okay by me if he doesn't come. *Dir sollte es doch egal sein, was sie von dir denkt.* It shouldn't worry you what she thinks of you. **8.** *subjunctive II, translation varies (possibility)* so etwas soll es geben *it is not unheard of* Es soll vorkommen, dass ich mich irre. It may be that I am wrong. *Sollte es möglich sein, dass er das nicht weiß?* Could it be possible that he doesn't know that? *Man sollte glauben, er hat noch nie eine Frau gesehen.* You would think that he had never seen a woman before. **9.** *subjunctive II in the event that, if, should* Sollte es regnen, findet das Fest im Haus statt. In the event that it rains the party will take place indoors. *Sollte ich mich täuschen, dann bitte ich um Verzeihung.* If I am mistaken, I apologize. *Sollte er anrufen, sag ihm bitte, dass ich zurückrufe.* Should he call please tell him that I'll ring back. **10.** *pres tense, translation varies (stating sb else's view)* jd/etw. soll etw. sein *sb/sth is supposed to be sth* ◇ *Das soll gut gegen Husten sein.* ♦ *Dort soll es sehr schön sein.* Wer soll das sein? Who is that supposed to be? *Die Steuern sollen schon wieder erhöht werden.* Taxes are supposed to be raised again. *Helena soll sehr schön gewesen sein.* Helena was said to be very beautiful. jd/etw. soll etw. gut/schlecht können *sb is said to be able to do sth well/badly* ◇ *Er soll sehr gut singen können.* **11.** *translation varies (fatefulness)* Er sollte sie nie wiedersehen. He was never to see her again. *Es hat offensichtlich nicht sollen sein.* It was obviously not to be. *Es sollten Jahre vergehen, bis/bevor ...* Years were to pass until ...

② **sol·len²** ['zɔlən] <soll, sollte, hat gesollt> [intr v] **1.** should *(do sth)* ◇ *Du sollst sofort nach Hause.* ♦ *Ich hätte heute eigentlich zum Zahnarzt gesollt.* ♦ *„Ob ich ihm meine Meinung sagen soll?" — „Das solltest du lieber nicht."* Soll der Fernseher in diese Ecke? Should the television go in this corner? **2.** *translation varies (purpose)* Ich bin eingeladen, aber was soll ich denn dort? I have been invited round, but what am I supposed to do there? *Was der Unsinn/Lärm?* What's all this nonsense/noise? *Was soll das?* Hey, stop it!

⊛ **was soll's** *(fam)* what the heck, what the hell ◇ *Ach, was soll's, dann verliere ich halt mal.*

so·lo ['zo:lo] [adj, adv] *no comp/superl; when used as an adj, not before ns* on your own ◇ *Anna ist jetzt wieder solo.* ♦ *Sie kam solo zur Party.* [adv] MUS solo ◇ *solo singen/spielen*

so·mit [zo'mɪt, 'zo:mɪt] [adv] thus, therefore ◇ *Er hat gute Noten, somit kann er aufs Gymnasium.* ⊖demnach, also

Som·mer ['zɔmɐ] der <-s, -> summer ◇ *Im Sommer fahren wir ans Meer.* ♦ *ein heißer Sommer* Bald wird es Sommer. Summer is coming soon.

Som·mer·fe·ri·en ['zɔmɐfe:rjən] die <-> *only pl*

summer holidays

Som·mer·zeit ['zɔmɐtsaet] die <–> no pl **1.** summertime ◊ Besonders schön ist es hier während der Sommerzeit. **2.** (on clocks) summer time, daylight saving time ◊ die Uhren von Sommerzeit auf Winterzeit umstellen

② **Son·der·…** ['zɔndɐ] prefix **1.** special … ◊ ein Sonderangebot ♦ für etw. eine Sondergenehmigung brauchen Sondermüll hazardous waste **2.** custommade … ◊ eine Sonderanfertigung ♦ ein Sondermodell

Son·der·an·ge·bot ['zɔndɐ|angəbo:t] das <–(e)s, –e> special offer ◊ Spargel gibt es zurzeit im Sonderangebot.

son·der·bar ['zɔndɐbaːʳ] adj, adv strange(ly), peculiar(ly), odd(ly) ◊ Er ist heute so sonderbar. ♦ Das ist aber eine sonderbare Entschuldigung. ♦ Es ist so sonderbar still. ⊜seltsam, eigenartig, merkwürdig, komisch

Son·der·fall ['zɔndɐfal] der <–(e)s, Sonderfälle> special case ◊ Hierbei handelt es sich um einen Sonderfall.

② **son·dern** ['zɔndɐn] conjunc but ◊ Er will nicht Chemie studieren, sondern zuerst eine Lehre machen. ♦ Komm lieber nicht heute, sondern erst morgen.

Son·der·preis ['zɔndɐpraes] der <–es, –e> special price ◊ etw. zu einem Sonderpreis verkaufen

Son·der·schu·le ['zɔndɐʃuːlə] die <–, –n> special needs school ◊ auf die Sonderschule gehen

② **Sonn·a·bend** ['zɔn|aːbmt, 'zɔn|aːbənt] der <–s, –e> (regional) Saturday ⊜Samstag → Montag

sonn·a·bends ['zɔn|aːbmts, 'zɔn|aːbənts] adv (regional) on Saturdays, on a Saturday ⊜samstags → montags

② **Son·ne** ['zɔnə] die <–, –n> sun ◊ Diese Pflanze braucht viel Sonne. ♦ Wann geht morgen die Sonne auf/unter?
 ⊚ sich dat die Sonne auf den Pelz brennen/scheinen lassen (fam) soak up the sun

son·nen ['zɔnən] ref v +haben sich sonnen sunbathe

Son·nen·auf·gang ['zɔnən|aofgaŋ] der <–(e)s, Sonnenaufgänge> sunrise ◊ Bei Sonnenaufgang fuhren wir los. ⊜Sonnenuntergang

Son·nen·brand ['zɔnənbrant] der <–(e)s, Sonnenbrände> sunburn ◊ einen Sonnenbrand bekommen

Son·nen·bril·le ['zɔnənbrɪlə] die <–, –n> (pair of) sunglasses ◊ eine Sonnenbrille aufsetzen

Son·nen·schirm ['zɔnənʃɪʳm] der <–(e)s, –e> sunshade ◊ sich unter den Sonnenschirm setzen

Son·nen·un·ter·gang ['zɔnən|ʊntɐgaŋ] der <–(e)s, Sonnenuntergänge> sunset ◊ Wir sollten vor Sonnenuntergang zurück sein. ⊜Sonnenaufgang

son·nig ['zɔnɪç] adj **1.** sunny ◊ ein sonniges Plätzchen ♦ Morgen soll es sonnig werden. **2.** mostly before ns cheerful ◊ ein sonniges Wesen haben

② **Sonn·tag** ['zɔntaːk] der <–(e)s, –e> Sunday → Montag

sonn·tags ['zɔntaːks] adv on Sundays, on a Sunday → montags

② **sonst** [zɔnst] adv **1.** else ◊ Paul war da, aber sonst keiner. ♦ Was hast du sonst noch zum Geburtstag bekommen? **2.** otherwise ◊ Beeil dich,

sonst kommen wir zu spät. ♦ Das Wetter war scheußlich, aber sonst war es ein toller Urlaub. ⊜ansonsten **3.** usually ◊ Der sonst so kluge Andreas wusste hier auch keine Lösung. ♦ Er übersetzt sonst viel besser.

sons·tig ['zɔnstɪç] adj no comp/superl, only before ns other ◊ Hosen, Pullis und sonstige Bekleidungsstücke

so·oft [zoˈ|ɔft] conjunc whenever ◊ Sooft ich ihn sehe, fragt er nach dir.

② **Sor·ge** ['zɔʳgə] die <–, –n> **1.** most pl trouble ◊ finanzielle Sorgen haben ♦ Sie erzählt ihm all ihre Sorgen. **2.** worry ◊ Sie war vor Sorge ganz außer sich. ♦ sich um ein krankes Kind sich dat um jdn/etw. Sorgen machen worry about sb/sth, be worried about sb/sth **3.** no pl care ◊ Die Sorge für ihre alte kranke Mutter nimmt sie ganz in Anspruch.
 ⊚ keine Sorge don't worry, no worries

② **sor·gen** ['zɔʳgŋ] intr v +haben **1.** für jdn/ein Tier sorgen take care of sb/an animal, look after sb/an animal ◊ gut/schlecht für seine Kinder sorgen ♦ Wer sorgt für den Hund, wenn wir weg sind? **2.** für etw. sorgen ensure sth, see to sth ◊ Die Polizei sorgt für Ruhe und Ordnung. ♦ Ich werde dafür sorgen, dass das nicht noch einmal passiert. **3.** für etw. sorgen provide sth, take care of sth ◊ Jutta sorgt für die Getränke.
 ref v +haben sich (um jdn/etw./wegen etw.) sorgen worry about sb/sth ◊ Ich sorge mich um deine Gesundheit.

Sorg·falt ['zɔʳkfalt] die <–> no pl care ◊ mit großer Sorgfalt arbeiten

sorg·fäl·tig ['zɔʳkfɛltɪç] adj, adv careful(ly), meticulous(ly) ◊ Als sorgfältiger Mensch überprüfe ich das lieber noch einmal. ♦ Franz ist sehr sorgfältig. eine sorgfältige Arbeit a job done with care sorgfältig arbeiten work with care seine Kleider sorgfältig zusammenlegen fold your clothes neatly ⊜genau ⊝nachlässig, schlampig

Sor·te ['zɔʳtə] die <–, –n> sort, kind, type ◊ Wir haben mehrere Sorten Käse. ♦ Die Sorte Mensch kenne ich genau. ⊜Art

sor·tie·ren [zɔʳˈtiːrən] <sortiert, sortierte, hat sortiert> tr v sort ◊ Stichwörter alphabetisch sortieren ♦ seine Urlaubsfotos sortieren; (goods) grade ◊ Eier nach Größe sortieren

Sor·ti·ment [zɔʳtiˈmɛnt] das <–(e)s, –e> assortment, range etw. ins Sortiment nehmen introduce sth to your range etw. aus dem Sortiment nehmen remove sth from your range einen Artikel im Sortiment haben stock an item

② **So·ße** ['zoːsə] die <–, –n> sauce ◊ fertige Soßen aus der Tüte; (for salad) dressing; (from or for cooked meat) gravy ◊ ein Stück Braten mit viel Soße

② **Sou·ve·nir** [suvəˈniːɐ̯] das <–s, –s> souvenir ◊ ein Souvenir aus Hawaii ⊜Andenken

sou·ve·rän [zuvəˈrɛːn, suvəˈrɛːn] adj **1.** self-assured ◊ Mein Chef ist nicht besonders souverän. ♦ ein souveräner Gegner **2.** POL sovereign ◊ ein souveräner Staat Die Bundesrepublik wurde 1955 souverän. The Federal Republic became a sovereign state in 1955. ⊜unabhängig adv eine schwierige Situation souverän meistern overcome a difficult situation in a self-assured way souverän

lächeln smile self-confidently *Unsere Mannschaft hat souverän gesiegt.* Our team had an effortless victory.

② **so·viel** [zo'fi:l] (conjunc) as far as ◊ *Soviel ich weiß, kommt er dieses Wochenende.*

so·weit [zo'vaet] (conjunc) as far as ◊ *Soweit ich das beurteilen kann, ist er sehr kompetent.*

so·wie [zo'vi:] (conjunc) **1.** as well as ◊ *Der Präsident sowie seine Gattin waren erschienen.* ⊜und **2.** as soon as ◊ *Ich rufe dich an, sowie ich nach Hause komme.* ⊜sobald

② **so·wie·so** [zovi'zo:, 'zo:vizo:] (adv) anyway, in any case ◊ *Erklär's ihm nicht, er versteht es ja sowieso nicht.* ♦ *Du kannst mir das mitgeben, ich muss sowieso zur Post.* ⊜ohnehin

② **so·wohl** [zo'vo:l] (conjunc) *(always sowohl ... als auch ...)* both ... and ..., ... as well as ... ◊ *Sie spricht sowohl Englisch als auch Spanisch.* „Willst du lieber reich oder glücklich sein?" — „Sowohl als auch!" "Would you rather be rich or happy?" — "Both!"

② **so·zi·al** [zo'tsja:l] (adj) **1.** *no comp/superl* social ◊ *soziale Gerechtigkeit* ♦ *aus schlechten sozialen Verhältnissen kommen* ♦ *soziale Einrichtungen/Berufe Die neuen Gesetze sind nicht sehr sozial.* The new laws don't particularly promote social harmony. *Der Staat ist in eine soziale Schieflage gekommen.* The state has got into difficulties in terms of its social policy. **2.** socially conscious, public-spirited ◊ *Er hat eine soziale Ader.* He is very public-spirited. *Ich habe heute meinen sozialen Tag.* I am in a charitable mood today. (adv) **1.** socially ◊ *sozial benachteiligte Gruppen* ♦ *Die Alten sollten sozial abgesichert sein.* **2.** socially, in a social way ◊ *sozial handeln* ein sozial denkender Mensch a socially minded person

So·zi·al·amt [zo'tsja:l|amt] das <-(e)s, Sozialämter> social security office ◊ *einen Antrag auf Wohngeld beim Sozialamt stellen*

② **So·zi·al·ar·bei·ter** [zo'tsja:l|a,baete] der <-s, ->, **So·zi·al·ar·bei·te·rin** [zo'tsja:l|a,baetərın] die <-, -nen> social worker ◊ *Die Gruppe wird von einem Sozialarbeiter betreut.* ♦ *Sie ist Sozialarbeiterin.*

So·zi·al·hil·fe [zo'tsja:l,hılfə] die <-> *no pl* income support, social welfare benefits ◊ *Sozialhilfe beantragen* ♦ *von Sozialhilfe leben*

So·zi·al·ver·si·che·rung [zo'tsja:l,fe,zıçəroŋ] die <-, -en> *(abbr SV)* national insurance, social security

The German *Sozialversicherung* is a statutory insurance providing benefits in the event of illness, accidents at work, occupational illness, occupational incapacity, disability, maternity, unemployment, retirement, and death. It is financed by contributions from employers, employees, and other insured persons, plus subsidies from the Federal Government. This does not apply to contributions for accident insurance which are paid by employers only. Social security benefits are not means-tested since claimants help to finance them through their own contributions and thereby acquire an entitlement to benefits. All employees are subject to compulsory insurance up to fixed income limits.

So·zi·al·ver·si·che·rungs·aus·weis [zo'tsja:lfe,zıçərʊŋs|aosvaes] der <-es, -e> national insurance card, social security card

In Germany every insured person is provided with a *Sozialversicherungsausweis* by their statutory pension insurance which they have to present to their employer and when claiming unemployment benefit. In certain jobs (construction work etc.), employees must carry their cards at all times.

So·zi·al·woh·nung [zo'tsja:l,vo:nʊŋ] die <-, -en> *publicly subsidised low-rent flat* ◊ *sich um eine Sozialwohnung bewerben*

Sozialwohnungen (the rough equivalent of council flats/housing projects) provide cheap housing for people on low incomes. Their building is subsidized by the government. Applicants for *Sozialwohnungen* need proof of entitlement, the so-called *Wohnberechtigungsschein (WBS)*, from their local housing department.

So·zi·o·lo·gie [zotsjolo'gi:] die <-> *no pl* sociology

so·zu·sa·gen [zotsu'za:gn, 'zo:tsuza:gn] (adv) so to speak, as it were ◊ *Das Gehirn ist sozusagen die Steuerzentrale des Körpers.*

Spa·ghet·ti, Spa·get·ti [ʃpa'gɛti:] die <-> *only pl* spaghetti ◊ *Spaghetti mit Tomatensoße*

Spalt [ʃpalt] der <-(e)s, -e> crack, gap, crevisse ◊ *ein Spalt in der Wand/im Felsen;* *(a door etc.)* etw. einen Spalt weit öffnen open sth slightly, open sth a crack einen Spalt weit offen stehen be slightly ajar

Spal·te ['ʃpaltə] die <-, -n> **1.** crevice, cleft, crack ◊ *eine Spalte im Felsen;* *(of a glacier)* crevasse **2.** *(of a table, newspaper etc.)* column ◊ *eine Tabelle mit fünf Spalten* ♦ *Der Bericht stand in der Spalte mit den Kurznachrichten.* **3.** *(Austr)* slice ◊ *Die Tomate waschen und in Spalten schneiden.*

Span·ge ['ʃpaŋə] die <-, -n> **1.** hairslide, barrette ◊ *Sie trug zwei Spangen im Haar.* **2.** *(for teeth)* braces ◊ *eine feste/herausnehmbare Spange* **3.** *(on clothes)* clasp ◊ *ein Umhang mit einer goldenen Spange*

Spa·ni·en ['ʃpa:njən] das <-s> *article only in combination with attribute, no pl* Spain → Deutschland

Spa·ni·er ['ʃpa:nje] der <-s, ->, **Spa·ni·e·rin** ['ʃpa:njərın] die <-, -nen> Spaniard → Deutsche

spa·nisch ['ʃpa:nıʃ] (adj) *mostly before ns* Spanish → deutsch
⊙ jdm spanisch vorkommen *(fam)* strike sb as odd

Spa·nisch ['ʃpa:nıʃ] das <-(s)> *no pl* Spanish → Deutsch

spann [ʃpan] *pret of* spinnen

span·nen ['ʃpanən] (tr v) +haben **1.** *(strings, a rope)* tighten ◊ *Die Violinistin spannt die Saiten ihrer Geige.;* *(a bow)* draw; *(a muscle)* flex **2.** stretch ◊ *ein Seil/Netz spannen;* *(a washing line)* put up etw. in einen Rahmen spannen mount sth on a frame etw. in einen Schraubstock spannen clamp sth in a vice **3.** ein Tier an/vor etw. (acc) spannen hitch an animal up to sth ◊ *die Pferde vor den Wagen spannen* **4.** *(a gun, camera)* cock (intr v) +haben *(clothes)* be tight ◊ *Das Kleid spannt am Bauch.;* *(skin)* be taut (ref v)

+**haben** 1. sich spannen tighten ◊ *Das Seil spannte sich.*; *(muscle)* tense ◊ *Beim Gewichtheben spannen sich die Armmuskel.* 2. sich über etw. [acc] spannen span sth ◊ *Der Viadukt spannt sich über das Tal.*
ⓔ **es spannen** *(esp SouthG, Austr, fam)* 1. catch on to it, get it ◊ *Jetzt hat er's endlich gespannt!* 2. get wise (to it) ◊ *Wenn wir abschreiben, spannt es unser Lehrer meist nicht.*

② **span·nend** ['ʃpanənt] [adj, adv] exciting(ly), thrilling(ly) ◊ *ein spannendes Buch* ♦ *Jetzt wird's spannend.* spannend schreiben/erzählen write in an exciting style ⊖langweilig
ⓔ **mach's nicht so spannend** don't keep me/us in suspense, get on with it

Span·nung ['ʃpanʊŋ] die <-, -en> 1. excitement, suspense ◊ *Die Spannung stieg mit jeder Minute.* einer Sache [dat] mit Spannung entgegensehen, mit/voller Spannung auf etw. [acc] warten await sth eagerly 2. tenseness ◊ *innere Spannung und Gereiztheit* 3. strain, stress ◊ *Er arbeitet den ganzen Tag unter Spannung.* 4. *(also fig)* tension ◊ *Das Seil sollte mehr Spannung haben.* ♦ *politische/internationale Spannungen* 5. PHYSICS voltage unter Spannung stehen be live

② **spa·ren** ['ʃpaːrən] [tr v] +**haben** 1. save ◊ *Geld/Energie/Wasser sparen* ♦ *Dieses Vorgehen wird uns viel Zeit sparen.*; *(money also)* put away ◊ *Ich spare jeden Monat zehn Euro.* bei etw. sparen save money on sth/doing sth ◊ *Wie kann ich beim Einkauf Geld sparen?* an etw. [dat] sparen save money on sth ◊ *Am Essen sollten man zuletzt sparen.* 2. sich [dat] etw. sparen save/spare yourself sth sich seine Worte/den (guten) Rat sparen keep your words/advice to yourself jd hätte sich das sparen können sb could have saved themselves the trouble ⊖sich etw. schenken [intr v] +**haben** 1. economize, make savings ◊ *Wenn wir ein Auto kaufen wollen, müssen wir jetzt sparen.* für etw. sparen save up for sth ◊ *für einen Urlaub sparen* an etw. [dat] sparen save on sth ◊ *Das Unternehmen spart an Personalkosten.* am falschen Ende sparen make false economies 2. mit etw. sparen be sparing with/in sth ◊ *Er ist eben so ein Typ, der mit Komplimenten spart.* nicht mit etw. sparen be generous with sth, use sth generously ◊ *Sie spart beim Kochen nicht mit Butter.*

Spar·gel ['ʃpaʳgl] der <-s, -> asparagus Spargel stechen cut/harvest asparagus

Spar·kas·se ['ʃpaːˈkasə] die <-, -n> savings bank ◊ *Er zahlt den Betrag auf sein Konto bei der Sparkasse ein.*

spär·lich ['ʃpɛːɡlɪç] [adj, adv] sparse(ly) ◊ *Gebiete mit spärlicher Vegetation* ♦ *Die Informationen dazu sind spärlich.* ♦ *eine spärlich möblierte Wohnung*; *(hair etc.)* thin(ly) ◊ *ein paar spärliche Haare*; clothing, scanty(-ily), skimpy(-ily) ◊ *Sie war nur spärlich bekleidet.*; *(meal)* meagre(ly); *(sandwich etc.)* spärlich belegt sein have a thin/meagre filling

② **spar·sam** ['ʃpaːˈzaːm] [adj, adv] 1. *(person)* thrifty(-ily) ◊ *Meine Frau ist sehr sparsam.* ♦ *Einem sparsameren Menschen würde das Geld reichen.* ♦ *Wir haben im Urlaub sehr sparsam gelebt.* sparsam wirtschaften economize sparsames Wirtschaften economizing, economising 2. sparsam (im Verbrauch) economical ◊

sparsamer Umgang mit Rohstoffen ♦ *Das Geschirrspülmittel ist sparsam im Verbrauch.* 3. mit etw. sparsam sein/umgehen, etw. sparsam verwenden be sparing with sth, use sth sparingly/economically ◊ *Sie ist sehr sparsam mit Lob.* ♦ *Sie verwendet die Schmerzmittel nur sparsam.* etw. sparsam auftragen apply sth sparingly 4. *(decoration etc.)* sparse(ly) ◊ *Die Innenausstattung des Hauses war sparsam.* ♦ *Die Wohnung war sehr sparsam möbliert.*

Spar·te ['ʃpaʳtə] die <-, -n> 1. area, field ◊ *eine profitable Sparte* ♦ *In welcher Sparte sind Sie beruflich tätig?* 2. *(newspaper)* section ◊ *die Sparte „Aktuelles"*

② **Spaß** [ʃpaːs] der <-es, Späße> 1. no pl fun ◊ *Die Gäste hatten auf der Feier viel Spaß.* ♦ *jdm den Spaß verderben* etw. macht jdm Spaß sb enjoys sth ◊ *Die Arbeit macht ihm keinen Spaß mehr.* Spaß an etw. [dat] haben enjoy sth ◊ *Er hat Spaß an seinem neuen Auto.* (ich wünsche dir/euch) viel Spaß have fun, enjoy yourself aus/zum Spaß for fun ◊ *Die Kinder haben sich zum Spaß verkleidet.* 2. joke, prank ◊ *Wir haben über die Späße des Clowns gelacht.* einen Spaß machen (make a) joke jd macht nur Spaß sb is just joking sich [dat] einen Spaß machen take delight in sth keinen Spaß verstehen not stand for any nonsense sich [dat] einen Spaß mit jdm erlauben play a joke on sb etw. im Spaß sagen say sth jokingly
ⓔ **aus (lauter) Spaß an der Freude** *(hum)* for the sheer fun of it **ein teurer Spaß** an expensive business **Spaß beiseite** joke apart **etw. ist kein Spaß mehr** sth is beyond a joke **was kostet der Spaß** *(fam)* what's the damage

② **spät** [ʃpɛːt] [adj, adv] <später, am spätesten> late ◊ *Es ist schon ziemlich spät.* ♦ *Das ist der späteste Abgabetermin, den ich Ihnen anbieten kann.* ♦ *So spät kannst du ihn nicht mehr anrufen.* ♦ *Das mache ich später.* zu spät kommen be late bis in die späte Nacht (hinein) until late at night die Werke der späten Klassik/des späten Barock etc. late classical/baroque etc. works the Werke des späten Beethoven etc. Beethoven's late(r) work (s)ein spätes Glück finden find happiness late in life ⊖früh → **später**

Spa·ten ['ʃpaːtn̩] der <-s, -> spade ◊ *mit einem Spaten ein Loch graben*

spä·ter ['ʃpɛːtə] *comp of* spät [adv] (at some point in the) future, later on ◊ *Eine spätere Übernahme durch den Mieter ist möglich.* ♦ *Aufgrund seiner Faulheit muss er später mit Ärger rechnen.* jdn auf später vertrösten put sb off jd will später (einmal) etw. werden sb wants to do sth later on/when they grow up ◊ *Sie möchte später einmal Tierärztin werden.*

spä·te·re ['ʃpɛːtərə] [adj] no comp/superl, only before ns <ein späterer ..., eine spätere ..., ein späterer ...> latter ◊ *Die meisten seiner Lieder entstanden erst in späteren Jahren.* ⊖frühere

spä·tes·tens ['ʃpɛːtəstn̩s, 'ʃpɛːtəstəns] [adv] at the latest ◊ *bis spätestens Ende des Monats* ♦ *spätestens am 1. September* ⊖frühestens

Spatz [ʃpats] der <-en or also -es, -en> sparrow
ⓔ **die Spatzen pfeifen es von den Dächern** *(fig)* said when sth is supposed to be a secret but is already widely known **besser ein Spatz in der**

Hand als eine Taube auf dem Dach a bird in the hand is worth two in the bush **(mein) Spatz** *(fam)* darling

Spätz·le [ˈʃpɛtslə] die <-> *only pl* Swabian pasta ◊ *Es gab Linsen mit Spätzle.*

spa·zie·ren [ʃpaˈtsiːrən] <spaziert, spazierte, ist spaziert> [intr v] stroll ◊ *Sie spazierten am Strand entlang.* spazieren gehen go for a walk/stroll ◊ *Sie geht zweimal am Tag mit dem Hund spazieren.* spazieren fahren go for a drive/ride etc.

Spa·zier·gang [ʃpaˈtsiːɡaŋ] der <-(e)s, Spaziergänge> walk, stroll ◊ *Er macht jeden Nachmittag einen Spaziergang.*

SPD [espeːˈdeː] die *(abbr of* Sozialdemokratische Partei Deutschlands*)* German Social Democrat Party

Originally a workers' party, the *SPD* has developed into a moderate, left of centre party advocating a regulated market economy and a strong welfare system.

Speck [ʃpɛk] der <-(e)s> *no pl* **1.** *(pork)* bacon fat ◊ *knusprig gebratener Speck* durchwachsener Speck streaky bacon **2.** *(hum) (of people)* fat, flab ◊ *Der Speck muss weg, darum gehe ich jetzt ins Fitnessstudio.* **3.** *(of whales, seals)* blubber ⊛ **mit Speck fängt man Mäuse** *(fig)* it takes a sprat to catch a mackerel **ran an den Speck** get down to it/work *(referring to food)* tuck in

Spe·di·ti·on [ʃpediˈtsioːn] die <-, -en> **1.** haulage company; *(for moving house)* removal company ◊ *Der Umzug wird von einer Spedition durchgeführt.* **2.** forwarding department **3.** carriage, transport ◊ *Die Firma ist auf die Spedition von Gefahrengütern spezialisiert.*

Spei·chel [ˈʃpaɪçl̩] der <-s> *no pl* saliva, spittle ◊ *Der Kuh lief Speichel aus dem Maul.*

Spei·cher [ˈʃpaɪçɐ] der <-s, -> **1.** warehouse, storehouse ◊ *Das Jahr war erfolgreich und die Speicher gefüllt.;* *(for grains)* silo, granary ⊜Lager **2.** *(SouthG)* loft, attic ◊ *Die alten Spielsachen brachten sie auf den Speicher.* ⊜Dachboden, Boden **3.** IT memory ◊ *den Speicher erweitern* ◆ *Der Computer hat für meine Zwecke zu wenig Speicher.*

② **spei·chern** [ˈʃpaɪçɐn] [tr v] +*haben* **1.** store ◊ *Das Gehirn kann große Mengen an Informationen speichern.* **2.** IT save, back up ◊ *Daten auf einer Diskette speichern* ⊜sichern **3.** accumulate, retain ◊ *Warme Luft kann mehr Feuchtigkeit speichern als kalte.* ⊜abgeben

② **Spei·se** [ˈʃpaɪzə] die <-, -n> dish ◊ *köstliche/raffinierte Speisen* Speisen und Getränke food and drink kalte und warme Speisen hot and cold dishes/meals

Spei·se·... [ˈʃpaɪzə] [prefix] expressing that sth is related to food, nutrition, cooking etc. ◊ *Speiseeis* ◆ *ein Zug mit Speisewagen*

Spei·se·kar·te [ˈʃpaɪzəkaʁtə] die <-, -n> menu ◊ *Sie wählte einen Salat aus der Speisekarte aus.*

Spek·ta·kel¹ [ʃpɛkˈtaːkl̩] der <-s, -> *most sing* *(fam)* row, rumpus ◊ *Was soll der Spektakel? Seid gefälligst leise!* ⊜Krawall

Spek·ta·kel² [ʃpɛkˈtaːkl̩, spɛkˈtaːkl̩] das <-s, -> *(also fig, also pej)* spectacle, show ◊ *ein buntes/unterhaltsames Spektakel* ◆ *Wann soll das*

Spektakel beginnen?; *(in the media etc.)* (media) circus ◊ *Die Verhandlung gegen Michael Jackson geriet zum Spektakel.*

spe·ku·lie·ren [ʃpekuˈliːrən] <spekuliert, spekulierte, hat spekuliert> [intr v] **1.** speculate ◊ *Er spekuliert an der Börse.* ◆ *Ich kann nur spekulieren, warum er es gemacht hat.* über etw. [acc] spekulieren speculate about sth mit etw. spekulieren speculate in sth ◊ *mit Aktien/Immobilien spekulieren* auf etw. [acc] spekulieren count on sth, speculate on sth ◊ *Sie spekuliert auf steigende Preise.* **2.** *(fam)* darauf spekulieren, etw. zu tun count on doing sth ◊ *Er spekuliert darauf, der Nachfolger seines Chefs zu werden.* darauf spekulieren, dass ... hope that ...

Spen·de [ˈʃpɛndə] die <-, -n> donation, contribution ◊ *eine Spende zugunsten Not leidender Kinder* ◆ *Spenden sammeln*

spen·den [ˈʃpɛndn̩] <spendet, spendete, hat gespendet> [tr+intr v] **1.** *(blood, money, organs)* give, donate ◊ *Knochenmark spenden* ◆ *Sie hat großzügig gespendet.* für jdn/etw. (etw.) spenden, jdm/einer Sache (etw.) spenden donate/contribute (sth) for/to sb/sth ◊ *der/für die Caritas Geld spenden* **2.** *(lofty, fig) (light, shade)* give ◊ *Die Lampe spendet Licht und Wärme.* ◆ *Der Sonnenschirm spendet Schatten.;* *(water etc.)* dispense; *(a blessing etc.)* bestow

spen·die·ren [ʃpɛnˈdiːrən] <spendiert, spendierte, hat spendiert> [tr v] *(fam)* (jdm) etw. spendieren buy/get (sb) sth ◊ *Er spendiert eine Runde Schnaps für alle.*

Sper·re [ˈʃpɛrə] die <-, -n> **1.** barrier ◊ *eine Sperre um das Baugelände errichten;* *(on the road)* roadblock **2.** SPORT *(in sport)* suspension ◊ *Der Spieler erhielt eine Sperre von sechs Wochen.* **3.** ECON *(of goods)* ban **4.** innerliche/psychische Sperre mental block ◊ *Er hat Angst vor Nähe und kann seine innerliche Sperre nicht überwinden.* **5.** TECHN locking device, lock-out ◊ *Eine Sperre im Handy verhindert seine Nutzung mit anderen Karten.*

sper·ren [ˈʃpɛrən] [tr v] +*haben* **1.** close (off) ◊ *eine Straße wegen Bauarbeiten sperren* ◆ *Die Innenstadt ist für den Verkehr gesperrt.* **2.** jdn/ein Tier in etw. [acc] sperren lock/shut sb/an animal into sth ◊ *Er hat das Kind in sein Zimmer gesperrt.* jdn ins Gefängnis sperren lock sb up **3.** *(a payment, cheque etc.)* stop ◊ *Die Bank hat den Scheck gesperrt.* ◆ *Sein Vater hat ihm das Taschengeld gesperrt.;* *(a card etc.)* lock, cancel; *(electricity, water etc.)* cut off, disconnect **4.** ban, prohibit ◊ *den Import/Export einer Ware sperren* jdm den Ausgang sperren confine sb to quarters/the barracks **5.** SPORT ban, suspend ◊ *Das Sportgericht sperrte ihn für sechs Wochen.* ◊ *Die Partei sperrte sich gegen die Reformpläne.*

Spe·sen [ˈʃpeːzn̩] die <-> *only pl* expenses ◊ *Ihre Spesen werden Ihnen selbstverständlich erstattet.* auf Spesen on expenses Spesen machen incur expenses ⊛ **außer Spesen nichts gewesen** *(hum)* a waste of time and effort

Spe·zi¹ [ˈʃpeːtsi] der <-s, -s> *(Austr, SouthG, fam)* pal, chum ◊ *mit ein paar Spezis in die Kneipe*

gehen

Spe·zi² [ˈʃpeːtsi:] *das* <–s, –s> *pl 'Spezi' when used with expressions of quantity a mix of cola and orange pop* ◊ *Sie bestellte zwei Spezi.*

② **Spe·zi·al·…** [ʃpeˈtsjaːl] (prefix) *special* … ◊ *eine Spezialanfertigung* ♦ *eine Spezialausbildung* ♦ *ein Spezialgeschäft für Fahrräder*

Spe·zi·a·list [ʃpetsiaˈlɪst] *der* <–en, –en>,
Spe·zi·a·lis·tin [ʃpetsiaˈlɪstɪn] *die* <–, –nen> *specialist* ◊ *Er konsultiert einen Spezialisten für Krebserkrankungen.* ♦ *Sie ist Spezialistin auf diesem Gebiet.*

spe·zi·ell [ʃpeˈtsjɛl] (adj, adv) *special(ly)* ◊ *eine spezielle Methode* ♦ *Dieser Fall ist sehr speziell.* ♦ *speziell ausgebildetes Personal*

② **Spie·gel** [ˈʃpiːgl̩] *der* <–s, –> **1.** *(also fig)* mirror ◊ *Sie betrachtet sich prüfend im Spiegel.* ein Spiegel … (gen) *a reflection of sth* ◊ *Die Politik ist ein Spiegel unserer Gesellschaft.* **2.** *(of water, substances in the blood)* level ◊ *Fällt der Spiegel des Alkohols ab, wird der Alkoholiker zittrig.*

Spie·gel·bild [ˈʃpiːgl̩bɪlt] *das* <–(e)s, Spiegelbilder> *(also fig)* reflection ◊ *Sie sah ihr Spiegelbild im Fenster.* ♦ *Kultur ist ein Spiegelbild der Gesellschaft.*

Spie·gel·ei [ˈʃpiːgl̩|ai̯e] *das* <–(e)s, –er> fried egg ◊ *sich ein Spiegelei braten*

spie·geln [ˈʃpiːgl̩n] (ref v) +*haben* **1.** *sich spiegeln* be reflected ◊ *In der Nacht spiegelt sich der Mond im Wasser.* ⊖*sich reflektieren* **2.** *(fig)* etw. spiegelt sich in jds Gesicht etc. sb's face etc. reflects sth (tr v) *(also fig)* reflect ◊ *Das klare Wasser spiegelt das Blau des Himmels.* ♦ *Sein Roman spiegelt die Zustände um die Jahrhundertwende.* ⊖*reflektieren* (intr v) **1.** shine, gleam ◊ *die Küche putzen, bis sie blitzt und spiegelt* ⊖glänzen **2.** be reflective, reflect the light ◊ *Der Bildschirm spiegelt bei ungünstigem Licht.* ⊖*reflektieren*

② **Spiel** [ʃpiːl] *das* <–(e)s, –e> **1.** *(also fig)* game ◊ *ein Spiel gewinnen/verlieren* ♦ *Für ihn ist die Liebe nur ein Spiel.* ♦ *Das ist ein riskantes Spiel.* **2.** sport match, game ◊ *Das Spiel endete unentschieden.* **3.** play(ing) ◊ *Die Kinder haben Spaß am/beim Spiel.* ⊚ ein Spiel mit dem Feuer playing with fire ein abgekartetes Spiel a fix (ein) leichtes Spiel haben have an easy job of it jd hat mit jdm (ein) leichtes Spiel sb is easy game for sb die Olympischen Spiele the Olympic Games jdn/etw. aus dem Spiel lassen leave sb/sth out of it etw. aufs Spiel setzen risk sth, put sth on the line auf dem Spiel stehen be at stake sein Spiel mit jdm treiben *(fig)* play games with sb

② **spie·len** [ˈʃpiːlən] (tr+intr v) +*haben* play ◊ *Er spielt mit seiner Eisenbahn.* ♦ *Sie spielen in der zweiten Bundesliga.* ♦ *Schach/Gitarre/Tennis spielen* ♦ *Sie spielt in dem Film eine Kommissarin.* ♦ *Spiel das Lied bitte noch mal.* gegen jdn spielen play sb ◊ *Im Finale spielt er gegen Gonzalez.* (tr v) jdn spielen play/act sb ◊ *Sie spielt gern die Chefin/große Dame.* den Beleidigten spielen act offended (intr v) **1.** play games ◊ *In unserer Familie wird viel gespielt.* **2.** *(um Geld)* spielen gamble um viel Geld spielen bet a lot of money **3.** mit jdm/etw. spielen play games with sb/sth ◊ *Er spielt mit ihren Gefühlen.* **4.** mit etw. spielen put sth at risk ◊

Wenn du das machst, spielst du mit deinem Leben. **5.** act, perform, feature ◊ *Wer spielt in dem Stück?* **6.** be set ◊ *Der Roman spielt im 18. Jahrhundert.* ⊚ etw. spielen lassen use sth ◊ *Er lässt bei den Damen gerne seinen Charme spielen.* seine Muskeln spielen lassen flex your muscles

Spie·ler [ˈʃpiːlɐ] *der* <–s, –>, **Spie·le·rin** [ˈʃpiːlərɪn] *die* <–, –nen> **1.** player ◊ *die beste Spielerin der Mannschaft* ♦ *Jeder Spieler erhält 13 Karten.* **2.** *(pej)* gambler

Spiel·film [ˈʃpiːlfɪlm] *der* <–(e)s, –e> TV feature film ◊ *sich einen Spielfilm im Fernsehen ansehen*

Spiel·platz [ˈʃpiːlplats] *der* <–es, Spielplätze> playground ◊ *Die Kinder spielen auf dem Spielplatz.*

Spiel·raum [ˈʃpiːlrau̯m] *der* <–(e)s, Spielräume> **1.** *(fig)* scope, room ◊ *der Fantasie viel/wenig Spielraum lassen* ♦ *Sie haben viel Spielraum für eigene Ideen.* **2.** leeway ◊ *wenig Spielraum für höhere Gebühren*

② **Spiel·zeug** [ˈʃpiːltsɔɪ̯k] *das* <–(e)s, –e> **1.** toy ◊ *Der Teddy war ihr liebstes Spielzeug.* **2.** *no pl* toys ◊ *viel/wenig Spielzeug haben* ♦ *pädagogisch wertvolles Spielzeug*

Spieß [ʃpiːs] *der* <–es, –e> **1.** spear ◊ *Sie gingen mit Schwertern und Spießen aufeinander los.* **2.** *(for roasting)* spit ◊ *Lamm am Spieß;* *(small)* skewer ⊚ wie am Spieß schreien *(fam)* scream your head off den Spieß umdrehen *(fam, fig)* turn the tables

Spi·nat [ʃpiˈnaːt] *der* <–(e)s, –e> spinach ◊ *Spiegeleier mit Spinat*

Spin·ne [ˈʃpɪnə] *die* <–, –n> spider ⊚ pfui Spinne *(fam)* yuck ⊖igitt

spin·nen [ˈʃpɪnən] <spinnt, spann, hat gesponnen> (intr v) *(fam, pej)* **1.** be crazy ◊ *He, lass das! Du spinnst wohl!* **2.** talk rubbish ◊ *Er spinnt manchmal ein wenig.* (tr+intr v) spin ◊ *Baumwolle zu Garn spinnen* ♦ *Die Spinne spinnt ein Netz.* ⊚ ich glaube, ich spinne *(fam)* I don't believe it

Spi·on¹ [ʃpiˈoːn] *der* <–s, –e> spyhole ◊ *eine Tür mit Spion* ♦ *durch den Spion schauen*

Spi·on² [ʃpiˈoːn] *der* <–s, –e>, **Spi·o·nin** [ʃpiˈoːnɪn] *die* <–, –nen> spy ◊ *Sie hat als Spionin für den KGB gearbeitet.* ♦ *Ein Spion muss unauffällig sein.*

spi·o·nie·ren [ʃpioˈniːrən] <spioniert, spionierte, hat spioniert> (intr v) **1.** spy ◊ *Sie wurde nach Russland geschickt, um zu spionieren.* **2.** *(fam, pej)* snoop (about) ◊ *Gib's doch zu, du hast in meinen Sachen spioniert!*

Spi·o·nin [ʃpiˈoːnɪn] → Spion

Spi·ra·le [ʃpiˈraːlə] *die* <–, –n> **1.** *(also fig)* spiral ◊ *Der Adler ließ sich in Spiralen in die Höhe tragen.* ♦ *ein Ornament in Form einer Spirale* ♦ *eine Spirale der Gewalt; (scientific)* helix **2.** coil ◊ *eine Feder in Form einer Spirale* ♦ *eine Spirale zur Empfängnisverhütung.*

② **Spi·tal** [ʃpiˈtaːl] *das* <–s, Spitäler> *(Austr, Swiss)* hospital ◊ *Das Baby ist im Spital zur Welt gekommen.*

② **spitz** [ʃpɪts] (adj) <spitzer, am spitzesten> **1.** pointed ◊ *ein spitzer Kirchturm* ♦ *Seine Nase war lang und spitz.; (pencil etc.)* sharp ein spitzer Ausschnitt a V-neck **2.** *(comment etc.)* cutting ◊ *Seine Kommentare wurden immer spitzer;*

(tongue) sharp ⊖scharf **3.** shrill ◊ *ein spitzer Schrei* **4.** *(fam)* haggard ◊ *Nach der Diät war er/sein Gesicht ganz spitz geworden.* [adv] **1.** spitz zulaufen taper/be tapered (to a point) **2.** *(comment etc.)* cuttingly ◊ *Sie hat seine Versuche, Gedichte zu schreiben, ziemlich spitz kommentiert.*

Spit·ze ['ʃpɪtsə] die <–, –n> **1.** point ◊ *Die Spitze des Bleistifts ist abgebrochen.*; *(of an arrow)* tip **2.** *(of a mountain, tower etc.)* top ◊ *Von der Spitze aus hat man eine wunderbare Aussicht.* **3.** *(of a row, train etc.)* head, front ◊ *der Wagen an der Spitze des Zuges* ♦ *Er ging an der Spitze und zeigte uns den Weg.* **4.** *(hierarchical)* head, top ◊ *Wer steht an der Spitze der Partei/Firma?* ♦ *sich zur Spitze vorkämpfen/emporarbeiten; (in sports)* lead ◊ *Welches Pferd liegt gerade an der Spitze?* an der Spitze der Tabelle stehen be top of the table sich an die Spitze setzen take the lead ⊖Führung **5.** dig, pointed remark ◊ *War das eine Spitze gegen mich?* ♦ *Sie amüsierten sich über die Spitzen des Kabarettisten.* **6.** lace ◊ *Unterwäsche aus Spitze* ♦ *eine mit Spitzen besetzte Tischdecke* ◉ die Spitze des Eisbergs the tip of the iceberg *(absolute/einsame)* Spitze sein *(fam)* be (really) great *(es mit)* etw. auf die Spitze treiben carry sth too far/to extremes

Spit·zer ['ʃpɪtsɐ] der <–s, –> *(abbr of* Bleistiftspitzer*)* pencil sharpener

Spitz·na·me ['ʃpɪtsnaːmə] der <–ns, –n> nickname ◊ *Kinder geben sich untereinander oft Spitznamen.*

Split·ter ['ʃplɪtɐ] der <–s, –> splinter, sliver ◊ *in winzige Splitter zerbrechen* ♦ *einen Splitter im Finger haben; (from a bomb etc.)* (piece of) shrapnel

SPÖ [ɛspeːˈløː] die *(Austr) (abbr of* Sozialdemokratische Partei Österreichs*)* Austrian Social Democrat Party

Originally founded in 1889 and re-established in 1945, the *SPÖ* is a left of centre party advocating a regulated market economy and a strong welfare system.

② **Sport** [ʃpɔrt] der <–(e)s> *no pl* **1.** sport ◊ *Sport ist gesund.* ♦ *Fußball ist Deutschlands beliebtester Sport.* Sport treiben do sport **2.** physical education, PE ◊ *Er unterrichtet Sport und Mathematik.* ◉ sich [dat] einen Sport aus etw. machen *(fam)* get a kick out of sth

Sport·ler ['ʃpɔrtlɐ] der <–s, –>, **Sport·le·rin** ['ʃpɔrtlərɪn] die <–, –nen> athlete ◊ *ein bekannter Sportler* ♦ *Als Sportlerin legt sie Wert auf gesunde Ernährung.*

② **sport·lich** ['ʃpɔrtlɪç] [adj, adv] **1.** *(person)* athletic, sporty ◊ *Er ist nicht sehr sportlich.* ♦ *Sie hat eine sportliche Figur.* sportlich aktiv/begabt sein be an active/a talented athlete **2.** sporting ◊ *Ihre sportlichen Leistungen sind ausgezeichnet.* ♦ *Der Spieler verhält sich sehr sportlich.; (behavio(u)r also)* sportsmanlike **3.** *(fig)* *(car, motorbike)* sporty sportlich fahren drive fast **4.** *(clothes, look etc.)* (smart) casual

Sport·platz ['ʃpɔrtplats] der <–es, Sportplätze> sports/playing field ◊ *zum Fußballspielen auf den Sportplatz gehen*

spot·ten ['ʃpɔtn̩] <spottet, spottete, hat gespottet> [intr v] +haben *(über jdn/etw.)* spotten mock *(sb/sth)*, poke fun *(at sb/sth)* ◊ *Spotte nur, dir wird es auch mal so gehen!* ♦ *Die Schüler spotten über ihre Lehrer.*

② **sprach** [ʃpraːx] pret of sprechen

② **Spra·che** ['ʃpraːxə] die <–, –n> **1.** language ◊ *Wie viele Sprachen sprichst du?* ♦ *ein Text in einfacher/gehobener Sprache* ♦ *die Sprache der Kunst/Musik; (of a group also)* jargon ◊ *die Sprache der Behörden/Juristen* ein Buch in englischer etc. Sprache an English etc. (language) book **2.** faculty of speech ◊ *Durch den Schock hat er die Sprache verloren.* **3.** *die Sprache auf jdn / etw. bringen* bring the conversation round to sb/sth etw. zur Sprache bringen bring sth up, raise sth zur Sprache kommen be raised, come up ◉ etw. spricht eine deutliche Sprache sth speaks for itself mit der Sprache herausrücken, raus mit der Sprache come out with it die Sprache verloren haben *(fam)* Hast du/Hat er etc. die Sprache verloren? Has the cat got your/his etc. tongue? etw. verschlägt jdm die Sprache sth takes sb's breath away jdm bleibt die Sprache weg *(fam)* sb is speechless

Sprach·füh·rer ['ʃpraːxfyːrɐ] der <–s, –> phrase book ◊ *Mithilfe des Sprachführers konnte er sich einigermaßen verständigen.*

Sprach·kennt·nis·se ['ʃpraːxkɛntnɪsə] die <–> *most pl* knowledge of a language/languages jds französische etc. Sprachkenntnisse sb's knowledge of French etc. gute Sprachkenntnisse in Englisch etc. good knowledge of English etc.

sprach·lich ['ʃpraːxlɪç] [adj] *no comp/superl; when used as an adj, mostly before ns* **1.** linguistic, language ◊ *eine sprachliche Minderheit; (mistake)* grammatical ◊ *sprachliche und inhaltliche Fehler* sprachlich korrekt (linguistically) correct **2.** stylistic ◊ *Die Metapher ist ein sprachliches Mittel.* sprachlich gut gestaltet, sprachlich von hoher Qualität (very) well written **3.** verbal ◊ *Kommunikation kann sprachlich oder mimisch sein.*

sprach·los ['ʃpraːxloːs] [adj] *no comp/superl* speechless, dumbfounded ◊ *Als sie das hörte, war sie erst einmal sprachlos.* ♦ *Die sprachlosen Zuschauer klatschten Beifall.* ♦ *Er hörte mir sprachlos zu.*

② **sprang** [ʃpraŋ] pret of springen

② **spre·chen** ['ʃprɛçn̩] <spricht, sprach, hat gesprochen> [intr v] **1.** speak ◊ *ein bisschen langsamer/lauter sprechen* ♦ *wegen Halsschmerzen kaum sprechen können* ♦ *gut über jdn/von jdm sprechen* ♦ *Ich spreche auch für meine Schwester/im Namen meiner Schwester.* ♦ *mit jdm deutsch/englisch sprechen* **2.** talk ◊ *sprechen können/lernen (mit jdm) (über jdn/etw.)* speak/learn to talk *(to sb/about sb/sth)* ◊ *Sie hört mir einfach nicht zu, sprich du doch mal mit ihr.* ♦ *Können wir über etwas anderes sprechen?* von jdm/etw. sprechen talk about sb/sth ◊ *Weißt du überhaupt, wovon du da sprichst?* jd spricht davon, dass zu tun; jd spricht davon, dass er etw. täte/tun würde sb talks of doing sth ◊ *Sie sprach davon, sich ein Boot zu kaufen.* ♦ *Er sprach davon, dass er einen neuen Job suche/suchen würde.* ⊖reden **3.** für jdn/etw. sprechen speak in

favour of sb/sth, speak in favor of sb/sth; *(stronger)* plead for sb/sth gegen etw. sprechen speak out against sth **4.** *(in a speech, lecture etc.)* von jdm/etw. sprechen talk of sb/sth, speak of sb/sth ◊ *Der Priester sprach zu uns von Nächstenliebe.* über jdn/etw. sprechen talk about sb/sth, speak about/on sb/sth **5.** etw. spricht aus jdm/etw. sb/sth is full of sth ◊ *Aus dir spricht doch nur der Neid!* ♦ *Aus seinem Brief sprach Misstrauen.* **6.** etw. spricht für jdn sth is one thing in sb's favour, sth is one thing in sb's favor ◊ *Deine Ehrlichkeit spricht für dich.* etw. spricht für etw. sth speaks in favour of sth, sth speaks in favor of sth ◊ *Die ausgezeichnete Qualität spricht für das Produkt.* etw. spricht gegen jdn/etw. sth speaks against sb/sth Die Fakten sprechen für sich selbst. The facts speak for themselves. **7.** *(probability)* manches/vieles spricht dafür, dass it seems likely/very likely that ◊ *Einiges spricht dafür, dass es morgen regnen wird. Seine Flucht spricht für seine Schuld. His running away suggests that he is guilty.; (probability)* manches/vieles spricht dagegen, dass it seems unlikely/very unlikely that ◊ *Vieles spricht dagegen, dass sich etwas ändern wird.* [tr v] **1.** speak ◊ *Sie haben einen Papagei, der ein paar Wörter spricht.* ♦ *mehrere Sprachen fließend sprechen* ♦ *Ich spreche leider kein Spanisch.* ♦ *ein gestelztes Deutsch sprechen* **2.** jdn sprechen speak to sb ◊ *„Kann ich bitte Herrn Meier sprechen?" Ist jd zu sprechen? Can I speak to/see sb?, Is sb available?* jd ist für niemanden zu sprechen sb isn't available, sb can't see anybody **3.** *(lofty)* say ◊ *Der Priester sprach: „Lasst uns beten."* ♦ *ein Gebet sprechen* ♦ *kein einziges Wort sprechen* ein Machtwort sprechen put your foot down **4.** jdn *(des Mordes/Betrugs etc.)* schuldig sprechen find sb guilty (of murder/fraud etc.) jdn heilig sprechen canonize sb jdn selig sprechen beatify sb

☻ auf jdn/etw. schlecht/nicht gut zu sprechen sein not have a good word to say about sb/sth

Spre·cher ['ʃprɛçɐ] der <-s, ->, **Spre·che·rin** ['ʃprɛçərɪn] die <-, -nen> **1.** spokesperson ◊ *ein Sprecher des Außenministeriums* ♦ *die innenpolitische Sprecherin der Partei; (masc also)* spokesman; *(fem also)* spokeswoman **2.** RADIO, TV announcer ◊ *ein professioneller Sprecher mit Radio- oder TV-Erfahrung; (of news)* newsreader, newscaster ◊ *als Sprecherin in der Nachrichtenabteilung der ARD arbeiten; (in films, radio plays etc.)* voice (actor) **3.** *(of a language)* speaker ◊ *ein einsprachiges Wörterbuch für fremdsprachliche/muttersprachliche Sprecher*

② **Sprech·stun·de** ['ʃprɛçʃtʊndə] die <-, -n> **1.** MED surgery (hour) **2.** SCHOOL *hour in which a teacher is available to talk to parents and guardians* ◊ *zu einem Lehrer in die Sprechstunde gehen/kommen*

spren·gen ['ʃprɛŋən] [tr v] +*haben* **1.** etw./jdn (in die Luft) sprengen blow sth/sb up ◊ *eine Brücke/ein Gebäude sprengen* **2.** *(esp fig)* break down ◊ *seine inneren Fesseln sprengen* ♦ *Glaube, der Grenzen sprengt* den Rahmen sprengen go beyond the scope **3.** *(a safe, door etc.)* bust open ◊ *ein Schloss mit Dynamit sprengen* **4.** etw. in etw. [acc] sprengen blast sth through/in sth ◊ *einen Tunnel in den Fels sprengen* **5.** sprinkle (with water) ◊ *den*

Rasen sprengen [intr v] +*haben/sein* **1.** +*haben* detonate ◊ *Vorsicht, wir sprengen bald.* **2.** +*sein (lofty) (on a horse)* gallop ◊ *Drei Reiter sprengten die Straße entlang.*

sprich [ʃprɪç] *imperative of* sprechen [adv] that is to say, i.e. ◊ *Er hat besonders viele wohlhabende, sprich Privatpatienten.* ♦ *Die große Mehrheit, sprich 82 %, war dafür.*

② **spricht** [ʃprɪçt] *pres of* sprechen

② **Sprich·wort** ['ʃprɪçvɔʳt] das <-(e)s, Sprichwörter> proverb, saying ◊ *Wie schon das Sprichwort sagt: Eine Hand wäscht die andere.*

② **sprin·gen** ['ʃprɪŋən] <springt, sprang, ist gesprungen> [intr v] **1.** jump ◊ *aus dem Stand/mit Anlauf drei Meter weit springen* ♦ *Wie hoch können Frösche springen?* ♦ *aus dem Bett/vor Freude in die Luft springen* ♦ *ins Wasser springen* Seil springen skip Trampolin springen trampoline **2.** *(also fig)* leap ◊ *Der Hund sprang bellend über den Platz.* ♦ *Der Zeiger der Uhr sprang auf die Zwölf.* ♦ *Der Zug sprang aus den Gleisen.* Die Ampel springt auf Grün The lights switch to green. **3.** crack ◊ *Das Eis ist an mehreren Stellen gesprungen.* **4.** in tausend Scherben/Stücke springen break into a thousand pieces, shatter

Sprin·ger¹ ['ʃprɪŋɐ] der <-s, -> knight ◊ *mit dem Springer einen Läufer schlagen* ⊖Pferd

Sprin·ger² ['ʃprɪŋɐ] der <-s, ->, **Sprin·ge·rin** ['ʃprɪŋərɪn] die <-, -nen> **1.** SPORT high jumper, long jumper, pole vaulter **2.** stand-in ◊ *als Springer im Zustelldienst der Post arbeiten* ♦ *Die Springerin blieb drei Monate.*

② **Sprit·ze** ['ʃprɪtsə] die <-, -n> **1.** MED injection ◊ *jdm eine schmerzstillende Spritze geben/verabreichen* ♦ *eine Spritze in den Arm bekommen* **2.** MED syringe ◊ *jdm mit der Spritze Blut abnehmen* **3.** *(used by firefighters)* hose **4.** spray ◊ *gegen Blattläuse zur Spritze greifen*

sprit·zen ['ʃprɪtsn̩] [tr v] +*haben* **1.** jdm/sich etw. spritzen give sb/yourself an injection of sth; *(drugs)* (sich [dat]) etw. spritzen inject yourself with sth, shoot up sth ◊ *Er spritzt (sich) seit Jahren Heroin.* (jdm) etw. (in die Vene/unter die Haut etc.) spritzen inject sth (into sb's vein/under sb's skin etc.) jdn spritzen give sb an injection ◊ *Er wurde mit Insulin gespritzt.* **2.** jdn/etw. nass spritzen splash sb/sth ◊ *jdn/etw. nass spritzen* sich [dat] Wasser aufs/ins Gesicht spritzen splash your face with water **3.** spray ◊ *sein Auto neu/blau etc. spritzen* ♦ *die Rosen mit Gift spritzen* [intr v] +*haben/sein* **1.** +*haben* give sb an injection ◊ *Hat der Arzt gespritzt?; (drugs)* inject yourself, shoot up ◊ *Sie nimmt zwar Drogen, aber sie spritzt nicht.* **2.** +*haben* splash about ◊ *mit Wasser/dem Gartenschlauch spritzen* ♦ *He, spritz nicht so!* **3.** +*haben (hot fat)* spit ◊ *Das Fett spritzte, als er das Fleisch in die Pfanne legte.* **4.** +*sein* irgendwohin spritzen spurt somewhere Blut spritzte aus der Wunde. Blood spurted from the wound. **5.** +*sein (fam)* (irgendwohin) spritzen run (somewhere) ◊ *Als die Lehrerin kam, spritzten die Kinder kichernd auseinander.*

Spruch [ʃprʊx] der <-(e)s, Sprüche> **1.** remark, comment ◊ *immer einen flotten Spruch auf Lager/parat haben* ♦ *sich jds ausländerfeindliche Sprüche*

A B C D E F G H I J K L M N O P Q R **S** T U V W X Y Z

anhören müssen; *(in advertising)* slogan ◇ *Sie werben mit den ewig gleichen, alten Sprüchen.* **2.** saying, adage ◇ *eine Sammlung von Sprüchen* **3.** poem ◇ *einen Spruch aufsagen/auswendig lernen*; quotation, quote ◇ *Sprüche aus der Bibel* **4.** LAW verdict, judg(e)ment ◇ *der Spruch des Bundesverfassungsgerichts* ⊖Urteil

ⓔ **(große) Sprüche klopfen/machen** *(fam, pej)* promise great things

spru·deln [ˈʃpruːdl̩n] [intr v] +*haben/sein* **1.** +*haben* bubble ◇ *Das Wasser sprudelt schon, es wird gleich kochen.* ♦ *Champagner sprudelte in den Gläsern.* **2.** +*sein* gush ◇ *Das Erdöl sprudelte aus dem Boden.* **3.** +*sein (fig)* flow ◇ *Jetzt sprudeln die Ideen wieder.*

sprü·hen [ˈʃpryːən] [tr v] +*haben* **1.** spray ◇ *Herbizide/Pestizide (auf die Felder) sprühen* jdm etw. ins Gesicht/in die Augen etc. sprühen spray sth into sb's face/eyes etc. **2.** *(also fig)* Funken sprühen throw up sparks; *(eyes)* flash [intr v] +*haben/sein* **1.** +*haben* spray; *(sparks)* fly ◇ *Der Schmied schlug auf das Eisen, dass die Funken sprühten.* **2.** +*sein* spurt ◇ *Die Gischt sprühte uns* [dat] *ins Gesicht.* **3.** +*haben (fig) (eyes)* (vor etw. [dat]) sprühen be flashing (with sth) ◇ *jds Augen sprühen (vor Begeisterung/Temperament/Wut etc.)*; *(person)* vor etw. [dat] sprühen be overflowing with sth ◇ *Er sprüht nur so vor Charme/Ideen/Temperament.*

ⓩ **Sprung** [ˈʃprʊŋ] der <-(e)s, Sprünge> **1.** *(also fig)* leap ◇ *mit großen Sprüngen hinter jdm hersetzen* ♦ *den Sprung in die Selbstständigkeit wagen*; dive ◇ *ein Sprung vom Zehnmeterbrett einen Sprung zur Seite machen* leap aside **2.** crack ◇ *Die Tasse hat einen Sprung.* ♦ *Im Spiegel sind ein paar Sprünge.*

ⓔ **einen Sprung in der Schüssel haben** *(fam)* have a screw loose, be mad, be crazy **ein Sprung ins Ungewisse/kalte Wasser** a leap into the unknown **keine großen Sprünge machen können** *(fam)* not be able to afford many luxuries **jdm auf die Sprünge helfen** *(fam)* give sb some help **auf einen (kurzen) Sprung hereinkommen/vorbeikommen** *(fam)* pop in for a while **auf dem Sprung sein** *(fam)* be on the go ◇ *Er ist immer auf dem Sprung, kommt nie zur Ruhe.* **auf dem Sprung sein, etw. zu tun** be about to do sth, be on the verge of doing sth **auf einen Sprung irgendwo sein** pop in somewhere

Sprung·brett [ˈʃprʊŋbrɛt] das <-(e)s, –er> *(also fig)* springboard ◇ *vom Sprungbrett abspringen und einen Salto machen* ♦ *Praktika als Sprungbrett ins Berufsleben nutzen*; *(for diving also)* diving board

sprung·haft [ˈʃprʊŋhaft] [adj] <sprunghafter, am sprunghaftesten> erratic ◇ *ein sprunghaftes Wesen haben* ♦ *Er ist sprunghaft und unberechenbar.* [adj, adv] sudden(ly), abrupt(ly) ◇ *Die Zunahme der Mitgliederzahlen war sprunghaft.* ♦ *eine sprunghafte Veränderung* ♦ *sprunghaft ansteigen/steigen/wachsen/zunehmen* ♦ *sich sprunghaft ändern/entwickeln*

SP Schweiz [ˌɛspe: ˈʃvaɛts] *(Swiss)* *(always* **die SP Schweiz***)* *(abbr of* Sozialdemokratische Partei der Schweiz*)* abbreviation of Social Democratic Party of Switzerland

---

The Social Democratic Party of Switzerland, which was formed in 1888, supports a democratic socialism, a socialist market economy, and the welfare state.

Spu·cke [ˈʃpʊkə] die <–> *no pl (fam)* spit ◇ *seinen Finger zum Umblättern mit Spucke anfeuchten* ⊖Speichel

ⓔ **jdm bleibt die Spucke weg** sb is speechless

spu·cken [ˈʃpʊkn̩] [tr+intr v] +*haben* **1.** spit ◇ *jdm ins Gesicht spucken* ♦ *einen Kaugummi/Kirschkern auf den Boden spucken* **2.** *(also fig)* spew ◇ *Mir ist so schlecht. Ich glaube, ich muss gleich spucken.* ♦ *Der Vulkan/Drache spuckte Feuer.*

Spuk [ʃpuːk] der <-(e)s, –e> *most sing* **1.** ghostly goings-on ◇ *Um ein Uhr war der ganze Spuk wieder vorbei.* **2.** *(fig)* strange business ◇ *Die Polizei machte dem Spuk ein Ende.*

ⓩ **spü·len** [ˈʃpyːlən] [tr v] +*haben* **1.** *(dishes)* wash (up) ◇ *das Geschirr von Hand spülen* ⊖abwaschen **2.** +*direction (also fig)* wash ◇ *Ein toter Wal wurde an Land gespült.* ♦ *mit dem Schlauch den Schlamm von den Stiefeln spülen* **3.** rinse ◇ *Wäsche waschen und spülen* [intr v] +*haben* **1.** wash (up) ◇ *Wenn du spülst, trockne ich ab.* **2.** flush (the toilet) ◇ *Vergiss nicht zu spülen, wenn du fertig bist.*; *(washing machine)* rinse

ⓩ **Spur** [ʃpuːɐ̯] die <-, –en> **1.** track(s), trail ◇ *auf der richtigen Spur sein* ♦ *jdm/einem Verbrechen auf die Spur kommen* ♦ *Seine Spur führt nach Amerika.* ♦ *die Spur eines Rehs verfolgen*; lead ◇ *Hat die Polizei schon eine erste/heiße Spur?* *(die)* Spuren sichern collect/secure evidence *von jdm/etw.* fehlt jede Spur there's no trace of sb/sth **2.** trace, mark ◇ *Das Trauma hat bei ihr deutliche Spuren hinterlassen.* ♦ *Spuren der Verwüstung* **3.** trace, touch ◇ *nicht die leiseste/keine Spur von Einsicht/Reue zeigen* ♦ *Am Essen fehlt noch eine Spur Knoblauch.*; *(of salt)* pinch ⊖Hauch **4.** lane ◇ *von der linken auf die rechte Spur wechseln* **5.** *(when driving)* course ◇ *Das Auto kann die Spur nicht halten.* **6.** *(between rails of a track, wheels of a train)* gauge **eine Kleinbahn mit schmaler Spur** a narrow gauge railway

spür·bar [ˈʃpyːɐ̯baːɐ̯] [adj, adv] *no comp/superl* noticeable(-ably) ◇ *eine spürbare Entlastung/Verbesserung* ♦ *Die Anspannung ist spürbar.* ♦ *Die Belastung hat spürbar nachgelassen/ist spürbar zurückgegangen.* ⊖merklich

spü·ren [ˈʃpyːrən] [tr v] +*haben* **1.** notice ◇ *Von dem Bürgerkrieg/Unwetter war dort kaum etwas zu spüren.* etw. zu spüren bekommen feel (the force of) sth ◇ *die Folgen von etw. am eigenen Leib zu spüren bekommen* jdn etw. spüren lassen show sb sth, make sb feel sth ◇ *Er hat mich seine Verachtung deutlich spüren lassen.* **2.** feel ◇ *den Fahrtwind im Gesicht spüren* ♦ *Sie spürte sofort, dass sie ihm vertrauen konnte.* ♦ *das Unheil kommen spüren*

ⓩ **Staat** [ʃtaːt] der <-(e)s, –en> **1.** state ◇ *ein demokratischer/totalitärer/unabhängiger Staat* ♦ *Er wohnt im Staat New York.* **2.** state, government ◇ *Steuern an den Staat abführen* ♦ *vom Staat finanziert/gefördert/subventioniert* ♦ *beim Staat angestellt sein/arbeiten* **3.** ZOO *(of ants, bees)* colony **Staaten bildende Insekten** insects that live in

colonies
⊛ in vollem/großem Staat *(fam, oldf)* in all your finery bei jdm mit etw./jdm keinen Staat machen können not be able to impress sb with sth/sb

② **staat·lich** ['ʃtaːtlɪç] adj *no comp/superl* state-owned ◊ *Der Rundfunk ist staatlich.* ♦ *staatliche Betriebe/Unternehmen privatisieren* adj, adv (by the) government, (by the) state ◊ *staatliche Beihilfen/Förderung/Zuschüsse beantragen* Diese Institution ist staatlich. This is a government institution staatlich geprüft/anerkannt (state-/government-)certified staatlich gefördert state-/government-assisted staatlich subventioniert (state-/government-)subsidized

② **Staats·an·ge·hö·rig·keit** ['ʃtaːtsˌangəˌhøːrɪçkaet] die <-, -en> nationality, citizenship ◊ *die britische Staatsangehörigkeit beantragen/bekommen/ erhalten/aufgeben/ablegen*

Staats·an·walt ['ʃtaːtsˌanvalt] der <-(e)s, Staatsanwälte>, **Staats·an·wäl·tin** ['ʃtaːtsˌanvɛltɪn] die <-, -nen> public prosecutor ◊ *Der Staatsanwalt erhob Anklage wegen Mordes.* ♦ *als Staatsanwältin tätig sein*

Staats·bür·ger ['ʃtaːtsbʏrˈgə] der <-s, ->, **Staats·bür·ge·rin** ['ʃtaːtsbʏrˈgərɪn] die <-, -nen> citizen ◊ *Sie ist deutsche Staatsbürgerin.* ♦ *Sie wurden wie Staatsbürger zweiter Klasse behandelt.*

Staats·e·xa·men ['ʃtaːtsɛˌksaːmən] das <-s, - or Staatsexamina> ◊ *das erste/zweite Staatsexamen machen/bestehen*

If you want to pursue a career in the public sector in Germany, you have to take a particular kind of exam: the *Staatsexamen* ('state examination'). The groups who take this exam include teachers, lawyers, chemists and doctors. In most cases, the first *Staatsexamen* is taken at the end of your university course, and the second after a subsequent period of practical training. Doctors and chemists, however, apply for a certificate entitling them to practise (the *Approbation*) instead of taking the second *Staatsexamen*.

Stab [ʃtaːp] der <-(e)s, Stäbe> **1.** stick ◊ *zum Wandern einen Stab mitnehmen* ♦ *mit dem Stab auf einen Fluss auf der Landkarte zeigen; (of a cage, window etc.)* bar ◊ *Bei diesem Gitterbett kann man einzelne Stäbe entfernen.* **2.** MUS baton ◊ *Der Dirigent klopfte mit dem Stab auf sein Pult.* **3.** *(abbr of* Zauberstab*)* (magic) wand ◊ *Der Zauberer richtete seinen Stab auf sie und sprach einen Zauberspruch.* **4.** REL *(abbr of* Bischofsstab*)* crosier, crozier **5.** SPORT pole **6.** *(of colleagues, experts etc.)* team, staff ◊ *Der Kanzler berät sich mit seinem Stab.* ♦ *über einen festen Stab von/an freien Mitarbeitern verfügen* **7.** MIL staff
⊛ den Stab über jdn/etw. brechen *(lofty)* condemn sb/sth

sta·bil [ʃtaˈbiːl] adj **1.** strong, robust, sturdy ◊ *eine stabile Stütze* ♦ *Ist die Konstruktion stabil genug, um dieser Belastung standzuhalten?* ♦ *psychisch nicht besonders stabil sein* ⊝schwach **2.** stable ◊ *Die politischen/wirtschaftlichen Verhältnisse dort sind relativ stabil.* ♦ *ein stabiler Wechselkurs* adv *(building, person)* stabil gebaut well built

sta·bi·li·sie·ren [ʃtabiliˈziːrən] <stabilisiert, stabilisierte, hat stabilisiert> tr v stabilize ◊ *jds Kreislauf stabilisieren* sich stabilisieren stabilize, become stable ◊ *Die Lage im Krisengebiet hat sich wieder stabilisiert.*

Sta·bi·li·tät [ʃtabiliˈtɛːt] die <-> *no pl* stability ◊ *die Stabilität einer Konstruktion prüfen* ♦ *die Stabilität des Friedens/einer Währung*

stach [ʃtaːx] *pret of* stechen

Sta·chel ['ʃtaxl̩] der <-s, -n> **1.** BOT prickle, thorn ◊ *Das Gestrüpp war voller Stacheln.* ♦ *die Stacheln der Distel* **2.** ZOO spine ◊ *die Stacheln des Igels/ Stachelschweins; (of a wasp, scorpion etc.)* sting
⊛ der Stachel sitzt tief the wounds remain

Sta·di·on ['ʃtaːdjɔn] das <-s, Stadien> stadium

Sta·di·um ['ʃtaːdjʊm] das <-s, Stadien> stage ◊ *eine Krankheit im fortgeschrittenen/frühen Stadium* ♦ *Die Entwicklung befindet sich jetzt in einem kritischen Stadium.*

② **Stadt** [ʃtat] die <-, Städte> **1.** town, city ◊ *Ein Zirkus ist in der Stadt.* ♦ *am Rande der Stadt wohnen* ♦ *Berlin ist keine geteilte Stadt mehr.* ♦ *Lebst du lieber in der Stadt oder auf dem Land?* kreisfreie Stadt *a town that is at the same time an administrative district* **2.** (town/city) council, municipality ◊ *als Gärtner bei der Stadt arbeiten* **3.** town in der Stadt in town in die Stadt fahren go into town
⊛ die Ewige Stadt the Eternal City die Goldene Stadt the Golden City die Heilige Stadt the Holy City

As a rule, the names of towns and cities in German are without articles (e.g. *Sie lebt in München.*). An article is used when the town/city name is accompanied by an attribute, e.g. an adjective *(im zeitgenössischen Berlin)* or a noun phrase *(das Paris der Nachkriegszeit)*. Town/city names are often prefixed by *die Stadt*: e.g. *die Stadt Köln*.

Stadt·bahn ['ʃtatbaːn] die <-, -en> *(abbr* S-Bahn*)* city railway (train), overground ◊ *die Berliner Stadtbahn* ♦ *mit der Stadtbahn fahren*

Stadt·hal·le ['ʃtathalə] die <-, -n> community hall ◊ *in der Stadthalle auftreten*

② **städ·tisch** ['ʃtɛ(ː)tɪʃ] adj *no comp/superl* **1.** town, city, municipal ◊ *die städtischen Behörden* städtische Angestellte/Bedienstete (town/city) council staff Das Krankenhaus ist städtisch. The hospital is owned/run by the town/city council. **2.** urban ◊ *Gemeinden mit städtischem Charakter* ♦ *Seine Kleidung war städtisch.* ⊝ländlich adv **1.** municipally städtisch verwaltet werden be run by the town/city council **2.** in an urban way ◊ *städtisch gekleidet sein* ⊝ländlich

Stadt·mit·te ['ʃtatmɪtə] die <-, -n> most sing town/city centre, downtown ◊ *die S-Bahn Richtung Stadtmitte* ⊝Innenstadt, Stadtzentrum

② **Stadt·plan** ['ʃtatplaːn] der <-(e)s, Stadtpläne> map (of a/the town/city)

② **Stadt·prä·si·dent** ['ʃtatprɛziˌdɛnt] der <-en, -en>, **Stadt·prä·si·den·tin** ['ʃtatprɛziˌdɛntɪn] die <-, -nen> *(Swiss)* mayor ◊ *die Wahl des Zürcher Stadtpräsidenten* Stadtpräsidentin mayoress ◊ *Sehr geehrte Frau Stadtpräsidentin, ...*

Stadt·rund·fahrt ['ʃtatrʊntfaːrt] die <-, -en> sight-

A B C D E F G H I J K L M N O P Q R S T U V W X Y Z

seeing tour (of a/the town/city) ◊ *eine Stadtrund-fahrt machen*

Stadt·wer·ke ['ʃtatvɛˈʁkə] <-> *only pl (always* die Stadtwerke) works department ◊ *Die Stadtwerke haben die Gaspreise erhöht.*

ⓩ **stahl** [ʃtaːl] *pret of* stehlen

Stahl [ʃtaːl] der <-(e)s, Stähle> steel ◊ *rostfreier Stahl* ♦ *Als Rennfahrer braucht man Nerven aus Stahl.*

Stall [ʃtal] der <-(e)s, Ställe> shed, barn ◊ *Bei ihnen stehen 20 Kühe im Stall.*; *(for horses)* stable(s); *(for pigs)* (pig)sty, (pig)pen ◊ *den Stall ausmisten*

Stamm [ʃtam] der <-(e)s, Stämme> **1.** BOT (tree) trunk ◊ *nach dem Fällen die Stämme von Ästen befreien* **2.** tribe ◊ *die zwölf Stämme Israels* ♦ *der Stamm der Apachen* **3.** core ◊ *zum Stamm des Teams gehören* einen großen Stamm treuer Kunden haben have a large number of regular customers **4.** BIO, BOT phylum **5.** LING group ◊ *Deutsch gehört zum Stamm der indogermanischen Sprachen.* **6.** LING *(of a word)* root

Stamm·buch ['ʃtambuːx] das <-(e)s, Stammbücher> *book in which documents concerning births, marriages, christenings and deaths within a particular family are kept* Ⓢ jdm etw. ins Stammbuch schreiben make sb take note of sth sich [dat] etw. ins Stammbuch schreiben make note of sth

stam·meln ['ʃtamln] [tr+intr v] +*haben* stammer ◊ *eine Liebeserklärung stammeln* ♦ *vor Angst/Aufregung zu stammeln anfangen*

stam·men ['ʃtamən] [intr v] +*haben* **1.** aus/von etw. stammen come from sth ◊ *Sie stammt aus einem schwierigen Elternhaus.* ♦ *Ursprünglich stammt die Kartoffel aus den Anden.* **2.** *temporal* aus/von etw. stammen date from sth ◊ *Die Fotos stammen von unserem Schwedenurlaub im letzten Jahr.* ♦ *Der Text stammt von 1968/aus dem Jahr 1968.* **3.** von jdm/etw. stammen be from sb/sth ◊ *Das Zitat stammt von Goethe.* ♦ *Die Narbe stammt von einer Blinddarmoperation.* Von wem stammt diese Idee/das Konzept? Who came up with this idea/concept? Woher stammen diese Probleme? What causes these problems?

Stamm·gast ['ʃtamgast] der <-(e)s, Stammgäste> regular ◊ *Stammgast in einem Hotel sein*

Stamm·tisch ['ʃtamtɪʃ] der <-(e)s, –e> **1.** social ◊ *sich jeden Mittwochabend zum Stammtisch treffen* **2.** regulars' table ◊ *Am Stammtisch wird immer heftig diskutiert/politisiert.*

> A German *Stammtisch* is a regular, informal gathering of like-minded people which usually takes place at a particular table in a pub or restaurant and where it is possible to make friends and discuss common interests.

ⓩ **stand** [ʃtant] *pret of* stehen

Stand [ʃtant] der <-(e)s, Stände> **1.** state der Stand der Dinge the way things stand etw. auf den letzten Stand bringen bring sth up to date auf dem neuesten Stand der Technik sein be state of the art **2.** level ◊ *Um acht Uhr erreichte das Hochwasser seinen höchsten Stand.* ♦ *Die Aktien stehen auf dem niedrigsten Stand seit Jahren.* **3.** stand ◊ *ein Stand mit Sonderangeboten in einem Kaufhaus*;

(in a market also) stall ◊ *Die Teilnehmer am Weihnachtsmarkt bauen schon ihre Stände auf.* **4.** *(outd)* class ◊ *als Adliger eine Frau von niederem Stand heiraten* ♦ *dem Stand der Bauern/Kaufleute etc. angehören* der dritte/vierte Stand the Third/Fourth estate die drei Stände the Three Estates **5.** marital status ☰Familienstand **6.** position ◊ *einen schlechten/schweren Stand bei seinen Kollegen/in der Klasse haben* **7.** sicherer/fester Stand hold, grip, support einer Sache [dat] einen festen Stand geben, für den sicheren Stand … [gen] sorgen stabilize sth Auf den glitschigen Felsen fand/hatte sie keinen sicheren Stand. On the slippery rocks her feet couldn't get a grip. ☰Halt **8.** *no pl* standing position ◊ *Er beschleunigt aus dem Stand von null auf hundert in zehn Sekunden.* ♦ *den Motor im Stand warmlaufen lassen* ein Sprung/Start aus dem Stand a standing jump/start

Ⓢ in den Stand der Ehe treten enter the state of matrimony jdn/etw. in den Stand setzen, etw. zu tun make it possible for sb/sth to do sth aus dem Stand (heraus) *(fam)* off the cuff, just like that

Stän·der ['ʃtɛndɐ] der <-s, –> **1.** rack, stand ◊ *sein Fahrrad in den Ständer am Bahnhof stellen* ♦ *ein Ständer für die Wäsche* **2.** *(rude)* stiffy ◊ *einen Ständer haben*

Stan·des·amt ['ʃtandəsˌamt] das <-(e)s, Standesämter> (civil) registry office

stand·fest ['ʃtantfɛst] [adj] <standfester, am standfestesten> **1.** stable, steady ◊ *ein standfestes Gerüst* ♦ *Das Regal ist sehr standfest.*; *(person)* nicht mehr besonders standfest sein be a bit shaky on your feet **2.** steadfast ◊ *Die Kinder bettelten sehr, aber er blieb standfest.* ♦ *Sie erwies sich als standfeste Verbündete.* **3.** reliable ◊ *selbst bei extremer Beanspruchung standfeste Bremsen* ♦ *Dieses Modell ist standfest und zuverlässig.* ☰zuverlässig

stand·hal·ten ['ʃtanthaltn] <hält stand, hielt stand, hat standgehalten> [intr v] **1.** jd hält jdm/einer Sache stand sb stands up to sb/sth ◊ *dem öffentlichen Druck standhalten und nicht zurücktreten* ♦ *den Angreifern nicht standhalten können* **2.** hold etw. hält einer Sache [dat] stand sth withstands sth ◊ *Die Mauer hat dem Druck nicht standgehalten und ist eingestürzt.* **3.** etw. hält einer Sache [dat] stand sth stands up to sth ◊ *Die These hat einer Überprüfung nicht standgehalten.*

stän·dig ['ʃtɛndɪç] [adj] *no comp/superl, only before ns* **1.** permanent, continuous ◊ *seinen ständigen Wohnsitz in Köln haben* ♦ *ständiges Mitglied eines Ausschusses sein* ☰dauernd **2.** *(esp pej)* constant ◊ *Diese ständigen Wiederholungen nerven mich.* ☰ewig, andauernd [adv] **1.** continuously ◊ *Die Zahl steigt/wächst ständig.* ♦ *einen Prozess ständig überwachen/beobachten* **2.** constantly ◊ *Sie schimpft ständig über ihre Nachbarn.*

Stand·ort ['ʃtantˌʔɔrt] der <-(e)s, –e> **1.** location ◊ *Unsere Stadt ist ein attraktiver Standort für große Unternehmen.* **2.** *(also fig)* position ◊ *seinen gegenwärtigen Standort an die Zentrale durchgeben* ♦ *seinen politischen Standort bestimmen* ☰Position **3.** MIL garrison

ⓩ **Stand·punkt** ['ʃtantpʊŋkt] der <-(e)s, –e> point of

view ◊ *Er vertritt den/steht auf dem Standpunkt, dass eine Neuerung nicht nötig ist.* ♦ *auf seinem Standpunkt beharren* ⊜Auffassung

Stan·ge ['ʃtaŋə] die <–, –n> **1.** pole ◊ *Die Bohnen ranken sich an den Stangen hoch.* ♦ *eine Einfahrt mit einer langen Stange versperren;* (for a bird) perch ◊ *Der Wellensittich sitzt auf seiner Stange und döst.;* (for clothing) rail ◊ *einen Kleiderbügel an die Stange hängen;* (of vegetables) stalk, stick ◊ *eine Stange Sellerie;* (of asparagus) spear; (of dynamite, salami) stick **2.** *eine Stange Zigaretten* 200 cigarettes **3.** (fam) *eine Stange (Geld)* loads (of money)
◉ *bei der Stange bleiben* stick at it **jdn bei der Stange halten** make sb stick at it, keep sb at it **jdm die Stange halten** stick by sb **von der Stange** (also pej) off the peg

Stän·gel ['ʃtɛŋl] der <–s, –> stem, stalk ◊ *Der Löwenzahn hat hohle Stängel.* ⊜Stiel

② **stank** [ʃtaŋk] *pret* of stinken

Sta·pel ['ʃta:pl] der <–s, –> (also fig) pile ◊ *ein Stapel Bücher/Handtücher/Holz/Papier* ♦ *Ich muss noch einen ganzen Stapel Briefe schreiben.*
◉ *etw. vom Stapel lassen* **1.** (fam, pej) (unwelcome jokes, remarks etc.) come out with sth ◊ *ein paar abgedroschene Witze vom Stapel lassen* **2.** (a ship) launch sth **vom Stapel laufen** (ship) be launched

sta·peln ['ʃta:pln] tr v +haben *etw.* stapeln stack sth, pile sth up ◊ *die Zeitschriften ordentlich in Kartons stapeln* sich stapeln pile up ◊ *Ich muss an die Arbeit, bei mir stapelt sich die Bügelwäsche.*

② **Star¹** [sta:ʳ] der <–s, –s> star ◊ *Sie war der Star des Abends.* ♦ *eine Show mit vielen berühmten Stars aus Film und Fernsehen*

Star² [ʃta:ʳ] der <–(e)s, –e> **1.** ZOO starling **2.** no pl MED (grauer) Star cataract(s) ◊ *am Star operiert werden* **3.** no pl MED (grüner) Star glaucoma

② **starb** [ʃtaʳp] *pret* of sterben

② **stark** [ʃtaʳk] adj <stärker, am stärksten> **1.** strong ◊ *ein starker Mann* ♦ *stark wie ein Bär/Löwe/Stier* ♦ *Iss das, damit du groß und stark wirst!* ♦ *starke Nerven haben/brauchen* ♦ *einen starken Charakter/ Willen haben* ♦ *eine starke Lobby* ♦ *starken Kaffee trinken* ♦ *Das Bier ist aber stark, wie viel Prozent hat es denn?* ♦ *eine 200 Mann starke Truppe* ⊜schwach **2.** (extreme) intense ◊ *Die Schmerzen waren sehr stark.* ♦ *Die Branche hofft auf ein starkes Wachstum der Umsätze.;* (clouds, rainfall, traffic) heavy ◊ *starke Bewölkung/Regenfälle* ♦ *Der Verkehr auf den Straßen war ziemlich stark.* **3.** thick ◊ *Burgen hatten sehr starke Mauern.* *ein vier Zentimeter starkes Seil* a rope four centimetres thick *ein 500 Seiten starkes Buch* a 500 page book ⊜dick ⊜dünn **4.** only before ns (smoker, drinker) heavy ◊ *ein starker Raucher* **5.** (fam, iron) *Das ist stark!, Das ist ein starkes Stück!* That's a bit rich!, That's a bit much! *sich* (dat) *ein starkes Stück leisten* surpass yourself **6.** (fam) great ◊ *ein starker Typ* ♦ *Das war echt stark, wie du das gemacht hast!* ⊜toll, großartig **7.** (euph) large, big ◊ *Er ist etwas stark geworden.* ♦ *Mode für stärkere Damen/Herren* ⊜dick ⊜schlank **8.** only before ns LING (verbs, nouns, adjectives) strong ◊ *„Gehen" ist ein starkes Verb.* ♦ *die starke Deklination eines Adjektivs* ⊜schwach adv **1.** very,

extremely, seriously ◊ *ein stark bewölkter Himmel* ♦ *Das Auto wurde bei dem Unfall stark beschädigt.* ♦ *Die Preise sind im letzten Monat ungewöhnlich stark gestiegen. Sie ähneln sich stark. They look very similar.* ⊜sehr **2.** in large numbers ◊ *In diesem Jahr sind die Frauen unter den Absolventen stärker vertreten. eine stark befahrene Straße* a busy road **3.** LING stark dekliniert/konjugiert in the strong declension/conjugation
◉ **sich für jdn/etw. stark machen** (fam) do your best for sb/sth, do what you can for sb/sth

Stär·ke ['ʃtɛʳkə] die <–, –n> **1.** intensity ◊ *Die Stärke des Sturms lässt schon wieder nach. ein Erdbeben der Stärke sechs auf der Richterskala an* earthquake measuring six on the Richter scale **2.** strength ◊ *Zuverlässigkeit ist ihre große Stärke.* ♦ *die Stärken und Schwächen eines Systems* ♦ *Es ist ein Zeichen von Stärke, Gefühle zuzulassen.* ⊜Schwäche **3.** no pl strength, power ◊ *militärische/wirtschaftliche Stärke* ⊜Macht **4.** seldom with the article, no pl CHEM starch ◊ *Getreide, Kartoffeln und Hülsenfrüchte enthalten besonders viel Stärke.* **5.** thickness ◊ *Bretter in verschiedenen Stärken* **6.** size ◊ *ein Heer mit einer Stärke von 20 000 Mann* a 20 000 man army

stär·ken ['ʃtɛʳkŋ] tr v +haben strengthen, fortify ◊ *jds Position stärken* ♦ *das Immunsystem/die Abwehrkräfte stärken* sich (mit etw.) stärken fortify yourself (with sth) ◊ *sich mit einem kleinen Imbiss stärken*

Stär·kung ['ʃtɛʳkʊŋ] die <–, –en> **1.** strengthening, fortification ◊ *Sie erhofft sich von den Wahlen eine Stärkung ihrer Position.* **2.** refreshment ◊ *ein Joghurt als kleine Stärkung zwischendurch*

starr [ʃtaʳ] adj ◊ *Die Glieder des Toten waren bereits starr.* ♦ *starr vor Schreck sein* ♦ *die starre Haltung der Regierung in einem Konflikt* ♦ *Das System ist viel zu starr.* starr vor Kälte stiff with (the) cold *ein starrer Blick* a fixed look, a stare adv fixedly ◊ *den Blick/die Augen starr aufs Ziel richten* starr geradeaus blicken

star·ren ['ʃtaʳən] intr v +haben **1.** stare ◊ *gebannt auf den Bildschirm starren* ♦ *Du sollst nicht so starren, das ist unhöflich.* **2.** vor Dreck/Schmutz starren be covered in dirt, be filthy

② **Start** [ʃtaʳt] der <–(e)s, –s> **1.** start ◊ *einen guten Start haben/hinlegen* ♦ *beim Start gut/schlecht wegkommen* ♦ *ein guter Start ins Berufsleben/ Leben* ♦ *Beim Start des Programms ist der Computer abgestürzt. den Start freigeben* give the start(ing) signal *ein fliegender Start* a flying start **2.** take-off ◊ *Der Start musste wegen Nebel verschoben werden. den Start freigeben* clear for take-off **3.** SPORT (in a race, competition) participation ◊ *seinen Start bei der Tour de France absagen* ⊜Teilnahme **4.** SPORT start, starting line ⊜Ziel
◉ **Start frei (für etw./jdn)** ready, steady, go (for sth/sb)

② **star·ten** ['ʃtaʳtn] <startet, startete, hat/ist gestartet> intr v +sein **1.** start ◊ *Wann soll die neue Serie starten?* ♦ *ins Berufsleben/neue Schuljahr starten* ♦ *in den Urlaub/nach Österreich etc. starten* go on holiday/to Austria etc. **2.** (plane) take off ◊ *Die Flugzeuge starten und landen.* ♦ *zum Jungfernflug starten;* (rocket) lift

off **3.** SPORT (bei/in etw. [dat]) starten take part (in sth) für etw./jdn starten represent sth/sb ◊ *für Spanien starten* [tr v] +*haben* etw. starten start sth ◊ *einen Versuch starten* ♦ *Bei der Kälte lässt sich mein Moped schlecht starten.*

② **Sta·ti·on** [ʃta'tsɪ̯oːn] die <-, -en> **1.** station, stop ◊ *Er ist an der letzten Station ausgestiegen.* ♦ *Wie viele Stationen sind es noch bis Hannover?* **2.** MED ward ◊ *von der Notaufnahme in die chirurgische Station verlegt werden* ♦ *die geschlossene Station der Psychiatrie* **3.** TECHN station ◊ *eine meteorologische/seismologische Station* **4.** *(in a life, career etc.)* stage ◊ *Stationen ihrer Karriere/ihrer Kindheit/ihres Lebens; (on a journey)* stop ◊ *Stockholm und Helsinki waren weitere Stationen unserer Reise.* irgendwo Station machen stop off somewhere

sta·ti·o·när [ʃtatsɪ̯o'nɛːɐ̯] adj *no comp/superl* **1.** *only before ns* MED in-patient ◊ *ein stationärer Aufenthalt/eine stationäre Behandlung im Krankenhaus* ⊖ambulant **2.** *mostly before ns* stationary ◊ *eine stationäre Anlage zur Ozonmessung* ♦ *Die Kamera ist stationär.* [adv] as an in-patient ◊ *stationär aufgenommen/behandelt werden*

sta·ti·o·nie·ren [ʃtatsɪ̯o'niːrən] <stationiert, stationierte, hat stationiert> [tr v] *(troops)* station ◊ *in einem Land Blauhelme/Friedenstruppen stationieren*

② **statt**[1] [ʃtat] [conjunc] instead of ◊ *Statt am Montag ist der Kurs in Zukunft am Dienstag.* ♦ *Er machte nach der Arbeit einen Spaziergang, statt gleich nach Hause zu gehen.* ⊖anstatt

② **statt**[2] [ʃtat] [prep] *sing nouns without article or attribute are not declined when following this prep, otherwise* [+gen] *or* [+dat] instead of, in place of ◊ *Statt der erhofften Belohnung bekam er nur einen Händedruck.* ♦ *Statt Äpfeln/der Äpfel kann man auch Birnen für den Kuchen verwenden.* ⊖anstatt, anstelle

statt·des·sen [ʃtat'dɛsn̩] [adv] instead ◊ *Wenn du keine Lust zum Tanzen hast, könnten wir ja stattdessen zum Essen gehen.*

② **statt|fin·den** ['ʃtatfɪndn̩] <findet statt, fand statt, hat stattgefunden> [intr v] take place ◊ *Wo/Wann soll denn das Fest stattfinden?* ♦ *Das Lernen findet im Kopf statt.*

② **Stau** [ʃtaʊ] der <-(e)s, -s or seldom -e> **1.** traffic jam ◊ *Auf der A8 Richtung München gibt es 14 Kilometer Stau.* ♦ *im Stau stehen/stecken* ♦ *ein Stau bildet sich/löst sich auf* ein langer Stau a long traffic jam **2.** *(of liquids)* damming-up ◊ *Das Regenwasser muss ohne Stau ablaufen.; (of data, blood)* blocking, blockage ◊ *ein Stau in der Datenübertragung* **3.** *(of people, things)* hold-up, jam ◊ *Bitte rechtzeitig kommen, sonst gibt es wieder Stau an den Kassen!*

Staub [ʃtaʊp] der <-(e)s> *no pl* dust ◊ *Eine dicke Schicht Staub lag auf den Regalen.* ♦ *zu Staub werden/zerfallen* Staub wischen do the dusting Staub saugen vaccum-clean

◉ viel Staub aufwirbeln cause a big stir sich aus dem Staub machen clear off, run off

stau·ben ['ʃtaʊbm̩] [intr v] +*haben* **1.** be dusty, become dusty ◊ *In der Trockenheit stauben die Straßen.; (dough)* become powdery **2.** swirl ◊ *Der Schnee staubte, als der Hubschrauber landete.*

[imp v] es staubt there is a lot of dust (in the air)

stau·big ['ʃtaʊbɪç] adj **1.** dusty ◊ *Im Archiv war es staubig.* ♦ *Hinter dem Auto bildete sich eine staubige Wolke.; (bands, car, clothes)* covered in dust ◊ *staubige Schuhe/Kleidung* **2.** *(fine-grained)* powdery ◊ *Der Rindenmulch trocknet aus und wird staubig.*

staub·sau·gen ['ʃtaʊpzaʊ̯ɡn̩] <staubsaugt, staubsaugte, hat gestaubsaugt> [tr+intr v] vacuum, hoover ◊ *das/im Wohnzimmer staubsaugen* ⊖saugen

Staub·sau·ger ['ʃtaʊpzaʊ̯ɡɐ] der <-s, -> vacuum cleaner, Hoover™

stau·en ['ʃtaʊən] [tr v] +*haben* dam (up) ◊ *einen Fluss (zu einem See) stauen* ♦ *Hier wird das Wasser gestaut und zur Stromerzeugung benutzt.* [ref v] +*haben* **1.** sich stauen come to a standstill, form a tailback ◊ *An den Grenzen staut sich der Verkehr.* **2.** *(liquids)* sich stauen accumulate, collect ◊ *Das Wasser staute sich am Biberdamm.* ♦ *Das Blut staut sich und es entstehen Gefäßknoten.* **3.** *(also fig)* build up ◊ *Alle diese Emotionen stauten sich seit Wochen in ihm.* ♦ *Am Alpenhauptkamm stauten sich die Wolken.* [imp v] es staut there is some congestion, traffic has become congested ◊ *Es staut auf folgenden Straßen: ...*

stau·nen ['ʃtaʊnən] [intr v] +*haben* (über etw. [acc]) staunen be amazed (at/by sth), be astonished (at/by sth) ◊ *Er war sprachlos; er konnte nur noch schauen und staunen.* ♦ *Du wirst staunen darüber, wie groß die Kinder geworden sind.* ♦ *Selbst Klimaexperten staunen über diesen Sommer.* (jdn) staunen lassen amaze sb, astonish sb ◊ *Das riesige Ölgemälde ließ so manchen Besucher staunen.*

◉ (über etw. [acc]) nicht schlecht staunen *(fam)* be quite amazed (at/by sth)

② **Steak** [steːk] das <-s, -s> steak ◊ *Sie hat ein Steak mit Pommes bestellt.*

ste·chen ['ʃtɛçn̩] <sticht, stach, hat gestochen> [tr+intr v] **1.** prick ◊ *Sein Bart sticht.* ♦ *Ich habe mir mit der Nadel in den Finger gestochen.* ♦ *Hast du dich am Kaktus gestochen?* **2.** *(bee, wasp, nettle)* sting ◊ *Aua! Mich hat etwas gestochen!; (gnat, mosquito)* bite **3.** *(a person)* stab ◊ *Er hat das/dem Opfer mehrmals in den Rücken gestochen.* ♦ *ein stechender Schmerz; (a knife)* plunge, thrust ◊ *jdm ein Messer ins Herz stechen; (a needle)* insert ◊ *Der Akupunkteur hat ihm mehrere Nadeln in den Rücken gestochen.; (an object)* pierce ◊ *mit einer Gabel mehrmals in den Teig stechen.* ♦ *ein Loch in eine Folie stechen* ♦ sich [dat] *Ohrlöcher stechen lassen* **4.** CARDS take (the trick) ◊ *Er hat meinen König mit dem Ass gestochen.* ♦ *Du hast gestochen. Spiel aus.; (with a trump)* trump [tr v] cut ◊ *Rasen/Torf/Spargel stechen* [imp v] es sticht sb gets a sharp pain ◊ *Es sticht jedes Mal, wenn ich huste.* [intr v] *(sun)* beat down ◊ *Die Sonne sticht heute so; ich bleibe lieber im Schatten.*

② **Steck·do·se** ['ʃtɛkdoːzə] die <-, -n> (wall) socket ◊ *den Stecker in die Steckdose stecken/aus der Steckdose ziehen*

② **ste·cken** ['ʃtɛkn̩] [tr v] +*haben* **1.** +*direction* put, stick ◊ *einen Brief in ein Kuvert stecken* ♦ *jdn ins Gefängnis/Altersheim stecken* ♦ sich [dat] *eine*

Blume in die Haare stecken ♦ *Der Hund steckte seinen Kopf durch den Zaun/unter die Decke.*; *(into sth also)* insert ◊ *einen Schlüssel ins Schloss stecken; (quietly)* slip ◊ *Er steckte das Geld heimlich in seine Tasche.* jdm/sich etw. irgendwohin stecken put sth on sb's/your sth ◊ *Er steckte ihr den Ring an den Finger.; (a brooch)* pin sth on sb's/your sth **2.** *(money, energy)* etw. in etw. `acc` stecken put sth into sth, invest sth in sth ◊ *In dieses Projekt habe ich viel Zeit und Energie gesteckt.* `intr v` +*haben* **1.** be stuck ◊ *Seit zwei Stunden stecken wir im Stau.; (bullet)* be lodged, be embedded stecken bleiben get stuck ◊ *Der Lift blieb stecken und das Licht ging aus.* ♦ *Viele Fahrzeuge blieben im Schnee stecken.* **2.** irgendwo stecken be somewhere ◊ *Ihre Füße steckten in hochhackigen Stiefeln.* ♦ *Wo steckt denn nur dieses Buch?* ♦ *Was steckt noch alles hinter diesem Vorfall?* ♦ *in Schwierigkeiten/einer Krise stecken* ♦ *mitten in der Ausbildung/den Vorbereitungen stecken* ◊ *In Blitzen stecken gewaltige Mengen an Energie.* ♦ *Wer steckt hinter dem Anschlag?* Ich weiß nicht, wo er den ganzen Tag steckt. I don't know where he gets to all day. Der Schlüssel steckt. The key is in the door/lock. etw. stecken lassen leave sth in ◊ *Er ließ den Schlüssel einfach stecken.* **3.** *(money, effort)* in etw. `dat` stecken have gone into sth ◊ *In diesem Projekt steckt eine Menge Geld.* **4.** jd/etw. steckt voller ... sb/sth is full of ... ◊ *Der Text steckt voller Fehler.* ♦ *Dieses Kind steckt voller Rätsel.*

② **Ste·cker** ['ʃtɛkɐ] der <-s, -> plug ◊ *den Stecker herausziehen/einstecken*

Steg [ʃteːk] der <-(e)s, -e> **1.** footbridge ◊ *ein Steg über einen Bach* ♦ *über einen Steg gehen* **2.** landing-stage, jetty ◊ *Sie saßen auf dem Steg und plantschten mit den Füßen im Wasser.* ♦ *das Boot am Steg festmachen* **3.** catwalk ◊ *Models in Abendkleidern spazierten über den Steg.* **4.** *(of a guitar, spectacles)* bridge **5.** footstrap ◊ *Skihosen mit Steg*

② **ste·hen** ['ʃteːən] <steht, stand, hat gestanden> `intr v` *in South G, Austr, Swiss often* +*sein* **1.** stand ◊ *gerade stehen* ♦ *Ich kann nicht mehr stehen, meine Füße tun weh!* ♦ *Es gab keine Plätze mehr, also mussten wir stehen.* ⊜*sitzen* **2.** be ◊ *Auf dem Hauptplatz des Dorfes steht eine Kirche.* ♦ *Die Bücher stehen im Regal.* ♦ *Auf wessen Seite stehst du eigentlich?* ♦ *jdm zur Verfügung/Wahl stehen* ♦ *Auf dem Programm steht eine zweistündige Wanderung.* ♦ *Unsere Mannschaft steht im Finale.* ♦ *an der Spitze einer Organisation stehen* ♦ *jdm/ einer Sache im Wege stehen* ♦ *Seit Stunden steht er schon im Stau.* ♦ *im Mittelpunkt/Vordergrund/ Hintergrund stehen* ♦ *in jds Schuld stehen* ♦ *Sie stehen immer noch in Kontakt zueinander.* ♦ *auf dem Spiel stehen* ♦ *unter Alkoholeinfluss/Druck stehen* ♦ *Das Medikament steht kurz vor der Markteinführung.* ♦ *Ihm stehen alle Wege offen.* ♦ *Die Wohnung steht leer.* ♦ *Die Chancen stehen gut.* zu etw. stehen be up for sth ◊ *zur Debatte/Diskussion stehen* ♦ *Das Haus steht zum Verkauf.; (a dilemma)* vor etw. `dat` stehen be facing sth ◊ *vor einer Aufgabe/Entscheidung stehen* ♦ *Die Fluggesellschaft steht kurz vor der Pleite.; (bus etc.)* be, wait ◊ *Der Bus steht schon an der Haltestelle.*

3. stand still, have stopped, be at a standstill, have come to a standstill ◊ *Ich weiß nicht, wie spät es ist. Meine Uhr steht.* ♦ *Während des Streiks standen alle Maschinen.* ♦ *Tür nicht öffnen, bevor der Zug steht.* **4.** *(text)* (geschrieben) stehen be (written) ◊ *Am Ende eines Satzes steht ein Punkt.* ♦ *auf der Liste stehen* ♦ *Das steht noch in den Sternen.* im Brief/auf dem Zettel steht ... the letter/note says ... Kannst du lesen, was da an der Tafel steht? Can you read what it says on the board? **5.** *(also fig) (scaffolding, part of a building, agreement etc.)* be in place ◊ *Das Gerüst steht schon; wir können mit der Renovierung beginnen.* ♦ *Der Kompromiss steht.* **6.** auf etw. `dat` stehen be at sth, be showing sth ◊ *Das Thermometer steht auf 30°.* ♦ *Der Zeiger der Uhr steht auf sechs.; (barometer)* be indicating ◊ *Das Barometer steht auf Sturm.* **7.** LAW *(penalty)* auf etw. `acc` stehen carry sth Auf Mord steht lebenslänglich. Murder carries a penalty of life imprisonment. **8.** für etw. stehen stand for sth ◊ *Unser Name steht für höchste Qualität.* ♦ *AGB steht für Allgemeine Geschäftsbedingungen.* **9.** zu jdm/etw. stehen stand by sb/sth ◊ *Sie stand trotz aller Schwierigkeiten zu ihm.* ♦ *Er steht zu seinem Wort.* jdm zur Seite stehen stand by sb **10.** jdm stehen suit sb ◊ *Das neue Kleid steht dir gut.* ♦ *Grün steht mir nicht.* `imp v` **1.** um jdn/etw. steht gut/schlecht things look good/bad for sb/sth Wie steht es eigentlich um seine Gesundheit? How are things looking as far as his health is concerned? **2.** SPORT be ◊ *Es steht 5:3 für die Gastmannschaft.*

⊛ **stehen bleiben 1.** stop, come to a standstill ◊ *Halt! Stehen bleiben!* ♦ *Sie bleiben kurz bei ihm stehen und unterhielten sich.* ♦ *Die Uhr ist stehen geblieben. (time)* stand still *(heart)* stop beating Nicht stehen bleiben! Keep moving! **2.** *(not leave)* stay ◊ *Bleib bitte hier stehen, bis ich zurück bin.* **3.** *(building, scaffolding etc.)* remain, be left/ there ◊ *Ich hoffe, dass das Haus noch so lange stehen bleibt.* ♦ *Nur die Grundmauern blieben stehen.* **4.** *(person who is talking, discussion)* stop, leave off ◊ *Wo bin ich stehen geblieben? Ah ja, deine Schulnoten.* etw. steht und fällt mit jdm/etw. the success of sth depends on sb/sth etw. stehen lassen **1.** leave sth ◊ *Er hat das Auto unverschlossen stehen gelassen.* ♦ *Den Teig über Nacht im Kühlschrank stehen lassen.* **2.** *(a statement)* accept sth ◊ *eine Behauptung so stehen lassen* jdn stehen lassen leave sb standing alles stehen und liegen lassen drop everything auf etw./jdn stehen *(fam)* be keen on sth/sb ◊ *Ich glaube, deine Schwester steht auf mich.* ♦ *Sie steht auf Rockmusik.*

② **steh·len** ['ʃteːlən] <stiehlt, stahl, hat gestohlen> `tr+intr v` steal ◊ *Mein Auto wurde gestohlen.* ♦ *Der Einbrecher hat wertvollen Schmuck gestohlen.* ♦ *Ich habe noch nie gestohlen.* ⊜*klauen* `tr v` *(fig)* jdm etw. stehlen rob sb of sth, steal sth from sb, deprive sb of sth ◊ *Dieses Regime hat einer ganzen Generation die Zukunft gestohlen.* ♦ *jdm die Zeit stehlen* jdm die Zeit waste sb's time `ref v` **1.** sich aus dem Haus/ins Zimmer etc. stehlen sneak/steal out of the house/into the room etc. **2.** sich aus etw. stehlen wriggle out of sth ◊ *So*

einfach kannst du dich nicht aus der Verantwortung stehlen.

◉ jd/etw. **kann jdm gestohlen bleiben** *(fam)* sb couldn't care less about sb/sth ◊ *Lasst mich in Ruhe, ihr könnt mir alle gestohlen bleiben!* ◆ *Das Geld kann mir gestohlen bleiben, ich brauche es nicht.*

steif [ʃtaef] ⟨adj, adv⟩ **1.** stiff(ly) ◊ *Mein Nacken ist so steif.* ◆ *eine steife Brise* ◆ *die Sahne steif schlagen* ◆ *Der Junge sitzt steif neben seiner Mutter.* ◆ *sich steif bewegen*; *(muscle)* tense; *(bodywork, chassis, leather)* strong ◊ *Schuhe aus steifem Leder* **2.** *(forced)* formal(ly) ◊ *eine steife Atmosphäre* ◆ *Er findet sie steif.* ◆ *Die Gäste standen etwas steif herum.* ⊜gezwungen ⊜locker ⟨adj⟩ *(fam) (penis)* erect, hard ◊ *Sein Glied wollte nicht steif werden.*

◉ **steif und fest behaupten/glauben, ...** *(fam)* insist/firmly believe that ...

② **stei·gen** [ˈʃtaeɡn̩] ⟨steigt, stieg, ist gestiegen⟩ ⟨intr v⟩ **1.** go up, increase ◊ *Die Preise/Kosten/Zinsen steigen.* ◆ *Die Temperaturen steigen im Laufe des Tages auf 25 Grad.* ◆ *Die Nachfrage nach Gas ist gestiegen.*; *(prospects)* look up ◊ *Seine Erfolgsaussichten steigen.* um etw. **steigen** increase by sth, rise by sth, go up by sth ◊ *Das Wasser stieg um zwei Zentimeter.* ⊜fallen, sinken **2.** *(balloon, hot air)* rise ◊ *Der Ballon stieg auf 1200 Meter.* ◆ *Rauch stieg in den Himmel.* einen **Drachen steigen lassen** fly a kite ⊜sinken **3.** climb, step ◊ *Er stieg von der Leiter.* ◆ *ins Wasser/in die Wanne steigen* auf etw. ⟨acc⟩ steigen climb (up) sth ◊ *auf einen Berg/Turm/Baum steigen* vom Berg ins Tal steigen climb down the mountain into the valley **4.** *(a vehicle)* in/auf etw. ⟨acc⟩ **steigen** get into/onto sth ◊ *ins Auto steigen* ◆ *in den Bus/Zug steigen* ◆ *aufs Fahrrad steigen* vom Pferd steigen mount (the horse) **5.** aus/von etw. **steigen** get out of/off sth ◊ *aus dem Flugzeug/Auto/Zug steigen* ◆ *vom Fahrrad steigen* vom Pferd steigen dismount **6.** *(fam) (festival, sporting event)* be ◊ *Wann steigt die Party?* **7.** *(fam)* auf etw. ⟨acc⟩ steigen step on sth, tread on sth ◊ *Steig mir nicht auf die Zehen!* aufs Gas steigen put your foot on the accelerator auf die Bremse steigen put your foot on the brake auf die Kupplung steigen depress the clutch ⊜treten

stei·gern [ˈʃtaeɡɐn] ⟨tr v⟩ +*haben* **1.** increase, raise ◊ *seinen Marktanteil um/auf 20 Prozent steigern* ◆ *das Arbeitstempo steigern* ⊜erhöhen ⊜senken **2.** LING compare ◊ *ein Adjektiv steigern* ⟨ref v⟩ +*haben* **1.** sich steigern increase, rise ◊ *Die Besucherzahlen haben sich gesteigert.* ◆ *Die Attraktivität des Produkts hat sich gesteigert.* ⊜zunehmen **2.** jd steigert sich sb improves ⊜jd verbessert sich

Stei·ge·rung [ˈʃtaeɡərʊŋ] die ⟨-, -en⟩ **1.** increase, rise ◊ *Das bedeutet eine deutliche Steigerung gegenüber dem Vorjahr.* eine Steigerung ... ⟨gen⟩ an increase in sth, a rise in sth ◊ *eine Steigerung der Effizienz/Produktivität* ◆ *eine Steigerung des Umsatzes um 15 Prozent* ⊜Erhöhung **2.** LING *(formation)* comparison ◊ *die Steigerung der Adjektive*; *(form)* comparative ◊ *„Lieber" ist die Steigerung von „gern".* **3.** improvement ◊ *Seine persönliche Steigerung war außerordentlich.*

Stei·gung [ˈʃtaeɡʊŋ] die ⟨-, -en⟩ **1.** slope, incline

◊ *An einer leichten Steigung blieb der Lastwagen stehen.* ◆ *eine Steigung überwinden/bewältigen* **2.** gradient ◊ *eine Straße mit einer leichten Steigung* ◆ *die Steigung der Kurve*

② **steil** [ʃtael] ⟨adj, adv⟩ steep(ly) ◊ *eine steile Treppe* ◆ *Der Abhang war sehr steil.* ◆ *eine steile Wachstumskurve* ◆ *eine steil abfallende Böschung* ◆ *Hier geht es wieder steil bergauf.* ⊜flach

② **Stein** [ʃtaen] der ⟨-(e)s, -e⟩ **1.** stone ◊ *etw. in Stein meißeln* ◆ *Steine ins Wasser werfen* ◆ *Er hat ein Herz aus Stein!*; *(fragment also)* rock; *(small)* pebble, stone ◊ *einen Stein im Schuh haben*; *(manufactured)* brick ◊ *ein solides Haus aus Stein* wie ein Stein zu Boden fallen drop like a stone **2.** jewel, gem ◊ *Sie trug einen Ring mit einem großen Stein.* **3.** gravestone, tombstone ◊ *Auf dem Stein stand nur der Name des Toten.*

◉ **Stein des Anstoßes** bone of contention jdm **fällt ein Stein vom Herzen** sth is a load off sb's mind jdm **fällt kein Stein aus der Krone** sth won't hurt sb einen/den **Stein ins Rollen bringen** start the ball rolling jdm/einer Sache **Steine in den Weg legen** make things difficult for sb/sth **Steine aus dem Weg räumen** smooth sb's path, smooth the way der **Stein der Weisen** the philosophers' stone **kein Stein blieb auf dem anderen 1.** everything was smashed to pieces, not a stone was left standing ◊ *Nach dem Erdbeben blieb im Dorf kein Stein auf dem anderen.* **2.** wholesale changes were made ◊ *Als der neue Chef kam, blieb im Unternehmen kein Stein auf dem anderen.* **(wie) in Stein gemeißelt** *(sein)* (be) carved in stone

Stein·bock [ˈʃtaenbɔk] der ⟨-(e)s, Steinböcke⟩ **1.** ZOO ibex **2.** ASTROL Capricorn **3.** *no pl* ASTRON Capricornus

Stein·zeit [ˈʃtaentsaet] die ⟨-⟩ *no pl* **1.** die Steinzeit the Stone Age ◊ *ein wertvoller Fund aus der frühen Steinzeit* **2.** *(fig, esp pej)* stone age, ancient history ◊ *Dieses Gesetz stammt ja noch aus der Steinzeit!*

② **Stel·le** [ˈʃtɛlə] die ⟨-, -n⟩ **1.** *(geographical)* place, location ◊ *An dieser Stelle stand früher ein Tempel.*; *(in relation to others also)* position ◊ *etw. an strategischer Stelle platzieren* ⊜Ort **2.** *(spatial, figurative)* place, spot ◊ *Diese Stelle ist durch hohe Sträucher uneinsichtlich.* ◆ *eine empfindliche/schmerzende Stelle* ◆ *Sie hat diese Stelle im Buch mit Leuchtstift markiert.*; *(fig also)* point ◊ *An dieser Stelle der Geschichte machte er eine Pause.* eine undichte/wunde Stelle a leak/sore an anderer Stelle elsewhere an jds Stelle in sb's place, in sb's position ◊ *An Stelle meiner Schwester kam ihr Mann.* ◆ *An Ihrer Stelle würde ich das nicht tun.* an Stelle einer ... ⟨gen⟩ instead of sth, in place of sth ◊ *An Stelle der erwarteten 50 000 Besucher kamen nur 30 000.* ◆ *An Stelle von Granit wird Stahl verwendet.* an jds/einer Sache Stelle treten take sb's/sth's place **3.** job ◊ *eine Stelle suchen/finden/ausschreiben* ◆ *eine Stelle als leitender Arzt antreten* ◆ *eine offene/freie Stelle besetzen* **4.** office, department ◊ *eine Stelle für interkulturelle Zusammenarbeit* ◊ *Der Plan wurde auch von höchster Stelle abgesegnet.* ◆ *die zuständige Stelle* **5.** *(sequence)* place ◊ *An erster/oberster Stelle steht die Qualität.* ◆ *an*

erster/zweiter/dritter etc. Stelle liegen/rangieren **6.** MATH figure, digit ◊ *die ersten drei Stellen der Codenummer; (after the decimal point)* place ◊ *Der Wert ist bis auf eine Stelle hinter dem Komma genau.*

⊙ **nicht von der Stelle kommen** make no progress, make no headway **zur Stelle sein 1.** be on the spot **2.** be there **auf der Stelle treten** not make any progress ◊ *Die Polizei tritt mit ihren Ermittlungen auf der Stelle. (economy)* be stagnant ◊ *Die Wirtschaft tritt seit Monaten auf der Stelle.* **auf der Stelle** on the spot, straight away, right away ◊ *Er erlitt einen Genickbruch und war auf der Stelle tot.* ◆ *Du gehst jetzt auf der Stelle ins Bett!* ⊜sofort

② **stel·len** ['ʃtɛlən] [tr v] +*haben* **1.** +*direction* put, place ◊ *Kannst du die Milch in den Kühlschrank stellen?* ◆ *eine Vase auf den Tisch stellen* ◆ *ein Foto ins Internet stellen* **2.** *(a demand, diagnosis)* make ◊ *eine Diagnose/Prognose stellen* ◆ *Ansprüche/Forderungen/Bedingungen stellen; (a horoscope)* draw up *jdm eine Frage stellen* ask sb a question *jdm eine Aufgabe stellen* set sb a task **3.** provide ◊ *Welche Partei stellt die Regierung/den Bürgermeister?* ◆ *Ein Dienstwagen wurde ihm gestellt.; (a bail)* put up **4.** *(an alarm, a trap)* set ◊ *den Wecker auf 7 Uhr stellen* ◆ *Die Weichen werden automatisch gestellt.* ◆ *Stell den Backofen auf 200°.* etw. lauter/höher stellen turn sth up ◊ *die Heizung höher stellen* etw. leiser/niedriger stellen turn sth down ◊ *den Fernseher/die Musik leiser stellen* **5.** *(a criminal)* catch ◊ *Die Polizei stellte einen Autoknacker.* **6.** *(food, drink)* etw kalt/warm stellen chill sth/keep sth warm **7.** jdn vor etw. [acc] stellen confront sb with sth ◊ *Du stellst mich vor eine schwierige Wahl/Entscheidung.* [ref v] **1.** sich irgendwohin stellen (go and) stand somewhere **2.** sich auf etw. [acc] stellen stand on sth ◊ *sich auf ein Bein/den Kopf stellen* ◆ *sich auf die Zehenspitzen stellen* **3.** *(a challenge etc.)* sich jdm/einer Sache [dat] stellen take up sth ◊ *sich einer Herausforderung/Aufgabe stellen; (the police, court)* face sth ◊ *sich dem Gericht/der Presse/Polizei stellen; (a responsibility)* face up to sth ◊ *sich der Verantwortung stellen müssen* **4.** sich dumm/taub/schlafend etc. stellen pretend to be stupid/deaf/asleep etc. **5.** sich gegen jdn/etw. stellen oppose sb/sth sich hinter jdn/etw. stellen support sb/sth Wie stellst du dich dazu? What do you think of it?

⊙ **auf sich (allein/selbst) gestellt sein** have to fend for yourself

stel·len·wei·se ['ʃtɛlənvaɛzə] [adj, adv] *no comp/superl* in places ◊ *niedrige Temperaturen bei stellenweisem Bodenfrost* ◆ *Stellenweise kann es kräftig regnen.* ◆ *Der Artikel ist stellenweise richtig beleidigend.*

② **Stel·lung** ['ʃtɛlʊŋ] die <-, -en> **1.** position ◊ *in aufrechter/gebückter Stellung* ◆ *In dieser Stellung ist das Gerät ausgeschaltet.* ◆ *Meine Stellung in dieser Frage ist dir bekannt.* ◆ *eine führende/dominierende/zentrale Stellung einnehmen* ◆ *Sind Sie schon lange in ihrer Stellung tätig?* ◆ *Die Truppen bezogen entlang der Grenze Stellung.* ◆ *Geschütze in Stellung bringen* **2.** (zu etw.) Stellung nehmen comment (on sth), give your opinion (on sth) ◊ *zu*

einem Thema/Vorwurf/einer Frage Stellung nehmen zu etw. Stellung beziehen take a view on sth, comment on sth in etw. [dat] Stellung beziehen take (up) a position on sth **3.** status, standing ◊ *die soziale/gesellschaftliche Stellung der Frau* ◆ *die rechtliche Stellung der Migranten*

Stel·lung·nah·me ['ʃtɛlʊŋnaːmə] die <-, -n> Stellungnahme (zu etw.) position (on sth), statement (on sth) ◊ *die Stellungnahme zum neuen Hochschulgesetz* ◆ *Die Stellungnahme der Kommission wird morgen bekannt gegeben.* ◆ *eine öffentliche/offizielle Stellungnahme abgeben*

stell·ver·tre·tend ['ʃtɛlfɛtreːtn̩t, 'ʃtɛlfɛtreːtənt] [adj] *no comp/superl, only before ns* deputy, assistant ◊ *der stellvertretende Kreisvorsitzende* [adv] in place of, on behalf of ◊ *Sie beschwerte sich stellvertretend für die ganze Klasse.*

Stell·ver·tre·ter ['ʃtɛlfɛtreːtɐ] der <-s, ->, **Stell·ver·tre·te·rin** ['ʃtɛlfɛtreːtərɪn] die <-, -nen> deputy, assistant, acting representative ◊ *der Stellvertreter des Innenministers/Bürgermeisters* ◆ *Sie ist meine Stellvertreterin.* ◆ *einen Stellvertreter bestimmen*

stem·men ['ʃtɛmən] [tr v] +*haben* **1.** chisel ◊ *ein Loch in die Wand stemmen* **2.** die Hände in die Seite/Hüften stemmen put your hands on your hips die Arme in die Seite/Hüften stemmen stand with your arms akimbo **3.** SPORT lift ◊ *Hanteln/Gewichte stemmen* [ref v] **1.** sich (gegen etw.) stemmen brace yourself (against sth) ◊ *Er stemmte sich gegen die Tür/den Wind. Die Esel stemmte sich mit den Hufen.* The donkey dug its heels in. **2.** *(fig)* resist ◊ *Die Konzerne stemmen sich gegen die geplante Reform.*

② **Stem·pel** ['ʃtɛmpl̩] der <-s, -> **1.** stamp ◊ *einen Stempel auf die Firmenadresse anfertigen lassen* ◆ *Er hat einen Stempel in seinen Pass bekommen.* ◆ *Das Manuskript trägt den Stempel der Staatsbibliothek.* **2.** *(on metal)* hallmark ◊ *Goldschmuck hat in der Regel einen Stempel.*

⊙ **einer Sache** [dat] **seinen Stempel aufdrücken** make your mark on sth

stem·peln ['ʃtɛmpl̩n] [tr v] +*haben* **1.** stamp ◊ *Die Maschine stempelt 35000 Kuverts pro Stunde.* ◆ *An der Grenze wurde ihr Pass gestempelt.* **2.** *(fig)* jdn/etw. zu etw. stempeln brand sb/sth as sth, mark sb/sth as sth ◊ *Die Presse stempelte ihn zu einem Verbrecher.*

⊙ **stempeln gehen** *(fam)* be on the dole, be on welfare

② **ster·ben** ['ʃtɛʳbm̩] <stirbt, starb, ist gestorben> [intr v] +*sein* ◊ *Er starb im Alter von 80 Jahren.* ◆ *Bei dem Unfall sind fünf Leute gestorben.* ◆ *Er ist eines natürlichen Todes gestorben.* ◆ *Die Opfer mussten einen qualvollen Tod sterben.* ◆ *Unsere Wälder sterben!* ◆ *Ihre Liebe ist vor langer Zeit gestorben.* an etw. [dat] sterben die of sth ◊ *an Hunger/den Folgen des Tabakkonsums sterben*

⊙ **für jdn gestorben sein** *(fig)* not exist as far as sb is concerned

sterb·lich ['ʃtɛʳplɪç] [adj] *no comp/superl* mortal ◊ *Alle Menschen sind sterblich.* ◆ *Zeus hatte zwei Kinder von sterblichen Müttern.* ◆ *Seine sterblichen Überreste wurden in seine Heimat überführt.*

Ste·re·o·an·la·ge ['ʃteːreoʔanlaːɡə] die <-, -n> stereo system

ste·ri·li·sie·ren [ʃterili'ziːrən] <sterilisiert, sterilisierte, hat sterilisiert> [tr v] sterilize ◊ *medizinische Instrumente sterilisieren* ♦ *Sie will keine Kinder mehr und hat sich sterilisieren lassen.*

ⓩ **Stern** [ʃtɛ'n] der <-(e)s, -e> star ◊ *Am Himmel war kein Stern zu sehen.* ♦ *der Stern von Bethlehem* ♦ *die Sterne auf der Europaflagge* ♦ *ein Hotel mit vier Sternen* ♦ *Die Sterne stehen günstig/schlecht.* ♦ *Er ist ein aufgehender Stern am Fußballhimmel.*

ⓢ **für jdn die Sterne vom Himmel holen** do anything for sb **unter einem/keinem guten Stern stehen** be destined to succeed/ill-starred **jds Stern geht auf/sinkt** sb's star is rising/on the wane **in den Sternen (geschrieben) stehen** be in the lap of the gods **wie von einem anderen Stern** from another planet

Stern·bild [ˈʃtɛ'nbɪlt] das <-(e)s, -er> constellation ◊ *Sirius gehört zum Sternbild „Großer Hund".*

Stern·chen [ˈʃtɛ'nçən] das <-s, -> **1.** starlet ◊ *Zur Preisverleihung erschienen viele Stars und Sternchen.* **2.** asterisk ◊ *Mit Sternchen gekennzeichnete Angaben sind freiwillig.*

Stern·zei·chen [ˈʃtɛ'ntsaeçn] das <-s, -> ASTROL sign of the zodiac, astrological sign ◊ *Mein Sternzeichen ist Widder.* ♦ *In/Unter welchem Sternzeichen bist du geboren?* ♦ *Welches Sternzeichen bist/hast du?*

ste·tig [ˈʃteːtɪç] [adj, adv] no comp/superl steady (-ily), continuous(ly) ◊ *eine stetige Entwicklung* ♦ *Der Rückgang war langsam, aber stetig.* ♦ *die stetig wachsende Zahl der Arbeitslosen*

stets [ˈʃteːts] [adv] always ◊ *In unserem Haus sind Sie ein stets willkommener Gast.* ♦ *Sie hat sich stets um ein gutes Verhältnis mit ihren Kollegen bemüht.*

Steu·er[1] [ˈʃtɔøɐ] das <-s, -> (of a vehicle) (steering-)wheel ◊ *am Steuer sitzen*; (of a ship) helm, tiller ◊ *das Steuer halten/übernehmen*

ⓢ **das Steuer in die Hand nehmen** take control

ⓩ **Steu·er**[2] [ˈʃtɔøɐ] die <-, -n> tax ◊ *Die Steuern sind nicht im Preis enthalten.* ♦ *Er zahlt 20 Prozent Steuern auf sein Bruttoeinkommen.* ♦ *eine Steuer erheben/einziehen/abführen*

Steu·er·be·ra·ter [ˈʃtɔøɐbəraːtɐ] der <-s, ->, **Steu·er·be·ra·te·rin** [ˈʃtɔøɐbəraːtərɪn] die <-, -nen> tax consultant ◊ *Sie ist Steuerberaterin von Beruf.* ♦ *Was hat dein Steuerberater gesagt?*

Steu·er·er·klä·rung [ˈʃtɔøɐʔɛklɛːrʊŋ] die <-, -en> tax return ◊ *eine Steuererklärung abgeben/einreichen*

steu·ern [ˈʃtɔøɐn] [tr v] +haben **1.** steer ◊ *ein Auto nach rechts/links steuern* ♦ *das Land auf einen stabilen politischen Kurs steuern* ♦ *ein Gespräch steuern*; (a ship also) navigate ◊ *Er steuerte das Schiff sicher in den Hafen.*; (an aircraft) fly, pilot ⊖lenken **2.** (an appliance, a process, development) control ◊ *Der Computer steuert den Prozessablauf/Fahrbetrieb.* ♦ *Einkauf, Personal und EDV werden zentral gesteuert.* ♦ *ein Gerät per Funk steuern* [intr v] +sein head for, be bound/heading for ◊ *Das Schiff steuerte in den Hafen/heimwärts.* ♦ *in eine Finanzkrise/in den Ruin steuern* ◊ *Die Firma steuert auf Erfolgskurs.*

Steu·e·rung [ˈʃtɔøɐrʊŋ] die <-, -en> **1.** (action) control ◊ *die Steuerung eines Gerätes/Prozesses* ♦

Die Steuerung erfolgt über eine Tastatur. **2.** (system) controls ◊ *Die Maschine verfügt über eine elektronische/automatische Steuerung.* ♦ *Die Steuerung des Flugzeugs versagte.*

Stich [ʃtɪç] der <-(e)s, -e> **1.** (with a knife) stab (wound) ◊ *jdm einen Stich versetzen* ♦ *Sie wurde durch einen Stich in den Hals schwer verletzt.*; (with a needle) prick **2.** sting, bite ◊ *Malaria wird durch den Stich einer Mücke übertragen.* **3.** stitch ◊ *Nur noch ein paar Stiche, dann ist die Hose fertig.* ♦ *Die Schnittwunde musste mit drei Stichen genäht werden.* **4.** CARDS trick ◊ *Er warf im dritten Stich den Karokönig ab.* **5.** (on copper) engraving **6.** stabbing pain ◊ *Sie hat einen Stich in der Brust gespürt.* **7.** tinge, shade ◊ *einen kleinen Stich ins Derbe haben* ♦ *Die Fotos haben einen Stich ins Grüne.*

ⓢ **etw. ist ein Stich ins Wespennest** sth stirs up a hornets' nest **einen Stich haben** (fam) **1.** (person) be round the twist **2.** (milk) have (slightly) gone off/be bad **jdn im Stich lassen** leave sb in the lurch

Stich·pro·be [ˈʃtɪçproːbə] die <-, -n> random sample ◊ *Stichproben machen/entnehmen*

sticht [ʃtɪçt] pres of stechen

Stich·wort [ˈʃtɪçvɔ't] das <-(e)s, -e or Stichwörter> **1.** pl 'Stichwörter' keyword ◊ *Geben Sie ein Stichwort ein und klicken Sie auf „Suchen".* ♦ *Was fällt euch zum Stichwort „Gesundheit" ein?* **2.** pl 'Stichwörter' entry, headword ◊ *Dieses Wörterbuch enthält etwa 20 000 Stichwörter.* **3.** pl 'Stichworte' cue ◊ *Sie liefert dem Komiker die Stichworte.* etw. in Stichworten festhalten make notes of sth

sti·cken [ˈʃtɪkn] [tr+intr v] +haben embroider ◊ *eine Tischdecke/Bettdecke sticken* ♦ *ein Monogramm auf etw.* [acc] *sticken* ♦ *beim Fernsehen sticken*

ⓩ **Stie·fel** [ˈʃtiːfl] der <-s, -> boot ◊ *hochhackige Stiefel*

ⓢ **zwei Paar Stiefel sein** (fam) be two different things **jdm die Stiefel lecken** (fam, pej) lick sb's boots **einen (ordentlichen/guten) Stiefel vertragen** (fam) be able to hold your drink **einen Stiefel** (fam, pej) a load of rubbish, a load of nonsense ◊ *Die hat hier vielleicht einen Stiefel zusammengeschrieben!*

Stief·kind [ˈʃtiːfkɪnt] das <-(e)s, -er> **1.** stepchild **2.** (fig) poor relation ◊ *Arbeitsschutz ist ein Stiefkind in vielen Betrieben.* sich als Stiefkind des Glücks fühlen have the impression that fortune never smiles upon you

Stief·mut·ter [ˈʃtiːfmʊtɐ] die <-, Stiefmütter> stepmother

Stief·müt·ter·chen [ˈʃtiːfmʏtɐçən] das <-s, -> pansy

Stief·schwes·ter [ˈʃtiːfʃvɛstɐ] die <-, -n> stepsister

Stief·va·ter [ˈʃtiːffaːtɐ] der <-s, Stiefväter> stepfather

ⓩ **stieg** [ʃtiːk] pret of steigen

ⓩ **Stie·ge** [ˈʃtiːgə] die <-, -n> **1.** narrow (wooden) staircase/stairs ◊ *Eine wacklige Stiege führte auf den Dachboden.* **2.** (Austr) (stairs) staircase

② **stiehlt** [ʃtiːlt] *pres of* stehlen

Stiel [ʃtiːl] der <-(e)s, -e> **1.** handle ◊ *ein Holz-schläger/Besen/Beil mit einem langen Stiel; (of a glass)* stem ◊ *ein Weinglas am Stiel halten; (of an ice lolly)* stick ◊ *Eis am Stiel; (of a broom)* broomstick **2.** stalk, stem ◊ *die Blätter von den Stielen der Rosen entfernen* ♦ *ein Blatt mit langem Stiel* ⊖Stängel

Stier [ʃtiːɐ] der <-(e)s, -e> **1.** *(cattle)* bull ⊖Bulle **2.** *no pl* ASTROL, ASTRON Taurus
◉ **den Stier bei den Hörnern packen** take the bull by the horns

Stier·kampf ['ʃtiːɐkampf] der <-(e)s, Stierkämpfe> bull-fight

stieß [ʃtiːs] *pret of* stoßen

Stift [ʃtɪft] der <-(e)s, -e> **1.** pen, ballpoint, biro™ ◊ *Ich habe keinen Stift dabei.; (wooden)* pencil ◊ *mit einem Stift schreiben/zeichnen; (coloured)* crayon; *(soft tip)* felt-tip, felt-tipped pen; *(cosmetics)* eye-liner pencil ◊ *die Augen mit einem schwarzen Stift betonen* **2.** TECHN pin, peg ◊ *den Stift in das gebohrte Loch stecken*

stif·ten ['ʃtɪftn̩] ⟨tr v⟩ +*haben* **1.** donate ◊ *Den For-schungspreis stiftete die Firma ...* ⊖spenden **2.** *(fam)* provide, supply ◊ *Mein Vater will die Getränke für die Party stiften.* ⊖spendieren **3.** cause ◊ *Verwirrung/Unordnung/Unruhe/Unfrieden stiften; (peace)* make **4.** found, establish ◊ *ein Kloster/eine Schule stiften* ⊖gründen
◉ **stiften gehen** *(fam)* make off

Stif·tung ['ʃtɪftʊŋ] die <-, -en> **1.** foundation ◊ *eine Stiftung einrichten/gründen* ♦ *eine private/gemeinnützige Stiftung* **2.** donation ◊ *Er bekommt monatlich 1000 Euro aus dieser Stiftung.*

> On 4th December 1964 the German government decided to set up the *Warentest* foundation, an independent institute in the private sector responsible for providing consumers with information on the quality and environmental compatibility of goods and services *(www.stiftung-warentest.de)*.

Stil [ʃtiːl, stiːl] der <-(e)s, -e> style ◊ *ein Kleid im Stil der 80er* ♦ *eine im gotischen Stil erbaute Kirche* ♦ *Die Band hat zu einem ganz eigenen Stil gefunden.* ♦ *ein Kavalier alten Stils* ♦ *eine mit Stil eingerichtete Wohnung* ♦ *Ich würde so was nicht machen, das ist nicht mein Stil.* ♦ *Schick, das hat Stil!*
◉ **im großen Stil 1.** *(lavishly)* in a big way ◊ *Er hat seinen 50. Geburtstag im großen Stil gefeiert.* **2.** *(sweeping)* on a grand scale ◊ *Entlassungen im großen Stil*

sti·lis·tisch [ʃtiˈlɪstɪʃ, stiˈlɪstɪʃ] ⟨adj, adv⟩ *no comp/superl; when used as an adj, only before ns* stylistic(ally) ◊ *eine stilistische Analyse* ♦ *stilisti-sche Schwächen/Merkmale/Mittel* ♦ *Diese Möbel passen stilistisch nicht zusammen.*

② **still** [ʃtɪl] ⟨adj, adv⟩ **1.** quiet(ly), silent(ly) ◊ *sich in eine stille Ecke zurückziehen* ♦ *Sei bitte mal einen Moment still.* ♦ *Du bist so still, fehlt dir was?* ♦ *in stiller Trauer* ♦ *still weinen* ♦ *Er lebt still und bescheiden.* ♦ *etw. still über sich ergehen lassen* etw. still dulden suffer sth in silence **2.** *when used as an adj, only before ns* secret(ly) ◊ *Sie hegte die stille Hoffnung, dass ...* ♦ *ein stiller Verehrer* ♦ *Er hat sie still verehrt.; (business partner, holding)*

dormant; *(reserves)* hidden ⟨adj⟩ *(without movement)* still ◊ *Die Luft war still.* ♦ *Das Kind saß still auf seinem Stuhl.* ♦ *Trinkst du lieber stilles Wasser oder sprudelndes?* Halte das Fernglas ganz still. Hold the binoculars completely still.; *(sea, lake, personality)* calm ◊ *Das Wasser/Meer war ganz still.* ♦ *Sie hat eine angenehm stille Art.* ♦ *einen stillen Urlaub verbringen*
◉ **im Stillen 1.** *(covertly)* secretly ◊ *Die Kollegen haben im Stillen ein Fest für sie vorbereitet.* **2.** *(anger, rage)* silently ◊ *Er sagte kein Wort zu den Vorwürfen, aber im Stillen kochte er vor Zorn.*

Stil·le ['ʃtɪlə] die <-> *no pl* **1.** quiet(ness), silence ◊ *Im Konzertsaal herrschte absolute Stille.* ♦ *eine unheimliche/beklemmende Stille* ♦ *die Stille der Nacht* ⊖Ruhe ⊖Lärm **2.** calm(ness) ◊ *die kühle Stille des Wassers* ♦ *die Stille der Natur*
◉ **in aller Stille** quietly, calmly Sie haben in aller Stille geheiratet. They had a quiet wedding.

stil·len ['ʃtɪlən] ⟨tr v⟩ +*haben* **1.** *(hunger, desire)* satisfy ◊ *den Hunger stillen* ♦ *die Gier nach etw. stillen* ♦ *jds Neugier stillen* ♦ *seinen Ehrgeiz stillen; (thirst)* quench **2.** MED stop ◊ *die Schmerzen stillen; (blood)* staunch ⟨tr+intr v⟩ breast-feed ◊ *ein Baby stillen* ♦ *Du sollst sie jetzt nicht stören, sie stillt gerade.*

still|hal·ten ['ʃtɪlhaltn̩] <hält still, hielt still, hat stillgehalten> ⟨intr v⟩ **1.** keep still ◊ *Bei diesem Rhythmus konnte keiner stillhalten.* **2.** keep quiet ◊ *Sie hat lange stillgehalten, aber jetzt erträgt sie das Unrecht nicht mehr.* ⊖sich wehren

still|le·gen ['ʃtɪleːgn̩] <legt still, legte still, hat stillgelegt> ⟨tr v⟩ +*haben* shut down ◊ *ein Werk/eine Fabrik/Maschine stilllegen; (production)* stop

still·schwei·gend ['ʃtɪlʃvaegn̩t, 'ʃtɪlʃvaegənt] ⟨adj, adv⟩ *no comp/superl; when used as an adj, only before n* tacit(ly), silent(ly) ◊ *eine stillschwei-gende Vertragsverlängerung* ♦ *stillschweigendes Einverständnis* ♦ *etw. stillschweigend hinnehmen/annehmen*

still|ste·hen ['ʃtɪlʃteːən] <steht still, stand still, hat stillgestanden> ⟨intr v⟩ *in South G, Austr, Swiss often +sein* **1.** have stopped, be at a standstill ◊ *Die Zeiger der Turmuhr stehen still.* ♦ *Die Maschine/Anlage/Fabrik/Produktion steht still.* ♦ *Heute steht das Telefon bei uns kaum still.; (time, heart)* stand still ◊ *Er hatte das Gefühl, als stünde die Zeit still.* **2.** MIL stand to attention Stillgestan-den! Attention!

Stimm·bruch ['ʃtɪmbrʊx] der <-(e)s> *no pl* breaking of the voice Der Junge ist gerade im Stimmbruch. The boy's voice is just breaking.

② **Stim·me** ['ʃtɪmə] die <-, -n> **1.** voice ◊ *eine tiefe/hohe/heisere/sanfte Stimme* ♦ *Sie entschuldigte sich mit leiser Stimme.* ♦ *Hör auf die Stimme deines Herzens.* ♦ *die Stimme des Volkes* ♦ *kritische Stimmen zur Gentechnik* **2.** MUS voice (part) ◊ *Ich singe die zweite Stimme.* **3.** vote ◊ *seine Stimme abgeben* ♦ *Wem hast du deine Stimme gegeben?* ♦ *Der Antrag wurde mit 50 zu 20 Stimmen angenommen.* sich der Stimme enthalten abstain

② **stim·men** ['ʃtɪmən] ⟨intr v⟩ +*haben* **1.** be right, be correct ◊ *Das Preis-Leistungs-Verhältnis muss stimmen.* ♦ *Die Kasse stimmt.* ♦ *Ich hab nachge-zählt, es stimmt ganz genau.* ♦ *Stimmt das, was*

A B C D E F G H I J K L M N O P Q R **S** T U V W X Y Z

er sagt? ♦ „Du heißt doch Anja?" — „Stimmt!";
(statement also) be true ◊ Das stimmt doch
überhaupt nicht! Du lügst! nicht stimmen be
wrong ◊ Die Rechnung stimmt nicht. ♦ Etwas
stimmt nicht mit meinem Computer. **2.** für/gegen
jdn/etw. stimmen vote for/against sb/sth ◊ Er hat
für die Grünen gestimmt. ♦ 27 Abgeordnete
stimmten für, 32 gegen den Antrag. mit Ja/Nein
stimmen vote in favour/vote against (tr v) +haben
1. jdn glücklich/traurig etc. stimmen make sb
(feel) happy/sad etc. ◊ Die Prognose stimmt uns
optimistisch. **2.** MUS tune ◊ ein Klavier stimmen
lassen

◉ stimmt so keep the change

stimm·haft ['ʃtɪmhaft] (adj) no comp/superl voiced
◊ b, d, und g sind stimmhafte Laute. ♦ Ist das s
hier stimmhaft? ⊖stimmlos (adv) stimmhaft ausgesprochen werden be voiced ⊖stimmlos

stimm·los ['ʃtɪmloːs] (adj) no comp/superl
voiceless, unvoiced ◊ p, t und k sind stimmlose
Laute. ♦ Im Auslaut ist das v stimmlos. ⊖stimm-
haft (adv) stimmlos ausgesprochen werden not be
voiced ⊖stimmhaft

Stimm·recht ['ʃtɪmrɛçt] das <-(e)s, -e> most sing
right to vote ◊ Aktien mit/ohne Stimmrecht ♦ von
seinem Stimmrecht Gebrauch machen

② **Stim·mung** ['ʃtɪmʊŋ] die <-, -en> **1.** (emotional
state, impact) mood ◊ Warum bist du heute (in)
so schlechter Stimmung? ♦ jdm die Stimmung
verderben ♦ Ich bin dazu nicht in der richtigen
Stimmung. ♦ Das Foto kann die Stimmung nicht
komplett wiedergeben.; (positive emotional state)
good mood ◊ jdn in Stimmung bringen ⊖Laune
2. no pl atmosphere ◊ Die Stimmung im Haus war
ungetrübt. ♦ Auf dem Fest herrschte gute/ausgelas-
sene Stimmung.; (level of confidence) morale ◊
Aufgrund der vielen Entlassungen war die
Stimmung unter den Mitarbeitern schlecht.;
(public) opinion, sentiment ◊ ausländerfeindliche
Stimmung ♦ Wie ist die Stimmung der Bürger zum
EU-Beitritt? für jdn/etw. Stimmung machen stir up
(public) opinion in favour of sb/sth, stir up
(public) opinion in favour of sb/sth gegen jdn/etw.
Stimmung machen stir up (public) opinion against
sb/sth ⊖Atmosphäre

Stimm·zet·tel ['ʃtɪmtsɛtl] der <-s, -> ballot paper

② **stin·ken** ['ʃtɪŋkŋ] <stinkt, stank, hat gestunken>
(intr v) **1.** stink ◊ stinkende Socken ◊ Der Käse
stinkt. ♦ Hier stinkt's! nach etw. stinken stink of
sth ◊ Das Zimmer hat nach Rauch gestunken.
2. (fam) (suspect) be fishy ◊ Hier stinkt etwas,
dem muss ich auf den Grund gehen! **3.** (fam) jdm
stinkt etw. sb is fed up about sth ◊ Es stinkt mir,
sie wieder vor dem Chef decken zu müssen.

◉ vor Faulheit stinken (pej) be bone idle vor
Geld stinken (pej) be stinking rich

Sti·pen·di·um ['ʃtiˈpɛndjʊm] das <-s, Stipendien>
grant ◊ sich um ein Stipendium bewerben ♦ ein Stipendium vergeben/bekommen

② **stirbt** ['ʃtɪrpt] pres of sterben

Stirn ['ʃtɪrn] die <-, -en> forehead, brow ◊ sich
den Schweiß von der Stirn wischen ♦ die Stirn
runzeln ♦ Sorgenfalten auf der Stirn haben ♦
Einige Locken fallen ihr in die Stirn.

◉ jdm/einer Sache die Stirn bieten stand up to
sb/sth (über etw. (acc)) die Stirn runzeln voice

your misgivings (about sth) jdm steht etw. auf
der Stirn geschrieben sth is written all over sb's
face, sth is etched on sb's face

stö·bern ['ʃtøːbɐn] (intr v) +haben irgendwo
stöbern rummage around/through somewhere ◊
auf dem Dachboden/im Bücherregal stöbern im
Internet stöbern search the net

② **Stock** [ʃtɔk] der <-(e)s, Stöcke> **1.** stick, cane ◊
jdn mit einem Stock schlagen ♦ mit einem Stock
im Feuer stochern ♦ am Stock gehen; (for elderly)
walking-stick; (in sports) hockey etc. stick; (for
skiing) ski pole/stick; (in billiards) cue **2.** (in a
building) storey, floor ◊ Wir wohnen im dritten
Stock. ♦ Sie wohnt einen Stock höher/tiefer als wir.
⊖Stockwerk, Etage **3.** (in a pot) pot plant; (of a
grape plant) vine ◊ Einige Trauben hängen noch
am Stock.

◉ über Stock und Stein up hill and down vale

Stock·werk ['ʃtɔkvɛ'k] das <-(e)s, -e> storey, floor
◊ das untere/oberste/dritte Stockwerk ⊖Stock,
Etage

② **Stoff** [ʃtɔf] der <-(e)s, -e> **1.** material, fabric,
cloth ◊ Sie haben Puppen aus Holz und Stoff
gebastelt. ♦ Sie hat fünf Meter Stoff für ihr Kleid
gekauft. ♦ ein leichter/bunter/glänzender/weicher
Stoff **2.** (chemical etc.) substance ◊ ein giftiger/
explosiver/biologisch abbaubarer Stoff ♦ Polyure-
than ist ein synthetischer Stoff. **3.** no pl subject
(matter), topic ◊ Die Gesundheitsreform liefert
Stoff für hitzige Diskussionen. ♦ genug Stoff für
öffentlichen Streit bieten ♦ Der Stoff des Films ist
immer noch aktuell.; (for a book, project)
material ◊ einen komplexen Stoff didaktisch gut
erklären ♦ Er musste den Stoff eines ganzen Schul-
jahres nachlernen. ♦ Ich sammle zurzeit Stoff für
meine Dissertation. **4.** (slang) (alcohol) booze ◊
Wir müssen für die Party noch Stoff besorgen.
5. (slang) dope ◊ Die Polizei hat den Stoff nicht
gefunden.

◉ der Stoff, aus dem etw. ist the stuff sth is
made of

stöh·nen ['ʃtøːnən] (intr v) +haben **1.** (vor im.
(dat)) stöhnen groan (with sth), moan (with sth) ◊
vor Lust/Erregung/Schmerz/Anstrengung stöhnen
2. über etw. (acc) stöhnen moan about sth ◊ Sie
stöhnte über den schlechten Service im Restaurant.

Stol·len ['ʃtɔlən] der <-s, -> **1.** gallery ◊ Die
Stollen wurden mit Stahlträgern im Rundbogen
gesichert. **2.** stollen

A stollen is a firm, oblong yeast cake that contains
nuts, orange and lemon peel, raisins and a lot of
butter, and which is baked at Christmas time.

stol·pern ['ʃtɔlpɐn] (intr v) +sein **1.** trip, stumble ◊
Sie stolperte und brach sich ein Bein. (über etw.
(acc)) stolpern fall (over sth) ◊ Der Jogger
stolperte über einen Stein. **2.** (fig) über etw. (acc)
stolpern come to grief over sth ◊ Der Politiker
stolperte über eine Finanzaffäre. **3.** (fig) über etw.
(acc) stolpern come across sth, stumble upon sth ◊
In einer Zeitschrift stolperte ich über einen Artikel
über einen ehemaligen Schulfreund.

② **stolz** [ʃtɔlts] (adj, adv) <stolzer, am stolzesten>
proud(ly) ◊ Sie war stolz, auf eigenen Füßen zu
stehen. ♦ die stolzen Besitzer eines Hauses ♦ Er ist

stolz wie ein römischer Kaiser. ♦ *Mit einem stolzen Blick wies sie ihn ab.* ♦ *Der Schauspieler blickte stolz auf das jubelnde Publikum.* auf jdn/etw. stolz sein be proud of sb/sth ◊ *Sie waren stolz auf ihren erfolgreichen Sohn.* ♦ *Sie war stolz auf ihre steile Karriere.* über etw. [acc] stolz sein be proud of sth [adj] *only before ns* impressive ◊ *stolze Leistungen*
Stolz [ʃtɔlts] der <-es> *no pl* **1.** pride ◊ *Er konnte seinen Stolz über den Sieg nicht verbergen.* etw. ist jds ganzer Stolz sth is sb's pride and joy **2.** pride, dignity ◊ *Das Leben in Armut konnte ihren Stolz nicht brechen.* **3.** *(pej)* (overweening) pride, arrogance ◊ *Sein Stolz wird ihn noch zu Fall bringen.*

stop·fen [ˈʃtɔpfn̩] [tr v] +*haben* **1.** stuff, shove ◊ *Er stopfte die Wäsche hastig in die Waschmaschine.* jdm/sich etw. in etw. [acc] stopfen stuff sth into sb's/your sth ◊ *Das Kind stopfte sich die Süßigkeiten in die Taschen.* **2.** fill (in) ◊ *Sie stopfte alle Löcher im Rasen mit Erde.* **3.** *(clothing etc.)* mend, darn ◊ *Sie stopfte ihre Strümpfe.* **4.** *(fig, esp pej)* plug, close ◊ *Der Staat wollte mit Steuererhöhungen die Haushaltslöcher stopfen.* ♦ *eine Sicherheitslücke stopfen* [intr v] +*haben* **1.** be very filling **2.** give you constipation ◊ *Bananen und Schokolade stopfen.*

stopp [ʃtɔp] [interj] stop (right there) ◊ *Stopp — ich möchte auch etwas sagen!* ♦ *Stopp — keinen Schritte weiter!*

Stopp [ʃtɔp] der <-s, -s> **1.** *no pl* halt, stop ◊ *Die Grünen fordern einen Stopp der Verhandlungen.; (on investments etc.)* freeze ◊ *Die Regierung beschloss einen Stopp der Investitionen.* Stopp einer Sache [dat] let's put an end to sth ◊ *Stopp dem Krieg/Vandalismus!* **2.** stop ◊ *Wie viele Stopps plant ihr auf eurer Tour?*

② **stop·pen** [ˈʃtɔpm̩] [tr+intr v] +*haben* stop ◊ *Die Polizei stoppte einen Transporter.* ♦ *Ein Wagen stoppte und der Fahrer sprach mich an.* [tr v] +*haben* **1.** stop, hold up ◊ *Das Projekt wurde wegen Geldmangel gestoppt.* ♦ *Die Flut muss gestoppt werden.* jd ist nicht mehr zu stoppen there's no stopping sb **2.** jdn stoppen time sb ◊ *Kannst du mich bei dem Rennen stoppen?* Es wird die Zeit gestoppt, die der Läufer für 2000 Meter braucht. The runner's time over 2000 metres is recorded.

Stopp·schild [ˈʃtɔpʃɪlt] das <-(e)s, -er> stop sign
Stöp·sel [ˈʃtœpsl̩] der <-s, -> stopper, plug ◊ *den Stöpsel aus der Flasche/Badewanne ziehen*; earplug ◊ *sich* [dat] *einen Stöpsel ins Ohr stecken*
Storch [ʃtɔrç] der <-(e)s, Störche>, **Stör·chin** [ˈʃtœrˌçɪn] die <-, -nen> stork
② **stö·ren** [ˈʃtøːrən] [tr v] +*haben* **1.** disturb ◊ *Ich möchte dich nicht stören, aber ich brauche deine Hilfe.* ♦ *jdn bei der Arbeit/beim Lesen stören* **2.** damage, interfere with ◊ *Nachtlärm stört das Immunsystem.* [intr v] +*haben* **1.** get in the way ◊ *Er wollte nicht länger stören, deshalb ging er.* ♦ *So viele Rechtschreibfehler stören sehr beim Lesen.* **2.** be a problem ◊ *Einige Bilder sind zwar etwas dunkel geraten, aber das stört nicht wirklich.* [imp v] +*haben* es stört jdn it annoys sb ◊ *Es stört ihn, dass die Nachbarn laut Musik hören.*
Stö·rung [ˈʃtøːrʊŋ] die <-, -en> **1.** disruption, disturbance ◊ *die Störung des Programmablaufs die/*

eine Störung des Gleichgewichts the/an imbalance ohne Störung without interruptions Entschuldigen Sie die Störung. Sorry to disturb you. **2.** *(on the telephone, television etc.)* interference **3.** MED disorder ◊ *psychische Störung* ♦ *eine Störung der Herzfunktion/Atmung* **4.** fault ◊ *Wegen einer technischen Störung kam der Zug mit Verspätung.* ♦ *eine Störung im Triebwerk des Flugzeugs*
Stoß [ʃtoːs] der <-es, Stöße> **1.** shove, push ◊ *ein Stoß mit den Ellenbogen/Fuß;* *(harder)* blow ◊ *jdm einen Stoß geben/versetzen* **2.** thrust, stab; *(in billiards)* shot **3.** *(when walking, running etc.)* impact ◊ *Stöße abfedern* ♦ *Seine Beine konnten den Stoß beim Sprung aus dieser Höhe kaum abfangen.; (during an earthquake)* tremor **4.** bang, crash ◊ *ein heftiger Stoß gegen die Wand* ♦ *Bei der Explosion gab es einen gewaltigen Stoß.* **5.** pile ◊ *Auf dem Schreibtisch lagen Stöße von Akten.* **6.** stroke ◊ *Sie schwamm einige Stöße vom Boot weg.* **7.** MIL attack
◉ tödlicher Stoß *(also fig)* fatal blow ◊ *Der Jäger versetzte dem Tier einen tödlichen Stoß.* ♦ *Die Affäre war ein tödlicher Stoß für seine politische Karriere.*
sto·ßen [ˈʃtoːsn̩] <stößt, stieß, hat/ist gestoßen> [intr v] +*sein* **1.** auf jdn stoßen run into sb ◊ *Letzte Woche bin ich in der Stadt auf einen alten Freund gestoßen.* auf etw. [acc] stoßen come across sth ◊ *Im Archiv stieß er auf interessante Dokumente.* **2.** auf etw. [acc] stoßen meet with sth ◊ *Dieser Vortrag stieß auf große Resonanz.* auf taube Ohren stoßen fall on deaf ears **3.** gegen etw. stoßen hit sth ◊ *Die Fahrradfahrerin stieß gegen den Pkw und stürzte.* **4.** an etw. [acc] stoßen adjoin sth, be attached to sth ◊ *Eine große Scheune stößt an das Haus.* [tr v] +*haben* **1.** jdn/etw. irgendwohin stoßen push sb/sth somewhere ◊ *Im letzten Moment konnte er das Kind noch zur Seite stoßen.* ♦ *Sie stießen das Auto von der Klippe.* **2.** sich/jdm etw. irgendwohin stoßen stick sth into your/sb's sth, jab sth into your/sb's sth ◊ *Er stieß mir seinen Ellbogen in die Rippen.* ♦ *Ich habe mir den Stock ins Auge gestoßen.* [ref v] +*haben* sich irgendwo stoßen hit your sth ◊ *Das Kind hat sich am Kopf gestoßen.*
Stoß·stan·ge [ˈʃtoːsʃtaŋə] die <-, -n> bumper
stößt [ʃtøːst] *pres of* stoßen
stot·tern [ˈʃtɔtɐn] [tr+intr v] +*haben* stutter, stammer ◊ *Vor Angst/Aufregung fing er an zu stottern.* ♦ *Er stotterte einen unverständlichen Satz.* [intr v] +*haben* **1.** have a stutter ◊ *Er stottert von klein auf.* **2.** *(engine, car)* splutter ◊ *Das Auto stotterte und blieb schließlich stehen.*
Str. [ˈʃtraːsə] die *(abbr of* Straße) St., Rd ◊ *Berliner Str. 7*
straf·bar [ˈʃtraːfbaːɐ̯] [adj] *no comp/superl* **1.** illegal ◊ *eine strafbare Handlung* ♦ *Dieses Verhalten ist strafbar.* **2.** sich strafbar machen commit an offence
② **Stra·fe** [ˈʃtraːfə] die <-, -n> **1.** LAW sentence ◊ *(gegen jdn) eine Strafe verhängen* ♦ *eine Strafe für etw. absitzen; (money)* fine ◊ *20 000 Euro Strafe zahlen auf etw.* [acc] steht Strafe sth is a criminal offence etw. unter Strafe stellen make sth a criminal offence **2.** punishment ◊ *Als Strafe musste er den ganzen Aufsatz noch einmal*

abschreiben. ♦ *Bekomme ich für diese Fehler eine Strafe?* **zur Strafe für etw.** as a punishment for sth

ⓔ **etw. ist eine echte Strafe** sth is hell, sth is an ordeal

stra·fen ['ʃtraːfn̩] ⟨tr v⟩ +*haben* **1.** *jdn/ein Tier (mit etw.) strafen* punish sb/an animal (with sth) ◊ *Sie strafte ihn mit eisigem Schweigen.* ♦ *Er strafte den Hund für seinen Ungehorsam mit einer Tracht Prügel.* **2.** curse ◊ *Mit dieser Krankheit ist sie vom Leben genug gestraft!* ♦ *Das Schicksal strafte sie mit Kinderlosigkeit.* **3. mit etw. (wirklich/echt) gestraft sein** sth is a (real) curse **mit jdm (wirklich/echt) gestraft sein** sb is the bane of sb's life, sb is a (real) curse ⟨intr v⟩ +*haben* dish out punishment(s) ◊ *Bei Fehlern strafen wir nie.*

straff [ʃtraf] ⟨adj⟩ **1.** taut ◊ *eine straffe Haut* ♦ *Ihr Körper war schlank und straff.* ♦ *eine straffe Schnur* ⓔschlaff **2.** *only before ns* strict, stringent ◊ *straffe Kontrolle der Kosten/Geldpolitik* ⟨adv⟩ **1.** taut ◊ *Das Gummiband muss straff gespannt sein.* **2.** strictly ◊ *eine straff geführte Organisation* **3. straff sitzen/anliegen** fit tightly

Straf·zet·tel ['ʃtraːfʦɛtl̩] der <-s, -> ticket ◊ *einen Strafzettel bekommen*

Strahl [ʃtraːl] der <-(e)s, -en> ray ◊ *Die Sonne verwöhnte uns mit ihren milden Strahlen.* ♦ *elektromagnetische Strahlen aussenden* ♦ *kosmische Strahlen; (of liquid, air)* jet ◊ *ein dünner Strahl Wasser*

strah·len ['ʃtraːlən] ⟨intr v⟩ +*haben* **1.** shine ◊ *Nach der Sanierung strahlt das Schloss in neuem Glanz.* ♦ *Am Nachmittag strahlte die Sonne.* **2.** beam ◊ *Sie strahlte vor Freude, als sie das hörte.* **3.** PHYSICS emit radioactivity ◊ *Plutonium strahlt mit einer Halbwertzeit von über 24 000 Jahren.* ♦ *Wie lange strahlt radioaktiver Müll?*

② **Strand** [ʃtrant] der <-(e)s, Strände> beach ◊ *am Strand liegen*

stra·pa·zie·ren [ʃtrapaˈtsiːrən] <strapaziert, strapazierte, hat strapaziert> ⟨tr v⟩ be/put a strain on ◊ *Die Kinder strapazieren ihre Mutter.* ♦ *Stress strapaziert die Nerven; (a subject)* flog sth to death **jds Nerven strapazieren** try sb's nerves ⓔschonen

② **Stra·ße** ['ʃtraːsə] die <-, -n> **1.** street, road ◊ *Durch den Ort führt eine enge Straße.* ♦ *eine stark befahrene Straße* ♦ *eine Straße sperren* ♦ *die nächste Straße links* ♦ *In welcher Straße wohnst du?* ♦ *Die fast 2000 Jahre alte Straße der Römer führt von Xanten nach Nimwegen.* **2.** strait(s) ◊ *die Straße von Gibraltar*

ⓔ **etw. auf der Straße finden** get sth for nothing **auf die Straße gehen 1.** take to the streets ◊ *Zehntausende Demonstranten gingen gegen den Irak-Krieg auf die Straße.* **2.** go onto the streets, go and live on the streets ◊ *Viele Obdachlose sind schon als Jugendliche auf die Straße gegangen.* **auf der Straße leben** live on the streets **jdn auf die Straße setzen 1.** throw sb out ◊ *Seine Eltern haben ihn einfach auf die Straße gesetzt.* **2.** give sb the sack ◊ *2000 Arbeiter wurden auf die Straße gesetzt.* **auf die Straße setzen (an animal)** abandon

② **Stra·ßen·bahn** ['ʃtraːsn̩baːn] die <-, -en> tram, streetcar

sträu·ben ['ʃtrɔɪbm̩] ⟨ref v⟩ +*haben* **1.** sich

sträuben, etw. zu tun refuse to do sth ◊ *Er sträubt sich, seine Fehler zuzugeben.* **sich gegen etw./jdn sträuben** refuse to accept sth/sb ◊ *Die Kinder sträubten sich gegen die neue Frau des Vaters.* **2. jdm sträuben sich die Haare** sb's hair stands on end **einem Tier sträubt sich das Fell** an animal raises its hackles ⟨tr v⟩ +*haben (animal)* **das Fell sträuben** raise its hackles

Strauch [ʃtraʊx] der <-(e)s, Sträucher> shrub, bush ◊ *Dieser Strauch trägt weiße Blüten.* ♦ *einen Strauch pflanzen/beschneiden*

Strauß¹ [ʃtraʊs] der <-es, -e> ostrich

Strauß² [ʃtraʊs] der <-es, Sträuße> bouquet, bunch (of flowers) ◊ *ein Strauß aus roten Rosen* ♦ *ein Strauß frisch geschnittene Blumen*

stre·ben ['ʃtreːbm̩] ⟨intr v⟩ +*haben/sein* **1.** +*haben* **nach etw. streben** strive for sth ◊ *Die römischen Provinzen strebten nach Unabhängigkeit.* **2.** +*sein (lofty)* **irgendwohin streben** head somewhere ◊ *Die Tänzer strebten auf das Parkett.* **in die Höhe streben** soar (aloft)

② **Stre·cke** ['ʃtrɛka] die <-, -n> **1.** route ◊ *Die Strecke am Rhein entlang ist besonders beliebt.* ♦ *Die Strecke der Rallye Monte Carlo gilt als eine der gefährlichsten.; (from A to B also)* way ◊ *Auf der Strecke von Düsseldorf nach Köln hatte ich einen Unfall.* **2.** stretch, section ◊ *Die Strecke ist bis morgen früh für den Verkehr gesperrt.* **3.** distance ◊ *Ich fahre die Strecke Heidelberg-Karlsruhe jeden Tag zweimal.* **4.** road ◊ *auf gerader/kurviger Strecke fahren* **5.** MATH line ◊ *der Mittelpunkt einer Strecke*

ⓔ **auf der Strecke bleiben** fall by the wayside **etw. auf der Strecke lassen 1.** neglect sth, forgo sth ◊ *Wer Karriere machen will, muss häufig seine Freizeitaktivitäten auf der Strecke lassen.* **2.** leave sth behind you ◊ *Beide sind älter geworden und haben Illusionen auf der Strecke gelassen.* **jdn auf der Strecke lassen 1.** neglect sb ◊ *Bei den Reformen dürfen Minderheiten nicht auf der Strecke gelassen werden.* **2.** leave sb behind, overtake sb ◊ *Wer sich durchsetzen will, muss andere auf der Strecke lassen.*

stre·cken ['ʃtrɛkŋ] ⟨tr v⟩ +*haben* **1.** stretch ◊ *Er streckte die Arme.* **sich strecken** stretch, have a stretch **2. den Kopf aus etw. strecken** stick your/its head out of sth **seinen Schwanz in die Höhe strecken** raise its tail **3.** *mostly passive* **etw. mit etw. strecken** dilute sth with sth; *(drugs)* cut sth with sth ◊ *Das Kokain wurde mit Staubzucker gestreckt.*

ⓔ **sich in die Länge strecken** → **Länge**

Streich [ʃtraɪç] der <-(e)s, -e> **1.** trick, prank **2.** coup ◊ *Der letzte Streich des Autoherstellers war ein preisgünstiger Sportwagen.*

ⓔ **jdm einen Streich spielen 1. etw. spielt jdm einen Streich** sth play tricks on sb ◊ *Meine Einbildung spielte mir einen Streich.* **2. jd spielt jdm einen Streich** sb plays a trick on sb ◊ *Die Jungen spielten dem Lehrer einen üblen Streich.* **auf einen Streich** in one go

strei·cheln ['ʃtraɪçl̩n] ⟨tr+intr v⟩ +*haben* stroke ◊ *Sie streichelte die Katze, die auf ihrem Schoß schlief.* **jdm über etw.** ⟨acc⟩ **streicheln** stroke sb's sth ◊ *Er streichelte mit der Hand über ihre Wange.*

strei·chen ['ʃtraɪçn̩] <streicht, strich, hat gestri-

chen> **trv 1.** paint ◇ *Sie haben das ganze Haus frisch streichen lassen.* **2.** spread ◇ *Butter/Honig auf das Brot streichen* **3.** etw. irgendwohin streichen brush sth somewhere ◇ *Er strich die Krümel von der Tischdecke.* ◆ *Sie strich ihm das Haar aus dem Gesicht.* **4.** abolish ◇ *Die Regierung will das Sterbegeld streichen.; (jobs)* cut ◇ *Die Firma will 600 Stellen streichen.* **5.** delete ◇ *Unzutreffendes bitte streichen.* jdn von der Gästeliste streichen cross sb's name off the guest list **6.** *(a flight, train etc.)* cancel **intrv 1.** (jdm/sich) (mit der Hand) über etw. acc streichen stroke (sb's/your) sth ◇ *Sie strich ihrem Sohn sanft über den Kopf.* ◆ *Er strich mit der Hand über die Kühlerhaube.* **2.** durch etw. streichen roam (around) somewhere ◇ *durch die Gegend/Wälder streichen* **3.** etw. durch ein Sieb streichen pass sth through a sieve ◇ *Streichen Sie die Himbeeren durch ein Sieb.*

② **Streich·holz** [ˈʃtraɛçhɔlts] das <–es, Streichhölzer> match ◇ *ein Streichholz anzünden* ⊖Zündholz

Strei·fe [ˈʃtraɛfə] die <–, –n> patrol ◇ *Während der Streife fanden die Soldaten eine Autobombe.* ◆ *auf Streife sein/gehen* ◆ *Auf Streife trägt die Polizistin eine Pistole.* ◆ *Die Streife folgte dem Fliehenden mit Blaulicht.*

strei·fen [ˈʃtraɛfn] **trv** +haben **1.** graze, scrape ◇ *Der Hubschrauber streifte das Dach eines Hochhauses.; (softer)* touch, brush ◇ *Du hast mich mit dem Ellbogen gestreift.* **2.** jds Blick streift jdn sb glances fleetingly at sb **3.** (jdm/sich) etw. von etw. streifen pull sth off (sb's/your) sth ◇ *Er streifte sich die Socken von den Füßen.* **4.** (jdm/sich) etw. über etw. acc streifen put sth on (sb's/your) sth ◇ *Er streifte ihr den Ring über den Finger.* etw. über den Kopf streifen pull sth over ◇ *Ihr war kalt und sie streifte sich ein Sweatshirt über den Kopf.* **5.** brush ◇ *Sie streifte sich die Haare aus der Stirn.* **intrv** +sein/haben **1.** +sein *(fig)* seinen Blick über etw. acc streifen lassen let your gaze wander over sth jds Blick streift über etw. acc sb scans sth ◇ *Ihr Blick streifte über den Fluss und die Weinberge.* **2.** +sein roam ◇ *Wir streiften durch die Felder.* **3.** +sein durch/über etw. acc streifen pass through/over sth ◇ *Ein leiser Wind streifte über die Hügel.* ◆ *Ihre Hand streifte über die Stirn des Kindes.* **4.** +haben (an etw. dat) streifen rub (against sth) ◇ *Der Hebel streift an der Kupplungsscheibe.*

Strei·fen [ˈʃtraɛfn] der <–s, –> **1.** stripe ◇ *ein Pullover mit schmalen Streifen* **2.** strip ◇ *etw. in Streifen schneiden* ◆ *ein Streifen Papier/Klebeband* ◆ *Links neben den Beeten ist ein Streifen Rasen.* **3.** *(fam)* film

② **Streik** [ʃtraɛk] der <–(e)s, –s> strike zum Streik aufrufen call a strike sich im Streik befinden be on strike

② **strei·ken** [ˈʃtraɛkn̩] **intrv** +haben **1.** strike, be on strike ◇ *Die Busfahrer streiken schon seit drei Tagen.; go on strike* **2.** *(fam)* pack up, have packed up ◇ *Der Fernseher streikt.*

② **Streit** [ʃtraɛt] der <–(e)s, –e> *most sing* dispute ◇ *eine heftiger/erbitterter Streit* ◆ *einen Streit anfangen/schlichten;* argument ◆ *Immer sucht er Streit! Streit über/um jdn/etw.* dispute over/about sth ◇ *der Streit um die Steuerpolitik* (mit jdm) in

Streit geraten get into an argument (with sb) (mit jdm) im Streit liegen be at odds (with sb)

◉ **einen Streit vom Zaun brechen** start a fight

② **strei·ten** [ˈʃtraɛtn̩] <streitet, stritt, hat gestritten> **intrv** (um jdn/etw.) streiten argue (about sb/sth) ◇ *Hört endlich auf zu streiten und vertragt euch wieder.* ◆ *Die frisch geschiedenen Eltern stritten um die Kinder.* über etw. acc streiten argue about sth ◇ *Psychologen streiten über die Auswirkungen von Gewalt im Fernsehen.* sie streiten sich they argue ◇ *Meine Brüder streiten sich schon wieder.* ◆ *Sie stritten sich über Politik.*

strei·tig [ˈʃtraɛtɪç] adj *seldom comp/superl* **1.** LAW court ◇ *das streitige Verfahren* ◆ *In diesem Verfahren ist streitig, wer schadenspflichtig ist.* **2.** controversial ◇ *ein streitiges Thema* ◆ *Diese Frage ist streitig.* ⊖umstritten, strittig

◉ **jdm etw. streitig machen** contest sb's (right to) sth ◇ *jdm seine Position/seinen Sieg streitig machen*

streng [ʃtrɛŋ] adj, adv **1.** strict(ly) ◇ *strenge Bestimmungen* ◆ *Die Gesetze sind streng in diesem Land.* ◆ *ein strenger Vater* ◆ *Die Anforderungen für Bewerber sind streng.* ◆ *strenge Maßstäbe anlegen* ◆ *Die viktorianische Erziehung war streng.* ◆ *eine strenge Auslegung der Gesetze* ◆ *ein streng hierarchischer Führungsstil* ◆ *streng verboten* ◆ *Anweisungen streng befolgen* ◆ *eine Diät streng einhalten* streng chronologisch geordnet in strict chronological order streng erzogen sein have a strict upbringing streng geheim top secret **2.** strict(ly), rigorous(ly) ◇ *eine strenge Kontrolle* ◆ *Die Diät für Gallenkranke ist sehr streng.* ◆ *etw./jdn streng bewachen* ◆ *etw. streng kontrollieren* **3.** stern(ly) ◇ *eine strenger Blick* ◆ *Ihre Miene ist streng.* ◆ *jdn streng ansehen* **4.** severe(ly) ◇ *eine strenge Buße* ◆ *Die Strafe für diese Tat ist streng.* ◆ *Zur Arbeit trug sie einen strengen Hosenanzug.* ◆ *jdn streng bestrafen* ◆ *ein streng geschnittener Mantel* **5.** *(odour)* strong(ly) ◇ *Im Zoo roch es streng nach Raubkatzen.* ◆ *ein streng riechender Fisch* adj harsh ◇ *ein strenger Frost* ◆ *Der Winter war streng.*

◉ **streng genommen** strictly speaking etw. **streng nehmen, es mit etw. streng nehmen** be very serious/strict about sth

Stress [ʃtrɛs] der <–es> *no pl* **1.** stress ◇ *Bei Stress hilft Sport und Bewegung.* unter Stress stehen/sein be under stress, be under a lot of pressure **2.** *(fam)* hassle, bother ◇ *Ich hab schon wieder Stress mit meinem Chef.* im Stress sein be too busy Mach keinen Stress! Chill out!

streu·en [ˈʃtrɔøən] **trv** +haben **1.** scatter, sprinkle ◇ *Sand/Samen streuen* ◆ *Parmesankäse auf die Spaghetti streuen; (on roads etc.)* Salz/Sand streuen put down salt/grit, spread salt/grit **2.** *(fig)* FIN distribute, spread ◇ *Vermögen/Gelder streuen* ◆ *Das Risikokapital wird auf viele Anleger gestreut.* **3.** *(fig) (rumours etc.)* spread **4.** PHYSICS disperse ◇ *Diese Linse streut das Licht, anstatt es zu bündeln.* **intrv** +haben **1.** *(on roads etc.)* put down salt/grit, spread salt/grit ◇ *Bei Glatteis wird hier nicht gestreut.* **2.** MED spread ◇ *Dieser Tumor muss entfernt werden, sonst streut er im Körper.* **3.** PHYSICS be dispersed, disperse ◇ *Das Licht streut in alle Richtungen.*

A B C D E F G H I J K L M N O P Q R S T U V W X Y Z

strich [ʃtrɪç] *pret of* streichen

Strich [ʃtrɪç] der <-(e)s, -e> **1.** line ◊ *ein dicker/ waagrechter/senkrechter Strich* ♦ *einen Strich zeichnen/ziehen; (between words)* hyphen **2.** *no pl* gegen den/mit dem Strich against/in the direction of hair growth ◊ *eine Katze gegen den Strich streicheln/bürsten* ♦ *den Bart gegen den/mit dem Strich rasieren* **3.** *no pl (slang)* game ◊ *Der Strich erscheint oft die letzte Lösung für drogenabhängige Frauen.* auf den Strich gehen be on the game

ⓢ **jdm einen Strich durch die Rechnung machen** put an end to sb's plans etw. geht jdm gegen den Strich sb hates (having to do) sth unter dem/unterm Strich on the whole ◊ *Unterm Strich haben wir ein gutes Geschäft gemacht.*

Strick [ʃtrɪk] der <-(e)s, -e> **1.** rope ◊ *einen Strick um etw. wickeln/schlingen* **2.** *no pl* knitwear ◊ *Dieses Jahr ist wieder klassischer Strick modern.*

ⓢ **an einem/am gleichen Strick ziehen** pull together wenn alle Stricke reißen if the worst comes to the worst

stri·cken [ˈʃtrɪkn̩] ⌈tr+intr v⌉ +haben knit ◊ *Socken stricken* ♦ *Ich stricke am liebsten mit Angorawolle.*

ⓩ **stritt** [ʃtrɪt] *pret of* streiten

strit·tig [ˈʃtrɪtɪç] ⌈adj⌉ controversial ◊ *eine strittige Frage* ♦ *Das Thema Tabakwerbung bleibt weiterhin strittig.* ⊖umstritten, streitig

Stroh [ʃtroː] das <-s> *no pl* straw ◊ *Weihnachtsschmuck aus Stroh*

ⓢ **Stroh im Kopf haben** be as thick as two short planks

Stroh·halm [ˈʃtroːhalm] der <-(e)s, -e> straw ◊ *am Strohhalm ziehen*

ⓢ **nach dem letzten/einem Strohhalm greifen, sich an einen Strohhalm klammern** clutch at straws

ⓩ **Strom** [ʃtroːm] der <-(e)s, Ströme> **1.** *no pl* electricity ◊ *Strom verbrauchen/sparen* ♦ *Strom aus Sonnenlicht gewinnen* ♦ *Heute fiel in der ganzen Stadt der Strom aus.* ♦ *Kupfer leitet Strom.* **2.** (large) river ◊ *Die Wolga ist der größte Strom Europas.* **3.** stream ◊ *ein Strom aus Lava* **4.** *(fig)* flow ◊ *ein Strom von Menschen in Panik* ♦ *ein Strom von Ideen/Gefühlen*

ⓢ **es regnet in Strömen** it's pouring down, it's chucking it down gegen den Strom schwimmen **1.** swim against the current/stream ◊ *Sie schwamm gegen den Strom und verärgerte so einige Kollegen.* **2.** swim against the current mit dem Strom schwimmen **1.** swim with the stream, go with the flow **2.** swim with the current unter Strom stehen/sein **1.** be buzzing ◊ *Das Finale stand bevor und die Spieler standen unter Strom.* **2.** be live ◊ *Der Zaun steht unter Strom.*

strö·men [ˈʃtrøːmən] ⌈intr v⌉ +sein **1.** irgendwohin strömen flow somewhere ◊ *Unser Blut strömt in einem Kreislauf.* ♦ *Der Regen strömte über ihr Gesicht.* ♦ *Von Russland her strömt kalte Luft zu uns.* **2.** *(fig)* irgendwohin strömen stream somewhere ◊ *Rund 30.000 Menschen strömen täglich in die Messehalle.* ♦ *Tausend Gedanken strömten durch ihren Kopf.*

Strö·mung [ˈʃtrøːmʊŋ] die <-, -en> **1.** current ◊ *die Strömung des Flusses/der Luft* ♦ *eine starke*

Strömung 2. *(fig)* trend, movement ◊ *neue Strömungen in der Geschichtswissenschaft*

Stru·del [ˈʃtruːdl̩] der <-s, -> **1.** strudel **2.** whirlpool ◊ *Im Fluss gibt es einige starke Strudel.* **3.** *(fig)* spiral, whirl ◊ *im Strudel der Sucht/des Abschwungs* ♦ *vom Strudel der Ereignisse verschlungen werden*

Struk·tur [ʃtrʊkˈtuːɐ̯] die <-, -en> structure ◊ *die hierarchische Struktur des Unternehmens* ♦ *die grammatische Struktur eines Satzes* ♦ *eine kristalline Struktur, (of fabric)* texture ◊ *die feine Struktur der Seide*

ⓩ **Strumpf** [ʃtrʊmpf] der <-(e)s, Strümpfe> sock; stocking ◊ *ein Paar Strümpfe aus Nylon*

Strumpf·ho·se [ˈʃtrʊmpfhoːzə] die <-, -n> tights ◊ *eine Strumpfhose aus Nylon*

Stu·be [ˈʃtuːbə] die <-, -n> **1.** *(oldf)* (living) room **2.** dormitory, barracks (room) ◊ *Meistens teilen sich vier bis sechs Soldaten eine Stube.*

ⓩ **Stück** [ʃtʏk] das <-(e)s, -e or -> **1.** *pl 'Stücke'* piece ◊ *etw. in Stücke schneiden/brechen; (small also)* bit; *(of a whole also)* part ◊ *ein Stück vom Puzzle; (of cake, bread also)* slice ◊ *ein großes Stück Brot/Kuchen* **2.** *pl 'Stück'* zwei etc. Stück (von etw.) two etc. (of sth) ◊ *Ich möchte drei Stück von diesen Äpfeln haben.* ⊜Exemplar **3.** *pl 'Stücke'* THEAT play ◊ *Das Stück kommt im Juni auf die Bühne.* **4.** *pl 'Stücke'* MUS piece ◊ *Er spielte ein Stück von Mozart.*

ⓢ **am/im Stück 1.** whole, in one piece ◊ *Salami am/im Stück kaufen* **2.** running, consecutively ◊ *Er arbeitet schon sechs Wochen am/im Stück.* **Stück für Stück** bit by bit

ⓩ **Stu·dent** [ʃtuˈdɛnt] der <-en, -en>, **Stu·den·tin** [ʃtuˈdɛntɪn] die <-, -nen> (university) student ◊ *Er ist Student an der Universität München.*

Stu·den·ten·aus·weis [ʃtuˈdɛntn̩|a͡ʊsva͡ɪs] der <-es, -e> student ID ◊ *ein elektronischer/internationaler Studentenausweis*

Stu·die [ˈʃtuːdi̯ə] die <-, -n> **1.** study ◊ *eine Studie durchführen/veröffentlichen* ♦ *eine empirische Studie* ♦ *eine Studie zur Energiewirtschaft* ♦ *eine Studie über Berufskrankheiten* ♦ *Sein Film ist eine Studie der oberen Gesellschaftsschichten.* **2.** ARTS sketch ◊ *eine Studie zu einer Plastik anfertigen*

Stu·di·en·platz [ˈʃtuːdi̯ənplats] der <-es, Studienplätze> (university/college) place

ⓩ **stu·die·ren** [ʃtuˈdiːrən] <studiert, studierte, hat studiert> ⌈intr v⌉ study, be a student ◊ *Er studiert schon seit zehn Semestern.* an einer Hochschule/Universität studieren go to a university ⌈tr v⌉ study ◊ *Informatik an der Universität studieren* ♦ *ein Buch/einen Bericht studieren* ♦ *das Paarungsverhalten von Gänsen studieren*

ⓩ **Stu·dio** [ˈʃtuːdi̯oː] das <-s, -s> studio ◊ *Alle Fotos wurden im Studio aufgenommen.* ♦ *Nur wenige Szenen konnten im Studio gedreht werden.* ♦ *ein Studio für orientalischen Tanz*

ⓩ **Stu·di·um** [ˈʃtuːdi̯ʊm] das <-s, Studien> **1.** (university) course ◊ *ein Studium der Mathematik an der Universität Heidelberg* ♦ *das Studium abbrechen/erfolgreich abschließen* **2.** *usually translated with a verb* Er konnte das Gerät erst nach einem sorgfältigen Studium der Gebrauchsanweisung benutzen. He was only able to use the machine after he had

A B C D E F G H I J K L M N O P Q R S T U V W X Y Z

studied the instructions carefully.

② **Stu·fe** ['ʃtuːfə] die <-, –n> **1.** step, stair ◇ *Vorsicht Stufe!* ✦ *zwei Stufen auf einmal nehmen* **2.** stage ◇ *die erste/nächste Stufe der ökologischen Steuerreform* ✦ *die letzte Stufe einer Ausbildung* **3.** level ◇ *Das Gebläse läuft auf der niedrigsten/höchsten Stufe.*

◉ *auf einer Stufe mit jdm/etw. stehen* be on a par with sb/sth

② **Stuhl** [ʃtuːl] der <-(e)s, Stühle> **1.** chair ◇ *auf einem Stuhl Platz nehmen* **2.** MED stool(s) ◇ *Blut im Stuhl kann auf ernsthafte Krankheiten hinweisen.*

◉ *der Apostolische/Heilige Stuhl* the Apostolic/Holy See *auf einem wackeligen Stuhl sitzen* be in a shaky position *fast vom Stuhl fallen (fam)* nearly fall off your chair *jdn vom Stuhl hauen (fam)* knock sb out *sich zwischen die/zwei Stühle setzen, zwischen den/allen Stühlen* be caught in a cleft stick

② **stumm** [ʃtʊm] adj *no comp/superl* **1.** speech-impaired ◇ *Sie ist schon von ihrer Geburt an stumm.* ✦ *ein stummes Kind* **2.** silent ◇ *stummer Protest* ✦ *Sie blieb den Rest des Abends stumm.* **3.** GEOG *(map)* mute ◇ *eine stumme Karte von Deutschland*

Stüm·per ['ʃtʏmpɐ] der <-s, –>, **Stüm·pe·rin** ['ʃtʏmpərɪn] die <-, –nen> bungler ◇ *Wie konnten Sie nur so einen Stümper einstellen?* ⊖Dilettant

stumpf [ʃtʊmpf] adj <stumpfer, am stumpfesten> **1.** blunt ◇ *ein stumpfes Messer* ✦ *Die Schere ist stumpf.* eine stumpfe Nase a snub nose ⊖scharf **2.** vacant ◇ *Sein Blick war stumpf.* ✦ *ein stumpfer Gesichtsausdruck*

② **Stun·de** ['ʃtʊndə] die <-, –n> **1.** hour ◇ *Die Fahrt dauerte vier Stunden.* ✦ *In zwei Stunden kommen die Gäste.* **2.** SCHOOL hour, lesson, period ◇ *Die erste Stunde haben wir Mathe.* **3.** hour, moment ◇ *Das war die schwerste Stunde seines Lebens.* ✦ *In einer schwachen Stunde wollte sie schon alles aufgeben.* ✦ *ein Partner für die schönsten Stunden des Lebens*

◉ *zu früher/später Stunde* early/late, at an early/late hour *jds letzte Stunde hat geschlagen* sb's time has come *jds letzte Stunde schlägt* sb dies, sb's last hour comes *die letzte Stunde einer Sache* gen schlägt it's the end of the line for sth *die Stunden zählen* count the hours *jds Stunden sind gezählt* sb's hours are numbered *die Stunden einer Sache* gen *sind gezählt* the hours of sth are numbered *die Stunde X* the hour of reckoning

Stun·den·ki·lo·me·ter ['ʃtʊndn̩kilo,meːtɐ] der <-s, –> *most pl* kilometres an/per hour, kilometers an/per hour ◇ *mit 120 Stundenkilometern fahren* ✦ *eine Geschwindigkeit von 150 Stundenkilometern*

Stun·den·plan ['ʃtʊndn̩plaːn] der <-(e)s, Stundenpläne> timetable, schedule ◇ *Was steht jetzt auf dem Stundenplan?* ✦ *ein voller Stundenplan*

stünd·lich ['ʃtʏntlɪç] adj, adv *no comp/superl; when used as an adj, only before noun* hourly, every hour ◇ *im stündlichen Wechsel* ✦ *Der Zug verkehrt stündlich.*

stur [ʃtuːɐ] adj obstinate, stubborn ◇ *Er blieb stur*

und gab nicht nach. ✦ *ein sturer Mensch sich stur stellen* dig your heels in

◉ *auf stur schalten* dig your heels in

② **Sturm** [ʃtʊrm] der <-(e)s, Stürme> **1.** *(also fig)* storm ◇ *Ein Sturm zieht auf.* ✦ *ein Sturm der Entrüstung* **2.** MIL assault *der Sturm auf die Bastille* the storming of the Bastille

◉ *jdn/etw. im Sturm erobern* take sb/sth by storm *gegen etw. Sturm laufen* be up in arms against sth *Sturm läuten* **1.** keep on ringing, keep your finger on the bell **2.** sound the storm warning

stür·men ['ʃtʏrmən] tr v +haben **1.** storm ◇ *Die Polizei stürmte das Gebäude.* **2.** *(fig)* make a rush for ◇ *Nach dem Schlusspfiff stürmten die Fans das Spielfeld.* intr v +sein +direction storm, rush ◇ *Die Kinder stürmten lachend in den Garten.* imp v +haben *es stürmt* it is blowing a gale, the winds are gale force

stür·misch ['ʃtʏrmɪʃ] adj stormy ◇ *Das Wetter bleibt stürmisch.* ✦ *ein stürmischer Tag* ✦ *Sie hatten eine stürmische Affäre.; (applause)* tumultuous; *(embrace)* passionate; *(greeting)* enthusiastic *es war eine stürmische Zeit* those were turbulent times adv *(greet, welcome)* enthusiastically; *(embrace)* passionately *Nicht so stürmisch!* Easy!

Sturz [ʃtʊrts] der <-(e)s, Stürze> fall ◇ *Er brach sich bei einem Sturz das Bein.* ✦ *der gewaltsame Sturz des Diktators* ✦ *ein überraschender Sturz der Börsenkurse*

② **stür·zen** ['ʃtʏrtsn̩] intr v +sein **1.** fall ◇ *vom Fahrrad stürzen* ✦ *Sie stürzte und verletzte sich am Knie.* **2.** +place rush, dash ◇ *Sie stürzte zur Tür und riss sie auf.* tr v +haben **1.** POL bring down, overthrow ◇ *Die Rebellen wollen den Präsidenten stürzen.* **2.** *jdn/etw. in etw.* acc *stürzen* plunge sb/sth into sth ◇ *ein Land ins Chaos/eine Krise stürzen* ✦ *jdn in den Ruin stürzen* ref v +haben **1.** *sich irgendwohin stürzen* hurl/throw yourself somewhere ◇ *Die Frau wollte sich in die Tiefe stürzen.* ✦ *Er stürzte sich gleich in die Arbeit.* **2.** *sich auf jdn/etw. stürzen* attack sb/sth, pounce on sb/sth ◇ *Mit einem Schrei stürzte sich der Mann auf ihn.* ✦ *Sie stürzte sich auf den Kuchen.; (further away)* make a dash for sb/sth, rush at sb/sth

Sturz·helm ['ʃtʊrtshɛlm] der <-(e)s, Sturzhelme> crash helmet ◇ *einen Sturzhelm tragen/aufsetzen/abnehmen*

Stu·te ['ʃtuːtə] die <-, –n> mare

Stüt·ze ['ʃtʏtsə] die <-, –n> *(also fig)* support, prop ◇ *Stützen aus Stahl* ✦ *Ihr Mann war ihr in der schweren Zeit eine wichtige Stütze.*

stüt·zen ['ʃtʏtsn̩] tr v +haben **1.** support, prop up ◇ *Die Decke wird von mehreren Balken gestützt.* ✦ *sich auf einen Stock stützen* **2.** *etw. auf etw.* acc *stützen* rest sth on sth ◇ *die Ellbogen auf den Tisch stützen* ref v +haben **1.** *sich auf etw.* acc *stützen* lean on sth, prop yourself up on sth, support yourself on sth ◇ *sich auf einen Stock stützen* **2.** *sich auf etw.* acc *stützen* be based on sth ◇ *Diese These stützt sich auf Forschungsergebnisse.*

Sub·jekt [zʊp'jɛkt, '– –] das <-(e)s, –e> **1.** *(tech)* GRAM subject ◇ *Das Subjekt des Satzes steht gewöhnlich im Nominativ.* **2.** *(pej)* character ◇ *ein verkommenes Subjekt*

A B C D E F G H I J K L M N O P Q R S T U V W X Y Z

sub·jek·tiv [zʊpjɛk'ti:f, '– – –] [adj, adv] subjective(ly) ◇ *ein rein subjektives Urteil* ✦ *Diese Sichtweise ist sehr subjektiv.* ✦ *subjektiv empfundene Lebensqualität* ⊖objektiv

Sub·stan·tiv ['zʊpstanti:f] *das <–s, –e>* noun ⊖Nomen, Hauptwort

Sub·stan·ti·vie·rung [zʊpstanti'vi:rʊŋ] *die <–, –en>* substantivation ⊖Nominalisierung

> In German, the verb can generally be substantivized, i.e. used as a noun. In such cases it takes *das* as its article and is written with a capital letter, e.g. *Gestern waren wir* wandern. Das Wandern *war sehr anstrengend.* When German verbs are turned into nouns, the article can be combined with a preposition, e.g. *Das Kind* trank Milch und verschluckte sich dabei. Das Kind verschluckte sich beim Trinken der Milch. Substantivized adjectives (participles) are always written with a capital letter, used with the definite or indefinite article, and generally declined in the same way as an attributive adjective, e.g. *der glückliche Mensch — der Glückliche; ein glücklicher Mensch — ein Glücklicher.* When used with the definite article in the plural, the noun ends in -**en**, but when used without the article it just ends in -**e**, e.g. *die Angestellten dieser Firma — Angestellte im Ruhestand.* Abstract and uncountable nouns can also be formed from an adjective. They take the article *das* and have no plural form, e.g. *gut — das Gute; schön — das Schöne.*

sub·tra·hie·ren [zʊptra'hi:rən] *<subtrahiert, subtrahierte, hat subtrahiert>* [tr+intr v] subtract ◇ *Wenn man drei von zehn subtrahiert, erhält man sieben.* ⊖abziehen ⊜addieren

Sub·ven·ti·on [zʊpvɛn'tsjo:n] *die <–, –en>* subsidy ◇ *Die EU will ihre Subventionen senken.*

Su·che ['zu:xə] *die <–>* *no pl* search die Suche nach jdm/etw. the search for sb/sth ◇ *auf die Suche gehen* ✦ *Er ist auf der Suche nach Arbeit.*

② **su·chen** ['zu:xn̩] [intr v] +*haben* look, search ◇ *Ich habe überall gesucht, den Schlüssel aber nicht gefunden.* jdn/etw. suchen, nach jdm/etw. suchen look for sb/sth, search for sb/sth ◇ *Wir suchen eine neue Wohnung.* ✦ *Die Firma sucht Mitarbeiter.* ✦ *nach einer Lösung suchen* ✦ *Sie suchte nach den richtigen Worten.*; *(a missed person)* try to trace sb; *(a criminal)* hunt (for) sb, track sb Sie wird von der Polizei gesucht. She is being hunted/wanted by the police. ⊖finden [tr v] +*haben* *(peace, advice, shelter etc.)* seek ◇ *Rat/Hilfe/Frieden suchen* ✦ *in einer Kirche Zuflucht suchen* ◉ **etw. irgendwo suchen** *(fam)* irgendwo nichts zu suchen haben have no business (being) somewhere ◇ *Mobiltelefone haben im Krankenhaus nichts zu suchen. Was suchst du denn hier?* What are you doing here? **seinesgleichen suchen** be unparalleled, have no equal

Sucht [zʊxt] *die <–, Süchte>* **1.** addiction ◇ *Tablettenmissbrauch kann zur Sucht führen.* **2.** die Sucht nach etw. obsessive desire for sth ◇ *die Sucht nach Vergnügen/Genuss/Erfolg*

süch·tig ['zʏçtɪç] [adj] *no comp/superl* **1.** addictive, addicted ◇ *Jede Droge macht irgendwann süchtig.* ✦ *ein süchtiger Spieler* ⊖abhängig **2.** süchtig nach addicted to ◇ *Er ist richtig süchtig nach Computer-*

spielen.

② **Süd** [zy:t] *without the article, invariable* **1.** +*prep* aus/von Süd from the south nach Süd to the south, southwards ⊖Süden ⊜Nord, Norden **2.** South ◇ *das Autobahnkreuz München Süd* ⊜Nord

② **Süd-...** [zy:t] [prefix] south ..., southern ... ◇ *die Südseite des Hauses* ✦ *der Südwind* ✦ *die Südhalbkugel der Erde* die Südländer, der Südländer the southerner; *(in names)* South ..., Southern ... ◇ *Südafrika* ✦ *Südeuropa* ⊜Nord...

② **Sü·den** ['zy:dn̩] *der <–s>* *no pl* south ◇ *im Süden der Stadt wohnen* ✦ *Urlaub im Süden machen* nach Süden to the south, southwards Züge in Richtung Süden southbound trains ⊖Norden

süd·lich¹ ['zy:tlɪç] [adj] *only before ns* **1.** south, southern ◇ *der südliche Teil Europas* ✦ *südliche Länder* ⊖nördlich **2.** *(wind, direction)* southerly aus südlicher Richtung from the south ⊖nördlich

süd·lich² ['zy:tlɪç] [prep] +*gen* +*dat* **1.** +*gen* south of ◇ *die Wohngebiete südlich der Stadt* ⊖nördlich **2.** *adverbial* +*dat* südlich von etw. south of sth ◇ *südlich der Themse* ⊖nördlich

Suf·fix ['zʊfɪks, – '–] *das <–es, –e>* suffix ⊖Präfix

② **Sum·me** ['zʊmə] *die <–, –n>* **1.** MATH sum, total ◇ *Die Summe aus vier und vier ergibt/ist acht.* **2.** *(of money)* sum, amount ◇ *Er hat dafür eine hohe Summe bezahlt.* ✦ *eine Summe von 30 Euro* ⊖Betrag

Sumpf [zʊmpf] *der <–(e)s, Sümpfe>* **1.** GEOL marsh, swamp ◇ *im Sumpf stecken bleiben* ✦ *die Sümpfe der Everglades* **2.** *(fig)* cesspit, cesspool ◇ *im Sumpf des Verbrechens*

Sün·de ['zʏndə] *die <–, –n>* sin ◇ *Du hast eine schwere Sünde begangen.* ✦ *jdm seine Sünden vergeben* ✦ *Es ist eine Sünde, wie viel Geld sie für Kleidung ausgibt.*

② **su·per** ['zu:pɐ] *(fam)* [adj] *invariable* super, great ◇ *eine super Leistung* ✦ *Die Stimmung war super.* ⊖toll, prima, klasse [adv] *invariable* really well ◇ *Das hast du super gemacht!* ⊖toll, prima, klasse

Su·per ['zu:pɐ] *das <–s>* *mostly used without the article, no pl* four-star ◇ *Er tankt stets Super.*

Su·per·la·tiv ['zu:pɐlati:f] *der <–s, –e>* **1.** GRAM superlative ◇ *Der Superlativ von „schön" ist „am schönsten".* → Komparativ **2.** superlative ◇ *ein Ereignis der Superlative box@* Adjektiv

② **Su·per·markt** ['zu:pɐmaʁkt] *der <–(e)s, Supermärkte>* supermarket ◇ *schnell etw. aus dem Supermarkt holen* ✦ *Sie arbeitet als Kassiererin im Supermarkt.*

② **Sup·pe** ['zʊpə] *die <–, –n>* soup ◇ *ein Teller Suppe* ✦ *als Vorspeise eine Suppe essen* ◉ **du musst die Suppe auslöffeln, die du dir eingebrockt hast** *(fam)* you have made your bed, now you must lie in it **jdm die Suppe versalzen** *(fam)* put a spoke in sb's wheel

sur·fen ['sœʁfn̩] [intr v] +*haben* surf ◇ *In den Ferien gehen wir surfen.*; *(with sail)* windsurf im Internet surfen surf the internet

② **süß** [zy:s] [adj, adv] *<süßer, am süßesten>* **1.** sweet(ly) ◇ *Der Tee ist mir zu süß.* ✦ *ein süßer Duft* ✦ *Er hat sich ganz süß um mich gekümmert.* süß duften/schmecken have a sweet scent/taste **2.** *(fam)* cute(ly) ◇ *Was für süße Hundebabys!* ✦ *Der Typ da drüben ist ja total süß!* ✦ *Seht nur, wie*

süß die Kätzchen miteinander spielen!
sü·ßen ['zy:sn] ⊏tr v⊐ *+haben* sweeten ◊ *Milch mit Honig süßen* ⊏intr v⊐ *+haben* use as a sweetener ◊ *Süßen Sie mit Süßstoff oder mit Zucker?*
Sü·ßig·keit ['zy:sɪçkaet] die <–, –en> *most pl* sweets ◊ *Süßigkeiten naschen*
Süß·stoff ['zy:sʃtɔf] der <–(e)s, –e> sweetener
SVP [ɛsfao'pe:] die *(Swiss) (abbr of* Schweizerische Volkspartei*)* SVP

> The *SVP*, or Swiss People's Party, was formed in 1971 as the result of a merger between two traditionalist parties. The party manifesto — which rests on predominantly Christian and Protestant principles — espouses liberalism, federalism, and conservatism. The party supports the free market economy and a combination of tradition and progress.

② **Sym·bol** [zʏm'bo:l] das <–s, –e> symbol ◊ *die Taube als Symbol des Friedens* ♦ *mathematische Symbole*
Sym·pa·thie [zʏmpa'ti:] die <–, –n> liking ◊ *Sie empfand auf Anhieb Sympathie für ihre Kollegin.*
② **sym·pa·thisch** [zʏm'pa:tɪʃ] ⊏adj⊐ nice, likeable ◊ *Er war mir auf Anhieb sympathisch.* ♦ *eine sympathische Stimme* ⊝unsympathisch
Sy·no·nym [zyno'ny:m] das <–s, –e *or* –a> synonym ⊝Antonym

> Language comes alive with variety. In order not to have to use the same word twice, people often prefer to opt for a slightly different alternative. Different words having the same or very similar meanings are referred to as **synonyms**. For example, the German words *Ausdruck* (expression) and *Begriff* (term) are synonyms.

② **Sys·tem** [zʏs'te:m] das <–s, –e> system ◊ *die Suche nach dem Fehler im System* ♦ *ein demokratisches/totalitäres System; (of/for doing sth also)* method ◊ *ein gut durchdachtes System*

> The political system of the Federal Republic of Germany is founded on a liberal, democratic state. Citizens elect deputies to the *Bundestag*, the German parliament, in open, secret ballots. They also elect the regional parliaments, and representatives of the people at municipal and regional level. The *Bundestag* enacts laws and elects the Federal Chancellor on the recommendation of the Federal President. The Federal Chancellor establishes policy directives and with these he forms the government. The regional states of Germany are represented in the *Bundesrat*, the second chamber, members being appointed by the regional governments. The *Bundesrat* participates in the legislative process, and in certain instances its assent is required. The authority of the state is upheld by three independent bodies: the Federal Government (executive); the *Bundestag* and *Bundesrat* (legislature); and the Federal Constitutional Court (judiciary), the latter being responsible for safeguarding the German Constitution, or the 'Basic Law'.

Sze·ne ['stse:nə] die <–, –n> **1.** scene ◊ *In der letzten Szene des Theaterstücks stirbt der Held.* ♦ *Als sie davon erfuhr, kam es zu einer hässlichen Szene.* **2.** FILM, THEAT set ◊ *Der Held betritt zum ersten Mal die Szene.*
⊛ (jdm) eine Szene machen make a scene sich in Szene setzen make yourself the centre of attention

A
B
C
D
E
F
G
H
I
J
K
L
M
N
O
P
Q
R
S
T
U
V
W
X
Y
Z

T

t, T [te:] das <–(s), –(s)> t, T ◊ *Dieses Wort wird mit einem kleinen t/großen T geschrieben.* ♦ *T wie Theodor*

Ta·bak ['ta:bak, ta'bak] der <–s, –e> *most sing* tobacco ◊ *Tabak anbauen/rauchen*

ta·bel·la·risch [tabɛ'la:rɪʃ] [adj] *no comp/superl* tabular ◊ *eine tabellarische Übersicht* ♦ *Der Lebenslauf sollte tabellarisch sein.* [adv] in tabular form ◊ *etw. tabellarisch auflisten/darstellen*

② **Ta·bel·le** [ta'bɛlə] die <–, –n> table ◊ *Zahlen in eine Tabelle eintragen* ♦ *eine Tabelle erstellen* ♦ *Die Mannschaft führt die Tabelle mit zwei Punkten Vorsprung an.*

Tab·lett [ta'blɛt] das <–(e)s, –s or –e> tray ◊ *Sie stellte das Geschirr auf ein Tablett.*

⊛ **jdm etw. auf einem silbernen Tablett servieren** hand sb sth on a (silver) plate

② **Tab·let·te** [ta'blɛtə] die <–, –n> tablet ♦ *eine Tablette gegen Kopfschmerzen schlucken/nehmen*

Ta·bu [ta'bu:] das <–s, –s> taboo ◊ *Das ist für sie ein Tabu.* ♦ *ein Tabu verletzen*

Ta·cho ['taxo:] der <–s, –s> *(fam) (abbr of* Tachometer*)* speedometer ◊ *Was zeigt der Tacho an?* 40 000 km auf dem Tacho haben have 40,000 km on the clock

Ta·cho·me·ter [taxo'me:tɐ] der *or* das <–s, –> → Tacho

Ta·del ['ta:dl] der <–s, –> *(lofty)* censure, reprimand ◊ *mehr Lob als Tadel aussprechen* ♦ *einen Tadel verdienen* ♦ *Es gab einen Tadel für mein vorschnelles Handeln.* ⊖Rüge ⊕Lob

② **Ta·fel** ['ta:fl] die <–, –n> **1.** school blackboard, whiteboard ◊ *etw. mit Kreide an die Tafel schreiben* **2.** table ◊ *Zur Hochzeit ist die Tafel festlich geschmückt.* **3.** bar ◊ *eine Tafel Schokolade* **4.** plate ◊ *Auf Tafel II sind die wichtigsten Raubvögel abgebildet.* **5.** board ◊ *Auf der Tafel stand „Heute frischer Fisch".; (memorial)* plaque

⊛ **die Tafel aufheben** *(form)* declare a meal over

② **Tag** [ta:k] der <–(e)s, –e> **1.** day ◊ *Was ist heute für ein Tag?* ♦ *vier Tage Urlaub haben* ♦ *Der Tag geht zu Ende.* ♦ *ein sonniger Tag* ♦ *jeden Tag* ♦ *Diese Kommode hat auch schon bessere Tage gesehen.* am/bei Tag by day **2.** *only pl (of a woman)* period ◊ *Sie hat ihre Tage.* ⊖Periode, Blutung **3.** über/unter Tage above/below ground ◊ *Kohle unter Tage abbauen*

⊛ **man soll den Tag nicht vor dem Abend loben** you shouldn't count your chickens before they're hatched **Tag der Deutschen Einheit** Day of German Unity **Tag der offenen Tür** open day **der Tag X** the day of reckoning ◊ *Vorbereitungen für den Tag X treffen* **guten Tag** good day, good afternoon **der Jüngste Tag** doomsday **einen schlechten Tag haben** have a bad day **ewig und drei Tage** *(fam)* for ever and a day **jds Tage (als etw.) sind gezählt** sb's days (as sth) are

numbered **an den Tag kommen** come to light **in den Tag hinein leben** live from day to day **etw. an den Tag legen** display sth ◊ *Er hat großen Fleiß an den Tag gelegt.* **von einem Tag auf den anderen** overnight **Tag für Tag** day after day

3rd October is the Day of German Unity, which commemorates the reunification of the GDR (German Democratic Republic) with the Federal Republic of Germany. It has been a public holiday in Germany since 1990.

Ta·ge·buch ['ta:gəbu:x] das <–(e)s, Tagebücher> diary ◊ *Sie führt seit Jahren (ein) Tagebuch.*

② **ta·ge·lang** ['ta:gəlaŋ] [adj] *no comp/superl, only before ns* lasting days ◊ *Es kam zu tagelangen Demonstrationen.* [adv] for days ◊ *Sie wartete tagelang vergeblich.*

ta·gen ['ta:gn̩] [intr v] *+haben* meet, sit ◊ *Der EU-Ministerrat tagt zum Thema Umweltschutz.*

Ta·ges·mut·ter ['ta:gəsmʊtɐ] die <–, Tagesmütter> childminder ◊ *Sie arbeitet als Tagesmutter.* ♦ *Meine Kinder sind vormittags bei ihrer Tagesmutter.*

A child-minder is paid to look after the children of working parents. As a nursery place cannot be guaranteed and day-nursery supervision is not suitable for every child, the child-minder represents an important alternative for working parents in Germany.

Ta·ges·ord·nung ['ta:gəsɔ'dnʊŋ] die <–, –en> *most sing* agenda ◊ *etw. auf die Tagesordnung setzen* ♦ *etw. steht auf der Tagesordnung*

⊛ **an der Tagesordnung sein** be the order of the day **zur Tagesordnung übergehen** carry on as normal

Ta·ges·zei·tung ['ta:gəstsaetʊŋ] die <–, –en> daily (paper) ◊ *eine Tageszeitung abonnieren*

② **täg·lich** ['tɛːklɪç] [adj] *no comp/superl; when used as an adj, only before ns* daily, on a daily basis ◊ *Lebensmittel für den täglichen Bedarf* ♦ *Diese Zeitung erscheint täglich.* ♦ *täglich acht Stunden arbeiten*

tags·ü·ber ['ta:ksly:bɐ] [adv] during the day ◊ *ein Kind tagsüber betreuen* ♦ *Tagsüber bin ich unter folgender Telefonnummer erreichbar: ...* ⊖nachts

Ta·gung ['ta:gʊŋ] die <–, –en> conference ◊ *auf einer Tagung sein* ♦ *eine Tagung zum Thema „Erziehung und Gewalt"*

Tail·le ['taljə] die <–, –n> waist ◊ *eine schlanke Taille haben*

Takt [takt] der <–(e)s, –e> **1.** time, beat ◊ *den Takt schlagen* ♦ *im Takt bleiben* **2.** bar ◊ *Nach den ersten Takten erkannten alle das Stück.* **3.** *no pl* tact ◊ *Sie hat manchmal überhaupt keinen Takt.* ⊖Feingefühl

② **Tal** [ta:l] das <–(e)s, Täler> valley ◊ *Tief unten im Tal konnte man die Häuser erkennen.*

② **tan·ken** ['taŋkn̩] [tr v] *+haben* put in ◊ *Sie hat 25*

Liter Diesel getankt.; (aircraft, racing car) refuel
[intr v] *+haben* **1.** get some more petrol, top up,
fill up ◇ *Wir müssen bei nächster Gelegenheit
tanken.* **2.** *(fig)* Kraft/Energie tanken recharge
your batteries *Sonne tanken* soak up the sun
3. *(fam, fig, hum)* get tanked up, down a few ◇
Der hat aber ordentlich getankt!

② **Tank·stel·le** ['taŋkʃtɛlə] die <–, –n> petrol station
Tan·ne ['tanə] die <–, –n> fir, pine ◇ *Im Wald
stehen viele Tannen.*

② **Tan·te** ['tantə] die <–, –n> **1.** aunt ◇ *Morgen
kommt Tante Berta zu Besuch.* **2.** *(fam, pej)*
woman ◇ *Das sind vielleicht komische Tanten!*

② **Tanz** [tants] der <–es, Tänze> **1.** dance ◇ *afrikanische Tänze* ◆ *In diesem Lokal ist samstags Tanz.*
zum Tanz aufspielen strike up a dance tune *jdn
zum Tanz auffordern/bitten* ask sb to dance
2. *(fam)* fuss ◇ *Mein Vater hat einen ziemlichen
Tanz aufgeführt, weil wir zu spät kamen.*
◉ der Tanz ums Goldene Kalb the love of
money, striving for riches ein Tanz auf dem
Vulkan playing with fire

② **tan·zen** ['tantsn̩] [tr+intr v] *+haben/with indication
of direction +sein* dance ◇ *Tanz doch mal mit ihr.*
◆ *Die Paare tanzten über das Parkett.* gut/schlecht
etc. tanzen be a good/bad etc. dancer *tanzen
gehen* go dancing *Samba/einen Foxtrott etc.
tanzen* do the samba/foxtrot etc. [intr v] *+sein (fig)*
dance ◇ *Schneeflocken tanzten durch die Luft.;
(boats etc.)* bob up and down, bob about

Tän·zer ['tɛntsɐ] der <–s, –>, **Tän·ze·rin**
['tɛntsərɪn] die <–, –nen> dancer ◇ *ein schlechter
Tänzer* ◆ *Sie ist Tänzerin an der Oper.*

Ta·pe·te [ta'peːtə] die <–, –n> wallpaper ◇ *fünf
Rollen Tapete*

ta·pe·zie·ren [tape'tsiːrən] <tapeziert, tapezierte,
hat tapeziert> [tr+intr v] (wall)paper ◇ *Wir haben
den Flur blau tapeziert.* tapezieren können know
how to put up wallpaper

tap·fer ['tapfɐ] [adj, adv] brave(ly) ◇ *Mein kleiner
Sohn war sehr tapfer beim Zahnarzt.* ◆ *tapfere
Krieger* ◆ *Sie lächelte tapfer.*

tap·pen ['tapn̩] [intr v] *+haben/sein; +sein* lumber
◇ *Unbeholfen tappten die jungen Bären durchs
Gras.* ◆ *Im Dunkeln tappte er vorsichtig zurück ins
Zimmer.*
◉ im Dunkeln/Finstern tappen be in the dark

② **Ta·rif** [ta'riːf] der <–s, –e> **1.** rate ◇ *abends zu
einem günstigeren Tarif telefonieren* **2.** rate (of
pay) ◇ *unter/über Tarif bezahlt werden*

ta·rif·lich [ta'riːflɪç] [adj] *no comp/superl, only
before ns* agreed ◇ *eine tarifliche Zusatzrente
bekommen* [adv] die tariflich festgelegte Arbeitszeit the agreed working hours *tariflich geregelt*
regulated by (a) contract *tariflich bezahlt werden*
be paid the standard wage

Ta·rif·ver·trag [ta'riːffɛrtraːk] der
<–(e)s, Tarifverträge> labour agreement, labor
agreement

tar·nen ['tarnən] [tr v] *+haben* disguise ◇ *sich mit
einer Perücke tarnen; (hide)* camouflage *etw./sich
als etw. tarnen* pass sth/yourself off as sth ◇ *Die
Einbrecher hatten sich als Handwerker getarnt.* ◆
Er versuchte, seine Tat als Unfall zu tarnen.

② **Ta·sche** ['taʃə] die <–, –n> **1.** *(also fig)* pocket ◇
Sie steckte die Hände in die Taschen. ◆ *Hast du*

das alles aus eigener Tasche bezahlt? **2.** bag ◇ *Sie
waren schwer mit Koffern und Taschen bepackt.* ◆
Der Dieb entriss ihr die Tasche.
◉ jdm auf der Tasche liegen *(fam)* live off sb
sich [dat] in die (eigene) Tasche lügen *(fam)* kid
yourself jdn in die Tasche stecken *(fam)* beat sb
hands down etw. in die eigene Tasche wirtschaften *(fam)* pocket sth in die eigene Tasche wirtschaften line your (own) pockets

② **Ta·schen·buch** ['taʃnbuːx] das
<–(e)s, Taschenbücher> paperback ◇ *Den Bestseller
gibt es jetzt auch als Taschenbuch.*

Ta·schen·dieb ['taʃndiːp] der <–(e)s, –e>,
Ta·schen·die·bin ['taʃndiːbɪn] die <–, –nen> pickpocket

Ta·schen·geld ['taʃŋɡɛlt] das <–(e)s, –er> *most
sing* pocket money ◇ *Sie bekommt fünf Euro
Taschengeld in der Woche.* ◆ *Der Lohn war kaum
mehr als ein Taschengeld.*

Ta·schen·lam·pe ['taʃnlampə] die <–, –n> torch,
flashlight ◇ *Sie leuchtete mit einer Taschenlampe
unter das Bett.*

Ta·schen·tuch ['taʃntuːx] das
<–(e)s, Taschentücher> handkerchief, hanky; *(dis-
posable)* tissue

② **Tas·se** ['tasə] die <–, –n> cup ◇ *eine Tasse Kaffee*
◆ *Die Tasse hat einen Sprung.*
◉ nicht alle Tassen im Schrank haben *(fam)*
have got a screw loose hoch die Tassen *(fam)*
cheers

② **Tas·ta·tur** [tasta'tuːɐ] die <–, –en> keyboard ◇
etw. über die Tastatur in den Computer eingeben

② **Tas·te** ['tastə] die <–, –n> button ◇ *Welche Taste
muss ich jetzt drücken?; (of a computer, piano
etc.)* key

tas·ten ['tastn̩] <tastet, tastete, hat getastet>
[intr v] *nach etw./jdm* tasten feel for sth/sb ◇ *Er
tastete im Dunkeln nach dem Lichtschalter.* [ref v]
sich irgendwohin tasten feel your way somewhere

② **tat** [taːt] *pret of* tun

② **Tat** [taːt] die <–, –en> **1.** deed ◇ *eine mutige Tat*
⊖Handlung **2.** crime ◇ *Weiß man schon, wer die
Tat begangen hat?* ⊖Verbrechen
◉ jdn auf frischer Tat ertappen catch sb red-
handed, catch sb in the act zur Tat schreiten act
etw. in die Tat umsetzen put sth into action in
der Tat indeed ◇ *„Ich habe meine Uhr
verloren." – „Das ist in der Tat schade."*

ta·ten·los ['taːtnloːs] [adj, adv] *no comp/superl;
when used as an adj, only before ns* idle(-ly) ◇
tatenlose Zuschauer ◆ *Das dürfen wir nicht
tatenlos hinnehmen!*

② **Tä·ter** ['tɛːtɐ] der <–s, –>, **Tä·te·rin** ['tɛːtərɪn] die
<–, –nen> culprit, perpetrator ◇ *Die Täter konnten
unerkannt entkommen.* der mutmaßliche Täter the
suspect ⊖Opfer

tä·tig ['tɛːtɪç] [adj] *no comp/superl* **1.** operating ◇
*international tätige Unternehmen (als etw.) tätig
sein* work (as sth) ◇ *freiberuflich tätig sein* ◆ *Er
ist als Arzt tätig.* in etw. [dat] tätig working in sth
◇ *im Außendienst tätige Mitarbeiter* **2.** active ◇
tätige Hilfe leisten ◆ *Dieser Vulkan ist nicht mehr
tätig.* tätig werden act ◇ *Sie wartete nicht auf
Hilfe von außen, sondern wurde selbst tätig.*

② **Tä·tig·keit** ['tɛːtɪçkaet] die <–, –en> **1.** work ◇ *die
Tätigkeit eines Rechtsanwalts* eine Tätigkeit

ausüben do a job Er geht keiner beruflichen Tätigkeit nach. He doesn't work. **2.** activity ◊ *Ich halte das Angeln für eine sehr entspannende Tätigkeit.*

tat·kräf·tig ['taːtkrɛftɪç] [adj, adv] energetic(ally) ◊ *Wir hatten viele tatkräftige Helfer.* ♦ *Die Arbeiter sind tatkräftig und verlässlich.* ♦ *bei etw. tatkräftig unterstützt werden*

Tä·to·wie·rung [tɛtoˈviːrʊŋ] die <-, -en> tattoo

Ⓣ **Tat·sa·che** ['taːtzaxə] die <-, -n> fact ◊ *Das ist keine Vermutung, sondern eine Tatsache.* ♦ *Entspricht es den Tatsachen, dass ...?*
⊛ **jdn vor vollendete Tatsachen stellen** present sb with a fait accompli

Ⓣ **tat·säch·lich** [taːtˈzɛçlɪç, '- - -] [adj, adv] *no comp/superl; when used as an adj, only before ns* actual(ly), real(ly) ◊ *Die tatsächliche Zahl der Opfer ist noch nicht bekannt.* ♦ *Er hat tatsächlich geglaubt, dass er damit durchkommt!* ♦ *Tatsächlich? Das kann ich mir nicht vorstellen!* ⊖wirklich

Tau¹ [tao] der <-(e)s> *no pl* dew ◊ *Das Gras war feucht vom Tau.*

Tau² [tao] das <-(e)s, -e> rope

Ⓣ **taub** [taop] [adj] *no comp/superl* **1.** deaf ◊ *Sie ist auf dem rechten Ohr taub.* ♦ *ein tauber Mann* sich taub stellen pretend not to hear für etw. taub sein be deaf to sth ◊ *Er war taub für die Anliegen seiner Mitarbeiter.* **2.** numb ◊ *Er hatte schon ganz taube Finger vor Kälte.* ♦ *Nach der Operation blieb sein Bein noch lange taub.* **3.** *(nut etc.)* empty

Tau·be¹ ['taobə] die <-, -n> zoo pigeon, dove

Tau·be² ['taobə] der/die <-n, die Tauben> *but: ein Tauber/eine Taube* deaf person ⊖Gehörlose

taub·stumm ['taopftʊm] [adj] *no comp/superl* deaf and dumb ◊ *ein taubstummes Kind* ♦ *Unser Nachbar ist taubstumm.*

tau·chen ['taoxn̩] [intr v] *+haben/sein* **1.** *+haben/ with direction +sein* dive ◊ *Im Urlaub gehen wir gerne tauchen.* ♦ *35 Meter tief tauchen; (with the head only)* duck under (water) nach etw. tauchen dive for sth **2.** *+haben* stay under (water) ◊ *Sie kann zwei Minuten lang tauchen.* **3.** *+sein (fig)* disappear ◊ *Die Wanderer tauchten ins Dunkel des Waldes.* [tr v] *+haben* **1.** jdn (unter Wasser) tauchen duck sb (under water) ◊ *Die Kinder spielten im Wasser und tauchten sich gegenseitig.* **2.** etw. in etw. [acc] tauchen dip sth in sth ◊ *Er tauchte die Feder in die Tinte.; (with more force)* plunge sth in sth ◊ *Sie tauchte ihr erhitztes Gesicht in kühlendes Wasser.* **3.** *(fig)* etw./jdn in etw. [acc] tauchen bathe sth/sb in sth ◊ *Scheinwerfer tauchten die Tanzfläche in farbiges Licht.; (in obscurity, darkness etc.)* shroud sth/sb in sth

tau·en ['taoən] [imp v] *+haben* es taut it is thawing [intr v] *+sein* melt ⊖schmelzen

Tau·fe ['taofə] die <-, -n> baptism, christening
⊛ **etw. aus der Taufe heben** launch sth

tau·fen ['taofn̩] [tr v] *+haben* **1.** *mostly passive* baptize ◊ *Meine Nichte ist noch nicht getauft.* **2.** jdn/ etw. (.../auf den Namen ...) taufen christen sb/sth (sth) ◊ *Sie wurde Elizabeth/auf den Namen Elisabeth getauft.*

tau·gen ['taogn̩] [intr v] *+haben* **1.** nichts taugen be good for nothing, be useless ◊ *Sie hat endlich gemerkt, dass er nichts taugt.* nicht viel/wenig taugen not be much good, be fairly useless ◊ *Die*

Pfanne war zwar teuer, taugt aber nicht viel. Taugt das was? Is it any good/use? **2.** zu/für etw. taugen be suitable for sth ◊ *Sein Verhalten taugt wenig dazu, mich zu überzeugen. Taugt er zum Soldaten?* Would he make a good soldier? als etw. taugen be suitable as sth ◊ *Das T-Shirt taugt nur noch als Putzlappen.*

tau·meln ['taoml̩n] [intr v] *+haben/sein* **1.** *+sein* stagger ◊ *Hustend taumelten sie aus dem brennenden Haus auf die Straße.* **2.** *+haben* sway ◊ *Der Betrunkene hat leicht getaumelt.*

Tausch [taoʃ] der <-(e)s, -e> *most sing* exchange ◊ *Er bietet Babysitten im Tausch gegen Nachhilfeunterricht.*

tau·schen ['taoʃn̩] [tr+intr v] *+haben* (etw.) (mit jdm) tauschen swap (sth) (with sb), swop (sth) (with sb), exchange (sth) (with sb) ◊ *Nach dem Spiel tauschten sie ihre Trikots.* ♦ *Ich bin zufrieden mit meinem Leben und würde mit niemandem tauschen wollen.* etw. gegen etw. tauschen swap sth for sth, swop sth for sth, exchange sth for sth ◊ *Tauschst du dein Zimmer gegen meines?*

täu·schen ['tɔøʃn̩] [ref v] *+haben* sich (in jdm/etw.) täuschen be wrong (about sb/sth), be mistaken (about sb/sth) ◊ *Ich habe mich in ihm getäuscht.* ♦ *Da täuschst du dich aber gewaltig!* ⊖sich irren [tr v] *+haben* jdn täuschen deceive sb wenn mich nicht alles täuscht unless I'm completely mistaken, if I'm right [intr v] *+haben* be deceptive ◊ *Der erste Eindruck täuscht oft.*

Täu·schung ['tɔøʃʊŋ] die <-, -en> **1.** delusion ◊ *Er gab sich der Täuschung hin, sie überzeugt zu haben.* einer Täuschung unterliegen delude yourself **2.** illusion ◊ *eine optische Täuschung* **3.** *(act of)* deception ◊ *eine raffinierte Täuschung*

tau·send ['taoznt, 'taozənt] [nmrl] **1.** (a/one) thousand ♦ vier **2.** *(fam)* hundreds of, so many ◊ *Sie hat immer tausend Änderungswünsche.* tausend Dank very many thanks
⊛ **tausend und abertausend** thousands and thousands (of)

> *Tausend* and *tausende* can also be written with a capital letter when used with indefinite expressions of quantity: *viele tausend/Tausend Besucher; tausende/Tausende von Malen.*

Tau·send¹ ['taoznt, 'taozənt] die <-, -en> (a/one) thousand ◊ *Die Zahl der Besucher hat die Tausend längst überschritten.*

Tau·send² ['taoznt, 'taozənt] das <-s, -e> (one) thousand ◊ *Mit dieser Kiste ist jetzt das zweite Tausend voll.*

Tau·sen·der ['taozn̩dɐ] der <-s, -> thousand ◊ *die Einer, Zehner, Hunderter und Tausender addieren*

Ⓣ **Tax·card** ['takskaːrt] die <-, -s> *(Swiss)* → Telefonkarte²

Ⓣ **Ta·xi** ['taksi] das <-s, -s> taxi ◊ *ein Taxi bestellen*

Ta·xi·fah·rer ['taksifaːrɐ] der <-s, ->,
Ta·xi·fah·re·rin ['taksifaːrərɪn] die <-, -nen> taxi driver ◊ *Sie arbeitet als Taxifahrerin.* ♦ *Der Taxifahrer half ihm mit seinem Koffer.*

Ⓣ **Team** [tiːm] das <-s, -s> team ◊ *Wir sind mittlerweile ein gut eingespieltes Team.*

Ⓣ **Tech·nik** ['tɛçnɪk] die <-, -en> **1.** *no pl* technology ◊ *auf dem neuesten Stand der Technik sein* **2.** technique ◊ *Welcher Technik hat sich der Autor*

hier bedient?

Tech·ni·ker ['tɛçnɪkɐ] *der* <-s, ->,
Tech·ni·ke·rin ['tɛçnɪkərɪn] *die* <-, -nen> technician ◊ *Sie ist staatlich geprüfte Technikerin für Elektrotechnik.* ♦ *Ich musste einen Techniker kommen lassen.* ♦ *Die brillante Technikerin begeisterte uns mit ihrem virtuosen Spiel.*

② **tech·nisch** ['tɛçnɪʃ] adj, adv *no comp/superl; when used as an adj, only before ns* technical(ly) ◊ *komplizierte technische Geräte* ♦ *Ist das denn technisch machbar? Sein Spiel war technisch perfekt.*

② **Tee** [te:] *der* <-s, -s> tea ◊ *Möchten Sie Tee oder Kaffee?* ♦ *Um diese Zeit sitzen sie beim Tee.*
Tee·beu·tel ['te:bɔɪtl̩] *der* <-s, -> tea bag
Tee·licht ['te:lɪçt] *das* <-(e)s, -er> tealight
Tee·löf·fel ['te:lœfl̩] *der* <-s, -> **1.** teaspoon **2.** teaspoon(ful) of ◊ *ein gestrichener Teelöffel Salz*
Teer [te:ɐ] *der* <-(e)s> *no pl* tar
Tee·wurst ['te:vʊɐst] *die* <-, Teewürste> *most sing* smoked or unsmoked German sausage spread ◊ *feine/grobe Teewurst*
Teich [taɪç] *der* <-(e)s, -e> pond ◊ *einen Teich anlegen* ♦ *Sie fütterten die Enten im Teich.*
◉ **der große Teich** *(fam, hum)* the pond, the Atlantic
Teig [taɪk] *der* <-(e)s, -e> dough ◊ *die Zutaten zu einem Teig verrühren*

② **Teil¹** [taɪl] *der* <-(e)s, -e> **1.** part ◊ *Das Schlafzimmer liegt im hinteren Teil des Hauses.* ♦ *Ein beträchtlicher Teil der Bevölkerung glaubt daran.* in zwei Teile zerbrochen broken in half, broken in two **2.** share ◊ *Ich will gerne meinen Teil zum Gelingen des Abends beitragen.* Teil an etw. dat haben share in sth **3.** zum Teil ◊ *Ich habe das Buch nur zum Teil gelesen.; (in expressions of time)* for part of the time ◊ *Das Wetter war zum Teil ziemlich regnerisch.* zum großen/größten Teil mostly, mainly
◉ **sich** dat **seinen Teil denken** have your thoughts about it/sth ich für meinen Teil personally, I

② **Teil²** [taɪl] *das* <-(e)s, -e> **1.** part ◊ *Dieses Teil muss ausgetauscht werden.* etw. in seine Teile zerlegen take sth apart **2.** *(fam)* thing ◊ *Wo hast du das Teil denn her?* Dieses Motorrad ist ein starkes Teil! This motorbike is a hot machine!

② **teil·...** [taɪl] prefix partly ..., part-... ◊ *eine teilautomatische Anlage* ♦ *eine teilmöblierte Wohnung*

② **Teil·...** [taɪl] prefix part-... ◊ *Teilzeit*; part of ◊ *Teilbetrag* ♦ *Teilbereich*
teil·bar ['taɪlbaːɐ] adj *no comp/superl* that can be divided (up) ◊ *eine teilbare Sporthalle; (numbers)* divisible ◊ *Zehn ist durch zwei und fünf teilbar.*
Teil·chen ['taɪlçən] *das* <-s, -> **1.** CHEM, PHYSICS particle ◊ *positiv geladene Teilchen* **2.** pastry ◊ *Zum Kaffee wurden süße Teilchen gereicht.*

② **tei·len** ['taɪlən] tr v +*haben* **1.** etw. (in etw. acc) teilen divide sth (into sth), split sth (into sth) ◊ *Ein Bach teilt das Grundstück in zwei Hälften.* ⊜trennen **2.** MATH etw. (durch etw.) teilen divide sth (by sth) ◊ *Kann man 126 durch 3 teilen?* ⊜malnehmen tr+intr v +*haben* share sth ◊ *Teil die Bonbons mit deiner Schwester.* ♦ *Wir teilen Ihre Auffassung, dass sich das ändern muss.* mit jdm

teilen share with sb sich dat etw. teilen share sth ref v +*haben* sich teilen divide ◊ *Im Delta teilt sich der Fluß in viele verschiedene Arme.*
Teil·ha·ber ['taɪlhaːbɐ] *der* <-s, ->,
Teil·ha·be·rin ['taɪlhaːbərɪn] *die* <-, -nen> ECON partner ◊ *Er war geschäftsführender Teilhaber des Verlags.* stiller Teilhaber sleeping partner, silent partner
Teil·nah·me ['taɪlnaːmə] *die* <-, -n> *most sing* die Teilnahme (an etw. dat) participation (in sth) ◊ *Er hat seine Teilnahme an dem Wettkampf abgesagt.; (at lessons, courses)* attendance (at sth)

② **teil·neh·men** ['taɪlneːmən] <nimmt teil, nahm teil, hat teilgenommen> intr v (an etw. dat) teilnehmen take part (in sth) ◊ *Die Mannschaft wird nicht an der Weltmeisterschaft teilnehmen.* ♦ *Jeder, der Lust hat, kann teilnehmen.; (lessons, courses etc.)* attend (sth) ◊ *Unsere Tochter kann wegen Krankheit heute nicht am Unterricht teilnehmen.*

② **Teil·neh·mer** ['taɪlneːmɐ] *der* <-s, ->,
Teil·neh·me·rin ['taɪlneːmərɪn] *die* <-, -nen> Teilnehmer (... gen), Teilnehmer (an etw. dat) participant (in sth) ◊ *Die Teilnehmer an der Studie wurden zu ihrem Konsumverhalten befragt.; (in a competition)* contestant (in sth), competitor (in sth) ◊ *Die Teilnehmer des Rennens laufen sich bereits warm.*
teils [taɪls] adv **1.** teils ..., teils ... partly ..., partly ... ◊ *Die Zuschauer wirkten teils verärgert, teils amüsiert.* **2.** in part ◊ *Ich fand den Film teils ziemlich langatmig.* ⊜zum Teil, teilweise
◉ **teils, teils** yes and no
teil·wei·se ['taɪlvaɪzə] adj *only before ns* partial ◊ *Ziel ist die teilweise Automatisierung dieses Ablaufs.* adv in part ◊ *Es kam zu teilweise erheblichen Verkehrsbehinderungen.; (in expressions of time)* for part of the time ◊ *Das Wetter war teilweise ziemlich regnerisch.* ⊜teils
Teil·zeit·ar·beit ['taɪltsaɪtʔarbaɪt] *die* <-> *no pl* part-time work, part-time jobs
Tel. [tele'foːnnʊmɐ] *(abbr of* Telefonnummer) tel. ◊ *Reisebüro Fritsch, Tel. 783549*

② **Te·le·fon** ['teːləfoːn, tele'foːn] *das* <-s, -e> (tele)phone ◊ *Er griff zum Telefon und rief seine Frau an.* am Telefon on the (tele)phone ◊ *Du wirst am Telefon verlangt.* ans Telefon gehen answer the (tele)phone

When German people pick up the phone, they tend to answer by giving their surnames, upon which the caller identifies him-/herself. They often say *Auf Wiederhören!* before hanging up.

② **Te·le·fon·buch** [tele'foːnbuːx] *das* <-(e)s, Telefonbücher> (tele)phone book, telephone directory ◊ *Meine Nummer steht im Telefonbuch.*

② **te·le·fo·nie·ren** [telefo'niːrən] <telefoniert, telefonierte, hat telefoniert> intr v (mit jdm) telefonieren be on the (tele)phone (to sb) ◊ *Er telefoniert schon seit Stunden mit seiner Freundin.; (call by telephone)* mit jdm telefonieren phone sb ◊ *Ich habe in dieser Angelegenheit mehrmals mit ihm telefoniert.* ins Ausland telefonieren phone abroad
te·le·fo·nisch [tele'foːnɪʃ] adj, adv *no comp/*

A B C D E F G H I J K L M N O P Q R S T U V W X Y Z

superl; when used as an adj, only before ns by (tele)phone ◊ *Termine nur nach telefonischer Voranmeldung.* ♦ *Sie haben mir telefonisch zugesagt.*

ⓩ **Te·le·fon·ka·bi·ne** [tele'fo:nka,bi:nə] die <-, -n> (tele)phone box, telephone kiosk, call box, (tele)phone booth ⊜Telefonzelle

ⓩ **Te·le·fon·kar·te** [tele'fo:nkaʳtə] die <-, -n> **1.** *(for mobile phones)* prepaid card, phonecard ◊ *ein Handy mit wiederaufladbarer Telefonkarte* **2.** *(for public phones)* phonecard ◊ *Wie viel Guthaben ist auf der Telefonkarte noch drauf?*

Te·le·fon·num·mer [tele'fo:nnʊmɐ] die <-, -n> telephone number ◊ *Informationen erhalten Sie unter folgender Telefonnummer: ...*

Te·le·fon·rech·nung [tele'fo:nrɛçnʊŋ] die <-, -en> (tele)phone bill

ⓩ **Te·le·fon·wert·kar·te** [tele'fo:nve:ɐ̯tkaʳtə] die <-, -n> *(Austr, form)* → Telefonkarte²

ⓩ **Te·le·fon·zel·le** [tele'fo:ntsɛlə] die <-, -n> (tele)phone box, telephone kiosk, call box, (tele)phone booth ◊ *Er hat von einer Telefonzelle aus angerufen.* ⊜Telefonkabine

ⓩ **Tel·ler** ['tɛlɐ] der <-s, -> plate ◊ *Sie häufte sich Kartoffeln und Gemüse auf den Teller.* ♦ *Sie aß zwei Teller Suppe.*

Tem·pel ['tɛmpl̩] der <-s, -> temple

Tem·pe·ra·ment [tɛmpəra'mɛnt] das <-(e)s, -e> **1.** temperament ◊ *Sie hat ein ausgesprochen cholerisches Temperament.* **2.** *no pl (lively disposition)* spirit ◊ *Er hat überhaupt kein Temperament.* vor Temperament sprühen be full of enthusiasm, be a real livewire

 ⊛ jds Temperament geht mit ihm durch sb loses his/her etc. temper

tem·pe·ra·ment·voll [tɛmpəra'mɛntfɔl] *[adj, adv]* exuberant(ly) ◊ *Meine Tochter ist ziemlich temperamentvoll.* ♦ *ein temperamentvolles Pferd* ♦ *Die Mannschaft spielte sehr temperamentvoll.*

ⓩ **Tem·pe·ra·tur** [tɛmpəra'tu:ɐ̯] die <-, -en> **1.** temperature ◊ *die Temperatur messen* ♦ *Die Temperatur lag knapp über dem Gefrierpunkt.* **2.** *no pl* MED a temperature ◊ *Er hat Temperatur.*

Tem·po ['tɛmpo] das <-s, -s> **1.** tempo, speed ◊ *das Tempo beschleunigen* **2.** speed limit ◊ *In diesem Wohnviertel gilt Tempo 30.*

 ⊛ Tempo *(fam)* hurry up, get a move on

Tem·po-30-Zo·ne [,tɛmpo'draɛsɪçtso:nə] die <-, -n> 30 kph zone ◊ *Das Gebiet um die Schule herum wurde zur Tempo-30-Zone erklärt.*

Tem·po·li·mit ['tɛmpo,lɪmɪt] das <-s, -s> speed limit ◊ *das Tempolimit überschreiten*

Ten·denz [tɛn'dɛnts] die <-, -en> trend ◊ *Die Tendenz geht dahin, ...;* *(inclination)* tendency ◊ *Er hat die Tendenz, verschwenderisch mit Geld umzugehen.*

ten·den·zi·ell [tɛndɛn'tsiɛl] *[adj]* *no comp/superl, only before ns* overall ◊ *eine tendenzielle Verschlechterung der Marktsituation* *[adv]* on the whole ◊ *eine tendenziell positive Entwicklung*

ten·die·ren [tɛn'di:rən] <tendiert, tendierte, hat tendiert> *[intr v]* zu etw. tendieren tend towards sth ◊ *„Welches Bild sollen wir nehmen?" — „Ich tendiere ehrlich zu diesem hier."* dazu tendieren, etw. zu tun tend to do sth ◊ *Ich tendiere dazu, ihr Recht zu geben.;* *(newspaper etc.)* irgendwohin tendieren be biased towards a certain direction,

lean towards a certain direction

 ⊛ gegen Null tendieren → Null

ⓩ **Ten·nis** ['tɛnɪs] das <-> *mostly used without the article, no pl* tennis ◊ *Sie spielt hervorragend Tennis.*

ⓩ **Tep·pich** ['tɛpɪç] der <-s, -e> carpet ◊ *ein mit Teppich ausgelegtes Zimmer,* *(smaller)* rug ◊ *Vor dem Kamin lag ein kostbarer Teppich.*

 ⊛ auf dem Teppich bleiben *(fam)* keep your feet on the ground

Tep·pich·bo·den ['tɛpɪçbo:dn̩] der <-s, Teppichböden> fitted carpet

ⓩ **Ter·min** [tɛɐ̯'mi:n] der <-s, -e> **1.** date ◊ *Die Ware wurde zum vereinbarten Termin geliefert.;* *(time limit)* deadline ◊ *den festgelegten Termin überschreiten* **2.** appointment ◊ *Um neun Uhr habe ich einen Termin beim Zahnarzt.*

Ter·min·ka·len·der [tɛɐ̯'mi:nka,lɛndɐ] der <-s, -> diary, datebook

Ter·rain [tɛ'rɛn, tɛ'rɛ̃:] das <-s, -s> *(also fig)* territory ◊ *auf heimischem Terrain* ♦ *Damit kenne ich mich nicht aus, das gehört nicht zu meinem Terrain.*

 ⊛ das Terrain sondieren **1.** *(fig)* sound things out, test the waters **2.** MIL reconnoitre the area

ⓩ **Ter·ras·se** [tɛ'rasə] die <-, -n> **1.** patio, terrace ◊ *Bei schönem Wetter grillen wir auf der Terrasse.* **2.** terrace ◊ *Reis auf bewässerten Terrassen anbauen*

Ter·ror ['tɛro:ɐ̯] der <-s> *no pl* **1.** terror ◊ *der Kampf gegen den internationalen Terror* ♦ *Sie verbreiteten Angst und Terror.* **2.** *(fam)* trouble ◊ *Wenn ich zu spät komme, macht mein Vater Terror.* ⊜Krach

Tes·ta·ment [tɛsta'mɛnt] das <-(e)s, -e> will ◊ *sein Testament machen*

tes·ten ['tɛstn̩] *[tr v]* +haben test ◊ *Neue Produkte werden getestet, bevor sie auf den Markt kommen.* ⊜prüfen

ⓩ **teu·er** ['tɔɥɐ] *[adj]* <teurer, am teuersten> <der/die/das teure ...> **1.** expensive ◊ *Er fährt ein teures Auto.* ♦ *Das Benzin ist schon wieder teurer geworden.* ⊜billig **2.** *(lofty, outd or hum)* dear ◊ *Da hast du Unrecht, teurer Freund!* ♦ *Seine Freiheit ist ihm lieb und teuer.* *[adv]* **1.** (für) etw. teuer bezahlen pay a high price for sth ◊ *Er hat (für) seine Dummheit teuer bezahlen müssen.* teuer erkauft bought at a high price **2.** at a high price ◊ *Sie konnten ihr altes Auto noch teuer verkaufen.*

 ⊛ jdn/jdm teuer zu stehen kommen cost sb dear

Teu·fel ['tɔɥfl̩] der <-s, -> **1.** *no pl* REL der Teufel the Devil, Satan ◊ *Man glaubte, sie sei vom Teufel besessen.* **2.** *(evil spirit)* demon ◊ *Wie von tausend Teufeln gehetzt stürzte er davon.* **3.** monster, devil ◊ *Das Kind ist ein wahrer Teufel.* ⊜Ungeheuer **4.** armer Teufel poor devil

 ⊛ den Teufel mit (dem) Beelzebub austreiben replace one evil with another der Teufel steckt im Detail it's always the little things that cause all the problems in Teufels Küche kommen *(fam)* get into a/one hell of a mess den Teufel an die Wand malen *(fam)* invite disaster, tempt fate hol's der Teufel bloody hell hol dich/ihn etc. der Teufel *(fam)* damn you/him etc. der Teufel ist los *(fam)* all hell is let loose auf Teufel

komm raus *(fam)* at no matter what cost **jdn reitet der/ein Teufel** *(fam)* sth gets into sb ◊ *Welcher Teufel hat dich denn geritten, als du ihm das erlaubt hast?* **des Teufels sein** *(fam)* be mad, have taken leave of your senses **zum/beim Teufel sein** *(fam)* be ruined, have had it **weiß der Teufel** *(fam)* God knows **den Teufel** *(fam, emph)* like hell ◊ *„Hat sie es zurückgezahlt?" — „Den Teufel hat sie!"* **pfui Teufel** *(fam, emph)* yuck, how disgusting **wie der Teufel** like the devil **zum Teufel** *(fam, emph)* **1.** (to) hell ◊ *Zum Teufel, jetzt ist es kaputt!* **wo zum Teufel** where the hell **woher/wie zum Teufel** how the hell ◊ *Woher zum Teufel soll ich denn das wissen?* **2.** jdn **zum Teufel wünschen** tell sb to go to hell

Teu·fels·kreis ['tɔɸfl̩skraɛs] der <-es, -e> *most sing* vicious circle ◊ *Sie versuchten, den Teufelskreis aus Armut und Krankheit zu durchbrechen.*

② **Text** [tɛkst] der <-(e)s, -e> text ◊ *einen Text verfassen/überarbeiten* ◆ *Die Zeitung druckte den kompletten Text der Regierungserklärung ab.*; *(of a play, film etc.)* script; *(of a song)* lyrics, words ◉ **weiter im Text** *(fam)* carry on

Tex·ti·li·e [tɛks'tiːliə] die <-, -n> textile ◊ *synthetische Textilien*

Text·ver·ar·bei·tung ['tɛkstfɛɐʔaˈbaɛtʊŋ] die <-, -en> word processing

TH [teːˈhaː] die *(abbr of* Technische Hochschule*)* technological university ◊ *Sie hat Informatik an der TH studiert.*

② **The·a·ter** [teˈaːtɐ] das <-s, -> **1.** theatre, theater ◊ *Er ist Schauspieler am Theater.* ◆ *Wir gehen heute ins Theater.* **Theater spielen** act **2.** ensemble ◊ *Das Theater ging auf Tournee.* **3.** *no pl (fam, pej)* fuss ◊ *Jetzt mach doch nicht so ein Theater wegen dem bisschen Arbeit!* ⊖Zirkus **4.** *no pl (fam, pej)* play-acting ◊ *Sie hat nicht wirklich geweint, das war nur Theater.* ⊖Show, Komödie

The·a·ter·stück [teˈaːtɐʃtʏk] das <-(e)s, -e> (stage) play ◊ *ein Theaterstück aufführen*

The·ke ['teːkə] die <-, -n> **1.** bar ◊ *Der Wirt stand hinter der Theke.* ⊖Tresen **2.** counter ◊ *Das Kind legte das Geld auf die Theke.* ⊖Tresen

② **The·ma** ['teːma] das <-s, Themen> **1.** subject, topic ◊ *Das Buch befasst sich mit dem Thema Rechtsextremismus.* ◆ *Über welche Themen habt ihr gesprochen?* **2.** theme ◉ **kein Thema sein 1.** *(fam)* go without saying **2.** not be an issue

Them·se ['tɛmzə] die <-> *no pl (always* die Themse*)* the Thames ◊ *eine Wohnung mit Blick auf die Themse*

The·o·lo·ge [teoˈloːgə] der <-n, -n>, **The·o·lo·gin** [teoˈloːgɪn] die <-, -nen> theologian ◊ *Sie ist Theologin.* ◆ *Dem Theologen wurde die kirchliche Lehrerlaubnis entzogen.*

The·o·rie [teoˈriː] die <-, -n> theory ◊ *die Integration in Theorie und Praxis* **eine Theorie über etw.** [acc]/**zu etw.** a theory about sth Theorie einer Sache [gen] theory of sth ◊ *Grundlagen und Theorie der Elektrotechnik* ◉ **graue Theorie** pure theory

The·ra·peut [teraˈpɔɥt] der <-en, -en>, **The·ra·peu·tin** [teraˈpɔɥtɪn] die <-, -nen> therapist ◊ *Sie ist Therapeutin für Suchterkrankungen.* ◆ *einen Therapeuten aufsuchen*

Ther·me ['tɛɐmə] die <-, -n> **1.** spa ◊ *Wir verbringen den Tag in der Therme.* **2.** *only pl (Roman)* bath

Ther·mo·me·ter [tɛɐmoˈmeːtɐ] das <-s, -> thermometer ◊ *Das Thermometer ist auf unter null Grad gefallen.* ◆ *Das Thermometer steht auf 25°C.*

The·se ['teːzə] die <-, -n> thesis, theory ◊ *eine These aufstellen/vertreten/beweisen*

Tun·fisch ['tuːnfɪʃ] der <-(e)s, -e> tuna ◊ *eine Dose Tunfisch in Öl*

Thü·rin·gen ['tyːrɪŋən] das <-s> *article only in combination with attribute, no pl* Thuringia box@ Land

> Area: 16,172 km²; population: approx. 2.43 million; regional capital: Erfurt.
> Thuringia was newly founded after German reunification in 1990. It is a richly wooded region that offers a lot of leisure time possibilities. It is a leading region in industrial terms, being the centre of German car manufacturing, microelectronics and optoelectronics. With its cities of Weimar, Jena and Eisenach as historical and cultural centres, the region also has a lot to offer in cultural terms.

Thy·mi·an ['tyːmiaːn] der <-s, -e> thyme

ti·cken ['tɪkŋ̍] [intr v] +*haben* tick ◊ *Ist die Uhr stehen geblieben oder tickt sie noch?* ◉ **nicht richtig ticken** *(fam)* be off your rocker, have lost your marbles

② **Ti·cket** ['tɪkət] das <-s, -s> ticket ◊ *beim Einchecken am Flughafen sein Ticket vorlegen*

② **tief** [tiːf] [adj] **1.** deep ◊ *Das Auto blieb im tiefen Schnee stecken.* ◆ *ein 12 Meter tiefer See* ◆ *eine Glocke mit tiefem Klang* ◆ *Das Regal ist 30 Zentimeter tief.*; *(fall)* long **im tiefsten ... in the depths of (the) ...** ◊ *Das sind ja Zustände wie im tiefsten Mittelalter!* ◆ *Sie hatten sich im tiefsten Wald verirrt.* **aus tiefstem Herzen/tiefster Seele** from the bottom of your heart/soul **in tiefer/tiefster Nacht** in the dead of night **2.** *(clouds, air pressure, temperature etc.)* low ◊ *Das Kleid hat einen tiefen Ausschnitt.* ◆ *In tieferen Lagen schmilzt jetzt schon der Schnee.* ◆ *Die Schuhabteilung ist zwei Etagen tiefer.* ⊖niedrig ⊖hoch **3.** *(feelings, crisis, sleep etc.)* deep ◊ *Die Nachricht stürzte sie in tiefe Verzweiflung.*; *(colours/colors also)* intense ◊ *Das Wasser war von einem tiefen Blau.* ⊖leicht [adv] **1.** *(also fig)* deep ◊ *Wenn wir noch tiefer graben, stoßen wir bald auf Wasser.* ◆ *Sie war tief in Gedanken versunken.* **bis tief in die Nacht** until deep into the night **tief gehend/greifend** profound ◊ *tief greifende Veränderungen* ◆ *tiefer gehende Kenntnisse* **tief sitzend/verwurzelt** deep-seated, deep-rooted **2.** low ◊ *Der Hubschrauber flog sehr tief.* **tief hängende Wolken/Zweige** low-hanging clouds/branches **ein tief ausgeschnittenes Kleid** a low-cut dress ⊖hoch **3.** deeply ◊ *Er war tief beeindruckt/gekränkt.* ◆ *tief durchatmen* ◉ **tief schürfend** *(fam)* profound

Tief [tiːf] das <-s, -s> low, depression ◊ *ein Tief über Norddeutschland* ⊖Hoch

Tie·fe ['tiːfə] die <-, -n> **1.** depth(s) ◊ *in die Tiefe stürzen* ◆ *Der See hat eine Tiefe von 100 Metern.* ◆ *in den Tiefen des Meeres* ◆ *Höhe, Breite und Tiefe eines Regals* ⊖Höhe **2.** *(fig)* die Tiefe ... [gen] the

depth of sth, the profundity of sth ◊ *Die Tiefe seiner Verzweiflung ist unermesslich.*

Tief·ga·ra·ge ['tiːfgaˌraːʒə] die <-, -n> underground car park, underground parking lot ◊ *Wir haben in der Tiefgarage des Supermarkts geparkt.*

② **Tier** [tiːɐ̯] das <-(e)s, -e> **1.** *(also pej)* animal ◊ *wilde Tiere* ♦ *Widerlich! Er benimmt sich wie ein Tier!*; *(domestic)* pet ◊ *Wir dürfen in unserer Wohnung keine Tiere halten.* **2.** *(fam)* ein hohes/ großes Tier a big shot/noise

⊚ zum Tier werden lose control, go wild

Tier·arzt ['tiːɐ̯ˌʔaːɐ̯t͡st] der <-(e)s, Tierärzte>, **Tier·ärz·tin** ['tiːɐ̯ˌʔɛɐ̯t͡stɪn] die <-, -nen> veterinary surgeon, vet ◊ *Ich muss mit dem Hund zum Tierarzt.* ♦ *Sie will Tierärztin werden.*

Tier·schutz·ver·ein ['tiːɐ̯ˌʃʊt͡sfɛˌʔaɛ̯n] der <-(e)s, -e> *society for the prevention of cruelty to animals*; *(in the UK)* ⊜RSPCA ◊ *Das Tierheim wird vom Tierschutzverein betrieben.*

til·gen ['tɪlɡn̩] [tr v] +haben **1.** FIN *(debts, a loan etc.)* pay off ◊ *einen Kredit innerhalb von drei Jahren tilgen* **2.** *(lofty)* *(shame, traces etc.)* wipe out ◊ *Diese Schuld kann nicht getilgt werden.*; *(text, faults etc.)* delete

Tin·te ['tɪntə] die <-, -n> ink ◊ *mit Tinte schreiben*

⊚ in der Tinte sitzen *(fam)* be in the soup

② **Tipp** [tɪp] der <-s, -s> *(fam)* tip ◊ *jdm einen (guten) Tipp geben* ♦ *Wie lautet dein Tipp für die Wahlen/das Rennen?*

② **tip·pen** ['tɪpm̩] [tr+intr v] +haben *(fam)* type ◊ *am Computer (einen Brief) tippen* [intr v] +haben **1.** +direction tap ◊ *Er tippte sich an die Stirn und sagte: „Du spinnst wohl?"* **2.** *(fam)* jd tippt auf jdn/etw. sb's bet is on sb/sth ◊ *Ich tippe auf 4:5 für Brasilien.* jd tippt darauf, dass sb's bet is that ◊ *Er tippt darauf, dass die Aktie steigt.*; *(the person, animal or thing to win a contest)* auf jdn/etw. tippen tip sb/sth to win ◊ *„Wer wird gewinnen?" — „Ich tippe auf Lance Armstrong."* **3.** *(fam)* do the pools/lottery ◊ *Hast du letzte Woche getippt?*

Tipp·feh·ler ['tɪpˌfeːlɐ] der <-s, -> typing error/ mistake ◊ *Die E-Mail war voller Tippfehler.*

② **Tisch** [tɪʃ] der <-(e)s, -e> **1.** table ◊ *Sie setzten sich an den Tisch und begannen zu essen.* ♦ *im Restaurant einen Tisch bestellen* **2.** bei Tisch at (the) table vor/nach Tisch before/after sb eats zu Tisch (gehen) go to lunch/dinner etc. ◊ *Er ist gerade zu Tisch. Zu Tisch! Dinner/Lunch etc. is ready!*

⊚ (bar) auf den Tisch *(fam)* in cash am grünen Tisch, vom grünen Tisch aus in theory, theoretically am runden Tisch in round-table talks ◊ *etw. am runden Tisch verhandeln* etw. unter den Tisch fallen lassen *(fam)* let sth go by the board etw. vom Tisch fegen/wischen *(fam)* brush sth aside auf den Tisch hauen *(fam)* take a hard line reinen Tisch machen *(fam)* come clean, sort things out ◊ *Er machte reinen Tisch und gestand ihr alles.* vom Tisch sein *(fam)* be out of the question ◊ *Diese Pläne sind wegen des Geldmangels fürs Erste vom Tisch.* sich (mit jdm) an einen Tisch setzen sit round a table (with sb) jdn über den Tisch ziehen *(fam)* outmanoeuvre sb

Tisch·ler ['tɪʃlɐ] der <-s, ->, **Tisch·le·rin** ['tɪʃlərɪn] die <-, -nen> carpenter, cabinetmaker ◊ *einen Schrank beim Tischler bauen lassen* ♦ *Sie arbeitet als Tischlerin.* ⊜Schreiner

Tisch·ten·nis ['tɪʃˌtɛnɪs] das <-> article only in combination with attribute, no pl table tennis, ping-pong ◊ *In der Pause spielen wir gern eine Runde Tischtennis.*

② **Ti·tel** ['tiːtl̩, 'tɪtl̩] der <-s, -> **1.** title ◊ *Das Buch trug den Titel „Erinnerungen".* ♦ *einen Titel gewinnen/verteidigen* ♦ *Er wurde mit dem Titel „Sportler des Jahres" ausgezeichnet.* **2.** *(piece of music)* number ◊ *Dieser Titel wird zurzeit sehr oft im Radio gespielt.*

Ti·tel·sei·te ['tiːtl̩ˌzaɛ̯tə, 'tɪtl̩ˌzaɛ̯tə] die <-, -n> **1.** front page ◊ *Mit diesem Skandal geriet sie wieder auf die Titelseiten.* **2.** title page ◊ *Auf der Titelseite des Buches war ein Vogel abgebildet.*

tja [tja(ː)] [interj] *(fam)* mostly at the beginning of a sentence well, yes ◊ *Tja, nun, was soll man dazu sagen?* ♦ *Tja, so ist das nun mal.*

to·ben ['toːbm̩] [intr v] +haben/sein **1.** +haben rage ◊ *„Der kann was erleben!", tobte sie.*; *(be very angry)* go mad ◊ *Deine Eltern werden toben, wenn sie das erfahren.*; *(with excitement)* +over etw. [dat] toben go wild (with sth) ◊ *Das Publikum tobte vor Begeisterung.* **2.** +haben; with direction +sein charge about ◊ *Die Kinder tobten fröhlich im Garten.* **3.** +haben/with direction +sein *(fig)* *(war, storm etc.)* rage ◊ *Stundenlang tobte ein Orkan ums Haus.* ♦ *In der Hauptstadt toben Straßenkämpfe zwischen Demonstranten und Polizei.*

② **Toch·ter** ['tɔxtɐ] die <-, Töchter> daughter ⊜Sohn

② **Tod** [toːt] der <-es, -e> **1.** death ◊ *eines natürlichen/gewaltsamen Todes sterben* ♦ *Der Arzt konnte nur noch den Tod feststellen.* zu Tode kommen, den Tod finden die, lose your life (für jdn/etw.) in den Tod gehen die (for sb/sth) **2.** *(also fam, also emph)* zu Tode to death ◊ *ein Tier zu Tode hetzen/prügeln* ♦ *Ich langweile/friere mich hier noch zu Tode!* ♦ *Du hast mich zu Tode erschreckt!*

⊚ der schwarze Tod the Black Death jdn/etw. auf den Tod nicht ausstehen/leiden können *(fam, emph)* not be able to stand/abide sb/sth sich [dat] den Tod holen *(fam)* catch your death (of cold) des Todes sein *(lofty, oldf or hum)* be doomed tausend Tode sterben *(fam, emph)* die a thousand deaths

To·des·op·fer ['toːdəsˌʔɔpfɐ] das <-s, -> fatality, casualty ◊ *Unter den Todesopfern sind auch Kinder.* etw. forderte Todesopfer sth claimed lives

To·des·stra·fe ['toːdəsˌʃtraːfə] die <-, -n> death penalty ◊ *Auf Mord steht dort die Todesstrafe.*

tod·krank ['toːtˈkraŋk] [adj] no comp/superl critically ill ◊ *ein todkranker Mann* ♦ *Sie war damals schon todkrank.*

② **töd·lich** ['tøːtlɪç] [adj] **1.** *(injuries, illness etc.)* fatal ◊ *tödliche Verletzungen erleiden; (poison, bite, shot)* lethal, deadly ◊ *Der Biss dieser Schlange ist tödlich.* ♦ *Dann traf sie ein tödlicher Schuss.* **2.** *(also fam, also emph)* *(boredom, work etc.)* deadly ◊ *Es herrschte tödliche Langeweile.* ♦ *Diese stupide Arbeit ist einfach tödlich.* [adv] **1.** fatally ◊ *Die Krankheit verläuft oft tödlich.*; *(shot, poison)* lethally ◊ *tödlich verletzt werden* ♦

In dieser Dosis wirkt das Gift tödlich. tödlich verunglücken be killed in an accident **2.** *(emph)* sich tödlich langweilen be bored to death tödlich beleidigt/gekränkt sein be mortally insulted

② **To·i·let·te** [toaˈlɛtə] die <–, –n> **1.** *(also lofty)* toilet, lavatory, restroom ◊ *zur Toilette gehen* ♦ *Ich muss auf die Toilette.* ⊖Klo, WC **2.** *no pl: getting yourself ready* Toilette machen get yourself ready *die morgendliche/abendliche Toilette* getting yourself ready in the morning/for bed

To·i·let·ten·pa·pier [toaˈlɛtn̩paˌpiːɐ̯] das <–s, –e> toilet paper ◊ *eine Rolle Toilettenpapier* ⊖Klopapier

② **to·le·rant** [toləˈrant] [adj] <toleranter, am tolerantesten> tolerant (gegenüber jdm/etw.) tolerant (towards sb/sth) ◊ *Er ist sehr tolerant gegenüber Andersdenkenden.* ♦ *eine tolerante Haltung* ⊖aufgeschlossen, liberal

② **toll** [tɔl] *(fam)* [adj] **1.** great, fantastic ◊ *Ich finde es toll, wie er sich um die Kinder kümmert.* ♦ *Auf der Party war eine tolle Stimmung.* ⊖prima, super, klasse **2.** amazing, crazy ◊ *Das ist ja eine tolle Story, so etwas habe ich noch nie gehört!* ⊖wild [adv] fantastically, terrifically ◊ *Er kann ganz toll Klavier spielen.* ♦ *Das hast du toll gemacht!* ⊖prima, super, klasse

② **To·ma·te** [toˈmaːtə] die <–, –n> tomato ◊ *Als Vorspeise gab es Mozzarella mit Tomaten.* *Er wurde vor Scham rot wie eine Tomate.* He went bright red with embarrassment.

Ton¹ [toːn] der <–(e)s, Töne> **1.** tone, sound ◊ *ein hoher/tiefer Ton* ♦ *Im Gespräch wurden auch kritische Töne laut.* **2.** word ◊ *keinen Ton herausbringen* ♦ *Wenn du nur einen Ton gesagt hättest, hätte ich dir doch geholfen!* ⊖Wort **3.** MUS note ◊ *Er trifft beim Singen nie den Ton.* **4.** *no pl* sound ◊ *Kannst du bitte den Ton lauter stellen?* **5.** shade, tone ◊ *ein Gemälde in hellen/düsteren Tönen* ⊛ der Ton macht die Musik it's not what you say but the way you say it nur große Töne *(fam, pej)* just big talk große Töne spucken *(fam, pej)* talk big zum guten Ton gehören be considered good form, be de rigueur in den höchsten Tönen to the skies ◊ *jdn/etw.* in den höchsten Tönen loben den Ton angeben have the greatest say hast du Töne *(fam)* can you believe it Ton in Ton colour-coordinated, color-coordinated

Ton² [toːn] der <–(e)s, –e> *seldom with the article, most sing* clay ◊ *Die Ziegel sind aus gebranntem Ton.*

tö·nen [ˈtøːnən] [intr v] +*haben* **1.** *(sounds)* come ◊ *Aus den Lautsprechern tönte sanfte Musik.*; *(bells)* ring ◊ *Vom Kirchturm tönten die Glocken.* ⊖klingen **2.** *(fam, pej)* boast ◊ *Er tönt oft von seinen Erfolgen.* [tr v] +*haben (your hair)* tin, colour, color ◊ *Sie hat sich die Haare rot getönt.*

Ton·ne [ˈtɔnə] die <–, –n> **1.** drum, barrel ◊ *Auf dem Fabrikgelände lagern viele Tonnen mit Chemikalien.; (for rain water)* water butt ⊖Fass **2.** *(for rubbish)* bin ◊ *Der Restmüll kommt in die graue Tonne.* ⊖Mülltonne **3.** *(abbr t)* ton, tonne ◊ *Der Lkw wiegt 260 Tonnen.* **4.** *(fam, pej)* fatty

② **Topf** [tɔpf] der <–(e)s, Töpfe> **1.** saucepan ◊ *Setz bitte einen Topf Wasser auf.* ♦ *Hast du die ganzen Topf Bohnen allein gegessen?; (for plants)* pot ◊ *Wir ziehen Küchenkräuter in Töpfen auf der Fensterbank.* **2.** jar ◊ *ein Topf (voll/mit) Honig/Schmalz*

3. potty ◊ *Tagsüber braucht er keine Windeln mehr, da geht er auf den Topf.* ⊛ in einen Topf werfen *(fam)* lump together

② **Top·fen** [ˈtɔpfn̩] der <–s> *no pl (SouthG, Austr)* ⊖*fromage frais* ◊ *Zum Nachtisch gab es einen mit Topfen und Marillen gefüllten Strudel.* ⊖Quark

Töp·fer [ˈtœpfɐ] der <–s, –>, **Töp·fe·rin** [ˈtœpfərɪn] die <–, –nen> potter ◊ *Er hat eine Lehre als Töpfer gemacht.* ♦ *Die Töpferin formte Vasen und Schalen.*

Tor [toːɐ̯] das <–(e)s, –e> **1.** SPORT goal ◊ *Das erste Tor fiel in der 32. Minute.* ♦ *Wer steht bei euch heute im Tor?* ein Tor schießen score a goal **2.** gate ◊ *Die Tore des Zoos schließen um 18 Uhr.; (of a barn, garage etc.)* door ◊ *Das Tor der Garage schließt sich automatisch.* vor den Toren *... [gen]* just outside *...*, at the gates of *...*

Tor·hü·ter [ˈtoːɐ̯hyːtɐ] der <–s, –>, **Tor·hü·te·rin** [ˈtoːɐ̯hyːtərɪn] die <–, –nen> goalkeeper, goalie ◊ *Unsere Torhüterin lässt nur selten einen Ball durch.* ♦ *Der Stürmer scheiterte an Torhüter Oliver Kahn.* ⊖Torwart

Tor·te [ˈtɔʁtə] die <–, –n> gateau, cake ◊ *Gleich schneidet das Hochzeitspaar die Torte an.*

German gateaux are usually round and made from a combination of fine dough and whipped cream or butter cream, and are often decorated with fruit and/or nuts. Germany and Austria are famous for their delicious cream cakes. A well-known speciality is the *Sachertorte* (a rich iced chocolate cake) from Austria. On Sundays and bank holidays, many families have gateau or cake in the afternoon.

Tor·wart [ˈtoːɐ̯vaʁt] der <–(e)s, –e>, **Tor·war·tin** [ˈtoːɐ̯vaʁtɪn] die <–, –nen> goalkeeper, goalie ◊ *Er ist seit Jahren Torwart der Nationalmannschaft.* ♦ *Die Torwartin konnte den Ball nicht halten.* ⊖Torhüter

② **tot** [toːt] [adj] *no comp/superl* **1.** *(also fig)* dead ◊ *ein toter Fisch* ♦ *Sie wurde in ihrer Wohnung tot aufgefunden.* ♦ *Er hatte einen Unfall und war auf der Stelle tot.* ♦ *Mitten im Gespräch war das Telefon plötzlich tot.* tot geboren stillborn **2.** *(capital, knowledge)* useless ◊ *Wenn du aus deinen Fähigkeiten nichts machst, sind sie nur totes Kapital.* ⊛ halb tot vor etw. [dat] *(fam)* half dead with sth

to·tal [toˈtaːl] [adj, adv] *no comp/superl, mostly before ns (also fam)* total(ly), complete(ly) ◊ *Die Stadt wurde vom Erdbeben total zerstört.* ♦ *Er fühlte sich total überfordert.* ♦ *eine totale Sonnenfinsternis* ♦ *Es herrschte das totale Chaos.* ♦ *Der Ausflug war eine totale Pleite!* ⊖völlig, vollständig, absolut

to·ta·li·tär [totaliˈtɛːɐ̯] *(pej)* [adj] totalitarian ◊ *ein totalitäres Regime* ♦ *Unter Franco war Spanien totalitär.* ⊖demokratisch [adv] in a totalitarian way ◊ *Das Land wird totalitär regiert.* ⊖demokratisch

To·te [ˈtoːtə] der/die <–n, die Toten> *but: ein Toter/ eine Tote* dead person ◊ *Bei dem Unglück gab es 20 Tote.* die Toten the dead ◊ *An Allerseelen wird der Toten gedacht.* ⊛ von den Toten auferstanden sein *(fam, hum)* be back in the land of the living, be back from the

A B C D E F G H I J K L M N O P Q R S T U V W X Y Z

dead **wie ein Toter/eine Tote schlafen** *(fam)* sleep like a log

② **tö·ten** ['tøːtn̩] <tötet, tötete, hat getötet> ⟨tr+intr v⟩ kill ◊ *Er tötete das Reh mit einem Schuss.* ♦ *Sie wurde bei einem Unfall getötet.* ♦ *Wenn Blicke töten könnten, hätte ich das Gespräch nicht überlebt.*

Tö·tung ['tøːtʊŋ] die <-, –en> *most sing* **1.** killing ◊ *Aufgrund der Seuchengefahr wurde die Tötung der Schweine angeordnet.* **2.** LAW Tötung auf Verlangen euthanasia fahrlässige Tötung death by/ as a result of negligence

② **Tou·rist** [tu'rɪst] der <-en, –en>, **Tou·ris·tin** [tu'rɪstɪn] die <-, –nen> tourist ◊ *Das Festival lockt Touristen aus aller Welt an.*

Tour·nee [tʊr'neː] die <-, –n> tour ◊ *Die Sängerin will demnächst in den USA auf Tournee gehen.*

② **Tra·di·ti·on** [tradi'tsi̯oːn] die <-, –en> tradition ◊ *Unsere Firma kann auf eine hundertjährige Tradition zurückblicken.* Tradition sein/haben be a tradition ◊ *Diese Treffen haben in unserer Familie Tradition.*

tra·di·ti·o·nell [traditsi̯o'nɛl] ⟨adj, adv⟩ traditional(ly) ◊ *die traditionelle Rollenverteilung zwischen Mann und Frau* ♦ *Er ist viel zu träge traditioneller als Deutsche.* ♦ *traditionelle afrikanische Tänze* ♦ *Die Arbeiter im Ruhrgebiet wählten traditionell sozialdemokratisch.*

② **traf** [traːf] *pret of* treffen

② **Tra·fik** [tra'fɪk] die <-, –en> *(Austr)* kiosk ◊ *eine kleine Trafik am Bahnhof*

Tra·ge ['traːgə] die <-, –n> stretcher ◊ *Die Sanitäter brachten ihn auf einer Trage zum Krankenwagen.*

trä·ge ['trɛːgə] ⟨adj, adv⟩ <träger, am trägsten> lethargic(ally) ◊ *Er ist viel zu träge, um sich nach einer neuen Arbeitsstelle umzusehen.* ♦ *ein träger Kater*

② **tra·gen** ['traːgn̩] <trägt, trug, hat getragen> ⟨tr+intr v⟩ **1.** carry ◊ *Trag die Einkäufe bitte gleich in die Küche.* ♦ *Die Strömung trug das Boot ans andere Ufer.* ♦ *Hilfst du mir bitte tragen?* schwer zu tragen haben be carrying a heavy load schwer an etw./jdm zu tragen haben find sb/sth very heavy to carry, have difficulty carrying sb/sth aus der Kurve getragen werden go off the bend **2.** take the weight of, support ◊ *Meinst du, das Boot trägt so viele Leute?* das Eis trägt noch nicht the ice is not thick enough to skate/walk etc. on yet eine tragende Wand a supporting wall **3.** produce, yield ◊ *Die Sträucher tragen dieses Jahr viele Beeren.* ♦ *Wenn deine Arbeit Früchte tragen soll, musst du dich noch mehr anstrengen.* **4.** ZOO *(animals)* carry (their young) ◊ *Hunde tragen durchschnittlich 63 Tage.* ⟨tr v⟩ **1.** *(clothes, jewellery etc.)* wear ◊ *Sie trägt gerne auffälligen Schmuck.* ♦ *Er muss im Büro Anzug und Krawatte tragen.* Trauer tragen be dressed in mourning ⊖anhaben **2.** *(your hair, a beard etc.)* wear, have ◊ *Soll ich mein Haar offen tragen oder hochstecken?* **3.** etw. irgendwie tragen carry your sth a certain way ◊ *Sie trägt den Kopf immer noch stolz erhoben.* **4.** *(weapons, papers etc.)* etw. (bei sich ⟨dat⟩) tragen carry sth (with you) ◊ *Ich trage meinen Ausweis immer bei mir.* ⊖bei sich haben **5.** *(lofty) (a name, title, an inscription, address)* have, bear ◊ *Bei dem*

Rennen trug er die Nummer 19. ⊖haben **6.** *(consequences, responsibility etc.)* bear, take ◊ *Wenn du das tust, musst du auch die Folgen tragen.* (die) Schuld (an etw. ⟨dat⟩) tragen be to blame (for sth) ⊖übernehmen, haben **7.** *(costs, damage)* bear, carry ◊ *Gemeinde und Staat tragen die Kosten für den Bau der Straße gemeinsam.* ⊖aufkommen **8.** *(sth unpleasant)* etw. irgendwie tragen bear sth a certain way, take sth a certain way ◊ *Trag's mit Fassung!* ♦ *Sie trägt ihr schweres Los mit Würde.* ⊖ertragen ⟨ref v⟩ **1.** *(lofty)* sich mit einer Sache tragen be contemplating sth ◊ *Sie tragen sich schon längere Zeit mit dem Gedanken, auszuwandern.* **2.** *(clothing, fabrics)* sich ... tragen be ... to wear ◊ *Seide trägt sich sehr angenehm.* **3.** sich (selbst) tragen cover your (own) costs ⓔ etw. zu tragen haben have sth to bear an etw. ⟨dat⟩ **(schwer)** zu tragen haben struggle with sth, find sth hard to bear zum Tragen kommen be effective ◊ *Die neue Regelung soll ab sofort zum Tragen kommen.* *(advantage, improvement)* become apparent

Trä·ger¹ ['trɛːgɐ] der <-s, –> **1.** strap ◊ *Ein Träger ihres Kleides war von der Schulter gerutscht.* **2.** *(for a bridge, roof etc.)* beam, girder ◊ *Die Konstruktion wird von zehn Trägern gestützt.* ⊖Pfeiler **3.** *(on a vehicle)* carrier ◊ *Das Boot transportieren wir mit einem Träger auf dem Dach.* ⊖Gepäckträger

Trä·ger² ['trɛːgɐ] der <-s, –>, **Trä·ge·rin** ['trɛːgərɪn] die <-, –nen> **1.** maintaining institution Die katholische Kirche ist Trägerin des Altenheimes. The old people's home is financed by the Catholic Church. **2.** porter ◊ *Sie gab dem Träger ein paar Dollar Trinkgeld.* ♦ *Er arbeitet als Träger am Bahnhof.*; *(on expeditions)* carrier **3.** *(of a stretcher, coffin)* bearer **4.** wearer ◊ *Augentropfen für Träger von harten Kontaktlinsen* **5.** holder ◊ *die diesjährige Trägerin des Friedensnobelpreises*; *(of a name, title etc.)* bearer; *(of genetic information, a virus etc.)* carrier ◊ *Gene sind die Träger der Erbinformation.*

tra·gisch ['traːgɪʃ] ⟨adj⟩ **1.** tragic ◊ *Er kam auf tragische Weise ums Leben.* ♦ *Am Ende muss der tragische Held des Romans scheitern. Sein Tod war tragisch für das ganze Land. His death was a tragedy for the whole land.* **2.** *(fam)* nicht (so) tragisch sein not be the end of the world ⟨adv⟩ **1.** tragisch enden/ausgehen end in tragedy, have a tragic end, end tragically **2.** *(fam)* etw. tragisch nehmen take sth seriously, take sth to heart

Tra·gö·die [tra'gøːdi̯ə] die <-, –n> tragedy ◊ *die Tragödie von Romeo und Julia* ♦ *Auf der Autobahn hat sich gestern eine Tragödie ereignet.*

② **trägt** [trɛːkt] *pres of* tragen

Trai·ner ['trɛːnɐ, 'trɛːnɐ] der <-s, –>, **Trai·ne·rin** ['trɛːnərɪn, 'trɛːnərɪn] die <-, –nen> coach, trainer ◊ *Der Verein hat für die nächste Saison einen neuen Trainer verpflichtet.* ♦ *als Trainerin arbeiten*

② **trai·nie·ren** [trɛ'niːrən, trɛ'niːrən] <trainiert, trai­nierte, hat trainiert> ⟨tr+intr v⟩ **1.** train ◊ *Wir haben hart für den Wettkampf trainiert.* ♦ *Übungen, mit denen man sein Gedächtnis trainieren kann* **2.** jdn/ mit jdm trainieren coach sb, train sb ◊ *Sie trainiert unsere Jugendmannschaft.*

② **Trai·ning** ['trɛːnɪŋ, 'trɛːnɪŋ] das <-s, –s> *most sing*

1. training ◊ *Er hat sich beim Training verletzt.* ✦ *Durch gezieltes Training können Rückenschmerzen verringert werden.* **2.** autogenes Training autogenic training

Trak·tor ['traktoːɐ̯] der <–s, –en> tractor ◊ *mit dem Traktor aufs Feld fahren*

② **Tram** [tram] die <–, –s> (SouthG, Austr, Swiss) tram ◊ *Die Preise für Tram und Bus sind erhöht worden.* ⊜Straßenbahn

tram·peln ['trampl̩n] [intr v] +haben/sein **1.** +haben stamp (your feet) ◊ *Sie klatschten und trampelten vor Begeisterung mit den Füßen.* **2.** +sein (pej) trample ◊ *Pass auf, trampel mir nicht auf die Füße!* [tr v] +haben jdn zu Tode trampeln trample sb to death

Trä·ne ['trɛːnə] die <–, –n> tear ◊ *in Tränen ausbrechen* ✦ *Sie erzählte ihm unter Tränen, was passiert war.* ✦ *Der Anblick rührte mich zu Tränen.*
⊛ jdm/etw. keine **Träne nachweinen** (fam) not shed any tears over sb/sth

② **trank** [traŋk] pret of trinken

tran·si·tiv ['tranzitiːf] [adj, adv] no comp/superl; when used as an adj, only before ns (verb) transitive(ly) ◊ *der transitive Gebrauch eines Verbs* ✦ *Manche Verben können sowohl intransitiv wie auch transitiv gebraucht werden.* ⊜intransitiv

② **Trans·port** [trans'pɔʁt] der <–(e)s, –e> **1.** transport(ation) ◊ *Die Ware wurde beim Transport beschädigt.* ✦ *der Transport von Tieren* **2.** consignment, shipment ◊ *Der erste Transport mit Hilfsgütern ist gestern angekommen.*

② **trans·por·tie·ren** [transpɔʁˈtiːʁən] <transportiert, transportierte, hat transportiert> [tr v] transport ◊ *Dieses Flugzeug transportiert Passagiere und Fracht.* [tr+intr v] (the film) wind on ◊ *Der Fotoapparat ist kaputt. Er transportiert (den Film) nicht.*

② **trat** [traːt] pret of treten

Trau·be ['traʊbə] die <–, –n> **1.** most pl grape ◊ *Es gibt weiße und blaue Trauben.* **2.** only pl bunch of grapes ◊ *An diesem Weinstock hängen viele Trauben.* **3.** (of people, objects etc.) bunch, cluster ◊ *Der Popstar hatte eine Traube von Fans um sich herum.* **4.** raceme

trau·en ['traʊən] [intr v] +haben jdm/einer Sache trauen trust sb/sth ◊ *Meinem Kollegen ist nicht zu trauen.* ✦ *Ich traue ihren Versprechungen nicht.* [ref v] +haben sich trauen dare ◊ *Traust du dich, von dieser Mauer zu springen?* Er traute sich nicht ins Wasser. He didn't dare go into the water. Trau dich, es kann nichts passieren. Be bold, nothing can happen. [tr v] +haben (registrar, priest etc.) jdn trauen marry sb ◊ *Dieser Pfarrer hat auch schon meine Eltern getraut.* sich trauen lassen get married

Trau·er ['traʊɐ] die <–> no pl **1.** grief, sorrow ◊ *die Trauer über den Tod eines geliebten Menschen* die Trauer um jdn the mourning for sb ⊜Freude **2.** mourning ◊ *Es wurde eine dreitägige Trauer angeordnet.* ✦ *Nach dem Tod ihres Mannes trug sie ein Jahr Trauer.*

trau·ern ['traʊɐn] [intr v] +haben um jdn trauern mourn for sb über etw. [acc] trauern mourn sth ◊ *Sie trauert über den Tod ihres Großvaters.*

② **Traum** [traʊm] der <–(e)s, Träume> dream ◊ *Im Traum sah er seine Mutter auf sich zukommen.* ✦ *Mein größter Traum ist es, den Mount Everest zu*

besteigen. ✦ *Diese Torte ist ein Traum aus Schokolade.* ✦ *ein Traum von einem Kleid*
⊛ **Träume sind Schäume** dreams are ephemeral nicht im Traum jd denkt nicht im Traum daran, etw. zu tun sb wouldn't dream of doing sth Es wäre ihm im Traum nicht eingefallen, dass sein Roman ein so großer Erfolg werden würde. He would never have dreamt that his novel would be such a great success.

② **Traum·...** [traʊm] [prefix] (fam) dream ..., ideal ... ◊ *Trauminsel* ✦ *Traumberuf* ✦ *Traumfrau*

② **träu·men** ['trɔʏmən] [tr+intr v] +haben dream ◊ *Du hast im Schlaf geschrien. Hast du schlecht geträumt?* ✦ *Er träumte, dass er durch die Prüfung gefallen sei.* von jdm/etw. träumen dream of sb/sth ◊ *In der Nacht träumte er von seinen Großeltern.* ✦ *Sie träumt davon, einmal in die Karibik zu fahren.* [intr v] +haben (be lost in a) daydream ◊ *Sie sah aus dem Fenster und träumte.*
⊛ sich [dat] etw. nicht/nie träumen lassen not/never have thought sth possible

② **trau·rig** ['traʊrɪç] [adj] **1.** (person, song, story) sad ◊ *traurige Menschen* ✦ *Dieses Lied macht mich traurig.* ✦ *Er war äußerst traurig über diese Nachricht.* ✦ *eine traurige Melodie* ✦ *Das Ende der Geschichte ist sehr traurig.* ⊜unglücklich ⊜fröhlich, froh **2.** pitiful, sad ◊ *eine traurige Gestalt* ✦ *Die Bilanz des Umweltgipfels ist eher traurig: ...* [adv] sadly ◊ *„Unsere Katze ist überfahren worden", sagte er traurig.* ✦ *Sie sah mich traurig an.* ⊜fröhlich

Trau·ung ['traʊʊŋ] die <–, –en> wedding (ceremony) ◊ *eine standesamtliche/kirchliche Trauung*

② **tref·fen** ['trɛfn̩] <trifft, traf, hat/ist getroffen> [tr+intr v] +haben hit ◊ *Der Pfeil traf genau/das Reh in den Hals.; (lightning)* strike ◊ *Der Baum wurde von einem Blitz getroffen.; (in a game of sports)* score ◊ *Nach einigen Torchancen traf er endlich zum 1:0.* [tr v] +haben **1.** jdn treffen, sich mit jdm treffen meet sb ◊ *Rate mal, wen ich getroffen habe!* ✦ *Sie traf sich mit ihrer Freundin in einem Restaurant.* sie treffen sich they meet (up) ◊ *Wir sollten uns mal wieder treffen.* **2.** etw. treffen capture sth ◊ *Sie treffen mit ihrer Musik genau den Zeitgeist.* jds Geschmack treffen be to sb's taste Der Maler hat ihn auf dem Porträt gut getroffen. The portrait is a good likeness of him. **3.** (feelings) hurt ◊ *Seine Worte haben mich tief getroffen.* ⊜verletzen **4.** affect ◊ *Die wirtschaftliche Flaute hat auch uns getroffen.* **5.** empty verb make, take ◊ *Maßnahmen/Vorbereitungen treffen* eine Anordnung treffen give an order **6.** es mit etw./jdm gut/schlecht treffen be lucky/unlucky with sth/sb ◊ *Mit meinem neuen Job/Chef habe ich es gut getroffen.* [intr v] +sein **1.** auf jdn/etw. treffen encounter sb/sth, come across sb/sth ◊ *Auf dem Straßenfest trafen wir auf meine Eltern.* ✦ *Nach einer Weile trafen wir auf eine breite Straße.* **2.** SPORT auf jdn treffen meet sb ◊ *Gleich in der ersten Runde trafen sie auf den Titelverteidiger.* [imp v] +haben es trifft sich gut, dass it is convenient that ◊ *Es trifft sich gut, dass du anrufst.*

Tref·fen ['trɛfn̩] das <–s, –> meeting ◊ *In Florenz fand ein Treffen der EU-Umweltminister statt.* ✦ *Das hat er mir bei unserem letzten Treffen erzählt.*

tref·fend ['trɛfn̩t, 'trɛfənt] [adj] apt, appropriate ◊ *eine treffende Beschreibung* ♦ *Die Bezeichnung war treffend.* [adv] aptly, in an apt manner, appropriately ◊ *etw. treffend bemerken/formulieren*

Treff·punkt ['trɛfpʊŋkt] der <–(e)s, –e> rendezvous, meeting place ◊ *Diese Kneipe ist ein beliebter Treffpunkt für Studenten.* ♦ *Er kam nicht zu dem vereinbarten Treffpunkt.*

⃝ **trei·ben** ['traɛbm̩] <treibt, trieb, hat/ist getrieben> [tr v] +*haben* **1.** +*direction* jdn/etw. irgendwohin treiben drive sb/sth somewhere ◊ *Es war schon dunkel, als sie die Tiere nach Hause trieben.* ♦ *Sie trieben die Pfosten für einen Zaun in den Boden. Die Strömung trieb das Boot aufs offene Meer hinaus.* The current took the boat out to sea. **2.** jdn zu etw. treiben drive sb to sth ◊ *Du treibst mich zur Verzweiflung!* jdn in den/zum Wahnsinn treiben drive sb mad jdn zur Weißglut treiben make sb apoplectic **3.** jdn dazu treiben, etw. zu tun drive sb to do sth ◊ *Ihr Ehrgeiz treibt sie dazu, das Abitur nachzuholen.* **4.** *(fam)* do ◊ *Was hast du am Wochenende getrieben?* **5.** *empty verb* Sport treiben do sport Handel treiben trade Schabernack/Unsinn treiben get up to all sorts of pranks/mischief Aufwand treiben be extravagant **6.** es zu schlimm/weit treiben go too far **7.** Knospen treiben bud **8.** etw. treiben drive sth ◊ *Die Maschine wird von Dampf getrieben.* [intr v] **1.** +*haben/sein* irgendwo treiben drift somewhere ◊ *Trockenes Laub trieb im Wind.; (in water also)* float somewhere **2.** +*sein and direction* irgendwohin treiben drift somewhere ◊ *Das Boot trieb aufs Meer und versank.* **3.** +*haben* bud ◊ *Der Apfelbaum treibt schon.*
⊛ **es mit jdm treiben** *(fam)* have it off with sb
Treib·stoff ['traɛpʃtɔf] der <–(e)s, –e> fuel ⊜Kraftstoff

⃝ **Trend** [trɛnt] der <–s, –s> trend ◊ *Wir hoffen, dass dieser positive Trend anhält.* ♦ *Es ist ein Trend zum Billigtourismus zu beobachten.*

⃝ **tren·nen** ['trɛnən] [tr v] +*haben* **1.** etw. von etw. trennen remove sth from sth, cut sth off sth ◊ *Trennen Sie das Fleisch vom Knochen.* **2.** separate ◊ *Ein Bach trennt die beiden Dörfer.* etw./jdn von etw./jdm trennen separate sth/sb from sth/sb ◊ *Diese Anlage trennt die festen von den flüssigen Stoffen.* ♦ *In dem Gedränge wurde das Kind von der Mutter getrennt.* ♦ *Wir wurden voneinander getrennt.* die Wahrheit von der Fiktion trennen distinguish between truth and fiction Uns trennen Welten! We are worlds apart! **3.** keep apart ◊ *Sie will ihre Arbeit und ihr Privatleben klar trennen.* [ref v] +*haben* **1.** sie trennen sich they part company ◊ *Wir stiegen gemeinsam aus dem Bus aus, dann trennten wir uns.* sich von jdm trennen split up with sb sich von etw. trennen leave sth ◊ *Er hat sich nach zehn Jahren von seiner Firma getrennt.* **2.** sich von etw. trennen part with sth ◊ *Ich werde mich wohl von meinem Auto trennen müssen.; (a bad idea etc.)* give sth up **3.** SPORT Die beiden Mannschaften trennten sich 1:0 It finished 1:0 between the two teams. Die beiden Mannschaften trennten sich unentschieden. It ended all square between the two sides. [tr+intr v] +*haben (a word)* divide ◊ *Wie trennt man „Zebra"?* am Zeilenende trennen split a word at the end of a line

⃝ **Trep·pe** ['trɛpə] die <–, –n> **1.** (flight of) stairs, staircase ◊ *Er ging die Treppe hinauf/hinunter.* ♦ *eine steile Treppe* **2.** floor ◊ *zwei Treppen über uns* ♦ *Müllers wohnen eine Treppe tiefer als wir.*

Trep·pen·haus ['trɛpm̩haɔs] das <–es, Treppenhäuser> stairwell, staircase im Treppenhaus on the stairs

Tre·sen ['tre:zn̩] der <–s, –> **1.** bar ◊ *Er saß am Tresen und trank ein Bier.* ⊜Theke **2.** counter ◊ *Auf dem Tresen des Reisebüros lagen bunte Broschüren.*

Tre·sor [tre'zo:ɐ̯] der <–s, –e> safe

⃝ **tre·ten** ['tre:tn̩] <tritt, trat, hat/ist getreten> [tr+intr v] +*haben* **1.** kick ◊ *Voller Zorn trat er gegen die Schranktür.* ♦ *Sie trat ihren Bruder in den Hintern.* **2.** auf die Bremse treten brake die Kupplung treten depress the clutch; *(on a bicycle)* in die Pedale treten pump the pedals; *(on a piano)* das Pedal treten depress the pedal [tr v] +*haben* **1.** Sie hat ihre Brille kaputt getreten. She trod on her glasses. etw. in etw. [acc] treten kick sth in sth ◊ *Er trat ein Loch in die Tür.* Irgendjemand hat eine Delle in mein Auto getreten. Someone has kicked my car and put a dent in it. **2.** *(a ball)* kick einen Eckball treten take a corner Er trat den Ball knapp neben das Tor. He shot just past the post. [intr v] +*sein/haben* **1.** +*sein* step ◊ *Er trat ins Freie.* ♦ *Treten Sie nach vorne.* ♦ *Sie trat ihm in den Weg.* **2.** +*sein* auf/in etw. [acc] treten tread on/in sth ◊ *in eine Scherbe treten* ♦ *Au! Du bist mir auf den Fuß getreten!* **3.** +*sein* in etw. [acc] treten enter into sth ◊ *in Verhandlungen treten* in Streik treten come out on strike in Funktion treten start operating **4.** +*haben* nach jdm/etw. treten aim a kick at sb/sth ◊ *Er trat nach dem Hund.* [ref v] *(injury)* sich [dat] etw. in etw. [acc] treten get sth stuck in sth ◊ *Sie hat sich einen Splitter in den Fuß getreten.*

⃝ **treu** [trɔø] [adj] <treuer, am treu(e)sten> **1.** loyal, devoted ◊ *ein treuer Freund* seinen Idealen treu bleiben remain true to your ideals; *(dog)* faithful **2.** faithful ◊ *eine treue Ehefrau* ♦ *Er kann einfach nicht treu sein.* ⊜untreu [adv] loyally ◊ *Er tut immer treu seine Pflicht.*

Treue ['trɔøə] die <–> *no pl* **1.** loyalty ◊ *Er hat seinem Verein immer die Treue gehalten.* ♦ *Wir bedanken uns bei unseren Kunden für ihre Treue.* **2.** faithfulness, fidelity ◊ *Er hatte Zweifel an ihrer Treue.* jdm Treue schwören vow to be faithful to sb ⊜Untreue

Tri·bü·ne [tri'by:nə] die <–, –n> **1.** *(in sports)* (grand)stand ◊ *Beim Endspiel saßen viele prominente Gäste auf der Tribüne.; (at a theatre)* seating in the auditorium **2.** *(at a conference)* rostrum ◊ *Der erste Redner betrat die Tribüne.*

Trich·ter ['trɪçtɐ] der <–s, –> **1.** funnel ◊ *Wasser mit Hilfe eines Trichters in eine Flasche gießen* **2.** crater ◊ *Die Bombe hinterließ einen Trichter von mehreren Metern Durchmesser.*
⊛ **auf den Trichter kommen** *(fam)* catch on

Trick [trɪk] der <–s, –s> **1.** trick ◊ *Der Zauberer verblüffte die Zuschauer mit seinen Tricks.* ♦ *Kaugummi kann man mit einem einfachen Trick von Kleidungsstücken entfernen.* **2.** *(a con man's)* ploy, dodge ◊ *Da bist du auf einen üblen Trick reingefallen.* ⊜Masche

Trick·film ['trɪkfɪlm] der <-(e)s, -e> animation (film), animated story; *(drawn also)* cartoon

ⓩ **trieb** [tri:p] *pret of* treiben

Trieb [tri:p] der <-(e)s, -e> **1.** urge, desire ◊ *Er hat einen zwanghaften Trieb zum Stehlen.* ✦ *Sie lässt sich von ihren Trieben bestimmen.* **2.** shoot ◊ *Bei dem Maifrost sind alle Triebe erfroren.*

ⓩ **trifft** [trɪft] *pres of* treffen

Tri·kot [tri'ko:] das <-s, -s> **1.** jersey, shirt ◊ *Nach dem Spiel tauschten die Spieler ihre Trikots.* **2.** leotard ◊ *ein Akrobat in einem roten Trikot*

ⓩ **trin·ken** ['trɪŋkn̩] <trinkt, trank, hat getrunken> [tr+intr v] drink ◊ *Er trank mit großen Schlucken.* ✦ *eine Tasse Kaffee trinken ◊ Kann ich bitte etwas zu trinken haben?* auf jdn/etw. trinken drink to sb/sth ◊ *Sie tranken ein Glas Sekt auf ihren Sohn.* ✦ *Sie tranken auf das Wohl der Braut.* [intr v] *(alcohol)* drink ◊ *Sie trinkt zu viel. Wenn sie getrunken hat, wird sie streitsüchtig.* When she's had a drink she gets argumentative.

ⓩ **Trink·geld** ['trɪŋkɡɛlt] das <-(e)s, -er> tip ◊ *ein großzügiges Trinkgeld geben*

> The service charge in Germany is included in the bill, but in restaurants and cafés it is customary to give an additional 10% or so as a tip. When small amounts are involved, for example when buying a coffee or paying for a taxi fare, the charge is rounded up. Only give a tip, however, if you are satisfied with the level of service.

Trink·was·ser ['trɪŋkvasɐ] das <-s, Trinkwässer> drinking water kein Trinkwasser not for drinking

ⓩ **tritt** [trɪt] *pres of* treten

Tritt [trɪt] der <-(e)s, -e> **1.** step ◊ *Er schritt mit festem Tritt zum Rednerpult. Er nahm zwei Stufen mit einem Tritt.* He bounded up two steps at once. **2.** kick ◊ *Sie versetzte ihm einen kräftigen Tritt ans Bein.* ⓔ **Tritt fassen** recover ◊ *Die Konjunktur hat wieder Tritt gefasst.*

tri·um·phie·ren [triʊm'fiːrən] <triumphiert, triumphierte, hat triumphiert> [intr v] +*haben* **1.** triumph ◊ *Am Ende triumphierte ein Außenseiter.* ✦ *Ihr Optimismus triumphierte über seinen Pessimismus.* **2.** rejoice ◊ *Er triumphierte, als seine Mannschaft die Meisterschaft gewann.* ⊜jubeln

ⓩ **tro·cken** ['trɔkn̩] [adj] **1.** dry ◊ *Zieh dir trockene Kleider an.* ✦ *sich* [dat] *die Haare trocken föhnen* ✦ *ein sehr trockener Sommer* ✦ *Er aß nur ein trockenes Brötchen.* ✦ *ein trockener Rotwein* ✦ *Ich finde Mathematik furchtbar trocken.* ✦ *Sein Humor ist sehr trocken.* Cornflakes/Frühstücksflocken trocken essen eat cornflakes/breakfast cereals without milk ein trockener Alkoholiker a dried out alcoholic **2.** no comp/superl *(fam) (small child)* potty-trained ◊ *Unser Jüngster ist noch nicht trocken.* [adv] **1.** Bitte trocken lagern. Please store in a dry environment. ⊜nass, feucht **2.** drily, in a dry manner ◊ *Er gestaltet seinen Unterricht sehr trocken.* ✦ *ein trocken abgefasster Bericht* **3.** *(joke etc.)* drily ◊ *Er sagte das so trocken, dass alle lachen mussten.* **4.** sich trocken rasieren use an electric razor ◊ *Rasierst du dich nass oder trocken?*

ⓩ **trock·nen** ['trɔknən] <trocknet, trocknete, hat/ist getrocknet> [tr v] +*haben* **1.** dry ◊ *Der Wind hat die Wäsche schnell getrocknet.* ✦ *Blumen trocknen* **2.** *(spilt liquid)* wipe, mop up ◊ *Er trocknete die verschüttete Milch von dem Buch.* [intr v] +*sein* dry ◊ *Diese Farbe trocknet ziemlich schnell.*

ⓩ **trö·deln** ['trøːdl̩n] [intr v] +*haben* dawdle ◊ *Katrin trödelte auf dem Weg zur Schule.* ✦ *Wie immer trödelte er beim Essen.* ⊜sich beeilen

Trom·mel ['trɔml] die <-, -n> **1.** MUS drum **2.** *(of a washing machine)* drum; *(of a revolver)* revolving breech

Trom·pe·te [trɔm'peːtə] die <-, -n> trumpet ◊ *Er spielt Trompete.* ✦ *Sie spielte ein Stück von Bach auf der Trompete.*

Tro·pen ['troːpn̩] die <-> only pl *(always die Tropen)* tropics

trop·fen ['trɔpfn̩] [tr v] +*haben* drip ◊ *Tropfen Sie das Medikament vorsichtig ins Auge.* [intr v] +*haben/sein* **1.** +*sein* drip ◊ *Der Honig tropft gleich vom Brötchen!* **2.** +*haben* be leaking ◊ *Der Boiler tropft.*

ⓩ **Trop·fen** ['trɔpfn̩] der <-s, -> **1.** drop ◊ *In meinem Auto ist kein Tropfen Benzin mehr.* ✦ *einige Tropfen Zitronensaft* **2.** only pl MED drops ◊ *Die Ärztin verschrieb ihm Tropfen gegen seinen Heuschnupfen.* ⓔ **ein Tropfen auf den heißen Stein sein** *(fam)* be a drop in the ocean

Trost [troːst] der <-(e)s> no pl comfort, consolation ◊ *Als/Zum Trost gab sie dem Kind ein paar Süßigkeiten.* ✦ *Er suchte Trost bei seiner Mutter.* jdm Trost zusprechen/spenden console sb, comfort sb etw. ist ein schwacher Trost sth is not much consolation ⓔ **nicht ganz/recht bei Trost sein** *(fam)* be out of your mind

trös·ten ['trøːstn̩] <tröstet, tröstete, hat getröstet> [tr v] comfort, console ◊ *Diese Worte werden ihn wohl kaum trösten.* ✦ *Er nahm sie in den Arm und tröstete sie.* sich mit etw./jdm trösten console yourself with sth/sb, get over sth with the help of sth/sb

ⓩ **Trot·toir** [trɔ'tŏaːr] das <-s, -e or -s> *(Swiss)* pavement

ⓩ **trotz** [trɔts] [prep] *sing nouns without article or attribute are not declined when following this prep, otherwise* [+gen] *or regional* [+dat] in spite of, despite ◊ *Trotz aller Kritik ist diese Fernsehsendung sehr beliebt.* ✦ *Wir haben trotz Regen und Sturm einen Spaziergang gemacht.*

ⓩ **trotz·dem** ['trɔtsdeːm] [adv] nevertheless, nonetheless, all the same ◊ *Wir sind sehr unterschiedlich, verstehen uns aber trotzdem gut.* ⊜dennoch

trot·zig ['trɔtsɪç] [adj, adv] defiant(ly) ◊ *eine trotzige Reaktion* ✦ *Unsere Tochter ist zurzeit sehr trotzig.* ✦ *„Das werde ich nicht tun!", sagte er trotzig.*

trüb [tryːp], **trü·be** ['tryːbə] [adj] <trüber, am trübsten> **1.** *(liquid)* cloudy ◊ *trüber Apfelsaft* ◊ *Die Linse ist trüb geworden.* ⊜klar **2.** *(light)* dim ◊ *im trüben Licht einer Laterne; (day etc.)* gloomy, dreary ◊ *ein trüber Novembertag* ✦ *Bis jetzt es ist nur trüb, es regnet aber noch nicht.* ⊜hell **3.** gloomy ◊ *trübe Gedanken* ✦ *Die Aussichten sind trübe.* ⊜heiter [adv] **1.** ein trübe beleuchteter Raum a dimly lit room ⊜hell **2.** gloomily ◊ *Er starrte trüb vor sich hin. Sie war trübe gestimmt.* She was in a gloomy mood. ⊜heiter

② **trug** [tru:k] *pret of* tragen

Tru·he ['tru:ə] die <-, –n> chest ◊ *eine hölzerne Truhe* ♦ *etw. in einer Truhe aufbewahren*

Trüm·mer ['trʏmɐ] die <-> *only pl* rubble, debris ◊ *die rauchenden Trümmer eines Gebäudes* in Trümmern liegen lie in ruins etw. in Trümmer legen reduce sth to rubble, flatten sth etw. in Trümmer schlagen smash sth to pieces

Trup·pe ['trʊpə] die <-, –n> **1.** unit *eine multinationale Truppe* a multinational force Truppen in einem Land stationieren station troops in a country Truppen aus einem Land abziehen withdraw troops from a country **2.** *no pl* troops ◊ *Die Truppe war demoralisiert.* **3.** *(performers)* troupe ◊ *eine Truppe mit zehn Tänzerinnen und Tänzern; (sportsmen)* team, squad **4.** *(fam)* group ◊ *eine Truppe unternehmungslustiger Leute*

Trut·hahn ['tru:tha:n] der <-(e)s, Truthähne>, **Pu·te** ['pu:tə] die <-, –n> turkey ◊ *Auf dem Bauernhof werden Puten gehalten.* ♦ *In Großbritannien isst man an Weihnachten Truthahn.*

Tsche·che ['tʃɛçə] der <-n, –n>, **Tsche·chin** ['tʃɛçɪn] die <-, –nen> Czech → Deutsche

Tsche·chi·en ['tʃɛçiən] das <-s> *article only in combination with attribute, no pl* Czech Republic → Deutschland

Tsche·chin ['tʃɛçɪn] *fem of* Tscheche

tsche·chisch ['tʃɛçɪʃ] [adj] *mostly before ns* Czech → deutsch

Tsche·chisch ['tʃɛçɪʃ] das <-(s)> *no pl* Czech → Deutsch

tschüs, tschüss [tʃy:s, tʃʏs] *(fam)* cheerio, bye ◊ *Tschüss, bis morgen!*

② **T-Shirt** ['ti:ʃœɐ̯t] das <-s, –s> T-shirt

TU [te:'u:] die *(abbr of* Technische Universität*)* ◊ *Sie studiert an der TU Dresden.*

Tu·be ['tu:bə] die <-, –n> tube ◊ *ein Tube Zahnpasta* ♦ *Senf aus der Tube*

② **Tuch**¹ [tu:x] das <-(e)s, Tücher> **1.** cloth, duster ◊ *Er nahm ein Tuch und wischte die verschüttete Milch auf.; (for washing-up)* dishcloth **2.** shawl, scarf ◊ *Sie hat sich ein Tuch um die Schultern gelegt.* ♦ *die Haare mit einem Tuch verhüllen* **3.** (dust)sheet ◊ *In der Fastenzeit werden alle Kreuze mit Tüchern verhüllt.* Sie wickelte ihr Kind in ein Tuch. She wrapped her child in a blanket.; *(for tables)* tablecloth

⊛ **ein rotes Tuch für jdn sein** *(fam)* be like a red rag to a bull to sb Dieser Politiker ist für viele ein rotes Tuch. This politician makes many people see red.

Tuch² [tu:x] das <-(e)s, –e> cloth, fabric ◊ *ein Mantel aus feinem Tuch* ⊖Stoff

tüch·tig ['tʏçtɪç] [adj] **1.** competent ◊ *eine tüchtige Geschäftsfrau* ♦ *Er ist sehr tüchtig in seinem Beruf.* **2.** *only before ns (fam)* huge, big ◊ *Er nahm einen tüchtigen Schluck.* eine tüchtige Tracht Prügel a mighty thrashing [adv] *(fam)* good and proper Das tut tüchtig weh. That really hurts. jdn tüchtig auslachen have a real good laugh at sb Greif tüchtig zu, es ist genügend da. Get stuck in, there is enough there.

Tü·cke ['tʏkə] die <-, –n> **1.** *no pl* malice ◊ *Seine Augen waren voller Tücke.* **2.** spiteful deed, malicious act ◊ *So eine fiese Tücke kannst wirklich nur du dir ausdenken!* **3.** hidden danger, pitfall ◊

Diese Aufgabe ist nicht ohne Tücke. Der Text steckt voller Tücken. The text is full of pitfalls.

Tu·gend ['tu:gn̩t, 'tu:gənt] die <-, –en> *no pl* virtue ◊ *Bescheidenheit gehört nicht gerade zu seinen Tugenden.* ♦ *Sie wurde wegen ihrer Schönheit und Tugend bewundert.* ⊖Laster

tum·meln ['tʊml̩n] [ref v] +*haben* **1.** sich irgendwo tummeln cavort about somewhere ◊ *Viele Skifahrer tummeln sich auf den Pisten.; (children)* romp about somewhere; *(fish)* dart about somewhere **2.** *(fam)* sich tummeln get a move on ◊ *Wir haben nicht viel Zeit. Tummelt euch also!* ⊖sich beeilen

② **tun** [tu:n] <tut, tat, hat getan> [tr v] **1.** do ◊ *Das habe ich für dich getan.* ♦ *Sie hat nichts zu tun.* ♦ *Er hat sein Bestes getan.* jdm nicht zwei Dinge gleichzeitig tun ♦ *Es gibt viel zu tun.* jdm sagen, was er tun soll tell sb what to do etwas gegen/für etw. tun do sth about/for sth ◊ *Du solltest etwas gegen deinen Husten tun.* ♦ *Diese Schule tut sehr viel für sozial schwächere Schüler.* **2.** *empty verb* Abbitte tun offer your apologies einen Schrei tun let out a cry **3.** jdm/sich etwas tun hurt sb/yourself, harm sb/yourself nichts tun be harmless ◊ *Eine Spinne tut doch nichts!* **4.** *(fam)* jdn/etw. irgendwohin tun put sb/sth somewhere ◊ *Tu bitte die Butter in den Kühlschrank.* Wir tun Max ab September in den Kindergarten. We are sending Max to nursery school from September. [intr v] +*subjunctive II* so tun, als ... act as if ... ◊ *Er tut so, als würde ihn das nicht interessieren.* Sie tut immer lieb und nett, aber ich traue ihr nicht. She always pretends to be kind and nice, but I don't trust her. [ref v] *(fam)* etwas/nichts/viel tut sich, es tut sich etwas/viel/nichts something/nothing/a lot is going on, something/nothing/a lot is happening ◊ *In den Verhandlungen tut sich endlich etwas.* ♦ *Es tut sich nichts auf dem Arbeitsmarkt. Was tut sich ...?* What is going on ...?, What is happening ...? ◊ *Was hat sich in der Sache getan?* [aux] *(fam)* **1.** Kochen tue ich nicht so gerne. I really don't like cooking. Sie kommt gleich, sie tut sich gerade umziehen. She'll be down in a minute, she's just getting changed. **2.** *as subjunctive II (SouthG)* Das täte ich an deiner Stelle anders machen. If I were you I'd do that differently.

⊛ **mit etw. nichts zu tun haben 1.** have nothing to do with sth ◊ *Er sagte, er habe mit dem Einbruch nichts zu tun.* **2.** not be involved in sth, not be responsible for sth ◊ *Mit der finanziellen Seite des Projekts habe ich nichts zu tun.* mit jdm/etw. nichts zu tun haben wollen not want anything to do with sb/sth es mit jdm/etw. zu tun bekommen/kriegen have to deal with sb/sth es mit der Angst zu tun bekommen get scared mit etw. ist es nicht getan sth is not enough mit jdm/etw. zu tun haben **1.** mit jdm zu tun haben have to do with sb, have contact with sb ◊ *Mit unseren Nachbarn haben wir nicht viel zu tun.* mit etw. zu tun haben be involved with/in sth ◊ *Sie hat beruflich mit Musik zu tun.* **2.** mit etw. zu tun haben have sth to do with sth ◊ *Das eine hat mit dem anderen nichts zu tun.* es mit jdm/etw. zu tun haben be dealing with sb/sth ◊ *Hier haben wir es mit einer chronischen Krankheit zu tun.* es tun *(fam)* **1.** suffice Du brauchst kein großes

Geschenk mitzubringen. Ein paar Blumen tun es auch. You don't need to bring a large present. A few flowers will do. **2.** work ◊ *Unser Fernseher ist zwar schon zehn Jahre alt, aber er tut es immer noch.*

Tun·fisch ['tuːnfɪʃ] → Thunfisch

⑦ **Tür** [tyːɐ̯] die <–, –en> door ◊ *eine Tür zumachen/ abschließen* ♦ *Da ist jemand an der Tür.* ♦ *zur Tür hereinkommen*
⊙ **zwischen Tür und Angel** *(fam)* in passing, fleeting(ly) ◊ *ein Gespräch zwischen Tür und Angel* **mit der Tür ins Haus fallen** *(fam)* come right out with it **einer Sache** ⎡dat⎤ **Tür und Tor öffnen** open the way to sth **offene Türen einrennen** *(fam)* preach to the converted **jdn vor die Tür setzen** *(fam)* **1.** *(an employee)* dismiss sb **2.** *(a partner etc.)* throw sb out **vor der Tür stehen** be just around the corner

Tür·ke ['tʏrkə] der <–n, –n>, **Tür·kin** ['tʏrkɪn] die <–, –nen> Turk → Deutsche

Tür·kei [tʏrˈkaɪ̯] <–> no pl (always die Türkei) Turkey ◊ *Im Sommer waren wir in der Türkei.* box@ Land

Tür·kin ['tʏrkɪn] fem of Türke

tür·kisch ['tʏrkɪʃ] ⎡adj⎤ mostly before ns Turkish → deutsch

Tür·kisch ['tʏrkɪʃ] das <–(s)> no pl Turkish → Deutsch

⑦ **Tür·klin·ke** ['tyːɐ̯klɪŋkə] die <–, –n> door-handle ◊ *die Türklinke herunterdrücken*

Turm [tʊrm] der <–(e)s, Türme> **1.** tower ◊ *Sie bestiegen den Turm und genossen die Aussicht.*; *(of a church also)* spire **2.** *(in chess)* castle, rook

tur·nen ['tʊrnən] ⎡tr+intr v⎤ +*haben* do gymnastics *Annika turnte einen hervorragenden Wettkampf.* Annika gave an outstanding performance at the gymnastic competition. **am Reck turnen** do exercises on the horizontal bars ⎡intr v⎤ +*sein* climb about ◊ *In der Pause turnten die Kinder über Tische und Bänke.*

Tur·nier [tʊrˈniːɐ̯] das <–s, –e> **1.** SPORT tournament, competition ◊ *ein Turnier gewinnen* **2.** HIST tournament ◊ *Ritter Kunibert war zum Turnier angetreten.*

Turn·schuh ['tʊrnʃuː] der <–(e)s, –e> trainer, sneaker, gym shoe; *(canvas also)* plimsoll

⑦ **Tür·schnal·le** ['tyːɐ̯ʃnalə] die <–, –n> *(Austr)* doorhandle

⑦ **Tü·te** ['tyːtə] die <–, –n> *(carrier)* bag ◊ *eine Tüte Gummibärchen* ♦ *Die Frau an der Kasse fragte, ob er eine Tüte wolle.*
⊙ **etw. kommt nicht in die Tüte** *(fam)* sth is not an option

TÜV [tʏf] der *(abbr of* Technischer Überwachungsverein*)* **1.** *technical inspection agency* ◊ *Das Gerät ist vom TÜV geprüft.* **2.** *(for vehicles)* MOT ◊ *Mein Auto ist nicht durch den TÜV gekommen.*

The *TÜV*, which has many centres in Germany, Austria and Switzerland, inspects and certifies technical equipment that might be hazardous to both people and the environment. All motor vehicles, for example, have to be tested by the *TÜV* on a regular basis. The *TÜV* is also responsible for driving tests.

TV[1] [teːˈfaʊ̯] *seldom with the article* das *(abbr of* Television*)* TV ◊ *Sportübertragungen im TV* ⊖Fernsehen

TV[2] [teːˈfaʊ̯] der *(abbr of* Turnverein*)* gymnastics club ◊ *Der TV Mosbach wurde mit 2:5 geschlagen.*

⑦ **Typ** [typ] der <–s, –en> **1.** type ◊ *Sie ist nicht mein Typ.* ♦ *Ich bin nicht der Typ, der Männer in der Disko anquatscht.* ♦ *Sie hat Diabetes Typ 2.* **2.** *(fam)* bloke, guy ◊ *ein cooler Typ* **3.** mark, series ◊ *ein Flugzeug vom Typ Airbus A310*
⊙ **dein Typ wird verlangt** *(fam)* you're wanted

⑦ **ty·pisch** ['typɪʃ] ⎡adj, adv⎤ typical(ly) ◊ *typische Merkmale* ♦ *Nadja hat ihren Schlüssel verloren? Das ist doch wieder mal typisch!* ♦ *Was ist Ihrer Meinung nach typisch deutsch?*

U

u, U [uː] das <−(s), −(s)> u, U ◊ *Dieses Wort wird mit einem kleinen u/großen U geschrieben.* ♦ *U wie Ulrich*

U [uː] die <−> *no pl (abbr of* U-Bahn) *(tube train line number)* U ◊ *Die U9 fährt zum Hauptbahnhof.*

ü, Ü [yː] das <−(s), −(s)> u umlaut, U umlaut ◊ *Dieses Wort wird mit einem kleinen ü/großen Ü geschrieben.* ♦ *Ü wie Übermut*

u. [ʊnt] *(abbr of* und) *and*

u. a.[1] [ʊnt 'andərəs] *(abbr of* und anderes) etc. ◊ *Wir verkaufen Hosen, Shorts, T-Shirts u. a.*

u. a.[2] [ˌʊnt 'andərəm] *(abbr of* unter anderem) *amongst other things* ◊ *Wir diskutierten u. a. über Politik.*

u. a.[3] [ʊnt 'andərə] *(abbr of* und andere) et al. ◊ *Herausgeber: Jens Maier u. a.*

U-Bahn ['uːbaːn] die <−, −en> *(abbr of* Untergrundbahn) *underground, tube, subway* ◊ *Sie fährt mit der U-Bahn zur Arbeit.*

ü·bel ['yːbl̩] adj, adv <übler, am übelsten> <der/die/das üble ...> bad(ly), nasty(-ily) ◊ *eine üble Erkältung* ♦ *Wir befinden uns in einer üblen Lage.* ♦ *Dieser Stadtteil ist besonders übel.* ♦ *Er hat sie übel beschimpft.* üble Nachrede defamation (of character) übel riechender Atem bad breath ⊛ nicht übel *(fam)* not bad jdm ist übel sb feels sick ◊ *Ihm war vom Autofahren übel.* übel nehmen jdm etw. übelnehmen feel offended by sb's sth ◊ *Deine Unzuverlässigkeit nehme ich dir sehr übel.* jdm übel nehmen, dass feel offended that sb

Ü·bel·keit ['yːbl̩kaet] die <−, −en> *most sing* nausea, sickness

ü·ben ['yːbm̩] tr+intr v +haben practise ◊ *Er will Pianist werden und übt deshalb täglich.* ♦ *Der Trainer ließ die Spieler Elfmeter üben.* ♦ *für den Ernstfall üben* tr v +haben **1.** *(lofty)* exercise ◊ Zurückhaltung/Toleranz üben Bescheidenheit üben show modesty **2.** *empty verb* Kritik an jdm üben criticise sb Selbstkritik üben criticise yourself Verzicht üben make do without Gerechtigkeit üben act justly

② **ü·ber**[1] ['yːbɐ] adv **1.** over, more than ◊ *ein Film von über drei Stunden Länge* ♦ *Diese Bluse hat über 100 € gekostet.* ⊜mehr als **2.** *after an expression of time* through(out) ◊ *Es hat die ganze Nacht über geregnet.* ⊜hindurch ⊛ über und über all over, completely ◊ *Das Kind hatte sich über und über mit Joghurt bekleckert.* ⊜ganz, völlig

ü·ber[2] ['yːbɐ] adj *no comp/superl, not before ns (fam)* **1.** über sein be left (over) ◊ *Ist noch Kuchen über?* ⊜übrig **2.** etw./jdn über haben have had enough of sth/sb ◊ *Am Anfang hat mir die Serie gut gefallen, aber jetzt habe ich sie über.* ⊜satt

② **ü·ber**[3] ['yːbɐ] *prep* with acc when expressing

motion towards a place, with dat when there is no or undirected motion **1.** +acc or +dat above, over ◊ *Das Bild hängt über dem Sofa.* ♦ *Ich betrachtete den Sternenhimmel über mir.* ♦ *Er hielt seine Hände über das Feuer, um sie zu wärmen.*; over ◊ *Die Hose hängt über den Stuhl.* ♦ *Er zog sich die Bettdecke über den Kopf. Der Fluss trat über die Ufer. The river broke its banks. Du darfst nicht über den Rand hinausschreiben. You're not allowed to write in the margins.* **2.** +acc or +dat across, over ◊ *eine Dampferfahrt über den Bodensee* ♦ *Er wohnt gleich über der Straße.* **3.** +acc through, via ◊ *über Bangkok nach Singapur fliegen* **4.** *temporal* +acc over ◊ *Wir waren über das Wochenende in Berlin.* ♦ *Über Nacht hat es geregnet.*; past ◊ *Bist du über dieses Alter nicht schon hinaus?* **5.** +dat above, over ◊ *Temperaturen über dem Gefrierpunkt* ♦ *Dieser Preis liegt weit über dem üblichen Marktpreis.* jd liebt jdn/etw. über alles, jd/etw. geht jdm über alles sb is particularly fond of sb/sth **6.** +acc on, about ◊ *ein Buch über die Alpen* **7.** +acc of ◊ *Er hat einen Kredit über 10 000 € aufgenommen.* **8.** +acc through ◊ *Das habe ich über Cornelia erfahren.* über Satellit by satellite **9.** +dat über (einer Tätigkeit) while (doing sth) ◊ *Über der Lektüre seines Buches schlief er ein.* ⊜bei **10.** +dat through, because of ◊ *Vergiss über der Arbeit deine Familie nicht!* ⊜wegen **11.** *used to link two identical nouns* +acc ... über ... ... upon ... ◊ *Es gab Probleme über Probleme.*

② **ü·ber·...**[1] ['yːbɐ] prefix +adj **1.** over... ◊ *überangepasst sein* ♦ *eine überkritische Beurteilung* **2.** very ... ◊ *Der Unterschied war überdeutlich zu erkennen.* ♦ *überglücklich sein* überbreite Lasten wide loads **3.** überbetrieblich industry-wide überparteilich all-party

ü·ber·...[2] ['yːbɐ] prefix +verb, unstressed and inseparable **1.** over... ◊ *Überanstrenge dich nicht!* jdn überfordern overtax sb, expect too much of sb sich an etw. dat überfressen eat too much sth **2.** out... ◊ *jdn/etw. überbieten* ♦ *Du bist überstimmt.* jdn überbrüllen shout sb down **3.** *translation varies* etw. übermalen paint over sth etw. überfluten flood sth Der Garten ist überwuchert. The garden is overgrown. **4.** etw. überfliegen fly over sth etw. überspringen jump over sth etw. überschreiten cross sth **5.** etw. übersehen overlook sth etw. überhören not hear sth

Ü·ber·... ['yːbɐ] prefix **1.** over... ◊ *die Überbeanspruchung* ♦ *die Überfischung der Meere* ♦ *die Überproduktion* **2.** super(-)... ◊ *ein Übervater*

② **ü·ber·all** [yːbɐ'al, '− − −] adv **1.** everywhere ◊ *Hier ist es überall schmutzig.* ♦ *Überall lauern Gefahren.* ⊜nirgends **2.** always ◊ *Er steckt überall seine Nase rein.* **3.** everybody, everyone sich überall bedanken thank everybody sich überall verabschieden say goodbye to everybody

ü·ber·ar·bei·ten [y:bɐˈʔaɐ̯baɛtn̩] <überarbeitet, überarbeitete, hat überarbeitet> [tr v] rework, revise ◊ *eine Internetseite überarbeiten* ♦ *einen Plan überarbeiten* [ref v] sich überarbeiten overwork ◊ *Hoffentlich überarbeitest du dich nicht.*

ü·ber·aus [ˈy:bɐʔaos, – ˈ–] [adv] *(lofty)* extremely, exceedingly ◊ *eine überaus erfolgreiche Ausstellung* ♦ *Ich bin Ihnen überaus dankbar.*

ü·ber·be·wer·ten [ˈy:bɐbəvɐˌtn̩] <überbewertet, überbewertete, hat überbewertet> [tr v] overrate, overplay, attach too much importance to ◊ *Diese Ergebnisse dürfen nicht überbewertet werden.*

ü·ber·bie·ten [y:bɐˈbi:tn̩] <überbietet, überbot, hat überboten> [tr v] **1.** *(at an auction)* jdn überbieten outbid sb **2.** beat, outdo ◊ *das Höchstgebot um 50 Euro überbieten* ♦ *den Weltrekord überbieten* ♦ *Das ist an Dummheit nicht zu überbieten!*

Ü·ber·blick [ˈy:bɐblɪk] der <-(e)s, -e> **1.** view ◊ *auf einen Berg klettern, um einen Überblick über die Gegend zu bekommen* **2.** *(fig)* overview ◊ *im Chaos den Überblick verlieren* ♦ *Das Buch gibt einen Überblick über die Geschichte des 20. Jahrhunderts.* ♦ *eine Liste mit allen Tarifen im Überblick*

ü·ber·brü·cken [y:bɐˈbrʏkn̩] <überbrückt, überbrückte, hat überbrückt> [tr v] survive ◊ *mehrere Wochen ohne Geld überbrücken müssen*; *(a period of time)* fill ◊ *Sie überbrückte die Pause mit Einkaufen.*

ü·ber·den·ken [y:bɐˈdɛŋkn̩] <überdenkt, überdachte, hat überdacht> [tr v] think over ◊ *eine Entscheidung noch einmal überdenken*

ü·ber·dies [y:bɐˈdi:s] [adv] **1.** *(on top)* what is more **2.** anyway, in any case ◊ *Im Tank ist kaum Benzin, und überdies springt der Wagen nicht an.*

ü·ber·drüs·sig [ˈy:bɐdrʏsɪç] [adj] *no comp/superl, not before ns* jds/einer Sache überdrüssig sein/werden be/get fed up with/of sb/sth, be/get tired of sb/sth ◊ *Er war des Wartens überdrüssig.* ♦ *Sie wurde seiner schnell überdrüssig.*

ü·ber·ei·len [y:bɐˈʔaelən] <übereilt, übereilte, hat übereilt> [tr v] rush, be too hasty with ◊ *eine Entscheidung nicht übereilen wollen*

ü·ber·ei·nan·der [y:bɐʔaeˈnandɐ] [adv] **1.** *(of things)* on top of each other/one another ◊ *Kisten übereinander stapeln mit übereinander geschlagenen Beinen with your legs crossed* **2.** *(of people)* about/at each other/one another ◊ *Sie schimpfen immer übereinander.*

Ü·ber·ein·kunft [y:bɐˈʔaenkʊnft] die <-, Übereinkünfte> agreement, understanding ◊ *eine Übereinkunft treffen* ♦ *eine Übereinkunft zwischen zwei Firmen erzielen*

ü·ber·ein|stim·men [y:bɐˈʔaenʃtɪmən] <stimmt überein, stimmte überein, hat übereingestimmt> [intr v] **1.** mit jdm (in etw.) übereinstimmen agree with sb (on/about sth) ◊ *Wir stimmen nicht in allen Punkten überein.* **2.** *(results, opinions)* agree, correspond ◊ *Unsere Ergebnisse stimmten nicht überein.* ⊜sich decken

② **ü·ber·fah·ren** [y:bɐˈfa:rən] <überfährt, überfuhr, hat überfahren> [tr v] **1.** *(a person, an animal)* run over, run down ◊ *eine Katze überfahren* ♦ *von einer Straßenbahn überfahren werden* **2.** *(the traffic lights, a stop sign)* go through **3.** *(fig)* steamroller, steam roll ◊ *jdn mit einem Vorschlag*

überfahren ♦ *sich (von jdm) überfahren fühlen*

Ü·ber·fahrt [ˈy:bɐfaːˀt] die <-, -en> crossing ◊ *eine stürmische Überfahrt* ♦ *Die Überfahrt nach Dublin dauerte vier Stunden.*

Ü·ber·fall [ˈy:bɐfal] der <-(e)s, Überfälle> attack, assault, mugging ◊ *ein brutaler/bewaffneter Überfall* ♦ *Er wurde bei dem Überfall verletzt.*; *(at a bank, garage etc.)* hold-up

ü·ber·fal·len [y:bɐˈfalən] <überfällt, überfiel, hat überfallen> [tr v] **1.** jdn überfallen mug sb, attack sb ◊ *Der Täter hatte die Frau auf offener Straße überfallen.* **2.** etw. überfallen hold sth up ◊ *eine Bank/einen Geldtransporter überfallen* **3.** jdn überfällt etw. sb is overcome by sth, sb is seized by sth ◊ *Mich überfiel panische Angst.*

ü·ber·fäl·lig [ˈy:bɐfɛlɪç] [adj] *no comp/superl* **1.** overdue ◊ *Ein neuer Anstrich war schon lange überfällig.* ♦ *längst überfällige Reformen* **2.** *not before ns* late, behind schedule ◊ *Das Flugzeug ist überfällig.*

ü·ber·flüs·sig [ˈy:bɐflʏsɪç] [adj] superfluous ◊ *etw. für überflüssig halten* ♦ *sich überflüssig vorkommen* ♦ *Das ist eine völlig überflüssige Diskussion.*; *(remark, comment also)* unnecessary ◊ *Diese Bemerkung war überflüssig.* überflüssige Pfunde loswerden wollen want to get rid of some excess pounds

ü·ber·for·dern [y:bɐˈfɔ(r)dɐn] <überfordert, überforderte, hat überfordert> [tr v] jdn/etw. überfordern demand too much of sb/sth, place excessive demands on sb/sth ◊ *Seine Mutter überfordert ihn.* ♦ *Der Job überfordert mich.*

ü·ber·füh·ren [y:bɐˈfy:rən] <überführt, überführte, hat überführt> [tr v] **1.** transport, convey ◊ *ein Fahrzeug nach Hamburg überführen* **2.** LAW jdn (einer Sache [gen]) überführen find sb guilty (of sth), convict sb (of sth) ◊ *Der Täter wurde (des Mordes) überführt.*

ü·ber·füllt [y:bɐˈfʏlt] [adj] <überfüllter, am überfülltesten> overcrowded, packed ◊ *Der Zug war völlig überfüllt.* ♦ *überfüllte Schulklassen*

Ü·ber·ga·be [ˈy:bɐga:bə] die <-, -n> handing over, handover ◊ *Die Übergabe des Lösegelds scheiterte.* ♦ *die Übergabe eines Hauses an den Käufer*

Ü·ber·gang [ˈy:bɐgaŋ] der <-(e)s, Übergänge> **1.** *(place)* crossing ◊ *Am nächsten Übergang überqueren sie die Bahnlinie.* **2.** *no pl (stage)* transition ◊ *der Übergang vom Studium ins Berufsleben* **3.** *no pl* change of the seasons sich [dat] einen Mantel für den Übergang kaufen buy yourself a coat for between seasons

ü·ber·ge·ben [y:bɐˈge:bm̩] <übergibt, übergab, hat übergeben> [tr v] **1.** hand over ◊ *Sie übergab ihm das Baby.* ♦ *den Täter der Polizei übergeben* **2.** jdm etw. übergeben place sth in the hands of sb ◊ *Der Fall wurde der Polizei übergeben.* [ref v] sich übergeben be sick ⊜spucken, brechen

ü·ber|ge·hen[1] [ˈy:bɐge:ən] <geht über, ging über, ist übergegangen> [intr v] **1.** *(a concerning topic)* zu etw. übergehen move on to sth, go on to sth ◊ *zum nächsten Tagesordnungspunkt übergehen* **2.** *(change your habits)* zu etw. übergehen take to sth ◊ *Mittlerweile bin ich dazu übergegangen, selbst zu kochen.* **3.** *(into a state)* in etw. [acc] übergehen turn into sth ◊ *Das Eis ging allmählich in Wasser über.* **4.** *(gradually)* in etw. [acc]

übergehen merge into sth ◇ *Das Blau ging in ein zartes Lila über.* **5.** in jds Besitz/auf jdn übergehen pass to sb ◇ *Das Vermögen ist auf ihren Ehemann übergegangen.*

ü·ber·ge·hen² [y:be'ge:ən] <übergeht, überging, hat übergangen> [tr v] **1.** etw./jdn übergehen ignore sth/sb ◇ *einen Einwand/eine Frage übergehen* ♦ *Sie überging ihn einfach.* **2.** jdn übergehen leave sb out, pass over sb ◇ *sich (von jdm) übergangen fühlen*

Ü·ber·ge·wicht ['y:bɐgəvɪçt] das <-(e)s> *no pl* **1.** MED excess weight ◇ *(15 Kilo) Übergewicht haben* **2.** (das) Übergewicht bekommen overbalance ◇ *Er kletterte aufs Fensterbrett, bekam (das) Übergewicht und fiel hinaus.*

② **ü·ber·haupt** [y:be'haopt] [adv] **1.** altogether ◇ *Er ist überhaupt sehr intelligent. Das war die erste Webcam überhaupt.* That was the first ever webcam. **2.** *in negations* überhaupt ... ... at all ◇ *Sie hat überhaupt keine Freunde.* ⊖gar **3.** *in questions* even ◇ *Hat er überhaupt einen Führerschein?* ♦ *Existiert dieser Vertrag überhaupt?* What's he doing here anyway? **4.** und überhaupt and anyway ◇ *Er war müde, und überhaupt, er hatte gar keine Zeit zum Ausgehen.* **5.** wenn überhaupt if at all ◇ *Wenn überhaupt, dann regnet es dort nur im Sommer.*

ü·ber·höht [y:be'hø:t] [adj] *no comp/superl* excessive ◇ *eine überhöhte Rechnung stellen; (prices also)* extortionate, exorbitant ◇ *Der Preis war überhöht.* überhöhte Geschwindigkeit speeding

② **ü·ber·ho·len** [y:be'ho:lən] <überholt, überholte, hat überholt> [tr+intr v] **1.** *(also fig)* overtake ◇ *einen Lkw überholen* ♦ *Als alles frei war, überholte sie.* ♦ *Sogar den Besten seiner Klasse hat er inzwischen überholt.* **2.** *(a vehicle, machine)* overhaul ◇ *Der Motor ist inzwischen überholt worden.*

ü·ber·holt [y:be'ho:lt] *past p of* überholen [adj] *no comp/superl* outdated ◇ *überholte Ansichten/ Theorien* ♦ *Dieser Ansatz ist inzwischen überholt.*

ü·ber·hö·ren [y:be'hø:rən] <überhört, hat überhört> [tr v] **1.** etw. überhören not hear sth ◇ *Er hatte das Klopfen überhört.* **2.** *(deliberately)* ignore ◇ *eine Bemerkung/Frage überhören* ♦ *Er hat meine Frage einfach überhört.*

ü·ber·las·sen¹ [y:be'lasn] <überlässt, überließ, hat überlassen> [tr v] **1.** *(permanently)* jdm etw. überlassen let sb have sth, give sb sth ◇ *jdm sein ganzes Vermögen überlassen* **2.** *(for a shorter period)* jdm etw. überlassen let sb use sth, give sb the use of sth ◇ *jdm seine Wohnung für ein paar Monate überlassen* **3.** *(so that sb can take care of sth)* jdm jdn/etw. überlassen leave sb/sth with sb ◇ *Sie hat das Kind ein paar Stunden den Großeltern überlassen.* **4.** *(a decision, an activity)* jdm etw. überlassen leave sth (up) to sb ◇ *Ich überließ ihm die Entscheidung.* ♦ *Es ist jedem selbst überlassen, was er abends macht.* alles/nichts dem Zufall überlassen leave everything/nothing to chance **5.** jdn jdm/einer Sache überlassen abandon sb to sb/sth, leave sb to sb/sth ◇ *jdn seinem Schicksal überlassen*

◉ jdn/etw. sich [dat] selbst überlassen *(not help)* leave sb/sth to their/its own devices leave sb/sth to fend for themselves/itself

ü·ber|las·sen² ['y:bɐlasn] <lässt über, ließ über,

hat übergelassen> [tr v] *(regional, fam)* leave (over) ◇ *Wir haben dir ein paar Bier übergelassen.*
⊖übrig lassen

ü·ber·las·tet [y:be'lastət] [adj] **1.** TECHN overloaded ◇ *Die Leitungen waren überlastet.* ♦ *Der überlastete Server wurde abgeschaltet.; (roads, routes)* congested **2.** *(person)* overworked, overstressed ◇ *Es gibt viele überlastete Lehrer.* ♦ *Die Mitarbeiter waren völlig überlastet.*

ü·ber|lau·fen¹ ['y:bɐlaofn] <läuft über, lief über, ist übergelaufen> [intr v] **1.** overflow ◇ *Die Badewanne ist übergelaufen.; (saucepan)* boil over ◇ *Pass auf, dass die Milch nicht überläuft.* **2.** *(also fig) (to the enemy, opposition)* go over ◇ *Er ist zur anderen Partei übergelaufen.*

ü·ber·lau·fen² [y:be'laofn] <überläuft, überlief, hat überlaufen> [intr v] **1.** *(feeling)* etw. überläuft jdn sth goes (right) through sb es überläuft jdn eiskalt a chill goes through sb ein Schauder überläuft jdn sb shudders **2.** überlaufen sein be overcrowded ◇ *Die Stadt ist im Sommer von Touristen überlaufen.*

ü·ber·le·ben [y:be'le:bn] <überlebt, überlebte, hat überlebt> [tr+intr v] (etw.) überleben survive (sth), get over sth ◇ *Wird er (die Operation) überleben?* ♦ *Diese Schande überlebe ich nicht!* [tr v] jdn überleben outlive sb ◇ *Sie überlebte ihren Ehemann um 15 Jahre.*

ü·ber·le·gen¹ [y:be'le:gn] <überlegt, überlegte, hat überlegt> [intr v] think (about sth) ◇ *Ich muss mal kurz überlegen.* ♦ *Er überlegte, wer es wohl gewesen sein könnte.* [tr v] (sich [dat]) etw. überlegen think about sth, consider sth ◇ *Sie wollte es sich noch überlegen.* ♦ *Es wäre zu überlegen, ob diese Anschaffung sinnvoll ist.* es sich [dat] anders überlegen change your mind

ü·ber·le·gen² [y:be'le:gn] [adj] (jdm) (an etw. [dat]) überlegen superior (to sb) (in sth) ◇ *Die Mannschaft war ihnen weit überlegen.* ♦ *ein an Ausdauer überlegener Gegner* [adv] in a sovereign way; *(win, lead)* convincingly ◇ *Die gegnerische Mannschaft hat überlegen gewonnen.*

Ü·ber·le·gung [y:be'le:gʊn] die <-, -en> consideration, thought ◇ *Nach sorgfältiger Überlegung hat er gekündigt.* eine Überlegung wert sein be worth consideration Überlegungen anstellen, wie man etw. machen könnte think about how sth could be done

ü·berm ['y:bɐm] [contract] *über + dem (fam)* **1.** over the ◇ *ein Flugzeugabsturz überm Bodensee* → über **2.** *with nominalized verbs, not to be split* while ◇ *Überm Nachdenken schlief ich ein.*

ü·ber·mä·ßig ['y:bɐmɛ:sɪç] [adj, adv] *no comp/ superl* excessive(ly) ◇ *Seine Ansprüche sind nicht übermäßig.* ♦ *übermäßige Kosten vermeiden* ♦ *übermäßig harte Strafe*

ü·ber·mit·teln [y:be'mɪtln] <übermittelt, übermittelte, hat übermittelt> [tr v] (jdm) etw. übermitteln convey sth (to sb), send (sb) sth ◇ *jdm eine Nachricht übermitteln* Meine Mutter ließ ihre Glückwünsche übermitteln. My mother sent her congratulations.; *(data)* etw. übermitteln transfer sth

② **ü·ber·mor·gen** ['y:bɐmɔʁgn] [adv] (on) the day after tomorrow, (on) the day after next ◇ *Übermorgen reisen wir ab.* übermorgen Abend (on) the evening after next

ü·ber·mü·tig ['y:bemy:tɪç] (adj, adv) exuberant(ly) ◊ *Sie war sehr übermütig.* ♦ *Es herrschte übermütige Stimmung.* ♦ *Er lachte übermütig.*

ü·bern ['y:ben] (contract) *über + den (fam)* **1.** over the ◊ *übern Zaun springen →* über **2.** *in certain idioms: look up the relevant idiom* ◊ *übern Berg sein*

ü·ber·nächs·te ['y:benɛ:çstə] (adj) *no comp/superl* **1.** *(temporal)* the ... after next ◊ *Wir wollten uns übernächste Woche treffen.* **2.** *(in space)* next but one ◊ *an der übernächsten Haltestelle aussteigen*

② **ü·ber·nach·ten** [y:be'naxtn̩] <übernachtet, übernachtete, hat übernachtet> (intr v) stay (the night) ◊ *bei einer Freundin/im Hotel übernachten*

Ü·ber·nach·tung [y:be'naxtʊŋ] die <-, -en> overnight stay ◊ *Eine/Die Übernachtung ohne Frühstück kostet 60 Euro.; (in a hotel, guesthouse etc. also)* night ◊ *Im Preis sind sieben Übernachtungen inbegriffen.* Übernachtung und Frühstück bed and breakfast

Ü·ber·nah·me ['y:bena:mə] die <-, -n> **1.** *no pl* takeover ◊ *Sie erwägen eine Übernahme der englischen Firma.* **2.** borrowing ◊ *Wörtliche Übernahmen aus dem Text sind zu kennzeichnen.*

② **ü·ber·neh·men** [y:be'ne:mən] <übernimmt, übernahm, hat übernommen.> (tr v) **1.** take on ◊ *die Praxis seines Vaters übernehmen* ♦ *die Verteidigung des Angeklagten übernehmen; (costs also)* take over ◊ *Das Arbeitsamt übernimmt die Kosten für den Kurs.; (an office also)* accept ◊ *ein Amt übernehmen* **2.** *(a business)* take over ◊ *eine hoch verschuldete Firma übernehmen* **3.** Gewähr/ Haftung übernehmen assume liability Garantie übernehmen (be able to) guarantee ◊ *für die Richtigkeit der Informationen keine Garantie übernehmen* Verantwortung übernehmen take responsibility **4.** *(an idea, a quotation)* take over, borrow ◊ *ein Zitat wörtlich übernehmen* (ref v) sich übernehmen take on too much, overdo it ◊ *sich finanziell übernehmen* ♦ *sich mit einem Projekt übernehmen*

ü·ber·prü·fen [y:be'pry:fn̩] <überprüft, hat überprüft> (tr v) check, examine ◊ *jds Angaben überprüfen* ♦ *Der Zoll hat 30 Lkws überprüft.*

② **ü·ber·que·ren** [y:be'kve:rən] <überquert, überquerte, hat überquert> (tr v) cross ◊ *einen Bach/ eine Straße überqueren*

② **ü·ber·ra·schen** [y:be'raʃn̩] <überrascht, überraschte, hat überrascht> (tr v) surprise ◊ *jdn mit einem Geschenk überraschen* ♦ *von einem Gewitter/Sturm überrascht werden*

Ü·ber·ra·schung [y:be'raʃʊŋ] die <-, -en> surprise ◊ *mit etw. für große Überraschung sorgen* ♦ *Zu ihrer Überraschung funktionierte der Fernseher noch.* ♦ *eine böse Überraschung erleben*

② **ü·ber·re·den** [y:be're:dn̩] <überredet, überredete, hat überredet> (tr v) persuade ◊ *Der Makler hat sie zum Kauf des Hauses überredet.* ♦ *Sie wollte ihn überreden, mit ihr ins Kino zu gehen.*

ü·ber·rei·chen [y:be'raeçn̩] <überreicht, hat überreicht> (tr v) jdm etw. überreichen present sb with sth ◊ *der Siegerin den Pokal überreichen* ♦ *jdm ein Geschenk überreichen*

Ü·ber·rest ['y:berɛst] der <-(e)s, -e> **1.** remnant ◊ *Überreste antiker Mauern* **2.** *(euph)* jds sterbliche Überreste sb's mortal remains

ü·bers ['y:bes] (contract) *über + das (fam)* **1.** over

the ◊ *übers Meer fliegen →* über **2.** about/on (the) ◊ *ein Buch übers Fliegen* ♦ *übers Wichtigste reden →* über **3.** *in certain idioms, not to be split:* look up the relevant idiom ◊ *jdn übers Ohr hauen*

ü·ber·schät·zen [y:be'ʃɛtsn̩] <überschätzt, überschätzte, hat überschätzt> (tr v) overestimate ◊ *seine Kräfte überschätzen* ♦ *ein Problem überschätzen* ⊜unterschätzen

ü·ber·schau·bar [y:be'ʃaoba:ʳ] (adj) **1.** manageable ◊ *eine überschaubare Gruppe von weniger als 30 Menschen; (text)* clear Das Kulturangebot der Stadt ist kaum überschaubar. It is scarcely possible to get an overview of what the city has to offer culturally. **2.** *(consequences, risk)* foreseeable ◊ *Die Konsequenzen sind nicht überschaubar.* ♦ *ein überschaubares Risiko eingehen* (adv) in a clear form, clearly ◊ *Daten überschaubar darstellen*

ü·ber·schla·gen [y:be'ʃla:gn̩] <überschlägt, überschlug, hat überschlagen> (tr v) make a rough estimate of, make a rough calculation of ◊ *die Kosten grob überschlagen* (ref v) **1.** sich überschlagen overturn ◊ *Das Auto hatte sich mehrmals überschlagen.* sich fast vor Begeisterung/Freude überschlagen jump for joy **2.** *(voice)* sich überschlagen crack ◊ *Ihre Stimme überschlug sich fast vor Aufregung.* **3.** *(events, news items)* sich überschlagen come thick and fast ◊ *Die Ereignisse überschlugen sich.*

ü·ber·schrei·ben [y:be'ʃraebm̩] <überschreibt, überschrieb, hat überschrieben> (tr v) **1.** entitle ◊ *einen Artikel mit „Kürzungen" überschreiben* **2.** jdm etw. überschreiben, etw. auf jdn überschreiben make sth over to sb, sign sth over to sb ◊ *Sie hat das Haus auf ihre Kinder überschrieben.* ♦ *seiner Frau den Bauernhof überschreiben* **3.** IT overwrite ◊ *gespeicherte Daten versehentlich überschreiben*

ü·ber·schrei·ten [y:be'ʃraetn̩] <überschreitet, überschritt, hat überschritten> (tr v) go over, exceed ◊ *die Höchstgeschwindigkeit deutlich überschreiten; (an age)* pass ◊ *Sie hat die 50 schon weit überschritten.; (authority, powers)* go beyond ◊ *Das überschreitet deine Befugnisse.*

② **Ü·ber·schrift** ['y:beʃrɪft] die <-, -en> title, heading ◊ *Wie lautet die Überschrift des Artikels?*

Ü·ber·schuss ['y:beʃʊs] der <-es, Überschüsse> **1.** *(financial)* profit ◊ *einen Überschuss von fünf Millionen Euro erzielen* **2.** *(amount)* surplus, excess ◊ *einen Überschuss an Arbeitskräften haben*

ü·ber·schwem·men [y:be'ʃvɛmən] <überschwemmt, überschwemmte, hat überschwemmt> (tr v) *(also fig)* flood ◊ *Der Fluss überschwemmte die Straße.* ♦ *Rom wird das ganze Jahr über von Touristen überschwemmt.*

ü·ber·se·hen [y:be'ze:ən] <übersieht, übersah, hat übersehen> (tr v) **1.** *(have a view)* look over, survey ◊ *Vom Aussichtsturm aus konnte man das ganze Dorf übersehen.* **2.** *(not see)* overlook ◊ *ein entgegenkommendes Auto übersehen* ♦ *ein paar Tippfehler übersehen* jdn übersehen miss sb **3.** ignore ◊ *Rechtschreibfehler wurden vom Lehrer großzügig übersehen.*

② **ü·ber·set·zen**[1] [y:be'zɛtsn̩] <übersetzt, übersetzte, hat übersetzt> (tr v) *(a text)* translate ◊ *Wer hat den Roman übersetzt?* ♦ *einen Text ins Spanische übersetzen*

A B C D E F G H I J K L M N O P Q R S T U V W X Y Z

ü·ber|set·zen[2] ['y:bɐˌzɛtsn̩] <setzt über, setzte über, hat/ist übergesetzt> [tr v] +*haben (in a boat)* ferry (across) ◊ *jdn mit einem Boot ans andere Ufer übersetzen* [intr v] +*haben/sein* cross (over) ◊ *Wir sind/haben an andere Ufer übergesetzt.*

Ü·ber·set·zung [y:bɐˈzɛtsʊŋ] die <-, -en> translation ◊ *bei der Übersetzung Fehler machen* ♦ *eine wörtliche Übersetzung*

Ü·ber·sicht ['y:bɐzɪçt] die <-, -en> **1.** *(of items, events)* overview, summary ◊ *eine detaillierte Übersicht über den Verlauf des Abends geben* **2.** *no pl (of the situation)* overview, perspective ◊ *die Übersicht verlieren* ♦ *sich Übersicht verschaffen*

ü·ber·sicht·lich ['y:bɐzɪçtlɪç] [adj] **1.** *(area, building)* well laid out ◊ *Das Gelände war nicht sehr übersichtlich.* ♦ *ein übersichtlicher Bahnhof* **2.** *(map, text)* clear ◊ *eine übersichtliche Straßenkarte* ♦ *Die Gebrauchsanleitung war sehr übersichtlich.* [adv] in a clear form, clearly ◊ *ein übersichtlich gestalteter Text*

② **ü·ber|sie·deln** ['y:bɐzi:dl̩n] <siedelt über, siedelte über, ist übergesiedelt> [intr v] move ◊ *von Berlin nach Wien übersiedeln* ♦ *Die Firma ist nach Frankreich übersiedelt.*

ü·ber·spie·len [y:bɐˈʃpi:lən] <überspielt, überspielte, hat überspielt> [tr v] **1.** *(hide)* cover up ◊ *Sie versuchte, ihre Unsicherheit zu überspielen.* ♦ *eine peinliche Situation überspielen* **2.** *(music, data etc.)* record ◊ *Kannst du mir diese Kassette überspielen?* ♦ *Daten auf einen PC überspielen*

ü·ber·sprin·gen[1] [y:bɐˈʃprɪŋən] <überspringt, übersprang, hat übersprungen> [tr v] **1.** jump over ◊ *einen Bach/eine Hürde überspringen; (a hurdle also)* clear **2.** *(leave out)* skip ◊ *das zweite Kapitel eines Buches überspringen* ♦ *Begabte Schüler können eine Klasse überspringen.*

ü·ber|sprin·gen[2] ['y:bɐʃprɪŋən] <springt über, sprang über, ist übergesprungen> [intr v] *(also fig)* auf etw. [acc] überspringen spread to sth ◊ *Kann dieser Erreger auf den Menschen überspringen?* Der Funke sprang auf das Heu über. The spark jumped onto the hay.

ü·ber·ste·hen[1] [y:bɐˈʃte:ən] <übersteht, überstand, hat überstanden> [tr v] *(time)* survive, get through ◊ *Das ist das einzige Haus, das den Krieg überstand.; (an operation)* come through ◊ *eine Operation gut überstehen* etw. heil überstehen survive sth in one piece

ü·ber|ste·hen[2] ['y:bɐʃte:ən] <steht über, stand über, hat/ist übergestanden> [intr v] stick out ◊ *Das Brett stand einen Meter über.*

ü·ber·stei·gen [y:bɐˈʃtaɛɡn̩] <übersteigt, überstieg, hat überstiegen> [tr v] exceed ◊ *Der Umsatz überstieg all unsere Erwartungen.* ♦ *Die Nachfrage überstieg das Angebot.*

② **Ü·ber·stun·de** ['y:bɐʃtʊndə] die <-, -n> *most pl* overtime ◊ *viele Überstunden machen* ♦ *Überstunden abbauen*

ü·ber·stür·zen [y:bɐˈʃtʏɐ̯tsn̩] <überstürzt, überstürzte, hat überstürzt> [tr v] rush (into) ◊ *Du solltest nichts überstürzen.* [ref v] *(events, news)* sich überstürzen come thick and fast ◊ *Die Ereignisse überstürzten sich.*

ü·ber·tra·gen [y:bɐˈtra:ɡn̩] <überträgt, übertrug, hat übertragen> [tr v] **1.** *(on TV, the radio)* broadcast, transmit ◊ *Die Sendung wurde live übertragen.* ♦ *Das ZDF überträgt alle drei Spiele.* **2.** translate ◊ *einen Roman/Text (vom Deutschen) ins Italienische übertragen* einen Text in Lautschrift übertragen make a phonetic transcription of a text **3.** etw. irgendwohin übertragen copy sth somewhere ◊ *Notizen in ein Heft übertragen* **4.** TECHN transmit ◊ *Die Antriebskraft wird auf die Räder übertragen.* ♦ *Daten übertragen* **5.** jdm etw. übertragen transfer sth to sb ◊ *jdm eine Aufgabe/ die Verantwortung übertragen* **6.** MED pass on, spread ◊ *Kann die Krankheit auf den Menschen übertragen werden?* **7.** etw. auf jdn/etw. übertragen transfer sth to sb/sth [ref v] *(also fig)* etw. überträgt sich (auf jdn) sth is passed on (to sb), sth spreads (to sb) ◊ *Kann sich diese Krankheit auf den Menschen übertragen?* ♦ *jds Begeisterung/ Nervosität überträgt sich auf jd anderen*

② **Ü·ber·tra·gung** [y:bɐˈtra:ɡʊŋ] die <-, -en> **1.** *(of data, sounds)* transmission ◊ *Die Übertragung des Schalls erfolgt durch Wellen.; (of a TV or radio programme also)* broadcast ◊ *Die Übertragung der Sendung war live.* **2.** translation ◊ *die Übertragung eines Textes aus dem Russischen/ins Russische; (into phonetics, a different script)* transcription **3.** *(of a method)* application, copying ◊ *Die Übertragung der Methode auf andere Bereiche erschien sinnvoll.* **4.** *(of responsibility, a title, rights)* transfer ◊ *der Übertragung der Leitung an jdn zustimmen* **5.** MED spread, transmission ◊ *die Übertragung einer Krankheit (auf jdn) verhindern*

ü·ber·tref·fen [y:bɐˈtrɛfn̩] <übertrifft, übertraf, hat übertroffen> [tr v] **1.** *(be better)* jd übertrifft jdn sb surpasses sb, sb does better than sb, sb beats sb ◊ *Der Schüler übertraf seinen Lehrer.* ⊖schlagen **2.** *(be higher)* etw. übertrifft etw. sth exceeds sth ◊ *Der Umsatz übertraf 15 Millionen Euro.* ♦ *Das Ergebnis übertraf unsere kühnsten Erwartungen.* **3.** jdn/etw. an etw. [dat] übertreffen surpass sb/sth in sth ◊ *seinen Bruder an Größe und Stärke übertreffen* ⊜ sich selbst übertreffen excel yourself

ü·ber·trei·ben [y:bɐˈtraɛbm̩] <übertreibt, übertrieb, hat übertrieben> [intr v] **1.** exaggerate ◊ *maßlos übertreiben* **2.** mit etw. übertreiben take sth too far ◊ *Ich finde, sie übertreibt mit dem Sparen.* [tr v] etw. übertreiben overdo (it with) sth ◊ *Du solltest die Diät nicht übertreiben.*

ü·ber·tre·ten[1] [y:bɐˈtre:tn̩] <übertritt, übertrat, hat übertreten> [tr v] *(a limit)* exceed, go over ◊ *die Geschwindigkeitsbegrenzung übertreten; (a law)* break, infringe

ü·ber|tre·ten[2] ['y:bɐtre:tn̩] <tritt über, trat über, ist übergetreten> [intr v] **1.** *(change adherence)* go over ◊ *zu einer anderen Partei übertreten* zum Islam übertreten convert to Islam **2.** SCHOOL go up, move ◊ *nach der vierten Klasse aufs/ins Gymnasium übertreten*

ü·ber·wa·chen [y:bɐˈvaxn̩] <überwacht, überwachte, hat überwacht> [tr v] **1.** *(watch)* keep under surveillance ◊ *Gefangene überwachen* ♦ *einen Geldautomaten mit einer Kamera überwachen* **2.** *(regulate)* monitor ◊ *Die Polizisten überwachten den Verkehr.*

ü·ber·wäl·ti·gen [y:bɐˈvɛltɪɡn̩] <überwältigt, überwältigte, hat überwältigt> [tr v] **1.** *(physically)*

overpower ◊ *Die Polizei konnte den Geiselnehmer überwältigen.* **2.** *(mentally)* overwhelm ◊ *Die Müdigkeit überwältigte ihn und er schlief ein.*

ü·ber·wand [ybeˈvant] *pret of* überwinden

② **ü·ber·wei·sen** [yːbeˈvaezn̩] <überweist, überwies, hat überwiesen> ⸤tr v⸥ **1.** *(money)* transfer ◊ *100 Euro auf ein Konto überweisen* **2.** MED refer ◊ *Sein Hausarzt überwies ihn an einen Spezialisten.*

ü·ber·wie·gen [yːbeˈviːgn̩] <überwiegt, überwog, hat überwogen> ⸤intr v⸥ predominate, prevail ◊ *Die Vorteile überwiegen deutlich.* ⊖dominieren ⸤tr v⸥ *etw.* überwiegt *etw.* sth is greater than sth, sth outweighs sth ◊ *Die Kosten überwogen die erzielten Erträge.*

ü·ber·win·den [yːbeˈvɪndn̩] <überwindet, überwand, hat überwunden> ⸤tr v⸥ overcome, get over ◊ *eine Gefahr/Krise überwinden* ♦ *seine Angst überwinden* ⊖bewältigen ⸤ref v⸥ *sich* überwinden force yourself ◊ *Er musste sich erst überwinden, doch dann klappte es ganz gut.* sich nicht überwinden können, etw. zu tun not be able to bring yourself to do sth

ü·ber·wun·den [ybeˈvʊndn̩] *past p of* überwinden

Ü·ber·zahl [ˈyːbetsaːl] die <–> *no pl* majority ◊ *in der Überzahl sein*

② **ü·ber·zeu·gen** [yːbeˈtsɔygn̩] <überzeugt, überzeugte, hat überzeugt> ⸤tr v⸥ **1.** *jdn (von etw.)* überzeugen persuade sb (of sth) ◊ *jdn von einem Plan überzeugen* **2.** *jd/etw.* überzeugt *jdn* sb finds sb/sth convincing ⸤intr v⸥ be convincing ◊ *Die Leistung der Schüler überzeugte nicht.* ⸤ref v⸥ *sich (von etw.)* überzeugen satisfy yourself (of sth), see (sth) for yourself

② **Ü·ber·zeu·gung** [yːbeˈtsɔygʊŋ] die <–, –en> **1.** *no pl* persuasion, persuading ◊ *Seine Studie diente der Überzeugung der Gegner.* **2.** *(strong belief, point of view)* conviction ◊ *aus religiöser Überzeugung handeln* ♦ *zu der Überzeugung gelangen, dass ...*

ü·ber·zie·hen [yːbeˈtsiːən] <überzieht, überzog, hat überzogen> ⸤tr v⸥ **1.** cover ◊ *Kekse mit Schokolade überziehen* ♦ *ein Sofa mit Stoff überziehen* die Betten frisch überziehen change the beds **2.** ein Konto überziehen overdraw your account, go overdrawn ◊ *sein Konto (um 2000 Euro) überziehen* ⸤tr+intr v⸥ *(time)* overrun ◊ *Der Moderator überzog (seine Sendezeit) um 15 Minuten.*

② **üb·lich** [ˈyːplɪç] ⸤adj⸥ usual, normal ◊ *nicht den üblichen Weg gehen* ♦ *Das ist in Frankreich so üblich.* ♦ *Wie üblich kam sie zu spät.*

② **üb·rig** [ˈyːbrɪç] ⸤adj⸥ *no comp/superl* der/die/das übrige ..., die übrigen ... the rest of the ... ◊ *Die übrige Strecke nach München schwiegen wir.* ♦ *Von dem übrigen Geld kaufte er Blumen.* übrig sein be left (over) ◊ *Es ist noch Suppe übrig.* übrig bleiben be left (over) ◊ *Ist vom Kuchen etwas übrig geblieben?* etw. übrig haben have got sth left jdm etw. übrig lassen leave sth for sb, leave sb sth ◊ *Wir haben ihr noch ein Bier übrig gelassen.* ⊛ jdm bleibt nichts anderes übrig, als ... sb has no choice but ... für etw. nichts übrig haben have got no interest in sth, not be very keen on sth für etw. viel übrig haben be very interested in sth, be very keen on sth **für jdn viel/etwas übrig haben** have got time/a lot of time for sb **für jdn wenig übrig haben** have got no time

for sb **zu wünschen übrig lassen 1.** nichts zu wünschen übrig lassen leave nothing to be desired, be perfect **2.** schwer/viel zu wünschen übrig lassen leave a lot to be desired

② **üb·ri·gens** [ˈyːbrɪɡn̩s, ˈyːbrɪɡəns] ⸤adv⸥ incidentally, by the way ◊ *Er heißt übrigens auch Christian.* ♦ *Übrigens hat unsere Mannschaft gestern gewonnen.*

② **Ü·bung** [ˈyːbʊŋ] die <–, –en> **1.** practice ◊ *Mit ein bisschen Übung kannst du bald ein Rad schlagen.* ♦ *Zeichnen erfordert viel Übung.* aus der Übung sein be out of practice in etw. ⸤dat⸥ keine Übung haben have got no experience of sth **2.** *(test)* exercise ◊ *ein paar zusätzliche Übungen zur Rechtschreibung machen* **3.** SPORT exercise ◊ *Diese Übung stärkt die Muskeln.* **4.** *(for an emergency)* practice, drill ◊ *Es brennt nicht wirklich. Es ist nur eine Übung.* ♦ *eine Übung durchführen* **5.** UNI seminar ◊ *an einer Übung in Linguistik teilnehmen*

② **U·fer** [ˈuːfe] das <–s, –> **1.** shore ◊ *ans gegenüberliegende Ufer schwimmen; (of a lake also)* side ◊ *am Ufer des Sees in der Sonne liegen; (of a river)* bank ◊ *Das Schiff legte am rechten Ufer des Flusses an.* **2.** *(river)* über die Ufer treten break its banks

② **Uhr** [uːɐ] die <–, –en> **1.** *(on the wall)* clock ◊ *Die Uhr im Wohnzimmer zeigte 11 Uhr.* ♦ *Diese Uhr geht nach/vor.* **2.** *(on the wrist)* watch ◊ *eine goldene Uhr tragen* ♦ *Auf seiner Uhr ist es halb zehn.* **3.** um drei/siebzehn etc. Uhr at three/five etc. (o'clock) ◊ *jeden Tag um acht Uhr aufstehen* ♦ *Der Laden hat von 9 Uhr bis 18 Uhr geöffnet.* null/vier etc. Uhr dreißig twelve/four etc. thirty ⊛ rund um die Uhr *(fam)* 24 hours a day

Uhr·zeit [ˈuːɐtsaet] die <–, –en> time ◊ *jdn nach der Uhrzeit fragen* ♦ *Um diese Uhrzeit schläft das Kind schon.* ♦ *Zu welcher Uhrzeit passierte der Unfall?*

In German, it is possible to answer the question 'what time is it?' in a number of ways. Somebody with a digital watch might say *dreizehn Uhr fünfzehn* ('one fifteen') or *zwölf Uhr zweiunddreißig* ('twelve thirty two'), whereas someone with an analogue watch might be more inclined to reply *Viertel nach eins* ('quarter past one') or *zwei nach halb eins* ('two minutes after half past twelve'). But watch out: in the South of Germany, people say *Viertel zwei* for one fifteen, which often leads to confusion between South and North Germans, and to North Germans being late for appointments (and sometimes even missing them). If you want to be sure of the time, then it is best to ask for it in exact figures.

U·kra·i·ne [ukraˈiːnə, uˈkraenə] <–> *no pl (always die Ukraine)* Ukraine ◊ *aus der Ukraine kommen/stammen* box@ Land

U·kra·i·ner [ukraˈiːnɐ, uˈkraenɐ] der <–s, –>, **U·kra·i·ne·rin** [ukraˈiːnərɪn, uˈkraenərɪn] die <–, –nen> Ukrainian → Deutsche

u·kra·i·nisch [ukraˈiːnɪʃ, uˈkraenɪʃ] ⸤adj⸥ *mostly before ns* Ukrainian → deutsch

U·kra·i·nisch [ukraˈiːnɪʃ, uˈkraenɪʃ] das <–(s)> *no pl* Ukrainian → Deutsch

② **um¹** [ʊm] ⸤adv⸥ **1.** um (die) ... getting on for ..., roughly ... ◊ *Es werden so um die 200 Leute*

kommen. ✦ *Die Reparatur wird um die 25 Euro kosten.* ⊜*ungefähr, etwa* **2.** *(fam) (break etc.)* over ◊ *So, die Pause ist um — macht euch wieder an die Arbeit. Ich sage dir Bescheid, wenn die Viertelstunde um ist.* I'll tell you when the fifteen minutes are up. ⊜*vorbei*

② **um²** [ʊm] (prep) (+acc) **1.** um etw. (herum) around sth ◊ *um das Haus gehen* ✦ *um die Ecke biegen* ✦ *Sie saßen um das Feuer herum.* Die Erde kreist um die Sonne. The earth orbits the sun. Er trug um den Arm die Binde um den Arm. He had a bandage on his arm. **2.** *(specific time)* um ... (Uhr) at ... (o' clock) ◊ *Ich bin spätestens um zehn (Uhr) wieder da.* **3.** um ... (herum) around ..., about ... ◊ *Ich mache heute so um sieben herum Schluss.* ✦ *Der Preis für diese Uhr liegt um 30 Euro.* **4.** mit Schimpfwörtern um sich werfen hurl abuse in all directions wild um sich schlagen lash out wildly Die traurige Stimmung griff (rasch) um sich. The sad atmosphere (quickly) spread. **5.** *(indicating a difference)* by ◊ *Sie hat sich um zehn Minuten verspätet.* ✦ *Ich habe mich um etwa einen Meter verschätzt.* ✦ *einen Preis um 25 Prozent reduzieren* **6.** *(regional) (indicating price)* Der Preis für diese Uhr liegt um 30 Euro. The price of this watch is 30 Euros. ⊜*bei* **7.** ... um ... ... after ... ◊ *Tag um Tag verging, ohne dass sich etwas änderte.* Schritt um Schritt step by step **8.** *(indicating a relationship)* for ◊ *jdn um etw. bitten* ✦ *um etw. kämpfen* ✦ *um jdn trauern* jdn um etw. beneiden envy sb sth jdn um etw. betrügen swindle sb out of sth der Skandal um das verseuchte Tierfutter the scandal involving the contaminated animal feed froh um etw. sein be pleased about sth

② **um³** [ʊm] (conjunc) **1.** +inf *(intention, consequence)* um zu ... (in order) to ... ◊ *Das tust du doch nur, um mich zu ärgern.* ✦ *Du brauchst 100 Punkte, um zu gewinnen.* **2.** with an adjective, +inf dumm/schlau/alt genug, um zu ... stupid/clever/old enough to ... ◊ *Er ist naiv genug, um das zu glauben.* ✦ *Sie ist reich genug, um sich so eine Urlaub leisten zu können.* zu schwach/klein/geizig, um zu ... too weak/small/stingy to ... ◊ *Sie war zu schwach, um aufzustehen.* **3.** +inf, only written *(subsequently)* um etw. zu tun and then did sth ◊ *Der Regen wurde immer schwächer, um schließlich ganz aufzuhören.*

um|...¹ [ʊm] (prefix) **1.** over ◊ *Wer hat das Rad umgeworfen?* ✦ *Er rannte mich um.* ✦ *jdn umfahren* **2.** translation varies *(change of place)* in eine andere Stadt umziehen move to a different town den Kaffee in eine andere Tasse umfüllen fill the coffee into a different cup **3.** re... ◊ *Wir bauen gerade um.* ✦ *eine Datei umbenennen* **4.** *(u-turn, circular movement)* around ◊ *Drehen Sie dort vorne um.* ✦ *Ein Gerücht geht um.* ✦ *Sieh dich mal um!*

um·...² [ʊm] (prefix) around ◊ *das Lenkrad fest umfassen* ✦ *Die Baustelle sollten wir umfahren.* ✦ *Können wir einen Konflikt umgehen?*

② **um·ar·men** [ʊm|'aʳmən] <umarmt, umarmte, hat umarmt> (tr v) jdn/etw. umarmen embrace sb/sth, hug sb/sth ◊ *Ich bin so glücklich, dass ich am liebsten die ganze Welt umarmen würde!* sich/einander umarmen embrace, hug ◊ *Nach ihrer Versöhnung umarmten sich die*

beiden Geschwister.

um|bau·en [ʊmbaʊ̯ən] <baut um, baute um, hat umgebaut> (tr v) etw. (in etw. (acc)/zu etw.) umbauen convert sth (into sth) ◊ *ein Haus umbauen* ✦ *die Terrasse zu einem Wintergarten umbauen* (intr v) do the/a conversion ◊ *Wir bauen für Sie um. Bitte entschuldigen Sie die dadurch entstehenden Unannehmlichkeiten.*

um|brin·gen ['ʊmbrɪŋən] <bringt um, brachte um, hat umgebracht> (tr v) *(fam)* kill, do in ◊ *Man sagt, er habe seine Frau umgebracht.* sich umbringen commit suicide, kill yourself
⊙ **nicht umzubringen sein** be indestructible jd/etw. bringt mich noch um *(fam)* sb/sth will be the death of me

um|den·ken ['ʊmdɛnkn̩] <denkt um, dachte um, hat umgedacht> (intr v) rethink, change your views ◊ *Wir müssen in der Sozialpolitik radikal umdenken.*

um|dre·hen ['ʊmdreːən] <dreht um, drehte um, hat/ist umgedreht> (tr v) +haben **1.** *(a key)* turn ◊ *den Schlüssel im Schloss umdrehen* jdm den Arm umdrehen twist sb's arm **2.** turn (over) ◊ *Er drehte das Blatt um und las, was auf der Rückseite stand.* **3.** *(pockets, trouser legs etc.)* turn inside out ◊ *Diese Hose sollte man vor dem Waschen umdrehen.* (intr v) +haben/sein *(fam)* turn around/back ◊ *Kurz vor dem Ziel mussten wir umdrehen.* ⊜*umkehren* (ref v) +haben sich (nach jdm/etw.) umdrehen turn round (to look at/face sb/sth) ◊ *Er drehte sich nach seinem Verfolger um.* Sie ist ein hübsches Mädchen, nach dem sich die Männer umdrehen. She is a pretty girl who can turn a few heads.

Um·dre·hung ['ʊm'dreːʊŋ] die <-, -en> revolution ◊ *eine halbe/volle Umdrehung* ✦ *Der Motor macht 4000 Umdrehungen pro Minute.*

um|fah·ren¹ ['ʊmfaːrən] <fährt um, fuhr um, hat umgefahren> (tr v) run over, knock down ◊ *ein Verkehrsschild umfahren* ✦ *Sie ist von einem Skifahrer umgefahren worden.*

um·fah·ren² [ʊm'faːrən] <umfährt, umfuhr, hat umfahren> (tr v) go round, drive round ◊ *ein Hindernis umfahren* ✦ *einen Stau weiträumig umfahren*

um|fal·len ['ʊmfalən] <fällt um, fiel um, ist umgefallen> (intr v) **1.** fall over ◊ *Pass auf, dass die teure Vase nicht umfällt.* ✦ *Sie ist mit ihrem Stuhl umgefallen.* ⊜*umkippen* **2.** *(sick person)* fall down, collapse ohnmächtig umfallen faint, pass out tot umfallen drop dead **3.** *(fam, pej)* do a U-turn ◊ *Wenn noch ein Konservativer umfällt, kommt das Gesetz nicht durch.*

Um·fang ['ʊmfaŋ] der <-(e)s, Umfänge> **1.** MATH circumference ◊ *den Umfang eines Kreises berechnen* ✦ *Der Stamm dieses Baumes hat einen Umfang von fast sechs Metern.*; *(of an area of land)* perimeter; *(of your stomach)* girth **2.** extent ◊ *Der Umfang des Schadens muss erst noch festgestellt werden.* ✦ *Der Umfang ihres Wissens ist erstaunlich.* ein Buch mit einem Umfang von über 1 200 Seiten a book containing over 1,200 pages Diese beiden Texte haben in etwa den gleichen Umfang. These two texts are roughly the same size. ⊜*Größe* **3.** in vollem Umfang fully, completely ◊ *Die Kosten*

werden in vollem Umfang erstattet. etw. in seinem vollen Umfang erkennen recognize the scope/full extent of sth; *(voice)* range

um·fang·reich ['ʊmfaŋraeç] [adj, adv] extensive(ly) ◊ *umfangreiche Ermittlungen anstellen* ♦ *Die Bibliothek ist sehr umfangreich.* ♦ *Sie haben auf diesem Gebiet umfangreich geforscht.*

um·fas·sen [ʊm'fasn̩] <umfasst, umfasste, hat umfasst> [tr v] **1.** *(book etc.)* etw. umfasst etw. sth contains sth, sth comprises sth ◊ *Das Buch umfasst etwa 450 Seiten.* ♦ *Das Werk umfasst acht Bände.* **2.** *(referring to the content)* etw. umfasst etw. sth includes sth, sth covers sth ◊ *Der erste Band umfasst das Früh- und Hochmittelalter.* **3.** etw. umfassen grasp sth ◊ *Sie umfasste das Geländer mit beiden Händen.; (sb's waist etc.)* put your arms around sth **4.** *(a garden etc.)* etw. (mit etw.) umfassen encircle sth (with sth)

um·fas·send [ʊm'fasn̩t, ʊm'fasənt] *pres p of* umfassen [adj, adv] **1.** full(y), complete(ly) ◊ *Der Angeklagte legte ein umfassendes Geständnis ab.* ♦ *Seine Beichte war ehrlich und umfassend.* ♦ *sich umfassend informieren* **2.** comprehensive(ly), extensive(ly) ◊ *Er verfügt über umfassende Kenntnisse auf diesem Gebiet.* ♦ *Sein Wissen ist sehr umfassend.* ♦ *Ich habe mich umfassend über sie erkundigt.*

Um·feld ['ʊmfɛlt] das <-(e)s, –er> *most sing* surroundings, sphere, environment ◊ *ein stabiles psychosoziales Umfeld* ♦ *Nachforschungen im politischen Umfeld einer Person anstellen*

Um·fra·ge ['ʊmfraːgə] die <-, –n> *(abbr of* Meinungsumfrage*)* survey ◊ *Die Umfrage hat ergeben, dass ...* ♦ *eine repräsentative Umfrage* ♦ *eine Umfrage durchführen; (political)* opinion poll

Um·gang ['ʊmgaŋ] der <-(e)s> *no pl* **1.** der Umgang (mit jdm) the contact (with sb) ◊ *Der Umgang mit den richtigen Leuten ist wichtig.* mit jdm Umgang haben/pflegen associate with sb **2.** company guten/schlechten Umgang haben keep good/bad company **3.** dealings geschickt im Umgang mit etw./jdm sein be skilful in dealing with/managing sth/sb Durch den Umgang mit alten Menschen ist sie nachdenklicher geworden. Dealing with the elderly has made her more pensive. Kinder sollten schon früh den richtigen Umgang mit Geld lernen. Children should be taught at an early age how to manage money. Durch einen sparsameren Umgang mit Energie könnten wir die Umwelt entlasten. By using energy more sparingly we could relieve pressure on the environment. ⊛ jd ist kein Umgang für jdn sb is not fit company for sb

um·gäng·lich ['ʊmgɛŋlɪç] [adj] obliging, friendly, pleasant-natured ◊ *ein umgänglicher Mensch/Typ* ♦ *Sie ist umgänglicher geworden.* ⊖verträglich ⊖schwierig

um·gangs·sprach·lich ['ʊmgaŋsʃpraːxlɪç] [adj, adv] *no comp/superl* colloquial(ly) ◊ *umgangssprachliche Wendungen* ♦ *Das Wort „kriegen" ist eher umgangssprachlich.* ♦ *Dieser Ausdruck wird nur umgangssprachlich verwendet.* [adv] colloquially, in a colloquial way ◊ *Umgangssprachlich ausgedrückt würde man sagen: „Ich hab die Schnauze voll!"*

um·ge·ben [ʊm'geːbm̩] <umgibt, umgab, hat umgeben> [tr v] etw. umgibt jdn/etw. sth surrounds sb/sth ◊ *Ein hoher Zaun umgibt das Haus.* ♦ *Plötzlich war er von neugierigen Menschen umgeben.* ♦ *Sie waren von völliger Dunkelheit umgeben.* etw./jdn mit etw./jdm umgeben surround sth/sb with sth/sb ◊ *Sie umgab sich gerne mit Künstlern.*

② **Um·ge·bung** [ʊm'geːbʊŋ] die <-, –en> **1.** surroundings, vicinity ◊ *Gibt es hier in der Umgebung einen Kinderspielplatz?* ♦ *Enten findet man meist in der Umgebung von Wasser.* ⊖Umkreis **2.** environment ◊ *Sie muss sich erst an die neue Umgebung gewöhnen.* ♦ *Tiere in ihrer natürlichen Umgebung beobachten*

um|ge·hen¹ ['ʊmgeːən] <geht um, ging um, ist umgegangen> [intr v] **1.** mit jdm/etw. (irgendwie) umgehen deal with sb/sth (in a certain manner), handle sb/sth (in a certain way) ◊ *Kannst du mit einer Kettensäge umgehen?* ♦ *Er kann gut mit Kindern/Tieren umgehen.* ♦ *sparsam/verschwenderisch mit Wasser umgehen* **2.** circulate, go round ◊ *Ein Gerücht geht um.* ♦ *Im Kindergarten gehen die Windpocken um.; (fear)* be spreading ◊ *Seit dem Mord geht in der Stadt die Angst um.* **3.** *(a ghost)* jd/etw. geht irgendwo um sb/sth haunts a location

um·ge·hen² [ʊm'geːən] <umgeht, umging, hat umgangen> [tr v] **1.** *(a traffic jam, an obstacle etc.)* go round, by-pass ◊ *Wir wollen versuchen, den Stau zu umgehen.* ♦ *ein Hindernis umgehen* **2.** *(an unpleasant event etc.)* avoid ◊ *Es lässt sich nicht umgehen, dass wir noch einmal zurückfahren.* ♦ *Die Erwähnung dieses Problems hat sie geschickt umgangen.* ⊖vermeiden **3.** *(a law, regulation etc.)* circumvent, evade ◊ *Er hat versucht, die Vorschriften zu umgehen.* Sie hat ihre Vorgesetzte einfach umgangen und die Entscheidung allein getroffen. She simply went over the heads of her superior and took the decision herself.

um·ge·hend ['ʊmgeːənt] [adj] *no comp/superl; only before ns* immediate, prompt ◊ *Wir bitten um umgehende Antwort/Zahlung.* [adv] immediately ◊ *Ich schicke Ihnen die Waren umgehend zu.; (in commercial correspondence)* by return ⊖prompt, sofort

um·ge·kehrt ['ʊmgəkeːɐt] *past p of* umkehren [adj] *no comp/superl* opposite, the other way round, vice versa ◊ *Der Wagen fuhr in umgekehrter Richtung zurück.* ♦ *Es war genau umgekehrt: Nicht er hat sie verlassen, sondern sie ihn.* in umgekehrter Reihenfolge in reverse order [adv] the other way round ◊ *Du musst das genau umgekehrt machen: Zuerst die negativen, dann die positiven Aspekte nennen.; the other way up* ◊ *Kann man diese Picknickdecke auch umgekehrt verwenden?* Meine neue Wendejacke kann ich auch umgekehrt anziehen. My new jacket is also reversible.

um|hän·gen ['ʊmhɛŋən] <hängt um, hängte um, hat umgehängt> [tr v] **1.** *(a picture etc.)* rehang; *(the washing etc.)* hang somewhere else **2.** jdm/sich etw. umhängen drape sth round sb/yourself ◊ *Komm, häng dir deinen Mantel um, dann wird dir wärmer.* jdm [dat] eine Kette umhängen put a chain round your neck sich [dat] eine Tasche umhängen sling a bag over your shoulder

um·her [ʊm'heːɐ] [adv] around, about ◊ *Die*

A B C D E F G H I J K L M N O P Q R S T U V W X Y Z

Trümmer lagen weit umher verstreut.

um·her|... [ʊmˈheːɐ̯] prefix around, about ◇ *Sie blickte umher, konnte ihn aber nicht entdecken.* ♦ *ziellos in der Gegend umherfahren* in einem Zimmer *umherlaufen* pace a room

Um·kehr [ˈʊmkeːɐ̯] die <-> no pl *(also fig)* turning back; *(religious)* changing of your ways jdn zur Umkehr bewegen/zwingen force sb to turn back, force sb into a U-turn ◇ *Die vielen Demonstrationen bewegten die Politiker zur Umkehr.*

um|keh·ren [ˈʊmkeːrən] <kehrt um, kehrte um, hat/ist umgekehrt> intr v +*sein (also fig)* turn back ◇ *Es wird schon bald dunkel — wir sollten umkehren.* ♦ *Kehr um, bevor es zu spät ist!* ⊖umdrehen tr v +*haben* **1.** *(a development, sequence etc.)* reverse ◇ *Diese Entwicklung lässt sich nicht umkehren.* ♦ *Warum kehren wir die Reihenfolge nicht einfach um?* sich umkehren be reversed ◇ *In Zukunft wird sich das Verhältnis von Rentnern und Arbeitnehmern nahezu umkehren.* **2.** *(a jacket, stockings etc.)* turn inside out ◇ *Er kehrte seine Hosentaschen um und leerte sie aus. Das Gehirn muss das Kopf stehende Bild auf der Netzhaut umkehren.* The brain has to turn the inverted image on the retina the right way up.

um|kip·pen [ˈʊmkɪpm̩] <kippt um, kippte um, hat/ist umgekippt> intr v +*sein* **1.** *(a glass, vase etc.)* tip over, overturn ◇ *Das Glas ist umgekippt.* ♦ *Pass auf, dass das Boot nicht umkippt. Er ist mit dem Stuhl umgekippt.* The chair toppled over with him on it. ⊖umfallen **2.** *(fam)* pass out ◇ *Bei der Hitze sind einige umgekippt.* **3.** *(fam) (atmosphere, mood)* turn, change ◇ *Die Stimmung im Saal kippte um;* *(voice)* crack **4.** BIO *(pond, lake etc.)* become polluted, become stagnant ◇ *Dieser Badesee kippt im Sommer bei hohen Temperaturen regelmäßig um.* tr v +*haben* knock over, overturn ◇ *Pass auf, dass du die Flasche nicht umkippst.* ⊖umwerfen

um|kom·men [ˈʊmkɔmən] <kommt um, kam um, ist umgekommen> intr v **1.** *(in an accident etc.)* die, be killed ◇ *Bei dem Zugunglück kamen über 100 Menschen um.* ⊖sterben ⊖überleben **2.** *(fam)* vor etw. dat umkommen die of sth ◇ *Ich komme um vor Hunger!*

Um·kreis [ˈʊmkraes] der <-es> no pl area, surroundings ◇ *Im ganzen Umkreis gibt es keinen Kinderarzt.* in einem Umkreis von 20 Kilometern within a radius of 20 kilometres im Umkreis der Stadt wohnen live in the immediate vicinity of the town jds engster Umkreis sb's inner circle ⊖Umgebung

um·krei·sen [ʊmˈkraezn̩] <umkreist, umkreiste, hat umkreist> tr v **1.** circle (around) ◇ *Die Hyänen umkreisten hungrig den Kadaver.; (planet, satellite)* orbit ◇ *Der Mond umkreist die Erde.* **2.** *(fig) (a problem, dilemma etc.)* revolve around ◇ *Seine Gedanken umkreisten immer nur ein Thema.*

Um·land [ˈʊmlant] das <-(e)s> no pl surrounding area ◇ *Viele Kinder aus dem Umland besuchen eine Schule in der Stadt.* ♦ *im Umland wohnen*

Um·lauf·bahn [ˈʊmlaofbaːn] die <-, –en> orbit ◇ *die Umlaufbahnen der Planeten*

Um·laut [ˈʊmlaot] der <-(e)s, –e> *(tech)* **1.** no pl *(sound)* vowel mutation ◇ *Das „äu" in „Mäuse"* ist der Umlaut des „au" in „Maus". **2.** *(letter)* mutated vowel, (vowel with an) umlaut ◇ *„Ä" ist ein Umlaut.*

um|le·gen [ˈʊmleːɡn̩] <legt um, legte um, hat umgelegt> tr v **1.** *(a lever)* turn, move ◇ *Bitte zum Einschalten den roten Hebel umlegen.* **2.** *(an appointment etc.)* change ◇ *Ich versuche, den Termin umzulegen.* **3.** *(a patient, telephone call etc.)* transfer ◇ *ein Telefongespräch umlegen* ein Kabel umlegen re-lay a cable **4.** jdm/sich etw. umlegen put sth round sb/yourself ◇ *Sie legte dem frierenden Kind eine Decke um.* **5.** *(costs etc.)* etw. auf jdn/etw. umlegen split sth between sb/sth, share sth between sb/sth ◇ *Die Heizkosten werden auf die Mieter umgelegt.* Legt man die 20 Krankheitsfälle auf 10 Jahre um, kommt man auf zwei Fälle pro Jahr. If the 20 cases of illness are spread over a 10 year period that works out at 2 cases per year. **6.** *(fam) (boxer, thug etc.)* jdn umlegen knock sb down, floor sb ◇ *Den lege ich doch mit der linken Hand um.* **7.** *(fam)* jdn umlegen do sb in, eliminate sb ◇ *Er weiß zu viel — leg ihn um!* ⊖töten

um|lei·ten [ˈʊmlaetn̩] <leitet um, leitete um, hat umgeleitet> tr v divert ♦ *Wegen der Demonstration leitet die Polizei den Verkehr um.* ♦ *einen Fluss umleiten* ♦ *Alle Anrufe werden automatisch zu ihrer Kollegin umgeleitet.*

ⓩ **Um·lei·tung** [ˈʊmlaetʊŋ] die <-, –en> diversion ◇ *Die Umleitung des Flusses gestaltete sich schwierig.* ♦ *Eine Umleitung des Verkehrs ist nicht zu vermeiden.* ein Umleitung fahren take a diversion

um·lie·gend [ˈʊmliːɡn̩t, ˈʊmliːɡənt] adj no comp/superl, only before ns surrounding ◇ *die Stadt und die umliegenden Dörfer*

um·rah·men [ʊmˈraːmən] <umrahmt, umrahmte, hat umrahmt> tr v **1.** *(the face etc.)* frame ◇ *Ein Bart umrahmte sein Gesicht.* **2.** give a musical accompaniment to ◇ *einen Vortrag mit Musik umrahmen*

um|räu·men [ˈʊmrɔʏmən] <räumt um, räumte um, hat umgeräumt> tr v **1.** move ◇ *Räumst du bitte deine Hemden in den anderen Kleiderschrank um?* **2.** *(a room)* rearrange the furniture ◇ *Sie haben ihr Wohnzimmer völlig umgeräumt.* Nächste Woche räumen wir den Keller um. We're going to change things around in the cellar next week. intr v rearrange things ◇ *Ich muss in der Garage mal wieder umräumen.*

um·rin·gen [ʊmˈrɪŋən] <umringt, umringte, hat umringt> tr v surround ◇ *Die Zuschauer umringten den Straßenkünstler.* ⊖umgeben

Um·riss [ˈʊmrɪs] der <-es, –e> **1.** outline, silhouette ◇ *Ich konnte nur die Umrisse des Mannes erkennen.* ♦ *Im Dunkeln zeichneten sich die Umrisse eines Hauses ab.* **2.** in (groben) Umrissen in outline eine Situation in groben Umrissen beschreiben describe a situation in rough detail **3.** *(fig)* feste Umrisse annehmen take shape ◇ *Allmählich nimmt die Idee feste Umrisse an.*

ⓩ **ums** [ʊms] contract *um + das* **1.** around the ◇ *Sie gingen ums Haus herum.* ♦ *Hier gibt es alles rund ums Fahrrad.* → um **2.** *in certain idioms: look up the relevant idiom* ◇ *es geht ums Ganze*

Um·satz [ˈʊmzats] der <-es, Umsätze> turnover ◇

Werbung hebt den Umsatz. ♦ *Das Restaurant macht einen Umsatz von etwa 900 Euro pro Tag.*
um|schal·ten ['ʊmʃaltn̩] <schaltet um, schaltete um, hat umgeschaltet> [tr+intr v] (auf etw. [acc]) umschalten switch (to sth), change (to sth) ◊ *Jetzt schalte doch nicht dauernd um — ich möchte den Film sehen!* ♦ *Die Ampel schaltete von Rot auf Grün um.* ♦ *ein Gerät auf Batteriebetrieb umschalten* [intr v] **1.** RADIO, TV *irgendwohin umschalten go over to somewhere* ◊ *Wir schalten jetzt ins Stadion um.* **2.** *(fam)* (auf etw. [acc]) umschalten change (to sth) ◊ *Es ist gar nicht so schwer, in England auf Linksverkehr umzuschalten.* auf eine andere Sprache umschalten switch to another language
Um·schlag ['ʊmʃlaːk] der <-(e)s, Umschläge> **1.** *(of a book etc.)* cover, jacket **2.** *(abbr of* Briefumschlag*)* envelope ◊ *ein Schreiben in den Umschlag stecken* ⊝Kuvert **3.** *most pl* MED compress, poultice ◊ *Sie machte ihm kalte Umschläge gegen das Fieber.* **4.** ein Umschlag (… [gen]) a (sudden) change (in sth) ◊ *ein plötzlicher Umschlag der Stimmung/des Wetters* ein Umschlag ins Gegenteil a sudden reversal **5.** *no pl* ECON transfer, trans-shipment ◊ *Wo sind die besten Standorte für den Umschlag der Waren?*
um·schlie·ßen [ʊm'ʃliːsn̩] <umschließt, umschloss, hat umschlossen> [tr v] **1.** etw. umschließt etw. sth surrounds sth ◊ *Eine Mauer umschließt das Grundstück.* ♦ *Eine dicke Schale umschließt die Frucht.* ⊝umgeben **2.** *(hands etc.)* etw. umschließen hold sth ◊ *Seine Finger umschlossen den kostbaren Edelstein.* **3.** *(person)* jdn irgendwie umschließen embrace sb in a certain way ◊ *Er umschloss sie mit beiden Armen und drückte sie an sich.* ⊝umarmen
um|schrei·ben¹ ['ʊmʃraebm̩] <schreibt um, schrieb um, hat umgeschrieben> [tr v] rewrite ◊ *Wir müssen das Drehbuch umschreiben.*
um·schrei·ben² [ʊm'ʃraebm̩] <umschreibt, umschrieb, hat umschrieben> [tr v] **1.** paraphrase ◊ *Er versuchte, den Begriff zu umschreiben.* **2.** outline ◊ *jds zukünftige Aufgaben genau umschreiben* ♦ *Umschreiben Sie bitte kurz, was Sie bisher gemacht haben.*
um|se·hen ['ʊmzeːən] <sieht sich um, sah sich um, hat sich umgesehen> [ref v] **1.** sich *(irgendwo)* umsehen look around ◊ *Sie sah sich neugierig im Zimmer um.* ♦ *Nein, ich möchte nichts kaufen, ich will mich nur mal umsehen.* **2.** *(a pursuer etc.)* sich nach jdm/etw. umsehen look round/back at sb/sth, turn round to look at sb/sth ◊ *Er sah sich suchend nach seiner Frau um.* **3.** sich nach etw. umsehen look around for sth ◊ *Ich sehe mich gerade nach einer neuen Wohnung um.*
⊛ jd wird sich noch umsehen sb is in for a big surprise
um|set·zen ['ʊmzɛtsn̩] <setzt um, setzte um, hat umgesetzt> [tr v] **1.** move ◊ *Wir müssen diesen Pfeiler umsetzen.* ♦ *Die Lehrerin hat den Schüler umgesetzt.* **2.** transplant, repot ◊ *Der Topf ist zu klein geworden; du solltest den Kaktus umsetzen.* **3.** etw. in etw. [acc] umsetzen convert sth into sth ◊ *Wasserkraft in Strom umsetzen* ⊝umwandeln **4.** transpose ◊ *Gefühle in Musik umsetzen*

5. *(fam)* *(money)* etw. in etw. [acc] umsetzen blow sth on sth ◊ *Er hat wieder einmal sein ganzes Taschengeld in Computerspiele umgesetzt.* **6.** etw. (in die Praxis) umsetzen put sth into practice ◊ *Wie können wir den Plan am besten umsetzen?* etw. (in die Tat) umsetzen translate sth into action **7.** ECON *(goods)* turn over, sell ◊ *Waren im Wert von über einer Million Euro umsetzen*
um·sich·tig ['ʊmzɪçtɪç] [adj, adv] circumspect(ly), prudent(ly) ◊ *eine umsichtige Mitarbeiterin* ♦ *Er war schon immer sehr umsichtig.* ♦ *Sie hat in dieser schwierigen Situation sehr umsichtig gehandelt.* ⊝besonnen ⊝leichtsinnig
② **um·so** ['ʊmzoː] [conjunc] **1.** je … umso the … the ◊ *Je größer ein Hund ist, umso mehr Futter braucht er.* ♦ *Je schneller man fährt, umso gefährlicher ist es.* ♦ *Je früher (er kommt), umso besser.* **2.** umso …, als all the (more) … as ◊ *Der Einführungskurs ist umso wichtiger, als viele Studenten nicht einmal über Grundkenntnisse verfügen.* umso … all the … (for that) ◊ *„Er bringt noch ein paar Freunde mit." — „Umso besser!"* ♦ *Nach seiner Krankheit ist es jetzt umso wichtiger, dass er sich schont.*
② **um·sonst** [ʊm'zɔnst] [adv] *no comp/superl* **1.** free (of charge) ◊ *In vielen Geschäften gibt es Tragetüten umsonst.* ♦ *Ich gebe Ihnen noch ein Pflegemittel umsonst dazu.* ⊝gratis, kostenlos **2.** for nothing ◊ *Umsonst mache ich das aber nicht.* ⊝unentgeltlich **3.** in vain, to no avail ◊ *Die ganze Arbeit war wieder einmal umsonst.* ♦ *Jetzt haben Sie sich leider umsonst bemüht.* ⊝vergeblich **4.** nicht umsonst not without reason ◊ *Ich habe dich nicht umsonst vor diesem Hund gewarnt — er hat schon einmal jemanden gebissen.*
Um·stand ['ʊmʃtant] der <-(e)s, Umstände> **1.** circumstance ◊ *Unter diesen Umständen kann ich nicht zulassen, dass du allein wegfährst.* unter (gar) keinen Umständen under no circumstances (whatsoever) den Umständen entsprechend in/under the circumstances ◊ *Ihrer Frau geht es den Umständen entsprechend gut.* mildernde Umstände mitigating/extenuating circumstances die näheren Umstände the details ein glücklicher Umstand a lucky chance unter Umständen possibly, perhaps ◊ *Unter Umständen haben wir eine Stelle für Sie frei.* unter allen Umständen at all costs, no matter what ◊ *Er muss unter allen Umständen heute noch bezahlen.* **2.** *only pl (in polite phrases)* Machen Sie sich/mach dir keine Umstände!, Nur keine Umstände! Don't go to any bother/trouble! etw. macht (jdm) wirklich/gar keine Umstände sth is no bother/trouble at all (for sb)
⊛ in anderen Umständen sein *(oldf)* be expecting
um·ständ·lich ['ʊmʃtɛntlɪç] [adj] **1.** *(preparations etc.)* laborious ◊ *umständliche Vorbereitungen; (person)* awkward ◊ *Werner ist ein furchtbar umständlicher Mensch. Sei doch nicht so umständlich!* Don't complicate everything! **2.** *(appliance etc.)* involved ◊ *Dieser Videorekorder ist mir viel zu umständlich.* ♦ *eine umständliche Methode* [adv] **1.** laboriously, at great length ◊ *Umständlich erklärte er den Passanten den Weg zum Bahnhof.* **2.** *(operation etc.)* in an involved way Diese Waschmaschine ist aber ziemlich umständlich zu

bedienen. Operating this washing machine is a rather involved process.

Um·stands·wort ['ʊmʃtantsvɔˀt] das <-(e)s, Umstandswörter> adverb ◊ *„Gestern" ist ein Umstandswort der Zeit.* ⊖Adverb

ⓩ **um|stei·gen** ['ʊmʃtaegn̩] <steigt um, stieg um, ist umgestiegen> [intr v] **1.** *(von etw.) (in etw.* [acc]*)* umsteigen change (from sth) (to sth) ◊ *Ich muss in Zürich umsteigen.* ◊ *von der U-Bahn in den Bus umsteigen* **2.** *(fam)* auf etw. [acc] umsteigen change to sth ◊ *Er ist vom Auto aufs Fahrrad umgestiegen.* ♦ *Spätestens nach dem zweiten Bier steige ich auf Mineralwasser um.*

um|stel·len¹ ['ʊmʃtɛlən] <stellt um, stellte um, hat umgestellt> [tr v] **1.** rearrange, change around ◊ *die Möbel umstellen* ◊ *Du solltest diese Sätze im Text ein wenig umstellen.* **2.** *(a lever, points etc.)* switch ◊ *einen Hebel umstellen* [tr+intr v] *(auf etw.* [acc]*)* umstellen change (to sth) ◊ *Ich habe meine Ernährung völlig umgestellt.* ♦ *die Uhr von Winterauf Sommerzeit umstellen* den Betrieb auf Computer umstellen computerize the operation [ref v] sich umstellen adjust to the new situation/circumstances/life etc. ◊ *Nach der Geburt der Zwillinge mussten wir uns ziemlich umstellen.* sich auf etw. [acc] umstellen adjust to sth ◊ *sich auf ein anderes Klima umstellen*

um·stel·len² [ʊm'ʃtɛlən] <umstellt, umstellte, hat umstellt> [tr v] surround ◊ *Die Polizei hat das Gebäude umstellt.* ⊖umringen

um|stim·men ['ʊmʃtɪmən] <stimmt um, stimmte um, hat umgestimmt> [tr v] jdn umstimmen change sb's mind ◊ *Wir haben alles versucht, aber wir konnten ihn nicht umstimmen.*

um·strit·ten [ʊm'ʃtrɪtn̩] [adj] controversial, disputed ◊ *eine umstrittene Methode* ◊ *Diese These ist in der Fachwelt umstritten.* ♦ *Er ist als Autor nach wie vor umstritten.* ⊖strittig

Um·sturz ['ʊmʃtʊˀts] der <-es, Umstürze> coup (d'état) ◊ *Er gelangte durch einen Umsturz an die Macht.*

um|stür·zen ['ʊmʃtyˀtsn̩] <stürzt um, stürzte um, hat/ist umgestürzt> [intr v] +*sein* overturn ◊ *Der Lkw kam ins Schleudern und stürzte um.; (tree)* blow down ◊ *Bei den Unwettern sind einige Bäume umgestürzt. Sie ist mit dem Stuhl umgestürzt.* The chair overturned with her on it. ⊖umfallen [tr v] +*haben* overturn, knock over ◊ *Rasend vor Wut stürzte er den Tisch um.* ⊖umwerfen

ⓩ **um|tau·schen** ['ʊmtaoʃn̩] <tauscht um, tauschte um, hat umgetauscht> [tr v] **1.** (jdm) etw. (gegen etw.) umtauschen (ex)change sth (for sth) ◊ *Wenn die Schuhe Ihrem Sohn nicht passen, können Sie sie gerne umtauschen.* ♦ *Das Geschäft hat mir das defekte Gerät problemlos gegen ein neues umgetauscht.* **2.** *(money)* (jdm) etw. (in etw. [acc]*)* umtauschen change sth (into sth), convert sth (into sth) ◊ *Ich möchte gerne Euro in Dollar umtauschen.* ♦ *Könnten Sie mir 100 Pfund in Euro umtauschen?*

um|wan·deln ['ʊmvandln̩] <wandelt um, wandelte um, hat umgewandelt> [tr v] etw. in etw. [acc]/zu etw. umwandeln convert sth into sth ◊ *Diese Turbinen wandeln Wasserkraft in Strom um.* ♦ *Mietwohnungen in Eigentumswohnungen umwandeln; (a sentence)* commute sth to sth ◊ *Seine Freiheits-*

strafe wurde in eine Geldstrafe umgewandelt.

⊙ **wie umgewandelt sein** be a changed person

Um·weg ['ʊmveːk] der <-(e)s, –e> detour ◊ *Sie mussten einen Umweg machen.* ♦ *Auf dem Heimweg sind wir einen Umweg über Regensburg gefahren.*

⊙ **auf Umwegen** by a circuitous route *(fig also)* in a roundabout way ◊ *Er erreichte sein Ziel auf Umwegen.* etw. auf Umwegen erfahren find sth out indirectly

ⓩ **Um·welt** ['ʊmvɛlt] die <–> *no pl* **1.** environment ◊ *Abgase belasten die Umwelt.* **2.** jds Umwelt those around sb ◊ *Er fühlt sich von seiner Umwelt nicht verstanden.*

um·welt·freund·lich ['ʊmvɛltfrɔøntlɪç] [adj] environmentally friendly ◊ *ein umweltfreundliches Waschmittel* ♦ *Diese Verpackung ist umweltfreundlich.* [adv] in an environmentally friendly way ◊ *Solaranlagen produzieren Strom besonders umweltfreundlich.*

Um·welt·schutz ['ʊmvɛltʃʊts] der <-es> *no pl* conservation, protection of the environment ◊ *Jeder Einzelne kann etwas zum Umweltschutz beitragen.*

um|wer·fen ['ʊmvɛˀfn̩] <wirft um, warf um, hat umgeworfen> [tr v] **1.** *(a vase, table etc.)* knock over ◊ *Wer hat die Vase umgeworfen?; (storm)* blow over ◊ *Der Sturm war so stark, dass er das Kind beinahe umwarf.* **2.** *(a coat, blanket)* jdm/ sich etw. umwerfen put sth round your shoulders/ sb ◊ *Er warf dem zitternden Kind eine Decke um.* **3.** *(fam)* jdn umwerfen upset sb, make sb lose it, really get to sb ◊ *Die Neuigkeit warf sie fast um.* ♦ *Mich wirft so leicht nichts um.* **4.** *(fam) (a plan etc.)* knock on the head ◊ *Sie hat ihre Pläne, die Wohnung zu renovieren, wieder umgeworfen.*

um·wer·fend ['ʊmvɛˀfn̩t, ˌʊmvɛˀfant] *pres p of* umwerfen [adj] fantastic, stunning ◊ *Das war ein umwerfendes Erlebnis.* ♦ *Dieses Kleid ist umwerfend!* [adv] fantastically (well) ◊ *Der Haupdarsteller hat umwerfend gespielt.* ♦ *Das Stück ist umwerfend komisch.*

ⓩ **um|zie·hen** ['ʊmtsiːən] <zieht um, zog um, hat/ist umgezogen> [intr v] +*sein* (irgendwohin) umziehen move (somewhere) ◊ *Wenn das Kind da ist, werden wir in eine größere Wohnung umziehen.* [tr v] +*haben* sich umziehen get changed, change ◊ *Nach der Arbeit zieht er sich immer um.* sich zum Sport umziehen put your kit on jdn umziehen change sb ◊ *Sie zog das Kind (zum Spielen) um.*

ⓩ **um zu** [ʊm tsuː] [conjunc] → um

Um·zug ['ʊmtsuːk] der <-(e)s, Umzüge> **1.** *(to a new place)* move ◊ *Der Umzug in die neue Wohnung wird etwa drei Tage dauern.* ♦ *jdm beim Umzug helfen* **2.** procession ◊ *ein festlicher Umzug der Schützenvereine*

ⓩ **un·...** [ʊn] [prefix] un... ♦ *Er ist nicht glücklich, sondern unglücklich.* ♦ *unattraktiv* ◊ *unbehandelt; in...* ◊ *unsicher; im...* ◊ *ungeduldig; dis...* ◊ *unehrlich*

un·ab·hän·gig ['ʊnʔaphɛŋɪç] [adj] **1.** *(von jdm/ etw.)* unabhängig independent (of sb/sth) ◊ *Sie möchte finanziell von ihrem Mann unabhängig sein.* ♦ *ein unabhängiger Richter* ♦ *Die ehemalige Kolonie ist seit zehn Jahren unabhängig.* sich von jdm/etw. unabhängig machen become independent

of sb/sth **2.** unabhängig davon, ob ... irrespective/ regardless of whether ... ◊ *Wir werden eine tolle Party feiern, unabhängig davon, ob er kommt oder nicht.* `[adj, adv]` unabhängig voneinander independent(ly) (from one another), seperate(ly) ◊ *Das sind zwei voneinander völlig unabhängige Ereignisse.*

Un·ab·hän·gig·keit [ˈʊn|apheŋɪçkaet] die <-> *no pl* Unabhängigkeit (von jdm/etw.) independence (from sb/sth) ◊ *Finanzielle Unabhängigkeit ist ihr sehr wichtig.* ✦ *Die Unabhängigkeit der Justiz muss gewährleistet sein.* ✦ *Kolonien in die Unabhängigkeit entlassen*

un·ab·läs·sig [ˈʊn|aplɛsɪç, – – '– –] `[adj, adv]` *no comp/superl, when used as an adj, only before ns* continual(ly), incessant(ly) ◊ *eine unablässige Wiederholung* ✦ *Sie redet wirklich unablässig.* ⊜ständig

un·an·ge·foch·ten [ˈʊn|angəfɔxtn̩] `[adj, adv]` *no comp/superl* unchallenged ◊ *Auf diesem Gebiet sind sie unangefochtener Marktführer.* ✦ *Seine Stellung ist unangefochten.* ✦ *unangefochten an der Spitze stehen*

un·an·ge·mes·sen [ˈʊn|angəmɛsn̩] `[adj, adv]` inappropriate(ly) ◊ *eine unangemessene Reaktion*; *(exceeding the normal)* excessive(ly) ◊ *Eine solche Forderung ist völlig unangemessen.* ✦ *Der Preis war unangemessen hoch.* ⊜angemessen

un·an·ge·nehm [ˈʊn|angəne:m] `[adj]` **1.** unpleasant ◊ *unangenehme Wahrheiten aussprechen* etw. ist jdm unangenehm sb doesn't like sth **2.** awkward, embarrassing ◊ *jdn in eine unangenehme Lage bringen* etw. ist jdm unangenehm sth is embarrassing for sb ◊ *Das Ganze war ihr äußerst unangenehm.* ⊜peinlich **3.** *(person)* unangenehm werden turn nasty ⊜böse `[adv]` **1.** unpleasantly ◊ *Heute ist es unangenehm schwül.* unangenehm auffallen stick out like a sore thumb sich unangenehm berührt fühlen, unangenehm berührt sein feel uncomfortable ⊜angenehm **2.** etw. berührt jdn unangenehm sth embarrasses sb ◊ *Sein übertriebenes Lob berührte mich unangenehm.* ⊜peinlich

un·an·nehm·bar [ˈʊn|anne:mba:ɐ̯] `[adj]` unacceptable ◊ *unannehmbare Forderungen stellen* ✦ *Das Angebot wurde als unannehmbar zurückgewiesen.*

Un·an·nehm·lich·keit [ˈʊn|anne:mlɪçkaet] die <-, –en> *most pl* trouble ◊ *jdm Unannehmlichkeiten bereiten*

un·an·stän·dig [ˈʊn|anʃtɛndɪç] `[adj, adv]` indecent(ly), rude(ly) ◊ *unanständige Witze* ✦ *Es ist geradezu unanständig, wie viel sie damit verdient!* ✦ *sich unanständig benehmen* ⊜obszön ⊜anständig

un·ap·pe·tit·lich [ˈʊn|apeti:tlɪç] `[adj, adv]` unappetizing ◊ *ein unappetitlicher Geruch* ✦ *Die Soße war kalt und unappetitlich.* ✦ *unappetitlich aussehen* ⊜widerlich ⊜lecker `[adj]` *(repugnant)* disgusting ◊ *Ich finde sein ungepflegtes Äußeres ziemlich unappetitlich.* ✦ *unappetitlich Bilder auf dem Internet*

un·auf·fäl·lig [ˈʊn|aʊffɛlɪç] `[adj, adv]` unobtrusive(ly), inconspicuous(ly), discreet(y) ◊ *Die Weinrebe hat unauffällige Blüten.* ✦ *Ihre Erscheinung ist eher unauffällig.* ✦ *Sie blieb unauffällig im Hintergrund.* ⊜auffällig

un·auf·halt·sam [ˈʊn|aʊfhaltza:m, – – '– –] `[adj, adv]` *no comp/superl* unstoppable(-ably), inex-

orable(-ably) ◊ *Die Entwicklung schien unaufhaltsam zu sein.* ✦ *Er trat einen scheinbar unaufhaltsamen Siegeszug an.* ✦ *Der Verfall schreitet unaufhaltsam voran.*

un·auf·hör·lich [ˈʊn|aʊfhøːɐ̯lɪç, – – '– –] `[adj, adv]` *no comp/superl; when used as an adj, only before ns* constant(ly), incessant(ly) ◊ *ein unaufhörlicher Kreislauf* ✦ *Die Arbeitslosenzahl wächst unaufhörlich.* ⊜unentwegt

un·aus·weich·lich [ˈʊn|aʊsvaeçlɪç, – – '– –] `[adj]` *no comp/superl* inevitable, unavoidable ◊ *Ein Krieg scheint unausweichlich geworden.* ✦ *unausweichliche Konsequenzen* ⊜unumgänglich

un·barm·her·zig [ˈʊnbaˈmhɛˈtsɪç] `[adj, adv]` *(also fig)* merciless(ly) ◊ *ein unbarmherziger Richter* ✦ *Sei doch nicht so unbarmherig!* ✦ *Die Sonne brannte unbarmherzig auf sie hinunter.*

un·be·ab·sich·tigt [ˈʊnbə|apzɪçtɪçt] `[adj, adv]` *no comp/superl* unintentional(ly) ◊ *eine unbeabsichtigte Folge* ✦ *Dieser Effekt ist eigentlich unbeabsichtigt.* ✦ *Aus seiner Waffe löste sich unbeabsichtigt ein Schuss.*

un·be·ach·tet [ˈʊnbə|axtət] `[adj]` *no comp/superl* unnoticed ◊ *Dieses Werk blieb jahrelang unbeachtet.* ✦ *ein lange Zeit unbeachtetes Phänomen* etw. unbeachtet lassen ignore sth

un·be·dacht [ˈʊnbədaxt] `[adj, adv]` *no comp/superl* thoughtless(ly), rash(ly) ◊ *Er bereute seine unbedachten Äußerungen.* ✦ *Das war ziemlich unbedacht von dir.* ✦ *Sie handelt oft unbedacht.* ⊜unüberlegt, gedankenlos

un·be·denk·lich [ˈʊnbədɛŋklɪç] `[adj]` safe ◊ *gesundheitlich unbedenkliche Baustoffe* ✦ *Dieses Produkt ist ökologisch völlig unbedenklich.* ⊜gefährlich

un·be·deu·tend [ˈʊnbədɔɡtn̩t, ˈʊnbədɔɡtənt] `[adj]` insignificant, minor ◊ *Sie spielt nur eine unbedeutende Nebenrolle.* ✦ *Diese Unterschiede sind völlig unbedeutend.* ⊜unerheblich ⊜wichtig

② **un·be·dingt** [ˈʊnbədɪŋt, – – '–] `[adv]` *no comp/ superl* really, absolutely ◊ *Er wollte unbedingt gewinnen.* ✦ *Ist das denn unbedingt nötig?* nicht unbedingt not necessarily unbedingt sein müssen be absolutely necessary `[adj]` absolute ◊ *Er fordert unbedingten Gehorsam.* ✦ *Unbedingte Voraussetzung dafür ist Folgendes: ...* ⊜uneingeschränkt

un·be·fan·gen [ˈʊnbəfaŋən] `[adj, adv]` **1.** *(concerning behaviour)* uninhibited(ly), natural(ly) ◊ *Sie war in seiner Gegenwart erstaunlich unbefangen.* ✦ *ganz unbefangen plaudern* ⊜ungezwungen **2.** *(concerning opinion)* impartial(ly) ◊ *ein unbefangener Beobachter* ⊜unbeteiligt

un·be·fris·tet [ˈʊnbəfrɪstət] `[adj, adv]` *no comp/ superl* permanent(ly), indefinite(ly) ◊ *eine unbefristete Aufenthaltserlaubnis* ✦ *Die Regelung ist unbefristet.* ✦ *Die Lizenz wurde unbefristet verlängert.*

un·be·fugt [ˈʊnbəfuːkt] `[adj]` *(form)* `[adj]` *no comp/ superl, mostly before ns* unauthorized ◊ *Diese Daten dürfen nicht in unbefugte Hände gelangen.* ⊜unberechtigt `[adv]` without authorization ◊ *ein Gelände unbefugt betreten* ⊜unerlaubt

un·be·greif·lich [ˈʊnbəgraeflɪç] `[adj]` incredible ◊ *Sie ging mit unbegreiflicher Naivität an die Sache heran.* (jdm) unbegreiflich incomprehensible (to sb), unimaginable (to sb) ◊ *Mir ist unbegreiflich, wie er das tun konnte.* ⊜unfassbar

un·be·grenzt [ˈʊnbəgrɛnt̩st] `[adj]` *no comp/superl*

unlimited, indefinite ◇ *Unsere Möglichkeiten sind nahezu unbegrenzt.* ✦ *für unbegrenzte Zeit* ⊖unendlich [adv] for an unlimited period, indefinitely ◇ *Ich bin leider nicht unbegrenzt belastbar.*

un·be·grün·det ['ʊnbəgryndət] [adj] *no comp/superl* groundless, unfounded, unwarranted ◇ *Der Verdacht erwies sich als unbegründet.* ✦ *unbegründete Eifersucht*

Un·be·ha·gen ['ʊnbəha:gn̩] das <–s> *no pl* unease ◇ *Mit wachsendem Unbehagen beobachtete sie die Entwicklung.*; *(physical)* discomfort jdm Unbehagen bereiten make sb uneasy ◇ *Diese Vorstellung bereitet mir ein gewisses Unbehagen.*

un·be·hol·fen ['ʊnbəhɔlfn̩] [adj, adv] awkward(ly), clumsy(-ily) ◇ *Seine Bewegungen wirken etwas unbeholfen.* ✦ *Das Kind machte ein paar unbeholfene Versuche, aufs Bett zu klettern.* ✦ *Die Welpen tappen noch recht unbeholfen herum.* ⊖ungeschickt

un·be·irrt ['ʊnbə|ɪ'rt] [adv] *no comp/superl* unperturbed ◇ *Er geht unbeirrt seinen Weg.*

un·be·kannt ['ʊnbəkant] [adj] <unbekannter, am unbekanntesten> unknown ◇ *Die Zahl der Opfer ist bislang unbekannt.* ✦ *Sie wollen das weitgehend unbekannte Gebiet erforschen.* etw./jd ist jdm unbekannt sth/sb is unknown to sb, sb has not heard of sth/sb; *(not used to)* unfamiliar ◇ *In unbekannter Umgebung ist er schüchtern.* ⊖bekannt [adv] „Empfänger unbekannt verzogen" "not known at this address"

un·be·küm·mert ['ʊnbəkʏmɐt] [adj] carefree, unconcerned ◇ *Er blieb trotz der Zwischenfälle völlig unbekümmert.* ✦ *Sie setzte eine betont unbekümmerte Miene auf.* [adv] in a carefree way ◇ *Er redete unbekümmert weiter.*

un·be·liebt ['ʊnbəli:pt] [adj] <unbeliebter, am unbeliebtesten> (bei jdm) unbeliebt unpopular (with sb) ◇ *Sie ist die unbeliebteste Lehrerin der ganzen Schule.* ✦ *Dieser Politiker ist beim Volk besonders unbeliebt.* ✦ *Du hast dich bei uns unbeliebt gemacht.* ⊖beliebt

un·be·merkt ['ʊnbəmɛ'rkt] [adj, adv] *no comp/superl* unnoticed ◇ *Sie konnte sich unbemerkt aus dem Haus schleichen.* ✦ *ein unbemerktes Problem* ✦ *Die Entwicklung blieb lange Zeit unbemerkt.*

un·be·o·bach·tet ['ʊnbə|o:baxtət] [adj] *no comp/superl* unobserved ◇ *Er fühlte sich unbeobachtet.* ✦ *In unbeobachteten Momenten weint er schon mal.*

un·be·quem ['ʊnbəkve:m] [adj] *(difficult)* awkward ◇ *unbequeme Fragen stellen* ✦ *Leute, die die Wahrheit sagen, sind oft unbequem.* [adj, adv] *(physically)* uncomfortable(-ably) ◇ *In so einer unbequemen Lage kann ich nicht einschlafen.* ✦ *Dieses Kleid ist furchtbar unbequem.* ✦ *unbequem sitzen* ⊖bequem

un·be·re·chen·bar ['ʊnbərɛçnba:ʳ] [adj] unpredictable ◇ *Wenn er trinkt, wird er immer unberechenbar.* ✦ *eine Katastrophe mit unberechenbaren Folgen*

un·be·rech·tigt ['ʊnbərɛçtɪçt] [adj] unjustified ◇ *unberechtigte Vorwürfe* ✦ *Er wies die Kritik als unberechtigt zurück.* [adv] without authorization, illegally ◇ *unberechtigt abgestellte Fahrzeuge* ⊖unbefugt

un·be·schreib·lich ['ʊnbəʃraɛplɪç, – – '– –] [adj, adv] *no comp/superl* indescribable(-ably) ◇

Von dort oben hatten wir eine unbeschreibliche Aussicht. ✦ *Deine Naivität ist wirklich unbeschreiblich.* ✦ *Das bedeutet mir unbeschreiblich viel.*

un·be·stän·dig ['ʊnbəʃtɛndɪç] [adj] changeable, inconsistent ◇ *unbeständiges Wetter* ✦ *Seine Leistungen sind recht unbeständig.* ⊖beständig

un·be·stimmt ['ʊnbəʃtɪmt] [adj] <unbestimmter, am unbestimmtesten> **1.** *(not known)* indefinite, unspecified ◇ *Damit kann eine unbestimmte Anzahl von Objekten verwaltet werden.* etw. auf unbestimmte Zeit vertagen adjourn sth indefinitely **2.** vague ◇ *Ich habe das unbestimmte Gefühl, dass da irgendetwas nicht stimmt.* ⊖vage **3.** *(not definite)* uncertain ◇ *Es ist noch unbestimmt, ob wir dazu Zeit haben werden.* ⊖ungewiss ⊖sicher **4.** LING indefinite ◇ *der unbestimmte Artikel* ⊖bestimmt

un·be·streit·bar ['ʊnbəʃtraɛtba:ʳ, – – '– –] [adj, adv] *seldom comp/superl* indisputable(-ably) ◇ *ein unbestreitbarer Vorteil* ✦ *Ihre Erfolge sind unbestreibar.* ✦ *Er ist unbestreitbar im Recht.*

un·be·strit·ten ['ʊnbəʃtrɪtn̩] [adj, adv] undisputed(ly) ◇ *Ihre Erfolge sind unbestritten.* ✦ *Trotz seiner unbestrittenen Verdienste wurde der Vorsitzende abgewählt.* ✦ *Der Hersteller ist unbestritten die Nummer 1 auf dem Markt.*

un·be·tei·ligt ['ʊnbətaɛlɪçt] [adj] *no comp/superl* *(not participating)* uninvolved ◇ *Für unbeteiligte Zuschauer sah das recht gefährlich aus.* ✦ *Ich blieb an dem Geschehen unbeteiligt.* ⊖passiv [adj, adv] *(emotionally)* indifferent(ly) ◇ *Solches Leid lässt mich nicht unbeteiligt.* ✦ *Sie machte ein unbeteiligtes Gesicht.* ✦ *völlig unbeteiligt zusehen* ⊖gleichgültig, unbewegt

un·be·weg·lich ['ʊnbəve:klɪç] [adj] **1.** *(with no movement)* motionless, stationary, fixed ◇ *Sein Gesicht blieb völlig unbeweglich.* ✦ *auf unbewegliche Ziele schießen* **2.** stiff ◇ *Ich bin ziemlich unbeweglich geworden.* ✦ *ein unbewegliches Gelenk* ⊖steif ⊖beweglich **3.** *mostly after ns (mentally)* inflexible ◇ *Er ist geistig ziemlich unbeweglich.* ⊖beweglich **4.** *only before ns (objects)* immovable ◇ *unbewegliche Güter* ⊖beweglich

un·be·wohnt ['ʊnbəvo:nt] [adj] *no comp/superl* **1.** *(building)* empty ◇ *Viele der Häuser sind heute unbewohnt.* **2.** *(area)* uninhabited ◇ *die unbewohnten Weiten der Antarktis* ✦ *Die Insel ist seit Jahren unbewohnt.* ⊖einsam

un·be·wusst ['ʊnbəvʊst] [adj] *no comp/superl* unconscious ◇ *Diese Vorgänge sind unbewusst und laufen automatisch ab.* ✦ *Sie hatte eine unbewusste Abneigung dagegen.* ⊖bewusst [adv] **1.** *(without knowing)* unconsciously ◇ *Er fürchtete sich unbewusst vor dem Erfolg.* ⊖bewusst **2.** *(without intention)* unintentionally ◇ *jdn unbewusst beleidigen* ⊖bewusst

un·be·zahl·bar ['ʊnbətsa:lba:ʳ] [adj] *no comp/superl* **1.** prohibitively expensive ◇ *Die Mieten sind unbezahlbar geworden.* ✦ *unbezahlbare Kostbarkeiten* **2.** *(precious)* priceless ◇ *unbezahlbare Gemälde* ✦ *Diese Erfahrung war einfach unbezahlbar!*

un·brauch·bar ['ʊnbraʊxba:ʳ] [adj] **1.** *(in a bad state)* unusable ◇ *Durch den Unfall ist der Helm unbrauchbar geworden.* ✦ *unbrauchbare Abfälle* **2.** *(very bad)* useless ◇ *Seine Beiträge waren*

völlig unbrauchbar. ⊖*brauchbar* **3.** *(for a certain purpose)* unsuitable ◊ *Für diesen Zweck ist Seide unbrauchbar.* ⊖*ungeeignet*

un·bü·ro·kra·tisch [ˈʊnbyrokraːtɪʃ] [adj] *(without red tape)* immediate, flexible ◊ *eine schnelle und unbürokratische Lösung* ♦ *Das Verfahren ist relativ unbürokratisch.* [adv] with a minimum of red tape ◊ *Wir wollen den Flutopfern schnell und unbürokratisch helfen.*

② **und** [ʊnt] [conjunc] **1.** and ◊ *jung, schön und reich* ♦ *Er klopfte und trat ein.* ♦ *Er kündigte, und das war gut so.* ♦ *Bitte sei so lieb und hilf mir tragen.* ♦ *Er kam näher und näher.* ♦ *Peter und liebevoll? Dass ich nicht lache!*; *(indifferent answer)* und? so?, what of it? ◊ *Sie konnte und konnte nicht couldn't* ◊ *Sie konnte und konnte den Fehler nicht finden.* **2.** *(vagueness)* zu der und der Zeit in such and such time so und so in such and such a way, such and such der und der such and such a person dann und dann on such and such a date, at such and such a time dies und das this and that **3.** MATH plus, and ◊ *Drei und vier ist sieben.* ⊖*plus* ⊖*weniger* **4.** *(abbr usw.)* und so weiter et cetera ◊ *Ich esse gern Kuchen, Kekse, Schokolade und so weiter.* und so weiter und so fort and so on and so forth und, und, und, und etc. etc. ◊ *Es gab Bier, Sekt, Wein und, und, und.* **5.** und Ähnliches and things like that ◊ *Sie liest gern historische Romane und Ähnliches.* und dergleichen and suchlike ◊ *Es gab Alkoholika wie Bier, Wein und dergleichen.* und andere/anderes (mehr) and other things

un·dank·bar [ˈʊndaŋkbaːʳ] [adj] **1.** *(person)* ungrateful ◊ *Diesem undankbaren Kerl helfe ich nicht mehr!* ♦ *Ich will ja nicht undankbar sein, aber ...* ⊖*dankbar* **2.** *(task)* thankless ◊ *Er musste die undankbare Rolle des Schiedsrichters spielen.* ⊖*dankbar*

un·denk·bar [ˈʊndɛŋkbaːʳ, – ' – –] [adj] unthinkable ◊ *So etwas wäre früher undenkbar gewesen.* ♦ *Das ist eine undenkbare Vorstellung!* ⊖*unmöglich* ⊖*denkbar*

un·deut·lich [ˈʊndɔʏtlɪç] [adj, adv] **1.** indistinct(ly) ◊ *undeutliche Konturen* ♦ *Die Umrisse der Gestalt waren sehr undeutlich.* ♦ *Ich konnte die Spuren nur undeutlich ausmachen.*; *(words)* unintelligible(-ibly) ◊ *Er stammelte ein paar undeutliche Worte.* ♦ *Sie spricht sehr undeutlich.*; *(writing)* illegible(-ibly) ◊ *Die Schrift war sehr undeutlich.* ♦ *undeutlich schreiben* ⊖*unklar* ⊖*deutlich* **2.** vague(ly) ◊ *Ich habe das undeutliche Gefühl, etwas vergessen zu haben.* ♦ *Diese Formulierung ist undeutlich.* ♦ *sich nur undeutlich an etw.* [acc] *erinnern können* ⊖*vage, ungenau* ⊖*deutlich*

un·dicht [ˈʊndɪçt] [adj] <undichter, am undichtesten> leaky, leaking ◊ *Das Dach ist undicht, es regnet herein.* eine undichte Stelle a leak ◊ *Die Luftmatratze muss eine undichte Stelle haben.* ♦ *Der Geheimdienst suchte nach der undichten Stelle.*

un·durch·sich·tig [ˈʊndʊʳçzɪçtɪç] [adj] **1.** *(substance)* opaque ◊ *Das Fenster im Bad ist undurchsichtig.* ♦ *undurchsichtige Strümpfe* ⊖*durchsichtig* **2.** *(pej)* obscure, shady ◊ *Er war in undurchsichtige Geschäfte verwickelt.*

un·e·he·lich [ˈʊnˌeːəlɪç] [adj] *no comp/superl (child)* illegitimate ◊ *ein uneheliches Kind* ♦ *Er ist*

unehelich.; *(mother)* unmarried ◊ *uneheliche Mütter* [adv] unehelich geboren sein be illegitimate

un·ei·gen·nüt·zig [ˈʊnˌaɪɡŋnʏtsɪç] [adj, adv] selfless(ly) ◊ *Er half ihr aus ganz uneigennützigen Gründen.* ♦ *Es war nicht uneigennützig, dass er dir seine Hilfe angeboten hat.* ♦ *uneigennützig handeln*

un·ein·ge·schränkt [ˈʊnˌaɪngəʃrɛŋkt] [adj, adv] *no comp/superl; when used as an adj, only before ns* unreserved(ly) ◊ *Sie erklärten ihre uneingeschränkte Solidarität mit den Streikenden.* ♦ *Ich kann dieses Gerät uneingeschränkt empfehlen.* ⊖*absolut, unbedingt*

un·ein·heit·lich [ˈʊnˌaɪnhaɛtlɪç] [adj, adv] inconsistent(ly) ◊ *Insgesamt ergibt sich ein uneinheitliches Bild.* ♦ *Die Tendenz war uneinheitlich.* ♦ *Diese Fälle sind uneinheitlich geregelt.* ⊖*unterschiedlich*

un·eins [ˈʊnˌaɛns] [adj] *no comp/superl, not before ns* uneins (über etw.* [acc]*) in disagreement (about sth) ◊ *Sie waren sich über die weitere Vorgehensweise uneins.*

un·end·lich [ʊnˈʔɛntlɪç] [adj, adv] *no comp/superl* endless(ly), infinite(ly) ◊ *die unendlichen Wälder Kanadas* ♦ *Meine Liebe zu dir ist unendlich.* ♦ *Die Zeit verging unendlich langsam.* unendlich viel an awful lot [adj] MATH infinite ◊ *eine unendliche Zahl/ Größe* gegen unendlich gehen go to infinity

un·ent·behr·lich [ˈʊnˌɛntbeˈɡlɪç, – – ' – –] [adj] unentbehrlich (für jdn/etw.) indispensable (to sb/ sth) ◊ *Ein Stadtplan ist für die Besichtigungstour unentbehrlich.* ♦ *Er ist mir eine unentbehrliche Hilfe.* sich unentbehrlich machen make yourself indispensable ⊖*unerlässlich*

un·ent·gelt·lich [ˈʊnˌɛntɡɛltlɪç] [adj] *no comp/ superl, mostly before ns* free ◊ *unentgeltliche Leistungen* [adv] free of charge ◊ *Die Räume wurden uns unentgeltlich zur Verfügung gestellt.* ⊖*kostenlos*

un·ent·schie·den [ˈʊnˌɛntʃiːdn̩] [adj] *no comp/ superl* **1.** undecided ◊ *unentschiedene Wähler* ♦ *Ich war noch unentschieden, ob ich gehen sollte oder nicht.* ⊖*unentschlossen* **2.** SPORT drawn ◊ *Auch in der Verlängerung blieb das Spiel unentschieden.* [adv] *no comp/superl* SPORT unentschieden enden end in a draw unentschieden spielen draw

Un·ent·schie·den [ˈʊnˌɛntʃiːdn̩] das <–s, –> draw ◊ *Für den 1. FC Köln reichte es nur zu einem Unentschieden.*

un·ent·schlos·sen [ˈʊnˌɛntʃlɔsn̩] [adj] undecided ◊ *eine Entscheidungshilfe für unentschlossene Käufer* ♦ *„Kommst du mit?" — „Ich weiß nicht, ich bin noch unentschlossen."* ⊖*unentschieden*

un·ent·wegt [ˈʊnˌɛntveːkt, – – '–] [adj, adv] *no comp/superl; when used as an adj, only before nouns* **1.** *(not stopping)* ceaseless(ly) ◊ *das unentwegte Brausen des Windes* ♦ *Bei uns klingelt heute unentwegt das Telefon.* ⊖*unaufhörlich* **2.** *(persevering)* tireless(ly) ◊ *Der Erfolg ist nur ihrem unentwegten Einsatz zu verdanken.* ♦ *Sie setzten sich unentwegt für die Rechte der Unterdrückten ein.* ⊖*unermüdlich, beharrlich*

un·er·bitt·lich [ˈʊnˌɛbɪtlɪç, – – ' – –] [adj, adv] relentless(ly) ◊ *mit unerbittlicher Härte vorgehen* ♦ *Darin ist er unerbittlich.* ♦ *Er trieb die Verhandlungen unerbittlich voran.*

un·er·fah·ren [ˈʊnˌɛfaːrən] [adj] unerfahren (in

A B C D E F G H I J K L M N O P Q R S T **U** V W X Y Z

etw. ⟨dat⟩ inexperienced (in sth) ◊ *ein unerfahrener junger Mensch* ♦ *In diesen Dingen bin ich ziemlich unerfahren.* ⊜erfahren

un·er·freu·lich [ˈʊn|ɛtfrɔøplɪç] ⟨adj, adv⟩ unpleasant(ly) ◊ *eine unerfreuliche Situation* ♦ *Sein Benehmen war ziemlich unerfreulich.* ♦ *Das Wetter war unerfreulich regnerisch.* ⊜unangenehm, schlecht ⊜erfreulich

un·er·heb·lich [ˈʊn|ehɛːplɪç] ⟨adj⟩ insignificant ◊ *ein nicht unerheblicher Schaden* ♦ *Die Unterschiede sind eigentlich unerheblich.* ⊜unbedeutend

un·er·kannt [ˈʊn|ekant] ⟨adj⟩ *no comp/superl* unrecognized ◊ *eine Problem, das lange unerkannt blieb* ♦ *unerkannte Krankheiten* ⟨adv⟩ without being recognized ◊ *Der Täter konnte unerkannt entkommen.*

un·er·klär·lich [ˈʊn|eklɛːglɪç, – – '– –] ⟨adj⟩ (jdm) unerklärlich inexplicable (to sb) ◊ *Es ist mir völlig unerklärlich, wie das geschehen konnte.* ♦ *ein unerklärliches Missverständnis*

un·er·läss·lich [ˈʊn|elɛslɪç, – – '– –] ⟨adj⟩ essential ◊ *Äußerste Sorgfalt ist bei dieser Arbeit unerlässlich.* ♦ *unerlässliche Voraussetzungen für etw.* ⊜unentbehrlich

un·er·laubt [ˈʊn|elaopt] ⟨adj⟩ *no comp/superl, only before ns* **1.** *(not allowed)* unauthorized ◊ *unerlaubtes Entfernen von der Truppe* ⊜unbefugt, unzulässig **2.** *(against the law)* illegal ◊ *An die Informationen sind sie mit unerlaubten Mitteln gekommen.* ⟨adv⟩ **1.** without authorization, without permission ◊ *Sie hat sich unerlaubt vom Unfallort entfernt.* ⊜unbefugt **2.** illegally ◊ *ein unerlaubt betriebenes Gewerbe*

un·er·le·digt [ˈʊn|ele:dɪçt] ⟨adj⟩ *no comp/superl* undone, unfinished ◊ *Zu Hause wartet jede Menge unerledigte Arbeit auf mich.* ♦ *Der Rest muss für heute unerledigt bleiben.*

un·er·mess·lich [ˈʊn|emɛslɪç, – – '– –] ⟨adj, adv⟩ immense(ly) ◊ *unermessliche Reichtümer* ♦ *Der Schaden wäre unermesslich.* ♦ *unermesslich wertvoll sein*

un·er·müd·lich [ˈʊn|emyːtlɪç, – – '– –] ⟨adj, adv⟩ tireless(ly) ◊ *der unermüdliche Einsatz der Helfer* ♦ *Sein Eifer schien unermüdlich.* ♦ *Sie kämpften unermüdlich für die Gleichberechtigung.*

un·er·reich·bar [ˈʊn|eraeçbaː] ⟨adj, adv⟩ *no comp/superl* out of reach ◊ *Der Federball landete in unerreichbarer Höhe auf einem Baum.* ♦ *Das oberste Regalbrett ist für mich unerreichbar.* ♦ *Putzmittel für Kinder unerreichbar lagern* in unerreichbarer Ferne liegen be way beyond reach ⟨adj⟩ **1.** unattainable ◊ *ein unerreichbarer Traum* ♦ *Dieses Ziel ist für mich unerreichbar.* **2.** inaccessible ◊ *Die Berghütte ist mit dem Auto unerreichbar.* **3.** *(fam)* unreachable, unobtainable ◊ *telefonisch unerreichbar sein*

un·er·schöpf·lich [ˈʊn|eʃœpflɪç, – – '– –] ⟨adj⟩ *no comp/superl* inexhaustible ◊ *Ihre Energie/Geduld ist unerschöpflich.* ♦ *ein unerschöpfliches Thema*

un·er·schüt·ter·lich [ˈʊn|eʃʏtɛlɪç, – – '– – –] ⟨adj, adv⟩ unshakeable(-ably) ◊ *Sein Optimismus ist unerschütterlich.* ♦ *ein unerschütterliches Selbstbewusstsein haben* ♦ *unerschütterlich an das Gute im Menschen glauben*

un·er·setz·lich [ˈʊn|ezɛtslɪç, – – '– –] ⟨adj⟩ *no comp/superl* **1.** irreplaceable ◊ *von unersetzlichem*

Wert sein ♦ *Der Teddy ist für die Kleine unersetzlich.* **2.** irreparable ◊ *ein unersetzlicher Verlust*

un·er·träg·lich [ˈʊn|etrɛːklɪç, – – '– – –] ⟨adj, adv⟩ unbearable(-ably) ◊ *unerträglicher Lärm* ♦ *Du bist heute mal wieder unerträglich!* ♦ *Es war unerträglich heiß.* jdm unerträglich unbearable for sb ◊ *Dieser Gedanke war mir unerträglich*

un·er·war·tet [ˈʊn|eva:tət] ⟨adj, adv⟩ *no comp/superl* unexpected(ly) ◊ *Ihr Besuch war unerwartet.* ♦ *Die Ereignisse nahmen eine unerwartete Wende.* ♦ *Der Anruf kam völlig unerwartet.*

un·er·wünscht [ˈʊn|evʏnʃt] ⟨adj⟩ *no comp/superl* unwelcome ◊ *ein Medikament mit unerwünschten Nebenwirkungen* Du bist hier unerwünscht! You're not welcome here. Kaugummikauen ist im Unterricht unerwünscht. You are not permitted to chew gum in class. Hunde unerwünscht. No dogs please.

un·fä·hig [ˈʊnfɛːɪç] ⟨adj⟩ **1.** *not before ns* unfähig, etw. zu tun incapable of doing sth, unable to do sth ◊ *Sie war unfähig, sich zu konzentrieren.* zu etw. ⟨dat⟩ unfähig incapable of sth ◊ *Zu einem Diebstahl wäre er unfähig.* **2.** incompetent ◊ *ein unfähiger Mitarbeiter* ♦ *Der neue Lehrer ist völlig unfähig.*

un·fair [ˈʊnfɛːɐ] ⟨adj, adv⟩ unfair(ly) ◊ *unfaire Methoden* ♦ *Das Spiel war unfair.* ♦ *Wer unfair kämpft, wird disqualifiziert.* unfair gegenüber jdm unfair(ly) to/towards sb ◊ *sich gegenüber jdm unfair verhalten* ⊜ungerecht

② **Un·fall** [ˈʊnfal] der <–(e)s, Unfälle> accident ◊ *einen Unfall haben* ♦ *ein schwerer/tragischer Unfall* ♦ *bei einem Unfall ums Leben kommen* einen Unfall bauen/verschulden cause an accident

un·fass·bar [ˈʊnfasbaːɐ, – '– –] ⟨adj, adv⟩ incredible(-ibly), incomprehensible(-ibly) ◊ *Dieses Unglück ist einfach unfassbar!* ♦ *jdm eine unfassbare Geschichte erzählen* ♦ *Diese Leute sind unfassbar arm.* ⊜unbegreiflich

un·frei·wil·lig [ˈʊnfraevɪlɪç] ⟨adj, adv⟩ *no comp/superl; when used as an adj, mostly before ns* **1.** involuntary(-ily) ◊ *eine unfreiwillige Pause* ♦ *Das Paar ist unfreiwillig kinderlos.* **2.** unintentional(ly) ◊ *die unfreiwillige Komik einer Situation* ♦ *Der Witz war unfreiwillig, aber dafür umso lustiger.* ♦ *unfreiwillig lachen müssen* ⊜unbeabsichtigt

un·freund·lich [ˈʊnfrɔøntlɪç] ⟨adj⟩ **1.** unfriendly ◊ *unfreundlich zu jdm sein* ♦ *eine unfreundliche Antwort bekommen* **2.** *(weather, place etc.)* unpleasant ◊ *Das Wetter bleibt unfreundlich.* ♦ *eine unfreundliche Gegend* ⟨adv⟩ in an unfriendly way ◊ *jdn unfreundlich begrüßen/behandeln* ⊜aufmerksam

Un·gar [ˈʊŋɡaːɐ] der <–n, –n>, **Un·ga·rin** die <–, –nen> Hungarian → Deutsche

un·ga·risch [ˈʊŋɡarɪʃ] ⟨adj⟩ *mostly before ns* Hungarian → deutsch

Un·ga·risch [ˈʊŋɡarɪʃ] das <–(s)> *no pl* Hungarian → Deutsch

Un·garn [ˈʊŋɡarn] das <–s> *article only in combination with attribute, no pl* Hungary → Deutschland

un·ge·ach·tet [ˈʊnɡə|axtət] ⟨prep⟩ +gen *(lofty)* despite, notwithstanding ◊ *Ungeachtet aller Bemühungen scheiterte das Projekt.* ⊜trotz

un·ge·bil·det [ˈʊnɡəbɪldət] ⟨adj⟩ uneducated ◊ *Er ist nicht dumm, nur ungebildet.* ♦ *ein ungebildeter*

Mensch ⊜gebildet

un·ge·dul·dig ['ʊngədʊldɪç] [adj, adv] impatient(ly)
◊ *Wo bleibt er nur? Langsam werde ich ungeduldig!* ♦ *ein ungeduldiger Kunde* ♦ *ungeduldig auf jdn/etw. warten*

un·ge·eig·net ['ʊngəlaegnət] [adj] unsuitable ◊ *Der Film ist für Kinder ungeeignet.* ♦ *ein ungeeigneter Bewerber* Er ist als Handwerker völlig ungeeignet. He is completely unsuited to be a craftsman. ⊜geeignet

② **un·ge·fähr** ['ʊngəfɛːɐ̯, – – '–] [adj, adv] *no comp/superl; when used as an adj, only before ns* approximate(ly), rough(ly) ◊ *ein ungefährer Wert* ♦ *Sie ist ungefähr so groß wie ich.* ♦ *Ich bin in ungefähr einer Stunde da.* sich [dat] etw. ungefähr vorstellen können have a rough idea of sth, be able to just about imagine sth ⊜genau, exakt, präzise
⊛ *etw. kommt nicht von ungefähr* sth is no accident so ungefähr *(fam)* more or less (wie) von ungefähr (as if) by chance

un·ge·fähr·lich ['ʊngəfɛːɐ̯lɪç] [adj] safe ◊ *Brennende Kerzen sind nicht ganz ungefährlich.*; *(illness)* harmless ◊ *eine für Menschen ungefährliche Krankheit*

un·ge·heu·er ['ʊngəhɔøɐ] [adj, adv] <ungeheurer, am ungeheuersten> <der/die/das ungeheure ...> *when used as an adj, mostly before ns* enormous(ly), immense(ly), tremendous(ly) ◊ *ein ungeheures Vermögen besitzen* ♦ *sich ungeheuer über ein Geschenk freuen*; *(pain, noise)* terrible (-ibly), dreadful(ly) ◊ *ungeheuer laut/schmerzhaft* ⊜unglaublich, außerordentlich
⊛ *ins Ungeheure steigen* be outrageous

Un·ge·heu·er ['ʊngəhɔøɐ] das <-s, -> monster ◊ *das Ungeheuer von Loch Ness* ♦ *Was ist er doch für ein Ungeheuer!*

un·ge·heu·er·lich ['ʊngəhɔøɐlɪç, – – '– – –] [adj] outrageous ◊ *Es ist ungeheuerlich, was er für Lügen erzählt!* ♦ *ungeheuerliche Vorwürfe*

un·ge·hin·dert ['ʊngəhɪndɐt] [adj, adv] *no comp/superl; when used as an adj, only before ns* unimpeded ◊ *ungehinderten Zugang zu etw. haben* ♦ *Das Feuer konnte sich ungehindert ausbreiten.*

un·ge·hor·sam ['ʊngəhoːɐ̯za:m] [adj] ungehorsam (gegenüber jdm) disobedient (to sb) ◊ *ein ungehorsames Kind* ♦ *Wenn du weiter so ungehorsam bist, gibt es kein Eis!*

un·ge·le·gen ['ʊngəleːgn̩] [adj, adv] *when used as an adj, only before ns* inconvenient, awkward ◊ *ein ungelegener Gast* (jdm) ungelegen kommen come at an inconvenient/awkward time (for sb) ◊ *Komme ich ungelegen?* ♦ *Der Regen kam ihnen äußerst ungelegen.*

un·ge·mein ['ʊngəmaen] [adj, adv] *no comp/superl; when used as an adj, only before ns* tremendous(ly) ◊ *Diese Lösung bringt ungemeine Vorteile.* ♦ *ein ungemein spannender Krimi* ♦ *sich ungemein über eine Panne ärgern* ⊜ungeheuer, unglaublich, unheimlich

un·ge·müt·lich ['ʊngəmyːtlɪç] [adj, adv] *(weather, light, atmosphere etc.)* unpleasant(ly) ◊ *Grelles Licht ist ungemütlich.* ♦ *eine ungemütliche Atmosphäre* ♦ *Draußen ist es ungemütlich kalt.*; *(seat, furnishings)* uncomfortable(-ably) ◊ *Die Wohnung ist ungemütlich (eingerichtet).*
⊛ *ungemütlich werden (fam)* get/turn nasty

un·ge·nau ['ʊngənao] [adj, adv] <ungenauer, am ungenauesten> **1.** inexact(ly), imprecise(ly), inaccurate(ly) ◊ *Wetterprognosen sind oft ungenau.* ♦ *ungenaue Informationen* ♦ *ein Thermometer, das die Werte nur ungenau anzeigt* ⊜präzise, exakt **2.** careless(ly) ◊ *eine ungenaue Arbeitsweise* ♦ *ungenau rechnen und zu einem falschen Ergebnis kommen*

un·ge·niert ['ʊnʒeniːɐ̯t] [adj] <ungenierter, am ungeniertesten> *mostly before ns* uninhibited, free and easy ◊ *der ungenierte Griff des Ministers in die Staatskasse* [adv] uninhibitedly, without inhibitions ◊ *laut und ungeniert gähnen/lachen*

un·ge·nü·gend ['ʊngəny:gn̩t, 'ʊngəny:gənt] [adj, adv] *no comp/superl* inadequate(ly), insufficient(ly) ◊ *Die Sicht ist bei dem Nebel ungenügend.* ♦ *aufgrund ungenügender Kenntnisse nicht eingestellt werden* ♦ *Seine Arbeit wird ungenügend bezahlt.* [adj] SCHOOL *(grade)* poor ◊ *eine Arbeit mit der Note „ungenügend" bewerten*

un·ge·recht ['ʊngərɛçt] [adj, adv] <ungerechter, am ungerechtesten> unjust(ly), unfair(ly) ◊ *eine ungerechte Strafe* ♦ *ungerecht gegenüber jdm sein* ♦ *sich ungerecht behandelt fühlen* ⊜unfair ⊜gerecht

un·gern ['ʊngɛʳn] [adv] etw. ungern tun not like/ dislike doing sth ◊ *ungern bügeln/putzen* ♦ *Sie lässt ihren Hund nur ungern allein.* „Leihst du mir deine neue Jacke?" — „Eher ungern." "Would you lend me your new jacket?" — " I'd rather not." ⊜gern

un·ge·schickt ['ʊngəʃɪkt] [adj, adv] <ungeschickter, am ungeschicktesten> **1.** clumsy(-ily) ◊ *Sie ist zu ungeschickt zum Nähen.* ♦ *ein ungeschickter Küchenjunge* ♦ *sich ungeschickt anstellen* ⊜geschickt **2.** awkward(ly) ◊ *eine ungeschickte Bewegung* ♦ *Die Formulierung war etwas ungeschickt.* ♦ *sich ungeschickt ausdrücken* ⊜geschickt **3.** unwise(ly) ◊ *ein ungeschicktes Vorgehen* ♦ *Es war etwas ungeschickt (von ihm), ihr das zu sagen.* ♦ *eine ungeschickt formulierte Frage* ⊜geschickt

un·ge·stört ['ʊngəʃtøːɐ̯t] [adj] *no comp/superl* undisturbed, uninterrupted ◊ *ungestörter Schlaf* ♦ *In meinem Zimmer sind wir ungestört.* [adv] in peace ◊ *Können wir uns irgendwo ungestört unterhalten?*

un·ge·straft ['ʊngəʃtraːft] [adj, adv] *no comp/superl* unpunished ◊ *Aufgrund mangelnder Beweise blieb der Mörder ungestraft.* ♦ *ein ungestraftes Verbrechen* ♦ *(noch einmal) ungestraft davonkommen*

un·ge·sund ['ʊngəzʊnt] [adj, adv] <ungesünder, am ungesündesten> unhealthy(-ily) ◊ *Zucker ist ungesund für die Zähne.* ♦ *eine ungesunde Gesichtsfarbe* ♦ *sich ungesund ernähren* Rauchen ist ungesund. Smoking is bad for your health. ⊜gesund
⊛ *allzu viel ist ungesund* one should never overdo things, you can have too much of a good thing

un·ge·wiss ['ʊngəvɪs] [adj] <ungewisser, am ungewissesten> *(also lofty)* uncertain ◊ *Das Schicksal der Geiseln ist ungewiss.* ♦ *Es ist noch ungewiss, ob sie kommt.* ♦ *eine ungewisse Entwicklung* ⊜unbestimmt

un·ge·wöhn·lich ['ʊngəvøːnlɪç] [adj, adv] unusual(ly) ◊ *Schnee ist zu dieser Jahreszeit eher*

ungewöhnlich. ♦ *eine ungewöhnliche Bitte haben* ♦ *ungewöhnlich gut gelaunt sein*; outstanding(ly), exceptional(ly) ◊ *eine Frau von ungewöhnlicher Schönheit* ♦ *ungewöhnlich begabt sein*

un·ge·wohnt ['ʊngəvoːnt] [adj] *no comp/superl* unfamiliar, strange ◊ *in ungewohnter Umgebung* ♦ *Es ist ganz ungewohnt, dich mit kurzen Haaren zu sehen.* [adv] unusually ◊ *ein ungewohnt milder Winter*

un·ge·wollt ['ʊngəvɔlt] [adj, adv] *no comp/superl* unintentional(ly) ◊ *Jede dritte Schwangerschaft ist ungewollt.* ♦ *ein Film voller ungewollter Komik* ♦ *jdn ungewollt beleidigen* ⊖gewollt

un·ge·zwun·gen ['ʊngətsvʊŋən] [adj, adv] casual(ly) ◊ *eine ungezwungene Unterhaltung führen* ♦ *Die Atmosphäre war locker und ungezwungen.* ♦ *ungezwungen miteinander plaudern* ⊖unbefangen

un·glaub·lich [ʊn'glaɔplɪç, '– – –] [adj, adv] unbelievable(-ably), incredible(-ibly) ◊ *unglaublichen Erfolg haben* ♦ *Die Geschichte ist unglaublich, aber wahr.* ♦ *Das ist ja eine unglaubliche Frechheit!* ♦ *unglaublich stolz auf jdn sein*

un·glaub·wür·dig ['ʊnglaɔpvʏrdɪç] [adj] untrustworthy, unreliable ◊ *eine unglaubwürdige Politik*; *(excuse)* implausible ◊ *Deine Entschuldigung ist unglaubwürdig.*

② **Un·glück** ['ʊnglʏk] das <-(e)s, –e> **1.** accident ◊ *ein schreckliches/tragisches Unglück* ♦ *Auf der Baustelle geschah gestern ein Unglück.* **2.** *no pl* bad luck ◊ *Eine schwarze Katze soll Unglück bringen.* ⊖Pech **3.** *no pl* misfortune, suffering ◊ *Die Seuche brachte Unglück über das Volk.* jdn/ sich ins Unglück stürzen bring ruin/disaster on sb/ yourself

⊛ **ein Unglück kommt selten allein** it never rains but it pours in **sein Unglück rennen** *(fam)* rush headlong into disaster **zu allem Unglück** to make matters worse

un·glück·lich ['ʊnglʏklɪç] [adj, adv] **1.** unhappy (-ily), sad(ly) ◊ *Ohne ihre Katze ist sie ganz unglücklich.* ♦ *einen unglücklichen Eindruck machen* ♦ *Sie sah ihn unglücklich an.* unglücklich über etw. [acc] sad/unhappy about sth ⊖traurig ⊖glücklich **2.** unfortunate(ly) ◊ *eine Verkettung unglücklicher Umstände* ♦ *Die Formulierung ist etwas unglücklich.* ♦ *ein unglücklich gewählter Termin* unglücklich enden/ausgehen turn out badly ⊖ungünstig **3.** awkward(ly) ◊ *Bei einem unglücklichen Fall brach er sich das Bein.* ♦ *unglücklich stürzen* ⊖ungeschickt

⊛ **unglücklich (in jdn) verliebt sein** be hopelessly in love (with sb)

un·gül·tig ['ʊngʏltɪç] [adj] *no comp/superl* **1.** invalid ◊ *ein ungültiger Ausweis* ♦ *Der Vertrag ist ohne Unterschrift ungültig.* **2.** void ◊ *eine Wahl wegen Betrugs für ungültig erklären* eine Ehe für ungültig erklären annul a marriage

un·güns·tig ['ʊngʏnstɪç] [adj, adv] unfavourable (-ably), unfavorable(-ably), bad(ly) ◊ *unter ungünstigen Voraussetzungen* ♦ *Die Gerüchte sind für sein Image denkbar ungünstig.* ♦ *Die erste Halbzeit verlief ungünstig für unsere Mannschaft.* ⊖günstig

un·halt·bar ['ʊnhaltbaːr] [adj] *seldom comp/superl* **1.** unbearable, intolerable ◊ *Die hygienischen Zustände dort sind unhaltbar.* ♦ *unhaltbare Arbeits-*

bedingungen ⊖unerträglich **2.** untenable ◊ *Forderungen/Vorwürfe als unhaltbar zurückweisen* ♦ *eine unhaltbare Theorie* [adj, adv] SPORT unstoppable (-ably) ◊ *Der Freistoß war für den Torhüter unhaltbar.* ♦ *ein unhaltbarer Schuss* ♦ *Der Ball flog unhaltbar ins Tor.*

Un·heil ['ʊnhael] das <-(e)s> *no pl (lofty)* disaster ◊ *Unheil anrichten/stiften* ♦ *ein Unheil bringender Tag* Unheil über jdn/etw. disaster upon sb/sth ◊ *Der Tornado brachte Unheil über das Land.* ⊖Unglück

un·heil·bar ['ʊnhaelbaːr] [adj, adv] *no comp/superl* incurable(-ably) ◊ *Aids ist noch immer unheilbar.* ♦ *an einer unheilbaren Krankheit leiden* ♦ *unheilbar krank sein*

② **un·heim·lich** ['ʊnhaemlɪç, – '– –] [adj] **1.** eerie, weird, strange ◊ *Nachts ist es im Wald ziemlich unheimlich.* ♦ *eine unheimliche Geschichte* jdm unheimlich sein give sb a weird/strange feeling, give sb the creeps etw. wird jdm unheimlich sb is getting a weird/strange feeling about sth, sth is giving sb the creeps **2.** jdm ist unheimlich (zumute) sb is frightened/scared [adj, adv] *when used as an adj, only before ns (fam)* terrific(ally), tremendous(ly), incredible(-ibly) ◊ *unheimliches Glück haben* ♦ *Das tut mir unheimlich Leid!* ♦ *unheimlich wichtig sein* ⊖ungemein, ungeheuer, unglaublich

un·höf·lich ['ʊnhøːflɪç] [adj, adv] impolite(ly), rude(ly) ◊ *Es wäre unhöflich, das Geschenk nicht anzunehmen.* ♦ *So ein unhöflicher Kerl!* ♦ *sich unhöflich benehmen* unhöflich zu/gegenüber jdm impolite/rude to(wards) sb ⊖höflich

u·ni [y'niː] [adj] *invariable; only before ns and adverbial* plain ◊ *Die Tischdecke gibt es gestreift, uni oder kariert.* ♦ *ein uni Hemd/T-Shirt* uni blau/ grün/rot plain blue/green/red ◊ *Der Stoff ist uni blau.* uni gefärbt in single-colour, in single-color ◊ *Die Kissen gibt es entweder uni gefärbt oder bunt.* ⊖einfarbig ⊖bunt, mehrfarbig

U·ni ['ʊni:, 'u:ni:] die <-, -s> *(fam) (abbr of* Universität*)* university ◊ *in die/zur Uni gehen* ♦ *an der Uni Augsburg studieren*

un·in·te·res·sant ['ʊn|ɪntərɛsant] [adj] <uninteressanter, am uninteressantesten> **1.** uninteresting ◊ *ein uninteressanter Mensch* ♦ *Deine Idee ist nicht uninteressant.* für jdn uninteressant sein be of no interest to sb ⊖unbedeutend ⊖interessant **2.** ECON (für jdn) uninteressant not attractive (to sb) ◊ *zu teuer und daher finanziell uninteressant* ♦ *einen für die Firma uninteressanten Auftrag ablehnen* ⊖interessant

② **U·ni·ver·si·tät** [univɛr'ziːtɛːt] die <-, -en> university ◊ *eine Universität besuchen* ♦ *Das Abitur berechtigt zum Studium an einer Universität.*

Un·kennt·nis ['ʊnkɛntnɪs] die <-> *no pl* Unkenntnis ... [gen], Unkenntnis über etw. [acc] ignorance of sth ◊ *Bei vielen herrscht über diese Regeln Unkenntnis.* ♦ *aus Unkenntnis einen Fehler machen*

un·klar ['ʊnklaːr] [adj] **1.** unclear ◊ *Die Ursache des Brandes ist bis heute unklar.* ♦ *eine unklare Aussage verdeutlichen* etw. ist jdm unklar sth is unclear to sb ⊖unverständlich **2.** blurred, hazy ◊ *Das Foto ist unklar.* ♦ *unklare Konturen* ⊖undeutlich, verschwommen

⊛ **im Unklaren bleiben/sein** remain/be unclear **im Unklaren lassen** leave it unclear ◊ *Der Autor*

lässt bis zur letzten Seite im Unklaren, wer der Mörder ist. **jdn (über etw.** [acc]**) im Unklaren lassen** keep sb guessing (about sth) **sich** [dat] **(über etw.** [acc]**) im Unklaren sein** be unclear/unsure (about sth)

Un·kos·ten ['ʊnkɔstn̩] die <–> only pl costs, expense(s) ◊ *hohe Unkosten haben* ◆ *die Unkosten decken*

◉ **sich (für jdn/etw.) in Unkosten stürzen** (fam) dig deep into your pockets (for sb/sth), really splash out (on sb/sth)

Un·kraut ['ʊnkraʊt] das <–(e)s, Unkräuter> most sing weeds ◊ *Zwischen den Salatpflanzen wächst das Unkraut.* **Unkraut jäten** do the/some weeding, weed

◉ **Unkraut vergeht nicht** (fam, hum) bad weeds grow tall, that sort go on for ever

un·längst ['ʊnlɛŋst] [adv] recently ◊ *Das geschah erst unlängst.* ◆ *Er hat unlängst beschlossen, mit dem Rauchen aufzuhören.* ⊖kürzlich

Un·men·ge ['ʊnmɛŋə] die <–, –n> (fam) enormous amount ◊ *Ich habe auf dem Seminar eine Unmenge gelernt.* **jd isst/trinkt Unmengen** sb eats/drinks enormous quantities **eine Unmenge von/an etw.** [dat], **eine Unmenge ...** [nom] an enormous amount of sth ◊ *Im Wald lag eine Unmenge von/an Müll herum.* **in Unmengen** in massive quantities ◊ *Kaffee sollte man nicht in Unmengen trinken.*

un·miss·ver·ständ·lich ['ʊnmɪsfɛʃtɛntlɪç, – – – '– –] [adj, adv] **1.** unambiguous(ly) ◊ *Die Botschaft des Textes ist unmissverständlich.* ◆ *eine unmissverständliche Aussage* ◆ *sich unmissverständlich ausdrücken* **2.** blunt(ly), frank(ly) ◊ *In einem unmissverständlichen Tonfall stellte sie ihn zur Rede.* ◆ *jdm unmissverständlich die Meinung sagen*

un·mit·tel·bar ['ʊnmɪtl̩baːʳ] [adj, adv] when used as an adj, only before ns **1.** direct(ly) ◊ *sich in unmittelbarer Gefahr befinden* ◆ *unmittelbar von etw. betroffen sein* **2.** immediate(ly) ◊ *ein Einkaufszentrum in unmittelbarer Nähe* ◆ *in der unmittelbaren Umgebung des Hotels* ◆ *ein Medikament unmittelbar vor dem Essen einnehmen; (when followed by a preposition also)* right ◊ *unmittelbar nach der Abfahrt etw.* steht unmittelbar bevor sth is almost upon us [adv] straight ◊ *Die Straße führt unmittelbar ins Stadtzentrum.*

un·mög·lich ['ʊnmøːklɪç, – '– –] [adj, adv] (also fam, pej) **1.** impossible(-ibly) ◊ *eine technisch unmögliche Reparatur* ◆ *Das ist völlig unmöglich!* ◆ *Hör auf, so zu schreien! Du bist unmöglich!* ◆ *sich unmöglich benehmen* **es ist jdm unmöglich, etw. zu tun** it is impossible for sb to do sth **jd/etw. kann unmöglich ...** sb/sth can't possibly ... ◊ *Er kann unmöglich der Mörder sein!* ◆ *Das kann unmöglich stimmen!* **2.** (appearance, dress etc.) ridiculous(ly) ◊ *ein unmögliches Outfit* ◆ *Diese Frisur sieht unmöglich aus.* ◆ *sich unmöglich kleiden*

◉ **sich (vor jdm) unmöglich machen** make a fool of yourself (in front of sb)

un·mo·ra·lisch ['ʊnmoraːlɪʃ] [adj, adv] immoral(ly) ◊ *ein unmoralisches Angebot* ◆ *Ist so ein Verhalten unmoralisch?* ◆ *unmoralisch handeln*

un·nütz ['ʊnnʏts] [adj] <unnützer, am unnützesten>

1. pointless ◊ *Es ist doch unnütz, sich darüber den Kopf zu zerbrechen!* ◆ *einen unnützen Versuch unternehmen* **2.** useless ◊ *In seiner Wohnung steht nur unnützes Zeug herum.* [adv] **1.** needlessly ◊ *unnütz Geld ausgeben* **2.** uselessly ◊ *Steh nicht so unnütz herum!*

un·nö·tig ['ʊnnøːtɪç] [adj, adv] unnecessary(-ily) ◊ *Ich halte diesen Streit für unnötig.* ◆ *sich unnötige Sorgen machen* ◆ *sich unnötig aufregen*

un·or·dent·lich ['ʊn|ɔʳdn̩tlɪç, 'ʊn|ɔʳdəntlɪç] [adj, adv] untidy(-ily) ◊ *ein unordentlicher Mensch* ◆ *Nach dem Umzug ist es hier noch etwas unordentlich.* ◆ *seine Sachen unordentlich herumliegen lassen* ⊖schlampig ⊖ordentlich

Un·ord·nung ['ʊn|ɔʳdnʊŋ] die <–> no pl mess ◊ *In der Küche herrscht Unordnung.* ◆ *eine schreckliche Unordnung hinterlassen* **in Unordnung** in a mess ◊ *Ihr Leben ist völlig in Unordnung geraten.* **etw. in Unordnung bringen** mess sth up ⊖Ordnung

un·per·sön·lich ['ʊnpɛʳzøːnlɪç] [adj, adv] **1.** impersonal(ly) ◊ *Geldgeschenke finde ich unpersönlich.* ◆ *ein unpersönliches Schreiben* ◆ *der unpersönliche Gebrauch von Verben* ◆ *Das Zimmer ist unpersönlich eingerichtet.* **2.** (not friendly) distant(ly) ◊ *ein distanziertes, unpersönliches Gespräch führen* ◆ *Ihr Verhältnis zueinander ist eher unpersönlich.* ⊖persönlich

un·pünkt·lich ['ʊnpʏŋktlɪç] [adj, adv] late ◊ *Der Zug ist jeden Morgen unpünktlich.* ◆ *eine unpünktliche Lieferung* ◆ *unpünktlich kommen* [adj] (person) unpunctual ◊ *ein unpünktlicher Mensch* ◆ *Sie ist schrecklich unpünktlich.*

un·recht ['ʊnrɛçt] [adj] no comp/superl (lofty) wrong ◊ *Stehlen ist unrecht.* ◆ *zum unrechten Zeitpunkt erscheinen*

◉ **etw. ist jdm unrecht** sb doesn't like sth ◊ *Es ist ihm unrecht, dass sie alleine in den Urlaub fährt.* **jdm unrecht tun** do sb an injustice

Un·recht ['ʊnrɛçt] das <–(e)s> no pl wrong ◊ *Ihr ist (ein) Unrecht geschehen.* ◆ *ein Unrecht begehen*

◉ **Unrecht bekommen** be shown to be in the wrong **jdm Unrecht geben** disagree with sb **Unrecht haben** be wrong **im Unrecht sein** be wrong **zu Unrecht** wrongly ◊ *jdn zu Unrecht beschuldigen/verdächtigen*

un·re·gel·mä·ßig ['ʊnreːgl̩mɛːsɪç] [adj, adv] irregular(ly) ◊ *unregelmäßige Arbeitszeiten* ◆ *Die Form der Blätter ist unregelmäßig.* ◆ *unregelmäßige Verben* ◆ *Sein Herz schlägt unregelmäßig.* ◆ *nur unregelmäßig zum Training kommen*

Un·ru·he ['ʊnruːə] die <–, –n> **1.** no pl anxiety, agitation ◊ *voller Unruhe auf und ab gehen* ◆ *etw. sorgt für erhebliche Unruhe* ⊖Ruhe **2.** no pl noise ◊ *Bei dieser Unruhe kann ich einfach nicht arbeiten!* ⊖Ruhe **3.** no pl unrest ◊ *Unruhe unter den Mitarbeitern stiften* ⊖Ruhe **4.** only pl Unruhen disturbances ◊ *Die Region wird von blutigen Unruhen erschüttert.*

un·ru·hig ['ʊnruːɪç] [adj] **1.** anxious, worried, agitated ◊ *unruhige Gedanken* ◆ *Als er um Mitternacht noch nicht zu Hause war, wurde sie unruhig.* ⊖ruhig **2.** restless ◊ *Die Nacht war ziemlich unruhig.* ◆ *in einer unruhigen Zeit leben* ⊖ruhig **3.** noisy ◊ *ein etwas unruhiges Hotel mit vielen jungen Gästen* ◆ *Hier ist es mir zu unruhig.* ⊖ruhig

4. *(pattern)* busy ◊ unruhige Farben ♦ Das Muster des Teppichs ist zu unruhig. ⊜ruhig **5.** *(sea)* rough ◊ ein unruhiges Gewässer ♦ Das Meer ist heute zu unruhig zum Schwimmen. ⊜ruhig [adv] **1.** anxiously, in agitation ◊ unruhig auf und ab gehen ⊜ruhig **2.** restlessly ◊ unruhig auf seinem Stuhl herumrutschen unruhig schlafen sleep badly ⊜ruhig

uns [ʊns] *dat and acc of* wir [ref pron] **1.** ourselves Sollen wir uns erst frisch machen? Shall we freshen up first? Wir halten uns an die Regeln. We're going to stick by the rules. **2.** *reciprocal* each other ◊ Wir hatten uns sehr lieb. Wir haben uns geschlagen. We had a fight. ⊜einander

un·schul·dig ['ʊnʃʊldɪç] [adj] innocent ◊ Ich bin unschuldig! ♦ ein unschuldiger Blick

② **un·ser** ['ʊnzɐ] [det] our ◊ Unser Vater geht mit uns in Kino. ♦ unsere neue Lehrerin ♦ unser Haus ♦ unsere Sachen

	m	f	nt	pl
nom	unser	unsere	unser	unsere
acc	unseren	unsere	unser	unsere
dat	unserem	unserer	unserem	unseren
gen	unseres	unserer	unseres	unserer

un·se·re ['ʊnzərə] → unser, unserer

② **un·se·rer** ['ʊnzərɐ] [poss pron] ours ◊ Euer Sohn ist gut erzogen, unserer leider nicht. ♦ „Wem gehört das rote Auto?" — „Das ist unseres." ♦ Sind diese Schlüssel unsere?

	m	f	nt	pl
nom	unserer	unsere	unseres	unsere
acc	unseren	unsere	unseres	unsere
dat	unserem	unserer	unserem	unseren
gen	-	-	-	-

un·se·res ['ʊnzərəs] → unserer

un·si·cher ['ʊnzɪçɐ] [adj] **1.** insecure, unconfident ◊ Er fühlt sich in ihrer Gegenwart sehr unsicher. ♦ mit unsicherer Stimme sprechen ⊜sicher **2.** unsafe, dangerous ◊ eine unsichere Technologie ♦ Hooligans machten die Stadt unsicher. ⊜sicher **3.** unstable ◊ Der Arbeitsmarkt bleibt unsicher. ♦ eine unsichere Angelegenheit ⊜sicher [adv] unconfidently, unsteadily ◊ Bei ihrem ersten Auftritt sang sie noch sehr unsicher. ⊜sicher

Un·sinn ['ʊnzɪn] der <-(e)s> *no pl* **1.** nonsense ◊ Was du da sagst, ist blanker Unsinn. ⊜Blödsinn, Quatsch **2.** mischief ◊ nur Unsinn im Kopf haben ♦ Unsinn treiben

un·sin·nig ['ʊnzɪnɪç] [adj, adv] outrageous(ly), ridiculous(ly) ◊ unsinnige Ausgaben ♦ in einer unsinnig großen Wohnung wohnen [adj] nonsensical ◊ unsinnige Vorschriften ♦ Was du da redest, ist doch völlig unsinnig. ⊜sinnvoll

un·tä·tig ['ʊntɛːtɪç] [adj, adv] *no comp/superl* idle (idly) ◊ Er hasst untätiges Warten. ♦ Die Regierung ist lange untätig geblieben. ♦ untätig herumsitzen

② **un·ten** ['ʊntn̩] [adv] **1.** down ◊ unten auf der Straße auf jdn warten ♦ unten am Bodensee ein Ferienhaus haben Er wohnt eine Treppe weiter unten. He lives one floor down. ⊜oben **2.** at the bottom ◊ Der Geldbeutel ist ganz unten in der Tasche. ♦ Die Flagge ist oben weiß und unten blau. ⊜oben **3.** *(in a lower position)* below ◊

Die Termine sind unten aufgelistet. ⊜oben

un·ter¹ ['ʊnte] [adv] under ◊ Für Kinder unter 12 Jahren verboten! ⊜über

un·ter² ['ʊnte] [prep] **1.** *with acc when expressing motion towards a place, with dat when there is no or undirected motion* [+acc] *or* [+dat] under, beneath ◊ Sie saßen unter einem Baum. ♦ Sie wohnen direkt unter uns.; *(covered by sth)* under ◊ Was trägst du unter dem Mantel? ♦ Das Kind kroch unter die Decke. seine Unterschrift unter einen Brief setzen add your signature to a letter ⊜über **2.** *temporal* [+dat] during ◊ Unter der Woche bin ich sehr beschäftigt. **3.** [+dat] *or* [+acc] *(with figures)* below, lower than ◊ Temperaturen unter null ♦ Die Beteiligung sank auf unter zehn Prozent. ⊜über **4.** [+dat] *(expressing circumstances)* in ◊ Er gestand unter Tränen, was er getan hatte. ♦ Sie steht unter Schock. unter großem Zeitdruck under great pressure of time unter Mordverdacht under suspicion of murder unter den/welchen Umständen under the/what circumstances **5.** *in combination with certain nouns, translation varies* [+acc] *or* [+dat] *(describing the condition in which sth is kept or under which sth is done)* jdn unter Druck setzen put sb under pressure ein Gebäude unter Denkmalschutz stellen make sth a listed building Ich helfe dir nur unter einer Voraussetzung/Bedingung: … I'll help you on one condition: … unter Verschluss under lock and key **6.** [+dat] by, through ◊ Sie rettete ihn unter Einsatz ihres Lebens. ♦ unter Anwendung von Gewalt **7.** [+dat] *or* [+acc] under ◊ die Berichte unter der Überschrift „Vermischtes" Sie erreichen uns unter der Nummer … You can reach us on the number … etw. unter das Motto … stellen give sth the name/title … **8.** [+dat] *or* [+acc] under ◊ eine Kommission unter dem Vorsitz des Außenministers ♦ Die Truppen wurden unter seinen Befehl gestellt. **9.** [+dat] *(giving cause)* under ◊ Sie brach unter der Belastung zusammen. unter etw. leiden suffer from sth **10.** [+dat] *(from)* among ◊ Ist einer unter euch, der mir das sagen kann? ♦ Unter den Briefen war keiner für dich. **11.** [+acc] into ◊ sich unters Volk mischen ♦ Zucker unter die Sahne rühren Du musst mehr unter die Leute gehen! You need to get out more!

⊛ **unter anderem** among other things ◊ Ich habe heute unter anderem zwei Bücher gekauft. **unter sich** on your/their etc. own ◊ Sie wollten unter sich bleiben. **unter uns** between you and me ◊ Unter uns gesagt: Ich finde ihn langweilig.

un·ter|…¹ ['ʊnte] [prefix] *+verb, stressed and separable* **1.** under… ◊ ein Handtuch unterlegen, damit der Boden nicht nass wird ♦ Im Schwimmbad tauchte er mich unter. **2.** *placing one thing underneath another, translation varies* Damit der Tisch nicht mehr wackelte, legte er ein Brettchen unter. He put a piece of wood under the table to stop it from wobbling. Halt die Hand unter, du kleckerst. Hold your hand under your food; you're making a mess.; *(boat, ship)* untergehen sink **3.** … in ◊ dem Futter Vitamine untermischen

un·ter…² ['ʊnte] [prefix] *inseparable* under… ◊ unterernährt ♦ unterbezahlt ♦ jdn unterfordern

un·ter·bre·chen [ʊntɐ'brɛçn̩] <unterbricht, unterbrach, hat unterbrochen> [tr+intr v] interrupt ◊ die

Fahrt mehrmals unterbrechen müssen ♦ eine Rede durch laute Zwischenrufe unterbrechen; (a meeting) break off ◊ eine Sitzung für eine halbe Stunde unterbrechen

un·ter|brin·gen ['ʊntəbrɪŋən] <bringt unter, brachte unter, hat untergebracht> [tr v] **1.** jdn/etw. irgendwo unterbringen find a place for sb/sth somewhere, find a place somewhere for sb/sth ◊ ein Kind in einem Kindergarten unterbringen ♦ Ich weiß nicht, wo ich den ganzen Kram unterbringen soll. **2.** jdn irgendwo unterbringen find sb a job somewhere ◊ Könntest du mich nicht in deiner Firma unterbringen? **3.** accommodate, put up ◊ Diese Pension kann zehn Gäste unterbringen.

② **un·ter·des·sen** [ʊntɐ'dɛsn] [adv] **1.** meanwhile, in the meantime ◊ Ich decke den Tisch; unterdessen kannst du die Weinflasche öffnen. ⊜inzwischen **2.** however, on the other hand ◊ Die Opposition sprach von Inkompetenz. Die Regierung verteidigte unterdessen ihr Vorgehen. ⊜indes, indessen

un·ter·drü·cken [ʊntɐ'drʏkŋ] <unterdrückt, unterdrückte, hat unterdrückt> [tr v] **1.** suppress ◊ das Lachen nicht unterdrücken können; (information also) withhold ◊ Beweismaterial unterdrücken **2.** (opponents to a regime) oppress ◊ Andersdenkende unterdrücken; (the discussion of a topic) suppress

② **un·te·re** ['ʊntərə] [adj] no comp, only before ns <ein unterer ..., eine untere ..., ein unteres ...> lower ◊ die unteren Stockwerke ♦ die untere Schicht der Gesellschaft ♦ die untere Donau

Un·ter·füh·rung [ʊntɐ'fyːrʊŋ] die <-, -en> subway, underpass ◊ die Unterführung benutzen

Un·ter·gang ['ʊntɐɡaŋ] der <-(e)s, Untergänge> **1.** (of the sun or moon) setting ◊ die Zeiten für Aufgang und Untergang des Mondes **2.** (of a ship) sinking ◊ der Untergang eines Öltankers **3.** downfall ◊ ein Unternehmen vor dem Untergang bewahren der Untergang des Römischen Reiches the Fall of the Roman Empire

un·ter|ge·hen ['ʊntɐɡeːən] <geht unter, ging unter, ist untergegangen> [intr v] **1.** (sun, moon) go down, set ◊ Die Sonne geht bald unter. ⊜aufgehen **2.** (ship) sink ◊ Das Schiff ging mit der gesamten Besatzung unter. ⊜auftauchen **3.** (decline) disappear ◊ Die Partei ist bei der letzten Wahl untergegangen. **4.** in etw. [dat] untergehen be swallowed up by sth, disappear in sth ◊ Seine Worte gingen im Lärm unter.

un·ter·ge·ord·net ['ʊntɐɡəˌʔɔrdnət] [adj] no comp/ superl **1.** subordinate, secondary ◊ untergeordnete Bedeutung haben ♦ Diese Debatte ist untergeordnet. ⊜sekundär **2.** GRAM subordinate ◊ ein untergeordneter Nebensatz [adv] on a subordinate level ◊ nur untergeordnet eine Rolle spielen

Un·ter·grund ['ʊntɐɡrʊnt] der <-(e)s, Untergründe> **1.** subsoil ◊ In der Tundra ist der Untergrund ständig gefroren. **2.** surface ◊ ein Aufkleber, der nur auf fettfreiem Untergrund haftet **3.** background ◊ weiße Schrift auf schwarzem Untergrund ⊜Grund **4.** no pl underground ◊ Der terroristische Untergrund operiert in kleinen Gruppen. viele Jahre im Untergrund verbringen spend many years (living) underground

Un·ter·grund·bahn ['ʊntɐɡrʊntbaːn] die <-, -en> (abbr U-Bahn) underground, subway ◊ mit der

Untergrundbahn zum Flughafen fahren; (in London) tube

un·ter·halb ['ʊntɐhalp] [prep] **1.** [+gen] underneath, below ◊ der Text unterhalb der Grafik ♦ Sie leben unterhalb der Armutsgrenze. ⊜oberhalb **2.** adverbial [+dat] unterhalb von below ◊ Sein Haus steht direkt unterhalb von meinem. ⊜oberhalb

Un·ter·halt ['ʊntɐhalt] der <-(e)s> no pl **1.** (money) living, keep ◊ seinen Unterhalt verdienen **2.** (payment) maintenance ◊ Unterhalt für seine geschiedene Frau zahlen **3.** upkeep, maintenance ◊ Der Unterhalt eines Schwimmbads ist sehr teuer.

② **un·ter·hal·ten** [ʊntɐ'haltn] <unterhält, unterhielt, hat unterhalten> [ref v] **1.** sich (mit jdm) (über etw. [acc]) unterhalten have a conversation (with sb) (about sth) ◊ sich mit jdm über seine Urlaubspläne unterhalten ♦ Wir haben uns nett miteinander unterhalten. **2.** sich gut/glänzend etc. unterhalten have a good/great etc. time [tr v] **1.** jdn unterhalten entertain sb ◊ Ein Clown unterhielt die kleinen Gäste. **2.** etw. unterhalten run sth ◊ Das Unternehmen unterhält eine Niederlassung in New York. **3.** (your family, dependants etc.) jdn unterhalten support sb ◊ Er muss hart arbeiten, um seine Familie zu unterhalten. **4.** (a relationship) keep up, maintain, continue ◊ Geschäftsbeziehungen unterhalten

② **Un·ter·hal·tung** [ʊntɐ'haltʊŋ] die <-, -en> **1.** conversation ◊ eine interessante Unterhaltung führen **2.** no pl entertainment ◊ für die musikalische Unterhaltung der Gäste sorgen **3.** no pl maintenance ◊ Die Gemeinde ist für die Unterhaltung des Kindergartens verantwortlich. ♦ die Unterhaltung freundschaftlicher Beziehungen

② **Un·ter·hemd** ['ʊntɐhɛmt] das <-(e)s, -en> vest, undershirt ◊ ein Unterhemd anziehen

② **Un·ter·ho·se** ['ʊntɐhoːzə] die <-, -n> briefs; (for women also) knickers; (for men also) (under)pants ◊ in Unterhosen herumlaufen ⊜Slip

un·ter|kom·men ['ʊntɐkɔmən] <kommt unter, kam unter, ist untergekommen> [intr v] **1.** irgendwo unterkommen stay somewhere ◊ bei Freunden oder Verwandten unterkommen **2.** (fam) irgendwo unterkommen get a job somewhere ◊ Meinst du, dass du mit deinem schlechten Abschluss irgendwo unterkommst? **3.** (fam) etw. kommt jdm unter sb experiences sth, sb comes across sth ◊ Ich arbeite hier seit zehn Jahren, aber so etwas ist mir noch nie untergekommen.

② **Un·ter·kunft** ['ʊntɐkʊnft] die <-, Unterkünfte> accommodation, place to stay ◊ eine Unterkunft für die Nacht suchen freie Unterkunft und Verpflegung bekommen get free board and lodging ⊜Bleibe

Un·ter·la·ge ['ʊntɐlaːɡə] die <-, -n> **1.** mat ◊ eine hitzebeständige Unterlage **2.** only pl document ◊ die Unterlagen für die Beantragung eines Passes

un·ter·las·sen [ʊntɐ'lasn] <unterlässt, unterließ, hat unterlassen> [tr v] **1.** etw. unterlassen refrain from (doing) sth **2.** omit, neglect ◊ Er hatte es unterlassen, sie ausreichend zu informieren.

un·ter|le·gen¹ ['ʊntɐleːɡn] <legt unter, legte unter, hat untergelegt> [tr v] (jdm) etw. unterlegen put sth underneath (sb) ◊ sich ein Kissen unterlegen

un·ter·le·gen² [ʊntɐˈleːgn̩] <unterlegt, unterlegte, hat unterlegt> [tr v] **1.** etw. irgendwie/mit etw. unterlegen accompany sth with sth ◊ *Texte mit schönen Bildern unterlegen* ein Wort im Text gelb unterlegen highlight a word in the text yellow **2.** A mit B unterlegen put B under A, line A with B ◊ *einen Sattel mit Schafsfell unterlegen*

un·ter·lie·gen [ʊntɐˈliːgn̩] <unterliegt, unterlag, ist unterlegen> [intr v] **1.** jdm/etw. unterliegen lose to sb/sth, be beaten by sb/sth, be defeated by sb/sth ◊ *seinem Gegner mit 1:2 unterliegen* **2.** einer Sache [dat] unterliegen be subject to sth, be influenced by sth ◊ *Die Preise unterliegen saisonalen Schwankungen.* **3.** *(taxes, regulations etc.)* einer Sache [dat] unterliegen be subject to sth, be liable to sth ◊ *Kontrollen unterliegen*

Un·ter·mie·ter [ˈʊntɐmiːtɐ] der <-s, ->, **Un·ter·mie·te·rin** [ˈʊntɐmiːtərɪn] die <-, –nen> lodger, subtenant

un·ter·neh·men [ʊntɐˈneːmən] <unternimmt, unternahm, hat unternommen> [tr v] do ◊ *Hast du Lust, etwas zu unternehmen? ♦ Warum hast du nichts dagegen unternommen?* einen Ausflug unternehmen go on a trip Anstrengungen unternehmen make efforts

Un·ter·neh·men [ʊntɐˈneːmən] das <-s, -> **1.** ECON business, firm ◊ *ein Unternehmen mit Sitz in Hamburg* ⊖Firma **2.** undertaking ◊ *ein aussichtsloses Unternehmen*

② **Un·ter·richt** [ˈʊntɐrɪçt] der <-(e)s *no pl* teaching ◊ *computergestützter Unterricht*; *(classes)* lessons ◊ *Sie nimmt Unterricht in Geige und Klavier.*

② **un·ter·rich·ten** [ʊntɐˈrɪçtn̩] <unterrichtet, unterrichtete, hat unterrichtet> [tr+intr v] SCHOOL teach ◊ *Sie unterrichtet Englisch. ♦ Er unterrichtet Erwachsene. ♦* an einer Fachhochschule unterrichten [tr v] jdn (über etw. [acc]/von etw.) unterrichten inform sb (of sth) ◊ *Bitte unterrichten Sie mich über alle Termine.* sich (über etw. [acc]) unterrichten inform yourself (about/of sth)

② **Un·ter·rock** [ˈʊntɐrɔk] der <-(e)s, Unterröcke> slip, petticoat ◊ *einen Unterrock tragen*

un·ter·sa·gen [ʊntɐˈzaːgn̩] <untersagt, untersagte, hat untersagt> [tr v] (jdm) etw. untersagen forbid (sb to do) sth, ban (sb from doing) sth ◊ *Der Vermieter untersagte ihr, Haustiere zu halten.* ⊖verbieten ⊖gestatten, erlauben

un·ter·schät·zen [ʊntɐˈʃɛtsn̩] <unterschätzt, unterschätzte, hat unterschätzt> [tr v] underestimate ◊ *ein Risiko unterschätzen* ⊖überschätzen

② **un·ter·schei·den** [ʊntɐˈʃaɛdn̩] <unterscheidet, unterschied, hat unterschieden> [tr v] **1.** etw./jdn von etw./jdm unterscheiden tell the difference between sth/sb and sth/sb, distinguish sth/sb from sth/sb ◊ *Kannst du einen Picasso von einem Miró unterscheiden? ♦ Die Zwillinge sind nicht voneinander zu unterscheiden.* **2.** differentiate between, make a distinction between ◊ *Bei dem Passwort müssen Sie Klein- und Großbuchstaben unterscheiden.* **3.** distinguish (between) ◊ *Man unterscheidet mehrere Arten von Forellen.* **4.** etw. unterscheidet jdn/etw. von jdm/etw. sth sets sb/sth apart from sb/sth, sth separates sb/sth from sb/sth ◊ *Seine blonden Haare unterscheiden ihn vom Rest der Familie.* **5.** make out, tell ◊ *Soweit ich das im Dunkeln unterscheiden konnte, waren es drei*

Männer. [intr v] unterscheiden zwischen make a distinction between ◊ *Man unterscheidet zwischen akuten und chronischen Krankheiten.* [ref v] sich von jdm/etw. unterscheiden differ from sb/sth ◊ *Wodurch unterscheidet sich das neue Modell vom alten?*

Un·ter·schen·kel [ˈʊntɐʃɛŋkl̩] der <-s, -> lower leg ◊ *sich am Unterschenkel verletzen*

② **Un·ter·schied** [ˈʊntɐʃiːt] der <-(e)s, -e> **1.** difference ◊ *Es gibt keinen Unterschied zwischen Bio- und Ökoprodukten.* **2.** distinction ◊ *Sie versucht, keinen Unterschied zwischen ihren Kindern zu machen.* im Unterschied zu jdm/etw. unlike sb/sth ◊ *Im Unterschied zu Jan kann Tom ausgezeichnet schwimmen.*
⊙ ein Unterschied wie Tag und Nacht as different as chalk and cheese

un·ter·schied·lich [ˈʊntɐʃiːtlɪç] [adj] different ◊ *unterschiedlicher Meinung sein*; *(varied)* diverse ◊ *Die Reaktionen auf die Ausstellung waren sehr unterschiedlich.* ⊝gleich [adv] in different ways, differently ◊ *Die beiden Gehirnhälften arbeiten sehr unterschiedlich. Die Schüler schnitten sehr unterschiedlich ab.* The pupils' marks varied considerably. ⊝gleich

② **un·ter·schrei·ben** [ʊntɐˈʃraɛbm̩] <unterschreibt, unterschrieb, hat unterschrieben> [tr+intr v] sign ◊ *ein Formular unterschreiben ♦ Unterschreiben Sie bitte hier.*

② **Un·ter·schrift** [ˈʊntɐʃrɪft] die <-, –en> signature ◊ *Die Unterschrift war gefälscht.* jdm etw. zur Unterschrift vorlegen give sb sth to sign seine Unterschrift unter etw. [acc] setzen sign sth, put your signature to sth

un·ters·te [ˈʊntɐstə] [superl] **1.** bottom ◊ *Die Stifte sind in der untersten Schublade.*; *(row of seats, in a cinema etc.)* front ◊ *Wir saßen im Kino in der untersten Reihe.* **2.** lowest ◊ *die unterste gerichtliche Instanz* → untere

② **un·ter·stüt·zen** [ʊntɐˈʃtʏtsn̩] <unterstützt, unterstützte, hat unterstützt> [tr v] support ◊ *das Rote Kreuz mit Spenden unterstützen ♦ jdn beim Wahlkampf unterstützen*

Un·ter·stüt·zung [ʊntɐˈʃtʏtsʊŋ] die <-, –en> **1.** *most sing* support ◊ *Dieser Kandidat hat unsere volle Unterstützung.* ein Verein zur Unterstützung von Flüchtlingskindern an association supporting the children of refugees **2.** (financial) aid ◊ *einem Kinderheim 12 000 Euro Unterstützung zusagen*

② **un·ter·su·chen** [ʊntɐˈzuːxn̩] <untersucht, untersuchte, hat untersucht> [tr v] **1.** investigate ◊ *Der Vorfall wird von der Polizei untersucht.* **2.** MED examine ◊ *zum Arzt gehen und sich gründlich untersuchen lassen*

② **Un·ter·su·chung** [ʊntɐˈzuːxʊŋ] die <-, –en> **1.** investigation ◊ *Die Untersuchung ergab menschliches Versagen als Unfallursache.* **2.** MED examination ◊ *eine ärztliche Untersuchung* **3.** *(scientific)* study ◊ *Eine kürzlich veröffentlichte Untersuchung hat ergeben, dass …*

② **Un·ter·wä·sche** [ˈʊntɐvɛʃə] die <-> *no pl* underwear, underclothes ◊ *frische Unterwäsche anziehen*

② **un·ter·wegs** [ʊntɐˈveːks] [adv] **1.** on the way ◊ *Ich habe unterwegs etwas gegessen.* **2.** away ◊ *dienstlich unterwegs sein* **3.** out (and about) ◊ *Sie ist*

seit heute Morgen um sieben unterwegs. ♦ *mit dem Fahrrad unterwegs sein*
un·ter·wer·fen [ʊntɐ'vɛʳfn̩] <unterwirft, unterwarf, hat unterworfen> [tr v] subjugate ◊ *ein Land unterwerfen* [ref v] **1.** sich (jdm) unterwerfen surrender (to sb) ◊ *sich dem Gegner bedingungslos unterwerfen* **2.** sich einer Sache [dat] unterwerfen submit to sth ◊ *sich bestimmten Regeln unterwerfen*
un·ter·zeich·nen [ʊntɐ'tsaeçnən] <unterzeichnet, unterzeichnete, hat unterzeichnet> [tr+intr v] *(form)* sign ◊ *Sind die Verträge unterzeichnet?* ♦ *Sie müssen noch unterzeichnen.*
Un·treue ['ʊntrɔøə] die <-> *no pl* **1.** infidelity ◊ *eheliche Untreue* ⊝Treue **2.** LAW embezzlement ◊ *gegen jdn Strafanzeige wegen Untreue erstatten*
un·ü·ber·legt ['ʊn|yːbɐleːkt] [adj] *no comp/superl* ill-considered ◊ *eine unüberlegte Äußerung* ♦ *Ich halte diese Reaktion für unüberlegt.* ⊝unbedacht [adv] without thinking ◊ *unüberlegt handeln* ⊝unbedacht
un·um·gäng·lich ['ʊn|ʊmgɛŋlɪç, – – '– –] [adj] essential, unavoidable ◊ *eine unumgängliche Voraussetzung* ♦ *Die Renovierung ist unumgänglich geworden.* ⊝unausweichlich [adv] vitally unumgänglich nötig/notwendig absolutely necessary
un·ver·ant·wort·lich ['ʊnfɛ|antvɔʳtlɪç] [adj, adv] irresponsible(-ibly) ◊ *eine unverantwortliche Bemerkung* ♦ *Es wäre unverantwortlich, weitere Schulden zu machen.* ♦ *unverantwortlich handeln*
un·ver·bind·lich ['ʊnfɛbɪntlɪç] [adj] *no comp/superl* **1.** not binding ◊ *eine unverbindliche Preisempfehlung* ♦ *Alle Hinweise sind rechtlich unverbindlich.* ⊝verbindlich **2.** non-committal ◊ *eine unverbindliche Antwort* ♦ *Das Gespräch blieb unverbindlich.* ⊝verbindlich [adv] **1.** without obligation ◊ *jdm Informationsmaterial kostenlos und unverbindlich zuschicken* ⊝verbindlich **2.** non-committally ◊ *Das Projekt sei recht interessant, sagte er unverbindlich.* ⊝verbindlich
un·ver·gess·lich ['ʊnfɛgɛslɪç] [adj, adv] unforgettable(-ably) ◊ *unvergessliche Momente* ♦ *Dieses Wochenende wird uns unvergesslich bleiben.* ♦ *ein unvergesslich schöner Urlaub*
un·ver·schämt ['ʊnfɛʃɛːmt] [adj, adv] <unverschämter, am unverschämtesten> **1.** impertinent(ly) ◊ *eine unverschämte Beleidigung* ♦ *Ich wollte nicht unverschämt sein.* ♦ *unverschämt grinsen/lügen* **2.** *(fam)* outrageous(ly) ◊ *unverschämte Forderungen stellen* ♦ *Die Preise in diesem Restaurant sind unverschämt.* ♦ *unverschämt teure Schuhe*
un·ver·ständ·lich ['ʊnfɛʃtɛntlɪç] [adj, adv] **1.** inaudible(-ibly) ◊ *eine unverständliche Aussprache* ♦ *Ihr Flüstern war unverständlich.* ♦ *Sie sprach unverständlich leise.* **2.** incomprehensible (-ibly) ◊ *ein unverständliches Problem* ♦ *Seine Reaktion war mir unverständlich.* ♦ *etw. unverständlich formulieren*
un·ver·züg·lich [ʊnfɛ'tsyːklɪç, '– – – –] [adj, adv] *no comp/superl; when used as an adj, only before*

ns immediate(ly) ◊ *die unverzügliche Freilassung der Gefangenen fordern* ♦ *Melden Sie alle Schäden unverzüglich.* ⊝augenblicklich
Un·wet·ter ['ʊnvɛtɐ] das <-s, –> storm ◊ *Bei dem schweren Unwetter kamen zwei Personen ums Leben.*
un·zu·frie·den ['ʊntsufriːdn̩] [adj] **1.** *not before ns* unhappy, not happy, not satisfied ◊ *Er war mit seiner Leistung unzufrieden.* ⊝zufrieden **2.** unhappy ◊ *Sie sieht unzufrieden aus.* ♦ *eine unzufriedene Miene* ⊝zufrieden
un·zu·läs·sig ['ʊntsuːlɛsɪç] [adj, adv] *no comp/ superl* improper(ly) ◊ *eine unzulässige Einmischung in interne Angelegenheiten* ♦ *Der Polizeisatz war unzulässig.* ♦ *staatliche Mittel unzulässig verwenden* etw. für unzulässig erklären declare sth inadmissible rechtlich unzulässig gespeicherte Daten illegally stored data ⊝zulässig
U·rin [u'riːn] der <-s> *no pl* urine ⊝Harn
Ur·kun·de ['uːɐkʊndə] die <-, –n> document ◊ *eine beglaubigte Urkunde*
② **Ur·laub** ['uːɐlaop] der <-(e)s, –e> holiday(s), vacation ◊ *eine Woche Urlaub haben* ♦ *in Spanien Urlaub machen* ♦ *in Urlaub fahren*
Ur·lau·ber ['uːɐlaobɐ] der <-s, –>, **Ur·lau·be·rin** ['uːɐlaobərɪn] die <-, –nen> holidaymaker, vacationer ◊ *Die Region zieht viele Urlauber an.*
② **Ur·sa·che** ['uːɐzaxə] die <-, –n> cause, reason ◊ *Das Auto geriet aus ungeklärter Ursache ins Schleudern.* ♦ *nach der Ursache des Brandes suchen* ⊝Grund ⊝Folge
④ keine Ursache don't mention it ◊ *„Danke für deine Hilfe!" — „Keine Ursache!"*
Ur·sprung ['uːɐʃprʊŋ] der <-(e)s, Ursprünge> origin(s) ◊ *der Ursprung des Lebens*
ur·sprüng·lich ['uːɐʃprʏŋlɪç] [adj] **1.** *no comp/ superl, only before ns* original ◊ *Die ursprüngliche Idee wurde aufgegeben.* **2.** natural, unspoilt ◊ *eine Welt von ursprünglicher Schönheit* ♦ *Neuseeland ist ursprünglich.* [adv] **1.** originally ◊ *Die Konferenz war ursprünglich für April geplant.* **2.** in its natural state, unspoilt ◊ *einen Strand ursprünglich belassen*
② **Ur·teil** ['ʊʳtael] das <-s, –e> **1.** LAW verdict ◊ *Der Richter fällte ein mildes Urteil.* **2.** judgement, judgment ◊ *ein vernichtendes Urteil über ein Buch fällen* ♦ *sich* [dat] *über etw./jdn ein Urteil bilden*
ur·tei·len ['ʊʳtaelən] [intr v] +*haben* judge ◊ *nicht nach dem Äußeren urteilen* ♦ *Dem Glanz nach zu urteilen ist das Hemd aus Seide.*
Ur·wald ['uːɐvalt] der <-(e)s, Urwälder> primeval forest ◊ *eine Expedition in den Urwald unternehmen*
USA [uː|ɛs|'aː] (*always* die USA) *(abbr of* United States of America*)* the USA, the US ◊ *Er ist in den USA geboren.*
usw. [ʊnt zoː 'vaetɐ] *(abbr of* und so weiter*)* etc. ◊ *Wir verkaufen Bücher, Zeitungen usw.*

V

v, V [fao] das <-(s), -(s)> v, V ◊ *Dieses Wort wird mit einem kleinen v/großen V geschrieben.* ♦ *V wie Viktor*

va·ge ['va:gə] [adj, adv] <vager, am vag(e)sten> vague(ly) ◊ *eine vage Vorstellung von etw. haben* ♦ *Die Angaben sind sehr vage.* ♦ *eine vage formulierte Vorschrift* ⊖unklar

Va·ri·an·te [va'rjantə] die <-, -n> version, variant ◊ *eine neue Variante des Internetwurms*

va·ri·ie·ren [vari'i:rən] <variiert, variierte, hat variiert> [tr+intr v] vary ◊ *Die Übernachtungspreise variieren je nach Saison.*

Va·se ['va:zə] die <-, -n> vase ◊ *Blumen in eine Vase stellen*

② **Va·ter** ['fa:tɐ] der <-s, Väter> **1.** *(also fig)* father ◊ *ein allein erziehender Vater* ♦ *Er gilt als der Vater des Computers.* zweifacher Vater sein be a/the father of two **2.** *no pl* REL Father ◊ *zum himmlischen Vater beten*

⊛ **der Heilige Vater** (the) Pope, the Holy Father

Va·ter·tag ['fa:tɐta:k] der <-(e)s, -e> *most sing* Father's Day

Father's Day in Germany traditionally coincides with Ascension Day, 10 days before Whitsun. To celebrate Father's Day in Germany, men often go out to the pub together in a group.

② **ve·ge·ta·risch** [vege'ta:rɪʃ] [adj] *no comp/superl* vegetarian ◊ *vegetarische Ernährung* ♦ *Dieses Gericht ist rein vegetarisch.* [adv] vegetarisch leben be a vegetarian vegetarisch kochen/essen cook/have a vegetarian meal sich vegetarisch ernähren have a vegetarian diet

② **Ve·lo** ['ve:lo:] das <-s, -s> *(Swiss) (abbr of Veloziped)* bicycle, bike ◊ *Velo fahren*

Ven·til [vɛn'ti:l] das <-s, -e> **1.** valve ◊ *ein undichtes Ventil* **2.** *(fig)* outlet ◊ *ein Ventil für seinen Frust suchen*

ver·... [fɛ] [prefix] *translation varies* **1.** *(change to a different condition)* sich vermehren multiply sich verbessern improve eine Tür verschließen lock a door verwandeln transform **2.** *(negative result)* mis... ◊ *Ich habe meine Brille verlegt.* ♦ *sich verrechnen* sich versprechen say something wrong by mistake sich verlaufen lose the way verschlafen oversleep **3.** *(movement away in space or time)* verreist sein be away on a journey einen Termin verschieben postpone an appointment verstreuen disperse **4.** *(expresses that sb dies, sth disintegrates)* verhungern starve to death verblühen wilt Briefe verbrennen burn letters **5.** *(expresses that sth is fused or amalgamated)* verknüpfen link vermischen mix up

② **ver·ab·re·den** [fɛ|'apre:dn̩] <verabredete, hat verabredet> [ref v] sich (mit jdm) verabreden arrange to meet (sb) ◊ *sich zum Abendessen verabreden* [tr v] etw. verabreden agree (on) sth ◊ *Es wurde verabredet, die Gespräche fortzusetzen.*

Ver·ab·re·dung [fɛ|'apre:dʊŋ] die <-, -en> **1.** *no pl* agreement ◊ *die Verabredung der genauen Arbeitseinteilung* **2.** appointment ◊ *eine wichtige Verabredung haben* nach Verabredung by appointment

② **ver·ab·schie·den** [fɛ|'apʃi:dn̩] <verabschiedet, verabschiedete, hat verabschiedet> [ref v] **1.** sich (von jdm) verabschieden say goodbye (to sb), part (with sb) ◊ *Wir verabschiedeten uns an der Bushaltestelle.* **2.** *(fig)* sich von etw. verabschieden part with sth ◊ *sich von einer Illusion verabschieden müssen* [tr v] **1.** jdn verabschieden say goodbye to sb, see sb off ◊ *Sie brachte ihre Mutter zur Tür und verabschiedete sie.* **2.** *(when sb leaves a place where they have worked)* jdn verabschieden say goodbye to sb, give sb a send-off ◊ *eine Kollegin in den Mutterschaftsurlaub verabschieden* **3.** approve ◊ *Die Partei verabschiedete ihr Wahlprogramm.*

ver·ach·ten [fɛ|'axtn̩] <verachtet, verachtete, hat verachtet> [tr v] despise ◊ *Er verachtet die Leute, die alles tun, um reich zu werden.*

⊛ **nicht zu verachten sein** *(fam)* be not to be sniffed at, be good

ver·all·ge·mei·nern [fɛ|algə'maɛnɐn] <verallgemeinert, verallgemeinerte, hat verallgemeinert> [tr+intr v] generalize, make a generalization ◊ *eine Erfahrung, die man nicht verallgemeinern kann* ♦ *Ich möchte nicht verallgemeinern.*

ver·al·ten [fɛ|'altn̩] <veraltet, veraltete, ist veraltet> [intr v] become obsolete ◊ *Theoretische Berufskenntnisse veralten rasch.*

② **ver·än·dern** [fɛ|'ɛndɐn] <verändert, veränderte, hat verändert> [tr v] change ◊ *Der Erfolg hat ihn verändert.* [ref v] **1.** sich verändern change, alter ◊ *Mein Leben hat sich von Grund auf verändert.* ⊖sich wandeln **2.** sich (beruflich) verändern change your job ◊ *Sie möchte sich beruflich verändern.*

Ver·än·de·rung [fɛ|'ɛndərʊŋ] die <-, -en> change ◊ *organisatorische Veränderungen vornehmen*

ver·ängs·ti·gen [fɛ|'ɛŋstɪgn̩] <verängstigt, verängstigte, hat verängstigt> [tr v] scare, frighten ◊ *mit Geistergeschichten die Kinder verängstigen*

ver·an·las·sen [fɛ|'anlasn̩] <veranlasst, veranlasste, hat veranlasst> [tr v] **1.** jdn zu etw. veranlassen make sb do sth ◊ *Dieses Buch hat mich zum Nachdenken veranlasst.* **2.** etw. veranlassen order sth, see to it that sth is done ◊ *Sie veranlasste eine Untersuchung des Falls.* ♦ *Er veranlasste, dass alle Unterlagen vernichtet wurden.* ⊖einleiten

⊛ **sich zu etw. veranlasst fühlen/sehen** feel compelled to do sth

ver·an·schau·li·chen [fɛ|'anʃaolɪçn̩] <veranschaulicht, veranschaulichte, hat veranschaulicht> [tr v] illustrate ◊ *Lassen Sie mich an einem Beispiel veranschaulichen, was ich meine.*

ver·an·stal·ten [fɛ|'anʃtaltn̩] <veranstaltet, veran-

staltete, hat veranstaltet> [tr v] **1.** hold, put on, organize ◊ *eine Konferenz/ein Konzert/einen Wettbewerb veranstalten* **2.** *(fam) (a fuss)* make ◊ *Sie hat einen richtigen Aufstand veranstaltet, nur weil ich eine Stunde zu spät kam.*

② **Ver·an·stal·tung** [fɛ|'anʃtaltʊŋ] die <-, -en> **1.** *no pl* organization ◊ *Daran sollten Sie bei der Veranstaltung eines Festes denken: ...* **2.** event ◊ *eine festliche Veranstaltung; (shorter event also)* function ◊ *Die Veranstaltung beginnt um 20 Uhr.*

ver·ant·wor·ten [fɛ|'antvɔʳtn̩] <verantwortet, verantwortete, hat verantwortet> [tr v] accept responsibility *einen Unfall zu verantworten haben* be responsible for an accident *etw. vor seinem Gewissen nicht verantworten können* not be able to reconcile sth with your conscience [ref v] *sich wegen etw.* [gen] verantworten answer for sth ◊ *sich vor Gericht wegen Betrugs verantworten müssen*

② **ver·ant·wort·lich** [fɛ|'antvɔʳtlɪç] [adj] *no comp/ superl* **1.** responsible ◊ *sich für jdn verantwortlich fühlen* ♦ *eine verantwortliche Position innehaben mit dem verantwortlichen Arzt sprechen* speak to the doctor in charge **2.** answerable ◊ *Das Unternehmen ist den Aktionären gegenüber verantwortlich.* **3.** jdn/etw. für etw. verantwortlich machen blame sth on sb/sth ◊ *Eine defekte Heizdecke wurde für den Brand verantwortlich gemacht.* [adv] **1.** für etw. verantwortlich zeichnen take official responsibility for sth **2.** responsibly ◊ *eine Aufgabe verantwortlich erledigen*

② **Ver·ant·wor·tung** [fɛ|'antvɔʳtʊŋ] die <-, -en> responsibility ◊ *die Verantwortung für etw. tragen* ♦ *für die Richtigkeit der Angaben keine Verantwortung übernehmen* jdn für etw. zur Verantwortung ziehen call sb to account for sth

ver·ar·bei·ten [fɛ|'aʳbaetn̩] <verarbeitet, verarbeitete, hat verarbeitet> [tr v] **1.** etw. (zu etw.) verarbeiten make sth (into sth) ◊ *Wir verarbeiten nur Naturprodukte.* ♦ *Bioabfall zu Kompost verarbeiten* **2.** use ◊ *Bei diesem Teig werden auf 500 Gramm Mehl vier Eier verarbeitet.* etw. literarisch verarbeiten turn sth into a book **3.** *(psychologically)* work through, process ◊ *ein schreckliches Erlebnis verarbeiten*

ver·är·gern [fɛ|'ɛʳgɐn] <verärgert, verärgerte, hat verärgert> [tr v] annoy ◊ *Wir sollten den Chef nicht unnötig verärgern.*

Ver·band [fɛ'bant] der <-(e)s, Verbände> **1.** MED bandage, dressing ◊ *jdm einen Verband anlegen* **2.** association ◊ *der Verband Deutscher Makler* **3.** MIL division ◊ *gepanzerte Verbände* **4.** alliance, union ◊ *Ihr Leben spielt sich im Verband der Familie ab.*

Ver·bands·zeug [fɛ'bantstsɔøk] das <-(e)s> *no pl* first-aid kit

ver·barg [fɛ'baʳk] *pret of* verbergen

ver·ber·gen [fɛ'bɛʳgn̩] <verbirgt, verbarg, hat verborgen> [tr v] hide, conceal ◊ *sein Gesicht in den Händen verbergen* ♦ *Ich glaube, sie hat etwas zu verbergen.* [ref v] sich irgendwo verbergen be hiding somewhere *Hinter seiner Arroganz verbirgt sich Unsicherheit.* His arrogance covers his insecurity. ⊜sich verstecken

② **ver·bes·sern** [fɛ'bɛsɐn] <verbessert, verbesserte, hat verbessert> [tr v] **1.** etw. verbessern improve

sth ◊ *seinen Umsatz im ersten Halbjahr deutlich verbessern* ⊜verschlechtern **2.** *(a mistake, piece of work etc.)* etw./jdn verbessern correct sth/sb ◊ *ein Diktat verbessern* ⊜korrigieren [ref v] **1.** *(when you have said something incorrect)* sich verbessern correct yourself ◊ *Erst gab sie die falsche Antwort, verbesserte sich dann aber.* **2.** sich verbessern improve yourself, improve your situation ◊ *Er ist in seinem Beruf unzufrieden und versucht, sich zu verbessern.* **3.** sich verbessern improve ◊ *Ihre Sprachkenntnisse haben sich erheblich verbessert.* ⊜sich verschlechtern

② **Ver·bes·se·rung** [fɛ'bɛsərʊŋ] die <-, -en> **1.** improvement ◊ *Vorschriften zur Verbesserung der Luftqualität* **2.** *(of a mistake, piece of work etc.)* correction ◊ *die Verbesserung eines Aufsatzes* ⊜Korrektur

ver·bie·gen [fɛ'biːgn̩] <verbiegt, verbog, hat verbogen> [tr v] **1.** bend ◊ *einen Löffel verbiegen* **2.** *(fig) (the truth)* distort, pervert ◊ *die Wahrheit verbiegen* [ref v] sich verbiegen bend (out of shape) ◊ *Der Nagel hat sich verbogen.* ⊛ sich nicht verbiegen lassen stay true to yourself

② **ver·bie·ten** [fɛ'biːtn̩] <verbietet, verbot, hat verboten> [tr v] **1.** (jdm) etw. verbieten forbid (sb to do) sth ◊ *Ich verbiete dir, so etwas zu sagen!* ♦ *jdm das Rauchen verbieten* ⊜untersagen ⊜erlauben **2.** etw. verbieten ban sth ◊ *einen Film verbieten* ⊜erlauben, genehmigen **3.** etw. verbietet etw. sth prohibits sth ◊ *Das verbietet der Anstand.* **4.** jdm das Haus verbieten ban sb from the house ◊ *Er verbot dem Freund seiner Tochter das Haus.* [ref v] etw. verbietet sich sth is out of the question

② **ver·bin·den** [fɛ'bɪndn̩] <verbindet, verband, hat verbunden> [tr v] **1.** MED bandage, dress ◊ *Die Hand muss verbunden werden.* jdn verbinden dress sb's wounds **2.** jdm die Augen verbinden blindfold sb **3.** join, connect, link ◊ *zwei Bretter mit einem Scharnier verbinden* ♦ *Die Brücke verbindet die Insel mit dem Festland.* ♦ *Eine besondere Liebe verbindet mich mit dieser Insel.* eine Geschäftsreise mit einem Besuch bei Verwandten verbinden combine a business trip with a visit to relatives **4.** *(ideas)* associate ◊ *Italien verbinde ich mit Sonne und Meer.* ⊜verknüpfen **5.** jdn mit jdm/etw. verbinden put sb through to sb/sth, connect sb with sb/sth ◊ *Verbinden Sie mich bitte mit der Personalabteilung.* [intr v] put sb through, connect sb ◊ *„Ich möchte mit Herrn Fuchs sprechen." — „Einen Moment, ich verbinde."* [ref v] **1.** sich verbinden join (together) ◊ *In dieser Organisation haben sich Arbeitnehmer desselben Berufs verbunden.* **2.** CHEM sich verbinden react ◊ *Kupfer verbindet sich mit Sauerstoff.* **3.** *(emotions)* be associated ◊ *Mit dieser Musik verbinden sich für mich schöne Erinnerungen.*

ver·bind·lich [fɛ'bɪntlɪç] [adj] **1.** pleasant ◊ *ein paar verbindliche Worte wechseln* ♦ *Er ist in der Regel nicht sehr verbindlich und diplomatisch.* ⊜unverbindlich **2.** binding ◊ *eine verbindliche Regelung* ♦ *Der Vertrag ist rechtlich verbindlich.* ⊜unverbindlich [adv] **1.** pleasantly ◊ *verbindlich lächeln* **2.** definitively, definitely ◊ *etw. verbindlich festlegen* verbindlich zusagen give a definite yes ⊜unverbindlich

ⓩ **Ver·bin·dung** [fɛ'bɪndʊn] die <-, –en> **1.** connection ◊ *eine Verbindung zwischen zwei Vorfällen sehen* ♦ *Sobald er den Hörer abnahm, war die Verbindung unterbrochen.* sich mit jdm in Verbindung setzen contact sb, get in touch with sb mit jdm in Verbindung bleiben keep/stay in touch with sb **2.** relationship ◊ *Zwischen den beiden besteht eine sehr liebevolle Verbindung.* **3.** union ◊ *die Verbindung zweier Unternehmen* **4.** CHEM compound ◊ *eine chemische Verbindung* **5.** UNI students' society, fraternity ◊ *einer Verbindung beitreten; (for women at US universities)* sorority box@ Studentenverbindung

◉ in Verbindung mit in conjunction with ◊ *Seine Verabschiedung findet in Verbindung mit der Weihnachtsfeier statt.*

ver·birgt [fɛ'bɪrkt] *pres of* verbergen

ver·blas·sen [fɛ'blasn̩] <verblasst, verblasste, ist verblasst> intr v *(also fig)* fade ◊ *Die Farbe ist mit den Jahren verblasst.* ♦ *Die Erinnerung an seine Großmutter verblasst allmählich.*

ver·blüf·fen [fɛ'blʏfn̩] <verblüfft, verblüffte, hat verblüfft> trv amaze ◊ *Er verblüffte das Publikum mit seinen Zaubertricks.* intr v be amazing ◊ *Dieses Gerät verblüfft durch seine einfache Handhabung.*

ver·bor·gen [fɛ'bɔrgn̩] *past p of* verbergen

ⓩ **Ver·bot** [fɛ'boːt] das <–(e)s, –e> ban ◊ *ein Verbot befolgen/missachten* ♦ *sich für ein Verbot von Kampfhunden aussprechen* gegen das Verbot des Arztes zur Arbeit gehen go to work even though your doctor has forbidden it

Ver·brauch [fɛ'braox] der <–(e)s> *no pl* consumption ◊ *Nahrungsmittel, die zum sofortigen Verbrauch bestimmt sind*

◉ sparsam im Verbrauch sein be very economical

ⓩ **ver·brau·chen** [fɛ'braoxn̩] <verbraucht, verbrauchte, hat verbraucht> trv use ◊ *beim Waschen viel Seife verbrauchen*

Ver·brau·cher [fɛ'braoxɐ] der <–s, –>, **Ver·brau·che·rin** [fɛ'braoxərɪn] die <–, –nen> consumer ◊ *ein Gesetz zum Schutz der Verbraucher*

ⓩ **Ver·bre·chen** [fɛ'brɛçn̩] das <–s, –> crime ◊ *einem Verbrechen zum Opfer fallen* ♦ *ein grausames Verbrechen begehen*

ⓩ **Ver·bre·cher** [fɛ'brɛçɐ] der <–s, –>, **Ver·bre·che·rin** [fɛ'brɛçərɪn] die <–, –nen> criminal ◊ *ein gefährlicher/skrupelloser Verbrecher* ♦ *Sie wurde wie eine Verbrecherin behandelt.*

ver·brei·ten [fɛ'braetn̩] <verbreitet, verbreitete, hat verbreitet> trv **1.** circulate ◊ *eine Pressemitteilung verbreiten* **2.** spread ◊ *einen üblen Gestank verbreiten* ♦ *Optimismus verbreiten* ♦ *Der Computervirus verbreitete sich weltweit.; (light)* shed ref v **1.** sich verbreiten become widespread ◊ *Diese Idee hat sich schnell verbreitet.* **2.** *(esp pej)* sich über etw. acc verbreiten hold forth on sth ◊ *Er verbreitete sich über sein Lieblingsthema, die Rosenzucht.*

ver·bren·nen [fɛ'brɛnən] <verbrennt, verbrannte, hat/ist verbrannt> trv +haben **1.** *(destroy)* burn ◊ *in einer Anlage Müll verbrennen; (a human body after death)* cremate ◊ *sich nach seinem Tod verbrennen lassen* sich verbrennen set yourself alight

2. *(hurt)* jdn/sich verbrennen burn sb/yourself ◊ *Au, du hast mich mit deiner Zigarette verbrannt!* sich am Herd verbrennen sich dat etw. (an etw. dat) verbrennen burn your sth ◊ *Ich habe mir die Zunge an der heißen Suppe verbrannt.* intr v +sein **1.** burn ◊ *Das Holz im Kamin ist verbrannt.* ♦ *Das Essen ist verbrannt.; (house)* burn down **2.** zu Asche verbrennen be reduced to ashes

ⓩ **ver·brin·gen** [fɛ'brɪnən] <verbringt, verbrachte, hat verbracht> trv spend ◊ *Wir haben die Ferien bei den Großeltern verbracht.* ♦ *Er verbringt seine Abende meist mit Fernsehen.*

ⓩ **Ver·dacht** [fɛ'daxt] der <–(e)s> *no pl* suspicion ◊ *Mein Verdacht hat sich bestätigt.* jdn in Verdacht haben suspect sb Verdacht schöpfen become suspicious ◊ *es besteht Verdacht auf Lungenentzündung* pneumonia is suspected

ver·däch·tig [fɛ'dɛçtɪç] adj, adv suspicious(ly) ◊ *ein verdächtiges Geräusch hören* ♦ *Im Kinderzimmer ist es verdächtig ruhig.* sich verdächtig machen arouse suspicion einer Sache gen verdächtig sein be suspected of sth ◊ *Er ist der Erpressung verdächtig.*

ⓩ **ver·däch·ti·gen** [fɛ'dɛçtɪgn̩] <verdächtigt, verdächtigte, hat verdächtigt> trv jdn (einer Sache gen) verdächtigen suspect sb (of sth) ◊ *jdn des Mordes verdächtigen* ♦ *Du verdächtigst doch nicht etwa mich?*

ver·dan·ken [fɛ'danŋ̍] <verdankt, verdankte, hat verdankt> trv jdm/einer Sache etw. verdanken owe sth to sb/sth ◊ *Ich verdanke meinem Vater viel.* ♦ *Ihrer schnellen Reaktion verdanke ich mein Leben.*

ver·darb [fɛ'darp] *pret of* verderben

ver·dau·en [fɛ'daoən] <verdaut, verdaute, hat verdaut> trv *(also fig)* digest ◊ *Fette Speisen sind schwer zu verdauen.* ♦ *Jetzt muss sie das Gelesene erst mal verdauen.; (a shock)* get over

ver·de·cken [fɛ'dɛkn̩] <verdeckt, verdeckte, hat verdeckt> trv hide, conceal, cover ◊ *Wolken verdeckten die Sonne.* ♦ *Der große Hut verdeckte ihr Gesicht.* jdn die Sicht verdecken block sb's view

ver·der·ben [fɛ'dɛrbm̩] <verdirbt, verdarb, hat/ist verdorben> intr v +sein go off ◊ *Leg das Fleisch in den Kühlschrank, damit es nicht verdirbt.* trv +haben **1.** sich dat etw. verderben ruin your sth ◊ *sich bei schlechtem Licht die Augen verderben* sich den Magen verderben eat something that disagrees with you **2.** *(joy, appetite)* jdm etw. verderben spoil sb's sth, ruin sb's sth ◊ *Der Regen hat uns den Ausflug verdorben.* ♦ *jdm den Appetit/ die gute Laune verderben* **3.** *(morals)* corrupt ◊ *Das viele Geld hat seinen Charakter verdorben.*

◉ es sich dat mit jdm verderben fall out of favour/favor with sb

ver·deut·li·chen [fɛ'dɔʏtlɪçn̩] <verdeutlicht, verdeutlichte, hat verdeutlicht> trv (jdm) etw. verdeutlichen clarify sth (for sb), explain sth (to sb) ◊ *etw. an einem Beispiel verdeutlichen*

ⓩ **ver·die·nen** [fɛ'diːnən] <verdient, verdiente, hat verdient> trv **1.** earn ◊ *Wie viel verdienst du im Monat?* ♦ *sich seinen Lebensunterhalt mit Klavierunterricht verdienen* **2.** deserve ◊ *Er verdient unseren Respekt.* jd hat es nicht anders verdient sb didn't deserve any better

Ver·dienst¹ [fɛ'diːnst] der <–(e)s, –e> **1.** earnings,

income ◊ *der monatliche Verdienst* **2.** profit ◊ *Dabei hat der Verkäufer kaum einen Verdienst gemacht.*

Ver·dienst² [fɛ'diːnst] *das* <–(e)s, –e> achievement, merit ◊ *Es ist hauptsächlich ihr Verdienst, dass das Buch so gut geworden ist.* jds Verdienst um etw. ist groß sb has made a huge contribution to sth für seine Verdienste geehrt werden be honoured/honored for your services

ver·dirbt [fɛ'dɪʳpt] *pres of* verderben

ver·dop·peln [fɛ'dɔpl̩n] <verdoppelt, verdoppelte, hat verdoppelt> ⓣⓡⓥ double ◊ *Ich verdopple Ihr Gehalt, wenn Sie bleiben.*; *(efforts)* redouble sich verdoppeln double ◊ *Unsere Ausgaben haben sich seit letztem Jahr verdoppelt.* ⊖halbieren

ver·dor·ben [fɛ'dɔʳbm̩] *past p of* verderben

ver·drän·gen [fɛ'drɛŋən] <verdrängt, verdrängte, hat verdrängt> ⓣⓡⓥ **1.** *(emotions, memories)* repress, suppress ◊ *Viele Gewaltopfer verdrängen das Erlebte.* „Hattest du nicht heute einen Zahnarzttermin?" — „Oje, den muss ich verdrängt haben." "Didn't you have a dental appointment today?" — "Oh dear, I must have put it out of my mind." **2.** replace, oust ◊ *Der Computer hat heutzutage die Schreibmaschine verdrängt.* jdn von seinem Posten verdrängen oust sb from their position

ver·dre·hen [fɛ'dreːən] <verdreht, verdrehte, hat verdreht> ⓣⓡⓥ *(also fig)* twist ◊ *die Wahrheit verdrehen* ♦ *Du verdrehst immer alles, was ich sage.* jdm den Arm verdrehen twist sb's arm die Augen verdrehen roll your eyes den Kopf verdrehen turn your head

ver·dün·nen [fɛ'dʏnən] <verdünnt, verdünnte, hat verdünnt> ⓣⓡⓥ etw. (mit etw.) verdünnen dilute sth (with sth) ◊ *Fruchtsaft mit Wasser verdünnen* ♦ *eine Säure verdünnen* den Teig mit Wasser verdünnen add water to the dough

② **Ver·ein** [fɛ'aen] *der* <–(e)s, –e> club, society, organization, association ◊ *einem Verein beitreten* ♦ *Ich bin in keinem Verein.*

A *Verein* is any organization that people have voluntarily joined for an extended period of time in order to pursue a common interest and commit themselves to certain organizational objectives and regulations. Political parties do not count among such organizations.

ver·ein·ba·ren [fɛ'aenbaːrən] <vereinbart, vereinbarte, hat vereinbart> ⓣⓡⓥ arrange, agree (on) ◊ *einen Termin vereinbaren* ♦ *Ich habe mit ihm vereinbart, dass wir uns morgen treffen.* ♦ *In einem Vertrag werden die Bedingungen vereinbart.* ⊙ etw. mit etw. vereinbaren können be able to reconcile sth with sth ◊ *Wie kannst du es mit deinem Gewissen vereinbaren, ihn so zu belügen?*

Ver·ein·ba·rung [fɛ'aenbaːrʊŋ] *die* <–, –en> agreement, arrangement ◊ *eine Vereinbarung mit jdm treffen* ♦ *sich nicht an eine Vereinbarung halten*

ver·ei·nen [fɛ'aenən] <vereint, vereinte, hat vereint> ⓣⓡⓥ unite ◊ *Er vereint Fleiß und Kreativität.* ♦ *Deutschland ist inzwischen wieder vereint.*; *(conflicting things also)* reconcile ◊ *Wie kann ich nur Beruf und Haushalt vereinen?*; *(forces)* combine ◊ *Wenn wir unsere Kräfte vereinen,*

können wir etwas bewegen. sich vereinen unite ◊ *Wir haben uns vereint, um gemeinsam für unser Ziel zu kämpfen.* In ihr vereinen sich Schönheit und Klugheit. She has both beauty and intelligence. In diesem Modell vereinen sich Eleganz und Funktionalität. This model combines elegance with functionality.

ver·ein·fa·chen [fɛ'aenfaxn̩] <vereinfacht, vereinfachte, hat vereinfacht> ⓣⓡⓥ etw. vereinfachen simplify sth, make sth easier ◊ *Geräte, die die Hausarbeit vereinfachen*

ver·ein·heit·li·chen [fɛ'aenhaetlɪçn̩] <vereinheitlicht, vereinheitlichte, hat vereinheitlicht> ⓣⓡⓥ standardize ◊ *die Vorschriften innerhalb der EU vereinheitlichen*

Ver·ei·ni·gung [fɛ'aenɪgʊŋ] *die* <–, –en> **1.** organization ◊ *eine Vereinigung zur Unterstützung krebskranker Kinder* ♦ *eine terroristische Vereinigung* **2.** fusion ◊ *die Vereinigung verschiedener Musikstile* die Vereinigung Deutschlands the unification of Germany

ver·ein·zelt [fɛ'aentsl̩t] ⓐⓓⓙ *no comp/superl, only before ns* isolated, scattered ◊ *In dieser Gegend wachsen nur ein paar vereinzelte Bäume.* ♦ *nur in vereinzelten Fällen* ⓐⓓⓥ occasionally ◊ *Im Neckar gibt es vereinzelt sogar Forellen.*

ver·eist [fɛ'aest] ⓐⓓⓙ *no comp/superl* icy, iced-up ◊ *auf der vereisten Fahrbahn ins Schleudern kommen* ♦ *Vorsicht, die Straßen sind vereist.*

ver·er·ben [fɛ'ɛʳbm̩] <vererbt, vererbte, hat vererbt> ⓣⓡⓥ **1.** jdm etw. vererben, etw. an jdn vererben leave sth to sb, bequeath sth to sb ◊ *Dieses Bild hat mir meine Tante vererbt.* ♦ *Sie hat all ihr Geld an die Kirche vererbt.* **2.** *(a defect, disease, genetic characteristic)* jdm etw. vererben pass sth on to sb ◊ *Er hat seinem Sohn seine Farbenblindheit/seine Liebe zur Kunst vererbt.*; *(disease)* sich vererben be hereditary

ver·fah·ren [fɛ'faːrən] <verfährt, verfuhr, hat/ist verfahren> ⓣⓡⓥ +*haben (petrol, money)* use (up) ◊ *pro Monat 50 Euro/50 Liter Benzin verfahren* ⓘⓝⓣⓡⓥ +*sein* act, proceed ◊ *Wie sollen wir in diesem Fall verfahren?* mit jdm härter verfahren deal more severely with sb ⓡⓔⓕⓥ +*haben* sich verfahren lose your way, take a wrong turning

② **Ver·fah·ren** [fɛ'faːrən] *das* <–s, –> **1.** process ◊ *ein neues Verfahren, um aus Müll Energie zu gewinnen* **2.** LAW proceedings ◊ *Die Staatsanwaltschaft wird gegen ihn ein Verfahren einleiten.* ♦ *Morgen wird das Verfahren in Sachen Schmider eröffnet.* ⊖Prozess

ver·fal·len [fɛ'falən] <verfällt, verfiel, ist verfallen> ⓘⓝⓣⓡⓥ **1.** decay, fall into disrepair ◊ *Das alte Gebäude verfällt immer mehr, seit es leer steht.* eine verfallene Burg a ruined castle; *(person)* decline ◊ *Es ist erschreckend, wie Großvater zusehends verfällt.* **2.** *(morals etc.)* decline ◊ *Verfällt die gesellschaftliche Moral?* **3.** *(ticket, voucher)* expire ◊ *Der Fahrschein verfällt nach Ablauf eines Jahres.*; *(claim)* lapse **4.** in etw. ⓐⓒⓒ verfallen sink into sth ◊ *in Depressionen verfallen*; *(into dialect)* lapse into sth **5.** auf etw. ⓐⓒⓒ verfallen hit upon sth, think of sth ◊ *Wie bist du denn auf die Idee verfallen, dir dort ein Haus zu kaufen?* **6.** jdm/einer Sache

verfallen fall victim to sb/sth der Trunksucht verfallen become addicted to drink jdm mit Haut und Haaren verfallen sein be head over heels in love with sb

ver·fas·sen [fɛ'fasn̩] <verfasst, verfasste, hat verfasst> [tr v] write, compose ◊ *einen Artikel/Aufsatz/Brief verfassen* ♦ *Wer hat dieses Gedicht verfasst?; (documents)* draw up

Ver·fas·ser [fɛ'fasɐ] der <−s, −>, **Ver·fas·se·rin** [fɛ'fasərɪn] die <−, −nen> author ◊ *Wer ist der Verfasser dieses Artikels?* ⊜Autor

Ver·fas·sung [fɛ'fasʊŋ] die <−, −en> 1. *no pl* state (of health/mind) ◊ *in guter/schlechter Verfassung sein* ♦ *Ich bin jetzt nicht in der Verfassung, mit dir darüber zu diskutieren.* 2. POL *(of a country)* constitution ◊ *Das Grundgesetz ist die Verfassung Deutschlands.* ♦ *gegen die Verfassung verstoßen*

ver·feh·len [fɛ'fe:lən] <verfehlt, verfehlte, hat verfehlt> [tr v] miss ◊ *Der Ball hat das Tor knapp verfehlt.* ♦ *Die Grünen haben ihr Wahlziel verfehlt.* das Thema verfehlen be totally off the subject den Zweck verfehlen not achieve its purpose seine Wirkung verfehlen fail to have any effect sie verfehlen sich/einander they miss each other ◊ *Wir wollten uns an der Säule treffen, haben uns aber verfehlt.* nicht zu verfehlen sein be impossible to miss

◉ **verfehlt sein** be inappropriate ◊ *Es wäre verfehlt, schon jetzt von einem Misserfolg zu sprechen.*

ver·fil·men [fɛ'fɪlmən] <verfilmt, verfilmte, hat verfilmt> [tr v] make a film of ◊ *einen Roman verfilmen* Thomas Manns ,Tod in Venedig' ist erfolgreich verfilmt worden. They made a successful film of Thomas Mann's 'Death in Venice'.

ver·fol·gen [fɛ'fɔlgn̩] <verfolgt, verfolgte, hat verfolgt> [tr v] 1. follow, pursue ◊ *Die Polizei verfolgte das Auto/den Mann.* ♦ *Als Star wird sie ständig von Reportern verfolgt.* ♦ *einen Plan/ein Ziel verfolgen* 2. *(idea, fear etc.)* etw. verfolgt jdn sb is haunted by sth, sb is plagued by sth Der Gedanke an einen Indienurlaub verfolgt mich schon lange. The thought of a holiday in India has been at the back of my mind for a long time. 3. follow ◊ *Er verfolgte jede ihrer Bewegungen.* ♦ *Wir sollten die weitere Entwicklung genau verfolgen.* 4. POL persecute ◊ *eine Minderheit verfolgen* 5. von etw. verfolgt sein be dogged by sth ◊ *vom Pech verfolgt sein* 6. LAW *(for an offence)* verfolgt werden be prosecuted strafrechtlich verfolgt werden be prosecuted under criminal law

ver·früht [fɛ'fry:t] [adj] *no comp/superl* premature ◊ *Was war der Grund für seine verfrühte Abreise?* ♦ *Es wäre verfrüht, jetzt schon ein Urteil abzugeben.*

ver·füg·bar [fɛ'fy:kba:ɐ] [adj] *no comp/superl* available ◊ *alle verfügbaren Mitarbeiter einsetzen* ♦ *Im Augenblick ist leider kein Personal verfügbar.*

ver·fü·gen [fɛ'fy:gn̩] <verfügt, verfügte, hat verfügt> [intr v] *(lofty)* 1. über etw. [acc] verfügen have sth at your disposal ◊ *nicht über die ausreichenden Mittel für etw. verfügen* jd kann frei über etw. [acc] verfügen sth is entirely at sb's disposal 2. über jdn verfügen have sb at your beck and call

über jds Zeit verfügen monopolize sb's time [tr v] *(form)* order ◊ *Die Richterin hat verfügt, dass er Unterhalt zahlen muss.*

Ver·fü·gung [fɛ'fy:gʊŋ] die <−, −en> 1. *(tech)* order, decree ◊ *Ein Hausdurchsuchungsbefehl ist eine amtliche Verfügung.* 2. jdm zur Vefügung stehen be at sb's disposal, be available to sb jdm etw. zur Verfügung stellen make sth available to sb freie Verfügung über etw. [acc] haben have free use of sth Bitte halten Sie sich zur Verfügung. Please remain available.

ver·füh·ren [fɛ'fy:rən] <verführt, verführte, hat verführt> [tr v] 1. jdn zu etw. verführen encourage sb to do sth ◊ *einen Jugendlichen zum Trinken verführen* ♦ *jdn dazu verführen, noch ein Stück Kuchen zu essen* 2. jdn verführen seduce sb ◊ *Er hat schon zahlreiche Frauen verführt.*

ver·füh·re·risch [fɛ'fy:rərɪʃ] [adj] tempting ◊ *Das Angebot ist sehr verführerisch.* ♦ *verführerische Düfte aus der Küche* [adj, adv] seductive(ly) ◊ *Ihre Pose war mehr als verführerisch.* ♦ *jdn verführerisch anblicken*

Ver·ga·be [fɛ'ga:bə] die <−> *no pl* allocation, awarding ◊ *Die Vergabe der Preise findet nächste Woche statt.* ♦ *über die Vergabe der Stipendien entscheiden*

② **Ver·gan·gen·heit** [fɛ'gaŋənhaet] die <−> *no pl* past ◊ *Über meine Vergangenheit möchte ich nicht sprechen. Ach, das ist doch längst Vergangenheit.* Oh, that's all in the past now. ⊜Zukunft

ver·gäng·lich [fɛ'gɛŋlɪç] [adj] *no comp/superl* transitory ◊ *Das Leben ist vergänglich.* ♦ *vergängliche Schönheit*

② **ver·gaß** [fɛ'ga:s] *pret of* vergessen

ver·ge·ben [fɛ'ge:bm̩] <vergibt, vergab, hat vergeben> [tr+intr v] jdm (etw.) vergeben forgive sb ((for) sth) ◊ *Sie hat ihm den Seitensprung nie vergeben.* ♦ *Kannst du mir noch einmal vergeben?* [tr v] allocate ◊ *Eine zentrale Stelle vergibt die Studienplätze.; (a prize)* award ◊ *Bei der Feier werden auch die Preise vergeben.* Die Stelle ist leider schon vergeben. Unfortunately, the job has already been taken.

② **ver·geb·lich** [fɛ'ge:plɪç] [adj] *no comp/superl* futile ◊ *Mein Versuch, sie davon abzubringen, war vergeblich.* ♦ *vergebliche Bemühungen* [adv] in vain ◊ *sich vergeblich um eine Stelle bemühen* ⊜umsonst

ver·ge·hen [fɛ'ge:ən] <vergeht, verging, ist/hat vergangen> [intr v] +*sein* 1. *(time)* pass, go by ◊ *Es vergeht kein Tag, an dem sie nicht an ihn denkt.; (pain)* wear off ◊ *Nachdem sie eine Tablette genommen hatte, waren die Schmerzen bald vergangen.* Die Zeit vergeht wie im Flug. Time flies. Die Zeit will nicht vergehen. Time is dragging. jdm ist die Lust an etw. [dat] vergangen sb doesn't feel like sth any more 2. vor etw. [dat] vergehen die of sth ◊ *Ich vergehe vor Durst!* ♦ *vor Angst/Neugier vergehen* +*haben* sich an jdm vergehen sexually abuse sb

Ver·ge·hen [fɛ'ge:ən] das <−s, −> crime, offence ◊ *Er ist wegen einiger Vergehen vorbestraft.*

② **ver·ges·sen** [fɛ'gɛsn̩] <vergisst, vergaß, hat vergessen> [tr v] forget ◊ *jds Geburtstag/Telefonnummer vergessen* ♦ *Jetzt habe ich vergessen, was ich sagen wollte.* ♦ *Oh nein, ich habe die Schlüssel vergessen!* seinen Schirm im Bus

vergessen leave your umbrella on the bus [ref v]
sich vergessen forget yourself ◊ *Verschwinde von
hier, ehe ich mich vergesse!*
◉ jdm etw. nie/nicht vergessen never/not forget
that sb did sth das/den/die kannst du
vergessen *(fam)* you can forget that/him/her
ver·gess·lich [fɛ'gɛslɪç] *[adj]* forgetful ◊ *Opa wird
immer vergesslicher.* ✦ *ein vergesslicher Mensch*
ver·ge·wal·ti·gen [fɛgə'valtɪgn̩] <vergewaltigt, vergewaltigte, hat vergewaltigt> [tr v] rape ◊ *Sie
wurde auf dem Weg nach Hause vergewaltigt.*
ver·ge·wis·sern [fɛgə'vɪsɐn] <vergewissert sich,
vergewisserte sich, hat sich vergewissert> [ref v]
sich vergewissern make sure ◊ *Sie vergewisserte
sich, dass auch wirklich alle Fenster geschlossen
waren.*
ver·gif·ten [fɛ'gɪftn̩] <vergiftet, vergiftete, hat
vergiftet> [tr v] **1.** poison ◊ *Ungeziefer vergiften* ✦
sich mit Tabletten vergiften **2.** *(the air, environment)* pollute ◊ *Abgase vergiften unsere Luft.;
(the atmosphere, a relationship)* sour ◊ *Der
Streit hatte unsere Beziehung vergiftet.* [ref v] sich
an etw. [dat] vergiften poisen yourself with sth ◊ *Er
hatte sich an selbst gesammelten Pilzen vergiftet.*
② **ver·gisst** [fɛ'gɪst] *pres of* vergessen
② **Ver·gleich** [fɛ'glaɛç] der <-(e)s, -e> **1.** comparison ◊ *Vergleiche zwischen zwei Personen anstellen
im Vergleich zu jdm/etw.* in comparison with sb/
sth, compared with sb/sth ◊ *Im Vergleich zu ihrer
Schwester kann sie wesentlich besser Englisch.*
2. LIT simile ◊ *„Schnell wie der Blitz" ist ein
Vergleich.* **3.** LAW settlement ◊ *Es kam zu einem
Vergleich und das Verfahren wurde eingestellt.*
◉ das ist (gar) kein Vergleich there is no comparison
ver·gleich·bar [fɛ'glaɛçbaːʳ] *[adj, adv]* no comp/
superl comparable(-ably) ◊ *eine vergleichbare
Stelle finden* ✦ *Ihre Leistung ist nicht mit der ihres
Bruders vergleichbar.* ✦ *ein vergleichbar attraktives
Angebot*
② **ver·glei·chen** [fɛ'glaɛçn̩] <vergleicht, verglich, hat
verglichen> [tr v] jdn/etw. (mit jdm/etw.) vergleichen compare sb/sth (with sb/sth) ◊ *eine Kopie
mit dem Original vergleichen* ✦ *vor dem Kauf die
Preise vergleichen* ✦ *Ich hasse es, wenn man mich
mit meiner Schwester vergleicht.* [ref v] sich vergleichen come to/reach a settlement ◊ *Der Richter
schlug vor, dass sich die Parteien vergleichen.*
ver·gnü·gen [fɛ'gnyːgn̩] <vergnügt sich, vergnügte
sich, hat sich vergnügt> [ref v] sich vergnügen
enjoy yourself, have a good time ◊ *Er vergnügte
sich während der Kur mit allen möglichen Frauen.*
② **Ver·gnü·gen** [fɛ'gnyːgn̩] das <-s, -> **1.** no pl
pleasure ◊ *Es ist ein Vergnügen, sie singen zu
hören.* ✦ *ein Buch mit großem Vergnügen lesen* ✦
etw. nur zum Vergnügen tun etw. macht/bereitet
jdm Vergnügen sb enjoys sth sich [dat] ein
Vergnügen daraus machen, etw. zu tun take a
pleasure in doing sth viel Vergnügen enjoy
yourself/yourselves **2.** fun ◊ *nichts für billige
Vergnügen übrig haben* sich ins Vergnügen stürzen
start having a good time, be out for a good time
◉ ein teures Vergnügen an expensive diversion
ver·gnügt [fɛ'gnyːkt] *past p of* vergnügen *[adj, adv]*
<vergnügter, am vergnügtesten> cheerful(ly) ◊ *ein
vergnügter Abend* ✦ *Sie war vergnügt und gut

gelaunt. ✦ *vergnügt lachen* ⊖fröhlich
ver·gra·ben [fɛ'graːbm̩] <vergräbt, vergrub, hat
vergraben> [tr v] bury ◊ *Der Hund hat einen
Knochen vergraben.* ✦ *Dort soll ein Schatz
vergraben sein.; (animal)* sich vergraben bury
itself [ref v] sich in etw. [acc] vergraben bury
yourself in sth, immerse yourself in sth ◊ *Sie
vergräbt sich in ihre Arbeit.*
② **ver·grö·ßern** [fɛ'grøːsɐn] <vergrößert, vergrößerte,
hat vergrößert> [tr+intr v] magnify ◊ *Diese Lupe vergrößert alles um 20 Prozent.* ✦ *Damit wird das
Problem ja noch vergrößert.; (a photograph, an
image etc.)* enlarge ◊ *Mit dem Kopierer können Sie
auch vergrößern und verkleinern.; (a company)*
expand; *(a house)* extend ◊ *ein Haus durch einen
Anbau vergrößern; (money, profits)* increase;
(town, business etc.) sich vergrößern expand;
(numbers) sich vergrößern increase ◊ *Die Zahl
der Mitarbeiter hat sich auf 30 vergrößert.* ⊖ver-
kleinern [ref v] sich vergrößern move to a bigger
place ◊ *Das Büro platzt aus allen Nähten, wir
müssen uns vergrößern.*
Ver·gü·tung [fɛ'gyːtʊŋ] die <-> no pl refund, reimbursement ◊ *die Vergütung der Reisekosten übernehmen; (for work)* payment, remuneration
② **ver·haf·ten** [fɛ'haftn̩] <verhaftet, verhaftete, hat
verhaftet> [tr v] arrest ◊ *Die Polizei hat einen Verdächtigen verhaftet.* ⊖festnehmen
② **ver·hal·ten** [fɛ'haltn̩] <verhält sich, verhielt sich,
hat sich verhalten> [ref v] **1.** sich (irgendwie)
verhalten behave (in a certain way) ◊ *So kannst
du dich ihr gegenüber doch nicht verhalten!* ✦ *sich
falsch/merkwürdig/richtig verhalten* ⊖sich
benehmen **2.** es/eine Sache verhält sich
(irgendwie) things are (a certain way) ◊ *In Wirklichkeit verhält es sich doch ganz anders.*
② **Ver·hal·ten** [fɛ'haltn̩] das <-s> no pl behaviour,
behavior ◊ *Ich verstehe ihr Verhalten nicht!* ✦ *das
Verhalten von Tieren studieren*
② **Ver·hält·nis** [fɛ'hɛltnɪs] das <-ses, -se> **1.** proportion, ratio, relation ◊ *Das Verhältnis zwischen
Einsatz und Bezahlung muss stimmen.* ✦ *zwei
Farben im Verhältnis drei zu eins mischen* **2.** relationship ◊ *ein gutes Verhältnis zu seinen Eltern
haben* **3.** *(sexual)* affair, relationship ◊ *Er soll ein
Verhältnis mit seiner Sekretärin haben.* **4.** only pl
situation, circumstances ◊ *die politischen Verhältnisse in diesem Land* über seine Verhältnisse
leben live beyond your means aus einfachen Verhältnissen kommen come from a humble background
ver·hält·nis·mä·ßig [fɛ'hɛltnɪsmɛːsɪç] *[adv]* relatively, comparatively ◊ *verhältnismäßig viel
verdienen* ✦ *ein verhältnismäßig einfacher Test*
⊖relativ, ziemlich
ver·han·deln [fɛ'handl̩n] <verhandelt, verhandelte,
hat verhandelt> [intr v] **1.** (über etw. [acc]) verhandeln negotiate (sth) ◊ *über die vertraglichen Bedingungen verhandeln* ✦ *Die beiden Staaten verhandeln noch.* **2.** LAW *(in court)* hold proceedings,
hold a trial ◊ *Gegen ihn wird wegen Steuerhinterziehung verhandelt.* [tr v] **1.** discuss ◊ *Wir sind uns so
weit einig, nur den Preis müssen wir noch verhandeln.* **2.** LAW *(in court)* try, hear ◊ *Sein Fall wird in
der ersten Instanz verhandelt.*
Ver·hand·lung [fɛ'handlʊŋ] die <-, -en> **1.** LAW

hearing, trial ◊ *Morgen findet die Verhandlung im Fall Schmider statt.* ♦ *eine nicht öffentliche Verhandlung* **2.** negotiation ◊ *mit jdm/einer Firma in Verhandlung stehen*

ver·hän·gen [fɛ'hɛŋən] <verhängt, verhängte, hat verhängt> [tr v] **1.** *(a fine, sentence, sanction)* impose ◊ *Der Richter hat die Höchststrafe verhängt.* den Ausnahmezustand über ein Land verhängen declare a state of emergency in a country **2.** *(a window, wall etc.)* etw. (mit etw.) verhängen cover sth (with sth) ◊ *die Fenster (mit schwarzen Tüchern) verhängen*

Ver·häng·nis [fɛ'hɛŋnɪs] das <–ses, –se> disaster ◊ *Von da an nahm das Verhängnis seinen Lauf.* jdm zum Verhängnis werden be sb's undoing

ver·har·ren [fɛ'harən] <verharrt, verharrte, hat verharrt> [intr v] *(lofty)* remain, stay ◊ *Die Katze verharrte bewegungslos vor ihrem Opfer.* bei seiner Meinung verharren adhere/stick to your opinion auf seiner Position verharren maintain your position

ver·hee·rend [fɛ'heːrənt] [adj, adv] **1.** disastrous(ly), catastrophic(ally) ◊ *verheerende Folgen für die Umwelt haben* ♦ *Eine Eskalation der Gewalt wäre verheerend.* verheerend aussehen look atrocious sich verheerend auswirken have a disastrous/catastrophic effect **2.** *(fam)* awful(ly), frightful(ly) ◊ *verheerende Lücken im Wortschatz haben* ♦ *Ihr Französisch ist verheerend.* ♦ *bei einer Prüfung verheerend abschneiden*; *(person)* verheerend aussehen look awful/dreadful

ver·hei·len [fɛ'haɛlən] <verheilt, verheilte, ist verheilt> [intr v] heal (up) ◊ *Die Wunde ist gut verheilt.*

ver·heim·li·chen [fɛ'haɛmlɪçn] <verheimlicht, verheimlichte, hat verheimlicht> [tr v] etw. verheimlichen conceal sth from sb, keep sth secret from sb ◊ *seinen Eltern eine schlechte Note verheimlichen*

② **ver·hei·ra·tet** [fɛ'haɛraːtət] [adj] no comp/superl married ◊ *Sie ist nicht verheiratet.* ♦ *ein verheirateter Mann* ⊝ledig

ver·hel·fen [fɛ'hɛlfn̩] <verhilft, verhalf, hat verholfen> [intr v] jdm zu etw. verhelfen help sb get sth ◊ *jdm zu einer Arbeitsstelle verhelfen* ♦ *jdm zu seinem Recht verhelfen*

② **ver·hin·dern** [fɛ'hɪndɐn] <verhindert, verhinderte, hat verhindert> [tr v] prevent ◊ *einen Unfall in letzter Minute verhindern* ♦ *Wie kann man verhindern, dass Schadstoffe ins Wasser gelangen?*

ver·hö·ren [fɛ'høːrən] <verhört, verhörte, hat verhört> [tr v] question, interrogate; *(in court)* examine ◊ *Der Richter verhörte den Angeklagten.* [ref v] sich verhören mishear sb ◊ *Ich dachte, er heißt Brunn, nicht Braun, aber da muss ich mich wohl verhört haben.*

ver·hun·gern [fɛ'hʊŋɐn] <verhungert, verhungerte, ist verhungert> [intr v] **1.** die of starvation ◊ *Überall auf der Welt verhungern täglich Kinder.* jdn verhungern lassen let sb starve (to death) **2.** *(fam)* be starving (hungry) ◊ *Ich verhungere, wann gibt es endlich was zu essen?* verhungert aussehen look half-starved

ver·hü·ten [fɛ'hyːtn̩] <verhütet, verhütete, hat verhütet> [tr v] prevent ◊ *ein Unglück verhüten* ♦ *eine Schwangerschaft verhüten* ♦ *Wir konnten das*

Schlimmste verhüten. [intr v] take precautions, use a contraceptive ◊ *Wie verhütet ihr?*

ver·ir·ren [fɛ'ɪrən] <verirrt sich, verirrte sich, hat sich verirrt> [ref v] **1.** sich (irgendwo) verirren get lost (somewhere) ◊ *sich im Wald verirren* ⊝sich verlaufen **2.** sich irgendwohin verirren stray into somewhere ◊ *Ein Vogel hatte sich in unseren Wintergarten verirrt.* ⊝sich verlaufen

Ver·kauf [fɛ'kaͻf] der <–(e)s, Verkäufe> **1.** sale ◊ *Dieses Gemälde steht nicht zum Verkauf.* ♦ etw. zum Verkauf anbieten ⊝Kauf **2.** no pl *(of a company)* sales department ◊ *im Verkauf tätig sein* ⊝Einkauf

② **ver·kau·fen** [fɛ'kaͻfn̩] <verkauft, verkaufte, hat verkauft> [tr v] *(also fig)* (jdm) etw. verkaufen sell sth (to sb) ◊ *Blumen auf dem Markt verkaufen* ♦ *Ich muss mir noch überlegen, wie ich meinem Chef diese Idee verkaufe.* zu verkaufen sein be for sale; *(goods)* sich verkaufen sell ◊ *Dieses Buch verkauft sich gut/schlecht.*; *(person)* sich verkaufen sell yourself ◊ *Als Selbstständiger muss man sich verkaufen können.*

Ver·käu·fer [fɛ'kͻøfɐ] der <–s, –>, **Ver·käu·fe·rin** [fɛ'kͻøfərɪn] die <–, –nen> **1.** sales/shop assistant, sales clerk ◊ *Die Verkäuferin hat mich sehr gut beraten.* ♦ *Er arbeitet als Verkäufer.* **2.** seller ◊ *Der Verkäufer des Autos hat mir diesen Mangel verschwiegen.*; *(professional)* salesman, saleswoman, salesperson ◊ *Thomas ist Verkäufer von Versicherungen.* ♦ *eine geschickte Verkäuferin* ⊝Käufer

② **Ver·kehr** [fɛ'keːɐ̯] der <–(e)s> no pl **1.** traffic ◊ *Um diese Zeit war noch wenig Verkehr.* ♦ *den Verkehr behindern* **2.** schriftlicher Verkehr correspondence diplomatischer Verkehr diplomatic relations **3.** *(sexual)* intercourse ◊ *mit jdm Verkehr haben* ⊝Geschlechtsverkehr

⊛ etw. in (den) Verkehr bringen put sth into circulation ◊ *Dieses Medikament darf nicht in Verkehr gebracht werden.* etw. aus dem Verkehr ziehen withdraw sth (from circulation)

ver·keh·ren [fɛ'keːrən] <verkehrt, verkehrte, hat/ist verkehrt> [intr v] **1.** +haben/sein *(bus, tram etc.)* run ◊ *Die U-Bahn verkehrt zwischen 5 und 24 Uhr.* ♦ *Dieser Bus verkehrt täglich.*; *(boat)* sail ◊ *Die Fähre verkehrt nur in den Sommermonaten.* **2.** +haben mit jdm verkehren associate with sb, mix with sb ◊ *Mit solchen Leuten verkehrt sie nicht.* mit jdm brieflich/schriftlich verkehren correspond with sb, communicate by letter with sb mit jdm geschäftlich verkehren have a business relationship with sb **3.** +haben in etw. [dat] verkehren frequent sth ◊ *In diesem Lokal verkehren viele Künstler.* [tr v] +haben etw. ins Gegenteil verkehren reverse sth [ref v] +haben sich in etw. [acc] verkehren turn into sth ◊ *Ihre Liebe verkehrte sich in Hass.* sich ins Gegenteil verkehren become reversed

② **Ver·kehrs·mit·tel** [fɛ'keːɐ̯smɪtl̩] das <–s, –> (means of) transport ◊ *Das Ticket gilt für alle öffentlichen Verkehrsmittel.*

② **Ver·kehrs·zei·chen** [fɛ'keːɐ̯stsaɛçn̩] das <–s, –> road sign ◊ *die Verkehrszeichen beachten*

ver·kehrt [fɛ'keːɐ̯t] past p of verkehren [adj, adv] <verkehrter, am verkehrtesten> wrong(ly) ◊ *Sie fuhr in die verkehrte Richtung.* ♦ *Es wäre verkehrt,*

wegzulaufen. ♦ *Er hat sehr viel verkehrt gemacht.*
verkehrt liegen be wrong ◊ *Mit deiner Schätzung
liegst du nicht verkehrt.*; *(clock)* verkehrt gehen
be wrong ⊜falsch ⊖richtig [adv] verkehrt herum
back to front ◊ *Das Baby hat den Schnuller
verkehrt herum in den Mund gesteckt.*; inside out ◊
Er hatte den Pulli verkehrt herum an.; upside down
◊ *Das Bild hängt ja verkehrt herum!*
ver·kla·gen [fɛ'klaːgn̩] <verklagt, verklagte, hat
verklagt> [tr v] sue ◊ *Er verklagte die Firma wegen
Vertragsbruchs.* ♦ *Sie verklagte die Universität auf
Schadenersatz.*
ver·klei·den [fɛ'klaɛdn̩] <verkleidet, verkleidete,
hat verkleidet> [tr v] 1. jdn als etw. verkleiden
dress sb up as sth ◊ *Die Mutter verkleidete ihn als
Cowboy.* sich als etw. verkleiden dress up as sth
sich verkleiden put on fancy dress verkleidet in
fancy dress ◊ *Wer möchte, kann verkleidet
kommen.* 2. cover ◊ *ein mit Marmor verkleidetes
Badezimmer* mit Holz verkleiden panel
Ver·klei·dung [fɛ'klaɛdʊŋ] die <-, -en>
1. costume 2. dressing up 3. disguise ◊ *In seiner
Verkleidung erkannte ihn niemand.* 4. panelling,
covering ◊ *eine Verkleidung aus Holz/Aluminium*
ver·klei·nern [fɛ'klaɛnɐn] <verkleinert, verkleinerte, hat verkleinert> [tr v] reduce ◊ *ein Foto/eine
Kopie verkleinern* ♦ *Der Chef wollte die Belegschaft
verkleinern.* ⊜vergrößern [ref v] sich verkleinern get
smaller, become smaller, shrink ◊ *Der Tumor verkleinerte sich.* ⊖sich vergrößern
Ver·klei·ne·rungs·form [fɛ'klaɛnərʊŋsfoˈm] die
<-, -en> diminutive ◊ *„Häuschen" ist die Verkleine-
rungsform von „Haus".*
ver·knei·fen [fɛ'knaɛfn̩] <verkneift sich, verkniff
sich, hat sich verkniffen> [ref v] sich [dat] etw. verkneifen suppress sth ◊ *Er verkniff sich die
Bemerkung.*
ver·knüp·fen [fɛ'knʏpfn̩] <verknüpft, verknüpfte,
hat verknüpft> [tr v] 1. (miteinander) verknüpfen
tie together ◊ *Er verknüpfte die beiden Schnüre
(miteinander).* 2. *(fig)* (miteinander) verknüpfen
combine ◊ *Ich konnte meine Reise nach Berlin mit
einem Besuch bei meiner Freundin verknüpfen.* ♦
*Sie verknüpft in diesem Artikel zwei interessante
Themen miteinander.* ⊜verbinden
ver·kom·men [fɛ'kɔmən] <verkommt, verkam, ist
verkommen> [intr v] 1. become run down ◊ *Das
Gebäude verkam immer mehr.*; *(person)* go to the
dogs ◊ *Deine Kinder verkommen und du schaust
zu!*; *(plants, garden)* run wild ◊ *Der Garten ist
völlig verkommen.* jdn/etw. verkommen lassen
neglect sb/sth ◊ *Meine Exfrau lässt unsere Kinder
verkommen.* ♦ *Warum lasst ihr euer Haus so
verkommen?* zu etw. verkommen degenerate into
sth ◊ *Die Produkte verkamen zur billigen Massen-
ware.* 2. *(food)* go bad ◊ *Die Speisen waren
verkommen.* etw. verkommen lassen let sth go to
waste
ver·kör·pern [fɛ'kœˈpɐn] <verkörpert, verkörperte,
hat verkörpert> [tr v] 1. embody ◊ *Dieser Star verkörpert den amerikanischen Traum.* 2. *(a figure in
a play, film etc.)* play ◊ *Er verkörpert in diesem
Film den jungen Goethe.*
ver·kraf·ten [fɛ'kraftn̩] <verkraftet, verkraftete,
hat verkraftet> [tr v] etw. verkraften cope with sth
◊ *Ihren Tod hat er nicht verkraftet.*

ver·kramp·fen [fɛ'krampfn̩] <verkrampft sich, verkrampfte sich, hat sich verkrampft> [ref v] sich verkrampfen tense up ◊ *Seine Muskeln verkrampften
sich.*
ver·krampft [fɛ'krampft] *past p of* verkrampfen
[adj, adv] <verkrampfter, am verkrampftesten>
seldom superl tense(ly) ◊ *ein verkrampftes Lächeln*
♦ *Er wurde im Laufe der Prüfung immer verkrampfter.* ♦ *Sie stand verkrampft vor dem Publikum.*
ver·küm·mern [fɛ'kʏmɐn] <verkümmert, verkümmerte, ist verkümmert> [intr v] 1. become stunted
◊ *Der Baum verkümmerte.* 2. go to waste ◊ *Sein
Talent verkümmerte.*
ver·kün·den [fɛ'kʏndn̩] <verkündet, verkündete,
hat verkündet> [tr v] announce ◊ *Der Minister verkündete seinen Rücktritt.*; *(a verdict)* give
ver·kür·zen [fɛ'kʏˈtsn̩] <verkürzt, verkürzte, hat
verkürzt> [tr v] 1. shorten ◊ *Er hat die Schnur um
20 cm verkürzt.* ♦ *Die Arbeitszeit wurde auf 35
Wochenstunden verkürzt.* den Abstand verkürzen
narrow the gap ⊜verlängern 2. *(a period of
time)* sich/jdm etw. verkürzen make sth pass
more quickly ◊ *Sie verkürzte sich das Warten mit
einer Zeitung.*
Ver·lag [fɛ'laːk] der <-(e)s, -e> publisher, publishing house ◊ *Er arbeitet bei einem Verlag.* In
welchem Verlag erscheint der Roman? Who is publishing the novel?
ver·la·gern [fɛ'laːgɐn] <verlagert, verlagerte, hat
verlagert> [tr v] 1. shift ◊ *Sie verlagerte das
Gewicht auf das linke Bein.* 2. transfer ◊ *Das Unternehmen will die Produktion ins Ausland verlagern.*
[ref v] 1. sich irgendwohin verlagern move
somewhere ◊ *Das Hoch verlagert sich weiter nach
Osten.* 2. *(fig)* sich (von etw. auf etw. [acc])/zu
etw. verlagern shift (from sth to sth) ◊ *Der Schwerpunkt der Diskussion hat sich inzwischen verlagert:
...* ♦ *Ihr Interesse verlagerte sich von Jazz zu
Swing.*
② **ver·lan·gen** [fɛ'laŋən] <verlangt, verlangte, hat
verlangt> [tr v] 1. demand ◊ *Die Arbeiter verlang-
ten mehr Lohn.*; *(less urgently)* ask for ◊ *Sie
verlangte die Rechnung.* 2. expect ◊ *Unser Lehrer
verlangt viel.* 3. *(as payment)* want ◊ *Sie
verlangte 5000 Euro für das Auto.* 4. require ◊
Diese Therapie verlangt viel Geduld. ⊜voraussetzen
5. ask to see ◊ *Sie verlangte den Chef.* ◊ *Der
Polizist verlangte die Ausweise.*; *(more urgently)*
demand to see am Telefon verlangt werden be
wanted on the phone [intr v] 1. nach jdm verlangen
want to speak to sb ◊ *Uwe ist am Telefon. Er
verlangt nach dir.* 2. *(lofty)* nach jdm/etw.
verlangen ask for sb/sth ◊ *Er verlangte nach einem
Schluck Wasser.*
Ver·lan·gen [fɛ'laŋən] das <-s> *no pl* *(lofty)*
1. desire ◊ *Er hatte das Verlangen, sie noch ein
letztes Mal zu sehen.*; *(for love)* longing; *(for a
cigarette, drink)* craving ◊ *Sie hatte ein starkes
Verlangen nach einer Zigarette.* 2. demand, request
◊ *Auf Verlangen des Käufers werden die Kleidungsstücke geändert.*
② **ver·län·gern** [fɛ'lɛŋɐn] <verlängert, verlängerte,
hat verlängert> [tr v] 1. lengthen ◊ *Er hat das Rohr
um 20 cm verlängert.* ⊜verkürzen 2. extend ◊ *Sie
verlängerten ihren Urlaub um eine Woche.* 3. renew
◊ *Die Firma verlängerte seinen Vertrag um weitere*

drei Jahre. [ref v] **1.** sich verlängern be prolonged ◊ *Die Rückfahrt verlängerte sich wegen des Staus um eine Stunde.* ⊖sich verkürzen **2.** sich verlängern get longer ◊ *Bei Glatteis verlängert sich der Bremsweg.*

ver·lang·sa·men [fɛ'laŋza:mən] <verlangsamt, verlangsamte, hat verlangsamt> [tr v] slow down ◊ *Der Regen verlangsamte die Ausbreitung des Brandes.* sich verlangsamen slow down ◊ *Das Tempo verlangsamte sich, als es bergauf ging.*

ver·las·sen¹ [fɛ'lasn̩] [adj, adv] lonely ◊ *Sie fühlte sich verlassen.* ♦ *ein alter, verlassener Mann* ♦ *Er saß verlassen auf dem Sofa.* einsam und verlassen all alone [adj] deserted, abandoned ◊ *ein verlassenes Haus*

② **ver·las·sen²** [fɛ'lasn̩] <verlässt, verließ, hat verlassen> [tr v] leave ◊ *Sie verließ den Raum.* ♦ *Sie verließ ihren Mann.* [ref v] sich auf jdn/etw. verlassen rely on sb/sth ◊ *Auf ihn kann man sich verlassen.* ♦ *Er verließ sich auf ihre Hilfe.* ♦ *Darauf kannst du dich verlassen!*

ver·läss·lich [fɛ'lɛslɪç] [adj, adv] reliable(-ably) ◊ *Er ist sehr verlässlich.* ♦ *eine verlässliche Quelle* ♦ *Das kann niemand verlässlich sagen.*

Ver·lauf [fɛ'laof] der <-(e)s, Verläufe> course ◊ *Das Wetter veränderte sich im Verlauf des Tages.* ♦ *Der Verlauf der Kurve war nicht abzuschätzen.*

ver·lau·fen [fɛ'laofn̩] <verläuft, verlief, hat/ist verlaufen> [ref v] +*haben* **1.** sich verlaufen lose your way, get lost ◊ *Er hat sich in der fremden Stadt verlaufen.* ⊖sich verirren **2.** sich verlaufen disperse ◊ *Die Menschenmenge hat sich inzwischen verlaufen.* ⊖sich zerstreuen [intr v] +*sein* **1.** run ◊ *Ihre Wimperntusche ist verlaufen.* ♦ *Die Straße verläuft parallel zur Autobahn.* **2.** go (off) ◊ *Der Tag verlief ganz anders als geplant.*

ver·lau·ten [fɛ'laotn̩] <verlautet, verlautete, ist verlautet> [intr v] etw. verlauten lassen announce sth [imp v] es verlautet it is reported ◊ *Es verlautet aus Regierungskreisen, dass der Minister zurücktreten wolle.* wie verlautet as reported ◊ *Wie aus Finanzkreisen verlautete, ...*

ver·le·gen¹ [fɛ'le:gn̩] [adj] embarrassed ◊ *Diese Frage machte ihn noch verlegener.* ♦ *Es herrschte verlegenes Schweigen.* [adv] in embarrassment, embarrassed ◊ *Verlegen sah sie ihn an.*

⊛ nie um etw. verlegen sein be never at a loss for sth ◊ *Sie war nie um eine Antwort/Ausrede verlegen.*

ver·le·gen² [fɛ'le:gn̩] <verlegt, verlegte, hat verlegt> [tr v] **1.** mislay ◊ *Sie hat ihren Schlüssel verlegt.* **2.** postpone ◊ *Der Vortrag wurde auf nächsten Samstag verlegt.* ⊖verschieben **3.** move, transfer ◊ *Das Unternehmen verlegte die Produktion in die USA.* ♦ *Die Patientin wurde auf eine andere Station verlegt.* **4.** *(tech)* *(a carpet, tracks etc.)* lay **5.** publish ◊ *Welcher Verlag verlegt dieses Buch?* [ref v] sich auf etw. [acc] verlegen take sth up ◊ *Der bekannte Theaterschauspieler hat sich neuerdings aufs Fernsehen verlegt.; (tactics)* resort to sth ◊ *Er verlegte sich aufs Leugnen.*

Ver·le·gen·heit [fɛ'le:gn̩haet] die <-, -en> **1.** *no pl* embarrassment ◊ *Er errötete vor Verlegenheit.* jdn in Verlegenheit bringen embarrass sb ◊ *Er brachte sie mit seiner Bemerkung in Verlegenheit.* **2.** embarrassing situation ◊ *Kannst du mir aus*

dieser Verlegenheit helfen? finanzielle Verlegenheit financial difficulty ◊ *Er geriet in finanzielle Verlegenheit.*

Ver·leih [fɛ'lae] der <-(e)s, -e> **1.** *no pl* hiring (out), renting (out) ◊ *der Verleih von Skiern* **2.** hire company ◊ *Er hat einen Verleih für Kinderfahrräder.*

ver·lei·hen [fɛ'laeən] <verleiht, verlieh, hat verliehen> [tr v] **1.** lend (out) ◊ *Ihr Auto verleiht sie grundsätzlich nicht.* **2.** award ◊ *Die Regierung verlieh ihr eine Medaille.* **3.** give, lend ◊ *Sie versuchte, ihren Worten Nachdruck zu verleihen.*

ver·lei·ten [fɛ'laetn̩] <verleitet, verleitete, hat verleitet> [tr v] jdn zu etw. verleiten lead sb to do sth, encourage sb to do sth ◊ *Seine Freunde haben ihn zum Trinken verleitet.*

ver·ler·nen [fɛ'lɛrnən] <verlernt, verlernte, hat verlernt> [tr v] etw. verlernen forget (how to do) sth ◊ *Fahrradfahren verlernt man nicht.* ♦ *Wir haben verlernt, sachlich miteinander zu diskutieren.*

ver·le·sen [fɛ'le:zn̩] <verliest, verlas, hat verlesen> [tr v] read out ◊ *Die Namen der Gewinner wurden verlesen.* [ref v] sich verlesen misread sth

② **ver·let·zen** [fɛ'lɛtsn̩] <verletzt, verletzte, hat verletzt> [tr v] **1.** jdn/sich verletzen injure sb/yourself ◊ *Er verletzte sich an einer Scherbe.* ♦ *Er wurde schwer/leicht verletzt.* jdm/sich etw. verletzen, jdn/sich an etw. [dat] verletzen injure your/sb's sth ◊ *Sie hat sich am Finger verletzt.* **2.** *(a law, the rules)* etw. verletzen violate sth, break sth ◊ *Gewisse Regeln dürfen nicht verletzt werden.* **3.** *(sb's feelings)* hurt ◊ *Ihre Bemerkung hat mich sehr verletzt.* ⊖treffen

ver·let·zend [fɛ'lɛtsn̩t, fɛ'lɛtsənt] *pres p of* verletzen [adj] hurtful ◊ *eine verletzende Bemerkung* ♦ *Das war sehr verletzend für ihn.*

ver·letz·lich [fɛ'lɛtslɪç] [adj] vulnerable ◊ *eine verletzliche Frau* ♦ *Er ist sehr verletzlich.*

② **Ver·let·zung** [fɛ'lɛtsoŋ] die <-, -en> **1.** injury ◊ *Sie erlitt schwere Verletzungen.* ♦ *Er hatte eine kleine Verletzung am Knie.* **2.** violation ◊ *eine Verletzung der Menschenrechte*

ver·leug·nen [fɛ'lɔøgnən] <verleugnet, verleugnete, hat verleugnet> [tr v] etw. verleugnen deny sth ◊ *Er verleugnete seine Herkunft.* jdn verleugnen disown sb ◊ *Er wurde von seinen Eltern verleugnet.* sich verleugnen lassen give instructions to say you are not in

② **ver·lie·ben** [fɛ'li:bm̩] <verliebt sich, verliebte sich, hat sich verliebt> [ref v] sich (in jdn) verlieben fall in love (with sb) ◊ *Sie hat sich in ihn verliebt.*

ver·liebt [fɛ'li:pt] *past p of* verlieben [adj] <verliebter, am verliebtesten> in love ◊ *Sie ist sehr verliebt.* ♦ *ein verliebtes Paar* ein verliebter Blick an amorous look [adv] with love ◊ *Er sah sie verliebt an.*

② **ver·lie·ren** [fɛ'li:rən] <verliert, verlor, hat verloren> [tr+intr v] lose ◊ *Ich habe mein Handy verloren.* ♦ *Sie verlor ihren Vater, als sie zehn war.* ♦ *Sie hat ihren Job verloren.* ♦ *Die Mannschaft hat 3:2 verloren.* ♦ *Er verlor sein ganzes Hab und Gut.* ♦ die Nerven/den Überblick verlieren verloren gehen go missing ◊ *Mein Ausweis ist verloren gegangen.*

⊛ irgendwo nichts verloren haben have no business to be somewhere ◊ *Du hast in meinem Zimmer nichts verloren!*

Ver·lie·rer [fɛ'liːrɐ] der <–s, –>, **Ver·lie·re·rin** [fɛ'liːrərɪn] die <–, –nen> loser ◊ *ein guter/schlechter Verlierer* ✦ *Er tröstete die Verliererin.* ⊜Sieger

② **ver·liert** [fɛ'liːɐt] *pres of* verlieren

Ver·lob·te [fɛ'loːptə] der/die <–n, die Verlobten> *but: ein Verlobter/eine Verlobte* der Verlobte the fiancé die Verlobte the fiancée die Verlobten the engaged couple *box@* Substantivierung

ver·lo·gen [fɛ'loːgn̩] [adj] *(pej)* hypocritical, two-faced ◊ *Er ist feige und verlogen.* ✦ *Er kritisierte ihre verlogene Haltung.*

② **ver·lor** [fɛ'loːɐ] *pret of* verlieren

② **ver·lo·ren** [fɛ'loːrən] *past p of* verlieren [adj] lost ◊ *eine verlorene Welt* ✦ *Die Verschütteten waren verloren.* ✦ *Ohne seine Mutter war er einfach verloren.*

② **Ver·lust** [fɛ'lʊst] der <–(e)s, –e> loss ◊ *Bei Verlust des Gepäcks bekommt man 500 Euro erstattet.* ✦ *Der Verlust ihres Bruders hat sie schwer getroffen.* ✦ *ein Verlust von fünf Millionen Euro* mit Verlust at a loss

ver·meh·ren [fɛ'meːrən] <vermehrt, vermehrte, hat vermehrt> [tr v] increase ◊ *Er wollte sein Geld vermehren.* sich vermehren increase ◊ *Ihre Aufgaben haben sich vermehrt.* [ref v] sich vermehren reproduce ◊ *Wie vermehren sich Schnecken?*; *(cells, bacteria)* multiply

ver·mei·den [fɛ'maedn̩] <vermeidet, vermied, hat vermieden> [tr v] avoid ◊ *Sie wollte Missverständnisse vermeiden.* ✦ *Er wollte es vermeiden, Aufmerksamkeit zu erregen.* sich nicht vermeiden lassen be unavoidable

ver·meint·lich [fɛ'maentlɪç] [adj, adv] *no comp/ superl; when used as an adj, only before ns* supposed(ly) ◊ *Er ignorierte vermeintliche Gefahren.* ✦ *ein vermeintlich einbruchsicheres Haus*

ver·mes·sen[1] [fɛ'mɛsn̩] <vermisst, vermaß, hat vermessen> [tr v] +*haben* measure ◊ *ein Zimmer vermessen*; *(an area of land)* survey

ver·mes·sen[2] [fɛ'mɛsn̩] [adj] presumptuous ◊ *ein vermessener Vorschlag* ✦ *Es wäre vermessen, das zu behaupten.*

② **ver·mie·ten** [fɛ'miːtn̩] <vermietet, vermietete, hat vermietet> [tr v] rent out, let (out) ◊ *Er vermietete das Zimmer an einen Studenten.*; *(cars, skis etc.)* hire (out), rent (out)

② **Ver·mie·ter** [fɛ'miːte] der <–s, –>, **Ver·mie·te·rin** [fɛ'miːtərɪn] die <–, –nen> 1. landlord, landlady ◊ *Der Vermieter erlaubt keine Haustiere.* 2. *sb who hires sth out* ◊ *Der Vermieter des Autos haftet für keinerlei Schäden.*

ver·min·dern [fɛ'mɪndɐn] <vermindert, verminderte, hat vermindert> [tr v] reduce ◊ *Sie verminderte das Tempo.*; *(responsibility)* diminish ◊ *verminderte Schuldfähigkeit* ⊜reduzieren [ref v] sich vermindern decrease, go down ◊ *Die Kosten verminderten sich um fünf Prozent.* ⊜sich reduzieren ⊜sich erhöhen

ver·mi·schen [fɛ'mɪʃn̩] <vermischt, vermischte, hat vermischt> [tr v] mix ◊ *Sie vermischte das Mehl mit dem Zucker.* sich mit etw. vermischen mix with sth sie vermischen sich they mix ◊ *Wasser und Öl vermischen sich nicht.* [ref v] *(fig)* sich mit etw. vermischen mingle with sth ◊ *Neugier vermischte sich mit der Angst vor dem Neuen.*

ver·mis·sen [fɛ'mɪsn̩] <vermisst, vermisste, hat

vermisst> [tr v] 1. miss ◊ *Ich vermisse meine Schwester sehr.* 2. not be able to find sth ◊ *Sie vermisste ihren Geldbeutel.* 3. vermisst werden be missing ◊ *Ein dreijähriges Kind wird vermisst.*

ver·mit·teln [fɛ'mɪtln̩] <vermittelt, vermittelte, hat vermittelt> [tr v] 1. jdm etw. vermitteln find sth for sb ◊ *Er wollte ihr einen neuen Job vermitteln.* jdn vermitteln find a job for sb 2. explain ◊ *Man konnte ihm nicht vermitteln, wie schwierig die Situation war.*; *(knowledge, information)* teach; *(a sense or feeling of sth)* give ◊ *Er versuchte, den Betroffenen Sicherheit zu vermitteln.* [intr v] mediate ◊ *Er bot an, in dem Konflikt zu vermitteln.* vermittelnd eingreifen intervene

Ver·mitt·ler [fɛ'mɪtlɐ] der <–s, –>, **Ver·mitt·le·rin** [fɛ'mɪtlərɪn] die <–, –nen> mediator ◊ *In diesem Streit tritt sie als Vermittlerin auf.* ✦ *ein neutraler Vermittler*

② **Ver·mitt·lung** [fɛ'mɪtlʊŋ] die <–, –en> 1. *mostly translated with a verb construction* agency ◊ *Im Internet gibt es eine Vermittlung für Au-Pairs.* Die Vermittlung von Arbeitslosen ist schwierig. It is difficult to find jobs for the unemployed. die Vermittlung von Häusern an Käufer finding buyers for houses 2. mediation ◊ *Unter Vermittlung des Papstes wurde ein Friede geschlossen.* 3. *(of knowledge, information)* passing on ◊ *die Vermittlung von Wissen und Kenntnissen* 4. telephone exchange; *(in a company)* switchboard; *(person)* operator

Ver·mö·gen [fɛ'møːgn̩] das <–s, –> fortune ◊ *Sein Vermögen beläuft sich auf 50 Millionen Dollar.* ✦ *Mit der Firma machte er ein Vermögen.*

ver·mö·gend [fɛ'møːgn̩t, fɛ'møːgənt] [adj] wealthy ◊ *Sie ist sehr vermögend.* ✦ *eine vermögende Familie* ⊜reich ⊜arm

② **ver·mu·ten** [fɛ'muːtn̩] <vermutet, vermutete, hat vermutet> [tr v] assume ◊ *Sie vermutete, dass er der Täter war.* jdn irgendwo vermuten believe sb to be somewhere ◊ *Ich vermute ihn in der Küche.*

ver·mut·lich [fɛ'muːtlɪç] [adj] *no comp/superl, only before ns* presumed, likely ◊ *Die vermutliche Todesursache war Herzversagen.* [adv] in all probability, in all likelihood ◊ *Die Entscheidung fällt vermutlich am Dienstag.* ⊜wahrscheinlich

Ver·mu·tung [fɛ'muːtʊŋ] die <–, –en> assumption ◊ *eine Vermutung äußern*

ver·nach·läs·si·gen [fɛ'naːxlɛsɪgn̩] <vernachlässigt, vernachlässigte, hat vernachlässigt> [tr v] 1. jdn/etw. vernachlässigen neglect sb/sth ◊ *Sie vernachlässigt das Kind.* ✦ *Er vernachlässigt seine Pflichten.* 2. *(not consider)* etw. vernachlässigen ignore sth ◊ *Wir dürfen diesen Aspekt nicht vernachlässigen.*

ver·neh·men [fɛ'neːmən] <vernimmt, vernahm, hat vernommen> [tr v] 1. examine ◊ *Sie wurde als Zeugin vom Gericht vernommen.*; *(by the police)* question 2. hear ◊ *Sie hatte ein leises Geräusch vernommen.* ✦ *Ich habe vernommen, dass er nach Berlin ziehen will.*

ver·nei·nen [fɛ'naenən] <verneint, verneinte, hat verneint> [tr v] 1. etw. verneinen answer sth in the negative ◊ *Sie verneinte die Frage.* verneinend den Kopf schütteln shake your head ⊜bejahen 2. deny ◊ *Ich kann dies weder verneinen noch bestätigen.* 3. reject ◊ *Er verneinte jeden Kontakt mit dem*

Mann. ⊖ablehnen

Ver·nei·nung [feˈnaɛnʊŋ] die <-, –en> **1.** denial **2.** LING negation ◊ *die Verneinung des Verbs* **3.** LING *(word)* negative ◊ *Kommt im Satz eine Verneinung vor?*

ver·nich·ten [feˈnɪçtn̩] <vernichtet, vernichtete, hat vernichtet> [tr v] +*haben* destroy ◊ *Sie vernichtete den Brief im Feuer.* ⊖zerstören

ver·nich·tend [feˈnɪçtn̩t, feˈnɪçtənt] *pres p of* vernichten [adj] devastating ◊ *Ihr Wahlergebnis war vernichtend.* ♦ *eine vernichtende Niederlage* [adv] *jdn vernichtend schlagen* thrash sb

Ver·nich·tung [feˈnɪçtʊŋ] die <-, –en> destruction; *(of people, pests)* extermination

Ver·nunft [feˈnʊnft] die <–> *no pl* reason, good sense ◊ *sich von der Vernunft leiten lassen* ⊙ *Vernunft annehmen* see sense, listen to reason *jdn zur Vernunft bringen* make sb see sense, make sb listen to reason *zur Vernunft kommen* come to your senses

② **ver·nünf·tig** [feˈnʏnftɪç] [adj, adv] **1.** sensible(-ibly) ◊ *eine vernünftige Frau* ♦ *Sei doch vernünftig!* ♦ *Er hat mir die Sache vernünftig erklärt.* **2.** *(fam)* proper(ly) ◊ *Zieh dir mal vernünftige Schuhe an!* ♦ *Kannst du die Formulare mal vernünftig ausfüllen?*

② **ver·öf·fent·li·chen** [feˈʔœfntlɪçn̩] <veröffentlicht, veröffentlichte, hat veröffentlicht> [tr v] publish ◊ *Das Buch wurde noch nicht veröffentlicht.* ♦ *Vom Täter wurde ein Foto veröffentlicht.; (a CD, DVD etc.)* release ⊖publizieren

Ver·öf·fent·li·chung [feˈʔœfntlɪçʊŋ] die <-, –en> publication ◊ *die Veröffentlichung eines Romans* ♦ *Was ist seine neueste Veröffentlichung?; (of a CD, DVD etc.)* release ⊖Publikation

ver·ord·nen [feˈʔɔʁdnən] <verordnet, verordnete, hat verordnet> [tr v] **1.** prescribe ◊ *Sie bekam Antibiotika verordnet.* ⊖verschreiben **2.** order ◊ *Das Ministerium hatte Stillschweigen verordnet.*

Ver·ord·nung [feˈʔɔʁdnʊŋ] die <-, –en> **1.** prescription ◊ *die Verordnung von Medikamenten* **2.** decree ◊ *Es wurde eine Verordnung erlassen.*

ver·pa·cken [feˈpakn̩] <verpackt, verpackte, hat verpackt> [tr v] **1.** pack **2.** wrap ◊ *Sie hat das Buch als Geschenk verpackt.*

Ver·pa·ckung [feˈpakʊŋ] die <-, –en> **1.** *no pl* packing; wrapping **2.** packaging ◊ *Porto und Verpackung kosten sechs Euro.*

② **ver·pas·sen** [feˈpasn̩] <verpasst, verpasste, hat verpasst> [tr v] **1.** miss ◊ *Er hat seinen Zug verpasst.* ♦ *Diese Gelegenheit hatte er verpasst.* **2.** *(fam) jdm etw. verpassen* give sb sth ◊ *Der Friseur verpasste ihm einen neuen Haarschnitt.*

Ver·pfle·gung [feˈpfleːgʊŋ] die <–> *no pl* **1.** feeding ◊ *Sie war für die Verpflegung der Gäste zuständig.* **2.** food ◊ *Er hatte dort freie Unterkunft und Verpflegung.*

ver·pflich·ten [feˈpflɪçtn̩] <verpflichtet, verpflichtete, hat verpflichtet> [tr v] **1.** *jdn zu etw. verpflichten; jdn verpflichten, etw. zu tun* oblige sb to do sth, put an obligation on sb to do sth ◊ *Niemand verpflichtet Sie dazu, Alkohol zu trinken. jdn zu nichts verpflichten* put sb under no obligation, put no obligation on sb ◊ *zum Schadenersatz verpflichtet werden* be ordered to pay damages **2.** *zu etw. verpflichtet sein; verpflichtet sein, etw. zu tun* be obliged to do sth ◊ *Er war zum Schweigen verpflich-*

tet. zu nichts verpflichtet sein be under no obligation **3.** *jdn verpflichten* engage sb ◊ *Ein neuer Manager wurde verpflichtet.; (a sportsperson)* sign sb [ref v] **1.** *sich zu etw. verpflichten; sich verpflichten, etw. zu tun* commit yourself to do sth ◊ *Er hatte sich zur Beseitigung des Schadens verpflichtet.* **2.** *sich verpflichten* sign ◊ *Der Spieler verpflichtete sich für fünf Jahre.*

Ver·pflich·tung [feˈpflɪçtʊŋ] die <-, –en> **1.** obligation, commitment ◊ *Sie hat große finanzielle Verpflichtungen.* **2.** appointment ◊ *die Verpflichtung einer neuen Trainerin; (of a sportsperson)* signing; *(of an artist)* engagement

ver·prü·geln [feˈpryːɡl̩n] <verprügelt, verprügelte, hat verprügelt> [tr v] beat ◊ *Sie verprügelte ihren Hund.* sie verprügelte sich *they beat each other up* ◊ *Die beiden Brüder verprügeln sich regelmäßig.*

Ver·rat [feˈraːt] der <-(e)s> *no pl* betrayal ◊ *der Verrat von Geheimnissen* ♦ *Ich empfand die Kritik als Verrat am Bürgermeister.; (in politics)* treason ◊ *Der Agent war wegen Verrats angeklagt.*

② **ver·ra·ten** [feˈraːtn̩] <verrät, verriet, hat verraten> [tr v] **1.** *etw./sich verraten* give sth/yourself away ◊ *ein Geheimnis verraten* ♦ *Mit dieser Bemerkung hat sie sich verraten. jdm etw. verraten* tell sb sth ◊ *Du darfst meiner Mutter nicht verraten, dass ich geraucht habe.* betray ◊ *Er hatte seinen Freund verraten.* **3.** show ◊ *Die Arbeit verrät eine enorme Sorgfalt.*

Ver·rä·ter [feˈrɛːte] der <–s, –>, **Ver·rä·te·rin** [feˈrɛːtərɪn] die <-, –en> traitor ◊ *Wer so etwas tut, ist ein Verräter!* ♦ *Er nannte sie eine Verräterin.*

ver·rech·nen [feˈʁɛçnən] <verrechnet, verrechnete, hat verrechnet> [tr v] *mostly passive* etw. (mit etw.) verrechnen deduct sth (from sth) ◊ *Die Anzahlung wird (mit dem Kaufpreis) verrechnet.* [ref v] **1.** *sich verrechnen* miscalculate, make a mistake (in your calculations) *sich um drei Euro etc. verrechnen* be out by three euros etc. **2.** *(fig) sich verrechnen* be wrong, be mistaken ◊ *Wenn du glaubst, dass ich zu dir zurückkomme, hast du dich verrechnet.*

② **ver·rei·sen** [feˈʁaɛzn̩] <verreist, verreiste, ist verreist> [intr v] go away ◊ *mehrere Male im Jahr verreisen* dienstlich/geschäftlich verreist sein be away on business

ver·rich·ten [feˈʁɪçtn̩] <verrichtet, verrichtete, hat verrichtet> [tr v] *(lofty)* carry out, perform ◊ *eine Arbeit/Aufgabe verrichten* seine Notdurft verrichten answer a call of nature

ver·rin·gern [feˈʁɪŋen] <verringert, verringerte, hat verringert> [tr v] reduce ◊ *einen Schuldenberg verringern* ♦ *Die Zahl der Unfälle konnte deutlich verringert werden.* [ref v] *sich verringern* go down ◊ *Die Zahl der Arbeitslosen hat sich verringert.; (prices also)* be reduced; *(strength, vision)* deteriorate ◊ *Opas Sehkraft verringert sich zunehmend.* ⊖sich reduzieren

② **ver·rückt** [feˈʁʏkt] [adj] <verrückter, am verrücktesten> *(fam)* **1.** *not before ns* verrückt *(vor etw.)* [dat] *werden* go mad (with sth), go crazy (with sth) ◊ *verrückt vor Angst/Schmerz werden* ♦ *Ich werde noch verrückt, wenn dieser Lärm nicht bald aufhört. jdn/sich verrückt machen* drive sb/yourself mad, drive sb/yourself crazy ⊖wahnsinnig **2.** mentally ill ◊ *jdn für verrückt erklären* ♦ *Der verrückte Mann ist jetzt in einer Nervenheilanstalt.*

3. crazy, weird ◊ *durch verrückte Klamotten auffallen* ♦ *Ihre Ideen sind immer total verrückt.* ♦ *Du bist verrückt, bei der Kälte hinauszugehen.* ⊛ **auf etw.** acc/**nach etw.** verrückt sein be mad on/about sth, be crazy about sth, love sth **auf jdn/nach jdm** verrückt sein be mad about sb, be crazy about sb **verrückt spielen 1.** *(not be normal)* act up, play up ◊ *Das Wetter spielt verrückt.* **2.** *(not function properly)* go mad, go crazy ◊ *Der Bordcomputer spielte plötzlich verrückt.* **ich werd verrückt** I don't believe it
Vers [fɛ*ɐ*s] der <-es, -e> **1.** LIT line ◊ *Diese Verse reimen sich nicht.* ♦ *eine Strophe mit vier Versen* etw. in Verse bringen/fassen put sth into verse **2.** LIT verse, stanza ◊ *einen Vers aufsagen* ♦ *einen Vers für die Schule auswendig lernen* **3.** REL verse ◊ *Der Pfarrer las aus dem ersten Buch Mose, Vers 11.*
ver·sa·gen [fɛ*ɐ*ˈzaːɡn̩] <versagt, versagte, hat versagt> intr v **1.** fail ◊ *Er hat im Leben/Beruf versagt.* ♦ *in der Prüfung (kläglich/völlig) versagen* **2.** *(equipment)* fail ◊ *Ein Lkw raste in eine Leitplanke, weil die Bremsen versagten.; (nerves, voice)* fail sb ◊ *Vor Aufregung versagten seine Nerven.* tr v *(lofty)* jdm etw. versagen refuse (to give/grant) sb sth, deny sb sth ◊ *jdm seine Unterstützung/einen Wunsch versagen* etw. bleibt jdm versagt sb is denied sth ref v *(lofty)* sich dat etw. versagen refuse sth ◊ *Magersüchtige versagen sich das Essen.*
ver·sam·meln [fɛ*ɐ*ˈzam(ə)ln̩] <versammelt, versammelte, hat versammelt> tr v jdn (irgendwo) versammeln gather sb (together) (somewhere), attract sb (somewhere) ◊ *eine Gruppe von Zuhörern um sich versammeln* ref v sich (irgendwo) versammeln gather ◊ *sich um das Lagerfeuer versammeln* ♦ *Tausende Demonstranten versammelten sich vor dem Rathaus.*
② **Ver·samm·lung** [fɛ*ɐ*ˈzamlʊŋ] die <-, -en> gathering, assembly, rally, convention ◊ *eine Versammlung abhalten/einberufen* ♦ *eine geheime/ öffentliche/politische Versammlung; (smaller)* meeting
Ver·sand [fɛ*ɐ*ˈzant] der <-(e)s> *no pl* **1.** dispatch ◊ *Der Versand erfolgt per Nachnahme.* etw. per Versand liefern dispatch sth, send sth by mail **2.** *(costs)* postage ◊ *Das Buch kostet inklusive Versand 30 Euro.* **3.** dispatch department ◊ *Die Computerspiele sind über unseren Versand erhältlich.*
② **ver·säu·men** [fɛ*ɐ*ˈzɔɪ̯mən] <versäumt, versäumte, hat versäumt> tr v miss ◊ *Ich darf diesen Termin auf keinen Fall versäumen.* ♦ *Sie war krank und hat deswegen den Unterricht versäumt.* ♦ *den Bus/ Zug versäumen; (a duty)* neglect (es) versäumen, etw. zu tun neglect to do sth, omit to do sth, fail to do sth ◊ *Ich habe (es) versäumt, mein Auto zum TÜV zu bringen.*
⊛ **nichts versäumen** not miss much **viel versäumen** miss out on a lot
ver·schaf·fen [fɛ*ɐ*ˈʃafn̩] <verschafft, verschaffte, hat verschafft> tr v jdm etw. verschaffen get sb sth, provide sb with sth ◊ *jdm einen Job verschaffen* sich dat etw. verschaffen get (yourself) sth ◊ *Ein Hacker hat sich Zugang zu meinem PC ver-*

schafft. ♦ *sich durch einen Kredit kurzfristig Geld verschaffen* ♦ *sich Anerkennung/Gehör/Respekt verschaffen*
⊛ **was verschafft mir/uns die Ehre/das Vergnügen** *(hum)* to what do I/we owe the hono(u)r/pleasure
ver·schär·fen [fɛ*ɐ*ˈʃɛ*ɐ*fn̩] <verschärft, verschärfte, hat verschärft> tr v **1.** *(the situation, a conflict)* worsen, intensify ◊ *Attentate haben die politische Lage verschärft.* ♦ *Glatteis verschärft die Unfallgefahr im Winter.* ⊖verschlimmern **2.** *(laws, checks)* tighten ◊ *die Drogenkontrollen/Waffengesetze verschärfen; (the speed)* increase ◊ *sein Tempo verschärfen, um das Rennen zu gewinnen* ref v sich verschärfen intensify ◊ *Der Wettbewerb verschärft sich.; (negative situation)* get worse ◊ *Die Situation auf dem Arbeitsmarkt verschärft sich.*
⊖sich verschlimmern
ver·schen·ken [fɛ*ɐ*ˈʃɛŋkn̩] <verschenkt, verschenkte, hat verschenkt> tr v **1.** etw. (an jdn) verschenken give sth away (to sb) ◊ *Junge Katzen zu verschenken!* ♦ *einen Gutschein an treue Kunden verschenken; (on a special occasion)* give sth (to sb) (as a present) ◊ *Zum Valentinstag werden oft Rosen verschenkt.* **2.** *(a victory)* give away ◊ *durch ein Eigentor den Sieg verschenken; (time)* lose ◊ *Wer bei Notfällen nicht sofort einen Arzt ruft, verschenkt wertvolle Zeit.*
ver·schi·cken [fɛ*ɐ*ˈʃɪkn̩] <verschickt, verschickte, hat verschickt> tr v etw. (an jdn) verschicken send (off) (to sb), send (sb) sth ◊ *einen Brief/ ein Paket (per Post) verschicken* ♦ *eine Einladung an alle Freunde verschicken* ♦ *eine E-Mail/SMS verschicken* ⊖abschicken, absenden, versenden
ver·schie·ben [fɛ*ɐ*ˈʃiːbm̩] <verschiebt, verschob, hat verschoben> tr v **1.** (auf etw. acc) verschieben postpone sth (until sth), put sth off (until sth) ◊ *einen Termin/Urlaub verschieben* ♦ *etw. auf einen anderen Tag verschieben* etw. um etw. verschieben postpone sth for sth, put sth off for sth ◊ *eine Reform um ein Jahr verschieben* sich (auf etw. acc) verschieben be postponed (until sth), be put off (until sth) ◊ *Das Konzert hat sich verschoben.* ♦ *Die Veröffentlichung des Buches verschiebt sich auf Mai.* sich um etw. verschieben be postponed for sth, be put off for sth *Das Programm verschiebt sich um 30 Minuten. The programme/ program is running thirty minutes late.* **2.** etw. (um etw.) verschieben move sth (by sth) ◊ *Möbel verschieben* ♦ *Die Symbole lassen sich auf dem Bildschirm verschieben.* sich (um etw.) verschieben shift (by sth) ◊ *Bei dem Unfall hat sich einer ihrer Wirbel verschoben.* **3.** *(fam) (drugs, weapons)* traffic in etw. ins Ausland verschieben smuggle sth abroad ref v sich verschieben shift, change ◊ *Das ökologische Gleichgewicht hat sich verschoben.* ♦ *Sobald man Kinder hat, verschieben sich die Prioritäten.* ⊖sich verlagern
② **ver·schie·den** [fɛ*ɐ*ˈʃiːdn̩] adj **1.** different ◊ *verschiedener Ansicht/Meinung sein* ♦ *verschiedene Richtungen einschlagen* ♦ *Wir haben uns getrennt, weil wir einfach verschieden sind.; (various)* diverse ◊ *Die Ursachen für Kopfschmerzen sind ganz verschieden.* verschieden von jdm/etw. sein be different from sb/sth, differ from sb/sth ◊ *Seine Lebensweise ist sehr verschieden von der seines*

Bruders.; *(tastes)* verschieden sein differ von Fall zu Fall verschieden sein differ from case to case ⊖unterschiedlich ⊕gleich **2.** *only before ns* several, a number of ◊ *Sie sind verschiedene Male umgezogen.* ♦ *verschiedene Dinge einkaufen* ⊖mehrere **3.** *only before ns* verschiedenste ... a range of ..., a variety of ... ◊ *Die Uhr gibt es in den verschiedensten Ausführungen.* ♦ *Menschen verschiedenster Herkunft* ⊖unterschiedlichste [adv] differently, in different ways ◊ *verschieden behandelte Milchtypen* verschieden groß/stark sein vary in height/strength verschieden gefärbt sein vary in colour/color; *(group of people)* verschieden zusammengesetzt sein be varied ⊖unterschiedlich ⊕gleich

⊛ **Verschiedenes** a number of things, a variety of things, a range of things ◊ *Das kann Verschiedenes bedeuten.* *(as a column in a newspaper, magazine)* miscellaneous

ver·schla·fen¹ [fɛ'ʃlaːfn̩] [adj, adv] half-asleep, sleepy(-ily) ◊ *noch ganz verschlafen sein* ♦ *Morgengymnastik für verschlafene Schüler* ♦ *sich* [dat] *verschlafen die Augen reiben* [adj] sleepy ◊ *durch die verschlafene Winterlandschaft spazieren* ♦ *Das Städtchen ist verschlafen und ruhig.*

ver·schla·fen² [fɛ'ʃlaːfn̩] <verschläft, verschlief, hat verschlafen> [intr v] oversleep ◊ *sich einen Wecker stellen, damit man morgens nicht verschläft* ♦ *zu spät zum Unterricht kommen, weil man verschlafen hat* [tr v] *(fam)* **1.** *(an appointment, occasion)* miss ◊ *einen Geburtstag/Termin verschlafen* **2.** den/einen Tag/Nachmittag verschlafen sleep through the/a day/afternoon

② **ver·schlech·tern** [fɛ'ʃlɛçtɐn] <verschlechtert, verschlechterte, hat verschlechtert> [tr v] etw. verschlechtern worsen sth ◊ *Zigarettenrauch verschlechtert die Raumluft.* ♦ *Diese Klausur hat meinen Notendurchschnitt verschlechtert.* ⊖verbessern [ref v] sich verschlechtern get worse, worsen, deteriorate ◊ *Das Wetter wird sich verschlechtern.* ♦ *sich in der Schule verschlechtern* ♦ *Ihre finanzielle Situation hat sich verschlechtert.* ⊖sich verbessern

ver·schlie·ßen [fɛ'ʃliːsn̩] <verschließt, verschloss, hat verschlossen> [tr v] **1.** etw. (mit etw.) verschließen seal sth (with sth) ◊ *einen Umschlag verschließen* ♦ *ein Glas (mit einem Deckel) verschließen* ⊖öffnen **2.** *(with a key)* lock ◊ *nachts die Tür verschließen* ♦ *Dieser Koffer lässt sich verschließen.* ⊖öffnen [ref v] **1.** sich einer Sache [dat] verschließen close yourself off to sth ◊ *alte Traditionen bewahren, ohne sich Neuem zu verschließen* ♦ *sich einem Anliegen/einer Bitte verschließen* **2.** sich (jdm) verschließen close yourself off (to sb) ◊ *Sie verschließt sich ihren Klassenkameraden.*

⊛ die Augen/Ohren vor etw. [dat] verschließen close your eyes/ears to sth ◊ *die Augen vor der Wahrheit verschließen*

ver·schlim·mern [fɛ'ʃlɪmɐn] <verschlimmert, verschlimmerte, hat verschlimmert> [tr v] etw. verschlimmern worsen sth, make sth worse ◊ *Ernteausfälle haben die Hungersnot verschlimmert.* [ref v] sich verschlimmern get worse, worsen, deteriorate ◊ *Sein Gesundheitszustand hat sich verschlimmert.* ♦ *Die Lage/Situation auf dem Arbeitsmarkt verschlimmert sich.* ⊖sich verschlechtern,

sich verschärfen ⊕sich verbessern

ver·schlos·sen [fɛ'ʃlɔsn̩] *past p of* verschließen [adj] **1.** *(person)* withdrawn ◊ *Sie wirkt ruhig und verschlossen.* ♦ *Er ist eher der verschlossene Typ, der keine Emotionen zeigt.* **2.** jdm verschlossen bleiben remain closed to sb ◊ *Was in seinem Inneren vorgeht, bleibt anderen verschlossen.*

ver·schlu·cken [fɛ'ʃlʊkn̩] <verschluckt, verschluckte, hat verschluckt> [tr v] **1.** *(objects, sounds, words)* swallow ◊ *aus Versehen ein Kaugummi/Kirschkern verschlucken* ♦ *Laute durch zu schnelles Reden verschlucken* **2.** *(make disappear)* swallow up ◊ *Finsternis verschluckte die Gestalten.* **3.** *(a noise)* muffle ◊ *Die Isolierung verschluckt den Lärm.* [ref v] sich (an etw. [dat]) verschlucken choke (on sth) ◊ *sich beim Essen (an einer Fischgräte) verschlucken*

Ver·schluss [fɛ'ʃlʊs] der <-es, Verschlüsse> **1.** *no pl* fastener ◊ *den Verschluss eines BHs/einer Kette öffnen*; *(of a bottle, container)* top, lid ◊ *Die Flasche hat einen kindersicheren Verschluss.* **2.** unter Verschluss under lock and key ◊ *Die Akten müssen unter Verschluss bleiben/aufbewahrt werden.* ♦ *wichtige Dokumente/Informationen unter Verschluss halten* **3.** MED blockage ◊ *der Verschluss einer Arterie/des Darms/eines Gefäßes*

ver·schmut·zen [fɛ'ʃmʊtsn̩] <verschmutzt, verschmutzte, hat/ist verschmutzt> [tr v] +*haben* **1.** etw. verschmutzen make sth dirty ◊ *mit dreckigen Schuhen den Teppich verschmutzen* **2.** *(the environment)* pollute, contaminate ◊ *die Luft/Umwelt verschmutzen* ♦ *Das Öl hat die Strände/das Meer verschmutzt.* [intr v] +*sein* get dirty ◊ *Die weiße Bluse verschmutzt schnell.*

ver·schol·len [fɛ'ʃɔlən] [adj] *no comp/superl* missing ◊ *ein verschollener Kunstgegenstand/Verwandter* im Krieg verschollen sein be missing in action, be lost in action

ver·scho·nen [fɛ'ʃoːnən] <verschont, verschonte, hat verschont> [tr v] **1.** spare ◊ *ein unschuldiges Opfer verschonen* ♦ *Der Orkan hat den südlichen Teil des Landes verschont.* **2.** von etw. verschont bleiben be spared (from) sth, escape sth ◊ *Der Kirchturm blieb von den Flammen weitgehend verschont.* **3.** jdn (mit etw.) verschonen spare sb (sth) ◊ *Verschone mich (damit/mit deinem Geschwätz)!*

② **ver·schrei·ben** [fɛ'ʃʀaɛ̯bm̩] <verschreibt, verschrieb, hat verschrieben> [tr v] **1.** MED (jdm) etw. verschreiben prescribe (sb) sth ◊ *Mein Arzt hat mir eine Kur/ein Schmerzmittel verschrieben.* ♦ *sich* [dat] *etw. gegen Bauchschmerzen verschreiben lassen* ⊖verordnen **2.** *(paper, ink)* get through ◊ *Er hat für seinen Roman viel Papier/Tinte verschrieben.* [ref v] **1.** *(lofty)* sich einer Sache [dat] verschreiben devote yourself to sth ◊ *sich ganz der Malerei/Musik verschreiben* **2.** sich verschreiben make a (spelling) mistake ◊ *Ich habe mich verschrieben; es muss „nett" heißen, nicht „mett".*

ver·schul·den [fɛ'ʃʊldn̩] <verschuldet, verschuldete, hat verschuldet> [tr v] *mostly written* cause, be responsible for, be to blame for ◊ *einen Schaden/Unfall verschulden* ♦ *Er hat seine Entlassung selbst verschuldet.* [ref v] sich (bei jdm/etw.) verschulden get into debt (with sb/sth) ◊ *sich bis über beide Ohren verschulden sich (mit 50 000*

Euro) verschulden run up debts (of 50,000 euros)
ver·schüt·ten [fɛ'ʃʏtn̩] <verschüttet, verschüttete,
hat verschüttet> [tr v] **1.** bury ◊ *Die Erdmassen
haben ganze Häuser verschüttet.* ✦ *Zwei Skifahrer
wurden von einer Lawine verschüttet.* ✦ *Bei einem
Erdbeben wurden mehrere Menschen verschüttet.*
2. spill ◊ *Mehl/Salz verschütten* ✦ *(ein Glas)
Wasser/Wein verschütten*
ver·schwand [fɛ'ʃvant] *pret of* verschwinden
ver·schwei·gen [fɛ'ʃvaɛɡn̩] <verschweigt, verschwieg, hat verschwiegen> [tr v] (jdm) etw. verschweigen hide sth (from sb) ◊ *Ich will dir mein
Geheimnis/die Wahrheit nicht länger verschweigen.*
ver·schwen·den [fɛ'ʃvɛndn̩] <verschwendet, verschwendete, hat verschwendet> [tr v] waste ◊ *viel
Energie/Platz/Zeit verschwenden* ✦ *keinen
Gedanken an jdn/etw. verschwenden*
ver·schwim·men [fɛ'ʃvɪmən] <verschwimmt, verschwamm, ist verschwommen> [intr v] blur ◊ *Die
Konturen der Berge verschwimmen im Nebel.* ✦ *Die
Buchstaben verschwammen vor ihren Augen.* ✦ *In
diesem Film verschwimmen die Grenzen zwischen
Realität und Fiktion.*
ver·schwin·den [fɛ'ʃvɪndn̩] <verschwindet, verschwand, ist verschwunden> [intr v] **1.** disappear ◊
Die Schmerzen sind endlich verschwunden. ✦ *Viele
seltene Tierarten drohen ganz zu verschwinden.* ✦
*Alte Traditionen verschwinden und werden durch
neue ersetzt.* ✦ *Er drehte sich um und verschwand
(durch den Ausgang).* ✦ *Der Regenwurm verschwand in der Erde.* ✦ *In der Garderobe verschwindet immer wieder Geld.* **2.** *mostly pres perf* vanish ◊
spurlos verschwunden sein ✦ *Er ist einfach verschwunden, ohne sich zu verabschieden.* **3.** *(fam,
euph)* jdn/etw. verschwinden lassen make sb/sth
disappear, get rid of sb/sth ◊ *Wer ließ den Zeugen
verschwinden? ✦ wichtige Akten/Beweise verschwinden lassen* **4.** *(fam, euph)* etw. verschwinden
lassen make off with sth, steal sth ◊ *beim Juwelier
ein paar Golduhren verschwinden lassen*
◉ **mal verschwinden (müssen)** *(fam, euph)*
(have to) go to the toilet, (have to) pay a visit **verschwinde** *(fam)* clear off, go away, get lost
ver·schwom·men [fɛ'ʃvɔmən] [adj] blurry, blurred
◊ *verschwommene Fotos/Konturen/Ränder; (ideas,
statement)* vague ◊ *Ihre Vorstellungen von der
Zukunft sind noch recht verschwommen.*
ver·schwö·ren [fɛ'ʃvøːrən] <verschwört sich,
verschwor sich, hat sich verschworen> [ref v] sich
(mit jdm) gegen jdn verschwören conspire (with
sb) against sb, plot (with sb) against sb ◊ *Die
Klasse hat sich gegen ihren strengen Lehrer verschworen. etw./jd verschwört sich gegen jdn sth/sb
conspires against sb* ◊ *Das Schicksal/Alle Welt
scheint sich gegen mich verschworen zu haben.*
ver·schwun·den [fɛ'ʃvɔndn̩] *past p of* verschwinden
Ver·se·hen [fɛ'zeːən] das <-s, -> mistake ◊ *Tut
mir Leid, das war ein Versehen.* ✦ *Mir ist ein
Versehen bei der Rechnung unterlaufen.* ✦ *Durch
ein Versehen wurden die Koffer vertauscht.* aus
Versehen by mistake
ver·se·hent·lich [fɛ'zeːəntlɪç] [adv] accidentally, by
accident, by mistake ◊ *versehentlich einen Beleg
wegwerfen* ✦ *versehentlich eine Tasse kaputtmachen* ⊖vorsätzlich [adj] *no comp/superl, only before*

ns accidental ◊ *Die Bank haftet nicht für eine versehentliche Doppelüberweisung.*
ver·sen·den [fɛ'zɛndn̩] <versendet, versandte/ver-
sendete, hat versandt/versendet> [tr v] (an
jdn) versenden send sth (to sb) ◊ *eine Datei als
Anhang versenden* ✦ *eine E-Mail/SMS versenden* ✦
Pressemitteilungen an Kunden versenden
⊖absenden, abschicken, versenden
ver·set·zen [fɛ'zɛtsn̩] <versetzt, versetzte, hat
versetzt> [tr v] **1.** etw. (irgendwohin) versetzen
move sth (to somewhere) ◊ *einen Baum versetzen*
✦ *die Wand/den Zaun um zwei Meter versetzen
lassen* **2.** jdn in etw. [acc] versetzen put sb in/into
sth ◊ *jdn in Narkose/Tiefschlaf versetzen; (with
emotions)* put sb in a state of sth ◊ *jdn in Angst/
Panik/Staunen versetzen* jdn/etw. in Alarmbereit-
schaft versetzen put sb/sth on alert **3.** *(to a
different time, world)* jdn in etw. [acc] versetzen
transport sb (in)to sth, take sb (in)to sth ◊ *jdn in
die Vergangenheit versetzen* ✦ *ein Film, der die
Zuschauer in eine andere Welt versetzt* **4.** *(a blow,
kick, shock)* jdm etw. versetzen give sb sth ◊ *jdm
einen Schlag/Stoß/Tritt versetzen* ✦ *Die schlimme
Nachricht hat ihm einen Schock versetzt.* **5.** *(to a
different workplace)* jdn versetzen transfer sb ◊
Sie will sich versetzen lassen. ✦ *ins Ausland/in
eine andere Filiale versetzt werden* **6.** *(substances)*
A mit B versetzen add B to A ◊ *Saft mit Wasser
versetzen* **7.** *passive* SCHOOL (in etw. [acc]) versetzt
werden advance (to sth), move up (to sth) ◊ *in die
fünfte Klasse versetzt werden* ✦ *Er wurde nicht
versetzt, weil er zwei Fünfen im Zeugnis hat.*
8. *(fam, pej)* jdn versetzen stand sb up ◊ *„Er ist
gar nicht gekommen?" — „Nein, er hat mich
einfach versetzt."* **9.** pawn ◊ *seinen Besitz/
Schmuck versetzen, um Geld zu bekommen* [ref v]
sich in jdn/etw. versetzen put yourself in sb's/sth's
position ◊ *sich gut in Kinder versetzen können* sich
in jds Lage/Situation versetzen put yourself in sb's
position/situation
② **ver·si·chern** [fɛ'zɪçɐn] <versichert, versicherte, hat
versichert> [tr v] **1.** (jdm) etw. versichern promise
(sb) sth, assure sb of sth ◊ *Er hat glaubhaft versichert, dass es so war.* **2.** jdn/sich/etw. (gegen
etw.) versichern insure sb/yourself/sth (against sth)
◊ *ein Haus gegen Feuer versichern* ✦ *sich zusätz-
lich/auf eigene Kosten versichern* ✦ *sein Fahrrad
gegen Diebstahl versichern lassen* ✦ *Die Haftpflichtversicherung versichert alle Personen- und Sach-
schäden.* [ref v] *(lofty)* sich einer Sache [gen] versichern be sure of sth ◊ *sich jds Hilfe/Unterstützung
versichern* ✦ *jdm nachspionieren, um sich seiner
Treue zu versichern*
② **Ver·si·cher·ten·kar·te** [fɛ'zɪçɐtn̩kaʀtə] die <-, -n>
insurance card ◊ *Bitte bringen Sie bei jedem Arzt-
besuch Ihre Versichertenkarte mit.*
② **Ver·si·che·rung** [fɛ'zɪçɐʊŋ] die <-, -en>
1. insurance ◊ *eine Versicherung abschließen/
kündigen* ✦ *Die Versicherung kostet 65 Euro im
Jahr.* ✦ *eine Versicherung gegen Berufsunfähigkeit/
Blitzschlag/Unfälle* **2.** insurance company ◊ *Die
Versicherung übernimmt/ersetzt den Unfallschaden.*
ver·söh·nen [fɛ'zøːnən] [tr v] **1.** jdn (mit jdm) versöhnen
reconcile sb (with sb) ◊ *Sie versuchte, die streitenden Parteien (miteinander) zu versöhnen.* sich (mit

jdm) **versöhnen** make up (with sb) *sich mit seinem Schicksal versöhnen* reconcile yourself to your fate **2.** *jdn (mit etw.) versöhnen* appease sb (with sth) ◊ *Kann ich dich mit einem Glas Wein versöhnen?*

ver·sor·gen [fɛˈzɔʁɡn̩] <versorgt, versorgte, hat versorgt> [tr v] **1.** *jdn/etw./sich mit etw. versorgen* supply sb/sth/yourself with sth ◊ *Der Brunnen versorgt das ganze Dorf mit Wasser.* ♦ *Ich versorge dich mit neuen Büchern.* ♦ *sich für die Reise mit Proviant versorgen* (mit etw.) *versorgt sein* have got enough (sth/of sth) ◊ *Mit Arbeit bin ich erst mal versorgt.* **2.** take care of, look after ◊ *den Haushalt alleine versorgen* ♦ *seinen alten Vater versorgen müssen* ♦ *im Stall die Pferde versorgen*

② **ver·spä·tet** [fɛˈʃpɛːtət] [adj, adv] *no comp/superl* delayed, late ◊ *Ist der Zug verspätet?* ♦ *verspätete Zahlungen* ♦ *verspätet eintreffen*

② **ver·spä·ten** [fɛˈʃpɛːtn̩] <verspätet sich, verspätete sich, hat sich verspätet> [ref v] *sich (um zwanzig Minuten/einen Tag) verspäten* be (twenty minutes/a day) late, be delayed (by twenty minutes/a day) ◊ *Ich werde mich etwas verspäten, weil ich im Stau stehe.*

② **Ver·spä·tung** [fɛˈʃpɛːtʊŋ] die <-, −en> delay ◊ *Bitte entschuldigt meine Verspätung!* ♦ *Mein Gehalt kam mit einem Monat Verspätung.* ♦ *Bahnreisende mussten heute mehrstündige Verspätungen in Kauf nehmen.* *Verspätung haben* be delayed

② **ver·spre·chen** [fɛˈʃpʁɛçn̩] <verspricht, versprach, hat versprochen> [tr v] **1.** *(jdm) etw. versprechen* promise (sb) sth ◊ *Er versprach, sich zu bessern.* ♦ *einem Kind ein Eis versprechen* ♦ *Versprich mir, dass du das nicht weitersagst.* ♦ *etw. hoch und heilig versprechen* **2.** *sich von jdm/etw.* [dat] *etw. versprechen* hope for sth from sb/sth ◊ *Was versprichst du dir von dieser Aktion?* **3.** *etw. verspricht etw.* sth promises sth ◊ *Das Wetter verspricht, gut zu werden.* ♦ *Das Programm verspricht einen amüsanten Abend.* [ref v] *sich versprechen* get your words mixed up ◊ *Sie war während des Vortrages so aufgeregt, dass sie sich ständig versprach.*

Ver·spre·chen [fɛˈʃpʁɛçn̩] das <-s, −> promise, pledge ◊ *ein Versprechen abgeben/brechen* ♦ *jdm sein Versprechen geben, dass man etw. tun wird*

Ver·stand [fɛˈʃtant] der <-(e)s> *no pl* reason, mind, brain ◊ *Drogen vernebeln den Verstand.* ♦ *Sie ist gewitzt und hat einen klaren/scharfen/wachen Verstand.* ♦ *seinen Verstand gebrauchen* ⊛ *jdn um den Verstand bringen, jdm den Verstand rauben (fam)* drive sb mad, drive sb crazy *bei Verstand sein (fam)* be in your right mind *den Verstand verlieren (also hum)* go mad, go crazy, lose your mind

ver·stän·di·gen [fɛˈʃtɛndɪɡn̩] <verständigt, verständigte, hat verständigt> [tr v] *jdn (über etw.* [acc]*/von etw.) verständigen* inform sb (of/about sth) ◊ *die Polizei von dem Einbruch verständigen* [ref v] **1.** *sich (mit jdm) (irgendwie) verständigen* communicate (with sb) (somehow) ◊ *sich über Funk/mit Zeichen verständigen* ♦ *sich mit Händen und Füßen verständigen* ♦ *sich auf Englisch verständigen* **2.** *sich (mit jdm) (über/auf etw.* [acc]*) verständigen* agree (with sb) (on sth) ◊ *sich über*

den Preis verständigen ♦ *Können wir uns darauf verständigen, dass ich das bezahle?*

ver·ständ·lich [fɛˈʃtɛntlɪç] [adj] **1.** intelligible, comprehensible, clear ◊ *Diese Technik ist für jedermann verständlich.* ♦ *auf eine verständliche Aussprache achten* ♦ *Sie redete laut und deutlich, sodass jedes Wort verständlich war.* *leicht/schwer etc. verständlich* easy/difficult etc. to understand ◊ *ein schwer verständlicher Dialekt* **2.** understandable ◊ *Es ist verständlich, dass sie enttäuscht ist.* ♦ *eine verständliche Reaktion* [adv] clearly, intelligibly ◊ *Fachbegriffe verständlich erklären* ♦ *etw. verständlich ausdrücken/formulieren* ♦ *Die Texte sind für Kinder verständlich geschrieben.* ⊛ *jdm etw. verständlich machen* explain sth to sb *sich (irgendwie) verständlich machen* communicate (somehow) ◊ *sich durch Rufen/Zeichen verständlich machen*

② **Ver·ständ·nis** [fɛˈʃtɛntnɪs] das <-ses, −se> *most sing* **1.** *Verständnis (für jdn/etw.)* understanding (for sb/sth), sympathy (for sb/sth) ◊ *jdm/einer Sache Verständnis entgegenbringen* ♦ *wenig/kein Verständnis für etw. haben/zeigen* ♦ *Wir bitten um Verständnis für die langen Wartezeiten.* **2.** *(lofty) (of a text) (das/ein) Verständnis …* [gen] understanding sth ◊ *Ist es für das Verständnis des Textes wichtig, etwas über den Autor zu wissen?*

ver·stär·ken [fɛˈʃtɛʁkn̩] <verstärkt, verstärkte, hat verstärkt> [tr v] **1.** intensify, increase ◊ *Anstrengungen/Bemühungen verstärken* ♦ *den Druck auf jdn verstärken* ♦ *Methan verstärkt den Treibhauseffekt.; (sound)* amplify ◊ *Das Hörgerät verstärkt den Schall.* **2.** *etw./sich (um jdn/mit jdm) verstärken* reinforce sth/itself (by sb) ◊ *eine Mauer/Wand verstärken* ♦ *die Truppen (um 800 Mann/mit Freiwilligen) verstärken* ♦ *Das Team hat sich durch die Neuzugänge auf zehn Mann verstärkt.* [ref v] *sich verstärken* intensify, be intensifying, grow, be growing ◊ *Der Druck hat sich verstärkt.* ♦ *Die Tendenz/Der Trend verstärkt sich.* ⊛ *etw. verstärkt tun* do sth intensively ◊ *verstärkt um Nachwuchs werben*

ver·staubt [fɛˈʃtaʊpt] [adj] *no comp/superl (pej)* outmoded ◊ *verstaubte Traditionen* ♦ *Seine Ansichten sind ziemlich verstaubt.* ♦ *Er findet Museen langweilig und verstaubt.*

Ver·steck [fɛˈʃtɛk] das <-(e)s, −e> hiding place ◊ *ein geheimes/gutes/sicheres Versteck* ♦ *Polizisten stürmten das Versteck der Terroristen.; (of drugs, weapons)* stash, cache ⊛ *(mit jdm) Versteck spielen (also fig)* play hide-and-seek (with sb)

② **ver·ste·cken** [fɛˈʃtɛkn̩] <versteckt, versteckte, hat versteckt> [tr v] *jdn/etw. (irgendwo) (vor jdm) verstecken* hide sb/sth (from sb) (somewhere) ◊ *Ostereier verstecken* ♦ *Süßigkeiten vor den Kindern im Schrank verstecken* ♦ *jdn vor der Polizei verstecken* *sich (irgendwo) (vor jdm) verstecken* hide (from sb) (somewhere) ◊ *sich hinter einer Maske verstecken* ♦ *Die Flüchtlinge verstecken sich in den Bergen.* ⊛ *sich (mit etw.) vor jdm nicht zu verstecken brauchen, sich (mit etw.) vor jdm nicht verstecken müssen (fam)* not need to hide (sth) from sb (mit jdm) *Verstecken spielen* play hide-and-

seek (with sb)

② **ver·ste·hen** [fɛˈʃteːən] <versteht, verstand, hat verstanden> ⟨tr v⟩ **1.** understand ◇ *einen Zusammenhang verstehen* ♦ *Hast du verstanden, worum es geht?* ♦ *Sein Dialekt ist kaum zu verstehen.* ♦ *jds Enttäuschung gut verstehen können* ♦ *Sie müssen schon verstehen, dass ich verärgert bin.* etw. unter etw. ⟨dat⟩ verstehen understand sth by sth ◇ *Was verstehst du unter Treue?* kein Wort/nichts verstehen können not be able to hear a word/anything jdn/etw. falsch verstehen misunderstand sb/sth etw. als etw. verstehen take sth as sth **2.** *(a profession, craft)* know a lot about ◇ *sein Fach/Handwerk verstehen* ♦ *Katrin versteht es, mit Tieren umzugehen.* etwas/nichts/viel von etw. verstehen know something/nothing/a lot about sth ⟨ref v⟩ **1.** sich (irgendwie) verstehen get on (in a certain way) ◇ *Wir verstehen uns (gut).* ♦ *Sie haben sich auf Anhieb verstanden.* sich mit jdm (irgendwie) verstehen get on with sb (in a certain way) ◇ *sich (blendend) mit seinen Eltern verstehen* **2.** sich auf etw. ⟨acc⟩ verstehen know a lot about sth, be good at sth ◇ *sich auf sein Handwerk verstehen* **3.** sich als jd/etw. verstehen regard yourself as sb/sth, see yourself as sb/sth ◇ *Er versteht sich als Künstler.* **4.** TRADE *(prices)* sich pro Person/Zimmer verstehen be per person/room sich inklusive Mehrwertsteuer/Lager verstehen include VAT *Die Preise verstehen sich in Euro. The prices are in euros.* ⟨intr v⟩ understand, get it ◇ *Das geht dich nichts an, (hast du) verstanden?* ♦ *Wenn ich recht verstanden habe, ist sie sauer.* ⊚ jdm etw. zu verstehen geben make sth quite clear to sb sich von selbst verstehen go without saying

ver·steu·ern [fɛˈʃtɔɪɐn] <versteuert, versteuerte, hat versteuert> ⟨tr v⟩ pay tax on ◇ *sein Einkommen versteuern*

ver·stim·men [fɛˈʃtɪmən] <verstimmt, verstimmte, hat verstimmt> ⟨tr v⟩ **1.** jdn verstimmen put sb in a bad mood, upset sb ◇ *Meine Bemerkung hat ihn verstimmt.* **2.** MUS etw. verstimmen put sth out of tune ◇ *eine Gitarre/Saite verstimmen* sich verstimmen get out of tune, go out of tune ◇ *Die Gitarre hat sich durch die Feuchtigkeit verstimmt.*

ver·stop·fen [fɛˈʃtɔpfn̩] <verstopft, verstopfte, hat verstopft> ⟨tr v⟩ etw. (mit etw.) verstopfen block sth (with sth) ◇ *eine verstopfte Nase* ♦ *Autos verstopfen die Straßen.* ♦ *seine Ohren mit Watte verstopfen* ⊚ verstopft sein be constipated

Ver·stop·fung [fɛˈʃtɔpfʊŋ] die <-, –en> **1.** blockage ◇ *ein Mittel, das Verstopfungen im Abfluss beseitigt/löst* **2.** MED constipation ◇ *an (akuter/chronischer) Verstopfung leiden* Verstopfung haben be constipated

Ver·stoß [fɛˈʃtoːs] der <–es, Verstöße> der/ein Verstoß (gegen etw.) the/a breach (of sth), the/an infringement (of sth) ◇ *einen Verstoß gegen die Regeln begehen* ♦ *ein Verstoß gegen den guten Geschmack; (against the law)* an offence ◇ *Bei schweren Verstößen droht der Entzug des Führerscheins.*

ver·sto·ßen [fɛˈʃtoːsn̩] <verstößt, verstieß, hat verstoßen> ⟨intr v⟩ gegen etw. verstoßen be in breach of sth, contravene sth ◇ *gegen das Urheber-*

recht verstoßen; *(the law, rules also)* break sth ◇ *gegen das Gesetz/die Regeln verstoßen* gegen die guten Sitten verstoßen be unacceptable ⟨tr v⟩ jdn verstoßen cast sb out, spurn sb, disown sb ◇ *von der Familie verstoßen werden*

ver·strei·chen [fɛˈʃtraɪçn̩] <verstreicht, verstrich, hat/ist verstrichen> ⟨tr v⟩ +haben spread ◇ *Butter auf einem Brot verstreichen* ♦ *Farbe mit einem Pinsel verstreichen* ⟨intr v⟩ +sein *(lofty)* pass ◇ *Die Zeit verstrich nur sehr langsam.* etw. verstreichen lassen let sth slip by ◇ *eine Frist/ein Ultimatum verstreichen lassen*

ver·stum·men [fɛˈʃtʊmən] <verstummt, verstummte, ist verstummt> ⟨intr v⟩ **1.** *(noise, music)* stop, cease, die away ◇ *Die Musik verstummte und der Vorhang fiel.* ♦ *Als der Redner die Bühne betrat, verstummten die Gespräche im Saal.* ♦ *Die Gerüchte verstummten mit der Zeit.* **2.** *(person, bird)* fall silent, go silent ◇ *vor Schreck verstummen* ♦ *Als ein Schuss fiel, verstummten die Vögel abrupt.*

② **Ver·such** [fɛˈzuːx] der <–(e)s, –e> **1.** try, attempt ◇ *ein geglückter Versuch* ♦ *einen Versuch wert sein* ♦ *einen Versuch machen/unternehmen/wagen* ♦ *Der Täter wollte fliehen, aber der Versuch scheiterte.* **2.** the/an experiment (on sb/sth) ◇ *ein klinischer/wissenschaftlicher Versuch* ♦ *Wissenschaftler haben in einem Versuch mit/an Ratten ein Gen entschlüsselt.* **3.** SPORT attempt ◇ *Beim Weitsprung hat jeder drei Versuche.*

② **ver·su·chen** [fɛˈzuːxn̩] <versucht, versuchte, hat versucht> ⟨tr v⟩ try, attempt ◇ *Er versucht sein Bestes.* ♦ *Sie versuchte ein Lächeln.* ♦ *Versuch mal, das Paket zu heben!* ♦ *„Ich kann das nicht." — „Versuch es wenigstens."* versuchen, etw. zu tun try to do sth, attempt to do sth ◇ *versuchen, sich zu ändern* ♦ *vergeblich/verzweifelt versuchen, jdn umzustimmen; (food)* try, taste ◇ *einen Kuchen versuchen* ♦ *Hast du die Soße schon versucht?* ⊖probieren, kosten ⟨intr v⟩ try it, taste it ◇ *Versuch doch mal, das schmeckt wirklich gut.* ⊖probieren, kosten ⟨ref v⟩ sich an/in etw. ⟨dat⟩ versuchen try your hand at sth, try yourself at sth ◇ *Sie versucht sich in der Politik.* ♦ *sich an der Kletterwand/am Klavier versuchen* sich als Maler/Autor versuchen try your hand as a painter/an author ⊚ versucht sein, etw. zu tun be tempted to do sth es mit etw. versuchen try sth ◇ *Wenn du nicht einschlafen kannst, versuch's doch mal mit warmer Milch.* es mit jdm versuchen give it a go with sb, give sb a chance es noch einmal mit jdm versuchen give it another go with sb, give sb another chance

ver·tau·schen [fɛˈtaʊʃn̩] <vertauscht, vertauschte, hat vertauscht> ⟨tr v⟩ **1.** etw. (mit etw.) vertauschen mix sth up (with sth) ◇ *Sie hat unsere Jacken vertauscht.* ♦ *den rechten Schuh mit dem linken vertauschen* **2.** etw. mit etw. vertauschen exchange sth for sth ◇ *den Lehrstuhl mit der Kanzel vertauschen und Priester werden*

ver·tei·di·gen [fɛˈtaɪdɪgn̩] <verteidigt, verteidigte, hat verteidigt> ⟨tr v⟩ defend ◇ *eine Burg gegen Feinde verteidigen* ♦ *seine Meinung verteidigen* ♦ *Der Angeklagte wird von Rechtsanwalt Müller verteidigt.* ♦ *seinen Titel verteidigen*

Ver·tei·di·gung [fɛ'taedɪɡʊŋ] die <–> no pl
defence, defense ◊ Diese Waffe benutze ich nur zur
Verteidigung. ◆ Was haben Sie zu Ihrer Verteidigung zu sagen? ◆ Die Verteidigung hat das Wort.
◆ Die Mannschaft zeigte Schwächen in der Verteidigung.

② **ver·tei·len** [fɛ'taelən] <verteilt, verteilte, hat
verteilt> [tr v] **1.** distribute ◊ Sie möchte das Geld
an die Armen verteilen. ◆ eine Last gleichmäßig
verteilen jdn/etw. auf etw. [acc] verteilen divide sb/
sth between/among sth ◊ Die Flüchtlinge werden
auf drei Lager verteilt. **2.** (an ointment, a cream)
spread [ref v] sich verteilen spread (out) ◊ Die Polizisten verteilten sich über den Park. ◆ Die Schüssel
fiel herunter, und ihr Inhalt verteilte sich auf dem
Boden.

ver·teu·ern [fɛ'tɔøɐn] <verteuert, verteuerte, hat
verteuert> [tr v] raise the price of ◊ Der schlechte
Eurokurs verteuert die Waren. [ref v] sich verteuern
go up in price ◊ Benzin hat sich stark verteuert.

ver·tie·fen [fɛ'tiːfn] <vertieft, vertiefte, hat
vertieft> [tr v] **1.** (knowledge, a friendship)
deepen, extend ◊ Ich möchte meine Sprachkenntnisse vertiefen. ◆ die Freundschaft zwischen zwei
Völkern vertiefen **2.** (a hole) make deeper, deepen
◊ Wir müssen das Loch für den Pfahl vertiefen.
3. in etw. [acc] vertieft sein be engrossed in sth ◊
Er war ganz in seine Arbeit vertieft. [ref v] **1.** sich
vertiefen deepen ◊ Die Falten auf seiner Stirn ver-
tieften sich. **2.** sich in etw. [acc] vertiefen become
absorbed in sth ◊ sich in ein Buch vertiefen

② **Ver·trag** [fɛ'traːk] der <–(e)s, Verträge> contract,
agreement ◊ einen Vertrag mit jdm schließen ◆
einen Vertrag unterzeichnen ◆ Sie ist bei einer Plattenfirma unter Vertrag.; (between countries)
treaty jdn unter Vertrag nehmen sign sb (up)

ver·tra·gen [fɛ'traːɡn] <verträgt, vertrug, hat
vertragen> [tr v] **1.** stand, take, tolerate ◊ Wie
verträgst du die Hitze? ◆ Sie verträgt keine Kritik.
2. (food, drink, medication) tolerate ◊ Sie
verträgt keinen Alkohol. einiges/viel vertragen hold
your drink [ref v] **1.** sich (mit jdm) vertragen get
on (with sb) ◊ Die beiden vertragen sich sehr gut.
◆ Sie verträgt sich nicht mit ihrer Schwiegermutter.
2. sich (mit jdm) wieder vertragen make up (with
sb) **3.** etw. verträgt sich mit etw. sth is compatible
with sth ◊ Dein Verhalten verträgt sich nicht mit
deiner beruflichen Stellung.; (colo(u)rs) etw.
verträgt sich mit etw. sth goes with sth Diese
beiden Farben vertragen sich nicht. These two
colours don't go together.

ver·träg·lich [fɛ'trɛːklɪç] [adj] **1.** (easily) digestible
◊ leicht verträgliche Speisen ein gut verträgliches
Medikament a medication without side-effects
2. (person, pet) easy-going ◊ Mein Opa war ein
sehr verträglicher Mensch. ◆ Der Hund ist lieb und
sehr verträglich. ⊖umgänglich

ver·trau·en [fɛ'traʊən] <vertraut, vertraute, hat
vertraut> [intr v] trust ◊ Ich vertraue dir blind. ◆
seinen Fähigkeiten vertrauen auf jdn/etw. vertrauen
trust in sb/sth ◊ auf Gott vertrauen ◆ Er vertraute auf
sein Glück. darauf vertrauen, dass trust that

② **Ver·trau·en** [fɛ'traʊən] das <–s> no pl Vertrauen
(in jdn/etw.) confidence (in sb/sth), faith (in sb/
sth) ◊ jds Vertrauen gewinnen Vertrauen (in jdn/zu
jdm) trust (in sb) ◊ Sie hat großes Vertrauen in

ihn/zu ihm. jdm/etw. Vertrauen entgegenbringen
trust in sb/sth jdn ins Vertrauen ziehen take sb
into your confidence im Vertrauen auf etw. [acc]
trusting in sth ◊ Im Vertrauen auf seine Kraft nahm
er das Projekt in Angriff. im Vertrauen in confidence ◊ jdm etw. im Vertrauen sagen

⊛ **Vertrauen ist gut, Kontrolle ist besser** (hum)
better safe than sorry

ver·trau·lich [fɛ'traʊlɪç] [adj, adv] **1.** confiden-
tial(ly) ◊ Die Sache ist streng vertraulich. ◆ eine
vertrauliche Unterredung ◆ Bitte behandeln Sie
diese Informationen vertraulich. **2.** chummy(-ily),
familiar(ly) ◊ in vertraulichem Ton miteinander
reden ◆ Sie wird schnell vertraulich. ◆ vertraulich
miteinander umgehen

ver·traut [fɛ'traʊt] past p of vertrauen [adj] <ver-
trauter, am vertrautesten> **1.** vertraut (mit jdm)
close (to sb), intimate (with sb) ◊ Sie wirken
ziemlich vertraut. ◆ vertrauten Umgang miteinander haben ◆ Ich fühlte mich schnell vertraut mit
ihm. **2.** vertraut (mit etw.) familiar (with sth) ◊ ein
vertrautes Gesicht ◆ Sind Sie mit der Bedienung
dieser Maschine vertraut? ⊖geläufig **3.** jdn/sich mit
etw. vertraut machen familiarize sb/yourself with sth

ver·trei·ben [fɛ'traebm] <vertreibt, vertrieb, hat
vertrieben> [tr v] **1.** jdn/etw. vertreiben drive sb/
sth away, drive sb/sth out ◊ Nach dem Krieg
wurden wir aus unserer Heimat vertrieben. ◆ Kaffee
vertreibt die Müdigkeit. **2.** ECON sell ◊ Dieses
Produkt wird im Fachhandel vertrieben. **3.** sich
[dat] die Zeit (mit etw.) vertreiben while away the
time (with sth/doing sth)

② **ver·tre·ten** [fɛ'treːtn] <vertritt, vertrat, hat
vertreten> [tr v] **1.** jdn vertreten stand in for sb ◊
Sie vertritt eine kranke Kollegin. **2.** jdn/etw.
vertreten represent sb/sth ◊ jds Interessen
vertreten ◆ Sie wird vor Gericht von ihrem Anwalt
vertreten. **3.** etw. vertreten be a/the sales
rep(resentative) for sth ◊ Er vertritt mehrere
Verlage in Bayern. **4.** (a point of view, an
opinion) hold, take, support ◊ Ich vertrete den
Standpunkt, dass diese Politik umweltfreundlich
ist. [ref v] **1.** sich [dat] den Fuß vertreten twist your
ankle **2.** sich [dat] die Beine vertreten (get up
and) stretch your legs

⊛ **irgendwo vertreten sein** be present
somewhere, be represented somewhere

② **Ver·tre·ter** [fɛ'treːtɐ] der <–s, –>, **Ver·tre·te·rin**
[fɛ'treːtərɪn] die <–, –nen> **1.** sales rep(resentative) ◊ ein Vertreter für Versicherungen ◆ Sie
arbeitet als Vertreterin. **2.** representative ◊ Die
Abgeordneten sind die Vertreter des Volkes. ◆
Vertreter aus Wirtschaft und Industrie **3.** (in sb's
absence) deputy

Ver·trieb [fɛ'triːp] der <–(e)s> no pl sales ◊ Sie
arbeitet seit Jahren im Vertrieb.; (selling) sale ◊
der Vertrieb von Büchern ⊖Einkauf

Ver·trie·be·ne [fɛ'triːbənə] der/die
<–n, die Vertriebenen> but: ein Vertriebener/eine Ver-
triebene displaced person

ver·un·glü·cken [fɛ'ʊnɡlʏkn] <verunglückt, verun-
glückte, ist verunglückt> [intr v] **1.** have an
accident, be involved in an accident ◊ Mein Sohn
ist mit dem Auto verunglückt. tödlich verunglücken
die in an accident **2.** (fam, hum) go wrong ◊ Der
Kuchen ist leider verunglückt.

ver·un·si·chern [fɐˈʔʊnzɪçɐn] <verunsichert, verun­sicherte, hat verunsichert> ⟨tr v⟩ *(always jdn verunsichern)* unsettle sb, make sb uncertain ◊ *Er versuchte, den Gegner zu verunsichern.* ✦ *Diese Mitteilung verunsicherte mich.*

ver·un·treu·en [fɐˈʔʊntrɔɔ̯ən] <veruntreut, verun­treute, hat veruntreut> ⟨tr v⟩ *mostly written* embezzle ◊ *Er hat große Summen veruntreut.*

② **ver·ur·sa·chen** [fɐˈʔuːɐ̯zaxn̩] <verursacht, verur­sachte, hat verursacht> ⟨tr v⟩ cause ◊ *Kosten/einen Unfall verursachen*

② **ver·ur·tei·len** [fɐˈʔʊɐ̯taɛ̯lən] <verurteilt, verurteilte, hat verurteilt> ⟨tr v⟩ **1.** LAW jdn (zu etw.) verurteilen sentence sb (to sth) ◊ *Er wurde zu zwei Jahren Haft verurteilt.* **2.** condemn ◊ *Ich verurteile sein Verhalten aufs Schärfste.* **3.** zu etw. verurteilt sein be condemned to (do) sth ◊ *Ich bin zum Schweigen verurteilt.* **4.** zu etw. verurteilt sein be doomed to sth ◊ *Dieser Plan ist von vornherein zum Scheitern verurteilt.*

ver·wal·ten [fɐˈvaltn̩] <verwaltet, verwaltete, hat verwaltet> ⟨tr v⟩ manage, administer ◊ *ein Vermögen verwalten*

② **Ver·wal·tung** [fɐˈvaltʊŋ] die <-, -en> **1.** administration ◊ *in der Verwaltung arbeiten* ✦ *Die Verwaltung befindet sich im Hauptgebäude.* **2.** *(of a building)* management ◊ *Dieses Gebäude steht unter staatlicher Verwaltung.*

ver·wan·deln [fɐˈvandl̩n] <verwandelt, verwan­delte, hat verwandelt> ⟨tr v⟩ **1.** jdn/etw. in etw./jdn verwandeln turn sb/sth into sth/sb, transform sb/ sth into sth/sb ◊ *Diese Maschine verwandelt Energie in Bewegung.* sich in etw./jdn verwandeln transform yourself into sth/sb, turn (yourself) into sth/sb ◊ *Im Märchen verwandelt sich der Frosch in einen Prinzen.* **2.** change ◊ *Die helle Farbe hat den Raum ganz verwandelt.* ✦ *Seit ihrer Scheidung ist sie wie verwandelt.* **3.** SPORT *(a penalty)* convert einen Freistoß/einen Eckball verwandeln score from a free kick/corner

② **ver·wandt** [fɐˈvant] ⟨adj⟩ *no comp/superl* **1.** related ◊ *Karin und ich sind entfernt miteinander verwandt.* ✦ *verwandte Schmetterlingsarten* **2.** similar ◊ *verwandte Fragestellungen*

② **Ver·wand·te** [fɐˈvantə] der/die <-n, die Verwandten> *but: ein Verwandter/eine Verwandte* relative, relation ◊ *ein naher Verwandter* ✦ *Freunde und Verwandte einladen*

Ver·wandt·schaft [fɐˈvantʃaft] die <-, -en> **1.** *no pl* relations, relatives ◊ *Zur Hochzeit laden wir die gesamte Verwandtschaft ein.* zur Verwandtschaft gehören be a relative, be a relation **2.** *(being related)* (blood) relationship ◊ *Zwischen ihm und mir besteht keinerlei Verwandtschaft.* **3.** *most sing* similarity ◊ *Zwischen beiden Problemen besteht eine gewisse Verwandtschaft.*

② **ver·wech·seln** [fɐˈvɛksl̩n] <verwechselt, verwech­selte, hat verwechselt> ⟨tr v⟩ jdn/etw. (mit jdn/ etw.) verwechseln get sth mixed up (with sb/ sth) ◊ *Er hat sie mit ihrer Schwester verwechselt.* ✦ *In der Eile verwechselten sie ihre Mäntel.*

ver·wei·gern [fɐˈvaɛ̯gɐn] <verweigert, verweigerte, hat verweigert> ⟨tr v⟩ **1.** etw. verweigern refuse to do sth ◊ *Ich verweigere meine Zustimmung!* ✦ *Die Soldaten verweigerten den Befehl.* etw. verweigert den Dienst sth won't work **2.** jdm etw. verweigern

deny sb sth, refuse sb sth ◊ *An der Grenze wurde ihm die Einreise verweigert.* **3.** (den Kriegsdienst/ Wehrdienst) verweigern be a conscientious objector

Ver·weis [fɐˈvaɛ̯s] der <-es, -e> **1.** reprimand ◊ *ein scharfer Verweis* ✦ *jdm einen Verweis erteilen* **2.** ein Verweis (auf etw. ⟨acc⟩) a reference (to sth) ◊ *ein Verweis auf Sekundärliteratur*

ver·wei·sen [fɐˈvaɛ̯zn̩] <verweist, verwies, hat verwiesen> ⟨tr+intr v⟩ **1.** auf etw./jdn verweisen, an etw./jdn verweisen refer to sth/sb ◊ *Sie hat mich auf ein Buch von Freud verwiesen.* ✦ *Darf ich Sie an meine Kollegin verweisen?* **2.** jdn des Landes verweisen expel sb from the country; *(in sports)* jdn vom Platz verweisen send sb off

② **ver·wen·den** [fɐˈvɛndn̩] <verwendet, verwendete/ verwandte, hat verwendet/verwandt> ⟨tr v⟩ use ◊ *Sie verwendet zum Kochen nur Butter.* ✦ *Die Verpackung kann man mehrmals verwenden.* Zeit für/auf etw. ⟨acc⟩ verwenden spend time on sth Zeit darauf verwenden, etw. zu tun spend time doing sth ⟨ref v⟩ *mostly written* sich für jdn/etw. verwenden use your influence on behalf of sb/sth ◊ *Ich werde mich dafür verwenden, dass Sie das Geld bald bekommen.*

ver·wer·ten [fɐˈveːɐ̯tn̩] <verwertet, verwertete, hat verwertet> ⟨tr v⟩ use, make use of ◊ *Diese Erfindung werden wir kommerziell verwerten.*

ver·wi·ckeln [fɐˈvɪkl̩n] <verwickelt, verwickelte, hat verwickelt> ⟨ref v⟩ sich (in etw. ⟨acc⟩/⟨dat⟩) verwickeln get tangled up (in sth) ◊ *Die Fäden haben sich verwickelt.* ✦ *Die Schnur des Drachens hat sich im Geäst verwickelt.* sich in Widersprüche verwickeln contradict yourself ⟨tr v⟩ jdn in etw. ⟨acc⟩ verwickeln involve sb in sth ◊ *Ich möchte nicht in diese Sache verwickelt werden.* ✦ *Die Truppen waren in schwere Kämpfe verwickelt.* ✦ *jdn in ein Gespräch verwickeln*

ver·wirk·li·chen [fɐˈvɪɐ̯klɪçn̩] <verwirklicht, verwirk­lichte, hat verwirklicht> ⟨tr v⟩ realize ◊ *eine Idee verwirklichen* ⊖realisieren ⟨ref v⟩ **1.** sich verwirklichen come true ◊ *Dieser Traum wird sich wohl niemals verwirklichen.* **2.** sich verwirklichen fulfil yourself ◊ *Sie möchte sich als Künstlerin verwirklichen.*

ver·wir·ren [fɐˈvɪrən] <verwirrt, verwirrte, hat verwirrt> ⟨tr v⟩ **1.** jdn verwirren confuse sb, bewilder sb ◊ *Die Frage verwirrte sie.* **2.** etw. verwirren tangle sth up ◊ *Fäden verwirren; (your hair)* ruffle (up)

② **ver·wit·wet** [fɐˈvɪtvət] ⟨adj⟩ *no comp/superl* widowed ◊ *Er ist seit sieben Jahren verwitwet.* ✦ *die verwitwete Frau Stein*

ver·wöh·nen [fɐˈvøːnən] <verwöhnt, verwöhnte, hat verwöhnt> ⟨tr v⟩ jdn verwöhnen spoil sb ◊ *Er verwöhnt seine Frau mit Geschenken.*

ver·wun·den [fɐˈvʊndn̩] <verwundet, verwundete, hat verwundet> ⟨tr v⟩ wound ◊ *Er hat das Reh mit einem Schuss verwundet.; (in an accident)* injure ◊ *Bei dem Unfall wurde sie am Kopf verwundet.*

ver·wun·dern [fɐˈvʊndɐn] <verwundert, verwun­derte, hat verwundert> ⟨tr v⟩ surprise, astonish ◊ *Es verwundert mich nicht im Geringsten, dass er wütend ist.*

ver·zau·bern [fɐˈtsaɔ̯bɐn] <verzaubert, verzau­berte, hat verzaubert> ⟨tr v⟩ **1.** jdn/etw. verzaubern cast a spell on sb/sth ◊ *Nachdem die Hexe sie ver*

zaubert hatte, fiel sie in tiefen Schlaf. *jdn/etw. in jdn/etw. verzaubern* turn sb/sth into sb/sth ◊ *Die Hexe hat den Prinzen in einen Raben verzaubert.* **2.** enchant ◊ *Ihr Anblick hat alle verzaubert.*

ver·zeich·nen [fɛ'tsaeçnən] <verzeichnet, verzeichnete, hat verzeichnet> ⟨tr v⟩ record ◊ *Verzeichnen Sie die Lösungen in der rechten Spalte.* ♦ *Fortschritte verzeichnen*

Ver·zeich·nis [fɛ'tsaeçnɪs] das <-ses, -se> list, catalogue, catalog, index ◊ *ein chronologisches Verzeichnis* ♦ *Legen Sie ein Verzeichnis aller Teilnehmer an.*

② **ver·zei·hen** [fɛ'tsaeən] <verzeiht, verzieh, hat verziehen> ⟨tr+intr v⟩ forgive ◊ *jdm eine Lüge verzeihen* ♦ *Sie wird mir nie verzeihen, dass ich sie belogen habe.* ♦ *Verzeihst du mir noch einmal? nicht zu verzeihen sein* be unforgivable ⊜*nachtragen*
Ⓔ **verzeihen Sie bitte, ...** (please) excuse me, ... ◊ *Verzeihen Sie bitte, darf ich mal kurz vorbei?*

② **Ver·zei·hung** [fɛ'tsaeʊŋ] die <-> *no pl* **1.** (jdn) um Verzeihung bitten apologize (to sb) ◊ *Ich bitte um Verzeihung für mein unhöfliches Verhalten.* ⊜*Entschuldigung* **2.** Verzeihung! Sorry! **3.** Verzeihung? Pardon?, Sorry? ⊜*Wie bitte?*

ver·zich·ten [fɛ'tsɪçtn] ⟨intr v⟩ **1.** (auf etw./jdn) verzichten do without (sth/sb) ◊ *Mein Beruf ist mir wichtig, deshalb verzichte ich auf Kinder.* **2.** (officially) auf etw. ⟨acc⟩ verzichten renounce sth ◊ *auf sein Recht/den Thron verzichten*

② **ver·zieh** [fɛ'tsiː] *pret of* verziehen
ver·zie·hen¹ [fɛ'tsiːən] <verzieht, verzog, hat verzogen> ⟨tr v⟩ **1.** (features) twist ◊ *den Mund zu einem Grinsen verziehen* ♦ *Er verzog keine Miene. das Gesicht verziehen* grimace, pull a face *sich verziehen* twist **2.** (fam) spoil ◊ *Verzieh doch die Kinder nicht so!* ⟨ref v⟩ **1.** sich verziehen warp, become distorted ◊ *Durch die Nässe haben sich die Fensterrahmen verzogen.*; (clothing) go out of shape **2.** (fam) (storm, fog) sich verziehen clear ◊ *Ich glaube, das Unwetter verzieht sich allmählich.* **3.** (fam) sich verziehen push off ◊ *Verzieh dich endlich!*

② **ver·zie·hen²** [fɛ'tsiːən] *past p of* verziehen
ver·zie·ren [fɛ'tsiːrən] <verziert, verzierte, hat verziert> ⟨tr v⟩ etw. (mit etw.) verzieren decorate sth (with sth) ◊ *eine Geburtstagstorte (mit Kerzen) verzieren.*

ver·zin·sen [fɛ'tsɪnzn] <verzinst, verzinste, hat verzinst> ⟨tr v⟩ pay interest on ◊ *Die Bank verzinst das Kapital mit 3%.* ⟨ref v⟩ etw. verzinst sich bears interest ◊ *Das Kapital verzinst sich gut.*

ver·zö·gern [fɛ'tsøːɡɐn] <verzögert, verzögerte, hat verzögert> ⟨tr v⟩ **1.** delay ◊ *Ein wichtiger Anruf verzögerte unsere Abfahrt. sich verzögern* be delayed ◊ *Die Ankunft des Zuges verzögert sich um 15 Minuten.* **2.** slow down ◊ *Er verzögerte seinen Schritt. sich verzögern* be slowed down ◊ *Die Gespräche verzögerten sich.*

ver·zol·len [fɛ'tsɔlən] <verzollt, verzollte, hat verzollt> ⟨tr v⟩ pay duty on, declare ◊ *Muss ich diese Zigaretten verzollen?* Haben Sie etwas zu verzollen? Have you anything to declare?

Ver·zug [fɛ'tsuːk] der <-(e)s> *no pl* delay ◊ *Wir werden das ohne Verzug erledigen. etw. duldet keinen Verzug* sth must not be delayed Verzug der

Zahlung delayed payment (mit etw.) in Verzug geraten/kommen fall behind (with sth), get behind (with sth) ◊ *Sie sind mit der Zahlung der Miete in Verzug geraten. (mit etw.) im Verzug sein* be behind (with sth)

ver·zwei·feln [fɛ'tsvaefl̩n] <verzweifelt, verzweifelte, ist verzweifelt> ⟨intr v⟩ (an jdm/etw.) verzweifeln despair (of sb/sth) ◊ *Ich verzweifle noch an seinem Starrsinn.*

VHS [faoha:'ɛs] die (abbr of Volkshochschule) ⊜*adult education centre* ◊ *Sie lernt Englisch an der VHS.* box⊛ Volkshochschule

② **Vi·de·o** ['viːdeo] das *or* der <-s, -s> video ◊ *Wollen wir uns für Samstag ein paar Videos ausleihen?* ◊ *Kennst du schon das neue Video von Britney?* etw. auf Video aufnehmen record sth on video, video sth

② **Vi·de·o·film** ['viːdeofɪlm] der <-(e)s, -e> video film, video movie ◊ *sich einen Videofilm ansehen*
Vi·de·o·ka·me·ra ['viːdeoˌkamera:] die <-, -s> video camera ◊ *etw. mit einer Videokamera filmen*
Vi·de·o·re·kor·der ['viːdeoreˌkɔʁde] der <-s, -> video recorder

Viech [fiːç] das <-(e)s, -er> (fam, esp pej) beast, animal ◊ *Schaff mir die Viecher vom Hals!*

② **Vieh** [fiː] das <-(e)s> *no pl* **1.** livestock ◊ *das Vieh versorgen* **2.** (abbr of Rindvieh) cattle ◊ *Der Bauer treibt das Vieh auf die Weide.* **3.** (fam, esp pej) beast, animal ◊ *Was ist denn das für ein widerliches Vieh?*
Ⓔ jdn wie ein Stück Vieh behandeln treat sb like an animal

② **viel¹** [fiːl] ⟨adv⟩ <mehr, am meisten> **1.** (fam) a lot ◊ *Sie gehen viel ins Theater.* ♦ *Säuglinge schlafen viel.* **2.** widely ◊ *Das ist ein viel gelesenes Buch. eine viel befahrene Straße* a very busy road **3.** (expressing a big difference) viel zu much too ◊ *Diese Hose ist mir viel zu eng. viel mehr/netter/schöner* much more/nicer/more beautiful ◊ *Er weiß viel mehr als ich.* ♦ *Ich finde dieses Auto viel schöner!*
Ⓔ so viel wie möglich as much as possible

② **viel²** [fiːl] ⟨det⟩ *before uncountable ns, indefinite and invariable* **1.** a lot of ◊ *Er braucht bei der Arbeit noch viel Hilfe.*; (in negative sentences, questions) much ◊ *Er trinkt nicht viel Alkohol.* ♦ *Wie viel Geld hat das gekostet?* zu viel too much ◊ *Das kostet zu viel Zeit.* ♦ *Mir wird die Arbeit mit dem großen Garten zu viel.* ⊜*wenig* **2.** Viel Erfolg! Good luck! Viel Vergnügen! Have fun! Vielen Dank! Thank you very much!

viel³ [fiːl] ⟨indef pron⟩ a lot ◊ *Sie hält viel von ihrem Bruder.*; (in negative sentences, questions) much ◊ *Du solltest nicht so viel trinken!* ♦ *Wie viel kostet das?* so viel (wie) as much as ◊ *Sie können vom Büffet essen, so viel Sie wollen.* ♦ *Er verdient doppelt so viel wie ich.* zu viel too much ◊ *Sie arbeitet zu viel.*
Ⓔ nicht viel von jdm haben not see much of sb ◊ *Seit seiner Beförderung habe ich nicht mehr viel von ihm. viel von jdm haben* be much like sb was zu viel ist, ist zu viel (fam) enough is enough zu viel kriegen (fam) be about to explode ein bisschen viel (fam) a bit much ◊ *Verlangst du da nicht ein bisschen viel?*

viel·deu·tig ['fiːldɔøtɪç] ⟨adj⟩ *no comp/superl* ambiguous ◊ *„Ton" ist im Deutschen ein vieldeuti-*

ger Begriff. ♦ Diese Aussage ist vieldeutig. ⊝mehrdeutig

vie·le ['fiːlə] [adj] indefinite, only before ns der/die/das viele all this/that ◊ Entschuldige den vielen Ärger. ♦ Es tut mir Leid um das viele Geld. die vielen all these/those ◊ Woher kommen die vielen Menschen?

vie·les ['fiːləs] [pron] a lot of things, many things ◊ Vieles ging von Anfang an schief. ♦ Das erklärt vieles.

vie·ler·lei ['fiːleˈlae] [det] invariable many different, all sorts of ◊ Es gibt hier vielerlei Arten von Insekten. ♦ Dafür gibt es vielerlei Gründe.

vie·ler·lei ['fiːleˈlae] [pron] invariable all sorts of things ◊ Ich habe vielerlei erfahren.

viel·fach ['fiːlfax] [adj] no comp/superl, only before ns multiple, many times over ◊ die vielfache Menge von etw. ♦ ein vielfacher Preisträger auf vielfachen Wunsch by popular request [adv] no comp/superl 1. many times ◊ Der Film wurde vielfach ausgezeichnet. ⊝mehrfach, mehrmals 2. (fam) frequently ◊ Diese Meinung findet man vielfach unter jungen Leuten.

Viel·falt ['fiːlfalt] die <–> no pl variety ◊ eine bunte Vielfalt aufweisen

viel·fäl·tig ['fiːlfɛltɪç] [adj] varied ◊ ein vielfältiges Freizeitangebot ♦ Die Spielmöglichkeiten für Kinder sind hier sehr vielfältig.

② **viel·leicht¹** [fiˈlaeçt] [adv] perhaps, maybe ◊ Vielleicht hat er ja Recht. ♦ „Gehst du heute Abend noch weg?" — „Vielleicht." ♦ ein Mann von vielleicht 70 Jahren

② **viel·leicht²** [fiˈlaeçt] [part] (fam) 1. (for emphasis and in questions to which a negative answer is expected) really ◊ Glaubst du vielleicht, ich bin ein Idiot? ♦ Ich war vielleicht aufgeregt! 2. (expressing impatience) how about ◊ Vielleicht wartest du mal, bis du an der Reihe bist! 3. (in polite requests) possibly ◊ Könnten Sie mir vielleicht sagen, wie spät es ist?

viel·mals ['fiːlmaːls] [adv] danke vielmals many thanks Ich bitte (Sie) vielmals um Entschuldigung! I am so sorry! vielmals grüßen lassen send your best regards

viel·mehr [fiːlˈmeːɐ, '– –] [adv] rather ◊ Das ist kein Scherz, sondern vielmehr eine ernste Angelegenheit.

viel·sa·gend ['fiːlzaːgn̩t] [adj, adv] meaningful(ly), knowing(ly) ◊ ein vielsagender Blick ♦ Sein Gesichtsausdruck war vielsagend. ♦ Sie lächelte vielsagend.

viel·sei·tig ['fiːlzaetɪç] [adj] 1. versatile ◊ eine vielseitige Künstlerin ♦ Diese Software ist nicht sehr vielseitig. 2. varied ◊ eine vielseitige Ausbildung ♦ Die Verwendungsmöglichkeiten dieses Geräts sind vielseitig. [adv] 1. vielseitig begabt sein have many talents 2. vielseitig einsetzbar have many uses

Viel·zahl ['fiːltsaːl] die <–> no pl multitude, large number ◊ eine Vielzahl möglicher Motive ♦ eine Vielzahl von Möglichkeiten

vier [fiːɐ] [nmrl] four ◊ Zwei plus zwei ist vier. ♦ Ich hätte gerne vier Brötchen. ♦ die vier Himmelsrichtungen ♦ vier Millionen Euro ♦ Meine kleine Tochter ist vier Jahre alt. ♦ Wann wird er vier? ♦ Wir treffen uns dann um vier am Bahnhof. ♦ Es ist schon Viertel nach vier. ♦ Sie haben vier zu drei

gewonnen. mit vier (Jahren) at (the age of) four ⊛ **alle viere von sich strecken** (fam) stretch out zu vieren/viert four of us/them ◊ Sie kommen zu viert.

Vier [fiːɐ] die <–, –en> 1. four ◊ Ist das eine Vier oder eine Neun? ♦ Er hat eine Vier gewürfelt. ♦ Die Vier hat gewonnen. 2. (fam) (bus, tram etc.) number four ◊ Am Hauptbahnhof steigen Sie dann in die Vier um. ♦ Wo hält denn bitte die Vier? ♦ Ich bin mit der Vier gefahren. 3. SCHOOL (grade) ⊝C ◊ Er hat fast lauter Vieren im Zeugnis. eine Vier schreiben get a C ⊝ausreichend box@ Note

Vier·eck ['fiːɐˌʔɛk] das <–(e)s, –e> 1. MATH quadrilateral, quadrangle ◊ Berechnen Sie die Fläche des Vierecks. 2. (fam) rectangle, square ◊ ein Viereck zeichnen ♦ Das Gebäude hat die Form eines Vierecks.

vier·e·ckig ['fiːɐˌʔɛkɪç] [adj] no comp/superl 1. quadrilateral 2. (fam) square, rectangular ◊ Der Garten hat einen viereckigen Grundriss. ♦ Unser Esstisch ist nicht rund, sondern viereckig.

vier·fach ['fiːɐfax] [adj, adv] when used as an adj, only before ns fourfold, four times ◊ die vierfache Menge Wasser ♦ der vierfache Weltmeister ♦ Der Benzinverbrauch ist in diesem Fall vierfach. ♦ Diese Abbildung ist vierfach vergrößert. ♦ etw. vierfach kopieren lassen eine vierfache Mutter a mother of four

vier·te ['fiːɐtə] [adj] <ein vierter ..., eine vierte ..., ein viertes ...> fourth ◊ Heute ist Freitag, der vierte Juni. ♦ Er kann die vierte Frage nicht beantworten. ♦ Das ist heute bereits das vierte Mal, dass er hier anruft. ♦ Wir wohnen im vierten Stock.

Vier·tel ['fɪrtl̩] das <–s, –> 1. quarter ◊ Ein Viertel der Zeit ist bereits vorbei. ♦ Fast drei Viertel der Bevölkerung sind gegen das neue Gesetz. ♦ Es ist nur noch ein Viertel des Kuchens übrig. Viertel nach quarter past ◊ Der Film beginnt um Viertel nach acht. Viertel vor quarter to ◊ Es ist Viertel vor fünf. 2. (abbr of Stadtviertel) part of town, area, quarter ◊ Wir wohnen in einem ruhigen Viertel. 3. (of wine) quarter of a litre, quarter of a liter ◊ ein Viertel Wein bestellen Er hat schon ein paar Viertel getrunken. He's had a few.

vier·teln ['fɪrtl̩n] [tr v] +haben etw. vierteln quarter sth, cut sth into four, divide sth into four ◊ Die Tomaten waschen, häuten und vierteln. ♦ Ich habe den Apfel für euch geviertelt.

Vier·tel·stun·de [fɪrtl̩ˈʃtʊndə] die <–, –n> quarter of an hour ◊ In einer Viertelstunde fängt der Film an.

vier·tens ['fiːɐtn̩s, 'fiːɐtəns] [adv] fourthly ◊ Erstens hat er keine Lust zum Verreisen, zweitens keine Zeit, drittens keine Begleitung und viertens kein Geld.

vier·zehn ['fɪrˈtseːn] [nmrl] fourteen → vier

vier·zig ['fɪrtsɪç] [nmrl] forty → vier

Vig·net·te [vɪnˈjɛtə] die <–, –n> vignette ⊝Pickerl

Before travelling on Austrian motorways and dual carriageways a Vignette (motorway vignette) has to be purchased. Only on the Brenner motorway are you still required to pay at a toll booth. In Switzerland, a vignette is needed by drivers on all motorways and roads marked with green and white signs.

Vil·la ['vɪla:] die <-, Villen> villa ◊ *in einer Villa wohnen*

vi·o·lett [vio'lɛt] [adj] purple, violet ◊ *eine Blume mit violetten Blüten* ♦ *Mein neues Kleid ist violett.*

Vi·ren ['vi:rən] *pl of* Virus

Vi·rus ['vi:rʊs] der *or* das <-, Viren> virus ◊ *Wurde die Infektion durch Viren oder Bakterien verursacht?* ♦ *Der Virus verbreitet sich über infizierte E-Mails.*

② **vis-à-vis**¹ [viza'vi:] [adv] vis-à-vis opposite ◊ *Komm, wir gehen ins Café vis-à-vis.* ♦ *Ich wohne gleich vis-à-vis vom Bahnhof.* ⊜gegenüber

② **vis-à-vis**² [viza'vi:] [prep] [+dat] vis-à-vis jdm/etw. opposite sb/sth ◊ *Das Café ist vis-à-vis dem Theater.* ♦ *Sie setzte sich mir vis-à-vis.* ⊜gegenüber

② **Vi·sum** ['vi:zʊm] das <-s, Visa *or* Visen> visa ◊ *Für die Einreise nach Indien brauchen Deutsche ein Visum.*

Vi·ta·min [vita'mi:n] das <-s, -e> vitamin ◊ *Im Winter braucht man viel Vitamin C.*

⊚ **Vitamin B** *(fam, hum)* connections

② **Vo·gel** ['fo:gl̩] der <-s, Vögel> **1.** zoo bird ◊ *Morgens weckt mich oft das Zwitschern der Vögel.* **2.** *(fam, also hum)* ein komischer/seltsamer Vogel an odd bird ein lustiger Vogel quite a character ⊚ *(mit etw.)* den Vogel abschießen *(fam)* take the biscuit (with sth) einen Vogel haben *(fam, pej)* be off your rocker jdm einen/den Vogel zeigen *(fam)* tap your forehead at sb

Vo·ka·bel [vo'ka:bl̩] die <-, -n> word Vokabeln vocabulary ◊ *Fragst du mich bitte die Vokabeln ab?* ⊜Wort

Vo·ka·bu·lar [vokabu'la:ʳ] das <-s, -e> *(lofty)* vocabulary ◊ *technisches Vokabular* ♦ *das Vokabular der Juristen* ⊜Wortschatz

Vo·kal [vo'ka:l] der <-s, -e> vowel ◊ *Das Wort „Delfin" enthält zwei Vokale.*

② **Volk** [fɔlk] das <-(e)s, Völker> **1.** people, nation ◊ *das deutsche/französische Volk* ♦ *die Völker Afrikas/Europas* ♦ *Der Bundestag wird vom Volk gewählt.* ⊜Bevölkerung **2.** *no pl (also fam)* people ◊ *Ein Teil des einfachen Volkes hielt am alten Glauben fest.* das gemeine Volk the common people ein Mann aus dem Volke a man of the people; *(fam also)* folk ◊ *Die Musik war eher was fürs junge Volk.* ⊜Leute

⊚ **das auserwählte Volk** REL the chosen people **etw. unters Volk bringen 1.** distribute/sell sth to the public ◊ *Er bringt sein Taschengeld immer schnell unters Volk.* **2.** spread sth to the public ◊ *Wer hat dieses Gerücht unters Volk gebracht?* **sich unters Volk mischen** mingle with the crowd

Volks·hoch·schu·le ['fɔlkshoːxʃuːlə] die <-, -n> *(abbr VHS)* ⊜adult education centre ◊ *Sie hat an der Volkshochschule einen Yogakurs gemacht.*

> The adult education centre is an educational establishment for adults with a diverse range of courses at good prices, including language acquisition, political education, vocational training, health, culture, and handicrafts, taught through lectures, group discussions, symposiums and workshops.

② **Volks·schu·le** ['fɔlksʃuːlə] die <-, -n> *(Austr)* primary school ◊ *Sie geht in die Volksschule.*

② **voll** [fɔl] [adj] **1.** *(also fig)* full ◊ *Du hast meine volle Unterstützung!* ♦ *Ich warte seit einer vollen Stunde auf dich!* ♦ *Dein Glas ist ja noch halb voll!* ♦ *Du bist voller geworden, bist du schwanger?* voll ... [gen], voll etw. full of ... ◊ *ein Regal voll alter Bücher* ♦ *ein Leben voll Kummer und Leid* **2.** *(on the surface)* voll (von/mit etw.) covered (in/with sth) ◊ *Das Hemd ist voll mit/von Flecken.* ♦ *Du bist ja ganz voll Dreck!* etw. voll schmieren scrawl all over sth Die Wand war voll geschmiert. There were smears all over the wall. jdn/etw. voll spritzen splash/spray sb/sth all over **3.** +verb etw. voll füllen/machen/tanken/laufen lassen fill sth up ◊ *Mach mein Glas bitte nicht so voll.* etw. voll laden load sth up completely etw. voll qualmen/schreiben fill sth with smoke/writing die Hosen voll machen mess your pants sich voll saugen become saturated **4.** +verb *(fam)* sich voll fressen, sich [dat] den Bauch voll schlagen stuff yourself, stuff your face sich voll laufen lassen/saufen get completely plastered/canned **5.** *(sound, voice)* full, rich ◊ *Dieses Instrument hat einen vollen Ton.* ♦ *Seine Stimme war voll und tief.* **6.** *(hair)* thick ◊ *Dein Haar ist voller geworden.* ♦ *volle Locken* ⊜dicht [adv] **1.** fully ◊ *ein voll besetzter Bus* ♦ *Das Gerät ist alt, aber voll funktionsfähig.* voll und ganz completely ⊜ganz, völlig **2.** voll arbeiten work full-time ◊ *Obwohl sie allein erziehend ist, arbeitet sie voll.* **3.** *(slang)* really ◊ *Die Party war voll langweilig!*

⊚ **brechend/gestopft voll** *(fam)* jam-packed **in die Vollen gehen** *(fam)* carry on as if there's no tomorrow **aus dem Vollen leben** live off the fat of the land **jdn nicht für voll nehmen** *(fam)* not take sb seriously **aus dem Vollen schöpfen** draw on abundant/plentiful resources **voll sein** *(fam)* **1.** be full up ◊ *Ich bin so voll, ich kann nichts mehr essen.* **2.** be plastered ◊ *Er war so voll, dass er sich hinterher an nichts erinnern konnte.*

voll·auf ['fɔlʔaʊf, – '-] [adv] completely, fully ◊ *Ich bin mit dem Ergebnis vollauf zufrieden.* vollauf genügen/reichen be quite enough ⊜völlig

voll·brin·gen [fɔl'brɪŋən] <vollbringt, vollbrachte, hat vollbracht> [tr v] *(lofty)* accomplish, achieve ◊ *Höchstleistungen/ein Kunststück vollbringen*

voll·en·den [fɔl'ɛndn̩] <vollendet, vollendete, hat vollendet> [tr v] complete, finish ◊ *Der Komponist konnte seine letzte Symphonie nicht mehr vollenden.* ♦ *Er hat gerade sein 60. Lebensjahr vollendet.*

voll·en·det [fɔl'ɛndət] *past p of* vollenden [adj] **1.** completed, finished ◊ *Sein Werk ist noch nicht vollendet.* ♦ *ein kürzlich vollendetes Projekt* ab dem vollendeten 18. Lebensjahr aged 18 and over bis zum vollendeten 12. Lebensjahr aged 12 and under **2.** perfect, accomplished ◊ *Er benahm sich wie ein vollendeter Gentleman.* ♦ *in vollendeter Harmonie* ⊜perfekt, vollkommen **3.** LAW consummated ◊ *wegen vollendeten Mordes/Betrugs angeklagt werden*

vol·ler ['fɔle] *comp of* voll [adj] *invariable; when followed by a noun without attribute, the noun remains uninflected; only before ns* **1.** [+gen] *(also fig)* full of, filled with ◊ *ein Korb voller Eier* ♦ *Sie war voller Energie.* ⊜voll **2.** [+gen] covered with ◊ *Du bist ja voller Dreck!* ⊜voll

② **völ·lig** ['fœlɪç] [adj, adv] *no comp/superl; when used*

as an adj, only before ns complete(ly), total(ly) ◊ *Dort herrschte völliges Chaos.* ✦ *Der Ort wurde vom Erdbeben völlig zerstört.* ✦ *Das kam für mich völlig überraschend.* ⊖total, vollkommen

voll·jäh·rig ['fɔljɛːrɪç] *adj no comp/superl* of age ◊ *Bist du denn schon volljährig? Sie haben zwei volljährige Kinder.* They have two adult children. volljährig werden come of age ⊖erwachsen, mündig ⊖minderjährig

voll·kom·men [fɔl'kɔmən, '– – –] adj, adv complete(ly), total(ly) ◊ *Das ist mir vollkommen egal.* ✦ *Die Gebrauchsanleitung war vollkommen unverständlich.* ✦ *Damit war unsere Niederlage vollkommen.* ✦ *Es herrschte vollkommene Ruhe.* ⊖völlig adj perfect ◊ *Sie lebten in vollkommener Harmonie.* ✦ *Unser Glück war nahezu vollkommen.* ⊖vollendet, perfekt

Voll·korn·brot ['fɔlkɔ'nbroːt] das <–(e)s, –e> wholemeal bread

Voll·macht ['fɔlmaxt] die <–, –en> **1.** eine Vollmacht (für/zu etw.) power of attorney (for sth) ◊ *Er erteilte seiner Frau eine Vollmacht für sein Konto.* ✦ *eine schriftliche Vollmacht vorlegen* **2.** authority ◊ *Ihr wurden weit reichende Vollmachten übertragen.*

Voll·mond ['fɔlmoːnt] der <–(e)s> *no pl* full moon ◊ *Bei Vollmond schlafe ich schlecht.*

Voll·pen·si·on ['fɔlpanˌzjoːn, 'fɔlpãziˌoːn] die <–> *no pl* full board ◊ *Wir haben zwei Wochen Vollpension gebucht.*

voll·stän·dig ['fɔlʃtɛndɪç] adj, adv full(y), complete(ly) ◊ *Ist die Liste jetzt vollständig?* ✦ *Bis zur vollständigen Heilung solltest du dich noch schonen.* ✦ *Ich bin noch nicht vollständig überzeugt davon.* ⊖komplett

Voll·tref·fer ['fɔltrɛfɐ] der <–s, –> *(also fig)* (direct) hit ◊ *Die Fabrik wurde im Krieg durch einen Volltreffer zerstört.* ✦ *Dieses Buch ist der absolute Volltreffer!*

voll·zäh·lig ['fɔltsɛːlɪç] adj *no comp/superl* complete ◊ *eine vollzählige Mannschaft* ✦ *Es fehlt nur noch Tom, dann sind wir vollzählig.* um vollzähliges Erscheinen bitten ask everyone to attend ⊖komplett adv *Die Mannschaft hatte sich vollzählig zum Training versammelt.* Every one of the team was present for training. vollzählig erscheinen turn out in full strength

vom [fɔm] contract *von + dem* **1.** from (the) ◊ *Er kommt gerade vom Arzt.* → von **2.** *with nominalized verbs, not to be split* from ◊ *vom Arbeiten müde sein* vom Radfahren begeistert sein be enthusiastic about cycling **3.** *in certain idioms, not to be split: look up the relevant idiom* ◊ *vom Regen in die Traufe kommen*

② **von** [fɔn] prep +dat **1.** from ◊ *Eine Kaltluftfront nähert sich von Norden.* ✦ *Von oben gesehen sieht alles so winzig aus.* ✦ *Das Baby ist vom Wickeltisch gefallen.* ✦ *ein Gesetz von 1910* von ... ab/ an/auf from ... (on) ◊ *Von hier ab wird der Weg steiler.* ✦ *Das habe ich von Anfang an gewusst!* ✦ *Das muss man von klein auf üben.* von ... aus from ... ◊ *Von der Hütte aus sind es noch zwei Kilometer.* von ... bis/nach/zu/auf ... from ... to ... ◊ *Wie weit ist es von der Fußgängerzone bis zum Zoo?* ✦ *Wir brauchen etwa eine Stunde von hier nach München.* Das kann man von heute

auf morgen lernen. You can't learn that overnight. von ... bis ... from ... until ... ◊ *Der Unterricht dauert von acht bis eins.* **2.** *in response to the question 'where?'* nördlich/östlich/links etc. von jdm/etw. to the north/east/left etc. of sb/sth ◊ *Italien liegt südlich von hier.* links/rechts von mir/ dir etc. on my/your etc. left/right **3.** of ◊ *der Verkauf von Waren* ✦ *ein Gewicht von zehn Gramm* ✦ *Sie lernte im Alter von sechs Jahren schwimmen.* ✦ *Exbundespräsident Richard von Weizsäcker* **4.** off ◊ *Kriegst du den Deckel von der Dose ab?* ✦ *Er nahm die Jacke vom Haken und zog sie an.* **5.** by ◊ *ein Krimi von Martha Grimes* ✦ *Er wurde vom Zug überfahren.* ✦ *Von wem wurde das Haus gebaut?* **6.** because of, by ◊ *Sie war von der Wanderung völlig erschöpft.* ✦ *Das kommt von deiner Faulheit!*

◉ **von jdm aus** as far as sb is concerned ◊ *Geh von mir aus früher nach Hause.* Von mir aus! If you like/want. **von sich aus** of your own accord

② **vor**[1] [foːɐ] prep **1.** *with acc when expressing motion towards a place, with dat when there is no or undirected motion* in front of ◊ *Er fuhr vor mir her, um mir den Weg zu zeigen.* ✦ *Er setzte sich vor den Fernseher.* ✦ *Er hat sie vor versammelter Mannschaft kritisiert.* Am nächsten Tag stand er vor unserer Haustür. The next day, he turned up at our door. die Vorhänge vors Fenster ziehen draw the curtains ⊖hinter **2.** *with acc when expressing motion towards a place, with dat when there is no or undirected motion* outside (of) ◊ *vor die Tür gehen* ✦ *Kurz vor der Stadt lag ein schöner Campingplatz.* ⊖in **3.** *in response to the question 'when?'* +dat ago, before ◊ *Ich habe ihn erst vor zwei Wochen getroffen.* ✦ *Vor langer Zeit lebte einmal ein König.* heute/morgen vor einer Woche etc. a week etc. ago today/tomorrow **4.** *in response to the question 'when?'* +dat *(when giving the time)* fünf vor zehn five to ten zehn vor halb twenty (minutes) past ⊖nach **5.** +dat ahead of, in front of ◊ *Er ging vor mir durchs Ziel.* ✦ *Wie viele sind denn noch vor dir dran?* Vorrang vor etw. haben take precedence over sth **6.** +dat *(giving a reason for an action or emotional state)* with ◊ *Er zitterte vor Angst.* ✦ *Ihr Gesicht war rot vor Wut.* Vor lauter Arbeit habe ich ganz vergessen, dich anzurufen. I was working so hard that I forgot to call you. **7.** *in combination with certain ns/adjs/verbs, translation varies* +dat Angst vor jdm/etw. haben be afraid of sb/sth Achtung/ Respekt vor jdm/etw. haben have respect sb/sth Warnung vor dem Hunde! Beware of the dog! vor jdm/etw. fliehen run away from sb/sth

vor[2] [foːɐ] adv forwards ◊ *einen Schritt vor machen* Freiwillige vor! Volunteers, one pace forward! ⊖zurück

◉ **vor sich hin 1.** vor sich hin dösen/rosten/vegetieren snooze/rust/vegetate away **2.** to oneself

Vor·an·mel·dung ['foːɐˌanmɛldʊŋ] die <–, –en> booking ◊ *Sprechstunde nur mit telefonischer Voranmeldung.* ✦ *Für einen Platz im Wohnheim gibt es schon viele Voranmeldungen.*

② **vo·raus** [fo'raʊs, 'foːraʊs] adv ahead ◊ *Volle Kraft voraus!* ✦ *Leonardo da Vinci war seiner Zeit weit voraus.* Er sprang mit dem Kopf voraus ins Wasser. He dived head first into the water. ⊖zurück

ⓥ **im Voraus** in advance ◊ *Er zahlte das Zimmer für eine Woche im Voraus.* ✦ *Vielen Dank im Voraus!* ⊝im Nachhinein

vo·raus|ge·hen [fo'raosgeːən] <geht voraus, ging voraus, ist vorausgegangen> ⟨intr v⟩ **1.** ⟨+dat⟩ go ahead ◊ *Geh schon mal voraus, ich komme gleich nach.* ✦ *Ich gehe (euch) voraus und zeige euch den Weg.* ⊝vorgehen **2.** ⟨+dat⟩ precede ◊ *Dem Frühling war ein harter Winter vorausgegangen.*

vo·raus·ge·setzt [fo'raosɡəzɛtst] *past p of* voraussetzen ⟨conjunc⟩ provided ◊ *Du kannst morgen anfangen, vorausgesetzt, du hast Zeit.* ✦ *Wir schaffen täglich 100 Kilometer, immer vorausgesetzt, dass das Wetter hält.*

Vo·raus·sa·ge [fo'raoszaːɡə] die <-, –n> eine Voraussage (über etw. ⟨acc⟩) a prediction (of/about sth) ◊ *Eine zuverlässige Voraussage über die Auswirkungen dieser Krise ist nicht möglich.*; *(for the weather)* eine Voraussage (für etw.) a forecast (for sth) ◊ *Und nun die Voraussagen für das Wochenende: ...* ⊝Vorhersage

vo·raus|se·hen [fo'raoszeːən] <sieht voraus, sah voraus, hat vorausgesehen> ⟨tr v⟩ foresee ◊ *Er sah seinen eigenen Tod voraus.* ✦ *Es war doch vorauszusehen, dass das passiert!* ⊝vorhersehen

vo·raus|set·zen [fo'raosˌzɛtsn̩] <setzt voraus, setzte voraus, hat vorausgesetzt> ⟨tr v⟩ **1.** assume ◊ *Dieses Wissen setze ich als bekannt voraus.* ✦ *Ihr Einverständnis vorausgesetzt, geben wir das so in Auftrag.* etw. stillschweigend/als selbstverständlich voraussetzen take sth for granted ⊝annehmen **2.** require ◊ *Wir setzen perfekte Englischkenntnisse voraus.* ⊝verlangen

ⓥ **Vo·raus·set·zung** [fo'raosˌzɛtsʊŋ] die <-, –en> **1.** condition ◊ *Hier wurden ideale Voraussetzungen für uns geschaffen.* ✦ *Unter solchen Voraussetzungen wirst du das kaum schaffen.* unter der Voraussetzung, dass on condition that; *(necessity)* eine Voraussetzung (für etw.) a prerequisite (for sth) die Voraussetzungen erfüllen meet the requirements ⊝Bedingung **2.** assumption ◊ *Du gehst da von völlig falschen Voraussetzungen aus.* ⊝Annahme

vo·raus·sicht·lich [fo'raosˌzɪçtlɪç] ⟨adv⟩ probably ◊ *Der Zug wird voraussichtlich pünktlich hier eintreffen.* ⟨adj⟩ only before ns anticipated, expected ◊ *Können Sie uns die voraussichtliche Höhe der Kosten bereits nennen?*

ⓥ **vor·bei** [foːɐ̯'bae] ⟨adv⟩ **1.** vorbei sein be over ◊ *Keine Angst, der Schmerz ist gleich vorbei!* ✦ *Zwischen uns ist es aus und vorbei!* vorbei ist vorbei what's past is past **2.** ein/zwei Uhr vorbei past one/two o' clock, gone one/two o' clock **3.** (an jdm/etw.) vorbei past (sb/sth) ◊ *Er wurde an mir vorbei nach vorne geschleudert.*

ⓥ **vor·bei|fah·ren** [foːɐ̯'baefaːrən] <fährt vorbei, fuhr vorbei, ist vorbeigefahren> ⟨intr v⟩ **1.** drive past, go past ◊ *Wir fuhren an einer Kirche vorbei.* **2.** *(fam)* bei jdm vorbeifahren stop off at sb's place ◊ *Soll ich nach dem Kino bei dir vorbeifahren?*

ⓥ **vor·bei|kom·men** [foːɐ̯'baekɔmən] <kommt vorbei, kam vorbei, ist vorbeigekommen> ⟨intr v⟩ **1.** pass ◊ *Kommen wir noch an einer Tankstelle vorbei?* **2.** drop in, come by ◊ *Komm doch morgen auf einen Kaffee vorbei!*

ⓥ **vor|be·rei·ten** ['foːɐ̯bəraetn̩] <bereitet vor,

bereitete vor, hat vorbereitet> ⟨tr v⟩ prepare ◊ *Er bereitet gerade sein Comeback vor.* ✦ *Die Reise war sorgfältig vorbereitet.* jdn/sich (auf etw. ⟨acc⟩) vorbereiten prepare sb/yourself (for sth) ◊ *sich gründlich auf eine Prüfung vorbereiten* ✦ *Ich bin auf alles vorbereitet.*

Vor·be·rei·tung ['foːɐ̯bəraetʊŋ] die <-, –en> Vorbereitung (auf etw. ⟨acc⟩/für etw.) preparation (for sth) ◊ *Eine Neuauflage ist bereits in Vorbereitung.* ✦ *Vorbereitungen für etw. treffen* ✦ *eine Aufgabensammlung zur Vorbereitung aufs Abitur*

vor·be·straft ['foːɐ̯bəʃtraːft] ⟨adj⟩ with a previous conviction, with previous convictions ◊ *Da er nicht vorbestraft war, kam er auf Bewährung frei.* ✦ *ein bereits wegen Körperverletzung vorbestrafter Angeklagter* einschlägig vorbestraft sein have previous convictions for a similar offence

vor|beu·gen ['foːɐ̯bɔøɡn̩] <beugt vor, beugte vor, hat vorgebeugt> ⟨intr v⟩ (einer Sache ⟨dat⟩) vorbeugen prevent (sth) ◊ *Wie kann man dem Missbrauch von Daten vorbeugen?* ⟨ref v⟩ sich vorbeugen lean forward, bend forward ◊ *Er beugte sich vor, um sein Gesicht im Spiegel zu betrachten.* ⟨tr v⟩ bend (forward) ◊ *Er beugte den Kopf vor und schaute aus dem Fenster.*

Vor·bild ['foːɐ̯bɪlt] das <-(e)s, –er> example, model ◊ *Das Management wurde nach japanischem Vorbild gestaltet.* ✦ *Du bist deiner Schwester kein gutes Vorbild.*; *(ideal)* role model ◊ *Albert Einstein ist sein großes Vorbild.* sich ⟨dat⟩ jdn/etw. zum Vorbild nehmen take sb/sth as a model, model yourself on sb/sth

vor|brin·gen ['foːɐ̯brɪŋən] <bringt vor, brachte vor, hat vorgebracht> ⟨tr v⟩ say ◊ *Einwände/Bedenken/Argumente vorbringen* ✦ *Was hast du zu deiner Entschuldigung vorzubringen?* ⊝vortragen

ⓥ **vor·de·re** ['foːɐ̯dərə] ⟨adj⟩ only before ns <ein vorderer ..., eine vordere ..., ein vorderes ...> front ◊ *Wir verließen das Haus durch den vorderen Eingang.*; *(in a competition)* die vorderen Plätze the top places die vorderste Reihe the front/first row an vorderster Front kämpfen fight right on the front line ⊝hintere

Vor·der·grund ['foːɐ̯dɐɡrʊnt] der <-(e)s, Vordergründe> **1.** *(fig)* im Vordergrund stehen be prominent/to the fore in den Vordergrund rücken/treten come to the fore etw. in den Vordergrund stellen give priority to sth ◊ *Du musst die positiven Aspekte mehr in den Vordergrund stellen.* sich in den Vordergrund drängen/schieben/spielen push yourself forward ⊝Hintergrund **2.** foreground ◊ *Was ist im Vordergrund des Bildes zu sehen?* ⊝Hintergrund

vor|drän·geln ['foːɐ̯drɛŋl̩n] <drängelt sich vor, drängelte sich vor, hat sich vorgedrängelt> ⟨ref v⟩ sich vordrängeln jump the queue ◊ *Er drängelte sich einfach vor.*

vor|drin·gen ['foːɐ̯drɪŋən] <dringt vor, drang vor, ist vorgedrungen> ⟨intr v⟩ advance ◊ *Das Feuer drang bis zu den Nachbarhäusern vor.* ✦ *Der Feind konnte bis zur Grenze vordringen.*

vor·ei·lig ['foːɐ̯aelɪç] ⟨adj, adv⟩ rash(ly) ◊ *voreilige Schlüsse ziehen* ✦ *Ihre Reaktion erwies sich als voreilig.* ✦ *Ich will nicht voreilig urteilen.*

vor|ent·hal·ten ['foːɐ̯ʔɛnthaltn̩] <enthält vor, enthielt vor, hat vorenthalten> ⟨tr v⟩ jdm etw. vor-

enthalten withhold sth from sb ◊ *Sie haben uns wichtige Informationen vorenthalten.* ⊖verweigern ⊕gewähren

vor·erst ['foːɐ̯|eˑɐ̯st] ⟨adv⟩ for the time being/ present ◊ *Die Grenze bleibt vorerst geschlossen.* ⊖vorläufig, fürs Erste, zunächst

Vor·fahr ['foːɐ̯faˑɐ̯] der ⟨-en, –en⟩, **Vor·fah·rin** ['foːɐ̯faːrɪn] die ⟨-, –nen⟩ *most pl* ancestor ◊ *Meine Vorfahren sind vor hundert Jahren hierher gezogen.* ⊖Nachkomme

② **Vor·fahrt** ['foːɐ̯faˑɐ̯t] die ⟨-⟩ *no pl* right of way ◊ *Wer hat hier Vorfahrt?* ✦ *Zu dem Unfall kam es, weil er mir die Vorfahrt nahm.*

Vor·fall ['foːɐ̯fal] der ⟨-(e)s, Vorfälle⟩ incident ◊ *Der Richter ließ sich den Vorfall von einem Zeugen schildern.*

vor|fin·den ['foːɐ̯fɪndn̩] ⟨findet vor, fand vor, hat vorgefunden⟩ ⟨tr v⟩ find ◊ *Bakterien finden dort ideale Lebensbedingungen vor.* ✦ *Ich fand sie weinend in ihrem Zimmer vor.*

vor|füh·ren ['foːɐ̯fyːrən] ⟨führt vor, führte vor, hat vorgeführt⟩ ⟨tr v⟩ **1.** perform ◊ *Die Gruppe führt Volkstänze vor.* ✦ *Der Physiklehrer hat heute ein Experiment vorgeführt.*; *(a film, slides etc.)* show ◊ *Hast du deine neue Frisur schon deinen Eltern vorgeführt?* **2.** demonstrate ◊ *Sie führte die verschiedenen Möglichkeiten anhand von Beispielen vor.* **3.** jdn/etw. jdm/irgendwo vorführen bring sb/ sth (forward) to sb/somewhere ◊ *sein Auto beim TÜV vorführen* jdn dem Richter vorführen bring sb before the judge

Vor·füh·rung ['foːɐ̯fyːrʊŋ] die ⟨-, –en⟩ performance, show ◊ *Die Vorführung am Abend ist bereits ausverkauft.*

Vor·ga·be ['foːɐ̯gaːbə] die ⟨-, –n⟩ *most pl* guideline ◊ *Welche gesetzlichen Vorgaben müssen erfüllt werden?* ✦ *kleine Vorgaben brauchen*

Vor·gang ['foːɐ̯gaŋ] der ⟨-(e)s, Vorgänge⟩ process ◊ *Im Gehirn laufen komplexe chemische Vorgänge ab.*; incident ◊ *Er wollte sich zu diesen Vorgängen nicht äußern.*

Vor·gän·ger ['foːɐ̯gɛŋɐ] der ⟨-s, –⟩, **Vor·gän·ge·rin** ['foːɐ̯gɛŋərɪn] die ⟨-, –nen⟩ predecessor ◊ *Ihr Vorgänger im Amt war 1998 verstorben.* ✦ *Anders als sein Vorgänger ist dieses Modell mit vier Airbags ausgestattet.* ⊖Nachfolger

Vor·gar·ten ['foːɐ̯gaˑɐ̯tn̩] der ⟨-s, Vorgärten⟩ front garden

vor|ge·ben ['foːɐ̯geːbm̩] ⟨gibt vor, gab vor, hat vorgegeben⟩ ⟨tr v⟩ **1.** (jdm) etw. vorgeben predetermine sth (for sb), preset sth (for sb) ◊ *Der Schlagzeuger gab der Band den Rhythmus vor.* ✦ *Wer gibt die Regeln vor?* ⊖festlegen, festsetzen **2.** *+infinitive construction with 'zu'* pretend ◊ *Sie gab vor, ihn nicht bemerkt zu haben.* ✦ *Um nicht in die Schule zu müssen, gab er vor, krank zu sein.* ⊖behaupten, vortäuschen **3.** SPORT jdm etw. vorgeben give sb sth ◊ *Ich gebe dir fünf Meter/ einen Vorsprung vor.*

vor|ge·hen ['foːɐ̯geːən] ⟨geht vor, ging vor, ist vorgegangen⟩ ⟨intr v⟩ **1.** happen ◊ *Er nahm nicht mehr wahr, was um ihn herum vorging.* in jdm/etw. vorgehen go on inside sb/sth ◊ *Sag mal, was geht eigentlich in deinem Kopf vor?* ⊖geschehen **2.** proceed ◊ *Wir sollten in Zukunft vorsichtiger vorgehen.* ✦ *Wie gehst du vor, wenn du so ein*

Projekt entwickelst? ⊖handeln **3.** gegen jdn/etw. vorgehen take action against sb/sth ◊ *Kann man gegen diese Entscheidung gerichtlich vorgehen?* ✦ *Wir müssen härter gegen Gewalttäter vorgehen.* **4.** be fast ◊ *Ich glaube, meine Uhr geht vor.* ⊖nachgehen **5.** have priority, come first ◊ *Im Moment muss bei dir die Schule vorgehen!* ⊖Vorrang haben **6.** *(fam)* go on ahead ◊ *Geh schon mal vor, ich komme gleich nach.* ✦ *Geh du bitte vor, du kennst den Weg.* ⊖vorausgehen

Vor·ge·setz·te ['foːɐ̯gəzɛtstə] der/die ⟨-n, die Vorgesetzten⟩ *but: ein Vorgesetzter/eine Vorgesetzte* superior ◊ *Sie ist meine direkte Vorgesetzte.* ✦ *Als Vorgesetzter trage ich die Verantwortung.* ⊖Chef ⊕Mitarbeiter *box@* Substantivierung

② **vor·ges·tern** ['foːɐ̯gɛstɐn] ⟨adv⟩ the day before yesterday ◊ *Vorgestern war ich in Bonn.* ✦ *Ich habe ihn seit vorgestern nicht mehr gesehen.*

② **vor|ha·ben** ['foːɐ̯haːbm̩] ⟨hat vor, hatte vor, hat vorgehabt⟩ ⟨tr v⟩ plan ◊ *Hast du am Wochenende schon etwas vor?* ✦ *Ich hatte eigentlich vor, früh ins Bett zu gehen.* Was hast du mit dem Geld vor? What are you going to do with the money? fest vorhaben, etw. zu tun be determined to do sth

vor|hal·ten ['foːɐ̯haltn̩] ⟨hält vor, hielt vor, hat vorgehalten⟩ ⟨tr v⟩ **1.** jdm etw. vorhalten reproach sb with sth, accuse sb of sth ◊ *Er musste sich mangelnde Sorgfalt vorhalten lassen.* ⊖vorwerfen **2.** hold up in front of sth ◊ *Halte die Hand vor, wenn du gähnst!* mit vorgehaltener Waffe/Pistole at gunpoint ⟨intr v⟩ *(fam)* last ◊ *Das muss jetzt aber mal eine Zeit lang vorhalten!* ⊖genügen, reichen, ausreichen

vor·han·den [foːɐ̯'handn̩] ⟨adj⟩ *no comp/superl* available, existing ◊ *Ist dafür noch genug Geld vorhanden?* ✦ *Die vorhandenen Parkplätze reichen nicht aus.*

② **Vor·hang** ['foːɐ̯haŋ] der ⟨-(e)s, Vorhänge⟩ curtain ◊ *Als es dunkel wurde, schloss sie die Vorhänge.* ✦ *Das Kind versteckte sich hinter dem Vorhang.* ⊛ der Eiserne Vorhang the Iron Curtain

② **vor·her** ['foːɐ̯heːɐ̯] ⟨adv⟩ beforehand, in advance ◊ *„Ich gebe meinen Aufsatz jetzt ab.“ — „Lies ihn dir vorher noch einmal durch.“* ✦ *Er hat seinen Besuch nicht vorher angekündigt.* ⊖davor, zuvor ⊕nachher

vor|herr·schen ['foːɐ̯hɛɐ̯ʃn̩] ⟨herrscht vor, herrschte vor, hat vorgeherrscht⟩ ⟨intr v⟩ predominate ◊ *In unseren Wäldern herrschen Fichten vor.* ⊖überwiegen, dominieren

Vor·her·sa·ge [foːɐ̯'heːɐ̯gaːgə] die ⟨-, –n⟩ forecast ◊ *„Wie ist die Vorhersage für morgen?“ — „Weiterhin regnerisch.“* eine Vorhersage (über etw. ⟨acc⟩) a prediction (of/about sth) ◊ *Ihre Vorhersage hat sich nicht bestätigt.* ⊖Voraussage

vor·her|se·hen [foːɐ̯'heːɐ̯zeːən] ⟨sieht vorher, sah vorher, hat vorhergesehen⟩ ⟨tr v⟩ foresee ◊ *Diese Entwicklung konnte niemand vorhersehen.* ✦ *Das Ende kam schneller als vorhergesehen.* ⊖absehen, voraussehen

② **vor·hin** [foːɐ̯'hɪn, '– –] ⟨adv⟩ **1.** a short time/while ago ◊ *Wo ist denn die Zeitung?* Sie war doch vorhin noch da? ✦ *Das sagtest du vorhin schon.* ⊖gerade, eben **2.** *(fam)* der Mann von vorhin the man who we saw/spoke to etc. a short time ago/

just now

② **vo·ri·ge** ['foːrɪgə] [adj] *no comp/superl, only before ns* <ein voriger ..., eine vorige ..., ein voriges ...> last, previous ◊ *Vorige Nacht war es sehr kalt.* ✦ *In der vorigen Saison lief das Geschäft besser.* ⊖nächste

Vor·jahr ['foːjaːʳ] das <-(e)s, –e> previous year, last year ◊ *Im Vorjahr war die Ernte besser.*

② **vor|kom·men** ['foːkɔmən] <kommt vor, kam vor, ist vorgekommen> [intr v] **1.** happen, occur ◊ *Es kam oft vor, dass er unpünktlich war.* ✦ *Besonders häufig kommen solche Unfälle bei Nebel vor.* ⊖geschehen, passieren **2.** be found ◊ *Dieser Schmetterling kommt bei uns nicht vor.* ✦ *In Märchen kommen oft Hexen vor.* ⊖auftreten **3.** jdm bekannt/lächerlich/seltsam etc. vorkommen seem familiar/ridiculous/strange etc. to sb ◊ *Die Geschichte kommt mir bekannt vor.* ✦ *Es kommt mir so vor, als hätte sich irgendetwas verändert.* ⊖erscheinen **4.** sich [dat] albern/schlau/wichtig etc. vorkommen feel silly/clever/important etc. ◊ *Er kam sich vor wie ein kompletter Idiot.* **5.** aus/hinter/unter/zwischen etw. [dat] vorkommen come out from behind/under/between sth ◊ *Die Sonne kommt wieder hinter den Wolken vor.*

Vor·la·ge ['foːlaːgə] die <-, –n> **1.** *no pl* presentation ◊ *Gegen Vorlage dieses Gutscheins erhalten Sie ein Gratisgetränk.* **2.** model ◊ *Diese Ereignisse dienten ihm als Vorlage für einen Roman.*

② **vor·läu·fig** ['foːlɔyfɪç] [adv] *no comp/superl* for the time being ◊ *Das ist die vorläufig letzte Folge der Serie.* ✦ *Du kannst vorläufig bei uns wohnen.* jdn vorläufig festnehmen detain sb temporarily ⊖vorerst [adj] temporary, provisional ◊ *Damit hat die Krise ihren vorläufigen Höhepunkt erreicht.* ✦ *Der Zeitplan ist nur vorläufig.*

vor|le·gen ['foːgleːgn̩] <legt vor, legte vor, hat vorgelegt> [tr v] **1.** present ◊ *Sie legte ein ärztliches Attest vor.* ✦ *Ergebnisse/einen Entwurf vorlegen* **2.** *(a record performance, high speed)* set

vor|le·sen ['foːgleːzn̩] <liest vor, las vor, hat vorgelesen> [tr+intr v] (jdm) (etw.) vorlesen read (sb) (sth) ◊ *Mama, liest du mir eine Geschichte vor?* ✦ *Was steht denn da? Lies doch mal vor!*

Vor·le·sung ['foːgleːzʊŋ] die <-, –en> lecture ◊ *Er hielt eine einstündige Vorlesung über Thomas Mann.*

vor·letz·te ['foːgletstə] [adj] *no comp/superl* <ein vorletzter ..., eine vorletzte ..., ein vorletztes ...> last but one, penultimate ◊ *Erst im vorletzten Kapitel erfährt man, wer sie ist.* vorletzte Woche/Nacht etc. the week/night before last

Vor·lie·be ['foːgliːbə] die <-, –n> preference, liking ◊ *Sie hat eine Vorliebe für Schokolade.* etw. mit Vorliebe tun prefer to do sth ◊ *Im Herbst arbeitet sie mit Vorliebe im Garten.*

vor|lie·gen ['foːgliːgn̩] <liegt vor, lag vor, hat vorgelegen> [intr v] **1.** [+dat] *(offers, results, documents)* be there, be available ◊ *Liegen die neuesten Zahlen schon vor?*; *(book)* be available jdm vorliegen be with sb, be/lie on sb's desk ◊ *Dem Staatsanwalt liegen neue Beweise vor.* im vorliegenden Fall in the present case **2.** *(error, illness, serious difficulties)* be (present), exist ◊ *Die Polizei stellte fest, dass keine Straftat vorlag.*

✦ *Hier muss ein Missverständnis vorliegen!* ✦ *Bei dem Patienten liegt ein Vitaminmangel vor.* **3.** etwas liegt gegen jdn vor *sb is a suspect* ◊ *Gegen Sie liegt nichts vor; Sie können gehen.* Gegen Sie liegt ein Haftbefehl vor! There is a warrant for your arrest! Was liegt gegen mich vor? What do I stand accused of?

vorm [foːm] [contract] *vor + dem (fam)* in front of ◊ *vorm Haus parken* Angst vorm Zahnarzt haben be afraid of the dentist → vor

vor|mer·ken ['foːmɛʳkn̩] <merkt vor, merkte vor, hat vorgemerkt> [tr v] jdn (für etw.) vormerken put sb down (for sth) ◊ *Ich habe Sie als Interessenten für die Wohnung vorgemerkt.* (sich [dat]) etw. vormerken make a note of sth ◊ *Ich habe mir den Termin vorgemerkt.*

Vor·mit·tag ['foːmɪtaːk] der <-(e)s, –e> morning ◊ *Morgen Vormittag soll es regnen.* ✦ *Am Vormittag schien die Sonne.* ✦ *im Lauf(e) des Vormittags*

vor·mit·tags ['foːmɪtaːks] [adv] in the morning ◊ *Vormittags sind die Kinder in der Schule.* ✦ *Er kam vormittags um zehn.*

② **vorn** [fɔʳn] [adv] **1.** at the front ◊ *Wir saßen ganz vorn, in der ersten Reihe.* ⊖hinten **2.** nach vorn to the front ◊ *Sieh beim Fahren nach vorn!* ⊖nach hinten **3.** da vorn just over there weiter vorn up ahead, a bit further on ⊖hinten **4.** von vorn from the front ◊ *Der Wind kam von vorn.* ✦ *Von vorn sieht das Haus recht hübsch aus.* ⊖von hinten **5.** von vorn from the beginning ◊ *Als er fertig war, fing er noch einmal von vorn an.* ✦ *Die Geschichte ist von vorn bis hinten gelogen.*

Vor·na·me ['foːnaːmə] der <-ns, –n> first/Christian name ◊ *Sie heißt mit zweitem Vornamen Maria.* ⊖Nachname, Familienname

vor·ne ['foːnə] [adv] → vorn

vor·nehm ['foːneːm] [adj, adv] **1.** exclusive(ly) ◊ *Die Gegend hier ist sehr vornehm.* ✦ *eine vornehme Villa* ✦ *vornehm wohnen*; *(clothes)* elegant(ly) ◊ *ein vornehm gekleideter Herr* ✦ *Im Smoking war er eine sehr vornehme Erscheinung.* **2.** *(also pej)* grand(ly) ◊ *Sein Auftritt wirkt sehr vornehm.* ✦ *Tu nicht so vornehm!* **3.** polite(ly) ◊ *vornehme Manieren* ✦ *Er hielt sich vornehm zurück.* ⊖fein, nobel [adj] distinguished, genteel ◊ *die vornehmsten Familien der Stadt*

vor|neh·men ['foːneːmən] <nimmt vor, nahm vor, hat vorgenommen> [tr v] *(form) (corrections, examinations, operations)* carry out, make ◊ *Änderungen an einem Text vornehmen* ✦ *Messungen vornehmen* ⊖durchführen [ref v] **1.** sich [dat] etw. vornehmen plan sth ◊ *Du hast dir dir aber viel Arbeit vorgenommen!* You really have taken on a lot of work there! ⊖beabsichtigen, planen **2.** *(fam)* sich [dat] jdn vornehmen give sb a talking-to

② **Vor·ort** ['foːʔɔʳt] der <-(e)s, –e> suburb ◊ *Wegen der hohen Mieten in der Stadt sind wir in einen Vorort gezogen.*

② **Vor·rang** ['foːraŋ] der <-(e)s> *no pl* pre-eminence ◊ *Sie wollte ihm den Vorrang in der Gruppe streitig machen.* Vorrang (vor jdm/etw.) priority (over sb/sth) ◊ *Sicherheit hat jetzt absoluten Vorrang vor allem anderen!* ✦ *Wir müssen diesem Projekt Vorrang einräumen.*

Vor·rat ['foːɡraːt] der <–(e)s, Vorräte> ein Vorrat (an etw. [dat]) a supply/stock (of sth) ◊ *Unser Vorrat an Holz reicht ein paar Jahre.* ✦ *Unsere Vorräte sind verbraucht.* etw. auf Vorrat kaufen/herstellen etc. stock up with/on sth ⊝Reserve

vor·rä·tig ['foːɡrɛːtɪç] [adj] no comp/superl in stock ◊ *Haben Sie diese Ware vorrätig?* ✦ *Die noch vorrätigen Äpfel sollten jetzt bald verkauft werden.*

vors [foːɐs] [contract] vor + das (fam) **1.** in front of ◊ *ein Schild vors Geschäft stellen* Gardinen vors Fenster ziehen draw the curtains → vor **2.** outside of ◊ *vors Haus gehen* → vor

Vor·satz ['foːɡzats] der <–es, Vorsätze> **1.** resolution, intention ◊ *Hast du gute Vorsätze fürs neue Jahr gefasst?* ⊝Absicht **2.** LAW mit/ohne Vorsatz with/without intent ◊ *Das Gericht entschied, der Beschuldigte habe mit Vorsatz gehandelt.*

vor·sätz·lich ['foːɡzɛtslɪç] [adj, adv] no comp/superl deliberate(ly) ◊ *ein vorsätzlicher Verstoß gegen die Regeln* ✦ *War das versehentlich oder vorsätzlich?* ✦ *Er hat vorsätzlich falsche Angaben gemacht.*; wilful(ly) ◊ *vorsätzliche Brandstiftung* ✦ *jdm vorsätzlich schaden* ⊝absichtlich, bewusst ⊝versehentlich

② **Vor·schlag** ['foːɡʃlaːk] der <–(e)s, Vorschläge> suggestion, proposal ◊ *Sie machte (uns) den Vorschlag, eine Pause einzulegen.* ✦ *Vorschlägen gegenüber aufgeschlossen sein* auf jds Vorschlag (hin) at sb's suggestion/proposal ⊝Anregung
⊛ **ein Vorschlag zur Güte** a conciliatory proposal

② **vor|schla·gen** ['foːɡʃlaːgn̩] <schlägt vor, schlug vor, hat vorgeschlagen> [trv] (jdm) etw. vorschlagen suggest/propose sth (to sb) ◊ *Er hat vorgeschlagen, dass wir einen Ausflug machen.* ✦ *Sie schlug ihm vor, ein Buch über seine Erlebnisse zu schreiben.* jdn für/als etw. vorschlagen propose sb for/as sth ◊ *Sie ist für den Friedensnobelpreis vorgeschlagen worden.* ✦ *Wer ist als Kandidat vorgeschlagen?*

② **Vor·schrift** ['foːɡʃrɪft] die <–, –en> regulation, rule ◊ *Ich muss mich an meine Vorschriften halten.* nach Vorschrift to rule ◊ *streng nach Vorschrift vorgehen* Von dir lasse ich mir keine Vorschriften machen! I don't take orders from you!

vor|se·hen ['foːɡzeːən] <sieht vor, sah vor, hat vorgesehen> [trv] **1.** plan ◊ *Was hast du zum Mittagessen vorgesehen?* ✦ *Das Treffen findet heute wie vorgesehen statt.* jdn/etw. für/als etw. vorsehen designate sb/sth for/as sth ◊ *Wer ist für diesen Posten vorgesehen?* **2.** provide for ◊ *Das Gesetz sieht für Brandstiftung Haftstrafen bis zu 15 Jahren vor.* ✦ *Ist dieser Fall im Vertrag vorgesehen?* [ref v] sich (vor jdm/etw.) vorsehen be careful (of sb/sth), be wary (of sb/sth) ◊ *Sieh dich vor, dass du dich nicht verrätst!* ✦ *Du musst dich vor ihm vorsehen, er ist gefährlich.* ⊝sich in Acht nehmen

② **Vor·sicht** ['foːɡzɪçt] die <–> no pl care, caution ◊ *In dieser Situation ist äußerste Vorsicht geboten.*; (exclamation) Vorsicht! Look out!; (on signs) Danger! ◊ *Vorsicht, Hochspannung!*

vor·sich·tig ['foːɡzɪçtɪç] [adj, adv] careful(ly), cautious(ly) ◊ *Sei bitte vorsichtig!* ✦ *ein vorsichtiger Autofahrer* ✦ *vorsichtiger Optimismus* ✦ *Wir müssen mit unseren Ressourcen vorsichtiger umgehen.*

Vor·sil·be ['foːɡzɪlbə] die <–, –n> prefix ⊝Präfix

Vor·sit·zen·de ['foːɡzɪtsn̩də] der/die <–n, die Vorsitzenden> but: ein Vorsitzender/eine Vorsitzende chairman, chairwoman

Vor·spei·se ['foːɡʃpaɛzə] die <–, –n> starter, hors d'oeuvre ◊ *Als Vorspeise gab es eine Suppe.* ⊝Nachspeise, Nachtisch, Dessert

Vor·sprung ['foːɡʃprʊŋ] der <–(e)s, Vorsprünge> **1.** lead ◊ *Er wurde mit zwei Sekunden Vorsprung Erster.* jdm einen Vorsprung geben give sb a start ⊝Rückstand **2.** (on a rock-face) ledge

Vor·stand ['foːɡʃtant] der <–(e)s, Vorstände> (of a company) board of directors ◊ *Sie wurde in den Vorstand gewählt.*; (of an organization) executive committee

② **vor|stel·len** ['foːɡʃtɛlən] <stellt vor, stellte vor, hat vorgestellt> [trv] **1.** jdn/sich (jdm) vorstellen introduce sb/yourself (to sb) ◊ *Darf ich mich vorstellen? Mein Name ist Tom Martin.* ✦ *Er stellte sie als seine Verlobte vor.* **2.** put the clock forward ◊ *Die Uhren werden heute eine Stunde vorgestellt.* ⊝zurückstellen [ref v] **1.** sich vorstellen come/go for an interview ◊ *Darf ich mich als freie Übersetzerin bei Ihnen vorstellen?* **2.** sich [dat] etw. vorstellen imagine sth ◊ *Ich kann mir gar nicht vorstellen, wie das gehen soll.* ✦ *Stell dir vor, ich habe es tatsächlich geschafft!* **3.** sich [dat] etw. vorstellen think of sth, have sth in mind ◊ *Ich habe mir vorgestellt, dass wir nach der Arbeit schön essen gehen.* ✦ *Welchen Preis hast du dir dafür vorgestellt?* **4.** sich [dat] etw. unter etw. [dat] vorstellen understand sth by sth ◊ *Das ist nicht das, was ich mir unter Gerechtigkeit vorstelle! Ich kann mir unter diesem Begriff nichts vorstellen.* This term doesn't mean anything to me.

② **Vor·stel·lung** ['foːɡʃtɛlʊŋ] die <–, –en> **1.** eine Vorstellung (von etw./jdm) an idea (of sth/sb) ◊ *Ich habe mir falsche Vorstellungen von dem Job gemacht.* sich [dat] keine Vorstellung machen have no idea ◊ *Du machst dir keine Vorstellung, wie langweilig das war!* jds Vorstellungen entsprechen be what sb had in mind **2.** (also fig) performance ◊ *Die Vorstellung war ausverkauft.* ✦ *Beim heutigen Rennen hat er eine ziemlich schwache Vorstellung geliefert.*; (at the cinema) showing **3.** introduction ◊ *die Begrüßung und Vorstellung der Gäste übernehmen*; (of a new product etc.) presentation **4.** imagination ◊ *Dieser Freund existiert nur in ihrer Vorstellung.* ✦ *Das geht über alle Vorstellung hinaus.* ⊝Fantasie

Vor·stel·lungs·ge·spräch ['foːɡʃtɛlʊŋsɡəʃprɛːç] das <–(e)s, –e> interview ◊ *zum Vorstellungsgespräch eingeladen werden*

vor|täu·schen ['foːɡtɔɡʃn̩] <täuscht vor, hat vorgetäuscht> [trv] (jdm) etw. vortäuschen feign sth (to sb) ◊ *Sie täuschte ihm Gleichgültigkeit vor.*; (a crime) fake ◊ *Der Raubüberfall war vorgetäuscht.*

② **Vor·teil** ['foːɡtaɛl] der <–(e)s, –e> **1.** advantage ◊ *Der große Vorteil (an) dieser Methode ist, dass man damit eine Sprache schneller lernt.* jdm gegenüber im Vorteil sein, sich jdm gegenüber im Vorteil befinden have an advantage over sb ⊝Vorzug, Plus ⊝Nachteil **2.** benefit ◊ *Sie ist immer nur auf ihren eigenen Vorteil bedacht.* ✦ *Er hat sich zu meinem Vorteil verrechnet.* ✦ *einen*

Vorteil aus etw. ziehen ⊖Nachteil, Schaden

ⓩ **Vor·trag** ['foːɐ̯traːk] der <-(e)s, Vorträge> talk, lecture ◊ *einen Vortrag über etw.* (acc) *halten* ✦ *Heute Abend gibt es einen Vortrag zum Thema „gesunde Ernährung".*

vor|tra·gen ['foːɐ̯traːɡn̩] <trägt vor, trug vor, hat vorgetragen> (tr v) **1.** (*a piece of music*) perform ◊ *Das Ensemble trug mittelalterliche Tänze vor.; (a poem)* recite ◊ *Er hat die „Bürgschaft" von Schiller auswendig vorgetragen.; (a song)* sing ⊖darbieten **2.** (*a request, doubts, demands*) (jdm) *etw.* vortragen present sth (to sb) ◊ *Er ging zum Lehrer und trug ihm die Bitte der Klasse vor.* ⊖etw. vorbringen

ⓩ **Vor·tritt** ['foːɐ̯trɪt] der <-(e)s> *no pl (always* jdm den Vortritt lassen*)* let sb go first ◊ *Er ließ ihr an der Kasse den Vortritt.*

vo·rü·ber·ge·hend [fo'ryːbɐɡeːənt] (adj, adv) *no comp/superl* temporary(-ily) ◊ *Das ist nur eine vorübergehende Erscheinung.* ✦ *Die Besserung ihres Zustands war leider nur vorübergehend.* ✦ *Wegen Umbau vorübergehend geschlossen!* ⊖dauerhaft

ⓩ **Vor·ur·teil** ['foːɐ̯ʊɐ̯taɛ̯l] das <-(e)s, -e> ein Vorurteil (gegen/über jdn/etw.) a prejudice (against/towards sb/sth) ◊ *Haben Sie etwa Vorurteile gegen Familien mit Kindern?* ✦ *Vorurteile abbauen*

Vor·ver·kauf ['foːɐ̯fɛkaɔ̯f] der <-(e)s, Vorverkäufe> advance sale ◊ *Habt ihr im Vorverkauf noch Karten bekommen?* ⊖Abendkasse

ⓩ **Vor·wahl** ['foːɐ̯vaːl] die <-, -en> **1.** dialling code ◊ *Welche Vorwahl hat Berlin?* ✦ *Die Vorwahl für Österreich ist 0043.* **2.** prefix number ◊ *Welche Vorwahl ist um diese Uhrzeit für Ferngespräche am günstigsten?* **3.** *most pl* POL preliminary election

Vor·wand ['foːɐ̯vant] der <-(e)s, Vorwände> pretext, excuse ◊ *Er blieb der Feier unter einem Vorwand fern.* ✦ *Das schlechte Wetter war ihr ein willkommener Vorwand, nicht im Garten zu arbeiten.* ⊖Ausrede

Vor·war·nung ['foːɐ̯varnʊŋ] die <-, -en> (advance) warning ◊ *Er schlug ihn ohne Vorwarnung nieder.*

ⓩ **vor·wärts** ['foːɐ̯vɛts] (adv) forward ◊ *Sie machte ein paar Schritte vorwärts.* ✦ *eine vorwärts weisende Entwicklung das Auto* vorwärts einparken park the car front first jdn/etw. vorwärts bringen allow sb/sth to make progress vorwärts gehen/kommen make progress ◊ *Zurzeit geht einfach nichts vorwärts.* ⊖rückwärts

vor|wei·sen ['foːɐ̯vaɛ̯zn̩] <weist vor, wies vor, hat vorgewiesen> (tr v) produce, show ◊ *Er musste an der Grenze seinen Pass vorweisen. etw.* vorweisen *können* have sth to show ◊ *Sie kann noch nicht viele Erfolge vorweisen.* ⊖vorzeigen

vor|wer·fen ['foːɐ̯vɛfn̩] <wirft vor, warf vor, hat vorgeworfen> (tr v) **1.** jdm etw. vorwerfen reproach

sb for sth, accuse sb of sth ◊ *Ihm wird vorgeworfen, Steuern hinterzogen zu haben.* ✦ *Ich habe mir nichts vorzuwerfen!* ⊖vorhalten **2.** *etw./jdn einem Tier (zum Fraß)* vorwerfen throw sth/sb to an animal (as food)

vor·wie·gend ['foːɐ̯viːɡn̩t, 'foːɐ̯viːɡənt] (adj, adv) *no comp/superl; when used as an adj, only before ns* main(ly), primary(-ily) ◊ *Das Wetter: vorwiegend heiter.* ✦ *Seine vorwiegende Tätigkeit bestand in Kundenkontakten.* ✦ *Das betrifft vorwiegend ältere Mitbürger.*

Vor·wort ['foːɐ̯vɔrt] das <-(e)s, -e or Vorwörter> foreword, preface

Vor·wurf ['foːɐ̯vʊrf] der <-(e)s> accusation ◊ *Sie wies alle Vorwürfe zurück.* jdm Vorwürfe/einen Vorwurf (wegen etw.) machen reproach sb (for sth) jdm etw. zum Vorwurf machen reproach sb with sth ◊ *Dass es nicht funktioniert hat, kann man ihm nicht zum Vorwurf machen!*

vor|zei·gen ['foːɐ̯tsaɛ̯ɡn̩] <zeigt vor, zeigte vor, hat vorgezeigt> (tr v) (jdm) etw. vorzeigen show sth (to sb) ◊ *Er musste den Polizisten seinen Ausweis vorzeigen.* ✦ *Zeig mal deine Hände vor: Sind die auch sauber?*

vor·zei·tig ['foːɐ̯tsaɛ̯tɪç] (adj, adv) *no comp/superl* premature(ly) ◊ *eine vorzeitige Pensionierung* ✦ *Die Ergebnisse wurden vorzeitig veröffentlicht.*

ⓩ **vor|zie·hen** ['foːɐ̯tsiːən] <zieht vor, zog vor, hat vorgezogen> (tr v) **1.** (jdm/etw.) jdn/etw. vorziehen prefer sb/sth (to sb/sth) ◊ *Schokolade ziehe ich anderen Süßigkeiten jederzeit vor.* ✦ *Sie zog es vor, nach Hause zu gehen.; (nepotistically)* favour sb/sth (over sb/sth), favor sb/sth (over sb/sth) ◊ *Ein Lehrer sollte keine Schüler haben, die er den anderen vorzieht.* ⊖jdn/etw. (gegenüber jdm/etw.) bevorzugen **2.** bring forward ◊ *Die geplante Steuerreform soll um ein Jahr vorgezogen werden.* vorgezogene Wahlen early elections **3.** give priority to ◊ *Weil er solche Schmerzen hatte, wurde er beim Arzt vorgezogen.* **4.** pull out from ◊ *Er zog eine Schachtel unter dem Bett vor.* **5.** (*a curtain*) draw ◊ *Es wird dunkel, zieh die Vorhänge vor!* ⊖zuziehen

Vor·zug ['foːɐ̯tsuːk] der <-(e)s, Vorzüge> **1.** advantage ◊ *Diese Lösung hat den großen Vorzug, preisgünstig zu sein.* ✦ *Ich weiß die Vorzüge meines Berufes zu schätzen.* ⊖Nachteil **2.** *no pl* jdm/etw. den Vorzug (vor jdm/etw.) geben give precedence to sb/sth (over sb/sth), prefer sb/sth (to sb/sth) ◊ *Welchem Kandidaten hat die Firma den Vorzug gegeben?*

vor·zugs·wei·se ['foːɐ̯tsuːksvaɛ̯zə] (adv) especially, particularly, preferably, primarily ◊ *Sie lernt vorzugsweise abends.* ✦ *Pilze findet man vorzugsweise im Wald.*

Vul·kan [vʊl'kaːn] der <-(e)s, -e> volcano ◊ *ein aktiver/erloschener Vulkan* ✦ *Der Vulkan spuckte glühende Lava.*

W

w, W [veː] das <–(s), –(s)> w, W ◊ *Dieses Wort
wird mit einem kleinen w/großen W geschrieben.* ♦
W wie Wilhelm
Waa·ge ['vaːɡə] die <–, –n> 1. scales ◊ *Wie
schwer bist du denn? Stell dich mal auf die
Waage!* 2. ASTROL, ASTRON Libra
◉ **etw. auf die Waage bringen** tip the scales at
sth ◊ *Er bringt fast 100 Kilo auf die Waage.* **sie
halten sich/einander die Waage** they balance
out/balance one another
② **waa·ge·recht** ['vaːɡərɛçt] [adj, adv] horizontal(ly) ◊
Die waagerechte Achse wird x-Achse genannt. ♦
Der Wasserspiegel ist immer waagerecht. ♦ *die
Arme waagerecht ausstrecken* ⊖senkrecht
② **wach** [vax] [adj] 1. *mostly after ns* awake ◊ *Bist du
schon wach?* ♦ *Er konnte sich nicht mehr wach
halten und schlief ein.* **wach werden** wake up jdn
wach machen wake sb up **jdn wach küssen/rütteln**
wake sb with a kiss/shake 2. alert, attentive ◊ *Sie
hat einen wachen Verstand.* ♦ *Seine Augen sind
wach und interessiert.*
◉ **eine Erinnerung wach halten** keep a memory
alive
Wa·che ['vaxə] die <–, –n> 1. *no pl* guard/sentry
duty ◊ *Wer übernimmt die nächste Wache?* **Wache
halten, auf Wache sein** be on guard/sentry duty
Wache schieben do sentry duty **Wache stehen**
stand on guard 2. guard, sentry ◊ *Vor dem Tor
standen zwei Wachen.* ♦ *Wache, führen Sie diesen
Mann ab!* ⊖Posten 3. police station ◊ *Er wurde
verhaftet und auf die Wache gebracht.* ⊖Revier
wa·chen ['vaxn̩] [intr v] +*haben* 1. über etw./jdn
wachen watch over sth/sb, keep an eye on sth/sb ◊
*Sie glaubt fest daran, dass ein Engel über sie
wacht.* ♦ *Das Bundesverfassungsgericht wacht
über die Einhaltung des Grundgesetzes.* 2. bei
jdm/an jds Seite wachen keep vigil at sb's bedside,
sit up with sb ◊ *Er wachte die ganze Nacht an
ihrer Seite.*
Wachs [vaks] das <–es, –e> *most sing* wax
◉ **Wachs in jds Hand/Händen sein** *(fig)* be
putty in sb's hands **weich wie Wachs** *(fig)*
become really amenable
wach·sam ['vaxzaːm] [adj, adv] vigilant(ly) ◊
wachsame Bürger ♦ *Sei etwas wachsamer!* ♦ *Er
beobachtete wachsam, was um ihn herum vorging.*
② **wach·sen** ['vaksn̩] <wächst, wuchs, ist gewachsen>
[intr v] grow ◊ *Du bist aber gewachsen!* ♦ *Bei
diesem Wetter wächst das Gras schnell.* ♦ *an einer
Aufgabe/Verantwortung wachsen* sich [dat] einen
Bart/die Haare wachsen lassen grow a beard/your
hair **jdm wächst ein Bart** sb grows a beard **einem
Tier wächst ein Geweih/Horn** an animal grows
antlers/a horn; *(number, danger, trouble also)*
increase ◊ *Der Umsatz ist im letzten Quartal um
15 Prozent gewachsen.* ♦ *Ihre Angst wuchs.*
② **wächst** [vɛksst] *pres of* wachsen
Wachs·tum ['vakstuːm] das <–s> *no pl* growth ◊

Kinder im Wachstum brauchen viel Kalzium. ♦ *das
Wachstum der Wirtschaft fördern*
Wäch·ter ['vɛçtɐ] der <–s, –>, **Wäch·te·rin**
['vɛçtərɪn] die <–, –nen> guard ◊ *Sie arbeitet als
Wächterin im Museum.* ♦ *Der Wächter schloss das
Tor ab.*
wa·cke·lig ['vakəlɪç] [adj] 1. wobbly ◊ *eine
wackelige Leiter* ♦ *Der Tisch ist wackelig.*; *(tooth)*
loose 2. *(fam)* shaky ◊ *Ihre finanzielle Lage war
wackelig.* ♦ *eine wackelige Koalition*
wa·ckeln ['vakl̩n] [intr v] +*baben* 1. wobble ◊ *Die
Leiter wackelte gefährlich, als er daran hochkletterte.*; *(tooth)* be loose 2. *(fam)* shake ◊ *Bei der
Explosion wackelten die Fensterscheiben.* ⊖beben
3. mit etw. wackeln wiggle your sth ◊ *Kannst du
mit den Ohren wackeln?* 4. *(fam, fig)* be shaky ◊
Wackelt Englands Thron? ♦ *Ihr Arbeitsplatz
wackelt bedrohlich.*
wack·lig ['vaklɪç] → wackelig
Wa·de ['vaːdə] die <–, –n> ANAT calf ◊ *Sie hatte
einen Krampf in der Wade.* ♦ *kräftige/dünne Waden*
② **Waf·fe** ['vafə] die <–, –n> 1. *(also fig)* weapon ◊
Tragen Sie eine Waffe bei sich? ♦ *atomare/biologische Waffen* ♦ *Ihre Schnelligkeit ist ihre stärkste
Waffe.* 2. gun, firearm ◊ *Mit vorgehaltener Waffe
forderte sie Geld.*
◉ **jdn mit seinen eigenen Waffen schlagen**
beat sb at their own game
Waf·fel ['vafl̩] die <–, –n> 1. waffle ◊ *Waffeln
backen* 2. wafer ◊ *eine Gebäckmischung mit
Keksen und Waffeln* 3. *(for ice cream)* cornet ◊
Wollen Sie das Eis im Becher oder in der Waffel?
⊖Eiswaffel
◉ **einen an der Waffel haben** *(slang)* be
crackers, be nuts
wa·gen ['vaːɡn̩] [tr v] +*baben* 1. etw. wagen;
wagen, etw. zu tun dare (to do) sth ◊ *Das hat
noch niemand gewagt!* ♦ *Du wagst es, mir zu
widersprechen?* 2. risk ◊ *Er wagte sein Leben für
sie.* ⊖riskieren [ref v] sich irgendwohin wagen
venture somewhere, dare (to) go somewhere ◊
Das Fotomodell wagte sich in die Welt des Pop. ♦
Wegen der Haie wagten sie sich nicht ins Wasser.
sich an etw. [acc] wagen tackle sth ◊ *Er wagte sich
an ein neues Projekt.* **sich nicht an etw.** [acc]
wagen not dare to tackle sth
② **Wa·gen** ['vaːɡn̩] der <–s, – *or regional* Wägen>
1. car ◊ *Der Wagen war ins Schleudern geraten.* ♦
aus dem Wagen steigen; *(for loads)* van 2. *(of a
train, tram)* carriage, car ◊ *ein Wagen der 1./2.
Klasse* 3. *(drawn by an animal)* wagon, cart,
coach ◊ *Die Pferde wurden vor den Wagen
gespannt.* 4. *(for babies)* pram, baby carriage,
pushchair, stroller ◊ *Das Baby lag in seinem
Wagen und schlief.*; *(for things)* (hand)cart ◊ *Er
zog einen Wagen voll Brennholz hinter sich her.*;
(for shopping, luggage) trolley
◉ **der Große Wagen** the Plough, the Big Dipper,

the Great Bear der Kleine Wagen the Little Dipper, the Little Bear

② **Wag·gon** [va'gɔŋ, va'gɔ̃ː] der <-s, -s> wagon, (freight) car, carriage ◊ *Ein weiterer Waggon wurde an den Zug angehängt.* ⊖Eisenbahnwagen

② **Wahl** [vaːl] die <-, -en> **1.** *most sing* choice ◊ *Das war eine gute Wahl!* ✦ *Er gewann eine Reise zu einem Ziel seiner Wahl.* ✦ jdn vor eine Wahl stellen give sb no choice ... ... is chosen eine/ seine Wahl treffen make a/your choice jdm die/ eine Wahl lassen leave (it up to) sb to choose jdm keine Wahl lassen leave sb no choice Welche Möglichkeiten stehen jetzt zur Wahl? Which possibilities do we have to choose from now? in die engere Wahl kommen be shortlisted **2.** POL election ◊ *freie Wahlen abhalten* ✦ *Nehmen Sie die Wahl an?* zur Wahl gehen go to vote sich zur Wahl stellen, zur Wahl antreten stand/run for election zur Wahl des Präsidenten antreten stand/run for president

◉ wer die Wahl hat, hat die Qual the greater the choice, the harder it is to decide

② **wäh·len** ['vɛːlən] [tr+intr v] +*haben* **1.** choose ◊ *Sie hat für ihr Gespräch einen günstigen Zeitpunkt gewählt.* ✦ *Ich wählte einen Ring als Geschenk.* unter/zwischen etw. [dat] wählen choose between sth ◊ *Sie können unter/zwischen fünf Farben wählen.* **2.** dial ◊ *Sie haben die falsche Nummer gewählt.* [tr v] +*haben* POL elect ◊ *Er wurde zum Kanzler gewählt.* ✦ *eine demokratisch gewählte Regierung* [intr v] +*haben* POL vote ◊ *Sie darf noch nicht wählen.*

wahl·los ['vaːlloːs] [adj, adv] no comp/superl indiscriminate(ly) ◊ *Die Anordnung war völlig wahllos.* ✦ *eine wahllose Aneinanderreihung* ✦ *Sie schossen wahllos in die Menge.*

Wahn·sinn ['vaːnzɪn] der <-s> no pl **1.** *(outd or emph)* MED insanity, madness ◊ *Sie war dem Wahnsinn nahe.* wie vom Wahnsinn gepackt like a madman/madwoman **2.** *(fam)* madness ◊ *Es wäre Wahnsinn, das zu tun.* **3.** *(fam, emph)* great, fantastic ◊ *Ich hab gewonnen! Ist das nicht (der reine) Wahnsinn?*

② **wahn·sin·nig** ['vaːnzɪnɪç] [adj] *(also fam)* insane, mad ◊ *Sie wurde fast wahnsinnig vor Schmerzen/ Furcht.* ✦ *Wer kam auf diese wahnsinnige Idee?* jdn wahnsinnig machen drive sb insane/mad ⊖verrückt [adj, adv] *when used as an adj, only before ns (fam, emph)* terrible(-ibly), incredible (-ibly) ◊ *Das hat uns wahnsinnigen Ärger gemacht.* ✦ *Sie freute sich wahnsinnig über das Geschenk.* wie wahnsinnig like mad ◊ *Sie schrie wie wahnsinnig.*

② **wahr** [vaːr] [adj] **1.** true ◊ *Ist das wirklich wahr?* ✦ *eine wahre Geschichte* wie wahr that's true wahr werden come true etw. wahr machen carry sth out ◊ *Er hat seine Drohung wahr gemacht und sie verlassen.* **2.** *only before ns* real ◊ *Du bist ein wahrer Freund!* ✦ *Es ist ein wahres Wunder, dass er überlebt hat.* ⊖richtig, echt **3.** *as a question tag, translation varies* Du bist nicht von hier, nicht wahr? You're not from round here, are you? Der Film war interessant, nicht wahr? The film was interesting, wasn't it?

◉ das darf/kann (doch) nicht wahr sein I don't believe it

② **wäh·rend¹** ['vɛːrənt] [conjunc] **1.** while ◊ *Während*

ich sprach, blickte er die ganze Zeit aus dem Fenster. **2.** whereas, while ◊ *Sie ist sehr groß, während ihre Brüder eher klein sind.* ⊖wohingegen

wäh·rend² ['vɛːrənt] [prep] +*gen* or *fam* +*dat* during ◊ *Ihr war während der Schwangerschaft oft übel.* ✦ *Während unserer Unterhaltung klingelte sein Handy.*

wahr·ha·ben ['vaːrhaːbm̩] <will wahrhaben, wollte wahrhaben, hat wahrhaben wollen> [tr v] *(always etw. wahrhaben wollen) mostly negated* want to accept sth ◊ *Sie will einfach nicht wahrhaben, dass alles vorbei ist.* ✦ *Er war kränker, als er es wahrhaben wollte.*

wahr·haf·tig [vaːrˈhaftɪç] [adv] *(lofty)* really ◊ *Es ist wahrhaftig ein Wunder, dass er überlebt hat.* ⊖wirklich

② **Wahr·heit** ['vaːrhaet] die <-, -en> truth ◊ *Sagt sie die Wahrheit?* in Wahrheit in reality ◊ *In Wahrheit war das alles ganz anders.* der Wahrheit entsprechen be in accordance with the truth

wahr|neh·men ['vaːrneːmən] <nimmt wahr, nahm wahr, hat wahrgenommen> [tr v] **1.** perceive, detect, notice ◊ *Sie nahm ein verdächtiges Geräusch wahr.* ✦ *Die Tiere schienen die Gefahr wahrzunehmen.* ✦ *Sie nimmt das Chaos gar nicht mehr wahr.* **2.** *(an offer, opportunity etc.)* take advantage of ◊ *Er nahm die Gelegenheit wahr zu verschwinden.* einen Termin wahrnehmen keep an appointment **3.** *(form) (a task, role, responsibilities)* perform, carry out ◊ *Er nahm im Vorstand die Aufgaben des Schriftführers wahr.* **4.** *(form) (sb's rights, interests)* look after ◊ *die Interessen eines Kindes wahrnehmen*

② **wahr·schein·lich** [vaːrˈʃaenlɪç, '— — —] [adj] likely, probable ◊ *Sie gilt als wahrscheinliche Nachfolgerin.* ✦ *Es ist nicht sehr wahrscheinlich, dass er noch einmal heiratet.* [adv] probably, in all likelihood ◊ *Wahrscheinlich kommt sie zu Fuß.* ⊖vermutlich

Wäh·rung ['vɛːrʊŋ] die <-, -en> currency ◊ *die europäische/brasilianische Währung* ✦ *eine starke/ harte Währung*

Wahr·zei·chen ['vaːrˈtsaeçn̩] das <-s, -> symbol, emblem; *(building)* landmark ◊ *Das Wahrzeichen Kölns ist der berühmte Dom.*

Wai·se ['vaezə] die <-n, -n> orphan ◊ *Das Kind war Waise.* (zur) Waise werden be orphaned box@ Substantivierung

Wal [vaːl] der <-(e)s, -e> whale

② **Wald** [valt] der <-(e)s, Wälder> wood(s), forest ◊ *Sie hatten sich im Wald verirrt.* ✦ *Ich war im Wald, Pilze sammeln.*

◉ jd sieht den Wald vor lauter Bäumen nicht sb can't see the wood for the trees ein Wald von etw. a forest of sth ◊ *ein Wald von Schildern*

Wal·nuss ['valnʊs] die <-, Walnüsse> walnut ◊ *eine Tüte gemahlene Walnüsse*

wäl·zen ['vɛltsn̩] [tr v] +*haben* **1.** roll ◊ *Er wälzte den Felsen zur Seite.* ✦ *Sie wälzte den Bewusstlosen auf die Seite.* sich in etw. [dat] wälzen roll (about) in sth ◊ *Der Hund wälzte sich im Sand.* sich auf die andere Seite wälzen roll over (onto the other side) sich schlaflos im Bett wälzen toss and turn **2.** *(in flour, breadcrumbs etc.)* coat ◊ *Schnitzel in Mehl wälzen* ⊖wenden **3.** *(fam) (books)* etw. wälzen pore over sth ◊ *Sie wälzte*

ein paar Reiseführer. ⊖studieren **4.** *(fam)* *(plans, problems)* turn over sth in your mind ◊ *Sie wälzen Pläne für den Umbau ihres Hauses.* etw. mit jdm wälzen discuss sth with sb ◊ *Ich habe keine Lust, ewig mit dir Probleme zu wälzen.* ⊖diskutieren **5.** *(fig)* *(the blame, responsibility)* etw. auf jdn wälzen shift sth onto sb ◊ *Sie wälzte die Schuld auf ihn.* ⊖schieben

Wal·zer ['valtsə] der <-s, -> waltz ◊ *Sie tanzten (einen) Walzer.*

ⓩ **Wand** [vant] die <-, Wände> *(also fig)* wall ◊ *An der Wand hing ein großes Bild.* ♦ *Er schlug einen Nagel in die Wand.* eine Wand ... gen, eine Wand von etw. a wall of sth ◊ *Er stieß an eine Wand des Schweigens.*

  ⊛ die eigenen vier Wände your own four walls weiß wie eine Wand as white as a sheet die Wände hochgehen go up the wall gegen eine Wand reden talk to a brick wall

Wan·del ['vandl̩] der <-s> *no pl* change ◊ *ein gesellschaftlicher Wandel*

wan·deln ['vandl̩n] *(lofty)* ref v +*haben* sich wandeln change ◊ *Die Orte wandelten sich allmählich zu Industriestädten.* intr v +*sein* stroll, saunter ◊ *Sie wandelten durch den Park.*

ⓩ **wan·dern** ['vandɐn] intr v +*sein* **1.** hike ◊ *Am nächsten Tag wanderten wir weiter.* wandern gehen go for a hike **2.** *(also fig)* wander ◊ *Sie wanderte unruhig durchs Haus.* ♦ *Sein Blick wanderte von einem zur anderen.* **3.** *(esp fam)* end up ◊ *Das Schreiben wanderte in den Papierkorb.* ♦ *Dafür wird er wohl ins Gefängnis wandern.*

Wan·de·rung ['vandərʊŋ] die <-, -en> long walk, hike ◊ *eine Wanderung machen*

wand·te ['vantə] *pret of* wenden

Wan·ge ['vaŋə] die <-, -n> *(lofty)* cheek ◊ *Er gab ihr einen Kuss auf die Wange.* ♦ *Sie hatte rosige Wangen.* ⊖Backe

wan·ken ['vaŋkŋ̍] intr v +*haben/sein* **1.** +*haben* sway, shake ◊ *Der Boden wankte.* **2.** +*sein* stagger ◊ *Er wankte zur Tür.*

ⓩ **wann** [van] adv when ◊ *Wann wurden Sie geboren?* ♦ *Seit wann trägt er eine Brille?* ♦ *Ich weiß nicht, wann der nächste Bus fährt.* wann immer whenever ◊ *Ich helfe, wann immer es nötig ist.*

Wan·ne ['vanə] die <-, -n> tub, bath tub ◊ *Die Flüssigkeit wird in einer Wanne aufgefangen.* ♦ *Sie lag lange in der Wanne.*

ⓩ **war** [vaːɐ̯] *pret of* sein

warb [varp] *pret of* werben

ⓩ **Wa·re** ['vaːrə] die <-, -n> good, product ◊ *abgepackte/importierte Waren* ♦ *Wann wird die Ware geliefert?*

  ⊛ heiße Ware *(slang)* illegal goods

> The singular form is often used to refer to a group of identical or connected products: *Obst und Gemüse sind verderbliche Ware.* (Fruit and vegetables are perishable goods.)

ⓩ **Wa·ren·haus** ['vaːrənhaos] das <-(e)s, Warenhäuser> *(oldf)* department store ⊖Kaufhaus

ⓩ **warf** [varf] *pret of* werfen

ⓩ **warm** [varm] adj, adv <wärmer, am wärmsten> **1.** warm(ly), hot ◊ *eine warme Mahlzeit* ♦ *Im*

Wohnzimmer war es sehr warm. ♦ *Die Decke hielt sie warm.* ♦ *ein warmes Gelb/Rot* ♦ *Sie bereiteten ihm einen warmen Empfang.* ♦ *Wie warm darf man das waschen?* etw. warm machen heat sth (up), warm sth (up) etw. warm halten/stellen keep sth warm/hot ◊ *Ich habe das Essen für dich warm gehalten.* etw. warm laufen lassen warm sth up jdm ist warm sb is warm/hot ◊ *Ist dir warm genug?* jdm wird (es) warm sb begins to feel warm/hot, sb is getting warm/hot warm essen have a hot meal ⊖kalt, kühl **2.** *(fam)* *(referring to rent)* including heating and services ◊ *Die Wohnung kostet warm 800 Euro.*

  ⊚ sich warm anziehen **1.** dress warmly **2.** *(fam)* brace yourself ◊ *Wenn du dich mit ihm messen willst, musst du dich aber warm anziehen!* sich dat jdn warm halten *(fam)* keep in with sb mit jdm warm werden *(fam)* warm to sb

ⓩ **Wär·me** ['vɛrmə] die <-> *no pl* warmth, heat ◊ *Wärme erzeugen* ♦ *Dieses Material leitet Wärme sehr gut.* ♦ *Er sprach mit großer Wärme.* ⊖Kälte

wär·men ['vɛrmən] tr v +*haben* warm (up) ◊ *Der Ofen wärmt unser ganzes Haus.* ♦ *Sie wärmte die Milch für das Baby.* sich wärmen warm yourself up; *(your hands, feet)* sich dat etw. wärmen warm your sth sich gegenseitig wärmen keep each other warm intr v +*haben* be warm, provide warmth ◊ *Trink das. Das wärmt.* ♦ *Im Winter wärmt die Sonne kaum noch.*

Wärm·fla·sche ['vɛrmflaʃə] die <-, -n> hot-water bottle ◊ *Sie füllte die Wärmflasche mit heißem Wasser.*

Warn·blink·an·la·ge ['varnblɪŋkʔanlaːɡə] die <-> *no pl* hazard lights ◊ *Nach dem Unfall schaltete sie die Warnblinkanlage ein.*

Warn·drei·eck ['varndraeʔɛk] das <-(e)s, -e> warning triangle ◊ *die Unfallstelle mit einem Warndreieck sichern*

ⓩ **war·nen** ['varnən] tr+intr v +*haben* (jdn) (vor etw.) warnen warn (sb) (of/about/against sth) ◊ *Du musst ihn warnen!* ♦ *Er warnte (sie) vor einem solchen Schritt.* (die Öffentlichkeit) vor etw. warnen issue a (public) warning about sth jdn vor jdm warnen warn sb about sb jdn davor warnen, etw. zu tun warn sb not to do sth

ⓩ **war·ten** ['vartn̩] <wartet, wartete, hat gewartet> intr v **1.** *(also fig)* (auf jdn/etw.) warten wait (for sb/sth) ◊ *Sie wartete auf ihren Bruder.* ♦ *Wir haben mit dem Essen auf dich gewartet.* ♦ *Auf mich wartet noch eine Menge Arbeit.* **2.** (lange) auf sich warten lassen be a long time coming ◊ *Der Aufschwung lässt ganz schön (lange) auf sich warten!* tr v service ◊ *Die Heizungsanlage muss regelmäßig gewartet werden.*

  ⊛ warte mal wait a minute, hold on ⊖Moment na warte just you wait ◊ *Na warte! Dafür werde ich mich rächen.*

War·te·zim·mer ['vartətsɪmɐ] das <-s, -> waiting room ◊ *Bitte nehmen Sie im Wartezimmer Platz.*

War·tung ['vartʊŋ] die <-, -en> servicing ◊ *Eine regelmäßige Wartung ist notwendig.*

ⓩ **war·um** [va'rʊm, 'vaːrʊm] adv why ◊ *Warum kommst du nicht mit?* ♦ *Ich weiß nicht, warum.* ♦ *Das ist der Grund, warum ich frage.* ⊖weshalb, weswegen

War·ze ['vartsə] die <-, -n> MED wart ◊ *Sie hatte*

eine Warze an der Fußsohle.

② **was¹** [vas] (adv) (fam) why, what … for ◇ *Was schaust du so?* ◆ *Was musstest du auch so viele Leute einladen!*

◉ **ach was** get away ◇ *Ach was! Das ist doch nur ein Kratzer.* ⊖Unsinn **na so was** well I never

② **was²** [vas] (interrog pron) what ◇ *Was hast du getan?* ◆ *Was genau ist/bedeutet MMS?* ◆ *Sie wunderte sich, was mit ihm los war.* ◆ *Um was geht es bei dem Spiel?* ◆ *Weißt du, an was mich das erinnert?* Was ist, wenn …? What if …? was für (ein/eine) what kind/sort of ◇ *Was für ein Vogel ist das?* ◆ *Was für Musik hörst du denn gern?* (rel pron) that, which ◇ *Das ist alles, was man braucht.* ◆ *Er wusste nicht mehr ein noch aus, was durchaus verständlich war.* (indef pron) (fam) something, anything ◇ *Hat er was davon gewusst?* ◆ *Tut doch was!* ein bisschen was a little bit; (+*adjectival noun*) was Besonderes/ Schlimmes etc. something special/bad etc. ⊖etwas

◉ **was auch immer** whatever ◇ *Was Sie auch immer wissen, sagen Sie es uns.*

Wasch·be·cken ['vaʃbɛkn̩] das <-s, -> washbasin, sink

② **Wä·sche** ['vɛʃə] die <-> no pl **1.** linen ◇ *ein Schrank voll Wäsche* **2.** washing, laundry ◇ *Er hängte die Wäsche auf.* (die) Wäsche waschen do the washing/laundry **3.** underwear ◇ *Sie zieht täglich frische Wäsche an.* ⊖Unterwäsche **4.** wash ◇ *Deine Socken sind alle in der Wäsche.* ◆ *Schon nach der ersten Wäsche war der Pulli eingelaufen.* bei der Wäsche von etw. when washing sth

◉ **dumm/blöd** etc. **aus der Wäsche gucken/ schauen** (fam) look stupid, look dumb **schmutzige Wäsche waschen** (pej) wash your dirty linen

② **wa·schen** ['vaʃn̩] <wäscht, wusch, hat gewaschen> (tr v) wash ◇ *sein Auto/einen Pulli waschen* ◆ *eine frisch gewaschene Bluse* sich waschen wash (yourself), have a wash sich/jdm etw. waschen wash your/sb's sth ◇ *Sie wusch sich die Hände.* ◆ *Er wusch dem Kind das Gesicht.* Wäsche waschen do the washing/laundry (intr v) do the washing/ laundry ◇ *Sie wäscht dreimal die Woche.*

◉ **etw., der/die/das sich gewaschen hat** an almighty sth

Wä·sche·trock·ner ['vɛʃətrɔknɐ] der <-s, -> **1.** (tumble-)dryer ◇ *Dieser Pulli darf nicht in den Wäschetrockner gegeben werden.* **2.** clothes horse, dryer

Wasch·lap·pen ['vaʃlapm̩] der <-s, -> **1.** flannel, facecloth, washcloth **2.** (fam, pej) (person) wimp ◇ *Was ist er nur für ein Waschlappen!*

Wasch·ma·schi·ne ['vaʃmaʃiːnə] die <-, -n> washing machine

② **Wasch·mit·tel** ['vaʃmɪtl̩] das <-s, -> washing powder, detergent ◇ *ein Waschmittel für Buntwäsche*

② **wäscht** [vɛʃt] pres of waschen

② **Was·ser** ['vasɐ] das <-s, -> (abbr H₂O) **1.** water ◇ *ein Glas Wasser trinken* ◆ *Warst du schon im Wasser?* unter Wasser stehen be flooded **2.** sweat ◇ *Das Wasser lief ihm über die Stirn.; (in the legs)* fluid; *(from the bladder)* urine Wasser lassen urinate

◉ **das Wasser steht jdm bis zum Hals** sb is up

to their neck in it **jdm läuft das Wasser im Mund zusammen** sb's mouth waters **ins Wasser fallen** (fam) be called off ◇ *Die Veranstaltung fällt ins Wasser.* **nahe am/ans Wasser gebaut haben** be a crybaby **mit allen Wassern gewaschen sein** be very crafty **sich über Wasser halten** keep your head above water **jd kann jdm nicht das Wasser reichen** sb can't hold a candle to sb

Was·ser·hahn ['vasɐhaːn] der <-(e)s, Wasserhähne> tap, faucet ◇ *den Wasserhahn aufdrehen/zudrehen*

wäs·se·rig ['vɛsərɪç] → wässrig

Was·ser·mann ['vasɐman] der <-(e)s, Wassermänner> **1.** ASTROL, ASTRON Aquarius **2.** MYTH *male water sprite*

wäss·rig ['vɛsrɪç] (adj) watery ◇ *eine wässrige Lösung* ◆ *Die Suppe hat nicht geschmeckt; sie war zu wässrig.* ◆ *Ihre Mutter hatte wässrige Augen.*

Watt¹ [vat] das <-(e)s, -en> GEOG mudflat(s) ◇ *Sie wanderten durchs Watt.*

Watt² [vat] das <-s, -> PHYSICS (abbr W) watt ◇ *eine Glühbirne mit 40 Watt*

Wat·te ['vatə] die <-> no pl cotton wool, cotton ◇ *Er steckte sich Watte in die Ohren.*

◉ **nicht aus Watte** be tough, be no softie

② **WC** [veːˈtseː] das (abbr of water closet) WC, toilet ◇ *Wo ist das WC, bitte?* ⊖Toilette, Klo

Web·sei·te ['vɛpzaɪtə] die <-, -n> IT web page ◇ *Die Webseite des Hueber-Verlags ist www.hueber.de.*

Wech·sel ['vɛksl̩] der <-s, -> **1.** change ◇ *Der Wechsel des Stromversorgers funktionierte ohne Probleme.* ◆ *ein rascher Wechsel zwischen warmen und kalten Temperaturen* **2.** im Wechsel mit jdm/ etw. alternately with sb/sth, in turn with sb/sth ◇ *Er hat im Wechsel mit seiner Schwester Küchendienst.* ⊖abwechselnd mit jdm/etw. **3.** SPORT substitution ◇ *Zwei Minuten nach dem Wechsel traf der Spieler das Tor.* **4.** FIN bill of exchange ◇ *Wann ist der Wechsel fällig?*

Wech·sel·geld ['vɛksl̩gɛlt] das <-(e)s> no pl change ◇ *Warten Sie, hier ist Ihr Wechselgeld.*

Wech·sel·kurs ['vɛksl̩kʊrs] der <-es, -e> exchange rate ◇ *Der Wechselkurs ist im Augenblick 1:1,27.*

② **wech·seln** ['vɛksl̩n] (tr v) +haben **1.** change ◇ *Wir müssen den Reifen wechseln.* ◆ *Er hat nur schnell sein Hemd gewechselt.* ◆ *Sie möchte den Beruf wechseln.* ◆ *den Anwalt wechseln; (money, currency)* etw. (in etw. (acc)) wechseln change sth (into sth) ◇ *Ich möchte gerne 100 Euro in Dollar wechseln.* ◆ *Wir müssen an der Grenze noch Geld wechseln.; (into smaller change)* jdm etw. in etw. (acc) wechseln change sth (into sth) for sb ◇ *Können Sie mir 20 Euro wechseln?* das Thema wechseln change the subject **2.** exchange ◇ *Sie wollte mit mir den Platz wechseln.* ◆ *Sie wechselten einen kurzen Blick.* (intr v) +haben/sein **1.** +haben change ◇ *Sie spürt es meist vorher, wenn das Wetter wechselt.* ◆ *Seine Stimmung wechselt häufig.* ◆ *Die Ampel wechselte von Grün auf Gelb.* **2.** +sein (irgendwohin) wechseln move (to somewhere) ◇ *Er ist ins Auswärtige Amt gewechselt.*

② **we·cken** ['vɛkn̩] (tr v) +haben **1.** wake ◇ *Weck mich morgen bitte um 6 Uhr.* ◆ *Er wurde durch einen*

A
B
C
D
E
F
G
H
I
J
K
L
M
N
O
P
Q
R
S
T
U
V
W
X
Y
Z

lauten Schrei geweckt. **2.** etw. (in/bei jdm) wecken arouse sth (in sb), awake sth (in sb) ◊ *Die verschlossene Tür weckte ihre Neugier.* ◆ *Das Foto hatte alte Erinnerungen in ihm geweckt.* Interesse bei jdm wecken arouse sb's interest

② **We·cker** [ˈvɛkɐ] der <–s, –> alarm clock ◊ *Stellst du den Wecker bitte auf 8 Uhr?* ◆ *Warum hat der Wecker heute Morgen nicht geklingelt/geläutet?*
  ⊚ jdm auf den Wecker gehen/fallen *(fam)* get on sb's nerves, get on sb's wick

② **we·der** [ˈveːdɐ] ⟨conjunc⟩ *(always weder ... noch ...)* neither ... nor ... ◊ *Dafür habe ich weder Zeit noch Geld.* weder noch neither ... ◊ *„Hast du Lust auf Kino oder Theater?" — „Weder noch."*

② **weg** [vɛk] ⟨adv⟩ **1.** weg sein be/have gone ◊ *Als wir am Bahnhof ankamen, war der Zug schon weg.* ◆ *Meine Kopfschmerzen sind weg.* ◆ *Mein Geldbeutel ist weg — jemand muss ihn gestohlen haben!*; *(on holiday)* be away ⊖fort **2.** *translation varies* Weg mit euch! Get out of here! Finger/Hände weg (von etw.) hands off (sth) Hand weg von der Waffe! Put down the gun! **3.** away ◊ *Ist der Bahnhof weit weg?* ⊖entfernt
  ⊚ schnell weg sein sell quickly, go quickly (ganz/völlig) weg sein (von jdm/etw.) *(fam)* be (completely/absolutely) bowled over (by sth/sb) ◊ *Er ist ganz weg von seiner neuen Englischlehrerin.* nichts wie weg let's get out of here ◊ *Die Bullen kommen, nichts wie weg!* weg sein *(fam)* be out of it ◊ *Nach dem Schlag auf den Kopf war ich erst mal fünf Minuten weg.*

② **Weg** [veːk] der <–(e)s, –e> **1.** way, distance ◊ *Bis zum Ziel ist es noch ein weiter Weg.* ◆ *Welches ist der kürzeste Weg zum Flughafen?* jdm auf halben Weg entgegenkommen meet sb halfway **2.** path ◊ *Ein schmaler Weg führte durch den Wald.* ◆ *Der Weg zum Gipfel war ziemlich steil.* ◆ *Führt der Weg am Fluss entlang?* **3.** *(also fig)* way ◊ *Ist das der richtige Weg zum Bahnhof?* ◆ *jdm den Weg zeigen* ◆ *nach dem Weg fragen* vom Weg abkommen lose your way auf dem Weg zu etw. on the way to sth ◊ *Ich bin auf dem Weg zur Arbeit.*; way ◊ *Wir werden einen Weg finden, dieses Problem zu lösen.* ◆ *Das muss auf dem schnellsten Weg erledigt werden.*; route ◊ *auf diplomatischem/schriftlichem Weg* **4.** der Weg zu etw. the road to sth, the path to sth ◊ *Der Weg zum Erfolg ist hart.*
  ⊚ sich auf dem Weg der Besserung befinden, auf dem Weg der Besserung sein be on the road to recovery auf dem besten Weg(e) sein, zu ... be (well) on the way to ... seine eigenen Wege gehen go your own way sich ⟨dat⟩ einen Weg (durch etw.) bahnen fight your way through (sth) jdm/etw. den Weg bereiten/ebnen smooth the way/path for sb/sth, smooth sb's/sth's way/path da führt kein Weg dran vorbei *(fam)* there's no way out of/around it jdm/einer Sache aus dem Weg gehen avoid sb/sth ◊ *Er geht allen Schwierigkeiten aus dem Weg.* ◆ *Seit unserem letzten Streit geht sie mir aus dem Weg.* seines Weges gehen *(lit)* continue on your way jdm über den Weg laufen *(fam)* bump into sb *(somebody or something unwelcome)* cross sb's path etw. in die Wege leiten get sth underway jd wird seinen Weg (schon) machen *(fam)* sb will be all right sich auf den Weg machen leave ◊ *Er machte*

sich um 6.30 Uhr auf den Weg zur Arbeit. etw. aus dem Weg räumen *(fam)* move sth out of the way, get rid of sth jdn aus dem Weg räumen *(fam)* get rid of sb, do away with sb (jdm) im Weg sein/stehen *(fam)* be in sb's/the way jdm nicht über den Weg trauen *(fam)* not trust sb as far as you can/could throw them, not trust sb an inch

② **weg|...** [vɛk] ⟨prefix⟩ **1.** ... away ◊ *Sie mussten drei der vier jungen Hunde weggeben.* ◆ *Legst du bitte das Messer weg?* ◆ *Der Vogel ist weggeflogen.* ◆ *Er drehte sich weg.* ◆ *Dieses alte Bier kannst du wegschütten.* etw. weglegen put sth aside/to one side ⊖fort... **2.** jdm etw. wegessen/wegtrinken eat/drink sth up so that there is none left for sb

② **we·gen** [ˈveːgn̩] ⟨prep⟩ *sing nouns without article or attribute are not declined when following this prep, otherwise* ⟨+gen⟩ *or fam* ⟨+dat⟩ **1.** *(giving reason)* because of ◊ *Wegen seiner Krankheit konnte er drei Wochen nicht zur Arbeit gehen.* ◆ *Wir müssen die Wanderung wegen des schlechten Wetters verschieben.* wegen Umbau(s) geschlossen closed for renovation jdn wegen Diebstahl(s) anzeigen report sb for theft ⊖aufgrund (von) **2.** *(concerning sth)* about ◊ *Ich rufe wegen Ihrer Anzeige an.* **3.** *(purpose)* for, because of ◊ *Sie hat es nur des Geldes wegen getan.* **4.** von ... wegen because of ... ◊ *etw. von Berufs wegen tun*; *(in the name of)* on behalf of ... ◊ *Folter von Staats wegen* **5.** *(fam)* wegen dir/mir/ihm etc. for your/my/his etc. sake ◊ *Wegen mir brauchst du dir keine Sorgen zu machen.*

weg|fah·ren [ˈvɛkfaːrən] <fährt weg, fuhr weg, hat/ist weggefahren> ⟨tr v⟩ +haben take away, transport ◊ *Der Verletzte wurde in einem Krankenwagen weggefahren.* ⟨intr v⟩ +sein **1.** leave ◊ *Wann wollt ihr von hier wieder wegfahren?* **2.** go away ◊ *Fahrt ihr in den Ferien weg?* **3.** etw. fährt jdm weg sth drives off/away ◊ *Jetzt ist mir der Zug vor der Nase weggefahren.*

weg|fal·len [ˈvɛkfalən] <fällt weg, fiel weg, ist weggefallen> ⟨intr v⟩ **1.** etw. fällt weg sth is lost, sb loses sth ◊ *Mit dem Tod ihrer Mutter fiel ihre wichtigste Stütze weg.* **2.** etw. kann wegfallen sth can go, sb can get rid of sth ◊ *Dieser Absatz kann wegfallen, da steht nichts Wichtiges drin.*

weg|ge·hen [ˈvɛkgeːən] <geht weg, ging weg, ist weggegangen> ⟨intr v⟩ **1.** go out ◊ *Gehst du heute Abend noch weg?*; go away, move ◊ *Geh mal bitte da weg, du stehst mir im Weg.* **2.** *(fam)* etw. geht weg sth goes away ◊ *Von diesen Tabletten gehen die Schmerzen schnell weg.* **3.** go away; *(mark, stain etc. also)* come out ◊ *Dieser Fleck geht nicht mehr weg.* **4.** etw. geht weg sells ◊ *Für diesen Preis geht der Wagen sofort weg.* **5.** *(fam)* *(money, salary etc.)* etw. geht für etw. weg sth goes on sth ◊ *Fast die Hälfte meines Gehalts geht für die Miete weg.*
  ⊚ geh mir bloß weg mit ... *(fam)* don't talk to me about ..., spare me ...

weg|kom·men [ˈvɛkkɔmən] <kommt weg, kam weg, ist weggekommen> ⟨intr v⟩ **1.** get away, get out ◊ *Wir müssen versuchen, hier wegzukommen.* **2.** *(fam)* von jdm/etw. wegkommen get over sb/sth ◊ *Er kommt von ihr nicht weg, denn sie ist die große Liebe seines Lebens.*; *(drugs, alcohol)* von

A B C D E F G H I J K L M N O P Q R S T U V W X Y Z

etw. wegkommen come off sth **3.** etw. kommt weg sth is going missing, sth is disappearing ◊ *Bei uns im Büro kommt ständig Geld weg.* **4.** jd kommt gut/schlecht bei etw. weg sb comes off well/badly in sth ◊ *Er ist bei dem Geschäft gut weggekommen.* **5.** *(fam)* über etw. [acc] nicht wegkommen not be able to get over sth ◊ *Er kommt über den Tod seiner Frau nicht weg.*

weg|lau·fen ['vɛklaʊfn̩] <läuft weg, lief weg, ist weggelaufen> [intr v] **1.** run away ◊ *Die Kinder laufen vor dem Hund weg.* **2.** *(fam)* jdm weglaufen leave sb ◊ *Ihm ist die Frau weggelaufen.*

ⓦ etw. läuft dir nicht weg you can do sth later, sth isn't going anywhere ◊ *Die Arbeit läuft dir nicht weg, jetzt komm erst mal zum Essen.*

weg|neh·men ['vɛkneːmən] <nimmt weg, nahm weg, hat weggenommen> [tr v] **1.** take away ◊ *Wie viele Eier bleiben von 16 übrig, wenn man 12 wegnimmt?* **2.** jdm etw. wegnehmen take sth away from sb ◊ *Wieso hast du deinem Bruder das Spielzeug weggenommen?* **3.** *(room, space)* take up ◊ *Dieser Schrank nimmt viel Platz weg.; (light)* block out, take away **4.** das Gas wegnehmen slow down, reduce your speed

weg|schau·en ['vɛkʃaʊən] <schaut weg, schaute weg, hat weggeschaut> *(regional)* look away, avert your eyes ◊ *Er schaute angewidert weg, als sie den Fisch ausnahm.* ⊝wegsehen

weg|schmei·ßen ['vɛkʃmaɪsn̩] <schmiss weg, schmiss weg, hat weggeschmissen> [tr v] *(fam)* **1.** throw away ◊ *Er hob den Lappen auf und schmiss ihn angeekelt wieder weg.* **2.** throw away, chuck away ◊ *Schmeiß doch endlich mal deine alten Schuhe weg.*

weg|se·hen ['vɛkzeːən] <sieht weg, sah weg, hat weggesehen> [intr v] look away, avert your eyes ◊ *verlegen wegsehen* ⊝wegschauen

weg|ste·cken ['vɛkʃtɛkn̩] <steckt weg, steckte weg, hat weggesteckt> [tr v] *(fam)* **1.** put away ◊ *Steck das Foto weg, das braucht dein Vater nicht zu sehen.* **2.** cope with, get over ◊ *Er hat den schrecklichen Unfall relativ gut weggesteckt.*

Weg·wei·ser ['veːkvaɪze] der <-s, -> sign(post) ◊ *Auf dem Wegweiser steht: München 28 km.*

weg|wer·fen ['vɛkvɛˈfn̩] <wirft weg, warf weg, hat weggeworfen> [tr v] **1.** put down, throw down ◊ *Sobald du ihn angezündet hast, musst du den Kracher wegwerfen.* **2.** throw away ◊ *Wirf doch endlich mal die alten Zeitschriften weg.* ♦ *Das ist doch weggeworfenes Geld!*

weg|zie·hen ['vɛktsiːən] <zieht weg, zog weg, hat/ ist weggezogen> [tr v] +*haben* pull away ◊ *Er zieht mir morgens immer die Bettdecke weg.* jdm den Stuhl unterm Hintern wegziehen pull sb's chair out from under them [intr v] +*sein* move away ◊ *Die Kloses sind letztes Jahr weggezogen.*

weh [veː] [adj] *only before n s* **1.** *(fam)* sore ◊ *Ich habe einen wehen Finger/Fuß.* **2.** *(lofty)* woeful ◊ *ein wehes Gefühl/Lächeln*

we·he ['veːə] [interj] wehe (jdm) woe betide (sb) ◊ *Wehe dir, wenn du nicht die Wahrheit sagst!* ♦ *Und wehe, jemand hat seine Hausaufgaben nicht gemacht!*

We·he ['veːə] die <-, -n> **1.** *most pl* MED contraction ◊ *Die Wehen kommen jetzt alle 5 Minuten.*

2. drift ◊ *Der Sturm hatte den Schnee zu einer großen Wehe aufgetürmt.*

we·hen ['veːən] [tr v] +*haben* etw. irgendwohin wehen blow sth somewhere ◊ *Der Wind hat die Blätter auf die Straße geweht.* [intr v] +*haben* **1.** *(wind, breeze)* weht (irgendwoher) sth is blowing (from somewhere) ◊ *Heute weht ein schwacher Wind (aus Norden).* ♦ *Eine kräftige Brise wehte ihm ins Gesicht.* **2.** wave, blow ◊ *Ihre Haare wehen im Wind.; (flag also)* fly ◊ *Von dem Gebäude wehte eine Fahne.*

Wehr·dienst ['veːgdiːnst] der <-(e)s> *no pl* military service ◊ *Wehrdienst leisten* ♦ *Er ist zum Wehrdienst einberufen/eingezogen worden.*

> In Germany, all male citizens must in principle do military service with the armed forces for several months after leaving school or college. Those who refuse to do military service are able to do community service instead, for example working as carers within social organizations.

weh·ren ['veːrən] [ref v] +*haben* **1.** sich (gegen jdn/etw.) wehren defend yourself (against sb/sth) ◊ *sich mit aller Kraft wehren* ♦ *Er wehrte sich heftig gegen diese Unterstellung.* **2.** sich gegen etw. wehren refuse to do sth ◊ *Er wehrte sich dagegen, die ganze Arbeit allein zu machen.*

ⓦ **weh|tun** ['veːtuːn] <tut weh, tat weh, hat wehgetan> [intr v] **1.** etw. tut (jdm) weh sth hurts (sb), (sb's) sth hurts ◊ *Wo tut es (dir) denn weh?* ♦ *Tut dir der Bauch immer noch weh?* ♦ *Der Stich hat kaum wehgetan.* ⊝etw. schmerzt jdn **2.** (jdm/ sich) wehtun hurt (sb/yourself) ◊ *Pass auf, dass du dir mit dem Messer nicht wehtust.* ♦ *Diese Bemerkung hat ihr sehr wehgetan.*

ⓦ **weib·lich** ['vaɪplɪç] [adj] **1.** *no comp/superl* female ◊ *ein Kind weiblichen Geschlechts* ♦ *Fünf der jungen Hunde sind weiblich, zwei männlich.* ♦ *Es meldete sich eine weibliche Stimme.* ⊝männlich **2.** feminine ◊ *Sie ist ein sehr weiblicher Typ.* ♦ *Diese emotionale Sichtweise gilt als typisch weiblich.* ♦ *Wörter auf -ung sind im Deutschen meist weiblich.* ⊝männlich

ⓦ **weich** [vaɪç] [adj] <weicher, am weich(e)sten> **1.** soft ◊ *Hast du das Fleisch schon weich geklopft?* ♦ *Diese Matratze ist mir zu weich.* ♦ *Für solche Verhandlungen ist er viel zu weich.* ♦ *weiche Gesichtszüge* ♦ *Die Violine hat einen weichen Klang.* ♦ *weiche Grüntöne* ♦ *eine weiche Landung* ◊ *Es wird darüber diskutiert, ob man weiche Drogen legalisieren sollte.* jd wird weich sb gives in, sb goes soft ◊ *Wenn du ihn lange genug bearbeitest, wird er weich.* ⊝hart **2.** soft, smooth ◊ *weiche Haut* ♦ *Das Leder ist schön weich.* ♦ *etw. ist weich wie Seide* ⊝rau **3.** *(fruit)* ripe ◊ *Die Birnen sollten für das Dessert nicht zu weich sein.* ♦ *Eine weiche Melone schmeckt besser als eine harte.* ⊝hart **4.** cooked, ready ◊ *Das Gemüse ist noch nicht weich.* ⊝gar **5.** ein weiches Gemüt/Herz haben be soft-hearted jdn weich stimmen soften sb's heart [adv] **1.** softly ◊ *Der Sessel ist weich gepolstert. Auf diesem Sofa sitzt man wunderbar weich.* This sofa is wonderfully soft. **2.** etw. weich kochen cook sth (until it is soft) ◊ *Gemüse weich kochen* ein Ei weich kochen soft boil an egg **3.** weich klingen have a soft sound **4.** softly, gently ◊ *weich landen* ♦

Er bremste weich ab. ⊖*sanft*
Wei·de ['vaɪdə] die <-, -n> **1.** pasture ◊ *die Kühe auf die Weide treiben* **2.** BOT willow ◊ *Die alte Weide am Fluss hat einen hohlen Stamm.*
② **wei·gern** ['vaɪgɐn] [ref v] +*haben* sich weigern(, etw. zu tun) refuse (to do sth) ◊ *sich beharrlich/ entschieden/standhaft weigern* ♦ *Die Soldaten haben sich geweigert, den Befehl zu befolgen.*
Weih·nach·ten ['vaɪnaxtn̩] *seldom with definite article 'das'* **1.** Christmas ◊ *Weihnachten feiern* ♦ *Schöne/Frohe Weihnachten und ein glückliches neues Jahr!* ♦ *Bald ist Weihnachten.* ♦ *Was hat du dieses Jahr zu Weihnachten bekommen?* ♦ *Was wünschst du dir zu Weihnachten?* ♦ *Ich weiß nicht, was ich meinen Eltern zu Weihnachten schenken soll.* **2.** Christmas Day ◊ *An Weihnachten selbst gibt es bei uns immer Pute.*
⊛ **grüne Weihnachten** *a Christmas without snow*

Christmas is the celebration of the birth of Christ. In Germany, families come together to give presents around the tree on Christmas Eve, the 24 December. Generally, practising Christians then go to Christmas Mass. The 25 December and 26 December are public holidays on which families join to eat and celebrate together.

Weih·nachts·mann ['vaɪnaxtsman] der <-(e)s, Weihnachtsmänner> Father Christmas, Santa Claus ◊ *Morgen kommt der Weihnachtsmann!*
Weih·nachts·markt ['vaɪnaxtsmaʁkt] der <-(e)s, Weihnachtsmärkte> Christmas market ◊ *über den Weihnachtsmarkt bummeln*

At Christmas time in Germany there are many Christmas markets, where you can buy festive craft gifts and specialities. At Christmas markets, it is common to drink mulled wine and eat hot waffles or potato fritters. The market in Nuremberg (the *Christkindlmarkt*), where you can buy Nuremberg spiced gingerbread (*Lebkuchen*), is particularly famous.

② **weil** [vaɪl] [conjunc] **1.** because ◊ *Er konnte nicht kommen, weil er krank war.* ♦ *„Warum hast du das nicht erledigt?" — „Weil ich keine Zeit hatte."* **2.** *(fam)* (just) because ◊ *„Wieso tust du das?" — „Weil!"* ⊖*darum*
Wei·le ['vaɪlə] die <-> *no pl* while ◊ *eine ganze/ geraume/kleine Weile* ♦ *Es wird wohl noch eine Weile dauern.*
② **Wein** [vaɪn] der <-(e)s, -e> **1.** wine ◊ *eine Flasche/ein Glas Wein* ♦ *Bringen Sie uns zweimal Wein, bitte!* ♦ *ein süßer/trockener Wein* ♦ *Welche Weine empfehlen Sie zum Essen?* **2.** BOT vine(s) ◊ *Der Wein blüht.* **3.** *no pl* grapes ◊ *Wein ernten/ lesen*
⊛ **junger Wein in alten Schläuchen** new wine in old bottles **im Wein ist Wahrheit** in vino veritas **jdm reinen Wein einschenken** tell sb the truth

Most of Germany's wine-growing regions are in the South West of the country. They include Baden, Franconia (*Franken*), Hessian Mountain Road (*Hessische Bergstraße*), Middle Rhine (*Mittelrhein*), Mosel-Saar-Ruwer, Nahe, Palatinate (*Pfalz*), Rheingau, Rhine-Hesse (*Rheinhessen*), Saale-Unstrut, Saxony (*Sachsen*) and Wurttem- ▶

▶ berg (*Baden-Württemberg*). The majority of grapes grown are white; but Germany also produces some fine (though less known) red wines.

② **wei·nen** ['vaɪnən] [intr v] +*haben* cry ◊ *bitterlich/ heftig/lautlos weinen* ♦ *Warum weinst du denn?* ♦ *vor Erschöpfung/Freude/Glück/Wut weinen* um jdn/ über etw. [acc] weinen cry over sb/sth [tr v] +*haben* cry, weep ◊ *Er weinte bittere Tränen um seinen Kameraden.* ♦ *Freudentränen weinen*
⊛ **etw. ist zum Weinen** *(fam)* sth is enough to make you cry/weep
Wein·trau·be ['vaɪntʁaʊbə] die <-, -n> *most pl* grape ◊ *blaue/weiße Weintrauben*
wei·se ['vaɪzə] [adj, adv] <weiser, am weisesten> wise(ly) ◊ *ein weiser alter Mann* ♦ *Sie ist mit den Jahren weiser geworden.* ♦ *weise handeln/urteilen*
Wei·se ['vaɪzə] die <-, -n> **1.** way ◊ *auf andere/ diese Weise* ♦ *Die Tasche ist auf geheimnisvolle Weise aus dem Auto verschwunden.* Art und Weise way ◊ *Auf diese Art und Weise wirst du bei ihr nichts erreichen. Das geschieht in der Weise, dass ... This is done by ..., This is achieved by ...* ⊖*Art* **2.** in gewisser Weise in some ways **3.** MUS tune, melody ◊ *eine alte/volkstümliche Weise singen/spielen*
wei·sen ['vaɪzn̩] <weist, wies, hat gewiesen> [tr v] **1.** *(lofty)* (jdm) etw. weisen show (sb) sth ◊ *jdm die Richtung/den Weg weisen* ⊖*zeigen* **2.** jdn aus/ von etw. weisen show sb out of sth ◊ *jdn aus dem Zimmer weisen; (from school etc.)* expel sb from sth **3.** etw. (weit) von sich weisen (firmly) reject sth ◊ *Er wies den Verdacht von sich.* [intr v] *(lofty)* irgendwohin weisen point somewhere ◊ *Er wies mit dem Finger zur Tür.* ⊖*deuten, zeigen*
Weis·heit ['vaɪshaɪt] die <-, -en> wisdom ◊ *die Weisheit des Alters* ♦ *eine alte chinesische Weisheit*
⊛ **mit seiner Weisheit am Ende sein** be at your wit's end **die Weisheit (auch) nicht (gerade) mit Löffeln gefressen/gegessen haben** *(fam, iron)* not be the sharpest tool in the box **nicht der Weisheit letzter Schluss** not the be all and end all, not an ideal solution **behalte deine Weisheit für dich** *(fam, iron)* you can keep your advice
weis|ma·chen ['vaɪsmaxn̩] <macht weis, machte weis, hat weisgemacht> [tr v] jdm etw. weismachen (wollen) (try to) make sb believe sth, (try to) tell sb sth ◊ *Du willst mir doch nicht etwa weismachen, dass du deinen eigenen Geburtstag vergessen hast! Das kannst du mir nicht weismachen., Das machst du mir nicht weis.* You can't expect me to believe that.
weiß¹ [vaɪs] [adj] <weißer, am weißesten> **1.** white ◊ *blendend weiße Zähne* ♦ *Mit diesem Waschmittel wird ihre Wäsche wieder strahlend weiß.* ♦ *weißer und roter Wein* ♦ *Er hat die Möbel weiß lackiert.* **2.** white, Caucasian ◊ *Das Opfer ist männlich, weiß und ca. 35 Jahre alt.* Menschen weißer Hautfarbe white people **3.** MED weiße Blutkörperchen white blood cells
② **weiß²** [vaɪs] *pres of* wissen
Weiß·bier ['vaɪsbiːɐ] das <-(e)s, -e> *pl 'Weißbier' when used with expressions of quantity* wheat beer ◊ *Zwei Weißbier, bitte!*

A
B
C
D
E
F
G
H
I
J
K
L
M
N
O
P
Q
R
S
T
U
V
W
X
Y
Z

Wei·ße¹ ['vaesə] der/die <-n, die Weißen> *but: ein Weißer/eine Weiße* white man/woman, person of Caucasian origin ◊ *Ein männlicher Weißer ist bei der Schießerei schwer verletzt worden.* die Weißen (the) white people, (the) whites *box@* Substantivierung

Wei·ße² ['vaesə] das <-n> *no pl* white ◊ *das Weiße vom Eigelb trennen box@* Farbe

Weiß·wein ['vaesvaen] der <-(e)s, -e> *pl 'Weißwein' when used with expressions of quantity* white wine ◊ *Wir empfehlen zu diesem Gericht einen trockenen Weißwein.*

② **weit** [vaet] [adj] <weiter, am weitesten>
1. (*journey, way etc.*) long ◊ *eine weite Reise* ♦ *Der Weg dorthin ist weit.*; far ◊ *Wie weit ist es bis dorthin?* ♦ *Das war bisher sein weitester Wurf.* von weit her from a long way away, from far away, from far and wide ◊ *Die Leute kamen von weit her, um das Wunderwerk zu bestaunen.* **2.** away ◊ *Der Ort liegt nur drei Kilometer weit von hier.* 25 Meter weit werfen throw a distance of 25 metres/meters **3.** (*clothing*) baggy, loose ◊ *Ist dir diese Hose nicht etwas zu weit?* ⊖eng **4.** large, wide ◊ *eine weite Öffnung* ⊖klein **5.** far ◊ *Wie weit ist er denn schon mit seinem Buch?* **6.** (*concept, term etc.*) broad ◊ *Wir sprechen hier von der Liebe im weiteren Sinne.* **7.** wide ◊ *ein weites Tal* [adv]
1. long ◊ *Es ist schon weit nach Mitternacht!* **2.** wide ◊ *eine weit geöffnete Tür* den Mund weit aufmachen open wide nicht weit entfernt not far away **3.** far ◊ *Die Krankheit ist schon zu weit fortgeschritten.* **4.** widely ◊ *ein weit gereister Mann* weit verbreitet widespread, common weit verzweigt extensive **5.** broadly ◊ *eine Vorschrift weit auslegen* **6.** a long way ◊ *etw. liegt weit zurück* **7.** +*comp* weit ... as much ... than ◊ *Er spielt weit besser als sie.* ⊖weitaus, viel, wesentlich
⊚ weit und breit for miles around so weit, so gut so far, so good es weit bringen go far ◊ *Er hat es im Leben weit gebracht.* das führt zu weit it's pointless jd ist zu weit gegangen sb has gone too far weit gehend → weitgehend das geht zu weit that's not on weit hergeholt irrelevant ◊ *Dieses Argument finde ich aber ein wenig weit hergeholt.* weit reichend → weitreichend bei weitem by far (and away) ⊖mit Abstand von weitem in the distance, from a long way away, from afar ◊ *Er konnte von weitem schon die Lichter der Stadt erkennen.*

weit·aus ['vaet|aos] [adv] far ◊ *Sie ist weitaus schneller als er.* ⊖mit Abstand

Wei·te ['vaetə] die <-, -n> **1.** expanse ◊ *die endlose Weite des Meeres/der Steppe* ⊖Enge **2.** distance ◊ *Er blickte in die Weite.* **3.** size, width ◊ *Bei dieser Hose ist die Weite verstellbar.* ♦ *Dieses Rohr gibt es in unterschiedlichen Weiten.*
⊚ die lichte Weite the inside width

② **wei·ter** ['vaetɐ] [adv] **1.** further, farther ◊ *Halt, nicht weiter!* **2.** else ◊ *Und was geschah weiter?* ♦ *Weiter weiß ich nichts darüber.* **3.** etw. weiter tun continue to do sth, carry on doing sth ◊ *Das Problem wird weiter bestehen.* ♦ *Wenn es weiter so stark regnet, bekommen wir eine Überschwemmung.* **4.** nichts weiter (als) nothing more (than), just ◊ *Das ist doch nichts weiter als dummes*

Gerede. ♦ *Er ist ein Feigling, nichts weiter.*
⊚ das ist nicht weiter schlimm it doesn't matter wenn es weiter nichts ist if that's all it is, if that's the only problem und so weiter and so on

wei·ter|bil·den ['vaetɐbɪldn] <bildet sich weiter, bildete sich weiter, hat sich weitergebildet> [ref v] sich weiterbilden continue your education ◊ *Sie möchte sich beruflich weiterbilden.*

② **Wei·ter·bil·dung** ['vaetɐbɪlduŋ] die <-, -en> continuing education, further training ◊ *sich um seine berufliche Weiterbildung kümmern* ⊖Fortbildung

② **wei·te·re** ['vaetərə] [adj] *only before ns* <ein weiterer ..., eine weitere ..., ein weiteres ...> further ◊ *Haben Sie noch weitere Fragen?* ♦ *Weitere Informationen finden Sie auf Seite 112.*
⊚ bis auf weiteres for the moment, for the time being ◊ *Sie können bis auf weiteres bei mir wohnen.* ⊖vorläufig, vorerst des Weiteren in addition, additionally, moreover, besides ⊖darüber hinaus ohne weiteres **1.** without any problems ◊ *Die Prüfung schaffst du doch ohne weiteres!* **2.** just like that ◊ *Du kannst dich doch nicht ohne weiteres bei den Leuten einladen!* **3.** easily, without hesitation ◊ *Dem würde ich nicht ohne weiteres zustimmen.*

② **wei·ter|fah·ren** ['vaetɐfaːrən] <fährt weiter, fuhr weiter, ist weitergefahren> [intr v] drive on, travel on ◊ *Nach einer kurzen Rast fuhren wir weiter.* ♦ *mit dem Zug nach Rom weiterfahren*

wei·ter|ge·ben ['vaetɐgeːbm] <gibt weiter, gab weiter, hat weitergegeben> [tr v] etw. (an jdn) weitergeben pass sth on (to sb) ◊ *Geben Sie dieses Schreiben bitte an Ihren Chef weiter.* ♦ *Dieses Rezept wurde von Generation zu Generation weitergegeben.*

wei·ter|ge·hen ['vaetɐgeːən] <geht weiter, ging weiter, ist weitergegangen> [intr v] **1.** carry on, go on ◊ *Nach einer kurzen Rast gingen sie weiter.* ♦ *Komm, lass uns weitergehen.* **2.** continue ◊ *Der Artikel geht auf der nächsten Seite weiter.* nicht mehr weitergehen stop ◊ *Plötzlich ging der Weg nicht mehr weiter.* [imp v] es geht weiter it goes on nicht mehr wissen, wie es weitergehen soll not know what to do, not know how to go on

wei·ter·hin ['vaetɐhɪn] [adv] **1.** etw. weiterhin bleiben remain sth ◊ *Er bleibt weiterhin skeptisch.*; (*question*) sich weiterhin stellen remain ⊖nicht mehr **2.** etw. weiterhin tun continue to do sth, carry on doing sth ◊ *Seine Eltern werden ihn weiterhin unterstützen.* jdm weiterhin alles Gute wünschen wish sb all the best (for the future) **3.** in addition, additionally, moreover, besides ◊ *Weiterhin müssen wir bedenken, dass dieses Projekt eine Menge Geld kosten wird.* ⊖außerdem, darüber hinaus

wei·ter|kom·men ['vaetɐkɔmən] <kommt weiter, kam weiter, ist weitergekommen> [intr v] **1.** go on ◊ *Ab hier kommen Sie nur noch zu Fuß weiter.* **2.** (mit etw.) weiterkommen make progress (with sth) ◊ *Er kommt mit seiner Arbeit nicht weiter.* ♦ *So kommen wir nicht weiter.*

wei·ter|ma·chen ['vaetɐmaxn] <macht weiter, machte weiter, hat weitergemacht> [intr v] (*fam*) (mit etw.) weitermachen carry on (with sth), continue (with sth) ◊ *Wenn du so weitermachst, kommst du bald in Schwierigkeiten.* ♦ *Er will mit*

dem Gitarrenunterricht weitermachen.

⊙ **mach nur so weiter** *(iron)* carry on like that

weit·ge·hend ['vaetgeːənt] [adj] <weiter gehend/ weitgehender, am weitestgehenden/weitgehendsten> **1.** comprehensive ◊ *weitgehende Reformen beschließen* ✦ *Diese Pläne sind sehr weitgehend.* **2.** *only before ns* almost complete, virtual ◊ *Wir versuchen, eine weitgehende Keimfreiheit zu erreichen.* [adv] almost completely ◊ *Der Platz war weitgehend menschenleer.*

weit·rei·chend ['vaetraeçn̩t, 'vaetraeçaeçn̩t] [adj] *no comp/superl* comprehensive, far-reaching ◊ *Er hat weitreichende Vollmachten vom Abteilungsleiter bekommen.* ✦ *Die Konsequenzen dieses Vorfalls sind ziemlich weitreichend.*

weit·sich·tig ['vaetzɪçtɪç] [adj] **1.** far-sighted ◊ *ein weitsichtiger Politiker* ✦ *Als Staatsmann ist er stets weitsichtig gewesen.* ⊛kurzsichtig **2.** MED long-sighted, far-sighted ◊ *Sie ist weitsichtig und braucht daher zum Lesen eine Brille.* ⊛kurzsichtig [adv] weitsichtig entscheiden make a far-sighted decision ⊛kurzsichtig

Wei·zen ['vaetsn̩] der <–s> *no pl* BOT wheat ◊ *Er baut auf seinen Feldern Weizen an.* ✦ *den Weizen ernten*

welch [vɛlç] [det] *in exclamations, invariable* **1.** welch ein/eine ... what a/an ... ◊ *Welch ein Blödmann er doch ist!* **2.** *before ns in place of the article (lofty)* what a/an ... ◊ *Welch Freude, dich hier zu treffen!*

⊘ **wel·cher¹** ['vɛlçɐ] [det] **1.** which ◊ *Auf welche Weise willst du das erreichen?* ✦ *Welches Auto ist deines?* ✦ *Welche Farben gefallen dir am besten? Welcher Mensch würde so etwas tun?* Who would do such a thing? **2.** *in exclamations* what (a/an) ◊ *Sieh nur, mit welchem Geschick sie das macht!* ✦ *Welcher Zufall, dass du auch hier bist!*

	m	f	nt	pl
nom	welcher	welche	welches	welche
acc	welchen	welche	welches	welche
dat	welchem	welcher	welchem	welchen
gen	welches	welcher	welches	welcher

⊘ **wel·cher²** ['vɛlçɐ] [interrog pron] which one ◊ *„Siehst du den Hund da drüben?" — „Welchen?"* ✦ *Es ist mir egal, welchen von beiden du nimmst.* [rel pron] which, who(m) ◊ *eine vor 50 Jahren entwickelte Methode, welche es ermöglicht, Krankheiten im Frühstadium zu erkennen* ✦ *Die Abteilung, für welche er verantwortlich war, wurde aufgelöst.* [indef pron] some, any ◊ *Ich gehe Brot kaufen. Brauchst du auch welches?* ✦ *Sind alle Kinder da oder fehlen noch welche?*

	m	f	nt	pl
nom	welcher	welche	welches	welche
acc	welchen	welche	welches	welche
dat	welchem	welcher	welchem	welchen
gen	-	-	-	-

wel·ken ['vɛlkn̩] [intr v] +*sein* **1.** etw. welkt sth is wilting ◊ *Schau, wie die Rosen welken schon.* **2.** *(lit)* fade ◊ *Ihre Schönheit begann zu welken.*

Wel·le ['vɛlə] die <–, –n> **1.** *(also fig)* wave ◊ *Ein Boot treibt auf der Welle fort* ◊ *von einer Welle fortgespült werden* ✦ *elektromagnetische Wellen* ◊ *Diese Meldung löste eine Welle von Protesten aus.*

✦ *eine Welle der Begeisterung/Hilfsbereitschaft* **2.** frequency ◊ *Dieser Radiosender sendet ab nächsten Montag auf einer anderen Welle.* ⊙ **grüne Welle** a traffic light setting which makes it possible for motorists to cross a sequence of traffic lights without stopping, provided they keep to a certain speed ◊ *Bei 60 km/h hat man auf dieser Strecke grüne Welle.* **hohe Wellen schlagen** cause a stir

Wel·pe ['vɛlpə] der <–n, –n> whelp, pup ◊ *Die Hündin hat sechs gesunde Welpen geworfen.*; *(young wolf, fox)* cub

⊘ **Welt** [vɛlt] die <–, –en> **1.** *no pl* world ◊ *die Welt umsegeln* ✦ *Brieffreunde aus/in der ganzen Welt haben* ✦ *Hier auf dem Land ist die Welt noch in Ordnung.* ✦ *Das Ereignis erschütterte die ganze Welt.* ✦ *die Welt der Medizin/der Mode* ✦ *die gelehrte/islamische Welt* ✦ *Lesen ist ihre Welt.* ✦ *Astronomen suchen nach fernen Welten.* **2.** ASTRON universe ◊ *eine Theorie über die Entstehung der Welt; (planet)* world ◊ *Besucher aus einer anderen Welt.*

⊙ **nobel geht die Welt zugrunde** *(hum)* talk about going out in style **eine verkehrte Welt** a topsy-turvy world **vornehm geht die Welt zugrunde** *(fam, iron)* live today as if there's no tomorrow **mit sich und der Welt zufrieden** content with life **nicht aus der Welt sein** *(fam)* not be a million miles away **nicht um alles in der Welt** not for anything in the world, not for anything on earth **für jdn bricht eine Welt zusammen** sb's whole world collapses **jdn zur Welt bringen** give birth to sb **von etw./davon geht die Welt nicht unter** sth/it is not the end of the world **das/so etwas hat die Welt noch nicht gesehen** *(fam)* this is out of this world, it is incredible **viel in der Welt herumkommen** travel the world **auf die/zur Welt kommen** be born ◊ *Das Kind kam gestern gesund und munter auf die/ zur Welt.* **was kostet die Welt** *(fam)* money is not an issue **in einer anderen Welt leben** live in a world of your own **Welten liegen zwischen ...** ... are worlds apart ◊ *Es liegen Welten zwischen den Geschwistern.* ✦ *Zwischen Theorie und Praxis liegen oft Welten.* **etw. aus der Welt schaffen** resolve sth, get sth sorted **eine Welt für sich sein** be a world on its own **die Welt nicht mehr verstehen** be at a loss to understand **alle Welt** everybody, the whole world **aus aller Welt** from all over the world **warum/wie/was/wo in aller Welt, warum/wie/was/wo um alles in der Welt** why/how/what/where on earth ◊ *Wo in aller Welt habe ich den Schlüssel hingelegt?* ✦ *Warum um alles in der Welt tut er das?*

Welt·an·schau·ung ['vɛlt|anʃaʊʊŋ] die <–, –en> view of the world, world view ◊ *Die beiden Philosophen haben völlig unterschiedliche Weltanschauungen.*

welt·be·rühmt ['vɛltbəryːmt] [adj] *no comp/superl* world-famous ◊ *ein weltberühmter Roman* ✦ *Der spektakuläre Fund machte den Geologen weltberühmt.*

welt·fremd ['vɛltfrɛmt] [adj] <weltfremder, am weltfremdesten> unworldly ◊ *ein weltfremder Romantiker* **Deine Lohnforderungen sind völlig weltfremd!** Your wage demands are totally unrealistic!

welt·lich [ˈvɛltlɪç] [adj] *no comp/superl* **1.** secular ◊ *weltliche Bauten/Kunst/Musik* ♦ *Die Universität ist weltlich und steht den Angehörigen aller Religionen offen.* **2.** *only before ns* worldly ◊ *weltliche Freuden/Genüsse*

Welt·meis·ter¹ [ˈvɛltmaɛstɐ] der <-s, –> Weltmeister (in etw. [dat]) world champions (in sth) ◊ *Die deutschen Damen wurden Weltmeister im Fußball.*

Welt·meis·ter² [ˈvɛltmaɛstɐ] der <-s, –>, **Welt·meis·te·rin** [ˈvɛltmaɛstərɪn] die <-, –nen> Weltmeister (in etw. [dat]) world champion (in sth) ◊ *Wird der amtierende Weltmeister seinen Titel verteidigen können?* ♦ *zweifacher Weltmeister im Boxen* ♦ *Er kann essen wie ein Weltmeister, ohne zuzunehmen.*

Welt·meis·ter·schaft [ˈvɛltmaɛstɐʃaft] die <-, –en> *(abbr* WM) **1.** world championship ◊ *sich für die Weltmeisterschaft qualifizieren* ♦ *an der Weltmeisterschaft im Taekwondo teilnehmen* **2.** *no pl* World Cup ◊ *ein Match/Turnier um die Weltmeisterschaft spielen* die Weltmeisterschaft im Boxen/Judo the boxing/judo World Cup

Welt·raum [ˈvɛltraɔm] der <-(e)s *no pl* space ◊ *den Weltraum erforschen* ♦ *einen Satelliten/eine Sonde in den Weltraum schießen*

welt·weit [ˈvɛltvaɛt] [adv] all over the world, throughout the world, worldwide ◊ *Das Ereignis erregte weltweit Aufsehen.* ♦ *der weltweit führende Anbieter/Hersteller von ...* ♦ *Weltweit gibt es über 20.000 Orchideenarten.* [adj] *no comp/superl, only before ns* worldwide, global ◊ *Naturgewalten können weltweite Katastrophen auslösen.* ♦ *der weltweite Kampf gegen den Terrorismus*

wem [ve:m] [pron] *dat of* wer

wen [ve:n] [pron] *acc of* wer

Wen·de [ˈvɛndə] die <-, –n> **1.** *no pl* turning point, change ◊ *eine Wende zum Guten/Besseren/Positiven* ♦ *eine politische Wende einleiten* ♦ *Das Geiseldrama hat eine unerwartete Wende genommen.* ⊜Wendung **2.** die Wende des Jahrhunderts the turn of the century um die Wende ... [gen] around the turn of ... ◊ *Die Kirche wurde um die Wende des 13. und 14. Jahrhunderts gebaut.* an der Wende zu etw. at the turn of sth ◊ *Was wird uns an der Wende zum dritten Jahrtausend erwarten?* **3.** SPORT an der Wende at the turnabout; *(manoeuvre)* turn ◊ *Beim Segeln gab Anselm den Befehl zur Wende.*

⊛ **die Wende** *the political and moral turnaround promised by Helmut Kohl of the CDU when he became the German chancellor in 1983* box⊛ Wiedervereinigung

wen·den [ˈvɛndn̩] <wendet, wendete/wandte, hat gewendet/gewandt> [ref v] **1.** *(also fig)* sich zu etw./jdm wenden turn to sth/sb ◊ *Sie wandte sich zur Tür.* ♦ *Er wandte sich zu mir und flüsterte mir etw. ins Ohr.* sich zum Gehen wenden turn to leave sich nach links/nach rechts wenden turn left/right sich (mit/um etw.) an jdn wenden turn to sb (with/for sth) ◊ *sich an jdn um Hilfe/Rat wenden* ♦ *Er wandte sich mit seiner Beschwerde an den Geschäftsführer.* **2.** *only pres* etw. wendet sich an jdn sth is addressed to sb, sth is directed at sb ◊ *Das Buch wendet sich vor allem an Erwachsene.* **3.** *wendete sich/hat sich gewendet* sich (in etw.

[acc]/zu etw.) wenden change (for sth) ◊ *Das Schicksal hat sich gewendet.* ♦ *Das Wetter hat sich nochmal zum Guten gewendet.* Ihre gute Laune wendete sich ins Gegenteil, als sie die Rechnung sah. Her good mood disappeared when she saw the bill. **4.** sich (mit etw.) gegen jdn/etw. wenden oppose sb/sth (with sth), turn against sb/sth (with sth) ◊ *Auf einmal haben sich seine Freunde gegen ihn gewandt.* ♦ *sich mit einem Bürgerentscheid gegen den Bau einer Straße wenden* [tr v] *wendete/hat gewendet* turn ◊ *sein Pferd wenden* ♦ *den Kopf zur Seite wenden; (onto the other side)* turn (over) ◊ *ein Blatt Papier/eine Seite wenden* ♦ *(an item of clothing)* turn inside out ◊ *eine Hose zum Waschen wenden* ♦ etw. in etw. [dat] wenden toss sth in sth ◊ *Das Fleisch in Eigelb und Paniermehl wenden.* **2.** den Blick zu jdm/etw. wenden look to(wards) sb/sth keinen Blick von jdm/etw. wenden not take your eyes off sb/sth **3.** *(lofty)* etw. von jdm wenden keep sth away from sb ◊ *das Pech/Ungück/Unheil von jdm wenden* [intr v] *wendete/hat gewendet* turn (around) ◊ *Ich musste wenden und zurückfahren.*

Wen·de·punkt [ˈvɛndəpʊŋkt] der <-(e)s, –e> **1.** turning point ◊ *Seine Karriere war an einem Wendepunkt angekommen.* **2.** MATH point of inflexion ◊ *der Wendepunkt einer mathematischen Kurve/der Sonne*

Wen·dung [ˈvɛndʊŋ] die <-, –en> **1.** turn ◊ *Der Krimi nahm eine überraschende Wendung.* ♦ *eine Wendung zum Besseren/Positiven/Schlechten* ♦ *eine Wendung um 180 Grad* ♦ *eine Wendung nach links/rechts* ⊜Wende **2.** GRAM expression, (turn of) phrase ◊ *umgangssprachliche Wendungen* **3.** *(of a road)* bend ◊ *Vorsicht, die Straße macht gleich eine scharfe Wendung nach links/rechts!* ⊜Kurve

② **we·nig¹** [ˈveːnɪç] [adv] *+adj or verb* **1.** not much, hardly ◊ *Sie kam wenig später.* ♦ *Er war wenig begeistert, als er das hörte.* zu wenig not enough, hardly ◊ *Sie ist müde, weil sie zu wenig geschlafen hat.* nicht wenig more than a little ◊ *Ich war nicht wenig enttäuscht/müde.* weniger rather less ◊ *Deine Ausreden interessieren mich eigentlich weniger.* **2.** rarely ◊ *Sie gehen wenig ins Theater.* ♦ *Er ist nur wenig krank. Du solltest so wenig wie möglich rauchen. You should smoke as little as possible.* ⊜selten **3.** sparsely ◊ *eine wenig besuchte Ausstellung Die Straße ist wenig befahren. The road is little used.* ⊜kaum **4.** ein wenig a little, a bit ◊ *Ein wenig schneller kannst du schon fahren.* ♦ *Ich ärgere mich ein wenig über ihn.*

② **we·nig²** [ˈveːnɪç] [det] *indefinite and invariable* **1.** *before uncountable ns* not much, little ◊ *Ich habe wenig Gutes gehört.* ♦ *wenig Zeit/Ahnung/Erfahrung/Geduld haben* zu wenig too little, not enough ◊ *zu wenig Geld verdienen* nicht (gerade) wenig quite a lot ◊ *Das hat nicht wenig Mühe gemacht.* ⊜viel **2.** *before pl ns* not many, few ◊ *Sie hat wenig Fehler gemacht.* ♦ *Der Käse hat wenig Kalorien.* zu wenig not enough, too few ◊ *Er hat zu wenig Freunde.* ⊜viele **3.** *as comp* weniger less, not as much/many ◊ *Du solltest weniger Schokolade essen.* ♦ *Laufen macht mir weniger Spaß als Fahren.* ⊜mehr

② **we·nig³** ['veːnɪç] [indef pron] *a little* ◇ *Sie haben nur wenig.* ◆ *Ich habe dem wenig hinzuzufügen.*
◉ **wenig von jdm haben 1.** *barely see sb* ◇ *Leo hat nur wenig von seiner Mutter, seit sie arbeitet.* **2.** *have little of sb* ◇ *Außer der Haarfarbe hat sie wenig von ihrem Vater.* **(das) wenige/Wenige** (the) *little* ◇ *Sie ist mit dem Wenigen, das sie hat, glücklich.* ◆ *sich mit wenigem begnügen* **die wenigsten** *only very few* ◇ *Die wenigsten interessieren sich für so was.*

we·ni·ge ['veːnɪgə] [adj] *indefinite, only before ns; before uncountable ns* der/die/das wenige *the small amount of …, what little … there is/was* ◇ *Das wenige Wasser verdunstet schnell.* ◆ *Sie gab mir die wenige Geld, das sie noch hatte.* Er muss sich die wenige Zeit gut einteilen. *The little time he has he must organize well.*

we·ni·ger ['veːnɪgɐ] *comp of* wenig [conjunc] weniger eins/zwei etc. *less one/two etc., take away one/two etc.* ◇ *Sechs weniger zwei gibt/ist/macht vier.* ⊜minus, weg ⊜und

we·ni·ges ['veːnɪgəs] [indef pron] (a) *little* ◇ *Es gibt nur weniges, was ihr nicht schmeckt.* ◆ *Ich bin mit wenigem zufrieden.*

we·nigs·tens ['veːnɪçstn̩s, 'veːnɪçstəns] [adv] **1.** *at least* ◇ *Hast du dich wenigstens entschuldigt?* ◆ *Kann ich wenigstens vorübergehend bei dir wohnen?* ◆ *Diese Lektion war bitter, aber wenigstens hat sie daraus gelernt.* ◆ *Die CD ist nicht gut, wenigstens hat er das behauptet.* ⊜zumindest **2.** *+figure* wenigstens … *at least …* ◇ *So ein Haus kostet wenigstens eine Million.* ◆ *Sie geht für wenigstens drei Jahre ins Ausland.* ⊜mindestens

② **wenn** [vɛn] [conjunc] **1.** *if* ◇ *Wenn es regnet, essen wir drinnen.* ◆ *Was ist, wenn was passiert?* ◆ *Wenn jemand nach mir fragt, dann sag, dass ich nicht da bin.* ◆ *Er braucht sich nicht zu wundern, wenn das schief geht.* wenn bloß/doch/nur *if only* ◇ *Wenn doch (nur) schon wieder Sommer wäre!* ⊜falls **2.** *(temporal)* when ◇ *Melde dich, wenn du fertig bist.* ◆ *Ich hole/rufe dich, wenn sie da ist.* **3.** *whenever, each time* ◇ *Wenn sie dieses Lied hört, wird sie traurig.* ◆ *Wenn ich mich bücke, tut mir der Rücken weh.*
◉ **wenn auch** *even though* ◇ *Wenn das Treffen auch nur kurz war, hatten wir viel Spaß.* ◆ *Die Wanderung war schön, wenn auch sehr anstrengend.*
Wenn [vɛn] *(always ohne Wenn und Aber)* without objection, without arguing ◇ *Er gehorchte ohne Wenn und Aber.*

wenn·gleich [vɛn'glaeç] [conjunc] *mostly written* although, even though ◇ *Die Arbeit war sehr gut, wenngleich noch nicht perfekt.* ◆ *Wenngleich die Wunde nicht mehr schmerzt, ist sie noch nicht ganz verheilt.* ⊜obwohl

② **wer** [veːɐ̯] [interrog pron] *(nominative)* who ◇ *Wer ist da?* ◆ *Ich frage mich, wer auf diesen Unfug gekommen ist.; (accusative)* who ◇ *Wen suchen Sie denn?* ◆ *Er weiß nicht, wen er bei Fragen anrufen kann.; (genitive)* whose ◇ *Wessen Stift ist das?* ◆ *Ich will sofort wissen, wessen Idee das war!; (dative)* (to/with) whom ◇ *Sie überlegt, wem sie alles Bescheid sagen soll.* ◆ *Mit wem spreche ich?* [indef pron] *(fam)* someone, somebody ◇ *Da hat wer für dich angerufen.* ◆ *Da ist wohl wer*

verliebt! ◆ *Ich bin schon bei wem eingeladen.* ◆ *Ich kenne wen, der dir helfen kann.; (in questions)* anybody ◇ *Ist da wer?* ⊜jemand
[rel pron] *(nominative, accusative, dative)* the person who, anyone/anybody who, whoever ◇ *Verloren ist, wer zu schnell aufgibt.* ◆ *Wer keinen Kaffee mag, kann auch Tee haben.* ◆ *Wen ich einlade, bestimme ich selbst.* ◆ *Wem zu kalt ist, der soll die Heizung aufdrehen.; (genitive)* the person (whom) ◇ *Wessen sie am meisten bedarf, ist ihr Kind.*

nom	wer
acc	wen
dat	wem
gen	wessen

wer·ben ['vɛʁbn̩] <wirbt, warb, hat geworben> [intr v] **1.** *advertise* ◇ *Diese Firma wirbt im Fernsehen.* ◆ *mit günstigen Preisen werben* für jdn/etw. werben *campaign for sb/sth, advertise for sb/sth* ◇ *Der Papst warb für den Frieden.* ◆ *Auf dem Plakat wird für Milch geworben.* **2.** um jdn/etw. werben *try to enlist sb/sth, seek to attract sb/sth* ◇ *um Aufträge werben* ◆ *Die Partei wirbt um Wähler.* ◆ *um Toleranz/Unterstützung/Vertrauen werben* um jds Gunst/Liebe werben *court sb's* favo(u)r/love [tr v] *(buyers, customers)* attract ◇ *Wer neue Abonnenten wirbt, bekommt eine Prämie.; (members etc.)* enlist ◇ *Interessenten für ein Projekt werben* ⊜gewinnen

② **Wer·bung** ['vɛʁbʊŋ] die <-, -en> **1.** *no pl* advertising ◇ *Geld für Werbung ausgeben* ◆ *Die Werbung zielt bewusst auf die jüngeren Konsumenten.* ◆ *indirekte Werbung betreiben;* publicity, advertising ◇ *Werbung für jdn/etw. machen* ⊜Reklame **2.** advertisement ◇ *Bitte keine Werbung einwerfen.* ⊜Reklame **3.** *translated with a verb construction* die Werbung … [gen] *attracting …, gaining …, the enrolment of …* ◇ *einen Bonus für die Werbung eines neuen Kunden/Mitglieds erhalten* die Werbung um jdn/etw. *the courting of sb/sth* die Werbung um die Gunst des Publikums *courting* favo(u)r *with the public*

Wer·de·gang ['veːɐ̯dəɡaŋ] der <-(e)s, Werdegänge> *career* ◇ *Ihr schulischer Werdegang verlief ohne Probleme.* ◆ *der Werdegang eines Künstlers/Politikers*

② **wer·den¹** ['veːɐ̯dn̩] <wird, wurde, ist geworden> [intr v] **1.** *+noun* etw. [nom] werden *become sth* ◇ *Mutter/Vater/Großvater werden* ◆ *Möchtest du meine Frau werden?* ◆ *Was möchtest du später mal werden?* ◆ *Er will Arzt werden.* ◆ *Ein Traum wird Wirklichkeit.* ◆ *Der Film wurde ein Welterfolg.* **2.** *+adj* get ◇ *Werd bald gesund!* ◆ *Das Essen wird kalt!* ◆ *Ihre Augen werden langsam schlecht.* krank werden *fall/become ill* alt/müde/vergesslich werden *become old/tired/forgetful* Das Wetter wird schlecht/schön. *The weather's turning/becoming bad/nice.* Das Wetter wird sonnig. *The weather's brightening up.* blind/rot/verrückt etc. werden *go blind/red/mad etc.* ◇ *Er wird schon ganz grau.* ◆ *Die Milch ist schlecht geworden.* **3.** *+indication of age* 18/35/50 werden *be* 18/35/50, *turn* 18/35/50 Er wurde nur 32 Jahre alt *He died already at the age of 32., He only reached the age of 32.* **4.** zu etw. werden *turn into sth, become sth* ◇ *Die Flüs-*

A B C D E F G H I J K L M N O P Q R S T U V **W** X Y Z

sigkeit wurde zu Gas. ♦ *Der mühsame Aufstieg wurde zur Qual.* ♦ *Das soll aber nicht zur Gewohnheit werden!* ♦ *Mit der Zeit wurde er zu einem guten Freund.* etw. wird aus etw./jdm sth/sb turns into sth, sth becomes of sth/sb ◊ *Aus ihrer Liebe ist Hass geworden.* ♦ *Aus der Raupe wurde ein Schmetterling.* ♦ *Aus dem faulen Lehrling wurde ein tüchtiger Schreiner.* ♦ *Was soll nur aus den Kindern werden, wenn ich sterbe?* ♦ *„Was ist eigentlich aus Tom geworden?"* — *„Der ist verheiratet und hat zwei Kinder!"* Was ist bloß aus … geworden? What has happened to …? aus jdm wird (et)was sb gets somewhere in life aus jdm wird nichts sb does not get anywhere in life aus etw. wird nichts you can forget about sth ◊ *Aus unserem Treffen wird nichts, denn er hat keine Zeit.* [imp v] **1.** *+noun or adj* es wird … it will be … ◊ *Es wird gleich 17 Uhr.* ♦ *Morgen soll es sehr warm werden.* ♦ *Bald wird es Frühling.* Es wird dunkel/spät/kalt. It is getting dark/late/cold. Es wird Abend. Evening is drawing in. Es wird Morgen/Tag. Dawn is breaking. Es wird alles anders. Everything will change. **2.** *+adj* jdm wird (es) … sb gets … ◊ *Ihm wurde (es) heiß/kalt.* ♦ *Plötzlich wurde ihr unheimlich.*

🄮 nicht mehr werden *(fam)* be damned, flip your lid ◊ *Das hast du wirklich getan? Ich werd nicht mehr!* (et)was/nichts werden *(fam)* turn out well/come to nothing ◊ *Der Braten/Kuchen wird was.* ♦ *Unser Plan ist leider nichts geworden.* etw. wird schon wieder *(fam)* everything will be okay/fine, sth will sort itself out ◊ *Mach dir nicht so viele Sorgen — das wird schon wieder!* was nicht ist, kann (ja) noch werden things can change das wird (et)was *(fam, iron)* that will be something wie jd werden get like sb, start to sound like sb ◊ *Hör auf, ständig alle zu kritisieren — du wirst schon wie dein Vater!*

🄮 **wer·den²** ['veːɐ̯dn̩] <wird, wurde, ist worden> [aux] **1.** *+inf (future)* Es wird bald regnen. It will rain soon. ◊ *Sie werden morgen verreisen.* ♦ *Er wird ab jetzt mehr Sport treiben.* ♦ *Ich werde zurück sein, wenn du da bist.* **2.** *+past p (future perfect)* getan/beendet etc. haben werden will have done/finished etc. ◊ *Bis heute Abend werde ich meine Arbeit geschafft haben.* gegangen/verschwunden etc. sein werden will have gone/disappeared etc. ◊ *Die Unordnung wird bis morgen wieder verschwunden sein.* **3.** *+inf (supposition, wish)* will ◊ *„Es hat geklingelt!"* —*„Das wird der Postbote sein!"* ♦ *Er wird doch an mich denken?* ♦ *Es wird schon alles gut gehen!* Das Hotel wird wohl teuer sein. The hotel will probably be expensive. Es wird doch nichts passiert sein, oder? Nothing will have happened, will it? **4.** *+past p (passive)* ausgelacht/beobachtet/gekauft etc. werden be laughed at/observed/bought etc. ◊ *Er ist angezeigt/verklagt worden.* ♦ *Mein Kuchen wird immer gern gegessen.* ♦ *Er wurde heute in der Schule bestraft.*; *(action in progress)* beobachtet/gebaut/verfolgt etc. werden be being watched/built/pursued etc. ◊ *Pass auf, wir werden überholt!* **5.** *subjunctive II, +inf (conditional)* would ◊ *Ich würde dir abraten, zuzusagen.* ♦ *Ich würde das an deiner Stelle nicht machen.* Würdest du so etwas tun? Would you do something like that? Würden Sie mir bitte helfen?

Would you help me please? **6.** *+past p (command)* Jetzt wird gearbeitet! Let's start working now! Im Unterricht wird nicht gegessen! There is no eating during lessons! Hier wird nicht getuschelt! Stop whispering! Wirst du nun endlich still sein? Keep quiet now!

🄮 **wer·fen** ['vɛrfn̩] <wirft, warf, hat geworfen> [tr+intr v] **1.** throw ◊ *Ich kann weiter werfen als du!* ♦ *Sie warf (den Ball) fast 50 Meter weit.* ♦ *Sie war so wütend, dass sie ihm einen Schuh an den Kopf warf.* ♦ sich verzweifelt in jds Arme/vor einen Zug werfen ein Produkt auf den Markt werfen launch a product onto the market; *(a coin, your hair, head)* toss ◊ *den Kopf in den Nacken werfen; (with force)* fling ◊ *Die Zuschauer warfen jubelnd ihre Arme in die Luft.* ♦ sich weinend aufs Bett/zu Boden werfen ♦ *Er wurde ins Gefängnis geworfen.* mit etw. (nach jdm/etw.) werfen throw sth (at sb/sth) ◊ *Man wirft nicht mit Steinen!* ♦ mit Schneebällen nach einem Auto werfen **2.** zoo give birth (to) ◊ *Hamster können mehrere Male im Jahr werfen.* ♦ *Junge/Welpen werfen* [tr v] **1.** *(a shadow, light)* cast ◊ *Die Bäume werfen lange Schatten.* ♦ *Der Mond warf ein bleiches Licht.* **2.** Blasen werfen bubble **3.** Falten werfen crease, get creased

Werft [vɛrft] die <-, -en> shipyard, dockyard

🄮 **Werk** [vɛrk] das <-(e)s, -e> **1.** work ◊ *Das Chaos im Büro ist das Werk von Einbrechern.* ♦ ein literarisches/wissenschaftliches Werk schreiben ♦ *„Romeo und Julia" ist ein Werk von Shakespeare.* **2.** no pl *(all creations of an artist)* works ◊ *das Leben und Werk Picassos* ♦ *Sein gesammeltes Werk umfasst 20 Bände.* **3.** factory, plant, works ◊ *Der Autohersteller muss mehrere Werke schließen.* ♦ als Mechaniker/Monteur in einem Werk arbeiten 🄮 das Diakonische Werk REL *the agency of the German Protestant Church responsible for social work* ein gutes Werk tun do a good deed ans Werk gehen, sich ans Werk machen get down to work am Werk sein be at work ab Werk ex works ◊ *direkt ab Werk einkaufen, um Geld zu sparen*

wer·keln ['vɛrkl̩n] [intr v] *+haben (fam)* (an etw. [dat]) werkeln potter around/about (with sth) ◊ *In ihrer Freizeit werkelt sie gerne im Garten/mit Holz.* ♦ *Er werkelt an einem Lenkdrachen.*

🄮 **Werk·statt** ['vɛrkʃtat] die <-, Werkstätten> **1.** *most sing* workshop ◊ *Schmuck aus eigener Werkstatt verkaufen* ♦ die Werkstatt eines Keramikers **2.** *most sing* garage ◊ *sein Auto in die Werkstatt bringen* ♦ *Das Auto muss dringend in die Werkstatt.*

Werk·tag ['vɛrktaːk] der <-(e)s, -e> working day, workday ◊ *Der Markt hat im Sommer jeden Werktag geöffnet.* ♦ *Dieser Zug verkehrt an Werktagen außer samstags.* ⊜Wochentag ⊜Feiertag

werk·tags ['vɛrktaːks] [adv] on weekdays ◊ *Die Läden haben ab jetzt werktags länger offen.*

🄮 **Werk·zeug** ['vɛrktsɔøk] das <-(e)s, -e> **1.** *no pl* tools ◊ *ein Auto/Schloss mit speziellem Werkzeug aufbrechen* ♦ *das richtige Werkzeug zum Tapezieren* **2.** *(also fig)* tool ◊ *ein Werkzeug benutzen* ♦ *Sprache ist das Werkzeug der Kommunikation.*

🄮 **wert** [veːɐ̯t] [adj] no comp/superl **1.** (jdm) etw. wert

sein be worth sth (to sb) ◇ *Irland ist eine Reise wert.* ♦ *Die Sache ist einen Versuch wert.* ♦ *Das Konzert war mir das Geld wert.* ♦ *Unsere Freundschaft/Sie ist mir eine Menge wert.* ♦ *Die Kette ist 200 Euro wert.* ♦ *Deine Hilfe ist sehr viel wert.* **2.** *(lofty)* einer Sache ⌐gen¬ wert sein deserve sth ◇ *Dieses Buch ist einer Erwähnung wert.* „Vielen Dank!" — „Nicht der Rede wert!" "Many thanks" — "Don't mention it!" jds nicht wert sein be unworthy of sb ◇ *Sie ist dieses Mannes nicht wert.*

② **Wert** [veːɐ̯t] der <-(e)s, -e> **1.** value ◇ *Edelsteine/ Vorzüge von unschätzbarem Wert* ♦ *Die Aktie gewinnt/verliert an Wert.* ♦ im Wert fallen/steigen ♦ *Der Wert der Sammlung beläuft sich auf/liegt bei 700 Euro.* ♦ *moralische/innere/ideelle Werte* im Wert von worth, to the value of ◇ *Schmuck im Wert von 3000 Euro erbeuten* **2.** *most sing* importance, value ◇ *Dieser Ring ist für mich von besonderem Wert.* ♦ *der literarische Wert eines Werks* **3.** *(of measurement)* result, value ◇ *einen Wert irgendwo ablesen* ♦ *einen mathematischen Wert berechnen* ♦ *jdm die Werte einer Blutuntersuchung mitteilen* **4.** *only pl* valuable objects, objects of value ◇ *Wurden bei dem Einbruch Bilder, Schmuck oder andere Werte gestohlen?* ⊚ keinen (gesteigerten) Wert auf etw. ⌐acc¬ legen *(fam)* set no (great) store by sth, attach no (great) importance to sth einer Sache ⌐dat¬ (großen/keinen) Wert beimessen/beilegen attach (great/no) value to sth (großen/viel) Wert auf etw. ⌐acc¬ legen set (great) store by sth, attach (great) importance to sth ◇ *Wert auf ein gepflegtes Äußeres legen* ♦ *viel Wert darauf legen, dass die Arbeit sorgfältig gemacht wird* das hat doch keinen Wert there is no point, it's a waste of time etw. (weit) unter Wert verkaufen sell sth for (far) less than its value

wer·ten [ˈveːɐ̯tn̩] <wertet, wertete, hat gewertet> ⌐tr+intr v¬ judge ◇ *Wie darf ich deine Aussage werten?* ♦ *Positiv zu werten ist die rege Teilnahme an der Veranstaltung.* ♦ *(an einer Diskussion teilnehmen, ohne zu werten; (in school)* rate, grade ◇ *eine Prüfung werten; (in sports)* award points, count ◇ *Der Wurf war ungültig und wurde nicht gewertet.; (in a quality test)* assess, evaluate etw. als etw. ⌐acc¬ werten rate sth as sth, evaluate sth as sth ◇ *eine Entwicklung as Erfolg werten*

Wer·tung [ˈveːɐ̯tʊŋ] die <-, -en> **1.** SPORT score ◇ *eine hohe Wertung erreichen* in die Wertung eingehen/kommen be counted **2.** SCHOOL grading ◇ *die Wertung einer Klassenarbeit/Prüfung* ♦ *die doppelte/einfache Wertung einer Klausur* in die Wertung eingehen be included in the grading **3.** *(in a quality test)* rating ◇ *Das Shampoo erhielt bei dem Test die Wertung „gut".* in die Wertung eingehen be assessed **4.** judgement, evaluation ◇ *Die Wertung des Sachverhalts ist Aufgabe des Richters.* ♦ *eine politische Wertung der Situation abgeben* ⊚ in der Wertung hinten/vorne liegen SPORT be in the lead/way behind

wert·voll [ˈveːɐ̯tfɔl] ⌐adj¬ valuable ◇ *eine wertvolle Uhr* ♦ *Nichts ist wertvoller als die Gesundheit.* ♦ *Das alles kostet mich nur wertvolle Zeit.* für jdn/ etw. wertvoll valuable to sb/sth ◇ *für den Körper*

wertvolle Vitamine ♦ *Der Hinweis war für die Polizei sehr wertvoll.*

We·sen [ˈveːzn̩] das <-s, -> **1.** *no pl* character, nature ◇ *Das Wesen des Hundes ist freundlich.* ♦ *ein einnehmendes/ernstes/stilles Wesen haben* ♦ *in seinem innersten Wesen einsam sein* ♦ *Es ist das Wesen der Forschung, Neues zu entdecken.* ♦ *Es gehört zum Wesen von Wörterbüchern, dass sie schnell veralten.* ⊜Natur **2.** being ◇ *Gott, das höchste Wesen* ♦ *Was für ein hilfloses Wesen ein Baby doch ist!* ♦ *Dürfen menschliche Wesen geklont werden?* ♦ *Dein Mann, das unbekannte Wesen!; (as a personality)* person ◇ *Sie ist ein liebenswürdiges Wesen.; (animal, alien)* creature ◇ *ein außerirdisches Wesen*

② **we·sent·lich** [ˈveːzn̩tlɪç, ˈveːzəntlɪç] ⌐adj¬ *(für jdn/ etw.)* wesentlich fundamental (to sb/sth), essential (to sb/sth) ◇ *ein wesentlicher Unterschied* ♦ *Vitamine als wesentlicher Bestandteil unserer Ernährung* ♦ *Deutschkenntnisse sind für diesen Job wesentlich.* ⌐adv¬ considerably, significantly ◇ *wesentlich zu etw. beitragen* ♦ *Sein Zustand hat sich wesentlich verbessert/verschlechtert.* ♦ *Es ist über Nacht nicht wesentlich kälter geworden.* ♦ *Sie ist wesentlich jünger als er.* ⊚ etwas/nichts Wesentliches something/nothing of importance das Wesentliche the essentials ◇ *sich/etw. auf das Wesentliche beschränken* im Wesentlichen in essence, essentially um ein Wesentliches *(lofty)* considerably, very ◇ *Er ist um ein Wesentliches jünger als sie.*

② **wes·halb** [vɛsˈhalp] ⌐adv¬ **1.** *interrogative* why ◇ *Weshalb ist das so?* ♦ *Weshalb funktioniert das nicht?* ♦ *„Ich fahre jetzt." — „Weshalb denn?"* ♦ *Ich frage mich, weshalb sie sich so aufregt.* ♦ *Ich weiß zwar nicht weshalb, aber der Kurs fällt aus.* ♦ *Den Grund, weshalb sie traurig ist, will sie nicht sagen.* ⊜warum, weswegen **2.** *relative* which is why ◇ *Sie sieht schlecht, weshalb sie eine Brille braucht.* ♦ *Es ist ein Unfall passiert, weshalb die Straße gesperrt wurde.* ⊜weswegen

Wes·pe [ˈvɛspə] die <-, -n> wasp ◇ *von einer Wespe gestochen werden*

② **wes·sen** [ˈvɛsn̩] ⌐pron¬ *gen of* wer

Wes·si [ˈvɛsiː] der <-s, -s> *(fam, also pej)* ◇ *Er ist ein typischer Wessi, der alles besser weiß.* ⊜Ossi

---

The word *Wessi* is a short form for 'West German', coined in East Germany. Even though it is not necessarily a derogatory term, it nevertheless expresses the reservations East Germans have about West Germans.

---

② **West** [vɛst] *without the article, invariable* **1.** *+prep* aus/von West from the west ◇ *Der Wind kommt aus West.* nach West to the west, westwards ◇ *ein Kurs von Ost nach West* ⊜Westen ⊜Ost, Osten **2.** West ◇ *das Freizeitzentrum West* ♦ *das Autobahnende München West* ⊜Ost **3.** West Germany, the West ◇ *Es kamen Besucher aus Ost und West.* ⊜Westdeutschland ⊜Ostdeutschland

② **West-...** [vɛst] ⌐prefix¬ west ..., western ... ◇ *der Westteil einer Stadt* ♦ *die Westgrenze eines Landes* ♦ *Westeuropäer/Westafrikaner sein* ♦ *Wind aus Westnordwest; (in names)* West ..., Western ... ◇ *Westdeutschland* ♦ *Westeuropa* ⊜Ost...

west·deutsch [ˈvɛstdɔʏt͡ʃ] ⌐adj¬ *mostly before ns*

A B C D E F G H I J K L M N O P Q R S T U V W X Y Z

West German ⊜ostdeutsch → deutsch

West·deut·sche ['vɛstdɔɐ̯tʃə] der/die
<–n, die Westdeutschen> *but: ein Westdeutscher/
eine Westdeutsche* West German ⊜Ostdeutsche →
Deutsche, Wessi

West·deutsch·land ['vɛstdɔɐ̯tʃlant] das <–(s)>
*article only in combination with attribute, no pl
(political)* West Germany ◊ *das Zusammenwach-
sen von Westdeutschland und Ostdeutschland
fördern; (geographical)* Western Germany ◊ *durch
Westdeutschland und Norddeutschland reisen*
⊜Ostdeutschland → Deutschland

Wes·te ['vɛstə] die <–, –n> **1.** waistcoat, vest ◊ *ein
Anzug mit Weste* ♦ *Er zog das Jackett aus, behielt
die Weste aber an.* **2.** cardigan ◊ *jdm eine Weste
stricken* ♦ *sich eine Weste überziehen, weil es kalt
ist*
Ⓔ *eine kugelsichere Weste* a bulletproof vest ♦
eine reine/saubere/weiße Weste haben have a
clean record

② **Wes·ten** ['vɛstn̩] der <–s> *no pl* **1.** west ◊ *Wo ist
Westen?* ♦ *Der Regen kommt aus Westen.* ♦ *nach
Westen fahren* nach Westen to the west, westwards
Züge in Richtung Westen westbound trains ⊜Osten
2. POL, HIST der Westen the West ◊ *Das Land hat
sich dem Westen geöffnet.* ♦ *die Fluchtbewegung
aus der DDR in den Westen* ⊜Osten

west·lich¹ ['vɛstlɪç] adj **1.** *only before ns* western
◊ *das westliche Mittelmeer* ♦ *im westlichen Teil der
Stadt* ⊜östlich **2.** *only before ns (wind,
direction)* westerly aus westlicher Richtung from
the West ⊜östlich **3.** Western ◊ *eine westliche
Religion* ⊜östlich **4.** HIST Western-bloc, West-bloc ◊
ein westlicher Geheimdienst ⊜östlich

west·lich² ['vɛstlɪç] prep **1.** +gen (to the) west
of ◊ *Westlich der Stadt ist eine Fabrik.* ♦ *im Wald
westlich der Ortschaft* ⊜östlich **2.** *adverbial* +dat
westlich von west of ◊ *Westlich von Mauritius ist
Afrika.* ♦ *westlich von München wohnen* ⊜östlich

wes·we·gen [vɛs'veːgn̩] adv **1.** *interrogative* why
◊ *Weswegen rufst du an?* ♦ *„Ich bin sauer."* —
„Weswegen denn?" ♦ *Das ist der Grund, weswegen
ich frage.* ♦ *Der Anlass, weswegen er bestraft
wurde, war ein Diebstahl.* ♦ *Ich begreife nicht,
weswegen er so schecht gelaunt ist.* ⊜warum,
weshalb **2.** *relative* which is why ◊ *Ich bin in einen
Stau geraten, weswegen ich zu spät bin.* ♦ *Sie ist
ohne Mütze Rad gefahren, weswegen sie jetzt
krank ist.* ⊜weshalb

Wett·be·werb ['vɛtbəvɛ'p] der <–(e)s, –e> competition ◊ *an einem Wettbewerb teilnehmen* ♦ *einen/
in einem Wettbewerb gewinnen* ♦ *mit jdm in Wettbewerb treten* ♦ *Die Firma konnte sich im internationalen Wettbewerb behaupten.*

wett·be·werbs·fä·hig ['vɛtbəvɛ'psfɛːɪç] adj competitive ◊ *ein wettbewerbsfähiges Angebot/Produkt*
♦ *international wettbewerbsfähig bleiben*

Wet·te ['vɛtə] die <–, –n> bet ◊ *(mit jdm) eine
Wette abschließen* ♦ *Nimmst du die Wette an?* ♦
eine Wette (gegen jdn) gewinnen/verlieren eine
Wette auf jdn/etw. a bet on sb/sth ◊ *eine Wette
auf das Pferd/den Spieler/die Zahl fünf* eine Wette
um etw. a bet for sth ◊ *eine Wette um zehn Euro/
ein Eis eingehen*
Ⓔ *jede Wette eingehen(, dass ...)* bet you
anything (that ...) *die Wette gilt (fam)* the bet is

on etw. (mit jdm) um die Wette tun (mit jdm)
um die Wette laufen have a race (with sb) *(mit
jdm) um die Wette schwimmen/trinken* have a
swimming/drinking competition (with sb) (mit jdm)
um die Wette arbeiten try to outdo (sb) at work

wet·ten ['vɛtn̩] <wettet, wettete, hat gewettet>
tr+intr v (mit jdm) (etw./um etw.) wetten bet (sb)
(sth) ◊ *mit jdm um Geld wetten* ♦ *Wollen wir
wetten?* ♦ *Worum/Um wie viel wetten wir?* ♦ *Ich
wette zehn Euro/eine Flasche Wein, dass es
morgen regnet.* ♦ *Ich wette, du lügst!* ♦ *Ich wette
mit dir, dass das nicht stimmt.* ♦ *Sie hat gegen ihn
gewettet.* ♦ *„Er wird es schaffen!"* — *„Ich wette
dagegen!"*; *(in sports, games)* auf jdn/etw.
wetten bet on sb/sth ◊ *auf ein Pferd wetten*
Ⓔ *auf etw.* acc *wetten können* be able to bet
on sth ◊ *Sie können darauf wetten, dass ich mich
beschweren werde!* *wetten, dass (fam)* it's a dead
cert, you can bet on it ◊ *Wetten, dass du dich
nicht traust?* ♦ *„Er kommt nicht."* — *„Wetten, dass
doch?"* so haben wir nicht gewettet *(fam)* that
was not the deal, that was not what we agreed

② **Wet·ter** ['vɛtɐ] das <–s> *no pl* weather ◊ *im
Urlaub gutes Wetter haben* ♦ *Wie wird das Wetter
am Wochenende?* ♦ *Wird das schöne Wetter
halten/anhalten?* ♦ *Bekleidung für jedes Wetter
einpacken* ♦ *Im April ist das Wetter sehr unbestän-
dig/wechselhaft.*

② **Wet·ter·be·richt** ['vɛtɐbərɪçt] der <–(e)s, –e>
weather forecast, weather report ◊ *Laut Wetterbericht soll es schön bleiben.* ♦ *Der Wetterbericht hat
für heute Regen angekündigt.* ⊜Wettervorhersage

wet·ter·fest ['vɛtɐfɛst] adj no comp/superl weatherproof, weather-resistant ◊ *wetterfeste Kleidung/
Schuhe* ♦ *Das Material ist wetterfest.* adv Holz
wetterfest imprägnieren weatherproof wood sich
zum Wandern wetterfest anziehen put weatherproof clothing on to go hiking

wet·tern ['vɛtɐn] intr v +haben curse ◊ *Anstatt
so zu wettern, könntest du eine Lösung vorschlagen.* gegen jdn/etw. wettern, über jdn/etw.
wettern loudly denounce sb/sth, rant about sb/sth
◊ *Die Opposition wetterte gegen den Kanzler.* ♦
über einen unfähigen Chef wettern

Wett·kampf ['vɛtkampf] der <–(e)s, Wettkämpfe>
competition ◊ *an einem Wettkampf teilnehmen* ♦
gegen jdn zum Wettkampf antreten ♦ *jdn zu einem
Wettkampf herausfordern* ♦ *einen Wettkampf
gewinnen/verlieren* den Wettkampf um jdn/etw. the
competition for sb/sth ◊ *ein Wettkampf um die
Goldmedaille/den Meistertitel*

Wett·streit ['vɛtʃtraet] der <–(e)s, –e> *most sing*
contest ◊ *einen Wettstreit austragen* ♦ *im Wettstreit der besten Sänger* ♦ *einen Wettstreit
zwischen Schülern und Lehrern veranstalten* im
Wettstreit mit jdm/etw. liegen, in Wettstreit mit
jdm/etw. treten be competing with sb/sth im Wettstreit gegeneinander antreten be competing
against each other

WG [veː'geː] die *(fam)* (abbr of Wohngemeinschaft)
group sharing accommodation ◊ *in eine WG
einziehen* ♦ *in einer WG leben*

wich aus [vɪç 'aos] *pret of* ausweichen

② **wich·tig** ['vɪçtɪç] adj important ◊ *eine wichtige
Frage.* ♦ *Tägliche Bewegung ist wichtig.* ♦ *Wichtig
ist, dass du es verstanden hast.* ♦ *die wichtigsten*

Nachrichten im Überblick wichtig für jdn/etw. important for sb/sth ◊ *Vorbilder sind für Jugendliche wichtig.* ♦ *Eine Karotte enthält viele für den Körper wichtige Vitamine.* jdm wichtig sein important to sb ◊ *Ihre Meinung ist ihm wichtig.* ♦ *Bin ich dir überhaupt wichtig?* ♦ *Meine Freizeit ist mir am wichtigsten.* (für jdn/etw.) (nur/nicht) halb so wichtig (only/not) half as important (to sb/sth) ◊ *Geld ist (für mich) nur halb so wichtig.* ⊛ sich/jdn/etw. (so/zu) wichtig nehmen take yourself/sb/sth (so/too) seriously ◊ *Nimm das doch jetzt nicht so wichtig!* ♦ *Sie nimmt sich und ihre Probleme zu wichtig.* sich (mit jdm/etw.) wichtig tun/machen, sich (dat) (mit jdm/etw.) wichtig vorkommen be pompous (about sb/sth), be full of yourself (because of sb/sth) ◊ *Mit seinem neuen Porsche macht/tut er sich (schon sehr) wichtig.*

wi·ckeln ['vɪk|n̩] (tr v) +*haben* **1.** etw. um etw. wickeln wrap sth around sth, wind sth around sth ◊ *Wickel dir doch einen Schal um den Hals!* eine Schnur um ein Paket wickeln tie a piece of string around a packet jdn/etw. in etw. (acc) wickeln wrap sb/sth in sth ◊ *Brote in Alufolie wickeln* ♦ *Er wickelte sich in seine Jacke und ging in die Kälte. Er wickelte sich aus seinem Schlafsack. He unwrapped himself from his sleeping bag.; (thread, leash)* sich um jdn/etw. wickeln wrap itself around sb/sth ◊ *Die Hundeleine hat sich um mein Bein gewickelt.* **2.** *(into a ball)* etw. (zu etw.) wickeln wind sth (into sth) ◊ *Garn/Wolle (zu einem Knäuel) wickeln; (onto a reel, spool)* etw. um/auf etw. (acc) wickeln wind sth round/onto sth ◊ *eine Schnur um eine Rolle wickeln* ♦ *einen Faden auf eine Spule wickeln* **3.** bandage ◊ *Das verletzte Bein/Knie muss gewickelt werden.* **4.** ein Baby/Kind wickeln change a baby's/child's nappy, change a baby's/child's diaper *Das Baby ist frisch gewickelt. The baby has just been changed.*

Wid·der ['vɪdɐ] der <-s, –> **1.** ZOO ram ◊ *Unter den fünf Schafen ist auch ein Widder.* **2.** ASTROL, ASTRON Aries

wi·der ['vidɐ] (prep) (+acc) *(lofty)* against ◊ *Sie kam wider Erwarten.* ♦ *Er musste wider Willen lachen.*

wi·der·fah·ren [vidɐ'faːrən] <widerfährt, widerfuhr, ist widerfahren> (intr v) *(lofty)* etw. widerfährt jdm sth happens to sb, sb experiences sth ◊ *Ihr ist Leid/Schlimmes/Unrecht widerfahren.* ♦ *Mir ist ein dummes Missgeschick widerfahren.*

wi·der·le·gen [vidɐ'leːgn̩] <widerlegt, widerlegte, hat widerlegt> (tr v) refute, disprove ◊ *einen Vorwurf widerlegen* ♦ *eine Hypothese/Theorie/These widerlegen*

wi·der·lich ['vidɐlɪç] (adj, adv) revolting(ly), disgusting(ly) ◊ *einen widerlichen Anblick bieten* ♦ *Diese Medizin schmeckt widerlich!* ♦ sich widerlich verhalten jdm widerlich sein be repulsive to sb ◊ *Fleisch ist ihm widerlich. Draußen ist es widerlich kalt und nass. It's awfully cold and wet outside.*

wi·der·ru·fen [vidɐ'ruːfn̩] <widerruft, widerrief, hat widerrufen> (tr v) retract, withdraw ◊ *eine Aussage/Behauptung/Erklärung widerrufen* ♦ *ein Urteil widerrufen; (a contract)* cancel ◊ *einen Vertrag innerhalb einer Frist von zehn Tagen widerrufen*

wi·der·set·zen [vidɐ'zɛtsn̩] <widersetzt sich, widersetzte sich, hat sich widersetzt> (ref v) sich jdm/etw. widersetzen oppose sb/sth ◊ *sich einem*

Befehl/Gesetz widersetzen sich einem Angriff widersetzen resist an attack

wi·der|spie·geln ['vidɐʃpiːgln̩] <spiegelt wider, spiegelte wider, hat widergespiegelt> (tr v) reflect ◊ *eine Umfrage, die die Meinung der Bürger widerspiegelt* ♦ *Der See spiegelt die Wolken wider.* sich widerspiegeln be reflected somewhere ◊ *In den Medien spiegelt sich die öffentliche Meinung wider.* ♦ *Die Sonne spiegelt sich im Wasser wider.* ⊜sich reflektieren

② **wi·der·spre·chen** [vidɐ'ʃprɛçn̩] <widerspricht, widersprach, hat widersprochen> (intr v) jdm/etw. widersprechen contradict sb/sth ◊ *Ich muss dir leider widersprechen.* ♦ *einer Aussage/Behauptung/Meinung widersprechen* ♦ *Ihre Äußerung/Behauptung widerspricht den Tatsachen.* die Behauptungen/Aussagen etc. widersprechen sich/einander the assertions/statements etc. contradict each other, the assertions/statements etc. are inconsistent ⊜zustimmen

Wi·der·spruch ['vidɐʃprʊx] der <-(e)s, Widersprüche> **1.** opposition, protest ◊ *auf Widerspruch stoßen* ♦ *Ihr Widerspruch war begründet.* ♦ *keinen Widerspruch dulden* **2.** contradiction ◊ *sich in Widersprüche verstricken* ♦ *Ist umweltfreundliche Kernenergie ein Widerspruch in sich?* ♦ *Es besteht ein krasser Widerspruch zwischen Theorie und Praxis.* im Widerspruch zu/mit etw. stehen/sein, sich im Widerspruch mit/zu etw. befinden contradict sth, be contrary to sth ◊ *Die Mieterhöhung steht im Widerspruch mit dem Vertrag.* **3.** LAW objection ◊ *Die Behörde hat den Widerspruch zurückgewiesen.* Widerspruch (gegen etw.) einlegen file an objection (to sth), lodge a protest (against sth)

wi·der·sprüch·lich ['vidɐʃprʏçlɪç] (adj) **1.** contradictory ◊ *Die Aussage des Zeugen war unklar und widersprüchlich.* ♦ *Die widersprüchlichen Meldungen sorgten für Verwirrung.* **2.** *with pl ns* inconsistent ◊ *widersprüchliche Interessen/Meinungen haben* ♦ *Die Beurteilungen der beiden Lehrer waren widersprüchlich.*

Wi·der·stand ['vidɐʃtant] der <-(e)s, Widerstände> **1.** *no pl* resistance ◊ *Er leistete schwachen/starken Widerstand.* ♦ *auf Widerstand stoßen* ♦ *aktiver/passiver Widerstand* ♦ *Sie sind verhaftet — Widerstand ist zwecklos!* ♦ *Die Uhr so lange aufziehen, bis ein Widerstand spürbar wird.* ♦ *den Widerstand berechnen/messen* Widerstand gegen jdn/etw. resistance to sb/sth ◊ *In der Klasse regt sich Widerstand gegen den Lehrer.* **2.** *most pl* opposition ◊ *beim geringsten Widerstand aufgeben* ♦ *große Widerstände überwinden, um sein Ziel zu erreichen* **3.** *no pl* resistance ◊ *sich dem Widerstand anschließen* **4.** TECHN resistor ◊ *einen Widerstand einbauen*

wi·der·ste·hen [vidɐ'ʃteːən] <widersteht, widerstand, hat widerstanden> (intr v) jdm/etw. widerstehen resist sb/sth ◊ *einer Versuchung widerstehen* ♦ *Ich kann seinem Charme/Süßigkeiten nicht widerstehen.; (a strain, an attack)* withstand sb/sth ◊ *Das Material kann Feuer 30 Minuten widerstehen.* ♦ *Sie konnte dem Druck nicht länger widerstehen und gab auf.*

wi·der·wil·lig ['vidɐvɪlɪç] (adj, adv) *no comp/superl* reluctant(ly), unwilling(ly) ◊ *ein widerwilliges Zuge-*

ständnis ♦ *Der Schüler ist widerwillig und faul.* ♦ *Widerwillig gab er mir das Geld zurück.*
wid·men ['vɪtmən] <widmet, widmete, hat gewidmet> ⎣tr v⎦ **1.** *jdm etw.* widmen *dedicate sth to sb* ◊ *seiner Frau ein Gedicht widmen* ♦ *Dieses Lied ist allen unglücklich Verliebten gewidmet.* **2.** *(time, attention)* *jdm/etw.* etw. widmen *give sth to sb/sth, devote sth to sb/sth* ◊ *jdm/etw. seine Aufmerksamkeit widmen* ♦ *Diesem Thema wurden in der Zeitung mehrere Artikel gewidmet.* ⎣ref v⎦ sich *jdm/etw.* widmen *devote yourself to sb/sth, attend to sb/sth* ◊ *sich wichtigen Dingen widmen* ♦ *sich seiner Arbeit/Familie widmen*
② **wie¹** [vi:] ⎣adv⎦ **1.** *how* ◊ *Wie geht es dir?* ♦ *Wie macht er das nur?* ♦ *Wie alt bist du?* ♦ *Wie schnell fährt das Auto?* ♦ *Er wollte wissen, wie es uns gefallen hat.* ♦ *Ich verstehe nicht, wie das funktioniert.* ♦ *Wie dumm von dir!* ♦ *Wie kommt sie dazu, so etwas zu tun?* ♦ *Wie soll ich das wissen?* wie viel *how much* ◊ *Wie viel verdienst du?* ♦ *Wie viel älter als ich bist du?* wie viele *how many* ◊ *Wie viele Äpfel soll ich kaufen?* Wie heißt du? *What's your name?* Wie spät/viel Uhr ist es? *What's the time?* Wie viel ist drei mal fünf? *What is three times five?* Wie ist er/sie/es denn so? *What's he/she/it like?* **2.** *in relative clauses to describe the manner in which sth is done* *the way (in which)*, *how* ◊ *Die Art, wie er denkt, ist unlogisch.* ♦ *Es ist unfair, wie sie über andere spricht.* **3.** *in relative clauses to describe the extent of sth* *as, to which* ◊ *Die Gewinne erhöhten sich im gleichen Umfang, wie die Kosten sanken.* ♦ *Die Firma konnte nicht in dem Umfang produzieren, wie zunächst geplant war.* ♦ *Das Ausmaß, wie die Preise steigen, verärgert die Kunden.* **4.** *(fam) (question tag)* ...,wie? *are you/is he etc.?, do you/does he etc.?* ◊ *Du magst ihn nicht, wie?*
◉ wie viel auch (immer) *no matter how much* ◊ *Das Kleid muss ich haben, wie viel auch immer das kostet.* wie dem auch sei, ... *in any case, ...; be that as it may, ...* ◊ *Wie dem auch sei, die Sache ist überstanden.* wie wär's mit etw. *(fam)* *how about sth* ◊ *Wie wär's mit einem Gläschen Wein?* wie ... auch *no matter how ...* ◊ *Wie ich es auch sage, sie versteht es nicht.* wie bitte **1.** *pardon, sorry* ◊ *Wie bitte? Ich hab dich gerade nicht verstanden!* **2.** *(fam)* *I beg your pardon* ◊ „*Ich habe dich betrogen!*“ — „*Wie bitte?*“
② **wie²** [vi:] ⎣conjunc⎦ **1.** *(comparative)* *as, like* ◊ *Sie sieht aus wie immer.* ♦ *Da geht es euch wie mir.* ♦ *Sie sind schlau wie ein Fuchs.* ♦ *Er ist so alt/dick/groß wie ich.* **2.** *(referring to sth)* *as* ◊ *Die Agenda ist wie folgt: ...* ♦ *Wie ich höre, gibt es was zu feiern.* ♦ *Sie verabredet, treffen wir uns um drei.* **3.** so (...), wie ... ... *just like ...* ◊ *Es verlief alles so, wie es geplant war.* ♦ *Er benimmt sich immer so, wie es ihm gerade passt.* **4.** *(enumerating)* *such as, like* ◊ *Es gab Beilagen wie Kartoffeln, Reis und Gemüse.* ♦ *Er treibt viel Sport wie Joggen und Radfahren.* **5.** both, as well as ◊ *Sie ist morgens wie abends müde.* ♦ *Die Sauna ist für Männer wie Frauen.* ⊖und auch **6.** *(with verbs of perception)* *that* ◊ *Er bemerkte, wie sie zornig wurde.* *Sie spürte, wie es langsam wärmer wurde.* *She noticed it gradually getting warmer.*
7. +*historical pres (fam)* *(on the point of) as*,

when ◊ *Wie ich gerade losgehe, fängt es an zu regnen.* ♦ *Wie ich mich hinlege, läutet das Telefon.* ⊖als
◉ wie du mir, so ich dir *tit for tat* wie wenn *as if* ◊ *Es war ein Knall, wie wenn etwas explodiert wäre.* ⊖als ob
② **wie·der¹** ['vi:de] ⎣adv⎦ **1.** *again* ◊ *endlich wieder sehen können* ♦ *Fahren wir nächstes Jahr wieder nach Frankreich?* ♦ *etw. wieder aufräumen* ♦ *sich wieder beruhigen* ♦ *Plötzlich ist es mir wieder eingefallen.* ♦ *Das darfst du nie wieder tun!* ♦ *Er hat sich verzählt und muss wieder anfangen.* mal wieder *once again* ◊ *Er hat sich mal wieder verspätet.* schon wieder *again* ◊ *Ich bin schon wieder erkältet.* immer wieder *time and time again, again and again* ◊ *Dieser Fehler passiert mir immer wieder.* **2.** re(-)... *Geld wieder anlegen reinvest money etw.* wieder aufbauen *rebuild sth, reconstruct sth* wieder gewählt werden *be re-elected*
◉ bald/gleich/sofort wieder da sein *be back in a minute*
② **wie·der²** ['vi:de] ⎣part⎦ **1.** *(fam)* *again* ◊ *Wie heißt sie gleich wieder? Das ist wieder typisch! That's typical, that is! Wie siehst du denn wieder aus! What on earth do you look like! Was ist denn nun schon wieder? What's the matter now?* **2.** auch wieder *on the other hand, there again* ◊ *Die Wanderung ist schön, dafür aber auch wieder schwierig. Das ist auch wieder wahr! That's true enough! So dramatisch ist das nun auch wieder nicht! It's not as dramatic as all that!*
② **wie·der|...** ['vi:de] ⎣prefix⎦ **1.** *back* ◊ *seine Freiheit wiedererlangen* ♦ *Ich möchte sofort mein Geld wiederhaben!* ♦ *Er war im Urlaub und ist heute wiedergekommen.* ⊖zurück... **2.** re- ◊ *eine Arbeit wiederaufnehmen* ♦ *einen Zustand wiederherstellen* ♦ *wiederverwertbares Material* **3.** again ◊ *ein Theaterstück wiederaufführen* ♦ *Verlorenes wiederfinden* ♦ *Wann werden wir uns wiedersehen?*
Wie·der·... ['vi:de] ⎣prefix⎦ re... ◊ *die Wiederwahl des Kanzlers* ♦ *die Wiedereröffnung eines Geschäfts* ♦ *die Wiederverwendung von Altpapier* ♦ *die Wiedervereinigung*
Wie·der·ga·be ['vi:dega:bə] die <-, -n> **1.** report, account ◊ *eine historisch korrekte Wiedergabe der Ereignisse* *eine wörtliche Wiedergabe a verbatim account die sinngemäße Wiedergabe einer Sache* (the) rough account of sth **2.** ARTS representation, reproduction ◊ *Die detailgetreue Wiedergabe ist bei dieser Malerei besonders wichtig.* ♦ *Der Fotograf bemühte sich um eine gestochen scharfe Wiedergabe.* **3.** TECHN playback ◊ *Software für die Wiedergabe von Videos* ♦ *Die Wiedergabe auf dem PC funktionierte nicht.*
wie·der|ge·ben ['vi:dege:bm] <gibt wieder, gab wieder, hat wiedergegeben> ⎣tr v⎦ **1.** give back, return ◊ *Gib mir bitte meinen Stift wieder.* ♦ *Ich möchte, dass du ihm das Geld wiedergibst.* **2.** report, give an account of ◊ *Das Buch gibt die Fakten unrichtig wieder. etw. sinngemäß wiedergeben give the gist of sth* **3.** express, render ◊ *Substantive werden im Englischen häufig mit einem Verb wiedergegeben.* **4.** *(sound, images, data)* reproduce ◊ *Dieser Bildschirm kann fast alle Farben wiedergeben.*; *(a computer file)* play back ◊ *Das Programm/Der PC kann die Datei nicht wie-*

dergeben.

wie·der|ho·len[1] ['viːdɐhoːlən] <holt wieder, holte wieder, hat wiedergeholt> [tr v] (sich [dat]) etw. wiederholen get sth back ◊ *Sie wollte sich ihr Geld wiederholen.*

② **wie·der·ho·len**[2] [viːdeˈhoːlən] <wiederholt, wiederholte, hat wiederholt> [tr v] **1.** repeat ◊ *Der Konzertmitschnitt wird im Radio wiederholt.* ♦ *Er wiederholte seine Bitte/Frage.* ♦ *Sie musste die 9. Klasse wiederholen.* **2.** *(an exam)* resit, retake ◊ *Die Prüfung kann zweimal wiederholt werden.* **3.** *(material, a lesson)* revise ◊ *Wir müssen alle Vokabeln wiederholen.* [ref v] **1.** sich wiederholen repeat yourself ◊ *Sie wiederholte sich ständig.* **2.** *(incident, catastrophe)* sich wiederholen repeat sth, happen again ◊ *Solch ein Unglück kann sich jederzeit wiederholen.*

wie·der·holt [viːdeˈhoːlt] *past p of* wiederholen[2] [adj, adv] *no comp/superl; when used as an adj, only before ns* repeated(ly) ◊ *wiederholtes Fehlen in der Schule* ♦ *Du bist wiederholt unangenehm aufgefallen.* zum wiederholten Male yet again

Wie·der·ho·lung [viːdeˈhoːlʊn] die <-, -en> repetition ◊ *Sie wollte eine Wiederholung des Fehlers vermeiden.*; *(on television)* repeat ◊ *Im Fernsehen kommen dauernd Wiederholungen.*; *(of material, a lesson)* revision ◊ *Die Wiederholung des Gelernten trainiert das Gedächtnis.*; *(of an exam)* eine Wiederholung der Prüfung a resit (examination)

② **Wie·der·hö·ren** ['viːdɐhøːrən] *(always* auf Wiederhören*)* goodbye

wie·der|keh·ren ['viːdekeːrən] <kehrt wieder, kehrte wieder, ist wiedergekehrt> [intr v] **1.** return, come back ◊ *Er ist aus dem Krieg nicht wiedergekehrt.* **2.** recur, be repeated ◊ *Dieses Problem kehrt immer wieder.* ♦ *ein wiederkehrendes Motiv des Romans*

wie·der|kom·men ['viːdekɔmən] <kommt wieder, kam wieder, ist wiedergekommen> [intr v] **1.** return, come back ◊ *Wann kommen sie vom Ausflug wieder?* ♦ *Sie wartet im Auto, bis er wiederkommt.* **2.** come back/again ◊ *Der Klempner kommt morgen wieder.* **3.** come again, come up ◊ *So bald kommt so ein Schnäppchen nicht wieder.*

wie·der|se·hen ['viːdeːzeːən] <sieht wieder, sah wieder, hat wiedergesehen> [tr v] **1.** jdn/etw. wiedersehen see sb/sth again ◊ *Ich habe ihn nie wiedergesehen.* ♦ *in einem Land/seine Heimat wiedersehen* sich wiedersehen see each other again, meet again ◊ *Es sollte noch zwei Jahre dauern, bis wir uns wiedersahen.* **2.** *(fam)* etw. wiedersehen get sth back ◊ *Der würde ich kein Geld geben. Das siehst du nie wieder!*

② **Wie·der·se·hen** ['viːdeːzeːən] das <-s> *no pl* **1.** reunion, meeting ◊ *ein unverhofftes/überraschendes Wiedersehen* **2.** (auf) Wiedersehen goodbye ◊ *„Auf Wiedersehen, Herr Huber."* ♦ *Sie musste ihm noch auf Wiedersehen sagen.*

Wie·der·ver·ei·ni·gung ['viːdefeɐˌʔaɪnɪɡʊn] die <-, -en> HIST reunification

On November 9th 1989, the Berlin Wall, symbol of a divided Germany, came down. In 1990, East and West Germany were reunified after having been divided since the end of World War II. German reunification was made possible by the ▶

▶ support of the Soviet leader Gorbachev. Representatives of the two German states, France, the United Kingdom, the USA and the Soviet Union signed the Two-Plus-Four Treaty that laid the foundations of a new unified Germany.

Wie·ge ['viːɡə] die <-, -n> *(also fig)* cradle ◊ *Sie legte das Baby in die Wiege.* ♦ *die Wiege der Zivilisation* ⦿ etw. wurde jdm in die Wiege gelegt sb was born with sth, sb has inherited sth ◊ *Wird Erfolg den Kindern in die Wiege gelegt?*

② **wie·gen**[1] ['viːɡŋ] <wiegt, wog, hat gewogen> [tr+intr v] weigh ◊ *Die Verkäuferin wog das Gemüse.* ♦ *Das Päckchen muss zuerst gewogen werden.* ♦ *Sie wiegt 62 Kilo.* sich wiegen weigh yourself zu viel wiegen be too heavy

wie·gen[2] ['viːɡŋ] <wiegt, wiegte, hat gewiegt> [tr v] rock (gently), sway ◊ *Sie wiegte das Kind in den Schlaf.* ⦿ sich in etw. [dat] wiegen sich in Sicherheit wiegen feel safe sich in der Zuversicht/Gewissheit wiegen, dass feel certain/confident that sich in der Hoffnung wiegen, dass nurture the hope that

wies [viːs] *pret of* weisen

② **Wie·se** ['viːzə] die <-, -n> meadow ◊ *Die Wiese war frisch gemäht.* ♦ *Die Kinder spielten auf der Wiese.* ⦿ auf der grünen Wiese in the countryside

② **wie·so** [viˈzoː] [adv] why ◊ *Wieso lügt er?* ♦ *Kannst du mir erklären, wieso das nicht funktioniert?* ♦ *Ich weiß auch nicht wieso.* ⊜warum, weshalb

② **wie viel** [viˈfiːl, ˈviːfiːl] → wie

wild [vɪlt] [adj, adv] <wilder, am wildesten> **1.** wild(ly) ◊ *wilde Tiere/Pflanzen* ♦ *wilde Spekulation* ♦ *Die Party war ausgesprochen wild.* ♦ *Sie tanzte wild durchs Zimmer.* wild lebend Tiere animals living in the wild; *(plants)* wild wachsend wild wild wuchernd rampant **2.** *(landscape)* rugged(ly) ◊ *eine wilde Landschaft* ♦ *Im Süden ist die Küste besonders wild.* ♦ *wild gezackte Felsformationen* **3.** *(determination, discussion, battle)* fierce(ly) ◊ *Mit wilder Entschlossenheit lief sie los.* ♦ *Sie lieferten sich eine wilde Schießerei mit der Polizei.* wild entschlossen with fierce determination [adj] *(child, hair)* unruly ◊ *eine wilde Frisur* ♦ *Unsere Tochter ist sehr wild.* ⦿ nicht so wild take it easy wild durcheinander brüllen/reden etc. shout/talk etc. at the same time wild um sich schlagen lash out

Wild [vɪlt] das <-(e)s> *no pl* game ◊ *Die Jäger schossen das Wild.* ♦ *Sie mag kein Wild.*

Wild·schwein ['vɪltʃvaɛn] das <-(e)s, -e> wild boar ◊ *Als Hauptgang gab es Wildschwein.*

② **will** [vɪl] *pres of* wollen[1], wollen[2]

Wil·le ['vɪlə] der <-n> *no pl* will ◊ *Er hat einen starken Willen.* ♦ *Gottes Wille* gegen jds Willen against sb's will/wishes ◊ *Er fuhr gegen den Willen seiner Eltern nach Rom.* den festen Willen haben, etw. zu tun be determined to do sth seinen Willen durchsetzen have your own way auf seinem Willen beharren insist on having your own way jdm seinen Willen lassen let sb have their own way guter Wille goodwill ◊ *Er zeigte guten Willen.* letzter Wille last will ◊ *Das war ihr letzter Wille.* ⦿ wider Willen against your will ein Held wider

Willen a reluctant hero

wil·len ['vɪlən] [prep] [+gen] *(always* **um einer Sache/jds willen)** for the sake of sth/sb, for sth's/ sb's sake ◊ *Um des Friedens willen lenkte er ein.* ♦ *Um ihres Bruders willen kam sie zur Party.*

wil·lens ['vɪləns] [adj] **willens sein, etw. zu tun** be willing/prepared to do sth ◊ *Sie war nicht willens, ihm zu folgen.*

wil·lig ['vɪlɪç] [adj, adv] **1.** *often pej when used before ns* willing(ly) ◊ *Er war nicht willig, das zu tun.* ♦ **ein williges Pferd** sich willig zeigen(, etw. zu tun) show (a) willingness (to do sth) **2.** obedient(ly) ◊ *Der Hund folgte ihr willig ins Haus.*

② **will·kom·men** [vɪl'kɔmən] [adj] welcome ◊ *Das war eine willkommene Abwechslung.* ♦ *Sie waren willkommene Gäste.* ♦ *Sie sind uns jederzeit willkommen!*

⊙ **jdn willkommen heißen** welcome sb ◊ *Er hieß die Gäste willkommen.* **(herzlich) willkommen** (a very warm) welcome **Seien Sie (herzlich) willkommen!** A very warm welcome to you!

will·kür·lich ['vɪlkyːɐ̯lɪç] [adj, adv] **1.** arbitrary(-ily) ◊ *willkürliche Gewalt* ♦ *Ausländer wurden willkürlich verhaftet.* **2.** random(ly) ◊ *Die Liste war willkürlich.* ♦ *eine willkürliche Einteilung* **3.** deliberate(ly) ◊ *Er handelte willkürlich.*; *(motions)* voluntary(-ily) ◊ *Willkürliche Bewegungen bereiteten dem Patienten Schwierigkeiten.* ♦ *Muskeln, die willkürlich bewegt werden können*

Wim·per ['vɪmpɐ] die <–, –n> (eye)lash ◊ *Sie hatte dunkle/dichte Wimpern.* ♦ *künstliche Wimpern*

⊙ **ohne mit der Wimper zu zucken** without batting an eyelid

Wim·pern·tu·sche ['vɪmpɐntʊʃə] die <–, –n> mascara ◊ *Wimperntusche auftragen* ♦ *Ihre Wimperntusche war ganz verlaufen.*

② **Wind** [vɪnt] der <–(e)s, –e> wind ◊ *Ein kalter Wind blies ihr ins Gesicht.* ♦ *Der Wind stand günstig.*

⊙ **jdm den Wind aus den Segeln nehmen** *(fam)* take the wind out of sb's sails **bei Wind und Wetter** in all weathers **viel Wind (um etw.) machen** *(fam)* make/create a fuss (about sth) **etw. in den Wind schlagen** turn a deaf ear to sth ◊ *Sie schlug alle Ratschläge in den Wind.* **etw. in den Wind schreiben** *(fam)* write sth off, kiss goodbye to sth ◊ *Das Geld kannst du in den Wind schreiben.*

Wind·beu·tel ['vɪntbɔɪ̯tl̩] der <–s, –> cream puff, profiterole ◊ *Er biss in den Windbeutel.*

Win·del ['vɪndl̩] die <–, –n> nappy, diaper ◊ *Sie wechselte die Windel des Babys.*

win·dig ['vɪndɪç] [adj] **1.** METEO windy ◊ *Heute ist es sehr windig.* ♦ *ein windiger Tag* **2.** shady, dodgy ◊ *ein windiger Geschäftsmann* ♦ *Er fiel auf das windige Angebot herein.*

Wind·po·cken ['vɪntpɔkn̩] die <–> *only pl; seldom with the article* chickenpox ◊ *Sie hatte Windpocken.*

Wind·schutz·schei·be ['vɪntʃʊtsʃaɛ̯bə] die <–, –n> windscreen, windshield ◊ *Die Windschutzscheibe war beschlagen.*

Wink [vɪŋk] der <–(e)s, –e> **1.** sign ◊ *Sie gab ihm einen Wink, ihr zu folgen.*; *(of the head)* nod **2.** *(also fig)* hint, tip ◊ *Sie hatte von ihm einen*

Wink bekommen.

⊙ **ein Wink des Schicksals** a sign from above **ein Wink mit dem Zaunpfahl** a broad hint

Win·kel ['vɪŋkl̩] der <–s, –> **1.** MATH angle ◊ *ein Winkel von 90 Grad* ♦ *ein rechter Winkel* **spitzer/stumpfer/gestreckter Winkel** an acute/ obtuse/a 180° angle **2.** *(tool)* square ◊ *Er nahm einen Winkel zu Hilfe.* **3.** *(also fig)* corner ◊ *Die Socken lagen im hintersten Winkel des Schranks.* ♦ *Er kennt jeden Winkel des Dorfes.* **4.** **toter Winkel** blind spot

② **win·ken** ['vɪŋkn̩] [intr v] +*haben* **1.** wave ◊ *Sie winkte (mit einem Taschentuch).* ♦ *Er winkte lachend in die Kamera.* **2.** jdm winken signal sb **dem Kellner/Ober/der Bedienung winken** beckon the waiter (over/ einem Taxi winken) hail a taxi **3.** etw. winkt sth is on offer ◊ *Es winken tolle Preise.* **etw. winkt jdm** sb can look forward to sth ◊ *Dem Gewinner winkt eine Karibikreise.* [tr v] +*haben* jdn zu sich winken beckon sb over ◊ *Er winkte das Kind zu sich.* **ein Fahrzeug/einen Fahrer an den Straßenrand winken** pull/wave a vehicle/ driver over (to the side of the road)

Win·ter ['vɪntɐ] der <–s, –> winter ◊ *Inzwischen war es Winter geworden.* ♦ *ein strenger Winter* ♦ *Im Winter ist es oft sehr kalt.*

win·ter·lich ['vɪntɐlɪç] [adj, adv] **1.** wintry, winter ◊ *Es herrschten winterliche Temperaturen.* ♦ *eine winterliche Landschaft* winterlich kalt cold and wintry **2.** winter ◊ *winterliche Kleidung* winterlich gekleidet wearing winter clothes

Win·zer ['vɪntsɐ] der <–s, –>, **Win·ze·rin** ['vɪntsərɪn] die <–, –nen> wine grower ◊ *Von Beruf war sie Winzerin.* ♦ *die kalifornischen Winzer*

win·zig ['vɪntsɪç] [adj] tiny, minute ◊ *ein winziges Handy* ♦ *Im Vergleich zu ihm wirkte ich winzig.* winzig klein tiny little ◊ *Ihm war ein winzig kleiner Fehler unterlaufen.* ⊙riesig

② **wir** [viːɐ̯] [pers pron] ◊ *Wir hörten einen Schrei.* ♦ *Das müssen wir uns ansehen.*

nom	wir
acc	uns
dat	uns
gen	unser

Wir·bel·säu·le ['vɪrbl̩zɔɪ̯lə] die <–, –n> spine, spinal column ⊙Rückgrat

wirbt [vɪrpt] *pres of* werben

② **wird** [vɪrt] *pres of* werden[1], werden[2]

② **wirft** [vɪrft] *pres of* werfen

wir·ken ['vɪrkn̩] [intr v] +*haben* **1.** work ◊ *Wie wirkt dieses Medikament?* ♦ *Diese Tabletten wirken bei mir nicht.* ansteckend/entspannend etc. wirken be contagious/relaxing etc. ◊ *Ihr Lachen wirkte ansteckend.* ♦ *Diese Musik wirkt entspannend.* **etw. auf sich wirken lassen** take sth in, let sth sink in ◊ *Sie ließ das Gemälde auf sich wirken.* **2.** *(lofty)* work ◊ *Sein Urgroßvater wirkte als Arzt und Chemiker.* **3.** appear, seem ◊ *Er wirkt sehr nett.* ♦ *Neben ihm wirkte ich sehr groß.* **4.** groß/warm etc. wirkend large/warm etc. looking ◊ *warm/natürlich wirkende Farben* **5.** *(make a positive impact)* work ◊ *Dieses Bild wirkt im Wohnzimmer besser als hier.*

② **wirk·lich** ['vɪrklɪç] [adj, adv] *seldom comp/superl* real(ly) ◊ *War er wirklich der Täter?* ♦ *Das ist kein wirklicher Verlust.* ♦ *Es gab keine wirkliche*

Alternative. ♦ *Dieser Film ist wirklich spannend.* ♦
Hat er das wirklich getan?

② **Wirk·lich·keit** ['vɪrklɪçkaet] die <-, -en> most
sing 1. reality ◊ *Die Wirklichkeit sah ein bisschen
anders aus. Wirklichkeit werden* come true
⊝Realität 2. in Wirklichkeit in reality ◊ *Die
schwarzen Stellen waren in Wirklichkeit Löcher.*

wirk·sam ['vɪrkza:m] adj, adv effective(ly) ◊
wirksame Sicherheitsmaßnahmen ♦ *ein wirksames
Medikament/Heilmittel* ♦ *Diese Arznei ist bei
Kindern mit Grippe wirksam.* ♦ *Wie kann man sich
wirksam vor dieser Krankheit schützen?*
     ⊛ **wirksam werden** take effect ◊ *Wann wird die
Kündigung wirksam?*

② **Wir·kung** ['vɪrkʊŋ] die <-, -en> 1. effect ◊ *Hat
das Urteil eine abschreckende Wirkung auf
mögliche Täter? Wirkung zeigen* be effective *eine
Wirkung bringen/erzielen* have an effect 2. effectiveness ◊ *Er bezweifelte die Wirkung des Medikaments.* 3. PHYSICS action ◊ *physikalische Kräfte und
ihre Wirkung*
     ⊛ **mit sofortiger Wirkung** with immediate effect
◊ *Sie wurde mit sofortiger Wirkung entlassen.* **mit
Wirkung vom ...** with effect from ... ◊ *Mit
Wirkung vom 1. März wird er Abteilungsleiter.*

wirr [vɪr] adj 1. tangled, tousled ◊ *Er brachte
seine wirre Frisur in Ordnung.* ♦ *Dein Haar ist ganz
wirr vom Wind.* 2. confused, incoherent, muddled ◊
wirre Gedanken ♦ *Die Gliederung wirkt wirr und
unübersichtlich. wirres Zeug reden* talk gibberish
jd ist wirr im Kopf sb is confused, sb's head is
reeling *jdn wirr machen* confuse sb adv
1. tangled, messily ◊ *Die Drähte lagen wirr auf
dem Boden.* ♦ *Auf dem Tisch lagen die Papiere wirr
durcheinander. Das Haar hing ihr wirr ins Gesicht.*
Her tangled hair hung in her face. 2. confusedly,
incoherently ◊ *ein wirr verfasster Text* die
Gedanken gehen jdm wirr im Kopf umher sb's
thoughts are confused
     ⊛ **wirr reden** talk gibberish **wirr durcheinander
reden/schreien** talk/shout at the same time

Wir·sing ['vɪrzɪŋ] der <-s> no pl savoy (cabbage)
◊ *Wirsing mag sie nicht.*

Wirt¹ [vɪrt] der <-(es), -e> BIO host ◊ *Der Erreger
benutzt normalerweise Tiere als Wirt.*

② **Wirt²** [vɪrt] der <-(e)s, -e>, **Wir·tin** ['vɪrtɪn] die
<-, -nen> landlord ◊ *Mein Vater ist Wirt.* ♦ *Der
Wirt brachte das Bier. Wirtin* landlady ◊ *Sie ist die
Wirtin des Gasthauses gegenüber.*

② **Wirt·schaft** ['vɪrtʃaft] die <-, -en> 1. economy ◊
Die Wirtschaft muss angekurbelt werden. ♦ *Die
deutsche Wirtschaft ist stark exportabhängig.*
2. (trade and) industry ◊ *Experten aus Wirtschaft
und Forschung diskutieren miteinander. die freie
Wirtschaft* the private sector 3. pub, inn ◊ *Er ging
in eine Wirtschaft und trank ein Bier.*

wirt·schaft·lich ['vɪrtʃaftlɪç] adj, adv 1. no comp/
superl; when used as an adj, only before ns
economic(ally) ◊ *Wie ist die derzeitige wirtschaftliche Situation?* ♦ *Ist das wirtschaftlich vertretbar?*
etw. wirtschaftlich nutzen use sth for economic
purposes 2. no comp/superl; when used as an adj,
only before ns financial(ly) ◊ *Der wirtschaftliche
Schaden war enorm.* ♦ *Sie sind wirtschaftlich
abhängig von den USA.* 3. economical(ly) ◊ *ein
wirtschaftliches Auto* ♦ *Diese Methode ist wirt-*

schaftlicher. ♦ *Wir sollten mit den Ressourcen wirtschaftlicher umgehen.*

Wirt·schafts·wun·der ['vɪrtʃaftsvʊnde] das <-s>
no pl (fam) HIST (Germany's) economic miracle

> The German *Wirtschaftswunder* of the years
> 1955–63 was made possible by West Germany's
> allegiance to the West and the energy, diligence
> and creativity of its people. At this time, produc-
> tion and export figures rose rapidly, unemploy-
> ment sank below one percent (in 1961), and
> West Germany prospered.

wi·schen ['vɪʃn] tr v +haben wipe ◊ *Er wischte
sich die Stirn.* ♦ *Sie wischte sich die Tränen von
den Wangen. Staub wischen* dust (nass) wischen
wash ◊ *Sie wischte den Fußboden/die Treppe.*

② **wis·sen** ['vɪsn] <weiß, wusste, hat gewusst>
tr+intr v no passive 1. know ◊ *Sie weiß recht viel.*
♦ *Weißt du eine Lösung?* ♦ *„Margit ist
schwanger." — „Ich weiß." von etw. wissen* know
about sth ◊ *Sie wusste von dem Vorfall.* ♦ *Hast du
davon gewusst? etw. von etw./über etw.* acc
wissen know sth about sth *viel/eine Menge über
etw.* acc *wissen* know a lot about sth *nichts von
etw./über etw.* acc *wissen* know nothing about/of
sth ◊ *Ich wusste nichts von seinen finanziellen
Schwierigkeiten. (über etw.* acc*) Bescheid wissen*
know (about sth) *jdn in Sicherheit/guten Händen
wissen* know that sb is safe/in good hands *sich
sicher/geborgen wissen* know you are safe/secure
◊ *In diesem Haus wusste sie sich geborgen.*
2. sich dat zu helfen wissen be able to take care
of yourself *sich zu behaupten/benehmen wissen*
know how to assert yourself/behave *nichts mit sich
anzufangen wissen* not know what to do with
yourself 3. noch wissen remember ◊ *Weißt du
noch, wie es damals war?* nicht mehr wissen not
remember ◊ *Ich weiß seinen Namen nicht mehr.*
     ⊛ **alles besser wissen** always know best **nicht,
dass ich wüsste** not that I'm aware of **nicht
mehr ein noch aus wissen, weder ein noch aus
wissen** be at your wits' end **jdn etw. wissen
lassen** let sb know sth, inform sb about sth ◊
*Lassen Sie mich wissen, wie Sie sich entschieden
haben. etw. zu schätzen wissen* appreciate sth ◊
Seine Hilfe weiß ich zu schätzen. **es wissen
wollen** (fam) put yourself to the test ◊ *Der dreima-
lige Weltmeister wollte es noch einmal wissen.* **von
jdm/etw. nichts wissen wollen** not be interested
in sb/sth ◊ *Sie wollte von diesen Gerüchten nichts
wissen.* **von jdm/etw. nichts mehr wissen
wollen** not want (to have) anything more to do
with sb/sth **was weiß ich** (fam) how should I
know **gewusst, wie** (fam) it's easy if you know
how

Wis·sen ['vɪsn] das <-s> no pl knowledge ◊ *tech-
nisches/psychologisches Wissen* ♦ *Sie gab ihr
Wissen an junge Leute weiter. über (ein) großes/
umfangreiches Wissen verfügen* be very knowledgeable *meines Wissens* to my knowledge ◊ *Meines
Wissens hält er sich zurzeit in Rom auf. mit/ohne
jds Wissen* with(out) sb's knowledge ◊ *Ohne ihr
Wissen lieh er sich das Auto.*

② **Wis·sen·schaft** ['vɪsnʃaft] die <-, -en> science ◊
Der aktuelle Stand der Wissenschaft zeigt, dass ...
♦ *die angewandten Wissenschaften* ♦ *Die Informa-*

tik ist eine recht junge Wissenschaft. ♦ Die Wissenschaft hat darauf noch keine Antwort gefunden.

wis·sen·schaft·lich ['vɪsn̩ʃaftlɪç] [adj, adv] scientific(ally) ◊ wissenschaftliche Methoden ♦ wissenschaftlich bewiesene Ergebnisse

wis·sens·wert ['vɪsn̩sveːɐ̯t] [adj] <wissenswerter, am wissenswertesten> wissenswert (sein) (be) worth knowing; (information, details etc.) valuable ◊ wissenswerte Informationen/Neuigkeiten wissenswert für jdn interesting for sb, relevant to sb ◊ Hier finden Sie alles, was für Eltern wissenswert ist.

Wit·te·rung ['vɪtərʊŋ] die <-, -en> 1. METEO weather ◊ Die Veranstaltung wurde wegen schlechter Witterung abgesagt. 2. (tech) scent die Witterung aufnehmen pick up the scent

Wit·wer ['vɪtvɐ] der <-s, ->, **Wit·we** ['vɪtvə] die <-, -n> widower, widow ◊ Er ist schon lange Witwer. ♦ eine junge Witwe Witwe/Witwer werden be widowed ◊ Sie wurde sehr früh Witwe.

ⓩ **Witz** [vɪts] der <-es, -e> 1. joke ◊ Sie erzählte einen Witz. ♦ Der Witz ist schon uralt. ♦ Das war nur ein Witz! ♦ Diese Geldsumme ist doch ein Witz! jd macht (wohl) Witze sb must be joking Soll das ein Witz sein? Are you joking? 2. wit ◊ Sein Witz gefällt mir. (viel) Witz haben be (very) witty beißender Witz cutting wit

wit·zig ['vɪtsɪç] [adj, adv] 1. funny(-ily) ◊ Sie ist total witzig. ♦ Das war eine witzige Geschichte. ♦ das witzigste Erlebnis meines Lebens witzig gemeint meant/intended as a joke sich witzig ausdrücken speak/write humorously 2. unusual(ly), imaginative(ly) ◊ Er trug witzige Klamotten. ♦ Diese Brille ist sehr witzig. ♦ ein witzig aufgemachtes Buch ein witziger Typ quite a character

WM [veːˈɛm] die (abbr of Weltmeisterschaft) world championship; (in football, soccer) World Cup ◊ Er nimmt an der WM teil. ♦ Sie erreichten das Halbfinale der WM.

ⓩ **wo¹** [voː] [adv] 1. interrogative, relative and spatial where ◊ Wo ist sie? ♦ Ich weiß nicht, wo er wohnt. ♦ In Wimbledon, wo er fünfmal erfolgreich war, hat er verloren. ♦ eine Stelle im See, wo es sehr flach ist ♦ Bleib, wo du bist! überall, wo wherever ◊ Überall, wo sie auftaucht, herrscht Chaos. 2. relative, temporal when ◊ Jetzt kommt die Jahreszeit, wo es wieder früh dunkel wird.

ⓩ **wo²** [voː] [conjunc] 1. wo (...) doch ... when ..., since ... ◊ Warum kaufst du ein neues Auto, wo doch das alte noch ganz gut läuft? ♦ Du solltest dich beeilen, wo du doch nicht viel Zeit hast. 2. wo ... doch even though ... ◊ Er verhielt sich ganz ruhig, wo er doch solche Schmerzen hatte. ♦ Sie hat das Match verloren, wo sie doch früher immer gewonnen hatte.

ⓩ **wo·(r)...** [voː(r)] [prefix] 1. interrogative what ◊ Wogegen ist er allergisch? ♦ Worüber möchtest du mit mir sprechen? 2. relative which ◊ Der Intendant wollte den Spielplan ändern, wogegen sich das Ensemble wehrte. ♦ Das ist etwas, worüber ich mit dir sprechen muss.

wo·an·ders [voˈʔandɐs] [adv] elsewhere, somewhere else ◊ Sie lebt/studiert/wohnt inzwischen woanders. ♦ Die wahren Gründe liegen woanders. mit seinen Gedanken (ganz) woanders sein be miles away

wo·bei [voˈbaɪ, ˈvoːbaɪ] [adv] with stress on the first syllable when seeking confirmation 1. interrogative, not translated directly Wobei wurde er/sie ertappt? What was he/she caught doing? 2. relative in/at/during which ◊ Letztes Jahr kam es zu einem Flugzeugabsturz, wobei es 40 Tote gab. 3. relative of/from which ◊ Angeboten wird das Auto in drei Ausstattungen, wobei die günstigste nur 9000 Euro kostet.

Wo·che ['vɔxə] die <-, -n> week ◊ Nächste Woche treffe ich mich mit Ute. ♦ diese/letzte/vorletzte Woche ♦ Einmal die Woche geht sie ins Fitnessstudio. ♦ Er lag eine Woche lang krank im Bett. unter der Woche during the week

Berlin's *Grüne Woche* is a trade fair promoting ecological agriculture. It attracts agricultural and horticultural businesses as well as political parties and organizations.

Wo·chen·en·de ['vɔxn̩ʔɛndə] das <-s, -n> weekend ◊ Hast du am Wochenende schon was vor? ♦ Kommendes Wochenende bekomme ich Besuch.

Wo·chen·markt ['vɔxn̩maˈkt] der <-(e)s, Wochenmärkte> (weekly) market ◊ Ich war heute Morgen auf dem Wochenmarkt.

Many German towns and cities have markets, so-called *Wochenmärkte* (not necessarily held just once a week), where consumers can buy food, flowers and other goods directly from the producers.

Wo·chen·tag ['vɔxn̩taːk] der <-(e)s, -e> 1. day of the week ◊ Welcher Wochentag ist heute? 2. weekday ◊ Die Serie läuft an jedem Wochentag um 18 Uhr. ♦ Der Feiertag fiel auf einen Wochentag.

wö·chent·lich ['vœçntlɪç, 'vœçəntlɪç] [adj] no comp/superl weekly ◊ eine wöchentliche Kolumne ♦ Die wöchentliche Arbeitszeit beträgt 37 Stunden. zweimal etc. wöchentlich twice etc. a week [adv] a/per week ◊ Er arbeitet wöchentlich 40 Stunden. ♦ Sie geht zweimal wöchentlich ins Fitnessstudio.

wo·durch [voˈdʊrç, ˈvoːdʊrç] [adv] with stress on the first syllable when seeking confirmation 1. interrogative how ◊ Wodurch hat er sich schuldig gemacht? ♦ Wodurch unterscheiden sich die beiden Fotos? 2. relative therefore, which means ◊ Er hatte viele kleine Jobs, wodurch er selten zu Hause war. Tu nichts, wodurch er sich bedroht fühlen könnte! Don't do anything that could make him feel threatened.

wo·für [voˈfyːɐ̯, ˈvoːfyːɐ̯] [adv] with stress on the first syllable when seeking confirmation 1. interrogative what ... for ◊ Wofür soll ich mich rechtfertigen? ♦ Wofür hat er sich entschieden? Wofür interessiert sie sich? What is she interested in? Wofür hat er sich entschieden? Which did he choose? 2. relative for which ◊ Er arbeitete drei Stunden, wofür er 50 Euro bekam.

ⓩ **wog** [voːk] pret of wiegen¹

Wo·ge ['voːgə] die <-, -n> (also fig) wave ◊ Eine gewaltige Woge ließ das Boot kentern. ♦ Die Woge der Begeisterung war unglaublich groß.

ⓩ **wo·her** [voˈheːɐ̯, ˈvoːheːɐ̯] [adv] with stress on the

first syllable when seeking confirmation; interrogative, relative where … from ◊ *Woher stammen Sie ursprünglich?* ♦ *Woher kommt dieser Geruch?* ♦ *Woher hast du das viele Geld?* ♦ *Er will prüfen, woher diese teuren Uhren kommen.* ♦ *Sie erzählte ihm über das Land, woher sie kam.*
◉ **(ach/aber) woher** *(fam)* not at all ◊ *„Bist du müde?" — „Ach woher!"*

② **wo·hin** [vo'hɪn, 'vo:hɪn] [adv] *with stress on the first syllable when seeking confirmation* **1.** *interrogative, relative* where (… to) ◊ *Wohin willst du?* ♦ *Sie wissen noch nicht, wohin die Reise geht.* ♦ *In Rom, wohin es ihn aus beruflichen Gründen verschlug, war er glücklich.* **2.** *indefinite* wherever ◊ *Wohin man auch blickte, sah man Blumen.* ♦ *Du darfst gehen, wohin du willst.*

wo·hin·ge·gen [vohɪn'ge:gŋ] [conjunc] whereas ◊ *Sie war sehr groß, wohingegen ihre Brüder eher klein sind.* ◉während

② **wohl¹** [vo:l] [adv] **1.** *(also lofty) (physically)* sich wohl fühlen feel well jdm ist nicht wohl sb doesn't feel well jdm wohl tun do sb good **2.** *(also lofty) (emotionally)* sich wohl fühlen be happy/at ease ◊ *Am wohlsten fühlt er sich zu Hause.* jdm ist bei etw. nicht ganz wohl sth makes sb feel uneasy **3.** well ◊ *Schlaf wohl.* ♦ *Das war eine wohl durchdachte Sache.* ♦ *Sie war sich den Folgen wohl bewusst.* leb(e) wohl farewell wohl bekomm's (to) your health ◊ *Hier Ihr Bier, wohl bekomm's!* **4.** wohl aber but ◊ *Er war nicht geschockt, wohl aber sehr erstaunt.* ♦ *Sie sprach einige wenige, wohl aber sehr wichtige Punkte an.* **5.** about ◊ *Es waren wohl 50 Gäste da.*
◉ **wohl oder übel** (whether you) like it or not ◊ *Er musste die 20 Euro wohl oder übel bezahlen.*

② **wohl²** [vo:l] [part] **1.** probably ◊ *Sie wird wohl bis 18 Uhr brauchen.* ◊ *„Kommt er auch auf die Party?" — „Wohl nicht."/„Sieht wohl so aus."* **2.** *(emph)* das kann man wohl sagen you can say that again Du spinnst wohl! You must be joking! Man wird wohl noch fragen dürfen! I was only asking! **3.** *(emph)* Willst/Wirst du wohl …! Will you …! ◊ *Willst du doch wohl still sein!* **4.** *in questions* was ist wohl … what might be … ◊ *Was ist wohl der Grund für diese Reaktion?* ob jd./etw. etw. wohl tut does sb/sth do sth, do you think sb/sth will do sth ◊ *Ob das Haus wohl stehen bleibt?* ob jd etw. wohl sollte should sb do sth ◊ *Ob wir ihn wohl warnen sollten?*

② **Wohl** [vo:l] das <-(e)s> *no pl* welfare, well-being ◊ *Ihr Wohl lag mir sehr am Herzen.* zu deinem eigenen Wohl for your own good das Wohl der Gesellschaft/Allgemeinheit the public good
◉ **für das leibliche/jds leibliches Wohl sorgen** provide food and drink (for sb) **auf jds Wohl anstoßen/trinken** toast sb ◊ *Sie stießen auf das Wohl des Brautpaars an.* **für jds Wohl sorgen** look after sb, feed sb ◊ *Für das Wohl der Gäste war bestens gesorgt.* **zum Wohl(e)** cheers

Wohl·fahrt ['vo:lfa:ɐt] die <-> *no pl (oldf)* **1.** *(also hum)* welfare services Wir sind doch nicht die Wohlfahrt! We're not a charity! **2.** welfare ◊ *die Wohlfahrt der Kinder/Gesellschaft*

wohl·ge·merkt ['vo:lgəmɛʁkt] [adv] mark/mind you ◊ *Sie verdient 4000 Euro, netto wohlgemerkt.* ♦ *Er ist wohlgemerkt nicht in den USA geboren.*

Wohl·stand ['vo:lʃtant] der <-(e)s> *no pl* prosperity, affluence ◊ *Er kam relativ schnell zu Wohlstand.* ♦ *Sie lebten im Wohlstand.*

Wohl·tat ['vo:lta:t] die <-, -en> **1.** good deed jdm eine Wohltat erweisen do sb a good deed **2.** delight ◊ *Die Massage war eine Wohltat für meinen geschundenen Körper.* ♦ *Es war eine Wohltat, faul in der Sonne zu liegen.* ◉Plage

wohl·tu·end ['vo:ltu:ənt] [adj, adv] pleasant(ly) ◊ *eine wohltuende Atmosphäre* ♦ *Ihre Worte waren wohltuend.* ♦ *Die Atmosphäre im Haus ist wohltuend ruhig.*; *(easing pain)* soothing wohltuend wirken have a soothing effect ◊ *Eukalyptus wirkt wohltuend auf die Atemwege.*

Wohl·wol·len ['vo:lvɔlən] das <-s> *no pl* goodwill ◊ *Meine Beförderung hängt von seinem Wohlwollen ab.* mit Wohlwollen favourably, favorably ◊ *jds Bewerbung mit Wohlwollen prüfen* jdm Wohlwollen entgegenbringen treat sb favourably

② **Wohn·block** ['vo:nblɔk] der <-(e)s, -s or Wohnblöcke> block of flats/apartments, apartment block/building

② **woh·nen** ['vo:nən] [intr v] +*haben* live ◊ *Er wohnt in der Liebigstr. 11.* ♦ *Sie wohnen im zweiten Stock.* ♦ *auf dem Land wohnen* zur Miete wohnen rent; *(for a short period)* stay ◊ *Wohnt ihr im Hotel?*

Wohn·ge·mein·schaft ['vo:ngəmaenʃaft] die <-, -en> *(abbr WG)* **1.** shared flat/apartment, flatshare, house-share ◊ *eine Wohngemeinschaft gründen/aufmachen* ♦ *Sie lebt in einer studentischen Wohngemeinschaft.* **2.** group sharing a tenancy ◊ *Vermieten Sie auch an Wohngemeinschaften?*

wohn·haft ['vo:nhaft] [adj] *no comp/superl (form)* resident ◊ *Sie ist wohnhaft in Mannheim.* ein im Ausland wohnhafter Rentner a pensioner who resides abroad

Wohn·heim ['vo:nhaem] das <-(e)s, -e> **1.** *(temporary)* hostel ◊ *ein Wohnheim für Flüchtlinge* ♦ *Wie viele Asylbewerber sind in dem Wohnheim untergebracht?*; *(permanent)* home ◊ *ein Wohnheim für Behinderte* **2.** *(for students)* hall (of residence), dorm(itory)

Wohn·kü·che ['vo:nkʏçə] die <-, -n> *kitchen with a living area*

Wohn·ort ['vo:nɔʁt] der <-(e)s, -e> home town, place of residence An unserem Wohnort gibt es keine Schule. There isn't a school where we live. Sie leben seit 30 Jahren am gleichen Wohnort. They have lived in the same place for the last 30 years.

Wohn·sitz ['vo:nzɪts] der <-es, -e> place of residence, domicile ◊ *seinen ständigen Wohnsitz im Ausland haben* ♦ *Sie hat ihren Wohnsitz nach Frankreich verlegt.* ohne festen Wohnsitz of no fixed abode

② **Woh·nung** ['vo:nʊŋ] die <-, -en> **1.** flat, apartment ◊ *Ich lebe in einer Wohnung mit zwei Zimmern, Küche und Bad* ♦ *Seine Wohnung ist im obersten Stockwerk.* ♦ *eine Wohnung mieten/suchen* **2.** freie Wohnung free accommodation

Wohn·zim·mer ['vo:ntsɪmɐ] das <-s, -> living room

Wolf [vɔlf] der <-(e)s, Wölfe>, **Wöl·fin** ['vœlfɪn] die <-, -nen> wolf ◊ *Wölfe leben in Rudeln mit strenger Rangordnung.*

A
B
C
D
E
F
G
H
I
J
K
L
M
N
O
P
Q
R
S
T
U
V
W
X
Y
Z

● **ein Wolf im Schafspelz** *(fig)* a wolf in sheep's clothing **etw. durch den Wolf drehen** mince sth, grind sth **wie durch den Wolf gedreht** *(slang, fig)* exhausted, done in ◇ *Nach der Auseinandersetzung fühlte sie sich wie durch den Wolf gedreht.* **mit den Wölfen heulen** *(fam, fig)* run with the pack **sich** [dat] **einen Wolf laufen** *(fam)* get sore between the legs by walking too much

② **Wol·ke** ['vɔlkə] die <-, –n> cloud ◇ *Wolken waren aufgezogen und verdüsterten den Himmel.* ♦ *Eine Wolke verdeckte die Sonne.*

● **aus allen Wolken fallen** *(fam, fig)* be horrified ◇ *Er fiel aus allen Wolken, als er die Rechnung las.* **(wie) auf Wolken schweben** *(fig)* be on cloud nine

② **Wol·le** ['vɔlə] die <-, –n> *most sing* wool ◇ *Socken aus reiner Wolle*

● **sich (mit jdm) in der Wolle haben** *(fam)* be arguing with sb, be at odds with sb **sich (mit jdm) in die Wolle kriegen** *(fam)* argue (with sb), come to blows (with sb) ◇ *Die beiden kriegen sich ständig in die Wolle.*

② **wol·len¹** ['vɔlən] <will, wollte, hat wollen> [modal v] +*inf* **1.** *(wish, request)* want ◇ *Sie wollen sich den Film unbedingt ansehen.* ♦ *Wir wollten dich bitten mitzukommen.; (in polite questions)* Willst du …?, Wollen Sie …? Would you like to …? **2.** *(intention)* intend, mean, want ◇ *Ich wollte dir nicht wehtun.* ♦ *Wollt ihr mir das etwa verbieten?* **3.** etw. will etw. (einfach) nicht tun sth will (just) not do sth ◇ *Das Fieber will einfach nicht sinken.* ♦ *Es wollte und wollte nicht aufhören zu regnen.* jdm will etw. einfach nicht gelingen sb just can't seem to get sth right **4.** jd will etw. getan haben sb claims to have done sth ◇ *Niemand will etwas davon gewusst haben.* jd will etw. sein sb claims to be sth ◇ *Dieser Idiot will ein Experte sein!* **5.** etw. will getan sein sth has to be done ◇ *So ein Projekt will ordentlich geplant sein.* **6.** *(emph) (impatience)* Willst du wohl …!, Wollt ihr wohl …! Will you …! ◇ *Willst du wohl still sein!* **7.** *(emph) (reinforcing)* Das will ich aber auch hoffen! I should hope so! Das will ich meinen! I should say so!

● **jd will nichts gegen etw./jdn gesagt haben** *(fam)* sb has got nothing against sth/sb

② **wol·len²** ['vɔlən] <will, wollte, hat gewollt> [tr v] **1.** want ◇ *Eltern wollen meist nur das Beste für ihre Kinder.* ♦ *Ohne es zu wollen, ist er in ein Abenteuer verwickelt worden.* jd will, dass jd etw. tut sb wants sb to do sth ◇ *Ich will, dass du tust, was ich sage!* jd will, dass etw. aufhört/passiert etc. sb wants sth to stop/happen etc. Ich wollte, du wärest hier! I wish you were here. **2.** intend, mean ◇ *Habe ich dich verletzt? Das wollte ich nicht.* [intr v] **1.** want ◇ *Wenn ihr wollt, können wir heute schwimmen gehen.* ♦ *Ob sie wollen oder nicht, die Kinder müssen zur Schule.* ♦ *„Geh ins Bett." — „Ich will aber nicht!"* nach Hause/ins Kino wollen want to go home/to the cinema **2.** *(fam)* etw. will nicht (mehr) sth has stopped working ◇ *Die Kaffeemaschine will nicht.*

● **jd kann jdm nichts wollen** *(fam)* sb can't touch sb, sb hasn't got a thing on sb ◇ *Die Polizei kann ihm nichts wollen, denn er hat ein Alibi.* **da ist nichts mehr zu wollen** *(fam)* there's nothing that sb can do

wo·mit [vo'mɪt, 'vo:mɪt] [adv] *with stress on the first syllable when seeking confirmation* **1.** *interrogative* what … with ◇ *Womit bezahlt er sein neues Auto?* ♦ *Womit wäscht man Seide?* Womit hat sie das verdient? What did she do to deserve that? **2.** *in relative clauses* whereby, with which ◇ *In der letzten Runde konnte er aufholen, womit er Zweiter wurde. Ihm gelingt einfach alles, womit er sich beschäftigt.* He succeeds at everything he does.

wo·mög·lich [vo'mø:klɪç] [adv] possibly ◇ *Es klingt ja absurd, aber er hat womöglich Recht.* ⊜eventuell, möglicherweise

wo·nach [vo'na:x, 'vo:na:x] [adv] *with stress on the first syllable when seeking confirmation* **1.** *interrogative* Wonach suchst ihr? What are you looking for? Wonach riecht es hier denn so seltsam? What's that funny smell? **2.** *relative* according to which ◇ *Berichte, wonach der Attentäter gefasst sei, haben sich als falsch erwiesen.*

wo·ran [vo'ran, 'vo:ran] [adv] *with stress on the first syllable when seeking confirmation* **1.** *interrogative* what … of ◇ *Woran denkst du?* ♦ *Woran ist er gestorben?* **2.** *relative* that ◇ *Das Leiden, woran er gestorben ist, ist nicht bekannt.* etwas, woran man sich orientieren kann a reference point

wo·rauf [vo'raof, 'vo:raof] [adv] *with stress on the first syllable when seeking confirmation* **1.** *interrogative* what … for ◇ *Worauf muss ich achten?* ♦ *Worauf wartest du?* **2.** *relative* that (… on) ◇ *Das ist etwas, worauf er sich freut.*

wo·rauf·hin [voraof'hɪn, 'vo:raofhɪn] [adv] *with stress on the first syllable when seeking confirmation* **1.** *in questions* on what grounds, why ◇ *Woraufhin hat er so reagiert?* **2.** *in relative clauses* whereupon ◇ *Ihm ging das Geld aus, woraufhin er seinen Freund um Hilfe bat.*

wo·raus [vo'raos, 'vo:raos] [adv] *with stress on the first syllable when seeking confirmation* **1.** *in questions* what … from ◇ *Woraus besteht das Material?* **2.** *in relative clauses* out of which, from which ◇ *Das Glas, woraus sie trinkt, hat einen Sprung.*

② **wor·den** ['vɔːdn] *past p of* werden²

wo·rin [vo'rɪn, 'vo:rɪn] [adv] *with stress on the first syllable when seeking confirmation* **1.** *in questions* what … (in) ◇ *Worin ist Calcium enthalten?* Worin liegt hier der Widerspruch? Where is the contradiction? Worin unterscheiden sich die Bilder? How do the pictures differ? **2.** *in relative clauses* in which ◇ *der Brief, worin man ihr das Ergebnis der Prüfung mitteilte*

② **Wort** [vɔrt] das <-(e)s, Wörter *or* –e> **1.** word ◇ *„Apfelsine" ist ein anderes Wort für „Orange".* ein Wort richtig/falsch aussprechen ♦ ein Wort buchstabieren/schreiben/übersetzen ♦ *An dem Gerede ist kein Wort wahr.* ♦ *Böse Worte sind zwischen uns gefallen.* ♦ *Das ist mein letztes Wort!* Wort für Wort word for word, verbatim ◇ *Die Schüler lesen den Text Wort für Wort.* ein treffendes Wort an appropriate word, a fitting expression **2.** *translation varies, no pl (in a (public) discussion)* jdn ums Wort bitten ask sb if you can speak/have your say jdm das Wort entziehen cut sb off das Wort ergreifen take the floor, begin to speak jdm das Wort erteilen let sb have their say,

give sb the floor jd hat das Wort it is sb's turn to speak/have their say sich zu Wort melden speak, take the floor jdm das Wort verbieten stop sb from having their say ⊚ in Wort und Bild in words and pictures das Wort Gottes REL the Bible ⊝Bibel, Heilige Schrift dein Wort in Gottes Ohr let's hope so ◊ *„Hoffentlich wird es bald Sommer!" — „Dein Wort in Gottes Ohr!"* jdm das Wort im Mund herumdrehen *(fig)* twist sb's words jdm das Wort aus dem Mund nehmen *(fig)* take the words out of sb's mouth in Wort und Schrift written and spoken Chinesisch in Wort und Schrift written and spoken Chinese ein geflügeltes Wort 1. a saying, a proverb ◊ *Auch hier gilt das geflügelte Wort: Gut Ding will Weile haben.* 2. a quotation, a quote ◊ *eine Sammlung geflügelter Worte Goethes* sein Wort brechen break your promise jdm ins Wort fallen interrupt sb ◊ *Kaum sprach sie, da fiel er ihr auch schon ins Wort.* jdm aufs Wort folgen/gehorchen/hören obey sb's every word ◊ *Der Hund folgte seinem Herrchen aufs Wort.* ein Wort gibt das andere one thing leads to another ◊ *Ein Wort gab das andere und bald prügelten sie sich.* sein Wort halten keep your promise das Wort an jdn richten address sb ein Wort mit jdm sprechen 1. speak to sb ◊ *Keiner sprach mit dem anderen ein Wort.* 2. have a word with sb ◊ *Kann ich mal wegen der Arbeitsaufteilung ein Wort mit dir sprechen?* kein Wort über etw./jdn verlieren not say anything about sth/sb auf ein Wort *(outd)* a word auf mein Wort I give you my word, I promise mit einem Wort in short, to put it briefly ◊ *Mit einem Wort: Er war ein Geizhals.*

> The plural of *Wort* is *Worte* for a sequence of words in context, e.g. when referring to a quotation, a speech, a book etc.: *die Worte des Korans, bewegende Worte.* When referring to unconnected words — as in a list, dictionary etc. — or to words as units of language, the plural is *Wörter*, e.g.: *ein Satz mit zehn Wörtern, Wörter buchstabieren.*

Wort·art ['vɔ't|aː't] die <–, –en> LING part of speech

Wort·bil·dung ['vɔ'tbɪldʊŋ] die <–, –en> LING word formation ◊ *ein Lehrwerk über Morphologie und Wortbildung* ♦ *Wortbildung durch Ableitung, Präfixe, Suffixe, Zusammensetzung etc.*

② **Wör·ter·buch** ['vœɐ'tebuːx] das <–(e)s, Wörterbücher> dictionary ◊ *ein Wort in einem Wörterbuch nachschlagen*

Wort·laut ['vɔ'tlaɔt] der <–(e)s, –e> wording ◊ *Kannst du dich noch an den ungefähren/genauen Wortlaut der Nachricht erinnern?* dem Wortlaut nach according to the wording im Wortlaut verbatim ◊ *Hier die Rede des Präsidenten im (vollen) Wortlaut: ...*

wört·lich ['vœɐ'tlɪç] [adj, adv] *no comp/superl; when used as an adj, only before ns* literal(ly) ◊ *eine wörtliche Übersetzung* ♦ *Ein „Tool" ist wörtlich übersetzt ein „Werkzeug".* ein wörtliches Zitat a (textual) quotation jdn wörtlich zitieren quote sb verbatim

Wort·schatz ['vɔ'tʃats] der <–es, Wortschätze> vocabulary ◊ *Sie liest viel, um ihren Wortschatz zu*

erweitern. ♦ *Er verfügt über einen umfangreichen Wortschatz.* ⊝Vokabular

Wort·stel·lung ['vɔ'tʃtɛlʊŋ] die <–, –en> LING word order, syntax ◊ *die Wortstellung im Fragesatz/im Deutschen* ⊝Satzstellung

wort·wört·lich ['vɔ't'vœɐ'tlɪç] [adj, adv] *no comp/superl; when used as an adj, mostly before ns* literal(ly) ◊ *die wortwörtliche Übersetzung eines Textes* ♦ *etw. wortwörtlich abschreiben*

wo·rü·ber [vo'ry:bɐ, 'vo:ry:bɐ] [adv] *with stress on the first syllable when seeking confirmation* 1. *interrogative* what ... about ◊ *Worüber sprecht ihr?* ♦ *Worüber lacht er?* 2. *relative* which ... about ◊ *Ich habe ein Problem, worüber ich mich ärgere.*

wo·rum [vo'rʊm, 'vo:rʊm] [adv] *with stress on the first syllable when seeking confirmation* 1. *interrogative, translation varies* Worum geht es hier? What's this about? Worum hat er dich betrogen? How much did he con you out of? Worum hat sie ihn gebeten? What did she ask him for? 2. *relative* that ◊ *Es gibt einiges, worum Sie sich kümmern muss.*

wo·von [vo'fɔn, 'vo:fɔn] [adv] *with stress on the first syllable when seeking confirmation* 1. *interrogative, translation varies* Wovon lebt er? What does he live on? Wovon sprichst du? What are you talking about? Wovon muss man 12 subtrahieren, um 15 zu erhalten? What do you subtract 12 from in order to get 15? 2. *relative* that ◊ *Das Geld, wovon sie leben, ist gestohlen.*

wo·vor [vo'fo:ɐ, 'vo:fo:ɐ] [adv] *with stress on the first syllable when seeking confirmation* 1. *interrogative, translation varies* Wovor hast du Angst/fürchtest du dich? What are you afraid of? Wovor läufst du davon? What are you running from? Wovor schützt diese Impfung? What does this inoculation protect against? 2. *relative* das, wovor ... what ... ◊ *Das, wovor er gewarnt hat, wird nun Wirklichkeit.*

wo·zu [vo'tsu:, 'vo:tsu:] [adv] *with stress on the first syllable when seeking confirmation* 1. *interrogative, translation varies* Wozu soll das gut sein? What's the point of that? Wozu die Mühe? Why bother?, What's the point? Wozu haben Sie sich entschlossen? What have you decided to do? Wozu passt die Bluse am besten? What does the shirt look best with? 2. *relative, translation varies* Sie muss heute arbeiten, wozu sie keine Lust hat. She's got to work today, which she doesn't want to do. Sie spielte Klavier, wozu sie auch selber sang. She played the piano and sang at the same time.

② **wuchs** [vuːks] *pret of* wachsen

Wucht [vʊxt] die <–> *no pl* force ◊ *die Wucht eines Schlages/Aufpralls* mit voller Wucht with full force ◊ *Sie warf den Ball mit voller Wucht gegen die Wand.*

⊚ **eine Wucht sein** *(fam)* be excellent

wüh·len ['vy:lən] [intr v] +*haben (also fig)* in etw. [dat] wühlen dig into sth ◊ *mit bloßen Händen in der Erde wühlen* Der Schmerz wühlte in seinen Eingeweiden. The pain gnawed at his innards.; *(in order to find sth)* in etw. [dat] (nach etw.) wühlen rummage around in sth (for sth) ◊ *Sie wühlte in der Schublade nach ihrem Schlüssel.* Die Reporter wühlten in seiner Vergangenheit. The reporters dug up his past. [tr v] dig ◊ *ein Loch in die Erde*

A
B
C
D
E
F
G
H
I
J
K
L
M
N
O
P
Q
R
S
T
U
V
W
X
Y
Z

wühlen Der Hund wühlte einen Knochen aus der Erde. The dog dug up a bone. [ref v] *(also fig)* sich durch etw. wühlen plough/plow through sth ◊ *Die Bagger wühlten sich durch den Boden.* ✦ *Ich wühlte mich durch die Menschenmenge.*

wund [vʊnt] [adj] <wunder, am wundesten> *(also fig)* sore ◊ *Der Po des Babys ist wund und gerötet.* ✦ *eine wunde Stelle am Knie* (jds) wunder Punkt (sb's) sore point ◊ *Mit deiner Kritik hast du seinen wunden Punkt getroffen.* sich wund laufen rub your feet raw ◊ *In den neuen Schuhen hat er sich wund gelaufen.* sich wund liegen get bedsores

② **Wun·de** ['vʊndə] die <–, –n> wound, cut ◊ *Der Junge hat eine Wunde an der Hand.* ✦ *Sie träufelte Jod auf die Wunde.* ✦ *Die Schwester verbindet die Wunde mit einem Verband.*

◉ **eine alte Wunde wieder aufreißen** *(fig)* open (up) old wounds **(jdm) tiefe Wunden schlagen** *(fig)* wound (sb) deeply

Wun·der ['vʊndɐ] das <–s, –> **1.** miracle ◊ *Es ist ein Wunder, dass sie noch lebt.* ✦ *Ich glaube nicht an Wunder.* (ein) Wunder tun work a miracle/miracles **2.** ein Wunder an etw. [dat] a miracle of sth ◊ *ein Wunder an Vollkommenheit*

◉ **ein/sein blaues Wunder erleben** *(fam)* get/have a nasty shock **Wunder wer/was** *(fam, pej)* really somebody/something ◊ *Sie sind so arrogant und meinen, Wunder wer sie sind!* ✦ *Sie bildet sich ein, dass sie Wunder was geleistet hat.* **Wunder wie** Er denkt immer, Wunder wie klug er ist. He thinks he's really clever.

② **wun·der·bar** ['vʊndɐbaːɐ̯] [adj] **1.** fantastic, wonderful ◊ *Die Landschaft ist einfach wunderbar!* ✦ *wunderbares Wetter* ⊖herrlich **2.** miraculous, amazing ◊ *Das Phänomen der Sonnenfinsternis ist wunderbar.* ✦ *die wunderbare Heilung des Aussätzigen* [adv] **1.** really well ◊ *Es hat alles wunderbar funktioniert.* ⊖großartig **2.** +adj *(fam)* really, wonderfully ◊ *Das Wasser war wunderbar warm.* ⊖sehr

② **wun·dern** ['vʊndɐn] [ref v] +haben **1.** sich (über jdn/etw.) wundern be surprised (at sb/sth), be amazed (at sb/sth) ◊ *Du wirst dich wundern, was noch alles auf dich zukommt!* ✦ *Der Gast wunderte sich über die unhöfliche Reaktion des Kellners.* **2.** sich wundern wonder ◊ *Ich wundere mich, was aus ihm geworden ist.* [tr v] jdn wundern surprise sb, amaze sb ◊ *Das seltsame Verhalten seines Freundes wundert ihn.*

wun·der·schön ['vʊndɐˈʃøːn] [adj] *no comp* **1.** very/really beautiful ◊ *Das Kleid ist wunderschön.* ✦ *eine wunderschöne Frau* **2.** wonderful, fantastic ◊ *Urlaubmachen ist wunderschön.* ✦ *Es ist wunderschön, im Zentrum der Stadt zu wohnen.* ⊖wundervoll, herrlich [adv] beautifully, wonderfully well ◊ *Die Kinder haben wunderschön miteinander gespielt.* ✦ *Die Blume hat wunderschön geblüht.* ⊖herrlich

wun·der·voll ['vʊndɐfɔl] [adj, adv] wonderful(ly), marvellous(ly) ◊ *Die Aussicht hier ist wundervoll!* ✦ *eine wundervolle Reise mit poetischen Bildern und vielen Überraschungen* ✦ *Sie hat wundervoll gesungen.* ✦ *Im Frühjahr ist die Natur so wundervoll grün.* ⊖wunderbar, herrlich

② **Wunsch** [vʊnʃ] der <–(e)s, Wünsche> **1.** wish, desire ◊ *Sie hat den Wunsch, zu malen.* ✦ *sich*

einen lang gehegten Wunsch erfüllen den Wunsch nach etw. [dat] haben want sth, wish for sth ◊ *Das Ehepaar hat den Wunsch nach Kindern.* nach Wunsch according to your wishes ◊ *ein Programm nach Wunsch ändern* auf Wunsch on/by request ◊ *Die Wiederholung erfolgt auf vielfachen Wunsch unserer Zuschauer.* **2.** *(on letters, cards)* mit den besten Wünschen best wishes

② **wün·schen** ['vʏnʃn̩] [tr v] +haben **1.** wish ◊ *Der Gast wünscht, um acht geweckt zu werden.* ✦ *Er ist unbeliebt und alle wünschen ihn weit fort von hier. Ja, bitte? Was wünschen Sie? Yes, what would you like? Ich wünschte, ...* I wish ... ◊ *Ich wünschte, es wäre alles schon vorbei!* sich [dat] etw. wünschen want sth, wish for sth ◊ *Sie wünscht mir nur fünf Minuten Ruhe.* ✦ *Sie hat alles, was man sich nur wünschen kann.* **2.** *(in polite phrases)* (jdm) gute Nacht/viel Erfolg/eine angenehme Reise wünschen wish sb good night/every success/a pleasant trip ◊ *Ich wünsche Ihnen gute Besserung!* I hope you get better soon. ✦ *Ich wünsche einen guten Appetit!* (I hope you) enjoy your meal. **3.** want, insist ◊ *Ich wünsche, dass du dein Zimmer aufräumst, haben wir uns verstanden?* ✦ *Ich wünsche, nicht unterbrochen zu werden!* ⊖verlangen

② **wur·de** ['vʊʁdə] *pret of* werden¹, werden²

Wür·de ['vʏʁdə] die <–, –n> **1.** dignity ◊ *Der Arzt bewahrt die Würde der Patienten.* ✦ *Ich fühle mich in meiner Würde gekränkt.* ◊ *Darauf zu antworten, war unter ihrer Würde.* ✦ *Er verlor das Spiel mit Würde.* in Würde alt werden grow old gracefully **2.** rank ◊ *Ihm wurde die Würde eines Ehrenbürgers verliehen.* ✦ *Er stieg zu höchsten Würden auf.*

◉ **unter aller Würde** disgraceful

wür·di·gen ['vʏʁdɪɡn̩] [tr v] +haben **1.** appreciate ◊ *Ihr Einsatz wurde nicht genügend gewürdigt.* etw. zu würdigen wissen appreciate sth ⊖schätzen **2.** pay tribute to ◊ *In seiner Rede würdigte der Bürgermeister die Leistung der Katastrophenhelfer.* **3.** jdn/etw. keines Blickes würdigen not deign to look at sb/sth

Wurf [vʊʁf] der <–(e)s, Würfe> **1.** throw ◊ *Er traf gleich beim ersten Wurf ins Tor.* ✦ *Beim nächsten Wurf würfelte sie eine Sechs.* zum Wurf ausholen take aim, get ready to throw **2.** zoo litter ◊ *ein Wurf von sieben Kätzchen*

Wür·fel ['vʏʁfl̩] der <–s, –> **1.** dice, die ◊ *Zu diesem Spiel braucht man zwei Würfel.* **2.** MATH cube ◊ *das Volumen eines Würfels* **3.** cube ◊ *ein paar Würfel Käse* etw. in Würfel schneiden cut sth into cubes, dice sth

◉ **die Würfel sind/der Würfel ist gefallen** *(fig)* the die is cast

wür·feln ['vʏʁfl̩n] [intr v] +haben **1.** throw (the dice/die) ◊ *Hast du schon gewürfelt?* **2.** play dice ◊ *Würfelt ihr um Geld?* [tr v] +haben **1.** throw ◊ *Wer eine Sechs würfelt, darf nochmal.* **2.** cut into cubes, dice ◊ *Fleisch für ein Gulasch würfeln*

Wurm [vʊʁm] der <–(e)s, Würmer> **1.** zoo worm ◊ *Der Hund hat Würmer.* ✦ *Würmer zum Angeln* **2.** *(fam)* maggot ◊ *Der Apfel hat einen Wurm.*

◉ **jdm die Würmer aus der Nase ziehen** *(fam, fig)* drag sth/it out of sb **irgendwo ist der Wurm**

drin *(fam, fig)* something is wrong/amiss somewhere

② **Wurst** [voʳst] die <–, Würste> **1.** sausage ◊ *Würste braten/grillen* ♦ *ein Brötchen mit Wurst*; sausage spread ◊ *Er strich sich Wurst aufs Brot.* **2.** sausage shape, roll ◊ *Den Teig zu einer Wurst rollen.*; *(faeces)* turd
⊛ **es geht um die Wurst** *(fam, fig)* the moment of truth has arrived ◊ *Die Endrunde hat begonnen, jetzt geht es um die Wurst!*

> In Germany, there are over 1,500 different types of sausage, warm (fried or boiled) or cold (usually served with bread). Each region sets great store by its sausages. Nuremberg grilled sausages, frankfurters und Regensburg sausages are particularly famous. Curried sausage (*Currywurst* — finely sliced sausage served with ketchup and dusted with curry powder) originated in Berlin. In shops, you can buy sausages in slices or by weight from the delicatessen counter.

Würst·chen [ˈvyʳstçən] das <–s, –> **1.** (small) sausage, chipolata ◊ *Würstchen mit Kartoffelsalat* ♦ *Würstchen grillen/heiß machen* Frankfurter Würstchen frankfurter Wiener Würstchen wiener **2.** *(fam, pej)* ein armes Würstchen a poor soul/devil **3.** *(fam, esp pej)* nobody ◊ *Was willst du von mir, du Würstchen?*

Wur·zel [ˈvoʳtsl] die <–, –n> **1.** *(also fig)* root ◊ *Der Baum hat kräftige Wurzeln.* ♦ *Unkraut mit den Wurzeln ausreißen* ♦ *die Wurzel eines Zahnes/Worts* ♦ *ein Problem an der Wurzel packen* ♦ *die Wurzel allen Übels; (of plants)* Wurzel fassen, Wurzeln schlagen take root ◊ *Auf dem felsigen Boden können größere Pflanzen kaum Wurzel fassen/Wurzeln schlagen.* **2.** MATH square root ◊ *Die Wurzel aus/von 16 ist 4.* die Wurzel aus etw. ziehen work out/calculate the square root of sth

⊛ etw. mit der Wurzel ausrotten *(fig)* eradicate sth ◊ *Er wollte das Übel mit der Wurzel ausrotten.*
Wurzeln schlagen 1. put down roots ◊ *Er hat mittlerweile hier in Deutschland Wurzeln geschlagen.* **2.** take root ◊ *Komm endlich, oder willst du hier Wurzeln schlagen?*

wür·zen [ˈvyʳtsn̩] tr v +haben *(also fig)* season, spice up ◊ *Das Fleisch mit Pfeffer und Salz würzen.* ♦ *Der Film ist mit witzigen Dialogen gewürzt.*

② **wusch** [vuːʃ] *pret of* waschen
② **wuss·te** [ˈvʊstə] *pret of* wissen
Wüs·te [ˈvyːstə] die <–, –n> GEOG desert ◊ *Die Karawane zog durch die Wüste.* ♦ *in der Wüste leben*
⊛ **jdn in die Wüste schicken** *(fam, fig)* send sb packing ◊ *Nach dem Skandal schickte ihn seine Partei in die Wüste.*
Wut [vuːt] die <–> *no pl* fury, rage ◊ *Sie wird knallrot im Gesicht, wenn sie in Wut gerät.* ♦ *Ich musste in ohnmächtiger Wut zusehen.* ♦ *Voller Wut schlug sie die Tür zu.* (auf jdn) (eine) Wut haben be furious/mad (with sb) ◊ *Hast du wegen gestern immer noch (eine) Wut auf mich?* ♦ *Wut im Bauch haben* vor Wut platzen go mad, go berserk
⊛ **vor Wut kochen** seethe with rage

② **wü·tend** [ˈvyːtn̩t, ˈvyːtənt] adj, adv angry(-ily), furious(ly) ◊ *Er ist wütend, weil sie gelogen hat.* ♦ *Solche Dummheit macht mich wütend!* ♦ *wütende Proteste* ♦ *„Du Schuft!", schrie sie ihn wütend an.* ♦ *ein wütend bellender Hund* wütend auf jdn sein be angry/furious with sb über etw. akk wütend sein be angry at/because of sth ◊ *Bist du wütend darüber, dass ich zu spät gekommen bin?* ⊖zornig adj *only before ns (storm, disease, anger, pain)* raging ◊ *Wütender Zorn flammt in ihm auf.* ♦ *Draußen tobte ein wütender Sturm.* ⊖heftig

X

x, X [ɪks] das <-, -> x, X ◇ *Dieses Wort wird mit einem kleinen x/großen X geschrieben.* ♦ *X wie Xanthippe*
ⓔ **jdm ein X für ein U vormachen** fool sb
x-fach ['ɪksfax] [adj] **1.** *only before ns (fam)* multiple ◇ *der x-fache Titelträger der Rallye* **2.** MATH n times die x-fache Menge n times the amount [adv] *(fam)* **1.** in a variety of ways ◇ *Der Treppenstuhl ist x-fach verstellbar.* **2.** a number of times, umpteen times ◇ *Er hat das Buch schon x-fach* gelesen.
x-mal ['ɪksmaːl] [adv] *(fam)* a number of times, umpteen times ◇ *Er hat x-mal gegen die Regel verstoßen.* ♦ *Sie musste x-mal operiert werden.*
x-te ['ɪkstə] [nmrl] *(fam)* umpteenth ◇ *die x-te Folge der Soap* ♦ *die x-te Neuauflage des Buchs* zum x-ten Mal for the nth time, for the umpteenth time Er spielte die x-te Zugabe. He played yet another encore.

Y

y, Y ['ʏpsilɔn] das <-(s), -(s)> y, Y ◇ *Dieses Wort wird mit einem kleinen y/großen Y geschrieben.* ♦ *Y wie Ypsilon*
Yp·si·lon ['ʏpsilɔn] das <-(s), -s> **1.** y, Y **2.** *(in the Greek alphabet)* upsilon

Z

z, Z [tsɛt] das <-(s), -(s)> z, Z ◇ *Dieses Wort wird mit einem kleinen z/großen Z geschrieben.* ♦ *Z wie Zacharias*

zäh [tsɛː] adj <zäher, am zäh(e)sten> **1.** *(person)* tough, hardy ◇ *ein zäher Kämpfer* ♦ *Marathonläufer müssen zäh sein.* **2.** *(meat)* tough ◇ *Das Fleisch ist ja noch zäh wie Leder!* **3.** *(liquid mass)* thick, viscous ◇ *Der Teig ist zäh und schwer.* ♦ *ein zäher Lavastrom* adv **1.** slowly, laboriously ◇ *Die Verhandlung kam nur zäh und stockend voran.* **2.** *(liquid mass)* thickly, viscously ◇ *ein zäh fließender Lavastrom*

⑦ **Zahl** [tsaːl] die <-, -en> number ◇ *die Zahlen 1 bis 10* ♦ *eine einstellige//mehrstellige Zahl* ♦ *eine gerade/ungerade Zahl* ♦ *die Wurzel einer Zahl berechnen* ♦ *Die Zahl der tödlichen Unfälle ist zurückgegangen.* an der Zahl in number ◇ *Die Studenten — 250 an der Zahl — verließen den Saal.* in großer Zahl in great numbers
⊛ **rote/schwarze Zahlen** the red/black ◇ *Die Firma ist in die roten Zahlen gekommen.* schwarze Zahlen schreiben be in the black

zahl·bar [ˈtsaːlbaːɐ] adj no comp/superl, not before ns *(tech)* payable ◇ *Rechnung zahlbar in drei Monatsraten* ⊜fällig

⑦ **zah·len** [ˈtsaːlən] tr+intr v +*haben* pay ◇ *Sie hat mir 75 Euro für den Schrank gezahlt.* ♦ *Wir müssen noch zahlen, bevor wir gehen.* ♦ *Die Versicherung zahlt in so einem Fall nicht.* ♦ *Er zahlt seine Angestellten sehr gut/schlecht.* ♦ *eine Rechnung/die Steuern/eine Strafe zahlen; (customs duty)* pay sth (on sth)
⊛ **bitte zahlen, zahlen bitte** could I/we have the bill, please

⑦ **zäh·len** [ˈtsɛːlən] tr+intr v +*haben* **1.** count ◇ *Die Lehrerin zählt ihre Schüler.* ♦ *Du solltest noch einmal zählen.* ♦ *Ich kann schon bis 100 zählen!* ♦ *In ihrem Job zählt nur Leistung.* ♦ *Sie zählt schon die Stunden bis zu ihrem Urlaub.* jdn/etw. zu etw. zählen count sb/sth as sth ◇ *Ich zähle ihn zu meinen Freunden.* **2.** *(also fig)* etw. zählt etw. sth is (worth) sth ◇ *Wie viele Punkte zählt das Ass?* intr v +*haben* **1.** *mostly negated* etw. zählt etw. counts ◇ *Der erste Versuch zählt nicht.* Wir machen erst ein Probespiel, danach zählt es. We'll have a practice game first, and then we'll play for real. **2.** *only written* etw. zählt ... sth has ... ◇ *Die Stadt zählt fast 30 000 Einwohner.* **3.** zu etw. zählen be (one of) sth, rank among sth ◇ *Er zählte damals zu den bekanntesten Schauspielern.* ♦ *Wale zählen zu den Säugetieren.* ⊜gehören **4.** auf jdn/etw. zählen (können) (be able to) count on sb/sth ◇ *Du kannst auf mich zählen.* ♦ *Kann ich auf deine Diskretion zählen?* ⊜mit jdm/etw. rechnen (können)

⑦ **zahl·reich** [ˈtsaːlraɪç] adj numerous ◇ *Solche Fälle sind zum Glück nicht sehr zahlreich.* ♦ *ihre zahlreichen Nachkommen; (family)* large Wir freuen uns auf Ihr zahlreiches Erscheinen. We look forward to seeing a large number of you. adv in large numbers ◇ *Ich freue mich sehr, dass ihr so zahlreich erscheint.*

Zah·lung [ˈtsaːlʊŋ] die <-, -en> payment ◇ *Die Zahlung erfolgt monatlich/per Scheck.* ♦ *Die Zahlung ist noch nicht auf meinem Konto angekommen.*
⊛ **(jdm) etw. in Zahlung geben** give (sb) sth in part-exchange etw. in Zahlung nehmen take sth in part-exchange

Zäh·lung [ˈtsɛːlʊŋ] die <-, -en> count ◇ *eine Zählung vornehmen; (of the population)* census

Zah·lungs·mit·tel [ˈtsaːlʊŋsmɪtl̩] das <-s, -> means of payment; *(legal tender)* currency ◇ *Das gesetzliche Zahlungsmittel in Portugal ist der Euro.*

Zahl·wort [ˈtsaːlvɔrt] das <-(e)s, Zahlwörter> numeral

zahm [tsaːm] adj **1.** tame ◇ *Wir haben ein zahmes Kaninchen zu Hause.; (not dangerous also)* docile ◇ *Keine Angst, das Pferd ist ganz zahm.* **2.** *(criticism, complaint)* mild ◇ *eine zahme Kritik* ♦ *Was er sagte, war ja noch zahm.* ⊜scharf

zäh·men [ˈtsɛːmən] tr v +*haben* **1.** ein Tier zähmen tame an animal **2.** *(lofty)* sich/etw. zähmen control yourself/your sth ◇ *Zähmen Sie sich, sonst müssen wir das Gespräch abbrechen!* Zähme deine Ungeduld!

⑦ **Zahn** [tsaːn] der <-(e)s, Zähne> **1.** tooth ◇ *sich die Zähne putzen* ♦ *Sie muss sich einen kranken Zahn behandeln/ziehen lassen.* ♦ *Der Hund knurrte und zeigte die Zähne.* **2.** *(of a stamp)* perforation; *(of a saw, comb)* tooth; *(of a leaf)* serration
⊛ **der Zahn der Zeit** the ravages of time **die dritten Zähne** *(fam, euph)* false teeth **einen ganz schönen Zahn draufhaben** *(fam)* be going at a fair (old) rate **sich** dat **an jdm/etw. die Zähne ausbeißen** have a hard time with sb/sth ◇ *An dieser Frage hat sich die Schüler die Zähne ausgebissen.* **bis an die Zähne bewaffnet** armed to the teeth **jdm auf den Zahn fühlen** sound sb out **jd klappert mit den Zähnen** sb's teeth are chattering **jdm die Zähne zeigen** *(fam)* show sb what you're made of **jdm den/diesen Zahn ziehen** *(fam)* quash that idea **einen Zahn zulegen** *(fam)* get a move on **die Zähne zusammenbeißen** *(fam)* grit your teeth

⑦ **Zahn·creme** [ˈtsaːnkreːm] die <-, -s> → Zahnpasta

Zahn·fleisch [ˈtsaːnflaɪʃ] das <-es> no pl gum(s) ◇ *Beim Putzen blutet mein Zahnfleisch.*
⊛ **auf dem Zahnfleisch gehen/kriechen** *(fam)* be on your knees

⑦ **Zahn·pas·ta** [ˈtsaːnpasta] die <-, -s or Zahnpasten> most sing toothpaste ◇ *eine Tube Zahnpasta* ⊜Zahncreme

Zan·ge [ˈtsaŋə] die <-, -n> **1.** (pair of) pliers ◇ *den Nagel mit einer Zange aus der Wand ziehen; (for cakes)* (pair of) tongs; *(used to deliver a*

baby) forceps **2.** *most pl* ZOO pincers ◊ *die Zangen des Krebses* ⊖Schere

◉ **jdn in der Zange haben** *(fam)* have got sb cornered **jdn in die Zange nehmen** *(fam)* put the screws on sb, give sb the third degree

zan·ken ['ʦaŋkn̩] ⌊ref+intr v⌋ +*haben* (sich) (um/ über etw. ⌊acc⌋) zanken quarrel (over/about sth) ◊ *Die beiden zanken ständig darüber, wer abwaschen muss.* ♦ *Er zankt sich mit dem Chef um die Kosten.* ♦ *Sie zankt wieder mal mit ihrer Mutter.* ♦ *Hört auf, euch zu zanken!*

Zäpf·chen ['ʦɛpfçən] das <-s, -> **1.** MED suppository ◊ *ein fiebersenkendes Zäpfchen nehmen* **2.** ANAT uvula

Zapf·säu·le ['ʦapfzɔɪlə] die <-, -n> petrol pump, gas pump ◊ *Ich habe an der Zapfsäule Nummer drei getankt.*

zap·peln ['ʦapln̩] ⌊intr v⌋ +*haben* wriggle, jiggle ◊ *Ein großer Fisch zappelte an der Angel.* ♦ *Hörst du bitte mal auf, mit den Beinen zu zappeln?*

◉ **jdn zappeln lassen** *(fam)* keep sb in suspense, keep sb guessing

zart [ʦaːɐt] ⌊adj⌋ <zarter, am zartesten> **1.** delicate ◊ *Ihre Arme/Finger wirken unheimlich zart und zerbrechlich.* ♦ *Im Frühjahr zeigen sich die ersten zarten Knospen.* ♦ *zarte Spitzen* ♦ *Dieser Stoff ist sehr weich und zart.* ♦ *Dieses Pflänzchen ist noch sehr zart.* **2.** soft ◊ *zarte Haut* **3.** *(meat, vegetables etc.)* tender ◊ *Ist das Fleisch auch schön zart?; (chocolate)* fine **4.** *(kiss, embrace)* tender ◊ *ein zarter Kuss auf die Wange* ♦ *Die Berührung war zart und schüchtern.* ⊖sanft ↔grob **5.** *(not intense and therefore pleasant to see, smell, hear)* delicate ◊ *ein zartes Blau* ♦ *ein zarter Duft* ♦ *Ihre Stimme klang weich und zart.* ⌊adv⌋ **1.** tenderly, gently ◊ *Sie küsste ihn zart auf die Wange.* ♦ *Er geht manchmal nicht gerade zart mit ihr um.* ⊖sanft **2.** *(of colo(u)r, sound, smell)* delicately, gently ◊ *ein zart getöntes Glas*

◉ **zart besaitet** *(esp hum)* highly strung, highstrung **zart besaitet sein** be highly strung, be highstrung

zärt·lich ['ʦɛːɐtlɪç] ⌊adj, adv⌋ **1.** tender(ly), affectionate(ly) ◊ *ein zärtlicher Kuss/Blick* ♦ *Du ist sehr zärtlich zu mir.* ♦ *Sie küssten sich zärtlich.* **2.** *(lofty) (father, wife etc.)* loving(ly) ◊ *eine zärtliche Ehefrau/Mutter* ♦ *Er ist als Vater sehr zärtlich.* ♦ *Du könntest mit den Kindern ruhig etwas zärtlicher umgehen.*

Zärt·lich·keit ['ʦɛːɐtlɪçkaɪt] die <-, -en> **1.** *no pl* tenderness, affection ◊ *Er empfand eine große Zärtlichkeit für sie.* ♦ *Sie sah ihn voll Zärtlichkeit an.* **2.** *most pl* intimacies ◊ *Sie tauschten Zärtlichkeiten aus.*

Zau·ber ['ʦaʊbɐ] der <-s> *no pl* **1.** spell ◊ *über jdn einen Zauber aussprechen* ♦ *Die Hexe wendete einen bösen Zauber an.* **2.** magic ◊ *Der verschneite Wald strahlt einen besonderen Zauber aus.* ♦ *Er ist ihrem Zauber erlegen.* **3.** *(fam, pej)* to-do, palaver, song and dance ◊ *Also diesen Zauber mache ich nicht mit.* ⊖Zirkus **4.** *(fam, pej)* stuff ◊ *Und was soll der ganze Zauber kosten?*

◉ **fauler Zauber** *(fam)* a scam

zau·bern ['ʦaʊbɐn] ⌊tr v⌋ +*haben* **1.** conjure up ◊ *Die Eingeborenen glauben, dass der Schamane Regen zaubern kann.* **einen Geist in eine Flasche**

zaubern put a genie into a bottle **2.** magic, produce ◊ *Ich zaubere nun ein Kaninchen aus dem Hut.* **3.** *(fig)* etw. (aus etw.) zaubern conjure sth up (out of sth) ◊ *Aus ein paar Resten hatte sie im Nu ein leckeres Abendessen gezaubert.* ⌊intr v⌋ +*haben* **1.** perform magic ◊ *Hexen können zaubern. Ich kann doch nicht zaubern! I can't perform miracles!* **2.** do conjuring tricks ◊ *Er zaubert in einem Zirkus.*

Zaun [ʦaʊn] der <-(e)s, Zäune> fence ◊ *ein hoher/ niedriger Zaun* ♦ *einen Zaun um etw. errichten/ ziehen*

◉ **einen Streit vom Zaun brechen** → Streit **ein lebender Zaun** a hedge

z. B. [ʦʊm 'baɛʃpiːl, ʦɛt 'beː] *(abbr zum Beispiel)* e.g. ◊ *Haustiere, z. B. Hunde, Katze oder Hamster*

ZDF [ʦɛtdeːʔɛf] das *(abbr of* Zweites Deutsches Fernsehen) ◊ *Was läuft heute Abend im ZDF?* ⊖das Zweite (Programm)

> *ZDF*, the second terrestrial channel in Germany, is broadcast from Mainz and is purely a television company. As a public-service broadcasting corporation financed by licence fees and advertising, which is restricted to certain hours, its remit is to provide people with a blend of education, culture and entertainment. Feature films are not interrupted by advertisements, as is the case with independent broadcasting organizations.

Zeb·ra·strei·fen ['ʦeːbraʃtraɛfn̩] der <-s, -> zebra crossing, pedestrian crossing ◊ *Kinder, benutzt immer den Zebrastreifen, wenn ihr über die Straße wollt!*

Ze·cke ['ʦɛka] die <-, -n> tick

Zeh [ʦeː] der <-s, -en> toe ◊ *der kleine/große Zeh* ♦ *Pass auf, dass du ihr beim Tanzen nicht dauernd auf die Zehen trittst!*

Zehe ['ʦeːə] die <-, -n> **1.** ANAT toe ◊ *die kleine/ große Zehe* ♦ *Er trat ihr versehentlich auf die Zehen.* **sich auf die Zehen stellen** stand on tiptoe **2.** BOT clove ◊ *Zerdrücken Sie eine halbe Zehe Knoblauch.*

◉ **jdm auf die Zehen treten 1.** tread on sb's toes **2.** hurry sb up

zehn [ʦeːn] ⌊nmrl⌋ ten → vier

Zeh·ner ['ʦeːnɐ] der <-s, -> **1.** *(fam)* ten **2.** *(fam) (banknote)* ten, tenner ◊ *Kannst du mir einen Zwanziger in zwei Zehner wechseln?* **3.** *(coin)* ten pence piece, ten cent piece ◊ *Nimmt dieser Münzautomat auch Zehner?* **4.** MATH ten ◊ *Nach den Einern addiert man die Zehner.*

⑦ **Zei·chen** ['ʦaɛçn̩] das <-s, -> **1.** sign ◊ *Er gab ihnen ein Zeichen, sich zu erheben.* ♦ *Das ist das Zeichen zum Aufbruch.* ♦ *Gehörlose verständigen sich durch Zeichen miteinander.* ♦ *Er hält es für ein Zeichen der Schwäche, wenn ein Mann weint.* ♦ *Das ist kein gutes Zeichen.* ♦ *Sie ist im Zeichen des Skorpions geboren.* zum Zeichen ... ⌊gen⌋ as a sign of sth ◊ *Reicht euch zum Zeichen der Versöhnung die Hände.* zum Zeichen, dass to show that ◊ *Zum Zeichen, dass wir in friedlicher Absicht kommen ...* **2.** symbol ◊ *Das ist das Zeichen für Pfund.* **3.** punctuation mark ◊ *Welches Zeichen steht am Ende einer Frage?*

◉ **die Zeichen der Zeit erkennen** recognize the

signs of the times **ein Zeichen setzen** set an example **(ganz) im Zeichen von etw. stehen**, **(ganz) im Zeichen ...** [gen] **stehen** be (completely) dominated by sth ◊ *Die ganze Stadt stand damals im Zeichen der Expo 2000.*

Zei·chen·set·zung ['ʦaeçnʦɛʦʊŋ] *die <-> no pl* punctuation ◊ *Er hat wieder einige Fehler bei der Zeichensetzung gemacht.* ⊖Interpunktion

ⓩ **zeich·nen** ['ʦaeçnən] [tr v] *+haben* **1.** jdn/etw. zeichnen draw sb/sth ◊ *Bitte zeichnen Sie mir bis morgen einen Entwurf.* ♦ *Ihr sollt das Haus nicht bunt ausmalen, sondern nur zeichnen.* **2.** schön/ungewöhnlich etc. gezeichnet sein have beautiful/unusual etc. markings ◊ *Das Fell der Katze ist wunderschön gezeichnet.* **3.** jd ist von etw. gezeichnet sth has left its mark on sb ◊ *Sie ist von der langen Krankheit deutlich gezeichnet.* **4.** sign ◊ *gezeichnet H. Bauer* ♦ *Aktien/einen Scheck zeichnen* [intr v] *+haben* **1.** gerne zeichnen like drawing Kannst du gut zeichnen? Are you good at drawing? *Er zeichnet schon eine ganze Weile an diesem Landschaftsbild.* He's been working on that landscape drawing for quite a long time now. **2.** *(form)* für etw. zeichnen be responsible for sth ◊ *Wer zeichnet für diesen Beitrag verantwortlich?*

ⓩ **Zeich·nung** ['ʦaeçnʊŋ] *die <-, -en>* **1.** drawing, illustration ◊ *Sieh nur die niedlichen Zeichnungen in diesem Kinderbuch!* ♦ *eine Zeichnung anfertigen/entwerfen* **2.** depiction, portrayal ◊ *die lebendige Zeichnung der Romanfiguren* **3.** *(on an animal)* markings ◊ *Der Tiger hat eine auffallende Zeichnung.* **4.** ECON signing ◊ *die Zeichnung von Aktien*

Zei·ge·fin·ger ['ʦaegəfɪŋɐ] *der <-s, ->* index finger, forefinger ◊ *Sie deutete mit dem Zeigefinger auf die Stelle.* ♦ *Er erhob warnend den Zeigefinger.*

ⓩ **zei·gen** ['ʦaegŋ] [tr v] *+haben* show ◊ *Zeig doch mal, was du da hast.* ♦ *Könnten Sie mir den Weg zum Bahnhof zeigen?* ♦ *Er hat mir gezeigt, wie man das Programm bedient.* ♦ *Ich möchte Ihnen gern meine Heimatstadt zeigen.* ♦ *Er zeigte seine Enttäuschung sehr deutlich.* ♦ *Du hast in dieser Situation großen Mut gezeigt.* ♦ *Dieses Foto zeigt meinen Vater im Alter von 14 Jahren.* ♦ *Das Thermometer zeigt fast 22 Grad unter null.* ♦ *Wir zeigen Ihnen heute den Spielfilm „Ben Hur";* *(clock)* say ◊ *Die Uhr zeigt fünf vor acht.; (film, play)* gezeigt werden be showing, be on ◊ *In der Oper wird im Moment „La Traviata" gezeigt. Erst die Zeit wird zeigen, wie dauerhaft diese Beziehung ist.* Only time will tell whether this relationship will last. [intr v] *+haben* (mit etw.) auf jdn/etw. zeigen point at sb/sth (with sth), point (sth) at sb ◊ *Du sollst doch nicht (mit dem Finger) auf andere Leute zeigen.* irgendwohin zeigen point in a certain direction ◊ *Er zeigte in Richtung Wald und sagte: „Dort ist der Mann verschwunden." ♦ Die Nadel des Kompasses zeigt immer nach Norden.* ⊖deuten, weisen [ref v] *+haben* **1.** sich (irgendwo) zeigen be seen (somewhere) ◊ *Der Filmstar zeigt sich kaum in der Öffentlichkeit. Los, zeig dich!* Come on, show yourself! **2.** etw. zeigt sich irgendwo sth appears somewhere, sth is somewhere ◊ *In seinem Gesicht zeigen sich bereits die ersten Falten.* ♦ *Am Himmel zeigte sich nicht eine einzige Wolke.* **3.** etw. zeigt sich becomes

apparent, sth transpires ◊ *Es wird sich erst noch zeigen, ob das eine gute Idee war.* ♦ *Die Folgen werden sich erst später zeigen.* ⊖etw. stellt sich heraus **4.** sich ... zeigen be ... ◊ *Meine Eltern haben sich wieder einmal sehr großzügig gezeigt.* ♦ *Er zeigte sich besorgt, als er von dem Unfall hörte.* sich von seiner besten Seite zeigen show your best side

⊚ **es jdm zeigen** *(fam)* show sb

Zei·ger ['ʦaegɐ] *der <-s, ->* **1.** *(of a clock)* hand der große/kleine Zeiger the big/small hand **2.** *(of a gauge)* indicator, pointer ◊ *Der Zeiger des Seismographen schlägt aus.*

ⓩ **Zei·le** ['ʦaelə] *die <-, -n>* line ◊ *Der Text ist nur wenige Zeilen lang.* ◊ *Du hast beim Lesen eine Zeile ausgelassen.* ♦ *jdm ein paar Zeilen schreiben*

ⓩ **Zeit** [ʦaet] *die <-, -en>* **1.** time ◊ *Die Zeit vergeht.* ♦ *Im Laufe der Zeit hat sie viele neue Freunde gefunden.* ♦ *Ich habe leider keine Zeit für dich.* ♦ *Du vergeudest deine Zeit.* ♦ *Leider habe ich noch nicht die Zeit gefunden, das zu tun.* ♦ *Die Zeit der Ernte ist gekommen.* ♦ *Ich habe in Hamburg eine sehr schöne Zeit verlebt.* ♦ *Die Zeit ist noch nicht reif für die Einführung dieses Systems.* ♦ *Sie haben für dieses Projekt genau zwei Wochen Zeit.* ♦ *die Zeit messen/nehmen/stoppen* ♦ *Er ist wieder eine gute Zeit gelaufen.* ♦ *Das waren finstere Zeiten.* ♦ *Können Sie mir die Zeit sagen?* ♦ *um 16.15 Uhr mitteleuropäischer Zeit* in letzter Zeit recently **2.** age, times ◊ *Die Diskriminierung von Frauen passt nicht in unsere Zeit.* ♦ *Diese Straße existierte schon zur Zeit der Römer.* in der heutigen Zeit nowadays **3.** LING tense ◊ *In welcher Zeit steht das Prädikat dieses Satzes?*

⊚ **spare in der Zeit, dann hast du in der Not** save for a rainy day **kommt Zeit, kommt Rat** the solution will come in time **die Zeit heilt alle Wunden** time is a great healer **seit ewigen Zeiten (nicht mehr)** *(fam)* (not) for ages **zu gegebener Zeit** in due course **es ist höchste Zeit, dass** it is high time that **in jüngster Zeit** recently **(ach) du liebe Zeit** *(fam)* (oh) my goodness **eine Zeit lang** for a while, for a time **die Zeit drängt** time is pressing **mit der Zeit gehen** move with the times **das hat Zeit** that can wait **es ist an der Zeit, dass** it is about time that, it is high time that **jdm läuft die Zeit davon** sb is running out of time **jdm Zeit lassen, etw. zu tun** give sb time to do sth **sich** [dat] **(bei/mit etw.) Zeit lassen** take your time (with/over sth) **sich** [dat] **die Zeit nehmen, etw. zu tun** take the time to do sth **sich** [dat] **für jdn/etw. Zeit nehmen** devote time to sb/sth **auf Zeit spielen** play for time **die Zeit totschlagen** *(fam)* kill time **keine Zeit verlieren dürfen** have got no time to lose **jdm (mit etw.) die Zeit vertreiben** make the time go quicker for sb (with/by doing sth) **sich (mit etw.) die Zeit vertreiben** pass the time (with/by doing sth) **es wird Zeit** it is (high) time ◊ *Es wird Zeit, dass du mal wieder zum Friseur gehst.* **alles zu seiner Zeit** all in good time **auf Zeit** for a limited period **ein Vertrag auf Zeit** a fixed-term contract **jdn auf Zeit einstellen** engage sb on a fixed-term contract, take sb on for a limited period **für alle Zeiten** for all time, for ever **zu meiner Zeit** in my day **mit der Zeit** in time ◊ *Mit der Zeit wurden die*

Schmerzen besser. **zu Zeiten** ... [gen] in ...'s time ◊ *Zu Zeiten Goethes fuhr man mit der Kutsche.*

Zeit·al·ter ['tsaet|alte] *das* <–s, –> age ◊ *Wir befinden uns im Zeitalter der Raumfahrt.*

zeit·ge·mäß ['tsaetgəmɛːs] [adj] up to date, contemporary ◊ *Diese Art der Fassadengestaltung ist heute nicht mehr zeitgemäß.* ♦ *eine zeitgemäßere Familienpolitik*

zeit·ge·nös·sisch ['tsaetgənœsɪʃ] [adj] *no comp/superl* contemporary ◊ *Mir wurde vorgeworfen, mein Stil sei nicht zeitgenössisch genug.* ♦ *ein hervorragendes Beispiel zeitgenössischer Kunst/Literatur* ♦ *historische und zeitgenössische Architektur* ♦ *Ein zeitgenössischer Kritiker beschrieb Goethe einmal so: ...*

zei·tig ['tsaetɪç] [adj] *only before ns* early ◊ *Sie hoffte auf eine zeitige Rückkehr ihres Mannes.* ♦ *Nach einem zeitigen Frühstück fuhren wir los.* [adv] early, in good time ◊ *Morgen müssen wir zeitig aufstehen.*

zeit·lich ['tsaetlɪç] [adj] *no comp/superl, only before ns* chronological, time ◊ *der zeitlichen Ablauf des Studiums* [adv] in terms of time *etw.* zeitlich auf zehn Minuten begrenzen restrict sth to ten minutes

Ⓔ **das Zeitliche segnen 1.** *(euph)* depart this world ◊ *Er hat doch schon vor Jahren das Zeitliche gesegnet.* **2.** *(hum)* give up the ghost ◊ *Nun hat der Regenschirm endgültig das Zeitliche gesegnet.*

zeit·los ['tsaetloːs] [adj] <zeitloser, am zeitlosesten> timeless ◊ *zeitlose Dichtung/Kunst* ♦ *Dieser Stil ist absolut zeitlos.* [adv] in a timeless way ◊ *eine Wohnung zeitlos und geschmackvoll einrichten* zeitlos elegant gekleidet sein be elegantly dressed in timeless clothes

Zeit·lu·pe ['tsaetluːpə] *die* <–> *mostly used without the article, no pl* slow motion ◊ *Beim Fussball werden wichtige Tore oft in Zeitlupe wiederholt.*

Zeit·punkt ['tsaetpʊŋkt] *der* <–(e)s, –e> moment, time ◊ *den richtigen Zeitpunkt verpassen/wählen* ♦ *Bis zu diesem Zeitpunkt hatte sie immer gedacht, dass ihr Mann ihr treu sei.* der Zeitpunkt einer Sache [gen] the time of sth ◊ *Zum Zeitpunkt seiner Ankunft war der Bahnhof menschenleer.* der Zeitpunkt für etw. the moment for sth ◊ *den geeigneten/passenden Zeitpunkt für etw. abwarten*

Zeit·raum ['tsaetraom] *der* <–(e)s, Zeiträume> period (of time) ◊ *über einen langen Zeitraum hinweg* ♦ *etw. umfasst einen Zeitraum von fünf Tagen/Wochen/Jahren*

Ⓩ **Zeit·schrift** ['tsaetʃrɪft] *die* <–, –en> magazine, periodical, journal ◊ *eine Zeitschrift abonnieren* ♦ *in einer Zeitschrift blättern/lesen* box@ Zeitung

Ⓩ **Zei·tung** ['tsaetʊŋ] *die* <–, –en> newspaper ◊ *eine lokale/regionale/überregionale Zeitung* ♦ *Er liest Zeitung.* ♦ *Was steht heute in der Zeitung?* ♦ *Sie arbeitet bei einer Zeitung.* ♦ *Sind Sie von der Zeitung?*

The daily paper with the highest circulation in Germany is the *Bild*, followed by the *Süddeutsche Zeitung* and the *Frankfurter Allgemeine Zeitung*. The best known weekly is probably *Die Zeit*. Launched in 1947, *Der Spiegel* was the only news magazine in circulation up until 1993; in ▶

▶ Germany, it has had competition from *Focus*. The magazine market with over 20,000 titles is a vast entity which covers a large number of ever more specialized fields. A fairly recent trend in the media landscape has been the emergence of periodicals sold by the homeless and unemployed.

zeit·wei·lig ['tsaetvaelɪç] [adj, adv] *no comp/superl; when used an an adj, only before ns* temporary (-ily) ◊ *zeitweilige Schwierigkeiten* ♦ *Dieses Produkt ist nur zeitweilig im Angebot.*

Zeit·wort ['tsaetvɔ˞t] *das* <–(e)s, Zeitwörter> verb ◊ *Es gibt im Deutschen starke und schwache Zeitwörter.*

Zel·le ['tsɛlə] *die* <–, –n> *(also fig)* cell ♦ *einen Gefangenen in seine Zelle bringen/führen* ♦ *Die Zellen teilen sich in regelmäßigen Abständen.* ♦ *die Zellen einer Honigwabe/Batterie* ♦ *eine Zelle des Widerstands bilden*

Ⓩ **Zelt** [tsɛlt] *das* <–(e)s, –e> tent ♦ *ein Zelt aufbauen/abbauen* ♦ *Im Zirkus errichtet sein Zelt auf der Wiese vor der Stadt.* ♦ *Die Nomaden wohnen in robusten Zelten aus Leder.*

Ⓔ **die/seine Zelte abbrechen** pull up roots **die/seine Zelte irgendwo aufschlagen** settle (down) somewhere, drop anchor somewhere

zel·ten ['tsɛltn̩] <zeltete, zeltete, hat gezeltet> [intr v] camp, go camping ◊ *Wir wollen im Urlaub an der Ostsee zelten.*

Ze·ment [tseˈmɛnt] *der* <–(e)s> *no pl* cement ◊ *Zement anrühren/mischen*

zen·sie·ren [tsɛnˈziːrən] <zensiert, zensierte, hat zensiert> [tr+intr v] **1.** *(in school)* mark, grade ◊ *Dieser Aufsatz wird nicht zensiert.* ♦ *Der Lehrer zensiert sehr milde/streng.* eine Arbeit mit „befriedigend" zensieren give a piece of work an average mark/grade ©benoten **2.** *(a text, film)* censor ◊ *Diese Szene des Films wurde in den USA zensiert.*

Zen·sur [tsɛnˈzuːr̯] *die* <–, –en> **1.** *no pl* censorship ◊ *In diesem Staat gibt es keine Zensur der Presse.* ♦ *Diese Filmszene ist der Zensur zum Opfer gefallen.* **2.** censors ◊ *Die Zensur hat dieses Buch/diesen Film verboten.* **3.** school mark, grade ◊ *eine schlechte Zensur in Chemie bekommen* ♦ *Er hat sehr gute Zensuren in allen Fächern.* ©Note

Zen·ti·me·ter [tsɛntiˈmeːte, '–––] *der or also das* <–s, –> centimetre, centimeter ◊ *Ich brauche 30 Zentimeter Stoff.* ♦ *ein Faden von 75 Zentimeter Länge*

Ⓩ **zen·tral** [tsɛnˈtraːl] [adj, adv] central(ly) ◊ *Dieser Parkplatz ist aber nicht sehr zentral.* ♦ *Das zentrale Thema des Romans ist die Suche nach Anerkennung.* ♦ *das zentrale Nervensystem* ♦ *unter zentraler Verwaltung stehen* ♦ *Unsere Praxis ist zentral gelegen.* ♦ *etw. zentral verwalten* Wir wohnen zentral. We live in a central location. Ihre Wohnung liegt sehr zentral. Her flat is very central. Dieses Hotel liegt zentraler. This hotel is more central.

Zent·ra·le [tsɛnˈtraːlə] *die* <–, –n> **1.** head office ◊ *die Zentrale einer Bank/Partei* **2.** information desk ◊ *Bei Rückfragen wenden Sie sich bitte direkt an die Zentrale.*

Ⓩ **Zent·rum** ['tsɛntrʊm] *das* <–s, Zentren> centre, center ◊ *Im Zentrum des Kreises befindet sich eine Münze.* ♦ *das Zentrum des Erdbebens* ♦ *Welcher Bus fährt ins Zentrum?* ♦ *Die Stadt ist das kultu-*

relle Zentrum der Region. ♦ *In unserem Stadtviertel soll ein neues Zentrum für die Jugend errichtet werden.* jd/etw. steht im Zentrum ... [gen] sb/sth is at the centre/center of sth im Zentrum der Aufmerksamkeit stehen be the centre/center of attention

zer·bre·chen [tsɛ'brɛçn̩] <zerbricht, zerbrach, hat/ist zerbrochen> [tr v] +*haben* **1.** break (into pieces) ◊ *Lisa hat aus Versehen ihre Brille zerbrochen.; (into two pieces)* break in two, break in half ◊ *Er zerbrach die Tablette und nahm eine Hälfte.* **2.** sich [dat] den Kopf (über etw./jdn) zerbrechen think hard (about sth/sb) ◊ *Er zerbrach sich den Kopf über eine Lösung des Problems.* [intr v] +*sein* **1.** break (up), shatter ◊ *Die Tasse fiel runter und zerbrach.* **2.** *(friendships, relationships etc.)* break up ◊ *Zerbricht das Bündnis zwischen den Parteien?* ♦ *Unter diesem Druck zerbrach die Familie.* an etw. [dat] zerbrechen break down because of sth ◊ *Ihre Ehe ist an seiner Untreue zerbrochen.* **3.** *(person)* an etw. [dat] zerbrechen be destroyed by sth ◊ *Er zerbricht noch am Kummer über den Tod seiner Frau.*

zer·brech·lich [tsɛ'brɛçlɪç] [adj] *(also fig)* fragile ◊ *zerbrechliche Knochen haben* ♦ *Ihr Glück war sehr zerbrechlich.; (person also)* frail ◊ *Sie wirkt sehr jung und zerbrechlich.* ⊜*zart*

zer·fal·len [tsɛ'falən] <zerfällt, zerfiel, ist zerfallen> [intr v] **1.** fall apart ◊ *Das unbewohnte Haus zerfällt allmählich.* zu etw./in etw. [acc] zerfallen break up into sth zu Asche zerfallen turn to ashes **2.** disintegrate ◊ *1991 zerfiel die Sowjetunion in Einzelstaaten.* **3.** CHEM decay ◊ *Ein Atom zerfällt, wenn sein Kern nicht stabil ist.* zu etw. zerfallen decay into sth

zer·klei·nern [tsɛ'klaɛnɐn] <zerkleinert, zerkleinerte, hat zerkleinert> [tr v] chop up ◊ *das Holz mit der Axt zerkleinern* ♦ *Wir zerkleinerten das Gemüse für den Eintopf.; (with your teeth)* chew up

zer·knirscht [tsɛ'knɪʁʃt] [adj] <zerknirschter, am zerknirschtesten> contrite ◊ *Der Angeklagte wirkte kleinlaut und zerknirscht.* ein zerknirschtes Gesicht machen look contrite [adv] contritely, full of remorse ◊ *Sichtbar zerknirscht bat sie um Entschuldigung.*

zer·le·gen [tsɛ'le:gn̩] <zerlegt, zerlegte, hat zerlegt> [tr v] **1.** etw. (in etw. [acc]) zerlegen break sth down (into sth) ◊ *Mit einem Prisma lässt sich Licht in seine Farben zerlegen.* ♦ *Enzyme zerlegen im Körper Fett und Zucker.; (machinery, furniture etc.)* etw. zerlegen, etw. in Einzelteile zerlegen take sth apart, dismantle sth ◊ *Der Schrank muss für den Umzug zerlegt werden.* **2.** etw. (in etw. [acc]) zerlegen cut sth up (into sth) ◊ *Der Metzger zerlegte das Schlachttier.*

zer·rei·ßen [tsɛ'raɛsn̩] <zerreißt, zerriss, hat/ist zerrissen> [tr v] +*haben* **1.** *(paper, a fabric etc.)* tear up, tear (in)to shreds ◊ *Papier in kleine Stücke zerreißen* ♦ *Er hat alle Briefe von ihr zerrissen.* eine Stromleitung zerreißen cut through a power line **2.** *(also fig)* jdn/etw. zerreißen tear sb/sth to pieces ◊ *Eine Explosion zerriss die Fabrik.* ♦ *Der Löwe hat eine Antilope zerrissen.* ♦ *Der Roman wurde von den Kritikern zerrissen.* jdm die Hand/den Arm zerreißen tear sb's hand/arm to pieces **3.** etw. zerreißen tear through sth ◊ *Plötzlich zerriss ein Blitz die Dunkelheit.; (the*

peace, silence) shatter sth ◊ *Ein Schrei zerriss die Stille.* **4.** *(clothing)* sich [dat] etw. (an etw. [dat]) zerreißen tear your sth (on sth) ◊ *Sie hat sich die Hose an einem Nagel zerrissen.* [intr v] +*sein* tear ◊ *Dieses Papier zerreißt leicht.; (a string of a musical instrument)* break ◊ *Dem Gitarristen ist eine Saite zerrissen.* [ref v] +*haben (fam)* sich (für jdn/etw.) zerreißen really put yourself out (for sb/sth) ◊ *Sie zerreißt sich für ihre Arbeit.*
⊙ jd kann sich nicht zerreißen *(fam)* sb can't be in two places at once

zer·ren ['tsɛʁən] [tr v] +*haben* **1.** jdn/etw. aus etw./in etw. [acc]/durch etw. zerren drag sb/sth out of/into/through sth ◊ *Ich muss ihn jeden Morgen aus dem Bett zerren.* ♦ *Der Mann wollte ein Mädchen ins Auto zerren und entführen.* **2.** sich [dat] etw. zerren pull sth ◊ *Er hat sich beim Sport eine Sehne gezerrt.* [intr v] +*haben* an jdm/etw. zerren tug at sb/sth ◊ *Der Hund zerrt an der Leine.*

zer·schla·gen¹ [tsɛ'ʃla:gn̩] [adj] *no comp/superl; not before ns* exhausted ◊ *Nach dem harten Arbeitstag fühlt er sich völlig zerschlagen.*

zer·schla·gen² [tsɛ'ʃla:gn̩] <zerschlägt, zerschlug, hat zerschlagen> [tr v] **1.** smash (up), shatter ◊ *Holz mit einer Axt zerschlagen* ♦ *Ein Stein hat die Windschutzscheibe zerschlagen.* **2.** *(a crime ring)* smash **3.** *(soldiers, an army etc.)* defeat [ref v] sich zerschlagen fall through ◊ *Sein Plan, in Urlaub zu fahren, hat sich aus Geldmangel zerschlagen.*

② **zer·stö·ren** [tsɛ'ʃtøːʁən] <zerstört, zerstörte, hat zerstört> [tr v] **1.** destroy ◊ *Die Häuser wurden durch ein Erdbeben zerstört.* ♦ *etw. mutwillig zerstören* ⊜*vernichten* **2.** *(sb's happiness, health, reputation, marriage)* destroy, ruin ◊ *Die Gerüchte werden seinen guten Ruf zerstören.; (hopes, illusions)* shatter

zer·streu·en [tsɛ'ʃtʁɔøən] <zerstreut, zerstreute, hat zerstreut> [tr v] **1.** dispel ◊ *Sie konnte seine Bedenken/Zweifel in der Diskussion zerstreuen.* **2.** jdn/sich zerstreuen distract sb/yourself, amuse sb/yourself ◊ *Er besuchte ein Konzert, um sich zu zerstreuen.* ♦ *Der Clown soll die Patienten im Krankenhaus zerstreuen.* **3.** disperse, scatter ◊ *Der Wind hat die Wolken zerstreut.* ♦ *Das Militär zerstreute die Menge mit Warnschüssen.; (light)* diffuse [ref v] sich zerstreuen disperse ◊ *Nach und nach zerstreuten sich die Gäste.* sich in alle Welt/Winde zerstreuen disperse in all directions

zer·streut [tsɛ'ʃtʁɔøt] *past p of* zerstreuen [adj, adv] <zerstreuter, am zerstreutesten> absent-minded(ly), distracted(ly) ◊ *ein zerstreuter Professor* ♦ *Sie ist manchmal etwas zerstreut.* ♦ *Er beantwortete zerstreut meine Frage und wandte sich sofort wieder ab.*

② **Zer·ti·fi·kat** [tsɛʁtifi'kaːt] das <-(e)s, -e> **1.** certificate ◊ *ein Zertifikat erhalten/ausstellen* ♦ *ein Zertifikat, das die Echtheit eines Produkts bescheinigt* **2.** FIN share, security ◊ *ein Zertifikat auflegen*

zer·trüm·mern [tsɛ'tʁʏmɐn] <zertrümmert, zertrümmerte, hat zertrümmert> [tr v] shatter, smash (up) ◊ *Nierensteine zertrümmern* ♦ *Rasend vor Wut hat sie das Mobiliar zertrümmert.* jdm etw. zertrümmern shatter sb's sth, smash sb's sth ◊ *Bei dem Unfall wurde ihm der Schädel zertrümmert.*

② **Zet·tel** ['tsɛtl̩] der <-s, -> **1.** piece of paper ◊ *etw.*

auf einen Zettel schreiben/notieren **2.** note ◇ *einen Zettel am schwarzen Brett anbringen;* (*to stop you forgetting sth also*) reminder **3.** form ◇ *Bitte füllen sie den anbei liegenden Zettel aus.*

ⓩ **Zeug** [tsɔɥk] *das* <-(e)s> *no pl* **1.** (*fam, esp pej*) stuff ◇ *billiges/unnützes Zeug* ◆ *Dieses Zeug schmeckt ja widerlich!* ⊖Dinge, Sachen **2.** (*fam, pej*) nonsense, rubbish ◇ *dummes/wirres Zeug reden* ◆ *Was hat er wieder für verrücktes Zeug angestellt?*

◉ *jdm (et)was am Zeug flicken* (*fam*) pin something on sb *das Zeug zu/für etw. haben* (*fam*) have got what it takes to be sth ◇ *Er hat das Zeug zum Star.* *das Zeug dazu, etw. zu tun* have got what it takes to do sth *was das Zeug hält* (*fam*) like mad, like nobody's business ◇ *Er arbeitet, was das Zeug hält.* *sich (für jdn/etw.) ins Zeug legen* (*fam*) go all out for it (for sb/sth) ◇ *Für die Prüfung wirst du dich ins Zeug legen müssen!*

ⓩ **Zeu·ge** [ˈtsɔɥɡə] *der* <-n, -n>, **Zeu·gin** [ˈtsɔɥɡɪn] *die* <-, -nen> witness ◇ *einen Zeugen verhören/befragen* ◆ *Sie wurde zufällig Zeugin des Gesprächs.* ◆ *einen Vertrag vor Zeugen unterschreiben* ◆ *Der mittelalterliche Ort ist ein Zeuge der Vergangenheit.*

zeu·gen [ˈtsɔɥɡn̩] [tr v] +*haben* BIO conceive ◇ *Ich wurde im Winter gezeugt.;* (*man*) father ◇ *Mit 90 zeugte er noch ein Kind.* [intr v] +*haben von etw. zeugen* be a sign of sth, be evidence of sth ◇ *Sein Verhalten zeugt nicht gerade von Intelligenz.* ◆ *Eine alte Burgruine zeugt von der Vergangenheit der Stadt.*

Zeu·gin [ˈtsɔɥɡɪn] *fem of* Zeuge

ⓩ **Zeug·nis** [ˈtsɔɥknɪs] *das* <-ses, -se> **1.** SCHOOL report ◇ *Morgen gibt es Zeugnisse.* ◆ *gute Noten im Zeugnis haben* **2.** reference, testimonial ◇ *jdm ein Zeugnis ausstellen* ◆ *das Zeugnis vom letzten Arbeitgeber* **3.** certificate ◇ *ein ärztliches/staatlich anerkanntes Zeugnis* **4.** (*lofty*) testimony ◇ *Ihre Bibliothek ist ein eindrucksvolles Zeugnis ihrer Bildung.* *ein beredtes Zeugnis* an eloquent testimony

Zie·ge [ˈtsiːɡə] *die* <-, -n> **1.** ZOO goat ◇ *Ziegen halten/hüten* ◆ *Die Ziege meckerte.* **2.** ZOO nanny goat ◇ *eine Ziege melken* **3.** (*fam, pej*) cow ◇ *Diese blöde Ziege!*

Zie·gel [ˈtsiːɡl̩] *der* <-s, -> **1.** brick ◇ *Der Eingang wurde mit Ziegeln zugemauert.* **2.** tile ◇ *ein mit roten Ziegeln gedecktes Dach*

ⓩ **zie·hen** [ˈtsiːən] <zieht, zog, hat/ist gezogen> [tr+intr v] +*haben* **1.** pull ◇ *Das Auto wurde aus dem Graben gezogen.* ◆ *Ich zog mir die Bettdecke über den Kopf.* ◆ *die Notbremse/Handbremse ziehen* ◆ *Du musst ziehen, nicht drücken.* ◆ *Er schob und ich zog.* *an etw./jdm ziehen* pull at sth/sb, tug at sth/sb ◇ *Der Hund zog an der Leine.* *jdn an etw.* [dat] *ziehen* pull sb's sth, tug at sb's sth ◇ *jdn an den Haaren ziehen;* (*with force*) drag sb/sth ◇ *Die Strömung zog ihn aufs offene Meer.* *jdn/etw. an sich* [acc] *ziehen* hug sb/sth (to you) ◇ *Er zog den Teddy an sich.* **2.** GAME (*a chessman*) move ◇ *beim Schach den Bauern zwei Felder weit ziehen* ◆ *Hast du schon gezogen?* **3.** (*a winning ticket, card, weapon*) draw ◇ *Er hat den Hauptgewinn gezogen.* ◆ *Jeder darf nur einmal ziehen.* ◆

ein Messer ziehen [tr v] +*haben* **1.** (*a vehicle*) etw. nach links/rechts/oben ziehen steer sth to the left/to the right/up ◇ *Der Pilot zog das Flugzeug nach oben.* **2.** *translation varies* (*describing facial expressions*) die Stirn in Falten ziehen wrinkle your forehead *eine Grimasse/ein Gesicht ziehen* pull a face *die Augenbrauen nach oben ziehen* raise your eyebrows *die Mundwinkel nach unten ziehen* turn down the corners of your mouth **3.** *etw. auf sich ziehen* attract sth ◇ *Hass/Aufmerksamkeit auf sich ziehen* **4.** *etw. nach sich ziehen* result in sth ◇ *Der Unfall zog hohe Kosten nach sich.;* (*repercussions, consequences*) have sth ◇ *Dein Verhalten wird ernste Folgen nach sich ziehen.* **5.** (*from a machine*) etw. (aus etw.) ziehen get sth (from sth), take sth (from sth) ◇ *einen Parkschein ziehen* ◆ *eine Schachtel Zigaretten aus einem Automaten ziehen* **6.** *etw. (aus etw.) ziehen* pull sth out (of sth), remove sth (from sth) ◇ *jdm einen Zahn ziehen* ◆ *Er zog den Stecker aus der Steckdose. etw. von etw. ziehen* take sth off sth ◇ *einen Ring vom Finger ziehen* **7.** (*a piece of clothing*) etw. über/unter etw. [acc] ziehen put sth on over/under sth ◇ *eine Strumpfhose unter die Hose ziehen* ◆ *Bei der Kälte solltest noch einen Pulli über das Hemd ziehen.* **8.** BOT grow ◇ *Sie will ein Bäumchen aus Samen ziehen.* selbst gezogen home-grown ◇ *Sind die Tomaten selbst gezogen oder gekauft?* **9.** (*a wire, cables etc.*) stretch ◇ *neue Kabel für einen Telefonanschluss ziehen;* (*a washing line*) put up etw. durch/in etw. [acc] ziehen put sth through sth, thread sth through sth ◇ *einen Faden durch ein Nadelloch ziehen* ◆ *Sie zog den Gürtel um die Hose.* **10.** *translation varies* einen Zaun/eine Mauer um einen Garten ziehen put a fence/wall around a garden *Gräben ziehen* dig trenches mit dem Pflug Furchen ziehen plough/plow furrows **11.** (*with a pen, pencil etc.*) draw ◇ *mit dem Lineal einen Strich ziehen* **12.** (*conclusions, comparisons*) draw ◇ *Ich zog aus seinem Verhalten den Schluss, dass er verärgert war.* [intr v] +*haben/sein* **1.** +*haben* (*vehicle*) nach links/rechts/oben ziehen pull to the left/to the right/up ◇ *Das Auto zieht stark nach rechts/links.* **2.** +*sein irgendwohin ziehen* move to somewhere ◇ *Er ist aufs Land gezogen.* ◆ *Sie zieht bald nach Berlin. Er ist zu seiner Freundin gezogen.* He has moved in with his girlfriend. ⊖umziehen **3.** +*sein, +direction durchs Land/nach Osten/flussabwärts ziehen* travel through the country/eastwards/watershipdown ◇ *Wanderer zogen durchs Land.;* (*animals*) migrate ◇ *Die Vögel ziehen nach Süden.;* (*smoke, clouds*) irgendwohin ziehen drift ◇ *Der Rauch zog nach oben.* **4.** +*haben an etw.* [dat] *ziehen* suck at sth ◇ *an einem Strohhalm ziehen* ◆ *Genüsslich zog er an seiner Pfeife.;* (*of a cigarette*) have a drag of sth **5.** +*haben* (*food*) (in etw. [dat]) *ziehen* soak (in sth), stand (in sth), marinade (in sth) ◇ *Der Knoblauch muss eine Woche in Olivenöl ziehen. etw. in heißem Wasser ziehen lassen* let sth simmer *den Tee ziehen lassen* let the tea brew/stand **6.** +*haben* (*car, engine*) accelerate, gather speed ◇ *Das Auto zieht gut/schlecht.* **7.** +*haben* (*trick, method etc.*) work ◇ *Diese Masche zieht bei mir nicht!* [imp v] +*haben* **1.** *es zieht* there's a draught, there's a

draft *es zieht jdm am Nacken/an den Beinen sb can feel a draught around their neck/legs* **2.** *es zieht jdm im Rücken/Arm sb has got a pain in their back/arm, sb's back/arm hurts* **3.** *es zieht jdn irgendwohin sb longs to go somewhere* ◊ *Mich zieht es ans Meer/nach Frankreich.* ⟨ref v⟩ +*haben* **1.** sich ziehen go on, drag (on) ◊ *Die Busfahrt zieht sich ganz schön!* ♦ *Das Fest zog sich bis in den frühen Morgen.* **2.** sich irgendwohin ziehen stretch somewhere ◊ *Die Berge ziehen sich bis zum Meer.* ♦ *Die Straße zog sich quer durch die Wüste.*

② **Ziel** [ʦiːl] *das* <-(e)s, -e> **1.** goal, aim ◊ *Sie hat ihre Ziele nicht erreicht.* ♦ *Was hatte diese Maßnahme zum Ziel?* ♦ *Ich habe mir zum Ziel gesetzt, den Mount Everest zu besteigen.* Welches Ziel verfolgt jd? What is sb's goal/purpose? Welches Ziel verfolgt etw.? What is the goal/purpose of sth? am Ziel seiner Träume sein have achieved your dream **2.** target ◊ *Die Fabrik bot dem Feind ein gutes Ziel.* ♦ *Der Schuss hat das Ziel getroffen/verfehlt.* **3.** destination ◊ *mit unbekanntem Ziel verreist sein* ♦ *Das Ziel unserer Fahrt war Hamburg.* **4.** SPORT finishing line, finish line ◊ *als Erster/Zweiter/Letzter etc. ins Ziel kommen/durchs Ziel gehen* ⊖Start
⊚ **über das Ziel hinausschießen** *(fam)* go too far

zie·len [ˈʦiːlən] ⟨intr v⟩ +*haben* **1.** (auf jdn/etw.) zielen aim (at sb/sth) ◊ *genau/gut/schlecht zielen* ♦ *Der Spieler zielte bei dem Freischuss zu tief.* **2.** *(advertising, criticisms)* auf jdn/etw. zielen be directed at sb/sth ◊ *Diese Werbung zielt auf junge Leute.; (actions)* be aimed at sb/sth ◊ *Die Reformen/Maßnahmen zielen auf eine Steuersenkung.*

② **ziem·lich** [ˈʦiːmlɪç] ⟨adv⟩ **1.** quite, rather ◊ *Sie sehen sich ziemlich oft.* ♦ *Ich bin ziemlich müde.* ⊖relativ, recht, verhältnismäßig **2.** really ◊ *„Findest du die Musik gut?" — „Ziemlich gut sogar!"* ♦ *Wir mussten uns ziemlich beeilen.* ⊖wirklich **3.** *(fam)* so ziemlich just about, pretty much ◊ *Ich habe die Arbeit so ziemlich geschafft.* ♦ *Wir haben so ziemlich die gleiche Schuhgröße.*

ziem·li·che [ˈʦiːmlɪçə] ⟨adj⟩ *no comp/superl, only before ns* <ein ziemlicher ..., eine ziemliche ..., ein ziemliches ...> *(fam)* considerable, quite a lot of ◊ *Sie hat ziemliche Schmerzen.* mit ziemlicher Sicherheit almost certainly ein ziemlicher.../eine ziemliche .../ein ziemliches ... quite a ... ◊ *Er ist ein ziemlicher Egoist.* ♦ *eine ziemliche Menge Leute* ♦ *ein ziemliches Problem haben*

zier·lich [ˈʦiːɐlɪç] ⟨adj, adv⟩ **1.** delicate(ly) ◊ *eine zierliche Figur haben* ♦ *eine zierlich gestaltete Halskette; (person)* of delicate build ◊ *zierlich gebaut/gewachsen sein; (woman also)* petite ⊖zart **2.** *(oldf) (of movements)* graceful(ly) ◊ *Sie hat einen zierlichen Gang.* ♦ *Die Bewegungen der Tänzerin sind zierlich.* ♦ *Sie schwebte zierlich übers Parkett.*

Zif·fer [ˈʦɪfɐ] *die* <-, -n> *(abbr Ziff.)* **1.** digit, figure ◊ *eine Zahl mit zwei Ziffern* die Ziffern einer Uhr the numbers on a watch arabische/römische Ziffern Arabic/Roman numerals **2.** clause, paragraph ◊ *Sie können gemäß Ziffer 2 des Vertrages kündigen.* ♦ *Was steht in Ziffer 5 der Verordnung?*

② **Zi·ga·ret·te** [ʦigaˈrɛtə] *die* <-, -n> cigarette ◊ *an einer Zigarette ziehen* ♦ *eine Zigarette ausdrücken* ♦ *Kannst du mir eine Zigarette geben?* ♦ *Sie raucht zwei Schachteln Zigaretten am Tag.*

② **Zim·mer** [ˈʦɪmɐ] *das* <-s, -> **1.** room ◊ *ein möbliertes Zimmer vermieten* ♦ *Geh auf/in dein Zimmer und mach deine Hausaufgaben!* ♦ *sich irgendwo ein Zimmer nehmen/mieten* ♦ *ein Zimmer reservieren/buchen* **2.** furnishings ◊ *Sie hat zum Geburtstag ein neues Zimmer bekommen.*

Zimt [ʦɪmt] *der* <-(e)s> *no pl* cinnamon ◊ *eine Stange Zimt* ♦ *Der Koch fügte noch (eine Prise) gemahlenen Zimt hinzu.*

② **Zins¹** [ʦɪns] *der* <-es, -en> *most pl* FIN interest ◊ *hohe/niedrige Zinsen bringen* ♦ *die Zinsen anheben/senken* ♦ *Wie viele Zinsen bekommt man auf/für ein Sparkonto?* ♦ *Für den Kredit werden monatlich 10,9 % Zinsen fällig.* mit Zins und Zinseszins with compound interest

Zins² [ʦɪns] *der* <-es, -e> *(SouthG, Austr, Swiss)* rent ◊ *Der Zins für die Wohnung beträgt monatlich 500 Euro.*

zir·ka [ˈʦɪrˈkaː] ⟨adv⟩ *(abbr ca.)* approximately, about, around ◊ *Er wiegt zirka 70 kg.* ♦ *Ich komme um zirka fünf Uhr.* ♦ *Sie ist in zirka einer halben Stunde zurück.* ⊖ungefähr, etwa ⊚exakt, genau

Zir·kel [ˈʦɪrkl̩] *der* <-s, -> **1.** compass, a pair of compasses ◊ *mit einem Zirkel einen Kreis ziehen/schlagen/zeichnen* **2.** *(of people)* circle ◊ *ein kleiner Zirkel von Experten* ♦ *Der literarische Zirkel trifft sich jeden Mittwoch um 19 Uhr.* ⊖Kreis

Zir·kus [ˈʦɪrkʊs] *der* <-, -se> **1.** circus ◊ *Er ist zum Zirkus gegangen und arbeitet jetzt als Clown.* ♦ *Wir gehen heute in den Zirkus.* **2.** *(fam, pej)* fuss ◊ *einen Zirkus um etw. machen* ⊖Theater, Zauber

zi·schen [ˈʦɪʃn̩] ⟨intr v⟩ +*haben/sein* **1.** +*haben* hiss ◊ *durch die Zähne zischen* ♦ *Es zischte laut, als sie die Dose öffnete.; (oil)* sizzle ◊ *Das Fett zischte, als sie das Steak in die Pfanne legte.* **2.** +*sein (fam)* irgendwohin zischen whizz somewhere ◊ *Der Sektkorken zischte durch den Raum.* ♦ *Sie ist schnell nach Hause gezischt, kommt aber gleich wieder.* ⟨tr v⟩ +*haben* hiss ◊ *„Lass mich in Ruhe!", zischte sie.*
⊚ **ein Bier/einen zischen** *(fam)* have a beer/a drink

Zi·tat [ʦiˈtaːt] *das* <-(e)s, -e> quotation, quote ◊ *Das Zitat „zwei Seelen wohnen ach in meiner Brust" stammt aus Goethes „Faust".*

zi·tie·ren [ʦiˈtiːrən] <zitiert, zitierte, hat zitiert> ⟨tr+intr v⟩ quote ◊ *jdn/etw. wörtlich zitieren* ♦ *einen Satz zitieren* ♦ *Hier zitiere ich den Präsidenten selbst: ... aus etw. zitieren quote from sth* ⟨tr v⟩ jdn irgendwohin zitieren summon sb to somewhere ◊ *jdn vor Gericht zitieren* ♦ *Er wurde aufs Finanzamt zitiert.*

② **Zit·ro·ne** [ʦiˈtroːnə] *die* <-, -n> **1.** lemon ◊ *eine Zitrone in Scheiben schneiden* **2.** lemon (juice) ◊ *Trinkst du den Tee mit Milch oder Zitrone?* heiße Zitrone hot lemon ⊖Zitronensaft
⊚ **jdn auspressen/ausquetschen wie eine Zitrone** *(fam)* **1.** squeeze sb dry ◊ *Die Polizei hat mich ausgequetscht wie eine Zitrone.* **2.** mercilessly exploit sb, bleed sb dry ◊ *Das Personal wird ausgepresst wie eine Zitrone.*

zit·tern ['tsɪtən] [intr v] +*haben* **1.** tremble, shake ◇ *Seine Hände zitterten.* ♦ *am ganzen Körper zittern* ♦ *vor Angst/Aufregung zittern* ♦ *Die Blätter zittern im Wind.* ♦ *Ihre Stimme zitterte vor Nervosität.*; *(when it is cold)* shiver **2.** vor etw./jdm zittern be terrified of sth/sb ◇ *Er zitterte vor der Prüfung/ seinem Angreifer.* um jdn/etw. zittern be worried sick about sb/sth ◇ *Sie zittert um ihre kranke Mutter.* für jdn zittern be worried sick about sb ◇ *Ob sie überlebt haben? Ich zittere für sie.*

Zi·vil·dienst [tsi'vi:ldi:nst] der <-(e)s *no pl* ◇ *Zivildienst leisten* ♦ *Nach dem Abitur wird er seinen Zivildienst machen.* ⊖Ersatzdienst

In Germany, young men are obliged to do military service. *Zivildienst* (often translated as **community service**) is a possible substitute. However, community service is only an option if you have submitted a written application and attended an interview in which you have given cogent reasons for not being able to reconcile military service with your ethical principles. In 2005, both community and military service last nine months.

Zi·vi·li·sa·ti·on [tsiviliza'tsjo:n] die <-, -en> civilization ◇ *die westliche/moderne/europäische Zivilisation* ♦ *Wir machten Urlaub fern der Zivilisation.* ⊖Kultur

② **zog** [tso:k] *pret of* ziehen

zö·gern ['tsø:gən] [intr v] +*haben* hesitate ◇ *einen Augenblick/Moment zögern* ♦ *Sie zögerte ein wenig, willigte dann aber ein.* ♦ *An deiner Stelle würde ich nicht zögern, dieses Angebot anzunehmen.* ohne zu zögern without hesitation/hesitating zögern, etw. zu tun hesitate to do sth mit einer Antwort zögern hesitate to reply mit seiner Entscheidung zögern hesitate to make a decision

Zoll¹ [tsɔl] der <-(e)s, Zölle> **1.** ECON Zoll (auf etw. [acc]/[dat]) customs duty (on sth) ◇ *Zoll für eine importierte Ware zahlen* ♦ *auf ausländische Waren Zoll erheben* **2.** *no pl (at an airport, port etc.)* der Zoll customs ◇ *am Flughafen durch den Zoll gehen* ♦ *Der Zoll hat 40 000 Stangen Zigaretten beschlagnahmt.*

Zoll² [tsɔl] der <-(e)s, -> *(also fig) (abbr ")* inch ◇ *Die Größe von Bildschirmen wird in Zoll gemessen.* ♦ *keinen Zoll nachgeben* ◉ **Zoll für Zoll ein Ehrenmann sein** be every inch a gentleman

zoll·frei ['tsɔlfraɛ] [adj, adv] *no comp/superl* duty-free ◇ *zollfreie Waren* ♦ *Die Ausfuhr von Zigaretten ist nicht zollfrei.* ♦ *etw. zollfrei in die EU einführen*

② **Zo·ne** ['tso:nə] die <-, -n> **1.** zone ◇ *eine besetzte/ atomwaffenfreie Zone* ♦ *Australien liegt in der tropischen Zone* ♦ *eine verkehrsfreie Zone* ♦ *eine Fahrkarte für zwei Zonen* **2.** *no pl (fam, esp pej)* HIST East (Germany) ◇ *Sie sind aus der Zone in den Westen geflüchtet.*

② **Zoo** [tso:] der <-s, -s> zoo ◇ *in den Zoo gehen*

Zopf [tsɔpf] der <-(e)s, Zöpfe> **1.** plait, braid ◇ *(jdm) Zöpfe flechten* ♦ *Ina trägt heute einen Zopf.* **2.** *(cake)* plait ◇ *einen Zopf backen* ◉ **ein alter Zopf** *(fam)* old hat

② **Zorn** [tsɔrn] der <-(e)s *no pl* anger, rage ◇ *in Zorn geraten* ♦ *jds Zorn erregen* ♦ *von Zorn erfüllt sein* ♦ *Außer sich vor Zorn/Voller Zorn knallte sie die*

Tür zu. ♦ *Als er die hohe Rechnung sah, packte ihn der Zorn.* Zorn auf jdn anger towards sb, rage towards sb ◇ *Zorn auf jdn haben* Zorn über etw. [acc] anger at/over sth, rage at/over sth ◇ *Ihr Zorn über seine Lügen ist unbeschreiblich.* ⊖Ärger

② **zor·nig** ['tsɔrnɪç] [adj] angry ◇ *Sein übermäßiger Stolz macht mich zornig.* ♦ *ein zorniger Leserbrief* zornig auf jdn angry with sb ◇ *Sie ist zornig auf ihren unpünktlichen Bruder.* zornig über etw. [acc] angry at/over sth ◇ *Er ist zornig über die gemeine Hinterhältigkeit.* ⊖wütend

② **zu¹** [tsu:] [adv] **1.** *before adj or adv* too ◇ *Das ist viel zu teuer.* ♦ *Du bist noch zu jung für den Film.* ♦ *Mach den Kaffee nicht wieder zu stark!* ♦ *Er fährt immer viel zu schnell in die Kurven.* ♦ *Es wäre zu schön, wenn das wahr wäre!* Ich wüsste zu gerne, was passiert ist! I'd love to know what happened! zu viel too much ◇ *Das wird mir langsam zu viel — ich brauche Ruhe.* ♦ *Nils hat Bauchweh, weil er immer zu viel Schokolade isst.* zu wenig not enough, too little ◇ *In der Suppe ist zu wenig Salz.* ♦ *Sie hat zu wenig geschlafen und ist nun sehr müde.* **2.** shut ◇ *Tür zu!* ♦ *Ab ins Bett und Augen zu!* zu sein be shut, be closed ◇ *Die Packung ist noch zu.* ♦ *Das Geschäft ist mittags zu.* ⊖geschlossen ⊖auf, offen **3.** *(fam)* zu sein be drunk ◇ *So wie der taumelt, ist er doch völlig zu!* ⊖betrunken **4.** *(fam) (nose, sinuses etc.)* zu sein be bunged up, be blocked ◇ *Ich krieg kaum Luft, meine Nase ist total zu!* ⊖verstopft **5.** nur (immer) zu go ahead, go on ◇ *„Kann ich noch Kekse nehmen?" — „Nur immer zu!"* ♦ *Nur zu, das schaffst du schon!*

② **zu²** [tsu:] [prep] +dat **1.** *in response to the question 'to where?'* to ◇ *Sie hatte auf dem Weg zur Arbeit einen Unfall.* ♦ *Willst du heute zu uns kommen?* ♦ *Ich muss noch zur Post/zum Friseur.* ♦ *zu einer Party/Feier gehen* **2.** *in response to the question 'where?'* on ◇ *Zu Ihrer Rechten/Linken sehen Sie den Louvre.* ♦ *Zu beiden Seiten des Weges erstrecken sich Felder.* zu Hause sein be at home **3.** *in response to the question 'when?'* at ◇ *Er ist zu jeder Zeit zu erreichen.* ♦ *Zu Anfang des Jahres schneit es oft.*; *(with dates)* on ◇ *Der Vertrag wurde zum 30. Juni gekündigt.* ♦ *Wir müssen zum Ersten des nächsten Monats die Bilanz erstellen. Wird das rechtzeitig zum Umzug fertig?* Will that be ready in time for the move? bis zum Ende der Woche until the end of the week zum Schluss in conclusion **4.** *(describing reason)* for ◇ *Zum Geburtstag bekam sie ein Fahrrad.* ♦ *Was wünschst du dir zu Weihnachten?* ♦ *Er nahm ein Medikament zur Beruhigung.* ♦ *Ich sage das nur zu deiner Information.* ♦ *Zum Arbeiten benötige ich einen Computer.* ein Fest zum 50. Jubiläum a golden jubilee/anniversary celebration Alles Gute zum Geburtstag! Happy Birthday! zu Ehren einer Person in sb's honour/ honor, in honour/honor of sb zum Tanzen gehen go dancing **5.** (in)to ◇ *Sie kann in ihrer Wut zum Drachen werden.* ♦ *Das Laub ist zu Erde geworden.* ♦ *Sie wurde zur Direktorin befördert.* jdn zum Lachen/Weinen bringen make sb laugh/cry **6.** *in response to the question 'how?'* on ◇ *zu Fuß gehen* ♦ *Sie kamen zu Pferd.* zu Wasser/Lande on sea/ land **7.** *(in statements of how many people there are in a group)* Zu zweit ist es doch schöner als

allein. It's nicer when there are two of you. Sie gingen zu dritt nebeneinander. The three of them walked along together. Wir sind heute nur zu viert. There are only four of us today. **8.** *(with prices)* at ◊ *Sie kaufte Kiwis zu je 20 Cent.* ♦ *Waren zu niedrigen/hohen Preisen anbieten* CDs zum halben Preis half-price CDs **9.** *(with quantities)* ein Sack Kartoffeln zu 5 kg a 5 kg bag of potatoes Flaschen zu 1,5 Litern 1.5 litre bottles zu 100 % biologisch abbaubar 100 % biologically degradable zur Hälfte/zu einem Drittel/Viertel aus etw. bestehen be half/a third/a quarter sth; *(with an indefinite quantity)* zu Hunderten/Tausenden in their hundreds/thousands zum Teil partly ◊ *Sie hat die Arbeit nur zum Teil geschafft.* **10.** *used to link two numbers* to ◊ *Die italienische Mannschaft siegte (mit) drei zu zwei.* ♦ *Die Chancen, dass wir gewinnen, stehen fünfzig zu fünfzig.* ♦ *Den Sirup im Verhältnis eins zu zehn mit Wasser mischen.* **11.** with ◊ *Zum Kaffee gab es Kuchen.* ♦ *Das gestreifte Hemd passt nicht zur karierten Hose.* Ich suche den Deckel zu diesem Glas. I'm looking for the lid to this jar. **12.** about ◊ *Der Zeuge wurde zu dem Unfall befragt.* ♦ *Zu diesem Thema steht ein Artikel in der Zeitung.* Was sagst du zu meinem Vorschlag? What do you say to my suggestion? ⊜über **13.** *with proper names, not translated* das Hotel „Zum goldenen Löwen" the Golden Lion Hotel der Dom zu Köln Cologne Cathedral **14.** *(in titles)* of ◊ *Friedrich Leopold, Graf zu Stolberg* ♦ *die Baronin von und zu Franckenstein* ◉ **zum Ersten, zum Zweiten(, zum Dritten ...)** firstly, secondly(, thirdly ...) ◊ *Zum Ersten ist Ihre Analyse unvollständig und zum Zweiten ist sie fehlerhaft.* **zum Ersten, zum Zweiten und zum Dritten** *(at an auction)* going, going, gone **zum Schreien/Weinen/Lachen etc.** sein be hilarious/pitiful/funny etc. ◊ *Dieser Typ ist einfach zum Schreien!*

② **zu³** [tsuː] ⌈conjunc⌉ **1.** +inf to ◊ *Ich habe viel zu tun.* ♦ *Es fängt an zu regnen.* ♦ *Es ist unmöglich, das zu schaffen.* aufhören, etw. zu tun stop doing sth zu verkaufen sein be for sale jd ist nicht zu sprechen you can't speak to sb nicht zu begreifen sein be unbelievable anstatt nichts zu tun, ... instead of doing nothing, ... ohne zu fragen without asking **2.** +pres p and noun to be ◊ *ein zu testendes Produkt* ♦ *eine zu erledigende Aufgabe* ♦ *Die zu begleichende Rechnung beläuft sich auf 100 Euro.*

② **zu|...** [tsuː] ⌈prefix⌉ +verb, stressed and separable **1.** ... (up) ◊ *Die Wunde heilt allmählich zu.* ♦ *die Schuhe zubinden* ♦ *eine Bluse zuknöpfen* zubleiben stay/remain shut ◊ *Das Fenster muss zubleiben.* etw. zubekommen get sth shut etw. zudrehen turn sth off ◊ *Hast du den Wasserhahn zugedreht?* **2.** ... over ◊ *eine Grube zuschütten* ♦ *Der See ist zugefroren.* **3.** *translation varies* etw. zugeben/zufügen add sth einem Zug zusteigen join a train sich einer Gruppe zugesellen join a group jdm Geld zuschießen give sb some money **4.** auf jdn/etw. zu... ... towards sb/sth ◊ *Sie rennen auf den Ausgang zu.* ♦ *Sie ging auf ihn zu.* etw. kommt auf jdn zu sb is faced with sth **5.** *describing an act performed firmly and quickly, translation varies* zufassen, zupacken grab hold zugreifen dig in ◊

Greift zu! Es ist genügend Pizza für alle da! zuschnappen, zubeißen take a firm bite zuschlagen hit out **6.** ... at ◊ *jdm zulächeln* ♦ *jdm zuwinken* ♦ *Sie nickte ihm auffordernd zu.* jdm zuprosten raise your glass to sb jdm zujubeln cheer sb **7.** jdm/einer Sache zusehen watch sb/sth jdm zuhören listen to sb sich einer Sache ⌈dat⌉ zuwenden turn (your attention) to sth **8.** jdm Arbeit zuteilen/zuweisen allocate work to sb jdm Geld zustecken give sb money jdm einen Brief zuschicken/zusenden send sb a letter **9.** einen Stift zuspitzen sharpen a pencil eine Mahlzeit zubereiten prepare a meal Sie schnitt den Stoff für eine Hose zu. She cut out the material for a pair of trousers. **10.** *(fam)* ... on, ... ahead ◊ *Nun mach zu, wir warten schon!* ♦ *Fahr endlich zu, die Ampel ist grün!*

Zu·be·hör ['tsuːbəhøːɐ] das <-(e)s, -e> *most sing* **1.** equipment, attachments ◊ *technisches Zubehör für die Stereoanlage* als Zubehör geliefert werden be included **2.** accessories ◊ *modisches Zubehör wie Haarschmuck*

zu|be·rei·ten ['tsuːbəraɛtn̩] <bereitet zu, bereitete zu, hat zubereitet> ⌈tr v⌉ *(food)* prepare, make ◊ *eine Mahlzeit zubereiten* ♦ *Wie wird der Fisch zubereitet?*

Zuc·chi·ni [tsʊ'kiːni] die <-, - *or fam* -s> BOT **1.** courgette, zucchini ◊ *Zum Essen gibt es gefüllte Zucchini.* **2.** courgette plant, zucchini plant

Zucht [tsʊxt] die <-, -en> BIO **1.** *no pl (of animals)* breeding ◊ *die Zucht bedrohter Tierarten; (of plants)* cultivation, growing ◊ *die Zucht von Bananen* **2.** *(of bacteria, cells)* growth **3.** breed ◊ *Die Schlangen stammen aus verschiedenen Zuchten.; (of horses)* stud ◊ *Der Reiterhof verkauft Pferde aus eigener/guter Zucht.* ◉ **Zucht und Ordnung** discipline and order

züch·ten ['tsʏçtn̩] <züchtet, züchtete, hat gezüchtet> ⌈tr v⌉ BIO **1.** *(animals)* breed ◊ *Schafe züchten* ♦ *Der Papagei ist selbst gezüchtet und daher sehr zahm.; (plants)* cultivate, grow **2.** *(bacteria, cells)* grow ◊ *Zellen in Zellkulturen züchten*

zu·cken ['tsʊkn̩] ⌈intr v⌉ +haben **1.** twitch ◊ *Die Pfoten des Hundes zuckten im Schlaf.* mit den Achseln/Schultern zucken shrug your shoulders **2.** *(a light, flames, shadows)* irgendwo(hin) zucken flicker somewhere ◊ *Blitze zuckten am Himmel.*

② **Zu·cker** ['tsʊkɐ] der <-s> *no pl* **1.** sugar ◊ *ein Teelöffel/Stück Zucker* ♦ *etw. mit Zucker süßen* ♦ *weißer/brauner Zucker* ♦ *Nimmst du Zucker in den Kaffee?* **2.** *(fam)* MED diabetes ◊ *Er hat Zucker.* an Zucker leiden

zu·ckern ['tsʊkɐn] ⌈tr v⌉ +haben sweeten ◊ *Schlagsahne zuckern* etw. ist zu stark gezuckert sth has got too much sugar in it, sth is too sweet ⊜süßen

zu·dem [tsu'deːm] ⌈adv⌉ *(lofty)* moreover, furthermore ◊ *Er ist reich und sieht zudem gut aus.*

zu|dre·hen ['tsuːdreːən] <dreht zu, drehte zu, hat zugedreht> ⌈tr v⌉ **1.** *(a tap, thermostat etc.)* turn off ◊ *den Wasserhahn zudrehen; (a lid, top etc. of sth)* close ◊ *den Verschluss einer Flasche zudrehen* ⊜schließen **2.** jdm/etw. etw. zudrehen turn your sth to sb/sth ◊ *jdm den Rücken zudrehen* ♦ *Er drehte das Gesicht der Sonne zu.* ⌈ref v⌉ sich jdm

zudrehen turn to sb ◊ *Der Redner drehte sich dem Publikum zu.*

zu·dring·lich ['tsu:drɪŋlɪç] [adj] pushy, tenacious ◊ *ein zudringlicher Vertreter* zudringlich werden make unwanted advances on/to sb, start to harass sb ◊ *Nach ein paar Gläsern Wein wurde er zudringlich.*

zu·ei·nan·der [tsu|ae'nandɐ] [adv] (to/with) each other, (to/with) one another ◊ *nett zueinander sein* ♦ *Wie ist ihr Verhältnis zueinander?* zueinander finden find each other zueinander halten stick together zueinander passen fit/go together

② **zu·erst** [tsu|'e:ɐst] [adv] **1.** first ◊ *zuerst an der Reihe sein* ♦ *Geh du zuerst!* ♦ *Was möchtest du zuerst machen?* **2.** at first ◊ *Ich dachte zuerst, dass sie älter wäre.* ♦ *Zuerst war er verärgert, doch dann lachte er.* ⊜zunächst, anfangs

Zu·fahrt ['tsu:fa:ɐt] die <-, -en> **1.** access (road) ◊ *die Zufahrt (zum Flughafen/Kloster) blockieren/ sperren* **2.** drive(way) ◊ *Jemand hatte die Zufahrt blockiert.*

② **Zu·fall** ['tsu:fal] der <-(e)s, Zufälle> chance, coincidence ◊ *Ich glaube nicht an Zufälle.* ♦ *Es ist kein Zufall, dass er diese Forderung stellte.* durch/per Zufall by chance, accidentally ◊ *durch/per Zufall von etw. erfahren* ein glücklicher Zufall a stroke of luck etw. dem Zufall überlassen leave sth to chance

zu|fal·len ['tsu:falən] <fällt zu, fiel zu, ist zugefallen> [intr v] **1.** *(door)* slam shut ◊ *Die Wohnungstür ist versehentlich zugefallen.* jdm fallen (beinahe) die Augen zu sb's eyelids are drooping **2.** *(prize, inheritance)* jdm zufallen go to sb ◊ *Der erste Preis fiel leider ihrer Rivalin zu.; (task, duty)* fall to sb ◊ *Diese schwere Aufgabe fiel ihm zu.*

② **zu·fäl·lig** ['tsu:fɛlɪç] [adj] accidental, coincidental ◊ *Ähnlichkeiten mit lebenden Personen sind rein zufällig.* ein zufälliger Fund a chance find/discovery eine zufällige Auswahl a random selection [adv] by chance, coincidentally, accidently ◊ *einen Fehler rein zufällig entdecken* etw. zufällig tun/wissen/ haben happen to do/know/have sth ◊ *Wissen Sie zufällig, wie viel Uhr es ist?* jdn zufällig treffen bump into sb

zu·fol·ge ['tsu:fɔlgə] [prep] *postpositive* [+dat] jdm/ einer Sache zufolge according to sb/sth ◊ *Presseberichten zufolge kam es bereits gestern zu einer Einigung.*

② **zu·frie·den** [tsu:'fri:dn̩] [adj, adv] **1.** contented(ly), happy(-ily) ◊ *zufriedene Gesichter* ♦ *Sie sah recht zufrieden aus.* ♦ *zufrieden lächeln* zufrieden mit jdm/etw. satisfied/happy/content with sb/sth ◊ *Bist du zufrieden mit ihr/dem Ergebnis?* zufrieden über etw. [acc] satisfied with sth ◊ *Er war über die Abstimmung nicht zufrieden.* jdn zufrieden stellen satisfy sb schwer zufrieden zu stellen sein be difficult to please sich mit etw. zufrieden geben be content with sth, accept sth sich (sehr) zufrieden über jdn/etw. äußern express your satisfaction with sb/sth ⊜unzufrieden **2.** jdn zufrieden lassen leave sb alone/in peace Lass mich endlich damit zufrieden! Stop going on about it!

② **Zug** [tsu:k] der <-(e)s, Züge> **1.** train ◊ *Sie nahm den Zug.* ♦ *mit dem Zug fahren* ♦ *Der Zug hatte Verspätung.* **2.** *(of people)* stream ◊ *Ein langer Zug von Vertriebenen bewegte sich in Richtung*

Grenze.; *(of demonstrators)* procession **3.** *(also fig) (strategic)* move ◊ *Du bist am Zug!* ♦ *jdn in fünf Zügen matt setzen* **4.** *(of air)* draught, draft ◊ *keinen Zug vertragen* **5.** *(from a cigarette)* puff, drag ◊ *Er zündete sich eine Zigarette an und nahm einen tiefen Zug.* **6.** *(from a bottle)* swig, gulp ◊ *einen Zug aus der Flasche nehmen* **7.** *(of a face)* feature ◊ *Sein Gesicht hat harte/weiche Züge.* **8.** trait, characteristic etw. ist ein/kein schöner Zug von jdm sth is nice/isn't very nice of sb etw. nimmt seltsame Züge an sth takes a strange turn ⊙ etw. in vollen Zügen genießen enjoy sth to the full zum Zug(e) kommen get a chance ◊ *Endlich kam er zum Zug und konnte auch mal etwas sagen.* in einem Zug in one go etw. in einem Zug lesen read sth without putting it down

Zu·ga·be ['tsu:ga:bə] die <-, -n> **1.** MUS encore ◊ *Die Band gab/spielte eine Zugabe.* **2.** extra, gift ◊ *Das Spiel gab es als Zugabe zu meinem Computer.* **3.** addition unter Zugabe von Zucker adding sugar

Zu·gang ['tsu:gaŋ] der <-(e)s, Zugänge> **1.** entrance ◊ *Alle Zugänge waren geschlossen.* **2.** no pl *(also fig)* access ◊ *freien Zugang zum Meer/zu den Akten haben.* ♦ *Der Zugang zum Internet ist derzeit nicht möglich.* Zugang verboten! No admittance. **3.** no pl *(fig)* Zugang zu etw./jdm haben be able to relate to sth/sb ◊ *Sie hat keinen Zugang zu ihren Schülern/zur Kunst.*

zu|ge·ben ['tsu:ge:bm̩] <gibt zu, gab zu, hat zugegeben> [tr v] **1.** add ◊ *Das Mehl muss man ganz zum Schluss zugeben.* ⊜hinzufügen **2.** admit (to), confess ◊ *Er hat zugegeben, sie ermordet zu haben.* ♦ *seinen Fehler zugeben* ♦ *Sie hat zugegeben, dass sie im Unrecht war.* ⊜gestehen, eingestehen ⊜leugnen

Zu·ge·ständ·nis ['tsu:gəʃtɛntnɪs] das <-ses, -se> concession ◊ *ein Zugeständnis an die Gewerkschaften* ♦ *keine Zugeständnisse machen*

zu|ge·ste·hen ['tsu:gəʃte:ən] <gesteht zu, gestand zu, hat zugestanden> [tr v] **1.** *(a right)* (jdm) etw. zugestehen grant (sb) sth ◊ *jdm das Recht zugestehen, etw. zu benutzen* ♦ *Den Universitäten wurde mehr Autonomie zugestanden.* ⊜verweigern **2.** etw. zugestehen admit sth jdm zugestehen, dass grant sb that ◊ *Ich muss Ihnen zugestehen, dass es sich um einen schwierigen Fall handelt.*

zü·gig ['tsy:gɪç] [adj, adv] swift(ly), speedy(-ily), rapid(ly) ◊ *eine zügige Realisierung der Reform* ♦ *einen Mordfall zügig aufklären* ♦ *eine Reform zügig durchsetzen; (speed)* brisk ◊ *Das Tempo war mir nicht zügig genug.*

zu·gleich [tsu:'glaeç] [adv] at the same time ◊ *Er lernt und hört zugleich Musik.* ♦ *Die Geschichte war komisch und informativ zugleich.* ♦ *Sie ist zugleich seine Frau und seine Trainerin.*

zu|grei·fen ['tsu:graefn̩] <greift zu, griff zu, hat zugegriffen> [intr v] **1.** help yourself ◊ *Greifen Sie zu! Es ist genug für alle da.* **2.** rush to buy ◊ *Die Anleger griffen beherzt zu.* bei einem Angebot zugreifen take up an offer **3.** auf etw. [acc] zugreifen access sth ◊ *auf Daten/Geld zugreifen können* ♦ *auf das Internet zugreifen*

zu·grun·de, zu Grun·de [tsu:'grʊndə] [adv] **1.** etw. liegt einer Sache [dat] zugrunde sth is based on sth ◊ *Dem Problem liegt ein Missverständnis zugrunde.* ♦ *Dem Film lag ein Roman zugrunde.* **2.** zugrunde

gehen perish ◇ *Die Maja-Kultur ist schon längst zugrunde gegangen.* ♦ *Das Vieh ging zugrunde.* **3.** etw./sich zugrunde richten destroy sth/yourself, ruin sth/yourself ◇ *Er wird sich mit dem Alkohol noch zugrunde richten.* ♦ *ein Unternehmen zugrunde richten*

zu·guns·ten, zu Guns·ten [ʦuˈɡʊnstn̩] (prep) (+gen) in favour of, in favor of ◇ *eine Versicherung zugunsten seiner Kinder abschließen* eine Sammlung zugunsten der Erdbebenopfer a collection for the earthquake victims

zu·gu·te [ʦuˈɡuːtə] (adv) **1.** jdm/einer Sache zugute kommen be an advantage to sb/sth ◇ *Der Mannschaft kam zugute, dass es kühl war.* ♦ *Ihm kam seine Erfahrung zugute.*; (money) benefit sb/sth, go to sb/sth ◇ *Der Erlös kommt dem Tierheim zugute.* **2.** jdm etw. zugute halten make allowances for sb's sth ◇ *Man muss ihm sein Alter zugute halten.* jdm zugute halten, dass er/sie … take into consideration the fact that sb … ◇ *Er hielt ihr zugute, dass sie gleich gestanden hatte.*

Ⓩ **Zu·hau·se** [ʦuˈhaʊzə] das <-s> *no pl* home ◇ *einem Hund ein neues Zuhause geben* ♦ *kein Zuhause haben*

Ⓩ **zu|hö·ren** [ˈʦuːhøːran] <hört zu, hörte zu, hat zugehört> (intr v) (jdm/einer Sache) zuhören listen (to sb/sth) ◇ *Hast du (mir) überhaupt zugehört?* ♦ *einem Gespräch schweigend zuhören*

zu|kom·men [ˈʦuːkoman] <kommt zu, kam zu, ist zugekommen> (intr v) **1.** auf jdn/etw. zukommen approach sb/sth, come towards/up to sb/sth ◇ *Sie kam lächelnd auf ihn zu.* ♦ *Er ist schon mehrmals auf sie zugekommen und hat um Rat gefragt.* **2.** *(fig)* etw. kommt auf jdn zu sth is in store for sb, sb will (have to) face sth ◇ *Auf ihn werden hohe Kosten zukommen.* ♦ *Welche Aufgaben kommen da auf mich zu?* **3.** *(lofty)* jdm etw. zukommen lassen give/send sb sth ◇ *Man ließ ihm eine Menge Trinkgeld zukommen.*

◉ etw. auf sich (acc) zukommen lassen take sth as it comes

Ⓩ **Zu·kunft** [ˈʦuːkʊnft] die <-> *no pl* future ◇ *Was erwartet mich in nächster Zukunft?* ♦ *besorgt in die Zukunft blicken* ♦ *Ihr steht eine großartige Zukunft bevor.* ♦ *In Zukunft will er mehr auf sein Gewicht achten.* mit/ohne Zukunft with/without a future ◇ *ein Beruf mit/ohne Zukunft* Zukunft haben have a future Ⓔ Vergangenheit

zu·künf·tig [ˈʦuːkʏnftɪç] (adj) no comp/superl, only before ns future ◇ *Das ist seine zukünftige Frau.* ♦ *zukünftige Ereignisse* (adv) in future ◇ *Zukünftig will sie sich stärker auf ihre Karriere konzentrieren.*

Zu·la·ge [ˈʦuːlaːɡə] die <-, -n> extra/additional pay ◇ *eine monatliche Zulage* ♦ *Diese Zulage soll gestrichen werden.*; *(from the government)* benefit, allowance Ⓔ Prämie

zu|las·sen [ˈʦuːlasn̩] <lässt zu, ließ zu, hat zugelassen> (tr v) **1.** allow ◇ *Wenn es das Wetter zulässt, wollen wir schwimmen gehen.* ♦ *Wir können nicht zulassen, dass das geschieht!* **2.** jdn zulassen admit sb ◇ *jdn nicht zur Prüfung zulassen* als Arzt/Ärztin zugelassen werden be registered as a physician als Anwalt/Anwältin zugelassen werden be called to the bar, be admitted as a barrister **3.** *(lofty)* etw. zulassen leave room for sth ◇ *Dieser Bericht lässt verschiedene Interpreta-*

tionen zu. **4.** *(fam)* etw. zulassen leave sth closed/shut/unopened ◇ *Lass bitte das Fenster/die Schublade zu!*

zu·läs·sig [ˈʦuːlɛsɪç] (adj) no comp/superl permissible ◇ *Diese Methode ist zulässig.* ♦ *zulässige Hilfsmittel*; *(lawsuit, complaint)* admissible ◇ *Das Gericht hat ihre Beschwerde für zulässig erklärt.* nicht mehr zulässig sein be outlawed/banned, be no longer permissible die zulässige Höchstgeschwindigkeit the speed limit Ⓔ unzulässig

zu·lei·de, zu Lei·de [ʦuˈlaɛdə] (adv) *(always jdm/etw. etwas/nichts zuleide tun)* hurt/harm sb/sth ◇ *Sie wollte dem Tier nichts zuleide tun.* ♦ *Hat er dir etwas zuleide getan?*

Ⓩ **zu·letzt** [ʦuˈlɛtst] (adv) **1.** last ◇ *Das Bad putze ich zuletzt.* ♦ *Er kam zuletzt.* ♦ *die zuletzt absolvierte Prüfung* ♦ *Wann warst du zuletzt im Urlaub?* **2.** in the end ◇ *Zuletzt konnte ihm niemand mehr helfen.* ♦ *Zuletzt verlor er das Match dann doch.*

◉ bis zuletzt until the end **nicht zuletzt** not least ◇ *Der Erfolg des Projekts ist nicht zuletzt von ihm abhängig.*

zu·lie·be [ʦuˈliːbə] (prep) *postpositive* (+dat) **1.** jdm zuliebe for sb('s sake) ◇ *Sie hat es ihm zuliebe getan.* **2.** einer Sache zuliebe for the sake of sth, because of sth ◇ *Dem Beruf zuliebe hat sie den Wohnort gewechselt.*

zum [ʦʊm] (contract) *zu + dem* **1.** to the ◇ *etw. zum Fest mitbringen* → zu **2.** *with nominalized verbs, not to be split* zum Arbeiten/Essen etc. for work(ing)/dinner etc. etw. ist nicht zum Lachen sth is not funny etw. ist zum Verzweifeln/Heulen sth is enough to make you despair/weep **3.** *in certain idioms, not to be split:* look up the relevant idiom ◇ *zum Glück*

Ⓩ **zu|ma·chen** [ˈʦuːmaxn̩] <macht zu, machte zu, hat zugemacht> (tr+intr v) *(fam)* close ◇ *das Fenster/die Tür/den Mantel zumachen* ♦ *Wann machen samstags die Geschäfte zu?*; close down ◇ *Die Polizei hat die Kneipe zugemacht.* ♦ *Dieser Laden musste zumachen.*; *(shoes)* fasten ◇ *Sie machte ihre Skischuhe zu.* Ⓔ schließen Ⓔ aufmachen

zu·mal¹ [ʦuˈmaːl] (adv) *(lofty)* particularly, especially ◇ *Alle waren begeistert, zumal die Fans.*

zu·mal² [ʦuˈmaːl] (conjunc) *mostly written (lofty)* paticularly/especially since ◇ *Ihm war es peinlich, zumal er wusste, dass er im Unrecht war.*

zu·meist [ʦuˈmaɛst] (adv) mostly, for the most part ◇ *Die zumeist weiblichen Fans waren begeistert.* ♦ *Die Kosten für den Versand trägt zumeist der Käufer.*

zu·min·dest [ʦuˈmɪndəst] (adv) at least ◇ *Du solltest es zumindest versuchen.* ♦ *Zumindest behauptete sie das im Interview.* Ⓔ wenigstens

zu·mu·te, zu Mu·te [ʦuˈmuːtə] (adv) jdm ist … zumute sb feels … ◇ *Wegen der Sache war ihm ganz elend zumute.* ♦ *Ihm war nicht wohl zumute.* jdm ist zum Lachen/Weinen zumute sb feels like laughing/crying

zu|mu·ten [ˈʦuːmuːtn̩] <mutet zu, mutete zu, hat zugemutet> (tr v) jdm etw. zumuten ask/expect sth of sb, expect sb to put up with sth jdm zumuten, etw. zu tun expect sb to do sth ◇ *Er wollte ihr nicht zumuten, so lange zu warten.* jdm zu viel zumuten ask/expect too much of sb sich zu viel zumuten overtax yourself

A B C D E F G H I J K L M N O P Q R S T U V W X Y **Z**

zu·nächst [ʦuˈnɛːçst] [adv] **1.** first ◇ *Du musst zunächst versuchen, den Fehler zu finden.* ⊜zuerst **2.** at first, initially ◇ *Zunächst konnte sie keinen Unterschied bemerken.* ⊜anfangs **3.** for the moment, for the time being ◇ *Damit wollte sie sich zunächst noch nicht befassen.* ⊜vorerst

Zu·nah·me [ˈʦuːnaːmə] die <–> *no pl* increase, rise ◇ *eine Zunahme der Kosten/Nachfrage* Zunahme (an Gewicht) weight increase ◇ *In der Schwangerschaft ist eine Zunahme von etwa zehn Kilogramm normal.*

zün·den [ˈʦʏndn̩] <zündet, zündete, hat gezündet> [tr v] +*haben* (explosives) detonate; (fireworks) let off; (a rocket) launch [intr v] +*haben* (explosives) go off ◇ *Die Bombe hat nicht gezündet.*; (engine) fire; (match) light

ⓩ **Zünd·holz** [ˈʦʏntholʦs] das <–es, Zündhölzer> match ◇ *ein brennendes Zündholz* ⊜Streichholz

ⓩ **zu|neh·men** [ˈʦuːneːmən] <nimmt zu, nahm zu, hat zugenommen> [intr v] **1.** put on weight ◇ *Er hat (leicht/stark/fünf Kilo) zugenommen.* im Gesicht zunehmen become fuller in the face ⊜abnehmen **2.** increase ◇ *Die Zahl der Anschläge hat deutlich zugenommen.* ♦ *Das Interesse an diesem Thema hat stark zugenommen.*; (disease) become more prevalent/widespread; (moon) wax ◇ *bei zunehmendem Mond* an etw. [dat] zunehmen increase in sth ◇ *Der Wind hatte an Stärke zugenommen.* an Gewicht zunehmen put on weight ⊜abnehmen

Zu·nei·gung [ˈʦuːnaɪɡʊn] die <–, –en> *most sing* affection ◇ *Ihre Zuneigung wurde nicht erwidert.* Zuneigung zu jdm fassen grow fond of sb (eine) große Zuneigung zu jdm empfinden feel a deep affection for sb ⊜Abneigung

Zun·ge [ˈʦʊnə] die <–, –n> tongue ◇ *sich am heißen Tee die Zunge verbrennen* ♦ *Dem Hund hing die Zunge aus dem Maul.* ♦ *Es gab gebratene/gedünstete Zunge.* ♦ *Die Zunge des Schuhs ist aus Leder.*

⊛ mit der Zunge anstoßen (fam) lisp sich [dat] auf die Zunge beißen bite your tongue jdm auf der Zunge liegen be on the tip of sb's tongue ◇ *Der Name/Das Wort liegt mir auf der Zunge.*

zu·nich·te [ʦuˈnɪçtə] *mostly written* etw. ist zunichte sth is shattered, sth is destroyed ◇ *All unsere Hoffnungen waren zunichte.* etw. zunichte machen wreck sth, ruin sth, shatter sth

zu|ord·nen [ˈʦuːʔɔrdnən] <ordnet zu, ordnete zu, hat zugeordnet> [tr v] **1.** etw. einer Sache [dat] zuordnen assign sth to sth ◇ *ein Tier einer Tierart zuordnen* **2.** (ownership) etw. kann jdm zugeordnet werden the owner of sth can be identified ◇ *Das gestohlene Fahrrad konnte keinem Besitzer zugeordnet werden.*

zur [ʦuːɐ̯] [contract] *zu + der* **1.** to the ◇ *Du gehörst zur ersten Gruppe.* ♦ *zur Tür gehen* → zu **2.** *in certain idioms, not to be split:* look up the relevant idiom ◇ *jdm zur Seite stehen*

zu·ran·de, zu Ran·de [ʦuˈrandə] [adv] (always (mit jdm/etw.) zurande/zu Rande kommen) cope (with sb/sth) ◇ *Ich komme ohne deine Hilfe ganz gut zurande.* ♦ *Wie kommst du mit der neuen Aufgabe zurande?* ⊜zurechtkommen

zu·ra·te, zu Ra·te [ʦuˈraːtə] [adv] (always jdn/etw. zurate/zu Rate ziehen) consult sb/sth ◇ *Wir*

haben einen Fachmann/Stadtplan zurate gezogen.

zu·recht|... [ʦuˈrɛçt] [prefix] **1.** *expressing that sth is brought into (the right) shape/reduced to (the right) size* etw. zurechtschneiden cut sth to size/shape etw. zurechtstutzen trim sth **2.** *expressing that sth is put into (its proper) place* (sich [dat]) etw. zurechtlegen lay sth out, prepare sth seine Brille zurechtrücken adjust your glasses

zu·recht|fin·den [ʦuˈrɛçtfɪndn̩] <findet sich zurecht, fand sich zurecht, hat sich zurechtgefunden> [ref v] sich zurechtfinden find your way ◇ *Sie fand sich (in der neuen Stadt) schnell zurecht.*

zu·recht|kom·men [ʦuˈrɛçtkɔmən] <kommt zurecht, kam zurecht, ist zurechtgekommen> [intr v] (mit jdm/etw.) zurechtkommen cope (with sb/sth) ◇ *mit einem Kind/einer Situation nicht mehr zurechtkommen* ♦ *Das ist sehr viel Arbeit. Kommst du allein zurecht?* ⊜zurande kommen, zu Rande kommen

ⓩ **zu·rück** [ʦuˈrʏk] [adv] **1.** back ◇ *Der Weg zurück kam ihr lang vor.* ♦ *etw. zurück an seinen Platz stellen* ♦ *Sie wird in einer Stunde zurück sein.* Zurück! Stand back! zurück an Absender return to sender mit Dank zurück returned with thanks **2.** (for) the return trip ◇ *Zurück brauchte er über eine Stunde.* ♦ *Zurück nahm er den Bus.* eine Fahrkarte nach München und zurück a return/round-trip ticket to Munich die Fahrt kostet hin und zurück ... the round-trip costs ... ⊜hin **3.** (fam) zurück sein be behind ◇ *ein Kind, das in seiner Entwicklung weit zurück ist*

ⓩ **zu·rück|...** [ʦuˈrʏk] [prefix] ... back ◇ *Sie flog am Sonntag nach Berlin zurück.* ♦ *Demonstranten zurückdrängen* ♦ *ein Buch zurückverlangen* ♦ *Sie winkte fröhlich zurück.* ♦ *gern an seine Studentenzeit zurückdenken*

zu·rück|blei·ben [ʦuˈrʏkblaɪbm̩] <bleibt zurück, blieb zurück, ist zurückgeblieben> [intr v] **1.** stay behind ◇ *allein in seinem Zimmer zurückbleiben* **2.** be left behind ◇ *Die Fahrräder blieben am Bahnhof zurück.* **3.** fall behind ◇ *Die Läuferin blieb allmählich hinter den anderen zurück.* **4.** be left, remain ◇ *Es blieb ein Fleck zurück.* ♦ *Bei ihr sind Narben zurückgeblieben.* an etw. [dat] bleibt ein Schaden zurück sth has suffered lasting damage **5.** stay back ◇ *Bitte bleiben Sie hinter der Absperrung zurück.* **6.** hinter etw. [dat] zurückbleiben fall short of sth ◇ *Das Angebot blieb weit hinter ihren Erwartungen zurück.*

ⓩ **zu·rück|fah·ren** [ʦuˈrʏkfaːrən] <fährt zurück, fuhr zurück, hat/ist zurückgefahren> [intr v] +*sein* **1.** go back, return ◇ *nach Hause/ins Hotel zurückfahren*; (by car) drive back; (on a bicycle) motorbike, ride back ⊜hinfahren **2.** mit dem Auto (ein Stückchen) zurückfahren reverse the car (a little) **3.** shrink back ◇ *vor Schreck zurückfahren* [tr v] +*haben* **1.** jdn zurückfahren drive sb back ⊜hinfahren **2.** reduce, cut back ◇ *Der Sender fährt seine Berichterstattung weiter zurück.* ♦ *die Ausgaben etwas zurückfahren*

ⓩ **zu·rück|ge·ben** [ʦuˈrʏkɡeːbm̩] <gibt zurück, gab zurück, hat zurückgegeben> [tr v] (also fig) (jdm) etw. zurückgeben give sth back (to sb), return sth (to sb) ◇ *jdm sein Geld zurückgeben* ♦ *einem Tier die Freiheit zurückgeben* jdm sein Selbstvertrauen zurückgeben restore sb's confidence

zu·rück·ge·blie·ben [ʦuˈrʏkɡəbliːbm̩] *past p of* zurückbleiben [adj] *(esp pej)* retarded ◊ *geistig zurückgeblieben sein* ♦ *ein etwas zurückgebliebenes Kind*

zu·rück|ge·hen [ʦuˈrʏkɡeːən] <geht zurück, ging zurück, ist zurückgegangen> [intr v] **1.** go back, return ◊ *Sollen wir zum Hotel zurückgehen?* ⊕hingehen **2.** go down, decrease ◊ *Der Umsatz/ Die Kriminalität ist zurückgegangen.* ⊕ansteigen **3.** step back ◊ *Könntest du ein Stückchen zurückgehen?* ⊕vorgehen **4.** etw. geht auf etw. [acc] zurück sth goes back to sth ◊ *„Tektonik" geht auf das griechische Wort „tekton" zurück.*

zu·rück|grei·fen [ʦuˈrʏkɡraefn̩] <greift zurück, griff zurück, hat zurückgegriffen> [intr v] auf jdn/ etw. zurückgreifen resort to sb/sth, fall back on sb/sth ◊ *auf bewährte Methoden zurückgreifen* ♦ *auf seine Reserven zurückgreifen müssen*

zu·rück|hal·ten [ʦuˈrʏkhaltn̩] <hält zurück, hielt zurück, hat zurückgehalten> [tr v] **1.** *(prevent from leaving)* jdn zurückhalten hold sb back ◊ *jdn am Arm zurückhalten* ♦ *Als sie gehen wollte, hielt er sie nicht zurück.; (hold in check)* keep sb back ◊ *aggressive Demonstranten zurückhalten* **2.** etw. zurückhalten withhold sth ◊ *die Wahlergebnisse zurückhalten; (tears, emotions also)* suppress sth ◊ *Sie konnte ihr Lachen nicht zurückhalten.* [ref v] **1.** sich zurückhalten control yourself, restrain yourself ◊ *Ich musste mich zurückhalten, damit ich ihm nicht die Meinung sagte.* ♦ *Er konnte sich nicht mehr zurückhalten und musste lachen.* **2.** *(when eating, drinking)* sich bei etw. zurückhalten go easy on sth ◊ *sich beim Nachtisch/Wein ein bisschen zurückhalten* **3.** *(criticism, opinions, suggestions)* sich mit etw. zurückhalten hold sth back ◊ *sich mit seiner Meinung/Kritik zurückhalten*

zu·rück|keh·ren [ʦuˈrʏkkeːrən] <kehrt zurück, kehrte zurück, ist zurückgekehrt> [intr v] *(lofty)* return, come back ◊ *aus dem Exil/Urlaub zurückkehren* ♦ *Allmählich kehrt sein Selbstbewusstsein zurück.* in die Heimat/zu jdm zurückkehren go back home/to sb ⊕zurückkommen

zu·rück|kom·men [ʦuˈrʏkkɔmən] <kommt zurück, kam zurück, ist zurückgekommen> [intr v] **1.** come back, return ◊ *aus Italien/aus dem Urlaub zurückkommen* ♦ *nach Deutschland zurückkommen* ♦ *vom Schwimmen zurückkommen* ⊕zurückkehren **2.** auf etw./jdn zurückkommen come back to sth/ sb ◊ *auf ein Angebot/Thema zurückkommen* ♦ *Ich werde später auf Sie zurückkommen.*

zu·rück|las·sen [ʦuˈrʏklasn̩] <lässt zurück, ließ zurück, hat zurückgelassen> [tr v] leave (behind) ◊ *versehentlich seinen Schal im Bus zurücklassen* ♦ *jdn allein zurücklassen* ♦ *Die Wunde hat eine Narbe zurückgelassen.*

zu·rück|le·gen [ʦuˈrʏkleːgn̩] <legt zurück, legte zurück, hat zurückgelegt> [tr v] **1.** etw. zurücklegen put sth back ◊ *die Briefe (in die Schublade) zurücklegen* **2.** *(money)* put away/aside ◊ *Geld für Notfälle zurücklegen* **3.** jdm etw. zurücklegen reserve sth for sb ◊ *Können Sie mir diesen Mantel bis morgen zurücklegen?* **4.** *(a distance)* cover ◊ *Die Läuferin hatte bereits 15 km zurückgelegt.* ♦ *durchschnittlich 120 km in der Stunde zurücklegen*

zu·rück|lie·gen [ʦuˈrʏkliːgn̩] <liegt zurück, lag

zurück, hat zurückgelegen> [intr v] *in South G, Austr, Swiss often +sein* **1.** etw. liegt eine Woche/ drei Jahre/lange etc. zurück sth took place/was a week/three years/long etc. ago **2.** SPORT be behind (um) zwei Tore/zehn Punkte etc. (hinter jdm) zurückliegen be two goals/ten points etc. behind (sb)

zu·rück|neh·men [ʦuˈrʏkneːmən] <nimmt zurück, nahm zurück, hat zurückgenommen> [tr v] take back ◊ *Dieses Geschäft nimmt sämtliche Verpackungen zurück.* ♦ *ein Versprechen wieder zurücknehmen; (an accusation, a complaint, remark)* withdraw ◊ *Ich nehme zurück, was ich vorhin gesagt habe, es war unfair.; (a decision)* reverse, revoke

zu·rück|schre·cken [ʦuˈrʏkʃrɛkn̩] <schreckt zurück, schreckte zurück, ist zurückgeschreckt> [intr v] **1.** shrink back ◊ *Als sie die Leiche sah, schreckte sie zurück.* **2.** vor etw. [dat] zurückschrecken shy away/shrink from sth ◊ *auch vor einem Mord nicht zurückschrecken* vor nichts zurückschrecken stop at nothing

zu·rück|ste·hen [ʦuˈrʏkʃteːən] <steht zurück, stand zurück, hat zurückgestanden> [intr v] *in South G, Austr, Swiss often +sein* (hinter jdm/etw.) zurückstehen (müssen) (have to) take second place (to sb/sth) ◊ *Das älteste Kind musste oft (hinter den anderen) zurückstehen.*

zu·rück|stel·len [ʦuˈrʏkʃtɛlən] <stellt zurück, stellte zurück, hat zurückgestellt> [tr v] **1.** put sth back ◊ *ein Buch ins Regal zurückstellen* ♦ *etw. an seinen Platz zurückstellen* ♦ *die Uhr zurückstellen* die Heizung zurückstellen turn down the radiator **2.** *(plans)* postpone

zu·rück|tre·ten [ʦuˈrʏktreːtn̩] <tritt zurück, trat zurück, ist zurückgetreten> [intr v] **1.** resign, step down ◊ *Der Präsident trat zurück.* ♦ *von einem Amt zurücktreten* **2.** step/stand back ◊ *von der Sicherheitslinie zurücktreten* einen Schritt zurücktreten take a step back **3.** von einem Kauf zurücktreten cancel a purchase von einem Vertrag zurücktreten withdraw from a contract **4.** (hinter etw. [dat] zurücktreten (müssen) (have to) take second place (to sth) ◊ *Die eigenen Interessen mussten hinter denen der Allgemeinheit zurücktreten.*

zu·rück|wei·sen [ʦuˈrʏkvaezn̩] <weist zurück, wies zurück, hat zurückgewiesen> [tr v] **1.** reject, turn down ◊ *Ihr Vorschlag wurde zurückgewiesen.* ♦ *Sie wies den Prinzen zurück und heiratete einen anderen.* **2.** repudiate ◊ *einen Vorwurf zurückweisen* **3.** turn away ◊ *Man wies den Flüchtling an der Grenze zurück.* [intr v] etw. weist zurück auf etw. [acc] zurückweisen refer to sth ◊ *Diese Romanfigur weist zurück auf die griechische Mythologie.*

zu·rück|zie·hen [ʦuˈrʏktsiːən] <zieht zurück, zog zurück, hat zurückgezogen> [tr v] **1.** pull/draw back ◊ *Sie zog die Vorhänge zurück.* ♦ *Er zog seine Tochter von der Straße zurück.* **2.** withdraw, cancel ◊ *Die Firma zog ihr Angebot zurück.* **3.** go back, return ◊ *Er zog wieder nach Hamburg zurück.* **4.** MIL withdraw, pull back ◊ *Die USA zogen gestern ihre Truppen zurück.* [ref v] **1.** sich zurückziehen retire ◊ *Ich ziehe mich jetzt für ein paar Stunden zurück.* sich aus/von etw. zurückziehen retire from sth ◊ *Sie hat sich aus der Politik zurückgezogen.* ♦ *Der Schauspieler zog sich von der Bühne zurück.*

2. MIL sich zurückziehen retreat

zur·zeit [ʦuːɐ̯'ʦaet] ⸢adv⸣ at present, currently ◊ *Sie wohnt zurzeit in Kassel.* ♦ *das zurzeit angebotene Programm* ♦ *Zurzeit ist er arbeitslos.*
⊜derzeit, gegenwärtig, momentan

Zu·sa·ge ['ʦuːzaːɡə] die <–, –n> **1.** confirmation, acceptance ◊ *eine unverbindliche Zusage* ♦ *Er hatte die Zusage der Bank, ihm einen Kredit zu geben.* eine feste Zusage a definite commitment; *(for a job, course)* eine Zusage (für etw.) bekommen be accepted (for sth) ◊ *eine Zusage für einen Praktikumsplatz bekommen* ⊜Absage **2.** promise, assurance ◊ *Wir wollen die Zusage, dass Sie bis übermorgen liefern.*

zu|sa·gen ['ʦuːzaːɡn̩] <sagt zu, sagte zu, hat zugesagt> ⸢tr+intr v⸣ **1.** accept ◊ *Ihm wurde die Stelle angeboten und er sagte zu.* fest zusagen confirm (your acceptance) ⊜absagen **2.** jdm zusagen appeal to sb ◊ *die Arbeit/Das Essen sagte ihm sehr zu.* ♦ *Der Bewerber hat ihr nicht zugesagt.* ⸢tr v⸣ **1.** etw. (fest) zusagen confirm sth ◊ *Sie hat ihre Teilnahme bereits (fest) zugesagt.* ⊜absagen **2.** jdm etw. zusagen promise sb sth, assure sb of sth ◊ *jdm Hilfe/Unterstützung zusagen*

Ⓩ **zu·sam·men** [ʦu'zamən] ⸢adv⸣ **1.** together ◊ *Wir fuhren alle zusammen nach Rom.* ♦ *zusammen spielen* ♦ *Wir waren das ganze Wochenende zusammen.* mit jdm zusammen sein be with sb **2.** *(as a couple)* mit jdm zusammen sein go out with sb ◊ *Sie ist nicht mehr mit ihm zusammen.* sie sind zusammen they are together, they are going out **3.** between us/you/them ◊ *Zusammen besitzen sie drei Autos.* etw. macht ..., etw. kostest zusammen ... sth comes to ... all together ◊ *Zusammen kostet/macht das 40 Euro.* alle/die beiden zusammen all/the two combined ◊ *Dieses Auto ist mehr wert als die beiden anderen zusammen.* **4.** *(in a greeting)* everybody ◊ *Hallo (alle) zusammen!*

Ⓩ **zu·sam·men|...** [ʦu'zamən] ⸢prefix⸣ **1.** together ◊ *Sie wollten für immer zusammenbleiben.* ♦ *Die Partei brachte nicht genug Stimmen zusammen.* ♦ *etw. zusammenkleben* **2.** expressing that sth is compressed etw. zusammendrücken crush sth, squash sth sich zusammenkauern cower, huddle; *(a knife, chair, umbrella)* etw. zusammenklappen fold sth (up) etw. zusammenknüllen crumple sth up **3.** *(fam)* expressing a collapse; *(building)* zusammenfallen, zusammenstürzen collapse, cave in; *(person)* collapse, break down **4.** expressing carelessness or superficiality etw. zusammenschreiben scribble sth down ◊ *schnell die Hausaufgaben zusammenschreiben* dummes Zeug zusammenreden talk nonsense, waffle

zu·sam·men|ar·bei·ten [ʦu'zamən|a'baetn̩] <arbeitet zusammen, arbeitete zusammen, hat zusammengearbeitet> ⸢intr v⸣ work together (with), cooperate, collaborate ◊ *Die beiden Firmen wollen enger zusammenarbeiten.*

zu·sam·men|bre·chen [ʦu'zamənbrɛçn̩] <bricht zusammen, brach zusammen, ist zusammengebrochen> ⸢intr v⸣ collapse ◊ *Die Brücke brach unter der Last zusammen.* ♦ *bewusstlos/vor Erschöpfung zusammenbrechen* ♦ *Das Telefonnetz ist zusammengebrochen.; (mentally)* break down ◊ *weinend zusammenbrechen; (traffic)* come to a standstill

für jdn bricht eine Welt zusammen sb's whole world collapses

zu·sam·men|brin·gen [ʦu'zamənbrɪŋən] <bringt zusammen, brachte zusammen, hat zusammengebracht> ⸢tr v⸣ **1.** *(money)* raise, get together ◊ *das Geld für ein neues Auto nicht zusammenbringen* **2.** *(fam)* *(a poem)* remember ◊ *Ich weiß nicht, ob ich das Lied noch zusammenbringe.* **3.** bring together, connect ◊ *die Enden der Stromkabel zusammenbringen* jdn/etw. mit jdm/etw. zusammenbringen bring sb/sth into contact with sb/sth ◊ *Ihre Tätigkeit als Journalistin bringt sie mit vielen Menschen zusammen.*

Ⓩ **zu·sam·men|fas·sen** [ʦu'zamənfasn̩] <fasst zusammen, fasste zusammen, hat zusammengefasst> ⸢tr v⸣ **1.** summarize, sum up ◊ *den Inhalt eines Romans kurz zusammenfassen* ♦ *das Wichtigste in einem Satz zusammenfassen* **2.** combine, unite ◊ *Einige Abteilungen wurden zusammengefasst.*

zu·sam·men|hal·ten [ʦu'zamənhaltn̩] <hält zusammen, hielt zusammen, hat zusammengehalten> ⸢tr+intr v⸣ hold together ◊ *Das Gehäuse wird durch Schrauben zusammengehalten.* ♦ *das Haar mit einem Band zusammenhalten* ⸢tr v⸣ sein Geld zusammenhalten hold on to your money ⸢intr v⸣ *(people)* sie halten zusammen they stick together

Ⓩ **Zu·sam·men·hang** [ʦu'zamənhaŋ] der <–(e)s, Zusammenhänge> **1.** connection, correlation ein Zusammenhang zwischen ... a connection/correlation between ... ◊ *Zwischen den beiden Vorfällen besteht ein enger Zusammenhang.* ♦ *Sie konnte keinen Zusammenhang zwischen den beiden Krankheiten feststellen.* in/im Zusammenhang mit etw. in connection with sth in Zusammenhang mit etw. stehen be connected to sth ◊ *Das steht in keinem Zusammenhang mit seiner Äußerung.* **2.** context ◊ *In diesem Zusammenhang fällt mir ein gutes Buch ein.* etw. aus dem Zusammenhang reißen take sth out of its context

zu·sam·men|hän·gen [ʦu'zamənhɛŋən] <hängt zusammen, hing zusammen, hat zusammengehangen> ⸢intr v⸣ **1.** mit etw. zusammenhängen be related to sth ◊ *sich für alles interessieren, was mit Musik zusammenhängt.* **2.** mit etw. zusammenhängen be the result of sth ◊ *Diese Entwicklung hängt mit den hohen Preisen zusammen.* etw. hängt damit zusammen, dass sth has to do with the fact that

zu·sam·men|le·gen [ʦu'zamənleːɡn̩] <legt zusammen, legte zusammen, hat zusammengelegt> ⸢tr v⸣ **1.** fold ◊ *Sie legt die Wäsche zusammen.* **2.** *(a company, workforce)* combine, merge ◊ *Die beiden Abteilungen werden zusammengelegt.* **3.** *(patients, schoolchildren etc.)* put together ◊ *8 Patienten werden in einen Raum zusammengelegt.* ⸢intr v⸣ +haben *(mehrere Personen)* legen (für etw.) zusammen *(several people)* club together (for sth), *(several people)* pool their money (for sth) ◊ *Alle Kollegen haben für eine Kaffeemaschine zusammengelegt.*

zu·sam·men|neh·men [ʦu'zaməneːmən] <nimmt zusammen, nahm zusammen, hat zusammengenommen> ⸢tr v⸣ **1.** wenn man alles zusammennimmt, alles zusammengenommen all in all **2.** *(courage, powers of judgement)* summon (up) ◊ *Er muss*

nur seinen ganzen Mut zusammennehmen und sie ansprechen.; (thoughts) collect ⟨ref v⟩ *sich zusammennehmen* pull yourself together, get a grip on yourself ◊ *Sie musste sich zusammennehmen, um nicht laut zu schreien.*

zu·sam·men|pas·sen [ˈʦuˈzamənpasn̩] ‹*passt zusammen, passte zusammen, hat zusammengepasst*› ⟨intr v⟩ *(people)* gut/schlecht zusammenpassen suit/not suit each other (well) ◊ *Die beiden passen sehr gut zusammen.; (things)* go/not go together (well) ◊ *Rot und Orange passen nicht gut zusammen.*

zu·sam·men|schlie·ßen [ˈʦuˈzamənʃliːsn̩] ‹*schließt zusammen, schloss zusammen, hat zusammengeschlossen*› ⟨tr v⟩ lock together ◊ *zwei Fahrräder zusammenschließen; (sb's hands)* secure ⟨ref v⟩ *sich (zu etw.) zusammenschließen* join together (to form sth) ◊ *Einige Bürger schlossen sich zusammen und gründeten einen Verein.; (businesses)* merge

zu·sam·men|set·zen [ˈʦuˈzamənʦɛtsn̩] ‹*setzt zusammen, setzte zusammen, hat zusammengesetzt*› ⟨tr v⟩ assemble, put together ◊ *Sie hat das Puzzle zusammengesetzt.* ⟨ref v⟩ **1.** etw. setzt sich aus jdm/etw. zusammen sth consists of sb/sth, sth is made up of sb/sth ◊ *Der Vorstand setzt sich aus 15 Mitgliedern zusammen.* ♦ *Eine Emulsion setzt sich aus Fett und Wasser zusammen.* **2.** sich zusammensetzen sit down (and talk) ◊ *Können wir uns deswegen mal zusammensetzen?* sich (mit jdm) zusammensetzen get together (with sb) ◊ *Die Minister wollen sich zu Verhandlungen zusammensetzen.*

zu·sam·men|stel·len [ˈʦuˈzamənʃtɛlən] ‹*stellt zusammen, stellte zusammen, hat zusammengestellt*› ⟨tr v⟩ **1.** *(a menu, programme)* put together, compile ◊ *ein Menü/Programm zusammenstellen* **2.** *(tables, chairs etc.)* put together ◊ *Sie haben die Tische zu einer großen Tafel zusammengestellt.* ⟨ref v⟩ sich zusammenstellen move (closer) together ◊ *Stellt euch für das Foto etwas enger zusammen.*

zu·sam·men|sto·ßen [ˈʦuˈzamənʃtoːsn̩] ‹*stößt zusammen, stieß zusammen, ist zusammengestoßen*› ⟨intr v⟩ **1.** (mit jdm/etw.) zusammenstoßen collide (with sb/sth) ◊ *Der BMW stieß frontal mit einem Lkw zusammen.* mit den Köpfen zusammenstoßen bang your heads together ◊ *Genau hier stoßen beide Grundstücke zusammen.* etw. stößt mit etw. zusammen sth adjoins sth

zu·sam·men|tra·gen [ˈʦuˈzamɛntraːgŋ̩] ‹*trägt zusammen, trug zusammen, hat zusammengetragen*› ⟨tr v⟩ *(also fig)* collect, gather together ◊ *Sie trugen Äste für ein Feuer zusammen.* ♦ *Material für einen Aufsatz zusammentragen.*

zu·sam·men|tref·fen [ˈʦuˈzamɛntrɛfn̩] ‹*trifft zusammen, traf zusammen, ist zusammengetroffen*› ⟨intr v⟩ **1.** (mit jdm) zusammentreffen meet (sb), meet up (with sb) ◊ *Sie trafen ganz zufällig auf dem Markt zusammen.* ⊜sich begegnen **2.** etw. trifft mit etw. zusammen sth coincides with sth ◊ *Mein Geburtstag trifft dieses Jahr mit Ostern zusammen.*

Zu·satz [ˈʦuːzats] *der ‹-es, Zusätze›* **1.** additive ◊ *Wurst ohne Geschmacksverstärker oder andere*

Zusätze **2.** addition ◊ *einen Zusatz in den Vertrag aufnehmen* ⊜Ergänzung **3.** *no pl* adding ◊ *Der Zusatz von chemischen Stoffen ist verboten.* ♦ *Diese Arznei wird unter Zusatz von Alkohol haltbar gemacht.*

zu·sätz·lich [ˈʦuːzɛtslɪç] ⟨adj⟩ *no comp/superl; only before ns* additional ◊ *zusätzliche Informationen* ⟨adv⟩ *no comp/superl* additionally, in addition ◊ *zusätzlich zum Kurs Einzelunterricht belegen*

② **zu|schau·en** [ˈʦuːʃaʊən] ‹*schaut zu, schaute zu, hat zugeschaut*› ⟨intr v⟩ *(Swiss, Austr, SouthG)* **1.** jdm/einer Sache zuschauen watch sb/sth ◊ *Schau deinem Bruder zu, wie er das macht!* jdm bei etw. zuschauen watch sb doing sth ◊ *Er schaut seiner Mutter beim Kochen zu.* ⊜zusehen **2.** stand and watch, look on ◊ *Sie mussten hilflos zuschauen, wie die Katze überfahren wurde.* ⊜zusehen, mit ansehen **3.** *(esp SouthG, Austr, Swiss)* zuschauen, dass see to it that ◊ *Schau zu, dass du endlich dein Zimmer aufräumst!*

Zu·schau·er [ˈʦuːʃaʊɐ] *der ‹-s, -›,*
Zu·schau·e·rin [ˈʦuːʃaʊərɪn] *die ‹-, -nen›* spectator; *(in a theatre/theater)* member of the audience die Zuschauer the spectators, the audience ◊ *Die Zuschauer klatschten begeistert.; (of an accident)* onlooker

Zu·schlag [ˈʦuːʃlaːk] *der ‹-(e)s, Zuschläge›* **1.** surcharge, supplementary charge ◊ *Für diesen Zug müssen Sie einen Zuschlag bezahlen.; (at work)* supplementary payment **2.** *(at an auction)* der Zuschlag erfolgt an jdn sold to sb ◊ *Der Zuschlag erfolgt an die Dame im roten Pullover.* jd erhält den Zuschlag für etw. sth goes to sb das höchste Gebot erhält den Zuschlag the highest bidder gets the lot **3.** contract ◊ *jdm den Zuschlag geben* ♦ *den Zuschlag erhalten* ⊜Auftrag

Zu·schuss [ˈʦuːʃʊs] *der ‹-es, Zuschüsse›* der/ein Zuschuss (für/zu etw.) the/a subsidy (for sth), the/a grant (for sth) ◊ *auf staatliche Zuschüsse angewiesen sein* ♦ *einen Zuschuss für ein Projekt beantragen*

zu|se·hen [ˈʦuːzeːən] ‹*sieht zu, sah zu, hat zugesehen*› ⟨intr v⟩ **1.** (jdm/einer Sache) zusehen watch (sb/sth) ◊ *Sie sah den Tänzern begeistert zu.* (jdm) bei etw. zusehen watch (sb doing) sth ◊ *Er sah seinem Vater interessiert bei der Arbeit zu.* ⊜zuschauen **2.** (bei etw.) zusehen stand and watch (sth), look on (as sth happens) ◊ *Hilflos muss sie zusehen, wie er ertrinkt.* ♦ *Ich will nicht tatenlos zusehen müssen!* ⊜mit ansehen, zuschauen **3.** zusehen, dass/ob/wie see (to it) that/whether/how ◊ *Seht zu, dass ihr nicht zu spät kommt!*

zu·se·hends [ˈʦuːzeːənts] ⟨adv⟩ **1.** visibly, noticeably ◊ *Es geht ihr zusehends besser.* **2.** more and more, increasingly ◊ *Dieses Thema gewinnt zusehends an Bedeutung.*

② **zu|sper·ren** [ˈʦuːʃpɛran] ‹*sperrt zu, sperrte zu, hat zugesperrt*› ⟨tr v⟩ *(SouthG, Austr)* lock ◊ *Ich habe vergessen, die Garage zuzusperren.* ⊜abschließen, absperren ⟨intr v⟩ lock up ◊ *Vergiss nicht zuzusperren, wenn du gehst.* ⊜abschließen, absperren

zu|spre·chen [ˈʦuːʃprɛçn̩] ‹*spricht zu, sprach zu, hat zugesprochen*› ⟨tr v⟩ **1.** jdm etw. zusprechen award sth to sb ◊ *Der Besitz wurde der Witwe zuge-*

A
B
C
D
E
F
G
H
I
J
K
L
M
N
O
P
Q
R
S
T
U
V
W
X
Y
Z

sprochen. **2.** *(courage, hope)* jdm/sich etw. zusprechen give sb/yourself sth ◊ *Er sprach ihr Mut zu.* [intr v] **1.** jdm gut/beruhigend etc. zusprechen talk nicely/soothingly etc. to sb ◊ *Sie sprach dem ängstlichen Kind beruhigend zu.* **2.** *(lofty) (food)* einer Sache [dat] (irgendwie) zusprechen tuck into sth (in a certain way) ◊ *Die Gäste sprachen den Speisen reichlich zu.*; *(drink)* get stuck into sth (in a certain way) ◊ *Gestern hat er dem Wein eifrig zugesprochen.*

② **Zu·stand** ['ʦu:ʃtant] der <-(e)s, Zustände> **1.** state ◊ *Ihr gesundheitlicher Zustand ist bedenklich.* ♦ *Im betrunkenen Zustand sollte man nicht fahren.* **2.** *(of a house, car)* condition, state ◊ *Das Haus war in einem ruinösen Zustand.* **3.** *most pl (social, economic)* Zustände conditions ◊ *Hier herrschen ja schlimme Zustände.* ♦ *die sozialen Zustände in einem Land* an unhaltbarer Zustand an intolerable situation

☺ **Zustände bekommen/kriegen** *(fam)* have a fit ◊ *Wenn ich deine Unordnung sehe, kriege ich Zustände!* **das ist doch kein Zustand** that's not right, that's not on

zu·stan·de, zu Stan·de [ʦu'ʃtandə] [adv] **1.** etw. zustande bringen achieve sth, manage sth ◊ *eine hervorragende Leistung zustande bringen* **2.** etw. kommt zustande sth materializes, sth comes about *Unter diesen Umständen kommt das Abkommen nicht zustande.* The agreement cannot be finalized under these circumstances.

zu·stän·dig ['ʦu:ʃtɛndɪç] [adj] *no comp/superl* (für jdn/etw.) zuständig responsible (for sb/sth), in charge (of sb/sth) ◊ *Wer ist der zuständige Beamte?* ♦ *Für diesen Bereich bin ich nicht zuständig.*

zu|ste·hen ['ʦu:ʃteːən] <steht zu, stand zu, hat zugestanden> [intr v] *in South G, Austr, Swiss often +sein* **1.** etw. steht jdm zu sb is entitled to sth ◊ *Wem steht das Erbe zu?* **2.** es steht jdm zu, etw. zu tun it is up to sb to do sth es steht jdm nicht zu, etw. zu tun it is not for sb to do sth ◊ *Es steht mir nicht zu, darüber zu urteilen.*

zu|stim·men ['ʦu:ʃtɪmən] <stimmt zu, stimmte zu, hat zugestimmt> [intr v] **1.** jdm zustimmen agree with sb ◊ *In diesem Punkt kann ich ihnen nicht zustimmen.* zustimmend nicken nod in agreement ⊖widersprechen **2.** einer Sache [dat] zustimmen agree to sth ◊ *einem Antrag mit knapper Mehrheit zustimmen* ⊖befürworten ⊖ablehnen

Zu·stim·mung ['ʦu:ʃtɪmʊŋ] die <-, -en> assent, consent ◊ *Der Chef muss noch seine Zustimmung dazu geben.*

zu·ta·ge, zu Ta·ge [ʦu'ta:gə] [adv] **1.** zutage kommen/treten come to light, be revealed, emerge ◊ *Allmählich kam die ganze Dimension der Katastrophe zutage.* **2.** etw. zutage bringen/fördern bring sth to light, reveal sth ◊ *Die Untersuchungen werden die Wahrheit zutage bringen.*

Zu·tat ['ʦu:ta:t] die <-, -en> *most pl* ingredient

zu|tei·len ['ʦu:tælən] <teilt zu, teilte zu, hat zugeteilt> [tr v] **1.** jdm etw. zuteilen allocate sb sth, allocate sth to sb ◊ *Jeder bekam eine Portion zugeteilt.* **2.** *(a task, role)* etw. zuteilen allot sb sth, allot sth to sb ◊ *Jeder bekam seine Rolle im Theaterstück zugeteilt.* **3.** *(a person)* jdn einer Sache [dat] zuteilen assign sb to sth ◊ *Welcher*

Einheit bist du zugeteilt worden?

zu·tiefst [ʦu'ti:fst] [adv] deeply ◊ *Solches Verhalten verachtet er zutiefst.*

zu|trau·en ['ʦu:traʊən] <traut zu, traute zu, hat zugetraut> [tr v] jdm/sich etw. zutrauen think sb/ yourself capable of sth ◊ *Traust du dir zu, die Party zu organisieren?* ♦ *Das hätte ich ihm nicht zugetraut!*

zu|tref·fen ['ʦu:trɛfn̩] <trifft zu, traf zu, hat zugetroffen> [intr v] **1.** be correct, be true ◊ *Diese Behauptung trifft nicht zu.* ⊖stimmen **2.** etw. trifft (auf jdn/etw.) zu sth applies (to sb/sth), sth is applicable (to sb/sth) ◊ *Diese Regel trifft hier nicht zu.* eine Beschreibung trifft auf jdn zu a description fits sb

zu·tref·fend ['ʦu:trɛfn̩t, 'ʦu:trɛfənt] [adj] accurate, appropriate ◊ *Der Vorwurf bestätigte sich als nicht zutreffend.* ♦ *eine zutreffende Bemerkung*

Zu·tref·fen·de ['ʦu:trɛfn̩də, 'ʦu:trɛfəndə] das Zutreffende what is appropriate Zutreffendes bitte ankreuzen/unterstreichen put a cross/underline where appropriate

Zu·tritt ['ʦu:trɪt] der <-(e)s> *no pl* admission, access ◊ *Zutritt für Unbefugte untersagt!* ♦ *jdm den Zutritt zu etw. verbieten*

② **zu·ver·läs·sig** ['ʦu:fɛlɛsɪç] [adj, adv] reliable(-ably) ◊ *ein sehr zuverlässiger Freund* ♦ *Dieser Kollege ist absolut zuverlässig.* ♦ *zuverlässig arbeiten*

zu·ver·sicht·lich ['ʦu:fɛzɪçtlɪç] [adj, adv] confident(ly), optimistic(ally) ◊ *Er ist zuversichtlich, dass sich die Situation bessern wird.* ♦ *Wir blicken zuversichtlich in die Zukunft.*

zu·vor [ʦu'fo:ɐ̯] [adv] before(hand) ◊ *die Woche zuvor* ♦ *Nie zuvor hat es hier so viel Schnee gegeben.* ⊖davor, vorher ⊖nachher, danach

Zu·wachs ['ʦu:vaks] der <-es> *no pl* growth ◊ *Die Firma konnte in diesem Jahr keinen Zuwachs verzeichnen.*

☺ **Zuwachs bekommen** have an addition to the family

Zu·wan·de·rer ['ʦu:vandərə] der <-s, ->, **Zu·wan·de·rin** ['ʦu:vandərɪn] die <-, -nen> immigrant

zu|wei·sen ['ʦu:vaezn̩] <weist zu, wies zu, hat zugewiesen> [tr v] assign, allocate ◊ *Welche Aufgabe hat man dir zugewiesen?* einen Platz/ Tisch zugewiesen bekommen be given a seat/table

zu|wen·den ['ʦu:vɛndn̩] <wendet zu, wandte/ wendete zu, hat zugewandt/zugewendet> [tr v] **1.** etw. jdm/einer Sache zuwenden turn sth to(wards) sb/sth ◊ *Pflanzen wenden ihre Blätter der Sonne zu.* sich jdm/einer Sache zuwenden turn to(wards) sb/sth ◊ *Sie wandte sich dem Herrn zu, der neben ihr saß.* jdm den Rücken zuwenden turn your back on sb **2.** etw./sich jdm/einer Sache zuwenden devote sth/yourself to sb/sth ◊ *Wir müssen uns nun neuen Aufgaben zuwenden.* einer Sache [dat] die Aufmerksamkeit zuwenden turn your attention to sth **3.** *(financial support)* jdm/ einer Sache etw. zuwenden give sth to sb/sth ◊ *Er hat dem Institut großzügige Spenden zugewendet.*

Zu·wen·dung ['ʦu:vɛndʊŋ] die <-, -en> **1.** *no pl* attention, care ◊ *Kleine Kinder brauchen viel Zuwendung.* **2.** *(financial support)* donation

zu·wi·der¹ ['ʦu:viːdə] [adv] **1.** jd/etw. ist jdm zuwider sb detests sb/sth, sb/sth is repugnant to sb

◊ *Oliven sind mir zuwider.* ✦ *Es ist mir zuwider, andere um Hilfe bitten zu müssen.* **2.** *(lofty)* etw. ist einer Sache* [dat] *zuwider sth conflicts with sth, sth is contrary to sth ◊ Die Entscheidung des Vorstands ist seinem Vorhaben zuwider.*

zu·wi·der² ['ʦu'viːdɐ] [prep] *postpositive* [+dat] contrary to, against ◊ *Aller Vernunft zuwider mischte er sich in den Streit ein.*

zu|zah·len ['ʦuːʦaːlən] <zahlte zu, hat zugezahlt> [tr v] 10 Euro etc. zuzahlen pay an additional 10 euros etc. [intr v] pay extra, pay a supplement/surcharge ◊ *Muss ich für diesen Zug zuzahlen?*

zu·zie·hen ['ʦuːʦiːən] <zieht zu, zog zu, hat/ist zugezogen> [tr v] +*haben* **1.** *(a door, bag)* close ◊ *die Tür zuziehen; (curtains)* draw; *(a zip)* do up **2.** *(an expert)* consult ◊ *Vielleicht müssen wir einen Experten zuziehen.* [intr v] +*sein* move here, move into the area ◊ *Die Familie ist neu zugezogen.* ✦ *Sie ist aus der Schweiz zugezogen.* [ref v] +*haben* **1.** der Himmel/es zieht sich zu the sky/it is clouding over **2.** sich [dat] etw. zuziehen incur sth ◊ *Pass auf, dass du dir nicht seinen Ärger zuziehst.; (an injury)* sustain sth; *(an illness)* contract sth

zu·züg·lich ['ʦuːʦyːklɪç] [prep] *sing nouns without article or attribute are not declined when following this prep, otherwise* [+gen] *or fam* [+dat] plus ◊ *Das Gerät kostet 250 Euro zuzüglich Mehrwertsteuer.*

ZVS ['ʦɛtfaʊ'ɛs] die *(abbr of* Zentralstelle für die Vergabe von Studienplätzen)

> The *ZVS*, the university central clearing organization in Dortmund, is responsible for allocating a specific number of places on courses at all state-run universities throughout the country. As the demand for these courses exceeds the number of places on offer, not every applicant is able to obtain a place straight away.

Ⓩ **zwang** ['ʦvaŋ] *pret of* zwingen

Zwang ['ʦvaŋ] der <-(e)s, Zwänge> **1.** force, pressure ◊ *auf jdn Zwang ausüben* unter Zwang stehen be under duress **2.** compulsion ◊ *unter einem inneren Zwang handeln* **3.** *most pl* constraint ◊ *von sozialen Zwängen beeinflusst sein; (to do sth)* obligation ◊ *Es besteht kein Zwang, etwas zu spenden.*

zwangs·läu·fig ['ʦvaŋsløʏfɪç] [adj, adv] *when used as an adj, only before ns* inevitable(-ably) ◊ *die zwangsläufigen Folgen einer Entscheidung* ✦ *In diesem Gebäude verirrt man sich zwangsläufig.*

zwan·zig ['ʦvanʦɪç] [nmrl] twenty → vier

Ⓩ **zwar** ['ʦvaːʳ] [part] admittedly ◊ *Es war zwar kalt, aber er ging ohne Mantel fort.*

ⓔ **und zwar** to be precise ◊ *Sie hat drei Hunde, und zwar einen Husky und zwei Terrier.*

Ⓩ **Zweck** ['ʦvɛk] der <-(e)s, -e> **1.** purpose ◊ *Die Maßnahme hat ihren Zweck nicht erfüllt.* ✦ *Was für einen Zweck soll das haben?* ✦ *Darf ich den Wagen auch für private Zwecke nutzen?*; ein guter Zweck, a good cause **2.** *no pl* es hat keinen/wenig Zweck, etw. zu tun there is no/not much point in doing sth

ⓔ **der Zweck heiligt die Mittel** the end justifies the means **(das ist ja) der Zweck der Übung** *(fam)* (that's) the whole point of the exercise

zweck·los ['ʦvɛkloːs] [adj] *no comp/superl* pointless, futile ◊ *Widerstand ist zwecklos.* ✦ *eine zwecklose Maßnahme*

zweck·mä·ßig ['ʦvɛkmɛːsɪç] [adj] **1.** *(equipment, clothing)* suitable ◊ *zweckmäßige Kleidung* ⓔpraktisch **2.** *(comment, action)* appropriate ◊ *Diese Bemerkung war nicht zweckmäßig.* ⓔhilfreich [adv] practically, in a practical way ◊ *eine Wohnung zweckmäßig einrichten*

zwecks ['ʦvɛks] [prep] *sing nouns without article or attribute are not declined when following this prep, otherwise* [+gen] *or fam* [+dat] for the purpose of ◊ *Ist eine Kündigung zwecks Lohnsenkung zulässig?*

zwei ['ʦvae] [nmrl] two → vier

ⓔ **für zwei** für zwei arbeiten do the work of two für zwei essen eat (enough) for two

Zwei ['ʦvae] die <-, -en> **1.** two → Vier 1. **2.** *(fam) (bus, tram etc.)* number two → Vier 2. **3.** SCHOOL *(grade)* ⓔB ◊ *Er hat fast lauter Zweien im Zeugnis.* ⓔgut *box*✦ Note

zwei·deu·tig ['ʦvaedɔʏtɪç] [adj, adv] **1.** ambiguous(ly) ◊ *zweideutige Antworten* ✦ *Diese Frage ist zweideutig.* ✦ *Diese These ist zweideutig formuliert.* ⓔeindeutig **2.** *(joke, remark)* suggestive(ly) ◊ *ein zweideutiger Witz*

zwei·er·lei ['ʦvaeɐlae] [adj] *invariable* two different ◊ *Dieser Satz hat zweierlei Bedeutung.* zweierlei Schuhe odd shoes

zwei·fach ['ʦvaefax] [adj] twofold die zweifache Menge double the amount ◊ *die zweifache Menge der üblichen Dosis* sie ist zweifache Großmutter she has two grandchildren in zweifacher Ausfertigung in duplicate ⓔdoppelt [adv] etw. zweifach vergrößern enlarge sth to twice its size etw. zweifach ausfertigen lassen have sth duplicated, have two copies made of sth den Faden zweifach nehmen double the thread ⓔdoppelt

Ⓩ **Zwei·fel** ['ʦvaefl] der <-s, -> Zweifel (an etw. [dat]) doubt (about sth) ◊ *Es gab nicht den geringsten Zweifel, dass er schuldig war.* ✦ *Sie hat ohne jeden Zweifel gelogen.* ich habe Zweifel an dieser Geschichte I have my doubts about this story. jdn über etw. [acc] im Zweifel lassen leave sb in doubt about sth etw. in Zweifel ziehen call sth into question sich [dat] über etw. [acc] im Zweifel sein be in two minds about sth etw. steht außer Zweifel sth is beyond (all) doubt

ⓔ **im Zweifel für den Angeklagten** *(also iron)* give the accused the benefit of the doubt

zwei·fel·haft ['ʦvaeflhaft] [adj] <zweifelhafter, am zweifelhaftesten> **1.** *before ns* uncertain, doubtful ◊ *Es ist zweifelhaft, ob er diese lange Reise antreten kann.* **2.** dubious, questionable ◊ *ein Mann von zweifelhaftem Ruf* ✦ *Diese Methode erscheint mir zweifelhaft.*

zwei·fel·los ['ʦvaefloːs] [adv] undoubtedly, without (a) doubt ◊ *Diese Antwort ist zweifellos richtig.* ✦ *Er ist zweifellos ihr Sohn.*

Ⓩ **zwei·feln** ['ʦvaefln] [intr v] +*haben* an jdm/etw. zweifeln doubt sb/sth ◊ *Zweifelst du daran, dass er aufrichtig ist?* daran zweifeln, dass doubt that an sich [dat] zweifeln doubt yourself

Zweig ['ʦvaek] der <-(e)s, -e> **1.** twig ◊ *Der Vogel sitzt auf einem Zweig.* **2.** *(of a field of knowledge)* branch ◊ *Optik und Mechanik sind Zweige der Physik.*

A
B
C
D
E
F
G
H
I
J
K
L
M
N
O
P
Q
R
S
T
U
V
W
X
Y
Z

ⓔ **auf keinen grünen Zweig kommen** get nowhere

zwei·mal ['tsvaema:l] [adv] twice ◊ *Er hat den Film schon zweimal gesehen.*

ⓔ **sich** [dat] **etw. nicht zweimal sagen lassen** not have to be told twice

zwei·spra·chig ['tsvaeʃpra:xɪç] [adj] *no comp/superl* **1.** *(person, dictionary etc.)* bilingual ◊ *Leo ist zweisprachig: Er spricht Französisch und Deutsch.* ♦ *die zweisprachigen Kinder eines Diplomaten* **2.** *(region)* having two languages ◊ *Irland ist in machen Regionen zweisprachig: Die Menschen sprechen Englisch und Gälisch. Kanada ist ein zweisprachiges Land. Canada is a country with two languages.* **3.** *(report, traffic sign, book)* in two languages ◊ *Die Verkehrsschilder in Katalonien sind zweisprachig: Spanisch und Katalonisch.* [adv] *no comp/superl* bilingually, speaking two languages ◊ *Er wächst zweisprachig auf.* ♦ *Sie möchte ihre Kinder zweisprachig erziehen.*

zweit [tsvaet] [nmrl] *(always* **zu zweit)** together ◊ *Wir fahren zu zweit in den Urlaub. Die Kiste könnt ihr zu zweit heben. You can lift the box between you. Die Täter waren zu zweit. There were two culprits.*

zwei·te ['tsvaetə] [adj] <ein zweiter ..., eine zweite ..., ein zweites ...> second → **vierte**

zwei·tens ['tsvaetns, 'tsvaetəns] [adv] second(ly) ◊ *Erstens hat er keine Lust zum Verreisen und zweitens kein Geld.*

zweit·ran·gig ['tsvaetraŋɪç] [adj] *no comp/superl* of secondary importance ◊ *Quantität ist zweitrangig; zuerst kommt Qualität.* **von zweitrangiger Bedeutung sein** be of secondary importance

Zwerg [tsvɛʳk] der <-(e)s, -e> *(also pej)* dwarf ⊖**Riese**

ⓩ **Zwetsch·ge** ['tsvɛtʃgə], **Zwetsch·ke** ['tsvɛtʃkə] die <-, -n> ⊖*damson* ◊ *fünf Kilo Zwetschgen*

zwi·cken ['tsvɪkŋ] [tr v] *+haben* **1.** etw. zwickt jdn sth pinches sb ◊ *Die Hose ist unbequem; sie zwickt mich am Bauch.* ⊖kneifen **2.** *(animal)* ein Tier zwickt jdn an animal nips sb ◊ *Der Hund hat mich gezwickt!* **3.** *(pain)* etw. zwickt jdn sth is troubling sb ◊ *Großvater zwickt mal wieder der Rücken.* [intr v] *+haben* **1.** *(clothing)* etw. zwickt sth is pinching ◊ *Der Rock zwickt am Bund.* ⊖kneifen **2.** give sb a nip ◊ *Können Fliegen zwicken?*

ⓩ **Zwie·bel** ['tsvi:bļ] die <-, -n> **1.** onion ◊ *eine Zwiebel in Ringe schneiden* **2.** BOT bulb ◊ *Du musst die Zwiebeln jetzt schon in die Erde pflanzen, wenn du im Sommer Blumen haben willst.*

Zwie·spalt ['tsvi:ʃpalt] der <-(e)s, Zwiespälte> *most sing* conflict ◊ *sich in einem inneren Zwiespalt befinden*

Zwil·ling ['tsvɪlɪŋ] der <-s, -e> **1.** twin ◊ *Meine beiden Schwestern sind Zwillinge.* **2.** ASTROL, ASTRON Gemini

ⓩ **zwin·gen** ['tsvɪŋən] <zwingt, zwang, hat gezwungen> [tr v] jdn zu etw. zwingen; jdn dazu zwingen, etw. zu tun force sb to do sth ◊ *Du kannst ihn nicht zwingen, dir seinen Wagen zu leihen.* ♦ *Die Umstände zwingen uns zu diesen Maßnahmen.* **sich zu etw. zwingen; sich dazu zwingen, etw. zu tun** force yourself to do sth ◊ *Er zwang sich zu einem Lächeln.* **sich zu etw.**

gezwungen sehen find yourself compelled/forced to do sth **jdn irgendwohin zwingen** force sb somewhere ◊ *Er zwang sie zurück ins Haus.*

ⓩ **zwi·schen** ['tsvɪʃŋ] [prep] **1.** *with acc when expressing motion towards a place, with dat when there is no or undirected motion* between ◊ *Er stand zwischen den beiden Mädchen.* ♦ *Der Abstand zwischen den beiden Läufern wird immer größer.* ♦ *zwischen Weihnachten und Neujahr* ♦ *zwischen Freund und Feind unterscheiden* ♦ *Die Post kommt zwischen 9 und 10 Uhr.* ♦ *Dieses Gerät kostet zwischen 100 und 150 Euro.* **2.** [+dat] among ◊ *Hast du schon zwischen den Briefen nachgesehen?* ⊖unter

zwi·schen·durch [tsvɪʃn'dʊʳç] [adv] in between ◊ *Hast du zwischendurch mal Zeit für mich?*; *(temporal also)* in the meantime ◊ *Waren Sie zwischendurch mal wieder beim Arzt?*

Zwi·schen·fall ['tsvɪʃnfal] der <-(e)s, Zwischenfälle> **1.** incident ◊ *Die Party verläuft bis jetzt ohne Zwischenfälle.* ♦ *ein unangenehmer Zwischenfall* **2.** Zwischenfälle clashes ◊ *Während der Demonstration kam es zu schweren Zwischenfällen.*

zwi·schen|lan·den ['tsvɪʃŋlandn] <landet zwischen, landete zwischen, ist zwischengelandet> [intr v] stop over/off ◊ *Auf unserem Flug nach Hawaii landeten wir in Los Angeles zwischen.*

Zwi·schen·prü·fung ['tsvɪʃnpry:fʊŋ] die <-, -en> intermediate examination ◊ *Sie hat nächste Woche Zwischenprüfung.*

Zwi·schen·zeit ['tsvɪʃntsaet] die <-, -en> *most sing* **1.** interim period ◊ *die Zwischenzeit sinnvoll nutzen* **2.** SPORT intermediate time ◊ *eine gute Zwischenzeit haben*

ⓔ **in der Zwischenzeit** in the meantime ⊖inzwischen, unterdessen

zwit·schern ['tsvɪtʃen] [tr+intr v] *+haben (also fig)* chirp, twitter ◊ *Der Vogel zwitscherte sein Lied.* ♦ *Hörst du die Vögel zwitschern?* ♦ *„Schatz, kauf mir doch die schöne Perlenkette", zwitscherte sie.*

ⓔ **einen zwitschern** *(fam)* have a drink

zwo [tsvo:] [nmrl] *(fam)* two → **vier**

zwölf [tsvœlf] [nmrl] twelve → **vier**

ⓔ **es ist fünf/kurz vor zwölf** we are approaching the eleventh hour, the hands of the clock are at five to midnight

Zyk·lus ['tsy:klʊs] der <-, Zyklen> **1.** cycle ◊ *der Zyklus der Jahreszeiten* ♦ *ein Zyklus von Geschichten rund um das Thema Abschied* **2.** MED menstrual cycle ◊ *Sie hat einen regelmäßigen Zyklus.*

Zy·lin·der [tsy'lɪndɐ, tsi'lɪndɐ] der <-s, -> **1.** MATH, TECHN cylinder **2.** top hat ◊ *in Frack und Zylinder erscheinen*

zy·nisch ['tsy:nɪʃ] [adj, adv] cynical(ly) ◊ *eine zynische Bemerkung* ♦ *Er ist immer so zynisch.* ♦ *„So ist das Leben nun einmal", bemerkte sie zynisch.*

Zy·pern ['tsy:pen] das <-s> *no pl; article only in combination with attribute* Cyprus ◊ *auf Zypern Urlaub machen* ♦ *Das schöne Zypern liebte sie sehr.*

Zyp·ri·ot [tsypri'o:t] der <-en, -en>, **Zyp·ri·o·tin** [tsypri'o:tɪn] die <-, -nen> Cypriot → **Deutsche**

zyp·ri·o·tisch [tsypri'o:tɪʃ] [adj] *mostly before ns* Cyprian, Cypriot ◊ *das zypriotische Pfund*

Declination

Declination of Determiners

DEFINITE ARTICLE AND DEMONSTRATIVE ARTICLE

		m		f		nt	
singular	nom	der	dieser	die	diese	das	dieses
	acc	den	diesen	die	diese	das	dieses
	dat	dem	diesem	der	dieser	dem	diesem
	gen	des	dieses	der	dieser	des	dieses

plural	nom	die	diese
	acc	die	diese
	dat	den	diesen
	gen	der	dieser

Likewise: *jeder, jener, sämtlicher, irgendwelcher* (singular and plural) and *alle, einzige* (plural only), when used as articles.

INDEFINITE ARTICLE, POSSESSIVE ARTICLE, NEGATIVE ARTICLE

		m			f			nt		
singular	nom	ein	mein	kein	eine	meine	keine	ein	mein	kein
	acc	einen	meinen	keinen	eine	meine	keine	ein	mein	kein
	dat	einem	meinem	keinem	einer	meiner	keiner	einem	meinem	keinem
	gen	eines	meines	keines	einer	meiner	keiner	eines	meines	keines

plural	nom	–	meine	keine
	acc	–	meine	keine
	dat	–	meinen	keinen
	gen	–	meiner	keiner

The plural forms are used without article.

Declination of pronouns

PERSONAL PRONOUNS

		1. person	2. person: address		3. person		
			informal	formal[1]	m	f	nt
singular	nom	ich	du	Sie	er	sie	es
	acc	mich	dich	Sie	ihn	sie	es
	dat	mir	dir	Ihnen	ihm	ihr	ihm
	gen	meiner	deiner	Ihrer	seiner	ihrer	seiner

plural	nom	wir	ihr	Sie	sie
	acc	uns	euch	Sie	sie
	dat	uns	euch	Ihnen	ihnen
	gen	unserer	eurer	Ihrer	ihrer

[1] The form of the 2. person used for formal address has the same spelling as the 3. person plural but is written with a capital.

The form of the 2. person used informally is used amongst children and young people, relatives and friends, often amongst workers and students, sometimes, too, amongst colleagues within an institution. In case of doubt, however, always use the formal form of address.

The personal pronouns in the 1. and 2. person always refer to people, 3. person pronouns can refer to people, things or events.

POSSESSIVE PRONOUNS

Possessive pronouns are used to replace a noun preceded by a possessive article: „Gehört das Auto deinem Vater?" „Nein, das ist mein(e)s." (= mein Auto)

<table>
<tr><td colspan="3"></td><td colspan="3">singular</td><td colspan="2">plural</td></tr>
<tr><td colspan="3"></td><td>m</td><td>f</td><td>nt</td><td></td></tr>
<tr><td rowspan="6">singular</td><td colspan="2">1. person</td><td>meiner</td><td>meine</td><td>mein(e)s</td><td>meine</td></tr>
<tr><td rowspan="2">2. person</td><td>informal</td><td>deiner</td><td>deine</td><td>dein(e)s</td><td>deine</td></tr>
<tr><td>formal</td><td>Ihrer</td><td>Ihre</td><td>Ihr(e)s</td><td>Ihre</td></tr>
<tr><td rowspan="3">3. person</td><td>m</td><td>seiner</td><td>seine</td><td>sein(e)s</td><td>seine</td></tr>
<tr><td>f</td><td>ihrer</td><td>ihre</td><td>ihr(e)s</td><td>ihre</td></tr>
<tr><td>nt</td><td>seiner</td><td>seine</td><td>sein(e)s</td><td>seine</td></tr>
<tr><td rowspan="3">plural</td><td colspan="2">1. person</td><td>unserer</td><td>unsere</td><td>unseres</td><td>unsere</td></tr>
<tr><td colspan="2">2. person</td><td>eurer</td><td>eure</td><td>eures</td><td>eure</td></tr>
<tr><td colspan="2">3. person</td><td>ihrer</td><td>ihre</td><td>ihres</td><td>ihre</td></tr>
</table>

Declination of possessive pronouns

		m	f	nt
singular	nom	meiner	meine	mein(e)s
	acc	meinen	meine	mein(e)s
	dat	meinem	meiner	meinem
	gen	–	–	–

plural	nom	meine
	acc	meine
	dat	meinen
	gen	–

DEMONSTRATIVE PRONOUNS

		m	f	nt
singular	nom	dieser	diese	dieses
	acc	diesen	diese	dieses
	dat	diesem	dieser	diesem
	gen	–	–	–

plural	nom	diese
	acc	diese
	dat	diesen
	gen	–

The declination of the demonstrative pronoun *dieser* is the same as that of the demonstrative article. *Jener* is also declined in the same way. These demonstrative pronouns do not normally occur in the genitive case.

		m	f	nt
singular	nom	derselbe	dieselbe	dasselbe
	acc	denselben	dieselbe	dasselbe
	dat	demselben	derselben	demselben
	gen	desselben	derselben	desselben

plural	nom	dieselben		
	acc	dieselben		
	dat	denselben		
	gen	derselben		

The demonstrative pronouns *der-/die-/dasselbe/dieselben* are declined in the same way as the definite article in the first part of the word, the ending following the declination pattern of adjectives. They refer to people, things or events that are the same as something previously mentioned.

Der-/die-/dasjenige/diejenigen are also declined in this way. These words refer to people, things or events to be mentioned or described in more detail in a following relative clause.

		m	f	nt
singular	nom	der	die	das
	acc	den	die	das
	dat	dem	der	dem
	gen	dessen	deren/derer	dessen

plural	nom	die		
	acc	die		
	dat	denen		
	gen	deren/derer		

The demonstrative pronouns *der, die, das* refer to people, things or events mentioned in a previous or following relative clause:

„Ist dein Auto kaputt?" – „Ja, das muss repariert werden."
Ich mag keine unehrlichen Leute. Mit denen möchte ich nicht zusammenarbeiten.

The demonstrative pronouns *der, die, das* have the same form as relative pronouns. Relative pronouns, however, introduce subordinate (relative) clauses:

„Kennst du den Film?" – „Nein, den kenne ich nicht." (= demonstrative pronoun)
Über einen Film, den ich nicht kenne, kann ich nichts sagen. (= relative pronoun)

If a demonstrative pronoun refers to an event, it is always neuter:

Er vergisst ständig ihren Geburtstag. Das gibt immer wieder Streit.

The demonstrative pronoun *das* is often used both in the singular and plural to introduce or to point out people:

Das sind Helmut und Gisela Müller, meine Nachbarn.
Siehst du die Frau da vorne? Das ist meine Chefin.

RELATIVE PRONOUNS

		m	f	nt
singular	nom	der	die	das
	acc	den	die	das
	dat	dem	der	dem
	gen	dessen	deren	dessen

plural	nom	die		
	acc	die		
	dat	denen		
	gen	deren/derer		

Relative pronouns introduce a subordinate (relative) clause that as a rule immediately follows the part of the sentence it refers to: Über einen Film, den ich nicht kenne, kann ich nichts sagen.

REFLEXIVE PRONOUNS

		accusative	*dative*
singular	ich	mich	mir
	du	dich	dir
	Sie	sich	
	er, sie, es	sich	

plural	wir	uns	
	ihr	euch	
	sie	sich	

Reflexive pronouns are part of the verb. As in other languages there is no rule as to whether a verb is reflexive or not. They just have to be learnt together with the reflexive pronouns.

INDEFINITE PRONOUNS

Indefinite pronouns are used to indicate that people or things are undefined or unknown or when nothing further is known about them.

nom	man	jemand	einer, -e, -(e)s	irgendwer	etwas/nichts
acc	einen	jemand(en)	einen, -e, -(e)s	irgendwen	etwas/nichts
dat	einem	jemand(em)	einem, -er, -em	irgendwem	–
gen	–	jemandes	–	–	–

		m	f	nt
singular	nom	jeder	jede	jedes
	acc	jeden	jede	jedes
	dat	jedem	jeder	jedem

plural	nom	alle		
	acc	alle		
	dat	allen		

Declination of adjectives

DECLINATION AFTER THE DEFINITE ARTICLE

		m			f			nt	
singular	nom	der	**junge**	Mann	die	**junge**	Frau	das	**kleine**	Kind
	acc	den	jungen	Mann	die	**junge**	Frau	das	**kleine**	Kind
	dat	dem	jungen	Mann	der	jungen	Frau	dem	kleinen	Kind
	gen	des	jungen	Mannes	der	jungen	Frau	des	kleinen	Kindes

		m			f			nt	
plural	nom	die	jungen	Männer	die	jungen	Frauen	die	kleinen	Kinder
	acc	die	jungen	Männer	die	jungen	Frauen	die	kleinen	Kinder
	dat	den	jungen	Männern	den	jungen	Frauen	den	kleinen	Kindern
	gen	der	jungen	Männer	der	jungen	Frauen	der	kleinen	Kinder

The five forms printed in bold type take the ending -*e*, all the others take -en.

DECLINATION AFTER THE INDEFINITE ARTICLE

		m			f			nt	
singular	nom	ein	**junger**	Mann	eine	**junge**	Frau	ein	**kleines**	Kind
	acc	einen	jungen	Mann	eine	**junge**	Frau	ein	**kleines**	Kind
	dat	einem	jungen	Mann	einer	jungen	Frau	einem	kleinen	Kind
	gen	eines	jungen	Mannes	einer	jungen	Frau	eines	kleinen	Kindes

		m			f			nt	
plural	nom		junge	Männer		junge	Frauen		kleine	Kinder
	acc		junge	Männer		junge	Frauen		kleine	Kinder
	dat		jungen	Männern		jungen	Frauen		kleinen	Kindern
	gen		junger	Männer		junger	Frauen		kleiner	Kinder

Singular: except for the five forms printed in bold type, all adjectives take the ending -*en*. Plural forms are used without the article.

DECLINATION AFTER THE POSSESSIVE ARTICLE AND NEGATIVE ARTICLE

		m			f			nt	
singular	nom	mein	**alter**	Freund	meine	**alte**	Freundin	mein	**altes**	Auto
	acc	meinen	alten	Freund	meine	**alte**	Freundin	mein	**altes**	Auto
	dat	meinem	alten	Freund	meiner	alten	Freundin	meinem	alten	Auto
	gen	meines	alten	Freundes	meiner	alten	Freundin	meines	alten	Autos

		m						nt	
plural	nom	meine	alten	Freunde	meine	alten	Freundinnen	meine	alten	Autos
	acc	meine	alten	Freunde	meine	alten	Freundinnen	meine	alten	Autos
	dat	meinen	alten	Freunden	meinen	alten	Freundinnen	meinen	alten	Autos
	gen	meiner	alten	Freunde	meiner	alten	Freundinnen	meiner	alten	Autos

In the singular the form of the adjective corresponds to the form after the indefinite article. In the plural all forms end in -*en*.

DECLINATION IN THE SINGULAR WITHOUT AN ARTICLE

		m		f		nt	
singular	nom	guter	Wein	klare	Luft	reines	Wasser
	acc	guten	Wein	klare	Luft	reines	Wasser
	dat	gutem	Wein	klarer	Luft	reinem	Wasser
	gen	gut**en**	Weines	klarer	Luft	rein**en**	Wassers

The adjectives take on the endings of the definite article, with the exception of the masculine and neuter genitive (ending -en).
This declination is often used with abstract nouns
- for indefinite quantities (materials and liquids):
Der Teller ist aus reinem Gold.
Auf dem Bauernhof gibt's frische Milch.
- for qualities and feelings (often with a preposition):
Alte Liebe rostet nicht.
Er kämpfte mit großem Mut und zäher Ausdauer für seine Überzeugung.

DECLINATION IN THE SINGULAR AND PLURAL WITHOUT AN ARTICLE

			m		f		nt	
singular	nom	Evas	**alter**	Lehrer	**alte**	Lehrerin	**altes**	Heft
	acc	Evas	alten	Lehrer	**alte**	Lehrerin	**altes**	Heft
	dat	Evas	altem	Lehrer	alter	Lehrerin	altem	Heft
	gen	Evas	–	–	–	–	–	–

			m		f		nt	
plural	nom	Evas	alte	Lehrer	alte	Lehrerinnen	alte	Hefte
	acc	Evas	alte	Lehrer	alte	Lehrerinnen	alte	Hefte
	dat	Evas	alten	Lehrern	alten	Lehrerinnen	alten	Heften
	gen	Evas	–	–	–	–	–	–

This declination is only used in certain exceptional cases
- after a genitive:
Ich habe mir Roberts neues Haus angesehen.
Wessen klugen Ratschlägen bist du gefolgt?
Der Nachbar, dessen reicher Onkel aus Amerika gekommen ist, ...
- after personal pronouns:
Du armes Kind!
mit uns schlecht bezahlten Hilfsarbeitern

Individual points and peculiarities
Adjectives ending in -el and -er lose an e:
dunkel: die dunkle Straße, edel: ein edler Wein, nobel: ein nobler Mensch, sauer: der saure Apfel, teuer: ein teures Auto
but: bitter: ein bitterer Geschmack, finster: die finstere Nacht.
hoch loses the c:
hoch: ein hohes Gebäude
Adjectives ending with -a are not declined:
eine rosa Blume, ein lila Kleid, prima Ideen.
Adjectives derived from place names take the ending -er. They are not declined and always written with a capital letter:

der Hamburger Hafen, in der Berliner S-Bahn, zum New Yorker Flughafen;
and: der Schweizer Käse.

Adjectives used as nouns are written with capital letters but declined as adjectives:
Bei meiner Ankunft habe ich etwas Unangenehmes erlebt.
Dabei hatte ich mit nichts Bösem gerechnet.

Declination of nouns

		m		f		nt	
singular	nom	der/ein	Vater	die/eine	Mutter	das/ein	Kind
	acc	den/einen	Vater	die/eine	Mutter	das/ein	Kind
	dat	dem/einem	Vater	der/einer	Mutter	dem/einem	Kind
	gen	des/eines	Vaters[1]	der/einer	Mutter	des/eines	Kindes[2]

[1] The genitive ending *-s* is used with nouns of more than one syllable: des Computers, des Kamins.

[2] *-es* is used mostly with single-syllable nouns: des Mannes, des Ortes, des Arztes.
-es must be used with nouns that end in *-s, -ss, -ß, -x, -z, -tz:* des Grases, des Komplexes, des Satzes.

		m		f		nt	
plural	nom	die/–	Väter	die/–	Mütter	die/–	Kinder
	acc	die/–	Väter	die/–	Mütter	die/–	Kinder
	dat[3]	den/–	Vätern	den/–	Müttern	den/–	Kindern
	gen	der/–[4]	Väter	der/–	Mütter	der/–	Kinder

[3] Nouns that add an *-s* in the plural do not have an *-n*:

	dat	den/–	Opas	den/–	CDs	den/–	Autos

[4] The genitive plural without an article is not commonly used.

THE N-DECLINATION

The n-declination is used for all masculine nouns that end in *-e* and several other masculine nouns as well. You can recognize these in the dictionary by their genitive ending *-en*.

singular	nom	der/ein	Mensch
	acc	den/einen	Menschen
	dat	dem/einem	Menschen
	gen	des/eines	Menschen

plural	nom	die/–	Menschen
	acc	die/–	Menschen
	dat	den/–	Menschen
	gen	der/–[5]	Menschen

[5] The genitive plural without an article is not in common use.

Comparison of adjectives and adverbs

General rules

	attributive adjective	*adverb*
	das **kalte** Wetter im Oktober	Im Oktober ist es oft schon **kalt**.
comparative	das **kältere** Wetter im November	Im November ist es meistens **kälter**.
superlative	der **kälteste** Januar seit zehn Jahren	Im Durchschnitt ist es im Januar am **kältesten**.

The *comparative* is formed by adding the ending -*er*. It is always followed by the word *als*.
An adjectival comparative used attributively has -*er* and the adjectival ending:
der stärkere Wind, ein leichteres Gewitter
An adverbial comparative has only -*er*:
In Hamburg regnete es stärker als in Hannover.

The *superlative* is always used together with the definite article and is formed by adding
-*st*. An adjectival superlative used attributively has -*st* and the adjectival ending:
der längste Tag des Jahres
An adverbial superlative is always formed with *am -sten*:
Am 22. Juli war die Sicht auf die Alpen am klarsten.

Exceptions

COMPARATIVE AND SUPERLATIVE WITH AN UMLAUT
arm, ärmer, am ärmsten/der ärmste
Likewise: alt, dumm, gesund, grob, hart, jung, kalt, klug, kurz, lang, scharf, stark, schwach, warm

ADJECTIVES WITH IRREGULAR COMPARISON

	attributive adjective	*adverb*
	das ho**he** Haus	es ist ho**ch**
comparative	das hö**here** Haus	es ist hö**her**
superlative	das hö**ch**ste Haus	es ist am hö**ch**sten
	das na**he** Ziel	es ist na**h**
comparative	das nä**here** Ziel	es ist nä**her**
superlative	das nä**ch**ste Ziel	es ist am nä**ch**sten
	die **gute** Art	es ist **gut**
comparative	die **bessere** Art	es ist **besser**
superlative	die **beste** Art	es ist am **besten**
	viele Angebote	es gibt viel
comparative	**mehr** Angebote[1]	es gibt **mehr**
superlative	die **meisten** Angebote	es gibt am **meisten**
		das tue ich gern
comparative		das tue ich **lieber**
superlative		das tue ich am **liebsten**

[1] *mehr* cannot be declined. It refers to an indefinite number or amount and has no article. *mehrere* on the other hand can be declined and refers to an indefinite number (= several, more than two): Ich musste mehrere Stunden beim Zahnarzt warten.

Adjectives ending in *-d, -t, -tz, -z, -sch, -ss* and *-ß* form the superlative by adding an extra *-e:*

wild	wilder	am wild**e**sten
breit	breiter	am breit**e**sten
stolz	stolzer	am stolz**e**sten
spitz	spitzer	am spitz**e**sten
heiß	heißer	am heiß**e**sten
krass	krasser	am krass**e**sten
hübsch	hübscher	am hübsch**e**sten

The same is true for adjectives derived from the past participle of weak verbs:

| vertraut | vertrauter | am vertrau**te**sten |
| beliebt | beliebter | am beliebt**e**sten |

The following are exceptions without the extra *-e:*

| groß | größer | am größten |

Adjectives ending in *-isch:* am komischsten
Adjectives derived from a present participle:

| bedeutend | bedeutender | am bedeutendsten |
| zutreffend | zutreffender | am zutreffendsten |

Adjectives derived from the past participle of weak verbs and ending in *-ert, -elt* or *-tet:*

begeistert	begeisterter	am begeistertsten
bekümmert	bekümmerter	am bekümmertsten
verzweifelt	verzweifelter	am verzweifeltsten
gefürchtet	gefürchteter	am gefürchtetsten

Adjectives ending in *-el* or *-er* lose an *e* in the comparative:

dunkel	der dunk**le** Keller	es wird dunk**le**r	es ist am dunkelsten
edel	der ed**le** Wein	er ist ed**le**r	er ist am edelsten
teuer	der teu**re** Mantel	er ist teu**re**r	er ist am teuersten

Forming sentences

Main clause

Word order in a German sentence follows certain established rules. The main verb or that part of the verb that is conjugated is placed second (position 2) and the second part (infinitive, past participle or separable prefix) at the end of the main clause. The other parts of the sentence can take up various positions. They differ, however, according to whether they are obligatory or optional parts of the sentence.

| position 0 | position 1 | position 2 | central positions | | | end |
			position 3	position 4	position 5	
	Mein Bruder	leiht	mir	morgen	sein Auto.	
	subject (nominative)		indirect object (dative)	temporal adverbial	direct object (accusative)	
	Unserer Schwester	möchte	er	es	nicht	leihen.
	indirect object (dative)		subject (nominative)	direct object (accusative)		infinitive
Aber	sein Motorrad	hat	er	ihr	gern	geliehen.
conjunction	direct object (accusative)		subject (nominative)	indirect object (dative)	adverbial of manner	past participle

The object(s), adverbials or other parts of the sentence may be placed at the beginning of the sentence in position 1 instead of the subject. The subject is then placed directly after the verb in position 3.

When placed centrally in the sentence after the verb the **indirect object** (in the dative) comes before the **direct object** (in the accusative). In the case of personal pronouns, the accusative comes before the dative. With other pronouns, however, the order remains the same.

Pronouns are placed in the central positions as far to the left as possible (position 3 or 4) if position 3 has been taken up by the subject. The correct sequence for pronouns is as follows:

nominative ▸ accusative ▸ dative whenever the accusative is a personal pronoun.
Bisher hat er es mir noch nie geliehen.

nominative ▸ dative ▸ accusative whenever the accusative is another kind of pronoun.
Vielleicht kann er mir seines leihen.

Adverbials (and other parts of a sentence) can be placed in position 1 or come in the central positions of the sentence. They may be placed anywhere in the central position; usually they follow the indirect object. In the case of several adverbials, their order is not fixed. As a rule, however, the following order is usually observed: temporal ▸ causal/concessive/conditional ▸ modal ▸ local – or more simply: time-manner-place.

In negative sentences, *nicht* is placed as near to the end as possible, but before the second part of the verb. It also comes before any adjunct that may be closely linked to the verb.
Der Film enttäuschte mich nicht.
Der Film hat mich nicht enttäuscht.
Ich erinnere mich nicht an die Handlung.

If only a part of the sentence is negated, *nicht* is placed directly before it:
Ich fahre nicht mit dem Bus zur Arbeit.

The main clause conjunctions *aber, denn, und, oder, sondern* are placed in position 0 at the very beginning before the sentence really starts, whereas *deshalb, trotzdem* take up position 1.

Subordinate clauses

In a subordinate clause position 1 is taken up by a connector (conjunction), position 2 by the subject, followed by the predicate at the end (with both parts of the verb if required). The other positions follow the rules given above for the middle parts of main clauses.

position 1	position 2			end	
				verb part 2	verb part 1
weil	er	ihr	eine Freude	machen	möchte.
conjunction	subject (nominative)	indirect object (dative)	direct object (accusative)	infinitive	conjugated verb

A subordinate clause may follow a main clause

main clause	subordinate clause
Ich mag ihn nicht,	weil er arrogant ist.

or be inserted in the middle of a main clause.

main clause	subordinate clause	main clause (continued)
Ich konnte den Mann,	der schnell weglief,	nicht richtig erkennen.

If the subordinate clause is placed at the beginning of a sentence, it takes over position 1 in the main clause order.

main clause		
position 1: subordinate clause	position 2: verb	...
Dass er morgen nicht hier ist,	hat	er mir nicht gesagt.

Conjunctions introducing subordinate clauses are:

als	falls	sofern
anstatt	indem	sooft
bevor	nachdem	statt
bis	obwohl	um ... zu
da	seit	während
damit	seitdem	weil
dass	sobald	wenn
ehe	sodass	wohingegen

Yes/no questions, imperatives and unreal conditionals without 'wenn'

In each of these types of sentence, position 1 remains unoccupied. The verb comes at the beginning of the sentence.

Leihst du mir dein Auto?

Sag mir bitte in Zukunft, wenn du nicht kommst!

Wäre der Mann nicht so schnell weggelaufen, hätte ich ihn bestimmt erkannt.

Spelling: the most important rules

Two words or one

Inseparable compound verbs are always written as one word:
schlussfolgern, langweilen, übersetzen, widersprechen.

Separable compound verbs are written as one word only in the infinitive, as participles and in subordinate clauses. Otherwise they are written as two words.
Ich dachte, der Zug fährt um 10 Uhr ab. Jetzt ärgere ich mich, weil der Zug schon um 9.55 Uhr abgefahren ist.
Am nächsten Kurs möchte ich unbedingt teilnehmen, denn auch Frau Meier nimmt daran teil.

Combinations with the verb *sein* are not regarded as compounds and are always written separately.

Compounds involving adjectives or participles are written as one word whenever:
▸ the first part of the compound represents a group of words:
  meterhoch (= einen/mehrere Meter hoch), tagelang (= mehrere Tage lang)
▸ the compound contains a linking -s-:
  altersschwach, wirkungsvoll
▸ one part of the compound cannot stand alone
  dreifach, mehrdeutig
▸ derivates of verbs are involved that would be written as one word:
  abfahrend, abgefahren, teilnehmend
▸ the adjectives are of equal importance:
  graugrün, taubstumm
▸ the first part strengthens or weakens the meaning:
  brandneu, stockkonservativ
▸ cardinal and ordinal numbers made up of several elements are involved:
  zweihundertneunzig, der fünfhunderttausendste Besucher
Compound nouns are written as one word:
der Montagmorgen, die Geburtstagsparty, das Wörterbuch, das Radfahren, der Jakobsweg

Derivatives from place names ending in -er are written separately from the following noun:
Hamburger Straße, Bremer Stadtmusikanten

The use of hyphens

A hyphen may be used to identify the constituent parts of compounds more clearly and to avoid words becoming too long and possible misunderstandings:
Anfänger-Sprachkurs, re-integrieren

Compounds involving single letters, abbreviations or numerals are written with a hyphen:
T-Shirt, Kfz-Werkstatt, der 20-Jährige

Suffixes have a hyphen only when preceded by a single letter:
x-mal, but: einmal

Compounds involving a numeral, a suffix and another word are written with a hyphen:
der 12er-Pack

Compound noun combinations with more than two elements are often written with hyphens:
der Erste-Hilfe-Kurs, 5-Zimmer-Wohnung

Capital letters

Initial capitals are used for
▸ headings and titles:
  Die Ästhetik des Widerstands

- the beginning of a sentence:
  Eines Morgens Anfang Mai stand ein junger Mann im schwarzen Anzug vor mir.
- the first word in direct speech:
  Sie rief mir noch zu: „Wir sehen uns um fünf!"
- all nouns and nominalizations:
  der Tisch, das Leben, das Lächeln, alles Gute
- the first part of a noun combination:
  Das ist zum Aus-der-Haut-Fahren.
  UV-Strahlung
- all proper names:
  Johann Wolfgang von Goethe, das Kap der Guten Hoffnung

Where proper names are involved, all words are written with an initial capital except for articles, prepositions and connectors, i.e.

- derivatives from place names ending in *-er:*
  der Hamburger Hafen
  However, adjectival derivatives from proper names ending in *-(i)sch* or other suffixes are
  written with small intital letters:
  die schweizerische Post, eine kafkaeske Erzählung
- the personal pronoun and appropriate possessive article/pronoun for formal address:
  „Herr Strauß, Sie haben Ihren Schlüssel liegen lassen."
  The pronouns and determiners for informal address on the other hand are written with
  small letters:
  „Und dein Zimmer, hast du das schon aufgeräumt?"
- official titles:
  der Erste Bürgermeister
- special days:
  der Erste Mai
- certain historical events or periods:
  der Dreißigjährige Krieg, das Frühe Mittelalter

Small letters are used for

- adverbs, prepositions and connectors ending in *-s* or *-ens:*
  abends, montags, falls, seitens
- the following prepositions: *dank, kraft, laut, statt, trotz, wegen, willen, zeit*
- the indefinite numerals *ein bisschen* and *ein paar:*
  ein bisschen Zeit, ein paar Minuten
- the numerical adjectives *viel, wenig, (der/die/das) eine, andere* in all inflected forms
- adjectives, participles and pronouns whose form is that of a noun but which refer to a noun
  that has gone before or that follows:
  Die beiden Männer trennten sich, der dicke ging nach links, der schlankere weiter
  geradeaus.
- adjectival derivatives from proper names ending in *-(i)sch* or other suffixes:
  das schillersche Werk, eine kafkaeske Erzählung
- superlatives with *am:*
  Er springt immer am höchsten, am schnellsten und am weitesten.
- pronouns (except for those used in formal address)
- certain established combinations of prepositions and adjectives:
  bis auf weiteres, seit langem
  Adjectives used as nouns, however, are written with capitals:
  Das ist ein Auto für Reiche.

Punctuation

The **full stop**

▸ comes at the end of a full sentence:
Er spielt mit dem Gedanken auszuwandern, wovor er sich aber auch fürchtet.

▸ is not used after headings, titles etc.

▸ is used after certain abbreviations:
z. B. (= zum Beispiel), Nr. (= Nummer)
Other abbreviations, however, do not have a full stop:
m (= Meter), g (= Gramm), Pkw (= Personenkraftwagen)

▸ is used to indicate an ordinal number:
der 20. November

An **exclamation mark** gives special emphasis to the content of a sentence:
„Jetzt ist endlich Schluss!"

A **question mark** is placed at the end of a direct question:
„Hast du eigentlich den Brief beantwortet? Nein? Wann willst du das endlich machen?"

The **comma**

▸ is used to separate a main clause from a subordinate clause. If the subordinate clause is placed within the main clause, commas are placed at the beginning and at the end of the subordinate clause:
Er kommt noch einmal, weil er heute nicht fertig geworden ist.
Er sagte mir, dass er nächste Woche wieder komme, und fuhr nach Hause.

▸ is placed between parts of a sentence, words or groups of words of equal importance:
Es ist spät geworden, ich muss morgen früh raus.

▸ need not be used if any of the following connectors are used to link parts of a sentence:
und, oder, beziehungsweise, sowie, wie, entweder ... oder, nicht ... noch, sowohl ... als (auch), weder ... noch. It may be used, however, if required to make things clearer.

▸ may be used in word groups involving infinitives, participles and adjectives to make the meaning clear:
Er missachtete mehrere Geschwindigkeitsbeschränkungen(,) um noch rechtzeitig anzukommen.

▸ is obligatory if the infinitive construction is introduced by a phrase upon which it depends (*es, davon* etc.):
Es wäre ein Fehler, jetzt unsere Pläne aufzugeben.

▸ separates additions and afterthoughts (in appositions):
Der Erfinder des Buchdrucks, Johannes Gutenberg, wurde zwischen 1397 und 1400 in Mainz geboren.
Wir treffen uns am Dienstag, den 23. September, um 19 Uhr.
In such cases, it is often left up to the writer to decide whether a comma is necessary or not.

▸ separates names of persons addressed, exclamations, comments and *Ja/Nein*:
„Anna, hast du heute schon deine Mutter angerufen?" – „Nein, das habe ich total vergessen!"

The **semicolon** is used to separate parts of a sentence or groups of words. Its effect is stronger than that of a comma but weaker than a full stop.

The **colon**

▸ introduces a summary or an addition: Onkel Paul, die Tanten und Oma Franziska: Alle waren zum großen Familienfest erschienen. In such cases either a comma or a dash would also be possible.

▸ is placed after a sentence introducing direct speech: Dann fragte er mit lauter Stimme: „Na, zufrieden?"

- introduces an enumeration: Ich habe an vielem Spaß: Lesen, Kino, Tanzen und Wandern

The **dash**
- is used to separate an addition or afterthought from the rest of the sentence. Its effect is stronger than that of a comma: Und morgen will sie – damit droht sie schon lange – zur Polizei gehen.
- introduces something additional or unexpected: Damit hatte niemand gerechnet – er lachte einfach nur.

Quotation marks
- are used to enclose direct speech or quotations. Punctuation marks belonging to the quotation remain inside, punctuation marks belonging to the accompanying text remain outside the quotation marks:

„Abgemacht?", fragte Harry.

The final full stop in the quotation is left out if it is followed by an accompanying sentence:

„Geht in Ordnung", antwortete sie ruhig.
- can be used to highlight or emphasize words or parts of a text: „Na" gehört zur Wortklasse der Partikel. Turgenjews „Vater und Söhne" würde ich gern mal wieder lesen.

A **forward slash** or **oblique** can be used to indicate that certain words or numbers etc. belong together:

Teilnehmer/Teilnehmerinnen.

In this dictionary the oblique is used to separate alternative elements from each other.

Separating words at the end of a line

Words of more than one syllable may be separated at the end of each syllable. The initial consonant of the separated syllable goes on to the new line:

kom-men, El-tern

Groups of letters that represent a single consonant *(ch, sch, ck, ph, th, rh, sh)* may not be separated:

Zu-cker

Compounds and words with a prefix or suffix are separated between the elements:

Pro-gramm, Lauf-zeit, auf-wärts, ängst-lich

Practice material

The German-English section

1 NEIGHBOURS

Find the words in the dictionary that immediately precede and follow the headword:

a	_angreifen_	Angriff	_Angst_
b		Bär	
c		EC-Karte	
d		heikel	
e		Mais	
f		OP	
g		sägen	
h		schmelzen	
i		Sünde	

2 WORD ORDER

Put the words in each line into alphabetical order using the same sorting system as the dictionary. Please read the short section on *Alphabetical Order* in the introduction (page 13) before you do this exercise. Finally, compare your results by looking at the order of the relevant dictionary entries. Do you know all these words?

a	☑ nehmen	☑ Nase	☑ neulich	☑ Neid	☑ nichts
b	☐ lachen	☐ Laden	☐ lächeln	☐ laden	☐ Lachs
c	☐ stellen	☐ Stiel	☐ stehlen	☐ Stall	☐ steil
d	☐ wieso	☐ weiß	☐ wessen	☐ Wissen	☐ weisen
e	☐ Münze	☐ Mund	☐ munter	☐ münden	☐ Mühe
f	☐ höher	☐ Hocker	☐ Höhe	☐ hoch	☐ Hochzeit

3 CORRECT SPELLING

Check in the dictionary if you are unsure.

a F or V? _V_ater

_____ieh

_____enster

b V or W? _____iese

_____illa

_____agen

c K or C? _____omputer

_____affee

_____reme

d K or Ch? _____rist

_____uvert

_____or

4 PLURALS

What is the plural form of these words? Look them up in the dictionary if you are not sure.

a ein Dach   rote _Dächer_____

b eine Katze   drei _____   g eine Burg   vier _____

c ein Sofa   zwei _____   h ein Zimmer   schöne _____

d ein Regal   fünf _____   i ein Platz   viele _____

e eine Freundin mehrere _____   j ein Kind   keine _____

f ein Apfel   zehn _____   k eine Spur   frische _____

5 THE RIGHT CASE

What case is it? If you are unsure about the case of the words printed in bold type, you can check in the section *Case* in the introduction (page 11). Whenever a headword is given in brackets, you will need to look up the dictionary entry.

a von etw. abhängig sein (von)   _etw. = dative_____

b **etw./jd** begeistert jdn   _____ / _____

c jdn von etw. abhalten *(von)*   _____

d einen Kuss auf **jds** Wange drücken   _____

e einer Sache große/keine Bedeutung beimessen *(Bedeutung)*   _____

f sich einer Sache bewusst sein *(bewusst)*   _____

g sich auf jdn/etw. beziehen *(beziehen)*   _____ / _____

6 HABEN OR SEIN?

Put the following sentences into the perfect tense. The dictionary will help you to find the right auxiliary verb.

a Wir begegnen im Park einem Wildschwein.

   _Wir sind im Park einem Wildschwein begegnet._____

b Tanja und Iris basteln eine Überraschung für ihre Mutter.

   _____

c Nach der Arbeit fährt Jürgen direkt nach Hause.

   _____

d Ich freue mich so sehr auf das Wochenende.

   _____

e Er traf einen alten Freund in der Stadt.

   _____

f Bleibt ihr noch lange auf der Party?

   _____

7 FINDING THE BASIC FORM

If you come across a word in a text that you don't know and you are unable to find it in the dictionary, the chances are that the word is an inflected form. After many headwords the dictionary lists its inflected forms or endings.

Find the basic form for the words in **bold** type.

a Im Finale **gewann** leider die andere Mannschaft. _gewinnen_

b Er **ging** mit seinem besten Freund ins Kino. _____ _____

c Unsere Chefin verfolgt ehrgeizige **Pläne**. _____

d Die Organisatoren **beschlossen**, die Veranstaltung wegen des schlechten Wetters

abzusagen. _____ _____

e Gut geführte Geschäfte **verhalfen** ihm zu Reichtum. _____

8 THE RIGHT MEANING

If while reading a text you find you have to look up an unknown word, do not be satisfied with the first meaning you find. Continue to read through the entries and sense groups until you find the one that fits your text best.

Try to find the right homograph, i.e. its numerical superscription (see also the section on *Homographs,* page 13) and/or the appropriate meaning, i. e. its Arabic numeral, for the words printed in bold type in the following sentences:

a Es ist schon sieben Uhr **durch** und sie wollte um sechs Uhr hier sein. _durch [1] 6._

b Das Hotel gehört zu einer großen **Kette**. _____

c Ich werde **wohl** nicht kommen können. _____

d Er **markierte** wieder mal den Starken. _____

e Die Aktienkurse sind in erheblichem **Maß** gestiegen. _____

f Leute von seinem **Schlag** sind einfach sympathisch! _____

g Mein **Kiefer** schmerzt. _____

9 ABBREVIATIONS

What do the following abbreviations mean?

a Bist du mit dem **ICE** gekommen? _Intercityexpresszug_

b Der **Lkw** wird gerade entladen. _____

c Elke studiert Kunst an der **FH**. _____

d Wir sind bei der **AOK** versichert. _____

e In Tübingen gibt es keinen **NC** für Geschichte. _____

f Beim Sport trage ich immer einen **BH**. _____

10 LOOKING UP IDIOMATIC PHRASES AND EXPRESSIONS

Each idiomatic phrase or expression in the dictionary is listed under a certain headword. The following hierarchical system is used: noun ▸ adjective ▸ adverb ▸ verb ▸ other parts of speech.

This means that a phrase or expression containing one or more nouns can be found under the first noun. If there is no noun in the phrase, it is listed under the first adjective. If neither noun nor adjective are present, an adverb is taken ... and so on. Try it out!

a   zwei Fliegen mit einer Klappe schlagen   *(go to) Fliege* _____

b   sich (für jdn/etw.) ins Zeug legen _____

c   jdn matt setzen _____

d   (bei etw.) seine Hände im Spiel haben _____

e   von oben bis unten _____

f   bei jdm nichts zu melden haben _____

g   jdm unter die Arme greifen _____

h   klein beigeben _____

i   etw./jdn gibt es wie Sand am Meer _____

11 UNDERSTANDING IDIOMS

Some expressions in German can be translated word for word into English. What do the following expressions mean? Look up the words in the dictionary and find the correct translation.

a   das Eis brechen   *break the ice* _____

b   dieselbe Sprache sprechen _____

c   von A bis Z _____

d   eine spitze Zunge haben _____

e   von etw. Wind bekommen _____

12 WORD FAMILIES

Working with a card index can be of great help when you want to learn new words. You can write all those words that belong to the same root or family on to one card.

Look for words in the dictionary that belong to those listed below. Find one noun or more with the same word root.

a   gesund   *Gesundheit* _____

b   erlauben _____

c   erziehen _____

d   unruhig _____

e   bauen _____

f   missverstehen _____

The English-German section

1 NEIGHBOURS

Try to find the words in the dictionary that immediately precede and follow the headword:

a ___authentic___ author ___authority___

b _____ knit _____

c _____ bracket _____

d _____ efficiency _____

e _____ crazy _____

f _____ franchise _____

g _____ classify _____

h _____ half board _____

i _____ draw[1] _____

2 WORD ORDER

Put the words in each line into alphabetical order, using the same sorting system as the dictionary.

a ⑤ landmark ③ land ④ landing ⑦ lamb ② lamp
b ☐ guilt ☐ giggle ☐ guidance ☐ guest ☐ gurgle
c ☐ interview ☐ interest ☐ intersect ☐ interrupt ☐ international(ly)
d ☐ mother ☐ muddy ☐ mush ☐ motif ☐ mother tongue
e ☐ previous ☐ privilege ☐ precision ☐ precise(ly) ☐ precious
f ☐ utmost ☐ utter ☐ uphill ☐ upheaval ☐ utility

3 PLURALS

Find the plural forms for the German translation of the following English headwords:

a library _Bibliotheken_

b horizon _____

c child _____

d computer _____

e bus _____

f hobby _____

g cardinal _____

h fish _____

i virus _____

4 MASCULINE – FEMININE

Most German occupations are not „neutral" – there are different forms for men and women. What are the masculine and feminine forms of the following occupations?

a   baker   _der Bäcker, die Bäckerin_

b   author   _____

c   dentist   _____

d   politician   _____

e   apprentice   _____

f   civil servant   _____

5 WHAT IS THE BEST TRANSLATION?

You want to translate something from English into German using the English–German section of the dictionary. You discover that many headwords don't have just the one translation but several. Which is the right one? The dictionary helps you by giving details of different constructions, differences in meaning, areas of knowledge and example sentences.

Fill in the gaps in the following sentences with the correct translation of the headwords given in brackets. In some cases you will need to add the article or pay close attention to declination and conjugation.

a   Ich habe beschlossen, als Bürgermeister zu _kandidieren_ . *(run)*

b   Wir haben den Termin auf nächste Woche _____ . *(move)*

c   Als ich zum Auto zurückkam, klemmte ein _____ hinter dem Scheibenwischer. *(ticket)*

d   Dieser Verlag hat einen guten _____ . *(name)*

e   Du bist aber ein _____ Kind! *(good)*

f   Bringst du mir _____ Bonbons vom Supermarkt mit? *(bag)*

g   Lesen Sie die Fragen _____ durch, bevor Sie antworten. *(carefully)*

h   Hoffentlich hält das _____ Wetter eine Weile an. *(nice)*

i   Das Projekt muss _____ Ende März abgeschlossen sein. *(by)*

j   Es waren _____ Unterschiede zu erkennen. *(distinct)*

k   In der ersten Reihe sind noch ein paar _____ frei. *(seat)*

6 THE RIGHT CASE

What case is it? Tick the correct box. If you don't know the answer, look up the appropriate construction in the dictionary.

a believe in **sth/sb**: Sie glaubt nicht mehr ☒ an den Weihnachtsmann. *(acc)*

☐ an dem Weihnachtsmann. *(dat)*

b collide with **sth**: Er prallte frontal ☐ auf das andere Auto. *(acc)*

☐ auf dem anderen Auto. *(dat)*

c advise **sb** to do sth: Die Lehrerin hat ☐ ihn geraten, sich mehr anzustrengen. *(acc)*

☐ ihm geraten, sich mehr anzustrengen. *(dat)*

d accuse sb of **sth**: Er wurde ☐ des Diebstahls beschuldigt. *(gen)*

☐ dem Diebstahl beschuldigt. *(dat)*

e pay **sb** a visit: Morgen besuche ich ☐ meinen Schwiegervater. *(acc)*

☐ meinem Schwiegervater. *(dat)*

f sth bends under **sth**: Die Tafel bog sich ☐ unter die Last der vielen Speisen. *(acc)*

☐ unter der Last der vielen Speisen. *(dat)*

g discontinue **sth**: Die Autofirma wird die Produktion ☐ dieses Wagens einstellen. *(gen)*

☐ diesem Wagen einstellen. *(dat)*

7 CLASSROOM ACTIVITY: PREPOSITIONS MEMORY

Form groups of four. Each person is a specialist for one English preposition, e.g. *for*. Each person thinks of four verbs commonly used with that particular preposition (e.g. wait for, thank for, hope for, go for ...) and looks up the German translation. They then write small cards with an example sentence in English, e.g. *I am waiting for the bus.* On another card they write the German translation *(Ich warte auf den Bus.).* All participants place their cards face down on the table. They now play a Memory game trying to find matching pairs by turning over single cards.

During the game, participants learn just how many translations a preposition can generate.

Further practice

1 ABBREVIATIONS

Match each abbreviation to the appropriate word. In the introduction at the front of the dictionary you will find a list of all abbreviations used.

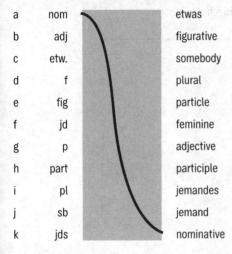

a	nom	etwas
b	adj	figurative
c	etw.	somebody
d	f	plural
e	fig	particle
f	jd	feminine
g	p	adjective
h	part	participle
i	pl	jemandes
j	sb	jemand
k	jds	nominative

2 PRONUNCIATION TRAINING

You really would like to pronounce the words you have just learnt properly? Then you should practise at home using the phonetic transcription to help you. If you are unsure about certain sounds, you can take advantage of our website:

`http://www.hueber.de/woertbuch/phonetik`

Listen to the correct pronunciation and imitate it. Further tips can be found in the introduction at the front of the dictionary under *Phonetics: a short introduction,* page 17.

3 OBTAINING INFORMATION

At the back of your dictionary you will find a list of sources that can be used to obtain further information about Germany, Austria, Switzerland, learning the German language, exams, extra materials and much more. Try out the various websites. Which one fits the following?

a   Sie möchten gern in Deutschland studieren

    und wollen sich über die Prüfung TestDaF informieren.   *www.testdaf.de*

b   Sie möchten sich über das politische System

    in Österreich informieren. _____

c   Sie interessieren sich für die Germanistikabteilung

    an der Universität Erlangen. _____

d Sie möchten wissen, wie viele Kantone es in der

   Schweiz gibt. _____

e Sie suchen jemanden, mit dem Sie auf Deutsch

   per E-Mail kommunizieren können. _____

f Sie möchten etwas über Lehrwerke für Deutsch als

   Fremdsprache herausfinden. _____

Letters and job applications

Private letters

<Sender>	Franz Schulz Neue Straße 5 12345 Musterhausen
<(Place and) Date>	(Musterhausen, den) 20. September 2003
<Form of address/salutation>	Liebe Frau Müller, Lieber Herr Maier, Liebe Andrea, Lieber Hans,
<Body>	...
<Greeting/final salutation> <Signature>	Herzliche Grüße Liebe Grüße Viele Grüße *(Ihr) Franz Schulz* *(Dein/dein) Franz*

   Private letters (letters to family members, friends and acquaintances) may have the sender's name and address at the top, but this is not strictly necessary. A very personal letter is best written by hand.
   The form of address with *Sie* (Frau/Herr + surname) or *Du/du* (first name) is chosen in accordance with your relationship to the recipient. If you are not writing to your family, a child, a fellow student etc., then it is better to use the *Sie* form – unless already agreed otherwise.

Official letters

A job application, for example.

<Sender>	Franz Schulz Neue Straße 5 12345 Musterhausen
<Postal address>	Ingenieurbüro Haller & Partner Herrn Stephan Neubert Berliner Ring 25 54321 Neustadt
<(Place and) Date>	(Musterhausen, den) 20. September 2003
<Reference>	Bewerbung als Bauingenieur
<Address/salutation>	Sehr geehrter Herr Neubert,
<Example text: purpose of letter>	besten Dank für das aufschlussreiche Telefongespräch heute Vormittag. Die Stelle eines Bauingenieurs, die Sie am Wochenende in der Neustädter Zeitung ausgeschrieben haben, interessiert mich sehr.
<Special mention>	Durch die drei Jahre Berufserfahrung bei der Stadtbau GmbH und meine Auslandspraktika fühle ich mich auf die Aufgabe in Ihrem Unternehmen gut vorbereitet und bin gespannt darauf, mich in ein neues Aufgabenfeld einzuarbeiten. Zum 1. Januar 2004 könnte ich bei Ihnen beginnen.
<Interview>	Für ein persönliches Gespräch stehe ich Ihnen natürlich zur Verfügung und freue mich schon darauf.
<Greeting/final salutation> <Signature>	Mit freundlichen Grüßen *Franz Schulz*

In an official letter, only the form of address with *„Sehr geehrte(r) ..."* is adequate. Any other would have the effect of being too familiar. In the first paragraph, the purpose of the letter should be stated. For the final greeting or salutation the form *„Mit freundlichen Grüßen"* is now standard. As an alternative *„Mit besten Grüßen"* may be used.

When applying for a job:

If a telephone number was included in the job advertisement, it is advisable before writing to telephone for further information. Prepare a list of pertinent questions beforehand. You will make a good impression by doing so, showing that you are motivated and able to take the initiative.

Under "Special mention" you should list the particular qualifications that make you suitable for the job and give the head of personnel good reason to invite you for an interview.

Curriculum vitae (CV)

<Name of sender>	Franz Schulz Neue Straße 5 12345 Musterhausen

Lebenslauf

Persönliche Daten

Geburtsdatum	22.11.1976
Geburtsort	Steinberg
Staatsangehörigkeit	deutsch
Familienstand	ledig

<These dates may also be listed in reverse order.>

Bildungsgang

1995	Abitur am Einstein-Gymnasium in Steinberg
1995–1999	Studium Bauingenieur an der TH Musterhausen
1999	Examen und Abschlussarbeit, Gesamtnote gut

Tätigkeiten

Okt.–Dez. 1999	Praktikum bei Bressoni in Mailand
Feb.–Mai 2000	Praktikum bei Dupont et Besson in Lyon
seit Juli 2000	Bauingenieur bei der Stadtbau GmbH

Sprachkenntnisse

Englisch
mündlich und schriftlich gut
Italienisch
mündlich gut, schriftlich ausreichend
Französisch
mündlich und schriftlich befriedigend

<Qualifications relevant to the job; possibly hobbies, if an advantage>

Weitere Qualifikationen

Computer	Fundierte Kenntnisse im Umgang mit 3D-CAD-Systemen
Fortbildungen	Sprachkurse Italienisch und Französisch Schulungen auf dem CAD-System „Architekt 3D" Bauleiter-Kurs bei der Bau-Akademie

<Date> Musterhausen, den 20. September 2003

<Signature> *Franz Schulz*

Numerals

Cardinal numbers

0	null	1000000	eine Million, -en
1	eins	1000000000	**eine Milliarde, -en**
2	zwei	1000000000000	**eine Billion, -en**
3	drei		The number 1, when placed before a noun,
4	vier		is declined like the indefinite article.
5	fünf		
6	sechs		

Ordinal numbers

7	sieben	1. der, die, das **erste**
8	acht	2. zweite
9	neun	3. **dritte**
10	zehn	4. vier**te**
11	elf	5. fünf**te**
12	zwölf	6. sechs**te**
13	dreizehn	7. **siebte**
14	vierzehn	8. ach**te**
15	fünfzehn	9. neun**te**
16	sechzehn	10. zehn**te**
17	siebzehn	11. elf**te**
18	achtzehn	19. neunzehn**te**
19	neunzehn	20. zwanzigste
20	zwanzig	21. einundzwanzig**ste**
21	einundzwanzig	99. neunundneunzig**ste**
22	zweiundzwanzig	100. hundertste
23	dreiundzwanzig	101. hundert**erste**
24	vierundzwanzig	1000. tausend**ste**
25	fünfundzwanzig	1001. tausend**erste**
26	sechsundzwanzig	Ordinal numbers are declined like adjec-
27	siebenundzwanzig	tives.
28	achtundzwanzig	

Fractions

29	neunundzwanzig	
30	dreißig	½ ein halb
40	vierzig	⅓ ein drittel
50	fünfzig	¼ ein viertel
60	sechzig	⅛ ein achtel
70	siebzig	⅔ zwei drittel
80	achtzig	¾ drei viertel
90	neunzig	1½ eineinhalb/anderthalb
100	(ein)hundert	3⅓ dreieindrittel
101	(ein)hunderteins	0,3 null Komma drei
110	(ein)hundertzehn	1,25 eins (Komma) fünfundzwanzig
1000	(ein)tausend	
2000	zweitausend	
10000	zehntausend	
100000	(ein)hunderttausend	

Weights and measures

Temperatures

20 °C	20 Grad (Celsius)
32 °F	32 Grad Fahrenheit
−10°	minus zehn Grad/zehn Grad unter Null
+4°	plus vier Grad/vier Grad über Null

CONVERSION C–F:

$C = (F − 32) \times 5 \div 9$

$F = (C \times 9 \div 5) + 32$

Length

1 mm	ein Millimeter
1 cm	ein Zentimeter
1 m	ein Meter
1,92 m	ein Meter zweiundneunzig/eins zweiundneunzig
1 km	ein Kilometer
50 km/h	fünfzig Kilometer pro Stunde/Stundenkilometer

Area

1 m²	ein Quadratmeter
1 a	ein Ar (= 100 m²)
1 ha	ein Hektar (= 10000 m²)
1 km²	ein Quadratkilometer

Volume

1 cm³	ein Kubikzentimeter
1 m³	ein Kubikmeter
1 ml	ein Milliliter (= 0,01 l)
1 cl	ein Zentiliter (= 0,1 l)
1 l	ein Liter
1 hl	ein Hektoliter (= 100 l)

Weight

1 g	ein Gramm
1 Pfd.	ein Pfund (= 500 g)
1 kg	ein Kilogramm
1 Ztr.	ein Zentner (in Germany = 50 kg)
1 q	ein Zentner (in Austria/Switzerland = 100 kg)
1 dz	ein Doppelzentner (in Germany = 100 kg)
1 t	eine Tonne (= 1000 kg)

Time

	formal	*informal*
9.05 Uhr	neun Uhr fünf	fünf nach neun
21.05 Uhr	einundzwanzig Uhr fünf	
9.15 Uhr	neun Uhr fünfzehn	Viertel nach neun
21.15 Uhr	einundzwanzig Uhr fünfzehn	viertel zehn
9.20 Uhr	neun Uhr zwanzig	zwanzig nach neun
21.20 Uhr	einundzwanzig Uhr zwanzig	
9.30 Uhr	neun Uhr dreißig	halb zehn
21.30 Uhr	einundzwanzig Uhr dreißig	
9.40 Uhr	neun Uhr vierzig	zwanzig vor zehn
21.40 Uhr	einundzwanzig Uhr vierzig	zehn nach halb zehn
9.45 Uhr	neun Uhr fünfundvierzig	Viertel vor zehn
21.45 Uhr	einundzwanzig Uhr fünfundvierzig	dreiviertel zehn
9.55 Uhr	neun Uhr fünfundfünfzig	fünf vor zehn
21.55 Uhr	einundzwanzig Uhr fünfundfünfzig	
12.00 Uhr	zwölf Uhr (Mittag)	
24.00 Uhr	vierundzwanzig Uhr (Mitternacht)	(um) zwölf
0.00 Uhr	null Uhr (Mitternacht)	

Geht die Uhr richtig? Es ist zehn Uhr.
Die Uhr geht nach.
Die Uhr geht (genau) richtig.
Die Uhr geht vor.
die Sekunde, -n
die Minute, -n
die Stunde, -n

Grammatical terminology

abbreviation	A letter or combination of letters forming a shortened version of a word (z. B. = zum Beispiel, Pkw = Personenkraftwagen, g = Gramm).
accusative	See *case.*
adjectival passive	A form of the passive with the conjugated form of *sein* and the past participle of the main verb. This particular form indicates a state: *Das Auto ist repariert und die Rechnung ist schon bezahlt.*
adjective	Adjectives describe the characteristics or qualities of a person, thing or event (*der alte Mann, das hellgrüne Auto, die korrekte Darstellung*). Adjectives are declined (see page 525).
adverb	Adverbs are not declined. They accompany a main verb (*Sie arbeitet schnell:* main verb in position 2, adverb after the verb. *Er lässt dich herzlich grüßen:* main verb at the end, adverb before the verb) or an adjective (*meine schnell arbeitende Kollegin*).
antonym	A word with the opposite meaning, e.g. *gut* ⊕ *schlecht.*
apposition	A noun or phrase in apposition follows the noun to which it belongs, separated by commas. As a rule it has the same case as the noun: *Johannes Gutenberg, der Erfinder des Buchdrucks mit beweglichen Lettern, starb 1468 in Mainz.*
article	The article in German indicates the gender (masculine: *der Stift,* feminine: *die Seite,* neuter: *das Buch*), number (singular: *der Vater,* plural: *die Väter*) and case (nominative: *der Mann,* accusative: *den Mann,* dative: *dem Mann,* genitive: *des Mannes*) of the following noun. There are the following kinds of article:

- definite article: *der Stift, die Seite, das Buch*
- demonstrative article: *dieser Stift, diese Seite, dieses Buch*
- indefinite article: *ein Stift, eine Seite, ein Buch*
- negative article: *kein Stift, keine Seite, kein Buch*
- possessive article: *mein Stift, meine Seite, mein Buch*

For the declination of the article see page 521.

attribute	An attributive adjective serves to describe or define a noun and is placed before it (*der schönste Tag*). An attributive genitive, on the other hand, follows the noun (*der schönste Tag meines Lebens*).
auxiliary verb	Haben: *Ich habe ihn heute noch nicht gesehen.* Sein: *Sie sind gestern in den Urlaub gefahren.* Werden: *Ich werde ihn morgen treffen. Das Auto wird repariert.*
cardinal numbers	Cardinal numbers indicate a particular number: *zwei Autos.* See also *numerals.*
case	In German there are four cases: nominative, accusative, dative and genitive. The genitive is used for the most part attributively and indicates possession or that something belongs to something or someone else (*die Werkstatt meiner Schwester*). Only very few verbs are followed by the genitive. If a verb can be followed by both accusative and dative cases, the accusative is often the object of the action and the dative its destination or goal: *Den Blumenstrauß schenkt er seiner Freundin.* The subject is in the nominative case.
causal	Explains the reason for something: *Wir bleiben heute zu Hause, weil es regnet.*

comparative	The second stage in the comparison of adjectives: schön (positive), schöner (comparative), der/die/das schönste/am schönsten (superlative).
conditional	Expresses a condition: Ich lese den Artikel, falls ich Zeit habe.
conjugation	Changes to the verb in accordance with the grammatical person: ich gehe, du gehst, er geht, wir gehen etc.
conjunction	A word that connects two main clauses or a main clause and a subordinate clause: Sie kommt morgen vorbei und bringt die Bücher mit. Ich kann nicht mitkommen, weil ich noch einen Arzttermin habe.
consecutive	Indicates order or sequence: Ich war so nervös, dass ich zitterte.
dative	See *case.*
declination	Refers to changes that occur with articles, adjectives and nouns according to case, gender and number.
demonstrative pronoun	See *pronoun.*
determiner	A word placed in front of a noun and not preceded by an article. Examples are *the, a, this, those, any, some;* most of their German counterparts are declined just like German adjectives.
diphthong	A sound made up of two vowels: *au, äu, ei* etc.
direct speech	Verbatim report of a statement indicated by quotation marks: Er meinte: „Ich habe morgen leider keine Zeit".
ending	Endings are determined by the conjugation of verbs (infinitive: geh-en, 3. person singular: er geh-t), the declination of adjectives (basic form: schön, nominative masculine: *der schön-e Mann, ein schön-er Mann*) and the declination of nouns (genitive: *des Mann-es,* plural: *Tisch-e*).
feminine	See *gender.*
future	See *tenses.*
gender	In German there are three genders – masculine: der Mond, feminine: die Sonne, neuter: das Wasser. In the singular, gender and case determine the required declination. In the plural no distinction is made between the genders.
genitive	See *case.*
imperative	Used to form a request or command. *Sie*-form: Bringen Sie mir doch bitte die Zeitschrift mit. *Du*-form: Räum jetzt endlich dein Zimmer auf! In an imperative sentence the verb comes at the beginning. The word *bitte,* however, may be placed before it: Bitte mach das Fenster zu.
imperfect tense	See *tenses.*
impersonal	The impersonal pronoun is *es.* It stands as a substitute in a sentence whenever the subject is unclear or non-existant: Es regnet. Impersonal verbs are used to describe the weather or changes in the time or the seasons. They too have no proper subject: blitzen, donnern etc.
indicative	See *mood.*
indirect speech	Non-verbatim report of a statement. In indirect speech use is usually made of the present subjunctive: Gestern sagte er zu mir, er habe keine Zeit.
infinitive	Basic form of a verb: lachen, stehen
infinitive construction	Über dieses Thema zu sprechen, ist mir unangenehm. Er ist stolz darauf, den Wettbewerb gewonnen zu haben. Er fuhr in die Stadt, um seine Freunde zu treffen.
interjection	An interjection gives expression to feelings: Hurra! Au!
intransitive	When a verb does not take an accusative object, it is called intransitive. Some verbs are always intransitive (Das Auto *steht* in der Garage.); other

verbs can be used either intransitively or transitively (Er kann nicht zum Telefon kommen, weil er gerade *lernt.*/Er *lernt* Vokabeln).

main clause   In the main clause the conjugated verb is placed in position 2, another part of the verb may come at the end: Morgen Abend möchte ich schwimmen gehen.

masculine   See *gender.*

modal verb   *Dürfen, können, lassen, müssen, sollen, wollen.* A modal verb is used in combination with a main verb to express possibility, need, permission, ability, etc. An example for ability: Er kann gut schwimmen.

mood   Grammatical concept to which both the *indicative* (i.e. the statement is true in reality) and the subjunctive belong (subjunctive I: the statement is neutral, i.e. the speaker neither confirms nor denies the truth or reality of the statement; subjunctive II: the statement does not correspond with reality). Indicative: Ich bin nicht reich und kann mir keine Kunstwerke leisten. Subjunctive I: Er sagt, er sei nicht reich und könne sich keine Kunstwerke leisten. Subjunctive II: Wenn ich reich wäre, würde ich mir einen Picasso kaufen. See also subjunctive.

morpheme   The smallest meaningful unit in a language. A morpheme can be a complete word: *Dieb, der* or *ein.* Alternatively, it may be a part of a word: *Mann-* and *-schaft* in *Mannschaft.*

neuter   See *gender.*

nominative   See *case.*

noun   All nouns in German are written with intitial capital letters. They are declined and usually appear together with articles: der Löffel, ein Messer, die Gabel.

number   Grammatical concept to which s*ingular* and *plural* belong.

numerals   Cardinal numbers indicate a certain number (zwei Autos). Ordinal numbers indicate a position within a sequence or order (der dritte Versuch). Indefinite numerals indicate an inexact or non-definable number (viele Leute).

object   A noun (and the words that accompany it) or pronoun in a clause with a specific function. It represents a person, thing or event at whom or which the action expressed by the verb is directed. In the following statement the verb *geben* takes an indirect object (dative – to whom is something being given?) and a direct object (accusative – what is being given?): Sie gibt ihrem Mann heute keinen Kuss, weil sie Streit mit ihm hat.

ordinal numbers Ordinal numbers indicate a particular position within an order or sequence (der dritte Versuch). See also *numerals.*

participles   Forms of a verb used as adjectives and adverbs and in forming the perfect, past perfect tenses and the passive. Present participle: abfahrend – der abfahrende Zug; schweigend – Er stand schweigend daneben. Past participle: abgefahren – der abgefahrene Zug, Der Zug ist abgefahren; geschwiegen – Er hat geschwiegen. The present participle is always regular (infinitive + d).

particle   A non-declinable word adding colour or emphasis to a statement: Das habe ich dir doch schon gestern gesagt. (= expressing impatience: „You should have remembered").

passive   The passive is formed with the appropriate form of the verb *werden* together with the past participle (Partizip II) of the main verb. The passive emphasizes the action rather than the person, either because the person is unknown or because in the context he or she is unimportant: Kaspar Hauser wurde 1833 in Ansbach ermordet.

past perfect	See *tenses*.
perfect	See *tenses*.
personal pronouns	Ich, du, er etc. See *pronouns*.
plural	A number indicating two or more people, things or events: die Dozentinnen, die Häuser, die Lügen.
possessive pronouns	Mein, dein, sein etc. See *pronouns*.
prefix	An additional intitial syllable at the beginning of a verb (ver-gehen), a noun (Un-abhängigkeit) or an adjective (il-legal).
preposition	Prepositions can be divided into groups: prepositions of place (Das Auto steht auf der Straße. Er wohnt in Bremen.), prepositions of time (Seit zwei Tagen ist sie wieder gesund. Bis morgen muss ich fertig sein.), prepositions of cause (Wegen der Zeitverschiebung kann sie nur nachts mit ihm telefonieren. Aus Langeweile sortiert er seine Bücher neu.), prepositions of manner (Dieses Schnitzel schmeckt, als wäre es aus Gummi. Ich fahre mit dem Zug.), prepositions of concession (Trotz des schlechten Wetters gehe ich zu Fuß.) and so-called final prepositions (Das ist für mich. Ich brauche das zum Malen.) Prepositions dictate the case of the noun that follows.
present tense	See *tenses*.
pronouns	Words that stand in the place of nouns:

- personal pronouns: Er (= Herr Schulze) ist heute nicht im Büro.
- demonstrative pronouns: Der/Dieser (= der grüne Pullover) gefällt mir besonders gut.
- possessive pronouns: Ich fahre heute das Auto meiner Frau, meines (= mein Auto) ist in der Werkstatt.
- reflexive pronouns: Das kann ich mir nicht vorstellen.
- relative pronouns: In einem berühmten Märchen kommt ein Wolf vor, der sich als Großmutter verkleidet. Relative pronouns introduce a subordinate clause. Gender and number are dictated by the noun to which they refer, case is governed by the verb in the relative clause.

questions	Direct yes/no questions: Hast du morgen Zeit? Direct when/where questions: Wann kommst du zurück? Indirect questions: Er fragte mich, ob ich Zeit habe/wann ich zurückkomme. In direct questions the verb comes first and the sentence ends with a question mark. Indirect questions are subordinate clauses and in the case of yes/no questions introduced by the word *ob*, in the case of when/where questions with the appropriate question word. There is no question mark.
reflexive	All reflexive verbs have an obligatory reflexive pronoun (see *pronouns*) in the accusative or dative. The reflexive pronoun and the subject of the sentence are identical: Im Urlaub möchte ich mich vor allem erholen.
relative clause	A subordinate clause that describes the noun to which it refers in more detail. Relative clauses are introduced by relative pronouns (see *pronouns*): In einem berühmten Märchen kommt ein Wolf vor, der sich als Großmutter verkleidet hat.
separable	Certain verbs consist of a main stem preceded by a preposition, adverb etc. called a prefix. When these verbs are conjugated, some tenses require the prefix to be separated from the stem. The verb is said to be separable. The separated prefix is placed at the end of the main clause as a second part of the verb: Mittwochabends geht sie immer mit ihren Freundinnen aus.
singular	A number indicating just one single person, thing or event: der Dozent, ein Haus, die Lüge.

subject A noun (and the words that accompany it) or pronoun in a clause with a specific function. It represents a person, thing or event from whom or which the action expressed by the verb originates. The subject takes the nominative case: Unser Haus soll im Herbst fertig werden. Kannst du morgen kommen? Impersonal verbs require the subject *es*: Es hat geschneit. See also impersonal.

subjunctive A form of the verb (mood) indicating how close a statement is to reality. The present subjunctive or subjunctive I *(Konjunktiv I)* is used for indirect speech: Er sagt, er habe morgen keine Zeit. This particular form is neutral and suggests nothing about whether the statement is true or not. The past subjunctive or subjunctive II *(Konjunktiv II)* is used in unreal conditional clauses: Wenn er Zeit hätte, würde er kommen. It indicates that the statement does not reflect reality.

suffix Additional syllable added to the end of a noun (Lieb-ling) or adjective (schrift-lich).

subordinate clause In a subordinate clause the conjugated verb comes at the end: ..., weil sie sich gestern ein neues Auto gekauft hat. As a rule subordinate clauses are dependent on main clauses and do not stand alone.

superlative Third stage in the comparison of adjectives: schön (positive), schöner (comparative), der/die/das schönste/am schönsten (superlative).

synonym A word with the same meaning, e.g. Zimmer/Raum.

temporal Verbs have several tenses. In German, the present tense *(Präsens)* indicates as a rule the present state of affairs and things of a permanent or timeless quality (Die Erde *ist* keine Scheibe). In combination with an indication of time it is used to refer to the future (*Nächsten Monat fahre ich nach Hamburg*). The preterite (*Präteritum:* Letztes Jahr *schneite* es im November nicht.) and the perfect tense (*Perfekt:* Es *hat geschneit.*) are both past tenses. The difference between them is mainly of a stylistic nature. In spoken German, the *Perfekt* is preferred. The past perfect tense *(Plusquamperfekt)* indicates a period of time before that described by the preterite or perfect tense (Nachdem das Gebäude fertig *geworden war,* stand es noch ein halbes Jahr leer.). The simple future tense *(Futur I)* is used to voice plans, resolutions, predictions, promises, and warnings for the time ahead (Im Mai *werden wir* in den Urlaub *fahren.*); the future perfect tense *(Futur II)* refers to an event or action that will have been completed in the future (Morgen Abend *werde* ich das fertig *gestellt haben.*). Instead of the simple future, the present tense is often used, and the perfect tense is often used instead of the future perfect.

transitive When a verb takes an accusative object, it is called transitive. Some verbs are always transitive (Ich *bitte dich* um deine Unterstützung.); other verbs can be used either transitively or intransitively (Ich *trinke keinen Alkohol.* Ich *trinke* schon lange nicht mehr).

Umlaut Ä, ö, ü.

verb The basic form is the infinitive (sehen). It is conjugated according to person and tense: du siehst, er sah, sie hat gesehen.

vowels A, e, i, o, u, ä, ö, ü.

A

a, A [noun] **1.** *(letter)* a, A [aː] das <–(s), –(s)> ◊ *Dieses Wort wird mit einem kleinen a/großen A geschrieben.* ♦ *A wie Anton* **2.** MUS A, a A [aː] das <–(s), –(s)> ◊ *Sie spielte ein A.* A minor a-Moll ['aːmɔl] A major A-Dur ['aːduːɐ̯]

a [det] **1.** ein [aɛn] eine ['aɛnə] ◊ *Ein Mann steigt aus dem Auto.* ♦ *Eine Frau wollte dich heute sprechen.* ♦ *Ein Kind fehlt heute im Unterricht.* ♦ *Kennst du eine Frau Müller?* → **ein²** **2.** pro [proː] ◊ *Ich bekomme 20 Anrufe pro Tag.* ♦ *11 Euro pro Stunde*

A¹ [noun] *(grade)* Eins [aɛns] die <–, –en> ◊ *Ich habe eine Eins bekommen.* box@ **Note**

A² *(road classification)* B [beː] ◊ *Stau auf der B 417*

AA (abbr of Alcoholics Anonymous) **1.** AA [a|'aː] *only pl* die ◊ *Sie geht zu den AA.* **2.** (abbr of Automobile Association) *britischer Autofahrerverein, ähnlich dem ADAC*

abandon [verb] **1.** *(leave helpless)* aussetzen ['aɔsztsn̩] +haben ◊ *Zur Urlaubszeit werden viele Tiere ausgesetzt.* **2.** *(a plan, project)* aufgeben ['aɔfgeːbm̩] <gibt auf, gab auf, hat aufgegeben> **3.** *(a place)* verlassen [fɛ'lasn̩] <verlässt, verließ, hat verlassen> ◊ *ein verlassenes Dorf* **4.** *(an object)* zurücklassen [tsu'rʏklasn̩] <lässt zurück, ließ zurück, hat zurückgelassen> ◊ *ein am Tatort zurückgelassenes Auto*

abbey [noun] Abtei [ap'taɛ] die <–, –en>

abbreviate [verb] abkürzen ['apkʏɐ̯tsn̩] +haben ◊ *In der Umgangssprache wird 'Abitur' zu 'Abi' abgekürzt.*

abbreviation [noun] Abkürzung ['apkʏɐ̯tsʊŋ] die <–, –en>

abduct [verb] entführen [ɛnt'fyːrən] <entführt, entführte, hat entführt> ◊ *Er wurde im Irak entführt.*

abduction [noun] Entführung [ɛnt'fyːrʊŋ] die <–, –en> ◊ *die Entführung eines Touristen*

ability [noun] Fähigkeit ['fɛːɪçkaɛt] die <–, –en> ◊ *Sie besitzt die Fähigkeit zu improvisieren.* ♦ *Ihre Fähigkeit als Rednerin steht außer Frage.*

able [adj] *(capable)* fähig ['fɛːɪç] ◊ *Er ist nicht einmal fähig, diese Maschine zu bedienen.; (having the possibility)* be able to do sth etw. tun können ['tuːn kœnən] <kann, konnte, hat können> ◊ *Leider konnte ich gestern nicht kommen.*

abnormal(ly) [adj, adv] **1.** *(due to an illness)* krankhaft ['kraŋkhaft] <krankhafter, am krankhaftesten> seldom comp/superl ◊ *eine krankhafte Störung des Essverhaltens* ♦ *Ein so hoher Blutzuckerwert gilt als krankhaft.* **2.** *(deviating from the ordinary)* anormal ['anɔ'maːl] seldom comp/superl ◊ *sich anormal verhalten*

abolish [verb] abschaffen ['apʃafn̩] +haben ◊ *Die Wehrpflicht soll abgeschafft werden.*

abolition [noun] Abschaffung ['apʃafʊŋ] die <–, –en> most sing ◊ *die Abschaffung der Todesstrafe*

abominable(-ably) [adj, adv] abscheulich [ap'ʃɔɪlɪç] ◊ *Du bist ein abscheulicher Schuft!* ♦ *Die Hitze war abscheulich.* ♦ *Er hat sich abscheulich aufgeführt.*

abortion [noun] Abtreibung ['aptraɛbʊŋ] die <–, –en>

about¹ [adv] **1.** *(approximately)* etwa ['ɛtvaː] ◊ *In Deutschland leben etwa 80 Millionen Menschen.; (with an expression of time)* (at/round) about gegen ['geːgn̩] +acc ◊ *Ich bin gegen drei Uhr nach Hause gekommen.* **2.** *(all around)* umher [ʊm'heːɐ̯] ◊ *Die Trümmer lagen weit umher verstreut.* **3.** *(expressing aimlessness, uncertainty, indecision, hesitation)* umher... [ʊm'heːɐ̯] walk about umherlaufen [ʊm'heːɐ̯laɔfn̩] <läuft umher, lief umher, ist umhergelaufen> ◊ *Er lief ziellos umher.* drive about umherfahren [ʊm'heːɐ̯faːrən] <fährt umher, fuhr umher, ist umhergefahren> ◊ *Sie fährt seit Stunden in der Stadt umher.; (expressing carelessness)* leave sth lying about etw. herumliegen lassen [hɛ'rʊmliːgn̩ lasn̩] <lässt, ließ, hat lassen> ◊ *Musst du immer deine Sachen herumliegen lassen?* **4.** *(almost, probably)* (just) about so ziemlich [zoː 'tsiːmlɪç] <Er hasst so ziemlich jeden.* ♦ *Sie ist so ziemlich im selben Alter wie du.* This is about as good as it gets. Besser geht's nicht.

⊚ be about da sein be about to do sth im Begriff sein, etw. zu tun

> 'About' may occur in phrasal verbs like 'come about' which have their own entries in the dictionary.

about² [prep] **1.** *(concerning sb/sth, dealing with sb/sth)* über ['yːbɐ] +acc ◊ *ein Buch über die Alpen* ♦ *Was hat er über mich gesagt?; (with certain verbs or idioms)* um [ʊm] +acc worry about sb sich um jdn Sorgen machen forget all about sb/sth jdn/etw. vollkommen vergessen [fɔl'kɔmən fɛ'gɛsn̩] <vergisst, vergaß, hat vergessen>; (because of)* wegen ['veːgn̩] sing nouns without article or attribute are not declined when following this prep, otherwise +gen ◊ *Ich rufe wegen Ihrer Anzeige an.* ♦ *wegen Krankheit fehlen* **2.** *(describing a characteristic)* an [an] +dat ◊ *Was ist das Wichtigste an einem Wörterbuch?* ♦ *Das gefällt mir so an dir!* **3.** *(with certain verbs: indicating undirected movement within a defined space)* umher... [ʊm'heːɐ̯] rush about sth irgendwo umhereilen [ʊm'heːɐ̯aɛlən] +sein ◊ *Er eilte im Zimmer umher.* wander about sth irgendwo umherwandeln [ʊm'heːɐ̯vandl̩n] +sein ◊ *Ziellos wandelte sie im Haus umher.*

⊚ do sth about sth etw. gegen etw. tun sth is about sth bei etw. geht es um etw. while you're about it wo du gerade dabei bist, wo Sie gerade dabei sind

above¹ [adj] *(mentioned before)* oben genannt [ˌoːbm̩ gə'nant] no comp/superl ◊ *Schreiben Sie an die oben genannte Adresse.*

above² [adv] **1.** *(higher up)* oben ['oːbm̩] ◊ *wie bereits oben erwähnt* ♦ *etw. von oben betrachten* **2.** *(with figures)* darüber [da'ryːbɐ] ◊ *Schiffe mit einer Länge von 60 Metern und darüber*

above³ [prep] **1.** *(higher than sb/sth)* über ['yːbɐ] with acc when expressing motion towards a place, with dat when there is no or undirected motion ◊ *Das Bild*

hängt über dem Sofa. ♦ *Sie hängte das Bild über das Sofa.* ♦ *Temperaturen über dem Gefrierpunkt* **2.** *(more than)* value sth above sth etw. mehr schätzen als etw. [meːɐ̯ ˈʃɛtsn̩ als] +haben love sth above anything else etw. über alles lieben [ˈyːbɐ ˈaləs ˈliːbm̩] +haben; *(most of all)* above all else vor allem [foːɐ̯ ˈaləm] ◊ *Vor allem musst du jetzt Ruhe bewahren.* ⊛ be above doing sth **1.** *(too good to do sth)* über etw. stehen **2.** *(too proud to do sth)* sich zu gut sein für etw. not be above sth sich [dat] für etw. nicht zu gut sein

abridge [verb] kürzen [ˈkʏʳtsn̩] +haben

abroad [adv] *(with motion)* ins Ausland [ɪns ˈaʊ̯slant] ◊ *ins Ausland fahren; (without motion)* im Ausland [ɪm ˈaʊ̯slant] ◊ *im Ausland leben*

abrupt(ly) [adj, adv] **1.** *(sudden)* plötzlich [ˈplœtslɪç] ◊ *Das Ende war etwas plötzlich.* ♦ *ein plötzlicher Wechsel* ♦ *plötzlich zurücktreten* **2.** *(brusque)* schroff [ʃrɔf] ◊ *eine schroffe Antwort* ♦ *jdn schroff behandeln* be abrupt with sb schroff zu jdm sein

absence [noun] **1.** *(non-presence)* Abwesenheit [ˈapveːznhaɪ̯t] die <-, -en> ◊ *In Abwesenheit des Direktors trifft sie die Entscheidungen.* ♦ *Schalten Sie bitte bei längerer Abwesenheit die Alarmanlage ein.; (from school, work)* Fehlzeit [ˈfeːltsaɪ̯t] die <-, -en> **2.** *(lack)* Fehlen [ˈfeːlən] das <-s> no pl ◊ *Die Firma beklagte das Fehlen von ausgebildeten Spezialisten.*

absent [adj] **1.** *(not present)* fehlend [ˈfeːlənt] only before ns ◊ *ein fehlender Schüler* be absent fehlen [ˈfeːlən] +haben ◊ *ohne Entschuldigung fehlen* be absent from school in der Schule fehlen sth is absent from sth einer Sache [gen] fehlt etw. **2.** *(distracted)* abwesend [ˈapveːznt] no comp/superl ◊ *Er wirkte abwesend.* ♦ *ein abwesender Gesichtsausdruck*

absent-minded(ly) [adj, adv] *(distracted)* geistesabwesend [ˈgaɪ̯stəsʔapveːznt] ◊ *einen geistesabwesenden Blick haben* ♦ *Sie sah mich geistesabwesend an.; (likely to forget things)* zerstreut [tsɛˈʃtrɔɪ̯t] <zerstreuter, am zerstreutesten> ◊ *ein zerstreuter Professor* ♦ *Sie ist manchmal etwas zerstreut.*

absolute [adj] **1.** *(sovereign, beginner)* absolut [apzoˈluːt] no comp/superl, only before ns ◊ *Sie war eine absolute Anfängerin.* **2.** *(impudence etc.)* ausgesprochen [ˈaʊ̯sgəʃprɔxn̩] no comp/superl, only before ns ◊ *Das ist eine ausgesprochene Frechheit!*

absolutely [adv] **1.** *(totally)* absolut [apzoˈluːt] no comp/superl *(emph)* ◊ *Dieser PC ist absolut veraltet.* ♦ *Das ist absolut unmöglich.* **2.** *(under all circumstances)* unbedingt [ˈʊnbədɪŋt] no comp/superl ◊ *Er wollte unbedingt gewinnen.* ♦ *Ist das denn unbedingt nötig?* ⊛ absolutely not auf gar keinen Fall

absorb [verb] **1.** *(a chemical; food, heat, an idea, information)* aufnehmen [ˈaʊ̯fneːmən] <nimmt auf, nahm auf, hat aufgenommen> ◊ *mit der Nahrung zahlreiche Schadstoffe aufnehmen* ♦ *Ich kann keine Informationen mehr aufnehmen.* sth is absorbed into sth etw. wird von etw. aufgenommen ◊ *Der Wirkstoff wurde schnell vom Blutkreislauf aufgenommen.; (a radar signal, sound, light, radiation)* absorbieren [apzɔʳˈbiːrən] <absorbiert, absorbierte, hat absorbiert> *(tech)* ◊ *Schwarze Farbe absorbiert Licht.* **2.** *(a group of people)* integrieren [ɪnteˈgriːrən] <integriert, integ-

rierte, hat integriert> ◊ *Die Einwanderer sind in die Bevölkerung integriert worden.* **3.** *(take all your attention)* absorb sb jdn im Bann halten [ɪm ˈban haltn̩] <hält, hielt, hat gehalten> **4.** *(an impact)* dämpfen [ˈdɛmpfn̩] +haben ◊ *Der Aufprall wurde durch den Schnee gedämpft.* **5.** *(a price increase, additional costs)* auffangen [ˈaʊ̯ffaŋən] <fängt auf, fing auf, hat aufgefangen> ◊ *Zusatzkosten auffangen* **6.** *(use up)* verschlingen [fɛˈʃlɪŋən] <verschlingt, verschlang, hat verschlungen> ◊ *Die Energiekosten verschlingen den Großteil des Budgets.*

absorbed → absorb [adj] be absorbed in sth in etw. [acc] vertieft sein [ɪn … feˈtiːft tsaɛ̯n] no comp/superl ◊ *Sie war so in ihre Lektüre vertieft, dass sie mich nicht kommen hörte.* He was completely absorbed. Er war ganz in Gedanken versunken.

absorption [noun] **1.** *(food, drink)* Aufnahme [ˈaʊ̯fnaːmə] die <-, -n> ◊ *die Aufnahme von Nahrung und Flüssigkeit durch den Körper* **2.** *(ethnic minorities)* Integration [ɪntegraˈtsɪ̯oːn] die <-, -en> most sing ◊ *die Integration von Ausländern in die deutsche Gesellschaft* **3.** *(deep concentration)* Selbstvergessenheit [ˈzɛlpstfɐˌgɛsnhaɪ̯t] die <-> no pl ◊ *Momente der Selbstvergessenheit*

abstract(ly) [adj, adv] abstrakt [apˈstrakt] <abstrakter, am abstraktesten> ◊ *abstrakte Malerei* ♦ *Diese Formulierung ist zu abstrakt.* ♦ *abstrakt denken*

absurd [adj] absurd [apˈzʊʳt] <absurder, am absurdesten> *(lofty)* ◊ *Das ist eine völlig absurde Argumentation!* ♦ *Das ist doch absurd, was Sie da sagen!*

abundance [noun] Fülle [ˈfʏlə] die <-> no pl ◊ *Zu diesem Thema gibt es eine Fülle von Material.* ⊛ in abundance in Hülle und Fülle

abundant(ly) [adj] reichlich [ˈraɛ̯çlɪç] when used as an adj, only before ns ◊ *eine reichliche Auswahl* sth is abundant somewhere etw. ist irgendwo reichlich vorhanden Food was abundant. Es gab reichlich zu essen.; *(wealth, resources)* groß [groːs] <größer, am größten> ◊ *großer Reichtum* have an abundant supply of sth etw. in großen Mengen haben an abundant supply of oil große Ölvorkommen

abuse¹ [noun] **1.** *(power, children)* Missbrauch [ˈmɪsbraʊ̯x] der <-(e)s, Missbräuche> ◊ *der Missbrauch von Macht und Einfluss* ♦ *der sexuelle Missbrauch von Kindern* abuse of drugs Medikamentenmissbrauch [medikaˈmɛntn̩mɪsbraʊ̯x] **2.** *(offensive words)* Beschimpfungen [bəˈʃɪmpfʊŋən] die <-> pl ◊ *wüste Beschimpfungen* give sb abuse jdn beschimpfen [bəˈʃɪmpfn̩] <beschimpft, beschimpfte, hat beschimpft>

abuse² [verb] **1.** *(a child, power)* missbrauchen [mɪsˈbraʊ̯xn̩] <missbraucht, missbrauchte, hat missbraucht> ◊ *Sie hat ihre Macht missbraucht.* abuse drugs Drogen nehmen [ˈdroːgn̩ neːmən] <nimmt, nahm, hat genommen> **2.** *(use offensive words)* beschimpfen [bəˈʃɪmpfn̩] <beschimpft, beschimpfte, hat beschimpft> ◊ *Er beschimpfte sie öffentlich.*

abusive [adj] **1.** *(verbally)* beleidigend [bəˈlaɪ̯dɪɡn̩t] ◊ *eine beleidigende Äußerung* ♦ *Werden Sie bitte nicht beleidigend!* **2.** *(violent)* gewalttätig [ɡəˈvalttɛːtɪç] ◊ *ein gewalttätiger Ehemann* get abusive gewalttätig werden [ɡəˈvalttɛːtɪç veːɐ̯dn̩] +sein

abyss [noun] Abgrund [ˈapɡrʊnt] der <-(e)s, Abgründe> ◊ *Sie ist in einen Abgrund gestürzt.* ♦ *die Abgründe der Seele*

academic¹ [noun] **1.** *(teacher)* Dozent [doˈtsɛnt] der

<-en, -en> ♀Dozentin [do'tsɛntɪn] die <-, -nen> ◊ *Er ist Dozent von Beruf.* ♦ *Wer ist hier die Dozentin für Medienwissenschaft?* **2.** *(working in research)* Wissenschaftler ['vɪsn̩ʃaftlɐ] der <-s, -> ♀Wissenschaftlerin ['vɪsn̩ʃaftlərɪn] die <-, -nen> ◊ *Er ist ein anerkannter Wissenschaftler.* ♦ *Sie arbeitet als Wissenschaftlerin an der Universität.*

academic² [adj] **1.** *(title, career, discussion)* akademisch [aka'de:mɪʃ] no comp/superl ◊ *Diese Diskussion ist rein akademisch.* **2.** *(intellectual)* intellektuell [ɪntɛlɛktu|'ɛl] ◊ *Sie ist mir zu intellektuell.* ♦ *ein intellektueller Typ*

academically [adv] **1.** *(at school)* sb performs well/poorly academically jds schulische Leistungen sind gut/schwach [ʃuːlɪʃə ˌlaɪstʊŋən zɪnt 'guːt/'ʃvax]; *(at university)* jds akademische Leistungen sind gut/schwach [aka,deːmɪʃə ˌlaɪstʊŋən zɪnt 'guːt/'ʃvax] struggle academically sich mit dem Lernen schwer tun [mɪt deːm ˌlɛʁnən 'ʃveːɐ̯ tuːn] <tut sich, tat sich, hat sich getan> **2.** *(concerning the intellect)* intellektuell [ɪntɛlɛktu|'ɛl] ◊ *Sie ist eher intellektuell veranlagt.* academically gifted intellektuell begabt

academy [noun] Akademie [akade'miː] die <-, -n> at the academy auf der Akademie

accelerate [verb] beschleunigen [bə'ʃla̯ɔ̯nɪgn̩] <beschleunigt, beschleunigte, hat beschleunigt> ◊ *Das Motorrad beschleunigt in zehn Sekunden von 0 auf 110 km/h.* ♦ *Viel Sonne beschleunigt das Heranreifen der Tomaten.*

accelerator [noun] Gaspedal ['gaːspeˌdaːl] das <-(e)s, -e> ◊ *aufs Gaspedal treten* ♦ *den Fuß vom Gaspedal nehmen*

accent [noun] **1.** *(pronunciation, mark, stress)* Akzent [ak'tsɛnt] der <-, -e> ◊ *Er hat einen starken schwäbischen Akzent.* ♦ *Dieses Wort hat einen Akzent auf dem ,e'.* ♦ *Der Akzent liegt auf der zweiten Silbe.* **2.** *(emphasis)* accent on sth Betonung ... [gen] [bə'toːnʊŋ] die <-> ◊ *eine Therapie mit Betonung der Krankengymnastik*

accentuate [verb] betonen [bə'toːnən] <betont, betonte, hat betont> ◊ *Das enge Kleid betont ihre gute Figur.*

accept [verb] **1.** *(a person, credit card, character trait)* akzeptieren [aktsɛp'tiːrən] <akzeptiert, akzeptierte, hat akzeptiert> ◊ *Wir akzeptieren alle gängigen Kreditkarten.* ♦ *Sie akzeptiert ihn mit all seinen Schwächen.* **2.** *(recognize)* anerkennen ['an|ɛknən] <erkennt an, erkannte an, hat anerkannt> ◊ *die Regeln anerkennen* **3.** *(take sth offered)* annehmen ['anneːmən] <nimmt an, nahm an, hat angenommen> ◊ *So viel Geld kann ich nicht annehmen.* ♦ *eine Einladung annehmen* **4.** *(a compromise, an obligation)* eingehen ['aɪ̯ŋeːən] <geht ein, ging ein, ist eingegangen> ◊ *Bei der Qualität gehe ich keine Kompromisse ein.* ♦ *Verpflichtungen eingehen* **5.** *(receive)* entgegennehmen [ɛnt'geːɡn̩eːmən] <nimmt entgegen, nahm entgegen, hat entgegengenommen> ◊ *Ich nahm für meinen Nachbarn ein Päckchen entgegen.* ♦ *einen Anruf entgegennehmen* **6.** *(a loss, criticism, loosing)* hinnehmen ['hɪnneːmən] <nimmt hin, nahm hin, hat hingenommen> ◊ *Die Mannschaft hat die Niederlage gelassen hingenommen.*; *(refuse to acknowledge)* not want to accept sth etw. nicht wahrhaben wollen [nɪçt 'vaːʁhaːbm̩ vɔlən] <will, wollte, hat wollen> ◊ *Er will einfach nicht wahrhaben, dass sie ihn verlassen hat.* **7.** *(take on)* übernehmen [ybɐ'neːmən]

<übernimmt, übernahm, hat übernommen> ◊ *ein Amt übernehmen* ♦ *Wer übernimmt die Aufgabe?* **8.** *(agree to sth)* zusagen ['tsuːzaːgn̩] +haben ◊ *Ihm wurde die Stelle angeboten und er sagte zu.* **9.** *(be accountable for)* accept responsibility for sth die Verantwortung für etw. übernehmen [diː fɐ|ˈantvɔʁtʊŋ fyːɐ̯ ... ybeˌneːmən] <übernimmt, übernahm, hat übernommen> ◊ *Wer übernimmt die Verantwortung für den Fehler?*

acceptable [adj] akzeptabel [aktsɛp'taːbl̩] <akzeptabler, am akzeptabelsten> <der/die/das akzeptable ...> ◊ *Das ist eine akzeptable Leistung.* ♦ *Die Lösung wurde als akzeptabel angesehen.* socially acceptable salonfähig [za'lɔnfɛːɪç] ◊ *salonfähiges Benehmen*

acceptance [noun] **1.** *(of a person)* Akzeptanz [aktsɛp'tants] die <-> no pl ◊ *die Akzeptanz Andersdenkender* **2.** *(of an offer, decision, plan)* Annahme ['annaːmə] die <-, -n> ◊ *die Annahme von Kleinanzeigen* ♦ *die Annahme des Friedensplans* ♦ *die Annahme eines Angebots* **3.** *(of sth undesirable)* Hinnahme ['hɪnnaːmə] die <-> no pl ◊ *die Hinnahme von Unrecht* **4.** *(agreement)* Zusage ['tsuːzaːgə] die <-, -n> ◊ *eine unverbindliche Zusage* ♦ *Er hatte die Zusage der Bank für den Kredit.*

accepted → accept [adj] allgemein anerkannt [ˌalgəmaɛn 'an|ɛkant] no comp/superl ◊ *allgemein anerkannte Werte*

access¹ [noun] **1.** *(to a person, information, education, the internet)* Zugang ['tsuːgaŋ] der <-(e)s> ◊ *Zugang zu jdm/etw. haben* ♦ *Der Zugang zum Internet ist derzeit nicht möglich.* gain access to sth Zugang zu etw. bekommen; *(to a building)* Zutritt ['tsuːtrɪt] der <-(e)s> ◊ *Zutritt verboten!*; *(by car)* Zufahrt ['tsuːfaːɐ̯t] die <-, -en> ◊ *Zufahrt zum Parkhaus über die Moltkestraße.* **2.** *(after a divorce)* right of access Umgangsrecht ['ʊmgaŋsʁɛçt] das <-(e)s, -e> ◊ *Bekommt der Vater Umgangsrecht?*

access² [verb] **1.** *(a computer file)* öffnen ['œfnən] +haben ◊ *Ich kann die Datei nicht öffnen.*; *(a piece of information)* access sth auf etw. [acc] zugreifen [aˌɔf ... ˌtsuːgraɛfn̩] <greift zu, griff zu, hat zugegriffen> ◊ *via Internet auf Daten zugreifen* **2.** access a road auf eine Straße fahren [aˌɔf aɛnə ˈʃtraːsə faːrən] <fährt, fuhr, ist gefahren>

accessible [adj] zugänglich ['tsuːgɛŋlɪç] ◊ *Die Informationen müssen leicht zugänglich gemacht werden.* ♦ *Dieses Museum ist für Rollstuhlfahrer nur schwer zugänglich.* ♦ *Er ist ein zugänglicher Typ.*; *(area, town etc.)* be easily accessible leicht zu erreichen sein [ˌlaɛçt tsuː ɛ'raɛçn̩ zaɛn] +sein ◊ *Die Skigebiete sind mit dem Auto leicht zu erreichen.*

accident [noun] **1.** *(misadventure)* Unfall ['ʊnfal] der <-(e)s, Unfälle> ◊ *einen Unfall haben* ♦ *ein schwerer Unfall* die in an accident bei einem Unfall ums Leben kommen **2.** *(catastrophy)* Unglück ['ʊnglʏk] das <-(e)s, -e> ◊ *Das Unglück forderte zwei Tote.*

⊚ **by accident** versehentlich

accidental [adj] **1.** *(inadvertent)* versehentlich [fɛ'zeːəntlɪç] no comp/superl, only before ns ◊ *eine versehentliche Weitergabe vertrauliche Informationen* **2.** *(by chance)* zufällig ['tsuːfɛlɪç] no comp/superl ◊ *Ähnlichkeiten mit lebenden Personen sind rein zufällig.* **3.** *(caused by an accident)* Unfall... ['ʊnfal] accidental death Unfalltod ['ʊnfaltoːt] der

<-(e)s, -e>
accidentally [adv] **1.** *(inadvertently)* versehentlich [fe'ze:əntlɪç] *no comp/superl* ◊ *Ich habe versehentlich das Glas zerbrochen.* **2.** *(by chance)* zufällig ['ʦuːfɛlɪç] *no comp/superl* ◊ *Er fand den Fehler rein zufällig.*

accident and emergency department [noun] Notaufnahme ['noːt|aofnaːmə] die <-, -n> ◊ *in die Notaufnahme eingeliefert werden*

accommodate [verb] **1.** *(take in for a while)* accommodate sb/sth jdn/etw. bei sich unterbringen [bae ... 'ʊntebrɪŋən] <bringt unter, brachte unter, hat untergebracht> ◊ *Für eine Nacht können wir dich schon bei uns unterbringen.* ♦ *Wir bringe deine Möbel gern für eine Weile bei mir unter.* **2.** *(have room for)* accommodate sb/sth für jdn/etw. Platz bieten [fyːɐ ... 'plats biːtn] <bietet, bot, hat geboten> ◊ *Diese Pension bietet Platz für zehn Gäste.* **3.** *(take account of)* berücksichtigen [bə'rʏkzɪçtɪgn] <berücksichtigt, berücksichtigte, hat berücksichtigt> ◊ *Wir müssen verschiedene Standpunkte berücksichtigen.* **4.** accommodate yourself to sth sich auf etw. [acc] einstellen [aof ... ,aenʃtɛlən] <stellt sich ein, stellte sich ein, hat sich eingestellt> ◊ *Er hat sich schnell auf die neue Situation eingestellt.*

accommodation [noun] **1.** *(place to stay)* Unterkunft ['ʊntekʊnft] die <-, Unterkünfte> ◊ *eine Unterkunft für die Nacht suchen* sth has accommodation for sb etw. bietet Platz für jdn [biːtət 'plats fyːɐ] <bietet, bot, hat geboten> ◊ *Das Appartement bietet Platz für sechs Personen.* **2.** *(agreement)* Verständigung [fɛ'ʃtɛndɪgʊŋ] die <-> no pl ◊ *eine Verständigung zwischen zwei Parteien erreichen*

accompaniment [noun] **1.** MUS Begleitung [bə'glaetʊŋ] die <-, -en> ◊ *Sie sang zur Begleitung des Orchesters.* **2.** *(food)* Beilage ['baelaːgə] die <-, -n> ◊ *Als Beilage gab es Reis.* **3.** *(simultaneous happening)* Begleiterscheinung [bə'glaet|ɐʃaenʊŋ] die <-, -en> ◊ *eine unvermeidliche Begleiterscheinung des technischen Fortschritts*

accompany [verb] begleiten [bə'glaetn] <begleitet, begleitete, hat begleitet> ◊ *Ihre Freundin begleitete sie zum Arzt.* ♦ *Sie sang und er begleitete sie auf dem Klavier.* ♦ *Heftige Proteste haben die Verhandlungen begleitet.* accompanying letter Begleitschreiben [bə'glaetʃraebn] das <-s, ->

accomplice [noun] Komplize [kɔm'pliːʦə] der <-n, -n> ♀Komplizin [kɔm'pliːʦɪn] die <-, -nen>

accomplish [verb] *(task, assignment, errand, mission)* ausführen ['aosfyːrən] +haben (lofty) ◊ *Wir haben die Aufgabe erfolgreich ausgeführt.* accomplish a lot viel erreichen ['fiːl ɛ,raeçn] <erreicht, erreichte, hat erreicht> ◊ *Zusammen können wir viel erreichen.* not accomplish much nicht viel erreichen

accomplished → **accomplish** [adj] **1.** *(perfect)* vollendet [fɔl|'ɛndət] ◊ *Er ist ein vollendeter Gentleman.* **2.** *(talented)* begabt [ba'gaːpt] <begabter, am begabtesten> ◊ *Sie ist eine begabte Pianistin.*

accord¹ [noun] Abkommen ['apkɔmən] das <-s, -> trade accord Handelsabkommen ['handls|apkɔmən] ⊛ **of your own accord** von selbst **in accord with** sb/sth im Einklang mit jdm/etw.

accord² [verb] accord sb sth, accord sth to sb jdm etw. gewähren [gə'vɛːrən] <gewährt, gewährte, hat gewährt> ◊ *jdm Privilegien gewähren* accord sb a warm welcome jdm einen herzlichen Empfang

bereiten [aenən hɛ'ʦlɪçn ɛm'pfaŋ bəraetn] <bereitet, bereitete, hat bereitet> accord sb/sth recognition jdm/etw. Anerkennung zuteil werden lassen ['an|ekenʊŋ ʦu,tael veːɐdn lasn] <lässt, ließ, hat lassen> *(lofty)* sth is accorded priority etw. hat Priorität [hat prioriˈtɛːt] +haben accord importance to sth etw. wichtig nehmen ['vɪçtɪç neːmən] <nimmt, nahm, hat genommen>
• **accord with** [phras v] accord with sth *(agree)* mit etw. übereinstimmen [mɪt ... ybeˈae]nʃtɪmən] +haben ◊ *Diese Behauptung stimmt mit den Tatsachen nicht überein.*

accordance [noun] in accordance with gemäß [gə'mɛːs] *sing nouns without article or attribute are not declined when following this prep, otherwise* [+dat] ◊ *gemäß Artikel 81 der Verfassung* ♦ *Seinem Wunsch gemäß gab es keine Feier.*

according to [prep] **1.** *(in accordance with)* entsprechend [ɛnt'ʃprɛçnt] *mostly postpositive* [+dat] ◊ *jdn seinen Begabungen entsprechend fördern* ♦ *etw. entsprechend den Regeln tun; (following a certain plan, system etc.)* nach [naːx] [+dat] ◊ *etw. nach dem Alphabet sortieren* ♦ *Die Liste ist nach Autoren geordnet.* go according to plan nach Plan verlaufen [naːx 'plaːn fe,laofn] <verläuft, verlief, ist verlaufen> **2.** *(quoting sb/sth)* laut [laot] *sing nouns without article or attribute are not declined when following this prep, otherwise* [+gen] ◊ *Laut Kanzler hat die Opposition kein Konzept.* ♦ *Laut eines Berichtes aus der Forschungsabteilung wurden gute Fortschritte gemacht.*

accordingly [adv] **1.** *(consequently)* demnach ['deːmnaːx] *(form)* ◊ *Sie arbeitet schon lange hier und hat demnach viel Erfahrung.* **2.** *(appropriately)* entsprechend [ɛnt'ʃprɛçnt] ◊ *Du musst beobachten, was passiert und dann entsprechend reagieren.*

account [noun] **1.** *(at a bank)* Konto ['kɔnto] das <-s, Konten> ◊ *ein Konto eröffnen* ♦ *Geld vom Konto abheben* **2.** *(of a business)* accounts Geschäftsbücher [gə'ʃɛftsbyːçe] die <-> only pl ◊ *die Geschäftsbücher überprüfen; (department)* Buchhaltung ['buːxhaltʊŋ] die <-, -en> **3.** *(with a shop)* Kreditkonto [kre'diːt,kɔnto] das <-s, Kreditkonten>; *(record)* Rechnung ['rɛçnʊŋ] die <-, -en> settle your account seine Rechnung zahlen **4.** *(customer)* Stammkunde ['ʃtamkʊndə] der <-n, -n> **5.** *(with an internet provider)* email account E-Mail-Konto ['iːmeːl,kɔnto] das <-, E-Mail-Konten> **6.** *(description)* Beschreibung [bə'ʃraebʊŋ] die <-, -en> ◊ *eine Beschreibung des Tathergangs* eyewitness report Augenzeugenbericht ['aogn̩ʦɔygn̩bərɪçt] der <-s, -e> give an account of sth über etw. [acc] berichten [yːbe ... bə,rɪçtn] <berichtet, berichtete, hat berichtet> ⊛ **of no/little account** ohne Bedeutung **hold sb to account** jdn zur Rechenschaft ziehen **take sth into account** etw. berücksichtigen **on my/his/her etc. account** meinetwegen/seinetwegen/ihretwegen etc. **by/from all accounts** nach allem, was man hört **on no account, not on any account** keinesfalls

accountable [adj] accountable (to sb) (jdm gegenüber) verantwortlich [fɛ'antvɔ'tlɪç] *no comp/ superl* ◊ *Wer ist für dieses Projekt verantwortlich?* ♦ *Politiker sind ihren Wählern gegenüber verantwortlich.*

accountability [noun] accountability (to sb) Verant-

wortlichkeit (gegenüber jdm) [fɛ|'antvɔʳtlɪçka͜et] die
<-, -en>

accountant [noun] Buchhalter ['buːxhaltɐ] der
<-s, -> ♀Buchhalterin ['buːxhaltərɪn] die
<-, -nen> ◊ *Hast du den neuen Buchhalter schon
gesehen?* ♦ *Sie arbeitet als Buchhalterin bei einer
großen Firma.*

account for [verb] **1.** *(be the reason)* account for sth
für etw. verantwortlich sein
[fyːɐ̯ ... fɛ|'antvɔʳtlɪç za͜en] +*sein* ◊ *Der hohe Ölpreis
ist für den Anstieg der Produktionskosten verantwortlich.* **2.** *(be a certain part of)* account for sth etw.
ausmachen ['a͜osmaxn̩] +*haben* ◊ *Das Korrigieren von
Fehlern macht die Hälfte meiner Arbeitszeit aus.*
3. *(explain)* account for sth Rechenschaft für etw.
ablegen ['rɛçn̩ʃaft fyːɐ̯ ... apleːɡn̩] +*haben* (lofty) ◊
Rechenschaft für sein Verhalten/eine Tat ablegen
4. *(you know where sb is)* sb is accounted for jds
Verbleib ist bekannt [fɛˌbla͜ep ɪst bə'kant] +*sein* sb
isn't accounted for jds Verbleib ist unbekannt

accounting [noun] Buchhaltung ['buːxhaltʊŋ] die
<-, -en>

accredited [adj] **1.** *(recognized)* anerkannt ['an|ɛkant]
<anerkannter, am anerkanntesten> *seldom comp* ◊ *ein
EU-weit anerkannter Ausbildungsgang* ♦ *Dieser Studi-
enabschluss ist allgemein anerkannt.* **2.** *(diplomat)*
accredited (to a country) (in einem Land) akkredi-
tiert [(ɪn aɪnəm lant) akredi'tiːɐ̯t] *mostly before ns* ◊
in Deutschland akkreditierte Botschafter

accumulate [verb] *(a sum of money, number of
objects)* accumulate sth etw. anhäufen ['anhɔ͜øfn̩]
+*haben* ◊ *Sie hatten ein Vermögen angehäuft.* sth
accumulates etw. häuft sich an ◊ *Inzwischen haben
sich bei mir viele Bücher angehäuft.; (experience,
data etc.)* accumulate sth etw. sammeln ['zaml̩n]
+*haben* ◊ *Daten sammeln; (evidence)* sth is accumu-
lating etw. häuft sich ['hɔ͜øft zɪç] +*haben* ◊
Anzeichen für eine Klimaveränderung häufen sich.

accumulation [noun] Anhäufung ['anhɔ͜øfʊŋ] die
<-, -en> ◊ *eine Anhäufung von Giftstoffen im
Körper*

accuracy [noun] **1.** *(precision)* Genauigkeit
[gə'na͜oɪçka͜et] die <-> *no pl* ◊ *ein Messgerät mit
hoher Genauigkeit* ♦ *Dies sollte der Genauigkeit
halber erwähnt werden.* **2.** *(correctness)* Richtigkeit
['rɪçtɪçka͜et] die <-> *no pl* ◊ *die Richtigkeit der
Angaben*

accurate(ly) [adj, adv] **1.** *(correct)* zutreffend
['tsuːtrɛfn̩t] ◊ *Der Vorwurf erwies sich als nicht
zutreffend.* ♦ *eine zutreffende Bemerkung* ♦ *etw.
zutreffend bemerken* **2.** *(exact)* genau [gə'na͜o]
<genauer, am genau(e)sten> ◊ *Können Sie mir bitte
genauere Informationen geben?* ♦ *Diese Beschreibung ist nicht genau genug.* ♦ *genau arbeiten*

accusation [noun] Anschuldigung ['anʃʊldɪgʊŋ] die
<-, -en> ◊ *Er hat alle Anschuldigungen zurückge-
wiesen.*

accusative [noun] Akkusativ ['akuzatiːf] der <-s, -e>
◊ *Welches Wort steht im Akkusativ?*

accuse [verb] **1.** *(blame)* accuse sb of sth jdn einer
Sache [gen] beschuldigen [bə'ʃʊldɪgn̩] <beschuldigt,
beschuldigte, hat beschuldigt> (lofty) ◊ *Er beschuldigte sie mangelnder Sorgfalt.* **2.** *(at court)* accuse sb
of sth jdn wegen etw. [gen] anklagen
[veːɐ̯gn̩ ... ˌanklaːgn̩] +*haben* ◊ *Sie ist wegen Mordes
angeklagt.* ♦ *Man klagte ihn wegen Steuerhinterzie-*

bung an.

accused → accuse [noun] Angeklagte ['angəklaːtə]
der/die <-n, die Angeklagten> *but: ein Angeklagter/
eine Angeklagte* ◊ *Der Angeklagte hat seine Unschuld
bewiesen.* ♦ *Die Angeklagte verlor den Prozess.*

ace[1] [noun] Ass [as] das <-es, -e> ◊ *Sie spielte ein
Ass aus.* ♦ *Ich beendete das Match mit einem Ass.* ♦
Auf seinem Gebiet ist er ein Ass.

ace[2] [adj] super ['zuːpɐ] *invariable (fam)* ◊ *ein super
Tattoo* ♦ *Die CD ist echt super.*

achieve [verb] **1.** *(an aim, objective, effect)* erreichen
[ɛ'ra͜eçn̩] <erreicht, erreichte, hat erreicht> ◊ *Was
willst du damit erreichen?; (a success, profit)*
erzielen [ɛ'tsiːlən] <erzielt, erzielte, hat erzielt> ◊
einen Erfolg/Gewinn erzielen achieve fame/independ-
ence Ruhm/Unabhängigkeit erlangen
['ruːm/'ʊn|aphɛŋɪçka͜et ɛlaŋən] <erlangt, erlangte, hat
erlangt>; (a top performance, miracle) vollbringen
[fɔl'brɪŋən] <vollbringt, vollbrachte, hat vollbracht>
(lofty) ◊ *Höchstleistungen/ein Wunder vollbringen*
2. *(get results through hard work)* leisten ['la͜estn̩]
<leistet, leistete, hat geleistet> ◊ *Er hat das Gefühl,
nicht genug zu leisten.*

achievement [noun] **1.** *(performance)* Leistung
['la͜estʊŋ] die <-, -en> ◊ *Dieser Aufsatz ist eine her-
vorragende/schwache Leistung.* **2.** *(merit)* Verdienst
[fɛ'diːnst] das <-(e)s, -e> ◊ *Es ist ihr Verdienst,
dass das Buch so gut geworden ist.*

acid [noun] Säure ['zɔ͜ørə] die <-, -n>

acknowledge [verb] **1.** *(recognize)* anerkennen
['an|ɛkɛnən] <erkennt an, erkannte an, hat anerkannt>
◊ *Sie erkennt an, dass er sich bemüht hat.* acknowledge sb/sth as being sth/to be sth jdn/etw. als etw.
[acc] anerkennen **2.** *(admit)* zugeben ['tsuːgeːbm̩]
<gibt zu, gab zu, hat zugegeben> ◊ *Sie will ihren
Fehler einfach nicht zugeben.* **3.** *(say you received
sth)* acknowledge (receipt of) sth den Empfang ...
[gen] bestätigen [deːn ɛmˌpfaŋ ... bə'ʃtɛːtɪgn̩]
<bestätigt, bestätigte, hat bestätigt> ◊ *Sie ließ sich den
Empfang des Pakets bestätigen.* **4.** *(by greeting)*
acknowledge sb, acknowledge sb's presence jdn
grüßen ['gryːsn̩] +*haben* ◊ *Er grüßte sie mit einem
Nicken.* ♦ *Hat sie dich gegrüßt?*

acknowledgement [noun] **1.** *(recognition)* Anerken-
nung ['an|ɛkɛnʊŋ] die <-, -en> there is universal
acknowledgement that es wird allgemein
anerkannt, dass [ɛs vɪʳt algəma͜en 'an|ɛkant das] ◊
2. *(of a crime, blame, failure)* Eingeständnis
['a͜engəʃtɛntnɪs] das <-ses, -se> ◊ *Ist das ein Eingeständnis deiner Schuld?* **3.** *(of receipt)* Empfangsbestätigung [ɛm'pfaŋsbəˌʃtɛːtɪgʊŋ] die <-, -en> ◊ *eine
Empfangsbestätigung für einen Brief* **4.** *(thanks)*
Dank [daŋk] der <-es> *no pl* express your acknowledgement to sb jdm seinen Dank aussprechen; (in
a book) acknowledgements Danksagungen
['daŋkzaːgʊŋən] die <-> *pl*
⊛ in acknowledgement zum Gruß ◊ *Als ich
hereinkam, nickte er zum Gruß.*

acoustic [adj] akustisch [a'kʊstɪʃ] *no comp/superl* ◊
ein akustisches Signal

acquaintance [noun] **1.** *(person you know)* Bekannte
[bə'kantə] der/die <-n, die Bekannten> *but: ein
Bekannter/eine Bekannte* ◊ *Sie hat viele Bekannte,
aber wenig Freunde.* **2.** *(knowledge of a person)*
Bekanntschaft [bə'kantʃaft] die <-, -en> ◊ „*Kennen
Sie Herrn Anders?*" — „*Ja, ich habe seine Bekannt-*

A

B

C

D

E

F

G

H

I

J

K

L

M

N

O

P

Q

R

S

T

U

V

W

X

Y

Z

A
B
C
D
E
F
G
H
I
J
K
L
M
N
O
P
Q
R
S
T
U
V
W
X
Y
Z

schaft schon gemacht." **3.** *(with a subject etc.)*
acquaintance with sth Kenntnis von etw.
['kɛntnɪs fɔn] die <-, -es>

acquire |verb| **1.** *(buy, get)* erwerben [e'vɛ'bm̩]
<erwirbt, erwarb, hat erworben> ◊ *Mit dieser Prüfung*
erwerben Sie die Berechtigung, Leute auszubilden.;
(a skill, knowledge etc.) sich aneignen ['an|aegnən]
<eignet sich an, eignete sich an, hat sich angeeignet>
◊ *Ich möchte mir Grundkenntnisse des Deutschen*
aneignen. ♦ *Er hat sich das nötige Wissen selbststän-*
dig angeeignet. **2.** *(a disease)* acquire sth sich mit
etw. anstecken [mɪt ... ˌanʃtɛkŋ̍] +haben ◊ *Ich habe*
mich mit der Grippe angesteckt. **3.** *(get to like)*
acquire a taste for sth an etw. |dat|
finden [gə'ʃmak an ... fɪndn̩] <findet, fand, hat
gefunden> sth is an acquired taste etw. ist gewöhn-
nungsbedürftig [ɪst ɡə'vøːnʊŋsbədʏˈftɪç]; *(get used*
to) acquire the habit of doing sth sich daran
gewöhnen, etw. zu tun [daran ɡə'vøːnən ... tsuː]
<gewöhnt sich, gewöhnte sich, hat sich gewöhnt>

acquisition |noun| **1.** *(of knowledge, property, a*
company) Erwerb [e'vɛ'p] der <-(e)s, -e> *most sing*
acquisition of property Erwerb vom Eigentum acqui-
sition of language Spracherwerb ['ʃpraːx|evɛ'p]
2. *(object you buy)* Anschaffung ['anʃafʊŋ] die
<-, -en> ◊ *eine größere Anschaffung planen* ♦ *Der*
Drucker war eine gute Anschaffung.

acquit |verb| acquit sb (of sth) jdn (von etw.) frei-
sprechen ['fraeʃprɛçn̩] <spricht frei, sprach frei, hat
freigesprochen> ◊ *Sie wurde aus Mangel an*
Beweisen freigesprochen. ♦ *Er wurde vom Vorwurf*
der Körperverletzung freigesprochen.

acre |noun| *eine Maßeinheit von 4047m²*

acrobat |noun| Akrobat [akro'baːt] der <-en, -en>
♀Akrobatin [akro'baːtɪn] die <-, -nen> ◊ *Er ist ein*
berühmter Akrobat. ♦ *Sie arbeitet als Akrobatin im*
Zirkus.

across¹ |adv| **1.** *(to the other side towards the speaker)*
herüber... [hɛ'ryːbɐ] come across herüberkommen
[hɛ'ryːbɐkɔmən] <kommt herüber, kam herüber, ist
herübergekommen> ◊ *Komm doch kurz herüber!*
2. *(to the other side away from the speaker)*
hinüber... [hɪ'nyːbɐ] look across hinübersehen
[hɪ'nyːbɐzeːən] <sieht hinüber, sah hinüber, hat hinü-
bergesehen> ◊ *Sieh mal zur anderen Seite hinüber,*
wer da steht. **3.** *(being on the other side)* drüben
['dryːbm̩] ◊ *Alle waren endlich drüben.* **4.** *(as a*
diameter) sth is ... across etw. hat einen Durchmesser von ... [hat aenan 'dʊʁçmɛsɐ fɔn] +haben ◊ *Der*
Krater hat einen Durchmesser von einem Kilometer.
5. *(in crosswords)* waagerecht ['vaːgəʁɛçt] ◊ *Was ist*
11 waagerecht?

'Across' often occurs in phrasal verbs like 'get
across' or 'come across' which have their own
entries in the dictionary.

across² |prep| **1.** *(moving from one side to the other,*
over a surface/space) über ['yːbɐ] +acc ◊ *eine Dampf-*
ferfahrt über den Bodensee ♦ *über die Grenze fahren*
walk across the road die Straße überqueren
[diː 'ʃtraːsə yːbɐ'kveːrən] <überquert, überquerte, hat
überquert> **2.** *(on the other side of)* across sth auf
der anderen Seite ... |gen| [aof deːɐ 'andərən 'zaɪtə]
◊ *auf der anderen Seite der Grenze/des Saales*
across the road gegenüber [geːgŋ̍'yːbɐ] ◊ *Die*
Apotheke ist gleich gegenüber. **3.** *(including many*

people/things) across the country im ganzen Land
[ɪm 'gantsən lant] across the population in der
gesamten Bevölkerung
[ɪn deːɐ gə'zamtən bə'fœlkərʊŋ]

act¹ |noun| **1.** *(deed)* Tat [taːt] die <-, -en> ◊ *eine kri-*
minelle Tat act of violence Gewalttat [gə'valttaːt] be
in the act of doing sth gerade dabei sein, etw. zu
tun [gəraːdə da'bae zaen ... tsuː] +sein ◊ *Ich war*
gerade dabei, ins Bett zu gehen, als es klingelte.
catch sb in the act jdn ertappen [e'tapm̩] <ertappt,
ertappte, hat ertappt> catch sb in the act of doing
sth jdn dabei ertappen, wie er etw. tut **2.** *(behavio(u)r)* Theater [te|'aːtɐ] das <-s> *no pl*
(pej) ◊ *Bitte hör mit dem Theater auf!* ♦ *Das ist doch*
alles nur Theater! put on an act Theater spielen
3. *(part of a performance)* Nummer ['nʊmɐ] die
<-, -n> ◊ *eine Nummer einstudieren/vorführen*
4. *(part of a play)* Akt [akt] der <-(e)s, -e> ◊ *ein*
Drama in fünf Akten **5.** LAW Gesetz [gə'zɛts] das
<-es, -e>; *(in compound ns)* ... act ...gesetz
[gə'zɛts] Data Protection Act Datenschutzgesetz
['daːtnʃʊtsgəzɛts]

act² |verb| **1.** *(do sth)* handeln ['handl̩n] +haben ◊ *Er*
hat vollkommen unverantwortlich gehandelt.;
(behave) act like a child/idiot sich wie ein Kind/
Idiot benehmen [vi: aen 'kɪnt/i'djoːt bəne:mən]
<benimmt sich, benahm sich, hat sich benommen> ◊
Du benimmst dich wie ein Kleinkind! **2.** *(in a play, a*
part) spielen ['ʃpiːlən] +haben ◊ *Wer spielt in dem*
Stück? ♦ *Sie spielte das Gretchen.* **3.** *(function as)* act
as sb als jd fungieren [als ... fʊŋiːrən] <fungiert,
fungierte, hat fungiert> ◊ *Tom fungierte als Schieds-*
richter. **4.** *(have an effect)* act as sth als etw. |nom|
wirken [als ... vɪ'kŋ̍] +haben ◊ *Diese Substanz wirkt*
als Katalysator.

action |noun| **1.** *(measure)* Maßnahme ['maːsnaːmə]
die <-, -n> take action Maßnahmen ergreifen
course of action Vorgehensweise ['foːgeːənsvaezə]
die <-, -n> **2.** *(strike)* industrial action Arbeitskampf ['aːbaetskampf] der <-(e)s, Arbeitskämpfe>
3. LAW *(legal)* action Klage ['klaːgə] die <-, -n> ◊
Ich werde Klage gegen Sie einreichen. take legal
action klagen ['klaːgŋ̍] +haben **4.** *(deed, plot)*
Handlung ['handlʊŋ] die <-, -en> ◊ *Wie können Sie*
diese Handlung verantworten? ♦ *Der Film enthält*
keine durchgehende Handlung. **5.** *(movement of a*
body part) Bewegung [bə'veːgʊŋ] die <-, -en> reflex
action Reflexbewegung [re'flɛksbəveːgʊŋ] **6.** *(effect)*
Wirkung ['vɪ'kʊŋ] die <-, -en> ◊ *die Wirkung von*
Nikotin auf das Gehirn **7.** TECHN *(of a machine)*
Betrieb [bə'triːp] der <-s> **8.** MIL Kampfhandlung
['kampfhandlʊŋ] die <-, Kampfhandlungen> be killed
in action im Krieg fallen [ɪm 'kriːk ˌfalən] <fällt, fiel,
ist gefallen>

ⓔ **actions speak louder than words** Taten
sprechen lauter als Worte **there is action**
somwhere irgendwo ist etwas los

activate |verb| in Gang setzen [ɪn 'gaŋ zɛtsn̩] +haben
active(ly) |adj, adv| aktiv [ak'tiːf] ◊ *Dieser Vulkan ist*
nicht mehr aktiv. ♦ *ein aktives Mitglied des Vereins*
♦ *aktiv an etw.* |dat| *mitwirken*

activist |noun| Aktivist [akti'vɪst] der <-en, -en> ♀Ak-
tivistin [akti'vɪstɪn] die <-, -nen>

activity |noun| **1.** *(pastime)* Beschäftigung [bə'ʃɛftɪgʊŋ]
die <-, -en> ◊ *Wenn dir langweilig ist, such dir*
eine sinnvolle Beschäftigung. **2.** *(more specific*

pursuit) Tätigkeit ['tɛːtɪçkaet] die <–, –en> ◊ *Ich halte das Angeln für eine sehr entspannende Tätigkeit.* economic activity Wirtschaftstätigkeit ['vɪrtʃaftstɛːtɪçkaet] criminal activity Straftat ['ʃtraːftaːt] die <–, –en> human activity menschlicher Einfluss [ˌmɛnʃlɪçe 'aenflʊs] sth is the result of human activity etw. ist auf menschlichen Einfluss zurückzuführen

actor [noun] Schauspieler ['ʃaoʃpiːle] der <–s, –> ♀Schauspielerin ['ʃaoʃpiːlərɪn] die <–, –nen> ◊ *Brad Pitt ist ein guter Schauspieler.*

actress [noun] Schauspielerin ['ʃaoʃpiːlərɪn] die <–, –nen> ◊ *Nicole Kidman, eine berühmte Schauspielerin*

actual [adj] tatsächlich [taːt'zɛçlɪç] *no comp/superl, only before n* ◊ *Die tatsächliche Anzahl der Opfer ist nicht bekannt.*; *(problem, purpose, question)* eigentlich ['aeɡŋ̩tlɪç] *no comp/superl, only before ns* ◊ *das eigentliche Problem* actual facts objektive Tatsachen [ˌɔpjɛktiːvə 'taːtzaxŋ̩]

actually¹ [adv] tatsächlich [taːt'zɛçlɪç] *no comp/superl* ◊ *Ist das tatsächlich passiert oder bloß erfunden?*; *(signalling agreement)* eigentlich ['aeɡŋ̩tlɪç] *no comp/superl* ◊ *Eigentlich hat er Recht.*

actually² [part] **1.** *(reinforcing)* auch [aox] ◊ *Wir dachten, es sei ein Unfall passiert und so war es dann auch.* ♦ *Er fühlte sich gut, und man sah es ihm auch an.* **2.** *(conceding)* eigentlich ['aeɡŋ̩tlɪç] ◊ *Eigentlich ist es doch ganz schön hier.* **3.** *(esp iron)* wirklich ['vɪrklɪç] ◊ *Hat er wirklich geglaubt, dass es klappen könnte?*

acute(ly) [adj, adv] **1.** *(extreme, immediate)* akut [a'kuːt] <akuter, am akutesten> *seldom comp/superl* ◊ *eine akute Bronchitis* ♦ *in akuter Lebensgefahr schweben* ♦ *Die Geldnot ist akut.* ♦ *4000 Arbeitsplätze sind akut gefährdet.* **2.** *(precise, exact)* genau [ɡə'nao] <genauer, am genau(e)sten> ◊ *seine genaue Beobachtungsgabe* ♦ *sich einer Sache* [gen] *genau bewusst sein*; *(senses)* scharf [ʃaʳf] <schärfer, am schärfsten> ◊ *Ihr Geruchssinn ist scharf.* **3.** *(angle)* spitz [ʃpɪts] <spitzer, am spitzesten> acutely angled mit spitzem Winkel

ad [noun] **1.** *(in a paper)* Anzeige ['antsaeɡə] die <–, –n> ◊ *eine Anzeige aufgeben* **2.** *(on TV)* Werbespot ['vɛʳbəspɔt] der <–s, –s> ads Werbung ['vɛʳbʊŋ] die <–, –en> most sing ◊ *In diesem Programm kommt zu viel Werbung.*

AD n. Chr. [naːx 'krɪstʊs] ◊ *im 8. Jahrhundert n. Chr.*

adapt [verb] **1.** *(change in order to deal with a new situation)* anpassen ['anpasn̩] +haben adapt sth to sth etw. einer Sache [gen] anpassen ◊ *seine Kleidung der Jahreszeit anpassen* adapt sth for sb etw. jds Bedürfnissen anpassen, etw. den Bedürfnissen von jdm anpassen ◊ *ein Gebäude den Bedürfnissen von Behinderten anpassen* sb adapts jd passt sich an sb adapts to sth jd passt sich einer Sache [dat] an ◊ *Er passte sich der neuen Situation gut an.* adapt sth for sth etw. auf etw. [acc] abstimmen [aof ... ˌapʃtɪmən] +haben **2.** *(literature)* bearbeiten [bə'aʳbaetn̩] <bearbeitet, bearbeitete, hat bearbeitet> ◊ *einen Roman für die Verfilmung bearbeiten*

adaptation [noun] **1.** *(change in sth)* Anpassung ['anpasʊŋ] die <–, –en> ◊ *Anpassung in der Schule* (the) adaptation to sth die Anpassung an etw. [acc] ◊ *die Anpassung einer Tierart an die Umwelt* **2.** *(of machinery, equipment etc.)* Umstellung ['ʊmʃtɛlʊŋ] die

<–, –en> ◊ *die Umstellung eines Computersystems* (the) adaptation of sth for sth die Umstellung ... [gen] auf etw. [acc] ◊ *die Umstellung der Uhr auf die Sommerzeit* **3.** *(of buildings)* Umbau ['ʊmbao] der <–(e)s, –ten> ◊ *der behindertengerechte Umbau einer Wohnung* **4.** *(of literature)* Bearbeitung [bə'aʳbaetʊŋ] die <–, –en> ◊ *die Bearbeitung eines Theaterstücks* **5.** FILM, TV Verfilmung [fe'fɪlmʊŋ] die <–, –en> ◊ *die Verfilmung eines Romans*

add [verb] **1.** *(a comment, detail, an ingredient)* hinzufügen [hɪn'tsuːfyːɡn̩] +haben ◊ *Ich möchte noch hinzufügen, dass ...* ♦ *Fügen Sie zwei Esslöffel Zucker hinzu.* **2.** MATH addieren [a'diːrən] <addiert, addierte, hat addiert> ◊ *Was bekommt man, wenn man 134 und 17 addiert?* **3.** *(corrections, improvements)* vornehmen ['foːɡneːmən] <nimmt vor, nahm vor, hat vorgenommen> ◊ *Sie nahm am Text wichtige Änderungen vor.* **4.** *(give sth a special quality)* add sth to sth einer Sache [acc] verleihen [fe'laeən] <verleiht, verlieh, hat verliehen> ◊ *Das Collier verlieh ihrer Garderobe einen besonderen Glanz.*

• **add up** [phras v] **1.** *(numbers)* add sth up etw. addieren [a'diːrən] <addiert, addierte, hat addiert> ◊ *Addieren Sie die zwei Werte.* ♦ *Zahlen addieren* **2.** *(mount up)* sich summieren [zʊ'miːrən] <summiert sich, summierte sich, hat sich summiert> ◊ *All diese Ausgaben summieren sich.* **3.** *(amount)* add up to sth sich auf etw. [acc] belaufen [aof ... bəlaofn̩] <beläuft sich, belief sich, hat sich belaufen> ◊ *Ihre Spesen belaufen sich auf 5000 Euro.* **4.** *(result)* add up to sth auf etw. [acc] hinauslaufen [aof ... hɪˌnaoslaofn̩] <läuft hinaus, lief hinaus, ist hinausgelaufen> ◊ *Die vielen Änderungen liefen auf viel Arbeit hinaus.*

◉ sth doesn't add up mit etw. stimmt etw. nicht

added → **add** [adj] zusätzlich ['tsuːzɛtslɪç] *no comp/superl, only before ns* ◊ *ein zusätzlicher Vorteil*

addicted [adj] süchtig ['zʏçtɪç] ◊ *Jede Droge macht irgendwann süchtig.* ♦ *ein süchtiger Spieler* be addicted to sth nach etw. süchtig sein

addiction [noun] Sucht [zʊxt] die <–, Süchte> ◊ *Tablettenmissbrauch kann zur Sucht führen.* addiction to heroin Heroinsucht [hero'iːnzʊxt]

addition [noun] **1.** *(sth that is added to sth)* addition (to sth) Erweiterung (... [gen]) [ɐ'vaetərʊŋ] die <–, –en> ◊ *eine Erweiterung unseres Warenangebots* **2.** *(in the US: to a building)* addition (to sth) Anbau (an etw. [acc]) ['anbao (an ...)] der <–, –ten> ◊ *ein Anbau an das Hauptgebäude* **3.** *(process of adding sth)* addition of sth Zugabe ... [gen]/von etw. ['tsuːɡaːbə ... vɔn] die <–, –n> ◊ *die Zugabe von Zucker bei Säften* **4.** *(to a text)* Zusatz ['tsuːzats] der <–es, Zusätze> ◊ *einen Zusatz in den Vertrag aufnehmen* **5.** MATH Addition [adi'tsjoːn] die <–, –en>

◉ in addition (und) außerdem ◊ *Er hat gelogen; außerdem hat er gestohlen.* in addition to sth neben etw. [dat] ◊ *Neben Deutsch lerne ich noch Italienisch.* in addition to doing sth außer etw. zu tun ◊ *Außer im Internet zu chatten, kann man auch einem Verein beitreten, um Leute kennen zu lernen.* in addition to this außerdem ◊ *Ich treibe viel Sport, außerdem ernähre ich mich gesund.*

additional [adj] zusätzlich ['tsuːzɛtslɪç] *no comp/superl, only before ns* ◊ *zusätzliche Informationen*

additionally [adv] **1.** *(moreover)* außerdem

A
B
C
D
E
F
G
H
I
J
K
L
M
N
O
P
Q
R
S
T
U
V
W
X
Y
Z

['aʊsəde:m] ◊ *Sie hat ein festes Gehalt; außerdem bekommt sie einen Bonus für besonders gute Leistungen.* **2.** *(intensifying)* zusätzlich ['tsu:zɛtslɪç] *no comp/superl* ◊ *Diese neue Aufgabe belastete sie zusätzlich.*

address¹ [noun] **1.** *(postal, email, web site)* Adresse [a'drɛsə] die <–, –n> ◊ *Bitte geben Sie Ihre Adresse an.* ♦ *Seine Adresse hat sich geändert.* **2.** *(speech)* Ansprache ['anʃpra:xə] die <–, –n> ◊ *eine feierliche Ansprache*

address² [verb] **1.** *(a letter)* adressieren [adrɛ'si:rən] <adressiert, adressierte, hat adressiert> ◊ *einen Brief adressieren* address sth to sb etw. an jdn adressieren ◊ *Der Brief ist an dich adressiert.* **2.** *(a question, complaint, remark)* address sth to sb/sth etw. an jdn/etw. richten [an ... rɪçtn̩] <richtet, richtete, hat gerichtet> ◊ *eine Beschwerde an eine Behörde richten* **3.** *(a group of people)* address sb zu/vor jdm sprechen ['ʃpu:/fo:ɐ̯ ... ʃprɛçn̩] <spricht, sprach, hat gesprochen> ◊ *zu einer Versammlung sprechen* **4.** *(appellation)* address sb as sth jdn als etw. [nom] anreden [als ... ˌanre:dn̩] <redet an, redete an, hat angeredet> ◊ *Er hat ihn als Herr Doktor angeredet.*

adequate(ly) [adj, adv] **1.** *(appropriate)* angemessen ['angəmɛsn̩] ◊ *eine angemessene Entschädigung zahlen* ♦ *Der Preis war durchaus angemessen.* ♦ *angemessen reagieren* **2.** *(satisfactory)* ausreichend ['aʊsraɪçn̩t] *seldom comp/superl* ◊ *Der Proviant war ausreichend.; (evidence)* hinreichend ['hɪnraɪçn̩t] *seldom comp/superl* ◊ *Es lag ein hinreichender Tatverdacht vor.* ♦ *Das ist noch nicht hinreichend bewiesen.*

adhesive [noun] Klebstoff ['kle:pʃtɔf] der <–(e)s, –e>

ad hoc [adj, adv] kurzfristig ['kʊɐ̯tsfrɪstɪç] *when used as an adj, only before ns* ◊ *eine kurzfristige Kündigung* ♦ *Sie entschlossen sich kurzfristig, ihn zu besuchen.*

adjacent [adj] be adjacent to sth an etw. [acc] grenzen [an ... grɛntsn̩] +haben ◊ *An das Haus grenzt ein Park.*

adjective [noun] Adjektiv ['atjɛkti:f] das <–s, –e>

adjoin [verb] adjoin sth an etw. [acc] grenzen [an ... grɛntsn̩] ◊ *An den Garten grenzt eine Wiese.* adjoin each other aneinander grenzen ◊ *Genau hier grenzen beide Grundstücke aneinander.*

adjust [verb] **1.** *(a mechanism, an engine etc.)* (richtig) einstellen [(ˌrɪçtɪç) 'aɪnʃtɛlən] +haben ◊ *den Motor einstellen; (your hair, clothes)* richten ['rɪçtn̩] <richtet, richtete, hat gerichtet> ◊ *seine Frisur/ Kravatte richten* **2.** adjust (sth to sth) (etw. an etw. [acc]) anpassen ['anpasn̩] +haben ◊ *Die Löhne wurden (an die Inflationsrate) angepasst.* **3.** *(become accustomed to sth)* adjust to sth sich an etw. [acc] gewöhnen [an ... gə.vø:nən] ◊ *Die Augen gewöhnen sich an die Dunkelheit.* ♦ *sich an neue Lebensumstände gewöhnen; (change in order to fit in with sth)* sich auf etw. [acc] einstellen [aʊf ... ˌaɪnʃtɛlən] +haben ◊ *Die Firma hat sich auf die veränderte Wirtschaftslage eingestellt.*

adjustment [noun] **1.** *(to new circumstances)* adjustment (to sth) Anpassung (an etw. [acc]) ['anpasʊŋ] die <–, –en> *most sing* ◊ *Die Anpassung an die neuen Arbeitsbedingungen fällt mir schwer.* a seasonal adjustment in price eine saisonal bedingte Anpassung der Preise **2.** *(of engines, machines)* Einstellung ['aɪnʃtɛlʊŋ] die <–, –en> *most sing* ◊ *die Einstellung der Maschinen* **3.** *(text)* adjustment (to

sth) Änderung (an etw. [dat]) ['ɛndərʊŋ] die <–, –en> ◊ *An dem Vertrag müssen noch ein paar Änderungen vorgenommen werden.* make an adjustment to a dress ein Kleid ändern [aɛn klaɛt 'ɛndən] +haben

administer [verb] **1.** *(organize, be in charge of)* verwalten [fɛ'valtn̩] <verwaltet, verwaltete, hat verwaltet> ◊ *ein System verwalten* ♦ *Wer verwaltet die Akten von A bis F?* **2.** *(a drug)* verabreichen [fɛ|'apraɛçn̩] <verabreicht, verabreichte, hat verabreicht> ◊ *Der Arzt verabreichte ihr eine Spritze.*

administration [noun] **1.** *(of a company, an institution)* Verwaltung [fɛ'valtʊŋ] die <–, –en> ◊ *Einsparungen in der öffentlichen Verwaltung* ♦ *in der Verwaltung arbeiten* ♦ *Die Verwaltung befindet sich im Hauptgebäude.* **2.** *(of a country)* Regierung [re'gi:rʊŋ] die <–, –en> ◊ *die Regierung der USA* **3.** *(of a drug)* Verabreichung [fɛ|'apraɛçʊŋ] die <–, –en> *most sing* ◊ *die Verabreichung von Antibiotika*

administrative [adj] administrativ [atmɪnɪstra'ti:f] *no comp/superl* ◊ *administrative Aufgaben;* Verwaltungs... [fɛ'valtʊŋs] administrative work Verwaltungsarbeit [fɛ'valtʊŋsar̩baɛt] der <–, –en>

administrator [noun] **1.** *(of a company, an authority)* Verwaltungsangestellte [fɛ'valtʊŋsanɡəˌʃtɛltə] der/die <–n, die Verwaltungsangestellten> *but: ein Verwaltungsangestellter/eine Verwaltungsangestellte* ◊ *ein Verwaltungsangestellter bei der Gemeinde* **2.** *(in a special field)* Sachbearbeiter ['zaxbər̩,a'baɛtə] der <–s, –> ♀Sachbearbeiterin ['zaxbəˌa'baɛtərɪn] die <–, –nen> ◊ *Erist Sachbearbeiter bei einer Krankenkasse.* ♦ *die zuständige Sachbearbeiterin*

admiration [noun] Bewunderung [bə'vʊndərʊŋ] die <–, –en> *most sing* ◊ *Sie haben unsere Bewunderung verdient.* in admiration voller Bewunderung

admire [verb] bewundern [bə'vʊndən] <bewundert, hat bewundert> ◊ *Ich bewundere dich für deine Geduld.* ♦ *Er bewunderte ihren Mut.*

admissible [adj] zulässig ['tsu:lɛsɪç] *no comp/superl* ◊ *Das Gericht hat ihre Beschwerde für zulässig erklärt.*

admission [noun] **1.** *(of patients, students, refugees)* Aufnahme ['aʊfna:mə] die <–, –n> ◊ *die stationäre Aufnahme von Patienten* ♦ *die Aufnahme neuer Schüler* **2.** *(fee)* Eintritt ['aɛntrɪt] der <–(e)s, –e> ◊ *Der Eintritt ist mir zu teuer.* **3.** *(to a place)* Zutritt ['tsu:trɪt] der <–(e)s> *no pl* ◊ *jdm den Zutritt zu etw. verbieten* **4.** *(of a mistake, guilt)* Eingeständnis ['aɛngəʃtɛntnɪs] das <–ses, –se> ◊ *das Eingeständnis einer Schuld*

admit [verb] **1.** *(a mistake, disappointment)* zugeben ['tsu:ge:bm] <gibt zu, gab zu, hat zugegeben> ◊ *Er gab seinen Fehler zu.* sb admits (that) jd gibt zu, dass ◊ *Sie gab zu, dass ihr Verhalten falsch war.* sb admits to doing sth jd gibt zu, etw. zu tun ◊ *Sie gibt zu, nervös zu sein.* **2.** *(refugees, members, students, patients)* aufnehmen ['aʊfne:mən] <nimmt auf, nahm auf, hat aufgenommen> ◊ *Wir können keine weiteren Patienten aufnehmen.* admit sb to sth jdn in etw. [acc] aufnehmen ◊ *Mitglieder in einen Verein aufnehmen* admit sb to hospital jdn ins Krankenhaus einliefern [ɪns 'kraŋkŋ̩haʊs ˌaɛnli:fən] +haben **3.** *(to a theatre, cinema etc.)* einlassen ['aɛnlasn̩] <lässt ein, ließ ein, hat eingelassen> ◊ *Zuspätkommende werden erst in der Pause eingelassen.* admit sb to sth jdn in etw. [acc] einlassen ◊ *jdn in einen Konzertsaal einlassen*

admittedly [adv] zugegebenermaßen
[,tsʊˈgəgeːbənəˈmaːsn̩] ◊ *Ich könnte zugegebenermaßen härter arbeiten, aber ich habe keine Lust.* ♦ *Sie
ist zugegebenermaßen die schönste Frau, die ich
kenne.*

adopt [verb] **1.** *(a child)* adoptieren [adɔpˈtiːrən]
<adoptiert, adoptierte, hat adoptiert> ◊ *ein Kind adop-
tieren* **2.** *(a nationality, name, belief, proposal)*
annehmen [ˈanneːmən] <nimmt an, nahm an, hat
angenommen> ◊ *einen neuen Namen annehmen* ♦
Ich nehme den Vorschlag an.; (a plan, method etc.)
übernehmen [ybeˈneːmən] <übernimmt, übernahm,
hat übernommen> ◊ *eine Strategie übernehmen*
adopt a country *(as your home)* ein Land zu seiner
Wahlheimat machen [tsuː ... ˈvaːlhaemaːt maxn̩] **3.** *(a
position, point of view)* einnehmen [ˈaenneːmən]
<nimmt ein, nahm ein, hat eingenommen> ◊ *Er
nimmt in dieser Diskussion einen sehr harten Standpunkt ein.*

adoption [noun] **1.** *(of a child)* adoption Adoption
[adɔpˈtsjoːn] die <-, -en> ◊ *die Adoption eines
Babys* **2.** *(of a plan, method etc.)* adoption of sth
Übernahme ... [gen] [ˈyːbenaːmə] die <-, -n> ◊ *die
Übernahme einer Strategie*

adult¹ [noun] Erwachsene [eˈvaksənə] der/die
<-n, die Erwachsenen> *but: ein Erwachsener/eine
Erwachsene* ◊ *Der Film ist nur für Erwachsene freigegeben.* sb is an adult jd ist erwachsen

adult² [adj] **1.** *(people)* erwachsen [eˈvaksn̩] ◊ *ein
erwachsener Mann* **2.** *(literature, films)* erotisch
[eˈroːtɪʃ] ◊ *erotische Literatur; (pornographic)*
Porno... [ˈpɔrno] ◊ *ein Pornofilm* adult film/movie
Pornofilm [ˈpɔrnofɪlm] der <-(e)s, -e>

advance¹ [noun] **1.** *(development)* advance of/in sth
Fortschritt in etw. [dat] Fortschritt ... [gen] [ˈfɔrtʃrɪt]
der <-(e)s, -e> ◊ *Fortschritte in der Medizin* ♦ *der
Fortschritt der Gentechnologie* **2.** *(payment)*
Vorschuss [ˈfoːɐʃʊs] der <-es, Vorschüsse> ◊
*Könnten Sie mir auf mein nächstes Gehalt einen
Vorschuss geben?* **3.** *(of an army)* Vorrücken
[ˈfoːɐrʏkn̩] das <-s> no pl ◊ *das Vorrücken der
Truppen* **4.** *(esp sexual)* advances Annäherungsversuch [ˈannɛːərʊŋsfezuːx] der <-(e)s, -e> *most pl* ◊
vergebliche Annäherungsversuche make advances to
sb einen Annäherungsversuch bei jdm machen
⊛ in advance vorher ◊ *Er hat seinen Besuch nicht
vorher angekündigt.* pay in advance im Voraus
bezahlen

advance² [verb] **1.** *(person)* advance towards sb/sth
auf jdn/etw. zugehen [aof ... ˌtsuːgeːən] <geht zu,
ging zu, ist zugegangen> ◊ *Sie ging langsam auf ihn
zu.; (army)* advance on sth *(auf etw.* [acc])
vorrücken [ˈfoːɐrʏkn̩] *+sein* ◊ *Die Armee ist auf die
Stadt vorgerückt.* **2.** *(fire, enemy)* vordringen
[ˈfoːɐdrɪŋən] <dringt vor, drang vor, ist vorgedrungen>
◊ *Das Feuer drang bis in den Keller vor.* **3.** *(science,
technology)* Fortschritte machen [ˈfɔrtʃrɪtə maxn̩] ◊
*Die Informationstechnologie hat große Fortschritte
gemacht.* **4.** *(disease)* fortschreiten [ˈfɔrtʃraetn̩]
<schreitet fort, schritt fort, ist fortgeschritten> ◊ *Wie
weit war der Krebs fortgeschritten?* **5.** *(peace, your
career)* fördern [ˈfœrden] *+haben* ◊ *seine Karriere
fördern* ♦ *den Weltfrieden fördern* **6.** *(an opinion,
theory)* darlegen [ˈdaːɐleːgn̩] *+haben* ◊ *Er legte seine
Theorie in einem Buch dar.* **7.** *(money)* vorschießen
[ˈfoːɐʃiːsn̩] <schießt vor, schoss vor, hat vorgeschos-

sen> *(fam)* ◊ *Soll ich dir die Summe vorschießen?*

advanced → **advance²** [adj] **1.** *(country, technology,
science)* fortschrittlich [ˈfɔrtʃrɪtlɪç] ◊ *fortschrittliche
Länder* ♦ *Das französische Eisenbahnnetz ist sehr
fortschrittlich.* **2.** *(student, disease, development)* fortgeschritten [ˈfɔrtgəʃrɪtn̩] ◊ *ein fortgeschrittener
Schüler* ♦ *Die Entwicklung ist so weit fortgeschritten,
dass ...*

advantage [noun] Vorteil [ˈfoːɐtael] der <-(e)s, -e> ◊
*Der große Vorteil an dieser Methode ist ihre
Effizienz.* have an advantage over sb/sth einen
Vorteil gegenüber jdm/etw. haben be at an
advantage im Vorteil sein sth gives sb an
advantage etw. ist ein Vorteil für jdn gain
advantage sich Vorteile verschaffen
⊛ show sb to good/best advantage jds Vorzüge
betonen show sth to good/best advantage die
Vorzüge ... [gen] betonen use sth to good/best
advantage etw. richtig/optimal nutzen take
advantage of **1.** take advantage of sth etw. nutzen
◊ *Wir haben den Schnee zum Skifahren genutzt.*
2. *(immorally)* take advantage of sb/sth jdn/etw.
ausnutzen ◊ *Die Betrügerin nutzte ihn/seine Leicht-
gläubigkeit aus.*

adventure [noun] Abenteuer [ˈaːbm̩tɔøɐ] das <-s, ->
◊ *Er hatte einige gefährliche Abenteuer zu bestehen.*
♦ *Die Fahrt durch die Wüste war ein echtes
Abenteuer.*

adverb [noun] Adverb [atˈvɛrp] das <-s, -ien> ◊
Adverbien sind im Deutschen unveränderlich. ♦
'*Gestern*' *ist ein Adverb der Zeit.*

adverse(ly) [adj, adv] **1.** *(negative)* ablehnend
[ˈapleːnant] ◊ *eine ablehnende Antwort* ♦ *Die allgemeine Reaktion der Öffentlichkeit auf den Vorschlag
war ablehnend.* ♦ *ablehnend reagieren*
2. *(unfavo(u)rable)* ungünstig [ˈʊngʏnstɪç] ◊ *Die
Arbeitszeiten sind ungünstig.* ♦ *ungünstige Bedingungen* have an adverse effect on sth/sb sich
ungünstig auf etw./jdn auswirken ◊ *Alkohol wirkt
sich ungünstig auf die Reaktionszeit aus.*

advertise [verb] **1.** *(in a newspaper)* advertise sth etw.
in die Zeitung setzen [ɪn diː ˈtsaetʊŋ zɛtsn̩] *+haben* ◊
*Hast du deine Wohnung schon in die Zeitung
gesetzt?* sb advertises jd gibt eine Anzeige auf
[gipt aenə ˈantsaegə aof] <gibt auf, gab auf, hat aufge-
geben> **2.** *(attract attention)* werben [ˈvɛrbm̩] <wirbt,
warb, hat geworben> ◊ *Diese Firma wirbt im
Fernsehen.* ♦ *mit günstigen Preisen werben* advertise
sth für etw. werben

advertisement [noun] **1.** *(in a newspaper)* Anzeige
[ˈantsaegə] die <-, -n> ◊ *Er meldete sich auf unsere
Anzeige hin.* ♦ *eine Anzeige aufgeben* **2.** *(on TV)*
Werbespot [ˈvɛrbəspɔt] der <-s, -s>

advertising → **advertise** [noun] Werbung [ˈvɛrbʊŋ] die
<-, -en> ◊ *Geld für Werbung ausgeben* ♦ *Die
Werbung zielt bewusst auf die jüngeren Konsumenten.*

advice [noun] **1.** *(sb's opinion or recommendation)* Rat
[raːt] der <-(e)s, Räte> ◊ *Der Patient hörte nicht
auf den Rat des Arztes.* take sb's advice jds Rat
befolgen **2.** *(professional)* Beratung [bəˈraːtʊŋ] die
<-, -en> ◊ *ärztliche Beratung* take legal advice sich
juristisch beraten lassen [juˈrɪstɪʃ bəraːtn̩ lasn̩]
<lässt sich, ließ sich, hat sich lassen>

advisable [adj] ratsam [ˈraːtzaːm] ◊ *Es ist ratsam,
einen Regenschirm mitzunehmen.* ♦ *ratsame*

Impfungen für Globetrotter

advise [verb] 1. *(give information or an opinion)* beraten [bə'ra:tn̩] <berät, beriet, hat beraten> ◊ *Der Anwalt hat mich gut beraten.* advise sb on sth jdn in etw. [dat] beraten ◊ *Er berät die Regierung in Gesundheitsfragen.* 2. advise sb to do sth jdm raten, etw. zu tun ['ra:tn̩ ... t͡su:] <rät, riet, hat geraten> ◊ *Der Arzt riet ihr, sich auszuruhen.* advise against sth von etw. abraten [fɔn ... 'apra:tn̩] <rät ab, riet ab, hat abgeraten> ◊ *Mein Arzt hat mir von einer Operation abgeraten.*

adviser, advisor [noun] 1. Berater [bə'ra:tɐ] der <-s, -> ♀Beraterin [bə'ra:tərɪn] die <-, -nen> ◊ *Frau Krause ist Ihre Beraterin in Anlagefragen.* 2. *(in government, an organisation)* Referent [refe'rɛnt] der <-en, -en> ♀Referentin [refe'rɛntɪn] die <-, -nen> ◊ *die zuständige Referentin für den Bereich der Umweltpolitik* ✦ *der persönliche Referent des Regierungspräsidenten*

advisory [adj] beratend [bə'ra:tn̩t] no comp/superl, mostly before ns ◊ *Sie hat eine beratende Funktion inne.* advisory committee Beratungskommission [bə'ra:tʊŋskɔmɪˌsi̯o:n] die <-, -en>

advocate¹ [noun] 1. *(of a cause, for people)* Fürsprecher ['fy:ɡʃprɛçɐ] der <-s, -> ♀Fürsprecherin ['fy:ɡʃprɛçərɪn] die <-, -nen> ◊ *Die Ärztelobby hat einflussreiche Fürsprecher im Gesundheitsministerium.* ✦ *ein Fürsprecher der Armen* 2. *(lawyer)* Anwalt ['anvalt] der <-(e)s, Anwälte> ♀Anwältin ['anvɛltɪn] die <-, -nen>

advocate² [verb] eintreten für ['a̯entre:tn̩ fy:ɐ̯] <tritt ein, trat ein, ist eingetreten> ◊ *Die Regierung tritt für ein Umdenken in der Gesundheitspolitik ein.*

aerial [noun] Antenne [an'tɛnə] die <-, -n>

aeroplane [noun] Flugzeug ['flu:kt͡sɔɪ̯k] das <-(e)s, -e>

aesthetic [adj] ästhetisch [ɛs'te:tɪʃ] ◊ *eine ästhetische Erfahrung* ✦ *Dieses Design ist nicht sehr ästhetisch.*

affair [noun] 1. *(matter)* Angelegenheit ['angəleˌɡn̩ha̯et] die <-, -en> ◊ *Für diese Angelegenheit ist mein Kollege zuständig.* ✦ *Betrug ist eine ernste Angelegenheit.* 2. *(private)* affairs Angelegenheit ['angəleˌɡn̩ha̯et] die <-, -en> most pl ◊ *Misch dich nicht in meine Angelegenheiten ein!* 3. POL foreign affairs Außenpolitik ['a̯osn̩poliˌti:k] die <-, -en> most sing current affairs Tagespolitik 4. *(sexual, criminal or immoral)* Affäre [a'fɛ:rə] die <-, -n> ◊ *Sie hat eine Affäre mit einem jüngeren Mann.* ✦ *Der ehemalige Kanzler war in diese Affäre verwickelt.*

affect [verb] 1. *(influence)* beeinflussen [bəˈʔa̯enflʊsn̩] <beeinflusst, beeinflusste, hat beeinflusst> ◊ *das Wachstum beeinflussen* ✦ *eine Entscheidung beeinflussen* 2. *(hit, target)* betreffen [bə'trɛfn̩] <betrifft, betraf, hat betroffen> ◊ *Mumps ist eine Krankheit, die vor allem Kinder betrifft.* ✦ *Die Inseln wurden von dem Erdbeben besonders betroffen.* 3. *(have an emotional impact on)* ergreifen [ɐ̯'ɡra̯efn̩] <ergreift, ergriff, hat ergriffen> ◊ *Ihre Rede hat uns zutiefst ergriffen.* ✦ *von einer Musik ergriffen sein* affect sb badly jdn sehr mitnehmen [ze:ɐ̯ 'mɪtne:mən] <nimmt mit, nahm mit, hat mitgenommen> ◊ *Die Scheidung der Eltern hat den Jungen sehr mitgenommen.* 4. *(pretend)* vortäuschen ['fo:ɐ̯tɔʏ̯ʃn̩] +haben ◊ *Er täuschte Desinteresse vor.*

affection [noun] Zuneigung ['t͡su:na̯eɡʊŋ] die <-, -en> most sing ◊ *Er empfand große Zuneigung für sie.* ✦

Ihre Zuneigung wurde nicht erwidert.

affectionate(ly) [adj, adv] liebevoll ['li:bəfɔl] ◊ *Sie warf ihm einen liebevollen Blick zu.* ✦ *Dein Umgang mit Kindern ist sehr liebevoll.* ✦ *Er sah mich liebevoll an.*

affinity [noun] 1. *(connection)* Verwandtschaft [fɛ'vantʃaft] die <-, -en> ◊ *die Verwandtschaft zwischen Schimpansen und Menschen* ✦ *die Verwandtschaft zwischen Fotografie und Malerei* 2. *(sympathy, liking)* Verbundenheit [fɛ'bʊndn̩ha̯et] die <-> no pl ◊ *Sie fühlte eine große Verbundenheit mit ihm.* 3. *(natural inclination)* have an affinity to sth sich zu etw. hingezogen fühlen [t͡su:... ˌhɪŋɡət͡so:ɡn̩ fy:lən] +haben

affirmative [adj] positiv ['po:ziti:f] ◊ *ein positives Resultat* ✦ *Der Bescheid war positiv.*

affluence [noun] Wohlstand ['vo:lʃtant] der <-(e)s> no pl ◊ *Sie lebten im Wohlstand.*

afford [verb] be able to afford sth sich etw. leisten können ['la̯estn̩ kœnən] <kann, konnte, hat können> ◊ *Er kann sich das neue Auto sicher leisten.* sb can afford to do sth jd kann es sich leisten, etw. zu tun ◊ *Ich kann es mir nicht leisten, den ganzen Tag zu faulenzen.*

affordable [adj] erschwinglich [ɐ̯'ʃvɪŋlɪç] ◊ *Wohnungen sind in dieser Gegend noch erschwinglich.* ✦ *Autos zu erschwinglichen Preisen*

afraid [adj] 1. *(expressing fear)* be afraid Angst haben ['aŋst ha:bm̩] ◊ *Hab keine Angst, der Hund beißt nicht!* be afraid of sb/sth vor jdm/etw. Angst haben ◊ *Er hat Angst vor dem Lehrer.* ✦ *Ich habe Angst vor Prüfungen.* be afraid of doing sth, be afraid to do sth Angst (davor) haben, etw. zu tun ◊ *Hab keine Angst, Fragen zu stellen.* ✦ *Er hat Angst davor, sich zu blamieren.* 2. *(expressing regret)* I'm afraid (that) leider [ˈla̯edɐ] ◊ *Leider kann ich Ihnen nicht helfen.* I'm afraid so. Ich fürchte ja. [ɪç fʏ'çtə 'ja:] I'm afraid not. Ich fürchte nein.

Africa [noun] Afrika ['a:frika] das <-s> article only in combination with attribute, no pl → Germany

African¹ [noun] Afrikaner [afri'ka:nɐ] der <-s, -> ♀Afrikanerin [afri'ka:nərɪn] die <-, -nen> → German¹ 1.

African² [adj] afrikanisch [afri'ka:nɪʃ] → German²

after¹ [adv] 1. *(following sth)* danach [da'na:x] He had an accident and died soon after. Er hatte einen Unfall und starb kurz danach.; *(with specified indication of time)* später ['ʃpɛ:tɐ] ◊ *Er hatte einen Unfall und starb zwei Tage später.* 2. *(behind sb/sth)* nach... [na:x] go after sb jdm nachgehen ['na:xɡe:ən] <geht nach, ging nach, ist nachgegangen> drive after sb jdm nachfahren ['na:xfa:rən] <fährt nach, fuhr nach, ist nachgefahren>

after² [prep] *(temporal)* nach [na:x] +dat ◊ *Sie hat gleich nach Erhalt der Rechnung bezahlt.*; *(directly following sth)* auf [a̯of] +acc ◊ *Auf den Schnee folgte Straßenglätte.* ✦ *Es häufte sich Fehler auf Fehler.*; *(spatial)* hinter ['hɪntɐ] +dat ◊ *Er kam knapp hinter dem Ersten ins Ziel.* ✦ *Kurz hinter der Grenze streikte der Motor.*

Ⓔ after all 1. *(in spite of what was expected)* doch ◊ *Er wollte mir nicht helfen, aber dann doch nicht getan.* 2. *(when referring to sth obvious)* schließlich ◊ *Ich kann mich schließlich nicht um alles kümmern.* 3. *(when giving an explanation or reason for sth)* auch ◊ *Ich bin sehr müde; es ist ja auch*

schon spät.

after³ conjunc nachdem [na:x'de:m] ◊ *Nachdem sie die Zähne geputzt hatte, ging sie schlafen.*

afternoon noun Nachmittag ['na:xmɪta:k] der <-(e)s, -e> ◊ *Ich habe heute Nachmittag frei.* in the afternoon nachmittags ['na:xmɪta:ks] ◊ *Wir machen nachmittags immer eine Kaffeepause.*

after-school club noun Hort [hɔʳt] der <-(e)s, -e> ◊ *Seit ich berufstätig bin, geht mein Sohn in den Hort.*

afterwards adv danach [da'na:x] ◊ *Zuerst regnete es, aber danach schien die Sonne.*

again¹ adv **1.** *(referring to a new start)* noch einmal [nɔx 'aɛnma:l] ◊ *Das Programm ist abgestürzt; jetzt kann ich alles noch einmal schreiben.* wieder ganz von vorn [ˌvi:dɐ gants fɔn 'fɔʳn] ◊ *Jetzt muss ich wieder ganz von vorn anfangen!* **2.** *(referring to sth that is a repetition of sth)* wieder ['vi:dɐ] ◊ *Fahren wir nächstes Jahr wieder nach Frankreich?* ♦ *Er bat sich wieder beruhigt.* ♦ *Das darfst du nie wieder tun!* again and again, time and again immer wieder
⊛ then again andererseits

again² part *(fam)* noch (gleich) [nɔx (glaɛç)] ◊ *Wie heißt sie noch (gleich)?*

against prep **1.** gegen ['ge:gŋ] +acc ◊ *Sie schwamm gegen die Strömung.* ♦ *Er wurde gegen Grippe geimpft.* ♦ *Morgen spielen sie gegen Bayern München.* ♦ *gegen meinen Willen/Wunsch* ♦ *Sie ist gegen Abtreibung.* ♦ *Anschuldigungen gegen jdn* Foulspiel ist gegen die Regeln. against each other gegeneinander [ge:gŋ|ae'nandɐ] ◊ *Es treten jeweils zwei Mannschaften gegeneinander an.* ♦ *Sie hat die Vor- und Nachteile gegeneinander abgewogen.* against it/this dagegen [da'ge:gŋ] ◊ *Bist du dafür oder dagegen?* ♦ *Was spricht eigentlich dagegen?* **2.** *(in contrast or relation to)* (as) against gegenüber [ge:gŋ'|y:bɐ] +dat ◊ *Unser Gewinn betrug 292 Mio. gegenüber 279 Mio. im Vorjahr.*

age¹ noun **1.** *(of a person)* Alter ['altɐ] das <-s, -> most sing ◊ *Ich schätze sein Alter auf 55 Jahre.* be sb's age in jds Alter sein at sb's age in jds Alter ◊ *In deinem Alter habe ich noch keinen Alkohol getrunken.* at the age of im Alter von ◊ *Er starb im Alter von 35 Jahren.* with age mit dem Alter ◊ *Mit dem Alter kommt Erfahrung.* well advanced in age betagt [bə'ta:kt] *(lofty)* ◊ *ein betagter Herr* ♦ *Meine Oma ist schon sehr betagt.* **2.** *(era)* Zeitalter ['tsaet|altɐ] das <-s, -> ◊ *im Zeitalter der Computertechnik*
⊛ (for) ages eine Ewigkeit *(fam)* ◊ *Wir haben uns ja eine Ewigkeit nicht gesehen!* of age volljährig ◊ *Ist deine Tochter schon volljährig?* under age minderjährig ◊ *Er ist noch minderjährig.*

age² verb **1.** *(become older)* altern ['altɐn] +sein ◊ *Sie ist sehr gealtert, seit ich sie zuletzt gesehen habe.* ♦ *Kunststoff altert und wird spröde.* **2.** *(make older)* altern lassen ['altɐn lasn] <lässt, ließ, hat lassen> ◊ *Sonnenbaden lässt die Haut vorzeitig altern.*

aged → **age²** adj **1.** *(of a particular age)* alt [alt] ◊ *Ich bin 40 Jahre alt.* a boy aged 12 ein zwölfjähriger Junge [aen ˌtsvœlfjɛːrɪgɐ 'jʊŋə] **2.** *(elderly)* betagt [bə'ta:kt] <betagter, am betagtesten> *(lofty)* ◊ *ein betagter Herr* ♦ *Meine Oma ist sehr betagt.*

agency noun **1.** *(company)* Agentur [agɛn'tu:ɐ] die <-, -en> ◊ *eine Agentur für Models* **2.** *(department*

that works for the government) government agency Regierungsstelle [re'gi:rʊŋsʃtɛlə] die <-, -n> intelligence agency Nachrichtendienst ['na:xrɪçtn̩di:nst] der <-(e)s, -e> ◊ *housing benefit agency* Wohngeldamt ['vo:ngɛlt|amt] das <-(e)s, Wohngeldämter>
⊛ through sb's agency durch jds Vermittlung ◊ *Durch seine Vermittlung habe ich einen neuen Job gefunden.*

agenda noun Tagesordnung ['ta:gəs|ɔʳdnʊŋ] die <-, -en> most sing ◊ *etw. auf die Tagesordnung setzen* ♦ *etw. steht auf der Tagesordnung*
⊛ have a hidden agenda heimliche Ziele verfolgen

agent noun **1.** *(person)* Agent [a'gɛnt] der <-s, -en> ♀Agentin [a'gɛntɪn] die <-, -nen> ◊ *eine Agentin des KGB* ♦ *Er ist als Agent für Schriftsteller tätig.* ♦ *Die Agentin verschaffte ihr ein neues Engagement.* **2.** CHEM cleaning agent Putzmittel ['pʊtsmɪtl̩] das <-s, -> chemical agent chemische Substanz [ˌçe:mɪʃə zʊp'stants] die <-, -en>

aggression noun Aggression [agrɛ'sjo:n] die <-, -en> ◊ *Aggressionen gegen jdn haben*

aggressive(ly) adj, adv **1.** *(nature, behavio(u)r)* aggressiv [agrɛ'si:f] ◊ *Computerspiele können aggressiv machen.* ♦ *aggressiv reagieren* ♦ *eine aggressive Fahrweise* **2.** *(strategy, in sports)* offensiv [ɔfɛn'zi:f] ◊ *ein offensiver Kampf* ♦ *Sein Fußballspiel war offensiv.* ♦ *offensiv auftreten*

agitate verb **1.** POL agitieren [agi'ti:rən] <agitiert, agitierte, hat agitiert> ◊ *gegen die Regierung/für mehr Freiheit agitieren* **2.** *(emotionally)* erregen [ɛ're:gŋ] <erregt, erregte, hat erregt> ◊ *Der Streit erregte ihn sehr.*

agitated → **agitate** adj unruhig ['ʊnru:ɪç] ◊ *unruhiger Schlaf* ♦ *Als er um Mitternacht noch nicht zu Hause war, wurde sie unruhig.*

agitation noun **1.** *(restlessness)* Unruhe ['ʊnru:ə] die <-, -n> most sing ◊ *etw. sorgt für erhebliche Unruhe* in agitation unruhig ['ʊnru:ɪç] ◊ *unruhig auf und ab gehen* **2.** POL Agitation [agita'tsjo:n] die <-, -en> ◊ *Agitation gegen die Regierung*

ago adv vor [fo:ɐ] placed before the noun +dat ◊ *Ich habe ihn vor zwei Wochen getroffen.* long ago vor langer Zeit ◊ *Vor langer Zeit lebte ein König.*

agony noun Qualen ['kva:lən] die <-> only pl be in agony Qualen erleiden die in agony qualvoll sterben [ˌkva:lfɔl 'ʃtɛʳbm̩] <stirbt, starb, ist gestorben>

agree verb **1.** *(share an opinion)* zustimmen ['tsu:ʃtɪmən] +haben ◊ *„Ich habe ihm einen Vorschlag gemacht." —„Hat er zugestimmt?"* agree with sb/sth jdm/einer Sache zustimmen ◊ *In dieser Sache stimme ich Ihnen zu.* ♦ *Ich kann dieser Aussage nicht zustimmen.* **2.** *(accept sth)* einverstanden sein ['aenfɛʃtandn̩ zaen] +sein ◊ *„Haben sie den Antrag abgelehnt?" — „Nein, sie waren einverstanden."* agree to sth mit etw. einverstanden sein agree to do sth damit einverstanden sein, etw. zu tun ◊ *Wären Sie damit einverstanden, mehr zu arbeiten?* **3.** *(come to an understanding about sth)* agree on sth sich über etw. acc einigen [y:bɐ ... 'aenɪgŋ] +haben ◊ *sich über einen Vertrag einigen* **4.** *(decide on a time, date etc.)* agree (on) sth etw. vereinbaren [fɛʳ'aenba:rən] <vereinbart, vereinbarte, hat vereinbart> ◊ *einen Termin beim Zahnarzt vereinbaren* ♦ *Ich habe mit ihm vereinbart, dass wir uns um 14 Uhr treffen.* **5.** *(harmonize)* übereinstimmen [ybɐ|'aenʃtɪmən] +haben ◊ *Unsere Ergebnisse*

stimmten nicht überein. ♦ *Das Adjektiv muss mit dem Substantiv übereinstimmen.*

⊛ **sth agrees with sb** *(food, drink)* etw. bekommt jdm

agreed → agree [adj] **1.** *(already established)* vereinbart [fɛˈʔaɛnbaːrt] no comp/superl ◊ *die vereinbarte Summe* **2.** *(people)* **be agreed (about sth)** sich (über etw. [acc]) einig sein [ˈaɛnɪç ˈzaɛn] +sein ◊ *Sie sind sich über ihre Pläne einig.*

agreement [noun] **1.** *(upon request)* Einverständnis [ˈaɛnfɛʃtɛntnɪs] das <-ses, -se> most sing ◊ *Sie haben um unser Einverständnis gebeten.* **2.** *(between people)* Vereinbarung [fɛˈʔaɛnbaːrʊŋ] die <-, -en> ◊ *sich an eine Vereinbarung halten* ♦ *eine mündliche Vereinbarung* **have an agreement with sb** eine Vereinbarung mit jdm getroffen haben; *(process of agreeing)* Übereinkunft [ybɛˈʔaɛnkʊnft] die <-, Übereinkünfte> ◊ *eine Übereinkunft zwischen zwei Firmen* **reach an agreement** eine Übereinkunft erzielen **3.** POL Abkommen [ˈapkɔmən] das <-s, -> ◊ *mit jdm ein Abkommen schließen*

⊛ **be in agreement (on sth)** (über etw. [acc]) einer Meinung sein **come to an agreement** sich einigen ◊ *Konnten die Delegierten sich einigen?*

agricultural [adj] landwirtschaftlich [ˈlantvɪrtʃaftlɪç] no comp/superl, mostly before ns ◊ *die landwirtschaftliche Nutzung einer Fläche* **agricultural policy** Agrarpolitik [aˈgraːrpoliˌtiːk] die <-, -en> most sing

agriculture [noun] Landwirtschaft [ˈlantvɪrtʃaft] die <-> most sing

ahead [adv] **1.** *(in front)* voraus [foˈraɵs] ◊ *Bitte fahren Sie voraus.* ♦ *Er ist seinen Mitschülern in Mathematik weit voraus.* **keep/stay ahead** in Führung bleiben [ɪn ˈfyːrʊŋ blaɛbm̩] <bleibt, blieb, ist geblieben> **get ahead** vorwärts kommen [ˈfoːɐ̯vɛrts kɔmən] <kommt, kam, ist gekommen> **straight ahead** geradeaus [gəraˈdəˈaɵs] **2.** *(with the future in mind)* voraus... [foˈraɵs] **look ahead** vorausschauen [foˈraɵsʃaɵən] +haben ◊ *Wir müssen in der Umweltpolitik vorausschauen.* **plan ahead** vorausplanen [foˈraɵsplaːnən] +haben ◊ *Er hat perfekt vorausgeplant.*

> 'Ahead' may occur in phrasal verbs like 'get ahead' which have their own entries in the dictionary.

ahead of [prep] vor [foːɐ̯] [+dat] ◊ *Er ging vor mir durchs Ziel.* **ahead of your time** seiner Zeit voraus [zaɛne tsaɛt foˈraɵs] ◊ *Leonardo da Vinci war seiner Zeit weit voraus.*

aid¹ [noun] Hilfe [ˈhɪlfə] die <-> no pl ◊ *Die Bevölkerung benötigt humanitäre Hilfe.* ♦ *finanzielle Hilfe vom Staat* **come to sb's aid** jdm zu Hilfe kommen **with the aid of sth** mithilfe ... [gen] [mɪtˈhɪlfə] **mithilfe von** [mɪtˈhɪlfə fɔn] [+gen] ◊ *Mithilfe eines Taschenrechners löste ich die Aufgabe.* ♦ *mithilfe von Tests die besten Bewerber aussuchen*

aid² [verb] unterstützen [ʊntɐˈʃtʏtsn̩] <unterstützt, unterstützte, hat unterstützt> ◊ *Dieses Medikament unterstützt den Kreislauf.* ♦ *Wir werden Sie bei Ihrer Arbeit gern unterstützen.*

AIDS, Aids [noun] Aids [eːts] das <-> no pl ◊ *Viele Kinder in Afrika sind mit Aids infiziert.*

aim¹ [noun] Ziel [tsiːl] das <-(e)s, -e> A is the aim of B B hat A zum Ziel ◊ *Was hatte diese Aktion zum Ziel?* **achieve your aims** seine Ziele erreichen

⊛ **take aim (at sth)** (auf etw. [acc]) zielen ◊ *Er*

zielte auf die Enten und schoss.

aim² [verb] **1.** *(have an intention/purpose)* **aim to do sth** beabsichtigen, etw. zu tun [bəˈʔapzɪçtɪgn̩ ... tuːn] <beabsichtigt, beabsichtigte, hat beabsichtigt> ◊ *Er beabsichtigt, sein Studium im Jahr 2007 abzuschließen.* **be aimed at sth** auf etw. [acc] abzielen [aɵf ... ˌaptsiːlən] +haben **be aimed at doing sth** darauf abzielen, etw. zu tun ◊ *Sein Verhalten zielt darauf ab, andere zu provozieren.* **be aimed at sb** für jdn gedacht sein [fyːɐ̯ ... gəˌdaxt zaɛn] ◊ *Dieses Buch ist besonders für junge Leser gedacht.* **aim for sth** etw. anstreben [ˈanʃtreːbm̩] +haben ◊ *Sie strebt eine Stelle in der Verwaltung an.* **2.** *(a gun)* anlegen [ˈanleːgn̩] +haben ◊ *Er legte an und feuerte.* **aim at sb/sth** auf jdn/etw. zielen [aɵf ... tsiːlən] +haben ◊ *Er zielte auf das Tor.* **aim sth at sb** mit etw. auf jdn zielen ◊ *Sie zielte mit der Pistole auf den Verbrecher.*

air¹ [noun] **1.** *(what we breathe, what surrounds everything)* Luft [lʊft] die <-, Lüfte> ◊ *frische Luft hereinlassen* ♦ *Sie warf den Ball in die Luft.* ♦ *nach Luft ringen* **2.** *(appearance, impression)* **air of confidence** selbstsicheres Auftreten [ˌzɛlpstzɪçərəs ˈaɵftreːtn̩] das <-s> no pl ◊ *Ihr selbstsicheres Auftreten beeindruckt alle.* **lend an air of importance to sth** einer Sache [dat] Gewicht verleihen [gəˈvɪçt fɛlaɛən] ◊ *Der Artikel verlieh dem Thema Umweltschutz zusätzliches Gewicht.* **3.** *(atmosphere)* **an air of doom** Untergangsstimmung [ˈʊntɐgaŋsʃtɪmʊŋ] <-> no pl ◊ *In der gesamten Abteilung herrschte Untergangsstimmung.* **an air of uncertainty** eine gewisse Unsicherheit [aɛnə gəvɪsə ˈʊnzɪçɐhaɛt] <-> no pl **have an air of mystery (about them/it)** etwas Mysteriöses an sich haben [ɛtvas mysteˈrjøːzəs an ... haːbm̩] **4.** *(behavio(u)r)* **airs (and graces)** Gehabe [gəˈhaːbə] das <-s> no pl ◊ *Er nervt mich mit seinem Gehabe.* **put on airs** vornehm tun ◊ *Sie tut immer so vornehm.*

⊛ **be up in the air** in der Luft hängen **disappear into thin air** sich in Luft auflösen **off (the) air** nicht mehr auf Sendung ◊ *Du kannst jetzt husten — wir sind nicht mehr auf Sendung.* **on (the) air** auf Sendung

air² [verb] **1.** *(your views, problems, complaints)* darlegen [ˈdaːrleːgn̩] +haben ◊ *In diesem Papier legt der Politiker seine persönliche Meinung dar.* **2.** *(your clothes, a room)* lüften [ˈlʏftn̩] +haben ◊ *die Wohnung bei Betten lüften*

air conditioning [noun] Klimaanlage [ˈkliːmaˌanlaːgə] die <-, -n> ◊ *Hat der Wagen eine Klimaanlage?* ♦ *die Klimaanlage einschalten*

aircraft [noun] Flugzeug [ˈfluːktsɔɵk] das <-(e)s, -e> ◊ *Das Flugzeug ist gelandet.*

air force [noun] Luftwaffe [ˈlʊftvafə] die <-, -n>

airline [noun] Fluggesellschaft [ˈfluːkgəzɛlʃaft] die <-, -en>

airmail [noun] Luftpost [ˈlʊftpɔst] die <-> no pl ◊ *Ich schicke den Brief per Luftpost.*

airplane → plane

airport [noun] Flughafen [ˈfluːkhaːfn̩] der <-s, Flughäfen> ◊ *Wir müssen zwei Stunden vor Abflug am Flughafen sein.*

aisle [noun] Gang [gaŋ] der <-(e)s, Gänge> ◊ *im Flugzeug am Gang sitzen*

alarm¹ [noun] **1.** *(concern, worry)* Sorge [ˈzɔrgə] die <-, -n> ◊ *Sie war voller Sorge.* ♦ *"Ist sie krank?" — "Kein Grund zur Sorge. Es geht ihr schon*

besser." **2.** *(warning sound)* Alarm [a'la^rm] der <— (e)s, —e> ◊ *Die Diebstahlsicherung löste sofort Alarm aus.* ✦ *falscher Alarm* raise/sound the alarm Alarm schlagen **3.** *(device)* Alarmanlage [a'la^rm|anla:gə] die <—, —n> ◊ *Hat das Haus eine Alarmanlage?* fire alarm Feuermelder ['fɔøemɛldɐ] der <—s, —>

alarm² [verb] beunruhigen [bə|'ʊnru:ɪgn̩] <beunruhigt, beunruhigte, hat beunruhigt> ◊ *Es beunruhigt mich etwas, dass sie so lange weg ist.* ✦ *Der Brief des Anwalts beunruhigte sie zutiefst.*

alarm clock [noun] Wecker ['vɛkɐ] der <—s, —> ◊ *Stellst du den Wecker bitte auf 8 Uhr?* ✦ *Der Wecker klingelt.*

alarming(ly) [adj, adv] alarmierend [ala^r'mi:rənt] ◊ *eine alarmierende Entwicklung* ✦ *Der Anstieg der Arbeitslosigkeit ist alarmierend.* ✦ *eine alarmierend hobe Konzentration von Giften*

albeit [conjunc] wenn auch [vɛn aọx] ◊ *Sie machte sich, wenn auch widerwillig, an die Arbeit.*

album [noun] Album ['albʊm] das <—s, Alben> ◊ *Wann erscheint das neue Album von Madonna?* ✦ *Ich muss die Urlaubsfotos noch ins Album kleben.*

alcohol [noun] Alkohol ['alkoho:l] der <—s, tech —e> *most sing* ◊ *Er trinkt keinen Alkohol.* ✦ *Desinfizieren Sie die Hautstelle mit Alkohol!*

alcoholic¹ [noun] Alkoholiker [alko'ho:lɪkɐ] der <—s, —> ♀Alkoholikerin [alko'ho:lɪkərɪn] die <—, —nen> ◊ *Sie ist Alkoholikerin.*

alcoholic² [adj] alkoholisch [alko'ho:lɪʃ] *no comp/ superl* ◊ *alkoholische Getränke*

Alcoholics Anonymous [noun] Anonyme Alkoholiker [ano,ny:mə alko'ho:lɪkɐ] die <Anonymen Alkoholiker> *only pl* ◊ *Sie geht jeden Donnerstag zum Treffen der Anonymen Alkoholiker.*

alert¹ [noun] Alarm [a'la^rm] der <— (e)s, —e> trigger an alert Alarm auslösen ◊ *Eine Giftwolke löste Alarm aus.* be on alert alarmbereit sein [a'la^rmbəraɛt zaɛn] ◊ *Die Sicherheitskräfte waren alarmbereit.* red alert Alarmstufe rot [a,la^rmʃtu:fə 'ro:t] die <—> *no pl* ⊛ be on the alert auf der Hut sein

alert² [adj] **1.** *(intelligent, bright)* wach [vax] ◊ *Sie hat einen wachen Verstand.* ✦ *Sein Blick wirkt wach und interessiert.* **2.** *(attentive, aware)* aufmerksam ['aọfmɛ^rkza:m] ◊ *Eltern müssen sehr aufmerksam sein, wenn kleine Kinder in der Küche spielen.* be alert to sth/sb auf etw./jdn achten [aọf ... ,axtn̩] ◊ *Du solltest auf Stresssymptome achten.*

alert³ [verb] **1.** *(the police, fire service etc.)* alarmieren [ala^r'mi:rən] <alarmiert, alarmierte, hat alarmiert> ◊ *Als er an den Unfallort kam, alarmierte er sofort die Polizei.* **2.** *(tell about a possible danger)* alert sb to sth jdn auf etw. [acc] hinweisen [aọf ... ,hɪnvaẹzn̩] <weist hin, wies hin, hat hingewiesen> ◊ *jdn auf eine Gefahr hinweisen* alert sb to the fact that jdn darauf hinweisen

A levels [noun] Abitur [abi'tu:ɐ] das <—s, —e> *most sing* ◊ *Nur wer das Abitur hat, kann studieren.* take your A levels Abitur machen ◊ *Er hat 1998 Abitur gemacht.*

alien¹ [noun] **1.** *(in the US: foreigner)* Ausländer ['aọslɛndɐ] der <—s, —> ♀Ausländerin ['aọslɛndərɪn] die <—, —nen> ◊ *Als Ausländer ist man bei der Arbeitssuche oft im Nachteil.* **2.** *(extraterrestrial)* Außerirdische ['aọse|ɪ^rdɪʃə] der/die

<—n, die Außerirdischen> *but: ein Außerirdischer/eine Außerirdische* ◊ *E. T. war ein Außerirdischer.*

alien² [adj] **1.** *(foreign)* ausländisch ['aọslɛndɪʃ] *no comp/superl* ◊ *ausländische Arbeitnehmer* **2.** *(extraterrestial)* außerirdisch ['aọse|ɪ^rdɪʃ] *no comp/superl* ◊ *In dem Film geht es um eine Invasion außerirdischer Wesen.* **3.** *(unfamiliar)* fremd [frɛmt] <fremder, am fremdesten> ◊ *eine fremde Kultur* be/become alien to sb jdm fremd sein/werden ◊ *Die Heimat war ihm fremd geworden.*

alike [adv] **1.** *(in the same way)* gleich [glaẹç] ◊ *Man kann nicht erwarten, dass alle Menschen gleich denken.* ✦ *Die Zwillinge ziehen sich gleich an.* **2.** *(equally valid for several persons/things)* gleichermaßen ['glaẹçema:sn̩] ◊ *Der Film gefiel Männern wie Frauen gleichermaßen.*

alive [adj] lebendig [le'bɛndɪç] ◊ *Gegen Abend wird der Marktplatz wieder lebendig.* ✦ *Einige Opfer wurden noch lebendig aufgefunden.* ✦ *In diesem Dorf sind die alten Traditionen noch sehr lebendig.* be buried/burned alive lebendig begraben/verbrannt werden be (still) alive (noch) am Leben sein [(nɔx) am 'le:bm̩ zaẹn] +sein ◊ *Ist deine Oma noch am Leben?* stay alive am Leben bleiben [am 'le:bm̩ blaẹbm̩] <bleibt, blieb, ist geblieben> keep sth alive etw. aufrechterhalten ['aọfrɛçt|ehaltn̩] <erhält aufrecht, erhielt aufrecht, hat aufrechterhalten> ◊ *Dieser alte Brauch sollte aufrechterhalten werden.* alive with erfüllt von [e'fʏlt fɔn] ◊ *Das Haus war erfüllt von Kinderlachen.* ⊛ alive and kicking gesund und munter

all¹ [adv] **1.** *(completely)* ganz [gants] ◊ *Sie war ganz glücklich.* ✦ *Die Braut war ganz in Weiß gekleidet.* **2.** *(without any exception)* sämtlich ['zɛmtlɪç] ◊ *Seine Vorfahren waren sämtlich erfolgreiche Geschäftsleute.* ✦ *Die Vorstellungen waren sämtlich ausverkauft.* ⊛ all along von Anfang an ◊ *Das habe ich von Anfang an befürchtet.* all around **1.** *(in the surroundings)* ringsherum ◊ *Ringsherum herrschte große Aufregung.* **2.** *(around sth)* rundum ◊ *Inseln sind rundum von Wasser umgeben.* all but fast ◊ *Er wäre fast abgestürzt.* all in all alles in allem ◊ *Mit dem Faulenzen ist es ab heute aus und vorbei.* **2.** *(everywhere)* überall ◊ *Er war überall im Gesicht mit Farbe beschmiert.* **3.** *(on every part of your body)* am ganzen Körper ◊ *Es juckte mich am ganzen Körper.* all too allzu all by yourself ganz allein

all² [det] **1.** *(every one of several)* alle ['alə] *before countable ns* ◊ *Nicht alle Fehler sind schlimm.* all sorts of allerlei [ale'laẹ] ◊ *Es gab allerlei Gerüchte um den Star.* **2.** *(the entirety of sth)* all the ... der/ die/das ganze ... [de:ɐ/di:/das 'gantsə] *before uncountable ns* ◊ *Er hat das ganze Geld verloren.* **3.** *(predeterminer)* all [al] ◊ *mit all unseren Kräften* ✦ *All die Menschen machen mir Angst.* ⊛ ... of all things/people ausgerechnet ... ◊ *Ausgerechnet er ist befördert worden!*

all³ [pron] **1.** *(everything)* alles ['aləs] ◊ *Draußen blieb alles ruhig.* ✦ *Das stimmt alles nicht!* the best of all am besten [am 'bɛstn̩] ◊ *Er hat die Aufgabe am besten gelöst.* the happiest of all am glücklichsten [am 'glʏklɪçstn̩] ◊ *Bei dir bin ich am glücklichsten.* the most of all am meisten [am 'maẹstn̩] ◊ *Klassi-*

sche Musik liebt sie am meisten. **2.** *(of a group of people or things)* all of the ... **alle** ... ['alə] *before countable ns* ◊ *Alle Mitarbeiter streikten.* all of us **wir alle** [viːɐ̯ 'alə] ◊ *Wir alle wollen mehr Freizeit.* ♦ *Wir sind alle dafür verantwortlich.* all of you **ihr/Sie alle** ◊ *Ich möchte euch allen danken.* ♦ *Sie sind alle zu spät gekommen.* all of those who **all diejenigen, die** [al 'diːjeːnɪɡn̩ diː]; *(the whole of a thing)* all of ... **der/die/das ganze ...** [deːɐ̯/diː/das 'gantsə] *before uncountable ns* ◊ *Er hat den ganzen Zucker verschüttet.*

◉ **at all überhaupt** ◊ *Sie hat überhaupt keine Ahnung von Astronomie.*

all-day adj **ganztägig** ['gantsteːɡɪç] ◊ *eine ganztägige Veranstaltung*

allegation noun **Anschuldigung** ['anʃʊldɪɡʊŋ] die <-, -en> ◊ *Ich weise diese Anschuldigungen zurück!*

allege verb **behaupten** [bə'haoptn̩] <behauptet, behauptete, hat behauptet> ◊ *Wer hat das behauptet?* ♦ *Sie behauptet, jemand habe ihre Handtasche gestohlen.* be alleged to have done sth **angeblich etw. getan haben** ◊ *Er hat angeblich versucht, seine Frau umzubringen.*

alleged(ly) adj, adv **angeblich** ['angeːplɪç] *no comp/ superl; when used as an adj, only before ns* ◊ *ein angeblicher Spion* ♦ *Sie war angeblich krank.*

allergic adj **allergisch** [a'lɛrɡɪʃ] *seldom comp/superl* ◊ *eine allergische Reaktion auf Katzenhaare*
◉ **be allergic to sth** **1.** *(to a substance)* **allergisch gegen etw. sein** ◊ *Er ist gegen Hausstaub allergisch.* **2.** *(to unpleasant behaviour, character traits)* **allergisch auf etw.** acc **reagieren** ◊ *Auf Dummheit reagiere ich allergisch.*

alley noun **Gasse** ['gasə] die <-, -n> ◊ *durch eine enge Gasse fahren*

alliance noun **Bündnis** ['bʏntnɪs] das <-ses, -se> ◊ *Sie schlossen ein Bündnis.* ♦ *Sie gingen ein Bündnis mit Frankreich ein.* ♦ *ein Bündnis gegen Rassismus*

allied adj **1.** *(related)* **verwandt** [fɛ'vant] ◊ *Umweltschutz und verwandte Themen* **2.** *(working together)* **verbündet** [fɛ'bʏndət] ◊ *verbündete Staaten/Unternehmen* **3.** *(connected)* **allied with verbunden mit** [fɛ'bʊndn̩ mɪt] ◊ *Die Krankheit verursacht hohes Fieber, verbunden mit Kopfschmerzen.* ♦ *ein mit dem Wetter verbundenes Phänomen*
◉ **the Allied forces die Alliierten** ◊ *die Landung der Alliierten in der Normandie*

all-inclusive adj **Pauschal...** [pao'ʃaːl] all-inclusive holiday **Pauschalurlaub** [pao'ʃaːlǀuːɐ̯laop] der <-(e)s, -e> all-inclusive price **Pauschalpreis** [pao'ʃaːlpraes] der <-(e)s, -e>

allocate verb **1.** *(a task)* **zuweisen** ['tsuːvaezn̩] <weist zu, wies zu, hat zugewiesen> ◊ *Welche Aufgabe hat man dir zugewiesen?* **2.** *(a vacancy, money)* **vergeben** [fɛ'ɡeːbm̩] <vergibt, vergab, hat vergeben> ◊ *Eine zentrale Stelle vergibt die Studienplätze.*

allocation noun **1.** *(amount, share)* **Zuteilung** ['tsuːtaelʊŋ] die <-, -en> ◊ *Hast du deine Zuteilung an Proviant schon bekommen?* **2.** *(process of allocating)* **Vergabe** [fɛ'ɡaːbə] die <-> *no pl* ◊ *Die Vergabe der Preise findet nächste Woche statt.* ♦ *über die Vergabe der Stipendien entscheiden*

allow verb **1.** *(give permission)* **erlauben** [ɛ'laobm̩] <erlaubt, erlaubte, hat erlaubt> ◊ *Rauchen ist hier nicht erlaubt.* allow sb to do sth **jdm erlauben, etw. zu tun** ◊ *Meine Eltern erlauben mir, bis 11 Uhr*

abends auszubleiben. **2.** *(let sth happen)* **lassen** ['lasn̩] <lässt, ließ, hat lassen> ◊ *den Tee fünf Minuten ziehen lassen* ♦ *Lässt du mich bitte ausreden?* **3.** *(calculate)* **rechnen** ['rɛçnən] +haben ◊ *Ich habe für jeden Gast zwei Stücke Fleisch gerechnet.* **4.** *(tolerate, accept)* **zulassen** ['tsuːlasn̩] <lässt zu, ließ zu, hat zugelassen> ◊ *Wir können nicht zulassen, dass so etwas geschieht!* ♦ *Diese Beweise werden vom Gericht nicht zugelassen.*
• **allow for** phras v **einplanen** ['aenplaːnən] +haben ◊ *Den Stau hatte ich natürlich nicht eingeplant.*

allowance noun **1.** *(amount of money)* **finanzielle Unterstützung** [finan͜tsjɛlə ʊntɐ'ʃtʏtsʊŋ] die <-> *no pl* housing allowance **Wohngeld** ['voːnɡɛlt] das <-(e)s, -er> Jobseeker's Allowance **Arbeitslosenunterstützung** ['aʁbaetsloːzn̩ʊntɐʃtʏtsʊŋ] die <-> *no pl* **2.** tax allowance **Steuerfreibetrag** [ʃtɔøɐ'fʁaebətraːk] der <-(e)s, Steuerfreibeträge> ◊ *Wie hoch ist der Steuerfreibetrag für allein Erziehende?* **3.** *(officially determined limit)* luggage allowance **Höchstgewicht für Gepäck** ['høːçstɡəvɪçt fyːɐ̯ ɡəˌpɛk] das <-(e)s, -e> daily recommended allowance **empfohlener Tagesbedarf** [ɛmˌpfoːlənɐ 'taːɡəsbədaʁf] der <-(e)s> *no pl* ◊ *Wie hoch ist der empfohlene Tagesbedarf an Vitamin A?*
◉ **make allowance(s)** *(tolerate unpleasant circumstances)* **Zugeständnisse machen** ◊ *Aufgrund der Renovierungsarbeiten mussten sie einige Zugeständnisse machen.* make allowance(s) for sth *(consider sth)* **etw. berücksichtigen** ◊ *Haben Sie die Kosten für die Instandhaltung berücksichtigt?*

all right¹ adj, adv **1.** *(satisfactory)* **okay** [o'keː] *no comp/superl; when used as an adj, not before ns* *(fam)* ◊ *Unsere neuen Nachbarn sind okay.* ♦ *Die Mannschaft hat gestern ganz okay gespielt.* get on all right with sb **mit jdm schon klarkommen** [mɪt ... ʃoːn 'klaːˈkɔmən] <kommt klar, kam klar, ist klargekommen> ◊ *Ich komme mit dem neuen Chef schon klar.* **2.** *(quite successful)* **go all right gut laufen** ['ɡuːt ˌlaofn̩] <läuft, lief, ist gelaufen> ◊ *Ist die Prüfung gut gelaufen?* ♦ „Wie war's denn?" — „Es lief gut." do all right in a test **in einem Test gut abschneiden** [ɪn aenəm tɛst ˌɡuːt 'apʃnaedn̩] <schneidet ab, schnitt ab, hat abgeschnitten> do all right for yourself **erfolgreich sein** [ɛ'fɔlkʁaeç zaen] +sein **3.** *(asking for or giving permission)* **in Ordnung** [ɪn 'ɔʁdnʊŋ] ◊ *Ist es in Ordnung, wenn ich kurz zur Post gehe?* **4.** *(healthy)* Are you all right? **Geht es Ihnen/dir gut?** [ˌɡeːt ɛs iːnən/diːɐ̯ 'ɡuːt]; *(unharmed)* Are you all right? **Ist Ihnen/dir etwas passiert?** [ɪst iːnən/diːɐ̯ ɛtvas pa'siːɐ̯t] **5.** *(confirming a statement which is then qualified)* **schon** [ʃoːn] ◊ *Sie ist schon hübsch, aber nicht mein Typ.* ♦ *Diese Aufgabe ist schon schwer, aber ich schaffe das schon.*
◉ **everything is going to be all right es wird alles gut** ◊ *Hab keine Angst — es wird alles gut.* that's all right **1.** *(polite response when sb thanks you for sth)* **gern geschehen** ◊ *Vielen herzlichen Dank für die Hilfe! — Gern geschehen!* **2.** *(forgiving response when sb apologizes to you)* **schon gut** ◊ *Das tut mir Leid! — Schon gut!*

all right² interj *(agreeing to sth or checking agreement)* **in Ordnung** [ɪn 'ɔʁdnʊŋ] ◊ „Darf ich Ihr Telefon benutzen?" — „In Ordnung." ♦ *Ich komme dann so gegen 20 Uhr, in Ordnung?*; *(used when*

getting sb's attention, giving in, admitting sth) schön [ʃøːn] ◊ *Schön, dann fangen wir an.* ♦ *Na schön, wenn du darauf bestehst.*

All Saints' Day (noun) Allerheiligen ['alɐˌhaɛlɪɡn̩] *seldom with definite article 'das'* ◊ *An Allerheiligen geben wir auf den Friedhof.*

All Souls' Day (noun) Allerseelen ['alɐˌzeːlən] *seldom with definite article 'das'* ◊ *An Allerseelen besuchte er das Grab seiner Eltern.*

ally (noun) Verbündete [fɛ'bʏndətə] der/die <–n, die Verbündeten> *but: ein Verbündeter/eine Verbündete* ◊ *Tina ist meine engste Verbündete gegen den Chef.* ♦ *Hast du in Tom einen Verbündeten gefunden?* ♦ *Amerika und seine Verbündeten* ◉ the **Allies** die Alliierten ◊ *Die Alliierten haben das Land aufgeteilt.*

almond (noun) Mandel ['mandl̩] die <–, –n> ◊ *eine Tüte gebrannte Mandeln*

almost (adv) fast [fast] ◊ *Die Flasche ist fast leer.* ♦ *Fast tausend Personen kamen.* ♦ *Ich bin fast fertig.* ♦ *Eine Lösung des Konflikts erscheint fast unmöglich.* He almost fell. Er wäre fast hingefallen. He almost won. Er hätte fast gewonnen.

alone¹ (adj) *(by yourself)* allein [a'laɛn] alleine [a'laɛnə] *no comp/superl, not before ns* ◊ *Bist du allein zu Hause?* ◉ feel alone sich einsam fühlen leave/let sb **alone** jdn in Ruhe lassen leave/let sth **alone** etw. sein lassen

alone² (adv) allein [a'laɛn] *no comp/superl* ◊ *Ich lebe allein.* ♦ *Schon allein vom Geruch wird mir schlecht.* ♦ *Er allein kann diese Entscheidung treffen.*

along¹ (adv) *(with sb)* mit... [mɪt] bring sth **along** etw. mitbringen ['mɪtbrɪŋən] <bringt mit, brachte mit, hat mitgebracht> ◊ *Bringst du deine Gitarre mit?* come **along** (with sb) (mit jdm) mitkommen ['mɪtkɔmən] <kommt mit, kam mit, ist mitgekommen> ◊ *Kommst du (mit uns) mit zum Straßenfest?* take sth **along** etw. mitnehmen ['mɪtneːmən] <nimmt mit, nahm mit, hat mitgenommen> ◊ *Nimm einen Schirm mit, es könnte regnen.; (alone)* go along hingehen ['hɪŋɡeːən] <geht hin, ging hin, ist hingegangen> ◊ *Nebenan ist ein Gartenfest; ich werde auch mal hingehen.* be/come **along** kommen [kɔmən] <kommt, kam, ist gekommen> ◊ *Die Polizei muss jeden Augenblick kommen.* ♦ *Ich komme gleich!*

> 'Along' often occurs in phrasal verbs like 'get along' or 'go along' which have their own entries in the dictionary.

along² (prep) 1. *(the whole length of sth)* entlang [ɛnt'laŋ] *with acc when used after a noun, otherwise with dat* ◊ *immer die Straße entlang in Richtung Norden* ♦ *ein Weg entlang dem Rheinufer; (with certain verbs)* entlang... [ɛnt'laŋ] drive along sth etw. entlangfahren [ɛnt'laŋfaːrən] +*sein* ◊ *Fahren Sie immer die Küste entlang!* 2. *(along the sides of sth)* längs [lɛŋs] +gen ◊ *Sie bauten Dutzende von Villen längs des Flusses.*

alongside¹ (adv) nebenher... [neːbm̩'heːɐ] stroll alongside nebenherlaufen [neːbm̩'heːɐˌglaofn̩] <läuft nebenher, lief nebenher, ist nebenhergelaufen> ◊ *Er ging spazieren und sein Hund lief nebenher.*

alongside² (prep) *(close to, in comparison with, in addition to)* neben ['neːbm̩] +dat ◊ *Neben ihm habe ich noch zwei weitere Mitarbeiter.* ♦ *Der Radweg*

verläuft direkt neben der Straße. ♦ *Hier leben Raubkatzen friedlich neben Wölfen.; (in the company of, working with)* an der Seite von [an deːɐ 'zaɛtə fɔn] +dat ◊ *In diesem Film spielte Julia Roberts an der Seite von Richard Gere.*

along with (prep) mit [mɪt] +dat ◊ *Er war mit seinem Sohn erschienen.* ♦ *Das Haus wird mit dem Pferdestall verkauft.*

aloud (adv) laut [laot] <lauter, am lautesten> ◊ *Könntest du das bitte laut vorlesen?*

Alps (noun) Alpen ['alpn̩] die <–> *only pl* ◊ *ein Urlaub in den Alpen* ♦ *die Schweizer Alpen*

alphabet (noun) Alphabet [alfa'beːt] das <–(e)s, –e> ◊ *das hebräische Alphabet*

alphabetical(ly) (adj, adv) alphabetisch [alfa'beːtɪʃ] *no comp/superl* ◊ *in alphabetischer Reihenfolge* ♦ *Der Index ist alphabetisch.* ♦ *alphabetisch geordnet*

already (adv) schon [ʃoːn] ◊ *Er ist erst 26 Jahre alt und hat schon seinen Doktor gemacht.* ♦ *Was? Es ist schon 11 Uhr?* ♦ *Ich warte schon seit Stunden.*

alright → all right

also (adv) auch [aox] ◊ *Es ist auch möglich, mit Karte zu zahlen.* ♦ *Er musste auch noch für die Busfahrt aufkommen.* ♦ *Warst du auch auf der Party?* ♦ *Mein Sohn hat diese Krankheit auch schon gehabt.* not only ... but also nicht nur ..., sondern auch ◊ *Sie ist nicht nur eine gute Schauspielerin, sondern auch eine begabte Sängerin.*

alter (verb) ändern ['ɛndɐn] <ändert, änderte, hat geändert> +haben ◊ *Wir müssen unser Firmenkonzept ändern.* ♦ *ein Kleid ändern lassen* sich altern etw. ändern sich ◊ *Die Lage hat sich inzwischen geändert.*

alteration (noun) Änderung ['ɛndərʊŋ] die <–, –en> ◊ *Die Gemeinde beschloss eine Änderung des Bauplans.* ♦ *Sie ließ ein paar Änderungen am Kleid vornehmen.*

alternative (noun) Alternative [altɛna'tiːvə] die <–, –n> ◊ *Ich weiß dazu keine Alternative.*

alternative(ly) (adj, adv) alternativ [altɛna'tiːf] *no comp/superl* ◊ *Gibt es eine alternative Methode, falls diese nicht funktionieren?* ♦ *Alternativ können Sie dieses Formular verwenden.* ♦ *alternative Medizin* the only alternative possibility die einzige Alternative [diː ˌaɛnʦɪɡə altɛna'tiːvə] <–>

although (conjunc) obwohl [ɔp'voːl] ◊ *Obwohl sie krank ist geht sie zur Arbeit.* ♦ *Er friert, obwohl er einen Pulli anhat.*

altitude (noun) Höhe ['høːə] die <–, –n> ◊ *Das Flugzeug gewann allmählich an Höhe.* ♦ *Mit über 4000 Metern Höhe ist dies der höchste Berg des Landes.* at an altitude of 2000 meters in einer Höhe von 2000 Metern

altogether (adv) 1. *(totally)* vollkommen [fɔl'kɔmən] *no comp/superl* ◊ *Sie hatte unsere Verabredung vollkommen vergessen.* ♦ *Das ist eine vollkommen neue Sichtweise* 2. *(including everyone/everything)* insgesamt [ɪnsɡə'zamt] ◊ *Insgesamt beschäftigt der Konzern 9000 Mitarbeiter.* ♦ *Es war insgesamt ein sehr schöner Abend.* ◉ not altogether 1. *(not completely)* nicht ganz ◊ *Da hast du nicht ganz Unrecht.* 2. *(not very)* nicht übermäßig ◊ *Sie war nicht übermäßig erstaunt, als er entlassen wurde.*

aluminium (noun) Aluminium [alu'miːni̯ʊm] das <–s> *no pl* ◊ *eine Milchkanne aus Aluminium*

always [adv] immer ['ɪmɐ] ◊ *Er fährt immer mit dem Fahrrad zur Arbeit.* ✦ *Das haben wir schon immer so gemacht.* ✦ *Du kannst mich immer anrufen.* ⊛ *as always* wie immer ◊ *you could always … du könntest doch auch …*

am → **be** [verb] *I am* ich bin [ɪç bɪn] ◊ *Ich bin 14 Jahre alt.* ✦ *Ich bin traurig.*

a.m. *(until around 10 a.m.)* morgens ['mɔrgn̩s] ◊ *Ich habe um 8 Uhr morgens einen Termin beim Arzt.; (from around 10 a.m. to midday)* vormittags ['foːɐmɪtaːks] ◊ *Es geht um 11 Uhr vormittags los.*

> In German it is common to use the 24-hour clock to differentiate between a.m. and p.m.

amass [verb] *(information)* zusammentragen [tsu'zamn̩traːgn̩] <trägt zusammen, trug zusammen, hat zusammengetragen> ◊ *Er hat eine Menge Informationen zusammengetragen.; (money)* anhäufen ['anhɔɪfn̩] +haben ◊ *Über die Jahre häufte er ein riesiges Vermögen an.*

amateur¹ [noun] **1.** *(sb who is not a professional)* Amateur [ama'tøːɐ] der <-s, -e> ♀Amateurin [ama'tøːrɪn] die <-, -nen> ◊ *ein von einem Amateur gedrehter Videofilm* **2.** *(sb who is not very good at sth)* Dilettant [dilɛ'tant] der <-en, -en> ♀Dilettantin [dilɛ'tantɪn] die <-, -nen> *(pej)* ◊ *Da waren wieder Dilettanten am Werk!*

amateur² [adj] **1.** *(describing a spare time activity)* Hobby… ['hɔbi] *amateur photographer* Hobbyfotograf ['hɔbi:foto,graːf] der <-en, -en> ♀Hobbyfotografin ['hɔbi:foto,graːfɪn] die <-, -nen>; *(theatrical)* Laien… ['laɛn] *amateur actor* Laiendarsteller ['laɛn:daːrˌʃtɛlɐ] der <-s, -> ♀Laiendarstellerin ['laɛn,daːrˌʃtɛlərɪn] die <-, -nen> **2.** *(not well done)* dilettantisch [dilɛ'tantɪʃ] *(pej)* ◊ *eine dilettantische Arbeit*

amaze [verb] verblüffen [fɛ'blʏfn̩] <verblüfft, verblüffte, hat verblüfft> ◊ *Er verblüffte den Lehrer mit seinem Wissen.*

amazement [noun] Erstaunen [e'ʃtaʊnən] das <-s> no pl ◊ *Diese Aussage rief Erstaunen hervor.* ✦ *Mit großem Erstaunen hörte ich ihr zu.* *to sb's amazement* zu jds Erstaunen ◊ *Zu meinem Erstaunen hat er sich gar nicht beklagt.* *in amazement* erstaunt [e'ʃtaʊnt] ◊ *Er sah mich erstaunt an.*

amazing [adj] **1.** *(astonishing)* erstaunlich [e'ʃtaʊnlɪç] ◊ *Es ist schon erstaunlich, wofür manche Leute ihr Geld ausgeben.* ✦ *erstaunliche Leistungen* **2.** *(great, fantastic)* toll [tɔl] *(fam)* ◊ *Was für ein tolles Dessert!* ✦ *Diese Story ist einfach toll!*

amazingly [adv] erstaunlich [e'ʃtaʊnlɪç] ◊ *Er ist für sein Alter noch erstaunlich fit.*

ambassador [noun] Botschafter ['boːtʃaftɐ] der <-s, -> ♀Botschafterin ['boːtʃaftərɪn] die <-, -nen> ◊ *der ehemalige Schweizer Botschafter* ✦ *Sie war Botschafterin der Tschechischen Republik in Australien.* ✦ *Franz Beckenbauer, Botschafter des Fußballsports*

ambiguity [noun] *(sth that allows more than one interpretation)* Mehrdeutigkeit ['meːɐdɔɪtɪçkaɛt] die <-, -en> ◊ *die Mehrdeutigkeit einer Äußerung; (sth that is difficult to understand)* Unklarheit ['ʊnklaːrhaɛt] die <-, -en> ◊ *Der Artikel enthält einige Unklarheiten.*

ambiguous(ly) [adj, adv] *(allowing more than one interpretation)* mehrdeutig ['meːɐdɔɪtɪç] *seldom comp/* superl ◊ *ein mehrdeutiger Titel* ✦ *Die Bilder des Künstlers sind mehrdeutig.* ✦ *mehrdeutig gemeint sein; (difficult to understand)* unklar ['ʊnklaːr] ◊ *eine unklare Anweisung* ✦ *etw. unklar formulieren*

ambition [noun] **1.** *(aim)* Ambition [ambi'tsjoːn] die <-, -en> most pl ◊ *Du hast keinerlei künstlerische Ambitionen.; (more specific goal)* Ziel [tsiːl] das <-(e)s, -e> ◊ *Mit 35 hat er alle seine Ziele erreicht.* ✦ *Mein Ziel ist es, mich nach dem Studium selbstständig zu machen.* **2.** *(eagerness to achieve)* Ehrgeiz ['eːɐgaɛts] der <-es> no pl ◊ *Ihm fehlt der Ehrgeiz, um Karriere zu machen.*

ambitious(ly) [adj, adv] ehrgeizig ['eːɐgaɛtsɪç] ◊ *Er ist sehr ehrgeizig.* ✦ *ein ehrgeiziges Projekt* ✦ *sich zielstrebig und ehrgeizig hocharbeiten*

ambulance [noun] Krankenwagen ['krankn̩vaːgn̩] der <-s, -> ◊ *Rufen Sie einen Krankenwagen!* ✦ *Sie wurde mit dem Krankenwagen in die Klinik gebracht.*

amend [verb] ändern ['ɛndɐn] <ändert, änderte, hat geändert> +haben ◊ *die Verfassung ändern* ✦ *Das Gesetz muss geändert werden.*

amendment [noun] Änderung ['ɛndərʊŋ] die <-, -en> ◊ *eine Änderung des Gesetzes vorschlagen* ✦ *Ich werde an dem Text einige Änderungen vornehmen.; (of the US constitution)* Amendment [ɛ'mɛntmənt] das <-s, -s> ◊ *das erste/zweite Amendment*

America [noun] Amerika [a'meːrika] das <-s> *article only in combination with attribute, no pl* → **Germany**

American¹ [noun] Amerikaner [ameri'kaːnɐ] der <-s, -> ♀Amerikanerin [ameri'kaːnərɪn] die <-, -nen> → **German¹** **1.**

American² [adj] amerikanisch [ameri'kaːnɪʃ] → **German²**

American English [noun] amerikanische Englisch [ameri'kaːnɪʃə ˌɛŋlɪʃ] das <amerikanischen Englischs> no pl → **German²**

amiable [adj] liebenswürdig ['liːbm̩svʏrdɪç] ◊ *eine liebenswürdige Person* ✦ *Er war schon immer liebenswürdig.*

amiably [adv] liebenswürdigerweise ['liːbm̩svʏrdɪgɐvaɛzə] ◊ *Sie hat sich liebenswürdigerweise bereit erklärt, uns zu helfen.*

amid [prep] **1.** *(under certain circumstances, surrounded by sth)* inmitten [ɪn'mɪtn̩] +gen ◊ *Inmitten der Unruhe rauchte er gemütlich seine Pfeife.* ✦ *Das Dorf liegt inmitten grüner Wiesen.* **2.** *(accompanied by a certain noise)* unter ['ʊntɐ] +dat ◊ *Unter lautem Applaus betrat der Star die Bühne.*

among [prep] **1.** *(shared by or affecting a certain group of people)* unter ['ʊntɐ] +dat ◊ *Wir sind hier unter Freunden.* ✦ *Auch unter Ärzten gibt es Raucher.* ✦ *Die Nachricht verbreitete sich schnell unter den Dorfbewohnern.* ✦ *Die Schokolade muss unter den Kindern aufgeteilt werden.* *among other things* unter anderem ◊ *Er erzählte unter anderem von seiner Studienzeit in London.* **2.** *(in the middle of or between people or things)* zwischen ['tsvɪʃn̩] +dat ◊ *Er stand zwischen den Fans.* ✦ *Hast du schon zwischen den Briefen nachgesehen?*

amount [noun] **1.** Menge ['mɛŋə] die <-, -n> ◊ *Da kommt eine ganze Menge Arbeit auf uns zu.* ✦ *Der Körper benötigt nur winzige Mengen dieses Vitamins.* *a small amount of* wenig ['veːnɪç] ◊ *Er hat wenig Zeit zur Verfügung.* *a large amount of* viel [fiːl] ◊ *Für dieses Hobby braucht man viel Geld.* **2.** *(of*

money) Betrag [bə'tra:k] der <–(e)s, Beträge> ◊ *Bitte überweisen Sie den Betrag auf mein Konto.* ✦ *ein hoher/niedriger Betrag* ◉ *no amount of ... kein ... der Welt* ◊ *Kein Geld der Welt kann diese Erfahrung ersetzen.*

amount to [verb] **1.** *(be equivalent to)* amount to sth einer Sache [dat] gleichkommen ['glaeçkɔmən] <kommt gleich, kam gleich, ist gleichgekommen> ◊ *Sein Schweigen kommt einem Geständnis gleich.* **2.** *(make up the sum of)* betragen [bə'tra:gn̩] <beträgt, betrug, hat betragen> ◊ *Die Kosten betragen etwa 500 Euro.*

ample [adj] **1.** *(more than enough)* reichlich ['ra̯eçlɪç] ◊ *eine reichliche Auswahl* ✦ *Die Portionen waren mehr als reichlich.* **2.** *(describing sb's body)* üppig ['ʏpɪç] ◊ *eine Frau mit üppiger Figur*

amuse [verb] **1.** *(delight)* amüsieren [amy'zi:rən] <amüsiert, amüsierte, hat amüsiert> ◊ *Der Gedanke amüsierte mich sehr.* **2.** *(entertain)* unterhalten [ʊntɐ'haltn̩] <unterhält, unterhielt, hat unterhalten> ◊ *Der Clown unterhält sein Publikum mit allerlei Späßen.* amuse yourself (by doing/with sth) sich (mit etw.) beschäftigen [bə'ʃɛftɪɡn̩] <beschäftigt sich, beschäftigte sich, hat sich beschäftigt> ◊ *Unser kleiner Sohn kann sich gut allein beschäftigen.* ✦ *Ich habe mich in der Zwischenzeit mit Zeitunglesen beschäftigt.*

amusement [noun] **1.** *(pleasure)* Vergnügen [fɛ'gny:gn̩] das <–s, –> most sing ◊ *etw. zum Vergnügen tun* ✦ *Zu unser aller Vergnügen las er ein witziges Gedicht vor.* **2.** *(entertainment)* Unterhaltung [ʊntɐ'haltʊŋ] die <–> no pl ◊ *Wer ist für die Unterhaltung auf der Party zuständig?* for sb's amusement zu jds Unterhaltung ◊ *Zur Unterhaltung der Kinder wurde ein Clown engagiert.* **3.** *(at a fair or an amusement park)* Attraktion [atrak'tsi̯o:n] die <–, –en> ◊ *ein Freizeitpark mit vielen Attraktionen*

amusing(ly) [adj, adv] amüsant [amy'zant] <amüsanter, am amüsantesten> ◊ *eine amüsante Anekdote* ✦ *Der Vorfall war recht amüsant.* ✦ *Die Geschichte ist amüsant erzählt.*

an → a

anaesthetic, anesthetic [noun] Narkose [naʁ'ko:zə] die <–, –n> ◊ *Die Wirkung der Narkose setzte sehr schnell ein.* general anaesthetic Vollnarkose ['fɔlnaʁˌko:zə] local anaesthetic örtliche Betäubung [ˌœʁtlɪçə bə'tɔɔbʊŋ] die <–, –en> most sing

anaesthetize, anesthetize [verb] betäuben [bə'tɔɔbm̩] <betäubt, betäubte, hat betäubt> ◊ *Vor dem Eingriff wurde der Zahn betäubt.*

analogy [noun] Vergleich [fɛ'glae̯ç] der <–(e)s, –e> ◊ *Anhand eines Vergleiches mit dem menschlichen Gehirn erklärte er die Funktionen eines Computers.* draw an analogy einen Vergleich ziehen ◊ *einen Vergleich zwischen der menschlichen Gesellschaft und einem Ameisenstaat ziehen*

analyse, analyze [verb] analysieren [analy'zi:rən] <analysiert, analysierte, hat analysiert> ◊ *Der Fall muss eingehend analysiert werden.* ✦ *Bodenproben im Labor analysieren*

analysis [noun] Analyse [ana'ly:zə] die <–, –n> ◊ *eine eingehende Analyse des Problems* ✦ *Ist die Analyse der Wasserproben schon abgeschlossen?* ✦ *Ihre Analyse beim Psychotherapeuten zeigt erste Erfolge.* ◉ *in the final/last analysis* letztens Endes ◊ *Letztens Endes teilen alle Menschen das gleiche*

Schicksal.

analyst [noun] **1.** *(sb who examines sth carefully)* Analytiker [ana'ly:tɪkɐ] der <–s, –> ♀Analytikerin [ana'ly:tɪkərɪn] die <–, –nen> system analyst Systemanalytiker [zʏs'te:mǀanaly:tɪkɐ] Systemanalytikerin [zʏs'te:mǀanaly:tɪkərɪn]; *(of the stock market)* Analyst [ana'lʏst] der <–en, –en> ♀Analystin [ana'lʏstɪn] die <–, –nen> ◊ *Diese Aktie wird von Analysten empfohlen.* **2.** MED Psychoanalytiker [ˌpsyçoǀana'ly:tɪkɐ] der <–s, –> ♀Psychoanalytikerin [ˌpsyçoǀana'ly:tɪkərɪn] die <–, –nen> ◊ *bei einem Psychoanalytiker in Behandlung sein* ✦ *zu einem Psychoanalytiker gehen*

analyze → analyse

ancestor [noun] **1.** *(of a person)* Vorfahr ['fo:gfaːʁ] der <–en, –en> ♀Vorfahrin ['fo:gfaːrɪn] die <–, –nen> most pl ◊ *Seine Vorfahren stammten aus Skandinavien.* **2.** *(fig) (of a thing)* Vorläufer ['fo:g̩lɔɔfɐ] der <–s, –> ♀Vorläuferin ['fo:g̩lɔɔfərɪn] die <–, –nen> ◊ *Die Europäische Gemeinschaft war die Vorläuferin der EU.*

anchor¹ [noun] **1.** SHIP Anker ['aŋkɐ] der <–s, –> ◊ *Er warf den Anker aus.* lie at anchor vor Anker liegen ◊ *Die Segelyacht liegt im Hafen vor Anker.* **2.** TV *(in the US: TV or radio presenter)* Nachrichtensprecher ['na:xrɪçtn̩ʃprɛçɐ] der <–s, –> ♀Nachrichtensprecherin ['na:xrɪçtn̩ʃprɛçərɪn] die <–, –nen> ◊ *Der Nachrichtensprecher hat sich versprochen.* ✦ *Sie ist Nachrichtensprecherin beim WDR.*

anchor² [verb] **1.** SHIP ankern ['aŋkɐn] +haben ◊ *Das Boot ankerte vor der Insel.* ✦ *Wir ankerten in der Bucht.* anchor sth mit etw. vor Anker gehen [mɪt ... fo:ɐ̯ 'aŋkɐ ge:ən] <gehen, ging, ist gegangen> ◊ *Wir gingen mit dem Boot im Hafen vor Anker.* **2.** TV *(in the US: a TV or radio programme)* präsentieren [prɛzɛn'ti:rən] <präsentiert, präsentierte, hat präsentiert> **3.** *(fix)* verankern [fɛǀ'aŋkɐn] <verankert, verankerte, hat verankert> anchor (sth) in sth (etw.) in etw. [dat] verankern ◊ *den Tierschutz in der Verfassung verankern* be anchored to sth mit etw. verankert sein

ancient [adj] **1.** *(fam) (very old)* uralt ['u:ǀalt] no comp/superl ◊ *Meine Kleider sind alle uralt* **2.** HIST alt [alt] <älter, älteste> only before ns ◊ *die alten Römer*

and [conjunc] und [ʊnt] ◊ *jung, schön und reich* ✦ *Du und ich werden jetzt den Tisch decken.* ✦ *Wir unterhielten uns und tranken Kaffee.* ✦ *Er kündigte, und das war gut so.* ✦ *Und was machen wir morgen?* ✦ *Er kam näher und näher.* ✦ *Drei und vier ist sieben.*

anesthetize → anaesthetize

angel [noun] Engel ['ɛŋl̩] der <–s, –>

anger¹ [noun] Wut [vuːt] die <–> no pl feel anger wütend sein ['vy:tn̩t zaɛn]

anger² [verb] verärgern [fɛǀ'ɛ'gɐn] <verärgerte, verärgert> ◊ *Die hohen Preise verärgerten die Kunden.*

angle [noun] **1.** MATH Winkel ['vɪŋkl̩] der <–s, –> ◊ *ein rechter Winkel* **2.** *(point of view)* Blickwinkel ['blɪkvɪŋkl̩] der <–s, –> ◊ *etw. aus einem anderen Blickwinkel betrachten*

angry(-ily) [adj, adv] wütend ['vy:tn̩t] ◊ *So viel Dummheit macht mich wütend!* ✦ *wütende Proteste* ✦ *„Du Schuft!", schrie sie ihn wütend an.*

anguish [noun] Schmerz [ʃmɛʁ͡ts] der <–es, –en> ◊ *Der Schmerz überwältigte sie.*

angular [adj] *(face, handwriting)* kantig ['kantɪç] ◊ *eine*

A
B
C
D
E
F
G
H
I
J
K
L
M
N
O
P
Q
R
S
T
U
V
W
X
Y
Z

kantige Schrift ♦ *Sein Gesicht ist kantig.; (body)*
knochig ['knɔxɪç] ◊ *ein knochiger Körperbau* ♦ *Er ist
ziemlich knochig.*

animal [noun] Tier [tiːɐ̯] das <–(e)s, –e> ◊ *wilde Tiere
in Afrika* ♦ *Widerlich! Er benimmt sich wie ein Tier!*

animate [verb] 1. *(make a picture move, encourage sb
to do sth)* animieren [ani'miːrən] <animiert,
animierte, hat animiert> ◊ *die Figuren eines Trick-
films animieren* animate sb to do sth jdn dazu
animieren, etw. zu tun ◊ *Die Werbung animierte
mich dazu, das Buch zu kaufen.* 2. *(stimulate)*
beleben [bə'leːbm̩] <belebt, belebte, hat belebt> ◊ *Leidenschaft belebt den Geist.*

animation (film) [noun] FILM Trickfilm ['trɪkfɪlm] der
<–(e)s, –e>

ankle [noun] Knöchel ['knœçl̩] der <–s, –>

anniversary [noun] Jahrestag ['jaːrəstaːk] das
<–(e)s, –e> ◊ *der 15. Jahrestag der deutschen
Einheit* wedding anniversary Hochzeitstag
['hɔxtsaɛ̯tstaːk] der <–(e)s, –e>

annotation [noun] Anmerkung ['anmɛrkʊŋ] die
<–, –en>

announce [verb] 1. *(give advance notice)* ankündigen
['ankʏndɪɡn̩] +haben ◊ *Sie kündigte ihren Besuch für
kommende Woche an.* 2. *(doubts, interest)* anmelden
['anmɛldn̩] <meldet an, meldete an, hat angemeldet> ◊
Ich meldete meine Bedenken an. 3. *(publicly)*
bekannt geben [bə'kant geːbm̩] <gibt, gab, hat
gegeben>

announcement [noun] Bekanntgabe [bə'kant] die
<–, –en> ◊ *die Bekanntgabe der Wahlergebnisse;
(over the TV, radio, loudspeaker also)* Durchsage
['dʊrçzaːɡə] die <–, –n> ◊ *Es erfolgte eine Durchsage
per Lautsprecher.* make an announcement that ...
bekannt geben, dass ... [bə'kant geːbm̩ das] <gibt,
gab, hat gegeben> ◊ *Sie gaben bekannt, dass sie bald
heiraten würden.*

annoy [verb] 1. *(irritate)* ärgern ['ɛrɡən] +haben ◊ *Ihr
Benehmen ärgerte ihn.* ♦ *Ärgert es dich, wenn du
Fehler machst?* 2. *(make sb angry)* annoy sb jdn
verärgern [fɛɐ̯'ɛrɡən] <verärgert, verärgerte, hat
verärgert>

annoyed → annoy [adj] be/get annoyed (with sb/
about sth), be/get annoyed (at sb/sth) sich (über
jdn/etw.) ärgern ['ɛrɡən] +haben ◊ *Ich ärgere mich
ziemlich über ihn.* be annoyed with/at yourself sich
über sich selbst ärgern be annoyed that ... sich
ärgern, dass ... ◊ *Ärgerst du dich, dass es regnet?*
be annoyed to find that sth has happened sich
darüber ärgern, dass etw. passiert ist

annoying [adj] 1. *(making you angry)* ärgerlich
['ɛrɡəlɪç] ◊ *Der Vorfall war sehr ärgerlich.* ♦ *ein paar
ärgerliche Fehler* 2. *(making you impatient)* lästig
['lɛstɪç] ◊ *lästige Fragen* ♦ *Die Mücken hier sind
wirklich lästig.*

annual(ly) [adj, adv] 1. *(taking place once a year)*
jährlich ['jɛːɡlɪç] *when used as an adj, only before ns*
◊ *unser jährliches Treffen* ♦ *Sie treffen sich jährlich
auf dem Kongress.* 2. *(applying to a period of one
year)* Jahres... ['jaːrəs] ◊ *die Jahreshauptversamm-
lung* ♦ *der Jahresbericht*

annuity [noun] 1. *(regular payment to sb)* Leibrente
['laɛ̯prɛntə] die <–, –n> ◊ *Die Versicherung zahlt der
Witwe eine Leibrente.* 2. *(investment)* Rentenversicherung ['rɛntn̩fɛˌtsɪçərʊŋ] die <–, –en> ◊ *in eine Rentenversicherung einzahlen*

anonymous(ly) [adj, adv] anonym [ano'nyːm] ◊ *Die
Anzeige war anonym.* ♦ *Jemand hat ihn anonym
angerufen.* ♦ *eine anonyme Atmosphäre*

another¹ [det] *(an additonal)* noch ein/eine
[nɔx aɛ̯n/aɛ̯nə] ◊ *Sie hat noch eine Frage.* The
institute needs another 11 lecturers. Das Institut
braucht noch 11 weitere Dozenten. another time
ein anderes Mal ◊ *Wir werden darüber ein anderes
Mal reden.* yet another schon wieder ein/eine
[ʃɔn 'viːdɐ aɛ̯n/aɛ̯nə] ◊ *Es gab schon wieder einen
Skandal.; (a second)* ein zweiter [aɛ̯n 'tsvaɛ̯tɐ] eine
zweite [aɛ̯nə 'tsvaɛ̯tə] ein zweites [aɛ̯n 'tsvaɛ̯təs] ◊
Sie sehen in ihm einen zweiten Einstein. Lisa is
great. You won't find another woman like her! Lisa
ist toll. So eine Frau findest du nie wieder!

another² [pron] ein anderer [aɛ̯n 'andərɐ] eine andere
[aɛ̯nə 'andərə] ein anderes [aɛ̯n 'andərəs] ◊ *Ein
anderer trat in ihr Leben.* ♦ *Er heiratete eine
andere.* another (like this/that) noch (so) einer/
eine/eins ['nɔx (zoː) aɛ̯nɐ/aɛ̯nə/aɛ̯ns] ◊ *Der Cocktail
war super, ich möchte noch einen haben!*
ⓔ for one another füreinander ◊ *Wir haben nie
genug Zeit füreinander.*

answer¹ [noun] 1. *(reply)* Antwort ['antvɔrt] die
<–, –en> ◊ *Sie wollte ihm keine Antwort auf seine
Frage geben.* ♦ *Krieg ist die falsche Antwort auf
Konflikte.* owe sb an answer jdm eine Antwort
schuldig sein 2. *(solution)* Lösung ['løːzʊŋ] die
<–, –en> ◊ *Die Lösungen der Aufgaben stehen
hinten im Buch.* get the answer right/wrong die
Aufgabe richtig/falsch lösen
[diː ˌaʊ̯fɡaːbə 'rɪçtɪç/'falʃ løːzn̩] ◊ *Habe ich alle
Aufgaben richtig gelöst?*

answer² [verb] 1. *(reply)* answer (sb) (jdm) antworten
['antvɔrtn̩] +haben ◊ *Als er gefragt wurde, antwortete
er nicht.* ♦ *Warum antwortest du mir nicht?* answer
sth etw. beantworten [bə'antvɔrtn̩] <beantwortet,
beantwortete, hat beantwortet> ◊ *einen Brief/eine
Frage beantworten* 2. answer an advertisement sich
auf eine Anzeige melden [aʊ̯f aɛ̯nə 'antsaɛ̯ɡə mɛldn̩]
<meldet sich, meldet sich, hat sich gemeldet>; (a
call)* answer the phone ans Telefon gehen
[ans 'teːlɛfoːn ɡeːən] <geht, ging, ist gegangen>
answer the door die Tür öffnen [diː 'tyːɐ̯ ˌœfnən]
<öffnet, öffnete, hat geöffnet>
• **answer back** [phras v] answer (sb) back (jdm)
widersprechen [viːdɐ'ʃprɛçn̩] <widerspricht, widersprach, hat widersprochen> ◊ *Widersprich (mir)
nicht immer!*
• **answer for** [phras v] 1. answer for sth für etw.
[acc] die Verantwortung übernehmen
[fyːɐ̯ ... diː fɛɐ̯'antvɔrtʊŋ ybɐˌneːmən] <übernimmt,
übernahm, hat übernommen> ◊ *Der Fahrer übernahm
die Verantwortung für den Unfall.* 2. answer for sb
für jdn sprechen [fyːɐ̯ ... ʃprɛçn̩] +haben ◊ *In
meiner Abwesenheit sprach er für mich.* I can't
answer for the others. Ich kann nur für mich
sprechen.
• **answer to** [phras v] 1. *(be accountable to sb)*
answer to sb jdm Rechenschaft ablegen
['rɛçn̩ʃaft ˌapleːɡn̩] +haben ◊ *Der Vorstand legt den
Aktionären Rechenschaft ab.* 2. *(be called)* answer to
the name of ... auf den Namen ... hören
[aʊ̯f deːn naːmən ... høːrən] +haben ◊ *Die Katze hört
auf den Namen Susi.*

answerable [adj] be answerable to sb sich jdm

gegenüber verantworten müssen
[geː'gɦyːbɐ fɛɐ'antvɔʳtn̩ mʏsn̩] <muss, musste, hat
müssen> ◊ *In einer Demokratie muss sich die
Regierung dem Volk gegenüber verantworten.* answerable for sb/sth **für jdn/etw. verantwortlich**
[fyːɐ ... fɛɐ,antvɔʳtlɪç] ◊ *Eltern sind für ihre Kinder
verantwortlich.*

answerphone (noun) Anrufbeantworter
['anruːfbəl,antvɔʳtə] der <–s, –>
ant (noun) Ameise ['aːmaezə] die <–, –n>
antibody (noun) Antikörper ['antikœʳpɐ] der <–s, –>
most pl
anticipate (verb) **1.** *(expect)* erwarten [e'vaʳtn̩]
<erwartet, erwartete, hat erwartet> ◊ *Ich bin früher
mit der Arbeit fertig geworden als erwartet.* anticipate sth eagerly **etw. gespannt erwarten** anticipate
sb/sth doing sth **erwarten, dass jd/etw. etw. tut** ◊
Wir erwarten, dass der Umsatz sich verdoppelt.
2. *(foresee)* voraussehen [fo'raɔszeːən] <sieht voraus,
sah voraus, hat vorausgesehen> ◊ *Diese Entwicklung
konnten wir nicht voraussehen.*
anticipation (noun) *(expectation that sth will happen)*
Erwartung [e'vaʳtʊŋ] die <–, –en> ◊ *Voller
Erwartung rannte sie zum Briefkasten.* ◆ *In
Erwartung eines Aufschwungs stiegen die Kurse.*
thrill of anticipation **freudige Erregung**
[frɔɡdɪɡə e'reːgʊŋ] die <–> *no pl*
antipathy (noun) Abneigung ['apnaegʊŋ] die <–, –en>
◊ *Er hat mich seine Abneigung spüren lassen.*
antipathy to/towards sb/sth **Abneigung gegen jdn/
etw.** ◊ *Er hat eine Abneigung gegen laute Musik.*
antique¹ (noun) Antiquität [antikvi'tɛːt] die <–, –en>
antique² (adj) antik [an'tiːk] ◊ *Der Schrank ist antik.*
◆ *eine antike Uhr*
antonym (noun) Antonym [anto'nyːm] das <–s, –e>
anxiety (noun) **1.** *(worried feeling)* Besorgnis
[bə'zɔʳknɪs] die <–, –se> *most sing* ◊ *wachsende
Besorgnis über die Schließung von Firmen*
2. *(extreme nervousness, panic)* Angst ['aŋst] die
<–, Ängste> ◊ *Stress kann Ängste auslösen.*
3. *((nervous) attempts)* Bemühen [bə'myːən] <–s> *no
pl* ◊ *jds Bemühen, es allen recht zu machen*
anxious(ly) (adj, adv) **1.** *(concerned, worried)* besorgt
[bə'zɔʳkt] <besorgter, am besorgtesten> ◊ *Die
besorgten Eltern riefen die Polizei.* ◆ *Sie sahen sich
besorgt an.* be anxious about sth **wegen etw.** (gen)
besorgt sein be anxious about sb **sich** (dat) **Sorgen
um jdn machen** ['zɔʳgɦ ʊm ... maxn̩] +*haben* make
sb anxious **jdn beunruhigen** [bə'ʊnruːɪɡɦ] <beunru-
higt, beunruhigte, hat beunruhigt>; *(in worried anticipation)* bang [baŋ] <banger/bänger, am bangsten/
bängsten> *seldom comp/superl; when used as an adj,
mostly before ns* ◊ *Nach einigen bangen Minuten
kam die Entwarnung.* ◆ *Die Studenten warteten
bang auf ihre Prüfungsergebnisse.* **2.** *(wanting sth
very much)* be anxious to do sth **unbedingt etw. tun
wollen** [ʊnbədɪŋt ... vɔlən] <will, wollte, hat wollen>
◊ *Er wollte unbedingt nach Hause gehen.* be anxious
that **sehr darauf achten, dass** [zeːɐ daraɔf 'axtn̩ das]
+*haben* ◊ *Wir achten sehr darauf, dass sich unsere
Mitarbeiter wohl fühlen.* be anxious for sth, wait for
sth anxiously **ungeduldig auf etw.** (acc) **warten**
[,ʊngədʊldɪç aɔf ... ,vaʳtn̩] +*haben* ◊ *Sie warteten
ungeduldig auf ein Lebenszeichen von ihm.*
any¹ (adv) **1.** *(emph) (before comparatives: not translated)* any better/faster/wiser etc. **besser/schneller/**

klüger etc. ['bɛsɐ/'ʃnɛlɐ/'klyːgɐ] ◊ *Ist dein neues
Auto schneller als das alte?* ◆ *Geht es dir jetzt besser?*
If you get any fatter, your trousers won't fit you any
more. **Wenn du noch dicker wirst, passen dir die
Hosen nicht mehr.** **2.** *(expressing that sth has
ended)* not ... any more/longer **nicht mehr**
[nɪçt meːɐ] ◊ *Ich arbeite nicht mehr für diese Firma.*
3. be any good **etwas taugen** [ɛtvas 'taɔgɦ] +*haben*
◊ *Taugt die neue Kollegin etwas?* sb/sth isn't any
good **jd/etw. taugt nichts** be any use **etwas nutzen**
[ɛtvas 'nʊtsn̩] +*haben* ◊ *Würde es etwas nutzen,
wenn ich mal mit ihm rede?* not be any use **nichts
nutzen**
any² (det) **1.** *(in questions before uncountable ns)* etwas
['ɛtvas] ◊ *Ist noch etwas Tee da?; (before countable
pl ns)* ein paar [aen paːɐ] ◊ *Haben Sie ein paar
Münzen für mich?; (in negatives)* not ... any **kein**
[kaen] **keine** ['kaenə] ◊ *Ich habe kein Geld mitgenommen.* ◆ *Es sind keine Kekse mehr da.* **2.** *(every)* jeder
['jeːdɐ] jede ['jeːdə] jedes ['jeːdəs] ◊ *Du kannst zu
jeder Stunde anrufen.* ◆ *Das kann doch jedes Kind!*
3. *(predeterminer)* any other **jeder andere**
[jeːdɐ 'andərə] **jede andere** [jeːdə 'andərə] **jedes
andere** [jeːdəs 'andərə] ◊ *Jeder andere Tag wäre mir
lieber.*
any³ (indef pron) **1.** *(in questions)* welcher ['vɛlçɐ]
welche ['vɛlçə] welches ['vɛlçəs] ◊ *Wir brauchen
Geld. Hast du welches?* ◆ *Kamen welche von deinen
Verwandten zu Besuch?* **2.** *(in negatives)* not ...any
keiner ['kaenɐ] **keine** ['kaenə] **keins** [kaens] ◊ *„Gib
mir mal die Milch!" — „Wir haben keine mehr."* ◆
Ich gebe Brot kaufen. Es ist keins mehr da. **3.** *(one
of several)* any of ... **einer/eine/eines ...** (gen)
['aenɐ/'aenə/'aenəs] ◊ *Hast du schon mal eines
seiner Bücher gelesen?* It was the first time any of
us ever heard of him. **Keiner von uns hatte je zuvor
von ihm gehört.**
anybody (indef pron) **1.** *(in questions and conditional
sentences)* jemand ['jeːmant] ◊ *Hat jemand meinen
Bleistift gesehen?* ◆ *Ist da jemand?; (in negative
sentences)* niemand ['niːmant] ◊ *Ich will niemanden
beschuldigen.* **2.** *(any person)* jeder ['jeːdɐ] ◊ *Das
kann jedem mal passieren.* ◆ *Jeder ist hier willkommen.*
⊛ not just anybody *(emph)* **nicht irgendjemand**
anyhow (adv) **1.** *(in spite of sth)* trotzdem ['trɔtsdeːm]
◊ *Wir hatten eine Autopanne, sind aber trotzdem
sicher ans Ziel gekommen.* **2.** *(qualifying a
statement)* jedenfalls ['jeːdn̩fals] ◊ *Ich habe keine
Lust zu joggen, jedenfalls nicht jetzt.* **3.** *(returning to
an earlier subject, concluding a conversation)* wie
dem auch sei [viː deːm aɔx 'zae] ◊ *Wie dem auch
sei, ich muss jetzt gehen.* **4.** *(signalling that sth is
not important)* sowieso [zovi'zoː] ◊ *Sie würden von
ihm sowieso keine Hilfe annehmen.* **5.** *(haphazardly)*
(just) anyhow **einfach irgendwie** [aenfax 'ɪʳgɦt'viː] ◊
*Sie warf die Kleider einfach irgendwie in den
Schrank.*
anymore (adv) *(in negatives)* nicht mehr [nɪçt meːɐ] ◊
Sie wohnt nicht mehr hier.
anyone (indef pron) **1.** *(non-specified person: in
questions and conditional sentences)* jemand
['jeːmant] ◊ *Hast du das jemandem erzählt?* ◆ *Ich
wäre froh, wenn mir jemand helfen könnte.* anyone
else **noch jemand** ◊ *Kommt noch jemand mit?; (in
negative sentences)* niemand ['niːmant] ◊ *Ich möchte*

ja niemanden beleidigen, aber … **2.** *(any person, no matter who)* jeder ['je:dɐ] ◊ *Das kann jedem mal passieren.* ◆ *Jeder ist hier willkommen.* just anyone irgendwer ['ɪrɡn̩t've:ɐ̯] ◊ *Ich kann doch nicht einfach irgendwem vertrauen!*

anything indef pron **1.** *(in questions)* etwas ['ɛtvas] ◊ *Möchtest du etwas zu trinken?* **2.** *(something unspecified)* irgendetwas ['ɪrɡn̩t|'ɛtvas] ◊ *Hast du ihm irgendetwas darüber erzählt?* not (…) anything nichts [nɪçts] ◊ *Ich habe noch nichts gegessen.*

anyway adv **1.** *(in any case)* sowieso [zovi'zo:] ◊ *Du kannst mir das mitgeben, ich muss sowieso zur Post.* **2.** *(besides)* außerdem ['aɔ̯sede:m] ◊ *Im Tank ist kaum Benzin, und außerdem springt der Wagen nicht an.* **3.** *(returning to an earlier subject, concluding a conversation)* wie dem auch sei [vi: de:m aɔx 'zaɛ̯] ◊ *Wie dem auch sei, jetzt ist sie gekommen.* **4.** *(qualifying a statement)* jedenfalls ['je:dn̩fals] ◊ *Er wird nicht zur Arbeit gehen, jedenfalls nicht, solange er Fieber hat.*

anywhere adv **1.** *(in any place)* irgendwo ['ɪrɡn̩t'vo:] ◊ *Gibt es hier irgendwo eine Apotheke?*; *(to any place)* irgendwohin ['ɪrɡn̩tvo'hɪn] ◊ *„Wohin fahrt ihr im Urlaub?" — „Irgendwohin, Hauptsache, weg."* **2.** *(no matter where)* wo [vo:] ◊ *Sie kann sitzen, wo sie möchte.*; *(no matter where to)* wohin [vo'hɪn] ◊ *Ich gehe, wohin ich möchte.* You can go anywhere you like — nobody wants to help. Egal, wo man sich hinwendet, keiner will helfen. **3.** not anywhere else nirgendwo anders [ˌnɪrɡn̩t'vo: 'andɐs] ◊ *Diese Qualität ist nirgendwo anders zu finden.*
⊛ not be getting anywhere nicht weiterkommen sth won't get sb anywhere etw. wird jdm nicht weiterhelfen

apart¹ adj be … apart … voneinander entfernt sein [fɔn|aɛ̯nandɐ ɛnt'fɛrnt zaɛ̯n] ◊ *Die beiden Dörfer sind 11 km voneinander entfernt.*

apart² adv **1.** *(seperate)* auseinander [aɔ̯s|aɛ̯'nandɐ] ◊ *Stehen die Stühle weit genug auseinander?* ◆ *Das Regal fällt schon auseinander.* ◆ *Wir haben uns auseinander gelebt.* be/live apart getrennt sein/leben [ɡə'trɛnt zaɛ̯n/le:bm̩] ◊ *Wir leben seit mehr als einem Jahr getrennt.* **2.** *(spatial, alone)* abseits ['apzaɛ̯ts] ◊ *Sie saß abseits und las ein Buch.* apart from abseits ['apzaɛ̯ts] +gen ◊ *Er stand abseits der Gruppe.* **3.** *(referring to a distance)* …. apart in einem Abstand von … [ɪn aɛ̯nam 'apʃtant fɔn] ◊ *in einem Abstand von 15 cm* **4.** *(temporal)* two events 50 year apart zwei Ereignisse, zwischen denen 50 Jahre liegen [tsvaɛ̯ ɛ|'aɛ̯ɡnɪsə tsvɪʃn̩ de:nən ,fʏnftsɪç 'jaːrə li:ɡn̩] ◊ *They are 20 years apart in age. Der Altersunterschied zwischen ihnen beträgt 20 Jahre.*
⊛ apart from sth/sb außer etw./jdm ◊ *Ich arbeite jeden Tag außer sonntags.* sth sets sb/sth apart from sb/sth jdn/etw. hebt sich durch etw. von jdm/etw. ab ◊ *Er hebt sich durch seine Kreativität von allen anderen ab.* sth/sb apart mal abgesehen von etw./jdm ◊ *Mal abgesehen von diesem Problem ist alles in Ordnung.*

apartment noun Wohnung ['vo:nʊŋ] die <-, -en> ◊ *Ich lebe in einer Wohnung mit zwei Zimmern, Küche und Bad.* ◆ *Seine Wohnung ist im obersten Stockwerk.* ◆ *eine Wohnung mieten/suchen*

ape noun Affe ['afə] der <-n, -n>

apologize verb sich entschuldigen [ɛnt'ʃʊldɪɡn̩] <entschuldigt sich, entschuldigte sich, hat sich entschuldigt> ◊ *Die Kinder haben sich entschuldigt.* ◆ *Er hat sich für sein schlechtes Benehmen entschuldigt.* ◆ *Du solltest dich entschuldigen!* apologize to sb sich bei jdm entschuldigen ◊ *Er entschuldigte sich bei seinen Nachbarn für den Lärm.*

apology noun **1.** *(asking for forgiveness)* Entschuldigung [ɛnt'ʃʊldɪɡʊŋ] die <-, -en> ◊ *Sie nahm seine Entschuldigung an.* my apologies ich bitte um Entschuldigung make an apology sich entschuldigen [ɛnt'ʃʊldɪɡn̩] <entschuldigt sich, entschuldigte sich, hat sich entschuldigt> ◊ *Sie entschuldigte sich für ihr Verhalten.* **2.** *(official justification)* apology (for sth) Rechtfertigung (… gen) ['rɛçtfɛr'tɪɡʊŋ] die <-, -en> ◊ *Dieses Buch ist eine Rechtfertigung seiner Taten.*
⊛ make no apologies for sth **1.** *(not explain your reasons)* sich nicht für etw. rechtfertigen I make no apologies for sth ich muss mich nicht für etw. rechtfertigen **2.** *(not say you are sorry)* sich für etw. nicht entschuldigen an apology for sb/sth ein erbärmliches Exemplar von jdm/etw. ◊ *Was ist denn das für ein erbärmliches Exemplar von Auto?*

appalling(ly) adj, adv erbärmlich [ɛ'bɛrmlɪç] ◊ *Beide Mannschaften boten eine erbärmliche Vorstellung.* ◆ *Die Luftqualität ist erbärmlich.* ◆ *Er hat bei der Prüfung erbärmlich abgeschnitten.*

apparent adj **1.** *(clear, obvious)* offensichtlich ['ɔfn̩zɪçtlɪç] ◊ *eine offensichtliche Lüge* ◆ *Der Misserfolg der Reform war offensichtlich.* it is apparent … es zeigt sich … [ɛs 'tsaɛ̯kt zɪç] ◊ *Es zeigte sich aus Untersuchungen, dass viele Krankheiten psychosomatisch sind.* it becomes apparent that … es wird deutlich, dass … [ɛs vɪrt 'dɔɤ̯tlɪç das] **2.** *(seeming)* scheinbar ['ʃaɛ̯nba:r] no comp/superl, mostly before ns ◊ *Dieser scheinbare Widerspruch lässt sich schnell erklären.*

apparently adv offenbar ['ɔfn̩ba:r] no comp/superl ◊ *Er ist offenbar gut gelaunt.*

appeal¹ noun **1.** *(plea, request)* Aufruf ['aɔ̯fru:f] der <-(e)s, -e> ◊ *einen Aufruf veröffentlichen/unterzeichnen* ◆ *einem Aufruf folgen* appeal for donations Spendenaufruf ['ʃpɛndn̩|aɔ̯fru:f] appeal for help Bitte um Hilfe [ˌbɪtə ʊm 'hɪlfə] die <-, -n> appeal for peace Friedensappell ['fri:dn̩sap,ɛl] der <-s, -e> launch an appeal (to sb) einen Aufruf (an jdn) um etw. bitten [ʊm … ,bɪtn̩] ◊ *Sie baten die UN um Unterstützung.* **2.** *(attraction)* Reiz [raɛ̯ts] der <-es, -e> hold great appeal for sb einen großen Reiz auf jdn ausüben ◊ *Mallorca übt einen großen Reiz auf Touristen aus.* have popular appeal sehr beliebt sein [ze:ɐ̯ bə'li:pt zaɛ̯n] **3.** LAW Einspruch ['aɛ̯nʃprʊx] der <-(e)s, Einsprüche> lodge an appeal against sth Einspruch gegen etw. einlegen

appeal² verb **1.** *(plea)* appeal (to sb) for sth (jdn) um etw. bitten [ʊm … ,bɪtn̩] <bittet, bat, hat gebeten> ◊ *Die Polizei bittet die Bevölkerung um Informationen.* appeal to sb's common sense an jds gesunden Menschenverstand appellieren [an … ɡəzʊndn̩ 'mɛnʃn̩fɛɐ̯ʃtant apɛ,li:rən] <appelliert, appellierte, hat appelliert> **2.** *(leave a positive impression)* appeal to sb jdn ansprechen ['anʃprɛçn̩] <spricht an, sprach an, hat angesprochen> ◊ *Diese Art von Kunst spricht mich überhaupt nicht an.* **3.** LAW

appeal against sth Einspruch gegen etw. einlegen [əˈpiːl] ... əˌpiːlɪŋ] +haben ◊ *Sie legte Einspruch gegen das Urteil ein.*

appear (verb) **1.** *(seem)* scheinen [ˈʃaɪnən] <scheint, schien, hat geschienen> ◊ *Diese Erklärung scheint mir plausibel.* ◆ *Der Hund scheint durstig zu sein.* ◆ *Das Baby scheint zu schlafen.* **2.** *(arrive, become visible, be published, be involved in a court case)* erscheinen [ɛˈʃaɪnən] <erscheint, erschien, ist erschienen> ◊ *Sie ist heute nicht zur Arbeit erschienen.* ◆ *Das Buch ist 2005 erschienen.* appear in court vor Gericht erscheinen **3.** *(in front of an audience)* auftreten [ˈaʊftreːtn̩] <tritt auf, trat auf, ist aufgetreten> ◊ *In diesem Film tritt er als kaltblütiger Killer auf.* **4.** *(make a particular impression)* wirken [ˈvɪrkn̩] +haben ◊ *Er wirkt sehr nett.* **5.** *(emerge)* aufkommen [ˈaʊfkɔmən] <kommt auf, kam auf, ist aufgekommen> ◊ *Eine neue Mode kommt auf.*

appearance (noun) **1.** *(looks, clothes etc.)* Erscheinung [ɛˈʃaɪnʊŋ] die <-, -en> ◊ *Er legt viel Wert auf seine äußere Erscheinung.* **2.** *(impression, often false)* Anschein [ˈanʃaɪn] der <-s> no pl give the appearance of sth den Anschein ... (gen) erwecken ◊ *Der Garten erweckte den Anschein liebevoller Pflege.* to all appearances allem Anschein nach **3.** *(arrival, first signs of sth)* Erscheinen [ɛˈʃaɪnən] das <-s> no pl ◊ *Ihr plötzliches Erscheinen überrascht mich.* court appearance Erscheinen vor Gericht [ɛˌʃaɪnən foːɐ̯ ɡəˈrɪçt] make an appearance in court vor Gericht erscheinen [foːɐ̯ ɡəˈrɪçt ɛˌʃaɪnən] <erscheint, erschien, ist erschienen>; *(of a disease, symptoms)* Auftreten [ˈaʊftreːtn̩] das <-s> no pl ◊ *das Auftreten einer Krankheit* at the appearance of sth wenn etw. auftritt [vɛn ... ˌaʊftrɪtt] <tritt auf, trat auf, ist aufgetreten> ◊ *Wenn diese Symptome auftreten, sollte man sofort den Arzt aufsuchen.* **4.** *(face, image)* Gesicht [ɡəˈzɪçt] das <-(e)s, -er> ◊ *Die Internetseite der Firma hat ein neues Gesicht bekommen.* **5.** *(on TV, a stage etc.)* Auftritt [ˈaʊftrɪt] der <-(e)s, -e> ◊ *Ihren ersten öffentlichen Auftritt hatte sie schon mit zwölf.* make an appearance auftreten [ˈaʊftreːtn̩] <tritt auf, trat auf, ist aufgetreten>
◉ appearances are deceptive der Schein trügt keep up appearances den Schein wahren put in an appearance sich sehen lassen

appendicitis (noun) Blinddarmentzündung [ˈblɪntdaʳmˌɛntsʏndʊŋ] die <-, -en>

appendix (noun) **1.** *(to a text)* Anhang [ˈanhaŋ] der <-(e)s, Anhänge> **2.** ANAT Blinddarm [ˈblɪntdaʳm] der <-(e)s, Blinddärme>

appetite (noun) **1.** Appetit [apeˈtiːt] der <-s> no pl ◊ *Bewegung regt den Appetit an.* **2.** *(fig)* appetite for sth Verlangen nach etw. [fɛˈlaŋən naːx] das <-s> no pl ◊ *sein Verlangen nach Macht*

applaud (verb) **1.** *(clap hands)* klatschen [ˈklatʃn̩] +haben ◊ *Das Publikum hat begeistert geklatscht.* **2.** *(praise)* loben [ˈloːbn̩] +haben ◊ *Die Mannschaft wurde für ihren Einsatz gelobt.* **3.** *(welcome)* begrüßen [bəˈɡryːsn̩] <begrüßt, begrüßte, hat begrüßt> ◊ *Die Öffentlichkeit begrüßte die Entscheidung der Regierung.*

applause (noun) Beifall [ˈbaɪfal] der <-(e)s> no pl ◊ *tosender Beifall* ◆ *Es gab viel Beifall für seine Rede.*

apple (noun) Apfel [ˈapfl̩] der <-s, Äpfel>
◉ the apple of sb's eye jds Liebling

appliance (noun) Gerät [ɡəˈrɛːt] das <-(e)s, -e>

applicable (adj) be applicable (to sb/sth) (für jdn/ etw.) gelten [ˈɡɛltn̩] <gilt, galt, hat gegolten> ◊ *Diese Richtlinie gilt nicht für Verträge.* applicable law geltendes Recht

applicant (noun) **1.** *(for a position)* Bewerber [bəˈvɛʳbɐ] der <-s, -> ♀Bewerberin [bəˈvɛʳbərɪn] die <-, -nen> ◊ *einen Bewerber zum Vorstellungsgespräch einladen* **2.** *(for a loan, financial assistance)* Antragsteller [ˈantraːkʃtɛlɐ] der <-s, -> ♀Antragstellerin [ˈantraːkʃtɛlərɪn] die <-, -nen> ◊ *Nur ein Teil der Antragsteller bekommt Sozialhilfe.*

application (noun) **1.** *(for a job, position etc.)* Bewerbung [bəˈvɛʳbʊŋ] die <-, -en> ◊ *eine Bewerbung um eine Stelle* ◆ *ihre Bewerbung als Redakteurin* **2.** *(use of sth, software)* Anwendung [ˈanvɛndʊŋ] die <-, -en> ◊ *die Anwendung der Methode auf andere Bereiche* ◆ *Bitte schließen Sie alle Anwendungen.* **3.** *(of paint etc.)* Auftragen [ˈaʊftraːɡn̩] das <-s> no pl ◊ *das Auftragen der Farbe* ◆ *die Oberfläche*

apply (verb) **1.** *(for a job, position)* apply (to sb/sth) for sth sich (bei jdm/etw.) um etw. bewerben [ʊm ... bəˌvɛʳbm̩] <bewirbt sich, bewarb sich, hat sich beworben> ◊ *Sie hat sich bei der Post um eine Stelle beworben.* **2.** *(for a passport etc.)* apply (to sb) for sth etw. (bei jdm) beantragen [bəˈʔantraːɡn̩] <beantragt, beantragte, hat beantragt> ◊ *einen Reisepass beantragen* **3.** *(be relevant for)* apply to sb/sth für jdn/etw. gelten [fyːɐ̯ ... ɡɛltn̩] <gilt, galt, hat gegolten> ◊ *Die Ermäßigung gilt nur für Kinder unter 12 Jahren.* **4.** *(a law, science)* anwenden [ˈanvɛndn̩] <wendet an, wendete/wandte an, hat angewendet/angewandt> ◊ *ein Verfahren anwenden* apply sth to sth etw. auf etw. (acc) anwenden applied mathematics angewandte Mathematik **5.** *(your knowledge, expertise)* anbringen [ˈanbrɪŋən] <bringt an, brachte an, hat angebracht> ◊ *Er konnte sein Wissen in der Prüfung gar nicht anbringen.* **6.** *(use physical force)* apply the brakes bremsen [ˈbrɛmzn̩] +haben ◊ *vorsichtig bremsen* apply pressure to sth auf etw. (acc) drücken [aʊf ... ˌdrʏkn̩] +haben **7.** *(sth to a surface)* apply sth (to sth) etw. (auf etw. (acc)) auftragen [ˈaʊftraːɡn̩] <trägt auf, trug auf, hat aufgetragen> ◊ *Klebstoff/Lack auftragen* **8.** *(a bandage, dressing)* anlegen [ˈanleːɡn̩] +haben ◊ *einen Verband anlegen* **9.** apply yourself (to sth) sich (dat) (mit etw.) Mühe geben [ˈmyːə ɡeːbm̩] <gibt sich, gab sich, hat sich gegeben>

appoint (verb) **1.** *(sb to a position)* appoint sb (as) sth jdn zu etw. ernennen [ʦuː ... ɛnɛnən] <ernennt, ernannte, hat ernannt> ◊ *Man hat ihn zum Professor ernannt.* appoint sb to the board of directors jdn zum Vorstandsmitglied ernennen **2.** *(a time, place)* bestimmen [bəˈʃtɪmən] <bestimmt, bestimmte, hat bestimmt> ◊ *Ort und Zeit des Treffens bestimmen*

appointed → **appoint** (adj) well/badly appointed gut/ schlecht ausgestattet [ɡuːt/ˈʃlɛçt ˌaʊsɡəˈʃtatət] no comp/superl ◊ *ein schlecht ausgestattetes Büro*

appointment (noun) **1.** *(professional or official meeting)* Termin [tɛʳˈmiːn] der <-s, -e> ◊ *ein Termin mit einem Geschäftspartner* ◆ *Um neun Uhr habe ich einen Termin beim Zahnarzt.* keep an appointment einen Termin einhalten **2.** *(of sb to a position)* appointment as Ernennung zu [ɛˈnɛnʊŋ ʦuː] die <-, -en> ◊ *seine Ernennung zum*

Direktor appointment to sth Berufung in etw. [acc]
[bəˈruːfʊŋ ɪn] die <-, -en> ◊ *ihre Berufung in den Vorstand* **3.** (job vacancy, position) Stelle [ˈʃtɛlə] die <-, -en>

appraisal [noun] **1.** Beurteilung [bəˈʊ̯ɔɐ̯taɪ̯lʊŋ] die <-, -en> ◊ *eine Beurteilung der Wirtschaftslage* **2.** (in the UK) Mitarbeitergespräch [ˈmɪtlaˈbaɛtɐɡəʃprɛːç] das <-(e)s, -e>

appraise [verb] beurteilen [bəˈʊ̯ɔɐ̯taɪ̯lən] <beurteilt, beurteilte, hat beurteilt> ◊ *Am Ende des Jahres wird jeder Angestellte beurteilt.*

appreciate [verb] **1.** (understand) verstehen [fɛˈʃteːən] <versteht, verstand, hat verstanden> ◊ *Er versteht das Ausmaß dieses Problems erst jetzt.* **2.** (recognize a quality or virtue, be grateful) zu schätzen wissen [tsu: ˈʃɛtsn̩ vɪsn̩] <weiß, wusste, hat gewusst> ◊ *Sie weiß guten Wein zu schätzen.* **3.** (give (official) recognition to) würdigen [ˈvʏɐ̯dɪɡŋ̍] +haben ◊ *Unser Einsatz wurde nicht genügend gewürdigt.* **4.** (gain in value) im Wert steigen [ɪm ˌveːɐ̯t ˈʃtaɪ̯ɡŋ̍] <steigt, stieg, ist gestiegen>

appreciation [noun] **1.** (gratitude, respect) Anerkennung [ˈan|ɛkɛnʊŋ] die <-> ◊ *jdm seine Anerkennung ausdrücken* ✦ *Der Preis wurde ihr in Anerkennung ihrer Verdienste verliehen.* **2.** (understanding) (sb's) appreciation of sth (jds) Sinn für etw. [zɪn fyːɐ̯] der <-s> ◊ *Mir fehlt leider der Sinn für Poesie.*; (awareness) (jds) Bewusstsein für etw. [bəˈvʊstzaɪ̯n fyːɐ̯] das <-> ◊ *Der Autor will das Bewusstsein der Leser für diese Problematik fördern.* **3.** (increase in value) Wertsteigerung [ˈveːɐ̯tʃtaɪ̯ɡərʊŋ] die <-, -en>

apprehend [verb] (arrest) fassen [ˈfasn̩] +haben ◊ *Sie wurde an der Grenze gefasst.*

apprehensive(ly) [adj, adv] besorgt [bəˈzɔɐ̯kt] <besorgter, am besorgtesten> ◊ *ein besorgter Blick* ✦ *„Ich muss doch nicht allein hingehen, oder?", fragte sie besorgt.* apprehensive of sth besorgt wegen etw. [gen] ◊ *Sie war sehr besorgt wegen der Operation.*

apprentice [noun] Lehrling [ˈleːɐ̯lɪŋ] der <-s, -e> ◊ *Lehrlinge ausbilden* ✦ *Er ist Lehrling in einer Bäckerei.*

apprenticeship [noun] **1.** (period of training) Lehre [ˈleːrə] die <-, -n> ◊ *eine dreijährige Lehre* serve an apprenticeship eine Lehre machen ◊ *Ich habe eine Lehre als Bäckerin gemacht.* **2.** (training place) Lehrstelle [ˈleːɐ̯ʃtɛlə] die <-, -n> ◊ *eine Lehrstelle bekommen/suchen*

approach¹ [noun] **1.** (to a task, topic etc.) Ansatz [ˈanzats] der <-es, Ansätze> ◊ *ein neuer Ansatz zur Lösung internationaler Probleme* **2.** (spatial or temporal) Herannahen [hɛˈrannaːən] das <-s> no pl ◊ *das Herannahen des Sturms*; (of a plane) Landeanflug [ˈlandə|anfluːk] der <-(e)s, Landeanflüge> **3.** (access) Zugang [ˈtsuːɡaŋ] der <-(e)s, Zugänge> ◊ *Alle Zugänge zum Haus waren blockiert.*; (road) Zufahrtsstraße [ˈtsuːfaːɐ̯tsʃtraːsə] die <-, -n> **4.** (appeal to sb, offer sb sth) make an approach to sb sich an jdn wenden [an ... vɛndn̩] +haben **5.** (advance on sb of the opposite sex) make approaches to sb Annäherungsversuche bei jdm machen [ˈannɛːərʊŋsfɛzuːxə baɪ ... maxn̩]

approach² [verb] **1.** (come close(r)) approach (sb/sth) sich (jdm/einer Sache) nähern [ˈnɛːɐn] +haben ◊ *Wir näherten uns der Stadt.* ✦ *Der Frühling nähert sich mit schnellen Schritten.* The temperature

approached 40°. Die Temperaturen näherten sich der 40°-Marke.; (storm) heranziehen [hɛˈrantsiːən] <zieht heran, zog heran, ist herangezogen> ◊ *Ein Unwetter/Gewitter zog heran.* **2.** (ask sb for sth, offer sb sth) approach sb (about sth) sich (wegen etw.) [gen] an jdn wenden [an ... vɛndn̩] <wendet sich, wendete/wandte, hat sich gewendet/gewandt> ◊ *Er hat sich wegen dieser Sache an mich gewendet.* **3.** (deal with) angehen [ˈangeːən] <geht an, ging an, hat angegangen> ◊ *Probleme gemeinsam angehen* ✦ *Er ging das Rennen locker an.* **4.** (almost reach a certain quality, talent etc.) approach sth an etw. [acc] heranreichen können [an ... hɛˈranraɪ̯çn̩ kœnən] <kann, konnte, hat können> mostly in the negative ◊ *An seine Leistung kann niemand heranreichen.*

appropriate [adj] **1.** (suitable) angebracht [ˈangəbraxt] <angebrachter, am angebrachtesten> ◊ *Hier ist Vorsicht angebracht.* ✦ *angebrachtes Verhalten* if appropriate gegebenenfalls [ɡəˈɡeːbənənfals] (lofty) ◊ *Er wird gegebenenfalls rechtliche Schritte einleiten.*; (required in a certain situation) entsprechend [ɛntˈʃprɛçn̩t] ◊ *Zur Wiederholung der Prüfung müssen Sie den entsprechenden Antrag stellen.* **2.** (to be expected in the light of what has gone before) dementsprechend [ˈdeːm|ɛntˈʃprɛçn̩t] no comp/superl, mostly before ns ◊ *Er hat mich blöd angeredet und eine dementsprechende Antwort bekommen.* **3.** (correct, of a decision, method, moment etc.) richtig [ˈrɪçtɪç] ◊ *Wäre es nicht richtiger, ihr die Entscheidung zu überlassen?* ✦ *Sie hatte die richtigen Argumente.* the appropriate time der richtige Augenblick **4.** (of a remark, description: well articulated) treffend [ˈtrɛfn̩t] ◊ *eine treffende Beschreibung* ✦ *Die Bezeichnung war sehr treffend.*; (of an accusation, observation: justified) zutreffend [ˈtsuːtrɛfn̩t] ◊ *Der Vorwurf erwies sich als nicht zutreffend.* ✦ *eine zutreffende Bemerkung* **5.** (sum of money) angemessen [ˈangəmɛsn̩] ◊ *eine angemessene Entschädigung zahlen* ✦ *Der Preis war durchaus angemessen.*

appropriately [adv] **1.** (suitably, to an acceptable standard) angemessen [ˈangəmɛsn̩] ◊ *jdn angemessen entschädigen* **2.** (suitably and concisely articulated) treffend [ˈtrɛfn̩t] ◊ *etw. treffend bemerken/formulieren*

approval [noun] **1.** (agreement) Zustimmung [ˈtsuːʃtɪmʊŋ] die <-> give your agreement seine Zustimmung erteilen meet with sb's approval jds Zustimmung finden nod of approval zustimmendes Nicken [ˌtsuːʃtɪmən̩dəs ˈnɪkn̩] <-s> no pl **2.** (positive feeling towards sb) Anerkennung [ˈan|ɛkɛnʊŋ] die <-> ◊ *Liebe und Anerkennung seiner Eltern blieben ihm versagt.* **3.** (official permission) Genehmigung [ɡəˈneːmɪɡʊŋ] die <-, -en> ◊ *einen Antrag zur Genehmigung einreichen* give/grant approval to sth die Genehmigung für etw. erteilen be subject to sb's approval von jdm genehmigt werden müssen [fɔn ... ɡəˈneːmɪçt veːɐ̯dn̩ mʏsn̩] <muss, musste, hat müssen>

approve [verb] **1.** (agree) approve (of sth) (mit etw.) einverstanden sein [ˈaɛnfɛʃtandn̩ zaɛn] +haben ◊ *Sie ist nicht einverstanden.* ✦ *Bist du mit meiner Wahl einverstanden?* approve of sb doing sth damit einverstanden sein, dass jd etw. tut; (support a project, an idea etc.) approve of sth etw. befürworten [bəˈfyːɐ̯vɔɐ̯tn̩] <befürwortet, befürwortete, hat befürwortet> ◊ *ein Projekt/einen Plan/eine Idee befürworten*

2. *(give official permission to sth)* genehmigen [gə'neːmɪɡn̩] +haben ◊ *Die Behörde hat den Antrag/ Etat genehmigt.*; *(parliament, party)* verabschieden [fɐˈʔapʃiːdn̩] <verabschiedet, verabschiedete, hat verabschiedet> ◊ *Die Partei verabschiedete ihr Wahlprogramm.*

approximate(ly) [adj, adv] *(used with figures, amounts)* ungefähr [ˈʊŋɡəfɛːɐ̯] no comp/superl; when used as an adj, only before ns ◊ *eine ungefähre Angabe* ♦ *Er wiegt ungefähr 80 kg.*

apricot [noun] Aprikose [apriˈkoːzə] die <-, -n>

April [noun] April [aˈprɪl] der <-(s), -e> most sing → **January**

ⓟ play an April fool's joke on sb, play an April fool on sb jdn in den April schicken

apron [noun] **1.** *(item of clothing)* Schürze [ˈʃʏɐ̯tsə] die <-, -n> ◊ *Der Fleischer band sich eine Schürze um.* **2.** THEAT Rampe [ˈrampə] die <-, -n> ◊ *Der Sänger trat bis nah an die Rampe vor.* **3.** AVIAT Vorfeld [ˈfoːɐ̯fɛlt] das <-(e)s, -er> ◊ *Ein Flugzeug wartet auf dem Vorfeld.*

apt(ly) [adj, adv] treffend [ˈtrɛfn̩t] ◊ *eine treffende Beschreibung* ♦ *Die Bezeichnung war treffend.* ♦ *etw. treffend bemerken/formulieren*

aquarium [noun] Aquarium [aˈkvaːrjʊm] das <-s, Aquarien>

Aquarius [noun] Wassermann [ˈvasɐman] der <-(e)s, Wassermänner>

Arab [noun] Araber [ˈarabɐ] der <-s, -> ♀Araberin [ˈarabərɪn] die <-, -nen> → **German¹** 1.

Arabic¹ [noun] Arabisch [aˈraːbɪʃ] das <-(s)> no pl → **German¹** 2.

Arabic² [adj] arabisch [aˈraːbɪʃ] → **German²**

arbitrary(-ily) [adj, adv] **1.** *(chosen for no particular reason)* beliebig [bəˈliːbɪç] no comp/superl ◊ *ein beliebiges Beispiel* ♦ *Die Reihenfolge der Zahlen ist beliebig.* ♦ *etw./jdn beliebig auswählen können* **2.** *(esp pej) (unfair(ly))* willkürlich [ˈvɪlkyːɐ̯lɪç] when used as an adj, mostly before ns ◊ *willkürliche Verhaftungen* ♦ *etw. willkürlich entscheiden*

arc [noun] Bogen [ˈboːɡn̩] der <-s, - or regional Bögen>

arcade [noun] Passage [paˈsaːʒə] die <-, -n>

arch¹ [noun] Bogen [ˈboːɡn̩] der <-s, - or regional Bögen> ◊ *ein Bogen im gotischen Stil*

arch² [verb] wölben [ˈvœlbm̩] +haben ◊ *Die Lupe wölbt das Bild ein wenig.* sth arches etw. wölbt sich ◊ *Über uns wölbten sich die Äste der alten Buchen.*

arch(ly) [adj, adv] schelmisch [ˈʃɛlmɪʃ] ◊ *ein schelmisches Grinsen* ♦ *Er lächelte sie schelmisch an.*

archaeological(ly) [adj, adv] archäologisch [aʁçɛoˈloːɡɪʃ] no comp/superl ◊ *archäologische Ausgrabungen* ♦ *eine archäologisch belegte Epoche*

archaeologist [noun] Archäologe [aʁçɛoˈloːɡə] der <-n, -n> ♀Archäologin [aʁçɛoˈloːɡɪn] die <-, -nen> ◊ *Der Archäologe legte eine Grabstätte frei.* ♦ *Sie ist Archäologin.*

archaeology [noun] Archäologie [aʁçɛoloˈɡiː] die <-, -n>

architect [noun] **1.** Architekt [aʁçiˈtɛkt] der <-en, -e> ♀Architektin [aʁçiˈtɛktɪn] die <-, -nen> ◊ *Mein Bruder ist Architekt.* ♦ *eine berühmte Architektin* **2.** *(fig) (creator)* architect of sth treibende Kraft hinter etw. [ˌtraɪbəndə ˈkraft hɪntɐ] die <-, Kräfte> ◊ *die treibende Kraft hinter der Ostpolitik*

architecture [noun] **1.** *(design of buildings, university course)* Architektur [aʁçitɛkˈtuːɐ̯] die <-, -en> **2.** IT database architecture Datenbankstruktur [ˈdaːtn̩baŋkʃtrʊkˌtuːɐ̯] die <-, -en> system architecture Systemstruktur [zʏsˈteːmʃtrʊkˌtuːɐ̯]

archive [noun] Archiv [aʁˈçiːf] das <-s, -e>

area [noun] **1.** *(domain, region)* Gebiet [ɡəˈbiːt] das <-(e)s, -e> ◊ *Auf diesem Gebiet kenne ich mich nicht so gut aus.* ♦ *die ländlichen Gebiete Chinas* area of interest Interessengebiet [ɪntəˈrɛsŋɡəbiːt]; *(neighbo(u)rhood)* Gegend [ˈɡeːɡn̩t] die <-, -en> ◊ *Er kommt auch aus dieser Gegend.* ♦ *Wir wohnen in einer ruhigen Gegend.*; *(with particular purpose, of skin)* Bereich [bəˈraɪç] der <-(e)s, -e> ◊ *Bitte parken Sie im markierten Bereich.* **2.** *(size)* Fläche [ˈflɛçə] die <-, -n> ◊ *ein Grundstück mit einer Fläche von zwei Hektar*

arena [noun] Arena [aˈreːna] die <-, Arenen> ◊ *eine überdachte Arena für sportliche Wettkämpfe* ♦ *Die Artisten zeigten in der Arena ihre Kunststücke.* ♦ *die politische Arena betreten* arena of war Kriegsschauplatz [ˈkriːksʃaʊplats] der <-es, Kriegsschauplätze>

argue [verb] **1.** *(fight)* (sich) streiten [ˈʃtraɪtn̩] <streitet, stritt, hat gestritten> ◊ *Die beiden Jungen streiten ständig.* ♦ *Ich mag mich nicht schon wieder streiten.* ♦ *Er hat mit seiner Frau über die Finanzen gestritten.* **2.** *(discuss)* argue sth etw. diskutieren [dɪskuˈtiːrən] <diskutiert, diskutierte, hat diskutiert> ◊ *unterschiedliche Ansichten diskutieren* **3.** *(present reasons)* argumentieren [aʁɡumɛnˈtiːrən] <argumentiert, argumentierte, hat argumentiert> ◊ *Sie argumentierte, dass das Haus renovierungsbedürftig sei.* ♦ *Er argumentierte gegen eine Verlängerung der Arbeitszeit.*

ⓟ argue sb out of/into sth jdm etw. ausreden/ einreden argue without arguing ohne Widerworte

argument [noun] **1.** *(quarrel)* Streit [ʃtraɪt] der <-(e)s, -e> ◊ *ein erbitterter Streit* ♦ *Vermeiden Sie Streit über dieses Thema.* have an argument (with sb) (mit jdm) Streit haben ◊ *Sie hatte Streit mit ihrem Mann.*; *(debate)* Diskussion [dɪskuˈsi̯oːn] die <-, -en> ◊ *eine Diskussion über die Reform des Rentensystems* **2.** *(reason)* Argument [aʁɡuˈmɛnt] das <-(e)s, -e> ◊ *ein gewichtiges Argument* ♦ *Dieses Argument überzeugt mich.*

Aries [noun] Widder [ˈvɪdɐ] der <-s, ->

arise [verb] **1.** *(problem, question)* auftauchen [ˈaʊftaʊxn̩] +sein ◊ *Es ist da ein Problem aufgetaucht.* ♦ *Wenn noch irgendwelche Fragen auftauchen sollten, …*; *(mistake)* auftreten [ˈaʊftreːtn̩] <tritt auf, trat auf, ist aufgetreten> ◊ *Ist dieser Fehler schon oft aufgetreten?*; *(result)* arise from/out of sth sich aus etw. ergeben [aʊs … ɐˈɡeːbm̩] <ergibt sich, ergab sich, hat sich ergeben> ◊ *Aus dem Treffen haben sich ein paar interessante Möglichkeiten ergeben.* **2.** *(lit) (get or stand up)* sich erheben [ɛˈheːbm̩] <erhebt sich, erhob sich, hat sich erhoben> *(lit)* ◊ *Der König erhob sich und rief nach seinem Diener.*

arithmetic [noun] **1.** *(part of mathematics)* Rechnen [ˈrɛçnən] das <-s> no pl ◊ *Heute haben wir in der ersten Stunde Rechnen.* **2.** *(calculation)* Rechnung [ˈrɛçnʊŋ] die <-, -en> ◊ *Wenn meine Rechnung stimmt, bleiben 27 Euro übrig.*

arm¹ [noun] **1.** *(of a human body, machine, river)* Arm [aʁm] der <-(e)s, -e> ◊ *Sie breitete die Arme aus und rief: „Herzlich willkommen!"* ♦ *Er klemmte sich*

die Zeitung unter den Arm. ♦ *Sie gingen Arm in Arm spazieren.* ♦ *ein Leuchter mit acht Armen* ♦ *Der Fluss teilt sich in drei Arme.* in sb's arms im Arm ◊ *Sie hielt ein Baby im Arm.* fold/cross your arms die Arme verschränken ◊ *Sie hatte die Arme verschränkt.* take sb in your arms jdn in die Arme nehmen **2.** *(of a chair)* Armlehne ['aˈmleːnə] die <-, –n> ◊ *ein Sessel mit Armlehnen* **3.** *(of clothes)* Ärmel ['ɛˈml] der <-s, –> ◊ *eine Bluse ohne Ärmel*

arm² [verb] **1.** *(with weapons)* arm sb/yourself with sth jdn/sich mit etw. bewaffnen [mɪt … bə,vafnən] <bewaffnet, bewaffnete, hat bewaffnet> ◊ *Sie bewaffneten sich mit Steinen und Stöcken.* **2.** *(with arguments etc.)* arm yourself with sth etw. parat haben [paˈraːt haːbm̩] +haben ◊ *Du solltest eine gute Entschuldigung parat haben, wenn du zum Chef gehst.*

armchair [noun] Sessel ['zɛsl̩] der <-s, –> ◊ *im Sessel vor dem Fernseher sitzen*

armed forces [noun] Streitkräfte ['ʃtraɛtkrɛftə] die <-> pl ◊ *den Oberbefehl über die Streitkräfte haben*

armpit [noun] Achsel ['aksl̩] die <-, –n> ◊ *unter der Achsel Fieber messen*

arms [noun] Waffen ['vafn̩] die <-> pl ◊ *Handel mit Waffen betreiben* lay down arms die Waffen niederlegen ◊ *Nach erbittertem Kampf legten beide Parteien die Waffen nieder.*

army [noun] **1.** Armee [aˈrmeː] die <-, –n> ◊ *Ihr Mann ist bei der Armee.* army of rescue workers Hilfstrupp ['hɪlfstrʊp] der <-s, –s> **2.** *(fig) (great number)* Heer [heːɐ] das <-(e)s, –e> ◊ *ein Heer von Arbeitslosen*

A-road [noun] Bundesstraße ['bʊndəsˌʃtraːsə] die <-, –n> ◊ *Die Bundesstraße 383 war blockiert.*

aroma [noun] Duft [dʊft] der <-(e)s, Düfte> ◊ *der Duft von frisch gebackenem Kuchen* ♦ *Die Nelken verströmten einen wunderbaren Duft.*

around¹ [adv] **1.** *(expressing circular movement, circular order)* herum [hɛˈrʊm] ◊ *Die Trümmer lagen weit herum verstreut.* all around ringsherum ['rɪŋshɛˈrʊm] ◊ *ein Haus mit Garten ringsherum* from all around von überallher [fɒn ybɛˈlaˈlʔheːɐ̯]; *(expressing circular movement, circular order, change of direction, aimlessness, indecision)* herum… [hɛˈrʊm] look around herumschauen [hɛˈrʊmʃaʊən] +haben ◊ *Sie schaute in der Halle herum, konnte ihn aber nirgends entdecken.* drive around herumfahren [hɛˈrʊmfaːrən] <fährt herum, fuhr herum, ist herumgefahren> ◊ *ziellos in der Gegend herumfahren; (referring to U-turn)* um… [ʊm] turn around (sich) umdrehen ['ʊmdreːən] +haben ◊ *Dreben Sie dort vorne um.* ♦ *Dreh dich mal um!* ♦ *Er drehte das Blatt um, um den Text zu lesen.* **2.** *(approximately: referring to figures)* etwa ['ɛtva:] ◊ *Es waren etwa 20 Gäste anwesend.* ♦ *Er ist etwa 35 Jahre alt.; (referring to time)* gegen ['geːgŋ̩] [+acc] ◊ *Gegen 20 Uhr wollen wir in Wien sein.* ♦ *Gegen Morgen kam ein Sturm auf.*

⊚ the biggest/fastest etc. … around der/die/das größte/schnellste etc. … überhaupt ◊ *das beste Chinarestaurant überhaupt* be around da sein ◊ *Ist Michael da?* ♦ *Als er sie am meisten brauchte, war sie nicht da.*

'Around' often occurs in phrasal verbs like 'get around' or 'turn around' which have their own entries in the dictionary.

---

around² [prep] **1.** *(around the outer sides of sth, encir-*

cling sth)* um [ʊm] [+acc] ◊ *Die Erde dreht sich um die Sonne.* ♦ *Das Auto fährt um die Ecke.* ♦ *Die Kinder versammelten sich um die Lehrerin.* somewhere around irgendwo in der Gegend von [ˌɪrˈgŋ̩t|ˌvo: ɪn deːɐ̯ ˌgeˈgŋ̩t fɒn] ◊ *Er wohnt irgendwo in der Gegend von Hamburg.* around that/it darum [daˈrʊm] ◊ *ein Schloss mit einem Park darum; (with certain verbs: encircling sth)* … around sth um etw. herum… [ʊm … hɛˈrʊm] sit around sth um etw. herumsitzen [ʊm … hɛˈrʊmzɪtsn̩] <sitzt herum, saß herum, hat herumgesessen> ◊ *Wir saßen alle um das Feuer herum.* walk around sth um etw. herumgehen [ʊm … hɛˈrʊmgeːən] <geht herum, ging herum, ist herumgegangen> ◊ *Sie gingen um das Auto herum.* **2.** A is focused/based around B B bildet den Mittelpunkt … [gen]/von A ['bɪldət deːn 'mɪtl̩pʊŋkt …/vɒn] +haben ◊ *Die Feuerstelle bildete den Mittelpunkt des Stammeslebens.* ♦ *Die komischen Dialoge bilden den Mittelpunkt von Peter Sellers' Inszenierung.* **3.** *(in various places all over an area)* around the country/ Europe überall im Land/in Europa [yːbɐˈʔal ɪm lant/ɪn ɔøˈroːpaː] ◊ *Die Volkshochschule gibt es überall in Deutschland.* **4.** *(everywhere within a certain area)* look around the house sich im ganzen Haus umsehen [zɪç ɪm 'gantsən haʊs 'ʊmzeːən] <sieht sich um, sah sich um, hat sich umgesehen> go around the building das ganze Gebäude absuchen [das 'gantsə gəˈbɒɪdə apˈzuːxn̩] +haben

arouse [verb] **1.** *(sympathy, anger etc., sexually)* erregen [ɛˈreːgŋ̩] <erregt, erregte, hat erregt> ◊ *jds Mitleid/Zorn etc. erregen* ♦ *Ihr Versprecher erregte allgemeine Heiterkeit.* **2.** *(lit) (wake up)* aufwecken ['aʊfvɛkn̩] +haben ◊ *Der Lärm weckte ihn auf.*

arrange [verb] **1.** *(a date etc.)* vereinbaren [fɛˈʔaɛnbaːrən] <vereinbart, vereinbarte, hat vereinbart> ◊ *einen Termin vereinbaren* ♦ *Ich habe mit ihm vereinbart, dass wir uns morgen treffen.* ♦ *In einem Vertrag werden die Bedingungen vereinbart.* **2.** *(organize, a piece of music)* arrangieren [araŋˈʒiːrən] <arrangiert, arrangierte, hat arrangiert> ◊ *eine Hochzeit arrangieren* ♦ *Ich arrangiere für Sie ein Treffen mit ihm.* ♦ *Wir fliegen am Sonntag los — ich habe bereits alles arrangiert.* ♦ *Er hat das Stück für Klavier arrangiert.; (details)* regeln ['reːgl̩n] <regelt, regelte, hat geregelt> arrange for a taxi ein Taxi besorgen [ɛɪn 'taksi: bəˌzɔˈgŋ̩] <besorgt, besorgte, hat besorgt> **3.** *(put in a certain order)* anordnen ['anʔɔˈdnən] <ordnet an, ordnete an, hat angeordnet> ◊ *Stühle um einen Tisch anordnen* ♦ *Sie hat die Bilder von links nach rechts angeordnet.*

arrangement [noun] **1.** *(agreement)* Vereinbarung [fɛˈʔaɛnbaːrʊŋ] die <-, –en> ◊ *eine Vereinbarung mit jdm haben* by arrangement nach Vereinbarung make an arrangement eine Vereinbarung treffen come to an arrangement eine Regelung finden [aɛnə 'reːgəlʊŋ fɪndn̩] <findet, fand, hat gefunden> **2.** *(scheduling and co-ordinating)* Vorbereitungen ['foːɐ̯bəraɛtʊŋən] die <-> pl ◊ *Wie laufen die Vorbereitungen für eure Hochzeit?* **3.** *(grouping)* Anordnung ['anʔɔˈdnʊŋ] die <-, –en> ◊ *Mir gefällt die Anordnung der Möbel nicht.* **4.** mus Arrangement [araŋʒəˈmãː] das <-s, –s> ◊ *ein Arrangement für Gitarre*

array [noun] **1.** *(collection, arrangement)* Reihe ['raɛə] die <-, –n> ◊ *eine Reihe berühmter Künstler* ♦ *eine*

eindrucksvolle Reihe von teuren Produkten ♦ eine Reihe von Solarkollektoren auf dem Dach installieren 2. (lit) (dress) Staat [ʃtaːt] der <-(e)s> no pl (lofty) ◊ Er kam in vollem Staat.

arrest¹ [noun] (of a suspect) Festnahme ['fɛstnaːmə] die <-, -n> ◊ Er leistete bei seiner Festnahme keinen Widerstand. be under arrest festgenommen sein ['fɛstɡənɔmən zaɛn] +sein ◊ Er ist vorläufig festgenommen.; (with a warrant) Verhaftung [fɛ'haftʊŋ] die <-, -en> ◊ Der Staatsanwalt ordnete die Verhaftung des Mannes an. ♦ Die Polizei hofft, dass es bald zu einer Verhaftung des Mörders kommt. be under arrest verhaftet sein [fɛ'haftət zaɛn] +sein ◊ „Sie sind verhaftet. Kommen Sie bitte mit", sagte der Polizist.

arrest² [verb] 1. (a suspect) festnehmen ['fɛstneːmən] <nimmt fest, nahm fest, hat festgenommen> ◊ Die Polizei hat sie vorübergehend festgenommen. ♦ Der Täter ließ sich widerstandslos festnehmen. arrest sb for sth jdn wegen etw. festnehmen 2. (with a warrant) verhaften [fɛ'haftn̩] <verhaftet, verhaftete, hat verhaftet> ◊ Die Polizei hat gestern einen der Entführer verhaftet. arrest sb for sth jdn wegen etw. verhaften ◊ Er wurde wegen Drogenbesitzes verhaftet. 3. (form) (stop spreading, slow down) arrest sth einer Sache [dat] Einhalt gebieten ['aɛnhalt ɡəbiːtn̩] <gebietet, gebot, hat geboten> (form) ◊ Nichts konnte dem Verlauf der Krankheit Einhalt gebieten. 4. (form) arrest sb's attention jds Aufmerksamkeit erregen ['aɔfmɛɐ̯kzaːmkaɛt ɛˌreːɡn̩] <erregt, erregte, hat erregt> ◊ Das Plakat hatte die Aufmerksamkeit des Publikums erregt.

arrival [noun] 1. (of a plane, person, baby etc.) Ankunft ['ankʊnft] die <-, Ankünfte> ◊ Fahrplanmäßige Ankunft in Genf ist um 8.30 Uhr. on sb's arrival bei jds Ankunft arrivals Sieh bitte auf der Anzeigetafel unter „Ankunft" nach, wann das Flugzeug landet. 2. (a new person) (new) arrival Neuankömmling ['nɔø|ankœmlɪŋ] der <-s, -e> ◊ Der Vorsitzende begrüßte die Neuankömmlinge.

arrive [verb] 1. (train, person etc.) ankommen ['ankɔmən] <kommt an, kam an, ist angekommen> ◊ Wann kommt dein Zug an? ♦ Bist du pünktlich in London angekommen? ♦ Der Brief ist nie bei ihm angekommen.; (information) erreichen [ɛ'raɛçn̩] <erreicht, erreichte, hat erreicht> ◊ Soeben erreicht uns die Information, dass der Präsident gestorben ist. 2. (start a job, start to exist) kommen ['kɔmən] <kommt, kam, ist gekommen> ◊ Mit 24 Jahren kam sie als Referendarin an diese Schule. ♦ Im März kommen die ersten Blumen. a baby arrives ein Baby kommt auf die Welt
ⓔ you've finally arrived jd hat es geschafft ◊ Wenn du mal dein eigenes Büro mit Sekretärin hast, dann hast du es geschafft.
• **arrive at** [phras v] arrive at sth zu etw. gelangen [tsu: ... ɡəlaŋən] +sein ◊ Wie bist du zu diesem Resultat gelangt?

arrogance [noun] Arroganz [aro'ɡants] die <-> no pl ◊ Mit seiner Arroganz schafft er sich keine Freunde.

arrogant(ly) [adj, adv] arrogant [aro'ɡant] <arroganter, am arrogantesten> ◊ Sie hielt ihn für arrogant. ♦ eine arrogante Bemerkung machen ♦ Arrogant sah sie auf ihn herab.

arrow [noun] Pfeil [pfaɛl] der <-(e)s, -e> ◊ Der Pfeil traf ihn im Rücken. ♦ Der Pfeil verweist auf ein

anderes Stichwort. ♦ den roten Pfeilen folgen

arse [noun] Arsch [aˈrʃ] der <-(e)s, Ärsche> (rude, also pej)
ⓔ kiss my arse leck mich am Arsch move your arse beweg deinen Arsch my arse das soll wohl ein Witz sein

arsehole [noun] Arschloch ['aˈrʃlɔx] das <-(e)s, Arschlöcher> (rude, pej) ◊ Er ist wirklich ein Arschloch!

arson [noun] Brandstiftung ['brantʃtɪftʊŋ] die <-, -en> ◊ wegen schwerer Brandstiftung verurteilt werden

art [noun] 1. (painting etc., activity of creating sth, subject, skill) Kunst [kʊnst] die <-, Künste> ◊ das Institut für moderne Kunst ♦ Er hat Kunst und Geschichte studiert. ♦ Kochen ist eine Kunst. the arts die schönen Künste the fine arts die bildenden Künste 2. UNI arts Geisteswissenschaften ['ɡaɛstəsvɪsnʃaftn̩] die <-> pl ◊ das Institut für Geisteswissenschaften
ⓔ there's an art to doing sth es gehört ein gewisses Geschick dazu, etw. zu tun

artful(ly) [adj, adv] raffiniert [rafi'niːɐ̯t] <raffinierter, am raffiniertesten> ◊ Der Täter war sehr raffiniert. ♦ ein raffinierter Trick ♦ Die Einbrecher sind äußerst raffiniert vorgegangen.

article [noun] 1. (in a newspaper etc., item, of a constitution, in grammar) Artikel [aˈrtɪkl̩] der <-s, -> ◊ Hast du den Artikel über Atomkraft gelesen? ♦ der Import indischer Artikel ♦ Artikel 3 Absatz 2 des Grundgesetzes ♦ Bei Städtenamen ohne Attribut steht im Deutschen kein Artikel. 2. LAW do your articles sein Referendariat machen [zaɛn referɛnda'riːat maxn̩] +haben ◊ Er macht gerade sein Referendariat in einer Anwaltskanzlei.

articulate [verb] artikulieren [a'rtiku'liːrən] <artikuliert, hat artikuliert> ◊ Es fällt ihr schwer, ihre Gefühle zu artikulieren. ♦ Der Kleine artikuliert für sein Alter schon recht gut.

artificial(ly) [adj, adv] künstlich ['kʏnstlɪç] ◊ künstliche Blumen ♦ Ihr Lachen wirkte künstlich. ♦ Die Patientin wird künstlich ernährt.

artist [noun] Künstler ['kʏnstlɐ] der <-s, -> ♀Künstlerin ['kʏnstlərɪn] die <-, -nen> ◊ der berühmte Künstler Vincent van Gogh ♦ Ihre Tochter ist Künstlerin.

artistic(ally) [adj, adv] 1. (referring to art) künstlerisch ['kʏnstlərɪʃ] no comp/superl ◊ Sie hat großes künstlerisches Talent. ♦ künstlerisch veranlagt sein 2. (tasteful) kunstvoll ['kʊnstfɔl] mostly before ns ◊ kunstvoller Blumenschmuck ♦ kunstvoll arrangiert

as¹ [adv] as ... as so ... wie [zoː ... viː] ◊ Er ist nicht so erfolgreich wie sein Vater. ♦ Sie sieht so aus wie immer. half/twice/three times/not etc. as much as halb/doppelt/dreimal/nicht etc. so viel wie ◊ Er isst fast doppelt so viel wie sie. the same ... as derselbe/dieselbe/dasselbe ... wie ◊ Sie hat dieselbe Frisur wie ihre Mutter. as ... as usual/possible etc. so ...wie üblich/möglich etc. ◊ Bitte kommen Sie so früh wie möglich! just as ebenso ['eːbmzoː] ◊ Disziplin ist beim Sport ebenso wichtig wie Ausdauer.

as² [prep] (in a particular role or function) als [als] [+acc] ◊ Sie arbeitet als Lehrerin. ♦ Als Kind wollte er Pilot werden. ♦ Es ist seine Aufgabe als Hausmeister, die Wege zu kehren. ♦ Ich als die Ältere gebe dir den guten Rat, ... ♦ Ich betrachte ihn als meinen

Freund.

as³ conjunc **1.** *(referring to a known fact, in the same way)* wie [viː] ◊ *Die Agenda ist wie folgt: ...* ♦ *Wie ich höre, gibt es was zu feiern.* ♦ *Wie verabredet treffen wir uns um drei.* ♦ *Ich habe es so gemacht, wie du gesagt hast.* ♦ *Mach das bitte, wie du möchtest.* as is/does/has etc. wie ◊ *Er benutzt den Bus, wie fast alle seine Kollegen.* as usual wie üblich ◊ *Sie kam wie üblich zehn Minuten zu spät.* **2.** *(when)* als [als] ◊ *Als er zur Tür ging, klingelte das Telefon.* just as gerade als ◊ *Gerade als er die Nachrichten einschalten wollte, klopfte es an die Tür.* **3.** as soon as sobald [zoˈbalt] ◊ *Bitte sag Bescheid, sobald du etwas Neues erfährst.* **4.** *(because)* da [daː] ◊ *Er machte einen Sprachkurs, da er sein Spanisch verbessern wollte.* ♦ *Da er kein Geld hat, kann er nicht in den Urlaub fahren.* **5.** *(although)* obwohl [ɔpˈvoːl] ◊ *Ich ging draußen spazieren, obwohl es in Strömen regnete.* rich/stupid etc. as sb is ... obwohl jd reich/dumm etc. ist ◊ *Obwohl er Talent hat, wurde er nicht genommen.* strange as it may seem obwohl es seltsam erscheinen mag ⦿ as it were gewissermaßen ◊ *Er bekam den Job gewissermaßen aus heiterem Himmel.* as for ... was ... betrifft ◊ *Was die Schule betrifft, so hat unsere Tochter im Moment keine Probleme.* as if als ob as of, as from ab ◊ *Ab heute müssen alle Urlaubsanträge von mir genehmigt werden.* as to sth *(form)* was etw./jdn betrifft *(form)* ◊ *Was dieses Problem betrifft, wird sich eine Lösung finden.*

ascend verb *(a mountain etc.)* erklimmen [eˈklɪmən] <erklimmt, erklomm, hat erklommen> *(lit)* ◊ *eine Felswand erklimmen; (plane, in a job)* aufsteigen [ˈa͜ofʃta͜eɡn̩] <steigt auf, stieg auf, ist aufgestiegen> ◊ *Langsam stieg das Flugzeug auf und verschwand in den Wolken.* ♦ *Er ist zum Abteilungsleiter aufgestiegen.; (road)* ansteigen [ˈanʃta͜eɡn̩] <steigt an, stieg an, ist angestiegen> ◊ *Hier steigt der Wanderweg bis zum Gipfel stark an.*

ascent noun Aufstieg [ˈa͜ofʃtiːk] der <-(e)s, -e> ◊ *ein beschwerlicher Aufstieg* ♦ *der Aufstieg eines Schauspielers zum Weltstar*

ascertain verb ermitteln [ɛˈmɪtl̩n] <ermittelt, ermittelte, hat ermittelt> ◊ *Die Polizei hat ermittelt, dass der Verdächtige zur Tatzeit am Tatort war.* ♦ *Man versuchte, die Ursache des Unfalls zu ermitteln.*

ash noun **1.** *(from fire)* Asche [ˈaʃə] die <-> no pl ◊ *zu Asche verbrennen* sb's ashes jds Asche **2.** *(tree, wood)* Esche [ˈɛʃə] die <-, -n> ◊ *In unserem Garten steht eine Esche.* ♦ *Möbel aus Esche*

ashamed(ly) adj, adv beschämt [bəˈʃɛːmt] <beschämter, am beschämtesten> ◊ *Beschämt blickte sie zu Boden.* ♦ *Sie fühlte sich beschämt.* be ashamed (of sth) sich (wegen etw.) schämen [ˈʃɛːmən] +haben ◊ *Du solltest dich wegen deines gestrigen Verhaltens schämen!* be ashamed to do sth sich schämen, etw. zu tun ◊ *Sie schämte sich, seinen Eltern von seinem Misserfolg zu erzählen.* be ashamed of sb sich für jdn schämen

Asia noun Asien [ˈaːzi̯ən] das <-s> article only in combination with attribute, no pl → **Germany**

Asian¹ noun **1.** *(sb from Asia)* Asiat [aˈzi̯aːt] der <-en, -en> ♀Asiatin [aˈzi̯aːtɪn] die <-, -nen> **2.** *(in the UK also: sb from India)* Inder [ˈɪndɐ] der <-s, -> ♀Inderin [ˈɪndərɪn] die <-, -nen> → **German¹** **1.**

Asian² adj asiatisch [aˈzi̯aːtɪʃ] → **German²**

aside adv **1.** *(away)* beiseite [ba͜eˈza͜etə] ◊ *Er legte den Stift beiseite und sah von seinem Manuskript auf.* ♦ *ein Thema beiseite lassen* turn aside sich abwenden [ˈapvɛndn̩] <wendet sich ab, wendete/wandte sich ab, hat sich abgewendet/abgewandt> ◊ *Sie wollte mit ihm reden, doch er wandte sich ab.* **2.** *(esp in the US: apart from)* aside from außer [ˈa͜osə] +dat ◊ *Außer einem Stück Brot habe ich noch nichts gegessen.*

ask verb **1.** *(inquire)* fragen [ˈfraːɡn̩] +haben ◊ *Ich wollte dich fragen, ob du mit ins Kino kommst.* ♦ *Er fragte nicht, warum.* ♦ *Wie viel verdienen Sie, wenn ich fragen darf?* ask a question eine Frage stellen [a͜enə ˈfraːɡə ʃtɛln̩] +haben **2.** *(request)* bitten [ˈbɪtn̩] <bittet, bat, hat gebeten> ◊ *Er bat sie, ihm zu helfen.* ♦ *Der Künstler bittet darum, nicht genannt zu werden.* ask (sb) for sth (jdn) um etw. bitten ◊ *Er bat die Gastgeberin um ein Glas Wasser.* ask sb's permission/advice etc. jdn um Erlaubnis/Rat etc. bitten **3.** *(a price etc.)* verlangen [fɛˈlaŋən] <verlangt, verlangte, hat verlangt> ◊ *Er verlangt über 15 000 Euro für den Wagen.* ♦ *Du verlangst zu viel von mir!* ask to see sb/sth jdn/etw. verlangen ◊ *Sie verlangte den Chef.* **4.** *(invite)* einladen [ˈa͜enlaːdn̩] <lädt ein, lud ein, hat eingeladen> ◊ *Ich habe die Nachbarn zum Essen eingeladen.* ♦ *Sie lud ihn ein, über Nacht zu bleiben.* ask sb in jdn hereinbitten [hɛˈra͜enbɪtn̩] <bittet herein, bat herein, hat hereingebeten> ⦿ **Don't ask!** Frag bloß nicht! ◊ *"Wie war die Party gestern?" — "Frag bloß nicht!"* Who asked you? Wer hat dich gefragt? for the asking auf Anfrage free for the asking umsonst zu haben

asleep adj **1.** *(person, animal)* be (fast) asleep (fest) schlafen [(fɛst) ˈʃlaːfn̩] <schläft, schlief, hat geschlafen> ◊ *Als sie nach Hause kam, schlief er bereits.* fall asleep einschlafen [ˈa͜enʃlaːfn̩] +sein ◊ *Nach der anstrengenden Reise schlief sie rasch ein.* **2.** *(arm, leg etc.: numb)* eingeschlafen [ˈa͜enɡəʃlaːfn̩] no comp/superl ◊ *Mein Arm ist eingeschlafen.*

asparagus noun Spargel [ˈʃpaːɡl̩] der <-s, -> most sing ◊ *Spargel mit Salzkartoffeln und gekochtem Schinken* ♦ *Ich esse sehr gern Spargel.*

aspect noun **1.** *(of a subject, in grammar)* Aspekt [asˈpɛkt] der <-(e)s, -e> ◊ *Unter dem Aspekt habe ich die Sache noch gar nicht betrachtet.* ♦ *Der progressive Aspekt wird im Englischen durch die ing-Form ausgedrückt.* What about the security aspect? Was ist mit der Sicherheit? **2.** *(of a building)* have a southerly etc. aspect Südlage etc. haben [ˈzyːtlaːɡə haːbn̩] +haben ◊ *Alle Fenster des Wohnzimmers haben Südlage.* **3.** *(form) (appearance)* Anblick [ˈanblɪk] der <-(e)s, -e> ◊ *Der nasse Hund bot einen kläglichen Anblick.*

aspiration noun Aspiration [aspiraˈtsi̯oːn] die <-, -en> *(lofty)* ◊ *Sie hatte schon lange Aspirationen auf das Amt der Bürgermeisterin.* ♦ *Im Französischen findet sich die Aspiration sehr selten.*

ass noun **1.** *(bottom)* Arsch [aˑʃ] der <-(e)s, Ärsche> *(rude, also pej)* ◊ *Er fragen beim Skifahren voll auf den Arsch gefallen.* ♦ *Los, beweg deinen Arsch!* **2.** *(oldf) (donkey, stupid person)* Esel [ˈeːzl̩] der <-s, -> *(fam, pej)* ◊ *So ein blöder Esel!* ⦿ my ass dass ich nicht lache ◊ *Das soll ein Diamant sein? Dass ich nicht lache!*

assassination [noun] Attentat ['atnta:t] das <-s, -e>
◊ *Auf den Minister wurde ein Attentat verübt.* assassination attempt Attentatsversuch ['atnta:tsfezu:x]
der <-(e)s, -e> ◊ *Seit dem Attentatsversuch hat der
Präsident die Anzahl seiner Leibwächter verdoppelt.*

assault[1] [noun] **1.** *(mugging)* Überfall ['y:befal] der
<-(e)s, Überfälle> ◊ *einen Überfall auf jdn begehen*
assault (and battery) Körperverletzung
['kœɐ̯pefelɛtsʊn] die <-, -en> *most sing* ◊ *Er wurde
wegen schwerer Körperverletzung angeklagt.* **2.** MIL
Angriff ['angrɪf] der <-(e)s, Angriffe> ◊ *einen
Angriff auf/gegen feindliche Stellungen fliegen* ✦
einen Angriff abwehren ✦ *Der Politiker sah sich
heftigen Angriffen ausgesetzt.*

assault[2] [verb] *(attack)* überfallen [ybɐ̯'falən]
<überfällt, überfiel, hat überfallen> ◊ *Sie wurde auf
der Straße überfallen.* assault sb sexually sich an
jdm vergehen [an ... fe̯ɐ̯ge:ən] <vergeht sich, verging
sich, hat sich vergangen>

assemble [verb] **1.** *(furniture, a device)* zusammenbauen [tsu'zamənbaʊən] +haben ◊ *einen Schrank
zusammenbauen* **2.** *(a jigsaw, mosaic)* zusammensetzen [tsu'zamənzɛtsn̩] +haben ◊ *Er setzte ein schwieriges Puzzle zusammen.* **3.** *(people)* versammeln
[fɐ̯'zamln̩] <versammelt, versammelte, hat versammelt>
◊ *Er versammelte alle Familienmitglieder um sich.*
sb assembles jd versammelt sich ◊ *Die Kinder versammelten sich in der Aula.; (a team for a special
purpose)* zusammenstellen [tsu'zamənʃtɛlən] +haben
◊ *Er stellte ein Expertenteam zusammen, um das
Problem zu lösen.*

assembly [noun] **1.** *(gathering of people, Parliament)*
Versammlung [fɐ̯'zamlʊn] die <-, -en> ◊ *eine Versammlung einberufen* ✦ *sich mit einer Rede an die
Versammlung wenden* the French National Assembly
die französische Nationalversammlung
[di: fran͜tsø:zɪʃə natsi̯o'na:lfɛɐ̯zamlʊn] morning
assembly morgendliche Schulversammlung
[ˌmɔɐ̯g̊n̩tlɪçə 'ʃu:lfɛɐ̯zamlʊn] freedom of assembly Versammlungsfreiheit [fɐ̯'zamlʊnsfra̯ehaɛt] die <-> *no
pl* **2.** *(of a machine etc.)* Montage [mɔn'ta:ʒə] die
<-, -n> ◊ *Wir übernehmen die Montage von PCs.;
(thing assembled)* Konstruktion [kɔnstrʊk'tsi̯o:n] die
<-, -en> ◊ *eine komplizierte Konstruktion*

assent [noun] Zustimmung ['tsu:ʃtɪmʊn] die <-, -en>
◊ *Der Chef muss noch seine Zustimmung dazu
geben.*

assert [verb] behaupten [bə'haʊptn̩] <behauptet,
behauptete, hat behauptet> ◊ *Sie behauptet, dass sie
die Akten nicht gesehen hat.* ✦ *Sie hat ihren Standpunkt in dieser Frage behauptet.* assert yourself sich
behaupten ◊ *Er muss lernen, sich beim Spielen mit
anderen Kindern zu behaupten.* assert your
innocence seine Unschuld beteuern
[zaɛnə 'ʊnʃʊlt bətɔ̯ɐ̯n] <beteuert, beteuerte, hat
beteuert> assert your authority seine Autorität
geltend machen [zaɛnə a̯otori'tɛ:t ˌgɛltn̩t maxn̩]
+haben

assertion [noun] Behauptung [bə'haʊptʊn] die
<-, -en> ◊ *Wer hat diese Behauptung aufgestellt?* ✦
*Seine Behauptung, ich hätte ihn geschlagen, ist nicht
wahr.*

assess [verb] **1.** *(judge)* einschätzen ['aɛnʃɛtsn̩] +haben
◊ *Er versuchte, die Situation schnell einzuschätzen.*
✦ *Wie schätzt du den neuen Kollegen ein?* **2.** *(value)*
schätzen ['ʃɛtsn̩] +haben ◊ *Ein Fachmann soll den*

Wert des Grundstücks schätzen.

assessment [noun] **1.** *(judgement)* Beurteilung
[bə'ʊ'ɐ̯taɛlʊn] die <-, -en> ◊ *die Beurteilung eines
Menschen* ✦ *Was sind die Kriterien zur Beurteilung
dieser Arbeit?* **2.** *(evaluation)* Schätzung ['ʃɛtsʊn] die
<-, -en> ◊ *eine Schätzung des Wertes vornehmen*

asset [noun] **1.** *(benefit)* Kapital [kapi'ta:l] das <-s> *no
pl* ◊ *Gesundheit ist ein großes Kapital.* ✦ *Sie kann
aus ihrem Aussehen kein Kapital schlagen.*
2. *(property)* assets Vermögen [fɛ'mø:gn̩] das
<-s, -> *most sing* ◊ *Sein Vermögen beläuft sich auf
rund eine Million Euro.*

asshole [noun] Arschloch ['a'ɐ̯ʃlɔx] das
<-(e)s, Arschlöcher> *(rude, pej)* ◊ *So ein Arschloch!*
→ arsehole

assign [verb] **1.** *(give sb a task etc.)* assign sb to sth
jdn mit etw. betrauen [mɪt ... bə̯traʊən] <betraut,
betraute, hat betraut> ◊ *Er wurde mit der Leitung der
Ermittlungen betraut.; (allot)* assign sth to sb jdm
etw. zuweisen ['tsu:vaɛzn̩] <weist zu, wies zu, hat zugewiesen> ◊ *Welche Aufgabe hat man dir zugewiesen?;
(determine where sb belongs)* assign sb to sth/sb jdn
einer Sache/jdm zuteilen ['tsu:taɛlən] +haben ◊ *Sie
wurde dem Kurs für Fortgeschrittene zugeteilt.*
2. *(appoint)* assign sb to sth jdn irgendwohin
berufen [bə'ru:fn̩] <beruft, berief, hat berufen> ◊ *Man
hat sie an eine andere Schule berufen.* ✦ *Er wurde
zum Botschafter berufen.* **3.** *(a time, date)* festsetzen
['fɛstzɛtsn̩] +haben ◊ *Der Chef hat eine Frist von fünf
Tagen für den Abschluss des Projekts festgesetzt.*
4. LAW übereignen [ybɐ̯'aɛgnən] <übereignet, übereignete, hat übereignet> ◊ *Er hat seine Villa dem
Obdachlosenheim übereignet.*

assignment [noun] **1.** *(task)* Aufgabe ['aʊfga:bə] die
<-, -n> ◊ *Ihre erste Aufgabe als Journalistin war,
einen Politiker zu interviewen.* ✦ *Bitte geben Sie die
fertigen Aufgaben bis zum 15. November ab.*
2. *(allotment)* Zuteilung ['tsu:taɛlʊn] die <-, -en> ◊
die Zuteilung der Gelder überwachen **3.** LAW Übereignung [ybɐ̯'aɛgnʊn] die <-, -en> *most sing* ◊ *Die
Übereignung des Besitzes erfolgt nächsten Monat.*

assist [verb] *(help)* helfen ['hɛlfn̩] <hilft, half, hat
geholfen> ◊ *Dieser Hinweis könnte der Polizei
helfen, den Täter zu fassen.* ✦ *Könnten Sie mir bitte
kurz helfen?* assist (sb) in/with sth (jdm) bei etw.
helfen ◊ *Einige Freiwillige halfen bei der Bergung
der Verletzten.; (act as an assistant)* assistieren
[asis'ti:rən] <assistiert, assistierte, hat assistiert> ◊ *Die
Krankenschwester assistierte dem Chirurgen.*

assistance [noun] Hilfe ['hɪlfə] die <-, -n> *most sing*
◊ *jdm finanzielle Hilfe anbieten* ✦ *Er konnte nur
mit der Hilfe seiner Frau die Treppe hinaufsteigen.*
come to sb's assistance jdm zu Hilfe kommen be
of assistance behilflich sein [bə'hɪlflɪç zaɛn] +sein ◊
Kann ich irgendwie behilflich sein?

assistant[1] [noun] Assistent [asɪs'tɛnt] der <-en, -en>
♀Assistentin [asɪs'tɛntɪn] die <-, -nen> ◊ *Bitte
wenden Sie sich an meine Assistentin.* ✦ *Ich arbeite
als persönlicher Assistent eines Abteilungsleiters.*

assistant[2] [adj] stellvertretend ['ʃtɛlfɛɐ̯tre:tn̩t] *no
comp/superl, only before ns* ◊ *der stellvertretende
Direktor* ✦ *Bitte wenden Sie sich an den stellvertretenden Geschäftsführer.*

associate[1] [noun] **1.** ECON Partner ['pa'ɐ̯tnɐ] der
<-s, -> ♀Partnerin ['pa'ɐ̯tnərɪn] die <-, -nen> ◊
Die beiden Unternehmer sind seit vielen Jahren

Partner. business associate Geschäftspartner [gə'ʃɛftspaˈtnɐ] **2.** *(member)* außerordentliches Mitglied [,aoseloˈrdn̩tlɪçəs 'mɪtgliːt] <–(e)s, –er> ◊ *Er ist außerordentliches Mitglied in dem Verein.*

associate² ⟨verb⟩ **1.** *(link)* associate sth with sb/sth etw. mit jdm/etw. assoziieren [mɪt ... asotsiˈiːrən] <assoziiert, assoziierte, hat assoziiert> ◊ *Mit Italien assoziiere ich Sonne, Meer, Wein und Pasta.* ✦ *Viele Menschen assoziieren mit Schlangen Bösartigkeit, obwohl das nicht stimmt.* be associated with sth mit etw. verbunden sein [mɪt ... fɐˌbʊndn̩ zaɐn] +*sein* ◊ *Diese Krankheit ist häufig mit Kopfschmerzen verbunden.* **2.** *(meet)* associate with sb mit jdm verkehren [mɪt ... fɐˌkeːrən] <verkehrt, verkehrte, ist verkehrt> ◊ *Während seiner Zeit in London verkehrte er mit einigen bekannten Künstlern.*

association ⟨noun⟩ **1.** *(group)* Verband [fɐˈbant] der <–(e)s, Verbände> ◊ *der Verband Deutscher Makler* ✦ *sich zu einem Verband zusammenschließen; (in names also)* Bund [bʊnt] der <–(e)s, Bünde> ◊ *der Bund für Umwelt und Naturschutz* **2.** *(connection with people, things)* Verbindung [fɐˈbɪndʊŋ] die <–, –en> ◊ *Ihm konnten Verbindungen zur Drogenmafia nachgewiesen werden.* ✦ *Es besteht eine eindeutige Verbindung zwischen Rauchen und Lungenkrebs.; (thought)* Assoziation [asotsiaˈtsi̯oːn] die <–, –en> ◊ *Das Bild rief unangenehme Assoziationen in ihm hervor.*

ⓔ in association with **1.** *(with the assistance of)* in Zusammenarbeit mit ◊ *Das Buch ist in Zusammenarbeit mit zahlreichen Fachleuten entstanden.* **2.** *(together with)* im Zusammenhang mit ◊ *Halsschmerzen treten häufig im Zusammenhang mit einer Erkältung auf.*

assume ⟨verb⟩ **1.** *(suppose)* annehmen ['anneːmən] <nimmt an, nahm an, hat angenommen> ◊ *Ist anzunehmen, dass es Ärger gibt?* ✦ *Nehmen wir mal an, du wirst krank ...; (presuppose)* voraussetzen [foˈraɔszɛtsn̩] +*haben* ◊ *Dieses Wissen setze ich als bekannt voraus.* **2.** *(responsibility, power)* übernehmen [ybɐˈneːmən] <übernimmt, übernahm, hat übernommen> ◊ *Übernehmen Sie dafür die Verantwortung?* ✦ *die Kontrolle über etw.* ⟨acc⟩ *übernehmen* **3.** *(a position, shape etc.)* einnehmen ['aɪnneːmən] <nimmt ein, nahm ein, hat eingenommen> ◊ *Die Balletttänzerin nahm die erste Position ein.* ✦ *Das Tier nahm seine Schlafstellung ein.* assume greater importance an Bedeutung gewinnen [an bəˈdɔɔtʊŋ ɡəˌvɪnən] <gewinnt, gewann, hat gewonnen> ◊ *Die Rolle der Väter gewinnt in der Kindererziehung an Bedeutung.* assume an air of innocence etc. eine unschuldige etc. Miene aufsetzen [aɛnə ˌʊnʃʊldɪɡə 'miːnə aɔfzɛtsn̩] +*haben* ◊ *Sie setzte eine unschuldige Miene auf, als man sie fragte, wer das Glas zerbrochen habe.*

assumption ⟨noun⟩ **1.** *(hypothesis)* Annahme ['anaːmə] die <–, –n> ◊ *Es besteht kein Grund zu der Annahme, dass ...* ✦ *Er ging von falschen Annahmen aus.; (presupposition)* Voraussetzung [foˈraɔszɛtsʊŋ] die <–, –en> go on the assumption that von der Voraussetzung ausgehen, dass **2.** *(of power, responsibility)* Übernahme ['yːbɐnaːmə] die <–, –n> *most sing* ◊ *sich auf die Übernahme des Amtes vorbereiten* ✦ *die Übernahme bestimmter Rechte und Pflichten*

assurance ⟨noun⟩ **1.** *(self-confidence, certainty)* Zuver-

sicht ['tsuːfɛɐzɪçt] die <–> no pl ◊ *„Er wird sicher bald wieder gesund", sagte sie voller Zuversicht.* ✦ *Mir fehlt es oft an Zuversicht.* **2.** *(promise)* Zusicherung ['tsuːzɪçərʊŋ] die <–, –en> ◊ *Nordkorea will die Zusicherung, dass die USA das Land nicht angreifen.* ✦ *eine schriftliche Zusicherung* **3.** *(esp in the UK)* life assurance Lebensversicherung ['leːbm̩sfɛɐˌzɪçərʊŋ] die <–, –en> ◊ *Er hat eine Lebensversicherung abgeschlossen.*

assure ⟨verb⟩ **1.** *(say with confidence)* assure sb that jdm versichern, dass [feˈzɪçɐn das] <versichert, versicherte, hat versichert> ◊ *Ich versichere Ihnen, dass ich alles tun werde, um Ihnen zu helfen.* **2.** *(make certain of)* assure sth etw. sichern ['zɪçɐn] +*haben* ◊ *Diese Maßnahmen werden den Erfolg des Projekts sichern.* ✦ *seine Zukunft sichern* **3.** assure yourself of sth sich von etw. überzeugen [fɔn ... yːbɐˌtsɔɔɡn̩] <überzeugt sich, überzeugte sich, hat sich überzeugt> ◊ *Ich möchte mich von der Qualität dieses Produkts überzeugen.*

astonish ⟨verb⟩ erstaunen [ɛˈʃtaɔnən] <erstaunt, hat erstaunt> ◊ *Es erstaunt mich nicht im Geringsten, dass er wütend ist.*

astonishing(ly) ⟨adj, adv⟩ erstaunlich [ɛˈʃtaɔnlɪç] ◊ *erstaunliche Leistungen vollbringen* ✦ *Seine Fähigkeit, andere zu überzeugen, ist erstaunlich.* ✦ *Er ist für sein Alter erstaunlich fit.*

astonishment ⟨noun⟩ Erstaunen [ɛˈʃtaɔnən] das <–s> no pl ◊ *Der Anblick des dressierten Seehunds versetzte sie in Erstaunen.* ✦ *Zu meinem Erstaunen hat er sich gar nicht beklagt.* in astonishment erstaunt [ɛˈʃtaɔnt] ✦ *erstauntesten> ◊ „Und du bekommst tatsächlich ab Januar mehr Gehalt?", fragte sie erstaunt.*

astrology ⟨noun⟩ Astrologie [astrolo'giː] die <–> no pl ◊ *Ich glaube nicht an Astrologie.*

astronomy ⟨noun⟩ Astronomie [astrono'miː] die <–> no pl ◊ *Er interessiert sich für Physik und Astronomie.*

astute(ly) ⟨adj, adv⟩ schlau [ʃlaɔ] ◊ *ein schlauer Geschäftsmann* ✦ *Das hat sie sehr schlau geplant.*

asylum ⟨noun⟩ **1.** *(protection)* Asyl [aˈzyːl] das <–s> no pl ◊ *politisches Asyl* seek asylum Asyl beantragen ◊ *Sie hat in Deutschland Asyl beantragt.* grant asylum Asyl gewähren ◊ *Man wird den Flüchtlingen Asyl gewähren.* **2.** *(oldf)* *(for lunatics)* Anstalt ['anʃtalt] die <–, –en> *(esp euph)* ◊ *jdn in eine Anstalt einliefern*

asylum seeker ⟨noun⟩ Asylbewerber [aˈzyːlbəvɛrˈbe] der <–s, –> ♀Asylbewerberin [aˈzyːlbəvɛːˈbərɪn] die <–, –nen> ◊ *als Asylbewerber anerkannt werden* ✦ *ein Heim für Asylbewerber*

at ⟨prep⟩ **1.** *(describing the position of sb/sth)* an [an] +*dat* ◊ *Sie blieb an der Kreuzung stehen.* ✦ *Wir treffen uns am Bahnhof.; (at sb's house, premises)* at sb's bei jdm [baɛ] +*dat* ◊ *Wir treffen uns bei Eva.* at the doctor's/hairdresser's beim Arzt/Friseur at home zu Hause [tsuː 'haɔzə]; *(in a certain town, city)* in [ɪn] +*dat* ◊ *Dieser Zug hält nicht in Augsburg.* **2.** *(attending sth, participating in sth)* auf [aɔf] +*dat* ◊ *Warst du gestern auch auf dem Konzert/der Tagung?* ✦ *Warst du auf ihrer Hochzeit?* ✦ *Du bist auf derselben Schule wie ich.* ✦ *Sie war gerade auf der Post.; (attending a university)* an [an] +*dat* ◊ *Er studiert Informatik an der Universität München.* **3.** *(having a meal, working)* bei [baɛ] +*dat* ◊ *Er ist gerade am Abendessen.* ✦ *Beim Frühstück erzählte*

sie nur von der Arbeit. ♦ *Stör sie nicht bei der Arbeit.* **4.** *(with times)* um [ʊm] `+acc` ◊ *Die Nachrichten beginnen um 20 Uhr.* ♦ *Um diese Zeit kann man nirgends mehr anrufen.; (during the weekend, a holiday)* an [an] `+dat` ◊ *Was machst du am Wochenende?* ♦ *Wollt ihr uns an Weihnachten besuchen?* at the beginning/end of am Anfang/Ende ... `gen` ◊ *Wir befinden uns am Anfang des dritten Jahrtausends.* ♦ *Am Ende der Tagung verabschiedeten sich die Teilnehmer.* at present im Moment [ɪm moˈmɛnt] ◊ *Leider habe ich im Moment keine Zeit.* at the time damals [ˈdaːmaːls] ◊ *Als Student lebte er in Paris; damals war er mit Michelle zusammen.* at any time jederzeit [ˈjeːdɐˈtsaet] ◊ *Ich bin jederzeit erreichbar.* at night nachts [naxts] ◊ *Nachts kann es in der Wüste ziemlich kalt werden.* at dawn bei Tagesanbruch [baeˈtaːɡəsˌanbrʊx] ◊ *Sie stand bei Tagesanbruch auf.* **5.** *(when talking about sb's age)* mit [mɪt] `+dat` ◊ *Sie hat mit 21 geheiratet.* at sb's death bei jds Tod [baeː ... toːt] ◊ *Bei seinem Tod war er 101 Jahre alt.* **6.** *(when describing a reaction or response to sth)* über [ˈyːbɐ] `+acc` ◊ *Keiner lacht über deine Witze!* ♦ *Sie ärgerte sich über seine Unpünktlichkeit.* **7.** *(with prices)* zu [tsuː] `+dat` ◊ *Sie kaufte Kiwis zu je 20 Cent.* ♦ *Waren zu niedrigen/hohen Preisen anbieten; (with temperatures, speeds)* bei [bae] `+dat` ◊ *Wasser gefriert bei null Grad Celsius.* ♦ *Bei 180 km/h trug es den Wagen aus der Kurve.* **8.** *(when describing the target of sth)* auf [aʊf] `+acc` ◊ *Der Jäger zielte auf das Herz des Tieres.* ♦ *Er richtete die Waffe auf den Einbrecher.* ♦ *Sie starrte gebannt auf den Bildschirm.; (when describing an attempt to hit or reach sth/sb)* nach [naːx] `+dat` ◊ *Er griff nach dem Seil.* ♦ *Das Pferd trat nach dem Reiter.* **9.** *(when describing a talent or skill)* in [ɪn] `+dat` good/bad at gut/schlecht in ◊ *Sie ist gut in Physik.* an expert at (ein) Experte in, (eine) Expertin in ◊ *Er ist ein Experte in der Fischzucht.* ♦ *Sie ist Expertin im Kochen.* **10.** *(with phone numbers)* unter [ˈʊntɐ] `+dat` ◊ *Sie erreichen uns tagsüber unter 20575.* ⊙ at sb's request/invitation etc. auf jds Bitte/Einladung etc. ♦ *können while you're at it es einfach nicht lassen können while you're at it wenn du schon dabei bist*

athlete `noun` Sportler [ˈʃpɔʁtlɐ] der <-s, -> ♀Sportlerin [ˈʃpɔʁtlərɪn] die <-, -nen> ◊ *Der prominente Sportler hat bereits mehrere Medaillen gewonnen.* ♦ *Als Sportlerin legt sie Wert auf gesunde Ernährung.* a natural athlete der geborene Sportler, die geborene Sportlerin ◊ *Er ist der geborene Sportler.*

athletic `adj` **1.** *(good at sports)* sportlich [ˈʃpɔʁtlɪç] ◊ *Er ist sportlich und spielt gern Basketball.* ♦ *Sie hat eine sportliche Figur.* **2.** *(referring to athletics)* leichtathletisch [ˈlaeçtatˌleːtɪʃ] no comp/superl, only before ns ◊ *leichtathletische Wettkämpfe;* Leichtathletik... [ˈlaeçtatˌleːtɪk] athletic club Leichtathletikverein [ˈlaeçtatleːtɪkfɐˌaen] der <-s, -e>

athletics `noun` **1.** *(in the UK: running, jumping, throwing)* Leichtathletik [ˈlaeçtatˌleːtɪk] die <-> no pl ◊ *Die Leichtathletik umfasst mehrere Disziplinen.* **2.** *(in the US: sports)* Sport [ʃpɔʁt] der <-(e)s> no pl ◊ *Sie treibt gern Sport.*

ATM, ATM machine Geldautomat [ˈɡɛltʔaʊtoˌmaːt] der <-en, -en> ◊ *Ich habe mir am Geldautomaten 300 Euro geholt.*

atmosphere `noun` Atmosphäre [atmoˈsfɛːrə] die <->

no pl ◊ *Die Raumfähre verglühte beim Eintritt in die Atmosphäre.* ♦ *Auf der Party herrschte eine ungezwungene Atmosphäre.*

atom `noun` Atom [aˈtoːm] das <-s, -e> ◊ *die Spaltung von Atomen* oxygen atom Sauerstoffatom [ˈzaʊɐˌʃtɔf|aˌtoːm] ◊ *Wasser besteht aus zwei Wasserstoffatomen und einem Sauerstoffatom.* ⊙ not an atom of sense kein Funken Verstand ◊ *Er hat keinen Funken Verstand.* not an atom of truth kein Körnchen Wahrheit

atomic `adj` Atom... [aˈtoːm] atomic energy Atomenergie [aˈtoːmˌenɛɐˌɡiː] die <-> no pl ◊ *die friedliche Nutzung der Atomenergie* atomic age Atomzeitalter [aˈtoːmtsaetˌʔaltɐ] das <-s> no pl ◊ *Wir leben im Atomzeitalter.*

attack `verb` **1.** *(fix)* befestigen [bəˈfɛstɪɡn] <befestigt, befestigte, hat befestigt> ◊ *die Hundeleine am Halsband befestigen* ♦ *ein Plakat an der Wand befestigen; (a document to a letter)* beifügen [ˈbaefyːɡn] +haben ◊ *Die aktuellen Preislisten füge ich bei.; (connect machines)* anschließen [ˈanʃliːsn̩] <schließt an, schloss an, hat angeschlossen> ◊ *Er schloss den Drucker an den Computer an.* **2.** *(assign)* zuteilen [ˈtsuːtaelən] +haben, mostly passive ◊ *Sie wurde der Abteilung für Sicherheitsfragen zugeteilt.* ⊙ attach yourself to sth/sb sich jdm/etw. anschließen

attached → attach `adj` **1.** *(document)* beiliegend [ˈbaelɪɡn̩t] no comp/superl ◊ *Bitte füllen Sie beiliegendes Formular aus.* ♦ *Beiliegend finden Sie die angeforderten Unterlagen.* **2.** *(be fond of)* be attached to sb/sth an jdm/etw. hängen [an ... ˌhɛŋən] <hängt, hing, hat gehangen> ◊ *Sie hängt an ihrem Großvater.* ♦ *Er möchte das alte Landhaus nicht verkaufen, weil er sehr daran hängt.* **3.** *(connected)* verbunden [fɛˈbʊndn̩] ◊ *Der Park ist direkt mit dem Altenheim verbunden.* ♦ *Mit dieser Aufgabe ist ein gewisses Risiko verbunden.*

attachment `noun` **1.** *(tool)* Zubehör [ˈtsuːbəhøːɐ] das <-(e)s, -e> most sing ◊ *Er hat technisches Zubehör für die Stereoanlage bestellt.* **2.** *(document)* Anlage [ˈanlaːɡə] die <-, -n> ◊ *Als Anlage übersende ich Ihnen meinen Lebenslauf.* ♦ *die Anlage einer E-Mail öffnen* **3.** *(affection)* Zuneigung [ˈtsuːnaeɡʊn] die <-, -en> most sing ◊ *Er empfand eine starke Zuneigung für die Freundin seiner Schwester.; (loyalty)* Verbundenheit [fɛˈbʊndn̩haet] die <-, -en> most sing ◊ *Zwischen den beiden Ländern besteht eine enge Verbundenheit.* **4.** *(fixture)* Befestigung [bəˈfɛstɪɡʊn] die <-, -en> most sing ◊ *Das Regal steht auch ohne Befestigung an der Wand sicher.*

attack¹ `noun` **1.** *(aggression, criticism, in sport)* Angriff [ˈanɡrɪf] der <-(e)s, -e> ◊ *einen Angriff abwehren* ♦ *ein Angriff auf die Familienpolitik der Regierung* ♦ *Beim nächsten Angriff hatten sie eine Torchance.* be under attack unter Beschuss stehen [ʊntɐ bəˈʃʊs ʃteːən] <steht, stand, hat gestanden> launch an attack on sb/sth jdn angreifen [ˈanɡraefn̩] <greift an, griff an, hat angegriffen> ◊ *Die Armee griff die Stadt am frühen Morgen an.* sexual attack sexueller Übergriff [zɛksuˌɛlɐ ˈyːbɐɡrɪf] <-(e)s, -e> **2.** *(fit etc.)* Anfall [ˈanfal] der <-(e)s, Anfälle> ◊ *Er bekam einen hysterischen Anfall.* ♦ *ein plötzlicher Anfall von Panik* ♦ *Patienten mit Asthma müssen bei einem Anfall sofort ein Medikament nehmen.*

attack² `verb` **1.** *(assault, criticize, damage, in sport)*

angreifen ['angra͜ifn̩] <greift an, griff an, hat angegriffen> ◊ *Napoleon griff Russland 1812 an.* ✦ *Sie wurde von zwei Unbekannten tätlich angegriffen.* ✦ *Der Kritiker hat die Sängerin öffentlich angegriffen.* ✦ *Das Salz hat das Metall angegriffen.* **2.** *(a problem)* in **Angriff nehmen** [ɪn 'angrɪf ne:mən] <nimmt, nahm, hat genommen> ◊ *Wir sollten das Problem endlich in Angriff nehmen.*

attacker [noun] **Angreifer** ['angra͜ifɐ] der <-s, -> ♀**Angreiferin** ['angra͜ifərɪn] die <-, -nen> ◊ *Es gelang ihr, den Angreifer abzuwehren.* ✦ *Die Angreifer waren zahlenmäßig überlegen.*

attain [verb] *(a rank, certain dimensions, an age, aim etc.)* **erreichen** [ɛ'ra͜içn̩] <erreicht, erreichte, hat erreicht> ◊ *Diese Schlange erreicht eine Länge von bis zu acht Metern.* ✦ *Er hat sein Ziel endlich erreicht.; (prosperity, power etc.)* attain sth zu etw. **gelangen** [tsu: ... gəlaŋən] <gelangt, gelangte, ist gelangt> ◊ *Er war in den letzten Jahren zu großem Reichtum gelangt.*

attainment [noun] **1.** *(of an aim, a level)* **Erreichen** [ɛ'ra͜içn̩] das <-s> no pl ◊ *Das Erreichen einer bestimmten Punktzahl ist Voraussetzung für die Zulassung.; (of knowledge, happiness etc.)* **Erlangen** [ɛ'laŋən] das <-s> no pl ◊ *Das Erlangen von Wissen sollte nicht das einzige Ziel eines Studiums sein.* **2.** *(accomplishment)* **Leistung** ['la͜istʊŋ] die <-, -en> ◊ *Seine schulischen Leistungen sind sehr gut.*

attempt¹ [noun] **Versuch** [fɛ'zu:x] der <-(e)s, -e> ◊ *ein geglückter Versuch* ✦ *einen Versuch wert sein* ✦ *Das Tier machte einen letzten Versuch, sich aus der Falle zu befreien.* ✦ *Beim dritten Versuch schaffte er die Prüfung endlich.* assassination attempt **Mordversuch** ['mɔɐ̯tfezu:x] suicide attempt **Selbstmordversuch** ['zɛlpstmɔɐ̯tfezu:x] attempt on sb's life **Anschlag** ['anʃla:k] der <-(e)s, Anschläge> ◊ *Der Präsident überlebte den Anschlag schwer verletzt.*

attempt² [verb] **versuchen** [fɛ'zu:xn̩] <versucht, versuchte, hat versucht> ◊ *Er versuchte, ihr die Situation zu erklären.* ✦ *Sie versuchte ein Lächeln.*

attend [verb] **1.** *(a meeting, school, course etc.)* **besuchen** [bə'zu:xn̩] <besucht, besuchte, hat besucht> ◊ *Sie besucht einen Kurs an der Volkshochschule.* ✦ *Ich habe neun Jahre lang das Gymnasium besucht.* ✦ *ein Konzert besuchen* attend class am Unterricht **teilnehmen** [am 'ʊntɐrɪçt ˌta͜ilne:mən] <nimmt teil, nahm teil, hat teilgenommen> ◊ *Unsere Tochter kann wegen Krankheit heute nicht am Unterricht teilnehmen.* **2.** *(care for)* **behandeln** [bə'handl̩n] <behandelt, behandelte, hat behandelt> ◊ *Sie wird von den besten Ärzten behandelt.* **3.** *(accompany)* **begleiten** [bə'gla͜itn̩] <begleitet, begleitete, hat begleitet> ◊ *Die Symptome werden von allgemeiner Müdigkeit begleitet.* **4.** *(pay attention to)* attend to sb/sth jdm/einer Sache Aufmerksamkeit **schenken** ['a͜ʊfmɛɐ̯kza:mka͜it ʃɛŋkn̩] +haben ◊ *Sie beklagte sich, dass ihr niemand Aufmerksamkeit schenkte.* **5.** *(serve)* attend to sb jdn **bedienen** [bə'di:nən] <bedient, bediente, hat bedient> ◊ *Wir wurden von einem sehr freundlichen Kellner bedient.*

attendance [noun] **1.** *(number of people)* **Teilnehmerzahl** ['ta͜ilne:mɐtsa:l] die <-, -en> ◊ *Auch bei den diesjährigen Festspielen erreichte die Teilnehmerzahl wieder Rekordhöhe.* church attendance die Zahl der **Kirchenbesucher** [di: ˌtsa:l de:ɐ̯ 'kɪɐ̯çn̩bəzu:xɐ] ◊ *Die Zahl der Kirchenbesucher ist stark gesunken.*

2. *(regular visit)* **Besuch** [bə'zu:x] der <-(e)s, -e> ◊ *Der Besuch dieses Sprachkurses hat ihr sehr geholfen.; (presence)* **Anwesenheit** ['anve:zn̩ha͜it] die <-> no pl ◊ *Die Anwesenheit Ihres Kindes ist Pflicht.* attendance record **Anwesenheitsliste** ['anve:zn̩ha͜itslɪstə] die <-, -n> ◊ *Sie steht nicht auf der Anwesenheitsliste der letzten Woche.*

☞ be in attendance at sth bei etw. anwesend sein be in attendance on sb jdn bedienen

attention [noun] **1.** *(interest, care)* **Aufmerksamkeit** ['a͜ʊfmɛɐ̯kza:mka͜it] die <-> no pl ◊ *Dürfte ich um Ihre Aufmerksamkeit bitten?* ✦ *jdm seine ungeteilte Aufmerksamkeit schenken* ✦ *Ihre Bemühungen verdienen unsere Aufmerksamkeit.* attract sb's attention jds Aufmerksamkeit **erregen** turn sb's attention to sth jds Aufmerksamkeit auf etw. [acc] **lenken** turn your attention to sb/sth seine Aufmerksamkeit auf jdn/etw. **richten** hold sb's attention jdn **fesseln** ['fɛsl̩n] +haben ◊ *Der Bericht fesselte ihn von Anfang bis Ende.* pay attention **aufpassen** ['a͜ʊfpasn̩] +haben ◊ *Was war das? Ich habe gerade nicht aufgepasst.* **2.** *(kindnesses)* attentions **Aufmerksamkeitsbezeugungen** ['a͜ʊfmɛɐ̯kza:mka͜itsbəˌtsɔøgʊŋən] die <-> pl

☞ stand to attention MIL stillstehen

attentive(ly) [adj, adv] **aufmerksam** ['a͜ʊfmɛɐ̯kza:m] ◊ *Dieser Schüler ist besonders aufmerksam.* ✦ *ein aufmerksamer Beobachter* ✦ *die Geschehnisse aufmerksam verfolgen* ✦ *Das Personal in dem Hotel ist sehr aufmerksam und höflich.* be attentive to sth sich um etw. **kümmern** [ʊm ... ˌkʏmən] <kümmert sich, kümmerte, hat sich gekümmert> ◊ *Die Bediensteten kümmern sich um alle Bedürfnisse der Königin.*

attic [noun] **Dachboden** ['daxbo:dn̩] der <-s, Dachböden> ◊ *etw. auf dem Dachboden verstauen*

attitude [noun] **1.** *(way of thinking)* **Einstellung** ['a͜inʃtɛlʊŋ] die <-, -en> most sing ◊ *Ich bin mit Ihrer Einstellung nicht einverstanden.* ✦ *Die Einstellung gegenüber behinderten Menschen hat sich gewandelt.* **2.** *(way of acting, position of body)* **Haltung** ['haltʊŋ] die <-, -en> ◊ *die Haltung der Regierung gegenüber dem Irak-Krieg* ✦ *eine abwehrende Haltung einnehmen*

attorney [noun] **Rechtsanwalt** ['rɛçtsˌanvalt] der <-(e)s, Rechtsanwälte> ♀**Rechtsanwältin** ['rɛçtsˌanvɛltɪn] die <-, -nen> ◊ *Er ist Rechtsanwalt und Notar.* ✦ *Sie arbeitet als Rechtsanwältin in einer Kanzlei.* ✦ *Ich nehme mir einen Rechtsanwalt und verklage Sie!*

attract [verb] *(visitors, insects, magnet, sexually)* **anziehen** ['antsi:ən] <zieht an, zog an, hat angezogen> ◊ *Das Licht auf der Terrasse zieht die Motten an.* ◊ *Die Ausstellung zog Besucher aus der ganzen Welt an.* ✦ *Der Magnet zieht Eisenspäne an.* be attracted to sb sich zu jdm hingezogen fühlen [tsu: ... 'hɪngətso:gn̩ fy:lən] +haben ◊ *Er fühlte sich zu ihr hingezogen.; (interest, attention etc.)* auf sich [acc] **ziehen** ['a͜ʊf ... ˌtsi:ən] <zieht, zog, hat gezogen> ◊ *Das Werbeplakat zieht die Aufmerksamkeit der Passanten auf sich.*

attraction [noun] **1.** *(interesting thing)* **Attraktion** [atrak'tsjo:n] die <-, -en> ◊ *Die Stadt hat viele Attraktionen zu bieten.* **2.** *(reason for liking sth)* **Reiz** [ra͜its] der <-(e)s, -e> ◊ *Worin besteht der besondere Reiz des Skifahrens?* **3.** *(feeling of liking*

sb, of a magnet etc.) Anziehungskraft
['antsiːʊŋskraft] die <-, Anziehungskräfte> ◊ *Sie
schien eine unwiderstehliche Anziehungskraft auf
ihn auszuüben.* ♦ *Hier wirken elektrische Anziehungs-
kräfte.*

attractive [adj] *(person, offer)* attraktiv [atrakˈtiːf] ◊ *Sie
ist sehr attraktiv.* ♦ *ein attraktives Angebot; (house,
picture, dress, place etc.)* reizvoll ['raetsfɔl] ◊ *Die
Landschaft dort ist sehr reizvoll.* ♦ *ein reizvolles
Kleid*

attribute¹ [noun] Eigenschaft ['aeɡɦʃaft] die <-, -en>
◊ *Welche Eigenschaften sollte ein geeigneter
Bewerber haben?*

attribute² [verb] **1.** *(consider sth to be the cause of
sth)* attribute sth to sth. auf etw. [acc] zurückführen [aof ... tsuˌrʏkfyːrən] +haben ◊ *Man führt seine
Verhaltensstörung auf Probleme im Elternhaus
zurück.* **2.** *(a quotation, quality)* attribute sth to sb
jdm etw. zuschreiben ['tsuːʃraebm̩] <schreibt zu,
schrieb zu, hat zugeschrieben> ◊ *Dieser Ausspruch
wird Shakespeare zugeschrieben.*

auction [noun] Versteigerung [feˈʃtaeɡarʊn] die
<-, -en> ◊ *etw. bei einer Versteigerung kaufen* be
up for auction versteigert werden [feˈʃtaeɡet veːɐdn̩]
<wird, wurde, ist worden> ◊ *Das Bild wurde für
2000 Euro versteigert.*

audience [noun] **1.** *(viewers)* Zuschauer ['tsuːʃaoe] die
<-> pl ◊ *Die Zuschauer klatschten Beifall.* an
audience of 2000 people 2000 Zuschauer;
(listeners) Zuhörer ['tsuːhøːre] die <-> pl ◊ *Diese
Sendung ist bei den Zuschauern beliebt.; (readers)*
Leser ['leːze] die <-> pl ◊ *Der Autor entführt in
diesem Buch seine Leser ins Mittelalter.* target
audience Zielpublikum ['tsiːlpuːblikʊm] das <-s> no
pl **2.** *(meeting with a king, queen etc.)* Audienz
[aoˈdjɛnts] die <-, -en> ◊ *eine Audienz bei der
Königin* ♦ *eine Audienz geben*

audit¹ [noun] *(examination)* Prüfung ['pryːfʊŋ] die
<-, -en>; *(of finances)* Rechnungsprüfung
['rɛçnʊŋspryːfʊŋ] ◊ *eine Rechnungsprüfung
vornehmen*

audit² [verb] **1.** *(examine)* prüfen ['pryːfn̩] +haben ◊ *die
Bücher prüfen* audit the credit worthiness of a
company die Kreditwürdigkeit einer Firma prüfen
2. *(in the US: attend a college course without taking
an examination)* Gasthörer sein ['gasthøːre zaen]
Gasthörerin sein ['gasthøːrərɪn zaen] +sein ◊ *Ich bin
Gasthörer an der Universität.*

auditor [noun] **1.** FIN Rechnungsprüfer ['rɛçnʊŋspryːfe]
der <-s, -> ♀Rechnungsprüferin ['rɛçnʊŋspryːfərɪn]
die <-, -nen> ◊ *Nächste Woche kommt der Rechnungsprüfer.* ♦ *Sie arbeitet als Rechnungsprüferin.*
2. *(in the US: sb who attends a college course
without taking an examination)* Gasthörer ['gasthøːre]
der <-s, -> ♀Gasthörerin ['gasthøːrərɪn] die
<-, -nen> ◊ *Sie nahm als Gasthörerin an der
Vorlesung teil.*

auditorium [noun] **1.** *(in a cinema, theatre)* Zuschauerraum ['tsuːʃaoeraom] der <-(e)s, Zuschauerräume>
◊ *Im Zuschauerraum ging das Licht aus.* **2.** *(building)*
Saalbau ['zaːlbao] der <-(e)s, -ten> **3.** *(room for
meetings)* Saal [zaːl] der <-(e)s, Säle>; *(room for
lectures)* Hörsaal ['høːɐzaːl]

August [noun] August [aoˈɡʊst] der <- or -(e)s, -e>
most sing → **January**

a umlaut, A umlaut [noun] ä, Ä [ɛː] das

<-(s), -(s)> ◊ *Dieses Wort wird mit einem kleinen
ä/großen Ä geschrieben.* ♦ *Ä wie Ärger*

aunt [noun] Tante ['tantə] die <-, -n>

Australia [noun] Australien [aosˈtraːljən] das <-s>
article only in combination with attribute, no pl →
Germany

Australian¹ [noun] Australier [aosˈtraːljɐ] der <-s, ->
♀Australierin [aosˈtraːljərɪn] die <-, -nen> →
German¹ 1.

Australian² [adj] australisch [aosˈtraːlɪʃ] *mostly before
ns* → **German²**

Austria [noun] Österreich ['øːstəraeç] das <-s> *article
only in combination with attribute, no pl* → **Germany**

Austrian¹ [noun] Österreicher ['øːstəraeçe] der
<-s, -> ♀Österreicherin ['øːstəraeçərɪn] der
<-, -nen> → **German¹ 1.**

Austrian² [adj] österreichisch ['øːstəraeçɪʃ] →
German²

authentic [adj] authentisch [aoˈtɛntɪʃ] ◊ *eine authenti-
sche Geschichte* ♦ *Ist dieser Film über Gandhi
authentisch?*

author [noun] Autor ['aotoːɐ] der <-s, -en> ♀Autorin
[aoˈtoːrɪn] die <-, -nen> ◊ *Sie arbeitet als Autorin
für einen Schulbuchverlag.* ♦ *Er ist ein berühmter
Autor.*

authority [noun] **1.** *(power to influence others, person
with power and knowledge)* Autorität [aotoriˈtɛːt] die
<-> no pl ◊ *Wer befehlen will, muss Autorität
haben.* ♦ *Sie ist eine Autorität auf dem Gebiet der
Gentechnologie.* lack authority es an Autorität fehlen
lassen; *(with expertise)* do sth with authority etw. mit
Sachkenntnis tun [mɪt ˈzaxkɛntnɪs] ◊ *Dieses Buch ist
mit großer Sachkenntnis geschrieben.* **2.** *(official permission)* Befugnis [bəˈfuːknɪs] die <-, -se> *(form)* ◊
*die Befugnis zur Abnahme von Hochschulprüfungen
an Universitäten* overstep your authority seine Befugnisse überschreiten **3.** *(institution)* Behörde
[bəˈhøːɐdə] die <-, -n> ◊ *Welche Behörde ist für
diese Genehmigung zuständig?* take your complaint
to the authority sich bei der Behörde beschweren
◉ **have sth on good authority** aus zuverlässiger Quelle haben

authorization [noun] Genehmigung [ɡəˈneːmɪgʊŋ] die
<-, -en> ◊ *Haben Sie eine schriftliche Genehmi-
gung?*

authorize [verb] authorize sb to do sth jdn dazu
ermächtigen, etw. zu tun [datsu: ɛˈmɛçtɪgn̩ ... tsuː]
<ermächtigt, ermächtigte, hat ermächtigt> ◊ *Ich habe
ihn dazu ermächtigt, in meinem Namen zu handeln.*
authorize sth etw. genehmigen [ɡəˈneːmɪgn̩] ◊ *Die
Behörde hat den Antrag genehmigt.*

authorized [verb] → authorize [adj] *(officially
empowered)* befugt [bəˈfuːkt] *no comp/superl (form)* ◊
Zutritt nur für befugte Personen! ♦ *Ich bin nicht
befugt, Informationen zu geben.*

automatic(ally) [adj, adv] automatisch [aotoˈmaːtɪʃ] *no
comp/superl; when used as an adj, mostly before ns*
◊ *automatische Türen* ♦ *ein Vertrag, der sich automatisch verlängert*

autonomous(ly) [adj, adv] autonom [aotoˈnoːm] ◊ *ein
autonomer Staat* ♦ *Diese Region ist autonom.* ♦
autonom handeln

autonomy [noun] Autonomie [aotonoˈmiː] die <-, -n>
◊ *Sie fordern Autonomie für ihre Region.*

autumn [noun] Herbst [hɛʳpst] der <-(e)s, -e> ◊ *Im*

A B C D E F G H I J K L M N O P Q R S T U V W X Y Z

Herbst 1998 zog sie nach Berlin. ◆ *Es wird allmäh-lich Herbst.*

auxiliary [noun] **1.** GRAM Hilfsverb ['hɪlfsvɛ'p] das <-s, -en> ◊ *Verben mit dem Hilfsverb „haben"* **2.** *(worker)* Hilfskraft ['hɪlfskraft] die <-, Hilfskräfte> ◊ *Er arbeitet als Hilfskraft.* ◆ *Wir brauchen eine Hilfs-kraft.*

availability [noun] Verfügbarkeit [fe'fy:kba:'kaet] die <-, -en> *(form)* ◊ *Wie steht es mit Ihrer Verfügbar-keit am Samstag?* the availability of sth die Verfüg-barkeit ... [gen]/von etw. ◊ *die Verfügbarkeit neuer Gelder* ◆ *die Verfügbarkeit von Kapital*

available [adj] **1.** TRADE *(for sale)* erhältlich [e'hɛltlɪç] no comp/superl ◊ *Die Zusatzteile sind nur im Fach-handel erhältlich.*; *(sth can be supplied)* lieferbar ['li:fɛba:'] no comp/superl ◊ *ein lieferbarer Artikel* ◆ *Das Buch ist zurzeit nicht lieferbar.* **2.** *(at sb's disposal)* verfügbar [fe'fy:kba:'] no comp/superl ◊ *alle verfügbaren Mitarbeiter einsetzen* ◆ *Im Augenblick ist leider kein Personal verfügbar.* not be available for comment für einen Kommentar nicht zur Verfügung stehen [fy:ɐ̯ aːnən kɔmɛn,taː'ɐ̯ nɪçt ʦuːɐ̯ fe'fy:ɡʊŋ ʃteːən] <steht, stand, hat gestanden> be available to talk to sb jdm für ein Gespräch zur Verfügung stehen **3.** *(single, not married)* be available noch zu haben sein [nɔx ʦuː 'haːbm̩ zaⁱn] ◊ *Ist dein Bruder noch zu haben?*

avalanche [noun] Lawine [la'vi:nə] die <-, -n> ◊ *eine Lawine von Bewerbungen* be buried by an avalanche von einer Lawine verschüttet werden

avenue [noun] **1.** *(road)* Allee [a'le:] die <-, -n> **2.** *(alternative)* Möglichkeit ['mø:klɪçkaet] die <-, -en> ◊ *Wir haben keine andere Möglichkeit mehr, als einen Kredit aufzunehmen.* explore every possible avenue alle Möglichkeiten bedenken

average¹ [noun] Durchschnitt ['dʊ'çʃnɪt] der <-(e)s, -e> most sing ◊ *Das neue Album der Gruppe ist nur Durchschnitt.* ◆ *Beim Abitur erreichte sie einen Durchschnitt von 1,8.* be above/below average über/unter dem Durchschnitt liegen on average durchschnittlich ['dʊ'çʃnɪtlɪç] ◊ *Die Preise sind um durchschnittlich zehn Prozent gestiegen.* an average of ... durchschnittlich ... ◊ *Sie verdient durchschnittlich 3000 Euro im Monat.*

average² [adj] durchschnittlich ['dʊ'çʃnɪtlɪç] ◊ *Ihre Leistungen sind durchschnittlich.* ◆ *der durchschnitt-liche Stundenlohn eines Arbeiters* be about average height von durchschnittlicher Größe sein average person Durchschnittsbürger ['dʊ'çʃnɪtsbʏ'ɡe] der <-s, -> ♀Durchschnittsbürgerin ['dʊ'çʃnɪtsbʏ'ɡərɪn] die <-, -nen>

aversion [noun] Abneigung ['apnaeɡʊn] die <-, -en> ◊ *Er hat mich seine Abneigung spüren lassen.* ◆ *eine Abneigung gegen etw.*

avert [verb] abwenden ['apvɛndn̩] <wendet ab, wendete ab/wandte ab, hat abgewendet/abgewandt> ◊ *Wie kann man einen weiteren Krieg abwenden?* avert your face/gaze (from sth/sb) sein Gesicht/seinen Blick (von etw./jdm) abwenden ◊ *Sein Gesicht hatte er abgewandt.* ◆ *Sie wendete ihren Blick von mir ab.*

aviation [noun] die Luftfahrt [di: 'lʊftfaː'ɐ̯t] <--> no pl ◊ *Berufe in der Luftfahrt*

avoid [verb] **1.** *(in order not to encounter sb/sth)* avoid sb/sth jdm/etw. ausweichen ['aosvaeçn̩] <weicht aus, wich aus, ist ausgewichen> ◊ *Ich bremste, um dem*

Radfahrer auszuweichen. ◆ *Sie versuchte, seinen Fragen auszuweichen.* **2.** *(stay away from sth)* avoid sth etw. meiden ['maednn̩] <meidet, mied, hat gemieden> ◊ *Diese Gegend sollte man nachts meiden.* ◆ *Meiden Sie Alkohol, solange Sie dieses Medikament einnehmen!* avoid doing sth es vermeiden, etw. zu tun [ɛs fe'maednn̩ ... ʦu:] <vermeidet, vermied, hat vermieden> ◊ *Vermeiden Sie es, zu viel Fett zu essen!*; *(stay away from sb)* avoid sb jdm aus dem Weg gehen [aos deːm 've:k ge:ən] <geht, ging, ist gegangen> ◊ *Du gehst ihm besser aus dem Weg, wenn du keinen Ärger willst.* **3.** *(prevent sth)* avoid sth etw. vermeiden [fe'maednn̩] <vermeidet, vermied, hat vermieden> ◊ *Sie wollte Missverständ-nisse vermeiden.* ◆ *Konflikte lassen sich nicht immer vermeiden.* avoid doing sth es vermeiden, etw. zu tun ◊ *Er wollte es vermeiden, Aufmerksamkeit zu erregen.*

await [verb] await sth auf etw. [acc] warten [aof ... ,vaˀtn̩] +haben ◊ *Ich habe lange auf deinen Besuch gewartet.*

awake¹ [adj] wach [vax] no comp/superl, mostly after ns ◊ *Ich habe vor Sorge die halbe Nacht wach gelegen.* ◆ *Er konnte sich nicht mehr wach halten.* wide awake hellwach ['hɛl'vax] no comp/superl

awake² [verb] **1.** sb awakes jd erwacht [e'vaxt] <erwachte, ist erwacht> *(lofty)* ◊ *Er erwachte aus seinem Schlaf.* **2.** *(a person, memories, feelings)* awake sb/sth jdn/etw. wecken ['vɛkn̩] +haben ◊ *Die alten Fotos weckten viele Erinnerungen.* awake sb from sth jdn aus etw. [dat] wecken ◊ *Das Handy weckte ihn aus seinen Gedanken.*

awaken [verb] **1.** *(a person, sb's curiosity, interest etc.)* awaken sb/sth jdn/etw. erwecken [e'vɛkn̩] <erweckt, erweckte, hat erweckt> *(lofty)* ◊ *Der Buchtitel erweckte meine Neugier.* awake sb from sth jdn aus etw. [dat] erwecken ◊ *Er erweckte sie aus ihrem Schlaf.* **2.** sb awakens jd erwacht [e'vaxt] <erwachte, ist erwacht> *(lofty)* ◊ *Am Morgen erwachte sie mit Kopfweh.* awake from sth aus etw. [dat] erwachen ◊ *Ich erwachte aus einem Traum.*

award¹ [noun] **1.** *(for an achievement)* Auszeichnung ['aostsaeçnʊn] die <-, -en> ◊ *Sie erhielt eine Aus-zeichnung für ihre außerordentlichen Leistungen.* **2.** *(grant, bursary)* Stipendium [ʃti'pɛndjʊm] das <-s, Stipendien> apply for an award sich um ein Sti-pendium bewerben **3.** *(compensation)* Entschädi-gung [ɛntˈʃɛːdɪɡʊn] die <-, -en> ◊ *Sie erhielt eine Entschädigung von 250 Euro.*

award² [verb] **1.** *(a prize, medal, scholarship)* verleihen [fe'laeən] <verleiht, verlieh, hat verliehen> award sb sth, award sth to sb jdm etw. verleihen, etw. an jdn verleihen ◊ *Die Regierung verlieh ihr einen Orden.* ◆ *An wen wurde der Nobelpreis für Medizin verliehen?* **2.** LAW *(damages, the custody of a child)* zusprechen ['ʦuːʃprɛçn̩] <spricht zu, sprach zu, hat zugesprochen> ◊ *Das Gericht sprach ihr das Sorgerecht für ihre Tochter zu.*

aware [adj] bewusst [bə'vʊst] <bewusster, am bewuss-testen> ◊ *Die Verbraucher sind beim Kauf von Lebensmitteln bewusster geworden.* ◆ *ein politisch bewusster Mann* be aware of sth sich [dat] einer Sache [gen] bewusst sein ◊ *Ich bin mir keiner Schuld bewusst.* environmentally aware umweltbe-wusst ['ʊmvɛltbəvʊst] <umweltbewusster, am umwelt-bewusstesten> be aware that wissen, dass

['vɪsn̩ das] <weiß, wusste, hat gewusst> ◊ *Wissen Sie,
dass Sie sich bei der Behörde melden müssen?*
◉ not that I'm aware of nicht dass ich wüsste
awareness ⌊noun⌋ 1. *(mental state of knowing)*
Bewusstsein [bə'vʊstzə̯ən] das <-s> no pl awareness
of sth Bewusstsein für etw. ◊ *das Bewusstsein für
ein Problem* raise awareness for sth das Bewusstsein für etw. schärfen lack of awareness mangelndes Bewusstsein ◊ *ein mangelndes Bewusstsein für
Gefahren* increased awareness geschärftes Bewusstsein 2. *(sense of sth)* awareness of sth Gefühl für
etw. [gə'fyːl fyːɐ̯] das <-s> ◊ *kein Gefühl für Zeit
und Raum haben*
away ⌊adv⌋ 1. *(in a different direction or place)* weg...
[vɛk] put sth away etw. weglegen ['vɛkleːgn̩] +haben
◊ *Leg das Messer weg!* fly away wegfliegen ['vɛkfliːgn̩]
<fliegt weg, flog weg, ist weggeflogen> ◊ *Der Vogel ist
weggeflogen.* turn away sich wegdrehen ['vɛkdreːən]
+haben ◊ *Dreh dich nicht weg, wenn ich mit dir
rede!* 2. *(absent)* weg [vɛk] ◊ *Ich werde zwei Wochen
weg sein.* far away weit weg ◊ *Australien ist weit
weg.* be away on business dienstlich unterwegs sein
[ˌdiːnstlɪç ʊntə'veːks zə̯ən] 3. *(+indication of distance)*
entfernt [ɛnt'fɛʳnt] no comp/superl ◊ *Bonn liegt 60
km entfernt.* 4. *(expressing the start of an activity)*
ask/chat/shoot away loslegen ['loːsleːgn̩] +haben ◊
„*Ich habe noch einige Fragen.*" — „*Dann leg mal
los!*" ◆ „*Loggen Sie sich in den Chat ein und legen
Sie los!*"; *(start shooting with a gun)* shoot away (at
sth) (auf etw. ⌊acc⌋) losschießen ['loːsʃiːsn̩] <schießt
los, schoss los, hat losgeschossen> 5. *(describing an
activity that continues for a long time)* work away
fleißig arbeiten [ˌflaɛ̯sɪç 'aʳbaɛ̯tn̩] +haben ◊ *Er
arbeitete fleißig an seinem Aufsatz.* chat away
plaudern ['plaʊ̯dɐn] +haben ◊ *Wir plauderten stundenlang am Telefon.* 6. *(temporal)* sth is three
hours/not far away etw. ist in drei Stunden/bald
[ɪst ɪn draɛ̯ 'ʃtʊndn̩/'balt] +sein ◊ *Der Termin ist in
drei Stunden.* ◆ *Bald ist Weihnachten.* 7. sport be/
play away to sb bei jdm auswärts spielen
[baɛ̯ ... ˌaɒsvɛʳts ʃpiːlən] +haben ◊ *Die Kölner spielten
auswärts beim Titelverteidiger München.*

'Away' often occurs in phrasal verbs like 'get away'
or 'put away' which have their own entries in the dictionary.

away game ⌊noun⌋ Auswärtsspiel ['aɒsvɛʳtsʃpiːl] das
<-(e)s, -e>
awful ⌊adj⌋ *(terrible, dreadful)* furchtbar ['fʊʳçtbaːʳ] ◊
eine Tat mit furchtbaren Folgen ◆ *Die Schmerzen
sind furchtbar.; (bad, of poor quality)* schlecht [ʃlɛçt]
<schlechter, am schlechtesten> ◊ *ein schlechter Arzt*
feel awful sich schlecht fühlen be awful at sth in
etw. ⌊dat⌋ schlecht sein ◊ *Er ist schlecht in Mathe.*
have the awful feeling that das unangenehme
Gefühl haben, dass
[das ˌʊn|angəneːmə gə'fyːl haːbm̩ das]
awfully ⌊adv⌋ furchtbar ['fʊʳçtbaːʳ] no comp/superl ◊
Das ist furchtbar nett von dir! ◆ *Er hat sich
furchtbar aufgeregt.*
awkward ⌊adj⌋ 1. *(clumsy)* ungeschickt ['ʊngəʃɪkt]
<ungeschickter, am ungeschicktesten> ◊ *eine unge-
schickte Bewegung* ◆ *Die Formulierungen waren
ungeschickt.; (fall)* unglücklich ['ʊnglʏklɪç] *mostly
before ns* ◊ *Bei einem unglücklichen Fall brach er
sich das Bein.* 2. *(embarrassing)* unangenehm
['ʊn|angəneːm] ◊ *jdn in eine unangenehme Lage
bringen* ◆ *Es ist unangenehm, sich entschuldigen zu
müssen.* sb feels awkward about doing sth es ist
jdm unangenehm, etw. zu tun ◊ *Es war ihm unangenehm, sie nach ihrem Namen zu fragen.* 3. *(difficult)*
unbequem ['ʊnbəkveːm] ◊ *unbequeme Fragen stellen*
◆ *Sie war dem Chef unbequem geworden.* sth is
awkward to transport etw. ist schwierig zu transportieren [ɪst ʃviːrɪç tsu: transpɔʳ'tiːrən] +sein ◊ *Ohne
Rollen ist der Koffer schwierig zu transportieren.*
awkwardly ⌊adv⌋ 1. *(clumsily)* ungeschickt ['ʊngəʃɪkt]
<ungeschickter, am ungeschicktesten> ◊ *sich unge-
schickt ausdrücken; (with bad consequences)*
unglücklich ['ʊnglʏklɪç] ◊ *Er war unglücklich
gestürzt.* 2. *(in an embarrassed way)* verlegen
[fɛ'leːgn̩] ◊ *Verlegen blickte er zu Boden.*
axe[1] ⌊noun⌋ Axt [akst] die <-, Äxte> ◊ *einen Baum mit
der Axt fällen*
◉ give sb the axe jdn entlassen give sth the axe
etw. streichen
axe[2] ⌊verb⌋ streichen ['ʃtraɛ̯çn̩] <streicht, strich, hat
gestrichen> ◊ *Viele Stellen wurden gestrichen.*
axis ⌊noun⌋ Achse ['aksə] die <-, -n> ◊ *Der Planet
dreht sich um die eigene Achse.* ◆ *die Achse Berlin–
Paris*

A
B
C
D
E
F
G
H
I
J
K
L
M
N
O
P
Q
R
S
T
U
V
W
X
Y
Z

B

b, B (noun) **1.** *(letter)* b, B [beː] das <–(s), –(s)> ◊ *Dieses Wort wird mit einem kleinen b/großen B geschrieben.* ♦ *B wie Berta* **2.** MUS B h, H [haː] das <–(s), –(s)> ◊ *Spielen Sie bitte ein h!* B minor h-Moll ['haːmɔl] B major H-Dur ['haːduːɐ̯]

B (noun) *(grade)* Zwei [tsvaɛ̯] die <–, –en> ◊ *Sie hat eine Zwei geschrieben.* ♦ *Er hat fast lauter Zweien im Zeugnis.* box@ **Note**

babble (verb) **1.** *(talk)* plappern ['plapɐn] +haben *(fam, pej)* ◊ *Was plappert er da ständig ins Mikrofon?* ♦ *Sie plappert die ganze Zeit.* **2.** *(baby)* brabbeln ['brabl̩n] +haben ◊ *Das Baby brabbelte lustig vor sich hin.* **3.** *(stream, fountain)* plätschern ['plɛtʃɐn] +haben ◊ *Im Park plätscherte ein Springbrunnen.*

baby (noun) **1.** *(child)* Baby ['beːbiː] das <–s, –s> ◊ *Ich erwarte ein Baby.* have a baby ein Kind bekommen [aɛ̯n 'kɪnt bəkɔmən] <bekommt, bekam, hat bekommen> ◊ *Sie bekommt bald ihr erstes Kind.* **2.** *(animal)* Junge ['jʊŋə] das <–n, –n> *but: ein Junges* ◊ *Die Katze hat vier Junge.* **3.** *(form of address)* Schätzchen ['ʃɛtsçən] das <–s, –> ◊ *Hallo Schätzchen, wie wär's mit uns beiden?*
⊛ throw the baby out with the bathwater das Kind mit dem Bade ausschütten be such a baby sich wie ein Baby benehmen don't be such a baby stell dich nicht so an

baby carriage (noun) Kinderwagen ['kɪndɐvaːgn̩] der <–s, –> ◊ *Schieb du mal den Kinderwagen!*

back¹ (noun) **1.** ANAT Rücken ['rʏkn̩] der <–s, –> ◊ *auf dem Rücken liegen* ♦ *jdm den Rücken zuwenden* lower back Kreuz [krɔɛ̯ts] das <–es> ◊ *Mir tut das Kreuz weh.* back of the neck Nacken ['nakn̩] der <–s, –> **2.** *(of a car)* Heck [hɛk] das <–(e)s, –s oder –e> **3.** *(of a building, document etc.)* Rückseite ['rʏkzaɛ̯tə] die <–, –n> ◊ *auf der Rückseite des Fragebogens unterschreiben* The bus station is round the back of the square. Der Busbahnhof ist an der Rückseite des Platzes. The children are playing round the back. Die Kinder spielen hinter dem Haus. go round the back hintenherum gehen ['hɪntn̩hɛrʊm geːən] <geht, ging, ist gegangen> in/at the back hinten ['hɪntn̩] +dat ◊ *Das Inhaltsverzeichnis ist hinten.*
⊛ in the back of your mind im Hinterkopf be glad to see the back of sb/sth froh sein, jdn/etw. los zu sein get off sb's back jdn in Ruhe lassen

back² (adj) **1.** *(furthest away from you)* hintere ['hɪntərə] no comp/superl, only before ns <ein hinterer ..., eine hintere ...> ◊ *die hintere Stoßstange* back row hinterste Reihe [,hɪntəstə 'raɛ̯ə] die <–, –n> ◊ *in der hintersten Reihe sitzen* back tooth Backenzahn ['bakn̩tsaːn] der <–(e)s, Backenzähne> **2.** *(wages, rent)* ausstehend ['aʊ̯sʃteːənt] no comp/superl ◊ *ausstehender Lohn*

back³ (adv) zurück ['tsu'rʏk] ◊ *Der Weg zurück kam ihr lang vor.* ♦ *Sie wird in einer Stunde zurück sein.*; *(with certain verbs)* zurück... ['tsu'rʏk] demand sth back etw. zurückverlangen [tsu'rʏkfəlaŋən] <verlangt zurück, verlangte zurück, hat zurückverlangt> ◊ *ein Buch zurückverlangen* fly back zurückfliegen [tsu'rʏkfliːgn̩] <fliegt zurück, flog zurück, ist zurückgeflogen> ◊ *Sie flog am Sonntag nach Berlin zurück.* think back zurückdenken [tsu'rʏkdɛŋkn̩] <denkt zurück, dachte zurück, hat zurückgedacht> ◊ *Er dachte gern an seine Kindheit zurück.*
⊛ back and forth hin und her

'Back' often occurs in phrasal verbs like 'get back' or 'put back' which have their own entries in the dictionary.

back⁴ (verb) **1.** *(support)* back sb (on sth) jdn (in etw. dat) unterstützen [ʊntɐˈʃtʏtsn̩] <unterstützt, unterstützte, hat unterstützt> ◊ *Diesen Vorschlag kann ich nicht unterstützen.* ♦ *Wer unterstützt Sie finanziell?* **2.** *(walk backwards)* rückwärts gehen ['rʏkvɛɐ̯ts geːən] <geht, ging, ist gegangen> ◊ *Sie ging rückwärts aus dem Zimmer und verbeugte sich wiederholt.* **3.** *(a car)* zurücksetzen [tsu'rʏkzɛtsn̩] +haben ◊ *Ich setzte (den Wagen) noch ein wenig zurück.* **4.** *(make sb move backwards)* back sb somewhere jdn irgendwohin drängen ['drɛŋən] +haben ◊ *Sie drängte mich in eine Ecke, um mit mir zu reden.* **5.** *(bet on sb/sth)* back sb/sth auf jdn/etw. setzen [aɔf ... zɛtsn̩] +haben ◊ *Ich setze auf Pferd Nummer drei.* **6.** *(adjoin sth at the back)* A is backed by B B liegt direkt hinter A [liːkt dɪˌrɛkt 'hɪntɐ] <lag, hat gelegen> ◊ *Direkt hinter dem Gebäude liegt ein großer Hof.* **7.** *(musician)* begleiten [bə'glaɛ̯tn̩] <begleitet, begleitete, hat begleitet> ◊ *Die Sängerin wurde von ihrer Band begleitet.*
• **back away** (phras v) back away (from sb/sth) (vor jdm/etw.) zurückweichen [tsu'rʏkvaɛ̯çn̩] <weicht zurück, wich zurück, ist zurückgewichen> ◊ *Ängstlich wich sie vor dem Hund zurück.*
• **back down** (phras v) back down (on sth) (in etw. dat) nachgeben ['naːxgeːbm̩] <gibt nach, gab nach, hat nachgegeben> ◊ *Einer von euch beiden muss nachgeben.* ♦ *Ich werde in dieser Sache nicht nachgeben.*
• **back off** (phras v) **1.** *(move backwards)* zurückweichen [tsu'rʏkvaɛ̯çn̩] <weicht zurück, wich zurück, ist zurückgewichen> ◊ *Sie wichen zurück, als sie den Hund sahen.* **2.** *(cease pursuing sth)* back off from sth von etw. ablassen [fɔn ... 'aplasn̩] <lässt ab, ließ ab, hat abgelassen> ◊ *Der Minister will von seiner Friedenspolitik nicht ablassen.* **3.** *(leave alone)* back off from sth jdn in Ruhe lassen [ɪn 'ruːə lasn̩] <lässt, ließ, hat gelassen> ◊ *Lass mich in Ruhe!*
• **back onto** (phras v) back onto sth hinten an etw. dat grenzen [hɪntn̩ an ... grɛntsn̩] +haben ◊ *Das Grundstück grenzt hinten an einen Wald.*
• **back out** (phras v) back out (of sth) **1.** *(not face sth)* (vor etw. dat) kneifen ['knaɛ̯fn̩] <kneift, kniff, hat gekniffen> *(fam)* ◊ *Sie hat vor der Klausur gekniffen.* ♦ *Du wolltest dich doch beschweren! Warum kneifst du jetzt?* **2.** *(of a contract, deal,*

agreement etc.) (aus etw.) aussteigen ['aʊsftaɛgn̩]
<steigt aus, stieg aus, ist ausgestiegen> *(fam)* ◊ *aus
einem Vertrag aussteigen*
• **back up** [phras v] **1.** *(support sb)* back sb up jdn
unterstützen [ʊntɐ'ftʏtsn̩] <unterstützt, unterstützte, hat
unterstützt> ◊ *Falls man dir Schwierigkeiten machen
sollte, unterstütze ich dich natürlich.* **2.** *(prove,
provide evidence of sth)* back sth up etw. untermauern [ʊntɐ'maʊ̯ɐn] <untermauert, untermauerte, hat
untermauert> ◊ *Er untermauerte seine Behauptung
mit einigen Beispielen.* **3.** ɪт back sth up eine Sicherungskopie von etw. erstellen
[aɛnə 'zɪçɐrʊŋsko,piː fɔn ... e.ftɛlən] <erstellt,
erstellte, hat erstellt> ◊ *Von dieser Datei muss eine
Sicherungskopie erstellt werden.* **4.** *(traffic, water)*
sich stauen ['ftaʊ̯ən] +haben ◊ *Der Verkehr staut sich
in beide Richtungen.; (sink, toilet, drain)* verstopft
sein [fɛ'ftɔpft zaɛn] +sein ◊ *Der Abfluss ist verstopft.;
(work, orders)* sth is backing up etw. staut sich auf
[ftaɔt zɪç 'aʊf] +haben ◊ *In unserer Firma stauen
sich die Aufträge auf.* sth is backed up etw. hat sich
aufgestaut **5.** *(move backwards)* zurücktreten
[tsʊ'rʏktreːtn̩] <tritt zurück, trat zurück, ist zurückgetre-
ten> ◊ *Treten Sie bitte zurück! Der Zug fährt ein.; (a
car)* zurücksetzen [tsʊ'rʏkzɛtsn̩] +haben ◊ *Du kannst
noch zurücksetzen.* ◆ *Ich setzte das Auto ein wenig
zurück.*
backbone [noun] Rückgrat ['rʏkgraːt] das <-(e)s, -e>
most sing ◊ *sich* [dat] *das Rückgrat brechen* ◆ *Dir
fehlt einfach das Rückgrat, um dich durchzusetzen.*
be the backbone of sth das Rückgrat ... [gen] sein
◊ *Kleinere und mittlere Unternehmen sind das
Rückgrat unserer Wirtschaft.*
back door [noun] **1.** *(of a building)* Hintereingang
['hɪntɐ,aɛŋgaŋ] der <-s, Hintereingänge> ◊ *Die Angestellten des Hotels nehmen den Hintereingang.*
2. *(fig) (dishonest route)* Hintertür ['hɪntɐtyːɐ̯] die
<-> no pl ◊ *Die Regierung versucht, durch die
Hintertür die Steuern zu erhöhen.*
background [noun] **1.** *(space behind sth, less
important position, underlying reasons)* Hintergrund
['hɪntɐgrʊnt] der <-(e)s, Hintergründe> ◊ *Im Hintergrund hörte sie Kinderstimmen.* ◆ *Sie fühlte sich in
den Hintergrund gedrängt.* the background to sth
der Hintergrund ... [gen] ◊ *Kennen Sie die Hintergründe dieses Mordes?* **2.** *(in paintings, on photos
etc.)* Untergrund ['ʊntɐgrʊnt] der
<-(e)s, Untergründe> ◊ *Der Untergrund des Bildes
ist schwarz.* ◆ *Auf dunklem Untergrund sieht man
Weiß am besten.* **3.** *(of a person)* Herkunft
['heːɐ̯kʊnft] die <-, Herkünfte> most sing ◊ *Sie ist
stolz auf ihre jüdische Herkunft.* be from an aristo-
cratic/a Muslim/ Spanish background adliger/musli-
mischer/spanischer Herkunft sein **4.** *(education,
training)* Ausbildung ['aʊsbɪldʊŋ] die <-, -en> ◊
Personen mit musikalischer Ausbildung.
backing [noun] **1.** *(support)* Unterstützung
[ʊntɐ'ftʏtsʊŋ] die <-> no pl with the backing of sb/
sth mit Unterstützung ... [gen] ◊ *Das Gesetz wurde
mit Unterstützung der Opposition verabschiedet.*
have the backing of sb/sth von jdm/etw. unterstützt
werden [fɔn ... ʊntɐ.ftʏtst veːɐ̯dn̩] <wird, wurde, ist
worden> **2.** *(music)* Begleitung [bə'glaɛtʊŋ] die
<-, -en> ◊ *die musikalische Begleitung* backing
group Begleitband [bə'glaɛtbant] die <-, -s>
backing singer Backgroundsänger ['bɛkgraʊntzɛŋɐ]

der <-s, -> ♀Backgroundsängerin
['bɛkgraʊntzɛŋərɪn] die <-, -nen>
backpack [noun] Rucksack ['rʊkzak] der
<-(e)s, Rucksäcke> ◊ *seinen Rucksack packen*
backrest [noun] Rückenlehne ['rʏkn̩leːnə] die <-, -n>
◊ *die Rückenlehne des Autositzes verstellen*
back seat [noun] Rücksitz ['rʏkzɪts] der <-es, -e> ◊
auf dem Rücksitz sitzen
backside [noun] Hintern ['hɪntɐn] der <-s, -> *(fam)* ◊
Vom Radfahren tut mir der Hintern weh.
backward¹, backwards [adj] **1.** *(spatial, temporal)*
zurück [tsʊ'rʏk] ◊ *ein Blick zurück* ◆ *ein Schritt
zurück in die Steinzeit* backward movement Rück-
wärtsbewegung ['rʏkvɛ'ɐ̯sbəveːgʊŋ] die <-, -en> **2.**
(in development) rückständig ['rʏkftɛndɪç] ◊ *eine
rückständige Gesellschaft* ◆ *Das Land ist in dieser
Beziehung sehr rückständig.*
backward², backwards [adv] **1.** *(direction)*
rückwärts ['rʏkvɛ'ɐ̯ts] ◊ *Er ging drei Schritte
rückwärts.* ◆ *Ich zähle von zehn an rückwärts.;
(behind you)* look backwards sich umsehen
['ʊmzeːən] <sieht sich um, sah sich um, hat sich
umgesehen> **2.** *(in time, development)* zurück
[tsʊ'rʏk] ◊ *ein Blick zurück in die Vergangenheit* ◆
Dieses Gesetz ist ein Schritt zurück. look backwards
zurückblicken [tsʊ'rʏkblɪkn̩] +haben; *(regress)* move
backwards Rückschritte machen ['rʏkfrɪtə maxn̩]
+haben **3.** *(back to front)* verkehrt herum
[fɛ'keːɐ̯t hɛrʊm] You put your sweater on backwards.
Du hast den Pullover verkehrt herum an.
⊛ **backwards and forwards** hin und her
bacon [noun] Speck [ʃpɛk] der <-(e)s, -e> most sing
◊ *Eier mit Speck*
bacteria [noun] Bakterien [bak'teːriən] die <-> pl
Diese Krankheit wird durch Bakterien verursacht.
bad [adj] **1.** *(not good)* schlecht [ʃlɛçt] <schlechter, am
schlechtesten> ◊ *schlechte Nachrichten für jdn haben*
◆ *Das Wetter ist schlecht.* ◆ *Das ist gar keine so
schlechte Idee!* ◆ *ein schlechter Schwimmer sein* ◆ *Er
ist durch und durch schlecht.* **2.** *(naughty)* unartig
['ʊn|aːɐ̯tɪç] ◊ *Lukas war unartig und muss in seinem
Zimmer bleiben.* ◆ *ein unartiges Kind* **3.** *(pain,
accident, situation)* schlimm [ʃlɪm] ◊ *Sind die
Schmerzen schlimm?* ◆ *Sie hat einen schlimmen
Unfall gehabt.* sth goes from bad to worse etw. wird
immer schlimmer
⊛ **too bad 1.** *(expressing sympathy)* schade
2. *(expressing indifference)* Pech
badge [noun] **1.** *(button with a pin)* Anstecker
['anʃtɛkɐ] der <-s, -> **2.** name badge Namensschild
['naːmənsʃɪlt] das <-(e)s, -er>; *(a police officer's)*
(police) badge Dienstmarke ['diːnstmaʳkə] die
<-, -n> ◊ *Der Polizist zeigte seine Dienstmarke.*
3. *(mark of sb's achievements)* Abzeichen ['aptsaɛçn̩]
das <-s, -> ◊ *ein militärisches Abzeichen*
⊛ **a badge of sth** *(symbol)* ein Zeichen ... [gen] ◊
ein Zeichen der Schande a badge if hono(u)r eine
Ehrenauszeichnung
badly [adv] **1.** *(not well)* schlecht [ʃlɛçt] <schlechter,
am schlechtesten> ◊ *jdn schlecht behandeln* ◆
schlecht informiert sein ◆ *ein schlecht bezahlter Job*
2. *(severely)* schlimm [ʃlɪm] ◆ *Er hat sich schlimm
wehgetan.* **3.** *(very much)* sehr [zeːɐ̯] ◊ *Sie vermisst
ihn sehr.* ◆ *Er litt sehr unter der Trennung.;
(urgently)* unbedingt ['ʊnbadɪŋt] no comp/superl ◊
Sie brauchen unbedingt Hilfe. ◆ *Ich wollte diesen Job*

A
B
C
D
E
F
G
H
I
J
K
L
M
N
O
P
Q
R
S
T
U
V
W
X
Y
Z

A
B
C
D
E
F
G
H
I
J
K
L
M
N
O
P
Q
R
S
T
U
V
W
X
Y
Z

unbedingt.
badminton ⸤noun⸥ Federball ['fe:dɛbal] der <-(e)s>
no pl ◊ Sie spielten Federball.; *(as a competetive
sport)* Badminton ['bɛtmɪntn̩] das <-s> *no pl*
bad-tempered ⸤adj⸥ schlecht gelaunt [ˌʃlɛçt gə'laʊnt]
<schlechter gelaunt, am schlechtesten gelaunt> ◊ *ein
schlecht gelauntes Kind ♦ Heute ist er noch schlechter gelaunt.*
baffled ⸤adj⸥ ratlos ['ra:tlo:s] <ratloser, am ratlosesten>
◊ *Die Ärzte sind in seinem Fall völlig ratlos. ♦ Er
warf mir einen ratlosen Blick zu.*
bag ⸤noun⸥ 1. *(for carrying things)* Tasche ['taʃə] die
<-, −n> ◊ *Sie trug eine Tasche über der Schulter.*;
(tied with string) Beutel ['bɔʏtl̩] der <-s, −> ◊ *Er
steckte seine Sportsachen in den Beutel.*
2. *(packaging, carrier bag)* Tüte ['ty:tə] die <-, −n>
◊ *eine Tüte Gummibärchen ♦ Die Frau an der Kasse
fragte, ob er eine Tüte wolle.*
⊛ be a bag of bones nur Haut und Knochen sein
have bags under your eyes Ringe unter den Augen
haben sth is in the bag jd hat etw. in der Tasche
baggage ⸤noun⸥ Gepäck [gə'pɛk] das <-(e)s> *no pl ◊
mit leichtem Gepäck reisen ♦ Sie können Ihr Gepäck
am Schalter aufgeben.*
⊛ emotional baggage emotionaler Ballast
baggy ⸤adj⸥ weit [vaɪt] <weiter, am weitesten> ◊ *Ist dir
diese Hose nicht etwas zu weit? ♦ ein weites Hemd*
baguette ⸤noun⸥ Baguette [ba'gɛt] das <-s, −s>
bail ⸤noun⸥ Kaution [kaʊ'tsjo:n] die <-, −en> ◊ *Sie kam
auf Kaution frei.*
bail out ⸤verb⸥ 1. LAW *(pay for sb's release)* bail sb out
die Kaution für jdn stellen
[di: kaʊˌtsjo:n fy:g ... ʃtɛlən] +haben ◊ *Wer hat die
Kaution für den Angeklagten gestellt?*; *(be able to get
sb released by bail)* in auf Kaution freibekommen
[aʊf kaʊˌtsjo:n 'fraɪbəkɔmən] <bekommt frei, bekam
frei, hat freibekommen> ◊ *Ich konnte Sie auf Kaution
freibekommen.* 2. *(save)* bail sb/sth out jdn/etw.
retten ['rɛtn̩] +haben ◊ *Das nächste Mal wird die
Regierung den Autohersteller nicht mehr retten
können.*
bake ⸤verb⸥ backen ['bakn̩] <backt/bäckt, backte/buk,
hat gebacken> ◊ *Brot backen ♦ Ich backe jeden
Sonntag.*
baker ⸤noun⸥ 1. *(person)* Bäcker ['bɛkɐ] der <-s, −>
♀Bäckerin ['bɛkərɪn] die <-, −nen> ◊ *Er wurde
Bäcker wie sein Vater. ♦ Die Bäckerin schiebt das
Brot in den Ofen.* 2. *(shop)* baker's Bäckerei
[bɛkə'raɪ] die <-, −en>
baking tray ⸤noun⸥ Backblech ['bakblɛç] das
<-(e)s, −e>
balance¹ ⸤noun⸥ 1. *(stability, stable or even condition)*
Gleichgewicht ['glaɪçgəvɪçt] das <-(e)s> *no pl ◊ jds
seelisches Gleichgewicht* lose your balance das
Gleichgewicht verlieren strike the balance between
... and ... das Gleichgewicht zwischen ... und ...
finden ◊ *das Gleichgewicht zwischen Beruf und Privatleben finden;* *(biological)* (sense of) balance
Gleichgewichtssinn ['glaɪçgəvɪçtszɪn] der <-(e)s>
no pl 2. FIN *(of an account)* Guthaben ['gu:tha:bm̩]
das <-s, −> ◊ *Er hat ein Guthaben von 5000 Euro
auf dem Konto.* 3. FIN *(money owed)* Restbetrag
['rɛstbətra:k] der <-(e)s, −e, Restbeträge> ◊ *Der Restbetrag ist bis zum Jahresende zu zahlen.*
⊛ hang in the balance in der Schwebe sein on
balance alles in allem

balance² ⸤verb⸥ 1. *(hold yourself or sth steady)* balan-
cieren [balaŋ'si:rən] <balanciert, balancierte, hat/ist
balanciert> *transitive use +haben/intransitive use
+sein ◊ Sie hat einen Teller auf dem Finger balanciert. ♦ Der Artist ist auf einem Seil balanciert.*
2. *(find a compromise between opposing needs)*
balance sth etw. in Einklang bringen
[ɪn 'aɪnklaŋ brɪŋən] <bringt, brachte, hat gebracht> ◊
*Wir müssen die Wünsche aller unserer Kinder in
Einklang bringen. ♦ Wie kann man Gefühl und
Verstand in Einklang bringen?* balance sth with sth
etw. mit etw. in Einklang bringen 3. *(consider, weigh
up)* balance sth against sth etw. und etw. gegeneinander abwägen [ʊnt ... ge:gɦ]aenande 'apvɛ:gɦ]
<wägt ab, wog/wägte ab, hat abgewogen/abgewägt> ◊
*Man sollte Vor- und Nachteile gegeneinander
abwägen* 4. *(offset, counteract)* balance sth by sth
etw. durch etw. ausgleichen [dʊrç ... ˌaʊsglaeçn̩]
<gleicht aus, glich aus, hat ausgeglichen> ◊ *Fehlendes
Licht kann man manchmal durch helle Farben ausgleichen.*
• **balance out** ⸤phras v⸥ ausgleichen ['aʊsglaeçn̩]
<gleicht aus, glich aus, hat ausgeglichen> ◊ *Wie
könnte man diese Nachteile ausgleichen?*
balanced → **balance²** ⸤adj⸥ 1. *(person)* ausgeglichen
['aʊsgəglɪçn̩] ◊ *ein ausgeglichener Mensch ♦ Sie ist
sehr ausgeglichen.* 2. *(thing)* ausgewogen
['aʊsgəvo:gɦ] ◊ *eine ausgewogene Berichterstattung ♦
Seine Ernährung ist ausgewogen.*
balance sheet ⸤noun⸥ Bilanz [bi'lants] die <-, −en> ◊
eine negative/positive Bilanz
balcony ⸤noun⸥ Balkon [bal'kɔn, bal'ko:n] der
<-s, −s or −e> ◊ *Wir frühstücken auf dem Balkon.*
bald ⸤adj⸥ 1. *(without hair)* kahl [ka:l] ◊ *ein kahler
Schädel ♦ Sein Kopf ist fast kahl.*; *(person)* be bald
eine Glatze haben [aɪnə 'glatsə ha:bm̩] ◊ *Rolf hatte
schon mit 30 eine Glatze.* go bald eine Glatze
bekommen [aɪnə 'glatsə bəkɔmən] <bekommt,
bekam, hat bekommen> 2. *(tyre)* abgefahren
['apgəfa:rən] ◊ *abgefahrene Reifen ♦ Die Reifen an
Ihrem Wagen sind ganz abgefahren.* 3. *(statement,
fact etc.)* unverblümt ['ʊnfəbly:mt] <unverblümter,
am unverblümtesten> ◊ *eine unverblümte Äußerung*
ball ⸤noun⸥ 1. *(object, game, dance)* Ball [bal] der
<-(e)s, Bälle> ◊ *Die Katze spielte mit einem Ball. ♦
Als Kinder haben wir oft Ball gespielt. ♦ Heute Abend
gehe ich auf einen Ball.* 2. SPORT *(passing a ball in a
game)* Pass [pas] der <-es, Pässe> ◊ *ein Pass zum
Mitspieler* 3. *(globe, sphere)* Kugel ['ku:gl̩] die
<-, −n> ◊ *Die Welt ist eine Kugel.*
⊛ the ball is in sb's court jd ist am Zug carry the
ball die Verantwortung tragen get the ball rolling
den Stein ins Rollen bringen get on the ball bei der
Sache
ballet ⸤noun⸥ Ballett [ba'lɛt] das <-(e)s, −e> ◊ *Ballett
tanzen ♦ ein Ballett von Tschaikowsky ♦ das Ballett
der Staatsoper Moskau*
balloon ⸤noun⸥ Ballon [ba'lɔn] der <-s, −s> hot air
balloon Heißluftballon ['haɪslʊftbaˌlɔn]; *(toy, decoration)* Luftballon ['lʊftbaˌlɔn]
ballot ⸤noun⸥ 1. *(process of voting)* Abstimmung
['apʃtɪmʊŋ] die <-, −en> ◊ *eine geheime Abstimmung* 2. *(votes in an election)* Stimmen ['ʃtɪmən] die
<−> *pl ◊ die Mehrheit der Stimmen* 3. *(paper on
which to record your vote)* Stimmzettel ['ʃtɪmtsɛtl̩] der
<-s, −>

ballot paper [noun] Stimmzettel ['ʃtɪmtsɛtl̩] der <-s, -> ◊ *die Stimmzettel auszählen* ♦ *Ich habe meinen Stimmzettel abgegeben.*

ballpoint pen [noun] Kugelschreiber ['ku:glʃraebɐ] der <-s, -> ◊ *mit Kugelschreiber schreiben*

balls [noun] 1. *(testicles)* Eier ['aeɐ] die <-> pl *(rude)* 2. *(courage)* Schneid [ʃnaet] der <-s> no pl ◊ *Ihm fehlt einfach der Schneid!*

Baltic (Sea) [noun] Ostsee ['ɔstze:] die <-> ◊ *Ferien an der Ostsee machen*

ban¹ [noun] 1. *(prohibition)* Verbot [fɛ'bo:t] das <-(e)s, -e> ◊ *sich für ein Verbot von Kampfhunden einsetzen* lift a ban *ein Verbot aufheben* impose a ban *ein Verbot aussprechen* ban on smoking *Rauchverbot* ['raoxfɛbo:t] ban on imports of sth *Importverbot für etw.* [ɪm'pɔʳtfɛbo:t fy:g] ◊ *ein Importverbot für Geflügel* 2. SPORT Sperre ['ʃpɛrə] die <-, -n> ◊ *Gegen den Athleten wurde eine dreimonatige Sperre verhängt.*

ban² [verb] 1. *(prohibit)* verbieten [fɛ'bi:tn̩] <verbietet, verbot, hat verboten> ◊ *den Import/Export einer Ware verbieten* ♦ *In dieser Firma ist das Rauchen verboten.* 2. SPORT sperren ['ʃpɛrən] +haben ◊ *Das Sportgericht sperrte ihn für sechs Wochen.*

banal [adj] banal [ba'na:l] ◊ *eine banale Bemerkung* ♦ *Dieses Buch ist mir zu banal.*

banana [noun] Banane [ba'na:nə] die <-, -n>

band [noun] 1. *(group of musicians)* Band [bɛnt] die <-, -s> ◊ *Er ist Gitarrist in einer Band.* 2. *(group of people)* band of ... Schar [gen] [ʃa:ʳ] die <-, -en> ◊ *eine Schar Neugieriger* 3. *(piece of cloth)* Band [bant] das <-es, Bänder> ◊ *Ihr Haar war mit einem Band zusammengebunden.* 4. *(of colo(u)r)* Streifen ['ʃtraefn̩] der <-s, -> ◊ *Das Männchen hat einen gelben Streifen am Hinterkopf.*

bandage¹ [noun] Verband [fɛ'bant] der <-(e)s, Verbände> ◊ *einen Verband anlegen*

bandage² [verb] verbinden [fɛ'bɪndn̩] <verbindet, verband, hat verbunden> ◊ *Die Hand muss verbunden werden.*

bang¹ [noun] 1. *(single blow)* Schlag [ʃla:k] der <-(e)s, Schläge> ◊ *einen Schlag auf den Kopf bekommen* 2. *(noise)* Knall [knal] der <-(e)s, -e> most sing ◊ *Mit einem lauten Knall fiel das Brett zu Boden.* ◉ go off with a bang *in voller Erfolg sein*

bang² [verb] 1. *(thump, strike noisily)* schlagen ['ʃla:gn̩] <schlägt, schlug, hat geschlagen> ◊ *gegen ein Fenster schlagen* ♦ *die Trommeln schlagen* bang your head on/against sth *mit dem Kopf auf/gegen etw.* [acc] schlagen; *(a telephone receiver)* bang down *hinknallen* ['hɪnknalən] +haben ◊ *Er knallte den Hörer hin.* 2. *(a door, window)* bang (shut) *zuschlagen* ['tsu:ʃla:gn̩] <schlägt zu, schlug zu, hat/ist zugeschlagen> transitive use +haben/intransitive use +sein ◊ *Wütend hat sie die Tür zugeschlagen.* ♦ *Das Fenster ist zugeschlagen.* 3. *(rude)* bang sb *jdn vögeln* ['fø:gln̩] +haben *(rude)* • bang on [phras v] bang on about sth *sich über etw.* [acc] *auslassen* [y:bɐ ... ˌaoszɡəlasn̩] <lässt sich aus, ließ sich aus, hat sich ausgelassen> *(fam)* ◊ *Sie hat sich stundenlang über meine schlechte Erziehung ausgelassen.*

banger [noun] 1. *(fam)* Würstchen ['vʏʳstçən] das <-s, -> ◊ *Es gab Würstchen und Sauerkraut.* 2. *(fam, pej) (car)* old banger *alte Karre* [ˌaltə 'karə]

die <-, -n> *(fam)* 3. *(firework)* Kracher ['kraxɐ] der <-s, -> ◊ *einen Kracher zünden*

bangs → fringe 1.

banister [noun] Geländer [gə'lɛndɐ] das <-s, -> ◊ *sich an/gegen das Geländer lehnen*

bank [noun] 1. *(financial institute)* Bank [baŋk] die <-, -en> ◊ *All mein Erspartes ist auf der Bank.* ♦ *Ich muss noch auf die Bank.* 2. *(of a river)* Ufer ['u:fɐ] das <-s, -> ◊ *Das Schiff legte am linken Ufer des Flusses an.* 3. *(supply of sth, storage, in compound ns)* ... bank ...bank [baŋk] die <-, -en> data bank *Datenbank* organ bank *Organbank* bottle bank *Glascontainer* ['gla:skɔnˌte:nɐ] der <-s, -> 4. bank of fog/fog bank *Nebelbank* ['ne:blbaŋk] die <-, Nebelbänke> bank of cloud/cloud bank *Wolkenbank* ['vɔlkn̩baŋk] die <-, Wolkenbänke>

bank account [noun] Bankkonto ['baŋkkɔnto:] das <-s, Bankkonten> ◊ *ein Bankkonto eröffnen*

bank balance [noun] Kontostand ['kɔntoʃtant] der <-(e)s, Kontostände>

banker [noun] Banker ['bɛŋkɐ] der <-s, -> ♀Bankerin ['bɛŋkərɪn] die <-, -nen> ◊ *Sie ist Bankerin bei einer Investmentbank.* ♦ *Diese Aktien hat mir der Banker empfohlen.*

bank holiday [noun] Feiertag ['faeɐta:k] der <-(e)s, -e>

banking [noun] 1. *(transactions)* Bankgeschäft ['baŋkɡəʃɛft] das <-(e)s, -e> most pl ◊ *seine Bankgeschäfte am Telefon erledigen* 2. *(industry)* Bankwesen ['baŋkve:zn̩] das <-s> no pl ◊ *Kundenorientierung im Bankwesen*

banknote [noun] Geldschein ['gɛltʃaen] der <-(e)s, -e>

bankrupt [adj] bankrott [baŋ'krɔt] no comp/superl ◊ *Die Firma ist bankrott.* ♦ *eine moralisch bankrotte Gesellschaft* go bankrupt *Konkurs machen* [kɔn'kʊʳs maxn̩] +haben ◊ *Unsere Firma hat Konkurs gemacht.*

bankruptcy [noun] Konkurs [kɔn'kʊʳs] der <-es, -e>

bank statement [noun] Kontoauszug ['kɔntoˌaostsu:k] der <-(e)s, Kontoauszüge> ◊ *Ich lasse mir einen Kontoauszug ausdrucken.*

banner [noun] Banner ['banɐ] das <-s, -> ◊ *ein Banner auf einer Website platzieren* ♦ *unter dem Banner der Freiheit*

banquet [noun] Bankett [baŋ'kɛt] das <-(e)s, -e>

baptism [noun] Taufe ['taofə] die <-, -n>

baptize [verb] taufen ['taofn̩] +haben ◊ *ein Kind taufen lassen* ♦ *Er wurde auf den Namen Andreas getauft.*

bar¹ [noun] 1. *(place for drinking)* Bar [ba:ʳ] die <-, -s> ◊ *Sie stand an der Bar und unterhielt sich.* ♦ *Wir haben uns in der Bar des Hotels getroffen.* 2. *(of a cage, window etc.)* Stab [ʃta:p] der <-(e)s, Stäbe> ◊ *Bei diesem Gitterbett kann man einzelne Stäbe entfernen.; (in front of a window, door etc.)* bars Gitter ['gɪtɐ] das <-s, -> ◊ *ein eisernes Gitter* 3. *(of gold, silver)* Barren ['barən] der <-s, -> ◊ *ein Barren Gold; (of soap)* Stück [ʃtʏk] das <-(e)s, -e> ◊ *ein Stück Seife; (of chocolate)* Riegel ['ri:gl̩] der <-s, -> ◊ *Er hatte Lust auf einen Riegel Schokolade.; (big and flat piece of chocolate)* Tafel ['ta:fl̩] die <-, -n> ◊ *Eine Tafel Schokolade wiegt 100 Gramm.* 4. *(in football, high jump, pole vault)* Latte ['latə] die <-, -n> ◊ *Sie legte die Latte auf 1,80 m.* ♦ *Er schoss den Ball gegen die Latte.* 5. *(on*

A
B
C
D
E
F
G
H
I
J
K
L
M
N
O
P
Q
R
S
T
U
V
W
X
Y
Z

a computer screen) Leiste ['laestə] die <-, -n>
6. MUS Takt [takt] der <-(e)s, -e> ◊ *Nach den
ersten Takten erkannten alle das Stück.* **7.** LAW
Gerichtshof [gə'rɪçtshoːf] der <-(e)s, Gerichtshöfe>
⊛ behind bars hinter Gittern **be called to the bar**
die Zulassung als Anwalt vor Gericht bekommen
bar² [verb] **1.** *(with a bolt)* verriegeln [fɛ'riːg|n] <verrie-
gelt, verriegelte, hat verriegelt> ◊ *alle Türen verriegeln*
2. *(block)* versperren [fɛ'ʃpɛrən] <versperrt, versperrte, hat versperrt> ◊ *jdm den Weg versperren*
3. *(prohibit)* verbieten [fɛ'biːtn] <verbietet, verbot, hat
verboten> ◊ *Das Gesetz verbietet die Diskriminierung von Minderheiten.* **bar sb from doing sth** jdn
daran hindern, etw. zu tun [daran 'hɪndən ... tsuː]
+haben ◊ *Er wurde daran gehindert, in das Land ein-
zureisen.; (person)* **be barred** keinen Zutritt haben
[kaenən 'tsuːtrɪt haːbm̩] +haben ◊ *Minderjährige
haben in diesem Lokal keinen Zutritt.*
barbecue¹ [noun] *(occasion)* Grillparty ['grɪlpaːˈtiː] die
<-, -s> ◊ *die Nachbarn zu einer Grillparty einladen*
have a barbecue grillen ['grɪlən] +haben; *(grid)* Grill
[grɪl] der <-s, -s> ◊ *Die Würstchen brutzelten auf
dem Grill.*
barbecue² [verb] grillen ['grɪlən] +haben ◊ *Würstchen
grillen*
barber [noun] Friseur [fri'zøːɐ̯] der <-s, -e> ♀Friseu-
rin [fri'zøːrɪn] die <-, -nen> ◊ *Sie ist Friseurin.* ✦
Kannst du mir einen guten Friseur empfehlen?
bare¹ [adj] **1.** *(room, tree etc.)* kahl [kaːl] ◊ *Die Räume
waren kahl.* ✦ *kahle Bäume im Winter* **2.** *(skin, floor,
wall, facts)* nackt [nakt] <nackter, am nacktesten> ◊
auf dem nackten Boden schlafen ✦ *nackte Tatsachen*
✦ *Ihre Schultern waren nackt.*
bare² [verb] *(a part of your body)* entblößen
[ɛnt'bløːsn̩] <entblößt, entblößte, hat entblößt> ◊ *Er
entblößte den rechten Arm.; (your teeth)* blecken
['blɛkn̩] +haben ◊ *Der Hund bleckte die Zähne.*
barefoot [adj, adv] barfuß ['baːˈfuːs] *invariable; when
used as an adj, only after ns* ◊ *Bist du bei dieser
Kälte barfuß?* ✦ *barfuß gehen/laufen*
barely [adv] kaum [kaom] *no comp/superl* ◊ *Ich kann
die Musik kaum hören.* ✦ *Ich kenne sie kaum.* ✦ *Als
er starb, war er kaum dreißig.*
bargain¹ [noun] **1.** *(cheap item)* Schnäppchen
['ʃnɛpçən] das <-s, -> *(fam)* ◊ *Mein neuer Computer
war ein echtes Schnäppchen.* **2.** *(agreement, deal)*
Abmachung ['apmaxʊŋ] die <-, -en> ◊ *Wir haben
eine Abmachung, dass wir uns bei der Arbeit abwechseln.* **strike a bargain** eine Abmachung treffen
⊛ **into the bargain** (noch) dazu ◊ *Es war eiskalt,
und noch dazu hatte ich meinen Schal vergessen.*
bargain² [verb] handeln ['handl̩n] +haben ◊ *Wenn man
handelt, bekommt man vieles billiger.*
⊛ **more than sb bargained for 1.** *(worse than sb
expected)* mehr als jdm lieb ist **2.** *(better than sb
expected)* mehr, als jd erwartet hat
• **bargain on** [phras v] not bargain on sth nicht mit
etw. rechnen [nɪçt mɪt ... ˈrɛçnən] ◊ *Wir hatten
nicht mit Regen gerechnet.* not bargain on sb being/
doing sth nicht damit rechnen, dass jd etw. ist/tut
bark¹ [noun] **1.** *(of a tree)* Rinde ['rɪndə] die <-, -n>
2. *(of a dog)* Bellen ['bɛlən] das <-s> *no pl* ◊ *Der
Einbrecher hörte ein Bellen und rannte fort.*
bark² [verb] bellen ['bɛlən] +haben ◊ *Sie hörten
irgendwo einen Hund bellen.* ✦ *Der Offizier bellte
seine Befehle.*

barn [noun] **1.** *(for grain, straw)* Scheune ['ʃɔʏnə] die
<-, -n> ◊ *In der Scheune lagert Stroh.; (for
machines)* Schuppen ['ʃʊpm̩] der <-s, -> ◊ *Der
Traktor steht im Schuppen.* **2.** *(for animals)* Stall
[ʃtal] der <-(e)s, Ställe> ◊ *Bei uns stehen 20 Kühe
im Stall.*
barracks [noun] Kaserne [ka'zɛˈnə] die <-, -n> ◊ *In
der Kaserne leben 3000 Soldaten.*
barrel [noun] **1.** *(for liquids)* Fass [fas] das
<-es, Fässer> ◊ *Das Bier wurde in Fässer abgefüllt.*
✦ *ein Fass mit Chemikalien* **2.** *(of a gun)* Lauf [laof]
der <-(e)s, Läufe> ◊ *Die Kugel war im Lauf stecken
geblieben.* **3.** *(unit of oil)* Barrel ['bɛrəl] das <-s, -s>
◊ *ein Barrel Rohöl*
barren [adj] **1.** *(soil, landscape etc.)* karg [ka'k]
<karger/kärger, am kargsten/kärgsten> ◊ *ein karger
Landstrich* ✦ *Der Boden hier ist karg.* **2.** *(tree,
female, discussion etc.)* unfruchtbar ['ʊnfrʊxtbaːˈ]
seldom comp/superl ◊ *Diese Pflanze ist unfruchtbar.*
✦ *eine unfruchtbare Diskussion*
barrier [noun] **1.** *(device for keeping sb/sth out)* Absperrung ['apʃpɛrʊŋ] die <-, -en> ◊ *eine Absperrung um
das Gelände errichten* **2.** *(bar)* Schranke ['ʃraŋkə] die
<-, -n> ◊ *ein Bahnübergang mit Schranke* **3.** *(on a
pitch)* Bande ['bandə] die <-, -n> ◊ *Der Eishockeyspieler prallte gegen die Bande.* **4.** *(fig) (obstacle)*
Barriere [ba'rjɛːˈrə] die <-, -n> *(esp fig)*
barrister [noun] Rechtsanwalt ['rɛçtsˌanvalt] der
<-(e)s, Rechtsanwälte> ♀Rechtsanwältin
['rɛçtsˌanvɛltɪn] die <-, -nen> ◊ *Sie arbeitet als
Rechtsanwältin in einer Kanzlei.* ✦ *Ich nehme mir
einen Rechtsanwalt und verklage Sie!*
barter [verb] *(goods)* tauschen ['taoʃn̩] +haben ◊ *Waren
tauschen* **barter sth for sth** etw. gegen etw. tauschen
barter with sb mit jdm handeln [mɪt ... ˌhandl̩n]
+haben ◊ *mit den Einheimischen handeln*
base¹ [noun] **1.** *(foundation, for military actions etc.,
main ingredient, of a theory, in maths)* Basis ['baːzɪs]
die <-, Basen> ◊ *eine Basis für militärische
Aktionen* **2.** *(bottom, of a monument, cliff)* Fuß [fuːs]
der <-es, Füße> ◊ *am Fuß des Denkmals; (of a
house, cupboard)* Sockel ['zɔkl̩] der <-s, -> **3.** *(of
the neck, nose etc.)* Ansatz ['anzats] der
<-es, Ansätze>
base² [adj] nieder ['niːde] *only before ns* ◊ *niedere
Instinkte*
base³ [verb] *(company, organization etc.)* be based
seinen Sitz haben [zaenən 'zɪts haːbm̩] +haben ◊ *Die
Firma hat ihren Sitz in Paris.; (army)* seinen Stütz-
punkt haben [zaenən 'ʃtʏtspʊŋkt haːbm̩] +haben
• **base on** [phras v] be based on sth auf etw. [dat]
basieren [aof ... ba.ziːrən] <basiert, basierte, hat
basiert> ◊ *Der Roman basiert auf Tatsachen.*
based → base [adj] *(company, organization etc.)*
ansässig ['anzɛsɪç] *no comp/superl* ◊ *eine in Köln
ansässige Firma* ✦ *Das Unternehmen ist in Paris
ansässig.*
basement [noun] Kellergeschoss ['kɛlɐgəʃɔs] das
<-es, -e>
basic [adj] Grund... [grʊnt] basic principle Grundprinzip ['grʊntprɪnˌtsip] das <-s, -ien> basic salary
Grundgehalt ['grʊntgəhalt] das
<-(e)s, Grundgehälter> basic need Grundbedürfnis
['grʊntbədɐˈfnɪs] das <-ses, -se> *most sing*
basically [adv] **1.** *(essentially)* im Wesentlichen
[ɪm 'veːzn̩tlɪçn̩] ◊ *Dieses Buch ist im Wesentlichen*

ein Bildungsroman. **2.** *(fundamentally)* im Grunde [ɪm 'ɡrʊndə] ◊ *Im Grunde interessiert mich dieses Thema nicht.*

basil [noun] Basilikum [ba'ziːlikʊm] das <-s> *no pl*

basin [noun] **1.** *(in the bathroom)* Waschbecken ['vaʃbɛkn̩] das <-s, -> ◊ *sich beim Zähneputzen über das Waschbecken beugen* **2.** GEOG *(large hollow)* Kessel ['kɛsl̩] der <-s, -> ◊ *Die Stadt liegt in einem Kessel.; (in geographical names)* Becken ['bɛkn̩] das <-s, -> ◊ *Im Wiener Becken wird Erdöl gefördert.* **3.** *(vessel)* Schüssel ['ʃʏsl̩] die <-, -n> ◊ *etw. in einer Schüssel servieren*

basis [noun] Basis ['baːzɪs] die <-, Basen> ◊ *Vertrauen bildet die Basis jeder Beziehung.*
⊛ on a daily basis täglich **on a regular basis** regelmäßig

basket [noun] Korb [kɔʳp] der <-(e)s, Körbe>

bass [noun] **1.** MUS *(voice, tone, instrument)* Bass [bas] der <-es, Bässe> **2.** ZOO Barsch [baʳʃ] der <-(e)s, -e>

bastard [noun] *(slang) (pityable or horrible man)* Schwein [ʃvaen] das <-(e)s, -e> *(fam)* ◊ *Armes Schwein!* ♦ *Du Schwein!*

bat [noun] **1.** ZOO Fledermaus ['fleːdɐmaos] die <-, Fledermäuse> **2.** *(in baseball, cricket, table tennis)* Schläger ['ʃlɛːɡɐ] der <-s, ->

batch [noun] batch of sth **1.** *(of things)* Schwung [gen] [ʃvʊŋ] der <-(e)s, Schwünge> *(fam)* ◊ *ein Schwung Fotos; (of people)* Trupp ... [gen] ['trʊp] der <-s, -s> ◊ *ein Trupp lauter Schulkinder* **2.** *(of products, goods)* Ladung ... [gen] ['laːdʊŋ] die <-, -en> ◊ *eine Ladung leerer Bierkästen* **3.** *(of documents, papers, books, files)* Stapel ... [gen] ['ʃtaːpl̩] der <-s, -> ◊ *ein Stapel neuer Bücher*

bath [noun] **1.** *(process)* Bad [baːt] das <-(e)s, Bäder> ◊ *medizinische Bäder* ♦ *Ich lasse mir ein Bad ein.* have/take a bath baden ['baːdn̩] +haben ◊ *Sie badet jeden Abend.* **2.** *(container)* Wanne ['vanə] die <-, -n> ◊ *Sie lag lange in der Wanne.* **3.** *(public place)* baths Hallenbad ['halənbaːt] das <-(e)s, Hallenbäder> ◊ *ins Hallenbad gehen*

bathe [verb] baden ['baːdn̩] +haben ◊ *im Meer baden* ♦ *ein Baby baden* ♦ *einen entzündeten Finger in Kamillenlösung baden*

bathroom [noun] Bad [baːt] das <-(e)s, Bäder> ◊ *Ist das Bad frei?*

bathtub [noun] Badewanne ['baːdəvanə] die <-, -n>

batter [noun] **1.** *(in cooking)* Teig [taek] der <-(e)s, -e> ◊ *den Teig rühren* **2.** *(in baseball, cricket etc.)* Schläger ['ʃlɛːɡɐ] der <-s, -> ♀Schlägerin ['ʃlɛːɡərɪn] die <-, -nen>

battery [noun] Batterie [batə'riː] die <-, -n> ◊ *eine neue Batterie für den Wecker* ♦ *Hühner in Batterien halten* ♦ *eine ganze Batterie von Tests durchführen*

battle¹ [noun] **1.** *(between armies, in a discussion)* Schlacht [ʃlaxt] die <-, -en> ◊ *die Schlacht um Stalingrad/von Waterloo* ♦ *Die Diskussionsteilnehmer lieferten sich eine heiße Schlacht.* **2.** *(ongoing struggle)* Kampf [kampf] der <-(e)s, Kämpfe> *(esp fig)* ◊ *der Kampf der Geschlechter* ♦ *der Kampf gegen den Krebs*

battle² [verb] kämpfen ['kɛmpfn̩] +haben ◊ *Ich habe gekämpft und gewonnen.* battle (against) sth/sb gegen etw./jdn kämpfen ◊ *gegen das organisierte Verbrechen/den Feind kämpfen* battle with sth mit etw. kämpfen ◊ *mit einem Problem kämpfen* battle

for sth um etw. kämpfen ◊ *um den Sieg kämpfen*

bawl [verb] brüllen ['brʏlən] +haben *(pej)* ◊ *Hör auf zu brüllen. So schlimm war das nicht!* bawl at sb jd anbrüllen ['anbrʏlən] +haben ◊ *„Lass das!", brüllte sie ihn an.*

bay [noun] Bucht [bʊxt] die <-, -en>

bazaar [noun] Basar [ba'zaːʳ] der <-s, -e>

be [verb] **1.** sein [zaen] <ist, war, ist gewesen> ◊ *Ich bin nicht von hier.* ♦ *Bist du hungrig?* ♦ *Er ist Lehrer von Beruf.* ♦ *Wir sind Deutsche.* ♦ *Wo seid ihr denn alle?* ♦ *Sind das deine Kinder?* ♦ *Ihr Geburtstag war gestern.* ♦ *Was ist? Du guckst so traurig.* ♦ *Heute ist der 31. August.* ♦ *Wie viel Uhr ist es?* ♦ *Vier plus vier ist acht.* ♦ *Der Patient ist außer Gefahr.* ♦ *Damals war Krieg in Polen.* Have you ever been to Berne? Warst du schon einmal in Bern? there is/are es gibt [ɛs giːpt] <gibt, gab, hat gegeben> ◊ *Gibt es tatsächlich keinen Ausweg?* ♦ *Es gibt viele Neuigkeiten.* ♦ *Wird es Krieg geben?* How much is that? Wie viel macht das? That is 25 dollars, please. Das macht zusammen 25 Dollar. **2.** *(distance, measurement)* betragen [bə'traːgn̩] <beträgt, betrug, hat betragen> ◊ *Die Entfernung beträgt 10 Kilometer.* **3.** *(auxiliary in the progressive tense)* be laughing/sitting/kissing etc. gerade lachen/sitzen/küssen etc. [gəraːdə 'laxn̩/'zɪtsn̩/'kʏsn̩] Standard German has no proper progressive tense; it can be expressed with the help of the adverb 'gerade' (=at this moment). ◊ *Ich esse gerade. Ruf später noch mal an.* ♦ *Wir saßen gerade vor dem Fernseher, als wir plötzlich ein lautes Geräusch hörten.* **4.** *(auxiliary in the passive)* werden ['veːɐdn̩] <wird, wurde, ist worden> ◊ *Sie wird in Englisch geprüft.* ♦ *Der Igel wurde von einem Auto überfahren.* ♦ *Das Haus ist durch ein Feuer zerstört worden.* **5.** *(auxiliary in the adjectival passive)* sein [zaen] <ist, war, ist gewesen> ◊ *Das Geschäft ist geschlossen.* ♦ *Das Mittagessen ist gekocht.*
⊛ been there, done that kenne ich alles schon be that as it may wie dem auch sei if sb were to write/walk/help etc. (expressing a condition) wenn jd schreiben/laufen/helfen etc. würde sb/sth is to do sth (expressing an expectation, order) jd/etw. soll etw. tun ◊ *Was sollen wir bloß machen?* ♦ *Die Hochzeit soll am 1. Mai stattfinden.* ♦ *Du solltest das möglichst bald tun.* be with sb (be able to grasp) jdm folgen können be with it **1.** (be modern, trendy) up to date sein **2.** (be able to grasp) voll da sein

beach [noun] Strand [ʃtrant] der <-(e)s, Strände> ◊ *am Strand liegen*

bead [noun] Perle ['pɛʳlə] die <-, -n> ◊ *Die Perlen meiner Kette sind aus Glas.*

beak [noun] **1.** *(of a bird)* Schnabel ['ʃnaːbl̩] der <-s, Schnäbel> ◊ *Der Vogel hatte einen Wurm im Schnabel.* **2.** *(fam, pej) (nose)* Zinken ['tsɪŋkn̩] der <-s, -> *(fam, pej)*

beaker [noun] **1.** *(for drinking)* Becher ['bɛçɐ] der <-s, -> ◊ *aus dem Becher trinken* **2.** CHEM Becherglas ['bɛçɐglaːs] das <-es, Bechergläser>

beam¹ [noun] **1.** *(piece of wood, apparatus in gymnastics)* Balken ['balkn̩] der <-s, -> ◊ *ein tragender Balken* ♦ *die Decke mit Balken abstützen* ♦ *am Balken turnen* **2.** *(of light)* Strahl [ʃtraːl] der <-(e)s, -en> ◊ *der Strahl einer Taschenlampe; (of a vehicle's lights)* full beam Fernlicht ['fɛʳnlɪçt] das

<-(e)s> no pl ◊ *das Fernlicht einschalten*
beam² [verb] *(sun, happy person)* strahlen ['ʃtraːlən]
+haben ◊ *Sie strahlte vor Freude, als sie das hörte.* ✦
Die Sonne strahlte hell.

bean [noun] Bohne ['boːnə] die <-, -n> ◊ *Lamm mit
Bohnen* ✦ *Bohnen pflanzen* ✦ *Kaffee aus frischen
Bohnen*

bear¹ [noun] Bär [bɛːɐ̯] der <-en, -en>

bear² [verb] **1.** *(tolerate, endure)* ertragen [ɛ'traːgn̩]
<erträgt, ertrug, hat ertragen> ◊ *Ich kann die
Schmerzen kaum noch ertragen.* ✦ *Sie erträgt ihr
Schicksal mit Gleichmut.* **2.** *(the costs, consequences
of sth, a name, an address etc.)* tragen ['traːgn̩]
<trägt, trug, hat getragen> ◊ *Gemeinde und Staat
tragen die Kosten für den Bau der Straße
gemeinsam.* ✦ *Der Brief trug die Unterschrift des
Kanzlers.* **3.** *(a child)* gebären [gə'bɛːrən] <gebiert,
gebar, hat geboren> *(lofty)*
• **bear with** [phras v] bear with sb/sth Geduld mit
jdm/etw. haben [gə'dʊlt mɪt ... 'haːbm̩] +haben ◊ *Ich
weiß, sie ist zur Zeit sehr gereizt. Hab etwas Geduld
mit ihr!*
⊛ bear with me/us einen Moment bitte

beard [noun] Bart [baːɐ̯t] der <-(e)s, Bärte> ◊ *Er trägt
einen Bart.* ✦ *Tom lässt sich einen Bart wachsen.*

bearer [noun] *(of a stretcher, coffin, name, title)* Träger
['trɛːgɐ] der <-s, -> ♀Trägerin ['trɛːgərɪn] die
<-, -nen> ◊ *Am Grab angekommen, setzten die
Träger den Sarg ab.* ✦ *Sie ist Trägerin eines
berühmten Namens.*; *(of a letter, cheque, news)* Überbringer [ybɐ'brɪŋɐ] der <-s, -> ♀Überbringerin
[ybɐ'brɪŋərɪn] die <- or -nen> ◊ *der Überbringer
einer Nachricht*

bearing [noun] **1.** *(way you control your body)* sb's
bearing jds Haltung ['haltʊŋ] die <-, -en> most sing
◊ *Ich konnte ihn an seiner Haltung erkennen.*
2. Lager ['laːgɐ] das <-s, ->
⊛ find your bearings sich orientieren ◊ *Er musste
sich im Nebel erst orientieren.* have some bearing/
no bearing on sth Einfluss/keinen Einfluss auf etw.
[acc] haben take a bearing seine Position
bestimmen ◊ *Mit Hilfe der Karte konnte ich meine
Position bestimmen.*

beast [noun] **1.** *(ferocious animal or person)* Bestie
['bɛstjə] die <-, -n> ◊ *Eine wilde Bestie fiel die
Schafe an.* **2.** *(domestic animal)* Tier [tiːɐ̯] das
<-(e)s, -e> ◊ *die Tiere in den Ställen* **3.** *(scheming
person)* Biest [biːst] das <-es, -er> *(fam, pej)* ◊ *Du
bist ein echtes Biest!*

beat¹ [noun] **1.** *(of the heart, pulse etc.)* Schlag [ʃlaːk]
der <-(e)s, Schläge> ◊ *ein Puls von 70 Schlägen in
der Minute* **2.** mus Takt [takt] der <-(e)s, -e> ◊ *den
Takt schlagen* ✦ *im Takt bleiben* **3.** *(of a police
officer)* Runde ['rʊndə] die <-, -n>

beat² [verb] **1.** *(hit, defeat, mix)* schlagen ['ʃlaːgn̩]
<schlägt, schlug, hat geschlagen> ◊ *Sie nahm sich
vor, ihre Kinder nie zu schlagen.* ✦ *Sie schlug die
anderen Läuferinnen um Längen.* ✦ *Wenn ich sie
sehe, schlägt mein Herz immer höher/schneller.* ✦
Eier schaumig schlagen beat against/on/at sth
gegen etw. schlagen; *(a carpet, meat)* klopfen
['klɔpfn̩] +haben ◊ *Schnitzel/Teppiche klopfen*
2. *(surpass, outdo)* übertreffen [ybɐ'trɛfn̩] <übertrifft,
übertraf, hat übertroffen> ◊ *Diese Aussage kann an
Dummheit nicht übertroffen werden.*; *(a record)*
brechen ['brɛçn̩] <bricht, brach, hat gebrochen> ◊

den Weltrekord brechen
⊛ you can't beat sth es gibt nichts Besseres als
etw. ◊ *Es gibt nichts Besseres als ein gutes Buch.*
beat sb to it jdm zuvorkommen
• **beat down** [phras v] **1.** *(sun)* stechen ['ʃtɛçn̩]
<sticht, stach, hat gestochen> ◊ *Die Sonne sticht
heute so; ich bleibe lieber im Schatten.* **2.** *(rain)*
prasseln ['prasl̩n] +haben/sein ◊ *Der Regen prasselte
auf das Dach.*
• **beat off** [phras v] **1.** *(person, an attack, a dog)*
beat sb/sth/an animal off jdn/etw./ein Tier
abwehren ['apveːrən] +haben ◊ *Er wehrte den
Angriff/Hund mit einem Stock ab.*; *(an army)* zurückschlagen [tsu'rʏkʃlaːgn̩] <schlägt zurück, schlug
zurück, hat zurückgeschlagen> ◊ *Napoleon schlug die
deutschen Armeen zurück.* **2.** *(the competition)* beat
sb off jdn abhängen ['aphɛŋən] +haben ◊ *Er hängte
die Konkurrenz ab.*
• **beat up** [phras v] beat sb up jdn zusammenschlagen [tsu'zamənʃlaːgn̩] <schlägt zusammen, schlug
zusammen, hat zusammengeschlagen>

beating [noun] **1.** *(series of blows)* Prügel ['pryːgl̩] die
<-> only pl ◊ *jdm Prügel verabreichen* **2.** *(defeat)*
Niederlage ['niːdɐlaːgə] die <-, -n> take a beating
eine Niederlage erleiden ◊ *Die Partei erlitt bei den
Wahlen eine Niederlage.*

beautiful(ly) [adj, adv] schön [ʃøːn] ◊ *eine schöne
Landschaft* ✦ *Ich finde seine Augen so schön.* ✦ *Sie
hat sehr schön gesungen.*

beauty [noun] Schönheit ['ʃøːnhaɛt] die <-, -en> ◊
eine Landschaft von außergewöhnlicher Schönheit ✦
Sie war eine echte Schönheit.
⊛ beauty is in the eye of the beholder Schönheit
liegt im Auge des Betrachters

because [conjunc] weil [vaɛl] ◊ *Er konnte nicht
kommen, weil er krank war.* ◊ *„Warum hast du das
nicht erledigt?" — „Weil ich keine Zeit hatte."*
because of sb wegen jdm ['veːgn̩] +dat *(fam)* ◊
Wegen dir komme ich zu spät zur Arbeit. because of
sth wegen etw. [gen] ['veːgn̩] sing nouns without
article or attribute are not declined when following
this prep, otherwise +gen ◊ *Wegen des schlechten
Wetters blieb sie zu Hause.* ✦ *wegen Krankheit fehlen*

become [verb] **1.** *(change into a different condition,
obtain a profession)* werden ['veːɐ̯dn̩] <wird, wurde,
ist geworden> ◊ *Sie ist plötzlich krank geworden.* ✦
Er wurde wütend. ✦ *Ich möchte mal Lehrer werden.*
what will become of sb/sth was wird aus jdm/etw.
◊ *Was wird aus mir, wenn ich arbeitslos werde?*
2. *(look good on sb)* become sb jdm (gut) stehen
[('juːt) 'ʃteːən] <steht, stand, hat gestanden> ◊ *Der
Anzug steht dir (gut).*

bed [noun] Bett [bɛt] das <-(e)s, -en> go to bed ins
Bett gehen put sb to bed jdn ins Bett bringen make
the bed das Bett machen make up a bed for sb jdm
ein Bett herrichten
⊛ get out of bed on the wrong side mit dem
linken Fuß aufstehen jump/get into bed with sb
mit jdm ins Bett gehen sb has made their bed and
now they must lie in it wie man sich bettet, so
liegt man

bedroom [noun] Schlafzimmer ['ʃlaːftsɪmɐ] das
<-s, ->

bedside table [noun] Nachttisch ['naxttɪʃ] der
<-(e)s, -e>

bee [noun] Biene ['biːnə] die <-, -n>

⊕ **have a bee in your bonnet** einen Tick haben
think you are the bee's knees sich für den
Größten/die Größte halten
beef [noun] Rindfleisch ['rɪntflaeʃ] das <–(e)s> no pl
beep [verb] 1. *(alarm clock, answerphone, microwave
etc.)* piepsen ['piːpsn̩] +haben ◊ *Die Eieruhr piepst.*
2. beep your horn hupen ['huːpm̩] +haben *The horn
beeped.* Es hupte.
beer [noun] Bier [biːɐ̯] das <–(e)s, –e> pl *'Bier'* when
used with expressions of quantity ◊ *In Deutschland
gibt es viele verschiedene Biere.* ♦ *helles/dunkles Bier*
♦ *Zwei Bier bitte!*
beetle [noun] Käfer ['kɛːfɐ] der <–s, –>
before¹ [adv] zuvor [ʦu'foːɐ̯] ◊ *die Woche zuvor* ♦ *Nie
zuvor hat es hier so viel geschneit.*
before² [prep] vor [foːɐ̯] with acc when expressing
motion towards a place, with dat when there is no or
undirected motion ◊ *sich vor jdn/etw. stellen* ♦ *vor
der Tür stehen* ♦ *Arbeit kommt vor dem Vergnügen.*
before the court vor Gericht; *(referring to sth previously mentioned)* before (that) davor [da'foːɐ̯] ◊ *Wir
waren im Kino, und davor waren wir einkaufen.* ♦
Was haben Sie am Tag davor gemacht? before long
bald [balt] ◊ *Bald werden die Prüfungsergebnisse
bekannt gemacht.* the day before yesterday vorgestern ['foːɐ̯gɛstɐn] the year before letztes Jahr
[ˌlɛtstəs 'jaːɐ̯] the year before last vorletztes Jahr
[ˌfoːɐ̯lɛtstəs 'jaːɐ̯]
before³ [conjunc] bevor [bə'foːɐ̯] ◊ *Bevor ich mit der
Arbeit anfange, muss ich noch schnell telefonieren.* ♦
Das war, bevor ich ihn kennen lernte.
beforehand [adv] vorher ['foːɐ̯heːɐ̯] ◊ *Er hat seinen
Besuch vorher angekündigt.*
beg [verb] 1. *(ask)* beg (for sth) (um etw.) bitten
['bɪtn̩] <bittet, bat, hat gebeten> ◊ *Kann ich Sie um
einen Gefallen bitten?* ♦ *Er bat darum, sich zu ihnen
setzen zu dürfen.; (desperately)* beg (for sth) (um
etw.) flehen ['fleːən] +haben ◊ *um Gnade flehen* beg
sb (for sth) jdn (um etw.) anflehen ['anfleːən]
+haben ◊ *Sie flehte mich um Hilfe an.* beg sb to do
sth jdn anflehen, etw. zu tun ◊ *Er flehte sie an, ihn
nicht zu verlassen.* **2.** *(for money, food etc.)* beg (for
sth) (um etw.) betteln ['bɛtln̩] +haben ◊ *auf der
Straße betteln* ♦ *Der Hund bettelte um Futter.* beg
sth from sb jdn um etw. anbetteln [ʊm ... ˌanbɛtln̩]
+haben ◊ *Er bettelte mich um Geld an.*
⊕ **I beg to differ** da bin ich anderer Meinung
begin [verb] 1. *(start)* anfangen ['anfaŋən] <fängt an,
fing an, hat angefangen> ◊ *Er fing zu weinen an.* ♦
Fangt schon mal an; das Essen wird kalt. ♦ *Sie
wollte ein neues Leben anfangen.* ♦ *Der Tag fing
schon hektisch an.* ♦ *Hinter diesem Berg fängt die
Schweiz an.* ♦ *Der Film fängt um 16 Uhr an.*
2. *(negotiations, talks)* aufnehmen ['aofneːmən]
<nimmt auf, nahm auf, hat aufgenommen> *(form)* ◊
Die Verhandlungen wurden bald aufgenommen.
⊕ **not be able to begin to understand** nicht
einmal ansatzweise verstehen können **to begin
with** zunächst ◊ *Zunächst müssen wir folgendes
Problem erörtern: ...*
beginner [noun] Anfänger ['anfɛŋɐ] der <–s, –> ♀An-
fängerin ['anfɛŋərɪn] die <–, –nen> ◊ *Deutschkurse
für Anfänger* ♦ *Beim Autofahren bin ich noch
absolute Anfängerin.*
beginning [noun] Anfang ['anfaŋ] der
<–(e)s, Anfänge> ◊ *ein vielversprechender Anfang* ♦

der Anfang einer langen Erfolgsgeschichte in the
beginning am Anfang at the beginning of the month
Anfang des Monats at the beginning of May Anfang
Mai
⊕ **the beginnings of sth 1.** *(first signs of sth)* die
ersten Anzeichen ... [gen] ◊ *Die ersten Anzeichen
seiner Krankheit zeigten sich vor zwei Monaten.*
2. *(start of sth)* die Anfänge ... [gen] ◊ *Die Partei
hatte in ihren Anfängen viele Anhänger.*
behalf [noun] 1. *(as a spokesman, representative)* on
behalf of sb/sth, on sb's/sth's behalf für jdn/etw.
[fyːɐ̯] [+acc] ◊ *Wir sammeln Geld für einen gemeinnüt-
zigen Verein.* ♦ *Ich rufe für meine Schwester an; sie
ist krank.; (more formal)* im Namen ... [gen]
[ɪm 'naːmən] ◊ *ein Appell im Namen der Schwachen*
2. *(because of sb, about sb)* on sb's behalf, on
behalf of sb um jdn [ʊm] [+acc] ◊ *sich um jdn Sorgen
machen*
behave [verb] 1. *(conduct yourself in a certain way)*
sich verhalten [fɛ'haltn̩] <verhält sich, verhielt sich,
hat sich verhalten> ◊ *Du hast dich ganz richtig
verhalten.* ♦ *Wie verhält sich diese Substanz bei
hohen Temperaturen?* **2.** *(show good manners)*
behave (yourself) sich benehmen [bə'neːmən]
<benimmt sich, benahm sich, hat sich benommen> ◊
Benimm dich! ♦ *Kannst du dich nicht anständig
benehmen?*
behaviour, behavior [noun] Verhalten [fɛ'haltn̩] das
<–s> no pl
behind¹ [noun] Hintern ['hɪntɐn] der <–s, –> *(fam)*
behind² [adv] 1. *(spatial)* dahinter [da'hɪntɐ] ◊ *Er ging
voran und ich folgte kurz dahinter.* follow a short
distance behind in kurzem Abstand folgen
[ɪn ˌkʊrʦm̩ 'apʃtant ˌfɔlgn̩] +sein ◊ *Der Favorit führte
das Feld und die anderen Läufer folgten in kurzem
Abstand.* from behind von hinten [fɔn 'hɪntn̩] ◊ *Ich
habe sie nur von hinten gesehen.* ♦ *Jemand sprach
mich von hinten an.* **2.** *(less advanced)* be (lagging)
behind hinterherhinken [hɪntɐheːˈhɪŋkn̩] +sein ◊
*Das Land hinkt in seiner wirtschaftlichen Entwick-
lung hinterher.* **3.** *(late)* be behind with mit etw.
im Rückstand sein [mɪt ... ɪm 'rʏkʃtant ʦaen] +sein
4. *(less successful)* be behind zurückliegen
[ʦu'rʏkliːgn̩] <liegt zurück, lag zurück, hat zurückgele-
gen> ◊ *Die Partei liegt 20 Prozentpunkte zurück.* be
far behind weit abgeschlagen sein
[vaet 'apgəʃlaːgn̩ zaen] +sein a step behind einen
Schritt hinterher [aenən ʃrɪt hɪnteˈheːɐ̯] ◊ *Egal wie
sehr ich mich anstrenge, ich bin immer einen
Schritt hinterher.*

> 'Behind' often occurs with verbs or in phrasal verbs
> like 'leave behind' or 'get behind' which have their
> own entries in the dictionary.

behind³ [prep] 1. *(at the back of, in the past, causing
or supporting)* hinter ['hɪntɐ] with acc when expressing motion towards a place, with dat when there is
no or undirected motion ◊ *Stell das Fahrrad hinter
das Haus!* ♦ *Der Parkplatz ist hinter dem Gebäude.* ♦
Die Schulzeit liegt schon lange hinter mir. ♦ *Er
stellte sich hinter seine Tochter.* ♦ *Man vermutet die
Mafia hinter dem Verbrechen.* be behind sb/sth
hinter jdm/etw. stehen ◊ *Die Kirche steht direkt
hinter dem Rathaus.* ♦ *Als ihr Chef sie kritisierte,
standen alle Kollegen hinter ihr.* behind that/it
dahinter [da'hɪntɐ] ◊ *Das ist das Kino; dahinter sind*

Parkplätze. ♦ *Die Idee dahinter ist einfach.* **2.** *(be less successful than)* be behind sb **hinter jdm zurückliegen** [hɪntɐ ... ˈtsuˌrʏkliːɡn̩] <liegt zurück, lag zurück, hat zurückgelegen> ◊ *Der Kandidat liegt weit hinter seinem Konkurrenten zurück.*; *(be less advanced than)* be behind sb/sth **jdm/etw. hinterherhinken** [hɪntɐˈheːɐ̯hɪŋkn̩] +*sein* ◊ *Die Firma hinkt der Konkurrenz hinterher.* be behind the times **der Zeit hinterherhinken**

being [noun] *(person, spirit)* Wesen [ˈveːzn̩] das <–s, –> ◊ *Was für ein hilfloses Wesen ein Baby doch ist!* ♦ *Dein Mann, das unbekannte Wesen!* the supreme being **das höchste Wesen** *(living)* being **Lebewesen** [ˈleːbəveːzn̩] das <–s, –> ◊ *Sollte man das Klonen von Lebewesen verbieten?*

 ⊛ sb's innermost being **jds Innerstes** ◊ *Sie enthüllte mir ihr Innerstes.* ♦ *Er fühlte eine große Traurigkeit in seinem Innersten.*

belch [verb] aufstoßen [ˈaʊ̯fʃtoːsn̩] <stößt auf, stieß auf, hat aufgestoßen>

Belgian[1] [noun] Belgier [ˈbɛlɡiɐ] der <–s, –> ♀Belgierin [ˈbɛlɡiərɪn] die <–, –nen> → **German**[1] **1.**

Belgian[2] [adj] belgisch [ˈbɛlɡɪʃ] *mostly before ns* ◊ *belgische Waffeln*

Belgium [noun] Belgien [ˈbɛlɡiən] das <–s> *article only in combination with attribute, no pl* → **Germany**

belief [noun] **1.** *(strong feeling that sth is true)* Glaube [ˈɡlaʊ̯bə] der <–ns> *no pl* ◊ *Wir ließen sie in dem Glauben, dass sie mitkommen würde.* belief in sth/sb **Vertrauen in etw./jdn** [fɛˈtraʊ̯ən ɪn] das <–s> *no pl* ◊ *unser Vertrauen in die Politik* **2.** *(conviction)* Überzeugung [ybɐˈtsɔɡɡʊŋ] die <–, –en> ◊ *Es ist meine feste Überzeugung, dass wir jetzt handeln müssen.*

 ⊛ beyond belief **unglaublich**

believe [verb] glauben [ˈɡlaʊ̯bm̩] +*haben* ◊ *Glauben Sie, dass er die Wahl gewinnt?* ♦ *Du darfst nicht alles glauben, was er dir erzählt.* ♦ *Ich glaube ihr nicht.* ♦ *Das glaube ich dir nicht!* believe it or not **ob du es glaubst oder nicht** find it hard to believe that **kaum glauben können, dass** lead sb to believe sth **jdm etw. weismachen** [ˈvaɪ̯smaxn̩] +*haben* lead sb to believe that **jdm weismachen, dass** ◊ *Er hat ihnen weisgemacht, dass sie dabei schnell reich würden.*; *(assumed)* believe sb/sth to be sth **davon ausgehen, dass jd/etw. etw. ist** [dafɔn ˈaʊ̯sɡeːən ... ɪst] <geht aus, ging aus, ist ausgegangen> ◊ *Man geht davon aus, dass die Vermisste tot ist.* it is widely believed **vermutlich** [fɛˈmuːtlɪç] ◊ *Vermutlich sind die Vermissten in der Flut umgekommen.*

 ⊛ I don't believe it! **1.** *(surprised)* kaum zu glauben! **2.** *(annoyed)* es ist nicht zu fassen ◊ *Es ist nicht zu fassen — er hat schon wieder gelogen!* don't you believe it **lass dir keinen Bären aufbinden** not believe your eyes/ears **seinen Augen/Ohren kaum trauen können** would you believe it **stell dir das vor**

 • believe in [phras v] **1.** *(miracles, God)* believe in sth/sb **an etw./jdn glauben** [an ... ˌɡlaʊ̯bm̩] +*haben* ◊ *Ich glaube nicht an ein Leben nach dem Tod.* ♦ *Glaubst du an Gott?* stop believing in sb **den Glauben an jdn verlieren** [deːn ˌɡlaʊ̯bm̩ an ... fɛˈliːrən] <verliert, verlor, hat verloren> **2.** *(a cause, conviction)* believe in sth **für etw. sein** [fyːɐ̯... zaɪn] +*sein* ◊ *Bist du für Schuluniformen?* not believe in sth **nichts von etw. halten**

[ˌnɪçts fɔn ... ˈhaltn̩] <hält, hielt, hat gehalten> ◊ *Er hält nichts von der Ehe.*

belittle [verb] [hɛˈrapzɛtsn̩] +*haben* ◊ *Er setzt immer ihre Fähigkeiten seiner Kollegin herab.*

bell [noun] **1.** *(in churches, a cow's etc.)* Glocke [ˈɡlɔkə] die <–, –n> ◊ *Um Mitternacht läuteten sie feierlich die Glocken.* **2.** *(on a door, bicycle)* Klingel [ˈklɪŋl̩] die <–, –n> ◊ *Das Fahrrad hatte keine Klingel.* ring the bell **klingeln** [ˈklɪŋln̩] ◊ *Sie klingelte und die Tür öffnete sich.* The bell is ringing. **Es klingelt.**

 ⊛ bells and whistles **Extras** ◊ *ein neuer Wagen mit vielen Extras* give sb a bell **jdn anrufen** sth rings a bell **etw. kommt jdm bekannt vor**

bellow [verb] brüllen [ˈbrʏln̩] +*haben* ◊ *Der Stier brüllte wütend.* ♦ *„Mach die Musik leiser!", brüllte er.*

belly [noun] Bauch [baʊ̯x] der <–(e)s, Bäuche> ◊ *Ich schlafe auf dem Bauch.* ♦ *Mir tut der Bauch weh.*

bellyache [noun] Bauchschmerzen [ˈbaʊ̯xʃmɛrtsn̩] die <–> *only pl* ◊ *Ich habe Bauchschmerzen.*

belly button [noun] Nabel [ˈnaːbl̩] der <–s, –>

belong [verb] **1.** *(object: have its place)* belong somewhere **irgendwohin gehören** [ɡəˈhøːrən] +*haben* ◊ *Der Hund gehört nicht auf das Sofa!* ♦ *Die Gläser gehören hierhin.* **2.** *(person: feel at home)* belong somewhere **irgendwo hingehören** [ˈhɪnɡəhøːrən] +*haben* ◊ *Er weiß nicht, wo er hingehört.*

 • belong to [phras v] **1.** *(be owned, controlled by sb/ sth)* sth belongs to sb/sth **etw. gehört jdm/etw.** [ɡəˈhøːɐ̯t] <gehört, gehörte, hat gehört> ◊ *Wem gehört diese Tasche?* ♦ *Die Zukunft gehört der Jugend.* sth belongs to sb **jd gehört zu jdm** ◊ *Die Kinder gehören zu mir.* **2.** *(be a member of an organization, group etc.)* belong to sth **einer Sache** [dat] **angehören** [ˈanɡəhøːrən] <gehört an, gehörte an, hat angehört> ◊ *Sie gehört dem Schachklub an.* ♦ *Der Wolf gehört der Familie der Hunde an.*

belongings [noun] Sachen [ˈzaxn̩] die <–> pl *(fam)* ◊ *Sie packte ihre Sachen und reiste ab.* personal belongings **persönliches Eigentum** [pɛɐ̯ˌzøːnlɪçəs ˈaɪ̯ɡn̩tuːm] <–s> *no pl* ◊ *Schützen Sie Ihr persönliches Eigentum.* ♦ *Die Versicherung haftet für das persönliche Eigentum des Reisenden.*; *(when you don't own a lot)* sb's few belongings **jds Habseligkeiten** [ˈhaːpzeːlɪçkaɪ̯tn̩] die <–> pl ◊ *Im Zelt packt sie ihre Habseligkeiten aus.*

below[1] [adv] **1.** *(in a lower position)* unten [ˈʊntn̩] ◊ siehe unten **2.** SHIP unter Deck [ʊntɐ ˈdɛk]

In German it is not possible to make statements such as 'in the flat below' or 'at the lake below' without specifying the point of reference, so you have to say 'the flat below us' or 'the lake below them' etc.: *In der Wohnung unter uns gab es Streit.* (In the flat 'below (us)' there was a row taking place.) — *Sie sah aus dem Fenster auf den Garten darunter.* (She looked out of the window at the garden 'below (it)')

below[2] [prep] unter [ˈʊntə] *with acc when expressing a drop in sth, with dat when there is stagnation* ◊ *Temperaturen unter null* ♦ *Seine Leistungen liegen unter dem Durchschnitt.* ♦ *Der Aktienindex fiel unter die Marke von 2300 Punkten.* below that/it **darunter** [daˈrʊntɐ] ◊ *Gestern betrug die Besucherzahl 3000; heute lag sie weit darunter.* ♦ *An der Wand hing ein Bild; darunter stand ein altes Sofa.*

belt [noun] Gürtel [ˈɡʏrtl̩] der <–s, –> ◊ *ein schwarzer*

Gürtel in Karate ♦ *Er trägt einen Gürtel.* ♦ *ein Gürtel aus Bäumen und Sträuchern* green belt Grüngürtel ['gry:ngʏ'tl] commuter belt Einzugsbereich ['aɛntsu:ksbəraɛç] der <–(e)s, –e> ◊ *der Einzugbereich Londons*
ⓔ **below the belt** unter der Gürtellinie
bench ⓝⓞⓤⓝ **1.** *(seat)* Bank [baŋk] die <–, Bänke> ◊ *Auf der Bank im Park saß ein Liebespärchen.* **2.** *(in workshops, factories)* Werkbank ['vɛ'kbaŋk] die <–, Werkbänke> ◊ *an der Werkbank arbeiten* **3.** SPORT the bench die Ersatzbank [di: ɐ'zatsbaŋk] <–, Ersatzbänke> ◊ *auf der Ersatzbank sitzen* **4.** POL *(in the British parliament)* the benches *die Bänke, auf denen die Abgeordneten im britischen Parlament sitzen* **5.** *(office of a judge)* the bench das Richteramt [das 'rɪçtɛˌamt] <–(e)s> be appointed to the bench ins Richteramt berufen werden
bend¹ ⓝⓞⓤⓝ **1.** *(of a road)* Kurve ['kʊ'və] die <–, –n> ◊ *eine scharfe Kurve* ♦ *Er raste um die Kurve.* round a bend um eine Kurve fahren a tight bend eine scharfe Kurve; *(of a river)* Biegung ['bi:gʊn] die <–, –en> ◊ *An dieser Stelle macht der Rhein eine Biegung.* **2.** *(movement, exercise)* Rumpfbeuge ['rʊmpfbɔɡɡə] die <–, –n>
ⓔ **be/go round the bend** verrückt sein/werden drive sb round the bend jdn verrückt machen
bend² ⓥⓔⓡⓑ **1.** *(stoop)* bend (forwards/down/over) sich bücken ['bʏkn̩] +haben ◊ *Er bückte sich und hob den Stift auf.* be bent double sich krümmen ['krʏmən] +haben ◊ *Sie krümmte sich vor Schmerzen.* **2.** *(lean forward)* bend sth forward etw. vorbeugen ['fo:ɛbɔɡɡn̩] +haben ◊ *Er beugte den Kopf vor und schaute aus dem Fenster.* sb bends forward jd beugt sich vor ◊ *Du musst dich vorbeugen, wenn du etwas sehen willst.* **3.** *(make/become curved or folded)* bend sth etw. biegen ['bi:gn̩] <biegt, bog, hat gebogen> ◊ *Er hat den Draht u-förmig gebogen.* sth bends (under sth) etw biegt sich (unter etw. ⓓⓐⓣ) ◊ *Die Äste bogen sich unter dem Gewicht der Äpfel.* **4.** *(your head, arm, leg)* bend sth etw. beugen ['bɔɡɡn̩] +haben ◊ *Sie hatten die Köpfe über ihre Bücher gebeugt.* ♦ *Er konnte den Arm nicht mehr beugen.* **5.** *(fold and break)* knicken ['knɪkn̩] +haben ◊ *Der Umschlag darf nicht geknickt werden.* bend a tree einen Baum umknicken [aɛnən 'baɔm ˌʊmknɪkn̩] +haben ◊ *Der Sturm hat viele Bäume umgeknickt.* **6.** *(road, river)* sth bends etw. macht eine Biegung [maxt aɛnə 'bi:gʊn] +haben ◊ *Hier macht der Fluss eine Biegung nach rechts.* **7.** *(distort the shape of sth)* bend sth etw. verbiegen [fɛ'bi:gn̩] <verbiegt, verbog, hat verbogen> ◊ *einen Löffel verbiegen* sth bends etw verbiegt sich
beneath¹ ⓐⓓⓥ darunter [da'rʊntɛ] ◊ *Wir wohnen im ersten Stock; darunter ist eine Bäckerei.*
beneath² ⓟⓡⓔⓟ unter ['ʊntɛ] with acc when expressing motion towards a place, with dat when there is no or undirected motion ◊ *Sie setzten sich unter einen Baum.* ♦ *Ihr wohnt direkt unter mir.* pull sth out from beneath sth etw. unter etw. ⓓⓐⓣ hervorziehen ◊ *Sie zog ein Messer unter ihrem Mantel hervor.* come out from beneath sth unter etw. ⓓⓐⓣ hervorkommen
ⓔ **beneath sb** *(undignified)* unter jds Würde
beneficial ⓐⓓⓙ günstig ['gʏnstɪç] ◊ *ein günstiges Klima für Investitionen* be beneficial to sth sich

günstig auf etw. ⓐⓒⓒ auswirken ◊ *Diese Reformen wirken sich günstig auf die Konjunktur aus.* be beneficial to sb für jdn von Nutzen sein [fy:ɐ ... fɔn 'nʊtsn̩ zaɛn] +sein ◊ *War diese Therapie für Sie von Nutzen?* mutually beneficial für beide Seiten von Vorteil [fy:ɐ ˌbaɛdə ˌzaɛtn̩ fɔn 'fo:ɐtaɛl]; *(for your health)* gesundheitsfördernd [gə'zʊnthaɛtsfœ'dent] mostly before ns ◊ *die gesundheitsfördernde Wirkung von Rotwein*
beneficially ⓐⓓⓥ günstig ['gʏnstɪç] ◊ *etw. günstig beeinflussen*
beneficiary ⓝⓞⓤⓝ **1.** *(person who inherits sth)* Erbe ['ɛ'bə] der <–n, –n> ♀Erbin ['ɛ'bɪn] die <–, –nen> **2.** *(person who benefits from sth)* Nutznießer ['nʊtsni:sɛ] der <–s, –> ♀Nutznießerin ['nʊtsni:sərɪn] die <–, –nen>
benefit¹ ⓝⓞⓤⓝ **1.** *(advantage)* Vorteil ['fo:ɐtaɛl] der <–(e)s, –e> ◊ *Sie ist immer nur auf ihren eigenen Vorteil bedacht.* ♦ *Er hat sich zu meinem Vorteil verrechnet.* ♦ *für jdn/etw. von Vorteil sein* derive a benefit from sth einen Vorteil aus etw. ziehen for sb's benefit für jdn [fy:ɐ] ◊ *Für mich erklärte sie alles noch einmal.* **2.** *(from the government)* Unterstützung [ʊntɛ'ʃtʏtsʊn] die <–, –en> ◊ *Die Unterstützung für Arbeitslose wurde drastisch gekürzt.* be on benefit Unterstützung beziehen child benefit Kindergeld ['kɪndɡɛlt] das <–(e)s> no pl housing benefit Wohngeld ['vo:nɡɛlt] das <–, –en> **3.** *(from an insurance company)* Leistung ['laɛstʊn] die <–, –en> **4.** *(from your employer)* Vergünstigung [fɛ'gʏnstɪgʊn] die <–, –en> ◊ *Vergünstigungen wie ein Firmenwagen, ein Handy etc.* **5.** *(event)* Benefizveranstaltung [bena'fi:tsfɛˌanʃtaltʊn] die <–, –en> benefit concert Benefizkonzert [bena'fi:tskɔnˌtsɛ't] das <–(e)s, –e>
ⓔ **give sb the benefit of the doubt** im Zweifelsfall zu jds Gunsten entscheiden
benefit² ⓥⓔⓡⓑ *(get help or an advantage from sth)* benefit (from sth), stand to benefit (from sth) (von etw.) profitieren [profi'ti:rən] <profitiert, profitierte, hat profitiert> ◊ *Das ganze Land hat von den Investitionen profitiert.* ♦ *Wer profitiert davon?;* *(help sb/sth)* benefit sb/sth jdm/etw. nützen ['nʏtsn̩] +haben ◊ *Das neue Steuergesetz nützt vor allem den Reichen.*
benevolent ⓐⓓⓙ **1.** *(sympathetic)* wohlwollend ['vo:lvolənt] mostly before ns ◊ *ein wohlwollendes Lächeln; (ruler, deity)* gütig ['gy:tɪç] ◊ *Gott ist gütig.* **2.** *(charitable)* wohltätig ['vo:ltɛ:tɪç] mostly before ns ◊ *eine wohltätige Stiftung*
benevolently ⓐⓓⓥ wohlwollend ['vo:lvolənt] ◊ *Er lächelte ihm wohlwollend zu.*
benign ⓐⓓⓙ **1.** *(not malignant)* gutartig ['gu:t|a:'tɪç] ◊ *ein gutartiger Tumor* ♦ *Das Geschwür ist gutartig.* **2.** *(kind)* gütig ['gy:tɪç] ◊ *ein gütiger alter Herr*
bent → **bend²** ⓐⓓⓙ *(corrupt)* korrupt [kɔ'rʊpt] <korrupter, am korruptesten> ◊ *ein korrupter Polizist*
ⓔ **be bent on (doing) sth** etw. unbedingt (tun) wollen
berry ⓝⓞⓤⓝ Beere ['be:rə] die <–, –n>
beside ⓟⓡⓔⓟ **1.** *(next to)* neben ['ne:bn̩] with acc when expressing motion towards a place, with dat when there is no or undirected motion ◊ *Er setzte sich neben mich.* ♦ *Wer steht neben ihr?;* *(with certain ns, next to)* an [an] ⓓⓐⓣ ◊ *ein schöner Platz am Ufer* **2.** *(compared with)* verglichen mit [fɛ'glɪçn̩ mɪt] ⓓⓐⓣ

A B C D E F G H I J K L M N O P Q R S T U V W X Y Z

◊ *Verglichen mit Peter werde ich schlecht bezahlt.*
3. *(apart from, in addition to)* neben ['neːbm̩] +dat ◊ *Neben Goethe wurden noch andere berühmte Dichter besprochen.*

ⓔ **beside yourself (with sth)** (vor etw.) ganz außer sich ◊ *Er war vor Wut ganz außer sich.*

besides¹ adv außerdem ['aosedeːm] ◊ *Sie spielt Geige und außerdem Klavier.* ♦ *Außerdem müssen wir bedenken, dass dieses Projekt teuer wird.* **and lots more besides** und noch vieles mehr [ʊnt nɔx fiːləs 'meːɐ]

besides² prep außer ['aosɐ] +dat ◊ *Außer Anna und Dirk waren auch noch Andreas und Jule da.* **besides that** außerdem ['aosedeːm] ◊ *Sie arbeitet als Journalistin; außerdem schreibt sie Kurzgeschichten.* **besides being sth, sb is … ** jd ist nicht nur etw., sondern auch … [ɪst nɪçt nuːɐ … zɔndɐn aox] ◊ *Er ist nicht nur mein Kollege, sondern auch ein guter Freund.* **besides doing sth, sb …** jd tut nicht nur etw., sondern … auch … ◊ *Sie malt nicht nur, sondern spielt auch Klavier.*

besiege verb **1.** *(surround with troops, gather round)* belagern [bə'laːgɐn] <belagert, belagerte, hat belagert> ◊ *eine Burg belagern* ♦ *Tausende Fans belagerten nach dem Konzert den Bühnenausgang.* **2.** *(inundate with requests etc.)* **besiege sb/sth with sth** jdn/etw. mit etw. überschütten [mɪt … ybɐˌʃytn̩] <überschüttet, überschüttete, hat überschüttet> ◊ *Wir sind mit Anfragen überschüttet worden.*

best¹ noun **1.** *(abstract)* Beste ['bɛstə] das <–n> no pl ◊ *Für sie ist nur das Beste gut genug.* ♦ *Ich werde mein Bestes tun.* **the best of everything** von allem nur das Beste **2.** *(person)* Beste ['bɛstə] der/die <–n, –n> ◊ *Mutter ist die Beste!* ♦ *Er war der Beste von allen.* ♦ *Die Besten kommen in die nächste Runde.*

ⓔ **be simply/absolutely the best** einsame Spitze sein **all the best** alles Gute **at best** bestenfalls **at sb's best** in Hochform

best² adj beste ['bɛstə] *mostly before ns* <jds bester …, jds beste …, jds bestes …> ◊ *Mein bester Freund heißt Max.* ♦ *Er erfreut sich bester Gesundheit.* ♦ *Meine Kondition ist nicht gerade die beste.* ♦ *ein Produkt von bester Qualität* **make the best use of sth** etw. so gut wie möglich nutzen [zoː ˌguːt viː 'møːklɪç ˌnʊtsn̩] ◊ *Ich möchte meine Zeit hier so gut wie möglich nutzen.*

ⓔ **at the best of times** selbst an guten Tagen

best³ adv **1.** *(with the most effective outcome, most suitable, most pleasing)* am besten [am 'bɛstn̩] ◊ *Morgens kann ich am besten arbeiten.* ♦ *Was hat dir am besten gefallen?* ♦ *Wir sollten das tun, was für die Kinder am besten ist.* **do sth as best you can** etw. so gut machen, wie man kann [zoː 'guːt maxn̩ viː man 'kan] **2.** *(preferred)* am liebsten [am 'liːpstn̩] <am liebsten> etw. am liebsten haben ◊ *Welche Musik hast du am liebsten?* **best known** bekannteste [bə'kantəstə] ◊ *Spielbergs bekanntester Film* **best loved** beliebteste [bə'liːptəstə] ◊ *eine seiner beliebtesten Melodien*

ⓔ **sb had best do sth** am besten tut jd etw. ◊ *Am besten Sie kommen mit mir! Ich kenne den Weg.* **like doing sth best** etw. am liebsten tun ◊ *Martin spielt am liebsten Schach.*

bestow verb **bestow sth on sb 1.** *(a present, property, love)* jdm etw. schenken ['ʃɛŋkn̩] +haben ◊

Er schenkte ihr seine ganze Liebe. **2.** *(a right, medal, an honour)* jdm etw. verleihen [fɛ'laeən] <verleiht, verlieh, hat verliehen> ◊ *Ihr wurde das Recht verliehen, sich „Lady" zu nennen.*

best-seller noun **1.** *(book)* Bestseller ['bɛstsɛlɐ] der <–s, –> ◊ *Sie hat schon drei Bestseller geschrieben.* **2.** *(product)* Verkaufsschlager [fɛ'kaofsˌʃlaːgɐ] der <–s, –> ◊ *Dieses Modell ist unser absoluter Verkaufsschlager.*

bet¹ noun Wette ['vɛtə] die <–, –n> ◊ *Nimmst du die Wette an?* ♦ **eine Wette gegen jdn gewinnen/verlieren** take a bet **eine Wette abschließen** place a bet on **sth auf etw.** acc setzen [aof … zɛtsn̩] +haben ◊ *Er setzte auf rot.*

ⓔ **the/sb's best bet** das Beste **a good bet** ein guter Tipp **it's a safe bet that** man kann wohl davon ausgehen, dass

bet² verb *(gamble)* bet (sth) (on sth) (etw.) (auf etw. acc) wetten ['vɛtn̩] +haben ◊ *Wollen wir wetten? Ich wette, dass er durchfällt!* ♦ *Er hat 100 Euro auf ein Pferd gewettet.* **bet sb (sth)** mit jdm (um etw.) wetten; *(hope for sth)* **be betting on sth** auf etw. acc setzen [aof … zɛtsn̩] +haben ◊ *Sie haben darauf gesetzt, dass die Aktienkurse weiter steigen.*

ⓔ **don't bet on it, I wouldn't bet on it** da wäre ich mir nicht so sicher **I bet, I'll bet** das glaube ich dir **you bet und ob** ◊ *„Gehst du heute schwimmen?" — „Und ob! Bei der Hitze auf jeden Fall."*

betray verb **1.** *(a country, friend, secret)* verraten [fɛ'raːtn̩] <verrät, verriet, hat verraten> ◊ *Er hatte den Freund verraten.* **betray your beliefs/principles** seinen Prinzipien untreu werden [zaenən prɪnˌtsiːpiən 'ʊntrɔø veːɐdn̩] +sein **2.** *(sb's trust)* missbrauchen [mɪs'braoxn̩] <missbraucht, missbrauchte, hat missbraucht> ◊ *Du hast mein Vertrauen missbraucht.*

betrayal noun **1.** *(of a country, friend, secret)* Verrat [fɛ'raːt] der <–(e)s> no pl ◊ *Ich empfand die Kritik als Verrat am Bürgermeister.* **2.** *(of convictions)* Bruch [brʊx] der <–(e)s, Brüche> **betrayal of sth** Bruch mit etw. ◊ *ein Bruch mit seinen Prinzipien* **betrayal of trust** Vertrauensbruch [fɛ'traoənsbrʊx]

better adj, adv **1.** *(of superior quality, more advantageous)* besser ['bɛsɐ] ◊ *Er hat einen besseren Computer als ich.* ♦ *Ich hoffe, dass das Wetter bald besser wird.* ♦ *Dieses Hotel ist besser ausgestattet.* ♦ *Du solltest jetzt besser gehen.* **sth is no/little better (than)** etw. ist auch nicht/kaum besser (als) ◊ *Die Wahrheit zu verschweigen ist kaum besser als zu lügen.* **deserve better** etwas Besseres verdient haben **sb is better** jdm geht es besser **the sooner/bigger etc. the better** je schneller/größer etc., desto besser; *(improve)* **get better** sich verbessern [fɛ'bɛsɐn] <verbessert, verbesserte, hat verbessert> ◊ *Die Lage hat sich erheblich verbessert.; (healthier)* **get better** gesund werden [gə'zʊnt veːɐdn̩] +sein **better for sb** gesünder [gə'zʏndɐ] ◊ *Frisches Gemüse ist gesünder.* **2.** *(more)* **like sb/sth better** jdn/etw. lieber haben ['liːbɐ haːbm̩] +haben **better known** bekannter [bə'kantɐ]

ⓔ **all the better** umso besser **get better soon** gute Besserung **be better off 1.** *(in an improved situation)* besser dran sein **2.** *(financially)* reicher sein **sb had better do sth** jd tut am besten etw. ◊

Morgen gibt es einen Test. Wir bereiten uns am besten gründlich vor.
between¹ [adv] in between **1.** *(spatial)* dazwischen [dəˈtsvɪʃn] ◊ *Auf dem Foto stehen meine Eltern hinten, die Kinder vorn und die Großeltern dazwischen.* **2.** *(temporal)* zwischendurch [ˈtsvɪʃnˈdʊʳç] ◊ *Hast du zwischendurch mal Zeit für mich?*
between² [prep] zwischen [ˈtsvɪʃn] with acc when expressing motion towards a place, with dat when there is no or undirected motion ◊ *Der Junge drängte sich zwischen seine Eltern.* ♦ *Ich stand zwischen meinem Vater und meiner Mutter.* ♦ *zwischen Weihnachten und Neujahr* ♦ *der Unterschied zwischen Gut und Böse*
⊚ between us/you/them *(put together)* zusammen ◊ *Zusammen besitzen sie drei Autos.* between you and me, between ourselves unter uns gesagt
beverage [noun] Getränk [gəˈtrɛŋk] das <-(e)s, -e>
beyond¹ [adv] darüber hinaus [daryːbeˈhɪˈnaʊs] ◊ *Der Einfluss der Römer erstreckte sich über ganz Europa und darüber hinaus.*
beyond² [prep] **1.** *(on the other side of)* jenseits [ˈjeːnzaɛ̯ts] [+gen] ◊ *die Welt jenseits der Gefängnismauern* **2.** *(outside, not within the limits of)* über ... [acc] hinaus [yːbe ... hɪˈnaʊs] ◊ *Sein Ruf hatte sich weit über die Landesgrenzen hinaus verbreitet.* **3.** *(except)* außer [ˈaʊsɐ] [+dat] ◊ *Sie hatte kein Einkommen außer ihrer kleinen Rente.* **4.** *(over, above)* über [ˈyːbɐ] [+acc] ◊ *Die Inflationsrate war auf über 10 Prozent gestiegen.*
⊚ be beyond sb **1.** *(too difficult)* zu schwierig für jdn sein **2.** *(hard to understand)* it's beyond me why ... ich kann nicht begreifen, warum ... be beyond sth sb/sth is beyond help für jdn/etw. kommt jede Hilfe zu spät sb/sth is beyond control jd/etw. ist völlig außer Kontrolle sth is beyond repair etw. kann nicht mehr repariert werden
bias [noun] **1.** *(prejudice)* bias (against sb/sth) Voreingenommenheit (gegenüber jdm/etw.) [ˈfoːɐ̯|aɛ̯ŋɡənɔmənhaɛ̯t] die <-> ◊ *die Voreingenommenheit gegenüber anderen Kulturen* have a bias against sb/sth gegenüber jdm/etw. voreingenommen sein [ɡəˈøːyˈbeː ... ˈfoːɐ̯|aɛ̯ŋɡənɔmən zaɛ̯n] [+sein] without bias unvoreingenommen [ˈʊnfoːɐ̯|aɛ̯ŋɡənɔmən]; *(discrimination)* bias against sb/sth Benachteiligung ... [gen] die <-, -en> ◊ *die Benachteiligung älterer Arbeitnehmer*; *(preference)* bias towards sb/sth Bevorzugung ... [gen] [bəˈfoːɐ̯ts uːgʊn] die <-, -en> ◊ *die Bevorzugung umweltfreundlicher Technologien* have a bias towards sth jdn/etw. bevorzugen [bəˈfoːɐ̯ts uːgn] <bevorzugt, bevorzugte, hat bevorzugt> **2.** *(tendency)* bias (towards sth) Schwerpunkt (auf etw. [dat]) [ˈʃveːɐ̯pʊŋkt] der <-(e)s, -e> ◊ *ein Gymnasium mit sprachlichem Schwerpunkt* ♦ *ein Überblick über die japanische Kultur mit dem Schwerpunkt auf Literatur*
bib [noun] Latz [lats] der <-es, Lätze> ◊ *Sie band dem Kind einen Latz um.* ♦ *eine Hose mit Latz*
bible [noun] Bibel [ˈbiːbl] die <-, -n>
⊚ the Holy Bible die Heilige Schrift
bicycle [noun] Fahrrad [ˈfaːʳraːt] das <-(e)s, Fahrräder> ◊ *Er fuhr mit dem Fahrrad zur Schule.* ♦ *Sie kann nicht Fahrrad fahren.*
bid¹ [noun] **1.** *(at auctions)* Gebot [gəˈboːt] das <-(e)s, -e> ◊ *ein Gebot abgeben* **2.** *(offer)* Angebot

[ˈangəboːt] das <-(e)s, -e> ◊ *Diese Firma hat uns das beste Angebot gemacht.* takeover bid Übernahmeangebot [ˈyːbɐnaːmə|angəboːt] **3.** *(attempt)* bid to do sth Versuch, etw. zu tun [fɛˈzuːx ... tuː] der <-(e)s, -e> ◊ *Der Versuch, die Schule zu retten, war gelungen.* **4.** *(for a post)* Kandidatur [kandidaˈtuːɐ̯] die <-, -en> sb's bid for an office jds Kandidatur für ein Amt
bid² [verb] **1.** *(at an auction)* bieten [ˈbiːtn] <bietet, bot, hat geboten> ◊ *Das ist mir zu teuer; ich biete nicht mehr.* ♦ *Er bot 300 Euro für das Bild.* **2.** *(for a job etc.)* bid for sth sich um etw. bewerben [ʊm ... bəˌvɛˈbm] <bewirbt sich, bewarb sich, hat sich beworben> ◊ *Mehrere Bauunternehmen bewarben sich um den Auftrag.*
big [adj] **1.** *(large in size, amount or degree, elder, nearing adulthood)* groß [ɡroːs] <größer, am größten> ◊ *ein großes Haus* ♦ *Die Schuhe sind mir zu groß.* ♦ *Sie haben ganz große Probleme.* ♦ *Ich bin ein großer Fan von ihr.* ♦ *meine große Schwester* ♦ *Du bist doch schon ein großer Junge!* a big success ein Riesenerfolg [aen ˈriːznʲeˈfɔlk] <-(e)s, -e> a big smile ein strahlendes Lächeln [aen ˈʃtraːləndəs ˈlɛçln] <-s> no pl **2.** *(heavy)* kräftig [ˈkrɛftɪç] ◊ *ein kräftiger Mann* ♦ *Sie ist ziemlich kräftig.; (fat)* dick [dɪk] ◊ *einen dicken Bauch haben* **3.** *(important)* wichtig [ˈvɪçtɪç] ◊ *Nächste Woche haben wir ein wichtiges Spiel.* **4.** *(popular)* beliebt [bəˈliːpt] <beliebter, am beliebtesten> ◊ *Diese Gruppe ist in Japan sehr beliebt.; (successful)* erfolgreich [eˈfɔlkraeç] ◊ *erfolgreiche Geschäftsleute*
big wheel [noun] Riesenrad [ˈriːznraːt] das <-(e)s, Riesenräder>
bike [noun] Rad [raːt] das <-(e)s, Räder> ◊ *Sie lernt gerade Rad fahren.* ♦ *Wir nehmen die Räder in den Urlaub mit.*
⊚ on your bike mach die Fliege *(fam)*
bilberry [noun] Heidelbeere [ˈhaedlbeːrə] die <-, -n>
bile [noun] Galle [ˈgalə] die <-, -n>
bilingual(ly) [adj, adv] zweisprachig [ˈtsvaeʃpraːxɪç] no comp/superl ◊ *ein zweisprachiges Wörterbuch* ♦ *Seine Tochter ist zweisprachig: Sie spricht Französisch und Deutsch.* ♦ *zweisprachig aufwachsen*
bill [noun] **1.** *(for services, goods)* Rechnung [ˈrɛçnʊŋ] die <-, -en> ◊ *Lass mich die Rechnung bezahlen.* ♦ *eine Rechnung über 100 Euro* **2.** *(banknote)* Schein [ʃaen] der <-(e)s, -e> ◊ *Der Automat nimmt Münzen und Scheine.* **3.** LAW *(in parliament)* Gesetzesentwurf [gəˈzɛtsəs|ɛntvʊˈf] der <-(e)s, Gesetzesentwürfe> pass a bill ein Gesetz verabschieden [aen gəˈzɛts feˌapʃiːdn] <verabschiedet, verabschiedete, hat verabschiedet> **4.** *(poster)* Plakat [plaˈkaːt] das <-(e)s, -e> ◊ *ein Plakat ankleben/aufhängen* **5.** *(beak)* Schnabel [ˈʃnaːbl] der <-s, Schnäbel>
⊚ fill/fit the bill für den/die/das Richtige sein top the bill die Hauptattraktion sein
billion [noun] **1.** *(a thousand million)* Milliarde [mɪˈli̯aːdə] die <-, -n> ◊ *Er besitzt Milliarden.* in a billion years in einer Milliarde Jahren **2.** *(oldf) (in the UK: a million million)* Billion [bɪˈli̯oːn] die <-, -en> ◊ *Billionen von Wassertropfen*
⊚ billions of times tausendmal
bill of exchange [noun] Wechsel [ˈvɛksl] der <-s, ->
bin [noun] **1.** *(for rubbish, small)* Mülleimer [ˈmʏl|aemɐ] der <-s, ->; *(big)* Mülltonne [ˈmʏltɔnə] die <-, -n>

2. *(for storage)* Tonne ['tɔnə] die <–, –n> ◊ *eine Tonne mit Giftstoffen*

bind [verb] **1.** *(a book, papers, a sauce etc.)* binden ['bɪndn] <bindet, band, hat gebunden> ◊ *ein Buch binden lassen* ♦ *Binden Sie die Soße mit Mehl!* bind together zusammenbinden [tsu'zamənbɪndn̩] ◊ *Sie band die alten Zeitungen zusammen.* **2.** *(a prisoner, hands etc.)* fesseln ['fɛsl̩n] +haben ◊ *Sie fesselten den Gefangenen mit einem Seil an den Stuhl.* bound and gagged gefesselt und geknebelt **3.** *(a wound)* bind (up) verbinden [fɛ'bɪndn̩] <verbindet, verband, hat verbunden> **4.** *(unite)* bind sb together jdn verbinden [fɛ'bɪndn̩] <verbindet, verband, hat verbunden> ◊ *Der Kummer über die verlorenen Kinder verband sie.* **5.** *(oblige)* bind sb to do sth jdn verpflichten, etw. zu tun [fɛ'pflɪçtn̩ ... tsuː] <verpflichtet, verpflichtete, hat verpflichtet> ◊ *Dieser Vertrag verpflichtet Sie dazu, die Wohnung beim Auszug zu renovieren.*

binding ← bind [adj] verbindlich [fɛ'bɪntlɪç] ◊ *eine verbindliche Abmachung* binding (on/upon sb/sth) (für jdn/etw.) verbindlich ◊ *Ist diese Regel für alle Teilnehmer verbindlich?*

binoculars [noun] Fernglas ['fɛˈŋglaːs] das <–s, Ferngläser> ◊ *Sie beobachtete die Vögel mit dem Fernglas.*

bio... [prefix] **1.** *(with adjectives)* bio... ['biːoː] ◊ *ein biochemischer Prozess* **2.** *(with nouns)* Bio... ['biːoː] ◊ *Biosphäre*

biography [noun] Biografie [biogra'fiː] die <–, –n>

biological [adj] **1.** *(relating to biology)* biologisch [bio'loːgɪʃ] no comp/superl, mostly before ns ◊ *biologische Merkmale* be biological biologische Ursachen haben ◊ *Haben Depressionen biologische Ursachen?* **2.** *(mother, father)* leiblich ['laɛplɪç] no comp/superl, only before ns ◊ *die leiblichen Eltern*

biologically [adj] biologisch [bio'loːgɪʃ] no comp/superl ◊ *biologisch aktiv*

biologist [noun] Biologe [bio'loːgə] der <–n, –n> ♀Biologin [bio'loːgɪn] die <–, –nen> ◊ *Er ist ein berühmter Biologe.* ♦ *Sie ist Biologin von Beruf.*

biology [noun] Biologie [biolo'giː] die <–> no pl ◊ *Biologie studieren* ♦ *die Biologie der Honigbiene*

birch [noun] Birke ['bɪrkə] die <–, –n>

bird [noun] **1.** *(animal)* Vogel ['foːgl] der <–s, Vögel> ◊ *Im Herbst ziehen viele Vögel nach Süden.* **2.** *(young woman)* Braut [braɔt] die <–, Bräute> *(slang)* ◊ *eine heiße Braut*
ⓔ be strictly for the birds reine Zeitverschwendung sein a bird in the hand is worth two in the bush der Spatz in der Hand ist besser als die Taube auf dem Dach the bird has flown der Vogel ist ausgeflogen

biro™ [noun] Kugelschreiber ['kuːgl̩ʃraɛbe] der <–s, –> ◊ *mit Kugelschreiber schreiben*

birth [noun] **1.** *(event)* Geburt [gə'buːgt] die <–, –en> ◊ *Bei der Geburt ihres zweiten Kindes war sie 36 Jahre alt.* ♦ *An Weihnachten wird Christi Geburt gefeiert.* ♦ *Sie ist von Geburt an blind.* a Swede etc. by birth ein gebürtiger Schwede etc. [aɛn gəbʏˈtɪgɐ 'ʃveːdɐ] a Swede etc. by birth eine gebürtige Schwedin etc. [aɛnə gəbʏˈtɪgɐ 'ʃveːdɪn]; *(process of giving birth)* Entbindung [ɛnt'bɪndʊŋ] die <–, –en> ◊ *eine Entbindung durch Kaiserschnitt* give birth to sb jdn gebären [gə'bɛːrən] <gebiert, gebar, hat geboren> ◊ *Sie hat gestern einen Jungen geboren.* **2.** *(fig) (of an*

idea, institution) Entstehung [ɛnt'ʃteːʊŋ] die <–, –en> give birth to sth zur Entstehung ... [gen] führen

birth certificate [noun] Geburtsurkunde [gə'buːgts|uːgkʊndə] die <–, –n>

birthday [noun] Geburtstag [gə'buːgtstaːk] der <–(e)s, –e> ◊ *Er feiert heute seinen 80. Geburtstag.* ♦ *Sie hat morgen Geburtstag.* wish sb a happy birthday jdm zum Geburtstag gratulieren birthday card Geburtstagskarte [gə'buːgtstaːkskaˈtə] die <–, –n> birthday present Geburtstagsgeschenk [gə'buːgtstaːksgəʃɛŋk] das <–s, –e>
ⓔ happy birthday herzlichen Glückwunsch zum Geburtstag

birthmark [noun] Muttermal ['mʊtemaːl] das <–s, –e>

biscuit [noun] **1.** *(in the UK: small pastry, homemade)* Plätzchen ['plɛtsçən] das <–s, –> ◊ *Sie haben Plätzchen gebacken.; (from the shops)* Keks [keːks] der <–es, –e> **2.** *(in the US: bread roll)* Brötchen ['brøːtsçən] das <–s, –>
ⓔ take the biscuit wirklich die Höhe sein

bishop [noun] **1.** REL Bischof ['bɪʃɔf] der <–s, Bischöfe> ♀Bischöfin ['bɪʃœfɪn] die <–, –nen> ◊ *jdn zum Bischof weihen* **2.** CHESS Läufer ['lɔøfe] der <–s, –>

bit [noun] **1.** *(small amount, short period)* a bit ein bisschen [aɛn 'bɪsçən] ◊ *Ich bin ein bisschen müde.* ♦ *Du musst ein bisschen warten.* not one little bit kein bisschen a bit of etwas ['ɛtvas] ◊ *Mit etwas Glück schaffen wir es noch.* for a bit eine Zeit lang [aɛnə 'tsaɛt laŋ] ◊ *Du kannst eine Zeit lang bei uns wohnen.* in a bit gleich [glaɛç] ◊ *Ich mache die Hausaufgaben gleich.* **2.** *(piece)* Stück [ʃtʏk] das <–(e)s, –e or –> ◊ *ein Stück Brot; (smaller)* Stückchen ['ʃtʏkçən] das <–s, –> ◊ *Möchtest du ein Stückchen von meinem Kuchen probieren?* **3.** *(of a jigsaw puzzle etc.)* Teil [taɛl] das <–(e)s, –e> ◊ *Dem Puzzle fehlen ein paar Teile.; (in a film, book, story)* Stelle ['ʃtɛlə] die <–, –n> ◊ *die beste Stelle im Film; (of a job)* Aspekt [as'pɛkt] der <–(e)s, –e> ◊ *Dieser Aspekt meiner Arbeit gefällt mir nicht so gut.* **4.** IT Bit [bɪt] das <–(s), –(s)> **5.** *(part of a bridle)* Gebiss [gə'bɪs] das <–es, –e> ◊ *Er schob dem Pferd das Gebiss ins Maul.* **6.** *(tool)* Bohrer ['boːrɐ] der <–s, –>
ⓔ a bit on the side eine Affäre be a bit of all right nicht schlecht sein quite a bit (of) ziemlich viel ◊ *Er hat ziemlich viel abgenommen.* ♦ *Das hat mich ziemlich viel Mühe gekostet.* do your bit seinen Teil beitragen bit by bit nach und nach

bitch [noun] **1.** *(dog)* Hündin ['hʏndɪn] die <–, –nen> **2.** *(woman)* Miststück ['mɪstʃtʏk] das <–(e)s, –e> *(fam, pej)*

bite¹ [noun] **1.** *(act of biting)* Biss [bɪs] der <–es, –e> give sb a bite jdn beißen ['baɛsn̩] <beißt, biss, hat gebissen> ◊ *Der Hund biss ihn ins Bein.; (wound)* Bisswunde ['bɪsvʊndə] die <–, –(n)>; *(by an insect)* Stich [ʃtɪç] der <–(e)s, –e> ◊ *Die Stiche entzündeten sich.* **2.** *(small piece of food)* Bissen ['bɪsn̩] der <–s, –> ◊ *Nach dem ersten Bissen war sie schon satt.* have a bite of sth von etw. abbeißen [fɔn ... ˌapbaɛsn̩] <beißt ab, biss ab, hat abgebissen> ◊ *Darf ich mal von deinem Brot abbeißen?* **3.** *(snack)* a bite (to eat) eine Kleinigkeit (zu essen) [aɛnə 'klaɛnɪçkaɛt] die <–, –en> have a bite to eat eine Kleinigkeit essen **4.** *(strong taste)* Schärfe

['ʃɛˈfə] die <–> no pl ◊ *Der Curry hat echte Schärfe.*
♦ *Die Schärfe der Soße kann man mit Sahne mildern.*
bite² ⟨verb⟩ **1.** *(with teeth)* beißen ['baɛsn] <beißt, biss, hat gebissen> ◊ *Eine Schlange hat ihn gebissen.* ♦ *Komm doch näher, der Hund beißt nicht!* ♦ *Er biss in sein Brot.* bite your nails an den Nägeln kauen [an deːn 'nɛːgln ˌkaʊən] +haben **2.** *(fish)* anbeißen ['anbaɛsn] <beißt an, biss an, hat angebissen> ◊ *Die Fische wollen heute nicht anbeißen.* **3.** *(insect)* stechen ['ʃtɛçn] <sticht, stach, hat gestochen> ⑳ once bitten twice shy ein gebranntes Kind scheut das Feuer
biting → ² ⟨adj⟩ scharf [ʃaˈf] <schärfer, am schärfsten> *mostly before ns* ◊ *scharfe Kritik* ♦ *ein scharfer Wind*
bitter ⟨adj⟩ **1.** *(taste, disappointment)* bitter ['bɪtɐ] ◊ *Das Medikament schmeckt sehr bitter.* ♦ *eine bittere Enttäuschung* a bitter blow ein schwerer Schlag [aɛn ˌʃveːrə 'ʃlaːk] <–(e)s, Schläge> **2.** *(angry and disappointed, upset)* verbittert [fɛ'bɪtɐt] ◊ *Sie hat einen verbitterten Zug um den Mund.* be bitter *(about sth)* (über etw. ⟨acc⟩) verbittert sein **3.** *(wind)* bitterkalt ['bɪtɐˈkalt] *no comp/superl* ◊ *ein bitterkalter Wind* **4.** *(critic, opposition, fight)* erbittert [ɛ'bɪtɐt] ◊ *auf erbitterte Kritik stoßen*
bitterly ⟨adv⟩ **1.** *(complain, disappoint)* bitter ['bɪtɐ] ◊ *Du hast mich bitter enttäuscht.* **2.** *(oppose, fight)* erbittert [ɛ'bɪtɐt] ◊ *erbittert kämpfen* **3.** bitterly cold bitterkalt ['bɪtɐˈkalt]
bitterness ⟨noun⟩ **1.** *(of taste)* bitterer Geschmack [ˌbɪtərə ɡə'ʃmak] <–, bittere Geschmäcke> ◊ *der bittere Geschmack der Schokolade* **2.** *(of disposition)* Verbitterung [fɛ'bɪtərʊŋ] die <–> no pl ◊ *Seine Verbitterung über ihren Verrat war groß.* **3.** *(of the wind)* Schärfe ['ʃɛˈfə] die <–> no pl ◊ *Die Schärfe des Windes tat web.*
bizarre ⟨adj⟩ *(event, coincidence)* seltsam ['zɛltzaːm] ◊ *ein seltsamer Zufall* ♦ *Das ist wirklich seltsam.*
black¹
⑳ in the black in den schwarzen Zahlen
black² ⟨adj⟩ **1.** *(colo(u)r)* schwarz [ʃvaˈts] <schwärzer, am schwärzesten> ◊ *schwarzes Haar* ♦ *Deine Fingernägel sind ja ganz schwarz.* ♦ *Sie trinkt am liebsten schwarzen Kaffee.* ♦ *schwarzer Humor* ♦ *Sie hat ihr Zimmer schwarz gestrichen.* **2.** *(look, mood)* finster ['fɪnstɐ] ◊ *ein finsterer Blick*
blackboard ⟨noun⟩ Tafel ['taːfl] die <–, –n> ◊ *Wer möchte an der Tafel vorrechnen?*
blackmail ⟨verb⟩ erpressen [ɛ'prɛsn] <erpresst, erpresste, hat erpresst> ◊ *Jemand hat versucht, ihn mit den Fotos zu erpressen.* ♦ *Wir lassen uns nicht erpressen.* blackmail sb into doing sth jdn durch Erpressung dazu zwingen, etw. zu tun [dʊ'ç ɛˌprɛsʊŋ daːtsuː 'tsvɪŋən ... tsuː] <zwingt, zwang, hat gezwungen>
bladder ⟨noun⟩ Blase ['blaːzə] die <–, –n> ◊ *eine empfindliche Blase haben*
blade ⟨noun⟩ **1.** *(of a knife etc.)* Klinge ['klɪŋə] die <–, –n> ◊ *Das Schwert hatte eine stumpfe Klinge.* **2.** *(on an ice-skate)* Kufe ['kuːfə] die <–, –n> **3.** *(of grass, wheat etc.)* Halm [halm] der <–(e)s, –e> blade of grass Grashalm ['graːshalm] **4.** *(of a propeller, helicopter)* Flügel ['flyːgl] der <–s, –> **5.** *(of an oar)* Blatt [blat] das <–(e)s, Blätter>
blame¹ ⟨noun⟩ blame (for sth) Schuld (an etw. ⟨dat⟩) [ʃʊlt] die <–> no pl get the blame for sth die

Schuld an etw. ⟨dat⟩ zugeschoben bekommen lay the blame on sb jdm die Schuld geben take the blame der Verantwortung übernehmen [diː fɛ|'antvɔˈtʊŋ ybɐˌneːmən] <übernimmt, übernahm, hat übernommen>
blame² ⟨verb⟩ blame sb/sth (for sth) jdm/einer Sache die Schuld (an etw. ⟨dat⟩) geben [diː 'ʃʊlt ɡeːbm̩] <gibt, gab, hat gegeben> ◊ *Sie geben den Lehrern die Schuld an den schlechten Leistungen der Schüler.* blame sth on sb/sth die Schuld für etw. auf jdn/etw. schieben [diː ʃʊlt fyːɐ ... aofˌ ... ʃiːbm̩] <schiebt, schob, hat geschoben> be to blame (for sth) (für etw.) verantwortlich sein [fɛ|'antvɔˈtlɪç zaɛn] +sein ♦ don't blame me beschwer dich nicht bei mir I don't blame you das kann ich dir/Ihnen nicht verdenken you have only got yourself to blame das ist deine/Ihre eigene Schuld
blank¹ ⟨noun⟩ **1.** *(on a form)* leeres Feld [ˌleːrəs 'fɛlt] <–(e)s, –er> **2.** *(gun cartridge)* Platzpatrone ['platspaˌtroːnə] die <–, –n> **3.** *(in a raffle)* Niete ['niːtə] die <–, –n> ◊ *Ich habe nur Nieten gezogen.*
blank² ⟨adj⟩ **1.** *(sheet, wall, tape, disc)* leer [leːɐ] ◊ *ein leeres Blatt Papier* ♦ *Die Kassette ist leer.; (screen)* schwarz [ʃvaˈts] ◊ *ein schwarzer Bildschirm* go blank schwarz werden; (on a form) leave sth blank etw. nicht ausfüllen [nɪçt 'aosfʏlən] +haben **2.** *(showing no emotion)* ausdruckslos ['aosdrʊksloːs] <ausdrucksloser, am ausdruckslosesten> ◊ *ausdruckslose Augen* ♦ *Sein Gesicht war völlig ausdruckslos.; (baffled)* verdutzt [fɛ'dʊtst] <verdutzter, am verdutztesten> ◊ *sein verdutzter Gesichtsausdruck*
blanket ⟨noun⟩ Decke ['dɛkə] die <–, –n> ◊ *Sie wickelte sich in die Decke und schlief ein.* blanket of clouds Wolkendecke ['vɔlkn̩dɛkə] blanket of snow Schneedecke ['ʃneːdɛkə]
⑳ blanket of secrecy Mantel der Verschwiegenheit
blare ⟨verb⟩ blare (out) plärren ['plɛrən] +haben (pej) sth blares out sth, sth blares from sth etw. plärrt aus etw. ◊ *Rockmusik plärrte aus dem Radio.* with their horns blaring laut hupend [ˌlaot 'huːpm̩t]
blast¹ ⟨noun⟩ **1.** *(of a bomb)* Explosion [ɛksplo'zjoːn] die <–, –en> ◊ *Bei der Explosion kamen zehn Menschen ums Leben.* **2.** *(current)* blast of wind Windstoß ['vɪntʃtoːs] der <–es, Windstöße> blast of cold air kalter Luftzug [ˌkaltə 'lʊftsuːk] <–(e)s, Luftzüge> **3.** *(sound)* Tuten ['tuːtn̩] das <–s> ◊ *das Tuten eines Schiffes; (of a siren etc.)* let out a short blast kurz tuten [kʊˈts 'tuːtn̩] +haben
⑳ a blast of criticism scharfe Kritik a blast of music schallende Musik
blast² ⟨verb⟩ **1.** *(destroy)* zerstören [tsɛˈʃtøːrən] <zerstört, zerstörte, hat zerstört> ◊ *Eine Autobombe zerstörte die Polizeiwache.; (blow up)* blast through sth. sprengen ['ʃprɛŋən] +haben ◊ *Die Armee sprengte die Absperrungen.* blast a hole in sth ein Loch in etw. ⟨acc⟩ sprengen; (shoot sb) blast sb away jdn wegpusten ['vɛkpuːstn̩] <pustet weg, pustete weg, hat weggepustet> (fam) **2.** *(rain)* prasseln ['prasln̩] <prasselte, hat geprasselt> +haben ◊ *Regen prasselte gegen die Windschutzscheibe.* **3.** *(music)* blast out plärren ['plɛrən] +haben ◊ *Aus dem Autoradio plärrte laute Musik.; (hoot)* blast your horn laut hupen [ˌlaot 'huːpm̩] +haben **4.** *(criticize)* blast sb/sth jdn/etw. heruntermachen [hɛ'rʊntɐmaxn̩] +haben (fam) ◊ *einen Vorschlag heruntermachen* **5.** *(a ball)* knallen ['knalən] +haben (fam)

◊ *Sie knallte den Ball ins Tor.*

⊛ **blast** it verflixt ◊ *Verflixt, ich habe meinen Schlüssel verloren!*

blatant [adj] offensichtlich ['ɔfṇzɪçtlɪç] ◊ *eine ganz offensichtliche Verletzung unserer Rechte*; (lie, fraud) glatt [glat] no comp/superl; (attempt, provocation, plagiarism) dreist [draest] <dreister, dreisteste> sth is a blatant rip-off (of sth) etw. ist dreist (bei etw.) abgekupfert

blaze[1] [noun] **1.** (fire) Feuersbrunst ['fɔøesbrʊnst] die <–, Feuersbrünste> ◊ *Er starb in einer Feuersbrunst.* **2.** (a lot of sth) blaze of colo(u)r Farbenmeer ['fa'bṃme:ɐ] das <–(e)s, –e> blaze of light Lichtermeer ['lɪçteme:ɐ] blaze of publicity großes Aufsehen [gro:səs 'aofze:ən] <–> no pl ◊ *Die Ausstellung wurde unter großem Aufsehen eröffnet.*

⊛ in a blaze of glory mit Glanz und Gloria

blaze[2] [verb] **1.** (fire) brennen ['brɛnən] <brennt, brannte, hat gebrannt> ◊ *Das Feuer brannte die ganze Nacht.*; (sun) blaze down on sb auf jdn niederbrennen [aof ... ˌni:debrɛnən] ◊ *Die Sonne brannte auf uns nieder.* **2.** (lights, colo(u)rs) erstrahlen [ɛ'ʃtra:lən] <erstrahlt, erstrahlte, ist erstrahlt> ◊ *In der Stadt erstrahlten die Lichter.* blaze with colo(u)r in hellen Farben erstrahlen [ɪn hɛlən 'fa'bṃ ɛʃtra:lən] **3.** (eyes) blitzen ['blɪtsṇ] +haben blaze with anger ärgerlich blitzen

blazing → **blaze**[2] [adj] **1.** (flame, fire, torch) lodernd ['lo:dent] ◊ *lodernde Flammen*; (sun) prall [pral] ◊ *Leg dich nicht in die pralle Sonne.* blazing hot glühend heiß [ˌgly:ənt 'haes] no comp/superl ◊ *ein glühend heißer Sommer* ♦ *Der Asphalt war glühend heiß.* **2.** (fig) (start, success) glänzend ['glɛntsṇt] ◊ *ein glänzender Erfolg* be off to a blazing start einen glänzenden Anfang gemacht haben; (row) heftig ['hɛftɪç] ◊ *ein heftiger Streit*

bleak [adj] **1.** (future, look) düster ['dy:ste] ◊ *Die Zukunft sieht ziemlich düster aus.* ♦ *ein düsterer Gesichtsausdruck* paint a bleak picture of sth etw. in düsteren Farben schildern **2.** (weather, suroundings) trostlos ['tro:stlo:s] <trostloser, am trostlosesten> ◊ *trostloses Regenwetter* ♦ *Die Stadt wirkt ziemlich trostlos.*; (barren) öde ['ø:də] <öder, am ödesten> ◊ *eine öde Landschaft*

bleat [verb] **1.** (goat) meckern ['mɛken] <meckerte, hat gemeckert> +haben; (sheep) blöken ['blø:kṇ] +haben **2.** (complain) jammern ['jamen] <jammerte, hat gejammert> +haben ◊ *über etw.* [acc] *jammern*

bleed [verb] **1.** bluten ['blu:tṇ] <blutet, blutete, hat geblutet> ◊ *Die Wunde blutet immer noch.* ♦ *Er blutete stark.* bleed from sth aus etw. bluten ◊ *Sie blutete aus der Nase.* bleed to death verbluten [fe'blu:tṇ] <verblutet, verblutete, ist verblutet> **2.** bleed sb for sth jdm etw. abknöpfen ['apknœpfṇ] +haben ◊ *Ich knöpfte ihm 50 Euro ab.* bleed sb dry jdm alles abknöpfen **3.** (colo(u)r) abfärben ['apfɛ:bṃ] +haben ◊ *Das Blau von dem neuen T-Shirt hat abgefärbt.* **4.** (a radiator) entlüften [ɛnt'lʏftṇ] <entlüftet, entlüftete, hat entlüftet> ◊ *den Heizkörper entlüften*

bleeding [noun] Blutung ['blu:tʊŋ] die <–, –en> ◊ *eine Blutung stillen* ♦ *innere Blutungen*

blemish [noun] (sth that spoils sth) Makel ['ma:kḷ] der <–s, –> ◊ *ein äußerer Makel* ♦ *ein Makel in jds Biografie*; (stain) Fleck [flɛk] der <–(e)s, –en> ◊ *Flecken auf der Haut*

blend [noun] Mischung ['mɪʃʊŋ] die <–, –en> ◊ *eine Mischung erlesener Kaffeesorten*

bless [verb] segnen ['ze:gnən] +haben ◊ *die Ernte segnen* ♦ *Gott segne dich!* be blessed with sth mit etw. gesegnet sein; (consecrate) weihen ['vaeən] +haben

⊛ **bless you** Gesundheit

blessing [noun] Segen ['ze:gṇ] der <–s, –> ◊ *Das gute Wetter ist ein Segen für die Bauern.* ♦ um Gottes Segen bitten give sb/sth your blessing jdm/etw. seinen Segen geben ◊ *Der Chef hat dem neuen Projekt seinen Segen gegeben.* with sb's blessing mit jds Zustimmung [mɪt ... 'tsu:ʃtɪmʊŋ] die <–> no pl ⊛ a blessing in disguise schließlich doch ein Segen

blind[1] [adj] **1.** (person) blind [blɪnt] <blinder, am blindesten> ◊ *Sie ist von Geburt an blind.* ♦ *Er ist auf einem Auge blind.* ♦ *In seiner blinden Wut hat er alles zerschlagen.* go blind erblinden [e'blɪndṇ] <erblindet, erblindete, ist erblindet>; (unable to realize the truth) be blind to sth etw. nicht sehen [nɪçt 'ze:ən] <sieht, sah, hat gesehen> ◊ *Er sieht die Probleme nicht.* **2.** (bend) unübersichtlich ['ʊnly:bezɪçtlɪç] ◊ *eine unübersichtliche Kurve*

blind[2] [verb] **1.** (make sb unable to see or realize) blenden ['blɛndṇ] <blendet, blendete, hat geblendet> ◊ *Die Sonne blendete sie.* ♦ *Er hat sich von dem vielen Geld blenden lassen.* blind sb to sth jdn für etw. blind machen [fy:ɐ ... 'blɪnt maxṇ] +haben ◊ *Seine Liebe machte ihn blind für ihre Fehler.* **2.** (lose your eyesight) be blinded in sth bei etw. sein Augenlicht verlieren [bae ... zaen 'aoglɪçt fe,li:rən] <verliert, verlor, hat verloren> ◊ *bei einem Autounfall sein Augenlicht verlieren*

blindfold [noun] Augenbinde ['aoglbɪndə] die <–, –n>

blindly [adv] **1.** (without thinking) blind [blɪnt] <blinder, am blindesten> ◊ *Du solltest ihr nicht blind vertrauen.* **2.** (in a rage) wie blind [vi: 'blɪnt] ◊ *Sie schlug wie blind auf ihn ein.*

blink [verb] **1.** (close your eyes briefly) blink (your eyes) blinzeln ['blɪntsḷn] +haben blink away the tears die Tränen zurückhalten [di: 'trɛ:nən tsu,rʏkhaltṇ] <hält zurück, hielt zurück, hat zurückgehalten> **2.** (light) blinken ['blɪŋkṇ] +haben ◊ *An deinem PC blinkt ein Lämpchen.*

blister [noun] Blase ['bla:zə] die <–, –n> ◊ *Ich habe mir Blasen gelaufen.*

bloc [noun] Block [blɔk] der <–(e)s, Blöcke> ◊ *der kommunistische Block*

block[1] [noun] **1.** (of houses, text, stone, ice, wood) Block [blɔk] der <–(e)s, –e or Blöcke> ◊ *Sie wohnt in einem Block mit sechs Etagen.* ♦ *Ich gehe mal kurz mit dem Hund um den Block.* ♦ *Blöcke aus dem Eis schlagen* block of flats/apartments Wohnblock ['vo:nblɔk]; (smaller, of wood) Klotz [klɔts] der <–es, Klötze> ◊ *die Tür mit einem Klotz aufhalten* **2.** (obstacle, impediment) Hindernis ['hɪndenɪs] das <–ses, –se> ◊ *Bequemlichkeit ist das größte Hindernis auf dem Weg zum Erfolg.*; (blockage) Verstopfung [fe'ʃtɔpfʊŋ] die <–, –en> ◊ *eine Verstopfung der Wasserleitung* mental block geistige Blockade [ˌgaestɪgə blɔ'ka:də] die <–, –n> most sing **3.** (period of time) Zeitraum ['tsaetraom] der <–(e)s, Zeiträume> a four-hour block ein Zeitraum von vier Stunden

⊛ put a block on sth einer Sache [dat] einen

Riegel vorschieben

block² [verb] **1.** *(obstruct)* blockieren [blɔ'kiːrən] <blockiert, blockierte, hat blockiert> ◊ *Der Kran blockierte die Straße.* ♦ *Die Opposition blockiert die Reformen.; (a punch)* abfangen ['apfaŋən] <fängt ab, fing ab, hat abgefangen> ◊ *Er fing den Schlag mit seinem Unterarm ab.* block sb's sth jdm etw. versperren [fɛ'ʃpɛrən] <versperrt, versperrte, hat versperrt> ◊ *Setz dich bitte hin; du versperrst mir die Sicht.* **2.** ɪɪ *(highlight)* markieren [maʳ'kiːrən] <markiert, markierte, hat markiert> ◊ *einen Absatz markieren*

• **block in** [phras v] block sb/sth in *(a driver or vehicle)* jdn/etw. einkeilen ['aɛnkaɛlən] +haben ◊ *Unser Wagen war in der engen Parklücke eingekeilt.*

• **block off** [phras v] block sth off etw. blockieren [blɔ'kiːrən] <blockiert, blockierte, hat blockiert> ◊ *Geröll blockierte die Straße.*

• **block out** [phras v] block sth out **1.** *(light, noise)* etw. abhalten ['aphaltn] <hält ab, hielt ab, hat abgehalten> ◊ *Der dünne Vorhang hält nicht genug Licht ab.; (more than desired)* etw. wegnehmen ['vɛkneːmən] <nimmt weg, nahm weg, hat weggenommen> ◊ *Die alte Eiche vor dem Fenster nimmt viel Licht weg.* **2.** *(a thought, memory)* etw. verdrängen [fɛ'drɛŋən] <verdrängt, verdrängte, hat verdrängt> ◊ *Sie hat diese Erinnerung verdrängt.* **3.** *(give an outline of)* etw. skizzieren [skɪ'tsiːrən] <skizziert, skizzierte, hat skizziert> ◊ *Ich skizziere kurz, worum es geht.*

blockade [verb] blockieren [blɔ'kiːrən] <blockiert, blockierte, hat blockiert> ◊ *Die Schiffe blockierten den Hafen.*

blockage [noun] Verstopfung [fɛ'ʃtɔpfʊŋ] die <-, -en> ◊ *eine Verstopfung im Abfluss* ♦ *die Verstopfung eines Blutgefäßes*

bloke [noun] Typ [tyːp] der <-s, -en> *(fam)* ◊ *Wer ist der Typ da neben Birgit?*

blonde¹ [adj] blond [blɔnt] <blonder, am blondesten> seldom comp/superl ◊ *Mein Mann ist blond.* ♦ *blondes Haar*

blonde² [noun] Blondine [blɔn'diːnə] die <-, -n> ◊ *eine attraktive Blondine*

blood [noun] Blut [bluːt] das <-(e)s> *no pl* ◊ *Du hast Blut an deinem Hemd.* ♦ *Sie hat spanisches Blut in den Adern.* give blood Blut spenden

◉ sb has blood on their hands an jds Händen klebt Blut bad blood böses Blut in cold blood kaltblütig make your blood run cold jdm das Blut in den Adern gefrieren lassen (the) new blood (der) Nachwuchs sth is in your blood etw. liegt jdm im Blut spill blood Blut vergießen

blood pressure [noun] Blutdruck ['bluːtdrʊk] der <-(e)s> *no pl* ◊ *den Blutdruck messen*

blood vessel [noun] Blutgefäß ['bluːtgəfɛːs] das <-es, -e>

bloody¹ [adj] **1.** *(expression of anger or irritation)* Scheiß... [ʃaɛs] *(rude)* the bloody door die Scheißtür [diː 'ʃaɛs'tyːɐ̯] <-, -en> *(rude)* **2.** *(covered in blood, involving the loss of blood)* blutig ['bluːtɪç] ◊ *Der Verband war ganz blutig.* ♦ *blutige Auseinandersetzungen*

bloody² [adv] scheiß... [ʃaɛs...] *(rude)* bloody cold scheißkalt ['ʃaɛs'kalt] *(rude)*

bloom [noun] **1.** *(of flowers)* Blüte ['blyːtə] die <-, -n> ◊ *Der Baum hatte rosa Blüten.* ♦ *die Blüte der Man-*

delbäume im Frühjahr ♦ *Die Blumen standen in voller Blüte.* ♦ *Sie starb in der Blüte ihrer Jugend.* **2.** *(of sb's skin)* rosiger Schimmer [ˌroːzɪgɐ 'ʃɪmɐ] der <-s> *no pl* ◊ *Ein rosiger Schimmer lag auf ihren Wangen.*

blossom [noun] Blüte ['blyːtə] die <-, -n> ◊ *Der Baum hat gelbe Blüten.* ♦ *Der Kirschbaum steht in voller Blüte.*

blotchy [adj] fleckig ['flɛkɪç] ◊ *ein fleckiges Gesicht* ♦ *Meine Haut war fleckig.*

blouse [noun] Bluse ['bluːzə] die <-, -n> ◊ *eine kurzärmelige Bluse*

blow¹ [noun] Schlag [ʃlaːk] der <-(e)s, Schläge> ◊ *Er gab ihm einen heftigen Schlag auf den Kopf.* ♦ *Der Tod ihres Vaters war ein schwerer Schlag für sie.*

◉ trade blows sich prügeln

blow² [verb] **1.** *(wind, breeze, waft, object in the wind)* wehen ['veːən] +haben ◊ *Der Wind weht heute stärker als gestern.* ♦ *Mein Hut wurde ins Wasser geweht.* ♦ *Ihre Haare wehten im Wind.* blow in hereinwehen [hɛ'raɛnveːən] transitive use +haben/ intransitive use +sein ◊ *Der Wind hat die Blätter hereingeweht.* ♦ *Ein kühler Luftzug wehte zur Tür herein.* **2.** *(with your lips)* blasen ['blaːzn] <bläst, blies, hat geblasen> ◊ *blasen, damit die Suppe abkühlt* ♦ *ins Horn blasen* blow the whistle pfeifen ['pfaɛfn] <pfeift, pfiff, hat gepfiffen> ◊ *Der Schiedsrichter pfiff.* blow sth off etw. wegblasen ['vɛkblaːzn] <bläst weg, blies weg, hat weggeblasen> ◊ *Sie blies den Staub weg.* **3.** *(electrical device)* durchbrennen ['dʊrçbrɛnən] <brennt durch, brannte durch, ist durchgebrannt> ◊ *Die Glühbirne ist durchgebrannt.* **4.** *(tyre)* platzen ['platsn] +sein ◊ *Mitten auf der Autobahn platzte der Vorderreifen.* **5.** *(an opportunity)* vermasseln [fɛ'masln] <vermasselt, vermasselte, hat vermasselt> *(fam)* ◊ *Ich glaub, ich hab die Prüfung vermasselt.* **6.** *(money)* verpulvern [fɛ'pʊlfɐn] <verpulvert, verpulverte, hat verpulvert> *(fam)* ◊ *Sie hat schon ihr ganzes Taschengeld verpulvert.* **7.** *(in the US)* blow this joint von hier verschwinden [fɔn hiːɐ̯ fɛ'ʃvɪndn] <verschwindet, verschwand, ist verschwunden> ◊ *Wir verschwinden jetzt besser von hier!*

◉ blow it Mist *(fam)* blow me **1.** *(expressing surprise)* mich trifft der Schlag *(fam)* **2.** *(expressing anger)* Mist *(fam)*

• **blow apart** [phras v] **1.** *(a building, car)* in die Luft sprengen [ɪn diː 'lʊft ʃprɛŋən] +haben **2.** *(a myth, misconception, belief)* zerstören [tsɛ'ʃtøːrən] <zerstört, zerstörte, hat zerstört> ◊ *Er hat meinen Glauben an das Gute im Menschen zerstört.*

• **blow away** [phras v] **1.** sth blows away etw. fliegt weg [fliːkt 'vɛk] <fliegt weg, flog weg, ist weggeflogen> ◊ *Der Wind war so stark, dass meine Zeitung wegflog.* blow sth away etw. wegblasen ['vɛkblaːzn] <bläst weg, blies weg, hat weggeblasen> ◊ *Er blies den Staub weg.* **2.** *(kill)* blow sb away jdn abknallen ['apknalən] +haben *(fam)* ◊ *Hat die Mafia den Richter abgeknallt?*

• **blow down** [phras v] sth blows down etw. stürzt um [ʃtyʳtst 'ʊm] +sein ◊ *Bei dem Sturm stürzten mehrere Bäume um.* blow sth down etw. umwehen ['ʊmveːən] +haben ◊ *Der Sturm wehte mehrere Bäume um.*

• **blow in** [phras v] *(a window)* blow sth in etw. eindrücken ['aɛndrʏkn̩] +haben ◊ *Der Windstoß drückte*

A

B

C

D

E

F

G

H

I

J

K

L

M

N

O

P

Q

R

S

T

U

V

W

X

Y

Z

ein Fenster ein. sth blows in etw. wird eingedrückt ◊ *Bei der Explosion wurden die Fenster eingedrückt.* → **blow²** 1.
• **blow off** (phras v) 1. *(in the wind)* sth blows off etw. fliegt weg [fli:kt 'vɛk] <fliegt weg, flog weg, ist weggeflogen> ◊ *Der Wind war so stark, dass mein Hut wegflog.* blow sth off etw. wegblasen ['vɛkblaːzn̩] <bläst weg, blies weg, hat weggeblasen> ◊ *Der Sturm hat doch tatsächlich das Dach weggeblasen!* 2. *(in an explosion)* blow sth off etw. abreißen ['apraesn̩] <reißt ab, riss ab, hat abgerissen> ◊ *Die Handgranate riss ihm den Arm ab.*
• **blow out** (phras v) 1. *(a flame)* blow sth out etw. ausblasen ['aosblaːzn̩] <bläst aus, blies aus, hat ausgeblasen> ◊ *Sie blies die Kerzen aus.* sth blows out etw. geht aus [geːt 'aos] <geht aus, ging aus, ist ausgegangen> ◊ *Von dem Luftzug ging die Kerze aus.* 2. *(burst)* sth blows out etw. zerspringt [tsɛ'ʃprɪŋt] <zerspringt, zersprang, ist zersprungen> ◊ *Durch die Wucht der Explosion zersprangen alle Fenster.* blow sth out etw. zerspringen lassen ◊ *Die Druckwelle ließ die Scheiben zerspringen.*
• **blow over** (phras v) 1. *(in the wind)* sth blows over etw. stürzt um [ʃtʏ'tst 'ʊm] +sein ◊ *Im Wald sind mehrere Bäume umgestürzt.* blow sth/sb over etw./ jdn umwehen ['ʊmveːən] +haben ◊ *Der Sturm wehte mich fast um.* 2. *(storm, excitement, trouble)* sich legen ['leːgn̩] +haben ◊ *Ich glaube, der Sturm hat sich gelegt.* ♦ *Die Aufregung wird sich bald wieder gelegt haben.*
• **blow up** (phras v) 1. *(in an explosion)* blow sth up etw. in die Luft sprengen [ɪn diː 'lʊft ʃprɛŋən] +haben ◊ *Bei dem Anschlag wurde ein Gebäude in die Luft gesprengt.* sth blows up etw. explodiert [ɛksplo'diːɐ̯t] <explodiert, explodierte, ist explodiert> ◊ *Das Auto explodierte und brannte völlig aus.* 2. *(lose your patience)* explodieren [ɛksplo'diːrən] <explodiert, explodierte, ist explodiert> ◊ *Plötzlich explodierte sie und schrie: „Ruhe!"* 3. *(fill with air)* aufblasen ['aofblaːzn̩] <bläst auf, blies auf, hat aufgeblasen> 4. *(wind, storm)* aufkommen ['aofkɔmən] <kommt auf, kam auf, ist aufgekommen> ◊ *Als ein Sturm aufkam, gingen wir ins Haus.* 5. *(argument, problem, crisis)* ausbrechen ['aosbrɛçn̩] <bricht aus, brach aus, ist ausgebrochen> ◊ *Dann brach eine nationale Krise aus.* 6. *(a photograph, image)* vergrößern [fɐ'grøːsən] <vergrößert, vergrößerte, hat vergrößert> have a picture blown up ein Bild vergrößern lassen

blow-dry (verb) föhnen ['føːnən] +haben ◊ *Ich habe mir die Haare geföhnt.*

blue¹
☉ **out of the blue** aus heiterem Himmel

blue² (adj) 1. *(colo(u)r)* blau [blao] ◊ *Er hat blaue Augen.* ♦ *Der Himmel ist blau.* blue with cold blau vor Kälte 2. *(sad)* trübsinnig ['tryːpzɪnɪç] ◊ *Der graue Himmel macht mich trübsinnig.*

blueberry (noun) Heidelbeere ['haedl̩beːrə] die <-, -n> ◊ *Heidelbeeren pflücken*

blue-eyed (adj) blauäugig ['blao|ɔøɡɪç] no comp/ superl ◊ *ein blauäugiges Kind* ♦ *Nicht alle Schweden sind blond und blauäugig.*

blueprint (noun) 1. *(plan)* Entwurf [ɛnt'vʊrf] der <-(e)s, Entwürfe> ◊ *einen Entwurf für eine Reform vorlegen* 2. *(for a building or machine)* Blaupause ['blaopaozə] die <-, -n>

blunt (adj) 1. *(answer, language)* unverblümt ['ʊnfɛblyːmt] <unverblümter, am unverblümtesten> ◊ *eine unverblümte Antwort* ♦ *Ihre Sprache war unverblümt.* 2. *(knife, scissors, pencil)* stumpf [ʃtʊmpf] ◊ *Die Schere ist stumpf.* ♦ *ein stumpfer Bleistift*

bluntly (adv) *(answer, language)* unverblümt ['ʊnfɛblyːmt] <unverblümter, am unverblümtesten> ◊ *Sie sagte ihm unverblümt ihre Meinung.*

blur (verb) 1. *(lose definition)* verschwimmen [fɐ'ʃvɪmən] <verschwimmt, verschwamm, ist verschwommen> ◊ *Die Buchstaben verschwammen vor ihren Augen.* ♦ *Die Erinnerungen verschwimmen mit der Zeit.* 2. *(make sth unclear)* blur sth etw. verwischen [fɐ'vɪʃn̩] <verwischt, verwischte, hat verwischt> ◊ *Der Autor verwischt die Grenzen zwischen Realität und Fiktion.*

blurry (adj) verschwommen [fɐ'ʃvɔmən] ◊ *Das Foto ist verschwommen* ♦ *verschwommene Erinnerungen*

blush (verb) erröten [ɛ'røːtn̩] <errötet, errötete, ist errötet> ◊ *Als er sie ansprach, errötete sie.*

blusher (noun) Rouge [ruːʃ] das <-, -s> most sing ◊ *Rouge mit einem Pinsel auftragen*

board¹ (noun) 1. *(piece of wood or hard material)* Brett [brɛt] das <-(e)s, -er> ◊ *aus Brettern ein Regal bauen* ♦ *Schach wird auf einem Brett mit 64 Feldern gespielt.* 2. *(with departures, arrivals, names etc.)* Tafel ['taːfl̩] die <-, -n> ◊ *Mein Flug steht noch nicht auf der Tafel.*; *(for pinning up notices)* Anschlagbrett ['anʃlaːkbrɛt] das <-(e)s, -er>; *(printed or painted sign)* Schild [ʃɪlt] das <-(e)s, -er> ◊ *Auf dem Schild stand „Betreten verboten".* 3. *(group of people)* Ausschuss ['aosʃʊs] der <-es, Ausschüsse> ◊ *Mitglied eines Ausschusses von Experten sein* ♦ *in einen Ausschuss gewählt werden* board of directors Vorstand ['foːɐ̯ʃtant] der <-(e)s, Vorstände> ◊ *Sie wurde in den Vorstand der Firma gewählt.* board of trustees Kuratorium [kura'toːrjʊm] das <-s, Kuratorien> ◊ *das Kuratorium der Universität/ des Museums* advisory board Beirat ['baeraːt] der <-(e)s, Beiräte> ◊ *der wissenschaftliche Beirat* school board Schulamt ['ʃuːlamt] das <-(e)s, Schulämter> 4. *(meals and lodging)* Verpflegung und Unterkunft [fɐ'pfleːgʊŋ ʊnt 'ʊntɐkʊnft] die <-> no pl ◊ *gegen Verpflegung und Unterkunft arbeiten* full board Vollpension ['fɔlpaŋˌzjoːn] die <-> no pl ◊ *Was kostet ein Doppelzimmer mit Vollpension?* half board Halbpension ['halppaŋˌzjoːn] die <-> no pl

☉ **on board** an Bord **sweep the board** alle Preise abräumen *(fam)* **take sth on board** etw. beherzigen

board² (verb) 1. *(a ship, plane)* board sth an Bord ... (gen) gehen [an 'boːɐ̯t ... geː|ən] <geht, ging, ist gegangen> ◊ *Wir gingen gegen 16 Uhr an Bord des Schiffes.* The ship is boarding. Die Passagiere gehen jetzt an Bord. Flight 234 now boarding at Gate 3. Die Passagiere des Fluges 234 werden gebeten, sich zum Flugsteig 3 zu begeben.; *(a train, bus)* etw. besteigen [bə'ʃtaeɡn̩] besteigt, bestieg, hat bestiegen> ◊ *Er bestieg den Zug und nahm in einem Abteil Platz.* sb boards jd steigt in [ʃtaeɡt aen] <steigt ein, stieg ein, ist eingestiegen> ◊ *Wir waren kaum eingestiegen, da fuhr der Zug schon los.* 2. *(at sb's house)* in Pension wohnen [ʃn paˈzjoːn voːnən] +haben ◊ *Sie wohnt bei einer alten Dame in Pension.*; *(at a school)* Internatsschüler sein [ɪntɐˈnaːtsʃyːlɐ zaen] Internatsschülerin sein

[ɪntɐˈnaːtsyːlərɪn zaɐn] +sein ◊ *Tina ist Internats-*
schülerin einer Schule in London.

boarding [noun] *(of a floor)* Dielen ['diːlən] die <-> pl
◊ *ein Geheimfach unter den Dielen; (on the wall)*
Täfelung ['tɛːfəlʊŋ] die <-, -en>; *(for concrete etc.)*
Verschalung [fɐˈʃaːlʊŋ] die <-, -en>

boarding school [noun] Internat [ɪntɐˈnaːt] das
<-(e)s, -e> ◊ *Sie ging auf ein Internat in der*
Schweiz.

boast [verb] **1.** *(show off)* prahlen ['praːlən] +haben ◊
Der kleine Junge prablte, dass er schon lesen könne.
boast of/about sth mit etw. prahlen **2.** *(possess)*
sich einer Sache [gen] rühmen können
['ryːmən kœnən] <kann, konnte, hat können> ◊
Irland kann sich der atemberaubenden Cliffs of
Moher rühmen.

boat [noun] Boot [boːt] das <-(e)s, -e> ◊ *ins Boot*
steigen
  ◉ **be in the same boat** im selben Boot sitzen **by**
boat *(boat)* mit dem Boot *(ship)* mit dem Schiff
(ferry) mit der Fähre

bob up and down [verb] auf und ab tanzen
[ˌaɔf ʊnt ˈap tantsn̩] +sein ◊ *Papierschiffchen tanzten*
auf den Wellen auf und ab.

bodily [adj] körperlich ['kœʳpɐlɪç] no comp/superl,
only before ns ◊ *körperliche Bedürfnisse* bodily harm
Körperverletzung ['kœʳpɐfɛlɛtsʊŋ] die <-> no pl ◊
Er wurde wegen Körperverletzung angezeigt. bodily
fluid Körperflüssigkeit ['kœʳpɐflʏsɪçkaɛt] die
<-, -en>

body [noun] **1.** *(the whole physical structure, the main*
part) Körper ['kœʳpɐ] der <-s, -> ◊ *ein athletischer*
Körper ♦ *die Arme an den Körper anlegen* upper
body Oberkörper ['oːbekœʳpɐ] ◊ *Er hat einen musku-*
lösen Oberkörper. lower body Unterkörper
['ʊntekœʳpɐ] body weight Körpergewicht
['kœʳpɐgəvɪçt] das <-(e)s> no pl body fat Körperfett
['kœʳpɐfɛt] das <-(e)s> no pl ◊ **2.** *(corpse)* Leiche
['laɛçə] die <-, -n> ◊ *die Leiche eines Soldaten*
3. *(group of people)* Gruppe ['grʊpə] die <-, -n> ◊
Eine Gruppe von Experten wird sich mit dem Fall
befassen. **4.** *(representing a group of organizations)*
Verband [fɛˈbant] der <-(e)s, Verbände> ◊ *der*
Verband der Internet-Wirtschaft in Deutschland professional body Berufsverband [bəˈruːfsfɐbant] der
<-(e)s, Berufsverbände> ruling body Führungsorgan
['fyːrʊŋsloʳgaːn] das <-s, -e> ◊ **5.** *(of facts,*
knowledge) Sammlung ['zamlʊŋ] die <-, -en> body
of data Datensammlung ['daːtn̩zamlʊŋ] body of
evidence Beweismaterial [bəˈvaɛsmateˌrjaːl] das
<-s, -ien> ◊ *das Beweismaterial zu diesem Fall*
6. *(of a plane, ship)* Rumpf [rʊmpf] der
<-(e)s, Rümpfe> most sing; *(of a building)* Haupt-
trakt ['haɔpttrakt] der <-(e)s, -e> ◊ *Der Speisesaal*
befindet sich im Haupttrakt des Gebäudes.; (of a
book, text) Hauptteil ['haɔpttaɛl] der <-(e)s, -e> ◊
Dieser Aspekt wird erst im Hauptteil des Buches
erwähnt. **7.** *(clothing)* Body ['bɔdi] der <-s, -s> ◊
Sie trug einen schwarzen Body. **8.** *(of hair)* Volumen
[voˈluːmən] das <-s> no pl ◊ *dem Haar mehr*
Volumen verleihen
  ◉ **in a body** geschlossen **body and soul** mit Leib
und Seele

bodyguard [noun] Leibwächter ['laɛpvɛçtɐ] der
<-s, -> ♀Leibwächterin ['laɛpvɛçtərɪn] die
<-, -nen> ◊ *Der Star hatte seine Leibwächter dabei.*

♦ *Sie arbeitet als Leibwächterin.*

bodywork [noun] Karosserie [karɔsəˈriː] die <-, -n> ◊
Die Karosserie muss neu lackiert werden.

bog [noun] **1.** *(wet ground)* Moor [moːɐ̯] das
<-(e)s, -e> ◊ *im Moor versinken* **2.** *(in the UK)* Klo
[kloː] das <-s, -s>

boil [verb] *(water, food, clothes)* kochen ['kɔxn̩] +haben
◊ *Kocht das Wasser schon?* ♦ *Soll ich die Eier kochen*
oder braten? **vor Wut kochen** put sth on to boil
etw. zum Kochen bringen **The pot boiled dry.** Das
Wasser ist verkocht. boil the kettle Wasser
aufsetzen ['vasɐ aɔfzɛtsn̩] +haben
  ● **boil down** [phras v] **1.** boil sth down to sth etw.
auf etw. [acc] reduzieren [aɔf ... reduˌtsiːrən]
<reduziert, reduzierte, hat reduziert> ◊ *Der Bericht*
wurde auf einen kurzen Artikel reduziert. **2.** sth
boils down to sth etw. läuft auf etw. [acc] hinaus
[lɔɔft aɔf ... hɪˌnaɔs] <läuft hinaus, lief hinaus, ist
hinausgelaufen>
  ● **boil over** [phras v] **1.** *(milk, potatoes etc.)* überko-
chen ['yːbekɔxn̩] +sein ◊ *Pass auf, die Milch kocht*
gleich über! **2.** *(emotions, tension)* den Siedepunkt
erreichen [deːn ˈziːdəpʊŋkt ɛˌraɛçn̩] <erreichen,
erreichte, hat erreicht> ◊ *Die politischen Spannungen*
erreichten den Siedepunkt.

boiler [noun] *(domestic)* Boiler ['bɔɔlɐ] der <-s, -> ◊
Sie stellte den Boiler im Bad an.; (of an engine)
Kessel ['kɛsl̩] der <-s, -> ◊ *den Kessel beheizen*

bold [adj] **1.** *(daring)* kühn [kyːn] ◊ *Das war ein*
kühnes Experiment. ♦ *Seine Thesen sind sehr kühn.*
2. *(colo(u)rs)* kräftig ['krɛftɪç] ◊ *ein kräftiges Rot*
3. in bold type fett gedruckt ['fɛt gədrʊkt] ◊ *Die*
Überschrift ist fett gedruckt.

bolt¹ [noun] **1.** *(on a door)* Riegel ['riːgl̩] der <-s, -> ◊
Sie schob den Riegel zurück und öffnete das Tor.
2. bolt *(of lightning)* Blitz [blɪts] der <-es, -e> ◊
Der Blitz hat in den Baum eingeschlagen. as/like a
bolt from/out of the blue wie ein Blitz aus
heiterem Himmel It came as/was a bolt from the
blue. Es kam/geschah völlig überraschend. **3.** *(con-*
necting piece, arrow for a crossbow) Bolzen ['bɔltsn̩]
der <-s, -> ◊ *die Mutter auf den Bolzen schrauben*
4. *(of fabric)* Ballen ['balən] der <-s, -> ◊ *ein*
Ballen Seide
  ◉ **make a bolt for sth** einen Satz zu etw. machen

bolt² [verb] **1.** *(a door, window)* verriegeln [fɛˈriːgl̩n]
<verriegelt, verriegelte, hat verriegelt> ◊ *Vergiss nicht,*
die Fenster zu verriegeln! **2.** bolt sth to sth etw. an
etw. [acc] schrauben [an ... ʃraɔbm̩] +haben ◊ *Er*
schraubte das Regal an die Wand. bolt things
together Dinge miteinander verschrauben
[mɪtˌaɛnandɐ fɛˈʃraɔbm̩] <verschraubt, verschraubte,
hat verschraubt> ◊ *zwei Teile fest miteinander ver-*
schrauben **3.** *(run away)* fliehen ['fliːən] <fliehen,*
*floh, ist geflohen> ◊ *Zwei der Gefangenen waren*
geflohen.; (horse) durchgehen ['dʊʳçgeːən] <geht*
*durch, ging durch, ist durchgegangen> ◊ *Das Pferd*
ging durch, den Reiterin stürzte. **4.** *(rush towards)*
bolt for/to/towards sth zu etw. stürzen
[tsuː: ... ʃtʏʳtsn̩] +sein ◊ *Als es klopfte, stürzte sie zur*
Tür. **5.** *(your food)* bolt sth *(down)* hinunterschlin-
gen [hɪˈnʊntɐʃlɪŋən] <schlingt hinunter, schlang
hinunter, hat hinuntergeschlungen> ◊ *Er schlang das*
Essen hinunter und verschwand wieder.

bomb¹ [noun] Bombe ['bɔmbə] die <-, -n> ◊ *eine*
Bombe zünden ♦ *(aus dem Flugzeug)* Bomben auf

eine Stadt abwerfen plant a bomb *eine Bombe legen* bomb attack Bombenanschlag ['bɔmbm̩|anʃlaːk] der <-(e)s, Bombenanschläge> bomb explosion Bombenexplosion ['bɔmbm̩|ɛksploˌzjoːn] die <-, –en>
⊛ **go like a bomb 1.** *(be very fast)* abgehen wie eine Rakete *(fam)* **2.** *(be a success)* ein Bombenerfolg sein *(fam)*

bomb² ⟨verb⟩ *(from the air)* bombardieren [bɔmbaʳˈdiːrən] <bombardiert, bombardierte, hat bombardiert> ◊ *Flugzeuge bombardierten die Stadt.;* *(not from the air)* bomb sb/sth einen Bombenanschlag auf jdn/etw. verüben [ˈaənən ˈbɔmbm̩|anʃlaːk aᴐf ... fɛ|yˈbm̩] <verübt, verübte, hat verübt> ◊ *Bombenanschläge auf Regierungsgebäude verüben*

bombard ⟨verb⟩ bombardieren [bɔmbaʳˈdiːrən] <bombardiert, bombardierte, hat bombardiert> ◊ *einen Redner mit Fragen/Tomaten bombardieren* ♦ *eine Stadt bombardieren*

bomber ⟨noun⟩ **1.** *(person)* Bombenleger [ˈbɔmbm̩leːɡe] der <-s, –> ♀Bombenlegerin [ˈbɔmbm̩leːɡərɪn] die <-, –nen> ◊ *Der Bombenleger wurde gefasst.* **2.** *(aircraft)* Bomber [ˈbɔmbe] der <-s, –> ◊ *die Bomber über Berlin*

bond ⟨noun⟩ **1.** *(between people, atoms)* Bindung [ˈbɪndʊn] die <-, –en> ◊ *Er hat eine enge Bindung an seine Mutter.* ♦ *Die Metallatome gehen eine feste Bindung ein.* **2.** FIN Anleihe [ˈanlaᴇə] die <-, –n> government bond Staatsanleihe [ˈʃtaːts|anlaᴇə] **3.** *(agreement)* Übereinkommen [ybeˈ|aənkɔmən] das <-s, –> enter into a bond with sb mit jdm ein Übereinkommen treffen **4.** *(adhesion)* Haftung [ˈhaftʊn] die <-, –en> most sing ◊ *zur besseren Haftung die Oberfläche anfeuchten* **5.** *(also fig) (fetters)* bonds Fesseln [ˈfɛsl̩n] die <-> pl ◊ *Sie bekamen Fesseln angelegt.* ♦ *sich aus den Fesseln einer unglücklichen Ehe befreien* **6.** LAW *(in the US)* Kaution [kaʊˈtsjoːn] die <-, –en> ◊ *eine Kaution festsetzen/hinterlegen*

bone ⟨noun⟩ *(of a person, an animal)* Knochen [ˈknɔxn̩] der <-s, –> ◊ *Sie gab dem Hund einen Knochen.* ♦ *Bei dem Sturz brach ich mir mehrere Knochen.* ♦ *eine Schnitzerei aus Knochen; (of fish)* Gräte [ˈɡrɛːtə] die <-, –n> ◊ *Pass auf, dass du keine Gräten verschluckst!*
⊛ **the bone of contention** der Zankapfel **frozen to the bone** völlig durchgefroren **feel sth in your bones** etw. in den Knochen spüren **make no bones about sth** mit etw. nicht hinterm Berg halten **have a bone to pick with sb** mit jdm ein Hühnchen zu rupfen haben

bone marrow ⟨noun⟩ Knochenmark [ˈknɔxn̩maʳk] das <-(e)s> no pl

bonus ⟨noun⟩ **1.** *(sth extra)* Bonus [ˈboːnʊs] der <-ses, –se> ◊ *Als Bonus erhalten Sie eine kostenlose Kinokarte.* **2.** *(on top of your salary)* Prämie [ˈprɛːmjə] die <-, –n> ◊ *Wenn Sie Ihre Ziele erreichen, bekommen Sie eine Prämie.* Christmas bonus Weihnachtsgratifikation [ˈvaənaxtsɡratifikaˌtsjoːn] die <-, –en> **3.** no-claims bonus Schadensfreiheitsrabatt [ˌʃaːdn̩|ɛzatsˈfraᴇhaᴇtsraˌbat] der <-(e)s, –e>

book¹ ⟨noun⟩ **1.** *(bound and printed pages)* Buch [buːx] das <-(e)s, Bücher> ◊ *Er schreibt ein Buch über seine Reisen.* address book Adressbuch [aˈdrɛsbuːx]

2. *(of stamps, matches)* Heftchen [ˈhɛftçən] das <-s, –> ◊ *eine Briefmarke aus dem Heftchen entnehmen* book of matches Streichholzheftchen [ˈʃtraᴇçhɔltsheftçən]; *(of tickets)* Block [blɔk] der <-(e)s, Blöcke> ◊ *eine Karte vom Block abreißen* **3.** FIN the books die Bücher [diː ˈbyːçɐ] <-> only pl ◊ *Morgen kommt jemand vom Finanzamt, um die Bücher zu prüfen.* do the books for sb jdm die Bücher führen balance the books Bilanz machen [biˈlants maxn̩] +haben
⊛ **be in sb's bad books** bei jdm in Ungnade gefallen sein **a closed book** ein Buch mit sieben Siegeln **get into sb's good books** sich bei jdm beliebt machen **an open book** ein offenes Buch **by the book** nach Vorschrift

book² ⟨verb⟩ **1.** *(a table, tickets)* bestellen [bəˈʃtɛlən] <bestellt, bestellte, hat bestellt> ◊ *Meine Sekretärin hat für mich ein Zimmer bestellt.; (a holiday, trip, flight)* buchen [ˈbuːxn̩] +haben ◊ *eine Reise/ein Hotel buchen* fully booked ausgebucht [ˈaʊsɡəbuːxt] no comp/superl ◊ *Der Flug ist bereits ausgebucht.; (a performer, entertainer)* engagieren [anɡaˈʒiːrən] <engagiert, engagierte, hat engagiert> ◊ *Wir haben für den Abend eine Sängerin engagiert.* **2.** *(police)* book sb jdn für etw. drankriegen [fyːɐ ... ˌdrankriːɡn̩] +haben/haben
• **book in** ⟨phras v⟩ **1.** *(make a room reservation)* book sb in at a hotel ein Hotelzimmer für jdn reservieren [aən hoˌtɛltsɪmɐ fyːɐ ... rezeʳˌviːrən] <reserviert, reservierte, hat reserviert> ◊ *Wir haben ein Zimmer im Bahnhofshotel für Sie reserviert.* book sb in at a hospital jdn in einem Krankenhaus anmelden [ɪn aənəm ˈkraŋkn̩haʊs ˌanmɛldn̩] <meldet an, meldete an, hat angemeldet> **2.** *(register)* sb books in jd meldet sich an [mɛldət ... an] <meldete sich an, hat sich angemeldet> ◊ *Ich werde mich gleich an der Rezeption anmelden.*

booking ⟨noun⟩ *(of a table, ticket)* Bestellung [bəˈʃtɛlʊn] die <-, –en> ◊ *Die Bestellung der Karten ist telefonisch möglich.; (of a holiday, trip, flight)* Buchung [ˈbuːxʊn] die <-, –en> ◊ *Wir bitten um rechtzeitige Buchung Ihrer Reise.*

bookkeeping ⟨noun⟩ Buchhaltung [ˈbuːxhaltʊn] die <-, –en> most sing ◊ *Der Steuerberater macht für mich die Buchhaltung.*

booklet ⟨noun⟩ Broschüre [brɔˈʃyːrə] die <-, –n> ◊ *eine Broschüre über Aids*

bookshop ⟨noun⟩ Buchhandlung [ˈbuːxhandlʊn] die <-, –en>

boom¹ ⟨noun⟩ **1.** *(improvement, increase in popularity)* Boom [buːm] der <-s, –s> ◊ *ein wirtschaftlicher/konjunktureller Boom* ♦ *Dieser Sport erlebt derzeit einen regelrechten Boom.* **2.** *(lasting noise of a motor, machine, plane etc.)* Dröhnen [ˈdrøːnən] das <-s> no pl; *(of explosions, shots, waves etc.)* Donnern [ˈdɔnɐn] das <-s> no pl ◊ *das Donnern der Wellen gegen die Hafenmauer; (bang)* Knall [knal] der <-(e)s, –e> most sing ◊ *Es gab einen lauten Knall und das Licht ging aus.*

boom² ⟨verb⟩ **1.** *(be successful)* boomen [ˈbuːmən] +haben *(fam)* ◊ *Die Wirtschaft des Landes boomt.* **2.** *(make a loud noise)* dröhnen [ˈdrøːnən] +haben ◊ *Sein Lachen dröhnt durch den Flur.* ♦ *Von fern hörte man ein Flugzeug dröhnen.*

boost¹ ⟨noun⟩ Auftrieb [ˈaʊftriːp] der <-(e)s> no pl give sb a boost jdm neuen Auftrieb geben be a

boost for sth einer Sache [dat] Auftrieb geben
boost² [verb] *(promote, strengthen)* ankurbeln
['anku^rb|n] <kurbelt an, kurbelte an, hat angekurbelt>
◊ *Sinkende Ölpreise kurbeln die Wirtschaft an.*; *(increase)* erhöhen [e'høːən] <erhöht, erhöhte, hat erhöht> ◊ *den Bekanntheitsgrad eines Produkts erhöhen* ♦ *Dieses Medikament erhöht den Blutdruck.*
boost (the) morale die Moral heben
[diː moˈraːl ˌheːbm̩] <hebt, hob, hat gehoben>
boot [noun] **1.** *(footwear)* Stiefel [ˈʃtiːfl̩] der <-s, -> ◊ *Er trug schwarze Stiefel aus Leder.* **2.** *(of a car)* Kofferraum [ˈkɔferaom] der <-(e)s, Kofferräume> ◊ *das Gepäck im Kofferraum verstauen*
🄳 the boot is on the other foot es ist genau umgekehrt too big for your boots größenwahnsinnig be given the boot an die Luft gesetzt werden *(fam)*
booty [noun] Beute [ˈbɔytə] die <-> no pl ◊ *Der Einbrecher entkam mit 1000 Euro Beute.*
booze¹ [noun] Alk [alk] der <-s> no pl *(fam)* ◊ *Wer sorgt für den Alk heute Abend?*
booze² [verb] saufen [ˈzaofn̩] <säuft, soff, hat gesoffen> *(fam, esp pej)* ◊ *Sie haben auf der Party ordentlich gesoffen.*
border [noun] **1.** *(between countries)* Grenze [ˈɡrɛntsə] die <-, -n> ◊ *die Grenze zwischen Deutschland und Polen* ♦ *Waffen über die Grenze schmuggeln* on the border an der Grenze cross the border die Grenze überschreiten **2.** *(band for decoration)* Bordüre [bɔrˈdyːrə] die <-, -n> ◊ *eine Tischdecke mit einer geblümten Bordüre; (around a lawn)* Rabatte [raˈbatə] die <-, -n> ◊ *die Rabatten mit Ziersträuchern bepflanzen; (margin)* Rand [rant] der <-(e)s, Ränder> ◊ *ein Trauerbrief mit schwarzem Rand*
bore [verb] **1.** *(be uninteresting)* langweilen [ˈlaŋvaelən] +haben ◊ *Das Theaterstück langweilte ihn.* ♦ *Er hat mich mit seinen endlosen Ausführungen gelangweilt.* **2.** *(drill)* bohren [ˈboːrən] +haben ◊ *Er bohrte ein Loch in die Wand.* ♦ *Die Handwerker hämmerten und bohrten den ganzen Tag.*
bored → bore [adj] gelangweilt [ɡəˈlaŋvaelt] <gelangweilter, am gelangweiltesten> ◊ *Sie hörten mit gelangweilter Miene zu.* ♦ *Das Publikum wirkte gelangweilt.* be bored sich langweilen [ˈlaŋvaelən] +haben be bored stiff/rigid/silly sich zu Tode langweilen get bored with sth etw. leid sein [laet zaen] +sein ◊ *Allmählich wurde sie seineVorwürfe leid.*
boredom [noun] Langeweile [laŋəˈvaelə] die <-> no pl ◊ *Aus Langeweile blätterte sie in einer Zeitschrift.* ♦ *über Langeweile klagen*
boring → bore [adj] langweilig [ˈlaŋvaeliç] ◊ *eine langweilige Geschichte* ♦ *Ich finde ihn eher langweilig.* ♦ *Alleine zu laufen ist ihr zu langweilig.*
born [adj] geboren [ɡəˈboːrən] no comp/superl ◊ *in Hamburg/an einem Sonntag/blind geboren sein* ♦ *ein geborener Künstler sein* He was born to be a singer. Er ist zum Sänger geboren.
🄳 I wasn't born yesterday ich bin doch nicht von gestern
borough [noun] Bezirk [bəˈtsɪrˀk] der <-(e)s, -e> ◊ *Er wohnt im selben Bezirk wie sie.*
borrow [verb] **1.** *(objects, money)* borrow sth (from sb) sich [dat] etw. (von jdm) leihen [ˈlaeən] <leiht sich, lieh sich, hat sich geliehen> ◊ *Kann ich mir dein Taschenmesser leihen?* ♦ *Ich habe mir 10 000 Euro*

von der Bank geliehen.; *(from a library)* ausleihen [ˈaoslaeən] <leiht aus, lieh aus, hat ausgeliehen> ◊ *Sie leiht jeden Monat mehrere Bücher aus.* **2.** *(an idea, a quotation)* übernehmen [ybeˈneːmən] <übernimmt, übernahm, hat übernommen> ◊ *Dieses Zitat hat er wörtlich übernommen.* **3.** LING *(a word)* entlehnen [ɛntˈleːnən] <entlehnt, entlehnte, hat entlehnt> ◊ *aus dem Lateinischen entlehnte Wörter*
borrowing [noun] **1.** FIN *(of money)* Kreditaufnahme [kreˈdiːtlaofnaːmə] die <-, -n> ◊ *eine Kreditaufnahme in Millionenhöhe; (money borrowed)* borrowings Fremdmittel [ˈfrɛmtmɪtl̩] die <-> pl The company has borrowings of 32 million. Die Firma hat 32 Millionen Schulden. The company has no borrowings. Die Firma ist schuldenfrei. **2.** *(quotation)* Zitat [tsiˈtaːt] das <-(e)s, -e> **3.** LING *(from a language, word)* Lehnwort [leːnvɔrˀt] das <-(e)s, Lehnwörter> ◊ *E-Mail ist ein Lehnwort aus dem Englischen.*
bosom [noun] ANAT Busen [ˈbuːzn̩] der <-s, -> ◊ *Sie hat einen großen Busen.*
🄳 in the bosom of your family im Schoß der Familie bosom friend *(male)* Busenfreund *(female)* Busenfreundin
boss [noun] **1.** *(at work)* Chef [ʃɛf] der <-s, -s> ♀Chefin [ˈʃɛfɪn] die <-, -nen> ◊ *Sie ist Uwes Chefin.* ♦ *Sie bekommen einen neuen Chef.* **2.** *(fam) (person who tells others what to do)* Boss [bɔs] der <-es, -e> *(fam)* ◊ *Okay, du bist der Boss. Machen wir es, wie du willst.*
both¹ [det] beide [ˈbaedə] ◊ *Beide Programme sind gleich gut.* ♦ *Ein Kind braucht beide Eltern.* ♦ *auf beiden Seiten des Flusses* both his sons seine beiden Söhne
both² [pron] **1.** *(two people or things)* both (of them) beide [ˈbaedə] ◊ *Ich stehe mit beiden in Kontakt.* ◊ *Da sind zwei Artikel. Machen Sie von beiden Kopien.* **2.** *(one thing as well as the other)* beides [ˈbaedəs] +verb in the sing ◊ *Lesen oder Spielen – beides ist schön.*
🄳 both ... and ... sowohl ... als auch ... ◊ *Er spricht sowohl Englisch als auch Spanisch.* be both ... and ... und ... sein ◊ *Sie ist schön und intelligent.* you and me both wir (...) beide ◊ *Wir haben beide das gleiche Problem.*
bother¹ [noun] **1.** *(problems, trouble)* Ärger [ˈɛrgɐ] der <-s> no pl ◊ *jdm eine Menge Ärger ersparen/machen* no pl *(annoying person or thing)* Plage [ˈplaːgə] die <-, -n> most sing ◊ *Du bist manchmal eine richtige Plage!*
🄳 sth is a bother for sb etw. macht jdm Umstände no bother kein Problem
bother² [verb] **1.** *(do sth unpleasant or pointless)* bother to do sth sich [dat] die Mühe machen, etw. zu tun [diː ˈmyːə maxn̩ ... tsuː] +haben ◊ *Er hat sich gar nicht erst die Mühe gemacht, das Buch zu lesen.*; *(concern yourself with sth/sb)* bother with sth/sb sich mit etw./jdm abgeben [mɪt ... ˈapgeːbm̩] <gibt sich ab, gab sich ab, hat sich abgegeben> ◊ *Mit solchen Idioten gebe ich mich nicht ab.* **2.** *(disturb, annoy)* bother sb jdn stören [ˈʃtøːrən] +haben ◊ *Stört Sie der Lärm?* ♦ *Darf ich dich mal kurz stören?* **3.** *(worry)* bother sb jdm Sorgen machen [ˈzɔrgn̩ maxn̩] +haben ◊ *Seine Schweigsamkeit machte ihr allmählich Sorgen.* sb is not bothered by sth etw. macht jdm nichts aus [maxt ... ˌnɪçts ˈaos] +haben

4. *(cause pain)* bother sb jdm zu schaffen machen ['tsu: 'ʃafn̩ maxn̩] +haben ◊ *Sein Rücken macht ihm wieder zu schaffen.* **5.** *(molest)* belästigen [bə'lɛstɪgn̩] <belästigt, belästigte, hat belästigt> ◊ *Hat der Kerl Sie belästigt?*

▣ **sb can't be bothered** jd hat keine Lust don't bother nicht nötig

bottle¹ [noun] **1.** *(container for/of liquid)* Flasche ['flaʃə] die <-, -n> ◊ *Sie trank das Bier direkt aus der Flasche.* ♦ *Hast du etwa die ganze Flasche allein getrunken?* ♦ *Er gibt gerade dem Baby die Flasche.* ♦ *Ich mache eine Flasche Wein auf.* **2.** *(fam) (courage)* Mumm [mʊm] der <-s> no pl ◊ *Er hatte nicht den Mumm, sich zu beschweren.*

▣ **hit the bottle** zur Flasche greifen

bottle² [verb] *(liquids)* abfüllen ['apfʏlən] +haben ◊ *50 000 Flaschen Saft werden hier jährlich abgefüllt.; (fruit, vegetables)* einwecken ['aɛnvɛkn̩] +haben ◊ *Sie weckt jedes Jahr Aprikosen ein.*

bottle opener [noun] Flaschenöffner ['flaʃn̩œfnə] der <-s, ->

bottom¹ [noun] **1.** *(the lowest part of a a container, mountain, page: under the text)* Fuß [fuːs] der <-es, Füße> most sing ◊ *Am Fuß des Berges steht ein Haus.* ♦ *Bitte lesen Sie die Anmerkungen am Fuß der Seite.; (of a page: part of the text)* Ende ['ɛndə] das <-s, -n> ◊ *die letzte Zeile am Ende der Seite; (of a screen, wall)* unteres Ende [ˌʊntərəs 'ɛndə] ◊ *Klicken Sie auf das Symbol am unteren Ende des Bildschirms.; (of a container)* Boden ['boːdn̩] der <-s, Böden> ◊ *Ich habe das auf dem Boden der Truhe gefunden.; (of the ocean, a lake)* Grund [grʊnt] der <-(e)s, Gründe> most sing ◊ *Das Schiff liegt jetzt auf dem Grund des Meeres.* **2.** *(of a road, garden)* Ende ['ɛndə] das <-s, -n> ◊ *ein Schuppen am Ende des Gartens* **3.** bottom of the league Tabellenende [ta'bɛlən|ɛndə] das <-s> no pl ◊ *die Mannschaft am Tabellenende* be at the bottom of the class der/die Letzte in der Klasse sein [deːɐ̯/diː 'lɛtstə ɪn deːɐ̯ ˌklasə zaɛn] der/die <-n, die Letzten> only with the definite article ◊ *Sie ist die Letzte in der Klasse.* **4.** ANAT *(backside)* Hintern ['hɪntən] der <-s, -> *(fam)* ◊ *Er fiel auf den Hintern.* **5.** *(of a pyjama, jogging suit)* bottoms Hose ['hoːzə] die <-, -n> ◊ *Wo ist die Hose meines Schlafanzugs?*

▣ **from the bottom of my heart** aus tiefstem Herzen be at the bottom of sth hinter etw. [dat] stecken get to the bottom of sth einer Sache [dat] auf den Grund gehen

bottom² [adj] **1.** *(lowest of several)* unterste ['ʊntəstə] no comp/superl, only before ns ◊ *Vorsicht, die unterste Stufe ist rutschig!; (lowest of two)* untere ['ʊntərə] no comp/superl, only before ns ◊ *Drücken Sie bitte auf den linken unteren Knopf.* **2.** *(lowest in a hierarchy)* schlechteste ['ʃlɛçtəstə] no comp/superl, only before ns ◊ *die schlechteste Mannschaft*

bough [noun] Ast [ast] der <-(e)s, Äste> ◊ *Der Affe schwang sich von Ast zu Ast.*

boulder [noun] Felsen ['fɛlzn̩] der <-s, ->

bounce [verb] **1.** *(strike a surface)* springen ['ʃprɪŋən] <sprang, sprang, ist gesprungen> ◊ *Der Ball sprang sofort ins Netz.* ♦ *Die Kinder sprangen aufgeregt auf und ab.* bounce off sth von etw. springen ◊ *Der Ball sprang von seinem Fuß ins Tor.* Stop bouncing on the sofa! Hör auf, auf dem Sofa herumzuspringen!

bounce a/the ball einen/den Ball dribbeln [aɛnən/deːn 'bal ˌdrɪbl̩n] +haben ◊ *Sie dribbelte den Ball an der Gegnerin vorbei.* **2.** *(move up and down)* schaukeln ['ʃaɔkl̩n] +haben ◊ *Er schaukelte das Baby auf den Knien.* ♦ *Der Wagen hat ganz schön geschaukelt.* She bounced the child up and down on her knee. Sie ließ das Kind auf den Knien reiten. **3.** FIN *(cheque)* platzen ['platsn̩] +sein *(fam)* ◊ *Der Scheck ist geplatzt.* **4.** IT *(e-mail)* nicht zugestellt werden können [nɪçt 'tsuːgəʃtɛlt veːɐ̯dn̩ kœnan] <kann, konnte, hat können> ◊ *Die Mail konnte leider nicht zugestellt werden.*

● **bounce back** [phras v] *(recover)* sich erholen [ɛ'hoːlən] <erholt sich, erholte sich, hat sich erholt> ◊ *Die Wirtschaft hat sich nun wieder erholt.*

bound → bind [adj] **1.** *(sb is sure to do sth)* sb is bound to do sth jd wird bestimmt etw. tun [vɪɐ̯t bə'ʃtɪmt] ◊ *Sie wird bestimmt fragen, wo du gewesen bist.* **2.** *(obliged)* verpflichtet [fɛ'pflɪçtət] no comp/superl be bound (by sth) to do sth *(durch etw.)* verpflichtet sein, etw. zu tun feel bound to do sth sich verpflichtet fühlen, etw. zu tun **3.** *(book)* gebunden [gə'bʊndn̩] no comp/superl ◊ *eine gebundene Ausgabe des Romans*

● **bound for** auf dem Weg nach

boundary [noun] Grenze ['grɛntsə] die <-, -n> ◊ *Die Grenze ihres Reiches verlief entlang des Flusses.* ♦ *Seine Spielleidenschaft kennt keine Grenzen.*

boundary wall Grenzmauer ['grɛntsmaɔə] die <-, -n>

bouquet [noun] **1.** *(of flowers)* Strauß [ʃtraɔs] der <-, Sträuße> ◊ *ein Strauß roter Rosen* **2.** *(of wine)* Blume ['bluːmə] die <-, -n>

bourgeois¹ [noun] Spießer ['ʃpiːsɐ] der <-s, -> ♀ Spießerin ['ʃpiːsərɪn] die <-, -nen> *(pej)*

bourgeois² [adj] **1.** *(typically middle-class)* spießig ['ʃpiːsɪç] *(pej)* ◊ *ihre spießigen Eltern* ♦ *Sie fand ihn zu spießig.* **2.** *(middle-class)* bürgerlich ['bʏɐ̯gəlɪç] no comp/superl ◊ *aus bürgerlichen Kreisen stammen*

bow¹ [noun] **1.** *(for shooting or playing a musical instrument)* Bogen ['boːgn̩] der <-s, -> ◊ *Er spannte den Bogen und zielte sorgfältig.* ♦ *mit dem Bogen über die Saiten einer Geige streichen* **2.** *(knot)* Schleife ['ʃlaɛfə] die <-, -n> ◊ *eine Schleife binden*

bow² [noun] Verbeugung [fɛ'bɔɔgʊŋ] die <-, -en> take a bow sich verbeugen [fɛ'bɔɔgn̩] <verbeugt sich, verbeugte sich, hat sich verbeugt>

bow³ [verb] **1.** *(as a sign of respect)* sich verbeugen [fɛ'bɔɔgn̩] <verbeugt sich, verbeugte sich, hat sich verbeugt> ◊ *Er verbeugte sich tief vor der Königin.* **2.** bow one's head den Kopf senken [deːn 'kɔpf ˌzɛŋkn̩] +haben ◊ *Sie senkte den Kopf und begann zu weinen.*

▣ **with head bowed** mit gesenktem Kopf with shoulders bowed mit gebeugten Schultern

● **bow to** [phras v] bow to sth/sb sich jdm/einer Sache beugen ['bɔɔgn̩] +haben ◊ *Ich beuge mich der Mehrheit.* ♦ *Die Familie musste sich dem Willen des Vaters beugen.*

bowel [noun] Darm [da'm] der <-(e)s, Därme> empty your bowels den Darm entleeren

● **the bowels of sth** das Innere ... [gen] ◊ *Gestein aus dem Inneren der Erde*

bowl¹ [noun] *(larger, deep)* Schüssel ['ʃʏsl̩] die <-, -n> ◊ *die Schüsseln mit dem Essen auftragen* ♦ *das Geschirr in einer Schüssel spülen; (smaller, more*

shallow, to drink from) Schale ['ʃaːlə] die <–, –n> ◊ *das Obst in eine Schale legen; (to eat from)* soup bowl Suppenteller ['zʊpm̩tɛlɐ] der <–s, –> sugar bowl Zuckerdose ['tsʊkedoːzə] die <–, –n>

bowl² [verb] **1.** SPORT *(in bowling)* rollen lassen ['rɔlən lasn̩] <lässt, ließ, hat lassen> ◊ *die Kugel rollen lassen* **2.** *(in cricket)* werfen ['vɛʳfn̩] <wirft, warf, hat geworfen> ◊ *Hast du schon geworfen?* ♦ *Er warf den Ball.*

bowler [noun] **1.** *(in bowls or bowling)* Bowlingspieler ['boːlɪŋʃpiːlɐ] der <–s, –> ♀Bowlingspielerin ['boːlɪŋʃpiːlərɪn] die <–, –nen> **2.** *(in cricket)* Werfer ['vɛʳfɐ] der <–s, –> ♀Werferin ['vɛʳfərɪn] die <–, –nen>

bowler hat [noun] Melone [meˈloːnə] die <–, –n> ◊ *eine Melone tragen*

bow tie [noun] Fliege ['fliːgə] die <–, –n> ◊ *Er erschien im Frack mit schwarzer Fliege.*

box¹ [noun] **1.** *(container, for horses)* Box [bɔks] die <–, –en> ◊ *Er holte ein Brötchen aus der mitgebrachten Box.* ♦ *Sie brachte das Pferd in seine Box.; (of chocolates, matches, for hats)* Schachtel ['ʃaxtl̩] die <–, –n> ◊ *eine Schachtel Pralinen/Streichhölzer.* ♦ *etw. in einer Schachtel aufbewahren; (wooden)* Kiste ['kɪstə] die <–, –n> ◊ *Das Kind räumte seine Spielsachen in die Kiste.* **2.** *(on a document)* Feld [fɛlt] das <–(e)s, –er> ◊ *Bitte füllen Sie alle Felder vollständig aus.* **3.** *(TV)* the box der Kasten [deːɐ̯ 'kastn̩] <–s, Kästen> *(fam, esp pej)* ◊ *Mach endlich den Kasten aus!* **4.** *(in the theatre, cinema)* Loge ['loːʒə] die <–, –n> ◊ *Plätze in der Loge* **5.** *(fam) (coffin)* Sarg [zaʳk] der <–(e)s, Särge> ◊ *Die Leiche lag im Sarg.*

box² [verb] **1.** SPORT boxen ['bɔksn̩] +haben ◊ *Er boxt hervorragend.* **2.** *(put into a box)* box sth etw. (in einer Schachtel) verpacken [(ɪn aɛnɐ 'ʃaxtl̩) fɐˈpakn̩] <verpackt, verpackte, hat verpackt>

boxing [noun] Boxen ['bɔksn̩] das <–s> no pl ◊ *Ist Boxen ein gefährlicher Sport?*

box office [noun] *(in a cinema, theatre)* Kasse ['kasə] die <–, –n> ◊ *Holen Sie die reservierten Karten an der Kasse ab!; (on the evening of the performance)* Abendkasse ['aːbm̩tkasə] die <–, –n> most sing ◊ *An der Abendkasse beträgt der Eintritt 10 Euro.*
◉ fail at the box office ein Flop sein take ... at the box office ... einspielen

boxroom [noun] *(small room)* kleines Zimmer [ˌklaɛnəs 'tsɪmɐ] <–s, –> ◊ *Ich habe das kleine Zimmer renoviert.; (for storing things)* Abstellkammer ['apʃtɛlkamɐ] die <–, –n>

boy [noun] **1.** *(young male, familiar address for a man)* Junge ['jʊŋə] der <–n, –n> ◊ *Ist das Baby ein Junge oder ein Mädchen?* ♦ *ein neunjähriger Junge* ♦ *Na, wie geht's, alter Junge?* **2.** *(fam) (group of men)* the boys die Jungs [diː 'jʊŋs] <–> pl *(fam)* ◊ *Die Jungs gehen heute zum Fußball.*
◉ boys will be boys Jungs sind nun mal so

boycott [verb] boykottieren [bɔykɔˈtiːrən] <boykottiert, boykottierte, hat boykottiert> ◊ *Wahlen boykottieren*

boyfriend [noun] Freund [frɔɪnt] der <–(e)s, –e> ◊ *Kommst du mit deinem Freund?*

bra [noun] BH [beːˈhaː] der <–(s), –(s)> *(fam)* ◊ *einen BH tragen*

brace [noun] **1.** *(for teeth)* Zahnspange ['tsaːnʃpaŋə] die <–, –n> ◊ *eine feste/herausnehmbare Zahnspange* **2.** MED *(for supporting an injured part of the body)*

Schiene ['ʃiːnə] die <–, –n> ◊ *Sie trägt den gebrochenen Arm in einer Schiene.* **3.** *(curly bracket)* geschweifte Klammer [gəˌʃvaɛftə 'klamɐ] die <–, –n> **4.** *(item of clothing)* braces Hosenträger ['hoːzn̩trɛːgɐ] die <–> pl ◊ *Er trägt lieber Hosenträger als einen Gürtel.*

bracket [noun] **1.** *(punctuation mark)* Klammer ['klamɐ] die <–, –n> ◊ *Das Wort steht in Klammern.* **2.** *(group, according to income, age)* Gruppe ['grʊpə] die <–, –n> ◊ *Sie gehört zur Gruppe der Besserverdienenden.; (according to tax, price)* Klasse ['klasə] die <–, –n> ◊ *Steuerlich ist sie in derselben Klasse wie er.* **3.** *(supporting device)* Winkelträger ['vɪŋkl̩trɛːgɐ] der <–s, –>

braid [noun] **1.** *(trimming)* Borte ['bɔʳtə] die <–, –n> ◊ *ein Kleid mit Borte* **2.** *(in the US: plait)* Zopf [tsɔpf] der <–(e)s, Zöpfe> ◊ *Ina trägt heute einen Zopf.*

brain [noun] **1.** ANAT Gehirn [gəˈhɪʳn] das <–(e)s, –e> ◊ *Das Gehirn ist das komplexeste Organ des Körpers.* **2.** *(intellectual capacity)* Verstand [fɐˈʃtant] der <–(e)s> no pl ◊ *Sie hat einen scharfen Verstand.* ♦ *seinen Verstand gebrauchen*
◉ be the brains am besten Bescheid wissen have brains intelligent sein pick sb's brains jdn über etw. [acc] ausquetschen rack your brain(s) sich [dat] das Gehirn zermartern

braise [verb] schmoren ['ʃmoːrən] +haben ◊ *einen Braten im eigenen Saft schmoren*

brake¹ [noun] **1.** *(of a vehicle)* Bremse ['brɛmzə] die <–, –n> ◊ *Die Bremsen haben versagt.* ♦ *schlechte Bremsen an einem Fahrrad* slam on the brakes voll auf die Bremse treten **2.** *(fig) (slow sth down)* put a brake on sth etw. bremsen ['brɛmzn̩] +haben ◊ *Der hohe Ölpreis hat das Wirtschaftswachstum stark gebremst.* act as a brake on sth als Bremse wirken [als 'brɛmzə vɪʳkn̩] +haben

brake² [verb] bremsen ['brɛmzn̩] +haben ◊ *Als er das Kind auf die Straße laufen sah, bremste er scharf.* ♦ *das Auto bremsen* brake the car to a halt das Auto zum Stillstand bringen [das ˌaoto: tsʊm 'ʃtɪlʃtant brɪŋən] <bringt, brachte, hat gebracht>

branch¹ [noun] **1.** BOT Ast [ast] der <–(e)s, Äste> ◊ *Der Affe schwang sich von Ast zu Ast.* **2.** *(of an organization, a company)* Filiale [fiˈljaːlə] die <–, –n> ◊ *eine Filiale eröffnen/schließen* **3.** *(field of knowledge, study)* Zweig [tsvaɛk] der <–(e)s, –e> ◊ *Optik und Mechanik sind Zweige der Physik.* **4.** *(of a river)* Arm [aʳm] der <–(e)s, –e> ◊ *Der Fluss teilt sich an der Mündung in zwei Arme.*

branch² [verb] *(divide into two parts)* sich gabeln ['gaːbl̩n] +haben ◊ *Dort vorn gabelt sich die Straße/der Fluss.; (divide into more than two parts)* branch into sth sich in etw. [acc] verzweigen [ɪn ... fɐˌtsvaɛgn̩] <verzweigt sich, verzweigte sich, hat sich verzweigt> ◊ *Der Fluss verzweigt sich in ein Delta.*
• branch off [phras v.] **1.** *(street, path, person)* abzweigen ['aptsvaɛgn̩] +sein ◊ *Diese Straße zweigt von der Hauptstraße ab.* ♦ *Wir sind vom Weg abgezweigt.* **2.** *(separate yourself from a group)* sich absondern ['apzɔndɐn] <sondert sich ab, sonderte sich ab, hat sich abgesondert> ◊ *Einige Schüler sonderten sich von der Klasse ab, um zusammen zu lernen.*

brand¹ [noun] **1.** *(of products)* Marke ['maʳkə] die

<-, -n> ◊ *Ich trinke oft Sekt, aber diese Marke kenne ich noch nicht.* **2.** *(characteristic version of sth)* Art [aːʳt] die <-, -en> *most sing* ◊ *Er hat seine eigene Art von Humor.* **3.** *(mark on cattle)* Brandzeichen ['brantˌsaɛçn̩] das <-s, -> ◊ *ein mit einem Brandzeichen gekennzeichnetes Rind*

brand² [verb] **1.** *(a person, thing)* brandmarken ['brantmaʳkn̩] +haben ◊ *Viele Athleten werden zu Unrecht als Dopingsünder gebrandmarkt.* **2.** *(products)* mit einem Warenzeichen versehen [mɪt aɛnəm 'vaːrənsaɛçn̩ fɛzeːən] <versieht, versah, hat versehen> **3.** *(cattle)* mit einem Brandzeichen kennzeichnen [mɪt aɛnəm 'brantˌsaɛçn̩ kɛntsaɛçnən] +haben ◊ *Die Rinder werden mit dem Brandzeichen ihres Besitzers gekennzeichnet.*

brandy [noun] Weinbrand ['vaɛnbrant] der <-(e)s, Weinbrände> ◊ *eine Flasche Weinbrand*

brass [noun] **1.** *(metal)* Messing ['mɛsɪŋ] das <-s> *no pl* ◊ *ein Rohr aus Messing* **2.** *(plaque)* Messingschild ['mɛsɪŋʃɪlt] das <-(e)s, -er> ◊ *Neben der Tür hängt ein Messingschild mit dem Namen der Firma.* **3.** MUS *(musicians)* Blechbläser ['blɛçblɛːzɐ] die <-> *pl* ◊ *ein Stück für Blechbläser und Schlagzeug* ◆ *Die Blechbläser haben in dieser Sinfonie viel zu spielen.* **4.** *(fam, also pej)* top brass hohes Tier [ˌhoːəs 'tiːɐ] <-(e)s, -e> ◊ *Sie war ein ganz hohes Tier bei der Staatssicherheit.*

brave(ly) [adj, adv] **1.** *(courageous)* mutig ['muːtɪç] ◊ *Der Soldat galt als mutig und furchtlos.* ◆ *eine mutige Passantin* ◆ *Trotz ihrer Angst hat sie mutig gehandelt.* **2.** *(enduring pain, fear)* tapfer ['tapfɐ] ◊ *Der kleine Leo war sehr tapfer beim Zahnarzt.* ◆ *Du bist ein tapferes Kind.* ◆ *Trotz der Schmerzen lächelte sie tapfer.*

brawl [noun] Schlägerei [ʃlɛːɡəˈraɛ] die <-, -en> ◊ *eine Schlägerei anzetteln* ◆ *in eine Schlägerei geraten*

brazen [adj] dreist [draɛst] <dreister, am dreistesten> ◊ *Das war ganz schön dreist von ihm.* ◆ *dreiste Forderungen* ◆ *Die Autodiebe werden immer dreister.*

Brazil [noun] Brasilien [braˈziːljən] das <-s> *article only in combination with attribute, no pl* → **Germany**

Brazilian¹ [noun] Brasilianer [braziˈljaːne] der <-s, -> ♀Brasilianerin [braziˈljaːnərɪn] die <- *or* -nen> → **German¹** 1.

Brazilian² [adj] brasilianisch [braziˈljaːnɪʃ] → **German²**

breach¹ [noun] **1.** *(of a law, rule, of etiquette)* breach of sth Verstoß gegen etw. [fɛˈʃtoːs ɡeːɡn̩] der <-es, Verstöße> ◊ *Ein Verstoß gegen das Gesetz wird hart bestraft.* be in breach of sth gegen etw. verstoßen [ɡeːɡn̩ ... fɛˌʃtoːsn̩] <verstößt, verstieß, hat verstoßen> ◊ *gegen die Regeln verstoßen* breach of contract Vertragsbruch [fɛˈtraːksbrʊx] der <-(e)s, Vertragsbrüche> ◊ *Wenn Sie nicht fristgemäß zahlen, begehen Sie einen Vertragsbruch.* **2.** *(in a relationship)* Bruch [brʊx] der <-(e)s, Brüche> ◊ *Die anhaltenden Auseinandersetzungen führten zum Bruch mit der Partei.* **3.** breach of confidence Vertrauensbruch [fɛˈtraɔənsbrʊx] der <-(e)s, Vertrauensbrüche> **4.** breach of the peace öffentliche Ruhestörung [ˌœfn̩tlɪçə 'ruːəʃtøːrʊŋ] die <-, -en>

breach² [verb] **1.** *(rules, regulations)* breach sth gegen etw. verstoßen [ɡeːɡn̩ ... fɛˌʃtoːsn̩] <verstößt, verstieß, hat verstoßen> ◊ *Er hat gegen die Spielregeln*

verstoßen. **2.** *(a wall, defences, security etc.)* durchbrechen [dʊʳçˈbrɛçn̩] <durchbricht, durchbrach, hat durchbrochen> ◊ *Die Demonstranten durchbrachen die Polizeibarrikaden.*

bread [noun] Brot [broːt] das <-(e)s, -e> ◊ *Wir essen lieber dunkles Brot und selten Brötchen.* ◆ *Brot backen*

● **know which side your bread is buttered** wissen, wo es was zu holen gibt

break¹ [noun] **1.** *(rest, pause)* Pause ['paɔzə] die <-, -n> ◊ *Nach der Pause geht der Film weiter.* ◆ *Eben hat es zur Pause geklingelt.* ◆ *Ich brauche ein Pause vom Alltag.* take a break eine Pause machen **2.** *(with what has gone before)* break (with sth/sb) Bruch (mit etw./jdm) [brʊx] der <-(e)s, Brüche> ◊ *ein Bruch mit der Vergangenheit* ◆ *Nach einem Streit kam es zum Bruch mit seiner Familie.* **3.** *(place where sth is broken)* Bruchstelle ['brʊxʃtɛlə] die <-, -n> ◊ *An der Bruchstelle hatte sich eine Bluterguss gebildet.* ◆ *Durch die Bruchstelle an der Leitung trat Gas aus.* **4.** *(time off, in compound ns)* ... break ...ferien ['feːrjən] die <-> *only pl* summer break Sommerferien ['zɔməfɛːrjən] ◊ *Wann fangen die Sommerferien an?* Christmas break Weihnachtsferien ['vaɛnaxtsfɛːrjən] ◊ *In den Weihnachtsferien fahre ich zu meinen Eltern.* short break Kurzurlaub ['kʊʳtsluːɡlaɔp] der <-(e)s, -e> ◊ *sing* **5.** *(opportunity)* big break großer Durchbruch [groːsɐ 'dʊʳçbrʊx] der <-(e)s *or* Durchbrüche> ◊ *Mit dieser Single hat sie den großen Durchbruch geschafft.*

● **have a good/bad break** Glück/Pech haben *(fam)* **give sb a break 1.** *(get off sb's back)* jdn in Ruhe lassen **2.** *(give sb a rest from sth)* jdm eine Auszeit gönnen **make a break for sth** auf etw. [acc] losrennen

break² [verb] **1.** *(also fig)* (separate, sever, violate, surpass) brechen ['brɛçn̩] <bricht, brach, hat/ist gebrochen> *transitive use* +haben/intransitive use +sein ◊ *Er brach den Stock in zwei Teile.* ◆ *Das Stuhlbein brach.* ◆ *Du hast mir den Arm gebrochen!* ◆ *einen Vertrag/sein Wort brechen* ◆ *Sie hat mir das Herz gebrochen.* ◆ *den Weltrekord brechen; (into many pieces)* zerbrechen [tsɛˈbrɛçn̩] <zerbricht, zerbrach, hat/ist zerbrochen> *transitive use* +haben/ *intransitive use* +sein ◊ *Max hat sein Spielzeugauto zerbrochen.* ◆ *Die Fensterscheibe zerbrach.; (string of a musical instrument)* sth breaks etw. reißt [raɛst] <riss, ist gerissen> ◊ *Dem Gitarristen ist eine Saite gerissen.* break sth in half etw. mitten durchbrechen [mɪtn̩ 'dʊʳçbrɛçn̩] +haben ◊ *Er brach das Brot mitten durch und gab ihr eine Hälfte.* **2.** *(machine, appliance)* sth breaks etw. geht kaputt [ɡeːt ka'pʊt] <geht kaputt, ging kaputt, ist kaputtgegangen> ◊ *Die Waschmaschine ist schon wieder kaputtgegangen.; (destroy)* break sth etw. kaputtmachen [ka'pʊtmaxn̩] +haben ◊ *Ich glaube, ich habe das Radio kaputtgemacht.* **3.** *(news)* sth breaks etw. wird bekannt [vɪʳt bə'kant] <wird, ist> ◊ *Sollte der Skandal jemals bekannt werden, wird er gefeuert.* break the news that bekannt geben, dass [bə'kant ɡeːbm̩ das] <gibt, gab, hat gegeben> break sth to sb jdm etw. sagen ['zaːɡn̩] +haben ◊ *Wie soll ich ihr nur sagen, dass ihr Mann verunglückt ist?* **4.** *(pause)* Schluss machen ['ʃlʊs maxn̩] +haben ◊ *Wir machen jetzt Schluss und setzen die Diskussion in zwei Stunden*

fort. **5.** *(a bad or unpleasant situation)* break sth etw. beenden [bə'lɛndn̩] <beendet, beendete, hat beendet> ◊ *Die Betriebsleitung konnte den Streik nicht beenden.* break the cycle of poverty/violence den Kreislauf der Armut/Gewalt durchbrechen [de:n ˌkraɛslaof de:ɐ̯ 'aɐ̯muːt/gə'valt dʊɐ̯ç,brɛçn̩] <durchbricht, durchbrach, hat durchbrochen> **6.** *(day)* anbrechen ['anbrɛçn̩] <bricht an, brach an, ist angebrochen> ◊ *Der neue Tag bricht an.* **7.** *(storm)* losbrechen ['lo:sbrɛçn̩] <bricht los, brach los, ist losgebrochen> ◊ *Plötzlich brach der Sturm los.* **8.** sb's voice breaks jd kommt in den Stimmbruch [kɔmt ɪn de:n 'ʃtɪmbrʊx] <kam, ist gekommen>
• **break away** ⌐phras v⌐ **1.** *(escape)* break away (from sb/sth) sich (von jdm/etw.) losreißen ['lo:sraɛsn̩] <reißt sich los, riss sich los, hat sich losgerissen> ◊ *Der Gefangene riss sich plötzlich los und entkam.* ♦ *Sie kann sich einfach nicht von ihm losreißen.* **2.** *(leave, separate)* break away (from sb/ sth) sich (von jdm/etw.) trennen ['trɛnən] +haben ◊ *Sie trennte sich nach 20 Jahren Ehe von ihrem Mann.* ♦ *Er hat sich von der Partei getrennt.* **3.** *(come off)* abbrechen ['apbrɛçn̩] <bricht ab, brach ab, ist abgebrochen> ◊ *Der Henkel brach ab und die Tasse fiel auf den Boden.*
• **break down** ⌐phras v⌐ **1.** *(machine, power)* ausfallen ['aosfalən] <fällt aus, fiel aus, ist ausgefallen> ◊ *Der Strom ist ausgefallen.* **2.** *(system, organization, person)* zusammenbrechen [tsu'zamənbrɛçn̩] <bricht zusammen, brach zusammen, ist zusammengebrochen> ◊ *Am Montag brach die Funkverbindung zusammen.* ♦ *Sie brach weinend zusammen.* **3.** *(negotiations, peace talks etc.)* scheitern ['ʃaɛtən] <scheitert, scheiterte, ist gescheitert> ◊ *Die Verhandlungen sind gescheitert.* **4.** *(negative feelings, difficulties, chemical substances)* abbauen ['apbaoən] +haben ◊ *Der Schüleraustausch soll Vorurteile abbauen.* ♦ *Wie können Aggressionen abgebaut werden?* ♦ *Mit Hilfe dieses Enzyms wird Stärke abgebaut.* **5.** *(costs, expenditure)* aufschlüsseln ['aofʃlʏsl̩n] <schlüsselt auf, schlüsselte auf, hat aufgeschlüsselt> ◊ *die Personalkosten aufschlüsseln* **6.** *(a door)* eintreten ['aɛntreːtn̩] <tritt ein, trat ein, hat eingetreten> ◊ *Die Feuerwehr musste die Haustür eintreten.; (a wall)* einreißen ['aɛnraɛsn̩] <reißt ein, riss ein, hat eingerissen> ◊ *eine Mauer einreißen*
• **break in** ⌐phras v⌐ **1.** *(enter illegally)* einbrechen ['aɛnbrɛçn̩] <bricht ein, brach ein, ist eingebrochen> ◊ *In unser Haus ist eingebrochen worden.; (a door)* aufbrechen ['aofbrɛçn̩] <bricht auf, brach auf, hat aufgebrochen> ◊ *Jemand hat unser Garagentor aufgebrochen.* **2.** *(interrupt)* unterbrechen [ʊntɐ'brɛçn̩] <unterbricht, unterbrach, hat unterbrochen> ◊ *„Gert", unterbrach er, „ich muss dir etwas sagen."* **3.** *(a new employee etc.)* break sb in jdn einarbeiten ['aɛn|aɐ̯baɛtn̩] <arbeitet ein, arbeitete ein, hat eingearbeitet> ◊ *Der Meister arbeitet die Lehrlinge ein.* **4.** *(shoes)* einlaufen ['aɛnlaofn̩] <läuft ein, lief ein, hat eingelaufen> ◊ *Ich muss die neuen Schuhe noch einlaufen.*
• **break into** ⌐phras v⌐ **1.** *(a building)* break into sth in etw. ⌐acc⌐ einbrechen [ɪn ... ˌaɛnbrɛçn̩] <bricht ein, brach ein, ist eingebrochen> ◊ *Am Mittwoch wurde in die Bank eingebrochen.; (a car, safe)* break into sth etw. aufbrechen ['aofbrɛçn̩] <bricht auf, brach auf, hat aufgebrochen> ◊ *Jemand hat den Safe*

aufgebrochen und 8000 Euro gestohlen. **2.** *(start sth suddenly)* break into a run loslaufen ['lo:slaofn̩] <läuft los, lief los, ist losgelaufen> break into laughter loslachen ['lo:slaxn̩] +haben break into applause zu applaudieren beginnen [tsu: aplao'di:rən bəgɪnən] <beginnt, begann, hat begonnen> ◊ *Das Publikum begann zu applaudieren.* **3.** *(savings, rations etc.)* anbrechen ['anbrɛçn̩] <bricht an, brach an, hat angebrochen> ◊ *Ich möchte meine Ersparnisse nicht anbrechen.* **4.** *(interrupt)* unterbrechen [ʊntɐ'brɛçn̩] <unterbricht, unterbrach, hat unterbrochen> ◊ *Ein lautes Geräusch unterbrach die Stille.* **5.** *(start to have success in sth)* break into sth sich ⌐dat⌐ einen Namen bei/auf etw. ⌐dat⌐ machen [aɛnən ˌnaːmən baɛ/aof ... maxn̩] +haben ◊ *Sie machte sich einen Namen beim Theater.* ♦ *Wie macht man sich auf diesem Markt einen Namen?*
• **break off** ⌐phras v⌐ **1.** *(stop, become severed)* abbrechen ['apbrɛçn̩] <bricht ab, brach ab, hat/ist abgebrochen> *transitive use +haben/intransitive use +sein* ◊ *Er hat seine Ausbildung abgebrochen.* ♦ *Der Präsident brach seinen Urlaub vorzeitig ab.* ♦ *Der Kontakt zwischen den beiden ist abgebrochen.* ♦ *Sie brach ein Stück Baguette ab und gab es mir.* **2.** *(an engagement)* auflösen ['aofløːzn̩] +haben ◊ *Sie löste die Verlobung auf.* **3.** *(stop temporarily)* unterbrechen [ʊntɐ'brɛçn̩] <unterbricht, unterbrach, hat unterbrochen> ◊ *Die Sitzung wurde für eine halbe Stunde unterbrochen.*
• **break out** ⌐phras v⌐ ausbrechen ['aosbrɛçn̩] <bricht aus, brach aus, ist ausgebrochen> ◊ *Zwei Gefangene sind aus dem Gefängnis ausgebrochen.* ♦ *Das Feuer ist im dritten Stock ausgebrochen.* ♦ *Ein Krieg brach aus.*
• **break through** ⌐phras v⌐ **1.** *(a barrier)* durchbrechen [dʊɐ̯ç'brɛçn̩] <durchbricht, durchbrach, hat durchbrochen> ◊ *Die Demonstranten durchbrachen die Absperrung.* **2.** *(sun, light)* break through sth durch etw. brechen [dʊɐ̯ç ... ˌbrɛçn̩] <bricht, brach, ist gebrochen> ◊ *Endlich brach die Sonne durch die Wolken.* **3.** *(a negative attitude)* überwinden [ybɐ'vɪndn̩] <überwindet, überwand, hat überwunden> ◊ *Wie können wir unsere Vorurteile überwinden?*
• **break up** ⌐phras v⌐ **1.** *(fall apart)* auseinander brechen [aos|aɛ'nande brɛçn̩] <bricht, brach, ist gebrochen> ◊ *Das Flugzeug brach mitten in der Luft auseinander.* **2.** break sth up into squares etw. in Vierecke brechen [ɪn 'fiːɐ̯ɛkə ˌbrɛçn̩] <bricht, brach, hat gebrochen> break sth up into two pieces etw. in zwei Teile brechen [ɪn tsvaɛ 'taɛlə ˌbrɛçn̩] **3.** *(destroy, ruin)* break sth up etw. zerstören [tsɐ'ʃtøːrən] <zerstört, zerstörte, hat zerstört> ◊ *Eifersucht zerstört eine Beziehung.; (come to an end, be destroyed)* sth breaks up etw. zerbricht [tsɛ'brɪçt] <zerbrach, ist zerbrochen> ◊ *Unter diesem Druck zerbrach die Familie.* **4.** *(end a relationship)* break up with sb sich von jdm trennen [fɔn ... ˌtrɛnən] +haben ◊ *Er trennte sich nach dreijähriger Ehe von ihr.* **5.** *(talks, negotiations)* break sth up etw. beenden [bə'lɛndn̩] <beendet, beendete, hat beendet> ◊ *Die Direktorin beendete die Sitzung.; (talks, negotiations, school)* sth breaks up etw. endet ['ɛndət] <endete, hat geendet> ◊ *Die Sitzung endete erst weit nach Mitternacht.* ♦ *Wann endet das Semester/das Schuljahr?* **6.** *(disband)* break sth up etw. auflösen ['aofløːzn̩] +haben ◊ *Die Polizei löste die Demonstra-*

A
B
C
D
E
F
G
H
I
J
K
L
M
N
O
P
Q
R
S
T
U
V
W
X
Y
Z

tion auf. sth breaks up etw. löst sich auf ◊ *Die Demonstration löste sich gegen 18 Uhr auf.* break sb up jdn auseinander treiben [ao̯s|a̯e'nandə tra̯ebm̩] <treibt, trieb, hat getrieben> ◊ *Die Polizei trieb die Demonstranten auseinander.*

breakdown [noun] **1.** *(of a system, person, an organization)* Zusammenbruch [ʦu'samənbrʊx] der <-(e)s, Zusammenbrüche> ◊ *der Zusammenbruch des Funknetzes* ♦ *Sie erholte sich nur schwer von ihrem Zusammenbruch.* **2.** *(of a machine)* Ausfall ['ao̯sfal] der <-(e)s, Ausfälle> ◊ *der Ausfall eines Triebwerks; (of a vehicle)* Panne ['panə] die <-, -n> ◊ *Der Bus hatte eine Panne.* ♦ *mit einer Panne liegen bleiben* **3.** *(of expenditure, figures)* Aufschlüsselung ['ao̯fʃlʏsəlʊŋ] die <-, -en> ◊ *eine Aufschlüsselung der Kosten* **4.** CHEM *(chemical process)* Abbau ['apba̯o̯] der <-(e)s> no pl ◊ *der Abbau von Zucker/ Stärke*

breakfast [noun] Frühstück ['fry:ʃtʏk] das <-s, -e> ◊ *Eine Übernachtung mit Frühstück kostet 50 Euro.* ♦ *Was gibt es zum Frühstück?*

break-in [noun] Einbruch ['a̯enbrʊx] der <-(e)s, Einbrüche> ◊ *Bei einem Einbruch in ein Privathaus wurden 5000 Euro gestohlen.*

breakout [noun] Ausbruch ['ao̯sbrʊx] der <-(e)s, Ausbrüche> ◊ *sein Ausbruch aus dem Gefängnis*

breakthrough [noun] Durchbruch ['dʊr̯çbrʊx] der <-(e)s, Durchbrüche> ◊ *Die Rolle des Hamlet hat ihm zum Durchbruch verholfen.* ♦ *Der Fund des Knochens war ein Durchbruch für die Forscher.*

break-up [noun] **1.** *(of a marriage)* Scheitern ['ʃa̯eten] das <-(e)s> no pl ◊ *Sie konnte das Scheitern ihrer Ehe nie ganz verwinden.* **2.** *(of an empire)* Zerfall [ʦe'fal] der <-(e)s> no pl ◊ *der Zerfall der Sowjetunion*

breast [noun] Brust [brʊst] die <-, Brüste> ◊ *dem Baby die Brust geben* ♦ *Bei dieser Vogelart hat das Männchen eine rote Brust.*

breast-feed [verb] stillen ['ʃtɪlən] +haben ◊ *ein Baby stillen* ♦ *Stör sie jetzt nicht, sie stillt gerade.*

breath [noun] Atem ['a:təm] der <-s> no pl ◊ *Sie holte tief Atem.* ♦ *Ich bin vom Laufen außer Atem.*
◉ a breath of air ein Lufthauch

breathe [verb] **1.** *(in and out)* atmen ['a:tmən] +haben ◊ *Er atmete durch den Mund.* ♦ *Atmet er noch?* **2.** *(only in)* einatmen ['a̯en|a:tmən] <atmet ein, atmete ein, hat eingeatmet> ◊ *Ich möchte den Zigarettenqualm nicht einatmen.* **3.** *(whisper)* hauchen ['hao̯xn̩] +haben ◊ *Sie beugte sich zu ihm hinunter und hauchte ihm etwas ins Ohr.*
• breathe in [phras v] einatmen ['a̯en|a:tmən] <atmet ein, atmete ein, hat eingeatmet> ◊ *Er atmete gierig den Rauch einer Zigarette ein.* ♦ *Atmen Sie bitte tief ein und halten Sie die Luft an!*
• breathe out [phras v] ausatmen ['ao̯s|a:tmən] <atmet aus, atmete aus, hat ausgeatmet> ◊ *Atmen Sie nun ruhig aus!* ♦ *die verbrauchte Luft ausatmen*

breathing [noun] *(respiration)* Atmung ['a:tmʊŋ] die <-> no pl ◊ *Er hat eine unregelmäßige Atmung.*

breathless [adj] **1.** *(out of breath, without breathing)* atemlos ['a:təmlo:s] <atemloser, am atemlosesten> ◊ *Es herrschte atemlose Stille.* be breathless with sth vor etw. atemlos sein ◊ *Sie war atemlos vor Angst.* sth leaves sb breathless etw. verschlägt jdm den Atem [fɐʃlɛ:kt ... de:n 'a:təm] <verschlug, hat verschla-

gen> at a breathless pace mit atemberaubender Schnelligkeit [mɪt ˌa:təmbə'ra̯obm̩də 'ʃnɛlɪçka̯et] **2.** *(very fast)* rasant [ra'zant] <rasanter, am rasantesten> ◊ *ein rasanter Film* ♦ *Das Tempo war rasant.* **3.** *(without air, stuffy)* stickig ['ʃtɪkɪç] ◊ *eine kleines, stickiges Zimmer* ♦ *Hier ist es ziemlich stickig.*

breathlessly [adv] **1.** *(out of breath, without breathing)* atemlos ['a:təmlo:s] <atemloser, am atemlosesten> ◊ *Sie börten ihn atemlos zu.* **2.** *(very fast)* rasant [ra'zant] <rasanter, am rasantesten> ◊ *Dieser Film ist rasant inszeniert.*

breathtaking [adj] atemberaubend ['a:təmbə,ra̯obm̩t] ◊ *ein atemberaubender Blick auf die Berge* ♦ *Die Aussicht war atemberaubend.*

breed¹ [noun] **1.** *(of animal)* Rasse ['rasə] die <-, -n> ◊ *Das Pferd ist von edler Rasse.* breed of dog Hunderasse ['hʊndərasə] breed of cat Katzenrasse ['katsn̩rasə] **2.** *(of plant)* Sorte ['zɔr̯tə] die <-, -n> ◊ *Diese Sorte blüht im August.* breed of rose Rosensorte ['ro:zn̩zɔr̯tə] breed of tulip Tulpensorte ['tʊlpm̩zɔr̯tə]

breed² [verb] **1.** *(animals, plants)* züchten ['tsʏçtn̩] +haben ◊ *Ich züchte Schafe/Rosen.* **2.** *(have young: birds)* brüten ['bry:tn̩] +haben ◊ *Die Störche haben in diesem Jahr erfolgreich gebrütet.; (mammals)* Junge bekommen ['jʊŋə bəkɔmən] <bekommt, bekam, hat bekommen> ◊ *Haben eure Hamster schon Junge bekommen?* **3.** *(fig) (cause or produce sth)* schaffen ['ʃafn̩] +haben ◊ *Jede Lüge schafft neues Misstrauen.*

breeding [noun] *(of animals, plants)* Zucht [ʦʊxt] die <-, -en> ◊ *die Zucht bedrohter Tierarten*

breeze [noun] Brise ['bri:zə] die <-, -n> ◊ *Abends wehte eine frische Brise.*
◉ be a breeze kinderleicht sein

brewery [noun] Brauerei [bra̯oə'ra̯e] die <-, -en>

bribery [noun] Bestechung [bə'ʃtɛçʊŋ] die <-> no pl ◊ *aktive/passive Bestechung* be open to bribery bestechlich sein [bə'ʃtɛçlɪç za̯en] +sein

brick [noun] **1.** *(for building)* Backstein ['bakʃta̯en] der <-(e)s, -e> ◊ *ein solides Haus aus Backstein* ♦ *Backsteine gebraucht kaufen* **2.** *(children's toy)* Bauklotz ['ba̯oklɔts] der <-es, Bauklötze> ◊ *Unser Sohn spielt gern mit seinen neuen Bauklötzen.*
◉ come up against a brick wall plötzlich vor einer Mauer stehen it's like talking to a brick wall da kann man ja gleich gegen die Wand reden drop a brick ins Fettnäpfchen treten

bricklayer [noun] Maurer ['ma̯orɐ] der <-s, -> ♀Maurerin ['ma̯orərɪn] die <-, -nen> ◊ *Er ist Maurer von Beruf.* ♦ *Der Maurer ist mit seiner Arbeit noch nicht fertig.*

bride [noun] Braut [bra̯ot] die <-, Bräute> ◊ *Sie dürfen die Braut jetzt küssen.*

bridegroom [noun] Bräutigam ['brɔøtɪgam] der <-s, -e>

bridesmaid [noun] Brautjungfer ['bra̯otjʊŋfɐ] die <-, -n>

bridge¹ [noun] Brücke ['brʏkə] die <-, -n> ◊ *über eine Brücke gehen/fahren* ♦ *Der Zahnarzt hat ihr eine Brücke eingesetzt.* ♦ *Wir wollen Brücken zwischen den Völkern bauen.* ♦ *Der Kapitän ist auf der Brücke.*

brief¹ [noun] **1.** *(instructions)* Anweisungen ['anva̯ezʊŋən] die <-> only pl ◊ *Ich muss mich strikt an die Anweisungen halten.* sb's brief is to do sth jd ist angewiesen, etw. zu tun [ɪst 'angəvi:zn̩ ... ʦu:]

+sein ◊ *Ich bin angewiesen, die Informationen zu
überprüfen.* **2.** LAW *(in the UK: case for a barrister)*
*ein detailliertes Mandat an einen Anwalt; (in the
US: legal document) ein Dokument, das die
Beweislage für das Gericht zusammenfasst*

brief² [verb] brief sb on sth jdn über etw. [acc] informieren [y:bɐ ... ɪnfɐˈmiːrən] <informiert, informierte,
hat informiert> ◊ *Jörg hat mich über alle Details
informiert.*

brief(ly) [adj, adv] kurz [kʊɐ̯ts] <kürzer, am kürzesten>
◊ *Der Aufsatz ist zu kurz.* ♦ *ein kurzer Aufenthalt in
Berlin* ♦ *Sie schilderte kurz, was geschehen war.*
keep it brief sich kurz fassen ◊ *Fassen Sie sich
kurz! Ich habe wenig Zeit.*
◉ be brief kurz angebunden sein in brief kurz
gesagt

briefcase [noun] Aktentasche [ˈaktn̩taʃə] die <-, -n>
◊ *Er öffnete die Aktentasche und nahm einen
Ordner heraus.*

briefs [noun] Unterhose [ˈʊntɐhoːzə] die <-, -n> can
be used in the pl or sing ◊ *Sie zog eine Unterhose
an.* ♦ *Er zog die Unterhosen aus.* a pair of briefs
eine Unterhose

bright [adj] **1.** *(full of light)* hell [hɛl] ◊ *ein helles
Zimmer* ♦ *Dank der großen Fenster sind die Räume
sehr hell.* **2.** *(colo(u)r, eyes)* leuchtend [ˈlɔɡçtn̩t] ◊ *ein
leuchtend blauer Himmel* ♦ *Er sah mich mit leuch-
tenden Augen an.* ♦ *Das Rot ist mir zu leuchtend.*
3. *(weather, day)* heiter [ˈhaetɐ] ◊ *ein heiterer Tag* ♦
Das Wetter war heiter und kühl. **4.** *(person)* aufgeweckt [ˈaofɡəvɛkt] <aufgeweckter, am aufgewecktes-
ten> ◊ *ein aufgeweckter Schüler* ♦ *Sie ist wirklich
sehr aufgeweckt.* **5.** *(idea, future)* glänzend [ˈɡlɛntsn̩t]
◊ *Die Idee ist wirklich glänzend!* ♦ *Der Sängerin
steht eine glänzende Karriere bevor.* **6.** *(smile)*
strahlend [ˈʃtraːlənt] ◊ *ein strahlendes Lächeln* sb's
smile is bright jd hat ein strahlendes Lächeln give
sb a bright smile jd anstrahlen [ˈanʃtraːlən] +haben

brightly [adv] **1.** *(full of light)* hell [hɛl] ◊ *hell
leuchten/strahlen* **2.** *(describing colo(u)rs, eyes)*
leuchtend [ˈlɔɡçtn̩t] ◊ *Beim Fasan ist das Männchen
leuchtend gefärbt.* **3.** *(cheerfully)* fröhlich [ˈfrøːlɪç] ◊
fröhlich strahlen

brightness [noun] **1.** *(gleam, brilliance)* Glanz [ɡlants]
der <-es> no pl ◊ *der strahlende Glanz der Sonne*
2. *(property of being full of light)* Helligkeit
[ˈhɛlɪçkaet] die <-, -en> most sing ◊ *Die Helligkeit
der Sonne schadet den Augen.*

brilliance [noun] **1.** *(brightness)* Glanz [ɡlants] der
<-es> no pl ◊ *der strahlende Glanz der Sonne*
2. *(great talent, intelligence)* Genialität [ɡenjaliˈtɛːt]
die <-> no pl ◊ *die Genialität Einsteins*

brilliant(ly) [adj, adv] **1.** *(very intelligent, skilful)* genial
[ɡeˈnjaːl] ◊ *Deine Idee ist einfach genial!* ♦ *Albert
Einstein war ein genialer Wissenschaftler.* ♦ *genial
erdacht* **2.** *(excellent and with class)* großartig
[ˈɡroːsˌaɐ̯tɪç] ◊ *eine großartige Schauspielerin* ♦
Diese Leistung ist wirklich großartig. ♦ *großartig
inszeniert* **3.** *(fam) (very good, nice)* prima [ˈpriːma]
invariable *(fam)* ◊ *eine prima Stimmung* ♦ *Das
Wetter war prima.* ♦ *Ich komme prima mit ihm
zurecht.* **4.** *(gleaming, bright)* glänzend [ˈɡlɛntsn̩t] ◊
eine glänzende Oberfläche be brilliant glänzen
[ˈɡlɛntsn̩] +haben ◊ *Nach dem Polieren glänzte die
Granitplatte.* The sun shone brilliantly. Die Sonne
strahlte.

brim [noun] Rand [rant] der <-(e)s, Ränder> ◊ *Der
Weg auf dem Rand des Kraters ist brüchig.* full to
the brim randvoll [ˈrantfɔl] no comp/superl

bring [verb] **1.** *(take along, come with)* bring sth/sb
(along) etw./jdn mitbringen [ˈmɪtbrɪŋən] <bringt mit,
brachte mit, hat mitgebracht> ◊ *Ich hab dir eine CD
mitgebracht.* ♦ *Kann ich meinen Freund mitbringen?; (fetch sth)* bring sb sth jdm etw. bringen
[ˈbrɪŋən] <bringt, brachte, hat gebracht> +haben ◊ *Ich
bringe Ihnen sofort die Getränke.* **2.** *(result in, entail)*
sth brings sth etw. bringt etw. [brɪŋt] <brachte, hat
gebracht> ◊ *Mach das nicht; das bringt bloß Ärger.* ♦
Seine Politik hat dem Land Wohlstand gebracht.
3. *(cause sb to be in a certain place)* bring sb
somewhere jdn irgendwohin führen [ˈfyːrən] +haben
◊ *Was führt Sie in diese Gegend?*
◉ bring yourself to do sth es über sich [acc]
bringen, etw. zu tun
• **bring about** [phras v] bring sth about **1.** *(cause
sth to happen)* etw. bewirken [bəˈvɪʁkn̩] <bewirkt,
bewirkte, hat bewirkt> ◊ *Seine Worte haben ein
Umdenken bewirkt.* ♦ *Liebe kann viel bewirken.*
2. *(bring sth into existence)* etw. herbeiführen
[hɛˈbaefyːrən] +haben ◊ *Neuwahlen sind der einzige
Weg, um eine politische Wende herbeizuführen.* **3.** *(a
dangerous or unpleasant situation)* etw. heraufbeschwören [hɛˈraofbəʃvøːrən] <beschwört herauf,
beschwor herauf, hat heraufbeschworen> ◊ *einen
Skandal/Streit/Krieg heraufbeschwören*
• **bring back** [phras v] **1.** *(return to a person or
place)* bring sb/sth back etw./jdn zurückbringen
[tsuˈʁʏkbrɪŋən] <bringt zurück, brachte zurück, hat
zurückgebracht> ◊ *Der Pfleger brachte den Patienten
zurück in sein Zimmer.* bring sb/sth back to sb jdm
jd/etw. zurückbringen ◊ *Hat Edith dir schon deinen
Koffer zurückgebracht?* bring sb back to sth jdn zu
etw. zurückbringen ◊ *Das bringt uns zurück zu der
Frage, wie ...* **2.** *(feelings, memories)* bring sth back
etw. wecken [ˈvɛkn̩] +haben ◊ *Das Klassentreffen hat
wieder alte Erinnerungen geweckt.* **3.** *(a present,
souvenir, news)* bring sth back etw. mitbringen
[ˈmɪtbrɪŋən] <bringt mit, brachte mit, hat mitge-
bracht> ◊ *Hast du Neuigkeiten mitgebracht?* ♦ *Ich
hab dir eine Kleinigkeit aus Italien mitgebracht.*
4. *(restore sb to a former position)* bring sb back jdn
wieder einsetzen [viːdɐ ˈaenzɛtsn̩] +haben ◊ *Er wurde
in sein früheres Amt wieder eingesetzt.; (reintroduce
sth)* bring sth back etw. wieder einführen
[viːdɐ ˈaenfyːrən] +haben ◊ *Mehrere Staaten haben
die Todesstrafe wieder eingeführt.* **5.** *(restore sb to a
former condition)* bring sb back to life/health jdn
wieder lebendig/gesund machen
[viːdɐ ˈlɛbɛndɪç/ɡəˈzʊnt maxn̩] +haben
• **bring down** [phras v] **1.** *(a government, politician)*
bring sth/sb down etw./jdn stürzen [ˈʃtʏɐ̯tsn̩] +haben
◊ *Die Rebellen wollen die Regierung/den Präsidenten
stürzen.* **2.** *(prices, costs etc.)* bring sth down etw.
senken [ˈzɛŋkn̩] +haben ◊ *Die Personalkosten müssen
gesenkt werden.* **3.** *(make fall to the ground)* bring sb
down jdn zu Fall bringen [tsuː ˈfal brɪŋən] <bringt,
brachte, hat gebracht> ◊ *Er brachte seinen Gegner
schon in der ersten Runde zu Fall.* bring sth down
etw. umstürzen lassen [ˈʊmʃtʏɐ̯tsn̩ lasn̩] <lässt, ließ,
hat lassen> ◊ *Der Sturm ließ die Bäume umstürzen.*
4. *(kill by shooting)* bring sb down niederschießen
[ˈniːdɐʃiːsn̩] <schießt nieder, schoss nieder, hat nieder-

geschossen>*; (a bird, plane)* bring an animal/sth down eine Tier/etw. abschießen ['apʃiːsn̩] <schießt ab, schoss ab, hat abgeschossen> ◊ *Der Hubschrauber wurde abgeschossen.*

• **bring forward** phras v bring sth forward **1.** *(make sth happen earlier than expected)* etw. vorziehen ['foːɡtsiːən] <zieht vor, zog vor, hat vorgezogen> ◊ *Die geplante Steuerreform soll um ein Jahr vorgezogen werden.* **2.** *(announce proposals, plans etc.)* etw. bekannt geben [bəˈkant ɡeːbm̩] <gibt, gab, hat gegeben> ◊ *Der Regierungssprecher gab am Abend den neuen Gesetzentwurf bekannt.*

• **bring in** phras v **1.** bring in an expert einen Experten einschalten [aɛnən ɛksˈpɛʁtn̩ aɛnʃaltn̩] eine Expertin einschalten [aɛnə ɛksˈpɛʁtɪn aɛnʃaltn̩] <schaltet ein, schaltete ein, hat eingeschaltet> ◊ *Es wird Zeit, einen Experten einzuschalten.* bring in new talent neue Talente finden [ˌnɔøə taˈlɛntə fɪndn̩] <findet, fand, hat gefunden> ◊ *Die Firma möchte neue Talente für diese Aufgabe finden.* **2.** LAW *(a bill)* bring sth in etw. einbringen ['aɛnbrɪŋən] <bringt ein, brachte ein, hat eingebracht> ◊ *eine Vorlage für ein neues Gesetz einbringen* bring in a verdict ein Urteil fällen [aɛn ˈʊʁtaɛl fɛlən] +haben bring in a verdict of guilty jdn schuldig sprechen ['ʃʊldɪç ʃprɛçn̩] <spricht, sprach, hat gesprochen> bring in a verdict of not guilty jdn freisprechen ['fraɛʃprɛçn̩] <spricht frei, sprach frei, hat freigesprochen> **3.** *(introduce: new fashions, customs, rules)* bring sth in etw. einführen ['aɛnfyːrən] +haben ◊ *Dieser Brauch wurde vor rund 100 Jahren eingeführt.; (reforms)* etw. umsetzen ['ʊmzɛtsn̩] +haben ◊ *Wann werden die Gesundheitsreformen umgesetzt?* **4.** *(the harvest)* brings sth in etw. einbringen ['aɛnbrɪŋən] <bringt ein, brachte ein, hat eingebracht> ◊ *Die Ernte muss vor dem Regen eingebracht werden.*

• **bring on** phras v *(cause sth unpleasant)* bring sth on etw. auslösen ['aɔsløːzn̩] +haben ◊ *Was hat diese Krankheit ausgelöst?*

• **bring out** phras v bring sth out **1.** *(produce sth, fetch sth to take it outdoors)* etw.herausbringen [hɛˈraɔsbrɪŋən] <bringt heraus, brachte heraus, hat herausgebracht> ◊ *Der Autor bringt bald seinen vierten Roman heraus.* ♦ *Sie brachte vor Angst keinen Ton heraus.* ♦ *Bring bitte das Fleisch heraus; wir grillen jetzt.* **2.** *(make sth appear, show)* etw. zum Vorschein bringen [tsʊm ˈfoːɐ̯ʃaɛn brɪŋən] <bringt, brachte, hat gebracht> ◊ *Manchmal bringt die Not das Beste im Menschen zum Vorschein.* **3.** *(emphasize)* etw. hervorheben [hɛˈfoːɐ̯heːbm̩] <hebt hervor, hob hervor, hat hervorgehoben> ◊ *In seiner Rede hob er den engagierten Einsatz vieler freiwilliger Helfer hervor.*

• **bring together** phras v zusammenbringen [tsʊˈzamənbrɪŋən] <bringt zusammen, brachte zusammen, hat zusammengebracht> ◊ *die Enden der Stromkabel zusammenbringen* ♦ *Seine Arbeit hat ihn mit den unterschiedlichsten Menschen zusammengebracht.*

• **bring up** phras v **1.** *(children)* bring sb up jdn großziehen ['ɡroːstsiːən] <zieht groß, zog groß, hat großgezogen> ◊ *Sie hat fünf Söhne großgezogen.; (young animals)* aufziehen ['aɔftsiːən] <zieht auf, zog auf, hat aufgezogen> ◊ *Orang-Utans ziehen nur alle sieben bis acht Jahre ein Junges auf.* **2.** *(teach sb sth)* bring sb up to be sth jdn zu etw. erziehen

[tsuː: ... ɐ̯ˌtsiːən] <erzieht, erzog, hat erzogen> ◊ *Sie hat ihren Sohn zu großer Toleranz erzogen.* **3.** *(raise, mention)* bring sth up etw. ansprechen ['anʃprɛçn̩] <spricht an, sprach an, hat angesprochen> ◊ *Ich finde, du solltest das Problem ansprechen.* **4.** *(vomit)* bring sth up etw. brechen ['brɛçn̩] <bricht, brach, hat gebrochen> ◊ *Blut brechen*

brink noun Rand [rant] der <-(e)s, Ränder> to the brink of war bis an den Rand eines Krieges brink of the rock Felsrand ['fɛlsrant] be on the brink of (doing) sth kurz vor etw. stehen [kʊʁts foːɐ̯ ... ʃteːən] <steht, stand, hat gestanden> ◊ *Die Wissenschaftler stehen kurz vor der Entschlüsselung des Rätsels.*

brisk adj **1.** *(quick)* flott [flɔt] <flotter, am flottesten> ◊ *Das Tempo war mir nicht flott genug.* ♦ *mit flottem Schritt* **2.** *(abrupt)* schroff [ʃrɔf] ◊ *Er hat eine schroffe Art.* ♦ *Ihr Antwort fiel etwas schroff aus.* **3.** *(business, voting)* rege ['reːɡə] ◊ *Es herrschte reger Betrieb im Kaufhaus.* ♦ *eine rege Wahlbeteiligung* **4.** *(wind, weather)* frisch [frɪʃ] <frischer, am frischesten> ◊ *Am Abend kam ein frischer Wind auf.* ♦ *Die Brise war frisch.*

briskly adv **1.** *(quickly)* flott [flɔt] <flotter, am flottesten> ◊ *Sie liefen recht flott.* **2.** *(abruptly)* schroff [ʃrɔf] ◊ *„Gehen wir!", sagte sie schroff.*

Brit noun Brite ['briːtə] der <-n, -n> ♀Britin ['briːtɪn] die <-, -nen> → German[1]

British adj britisch ['briːtɪʃ] ◊ *britisches Englisch sprechen* the British die Briten [diː 'briːtn̩] <-> pl → German[2]

Briton noun Brite ['briːtə] der <-n, -n> ♀Britin ['briːtɪn] die <-, -nen> → German[1] **1.**

brittle adj **1.** *(hair, bones, nails)* brüchig ['brʏçɪç] ◊ *brüchige Fingernägel* ♦ *Im Alter wird die Knochensubstanz brüchig.* **2.** *(confidence)* schwach [ʃvax] <schwächer, am schwächsten> ◊ *ein schwaches Selbstbewusstsein haben; (relationship, situation)* zerbrechlich [tsɛˈbrɛçlɪç] ◊ *eine zerbrechliche Beziehung; (nerves)* empfindlich [ɛmˈpfɪntlɪç] ◊ *Warum sind deine Nerven so empfindlich?* **3.** *(sound, voice)* schrill [ʃrɪl] ◊ *ein schriller Ton* ♦ *Ihre Stimme ist furchtbar schrill.*

broad(ly) adj, adv **1.** *(street, shoulders, range, spectrum, smile, dialect)* breit [braɛt] <breiter, am breitesten> ◊ *breite Schultern* ♦ *ein breites Grinsen/Lächeln* ♦ *die Vokale breit aussprechen* **2.** *(concept, term)* weit [vaɛt] <weiter, am weitesten> when used as an adj, only before ns ◊ *Wir sprechen hier von der Liebe im weiteren Sinne.* ♦ *eine Vorschrift weit auslegen* **3.** *(theory)* umfassend [ʊmˈfasnt] ◊ *eine umfassende Theorie* ♦ *Das Kursangebot ist umfassend und ♦ eine umfassend angelegte Sicherheitspolitik* **4.** *(without details, rough)* grob [groːp] <gröber, am gröbsten> ◊ *eine grobe Zusammenfassung geben* ♦ *etw. entspricht nur grob den Vorstellungen* draw/paint sth in broad strokes etw. in groben Zügen umreißen

broadcast¹ noun **1.** *(TV or radio programme)* Sendung ['zɛndʊŋ] die <-, -en> ◊ *Diese Sendung kommt jeden Montag um 20 Uhr.* **2.** *(process of broadcasting sth)* Übertragung [ybeˈtraːɡʊŋ] die <-, -en> ◊ *Die Übertragung der Sendung war live.*

broadcast² verb **1.** *(on a TV or radio programme)* senden ['zɛndn̩] +haben ◊ *stündlich Nachrichten senden* **2.** *(an event, a football match etc.)* übertragen [ybeˈtraːɡn̩] <überträgt, übertrug, hat übertragen>

◊ *Das Konzert wurde live übertragen.* ✦ *Der Fernseh-sender überträgt alle drei Spiele.* **3.** *(a secret)* ausposaunen* ['a͜ʊspozaʊnən] <posaunt aus, posaunte aus, hat ausposaunt> *(fam, pej)* ◊ *Du musst ja nicht alles gleich ausposaunen!*

broadcasting station [noun] Sender ['zɛndə] der <-s, -> ◊ *ein kommerzieller Sender*

broaden [verb] **1.** *(make wider)* broaden sth etw. ver-breitern [fe'bra͜ɛtən] <verbreitert, verbreiterte, hat ver-breitert> ◊ *Dieser schmale Weg muss schnellstens ver-breitert werden.; (become wider)* sth broadens etw. wird breiter [wɪr't 'bra͜ɛtə] +sein ◊ *Nach einigen Metern wurde die Straße breiter.* **2.** *(fig) (make sth more extensive)* erweitern [e'va͜ɛtən] <erweitert, erwei-terte, hat erweitert> ◊ *Ich will mein Wissen auf diesem Gebiet erheblich erweitern.* broaden your horizons seinen Horizont erweitern sth broadens the mind etw. bildet ['bɪldət] <bildete, hat gebildet> ◊ *Reisen bildet ungemein.*

brochure [noun] **1.** *(containing information)* Broschüre [bro'ʃy:rə] die <-, -n> ◊ *eine Broschüre über das Museum* **2.** *(for advertising purposes)* Prospekt [pro'spɛkt] der <-(e)s, -e> ◊ *Laut Prospekt ist das Hotel direkt am Meer.* ✦ *einen Prospekt anfordern*

broken → **break²** [adj] **1.** *(bone, language, heart, spirit, person)* gebrochen [gə'brɔxn] *no comp/superl* ◊ *Das Bein war gebrochen.* ✦ *Sie starb 1920 als gebro-chene Frau.* ✦ *Er sprach ein gebrochenes Deutsch.* **2.** *(machine, equipment)* kaputt [ka'pʊt] *no comp/ superl* ◊ *ein kaputtes Radio* ✦ *Der Fahrstuhl ist kaputt.* **3.** *(home, relationship)* zerrüttet [tsɛ'rʏtət] ◊ *aus zerrütteten Familienverhältnissen kommen* ✦ *eine zerrüttete Ehe* **4.** *(line)* gestrichelt [gə'ʃtrɪçl̩t] *no comp/superl* ◊ *eine gestrichelte Linie*

broker [noun] Makler ['ma:klɐ] der <-s, -> ♀Maklerin ['ma:klərɪn] die <-, -nen> ◊ *Sie arbeitet in Köln als Maklerin.* ✦ *ein Haus durch einen Makler finden*

bronze¹ [noun] *(metal)* Bronze ['brɔŋsə] die <-, -n> *most sing* ◊ *eine Statue aus Bronze* ⊕ win Bronze Bronze holen

bronze² [adj] **1.** *(made of bronze)* bronzen ['brɔŋsn̩] *no comp/superl* ◊ *ein bronzenes Gefäß* **2.** *(bronze-coloured)* bronzefarben ['brɔŋsəfaʳbm̩] ◊ *eine bronze-farbene Kette/Bluse*

brood [verb] brüten ['bry:tn̩] +haben ◊ *Sieh mal, da sitzt ein Vogel im Nest und brütet.* ✦ *Er brütet schon tagelang über seinen neuen Plänen.*

broom [noun] **1.** *(for sweeping)* Besen ['be:zn̩] der <-s, -> ◊ *den Boden mit einem Besen fegen* **2.** BOT Ginster ['gɪnstɐ] der <-s, ->

broomstick [noun] Besenstiel ['be:zn̩ʃti:l] der <-(e)s, -e>

brothel [noun] Bordell [bɔʳ'dɛl] das <-s, -e>

brother [noun] Bruder ['bru:dɐ] der <-s, Brüder> ◊ *Ich habe drei Brüder und eine Schwester.* ✦ *Bruder Franziskus sprach mit den Tieren.* brothers and/or sisters Geschwister [gə'ʃvɪstɐ] die <-> *only pl* ◊ *Ich habe vier Geschwister.*

brother-in-law [noun] Schwager ['ʃva:gɐ] der <-s, Schwäger>

brow [noun] **1.** *(forehead)* Stirn [ʃtɪʳn] die <-, -en> ◊ *die Stirn runzeln* **2.** *(eyebrow)* Braue ['bra͜ʊə] die <-, -n> *most pl* ◊ *die Brauen heben* **3.** *(of a hill)* Kuppe ['kʊpə] die <-, -n> ◊ *Auf der Kuppe des*

Berges machten sie eine Pause.

brown [adj] braun [bra͜ʊn] ◊ *Er hat braunes Haar.* ✦ *Er hat den Zaun braun gestrichen.* ✦ *Sie war ganz braun, als sie aus dem Urlaub zurückkam.*

browse [verb] **1.** IT durchsuchen [dʊʳç'zu:xn̩] <durch-sucht, durchsuchte, hat durchsucht> ◊ *das Internet durchsuchen* **2.** *(in a shop)* sich umsehen ['ʊmze:ən] <sieht sich um, sah sich um, hat sich umgesehen> ◊ „*Kann ich Ihnen helfen?" — "Nein danke, ich sehe mich erst mal um."* **3.** *(in books, newspapers)* browse (through) sth in etw. blättern ['blɛtɐn] +haben *(fam)* ◊ *Er blättert gerade in der Zeitung.*

bruise¹ [noun] **1.** *(contusion)* Prellung ['prɛlʊŋ] die <-, -en> ◊ *Ich habe mir bei dem Sturz mehrere Prellungen zugezogen.; (less serious)* blauer Fleck [bla͜ʊə 'flɛk] <-(e)s, -e> ◊ *Der blaue Fleck stammt von einem Sturz.* **2.** *(on fruit)* Druckstelle ['drʊkʃtɛlə] die <-, -n> ◊ *Die Äpfel haben aber schon viele Druckstellen!*

bruise² [verb] **1.** *(injure)* bruise yourself einen blauen Fleck/blaue Flecken bekommen [a͜ɛnən bla͜ʊən 'flɛk/bla͜ʊə 'flɛkn̩ bəkɔmən] <bekommt, bekam, hat bekommen> bruise easily schnell blaue Flecken bekommen bruise sb jdm einen blauen Fleck/blaue Flecken verpassen [a͜ɛnən bla͜ʊən 'flɛk/bla͜ʊə 'flɛkn̩ fe'pasn̩] <verpasst, verpasste, hat verpasst> **2.** *(fruit)* bruise sth etw. beschädigen [bə'ʃɛ:dɪgn̩] <beschädigt, beschädigte, hat beschädigt> ◊ *Das Obst ist durch den Transport beschädigt worden.* sth bruises etw. bekommt eine Druckstelle/Druckstellen [bəkɔmt a͜ɛnə 'drʊkʃtɛlə/'drʊkʃtɛlən] <bekam, hat bekommen> ◊ *Die Birnen haben beim Transport viele Druckstellen bekommen.* **3.** *(sb's reputation)* schädigen ['ʃɛ:dɪgn̩] +haben ◊ *jds Ruf schädigen* ⊕ feel bruised angeschlagen sein

brush¹ [noun] **1.** *(for hair, for cleaning)* Bürste ['bʏʳstə] die <-, -n> ◊ *Kamm und Bürste einpacken* ✦ *Er schrubbte seine Fingernägel mit einer Bürste.* **2.** *(for painting)* Pinsel ['pɪnzl̩] der <-s, -> **3.** *(incident, quarrel)* Zusammenstoß [tsu'zamənʃto:s] der <-es, Zusammenstöße> ◊ *Die Polizei befürchtet Zusammenstöße zwischen Links- und Rechtsradika-len.* have a brush with sb mit jdm aneinander geraten [mɪt ... anla͜ɛ'nande gəra:tn̩] <gerät, geriet, ist geraten>

brush² [verb] **1.** *(your hair, sth that is dirty or dusty)* bürsten ['bʏʳstn̩] +haben ◊ *Ich muss noch mein Haar bürsten, dann komme ich.; (your teeth)* putzen ['pʊtsn̩] +haben ◊ *Hast du heute schon deine Zähne geputzt?* **2.** *(touch sb/sth for a short time)* streifen ['ʃtra͜ɛfn̩] +haben ◊ *Du hast mich mit dem Ellbogen gestreift.* ✦ *Sie streifte sich das Haar aus der Stirn.* **3.** *(sweep, with your hand, a cloth)* wischen ['vɪʃn̩] +haben ◊ *Uta wischte sich schnell die Tränen aus dem Gesicht.* ✦ *die Küche/Treppe wischen; (with broom)* fegen ['fe:gn̩] +haben ◊ *den Hausflur fegen*

Brussels sprouts [noun] Rosenkohl ['ro:znko:l] der <-(e)s *no pl* ◊ *Was kostet der Rosenkohl?*

brutal(ly) [adj, adv] brutal [bru'ta:l] ◊ *Der Wettbewerb war brutal.* ✦ *ein brutaler Bursche* ✦ *jdn brutal miss-handeln*

bubble¹ [noun] **1.** *(filled with air or gas)* Blase ['bla:zə] die <-, -n> ◊ *Die Blase steigt auf und platzt.; (soap bubble)* Seifenblase ['za͜ɛfnbla:zə] blow bubbles Sei-fenblasen machen ['za͜ɛfnbla:zn̩ ˌmaxn̩] +haben **2.** *(in*

a cartoon) Sprechblase [ˈʃprɛçblaːzə] die <–, –n>
ⓔ **burst sb's bubble** jds Illusionen zerstören
bubble² ⟨verb⟩ *(quickly)* sprudeln [ˈʃpruːdl̩n] +haben ◊
Das Wasser sprudelt schon; es wird gleich kochen.;
(slowly) blubbern [ˈblʊbɐn] +haben ◊ *Das Käsefondue*
blubbert im Topf.
buck ⟨noun⟩ **1.** *(male deer, rabbit, goat)* Bock [bɔk] der
<–(e)s, Böcke> **2.** *(dollar)* Dollar [ˈdɔlaʳ] der
<–s, –s> pl *'Dollar' when used with expressions of*
quantity make a buck Geld machen [ˈɡɛlt maxn̩]
+haben *(fam)* ◊ *Leute, die schnelles Geld machen*
wollen
bucket ⟨noun⟩ Eimer [ˈaɛmɐ] der <–s, –> ◊ *einen*
Eimer voll Wasser laufen lassen ◆ *ein Eimer Wasser*
by the bucket eimerweise [ˈaɛmɐvaɛzə] ◊ *Sie trinkt*
eimerweise Kaffee.
ⓔ **kick the bucket** den Löffel abgeben *(fam)*
buckets of sth jede Menge … ⟨acc⟩ *(fam)* ◊ *jede*
Menge Geld
bucketful ⟨noun⟩ Eimer [ˈaɛmɐ] der <–s, –> ◊ *ein*
Eimer Wasser zum Putzen bucketfuls Unmengen
[ˈʊnmɛŋən] die <–> pl ◊ *Das kostet Unmengen Geld.*
buckle ⟨noun⟩ Schnalle [ˈʃnalə] die <–, –n>
bud¹ ⟨noun⟩ Knospe [ˈknɔspə] die <–, –n>
ⓔ **nip sth in the bud** etw. im Keim ersticken
bud² ⟨verb⟩ knospen [ˈknɔspm̩] +haben
Buddhism ⟨noun⟩ Buddhismus [bʊˈdɪsmʊs] der <–>
no pl ◊ *Im Buddhismus spielt Meditation eine große*
Rolle.
Buddhist¹ ⟨noun⟩ Buddhist [] der <–en, –en> ♀Bud-
dhistin [] die <–, –nen> ◊ *Er wuchs als Buddhist auf.*
be a Buddhist Buddhist/Buddhistin sein
Buddhist² ⟨adj⟩ buddhistisch [] ◊ *die buddhistische*
Lehre ◆ *Ein großer Teil der Bevölkerung ist buddhis-*
tisch.
buddy ⟨noun⟩ Kumpel [ˈkʊmpl̩] der <–s, –(s)> *(fam)*
budgerigar ⟨noun⟩ Wellensittich [ˈvɛlənzɪtɪç] der
<–s, –e>
budget ⟨noun⟩ **1.** *(available funds)* Budget [bʏˈdʒeː] das
<–s, –s> ◊ *Ich habe nur ein beschränktes Budget*
zur Verfügung. **2.** *(state of sb's/sth's finances)*
Haushalt [ˈhaʊshalt] der <–(e)s, –e> ◊ *den Haushalt*
beraten/beschließen/verabschieden
buffet ⟨noun⟩ **1.** *(meal)* Büffet [bʏˈfeː] das <–s, –s> ◊
ein kaltes/warmes Büffet **2.** *(station café)* Imbiss-
stand [ˈɪmbɪsʃtant] der <–(e)s, Imbissstände> **3.** *(on*
a train) Speisewagen [ˈʃpaɛzəvaːɡn̩] der <–s, –>; *(on*
a boat) Bordrestaurant [ˈbɔʁtʁestoˌʁaŋ] das <–s, –s>
bug¹ ⟨noun⟩ **1.** *(illness)* Virus [ˈviːrʊs] das <–> no pl ◊
ein Virus aufschnappen **2.** *(in software)* Fehler
[ˈfeːlɐ] der <–s, –> **3.** *(for recording conversations)*
Wanze [ˈvantsə] die <–, –n> **4.** *(insect)* Insekt
[ɪnˈzɛkt] das <–s, –en>
bug² ⟨verb⟩ **1.** *(secretly listen with the help of a bug)*
abhören [ˈaphøːʁən] +haben ◊ *Mein Telefon wird*
abgehört. **2.** *(install a bug)* eine Wanze installieren
[aɛnə ˈvantsə ɪnstaˌliːʁən] <installiert, installierte, hat
installiert> **3.** *(annoy)* nerven [ˈnɛʳfn̩] +haben *(fam)* ◊
Hör auf zu nerven, ich mach's ja gleich! ◆ *Es nervt*
sie, dass er immer Sachen herumliegen lässt.
build¹ ⟨noun⟩ Körperbau [ˈkœʳpebaʊ] der <–(e)s> no
pl ◊ *ein kräftiger Körperbau* be of … build einen …
Körperbau haben ◊ *Julia hat einen zierlichen*
Körperbau.
build² ⟨verb⟩ **1.** *(make, erect)* bauen [ˈbaʊən] +haben ◊
ein Haus/eine Straße bauen ◆ *Eine Amsel baute in der*

Hecke ihr Nest gebaut. ◆ *Meine Eltern wollen bauen.*
build an extension anbauen [ˈanbaʊən] +haben
2. *(fig) (develop)* aufbauen [ˈaʊfbaʊən] +haben ◊ *Sie*
hat das Unternehmen aus dem Nichts aufgebaut.
• **build in, build into** ⟨phras v⟩ **1.** *(install)* einbauen
[ˈaɛnbaʊən] ◊ *Die neuen Fenster werden nächste*
Woche eingebaut. ◆ *sich zwei weitere Schränke in*
die Küche einbauen lassen **2.** *(fig) (integrate)* mit
einbauen [mɪt ˈaɛnbaʊən] ◊ *Eine Lebensversicherung*
kann in die Finanzierung mit eingebaut werden.
• **build on, build onto** ⟨phras v⟩ **1.** *(attach to a*
building) build sth on(to sth) etw. (an etw. ⟨acc⟩)
anbauen [an … ˈanbaʊən] +haben ◊ *einen Wintergar-*
ten anbauen ◆ *einen Wintergarten an ein Haus*
anbauen **2.** *(add to sth)* build sth on sth etw. auf
etw. ⟨acc⟩ aufbauen [aɔf … ˌaʊfbaʊən] +haben ◊
Werte auf Traditionen aufbauen
• **build up** ⟨phras v⟩ **1.** *(become more)* sich
ansammeln [ˈanzaml̩n] +haben ◊ *Nach und nach*
sammelte sich eine Menschenmenge an.; (a deposit
of sth) sich ablagern [ˈapla:ɡɐn] +haben ◊ *In den*
Gelenken lagert sich Kalk ab. **2.** *(increase, improve)*
build sth up etw. aufbauen [ˈaʊfbaʊən] +haben ◊ *jds*
Kräfte aufbauen **3.** *(anticipate sth)* build up to sth
sich zu etw. steigern [tsu: … ˈʃtaɛɡɐn] <steigert sich,
steigerte sich, hat sich gesteigert> ◊ *Die Musik*
steigerte sich zu einem Forte.
builder ⟨noun⟩ **1.** *(worker)* Bauarbeiter [ˈbaʊɐˌbaɛtɐ]
der <–s, –> ♀Bauarbeiterin [ˈbaʊɐˌbaɛtərɪn] die
<–, –nen> ◊ *ein arbeitsloser Bauarbeiter* ◆ *Sie hat*
einen Job als Bauarbeiterin. **2.** *(contractor)* Bauunternehmer [ˈbaʊʊntəˌneːmɐ] der <–s, –> ♀Bauunter-
nehmerin [ˈbaʊʊntəˌneːmərɪn] die <–, –nen> ◊ *Er*
ist selbstständiger Bauunternehmer. ◆ *eine erfolgrei-*
che Bauunternehmerin
building ⟨noun⟩ **1.** *(structure)* Gebäude [ɡəˈbɔɪdə] das
<–s, –> ◊ *ein öffentliches Gebäude* **2.** *(process)* Bau
[baʊ] der <–(e)s> no pl ◊ *der Bau eines Hauses* ◆
Die Brücke befindet sich noch im Bau.
building block ⟨noun⟩ **1.** *(for children)* Bauklotz
[ˈbaʊklɔts] der <–es, Bauklötze> ◊ *mit Bauklötzen*
spielen **2.** *(basic element of sth)* Baustein [ˈbaʊʃtaɛn]
der <–(e)s, –e> ◊ *die Familie als Baustein der*
Gesellschaft
building site ⟨noun⟩ Baustelle [ˈbaʊʃtɛlə] die <–, –n>
◊ *Er arbeitet auf einer Baustelle.*
built-up ⟨adj⟩ bebaut [bəˈbaʊt] no comp/superl ◊ *ein*
stark bebautes Gebiet; (part of a town or city)
geschlossen [ɡəˈʃlɔsn̩] no comp/superl, only before n
◊ *innerhalb geschlossener Ortschaften*
bulb ⟨noun⟩ **1.** *(part of a plant)* Zwiebel [ˈtsviːbl̩] die
<–, –n> ◊ *Zwiebeln stecken* **2.** *(to give light)* Birne
[ˈbɪʳnə] die <–, –n> ◊ *eine Birne auswechseln*
Bulgaria ⟨noun⟩ Bulgarien [bʊlˈɡaːrjən] das
article only in combination with attribute, no pl →
Germany
Bulgarian¹ ⟨noun⟩ **1.** Bulgare [bʊlˈɡaːrə] der <–n, –n>
♀Bulgarin [bʊlˈɡaːrɪn] die <–, –nen> → **German¹**
1. 2. Bulgarisch [bʊlˈɡaːrɪʃ] das <–(s)> no pl →
German¹ 2.
Bulgarian² ⟨adj⟩ bulgarisch [bʊlˈɡaːrɪʃ] → **German²**
bulging ⟨adj⟩ prall gefüllt [ˌpral ɡəˈfʏlt] <praller gefüllt,
am prallsten gefüllt> ◊ *prall gefüllte Taschen* ◆ *Ihr*
Terminkalender ist prall gefüllt.
bulk ⟨noun⟩ Masse [ˈmasə] die <–, –n>
ⓔ **in bulk** in großen Mengen the bulk of … der

Großteil … gen

bull noun *(male elephant, whale)* Bulle ['bʊlə] der <-n, -n>; *(male cow)* Stier [ʃtiːɐ] der <-(e)s, -e> ⊛ **like a bull in a china shop** wie ein Elefant im Porzellanladen

bullet noun Kugel ['kuːgl̩] die <-, -n>

bulletin noun **1.** *(news)* Kurznachrichten ['kʊ*ɐ*tsnaːxrɪçtn̩] die <-> pl ◊ *die Kurznachrichten um 12.30 Uhr* **2.** *(official statement)* Bulletin [bʏl'tɛ̃ː] das <-s, -s> ◊ *ein Bulletin herausgeben*

bullfight noun Stierkampf ['ʃtiːɐkampf] der <-(e)s, Stierkämpfe>

bullshit noun Scheiße ['ʃaɛsə] die <-> no pl *(rude)*

bum noun Hintern ['hɪntɐn] der <-s, -> *(fam)*

bump¹ noun **1.** *(injury)* Beule ['bɔɛlə] die <-, -n> **2.** *(in the road)* Unebenheit ['ʊn|eːbm̩haɛt] die <-, -en> **3.** *(dull sound)* dumpfer Schlag [dʊmpfɐ 'ʃlaːk] <-(e)s, Schläge> ◊ *Ich hörte einen dumpfen Schlag.*

bump² verb **1.** *(hit, strike)* stoßen ['ʃtoːsn̩] <stößt, stieß, hat/ist gestoßen> *transitive use +haben/intransitive use +sein* ◊ *Die Boote stoßen gegen die Kaimauer.* bump your sth sich dat etw. stoßen ◊ *Au, ich habe mir den Kopf gestoßen!* bump yourself sich stoßen ◊ *Vorsicht, stoß dich nicht!* bump into sth an etw. acc stoßen [an … 'ʃtoːsn̩] <stößt, stieß, ist gestoßen> ◊ *Als er aus der Garage fuhr, stieß er an den Mülleimer.* bump into sb jdn anrempeln ['anrɛmpl̩n] +haben ◊ *Jemand rempelte mich von hinten an.* **2.** *(move slowly or awkwardly)* rumpeln ['rʊmpl̩n] +haben ◊ *Der Wagen rumpelte über das Kopfsteinpflaster.*
• **bump into** phras v *(meet sb)* bump into sb jdn zufällig treffen [ˌtsuːfɛlɪç 'trɛfn̩] <trifft, traf, hat getroffen> ◊ *Auf dem Heimweg traf ich zufällig Eva.* → bump² **1.**
• **bump off** phras v bump sb off jdn umlegen ['ʊmleːgn̩] +haben *(fam)*

bumper noun Stoßstange ['ʃtoːsʃtaŋə] die <-, -n>

bun noun **1.** *(roll)* Brötchen ['brøːtçən] das <-s, -> **2.** *(hairstyle)* Knoten ['knoːtn̩] der <-s, ->

bunch noun **1.** *(bundle)* Bund [bʊnt] das <-(e)s, -e> ◊ *ein Bund Radieschen* bunch of keys Schlüsselbund ['ʃlʏsl̩bʊnt] der <-(e)s, -e>; *(of flowers)* Strauß [ʃtraɔs] der <-es, Sträuße> ◊ *ein Strauß Rosen* **2.** *(growing together)* Büschel ['bʏʃl̩] das <-s, -> ◊ *jdm ein Büschel Haare ausreißen* ♦ *ein Büschel Kirschen* bunch of grapes Traube ['traɔbə] die <-, -n> **3.** *(of people)* Haufen ['haɔfn̩] der <-s> no pl ◊ *Sie sind ein lustiger Haufen.* **4.** *(hairstyle)* bunches Rattenschwänze ['ratn̩ʃvɛntsə] die <-> pl ⊛ **a bunch (of sth)** *(a lot)* ein Haufen (… nom) *(fam)* ◊ *ein Haufen Arbeit*

bundle noun **1.** *(tied or fastened together)* Bündel ['bʏndl̩] das <-s, -> ◊ *ein Bündel Briefe* **2.** *(sold or offered together)* Paket [pa'keːt] das <-(e)s, -e> ◊ *ein Paket von Maßnahmen* **3.** *(person)* a bundle of sth ein Ausbund an etw. dat [aɛn 'aɔsbʊnt an] <-(e)s, Ausbünde> *most sing* ◊ *Tim ist ein Ausbund an Fröhlichkeit.* a bundle of nerves furchtbar nervös [ˌfʊ*ɐ*çtbaːɐ nɛr'vøːs] *no comp/superl* ◊ *Vor der Prüfung war sie furchtbar nervös.*
• **bundle up** verb bündeln ['bʏndl̩n] +haben ◊ *Zeitungen für die Altpapiersammlung bündeln*

bung verb schmeißen ['ʃmaɛsn̩] <schmeißt, schmiss, hat geschmissen> *(fam)* ◊ *seine Tasche in die Ecke*

schmeißen

bungalow noun Bungalow ['bʊŋgaloː] der <-s, -s>

bungler noun Pfuscher ['pfʊʃɐ] der <-s, -> ♀Pfuscherin ['pfʊʃərɪn] die <-, -nen> *(pej)*

bunker noun Bunker ['bʊŋkɐ] der <-s, ->

burden¹ noun Last [last] die <-, -en> ◊ *die Last der Verantwortung* become a burden to sb jdm zur Last fallen ◊ *Ich möchte euch nicht zur Last fallen.*

burden² verb belasten [bə'lastn̩] <belastet, belastete, hat belastet> ◊ *Eine schwere Schuld belastete ihr Gewissen.* ♦ *Er wollte uns nicht damit belasten.*

bureau noun **1.** *(writing table)* Sekretär [zekre'tɛːɐ] der <-s, -e> **2.** *(chest of drawers)* Kommode [kɔ'moːdə] die <-, -n> **3.** *(office, organization)* Büro [by'roː] das <-s, -s> **4.** *(government department)* Behörde [bə'høːɐdə] die <-, -n>

bureaucracy noun Bürokratie [byrokra'tiː] die <-, -n> ◊ *Sie klagte über zu viel Bürokratie.* ♦ *die Brüsseler Bürokratie*

bureaucratic adj bürokratisch [byro'kraːtɪʃ] ◊ *hoher bürokratischer Aufwand* ♦ *Das ganze System ist ungeheuer bürokratisch.*

burglar noun Einbrecher ['aɛnbrɛçɐ] der <-s, -> ♀Einbrecherin ['aɛnbrɛçərɪn] die <-, -nen>

burglary noun Einbruch ['aɛnbrʊx] der <-(e)s, Einbrüche> ◊ *Bei dem Einbruch wurden 5000 Euro gestohlen.*

burial noun **1.** *(of sb's body)* Bestattung [bə'ʃtatʊŋ] die <-, -en> ◊ *Die Bestattung fand im engsten Familienkreis statt.* **2.** *(of objects)* Vergraben [fɛ'graːbm̩] das <-s> no pl ◊ *das Vergraben von Abfällen*

burn¹ noun **1.** *(injury)* Verbrennung [fɛ'brɛnʊŋ] die <-, -en> ◊ *schwere Verbrennungen erleiden* ♦ *eine Verbrennung zweiten Grades* **2.** *(mark)* Brandfleck ['brantflɛk] der <-(e)s, -e>

burn² verb **1.** *(also fig) (produce light or heat, be on fire, cause damage, hurt, copy onto a CD)* brennen ['brɛnən] <brennt, brannte, hat gebrannt> ◊ *Im Kamin brannte ein warmes Feuer.* ♦ *Das Haus brannte.* ♦ *ein Loch in die Tischdecke brennen* ♦ *auf der Haut brennen* ♦ *Sein Gesicht brannte vor Scham.* ♦ *Sie brannte vor Neugier.* ♦ *Kannst du mir das auf eine CD brennen?* **2.** *(reduce or be reduced to cinders, use up, injure)* verbrennen [fɛ'brɛnən] <verbrennt, verbrannte, hat/ist verbrannt> *transitive and reflexive use +haben/intransitive use +sein* ◊ *Das Holz ist völlig verbrannt.* ♦ *Müll/Kalorien verbrennen* burn your sth sich dat etw. verbrennen ◊ *Ich habe mir die Hand verbrannt.* burn yourself sich verbrennen ◊ *Ich habe mich am Bügeleisen verbrannt.* **3.** *(food)* anbrennen ['anbrɛnən] <brennt an, brannte an, ist angebrannt> ◊ *Das Essen ist angebrannt.* ♦ *Lass das Gemüse nicht anbrennen!*
• **burn down** phras v **1.** *(destroy or be destroyed by fire)* abbrennen ['apbrɛnən] <brennt ab, brannte ab, hat/ist abgebrannt> *transitive use +haben/intransitive use +sein* ◊ *Die Kirche ist abgebrannt.* ♦ *Er hat das Haus abgebrannt.* **2.** *(fire, flame)* sth burns down etw. brennt herunter [brɛnt hɛ'rʊntɐ] <brannte herunter, ist heruntergebrannt> ◊ *Das Kaminfeuer brannte langsam herunter.* ♦ *Lass die Kerze nicht ganz herunterbrennen!*
• **burn off** phras v burn sth off **1.** *(remove)* etw. abbrennen ['apbrɛnən] <brennt ab, brannte ab, hat abgebrannt> ◊ *Unkraut abbrennen* **2.** *(use up)* etw.

verbrauchen [fɛ'braͅoxn̩] <verbraucht, verbrauchte, hat verbraucht> ◊ *Kalorien/Energie verbrauchen*

• **burn up** (phras v) **1.** *(be consumed or destroyed by fire)* sth burns up etw. verbrennt [fɛ'brɛnt] <verbrannte, ist verbrannt> ◊ *Die Holzscheite sind verbrannt.; (building)* brennt ab [brɛnt 'ap] <brannte ab, ist abgebrannt> ◊ *Das Haus ist völlig abgebrannt.; (meteorite etc.)* verglüht [fɛ'glyːt] <verglühte, ist verglüht> ◊ *beim Eintritt in die Atmosphäre verglühen* **2.** *(use up)* burn sth up etw. verbrauchen [fɛ'braͅoxn̩] <verbraucht, verbrauchte, hat verbraucht> ◊ *Kalorien/Energie verbrauchen*

⊙ sb is burning up **1.** *(because it's hot)* jd kommt um vor Hitze **2.** *(because of an illness or overexertion)* jd glüht

burning (adj) **1.** *(on fire, painful, intensive)* brennend ['brɛnənt] *only before ns* ◊ *ein brennendes Gebäude* ♦ *eine brennende Frage* ♦ *brennender Schmerz* **2.** *(very hot)* glühend ['glyːənt] *only before ns* ◊ *die glühende Wüstensonne*

burp (verb) aufstoßen ['aͅofʃtoːsn̩] <stößt auf, stieß auf, hat aufgestoßen> ◊ *Ich musste plötzlich aufstoßen.* Don't forget to burp the baby. Vergiss nicht/ Vergessen Sie nicht, das Baby aufstoßen zu lassen.

burrow (noun) Bau [baͅo] der <-(e)s, -e>

burst¹ (noun) **1.** *(of emotion, energy)* Anfall ['anfal] der <-(e)s, Anfälle> ◊ *In einem Anfall von Heißhunger aß er alles auf.; (of activity)* Schub ['ʃuːp] der <-(e)s, Schübe> ◊ *Die Entwicklung verlief in Schüben.* The sun erupts into a major burst of activity every 11 years. Alle 11 Jahre zeigt die Sonne einen plötzlichen Aktivitätsschub. burst of growth Wachstumsschub ['vaksstuːmsʃuːp] burst of emotion Gefühlsausbruch [gə'fyːls|aͅosbrͅox] der <-(e)s, Gefühlsausbrüche> burst of speed Spurt [ʃpͅoʳt] der <-s, -s> ◊ *Er holte sie mit einem kurzen Spurt ein.* put on a burst of speed einen Spurt einlegen **2.** burst of applause Beifallssturm ['baͅefalsʃtoͅm] der <-(e)s, Beifallsstürme> burst of (gun)fire Salve ['zalvə] die <-, -n> ◊ *eine Salve aus dem Maschinengewehr abgeben* **3.** *(process of bursting)* Bruch [brͅox] der <-(e)s, Brüche> ◊ *ein Bruch in der Wasserleitung*

burst² (verb) **1.** *(balloon, tyre)* platzen ['platsn̩] +sein ◊ *Der Luftballon platzte mit einem lauten Knall.; (dam)* brechen ['brɛçn̩] <bricht, brach, ist gebrochen> burst sth etw. platzen lassen ['platsn̩ lasn̩] <lässt, ließ, hat lassen> ◊ *Er ließ den Luftballon platzen.* **2.** *(bomb)* explodieren [ɛksploˈdiːrən] <explodiert, explodierte, ist explodiert> ◊ *In der Innenstadt explodierte eine Autobombe.*

• **burst into** (phras v) burst into sth **1.** *(do sth suddenly)* in etw. (acc) ausbrechen [ɪn ... ˌaͅosbrɛçn̩] <bricht aus, brach aus, ist ausgebrochen> ◊ *Er brach plötzlich in Tränen aus.* **2.** *(go somewhere quickly)* in etw. (acc) platzen [ɪn ... ˌplatsn̩] +sein ◊ *Sie platzte in die Küche und verlangte etwas zu essen.*

• **burst open** (phras v) burst open aufspringen ['aͅofʃprɪŋən] <springt auf, sprang auf, ist aufgesprungen> ◊ *Die Tür sprang plötzlich auf.*

• **burst out** (phras v) *(say sth suddenly)* herausplatzen [hɛ'raͅosplatsn̩] +sein ◊ *„Ich hasse euch alle!", platzte sie heraus.; (do sth suddenly)* burst out laughing/crying etc. in Gelächter/Tränen etc. ausbrechen [ɪn gə'lɛçtɐ/'trɛːnən aͅosbrɛçn̩] <bricht aus, brach aus, ist ausgebrochen> ◊ *Er brach in schallen-*

des Gelächter aus.

bury (verb) **1.** *(a dead body)* begraben [bə'graːbm̩] <begräbt, begrub, hat begraben> ◊ *Der Verstorbene wird am Freitag begraben.* **2.** *(an object)* vergraben [fɛ'graːbm̩] <vergräbt, vergrub, hat vergraben> ◊ *Der Hund hat einen Knochen vergraben.* **3.** *(avalanche, landslide etc.)* verschütten [fɛ'ʃytn̩] <verschüttet, verschüttete, hat verschüttet> ◊ *Zwei Skifahrer wurden von einer Lawine verschüttet.* ♦ *Die Erdmassen haben ganze Häuser verschüttet.*

bus (noun) Bus [bͅos] der <-ses, -se> ◊ *Willst du nicht lieber den Bus nehmen?* ♦ *den Bus verpassen* by bus mit dem Bus ◊ *Ich fuhr mit dem Bus in die Stadt.*

bush (noun) Busch [bͅoʃ] der <-es, Büsche> ◊ *Bäume und Büsche säumen den Schulhof.* ♦ *eine Safari durch den afrikanischen Busch* bushes Gebüsch [gə'byʃ] das <-(e)s> sing ◊ *Die Beute hatte er im Gebüsch versteckt.*

⊙ beat about/around the bush um den heißen Brei herumreden *(fam)*

business (noun) **1.** *(dealings, transactions, shop)* Geschäft [gə'ʃɛft] das <-(e)s, -e> ◊ *Das Geschäft läuft zurzeit gut.* ♦ *Sie hat ein eigenes Geschäft.* do business with sb mit jdm Geschäfte machen be away on business dienstlich unterwegs sein [ˌdiːnstlɪç ͅontɐˈveːks zaͅen] +sein for business reasons aus geschäftlichen Gründen [aͅos gə'ʃɛftlɪçn̩ 'grͅyndn̩] business partner Geschäftspartner [gə'ʃɛftspaͅetnɐ] der <-s, -> ♀ Geschäftspartnerin [gə'ʃɛftspaͅetnͅerɪn] die <-, -nen> fashion business Modegeschäft ['moːdəgəʃɛft] das <-(e)s, -e> **2.** *(company)* Firma ['fɪrmaː] die <-, Firmen> ◊ *kleine und mittelständische Firmen* **3.** *(affair, matter)* Angelegenheit ['angəleːgn̩haͅet] die <-, -en> ◊ *Die ganze Angelegenheit dauerte etwa drei Stunden.* mind your own business sich um seine eigenen Angelegenheiten kümmern

⊙ get down to business zur Sache kommen go about your business seinen Geschäften nachgehen go out of business Pleite machen like nobody's business wie verrückt

businessman (noun) Geschäftsmann [gə'ʃɛftsman] der <-(e)s, Geschäftsleute *or seldom* Geschäftsmänner> ◊ *Er ist ein erfolgreicher Geschäftsmann.* ♦ *Als Geschäftsmann kenne ich mich mit Kundenbetreuung gut aus.*

business park (noun) Gewerbegebiet [gə'vɛʳbəgəbiːt] das <-(e)s, -e>

businesswoman (noun) Geschäftsfrau [gə'ʃɛftsfraͅo] die <-, -en> ◊ *Sie ist eine erfolgreiche Geschäftsfrau.* ♦ *Mit Zahlen kenne ich mich aus; schließlich bin ich Geschäftsfrau.*

bus stop (noun) Bushaltestelle ['bͅoshaltəʃtɛlə] die <-, -n>

bust¹ (noun) Büste ['bʏstə] die <-, -n>

bust² (verb) **1.** *(a lock, safe)* bust (open) aufbrechen ['aͅofbrɛçn̩] <bricht auf, brach auf, hat aufgebrochen> ◊ *Die Einbrecher brachen die Tür auf.; (with an explosive)* bust (open/up) sprengen ['ʃprɛŋən] +haben ◊ *einen Tunnel in den Berg sprengen* **2.** *(break a bone)* bust your sth sich (dat) etw. brechen [zɪç ... 'brɛçn̩] <bricht, brach, hat gebrochen> ◊ *Ich habe mir den Knöchel gebrochen.; (hurt sth)* verletzen [fɛ'lɛtsn̩] <verletzt, verletzte, hat verletzt> bust your sth sich an etw. (dat) verletzen ◊ *Ich habe mich am Knie verletzt.* **3.** *(get damaged)* go bust kaputtgehen [ka'pͅotgeːən] <geht kaputt, ging kaputt,*

ist kaputtgegangen> ◊ *Unser Fernseher ist kaputtge-gangen.* **4.** *(police, a person)* hochnehmen ['hoːxneːmən] <nimmt hoch, nahm hoch, hat hochge-nommen> *(slang)* ◊ *jdn wegen Drogenbesitz hochneh-men; (a place)* eine Razzia in etw. ⌈dat⌉ machen [aena 'ratsja: ɪn … maxn̩] +haben The police busted the bar. Die Polizei hat eine Razzia in der Bar gemacht. **5.** *(stop an event, a meeting)* sprengen ['ʃprɛŋən] +haben ◊ *eine Versammlung sprengen*

bustle ⌈noun⌉ Betrieb [bə'triːp] der <-(e)s> no pl ◊ *In der Stadt war heute viel Betrieb.*

bustling ⌈adj⌉ rege ['reːgə] <reger, regste> ◊ *In der Altstadt herrscht reges Leben.*

busy ⌈adj⌉ **1.** *(with a lot to do)* beschäftigt [bə'ʃɛftɪçt] ◊ *Ich kann nicht kommen, ich bin gerade beschäftigt.* ♦ *ein viel beschäftigter Manager* be busy doing sth mit etw. beschäftigt sein ◊ *Sie war mit der Vorberei-tung des Treffens beschäftigt.* ♦ *Er ist damit beschäf-tigt, das Protokoll zu schreiben.* **2.** *(active)* rege ['reːgə] <reger, regste> ◊ *Unsere Spendensammler waren sehr rege.* **3.** *(full of people)* voll [fɔl] ◊ *ein volles Wartezimmer* ♦ *Diese Kneipe ist immer voll.; (streets)* belebt [bə'leːpt] <belebter, belebteste> ◊ *eine belebte Straße* ♦ *Die Autobahn war auch nachts noch sehr belebt.* **4.** *(telephone)* besetzt [bə'zɛtst] no comp/superl ◊ *Der Anschluss ist dauernd besetzt.* ♦ *eine seit Stunden besetzte Leitung* **5.** *(pattern)* unruhig ['ʊnruːɪç] ◊ *unruhige Farben* ♦ *Dieser Teppich ist zu unruhig.*

but¹ ⌈adv⌉ nur [nuːɐ̯] ◊ *Wir können nur hoffen, dass es ihm bald besser geht.*

but² ⌈conjunc⌉ **1.** *(expressing a contrast, contradiction or reservation)* aber ['aːbɐ] ◊ *Alle saßen, aber er wollte unbedingt stehen.* ♦ *Gut, aber heute schaffe ich das nicht mehr.* ♦ *Aber wieso nur?; (after a negation)* sondern ['zɔndɐn] ◊ *Nicht er, sondern sie hat das gesagt.* ♦ *Er will nicht studieren, sondern eine Lehre machen.* **2.** *(except)* außer ['aʊsɐ] ◊ *Hier gibt es nichts außer Hotels und Nachtclubs.* ♦ *Das weiß niemand außer mir.*

butcher ⌈noun⌉ Fleischer ['flaeʃɐ] der <-s, -> ♀Flei-scherin ['flaeʃərɪn] die <-, -nen> ◊ *Er ist Fleischer von Beruf.* ♦ *Die Fleischerin schneidet zwei Steaks ab.*

butter ⌈noun⌉ Butter ['bʊtɐ] die <-> no pl
 ◉ **butter wouldn't melt in sb's mouth** jd sieht aus, als könne er kein Wässerchen trüben

butterfly ⌈noun⌉ Schmetterling ['ʃmɛtɐlɪŋ] der <-s, -e> ◊ *ein bunter Schmetterling* ♦ *die 100 m Schmetterling in neuer Rekordzeit schwimmen*
 ◉ **have butterflies in your stomach** ein flaues Gefühl im Bauch haben

button ⌈noun⌉ **1.** *(on clothing)* Knopf [knɔpf] der <-(e)s, Knöpfe> ◊ *einen Knopf annähen* **2.** *(on a machine, round)* Knopf [knɔpf] der <-(e), Knöpfe> ◊ *einen Knopf drücken; (rectangular)* Taste ['tastə] die <-, -n> ◊ *Welche Taste muss ich jetzt drücken?* **3.** *(badge)* Button ['batn̩] der <-s, -s> ◊ *einen Button am Pullover tragen*
 ◉ **bright as a button 1.** *(clever)* blitzgescheit **2.** *(lively)* aufgeweckt **push sb's buttons** jdn provo-zieren

buy¹ ⌈noun⌉ Kauf [kaof] der <-(e)s, Käufe> ◊ *Mit diesem Auto hast du einen schlechten/guten Kauf gemacht.*

buy² ⌈verb⌉ **1.** *(exchange for money, bribe)* kaufen

['kaofn̩] +haben ◊ *ein Auto kaufen* ♦ *Sie kaufte sich/ ihm ein Eis.* ♦ *Der Schiedsrichter ist doch gekauft!* the best money can buy das Beste, was man für Geld kaufen kann buy sth off sb jdm etw. abkaufen ['apkaofn̩] +haben ◊ *Das Motorrad habe ich einem Freund abgekauft.* **2.** *(acquire with difficulty)* erkaufen [e'kaofn̩] <erkauft, erkaufte, hat erkauft> ◊ *jds Zustimmung mit Zugeständnissen erkaufen* buy time Zeit gewinnen ['tsaet gəvɪnən] <gewinnt, gewann, hat gewonnen> **3.** *(believe)* abkaufen ['apkaofn̩] +haben *(fam)* ◊ *Hat er dir diese lahme Ausrede abgekauft?*
 • **buy into** ⌈phras v⌉ buy into sth sich in etw. ⌈acc⌉ einkaufen [ɪn … 'aenkaofn̩] +haben ◊ *Sie hat sich mit 20 000 Euro in die Firma eingekauft.*
 • **buy off** ⌈phras v⌉ buy sb off jdn kaufen ['kaofn̩] +haben *(fam)* ◊ *Der Schiedsrichter ist doch gekauft!*
 • **buy out** ⌈phras v⌉ buy sb out **1.** *(a business partner)* jdn auszahlen ['aostsaːlən] +haben **2.** *(so that sb can leave sth)* loskaufen ['loːskaofn̩] +haben
 • **buy up** ⌈phras v⌉ buy sth up etw. aufkaufen ['aofkaofn̩] +haben ◊ *Die Firma wurde von der Kon-kurrenz aufgekauft.*

buyer ⌈noun⌉ Käufer ['kɔøfɐ] der <-s, -> ♀Käuferin ['kɔøfərɪn] die <-, -nen>

buying department ⌈noun⌉ Einkauf ['aenkaof] der <-(e)s> no pl ◊ *im Einkauf tätig sein/arbeiten*

buzz ⌈verb⌉ **1.** *(make a sound, insects, machines)* summen ['zʊmən] +haben ◊ *Im Garten summten Bienen.* ♦ *Die Maschinen summten leise.; (head, ears)* dröhnen ['drøːnən] +haben ◊ *Meine Ohren dröhnten von dem Krach.* **2.** *(bee, fly etc.)* summen ['zʊmən] +sein ◊ *Eine dicke Fliege summte ihm um den Kopf.* **3.** *(use a buzzer)* den Summer betätigen [deːn 'zʊmɐ bətɛːtɪgn̩] <betätigt, betätigte, hat betätigt> ◊ *Betätigen Sie den Summer, wenn Sie die Antwort wissen.* She buzzed her secretary. Sie betätigte den Summer, um ihren Sekretär zu rufen. **4.** *(be busy, full of sth)* schwirren ['ʃvɪrən] +haben ◊ *Sein Kopf schwirrte vor Ideen.*

by¹ ⌈adv⌉ **1.** vorbei… [foːɐ̯'bae] stop by vorbei-schauen [foːɐ̯'baeʃaoən] +haben ◊ *Ich schaue vorbei, wenn ich Zeit habe.* drive by vorbeifahren [foːɐ̯'baefaːrən] <fährt vorbei, fuhr vorbei, ist vorbeige-fahren> ◊ *Vorhin ist ein Zug vorbeigefahren.* **2.** *(time)* fly by wie im Fluge vergehen [vɪ: ɪm 'fluːgə fɛɐ̯geːən] <vergeht, verging, ist vergangen>
 ◉ **by and large** im Großen und Ganzen

'By' often occurs in phrasal verbs like 'drop by' or 'come by' which have their own entries in the diction-ary.

by² ⌈prep⌉ **1.** *(stating who or what does sth, after passive verbs)* von [fɔn] +dat ◊ *Er wurde von einem Zug überfahren.* ♦ *Sie war von der Wanderung völlig erschöpft.* ♦ *ein Krimi von Martha Grimes* **2.** *(by means or way of, through)* durch [dʊʳç] +acc ◊ *ein Problem durch geschicktes Vorgehen lösen* ♦ *Alte Programme werden durch neue ersetzt.* ♦ *Die Katze kam durch das Fenster herein.* He calmed the baby by stroking its back. Er beruhigte das Baby, indem er ihm den Rücken streichelte.; *(using a bus/car/ train, your hand, a machine etc.)* mit [mɪt] +dat ◊ *mit dem Taxi/Bus fahren* ♦ *einen Brief mit der Hand schreiben* ♦ *mit einem Scheck zahlen* by air mit dem

Flugzeug; *(using a particular route or street)* auf [a͜of] ⊞dat ◊ *Wir sind auf der A7/einer anderen Route gekommen.* by sea/land zu Wasser/Lande [tu: 'vasɐ/'landə]; *(using the phone or postal service)* per [pɛr] ⊞acc ◊ *Ich sag dir per SMS Bescheid.* ✦ *Bestellungen per Telefon; (by sb's voice, their hand, name or looks)* an [an] ⊞dat ◊ *Er nahm mich an der Hand und führte mich zur Tür.* I recognized him by his voice Ich habe ihn an der Stimme erkannt. She took me by the hand. Sie nahm mich an der Hand. I know him by name/sight. Ich kenne ihn dem Namen nach/vom Sehen. **3.** *(before, not later than)* bis [bɪs] ⊞acc ◊ *Bis Freitag sollte das fertig sein.* ✦ *Bis 18 Uhr bin ich längst zurück.* By the time you read this I will have left. Wenn du dies liest, werde ich schon weg sein. by then mittlerweile ['mɪtlɐ'vaɪlə] ◊ *Mittlerweile wussten alle Bescheid.* **4.** *(during, at the time of)* bei [ba͜e] ⊞dat ◊ *bei Tag/*

Nacht arbeiten ✦ *Wir wollen bei Einbruch der Nacht wieder zurück sein.* **5.** *(indicating a difference)* um [ʊm] ⊞acc ◊ *einen Preis um 25% reduzieren* **6.** *(near, next to)* an [an] ⊞dat ◊ *Er stand an der Tür.* ✦ *Wir wohnen direkt am Meer.* **7.** *(in measurements, multiplications)* mal [ma:l] ◊ *Die Fläche ist vier mal vier Meter groß.* ✦ *Zwei mal drei ist sechs.; (in divisions)* durch [dʊrç] ⊞acc ◊ *Sechs (geteilt) durch zwei ist drei.* ✦ *Kann man 213 durch 3 teilen?*

bye ⟨interj⟩ tschüss [tʃʏs] *only spoken (fam)* ◊ *Tschüss, bis morgen!*

bypass¹ ⟨noun⟩ **1.** *(road)* Umgehungsstraße [ʊm'ge:ʊnsʃtra:sə] die <-, -n> ◊ *Auf der Umgehungsstraße ist Stau.* **2.** MED Bypass ['baɛpas] der <-(es), Bypässe>

bypass² ⟨verb⟩ umgehen [ʊm'ge:ən] <umgeht, umging, hat umgangen> ◊ *Wir wollen versuchen, den Stau zu umgehen.* ✦ *Probleme umgehen*

A
B
C
D
E
F
G
H
I
J
K
L
M
N
O
P
Q
R
S
T
U
V
W
X
Y
Z

C

c, C [noun] **1.** *(letter)* c, C [tseː] das <-(s), -(s)> ◊ *ein kleines c/großes C* ♦ *C wie Cäsar* **2.** MUS C c, C [tseː] das <-(s), -(s)> ◊ *Er spielte ein C.* C minor c-Moll ['tseːmɔl] C major C-Dur ['tseːduːɐ̯] **C** [noun] *(grade)* ☺*Drei* [draɐ̯] die <-, -en> ◊ *Er hat fast lauter Dreien im Zeugnis.* box@ Note

cab [noun] **1.** *(taxi)* Taxi ['taksi] das <-s, -s> ◊ *ein Taxi rufen* ♦ *mit dem Taxi fahren* **2.** *(of a lorry)* Fahrerkabine ['faːrekaˌbiːnə] die <-, -n>

cabbage [noun] Kohl [koːl] der <-(e)s> no pl

cabin [noun] **1.** *(on a boat)* Kabine [ka'biːnə] die <-, -n> **2.** *(on a plane)* Passagierraum [pasa'ʒiːɐ̯raʊ̯m] der <-(e)s, Passagierräume> **3.** *(hut)* Hütte ['hʏtə] die <-, -n>

cabinet [noun] **1.** POL Kabinett [kabi'nɛt] das <-s, -e> **2.** *(piece of furniture)* Schrank [ʃraŋk] der <-(e)s, Schränke>

cable [noun] **1.** *(for electricity)* Kabel ['kaːbl̩] das <-s, -> ◊ *ein Kabel verlegen* **2.** *(metal rope)* Drahtseil ['draːtsaɪ̯l] das <-(e)s, -e> **3.** *(television)* Kabelfernsehen ['kaːbl̩fɛʁnzeːən] das <-s> no pl

cable railway [noun] Drahtseilbahn ['draːtsaɪ̯lbaːn] die <-, -en>

café [noun] **1.** *(mainly for having coffee or tea and cakes)* Café [ka'feː] das <-s, -s> ◊ *sich nachmittags mit Freunden im Café treffen* **2.** *(mainly for cheap meals)* Imbissstube ['ɪmbɪsʃtuːbə] die <-, -n> ◊ *mittags nur schnell in die Imbissstube gehen*

cafeteria [noun] Cafeteria [kafeteˈriːaː] die <-, -s or Cafeterien>

cage [noun] Käfig ['kɛːfɪç] der <-s, -e>

cake [noun] Kuchen ['kuːxn̩] der <-s, -> ◊ *Möchten Sie noch ein Stück Kuchen?* ♦ *Am Nachmittag gab es Kaffee und Kuchen.*
☻ **you can't have your cake and eat it** man kann nicht alles haben

calcium [noun] Kalzium ['kaltsjʊm] das <-s> no pl

calculate [verb] **1.** *(work out using mathematics)* ausrechnen ['aʊ̯sʁɛçnən] <rechnet aus, rechnete aus, hat ausgerechnet> ◊ *die Kosten von etw. ausrechnen* **2.** *(judge, estimate)* abschätzen ['apʃɛtsn̩] +haben ◊ *Die Auswirkungen der Entscheidung sind schwierig abzuschätzen.* **3.** *(have a certain intention)* be calculated to do sth auf etw. [acc] abzielen [aʊ̯f ... ˌaptsiːlən] +haben ◊ *Die Reform zielt darauf ab, die Arbeitslosenzahl zu senken.*

calculation [noun] **1.** *(mathematical or when planning a project)* Berechnung [bə'ʁɛçnʊŋ] die <-, -en> ◊ *die Berechnung einer Kreisfläche* ♦ *Alles, was sie tut, ist reine Berechnung.* **2.** *(judgement, estimate)* Schätzung ['ʃɛtsʊŋ] die <-, -en> ◊ *Nach meiner Schätzung waren ungefähr 1000 Zuschauer da.*

calculator [noun] Taschenrechner ['taʃn̩ʁɛçnɐ] der <-s, ->

calendar [noun] Kalender [ka'lɛndɐ] der <-s, -> ◊ *einen Termin in den Kalender eintragen*

calf [noun] **1.** *(young cow)* Kalb [kalp] das <-(e)s, Kälber> **2.** *(part of the leg)* Wade ['vaːdə] die <-, -n>

call¹ [noun] **1.** *(phone call)* Anruf ['anʁuːf] der <-(e)s, -e> ◊ *einen wichtigen Anruf erwarten* take a call einen Anruf entgegennehmen give sb a call jdn anrufen ['anʁuːfn̩] <ruft an, rief an, hat angerufen> make a call anrufen ['anʁuːfn̩] <ruft an, rief an, hat angerufen> I have to make another call. Ich muss noch jemanden anrufen. return sb's call jdn zurückrufen [tsu'ʁʏkʁuːfn̩] <ruft zurück, rief zurück, hat zurückgerufen> incoming call *ein Anruf, der entgegengenommen wird oder wurde* outgoing call *ein Anruf, den man tätigt oder schon getätigt hat* **2.** *(sound)* Ruf [ʁuːf] der <-(e)s, -e> ◊ *der Ruf eines Vogels* call for help Hilferuf ['hɪlfəʁuːf] ◊ *Aus dem brennenden Haus drang ein Hilferuf.* **3.** *(request)* call (for sth) Ruf *(nach etw.)* [ʁuːf] ◊ *Sofort wurden Rufe nach seinem Rücktritt laut.* call to sb to do sth Aufruf an jdn, etw. zu tun [ˌanʁuːf an ... tsuː] **4.** *(visit)* Besuch [bə'zuːx] der <-(e)s, -e> pay a call on sb, pay sb a call jdn besuchen [bə'zuːxn̩] +haben ◊ *Ich will heute meine Tante besuchen.* **5.** *(at the airport)* Aufruf ['aʊ̯fʁuːf] der <-(e)s, -e> ◊ *Letzter Aufruf für Flug LH 345 nach Amsterdam!* **6.** *(decision)* Entscheidung [ɛnt'ʃaɪ̯dʊŋ] die <-, -en> ◊ *Das ist deine Entscheidung!* make the call die Entscheidung treffen **7.** *(for a product)* call (for sth) Nachfrage *(nach etw.)* ['naːxfʁaːgə] die <-> no pl ◊ *Hier besteht keine große Nachfrage nach Kaviar.* **8.** *(sth needing your resources)* be/have a call on sb's time jds Zeit beanspruchen ['tsaɪ̯t bəˌanʃpʁʊxn̩] <beansprucht, beanspruchte, hat beansprucht> ◊ *Die kranke Mutter beansprucht ihre Zeit.* call on sb's finances finanzielle Belastung [finanˌtsjɛlə bə'lastʊŋ] die <-, -en>
☻ **go beyond the call of duty** mehr als nur seine Pflicht tun **have first call on sth** bei etw. an erster Stelle stehen **be on call** Bereitschaftsdienst haben

call² [verb] **1.** *(use a name for, describe)* nennen ['nɛnən] <nennt, nannte, hat genannt> ◊ *Wie wollt ihr euer Kind nennen?* ♦ *Wie nennt man diese Methode?* call yourself sth sich etw. nennen ◊ *Er hat kein Recht, sich Sozialist zu nennen.* be called ... ... heißen ['haɪ̯sn̩] <heißt, hieß, hat geheißen> ◊ *Wie heißt deine Mutter?* call sb by their surname/nickname jdn mit Nachnamen/mit seinem Spitznamen anreden [mɪt 'naːxnaːmən/mɪt zaɪ̯nəm 'ʃpɪtsnaːmən ˌanʁeːdn̩] <redet an, redete an, hat angeredet> ◊ *Seine Freunde reden ihn nur mit seinem Spitznamen an.* call sb/sth sth jdn/etw. als etw. [acc] bezeichnen [als ... bəˌtsaɪ̯çnən] <bezeichnet, bezeichnete, hat bezeichnet> ◊ *Ich würde diesen Konflikt als Bürgerkrieg bezeichnen.* call sb names jdn beschimpfen [bə'ʃɪmpfn̩] <beschimpft, beschimpfte, hat beschimpft> ◊ *Die anderen Kinder beschimpfen ihn immer.* let's call it ... also sagen wir mal ... [alzo: 'zaːgn̩ viːɐ̯ maːl] ◊ *Du schuldest mir 5,35 Euro – also sagen wir mal 5 Euro.* **2.** *(telephone)*

anrufen ['anruːfn̩] <ruft an, rief an, hat angerufen> ◊ *Sie hat ihn im Büro angerufen.* ♦ *Bitte rufen Sie erst nach 19 Uhr an.* ♦ *Ich muss mal kurz bei der Bank anrufen.* **3.** *(shout, demand sb)* rufen ['ruːfn̩] <ruft, rief, hat gerufen> ◊ *Hast du (mich) gerufen?* ♦ *Im Dunkeln rief eine Eule.* ♦ *Er wurde ans Telefon gerufen.* ♦ *die Polizei/einen Krankenwagen/ein Taxi rufen* call to sb to do sth jdm zurufen, dass er/sie etc. etw. tun solle ['ʦuːruːfn̩ das eːɡ/ziː ... ˌʦolə] <ruft zu, rief zu, hat zugerufen> ◊ *Er rief dem Fahrer zu, dass er anhalten solle.* call to sb for sth jdm zurufen, dass man etw. (haben) wolle ◊ *Sie rief dem Kellner zu, dass sie noch ein Bier wolle.* **4.** *(to a court)* vorladen ['foːɐ̯laːdn̩] <lädt vor, lud vor, hat vorgeladen> ◊ *Sie wurde als Zeugin vorgeladen.* **5.** *(a name, flight)* aufrufen ['aʊfruːfn̩] <ruft auf, rief auf, hat aufgerufen> ◊ *Der Flug wird in einer halben Stunde aufgerufen.* **6.** *(a meeting, conference etc.)* einberufen ['aɛnbəruːfn̩] <beruft ein, berief ein, hat einberufen> ◊ *Auf Wunsch der Leiterin wurde eine Besprechung einberufen.; (an election)* ausschreiben ['aʊsʃʁaɪbm̩] <schreibt aus, schrieb aus, hat ausgeschrieben> ◊ *Für Ende März wurden Neuwahlen ausgeschrieben.* **7.** *(visit)* call (in/round) vorbeikommen [foːɐ̯ˈbaɛkɔmən] <kommt vorbei, kam vorbei, ist vorbeigekommen> ◊ *Ich komme bald mal bei dir vorbei.*

● **call at** phras v call at sth irgendwo halten ['haltn̩] <hält, hielt, hat gehalten> ◊ *Hält der Bus am Bahnhof?* ♦ *Der Zug hält in Birmingham und Oxford.*

● **call back** phras v **1.** *(telephone again)* zurückrufen [ʦuˈrʏkruːfn̩] <ruft zurück, rief zurück, hat zurückgerufen> ◊ *Sie ruft (mich) in einer Stunde zurück.* **2.** *(visit again)* noch einmal vorbeikommen [nɔx aɛnmaːl foːɐ̯ˈbaɛkɔmən] <kommt vorbei, kam vorbei, ist vorbeigekommen> ◊ *Komm doch bald noch einmal vorbei!*

● **call for** phras v **1.** *(demand)* fordern ['fɔʁdɐn] <fordert, forderte, hat gefordert> ◊ *Die Opposition forderte seinen Rücktritt.* **2.** *(collect)* abholen ['aphoːlən] +haben ◊ *Ich hole dich um 18 Uhr ab.*

● **call in** phras v **1.** *(visit)* call in (on sb) (bei jdm) vorbeigehen [foːɐ̯ˈbaɛɡeːən] <geht vorbei, ging vorbei, ist vorbeigegangen> ◊ *Ich gehe heute Abend bei Anna vorbei.* **2.** *(ask to come)* call sb in jdn kommen lassen ['kɔmən lasn̩] <lässt, ließ, hat lassen> ◊ *Der Chef hat mich kommen lassen, um mit mir zu reden.; (the police)* jdn rufen ['ruːfn̩] <ruft, rief, hat gerufen> ◊ *Wenn jetzt nicht gleich Ruhe ist, rufe ich die Polizei!* **3.** *(telephone a radio or TV station)* (beim Sender) anrufen [(baɛm ˌzɛndɐ) 'anruːfn̩] <ruft an, rief an, hat angerufen> ◊ *Sie rief beim Sender an, um ihre Meinung zu dem Thema zu sagen.* **4.** *(telephone your place of work)* (im Büro) anrufen [(ɪm byˌroː) 'anruːfn̩] <ruft an, rief an, hat angerufen> ◊ *Wenn er auf Geschäftsreise ist, ruft er jeden Morgen im Büro an.* call in sick sich krankmelden ['krankmɛldn̩] <meldet sich krank, meldete sich krank, hat sich krankgemeldet> ◊ *Heute Morgen haben sich schon drei Mitarbeiter krankgemeldet.*

● **call off** phras v call sth off **1.** *(cancel)* etw. absagen ['apzaːgn̩] +haben ◊ *Sie sagte das Konzert ab.* **2.** *(a match, search)* etw. abbrechen ['apbʁɛçn̩] <bricht ab, brach ab, hat abgebrochen> ◊ *Wegen Regen musste das Rennen abgebrochen werden.*

● **call on** phras v **1.** *(ask)* call on sb/sth to do sth

jdn/etw. dazu aufrufen, etw. zu tun [daːʦu: 'aʊfruːfn̩ ... ʦu:] <ruft auf, rief auf, hat aufgerufen> ◊ *Sie riefen die Regierung dazu auf, die Todesstrafe abzuschaffen.* **2.** *(visit)* call on sb jdn besuchen [bəˈzuːxn̩] <besucht, besuchte, hat besucht> ◊ *Auf dem Rückweg haben wir Alex besucht.*

● **call up** phras v **1.** *(in the US: telephone)* call (sb) up (jdn) anrufen ['anruːfn̩] <ruft an, rief an, hat angerufen> ◊ *Sie hat (ihn) gestern angerufen.* **2.** *(to the armed forces)* call sb up jdn einberufen ['aɛnbəruːfn̩] <beruft ein, berief ein, hat einberufen> ◊ *Alle 18-Jährigen werden einberufen.* **3.** *(as part of a team)* call sb up jdn aufstellen ['aʊfʃtɛlən] +haben ◊ *Warum wurde er für dieses Spiel nicht wieder aufgestellt?* **4.** *(information in a computer)* call sth up etw. abrufen ['apruːfn̩] <ruft ab, rief ab, hat abgerufen> ◊ *Daten abrufen; (a menu)* etw. aufrufen ['aʊfruːfn̩] <ruft auf, rief auf, hat aufgerufen> ◊ *etw. mit Doppelklick aufrufen*

call box noun **1.** *(in the UK: cabin with a public phone)* Telefonzelle [teleˈfoːnʦɛlə] die <-, -n> ◊ *Er hat von einer Telefonzelle aus angerufen.* **2.** *(in the US: emergency phone on the roadside)* Notrufsäule ['noːtruːfzɔʏlə] die <-, -n>

called → call² adv *(introducing sb's name)* namens ['naːmən̩s] ◊ *Dort traf sie einen Mann namens Otto.*

caller noun **1.** *(person making a phone call)* Anrufer ['anruːfɐ] der <-s, -> ♀Anruferin ['anruːfərɪn] die <-, -nen> ◊ *Der Anrufer hat seinen Namen nicht gesagt.* **2.** *(visitor)* Besucher [bəˈzuːxɐ] der <-s, -> ♀Besucherin [bəˈzuːxərɪn] die <-, -nen> ◊ *Ich freue mich auch über unangemeldete Besucher.*

calm¹ noun **1.** *(calm state)* Ruhe ['ruːə] die <-> no pl ◊ *Sie antwortete mit ihrer gewohnten Ruhe.* **2.** *(lack of wind)* Flaute ['flaʊtə] die <-, -n> ◉ **the calm before the storm** die Ruhe vor dem Sturm

calm² verb beruhigen [bəˈruːɪɡn̩] <beruhigt, beruhigte, hat beruhigt> ◊ *Er versuchte, das schreiende Kind zu beruhigen.* ♦ *Diese Maßnahmen sollen die Lage beruhigen.*

calm(ly) adj, adv ruhig ['ruːɪç] ◊ *Sie hat eine angenehm ruhige Art.* ♦ *Das Meer war ziemlich ruhig.* ♦ *ruhig auf dem Boden liegen* ♦ *Versuche, bei dem Gespräch ganz ruhig zu bleiben.*

calorie noun Kalorie [kaloˈriː] die <-, -n> ◊ *Dieser Müsliriegel hat 130 Kalorien.*

camera noun Kamera ['kaməra] die <-, -s> ◊ *Sie macht mit seiner Kamera schöne Fotos.* ♦ *Der Minister machte vor laufender Kamera eine dumme Bemerkung.*

camp¹ noun **1.** *(also fig) (for holidays, soldiers, prisoners)* Lager ['laːgɐ] das <-s, -> ◊ *das Lager der Soldaten* ♦ *Ich halte es mit den Umweltschützern. Zu welchem Lager gehören Sie?* refugee camp Flüchtlingslager ['flʏçtlɪŋslaːgɐ] **2.** *(for children's holidays)* Ferienlager ['feːrɪənlaːgɐ] das <-s, -> ◊ *Die Kinder fuhren jeden Sommer in ein Ferienlager.* ◉ **break camp** sein Lager abbrechen **set up camp** sein Lager aufschlagen

camp² verb **1.** *(in a tent)* zelten ['ʦɛltn̩] +haben ◊ *Sie wollen im Urlaub wieder an der Ostsee zelten.* **2.** *(paparazzi, fans)* camp (out) lagern ['laːgɐn] <lagert, lagerte, hat gelagert> ◊ *Vor seinem Haus lagerten Dutzende von Journalisten.*

campaign¹ noun **1.** *(for publicity)* Kampagne

[kamˈpanjə] die <–, –n> ◊ *eine Kampagne für gesunde Ernährung* advertising campaign Werbekampagne [ˈvɛrbəkamˌpanjə] 2. *(of a political party)* (election) campaign Wahlkampf [ˈvaːlkampf] der <–(e)s, Wahlkämpfe> ◊ *Wie wird der Wahlkampf finanziert?* 3. *(of an army)* Feldzug [ˈfɛlttsuːk] der <–(e)s, Feldzüge>

campaign² ⟨verb⟩ 1. *(fight)* campaign for/against sth für/gegen etw. kämpfen [fyːɛ/geːgn̩] ... ,kɛmpfn̩] +haben ◊ *Alle Eltern haben gegen die Schließung der Schule gekämpft.* 2. *(to win an election)* Wahlkampf machen [ˈvaːlkampf maxn̩] +haben ◊ *Die Partei hat besonders in den Großstädten intensiv Wahlkampf gemacht.*

camping ⟨noun⟩ Camping [ˈkɛmpɪŋ] das <–s> no pl ◊ *Sie fahren zum Camping nach Frankreich.*; *(in a tent)* Zelten [ˈtsɛltn̩] das <–s> no pl ◊ *Wir hatten viel Spaß beim Zelten.* go camping zelten gehen

campus ⟨noun⟩ Campus [ˈkampʊs] der <–, –>

can¹ ⟨noun⟩ 1. *(for food, drinks)* Dose [ˈdoːzə] die <–, –n> ◊ *Auf dem Tisch standen zwei Dosen Bier.* ♦ *Champignons aus der Dose* ♦ *Tee in einer Dose aufbewahren* spray can Spraydose [ˈʃpreːdoːzə] 2. *(large container for liquids)* Kanister [kaˈnɪstɐ] der <–s, –> ◊ *ein Kanister mit Benzin;* *(for paint)* Topf [tɔpf] der <–(e)s, Töpfe> ◊ *Wir brauchen noch zwei Töpfe Wandfarbe.* 3. *(slang)* *(prison)* Knast [knast] der <–(e)s, Knäste or –e> most sing (slang) ◊ *Er sitzt im Knast.*
⊙ open a can of worms in ein Wespennest stechen carry the can for sth seinen Kopf für etw. hinhalten

can² ⟨verb⟩ 1. *(modal: expressing ability, possibility, surprise)* sb can do sth jd kann etw. tun [kan] <konnte, hat können> ◊ *Kannst du schwimmen?* ♦ *Ich kann jetzt nicht kommen.* ♦ *Wie kann man da noch widerstehen?* ♦ *Hier kann es im Winter sehr kalt werden.* ♦ *Können Sie mir sagen, wie ich zum Bahnhof komme?* ♦ *Kann ich noch ein Stück Kuchen haben?* ♦ *Wie kannst du nur so etwas sagen?* ♦ *Wie konntest du das nur tun!* I cannot tell you how relieved I am. Ich kann dir gar nicht sagen, wie erleichtert ich bin. We couldn't afford a car at the time. Wir konnten uns damals kein Auto leisten. I couldn't help smiling. Ich musste einfach lächeln. 2. *(modal: giving or requesting permission)* dürfen [ˈdʏrfn̩] <darf, durfte, hat dürfen> ◊ *Du darfst es dir ausleihen.* ♦ *Mein Sohn ist Diabetiker — er darf nur ein ganz kleines Stück Kuchen haben.* ♦ *Darf man den Patienten schon besuchen?* You cannot smoke here. Hier darf man nicht rauchen. They can't come in. Sie dürfen nicht hereinkommen. 3. *(as a question tag)* can't you/he etc.?, can you/he etc.? oder? [ˈoːdɐ] ◊ *Das können wir ihm nicht sagen, oder?*
⊙ cannot help sth etw. nicht ändern können

Canada ⟨noun⟩ Kanada [ˈkanada] das <–s> *article only in combination with attribute, no pl* → **Germany**

Canadian¹ ⟨noun⟩ Kanadier [kaˈnaːdiɐ] der <–s, –> ♀Kanadierin [kaˈnaːdiərɪn] die <–, –nen> → **German¹** 1.

Canadian² ⟨adj⟩ kanadisch [kaˈnaːdɪʃ] → **German²**

canal ⟨noun⟩ Kanal [kaˈnaːl] der <–s, Kanäle> ◊ *Main und Donau sind durch einen Kanal verbunden.* ♦ *Der Verdauungstrakt ist ein langer Kanal.*

cancel ⟨verb⟩ 1. *(an event)* absagen [ˈapzaːgn̩] +haben

◊ *eine Veranstaltung absagen* ♦ *Wie viele der Gäste haben abgesagt?* 2. *(a flight, train etc.)* streichen [ˈʃtraeçn̩] <streicht, strich, hat gestrichen> ◊ *Die Fluggesellschaft musste mehrere Flüge streichen.* 3. *(a subscription, contract)* kündigen [ˈkʏndɪgn̩] +haben; *(a debt)* erlassen [ɛˈlasn̩] <erlässt, erließ, hat erlassen> ◊ *Dem Land wurden die Schulden erlassen.* 4. *(a ticket)* entwerten [ɛntˈveːɐtn̩] <entwertet, hat entwertet> ◊ *den Fahrschein entwerten; (a stamp)* abstempeln [ˈapʃtɛmpl̩n] <stempelt ab, stempelte ab, hat abgestempelt> ◊ *Die Briefmarke ist gar nicht abgestempelt worden.; (a cheque)* ungültig machen [ˈʊnɡʏltɪç maxn̩] +haben ◊ *einen Scheck durch mehrmaliges Durchstreichen ungültig machen* 5. *(a payment, an order etc.)* stornieren [ʃtɔˈniːrən] <storniert, stornierte, hat storniert> ◊ *einen Auftrag stornieren*

cancellation ⟨noun⟩ 1. *(of an event)* Ausfall [ˈaosfal] der <–(e)s, Ausfälle> ◊ *Bei Ausfall wird das Spiel als unentschieden gewertet.* 2. *(of an appointment, a seat in the theatre etc.)* Absage [ˈapzaːgə] die <–, –n> ◊ *Wegen einer Absage habe ich heute kurzfristig einen Termin bekommen.; (a ticket that has been returned)* eine Karte, *die zurückgegeben wurde* 3. *(of a contract)* Kündigung [ˈkʏndɪgʊŋ] die <–, –en> ◊ *Sie entschieden sich für die Kündigung des Vertrags.* 4. *(of a payment, an order)* Stornierung [ʃtɔˈniːrʊŋ] die <–, –en> ◊ *die Stornierung eines Auftrags*

cancer ⟨noun⟩ 1. MED Krebs [kreːps] der <–es> no pl ◊ *an Krebs erkranken/sterben* lung cancer Lungenkrebs [ˈlʊŋənkreːps] cancer of the colon Darmkrebs [ˈdarmkreːps] 2. *(fig) (widespread problem)* Krebsgeschwür [ˈkreːpsɡəʃvyːɐ] das <–s, –e> ◊ *das Krebsgeschwür der Korruption* 3. ASTROL Cancer Krebs [kreːps] der <–es, –e>

candidate ⟨noun⟩ 1. *(in an election, for an award)* Kandidat [kandiˈdaːt] der <–en, –en> ♀Kandidatin [kandiˈdaːtɪn] die <–, –nen> ◊ *der Kandidat der SPD* 2. *(for a job)* Bewerber [bəˈvɛrbɐ] der <–s, –> ♀Bewerberin [bəˈvɛrbərɪn] die <–, –nen> ◊ *Es gab zwei Bewerber für die Stelle.* 3. *(suitable person for sth)* sb is a good candidate for sth etw. ist das Richtige für jdn [ɪst das ˈrɪçtɪgə fyːɐ] *+sein* ◊ *Ist diese Therapie das Richtige für mich?* He is a prime candidate for lung cancer/a heart attack Es ist sehr wahrscheinlich, dass er Lungenkrebs/einen Herzanfall bekommt. She is a prime candidate for this post/task. Sie eignet sich hervorragend für diesen Posten/diese Aufgabe. 4. *(in an examination)* Prüfling [ˈpryːflɪŋ] der <–s, –e> ◊ *Alle Prüflinge haben bestanden.*

candle ⟨noun⟩ Kerze [ˈkɛrtsə] die <–, –n> ◊ *eine Kerze anzünden*

candy ⟨noun⟩ 1. *(in the US: sweets)* Süßigkeiten [ˈzyːsɪçkaetn̩] die <–> pl ◊ *Sie isst gern Süßigkeiten.* 2. *(a sweet)* Bonbon [bɔŋˈbɔŋ] das <–s, –s> ◊ *Er lutschte ein Bonbon.*

cane ⟨noun⟩ 1. *(stem of a plant)* Rohr [roːɐ] das <–(e)s, –e> ◊ *ein Korb aus Rohr* 2. *(stick)* Stock [ʃtɔk] der <–(e)s, Stöcke> ◊ *jdn mit einem Stock schlagen* ♦ *Der alte Mann ging am Stock.* 3. *(punishment)* the cane die Prügelstrafe [di: ˈpryːgl̩ʃtraːfə] ◊ *Die Prügelstrafe wurde schon vor vielen Jahren abgeschafft.*

canister ⟨noun⟩ 1. *(for liquids)* Kanister [kaˈnɪstɐ] der

<-s, -> ◊ *ein Kanister mit Benzin* **2.** *(for storing food)* Dose ['do:zə] die <-, -n> ◊ *Den Kaffee bewahren wir in dieser Dose auf.*

cannon [noun] Kanone [ka'no:nə] die <-, -n> ◊ *eine Kanone laden/zünden*

cannot → can²

canoe [noun] Kanu ['ka:nu:] das <-s, -s>

can opener [noun] Dosenöffner ['do:zn̩|œfnɐ] der <-s, -> ◊ *ein elektrischer Dosenöffner*

can't → can²

canteen [noun] **1.** *(restaurant)* Kantine [kan'ti:nə] die <-, -n> ◊ *Mittags isst er in der Kantine.* **2.** *(water bottle)* Feldflasche ['fɛltflaʃə] die <-, -n> **3.** *(for cutlery)* canteen (of cutlery) Besteckkasten [bə'ʃtɛkkastn̩] der <-s, Besteckkästen>

canton [noun] Kanton [kan'to:n] der <-s, -e> ◊ *Andreas lebt im Kanton Zürich.*

canvas [noun] **1.** *(for sails, tents, shoes)* Segeltuch ['ze:gl̩tu:x] das <-(e)s, -e> most sing ◊ *Schuhe aus Segeltuch* **2.** *(for paintings)* Leinwand ['laɛnvant] die <-, Leinwände> ◊ *Bilder in Öl auf Leinwand* **3.** *(oil painting)* Ölgemälde ['ø:lgəmɛ:ldə] das <-s, -> ◊ *ein teures Ölgemälde*

⊛ **under canvas** im Zelt

cap¹ [noun] **1.** *(against the cold)* Mütze ['mʏtsə] die <-, -n> ◊ *Setz eine Mütze auf, draußen ist es kalt.*; *(for swimming)* Bademütze ['ba:dəmʏtsə] peaked cap Schirmmütze ['ʃɪrmmʏtsə] **2.** *(to protect your hair)* Haube ['haɔbə] die <-, -n> ◊ *Beim Duschen setzt sie immer eine Haube auf.* nurse's cap Schwesternhaube ['ʃvɛstɐnhaɔbə] **3.** *(cover)* Verschluss [fɛ'ʃlʊs] der <-es, Verschlüsse> ◊ *den Verschluss wieder auf die Flasche schrauben;* *(lid)* Deckel ['dɛkl̩] der <-s, -> ◊ *der Deckel eines Marmeladenglases* **4.** *(financial limit)* Obergrenze ['o:bɐgrɛntsə] die <-, -n> ◊ *Es wurde eine Obergrenze von 50 Euro festgelegt.* spending cap Höchstsatz für die Ausgaben ['hø:çstzats fy:ɐ di: ,aɔsga:bm̩] der <-es, Höchstsätze> ◊ *einen Höchstsatz für die Ausgaben für Soziales festlegen* **5.** *(for a tooth)* Krone ['kro:nə] die <-, -n>

cap² [verb] **1.** *(set a financial limit)* cap sth (at sth) etw. (maximal auf etw. [acc]) beschränken [(maksi'ma:l aɔf ...) ‚aɛnʃrɛŋkŋ̩] <beschränkt, beschränkte, hat beschränkt> ◊ *Die Steuererhöhung wurde auf maximal zwei Prozent beschränkt.* **2.** *(surpass what has gone before)* krönen ['krø:nən] +haben ◊ *Sein zweites Tor krönte seine Leistung an diesem Abend.* **3.** *(a tooth)* überkronen [ybe'kro:nən] <überkront, überkronte, hat überkront> have a tooth capped sich [dat] einen Zahn überkronen lassen **4.** *(cover)* cap sth with/in sth etw. mit etw. bedecken [mɪt ... bə,dɛkŋ̩] <bedeckt, bedeckte, hat bedeckt>; *(mostly stative passive)* capped with/in sth mit etw. bedeckt [mɪt ... bə,dɛkt] ◊ *Die Gipfel der Berge waren mit Schnee bedeckt.*

capability [noun] **1.** *(ability)* Fähigkeit ['fɛ:ɪçkaɛt] die <-, -en> ◊ *Ich möchte meine Fähigkeiten unter Beweis stellen* have the capability dazu fähig sein [da:tsu: 'fɛ:ɪç zaɛn] +sein ◊ *Vielleicht gewinnt sie — sie ist auf jeden Fall dazu fähig.* have the capability to do sth etw. tun können ['kœnən] <kann, konnte, hat können> ◊ *Der Zug kann eine Geschwindigkeit von 300 km/h erreichen.* have the capability of doing sth das Potenzial dazu haben, etw. zu tun [das potɛn'tsja:l da:tsu: ha:bm̩ tsu:] +haben ◊ *Er hat*

das Potenzial dazu, ein guter Lehrer zu werden. **2.** MIL Potenzial [potɛn'tsja:l] das <-s, -e> ◊ *das militärische Potenzial des Landes*

capable [adj] fähig ['fɛ:ɪç] ◊ *Ich halte sie für ausgesprochen fähig.* be capable of sth zu etw. fähig sein ◊ *Er ist zu allem fähig.* be capable of doing sth etw. tun können ['kœnən] <kann, konnte, hat können> ◊ *Ich kann diese Maschine nicht bedienen.*

capably [adv] kompetent [kɔmpe'tɛnt] <kompetenter, am kompetentesten> ◊ *Das Buch behandelt komplexe Fragen sehr kompetent.*

capacity [noun] **1.** *(of a container)* Fassungsvermögen ['fasʊŋsfɛmø:gŋ̩] das <-s> no pl ◊ *Das Fassungsvermögen des Tanks beträgt 150 Liter.;* *(of a stadium, hall etc.)* Kapazität [kapatsi'tɛ:t] die <-, -en> most sing ◊ *Das Stadion hat eine Kapazität von 60 000 Zuschauern.* a seating capacity of 800 800 Sitzplätze [,axthʊndɐt 'zɪtsplɛtsə] full to capacity voll bis auf den letzten Platz [,fɔl bɪs aɔf de:n ,lɛtstn̩ 'plats] a capacity crowd ein volles Haus [aɛn ,fɔləs 'haɔs] **2.** *(of a company, computer, plant)* Kapazität [kapatsi'tɛ:t] die <-, -en> most sing ◊ *freie Kapazitäten haben* ♦ *Die Firma hat ihre Kapazität erweitert.* ♦ *die Kapazität eines Rechners at full capacity mit voller Kapazität* ◊ *Die Anlage arbeitet mit voller Kapazität.* **3.** *(of an engine)* Leistung ['laɛstʊŋ] die <-, -en> ◊ *ein Motor mit 80 PS Leistung* **4.** *(ability)* Fähigkeit ['fɛ:ɪçkaɛt] die <-, -en> have a tremendous capacity for work sehr leistungsfähig sein [ze:ɐ 'laɛstʊŋsfɛ:ɪç zaɛn] +sein

⊛ **in your capacity as** in seiner Eigenschaft als ◊ *Ich bin in meiner Eigenschaft als Betriebsratsvorsitzender hier.* in an advisory capacity in beratender Funktion in a private capacity privat in a professional capacity in beruflicher Eigenschaft

cape [noun] **1.** *(headland)* Kap [kap] das <-s, -s> ◊ *Sie umsegelten das Kap.* **2.** *(cloak)* Umhang ['ʊmhaŋ] der <-(e)s, Umhänge>

capital¹ [noun] **1.** capital (city) Hauptstadt ['haɔptʃtat] die <-, Hauptstädte> ◊ *Rom, die Hauptstadt Italiens* ♦ *Paris ist die Hauptstadt der Mode und der Künste.* **2.** capital (letter) Großbuchstabe ['gro:sbu:xʃta:bə] der <-ns, -n> ◊ *Notieren Sie hier Ihren Namen in Großbuchstaben.* write sth with a capital etw. großschreiben ['gro:sʃraɛbm̩] <schreibt groß, schrieb groß, hat großgeschrieben> ◊ *Im Deutschen schreibt man alle Substantive groß.* **3.** FIN *(money, property)* Kapital [kapi'ta:l] das <-s, -e or also -ien> ◊ *verfügbares Kapital* ♦ *Kapital Gewinn bringend anlegen*

⊛ **make capital of sth** Kapital aus etw. schlagen

capital² [adj] *(letter)* groß [gro:s] no comp/superl ◊ *Wann schreibt man „Deutsch" mit großem D?*

capitalism [noun] Kapitalismus [kapita'lɪsmʊs] der <-> no pl

capitalist¹ [noun] Kapitalist [kapita'lɪst] der <-en, -en> ♀Kapitalistin [kapita'lɪstɪn] die <-, -nen>

capitalist² [adj] kapitalistisch [kapita'lɪstɪʃ] ◊ *ein kapitalistisches Land* ♦ *Die Wirtschaftsform dort ist kapitalistisch.*

capitalize [verb] **1.** *(write in capital letters)* in Großbuchstaben schreiben [ɪn 'gro:sbu:xʃta:bm̩ ʃraɛbm̩] <schreibt, schrieb, hat geschrieben> ◊ *Bitte schreiben Sie Ihren Namen in Großbuchstaben.;* *(start with a*

capital letter) großschreiben ['gro:ʃraebm̩] <schreibt groß, schrieb groß, hat großgeschrieben> ◊ *Im Deutschen schreibt man Nomen groß.* **2.** *(sell)* zu Kapital machen [tsu: kapi'ta:l maxn̩] +haben ◊ *Er wollte seine Wertpapiere zu Kapital machen.*
• **capitalize on** ⟨phras v⟩ capitalize on sth Kapital aus etw. schlagen [kapi'ta:l aos ... ʃla:gn̩] <schlägt, schlug, hat geschlagen> ◊ *Man sollte nicht aus der Not anderer Kapital schlagen.*

capitulate ⟨verb⟩ **1.** *(stop opposing sth)* capitulate (to sth) (einer Sache ⟨dat⟩) nachgeben ['na:xge:bm̩] <gibt nach, gab nach, hat nachgegeben> ◊ *Sie gaben den Forderungen der Terroristen nach.* **2.** *(surrender)* kapitulieren [kapitu'li:rən] <kapituliert, kapitulierte, hat kapituliert> ◊ *Schließlich haben sie vor dem Feind kapituliert.*

Capricorn, Capricornus ⟨noun⟩ Steinbock ['ʃtaenbɔk] der <-(e)s, Steinböcke>

capsule ⟨noun⟩ **1.** *(drug, membrane)* Kapsel ['kapsl̩] die <-, -n> ◊ *Das Medikament wird in Kapseln verabreicht.* ♦ *die Kapsel des Schultergelenks* **2.** *(of a space vehicle)* Raumkapsel ['raomkapsl̩] die <-, -n>

captain ⟨noun⟩ **1.** *(of a ship, plane, team)* Kapitän [kapi'tɛ:n] der <-s, -e> ♀Kapitänin [kapi'tɛ:nɪn] die <-, -nen> ◊ *Er ist der neue Kapitän des Dampfers.* ♦ *Sie ist Kapitänin der Volleyballdamen.* **2.** *(officer)* Hauptmann ['haoptman] der <-(e)s, Hauptleute>; *(in the navy)* Kapitän zur See [kapi,tɛ:n tsu:g 'ze:] der <-s zur See, -e zur See> ♀Kapitänin zur See [kapi'tɛ:nɪn tsu:g 'ze:] die <- zur See, -nen zur See>

captivate ⟨verb⟩ faszinieren [fastsi'ni:rən] <fasziniert, faszinierte, hat fasziniert> ◊ *Die Stimme des Sängers faszinierte das Publikum.*

capture ⟨verb⟩ **1.** *(a person)* gefangen nehmen [gə'faŋən ne:mən] <nimmt, nahm, hat genommen> ◊ *Sie wurden entweder getötet oder gefangen genommen.;* *(an animal)* einfangen ['aenfaŋən] <fängt ein, fing ein, hat eingefangen> ◊ *streunende Katzen einfangen und ins Tierheim bringen* **2.** *(a town, country)* erobern [ɛ|'o:ben] <erobert, eroberte, hat erobert> ◊ *eine Festung/Stadt erobern* **3.** *(a share of the market, vote)* capture sth sich ⟨dat⟩ etw. erobern [ɛ|'o:bən] <erobert sich, eroberte sich, hat sich erobert> ◊ *Die Japaner haben sich einen Marktanteil von 50 Prozent erobert.* **4.** *(a mood)* einfangen ['aenfaŋən] <fängt ein, fing ein, hat eingefangen> ◊ *Der Film fängt die Atmosphäre der Nachkriegszeit ganz hervorragend ein.* **5.** *(record an event)* festhalten ['fɛsthaltn̩] <hält fest, hielt fest, hat festgehalten> ◊ *Der Zwischenfall wurde von einem Kameramann festgehalten.* **6.** *(information)* erfassen [ɛ'fasn̩] <erfasst, erfasste, hat erfasst> ◊ *Daten erfassen*

car ⟨noun⟩ **1.** *(motor car)* Auto ['aoto:] das <-s, -s> ◊ *Ich kann nicht Auto fahren.* ♦ *Kann ich dich ein Stück im Auto mitnehmen?* ♦ *Er stieg aus dem Auto.* by car mit dem Auto **2.** *(in the US: carriage of a train)* Wagen ['va:gn̩] der <-s, -> ◊ *Ich stieg in den hinteren/vorderen Wagen ein.* sleeping car Schlafwagen ['ʃla:fva:gn̩]

caravan ⟨noun⟩ **1.** *(for holidays)* Wohnwagen ['vo:nva:gn̩] der <-s, -> **2.** *(in the desert)* Karawane [kara'va:nə] die <-, -n>

carbon ⟨noun⟩ Kohlenstoff ['ko:lənʃtɔf] der <-(e)s> no pl

carbon dioxide ⟨noun⟩ Kohlendioxid [,ko:lən'di:|ɔksi:t] das <-(e)s> *seldom with the article, no pl*

car boot sale ⟨noun⟩ *ein Flohmarkt, auf dem man seine Waren aus dem Kofferraum heraus verkauft*

card ⟨noun⟩ **1.** *(thick stiff paper)* Karton [ka'tɔŋ] der <-s, -s> ◊ *Zum Basteln brauche ich einen Bogen roten Karton.* ♦ *eine Verpackung aus festem Karton* **2.** *(greetings card, postcard, business card, bank card, in a computer)* Karte ['ka'tə] die <-, -n> ◊ *Ich schreibe dir eine Karte aus Paris.* ♦ *Könnte ich Ihre Karte haben?* ♦ *Sie können auch mit Karte bezahlen.* ♦ *die Karte in den Steckplatz stecken* a card says sth auf einer Karte steht etw. ◊ *Auf der Karte stand: „Herzlichen Glückwunsch zum Geburtstag".* Christmas card Weihnachtskarte ['vaenaxtska'tə] **3.** *(playing card)* Spielkarte ['ʃpi:lka'tə] die <-, -n> ◊ *Er hat immer seine Spielkarten dabei.* a pack of cards ein Satz Spielkarten **4.** *(game)* cards Kartenspielen ['ka'tnʃpi:lən] das <-s> no pl ◊ *Beim Kartenspielen gewinne ich nie.* play cards Karten spielen ['ka'tn ʃpi:lən] +haben game of cards Kartenspiel ['ka'tnʃpi:l] das <-(e)s, -e> ◊ *Sie haben immer Zeit für ein Kartenspiel.* **5.** *(with information)* Ausweis ['aosvaes] der <-es, -e> ◊ *Ohne Ihren Ausweis können Sie keine Bücher ausleihen.* membership card Mitgliedsausweis ['mɪtgli:tsaosvaes] **6.** *(list of sports events)* Programm [pro'gram] das <-s, -e> ◊ *Heute stehen sechs Rennen auf dem Programm.* **7.** *(advantage)* Trumpf [trompf] der <-(e)s, Trümpfe> sb's strongest card jds stärkster Trumpf
⊚ have a card up your sleeve einen Trumpf im Ärmel haben hold all the cards alle Trümpfe in der Hand haben keep your cards close to your chest sich bedeckt halten lay your cards on the table die Karten auf den Tisch legen

cardboard ⟨noun⟩ Pappe ['papə] die <-, -n> ◊ *Verpackungen aus Pappe; (thinner)* Karton [ka'tɔŋ] der <-s, -s>

cardboard box ⟨noun⟩ Pappkarton ['papka,tɔŋ] der <-s, -s> ◊ *Der PC war in einem Pappkarton verpackt.*

cardigan ⟨noun⟩ Strickjacke ['ʃtrɪkjakə] die <-, -n>

cardinal ⟨noun⟩ Kardinal [ka'di'na:l] der <-s, Kardinäle>

card index ⟨noun⟩ Kartei [ka'tae] die <-, -en> ◊ *Die Namen aller Kunden stehen in der Kartei.*

care[1] ⟨noun⟩ **1.** *(effort and attention)* Sorgfalt ['zɔ'kfalt] die <-> no pl ◊ *mit großer Sorgfalt arbeiten* handle sth with care etw. vorsichtig behandeln ['fo:gzɪçtɪç bə,handl̩n] <behandelt, behandelte, hat behandelt> **2.** *(looking after sb)* Betreuung [bə'trɔyʊŋ] die <-> no pl ◊ *Wir legen großen Wert auf die Betreuung unserer Fluggäste.* ♦ *Sie ist auf ärztliche Betreuung angewiesen.* in sb's care in jds Obhut [ɪn ... 'ɔphu:t] ◊ *Sie hat die Kinder in meiner Obhut gelassen.* **3.** *(treatment)* Behandlung [bə'handlʊŋ] die <-, -en> ◊ *Die Versicherung zahlt auch für eine zahnärztliche Behandlung.* ♦ *Das Krankenhaus hat sich auf die Behandlung von Herzkranken spezialisiert.* medical care medizinische Versorgung [medi,tsi:nɪʃə fe'zɔ'gʊŋ] die <-> no pl ◊ *Wie ist denn die medizinische Versorgung in Portugal?* be in need of hospital care im Krankenhaus versorgt werden müssen [ɪm 'kraŋkhaos fe,zɔ'kt ve:gdn̩ mʏsn̩] <muss, musste, hat müssen> **4.** *(foster care for children)* staatliche

A
B
C
D
E
F
G
H
I
J
K
L
M
N
O
P
Q
R
S
T
U
V
W
X
Y
Z

Fürsorge [ˌʃtaːtlɪçə ˈfyːɐ̯zoˀɡə] die <-> no pl ◊ *Kinder in staatlicher Fürsorge* take sb into care jdn in Pflege nehmen [ɪn ˈpfleːɡə neːmən] <nimmt, nahm, hat genommen> place sb into care jdn in Pflege geben [ɪn ˈpfleːɡə ɡeːbm̩] <gibt, gab, hat gegeben> **5.** *(of your skin, a car etc.)* Pflege [ˈpfleːɡə] die <-> no pl ◊ *Die Pflege der Zähne ist wichtig.* **6.** *(worry)* Sorge [ˈzɔˀɡə] die <-, -n> most pl not have a care in the world überhaupt keine Sorgen haben ⓔ care to bei ◊ *Adressiere den Brief an Anna Schmidt, bei Familie Meier.* take care **1.** *(be careful)* aufpassen ◊ *Pass auf, dass du nicht hinfällst!* take care to do sth darauf achten, dass man etw. tut ◊ *Bitte achten Sie darauf, dass Sie nicht auf die Kabel treten.* *(be careful to handle sth properly)* take care with sth sorgfältig mit etw. umgehen ◊ *Im Sommer sollte man mit Fleisch sorgfältig umgehen.* **2.** *(for saying goodbye)* Take care! Tschüs! take care of sb/sth sich um jdn/etw. kümmern

care² [verb] A cares about B B bedeutet A [dat] viel [bə,dʊɡtət ... ˈfiːl] <bedeutet, bedeutete, hat bedeutet> ◊ *Er bedeutet mir wirklich viel.* sb does not care for sb jd bedeutet jdm nichts care about sth Wert auf etw. [acc] legen [ˌveːɐ̯t aͦf ... leːɡn̩] +haben ◊ *Ich lege Wert auf eine gute Ausbildung.* not care about sth keinen Wert auf etw. [acc] legen ◊ *Er legt keinen Wert auf Reichtum.* sb cares what/why es interessiert jdn, was/warum [ɛs ɪntərɛˈsiːɐ̯t ... vas/varʊm] <interessiert, interessierte, hat interessiert> ◊ *Natürlich interessiert es mich, was an der Schule passiert.* sb cares deeply about sth etw. liegt jdm sehr am Herzen [liːkt ... zeːɐ̯ am ˈhɛˀtsn̩] <lag, hat gelegen> She genuinely doesn't care. Es ist ihr wirklich egal. sb doesn't care either way es ist jdm gleich [ɛs ɪst ... ˈglaͤç] +sein sb cares enough to do sth jdm ist etw. so wichtig, dass er/sie etw. tut [ɪst ... ˌzoː ˈvɪçtɪç das] +sein I love cars. I care enough to spend all my money on them. Ich liebe Autos. Sie sind mir so wichtig, dass ich all mein Geld dafür ausgebe. Only he cares enough to help improve the situation. Nur ihm ist die Situation so wichtig, dass er dabei hilft, sie zu verbessern. ⓔ sb couldn't care less es ist jdm ganz egal see if I care das ist mir völlig egal would sb care for sth hätte jd gern etw. ◊ *Hätten Sie gern eine Tasse Kaffee?* for all sb cares was jdn angeht ◊ *Was mich angeht, kann er ruhig verschwinden.* who cares wen störts

• **care for** [phras v] **1.** *(like)* care for sb jdn mögen [ˈmøːɡn̩] <mag, mochte, hat gemocht> ◊ *Er mochte sie wirklich gern.* **2.** *(look after an ill person, a garment)* care for sb/sth jdn/etw. pflegen [ˈpfleːɡn̩] +haben ◊ *Sie pflegt ihre kranke Mutter.* ♦ *Wenn Sie diesen Pullover richtig pflegen, bleibt er lange schön.*; *(provide food for, keep clean on a regular basis)* care for sb/an animal sich um jdn/ein Tier kümmern [ʊm ... ˌkʏmən] <kümmert sich, kümmerte sich, hat sich gekümmert> ◊ *Kinder sollen lernen, sich um ihre Haustiere zu kümmern.*

career [noun] **1.** *(job, profession)* Beruf [bəˈruːf] der <-(e)s, -e> ◊ *Welchen Beruf möchte er wählen?* ♦ *den Beruf wechseln* ♦ *Beruf und Familie miteinander vereinbaren* **2.** *(personal or professional development)* Laufbahn [ˈlaͦfbaːn] die <-, -en> ◊ *eine künstlerische Laufbahn einschlagen* ♦ *Die Verletzung bedeutete das Ende seiner Laufbahn als Tänzer.*; *(suc-*

cessful) Karriere [kaˈrjeːrə] die <-, -n> ◊ *1950 stand sie auf dem Höhepunkt ihrer Karriere.*

carefree [adj] *(person)* unbekümmert [ˈʊnbəkʏmɐt] ◊ *Er blieb trotz allem völlig unbekümmert.* ♦ *ein unbekümmertes Lachen;* *(time)* sorgenfrei [ˈzɔˀɡn̩fraͤ] no comp/superl ◊ *Sie erinnerte sich an ihre sorgenfreie Studienzeit.* ♦ *Die Schulferien waren sorgenfrei.*

careful(ly) [adj, adv] **1.** *(cautious)* vorsichtig [ˈfoːɐ̯zɪçtɪç] ◊ *Sei bitte vorsichtig!* ♦ *ein vorsichtiger Autofahrer* ♦ *Vorsichtig kehrte ich das zerbrochene Glas auf.* be careful with sth vorsichtig mit etw. umgehen Be careful! Vorsicht! **2.** *(involving effort and attention)* sorgfältig [ˈzɔˀfɛltɪç] ◊ *eine sorgfältige Korrekturleserin* ♦ *Du bist nicht sorgfältig genug.* ♦ *ein sorgfältig formulierter Brief* be careful that darauf achten, dass [daraͦf ˈaxtn̩ das] +haben ◊ *Achten Sie darauf, dass Sie Medikamente für Kinder unzugänglich aufbewahren.* be careful to do sth darauf achten, dass man etw. tut **3.** *(thrifty)* sparsam [ˈʃpaːˀzaːm] ◊ *eine sparsame Hausfrau* ♦ *Wir sollten sparsamer sein, sonst reicht das Geld nicht.* ♦ *Studenten müssen sparsam leben.* be careful with (your) money sparsam sein

careless(ly) [adj, adv] **1.** *(negligent)* nachlässig [ˈnaːxlɛsɪç] ◊ *Bei der nachlässigen Kontrolle wurde der Fehler übersehen.* ♦ *Er war in letzter Zeit sehr nachlässig bei der Arbeit.* ♦ *Diese Regelung wird zu nachlässig gehandhabt.* be careless about sth nachlässig mit etw. umgehen **2.** *(thoughtless)* leichtfertig [ˈlaͤçtfeˀtɪç] ◊ *eine leichtfertige Art haben* ♦ *Sie ist leichtfertig und verantwortungslos.* ♦ *Er hat seine letzte Chance leichtfertig vertan.*; *(irresponsible)* leichtsinnig [ˈlaͤçtzɪnɪç] ◊ *ein leichtsinniger Umgang mit Feuer* ♦ *Als nichts passierte, wurde sie leichtsinnig.* ♦ *leichtsinnig mit Geld umgehen*

carer [noun] **1.** *(person looking after sb)* Betreuer [bəˈtrɔ̯ͦɐ] der <-s, -> ♀Betreuerin [bəˈtrɔ̯ͦɐrɪn] die <-, -nen> ◊ *Bei dem Ausflug fahren mehrere Betreuer mit.* **2.** *(in a home, hospital, zoo)* Pfleger [ˈpfleːɡɐ] der <-s, -> ♀Pflegerin [ˈpfleːɡərɪn] die <-, -nen> ◊ *Er arbeitet als Pfleger im Altersheim.* ♦ *Sie wird von einer netten Pflegerin betreut.*

caretaker [noun] Hausmeister [ˈhaͦsmaͤstɐ] der <-s, -> ♀Hausmeisterin [ˈhaͦsmaͤstərɪn] die <-, -nen> ◊ *Er ist Hausmeister an einer Schule.* ♦ *Sie arbeitet als Hausmeisterin.*

cargo [noun] Fracht [fraxt] die <-, -en> ◊ *eine kostbare Fracht geladen haben* cargo ship Frachtschiff [ˈfraxtʃɪf] das <-(e)s, -e>

Caribbean¹ [noun] Karibik [kaˈriːbɪk] die <-> no pl ◊ *Urlaub in der Karibik machen*

Caribbean² [adj] karibisch [kaˈriːbɪʃ] mostly before ns ◊ *karibische Musik* ♦ *Dieses Essen ist typisch karibisch.*

caricature [noun] Karikatur [karikaˈtuːɐ̯] die <-, -en>

carnation [noun] Nelke [ˈnɛlkə] die <-, -n>

carnival [noun] *(festival)* Volksfest [ˈfɔlksfɛst] das <-(e)s, -e>; *(before Lent)* Karneval [ˈkaˀnaval] der <-s, -e or -s> ◊ *Karneval feiern*

carol [noun] Lied [liːt] das <-(e)s, -er> Christmas carol Weihnachtslied [ˈvaͤnaxtsliːt]

carousel [noun] **1.** *(for luggage at the airport)* Band [bant] das <-(e)s, Bänder> **2.** *(in the US: roundabout)* Karussell [karʊˈsɛl] das <-s, -s or -e> ◊ *Die Kinder fahren Karussell.*

car park [noun] **1.** *(area)* Parkplatz [ˈpaˀkplats] der

<es, Parkplätze> ◊ *ein bewachter Parkplatz;*
(building) Parkhaus ['parkhaos] das
<es, Parkhäuser> ◊ *Die Parkhäuser in der Innenstadt sind teuer.* **2.** underground car park Tiefgarage
['tiːfgaˌraːʒə] die <-, -n> ◊ *Wir haben in der Tiefgarage des Supermarkts geparkt.*

carpenter [noun] Schreiner ['ʃraenɐ] der <-s, ->
♀Schreinerin ['ʃraenərɪn] die <-, -nen> ◊ *Sie ist Schreinerin.* ◆ *Der Schreiner arbeitet mit Holz.*

carpet [noun] Teppich ['tɛpɪç] der <-s, -e> ◊ *Im Wohnzimmer lagen wertvolle Teppiche.* fitted carpet
Teppichboden ['tɛpɪçboːdn̩] der <-s, Teppichböden>
◊ *ein mit Teppichboden ausgelegtes Zimmer*

carriage [noun] **1.** *(horse-drawn)* Kutsche ['kʊtʃə] die
<-, -n> **2.** *(of a train, typewriter)* Wagen ['vaːgn̩] der
<-s, -> ◊ *ein Wagen der 1./2. Klasse* **3.** *(transport of goods)* Beförderung [bəˈfœrdərʊŋ] die <-, -en> ◊
die Beförderung von explosiven Stoffen **4.** *(price)*
Fracht [fraxt] die <-, -en> ◊ *Die Fracht beträgt 300 Euro.*

carriageway [noun] Fahrbahn ['faːrbaːn] die <-, -en>
◊ *die Fahrbahn überqueren*

carrier [noun] **1.** *(company)* Transportunternehmen
[transˈpɔrtʔʊntɐˌneːmən] das <-s, -> **2.** *(vehicle)*
Transporter [transˈpɔrtɐ] der <-s, ->; *(ship)* Transportschiff [transˈpɔrtʃɪf] das <-(e)s, -e> **3.** *(of a disease)* Überträger [ybɐˈtrɛːgɐ] der <-s, -> ♀Überträgerin [ybɐˈtrɛːgərɪn] die <-, -nen> ◊ *Welches Insekt ist der Überträger von Malaria?* **4.** *(for shopping)* carrier *(bag)* Einkaufstüte ['aenkaofstyːtə]
die <-, -n> ◊ *Ich packe alles in die Einkaufstüte.*
5. *(on a bicycle)* Gepäckträger [gəˈpɛktrɛːgɐ] der
<-s, -> ◊ *Das Fahrrad hatte keinen Gepäckträger.*

carrier bag [noun] Einkaufstüte ['aenkaofstyːtə] die
<-, -n> ◊ *Waren in eine Einkaufstüte packen*

carrot [noun] Karotte [ka'rɔtə] die <-, -n>
☞ **carrot and stick** Zuckerbrot und Peitsche

carry [verb] **1.** *(also fig)* (lift, transport, take on, support)* tragen ['traːgn̩] <trägt, trug, hat getragen> ◊
Die Strömung trug das Boot ans andere Ufer. ◆ *Der Polizist trug keine Waffe.* ◆ *Die Eltern tragen die Verantwortung.* ◆ *Trägt die Brücke das Gewicht?* ◆ *Alle Kinder trugen schwere Koffer.* **2.** carry sth with you
etw. bei sich haben ['bae ... haːbm̩] +haben ◊ *Ich habe nie viel Bargeld bei mir.* **3.** *(a lot of people, goods)* befördern [bəˈfœrdɐn] <befördert, beförderte, hat befördert> ◊ *Waren/Güter mit der Bahn befördern* ◆ *In dem Bus können 40 Personen befördert werden.* A plane carrying 150 passengers has crashed. Ein Flugzeug mit 150 Passagieren an Bord ist abgestürzt. carry a disease etw. mit sich führen ['mɪt ... fyːrən] +haben *(esp form)* ◊ *Die Lawine führte Geröll mit sich.; (signal, data)* be carried along sth durch etw. geleitet werden
[dʊrç ... gəˌlaetət veːɐ̯dn̩] <wird, wurde, ist worden>
◊ *Wie werden Signale durch die Nervenbahnen geleitet?; (on a conveyor belt etc.)* be carried along sth auf etw. [dat] befördert werden
[aof ... baˌfœrdət veːɐ̯dn̩] ◊ *Die Waren werden auf einem Band befördert.* **4.** carry a disease Überträger einer Krankheit [gen] sein
[ybeˌtrɛːgə aene ˈkraŋkhaet zaen] +sein **5.** *(a feeling)*
mit sich [dat] herumtragen [mɪt ... hɛˈrʊmtraːgn̩]
<trägt herum, trug herum, hat herumgetragen> ◊ *Er trug immer Schuldgefühle mit sich herum.* **6.** *(an article, a story)* bringen ['brɪŋən] <bringt, brachte, hat

gebracht> ◊ *Alle Zeitungen brachten die Story auf der ersten Seite.* **7.** *(a guarantee)* haben ['haːbm̩]
+haben ◊ *Der Kühlschrank hat ein Jahr Garantie.*
☞ **carry yourself well** eine gute Haltung haben
• **carry away** [phras v] carry sb away jdn mitreißen
['mɪtraesn̩] <reißt mit, riss mit, hat mitgerissen> ◊ *Mit seiner Ansprache hat er alle Zuhörer mitgerissen.*
☞ **get carried away (by sth)** sich (von etw.)
mitreißen lassen
• **carry off** [phras v] carry sth off **1.** *(a role)* etw.
meistern ['maesten] +haben ◊ *Er hat die schwierige Rolle gemeistert.* **2.** *(a prize)* etw. gewinnen
[gəˈvɪnən] <gewinnt, gewann, hat gewonnen> ◊ *Die Franzosen haben viele Medaillen gewonnen.*
• **carry on** [phras v] **1.** *(continue)* weitermachen
['vaetemaxn̩] +haben *(fam)* ◊ *Mach so weiter wie bisher!* ◆ *Du kannst mit deiner Arbeit weitermachen.* carry on reading weiterlesen ['vaeteleːzn̩]
+haben carry on playing weiterspielen ['vaeteʃpiːlən]
+haben carry on laughing weiterlachen ['vaetelaxn̩]
+haben **2.** *(continue walking)* weitergehen
['vaetegeːən] <geht weiter, ging weiter, ist weitergegangen> ◊ *Gehen Sie geradeaus weiter bis zur Ampel!*
3. *(continue sth that someone else started)* weiterführen ['vaetefyːrən] +haben ◊ *Er führt die Arbeit seines Vaters weiter.*
• **carry out** [phras v] carry sth out **1.** *(a piece of work, repair)* etw. ausführen ['aosfyːrən] +haben ◊
Die Reparatur ist zu unserer Zufriedenheit ausgeführt worden.; (an investigation, experiment, a project) etw. durchführen ['dʊrçfyːrən] +haben ◊ *Wir werden eine Untersuchung durchführen.* **2.** *(an instruction)* etw. befolgen [bəˈfɔlgn̩] <befolgt, befolgte, hat befolgt> ◊ *Ich erwarte, dass Sie meine Anweisungen genau befolgen.; (a promise, an obligation)* etw.
erfüllen [ɛ'fʏlən] <erfüllt, erfüllte, hat erfüllt> ◊ *Sie hat ihr Versprechen nicht erfüllt.*

cart [noun] **1.** *(drawn by horses)* Karren ['karən] der
<-s, -> ◊ *ein von Pferden gezogener Karren* **2.** *(in the US: for shopping)* Einkaufswagen ['aenkaofsvaːgn̩]
der <-s, -> **3.** *(in the US: for serving food)* Servierwagen [zɛˈviːɐ̯vaːgn̩] der <-s, ->

carton [noun] **1.** *(for food)* Packung ['pakʊŋ] die
<-, -en> ◊ *eine Packung Milch/Orangensaft*
2. *(larger and for goods)* Karton [kaˈtɔŋ] der
<-s, -s> ◊ *etw. in Kartons verpacken; (of cigarettes)*
Stange ['ʃtaŋə] die <-, -n> ◊ *eine Stange Zigaretten*

cartoon [noun] **1.** *(drawing)* Karikatur [karikaˈtuːɐ̯] die
<-, -en> **2.** *(series of drawings)* Comicstrip
['kɔmɪkstrɪp] der <-s, -s> **3.** *(film)* Trickfilm
['trɪkfɪlm] der <-s, -e>

cartridge [noun] **1.** *(for a firearm, fountain pen, printer)*
Patrone [pa'troːnə] die <-, -n> **2.** *(for a film, tape)*
Kassette [ka'sɛtə] die <-, -n>

carve [verb] **1.** *(wood)* schnitzen ['ʃnɪtsn̩] +haben ◊ *Alle Jungen schnitzen gern.* ◆ *Sie schnitzten ein Herz in den Baum.; (stone)* hauen ['haoən] <haut, haute, hat gehauen> ◊ *eine in Stein gehauene Inschrift* **2.** *(a roast etc.)* aufschneiden ['aofʃnaedn̩] <schneidet auf, schnitt auf, hat aufgeschnitten> ◊ *Sie schnitt den Braten auf.*

case [noun] **1.** *(instance, situation, disease, patient, client, crime)* Fall [fal] der <-(e)s, Fälle> ◊ *Das ist ein typischer Fall von Irreführung des Kunden.* ◆ *Das ist von Fall zu Fall verschieden.* ◆ *In deinem Fall machen wir eine Ausnahme.* ◆ *ein Fall von Cholera* ◆

A
B
C
D
E
F
G
H
I
J
K
L
M
N
O
P
Q
R
S
T
U
V
W
X
Y
Z

Die leichten Fälle werden ambulant behandelt. ♦
Jeder Sozialarbeiter betreut 30 Fälle. ♦ *Die Polizei
versucht, den Fall aufzuklären.* as is the case for …
wie es für … der Fall ist it is the case that es ist
so, dass [ɛs ɪst 'zoː das] ◊ *Ist es nicht so, dass Sie
Angst haben?* it's a case of … hier kann man nur
sagen … [hiːɐ̯ kan man nuːɐ̯ 'zaːɡn̩] ◊ *Hier kann
man nur sagen: Was ich nicht weiß, macht mich
nicht heiß.* in that case, if that's the case wenn das
so ist [vɛn das 'zoː ɪst] ◊ *Wenn das so ist, brauche
ich mir ja keine Sorgen zu machen.* as the case
may be je nachdem [je: naːx'deːm] 2. *(legal action)*
Fall [fal] der <-(e)s, Fälle>; *(court case)* Prozess
[proˈtsɛs] der <-es, -e> ◊ *einen Prozess gewinnen/
verlieren* have a case Aussichten haben, den
Prozess zu gewinnen the case for the prosecution
die Anklage [di: 'ankla:gə] the case for the defence
die Verteidigung [di: fɐ'taedɪɡʊŋ] 3. *(reasons, facts)*
the case *(for/against)* die Argumente *(für/gegen)*
[di: aʁɡu'mɛntə] <-> pl ◊ *Es gibt gute Argumente für
eine militärische Intervention.* state your case seine
Argumente vorbringen make a case for sth
Argumente für etw. vorbringen 4. *(container, box)*
Kiste ['kɪstə] die <-, -n> ◊ *eine Kiste Wein; (for
glasses)* Etui [ɛt'vi:] das <-s, -s> ◊ *die Brille ins
Etui legen; (of a watch)* Gehäuse [gə'hɔɪzə] das
<-s, -> ◊ *eine Uhr mit wasserdichtem Gehäuse; (in
a shop, museum)* Schaukasten ['ʃaokastn̩] der
<-s, Schaukästen>; *(suitcase)* Koffer ['kɔfɐ] der
<-s, -> 5. *(in grammar)* Fall [fal] der <-(e)s, Fälle>
◊ *Der Dativ ist der 3. Fall.*
➋ a case in point ein gutes Beispiel dafür in any
case 1. *(whatever happens)* auf jeden Fall
2. *(moreover)* außerdem … sowieso ◊ *Motorradfahren ist gefährlich. Außerdem habe ich sowieso
keinen Führerschein.* in case falls ◊ *Falls du mich
brauchst, helfe ich dir gern.* just in case für alle
Fälle in case of bei ◊ *Bei schlechtem Wetter fällt
das Spiel aus.*
cash[1] [noun] 1. *(coins, notes)* Bargeld ['baːɐ̯gɛlt] das
<-(e)s> no pl ◊ *Ich habe kein Bargeld bei mir.* in
cash in bar [ɪn 'baːɐ̯] ◊ *Er hat in bar bezahlt.*
2. *(money)* Geld [gɛlt] das <-(e)s> no pl ◊ *Ich
brauche unbedingt Geld.* short of cash knapp bei
Kasse [ˌknap bae 'kasə] ◊ *Er ist zurzeit ziemlich
knapp bei Kasse.*
cash[2] [verb] *(a cheque)* einlösen ['aenløːzn̩] +haben ◊
Sie ging zur Bank, um einen Scheck einzulösen.
• **cash in** [phras v] 1. cash in on sth aus etw. Kapital
schlagen [aos … kapiˈtaːl ʃlaːgn̩] <schlägt, schlug, hat
geschlagen> 2. *(a policy, share option)* cash sth in
sich [dat] etw. auszahlen lassen ['aostsaːlən lasn̩]
<lässt sich, ließ sich, hat sich … lassen>; *(a coupon,
voucher)* einlösen ['aenløːzn̩] +haben
• **cash up** [phras v] Kasse machen ['kasə maxn̩]
+haben ◊ *Jeden Abend machten sie Kasse.*
cashdesk [noun] Kasse ['kasə] die <-, -n> ◊ *die Ware
an der Kasse bezahlen*
cash machine [noun] Geldautomat ['gɛlt|aoto̯maːt]
der <-en, -en> ◊ *Wo gibt es hier einen Geldautomaten?*
cassette [noun] Kassette [ka'sɛtə] die <-, -n> ◊ *eine
Kassette anhören/einlegen*
cassette recorder [noun] Kassettenrekorder
[ka'sɛtn̩reˌkɔ̯ɐ̯də] der <-s, -> ◊ *den Kassettenrekorder einschalten/ausschalten*

cast[1] [noun] 1. *(of actors)* Besetzung [bə'zɛtsʊŋ] die
<-, -en> most sing ◊ *eine ungewöhnliche Besetzung*
2. *(for broken limbs)* Gipsverband ['gɪpsfɛbant] der
<-(e)s, Gipsverbände> ◊ *Sie musste sechs Wochen
lang einen Gipsverband tragen.* 3. *(model)* Abdruck
['apdrʊk] der <-(e)s, Abdrücke> ◊ *Er hat einen
Abdruck seiner Hand gießen lassen.*
cast[2] [verb] 1. *(a stone, shadow, light)* werfen ['vɛ̯ɐ̯fn̩]
<wirft, warf, hat geworfen> ◊ *einen Stein werfen* ♦
Die Bäume werfen lange Schatten. 2. *(a vote)*
abgeben ['apge:bm̩] <gibt ab, gab ab, hat abgegeben>
◊ *150 gültige Stimmen wurden abgegeben.* 3. FILM,
THEAT cast sb as sb die Rolle … [gen] mit jdm
besetzen [di: ˌrɔlə … mɪt … bəzɛtsn̩] <besetzt,
besetzte, hat besetzt> ◊ *Die Rolle des Tom Ripley
wurde mit Matt Damon besetzt.* be cast in the role
of sb die Rolle … [gen] bekommen
[di: ˌrɔlə … bəkɔmən] <bekommt, bekam, hat
bekommen> 4. *(a sculpture)* gießen ['giːsn̩] <gießt,
goss, hat gegossen> ◊ *eine Skulptur aus Bronze
gießen*
castle [noun] 1. *(fortified)* Burg [bʊ̯ɐ̯k] die <-, -en> ◊
Schlösser und Burgen in Sachsen ♦ *Die Feinde bela-
gerten/stürmten die Burg.* 2. *(mansion)* Schloss [ʃlɔs]
das <-es, Schlösser> ◊ *Schloss Neuschwanstein* ♦ *Der
Königssohn führte die Prinzessin beim auf sein
Schloss.* 3. CHESS Turm [tʊ̯ɐ̯m] der <-(e)s, Türme> ◊
den Turm schlagen
casual(ly) [adj, adv] 1. *(atmosphere, character)* ungezwungen ['ʊngətsvʊŋən] ◊ *Die Atmosphäre war ungezwungen.* ♦ *eine ungezwungene Art haben* ♦ *ungezwungen plaudern; (clothes etc.)* leger [le'ʒeːɐ̯] ◊
Seine Kleidung ist recht leger. ♦ *eine legere Haltung*
♦ *Sie kleidet sich sehr leger.* 2. *(question, comment)*
beiläufig ['baelɔɪfɪç] seldom comp/superl ◊ *eine beiläufige Bemerkung machen* ◊ *Die Frage war eher
beiläufig.* ♦ *etw. beiläufig erwähnen* 3. *(attitude,
view, pattern)* locker ['lɔkɐ] ◊ *eine lockere Einstellung zu etw. haben* casually arranged in lockerer
Anordnung [ɪn ˌlɔkərə 'an|o̯ɐ̯dnʊŋ]
casualty [noun] *(injured)* Verletzte [fɛ'lɛtstə] der/die
<-n, Schlösser> ◊ *but: ein Verletzter/eine Verletzte*
◊ *Bei dem Unfall gab es keine Verletzten.; (killed)*
Todesopfer ['toːdəs|ɔpfɐ] das <-s, -> ◊ *Unter den
Todesopfern sind auch Kinder.*
➋ be a casualty of sth einer Sache [dat] zum Opfer
fallen
casualty department [noun] Notaufnahme
['noːt|aofnaːmə] die <-, -n> ◊ *jdn in die Notauf-
nahme einliefern*
cat [noun] Katze ['katsə] die <-, -n>
➋ let the cat out of the bag die Katze aus dem
Sack lassen when the cat's away the mice will
play wenn die Katze aus dem Haus ist, tanzen die
Mäuse put the cat among the pigeons für
Aufregung sorgen Has the cat got your tongue?
Hat es dir/Ihnen/euch die Sprache verschlagen?
catalogue [noun] Katalog [kata'lo:k] der <-(e)s, -e> ◊
der Katalog einer Bibliothek/Ausstellung
➋ a catalogue of disasters eine Unglücksserie a
catalogue of errors eine ganze Reihe von Fehlern
catastrophe [noun] Katastrophe [katas'tro:fə] die
<-, -n>
catastrophic(ally) [adj, adv] katastrophal
[katastro'fa:l] ◊ *katastrophale Auswirkungen auf die
Umwelt haben* ♦ *Eine Eskalation der Gewalt wäre*

für das Land katastrophal. ♦ *Er hat katastrophal versagt.*

catch¹ [noun] **1.** *(of sth desirable, of fish)* Fang [faŋ] der <–(e)s> *no pl* ◊ *Die neue Managerin war ein guter Fang für die Firma.* ♦ *Der Fang wird auf dem Fischmarkt verkauft.; (animal hunted for food)* Beute ['bɔɡtə] die <–> *no pl* **2.** SPORT *(of a ball)* make a catch einen Ball fangen [aenən 'bal ˌfaŋən] <fängt, fing, hat gefangen> *That was a good catch!* Großartig gefangen! **3.** *(hidden problem)* Haken ['ha:kɳ] der <–s, –> ◊ *Die Sache muss einen Haken haben.* **4.** *(to close sth)* Verschluss [fɛ'ʃlʊs] der <–es, Verschlüsse> safety catch Sicherung ['zɪçərʊŋ] die <–, –en>

catch² [verb] **1.** fangen ['faŋən] <fängt, fing, hat gefangen> ◊ *Mit Speck fängt man Mäuse.* ♦ *Fang den Ball!; (a criminal also)* fassen ['fasɳ] +haben ◊ *Der Einbrecher wurde gefasst.; (light, a mood, an escaped animal)* einfangen ['aenfaŋən] <fängt ein, fing ein, hat eingefangen> ◊ *Das Foto fing die Stimmung gut ein.* catch hold of sth/sb etw./jdn packen ['pakɳ] +haben catch sb by the wrist/sleeve etc. jdn am Handgelenk/Ärmel etc. packen **2.** *(a train, bus)* erreichen [ɛ'raeçn] <erreicht, erreichte, hat erreicht> ◊ *Wenn du den Zug erreichen möchtest, musst du jetzt gehen.* **3.** *(prevent from falling to the ground)* auffangen ['aɔffaŋən] <fängt auf, fing auf, hat aufgefangen> ◊ *Als ich fiel, fing er mich auf.* **4.** *(avalanche, flood)* erfassen [ɛ'fasɳ] <erfasst, erfasste, hat erfasst> ◊ *Ein Skifahrer wurde von einer Lawine erfasst und verschüttet.* **5.** catch sb doing sth jdn dabei ertappen, wie er etw. tut [dabae ɛ'tapm vi:] <ertappt, ertappte, hat ertappt> ◊ *Er ertappte sie dabei, wie sie ihn beobachtete.* catch sb in the act jdn auf frischer Tat ertappen **6.** *(a disease)* catch sth (from sb) sich (bei jdm) mit etw. anstecken [mɪt ... ˌanʃtɛkɳ] +haben ◊ *Sie hat sich (bei ihrer Schwester) mit Grippe angesteckt.* catch a cold sich erkälten [ɛ'kɛltɳ] <erkältet sich, erkältete sich, hat sich erkältet> **7.** *(understand)* verstehen [fɛ'ʃteːən] <versteht, verstand, hat verstanden> ◊ *Entschuldigung, ich habe Ihren Namen nicht verstanden.* **8.** *(contact)* erwischen [ɛ'vɪʃn] <erwischt, erwischte, hat erwischt> *(fam)* ◊ *jdn im Büro/zu Hause erwischen* **9.** *(in a storm, traffic jam etc.)* be caught in sth in etw. [acc] geraten [ɪn ... gəra:tɳ] <gerät, geriet, ist geraten> ◊ *in einen Sturm/Stau geraten* **10.** *(on a nail, branch etc.)* catch on sth an etw. [dat] hängen bleiben [an ... ˌhɛŋən blaebm] <bleibt, blieb, ist geblieben> ◊ *Ihr Haar ist an einem Zweig hängen geblieben.* catch sth on sth mit etw. an etw. [dat] hängen bleiben ◊ *mit dem Ärmel an einem Nagel hängen bleiben* **11.** catch fire Feuer fangen ['fɔøɐ faŋən] <fängt, fing, hat gefangen>

• **catch on** [phras v] **1.** *(pursuers)* aufholen ['aɔfhoːlən] +haben ◊ *Beeil dich, die anderen holen auf!* **2.** *(lost time, things to learn)* catch up on sth etw. nachholen ['na:xhoːlən] +haben ◊ *Sie arbeitete hart, um den verpassten Unterrichtsstoff nachzuholen.* **3.** *(get where sb/sth else is)* catch up with sb/ sth jdn/etw. einholen ['aenhoːlən] +haben ◊ *Er ging so schnell, dass ich ihn kaum einholen konnte.* ♦ *Ist unser Rückstand noch einzuholen?*

categorically [adv] kategorisch [kate'goːrɪʃ] *no comp/ superl* ◊ *Er sagt kategorisch zu allem „nein".* ♦ *Die Bevölkerung war kategorisch gegen den Krieg.*

category [noun] Kategorie [kategoˈriː] die <–, –n> ◊ *einer Kategorie angehören*

cater [verb] Speisen und Getränke liefern [ˈʃpaezɳ ʊnt gəˈtrɛŋkə liːfən] +haben
• **cater for** [phras v] **1.** *(address specific needs)* cater for sb sich um jds Bedürfnisse kümmern [ʊm ... bəˌdyˈfnɪsə kymən] +haben ◊ *Diese Schule kümmert sich um die Bedürfnisse von Behinderten.* **2.** *(have room for)* cater for sb fassen ['fasɳ] +haben ◊ *Das Theater fasst 500 Zuschauer.* **3.** *(provide food and drink)* cater for sb Speisen und Getränke für jdn liefern [ˈʃpaezɳ ʊnt gəˌtrɛŋkə fyːɐ ... liːfən] +haben **4.** *(enable, facilitate)* cater for sth etw. ermöglichen [ɛ'møːklɪçn] <ermöglicht, ermöglichte, hat ermöglicht> ◊ *Diese Software ermöglicht eine statistische Analyse.* **5.** *(leisure activities and sports)* cater for sth etw. anbieten ['anbiːtɳ] <bietet an, bot an, hat angeboten> ◊ *Der Verein bietet auch Volleyball an.*
• **cater to** [phras v] cater to sb sich an jdn wenden [an ... vɛndɳ] <wendet sich, wendete/wandte sich, hat sich gewendet/gewandt> ◊ *Diese Sendung wendet sich an Kinder unter 12.*

catering [noun] Gastronomie [gastronoˈmiː] die <–> *no pl (tech)* ◊ *in der Gastronomie tätig sein* do the catering (die) Speisen und Getränke liefern [(diː) ˈʃpaezɳ ʊnt gəˈtrɛŋkə liːfən] +haben ◊ *Wer liefert die Speisen und Getränke für die Veranstaltung?*

caterpillar [noun] Raupe [ˈraɔpə] die <–, –n>

cathedral [noun] Dom [doːm] der <–(e)s, –e> ◊ *der Kölner Dom*

Catholic¹ [noun] Katholik [katoˈliːk] der <–en, –en> ♀Katholikin [katoˈliːkɪn] die <–, –nen> be a Catholic Katholik/Katholikin sein

Catholic² [adj] katholisch [kaˈtoːlɪʃ] ◊ *Seine ganze Familie ist katholisch.* ♦ *die katholische Kirche*

cattle [noun] Rindvieh [ˈrɪntfiː] das <–(e)s> *no pl* dairy cattle Milchvieh [ˈmɪlçfiː]

Caucasian [adj] **1.** *(having white skin)* weiß [vaes] *no comp/superl* ◊ *Das Opfer ist männlich, weiß und zirka 35 Jahre alt.* **2.** *(not Negroid or Mongoloid)* kaukasisch [kaɔˈkaːzɪʃ] *no comp/superl*

cauliflower [noun] Blumenkohl [ˈbluːmənkoːl] der <–(e)s> *no pl*

causal [adj] kausal [kaɔˈzaːl] *no comp/superl* ◊ *ein kausaler Zusammenhang; (in compound ns)* Kausal... [kaɔˈzaːl] causal clause Kausalsatz [kaɔˈzaːlzats] der <–es, Kausalsätze> ◊ *Die Konjunktion „weil" leitet einen Kausalsatz ein.*

cause¹ [noun] **1.** *(sth responsible for or triggering sth)* Ursache [ˈuːɐzaxə] die <–, –n> ◊ *Das Auto geriet aus bisher ungeklärter Ursache ins Schleudern.; (a specific behavio(u)r or emotion)* Anlass [ˈanlas] der <–es, Anlässe> ◊ *Was war der Anlass zu diesem Streit?* cause for concern Anlass zur Sorge **2.** *(ideal you defend)* Sache [ˈzaxə] die <–, –n> ◊ *für eine*

gerechte Sache kämpfen

cause² [verb] *(an accident, trouble, work, costs)* verursachen [fɐˈʔuːɐ̯zaxn̩] <verursacht, verursachte, hat verursacht> ◊ *Sie hat durch Unachtsamkeit einen Unfall verursacht.; (a bloodbath, disaster)* anrichten [ˈanrɪçtn̩] <richtet an, richtete an, hat angerichtet> ◊ *Der Sturm hat große Verwüstungen angerichtet.; (confusion, unrest)* stiften [ˈʃtɪftn̩] <stiftet, stiftete, hat gestiftet> ◊ *Verwirrung/Unruhe stiften; (a fire, reaction)* auslösen [ˈaʊ̯sløːzn̩] +haben ◊ *einen Brand auslösen* ✦ *Diese Aussage hat unterschiedliche Reaktionen ausgelöst.*

caution [noun] **1.** *(circumspection)* Vorsicht [ˈfoːɐ̯zɪçt] die <-> *no pl* ◊ *Sie mahnte zu größerer Vorsicht.* **2.** *(official warning)* Verwarnung [fɐˈvarnʊŋ] die <-, -en> *give sb a caution* jdm eine Verwarnung erteilen

cautious(ly) [adj, adv] vorsichtig [ˈfoːɐ̯zɪçtɪç] ◊ *Sie war so vorsichtig, die Unterlagen noch einmal zu überprüfen.* ✦ *Ich machte ein paar vorsichtige Schritte auf den Hund zu.* ✦ *die Tür vorsichtig öffnen*

cave [noun] Höhle [ˈhøːlə] die <-, -n>

cave in [verb] *(roof, surface)* einbrechen [ˈaɪ̯nbrɛçn̩] <bricht ein, brach ein, ist eingebrochen> ◊ *Das Dach ist unter der Schneelast eingebrochen.*

cavern [noun] Höhle [ˈhøːlə] die <-, -n>

cavity [noun] Hohlraum [ˈhoːlraʊ̯m] der <-(e)s, Hohlräume>; *(in a tooth)* Loch [lɔx] das <-(e)s, Löcher> *chest cavity* Brusthöhle [ˈbrʊsthøːlə] die <-, -n>

CD [noun] CD [tseːˈdeː] die <-, -s>

CD-ROM [noun] CD-ROM [tseːdeːˈrɔm] die <-, -s>

cease [verb] **1.** *(stop existing or happening)* aufhören [ˈaʊ̯fhøːrən] +haben ◊ *Der Regen/Die Musik hat aufgehört.* *cease doing sth, cease to do sth* aufhören, etw. zu tun ◊ *Er hörte auf, sie anzusehen.* *sth has ceased to exist* etw. gibt es nicht mehr [ˈɡiːpt ɛs nɪçt meːɐ̯] <gibt, gab, hat gegeben> ◊ *Das alte Jugoslawien gibt es nicht mehr.; (conversation)* verstummen [fɐˈʃtʊmən] <verstummt, verstummte, ist verstummt> ◊ *Die Gerüchte verstummten mit der Zeit.* **2.** *(the production, firing)* einstellen [ˈaɪ̯nʃtɛlən] +haben ◊ *die Produktion/das Feuer einstellen* ◉ *sth never ceases to amaze sb* jd ist immer wieder erstaunt über etw. [acc]

ceaseless(ly) [adj, adv] unentwegt [ˈʊnʔɛntveːkt] *no comp/superl; when used as an adj, only before ns* ◊ *das unentwegte Wogen des Meeres* ✦ *Bei uns klingelt unentwegt das Telefon.*

ceiling [noun] Decke [ˈdɛkə] die <-, -n> ◊ *Eine Glühbirne hing von der Decke herab.*

celebrate [verb] feiern [ˈfaɪ̯ɐn] +haben ◊ *Wie feierst du Weihnachten?* ✦ *Das muss gefeiert werden!*

celebration [noun] Feier [ˈfaɪ̯ɐ] die <-, -n> ◊ *Warst du auf der Feier?* *in celebration of sth* zur Feier … [gen] ◊ *ein Feuerwerk zur Feier der Geburt des Prinzen von Wales* in celebration of sb zu Ehren von jdm [tsuː ˈeːrən fɔn] ◊ *ein Symposium zu Ehren von Thomas Mann*

celebrity [noun] Berühmtheit [bəˈryːmthaɪ̯t] die <-, -en>

cell [noun] Zelle [ˈtsɛlə] die <-, -n> ◊ *einen Gefangenen in seine Zelle bringen/führen* ✦ *Dieses Gift greift die Zellen an und zerstört sie.* ✦ *die Zellen einer Batterie*

cellar [noun] Keller [ˈkɛlɐ] der <-s, ->

cellphone [noun] Handy [ˈhɛndi] das <-s, -s>

cement [noun] Zement [tseˈmɛnt] der <-(e)s> *no pl*

cemetery [noun] Friedhof [ˈfriːthoːf] der <-(e)s, Friedhöfe>

center → centre

centimetre, centimeter [noun] Zentimeter [tsɛntiˈmeːtɐ] der *or also* das <-s, -> ◊ *Ich brauche 30 Zentimeter Stoff.* ✦ *ein Faden von 75 Zentimeter Länge*

Central America [noun] Mittelamerika [ˈmɪtl̩ʔaˌmeːrikaː] das <-s> *article only in combination with attribute, no pl* → **Germany**

Central Europe [noun] Mitteleuropa [ˈmɪtl̩ʔɔɪ̯ˌroːpaː] das <-s> *article only in combination with attribute, no pl* → **Germany**

central(ly) [adj, adv] zentral [tsɛnˈtraːl] ◊ *Dieser Parkplatz ist aber nicht sehr zentral.* ✦ *Dieses Problem ist von zentraler Bedeutung.* ✦ *etw. zentral verwalten*

centre¹, center [noun] **1.** *(middle, important place, of a city, for sports, culture etc.)* Zentrum [ˈtsɛntrʊm] das <-s, Zentren> ◊ *das Zentrum des Erdbebens* ✦ *Welcher Bus fährt ins Zentrum?* ✦ *ein Zentrum, in dem Jugendliche sich treffen können; (in geometry)* Mittelpunkt [ˈmɪtl̩pʊŋkt] der <-(e)s, -e> ◊ *der Mittelpunkt eines Kreises* **2.** *(of the political spectrum)* Mitte [ˈmɪtə] die <-, -n> *most sing* ◊ *eine Partei der Mitte* **3.** SPORT Mittelfeldspieler [ˈmɪtl̩fɛltʃpiːlɐ] der <-s, -> ♀Mittelfeldspielerin [ˈmɪtl̩fɛltʃpiːlərɪn] die <-, -nen>

centre², center [verb] zentrieren [tsɛnˈtriːrən] <zentriert, zentrierte, hat zentriert> ◊ *eine Überschrift zentrieren*

● **centre around, center around** [phras v] *centre around sth,* be centred around sth sich auf etw. [acc] konzentrieren [aʊ̯f … kɔntsɛnˌtriːrən] <konzentriert sich, konzentrierte sich, hat sich konzentriert> ◊ *Die Diskussion konzentrierte sich auf die Umweltpolitik.*

century [noun] Jahrhundert [jaːɐ̯ˈhʊndɐt] das <-s, -e>

cereal [noun] Getreide [ɡəˈtraɪ̯də] das <-s, -> ◊ *Getreide anbauen* ✦ *Erzeugnisse aus Getreide*

ceremony [noun] Zeremonie [tseremoˈniː] die <-, -n> ◉ *in a ceremony* **1.** *(during an official reception)* bei einem Festakt **2.** *(during a ritual)* in einer Zeremonie

certain¹ [adj] **1.** *(sure)* be certain, know for certain *(sich* [dat]) sicher sein [ˈzɪçɐ zaɪ̯n] +sein ◊ *Ich bin sicher, dass er uns helfen kann.* ✦ *Bist du dir sicher, dass sie noch kommt?* *be certain of/about sth* sich [dat] einer Sache [gen] sicher sein ◊ *Er war sich ihrer Liebe sicher.* *make certain that …* sich vergewissern, etw. [fega'vɪsən das] <vergewissert sich, vergewisserte sich, hat sich vergewissert> ◊ *sich vergewissern, dass alles in Ordnung ist* **2.** *(inevitable)* sicher [ˈzɪçɐ] ◊ *der sichere Tod* sth is certain etw. steht fest [ʃteːt ˈfɛst] <steht fest, stand fest, hat festgestanden> ◊ *Es steht fest, dass Gewalt Gegengewalt erzeugt.*

certain² [det] **1.** *(referring to sth/sb without being specific)* bestimmt [bəˈʃtɪmt] *no comp/superl, only before ns* ◊ *Bestimmte Grundregeln müssen festgelegt werden.* **2.** *(referring to sth/sb not quite known or defined)* gewiss [ɡəˈvɪs] *no comp/superl, only before ns* ◊ *Ein gewisser Fred hat angerufen.*

certainly [adv] **1.** *(surely, admitting, confirming, in a*

reply) sicher ['zɪçɐ] ◊ *Diese Kritik ist sicher berechtigt.* ♦ *Sicher regnet es morgen wieder.* **2.** *(in a reply: expressing irritation)* allerdings ['alɐdɪŋs] ◊ *„Kennst du ihn?"* — *„Allerdings!"* **3.** *(in a retort, expressing defiance)* certainly not bestimmt nicht [bə'ʃtɪmt ,nɪçt] ◊ *„Wirst du dich bei ihr entschuldigen?"* — *„Bestimmt nicht!"*

certainty ⟨noun⟩ Gewissheit [gə'vɪshaɛt] die <-, -en> ◊ *Ich hatte die Gewissheit, dass sie noch lebte.* with certainty mit Sicherheit [mɪt 'zɪçɐhaɛt] ◊ *Das kann ich noch nicht mit Sicherheit sagen.*

certificate ⟨noun⟩ **1.** *(by an authority)* birth certificate Geburtsurkunde [gə'buːɐtsˌlu:ɐkʊndə] die <-, -n> health certificate Gesundheitszeugnis [gə'zʊnthaɛtsˌtsɔɡknɪs] das <-ses, -se> doctor's certificate Attest [a'tɛst] das <-(e)s, -e>; *(of authenticity)* Zertifikat [tsɛ'tifi'kaːt] das <-(e)s, -e> ◊ *ein Zertifikat, das die Echtheit eines Produkts bescheinigt* **2.** *(school)* Zeugnis ['tsɔɡknɪs] das <-ses, -se> ◊ *ein staatlich anerkanntes Zeugnis; (degree, vocational training)* Diplom [di'ploːm] das <-s, -e>; *(for a university seminar, course)* Schein [ʃaɛn] der <-(e)s, -e> ◊ *Ich habe in diesem Semester die letzten Scheine gemacht.; (for a language exam)* Zertifikat [tsɛ'tifi'kaːt] das <-(e)s, -e> ◊ *Das Zertifikat Deutsch ist international anerkannt.*

certify ⟨verb⟩ **1.** *(a report etc.)* (amtlich) bestätigen [(ˌamtlɪç) bə'ʃtɛːtɪɡn̩] <bestätigt, bestätigte, hat bestätigt> ◊ *ein Wahlergebnis (amtlich) bestätigen; (a procedure, company, quality)* zertifizieren [tsɛ'tifi'tsiːrən] <zertifiziert, zertifizierte, hat zertifiziert> ◊ *ein Unternehmen zertifizieren; (a product, food etc.)* certify sth as safe die Unbedenklichkeit ... ⟨gen⟩ bescheinigen [di: 'ʊnbədɛnklɪçkaɛt ... bəˌʃaɛnɪɡn̩] <bescheinigt, bescheinigte, hat bescheinigt> **2.** *(a document, copy, signature)* beglaubigen [bə'glaɔbɪɡn̩] <beglaubigt, beglaubigte, hat beglaubigt> ◊ *eine Kopie/Übersetzung beglaubigen lassen* **3.** MED certify sb (insane) jdn für unzurechnungsfähig erklären [fyːɐ 'ʊntsuːreçnʊŋsfɛːɪç ɐ'klɛːrən] <erklärt, erklärte, hat erklärt> certify sb's death einen Totenschein für jdn ausstellen [aɛnən 'toːtnʃaɛn fyːɐ ... ˌaɔsʃtɛlən] +haben

CET **MEZ** [ɛmˌeːˈtsɛt] die ◊ *Es geschah um 15 Uhr MEZ.*

chain¹ ⟨noun⟩ **1.** *(of metal rings, businesses, people)* Kette ['kɛtə] die <-, -n> ◊ *eine goldene Kette mit Anhänger* ♦ *Der Hofhund zerrte an seiner Kette.* ♦ *Dieser Supermarkt gehört zu einer deutschen Kette.* ♦ *Die Menschen bildeten bei der Demonstration eine Kette.* **2.** *(fetters)* chains Fesseln ['fɛsln̩] die <-> pl ◊ *die Fesseln des Alltags/der Konvention*

chain² ⟨verb⟩ in Ketten legen [ɪn 'kɛtn leːɡn̩] +haben ◊ *Sie legten die Gefangenen in Ketten.* chain sb/sth to sth jdn/etw. an etw. ⟨acc⟩ ketten [an ... ˌkɛtn̩] <kettet, kettete, hat gekettet> ◊ *Er kettete ihn an den Stuhl.* • **chain up** ⟨phras v⟩ chain sth/sb up jdn anketten ['ankɛtn̩] <kettet an, kettete an, hat angekettet> ◊ *ein Fahrrad anketten*

chair¹ ⟨noun⟩ **1.** *(piece of furniture)* Stuhl [ʃtuːl] der <-(e)s, Stühle> ◊ *sich auf einen Stuhl setzen* **2.** *(of a meeting, discussion etc.)* Leiter ['laɛtɐ] der <-s, -> ♀Leiterin ['laɛtərɪn] die <-, -nen> ◊ *die Leiterin der Kommission* **3.** *(at a university)* Lehrstuhl ['leːɐʃtuːl] der <-(e)s, Lehrstühle> ◊ *der Lehrstuhl für Physik*

chair² ⟨verb⟩ *(a discussion, meeting etc.)* leiten ['laɛtn̩] <leitet, leitete, hat geleitet> ◊ *eine Diskussion/einen Ausschuss leiten*

chairman ⟨noun⟩ Vorsitzende ['foːɐzɪtsndə] der <-n, die Vorsitzenden> but: ein Vorsitzender ◊ *Der Vorsitzende der Partei trat gestern zurück.* ♦ *Er ist Vorsitzender des Verwaltungsrats.*

chairwoman ⟨noun⟩ Vorsitzende ['foːɐzɪtsndə] die <-n, die Vorsitzenden> but: eine Vorsitzende ◊ *die Vorsitzende der Kommission* ♦ *Sie ist Vorsitzende der Partei.*

chalk ⟨noun⟩ Kreide ['kraɛdə] die <-, -n> ◊ *mit Kreide an die Tafel schreiben* ♦ *Die weißen Felsen bestehen aus Kreide.* ⓔ (like) chalk and cheese so verschieden wie Tag und Nacht

challenge¹ ⟨noun⟩ **1.** *(of a problem, task, to a contest)* Herausforderung [hɛ'raɔsfɔ'dərʊŋ] die <-, -en> ◊ *eine Herausforderung annehmen* ♦ *etw. stellt eine Herausforderung dar* face a challenge vor einer Herausforderung stehen **2.** *(a theory, doctrine, decision)* pose a challenge to sth etw. infrage stellen [ɪn'fraːɡə ʃtɛlən] +haben ◊ *Neue Erkenntnisse stellen die Theorie infrage.* **3.** LAW legal challenge (to sth) Klage (gegen etw.) ['klaːɡə] die <-, -n> ◊ *eine Klage gegen Genpatente*

challenge² ⟨verb⟩ **1.** *(a theory, doctrine, decision, sb's authority)* infrage stellen [ɪn'fraːɡə ʃtɛlən] +haben ◊ *jds Autorität infrage stellen; (oppose a person, an opinion)* challenge sb/sth jdm/einer Sache widersprechen [viːdɐ'ʃpreçn̩] <widerspricht, widersprach, hat widersprochen> challenge sb on sth jdm in etw. ⟨dat⟩ widersprechen **2.** *(to a contest, fight)* challenge sb (to sth) jdn (zu etw.) herausfordern [hɛ'raɔsfɔ'dɐn] <fordert heraus, forderte heraus, hat herausgefordert> ◊ *jdn zu einem Spiel/Kampf herausfordern* ♦ *seinen Gegner herausfordern* challenge sb to do sth jdn dazu herausfordern, etw. zu tun

chamber ⟨noun⟩ **1.** *(of a house, machinery, gun, the body)* Kammer ['kamə] die <-, -n> ◊ *Ich wohnte in einer Kammer unter dem Dach.* ♦ *Das menschliche Herz hat zwei Kammern.* torture chamber Folterkammer ['fɔltɐkamə] **2.** *(for meetings)* Sitzungssaal ['zɪtsʊŋszaːl] der <-(e)s, Sitzungssäle> Lower Chamber Unterhaus ['ʊntɐhaɔs] das <-es> no pl Upper Chamber Oberhaus ['oːbɐhaɔs] das <-es> no pl

chamber of industry and commerce ⟨noun⟩ Industrie- und Handelskammer [ɪndʊsˌtriː ʊnt 'handl̩skamə] die <-, -n>

champagne ⟨noun⟩ Champagner [ʃam'panjə] der <-s, ->

champion ⟨noun⟩ **1.** *(of a contest)* Meister ['maɛstə] der <-s, -> ♀Meisterin ['maɛstərɪn] die <-, -nen> ◊ *Sie ist deutsche Meisterin im Eiskunstlauf.* **2.** *(of a cause)* Verfechter [fɛ'fɛçtə] der <-s, -> ♀Verfechterin [fɛ'fɛçtərɪn] die <-, -nen> ◊ *Er ist ein Verfechter der sozialen Marktwirtschaft.; (of people)* Anwalt ['anvalt] der <-(e)s, Anwälte> ♀Anwältin ['anvɛltɪn] die <-, -nen> ◊ *eine Anwältin der Armen und Unterdrückten*

championship ⟨noun⟩ **1.** *(in a contest)* Meisterschaft ['maɛstəʃaft] die <-, -en> ◊ *die deutschen Meisterschaften im Kunstturnen* **2.** *(for a cause, people)* championship (of sb/sth) Engagement (für jdn/etw.) [aŋɡaʒə'maŋ] das <-s> no pl ◊ *jds Engagement für die Armen/soziale Gerechtigkeit*

A B C D E F G H I J K L M N O P Q R S T U V W X Y Z

A
B
C
D
E
F
G
H
I
J
K
L
M
N
O
P
Q
R
S
T
U
V
W
X
Y
Z

chance [noun] **1.** *(opportunity)* Gelegenheit [gə'le:gɲhaet] die <-, -en> ◊ *Sie nutzte die Gelegenheit, sich auszuruhen.* ◆ *Es gab kaum Gelegenheit für ein ernstes Gespräch.* given the chance wenn jd die Gelegenheit hätte **2.** *(possibility)* Möglichkeit ['mø:klɪçkaet] die <-, -en> ◊ *Besteht die Möglichkeit, dass er sich verirrt hat?*; *(probability)* Wahrscheinlichkeit [va:"ɲaenlɪçkaet] die <-, -en> most sing ◊ *Die Wahrscheinlichkeit, dass es heute regnet, ist sehr gering.* **3.** *(prospect)* Chance ['ʃaŋs(ə)] die <-, -n> ◊ *Sie bekam eine zweite Chance.* ◆ *gute Chancen im Beruf haben* blow your chance seine Chance vertun not stand a chance keine Chance haben be in with a chance eine Chance haben ◊ *Glaubst du, du hast eine Chance, im Lotto zu gewinnen?* **4.** *(coincidence)* Zufall ['tsu:fal] der <-(e)s, Zufälle> ◊ *Ich glaube nicht an Zufälle.* ◆ *Es ist kein Zufall, dass er diese Forderung stellte.* by chance zufällig ['tsu:fɛlɪç]

⊛ **take a chance** ein Risiko eingehen take a chance on sth es bei etw. auf einen Versuch ankommen lassen by any chance *(in questions, only spoken)* zufällig any chance of sth *(when asking for sth)* Any chance of a cup of coffee? Hast du eine Tasse Kaffee für mich? on the off chance that in der Hoffnung, dass

chancellor [noun] **1.** POL *(in Germany, Austria)* Bundeskanzler ['bʊndəskantslɐ] der <-s, -> ♀Bundeskanzlerin ['bʊndəskantslərɪn] die <-, -nen> ◊ *Der Bundeskanzler spricht heute in München.* ◆ *Sie will Bundeskanzlerin werden.* **2.** UNI, POL Kanzler ['kantslɐ] der <-s, -> ♀Kanzlerin ['kantslərɪn] die <-, -nen> ◊ *die Kanzlerin der Universität Heidelberg* Chancellor of the Exchequer Finanzminister [fi'nantsmi,nɪstɐ] der <-s, -> ♀Finanzministerin [fi'nantsmi,nɪstərɪn] die <-, -nen>; *(in the UK)* Schatzkanzler ['ʃatskantslɐ] Schatzkanzlerin ['ʃatskantslərɪn]

change¹ [noun] **1.** *(of a plan, name, address, law, view, lifestyle)* Änderung ['ɛndərʊŋ] die <-, -en> ◊ *Er beschloss eine Änderung des Plans.* make a change eine Änderung vornehmen; *(stronger)* Veränderung [fɛl'ɛndərʊŋ] die <-, -en> ◊ *Große Veränderungen sind vor sich gegangen.* **2.** *(from one thing to another)* Wechsel ['vɛksl] der <-s, -> ◊ *der Wechsel der Jahreszeiten* ◆ *ein rascher Wechsel zwischen warmen und kalten Temperaturen* **3.** *(of routine)* Abwechslung ['apvɛkslʊŋ] die <-, -en> most sing ◊ *Ein Urlaub an der See wäre eine schöne Abwechslung.* for a change zur Abwechslung ◊ *Zur Abwechslung kannst du mal abspülen.* **4.** *(coins)* Kleingeld ['klaengɛlt] das <-(e)s> no pl ◊ *Ich habe leider kein Kleingeld.*; *(after paying for sth)* Wechselgeld ['vɛksl̩gɛlt] das <-(e)s> no pl ◊ *Warten Sie, hier ist Ihr Wechselgeld.* **5.** a change of clothes Kleidung zum Wechseln [,klaedʊŋ tsʊm 'vɛksl̩n] die <-> no pl

⊛ **change of heart** Sinneswandel change of scene neue Umgebung

change² [verb] **1.** *(a rule, direction, opinion, appointment)* ändern ['ɛndɐn] +haben ◊ *Der Wind hat seine Richtung geändert.* ◆ *Der Termin war nicht mehr zu ändern.* sb changes jd ändert sich ◊ *Der Streit versprach sie, sich zu ändern.*; *(stronger)* jd verändert sich [fɛl'ɛndɐt] <verändert sich, veränderte sich, hat sich verändert> ◊ *Nach ihrem Tod hat er sich sehr verändert.* sth changes sb etw. verändert

jdn ◊ *Der Erfolg hat sie verändert.* ◆ *Du bist ganz verändert.*; *(transform)* change sth etw. verwandeln [fɛl'vandl̩n] <verwandelt, verwandelte, hat verwandelt> ◊ *Die helle Farbe hat den Raum verwandelt.* **2.** *(exchange for sth else, your job, an item of clothing, a service, bank note, currency, light bulb etc.)* wechseln ['vɛksl̩n] +haben ◊ *eine Batterie/Glühbirne wechseln* ◆ *Er hat nur schnell sein Hemd gewechselt.* ◆ *Sie möchte den Beruf wechseln.* ◆ *den Anwalt wechseln* ◆ *Euro in Dollar wechseln* change colo(u)r die Farbe wechseln ◊ *Die Ampel wechselte von Grün auf Gelb.* change to sth/sb zu etw. wechseln [tsu: ... ,vɛksl̩n] +sein ◊ *Viele Verbraucher sind zu anderen Stromversorgern gewechselt.* **3.** *(put on different clothes)* sb changes jd zieht sich um [tsi:t ... 'ʊm] <zog sich um, hat sich umgezogen> ◊ *Er zieht sich vor dem Essen um.* sb changes into sth jd zieht etw. an [tsi:t ... 'an] <zog an, hat angezogen> ◊ *ein frisches Hemd anziehen* **4.** *(train, bus etc.)* umsteigen ['ʊmʃtaeg̍n] <steigt um, stieg um, ist umgestiegen> ◊ *Wir müssen in Hannover umsteigen.* change to sth in etw. [acc] umsteigen ◊ *Am Busbahnhof steige ich in den Bus nach London um.*

• **change around** [phras v] change sth around etw. umstellen ['ʊmʃtɛlən] +haben ◊ *Ich habe im Wohnzimmer die Möbel umgestellt.*

• **change into** [phras v] change into sth/sb sich in etw./jdn verwandeln [ɪn ... fɛ,vandl̩n] <verwandelt sich, verwandelte sich, hat sich verwandelt> ◊ *Zeus verwandelte sich in einen Stier.* ◆ *Wenn man Wasser erhitzt, verwandelt es sich in Dampf.*

• **change over** [phras v] change over (to sth) (zu etw.) überwechseln ['y:bɐvɛksl̩n] <wechselt über, wechselte über, ist übergewechselt> ◊ *Deutschland ist von der D-Mark zum Euro übergewechselt.*

changeable [adj] unbeständig ['ʊnbəʃtɛndɪç] ◊ *unbeständiges Wetter* ◆ *Seine Leistungen sind recht unbeständig.*

channel [noun] **1.** *(for information, for water, radio/TV frequency)* Kanal [ka'na:l] der <-s, Kanäle> ◊ *Auf welchem Kanal sendet Antenne 1?* ◆ *Wir müssen diese Informationen über die richtigen Kanäle weiterleiten.* **2.** TV, RADIO *(broadcasting service)* Programm [pro'gram] das <-(e)s, -e> ◊ *Der Krimi kommt im ersten Programm.*

⊛ **the Channel** der Ärmelkanal

chaos [noun] Chaos ['ka:ɔs] das <-> no pl ◊ *Chaos verursachen* be in chaos ein Chaos sein ◊ *Damals war mein Leben ein einziges Chaos.*

chapel [noun] Kapelle [ka'pɛlə] die <-, -n>

chapter [noun] **1.** *(of a book, sb's life, a church)* Kapitel [ka'pɪtl̩] das <-s, -> ◊ *Der Roman hat 25 Kapitel.* ◆ *Das ist ein dunkles Kapitel in seinem Leben.* **2.** *(in the US: part of a large organization)* Sektion [zɛk'tsi̯o:n] die <-, -en>

character [noun] **1.** *(nature, qualities)* Charakter [ka'raktɐ] der <-s, -e> ◊ *Er hat einen guten Charakter.* ◆ *Die Mitgliedsbeiträge haben eher symbolischen Charakter.* ◆ *Der Ort hat noch immer einen dörflichen Charakter.* in character typisch (für jdn) ['ty:pɪʃ] out of character untypisch (für jdn) ['ʊnty:pɪʃ] ◊ *Dieses Verhalten ist untypisch für ihn.* **2.** *(sb's reputation)* Ruf [ru:f] der <-(e)s> no pl ◊ *ein Mann von gutem Ruf* **3.** *(in a book, film)* Figur [fi'gu:ɐ] die <-, -en> ◊ *Fast alle Figuren des Romans waren Männer.* **4.** *(extraordinary person)* Persönlich-

keit [pɛrˈzøːnlɪçkaet] die <-, –en> ◊ *Mutter Theresa war eine außergewöhnliche Persönlichkeit.; (excentric or loveable person)* Original [origiˈnaːl] das <-s, –e> ◊ *Mein Opa war ein richtiges Original.* **5.** *(suspicious or immoral individual)* Subjekt [zʊpˈjɛkt] das <-(e)s, –e> *(pej)* ◊ *ein verkommenes Subjekt*

characteristic[1] [noun] **1.** *(inherent)* Eigenschaft [ˈaegŋʃaft] die <-, –en> ◊ *Zu ihren bemerkenswertesten Eigenschaften gehört ihr Mut.* **2.** *(external)* Merkmal [ˈmɛrkmaːl] das <-s, –e> ◊ *ein auffälliges/ typisches/wesentliches Merkmal*

characteristic[2] [adj] charakteristisch [karakteˈrɪstɪʃ] ◊ *das charakteristische Aroma von gebrannten Mandeln* ♦ *Diese Reaktion ist charakteristisch für ihn.*

characterize [verb] **1.** *(the nature of sth)* prägen [ˈprɛːgŋ] +haben ◊ *Zahlreiche Kanäle prägen das Stadtbild Amsterdams.* **2.** characterize sb/sth as sb/ sth jdn/etw. als jdn/etw. beschreiben [als ... bəˌʃraebm̩] <beschreibt, beschrieb, hat beschrieben> ◊ *Sein ehemaliger Professor beschrieb den Präsidenten als oberflächlich.*

charge[1] [noun] **1.** *(for most services, admission etc.)* Preis [praes] der <-es, –e> ◊ *Mein Preis beträgt 35 Euro die Stunde.; (payable to authorities, banks, for electricity, telephone etc.)* Gebühr [gəˈbyːɐ] die <-, –en> ◊ *Die Bank erhebt eine Gebühr für Überweisungen.* free of charge kostenlos [ˈkɔstn̩loːs] *no comp/superl* extra charge Aufpreis [ˈaofpraes] der <-es, –e> **2.** LAW *(by a public prosecutor)* Anklage [ˈanklaːgə] die <-, –n> charge of sth Anklage wegen etw. ◊ *eine Anklage wegen Mordes/Diebstahls etc.; (by a member of the public)* Anzeige [ˈantsaegə] die <-, –n> press charges (against sb) (gegen jdn) Anzeige erstatten ◊ *Ich werde Anzeige gegen Sie erstatten.* **3.** *(accusation)* Vorwurf [ˈfoːɐvʊrf] der <-(e)s, Vorwürfe> ◊ *Er wies den Vorwurf des Rassismus zurück.* **4.** *(by an army, animal)* Angriff [ˈangrɪf] der <-(e)s, –e> **5.** *(of electricity, explosives)* Ladung [ˈlaːdʊŋ] die <-, –en> ◊ *eine Ladung Dynamit* ♦ *Elektronen haben eine elektrische Ladung.* ◉ take charge of sth etw. übernehmen ◊ *die Geschäftsleitung übernehmen* in charge be in charge (of sth/sb) die Verantwortung (für etw./jdn) haben put sb in charge of sth/sb) jdm die Verantwortung (für etw./jdn) übertragen in sb's charge in jds Obhut ◊ *die Kinder/Juwelen in ihrer Obhut*

charge[2] [verb] **1.** *(request payment)* charge (sb) Geld (von jdm) verlangen [ˈgɛlt fɛˌlaŋən] <verlangt, verlangte, hat verlangt> ◊ *Hat sie Geld (von dir) verlangt?* charge (sb) for sth (jdm) etw. berechnen [bəˈrɛçnən] <berechnet, berechnete, hat berechnet> ◊ *Der Optiker hat (mir) die Reparatur nicht berechnet.* charge (sb) sth (jdm) etw. berechnen ◊ *(jdm) 20 Euro/eine Gebühr berechnen* be charged at ... ... kosten [ˈkɔstn̩] <kostet, kostete, hat gekostet> ◊ *Alle Anrufe kosten 1,86 Euro pro Minute.* charge sth to sb jdm etw. in Rechnung stellen [ɪn ˈrɛçnʊŋ ʃtɛlən] +haben charge sth to an account ein Konto mit etw. belasten [aen ˌkɔnto: mɪt ... bəˌlastn̩] <belastet, belastete, hat belastet> **2.** LAW charge sb (with sth) jdn (wegen etw.) anklagen [ˈanklaːgŋ] +haben ◊ *Er wurde wegen Mordes angeklagt.* **3.** *(accuse)* charge sb with sth jdm etw. vorwerfen [ˈfoːɐvɛrfŋ] <wirft

vor, warf vor, hat vorgeworfen> ◊ *jdm einen Regelverstoß vorwerfen* charge sb with doing sth jdm vorwerfen, etw. getan zu haben **4.** *(with power)* laden [ˈlaːdn̩] <lädt, lud, hat geladen> ◊ *Hast du die Akkus geladen?* **5.** *(attack)* charge (at sb/sth) (jdn/ etw). angreifen [ˈangraefŋ] <greift an, griff an, hat angegriffen> ◊ *Der Stier hat den Torero angegriffen.* • charge about [phras v] toben [ˈtoːbm̩] +haben/with indication of direction +sein ◊ *Die Kinder haben den ganzen Tag im Garten getobt.*

charity [noun] **1.** *(organization)* Wohltätigkeitsverein [ˈvoːltɛːtɪçkaetsfɛˌaen] der <-(e)s, –e> **2.** *(act, intention)* wohltätiger Zweck [ˌvoːltɛːtɪgɐ ˈtsvɛk] <-(e)s, –e> ◊ *Die Veranstaltung dient einem wohltätigen Zweck.* give to charity für wohltätige Zwecke spenden charity event Wohltätigkeitsveranstaltung [ˈvoːltɛːtɪçkaetsfɛˌanʃtaltʊŋ] die <-, –en> ⓔ charity begins at home *man sollte sich zuerst um die Bedürfnisse der Menschen kümmern, mit denen man unmittelbar zusammenlebt*

charm [noun] **1.** *(quality)* Reiz [raets] der <-es, –e> *most sing* ◊ *Seine Romane haben nach all den Jahren nichts von ihrem Reiz verloren.; (of a person)* Charme [ʃarm] der <-s> *no pl* ◊ *Sie ist seinem Charme erlegen.* turn on the charm seinen Charme spielen lassen **2.** *(object bringing luck)* Glücksbringer [ˈglʏksbrɪŋɐ] der <-s, –> ◊ *eine Kette mit einem Glücksbringer* ⓔ work like a charm Wunder wirken

charming(ly) [adj, adv] *(very pleasant, attractive)* reizend [ˈraetsn̩t] ◊ *eine reizende Wohnung in der Altstadt* ♦ *Du überlässt mir den Abwasch? Wie reizend von dir!* ♦ *Sie war ganz reizend gekleidet.; (with the intention to enchant)* charmant [ʃarˈmant] <charmanter, am charmantesten> ◊ *Er war sehr charmant.* ♦ *ein charmantes Lächeln* ♦ *Sie lächelte charmant.*

chart[1] [noun] **1.** *(list)* Tabelle [taˈbɛlə] die <-, –n> ◊ *die Tabelle mit den Daten; (graph)* Diagramm [diaˈgram] das <-s, –e> ◊ *ein Diagramm erstellen* **2.** *(map)* Karte [ˈkaʀtə] die <-, –n> naval chart Seekarte [ˈzeːkaʀtə] ⓔ the charts die Charts

chart[2] [verb] **1.** *(record)* erfassen [ɛˈfasn̩] <erfasst, erfasste, hat erfasst> ◊ *Veränderungen erfassen* **2.** GEOG *(make a map)* kartografieren [kaʀtograˈfiːrən] <kartografiert, kartografierte, hat kartografiert> *(tech)* ◊ *eine Region kartografieren*

charter [noun] **1.** *(rules)* Charta [ˈkaʀta:] die <-, –s> ◊ *die Charta der Menschenrechte* **2.** *(of a plane, ship)* Charter [ˈtʃaʀtə] der <-s, –s> ◊ *der Charter eines Flugzeugs* charter flight Charterflug [ˈtʃaʀteʀfluːk] der <-(e)s, Charterflüge> **3.** LAW bank charter Bankenkonzession [ˈbaŋkjkɔntsɛˌsjoːn] die <-, –en>

chase[1] [noun] Jagd [jaːkt] die <-, –en> ◊ *Jagd auf Verbrecher machen* give chase to sb jds Verfolgung aufnehmen [fɛˈfɔlgʊŋ ˌaofneːmən] <nimmt auf, nahm auf, hat aufgenommen> ◊ *Die Polizei nahm die Verfolgung des Verbrechers auf.*

chase[2] [verb] jagen [ˈjaːgŋ] +haben ◊ *Verbrecher jagen* chase away verjagen [fɛˈjaːgŋ] <verjagt, verjagte, hat verjagt> ◊ *einen Hund verjagen* chase after sth/sb jdm/etw. hinterherjagen [hɪntɐˈheːɐjaːgŋ] +sein ◊ *Der Spieler jagte dem Ball hinterher.*

chat[1] [noun] Unterhaltung [ʊntɐˈhaltʊŋ] die <-, –en> ◊ *Wir hatten eine nette kleine Unterhaltung.;*

(internet) Chat [tʃɛt] der <-s, -s> have a chat with sb mit jdm plaudern [mɪt ... ˈplaʊdən] +haben for a chat um ein wenig (mit jdm) zu plaudern [ʊm aɛn ˌveːnɪç ʦu: ˈplaʊdən] ◊ *Sie rief ihre Freundin an, um ein wenig mit ihr zu plaudern.* **chat²** ⟨verb⟩ **1.** *(talk)* plaudern [ˈplaʊdən] +haben ◊ *Wir plauderten angeregt über das Wetter.* **2.** IT chatten [ˈtʃɛtn̩] <chattet, chattete, hat gechattet> ◊ *Anstatt sich mal wieder mit Freunden zu treffen, chattet er nur noch.*

• **chat up** ⟨phras v⟩ chat sb up jdn anquatschen [ˈankvatʃn̩] +haben *(fam)*

chauffeur ⟨noun⟩ Chauffeur [ʃɔˈføːɐ̯] der <-s, -e> ♀Chauffeurin [ʃɔˈføːrɪn] die <-, -nen> ◊ *eine Limousine mit Chauffeur mieten* ♦ *Die Chauffeurin fuhr sie in die Stadt.*

cheap ⟨adj⟩ **1.** *(inexpensive, of poor quality, despicable)* billig [ˈbɪlɪç] ◊ *Wohnungen in München sind nicht gerade billig.* ♦ *billig einkaufen* ♦ *Das ist doch eine ganz billige Ausrede.* a cheap trick ein billiger Trick Under his dictatorship life was cheap. Während seiner Diktatur zählte ein Menschenleben nicht viel. **2.** *(miserly)* geizig [ˈɡaɛ̯tsɪç]
ⓔ on the cheap für einen Pappenstiel
cheaply ⟨adv⟩ günstig [ˈɡʏnstɪç] ◊ *günstig reisen*
cheat ⟨verb⟩ **1.** *(in a game, exam)* mogeln [ˈmoːɡl̩n] +haben *(fam)* ◊ *beim Kartenspiel mogeln* **2.** *(deceive, commit adultery)* betrügen [bəˈtryːɡn̩] <betrügt, betrog, hat betrogen> ◊ *Der Verkäufer hat uns betrogen.* ♦ *Sie gab zu, ihren Mann mehrmals betrogen zu haben.* cheat sb (out) of sth jdn um etw. betrügen ◊ *Man hat die Rentnerin um ihre gesamten Ersparnisse betrogen.*
• **cheat on** ⟨phras v⟩ cheat on sb jdn betrügen [bəˈtryːɡn̩] <betrügt, betrog, hat betrogen> ◊ *Er hat seine Frau schon oft betrogen.*; *(esp in the US)* cheat on sth bei etw. betrügen [bae ... bəˈtryːɡn̩] ◊ *Sie hat bei der Steuererklärung betrogen.*

check¹ ⟨noun⟩ **1.** *(inspection)* Kontrolle [kɔnˈtrɔlə] die <-, -n> ◊ *Wann ist die nächste Kontrolle des Reifendrucks fällig?* make a check on sb/sth bei jdm /etw. eine Kontrolle durchführen act as a check on sth etw. unter Kontrolle halten **2.** POL checks and balances Gewaltenteilung [ɡəˈvaltn̩taɛ̯lʊŋ] die <-> no pl **3.** *(examination of sb's health)* Vorsorgeuntersuchung [ˈfoːɐ̯zoːɐ̯ɡəlʊntɐˌzuːxʊŋ] die <-, -en> ◊ *Sie muss demnächst wieder zur Vorsorgeuntersuchung gehen.* **4.** *(pattern)* Karo [ˈkaːro:] das <-s, -s> ◊ *ein Hemd mit weißen und roten Karos* **5.** *(in chess)* Schach [ʃax] das <-s> no pl ◊ *Sein König befindet sich im Schach.* **6.** *(amount to pay in a restaurant)* Rechnung [ˈrɛçnʊŋ] die <-, -en> ◊ *Bringen Sie uns bitte die Rechnung?* **7.** FIN *(means of payment)* Scheck [ʃɛk] der <-s, -s> ◊ *Zahlen Sie bar oder mit Scheck?* **8.** *(written symbol)* Haken [ˈhaːkn̩] der <-s, ->
ⓔ keep/hold sb/sth in check jdn/etw. in Schach halten
check² ⟨verb⟩ **1.** *(inspect, examine)* überprüfen [ybɐˈpryːfn̩] <überprüft, überprüfte, hat überprüft> ◊ *den Reifendruck überprüfen* ♦ *Der Grenzbeamte überprüfte die Ausweise.* check sth for sth etw. auf etw. ⟨acc⟩ hin überprüfen ◊ *Nach dem Sturz überprüfte er das Motorrad auf Beschädigungen hin.* **2.** *(make sure)* nachsehen [ˈnaːxzeːən] <sieht nach, sah nach, hat nachgesehen> ◊ *Hast du nachgesehen,*

ob alle Fenster zu sind? **3.** *(a process, development etc.)* aufhalten [ˈaʊfhaltn̩] <hält auf, hielt auf, hat aufgehalten> ◊ *die Verbreitung einer Krankheit aufhalten* check yourself sich zurückhalten [ʦuˈrʏkhaltn̩] <hält sich zurück, hielt sich zurück, hat sich zurückgehalten> ◊ *Sie wollte ihm das Geheimnis schon verraten, hielt sich dann aber doch zurück.*
• **check against** ⟨phras v⟩ check sth against sth die Übereinstimmung von etw. mit etw. prüfen [di: ybeˌaɛnʃtmʊŋ fɔn ... mɪt ... ˌpryːfn̩] +haben ◊ *Er prüfte die Übereinstimmung des Fingerabdrucks mit den Einträgen in der Datenbank.*
• **check in** ⟨phras v⟩ **1.** *(to a hotel)* sich anmelden [ˈanmɛldn̩] <meldet sich an, meldete sich an, hat sich angemeldet> ◊ *Haben Sie sich schon an der Rezeption angemeldet?* check sb in jdn irgendwo anmelden **2.** *(at an airport)* einchecken [ˈaɛ̯ntʃɛkn̩] +haben ◊ *Die Fluggäste können an diesem Schalter einchecken.* ♦ *Ich habe die Koffer schon eingecheckt.* ♦ *Die Dame der Fluggesellschaft checkte uns ein.*
• **check into** ⟨phras v⟩ **1.** *(a hotel)* sich irgendwo anmelden [ˈanmɛldn̩] <meldet sich an, meldete sich an, hat sich angemeldet> ◊ *Wir konnten uns erst sehr spät im Hotel anmelden.* **2.** *(to find out more about sth)* check into sth etw. überprüfen [ybeˈpryːfn̩] <überprüft, überprüfte, hat überprüft> ◊ *Würdest du die Angebote nochmal überprüfen?*
• **check on** ⟨phras v⟩ check on sb/sth nach jdm/etw. sehen [naːx ... zeːən] <sieht, sah, hat gesehen> ◊ *Kannst du bitte mal nach dem Baby sehen?*
• **check off** ⟨phras v⟩ check sth off etw. abhaken [ˈaphaːkn̩] +haben ◊ *Sie hakte die erledigten Aufgaben auf der Liste ab.*
• **check out** ⟨phras v⟩ **1.** *(of a hotel)* abreisen [ˈapraɛ̯zn̩] +sein ◊ *Die Gäste reisen morgen um elf Uhr ab.* **2.** *(pay for sth)* bezahlen [bəˈʦaːlən] <bezahlt, bezahlte, hat bezahlt> ◊ *Sie müssen erst bezahlen, bevor Sie die Verpackung öffnen.* **3.** *(examine)* überprüfen [ybeˈpryːfn̩] <überprüft, überprüfte, hat überprüft> ◊ *einen Verdächtigen/jds Gesundheitszustand überprüfen*
• **check up on** ⟨phras v⟩ check up on sb jdn überprüfen [ybeˈpryːfn̩] <überprüft, überprüfte, hat überprüft> ◊ *Die Polizei hat den Verdächtigen überprüft.*

checkers ⟨noun⟩ Dame [ˈdaːmə] das <-> *article only in combination with attribute, no pl* ◊ *Dame spielen*
cheek ⟨noun⟩ **1.** *(part of the body)* Backe [ˈbakə] die <-, -n> ◊ *jdm einen Kuss auf die Backe geben* **2.** *(impertinence)* Frechheit [ˈfrɛçhaɛ̯t] die <-, -en> ◊ *Sein Artikel ist eine absolute Frechheit.* have the cheek to do sth die Frechheit haben, etw. zu tun
ⓔ cheek to cheek Wange an Wange turn the other cheek die andere Wange hinhalten
cheeky(-ily) ⟨adj, adv⟩ frech [frɛç] ◊ *ein freches Grinsen* ♦ *Sei nicht so frech!* ♦ *Der Kleine grinste frech und sauste davon.*
cheep ⟨verb⟩ piepsen [ˈpiːpsn̩] +haben
cheer¹ ⟨noun⟩ **1.** *(applause)* Beifallsruf [ˈbaɛ̯falsruːf] der <-(e)s, -e> ◊ *Aus der Menge ertönten laute Beifallsrufe.* three cheers for ein dreifaches Hurra für [aɛn ˌdraɛ̯faxəs huˈraː fy:ɡ] ◊ *Ein dreifaches Hurra für den glücklichen Gewinner Tim!* **2.** *(merriment)* Aufmunterung [ˈaʊfmʊntərʊŋ] die <-, -en> ◊ *Worte der Aufmunterung* be full of good cheer guter Dinge sein [ɡuːtɐ ˈdɪŋə zaɛn] +sein bring cheer to sb jdn

aufmuntern ['aʊfmʊntɐn] <muntert auf, munterte auf, hat aufgemuntert> ◊ *Deine lieben Worte haben mich aufgemuntert.*

cheer² [verb] **1.** *(applaud)* jubeln ['juːbln̩] +haben ◊ *Die Zuschauer jubelten auf der Tribüne.* cheer sb jdm zujubeln ['tsuːjuːbln̩] +haben ◊ *Die Menge jubelte dem Präsidenten zu.* **2.** *(be made happy)* be cheered erfreut sein [ɛ'frɔʏt tsaˑɛn] +sein ◊ *Er schien über die Neuigkeit sehr erfreut zu sein.*

cheerful(ly) [adj, adv] **1.** *(merry(-ily))* fröhlich ['frøːlɪç] ◊ *Überall sah man fröhliche Gesichter.* ◆ *Du siehst ja so fröhlich aus!* ◆ *Er lachte fröhlich.* **2.** *(pleasant(ly))* freundlich ['frɔʏntlɪç] ◊ *ein freundlicher, warmer Gelbton* ◆ *Der Raum ist hell und freundlich eingerichtet.* ◆ *Das Zimmer wirkte sehr freundlich.*

cheering [noun] Beifall ['baɛfal] der <-(e)s> *no pl* ◊ *Es gab viel Beifall für seine Rede.*

cheerio [interj] tschüss [tʃʏs] *only spoken (fam)* ◊ *Tschüss, bis morgen!*

cheers [interj] **1.** *(before drinking alcohol)* prost [proːst] ◊ *Prost allerseits!* **2.** *(thanks)* danke ['daŋkə] ◊ *„Hier ist dein Kaffee." — „Danke!"* **3.** *(goodbye)* tschüss [tʃʏs] *only spoken (fam)* ◊ *Tschüss, bis später!*

cheese [noun] Käse ['kɛːzə] der <-s, -> ◊ *Sie belegt ihr Brötchen mit Käse.* sliced cheese Schnittkäse ['ʃnɪtkɛːzə]
◉ **say cheese** bitte recht freundlich

cheesecake [noun] Käsekuchen ['kɛːzəkuːxn̩] der <-s, ->

chef [noun] Koch [kɔx] der <-(e)s, Köche> ♀Köchin ['kœçɪn] die <-, -nen> ◊ *Sie ist Köchin in einem Restaurant in München.* ◆ *Kompliment an den Koch für das Dessert!*

chemical [noun] Chemikalie [çemi'kaːliə] die <-, -n> *most pl* ◊ *Vorsicht beim Umgang mit giftigen Chemikalien!* chemicals in food Chemie in Lebensmitteln [çe,miː ɪn 'leːbm̩sm̩ɪtl̩n] die <—> *no pl*

chemical(ly) [adj, adv] chemisch ['çeːmɪʃ] *no comp/ superl; when used as an adj, mostly before ns* ◊ *eine chemische Reaktion* ◆ *ohne chemische Zusätze* ◆ *einen Anzug chemisch reinigen lassen*

chemist [noun] **1.** *(shop for medicines)* Apotheke [apo'teːkə] die <-, -n> ◊ *Schmerzmittel aus der Apotheke holen; (shop for toiletries)* Drogerie [drogə'riː] die <-, -n> ◊ *Bringst du mir aus der Drogerie Duschgel mit?* **2.** *(sb who sells medicines)* Apotheker [apo'teːkɐ] der <-s, -> ♀Apothekerin [apo'teːkərɪn] die <-, -nen> ◊ *Er ist Apotheker.* ◆ *Die Apothekerin hat mir zu diesem Medikament geraten.; (sb who sells toiletries)* Drogist [dro'gɪst] der <-en, -en> ♀Drogistin [dro'gɪstɪn] die <-, -nen> ◊ *Sie arbeitet als Drogistin.* ◆ *Der Drogist hat mir diese Handcreme empfohlen.* **3.** *(sb who works with chemicals)* Chemiker ['çeːmɪkɐ] der <-s, -> ♀Chemikerin ['çeːmɪkərɪn] die <-, -nen> ◊ *Sie ist Chemikerin bei der BASF.* ◆ *der berühmte Chemiker Justus Liebig*

chemistry [noun] Chemie [çe'miː] die <—> *no pl* ◊ *die anorganische/organische Chemie* ◆ *Sie hat in Chemie eine Zwei.* ◆ *Zwischen den beiden hat die Chemie von Anfang an nicht gestimmt.*

cheque [noun] Scheck [ʃɛk] der <-s, -s> ◊ *einen Scheck ausstellen* a cheque for ... ein Scheck über ... [acc] ◊ *ein Scheck über 100 Euro* by cheque mit Scheck ◊ *Zahlen Sie bar oder mit Scheck?*

cheque guarantee card [noun] Scheckkarte

['ʃɛkaˑtə] die <-, -n>

cherry [noun] Kirsche ['kɪrʃə] die <-, -n> ◊ *ein Kuchen mit Kirschen* ◆ *In ihrem Garten steht eine Kirsche.* ◆ *Möbel aus Kirsche*

chess [noun] Schach [ʃax] das <-s> *no pl* ◊ *Schach spielen*

chessboard [noun] Schachbrett ['ʃaxbrɛt] das <-(e)s, -er>

chest [noun] **1.** ANAT Brust [brʊst] die <-, Brüste> ◊ *eine behaarte Brust haben* ◆ *jdn an seine Brust drücken* have a bad chest Probleme mit den Bronchien haben [pro,bleːmə mɪt deːn 'brɔnçiən haːbm̩] +haben **2.** *(piece of furniture)* Truhe ['truːə] die <-, -n> ◊ *etw. in einer Truhe aufbewahren*

chest of drawers [noun] Kommode [kɔ'moːdə] die <-, -n>

chew [verb] kauen ['kaʊən] +haben ◊ *Winfried kaut unentwegt Kaugummi.* ◆ *Du solltest gründlicher kauen.*
● **chew up** [phras v] chew sth up **1.** *(with your teeth)* etw. zerkauen ['tsɛ'kaʊən] <zerkaut, zerkaute, hat zerkaut> ◊ *Der Hund hat den Knochen zerkaut.* **2.** *(destroy)* etw. übel zurichten [,yːbl̩ 'tsuːrɪçtn̩] <richtet zu, richtete zu, hat zugerichtet> ◊ *Die Maschine hatte seinen Arm übel zugerichtet.*

chewing gum [noun] Kaugummi ['kaʊɡʊmiː] der *or also* das <-s, -s> ◊ *Er kaut Kaugummi.*

chic [adj] schick [ʃɪk] ◊ *ein schickes Kleid* ◆ *Du siehst aber heute schick aus!*

chick [noun] Küken ['kyːkn̩] das <-s, ->

chicken [noun] **1.** *(bird, meat of this bird)* Huhn [huːn] das <-(e)s, Hühner> ◊ *Dieser Bauer hält Hühner.* ◆ *Er isst nicht gern Huhn.* roast chicken Hähnchen ['hɛːnçən] das <-s, -> **2.** *(coward)* Feigling ['faɛklɪŋ] der <-s, -e> ◊ *Sei kein Feigling!*

chicken out [verb] kneifen ['knaɛfn̩] <kneift, kniff, hat gekniffen> *(fam)* ◊ *Sie hat vor der Klausur gekniffen.*

chickenpox [noun] Windpocken ['vɪntpɔkn̩] die <—> *only pl*

chief¹ [noun] **1.** *(of an organization, department etc.)* Leiter ['laɛtɐ] der <-s, -> ♀Leiterin ['laɛtərɪn] die <-, -nen> ◊ *Ist der neue Leiter der Abteilung schon da?* ◆ *Sie war vorher Leiterin unserer Abteilung.; (boss)* Chef [ʃɛf] der <-s, -s> ♀Chefin ['ʃɛfɪn] die <-, -nen> chief of police Polizeichef [poli'tsaɛʃɛf] chief of staff Stabschef ['ʃtaːpsʃɛf] chief of state Staatschef ['ʃtaːtsʃɛf] **2.** *(of a gang)* Anführer ['anfyːrɐ] der <-s, -> ♀Anführerin ['anfyːrərɪn] die <-, -nen> ◊ *Der Anführer der Bande ist untergetaucht.* **3.** *(of a tribe)* Häuptling ['hɔʏptlɪŋ] der <-s, -e> ♀Häuptlingin ['hɔʏptlɪŋɪn] die <-, -nen> ◊ *der Häuptling der Apachen*

chief² [adj] **1.** *(main)* Haupt... [haʊpt] ◊ *der Hauptgrund für das Unglück* ◆ *Das Geld ist im Moment unser Hauptproblem.* **2.** *(leading)* Ober... ['oːbɐ] ◊ *ein Oberförster/Oberkellner/Oberschulrat*

chief executive [noun] Generaldirektor [genəra'ldɪ,rɛktoːɐ] der <-s, -en> ♀Generaldirektorin [genəra'ldɪrɛk,toːrɪn] die <-, -nen> ◊ *Er ist Generaldirektor bei Siemens.* ◆ *Was sagt denn der Generaldirektor zu diesem Vorschlag?*

chiefly [adv] hauptsächlich ['haʊptzɛçlɪç] ◊ *Wir verkaufen hauptsächlich Damenbekleidung.*

child [noun] Kind [kɪnt] das <-(e)s, -er> ◊ *Du benimmst dich wie ein kleines Kind.* ◆ *Sie ist ein*

Kind der Sechzigerjahre. only child Einzelkind
['aents|kɪnt]; *(in compound ns)* Kinder... ['kɪnde]
child labour Kinderarbeit ['kɪnde|aʳbaet] die <–> *no
pl* child seat Kindersitz ['kɪndezɪts] der <–es, –e>;
(be a mother/father) have children Kinder haben
['kɪnde ha:bm̩] +*haben; (give birth)* have children
Kinder bekommen ['kɪnde bəkɔmən] <bekommt,
bekam, hat bekommen>
🅐 child's play ein Kinderspiel
childhood (noun) Kindheit ['kɪnthaet] die <–, –en>
*most sing ◊ Sie hatte eine glückliche/unbeschwerte
Kindheit. ♦ Er hat seine Kindheit auf dem Land
verbracht.*
childminder (noun) Tagesmutter ['ta:gəsmʊte] die
<–, Tagesmütter> *◊ Sie arbeitet als Tagesmutter. ♦
Meine Kinder sind vormittags bei einer Tagesmutter.*
Chile (noun) Chile ['tʃi:le:] das <–s> *article only in combination with attribute, no pl* → **Germany**
Chilean¹ (noun) Chilene [tʃi'le:nə] der <–n, –n>
♀Chilenin [tʃi'le:nɪn] die <–, –nen> → **German¹** 1.
Chilean² (adj) chilenisch [tʃi'le:nɪʃ] *mostly before ns* →
German²
chill¹ (noun) 1. *(coolness)* Frische ['frɪʃə] die <–> *no pl
◊ die Frische des Herbstes* There's quite a chill in the
air. Es ist ziemlich frisch. take the chill off sth etw.
erwärmen [e'veʳmən] <erwärmt, erwärmte, hat
erwärmt> *◊ Die Sonne hat das Wasser ein wenig
erwärmt.* 2. *(illness)* Erkältung [e'kɛltʊŋ] die
<–, –en> *◊ Sie hat eine Erkältung.* catch a chill sich
verkühlen [fe'ky:lən] <verkühlt sich, verkühlte sich,
hat sich verkühlt> 3. *(of fear, horror etc.)* Frösteln
['frœstl̩n] das <–s> *no pl ◊ Ein Frösteln überkam
sie, als sie die schrecklichen Bilder im Fernsehen
sah.* sth sends a chill down sb's spine bei etw. läuft
es jdm kalt den Rücken herunter *◊ Beim Anblick
des toten Hundes lief es ihm kalt den Rücken
herunter.*
chill² (verb) 1. *(make cooler)* kühlen ['ky:lən] +*haben ◊
im Kühlschrank ein paar Dosen Bier kühlen*
2. *(terrify)* erschrecken [e'ʃrekŋ̍] <erschreckt,
erschreckte, hat erschreckt> *◊ Das unheimliche
Geräusch erschreckte alle zutiefst.* 3. *(friendship,
relations)* abkühlen ['apky:lən] +*sein ◊ Nach dem Zwischenfall kühlten die Beziehungen zwischen den
beiden Staaten merklich ab.*
🅐 sb is chilled to the bone 1. *(sb is very cold)* jdm
geht die Kälte bis auf die Knochen 2. *(sb is terrified
by sth)* sb is chilled to the bone by sth etw. lässt
jdm das Blut in den Adern gefrieren
• chill out (phras v) relaxen [ri'lɛksn̩] <relaxt, relaxte,
hat relaxt> *(fam)*
chilly (adj) 1. *(quite cold)* frisch [frɪʃ] <frischer, am fri-
schesten> *◊ Es wehte ein frischer Wind. ♦ Abends
kann es hier frisch werden.* 2. *(unfriendly)* kühl [ky:l]
*◊ Ihr Lächeln wirkte kühl und reserviert. ♦ ein
kühler Blick*
chimney (noun) Schornstein ['ʃoʳnʃtaen] der
<–(e)s, –e>
chin (noun) Kinn [kɪn] das <–(e)s, –e>
🅐 chin up Kopf hoch
china (noun) Porzellan [pɔʳtsɛ'la:n] das <–s, –e> *most
sing ◊ Geschirr/eine Figur aus Porzellan ♦ das teure
Porzellan in der Vitrine* a china jug ein Porzellan-
krug
China (noun) China ['çi:na] das <–s> *article only in
combination with attribute, no pl* → **Germany**

Chinese¹ (noun) 1. *(inhabitant)* Chinese [çi'ne:zə] der
<–n, –n> ♀Chinesin [çi'ne:zɪn] die <–, –nen> →
German¹ 1. 2. *(language)* Chinesisch [çi'ne:zɪʃ] das
<–(s)> *no pl* → **German¹** 2.
Chinese² (adj) chinesisch [çi'ne:zɪʃ] → **German²**
chip¹ (noun) 1. *(food)* chips Pommes frites [pɔm'frɪt(s)]
die <–> *pl ◊ eine Portion Pommes frites mit
Ketschup ♦ Hähnchen mit Pommes frites* 2. *(for
computers, gambling)* Chip [tʃɪp] der <–s, –s> *◊ die
auf dem Chip gespeicherten Daten ♦ Er hat seine
ganzen Chips verspielt.* 3. *(of glass)* Splitter ['ʃplɪte]
der <–s, –> *◊ Vorsicht, hier liegen überall Splitter!;
(of wood)* Span [ʃpa:n] der <–(e)s, Späne> *most pl*
wood chips Holzspäne ['hɔltsʃpɛ:nə]
🅐 a chip off the old block *(just like the father)*
ganz der Vater *(just like the mother)* ganz die Mutter
have a chip on your shoulder about sth wegen
etw. Komplexe haben
chip² (verb) 1. *(damage)* anschlagen ['anʃla:gŋ̍]
<schlägt an, schlug an, hat angeschlagen> *◊ beim
Spülen eine Tasse anschlagen* 2. sport *(in golf)* hoch-
schlagen ['ho:xʃla:gŋ̍] <schlägt hoch, schlug hoch, hat
hochgeschlagen>; *(in football)* chip the ball *(over sb/
sth)* den Ball *(über jdn/etw)*. heben
[de:n 'bal ˌhe:bm̩] <hebt, hob, hat gehoben> 3. chip
potatoes Kartoffeln in schmale Streifen schneiden
[kaʳˌtɔfl̩n ɪn ʃma:lə 'ʃtraefn̩ ʃnaedn̩] <schneidet, schnitt,
hat geschnitten>
• chip in (phras v) 1. *(join a conversation)* sich einschalten ['aenʃaltn̩] <schaltet sich ein, schaltete sich
ein, hat sich eingeschaltet> *◊ Als die Kinder aufeinander losgingen, schaltete sich der Vater ein.* 2. *(give
money)* chip sth in etw. beisteuern ['baeʃtɔgen]
<steuert bei, steuerte bei, hat beigesteuert> *◊ Ich habe
eine große Summe zum Kauf des Hauses beigesteu-
ert.* Would you like to chip in? Möchtest du gerne
etwas beisteuern?
• chip off (phras v) 1. chip sth off etw. abschlagen
['apʃla:gŋ̍] <schlägt ab, schlug ab, hat abgeschlagen> *◊
den Putz von den Wänden abschlagen* 2. sth chips
off etw. geht ab [ge:t ap] <ging ab, ist abgegangen>
*◊ Wir müssen streichen; die alte Farbe geht überall
ab.*
chirp (verb) zwitschern ['tsvɪtʃeʳn] +*haben*
chives (noun) Schnittlauch ['ʃnɪtlaox] der <–(e)s> *no
pl*
chocolate (noun) 1. *(food made from cocoa, drink)*
Schokolade [ʃoko'la:də] die <–, –n> *most sing ◊
eine Tafel/ein Riegel Schokolade ♦ ein mit Schokolade überzogener Kuchen ♦ Sie trank eine heiße Schokolade.* chocolate cake Schokoladenkuchen
[ʃoko'la:dŋ̍ku:xn̩] der <–s, –> 2. *(small sweet)*
Praline [pra'li:nə] die <–, –n> *◊ eine Schachtel
Pralinen*
choice (noun) 1. *(process of selecting and its result,
thing chosen)* Wahl [va:l] die <–, –en> *most sing ◊
Das war eine gute Wahl. ♦ Sie haben ihn vor die
Wahl gestellt, selbst zu kündigen oder entlassen zu
werden.* sb's first/second choice jds erste/zweite
Wahl *◊ Die Universität Bonn wäre meine erste Wahl
gewesen.* of your choice deiner/Ihrer Wahl *◊
Gewinnen Sie eine Reise zu einem Ziel Ihrer Wahl!*
be given the choice die Wahl haben *◊ Wenn du die
Wahl hättest, welches Auto würdest du nehmen?* have
no choice keine *(andere)* Wahl haben make a
choice eine Wahl treffen choice between Wahl

zwischen ◊ *Sie haben die Wahl zwischen fünf ver-schiedenen Modellen.* **2.** *(selection, range)* Auswahl ['aʊsvaːl] die <-> *no pl* ◊ *Das Lokal bietet seinen Gästen eine Auswahl erlesener Speisen.* a wide choice eine große Auswahl ◊ *Paris hat eine große Auswahl an Sehenswürdigkeiten zu bieten.*
⊚ **by choice** freiwillig

choir [noun] Chor [koːɐ̯] der <-(e)s, Chöre> ◊ *Sie singt in einem gemischten Chor.*

choke [verb] **1.** *(be unable to breathe)* ersticken [ɛ'ʃtɪkŋ] <erstickt, erstickte, ist erstickt> ◊ *Wir glaubten in dem dicken Rauch ersticken zu müssen.* choke on sth an etw. [dat] ersticken ◊ *Das Kind wäre fast an einem Bonbon erstickt.* in a voice choked with sobs mit tränenerstickter Stimme [mɪt ˌtrɛːnən|ɛʃtɪktɐ 'ʃtɪmə] **2.** *(strangle, make coughing sounds)* würgen ['vʏɐ̯gŋ] +haben ◊ *Der Täter würgte sein Opfer, bis es sich nicht mehr bewegte.* ◆ *Er verschluckte sich an einem Stück Fleisch und begann zu würgen.* choke sb to death jdn erwürgen [ɛ'vʏɐ̯gŋ] <erwürgt, erwürgte, hat erwürgt> choke to death (on sth) (an etw. [dat]) ersticken [ɛ'ʃtɪkŋ] <erstickt, erstickte, hat erstickt>

choose [verb] **1.** *(select)* wählen ['vɛːlən] +haben ◊ *Sie hat für ihr Gespräch einen günstigen Zeitpunkt gewählt.* ◆ *Ich wählte einen Ring als Geschenk.* ◆ *Er kann wählen, was er tun will.* choose from wählen aus ◊ *Sie können aus einem breiten Angebot an Stoffen wählen.* choose between wählen zwischen ◊ *Hoffentlich muss ich niemals zwischen Familie und Beruf wählen.* choose sth/sb as ... etw./jdn zu ... wählen ◊ *Sie wählten ihn zu ihrem Anführer.; (select from among a given number)* auswählen ['aʊsvɛːlən] +haben ◊ *Welcher der Bewerber wurde ausgewählt?* ◆ *Die Zutaten wurden mit Sorgfalt ausgewählt.* choose sb/sth out of ... jdn/etw. aus ... auswählen ◊ *Die Jury hat aus allen Einsendungen mein Bild ausge-wählt.* **2.** *(prefer)* choose to do sth es vorziehen, etw. zu tun [ɛs 'foːɐ̯tsiːən ... tsuː] <zieht vor, zog vor, hat vorgezogen> ◊ *Sie zieht es vor, allein zu leben.*
⊚ **there is nothing/little to choose between them** sie sind gleich gut

chop¹ [noun] **1.** *(meat)* Kotelett [kɔt'lɛt] das <-s, -s> **2.** *(blow with the hand)* Schlag [ʃlaːk] der <-(e)s, Schläge> karate chop Karateschlag [ka'raːtəʃlaːk] ◊ *Er versetzte dem Gegner einen Karate-schlag ins Genick.*
⊚ **get the chop** rausgeschmissen werden

chop² [verb] **1.** *(cut up)* klein schneiden ['klaɪn ʃnaɪdŋ] <schneidet, schnitt, hat geschnitten> ◊ *Fleisch klein schneiden* chop sth into sth etw. in etw. [acc] schneiden ◊ *die Kartoffeln in Würfel schneiden; (wood)* hacken ['hakŋ] +haben ◊ *für den Winter Holz hacken* chop one's way through sth sich [dat] einen Weg durch etw. schlagen [aɛnən ˌveːk dʊɐ̯ç ... ʃlaːgŋ] <schlägt, schlug, hat geschlagen> ◊ *Sie schlugen sich einen Weg durch das Unterholz.* **2.** *(reduce an amount)* kürzen ['kʏɐ̯tsn̩] +haben ◊ *die Ausgaben um 30 Prozent kürzen* **3.** *(hit sb/sth with your hand)* chop sb/sth jdm/etw. einen Schlag versetzen [aɛnən 'ʃlaːk fɛzɛtsn̩] <versetzt, versetzte, hat versetzt>

• **chop down** [phras v] chop sth down etw. fällen ['fɛlən] +haben ◊ *Die alte Eiche am Stadtrand wird gefällt.*

• **chop off** [phras v] chop sth off etw. abhacken

['aphakŋ] +haben

• **chop up** [phras v] chop sth up etw. zerkleinern [tsɐ'klaɛnɐn] <zerkleinert, zerkleinerte, hat zerklei-nert>

choppy [adj] bewegt [bə've:kt] <bewegter, am bewegtes-ten> ◊ *Das Boot schaukelte auf dem bewegten Wasser.* ◆ *Die See ist heute sehr bewegt.*

chord [noun] **1.** MUS Akkord [a'kɔrt] der <-(e)s, -e> ◊ *einen Akkord anschlagen* **2.** MATH Sehne ['zeːnə] die <-, -n>
⊚ **strike a chord (with sb)** (bei jdm) auf Verständ-nis stoßen

chore [noun] **1.** *(household)* chores Hausarbeit ['haʊslaˌbaɛt] die <-, -en> ◊ *Du gehst erst spielen, wenn du die Hausarbeit erledigt hast!* **2.** *(disagrea-ble job)* Plage ['plaːgə] die <-, -n> ◊ *Früher war das Wäschewaschen eine rechte Plage.*

chorus [noun] **1.** *(of a song)* Refrain [re'frɛ̃] der <-s, -s> ◊ *Beim Refrain bitte alle mitsingen!* **2.** *(group of people, piece of music)* Chor [koːɐ̯] der <-(e)s, Chöre> ◊ *Sie singt im Chor.* ◆ *einen vier-stimmigen Chor komponieren* ◆ *der Chor in der antiken Tragödie* in chorus im Chor ◊ *„Wir haben Hunger!", riefen alle im Chor.*

chosen → **choose** [adj] auserwählt ['aʊslɛvɛːlt] *no comp/superl* ◊ *das auserwählte Volk* ◆ *Sie fühlte sich auserwählt, ihn zu retten.*

Christ [noun] Christus ['krɪstʊs] der <Christi> *article only in combination with attribute, no pl* ◊ *der Tod/ die Auferstehung Christi* ◆ *Christus ist von den Toten auferstanden.*
⊚ **for Christ's sake** um Himmels willen

christen [verb] taufen ['taʊfn̩] +haben ◊ *Er wurde auf den Namen Andreas getauft.* ◆ *ein Kind taufen lassen*

christening [noun] Taufe ['taʊfə] die <-, -n> ◊ *die Taufe empfangen*

Christian¹ [noun] Christ [krɪst] der <-en, -en> ♀Christin ['krɪstɪn] die <-, -nen> be a Christian Christ/Christin sein

Christian² [adj] christlich ['krɪstlɪç] *seldom comp/ superl* ◊ *der christliche Glaube* ◆ *Ich finde sein Verhalten nicht sehr christlich.*

Christianity [noun] Christentum ['krɪstn̩tuːm] das <-s> *no pl*

Christian name [noun] Vorname ['foːɐ̯naːmə] der <-n, -n> ◊ *Sie heißt mit zweitem Vornamen Maria.* ◆ *Michael ist einer der beliebtesten deutschen Vornamen.*

Christmas [noun] Weihnachten ['vaɛnaxtn̩] *seldom with definite article 'das'* ◊ *Frohe Weihnachten und ein glückliches neues Jahr!* for Christmas zu Weih-nachten

Christmas Day [noun] erster Weihnachtsfeiertag [ˌeːɐ̯stɐ 'vaɛnaxtsfaɛɐtaːk] <-> ◊ *Der 25. Dezember ist der erste Weihnachtsfeiertag.*

Christmas Eve [noun] Heiligabend [haɛlɪç'|aːbm̩t] der <-s, -e> *most sing* ◊ *An Heiligabend versammelt sich die Familie vor dem Weihnachtsbaum.*

chronic [adj] **1.** *(illness, problem)* chronisch ['kroːnɪʃ] *no comp/superl* ◊ *Dieses Leiden kann chronisch werden.* ◆ *Er ist ein chronischer Lügner.* **2.** *(fam) (very bad)* miserabel [mizə'raːbl̩] <miserabler, am miserabelsten> <der/die/das miserable ...> ◊ *Das Theaterstück war einfach miserabel!*

chronological(ly) [adj, adv] chronologisch

[krono'lo:gɪʃ] *no comp/superl* ◊ *der chronologische Ablauf von Ereignissen* ♦ *Die Reihenfolge ist chronologisch.* ♦ *chronologisch geordnet*

chubby [adj] pummelig ['pʊməlɪç] ◊ *ein pummeliges Baby* ♦ *Als Kind war sie recht pummelig.* chubby cheeks Pausbacken ['paʊsbakn̩] die <−> *pl*

chuck [verb] 1. *(throw)* schmeißen ['ʃmaɛsn̩] <schmeißt, schmiss, hat geschmissen> *(fam)* ◊ *Schmeiß mal den Ball zu mir!* ♦ *Du sollst deine Schultasche nicht in die Ecke schmeißen!* 2. *(dispose of)* wegschmeißen ['vɛkʃmaɛsn̩] <schmeißt weg, schmiss weg, hat weggeschmissen> *(fam)* ◊ *Das brauche ich nicht mehr, du kannst es wegschmeißen.* 3. chuck sb mit jdm Schluss machen [mɪt ... 'ʃlʊs maxn̩] +haben *(fam)*
• **chuck away** [phras v] chuck sth away etw. wegschmeißen ['vɛkʃmaɛsn̩] <schmeißt weg, schmiss weg, hat weggeschmissen> *(fam)* ◊ *Schmeiß doch endlich mal diese alten Schuhe weg!* chuck away money Geld aus dem Fenster schmeißen [,gɛlt aʊs de:m 'fɛnstɐ ʃmaɛsn̩] <schmeißt, schmiss, hat geschmissen> *(fam)*
• **chuck in** [phras v] chuck sth in etw. hinschmeißen ['hɪnʃmaɛsn̩] <schmeißt hin, schmiss hin, hat hingeschmissen> *(fam)* ◊ *die Arbeit/Schule hinschmeißen*

chunk [noun] 1. *(large piece of sth)* Brocken ['brɔkn̩] der <−s, −> ◊ *jdm einen Brocken Brot geben* 2. *(of money)* Batzen ['batsn̩] der <−s, −> ◊ *Der Wagen hat einen schönen Batzen Geld gekostet.*

church [noun] 1. Kirche ['kɪrçə] die <−, −n> ◊ *eine gotische Kirche* go to church in die/zur Kirche gehen ◊ *Sie geht jeden Sonntag zur Kirche.* get married in church kirchlich heiraten ['kɪrçlɪç ,haɛra:tn̩] +haben church choir Kirchenchor ['kɪrçn̩ko:g] der <−(e)s, Kirchenchöre> 2. the Church die Kirche [di: 'kɪrçə] <−, −n> ◊ *die Trennung von Kirche und Staat*

churn [verb] 1. *(milk)* churn sth into sth etw. zu etw. schlagen [tsu: ... ʃla:gn̩] <schlägt, schlug, hat geschlagen> ◊ *Sie schlug die Sahne zu Butter.* 2. sb's stomach churns jdm dreht sich der Magen um [dreːt stɪç deːg 'maːgn̩ ʊm] +haben 3. sb's mind churns jds Gedanken überschlagen sich [gə,daŋkn̩ ybɐ'ʃlaːgn̩ zɪç] <überschlägt sich, überschlug sich, hat sich überschlagen>
• **churn out** [phras v] churn sth out etw. produzieren [produ'tsiːrən] <produziert, produzierte, hat produziert> *(pej)* ◊ *Sie produziert einen Roman nach dem anderen.*

cigarette [noun] Zigarette [tsiga'rɛtə] die <−, −n>
cigarette lighter [noun] Feuerzeug ['fɔɛtsɔɛk] das <−(e)s, −e>

cinema [noun] 1. *(building)* Kino ['kiːnoː] das <−s, −s> ◊ *Wir treffen uns um acht vor dem Kino.* go to the cinema ins Kino gehen 2. *(film business)* Film [fɪlm] der <−(e)s *no pl* ◊ *Er ist ein Star des deutschen Films.*

cinnamon [noun] Zimt [tsɪmt] der <−(e)s *no pl* ◊ *eine Stange Zimt*

circle[1] [noun] Kreis [kraɛs] der <−es, −e> ◊ *einen Kreis zeichnen* ♦ *ein kleiner Kreis von Experten* in a circle im Kreis ◊ *die Stühle im Kreis aufstellen* form a circle einen Kreis bilden circle of friends Freundeskreis ['frɔɛndəskraɛs] der <−es, −e> *most sing* ⊚ the circle der Rang ◊ *Wir hatten einen Platz im zweiten Rang.* go around in circles sich im Kreis bewegen

circle[2] [verb] 1. *(in the air)* kreisen ['kraɛzn̩] +haben/sein ◊ *Am Himmel kreisten die Geier.* circle (around) sb/sth jdn/etw. umkreisen [ʊm'kraɛzn̩] <umkreist, umkreiste, hat umkreist> ◊ *Die Hyänen umkreisten hungrig den Kadaver.* 2. *(loop around)* umschlingen [ʊm'ʃlɪŋən] <umschlingt, umschlang, hat umschlungen> ◊ *Er umschlang ihre Taille.* 3. *(draw a circle)* einkreisen ['aɛnkraɛzn̩] +haben ◊ *Ich habe die wichtigen Punkte rot eingekreist.*

circuit [noun] 1. *(series of places)* Tournee [tʊr'neː] die <−, −n> on the club circuit auf Tournee durch die Nachtklubs travel the circuit auf Tournee sein ◊ *Die Band ist schon seit einem Jahr auf Tournee.* 2. *(in a race, around a place)* Runde ['rʊndə] die <−, −n> ◊ *fünf Runden laufen* ♦ *Wir drehten vor dem Abendessen noch eine Runde im Park.* 3. TECHN Schaltung ['ʃaltʊŋ] die <−, −en> ◊ *eine einfache Schaltung für die Stromversorgung* short circuit Kurzschluss ['kʊrtsʃlʊs] der <−es, Kurzschlüsse> ◊ *Es gab einen Kurzschluss und das Licht ging aus.*

circular[1] [noun] Rundschreiben ['rʊntʃraɛbm̩] das <−s, −>

circular[2] [adj] 1. *(in the form of a circle)* rund [rʊnt] *no comp/superl* ◊ *ein rundes Gebäude* circular tour Rundfahrt ['rʊntfaːrt] die <−, −en> 2. circular argument Zirkelschluss ['tsɪrkl̩ʃlʊs] der <−es, Zirkelschlüsse> 3. circular letter Rundbrief ['rʊntbriːf] der <−(e)s, −e>

circulate [verb] 1. *(spread, become known)* sich verbreiten [fɐ'braɛtn̩] <verbreitet sich, verbreitete sich, hat sich verbreitet> ◊ *Die Neuigkeit hat sich rasch verbreitet.* 2. *(make known)* in Umlauf bringen [ɪn 'ʊmlaʊf brɪŋən] <bringt, brachte, hat gebracht> ◊ *ein Schreiben in Umlauf bringen* 3. *(blood, air etc.)* zirkulieren [tsɪrku'liːrən] <zirkuliert, zirkulierte, hat zirkuliert> ◊ *Das Blut zirkuliert in den Adern.* circulate sth etw. zirkulieren lassen ◊ *Der Ventilator lässt die Luft im Raum zirkulieren.* 4. *(at a social gathering)* die Runde machen [di: 'rʊndə maxn̩] +haben ◊ *Ich habe auf Peters Party gestern mal die Runde gemacht und viele nette Leute kennen gelernt.*

circulation [noun] 1. *(of blood)* Kreislauf ['kraɛslaʊf] der <−(e)s, Kreisläufe> ◊ *den Kreislauf in Schwung bringen* air circulation Luftzirkulation ['lʊfttsɪrkula,tsjoːn] die <−, −en> *most sing* 2. *(of a newspaper)* Auflage ['aʊflaːgə] die <−, −n> ◊ *Die Zeitschrift erscheint in einer Auflage von 800 000 Stück.* 3. *(of money, currency)* Umlauf ['ʊmlaʊf] der <−(e)s *no pl* in circulation in/im Umlauf ◊ *Diese Münze ist schon lange nicht mehr im Umlauf.* put sth into circulation etw. in Umlauf bringen ◊ *Falschgeld in Umlauf bringen*

circumference [noun] Umfang ['ʊmfaŋ] der <−(e)s, Umfänge> ◊ *den Umfang eines Kreises berechnen*

circumstance [noun] 1. *(particular condition)* Umstand ['ʊmʃtant] der <−(e)s, Umstände> *most pl* ◊ *Die Umstände, die zu dem Unfall führten, müssen noch geklärt werden.* under/in ... circumstances unter ... Umständen ◊ *Unter diesen Umständen kann ich nicht zulassen, dass du allein wegfährst.* not under/in any circumstances, under no circumstances unter keinen Umständen under normal circumstances normalerweise ['nɔr'maːlɐvaɛzə] ◊ *Normalerweise geht sie um 11 Uhr ins Bett.* ♦ *Wo ist er bloß? Normaler-*

weise müsste er schon da sein. **2.** *(financial conditions, external conditions)* circumstances Verhältnisse [fɛ'hɛltnɪsə] die <-> pl ◊ *in geordneten Verhältnissen leben* family circumstances Familienverhältnisse [fa'miːljənfɛhɛltnɪsə] ◊ *aus schwierigen Familienverhältnissen stammen* a victim of circumstance ein Opfer der Verhältnisse [aen ˌɔpfe deːɐ fɛ'hɛltnɪsə] ◊ *Er wurde ein Opfer der politischen Verhältnisse.* ◉ due to unforeseen circumstances aufgrund unvorhergesehener Umstände

circumvent [verb] **1.** umgehen [ʊm'geːən] <umgeht, umging, hat umgangen> ◊ *ein Verbot umgehen* **2.** *(motorist)* umfahren [ʊm'faːrən] <umfährt, umfuhr, hat umfahren> ◊ *eine gesperrte Straße umfahren; (pedestrian)* umgehen [ʊm'geːən] <umgeht, umging, hat umgangen>

circus [noun] **1.** *(show with animals and clowns etc., big fuss)* Zirkus ['tsɪrkʊs] der <-, -se> ◊ *Wir gehen heute in den Zirkus.* media circus Medienzirkus ['meːdjəntsɪrkʊs] **2.** HIST *(in ancient Rome)* Arena [a'reːna] die <-, Arenen> ◊ *Die Gladiatoren kämpften in der Arena.* **3.** *(road intersection)* (runder) Platz [(rʊnde) plats] der <-es, Plätze> ◊ *Acht Straßen laufen auf den runden Platz zu.*

cite [verb] **1.** *(quote)* zitieren ['tsi'tiːrən] <zitiert, zitierte, hat zitiert> ◊ *Er zitierte ein Gedicht von Goethe.* ♦ *jdn/etw. in einer wissenschaftlichen Arbeit zitieren* **2.** *(mention)* nennen ['nɛnən] <nennt, nannte, hat genannt> ◊ *Nenn (mir) bitte ein Beispiel dafür.* ♦ *Ich kann Ihnen mehrere Fälle nennen, in denen so vorgegangen wurde.; (as an example/explanation)* anführen ['anfyːrən] +haben ◊ *Sie führte das als Beispiel an.* **3.** *(name sb, in favo(u)rable terms)* cite sb as sth jdn als etw. [acc] preisen [als ... praezn] <preist, pries, hat gepriesen> ◊ *Man preist ihn als einen Kenner moderner Kunst.* **4.** LAW *(in the US: in court)* vorladen ['foːɐglaːdn] <lädt vor, lud vor, hat vorgeladen> ◊ *Das Gericht hat sie als Zeugin vorgeladen.*

citizen [noun] Bürger ['bʏrge] der <-s, -> ♀Bürgerin ['bʏrgərɪn] die <-, -nen> ◊ *die Bürger Kölns/ Spaniens/der EU; (of a country: having certain rights and duties)* Staatsbürger ['ʃtaːtsbʏrge] Staatsbürgerin ['ʃtaːtsbʏrgərɪn] ◊ *Sie ist deutsche Staatsbürgerin.*

citizenship [noun] Staatsangehörigkeit ['ʃtaːtsˌangəˌhøːrɪçkaet] die <-, -en> ◊ *die britische Staatsangehörigkeit beantragen/erhalten/aufgeben* ♦ *die doppelte Staatsangehörigkeit*

city[1] [noun] **1.** *(very large town)* Großstadt ['groːsʃtat] die <-, Großstädte> **2.** *(urban area)* Stadt [ʃtat] die <-, Städte> ◊ *Lebst du lieber in der Stadt oder auf dem Land?*

city[2] [adj] städtisch ['ʃtɛ(ː)tɪʃ] no comp/superl ◊ *die städtischen Behörden*

city centre, city center [noun] *(part of town or city where shops and businesses are concentrated)* Innenstadt ['ɪnənʃtat] die <-, Innenstädte> ◊ *die Fußgängerzone in der Münchener Innenstadt; (geographical middle of a town or city)* Stadtmitte ['ʃtatmɪtə] die <-, -n> most sing ◊ *die S-Bahn Richtung Stadtmitte*

city hall [noun] **1.** *(building)* Rathaus ['raːthaos] das <-es, Rathäuser> ◊ *zum Rathaus gehen* **2.** *(administration)* Stadtverwaltung ['ʃtatfɛvaltʊŋ] die <-, -en> ◊ *bei der Stadtverwaltung arbeiten*

civic [adj] **1.** *(relating to a town or city)* städtisch ['ʃtɛ(ː)tɪʃ] no comp/superl ◊ *die städtischen Behörden*

2. *(relating to the people of a town or city)* staatsbürgerlich ['ʃtaːtsbʏˈgelɪç] no comp/superl ◊ *die staatsbürgerlichen Rechte und Pflichten*

civil [adj] **1.** *(relating to (ordinary) people)* zivil [tsi'viːl] no comp/superl, mostly before ns ◊ *das zivile Gesundheitswesen* ♦ *die zivile Gerichtsbarkeit* civil proceedings Zivilverfahren [tsi'viːlfɛfaːrən] das <-s, -> **2.** *(relating to the people of a particular country)* bürgerlich ['bʏˈgelɪç] no comp/superl, only before ns ◊ *die bürgerlichen Rechte* civil code bürgerliches Gesetzbuch **3.** *(polite)* höflich ['høːflɪç] ◊ *ein höfliches Benehmen* ♦ *Das war nicht sehr höflich.* **4.** *(wedding)* standesamtlich ['ʃtandəsˌamtlɪç] no comp/superl, only before ns ◊ *eine standesamtliche Trauung*

civilly [adv] höflich ['høːflɪç] ◊ *Er hat sich sehr höflich verhalten.*

civilian[1] [noun] MIL Zivilist [tsivi'lɪst] der <-en, -en> ♀Zivilistin [tsivi'lɪstɪn] die <-, -nen> ◊ *Bei den Kämpfen wurden auch unschuldige Zivilsten getötet.*

civilian[2] [adj] Zivil... [tsi'viːl] civilian population Zivilbevölkerung [tsi'viːlbəˌfœlkərʊŋ] die <-> no pl

civilization [noun] Zivilisation [tsiviliza'tsjoːn] die <-, -en> ◊ *die westliche/moderne/abendländische Zivilisation* ♦ *Urlaub in der Wildnis fern der Zivilisation*

civilized [adj] **1.** *(highly-developed, advanced, polite)* zivilisiert [tsivili'ziːɐt] <zivilisierter, am zivilisiertesten> ◊ *ein zivilisiertes Land* ♦ *Sein Benehmen kann man kaum als zivilisiert bezeichnen.* **2.** *(refined)* gepflegt [gə'pfleːkt] <gepflegter, am gepflegtesten> ◊ *gepflegte Gastlichkeit/Atmosphäre* ♦ *Das Ambiente des Cafés ist sehr gepflegt.*

civil servant [noun] Beamte [bə'amtə] der <-n, die Beamten> ♀Beamtin [bə'amtɪn] die <-, -nen> but: ein Beamter/eine Beamtin ◊ *ein beim Finanzamt angestellter Beamter* ♦ *Frau Sachs ist Beamtin.* ♦ *In Deutschland sind Lehrer Beamte.*

civil war [noun] Bürgerkrieg ['bʏˈgekriːk] der <-(e)s, -e>

claim[1] [noun] **1.** *(assertion)* Behauptung [bə'haoptʊŋ] die <-, -en> ◊ *eine Behauptung aufstellen/beweisen* ♦ *Seine Behauptung, ich hätte ihn geschlagen, ist nicht wahr.* **2.** *(to property, sb's attention, gratitude etc.)* claim to/on sth Anspruch auf etw. [acc] ['anʃprʊx aof] der <-(e)s, Ansprüche> ◊ *Anspruch auf ein Gebiet erheben* ♦ *Er hat Anspruch auf meine Dankbarkeit.* claim to fame Anspruch auf Berühmtheit claim for damages Anspruch auf Schadenersatz **3.** *(request for money)* Forderung ['fɔˈdərʊŋ] die <-, -en> *(tech)* ◊ *Die Forderungen der Gläubiger an die Firma konnten nicht erfüllt werden.* ◉ make no claim to be sth/sb nicht vorgeben, etw./jd zu sein ◊ *Ich gebe nicht vor, ein Experte zu sein.*

claim[2] [verb] **1.** *(state that sth is true)* behaupten [bə'haoptn] <behauptet, behauptete, hat behauptet> ◊ *Er behauptet, er habe keinen Fehler gemacht.* ♦ *Sie behauptet steif und fest, dich dort gesehen zu haben.* ♦ *Ich behaupte nicht, dass ich Recht habe.* **2.** *(state that sth is yours)* claim sth Anspruch auf etw. [acc] erheben [ˌanʃprʊx aof ... ɛhe:bm] <erhebt, erhob, hat erhoben> ◊ *Anspruch auf ein Territorium/einen Anteil erheben* ♦ *Beide Gegner erhoben Anspruch auf den Sieg.* claim responsibility for sth die Verantwortung für etw. übernehmen

[diː feˈʔantvɔˈtʊŋ fyːɐ̯ ... ybɐˌneːmən] <übernimmt, übernahm, hat übernommen> 3. *(request, result in the loss of)* fordern [ˈfɔʁdɐn] +haben ◊ *Sie forderte ihr Geld von ihm.* ♦ *eine Lohnerhöhung fordern* ♦ *Das Unglück forderte fünf Todesopfer.* 4. *(a service, credit, sb's attention/time)* in Anspruch nehmen [ɪn ˈanʃpʁʊx neːmən] <nimmt, nahm, hat genommen> ◊ *Dieser Service kann zehn Jahre lang kostenlos in Anspruch genommen werden.* ♦ *Die Pflege der Tiere nahm viel Zeit in Anspruch.* claim on your insurance seine Versicherung in Anspruch nehmen 5. *(asylum, benefits)* beantragen [bəˈʔantʁaːɡn̩] <beantragt, beantragte, hat beantragt> ◊ *Hast du Arbeitslosengeld beantragt?* 6. *(baggage, lost property)* abholen [ˈaphoːlən] +haben ◊ *Fundgegenstände, die nicht abgeholt werden, werden versteigert.* ♦ *Er holte seinen Koffer ab.* 7. claim sth against sb jdn einer Sache [gen] beschuldigen [bəˈʃʊldɪɡn̩] <beschuldigt, beschuldigte, hat beschuldigt> ◊ *Sie beschuldigten sich gegenseitig schwerer Kriegsverbrechen.* 8. *(win)* gewinnen [ɡəˈvɪnən] <gewinnt, gewann, hat gewonnen> ◊ *Die Weltranglistenerste hat ihren vierten Titel gewonnen.*

clap¹ [noun] 1. *(applause)* Applaus [aˈplaʊ̯s] der <-(e)s no pl ◊ *Wie wäre es mit einem Applaus für die Gäste?* 2. *(blow)* Klaps [klaps] der <-es, -e> ◊ *dem Baby einen Klaps auf den Rücken geben* 3. clap of thunder Donnerschlag [ˈdɔnɐʃlaːk] der <-(e)s, Donnerschläge>

clap² [verb] 1. *(applaud)* klatschen [ˈklatʃn̩] +haben ◊ *Das Publikum hat begeistert geklatscht.* clap your hands in die Hände klatschen 2. *(slap)* schlagen [ˈʃlaːɡn̩] <schlägt, schlug, hat geschlagen> ◊ *jdm freundschaftlich auf die Schulter schlagen* clap your hand to your mouth/brow die Hand vor den Mund/ an die Stirn schlagen clap your hands over/to your eyes die Hände vors Gesicht schlagen clap your hands over your ears sich [dat] die Ohren zuhalten [diː ˈoːʁən ˌtsuːˈhaltn̩] <hält zu, hielt zu, hat zugehalten> 3. clap sb in prison jdn ins Gefängnis werfen [ɪns ɡəˈfɛŋnɪs vɛʁfn̩] <wirft, warf, hat geworfen>

clarification [noun] 1. *(explanation, information)* Aufklärung [ˈaʊ̯fklɛːʁʊŋ] die <-, -en> ◊ *um Aufklärung bitten* clarification on sth Erläuterungen zu etw. [ɛʁˈlɔɪ̯təʁʊŋən tsuː] die <-> pl 2. *(also fig)* *(process of making sth clearer)* Klärung [ˈklɛːʁʊŋ] die <-, -en> ◊ *die Klärung von Abwässern* ♦ *die Klärung einer Frage*

clarify [verb] klären [ˈklɛːʁən] +haben ◊ *Anwässer klären* ♦ *eine Frage mit dem Chef klären* ♦ *Ich muss erst klären, was wir machen sollen.*

clarinet [noun] Klarinette [klaʁiˈnɛta] die <-, -n>

clarity [noun] Klarheit [ˈklaːʁhaɪ̯t] die <-> no pl ◊ *die Klarheit ihrer Stimme* ♦ *die Klarheit des Wassers* ◊ *Diese Frage kann nicht mit absoluter Klarheit beantwortet werden.*

clash¹ [noun] 1. *(meeting in conflict)* Zusammenstoß [tsuˈzamənʃtoːs] der <-es, Zusammenstöße> ◊ *Zusammenstöße zwischen Polizei und Demonstrierenden;* *(disagreement)* Auseinandersetzung [aʊ̯sʔaɪ̯ˈnandɐˌzɛtsʊŋ] die <-, -en> ◊ *Er hatte eine Auseinandersetzung mit seiner Frau über die Erziehung der Kinder.; (ethnic, armed, military)* Konflikt [kɔnˈflɪkt] der <-(e)s, -e> ◊ *ethnische Konflikte in Afrika* clash of interests Interessenskonflikt [ɪntəˈʁɛsn̩skɔnˌflɪkt] 2. *(of metal objects)* Aneinanderschlagen [anʔaɪ̯ˈnandɐʃlaːɡn̩] das <-s> no pl

◊ *das Aneinanderschlagen der Schwerter* 3. *(between incompatible things)* Unvereinbarkeit [ˈʊnfɛɐ̯ʔaɪ̯nbaːɐ̯ˌkaɪ̯t] die <-, -en> ◊ *die Unvereinbarkeit ihrer Standpunkte* 4. *(of personalities, colo(u)rs)* Unverträglichkeit [ˈʊnfɛɐ̯tʁɛːklɪçkaɪ̯t] die <-, -en> ◊ *Unverträglichkeit der Charaktere* 5. *(of simultaneous things)* Überschneidung [ybɐˈʃnaɪ̯dʊŋ] die <-, -en> ◊ *Überschneidungen zwischen Veranstaltungen vermeiden*

clash² [verb] 1. *(fight, quarrel)* aneinander geraten [anʔaɪ̯ˈnandɐ ɡəʁaːtn̩] <gerät, geriet, ist geraten> ◊ *mit den Nachbarn aneinander geraten* 2. *(happen at the same time)* sth clashes with sth etw. überschneidet sich mit etw. [ybɐˈʃnaɪ̯dət zɪç mɪt] <überschneidet, überschnitt, hat überschnitten> ◊ *Die Party überschneidet sich mit der Theatervorstellung.* 3. *(fam)* *(be incompatible)* aufeinander prallen [aʊ̯fʔaɪ̯ˈnandə pʁalən] +sein ◊ *wenn Welten/Kulturen/ Standpunkte aufeinander prallen; (colo(u)rs)* sich beißen [ˈbaɪ̯sn̩] <beißt sich, biss sich, hat sich gebissen> ◊ *Die Farben beißen sich.* 4. *(metal objects)* schlagen [ˈʃlaːɡn̩] <schlägt, schlug, ist/hat geschlagen> transitive use +haben/intransitive use +sein Their swords clashed. Ihre Schwerter schlugen aneinander. He clashed two dustbin lids. Er schlug zwei Mülltonnendeckel gegeneinander. They clashed their swords. Sie schlugen mit ihren Schwertern aufeinander ein.

clasp¹ [noun] 1. *(on clothes)* Spange [ˈʃpaŋə] die <-, -n> ◊ *ein Umhang mit goldener Spange* 2. *(grasp)* Griff [ɡʁɪf] der <-(e)s, -e> ◊ *Sein Griff um ihren Arm wurde fester.*

clasp² [verb] 1. *(hold tightly)* clasp drücken [ˈdʁʏkn̩] +haben ◊ *jdm zur Begrüßung die Hand drücken* ♦ *Die Mutter drückte ihre Kinder an sich.* ♦ *Er drückte ein Taschentuch auf die Wunde.; (in fear of falling etc.)* umklammern [ʊmˈklamɐn] <umklammert, umklammerte, hat umklammert> ◊ *Sie umklammerte das Geländer.* clasp your hands die Hände verschränken [diː ˈhɛndə fɛˌʃʁɛŋkn̩] <verschränkt, verschränkte, hat verschränkte> ◊ *die Hände im Schoß/ hinter dem Kopf verschränken* 2. *(close, fasten)* schließen [ˈʃliːsn̩] <schließt, schloss, hat geschlossen> ◊ *Sie schließt die Schnalle ihres Gürtels.*

class [noun] 1. *(reputation, style)* Format [fɔʁˈmaːt] das <-(e)s no pl ◊ *Sie hat als Designerin internationales Format.* ♦ *Er ist ein Mann von internationalem Format.* have (no) class (kein) Format haben 2. *(group or category of people/things)* Klasse [ˈklasə] die <-, -n> ◊ *Bernd ist in derselben Klasse wie Daniel.* ♦ *die unteren sozialen Klassen* ♦ *Eine Fahrkarte zweiter Klasse kostet 35 Euro.* ♦ *Der Mensch gehört zur Klasse der Säugetiere.* 3. *(social or professional group)* Stand [ʃtant] der <-(e)s, Stände> *(outd)* ◊ *als Adliger eine Frau von niederem Stand heiraten* ♦ *dem Stand der Bauern angehören* 4. *(lesson)* Unterrichtsstunde [ˈʊntɐʁɪçtsʃtʊndə] die <-, -n>; *(in compound ns)* ... class ...stunde [ˈʃtʊndə] German class Deutschstunde [ˈdɔɪ̯tʃʃtʊndə]

⊚ sb/sth is in a different class from sb/sth man kann jdn/etw. nicht mit jdm/etw. vergleichen ◊ *Dieses Luxusmodell kann man einfach nicht mit anderen Autos vergleichen.* not be in the same class as sb/sth nicht die Klasse von jdm/etw. haben ◊ *Er ist gut, aber er hat nicht die Klasse von Rembrandt.* be in a class of your own eine Klasse

für sich sein

classic[1] [noun] Klassiker ['klasɪke] der <-s, -> ◇ *Der Film ist ein Klassiker.*

classic[2] [adj] klassisch ['klasɪʃ] ◇ *Bauwerke von klassischer Schönheit* ◆ *Dieser Fehler ist geradezu klassisch.*

classical [adj] klassisch ['klasɪʃ] no comp/superl ◇ *Sagen des klassischen Altertums* ◆ *Sie hört gern klassische Musik.*

classicism [noun] Klassik ['klasɪk] die <-> no pl ◇ *ein Vertreter der deutschen Klassik*

classification [noun] (process of grouping) Klassifizierung [klasifi'tsiːrʊŋ] die <-, -en> ◇ *die Klassifizierung von Weinen*

classify [verb] classifiy sb/sth as sth jdn/etw. als etw. einstufen [als … ˌaɛnʃtuːfn] +haben ◇ *Meine Kollegen stufen mich als konservativ ein.* ◆ *Wird Alkohol als Droge eingestuft?* classify sth according to sth etw. nach etw. ordnen [naːx … ˌɔ'dnən] +haben ◇ *Bücher nach Sachgebieten ordnen*

classmate [noun] Mitschüler ['mɪtʃyːle] der <-s, -> ♀Mitschülerin ['mɪtʃyːlərɪn] die <-, -nen>

classroom [noun] Klassenzimmer ['klasn̩tsɪme] das <-s, ->

classy(-ily) [adj, adv] 1. (exquisite(ly)) edel ['eːdl̩] <edler, am edelsten> <der/die/das edle …> ◇ *Dieses Brautkleid ist echt edel.* ◆ *Dieser Wein ist ein edler Tropfen.* ◆ *ein edel ausgestattetes Auto* 2. (stylish(ly), expensive(ly)) nobel ['noːbl̩] <nobler, am nobelsten> <der/die/das noble …> ◇ *ein nobles Hotel* ◆ *Sie war immer sehr nobel gekleidet.*

clatter [verb] 1. (pots and pans, hooves) klappern ['klapen] +haben ◇ *Man konnte Hufe hören, die über die Straße klapperten.* 2. (move noisily) poltern ['pɔlten] +haben/with indication of direction +sein ◇ *Poltert nicht so laut auf der Treppe!* ◆ *Die Kisten polterten vom Lkw auf die Fahrbahn.*

clause [noun] 1. GRAM Satz [zats] der <-(e)s, Sätze> main clause Hauptsatz ['haɔptzats] subordinate clause Nebensatz ['neːbm̩zats] relative clause Relativsatz [rela'tiːfzats] 2. LAW (of a contract) Klausel ['klaɔzl̩] die <-, -n> ◇ *Der Vertrag enthält eine Klausel, wonach der Mieter verpflichtet ist, …*

claw [noun] 1. (of crabs) Schere ['ʃeːrə] die <-, -n> 2. (smaller, of cats, dogs, birds) Kralle ['kralə] die <-, -n> ◇ *Die Katze zeigte ihre Krallen.*; (bigger, of lions, tigers, tools) Klaue ['klaɔə] die <-, -n>

clay [noun] 1. (type of soil) Lehm [leːm] der <-(e)s, -e> most sing; (for pottery) Ton [toːn] der <-(e)s, -e> most sing ◇ *Die Ziegel sind aus gebranntem Ton.* mode(l)ling clay Knetmasse ['kneːtmasə] die <-, -n> 2. SPORT (in tennis) Sandplatz ['zantplats] der <-(e)s, Sandplätze> ◇ *auf einem Sandplatz spielen*

clean[1] [adj] 1. (also fig) (not dirty, spotless, fair, innocent) sauber ['zaɔbe] ◇ *Er zog ein sauberes Hemd an.* ◆ *das Haus sauber halten* ◆ *Das war ein sauberer Kampf.* ◆ *eine saubere Arbeit ohne Fehler*; (conscience) rein [raɛn] ◇ *ein reines Gewissen haben* have a clean record unbescholten sein ['ʊnbəʃɔltn̩ zaɛn] +sein 2. (linen, clothes, smell) frisch [frɪʃ] <frischer, am frischesten> ◇ *Die Bettwäsche ist frisch.* ◆ *frische Unterwäsche anziehen* 3. (liquids, lines, shapes) klar [klaːɐ̯] ◇ *Das Wasser in diesem See ist sehr klar.* ◆ *eine klare Linie/Form* 4. (piece of paper) leer [leːɐ̯] no comp/superl ◇ *ein leeres Blatt*

nehmen 5. (dog: trained not to soil the house) stubenrein ['ʃtuːbm̩raɛn] no comp/superl ◇ *Ist euer Terrier schon stubenrein?* ◆ *ein stubenreiner Hund*

◉ come clean auspacken ['aɔspakn̩] ◇ *„Pack endlich aus! Wo ist das Geld?"*

clean[2] [verb] 1. (a floor, house, window, shoes, teeth with brush) putzen ['pʊtsn̩] +haben ◇ *die Fenster putzen* ◆ *Hier muss mal wieder geputzt werden.*; (air, sewage, your skin, teeth) reinigen ['raɛnɪɡn̩] +haben ◇ *die Zähne mit Zahnseide reinigen* ◇ *Abluft mit Filtern reinigen*; (a wound, beach) säubern ['zɔɪben] +haben ◇ *Der Strand wird täglich von Unrat gesäubert.* ◆ *Der Arzt säuberte die Wunde.* clean sth off (sth) etw. (von etw.) abputzen ['appʊtsn̩] +haben ◇ *Putz den Schmutz von den Schuhen ab!* 2. (fish, animals) ausnehmen ['aɔsneːmən] <nimmt aus, nahm aus, hat ausgenommen> ◇ *die Fische sofort nach dem Fangen ausnehmen*

• **clean out** [phras v] 1. clean sth out etw. sauber machen ['zaɔbe maxn̩] +haben ◇ *die Garage sauber machen* 2. clean sb out jdn ausnehmen ['aɔsneːmən] <nimmt aus, nahm aus, hat ausgenommen> (fam, pej) ◇ *jdn beim Kartenspielen ausnehmen*

• **clean up** [phras v] aufräumen ['aɔfrɔɪmən] +haben ◇ *Räum endlich dein Zimmer auf!*

cleaner [noun] 1. (in private households) Putzhilfe ['pʊtshɪlfə] die <-, -n> She had to work as a cleaner to support her family. Sie musste putzen gehen, um ihre Familie zu ernähren.; (in offices) Raumpfleger ['raɔmpfleːɡe] der <-s, -> ♀Raumpflegerin ['raɔmpfleːɡərɪn] die <-, -nen> (also euph) 2. (chemical substance) Reiniger ['raɛnɪɡe] der <-s, -> ◇ *Welchen Reiniger nimmst du für die Toilette?* 3. (dry) cleaners Reinigung ['raɛnɪɡʊŋ] die <-> sg ◇ *einen Anzug in die Reinigung bringen*

◉ take sb to the cleaners 1. (exploit sb financially) jdn ausnehmen (fam) 2. (defeat sb in a game or contest) jdn haushoch schlagen

cleanliness [noun] 1. (of a person, animal) Reinlichkeit ['raɛnlɪçkaɛt] die <-> no pl ◇ *Katzen sind für ihre Reinlichkeit bekannt.* 2. (of a thing) Sauberkeit ['zaɔbekaɛt] die <-> no pl

cleanness [noun] Sauberkeit ['zaɔbekaɛt] die <-> no pl

cleanse [verb] 1. (your skin, teeth) reinigen ['raɛnɪɡn̩] +haben ◇ *Sie reinigt abends ihre Haut mit einem Gesichtswasser.*; (a wound, country, town) säubern ['zɔɪbən] +haben ◇ *Der Arzt säuberte die Wunde.* ◆ *ein Gebiet von Feinden säubern* 2. cleanse sth/sb of sth etw./jdn von etw. befreien [fɔn … bəˌfraɛən] <befreit, befreite, hat befreit> ◇ *Honig durch Schleudern von Verunreinigungen befreien* ◆ *jdn von Schuldgefühlen befreien* 3. (make spiritually clean) läutern ['lɔɪten] +haben ◇ *ein durch Buße geläuterter Sünder*

clear[1] [adj] 1. (obvious, unmistakable, having or leaving no doubt) klar [klaːɐ̯] ◇ *einen klaren Vorsprung haben* ◆ *Der Fall ist vollkommen klar.* ◆ *Ist das jetzt klar?* make yourself clear sich klar ausdrücken be clear (in your mind) about/on sth sich [dat] über etw. [acc] klar sein ◇ *Bist du dir über die Konsequenzen klar?* ◆ *Sie war sich klar darüber, wie es weitergehen sollte.* get it/become clear in your mind that sich [dat] klar machen, dass ◇ *Du musst dir klar machen, dass es so nicht weitergeht.*; (easy to

see or understand) deutlich ['dɔɡtlɪç] ◊ *deutliche Fortschritte machen* ✦ *Sein Hinweis war recht deutlich.* make sth clear jdm etw. (klar und) deutlich sagen/ zeigen ◊ *Sie zeigte ihm deutlich, dass sie gekränkt war.* ✦ *Du musst es ihr klar und deutlich sagen, wenn sie gehen soll.* in a clear voice deutlich ◊ *Sprich bitte laut und deutlich.* get sth clear etw. klarstellen ['klaːrʃtɛlən] <stellt klar, stellte klar, hat klargestellt> ◊ *Lass uns das endlich klarstellen: Magst du ihn oder nicht?* **2.** (unblocked, free from sth) frei [fraɛ] no comp/superl ◊ *Ist die Straße jetzt wieder frei?* ✦ *freie Sicht aufs Meer haben* have a clear run freie Fahrt haben clear of sth frei von etw. ◊ *sich frei von Schuld fühlen* ✦ *Das Beet ist wieder frei von Unkraut.*; (skin, conscience) rein [raɛn] ◊ *Sie hat eine reine Haut.* ✦ *Das kann ich mit reinem Gewissen sagen.* free of debt schuldenfrei ['ʃʊldn̩fraɛ] keep clear freihalten ['fraɛhaltn̩] <hält frei, hielt frei, hat freigehalten> ◊ *Auf dem Schild stand: „Ausfahrt freihalten!"* keep the day clear sich [dat] den Tag freihalten **3.** (water, air, sky, eyes) klar [klaːr] ◊ *Die Luft war frisch und klar.* ✦ *Der See hat sehr klares Wasser.*

clear² [verb] **1.** (empty, remove) clear sth etw. räumen ['rɔɡmən] +haben ◊ *Wir räumen unser Teppichlager.* ✦ *Die Demonstranten wurden aufgefordert, die Straße zu räumen.* ✦ *Die Polizei räumte das Gebäude und nahm die Besetzer fest.* ✦ *Die Mieter müssen den Schnee selbst räumen.*; (the table) abräumen ['apʀɔɡmən] +haben ◊ *Räum bitte den Tisch/das Geschirr ab!* clear sth of sth etw. von etw. befreien [fɔn ... bə,fraɛən] <befreit, befreite, hat befreit> ◊ *die Beete vom Unkraut befreien* sth clears etw. leert sich ['leːɐt zɪç] +haben ◊ *Nach dem Unterricht lehrte sich das Klassenzimmer.* **2.** (mind, head, your thoughts) clear sth leeren ['leːrən] +haben ◊ *Leeren Sie den Kopf und entspannen Sie sich!* sth clears etw. wird klar [vɪrt 'klaːr] +sein ◊ *Mein Kopf wurde wieder klar.* **3.** (allow to be used or take place: plane or flight) clear sth for sth etw. für etw. freigeben [fyːɡ ... ˌfraɛɡeːbm̩] <gibt frei, gab frei, hat freigegeben> ◊ *ein Flugzeug für den Abflug freigeben* ✦ *Der Flug wurde für 19 Uhr freigegeben.*; (a drug) etw. für etw. zulassen [fyːɡ ... ˌtsuːlasn̩] <lässt zu, ließ zu, hat zugelassen> **4.** (discuss to clarify) clear sth with sb etw. mit jdm klären [mɪt ... 'klɛːrən] +haben ◊ *Haben Sie das Thema schon mit Ihrem Chef geklärt?* **5.** (mist, fog) sth clears etw. lichtet sich ['lɪçtət zɪç] <lichtete sich, hat sich gelichtet> ◊ *Der Nebel lichtete sich allmählich.* **6.** (a cheque) clear sth etw. verrechnen [fɛ'rɛçnən] <verrechnet, verrechnete, hat verrechnet> ◊ *Die Bank hat den Scheck verrechnet.* sth clears verrechnet werden [fɛ'rɛçnət veːɡdn̩] <wird, wurde, ist worden> ◊ *Ist der Scheck schon verrechnet worden?* **7.** (manage to avoid an impact, not collide with or hit) clear sth etw. verfehlen [fɛ'feːlən] <verfehlt, verfehlte, hat verfehlt> ◊ *Unser Auto verfehlte die Mauer um wenige Zentimeter.* **8.** (a hurdle etc.: by jumping) überspringen [ybeʃprɪŋən] <überspringt, übersprang, hat übersprungen> ◊ *Das Pferd übersprang den Zaun mühelos.* **9.** (the land, forest) roden ['roːdn̩] <rodet, rodete, hat gerodet> ◊ *den Wald roden* **10.** (a debt) begleichen [bə'glaɛçn̩] <begleicht, beglich, hat beglichen> ◊ *seine Schulden begleichen* **11.** (a path) schlagen ['ʃlaːɡn̩] <schlägt, schlug, hat geschlagen> ◊ *eine Bresche/*

Schneise in den Wald schlagen **12.** LAW (a defendant) clear sb jdn freisprechen ['fraɛʃprɛçn̩] <spricht frei, sprach frei, hat freigesprochen> clear sb of sth jdn vom Verwurf einer Sache [gen] freisprechen ◊ *Er wurde vom Vorwurf des Kindesmissbrauchs freigesprochen.*

● **clear away** [phras v] clear sth away (remove, get rid of) etw. beseitigen [bə'zaɛtıɡn̩] <beseitigt, beseitigte, hat beseitigt> ◊ *den Müll beseitigen*; (remove in order to tidy) etw. wegräumen ['vɛkrɔɡmən] +haben ◊ *Wer räumt die Werkzeuge weg?*; (the dishes) abräumen ['apʀɔɡmən] +haben ◊ *Räumst du bitte das Geschirr ab?*

● **clear off** [phras v] abhauen ['aphaɔən] <haut ab, haute ab, ist abgehauen> (fam) ◊ *Hau bloß ab!*

● **clear up** [phras v] **1.** (tidy up) clear sth up etw. aufräumen ['aɔfrɔɡmən] +haben ◊ *Ich muss mal (meinen Schreibtisch) aufräumen.* ✦ *Räum bitte deine Schulsachen auf!*; (clear away) etw. beseitigen [bə'zaɛtıɡn̩] <beseitigt, beseitigte, hat beseitigt> ◊ *die Scherben/den Müll beseitigen* ✦ *Könntest du mal dieses Chaos beseitigen?* **2.** (ailment, storm) nachlassen ['naːxlasn̩] <lässt nach, ließ nach, hat nachgelassen> ◊ *Der quälende Husten ließ endlich nach.* **3.** (a problem, mystery) clear sth up etw. klären ['klɛːrən] +haben ◊ *Eine Reihe von Fragen muss geklärt werden.*; (a crime) etw. aufklären ['aɔfklɛːrən] +haben ◊ *Der Mord wurde nie aufgeklärt.* **4.** (weather) aufklaren ['aɔfklaːrən] +haben ◊ *Das Wetter klarte auf, und die Sonne kam hervor.*

clearance [noun] **1.** (permission to use/do etc.) Freigabe ['fraɛɡaːbə] die <–, –n> ◊ *Wir warten noch auf die Freigabe der Mittel.* clearance to land Landeerlaubnis ['landəlɛ,laɔpnɪs] die <–> no pl **2.** (free space) Spielraum ['ʃpiːlraɔm] der <–(e)s, Spielräume> ◊ *genügend Spielraum lassen*; (between things) Abstand ['apʃtant] der <–(e)s, Abstände> ◊ *ausreichenden Abstand einhalten* **3.** (process of removing sth) Beseitigung [bə'zaɛtıɡʊŋ] die <–, –en> ◊ *die Beseitigung von Hindernissen* **4.** (process of unblocking/emptying sth) Räumung ['rɔɡmʊŋ] die <–, –en> ◊ *Sonderangebote wegen Räumung unseres Lagers!*; (of a house, garage etc.) Entrümpelung [ɛnt'rʏmpəlʊŋ] die <–, –en> **5.** SPORT (defence) Abwehr ['apveːɡ] die <–> no pl ◊ *den Ball bei der Abwehr mit der Hand berühren* **6.** FIN (of a cheque) Verrechnung [fɛ'rɛçnʊŋ] die <–> no pl

clear-cut [adj] klar [klaːr] ◊ *Das Ergebnis war nicht so klar wie erwartet.*

clearing [noun] Lichtung ['lɪçtʊŋ] die <–, –en> ◊ *Die Rehe grasen friedlich auf der Lichtung.*

clearly [adv] **1.** klar [klaːr] ◊ *etw. klar erkennen* ✦ *Er war ihr klar unterlegen.* ✦ *nicht klar denken können*; (without doubt) eindeutig ['aɛndɔɡtıç] ◊ *Sie konnte den Täter eindeutig identifizieren.* say sth clearly etw. deutlich sagen [,dɔɡtlıç 'zaːɡn̩] **2.** (plainly) offensichtlich ['ɔfnzɪçtlɪç] ◊ *Er hat offensichtlich keine Lust, mitzukommen.*

clergy [noun] Klerus ['kleːrʊs] der <–> no pl

clerical [adj] **1.** (relating to priests) geistlich ['gaɛstlɪç] no comp/superl, only before ns ◊ *ein geistlicher Beruf* **2.** (in an office) clerical work Büroarbeit [by'roːʔaɐ̯baɛt] die <–, –en>

clerk [noun] **1.** (administrator) Büroangestellte [by'roːʔaŋgəʃtɛltə] der/die <–n, die Büroangestellten>

but: *ein Büroangestellter/eine Büroangestellte* ◊ *Der Büroangestellte arbeitet fünf Tage pro Woche.* ✦ *Sie arbeitet als Büroangestellte bei der Firma.* **2.** *(in the US: salesperson)* Verkäufer [fɛ'kɔ:fɐ] der <–s, –> ♀Verkäuferin [fɛ'kɔ:fərɪn] die <–, –nen> ◊ *Er arbeitet schon seit 10 Jahren als Verkäufer.* ✦ *Sie ist als Verkäuferin in einem Modehaus tätig.* **3.** *(in the US: receptionist)* Hotelangestellte [ho'tɛlˌaŋɡəˌʃtɛltə] der/die <–n, die Hotelangestellten> *but: ein Hotelangestellter/eine Hotelangestellte* ◊ *Sie arbeitet als Hotelangestellte im Hilton.* ✦ *Der Hotelangestellte muss auch andere Arbeiten erledigen.*

clever(ly) [adj, adv] **1.** *(skilful(ly), shrewd(ly))* geschickt [ɡə'ʃɪkt] <geschickter, am geschicktesten> ◊ *eine geschickte Taktik* ✦ *Das war sehr geschickt von dir.* ◊ *sich geschickt aus der Affäre ziehen* **2.** *(intelligent(ly))* klug [klu:k] <klüger, am klügsten> ◊ *Sie ist sehr klug.* ✦ *eine kluge Antwort* ✦ *Er hat das Problem klug gelöst.*

cliché [noun] **1.** *(stereotype)* Klischee [kli'ʃe:] das <–s, –s> ◊ *ein Horrorfilm, der alle Klischees bedient* **2.** *(meaningless phrase)* Phrase ['fra:zə] die <–, –n> ◊ *eine abgedroschene/hohle/leere Phrase*

click¹ [noun] **1.** *(sound)* Klicken ['klɪkn̩] das <–s, –> **2.** *(with the mouse)* Klick [klɪk] der <–s, –s> ◊ *mit ein paar Klicks zum Ziel* double click Doppelklick ['dɔplˌklɪk]

click² [verb] klicken ['klɪkn̩] +haben ◊ *Sie klickte auf das Symbol.* ✦ *Man hörte die Fotoapparate klicken.* click shut einschnappen ['aɛnˌʃnapm̩] +haben ◊ *Die Tür schnappte ein.*
⊚ it's just clicked ich hab's *(fam)* click with sb mit jdm gut auskommen

client [noun] **1.** *(of a therapist)* Klient [kli'ɛnt] der <–en, –en> ♀Klientin [kli'ɛntɪn] die <–, –nen> ◊ *eine Gruppentherapie mit sechs Klienten* **2.** *(of a barrister)* Mandant [man'dant] der <–en, –en> ♀Mandantin [man'dantɪn] die <–, –nen> ◊ *Er glaubt an die Unschuld seines Mandanten.* **3.** ɪᴛ *(computer, programme)* Client ['klaɛənt] der <–en, –en> ◊ *Die Verbindung zwischen Client und Server ist unterbrochen.*

clientele [noun] Kundschaft ['kʊntʃaft] die <–, –en>

cliff [noun] *(on the coast)* Klippe ['klɪpə] die <–, –n> ◊ *Das Schiff zerschellte an der Klippe.*; *(in the mountains)* Fels [fɛls] der <–en(s), –en> *(lofty)* ◊ *ein schroffer/steiler Fels*

climate [noun] *(also fig)* Klima ['kli:ma:] das <–s, –ta> *most sing*

climax [noun] **1.** *(of a story, an event)* Höhepunkt ['hø:əpʊŋkt] der <–(e)s, –e> ◊ *Die Veranstaltung erreichte ihren Höhepunkt.* **2.** *(sexual)* Orgasmus [ɔr'ɡasmʊs] der <–, Orgasmen>

climb¹ [noun] **1.** *(ascent)* Aufstieg ['aɔfʃti:k] der <–(e)s, –e> ◊ *sozialer/beruflicher Aufstieg* ✦ *Nach dreistündigem Aufstieg erreichten sie den Gipfel.* **2.** *(of prices, temperature)* Ansteigen ['anʃtaɛɡn̩] das <–s> no pl ◊ *Die erhöhte Nachfrage führte zu einem Ansteigen der Preise.*

climb² [verb] **1.** *(using your hands and feet)* klettern ['klɛtɐn] +sein ◊ *Sie kletterten über den Zaun.* ✦ *aus dem Fenster klettern* climb sth auf etw. [acc] klettern ◊ *Die Katze kletterte auf den Baum.* climbing plant Kletterpflanze ['klɛtɐpflantsə] die <–, –n> **2.** *(walk or move somewhere)* steigen ['ʃtaɛɡn̩] <steigt, stieg, ist gestiegen> ◊ *ins Wasser/in die Wanne steigen* ✦ *auf*

einen Berg steigen ✦ *Das Flugzeug stieg auf 10 000 m Höhe.* ✦ *Die Preise sind gestiegen.*; *(towards the speaker)* climb down heruntersteigen [hɛ'rʊntɐˌʃtaɛɡn̩] ◊ *Sie stieg wieder vom Dach herunter.*; *(away from the speaker)* climb down hinuntersteigen [hɪ'nʊntɐˌʃtaɛɡn̩] ◊ *Er stieg in den Schacht hinunter.* **3.** *(road)* ansteigen ['anʃtaɛɡn̩] <steigt an, stieg an, ist angestiegen> **4.** *(person, be successful)* aufsteigen ['aɔfʃtaɛɡn̩] <steigt auf, stieg auf, ist aufgestiegen> ◊ *beruflich/sozial aufsteigen* climb the career ladder die Karriereleiter erklimmen [di: ka'rie:rəlaɛtɐ ɛklɪmən] <erklimmt, erklomm, hat erklommen>
• **climb down** [phras v] *(fig)* einlenken ['aɛnlɛŋkn̩] +haben ◊ *Schließlich lenkte er ein und entschuldigte sich.*

climber [noun] **1.** *(person)* Bergsteiger ['bɛrkʃtaɛɡɐ] der <–s, –> ♀Bergsteigerin ['bɛrkʃtaɛɡərɪn] die <–, –nen> **2.** *(plant)* Kletterpflanze ['klɛtɐpflantsə] die <–, –n>

cling [verb] **1.** cling (to sb/sth) sich (an jdn/etw.) klammern ['klamen] <klammert, klammerte, hat geklammert> ◊ *Sie klammerte sich an seinen Arm.* ✦ *Er klammert sich an sein Amt.* **2.** *(clothes)* eng anliegen [ˌɛŋ 'anli:ɡn̩] <liegt an, lag an, hat angelegen>

cling film [noun] Frischhaltefolie ['frɪʃhaltəfo:ljə] die <–, –n>

clinic [noun] **1.** *(special hospital)* Klinik ['kli:nɪk] die <–, –en> ◊ *eine psychiatrische Klinik* **2.** *(special class or course)* Seminar [zemi'na:r] das <–s, –e> ◊ *ein Seminar zum Thema Medienkunde*

clinical(ly) [adj, adv] **1.** *(relating to hospital patients or illnesses)* klinisch ['kli:nɪʃ] no comp/superl when used as an adj, mostly before ns ◊ *klinische Tests durchführen* ✦ *klinische Symptome* ✦ *Der Patient war klinisch tot.* **2.** *(matter-of-fact)* nüchtern ['nʏçtɐn] ◊ *ein nüchterner Bericht* ✦ *Sein Stil ist recht nüchtern.* ✦ *eine Sache nüchtern betrachten*

clip¹ [noun] **1.** *(for paper, hair)* Klammer ['klamɐ] die <–, –n>; *(on an earring, for cables)* Klipp [klɪp] der <–s, –s> **2.** *(from a film)* Ausschnitt ['aɔsʃnɪt] der <–(e)s, –e> video clip Videoclip ['vi:deoklɪp] der <–s, –s> **3.** *(top of a bottle)* Bügel ['by:ɡl̩] der <–s, –> ◊ *Bierflaschen mit Bügeln* **4.** clip around the ear Ohrfeige ['o:ɐfaɛɡə] die <–, –n>

clip² [verb] schneiden ['ʃnaɛdn̩] <schneidet, schnitt, hat geschnitten> ◊ *jdm die Haare schneiden* ✦ *die Kurven schneiden*

clique [noun] Clique ['klɪkə] die <–, –n> *(pej)*

cloak [noun] **1.** *(item of clothing)* Umhang ['ʊmhaŋ] der <–(e)s, Umhänge> **2.** *(fig)* *(sth which hides sth)* Deckmantel ['dɛkmantl̩] der <–s, Deckmäntel> *most pl* ◊ *Die Bande operiert unter dem Deckmantel der Legalität.* under the cloak of darkness im Schutz der Dunkelheit [ɪm ˌʃʊts de:ɐ 'dʊŋkl̩haɛt]

cloakroom [noun] **1.** *(for coats)* Garderobe [ɡa'də'ro:bə] die <–, –n> ◊ *seinen Mantel an der Garderobe abgeben/in der Garderobe lassen* **2.** *(toilet, bathroom)* Toilette [tɔa'lɛtə] die <–, –n>

clock [noun] Uhr [u:ɐ] die <–, –en> ◊ *Die Uhr im Wohnzimmer schlug Mitternacht.* ✦ *Diese Uhr geht nach/vor.* put the clocks forward die Uhren vorstellen
⊚ the clock is ticking die Zeit läuft work against the clock gegen die Zeit arbeiten round the clock

rund um die Uhr

close¹ [noun] *(conclusion)* Abschluss ['apʃlʊs] der <–es, Abschlüsse> ◊ *der Abschluss der Verhandlungen* ♦ *ein Feuerwerk zum krönenden Abschluss des Tages; (end)* Ende ['ɛndə] das <–s> *no pl* at the close of sth am Ende … [gen] ◊ *am Ende des Tages/ Jahres/Monats* draw/come to a close zu Ende gehen at the close of business bei Geschäftsschluss [baɛ gə'ʃɛftsʃlʊs]

close² [adj] **1.** *(temporal, spatial, relative)* nah [naː] nahe ['naːə] <näher, am nächsten> ◊ *Das Ende ist nah!* ♦ *Wo ist bitte die nächste Tankstelle?* ♦ *die nächsten Angehörigen verständigen* ♦ *den Tränen nahe sein* in close proximity to sth nahe bei etw. be close together nah beieinander liegen ◊ *Ihre Augen/ Die Termine liegen nah beieinander.* be close to sb jdm nahe stehen ◊ *Sie steht ihrem Bruder sehr nahe.; (spatial)* be close nicht weit sein [nɪçt 'vaɛt zaɛn] ◊ *Wir können zu Fuß gehen, es ist nicht weit.* be close to sth nicht weit von etw. sein ◊ *Der Bahnhof ist nicht weit vom Hotel.* at close quarters aus der Nähe [aʊs deːɐ̯ 'nɛːə] be close to death/collapse dem Tode/Zusammenbruch nahe sein [deːm ˌtoːdə/tsuˌzamənbrʊx 'naːə zaɛn] +sein ◊ *Sie war dem Tode nahe.* **2.** *(friends, relationship, cooperation, contact)* eng [ɛŋ] ◊ *Ihre Beziehung ist recht eng.* ♦ *in enger Verbindung bleiben* They are close friends. Sie sind eng befreundet. **3.** *(careful, precise)* genau [gə'naʊ] <genauer, am genauesten> ◊ *eine genaue Untersuchung* take a close look at sth/ sb sich [dat] etw./jdn genau ansehen keep a close eye on sth/sb etw./jdn genau im Auge behalten **4.** *(very similar)* close (to sth) (einer Sache [dat]) sehr ähnlich [zeːɐ̯ 'ɛːnlɪç] ◊ *Es ist nicht ganz der Farbton, aber sehr ähnlich.* bear a close resemblance to sb/sth jdm/etw. sehr ähnlich sehen/sein sth ist the closest thing to sth etw. kommt einer Sache [dat] am nächsten [kɔmt … am 'nɛːçstn̩] <kommt, kam, ist gekommen> **5.** *(escape, call, contest)* knapp [knap] ◊ *ein knappes Entkommen* ♦ *Das war knapp!* by a close vote mit knapper Mehrheit win/lose by a close margin knapp gewinnen/verlieren She was a close second. Sie hat nur knapp verloren. She won, with Peter a close second. Sie gewann knapp vor Peter. **6.** *(air)* stickig ['ʃtɪkɪç] ◊ *Die Luft im Schlafzimmer war stickig.* **7.** *(person: introvert)* verschlossen [fɛ'ʃlɔsn̩] <verschlossener, am verschlossensten> ◊ *ein verschlossener Mensch* ♦ *Du warst schon immer sehr verschlossen.* **8.** *(haircut)* kurz [kʊ'ts] <kürzer, am kürzesten> ◊ *ein sehr kurzer Haarschnitt* a man with a close shave ein glatt rasierter Mann [aɛn ˌglat raziːɐ̯tə 'man]

close³ [adv] **1.** *(spatial, temporal)* nah [naː] <näher, am nächsten> ◊ *Die Prüfungen rückten näher.* ♦ *Geh nicht so nah an den Abgrund.* close to sth bei etw. [baɛ] +dat ◊ *Ludwigsburg liegt bei Stuttgart.* ♦ *Bleib bitte beim Gepäck.* She held the baby close to her. Sie drückte das Baby an sich. **2.** *(nearly)* fast [fast] ◊ *Er kam fast auf hundert Punkte.*
 ⊚ close by/close at hand **1.** *(spatial)* (ganz) in der/jds Nähe ◊ *Bleib bitte in meiner Nähe!* **2.** *(temporal)* nah ◊ *Halte aus, die Rettung ist nah!* close up/up close **1.** *(at/from a short distance)* aus der Nähe ◊ *Das muss ich mir aus der Nähe ansehen.* **2.** *(to a short distance)* nah ◊ *Geh nicht so nah ans*

Feuer!

close⁴ [verb] **1.** *(shut or shut down, end)* schließen ['ʃliːsn̩] <schließt, schloss, hat geschlossen> ◊ *ein Fenster/die Augen schließen* ♦ *eine Grenze/einen Koffer/eine Lücke schließen* ♦ *vor der Installation eines Programms alle anderen Anwendungen schließen* ♦ *Die Verhandlung ist hiermit geschlossen.* ♦ *Wir/Die Wahllokale schließen um 20 Uhr.* ♦ *Sie schloss mit den Worten: … ♦ Das Fest schloss mit einem Feuerwerk.* ♦ *Die Schubladen mussten leider schließen.; (a book, coat, zipper)* zumachen ['tsuːmaxn̩] +haben *(fam)* ◊ *Mach deinen Mantel zu, es ist kalt.* **2.** *(conclude a deal)* abschließen ['apʃliːsn̩] <schließt ab, schloss ab, hat abgeschlossen> ◊ *Ich will unbedingt das Geschäft noch abschließen.* **3.** *(conclude the day, evening)* close sth with sth etw. mit etw. beschließen [mɪt … bə'ʃliːsn̩] <beschließt, beschloss, hat beschlossen> *(lofty)* ◊ *den Abend mit einem Glas Wein beschließen* **4.** *(give up an account)* auflösen ['aʊflø:zn̩] +haben ◊ *Ich habe mein Konto bei dieser Bank aufgelöst.* **5.** *(catch up)* close on sb die Distanz zu jdm verringern [diː dɪsˌtants tsu… fɛ'rɪŋɐn] <verringert, verringerte, hat verringert> ◊ *In der letzten Runde konnte er die Distanz zum Favoriten verringern.* close the gap aufholen ['aʊfhoːlən] +haben ◊ *Meinst du, er holt noch auf?* **6.** *(wound)* sth closes etw. schließt sich ['ʃliːst zɪç] <schloss sich, hat sich geschlossen> ◊ *Die Wunde schloss sich nach kurzer Zeit.* close sth etw. schließen ◊ *Die Ärztin schloss die Wunde mit Klammern.*
 • **close down** [phras v] *(business)* schließen ['ʃliːsn̩] <schließt, schloss, hat geschlossen> ◊ *Das Museum wurde aus Kostengründen geschlossen.* ♦ *Der Bäcker musste leider schließen.*
 • **close in** [phras v] **1.** *(come closer)* close in on sb/ sth sich jdm/etw. nähern ['nɛːɐn] +haben ◊ *Sie näherten sich dem Hund vorsichtig von allen Seiten.* **2.** *(darkness, night)* hereinbrechen [hɛ'raɛnbrɛçn̩] <bricht herein, brach herein, ist hereingebrochen> ◊ *Die Dunkelheit brach über uns herein.* **3.** *(days)* kürzer werden [kʏ'tsɐ veːɐ̯dn̩] <wird, wurde, ist geworden> ◊ *Es wird Winter, die Tage werden kürzer.*
 • **close off** [phras v] close sth off **1.** *(separate with a barrier)* etw. abgrenzen ['apgrɛntsn̩] +haben ◊ *Er grenzte sein Grundstück mit einer Hecke ab.* **2.** *(a street, an area, a crime or accident scene)* absperren ['apʃpɛrən] +haben ◊ *Das gefährdete Gebiet wurde weiträumig abgesperrt.*
 • **close up** [phras v] **1.** *(a shop etc.)* schließen ['ʃliːsn̩] <schließt, schloss, hat geschlossen> ◊ *Das Museum schließt um sechs.* ♦ *Wir schließen das Geschäft in fünf Minuten.; (with a key)* abschließen ['apʃliːsn̩] <schließt ab, schloss ab, hat abgeschlossen> ◊ *Schließ bitte ab, wenn du gehst.* **2.** *(stop communicating)* sb closes up jd wird unzugänglich [vɪ't 'ʊntsugɛnlɪç] +sein ◊ *Jedes Mal, wenn ich dich auf dieses Thema ansprache, wird sie unzugänglich.*

closely [adv] **1.** *(separated by very little distance)* dicht [dɪçt] <dichter, am dichtesten> ◊ *Der Wagen fuhr dicht an ihm vorbei.* ♦ *Er kam dicht gefolgt von Roland ins Ziel.* closely miss sb jdn knapp verfehlen [knap fɛ'feːlən] <verfehlt, verfehlte, hat verfehlt> ◊ *Die Kugel verfehlte ihn knapp.*
 2. *(carefully, precisely)* genau [gə'naʊ] <genauer, am genauesten> ◊ *etw. genau prüfen* **3.** *(having links,*

characterized by an exchange of ideas and personal contact) eng [ɛŋ] ◊ *Wir wollen künftig enger zusammenarbeiten.* ◆ *Der Erfolg hängt eng mit der Motivation der Mitarbeiter zusammen.* ◆ *eng befreundet*

closeness [noun] Nähe ['nɛːə] die <–> *no pl* ◊ *ein Bedürfnis nach mehr Nähe haben*

closet [noun] Schrank [ʃraŋk] der <–(e)s, Schränke> ◊ *Sie verstaute ihre Kleidung im Schrank.*

◉ **come out of the closet** sich nicht länger verstecken

closure [noun] 1. *(of a factory, hospital etc.)* Schließung ['ʃliːsʊŋ] die <–, –en> ◊ *die Schließung der Bergwerke* 2. *(end of sth)* Schluss [ʃlʊs] der <–es, Schlüsse> ◊ *der Schluss der Debatte*

cloth [noun] 1. *(piece of material: wet)* Lappen ['lapm̩] der <–s, –> ◊ *Nimm einen Lappen und wisch das weg.; (dry: for dusting)* Tuch [tuːx] das <–(e)s, Tücher> ◊ *Die Tücher aus Mikrofaser sind wunderbar zum Putzen.* 2. *(textile)* Stoff [ʃtɔf] der <–(e)s, –e> ◊ *Sie hat fünf Meter Stoff für ihr Kleid gekauft.; (used in bookbinding)* Leinen ['laɛnən] das <–s> *no pl* ◊ *Der Bucheinband ist aus Leinen.*

clothes [noun] *(in general)* Kleidung ['klaɛdʊŋ] die <–> *no pl* ◊ *Sie bevorzugt sportliche Kleidung.; (that you wear)* Kleider ['klaɛdɐ] die <–> *only pl* ◊ *seine Kleider ausziehen* ◆ *Er hatte warme Kleider an.*
evening clothes Abendkleidung ['aːbm̩tklaɛdʊŋ]
maternity clothes Umstandskleidung ['ʊmʃtantsklaɛdʊŋ]

clothes hanger [noun] Kleiderbügel ['klaɛdɐbyːgl̩] der <–s, –>

clothes line [noun] Wäscheleine ['vɛʃəlaɛnə] die <–, –n> ◊ *etw. an/auf die Wäscheleine hängen*

clothes peg [noun] Wäscheklammer ['vɛʃəklamɐ] die <–, –n>

clothespin [noun] Wäscheklammer ['vɛʃəklamɐ] die <–, –n>

clothing [noun] 1. *(in general)* Kleidung ['klaɛdʊŋ] die <–> *no pl* ◊ *Er bevorzugt sportliche Kleidung.* 2. *(the clothes sb owns/wears)* Garderobe [garˈdeˈroːbə] die <–, –n> ◊ *Sie schneidert ihre Garderobe selbst.*

cloud¹ [noun] *(also fig)* Wolke ['vɔlkə] die <–, –n> ◊ *Wolken zogen auf.* ◆ *Dunkle Wolken werfen Schatten über seinen Besuch.* cloud of dust Staubwolke ['ʃtaɔpvɔlkə] cloud of smoke Rauchwolke ['raɔxvɔlkə]

◉ **on cloud nine** im siebten Himmel

cloud² [verb] 1. *(sky)* sich bewölken [zɪç bəˈvœlkn̩] <bewölkt sich, bewölkte sich, hat sich bewölkt> ◊ *Der Himmel bewölkte sich.* 2. *(also fig) (cast a shadow over, make unclear)* trüben ['tryːbm̩] +haben ◊ *Der Schlamm trübt das Wasser.* ◆ *Ein Streit trübte die Atmosphäre.* ◆ *jds Urteilsvermögen trüben*

• **cloud over** [phras v] 1. *(sky)* sich bewölken [zɪç bəˈvœlkn̩] <bewölkt sich, bewölkte sich, hat sich bewölkt> ◊ *Der Himmel bewölkte sich.* 2. *(sb's face)* sich verdüstern [zɪç fɛˈdyːstɐn] <verdüstert sich, verdüsterte sich, hat sich verdüstert>

cloudy [adj] 1. *(overcast)* bewölkt [bəˈvœlkt] <bewölkter, am bewölktesten> ◊ *Der Himmel ist heute bewölkt* ◆ *ein bewölkter Tag* 2. *(not clear)* trüb [tryːp] trübe ['tryːbə] <trüber, am trübsten> ◊ *trübes Wasser* ◆ *Die Linse ist trüb geworden.*

clove [noun] 1. *(spice)* Nelke ['nɛlkə] die <–, –n> ◊ *den Schweinebraten mit Nelken spicken* 2. *(of garlic)* Zehe ['tseːə] die <–, –n>

club [noun] 1. *(society, nightclub, bookclub)* Klub, Club [klʊp] der <–s, –s> ◊ *einem Klub beitreten* ◆ *Mitglied in einem Klub sein* ◆ *ein Club, wo man Salsa tanzen kann; (sports team)* Verein [fɛˈʔaɛn] der <–s, –e> 2. *(for playing golf, baseball etc.)* Schläger ['ʃlɛːgɐ] der <–s, –> 3. *(weapon)* Knüppel ['knʏpl̩] der <–s, –> 4. CARDS Kreuz [krɔɛts] das <–es, –> ◊ *Wie viele Kreuz hast du?* ◆ *Kreuz ist Trumpf*

◉ **join the club** willkommen im Club

clue [noun] 1. *(piece of evidence)* Anhaltspunkt ['anhaltspʊŋkt] der <–(e)s, –e> ◊ *Es gibt keinerlei Anhaltspunkte für ein Fremdverschulden.* 2. *(hint)* Hinweis ['hɪnvaɛs] der <–es, –e> ◊ *Komm, gib mir doch einen Hinweis!*

◉ **not have a clue, haven't got a clue** keine Ahnung haben

clumsy(-ily) [adj, adv] 1. *(awkward(ly))* unbeholfen ['ʊnbəhɔlfn̩] ◊ *Seine Bewegungen wirken etwas unbeholfen.* ◆ *Das Kind machte unbeholfene Versuche, aufs Bett zu klettern.* ◆ *Die Welpen tapsen noch recht unbeholfen herum.* 2. *(lacking (manual) skill)* ungeschickt ['ʊngəʃɪkt] <ungeschickter, am ungeschicktesten> ◊ *Sie ist zu ungeschickt zum Nähen.* ◆ *ein ungeschickter Küchenjunge* ◆ *sich ungeschickt anstellen* 3. *(ineffectual(ly))* hilflos ['hɪlfloːs] <hilfloser, am hilflosesten> ◊ *hilflose Versuche* ◆ *hilflos reagieren*

cluster [noun] 1. *(of people, objects etc.)* Traube ['traɔbə] die <–, –n> ◊ *Eine Traube von Fans umlagerte den Star.* 2. *(concentration, simultaneous occurrence of sth)* Cluster ['klastɐ] der <–s, –> *(tech)* ◊ *ein Cluster von drei Datenbankservern/Elektronen*

clutch¹ [noun] 1. TECHN *(in a motor vehicle)* Kupplung ['kʊplʊŋ] die <–, –en> ◊ *die Kupplung treten/kommen lassen* 2. *(tight grasp)* Umklammerung [ʊmˈklamərʊŋ] die <–, –en> ◊ *Sie versuchte, sich aus der Umklammerung ihrer Mutter zu lösen.* 3. *(fig) (control)* Klauen ['klaɔən] die <–> *pl (pej)* ◊ *jdn den Klauen einer Sekte entreißen* 4. *(of eggs or chicks)* Gelege [gəˈleːgə] das <–s, –> ◊ *Das Gelege besteht aus 25 bis 90 Eiern.*

clutch² [verb] 1. *(hold tightly to yourself)* clutch sth etw. an sich [acc] drücken ['an ... drʏkn̩] +haben ◊ *Sie drückte ihr Kind/die Tasche an sich.* 2. *(take hold of sth)* clutch at sth nach etw. greifen [naːx ... graɛfn̩] <greift, griff, hat gegriffen> ◊ *Er stolperte und griff nach dem Türrahmen.*

coach¹ [noun] 1. *(bus)* Bus [bʊs] der <–ses, –se> ◊ *den Bus nehmen; (for longer journeys)* Reisebus ['raɛzəbʊs] 2. *(drawn by horses)* Kutsche ['kʊtʃə] die <–, –n> ◊ *mit der Kutsche fahren* 3. SPORT Trainer ['trɛːnɐ] der <–s, –> ♀Trainerin ['trɛːnərɪn] die <–, –nen> ◊ *Der Fußballverein hat einen neuen Trainer verpflichtet.* ◆ *Sie ist Trainerin der Handballmannschaft.* 4. *(sb who teaches specific skills)* ... coach ...lehrer ['leːrɐ] der <–s, –> ♀...lehrerin ['leːrərɪn] die <–, –nen> dance coach Tanzlehrer ['tantsleːrɐ] Tanzlehrerin ['tantsleːrərɪn]; *(for school subjects)* Nachhilfelehrer ['naːxhɪlfəleːrɐ] Nachhilfelehrerin ['naːxhɪlfələrərɪn]

coach² [verb] 1. *(a sports team)* trainieren [trɛˈniːrən] <trainiert, trainierte, hat trainiert> ◊ *eine Mannschaft trainieren* 2. *(teach specific skills)* coach (sb in sth) (jdm in etw. [dat]) Unterricht geben ['ʊntɐrɪçt geːbm̩] <gibt, gab, hat gegeben> ◊ *Sie gibt*

mir Unterricht in Mathematik. He coaches us in German. *Er gibt uns Deutschunterricht.* **3.** *(prepare for a certain situation)* vorbereiten ['foːgbəraetn̩] <bereitet vor, bereitete vor, hat vorbereitet> ◊ *Man hat ihn auf das Verhör vor Gericht vorbereitet.*

coal ⟨noun⟩ Kohle ['koːlə] die <–, –n> ◊ *Hier wird Kohle abgebaut.*

When referring to individual pieces of coal, the plural form is appropriate: *Sie legte noch ein paar Kohlen nach.*

coalition ⟨noun⟩ Koalition [koali'tsi̯oːn] die <–, –en>

coarse(ly) ⟨adj, adv⟩ **1.** *(vulgar(ly), offensive(ly), rough(ly))* derb [dɛʳp] ◊ *derbes Leder* ♦ *Sein Humor ist recht derb.* ♦ *Er drückt sich oft sehr derb aus.* **2.** *(rough(ly))* grob [groːp] <gröber, am gröbsten> ◊ *grober Sand* ♦ *grob gemahlenes Mehl*

coast ⟨noun⟩ Küste ['kʏstə] die <–, –n> ◊ *die Küste Kents* on the coast an der Küste ⊛ the coast is clear die Luft ist rein *(fam)*

coastal ⟨adj⟩ Küsten... ['kʏstn̩] coastal area Küstengebiet ['kʏstn̩gəbiːt] das <–(e)s, –e> coastal town Küstenstadt ['kʏstn̩ʃtat] die <–, Küstenstädte>

coat[1] ⟨noun⟩ **1.** *(piece of clothing, short)* Jacke ['jakə] die <–, –n>; *(long)* Mantel ['mantl̩] der <–s, Mäntel> ◊ *Kann ich Ihnen in den Mantel helfen?* **2.** *(layer of sth)* Schicht [ʃɪçt] die <–, –en> ◊ *eine neue Schicht Farbe auftragen*

coat[2] ⟨verb⟩ überziehen [ybɐ'tsiːən] <überzieht, überzog, hat überzogen> ◊ *Plätzchen mit Kuvertüre überziehen; (in flour, breadcrumbs)* wälzen ['vɛltsn̩] +haben ◊ *Schnitzel in Paniermehl wälzen*

coat hanger ⟨noun⟩ Kleiderbügel ['klaedɐbyːgl̩] der <–s, –>

coating ⟨noun⟩ *(layer of sth)* Schicht [ʃɪçt] die <–, –en> ◊ *mit einer Schicht aus Staub und Schmutz bedeckt; (protective and permanent)* Beschichtung [bə'ʃɪçtʊŋ] die <–, –en> ◊ *Bei der Pfanne geht die Beschichtung ab.*

cocaine ⟨noun⟩ Kokain [koka'iːn] das <–s> no pl

cock ⟨noun⟩ **1.** *(male chicken)* Hahn [haːn] der <–(e)s, Hähne> ◊ *Der Hahn kräht.* **2.** *(penis)* Schwanz [ʃvants] der <–es, Schwänze> *(rude)*

cocoa ⟨noun⟩ Kakao [ka'kao] der <–s, –s> pl 'Kakao' when used with expressions of quantity ◊ *eine Tasse Kakao* ♦ *Bringen sie uns bitte zwei Kakao.*

cocoa powder ⟨noun⟩ Kakaopulver [ka'kaopʊlfɐ] das <–s, –>

code[1] ⟨noun⟩ **1.** *(for secret messages)* Code [koːt] der <–s, –s> ◊ *ein geheimer Code* crack/break a code einen Code knacken **2.** *(set of rules)* Kodex ['koːdɛks] der <–es or –, –e or lofty Kodizes> ◊ *ein strenger Kodex* code of conduct Verhaltensregel [fɐ'haltn̩sreːgl̩] die <–, –n> most pl **3.** *(set of numbers)* Zahlenkombination ['tsaːlənkɔmbinatsi̯oːn] die <–, –en> ◊ *die Zahlenkombination eines Safes* **4.** *(telephone)* Vorwahl ['foːɐvaːl] die <–, –en> ◊ *Die Vorwahl für Deutschland ist 0049.* ♦ *Welche Vorwahl hat Hanau?*

code[2] ⟨verb⟩ **1.** *(mark)* kennzeichnen ['kɛntsaeçnən] <kennzeichnet, kennzeichnete, hat gekennzeichnet> ◊ *etw. mit verschiedenen Farben kennzeichnen* **2.** *(encode)* kodieren [ko'diːrən] <kodiert, kodierte, hat kodiert> ◊ *eine Nachricht kodieren*

coffee ⟨noun⟩ Kaffee ['kafeː] der <–s, –s> pl 'Kaffee' when used with expressions of quantity ◊ *eine Tasse*

Kaffee ♦ *Sie bestellten zwei Kaffee.*

coffin ⟨noun⟩ Sarg [zaʳk] der <–(e)s, Särge>

cognitive ⟨adj⟩ kognitiv [kɔgni'tiːf] no comp/superl, mostly before ns ◊ *kognitive Fähigkeiten*

coherent ⟨adj⟩ schlüssig ['ʃlʏsɪç] ◊ *ein schlüssiges Konzept* ♦ *Diese Argumentation ist nicht schlüssig.*

cohesion ⟨noun⟩ Geschlossenheit [gə'ʃlɔsn̩haet] die <–> no pl

coil ⟨noun⟩ Spirale [ʃpi'raːlə] die <–, –n> ◊ *eine Feder in Form einer Spirale* ♦ *eine Spirale zur Empfängnisverhütung*

coin ⟨noun⟩ Münze ['mʏntsə] die <–, –n> flip/toss a coin eine Münze werfen

coincide ⟨verb⟩ **1.** *(temporal)* zusammenfallen [tsu'zamənfalən] <fällt zusammen, fiel zusammen, ist zusammengefallen> ◊ *Dieses Jahr fällt mein Geburtstag mit Ostern zusammen.* **2.** *(in content etc.)* übereinstimmen [ybɐ'aenʃtɪmən] +haben ◊ *Die Aussagen der Zeugen stimmten miteinander überein.*

coincidence ⟨noun⟩ Zufall ['tsuːfal] der <–(e)s, Zufälle> ◊ *Dass ich den Job bekommen habe, war reiner Zufall.* by coincidence zufällig ['tsuːfɛlɪç]

coincidental(ly) ⟨adj, adv⟩ zufällig ['tsuːfɛlɪç] ◊ *Ähnlichkeiten mit lebenden Personen sind rein zufällig.* ♦ *eine zufällige Begegnung* ♦ *einen Fehler zufällig entdecken*

cola, Coke™ ⟨noun⟩ Cola ['koːla] die <–, –s> pl 'Cola' when used with expressions of quantity ◊ *Bringen Sie uns bitte zwei Cola!* ♦ *ein Glas Cola*

cold[1] ⟨noun⟩ **1.** *(illness)* Erkältung [ɛɐ'kɛltʊŋ] die <–, –en> ◊ *eine schwere/leichte Erkältung.* catch a cold sich erkälten [ɛ'kɛltn̩] <erkältet sich, erkältete sich, hat sich erkältet> ◊ *Sie hat sich beim Baden erkältet.* **2.** *(low temperature)* Kälte ['kɛltə] die <–> no pl ◊ *Bei dieser Kälte mag ich nicht aus dem Haus.* ⊛ leave sb out in the cold jdn links liegen lassen

cold[2] ⟨adj⟩ **1.** *(temperature, colo(u)r)* kalt [kalt] <kälter, am kältesten> ◊ *Heute ist es kalt.* ♦ *Das Essen wird kalt.* ♦ *Blau ist eine kalte Farbe.* ♦ *warme und kalte Speisen* Are you cold? Ist dir kalt? freezing cold eiskalt ['aeskalt] no comp/superl feel cold frieren ['friːrən] <friert, fror, hat gefroren> **2.** *(unfriendly)* kühl [kyːl] ◊ *ein kühler Empfang* ♦ *Er war sehr kühl zu mir.* ⊛ out cold ohnmächtig

coldly ⟨adv⟩ kühl [kyːl] ◊ *In dieser brenzligen Situation reagierte sie kühl.*

coldness ⟨noun⟩ Kälte ['kɛltə] die <–> no pl ◊ *In ihrer Stimme lag Kälte.*

collaborate ⟨verb⟩ zusammenarbeiten [tsu'zamən|aʳbaetn̩] <arbeitet zusammen, arbeitete zusammen, hat zusammengearbeitet> ◊ *Die beiden Firmen wollen enger zusammenarbeiten.* ♦ *Er hat bei der Planung mit mir zusammengearbeitet.; (derogatory)* kollaborieren [kɔlabo'riːrən] <kollaboriert, kollaborierte, hat kollaboriert> ◊ *mit der Mafia kollaborieren*

collaboration ⟨noun⟩ **1.** *(working together)* Zusammenarbeit [tsu'zamən|aʳbaet] die <–, –en> ◊ *Dieses Buch ist in Zusammenarbeit mit Lehrern entstanden.; (derogatory)* Kollaboration [kɔlabora'tsi̯oːn] die <–, –en> ◊ *Er wurde der Kollaboration mit dem Feind verdächtigt.* **2.** *(product)* Gemeinschaftsprodukt [gə'maenʃaftsproˌdʊkt] das <–(e)s, –e> ◊ *Dieses*

Flugzeug ist ein Gemeinschaftsprodukt mehrerer Unternehmen.; (TV or radio programme) Gemeinschaftsproduktion [gə'maenʃaftsprodʊk͜tsjoːn] die <–, –en> ◊ *eine Gemeinschaftsproduktion von ARD und ZDF*

collaborator [noun] *(co-worker)* Mitarbeiter ['mɪt|a'baɐ̯tɐ] der <–s, –> ♀Mitarbeiterin ['mɪt|a'baɐ̯tɐrɪn] die <–, –nen>; *(derogatory)* Kollaborateur [kɔlabora'tøːɐ̯] der <–s, –e> ♀Kollaborateurin [kɔlabora'tøːrɪn] die <–, –nen>

collapse¹ [noun] **1.** *(of a system, of the body)* Zusammenbruch [tsu'zamənbrʊx] der <–(e)s, Zusammenbrüche> ◊ *Dem staatlichen Gesundheitssystem droht der Zusammenbruch.* ♦ *Er erlitt einen Zusammenbruch und verlor das Bewusstsein.* be on the point of collapse kurz vor dem Zusammenbruch stehen; *(of negotiations, plans etc.)* Scheitern ['ʃaetən] das <–s> no pl ◊ *das Scheitern einer Reform* **2.** *(of a building)* Einsturz ['aenʃtʊ'ts] der <–es, Einstürze> ◊ *Beim Einsturz des Hotels starben viele Menschen.* **3.** *(sudden decline)* Einbruch ['aenbrʊx] der <–(e)s, Einbrüche> ◊ *Der Export hat einen dramatischen Einbruch erlitten.*

collapse² [verb] **1.** *(roof, building etc.)* einstürzen ['aenʃtʏ'tsn] +sein ◊ *Das Gebäude ist eingestürzt.* **2.** *(person, system)* zusammenbrechen [tsu'zamənbrɛçn] <bricht zusammen, brach zusammen, ist zusammengebrochen> ◊ *ohnmächtig zusammenbrechen* ♦ *Das Telefonnetz ist zusammengebrochen.; (sit or lie down)* sich fallen lassen ['falən lasn] <lässt sich fallen, ließ sich fallen, hat sich fallen lassen> ◊ *Erschöpft ließ er sich aufs Sofa fallen.* **3.** *(fold)* collapse into etw. zusammenklappen [tsu'zamənklapm] +haben ◊ *Sie klappte den Liegestuhl zusammen.* sth collapses etw. lässt sich zusammenklappen ◊ *Diese Stühle lassen sich zusammenklappen.* **4.** collapse into laughter in Lachen ausbrechen [ɪn 'laxn aosbrɛçn] <bricht aus, brach aus, ist ausgebrochen> ◊ *Sie brach spontan in Lachen aus.*

collar [noun] **1.** *(on a piece of clothing)* Kragen ['kraːgṇ] der <–s, –> ◊ *Er schlug den Kragen hoch.* **2.** *(for an animal)* Halsband ['halsbant] das <–(e)s, Halsbänder> ◊ *Ihre Katze trägt ein Halsband.*

colleague [noun] Kollege [kɔ'leːgə] der <–n, –n> ♀Kollegin [kɔ'leːgɪn] die <–, –nen> ◊ *Er ist ein Kollege von mir.*

collect [verb] **1.** *(gather things or money)* sammeln ['zamln] +haben ◊ *Die Polizei sammelt Beweise.* ♦ *Tom sammelt Briefmarken.* ♦ *Wir sammeln für den Tierschutzverein.* **2.** *(pick sb/sth up)* abholen ['aphoːlən] +haben ◊ *Ich hole dich vom Bahnhof ab.* ♦ *Der Müll wird freitags abgeholt.* **3.** *(from an account)* einziehen ['aentsiːən] <zieht ein, zog ein, hat eingezogen> ◊ *Der Betrag wird vom Girokonto eingezogen.* **4.** *(people, come together)* sich versammeln [fɛ'zamln] <versammelt sich, versammelte sich, hat sich versammelt> ◊ *Die Demonstranten versammeln sich vor der Botschaft.* **5.** *(things, accumulate)* sich ansammeln ['anzamln] <sammelt sich an, sammelte sich an, hat sich angesammelt> ◊ *In der Lunge hatte sich Wasser angesammelt.*
ⓔ **collect yourself** sich sammeln
• **collect up** [phras v] collect sth up etw. einsammeln ['aenzamln] <sammelt ein, sammelte ein, hat eingesammelt>

collection [noun] **1.** *(of objects, money)* Sammlung ['zamlʊŋ] die <–, –en> ◊ *Er hat eine Sammlung antiker Münzen.* ♦ *eine Sammlung für die Erdbebenopfer* **2.** *(fashion)* Kollektion [kɔlɛk'tsjoːn] die <–, –en> ◊ *die neue Kollektion für den Winter* **3.** *(of rubbish)* Abholung ['apho:lʊŋ] die <–, –en> ◊ *den Müll am Abend vor der Abholung rausstellen; (of post)* Leerung ['leːrʊŋ] die <–, –en> ◊ *Die letzte Leerung ist um 18 Uhr.* **4.** *(of money owed)* Einzug ['aentsuːk] der <–(e)s, Einzüge> *most sing* ◊ *der Einzug der Beiträge* **5.** *(of people)* a collection of eine Ansammlung von [aenə 'anzamlʊŋ fɔn] der <–, –en> ◊ *eine Ansammlung von Exzentrikern*

collective(ly) [adj, adv] kollektiv [kɔlɛk'tiːf] *no comp/superl; when used as an adj, mostly before ns (tech)* ◊ *kollektive Schuld* ♦ *kollektiv bestraft werden/haften*; gemeinsam [gə'maenza:m] *no comp/superl; when used as an adj, mostly before ns* gemeinsame Verantwortung ♦ *Die Farm bewirtschaften sie gemeinsam.*

collector [noun] Sammler ['zamlɐ] der <–s, –> ♀Sammlerin ['zamlərɪn] die <–, –nen>

college [noun] **1.** *(in the UK, offering vocational courses)* Berufsschule [bə'ruːfsʃuːlə] die <–, –n> ◊ *Er geht zur Berufsschule.* at college on the Berufsschule **2.** *(in the US: university)* Hochschule ['hoːxʃuːlə] die <–, –n>

collide [verb] **1.** *(crash)* zusammenstoßen [tsu'zamənʃtoːsn] <stößt zusammen, stieß zusammen, ist zusammengestoßen> ◊ *Sie stießen mit den Köpfen zusammen.* ♦ *Die beiden Autos stießen frontal zusammen.* **2.** *(hit sth)* collide with sth auf etw. [aof ... ,aof] prallen [aof ... ,pralən] +sein ◊ *Der Lkw prallte auf eine Mauer.* **3.** *(argue, disagree)* aneinander geraten [an|ae'nande gəra:tn] <gerät, geriet, sind geraten> ◊ *Sie sind wieder einmal aneinander geraten.*

collision [noun] **1.** *(crash)* Zusammenstoß [tsu'zamənʃtoːs] der <–s, Zusammenstöße> ◊ *ein Zusammenstoß zwischen einem Motorroller und einem Pkw* head-on collision Frontalzusammenstoß [frɔn'taːltsu,zamənʃtoːs] be in collision with sth mit etw. zusammenstoßen [mɪt ... tsu,zamənʃtoːsn] <stößt zusammen, stieß zusammen, ist zusammengestoßen> ◊ *Das Motorrad war mit einem Lkw zusammengestoßen.* **2.** *(argument, disagreement)* Konflikt [kɔn'flɪkt] der <–(e)s, –e> ◊ *ein Konflikt zwischen Regierung und Parlament*

colloquial(ly) [adj, adv] umgangssprachlich ['ʊmgaŋsʃpraːxlɪç] *seldom comp/superl* ◊ *ein umgangssprachlicher Ausdruck* ♦ *Dieses Wort ist umgangssprachlich.* ♦ *Der Ausdruck wird nur umgangssprachlich verwendet.*

colon [noun] **1.** *(punctuation mark)* Doppelpunkt ['dɔplpʊŋkt] der <–(e)s, –e> **2.** *(intestine)* Dickdarm ['dɪkda'm] der <–(e)s, Dickdärme> *most sing*

colonel [noun] Oberst ['oːbest] der <–en *or* –s, –en *or* –e> ♀Oberstin ['oːbestɪn] die <–, –nen>

colonial [adj] kolonial [kolo'njaːl] *no comp/superl* ◊ *die koloniale Vergangenheit Großbritanniens* ♦ *Der Baustil ist vorwiegend kolonial.*

colony [noun] Kolonie [kolo'niː] die <–, –n> ◊ *eine ehemalige deutsche Kolonie* ♦ *Diese Vögel brüten in riesigen Kolonien.*

colour¹, **color** [noun] **1.** Farbe ['fa'bə] die <–, –n> ◊ *die Farbe Rot* ♦ *Schwarz, Rot und Gold sind die*

A
B
C
D
E
F
G
H
I
J
K
L
M
N
O
P
Q
R
S
T
U
V
W
X
Y
Z

Farben der deutschen Flagge. ✦ *Der Wind brachte frische Farbe in ihr Gesicht.* What colo(u)r are his eyes? Welche Farbe haben seine Augen? It became/was blue in colo(u)r. Es wurde/war blau. colo(u)r photograph Farbfotografie ['faˑpfotograˌfiː] die <-, -n> colo(u)r television Farbfernseher ['faˑpfɛˈnzeːɐ] der <-s, -> 2. *(of sb's skin)* Hautfarbe ['haͻtfaˑbə] die <-, -n> ◊ *Menschen aller Hautfarben* 3. *(for your hair, temporary)* Tönung ['tøːnʊŋ] die <-, -en>; *(permanent)* Farbe ['faˑbə] die <-, -n> ☞ nail your colo(u)rs to the mast sein Meinung kundtun add colo(u)r to sth Farbe in etw. [acc] bringen show your true colo(u)rs sein wahres Gesicht zeigen with flying colo(u)rs mit Bravour

colour², **color** [verb] 1. *(give sth a particular colo(u)r)* färben ['fɛˑbm̩] +haben ◊ *Ich möchte diese Bluse blau färben.* ✦ *Färbst du dir die Haare?*; *(using paint, crayons etc.)* anmalen ['anmaːlən] +haben 2. *(blush)* erröten [e'røːtn̩] <errötet, errötete, ist errötet> ◊ *Als er sie ansah, errötete sie.* 3. *(influence)* beeinflussen [bə'aɛnflʊsn̩] <beeinflusst, beeinflusste, hat beeinflusst> ◊ *Lass dich in deinem Urteil nicht von anderen beeinflussen.*

coloured, **colored** [adj] 1. *(not white or transparent)* farbig ['faˑbɪç] ◊ *Die Wand war nicht weiß, sondern farbig.* ✦ *farbiges Glas* 2. *(hair)* gefärbt [gə'fɛˑpt] no comp/superl ◊ *Mein Haar ist gefärbt.* ✦ *gefärbte Augenbrauen*

colourful(ly), **colorful(ly)** [adj, adv] 1. bunt [bʊnt] <bunter, am buntesten> ◊ *ein bunter Pulli* ✦ *Seine Welt ist bunt und fröhlich.* ✦ *eine bunt gemusterte Schürze*; *(sb's character, past)* schillernd ['ʃɪlɐnt] 2. *(language, positive)* anschaulich ['anʃaͻlɪç] ◊ *etw. anschaulich schildern; (negative)* drastisch ['drastɪʃ]

colouring, **coloring** [noun] 1. *(of eyes, hair)* Farbe ['faˑbə] die <-, -n> ◊ *Die Farbe ihrer Augen ist blau.; (of skin)* Teint [tɛn] der <-s, -s> ◊ *Sie hat einen sehr hellen Teint.; (of an animal or plant)* Färbung ['fɛˑbʊn] die <-, -en> ◊ *die Färbung des Gefieders* 2. *(substance)* Färbemittel ['fɛˑbəmɪt] das <-s, ->

column [noun] 1. ARCH Säule ['zͻɛlə] die <-, -n> ◊ *eine korinthische Säule* 2. *(of people, vehicles)* Kolonne [ko'lͻnə] die <-, -n> ◊ *eine Kolonne von Lkws* 3. *(thematic)* Rubrik [ru'briːk] die <-, -en> ◊ *Angebote in der Rubrik „Sonstiges"* 4. *(on a page)* Spalte ['ʃpaltə] die <-, -n> ◊ *eine Tabelle mit fünf Spalten*

coma [noun] Koma ['koːmaː] das <-s, -s> most sing ◊ *Er fiel ins Koma.*

comb¹ [noun] Kamm [kam] der <-(e)s, Kämme> ◊ *mit dem Kamm einen Scheitel ziehen* ✦ *Der Hahn hat einen roten Kamm.*

comb² [verb] 1. *(hair)* kämmen ['kɛmən] +haben comb your hair sich kämmen ◊ *Er hat sich nicht gekämmt.* 2. *(search sth)* durchkämmen [dʊçˈçkɛmən] <durchkämmt, durchkämmte, hat durchkämmt> ◊ *Die Polizei durchkämmte den Wald nach dem Vermissten.*

combat¹ [noun] Kampf [kampf] der <-es, Kämpfe> ◊ *der Kampf gegen Aids* killed in combat im Kampf gefallen

combat² [verb] bekämpfen [bə'kɛmpfn̩] <bekämpft, bekämpfte, hat bekämpft> ◊ *Wie kann man die Armut bekämpfen?*

combination [noun] Kombination [kͻmbinaˈtsjoːn] die

<-, -en> ◊ *Das Gerät ist eine Kombination aus Drucker und Kopierer.* ✦ *die Kombination für den Safe* in combination zusammen [tsu'zamən] ◊ *Diese Medikamente dürfen nicht zusammen genommen werden.* in combination with gepaart mit [gə'paːt mɪt] ◊ *Ausdauer, gepaart mit Talent, führt zum Erfolg.*

combine [verb] 1. *(join)* combine sth with sth etw. mit etw. verbinden [mɪt ... fɛˌbɪndn̩] <verbindet, verband, hat verbunden> ◊ *das Angenehme mit dem Nützlichen verbinden* combine things Dinge miteinander verbinden ◊ *Kann man beide Aufgaben miteinander verbinden?* sth combines with sth etw. verbindet sich mit etw. ◊ *Seine Freude verband sich mit Befürchtungen.* 2. *(groups, organizations)* sich zusammenschließen [tsu'zamənʃliːsn̩] <schließt sich zusammen, schloss sich zusammen, hat sich zusammengeschlossen> ◊ *Die beiden Vereine haben sich zusammengeschlossen.* 3. *(ingredients)* verrühren [fɛ'ryːrən] <verrührt, verrührte, hat verrührt> ◊ *die Zutaten in einer Schüssel (miteinander) verrühren*

combined ✦ combine [adj] gemeinsam [gə'maɛnzaːm] no comp/superl, only before ns ◊ *das gemeinsame Einkommen der Ehepartner*

come [verb] 1. *(person, object, wind, event etc.)* kommen ['kͻmən] <kommt, kam, ist gekommen> ◊ *Wir kamen früh nach Hause.* ◊ *Kommst du jetzt endlich?* ✦ *Der Lottogewinn kommt zur rechten Zeit.* ✦ *Die Erfahrung im Beruf kommt mit den Arbeitsjahren.* ✦ *zu einem Schluss/einer Entscheidung kommen* ✦ *Das habe ich kommen sehen!* It came as a relief/shock etc. (to me). Es war eine Erleichterung/ein Schock etc. (für mich). She came running into the house. Sie kam ins Haus gerannt. A truck came driving along. Ein Lkw kam angefahren. sth is yet to come etw. kommt erst ◊ *Das Beste kommt erst!* come what may was auch immer kommen mag come here herkommen ['heːɐkͻmən] <kommt her, kam her, ist hergekommen> ◊ *Komm doch bitte mal her und sieh dir das an!* come inside hereinkommen [hɛ'raɛnkͻmən] <kommt herein, kam herein, ist hereingekommen> ◊ *Sie kam aus dem Garten herein.* 2. *(products, be available)* colo(u)red sth comes in ... etw. gibt es in ... [gi:pt ɛs] <gibt, gab, hat gegeben> ◊ *Dieses Kleid gibt es in Rot und Blau.* ✦ *Dieses Auto gibt es mit vielen Extras.* ☞ as good/big etc. as they come so good as they come unglaublich gut sein *(referring to the importance of sth/sb)* be as big as they come unübertroffen sein as bad as they come unvorstellbar schlecht sein come to do sth etw. zu tun beginnen ◊ *Mit der Zeit begann ich, ihn zu lieben.* ✦ *Ich begann, ihn als Feind zu betrachten.* come to know 1. *(a person, country)* kennen lernen 2. *(a fact)* erfahren ◊ *Wann/Wie hast du von dem Unfall erfahren?* How do you come to know? Woher weißt du das? come to pass geschehen come to think of it *(introducing an afterthought)* wenn ich es mir recht überlege ◊ *E-Mails können ganz schön lästig sein. Wenn ich es mir recht überlege, Anrufe auch.* *(when sth crosses your mind)* da fällt mir ein ◊ *Hast du Durst? Da fällt mir ein, ich muss noch zum Getränkemarkt.* how come (...) warum (...) ◊ *Warum bist du so schlecht in der Schule?* to come *(future)* kommend ◊ *in den kommenden Jahren*

● **come about** [phras v] sth comes about es kommt

zu etw. [ɛs kɔmt ʦuː] <kommt, kam, ist gekommen>
◊ *Zu dem Unfall kam es durch Unachtsamkeit.*

• **come across** phras v **1.** *(from the other side of sth)* herüberkommen [hɛˈryːbɐkɔmən] <kommt herüber, kam herüber, ist herübergekommen> ◊ *Er kam zu uns herüber.* **2.** *(meet by chance)* zufällig treffen [ˌʦuːfɛlɪç ˈtrɛfn̩] <trifft, traf, hat getroffen> ◊ *Gestern habe ich zufällig Fabian im Supermarkt getroffen.; (find by chance)* zufällig finden [ˌʦuːfɛlɪç ˈfɪndn̩] <findet, fand, hat gefunden> ◊ *Dieses Buch habe ich zufällig in einem Antiquariat gefunden.* **3.** *(make an impression)* come across as (being) ... ... wirken [ˈvɪʁkn̩] +haben ◊ *Sie wirkt sehr selbstbewusst.* **4.** *(be clear, provide sth)* rüberkommen [ˈryːbɐkɔmən] <kommt rüber, kam rüber, ist rübergekommen> *(fam)* ◊ *Die Aussage des Films kam nicht gut rüber.* ♦ *Komm endlich mit dem Geld rüber!*

• **come after** phras v come after sb jdn verfolgen [fɛˈfɔlɡn̩] <verfolgt, verfolgte, hat verfolgt> ◊ *Der Dieb verfolgte sie.*

• **come along** phras v **1.** *(pass by)* vorbeikommen [foːɐ̯ˈbaɪkɔmən] <kommt vorbei, kam vorbei, ist vorbeigekommen> ◊ *Sie gab das Buch dem Ersten, der vorbeikam.* **2.** *(become available, come later)* kommen [ˈkɔmən] <kommt, kam, ist gekommen> ◊ *So eine Gelegenheit kommt nicht oft.* ♦ *Geh du schon mal. Ich komme, wenn ich fertig bin.* **3.** *(go somewhere with sb)* mitkommen [ˈmɪtkɔmən] <kommt mit, kam mit, ist mitgekommen> ◊ *Du gehst ins Schwimmbad? Warte, ich komme mit.* **4.** *(make progress)* Fortschritte machen [ˈfɔʁtʃʁɪtə maxn̩] +haben ◊ *Die Bauarbeiten machen gute Fortschritte.* ℗ be coming along with sth mit etw. vorankommen ◊ *Sie kommt mit ihrem Training gut voran.*

• **come at** phras v **1.** *(attack sb)* come at sb auf jdn losgehen [aof ... ˌloːsɡeːən] <geht los, ging los, ist losgegangen> ◊ *Der Kerl ist mit einem Messer auf mich losgegangen!* **2.** *(be directed at sb)* come at sb sich jdm stellen [ˈʃtɛlən] +haben ◊ *Diese Frage stellte sich ihm immer häufiger.; (information)* auf jdn einstürmen [aof ... ˌaenʃtʏrˈmən] +sein ◊ *Am Anfang stürmte eine Unmenge an Informationen auf uns ein.* **3.** *(approach or tackle sth)* come at sth etw. angehen [ˈanɡeːən] <geht an, ging an, ist angegangen> ◊ *Sie beschloss, das Problem anders anzugehen.*

• **come away** phras v **1.** *(become loose)* come away (from sth) sich lösen [ˈløːzn̩] +haben ◊ *Der Putz löste sich von den Wänden.* **2.** *(leave)* come away with sth mit etw. (nach Hause) gehen [mɪt ... (naːx ˈhaozə) ɡeːən] <geht, ging, ist gegangen> ◊ *Sie gingen mit dem Gefühl (nach Hause), dass es noch viel zu tun gab.*

• **come back** phras v **1.** *(return)* zurückkommen [ʦuˈrʏkkɔmən] <kommt zurück, kam zurück, ist zurückgekommen> ♦ *aus Italien/nach Deutschland zurückkommen* ♦ *vom Schwimmen zurückkommen* ♦ *Auf dieses Thema kommen wir später wieder zurück.; (sth that was lost)* zurückkehren [ʦuˈrʏkkeːrən] +sein ◊ *Allmählich kehrt sein Selbstbewusstsein/Gedächtnis zurück.* **2.** *(memory)* come back to sb jdm wieder einfallen [viːdɐ ˈaenfalən] <fällt ein, fiel ein, ist eingefallen> ◊ *Ich weiß es nicht mehr, aber es fällt mir bestimmt wieder ein.*

• **come by** phras v **1.** *(visit, drop in)* vorbeikommen [foːɐ̯ˈbaɛkɔmən] <kommt vorbei, kam vorbei, ist vorbei-

gekommen> ◊ *Komm doch morgen auf einen Kaffee vorbei.* **2.** *(acquire sth)* come by sth etw. bekommen [bəˈkɔmən] <bekommt, bekam, hat bekommen> ◊ *Woher habt ihr diese tolle Vase bekommen?* be hard to come by schwer zu bekommen sein ◊ *Dieser Job war schwer zu bekommen.*

• **come down** phras v **1.** *(descend)* herunterkommen [hɛˈrʊntɐkɔmən] <kommt herunter, kam herunter, ist heruntergekommen> ◊ *Er kam die Treppe herunter.* **2.** *(plane)* landen [ˈlandn̩] <landet, landete, ist gelandet>; *(crash)* abstürzen [ˈapʃtʏɐ̯ʦn̩] +sein ◊ *Das Flugzeug stürzte aus großer Höbe ab.* **3.** *(rain, snow etc.)* fallen [ˈfalən] <fällt, fiel, ist gefallen> ◊ *Gestern fiel starker Regen.* **4.** *(amount, level, price)* sinken [ˈzɪŋkn̩] <sinkt, sank, ist gesunken> ◊ *Die Preise sind in den letzten Jahren gesunken.* **5.** *(decide)* come down for/against sb/sth für/gegen jdn/etw. entscheiden [ˈfyːɐ̯/ˈɡeːɡn̩ ... ɛntˌʃaedn̩] <entscheidet, entschied, hat entschieden> ◊ *Es war unsicher, ob sie sich für oder gegen ihn entscheiden würde.* **6.** *(become ill)* come down with sth etw. bekommen [bəˈkɔmən] <bekommt, bekam, hat bekommen> ◊ *Er hat eine Erkältung bekommen.*

• **come for** phras v come for sb/sth abholen [ˈaphoːlən] +haben ◊ *Unsere Freunde holen uns um 8 Uhr ab.*

• **come forward** phras v **1.** sich melden [ˈmɛldn̩] +haben ◊ *Zeugen des Unfalls sollten sich bei der Polizei melden.* **2.** come forward with sth etw. anbieten [ˈanbiːtn̩] <bietet an, bot an, hat angeboten> ◊ *Sie haben ihre Hilfe angeboten.* ♦ *Er bietet ihnen Informationen an.*

• **come from** phras v *(from a country, family)* come from sth aus etw. kommen [aos ... kɔmən] <kommt, kam, ist gekommen> ◊ *Er kommt aus Italien/einer guten Familie.; (from an origin, cause)* von etw. kommen [fɔn ... kɔmən] +haben ◊ *Das Gift kommt von einer Kobra.* ♦ *Das kommt von deiner Ungeduld.*

• **come in** phras v **1.** *(enter)* hereinkommen [hɛˈraenkɔmən] <kommt herein, kam herein, ist hereingekommen> ◊ *Komm herein!* ♦ *Wir müssen zusehen, dass Geld hereinkommt.* ♦ *Immer mehr Nachrichten über die Flutwelle kamen herein.; (train, into the station)* einfahren [ˈaenfaːrən] <fährt ein, fuhr ein, ist eingefahren> ◊ *Der Regionalexpress nach Hannover fährt auf Gleis 2 ein.; (ship)* einlaufen [ˈaenlaofn̩] <läuft ein, lief ein, ist eingelaufen> ◊ *in den Hafen einlaufen* **2.** *(arrive)* eintreffen [ˈaentrɛfn̩] <trifft ein, traf ein, ist eingetroffen> ◊ *Ist der Zug/Brief schon eingetroffen?; (tide)* kommen [ˈkɔmən] <kommt, kam, ist gekommen> ◊ *In zwei Stunden kommt die Flut.* **3.** *(interject)* sich einschalten [ˈaenʃaltn̩] <schaltet sich ein, schaltete sich ein, hat sich eingeschaltet> ◊ *Ich möchte mich kurz einschalten und meine Bedenken äußern.* ℗ come in useful/handy nützlich sein ◊ *Ein Stück Papier und ein Stift sind immer nützlich.*

• **come into** phras v **1.** *(an inheritance)* erben [ˈɛʁbm̩] +haben ◊ *Er hat ein Vermögen geerbt.* **2.** come/not come into it eine/keine Rolle spielen [aenə/kaenə ˈrɔlə ʃpiːlən] +haben ◊ *Für sie spielt Geld keine Rolle.*

• **come of** phras v sth comes of sth aus etw. wird etw. [aos ... vɪɐ̯t ...] <wurde, ist geworden> ◊ *Trotz harter Arbeit ist aus dem Projekt nichts geworden.* I don't know what will come of it. Ich weiß nicht,

was daraus wird.
• **come off** [phras v] 1. *(fall off)* abgehen ['apge:ən] <geht ab, ging ab, ist abgegangen> ◊ *An meiner Jacke ist ein Knopf abgegangen.* 2. *(stop using or doing sth)* come off sth von etw. loskommen [fɔn ... ,loːskɔmən] <kommt los, kam los, ist losgekommen> *(fam)* ◊ *Er hat es geschafft, von den Drogen loszukommen.* 3. *(in a fight, competition)* come off well/badly etc. sich gut/schlecht etc. schlagen ['guːt/'ʃlɛçt ʃlaːgn̩] <schlägt sich, schlug sich, hat sich geschlagen> ◊ *Bei dem Lesewettbewerb hat er sich ganz gut geschlagen.*
⊚ **Oh, come off it!** Jetzt hör aber auf!
• **come on** [phras v] 1. *(electrical equipment)* angehen ['ange:ən] <geht an, ging an, ist angegangen> ◊ *Das Radio geht nicht mehr an.* 2. *(appear in a radio or TV programme)* im Radio/Fernsehen kommen [ɪm 'raːdjoː/'fɛ'nzeːən kɔmən] <kommt, kam, ist gekommen> 3. *(make progress)* vorankommen [foˈrankɔmən] <kommt voran, kam voran, ist vorangekommen> ◊ *Sie kommt mit ihrer Arbeit gut voran.*
⊚ **come on!** los! ◊ *Los, mach schon, wir verpassen sonst den Zug!*
• **come out** [phras v] 1. *(emerge, appear, become available or known)* herauskommen [hɛˈraʊskɔmən] <kommt heraus, kam heraus, ist herausgekommen> ◊ *Er kam mit einem Tablett auf die Terrasse heraus.* ♦ *Wann kommt dieser Film heraus?* ♦ *Ist inzwischen herausgekommen, wer es war?* 2. *(mark, stain etc.)* weggehen ['vɛkge:ən] <geht weg, ging weg, ist weggegangen> 3. *(tell people that you are gay)* sich outen ['aʊtn̩] <outet sich, outete sich, hat sich geoutet>
• **come over** [phras v] 1. *(move towards)* herüberkommen [hɛˈryːbɐkɔmən] <kommt herüber, kam herüber, ist herübergekommen> ◊ *Sie kam zu unserer Gruppe herüber.* ♦ *Kannst du mal ins Wohnzimmer herüberkommen?* 2. *(feelings)* come over sb jdn überkommen [ybɐˈkɔmən] <überkommt, überkam, hat überkommen> ◊ *Mich überkam ein Gefühl der Unzulänglichkeit.* I don't know what came over me. Ich weiß nicht, was über mich gekommen ist.
• **come round** [phras v] 1. *(event)* kommen ['kɔmən] <kommt, kam, ist gekommen> ◊ *Bald kommt wieder Weihnachten.* 2. *(regain consciousness)* wieder zu sich kommen [viːde 'tsu: ... kɔmən] <kommt, kam, ist gekommen> 3. *(visit sb)* bei jdm vorbeischauen [baɛ ... foːɐ̯,baɛʃaʊən] +haben *(fam)* ◊ *Sie schaute nach der Arbeit noch bei uns vorbei.*
• **come through** [phras v] 1. *(pass or get through)* durchkommen ['dʊɐ̯çkɔmən] <kommt durch, kam durch, ist durchgekommen> ◊ *Auf dem Heimweg kommen wir durch Mannheim durch.* ♦ *Durch das Loch kommt Wasser durch.* ♦ *Ich wollte ihn anrufen, aber ich bin nicht durchgekommen.*; *(penetrate)* durchdringen [dʊɐ̯çˈdrɪŋən] <durchdringt, durchdrang, hat durchdrungen> ◊ *Das Prasseln des Regens durchdrang die Stille.* 2. *(an operation, a bad experience)* überstehen [ybɐˈʃteːən] <übersteht, überstand, hat überstanden> ◊ *eine Operation gut überstehen*
• **come to** [phras v] 1. *(idea, thought etc.)* come to sb jdm kommen ['kɔmən] <kommt, kam, ist gekommen> ◊ *Wann ist dir diese Idee gekommen?* 2. *(reach a certain point)* come to sth zu etw. kommen ['tsu: ... kɔmən] <kommt, kam, ist gekommen> ◊ *Wenn es zum Krieg kommen sollte,*

werden wir eingreifen. 3. *(reach a total)* come to sth etw. ergeben [ɛˈgeːbm̩] <ergibt, ergab, hat ergeben> ◊ *Was ergibt 154 plus 217?*
• **come together** [phras v] 1. *(meet)* zusammenkommen [tsuˈzamənkɔmən] <kommt zusammen, kamen zusammen, sind zusammengekommen> ◊ *zu einem Gedankenaustausch zusammenkommen* 2. *(cooperate)* sich zusammentun [tsuˈzaməntuːn] <tun sich zusammen, taten sich zusammen, haben sich zusammengetan> ◊ *Mehrere Organisationen taten sich zusammen, um zu helfen.*
• **come under** [phras v] 1. *(under the microscope, scalpel etc.)* come under sth unter etw. [acc] kommen [ʊnte ... kɔmən] <kommt, kam, ist gekommen> ◊ *Wenn diese Behandlung nicht anschlägt, komme ich unter das Messer.*; *(under pressure)* unter etw. [acc] geraten [ʊnte ... gəraːtn̩] <gerät, geriet, ist geraten> ◊ *Sie gerät immer mehr unter Druck.* come under criticism in die Kritik geraten come under the spotlight ins Rampenlicht geraten come under fire unter Beschuss geraten come under attack angegriffen werden ['angəgrɪfn̩ veːɐ̯dn̩] <wird, wurde, ist worden> sth/sb comes under sb's control jd bringt etw./jdn unter seine Kontrolle [brɪŋt ... ʊnte zaɛnə kɔnˈtrɔlə] <bringt, brachte, hat gebracht> come under close scrutiny, come under the scanner einer genauen Prüfung unterzogen werden [aɛnə gənaʊən 'pryːfʊŋ ʊnte,tsoːgn̩ veːɐ̯dn̩] 2. *(under a category, law etc.)* come under sth unter etw. fallen [ʊnte ... falən] <fällt, fiel, ist gefallen> ◊ *Fällt dieser Fall unter die neuen Bestimmungen.*
• **come undone** [phras v] *(button, zip etc.)* aufgehen ['aʊfge:ən] <geht auf, ging auf, ist aufgegangen> *(fam)* ◊ *Der Knoten geht nicht mehr auf.*
• **come up** [phras v] 1. *(problem, question, difficulty etc.)* aufkommen ['aʊfkɔmən] <kommt auf, kam auf, ist aufgekommen> ◊ *eingreifen, wenn Probleme aufkommen; (keeping sb from sth)* jdm dazwischenkommen [daˈtsvɪʃn̩kɔmən] <kommt dazwischen, kam dazwischen, ist dazwischengekommen> ◊ *Ich wollte dich anrufen, aber mir ist etwas dazwischengekommen.* 2. *(in a discussion)* zur Sprache kommen [tsuːɐ̯ 'ʃpraːxə kɔmən] <kommt, kam, ist gekommen>; *(court case, topic)* behandelt werden [bəˈhandlt veːɐ̯dn̩] <wird, wurde, ist worden> ◊ *Dieser Fall wurde vor Gericht behandelt.; (in a lottery)* gezogen werden [gəˈtsoːgn̩ veːɐ̯dn̩] +sein ◊ *Meine Nummer wurde gezogen.* 3. *(event)* be coming up bald kommen [,balt 'kɔmən] <kommt, kam, ist gekommen> ◊ *Ihr neues Album kommt bald.* Christmas is coming up. Weihnachten steht vor der Tür. With his exams coming up he was very nervous. Wegen der bevorstehenden Prüfung war er sehr nervös. 4. *(person, come nearer)* come up to sb auf jdn zukommen [aʊf ... 'tsuːkɔmən] <kommt zu, kam zu, ist zugekommen> ◊ *Sie kam lächelnd auf mich zu.; (come to sb)* zu jdm kommen ['tsu: ... kɔmən] <kommt, kam, ist gekommen> ◊ *Er kam zu mir und legte mir die Hand auf die Schulter.* 5. *(person: up the stairs or a hill etc., food)* hochkommen ['hoːxkɔmən] <kommt hoch, kam hoch, ist hochgekommen> *(fam)* ◊ *Er kam langsam die Treppe hoch.* ♦ *Mir kam das Essen wieder hoch.* 6. *(job)* frei werden ['fraɛ veːɐ̯dn̩] +sein 7. *(sun, moon)* aufgehen ['aʊfge:ən] <geht auf, ging auf, ist auf-

gegangen> 8. *(seed)* aufgehen [ˈaɔfgeːən] <geht auf, ging auf, ist aufgegangen> ◊ *Der Samen ging nicht auf.; (plant)* herauskommen [hɛˈraɔskɔmən] <kommt heraus, kam heraus, ist herausgekommen> 9. come up to/as far as sth bis zu etw. reichen [bɪs tsuː: ... raeçn̩] +haben ◊ *Das Wasser reicht ihm bis zum Knie.*

• **come up against** [phras v] come up against sb/sth auf jdn/etw. stoßen [aɔf ... ʃtoːsn̩] <stößt, stieß, ist gestoßen> ◊ *Wir stießen auf ernste Probleme.*

• **come up with** [phras v] 1. *(an answer, idea, theory)* sb comes up with sth jd hat etw. [hat] +haben ◊ *Ich hatte die Idee, ins Kino zu fahren.; (a plan, something brilliant or stupid etc.)* jd denkt sich etw. aus [dɛŋkt ... aɔs] <dachte sich aus, hat sich ausgedacht> ◊ *Wir müssen uns einen Plan ausdenken.; (a name, address, reason, argument)* jdm fällt etw. ein [fɛlt ... aen] <fällt ein, fiel ein, ist eingefallen> ◊ *Mir fallen sofort viele Gründe ein, warum man Sport treiben sollte.* 2. *(in an internet search, data)* sth comes up with sth etw. findet etw. [ˈfɪndət] <fand, hat gefunden> ◊ *Die Suchmaschine fand 23 Webseiten zu diesem Stichwort.*

comeback [noun] 1. *(return to success)* Comeback [kamˈbɛk] das <-s, -s> ◊ *Sie feierte ein großes Comeback.* 2. *(quick answer)* Erwiderung [ɛˈviːdərʊŋ] die <-, -en> ◊ *Auf seine Anschuldigungen kamen heftige Erwiderungen.*

comedy [noun] 1. *(theatre play)* Komödie [koˈmøːdjə] die <-, -n> ◊ *Tragödie und Komödie sind Gattungen des Dramas.* 2. *(humorous film, often a serial)* Comedy [ˈkɔmədi] die <-, -s> ◊ *sich eine Comedy ansehen*

comfort¹ [noun] 1. *(physical ease)* Komfort [kɔmˈfoːɐ] der <-s> no pl ◊ *großen Komfort genießen* in comfort bequem [bəˈkveːm] ◊ *In dem Bett konnten bequem zwei Personen schlafen.* 2. *(consolation)* Trost [troːst] der <-(e)s> no pl ◊ *Zum Trost gab sie dem Kind ein paar Süßigkeiten.* ♦ *Er suchte bei seiner Mutter Trost.*

ⓔ **too close to comfort** beunruhigend nah

comfort² [verb] trösten [ˈtrøːstn̩] <tröstet, tröstete, hat getröstet> ◊ *Diese Worte werden ihn wohl kaum trösten.* ♦ *Er nahm sie in den Arm und tröstete sie.*

comfortable [adj] 1. *(clothing, chair)* bequem [bəˈkveːm] ◊ *bequeme Kleidung* ♦ *Ein Anorak ist in den Bergen bequemer als ein Mantel.* 2. *(atmosphere, room, pub)* gemütlich [gəˈmyːtlɪç] ◊ *ein gemütliches Lokal* make yourself comfortable es sich gemütlich machen 3. *(be happy with a situation)* be comfortable with sth zufrieden mit etw. sein [tsuˈfriːdn̩ mɪt ... tsaen] +sein ◊ *Sie war mit der neuen Sitzordnung sehr zufrieden.* feel comfortable about sth sich bei etw. wohl fühlen [baɛ ... ˈvoːl fyːlən] +haben ◊ *Ich fühle mich bei dieser Entscheidung nicht wohl.* 4. *(victory, lead)* deutlich [ˈdɔɔtlɪç] ◊ *mit deutlichem Vorsprung gewinnen*

comfortably [adv] 1. *(without physical effort or discomfort, with ease)* bequem [bəˈkveːm] ◊ *Liegst du auch bequem?* ♦ *Der Bahnhof ist bequem zu Fuß zu erreichen.* 2. *(cosily, offering all comforts)* gemütlich [gəˈmyːtlɪç] ◊ *eine gemütlich eingerichtete Wohnung* 3. *(pleasantly)* angenehm [ˈangəneːm] ◊ *ein angenehm kühler Tag* ♦ *Ich war angenehm erschöpft.*

comic¹ [noun] 1. *(book, strip)* Comic [ˈkɔmɪk] der <-s, -s> ◊ *gern Comics lesen* 2. *(person)* Komiker

[ˈkɔːmɪkɐ] der <-s, -> ♀Komikerin [ˈkɔːmɪkərɪn] die <-, -nen> ◊ *eine Karriere als Komiker* ♦ *Anke Engelke, eine bekannte Komikerin*

comic², **comical** [adj] komisch [ˈkɔːmɪʃ] ◊ *eine komische Geschichte* ♦ *Ich finde deine Scherze gar nicht komisch!*

coming [adj] kommend [ˈkɔmənt] no comp/superl ◊ *die kommende Preisverleihung*

comma [noun] Komma [ˈkɔmaː] das <-s, -s or lofty -ta> ◊ *ein Komma setzen*

command¹ [noun] 1. *(order, instruction)* Befehl [bəˈfeːl] der <-(e)s, -e> ◊ *Auf Befehl des Königs wurden die Rebellen begnadigt.* ♦ *Mit welchem Befehl kann man die Datei ausdrucken?* be under sb's command unter jds Befehl stehen 2. *(control, section of army)* Kommando [kɔˈmandoː] das <-s, -s> be in command (of sb/sth) das Kommando (über jdn/etw.) haben take command (of sth) das Kommando (über etw. [acc]) übernehmen in command befehlshabend [bəˈfeːlshaːbm̩t] no comp/superl, only before ns ◊ *der befehlshabende Offizier* 3. *(knowledge)* Kenntnisse [ˈkɛntnɪsə] die <-> pl ◊ *Dafür sind perfekte Kenntnisse in diesen Sprachen erforderlich.* He has no command of this language. *Er beherrscht diese Sprache nicht.* command of English Englischkenntnisse [ˈɛnlɪʃkɛntnɪsə]

command² [verb] befehlen [bəˈfeːlən] <befiehlt, befahl, hat befohlen> ◊ *„Stillgestanden!", befahl der Offizier.* ♦ *Der König hat befohlen, die Rebellen freizulassen.*

commander [noun] Offizier [ɔfiˈtsiːɐ] der <-s, -e> ♀Offizierin [ɔfiˈtsiːrɪn] die <-, -nen> ◊ *Er ist Offizier bei der Marine.*

commemorate [verb] jds/einer Sache gedenken [gəˈdɛŋkn̩] <gedenkt, gedachte, hat gedacht> *(lofty)* ◊ *der Toten gedenken*

commemoration [noun] Gedenken [gəˈdɛŋkn̩] das <-s, -> ◊ *ein Denkmal zum Gedenken an die Kriegsopfer*

commence [verb] beginnen [bəˈɡɪnən] <beginnt, begann, hat begonnen> ◊ *Das Seminar beginnt in wenigen Tagen.* ♦ *Wir haben die Übersetzung des Buches begonnen.*

commencement [noun] Aufnahme [ˈaɔfnaːmə] die <-, -n> *(lofty)* ◊ *die Aufnahme diplomatischer Beziehungen*

comment¹ [noun] 1. *(spoken or written remark on sth)* Anmerkung [ˈanmɛˈkʊŋ] die <-, -en> ◊ *eine Anmerkung machen* ♦ *Es gab auch ein paar kritische Anmerkungen.* 2. *(statement)* Äußerung [ˈɔɡsərʊŋ] die <-, -en> ◊ *eine unbedachte/verletzende Äußerung* ♦ *Die Zeitung zitierte eine Äußerung des Ministers, wonach ...* 3. *(observation, remark in general)* Bemerkung [bəˈmɛˈkʊŋ] die <-, -en> ◊ *eine unpassende Bemerkung* ♦ *Er hatte einige Bemerkungen an den Rand geschrieben.* 4. *(phrase, set of words)* Spruch [ʃprʊx] der <-(e)s, Sprüche> ◊ *sich jds ausländerfeindliche Sprüche anhören müssen*

comment² [verb] anmerken [ˈanmɛˈkn̩] +haben ◊ *Willst du dazu noch etwas anmerken?*

commentary [noun] Kommentar [kɔmɛnˈtaːˈ] der <-s, -e>

commentator [noun] Kommentator [kɔmɛnˈtaːtoːɐ] der <-s, -en> ♀Kommentatorin [kɔmɛntaˈtoːrɪn] die <-, -nen> ◊ *der Kommentator des Fußballspiels* ♦ *Sie arbeitet als Kommentatorin für den Sportkanal.*

commerce [noun] Handel [ˈhandl̩] der <-s> no pl

commercial [noun] Werbung ['vɛʳbʊŋ] die <-, -en>

commercial(ly) [adj, adv] kommerziell [kɔmɐˈt͡si̯ɛl] *seldom comp/superl ◊ kommerzielles Interesse an einer Sache haben ♦ Diese Art von Musik/Kunst ist ihm zu kommerziell. ♦ Die Räume werden kommerziell genutzt.*

commission¹ [noun] **1.** *(request for services)* Auftrag ['aʊftraːk] der <-(e)s, Aufträge> ◊ *Sie haben den Auftrag zum Ausbau des Bahnhofs bekommen.* **2.** *(group of people)* Kommission [kɔmɪˈsi̯oːn] die <-, -en> **3.** *(money earnt by selling sth)* Provision [proviˈzi̯oːn] die <-, -en> ◊ *eine Provision von 15 Prozent bekommen/erhalten*

Ⓔ out of commission außer Betrieb

commission² [verb] in Auftrag geben [ɪn ˈaʊftraːk geˈbm̩] <gibt, gab, hat gegeben> ◊ *Er gab ein Bild in Auftrag.*

commissioner [noun] **1.** *(senior official)* Abteilungsleiter [apˈtaɪlʊŋslaɪtɐ] der <-s, -> ♀Abteilungsleiterin [apˈtaɪlʊŋslaɪtərɪn] die <-, -nen> **2.** *(senior police officer)* Polizeipräsident [poliˈt͡saɛprɛziˌdɛnt] der <-en, -en> ♀Polizeipräsidentin [poliˈt͡saɛprɛziˌdɛntɪn] die <-, -nen>

commit [verb] **1.** *(a crime, suicide)* begehen [bəˈgeːən] <begeht, beging, hat begangen> ◊ *Selbstmord begehen* commit murder einen Mord begehen **2.** *((make) promise)* verpflichten [fɛˈp͡flɪçtn̩] <verpflichtete, hat verpflichtet> commit sb to sth jdn zu etw. verpflichten commit sb to doing sth jdn (dazu) verpflichten, etw. zu tun ◊ *Er verpflichtete mich dazu, Stillschweigen zu wahren.* commit to sth sich zu etw. verpflichten ◊ *Sie sich zu pünktlicher Zahlung verpflichten* commit to doing sth sich (dazu) verpflichten, etw. zu tun **3.** *(have a serious relationship)* sich binden ['bɪndn̩] <bindet sich, band sich, hat sich gebunden> ◊ *Ich bin noch nicht bereit, mich zu binden.* **4.** *(to a mental institution, prison)* commit sb (to sth) jdn in etw. [acc] einweisen ['aɛnvaɛzn̩] <weist ein, wies ein, hat eingewiesen> ◊ *Er wurde ins Gefängnis eingewiesen.* commit sb to trial jdn dem Gericht überstellen [deːm gəˈrɪçt ybɐˈʃtɛlən] <überstellt, überstellte, hat überstellt> **5.** *(money, resources)* commit sth to sth etw. für etw. zur Verfügung stellen [fyːɐ̯ ... t͡suːɡ fɛˌfyːgʊŋ ʃtɛlən] +haben ◊ *Gelder für den Bau einer Schule zur Verfügung stellen* **6.** *(entrust)* commit sb/sth to sb, commit sb/sth to sb's care jdm jdn/etw. anvertrauen ['anfɛtraʊ̯ən] <vertraut an, vertraute an, hat anvertraut> ◊ *jdm seine Kinder anvertrauen* commit sth to memory sich [dat] etw. einprägen ['aɛnprɛːɡn̩] +haben ◊ *Präg dir die Geheimzahl ein.* commit sth to paper/writing etw. zu Papier bringen [t͡suː paˈpiːɐ̯ brɪŋən] <bringt, brachte, hat gebracht> commit sth to the flames etw. den Flammen übergeben [deːn ˈflamən ybɐˌgeːbm̩] <übergibt, übergab, hat übergeben> *(lofty)*

commitment [noun] **1.** *(engagement, enthusiasm)* Einsatz ['aɛnzat͡s] der <-(e)s, Einsätze> ◊ *Sie zeigte vollen Einsatz.* **2.** *(obligation, debt)* Verpflichtung [fɛˈp͡flɪçtʊŋ] die <-, -en> ◊ *Sie fühlte ihm gegenüber eine Verpflichtung.* ♦ *Er hat große finanzielle Verpflichtungen.* fulfil/meet a commitment eine Verpflichtung erfüllen make/undertake a commitment eine Verpflichtung eingehen

committed → commit [adj] engagiert [aŋgaˈʒiːɐ̯t] <engagierter, am engagiertesten> ◊ *eine sehr engagierte Kollegin* ♦ *Er ist sehr engagiert.*

committee [noun] Ausschuss ['aʊsʃʊs] der <-es, Ausschüsse> ◊ *in einem Ausschuss sitzen*

commodity [noun] **1.** *(sth that can be bought and sold)* Ware ['vaːrə] die <-, -n> agricultural commodity landwirtschaftliches Erzeugnis [ˌlantvɪʳtʃaftlɪçəs ɛ'ts̮ɔɡknɪs] <-ses, -se> ◊ *landwirtschaftliche Erzeugnisse wie Mais, Tee und Reis* **2.** *(raw material)* Rohstoff ['roːʃtɔf] der <-(e)s, -e> ◊ *Rohstoffe wie Öl und Eisenerz* **3.** *(fig) (important or necessary thing)* Ressource [rɛˈsʊʳsə] die <-, -n> ◊ *Wissen ist unsere wichtigste Ressource.*

common [adj] **1.** *(widely used or practiced)* gängig ['gɛnɪç] ◊ *Wir akzeptieren alle gängigen Kreditkarten.* ♦ *Welche Arbeitszeiten sind in diesem Beruf gängig?* **2.** *(widespread)* häufig ['hɔɡfɪç] ◊ *eine häufige Krankheit* ♦ *Ist diese Erscheinung häufig?* **3.** *(shared)* gemeinsam [gəˈmaɛnzaːm] *no comp/superl ◊ eine gemeinsame Sprache sprechen ♦ Dieses Merkmal ist allen ihren Produkten gemeinsam. ♦ Sie haben ein gemeinsames Konto.* the common good das Gemeinwohl [das gəˈmaɛnvoːl] <-(e)s> *no pl* **4.** *(ordinary)* gemein [gəˈmaɛn] *no comp/superl, only before ns (tech, also oldf) ◊ das gemeine Volk ♦ der gemeine Rabe* **5.** *(vulgar)* gewöhnlich [gəˈvøːnlɪç] *(outd) ◊ eine gewöhnliche Ausdrucksweise ♦ Ich halte sie für ziemlich gewöhnlich.*

commonly [adv] allgemein [algəˈmaɛn] *no comp/ superl ◊ Vitamin D, allgemein bekannt als das „Sonnenschein-Vitamin"*

commonplace [adj] alltäglich [alˈtɛːklɪç] ◊ *eine alltägliche Erscheinung* ♦ *Konflikte sind inzwischen alltäglich geworden.*

Commons [noun] the (House of) Commons POL das britische Unterhaus [das ˌbrɪːtɪʃə ˈʊntɐhaʊs] <-es> *no pl ◊ der Vorsitzende des britischen Unterhauses*

commonwealth [noun] Commonwealth ['kɔmənvɛlθ] das <-> *no pl*

communal [adj] **1.** *(shared)* gemeinsam [gəˈmaɛnzaːm] *no comp/superl ◊ Jeweils vier Studentenzimmer haben eine gemeinsame Küche.* communal aerial Gemeinschaftsantenne [gəˈmaɛnʃafts|anˌtɛnə] die <-, -n> **2.** *(relating to a community)* kommunal [kɔmuˈnaːl] *no comp/superl ◊ die kommunale Wasserversorgung*

communicate [verb] **1.** *(make yourself understood)* sich verständigen [fɛˈʃtɛndɪgn̩] <verständigt sich, verständigte sich, hat sich verständigt> ◊ *sich ohne Worte verständigen* ♦ *Sie konnten sich mit den Engländern verständigen.* **2.** *(tell sb sth)* communicate sth to sb jdm etw. mitteilen ['mɪttaɛlən] +haben ◊ *Es wurde ihnen schriftlich mitgeteilt.* **3.** *(rooms)* miteinander verbunden sein [mɪt|aɛnandɐ fɛˈbʊndn̩ zaɛn] +sein ◊ *Küche und Esszimmer sind miteinander verbunden.*

communication [noun] **1.** *(by language, gestures etc.)* Kommunikation [kɔmunikaˈt͡si̯oːn] die <-> *no pl ◊ Die Kommunikation erfolgte über E-Mail und Telefon.* ♦ *nonverbale Kommunikation* He has no communication with the outside world. Er steht nicht mit der Außenwelt in Kontakt. They are in regular communication. Sie stehen in ständigem Kontakt. We still have no communication from him. Wir haben noch keine Nachricht von ihm. **2.** *(by technical means)* Übertragung [ybeˈtraːgʊŋ] die <-> *only pl ◊ die sichere Übertragung von Daten im Internet* **3.** *(for sending information)* communications Nachrichtentechnik ['naːxrɪçtn̩tɛçnɪk] die <-> sing

4. *(for transport)* Verkehrsweg [fɛ'keːɐ̯sveːk] der <-(e)s, -e> ◊ *gut ausgebaute Verkehrswege*

communicative [adj] mitteilsam ['mɪttaɪ̯lzaːm] ◊ *ein sehr mitteilsamer Mann*

Communion [noun] *(Protestant)* (Holy) Communion Abendmahl ['aːbm̩tmaːl] das <-(e)s> *no pl* ◊ *das Abendmahl empfangen; (Catholic)* Kommunion [kɔmu'njoːn] die <-> *no pl* ◊ *zur Kommunion gehen*

communism [noun] *(political theory)* Kommunismus [kɔmu'nɪsmʊs] der <-> *no pl*

communist[1] [noun] **1.** *(advocate of the political theory)* communist Kommunist [kɔmu'nɪst] der <-en, -en> ♀Kommunistin [kɔmu'nɪstɪn] die <-, -nen> **2.** *(party member)* Communist Kommunist [kɔmu'nɪst] der <-en, -en> ♀Kommunistin [kɔmu'nɪstɪn] die <-, -nen>

communist[2] [adj] kommunistisch [kɔmu'nɪstɪʃ] *no comp/superl* ◊ *einer kommunistischen Partei angehören* ♦ *als das Land noch kommunistisch war*

community [noun] **1.** *(of people, religion)* Gemeinde [gə'maɪ̯ndə] die <-, -n> ◊ *eine kleine, ländliche Gemeinde* ♦ *die jüdische Gemeinde Frankfurts* community member Gemeindemitglied [gə'maɪ̯ndəmɪtɡliːt] das <-(e)s, -er> community centre Gemeindezentrum [gə'maɪ̯ndətsɛntrʊm] das <-s, Gemeindezentren> **2.** *(group, feeling of belonging together)* Gemeinschaft [gə'maɪ̯nʃaft] die <-, -en> ◊ *Es gelang ihm nicht, sich in die Gemeinschaft der Klasse zu integrieren.* ♦ *die Gemeinschaft der Völker und Staaten* close-knit community enge Gemeinschaft; *(of monks)* Ordensgemeinschaft ['ɔrdn̩sɡəmaɪ̯nʃaft] ◊ *einer Ordensgemeinschaft angehören* sense of community Gemeinschaftssinn [gə'maɪ̯nʃaftsˌzɪn] der <-(e)s> *no pl* ethnic community Bevölkerungsgruppe [bə'fœlkərʊŋsɡrʊpə] die <-, -n> **3.** *(society)* the community die Gesellschaft [diː gə'zɛlʃaft] die <-, -en> ◊ *etw. für die Gesellschaft tun*

◉ the international community die Völkergemeinschaft

commute [verb] **1.** *(travel)* pendeln ['pɛndl̩n] +sein ◊ *zur Arbeit pendeln* **2.** LAW *(a sentence)* umwandeln ['ʊmvandl̩n] <wandelt um, wandelte um, hat umgewandelt> ◊ *Seine Freiheitsstrafe wurde in eine Geldstrafe umgewandelt.*

commuter [noun] Pendler ['pɛndlɐ] der <-s, -> ♀Pendlerin ['pɛndlərɪn] die <-, -nen> commuter train Pendlerzug ['pɛndlɐtsuːk] der <-(e)s, Pendlerzüge>

compact [adj] kompakt [kɔm'pakt] <kompakter, am kompaktesten> ◊ *Diese Kamera ist klein und kompakt.* ♦ *ein kompakter Text*

companion [noun] **1.** *(person with sb)* Begleiter [bə'ɡlaɪ̯tɐ] der <-s, -> ♀Begleiterin [bə'ɡlaɪ̯tərɪn] die <-, -nen> ◊ *Der Minister und seine Begleiter wurden herzlich begrüßt.* travelling companion Reisegefährte ['raɪ̯zəɡəfɛːɐ̯tə] der <-n, -n> ♀Reisegefährtin ['raɪ̯zəɡəfɛːɐ̯tɪn] die <-, -nen> ◊ *Er verabschiedete sich von seinem Reisegefährten.; (friend)* Freund [frɔɪ̯nt] der <-(e)s, -e> ♀Freundin ['frɔɪ̯ndɪn] die <-, -nen> ◊ *Der Hund war ihm 12 Jahre lang ein treuer Freund.* **2.** *(one of a pair of objects)* Pendant [paŋ'daŋ] das <-s, -s> ◊ *Wo ist nur das Pendant zu diesem Ohrring?* **3.** *(handbook)* Handbuch ['hantbuːx] das <-(e)s, Handbücher> ◊ *„Handbuch für den Aquarienfreund"*

company [noun] **1.** ECON *(enterprise)* Firma ['fɪrma:] die <-, Firmen> ◊ *eine eigene Firma gründen* ♦ *Die in Lübeck ansässige Firma ist berühmt für ihr Marzipan.* company car Firmenwagen ['fɪrmənvaːgn̩] der <-s, -> company policy Geschäftspolitik [ɡə'ʃɛftspoliˌtiːk] die <-> *no pl* oil company Ölgesellschaft ['øːlɡəzɛlʃaft] die <-, -en> publishing company Verlag [fɛ'laːk] der <-(e)s, -e> **2.** *(community)* Gesellschaft [ɡə'zɛlʃaft] die <-> *no pl* ◊ *in guter/schlechter Gesellschaft* ♦ *Sie suchte verstärkt seine Gesellschaft.* keep sb company jdm Gesellschaft leisten **3.** *(of actors)* Schauspieltruppe ['ʃaʊ̯ʃpiːltrʊpə] die <-, -n> ◊ *Seit zwei Jahren zieht sie mit einer Schauspieltruppe umher.; (of soldiers)* Kompanie [kɔmpa'niː] die <-, -n> ◊ *Die Kompanie ist angetreten.; (of a ship)* Besatzung [bə'zatsʊŋ] die <-, -en> ◊ *Die Besatzung des Schiffes versammelte sich an Deck.*

◉ be in mixed company es sind Damen anwesend ◊ *Keine schmutzigen Witze, bitte! Es sind Damen anwesend.* in the company of others in Gegenwart anderer ◊ *In Gegenwart anderer ist er sehr unsicher.* part company **1.** *(end a relationship, go separate ways)* sich trennen **2.** *(disagree)* jds Ansicht nicht teilen

comparable(-ably) [adj, adv] vergleichbar [fɛ'ɡlaɪ̯çbaːɐ̯] *no comp/superl* ◊ *eine vergleichbare Stelle finden* ♦ *Ihre Leistung ist nicht mit der ihres Bruders vergleichbar.* ♦ *ein vergleichbar attraktives Angebot*

comparative[1] [noun] Komparativ ['kɔmparatiːf] der <-s, -e> ◊ *„Besser" ist der Komparativ von „gut".*

comparative[2] [adj] **1.** *(relative)* relativ [rela'tiːf] *no comp/superl* ◊ *Er lebt seit Jahren in relativem Luxus.* **2.** *(comparing things)* vergleichend [fɛ'ɡlaɪ̯çn̩t] *no comp/superl, only before ns* ◊ *eine vergleichende Analyse* **3.** GRAM comparative form Komparativ ['kɔmparatiːf] der <-s, -e> ◊ *„Größer" ist der Komparativ von „groß".*

comparatively [adv] verhältnismäßig [fɛ'hɛltnɪsmɛːsɪç] *no comp/superl* ◊ *verhältnismäßig viel verdienen*

compare [verb] vergleichen [fɛ'ɡlaɪ̯çn̩] <vergleicht, verglich, hat verglichen> ◊ *Ich habe die beiden Dateien verglichen.* compare sb/sth to sb/sth jdn/etw. mit jdm/etw. vergleichen ◊ *Du sollst mich nicht mit meiner Schwester vergleichen.* sb/sth compares to jd/etw. lässt sich vergleichen mit ◊ *Nichts lässt sich mit der Schönheit des Himalaja vergleichen.* compare and contrast vergleichend gegenüberstellen [fɛ.ɡlaɪ̯çn̩t ɡeːɡn̩'yːbɐʃtɛlən] +haben ◊ *In meiner Arbeit versuche ich, die beiden Kurzgeschichten vergleichend gegenüberzustellen.* compared to im Vergleich zu [ɪm fɛ'ɡlaɪ̯ç tsuː] ◊ *Im Vergleich zu ihm bist du ein Zwerg.*

comparison [noun] **1.** *(process of contrasting things, contrast)* Vergleich [fɛ'ɡlaɪ̯ç] der <-(e)s, -e> ◊ *Ein Vergleich der beiden Bilder hat ergeben, dass eines davon eine Fälschung ist.* draw a comparison between ... einen Vergleich zwischen ... [dat] anstellen ◊ *Vergleiche zwischen zwei Personen anstellen* in comparison with im Vergleich zu ◊ *Im Vergleich zu anderen Männern hilft Rolf viel im Haushalt.* **2.** GRAM Steigerung ['ʃtaɪ̯ɡərʊŋ] die <-, -en> ◊ *die Steigerung der Adjektive*

◉ stand comparison einem Vergleich standhalten

there's no comparison das ist gar kein Vergleich

compartment [noun] **1.** *(for keeping things)* Fach [fax] das <-(e)s, Fächer> ◊ *das Gemüse im untersten Fach des Kühlschranks aufbewahren* **2.** *(in a train)* Abteil [ap'taɛl] das <-(e)s, -e> ◊ *Darf ich mich zu Ihnen ins Abteil setzen?*

compass [noun] **1.** *(for orientation)* Kompass ['kɔmpas] der <-es, -e> ◊ *Die Nadel des Kompasses zeigt immer nach Norden.* **2.** *(pair of)* compasses Zirkel ['tsɪrkl] der <-s, -> ◊ *mit einem Zirkel einen Kreis zeichnen* **3.** *(form) (range)* Umfang ['ʊmfaŋ] der <-(e)s> no pl ◊ *eine Stimme von erstaunlichem Umfang*

compassionate(ly) [adj, adv] mitfühlend ['mɪtfyːlənt] ◊ *ein mitfühlender Blick* ♦ *Er ist immer sehr mitfühlend.* ♦ *„Der arme Junge", sagte sie mitfühlend.*

compatible [adj] **1.** *(ideas etc.)* vereinbar [fɛ'|aɛnbaːʳ] no comp/superl ◊ *Dieser Vorschlag ist nicht mit meinen Prinzipien vereinbar.* **2.** IT kompatibel [kɔmpa'tiːbl] no comp/superl <der/die/das kompatible …> ◊ *Ist das Programm mit Windows kompatibel?* **3.** *(people)* be compatible zueinander passen [tsu|aɛˌnandɐ 'pasn̩] +haben ◊ *Nach einigen Monaten erkannten die beiden, dass sie nicht zueinander passten.*

compel [verb] compel sb to do sth jdn zwingen, etw. zu tun ['tsvɪŋən … tsuː] <zwingt, zwang, hat gezwungen> ◊ *Man zwang das Kind, schwere Arbeiten zu verrichten.* feel compelled to do sth sich dazu gezwungen sehen, etw. zu tun ◊ *Er sah sich dazu gezwungen, seinen Sohn anzuzeigen.*

compensate for [verb] **1.** *(a loss etc.)* ersetzen [ɛ'zɛtsn̩] <ersetzt, ersetzte, hat ersetzt> ◊ *Und wer wird uns diesen Verlust ersetzen?; (a fault, failing)* kompensieren [kɔmpɛn'ziːrən] <kompensiert, kompensierte, hat kompensiert> ◊ *Er versucht, seine Angst mit Dreistigkeit zu kompensieren.* **2.** *(pay money)* compensate sb for sth jdm für etw. Schadenersatz leisten [fyːɐ … 'ʃaːdn̩ˌezats laɛstn̩] <leistet, leistete, hat geleistet> ◊ *Die Firma will allen von dem Unglück betroffenen Arbeitern Schadenersatz leisten.*

compensation [noun] **1.** *(damages)* Schadenersatz ['ʃaːdn̩ˌezats] der <-es> no pl ◊ *Er forderte Schadenersatz für die zerbrochene Fensterscheibe.* pay compensation jdm Schadenersatz leisten **2.** *(advantage among disadvantages)* Ausgleich ['aosglaɛç] der <-(e)s, -e> most sing ◊ *Die ruhige Lage des Hotels ist ein kleiner Ausgleich dafür, dass es so weit vom Strand entfernt ist.* **3.** *(for a failing)* Kompensation [kɔmpɛnza'tsjoːn] die <-, -en> ◊ *Seine Aggressivität scheint eine Kompensation seiner Unsicherheit zu sein.*

compete [verb] **1.** *(in business etc.)* konkurrieren [kɔnkʊ'riːrən] <konkurriert, konkurrierte, hat konkurriert> ◊ *Auf dem Markt konkurrieren viele derartige Produkte.* compete with sb/sth mit jdm/etw. konkurrieren ◊ *Mit einem Unternehmen dieser Größe können wir nicht konkurrieren.* compete for sth um etw. konkurrieren ◊ *Zwei Bewerber konkurrieren um den Posten.* **2.** SPORT compete in sth an etw. [dat] teilnehmen [an … ˌtaɛlneːmən] <nimmt teil, nahm teil, hat teilgenommen> ◊ *Er wird nächstes Jahr an der Weltmeisterschaft teilnehmen.* compete with sb gegen jdn antreten [geːgn̩ … ˌantreːtn̩] <tritt an, trat an, ist angetreten> ◊ *Sie tritt gegen die besten Schwimmerinnen der Welt an.* compete for sth um

etw. kämpfen [ʊm … ˌkɛmpfn̩] +haben ◊ *um die Meisterschaft kämpfen* ⊛ sb/sth cannot compete with sb/sth jd/etw. kann sich nicht mit jdm/etw. messen ◊ *Dieser Film kann sich nicht mit dem Original messen.*

competence [noun] **1.** *(capability, skill)* Kompetenz [kɔmpe'tɛnts] die <-, -en> ◊ *Sie bewies große Kompetenz im Umgang mit Kunden.* **2.** LAW Zuständigkeit ['tsuːʃtɛndɪçkaɛt] die <-, -en> ◊ *Das fällt in die Zuständigkeit eines anderen Gerichts.*

competent [adj] **1.** *(capable)* fähig ['fɛːɪç] ◊ *ein fähiger Nachfolger* ♦ *Ich halte ihn für ausgesprochen fähig.* competent to do sth fähig, etw. zu tun ◊ *Halten Sie ihn für fähig, die Leitung der Abteilung zu übernehmen?* **2.** *(adequate)* angemessen ['angəmɛsn̩] ◊ *ein angemessenes Ergebnis* **3.** LAW *(court)* zuständig ['tsuːʃtɛndɪç] no comp/superl ◊ *sich an das zuständige Gericht wenden; (evidence etc.)* zulässig ['tsuːlɛsɪç] no comp/superl ◊ *Diese Beweise sind vor Gericht nicht zulässig.*

competently [adv] kompetent [kɔmpe'tɛnt] <kompetenter, am kompetentesten> ◊ *eine Abteilung kompetent leiten*

competition [noun] **1.** *(in business)* Konkurrenz [kɔnkʊ'rɛnts] die <-> no pl ◊ *Unser Buch steht nicht in Konkurrenz zu Fachbüchern.* ♦ *Er ist keine Konkurrenz für mich.* competition between … Konkurrenz unter … [dat] ◊ *Was kann man gegen die Konkurrenz unter Geschwistern tun?* competition for Konkurrenz um ◊ *Die Konkurrenz um Arbeitsplätze nimmt zu.* be in competition with sb mit jdm konkurrieren [mɪt … kɔnkʊ'riːrən] <konkurriert, konkurrierte, hat konkurriert> **2.** *(contest)* Wettbewerb ['vɛtbəvɛʳp] der <-s, -e> ◊ *einen Wettbewerb veranstalten* ♦ *an einem Wettbewerb teilnehmen* **3.** *(person, company)* the competition die Konkurrenz [diː kɔnkʊ'rɛnts] <-> no pl ◊ *Die Konkurrenz schläft nicht!*

competitive [adj] **1.** *(person, attitude)* vom Konkurrenzdenken geprägt [fɔm kɔnkʊ'rɛntsdɛŋkn̩ gə'prɛːkt] ◊ *Der Weltmarkt ist stark vom Konkurrenzdenken geprägt.;* Konkurrenz… [kɔnkʊ'rɛnts] competitive spirit Konkurrenzgeist [kɔnkʊ'rɛntsgaɛst] der <-(e)s> no pl competitive advantage Konkurrenzvorteil [kɔnkʊ'rɛntsfoːgtaɛl] der <-(e)s, -e> **2.** *(price, business)* wettbewerbsfähig ['vɛtbəvɛʳpsfɛːɪç] ◊ *ein wettbewerbsfähiges Angebot/Produkt* ♦ *international wettbewerbsfähig bleiben*

competitor [noun] **1.** *(in business)* Konkurrent [kɔnkʊ'rɛnt] der <-en, -en> ♀Konkurrentin [kɔnkʊ'rɛntɪn] die <-, -nen> **2.** *(in sports, contest)* Teilnehmer ['taɛlneːmɐ] der <-s, -> ♀Teilnehmerin ['taɛlneːmərɪn] die <-, -nen> ◊ *Die Teilnehmer des Rennens laufen sich bereits warm.*

compile [verb] **1.** *(statistics)* erstellen [e'ʃtɛlən] <erstellt, erstellte, hat erstellt> ◊ *Diese Statistik wurde von einem renommierten Institut erstellt.* **2.** *(a menu, agenda)* zusammenstellen [tsu'zamənʃtɛlən] +haben ◊ *ein Geburtstagsmenü zusammenstellen* **3.** IT kompilieren [kɔmpi'liːrən] <kompiliert, kompilierte, hat kompiliert> ◊ *ein Programm kompilieren*

complain [verb] **1.** sich beklagen [bə'klaːgn̩] <beklagt sich, beklagte sich, hat sich beklagt> ◊ *„Wie geht es Ihnen?" — „Ach, ich kann mich nicht beklagen."* ♦ *Er beklagt sich dauernd, dass er keine Zeit hat.* ♦ *Er*

beklagte sich über die vielen Überstunden. **2.** *(make a formal complaint)* complain about sth sich über etw. acc beschweren [yːbɐ ... bəˈʃveːrən] <beschwert sich, beschwerte sich, hat sich beschwert> ◊ *Ich werde mich bei Ihrem Chef über Sie beschweren!*
• **complain of** phras v complain of sth über etw. acc klagen [yːbɐ ... ˌklaːɡn̩] +haben ◊ *Er klagt seit Tagen über heftige Kopfschmerzen.*

complaint noun **1.** *(statement)* Beschwerde [bəˈʃveːɡdə] die <-, -n> ◊ *Beschwerden über die Lärmbelästigung erhalten* ◆ *Ihre Beschwerde werden wir sorgfältig prüfen.; (empty verb)* make a complaint sich beschweren [bəˈʃveːrən] <beschwert sich, beschwerte sich, hat sich beschwert> ◊ *Ich möchte mich bei Ihnen beschweren.* **2.** *(illness)* Beschwerden [bəˈʃveːɡdn̩] die <-> pl ◊ *Seit wann haben Sie diese Beschwerde?* ◆ *über Beschwerden im Oberbauch klagen*

complement¹ noun **1.** *(completion, in grammar)* Ergänzung [ɛˈɡɛntsʊŋ] die <-, -en> ◊ *Dieses Bild ist die perfekte Ergänzung zu unseren Stilmöbeln.* ◆ *ein Subjekt mit mehreren Ergänzungen* **2.** *(on a ship)* Besatzung [bəˈzatsʊŋ] die <-, -en> have a full complement of sth komplett sein [kɔmˈplɛt t͡saɛn] +sein ◊ *Unser Team ist noch nicht komplett.*

complement² verb ergänzen [ɛˈɡɛntsn̩] <ergänzt, ergänzte, hat ergänzt>

complementary adj zusammengehörig [t͡suˈzamənɡəhøːrɪç] no comp/superl ◊ *zwei zusammengehörige Teile* be complementary sich ergänzen [ɛˈɡɛntsn̩] <ergänzen sich, ergänzten sich, haben sich ergänzt> ◊ *Ihre Interessen ergänzen sich.*

complete¹ adj **1.** *(adding emphasis, including everything or everyone)* komplett [kɔmˈplɛt] no comp/superl ◊ *Dieser Plan war kompletter Wahnsinn.* ◆ *Ist die Gruppe komplett?* ◆ *Die komplette Namensliste hing aus.* ◆ *Unsere Geräte werden komplett mit Zubehör und Montageanleitung geliefert.* complete and utter absolut [apzoˈluːt] no comp/superl, only before ns ◊ *Du bist ein absoluter Versager!* **2.** *(finished)* fertig [ˈfɛʁtɪç] no comp/superl ◊ *Sein neuer Roman ist fast fertig.* ◆ *Wenn der Bericht fertig ist, geben Sie ihn bitte meiner Sekretärin.* ⊚ the complete sb/sth der/die/das perfekte ... ◊ *Er ist der perfekte Gärtner.* ◆ *das perfekte Make-up für dunkle Haut*

complete² verb **1.** *(finish)* beenden [bəˈɛndn̩] <beendet, beendete, hat beendet> ◊ *Im Sommer beendet er sein Studium.* ◆ *Das Projekt wurde erfolgreich beendet.; (add missing parts)* ergänzen [ɛˈɡɛntsn̩] <ergänzt, ergänzte, hat ergänzt> ◊ *Ergänzen Sie das Sprichwort: Viele Köche verderben den ...* ◆ *Das vorhandene Warenangebot soll sinnvoll ergänzt werden.* **2.** *(a questionnaire etc.)* ausfüllen [ˈaʊsfʏlən] +haben ◊ *Bitte füllen Sie dieses Formular aus.*

completely adv völlig [ˈfœlɪç] no comp/superl ◊ *Das kam für mich völlig überraschend.* ◆ *Das hatte ich völlig vergessen.*

completion noun **1.** *(finishing)* Abschluss [ˈapʃlʊs] der <-es, Abschlüsse> ◊ *Nach dem Abschluss seiner Ausbildung ging er zur Bundeswehr.* upon completion zum Abschluss ◊ *Zum Abschluss des Kurses erhalten alle Teilnehmer ein Zertifikat.* nearing completion kurz vor dem Abschluss ◊ *Die Wiederaufbauarbeiten stehen kurz vor dem Abschluss.* **2.** *(of questionnaire)* Ausfüllen [ˈaʊsfʏlən] das <-s> no pl

Nach dem Ausfüllen des Formulars senden Sie dieses bitte umgehend an uns zurück.

complex¹ noun *(of buildings, psychological, complicated system)* Komplex [kɔmˈplɛks] der <-es, -e> ◊ *Das Kloster ist ein weiträumiger Komplex.* ◆ *Wenn du ständig an ihm herumnörgelst, bekommt er noch Komplexe.* have a complex about sth wegen etw. einen Komplex haben ◊ *Sie hat einen Komplex wegen ihrer großen Nase.* inferiority complex Minderwertigkeitskomplex [ˈmɪndɐveːɐtɪçkaɛtskɔmˌplɛks]

complex² adj **1.** *(complicated)* komplex [kɔmˈplɛks] <komplexer, am komplexesten> ◊ *Diese Aufgabe ist äußerst komplex.* ◆ *ein komplexer Charakter* **2.** GRAM complex sentence Satzgefüge [ˈzat͡sɡəfyːɡə] das <-s, ->

complexion noun Teint [tɛŋ] der <-s, -s> ◊ *Du hast einen schönen Teint.*

complexity noun Komplexität [kɔmplɛksiˈtɛːt] die <-> no pl

compliance noun **1.** *(obedience)* compliance with sth Einhalten ... gen [ˈaɛnhaltn̩] das <-s> no pl ◊ *für das Einhalten der Vorschriften sorgen* in compliance with gemäß [ɡəˈmɛːs] +dat ◊ *gemäß internationalem Recht* **2.** *(submissiveness)* Unterwürfigkeit [ˈʊntɐvʏʁfɪçkaɛt] die <-> no pl ◊ *Ihre Unterwürfigkeit den Vorgesetzten gegenüber geht mir auf die Nerven.*

complicate verb komplizieren [kɔmpliˈt͡siːrən] <kompliziert, komplizierte, hat kompliziert> ◊ *Wir sollten das Verfahren nicht unnötig komplizieren.* ◆ *Das kompliziert die Sache ein wenig.*

complicated → **complicate** adj **1.** *(difficult)* kompliziert [kɔmpliˈt͡siːɐt] <komplizierter, am kompliziertesten> ◊ *Er ist ein komplizierter Mensch.* ◆ *Die Rechenaufgabe war kompliziert.* **2.** *(complex)* komplex [kɔmˈplɛks] <komplexer, am komplexesten> ◊ *Das menschliche Gehirn ist ein äußerst komplexes Organ.* ◊ *Diese Vorgänge sind recht komplex.*

complication noun Komplikation [kɔmplikaˈt͡sjoːn] die <-, -en> ◊ *Daraus ergeben sich einige Komplikationen.* ◆ *Die Geburt verlief ohne Komplikationen.*

compliment¹ noun *(flattering words)* Kompliment [kɔmpliˈmɛnt] das <-(e)s, -e> ◊ *Kompliment an den Koch — das Lamm war vorzüglich!* pay sb a compliment jdm ein Kompliment machen ◊ *Das ist das schönste Kompliment, das man mir jemals gemacht hat.*

compliment² verb compliment sb (on sth) jdm (zu etw.) ein Kompliment machen [aɛn kɔmpliˈmɛnt maxn̩] +haben ◊ *Er machte ihr ein Kompliment zu ihrer Frisur.*

comply with verb comply with sth **1.** *(a condition, prerequisite etc.)* erfüllen [ɛˈfʏlən] <erfüllt, erfüllte, hat erfüllt> ◊ *Erfüllen Sie die Voraussetzungen für das Studium?* ◆ *Diese Vertragsbedingung wurde nicht erfüllt.* **2.** *(a request)* einer Sache dat nachkommen [ˈnaːxkɔmən] <kommt nach, kam nach, ist nachgekommen> *(lofty)* ◊ *Er ist unserer Bitte nicht nachgekommen.*

component noun *(part, ingredient)* Bestandteil [bəˈʃtanttaɛl] der <-(e)s, -e> ◊ *Praktische Übungen sind ein Bestandteil des Sprachunterrichts.* ◆ *Das Brot enthält wertvolle pflanzliche Bestandteile.; (of a machine)* Teil [taɛl] das <-(e)s, -e> ◊ *Diese Maschine besteht aus 235 Teilen.*

compose verb **1.** *(a piece of music)* komponieren

[kɔmpoˈniːrən] <komponiert, komponierte, hat komponiert> ◊ *Dieses Lied hat er für seine Frau komponiert.; (a letter, poem)* verfassen [feˈfasn̩] <verfasst, verfasste, hat verfasst> ◊ *Wer hat dieses Gedicht verfasst?* **2.** *(form) (arrange)* arrangieren [araŋˈʒiːrən] <arrangiert, arrangierte, hat arrangiert> ◊ *Er versuchte, das Foto effektvoll zu arrangieren.* **3.** *(form) (constitute)* bilden [ˈbɪldn̩] <bildet, bildete, hat gebildet> ◊ *Subjekt und Prädikat bilden einen Satz.* be composed of sth aus etw. bestehen [aʊs ... bəˈʃteːən] <besteht, bestand, hat bestanden> ◊ *Wasser besteht aus Wasserstoff und Sauerstoff.* **4.** compose yourself sich sammeln [ˈzamɫn̩] <sammelt sich, sammelte sich, hat sich gesammelt> ◊ *Er versuchte, sich zu sammeln, und betrat das Büro.*

⊙ compose your thoughts Ordnung in seine Gedanken bringen

composed → compose [adj] gelassen [ɡəˈlasn̩] ◊ *Trotz des großen Drucks erschien sie sehr gelassen.* ◆ *ein gelassener Mann*

composer [noun] Komponist [kompoˈnɪst] der <–en, –en> ♀Komponistin [kompoˈnɪstɪn] die <–, –nen> ◊ *Mozart gehört zu den bekanntesten deutschen Komponisten.* ◆ *Wenn sie groß ist, möchte sie Komponistin werden.*

composition [noun] **1.** *(structure)* Zusammensetzung [tsuˈzamənzɛtsʊŋ] die <–, –en> ◊ *die chemische Zusammensetzung einer Substanz* ◆ *Ich bin mit der Zusammensetzung des Ausschusses nicht zufrieden.* **2.** *(in music, art)* Komposition [kompoziˈtsi̯oːn] die <–, –en> ◊ *Das ist eine wunderschöne Komposition.; (essay)* Aufsatz [ˈaʊfzats] der <–es, Aufsätze> ◊ *Schreibt bis morgen einen Aufsatz über dieses Thema!* **3.** *(of music)* Komponieren [kompoˈniːrən] das <–s> no pl ◊ *Das Komponieren des Stücks war nicht einfach für sie.; (of an essay, a poem)* Verfassen [feˈfasn̩] das <–s> no pl ◊ *Das Verfassen von Gedichten liegt ihm gar nicht.*

composure [noun] Beherrschung [bəˈhɛrʃʊŋ] die <–> no pl ◊ *Als der Hund auch noch die zweite Vase zerbrach, verlor sie die Beherrschung.*

compound¹ [noun] **1.** *(in chemistry)* Verbindung [feˈbɪndʊŋ] die <–, –en> ◊ *eine chemische Verbindung; (mixture: paste or lotion etc.)* Mischung [ˈmɪʃʊŋ] die <–, –en> **2.** *(with buildings)* Anlage [ˈanlaːɡə] die <–, –n> ◊ *Diese Anlage ist ausgesprochen kindgerecht.* **3.** GRAM Kompositum [kɔmˈpoːzitʊm] das <–s, Komposita> ◊ *„Winterpullover" ist ein Kompositum aus „Winter" und „Pullover".*

compound² [verb] **1.** *(aggravate)* verschlimmern [feˈʃlɪmɐn] <verschlimmert, verschlimmerte, hat verschlimmert> ◊ *Die starken Regenfälle verschlimmerten die Lage zusätzlich.* **2.** *(mix)* mischen [ˈmɪʃn̩] +haben ◊ *Wenn man diese beiden Substanzen mischt, entsteht eine explosive Flüssigkeit.* be compounded of sth aus etw. zusammensetzen [aʊs ... tsuˌzamənzɛtsn̩] +haben ◊ *Die Salbe setzt sich zusammen aus ...*

comprehend [verb] verstehen [feˈʃteːən] <versteht, verstand, hat verstanden> ◊ *Verstehst du, was das für mich bedeutet?* ◆ *einen mathematischen Zusammenhang verstehen* fully comprehend etw. gut verstehen

comprehensible [adj] verständlich [feˈʃtɛntlɪç] ◊ *Diese Technik ist für jedermann verständlich.* ◆ *ein*

verständliches Verhalten

comprehension [noun] **1.** *(ability to understand)* Verständnis [feˈʃtɛntnɪs] das <–ses> no pl ◊ *Die Anmerkungen sollen dem Leser das Verständnis des Textes erleichtern.; (knowledge, idea)* Vorstellung [ˈfoːɐ̯ʃtɛlʊŋ] die <–, –en> ◊ *Sie haben keine Vorstellung davon, was diese Menschen erdulden mussten.* without comprehension verständnislos [feˈʃtɛntnɪsloːs] <verständnisloser, am verständnislosesten> ◊ *Sie sah ihn verständnislos an.* be beyond sb's comprehension jdm unbegreiflich sein [ˈʊnbəɡraɛ̯flɪç zaɛ̯n] +sein ◊ *Es ist mir unbegreiflich, wie Menschen sich so etwas antun können.* **2.** SCHOOL reading comprehension Leseverstehen [ˈleːzəfeʃteːən] das <–s> no pl listening comprehension Hörverstehen [ˈhøːɐ̯feʃteːən] das <–s> no pl

comprehensive(ly) [adj, adv] **1.** *(extensive)* umfassend [ʊmˈfasn̩t] ◊ *Sein Wissen ist umfassend und fundiert.* ◆ *ein umfassendes Angebot an Spielwaren* ◆ umfassend über etw. [acc] berichten **2.** SCHOOL *(in the UK)* comprehensive school Gesamtschule [ɡəˈzamtʃuːlə] die <–, –n> **3.** comprehensive insurance Vollkaskoversicherung [ˈfɔlkaskofeˌzɪçərʊŋ] die <–, –en>

comprise [verb] *(consist of)* umfassen [ʊmˈfasn̩] <umfasst, umfasste, hat umfasst> ◊ *Die Wohnung umfasst drei Zimmer, eine Küche und zwei Bäder.; (form)* bilden [ˈbɪldn̩] <bildet, bildete, hat gebildet> ◊ *Frauen bilden einen hohen Anteil der Teilzeitarbeitenden.* be comprised of sth sich aus etw. zusammensetzen [aʊs ... tsuˌzamənzɛtsn̩] +haben ◊ *Die Bevölkerung des Landes setzt sich überwiegend aus Einwanderern zusammen.*

compromise¹ [noun] Kompromiss [kɔmproˈmɪs] der <–es, –e> ◊ *ein Kompromiss zwischen Arbeitgebern und Arbeitnehmern* reach a compromise einen Kompromiss schließen make a compromise Kompromisse machen compromise solution Kompromisslösung [kɔmproˈmɪsløːzʊŋ] die <–, –en>

compromise² [verb] **1.** *(make concessions)* compromise (on sth) einen Kompromiss (über etw. [acc]) schließen [aɛ̯nən kɔmproˈmɪs ʃliːsn̩] <schließt, schloss, hat geschlossen> ◊ *Am Ende schlossen sie einen Kompromiss über den Preis des Wagens.* **2.** *(imperil)* gefährden [ɡəˈfɛːɐ̯dn̩] <gefährdet, gefährdete, hat gefährdet> ◊ *Ohne Ampel ist die Sicherheit unserer Kinder gefährdet.* **3.** *(sb's position, reputation)* kompromittieren [kɔmprɔmɪˈtiːrən] <kompromittiert, kompromittierte, hat kompromittiert> ◊ *Seine politischen Gegner versuchten ihn zu kompromittieren.* compromise yourself sich kompromittieren ◊ *Durch diese Lüge hat sie sich kompromittiert.; (principles, beliefs)* verraten [feˈraːtn̩] <verrät, verriet, hat verraten> ◊ *Mit einer solchen Entscheidung würde er seine Prinzipien verraten.*

compulsion [noun] Zwang [tsvaŋ] der <–(e)s, Zwänge> ◊ *Er verspürte einen starken Zwang, ihr seine Sorgen anzuvertrauen.* ◆ *der Zwang der Gesetze* under compulsion unter Zwang ◊ *einen Vertrag unter Zwang unterschreiben*

compulsory [adj] obligatorisch [ɔbliɡaˈtoːrɪʃ] no comp/superl ◊ *An vielen britischen Schulen sind Uniformen obligatorisch.* ◆ *obligatorische Vorlesungen* Education is compulsory. Es besteht allgemeine Schulpflicht. compulsory subject Pflichtfach [ˈpflɪçtfax] das <–(e)s, Pflichtfächer>

compute [verb] berechnen [bə'rɛçnən] <berechnet, berechnete, hat berechnet> ◊ *Er berechnete den Betrag, der für die Renovierung anfallen würde.*

computer [noun] Computer [kɔm'pju:tɐ] der <–s, –> ◊ *am Computer arbeiten* ♦ *Daten in den Computer eingeben* ♦ *Fahr jetzt den Computer runter und komm zum Essen!* by computer per Computer ◊ *Reservierungen sind nur per Computer möglich.*
⊙ on computer auf dem PC

computer science [noun] Informatik [ɪnfɔrˈmaːtɪk] die <–> *no pl*

computing [noun] Informatik [ɪnfɔrˈmaːtɪk] die <–> *no pl* ◊ *Er interessiert sich sehr für Informatik.* be in computing in der Computerbranche sein [ɪn deːɐ̯ kɔmˈpjuːtebranʃə zaːɛ̯n] +sein

con [noun] 1. *(fam) (deception)* Schwindel ['ʃvɪndl̩] der <–s> *no pl (fam)* ◊ *Das Ganze war nichts als Schwindel.* ♦ *Schließlich flog der ganze Schwindel auf.* 2. *(fam) (prisoner)* Knastbruder ['knastbruːdɐ] der <–s, Knastbrüder> *(fam)*

con artist [noun] Schwindler ['ʃvɪndlɐ] der <–s, –> ♀Schwindlerin ['ʃvɪndlərɪn] die <–, –nen> *(fam)*

conceal [verb] *(prevent from being seen or known)* verbergen [fɐ'bɛrɡn̩] <verbirgt, verbarg, hat verborgen> ◊ *Sie konnte ihre Bewunderung nicht verbergen.* ♦ *Der große Hut verbarg ihr Gesicht.; (keep secret)* conceal sth from sb jdm etw. verheimlichen [fɐ'haɛ̯mlɪçn̩] <verheimlicht, verheimlichte, hat verheimlicht> ◊ *Er verheimlichte ihr seinen wahren Namen.*

concede [verb] 1. *(admit)* zugeben ['tsuːɡeːbm̩] <gibt zu, gab zu, hat zugegeben> ◊ *Sie musste zugeben, dass er gute Arbeit geleistet hatte.* 2. *(surrender)* kapitulieren [kapitu'liːrən] <kapituliert, kapitulierte, hat kapituliert> ◊ *In der neunten Runde kapitulierte der Gegner.* concede defeat sich geschlagen geben [ɡəˈʃlaːɡn̩ ɡeːbm̩] <gibt sich, gab sich, hat sich … gegeben> 3. *(give sth as a right)* concede sth to sb jdm etw. einräumen ['aɛ̯nrɔʏmən] +haben ◊ *Er räumte mir das Recht ein, vorzeitig zu kündigen.; (give sth unwillingly)* concede sth to sb etw. an jdn abtreten [an … 'aptreːtn̩] <tritt ab, trat ab, hat abgetreten> ◊ *Gebiete an Nachbarstaaten abtreten müssen* 4. SPORT concede a goal ein Tor kassieren [aɛ̯n 'tɔːɐ̯ kasiːrən] <kassiert, kassierte, hat kassiert>

conceited [adj] eingebildet ['aɛ̯nɡəbɪldət] *(pej)* ◊ *ein eingebildeter Typ* ♦ *Sie ist furchtbar eingebildet.*

conceivable [adj] denkbar ['dɛŋkbaːr] *no comp/superl* ◊ *ein denkbarer Kompromiss* ♦ *Es ist denkbar, dass er den Zug nicht erwischt hat.*

conceive [verb] 1. *(an idea)* conceive (of) sth auf etw. [acc] kommen [aɔf … ˌkɔmən] +haben ◊ *Wer ist als Erster auf die Idee gekommen, Fleisch über dem Feuer zu braten?; (plan)* etw. planen ['plaːnən] +haben ◊ *Diese Anlagen sind vor allem für Familien mit Kindern geplant worden.* 2. *(imagine)* sich [dat] vorstellen ['foːɐ̯ʃtɛlən] +haben ◊ *Ich kann mir ein Leben auf dem Mond nicht vorstellen.; (understand)* not be able to conceive what/why etc. nicht begreifen können, was/warum etc. [nɪçt bə'ɡraɛ̯fn̩ kœnən vas/varʊm] <kann, konnte, hat können> ◊ *Ich kann nicht begreifen, warum er das getan hat.* conceive of doing sth daran denken, etw. zu tun [daːran 'dɛŋkn̩ … tsuː] <denkt, dachte, hat gedacht> ◊ *Er würde niemals daran denken, seine Frau zu verlassen.* 3. MED *(become pregnant)*

empfangen [ɛm'pfaŋən] <empfängt, empfing, hat empfangen> ◊ *eine Behandlung für Frauen, die nicht empfangen können*

concentrate [verb] concentrate sth on sth etw. auf etw. [acc] konzentrieren [aɔf … kɔntsɛn,triːrən] <konzentriert, konzentrierte, hat konzentriert> ◊ *Konzentrieren Sie alle Ressourcen auf dieses Projekt.* sb concentrates (on sth) jd konzentriert sich (auf etw. [acc]) ◊ *Es ist zu laut hier — ich kann mich nicht konzentrieren.* concentrate your efforts/attention on sth seine Bemühungen/Aufmerksamkeit auf etw. [acc] konzentrieren be concentrated somewhere sich irgendwo konzentrieren ◊ *Die Bevölkerung konzentriert sich in den großen Ballungsräumen.*

concentrated [adj] 1. *(undiluted)* konzentriert [kɔntsɛn'triːɐ̯t] <konzentrierter, am konzentriertesten> ◊ *eine konzentrierte Säure* 2. *(with determination)* angestrengt ['anɡəʃtrɛŋt] <angestrengter, am angestrengtesten> ◊ *einen angestrengten Versuch machen, etwas zu erreichen*

concentration [noun] Konzentration [kɔntsɛntra'tsi̯oːn] die <–, –en> ◊ *Diese Arbeit erfordert äußerste Konzentration.* ♦ *Im Wasser wurden Giftstoffe in hohen Konzentrationen gefunden.*

concept [noun] *(notion)* Begriff [bə'ɡrɪf] der <–(e)s, –e> ◊ *der traditionelle Begriff der Ehe* ♦ *Jeglicher Begriff von Wahrheit ist relativ.* have no concept of sth sich keinen Begriff von etw. machen ◊ *Du machst dir keinBegriff davon, wie schlimm das war!* basic concept Grundbegriff ['ɡrʊntbəɡrɪf] ◊ *Wir lernen zunächst die Grundbegriffe der Psychologie.; (plan)* Konzept [kɔn'tsɛpt] das <–(e)s, –e> ◊ *Auf der Tagung stellte er sein neues Konzept zur Verbesserung der Verkaufszahlen vor.*

conception [noun] 1. *(idea)* conception (of sth) Vorstellung (von etw.) ['foːɐ̯ʃtɛlʊŋ] die <–, –en> ◊ *die christliche Vorstellung vom Leben nach dem Tod* ♦ *Du hast keine Vorstellung davon, wie das Leben in den Slums abläuft.* 2. *(of a book, theatre play, software etc.)* conception (of sth) Konzeption (...) [gen] [kɔntsɛp'tsi̯oːn] die <–, –en> ◊ *Die Konzeption des Romans fiel ihr nicht schwer, doch das Schreiben dauerte Monate.* 3. *(of an organization)* conception (of sth) Gründung (... [gen] ['ɡrʏndʊŋ] die <–, –en> ◊ *die Gründung eines Chors/Vereins* 4. MED *(of a child)* Empfängnis [ɛm'pfɛŋnɪs] die <–> *no pl* ◊ *Die Pille soll eine Empfängnis verhindern.*

conceptual [adj] begrifflich [bə'ɡrɪflɪç] *no comp/superl, only before ns* ◊ *auf begriffliche Klarheit achten* ♦ *begriffliches Denken* conceptual art abstrakte Kunst [ap,straktə 'kʊnst] die <–> *no pl*

concern[1] [noun] 1. *(worry)* Besorgnis [bə'zɔrknɪs] die <–, –se> *most sing* ◊ *Er äußerte seine Besorgnis über ihren Gesundheitszustand.* ♦ *Mit Besorgnis sah er seinen Prüfungsergebnissen entgegen.* raise concerns seine Besorgnis ausdrücken cause concern besorgniserregend sein [bə'zɔrknɪs,ʔɛrɛɡnt zaɛ̯n] +sein ◊ *Die Lage ist nach wie vor besorgniserregend.* 2. *(sth important)* Anliegen ['anliːɡn̩] das <–s, –> ◊ *Es ist uns ein Anliegen, dass die Gäste zufrieden sind.* main/major concern Hauptanliegen ['haɔptˌanliːɡn̩] ◊ *Unser Hauptanliegen ist die Ernährung der Flüchtlinge.* 3. *(interest in sb's welfare)* Fürsorge ['fyːɐ̯zɔrɡə] die <–> *no pl* ◊ *die liebevolle Fürsorge der Eltern für ihr Kind* 4. *(responsibility)* sb's concern jds Angelegen-

heit ['angǝlǝ:gn̩haet] die <–, –en> ◊ *Das ist meine Angelegenheit.* What concern is it of yours? *Was geht Sie das an?* **5.** *(of importance)* of concern to sb für jdn von Bedeutung [fy:ɡ ... fɔn bǝ'dɔɡtʊn] ◊ *Die Sicherheit seines Arbeitsplatzes ist für ihn von großer Bedeutung.* **6.** ECON *(company)* Konzern [kɔn'tsɛʳn] der <–(e)s, –e> ◊ *Er arbeitet bei einem großen Konzern.*

concern² [verb] **1.** *(worry)* concern sb jdm Sorgen machen ['zɔʳɡn̩ maxn̩] +haben ◊ *Seine schulischen Leistungen machen mir Sorgen.* be concerned about sth sich [dat] um etw. Sorgen machen ◊ *Sie macht sich Sorgen um ihren kranken Vater.* **2.** *(be about)* concern sth von etw. handeln [fɔn ... handl̩n] +haben ◊ *Die Geschichte handelt von den Abenteuern eines kleinen Jungen.* be concerned with sth sich mit etw. befassen [mɪt ... bǝfasn̩] <befasst sich, befasste sich, hat sich befasst> ◊ *Der Artikel befasst sich mit den neuen Möglichkeiten der künstlichen Befruchtung.* **3.** *(involve)* betreffen [bǝ'trɛfn̩] <betrifft, betraf, hat betroffen> ◊ *Alle Termine, die das Studium betreffen, stehen am schwarzen Brett.* ♦ *Umweltschutz betrifft uns alle!* as far as ... is concerned was ... betrifft ◊ *Was die Finanzierung betrifft, so machen Sie sich mal keine Sorgen.* **4.** *(pay attention)* sb is concerned with sth etw. interessiert jdn [ɪntǝrɛ'si:ɡt] <interessierte, hat interessiert> ◊ *Die Sorgen ihres Sohnes interessieren sie nicht.* concern yourself with sth sich mit etw. befassen [mɪt ... bǝ,fasn̩] <befasst sich, befasste sich, hat sich befasst> ◊ *Ich habe im Moment leider keine Zeit, mich mit dieser Angelegenheit zu befassen.*

ⓔ as far as I'm concerned was mich betrifft ◊ *Also was mich betrifft, können sie den Spielplatz hier ruhig bauen.*

concerning [prep] bezüglich [bǝ'tsy:klɪç] sing ns without article or attribute are not declined after this prep, otherwise [+gen] *(form)* ◊ *Ich hätte da eine Frage bezüglich der Finanzierung.*

concert [noun] Konzert [kɔn'tsɛʳt] das <–(e)s, –e> ◊ *Heute gehe ich ins Konzert.* in concert live [laef] ◊ *Heute Abend in der Olympiahalle: Sting live!*

concerted [adj] gemeinsam [gǝ'maenza:m] no comp/ superl, only before ns ◊ *Durch unsere gemeinsamen Bemühungen haben wir viel erreicht.* take concerted action gemeinsam vorgehen ◊ *gemeinsam gegen das organisierte Verbrechen vorgehen*

concerto [noun] Konzert [kɔn'tsɛʳt] das <–(e)s, –e>

concession [noun] **1.** *(compromise)* Zugeständnis ['tsu:gǝʃtɛntnɪs] das <–ses, –se> ◊ *jdm ein Zuge-ständnis abringen* ♦ *bereit sein, Zugeständnisse zu*

machen a concession to sb/sth ein Zugeständnis an jdn/etw. ◊ *Dieser Vorschlag ist ein Zugeständnis an die Gewerkschaften.* **2.** ECON Konzession [kɔntsɛ'sjo:n] die <–, –en> ◊ *Haben Sie eine Konzession für den Ausschank von Alkohol?* **3.** *(reduction)* Ermäßigung [ɛ'mɛ:sɪgʊn] die <–, –en> ◊ *Gibt es Ermäßigungen für Schüler?* tax concessions Steuervergünstigungen ['ʃtɔɡǝfǝ,gynstɪgʊnǝn] die <–> pl

concise(ly) [adj, adv] prägnant [prɛg'nant] <prägnanter, am prägnantesten> ◊ *eine prägnante Schilderung der Lage* ♦ *Sein Stil ist sachlich und prägnant.* ♦ *prägnant ausgedrückt* concise dictionary Handwör-terbuch ['hantvœ'tebu:x] das <–(e)s, Handwörterbücher>

conclude [verb] **1.** *(infer)* folgern ['fɔlgǝn] +haben ◊ *Er folgert aus den Worten seines Vorgesetzten, dass er sich noch mehr anstrengen muss.* **2.** *(form) (end)* schließen ['ʃli:sn̩] <schließt, schloss, hat geschlossen> ◊ *Die Veranstaltung schloss mit einem Feuerwerk.* ♦ *Sie schloss ihre Rede mit den Worten: ...; (bring to an end)* abschließen ['apʃli:sn̩] <schließt ab, schloss ab, hat abgeschlossen> ◊ *eine Lektion abschließen* ♦ *Wann schließt er seine Studien ab?* **3.** *(form) (a contract, deal)* abschließen ['apʃli:sn̩] <schließt ab, schloss ab, hat abgeschlossen> ◊ *einen Vertrag mit jdm abschließen*

conclusion [noun] **1.** *(inference)* Schlussfolgerung ['ʃlusfɔlgǝrʊn] die <–, –en> come to a conclusion zu einer Schlussfolgerung gelangen ◊ *Sie gelangten zu der Schlussfolgerung, dass Reformen nötig sind.* draw a conclusion eine Schlussfolgerung ziehen ◊ *Sie zog eine überraschend positive Schlussfolgerung.* **2.** *(end, agreement)* Abschluss ['apʃlus] der <–es, Abschlüsse> ◊ *Ein Feuerwerk war der krönende Abschluss des Festes.* ♦ *der Abschluss eines Kaufvertrags* ♦ *sein Studium zum Abschluss bringen* ⓔ sth is a foregone conclusion etw. scheint unaus-weichlich jump to a conclusion einen voreiligen Schluss ziehen in conclusion abschließend ◊ *Abschließend möchte ich Ihnen noch einmal herzlich für Ihr Interesse danken.*

concrete¹ [noun] Beton [be'tɔn] der <–s> no pl

concrete² [adj] **1.** *(made of concrete)* Beton... [be'tɔn] concrete floor Betonboden [be'tɔnbo:dn̩] der <–s, Betonböden> **2.** *(definite, specific)* konkret [kɔn'kre:t] <konkreter, am konkretesten> ◊ *Können Sie dazu ein konkretes Beispiel nennen?* ♦ *Wir planen ein Konzert, aber das ist noch nicht konkret.*

concussion [noun] Gehirnerschütterung [gǝ'hɪʳn̩ɛʃtǝrʊn] die <–, –en>

condemn [verb] **1.** *(disapprove, convict)* verurteilen [fɛʳ'ʊʳtaelǝn] <verurteilt, verurteilte, hat verurteilt> ◊ *Er wurde zu zehn Jahren Haft verurteilt.* ♦ *Die Gipsver-bände an beiden Armen verurteilen ihn zur Untätig-keit.* condemn sb for doing sth jdn verurteilen, weil er etw. getan hat ◊ *Er verurteilt mich, weil ich ihn im Stich gelassen habe.* **2.** *(a building)* für abbruchreif erklären [fy:ɡ 'apbrʊxraef ɛklɛ:rǝn] <erklärt, erklärte, hat erklärt>

condense [verb] **1.** *(a text)* kürzen ['kyʳtsn̩] +haben ◊ *einen Artikel kürzen* **2.** *(gas)* kondensieren [kɔndɛn'zi:rǝn] <kondensiert, kondensierte, hat konden-siert> ◊ *Wasserdampf kondensiert an den kalten Fensterscheiben.*

condition [noun] **1.** *(state, health)* Zustand ['tsu:ʃtant]

der <-(e)s, Zustände> ◊ *Das Haus war in einem verwahrlosten Zustand.* ♦ *Der Zustand des Patienten hat sich verbessert.* physical condition körperliche Verfassung [ˌkœˈpɐlɪçə feˈfasʊŋ] die <-> no pl ◊ *Trotz seines Alters ist er in ausgezeichneter körperlicher Verfassung.* **2.** *(situation, environment)* conditions Verhältnisse [feˈhɛltnɪsə] die <-> pl ◊ *in erschreckenden Verhältnissen leben* ♦ *Sie ist mit den örtlichen Verhältnissen bestens vertraut.* under difficult conditions unter schwierigen Bedingungen [ʊntə ˌʃviːrɪgn bəˈdɪŋʊŋən] working conditions Arbeitsbedingungen [ˈarbaɛtsbəˌdɪŋʊŋən] die <-> pl living conditions Wohnverhältnisse [ˈvoːnfeˌhɛltnɪsə] die <-> pl weather conditions Wetterlage [ˈvɛtɛlaːgə] die <-> sg **3.** *(prerequisite)* Bedingung [bəˈdɪŋʊŋ] die <-, -en> ◊ *Welche Bedingungen stellen der Erpresser?* on condition that unter der Bedingung, dass ◊ *Unter der Bedingung, dass du vorsichtig fährst, kannst du mein Auto nehmen.* meet conditions Bedingungen erfüllen **4.** *(health problem)* Beschwerden [bəˈʃveːɐdn] die <-> pl ◊ *gesundheitliche Beschwerden* heart condition Herzbeschwerden [ˈhɛrtsbəʃveːɐdn]

conditional [adj] **1.** *(relative)* bedingt [bəˈdɪŋt] no comp/superl, only before ns ◊ *eine bedingte Genehmigung erteilen* sth is conditional on sb doing etw. gilt unter der Voraussetzung, dass jd etw. tut [gɪlt ʊntə deːɐ foˈraozɛtsʊŋ das] <gilt, galt, hat gegolten> ◊ *Das Stellenangebot gilt unter der Voraussetzung, dass Sie die Abschlussprüfung bestehen.* **2.** GRAM konditional [kɔnditsjoˈnaːl] no comp/superl ◊ *„Falls" ist eine konditionale Konjunktion.* conditional clause Konditionalsatz [kɔnditsjoˈnaːlzats] der <-(e)s, Konditionalsätze>

condom [noun] Kondom [kɔnˈdoːm] das or der <-s, -e>

conduct¹ [noun] **1.** *(behavio(u)r)* Verhalten [feˈhaltn] das <-s> no pl ◊ *ein tadelloses Verhalten an den Tag legen* **2.** *(management)* Führung [ˈfyːrʊŋ] die <-, -en> most sing conduct of war Kriegsführung [ˈkriːksfyːrʊŋ] conduct of a trial Prozessführung [proˈtsɛsfyːrʊŋ]

conduct² [verb] **1.** *(manage, guide)* führen [ˈfyːrən] +haben ◊ *die Geschäfte einer Firma führen* ♦ *ein Gespräch/Interview mit jdm führen* ♦ *Der Reiseleiter führte uns durch die Katakomben.; (an experiment, investigation)* durchführen [ˈdʊˤçfyːrən] +haben ◊ *Die Forscher führten ein Experiment an Affen durch.* **2.** conduct yourself sich verhalten [feˈhaltn] <verhält sich, verhielt sich, hat sich verhalten> ◊ *Hat sie sich der Situation angemessen verhalten?* **3.** *(electricity, heat)* leiten [ˈlaɛtn] <leitet, leitete, hat geleitet> ◊ *Metalle leiten Strom.* **4.** MUS dirigieren [diriˈgiːrən] <dirigiert, dirigierte, hat dirigiert> ◊ *ein Orchester dirigieren* ♦ *Er dirigierte mit Taktstock.*

conductor [noun] **1.** *(of an orchestra)* Dirigent [diriˈgɛnt] der <-en, -en> ♀Dirigentin [diriˈgɛntɪn] die <-, -nen> ◊ *Der Dirigent hob den Taktstock.* ♦ *Sie ist Dirigentin in der Staatsoper.* **2.** *(on a train etc.)* Schaffner [ˈʃafnɐ] der <-s, -> ♀Schaffnerin [ˈʃafnərɪn] die <-, -nen> ◊ *Marco ist Schaffner bei der Deutschen Bahn.* ♦ *Er zeigte der Schaffnerin die Fahrkarte.* **3.** *(of electricity, heat)* Leiter [ˈlaɛtə] der <-s, -> ◊ *Metalle sind gute Leiter.*

cone [noun] **1.** MATH Kegel [ˈkeːgl] der <-s, -> ◊ *das Volumen eines Kegels berechnen* **2.** *(roadworks)* traffic cone Pylon [pyˈloːn] der <-en, -en> **3.** *(for ice-cream)* Tüte [ˈtyːtə] die <-, -n> ◊ *Zwei Kugeln Vanilleeis in der Tüte, bitte!* **4.** BOT Zapfen [ˈtsapfn] der <-s, -> ◊ *die Zapfen von Kiefern, Fichten und Tannen*

confectioner [noun] **1.** *(job)* Konditor [kɔnˈdiːtoːɐ] der <-s, -en> ♀Konditorin [kɔndiˈtoːrɪn] die <-, -nen> ◊ *Der Konditor überzieht die Torte mit Schokoladenguss.* ♦ *Sie ist gelernte Konditorin.* **2.** *(shop)* confectioner's Konditorei [kɔndiˈtoːɐ] der <-s, -en>

confederation [noun] *(alliance)* Bündnis [ˈbʏntnɪs] das <-ses, -se> ◊ *Mitglied eines Bündnisses werden; (association, of states also)* Bund [bʊnt] der <-(e)s, Bünde> ◊ *ein Bund zwischen drei Staaten*

confer [verb] **1.** *(a title)* verleihen [feˈlaɛən] <verleiht, verlieh, hat verliehen> ◊ *Man verlieh ihm die Ehrendoktorwürde.; (power)* übertragen [ybeˈtraːgn] <überträgt, übertrug, hat übertragen> ◊ *jdm bestimmte Rechte übertragen* **2.** *(talk)* confer with sb sich mit jdm beraten [mɪt ... bəˌraːtn] <berät sich, beriet sich, hat sich beraten> ◊ *Der Angeklagte möchte sich noch einmal mit seinem Anwalt beraten.*

conference [noun] **1.** *(meeting)* Konferenz [kɔnfeˈrɛnts] die <-, -en> ◊ *eine Konferenz zum Thema „Erziehung und Gewalt"* peace conference Friedenskonferenz [ˈfriːdnskɔnfeˌrɛnts] **2.** SPORT *(in the US)* Liga [ˈliːgaː] die <-, Ligen> ◊ *In welcher Liga spielt die Mannschaft?*
ⓔ be in conference in einer Besprechung sein

confess [verb] **1.** *(a crime)* gestehen [gəˈʃteːən] <gesteht, gestand, hat gestanden> ◊ *Sie gestand, dass er in den Überfall verwickelt war.* ♦ *Sie gestand ihm ihren Seitensprung.* confess to doing sth gestehen, etw. getan zu haben ◊ *Er hat gestanden, sie ermordet zu haben.* **2.** *(a mistake, your ignorance)* bekennen [bəˈkɛnən] <bekennt, bekannte, hat bekannt> ◊ *Er bekannte seinen Irrtum.* ♦ *Sie bekannte öffentlich, dass sie sich falsch verhalten hatte.* confess to doing sth bekennen, etw. zu tun; bekennen, etw. zu haben ◊ *Sie bekannte, eine Vorliebe für alte Liebesfilme zu haben.* **3.** REL beichten [ˈbaɛçtn] <beichtet, beichtete, hat gebeichtet> ◊ *Er beichtete dem Priester seine Sünden.*
ⓔ I must confess ich muss zugeben ◊ *Ich muss zugeben, dass ich zu wenig Zeit mit meinen Kindern verbringe.*

confession [noun] **1.** *(of guilt, a crime)* Geständnis [gəˈʃtɛntnɪs] das <-ses, -se> ◊ *ein umfassendes Geständnis ablegen* **2.** *(of a mistake)* Eingeständnis [ˈaɛngəʃtɛntnɪs] das <-ses, -se> ◊ *das Eingeständnis eines Irrtums* ♦ *Ihr Schweigen wirkte wie ein Eingeständnis ihres Versagens.* I have to make a confession. Ich muss dir/Ihnen etwas gestehen. **3.** REL *(of sins)* Beichte [ˈbaɛçtə] die <-, -n> ◊ *zur Beichte gehen* ♦ *die Beichte hören*

confide [verb] **1.** *(a secret, sth valuable)* confide sth to sb('s care) jdm etw. anvertrauen [ˈanfetraoən] <vertraut an, vertraute an, hat anvertraut> ◊ *Sie vertraute ihm ihre Sorgen an.* ♦ *Darf ich Ihnen meinen Schmuck anvertrauen, solange wir verreist sind?* **2.** *(trust)* confide in sb jdm vertrauen [feˈtraoən] <vertraut, vertraute, hat vertraut> ◊ *Sie wusste nicht, ob sie ihm vertrauen konnte.*

confidence [noun] **1.** *(self-assurance)* Selbstvertrauen [ˈzɛlpstfetraoən] das <-s> no pl ◊ *Ihm fehlt das*

Selbstvertrauen, diese schwierige Aufgabe anzupacken. give sb confidence jdm Selbstvertrauen schenken **2.** *(reliance, trust)* Vertrauen [fɛ'traoən] das <–s> no pl ◊ *Das Vertrauen in die Medizin scheint in den letzten Jahren gewachsen zu sein.* lose confidence in sb/sth das Vertrauen in jdn/etw. verlieren have confidence in sb/sth jdm/einer Sache vertrauen [fɛ'traoən] <vertraut, vertraute, hat vertraut> ◊ *Vertrauen Sie diesem Bericht?* ✦ *Ich vertraue meinen Mitarbeitern völlig.* inspire confidence einen Vertrauen erweckenden Eindruck machen [aenən fɛ,traoən evek)dn̩ 'aendrʊk maxn̩] +haben with confidence mit Sicherheit [mɪt 'zɪçɛhaet] ◊ *Wir können mit Sicherheit sagen, dass diese Krankheit nicht ansteckend ist.* **3.** *(secret)* vertrauliche Mitteilung [fɛ,traolɪçə 'mɪttaelʊŋ] die <–, –en> in confidence im Vertrauen [ɪm fɛ'traoən] ◊ *Sie sagte mir im Vertrauen, dass sie bald kündigen wird.*

confidential(ly) [adj, adv] vertraulich [fɛ'traolɪç] ◊ *Die Sache ist streng vertraulich.* ✦ *ein vertrauliches Gespräch* ✦ *Bitte behandeln Sie diese Informationen vertraulich!* confidential secretary Privatsekretär [pri'va:tzekre,tɛ:g] der <–s, –e> ♀Privatsekretärin [pri'va:tzekre,tɛ:rɪn] die <–, –nen>

confident(ly) [adj, adv] **1.** *(self-assured)* selbstbewusst ['zɛlpstbəvʊst] <selbstbewusster, am selbstbewusstesten> ◊ *ein selbstbewusstes Lächeln* ✦ *Sie wirkt äußerst selbstbewusst.* ✦ *selbstbewusst auftreten* **2.** *(sure)* zuversichtlich ['tsu:fezɪçtlɪç] ◊ *Er ist zuversichtlich, dass sich die Situation bessern wird.* ✦ *Wir blicken zuversichtlich in die Zukunft.* be confident of sth von etw. überzeugt sein [fɔn ... ybe'tsɔøkt zaen] +sein ◊ *Er ist vom Erfolg seines Plans überzeugt.*

configuration [noun] **1.** *(of molecules, parts of a machine)* Anordnung ['anlɔ'dnʊŋ] die <–, –en> ◊ *die Anordnung der Moleküle; (of the economy or other systems)* Ausrichtung ['aosrɪçtʊŋ] die <–, –en> ◊ *von der Ausrichtung der Wirtschaft verursachte Umweltprobleme* **2.** ɪт Konfiguration [kɔnfigura'tsĭo:n] die <–, –en> ◊ *die Konfiguration eines Rechners ändern*

confine [verb] **1.** *(limit)* be confined to sth sich auf etw. [acc] beschränken [aof ... bə,rɛŋkn̩] <beschränkt sich, beschränkte sich, hat sich beschränkt> ◊ *Die Ansteckungsgefahr beschränkt sich auf bestimmte Risikogruppen.* confine sth to etw. auf etw. [acc] beschränken ◊ *Wir müssen die Diskussion auf die wesentlichen Punkte beschränken.* confine yourself to doing sth sich darauf beschränken, etw. zu tun ◊ *Ich werde mich darauf beschränken, die wichtigsten Aspekte zu nennen.* **2.** *(keep in)* confine sb/sth to sth jdn/etw. in etw. [acc] sperren [ɪn ... ʃpɛrən] +haben ◊ *einen Hund in einen Zwinger sperren; (illness)* confine sb to sth jdn an etw. [acc] fesseln [an ... fɛsln̩] +haben ◊ *Die Krankheit fesselte ihn für Wochen ans Bett.* **3.** *(prevent from spreading)* eindämmen ['aendɛmən] +haben ◊ *einen Brand eindämmen*

confined → **confine** [adj] *(space)* eng [ɛŋ] ◊ *Die räumlichen Verhältnisse sind sehr eng.* ✦ *Sie leben auf engem Raum zusammen.; (atmosphere)* beengend [bə'ɛŋənt] ◊ *Er empfand das Übernachten im Zelt als sehr beengend.*

confinement [noun] **1.** *(in prison)* Haft [haft] die <–>

no pl ◊ *aus der Haft entlassen werden; (of an animal)* Gefangenschaft [gə'faŋənʃaft] die <–, –en> most sing ◊ *In Gefangenschaft pflanzen sich diese Tiere nur selten fort.* **2.** *(oldf) (childbirth)* Entbindung [ɛnt'bɪndʊŋ] die <–, –en> ◊ *Während der Entbindung kam es zu Komplikationen.*

confirm [verb] **1.** *(prove the truth, assure)* bestätigen [bə'ʃtɛːtɪɡn̩] <bestätigt, bestätigte, hat bestätigt> ◊ *Ich kann bestätigen, dass er das gesagt hat.* ✦ *Neue Forschungsergebnisse bestätigen diese Theorie.* ✦ *jdn im Amt bestätigen* ✦ *Das Untersuchungsergebnis bestätigte ihn in seinem Glauben, dass er krank war.; (repeat that sth is your opinion, intention)* bekräftigen [bə'krɛftɪɡn̩] <bekräftigt, bekräftigte, hat bekräftigt> ◊ *seine Absicht/Meinung bekräftigen* **2.** REL *(a Protestant)* konfirmieren [kɔnfɪr'mi:rən] <konfirmiert, konfirmierte, hat konfirmiert> mostly passive ◊ *Sie wird nächsten Sonntag konfirmiert; (a Roman Catholic)* firmen ['fɪrmən] +haben; mostly passive ◊ *Er wird nächsten Monat gefirmt.*

confirmation [noun] **1.** *(proof, assurance)* Bestätigung [bə'ʃtɛːtɪɡʊŋ] die <–, –en> ◊ *Wir warten noch auf die Bestätigung unserer Theorie.* ✦ *Sie erhalten eine schriftliche Bestätigung Ihrer Bestellung.* ✦ *die Bestätigung des Vorsitzenden im Amt* **2.** REL *(of a Protestant)* Konfirmation [kɔnfɪrma'tsĭo:n] die <–, –en>; *(of a Roman Catholic)* Firmung ['fɪrmʊŋ] die <–, –en>

confiscate [verb] beschlagnahmen [bə'ʃla:kna:mən] <beschlagnahmt, beschlagnahmte, hat beschlagnahmt> ◊ *gestohlene Ware/Waffen beschlagnahmen* confiscate sth from sb jdm etw. abnehmen ['apne:mən] <nimmt ab, nahm ab, hat abgenommen> ◊ *Der Polizist nahm ihm das Messer ab.*

conflict[1] [noun] Konflikt [kɔn'flɪkt] der <–(e)s, –e> ◊ *Sie versuchten, den Konflikt durch Verhandlungen beizulegen.* ✦ *sich in einem inneren Konflikt befinden* be in conflict with sb mit jdm in Konflikt haben ◊ *Er hat einen Konflikt mit seinem Chef, weil er sich weigert, Überstunden zu machen.* come into conflict with sb mit jdm in Konflikt geraten ◊ *Die Forscher gerieten in Konflikt mit den Einheimischen.* conflict of interests Interessenkonflikt [ɪntə'rɛsnkɔn,flɪkt]

conflict[2] [verb] conflict with sth zu etw. im Widerspruch stehen [tsu: ... ɪm 'vi:dɛʃprox ʃte:ən] <steht, stand, hat gestanden> ◊ *Die beiden Theorien stehen im Widerspruch zueinander.* conflicting opinions/advice widersprüchliche Meinungen/Ratschläge [,vi:dɛʃprʏçlɪçə 'maenʊŋən/'ra:tʃlɛːgə]

conform [verb] **1.** *(comply with)* conform to sth einer Sache [dat] entsprechen [ɛnt'ʃprɛçn̩] <entspricht, entsprach, hat entsprochen> ◊ *Entspricht dieses Spielzeug den Sicherheitsvorschriften?* ✦ *Sie entspricht nicht der Vorstellung, die man von einer typischen Großmutter hat.* conform to a law/rule sich an ein Gesetz/eine Regel halten [an aen gə'zɛts/aenə 're:gl̩ haltn̩] <hält sich, hielt sich, hat sich gehalten> **2.** *(socially)* sich anpassen ['anpasn̩] +haben ◊ *Schon als Kind wollte er sich nicht anpassen.*

confront [verb] **1.** *(face)* be confronted by sb/sth sich jdm/einer Sache gegenübersehen [ge:ɡn̩'y:beze:ən] <sieht sich gegenüber, sah sich gegenüber, hat sich gegenübergesehen> ◊ *Plötzlich sah sie sich einem Tiger gegenüber.; (a problem, decision, fear)* sich einer Sache [dat] stellen ['ʃtɛlən] +haben ◊ *Man*

muss sich seinen Problemen stellen, um sie zu lösen. **2.** *(bring face to face with)* confront sb with sth jdn mit etw. konfrontieren [mɪt ... kɔnfrɔn‚tiːrən] <konfrontiert, konfrontierte, hat konfrontiert> ◊ *Als man den Verdächtigen mit den Beweisen konfrontierte, gab er auf und gestand.* be confronted with sth vor etw. ⸤dat⸥ stehen [foːɐ̯ ... ʃteːən] <steht, stand, hat gestanden> ◊ *Sie steht vor der größten Krise ihres Lebens.* the problem confronting sb das Problem, vor dem jd steht ◊ *Die Probleme, vor denen die Partei steht, werden nicht leicht zu lösen sein.*

confrontation ⸤noun⸥ Konfrontation [kɔnfrɔnta'tsi̯oːn] die <-, –en>

confuse ⸤verb⸥ **1.** *(puzzle)* verwirren [fɛ'vɪrən] <verwirrt, verwirrte, hat verwirrt> ◊ *Die Frage schien ihn zu verwirren.* **2.** *(a situation)* noch komplizierter machen [nɔx kɔmpli'tsiːɡtɐ maxn̩] +haben ◊ *Die zusätzlichen Beweise machen den Fall noch komplizierter.* **3.** *(mix up)* verwechseln [fɛ'vɛksl̩n] <verwechselt, verwechselte, hat verwechselt> ◊ *Ich glaube, ich habe die beiden Schalter verwechselt.*

confused(ly) ⸤adj, adv⸥ **1.** *(puzzled, disorientated)* verwirrt [fɛ'vɪɐ̯t] <verwirrter, am verwirrtesten> ◊ *jdm einen verwirrten Blick zuwerfen* ♦ *Völlig verwirrt sah sie ihn an.* ♦ *Der alte Mann schien ein wenig verwirrt zu sein.* **2.** *(not clear)* wirr [vɪɐ̯] ◊ *wirre Gedanken* ♦ *Die Lage ist wirr und unübersichtlich.* ♦ *wirr daherreden*

confusion ⸤noun⸥ **1.** *(bewilderment)* Verwirrung [fɛ'vɪrʊŋ] die <-, –en> ◊ *Es herrscht Verwirrung darüber, wer nun der neue Chef wird.* ♦ *Seine Bemerkung verursachte große Verwirrung.* in confusion verwirrt [fɛ'vɪɐ̯t] <verwirrter, am verwirrtesten> ◊ *Verwirrt blickte er sie an.* **2.** *(disorder)* Durcheinander [dʊrçlae'nandɐ] das <–s> no pl ◊ *Nach der Explosion herrschte in dem Kaufhaus völliges Durcheinander.* in all the confusion in dem allgemeinen Durcheinander **3.** *(mixing up)* Verwechslung [fɛ'vɛkslʊŋ] die <-, –en> ◊ *Ich glaube, hier liegt eine Verwechslung vor: Mein Name ist nicht Hofmann.*

congenital ⸤adj⸥ angeboren ['angəboːrən] no comp/ superl ◊ *Sein Herzfehler ist angeboren.* ♦ *ein angeborenes Leiden*

congested ⸤adj⸥ verstopft [fɛ'ʃtɔpft] <verstopfter, am verstopftesten> seldom comp/superl ◊ *Die Straßen nach Süden waren völlig verstopft.* ♦ *eine verstopfte Nase*

congratulate ⸤verb⸥ gratulieren [gratu'liːrən] <gratuliert, gratulierte, hat gratuliert> ◊ *Ich gratuliere!* congratulate sb on sth jdm zu etw. gratulieren

congratulation ⸤noun⸥ Glückwunsch ['glʏkvʊnʃ] der <–(e)s, Glückwünsche> ◊ letter of congratulation Glückwunschbrief ['glʏkvʊnʃbriːf] der <–(e)s, –e> ⊛ **congratulations (on sth)** herzlichen Glückwunsch (zu etw.) ◊ *Herzlichen Glückwünsch zum bestandenen Examen!*

congregation ⸤noun⸥ Gemeinde [gə'maɪndə] die <-, –n> ◊ *die jüdische Gemeinde Berlins*

congress ⸤noun⸥ **1.** *(meeting of experts, politicians etc.)* Kongress [kɔn'grɛs] der <–es, –e> ◊ *der Wiener Kongress* ♦ *der Kongress der Augenärzte; (of a political party)* Parteitag [pɑr'taetaːk] der <–(e)s, –e> **2.** *(US legislature)* the Congress der Kongress [kɔn'grɛs] <–es> no pl

conjugate ⸤verb⸥ konjugieren [kɔnju'giːrən] <konjugiert, konjugierte, hat konjugiert> ◊ *lateinische Verben*

konjugieren a verb conjugates ein Verb wird konjugiert

conjunction ⸤noun⸥ Konjunktion [kɔnjʊŋk'tsi̯oːn] die <-, –en> ◊ *Die Teilsätze sind durch eine Konjunktion verbunden.* ⊛ **in conjunction with** in Verbindung mit ◊ *Qualität in Verbindung mit einem guten Preis*

conjure up ⸤verb⸥ **1.** *(produce by magic)* herbeizaubern [he'baetsaobən] +haben ◊ *Die Eingeborenen glauben, dass der Schamane Regen herbeizaubern kann.* conjure up a meal ein Essen auf den Tisch zaubern [æn 'ɛsn̩ aɔf deːn ‚tɪʃ tsaobən] +haben **2.** *(a spirit, memories)* beschwören [bə'ʃvøːrən] <beschwört, beschwor, hat beschworen> ◊ *Dämonen beschwören* ♦ *Immer wieder beschwor er die alten Zeiten.*

connect ⸤verb⸥ **1.** connect sb/sth (with/to sb/sth) jdn/ etw. (mit jdm/etw.) verbinden [fɛ'bɪndn̩] <verbindet, verband, hat verbunden> ◊ *zwei Bretter mit einem Scharnier verbinden* ♦ *Der Eurotunnel verbindet die Britischen Inseln mit dem europäischen Kontinent.* ♦ *Eine besondere Liebe verbindet mich mit dieser Insel.* ♦ *Ich verbinde Sie mit dem zuständigen Sachbearbeiter.* connect two things zwei Dinge miteinander verbinden **2.** *(to a machine, the mains, the telephone network)* connect (sth to/with sth) (etw. an etw. ⸤acc⸥ anschließen ['anʃliːsn̩] <schließt an, schloss an, hat angeschlossen> ◊ *Die Waschmaschine muss erst angeschlossen werden.* ♦ *Ich schließe den Schlauch an den Wasserhahn an.* **3.** *(relate)* connect sb/sth to/with sth jdn/etw. mit etw. in Verbindung bringen [mɪt ... in fɛ‚bɪndʊŋ brɪŋən] <bringt, brachte, hat gebracht> ◊ *jdn mit einem Verbrechen in Verbindung bringen* ♦ *das Virus, das mit dieser Infektion in Verbindung gebracht wird* **4.** *(get on well)* connect (with sb) sich (mit jdm) verstehen [fɛ'ʃteːən] <versteht sich, verstand sich, hat sich verstanden> ◊ *Wir haben uns gleich verstanden.* ♦ *Wie verstehen Sie sich mit dem neuen Kollegen?*

connection ⸤noun⸥ **1.** *(link)* Verbindung [fɛ'bɪndʊŋ] die <-, –en> ◊ *Die Verbindung zwischen Stuttgart und Birmingham wurde in den Flugplan aufgenommen.* ♦ *Sie hat Verbindungen zu Terroristen.* ♦ *Kurz nachdem er den Hörer abgenommen hatte, wurde die Verbindung unterbrochen.* **2.** *(link between facts, events)* Zusammenhang ['tsu'zamənhaŋ] der <–(e)s, Zusammenhänge> ◊ *Stehen die zwei Vorfälle in einem Zusammenhang?* ♦ *Er wird im Zusammenhang mit einem Mord gesucht.* **3.** *(means of communication, transport etc.)* Anschluss ['anʃlʊs] der <–es, Anschlüsse> ◊ *ein analoger/digitaler Anschluss* ♦ *Ihr Anschluss ist ständig besetzt.* connection to sth Anschluss an etw. ⸤acc⸥ ◊ *In Nürnberg haben wir Anschluss an den ICE nach Köln.* ♦ *Das Haus hat keinen Anschluss an die Kanalisation.* **4.** *(relationship with a person)* Beziehung [bə'tsi̯ʊŋ] die <-, –en> ◊ *eine Stelle durch Beziehungen bekommen* trade connection Handelsbeziehung ['handl̩sbatsiːʊŋ]

conquer ⸤verb⸥ **1.** *(a country, person)* erobern [ɛ'oːbən] <erobert, eroberte, hat erobert> ◊ *Die Römer haben viele Länder erobert.* ♦ *jds Herz erobern* **2.** *(an enemy, a disease, an addiction, fear)* besiegen [bə'ziːgn̩] <besiegt, besiegte, hat besiegt> ◊ *Sie besiegten die feindlichen Truppen.* ♦ *den Krebs/ seine Ängste besiegen* **3.** *(a mountain)* bezwingen

A
B
C
D
E
F
G
H
I
J
K
L
M
N
O
P
Q
R
S
T
U
V
W
X
Y
Z

[bə'tsvɪŋən] <bezwingt, bezwang, hat bezwungen> ◊ *Messner hat den Mount Everest mehrmals bezwungen.*

conquest [noun] **1.** *(process, person)* Eroberung [eɪ'oːbərʊŋ] die <-, -en> ◊ *die Eroberung neuer Märkte* ✦ *Napoleons Eroberungen in Europa* ✦ *Zu seinen Eroberungen sollen viele Filmstars gehört haben.* **2.** *(of a mountain)* Bezwingung [bə'tsvɪŋʊŋ] die <-, -en> ◊ *die Bezwingung des Nanga Parbat*

conscience [noun] Gewissen [gə'vɪsn] das <-s, -> *most sing* ◊ *Kannst du das mit deinem Gewissen vereinbaren?* a clear/guilty conscience ein gutes/ schlechtes Gewissen in good conscience guten Gewissens ease your conscience sein Gewissen beruhigen

conscientious(ly) [adj, adv] gewissenhaft [gə'vɪsnhaft] <gewissenhafter, am gewissenhaftesten> ◊ *Man dankte ihm für seine gewissenhafte Arbeit.* ✦ *Sie ist in allem, was sie tut, äußerst gewissenhaft.* ✦ *Ich hatte mich gewissenhaft auf die Prüfung vorbereitet.*

conscious(ly) [adj, adv] **1.** *(aware, deliberate)* bewusst [bə'vʊst] <bewusster, am bewusstesten> ◊ *eine bewusste Anstrengung* ✦ *Wir alle sind bewusst oder unbewusst an der Umweltverschmutzung beteiligt.* be conscious of sth sich [dat] einer Sache [gen] bewusst sein be conscious that sich [dat] bewusst sein, dass **2.** *(be awake)* be conscious bei Bewusstsein sein [baɛ bə'vʊstzaɛn zaɛn] +sein ◊ *Die Patientin war bei Bewusstsein.*

consciousness [noun] Bewusstsein [bə'vʊstzaɛn] das <-s> *no pl* ◊ *Manche Drogen scheinen das Bewusstsein zu erweitern.* ✦ *das geschichtliche/nationale/politische Bewusstsein* ✦ *das Bewusstsein verlieren/wiedererlangen*

consensus [noun] Konsens [kɔn'zɛns] der <-es, -e> *most sing* ◊ *der sozialstaatliche Konsens* reach a consensus zu einem Konsens kommen by consensus übereinstimmend [ybeɪ'aɛnʃtɪmənt] *no comp/superl* ◊ *etw. übereinstimmend beschließen*

consent¹ [noun] Einverständnis ['aɛnfeɐʃtɛntnɪs] das <-ses, -se> *most sing* ◊ *Sie haben um unser Einverständnis gebeten.* ✦ *mit/ohne jds Einverständnis* by mutual consent in gegenseitigem Einverständnis give (your) consent to sth sein Einverständnis zu etw. geben ◊ *Dazu werde ich nie mein Einverständnis geben.*

⊛ by general consent **1.** *(with all votes)* einstimmig ◊ *Der Antrag wurde einstimmig angenommen.* **2.** *(wish)* auf allgemeinen Wunsch ◊ *Der Film wird auf allgemeinen Wunsch wiederholt.*

consent² [verb] einwilligen ['aɛnvɪlɪgŋ] +haben ◊ *Nur wenn der Patient eingewilligt hat, kann er operiert werden.* consent to sth in etw. [acc] einwilligen ◊ *Hat er in ein Treffen eingewilligt?* consent to do sth einwilligen, etw. zu tun

consequence [noun] Folge ['fɔlgə] die <-, -n> ◊ *Die Folgen sind nicht abzusehen.* ✦ *Der Unfall hatte katastrophale Folgen.* accept the consequences die Folgen tragen as a consequence infolgedessen [ɪnfɔlgə'dɛsn] ◊ *Ich hatte Hunger und war infolgedessen schlecht gelaunt.*

⊛ of consequence von Bedeutung ◊ *eine Angelegenheit von großer Bedeutung* of no consequence bedeutungslos

consequently [adv] infolgedessen [ɪnfɔlgə'dɛsn] ◊ *Er ist krank und kann infolgedessen nicht mitfahren.*

conservation [noun] **1.** *(of the environment)* Umweltschutz ['ʊmvɛltʃʊts] der <-es> *no pl* ◊ *Jeder kann etwas zum Umweltschutz beitragen.*; *(protection of plants, animals, habitats)* Naturschutz [na'tuːɐʃʊts] der <-(e)s> *no pl* **2.** *(of energy)* Erhaltung [ɛ'haltʊŋ] die <-, -en> ◊ *die Erhaltung fossiler Energien*; *(in the home)* energy conservation Energiesparen [enɛɐ'giːʃpaːrən] das <-s> *no pl*

conservative¹ [noun] **1.** Konservative [kɔnzɛɐ'vaːtiːvə] der/die <-n, -n> *but:* ein Konservativer/eine Konservative ◊ *Der Erzbischof gilt als Konservativer.* **2.** *(member of the Conservative Party)* Conservative Konservative [kɔnzɛɐ'vaːtiːvə] der/die <-n, die Konservativen> *but:* ein Konservativer/eine Konservative ◊ *Die Konservativen haben bei der Wahl wenig Chancen.*

conservative² [adj] **1.** *(person, views, policy, dress etc.)* konservativ [kɔnzɛɐ'vaːtiːf] ◊ *eine konservative Frisur* ✦ *Seine Ansichten sind ziemlich konservativ.* **2.** Conservative der Konservativen Partei [deːɐ kɔnzɛɐ'vaːtiːvn paɐ'taɛ] *postpositive* ◊ *ein Gremium der Konservativen Partei* the Conservative Party die Konservative Partei **3.** *(estimate)* vorsichtig ['foːɐzɪçtɪç] *mostly before ns* ◊ *eine vorsichtige Schätzung*

conservatively [adv] **1.** *(dress etc.)* konservativ [kɔnzɛɐ'vaːtiːf] ◊ *Sie kleidet sich konservativ.* **2.** *(estimate)* vorsichtig ['foːɐzɪçtɪç] ◊ *vorsichtig geschätzt*

consider [verb] **1.** *(ponder, reflect)* überlegen [ybe'leːgŋ] <überlegt, überlegte, hat überlegt> ◊ *Er überlegte einen Augenblick.* ✦ *Sie überlegte, ob sie das Angebot annehmen sollte.* sb considers doing sth jd überlegt sich [dat], ob er/sie etw. tun sollte [ybe'leːkt ... ɔp eːɐ/ziː ... zɔltə] <überlegte sich, hat sich überlegt> ◊ *Ich überlegte mir, ob ich ein Taxi rufen sollte.* **2.** *(the consequences, sb's reactions or feelings)* consider sb/sth an jdn/etw. denken [an ... ˌdɛŋkŋ] <denkt, dachte, hat gedacht> ◊ *an die gesundheitlichen Folgen denken* ✦ *Ich muss an meine Eltern denken.* consider that daran denken, dass ◊ *Sie hat gar nicht daran gedacht, dass sie ihn verletzen könnte.* **3.** *(a candidate, an offer etc.)* consider sth/sb etw./jdn in Betracht ziehen [ɪn bə'traxt tsiːən] <zieht, zog, hat gezogen> ◊ *eine Bewerbung in Betracht ziehen* ✦ *Welcher Schauspieler wurde für die Rolle in Betracht gezogen?* **4.** *(discuss)* consider sth über etw. [acc] beraten [yːbɐ ... bə,raːtn] <berät, beriet, hat beraten> ◊ *Sie berieten über das Problem.* **5.** *(regard sb/sth as)* consider sb/sth ... jdn/etw. für ... halten [fyːɐ ... haltn] <hält, hielt, hat gehalten> ◊ *sich für ein Genie halten* ✦ *jdn für größenwahnsinnig halten* ✦ *Ich halte eine Entschuldigung für unvermeidlich.*; *(more formal)* jdn/etw. als ... betrachten [als ... bə,traxtn] <betrachtet, betrachtete, hat betrachtet> ◊ *Betrachten Sie unser Gespräch als beendet.* ✦ *Ich betrachte ihn trotz allem noch als Freund.*

⊛ all things considered alles in allem

considerable(-ably) [adj, adv] erheblich [ɛ'heːplɪç] *seldom comp/superl* ◊ *Sie hat erhebliche Fortschritte gemacht.* ✦ *Der Vorteil eines solchen Vorgehens ist erheblich.* ✦ *Er hat sich in der Schule erheblich verbessert.*

considerate(ly) [adj, adv] rücksichtsvoll ['rʏkzɪçtsfɔl] ◊ *Er ist ihr gegenüber sehr rücksichtsvoll.* ✦ *Sie ist*

eine rücksichtsvolle Fahrerin. ♦ *jdn rücksichtsvoll behandeln*

consideration [noun] **1.** *(thought, reflection)* Überlegung [ybə'le:gʊŋ] die <-, –en> ◊ *Nach reiflicher/sorgfältiger Überlegung hat er gekündigt.* ♦ *alle Umstände in seine Überlegungen einbeziehen* ♦ *(taking into account)* Berücksichtigung [bə'rʏkzɪçtɪgʊŋ] die <-> no pl ◊ *mangelnde Berücksichtigung der Zielgruppe* in consideration of sth unter Berücksichtigung ... [gen] take into consideration berücksichtigen [bə'rʏkzɪçtɪgn̩] <berücksichtigt, berücksichtigte, hat berücksichtigt> ◊ *Bei der Erstellung des Textes ist Folgendes zu berücksichtigen:* ... **3.** *(an application, claim etc.)* give consideration to sth etw. prüfen ['pry:fn̩] +haben ◊ *Wir haben Ihre Bewerbung eingebend geprüft.* **4.** *(caring about others)* Rücksicht ['rʏkzɪçt] die <-, –en> *most sing* ◊ *Behandeln Sie den Patienten mit Rücksicht.* out of consideration for sb aus Rücksicht gegenüber jdm show consideration for sb/sth auf jdn/etw. Rücksicht nehmen

considering¹ [prep] angesichts ['angəzɪçts] [+gen] ◊ *Was muss angesichts dieser Lage getan werden?* ♦ *Die Bürger sind angesichts der vielen Gewalttaten alarmiert.*

considering² [conjunc] considering how/that/what ... wenn man bedenkt, wie/dass/was ... [vɛn man bə'dɛŋkt vi:/das/vas] ◊ *Das Projekt ist gut gelungen, wenn man bedenkt, wie wenig Zeit wir hatten.* ♦ *Wenn man bedenkt, dass sie erst sechs ist, drückt sie sich sehr gut aus.*

consignment [noun] Lieferung ['li:fərʊŋ] die <-, –en> ◊ *Die Lieferung brauchte drei Tage.* ♦ *Der Wert der Lieferung beträgt 1000 Euro.*

consistency [noun] **1.** *(of a substance)* Konsistenz [kɔnzɪs'tɛnts] die <-, –en> ◊ *eine weiche/harte Konsistenz haben* **2.** *(constancy, steadiness)* Beständigkeit [bə'ʃtɛndɪçkaet] die <-> no pl ◊ *Beständigkeit bei der Arbeit*

consistent(ly) [adj, adv] **1.** *(logical)* konsequent [kɔnzə'kvɛnt] <konsequenter, am konsequentesten> ◊ *eine konsequente Umsetzung des Konzepts* ♦ *Sie führten den Ausbau der Firma konsequent fort.* ♦ *Er ist in dieser Hinsicht nicht konsequent genug.* be consistent in doing sth etw. konsequent tun **2.** *(uniform)* einheitlich ['aenhaetlɪç] ◊ *eine einheitliche Geschäftspolitik* ♦ *etw. bundesweit einheitlich regeln; (correspond with facts, data)* be consistent with sth mit etw. übereinstimmen [mɪt ... ybəl̩,aenʃtɪmən] +haben ◊ *Die Vorhersage stimmt nicht mit den tatsächlichen Verkaufszahlen überein.; (with laws, rules and regulations etc.)* sich mit etw. vereinbaren lassen [fe̜|'aenba:rən ,lasn̩] *<lässt sich, ließ sich, hat sich ... lassen>* ◊ *Diese Lebensweise lässt sich mit meinem Glauben nicht vereinbaren.*

consist in [verb] bestehen in [bə'ʃte:ən ɪn] <besteht, bestand, hat bestanden> ◊ *Ihre Aufgabe besteht in der Analyse eines kurzen Textes.* consist in doing sth darin bestehen, etw. zu tun ◊ *Erfolg besteht darin, sich gut zu verkaufen.*

consist of [verb] bestehen aus [bə'ʃte:ən aɒs] <besteht, bestand, hat bestanden> ◊ *Der Test besteht aus drei Teilen.* consist of doing sth daraus bestehen, etw. zu tun ◊ *Das Leben besteht daraus, Erfahrungen zu machen.*

consolation [noun] Trost [tro:st] der <-(e)s> no pl ◊

Zum Trost gab sie dem Kind ein Bonbon. ♦ *Es war ihr ein Trost, dass er bei ihr war.* ♦ *Er suchte Trost bei seiner Mutter.*

console [verb] trösten ['trø:stn̩] <tröstet, tröstete, hat getröstet> ◊ *Diese Worte werden ihn wohl kaum trösten.* ♦ *Er nahm sie in den Arm und tröstete sie.*

consolidate [verb] **1.** *(strengthen)* festigen ['fɛstɪgn̩] +haben ◊ *Würde das Baby ihre Beziehung festigen können?* **2.** *(merge)* konsolidieren [kɔnzoli'di:rən] <konsolidiert, konsolidierte, hat konsolidiert> ◊ *Schulden konsolidieren* sth consolidates etw. konsolidiert sich ◊ *Firmen müssen sich konsolidieren, um zu überleben.*

consonant [noun] Konsonant [kɔnzo'nant] der <–en, –en>

consortium [noun] Konsortium [kɔn'zɔʳtsjʊm] das <–s, Konsortien> *(form)*

conspicuous(ly) [adj, adv] auffällig ['aɒffɛlɪç] ◊ *auffälliges Verhalten* ♦ *Auffällig war, dass beide aus derselben Stadt stammten.* ♦ *sich auffällig benehmen*

conspiracy [noun] Verschwörung [fe'ʃvø:rʊŋ] die <-, –en> ◊ *eine Verschwörung, jdn zu ermorden* conspiracy against sb/sth Verschwörung gegen jdn/etw. ◊ *die Verschwörung gegen Cäsar*

constable [noun] Wachtmeister ['vaxtmaestɐ] der <–s, –> ♀Wachtmeisterin ['vaxtmaestərɪn] die <-, –nen>

constant(ly) [adj, adv] *(continuous)* unaufhörlich ['ʊn|aɒfhø:ɐlɪç] no comp/superl; when used as an adj, only before ns ◊ *ein unaufhörlicher Kreislauf* ♦ *Die Zahl der Arbeitslosen wächst unaufhörlich.; (repeated)* ständig ['ʃtɛndɪç] no comp/superl; when used as an adj, only before ns ◊ *Diese ständigen Wiederholungen nerven mich.* ♦ *Das ändert sich ständig.* ♦ *Sie schimpft ständig über ihre Nachbarn.*

constellation [noun] *(of people, objects, concepts)* Konstellation [kɔnstɛla'tsjo:n] die <-, –en> *(lofty)* ◊ *Die Band spielte zum letzten Mal in dieser Konstellation.; (of stars also)* Sternbild ['ʃtɛ'nbɪlt] das <–(e)s, –er> ◊ *Sirius gehört zum Sternbild Großer Hund.*

constipation [noun] Verstopfung [fe'ʃtɔpfʊŋ] die <-, –en> ◊ *an (akuter/chronischer) Verstopfung leiden*

constituency [noun] **1.** *(area)* Wahlkreis ['va:lkraes] der <–es, –e> **2.** *(voters)* Wählerschaft ['vɛ:leʃaft] die <-, –en>

constituent [noun] **1.** *(voter)* Wähler ['vɛ:le] der <–s, –> ♀Wählerin ['vɛ:lərɪn] die <-, –nen> ◊ *der Abgeordnete und seine Wähler* **2.** *(component, part)* Bestandteil [bə'ʃtanttael] der <–(e)s, –e> ◊ *die Bestandteile der Milch*

constitute [verb] **1.** *(make up)* bilden ['bɪldn̩] <bildet, bildete, hat gebildet> ◊ *die Länder, die die OPEC bilden* **2.** *(be)* darstellen ['da:ʳʃtɛlən] +haben ◊ *Die Erderwärmung stellt eine Gefahr für die Menschen dar.* **3.** *(establish)* gründen ['grʏndn̩] <gründet, gründete, hat gegründet> ◊ *eine Organisation gründen*

constitution [noun] *(basic laws of a state, sb's physical condition)* Verfassung [fe'fasʊŋ] die <-, –en> ◊ *Das Grundgesetz ist die Verfassung Deutschlands.* ♦ *jds geistige/körperliche Verfassung*

constitutional(ly) [adj, adv] **1.** LAW, POL *(abiding by the constitution)* verfassungsgemäß [fe'fasʊŋsɡəmɛ:s] no comp/superl ◊ *Das Gesetz ist verfassungsgemäß.* ♦

A B C D E F G H I J K L M N O P Q R S T U V W X Y Z

eine verfassungsgemäße Rentenreform ◆ *verfassungsgemäß handeln* **2.** LAW, POL *(guaranteed by the constitution)* verfassungsmäßig [fɛˈfasʊŋsmɛːsɪç] *no comp/ superl; when used as an adj, mostly before ns* ◊ *verfassungsmäßige Rechte* ◆ *die verfassungsmäßig verankerte Trennung von Kirche und Staat* **3.** MED konstitutionell [kɔnstitutsi̯oˈnɛl] *no comp/superl, mostly before ns (tech)* ◊ *eine konstitutionelle Schwäche der Verdauungsorgane*

constrain [verb] **1.** *(sb's freedom, power)* einschränken [ˈaɛnʃrɛŋkn̩] *+haben* ◊ *Ohne Auto ist meine Bewegungsfreiheit eingeschränkt.* ◆ *ein Gesetz, das die Macht der Polizei einschränkt; (a development, movement)* hemmen [ˈhɛmən] *+haben* ◊ *eine Entwicklung hemmen* **2.** *(force sb)* constrain sb to do sth jdn zwingen, etw. zu tun [ˈtsvɪŋən ... tsuː] <zwingt, zwang, hat gezwungen> ◊ *Seine Krankheit zwang ihn, die Arbeit aufzugeben.* feel constrained to do sth sich gezwungen sehen, etw. zu tun ◊ *Die Regierung sah sich gezwungen zu intervenieren.*

constraint [noun] Zwang [tsvaŋ] der <-(e)s, Zwänge> ◊ *In der Gesellschaft ist man vielen Zwängen ausgesetzt.* constraint on sth Einschränkung ... [gen] [ˈaɛnʃrɛŋkʊŋ] die <-, -en> ◊ *die Einschränkung der Regierungsmacht*

construct [verb] **1.** *(a building, road, machine)* bauen [ˈbaʊ̯ən] *+haben* ◊ *eine Brücke/Straße bauen* ◆ *Wir haben ein neues Auto gebaut.* **2.** *(put together)* erstellen [ɛˈʃtɛlən] <erstellt, erstellte, hat erstellt> ◊ *eine Website erstellen* ◆ *Erstellen Sie einen Plan, wie das Projekt ablaufen soll.; (a sentence)* bilden [ˈbɪldn̩] <bildet, bildete, hat gebildet> ◊ *Bilden Sie einen Satz im Perfekt.* **3.** *(an argument, essay)* aufbauen [ˈaʊ̯fbaʊ̯ən] *+haben* ◊ *Die Argumentation ist überzeugend aufgebaut.* ◆ *Wie baue ich den Aufsatz am besten auf?* **4.** MATH *(draw)* konstruieren [kɔnstruˈiːrən] <konstruiert, konstruierte, hat konstruiert> ◊ *Konstruieren Sie ein Dreieck mit gleichen Seiten.*

construction [noun] **1.** *(of buildings, roads, machines)* Bau [baʊ̯] der <-(e)s> no pl ◊ *Der Bau des Hauses wird ein Jahr dauern.* ◆ *Die Firma hat mit dem Bau eines neuen Autos begonnen.* under construction im Bau ◊ *Die Brücke befindet sich noch im Bau.* **2.** *(industry)* Baugewerbe [ˈbaʊ̯ɡəvɛrbə] das <-s> no pl ◊ *Er arbeitet im Baugewerbe.; (in compound ns)* construction ... Bau... [baʊ̯] construction company Bauunternehmen [ˈbaʊ̯ʊntɐneːmən] das <-s, -> construction work Bauarbeit [ˈbaʊ̯arbaɛt] die <-, -en> most pl ◊ *Die Bauarbeiten sind noch nicht beendet.* **3.** *(building, structure)* Gebäude [ɡəˈbɔɪ̯də] das <-s, -> ◊ *Westminster Abbey ist ein beeindruckendes Gebäude.; (bridge, tunnel)* Konstruktion [kɔnstrʊkˈtsi̯oːn] die <-, -nen> ◊ *Diese Brücke ist eine geniale Konstruktion.* **4.** *(development)* Aufbau [ˈaʊ̯fbaʊ̯] der <-(e)s> no pl under construction im Aufbau ◊ *Unser Onlineangebot befindet sich noch im Aufbau.* the construction of sth der Aufbau ... [gen] ◊ *Der Aufbau der Webseite ist fast abgeschlossen.* **5.** LING Fügung [ˈfyːɡʊŋ] die <-, -en> ◊ *eine feste/ idiomatische/präpositionale Fügung*

constructive [adj] konstruktiv [kɔnstrʊkˈtiːf] ◊ *konstruktive Kritik* ◆ *Deine Bemerkungen sind nicht sehr konstruktiv.*

consulate [noun] Konsulat [kɔnzuˈlaːt] das <-(e)s, -e> ◊ *aufs Konsulat gehen*

consult [verb] **1.** *(seek sb's advice, look sth up)* consult sb/sth jdn/etw. zu Rate ziehen [tsuː ˈraːtə tsiːən] <zieht, zog, hat gezogen> *(lofty)* ◊ *einen Anwalt/einen Stadtplan zu Rate ziehen; (a doctor)* konsultieren [kɔnzʊlˈtiːrən] <konsultiert, konsultierte, hat konsultiert> **2.** *(discuss sth with sb)* consult with sb sich mit jdm beraten [mɪt ... bəˌraːtn̩] <berät sich, beriet sich, hat sich beraten> ◊ *Die Regierung beriet sich mit verschiedenen Experten.* consult sb on sth etw. mit jdm beraten ◊ *Ich würde diese Entscheidung gern mit Ihnen beraten.*

consultant [noun] **1.** *(expert who gives advice)* Berater [bəˈraːtɐ] der <-s, -> ♀Beraterin [bəˈraːtərɪn] die <-, -nen> ◊ *Er arbeitet als Berater für eine große Firma.* ◆ *Morgen kommt eine Beraterin für Gesundheit am Arbeitsplatz.* **2.** MED *(senior doctor)* Facharzt [ˈfaxˌʔaʁtst] der <-es, Fachärzte> ♀Fachärztin [ˈfaxˌʔɛʁtstɪn] die <-, -nen> ◊ *Er ist Facharzt für Urologie.* ◆ *Sollte man eine Fachärztin für Psychiatrie einschalten?*

consultation [noun] **1.** *(discussion)* Absprache [ˈapʃpraːxə] die <-, -n> most sing ◊ *nach Absprache mit der Geschäftsleitung entscheiden* ◆ *Die Reform wurde in Absprache mit der Opposition beschlossen.* **2.** *(meeting with an advisor)* Beratungsgespräch [bəˈraːtʊŋsɡəʃprɛːç] das <-(e)s, -e> ◊ *ein Beratungsgespräch mit seinem Anwalt/Steuerberater haben; (with a doctor)* Konsultation [kɔnzʊltaˈtsi̯oːn] die <-, -en> hold consultations with sb sich mit jdm beraten [mɪt ... bəˌraːtn̩] <berät sich, beriet sich, hat sich beraten> ◊ *Die Regierung berät sich mit der Opposition.*

consume [verb] **1.** *(use sth up)* verbrauchen [fɛˈbraʊ̯xn̩] <verbraucht, verbrauchte, hat verbraucht> ◊ *Wir verbrauchen zu viel Strom.* ◆ *Wie viel Benzin verbraucht dein Auto?* **2.** *(eat, drink)* konsumieren [kɔnzuˈmiːrən] <konsumiert, konsumierte, hat konsumiert> ◊ *Konsumieren die Deutschen zu viel Fett?* ◆ *Alkohol sollte man nur in Maßen konsumieren.* **3.** *(destroy by fire)* zerstören [tsɛˈʃtøːrən] <zerstört, zerstörte, hat zerstört> ◊ *Das Gebäude wurde vom Feuer zerstört.* ◉ be consumed by/with sth sich vor etw. [dat] verzehren ◊ *Ich verzehrte mich vor Sehnsucht nach dir.*

consumer [noun] Verbraucher [fɛˈbraʊ̯xɐ] der <-s, -> ♀Verbraucherin [fɛˈbraʊ̯xərɪn] die <-, -nen> ◊ *Informationen für Verbraucher* consumer protection Verbraucherschutz [fɛˈbraʊ̯xɐʃʊts] der <-es> no pl

consumption [noun] **1.** *(of resources, energy etc.)* Verbrauch [fɛˈbraʊ̯x] der <-(e)s> no pl ◊ *Nahrungsmittel, die zum sofortigen Verbrauch bestimmt sind* energy consumption Energieverbrauch [enɛɐˈɡiːfɛbraʊ̯x] **2.** *(of goods, alcohol, cigarettes, drugs)* Konsum [kɔnˈzuːm] der <-s> ◊ *der Konsum illegaler Drogen* alcohol consumption Alkoholkonsum [ˈalkohoːlkɔnˌzuːm]; *(of food)* Verzehr [fɛˈtseːɐ] der <-s> no pl ◊ *sth is unfit for human consumption etw. ist nicht zum Verzehr geeignet*

contact¹ [noun] Kontakt [kɔnˈtakt] der <-(e)s, -e> ◊ *Sie hat den Kontakt zu mir abgebrochen.* ◆ *Kontakt mit jdm/etw. haben* ◆ *in Kontakt mit etw. kommen* ◆ *Kontakte in einer Firma haben* ◆ *ein elektrischer Kontakt* on contact with sth bei Kontakt mit etw. be in contact with sb mit jdm in Kontakt stehen they

are in contact sie stehen in Kontakt miteinander
lose contact (with sb) den Kontakt (zu jdm)
verlieren get in contact with sb sich mit jdm in Verbindung setzen [mɪt ... ɪn fe'bɪndʊŋ zɛtsn̩] +haben ◊
Ich werde mich mit Ihnen in Verbindung setzen.
contact² [verb] contact sb sich mit jdm in Verbindung setzen [mɪt ... ɪn fe'bɪndʊŋ zɛtsn̩] +haben ◊
*Haben Sie sich schon mit der Polizei in Verbindung
gesetzt?* try to contact sb versuchen, jdn zu
erreichen [fe'zuːxn̩ ... tsuː ɛ'raeçn̩] <versucht,
versuchte, hat versucht> ◊ *Ich habe den ganzen Tag
versucht, dich zu erreichen.* sb can contact sb jd
kann jdn erreichen [kan ... ɛ'raeçn̩] <konnte, hat
können>
contain [verb] **1.** *(have as contents)* enthalten
[ɛnt'haltn̩] <enthält, enthielt, hat enthalten> ◊ *Das
Buch enthält zahlreiche Abbildungen.* ◆ *Einige Nahrungsmittel enthalten Farbstoffe.* **2.** *(be surrounded)*
be contained by sth von etw. umgeben sein
[fɔn ... ʊm‚geːbm̩ zaen] +sein ◊ *Das Schloss war von
einem Graben umgeben.* **3.** *(your feelings)* verbergen
[fe'bɛrgŋ̩] <verbirgt, verbarg, hat verborgen> ◊ *Er
verbarg seine Wut hinter einem Lächeln.* be able to
contain yourself an sich [acc] halten können
['an ... haltn̩ kœnən] <kann, konnte, hat können> ◊
*Ich konnte nicht mehr an mich halten und lachte
los.; (a fire, an epidemic, costs)* eindämmen
['aendɛman] +haben ◊ *Die Feuerwehr versuchte, den
Brand einzudämmen.*
container [noun] *(box, receptacle)* Behälter [bə'hɛltɐ]
der <-s, -> ◊ *einen Behälter mit Wasser füllen* ◆
einen Behälter verschließen; (for cargo) Container
[kɔn'teːnɐ] der <-s, -> ◊ *Container auf ein Schiff
laden*
contaminate [verb] *(pollute)* verschmutzen [fe'ʃmʊtsn̩]
<verschmutzt, verschmutzte, hat verschmutzt> ◊ *die
Luft/Umwelt verschmutzen* ◆ *Das Öl hat die Strände
verschmutzt.; (with chemicals, radioactivity, bacteria)*
verseuchen [fe'zɔøçn̩] <verseucht, verseuchte, hat
verseucht> ◊ *Das Trinkwasser wurde verseucht.; (with
a disease, bad influence)* anstecken ['anʃtɛkŋ̩] +haben
◊ *Ich möchte Sie nicht mit meiner Grippe anstecken.*
◆ *Hat er dich mit seinem Zynismus angesteckt?*
contemplate [verb] contemplate sth über etw. [acc]
nachdenken [yːbe ... ‚naːxdɛŋkŋ̩] <denkt nach, dachte
nach, hat nachgedacht> ◊ *Er dachte über einen
langen Urlaub nach.* ◆ *über den Tod nachdenken*
contemplate doing sth darüber nachdenken, etw.
zu tun ◊ *Sie denkt darüber nach, sich zu bewerben.*
The consequences would be too dreadful to contemplate. Die Folgen wären nicht auszudenken. sb
doesn't even contemplate sth der Gedanke an etw.
[acc] kommt jdm überhaupt nicht
[deːɐ gə‚daŋkə an ... 'kɔmt ... ybe‚haopt nɪçt]
<kommt, kam, ist gekommen> ◊ *Der Gedanke an ein
Scheitern kommt ihm überhaupt nicht.*
contemporary¹ [noun] **1.** *(person living at the same
time)* Zeitgenosse ['tsaetgənɔsə] der <-n, -n> ♀Zeit-
genossin ['tsaetgənɔsɪn] die <-, -nen> ◊ *Salieri war
ein Zeitgenosse Mozarts.* **2.** *(sb of the same age)*
Altersgenosse ['altɐsgənɔsə] der <-n, -n> ♀Altersge-
nossin ['altɐsgənɔsɪn] die <-, -nen> ◊ *meine Alters-
genossen im Sportverein*
contemporary² [adj] zeitgenössisch ['tsaetgənœsɪʃ]
no comp/superl ◊ *eitgenössische Musik* ◆ *Sein Design
ist zeitgenössisch.* be contemporary with sth aus der

gleichen Zeit sein wie etw. sein
[aos deːɐ 'glaeçn̩ ‚tsaet zaen viː] +sein ◊ *Das Bild ist
aus der gleichen Zeit wie das Porzellan.*
contempt [noun] **1.** *(lack of respect)* Verachtung
[fe'axtʊŋ] die <-> *no pl* with utter contempt voller
Verachtung have (nothing but) contempt for sb/sth
(nichts als) Verachtung für jdn/etw. empfinden
treat sb/sth with contempt jdn/etw. mit Verachtung
strafen hold in contempt verachten [fe'axtn̩]
<verachtet, verachtete, hat verachtet> ◊ *Ich verachte
dich für deine Hinterhältigkeit.* beneath contempt
verachtenswert [fe'axtn̩sveːɐt] <verachtenswerter, am
verachtenswertesten> ◊ *Diese Tat ist verachtenswert.*
2. *(disregard)* Missachtung ['mɪs‚axtʊŋ] die <-> *no
pl* ◊ *die Missachtung internationalen Rechts* ◆ *Die
Missachtung der Autorität des Chefs führt zu Spannungen.; (indifference)* contempt for sb/sth Gleichgültigkeit gegenüber jdm/etw.
['glaeçgʏltɪçkaet ge:gŋ̩ly:be] die <-> *no pl* ◊ *deine
Gleichgültigkeit gegenüber den Gefühlen anderer*
◉ contempt of court Ungebühr vor Gericht *(tech)*
contend [verb] **1.** *(claim)* contend (that) behaupten,
(dass) [ba'haoptn̩] <behauptet, behauptete, hat
behauptet> +subjunctive ◊ *Er behauptet, dass er
Erster geworden ist.* ◆ *Sie behauptete, sie habe von
dem Vorfall nichts gewusst.* **2.** *(compete)* contend
(with sb) for sth (mit jdm) um etw. kämpfen
[ʊm ... ‚kɛmpfn̩] +haben ◊ *Die Mannschaften
kämpfen um den Pokal.*
● contend with [phras v] contend with sth mit etw.
kämpfen [mɪt ...‚kɛmpfn̩] +haben ◊ *mit Schwierigkeiten kämpfen* ◆ *Auf dem Fahrrad hatte ich mit dem
Wind zu kämpfen.*
content¹ [noun] **1.** *(sth contained within sth)*
content(s) Inhalt ['ɪnhalt] der <-(e)s, -e> *most sing*
◊ *ein Artikel mit brisantem Inhalt* ◆ *Sie leerte den
Inhalt ihrer Tasche auf den Tisch.; (of a room,
building)* Inventar [ɪnvɛn'taːɐ] das <-s, -e>
2. *(amount, portion, percentage)* Gehalt [gə'halt] der
<-(e)s, -e> *most sing* ◊ *der Gehalt an Alkohol im
Wein* sugar content Zuckergehalt ['tsʊkɐgəhalt]
3. *(list in the front of a book)* contents Inhaltsverzeichnis ['ɪnhaltsfetsaeçnɪs] das <-ses, -se>
content² [adj] zufrieden [tsu'friːdn̩] ◊ *eine zufriedene
Frau* ◆ *Er wirkte recht zufrieden.* ◆ zufrieden mit
etw. sein
◉ not content with doing sth nicht genug damit,
dass jd etw. tut ◊ *Nicht genug damit, dass er zu viel
trinkt — jetzt nimmt er auch noch Drogen!*
contented(ly) [adj, adv] zufrieden [tsu'friːdn̩] ◊ *zufriedene Gesichter* ◆ *Sie sah recht zufrieden aus.* ◆
zufrieden lächeln
contest¹ [noun] Wettstreit ['vɛtʃtraet] der <-(e)s, -e>
most sing ◊ *ein Wettstreit der besten Sänger* ◆ *einen
Wettstreit zwischen Schülern und Lehrern veranstalten* the contest for sth der Wettstreit um etw. ◊ *der
Wettstreit um die Goldmedaille*
contest² [verb] **1.** *(dispute)* anfechten ['anfɛçtn̩] <ficht
an, focht an, hat angefochten> ◊ *ein Testament
anfechten* **2.** *(in a competition)* contest sth um etw.
kämpfen [ʊm ... ‚kɛmpfn̩] +haben ◊ *um den Weltmeis-
tertitel kämpfen* **3.** *(a job, position)* contest sth für
etw. kandidieren [fyːɐ ... kandi‚diːrən] <kandidiert,
kandidierte, hat kandidiert> ◊ *Sie kandidierte für das
Amt der Bürgermeisterin.*
contestant [noun] *(in a competition)* Teilnehmer

(right margin index letters) A B **C** D E F G H I J K L M N O P Q R S T U V W X Y Z

['tɛlneːmɐ] der <–s, –> ♀Teilnehmerin
['tɛlneːmɐrɪn] die <–, –nen> ◊ *Die Teilnehmer des Rennens laufen sich bereits warm.* contestant in sth Teilnehmer an etw. [dat]; *(on a quiz show, in an election)* Kandidat [kandi'daːt] der <–en, –en> ♀Kandidatin [kandi'daːtɪn] die <–, –nen>

context [noun] Zusammenhang [tsu'zamənhaŋ] der <–(e)s, Zusammenhänge> ◊ *der historische Zusammenhang* ♦ *Was bedeutet das Wort in diesem Zusammenhang?* in context im Zusammenhang ◊ *Man muss das im Zusammenhang sehen.*

continent [noun] Kontinent [kɔnti'nɛnt] der <–(e)s, –e> ◊ *der afrikanische Kontinent*
⊙ the Continent das europäische Festland

continental [adj] 1. *(belonging or relating to a continent)* kontinental [kɔntinɛn'taːl] no comp/superl ◊ *das kontinentale Europa* ♦ *Das Klima in Russland ist kontinental.* 2. *(in the UK: belonging or relating to the European mainland)* continental Europe das europäische Festland [das əɡro,pɛːʃə 'fɛstlant] <–(e)s> continental breakfast kontinentales Frühstück [kɔntinɛn,taːləs 'fryːʃtʏk] <–s, –e> ◊ *Das kontinentale Frühstück ist eher karg.*

continual(ly) [adj, adv] ständig ['ʃtɛndɪç] no comp/superl; *when used as an adj, only before ns* ◊ *ständige Konflikte zwischen den Parteimitgliedern* ♦ *Er belästigt uns ständig mit dummen Fragen.*

continuation [noun] 1. *(continued existence)* continuation of sth Fortbestand ... [gen] ['fɔrtbəʃtant] der <–> no pl ◊ *der Fortbestand des menschlichen Lebens* ♦ *Der Fortbestand ihrer Ehe ist gefährdet.* 2. *(after an interruption)* continuation of sth Fortsetzung ... [gen] ['fɔrtzɛtsʊŋ] die <–, –en> ◊ *die Fortsetzung der Friedensverhandlungen* 3. *(of a road, contract)* continuation (of sth) Verlängerung (... [gen]) [fɛ'lɛŋərʊŋ] die <–, –en> ◊ *die Verlängerung der Dorfstraße* ♦ *Eine Verlängerung der Versicherung um bis zu zwei Jahre ist möglich.*

continue [verb] 1. continue doing sth weiter... ['vaɛtɐ] continue reading weiterlesen ['vaɛtəleːzn̩] <liest weiter, las weiter, hat weitergelesen> ◊ *Heute Abend möchte ich „Harry Potter" weiterlesen.* ♦ *Kann ich jetzt weiterlesen?* continue working weiterarbeiten ['vaɛtɐˌarbaɛtn̩] <arbeitet weiter, arbeitete weiter, hat weitergearbeitet> ◊ *Ich muss noch an meinem Referat weiterarbeiten.* ♦ *Arbeiten Sie ruhig weiter!* 2. *(carry on speaking)* continue (sth) (mit etw.) fortfahren ['fɔrtfaːrən] <fährt fort, fuhr fort, ist fortgefahren> ◊ *Die Moderatorin fuhr mit dem Interview fort.* ♦ *Entschuldigen Sie die Unterbrechung. Bitte fahren Sie fort!* 3. *(endure)* andauern ['andaʊən] +haben ◊ *Die Kämpfe dauern an.* ♦ *Wie lange wird dieser Zustand noch andauern?* 4. *(text, film)* weitergehen ['vaɛtəɡeːən] <geht weiter, ging weiter, ist weitergegangen> ◊ *Der Artikel geht auf der nächsten Seite weiter.* ♦ *Nach der Pause geht der Film weiter.* 5. *(carry on walking)* weiterlaufen ['vaɛtəlaʊfn̩] <läuft weiter, lief weiter, ist weitergelaufen> ◊ *Wir liefen den Weg weiter.* ♦ *Mir ist kalt. Ich möchte weiterlaufen.* 6. *(path, road)* weiterführen ['vaɛtəfyːrən] +haben ◊ *Der Weg führt 500 m weiter.* ♦ *Hier führt die Straße nicht mehr weiter.*
⊙ to be continued Fortsetzung folgt

continued → continue [adj] kontinuierlich [kɔntinu'iːɡlɪç] no comp/superl, mostly before ns ◊ *Wir danken Ihnen für Ihre kontinuierliche Unterstüt-*

zung.

continuing [adj] anhaltend ['anhaltn̩t] no comp/superl, only before ns ◊ *anhaltende Gespräche* continuing education Weiterbildung ['vaɛtebɪldʊŋ] die <–, –en> ◊ *Die Firma ermöglicht eine berufliche Weiterbildung.*

continuity [noun] Kontinuität [kɔntinui'tɛːt] die <–> no pl *(lofty)* ◊ *die Kontinuität der Beziehungen*

continuous [adj] 1. *(development, movement, process)* stetig ['ʃteːtɪç] no comp/superl ◊ *eine stetige Entwicklung* ♦ *Der Rückgang war langsam, aber stetig.*; *(line)* durchgehend ['dʊʁçɡeːənt] no comp/superl ◊ *Ziehen Sie eine durchgehende Linie von A nach B.* 2. LING continuous form Verlaufsform [fɛ'laʊfsfɔˑm] die <–, –en> ◊ *ein Verb in der Verlaufsform* past continuous Verlaufsform des Präteritums [fɛˌlaʊfsfɔˑm dɛs prɛˈteːritʊms] present continuous Verlaufsform des Präsens [fɛˌlaʊfsfɔˑm dɛs 'prɛːzəns]

Standard German does not have a regular continuous form. The context usually determines whether an action or event is still in progress or not. If you would like to emphasize that an action is going on at the time of speaking or at a specific time in the past or future, you can use an adverb like *gerade*: *Stör mich jetzt nicht! Siehst du nicht, dass ich gerade arbeite?* — 'Don't bother me now! Can't you see I'm working?'

continuously [adv] stetig ['ʃteːtɪç] no comp/superl ◊ *die stetig wachsende Zahl der Arbeitslosen*; *(rain)* ununterbrochen ['ʊnlʊntebrɔxn̩] no comp/superl ◊ *Es regnete ununterbrochen.*

contraception [noun] Empfängnisverhütung [ɛmp'fɛŋnɪsfɛhyːtʊŋ] die <–> no pl ◊ *natürliche Empfängnisverhütung* ♦ *die sicherste Form der Empfängnisverhütung*

contraceptive [noun] Verhütungsmittel [fɛ'hyːtʊŋsmɪtl̩] das <–s, –> use a contraceptive verhüten [fɛ'hyːtn̩] <verhütet, verhütete, hat verhütet> ◊ *Wer kein Kind bekommen möchte, sollte verhüten.*

contract[1] [noun] Vertrag [fɛ'traːk] der <–(e)s, Verträge> ◊ *einen Vertrag mit jdm schließen* ♦ *Ich möchte von dem Vertrag zurücktreten.* ♦ *einen Vertrag aufsetzen/unterzeichnen/brechen* under a contract nach einem Vertrag einen Vertrag haben ◊ *Ich hatte einen guten Vertrag mit einer Werbeagentur.* be under contract to sb/sth bei jdm/etw. unter Vertrag sein ◊ *Die Sängerin ist bei einer Plattenfirma unter Vertrag.* award sb the contract for sth jdm den Zuschlag für etw. geben [deːn ˌtsuːʃlaːk fyːɛ ... ɡeːbm̩] <gibt, gab, hat gegeben> ◊ *Den Zuschlag für das Bauprojekt gab man einer englischen Firma.*
⊙ take out a contract on sb einen Killer auf jdn ansetzen

contract[2] [verb] 1. *(shrink)* sich zusammenziehen [tsu'zaməntsiːən] <zieht sich zusammen, zog sich zusammen, hat sich zusammengezogen> ◊ *Das Material zieht sich bei der Abkühlung zusammen.* 2. *(tighten)* sich spannen ['ʃpanən] +haben ◊ *Der Muskel spannt sich.* 3. *(a disease, illness)* contract sth sich [dat] etw. zuziehen ['tsuːtsiːən] <zieht sich zu, zog sich zu, hat sich zugezogen> ◊ *Ich habe mir eine Grippe zugezogen.* 4. *(in a formal agreement)* contract sb to do sth jdn beauftragen, etw. zu tun [bə'laʊftraːɡn̩ ... tsuː] <beauftragt, beauftragte, hat

beauftragt>

contraction [noun] **1.** MED *(when giving birth)* Wehe ['ve:ə] die <-, -n> ◊ *Die Wehen kommen jetzt alle 5 Minuten.* **2.** *(of muscles, words)* Kontraktion [kɔntrak'tsjo:n] die <-, -en> ◊ *die Kontraktionen des Herzmuskels* ♦ *„Im" ist eine Kontraktion von „in" und „dem".* **3.** *(shrinking)* Schrumpfung ['ʃrʊmpfʊŋ] die <-, -en> ◊ *eine demographische Schrumpfung*

contractor [noun] Auftragnehmer ['aʊftra:kne:mɐ] der <-s, -> ♀Auftragnehmerin ['aʊftra:kne:mərɪn] die <-, -nen>

contractual [adj] vertraglich [fɛ'tra:klɪç] *no comp/ superl, only before ns* ◊ *vertragliche Verpflichtungen*

contradict [verb] widersprechen [vi:dɐ'ʃprɛçn̩] <widerspricht, widersprach, hat widersprochen> ◊ *Musst du immer widersprechen?* contradict sb/sth jdm/einer Sache widersprechen ◊ *Seine Aussage widersprach der des anderen Zeugen.* contradict yourself sich [dat] selbst widersprechen ◊ *Jetzt hast du dir selbst widersprochen!*

contradiction [noun] Widerspruch ['vi:dɐʃprʊx] der <-(e)s, Widersprüche> ◊ *sich in Widersprüche verstricken* ♦ *ein Widerspruch zwischen Theorie und Praxis* a contradiction in terms ein Widerspruch in sich

contradictory [adj] widersprüchlich ['vi:dɐʃprʏçlɪç] ◊ *Die Aussage des Zeugen war unklar und widersprüchlich.* ♦ *widersprüchliche Meldungen*

contrary¹ [noun] Gegenteil ['ge:gn̩taɪl] das <-(e)s, -e> on the contrary im Gegenteil evidence to the contrary Gegenbeweise ['ge:gn̩bəvaɪzə] die <-> *pl* claims to the contrary gegenteilige Behauptungen [,ge:gn̩taɪlɪgə bə'haʊptʊŋən] die <-> *pl* ◊ *Trotz gegenteiliger Behauptungen gibt der Minister sein Amt nicht auf.* proof to the contrary (of sth) Gegenbeweis (zu etw.) ['ge:gn̩bəvaɪs] der <-es, -e> ◊ *Gibt es Gegenbeweise zu dieser These?*

contrary² [adj] **1.** *(opposing)* entgegengesetzt [ɛnt'ge:gn̩gəzɛtst] *no comp/superl* ◊ *Er vertritt eine entgegengesetzte Meinung.* be contrary to sth einer Sache [dat] widersprechen [vi:dɐ'ʃprɛçn̩] <widerspricht, widersprach, hat widersprochen> contrary to ... entgegen ... [ɛnt'ge:gn̩] [+dat] ◊ *Entgegen ihren Behauptungen hatte sie nicht studiert.* contrary to popular belief entgegen der landläufigen Meinung **2.** *(person)* widerspenstig ['vi:dɐʃpɛnstɪç] ◊ *ein widerspenstiger Mensch*

contrast¹ [noun] **1.** *(difference)* Gegensatz ['ge:gn̩zats] der <-es, Gegensätze> ◊ *der Gegensatz zwischen Stadt und Land* in contrast (to sb/sth) im Gegensatz (zu jdm/etw.) be/stand in contrast to sth im Gegensatz zu etw. stehen ◊ *Dieses Ergebnis steht im Gegensatz zu früheren Erkenntnissen.* **2.** *(between colours, on a monitor)* Kontrast [kɔn'trast] der <-(e)s, -e> ◊ *der Kontrast von Rot und Grün* ♦ *den Kontrast am Fernseher einstellen*

contrast² [verb] **1.** *(stand out)* contrast (with sth) (mit etw.) kontrastieren [kɔntras'ti:rən] <kontrastiert, kontrastierte, hat kontrastiert> ◊ *Die schwarze Kleidung kontrastiert mit seiner blassen Haut.* **2.** *(juxtapose)* contrast sb/sth with sb/sth jdn/etw. mit jdm/etw. vergleichen [mɪt ... fɐˌglaɪçn̩] <vergleicht, verglich, hat verglichen> ◊ *die Theorie mit der Praxis vergleichen* ♦ *Vergleichen Sie die beiden Modelle miteinander.*

contribute [verb] **1.** contribute (sth) to sth (etw.) zu

etw. beitragen [tsu: ... ˌbaɪtra:gn̩] <trägt bei, trug bei, hat beigetragen> ◊ *zum Erfolg beitragen* ♦ *Was möchten Sie zu diesem Thema beitragen?; (money)* contribute sth (to sth) etw. (für etw.) beisteuern ['baɪʃtɔyɐn] +haben ◊ *Wir sammeln für einen neuen PC für die Schule. Möchten Sie etwas beisteuern?* ♦ *Ich möchte gern 20 Euro für Vaters Geschenk beisteuern.; (to a charity)* contribute (sth to sth) (etw. für etw.) spenden ['ʃpɛndn̩] <spendet, spendete, hat gespendet> **2.** *(to a paper, magazine)* contribute (sth) to sth (etw.) für etw. schreiben [fy:ɐ̯ ... ˈʃraɪbn̩] <schreibt, schrieb, hat geschrieben> ◊ *Er schreibt für die Tageszeitung.* ♦ *Möchten Sie einen Artikel für unser Blatt schreiben?*

contribution [noun] **1.** *(payment, story, article)* Beitrag ['baɪtra:k] der <-(e)s, Beiträge> ◊ *ein wertvoller Beitrag* ♦ *Beiträge zur Rentenversicherung* ♦ *Hast du seinen Beitrag in der Zeitung gelesen?* make a contribution (to sth) einen Beitrag (zu etw.) leisten ◊ *Mit dieser Reform wurde ein Beitrag zum Schutz der Menschenrechte geleistet.* **2.** *(to charity)* Spende ['ʃpɛndə] die <-, -n> ◊ *eine Spende zugunsten Not leidender Kinder* ♦ *Eine kleine Spende, bitte!* make a contribution (to sth) (für etw.) spenden ['ʃpɛndn̩] <spendet, spendete, hat gespendet>

contrite(ly) [adj, adv] zerknirscht [tsɐ'knɪrʃt] <zerknirschter, am zerknirschtesten> ◊ *Der Angeklagte wirkte kleinlaut und zerknirscht.* ♦ *eine zerknirschte Sünderin* ♦ *Sichtlich zerknirscht hat sie um Entschuldigung.*

control¹ [noun] **1.** *(check, limitation, influence)* Kontrolle [kɔn'trɔlə] die <-, -n> ◊ *etw. unter Kontrolle bringen* ♦ *die Kontrolle der Inflation* ♦ *die Kontrolle an der Grenze* be under sb's control jds Kontrolle unterstehen be beyond sb's control sich jds Kontrolle entziehen gain control of sth die Kontrolle über etw. [acc] gewinnen get out of control außer Kontrolle geraten ◊ *Die Situation geriet völlig außer Kontrolle.* have control of sth be in control of sth die Kontrolle über etw. [acc] haben lose control (of sth) die Kontrolle (über etw. [acc]) verlieren take control of sth die Kontrolle über etw. [acc] übernehmen **2.** TECHN, IT *(on a machine, vehicle etc.)* control(s) Steuerung ['ʃtɔyərʊŋ] die <-, -en> ◊ *die Steuerung eines Prozesses* ♦ *Die Steuerung erfolgt über eine Tastatur.* ♦ *Die Steuerung des Flugzeugs versagte.* remote control Fernsteuerung ['fɛɐ̯nʃtɔyərʊŋ] die ⊛ lose control *(lose your temper)* die Beherrschung verlieren

control² [verb] **1.** *(have power over, restrain)* kontrollieren [kɔntro'li:rən] <kontrolliert, kontrollierte, hat kontrolliert> ◊ *Wer kontrolliert die Medien?* ♦ *Das Gebiet wird von Soldaten kontrolliert.; (your temper)* beherrschen [bə'hɛɐ̯ʃn̩] <beherrscht, beherrschte, hat beherrscht> ◊ *Beherrschen Sie Ihre Wut!* control yourself sich beherrschen ◊ *Er musste sich beherrschen, um nicht zu lachen.* **2.** *(regulate)* regulieren [regu'li:rən] <reguliert, regulierte, hat reguliert> ◊ *ein Thermostat, der die Wärme reguliert* control each other sich gegenseitig regulieren ◊ *Angebot und Nachfrage regulieren sich gegenseitig.* **3.** *(an appliance, a process, development)* steuern ['ʃtɔyɐn] +haben ◊ *Der Computer steuert den Prozessablauf.* ♦ *ein Gerät per Funk steuern* **4.** *(a pest)* bekämpfen [bə'kɛmpfn̩] <bekämpft, bekämpfte, hat bekämpft> ◊

Manche Schädlinge kann man auch ohne Gift bekämpfen.

controller [noun] **1.** *(director)* Leiter ['lᴂete] der <–s, –> ♀Leiterin ['lᴂtərɪn] die <–, –nen> **2.** FIN Controller [kɔn'troːle] der <–s, –> ♀Controllerin [kɔn'troːlərɪn] die <–, –nen> ◊ *Der Controller ist für die Prognose verantwortlich.* ◆ *Sie ist als Controllerin in einem Verlag tätig.*

controversial [adj] umstritten [ʊm'ʃtrɪtn̩] ◊ *eine umstrittene Methode/Theorie* ◆ *Er ist als Autor nach wie vor umstritten.*

controversy [noun] Kontroverse [kɔntro'vɛɐ̯zə] die <–, –n> controversy over sth Kontroverse um etw. ◊ *die Kontroverse um die Atomenergie* spark controversy eine Kontroverse auslösen

convene [verb] **1.** *(a meeting, conference etc.)* convene sth etw. einberufen ['aɛnbəru:fn̩] <beruft ein, berief ein, hat einberufen> ◊ *Auf Wunsch der Leiterin wurde eine Besprechung einberufen.* **2.** *(gather, come together)* convene *(for sth)* sich *(für etw.)* versammeln [fɛ'zamln̩] <versammelt sich, versammelte sich, hat sich versammelt> ◊ *Die Partei hat sich versammelt, um den Wahlkampf zu planen.*

convenience [noun] **1.** *(object that makes life pleasant, comfort)* Annehmlichkeit ['anne:mlɪçkaɛt] die <–, –en> most pl ◊ *die Annehmlichkeiten der Großstadt* ◆ *eine Reihe von Annehmlichkeiten* **2.** *(ease)* enjoy the convenience of online shopping/ internet banking den bequemen Online-Einkauf genießen [de:n bə‚kve:mən 'ɔnlaen‚aenkaof gə‚ni:sn̩] <genießt, genoss, hat genossen> for convenience der Einfachheit halber [de:ɐ̯ 'aenfaxhaet halbe] ◊ *Der Einfachheit halber teilen wir die Kriterien in zwei Kategorien auf.* like the convenience of doing sth etw. gern tun, weil es bequem ist ['gɛ'n ... vael es bə'kve:m ɪst] ◊ *Ich zahle gern mit Kreditkarte, weil es bequem ist.* **3.** *(WC)* Bedürfnisanstalt [bə'dʏ'fnɪs‚anʃtalt] die <–, –en> *(form)* ⊛ be to sb's convenience jdm passen ◊ *Passt Ihnen der Termin?* at sb's convenience wann es jdm passt for your convenience für Sie ◊ *Hier liegen Handtücher für Sie bereit.*

convenient [adj] **1.** *(easy to use or do)* praktisch ['praktɪʃ] ◊ *ein praktischer Reiseführer* ◆ *Dieser Camcorder ist klein und praktisch.* **2.** *(in a good location)* günstig ['gʏnstɪç] ◊ *Sie wählten das Haus wegen seiner günstigen Lage.* **3.** *(iron) (excuse, opportunity)* willkommen [vɪl'kɔmən] ◊ *eine willkommene Ausrede*

conveniently [adv] **1.** *(in a practical way)* handlich ['hantlɪç] ◊ *Das Regal ist handlich verpackt.* **2.** *(in a good location)* günstig ['gʏnstɪç] ◊ *Das Hotel liegt günstig.* **3.** *(iron) (because it is advantageous for sb)* praktischerweise ['praktɪʃe'vaezə] no comp/superl ◊ *Er hat praktischerweise unseren Termin vergessen.*

convent [noun] Kloster ['klo:ste] das <–s, Klöster> ◊ *Sie ging für ein Jahr ins Kloster.*

convention [noun] **1.** *(agreement, tradition)* Konvention [kɔnvɛn'tsjo:n] die <–, –en> ◊ *die Genfer Konvention* ◆ *gegen gesellschaftliche Konventionen verstoßen* ◆ *Konventionen der Architektur/Erzählkunst* **2.** *(formal meeting)* Kongress [kɔn'grɛs] der <–es, –e> ◊ *einen Kongress abhalten/einberufen* ◆ *der Kongress der deutschen Zahnärzte*; *(less formal, of fans etc.)* Treffen ['trɛfn̩] das <–s, –> ◊ *das Treffen der Star-Trek-Fans*

conventional(ly) [adj, adv] konventionell [kɔnvɛntsjo'nɛl] ◊ *konventionelle Umgangsformen* ◆ *Seine Methoden sind konventionell.* ◆ *Sie kleidet sich sehr konventionell.*

conversation [noun] Gespräch [gə'ʃprɛ:ç] das <–(e)s, –e> ◊ *Er hat sie in ein Gespräch verwickelt.* have a conversation (with sb) ein Gespräch (mit jdm) führen ◊ *Wir führten ein langes Gespräch über Kunst/Politik.* get into conversation (with sb) (mit jdm) ins Gespräch kommen fall into conversation with sb ein Gespräch mit jdm anfangen strike up a conversation ein Gespräch mit jdm anknüpfen

conversely [adv] wiederum ['vi:dərʊm] no comp/ superl ◊ *Wenn das Produkt zu teuer ist, kauft es keiner. Verkauft man es wiederum zu billig, macht man keinen Gewinn.*

conversion [noun] **1.** *(change)* Umwandlung ['ʊmvandlʊŋ] die <–> no pl the conversion of sth (in)to sth die Umwandlung ... [gen]/von etw. in etw. [acc] ◊ *die Umwandlung analoger in digitale Signale* ◆ *die Umwandlung von Zucker in Alkohol* **2.** *(of currencies, units of measurement)* Umrechnung ['ʊmrɛçnʊŋ] die <–> no pl the conversion of sth (in)to sth die Umrechnung von etw. in etw. [acc] ◊ *die Umrechnung von Dollar in Euro* ◆ *die Umrechnung von Kilometern in Meilen* **3.** *(of a building, room)* Umbau ['ʊmbao] der <–(e)s, –ten> ◊ *der Umbau einer Scheune; (of a loft)* Ausbau ['aosbao] der <–(e)s, –ten> ◊ *der Ausbau des Dachbodens* **4.** REL Bekehrung [bə'ke:rʊŋ] die <–, –en> ◊ *seine Bekehrung zum Islam*

convert [verb] **1.** *(a measurement, currency)* convert (sth into sth) (etw. in etw. [acc]) umrechnen ['ʊmrɛçnən] <rechnet um, rechnete um, hat umgerechnet> ◊ *Meilen in Kilometer umrechnen* **2.** *(change, go over to)* convert to sth auf etw. [acc] umstellen [aof ... ‚ʊmʃtɛlən] +haben ◊ *Er stellt jetzt seinen Hof auf biologische Landwirtschaft um.* **3.** *(a loft, cellar)* convert sth (into sth) etw. (zu etw.) ausbauen ['aosbaoən] +haben ◊ *Sie haben den Dachboden zum Schlafzimmer ausgebaut.* **4.** REL convert sb (to sth) jdn (zu etw.) bekehren [bə'ke:rən] <bekehrt, bekehrte, hat bekehrt> **5.** REL sb converts (to sth) jd konvertiert (zu etw.) [kɔnvɛ''ti:gt] <konvertierte, ist konvertiert> ◊ *Er konvertierte zum Protestantismus.* **6.** SPORT *(a penalty etc.)* verwandeln [fɛ'vandln̩] <verwandelt, verwandelte, hat verwandelt> ◊ *einen Elfmeter verwandeln*

convey [verb] **1.** *(a feeling, an idea)* vermitteln [fɛ'mɪtln̩] <vermittelt, vermittelte, hat vermittelt> ◊ *jdm Hoffnung/Ruhe vermitteln* **2.** *(a message, greetings)* übermitteln [ybe'mɪtln̩] <übermittelt, übermittelte, hat übermittelt>; *(lofty)* ◊ *Übermitteln Sie ihm Grüße von mir!* **3.** *(goods, passengers)* befördern [bə'fœɐ̯den] <befördert, beförderte, hat befördert> *(form)* ◊ *Waren/Güter mit der Bahn befördern* ◆ *In dem Bus können 40 Personen befördert werden.* **4.** LAW *(a property)* convey sth to sb jdm etw. übertragen [ybe'tra:gn̩] <überträgt, übertrug, hat übertragen>

conveyance [noun] **1.** *(transport)* Beförderung [bə'fœ'dərʊŋ] die <–, –en> most sing *(form)* ◊ *die Beförderung gefährlicher Güter auf der Straße* **2.** *(vehicle)* Beförderungsmittel [bə'fœ'dərʊŋsmɪtl̩] das <–s, –> **3.** LAW *(of property)* Übertragung [ybe'tra:gʊŋ] die <–, –en> most sing

conveyer belt, conveyor belt [noun] Fließband

['fliːsbant] das <-(e)s, Fließbänder>

convict ⟨verb⟩ *(find guilty)* convict sb jdn schuldig sprechen ['ʃʊldɪç 'ʃprɛçn̩] <spricht, sprach, hat gesprochen> ◊ *Die Jury/Der Richter sprach die Angeklagte schuldig.; (sentence)* convict sb (of sth) jdn (wegen etw.) verurteilen [veːɡn̩] ... fɛ|,ʊʳtaelən] <verurteilt, verurteilte, hat verurteilt> ◊ *Er wurde wegen Mordes verurteilt.*

conviction ⟨noun⟩ 1. LAW Verurteilung [fɛ|'ʊʳtaelʊn] die <-, -en> ◊ *Die Öffentlichkeit erwartet die Verurteilung des Angeklagten.* with a previous conviction/convictions mit Vorstrafe/n [mɪt 'foːɡʃtraːfə/'foːɡʃtraːfn̩] ◊ *Personen mit Vorstrafen* have a previous conviction vorbestraft sein ['foːɡbəʃtraːft zaen] +sein ◊ *Der Täter war nicht vorbestraft.* 2. *(belief, point of view, self-confidence)* Überzeugung [ybɐ'tsɔøgʊn] die <-, -en> ◊ *aus religiöser Überzeugung handeln ◆ zu der Überzeugung gelangen, dass ... ◆ „Vielleicht finden wir ja doch eine Lösung", sagte er mit wenig Überzeugung.*

convince ⟨verb⟩ *(make sb believe sth is true)* überzeugen [ybɐ'tsɔøgn̩] <überzeugt, überzeugte, hat überzeugt> ◊ *Ihre Argumente haben mich nicht überzeugt. ◆ Er versuchte, sie von der Richtigkeit seiner Worte zu überzeugen.; (win over)* convince sb to do sth jdn dazu überreden, etw. zu tun [daˈtsuː ybɐˈreːdn̩... tsuː] <überredet, überredete, hat überredet> ◊ *Sie überredete ihn dazu, mit ihr ins Kino zu gehen.*

convincing(ly) → convince ⟨adj, adv⟩ 1. *(victory)* überlegen [ybɐ'leːgn̩] only before ns ◊ *ein überlegener Sieg ◆ Die gegnerische Mannschaft hat überlegen gespielt und gewonnen.* 2. *(arguments, performance)* überzeugend [ybɐ'tsɔøgn̩t] ◊ *ein überzeugender Schauspieler ◆ Ich finde seine Argumente nicht überzeugend. ◆ Der Redner sprach sehr überzeugend.*

cook¹ ⟨noun⟩ Koch [kɔx] der <-(e)s, Köche> ♀Köchin ['kœçɪn] die <-, -nen> ◊ *Sie ist eine begeisterte Köchin. ◆ Er ist Koch in einem kleinen Lokal.*

◉ **too many cooks spoil the broth** viele Köche verderben den Brei

cook² ⟨verb⟩ 1. *(prepare food, boil)* kochen ['kɔxn̩] +haben ◊ *Er kann nicht kochen. ◆ Sie hat ein tolles Abendessen gekocht. ◆ Wie lange müssen die Kartoffeln noch kochen?; (heat sth, be heated until ready)* garen ['gaːrən] +haben ◊ *das Fleisch langsam im Ofen garen* sth is cooking etw. gart cook sb sth, cook sth for sb jdm etw. machen ['maxn̩] +haben ◊ *Hast du Hunger? Ich könnte dir ein Steak machen.* 2. *(falsify)* frisieren [friˈziːrən] <frisiert, frisierte, hat frisiert> *(fam)* ◊ *Da hat wohl jemand die Bilanzen frisiert.*

◉ **what's cooking?** was ist los?

cooker ⟨noun⟩ Herd [heːɐ̯t] der <-(e)s, -e>

cookie ⟨noun⟩ 1. *(in the US: biscuit)* Keks [keːks] der <- or -es, -e> ◊ *leckere Kekse backen* 2. IT Cookie ['kʊki] das <-s, -s> ◊ *Cookies blockieren/zulassen*

◉ **that's the way the cookie crumbles** so ist das nun mal

cooking ⟨noun⟩ 1. *(process)* Kochen ['kɔxn̩] das <-s> no pl ◊ *Wer übernimmt heute das Kochen?* 2. *(food)* Küche ['kʏçə] die <-, -n> ◊ *italienische/vegetarische Küche*

cool¹ ⟨adj⟩ 1. *(temperature, behaviou(u)r, colo(u)r)* kühl [kyːl] ◊ *Morgen soll es kühl werden. ◆ kühle Getränke ◆ Seine Mutter war sehr kühl zu mir. ◆ Der Raum*

war in kühlen Blautönen gestrichen. store in a cool, dry place kühl und trocken lagern 2. *(thin or transparent, clothes)* luftig ['lʊftɪç] ◊ *Sie trug eine luftige Bluse. ◆ Diese Jacke ist luftig und bequem.* 3. *(calm)* ruhig ['ruːɪç] ◊ *eine ruhige, entspannte Atmosphäre* keep cool, play it cool ruhig bleiben ◊ *Trotz der allgemeinen Aufregung blieb sie ruhig.* 4. *(attractive, fashionable)* cool [kuːl] *(fam)* ◊ *Das sieht echt cool aus! ◆ Dein Freund ist ein cooler Typ.* 5. *(as much as)* glatt [glat] no comp/superl, only before ns *(fam)* ◊ *Sie verdient glatte 7000 Euro im Monat!*

cool² ⟨verb⟩ 1. *(make colder)* kühlen ['kyːlən] +haben ◊ *eine Wunde mit Eis kühlen; (become colder)* abkühlen ['apkyːlən] +sein ◊ *Wenn der Kuchen abgekühlt ist, kommt noch Sahne darauf.* 2. *(feeling)* sich legen ['leːgn̩] +haben ◊ *Ihre anfängliche Begeisterung legte sich rasch wieder.; (love)* abkühlen ['apkyːlən] +sein

● **cool down** ⟨phras v⟩ *(calm down)* sich abregen ['apreːgn̩] +haben *(fam)* ◊ *Nun reg dich mal wieder ab — so schlimm ist das auch nicht! →* cool² 1.

● **cool off** ⟨phras v⟩ 1. *(become colder)* abkühlen ['apkyːlən] +sein ◊ *Der Motor muss erst abkühlen.* The weather has cooled off. Es ist kühler geworden. cool yourself off sich abkühlen ['apkyːlən] +haben ◊ *Wir sprangen in den See, um uns abzukühlen.* 2. *(become less upset or hectic)* sich beruhigen [bəˈruːɪɡn̩] <beruhigt sich, beruhigte sich, hat sich beruhigt> ◊ *Warte erst einmal, bis der Chef sich wieder beruhigt hat. ◆ Die Lage wird sich schon wieder beruhigen.*

coolly ⟨adv⟩ 1. *(without getting upset)* besonnen [bəˈzɔnən] ◊ *Er reagierte auf die plötzliche Krise sehr besonnen.* 2. *(in an unfriendly way)* kühl [kyːl] ◊ *„Das geht Sie nichts an", erwiderte sie kühl.*

coolness ⟨noun⟩ Kühle ['kyːlə] die <-> no pl ◊ *die Kühle der Morgenluft ◆ Sie begegnete ihm mit zurückhaltender Kühle.*

cooperate ⟨verb⟩ 1. *(work together)* cooperate (with sb) (mit jdm) zusammenarbeiten [tsuˈzamənˌʔaʳbaetn̩] <arbeitet zusammen, arbeitete zusammen, hat zusammengearbeitet> ◊ *Wir arbeiten mit verschiedenen Organisationen zusammen.* 2. *(do what sb wants)* cooperate (with sb) (mit jdm) kooperieren [koopeˈriːrən] <kooperiert, kooperierte, hat kooperiert> ◊ *mit der Polizei kooperieren*

cooperation ⟨noun⟩ 1. *(working together)* Zusammenarbeit [tsuˈzamənʔaˌbaet] die <-> no pl ◊ *Dieses Buch ist in Zusammenarbeit mit der Universität Köln entstanden.* 2. *(help)* Mitarbeit [ˈmɪtʔaˌbaet] die <-> no pl ◊ *Wir danken Ihnen für Ihre Mitarbeit.*

cooperative ⟨adj⟩ 1. *(ready to do sth)* kooperativ [koopeˈraˌtiːf] ◊ *ein sehr kooperativer Mitarbeiter ◆ sich kooperativ zeigen* 2. *(based on cooperation)* gemeinsam [gəˈmaenzaːm] no comp/superl, only before ns ◊ *ein gemeinsames Forschungsprojekt der beiden Universitäten* 3. *(referring to a business with shared profits)* auf genossenschaftlicher Basis [aof gəˌnɔsn̩ʃaftlɪçɐ ˈbaːzɪs] ◊ *Landwirtschaft auf genossenschaftlicher Basis* cooperative society Genossenschaft [gəˈnɔsn̩ʃaft] die <-, -en>

coordinate ⟨verb⟩ koordinieren [koʔɔʳdiˈniːrən] <koordiniert, koordinierte, hat koordiniert> ◊ *Seine Aufgabe ist es, die Verteilung der Hilfsgüter zu koordinieren.*

coordination ⟨noun⟩ Koordination [koʔɔʳdinaˈtsjoːn] die <-, -en>

A B **C** D E F G H I J K L M N O P Q R S T U V W X Y Z

A
B
C
D
E
F
G
H
I
J
K
L
M
N
O
P
Q
R
S
T
U
V
W
X
Y
Z

cop[1] [noun] Sheriff [ˈʃerɪf] der <-s, -s> (fam, hum) ◊ *Gestern haben mich die Sheriffs angehalten.*; Bulle [ˈbʊlə] der <-n, -n> (slang, pej) ◊ *Die Bullen kommen!*

ⓔ be not much cop nicht gerade toll sein

cop[2] [verb] cop sth sich etw. einhandeln [ˈaɛnhandl̩n] <handelt sich ein, handelte sich ein, hat sich eingehandelt> ◊ *sich eine saftige Geldstrafe einhandeln*

ⓔ cop it 1. (in the UK: be killed) dran glauben müssen 2. (in the UK: be punished) was erleben können

• cop out [phras v] cop out (of sth) sich (vor etw. [dat]) drücken [ˈdrʏkn̩] +haben (fam) ◊ *Sie hat wieder mal versucht, sich vor der Verantwortung zu drücken.*

cope [verb] (be able to deal with) cope (with sb/sth) (mit jdm./etw.) zurechtkommen [tsuˈrɛçtkɔmən] <kommt zurecht, kam zurecht, ist zurechtgekommen> ◊ *Kommst du zurecht oder soll ich dir helfen?* ◆ *Ich komme mit den Kindern nicht mehr zurecht.*; (with a loss, problem, disease etc.) cope with sth etw. fertig werden [mɪt ... ˌfɛʁtɪç veːɐ̯dn̩] +sein ◊ *mit dem Tod eines Freundes fertig werden*

copper [noun] Kupfer [ˈkʊpfɐ] das <-s>

copy[1] [noun] 1. (duplicate) Kopie [koˈpiː] die <-, -n> ◊ *eine beglaubigte Kopie Ihrer Geburtsurkunde* ◆ *eine Kopie der Datei speichern* ◆ *Das ist kein echtes Rubensgemälde, sondern lediglich eine Kopie.* 2. (of a newspaper, book etc.) Exemplar [ɛksɛmˈplaːɐ̯] das <-s, -e> ◊ *Von seinem ersten Buch wurden über 500 000 Exemplare verkauft.* a copy of yesterday's newspaper eine Zeitung von gestern [aɛnə ˌtsaɛtʊŋ fɔn ˈɡɛstɐn] die <-, -en> 3. (piece of writing for a newspaper etc.) Artikel [aʁˈtɪkl̩] die <-s, -> ◊ *Bitte reichen Sie ihre Artikel bis Ende des Monats ein.* make good copy für die Presse interessant sein [fyːɐ̯ diː ˌprɛsə ɪntəˈrɛsant zaɛn] (advertising) copy Werbetext [ˈvɛʁbətɛkst] der <-(e)s, -e>

copy[2] [verb] 1. (a document, famous person, painting, method) kopieren [koˈpiːrən] <kopiert, kopierte, hat kopiert> ◊ *CDs kopieren* ◆ *Bitte kopieren Sie diese Liste für alle Teilnehmer.* ◆ *Diese Band kopiert die Beatles.* copy sth onto sth etw. auf etw. [acc] kopieren ◊ *Sie kopierte die Datei auf eine zweite Festplatte.* 2. (sb's actions) nachahmen [ˈnaːxʔaːmən] +haben ◊ *Ich ahmte die Bewegungen des Yogalehrers nach.* 3. (a drawing) abzeichnen [ˈaptsaɛçnən] <zeichnet ab, zeichnete ab, hat abgezeichnet> ◊ *ein Motiv abzeichnen* 4. (a text) copy sth (down/out) etw. abschreiben [ˈapʃraɛbm̩] <schreibt ab, schrieb ab, hat abgeschrieben> ◊ *Er hat in der Prüfung von seinem Nachbarn abgeschrieben.* ◆ *etw. von der Tafel abschreiben*

• copy in [phras v] copy sb in jdm eine Kopie schicken [aɛnə koˈpiː ʃɪkn̩] +haben ◊ *Mailen Sie dem Kunden eine Antwort und schicken Sie mir eine Kopie!*

copyright [noun] Urheberrecht [ˈuːɐ̯hebəʁɛçt] das <-(e)s, -e> ◊ *Das Urheberrecht für diese Fotos liegt beim Verlag.* protected by copyright urheberrechtlich geschützt [ˌuːɐ̯hebəʁɛçtlɪç ɡəˈʃʏtst] ◊ *Diese Bezeichnung ist urheberrechtlich geschützt.*

cord [noun] 1. (string) Schnur [ʃnuːɐ̯] die <-, Schnüre> ◊ *Sie wickelte die Schnur ums Päckchen.* ◆ *Er spannte eine Schnur zwischen den Bäumen.* 2. (for decoration, on clothes) Kordel [ˈkɔʁdl̩] die <-, -n> ◊

ein mit Kordeln verzierter Vorhang ◆ *Der Mönch trug eine Kordel um seine Taille.* 3. (in the US: flex) Kabel [ˈkaːbl̩] das <-s, ->

cordial(ly) [adj, adv] herzlich [ˈhɛʁtslɪç] ◊ *Der Empfang war sehr herzlich.* ◆ *eine herzliche Einladung* ◆ *Sie sind herzlich eingeladen!*

core[1] [noun] Kern [kɛʁn] der <-(e)s, -e> ◊ *Kommen wir zum Kern der Sache.* ◆ *Der innere Kern der Erde besteht zu über 75 Prozent aus Eisen.* sth lies at the core of the problem etw. ist der Kern des Problems

ⓔ to the core durch und durch

core[2] [adj] Kern... [kɛʁn] core curriculum Kernfächer [ˈkɛʁnfɛçɐ] die <-> pl core belief Glaubensgrundsatz [ˈɡlaɔbm̩sɡrʊntzats] der <-s, Glaubensgrundsätze>

cork [noun] 1. (of a bottle) Korken [ˈkɔʁkn̩] der <-s, -> ◊ *den Korken aus einer Weinflasche ziehen* 2. (material) Kork [kɔʁk] der <-(e)s, -e> most sing cork flooring Korkboden [ˈkɔʁkboːdn̩] der <-s, Korkböden>

corkscrew [noun] Korkenzieher [ˈkɔʁkn̩tsiːɐ] der <-s, ->

corn [noun] 1. (in the UK: cereals) Korn [kɔʁn] das <-(e)s> ◊ *Korn anbauen* ◆ *das Korn zu Mehl mahlen* 2. (in the US: maize) Mais [maɛs] der <-es> no pl ◊ *Isst du gern Mais?* corn oil Maisöl [ˈmaɛsˌʔøːl] das <-(e)s> 3. MED Hühnerauge [ˈhyːnɐˌʔaɔɡə] das <-s, -n>

corner [noun] 1. (of a table, street, an area, in a football match) Ecke [ˈɛkə] die <-, -n> ◊ *Er stieß sich an der Ecke des Schreibtischs.* ◆ *Die Stadtbücherei ist an der Ecke Bachstraße/Mozartstraße.* ◆ *In dieser Ecke Frankreichs kenne ich mich gut aus.* turn the corner um die Ecke biegen ◊ *Er sah den Fahrraddieb gerade noch um die Ecke biegen.*; (bend) Kurve [ˈkʊʁvə] die <-, -n> ◊ *die Kurven schneiden* 2. (remote or obscure place, edge of sb's eye, mouth) Winkel [ˈvɪŋkl̩] der <-s, -> ◊ *Die Socken lagen im hintersten Winkel des Schranks.* ◆ *Er kennt jeden Winkel des Dorfes.* corner of the eye Augenwinkel [ˈaɔɡn̩vɪŋkl̩] corner of the mouth Mundwinkel [ˈmʊntvɪŋkl̩] 3. (difficult situation) (tight) corner Enge [ˈɛŋə] die <-> no pl force sb into a corner jdn in die Enge treiben be in a corner in die Enge getrieben sein

ⓔ all four corners of the world die ganze Welt ◊ *Besucher aus der ganzen Welt kamen und bestaunten die Erfindung.* cut corners (on sth) 1. (do a shoddy job) (bei etw.) nachlässig arbeiten 2. (save money) (bei etw.) sparen have turned the corner über den Berg sein around the corner 1. (nearby) um die Ecke 2. (coming soon) vor der Tür ◊ *Der Winter steht vor der Tür.*

coroner [noun] Gerichtsmediziner [ɡəˈrɪçtsmediˌtsiːnɐ] der <-s, -> ♀Gerichtsmedizinerin [ɡəˈrɪçtsmediˌtsiːnərɪn] die <-, -nen> ◊ *Tom arbeitet als Gerichtsmediziner.* ◆ *Die Gerichtsmedizinerin stellte Tod durch Ertrinken fest.*

corporate [adj] 1. (concerning a firm) Firmen... [ˈfɪʁmən] corporate identity Firmenimage [ˈfɪʁmənˌɪmɪtʃ] das <-(s), -s> 2. (concerning a group) gemeinsam [ɡəˈmaɛnzaːm] no comp/superl, only before ns ◊ *über ein gemeinsames Vorgehen abstimmen*

corporation [noun] 1. (firm) Handelsgesellschaft [ˈhandl̩sɡəzɛlʃaft] die <-, -en> 2. (in the UK, of a

town etc.) Gemeinde [gə'maəndə] die <-, –n>

corps [noun] Korps [ko:g] das <-, ->

corpse [noun] Leiche ['laəçə] die <-, –n>

correct[1] [adj] korrekt [ko'rɛkt] <korrekter, am korrektesten> ◊ *die korrekte Lösung* ♦ *Mein Großvater war immer sehr korrekt.*

correct[2] [verb] *(show or say what is wrong, deal with a problem)* korrigieren [kɔri'gi:rən] <korrigiert, korrigierte, hat korrigiert> ◊ *eine Klassenarbeit korrigieren* ♦ *einen Sehfehler korrigieren* ♦ *den Kurs korrigieren; (take into account)* correct for sth etw. berücksichtigen [bə'rʏkzɪçtɪgn̩] <berücksichtigt, berücksichtigte, hat berücksichtigt> ◊ *Abweichungen berücksichtigen*

☞ **correct me if I'm wrong** irre ich mich ◊ *Irre ich mich oder habe ich Sie bereits gestern davon unterrichtet?* **I stand corrected** ich nehme alles zurück

correction [noun] Korrektur [kɔrɛk'tu:g] die <-, –en> ◊ *Korrekturen am Rand eintragen* ♦ *die Korrektur eines Schönheitsfehlers/des politischen Kurses* **make a correction** eine Korrektur vornehmen

correctly [adv] richtig ['rɪçtɪç] ◊ *Er hat ihren Namen richtig ausgesprochen.*

correlate [verb] *(two)* things correlate (zwei) Dinge stehen zueinander in Beziehung [(tsvae) ... ʃte:ən tsu|aenandɐ ɪn bə'tsi:ʊŋ] <steht, stand, hat gestanden> ◊ *Die beiden Werte stehen in keiner Beziehung zueinander.* **be correlated with sth** in Beziehung zu etw. stehen **correlate A with B** A zu B in Beziehung setzen [tsu: ... ɪn bə'tsi:ʊŋ zɛtsn̩] +haben ◊ *Man kann Krebs in eine Beziehung zum Zigarettenkonsum setzen.* **A correlates with B,** A is correlated with B es besteht ein direkter Zusammenhang zwischen A und B [dat] [ɛs baʃte:t aen di,rɛkte tsu'zamənhaŋ tsvɪʃn̩ ... ʊnt] <besteht, bestand, hat bestanden> ◊ *Besteht ein direkter Zusammenhang zwischen Spaß bei der Arbeit und der Kreativität der Mitarbeitenden?*

correlation [noun] Zusammenhang [tsu'zamənhaŋ] der <-(e)s, Zusammenhänge> ◊ *Alles weist auf einen engen Zusammenhang zwischen Rauchen und Krebs hin.*

correspond [verb] **1.** *(be the same)* übereinstimmen [ybɐ|'aenʃtɪmən] +haben ◊ *Unsere Ergebnisse stimmten nicht überein.* ♦ *Das Ergebnis stimmt nicht mit unseren Berechnungen überein.; (be related, be comparable)* correspond to sth einer Sache [dat] entsprechen [ɛnt'ʃprɛçn̩] <entspricht, entsprach, hat entsprochen> ◊ *Jeder Taste auf dem Klavier entspricht ein Ton.* ♦ *Das Testergebnis entspricht ziemlich genau unseren Erwartungen.* **2.** *(write to each other)* correspond with sb mit jdm korrespondieren [mɪt ... kɔrɛspɔn,di:rən] <korrespondiert, korrespondierte, hat korrespondiert> ◊ *Sie korrespondieren seit Jahren miteinander.*

correspondence [noun] **1.** *(letters)* Korrespondenz [kɔrɛspɔn'dɛnts] die <-, –en> ◊ *In diesem Ordner bewahre ich meine Korrespondenz auf.* **2.** *(correlation)* Zusammenhang [tsu'zamənhaŋ] der <-(e)s, Zusammenhänge> ◊ *Es besteht ein enger Zusammenhang zwischen Armut und Kriminalität.*

correspondent [noun] **1.** *(reporter)* Korrespondent [kɔrɛspɔn'dɛnt] der <-en, –en> ♀Korrespondentin [kɔrɛspɔn'dɛntɪn] die <-, –nen> ◊ *Er arbeitet als Korrespondent für die BBC.* ♦ *Die Korrespondentin berichtete aus dem Krisengebiet.* **2.** *(pen pal)* Brief-

freund ['bri:ffrɔʏnt] der <-(e)s, –e> ♀Brieffreundin ['bri:ffrɔʏndɪn] die <-, –nen> ◊ *Sie hat mehrere Briefreunde im Ausland.*

corresponding [adj] entsprechend [ɛnt'ʃprɛçnt] no comp/superl ◊ *Bei diesem Preis erwarte ich eine entsprechende Qualität.* ♦ *Die Arbeitslosigkeit ist derzeit höher als im entsprechenden Monat des Vorjahres.*

correspondingly [adv] dementsprechend ['de:m|ɛnt'ʃprɛçnt] no comp/superl ◊ *Dieses Haus ist größer und dementsprechend teurer.*

corridor [noun] **1.** *(of a building, land)* Korridor ['kɔridoːg] der <-s, –e> ◊ *Er ging den Korridor des Hotels entlang und suchte den Fitnessraum.* ♦ *Ein schmaler Korridor verbindet die beiden Teile des Landes.* **2.** *(in a train)* Gang [gaŋ] der <-(e)s, Gänge> ◊ *Der Schaffner kam den Gang entlang.*

☞ **the corridors of power** das Zentrum der Macht

corrupt[1] [adj] **1.** *(dishonest, immoral)* korrupt [kɔ'rʊpt] <korrupter, am korruptesten> ◊ *Das System ist korrupt.* ♦ *ein korrupter Politiker* **2.** IT defekt [de'fɛkt] no comp/superl ◊ *Die Datei ist defekt.* ♦ *defekte Software*

corrupt[2] [verb] **1.** *(make immoral, dishonest)* verderben [fɛ'dɛrbm̩] <verdirbt, verdarb, hat verdorben> +haben ◊ *Verdirbt Geld den Charakter?* **2.** IT beschädigen [bə'ʃɛ:dɪgn̩] <beschädigt, beschädigte, hat beschädigt> ◊ *eine Datei beschädigen*

corruption [noun] **1.** *(bribery)* Korruption [kɔrʊp'tsio:n] die <-, –en> most sing ◊ *Es besteht Verdacht auf Korruption.* **2.** *(of morals)* Verfall [fɛ'fal] der <-(e)s> no pl ◊ *der Verfall der Sitten* **3.** IT *(of data, software etc.)* Zerstörung [tsɛ'ʃtøːrʊŋ] die <-> ◊ *eine Zerstörung der Daten durch Viren* **4.** *(of a body)* Zersetzung [tsɛ'zɛtsʊŋ] die <-> no pl ◊ *Die Zersetzung einer Leiche beginnt unmittelbar nach dem Tod.*

cos → **because**

cosmetics [noun] Kosmetika [kɔs'me:tika:] die <-> pl ◊ *Benutzen Sie Kosmetika?*

cost[1] [noun] **1.** *(money to pay)* cost(s) Kosten ['kɔstn̩] die <-> only pl ◊ *Wer übernimmt die Kosten für die Reise?* ♦ *Es fallen hohe Kosten an.* ♦ *Dieser Betrag deckt gerade mal die Kosten für das Büro.* **running costs** Betriebskosten [bə'tri:pskɔstn̩] **cost of living** Lebenshaltungskosten ['le:bm̩shaltʊŋs,kɔstn̩] **at a cost of ...** für ... [fy:g] ◊ *Dieses Produkt ist für 12 Euro erhältlich.* **2.** *(fig)* **the social costs of sth** der Preis, den die Gesellschaft für etw. zahlen muss

☞ **count the cost of sth 1.** *(calculate what sth costs)* berechnen, wie viel etw. kostet ◊ *Hat man schon berechnet, wie viel der Transport kostet?* **2.** *(put up with the consequences)* mit den Folgen ... [gen] leben müssen ◊ *Jeder muss mit den Konsequenzen seiner Taten leben.* **at a cost um welchen Preis** ◊ *Sie hat die Stelle dann doch noch bekommen, aber um welchen Preis!* **at all costs um jeden Preis at cost zum Selbstkostenpreis** **at the cost of sth** auf Kosten ... [gen] ◊ *Tourismus auf Kosten der Umwelt*

cost[2] [verb] **1.** *(money, a life etc.)* kosten ['kɔstn̩] +haben ◊ *Der Anruf kostet 12 Cent pro Minute.* ♦ *viele Menschenleben kosten* ♦ *Diese Entscheidung kostete sie das Leben.* **2.** *(calculate)* cost sth die Kosten für etw. veranschlagen [di: ,kɔstn̩ fy:g ... fɛ|,anʃla:gn̩] <veranschlagt, veranschlagte, hat veranschlagt> ◊ *Wir müssen zuerst die Kosten für den geplanten Anbau veranschlagen.*

A B C D E F G H I J K L M N O P Q R S T U V W X Y Z

ⓔ **it'll cost sb das** wird jdn einiges kosten

costly ⟨adj⟩ **1.** *(high-priced)* kostspielig ['kɔstʃpiːlɪç] ◊ *Reiten ist ein kostspieliges Hobby.* ✦ *Schönheitsoperationen sind kostspielig.* **2.** *(mistake)* folgenschwer ['fɔlɡn̩ʃveːɐ̯] ◊ *ein folgenschwerer Fehler* ✦ *Der Sturz des Reiters war folgenschwer.*

costume ⟨noun⟩ **1.** *(at the theatre, fancy dress)* Kostüm [kɔs'tyːm] das <-s, -e> ◊ *Die Schauspieler trugen bereits ihre Kostüme.* **2.** *(historical, regional)* Tracht [traxt] die <-, -en> ◊ *Das Dirndl ist eine bayerische Tracht.* national costume Nationaltracht [natsi̯oˈnaːltraxt] **3.** *(in the UK: swim suit)* Badeanzug ['baːdəʔantsuːk] der <-(e)s, Badeanzüge>

cosy(-ily), cozy(-ily) ⟨adj, adv⟩ gemütlich [ɡə'myːtlɪç] ◊ *ein gemütliches Sofa* ✦ *Hier ist es sehr gemütlich.* ✦ *Wir saßen gemütlich vor dem Kamin.* warm and cosy mollig warm [mɔlɪç 'vaʁm] ◊ *Vor dem Feuer war es mollig warm.*

cottage ⟨noun⟩ Häuschen ['hɔɪ̯sçən] das <-s, ->

cotton ⟨noun⟩ **1.** *(plant, fibre, fabric)* Baumwolle ['baʊ̯mvɔlə] die <-> no pl ◊ *Baumwolle anbauen/pflücken* ✦ *eine Bluse aus reiner Baumwolle* cotton dress Baumwollkleid ['baʊ̯mvɔlklaɪ̯t] das <-(e)s, -er> **2.** *(in the UK: thread for sewing)* Garn [ɡaʁn] das <-(e)s, -e> ◊ *Garne für Handarbeiten* **3.** *(in the US, cotton wool)* Watte ['vatə] die <-> no pl ◊ *sich* ⟨dat⟩ *die Ohren mit Watte reinigen*

cotton wool ⟨noun⟩ Watte ['vatə] die <-> no pl

couch ⟨noun⟩ Couch [kaʊ̯tʃ] die <-, -s or also -en>

cough¹ ⟨noun⟩ **1.** MED Husten ['huːstn̩] der <-s> no pl ◊ *Ich habe Husten/einen starken Husten.* **2.** *(when clearing your throat)* Räuspern ['rɔɪ̯span] das <-s> no pl ◊ *Er ließ ein lautes Räuspern vernehmen.*

cough² ⟨verb⟩ husten ['huːstn̩] +haben ◊ *Er kann nachts nicht schlafen, weil er immerzu husten muss.* ✦ *Der Kranke hustete Blut.*
  • **cough up** ⟨phras v⟩ **1.** *(blood, mucus)* cough sth up etw. husten ['huːstn̩] +haben ◊ *Der Patient hustet zähen Schleim.* **2.** *(some money, information)* cough sth up etw. rausrücken ['ʁaʊ̯sʁʏkn̩] +haben *(fam)* ◊ *Nun los, rück das Geld schon raus.* sb coughs/doesn't cough up jd rückt etwas/nichts raus cough up for sth für etw. blechen [fyːɐ̯ ... ˌblɛçn̩] +haben *(fam)* ◊ *Und dein Vater darf dann wieder für den Schaden blechen, oder?*

could pret of can ⟨verb⟩ **1.** *(subjunctive of 'can', used when expressing possibility, making requests, offers, giving emphasis)* sb/sth could do sth jd/etw. könnte etw. tun ['kœntə] subjunctive II ◊ *Könnte ich mal Ihr Telefon benutzen?* ✦ *Könntest du bitte das Fenster schließen?* ✦ *Er ist immer so unordentlich — ich könnte ihn manchmal erwürgen!* ✦ *Ihr könntet uns ja im Winter mal besuchen kommen!* sb could always do sth jd kann immer noch etw. tun [kan 'ɪmɐ nɔx] <kann, konnte, hat können> ◊ *Wenn es nicht anders geht, könnt ihr immer noch im Zelt übernachten.; (expressing a possibility that did not materialize)* sb/sth could have been/done sth jd/etw. hätte etw. sein/tun können [hɛtə ... kœnan] ◊ *Er hätte gewinnen können, wenn er sich mehr angestrengt hätte.* ✦ *Es hätte so schön sein können, wenn er nicht dabei gewesen wäre.; (expressing a small possibility, presumption, doubt)* sb/sth could have done sth jd/etw. könnte etw. getan haben [kœntə ... haːbm̩] ◊ *Sie könnte den Betrug begangen haben, aber es gibt keine Beweise.* it could have

been sb/sth es könnte jd/etw. gewesen sein ◊ *Es könnte ein Unfall gewesen sein.* **2.** *(as a question tag)* couldn't you/he etc.?, could you/he etc.? oder? ['oːdɐ] ◊ *Sie könnte ihn wohl nicht fragen, oder?* ✦ *Wir könnten auf sie warten, oder?*

ⓔ **sth couldn't be better/worse etc.** etw. ist äußerst gut/schlecht etc. ◊ *Das Arbeitsklima in der neuen Firma ist äußerst schlecht.* sb could do with sth *(fam)* jd könnte etw. brauchen I couldn't wish for ... ich könnte mir keinen/keine/kein ... wünschen ◊ *Ich könnte mir keinen besseren Chef wünschen.*

couldn't → could

council ⟨noun⟩ Rat [raːt] der <-(e)s, Räte> ◊ *Er wurde in den Rat gewählt.* ✦ der Rat der Europäischen Union city council Stadtrat ['ʃtatʁaːt] Council of Europe Europarat [ɔɪ̯ˈʁoːpaʁaːt]

councillor ⟨noun⟩ Rat [raːt] der <-(e)s, Räte> ♀Rätin ['ʁɛːtɪn] die <-, -nen> ◊ *jdn zum Rat wählen* town councillor Stadtrat ['ʃtatʁaːt] Stadträtin ['ʃtatʁɛːtɪn]

counsel ⟨noun⟩ **1.** LAW Rechtsanwalt ['ʁɛçtsʔanvalt] der <-(e)s, Rechtsanwälte> ♀Rechtsanwältin ['ʁɛçtsʔanvɛltɪn] die <-, -nen> ◊ *sich vor Gericht von seinem Rechtsanwalt vertreten lassen* ✦ *Wärst du lieber Rechtsanwältin oder Richterin?* defence counsel Verteidiger [fɛ'taɪ̯dɪɡɐ] der <-s, -> ♀Verteidigerin [fɛ'taɪ̯dɪɡəʁɪn] die <-, -nen> **2.** *(recommendation)* Rat [raːt] der <-(e)s> ◊ *Darf ich Ihnen einen Rat geben?*

ⓔ **keep your own counsel** seine Meinung für sich behalten

counselling ⟨noun⟩ Beratung [bə'ʁaːtʊŋ] die <-, -en> debt counselling Schuldnerberatung ['ʃʊldnɐbəʁaːtʊŋ]

counsellor, counselor ⟨noun⟩ Berater [bə'ʁaːtɐ] der <-s, -> ♀Beraterin [bə'ʁaːtəʁɪn] die <-, -nen> ◊ *Sie sollten mit ihrer Tochter einmal zu einem Berater gehen.* ✦ *Sie arbeitet als Beraterin für Ehepaare.* marriage counsellor Eheberater ['eːəbəʁaːtɐ] Eheberaterin ['eːəbəʁaːtəʁɪn]

count¹ ⟨noun⟩ **1.** *(calculation)* Zählung ['tsɛːlʊŋ] die <-, -en> ◊ *eine Zählung vornehmen* ✦ *Bei der letzten Zählung hatte das Dorf 150 Einwohner weniger.* traffic count Verkehrszählung [fɛ'keːɐ̯stsɛːlʊŋ] for a count of ten bis jd bis zehn gezählt hat [bɪs ... bɪs 'tseːn ɡətsɛːlt hat] ◊ *Halt die Luft an, bis du bis zehn gezählt habe.* **2.** *(number)* Anzahl ['antsaːl] die <-, -en> most sing ◊ *die Anzahl der weißen Blutkörperchen im Blut bestimmen* pollen count Pollenbelastung ['pɔlənbəlastʊŋ] die <-, -en> **3.** LAW Anklagepunkt ['anklaːɡəpʊŋkt] der <-(e)s, -e> ◊ *Sie wurde in allen drei Anklagepunkten schuldig gesprochen.* **4.** *(nobleman)* count, Count Graf [ɡʁaːf] der <-en, -en> ◊ *der Graf von Monte Christo*

ⓔ **be out for the count** k.o. sein keep count of sth die Übersicht über etw. ⟨acc⟩ behalten lose count of sth die Übersicht über etw. ⟨acc⟩ verlieren ◊ *Sie hat die Übersicht über die Rechnungen verloren, die sie noch bezahlen muss.*

count² ⟨verb⟩ **1.** *(add up, be of importance, be valid)* zählen ['tsɛːlən] +haben ◊ *bis 100 zählen* ✦ *In ihrem Job zählt nur Leistung.* ✦ *Sie zählt schon die Stunden bis zu ihrem Urlaub.* ✦ *Die Mittagspause zählt nicht als Arbeitszeit.* count sb among sb/sth jdn zu jdm/etw. zählen ◊ *Ich zähle ihn zu meinen besten*

Freunden. count towards sth auf etw. ⟨acc⟩ angerechnet werden [aof ... ‚angərəçnət veːɐdn] ⟨wird, wurde, ist worden⟩ ◊ *Mündliche Leistungen werden auf das Prüfungsergebnis angerechnet.* **2.** *(be insignificant)* count for nothing nichts gelten [‚nɪçts 'gɛltn] ⟨gilt, galt, hat gegolten⟩ ◊ *Deine Meinung gilt hier nichts.* ⓔ make sth count aus etw. das Beste machen
• **count against** ⟨phras v⟩ count against sb/sth gegen jdn/etw. sprechen ['geːgn̩ ... ʃprɛçn̩] ⟨spricht, sprach, hat gesprochen⟩ ◊ *Die fehlende Auslandserfahrung spricht gegen den Bewerber.*
• **count down** ⟨phras v⟩ zählen ['tsɛːlən] +haben ◊ *Sie zählt die Tage bis zu ihrem Urlaub.*
• **count in** ⟨phras v⟩ count sb in mit jdm rechnen [mɪt ... ‚rɛçnən] +haben ◊ *Für das Grillfest am Wochenende kannst du mit mir rechnen.*
• **count on** ⟨phras v⟩ **1.** *(rely on)* count on sb sich auf jdn verlassen [aof ... fɛ‚lasn̩] ⟨verlässt sich, verließ sich, hat sich verlassen⟩ ◊ *Auf diesen Mitarbeiter kann man sich immer verlassen.* count on sb doing sth, count on sb to do sth sich darauf verlassen, dass jd etw. tut ◊ *Kann ich mich darauf verlassen, dass du pünktlich kommst?* **2.** *(expect)* count on sb/sth mit jdm/etw. rechnen [mɪt ... ‚rɛçnən] +haben ◊ *Die Veranstalter rechnen mit etwa 200 000 Besuchern.* ♦ *Wir hatten nicht mit Regen gerechnet.* count on sb/sth doing sth damit rechnen, dass jd/etw. etw. tut
• **count out** ⟨phras v⟩ **1.** *(calculate)* count sth out etw. abzählen ['aptsɛːlən] +haben ◊ *Zähl das Geld bitte genau ab.* **2.** *(exclude)* count sb out nicht mit jdm rechnen [‚nɪçt mɪt ... ‚rɛçnən] +haben ◊ *Für die Party am Samstag brauchst du nicht mit mir zu rechnen.* **3.** *(boxing)* auszählen ['aostsɛːlən] +haben ◊ *Der Ringrichter zählte ihn aus.*
• **count up** ⟨phras v⟩ zusammenzählen [tsu'zaməntsɛːlən] +haben ◊ *Er zählte die Beträge zusammen.*
counter[1] ⟨noun⟩ **1.** *(in a shop, bar)* Theke ['teːkə] die ⟨-, -n⟩ ◊ *Das Kind legte das abgezählte Geld auf die Theke.* cheese counter Käsetheke ['kɛːzətheːkə] **2.** *(in a bank, post office)* Schalter ['ʃaltɐ] der ⟨-s, -⟩ ◊ *Der Schalter ist nicht besetzt.* ♦ *am Schalter fragen* **3.** *(machine)* Zähler ['tsɛːlɐ] der ⟨-s, -⟩ ◊ *den Stand des Zählers überprüfen* **4.** GAME Spielstein ['ʃpiːlʃtaen] der ⟨-(e)s, -e⟩ ◊ *Möchtest du die schwarzen oder die weißen Spielsteine?* **5.** *(reply)* Entgegnung [ɛnt'geːgnʊŋ] die ⟨-, -en⟩ ◊ *eine schlagfertige Entgegnung*
ⓔ over the counter rezeptfrei under the counter unter dem Ladentisch
counter[2] ⟨verb⟩ **1.** *(defend yourself)* sich zur Wehr setzen [tsuːɐ 'veːɐ̯ zɛtsn̩] +haben ◊ *Wir müssen uns gegen diese Vorwürfe zur Wehr setzen.; (reply)* entgegnen [ɛnt'geːgnən] ⟨entgegnet, entgegnete, hat entgegnet⟩ ◊ *„Aber das stimmt doch gar nicht!", entgegnete er.* **2.** *(hinder)* counter sth einer Sache ⟨dat⟩ entgegenwirken [ɛnt'geːgn̩vɪrkn̩] +haben ◊ *Was kann man tun, um Vorurteilen entgegenzuwirken?*
counterfeit[1] ⟨adj⟩ gefälscht [gə'fɛlʃt] no comp/superl ◊ *gefälschte Banknoten in Umlauf bringen* ♦ *Dieses Produkt ist gefälscht.*
counterfeit[2] ⟨verb⟩ fälschen ['fɛlʃn̩] +haben ◊ *Banknoten fälschen*
counterfoil ⟨noun⟩ Kontrollabschnitt [kɔn'trɔl‚apʃnɪt] der ⟨-(e)s, -e⟩

counterpart ⟨noun⟩ Gegenstück ['geːgn̩ʃtʏk] das ⟨-(e)s, -e⟩
country ⟨noun⟩ **1.** *(nation, countryside)* Land [lant] das ⟨-es, Länder⟩ ◊ *In welchem Land sind Sie geboren?* ♦ *Das ganze Land war geschockt von den schrecklichen Ereignissen.* ♦ *Sie lebt lieber auf dem Land als in der Stadt.* ♦ *Das Land dort eignet sich gut für den Weinbau.* underdeveloped country Entwicklungsland [ɛnt'vɪklʊŋslant] mining country Bergbaugebiet ['bɛrkbaogəbiːt] das ⟨-(e)s, -e⟩ **2.** MUS Countrymusic ['kantri‚mjuːzɪk] die ⟨-⟩ no pl
country road ⟨noun⟩ Landstraße ['lantʃtraːsə] die ⟨-, -n⟩
countryside ⟨noun⟩ **1.** *(rural areas)* ländliche Regionen [‚lɛntlɪçə re'gioːnən] ⟨-⟩ pl ◊ *die Förderung ländlicher Regionen* in the countryside auf dem Land [aof deːm 'lant] **2.** *(landscape)* Landschaft ['lantʃaft] die ⟨-⟩ ◊ *die schöne Landschaft um Berlin*
countrywide ⟨adj, adv⟩ landesweit ['landəsvaet] no comp/superl; when used as an adj, only before ns ◊ *eine landesweite Kampagne* ♦ *Die Partei errang landesweit über 50 Prozent.*
county ⟨noun⟩ *(in the UK)* Grafschaft ['graːfʃaft] die ⟨-, -en⟩ ◊ *die Grafschaft Essex; (in the US)* Verwaltungsbezirk [fɛ'valtʊŋsbətsɪr̯k] der ⟨-(e)s, -e⟩ ◊ *Alaska ist in vier Verwaltungsbezirke aufgeteilt.*
coup ⟨noun⟩ **1.** POL coup (d'état) Umsturz ['ʊmʃtʊrts] der ⟨-es, Umstürze⟩ ◊ *Er gelangte durch einen Umsturz an die Macht.* stage a coup einen Umsturz herbeiführen a failed coup ein gescheiterter Umsturz attempted coup Umsturzversuch ['ʊmʃtʊ'tsfɛzuːx] der ⟨-(e)s, -e⟩ military coup Militärputsch [mili'tɛːɐ̯pʊtʃ] der ⟨-(e)s, -e⟩ **2.** *(successful action)* Coup [kuː] der ⟨-s, -s⟩ ◊ *Das war sein letzter großer Coup.* propaganda coup Werbeerfolg ['vɛrbə‚ɛfɔlk] der ⟨-(e)s, -e⟩
couple[1] ⟨noun⟩ **1.** a couple of ... zwei ... [tsvae] ◊ *Zwei Sportler drehten ihre Runden.* ♦ *Hast du mal zwei Minuten Zeit?; (in the US)* ein paar ... [aen 'paːɐ̯] invariable ◊ *Hast du ein paar Minuten Zeit?* **2.** *(two people belonging together)* Paar [paːɐ̯] das ⟨-(e)s, -e⟩ ◊ *ein verliebtes Paar* ♦ *Die Paare tanzten eng umschlungen.* married couple Ehepaar ['eːəpaːɐ̯]
couple[2] ⟨verb⟩ *(connect, combine)* verbinden [fɛ'bɪndn̩] ⟨verbindet, verband, hat verbunden⟩ couple sth with sth etw. mit etw. verbinden couple two things zwei Dinge miteinander verbinden coupled with verbunden mit ◊ *Frustration verbunden mit Aggression ist eine gefährliche Mischung.; (vehicles)* couple (sth to sth) etw. an etw. ⟨acc⟩ koppeln ['kɔpln̩] +haben ◊ *Der Anhänger ist an das Auto gekoppelt.*
coupling ⟨noun⟩ TECHN *(device)* Kupplung ['kʊplʊŋ] die ⟨-, -en⟩ ◊ *Er löste den Anhänger von der Kupplung.; (process)* Koppelung ['kɔpəlʊŋ] die ⟨-, -en⟩ ◊ *die Koppelung der Geräte*
coupon ⟨noun⟩ **1.** *(voucher)* Bon [bɔŋ] der ⟨-s, -s⟩ ◊ *ein Bon im Wert von zehn Euro; (for rations)* Marke ['maːkə] die ⟨-, -n⟩ ◊ *Marken für Brot und Zucker* food coupon Lebensmittelmarke ['leːbm̩smɪtl‚maːkə] **2.** *(detachable piece)* Abschnitt ['apʃnɪt] der ⟨-(e)s, -e⟩ ◊ *Schicken Sie den Abschnitt mit der Lösung an ...*
courage ⟨noun⟩ Mut [muːt] der ⟨-(e)s⟩ no pl ◊ *in einer Situation viel Mut beweisen* ♦ *Sie hatte nicht*

den Mut, ihn anzusprechen. ♦ *Es gehört Mut dazu, sich in eine Schlägerei einzumischen.* summon up (the) courage seinen ganzen Mut zusammennehmen take courage from sth sich durch etw. ermutigt fühlen [dʊʳç ... ɪˈmuːtɪçt fyːlən] +haben ◉ take your courage in both hands sich [dat] ein Herz nehmen

courageous(ly) [adj, adv] mutig [ˈmuːtɪç] ◊ *eine mutige Entscheidung ♦ mutig handeln*

courgette [noun] Zucchini [tsʊˈkiːni:] die <–, –> most pl

courier [noun] 1. *(messenger)* Kurier [kuˈriːɐ̯] der <–s, –e> ♀Kurierin [kuˈriːrɪn] die <–, –nen> ◊ *Er arbeitet als Kurier. ♦ Die Kurierin lieferte einen Brief ab.* 2. *(in the UK: tourist guide)* Reiseleiter [ˈraɛzalaɛtə] der <–s, –> ♀Reiseleiterin [ˈraɛzalaɛtərɪn] die <–, –nen> ◊ *Bei Problemen wenden Sie sich bitte an Ihren Reiseleiter. ♦ Als Reiseleiterin kommt sie viel herum.*

course¹ [noun] 1. *(for learners, of an aircraft, a ship)* Kurs [kʊʳs] der <–es, –e> ◊ *ein Kurs für Anfänger/ Fortgeschrittene ♦ vom Kurs abweichen* run a course einen Kurs anbieten ◊ *Die Volkshochschule bietet zahlreiche Kurse an.* be on course auf Kurs sein be off course vom Kurs abgekommen sein 2. *(of a river)* Lauf [laʊf] der <–(e)s, Läufe> ◊ *Sie folgten dem Lauf des Flusses.* 3. course of action Vorgehensweise [ˈfoːgeːənsvaɛzə] die <–, –n> ◊ *Was ist in so einem Fall die beste Vorgehensweise?* 4. *(progress)* Ablauf [ˈaplaʊf] der <–(e)s, Abläufe> ◊ *der reibungslose Ablauf des Programms* 5. *(of a meal)* Gang [gaŋ] der <–(e)s, Gänge> ◊ *ein Menü mit fünf Gängen* main course Hauptgang [ˈhaʊptgaŋ] 6. MED course of treatment Behandlung [bəˈhandlʊŋ] die <–, –en> ◊ *eine dreiwöchige Behandlung* a course of antibiotics eine Behandlung mit Antibiotika 7. SPORT *(route)* Strecke [ˈʃtrɛkə] die <–, –n> ◊ *Der letzte Teil der Strecke war sehr anstrengend.; (for horses)* Rennbahn [ˈrɛnbaːn] die <–, –en> *(golf)* course Golfplatz [ˈgɔlfplats] der <–es, Golfplätze> ◉ the course of events der Lauf der Dinge ◉ the course of history der Lauf der Geschichte be on course for sth auf etw. [acc] zusteuern ◊ *Die Firma steuert auf einen großen Gewinn zu.* let sth take its course einer Sache [dat] ihren Lauf lassen in the course of *(of time, a century, year, month)* im Laufe einer Sache [gen] ◊ *Du wirst dich im Laufe der Zeit an deine neuen Nachbarn gewöhnen. (of an operation, action)* in the course of sth/doing sth während einer Sache [gen]/jd etw. tut ◊ *Während der Vorlesung ging auf einmal die Tür auf. ♦ Während ich meinen ersten Roman schrieb, lebte ich völlig zurückgezogen.*

course² [adv] klar [klaːʳ] *(fam)* ◊ *"Kommst du auch mit ins Kino?" — "Klar!"* of course natürlich [naˈtyːɐ̯lɪç] ◊ *"Kommst du mit?" — "Natürlich!" ♦ Karin ist natürlich wieder zu spät gekommen.*

coursebook [noun] Lehrbuch [ˈleːɐ̯buːx] das <–(e)s, Lehrbücher>

court [noun] 1. LAW Gericht [gəˈrɪçt] das <–(e)s, –e> ◊ *Das Gericht zog sich zur Beratung zurück.* in court vor Gericht ◊ *vor Gericht als Zeuge aussagen ♦ vor Gericht erscheinen* go to court vor Gericht gehen ◊ *Ich werde wegen dieser Sache vor Gericht gehen.* court case Gerichtsverfahren [gəˈrɪçtsfɛfaːrən] das <–s, –> court order Gerichtsbeschluss

[gəˈrɪçtsbəʃlʊs] der <–es, Gerichtsbeschlüsse> court reporter Gerichtsschreiber [gəˈrɪçtsʃraɛbɐ] der <–s, –> ♀Gerichtsschreiberin [gəˈrɪçtsʃraɛbərɪn] die <–, –nen> 2. SPORT Platz [plats] der <–es, Plätze> ◊ *Beide Spieler waren bereits auf dem Platz.* tennis court Tennisplatz [ˈtɛnɪsplats] der <–es, Tennisplätze> 3. *(a monarch's residence, enclosed place)* Hof [hoːf] der <–(e)s, Höfe> ◊ *bei Hofe vorgestellt werden ♦ Die Kinder spielen im Hof.* ◉ pay court to sb jdn umwerben

courteous(ly) [adj, adv] höflich [ˈhøːflɪç] ◊ *Das Personal in diesem Lokal ist nicht sehr höflich. ♦ höfliches Auftreten ♦ Sie grüßte ihn höflich.*

courtesy [noun] Höflichkeit [ˈhøːflɪçkaɛt] die <–, –en> ◊ *Er zeichnet sich durch Zurückhaltung und Höflichkeit aus.* common courtesy ein Gebot der Höflichkeit it would be a courtesy to do sth man sollte höflicherweise etw. tun [man zɔltə ˈhøːflɪçə̯ˈvaɛzə] ◊ *Man sollte höflicherweise anrufen, bevor man jemanden besucht.; (expressing anger)* have the courtesy to do sth höflicherweise etw. tun [ˈhøːflɪçə̯ˈvaɛzə] ◊ *Könntest du höflicherweise mal deinen Mund halten?* ◉ courtesy of 1. *(prize etc.)* freundlicherweise zur Verfügung gestellt von ◊ *Der erste Preis sind zwei Eintrittskarten, freundlicherweise vom FC Köln zur Verfügung gestellt. (right)* mit freundlicher Genehmigung von ◊ *Die Bilder sind eine Leihgabe mit freundlicher Genehmigung der Nationalgalerie.* 2. *(as a result of)* dank [gen]/fam [dat] ◊ *Dank einer großzügigen Spende konnte die Schule gebaut werden.*

courthouse [noun] Gerichtsgebäude [gəˈrɪçtsgəbɔɔdə] das <–s, –>

court of law [noun] Gericht [gəˈrɪçt] das <–(e)s, –e>

courtyard [noun] Hof [hoːf] der <–(e)s, Höfe>

cousin [noun] Cousin [kuˈzɛŋ] der <–s, –s> ♀Cousine [kuˈziːnə] die <–, –n> ◊ *Mein Cousin kommt morgen zu Besuch. ♦ Ich habe vier Cousins und zwei Cousinen.*

cove [noun] Bucht [bʊxt] die <–, –en>

covenant [noun] 1. *(contract)* Abkommen [ˈapkəmən] das <–s, –> breach of covenant Vertragsbruch [fɛˈtraːksbrʊx] der <–(e)s, Vertragsbrüche> make a covenant with sb eine Vereinbarung mit jdm treffen [aɛnə fɛˈˈaɛnbaːrʊŋ mɪt ... trɛfn] <trifft, traf, hat getroffen> 2. *(to a charity)* Verpflichtung zu regelmäßigen Spenden [fɛˈpflɪçtʊŋ tsuː: reːglmɛːsɪç ˈʃpɛndn] die <–, –en> 3. REL *(promise)* Bund [bʊnt] der <–(e)s, Bünde> ◊ *einen Bund mit jdm schließen*

cover¹ [noun] 1. *(protective cover)* Hülle [ˈhʏlə] die <–, –n> ◊ *etw. in eine Hülle stecken; (for a letter, of a book, magazine)* Umschlag [ˈʊmʃlaːk] der <–(e)s, Umschläge> ◊ *Welches Foto soll auf den Umschlag?; (for a cushion, furniture)* Bezug [bəˈtsuːk] der <–(e)s, Bezüge> ◊ *neue Bezüge für die Kissen kaufen; (of a CD)* Cover [ˈkavɐ] das <–s, –> 2. *(sheets, blankets)* the covers die Bettdecke [di: ˈbɛtdɛkə] <–, –n> ◊ *Sie zog die Bettdecke hoch und schloss die Augen.* 3. *(in the UK: insurance)* Versicherungsschutz [fɛˈzɪçərʊŋsʃʊts] der <–es> no pl ◊ *In diesem Fall haben Sie keinen Versicherungsschutz.* 4. *(from the weather)* Schutz [ʃʊts] der <–es> no pl take cover Schutz suchen ◊ *Als es anfing zu regnen, haben wir in einer Hütte Schutz gesucht.* under cover of darkness/night im Schutz der Dunkelheit/ Nacht 5. *(protection)* Deckung [ˈdɛkʊŋ] die <–> no

pl break cover aus der Deckung kommen give (sb)
cover jdm Deckung geben ◊ *Der Soldat gab seinem*
Kameraden Deckung. **6.** *(in order to hide sth)*
Tarnung ['ta'nʊŋ] die <–, –en> ◊ *Diese Geschichte*
dient lediglich der Tarnung. blow sb's cover jds
Tarnung aufdecken **7.** *(in the UK: replacement)* Vertretung [fe'tre:tʊŋ] die <–, –en> ◊ *Wer übernimmt*
die Vertretung für den erkrankten Mitarbeiter?
holiday cover Urlaubsvertretung ['u:ɡlaopsfetre:tʊŋ]
8. mus Coverversion ['kaveve',zjo:n] die <–, –en> ◊
Die Coverversion gefällt mir fast besser als das
Original. **9.** *(at a restaurant)* Gedeck [ɡə'dɛk] das
<–(e)s, –e> ◊ *Das Gedeck kostet in deutschen*
Lokalen nichts.

◉ under separate cover mit getrennter Post work
under cover verdeckt arbeiten from cover to cover
von Anfang bis Ende ◊ *Ich habe das Buch von*
Anfang bis Ende gelesen.

cover² [verb] **1.** *(spread over sth, protect sth)*
bedecken [bə'dɛkn̩] <bedeckt, bedeckte, hat bedeckt>
◊ *Der erste Schnee bedeckt die Berge.* ♦ *Sie bedeckte*
ihr Haar mit einem Tuch. be covered with/by/in sth
mit etw. bedeckt sein ◊ *Die Regale waren mit*
weißen Laken/mit Staub bedeckt.; *(a hole, food)*
abdecken ['apdɛkn̩] +haben ◊ *ein Loch mit einem*
Brett abdecken **2.** *(have as a topic)* behandeln
[bə'handl̩n] <behandelt, behandelte, hat behandelt> ◊
Dieses Buch behandelt die Zeit zwischen den beiden
Weltkriegen.; *(a particular case)* abdecken ['apdɛkn̩]
+haben ◊ *Das Gesetz deckt diesen Fall nicht ab.*
3. *(press)* cover sth über etw. [acc] berichten
[y:be ... bə,rɪçtn̩] <berichtet, berichtete, hat berichtet>
◊ *Wir werden später ausführlich über diesen Fall*
berichten. **4.** *(costs, damages)* decken ['dɛkn̩]
+haben ◊ *die Nachfrage decken* ♦ *Der Schaden ist*
von der Versicherung gedeckt. **5.** *(provide insurance)*
versichern [fe'zɪçɐn] <versichert, versicherte, hat versi-
chert> *mostly in adjectival passive constructions* ◊
Diesen Fall müssen Sie gesondert versichern lassen.
cover sb against sth jdn gegen etw. versichern ◊
Sind Sie gegen Wasserschäden versichert? **6.** *(a*
distance) zurücklegen [tsu'rʏkle:ɡn̩] +haben ◊ *Die*
Läuferin hatte bereits 15 km zurückgelegt. ♦ *durch-*
schnittlich 120 km in der Stunde zurücklegen **7.** mus
covern ['kaven] +haben *(tech)* ◊ *Er hat den Elvis-Hit*
,Love me tender' gecovert. **8.** *(protect sb)* cover sb
jdm Deckung geben ['dɛkʊŋ ɡe:bm̩] <gibt, gab, hat
gegeben>; *(prevent an escape)* cover sth etw. sichern
['zɪçɐn] +haben ◊ *Zwei der Beamten sicherten die*
Hinterausgänge. **9.** sport decken ['dɛkn̩] +haben ◊
einen Spieler hautnah decken

● **cover for** [phras v] **1.** *(do sb's work)* vertreten
[fe'tre:tn̩] <vertritt, vertrat, hat vertreten> ◊ *Sie vertritt*
die Chefsekretärin. **2.** *(provide an alibi or protection)*
decken ['dɛkn̩] +haben ◊ *einen Komplizen decken*
● **cover up** [phras v] **1.** *(wrap up)* sich warm
anziehen [,va'm 'antsi:ən] <zieht sich an, zog sich an,
hat sich angezogen> ◊ *Sie hatten sich warm*
angezogen, bevor sie hinaus in den Schnee gingen.
2. *(not tell the truth)* cover sth up etw. vertuschen
[fe'tʊʃn̩] <vertuscht, vertuschte, hat vertuscht> ◊ *einen*
Fehler/Skandal vertuschen **3.** cover up for decken
['dɛkn̩] +haben ◊ *seine Komplizen decken* ♦ *Ich bin*
nicht bereit, deine Fehler weiterhin zu decken. →
cover² 1.

coverage [noun] **1.** *(reports)* Berichterstattung

[bə'rɪçtlɛʃtatʊŋ] die <–, –en> ◊ *eine sachliche*
Berichterstattung durch die Presse coverage of
Berichterstattung über sth gets extensive media
coverage über etw. [acc] wird ausführlich in den
Medien berichtet
[y:be ... vɪ't ,aosfy:ɐlɪç in de:n ,me:djən bə'rɪçtət] ◊
Über die Attentate wurde ausführlich in den Medien
berichtet. **2.** *(subject-matter)* offer good coverage of
etw. gut abdecken [,ɡu:t 'apdɛkn̩] +haben ◊ *Das*
Buch deckt dieses Thema gut ab. **3.** *(in the US:*
insurance) Versicherung [fe'zɪçərʊŋ] die <–, –en> ◊
Haben Sie eine ausreichende Versicherung für Hoch-
wasserschäden?

covered → **cover²** [adj] *(with a roof)* überdacht
[ybe'daxt] *no comp/superl* ◊ *überdachte Parkplätze*
covering [noun] **1.** *(layer)* Decke ['dɛkə] die <–, –n>
covering of snow Schneedecke ['ʃne:dɛkə] **2.** *(for the*
floor in a house) Belag [bə'la:k] der <–(e)s, Beläge>
◊ *Der Fußboden bekommt demnächst einen neuen*
Belag.
covet [verb] begehren [bə'ge:rən] +haben *(lofty)* ◊ *eine*
Auszeichnung begehren ♦ *Sie begehrt ihn seit ihrer*
ersten Begegnung.
cow [noun] Kuh [ku:] die <–, Kühe> ◊ *die Kühe melken*
♦ *Die Elefantenherde hat elf Kühe.* ♦ *Diese dumme*
Kuh geht mir auf die Nerven.
coward [noun] Feigling ['faɛklɪŋ] der <–s, –e>
cowardly [adj] feig [faɛk] feige ['faɛɡə] <feiger, am
feigsten> ◊ *Mein Bruder ist sehr feige.* ♦ *ein feiger*
Mord
cozy('-ily) → **cosy('-ily)**
crab [noun] **1.** *(animal)* Krabbe ['krabə] die <–, –n>;
(as food) Krebs [kre:ps] der <–es, –e> **2.** MED
(parasite) crabs Filzläuse ['fɪltslɔøzə] die <–> *pl*
3. *(sb who keeps complaining about things)* Nörgler
['nœrɡle] der <–s, –> ♀Nörglerin ['nœrɡlərɪn] die
<–, –nen>
crack¹ [noun] **1.** *(line, first sign of breakup)* Riss [rɪs]
der <–es, –e> ◊ *In der Mauer war ein Riss.* ♦ *Risse*
in der Allianz hairline crack Haarriss ['ha:'rɪs]; *(in*
glass, china) Sprung [ʃprʊŋ] der <–(e)s, Sprünge> ◊
Die Tasse hat einen Sprung.; *(in a relationship)*
Knacks [knaks] der <–es, –e> *most sing (fam)* cracks
start to appear in sth etw. bekommt einen Knacks
2. *(narrow opening)* Spalt [ʃpalt] der <–(e)s, –e> ◊
Sie spähte durch den Spalt im Vorhang nach
draußen. **3.** *(sound)* Knall [knal] der <–(e)s, –e> ◊
der Knall einer Peitsche **4.** *(drug)* crack (cocaine)
Crack [krɛk] das <–s> *no pl*

◉ at the crack of dawn im Morgengrauen fall
through the cracks durch das Netz fallen
crack² [verb] **1.** *(a bone)* crack sth sich [dat] etw.
anbrechen ['anbrɛçn̩] <bricht an, brach an, hat ange-
brochen> ◊ *Er hat sich [dat] das Nasenbein angebro-*
chen. **2.** *(ice)* brechen ['brɛçn̩] <bricht, brach, ist
gebrochen> ◊ *Vorsicht, das Eis bricht!*; *(china, glass*
etc.) sth cracks etw. bekommt einen Sprung
[bə,kɔmt ænən 'ʃprʊŋ] <bekam, hat bekommen> sth
is cracked etw. hat einen Sprung **3.** *(break open)*
crack (open) aufbrechen ['aofbrɛçn̩] <bricht auf,
brach auf, hat/ist aufgebrochen> *transitive use*
+haben/*intransitive use* +sein ◊ *Sie hat die Kokosnuss*
mit einem Hammer aufgebrochen. ♦ *Die Eierschale*
ist aufgebrochen und ein kleiner Vogel geschlüpft.; *(a*
nut) crack sth etw. knacken ['knakn̩] +haben; *(an*
egg) crack sth etw. aufschlagen ['aofʃla:ɡn̩] <schlägt

A
B
C
D
E
F
G
H
I
J
K
L
M
N
O
P
Q
R
S
T
U
V
W
X
Y
Z

auf, schlug auf, hat aufgeschlagen> **4.** *(make a loud noise)* **krachen** ['kraxn̩] +haben ◊ *Über uns krachte ein Donnerschlag.; (shot, pistol, whip)* **knallen** ['knalən] +haben ◊ *Ein Schuss knallte durch die Abenddämmerung.* **crack a whip** mit der Peitsche knallen **5.** *(make a crackling sound)* **knacken** ['knakn̩] +haben ◊ *Die Zweige knackten unter meinen Füßen.* **crack your knuckles** mit den Fingern knacken **6.** *(hit a part of your body)* **crack sth against sth** mit etw. gegen etw. stoßen [mɪt ... ge:gn̩ ... ʃto:sn̩] <stößt, stieß, ist gestoßen> ◊ *Er ist mit dem Kopf gegen die Tür gestoßen.; (hit sb)* **crack sb over the head with sth** jdm mit etw. auf den Kopf schlagen [mɪt ... aof de:n 'kɔpf ʃla:gn̩] <schlägt, schlug, hat geschlagen> ◊ *Sie schlug ihm mit dem Schirm auf den Kopf.* **7.** *(a code, case, problem)* **knacken** ['knakn̩] +haben *(fam)* ◊ *einen Code/Safe knacken* **8.** *(break down)* **zusammenbrechen** [tsu'zamənbreçn̩] <bricht zusammen, brach zusammen, ist zusammengebrochen> ◊ *Schließlich ist er unter dem Druck zusammengebrochen.* **9.** *(voice)* **umkippen** ['ʊmkɪpm̩] +sein ◊ *Ihre Stimme kippte plötzlich um.* **10.** *(crime)* **bekämpfen** [bə'kɛmpfn̩] <bekämpft, bekämpfte, hat bekämpft> ◊ *die Kriminalität bekämpfen*

⊛ **get cracking** sich ranhalten ◊ *Wenn du die Arbeit bis morgen schaffen willst, solltest du dich besser ranhalten.* **sb cracked it** jd hat es ◊ *Jetzt habe ichs! Die Lösung ist ganz einfach!*

• **crack down** [phras v] **crack down (on sb/sth)** (gegen jdn/etw.) hart durchgreifen [ˌhaʳt 'dʊʳçgraɪfn̩] <greift durch, griff durch, hat durchgegriffen> ◊ *Die Polizei greift jetzt hart gegen Drogenhandel durch.*

• **crack on** [phras v] **crack on (with sth)** sich (bei etw.) ranhalten ['ranhaltn̩] <hält sich ran, hielt sich ran, hat sich rangehalten> *(fam)* ◊ *Wenn wir heute noch fertig werden wollen, müssen wir uns ranhalten.*

• **crack up** [phras v] **1.** *(mentally)* einen Nervenzusammenbruch bekommen [aenən 'nɛʳfn̩tsuˌzamənbrʊx bəkɔmən] <bekommt, bekam, hat bekommen> ◊ *Er hat von dem Stress einen Nervenzusammenbruch bekommen.* **2.** *(with laughter)* in Gelächter ausbrechen [ɪn gə'lɛçtɐ aosbreçn̩] <bricht aus, brach aus, ist ausgebrochen> ◊ *Als sie ihn sahen, brachen sie in Gelächter aus.* **3.** *(make sb laugh)* **crack sb up** jdn zum Lachen bringen [tsʊm 'laxn̩ brɪŋən] <bringt, brachte, hat gebracht>

⊛ **sth is not all it's cracked up to be** etw. ist nicht so gut wie man immer sagt

cracked → **crack²** [adj] **1.** *(lips)* aufgesprungen ['aofgəʃprʊŋən] no comp/superl ◊ *Meine Lippen sind ganz trocken und aufgesprungen.* **2.** *(ice, leather, voice)* brüchig ['brʏçɪç] ◊ *Das Leder ist brüchig.* ♦ *Er sprach mit brüchiger Stimme.* **3.** *(wall, wood)* rissig ['rɪsɪç] ◊ *Das Holz war rissig.* ♦ *eine rissige alte Mauer*

crackle [verb] knistern ['knɪstɐn] +haben ◊ *Das Feuer knisterte im Kamin.* ♦ *eine knisternde Atmosphäre*

cradle [noun] **1.** *(also fig) (for a baby)* Wiege ['vi:gə] die <-, -n> ◊ *Sie legte das Baby in die Wiege.* ♦ *die Wiege der Zivilisation* **2.** *(for work on buildings)* Hängegerüst ['hɛŋəgaryst] das <-(e)s, -e> **3.** *(of an old-fashioned telephone)* Gabel ['ga:bl̩] die <-, -n> ◊

den Hörer auf die Gabel legen

⊛ **from the cradle 1.** von klein auf **2.** **from the cradle to the grave** von der Wiege bis zur Bahre ◊ *in the cradle* in frühester Kindheit

craft [noun] **1.** *(trade, skill)* Handwerk ['hantvɛʳk] das <-(e)s, -e> ◊ *das Handwerk des Töpfers/Schreiners* **2.** *(sth produced by hand)* **craft(s), arts and crafts** Kunsthandwerk ['kʊnsthantvɛʳk] das <-(e)s, -e> ◊ *Das Geschäft verkauft Kunsthandwerk aus Marokko.* **3.** *(boat)* Boot [bo:t] das <-(e)s, -e> **4.** *(aircraft)* Flugzeug ['flu:ktsɔøk] das <-(e)s, -e>; *(space vehicle)* Raumfahrzeug ['raomfa:ʳtsɔøk] das <-(e)s, -e>

craftily [adv] raffiniert [rafi'ni:ɐt] <raffinierter, am raffiniertesten> ◊ *raffiniert vorgehen*

craftsman [noun] Handwerker ['hantvɛʳkɐ] der <-s, -> ◊ *Er arbeitet als selbstständiger Handwerker.* ♦ *Ein guter Handwerker findet immer eine Stelle.*

craftsmanship [noun] **1.** *(skill)* Kunstfertigkeit ['kʊnstfeːʳtɪçkaet] die <-> no pl ◊ *die Kunstfertigkeit der Handwerker* **2.** *(quality)* handwerkliche Qualität [ˌhantvɛʳklɪçə kvali'tɛːt] die <-, -en> ◊ *die ausgezeichnete handwerkliche Qualität der Schnitzereien*

craftswoman [noun] Handwerkerin ['hantvɛʳkərɪn] die <-, -nen> ◊ *Sie will Handwerkerin werden.* ♦ *Sie ist eine ausgezeichnete Handwerkerin.*

crafty [adj] raffiniert [rafi'ni:ɐt] <raffinierter, am raffiniertesten> ◊ *Das war raffiniert von dir!* ♦ *ein raffinierter Trick*

cram [verb] **1.** *(put into a narrow space)* **cram sth into/under sth** etw. in/unter etw. [acc] stopfen [ɪn/ʊntɐ ... ʃtɔpfn̩] +haben ◊ *Wir stopften die Säcke unter die Bank.* **cram your mouth with sth, cram sth into your mouth** sich [dat] den Mund mit etw. voll stopfen ◊ *Er stopfte sich den Mund mit Keksen voll.* **People crammed the streets.** Die Straßen waren voller Menschen. **2.** *(revise)* pauken ['paokn̩] +haben *(fam)*

crammed → **cram** [adj] voll gestopft ['fɔl gəʃtɔpft] no comp/superl ◊ *Der kleine Raum war voll gestopft mit Flüchtlingen.* ♦ *ein voll gestopfter Koffer*

cramp [noun] **1.** *(muscle spasm)* Krampf [krampf] der <-(e)s, Krämpfe> ◊ *einen Krampf im Oberschenkel haben* **2.** *(menstrual)* **cramps** Regelschmerzen ['re:glʃmɛʳtsn̩] die <-> pl

cramped [adj] **1.** *(small, crowded)* eng [ɛŋ] ◊ *Es war sehr eng in dem Auto.* **live in cramped conditions** auf engstem Raum leben; *(prison)* überfüllt [ybeˈfʏlt] <überfüllter, am überfülltesten> ◊ *ein überfülltes Gefängnis* **2.** *(uncomfortable)* beengt [bə'ɛŋt] <beengter, am beengtesten> seldom comp/superl ◊ *Ich fühlte mich beengt und unwohl.*

crane¹ [noun] **1.** *(machine)* Kran [kra:n] der <-(e)s, Kräne> **2.** *(bird)* Kranich ['kra:nɪç] der <-s, -e>

crane² [verb] **crane (your neck)** den Hals recken [de:n 'hals rɛkn̩] +haben ◊ *Er musste den Hals recken, um die Bühne richtig zu sehen.*

crap [noun] **1.** *(sth that is of bad quality, nonsense)* Mist [mɪst] der <-s> no pl *(fam, pej)* ◊ *der Mist, den es in der Mensa zu essen gibt* ♦ *Im Fernsehen läuft am Wochenende nur Mist.* **2.** *(useless things)* Krempel ['krɛmpl̩] der <-s> no pl *(fam, pej)* ◊ *Meine Oma hat unglaublich viel Krempel in ihrer Wohnung.* **3.** *(solid body waste)* Scheiße ['ʃaesə] die <-> no pl

(rude) ◊ *Hier stinkt es nach Scheiße.* have a crap
scheißen ['ʃaɛsn̩] <scheißt, schiss, hat geschissen>
(rude)

crash[1] [noun] **1.** *(accident)* Unfall ['ʊnfal] der
<-(e)s, Unfälle> in a crash bei einem Unfall car
crash Autounfall ['aɔtoʊnfal] plane crash Flugzeug-
absturz ['fluːktsɔɡk|apʃtʊrˈts] der
<-es, Flugzeugabstürze> train crash Zugunglück
['tsuːk|ʊnɡlʏk] das <-(e)s, -e> head-on crash Fron-
talzusammenstoß [frɔnˈtaːltsuˌzamənʃtoːs] der
<-es, Frontalzusammenstöße> **2.** *(noise)* Krachen
['kraxn̩] das <-s> no pl ◊ *Aus der Küche hörte man
ein lautes Krachen.* **3.** *(of prices, the stock market, a
computer)* Absturz ['apʃtʊrˈts] der <-es, Abstürze> ◊
der Absturz der Börse in New York ♦ *Ein Absturz des
Systems ist so gut wie ausgeschlossen.* **4.** *(of a
business)* Zusammenbruch [tsuˈzamənbrʊx] der
<-(e)s, Zusammenbrüche> ◊ *der Zusammenbruch
eines Unternehmens*

crash[2] [verb] **1.** *(car, motorbike, driver, passengers)*
einen Unfall haben [aɛnən ˈʊnfal haːbm̩] +haben ◊
Wir hatten auf der Autobahn einen Unfall. crash
your car einen Unfall mit seinem Auto haben crash
into sth gegen etw. fahren [ɡeːɡn̩ ... faːrən] <fährt,
fuhr, ist gefahren> ◊ *Das Motorrad ist gegen einen
Baum gefahren.* **2.** *(plane, computer etc.)* abstürzen
['apʃtʏrˈtsn̩] +sein ◊ *Der PC ist abgestürzt.* crash your
plane mit seinem Flugzeug abstürzen crash into sth
in etw. [acc] stürzen [ɪn ... ʃtʏrˈtsn̩] +sein ◊ *Das
Flugzeug ist ins Meer gestürzt.* **3.** *(make a loud noise)*
krachen ['kraxn̩] +haben/with a word expressing
direction of movement +sein ◊ *Draußen krachte der
Donner.* ♦ *Das Tablett krachte zu Boden.*; *(wave)*
schlagen ['ʃlaːɡn̩] <schlägt, schlug, ist geschlagen> ◊
Die Wellen schlugen gegen die Felsen. **4.** *(company)*
zusammenbrechen [tsuˈzamənbrɛçn̩] <bricht
zusammen, brach zusammen, ist zusammengebrochen>
◊ *Unter dem Druck der Konkurrenz brach die Firma
zusammen.*

• **crash out** [phras v] einpennen ['aɛnpɛnən] +sein
(fam) ◊ *Penn nicht vor dem Fernseher ein!*

crash barrier [noun] Leitplanke ['laɛtplaŋkə] die
<-, -n>

crash helmet [noun] Sturzhelm ['ʃtʊrˈtshɛlm] der
<-(e)s, -e>

crate [noun] **1.** *(for goods)* Kiste ['kɪstə] die <-, -n> a
crate of bananas eine Kiste Bananen; *(for bottles)*
Kasten ['kastn̩] der <-s, Kästen> a crate of beer ein
Kasten Bier **2.** *(for animals)* Verschlag [fɛˈʃlaːk] der
<-(e)s, Verschläge>

crater [noun] Krater ['kraːtɐ] der <-s, ->

craving [noun] Verlangen [fɛˈlaŋən] das <-s> no pl
(lofty) ◊ *Sie hatte starkes Verlangen nach einer
Zigarette.*

crawl [verb] **1.** *(move with your body flat on the
ground, with difficulty)* crawl somewhere irgendwo
herumkriechen [hɛˈrʊmkriːçn̩] <kriecht herum, kroch
herum, ist herumgekrochen> ◊ *Verletzte krochen auf
dem Boden herum.*; *(+indication of direction)* irgendwohin kriechen ['kriːçn̩] <kriecht, kroch, ist
gekrochen> ◊ *Ich will jetzt nur noch ins Bett
kriechen.*; *(baby, insect)* krabbeln ['krabl̩n̩] +haben/
with a word expressing direction of movement +sein ◊
Kann die Kleine schon krabbeln? ♦ *Da krabbelt ein
Käfer.* **2.** *(vehicle)* im Schneckentempo fahren
[ɪm ˈʃnɛkn̩ˌtɛmpoː faːrən] <fährt, fuhr, ist gefahren> ◊

*Lastwagen fuhren im Schneckentempo durch den
Ortskern.* **3.** *(time)* crawl by sich dahinziehen
[daˈhɪntsiːən] <zieht sich dahin, zog sich dahin, hat
sich dahingezogen> ◊ *Der Winter war lang und die
Wochen zogen sich dahin.* **4.** *(ingratiate yourself)*
crawl to sb vor jdm kriechen [foːɐ̯ ... ˈkriːçn̩]
<kriecht, kroch, ist gekrochen> *(pej)* ◊ *Es ist ja nicht
auszuhalten, wie der vor dem Chef kriecht.*

⊛ be crawling with sb/sth von jdm/etw. wimmeln

crayon [noun] Wachsmalstift ['vaksmaːlʃtɪft] der
<-(e)s, -e>

crazy [adj] **1.** *(insane, obsessed)* verrückt [fɛˈrʏkt] <ver-
rückter, am verrücktesten> *(fam)* ◊ *eine verrückte
Idee* ♦ *Sie wäre verrückt, wenn sie das Angebot
ablehnen würde.* crazy about sb/sth verrückt nach
jdm/etw. like crazy wie verrückt ◊ *Sie schrie wie
verrückt.* drive sb crazy jdn verrückt machen
2. *(become angry or bored)* go crazy durchdrehen
['dʊrçdreːən] +haben/sein ◊ *Mein Vater dreht durch,
wenn er das erfährt.*; *(become excited)* go crazy
toben ['toːbm̩] +haben ◊ *Als er ein Tor schoss, tobten
die Zuschauer vor Begeisterung.*

creak [verb] **1.** *(wood)* knarren ['knarən] +haben ◊ *Der
Stuhl knarrte, als er sich hinsetzte.*; *(door)* quietschen ['kviːtʃn̩] +haben ◊ *Die Tür zum Wohnzimmer
quietscht.* **2.** *(system, method)* Schwächen zeigen
['ʃvɛçn̩ tsaɛɡn̩] +haben

cream [noun] **1.** *(made from milk)* Sahne ['zaːnə] die
<-> no pl ◊ *Erdbeeren mit Sahne* cream sauce
Sahnesoße ['zaːnəzoːsə] die <-, -n> cream cake Sah-
netörtchen ['zaːnətœrˈtçən] das <-s, -> cream of
tomato soup Tomatencremesuppe
[toˈmaːtn̩kreːmzʊpə] die <-, -n> **2.** *(for the skin)*
Creme [kreːm] die <-, -s> ◊ *Die Creme zieht schnell
ein.* sun cream Sonnencreme ['zɔnənkreːm]
3. *(colo(u)r)* Creme [kreːm] das <-, -s>

⊛ the cream of the crop die Besten the cream of
... die Elite unter ... [dat]

cream cheese [noun] Frischkäse ['frɪʃkɛːzə] der <-s>
no pl

crease [noun] Falte ['faltə] die <-, -n>

create [verb] **1.** *(sth new)* schaffen ['ʃafn̩] <schafft,
schuf, hat geschaffen> ◊ *ein Kunstwerk/neueArbeits-
plätze schaffen* ♦ *die Voraussetzungen für etw.
schaffen; (a hairstyle, dish, fashion etc.)* kreieren
[kreˈiːrən] <kreiert, kreierte, hat kreiert>; *(a garden,
computer file)* anlegen ['anleːɡn̩] +haben ◊ *Er legte
einen Gemüsegarten an.* **2.** REL erschaffen [ɛˈʃafn̩]
<erschafft, erschuf, hat erschaffen> ◊ *Laut Bibel hat
Gott die Welt in sechs Tagen erschaffen.* **3.** *(cause)*
erzeugen [ɛˈtsɔɡn̩] <erzeugt, erzeugte, hat erzeugt> ◊
*Die leise Hintergrundmusik erzeugte eine
angenehme Atmosphäre.* ♦ *Druck erzeugt Gegendruck.* create an impression einen Eindruck
machen [aɛnən ˈaɛndrʊk maxn̩] +haben **4.** *(give sb a
title)* create sb sth jdn zu etw. ernennen
[tsuː ... ɛnɛnən] <ernennt, ernannte, hat ernannt> ◊ *Er
wurde 1825 zum Marquis ernannt.*

creation [noun] **1.** *(of sth new)* Schaffung ['ʃafʊŋ] die
<-> no pl job creation die Schaffung von Arbeits-
plätzen; *(of a park, gardens etc.)* Anlage ['anlaːɡə]
die <-, -n> ◊ *Was muss man bei der Anlage eines
Teichs beachten?* **2.** *(work of art)* Kreation
[kreaˈtsɪoːn] die <-, -en> ◊ *Hast du seine neueste
Kreation gesehen?*; *(shaped form)* Gebilde [ɡəˈbɪldə]
das <-s, -> ◊ *Vogelnester sind kunstvolle Gebilde.*

3. REL the Creation die Schöpfung [diː 'ʃœpfʊŋ] <-> no pl

creative(ly) [adj, adv] kreativ [krea'tiːf] ◊ *Malen ist ein kreativer Vorgang.* ♦ *verschiedene Stilmittel kreativ einsetzen* ♦ *Meine Tochter ist sehr kreativ.* creative writer Schriftsteller ['ʃrɪftʃtɛlɐ] der <-s, -> ♀Schriftstellerin ['ʃrɪftʃtɛlərɪn] die <-, -nen>

creativity [noun] Kreativität [kreativi'tɛːt] die <-> no pl

creator [noun] Schöpfer ['ʃœpfɐ] der <-s, -> ♀Schöpferin ['ʃœpfərɪn] die <-, -nen> ◊ *Der Schöpfer dieses Begriffs war Karl Marx.* ♦ *Astrid Lindgren ist als Schöpferin von Pippi Langstrumpf bekannt.* the Creator der Schöpfer

creature [noun] **1.** (living thing) Lebewesen ['leːbəveːzn̩] das <-s, -> ◊ *Alle Lebewesen müssen sterben.* **2.** (strange or frightening being) Wesen ['veːzn̩] das <-s, -> ◊ *ein außerirdisches Wesen* **3.** (person, thing created) Geschöpf [gə'ʃœpf] das <-(e)s, -e> ◊ *Er hatte Mitleid mit dem armen Geschöpf.* ♦ *Vampire sind Geschöpfe der Fantasie.* **4.** (sb controlled by sb else) Marionette [marjo'nɛtə] die <-, -n> ◊ *Er ist eine Marionette der Ölindustrie.*

crèche, creche [noun] Kinderkrippe ['kɪndɐkrɪpə] die <-, -n>

credibility [noun] Glaubwürdigkeit ['glaopvʏrˈdɪçkaet] die <-> no pl ◊ *jds Glaubwürdigkeit untergraben* gain/lose credibility an Glaubwürdigkeit gewinnen/verlieren

credible [adj] **1.** (to be believed) glaubwürdig ['glaopvʏr'dɪç] ◊ *Er ist kein glaubwürdiger Zeuge.* ♦ *Ihre Aussage war glaubwürdig.* **2.** (likely to be successful or come true) ernst zu nehmend ['ɛrnst tsuː neːmənt] no comp/superl, only before ns ◊ *ein ernst zu nehmender Gegner* ♦ *ein ernst zu nehmendes Risiko;* (chance) reell [re'ɛl] only before ns ◊ *Sie hat eine reelle Chance zu gewinnen.*

credit¹ [noun] **1.** (arrangement to pay later) Kredit [kre'diːt] der <-s, -e> ◊ *Ich kaufe nicht gern auf Kredit.* give credit to sb jdm Kredit gewähren **2.** (praise, recognition) Anerkennung ['anˈɛkɛnʊŋ] die <-, -en> ◊ *Sie verdient Anerkennung dafür, dass sie ihn doch noch überzeugt hat.* take the credit for sth die Anerkennung für etw. erhalten ◊ *Immer erhält er die Anerkennung für meine Ideen.* **3.** (sum added to an account) Gutschrift ['guːtʃrɪft] die <-, -en> ◊ *eine Gutschrift in Höhe von 1000 Euro* The account is in credit. Das Konto weist ein Guthaben auf. **4.** (entitlement) Freibetrag ['fraebətraːk] der <-(e)s, Freibeträge> **5.** (at university, college etc.) ⊜Schein [ʃaen] der <-(e)s, -e> ◊ *Für diesen Kurs bekommt man einen Schein.* **6.** LIT, FILM (an author's or director's creations) Werk [vɛrk] das <-(e)s, -e> ◊ *Goethes Werk in 12 Bänden* ♦ *Zu ihren Werken gehören Filme wie ...* He has over 30 films to his credit. Sein Werk umfasst über 30 Filme.; (a crew member's) sb's credits include sth jd hat unter anderem an etw. [dat] mitgearbeitet [hat ʊntɐ andərəm an ... mɪtgəˈbaetət]; (an actor's) jd hat unter anderem in etw. [dat] mitgespielt [hat ʊntɐ andərəm ɪn ... mɪtgəʃpiːlt] **7.** (list of people who made a film) the opening credits der Vorspann [deːɐ 'foːɐʃpan] <-(e)s, Vorspänne> the closing credits der Nachspann [deːɐ 'naːxʃpan] <-(e)s, Nachspänne>

ⓔ credit where credit's due Ehre, wem Ehre gebührt be a credit to sb, do sb credit jdm Ehre machen give sb credit for sth jdm etw. zugute halten sb is better etc. than people give them credit for jd ist besser etc. als allgemein angenommen to sb's credit das muss man jdm lassen ◊ *Jane hat ihn sofort durchschaut, das muss man ihr lassen.*

credit² [verb] **1.** (an amount of money) credit sb/sth with sth, credit sth to sb/sth jdm/etw. etw. gutschreiben ['guːtʃraebm̩] <schreibt gut, schrieb gut, hat gutgeschrieben> ◊ *Die Summe wird morgen ihrem Konto gutgeschrieben* **2.** (believe) credit sth etw. glauben ['glaobm̩] +haben ◊ *Es ist kaum zu glauben, dass er einmal Schauspieler war.* Would you credit it? Kannst du das glauben? **3.** (ascribe sth to sb) credit sb with sth jdm etw. zuschreiben ['tsuːʃraebm̩] <schreibt zu, schrieb zu, hat zugeschrieben> ◊ *Diese Erfindung wird Leonardo da Vinci zugeschrieben.;* (ironic) credit sb with sth jdm etw. zutrauen ['tsuːtraoən] +haben ◊ *Ich hätte dir einen besseren Geschmack zugetraut!* **4.** (think that sth is responsible for sth) credit sth to sth etw. einer Sache [dat] zuschreiben ['tsuːʃraebm̩] <schreibt zu, schrieb zu, hat zugeschrieben> ◊ *Die Mannschaft schreibt ihren Erfolg der guten Vorbereitung zu.*

credit card [noun] Kreditkarte [kre'diːtkaˈtə] die <-, -n>

credit note [noun] Gutschein ['guːtʃaen] der <-(e)s, -e>

creditor [noun] Gläubiger ['glɔøbɪgɐ] der <-s, -> ♀Gläubigerin ['glɔøbɪgərɪn] die <-, -nen>

creed [noun] (faith) Glaubensrichtung ['glaobmsrɪçtʊŋ] die <-, -en> ◊ *Menschen aller Glaubensrichtungen;* (statement) Glaubensbekenntnis ['glaobmsbəkɛntnɪs] das <-ses, -se> ◊ *sein politisches Glaubensbekenntnis*

creep [verb] **1.** (go quietly) schleichen ['ʃlaeçn̩] <schleicht, schlich, ist geschlichen> ◊ *heimlich durch die Speisekammer schleichen* ♦ *auf Zehenspitzen durchs Haus schleichen* **2.** (make a slow movement) kriechen ['kriːçn̩] <kriecht, kroch, ist gekrochen> ◊ *Ihre Hand kroch über den Tisch.* ♦ *Ich sah zu, wie die Schatten langsam über die Wände krochen.* Dusk crept in. Es dämmerte. **3.** (smile, sensation) sich breit machen ['braet maxn̩] +haben ◊ *Ein Lächeln machte sich auf ihrem Gesicht breit.* **4.** (error, mistake) creep into sth sich in etw. [acc] einschleichen [ɪn ... 'aenʃlaeçn̩] <schleicht sich ein, schlich sich ein, hat sich eingeschlichen> ◊ *In deinen Aufsatz haben sich einige Fehler eingeschlichen.*

● **creep by** [phras v] dahinkriechen [da'hɪnkriːçn̩] <kriecht dahin, kroch dahin, ist dahingekrochen> ◊ *Die Minuten kriechen scheinbar endlos dahin.*

● **creep up** [phras v] **1.** ansteigen ['anʃtaegn̩] <steigt an, stieg an, ist angestiegen> ◊ *Die Zahl der Verletzten ist auf über 400 angestiegen.* **2.** sb creeps up on sb jd schleicht sich an jdn an [ʃlaeçt ... an ... ˌan] <schlich sich an, hat sich angeschlichen>

cremate [verb] einäschern ['aenɛʃɐn] <äschert ein, äscherte ein, hat eingeäschert>

crest [noun] **1.** (of a hill, wave) Kamm [kam] der <-(e)s, Kämme> **2.** (of a bird) Haube ['haobə] die <-, -n>; (of a cock) Kamm [kam] der <-(e)s, Kämme> **3.** (design, emblem) Wappen ['vapm̩] das <-s, -> ◊ *das königliche Wappen*

crevasse [noun] Spalte ['ʃpaltə] die <-, -n>

crew [noun] **1.** (on a ship, aircraft) Besatzung

[bə'zatsʊŋ] die <–, –en> ◊ *Bei dem Flugzeugabsturz kam die gesamte Besatzung ums Leben.* ambulance crew Krankenwagenbesatzung ['kraŋkn̩va:gŋbəzatsʊŋ] **2.** *(on a military vehicle, in a boat race)* Mannschaft ['manʃaft] die <–, –en> **3.** *(group working together)* Team [tiːm] das <–s, –s> film crew Filmteam ['fɪlmtiːm]

crib ⟨noun⟩ **1.** *(for animals, at Christmas)* Krippe ['krɪpə] die <–, –n> ◊ *In der Krippe war Heu für die Rehe.* ♦ *Unter dem Weihnachtsbaum war eine Krippe aufgebaut.* **2.** *(used for cheating)* Spickzettel ['ʃpɪktsɛtl̩] der <–s, –> ◊ *Er hatte einen Spickzettel dabei.* **3.** *(in the US: cot)* Kinderbett ['kɪndebɛt] das <–s, –en>

cricket ⟨noun⟩ **1.** sport Kricket ['krɪkət] das <–s> no pl **2.** *(insect)* Grille ['grɪlə] die <–, –n>

crime ⟨noun⟩ **1.** *(single illegal action)* Straftat ['ʃtraːftaːt] die <–, –en>; *(more serious)* Verbrechen [fe'brɛçn̩] das <–s, –> ◊ *Sie ist einem Verbrechen zum Opfer gefallen.* ♦ *ein Verbrechen gegen die Menschlichkeit* ♦ *Es ist doch kein Verbrechen, dass ich mal allein in den Urlaub fahren will.* commit a crime ein Verbrechen begehen solve a crime ein Verbrechen aufklären scene of the crime Tatort ['taːtlɔʁt] der <–(e)s, –e> **2.** *(criminality, crime as an abstract whole)* Kriminalität [krɪminaliˈtɛːt] die <–> no pl ◊ *organisierte Kriminalität* juvenile crime Jugendkriminalität ['juːgŋt̩krɪminaliˌtɛːt]

crime rate ⟨noun⟩ Kriminalität [krɪminaliˈtɛːt] die <–> no pl

criminal¹ ⟨noun⟩ *(sb who has committed a crime)* Straftäter ['ʃtraːftɛːtɐ] der <–s, –> ♀Straftäterin ['ʃtraːftɛːtərɪn] die <–, –nen> ◊ *ein verurteilter/rückfälliger Straftäter; (sb who has committed more serious crimes)* Verbrecher [fe'brɛçɐ] der <–s, –> ♀Verbrecherin [fe'brɛçərɪn] die <–, –nen> ◊ *ein gefährlicher/skrupelloser Verbrecher*

criminal² ⟨adj⟩ kriminell [krɪmi'nɛl] ◊ *Es ist kriminell, wie die Tiere dort behandelt werden.* ♦ *eine kriminelle Verschwendung* criminal offence Straftat ['ʃtraːftaːt] die <–, –en> criminal justice system Strafrechtssystem ['ʃtraːfrɛçtszʏsˌteːm] das <–s, –e> criminal investigation polizeiliche Untersuchung [poli,tsaelɪçə ʊntɐ'zuːxʊŋ] die <–, –en> face criminal charges einer Straftat ⟨gen⟩ angeklagt werden [aene 'ʃtraːftaːt ˌangəklaːkt veːɐdn̩] criminal proceedings Strafverfahren ['ʃtraːffeːfaːrən] das <–s, –> ◊ *ein Strafverfahren gegen jdn einleiten* criminal investigation department Kriminalpolizei [krɪmi'naːlˌpoliˌtsae] die <–, –en> most sing

criminal record ⟨noun⟩ Vorstrafenregister ['foːɐʃtraːfn̩reˌgɪstɐ] das <–s, –> have a criminal record vorbestraft sein ['foːɐbəʃtraːft zaen] +sein

crisis ⟨noun⟩ Krise ['kriːzə] die <–, –n> ◊ *eine finanzielle/wirtschaftliche/politische Krise* ♦ *Sie wird mit jeder Krise gut fertig.* ♦ *Der Kranke hat die Krise überwunden.* be in crisis sich in einer Krise befinden midlife crisis Midlife-Crisis ['mɪtlaefkraesɪs] die <–> no pl

crisp¹ ⟨noun⟩ Chip [tʃɪp] der <–s, –s> most pl

crisp² ⟨adj⟩ **1.** *(bacon, bread etc.)* knusprig ['knʊsprɪç] ◊ *knusprige Waffeln* ♦ *Das Speck ist sehr knusprig.; (apple, carrot etc.)* knackig ['knakɪç] ◊ *knackige Äpfel* ♦ *Die Möhren sind schön knackig.* **2.** *(shirt, paper, weather, day)* frisch [frɪʃ] ◊ *Ich zog ein frisches Hemd an.* ♦ *Draußen ist es ziemlich frisch*

heute. **3.** *(speech, writing)* deutlich ['dɔøtlɪç] ◊ *seine deutliche Sprache* ♦ *Die Antwort war deutlich.* **4.** *(movement)* scharf [ʃaˀf] <schärfer, am schärfsten> ◊ *ein scharfer Pass nach innen*

crispbread ⟨noun⟩ Knäckebrot ['knɛkəbroːt] das <–(e)s> no pl

criteria ⟨noun⟩ Kriterien [kri'teːrjən] die <–> pl ◊ *Was sind die Kriterien für die Auswahl der Patienten?* meet the criteria die Kriterien erfüllen

critic ⟨noun⟩ *(sb who criticizes sth, sb gives their opinion about sth)* Kritiker ['kriːtɪkɐ] der <–s, –> ♀Kritikerin ['kriːtɪkərɪn] die <–, –nen> ◊ *Sie ist eine der schärfsten Kritikerinnen der Regierungspolitik.* ♦ *Fast alle Kritiker haben den Film verrissen.* literary critic Literaturkritiker [lɪtəra'tuːɐkriːtɪkɐ] Literaturkritikerin [lɪtəra'tuːɐkriːtɪkərɪn]

critical(ly) ⟨adj, adv⟩ **1.** *(criticizing, careful, difficult)* kritisch ['kriːtɪʃ] ◊ *Sie ist immer sehr kritisch.* ♦ *Die Verhandlungen haben ein kritisches Stadium erreicht.* ♦ *ein kritischer Blick auf unsere Gesellschaft* ♦ *Die Kinder sollen lernen, kritisch zu denken.* be critical of sth etw. kritisieren [kriti'ziːrən] <kritisiert, kritisierte, hat kritisiert> ◊ *Man hat ihre Reaktion allgemein kritisiert.* **2.** *(very important)* critical (to) entscheidend (für) [ɛnt'ʃaednt] ◊ *ein entscheidender Faktor* ♦ *Die Besucherzahlen sind für unseren Erfolg entscheidend.* of critical importance, critically important von entscheidender Bedeutung **3.** *(very ill)* in Lebensgefahr [ɪn 'leːbn̩sgəfaːʴ] ◊ *Einige Unfallopfer sind immer noch in Lebensgefahr.* in a critical condition in einem kritischen Zustand [ɪn aenəm ˌkriːtɪʃn̩ 'tsuːʃtant] critically ill schwer krank [ʃveːg 'kraŋk] no comp/superl ◊ *ein schwer kranker Mann* ♦ *Sie war damals schon schwer krank.* **4.** critical acclaim gute Kritiken [ˌguːtə kri'tiːkŋ] die <–> pl ◊ *Ihre neueste Show hat gute Kritiken bekommen.* critically acclaimed von den Kritikern gelobt [fɔn deːn ˌkriːtɪkɐn gə'loːpt] ◊ *sein von den Kritikern gelobter Roman* be a critical success bei den Kritikern gut ankommen [bae deːn ˌkriːtɪkɐn ˌguːt 'ankɔmən] <kommt an, kam an, ist angekommen>

criticism ⟨noun⟩ **1.** *(negative opinion, profession)* criticism (of sb/sth) Kritik (an jdm/etw.) [kri'tiːk] die <–, –en> most sing ◊ *Er lässt keine Kritik an seiner Arbeit zu.* ♦ *Ihr Vorschlag stieß auf scharfe Kritik.* ♦ *Wir bitten um konstruktive Kritik.* literary criticism Literaturkritik [lɪtəra'tuːɐkriˌtiːk] attract criticism viel kritisiert werden [fiːl kriti'ziːɐt veːɐdn̩] <wird, wurde, ist worden> ◊ *Politiker werden immer viel kritisiert.* **2.** *(negative comment on one particular issue)* Kritikpunkt [kri'tiːkpʊŋkt] der <–(e)s, –e> ◊ *Er brachte auch einige Kritikpunkte vor.*

criticize ⟨verb⟩ **1.** *(have a negative opinion on)* kritisieren [kriti'ziːrən] <kritisiert, kritisierte, hat kritisiert> ◊ *Sie kritisiert gern.* ♦ *etw. offen kritisieren* ♦ *Sie wurde für ihre Äußerung scharf kritisiert.* criticize sb/sth for doing sth jdn/etw. kritisieren, weil er/es etw. tut ◊ *Er hat die geplante Reform kritisiert, weil sie nicht weit genug geht.* **2.** *(appraise, consider carefully)* kritisch beurteilen [ˌkriːtɪʃ bə'ʊˀtaelən] <beurteilt, beurteilte, hat beurteilt>

critique ⟨noun⟩ Kritik [kri'tiːk] die <–, –en>

croaky ⟨adj⟩ heiser ['haezɐ] ◊ *Ich bin ganz heiser vom vielen Sprechen.* ♦ *Warum hast du so eine heisere Stimme?*

crockery [noun] Geschirr [gə'ʃɪrʲ] das <-(e)s, -e>

crocodile [noun] Krokodil [kroko'diːl] das <-s, -e>

crook [noun] **1.** *(dishonest person)* Gauner ['gaonɐ] der <-s, -> ♀Gaunerin ['gaonərɪn] die <-, -nen> ◊ *Die Gauner erbeuteten über zwei Millionen Euro.* **2.** crook of your arm Armbeuge ['aʳmbɔøgə] die <-, -n> **3.** *(a shepherd's)* Hirtenstab ['hɪʳtn̩ʃtaːp] der <-(e)s, Hirtenstäbe>; *(a bishop's)* Bischofsstab ['bɪʃɔfsʃtaːp]

crooked(ly) [adj, adv] **1.** *(not straight)* schief [ʃiːf] ◊ *Sie hat schiefe Zähne.* ♦ *Ist das schief oder gerade?* ♦ *Deine Krawatte sitzt schief.; (bent)* krumm [krʊm] ◊ *eine krumme Wirbelsäule* ♦ *Sie findet ihre Nase zu krumm.* **2.** *(dishonest)* korrupt [kɔ'rʊpt] <korrupter, am korruptesten> ◊ *ein korrupter Politiker* ♦ *Ist er korrupt?*

crop¹ [noun] **1.** *(plant)* Feldfrucht ['fɛltfrʊxt] die <-, Feldfrüchte> ◊ *Feldfrüchte anbauen* cash crop Marktfrucht ['maʳktfrʊxt] genetically modified crops gentechnisch veränderte Pflanzen [,geːntɛçnɪʃ fɛ|,ɛndetə 'pflantsn̩] die <-> pl **2.** *(harvest for a particular year)* Ernte ['ɛʳntə] die <-, -n> bumper crop Rekordernte [re'kɔʳt|ɛʳntə] a good crop of potatoes eine gute Kartoffelernte [aenə ,guːtə kaʳ'tɔfl̩|ɛʳntə] crop failure eine Missernte [aenə 'mɪs|ɛʳntə] **3.** *(group of people or things)* crop *(of sth)* Gruppe *(von etw.)* ['grʊpə] die <-, -n> this year's crop of films/newcomers die Filme/Neulinge dieses Jahres [diː ,fɪlmə/,nɔøliŋə diːzəs 'jaːrəs] **4.** *(hairstyle)* Kurzhaarschnitt ['kʊʳtshaːʳʃnɪt] der <-(e)s, -e> **5.** *(for riding)* Reitgerte ['raetgɐ'tə] die <-, -n>

crop² [verb] **1.** *(a picture, photo)* zuschneiden ['tsuːʃnaedn̩] <schneidet zu, schnitt zu, hat zugeschnitten> ◊ *Mit dieser Software kann man Fotos drehen und zuschneiden.* **2.** *(sb's hair)* kurz schneiden ['kʊʳts ʃnaedn̩] <schneidet, schnitt, hat geschnitten> ◊ *Sie hat sich die Haare kurz schneiden lassen.*

• **crop up** [phras v] *(appear unexpectedly)* auftauchen ['aoftaoxn̩] +sein ◊ *Es ist da ein Problem aufgetaucht.; (name)* fallen ['falən] <fällt, fiel, ist gefallen> ◊ *Komisch, Alisons Name fällt immer wieder, wenn man sich mit ihm unterhält.*

ⓔ something's cropped up es ist etwas dazwischengekommen

cross¹ [noun] **1.** *(symbol, crucifix)* Kreuz [krɔøts] das <-es, -e> ◊ *etw. mit einem Kreuz markieren* ♦ *ein Kreuz um den Hals tragen* ♦ *Das Bild stellt Jesus am Kreuz dar.* **2.** *(animal, plant)* cross *(between)* Kreuzung *(aus)* ['krɔøtsʊŋ] die <-, -en> ◊ *Die Nektarine ist eine Kreuzung aus Pfirsich und Pflaume.* **3.** *(thing combining two different things)* cross *(between)* Mischung *(aus)* ['mɪʃʊŋ] die <-, -en> ◊ *Ihre Musik ist eine Mischung aus Jazz und Rock.* **4.** *(in football)* Querpass ['kveːʳpas] der <-es, Querpässe>

cross² [adj] cross *(with sb)* böse *(auf jdn)* ['bøːzə] <böser, am bösesten> *(fam)* ◊ *Bist du noch böse auf mich?* ♦ *jdm böse Blicke zuwerfen*

cross³ [verb] **1.** *(a road, river)* überqueren [ybɐ'kveːrən] <überquert, überquerte, hat überquert> ◊ *Wann kann ein Kind allein die Straße überqueren?* **2.** *(a room, an area)* durchqueren [dʊʳç'kveːrən] <durchquert, durchquerte, hat durchquert> ◊ *Sie durchquerte das Foyer und ging die Treppe hinauf.* cross to the window zum Fenster gehen [tsʊm 'fɛnstɐ geːən]

<geht, ging, ist gegangen> **3.** *(a border)* überschreiten [ybɐ'ʃraetn̩] <überschreitet, überschritt, hat überschritten> ◊ *Wir haben gerade die französische Grenze überschritten.* cross into ... die Grenze nach ... überschreiten ◊ *In der Nacht überschritten sie die Grenze nach Albanien.* **4.** *(a road, line)* sth crosses sth etw. kreuzt etw. [krɔøtst] +haben ◊ *Hier kreuzt die Autobahn eine alte Römerstraße.* two things cross zwei Dinge kreuzen sich ◊ *Wir treffen uns an der Stelle, wo die beiden Wege sich kreuzen.* **5.** *(two plants, animals)* cross sth *(with sth)* etw. *(mit etw.)* kreuzen ['krɔøtsn̩] +haben ◊ *Ist es möglich, ein Schaf mit einer Ziege zu kreuzen?* **6.** *(expression)* cross sb's face über jds Gesicht huschen [y:bɐ ... gə'zɪçt hʊʃn̩] +sein ◊ *Ein Lächeln huschte über ihr Gesicht.* cross sb's lips um jds Lippen spielen [ʊm ... 'lɪpn̩ ʃpiːlən] +haben ◊ *Ein leichtes Lächeln spielte um ihre Lippen.* **7.** *(in football)* einen Querpass spielen [aenən 'kveːʳpas ʃpiːlən] +haben **8.** *(oppose)* cross sb jdm widersprechen [viːdɐ'ʃprɛçn̩] <widerspricht, widersprach, hat widersprochen> ◊ *Niemand wagte ihm zu widersprechen.* **9.** *(religion)* cross yourself sich bekreuzigen [bə'krɔøtsɪgn̩] <bekreuzigt sich, bekreuzigte sich, hat sich bekreuzigt>

• **cross out** [phras v] cross sth out etw. durchstreichen [dʊʳçʃtraeçn̩] <streicht durch, strich durch, hat durchgestrichen> ◊ *Sie strich das Wort durch und schrieb ein anderes darüber.*

• **cross over** [phras v] überwechseln ['yːbɐvɛksl̩n] <wechselt über, wechselte über, ist übergewechselt> ◊ *Er ist zur Opposition übergewechselt.*

crossbar [noun] **1.** *(of a goalpost)* Latte ['latə] die <-, -n> ◊ *Der Ball traf die Latte.* **2.** *(of a bicycle)* Stange ['ʃtaŋə] die <-, -n>

crossbreed [noun] Kreuzung ['krɔøtsʊŋ] die <-, -en>

crossfire [noun] Kreuzfeuer ['krɔøtsfɔøɐ] das <-s, ->

crossing [noun] **1.** *(by boat)* Überfahrt ['yːbɐfaːʳt] die <-, -en> ◊ *eine stürmische Überfahrt* ♦ *Die Überfahrt nach Dublin dauerte vier Stunden.* **2.** *(place)* Übergang ['yːbɐgaŋ] der <-(e)s, Übergänge> ◊ *Beim nächsten Übergang überquerten sie die Bahnlinie.* pedestrian crossing Fußgängerübergang ['fuːsgɛŋɐ|yːbɐgaŋ]

crossroads [noun] **1.** *(place where roads meet)* Kreuzung ['krɔøtsʊŋ] die <-, -en> ◊ *an der Kreuzung links/rechts abbiegen* **2.** *(fig)* *(turning point in a development)* Scheideweg ['ʃaedəveːk] der <-(e)s, -e> ◊ *Sie steht am Scheideweg ihrer Karriere.*

cross section [noun] Querschnitt ['kveːɐ̯ʃnɪt] der <-(e)s, -e> ◊ *ein Querschnitt durch die Bevölkerung*

crossword, crossword puzzle [noun] Kreuzworträtsel ['krɔøtsvɔʳ'trɛːtsl̩] das <-s, ->

crotch → crutch³

crouch [verb] **1.** *(sit with bent knees)* hocken ['hɔkn̩] +haben ◊ *Er hockte stumm in einer Ecke.* crouch down in die Hocke gehen [ɪn diː 'hɔkə geːən] <geht, ging, ist gegangen> **2.** *(lean forwards)* crouch over sth sich über etw. [acc] beugen [y:bɐ ... bɔøgn̩] +haben ◊ *Die Männer beugten sich über die Karte.*

crowd¹ [noun] **1.** *(of people)* Menge ['mɛŋə] die <-, -n> ◊ *Der Mann verschwand in der Menge.* crowds of people Menschenmengen ['mɛnʃn̩mɛŋən] **2.** *(at an event)* Publikum ['puːblikʊm] das <-s> no

pl ◊ *Das Publikum war begeistert.* **3.** *(group of friends)* Clique ['klɪkə] die <-, -n> ◊ *Die ganze Clique traf sich im Freibad.*
⊛ follow the crowd mit der Herde laufen **stand out** in a crowd sich von der Masse abheben

crowd² [verb] **1.** *(move)* crowd round sb sich um jdn drängen [ʊm ... ˌdrɛŋən] +haben ◊ *Alle drängten sich um das Geburtstagskind.* crowd into sth sich in etw. [acc] drängen ◊ *Wir drängten uns mit den anderen in die Küche.* **2.** *(fill a place)* füllen ['fʏlən] +haben ◊ *Hunderte von Menschen füllten die Straßen.* **3.** *(thoughts, memories)* crowd sb's mind/head jdm nicht aus dem Kopf gehen [nɪçt aʊs deːm 'kɔpf geːən] <geht, ging, ist gegangen> ◊ *Die Bilder von dem Unfall gingen mir nicht aus dem Kopf.* **4.** *(stand too close)* crowd sb jdm zu nahe kommen [tsuː 'naːə kɔmən] <kommt, kam, ist gekommen> ◊ *Komm mir nicht zu nahe!*
• **crowd out** [phras v] verdrängen [fɛ'drɛŋən] <verdrängt, verdrängte, hat verdrängt> ◊ *Die Ureinwohner wurden von den Einwanderern verdrängt.*

crowded → **crowd²** [adj] *(bus, train, schedule, timetable)* voll [fɔl] ◊ *ein volles Programm* ♦ *Die U-Bahn ist mir zu voll.*

crown¹ [noun] **1.** *(decoration worn on your head, king or queen, treetop, tooth cover)* Krone ['kroːnə] die <-, -n> ◊ *Der König trug eine goldene Krone.* ♦ *das Verhältnis zwischen Parlament und Krone* ♦ *Die Eiche hatte eine dichte Krone.* ♦ *Der Zahnarzt passte die Krone an.* crown of flowers Blumenkranz ['bluːmənkrants] der <-es, Blumenkränze> **2.** *(government)* the Crown der Staat [deːɐ̯ 'ʃtaːt] <-(e)s> no pl **3.** SPORT *(title)* Titel ['tiːtl̩] der <-s, -> ◊ *seinen Titel verteidigen* **4.** *(of your head)* Scheitel ['ʃaɪtl̩] der <-s, -> **5.** *(of a hat)* Kopfteil ['kɔpftaɪl] das <-(e)s, -e> **6.** *(of a hill)* Kuppe ['kʊpə] die <-, -n> **7.** *(outd)* *(currency)* Krone ['kroːnə] die <-, -n>; *(in the UK: coin)* Fünfschillingstück [fʏnf'ʃɪlɪŋʃtʏk] das <-(e)s, -e>

crown² [verb] **1.** *(a king or queen)* krönen ['krøːnən] +haben **2.** *(a tooth)* überkronen [ybɐ'kroːnən] <überkront, überkronte, hat überkront>

crucial [adj] *(decisive)* entscheidend [ɛnt'ʃaɪdn̩t] ◊ *von entscheidender Bedeutung sein* ♦ *Die nächsten Tage sind entscheidend.; (important)* crucial (for/to) äußerst wichtig (für) [ˌɔʏsəst 'vɪçtɪç] no comp/ superl ◊ *Es ist äußerst wichtig, dass diese Kinder lesen lernen.* ♦ *Diese Mittel sind für die Forschung äußerst wichtig.*

crucifix [noun] Kruzifix ['kruːtsifɪks] das <-es, -e>

crude(ly) [adj, adv] **1.** *(basic)* simpel ['zɪmpl̩] <simpler, am simpelsten> ◊ *eine simple, selbst gebaute Bombe* ♦ *Die Konstruktion war simpel.* ♦ *ein simpel gebauter Stall* **2.** *(rough, imprecise)* grob [groːp] <gröber, am gröbsten> ◊ *eine grobe Skizze* ♦ *eine grob geschätzte Summe* ♦ *Die Zeichnung war ziemlich grob, aber man konnte ihn erkennen.* **3.** *(vulgar, offensive)* derb [dɛʁp] ◊ *ein derber Spaß* ♦ *Sein Humor ist recht derb.* ♦ *Er drückt sich oft sehr derb aus.*

crude oil [noun] Rohöl ['roːøːl] das <-(e)s, -e>

cruel(ly) [adj, adv] grausam ['graʊzaːm] ◊ *ein grausamer Mord* ♦ *Wie kann man nur so grausam zu einem Tier sein?* ♦ *jdn grausam foltern* a cruel blow ein schwerer Schlag [aɛn ˌʃveːrə 'ʃlaːk] der <-(e)s, Schläge>

⊛ **be cruel to be kind** jdm wehtun, um ihm in der Zukunft Leid zu ersparen

cruelty [noun] *(cruel behavio(u)r)* Grausamkeit ['graʊzaːmkaɛt] die <-, -en> ◊ *die Grausamkeit dieser Worte* ♦ *die Grausamkeiten, die er im Krieg miterlebt hatte* mental cruelty seelische Grausamkeit cruelty to children Kindesmisshandlung ['kɪndəsmɪshandlʊŋ] die <-, -en> cruelty to animals Tierquälerei [tiːɐ̯kvɛːlə'raɛ] die <-, -en>

cruise¹ [noun] Kreuzfahrt ['krɔʏtsfaːɐ̯t] die <-, -en>

cruise² [verb] **1.** *(on a ship)* cruise (sth) eine Kreuzfahrt (durch etw.) machen [aɛnə 'krɔʏtsfaːɐ̯t maxn̩] +haben ◊ *Sie machten eine Kreuzfahrt durch die Ostsee.* **2.** *(aircraft)* cruise at ... in einer Höhe von ... fliegen [ɪn aɛnə ˌhøːə fɔn ... fliːgn̩] <fliegt, flog, ist geflogen> ◊ *Wir fliegen jetzt in einer Höhe von 10 000 Metern.* **3.** *(drive around slowly, drive at a certain speed)* cruise sth durch etw. fahren [dʊʁç ... faːrən] <fährt, fuhr, ist gefahren> ◊ *langsam durch die Straßen fahren* cruise (at ...) (mit ...) fahren ◊ *Wir fuhren mit 120 km/h auf der Autobahn.*

crumb [noun] **1.** *(of bread, cake etc.)* Krümel ['kryːml̩] der <-s, -> ◊ *Er wischte die Krümel vom Tisch.* **2.** *(fig) (small amount of sth)* a few crumbs of praise ein kleines Lob [aɛn ˌklaɛnəs 'loːp] das <-(e)s> no pl their only crumb of comfort ihr einziger Trost [iːɐ̯ ˌaɛntsɪgə 'troːst] <-(e)s> no pl

crumble [verb] **1.** *(break into tiny pieces)* zerkrümeln [tsɛ'kryːml̩n] <zerkrümelt, zerkrümelte, hat/ist zerkrümelt> transitive use +haben/intransitive use +sein ◊ *Das Baby hat seinen Keks zerkrümelt.* ♦ *Der Kuchen zerkrümelte.* **2.** *(fall down)* abbröckeln ['apbrœkl̩n] +sein ◊ *Der Putz bröckelt schon ab.* ♦ *Abbröckelndes Gestein kann eine Lawine auslösen.* **3.** *(stop existing, disintegrate)* zerfallen [tsɛ'falən] <zerfällt, zerfiel, ist zerfallen> ◊ *Warum ist die Sowjetunion zerfallen?; (sb's determination)* schwinden ['ʃvɪndn̩] <schwindet, schwand, ist geschwunden> ◊ *Seine Entschlossenheit schwand, als die Waffe in ihrer Hand sah.*

crunchy [adj] *(biscuit, pastry etc.)* knusprig ['knʊsprɪç] ◊ *knusprige Waffeln* ♦ *Die Kekse sind knusprig.; (fruit, vegetables)* knackig ['knakɪç] ◊ *ein knackiger Salat* ♦ *Die Äpfel sind schön knackig.*

crush¹ [noun] **1.** *(crowd)* Gedränge [gə'drɛŋə] das <-s> no pl ◊ *Wir hatten Angst, sie in dem Gedränge zu verlieren.* **2.** *(infatuation)* crush (on sb) Schwärmerei (für jdn) [ʃvɛʁmə'raɛ] die <-, -en> have a crush on sb für jdn schwärmen [fyːɐ̯ ... ˌʃvɛʁmən] +haben

crush² [verb] **1.** *(damage, destroy)* zusammendrücken [tsu'zaməndrʏkn̩] +haben ◊ *Das Auto wurde bei dem Unfall zusammengedrückt.* crush sb to death jdn erdrücken [ɛɐ̯'drʏkn̩] <erdrückt, erdrückte, hat erdrückt> ◊ *Der Bauer wurde von einem Traktor erdrückt.* **2.** *(spices, ice)* zerstoßen [tsɛ'ʃtoːsn̩] <zerstößt, zerstieß, hat zerstoßen>; *(garlic)* pressen ['prɛsn̩] +haben **3.** *(an enemy, opponent)* vernichtend schlagen [fɛˌnɪçtn̩t 'ʃlaːgn̩] <schlägt, schlug, hat geschlagen> ◊ *Sie wurden von den Niederländern vernichtend geschlagen.; (a protest)* unterdrücken [ʊntə'drʏkn̩] <unterdrückt, unterdrückte, hat unterdrückt> ◊ *Jeder Protest gegen die Regierung wurde sofort unterdrückt.* **4.** *(upset, disappoint)* niederschmettern ['niːdɐʃmɛtɐn] +haben; *often in adjectival passive constructions* ◊ *Ich war völlig niedergeschmettert, weil ich nicht eingeladen war.* **5.** *(fabric)* crush

A
B
C
D
E
F
G
H
I
J
K
L
M
N
O
P
Q
R
S
T
U
V
W
X
Y
Z

sth etw. zerknittern [ʦɐ'knɪtən] <zerknittert, zerknitterte, hat zerknittert> ◊ *Sie blieb stehen, weil sie ihr Kleid nicht zerknittern wollte.* sth crushes etw. knittert ['knɪtət] +haben ◊ *Leinen knittert sehr leicht.*

crust [noun] **1.** *(hard outer layer)* Kruste ['krʊstə] die <-, -n> ◊ *Das Gebäck hat eine schöne braune Kruste.* ♦ *Auf der Wunde hatte sich eine Kruste gebildet.* crust of bread Brotkruste ['broːtkrʊstə] the Earth's crust die Erdkruste [diː 'eːɐ̯tkrʊstə] **2.** *(on a pie)* Teigdeckel ['taɛ̯kdɛkl] der <-s, ->

crusty [adj] **1.** *(crisp)* knusprig ['knʊsprɪç] ◊ *ein knuspriges frisches Brötchen* ♦ *Das französische Weißbrot ist besonders knusprig.* **2.** *(grumpy)* brummig ['brʊmɪç] *(fam)* ◊ *ein brummiger Kollege*

crutch [noun] **1.** *(for walking)* Krücke ['krʏkə] die <-, -n> ◊ *Sie stützte sich beim Gehen auf eine Krücke.* a pair of crutches zwei Krücken be on crutches an Krücken gehen **2.** *(fig)* need sb as a crutch auf jds Unterstützung angewiesen sein [aɔf ... ʊntɐ'ʃtʏtsʊŋ ˌaŋɡəviːzn̩ zaɛ̯n] +sein ◊ *Seit ihrer Krankheit war sie auf die Unterstützung der Kinder angewiesen.* use sth as a crutch ohne etw. nicht auskommen [oːnə ... nɪçt 'aɔskɔmən] <kommt aus, kam aus, ist ausgekommen> ◊ *Du kommst ja ohne Alkohol nicht mehr aus.* **3.** *(on trousers, body)* Schritt [ʃrɪt] der <-(e)s, -e> ◊ *Diese Hose spannt im Schritt.*

cry¹ [noun] **1.** *(sound expressing emotion or pain, utterance of a bird)* Schrei [ʃraɛ̯] der <-(e)s, -e> ◊ *Sie stieß einen empörten Schrei aus.* ♦ *der Schrei einer Möwe* cry of pain Schmerzensschrei ['ʃmɛɐ̯tsn̩sʃraɛ̯] give a cry schreien ['ʃraɛ̯ən] <schreit, schrie, hat geschrien> **2.** *(call)* Ruf [ruːf] der <-(e)s, -e> ◊ *der Ruf der Mutter nach ihrem Kind* cry for help Hilferuf ['hɪlfəruːf] **3.** *(howling)* Heulen ['hɔɡlən] das <-s> *no pl* ◊ *das Heulen eines Wolfs* **4.** *(emotional reaction)* Aufschrei ['aɔfʃraɛ̯] der <-(e)s, -e> ◊ *ein Aufschrei der Empörung* **5.** have a good cry sich ausweinen ['aɔsvaɛ̯nən] +haben ◊ *Hast du niemanden, bei dem du dich ausweinen kannst?*

cry² [verb] **1.** *(shed tears)* weinen ['vaɛ̯nən] +haben ◊ *bitterlich/heftig/lautlos weinen* ♦ *Freudentränen weinen* cry for sb/sth nach jdm/etw. weinen ◊ *Das Kind weinte nach seiner Mutter/seinem Schnuller.* cry over sb/sth um jdn/etw. weinen cry with pain/ happiness etc. vor Schmerzen/Glück etc. weinen cry tears of rage vor Wut weinen cry yourself to sleep sich in den Schlaf weinen **2.** *(call, shout)* rufen ['ruːfn̩] <ruft, rief, hat gerufen> ◊ *mit lauter Stimme rufen* ♦ *Sie riefen: „Bravo!"* ♦ *Wir riefen seinen Namen.* cry for help um Hilfe rufen cry sth in surprise etw. voller Überraschung rufen **3.** *(utter sounds of pain etc., shout loudly, bird: make a loud sound)* schreien ['ʃraɛ̯ən] <schreit, schrie, hat geschrien> ◊ *Das Baby hat die ganze Nacht geschrien.* ♦ *„Ruhe!", schrie sie.* ♦ *Er schrie ihren Namen.* ♦ *In der Ferne schrie eine Eule.; (wolf)* heulen ['hɔɡlən] +haben

crypt [noun] Gruft [ɡrʊft] die <-, Grüfte>

crystal [noun] **1.** *(substance in a regular shape)* Kristall [krɪs'tal] der <-s, -e> ice crystals Eiskristalle ['aɛ̯skrɪsˌtalə] **2.** *(quartz)* Bergkristall ['bɛɐ̯kkrɪsˌtal] der <-s, -e> **3.** *(glass, glassware)* Kristall [krɪs'tal] das <-s> *no pl* crystal bowl Kristallschale [krɪs'talʃaˌlə] die <-, -n>

cub [noun] Junge ['jʊŋə] das <-n, die Jungen> *but: ein Junges* ◊ *Die Bärin hatte ein Junges dabei.* ♦ *Das Junge war etwa ein Jahr alt.*

cube [noun] Würfel ['vʏ'fl] der <-s, -> ◊ *das Volumen eines Würfels* ♦ *das Brot in Würfel schneiden* ♦ *zwei Würfel Zucker* cubes of cheese Käsewürfel ['kɛːzəvʏ'fl]

cubicle [noun] Kabine [ka'biːnə] die <-, -n> shower cubicle Duschkabine ['duːʃka,biːnə]

cucumber [noun] Gurke ['ɡʊ'kə] die <-, -n>

cuddle [verb] schmusen ['ʃmuːzn̩] +haben ◊ *In der Ecke schmuste ein Pärchen.* cuddle sb jdn an sich [acc] drücken ['an ... drʏkn̩] +haben ◊ *Er nahm sie in den Arm und drückte sie an sich.*
• **cuddle up** [phras v] cuddle up to sb sich an jdn kuscheln [an ... ˌkʊʃln̩] +haben ◊ *Er kuschelte sich an seine Mutter.*

cue [noun] **1.** *(signal: spoken)* Stichwort ['ʃtɪçvɔ'ɐ̯t] das <-(e)s, Stichwörter> ◊ *Das war das Stichwort für meinen Auftritt.; (sign)* Zeichen ['ʦaɛ̯çn̩] das <-s, -> ◊ *Sein Gähnen war das Zeichen, die Party zu beenden.* **2.** *(for playing snooker, billiards)* Queue [køː] der <-s, -s>
ⓔ right on cue wie erwartet take your cue from sb sich nach jdm richten

cuff [noun] **1.** *(on a sleeve)* Manschette [man'ʃɛtə] die <-, -n> ◊ *ein Hemd mit breiten Manschetten* **2.** *(on trousers)* Aufschlag ['aɔfʃlaːk] der <-(e)s, Aufschläge> ◊ *eine Hose mit Aufschlägen*

culprit [noun] *(person)* Täter ['tɛːtɐ] der <-s, -> ♀Täterin ['tɛːtərɪn] die <-, -nen>
ⓔ be the culprit (be the cause of sth bad) schuld daran sein

cult [noun] **1.** *(religious)* Sekte ['zɛktə] die <-, -n> ◊ *Sie gehört zu einer merkwürdigen Sekte.* **2.** *(worship, object of admiration)* Kult [kʊlt] der <-(e)s, -e> ◊ *der Kult der Isis* ♦ *der Kult um Schönheit und Fitness*

cultivate [verb] **1.** *(a piece of land)* bebauen [bə'baɔən] <bebaut, bebaute, hat bebaut> ◊ *In der Steinzeit wurde dieses Land schon bebaut.* **2.** *(a crop, plant)* anbauen ['anbaɔən] +haben ◊ *Sie bauen Reis/Tomaten/Baumwolle/Tabak an.* **3.** *(a relationship, skill, or attitude)* kultivieren [kʊlti'viːrən] <kultiviert, kultivierte, hat kultiviert> ◊ *Er kultiviert sein Image/die Freundschaft mit dem Chef.*

cultivated → cultivate [adj] **1.** *(educated, refined)* kultiviert [kʊlti'viːɐ̯t] <kultivierter, am kultiviertesten> ◊ *eine kultivierte Umgebung* ♦ *Er ist nicht besonders kultiviert.* **2.** *(plant)* Zucht... [ʦʊxt] cultivated sort Zuchtsorte ['ʦʊxtzɔ'ɐ̯tə] die <-, -n>

cultivation [noun] **1.** *(of plants, crops)* Anbau ['anbaɔ] der <-(e)s> *no pl* ◊ *der Anbau von Zuckerrüben; (land)* be under cultivation landwirtschaftlich genutzt werden [ˌlantvɪ'ɐ̯tʃaftlɪç ɡə'nʊtst veːɐ̯dn̩] <wird, wurde, ist worden> **2.** *(of a relationship, skill, an attitude)* Kultivierung [kʊlti'viːrʊŋ] die <-> *no pl*

cultural [adj] kulturell [kʊltu'rɛl] *no comp/superl, mostly before ns* ◊ *kulturelle Unterschiede* ♦ *das kulturelle Leben in der Hauptstadt*

culture [noun] Kultur [kʊl'tuːɐ̯] die <-, -en> ◊ *die westliche Kultur*

cultured [adj] kultiviert [kʊlti'viːɐ̯t] <kultivierter, am kultiviertesten> ◊ *eine gepflegte und kultivierte Dame* ♦ *Ihr neuer Freund ist sehr kultiviert.*

cumulative [adj] Gesamt... [ɡə'zamt] cumulative dose Gesamtdosis [ɡə'zamtdoːzɪs] die <-, Gesamtdosen>

cumulative effect Gesamtwirkung [gə'zamtvɪˈkʊŋ] die <-, -en>

cunning(ly) ⟨adj, adv⟩ *(plan, trick)* raffiniert [rafi'niːɛt] <raffinierter, am raffiniertesten> ◊ *Ihr Plan war sehr raffiniert.* ♦ *ein raffinierter Trick* ♦ *Die Strategie war raffiniert ausgedacht.*

cup ⟨noun⟩ **1.** *(for coffee, tea etc.)* Tasse ['tasə] die <-, -n> ◊ *Die Tasse hat einen Sprung.* ♦ *Ich habe schon drei Tassen getrunken.* a cup of coffee eine Tasse Kaffee **2.** *(trophy, competition)* Pokal [po'kaːl] der <-s, -e> ◊ *Der Verbandspräsident übergab ihr den Pokal.* the Cup der Pokal ◊ *Sie sind aus dem Pokal ausgeschieden.* **3.** *(of a bra)* Körbchen ['kœrpçən] das <-s, -> **4.** *(drink, in compound ns)* fruit cup *Mischgetränk aus Alkohol und Fruchtsaft*
ⓔ in the cup of your hand in der hohlen Hand not sb's cup of tea nicht jds Fall *(fam)*

cupboard ⟨noun⟩ *(piece of furniture)* Schrank [ʃraŋk] der <-(e)s, Schränke> ◊ *Holst du mal das Geschirr aus dem Schrank?* ♦ *Ich habe die Hosen in den Schrank gelegt.; (small room)* Wandschrank ['vantʃraŋk] ◊ *ein begehbarer Wandschrank*

cure¹ ⟨noun⟩ **1.** MED *(remedy)* Heilmittel ['haɛlmɪtl] das <-s, -> ◊ *ein Heilmittel für/gegen eine Krankheit; (treatment)* Heilverfahren ['haɛlfefaːrən] das <-s, -> ◊ *ein neues Heilverfahren erproben; (restoration of health)* Heilung ['haɛlʊŋ] die <-, -en> most sing ◊ *Die Medizin brachte schnelle Heilung.* **2.** *(solution)* Mittel ['mɪtl] das <-s, -> ◊ *ein Mittel gegen die hohe Arbeitslosigkeit* miracle cure Wundermittel ['vʊndəmɪtl]

cure² ⟨verb⟩ **1.** *(a person, from an illness or bad habit)* heilen ['haɛlən] +haben ◊ *von einer Sucht/Krankheit geheilt werden* ♦ *Diese Krankheit kann man heute heilen.* ♦ *Meine Kinder heilten mich von meinem übertriebenen Ordnungssinn.* **2.** *(solve a problem)* cure sth einer Sache ⟨dat⟩ abhelfen ['aphɛlfn] <hilft ab, half ab, hat abgeholfen> ◊ *Wie können wir der hohen Arbeitslosigkeit abhelfen?* ♦ *einem Missstand abhelfen* **3.** *(foods: preserve)* haltbar machen ['haltbaːr maxn] +haben ◊ *Das Fleisch wird getrocknet und dadurch haltbar gemacht.; (dry)* trocknen ['trɔknən] <trocknet, trocknete, hat getrocknet> ◊ *Der Fisch wird anschließend getrocknet.; (salt)* pökeln ['pøːkln] +haben ◊ *Fleisch pökeln; (smoke)* räuchern ['rɔçən] +haben ◊ *Schinken räuchern*

curiosity ⟨noun⟩ **1.** *(inquisitiveness)* Neugier ['nɔɡiːɐ] die <-> no pl ◊ *seine Neugier befriedigen* ♦ *Ich platze vor Neugier auf deinen Freund.* idle curiosity reine Neugier ◊ *Ich habe die Tür aus reiner Neugier geöffnet.* **2.** *(strange object, person)* Kuriosität [kurjozi'tɛːt] die <-, -en> ◊ *Der Aw Boon Haw Garden in Hongkong ist eine Kuriosität.*
ⓔ curiosity killed the cat sei nicht so neugierig „*Was machst du denn da?" — „Sei nicht so neugierig!"*

curious ⟨adj⟩ **1.** *(inquisitive)* neugierig ['nɔɡiːrɪç] ◊ *neugierige Blicke* ♦ *Ich bin neugierig, ob er das schafft.* ♦ *Sie war neugierig zu erfahren, wie es das gemacht hatte.* **2.** *(strange)* seltsam ['zɛltzaːm] ◊ *Seine Geschichte ist seltsam.* ♦ *Was für eine seltsame Idee!*

curl¹ ⟨noun⟩ **1.** *(of hair)* Locke ['lɔkə] die <-, -n> ◊ *ein kleines Mädchen mit blonden Locken* **2.** curl of smoke Rauchkringel ['raʊxkrɪŋl] der <-s, -> ◊ *Er*

blies Rauchkringel in die Luft.
ⓔ with a curl of your lips mit gekräuselten Lippen

curl² ⟨verb⟩ **1.** *(hair)* curl sth etw. locken ['lɔkn] +haben have your hair curled sich ⟨dat⟩ beim Friseur die Haare locken lassen sth curls etw. lockt sich ◊ *Wenn meine Haare feucht werden, locken sie sich.* **2.** *(smoke, water, lips)* sich kräuseln ['krɔɡzln] +haben ◊ *Das Wasser kräuselte sich im Wind.* ♦ *Seine Lippen kräuselten sich spöttisch.; (ivy)* sich ranken ['raŋkn] +haben ◊ *Efeu rankte sich um den Baumstamm.; (road)* sich schlängeln ['ʃlɛŋln] +haben ◊ *Die Straße schlängelt sich durch grüne Landschaften.* **3.** *(paper)* sich wellen ['vɛlən] +haben ◊ *Die Seiten des alten Buches begannen sich zu wellen.*

curly ⟨adj⟩ *(hair)* lockig ['lɔkɪç] ◊ *lockiges Haar haben; (tail)* geringelt [ɡə'rɪŋlt] no comp/superl ◊ *Das Schwein hat einen geringelten Schwanz.; (writing, pattern)* verschnörkelt [fɛ'ʃnœrklt] ◊ *eine verschnörkelte Schrift*

currant ⟨noun⟩ **1.** *(dried fruit)* Korinthe [ko'rɪntə] die <-, -n> ◊ *Weihnachtsbrot mit Korinthen und Honig* **2.** *(red or black fruit)* Johannisbeere [jo'hanɪsbeːrə] die <-, -n> ◊ *Marmelade aus Erdbeeren und Johannisbeeren*

currency ⟨noun⟩ **1.** FIN *(system of money)* Währung ['vɛːrʊŋ] die <-, -en> ◊ *die britische Währung* ♦ *eine starke Währung; (money)* Geld [ɡɛlt] das <-(e)s> no pl ◊ *Wir hatten nur japanisches Geld bei uns.* Take some currency with you. Nimm/Nehmt auch Bargeld mit. **2.** *(prevalence)* Verbreitung [fɛ'braɛtʊŋ] die <-, -en> ◊ *eine Technologie, die weite Verbreitung gefunden hat* gain currency sich verbreiten [fɛ'braɛtn] <verbreitet sich, verbreitete sich, hat sich verbreitet> ◊ *Dieser Begriff hat sich in den USA rasch verbreitet.*

current¹ ⟨noun⟩ **1.** *(of water)* Strömung ['ʃtrøːmʊŋ] die <-, -en> ◊ *gegen die Strömung schwimmen* ♦ *eine starke Strömung; (of air)* Luftstrom ['lʊftʃtroːm] der <-(e)s, Luftströme> ◊ *sich vom Luftstrom nach oben tragen lassen.* TECHN *(electrical)* Strom [ʃtroːm] der <-(e)s, Ströme> ◊ *elektrischer Strom*
ⓔ current of popular opinion Strom der öffentlichen Meinung ◊ *gegen den Strom der öffentlichen Meinung anschwimmen*

current² ⟨adj⟩ **1.** *(present)* gegenwärtig ['ɡeːɡŋvɛˈtɪç] no comp/superl, only before ns ◊ *Die gegenwärtige Situation ist eher schlecht.* ♦ *der gegenwärtige Bundeskanzler; (week, month, research)* laufend ['laʊfn̩t] no comp/superl, only before ns ◊ *in der laufenden Woche* ♦ *Ausgaben im laufenden Monat; (opinion, theory)* verbreitet [fɛ'braɛtət] ◊ *eine weit verbreitete Theorie/Meinung; (word, spelling)* gebräuchlich [ɡə'brɔçlɪç] ◊ *ein gebräuchlicher Ausdruck* **2.** *(up-to-date, valid)* aktuell [aktu'ɛl] ◊ *Ist das Ihre aktuelle Adresse?* ♦ *Diese Genehmigung ist nicht mehr aktuell.*

current account ⟨noun⟩ Girokonto ['ʒiːroˌkonto:] das <-s, Girokonten> ◊ *Der Betrag wurde vom Girokonto abgebucht.*

currently ⟨adv⟩ zurzeit ['tsuːɐ̯'tsaɛt] ◊ *Sie wohnt zurzeit in Kassel.* ♦ *Zurzeit ist er arbeitslos.*

curriculum ⟨noun⟩ Lehrplan ['leːɐplaːn] der <-(e)s, Lehrpläne> ◊ *etw. auf den Lehrplan halten* be on the curriculum auf dem Lehrplan stehen

curriculum vitae ⟨noun⟩ Lebenslauf ['leːbm̩slaɔf] der <-(e)s, Lebensläufe> ◊ *ein tabellarischer Lebenslauf*

A
B
C
D
E
F
G
H
I
J
K
L
M
N
O
P
Q
R
S
T
U
V
W
X
Y
Z

♦ *Bitte senden Sie uns Ihren Lebenslauf mit Foto.*

curse [verb] *(swear)* sb curses jd **flucht** [fluːxt] +*haben* ◊ *laut fluchen* ♦ *Sie fluchte, weil sich das Tor nicht öffnen ließ.*; *(get angry about sth or sb, use magic powers)* curse sb/sth jdn/etw. **verfluchen** [fɛˈfluːxn̩] <verflucht, verfluchte, hat verflucht> ◊ *Eine böse Hexe hat den Prinzen verflucht.* ♦ *Er verfluchte seinen Wagen, der wieder einmal nicht ansprang.* curse yourself sich **verfluchen** Curse you/it! Verflucht!

curtain [noun] 1. *(for a window, in the theatre)* **Vorhang** [ˈfoːɡhaŋ] der <-(e)s, Vorhänge> ◊ *die Vorhänge zuziehen/öffnen* ♦ *Als die Vorführung zu Ende war, fiel der Vorhang.* 2. *(fig)* curtain of ... ...**wand** [vant] die <-, ...wände> curtain of mist/fog **Nebelwand** [ˈneːbl̩vant] ◊ *Eine Nebelwand versperrte uns plötzlich die Sicht.* curtain of flames **Flammenwand** [ˈflamənvant]

curve[1] [noun] *(of a road, graph)* **Kurve** [ˈkʊɐ̯və] die <-, -n> ◊ *in einer scharfen Kurve ins Schleudern geraten* ♦ *eine Kurve eischnen/berechnen*; *(of a river)* **Biegung** [ˈbiːɡʊŋ] die <-, -en> ◊ *Das Dorf ist gleich hinter der nächsten Biegung.*; *(of the body, a vase etc.)* **Rundung** [ˈrʊndʊŋ] die <-, -en> ◊ *die sanften Rundungen ihres Körpers*

curve[2] [verb] *(line, road etc.)* **einen Bogen machen** [aenən ˈboːɡn̩ maxn̩] +*haben* ◊ *Der Weg macht dort einen Bogen.* ♦ *Die Straße macht einen Bogen um die Stadt.* curve your lips/mouth into a smile die **Lippen/den Mund zu einem Lächeln verziehen** [diː ˌlɪpm̩/deːn ˌmʊnt tsuː aenəm ˈlɛçln̩ fɛtsiːən] <verzieht, verzog, hat verzogen> ◊ *Sie verzog die Lippen zu einem leichten Lächeln.*

curved → curve[2] [adj] *(not straight)* **gebogen** [ɡəˈboːɡn̩] ◊ *eine gebogene Linie zeichnen* ♦ *ein Vogel mit gebogenem Schnabel*; *(arch, surface)* **gewölbt** [ɡəˈvœlpt] <gewölbter, am gewölbtesten> ◊ *eine gewölbte Decke*

cushion [noun] 1. *(pillow)* **Kissen** [ˈkɪsn̩] das <-s, -> ◊ *Auf ihrem Sofa liegen viele bunte Kissen.* 2. TECHN *(of a hovercraft)* air cushion **Luftkissen** [ˈlʊftkɪsn̩] das <-s, -> 3. *(fig) (buffer)* **Polster** [ˈpɔlstɐ] das <-s, -> ◊ *ein Polster für schlechtere Zeiten* 4. GAME *(in billiards)* **Bande** [ˈbandə] die <-, -n> ◊ *gegen die Bande spielen*

custody [noun] 1. LAW *(of children)* **Sorgerecht** [ˈzɔʁɡəʁɛçt] das <-(e)s, -e> most sing ◊ *Dem Vater wurde das Sorgerecht entzogen.* ♦ *Die Eltern teilen sich das Sorgerecht für die Kinder.* 2. *(imprisonment)* **Haft** [haft] die <-> no pl ◊ *Der Tatverdächtige blieb in Haft.* take sb into custody jdn **verhaften** [fɛˈhaftn̩] <verhaftet, verhaftete, hat verhaftet> ◊ *Der Täter wurde noch am Tatort verhaftet.* 3. *(safe keeping, guardianship)* in sb's custody in jds **Obhut** [ɪn ... ˈɔphuːt] ◊ *Die Kinder sind zurzeit in der Obhut der Polizei.*

custom [noun] 1. *(tradition, convention)* **Brauch** [braʊx] der <-(e)s, Bräuche> ◊ *Bräuche pflegen* ♦ *Wie es in der Gegend Brauch ist, wurde die Braut entführt.* ♦ *Touristen werfen nach altem Brauch Münzen in den Brunnen.*; *(habit)* **Gewohnheit** [ɡəˈvoːnhaet] die <-, -en> ◊ *Wie es seine Gewohnheit war, stand er früh auf.* 2. ECON *(people buying from a shop)* **Kundschaft** [ˈkʊntʃaft] die <-> no pl ◊ *Die Fitnesscenter werben um Kundschaft.* get sb's custom jdn als **Kunden gewinnen** [als ˈkʊndn̩ ɡəvɪnən] <gewinnt, gewann, hat gewonnen>

customary [adj] **üblich** [ˈyːplɪç] ◊ *Es ist üblich, in Restaurants ein Trinkgeld zu geben.* ♦ *Sie antwortete mit ihrer üblichen Offenheit.*

customer [noun] **Kunde** [ˈkʊndə] der <-n, -n> ♀**Kundin** [ˈkʊndɪn] die <-, -nen> ◊ *einen Kunden bedienen* ♦ *sich um neue Kunden bemühen* ♦ *Diese Kundin möchte etwas reklamieren.*

⊙ an awkward customer ein schwieriger Typ *(fam)*

customer service (department) [noun] **Kundendienst** [ˈkʊndn̩diːnst] der <-(e)s, -e>

custom-made [adj] **nach Maß** [naːx ˈmaːs] ◊ *ein Anzug/Schuhe nach Maß* ♦ *eine Kücheneinrichtung nach Maß*

customs [noun] **Zoll** [tsɔl] der <-(e)s, Zölle> ◊ *Der Zoll hat Drogen im Auto gefunden.* ♦ *Wir müssen noch durch den Zoll.* ♦ *für etw. Zoll bezahlen*

cut[1] [noun] 1. *(wound, injury, act of cutting, fit of clothes, hairstyle)* **Schnitt** [ʃnɪt] der <-(e)s, -e> ◊ *Aus dem Schnitt in ihrer Hand quoll Blut.* ♦ *einen Schnitt in etw.* [acc] *machen* ♦ *Der Arzt durchtrennte mit zwei Schnitten den Nerv.* ♦ *Der Schnitt dieses Sakkos gefällt mir nicht.* ♦ *Der neue Schnitt steht ihr wirklich gut.* 2. *(reduction)* **Kürzung** [ˈkʏɐ̯tsʊŋ] die <-, -en> ◊ *Im Ausbildungsbereich wurden finanzielle Kürzungen vorgenommen.* ♦ *eine Kürzung des Gehalts hinnehmen müssen*; *(in prices, taxes)* **Senkung** [ˈzɛŋkʊŋ] die <-, -en> ◊ *eine Senkung der Steuern ankündigen* 3. *(act of cutting sb's hair)* **Schneiden** [ˈʃnaedn̩] das <-s> no pl ◊ *Einmal Schneiden und Föhnen, bitte!* 4. *(removal of parts of a text, film etc.)* **Streichung** [ˈʃtraeçʊŋ] die <-, -en> ◊ *Streichungen am Text vornehmen* ♦ *Die Streichung der zweiten Szene hat dem Theaterstück geschadet.* 5. FILM **Schnitt** [ʃnɪt] der <-(e)s, -e> ◊ *Die Schnitte im Film sind gut gesetzt und tragen zur Spannung bei.* ♦ *„Schnitt!", rief der Regisseur.* 6. *(of meat)* **Stück** [ʃtʏk] das <-(e)s, -e> ◊ *Sie legte ein Stück Fleisch auf den Teller.* ♦ *ein Stück von der Schulter* 7. *(fam) (share)* **Anteil** [ˈantael] der <-(e)s, -e> ◊ *einen Anteil von 15 Prozent verlangen*

cut[2] [verb] 1. *(use a knife, be sharp, hurt)* **schneiden** [ˈʃnaedn̩] <schneidet, schnitt, hat geschnitten> ◊ *Papier in Streifen schneiden* ♦ *einen Apfel in zwei Hälften schneiden* ♦ *ein Loch ins Tischtuch schneiden* ♦ *Diese Messer schneiden gut/schlecht.* have/get your hair cut sich [dat] die **Haare schneiden lassen** cut your/sb's (finger)nails sich/jdm die Fingernägel schneiden cut yourself sich **schneiden** cut your finger sich in den Finger schneiden; *(grass)* **mähen** [ˈmɛːən] +*haben* ◊ *den Rasen mähen*; *(a rope, thread, piece of paper)* **durchschneiden** [ˈdʊɐ̯çʃnaedn̩] <schneidet durch, schnitt durch, hat durchgeschnitten> ◊ *Er schnitt das Seil durch.* cut off **abschneiden** [ˈapʃnaedn̩] <schneidet ab, schnitt ab, hat abgeschnitten> ◊ *Schneide dir doch noch ein Stück Kuchen ab!*; *(a diamond, glass)* **schleifen** [ˈʃlaefn̩] <schleift, schliff, hat geschliffen> ◊ *Das Glas muss noch geschliffen werden.*; *(stone)* **hauen** [ˈhaʊən] <haut, haute, hat gehauen> ◊ *Stufen in den Fels hauen* cut open **aufschneiden** [ˈaʊfʃnaedn̩] <schneidet auf, schnitt auf, hat aufgeschnitten> ◊ *einen Sack aufschneiden* ♦ *Ich habe mir an den Scherben den Fuß aufgeschnitten.* cut sth out of sth etw. aus etw. **ausschneiden** [aʊs ... ˌaʊsʃnaedn̩] <schneidet aus, schnitt aus, hat ausgeschnitten> ◊ *Sie*

schnitt den Artikel aus der Zeitschrift aus. **2.** *(reduce prices, costs)* reduzieren [redu'tsiːrən] <reduziert, reduzierte, hat reduziert> ◊ *den Preis für ein Produkt reduzieren* ♦ *Ausgaben reduzieren; (reduce hours, time)* verkürzen [fɛ'kʏrtsn̩] <verkürzt, verkürzte, hat verkürzt> ◊ *die Arbeitszeit verkürzen; (drugs)* cut sth with sth etw. mit etw. strecken [mɪt ... ʃtrɛkn̩] +haben ◊ *Das Kokain wurde mit Staubzucker gestreckt.* **3.** IT ausschneiden ['aosʃnaedn̩] <schneidet aus, schnitt aus, hat ausgeschnitten> ◊ *Textelemente ausschneiden und woanders einfügen.* **4.** *(disconnect)* cut (off) abstellen ['apʃtɛlən] +haben ◊ *(jdm) den Strom abstellen* ♦ *Bitte stellen Sie den Motor ab!; (interrupt)* unterbrechen [ʊntɐ'brɛçn̩] <unterbricht, unterbrach, hat unterbrochen> ◊ *Die Sauerstoffzufuhr zum Gehirn wurde unterbrochen.* **5.** *(make shorter)* kürzen ['kʏrtsn̩] +haben ◊ *einen Vortrag um 15 Minuten kürzen* ♦ *Sie haben den Film erheblich gekürzt.; (delete)* herausstreichen [hɛ'raosʃtraeçn̩] <streicht heraus, strich heraus, hat herausgestrichen> ◊ *eine Szene aus einem Film herausstreichen* **6.** GAME cut the cards abheben ['apheːbm̩] <hebt ab, hob ab, hat abgehoben> ◊ *Du musst abheben.* **7.** *(divide an area)* teilen ['taelən] +haben ◊ *Der Fluss teilt das Tal.* **8.** *(a record)* machen ['maxn̩] +haben ◊ *Der Sänger hat eine neue CD gemacht.* **9.** *(intersect)* kreuzen ['krɔøtsn̩] +haben ◊ *An dieser Stelle kreuzt die Straße eine Bahnlinie.*

⊚ cut it es schaffen ◊ *Er hat es als Künstler geschafft.*

• **cut across** phras v cut across sth **1.** *(take a short cut)* quer über etw. acc gehen [kveːɐ yːbɐ ... geːən] <geht, ging, ist gegangen> ◊ *Wir sind quer über das Feld gegangen.* **2.** *(intersect)* kreuzen ['krɔøtsn̩] ◊ *Hier kreuzt die Hauptstraße eine Bahnlinie.* **3.** *(concern different groups)* sich durch etw. ziehen [dʊrç ... tsiːən] <zieht sich, zog sich, hat sich gezogen> ◊ *Die Angst vor Arbeitslosigkeit zieht sich durch alle Generationen.*

• **cut back** phras v **1.** *(reduce expenditure, staff etc.)* cut back (on) sth etw. reduzieren [redu'tsiːrən] <reduziert, reduzierte, hat reduziert> ◊ *Wir müssen unsere Ausgaben in Zukunft ein wenig reduzieren.* ♦ *die Anzahl der Angestellten reduzieren; (reduce hours, time)* etw. verkürzen [fɛ'kʏrtsn̩] <verkürzt, verkürzte, hat verkürzt> ◊ *die Arbeitszeit verkürzen* **2.** cut back on smoking/drinking weniger rauchen/trinken [ˌveːnɪgɐ 'raoxn̩/'trɪŋkn̩] **3.** *(a plant)* cut sth back etw. zurückschneiden [tsu'rʏkʃnaedn̩] <schneidet zurück, schnitt zurück, hat zurückgeschnitten> ◊ *Wir sollten die Sträucher ein wenig zurückschneiden.*

• **cut down** phras v **1.** *(reduce)* cut down (on) sth etw. reduzieren [redu'tsiːrən] <reduziert, reduzierte, hat reduziert> ◊ *ein Risiko/die Ausgaben reduzieren* ♦ *Er versucht, seinen Alkoholkonsum zu reduzieren.; (reduce hours, time)* etw. verkürzen [fɛ'kʏrtsn̩] <verkürzt, verkürzte, hat verkürzt> ◊ *die Arbeitszeit verkürzen* **2.** *(make shorter)* cut sth down etw. zusammenstreichen [tsu'zamənʃtraeçn̩] <streicht zusammen, strich zusammen, hat zusammengestrichen> ◊ *einen Text zusammenstreichen* **3.** *(a tree)* cut sth down etw. fällen ['fɛlən] +haben ◊ *Der Apfelbaum ist morsch und muss gefällt werden.* **4.** *(lit) (a person)* niederstrecken ['niːdɐʃtrɛkn̩] +haben (lit) ◊ *Er streckte den Feind mit dem Schwert nieder.*

• **cut in** phras v **1.** *(interrupt)* cut in (on sb/sth) (jdn/etw.) unterbrechen [ʊntɐ'brɛçn̩] <unterbricht, unterbrach, hat unterbrochen> ◊ *„Und warum ist das so?", unterbrach sie ihn.* **2.** *(after overtaking)* cut in on sb/sth jdn/etw. schneiden ['ʃnaedn̩] <schneidet, schnitt, hat geschnitten> ◊ *Der Minibus hat uns beim Überholen geschnitten.* **3.** *(start working when needed)* sich einschalten ['aenʃaltn̩] <schaltet sich ein, schaltete sich ein, hat sich eingeschaltet> ◊ *Wenn es kalt wird, schaltet sich die Heizung automatisch ein.* **4.** *(fam)* cut sb in on sth jdn an etw. dat beteiligen [an ... bə,taelɪgn̩] <beteiligt, beteiligte, hat beteiligt> ◊ *Sie haben ihn am Gewinn beteiligt.*

• **cut off** phras v **1.** *(separate sth from sth)* abschneiden ['apʃnaedn̩] <schneidet ab, schnitt ab, hat abgeschnitten> ◊ *Ich schneide das Fett vom Fleisch ab.* ♦ *Schneiden Sie mir bitte ein Stück Wurst ab?* ♦ *Die Polizei schnitt dem Dieb den Fluchtweg ab.* ♦ *Die Schneemassen haben das Dorf von der Außenwelt abgeschnitten.* **2.** *(disconnect)* abstellen ['apʃtɛlən] +haben ◊ *(jdm) den Strom abstellen* ♦ *Bitte stellen Sie den Motor ab.* **3.** *(interrupt)* unterbrechen [ʊntɐ'brɛçn̩] <unterbricht, unterbrach, hat unterbrochen> ◊ *Er hat mich mitten im Satz unterbrochen.* **4.** *(disinherit)* enterben [ɛnt|'ɛrbm̩] <enterbt, enterbte, hat enterbt> ◊ *Ihr Vater hat sie enterbt.* **5.** *(end a relationship)* cut sb off die Beziehung zu jdm abbrechen [diː bə,tsiːʊŋ tsu: ... 'apbrɛçn̩] <bricht ab, brach ab, hat abgebrochen> ◊ *Warum hat sie auf einmal die Beziehungen zu ihren Freundinnen abgebrochen?* **6.** *(on the phone)* be/get cut off unterbrochen werden [ʊntɐ'brɔxn̩ veːɐdn̩] <wird, wurde, ist worden> ◊ *Wir sind vorhin unterbrochen worden.* → cut² 1., cut² 4.

• **cut out** phras v **1.** *(remove by cutting, shape by cutting)* ausschneiden ['aosʃnaedn̩] <schneidet aus, schnitt aus, hat ausgeschnitten> ◊ *ein Foto aus der Zeitschrift ausschneiden* ♦ *aus Karton Dreiecke und Kreise ausschneiden* **2.** *(delete text)* cut sth out etw. herausstreichen [hɛ'raosʃtraeçn̩] <streicht heraus, strich heraus, hat herausgestrichen> ◊ *Text aus dem Manuskript herausstreichen; (delete material from a film)* etw. herausschneiden [hɛ'raosʃnaedn̩] <schneidet heraus, schnitt heraus, hat herausgeschnitten> ◊ *eine Szene aus einem Film herausschneiden* **3.** *(stop doing sth)* cut sth out mit etw. aufhören [mɪt ... ˌaofhøːrən] +haben ◊ *Er hat mit dem Rauchen/Trinken aufgehört.* Cut it out! Hör auf damit! **4.** *(light, noise)* cut sth out etw. abhalten ['aphaltn̩] <hält ab, hielt ab, hat abgehalten> ◊ *Die dicken Vorhänge halten das Licht ab.* **5.** *(exclude)* cut sb out of sth jdn von etw. ausschließen [fɔn ... 'aosʃliːsn̩] <schließt aus, schloss aus, hat ausgeschlossen> ◊ *Er wurde von dem Wettbewerb ausgeschlossen.* **6.** *(stop working)* aussetzen ['aoszɛtsn̩] +haben ◊ *Plötzlich setzte der Motor aus.*

⊚ be/not be cut out for sth wie/nicht geschaffen für etw. sein ◊ *Sie ist wie geschaffen für das politische Leben.* ♦ *Für diesen Beruf bin ich einfach nicht geschaffen.*

• **cut through** phras v **1.** *(take a short cut)* cut through sth quer durch etw. gehen [kveːɐ dʊrç ... geːən] <geht, ging, ist gegangen> ◊ *Sie gingen quer durch den Park/Wald.* **2.** cut a way/path through sth sich dat einen Weg/Pfad durch etw. bahnen [aenən ˌveːk/ˌpfaːt dʊrç ... baːnən] +haben →

cut² 1.

• **cut up** [phras v] **1.** *(separate into pieces)* klein schneiden [ˌklaɛn ˈʃnaɛdn̩] <schneidet, schnitt, hat geschnitten> ◊ *Ihre Mutter schnitt ihr das Fleisch klein.* **2.** *(after overtaking)* cut sb/sth up jdn/etw. schneiden [ˈʃnaɛdn̩] <schneidet, schnitt, hat geschnitten> ◊ *Er hat uns beim Überholen geschnitten.* **3.** *(fam)* *(in the US: be silly and noisy)* außer Rand und Band geraten [aosɐ ˌrant ʊnt ˈbant gɐraːtn̩] <gerät, geriet, ist geraten> ◊ *Kaum waren die Eltern weg, gerieten die Kinder außer Rand und Band.*

cutback [noun] Kürzung [ˈkʏˈtsʊŋ] die <-, -en> ◊ *eine Kürzung der Gehälter/Ausgaben beschließen* ✦ *Kürzungen bei bestimmten Leistungen vornehmen*

cute(ly) [adj, adv] **1.** *(nice, sweet)* süß [zyːs] <süßer, am süßesten> ◊ *Was für süße Hundebabys!* ✦ *Gestern hab' ich einen kennen gelernt — der ist total süß!* ✦ *Seht nur, wie süß die Kätzchen miteinander spielen!* **2.** *(fam)* *(in the US: shrewd)* gerissen [gɐˈrɪsn̩] ◊ *ein gerissener Anwalt* ✦ *Es war sehr gerissen, wie sie ihren Plan verwirklichte.* ✦ *Das hast du ganz schön gerissen gemacht!*

cutlery [noun] Besteck [bɐˈʃtɛk] das <-(e)s, -e>

cutlet [noun] Kotelett [kɔtˈlɛt] das <-s, -s> ◊ *ein Kotelett vom Kalb* ✦ *ein paniertes Kotelett*

cutting¹ [noun] **1.** *(from a newspaper)* Ausschnitt [ˈaosʃnɪt] der <-(e)s, -e> ◊ *ein Ausschnitt aus der heutigen Tageszeitung* **2.** *(from a plant)* Ableger [ˈapleːgɐ] der <-s, -> ◊ *Ableger von einer Pflanze ziehen* **3.** *(passage for a road, railway)* Durchstich [ˈdʊʳçʃtɪç] der <-(e)s, -e> ◊ *Der Durchstich wird nächstes Jahr fertig gestellt.*

cutting² [adj] scharf [ʃaʳf] <schärfer, am schärfsten> ◊ *eine scharfe Bemerkung machen* ✦ *ein scharfer Wind.*

CV [noun] Lebenslauf [ˈleːbn̩slaof] der <-(e)s, Lebensläufe> ◊ *ein tabellarischer Lebenslauf* ✦ *Bitte senden Sie uns Ihre Bewerbung mit Lebenslauf.*

cycle¹ [noun] **1.** *(recurring series of events)* Kreislauf [ˈkraɛslaof] der <-(e)s, Kreisläufe> ◊ *der Kreislauf des Lebens/der Jahreszeiten; (of a washing machine)* rinse cycle Schleudergang [ˈʃlɔɐdegaŋ] der <-(e)s, Schleudergänge> ◊ *Die Waschmaschine hat den Schleudergang noch nicht beendet.; (of poems, songs)* Zyklus [ˈtsyːklʊs] der <-, Zyklen> ◊ *ein Zyklus von Geschichten rund um das Thema Abschied* **2.** *(bicycle)* Rad [raːt] das <-(e)s, Räder> ◊ *Rad fahren* ✦ *Er hat sich ein neues Rad gekauft.*

cycle² [verb] mit dem Rad fahren [mɪt deːm ˈraːt faːrən] <fährt, fuhr, ist gefahren> ◊ *Sie fährt mit dem Rad zur Arbeit.*

cycle lane, cycle path [noun] Radweg [ˈraːtveːk] der <-(e)s, -e> ◊ *auf dem Radweg fahren* ✦ *den Radweg benutzen*

cycling [noun] Radfahren [ˈraːtfaːrən] das <-s> no pl ◊ *Meine Hobbys sind Wandern und Radfahren.* ✦ *Das Radfahren zählt zu den Ausdauersportarten.* He enjoys cycling. *Er fährt gern Rad.*

cyclist [noun] Radfahrer [ˈraːtfaːrɐ] der <-s, -> ♀Radfahrerin [ˈraːtfaːrərɪn] die <-, -nen> ◊ *Radfahrer sollten einen Helm tragen.* ✦ *Der Autofahrer übersah die Radfahrerin.*

cylinder [noun] Zylinder [tsyˈlɪndɐ] der <-s, -> ◊ *Der Motor hat vier Zylinder.* ✦ *die Oberfläche eines Zylinders berechnen*

cynical(ly) [adj, adv] zynisch [ˈtsyːnɪʃ] ◊ *eine zynische Bemerkung machen* ✦ *Sei doch nicht immer so zynisch!* ✦ *„So ist das Leben nun einmal", bemerkte er zynisch.*

Cypriot¹ [noun] Zypriot [tsypriˈoːt] der <-en, -en> ♀Zypriotin [tsypriˈoːtɪn] die <-, -nen> → **German¹ 1.**

Cypriot² [adj] zypriotisch [tsypriˈoːtɪʃ] *mostly before ns* ◊ *die zypriotische Pfund*

Cyprus [noun] Zypern [ˈtsyːpɐn] das <-(s)> *article only in combination with attribute, no pl* → **Germany**

Czech¹ [noun] **1.** *(inhabitant)* Tscheche [ˈtʃɛçə] der <-n, -n> ♀Tschechin [ˈtʃɛçɪn] die <-, -nen> → **German¹ 1.** **2.** *(language, subject)* Tschechisch [ˈtʃɛçɪʃ] das <-(s)> no pl → **German¹ 2.**

Czech² [adj] tschechisch [ˈtʃɛçɪʃ] → **German²**

Czech Republic [noun] Tschechische Republik [ˌtʃɛçɪʃə repuˈbliːk] die <Tschechischen Republik> no pl ◊ *Die Tschechische Republik grenzt an Deutschland.*

A
B
C
D
E
F
G
H
I
J
K
L
M
N
O
P
Q
R
S
T
U
V
W
X
Y
Z

D

d, D [noun] 1. *(letter)* d, D [deː] das <–(s), –(s)> ◊ *Das Wort wird mit einem kleinen d/großen D geschrieben.* ♦ *D wie Dora* 2. MUS D d, D [deː] das <–(s), –(s)> ◊ *Er spielte ein D.* D minor d-Moll ['deːmɔl] D major D-Dur ['deːduːɐ̯] D [noun] *(grade)* Vier [fiːɐ̯] die <–, –en> ◊ *Sie hat eine Vier in Deutsch.* box@ **Note**

dad [noun] Vater ['faːtɐ] der <–s, Väter> ◊ *Die Firma gehört meinem Vater.*; *(affectionately)* Papa ['papa(ː)] der <–s, –s> *(kidsp)* ◊ *„Papa, spielst du mit mir Ball?"*

daft [adj] blöd [bløːt] <blöder, am blödesten> ◊ *So eine blöde Idee!* ♦ *Du bist blöd genug, den gleichen Fehler nochmal zu machen.* ♦ *Kann man vom Computerspielen blöd werden?*
ⓔ be daft about sb/sth nach jdm/etw. verrückt sein

daily¹ [adj] 1. *(taking place every day, for every day)* täglich ['tɛːklɪç] *no comp/superl, only before ns* ◊ *tägliche Flüge nach Los Angeles* ♦ *Lebensmittel für den täglichen Bedarf* ♦ *Zähneputzen als tägliche Routine* 2. daily newspaper Tageszeitung ['taːgəstsaetʊŋ] die <–, –en> daily wage Tageslohn ['taːgəsloːn] der <–(e)s, Tageslöhne>

daily² [adv] täglich ['tɛːklɪç] *no comp/superl* ◊ *täglich frische Ware* ♦ *täglich acht Stunden arbeiten* ♦ *Sie besucht ihre kranke Mutter täglich.* ♦ *Nehmen Sie täglich drei Tabletten.*

dairy¹ [noun] 1. *(company, firm)* Molkerei [mɔlkə'rae] die <–, –en> ◊ *In der Molkerei wird die Milch weiterverarbeitet.* ♦ *Die Molkerei verkauft Käse aus der Region.* ♦ *in einer Molkerei arbeiten* 2. *(on a farm)* Milchkammer ['mɪlçkamɐ] die <–, –n> ◊ *In der Milchkammer wird die Milch entrahmt.* 3. *(foods containing milk)* Milchprodukte ['mɪlçproˌdʊktə] die <–> pl ◊ *Sie isst gern Milchprodukte.* 4. *(shop)* Milchgeschäft ['mɪlçgəʃɛft] das <–(e)s, –e> ◊ *Ich gehe noch schnell ins Milchgeschäft.*

dairy² [adj] *(in compound ns)* dairy ... Milch... [mɪlç] dairy product Milchprodukt ['mɪlçproˌdʊkt] das <–(e)s, –e> ◊ *Milchprodukte wie Butter, Käse und Quark* dairy cow Milchkuh ['mɪlçkuː] die <–, Milchkühe> ◊ *Milchkühe halten* dairy farming Milchviehhaltung ['mɪlçfiːhaltʊŋ] die <–> *no pl*

dam [noun] 1. *(across a river)* Damm [dam] der <–(e)s, Dämme> ◊ *einen Damm bauen* ♦ *Der Damm brach, und das ganze Dorf wurde überschwemmt.* 2. ZOO Muttertier ['mʊtɐtiːɐ̯] das <–(e)s, –e> ◊ *Das Muttertier versorgt seine Jungen.*

damage¹ [noun] 1. *(harm, negative effects)* Schaden ['ʃaːdn̩] der <–s, Schäden> ◊ *großen/irreparablen Schaden verursachen* ♦ *Er hat den Unfall ohne bleibende Schäden überstanden.* do damage Schaden anrichten do damage to sth einer Sache [dat] schaden ['ʃaːdn̩] <schadet, schadete, hat geschadet> ◊ *Der Skandal hat ihrem Ansehen in der Firma geschadet.* 2. LAW damages Schadenersatz ['ʃaːdn̩ˌʔezats] der <–es> *no pl* ◊ *Sie müssen Schaden-*

ersatz leisten. ♦ *eine Klage auf Schadenersatz*

damage² [verb] 1. *(cause physical or actual harm to)* beschädigen [bə'ʃɛːdɪgn̩] <beschädigt, beschädigte, hat beschädigt> ◊ *Wer hat mein Auto beschädigt?* ♦ *Bei der Explosion wurde das Gebäude stark beschädigt.* 2. *(have a bad effect on)* schädigen ['ʃɛːdɪgn̩] +haben ◊ *Alkohol schädigt die Leber.* ♦ *Das hat seinen Ruf geschädigt.*

damaging [adj] 1. *(causing psychological or physical harm)* schädlich ['ʃɛːtlɪç] ◊ *Rauchen ist schädlich für die Gesundheit.* ♦ *schädliche Substanzen* 2. *(disadvantageous)* nachteilig ['naːxtaelɪç] ◊ *eine nachteilige Wirkung* ♦ *Diese Bemerkung könnte nachteilig für sie sein.*

damn [verb] 1. *(condemn)* verurteilen [fɛ'ʔʊɐ̯taelən] <verurteilt, verurteilte, hat verurteilt> ◊ *eine Tat scharf verurteilen* ♦ *Die Gewerkschaft verurteilte das Verhalten der Regierung.; (strongly criticize)* verreißen [fɛ'raesn̩] <verreißt, verriss, hat verrissen> ◊ *Die Kritiker haben das Stück verrissen.* 2. REL verdammen [fɛ'damən] <verdammt, verdammte, hat verdammt> ◊ *Er glaubte, dass alle Sünder verdammt seien.*
ⓔ damn it *(fam)* verdammt noch mal

damp¹ [noun] Feuchtigkeit ['fɔøçtɪçkaet] die <–> *no pl* ◊ *Feuchtigkeit an den Wänden*

damp² [adj] feucht [fɔøçt] <feuchter, am feuchtesten> ◊ *Das Gras war immer noch feucht.* ♦ *Sie wischte den Tisch mit einem feuchten Tuch ab.*

dampen [verb] 1. *(make slightly wet)* befeuchten [bə'fɔøçtn̩] <befeuchtet, befeuchtete, hat befeuchtet> ◊ *einen Lappen befeuchten* ♦ *Das Gerät befeuchtet die Luft.* 2. *(sb's mood, spirits)* dämpfen ['dɛmpfn̩] +haben ◊ *Nichts konnte ihre Begeisterung dämpfen.*

dance¹ [noun] Tanz [tants] der <–es, Tänze> ◊ *Die Gruppe führte slawische Tänze vor.* ♦ *Darf ich um diesen Tanz bitten?* ♦ *Der Schützenverein lädt heute Abend zum Tanz.* ♦ *Das Orchester spielte einen Tanz.* ♦ *Gymnastik und Tanz unterrichten*

dance² [verb] *(move to music)* tanzen ['tantsn̩] +haben/ *with indication of direction* +sein ◊ *Möchten Sie tanzen?* ♦ *Hast du schon mal einen Tango getanzt?* ♦ *Insekten tanzten um die Lampe.* ♦ *Er war mit ihr bis zur Mitte des Saals getanzt.; (move lightly)* dance about herumtänzeln [hɛ'rʊmtɛntsl̩n] <tänzelt herum, ist herumgetänzelt> ◊ *Das Pferd tänzelte herum.*

dancer [noun] Tänzer ['tɛntsɐ] der <–s, –> ♀Tänzerin ['tɛntsərɪn] die <–, –nen> ◊ *Werner ist ein schlechter Tänzer.* ♦ *Sie ist Tänzerin beim Bolshoi Ballett.*

dancing [noun] Tanzen ['tantsn̩] das <–s> *no pl* ◊ *Das Tanzen hat sie durstig gemacht.* ♦ *Seine Hobbys sind Reiten und Tanzen.* dancing shoe Tanzschuh ['tantsʃuː] der <–(e)s, –e> *most pl* dancing course Tanzkurs ['tantskʊɐ̯s] der <–es, –e> dancing teacher Tanzlehrer ['tantsleːrɐ] der <–s, –> ♀Tanzlehrerin ['tantsleːrərɪn] die <–, –nen>

Dane [noun] Däne ['dɛːnə] der <–n, –n> ♀Dänin

['dɛːnɪn] die <–, –nen> → **German¹** 1.

danger [noun] Gefahr [gə'faːɐ] die <–, –en> ◊ *Der Patient ist außer Gefahr.* ♦ *Es besteht die Gefahr, dass der Behälter explodiert.* ♦ *Solche Hunde sind eine Gefahr für die Bevölkerung.* ♦ *Gefahren im Straßenverkehr* put sb/sth in danger jdn/etw. in Gefahr bringen be in danger of doing sth Gefahr laufen, etw. zu tun ◊ *Er läuft Gefahr, seine Arbeit zu verlieren.* pose a danger to sb/sth eine Gefahr für jdn/etw. darstellen "Danger!" "Achtung! Lebensgefahr!"

dangerous(ly) [adj, adv] gefährlich [gə'fɛːɐlɪç] ◊ *eine gefährliche Kurve* ♦ *Ist das Tier gefährlich?* ♦ *Es ist gefährlich, nachts allein durch den Wald zu gehen.* ♦ *gefährlich hohe Klippen* ♦ *Der Tiger kam ihm gefährlich nah.*

dangle [verb] sth/sb dangles etw./jd baumelt ['baʊmlt̩] +haben ◊ *Das Seil baumelt an einem Ast.* dangle sth etw. baumeln lassen ◊ *Ich saß auf der Mauer und ließ die Beine baumeln.*
⊛ keep/leave sb dangling jdn zappeln lassen dangle sth before/in front of sb jdm etw. in Aussicht stellen

Danish¹ [noun] (language, subject) Dänisch ['dɛːnɪʃ] das <–(s)> no pl → **German¹** 2.

Danish² [adj] dänisch ['dɛːnɪʃ] → **German²**

dare [verb] 1. (be confident enough) dare (to) do sth wagen, etw. zu tun ['vaːgn̩ ... tsuː] ◊ *Wir wagten nicht, ihm die Wahrheit zu sagen.* ♦ *Sie hatte nicht zu träumen gewagt, dass sie ansprechen würde.* How dare you! Was fällt dir ein! Don't you dare! Untersteh dich! 2. (face the risk of) dare sth etw. riskieren [rɪs'kiːrən] <riskiert, riskierte, hat riskiert> ◊ *Er hat sein Leben riskiert.* ♦ *Sie riskierte ein Lächeln.* 3. (challenge) dare sb to do sth jdn fragen, ob er/sie sich traut, etw. zu tun ['fraːgn̩ ɔp eːɐ'ziː ... traʊt ... tsuː] ◊ *Er fragte sie, ob sie sich trauen würde, von der Mauer zu springen.* She dared me to play. Sie forderte mich zu einem Spiel heraus. I dare you! Feigling! ◊ *Los, ruf sie einfach an! Feigling!*
⊛ I dare say ich glaube wohl ◊ *Ich glaube wohl, dass er auch dort sein wird.*

daring [adj] 1. (brave) kühn [kyːn] ◊ *eine kühne Rettungsaktion* ♦ *ein kühnes Experiment* ♦ *Das war sehr kühn von dir!* 2. (possibly offensive) gewagt [gə'vaːkt] <gewagter, am gewagtesten> ◊ *Einige Szenen im Film sind sehr gewagt.* ♦ *ein gewagtes Kleid*

dark¹ [noun] Dunkelheit ['dʊŋkl̩haet] die <–> no pl ◊ *In der Dunkelheit konnten wir den Einbrecher nicht sehen.* after/before dark nach/vor Einbruch der Dunkelheit in the dark im Dunkeln [ɪm 'dʊŋkl̩n] ◊ *Was machst du hier allein im Dunkeln?*
⊛ keep sb in the dark about sth jdn über etw. [acc] im Dunkeln lassen

dark² [adj] 1. (with no light, almost black) dunkel ['dʊŋkl̩] <dunkler, am dunkelsten> <der/die/das dunkle ...> ◊ *dunkle Wolken* ♦ *Im Zimmer ist es sehr dunkel.* ♦ *Er trug einen dunklen Anzug.* get/grow dark dunkel werden; (with black or brown hair) dunkelhaarig ['dʊŋkl̩haːrɪç] seldom comp/superl ◊ *eine dunkelhaarige Frau* dark blue dunkelblau ['dʊŋkl̩blaʊ] no comp/superl ◊ *eine dunkelblaue Bluse* 2. (unpleasant, wicked) finster ['fɪnstɐ] ◊ *Das ist eines der finstersten Kapitel der Geschichte.* ♦ *die finsteren Machenschaften der Mafia* 3. (gloomy, sad) düster ['dyːstɐ] ◊ *düstere Farben* ♦ *Die Erfolgsaussichten sind eher düster.*

darkly [adv] 1. (gloomily, sadly) düster ['dyːstɐ] ◊ *ein nur düster beleuchteter Raum* ♦ *düster dreinblicken* ♦ *"Das wird nicht gut gehen", sagte sie düster.* 2. (in a dark colo(u)r) dunkel ['dʊŋkl̩] <dunkler, am dunkelsten> ◊ *dunkel gekleidet sein* ♦ *eine dunkel getönte Brille*

darkness [noun] 1. (absence of light, dark colo(u)r) Dunkelheit ['dʊŋkl̩haet] die <–, –en> most sing ◊ *Ich habe das in der Dunkelheit nicht gesehen.* ♦ *Das Gebäude lag in völliger Dunkelheit.* ♦ *Dunkelheit brach herein.* 2. (lit) (evil) Finsternis ['fɪnstɐnɪs] die <–, –se> most sing ◊ *die Mächte/das Reich der Finsternis*

darling¹ [noun] 1. (form of address, person you love, very kind person) Schatz [ʃats] der <–es, Schätze> ◊ *Schatz, würdest du mal bitte kommen?* ♦ *Laurin ist unser kleiner Schatz.* ♦ *Sie sind ein Schatz! Vielen Dank!* 2. (favo(u)rite) Liebling ['liːplɪŋ] der <–s, –e> ◊ *der Liebling des Publikums* ♦ *Er ist der Liebling aller Frauen.*

darling² [adj] 1. (beloved) geliebt [gə'liːpt] <geliebter, am geliebtesten> only before ns ◊ *"Mein geliebter Richard, wie sehr hast du mir gefehlt!"* 2. (lovely, sweet) reizend ['raetsn̩t] ◊ *Das ist eine ganz reizende Tischdecke.* ♦ *Was für reizende Kätzchen!*

dart¹ [noun] 1. (used in sport, as a weapon) Pfeil [pfael] der <–(e)s, –e> ◊ *mit Pfeilen auf jdn schießen* 2. (sudden movement, jump) Satz [zats] der <–es, Sätze> ◊ *Als es klingelte, machte er einen Satz zur Tür.* 3. (in a piece of clothing) Abnäher ['apnɛːɐ] der <–s, –> ◊ *einen Abnäher machen*

dart² [verb] 1. (move very quickly) dart somewhere irgendwohin flitzen ['flɪtsn̩] +sein ◊ *Die Katze flitzte aus dem Zimmer.* dart into sth etw. [acc] stürzen [ɪn ... 'ʃtʏrtsn̩] +sein ◊ *Sie stürzte ins Zimmer und umarmte ihn.* 2. dart a glance at sth einen Blick auf etw. [acc] werfen [aenən ˌblɪk aof ... vɛ'rfn̩] <wirft, warf, hat geworfen> ◊ *Sie warf einen Blick auf die Uhr.* dart a glance at sb jdm einen Blick zuwerfen [aenən 'blɪk ˌtsuːvɛ'rfn̩] +haben ◊ *Er warf ihr einen nervösen Blick zu.*

dash¹ [noun] 1. (quick movement) make a dash for sb/sth auf jdn/etw. zustürzen [aof ... ˌtsuːʃtʏr'tsn̩] +sein ◊ *Er stürzte auf den Ausgang zu.* make a dash for freedom versuchen, zu entkommen [fe'zuːxn̩ tsuː ɛnt'kɔmən] <versucht, versuchte, hat versucht> make a dash for it rennen, so schnell jd kann ['rɛnən zoː ʃnɛl ... 'kan] <rennt, rannte, ist gerannt> ◊ *Sie riss sich los und rannte, so schnell sie konnte.* 2. (small amount) a dash of ... etwas ... ['ɛtvas] ◊ *Mit etwas Essig schmeckt die Soße pikanter.* 3. GRAM Gedankenstrich [gə'daŋkn̩ʃtrɪç] der <–(e)s, –e> ◊ *einen Gedankenstrich setzen* 4. (in morse code) Strich [ʃtrɪç] der <–(e)s, –e> ◊ *Lange Morsesignale werden durch Striche, kurze durch Punkte dargestellt.* 5. (fam) (dashboard) Armaturenbrett [arma'tuːrənbrɛt] das <–(e)s, –er> 6. (oldf) (style, energy) Elan [e'laːn] der <–s> no pl ◊ *mit viel Elan an etw. herangehen*

dash² [verb] 1. (move very quickly) dash somewhere irgendwohin sausen ['zaozn̩] +sein (fam) ◊ *Sie sauste zur Tür und riss sie auf.* 2. (throw using force) schleudern ['ʃlɔødɐn] +haben ◊ *Wütend schleuderte*

sie den Teller zu Boden.; (water) sth dashes against sth etw. peitscht gegen etw. [paɛʧt gɛːgn̩] +*sein* ◊ *Regen peitschte gegen die Scheiben.* **3.** *(sb's hopes)* zunichte machen [ʦuˈnɪçtə maxn̩] +*haben* ◊ *Die Diagnose machte alle seine Hoffnungen zunichte.*

⊚ **dash it (all)** verflixt *(fam)*

data [noun] Daten [ˈdaːtn̩] die <–, pl> ◊ *die aktuellen Daten zum Aktienmarkt* ♦ *Daten sammeln* ♦ *Daten in den Computer eingeben*

database [noun] Datenbank [ˈdaːtn̩baŋk] die <–, –en> ◊ *etw. in einer Datenbank erfassen* ♦ *eine Datenbank verwalten*

date¹ [noun] **1.** *(particular day, year etc.)* Datum [ˈdaːtʊm] das <–s, Daten> ◊ *Der Poststempel trägt das gestrige Datum.* ♦ *ein bedeutendes historisches Datum* ♦ *Bitte legen Sie ein Foto jüngeren Datums bei.* ♦ *Das genaue Datum steht noch nicht fest.* What's the date today? Welches Datum haben wir heute? date of birth Geburtsdatum [ɡəˈbuːɐ̯tsˌdaːtʊm]; *(of an appointment)* Termin [tɛrˈmiːn] der <–s, –e> ◊ *Die Ware wurde zum vereinbarten Termin geliefert.* set/fix a date einen Termin vereinbaren **2.** *(romantic meeting)* Verabredung [fɛlˈapreːdʊŋ] die <–, –en> ◊ *Sie hat eine Verabredung mit ihrem Freund.* Who's her date? Mit wem trifft sie sich? make a date with sb sich mit jdm verabreden [mɪt ... fɛlˌapreːdn̩] <verabredet sich, verabredete sich, hat sich verabredet> **3.** *(fruit)* Dattel [ˈdatl̩] die <–, –n>

date² [verb] **1.** *(write a date on sth, find out the age of sth)* datieren [daˈtiːrən] <datiert, datierte, hat datiert> ◊ *einen Brief auf den 16. Februar datieren* ♦ *Der Brief ist vom 1. Mai 1963 datiert.* ♦ *Die Archäologen konnten den Fund nicht datieren.* **2.** *(become old-fashioned)* aus der Mode kommen [aʊs deːɐ̯ ˈmoːdə kɔmən] <kommt, kam, ist gekommen> ◊ *Das Design des Kleides ist aus der Mode gekommen.* sth dates sb an etw. [dat] merkt man, wie alt jd ist [an ... ˈmɛrkt man viː ˈalt ... ɪst] +*haben* **3.** *(have a relationship with)* date sb mit jdm gehen [mɪt ... ˌgeːən] <geht, ging, ist gegangen> ◊ *Er geht schon seit einem Jahr mit ihr.*

dative [noun] Dativ [ˈdaːtiːf] der <–s, –e>

daughter [noun] Tochter [ˈtɔxtɐ] die <–, Töchter> ◊ *Ich habe einen Sohn und zwei Töchter.* ♦ *Sie war eine Tochter der Revolution.*

daughter-in-law [noun] Schwiegertochter [ˈʃviːgɐtɔxtɐ] die <–, Schwiegertöchter>

dawn¹ [noun] Morgendämmerung [ˈmɔrgn̩dɛmərʊŋ] die <–, –en> ◊ *Die Morgendämmerung bricht an.* at (the crack of) dawn im Morgengrauen [ɪm ˈmɔrgn̩graʊən] ◊ *Sie wollen im Morgengrauen aufbrechen.* from dawn till dusk von morgens bis abends [fɔn ˌmɔrgn̩s bɪs ˈaːbm̩ts] ◊ *Sie arbeiteten von morgens bis abends.*

⊚ **the dawn of sth** (der) Beginn ... [gen] ◊ *der Beginn des Lebens* **the dawn of time** der Anbeginn der Zeit

dawn² [verb] **1.** *(morning)* dämmern [ˈdɛmɐn] +*haben* ◊ *Als der Morgen dämmerte, stand ich auf.* The day is dawning. Es dämmert. The day dawned rainy. Der Tag begann mit Regen.; *(new age)* anbrechen [ˈanbrɛçn̩] <bricht an, brach an, ist angebrochen> ◊ *Eine neue Ära ist angebrochen.* **2.** *(be realized)* dawn on sb jdm dämmern [ˈdɛmən] +*haben* ◊ *Da dämmerte ihm, dass seine Kollegen dafür verantwort-*

lich waren.

day [noun] Tag [taːk] der <–(e)s, –e> ◊ *Was ist heute für ein Tag?* ♦ *Er sollte jeden Tag ein wenig spazieren gehen.* ♦ *Sie hat heute einen harten Tag gehabt.* ♦ *vier Tage Urlaub haben* ♦ *Es wird Tag.* ♦ *Der Tag geht zu Ende.* ♦ *ein regnerischer/sonniger Tag* ♦ *Es kommen auch wieder glückliche Tage.* ♦ *Erinnerungen aus früheren Tagen* all day den ganzen Tag one day eines Tages ◊ *Eines Tages wirst du mir dafür dankbar sein.* day by day von Tag zu Tag day of the week Wochentag [ˈvɔxn̩taːk] ◊ *Welcher Wochentag ist heute?* during the day, by day tagsüber [ˈtaːksˌyːbe] ◊ *ein Kind tagsüber betreuen* ♦ *Tagsüber bin ich unter folgender Telefonnummer erreichbar: ...* the day after next/tomorrow übermorgen [ˈyːbɐmɔˈgn̩] ◊ *Übermorgen reisen wir ab.* the day before yesterday vorgestern [ˈfoːɐɡɛstɐn] ◊ *Ich habe ihn seit vorgestern nicht mehr gesehen.*

⊚ **in the old days** früher ◊ *War früher tatsächlich alles besser?* **the other day** neulich **these days** heutzutage in those days damals

daylight [noun] Tageslicht [ˈtaːgəslɪçt] das <–(e)s> no pl ◊ *Das Tageslicht erhellte das Zimmer.* ♦ *Sie wollen noch bei Tageslicht zurückkehren.* It was still daylight. Es war noch hell.

⊚ **sb begins to see daylight** jdm geht ein Licht auf

daylight saving time, daylight savings [noun] Sommerzeit [ˈzɔmɐtsaɛt] die <–> no pl ◊ *die Uhren von Sommerzeit auf Winterzeit umstellen*

day nursery [noun] Kindertagesstätte [ˈkɪndɐˌtaːgəsʃtɛtə] die <–, –n>

daytime [noun] Tag [taːk] der <–(e)s> no pl ◊ *Während des Tages sitzt er gern im Garten.* ♦ *Ich kann bei Tag nicht schlafen.*

day-to-day [adj] täglich [ˈtɛːklɪç] no comp/superl, only before ns ◊ *Beide kümmerten sich um die tägliche Hausarbeit.*

dazzle [verb] blenden [ˈblɛndn̩] <blendet, blendete, hat geblendet> ◊ *Das grelle Licht blendet mich.* ♦ *Er blendete sie mit einem Taschenspiegel.* ♦ *Sie hat sich von den vielen Geld blenden lassen.*

deactivate [verb] *(alarm)* deaktivieren [deˈaktiˈviːrən] <deaktiviert, deaktivierte, hat deaktiviert> ◊ *Sie deaktivierten den Alarm.; (bombs)* entschärfen [ɛntˈʃɛrfn̩] <entschärft, entschärfte, hat entschärft> ◊ *Die Bombe ist entschärft worden.*

dead¹ [adj] **1.** *(person, town, appliance)* tot [toːt] no comp/superl ◊ *ein toter Fisch* ♦ *Mitten im Gespräch war das Telefon plötzlich tot.* ♦ *Die tote Strecke war von Unkraut überwuchert.* leave sb for dead jdn für tot halten und liegen lassen dead body Leiche [ˈlaɛçə] die <–, –n> strike dead erschlagen [ɛˈʃlaːgn̩] <erschlägt, erschlug, hat erschlagen> **2.** *(arm, leg)* taub [taʊp] ◊ *ein taubes Bein* go dead einschlafen [ˈaɛnʃlaːfn̩] <schläft ein, schlief ein, ist eingeschlafen> ◊ *Mein Bein ist eingeschlafen.* **3.** *(battery)* leer [leːɐ̯] ◊ *Die Batterien sind leer.* **4.** *(voice, eyes)* ausdruckslos [ˈaʊsdrʊksloːs] <ausdruckloser, am ausdruckslosesten> ◊ *Ihre Stimme war vollkommen ausdruckslos.* ♦ *Er sah sie mit ausdruckslosen Augen an.* **5.** *(complete, absolute)* absolut [apzoˈluːt] no comp/superl, only before ns ◊ *Es herrschte absolutes Schweigen.* dead centre genau in der Mitte [gəˌnaʊ in deːɐ̯ ˈmɪtə] ◊ *Der Pfeil traf die Scheibe genau in der Mitte.* dead stop Stillstand [ˈʃtɪlʃtant]

der <–(e)s> *no pl* ◊ *Ich bremste und der Wagen kam zum Stillstand.* ⊕ be a dead cert todsicher sein sb wouldn't be seen dead in sth jd würde nie im Leben etw. anziehen ◊ *Ich würde nie im Leben einen Minirock anziehen!* sb wouldn't be seen dead somewhere/with sb jd würde sich nie im Leben irgendwo/mit jdm sehen lassen ◊ *Ich würde mich nie im Leben mit ihm auf der Straße sehen lassen.* drop dead Leine ziehen *(fam)* ◊ *Zieh Leine!*

dead² ⟨adv⟩ 1. *(precisely)* genau [gə'naʊ] <genauer, am genauesten> ◊ *Der Schuss traf genau in die Mitte.* dead on time pünktlich auf die Minute ['pʏŋktlɪç ˌaʊf di: mi'nuːtə] 2. *(totally)* total [to'taːl] *no comp/superl (fam)* ◊ *Das geht total einfach/langsam.* ♦ *Meine Eltern sind total dagegen, dass ich mir ein Auto kaufe.* dead boring todlangweilig ['toːt'laŋvaɪlɪç] dead tired todmüde ['toːt'myːdə] be dead right absolut Recht haben ['apzoluːt ˌreçt haːbm̩] +haben be dead wrong völlig falsch liegen ['fœlɪç ˌfalʃ liːgŋ̩] <liegt, lag, hat gelegen> ⊕ be dead set on sth sich ⟨dat⟩ etw. in den Kopf gesetzt haben stop dead *(person)* erstarren *(vehicle)* zum Stillstand kommen sb/sth is stopped dead in their/its tracks jd/etw. wird gestoppt

dead end ⟨noun⟩ Sackgasse ['zakgasə] die <–, –n> ◊ *Die Verhandlungen gerieten in eine Sackgasse.*

deadline ⟨noun⟩ 1. *(time span)* Frist [frɪst] die <–, –en> ◊ *Sie haben ihm eine Frist von zwei Monaten gesetzt.* ♦ *Die Frist für die Bewerbungen läuft Ende Mai ab.* 2. *(time limit)* Termin [tɛr'miːn] der <–s, –e> meet a deadline einen Termin einhalten [aɛnən tɛr'miːn ˌaɛnhaltn̩] <hält ein, hielt ein, hat eingehalten> ◊ *Können Sie den Termin für die Doktorarbeit einhalten?* miss a deadline einen Termin nicht einhalten ◊ *Die Handwerker haben ihre Termine nicht eingehalten.*

deadly ⟨adj⟩ 1. *(poison, bite, weapon, boredom, work)* tödlich ['tøːtlɪç] *(also fam)* ◊ *eine tödliche Waffe* ♦ *Diese stupide Arbeit ist einfach tödlich.* 2. *(complete)* absolut ['fœlɪç] *no comp/superl* ◊ *Es herrschte völliges Schweigen.* ♦ *Sie hat das in völligem Ernst gesagt.*

deaf ⟨adj⟩ taub [taʊp] *seldom comp/superl* ◊ *Sie ist auf dem rechten Ohr taub.* ♦ *ein tauber Mann* deaf and dumb taubstumm ['taʊpʃtʊm] *no comp/superl* the deaf Gehörlose [gə'høːɐloːzə] ⊕ deaf to sth taub für etw.

deal¹ ⟨noun⟩ 1. *(profit)* Geschäft [gə'ʃɛft] das <–(e)s, –e> ◊ *Er hat mit dem Autokauf ein gutes Geschäft gemacht.* 2. *(agreement)* Handel ['handl] der <–s> *no pl* ◊ *Der Handel gilt!* strike a deal with sb einen Handel mit jdm abschließen ⊕ be a big deal ein großes Thema sein ◊ *Der Bau des Atomkraftwerks ist ein großes Thema.* it's no big deal es macht nichts a great deal of eine Menge … ⟨dat⟩ ◊ *Es gibt eine Menge Arbeit zu tun.* get a raw deal ungerecht behandelt werden it's sb's deal 1. *(sb's turn to distribute the cards)* jd gibt ◊ *Wer gibt in dieser Runde?* 2. *(sb's turn to put down a card)* jd ist mit dem Ablegen dran it's a deal abgemacht what is the deal was ist nun ◊ *Was ist nun — kommst du mit oder nicht?*

deal² ⟨verb⟩ 1. CARDS geben ['geːbm̩] <gibt, gab, hat gegeben> ◊ *Wer gibt? ♦ Du gibst.* 2. *(drugs)* dealen

['diːlən] +haben ◊ *Sie dealten mit Heroin.* • **deal in** ⟨phras v⟩ 1. *(goods)* deal in sth mit etw. handeln [mɪt … ˌhandl̩n] +haben ◊ *Er handelt mit Autos.* 2. *(include sb)* deal sb in mit jdm rechnen [mɪt … 'rɛçnən] <rechnet, rechnete, hat gerechnet> ◊ *„Wir haben am Samstag ein Fußballspiel." — „Du kannst mit mir rechnen!"* • **deal out** ⟨phras v⟩ *(blows, a punishment, cards)* austeilen ['aʊstaɛlən] +haben ◊ *Er hat einige Schläge ausgeteilt.* ♦ *Sie teilte die Karten aus.* • **deal with** ⟨phras v⟩ 1. *(a problem, situation, person)* deal with sb/sth sich um jdn/etw. kümmern [ʊm … ˌkʏmən] +haben ◊ *Sie mussten sich um die Unfallopfer kümmern.* 2. *(a personal situation)* deal with sth etw. verarbeiten [fɛ|a'baɛtn̩] <verarbeitet, verarbeitete, hat verarbeitet> ◊ *Sie hat ihren Verlust noch nicht verarbeitet.* 3. *(a company etc.)* deal with sb/sth mit jdm/etw. Handel treiben [mɪt … 'handl̩ traɛbm̩] <treibt, trieb, hat getrieben> ◊ *Wir treiben seit Jahren Handel mit dieser Firma.* 4. *(a subject, question)* deal with sth sich mit etw. befassen [mɪt … bə,fasn̩] <befasst sich, befasste sich, hat sich befasst> ◊ *Mit welchem Thema befasst sich das Buch? ♦ Der Film befasst sich mit der Todesstrafe.; (a topic at school)* etw. durchnehmen ['dʊrçneːmən] <nimmt durch, nahm durch, hat durchgenommen> ◊ *Wir nehmen heute den Konjunktiv durch.* 5. *(step by step)* deal with sth etw. abarbeiten ['ap|a'baɛtn̩] <arbeitet ab, arbeitete ab, hat abgearbeitet> ◊ *Diese Tagesordnungspunkte haben wir abgearbeitet.* ♦ *Bitte arbeiten Sie alle Anweisungen schrittweise ab!* 6. *(a conflict, controversy)* deal with sth etw. austragen ['aʊstraːgn̩] <trägt aus, trug aus, hat ausgetragen> ◊ *Der Streit wurde in aller Öffentlichkeit ausgetragen.*

dealer ⟨noun⟩ 1. *(goods)* Händler ['hɛndlɐ] der <–s, –> ♀Händlerin ['hɛndlərɪn] die <–, –nen> ◊ *eine Liste der nächstgelegenen Händler ♦ Sie ist Händlerin von Gebrauchtwaren.* 2. *(drugs)* Dealer ['diːlɐ] der <–s, –> ♀Dealerin ['diːlərɪn] die <–, –nen> 3. *(cards)* Geber ['geːbɐ] der <–s, –> ♀Geberin ['geːbərɪn] die <–, –nen>

dealing ⟨noun⟩ 1. *(interaction, also in business)* have dealings with sb/sth mit jdm/etw. zu tun haben [mɪt … tsu: 'tuːn haːbm̩] +haben ◊ *Sie war immer höflich, wenn ich mit ihr zu tun hatte.* ♦ *Hatten Sie nicht letztes Jahr geschäftlich mit dieser Firma zu tun?* in sb's dealings with sb wenn jd mit jdm zu tun hat 2. *(selling and buying goods)* Handel ['handl] der <–s> *no pl* ◊ *der Handel mit Drogen* 3. Geschäftsgebaren [gə'ʃɛftsgəbaːrən] das <–s> *no pl* ◊ *für ein zweifelhaftes Geschäftsgebaren bekannt sein*

dear¹ ⟨noun⟩ 1. *(form of address)* (my) dear mein Lieber [maɛnə 'liːbə] ◊ *Ich rufe dich später an, meine Liebe.* 2. *(person)* Schatz [ʃats] der <–es, Schätze> most sing *(fam)* ◊ *Die Pflegerin ist ein echter Schatz.* ⊕ be a dear and do sth sei so lieb und mach etw. ◊ *Sei so lieb und trag den Müll runter.*

dear² ⟨adj⟩ 1. *(form of address)* lieb [liːp] ◊ *Liebe Frau Lerch, …* ♦ *Mein lieber Schatz, …* 2. *(goods, prices)* teuer ['tɔɐ] <teurer, am teuersten> <der/die/das teure …> ◊ *Für diese Qualität ist das ein bisschen teuer.* pay a dear price teuer bezahlen

dear³ ⟨interj⟩ ach du meine Güte [ax du: 'maɛnə gyːtə] ◊ *Ach du meine Güte! Was soll ich jetzt bloß tun?*

dearly [adv] von ganzem Herzen [fɔn gantsm̩ ˈhɛɐ̯tsn̩] ◊ *Er liebt sie von ganzem Herzen.*

◉ cost sb dearly jdn teuer zu stehen kommen

death [noun] Tod der <-es, -e> ◊ *eines natürlichen/gewaltsamen Todes sterben* ♦ *nur knapp dem Tod entronnen sein* bleed to death verbluten [fɛˈbluːtn̩] <verblutet, verblutete, ist verblutet> ◊ *Bei dem Unfall ist sie fast verblutet.* freeze to death erfrieren [ɛˈfriːɾən] <erfriert, erfror, ist erfroren> ◊ *In diesem Winter sind bereits mehrere Menschen erfroren.* ♦ *Bei dem späten Frost erfroren fast sämtliche Kirschblüten.* starve to death verhungern [fɛˈhʊŋɐn] <verhungert, verhungerte, ist verhungert> ◊ *Wenn wir nicht bald etwas zu essen finden, werden wir verhungern.*

◉ be scared to death zu Tode erschrocken sein frighten sb to death jdn zu Tode erschrecken

death penalty [noun] Todesstrafe [ˈtoːdəsʃtraːfə] die <-, -n> ◊ *Auf Hochverrat steht die Todesstrafe.*

debate¹ [noun] 1. *(conversation)* Diskussion [dɪskʊˈsjoːn] die <-, -en> ◊ *ein Vortrag mit anschließender Diskussion* 2. POL Debatte [deˈbatə] die <-, -n> ◊ *eine Debatte über den Bundeshaushalt*

debate² [verb] 1. POL *(politics)* debattieren [debaˈtiːɾən] <debattiert, debattierte, hat debattiert> ◊ *Das Parlament debattierte die Finanzplanung für das nächste Jahr.* be hotly debated heiß diskutiert werden [haɛs dɪskuˈtiːɐt veːɐdn̩] <wird, wurde, ist worden> ◊ *Das Thema wurde heiß diskutiert.* 2. *(think about very carefully)* überlegen [ybɐˈleːgn̩] <überlegt, überlegte, hat überlegt> ◊ *Ich überlegte, ob ich mir das Buch kaufen sollte.* debate with yourself mit sich [dat] ringen [mɪt ... ˈɾɪŋən] <ringt, rang, hat gerungen> *(lofty)* ◊ *Ich rang mit mir, ob ich sie anrufen sollte.*

debit [verb] abbuchen [ˈapbuːxn̩] +haben ◊ *Der Betrag wird automatisch von seinem Konto abgebucht.*

debit card [noun] *(charge card)* Karte [ˈkaɐ̯tə] die <-, -n> ◊ *Zahlen Sie bar oder mit Karte?*

debris [noun] Trümmer [ˈtrʏmɐ] die <-> only pl ◊ *Er konnte nur noch tot aus den Trümmern geborgen werden.*

debt [noun] Schuld [ʃʊlt] die <-, -en> most pl ◊ *Schulden abbezahlen* ♦ *Wir haben Schulden bei unserer Bank.* owe a debt of gratitude to sb in jds Schuld stehen heavily in debt schwer verschuldet [ˌʃveːɐ̯ fɛˈʃʊldət]

debtor [noun] Schuldner [ˈʃʊldnɐ] der <-s, -> ♀Schuldnerin [ˈʃʊldnərɪn] die <-, -nen>

debut [noun] Debüt [deˈbyː] das <-s, -s>

decade [noun] Jahrzehnt [jaˈɐ̯ˈtseːnt] das <-(e)s, -e>

decaffeinated [adj] entkoffeiniert [ɛntkɔfeˈiˈniːɐt] no comp/superl

decay¹ [noun] 1. *(of plants, animals)* Verwesung [fɛˈveːzʊŋ] die <-> no pl ◊ *die Verwesung von Pflanzen* 2. *(of houses, morals)* Verfall [fɛˈfal] der <-s> no pl ◊ *Der Verfall der alten Bauernhäuser ist überall zu beobachten.* ♦ *der Verfall der Sitten*

decay² [verb] 1. *(building)* verfallen [fɛˈfalən] <verfällt, verfiel, ist verfallen> ◊ *Die alte Mühle verfällt immer mehr.* 2. *(power, quality)* nachlassen [ˈnaːxlasn̩] <lässt nach, ließ nach, hat nachgelassen> ◊ *Die Qualität der Produkte hat stark nachgelassen.*

deceive [verb] täuschen [ˈtɔʏʃn̩] +haben ◊ *Lass dich nicht täuschen; dieser Mann ist nicht ehrlich.* deceive yourself sich [dat] etw. vormachen

[ˈfoːɐ̯maxn̩] +haben ◊ *Mach dir nichts vor; sie wird dich verlassen.*

December [noun] Dezember [deˈtsɛmbɐ] der <-(s), -> most sing → **January**

decency [noun] Anstand [ˈanʃtant] der <-(e)s> no pl ◊ *Sie sollten den Anstand haben, Ihren Irrtum zuzugeben!* observe the decencies den Anstand wahren

decent(ly) [adj, adv] anständig [ˈanʃtɛndɪç] ◊ *Es war sehr anständig von ihm, dass er sich entschuldigt hat.* ♦ *Machen Sie mir bitte ein anständiges Angebot!* ♦ *sich anständig benehmen*

deception [noun] Betrug [bəˈtruːk] der <-(e)s> no pl

decide [verb] 1. *(come to a conclusion on a matter, judge or evaluate sth)* über etw. [acc] entscheiden [yːbɐ ... ɛntˈʃaɛdn̩] <entscheidet, entschied, hat entschieden> ◊ *Sie haben noch nicht über den Antrag entschieden.* decide between A or B sich für A oder B entscheiden ◊ *Wir mussten uns für einen Urlaub oder ein neues Auto entscheiden.*; *(resolve a game)* etw. entscheiden [ɛntˈʃaɛdn̩] ◊ *Das Tor in der 89. Minute entschied das Fußballspiel.*; *(determine what to do)* decide to do sth beschließen, etw. zu tun [bəˈʃliːsn̩ ... tsuː] <beschließt, beschloss, hat beschlossen> ◊ *Wir beschlossen, den Urlaub zu verlängern.* sth decides sb to do sth etw. bewegt jdn dazu, etw. zu tun [bəˈveːkt ... datsuː; ... tsuː] <bewegte, hat bewegt> ◊ *Das hohe Gehalt bewegte mich dazu, den Job anzunehmen.* 2. *(direction)* angeben [ˈangeːbm̩] <gibt an, gab an, hat angegeben> ◊ *Gib du die Richtung an.*

• **decide on** [phras v] beschließen [bəˈʃliːsn̩] <beschließt, beschloss, hat beschlossen> ◊ *Die Firma hat die Streichung von hundert Stellen beschlossen.*

decimal point [noun] Komma [ˈkɔma] das <-s, -s or -ta> ◊ *auf eine Stelle hinter dem Komma runden*

> In German speaking countries the comma is the symbol used in a decimal.

decision [noun] 1. *(selection of a course of action)* Entscheidung [ɛntˈʃaɛdʊŋ] die <-, -en> ◊ *Sie haben eine endgültige Entscheidung getroffen.* ♦ *Wann ist die Entscheidung gefallen?* reach a decision eine Entscheidung fällen 2. *(official)* Beschluss [bəˈʃlʊs] der <-es, Beschlüsse> *(esp form)* ◊ *jdn durch einstimmigen Beschluss zu etw. ernennen* 3. *(final decision)* Entschluss [ɛntˈʃlʊs] der <-es, Entschlüsse> ◊ *Ich bin zu dem Entschluss gekommen, dass ...* ♦ *Sie fasste einen spontanen Entschluss.*

decision-making [noun] Entscheidungsfindung [ɛntˈʃaɛdʊŋsfɪndʊŋ] die <-, -en> ◊ *der Prozess der Entscheidungsfindung*

decisive [adj] 1. *(part, victory)* maßgeblich [ˈmaːsgeːplɪç] ◊ *eine maßgebliche Rolle spielen* ♦ *Welches Kriterium ist maßgeblich?* 2. *(character, voice)* bestimmt [bəˈʃtɪmt] <bestimmter, am bestimmtesten> ◊ *Sie sagte das in einem sehr bestimmten Ton.* 3. *(person)* entscheidungsfreudig [ɛntˈʃaɛdʊŋsfrɔʏdɪç] ◊ *Er ist sehr entscheidungsfreudig.*

decisively [adv] maßgeblich [ˈmaːsgeːplɪç] ◊ *Von welchem Künstler wurde er maßgeblich beeinflusst?*

deck [noun] 1. *(of a ship)* Deck [dɛk] das <-(e)s, -s> ◊ *Der Kapitän ist gerade unter Deck.* ♦ *Sie hatten ihr Zimmer auf dem unteren Deck.* 2. *(in the US:*

wooden terrace) Terrasse [tɛ'rasə] die <-, –n> ◊ *Sie sitzen gern auf ihrer Terrasse.* **3.** *(of cards)* Kartenspiel ['ka'tn̩ʃpiːl] das <-(e)s, -e> ◊ *Sie benötigten ein neues Kartenspiel.* **4.** TECHN *(in compound ns)* ...deck [dɛk] tape deck Kassettendeck [ka'sɛtn̩dɛk] ⊙ **clear the deck** klar Schiff machen *(fam)*

declaration [noun] Erklärung [eˈklɛːrʊŋ] die <-, –en> ◊ *Sie verlas eine Erklärung.* tax declaration Steuererklärung ['ʃtɔøɐˌklɛːrʊŋ]

declare [verb] **1.** *(announce)* ankündigen ['anˌkʏndɪɡn̩] +haben ◊ *Der Minister kündigte sofortige Hilfe an.* **2.** *(proclaim)* erklären [eˈklɛːrən] <erklärt, erklärte, hat erklärt> declare war on a country einem Land den Krieg erklären declare sb/sth to be sth jdn/ etw. für/zu etw. erklären ◊ *Er wurde zum Helden des Tages erklärt.* **3.** *(income, address, in documents)* angeben ['angeːbn̩] <gibt an, gab an, hat angegeben> ◊ *eine falsche Adresse angeben* ♦ *seine Einnahmen angeben* **4.** *(in accounts)* ausweisen ['aʊsvaɪzn̩] <weist aus, wies aus, hat ausgewiesen> ◊ *Das Unternehmen weist in diesem Geschäftsjahr einen Verlust aus.* **5.** *(at the border)* deklarieren [dekla'riːrən] <deklariert, deklarierte, hat deklariert> ◊ *Muss ich diese Zigaretten deklarieren?*

declension [noun] Deklination [deklina'tsjoːn] die <-, –en> ◊ *die Deklination des Adjektivs*

decline¹ [noun] **1.** *(become less)* Rückgang ['rʏkɡaŋ] der <-(e)s> most sing ◊ *ein dramatischer Rückgang der Produktion* on the decline auf dem Rückzug [aʊf deːm 'rʏktsuːk] ◊ *Diese Tradition ist schon lange auf dem Rückzug.* **2.** *(morals)* Verfall [fɛ'fal] der <-(e)s> no pl ◊ *der moralische Verfall der Gesellschaft*

decline² [verb] **1.** *(numbers)* abnehmen ['apneːmən] <nimmt ab, nahm ab, hat abgenommen> ◊ *Die Schülerzahlen nehmen ab.* **2.** *(an invitation)* ablehnen ['apleːnən] +haben ◊ *Er lehnte ihre Einladung zum Kaffee ab.* **3.** *(a word)* deklinieren [dekli'niːrən] <dekliniert, deklinierte, hat dekliniert> ◊ *Deklinieren Sie „Hund".* **4.** *(health)* sich verschlechtern [fɛ'ʃlɛçtɐn] <verschlechtert sich, verschlechterte sich, hat sich verschlechtert> ◊ *Ihr Zustand hat sich verschlechtert.*

decor [noun] Ausstattung ['aʊsʃtatʊŋ] die <-, –en> most sing

decorate [verb] **1.** *(with decorations)* schmücken ['ʃmʏkn̩] +haben ◊ *Sie schmückte den Weihnachtsbaum.* ♦ *ein festlich geschmückter Saal* **2.** *(with paint)* streichen ['ʃtraɪçn̩] <streicht, strich, hat gestrichen> ◊ *das Zimmer neu streichen;* *(with wallpaper)* tapezieren [tape'tsiːrən] <tapeziert, tapezierte, hat tapeziert> ◊ *Sie tapezierte die Wände neu.* **3.** *(with a medal)* be decorated (with sth for sth) (mit etw. für etw.) ausgezeichnet werden ['aʊsɡətsaeçnət veːɐdn̩] <wird, wurde, ist worden> ◊ *Er wurde mit einer Tapferkeitsmedaille ausgezeichnet.*

decoration [noun] **1.** *(ornamentation)* Schmuck [ʃmʊk] der <-(e)s> no pl ◊ *Der einzige Schmuck des Gebäudes besteht aus den farbigen Kacheln.* **2.** *(process of painting)* Streichen ['ʃtraɪçn̩] das <-s> no pl; *(of putting wallpaper up)* Tapezieren [tape'tsiːrən] das <-s> no pl **3.** *(medal)* Auszeichnung ['aʊstsaeçnʊŋ] die <-, –en> ◊ *Er erhielt eine Auszeichnung.*

decorative [adj] dekorativ [dekora'tiːf] ◊ *eine dekorative Vase*

decrease¹ [noun] Rückgang ['rʏkɡaŋ] der <-(e)s, Rückgänge> ◊ *Der Rückgang der Arbeitslosenzahlen ist erfreulich.*

decrease² [verb] **1.** *(reduce)* abbauen ['apbaʊən] +haben ◊ *Die Firma baute Personal/Stellen/ihre Lagerbestände ab.* **2.** *(pressure)* nachlassen ['naːxlasn̩] <lässt nach, ließ nach, hat nachgelassen> ◊ *Der Druck auf die Regierung lässt nicht nach.* **3.** *(amount)* zurückgehen [tsu'rʏkɡeːən] <geht zurück, ging zurück, ist zurückgegangen> ◊ *Der Umsatz/Die Kriminalität ist zurückgegangen.*

decree¹ [noun] **1.** LAW Verfügung [fɛ'fyːɡʊŋ] die <-, –en> *(tech)* ◊ *eine amtliche Verfügung* **2.** POL Verordnung [fɛ'ɔʁdnʊŋ] die <-, –en> ◊ *Es wurde eine Verordnung erlassen.*

decree² [verb] verordnen [fɛ'ʔɔʁdnən] <verordnet, verordnete, hat verordnet> ◊ *Die Regierung verordnete ein Rauchverbot.*

dedicate [verb] *(devote yourself to)* widmen ['vɪtmən] <widmet, widmete, hat gewidmet> ◊ *Ich widme meinem Hobby viel Zeit.* dedicate yourself to sth sich einer Sache [dat] widmen ◊ *Sie widmete sich intensiv ihrer Arbeit.* dedicate sth to sb jdm etw. widmen ◊ *Er widmete ihr ein Gedicht.*

dedication [noun] **1.** *(total commitment)* Hingabe ['hɪnɡaːbə] die <-> no pl ◊ *Seine Aufgaben erfüllt er mit Hingabe.* **2.** *(in a book)* Widmung ['vɪtmʊŋ] die <-, –en> ◊ *Im Buch stand eine Widmung an ihre Eltern.*

deduce [verb] schließen ['ʃliːsn̩] <schließt, schloss, hat geschlossen> deduce sth from sth etw. aus etw. [dat] schließen ◊ *Er schloss daraus, dass ihr der Film gefallen hatte.*

deed [noun] **1.** *(an exploit, a feat)* Tat [taːt] die <-, –en> ◊ *jds gute Tat für heute* **2.** LAW *(document)* Besitzurkunde [bə'zɪtsˌlʊʁkʊndə] die <-, –en>

deem [verb] halten für ['haltn̩ fyːɐ] <hält, hielt, hat gehalten> deem sth necessary etw. für wichtig halten ◊ *Er hielt ihr Engagement für sehr wichtig.*

deep¹ [adj] **1.** *(river, valley, sound, emotions)* tief [tiːf] ◊ *Das Auto blieb im tiefen Schnee stecken.* ♦ *ein zehn Meter tiefer See* ♦ *eine Glocke mit tiefem Klang* ♦ *Wie tief ist das Regal?* **2.** *(colo(u)rs)* satt [zat] <satter, am sattesten> ◊ *ein sattes Rot* **3.** *(thoughts, person)* tiefgründig ['tiːfɡrʏndɪç]

deep² [adv] tief [tiːf] ◊ *Das Wrack liegt 100 Meter tief im Wasser.* ♦ *Wenn wir noch tiefer graben, stoßen wir bald auf Wasser.* ♦ *Sie war tief in Gedanken versunken.* ⊙ **deep down** im Innersten run/go deep tief gehen

deepen [verb] **1.** *(your knowledge, a friendship, hole, conflict)* vertiefen [fɛ'tiːfn̩] <vertieft, vertiefte, hat vertieft> ◊ *Ich möchte meine Sprachkenntnisse vertiefen.* ♦ *die Freundschaft zwischen zwei Völkern vertiefen* **2.** *(crisis)* sich zuspitzen ['tsuːʃpɪtsn̩] +haben ◊ *Der Konflikt im Irak spitzt sich zu.* **3.** *(voice)* tiefer werden ['tiːfɐ veːɐdn̩] +sein ◊ *Seine Stimme wurde tiefer.* **4.** *(colo(u)rs)* intensiver werden [ɪntɛn'ziːvɐ veːɐdn̩] +sein

deep freeze [noun] Gefriertruhe [ɡə'friːɡtruːə] die <-, –n>

deep-fry [verb] frittieren [frɪ'tiːrən] <frittiert, frittierte, hat frittiert>

deeply [adv] **1.** tief [tiːf] ◊ *Er war tief beeindruckt/ erschüttert/verunsichert/gekränkt.* ♦ *Du musst tief durchatmen.;* *(disappointed)* schwer [ʃveːɐ] ◊ *Du hast*

mich schwer enttäuscht. **2.** *(extremely)* zutiefst [tsu'ti:fst] *no comp/superl* ◊ *Solches Verhalten verachtet er zutiefst.*

deer ⸤noun⸥ Hirsch [hɪrʃ] der <-es, -e> ♀Reh [re:] das <-(e)s, -e>

default ⸤noun⸥ **1.** *(computer)* Voreinstellung ['fo:ɐ̯|aɛnʃtɛlʊŋ] die <-, -en> ◊ *Sie können die Voreinstellungen Ihres Computers verändern.* **2.** *(be too late)* Versäumnis [fɛ'zɔɜ̯mnɪs] das <-ses, -se> ⊛ by default automatisch

defeat[1] ⸤noun⸥ Niederlage ['ni:dɐla:gə] die <-, -n> ◊ *eine schwere Niederlage erleiden*

defeat[2] ⸤verb⸥ besiegen [bə'zi:gn̩] <besiegt, besiegte, hat besiegt> ◊ *Die Mannschaft besiegte den Gegner mit 3:0.* ⊛ sth defeats sb etw. ist jdm zu hoch

defect[1] ⸤noun⸥ Fehler ['fe:lɐ] der <-s, ->

defect[2] ⸤verb⸥ **1.** defect to another country sich in ein anderes Land absetzen [ɪn ... 'apzɛtsn̩] +*haben* ◊ *Heimlich setzte er sich nach Südamerika ab.* **2.** defect to sth/sb zu etw./jdm überlaufen [] <läuft über, lief über, ist übergelaufen> ◊ *Sie ist zur Opposition übergelaufen.*

defective ⸤adj⸥ fehlerhaft ['fe:lɐhaft] *no comp/superl* ◊ *eine fehlerhafte Diskette* ♦ *Die Verarbeitung war fehlerhaft.*

defence, defense ⸤noun⸥ **1.** *(military, in an argument, legal)* Verteidigung [fɛ'taɛ̯dɪgʊŋ] die <-> *no pl* ◊ *Diese Waffe benutze ich nur zur Verteidigung.* ♦ *Was haben Sie zu Ihrer Verteidigung zu sagen?* speak in sb's defence jdn verteidigen [fɛ'taɛ̯dɪgn̩] <verteidigt, verteidigte, hat verteidigt> **2.** *(in football)* Abwehr ['apveːɐ̯] die <-> *no pl* ◊ *Wer spielt in der Abwehr?* **3.** *(of the body)* Abwehrkräfte ['apveːɐ̯krɛftə] die <-> *only pl*

defend ⸤verb⸥ verteidigen [fɛ'taɛ̯dɪgn̩] <verteidigte, verteidigt> ◊ *eine Burg gegen Angreifer verteidigen* ♦ *seine Meinung verteidigen* ♦ *Der Angeklagte wird von Rechtsanwalt Müller verteidigt.* ♦ *seinen Titel/Vorsprung verteidigen* defend yourself (against sb/sth) sich (gegen jdn/etw.) wehren ['ve:rən] +*haben* ◊ *Sie wehrte sich gegen ihn.*

defendant ⸤noun⸥ Angeklagte ['angəkla:ktə] der/die <-n, die Angeklagten> but: ein Angeklagter/eine Angeklagte ◊ *Die Angeklagte wurde freigesprochen.*

defender ⸤noun⸥ Verteidiger [fɛ'taɛ̯dɪgɐ] der <-s, -> ♀Verteidigerin [fɛ'taɛ̯dɪgərɪn] die <-, -nen> ◊ *Die Verteidigerin des Angeklagten plädierte auf „nicht schuldig".* ♦ *Als Verteidiger hat er viele Mandanten.*

defense → defence

defensive ⸤adj⸥ defensiv [defɛn'zi:f] *no comp/superl* ◊ *defensiv bleiben* ♦ *eine defensive Haltung* become defensive in die Defensive gehen [ɪn di: defɛn'zi:və ge:ən] <geht, ging, ist gegangen>

defiant(ly) ⸤adj, adv⸥ trotzig ['trɔtsɪç] ◊ *ein trotziger Junge* ♦ *„Das werde ich nicht tun!", sagte er trotzig.*

deficiency ⸤noun⸥ **1.** *(lack)* Mangel ['maŋl̩] der <-s> *no pl* ◊ *Mangel an Vitaminen* **2.** *(weakness)* Schwäche ['ʃvɛçə] die <-, -n> ◊ *Die Schwächen des Programms können behoben werden.* mental deficiency Geistesschwäche ['gaɛstəsʃvɛçə]

deficit ⸤noun⸥ **1.** *(financial)* Defizit ['de:fitsɪt] das <-s, -s> ◊ *ein Defizit haben* ◊ *ein Defizit in Höhe von* ◊ *ein Defizit in Höhe von drei Millionen* **2.** *(lack or need of sth)* Mangel ['maŋl̩] der <-s, Mängel> nutritional deficit Ernährungsmangel

[ɛ'nɛːrʊŋsmaŋl̩] protein deficit Eiweißmangel ['aɛ̯vaɛsmaŋl̩]

define ⸤verb⸥ definieren [defi'ni:rən] <definiert, definierte, hat definiert> ◊ *Ziele/ein Wort definieren* define yourself by sth sich über etw. ⸤acc⸥ definieren ◊ *Sie definiert sich stark über ihren Beruf.*

definite ⸤adj⸥ **1.** *(particular)* bestimmt [bə'ʃtɪmt] *no comp/superl* definite ideas about sth ganz bestimmte Vorstellungen von etw. **2.** *(committed, clear)* endgültig ['ɛntgʏltɪç] *no comp/superl, only before* no ◊ *eine endgültige Antwort* sth is definite etw. steht fest [ʃteːt 'fɛst] <steht fest, stand fest, hat festgestanden> ◊ *Steht der Termin schon fest?* ⊛ be definite about sth **1.** *(have very clear ideas or opinons)* ganz bestimmte Vorstellungen von etw. haben ◊ *Ich hatte ganz bestimmte Vorstellungen davon, wie meine Karriere verlaufen sollte.* **2.** *(be very sure)* sich ⸤dat⸥ ganz sicher sein, was etw. angeht ◊ *Bist du dir ganz sicher, was die Adresse angeht?* **3.** *(really want to do sth)* be definite about doing sth etw. wirklich tun wollen ◊ *Willst du wirklich mit dem Rauchen aufhören?*

definitely ⸤adv⸥ **1.** *(to assure sb, expressing that you are positive about sth)* bestimmt [bə'ʃtɪmt] *no comp/superl* ◊ *Das hat er bestimmt nicht gesagt.* ♦ *Ich komme ganz bestimmt.* **2.** *(without a doubt, with finality)* definitiv [defini'ti:f] *no comp/superl* ◊ *Er hat definitiv gesagt, er wolle sich entschuldigen.* ♦ *Wir haben uns jetzt definitiv für einen Namen entschieden.*

definition ⸤noun⸥ **1.** *(statement of meaning)* Definition [defini'tsjo:n] die <-, -en> ◊ *Der Chef ist für die Definition der Ziele zuständig.* ♦ *die Definition von „Liebe"* by definition definitionsgemäß [defini'tsjo:nsgəmɛːs] **2.** ꜰᴏᴛᴏ Schärfe ['ʃɛrfə] die <-> *no pl* ◊ *die Schärfe einstellen*

definitive(ly) ⸤adj, adv⸥ endgültig ['ɛntgʏltɪç] *no comp/superl* ◊ *Ist diese Entscheidung endgültig?* ◊ *das endgültige Wahlergebnis* ♦ *Sie haben sich jetzt endgültig getrennt.*

defraud ⸤verb⸥ betrügen [bə'try:gn̩] <betrügt, betrog, hat betrogen> ◊ *Wer das Finanzamt betrügt, muss mit schweren Strafen rechnen.*

defrost ⸤verb⸥ **1.** *(food)* auftauen ['aoftao̯ən] *transitive use* +*haben/intransitive use* +*sein* ◊ *Er hat den Spinat in der Mikrowelle aufgetaut.* ♦ *Das Fleisch taut im Kühlschrank langsam auf.* **2.** *(fridge)* abtauen ['aptao̯ən] *transitive use* +*haben/intransitive use* +*sein* ◊ *Er taut den Kühlschrank ab.* ♦ *Der Kühlschrank taut ab.*

defuse ⸤verb⸥ entschärfen [ɛnt'ʃɛrfn̩] <entschärft, entschärft, hat entschärft> ◊ *einen Konflikt/Streit entschärfen* ◊ *einen Sprengsatz entschärfen*

defy ⸤verb⸥ **1.** *(an order, instruction)* missachten [mɪs'|axtn̩] <missachtet, missachtete, hat missachtet> ◊ *eine Anweisung missachten* **2.** defy description jeder Beschreibung spotten [je:de:ɐ̯ bə'ʃraɛbʊŋ ʃpɔtn̩] <spottet, spottete, hat gespottet> ◊ *Der Zustand auf dem Arbeitsmarkt spottet jeder Beschreibung.*

degree ⸤noun⸥ **1.** *(of temperature, angles, academic)* Grad [gra:t] der <-(e)s, -e or -> ◊ *Es herrschen Temperaturen um die 20 Grad plus.* ♦ *ein Winkel von 90 Grad* ♦ *Sie hat mehrere akademische Grade.* **2.** *(of education, training)* Abschluss ['apʃlʊs] der <-es, Abschlüsse> ◊ *Ich habe einen Abschluss in Psychologie.; (university)* Hochschulabschluss

['hoːxʃuːlˌlapʃlʊs] take a degree einen Hochschulab-schluss machen 3. *(of quality)* Maß [maːs] das <-es, -e> ◊ *Das trifft in geringem/hohem/besonde-rem Maße zu.* ♦ *Dazu gehört ein beträchtliches Maß an Mut.*

dejected [adj] niedergeschlagen ['niːdəgəʃlaˌgn̩] ◊ *ein niedergeschlagener Ausdruck* ♦ *Völlig niedergeschla-gen kamen die Verlierer nach Hause.* dejected mood Niedergeschlagenheit ['niːdəgəʃlaˌgŋ̩haɛt] die <-> no pl

delay¹ [noun] 1. *(of a plane, train, person)* Verspätung [fɛ'ʃpɛːtʊn] die <-, -en> ◊ *Bitte entschuldigt meine Verspätung!* ♦ *Mein Gehalt kam mit einem Monat Ver-spätung.* 2. *(in concluding a task)* Verzug [fɛ'tsuːk] der <-(e)s> no pl ◊ *Wir werden das ohne Verzug erledigen.* 3. *(deferment)* Aufschub [ˈaʊfʃuːp] der <-(e)s, Aufschübe> most sing ◊ *jdm Aufschub gewähren* ♦ *einen Aufschub der Entscheidung/ Gerichtsverhandlung erwirken*

delay² [verb] 1. *(arrival, departure)* sth is delayed etw. verzögert sich [fɛ'tsøːgɐt zɪç] <verzögerte sich, hat sich verzögert> ◊ *Die Abfahrt des Zuges verzögert sich um 20 Minuten.* The train is delayed. Der Zug hat Verspätung. 2. *(do sth at a later point in time)* delay sth etw. verschieben [fɛ'ʃiːbm̩] <verschiebt, verschob, hat verschoben> ◊ *Diesen Termin habe ich auf morgen verschoben.; (a decision)* aufschieben ['aʊfʃiːbm̩] <schiebt auf, schob auf, hat aufgeschoben> ◊ *Können wir diese Entscheidung noch aufschieben?* 3. *(hesitate)* zögern ['tsøːgɐn] +haben ◊ *Zögern Sie nicht länger, wenn Sie etwas tun wollen!* 4. *(slow down a process, development)* hinauszögern [hɪ'naʊstsøːgɐn] +haben ◊ *die Entwicklung einer Krankheit hinauszögern*

delegate¹ [noun] Delegierte [dele'giːgtə] der/die <-n, die Delegierten> but: ein Delegierter/eine Dele-gierte

delegate² [verb] delegieren [dele'giːrən] <delegiert, delegierte, hat delegiert> ◊ *Er delegierte einen Teil seiner Arbeit an seine Mitarbeiter.*

delegation [noun] 1. *(group of people)* Delegation [delega'tsjoːn] die <-, -en> ◊ *die deutsche Delega-tion* 2. *(of work)* Delegierung [dele'giːrʊn] die <-, -en> ◊ *die Delegierung von Aufgaben*

delete [verb] 1. *(cross out)* streichen ['ʃtraɛçn̩] <streicht, strich, hat gestrichen> ◊ *Unzutreffendes bitte streichen.* 2. *(computer)* löschen ['lœʃn̩] +haben ◊ *Daten löschen*

deliberate(ly) [adj, adv] 1. *(intentional)* absichtlich ['apzɪçtlɪç] no comp/superl ◊ *Entschuldigung, das war nicht absichtlich.* ♦ *ein absichtlicher Fehler* ♦ *Er hat sie absichtlich getreten.* 2. *(malicious)* mutwillig ['muːtvɪlɪç] no comp/superl ◊ *ein mutwilliges Vorgehen* ♦ *etw. mutwillig zerstören* 3. *(aware)* bewusst [bə'vʊst] <bewusster, am bewusstesten> ◊ *eine bewusste Lüge* ♦ *Sie entschied sich bewusst für eine Hausgeburt.*

delicate [adj] 1. *(skin, body, cloth, breeze, colo(u)rs, health, fragrance, voice)* zart [tsaːɐt] <zarter, am zartesten> ◊ *Dieses Pflänzchen ist noch sehr zart.* ♦ *ein zartes Blau* ♦ *ein zartes Stimmchen haben* 2. *(stomach and other organs)* empfindlich [ɛm'pfɪntlɪç] ◊ *Sie hat einen empfindlichen Magen.* 3. *(issue, question)* heikel ['haɛkl] <heikler, am hei-kelsten> <der/die/das heikle ...> ◊ *eine heikle Frage* ♦ *Dieses Thema ist mir zu heikel.* 4. *(handwriting,*

pattern, line) fein [faɛn] ◊ *eine Tapete mit feinen Mustern* ♦ *Die Handschrift ist sehr fein.*

delicately [adv] 1. *(with great skill and attention to detail)* fein [faɛn] ◊ *fein bemaltes Porzellan* ♦ *eine fein gearbeitete Brosche* 2. *(carefully)* vorsichtig ['foːɐzɪçtɪç] ◊ *etw. vorsichtig handhaben* 3. delicately colo(u)red in zarten Farben [ɪn ˌtsaːɐtn 'farbm̩] ◊ *Porzellan in zarten Farben* delicately flavo(u)red mit zartem Aroma [mɪt ˌtsaːɐtm a'roːmaː] ◊ *eine Teesorte mit zartem Aroma*

delicious(ly) [adj, adv] köstlich ['kœstlɪç] ◊ *ein köstli-ches Rezept* ♦ *Der Nachtisch war einfach köstlich.* ♦ *köstlich riechen*

delight¹ [noun] 1. *(happiness)* Freude ['frɔɡdə] die <-, -n> ◊ *Es ist mir eine große Freude, Sie hier begrüßen zu dürfen.* ♦ *die Freuden des Lebens genießen* to sb's delight zu jds großer Freude 2. *(relief)* Wohltat ['voːltaːt] die <-, -en> ◊ *Es war eine Wohltat, faul in der Sonne zu liegen.*

delight² [verb] delight sb jdn entzücken [ɛnt'tsʏkn̩] <entzückt, entzückte, hat entzückt> ◊ *Ihr Anblick entzückte mich.* to be delighted by sth von etw. entzückt sein ◊ *Ich war von der Idee entzückt.*
ⓘ sb is delighted *(when you are introduced)* sehr erfreut ◊ *„Darf ich Ihnen Frau Rieger vorstellen?"* — *„Sehr erfreut!"*

delightful [adj] entzückend [ɛnt'tsʏkn̩t] ◊ *ein entzü-ckendes Kleid* ♦ *Leonie ist wirklich entzückend.*

deliver [verb] 1. *(goods)* liefern ['liːfɐn] <liefert, lieferte, hat geliefert> ◊ *Wir liefern Ihre Möbel frei Haus.* ♦ *Wir liefern innerhalb von 24 Stunden.* 2. *(a message)* überbringen [ybɐ'brɪnən] <überbringt, über-brachte, hat überbracht> ◊ *Er überbrachte eine Nachricht.* 3. *(letters)* austragen ['aʊstraːgn̩] <trägt aus, trug aus, hat ausgetragen> ◊ *Briefe austragen* 4. *(in person)* abgeben ['apɡeːbm̩] <gibt ab, gab ab, hat abgegeben> ◊ *Der Junge hat ein Paket bei uns abgegeben.* 5. deliver a speech eine Rede halten [aɛnə 'reːdə haltn̩] <hält, hielt, hat gehalten> 6. deliver (sb) a blow jdm einen Schlag versetzen [aɛnən 'ʃlaːk fɛzɛtsn̩] <versetzt, versetzte, hat versetzt> ◊ *Er versetzte ihm einen Schlag.* 7. *(a baby)* entbinden [ɛnt'bɪndn̩] <entbindet, entband, hat entbunden> ◊ *Mein Kind wurde im Krankenhaus entbunden.*
• **deliver from** [phras v] deliver sb from sb/sth jdn aus etw. befreien [aʊs ... bə,fraɛən] <befreit, befreite, hat befreit> ◊ *jdn aus der Sklaverei befreien* ♦ *Sie wurden aus der Hände des Feindes befreit.*

delivery [noun] 1. *(of goods)* Lieferung ['liːfərʊn] die <-, -en> ◊ *Die Lieferung des Sofas erfolgt innerhalb von sechs Wochen.* free delivery Lieferung frei Haus 2. *(of a baby)* Geburt [gə'buːɐt] die <-, -en> ◊ *Es war eine leichte Geburt.* 3. *(of a speech)* Vortrags-technik ['foːɐtraːksˌtɛçnɪk] die <-, -en> 4. *(of a ball, with a bat)* Schlag [ʃlaːk] das <-(e)s, Schläge>; *(by kicking)* Schuss [ʃʊs] der <-es, Schüsse>; *(by throwing)* Wurf [vʊrf] der <-(e)s, Würfe>

delusion [noun] 1. *(illusion)* Illusion [ɪlu'zjoːn] die <-, -en> ◊ *die Illusion, dass man die Welt verbes-sern könne* optical delusion optische Täuschung [ˌɔptɪʃə 'tɔɡʃʊn] die <-, -en> 2. MED *(mental illness)* Wahnvorstellung ['vaːnfoːɐʃtɛlʊn] die <-, -en> ◊ *unter Wahnvorstellungen leiden*

demand¹ [noun] 1. *(insistent request to which sb feels entitled)* demand for Forderung nach ['fɔrdərʊn naːx]

die <–, –en> ◊ *jds Forderungen nach mehr Geld*
make a demand eine Forderung stellen meet sb's
demands jds Forderungen erfüllen 2. *(of a job, an
exam)* demands Anforderungen ['anfɔrdərʊŋən] die
<–> pl ◊ *Sie war den Anforderungen nicht
gewachsen.* make demands on sb/sth hohe Anforderungen an jdn/etw. stellen 3. *(firm but polite
request)* Verlangen [fɛ'laŋən] das <–s> no pl *(lofty)* ◊
*Auf mein Verlangen stellte man mir eine Bestätigung
aus.* 4. *(request, for goods)* Nachfrage ['naːxfraːgə]
die <–> no pl ◊ *Die Nachfrage nach Benzin steigt.* ✦
*Der Preis wird durch Angebot und Nachfrage
bestimmt.*
◉ by popular demand auf allgemeinen Wunsch
demand² ⌊verb⌋ 1. *(ask for)* verlangen [fɛ'laŋən]
<verlangt, verlangte, hat verlangt> ◊ *Die Firma
verlangt viel Engagement von ihren Angestellten.*
2. *(attention)* beanspruchen [bə'ʔanʃprʊxn̩] <bean-
sprucht, beanspruchte, hat beansprucht> ◊ *Das Kind
beansprucht ihre ganze Aufmerksamkeit.* 3. LAW beantragen [bə'ʔantraːgn̩] <beantragt, beantragte, hat
beantragt> ◊ *eine Unterbrechung der Verhandlung
beantragen*
demanding ⌊adj⌋ anspruchsvoll ['anʃprʊxsfɔl] ◊ *Der
Kunde war sehr anspruchsvoll.* ✦ *eine anspruchsvolle
Tätigkeit/Aufgabe* physically demanding schwer
[ʃveːɐ̯] ◊ *Gartenarbeit ist schwere Arbeit.* ✦ *Seine
Arbeit ist sehr schwer.*
democracy ⌊noun⌋ Demokratie [demokra'tiː] die
<–, –n>
democrat ⌊noun⌋ Demokrat [demo'kraːt] der
<–en, –en> ♀Demokratin [demo'kraːtɪn] die
<–, –nen>
democratic(ally) ⌊adj, adv⌋ demokratisch
[demo'kraːtɪʃ] ◊ *demokratische Wahlen* ✦ *Ich finde
das nicht demokratisch!* ✦ *ein demokratisch
gewählter Politiker*
demolish ⌊verb⌋ 1. *(deliberately, a building)* abbrechen
['apbrɛçn̩] <bricht ab, brach ab, hat abgebrochen> ◊
Das Gebäude wurde 1930 abgebrochen. 2. *(sb's confidence)* zerstören [tsɛ'ʃtøːrən] <zerstört, zerstörte, hat
zerstört> ◊ *Diese Erfahrung zerstörte mein Selbstvertrauen.* 3. *(food)* vertilgen [fɛ'tɪlgn̩] <vertilgt, vertilgte,
hat vertilgt> *(fam)* ◊ *Ich habe eine ganze Tafel Schokolade vertilgt.* 4. SPORT *(an opponent in sports)* vernichtend schlagen [fɛˌnɪçtn̩t 'ʃlaːgn̩] <schlägt, schlug,
hat geschlagen> ◊ *Unsere Mannschaft wurde vernichtend geschlagen.*
demolition ⌊noun⌋ 1. *(of a building)* Abriss ['aprɪs] der
<–es, –e> ◊ *Viele Häuser in der Altstadt sind vom
Abriss bedroht.* 2. *(of a team)* Niederlage ['niːdɐlaːgə]
die <–, –n> ◊ *Nach dem vierten Tor war unsere Niederlage perfekt.*
demon ⌊noun⌋ *(evil spirit)* Teufel ['tɔɣfl̩] der <–s, –> ◊
Wie von tausend Teufeln gehetzt stürzte er davon.
sb's inner demons *verborgene Ängste und Agres-
sionen, die einen Menschen beherrschen können*
demonstrate ⌊verb⌋ 1. *(show)* demonstrate sth to sb
jdm etw. vorführen ['foːɐ̯fyːrən] +haben ◊ *Sie führte
uns einen Roboter vor.* 2. *(prove)* demonstrate that
nachweisen, dass ['naːxvaɪ̯zn̩ das] <weist nach, wies
nach, hat nachgewiesen> ◊ *Er wies nach, dass der
Zellkern Proteine enthält.* sth was demonstrated to
be some wie wurde nachgewiesen, dass etw.
irgendwie ist ◊ *Es wurde nachgewiesen, dass
Rauchen gesundheitsschädlich ist.* 3. *(protest)*

demonstrieren [demɔn'striːrən] <demonstriert,
demonstrierte, hat demonstriert> ◊ *gegen den Krieg/
für den Frieden demonstrieren*
demonstration ⌊noun⌋ 1. *(showing)* Vorführung
['foːɐ̯fyːrʊŋ] die <–, –en> ◊ *die Vorführung neuer
Produkte* 2. *(protest)* Demonstration
[demɔnstra'tsi̯oːn] die <–, –en> ◊ *eine Demonstration gegen den Krieg/für den Frieden* 3. *(of feelings)*
Beweis [bə'vaɪ̯s] der <–es, –e> ◊ *ein Beweis meiner
Zuneigung* demonstration of sb's love Liebesbeweis
['liːbəsbəvaɪ̯s] der <–es, –e>
demonstrator ⌊noun⌋ 1. *(protester)* Demonstrant
[demɔn'strant] der <–en, –en> ♀Demonstrantin
[demɔn'strantɪn] die <–, –nen> ◊ *Die Demonstranten stürmten das Ministerium.* 2. *(instructor)*
Person, die etw. vorführt
den ⌊noun⌋ Höhle ['høːlə] die <–, –n> ◊ *Der Löwe verschwand in seiner Höhle.*
denial ⌊noun⌋ 1. *(of facts, problems, conflicts)*
Leugnung ['lɔɣgnʊŋ] die <–> no pl ◊ *die Leugnung
eines Problems; (of responsibility)* Ablehnung
['aple̯nʊŋ] die <–> no pl 2. *(of rights)* Verweigerung
[fɛ'vaɪ̯gərʊŋ] die <–> no pl ◊ *die Verweigerung des
Rechtes auf Arbeit* 3. offical denial Dementi
[de'mɛnti] das <–s, –s> issue an official denial ein
Dementi veröffentlichen
◉ be in denial verdrängen ◊ *Er verdrängt das
Unglück.*
Denmark ⌊noun⌋ Dänemark ['dɛːnəmaʁk] das <–s>
article only in combination with attribute, no pl ✦
Germany
denomination ⌊noun⌋ 1. *(religion)* Konfession
[kɔnfɛ'si̯oːn] die <–, –en> ◊ *Welcher Konfession
gehören Sie an?* 2. *(of a coin)* Wert [veːɐ̯t] der
<–(e)s, –e> ◊ *Münzen mit unterschiedlichen Werten*
denounce ⌊verb⌋ 1. *(criticism)* kritisieren [kriti'ziːrən]
<kritisiert, kritisierte, hat kritisiert> ◊ *Seine Politik
wurde häufig kritisiert.* 2. *(inform the police)* denun-
zieren [denʊn'tsiːrən] <denunziert, denunzierte, hat
denunziert> ◊ *Man hatte mich bei der Geheimpolizei
denunziert.*
dense ⌊adj⌋ 1. *(fog, traffic, population)* dicht [dɪçt]
<dichter, am dichtesten> ◊ *Der Nebel war sehr dicht.*
✦ *dichter Verkehr auf den Straßen* 2. *(stupid)* dumm
[dʊm] <dümmer, am dümmsten> ◊ *Er ist echt dumm.*
✦ *Dummer Kerl!*
densely ⌊adv⌋ dicht [dɪçt] <dichter, am dichtesten> ◊
ein dicht besiedeltes Land
density ⌊noun⌋ Dichte ['dɪçtə] die <–, –n> most sing
◊ *Wasser hat eine höhere Dichte als Luft.*
dent¹ ⌊noun⌋ Beule ['bɔɣlə] die <–, –n> ◊ *eine Beule
am Auto*
◉ make a dent in sth in Loch in etw. ⌊acc⌋ reißen
dent² ⌊verb⌋ 1. *(a car, bonnet, wing)* verbeulen
[fɛ'bɔɣlən] <verbeult, verbeulte, hat verbeult> ◊ *eine
Stoßstange verbeulen* 2. *(sb's pride, confidence)*
anknacksen ['anknaksn̩] +haben *(fam)* ◊ *Die Niederlage hat sein Ego angeknackst.*
dentist ⌊noun⌋ Zahnarzt ['tsaːnaʁt͡st] der
<–es, Zahnärzte> ♀Zahnärztin ['tsaːnɛɐ̯t͡stɪn] die
<–, –nen> ◊ *Seine Frau ist Zahnärztin.* ✦ *Kannst du
mir einen guten Zahnarzt empfehlen?* at the
dentist's beim Zahnarzt
deny ⌊verb⌋ 1. *(an accusation, a fact, claim)* bestreiten
[bə'ʃtraɪ̯tn̩] <bestreitet, bestritt, hat bestritten> ◊ *Sie
bestreitet diese Vorwürfe.* deny doing sth bestreiten,

etw. getan zu haben ◊ *Er bestreitet, das Geld gestohlen zu haben.* there's no denying sth etw. lässt sich nicht bestreiten there's no denying (that) es lässt sich nicht bestreiten, dass 2. *(a feeling, personal problem)* nicht wahrhaben wollen [nɪçt 'vaːʁhaːbm̩ vɔlən] <will, wollte, hat wollen> ◊ *Sie wollte ihre Krankheit nicht wahrhaben.* ♦ *Er will nicht wahrhaben, dass er abhängig ist.* 3. *(refuse)* deny sth to sb, deny sb sth jdm etw. verweigern [fɐ'vaɪ̯gən] <verweigert, verweigerte, hat verweigert> ◊ *Die Bank hat ihr den Kredit verweigert.*

deodorant (noun) Deodorant [deodo'rant] das <-s, -s or -e>

depart (verb) 1. *(go on a journey)* abreisen ['apʁaɪ̯zn̩] +sein ◊ *Sie sind gestern abgereist.* depart for Australia nach Australien abreisen 2. *(leave)* abfahren ['apfaːʁən] <fährt ab, fuhr ab, ist abgefahren> ◊ *Übermorgen fährt die Familie wieder ab.* ♦ *Der Zug fährt um 20 Uhr 15 ab.; (plane)* abfliegen ['apfliːgn̩] <fliegt ab, flog ab, ist abgeflogen> ◊ *Er/Die Maschine fliegt um sechs Uhr ab.*

department (noun) 1. *(of a company, hospital, shop)* Abteilung [ap'taɪ̯lʊŋ] die <-, -en> ◊ *Die Abteilung, in der er arbeitet, soll geschlossen werden.* ♦ *die Abteilung für Innere Medizin* toy department Spielzeugabteilung ['ʃpiːltsɔɪ̯k|aptaɪ̯lʊŋ] 2. POL *(of a state government)* Ministerium [mɪnɪs'teːʁi̯ʊm] das <-s, Ministerien> ◊ *das Ministerium für Umwelt und Naturschutz* Department of Health Gesundheitsministerium [ɡə'zʊndhaɪ̯tsmɪnɪs̩teːʁi̯ʊm] 3. *(of public administration)* Behörde [bə'høːʁdə] die <-, -n> ◊ *Welche Behörde ist für diese Genehmigung zuständig?* 4. UNI *(of a university)* Seminar [zemi'naːʁ] das <-s, -e> ◊ *das Anglistische Seminar der Universität Heidelberg* 5. GEOG *(French district)* Departement [depaʁtə'man] das <-s, -s> ◊ *das Departement Bouches-du-Rhône*

departmental (adj) Abteilungs... [ap'taɪ̯lʊŋs] departmental secretary Abteilungssekretärin [ap'taɪ̯lʊŋszekʁɛˌtɛːʁɪn] die <-, -nen>

department store (noun) Kaufhaus ['kaʊ̯fhaʊ̯s] das <-es, Kaufhäuser>

departure (noun) 1. *(from an organization, a job)* Abgang ['apɡaŋ] der <-(e)s, Abgänge> ◊ *Der Abgang des Ministers/Präsidenten erfolgte überraschend.; (on a journey)* Abreise ['apʁaɪ̯zə] die <-, -n> ◊ *Vor seiner Abreise verabschiedete er sich von seiner Familie.; (of a train, bus, ship)* Abfahrt ['apfaːʁt] die <-, -en> ◊ *Die Abfahrt des Zuges verzögerte sich um 15 Minuten.; (of a plane)* Abflug ['apfluːk] der <-(e)s, Abflüge> ◊ *Bitte seien Sie eine Stunde vor Abflug am Flughafen.* 2. *(change)* Richtung ['ʁɪçtʊŋ] die <-, -en> ◊ *Das ist eine neue Richtung für uns.* departure from sth Abkehr von etw. ['apkeːɐ̯ fɔn] die <-> no pl ◊ *eine radikale Abkehr von der Tradition*

depend (verb) it depends das kommt drauf an [das kɔmt dʁaʊ̯f 'an]

• **depend on** (phras v) 1. *(be affected by)* depend on sb/sth von jdm/etw. abhängen [fɔn ... ˌaphɛŋən] <hängt ab, hing ab, hat abgehangen> ◊ *Der Erfolg der Firma hängt von Ihrer Leistung ab.* 2. *(need)* depend on sb/sth auf jdn/etw. angewiesen sein [aɔf ... ˌangəviːzn̩ zaɛn] ◊ *Kinder sind auf die Fürsorge ihrer Eltern angewiesen.* depend on sb for sth auf jds etw. angewiesen sein ◊ *auf die Hilfe eines Freundes angewiesen sein* depend on sb to do

sth darauf angewiesen sein, dass jd etw. tut ◊ *Viele Familien sind darauf angewiesen, dass beide Elternteile arbeiten.* 3. *(rely on)* depend on sb sich auf jdn verlassen [aɔf ... fɐˌlasn̩] <verlässt sich, verließ sich, hat sich verlassen> ◊ *Sie können sich auf mich verlassen!*

ⓘ depending on je nach ◊ *Je nach Laune behandelt er den Hund gut oder schlecht.*

dependant, dependent (noun) abhängige Angehörige [ˌaphɛŋɪɡə 'angəhøːʁɪɡə] der/die <-n, die abhängigen Angehörigen> but: ein abhängiger Angehöriger/eine abhängige Angehörige, most pl ◊ *Haben Sie abhängige Angehörige?*

dependence, dependency (noun) dependence on sth Abhängigkeit von etw. ['aphɛŋɪçkaɛt fɔn] die <-, -en> ◊ *die Abhängigkeit von den Eltern* ♦ *die wirtschaftliche Abhängigkeit von einem anderen Land* alcohol dependence Alkoholabhängigkeit ['alkohoːl|ˌaphɛŋɪçkaɛt]

dependency (noun) Kolonie [kolo'niː] die <-, -n> ◊ *Das Land war früher eine französische Kolonie.*

dependent (adj) abhängig ['aphɛŋɪç] ◊ *ein Ehepaar ohne abhängige Kinder* be dependent on sb/sth von jdm/etw. abhängig sein ◊ *Sie ist finanziell von ihren Eltern abhängig.* ♦ *Der Preis des Kurses ist von der Anzahl der Teilnehmer abhängig.* → dependant

depict (verb) darstellen ['daːʃtɛlən] +haben ◊ *Dieses Gemälde stellt die Schwester des Künstlers dar.*

depiction (noun) Darstellung ['daːʃtɛlʊŋ] die <-, -en>

deplete (verb) erschöpfen [ɛ'ʃœpfn̩] <erschöpft, erschöpfte, hat erschöpft> ◊ *Ihre Vorräte waren erschöpft.*

deploy (verb) einsetzen ['aɛnzɛtsn̩] +haben ◊ *Die UNO setzt Hilfstruppen ein.*

deport (verb) abschieben ['apʃiːbm̩] <schiebt ab, schob ab, hat abgeschoben> ◊ *Der Flüchtling wurde in seine Heimat abgeschoben.*

deposit¹ (noun) 1. *(first instalment)* Anzahlung ['antsaːlʊŋ] die <-, -en> ◊ *Er machte eine Anzahlung von 50 Euro.; (as security)* Kaution [kaɔ'tsi̯oːn] die <-, -en> ◊ *eine Kaution an den Vermieter zahlen; (for bottles etc.)* Pfand [pfant] das <-(e)s, Pfänder> most sing ◊ *für etw. Pfand bezahlen* 2. FIN *(in a bank)* Einlage ['aɛnlaːɡə] die <-, -n> ◊ *eine Einlage von 750 Euro haben* 3. *(of a substance)* Ablagerung ['aplaːɡəʁʊŋ] die <-, -en> ◊ *Ablagerungen von Kalk/Fett*

deposit² (verb) 1. *(valuables, luggage)* deponieren [depo'niːʁən] <deponiert, deponierte, hat deponiert> ◊ *Gepäck in einem Schließfach deponieren* 2. FIN *(money)* einzahlen ['aɛntsaːlən] +haben ◊ *Sie zahlte 300 Euro auf ihr Sparbuch ein.* 3. GEOL *(a layer of sth)* ablagern ['aplaːɡɐn] <lagert ab, lagerte ab, hat abgelagert> ◊ *Das Meer lagert Sand ab, und so entsteht neues Land.*

depot (noun) 1. *(to store material)* Lager ['laːɡə] das <-s, -> ◊ *ein Lager für radioaktive Abfälle* 2. *(in the UK: place for keeping buses etc.)* Depot [de'poː] das <-s, -s> 3. *(in the US: station)* Bahnhof ['baːnhoːf] der <-(e)s, Bahnhöfe>

depress (verb) 1. *(sadden)* deprimieren [depri'miːʁən] <deprimiert, deprimierte, hat deprimiert> ◊ *Das Novemberwetter deprimiert mich jedes Jahr.* 2. *(weaken)* schwächen ['ʃvɛçn̩] +haben ◊ *das Immunsystem schwächen* ♦ *Die hohe Arbeitslosigkeit*

schwächt den Markt.

depressed → depress [adj] 1. *(sad)* deprimiert [dɛpri'miːɐ̯t] <deprimierter, am deprimiertesten> ◊ *Du siehst deprimiert aus. Was ist los?*; *(mentally ill)* be clinically depressed Depressionen haben [dɛprɛ'sjoːnən haːbm̩] +*haben* become clinically depressed Depressionen bekommen 2. *(economy etc.)* geschwächt [gə'ʃvɛçt] <geschwächter, am geschwächtesten> *seldom comp/superl* ◊ *eine geschwächte Konjunktur* ♦ *Die Wirtschaft ist immer noch geschwächt.*

depression [noun] 1. *(of the mind, economy)* Depression [dɛprɛ'sjoːn] die <–, – en> ◊ *Depressionen zählen zu den häufigsten Krankheiten.* ♦ *Das Land befindet sich in einer Depression.* suffer from depression an Depressionen leiden the Depression die Weltwirtschaftskrise [diː vɛlt'vɪɐ̯tʃaftskriːzə] die <–, –n> 2. METEO Tief [tiːf] das <–s, –s> ◊ *Für morgen wird ein Tief erwartet.* 3. *(in the ground)* Vertiefung [fɛɐ̯'tiːfʊŋ] die <–, –en> ◊ *eine Vertiefung im Boden*

deprivation [noun] 1. *(state)* Benachteiligung [bə'naːxtaɛl̩gʊŋ] die <–, –en> *most sing* ◊ *soziale/ wirtschaftliche Benachteiligung* 2. *(withdrawal)* Entzug [ɛnt'tsuːk] der <–(e)s> *no pl* ◊ *der Entzug einer Lizenz* ♦ *der Entzug von Privilegien* sleep deprivation Schlafentzug ['ʃlaːf|ɛnttsuːk]; *(lack, shortage)* Entbehrung [ɛnt'beːrʊŋ] die <–, –en> ◊ *die Entbehrungen des Krieges*

deprive [verb] *(take away)* deprive sb of sth jdm etw. entziehen [ɛnt'tsiːən] <entzieht, entzog, hat entzogen> ◊ *jdm seine Freiheit entziehen;* deprive sb of sth jdm etw. vorenthalten ['foːɐ̯|ɛnthaltn̩] <enthält vor, enthielt vor, hat vorenthalten> ◊ *Sie haben mir mein Erbe vorenthalten.*; *(lack)* sb is deprived of sth jdm fehlt es an etw. [dat] [feːlt ɛs an] +*haben* ◊ *Diesen Kindern fehlt es an Liebe.*

deprived → deprive [adj] benachteiligt [bə'naːxtaɛl̩çt] *no comp/superl* ◊ *Diese Menschen sind sozial benachteiligt.* ♦ *eine wirtschaftlich benachteiligte Region*

depth [noun] 1. *(dimension, intensity, profundity)* depth(s) Tiefe ['tiːfə] die <–, –n> ◊ *in die Tiefe stürzen* ♦ *Der See hat eine Tiefe von 100 Metern.* ♦ *Höhe, Breite und Tiefe eines Regals* ♦ *Der Verfilmung fehlt die Tiefe, die der Roman hat.* ♦ *die Tiefe seiner Stimme* ♦ *Mir gefällt die Tiefe des Blaus.* ... in depth ... tief [tiːf] ◊ *Das Becken ist drei Meter tief.* 2. *(extent of sth: of knowledge)* Umfang ['ʊmfaŋ] der <–(e)s> *no pl* ◊ *der Umfang seines Wissens;* *(of a crisis, catastrophe)* Ausmaß ['aʊsmaːs] das <–es, –e> ◊ *das Ausmaß der Krise*

⊚ be out of your depth 1. *(in water)* nicht mehr stehen können 2. *(in a difficult situation)* ins Schwimmen kommen in depth eingehend

deputy [noun] Stellvertreter ['ʃtɛlfɛɐ̯treːtɐ] der <–s, –> ♀Stellvertreterin ['ʃtɛlfɛɐ̯treːtərɪn] die <–, –nen> ◊ *der Stellvertreter des Bürgermeisters* ♦ *Sie ist meine Stellvertreterin.*; *(in compounds)* deputy ... stellvertretende ... ['ʃtɛlfɛɐ̯treːtn̩ə] *no comp/superl, only before ns* <but: ein stellvertretender ..., eine stellvertretende ..., ein stellvertretendes ...> ◊ *der/die stellvertretende Kreisvorsitzende* deputy (sheriff) Hilfssheriff ['hɪlfsʃɛrɪf] der <–s, –s>

deranged [adj] *(mentally)* deranged geisteskrank ['gaɛstəskraŋk] *no comp/superl* ◊ *eine geisteskranke Frau* ♦ *Der Mörder ist geisteskrank.*

---

derision [noun] Hohn [hoːn] der <–(e)s> *no pl* ◊ *Er erntete dafür nur Spott und Hohn.*

derive [verb] 1. *(get)* derive sth from sth etw. aus etw. gewinnen [aɔs ... gəvɪnən] <gewinnt, gewann, hat gewonnen> ◊ *Kunststoffe werden aus Erdöl gewonnen.* derive pleasure from sth Vergnügen an etw. [dat] haben [fɛ,gnyːgŋ̍ an ... haːbm̩] +*haben* ◊ *Kinder haben oft großes Vergnügen an kleinen Dingen.* 2. *(come from)* sth derives from sth etw. stammt von etw. [ʃtamt fɔn] +*haben* ◊ *Sein Reichtum stammt von einer Erbschaft.* 3. *(develop)* herleiten ['heːɐ̯laɛtn̩] <leitet her, leitete her, hat hergeleitet> ◊ *eine mathematische Formel herleiten* sth derives from sth, sth is derived from sth etw. leitet sich aus etw. her ◊ *Das Wort leitet sich aus dem Französischen her.*

descend [verb] 1. *(go down, person)* hinuntergehen [hɪ'nʊntɐgeːən] <geht hinunter, ging hinunter, ist hinuntergegangen> ◊ *ins Tal hinuntergehen* ♦ *Sie ging die Treppe hinunter.*; *(vehicle, lift)* hinunterfahren [hɪ'nʊntɐfaːrən] <fährt hinunter, fuhr hinunter, ist hinuntergefahren> ◊ *Der Wagen fuhr langsam die Straße hinunter.*; *(road, path)* abfallen ['apfalən] <fällt ab, fiel ab, ist abgefallen> ◊ *Der Hang fällt zum See hin steil ab.* 2. *(darkness)* hereinbrechen [hɛ'raɛnbrɛçn̩] <bricht herein, brach herein, ist hereingebrochen> ◊ *Im Dezember bricht die Dunkelheit früh herein.*

descendant [noun] Nachkomme ['naːxkɔmə] der <–n, –n> ◊ *ein direkter Nachkomme Karls des Großen*

descent [noun] 1. *(from mountain, of a plane)* Abstieg ['apʃtiːk] der <–(e)s, –e> ◊ *Der Abstieg vom Gipfel war nicht einfach.*; *(on skis)* Abfahrt ['apfaːɐ̯t] die <–, –en> ◊ *Das war eine rasante Abfahrt.*; *(of a slope, road)* Abfall ['apfal] der <–(e)s> *no pl* ◊ *der sanfte Abfall eines Hügels* 2. *(origin)* Herkunft ['heːɐ̯kʊnft] die <–, Herkünfte> *most sing* ◊ *Sie war jüdischer Herkunft.* 3. *(change to a worse condition)* Abstieg ['apʃtiːk] der <–(e)s, –e> ◊ *Ihr sozialer Abstieg war nicht mehr aufzuhalten.* descent into sth Abgleiten in etw. [acc] ['apglaɛtn̩ ɪn] das <–s> *no pl* ◊ *ein Land vor dem Abgleiten in die Anarchie bewahren*

describe [verb] beschreiben [bə'ʃraɛbm̩] <beschreibt, beschrieb, hat beschrieben> ◊ *Ich weiss nicht, wie ich das beschreiben soll.* ♦ *Man könnte sie als naiv beschreiben.* sb describes doing sth jd beschreibt, wie er etw. getan hat ◊ *Sie beschrieb, wie sie vor Wut seinen Wagen zerkratzt hatte.*

description [noun] Beschreibung [bə'ʃraɛbʊŋ] die <–, –en> ◊ *Er hat mir eine genaue Beschreibung von dir gegeben.*

⊚ beyond description unbeschreiblich ◊ *Die Tat war unbeschreiblich grausam.*

desert[1] [noun] Wüste ['vyːstə] die <–, –n>

desert[2] [verb] 1. *(abandon, leave)* verlassen [fɛ'lasn̩] <verlässt, verließ, hat verlassen> ◊ *Er hat seine Frau verlassen.* ♦ *Das Glück hat mich verlassen.* 2. MIL desertieren [dezɛɐ̯'tiːrən] <desertiert, desertierte, hat/ ist desertiert> ◊ *Der Soldat ist von seiner Truppe desertiert.*

deserted → desert[2] [adj] verlassen [fɛ'lasn̩] ◊ *ein verlassenes Haus* ♦ *Am Sonntag ist die Innenstadt ganz verlassen.*

deserve [verb] verdienen [fɛ'diːnən] <verdient,

verdiente, hat verdient> ◊ *Das hat er nicht verdient.* ♦
Sie verdient es, bestraft zu werden. ♦ *Diese Entscheidung verdient Respekt.* deserve better etwas
Besseres verdienen haben
design¹ [noun] **1.** *(shape, study)* Design [diˈzaɛn] das
<-s, -s> ◊ *Dein Handy hat ein tolles Design.* ♦
Design studieren; (of a building, book etc.) Entwurf
[ɛntˈvʊˀf] der <-(e)s, Entwürfe> ◊ *Der Architekt
zeichnete einen Entwurf für ein Mehrfamilienhaus.;
(of a car, machine)* Konstruktion [kɔnstrʊkˈtsʲoːn] die
<-, -en> ◊ *eine ganz neue Konstruktion* **2.** *(pattern)*
Muster [ˈmʊstɐ] das <-s, -> ◊ *ein Muster für einen
Teppich entwerfen* **3.** *(lit) (intention)* Plan [plaːn] der
<-(e)s, Pläne> ◊ *große Pläne haben*
◉ *have designs on sb/sth* hinter jdm/etw. her sein
(fam) by design mit Absicht
design² [verb] entwerfen [ɛntˈvɛˀfn̩] <entwirft, entwarf,
hat entworfen> ◊ *Das Gebäude wurde von einem
bekannten Architekten entworfen.*
◉ *be designed to do sth* etw. tun sollen ◊ *Dieses
Medikament soll die Abwehr stärken.* be designed
as sth als etw. gedacht sein ◊ *Das obere Stockwerk
war ursprünglich als Schlafbereich gedacht.* be
designed for sb/sth für jdn/etw. konzipiert sein ◊
Das Auto ist für Großfamilien konzipiert.
designate [verb] **1.** *(appoint)* designate sb (as sth) jdn
(zu etw.) ernennen [ɛˈnɛnən] <ernennt, ernannte, hat
ernannt> ◊ *jdn zum Minister ernennen* **2.** *(mark)*
kennzeichnen [ˈkɛntsaɛçnən] <kennzeichnet, kennzeichnete, hat gekennzeichnet> ◊ *Die Strecke wurde
mit grünen Pfeilen gekennzeichnet.*
designer [noun] *(of fashion, everyday items etc.)*
Designer [diˈzaɛnɐ] der <-s, -> ♀Designerin
[diˈzaɛnərɪn] die <-, -nen> ◊ *Sie ist Designerin.* of
machines Konstrukteur [kɔnstrʊkˈtøːɐ̯] der <-s, -e>
♀Konstrukteurin [kɔnstrʊkˈtøːrɪn] die <-, -nen> ◊
der Konstrukteur der ersten Nähmaschine
desirable [adj] **1.** *(progress, quality, result)* wünschenswert [ˈvʏnʃnsveːɐ̯t] <wünschenswerter, am wünschenswertesten> ◊ *eine wünschenswerte Eigenschaft* ♦ *Es
ist nicht wünschenswert, dass …* **2.** *(offer, house,
woman)* attraktiv [atrakˈtiːf] ◊ *Das ist ein attraktives
Angebot.* ♦ *Ich finde sie sehr attraktiv.*
desire¹ [noun] **1.** *(wish)* Wunsch [vʊnʃ] der
<-(e)s, Wünsche> ◊ *Sie hat den Wunsch zu malen.*
the desire for sth der Wunsch nach etw. ◊ *der
Wunsch nach Frieden.* sb's heart's desire jds Herzenswunsch [ˈhɛˀtsənsvʊnʃ] **2.** *(sexual)* Verlangen
[fɛˈlaŋən] das <-s, -> most sing ◊ *Er verspürte
starkes Verlangen nach ihr.*
desire² [verb] **1.** *(want)* wünschen [ˈvʏnʃn̩] +haben
desire sth sich [dat] etw. wünschen ◊ *sich Frieden
wünschen* desire sb to do sth wünschen, dass jd
etw. tut ◊ *Ich wünsche, dass Sie morgen um 8 Uhr
in mein Büro kommen.* leave much to be desired
viel zu wünschen übrig lassen ◊ *Die Pflege des
Gartens lässt viel zu wünschen übrig.* if sb so
desires wie jd wünscht ◊ *Wie Sie wünschen!* **2.** *(as
a sexual partner)* begehren [bəˈɡeːrən] <begehrt,
begehrte, hat begehrt>
desired → **desire** [adj] gewünscht [ɡəˈvʏnʃt] *no comp/
superl* ◊ *Meine Bemühungen hatten nicht den
gewünschten Erfolg.* ♦ *Diese Wirkung war nicht
gewünscht.*
◉ *if desired* auf Wunsch
desk [noun] **1.** *(personal)* Schreibtisch [ˈʃraɛptɪʃ] der

<-(e)s, -e> ◊ *Sie setzte sich an den Schreibtisch.* ♦
Die Akten liegen auf seinem Schreibtisch.; (in school)
Pult [pʊlt] das <-(e)s, -e> **2.** *(in a shop)* Kasse
[ˈkasə] die <-, -n> ◊ *Bitte bezahlen Sie an der
Kasse.; (in a hotel)* Empfang [ɛmˈpfaŋ] der
<-(e)s, Empfänge> ◊ *Am Empfang liegt eine
Nachricht für Sie.* information desk Information
[ɪnfɔɐ̯maˈtsʲoːn] die <-, -en> ◊ *Am besten erkundigen Sie sich bei der Information.*
desktop [noun] Desktop [ˈdɛsktɔp] der <-s, -s> ◊
Icons auf dem Desktop
despair [noun] Verzweiflung [fɛˈtsvaɛflʊŋ] die <-> no
pl ◊ *die wachsende Verzweiflung der Eingeschlossenen* ♦ *In seiner Verzweiflung rief er die Telefonseelsorge an.* be in despair verzweifelt sein
[fɛˈtsvaɛflt zaɛn] +sein ◊ *Sie war verzweifelt und
wusste nicht, was sie tun sollte.*
desperate(ly) [adj, adv] **1.** *(hopeless, severe)* verzweifelt [fɛˈtsvaɛflt] ◊ *Ich war völlig verzweifelt.* ♦ *die verzweifelte Lage der Bevölkerung* ♦ *verzweifelt
versuchen, etw. zu tun* **2.** be desperate for sth etw.
dringend brauchen [ˌdrɪŋənt ˈbraoxn̩] +haben ◊ *Die
Flüchtlinge brauchen dringend Lebensmittel.* be
desperate to do sth unbedingt etw. tun wollen
[ˌʊnbədɪŋt … voːlən] <will, wollte, hat wollen> ◊ *Er
wollte unbedingt wieder nach Hause fahren.*
despicable [adj] abscheulich [apˈʃɔɪlɪç] ◊ *ein
abscheuliches Verbrechen* ♦ *Was du getan hast, war
abscheulich.*
despise [verb] verachten [fɛˈʔaxtn̩] <verachtet, verachtete, hat verachtet> ◊ *Er verachtet Leute, die alles
tun, um reich zu werden.*
despite [prep] trotz [trɔts] +gen ◊ *Trotz aller Kritik ist
diese Fernsehsendung sehr beliebt.* ♦ *Wir haben trotz
des Regens einen Spaziergang gemacht.* despite the
fact that *(in spite of) (in school)* ◊ *Er ging zur Arbeit,
obwohl er krank war.*
◉ *despite yourself* wider Erwarten ◊ *Wider
Erwarten gefiel es ihr auf der Party ganz gut.*
dessert [noun] Nachtisch [ˈnaːxtɪʃ] der <-(e)s> no pl
◊ *Zum Nachtisch gab es Erdbeeren mit Schlagsahne.*
dessertspoon [noun] Dessertlöffel [dɛˈsɛɐ̯lœfl̩] der
<-s, ->
destination [noun] Ziel [tsiːl] das <-(e)s, -e> ◊ *Das
Ziel unserer Fahrt war Hamburg.* ♦ *Erst gegen Mitternacht erreichten sie ihr Ziel.* holiday destination
Reiseziel [ˈraɛzatsiːl]
destiny [noun] Schicksal [ˈʃɪksaːl] das <-s, -e> ◊ *Das
Schicksal nahm seinen Lauf.* ♦ *Was das Schicksal
wohl noch für uns bereithält?* shape your own
destiny sein Schicksal selbst bestimmen
destroy [verb] **1.** *(an object, a building, city, sb's life,
relationship, reputation, the environment)* zerstören
[tsɛˈʃtøːrən] <zerstört, zerstörte, hat zerstört> ◊ *etw.
mutwillig zerstören* ♦ *Die Häuser wurden durch ein
Erdbeben zerstört.* ♦ *Diese Frau hat meine Ehe
zerstört.; (a toy)* kaputtmachen [kaˈpʊtmaxn̩] ◊ *Max
hat sein Spielzeugauto kaputtgemacht.; (an enemy,
crops, pests, documents)* vernichten [fɛˈnɪçtn̩] <vernichtet, vernichtete, hat vernichtet> ◊ *Der Sturm hat
die Ernte vernichtet.* **2.** *(an animal)* einschläfern
[ˈaɛnʃlɛːfɐn] <schläfert ein, schläferte ein, hat eingeschläfert> ◊ *Das Tier ist gefährlich und muss eingeschläfert werden.*
destruction [noun] *(of an object, a building, city, the
environment)* Zerstörung [tsɛˈʃtøːrʊŋ] die <-, -en> ◊

Sie wollen etwas gegen die Zerstörung der Umwelt unternehmen.; *(of people, documents, a regime, an enemy)* Vernichtung [fɛ'nɪçtʊŋ] die <-, –en> *most sing* ◊ *Bitte sorgen Sie für die Vernichtung der Dokumente.*

detach [verb] **1.** *(remove)* detach sth (from sth) etw. (von etw.) abnehmen ['apneːmən] <nimmt ab, nahm ab, hat abgenommen> ◊ *die Kapuze von der Jacke abnehmen* sth detaches easily etw. lässt sich leicht abnehmen ◊ *Der Griff lässt sich leicht abnehmen, wenn er nicht gebraucht wird.*; *(a part of a document)* abtrennen ['aptrɛnən] +*haben* ◊ *Trennen Sie den Teilnahmeschein ab und senden Sie ihn an uns zurück.* **2.** detach yourself from sb/sth sich von jdm/etw. entfernen [fɔn ... ɛnt,fɛ'nən] <entfernt sich, entfernte sich, hat sich entfernt> ◊ *Sie hatte sich von der Gruppe entfernt.*; *(emotionally)* sich von jdm/etw. distanzieren [fɔn ... dɪstan,tsiːrən] <distanziert sich, distanzierte sich, hat sich distanziert> ◊ *Er hat sich von seinen alten Freunden distanziert.* **3.** MIL *(send)* abkommandieren ['apkɔmandiːrən] <kommandiert ab, kommandierte ab, hat abkommandiert> ◊ *Ein Teil der Einheit wurde an die Küste abkommandiert.*

detached → detach [adj] **1.** *(unbiased, unemotional)* distanziert [dɪstan'tsiːɡt] <distanzierter, am distanziertesten> ◊ *eine distanzierte Betrachtungsweise* ◊ *Er wirkte sehr distanziert.* **2.** detached house Einzelhaus ['aɛntslhaɔs] das <-es, Einzelhäuser>

detail¹ [noun] **1.** *(individual fact, item)* Einzelheit ['aɛntslhaɛt] die <-, –en> *most pl* ◊ *Erspare mir bitte die Einzelheiten!* ♦ *Nähere/weitere Einzelheiten sind nicht bekannt.*; *(regarding a person)* details Personalien [pɛ'zoːnaːliən] die <-> *pl* ◊ *Der Polizeibeamte nahm meine Personalien auf.* **2.** *(feature that is difficult to see)* Detail [de'taɛ] das <-s, –s> ◊ *auf Details achten* ♦ *ein Auge fürs Detail haben* **3.** *(part of a painting, picture)* Ausschnitt ['aɔsʃnɪt] der <-(e)s, –e> ◊ *Auf dem Plakat ist ein Ausschnitt aus van Goghs „Sonnenblumen" zu sehen.*

 go into detail ins Detail gehen in detail ausführlich ◊ *Er hat mir ausführlich erzählt, was er erlebt hat.*

detail² [verb] ausführlich beschreiben [,aɔsfyːɡlɪç bə'ʃraɛbm̩] <beschreibt, beschrieb, hat beschrieben> ◊ *Der Bericht beschreibt ausführlich die damit verbundenen Probleme.*

detailed → detail² [adj] ausführlich ['aɔsfyːɡlɪç] ◊ *ein ausführlicher Bericht* ♦ *Die Gebrauchsanweisung war nicht ausführlich genug.*

detain [verb] **1.** *(police)* festhalten ['fɛsthaltn̩] <hält fest, hielt fest, hat festgehalten> ◊ *Die Reporter wurden stundenlang festgehalten.* **2.** *(in hospital)* dabehalten ['daːbəhaltn̩] <behält da, behielt da, hat dabehalten> ◊ *Man behielt den Patienten vorsichtshalber über Nacht da.* **3.** *(delay)* aufhalten ['aɔfhaltn̩] <hält auf, hielt auf, hat aufgehalten> ◊ *Leider wurden wir unterwegs aufgehalten.*

detect [verb] **1.** *(discover)* entdecken [ɛnt'dɛkn̩] <entdeckt, entdeckte, hat entdeckt> ◊ *einen Fehler entdecken* ♦ *Der Tumor wurde zum Glück rechtzeitig entdeckt.*; *(a substance, pollutant)* nachweisen ['naːxvaɛzn̩] <weist nach, wies nach, hat nachgewiesen> ◊ *In vielen Produkten wurden Schadstoffe nachgewiesen.* **2.** *(with your senses)* wahrnehmen ['vaːneːmən] <nimmt wahr, nahm war, hat wahrgenommen> ◊ *Er nahm ein verdächtiges Geräusch wahr.* ♦

In seiner Stimme nahm sie eine Spur von Bedauern wahr.

detection [noun] **1.** *(discovery)* Entdeckung [ɛnt'dɛkʊŋ] die <-, –en> ◊ *die Entdeckung feindlicher U-Boote* **2.** *(work of a detective)* Ermittlungsarbeit [ɛ'mɪtlʊŋslaɾbaɛt] die <-, –en> ◊ *Die Ermittlungsarbeit im Fall Felix geht gut voran.*

detective [noun] **1.** *(police officer)* Kriminalbeamte [krɪmi'naːlbəamtə] der <–n> ♀Kriminalbeamtin [krɪmi'naːlbəamtɪn] die <-, –nen> *but*: ein Kriminalbeamter/eine Kriminalbeamtin ◊ *Ein Kriminalbeamter befragte die Zeugen.* ♦ *Sie ist Kriminalbeamtin.* **2.** *(private)* detective Detektiv [detɛk'tiːf] der <-s, –e> ♀Detektivin [detɛk'tiːvɪn] die <-, –nen> ◊ *einen Detektiv beauftragen* ♦ *Sie will später einmal Detektivin werden.* detective agency Detektivbüro [detɛk'tiːfbyˌroː] das <-s, –s> **3.** *(about a crime)* Kriminal... [krɪmi'naːl] detective story Kriminalgeschichte [krɪmi'naːlɡəʃɪçtə] die <-, –n>

detector [noun] Detektor [de'tɛktoːg] der <-s, –en> ◊ *ein Detektor für gefälschte Banknoten* lie detector Lügendetektor ['lyːɡn̩deˌtɛktoːg] ◊ *einen Test am Lügendetektor machen*

detention [noun] **1.** *(in a police station, prison)* Haft [haft] die <-> *no pl* ◊ *zwei Wochen in Haft verbringen* **2.** SCHOOL Nachsitzen ['naːxzɪtsn̩] das <-s> *no pl* be in detention nachsitzen müssen ['naːxzɪtsn̩ mʏsn̩] <muss, musste, hat müssen> ◊ *Zur Strafe musste sie nachsitzen.*

deter [verb] *(discourage)* abschrecken ['apʃrɛkn̩] +*haben* ◊ *Ich lasse mich nicht durch Drohungen abschrecken.*; *(prevent)* deter sb from sth jdn von etw. abhalten [fɔn ... ˌaphaltn̩] <hält ab, hielt ab, hat abgehalten> ◊ *Der Regen hielt uns nicht von einem Spaziergang ab.* deter sb from doing sth jdn davon abhalten, etw. zu tun

detergent [noun] *(for cleaning)* Reinigungsmittel ['raɛnɪɡʊŋsmɪtl̩] das <-s, –>; *(for washing clothes)* Waschmittel ['vaʃmɪtl̩] das <-s, –>

deteriorate [verb] *(weather, relationship, condition)* sich verschlechtern [fɛ'ʃlɛçtɐn] <verschlechtert sich, verschlechterte sich, hat sich verschlechtert> ◊ *Sein Sehvermögen hat sich verschlechtert.*; *(building)* deteriorate (into sth) (zu etw.) verfallen [fɛ'falən] <verfällt, verfiel, ist verfallen> ◊ *Das Gebäude verfällt zusehends.*; *(conflict, situation)* deteriorate into sth in etw. [acc] ausarten [ɪn ... ˌaɔslaɾtn̩] <artet aus, artete aus, ist ausgeartet> ◊ *Der Konflikt ist in einen bewaffneten Kampf ausgeartet.*

determination [noun] **1.** *(firmness)* Entschlossenheit [ɛnt'ʃlɔsnhaɛt] die <-> *no pl* ◊ *Sie setzte sich mit großer Entschlossenheit durch.* **2.** *(determining, calculating)* Bestimmung [bə'ʃtɪmʊŋ] die <-, –en> *most sing* ◊ *die Bestimmung des Kurses anhand der Sterne* **3.** *(deciding)* Festlegung ['fɛstleːɡʊŋ] die <-, –en> *most sing* ◊ *die Festlegung der Ziele*

determine [verb] **1.** *(fix, be a decisive factor)* bestimmen [bə'ʃtɪmən] <bestimmt, bestimmte, hat bestimmt> ◊ *Wir sollten unsere Ziele neu bestimmen.* ♦ *Den Preis bestimmen Angebot und Nachfrage.* **2.** *(discover)* feststellen ['fɛstʃtɛlən] <stellt fest, stellte fest, hat festgestellt> ◊ *feststellen, wer für den Unfall verantwortlich war*

determined(ly) → determine [adj, adv] *(person, action)* entschlossen [ɛnt'ʃlɔsn̩] ◊ *ein entschlossenes Vorgehen* ♦ *Ich bin fest entschlossen, nicht nachzuge-*

A B C D E F G H I J K L M N O P Q R S T U V W X Y Z

ben. ◆ *entschlossen handeln; (opposition, tone)* entschieden [ɛntˈʃiːdn̩] *when used as an adj, mostly before ns* ◊ *Sie sagte das in einem entschiedenen Ton.* ◆ *„Ihr geht den falschen Weg", sagte er entschieden.*

determiner ⟨noun⟩ Begleiter [bəˈɡlaɛtɐ] *der <-s, -en>* ◊ *Ein bestimmter Artikel ist ein Begleiter.*

deterrent ⟨noun⟩ Abschreckungsmittel [ˈapʃrɛkʊŋsmɪtl̩] *das <-s, -> ◊ ein Abschreckungsmittel gegen weitere Angriffe; (against insects)* Abwehrmittel [ˈapveːɐ̯mɪtl̩] *das <-s, ->*

detonate ⟨verb⟩ *(explode)* detonieren [detoˈniːrən] <detoniert, detonierte, ist detoniert> ◊ *Eine Granate ist detoniert.; (make explode)* detonate sth etw. zünden [ˈtsʏndn̩] *+haben* ◊ *einen Sprengsatz zünden*

detour ⟨noun⟩ Umweg [ˈʊmveːk] *der <-(e)s, -e> ◊ Sie mussten einen weiten Umweg machen.*

devalue ⟨verb⟩ abwerten [ˈapveːɐ̯tn̩] <wertet ab, wertete ab, hat abgewertet> ◊ *Der Dollar ist schon wieder abgewertet worden.*

devastate ⟨verb⟩ **1.** *(an area, city, crops)* verwüsten [fɐˈvyːstn̩] <verwüstet, verwüstete, hat verwüstet> ◊ *Der Sturm verwüstete ganze Landstriche.* **2.** *(a person)* erschüttern [ɛˈʃʏtɐn] <erschüttert, erschütterte, hat erschüttert> ◊ *Die Nachricht von ihrem Tod erschütterte ihre Familie.*

devastating → devastate ⟨adj⟩ **1.** *(causing a lot of damage)* verheerend [fɐˈheːrənt] ◊ *verheerende Auswirkungen* ◆ *Der Sturm war verheerend.* **2.** *(shocking)* erschütternd [ɛˈʃʏtɐnt] ◊ *eine erschütternde Nachricht* ◆ *Der Anblick war erschütternd.* **3.** *(very impressive)* umwerfend [ˈʊmvɛɐ̯fn̩t] *(fam)* ◊ *Er hat einen umwerfenden Charme.* ◆ *Sie ist einfach umwerfend!* **4.** *(defeat, argument)* vernichtend [fɐˈnɪçtn̩t] ◊ *Das Wahlergebnis war vernichtend.* ◆ *eine vernichtende Niederlage erleiden*

develop ⟨verb⟩ **1.** *(produce, create, grow, explain, make visible, begin to show)* develop sth etw. entwickeln [ɛntˈvɪkl̩n] <entwickelt, entwickelte, hat entwickelt> ◊ *einen neuen Impfstoff entwickeln* ◆ *Sie hat ihren eigenen Stil entwickelt.* ◆ *einen Film entwickeln lassen* sb/sth develops jd/etw. entwickelt sich ◊ *Manche Kinder entwickeln sich sehr langsam.* develop into sth sich zu etw. entwickeln ◊ *Ihre Beziehung entwickelte sich zu einer tiefen Freundschaft.* develop from sth sich aus etw. entwickeln ◊ *Aus den Knospen entwickeln sich die Blüten.* **2.** *(expand, increase, improve)* ausbauen [ˈaʊsbaʊən] *+haben* ◊ *die Infrastruktur/seine Kontakte ausbauen* **3.** MED *(a disease)* bekommen [bəˈkɔmən] <bekommt, bekam, hat bekommen> ◊ *Krebs/Diabetes bekommen* **4.** ECON *(land, an area)* erschließen [ɛˈʃliːsn̩] <erschließt, erschloss, hat erschlossen> ◊ *ein Gebiet als Bauland erschließen*

developer ⟨noun⟩ **1.** *(of land, real estate)* Bauunternehmer [ˈbaʊʊntɐˌneːmɐ] *der <-s, -> ♀*Bauunternehmerin [ˈbaʊʊntɐˌneːmərɪn] *die <-, -nen> ◊ Seine Mutter ist Bauunternehmerin.* ◆ *Mehrere Bauunternehmer sind an dem Gelände interessiert.* **2.** IT Entwickler [ɛntˈvɪklɐ] *der <-s, -> ♀*Entwicklerin [ɛntˈvɪklərɪn] *die <-, -nen> ◊ Sie ist Entwicklerin für Software.* ◆ *Die Firma sucht einen Entwickler.* **3.** CHEM Entwickler [ɛntˈvɪklɐ] *der <-s, ->*

developing country ⟨noun⟩ Entwicklungsland [ɛntˈvɪklʊŋslant] *das <-(e)s, Entwicklungsländer>*

development ⟨noun⟩ **1.** *(improvement, growth,*

creation, progress, putting forward, of photos) Entwicklung [ɛntˈvɪklʊŋ] *die <-, -en> ◊ die Entwicklung eines Kindes* ◆ *eine Entwicklung abwarten* ◆ *die rasende Entwicklung von Computern* **2.** *(of an area, site)* Erschließung [ɛˈʃliːsʊŋ] *die <-, -en> ◊ die Erschließung eines neuen Industriegebiets; (area with new houses)* (new) development Neubaugebiet [ˈnɔɞbaʊɡəbiːt] *das <-(e)s, -e>*

deviation ⟨noun⟩ Abweichung [ˈapvaɛçʊŋ] *die <-, -en> ◊ eine Abweichung von der Norm*

device ⟨noun⟩ **1.** *(machine, gadget)* Gerät [ɡəˈrɛːt] *das <-(e)s, -e> ◊ ein neues Gerät für die Herzdiagnostik; (extra fitment)* Vorrichtung [ˈfoːɐ̯rɪçtʊŋ] *die <-, -en> ◊ Das Gepäck lässt sich mit einer einfachen Vorrichtung gegen Diebstahl sichern.* **2.** *(explosive)* device Sprengkörper [ˈʃprɛŋkœˈpɐ] *der <-s, -> ◊ ein selbst gebastelter Sprengkörper* **3.** *(method, means)* Mittel [ˈmɪtl̩] *das <-s, -> ◊ Der Regisseur bedient sich unterschiedlicher filmischer Mittel.*

devil ⟨noun⟩ Teufel [ˈtɔɞfl̩] *der <-s, -> ◊ Dieses Kind ist ein wahrer Teufel.* ◆ *ein armer Teufel* the Devil der Teufel ◊ *vom Teufel besessen sein*

ⓘ talk of the devil wenn man vom Teufel spricht what/how/who etc. the devil was/wie/wer etc. zum Teufel *(fam)* ◊ *Was zum Teufel will der schon wieder hier?*

devise ⟨verb⟩ *(a plan, strategy)* entwerfen [ɛntˈvɛɐ̯fn̩] <entwirft, entwarf, hat entworfen> ◊ *ein Konzept entwerfen; (a way, method)* finden [ˈfɪndn̩] <findet, fand, hat gefunden> ◊ *einen Weg finden, um etw. zu erreichen*

devoted → devote to ⟨adj⟩ **1.** *(loving sb very much)* hingebungsvoll [ˈhɪngəˌbʊŋsfɔl] ◊ *ein hingebungsvoller Vater* They are devoted to each other. Sie lieben sich sehr. **2.** *(enthusiastic, loyal)* treu [trɔɞ] <treuer, am treu(e)sten> ◊ *Echte Fans sind treu.* ◆ *Du bist ein treuer Freund.*

devote to ⟨verb⟩ **1.** *(dedicate)* devote sth to sb/sth etw. jdm/etw. widmen [ˈvɪtmən] <widmet, widmete, hat gewidmet> ◊ *Sie hat ihr Leben der Forschung gewidmet.* devote yourself to sth sich einer Sache ⟨dat⟩ widmen ◊ *Er widmet sich ausgiebig der Malerei.* be devoted to sb/sth jdm/etw. gewidmet sein [ɡəˈvɪtmət zaɛn] *+sein* ◊ *Die Ausstellung ist Dali gewidmet.* ◆ *Sie widmet sich voll und ganz ihrer Arbeit.* **2.** *(use)* devote sth to sth etw. für etw. verwenden [fʏːɐ̯ ... fɛvɛndn̩] <verwendet, verwendete, hat verwendet> ◊ *Die Einnahmen werden für wohltätige Zwecke verwendet.*

devotion ⟨noun⟩ **1.** *(love, commitment)* Hingabe [ˈhɪŋɡaːbə] *die <-> no pl ◊ Sie pflegte ihre Tochter mit großer Hingabe.* **2.** *(devotion to duty* Pflichteifer [ˈpflɪçtˌaɛfɐ] *der <-s> no pl ◊ großen Pflichteifer zeigen*

devout ⟨adj⟩ fromm [frɔm] <frömmer/frommer, am frömmsten/frommsten> ◊ *Sie ist sehr fromm.* ◆ *ein frommer Christ*

dew ⟨noun⟩ Tau [taʊ] *der <-(e)s> no pl ◊ Das Gras war feucht vom Tau.*

dexterity ⟨noun⟩ Geschick [ɡəˈʃɪk] *das <-(e)s> no pl ◊ Mit großem Geschick setzte sie die Bauteile zusammen.*

dexterous(ly) ⟨adj, adv⟩ geschickt [ɡəˈʃɪkt] <geschickter, am geschicktesten> ◊ *Er ist sehr geschickt im Umgang mit Holz.* ◆ *Sie war eine geschickte Hand-*

werkerin. ♦ *Geschickt balancierte er das Tablett in die Küche.*

diabetes [noun] Diabetes [diaˈbeːtɛs] der <-> *no pl* ◊ *an Diabetes leiden* ♦ *Er hat Diabetes.*

diagnose [verb] feststellen [ˈfɛstʃtɛlən] +haben ◊ *eine Krankheit feststellen* ♦ *einen Fehler am Motor feststellen* diagnose sb with sth bei jdm etw. feststellen ◊ *Der Arzt stellte Lungenkrebs bei ihm fest.* diagnose sb as diabetic/depressed bei jdm Diabetes/eine Depression feststellen

diagnosis [noun] Diagnose [diaˈgnoːzə] die <-, -n> ◊ *Wie lautet Ihre Diagnose?* make a diagnosis eine Diagnose stellen

diagonal(ly) [adj, adv] diagonal [diagoˈnaːl] *no comp/ superl* ◊ *eine diagonale Linie* ♦ *Die Streifen auf dem Hemd sind diagonal.* ♦ *Sie gingen diagonal über den Platz.*

diagram [noun] Diagramm [diaˈgram] das <-s, -e> ◊ *etw. in einem Diagramm darstellen*

dial¹ [noun] 1. *(of a clock, watch)* Zifferblatt [ˈtsɪfɐblat] das <-(e)s, Zifferblätter> ◊ *eine Uhr mit einem blauen Zifferblatt; (of a meter)* Skala [ˈskaːlaː] die <-, Skalen *or* -s> ◊ *einen Wert auf der Skala ablesen* 2. *(of an appliance)* Einstellknopf [ˈaɛnʃtɛlknɔpf] der <-(e)s, Einstellknöpfe>; *(of a radio)* Einstellskala [ˈaɛnʃtɛlˌskaːlaː] die <-, Einstellskalen *or* -s> 3. *(of an old-fashioned telephone)* Wählscheibe [ˈvɛːlʃaɛbə] die <-, -n>

dial² [verb] wählen [ˈvɛːlən] +haben ◊ *Sie haben die falsche Nummer gewählt.* ♦ *Sie wählte, doch dann legte sie auf.*

dialect [noun] Dialekt [diaˈlɛkt] der <-(e)s, -e> ◊ *Texte und Lieder im Dialekt* ♦ *Dialekt sprechen*

dialling code [noun] Vorwahl [ˈfoːɐvaːl] die <-, -en> ◊ *Welche Vorwahl hat Berlin?* ♦ *Die Vorwahl für Österreich ist 0043.*

dialling tone [noun] Freizeichen [ˈfraɛtsaɛçn̩] das <-s, -> ◊ *Ich bekomme kein Freizeichen.*

dialogue [noun] Dialog [diaˈloːk] der <-(e)s, -e> ◊ *Ich fand die Dialoge im Film etwas steif.* ♦ *den Dialog suchen*

diameter [noun] Durchmesser [ˈdʊrçmɛsɐ] der <-s, -> ◊ *Wie berechnet man den Durchmesser eines Kreises?* be ... in diameter einen Durchmesser von ... haben ◊ *Das Rohr hat einen Durchmesser von 17 Zentimetern.*

diamond [noun] 1. *(precious stone)* Diamant [diaˈmant] der <-en, -en> ◊ *ein Collier mit Diamanten* 2. MATH *(rhombus)* Raute [ˈraɔtə] die <-, -n> ◊ *ein Verkehrsschild in Form einer Raute* 3. CARDS *(playing card, suit of playing cards)* diamond(s) Karo [ˈkaːroː] das <-s, -> ◊ *Sie spielte Karo.* ♦ *Wie viele Karo hast du?*

diaper [noun] Windel [ˈvɪndl̩] die <-, -n>

diarrhoea [noun] Durchfall [ˈdʊrçfal] der <-(e)s, Durchfälle> ◊ *Sie bekam im Urlaub starken Durchfall.*

diary [noun] 1. *(of personal experience)* Tagebuch [ˈtaːgəbuːx] das <-(e)s, Tagebücher> ◊ *Er hatte heimlich in ihrem Tagebuch gelesen.* keep a diary ein Tagebuch führen 2. *(for appointments)* Terminkalender [tɛrˈmiːnkaˌlɛndɐ] der <-s, -> ◊ *Ich werde in meinem Terminkalender nachsehen, ob der Tag noch frei ist.*

dice¹ [noun] 1. *(square object with six sides)* Würfel [ˈvʏrfl̩] der <-s, -> ◊ *Zu diesem Spiel braucht man zwei Würfel.* ♦ *Schneiden Sie die Karotten in kleine*

Würfel. 2. GAME Würfelspiel [ˈvʏrfl̩ʃpiːl] das <-(e)s, -e> ◊ *Er hat beim Würfelspiel viel Geld verloren.* play dice würfeln [ˈvʏrfl̩n] +haben ◊ *Würfelt ihr um Geld?*

dice² [verb] würfeln [ˈvʏrfl̩n] +haben ◊ *Fleisch für ein Gulasch würfeln*

ⓔ dice with death mit dem Tode spielen

dictate [verb] diktieren [dɪkˈtiːrən] <diktiert, diktierte, hat diktiert> ◊ *Du diktierst und ich tippe.* ♦ *Ich lasse mir nicht diktieren, was ich zu tun habe.* ♦ *die Preise diktieren* common sense dictates that die Vernunft gebietet, dass [diː fɐˌnʊnft gəˈbiːtat das]

dictation [noun] Diktat [dɪkˈtaːt] das <-(e)s, -e> ◊ *Welche Note hast du im Diktat?* ♦ *Sie rief die Sekretärin zum Diktat.* ♦ *sich dem Diktat des Siegers unterwerfen*

dictatorship [noun] Diktatur [dɪktaˈtuːɐ] die <-, -en> ◊ *Spanien unter der Diktatur Francos* ♦ *in einer Diktatur leben*

dictionary [noun] 1. *(of a language)* Wörterbuch [ˈvœrtɐbuːx] das <-(e)s, Wörterbücher> ◊ *ein Wort im Wörterbuch nachschlagen* ♦ *ein deutsch-französisches Wörterbuch* 2. *(about a subject)* Lexikon [ˈlɛksikɔn] das <-s, Lexika> ◊ *ein Lexikon der Literaturwissenschaft*

die¹ [noun] *(form)* Würfel [ˈvʏrfl̩] der <-s, -> → **dice**

ⓔ the die is cast die Würfel sind gefallen

die² [verb] 1. *(cease to exist)* sterben [ˈʃtɛrbm̩] <stirbt, starb, ist gestorben> ◊ *Er starb im Alter von 80 Jahren.* ♦ *Unsere Wälder sterben!* ♦ *Ihr Bruder ist jung gestorben.* die of sth an etw. [dat] sterben ◊ *Seine Frau starb an einem Herzinfarkt.* die a hero als Held sterben die a natural/violent death eines natürlichen/gewaltsamen Todes sterben; *(animal, plant)* eingehen [ˈaɛngeːən] <geht ein, ging ein, ist eingegangen> ◊ *Die Rosen sind eingegangen, weil sie keiner gegossen hat.* die of starvation verhungern [fɐˈhʊŋɐn] <verhungert, verhungerte, ist verhungert> die of suffocation ersticken [ɛˈʃtɪkn̩] <erstickt, erstickte, ist erstickt> 2. *(custom, tradition)* aussterben [ˈaɔsʃtɛrbm̩] <stirbt aus, starb aus, ist ausgestorben> ◊ *Die alten Bräuche sterben langsam aus.; (memory, feeling)* vergehen [fɐˈgeːən] <vergeht, verging, ist vergangen> ◊ *Meine Erinnerung an diese Zeit wird niemals vergehen.* 3. *(candle, fire)* ausgehen [ˈaɔsgeːən] <geht aus, ging aus, ist ausgegangen> 4. *(engine)* absterben [ˈapʃtɛrbm̩] <stirbt ab, starb ab, ist abgestorben> *(fam)* ◊ *Bei meinem Auto stirbt der Motor immer ab.*

ⓔ be dying of boredom/hunger etc. vor Langeweile/Hunger etc. sterben be dying to do sth darauf brennen, etw. zu tun be dying for sth etw. unbedingt brauchen

• **die away** [phras v] *(noise, music)* leiser werden [ˈlaɛzɐ veːɐdn̩] +sein ◊ *Die Musik wurde allmählich leiser.; (wind, emotion)* sich legen [zɪç ˈleːgn̩] +haben ◊ *Warten wir lieber ab, bis sich sein Zorn gelegt hat.*

• **die down** [phras v] *(noise, wind, emotion)* nachlassen [ˈnaːxlasn̩] <lässt nach, ließ nach, hat nachgelassen> ◊ *Das Geschrei ließ allmählich nach.; (fire)* herunterbrennen [hɛˈrʊntɐbrɛnən] <brennt herunter, brannte herunter, ist heruntergebrannt> ◊ *Ich warte, bis das Feuer heruntergebrannt ist.*

• **die out** [phras v] aussterben [ˈaɔsʃtɛrbm̩] <stirbt aus, starb aus, ist ausgestorben> ◊ *Stirbt dieser Brauch/ Dialekt aus?*

diesel [noun] Diesel ['diːzl̩] der <-s, -> most sing ◊ *Diesel tanken* ♦ *Er fährt einen alten Diesel.*

diet [noun] **1.** *(daily food)* Ernährung [eˈnɛːrʊŋ] die <-> no pl ◊ *auf eine ausgewogene Ernährung achten* have a diet of sth sich von etw. ernähren [fɔn … ɐˈnɛːrən] <ernährt sich, ernährte sich, hat sich ernährt> **2.** *(for slimming, health)* Diät [diˈɛːt] die <-, -en> ◊ *Diät halten müssen* ♦ *eine eiweißreiche Diät* be on a diet auf Diät sein ◊ *Sie ist schon wieder auf Diät.* go on a diet eine Diät machen ◊ *Er sollte mal eine Diät machen.* diet product Diätprodukt [diˈɛːtproˌdʊkt] das <-(e)s, -e> **3.** POL Reichstag ['raɛçstaːk] der <-(e)s, -e> ◊ *der japanische Reichstag* the Diet of Worms der Reichstag zu Worms

differ [verb] **1.** *(be different)* sich unterscheiden [ʊntɐˈʃaɛdn̩] <unterscheidet sich, unterschied sich, hat sich unterschieden> ◊ *Sitten und Gebräuche der beiden Länder unterscheiden sich stark.* ♦ *Das Männchen unterscheidet sich vom Weibchen in der Farbe.* **2.** *(disagree)* differ on/over sth unterschiedlicher Ansicht über etw. [acc] sein [ˌʊntɐʃiːtlɪçɐ ˈanzɪçt yːbɐ … zaɛn] +sein ◊ *Die Kritiker sind unterschiedlicher Ansicht über das Theaterstück.* differ with sb on/over sth über etw. [acc] anderer Meinung sein als jd [yːbɐ … ˈandərə ˌmaɛnʊŋ zaɛn als] ◊ *Ich bin über den Vorschlag anderer Meinung als Sie.*
⊚ opinions differ die Meinungen sind geteilt
agree to differ sich [dat] verschiedene Meinungen zugestehen **beg to differ** sich [dat] erlauben, anderer Meinung zu sein

difference [noun] **1.** *(dissimilarity)* Unterschied ['ʊntɐʃiːt] der <-(e)s, -e> ◊ *kulturelle Unterschiede* ♦ *Es gibt keinen Unterschied zwischen Bio- und Ökoprodukten.* tell the difference (between …) den Unterschied (zwischen … [dat]) erkennen ◊ *Sie konnte den Unterschied zwischen den beiden Pflanzen nicht erkennen.* age difference Altersunterschied ['altɐsˌʊntɐʃiːt] **2.** *(dissent)* differences Meinungsverschiedenheiten ['maɛnʊŋsfɐˌʃiːdn̩haɛtn̩] die <-> pl ◊ *Meinungsverschiedenheiten haben* ♦ *Sie haben ihre Meinungsverschiedenheiten beigelegt.*
⊚ difference of opinion Meinungsverschiedenheit
make a difference to sth sich auf etw. [acc] auswirken **make all the difference (to sb)** (für jdn) einen großen Unterschied machen **make a big difference** viel ausmachen **make no difference** keinen Unterschied machen

different [adj] **1.** *(not similar, various)* verschieden [fɛˈʃiːdn̩] no comp ◊ *verschiedene Kleider anprobieren* ♦ *Wir haben uns getrennt, weil wir einfach zu verschieden sind.* ♦ *fünf verschiedene Fahrräder* **2.** *(before sing ns)* andere ['andərə] no comp/superl <ein anderer …, eine andere …, ein anderes …> ◊ *Er ging in eine andere Richtung davon.* ♦ *Ich bin anderer Meinung.* something different etwas anderes [ɛtvas ˈandərəs]; *(not before ns)* anders ['andəs] ◊ *Er sieht ohne Bart ganz anders aus.* different from anders als ◊ *Sie ist anders als seine früheren Freundinnen.*
⊚ that's different das ist etwas anderes

differentiate [verb] **1.** *(discriminate)* differenzieren [dɪfərɛnˈtsiːrən] <differenziert, differenzierte, hat differenziert> ◊ *Wir müssen bei dieser Frage genau differenzieren.*; *(see the difference)* differentiate between

sth and sth zwischen etw. [dat] und etw. [dat] unterscheiden [tsvɪʃn̩ … ʊnt … ʊntɐʃaɛdn̩] <unterscheidet, unterschied, hat unterschieden> ◊ *Tiere können nicht zwischen Gut und Böse unterscheiden.* **2.** *(make sb/sth different)* differentiate sb/sth from sb/sth jdn/ etw. von jdm/etw. unterscheiden [fɔn … ʊntɐʃaɛdn̩] <unterscheidet, unterschied, hat unterschieden> ◊ *Was unterscheidet dieses Programm von den anderen?*

differently [adv] **1.** *(unconventionally)* anders ['andəs] ◊ *Wir machen das anders.* ♦ *Er denkt anders als die anderen.* **2.** *(not in the same way)* unterschiedlich ['ʊntɐʃiːtlɪç] ◊ *als Lehrer die Schüler unterschiedlich behandeln*

difficult [adj] schwierig ['ʃviːrɪç] ◊ *Das ist eine schwierige Frage.* ♦ *Die Klassenarbeit war sehr schwierig.* ♦ *Ich befinde mich in einer schwierigen Lage.* ♦ *Es ist schwierig, einen Termin bei diesem Arzt zu bekommen.* ♦ *Morgen ist es schwierig. Wie wär's mit Freitag?* sb finds it difficult to do sth es fällt jdm schwer, etw. zu tun [ɛs fɛlt … ˈʃveːɐ … tsuː] <fiel, ist gefallen> ◊ *Es fällt ihm schwer, seine Fehler zuzugeben.*
⊚ make life difficult for sb jdm das Leben schwer machen

difficulty [noun] Schwierigkeit ['ʃviːrɪçkaɛt] die <-, -en> ◊ *Das Projekt hat uns vor einige Schwierigkeiten gestellt.* ♦ *Haben Sie Schwierigkeiten mit dem Wagen?* ♦ *Sie hat die Aufgabe ohne Schwierigkeiten gelöst.* difficulty doing sth Schwierigkeiten bei etw. ◊ *Ich hatte Schwierigkeiten beim Einparken.* in difficulty in Schwierigkeiten ◊ *Er ist in finanziellen Schwierigkeiten.* get into difficulty in Schwierigkeiten geraten learning difficulties Lernschwierigkeiten ['lɛˀnʃviːrɪçkaɛtn̩] die <-> pl

dig¹ [noun] **1.** *(excavation)* Ausgrabung ['aʊsgraːbʊŋ] die <-, -en> ◊ *Bei den Ausgrabungen wurde eine römische Siedlung gefunden.* **2.** *(using your elbow or finger)* Stoß [ʃtoːs] der <-es, Stöße> ◊ *jdm einen Stoß in die Rippen versetzen* **3.** *(insinuation)* Spitze ['ʃpɪtsə] die <-, -n> ◊ *War das eine Spitze gegen mich?*

dig² [verb] **1.** *(make a hole, tunnel etc.)* graben ['graːbm̩] <gräbt, grub, hat gegraben> ◊ *einen Tunnel graben* ♦ *Hunde graben gern im Sand.* dig for sth nach etw. graben ◊ *Die Kinder gruben im Sand nach Muscheln.* **2.** *(investigate)* herumschnüffeln [hɛˈrʊmʃnʏfln̩] +haben ◊ *Dieser Reporter schnüffelt schon wieder herum.*
• **dig in** [phras v] **1.** *(put into the ground)* untergraben ['ʊntɐgraːbm̩] <gräbt unter, grub unter, hat untergraben> ◊ *den Dünger gut untergraben* dig yourself in sich eingraben ['aɛngraːbm̩] <gräbt sich ein, grub sich ein, hat sich eingegraben> ◊ *Die Soldaten erhielten den Befehl, sich einzugraben.* **2.** *(start eating)* reinhauen ['raɛnhaʊən] <haut rein, haute rein, hat reingehauen> *(fam)* ◊ *Es ist genug Pizza für alle da, also haut rein!*
• **dig into** [phras v] **1.** *(press)* sth digs into sth etw. schneidet in etw. [acc] ['ʃnaɛdət ɪn] <schnitt, hat geschnitten> ◊ *Die Fesseln schnitten in seine Handgelenke.* dig sth into sth etw. in etw. [acc] graben [ɪn … graːbm̩] <gräbt, grub, hat gegraben> ◊ *Sie grub ihre Fingernägel in seinen Arm.* **2.** *(mix)* dig sth into sth etw. in etw. [acc] eingraben [ɪn … ˌaɛngraːbm̩] <gräbt ein, grub ein, hat eingegraben> ◊ *Dünger in die Beete eingraben* **3.** *(search)* dig (your hand) into

sth in etw. ⟨dat⟩ kramen [ɪn … kraːmən] +haben ◊ *Er kramte in seiner Manteltasche und zog einen Zettel hervor.* **4.** *(spend)* dig into sth etw. antasten ['antastn̩] <tastet an, tastete an, hat angetastet> ◊ *Ich möchte unsere Ersparnisse nicht antasten.* **5.** *(investigate)* dig into sth in etw. ⟨dat⟩ wühlen [ɪn … vyːlən] +haben ◊ *in jds Vergangenheit wühlen*
* **dig out** ⟨phras v⟩ ausgraben ['a̯ʊsɡraːbm̩] <gräbt aus, grub aus, hat ausgegraben>
* **dig up** ⟨phras v⟩ **1.** *(remove from under the ground, discover)* ausgraben ['a̯ʊsɡraːbm̩] <gräbt aus, grub aus, hat ausgegraben> ◊ *einen Baum ausgraben* ♦ *Archäologen gruben die Überreste einer Siedlung aus.* ♦ *interessante Details aus jds Vergangenheit ausgraben* **2.** *(a road)* aufreißen ['a̯ʊfra̯esn̩] <reißt auf, riss auf, hat aufgerissen> ◊ *die Straße aufreißen und neue Rohre verlegen*
digest ⟨verb⟩ verdauen [fɛ'da̯ʊən] <verdaut, verdaute, hat verdaut> ◊ *Fette Speisen sind schwer zu verdauen.* ♦ *das Gelesene erst mal verdauen*
digger ⟨noun⟩ Bagger ['baɡɐ] der <-s, -> ◊ *mit einem Bagger eine Grube ausheben*
digit ⟨noun⟩ **1.** MATH Ziffer ['tsɪfɐ] die <-, -n> ◊ *eine Zahl mit zwei Ziffern* four-digit/five-digit etc. vierstellig/fünfstellig etc. ['fiːɐ̯ʃtɛlɪç/'fʏnfʃtɛlɪç] ◊ *Bitte geben Sie Ihre vierstellige PIN ein.* **2.** ANAT *(finger)* Finger ['fɪŋɐ] der <-s, ->; *(toe)* Zehe ['tseːə] die <-, -n>
digital ⟨adj⟩ **1.** *(using electronic signals)* digital [digi'taːl] no comp/superl ◊ *eine digitale Aufnahme* ♦ *Die Zukunft des Fernsehens ist digital.* **2.** *(clock, instrument)* digital … Digital… [digi'taːl] ◊ *digital* [digi'taːl] digital watch Digitaluhr [digi'taːlʔuːɐ̯] die <-, -en>
dignified ⟨adj⟩ **1.** *(calm, composed)* würdevoll ['vʏrdəfɔl] ◊ *Sein würdevolles Auftreten beeindruckte alle.* ♦ *Die Zeremonie war würdevoll.* **2.** *(awe-inspiring)* ehrwürdig ['eːɐ̯vʏrdɪç] ◊ *ein ehrwürdiges altes Herrenhaus* ♦ *Das Gebäude ist ehrwürdig.*
dignity ⟨noun⟩ Würde ['vʏrdə] die <-> no pl ◊ *seinem Schicksal mit Würde begegnen* ♦ *Ich fühle mich in meiner Würde gekränkt.* maintain your dignity seine Würde bewahren
⊛ **beneath your dignity** unter seiner Würde
dilate ⟨verb⟩ sich erweitern [zɪç ɛ'va̯etn̩] <erweitert sich, erweiterte sich, hat sich erweitert> ◊ *In der Dämmerung erweitern sich die Pupillen.*
dilemma ⟨noun⟩ Dilemma [di'lɛmaː] das <-s, -s or -ta> ◊ *Er sucht einen Ausweg aus dem Dilemma.* face a dilemma vor einem Dilemma stehen
diligence ⟨noun⟩ Fleiß [fla̯es] der <-es> no pl
dilute¹ ⟨verb⟩ **1.** *(a liquid)* verdünnen [fɛ'dʏnən] <verdünnt, verdünnte, hat verdünnt> ◊ *eine Säure verdünnen* ♦ *Orangensaft mit Wasser verdünnen* **2.** *(make sth less effective)* abschwächen ['apʃvɛçn̩] <schwächt ab, schwächte ab, hat abgeschwächt> ◊ *Seine Entschuldigung wurde durch seinen ironischen Ton abgeschwächt.*
dilute² ⟨adj⟩ verdünnt [fɛ'dʏnt] <verdünnter, am verdünntesten> seldom comp/superl ◊ *eine verdünnte Säure*
dim¹ ⟨adj⟩ **1.** *(light)* schwach [ʃvax] <schwächer, am schwächsten> ◊ *Sie las in dem schwachen Licht einer Lampe.* ♦ *Das Kerzenlicht war schwach und flackerte stark.* **2.** *(room)* dämmrig ['dɛmrɪç] ◊ *ein dämmriges Zimmer* ♦ *Die Kammer war dämmrig.* **3.** *(not clear)*

verschwommen [fɛ'ʃvɔmən] ◊ *Ihre Erinnerung an den Unfall ist verschwommen.* ♦ *eine verschwommene Vorstellung von etw. haben* **4.** *(stupid)* beschränkt [bə'ʃrɛŋkt] <beschränkter, am beschränktesten> ◊ *ein beschränkter Mensch* ♦ *Sie kommt mir manchmal etwas beschränkt vor.* **5.** *(prospects, chances)* düster ['dyːstɐ] ◊ *düstere Aussichten* ♦ *Seine Aussicht auf Erfolg sah zunehmend düster aus.*
⊛ **take a dim view of sb/sth** nicht viel von jdm/ etw. halten
dim² ⟨verb⟩ dim sth etw. dämpfen ['dɛmpfn̩] +haben ◊ *Könnten Sie das Licht ein wenig dämpfen?* sth dims etw. wird schwächer [vɪ'ːt 'ʃvɛçɐ] +sein ◊ *Der Schein des Feuers wurde schwächer.*
dimension ⟨noun⟩ Dimension [dimɛn'zi̯oːn] die <-, -en> ◊ *Dadurch erhält unser Projekt eine politische Dimension.* ♦ *Zeit, die vierte Dimension*
diminish ⟨verb⟩ **1.** *(become less)* sth diminishes etw. verringert sich [fɛ'rɪŋɐt zɪç] <verringerte sich, hat sich verringert> ◊ *Der Umsatz hat sich gegenüber dem Vorjahr verringert.* diminish sth etw. verringern ◊ *Lärm verringert die Lebensqualität.* **2.** *(emotion)* nachlassen ['naːxlasn̩] <lässt nach, ließ nach, hat nachgelassen> ◊ *Ihre Begeisterung ließ rasch nach.* **3.** *(hope, expectation)* dämpfen ['dɛmpfn̩] +haben ◊ *Die Prognosen dämpften die Erwartungen für das kommende Quartal.; (an achievement)* schmälern ['ʃmɛːlɐn] +haben ◊ *jds Verdienste schmälern*
diminutive ⟨noun⟩ LING Verkleinerungsform [fɛ'kla̯enərʊŋsfɔ'ːm] die <-, -en> ◊ *„Häuschen" ist die Verkleinerungsform von „Haus".*
dine ⟨verb⟩ speisen ['ʃpa̯ezn̩] +haben *(lofty)* ◊ *Sie speisten in einem vornehmen Lokal.*
* **dine out** ⟨phras v⟩ auswärts essen ['a̯ʊsvɛ'ːts ˌɛsn̩] <isst, aß, hat gegessen> ◊ *Er schlug ihr vor, wieder einmal auswärts zu essen.*
diner ⟨noun⟩ **1.** *(restaurant guest)* Gast [ɡast] der <-(e)s, Gäste> ◊ *ein Gast, der Stammkunde ist* **2.** *(in the US: small restaurant)* Imbiss ['ɪmbɪs] der <-es, -e> ◊ *einen Kleinigkeit im Imbiss essen*
dining room ⟨noun⟩ *(in a house)* Esszimmer ['ɛstsɪmɐ] das <-s, -> ◊ *im Esszimmer frühstücken; (in a hotel)* Speisesaal ['ʃpa̯ezazaːl] der <-(e)s, Speisesäle> ◊ *Das Frühstück wird im Speisesaal serviert.*
dinner ⟨noun⟩ **1.** *((main) meal)* Essen ['ɛsn̩] das <-s> no pl ◊ *Das Essen ist fertig.* ♦ *jdn zum Essen einladen* have dinner essen ['ɛsn̩] <isst, aß, hat gegessen> ◊ *Hast du schon gegessen?* **2.** *(evening meal)* Abendessen ['aːbm̩tʔɛsn̩] das <-s> no pl ◊ *Wann gibt es Abendessen?* have sth for dinner etw. zum Abendessen haben ♦ *Wir hatten Nudeln zum Abendessen.* **3.** *(meal eaten in the middle of day)* Mittagessen ['mɪtaːkˌɛsn̩] das <-s> no pl ◊ *Um 12 Uhr gibt es Mittagessen.* have sth for dinner etw. zum Mittagessen haben **4.** *(formal meal)* Festessen ['fɛstˌɛsn̩] das <-s, -> ◊ *ein Festessen zu Ehren des Bürgermeisters*
⊛ **go out to dinner 1.** *(at a restaurant)* essen gehen **2.** *(at sb's house)* zum Essen eingeladen sein **have dinner with sb 1.** *(at a restaurant)* mit jdm essen gehen **2.** *(at sb's house)* zu jdm zum Essen kommen
dip¹ ⟨noun⟩ **1.** *(swim)* go for a dip kurz schwimmen gehen [kʊ'ːts 'ʃvɪmən ɡeːən] <geht, ging, ist gegangen> ◊ *Es ist so heiß! Lass uns kurz im See schwimmen*

geben. **2.** *(drop)* dip in sth Abfall ... gen ['apfal] der <-(e)s> *no pl* ◊ *ein leichter Abfall der Börsenkurse* take a dip sinken ['zɪŋkn̩] <sinkt, sank, ist gesunken> ◊ *Die Zahl der Arbeitslosen ist im Sommer gesunken.* **3.** *(sauce)* Dip [dɪp] der <-s, -s> **4.** *(hollow)* Bodensenke ['boːdn̩zɛŋkə] die <-, -n> take a dip abfallen ['apfalən] <fällt ab, fiel ab, ist abgefallen> ◊ *Die Straße fällt nach der Kurve merklich ab.* **5.** *(for animals)* Desinfektionslösung [dɛs|ɪnfɛk'tsjoːnsløːzʊŋ] die <-, -en> ◊ *ein Tier in Desinfektionslösung baden*

dip² verb **1.** *(place in a liquid)* dip sth in(to) sth etw. in etw. acc tauchen [ɪn ... taoxn̩] +*haben* ◊ *den Fuß ins Wasser tauchen*; *(an animal)* in Desinfektionslösung baden [ɪn dɛs|ɪnfɛk'tsjoːnsløːzʊŋ baːdn̩] +*haben* ◊ *Schafe in Desinfektionslösung baden* **2.** *(lower)* dip sth etw. senken ['zɛŋkn̩] +*haben* ◊ *Er senkte den Kopf.* sth dips etw. fällt ab [fɛlt 'ap] <fiel ab, ist abgefallen> +*haben* ◊ *Die Straße führt erst bergauf und fällt dann wieder ab.* **3.** *(decrease, diminish)* sinken ['zɪŋkn̩] <sinkt, sank, ist gesunken> ◊ *Die Preise sind gesunken.*

diploma noun **1.** *(qualification)* Abschluss ['apʃlʊs] der <-es, Abschlüsse> ◊ *Ich habe einen Abschluss in Psychologie.* **2.** *(degree, course of study)* Diplom [di'ploːm] das <-s, -e> ◊ *Letztes Jahr hat sie ihr Diplom gemacht.*

diplomat noun Diplomat [diplo'maːt] der <-en, -en> ♀Diplomatin [diplo'maːtɪn] die <-, -nen> ◊ *Er ist Diplomat in London.* ◆ *Sie ist eine geborene Diplomatin.*

diplomatic adj diplomatisch [diplo'maːtɪʃ] ◊ *diplomatische Beziehungen* ◆ *Diese Antwort war nicht sehr diplomatisch.*

direct¹ adj **1.** *(route, link, descendant, light, remark)* direkt [di'rɛkt] <direkter, am direktesten> ◊ *Sie nahm den direkten Weg.* ◆ *Es besteht ein direkter Zusammenhang zwischen Rauchen und Lungenkrebs.* ◆ *ein direkter Nachkomme Napoleons* ◆ *Diese Frage ist mir zu direkt.* direct hit Volltreffer ['fɔltrɛfɐ] der <-s, -> **2.** *(danger, result, cause)* unmittelbar ['ʊnmɪtl̩baːɐ̯] *only before n* ◊ *sich in unmittelbarer Gefahr befinden* ◆ *unmittelbare Auswirkungen auf jdn/etw. haben* the direct opposite genau das Gegenteil [gənao das 'geːgn̩taɛl]

direct² adv direkt [di'rɛkt] <direkter, am direktesten> ◊ *Diese Maschine fliegt direkt nach Hamburg.*

direct³ verb **1.** *(aim)* richten ['rɪçtn̩] <richtet, richtete, hat gerichtet> ◊ *Meine Kritik war an ihn gerichtet.* ◆ *Wir richten unsere Bemühungen darauf, den Betroffenen rasch zu helfen.* **2.** *(manage, control)* leiten ['laɛtn̩] <leitet, leitete, hat geleitet> ◊ *eine Firma leiten* **3.** *(instruct)* anweisen ['anvaɛzn̩] <weist an, wies an, hat angewiesen> ◊ *Ich wurde angewiesen, Sie aus dem Saal zu begleiten.* **4.** *(a film, play)* direct sth bei etw. Regie führen [bae ... re'ʒiː fyːrən] +*haben* ◊ *Wer hat bei dem Film Regie geführt?* **5.** *(traffic)* regeln ['reːgln̩] +*haben* ◊ *Ein Polizist regelte den Verkehr.* direct sb somewhere jdm den Weg irgendwohin sagen [deːn veːk ... zaːgn̩] +*haben* ◊ *Können Sie mir den Weg zum Rathaus sagen?*

direct debit noun Einzugsermächtigung ['aɛntsuːks|ɛɐ̯mɛçtɪgʊŋ] die <-, -en> ◊ *jdm eine Einzugsermächtigung erteilen*

direction noun **1.** *(way)* Richtung ['rɪçtʊŋ] die <-, -en> ◊ *Der Wind weht aus nordwestlicher*

Richtung. ◆ *in die entgegengesetzte Richtung* ◆ *Er winkte ihr, aber sie sah nicht in seine Richtung.* ◆ *Die Reform ist ein Schritt in die richtige Richtung.* in the direction of Munich in Richtung München take a ... direction eine ... Richtung einschlagen ◊ *im Bereich Umweltpolitik eine völlig neue Richtung einschlagen* sense of direction Orientierungssinn [orjɛn'tiːrʊŋszɪn] der <-(e)s> *no pl* change of direction Richtungswechsel ['rɪçtʊŋsvɛksl̩] der <-s, -> **2.** *(purpose)* Ziel [tsiːl] das <-(e)s, -e> have a sense of direction ein Ziel im Leben haben **3.** *(instructions)* directions Anweisungen ['anvaɛzʊŋən] die <-> *pl* ◊ *Bitte folgen Sie den Anweisungen des Personals.* **4.** *(of an organization, a project etc.)* Leitung ['laɛtʊŋ] die <-, -en> *most sing* ◊ *Wer übernimmt die Leitung der Firma?* ◆ *das Orchester unter Leitung von Bettina Wöhrer* **5.** FILM, THEAT Regie [re'ʒiː] die <-> *no pl* ◊ *Er hat oft unter der Regie von Peter Zadek gespielt.*

directive noun Weisung ['vaɛzʊŋ] die <-, -en> ◊ *Weisungen erhalten*

directly adv **1.** *(without anything in between)* direkt [di'rɛkt] <direkter, am direktesten> ◊ *Diese Sendung wird direkt übertragen.* ◆ *ein Haus direkt am See* ◆ *Von dieser Entscheidung bin ich direkt betroffen.* **2.** *(immediately)* sofort [zo'fɔʁt] *no comp/superl* ◊ *Er kam sofort nach dem Unfall ins Krankenhaus.*

director noun **1.** FILM, THEAT Regisseur [reʒɪ'søːɐ̯] der <-s, -e> ♀Regisseurin [reʒɪ'søːrɪn] die <-, -nen> ◊ *Er ist Regisseur.* ◆ *die umstrittene Regisseurin Leni Riefenstahl* **2.** *(manager)* Direktor [di'rɛktoːɐ̯] der <-s, -en> ♀Direktorin [dɪrɛk'toːrɪn] die <-, -nen> ◊ *Die Direktorin des Museums eröffnete die Ausstellung.* ◆ *Er ist Direktor des Instituts.*; *(of a company, department, organization)* Leiter ['laɛtɐ] der <-s, -> ♀Leiterin ['laɛtərɪn] die <-, -nen> ◊ *der neue Leiter der Firma* ◆ *Sie ist Leiterin einer großen Abteilung.* personnel director Personalleiter [pɛɐ̯zo'naːllaɛtɐ] ♀Personalleiterin [pɛɐ̯zo'naːllaɛtərɪn] board of directors Direktorium [dɪrɛk'toːrjʊm] das <-s, Direktorien>

directory noun **1.** *(phone book)* Telefonbuch [tele'foːnbuːx] das <-(e)s, Telefonbücher> ◊ *Sein Name steht nicht im Telefonbuch.*; *(of an organization)* Mitarbeiterverzeichnis ['mɪt|aʁbaɛtɐfɐˌtsaɛçnɪs] das <-ses, -se>; *(alphabetical list)* Verzeichnis [fɛ'tsaɛçnɪs] das <-ses, -se> ◊ *ein Verzeichnis aller Restaurants der Stadt* **2.** IT *(folder)* Verzeichnis [fɛ'tsaɛçnɪs] das <-ses, -se> ◊ *ein neues Verzeichnis anlegen*

directory enquiries noun Auskunft ['aoskʊnft] die <-> *no pl* ◊ *Ruf doch mal die Auskunft an.*

dirt noun Schmutz [ʃmʊts] der <-es> *no pl* ◊ *Das Kind hat draußen im Schmutz gespielt.*
◉ treat sb like dirt jdn wie den letzten Dreck behandeln *(fam)*

dirty adj schmutzig ['ʃmʊtsɪç] ◊ *schmutziges Geschirr* ◆ *Deine Hände sind schmutzig.* ◆ *ein schmutziger Witz* ◆ *Er ist in schmutzige Geschäfte verwickelt.*
◉ give sb a dirty look jdm einen bösen Blick zuwerfen do the dirty on sb jdn reinlegen *(fam)*

disability noun Behinderung [bə'hɪndərʊŋ] die <-, -en> ◊ *Die Blinde hat gelernt, mit ihrer Behinderung zu leben.* disability benefit Behindertenunterstützung [bə'hɪndɐtn̩|ʊntɐˌʃtʏtsʊŋ] die <-> *no pl*

disabled adj behindert [bə'hɪndɐt] *no comp/superl*

ein behindertes Kind ♦ *geistig/körperlich behindert sein* severely disabled **schwerbehindert** [ˈʃveːɡbəhɪndɐt] *no comp/superl*

disabled person (noun) Behinderte [bəˈhɪndɐtə] der/die <–n, die Behinderten> *but: ein Behinderter/eine Behinderte* ◊ *eine Toilette für Behinderte*

disadvantage¹ (noun) Nachteil [ˈnaːxtaɪl] der <–(e)s, –e> ◊ *Der einzige Nachteil an diesem Hobby ist, dass es sehr teuer ist.* advantages and disadvantages **Vor- und Nachteile** be to sb's disadvantage **zu jds Nachteil sein** ◊ *Wenn Sie mitmachen, soll das nicht zu Ihrem Nachteil sein.* put sb at a disadvantage **jdn benachteiligen** [bəˈnaːxtaɪlɪɡn̩] <benachteiligt, benachteiligte, hat benachteiligt>

disadvantage² (verb) benachteiligen [bəˈnaːxtaɪlɪɡn̩] <benachteiligt, benachteiligte, hat benachteiligt> ◊ *Frauen werden in vielen Ländern immer noch benachteiligt.*

disagree (verb) **1.** *(have a different opinion)* nicht derselben Meinung sein [ˌnɪçt deːɐ̯ˈzɛlbm̩ ˈmaɪnʊŋ zaɪn] +sein ◊ *Seine Frau und er sind oft nicht derselben Meinung.* disagree on sth über etw. (acc) nicht derselben Meinung sein disagree with sb anderer Meinung sein als jd [ˈandərɐ ˌmaɪnʊŋ zaɪn als] +sein ◊ *Der Chef ist da aber völlig anderer Meinung als Sie.* disagree with sth mit etw. nicht einverstanden sein [mɪt ... ˌnɪçt ˈaɪnfɛʃtandn̩ zaɪn] +sein ◊ *Mit deinem Vorschlag bin ich überhaupt nicht einverstanden.* **2.** *(be different)* nicht übereinstimmen [ˌnɪçt ybeˈʔaɪnʃtɪmən] +haben ◊ *Die Forschungsergebnisse der beiden Teams stimmen nicht überein.* **3.** *(food)* disagree with sb jdm nicht bekommen [ˌnɪçt bəˈkɔmən] <bekommt, bekam, ist bekommen> ◊ *Fettes Fleisch bekommt mir nicht.*

disagreement (noun) **1.** *(different opinions)* Uneinigkeit [ˈʊnʔaɪnɪçkaɪt] die <–, –en> ◊ *Bei vielen Paaren besteht Uneinigkeit in der Frage der Kindererziehung.* disagreement over sth Uneinigkeit über etw. (acc) ◊ *Es herrscht Uneinigkeit darüber, wer die Kosten übernehmen soll.* **2.** *(discrepancy)* Diskrepanz [dɪskreˈpant͡s] die <–, –en> ◊ *eine deutliche Diskrepanz zwischen Theorie und Praxis*

disappear (verb) verschwinden [fɛˈʃvɪndn̩] <verschwindet, verschwand, ist verschwunden> ◊ *Er drehte sich um und verschwand durch den Ausgang.* ♦ *Die Schmerzen sind plötzlich verschwunden.* ♦ *Mein Geldbeutel ist spurlos verschwunden.* disappear without trace spurlos verschwinden

disappearance (noun) Verschwinden [fɛˈʃvɪndn̩] das <–s> no pl ◊ *Seit ihrem Verschwinden sind Monate vergangen.*

disappoint (verb) enttäuschen [ɛnˈtɔɪʃn̩] <enttäuscht, enttäuschte, hat enttäuscht> ◊ *Du hast mich sehr enttäuscht.* ♦ *Sie enttäuschte unsere Erwartungen nicht.*

disappointed → disappoint (adj) enttäuscht [ɛnˈtɔɪʃt] disappointed at sth über etw. (acc) sein disappointed in sb von jdm enttäuscht sein

disappointment (noun) Enttäuschung [ɛnˈtɔɪʃʊŋ] die <–, –en> ◊ *Man konnte ihm seine Enttäuschung ansehen.* ♦ *Der Abstieg der Mannschaft war eine bittere Enttäuschung.* disappointment with sth Enttäuschung über etw. (acc)

disapproval (noun) Missbilligung [ˈmɪsbɪlɪɡʊŋ] die <–> no pl ◊ *Sie zeigte ihre Missbilligung deutlich.* in disapproval missbilligend [mɪsˈbɪlɪɡn̩t] ◊ *Sein Vater*

schüttelte missbilligend den Kopf.

disapprove (verb) dagegen sein [daˈɡeːɡn̩ zaɪn] +sein ◊ *Egal, was ich sage, er ist immer dagegen.* disapprove of sth etw. ablehnen [ˈaplɛːnən] +haben ◊ *Sie lehnt grundsätzlich jeden Vorschlag ab, den ich mache.*

disaster (noun) *(accident)* Unglück [ˈʊnɡlʏk] das <–(e)s, –e> ◊ *In der Fabrik ereignete sich ein Unglück.; (catastrophe, failure)* Katastrophe [katasˈtroːfə] die <–, –n> ◊ *Eine erneute Dürreperiode wäre eine Katastrophe für die Bauern.* ♦ *Der Ausflug der jungen Leute endete in einer Katastrophe.* ♦ *Meine Mathearbeit ist eine Katastrophe: Null Punkte!* natural disaster Naturkatastrophe [naˈtuːɐ̯katastroːfə]

disastrous(ly) (adj, adv) katastrophal [katastroˈfaːl] ◊ *katastrophale Folgen für die Umwelt haben* ♦ *Eine Eskalation der Gewalt wäre katastrophal.* ♦ *Meine Führerscheinprüfung ist katastrophal gelaufen.*

disc, disk (noun) **1.** *(round, flat object)* Scheibe [ˈʃaɪbə] die <–, –n> ◊ *Früher dachten die Menschen, die Erde sei eine Scheibe.* **2.** IT *(floppy)* disk/disc Diskette [dɪsˈkɛtə] die <–, –n> ◊ *Ich bringe Ihnen eine Diskette mit den Dateien mit.* (hard) disk/disc Festplatte [ˈfɛstplatə] die <–, –n> **3.** ANAT Bandscheibe [ˈbantʃaɪbə] die <–, –n> slipped disc Bandscheibenvorfall [ˈbantʃaɪbm̩foːɡfal] der <–(e)s, Bandscheibenvorfälle> ◊ *Er muss wegen eines Bandscheibenvorfalls operiert werden.* **4.** *(for music)* CD [tseˈdeː] die <–, –s> ◊ *Hast du die neue CD von Madonna schon?*

discard (verb) wegwerfen [ˈvɛkvɛɐ̯fn̩] <wirft weg, warf weg, hat weggeworfen> ◊ *die Verpackung wegwerfen*

discharge¹ (noun) **1.** *(from a hospital, prison)* Entlassung [ɛntˈlasʊŋ] die <–, –en> ◊ *Nach seiner Entlassung aus dem Krankenhaus fuhr er sofort nach Hause.* **2.** *(of a liquid, gas)* Ausströmen [ˈaosˌʃtrøːmən] das <–s> no pl ◊ *das Ausströmen des Gases aus der Leitung; (from a part of the body)* Ausfluss [ˈaosflʊs] der <–es, Ausflüsse> ◊ *Ausfluss aus der Scheide* **3.** *(of a duty)* Erfüllung [eˈfʏlʊŋ] die <–, –en> most sing ◊ *Er bestand auf der Erfüllung seiner Pflicht.* **4.** *(of a gun)* Abfeuern [ˈapfɔɪɐn] das <–s> no pl ◊ *das Abfeuern einer Schusswaffe* **5.** *(of debts)* Begleichung [bəˈɡlaɪçʊŋ] die <–> no pl ◊ *auf die Begleichung einer Schuld warten* **6.** TECHN *(of electricity)* Entladung [ɛntˈlaːdʊŋ] die <–, –en> ◊ *Es kam zu einer heftigen Entladung.*

discharge² (verb) **1.** *(a patient, inmate)* entlassen [ɛntˈlasn̩] <entlässt, entließ, hat entlassen> ◊ *Er wurde vorzeitig aus der Haft entlassen.* ♦ *Man hat die Patientin heute morgen entlassen.; (sb accused of a crime)* freisprechen [ˈfraɪ͡ʃprɛçn̩] <spricht frei, sprach frei, hat freigesprochen> ◊ *Der Angeklagte wurde freigesprochen.* **2.** *(a liquid, gas)* discharge sth somewhere etw. irgendwohin strömen lassen [ˈʃtrøːmən ˌlasn̩] <lässt, ließ, hat gelassen> ◊ *Abwässer ins Meer strömen lassen* etw. is discharged (from sth) etw. strömt (aus etw. (dat)) aus [ˈʃtrøːmt ˈaos] +sein ◊ *Aus dem Tanker strömt Öl ins Meer aus.* **3.** *(a function, duty)* erfüllen [eˈfʏlən] <erfüllt, erfüllte, hat erfüllt> ◊ *seine Pflicht treu erfüllen* **4.** *(a gun)* abfeuern [ˈapfɔɪɐn] +haben ◊ *Er lud die Pistole und feuerte sie ab.* **5.** *(a debt)* begleichen [bəˈɡlaɪçn̩] <begleicht, beglich, hat beglichen> ◊ *Sein Vater musste die Schuld für ihn begleichen.* **6.** TECHN *(a*

battery) entladen [ɛntˈlaːdn̩] <entlädt, entlud, hat entladen>

disciple [noun] **1.** Anhänger [ˈanhɛŋɐ] der <-s, -> ♀Anhängerin [ˈanhɛŋərɪn] die <-, –nen> **2.** REL Jünger [ˈjʏŋə] der <-s, –>

disciplinary [adj] disziplinarisch [dɪstsipliˈnaːrɪʃ] no comp/superl ◊ *disziplinarische Maßnahmen gegen einen Schüler ergreifen* disciplinary proceedings Disziplinarverfahren [dɪstsipliˈnaːʳfeːfaːrən] das <-s, -> most sing

discipline¹ [noun] Disziplin [dɪstsiˈpliːn] die <-, –en> ◊ *Unser Lehrer legt viel Wert auf Disziplin.* ◆ *Es fällt ihr schwer, die Disziplin in der Gruppe aufrechtzuerhalten.* ◆ *Die Anatomie ist eine selbstständige Disziplin der Medizin.*

discipline² [verb] bestrafen [bəˈʃtraːfn̩] <bestraft, bestrafte, hat bestraft> ◊ *Eltern sollten ihre Kinder nicht zu oft bestrafen.*

ⓔ discipline yourself to do sth sich dazu zwingen, etw. zu tun

disclose [verb] *(facts, information)* bekannt geben [bəˈkant geːbm̩] <gibt, gab, hat gegeben> ◊ *bekannt geben, wo das Kraftwerk gebaut werden soll;* *(secrets)* preisgeben [ˈpraesgeːbm̩] +haben ◊ *Sie gab den Namen des Vaters nicht preis.*

disclosure [noun] *(of information)* Bekanntgabe [bəˈkantgaːbə] die <-, –n> most sing ◊ *Die Medien fordern eine Bekanntgabe der Ergebnisse der Studie.;* *(of secrets)* Enthüllung [ɛntˈhʏlʊŋ] die <-, –en> ◊ *Die Enthüllungen aus seinem Privatleben beendeten seine politische Karriere.*

disco [noun] **1.** *(venue)* Disko [ˈdɪskoː] die <-, –s> ◊ *in die Disko gehen* **2.** disco *(music)* Diskomusik [ˈdɪskomuˌziːk] die <-> no pl

discomfort [noun] **1.** *(slight pain)* leichte Schmerzen [ˌlaeçtə ˈʃmɛʳtsn̩] die <-> pl ◊ *bei der Zahnbehandlung leichte Schmerzen spüren* **2.** *(feeling of uneasiness)* Unbehagen [ˈʊnbəhaːgn̩] das <-s> no pl ◊ *Sie empfand in der Gegenwart des Fremden großes Unbehagen.*

disconnect [verb] **1.** *(electricity, water etc.)* abstellen [ˈapʃtɛlən] +haben ◊ *Weil er seine Rechnung nicht bezahlt hat, wurde ihm der Strom abgestellt.* **2.** *(electrical device)* ausstecken [ˈaosʃtɛkn̩] +haben ◊ *Bitte stecken Sie das Gerät aus, bevor Sie das Gehäuse öffnen.* **3.** *(telephone)* unterbrechen [ʊntɐˈbrɛçn̩] <unterbricht, unterbrach, hat unterbrochen> ◊ *Wir wurden bereits mehrmals unterbrochen; irgendetwas stimmt mit dem Anschluss nicht.*

discontinue [verb] *(finish)* beenden [bəˈʔɛndn̩] <beendet, beendete, hat beendet> ◊ *eine Behandlung beenden* ◆ *Ich möchte das Abonnement zum nächstmöglichen Zeitpunkt beenden.; (a product)* discontinue sth die Produktion ... [gen] einstellen [diː proˈdʊkˌtsjoːn ... ˌaenˈʃtɛlən] +haben ◊ *Es tut uns Leid, aber die Produktion dieses Artikels wurde eingestellt.*

discount¹ [noun] Rabatt [raˈbat] der <-(e)s, -e> ◊ *Auf Lederwaren gibt es heute 15% Rabatt.* at a discount zu herabgesetzten Preisen [tsuː hɛˌrapgəzɛtstn̩ ˈpraezn̩]

discount² [verb] **1.** *(a price)* herabsetzen [hɛˈrapzɛtsn̩] +haben ◊ *Zum Ende der Saison haben die Geschäfte die Preise stark herabgesetzt.* **2.** *(a possibility)* ausschließen [ˈaosʃliːsn̩] <schließt aus, schloss aus, hat ausgeschlossen> ◊ *Die Kripo schließt die Möglichkeit*

aus, dass es sich um eine Entführung handelt.

discourage [verb] **1.** *(hinder, prevent)* verhindern [fɐˈhɪndɐn] <verhindert, verhinderte, hat verhindert> ◊ *Wie kann man den Drogenkonsum Jugendlicher verhindern?; (deter)* abwehren [ˈapveːrən] +haben ◊ *eine Schutzvorrichtung, die Einbrecher abwehren soll; (dissuade)* discourage sb from doing sth jdn davon abhalten, etw. zu tun [dafɔn ˈaphaltn̩ ... tsuː] <hält ab, hielt ab, hat abgehalten> ◊ *jdn davon abhalten, eine gefährliche Expedition durchzuführen* **2.** *(dishearten)* entmutigen [ɛntˈmuːtɪgn̩] <entmutigt, entmutigte, hat entmutigt> ◊ *Er lässt sich viel zu schnell entmutigen.*

discourse [noun] Diskurs [dɪsˈkuʳs] der <-es, -e> ◊ *ein Diskurs über moderne Kommunikationsmethoden* ◆ *einen Diskurs mit jdm führen*

discover [verb] **1.** *(find out)* herausfinden [hɛˈraosfɪndn̩] <findet heraus, fand heraus, hat herausgefunden> ◊ *die Wahrheit herausfinden* ◆ *herausfinden, ob eine Substanz giftig ist* **2.** *(find sth that was missing, hidden, not known)* entdecken [ɛntˈdɛkn̩] <entdeckt, entdeckte, hat entdeckt> ◊ *die Schönheiten eines Landes entdecken* ◆ *Wann wurde sie als Sängerin entdeckt?* ◆ *Marie Curie entdeckte das Radium.*

discovery [noun] Entdeckung [ɛntˈdɛkʊŋ] die <-, –en> ◊ *die Entdeckung des Penicillins* ◆ *Er machte eine grausige Entdeckung.*

discreet(ly) [adj, adv] **1.** *(tactful, unobtrusive(ly))* diskret [dɪsˈkreːt] <diskreter, am diskretesten> ◊ *Sie war sehr diskret.* ◆ *ein diskreter Hinweis* ◆ *Er schwieg diskret.* **2.** *(tasteful)* dezent [deˈtsent] <dezenter, am dezentesten> ◊ *ihr dezentes Make-up* ◆ *Das Muster war sehr dezent.* ◆ *dezent geschminkt sein*

discretion [noun] **1.** *(freedom to decide)* Ermessen [ɛˈmɛsn̩] das <-s> no pl ◊ *Das Strafmaß liegt im Ermessen des Gerichts.* at sb's discretion nach jds Ermessen ◊ *Er kann nach seinem Ermessen entscheiden, ob ...* use your own discretion nach eigenem Ermessen handeln **2.** *(tact)* Diskretion [dɪskreˈtsjoːn] die <-> no pl ◊ *einen Fall mit äußerster Diskretion behandeln*

discriminate [verb] **1.** *(make an unfair distinction)* Unterschiede machen [ˈʊntəʃiːdə maxn̩] +haben ◊ *Es dürfen keine Unterschiede aufgrund der Hautfarbe gemacht werden.* ◆ *Unterschiede zwischen Männern und Frauen machen* discriminate against sb jdn diskriminieren [dɪskrimiˈniːrən] <diskriminiert, diskriminierte, hat diskriminiert> ◊ *In vielen Ländern werden Frauen nach wie vor diskriminiert.* **2.** *(distinguish)* unterscheiden [ʊntəˈʃaedn̩] <unterscheidet, unterschied, hat unterschieden> ◊ *einen Pilz von einem anderen unterscheiden* ◆ *zwischen Gut und Böse unterscheiden können*

discrimination [noun] **1.** *(unfair treatment)* Diskriminierung [dɪskrimiˈniːrʊŋ] die <-, –en> most sing ◊ *sexuelle Diskriminierung* ◆ *Sein Verhalten grenzt an Diskriminierung.* discrimination against sb Diskriminierung von jdm ◊ *die Diskriminierung von Behinderten* discrimination on the grounds of ... eine Diskriminierung aufgrund ... [gen] ◊ *Frauen wehren sich gegen eine Diskriminierung aufgrund ihres Geschlechts.* racial discrimination Rassendiskriminierung [ˈrasnˌdɪskrimiˌniːrʊŋ] **2.** *(capacity to differentiate)* Urteilsvermögen [ˈʊʳtaelsfɛmøːgn̩] das <-s> no

pl ◊ *sein Urteilsvermögen einsetzen, um etw. zu bewerten*

discuss verb **1.** *(talk about)* besprechen [bəˈʃprɛçn] <bespricht, besprach, hat besprochen> ◊ *Alles Weitere besprechen wir morgen.* ♦ *Haben Sie das schon mit dem Chef besprochen?* ♦ *Wir sollten in Ruhe besprechen, wie wir das Problem lösen können.*; *(exchange opinions)* diskutieren [dɪskuˈtiːrən] <diskutiert, diskutierte, hat diskutiert> ◊ *Ich möchte das nicht weiter diskutieren.* discuss sth with sb mit jdm über etw. acc diskutieren ◊ *Wir diskutierten lange über die Vor- und Nachteile des Vorschlags.* **2.** *(consider in detail, in writing)* erörtern [ɛ|ˈœɐtɐn] <erörtert, erörterte, hat erörtert> ◊ *eine Frage erörtern* ♦ *Erörtern Sie die Vor- und Nachteile des Verfahrens.*

discussion noun **1.** *(talk, debate)* Diskussion [dɪskʊˈsjoːn] die <-, -en> ◊ *Sie führte wieder mal eine lange Diskussion mit ihrem Vater.* ♦ *ein Vortrag mit anschließender Diskussion* ♦ *Das Urteil hatte heftige Diskussionen ausgelöst.* sth is under discussion über etw. acc wird diskutiert [yːbɐ ... vɪ̣ɐt dɪskuˈtiːɐt] ◊ *Über eine Reform des Rentensystems wird derzeit diskutiert.* **2.** *(written analysis)* Erörterung [ɛ|ˈœɐtərʊŋ] die <-, -en> ◊ *Der Bericht enthält auch eine Erörterung dieses Problems.*

disease noun Krankheit [ˈkraŋkhaɛt] die <-, -en> ◊ *eine ansteckende Krankheit haben* ♦ *Diese Substanz kann Krankheiten verursachen.* ♦ *Zeitmangel ist eine Krankheit unserer Gesellschaft.*

disgrace noun Schande [ˈʃandə] die <-> no pl ◊ *Sein Verbrechen brachte Schande über das ganze Dorf.* ♦ *Zu meiner Schande muss ich gestehen, dass ich gelogen habe.* be a disgrace to sth eine Schande für etw. sein ◊ *Sein Verhalten ist eine Schande für die ganze Familie.*

disguise¹ noun **1.** *(clothing)* Verkleidung [fɛˈklaɛdʊŋ] die <-, -en> ◊ *In seiner Verkleidung erkannte ihn niemand.* in disguise verkleidet [fɛˈklaɛdət] no comp/superl ◊ *Er kam verkleidet.* **2.** *(cover)* Tarnung [ˈtaɐnʊŋ] die <-, -en> ◊ *Seine Ausgelassenheit dient nur als Tarnung.*

disguise² verb **1.** *(a fact, intention, feeling)* verbergen [fɛˈbɛˈgn̩] <verbirgt, verbarg, hat verborgen> ◊ *Ein Lächeln sollte seine Unsicherheit verbergen.*; *(your voice)* verstellen [fɛˈʃtɛlən] <verstellt, verstellte, hat verstellt> ◊ *Der Täter verstellte am Telefon seine Stimme.* **2.** *(dress up)* disguise yourself (as sb/sth) sich (als jd/etw.) verkleiden [fɛˈklaɛdn̩] <verkleidet sich, verkleidete sich, hat sich verkleidet> ◊ *Sie hat sich als Mann verkleidet.* disguised as sth als jd/etw. verkleidet ◊ *Er betrat als Elvis Presley verkleidet die Bühne.* **3.** *(with the intention to deceive)* disguise sth/sb (as sth/sb) etw./jdn (als etw./jdn) tarnen [ˈtaɐnən] +haben ◊ *Man hatte die Herointüten als Zuckerpäckchen getarnt.* disguised as sb/sth als jd/etw. getarnt ◊ *ein als Reporter getarnter Spion*

disgust¹ noun Ekel [ˈeːkl̩] der <-s> no pl ◊ *Ekel vor Schnecken empfinden* in disgust voller Ekel ◊ *Voller Ekel wandte sie sich ab.*

disgust² verb anekeln [ˈanˈeːkl̩n] <ekelt an, ekelte an, hat angeekelt> ◊ *Muscheln ekeln mich an.* ♦ *Ihre heuchlerische Freundlichkeit ekelte ihn an.*

disgusting adj ekelhaft [ˈeːkl̩haft] <ekelhafter, am ekelhaftesten> ◊ *ein ekelhafter Geruch* ♦ *Ich finde*

sein Benehmen ziemlich ekelhaft.

dish noun **1.** *(container)* Schale [ˈʃaːlə] die <-, -n> ◊ *eine Schale mit Obst auf den Tisch stellen* soap dish Seifenschale [ˈzaɛfn̩ʃaːlə] **2.** *(meal)* Gericht [gəˈrɪçt] das <-(e)s, -e> ◊ *ein typisch italienisches Gericht* ♦ *Haben Sie auch vegetarische Gerichte?* dish of the day Tagesgericht [ˈtaːgəsgərɪçt] **3.** dishes Geschirr [gəˈʃɪr] das <-(e)s, -e> most sing ◊ *Sie kaufte neues Geschirr und Besteck.* do the dishes das Geschirr spülen **4.** TV Schüssel [ˈʃʏsl̩] die <-, -n> ◊ *Hier sieht man auf fast jedem Dach eine Schüssel.* satellite dish Satellitenschüssel [zatɛˈliːtn̩ʃʏsl̩]

dishcloth noun *(for washing-up)* Spüllappen [ˈʃpyːllapm̩] der <-s, ->; *(for drying)* Geschirrtuch [gəˈʃɪrtuːx] das <-(e)s, -tücher>

dishonest(ly) adj, adv unredlich [ˈʊnreːtlɪç] ◊ *unredliche Methoden* ♦ *Es wäre unredlich, etwas zu versprechen, was man nicht halten kann.* ♦ *unredlich handeln*

dishwasher noun **1.** *(machine)* Spülmaschine [ˈʃpyːlmaˌʃiːnə] die <-, -n> ◊ *Sie räumte die Spülmaschine ein/aus.* **2.** *(person)* Tellerwäscher [ˈtɛlevɛʃe] der <-s, -> ♀Tellerwäscherin [ˈtɛlevɛʃərɪn] die <-, -nen> ◊ *Angeblich hat er einst als Tellerwäscher angefangen.*

disinfect verb desinfizieren [dɛs|ɪnfiˈtsiːrən] <desinfiziert, desinfizierte, hat desinfiziert>

disinfectant noun Desinfektionsmittel [dɛs|ɪnfɛkˈtsjoːnsmɪtl̩] das <-s, ->

disintegrate verb zerfallen [tsɛˈfalən] <zerfällt, zerfiel, ist zerfallen> ◊ *Im Lauf der Jahrtausende ist der Fels immer mehr zerfallen.* ♦ *1991 zerfiel die Sowjetunion.*

disk US variant for **disc**

dislike¹ noun Abneigung [ˈapnaɛgʊŋ] die <-, -en> dislike for/of sb/sth Abneigung gegen jdn/etw. ◊ *Er hat eine Abneigung gegen seinen neuen Chef.* likes and dislikes Vorlieben und Abneigungen take an instant dislike to sb/sth jdn/etw. von Anfang an nicht mögen [fɔn ˌanfaŋ ʔan nɪçt ˌmøːgn̩] <mag, mochte, hat gemocht>

dislike² verb dislike sb/sth etw. nicht mögen [nɪçt ˈmøːgn̩] <mag, mochte, hat gemocht> ◊ *Er mochte sie überhaupt nicht.* ♦ *Katzen mögen es nicht, wenn ihr Fell nass wird.* dislike doing sth etw. nicht gern tun [nɪçt ˈgɛrn] ◊ *Ich stehe nicht gern auf, wenn es draußen noch dunkel ist.*

dismal adj **1.** *(depressing)* trostlos [ˈtroːstloːs] <trostloser, am trostlosesten> ◊ *Das Leben in dem Flüchtlingslager war wirklich trostlos.* ♦ *eine trostlose Gegend* **2.** *(really bad)* katastrophal [katastroˈfaːl] ◊ *eine katastrophale Vorstellung* ♦ *Die Aufführung war katastrophal.*

dismantle verb **1.** *(take apart)* auseinander nehmen [aʊs|aɛˈnandɐ neːmən] <nimmt, nahm, hat genommen> ◊ *Die Möbel lassen sich zum Transport leicht auseinander nehmen.* **2.** *(abolish)* abschaffen [ˈapʃafn̩] +haben ◊ *Die Regierung schaffte Steuervorteile ab.*; *(slowly)* abbauen [ˈapbaʊən] +haben ◊ *Wie kann die unnötige Bürokratie abgebaut werden?*

dismiss verb **1.** *(a claim, an idea)* ablehnen [ˈapleːnən] +haben ◊ *Sie lehnte seinen Vorschlag ab.* dismiss sth as sth etw. als etw. abtun [als ... ˌaptuːn] <tut ab, tat ab, hat abgetan> ◊ *Er tat die Geschichte als Gerücht ab.* dismiss sth out of hand etw. von der Hand weisen

[fɔn deːɐ̯ 'hant vaɛ̯zn̩] <weist, wies, hat gewiesen> ◊ *Es lässt sich nicht von der Hand weisen, dass es ein Problem gibt.* **2.** *(sack, allow sb to leave)* entlassen [ɛnt'lasn̩] <entlässt, entließ, hat entlassen> ◊ *In der Firma sind zehn Mitarbeiter entlassen worden.* ♦ *Die Lehrerin entließ die Klasse.* dismiss sb for sth jdn wegen etw. entlassen ◊ *Er wurde wegen Unterschlagung entlassen.* dismiss sb from a job jdn aus einem Arbeitsverhältnis entlassen **3.** *(a case, an appeal)* abweisen ['apvaɛ̯zn̩] <weist ab, wies ab, hat abgewiesen> ◊ *Der Richter wies die Klage ab.*

dismissal [noun] **1.** *(sacking, permission to leave)* Entlassung [ɛnt'lasʊŋ] die <-, -en> ◊ *Die Korruptionsaffäre hatte fünf Entlassungen zur Folge.* ♦ *die Entlassung der Geschworenen* unfair dismissal ungerechtfertigte Entlassung **2.** *(of a claim, an idea)* Ablehnung ['apleːnʊŋ] die <-, -en> ◊ *die Ablehnung von Studiengebühren* **3.** *(of a case, an appeal)* Abweisung ['apvaɛ̯zʊŋ] die <-, -en> ◊ *die Abweisung seiner Klage*

disorder [noun] **1.** *(illness)* Störung ['ʃtøːrʊŋ] die <-, -en> ◊ *eine psychische Störung* skin disorder Hautkrankheit ['haʊ̯tkraŋkhaɛ̯t] die <-, -en> stomach disorder Magenbeschwerden ['maːɡn̩bəʃveːɐ̯dn̩] die <-> pl **2.** *(unrest)* Unruhen ['ʊnruːən] die <-> pl civil disorder Unruhen in der Bevölkerung public disorder Störung der öffentlichen Ordnung [ʃtøːrʊŋ deːɐ̯ œfn̩tlɪçn̩ 'ɔ'dnʊŋ] die <-, -en> **3.** *(untidyness)* Unordnung ['ʊn|ɔ'dnʊŋ] die <-> no pl ◊ *Auf dem Schreibtisch war alles in Unordnung.*

dispatch [verb] **1.** *(send)* schicken ['ʃɪkn̩] +haben ◊ *ein Paket/eine Nachricht schicken* ♦ *100 Polizisten wurden in das Krisengebiet geschickt.* **2.** *(kill)* töten ['tøːtn̩] <tötet, tötete, hat getötet> ◊ *Er tötete den Hirsch mit einem gezielten Schuss.* **3.** *(deal with)* erledigen [ɛ'leːdɪɡn̩] <erledigt, erledigte, hat erledigt> *(fam)* ◊ *Der Boxer hat seinen Gegner in wenigen Minuten erledigt.*

dispensing chemist [noun] Apotheker [apo'teːke] der <-s, -> ♀Apothekerin [apo'teːkərɪn] die <-, -nen> ◊ *Sie ist Apothekerin.* ♦ *Dieses Mittel hat mir der Apotheker empfohlen.*

disperse [verb] **1.** *(separate)* zerstreuen [tsɐ'ʃtrɔɡ̯ən] <zerstreut, zerstreute, hat zerstreut> ◊ *Das Militär zerstreute die Menge mit Warnschüssen.* sth disperses etw. zerstreut sich ◊ *Die Gruppe zerstreute sich.* **2.** *(spread)* verbreiten [fɐ'braɛ̯tn̩] <verbreitet, verbreitete, hat verbreitet> ◊ *Die Samen werden von Vögeln verbreitet.* sth disperses etw. verbreitet sich ◊ *Die Giftwolke verbreitete sich schnell über der ganzen Stadt.*

displace [verb] **1.** *(force to leave)* displace sb jdn vertreiben [fɐ'traɛ̯bm̩] <vertreibt, vertrieb, hat vertrieben> ◊ *Sie wurden aus ihrer Heimat vertrieben.* **2.** *(take the place of)* displace sth an die Stelle ... [gen] treten [an diː ʃtɛlə ... treːtn̩] <tritt, trat, ist getreten> ◊ *Staatliche Gelder sind an die Stelle privater Investitionen getreten.* **3.** *(air, water etc.)* verdrängen [fɐ'drɛŋən] <verdrängt, verdrängte, hat verdrängt>

displaced person [noun] Vertriebene [fɐ'triːbənə] der/die <-n, die Vertriebenen> *but: ein Vertriebener/eine Vertriebene*

display¹ [noun] **1.** *(in a shop window)* Auslage ['aʊ̯slaːɡə] die <-, -n> ◊ *sich* [dat] *die Auslagen in* den Schaufenstern ansehen; *(in a museum etc.)* Ausstellung ['aʊ̯sʃtɛlʊŋ] die <-, -en> put sth on display etw. ausstellen ['aʊ̯sʃtɛlən] +haben be on display ausgestellt werden ◊ *Ihre Arbeiten werden zurzeit im Foyer der Sparkasse ausgestellt.* **2.** *(show)* Vorführung ['foːɐ̯fyːrʊŋ] die <-, -en> firework display Feuerwerk ['fɔɡ̯ɐveˈk] das <-(e)s, -e> **3.** *(of feelings etc.)* Zurschaustellung [tsuːɐ̯'ʃaʊ̯ʃtɛlʊŋ] die <-, -en> ◊ *Sie hasste die Zurschaustellung von Gefühlen.* **4.** *(showing information)* Anzeige ['antsaɛ̯ɡə] die <-, -n> ◊ *Die Waage hat eine digitale Anzeige.*; *(screen)* Monitor ['moːnitoːɐ̯] der <-s, -en> ◊ *der Monitor eines Computers*

display² [verb] **1.** *(put sth on show)* ausstellen ['aʊ̯sʃtɛlən] +haben ◊ *Sie stellen im Schaufenster gerade Spielsachen aus.*; *(by hanging it up)* etw. aushängen ['aʊ̯shɛŋən] +haben ◊ *Sie hängte das Plakat am schwarzen Brett aus.* **2.** *(a feeling, talent, an attitude)* zeigen ['tsaɛ̯ɡn̩] +haben ◊ *Schon früh zeigte er sein Talent als Dichter.* **3.** *(on a screen)* anzeigen ['antsaɛ̯ɡn̩] +haben ◊ *Der Computer zeigte eine Fehlermeldung an.*

disposable [adj] **1.** *(products)* Einweg... ['aɛ̯nveˈk] disposable nappy/diaper Einwegwindel ['aɛ̯nveːkvɪndl̩] die <-, -n> **2.** *(income, funds)* verfügbar [fɛ'fyːkbaːˈ] no comp/superl ◊ *verfügbares Einkommen* ♦ *Die investierten Gelder sind nicht sofort verfügbar.*

disposal [noun] *(of waste, objects beyond use)* Entsorgung [ɛnt'zɔˈɡʊŋ] die <-, -en> ◊ *die Entsorgung abgelaufener Medikamente/von Atommüll; (of a person, body, evidence)* Beseitigung [bə'zaɛ̯tɪɡʊŋ] die <-> no pl ◊ *die Beseitigung der Leiche* ☞ **at sb's disposal** be at sb's disposal jdm zur Verfügung stehen put sth at sb's disposal jdm etw. zur Verfügung stellen

dispose of [verb] **1.** *(waste, objects beyond use)* entsorgen [ɛnt'zɔˈɡn̩] <entsorgt, entsorgte, hat entsorgt> ◊ *Müll/alte Zeitungen entsorgen; (a body, evidence, a problem)* beseitigen [bə'zaɛ̯tɪɡn̩] <beseitigt, beseitigte, hat beseitigt> ◊ *Das kleine Problem hatten wir schnell beseitigt.; (a witness)* verschwinden lassen [fɐ'ʃvɪndn̩ lasn̩] <lässt, ließ, hat lassen> **2.** *(in a competition)* schlagen ['ʃlaːɡn̩] <schlägt, schlug, hat geschlagen> ◊ *Die Nationalelf hat die italienische Mannschaft geschlagen.*

disposition [noun] **1.** *(character)* Wesen ['veːzn̩] das <-s, -> ◊ *Er ist für sein freundliches Wesen bekannt.* of a nervous disposition ängstlich ['ɛŋstlɪç] ◊ *Ich bin nicht ängstlich.* ♦ *Der Film ist für ängstliche Kinder völlig ungeeignet.* **2.** *(tendency)* disposition (towards sth) Neigung (zu etw.) ['naɛ̯ɡʊŋ] die <-, -en> ◊ *eine Neigung zur Kriminalität zeigen* have a disposition to do sth dazu neigen, etw. zu tun [daˈtsuː 'naɛ̯ɡn̩ ... tsuː] +haben ◊ *Er neigt dazu, unnötige Risiken einzugehen.*

disprove [verb] widerlegen [viːdɐ'leːɡn̩] <widerlegt, widerlegte, hat widerlegt> ◊ *eine Theorie widerlegen*

dispute¹ [noun] Auseinandersetzung [aʊ̯s|aˈnandɐzɛtsʊŋ] die <-, -en> ◊ *Es kam zu einer Auseinandersetzung mit dem Schiedsrichter.* dispute over sth Auseinandersetzung um etw. ◊ *eine Auseinandersetzung um die Höhe der Rechnung* be in dispute with sb eine Auseinandersetzung mit jdm haben ☞ **be beyond dispute** außer Frage stehen in dispute, open to dispute umstritten

dispute² [verb] **1.** *(deny)* bestreiten [bə'ʃtraɛtn̩]
<bestreitet, bestritt, hat bestritten> ◊ *Diese Tatsache
will ich auch gar nicht bestreiten.* **2.** *(question)*
anfechten ['anfɛçtn̩] <ficht an, focht an, hat angefoch-
ten> ◊ *Das Wahlergebnis wurde sofort von der Opposition angefochten.*

disputed → **dispute²** [adj] umstritten [ʊm'ʃtrɪtn̩] ◊
das umstrittene Gebiet ♦ *Diese These ist in der
Fachwelt heiß umstritten.*

disqualify [verb] ausschließen ['aɔsʃliːsn̩] <schließt
aus, schloss aus, hat ausgeschlossen> disqualify sb
from sth (for sth) jdn (wegen etw.) von etw.
auschließen ◊ *Der Athlet wurde wegen Dopings vom
Wettkampf ausgeschlossen.* disqualify sb from driving
jdm den Führerschein entziehen
[deːn 'fyːrəʃaɛn ɛnt͡siːən] <entzieht, entzog, hat
entzogen> ◊ *Mir wurde für ein Jahr der Führerschein
entzogen.* disqualify sb from voting jdm das
Wahlrecht entziehen

disrupt [verb] stören ['ʃtøːrən] +haben ◊ *Demonstranten versuchten, die Konferenz zu stören.*

disruption [noun] *(interruption)* disruption (to sth)
Störung (... [gen]) ['ʃtøːrʊn] die <–, –en> ◊ *eine
Störung des Programmablaufs/Zugverkehrs*; *(delay)*
disruption (to sb) Verzögerung (für jdn)
[fɛ'tsøːɡərʊn] die <–, –en> ◊ *Es kam zu stundenlan-
gen Verzögerungen für die Bahnreisenden.*

dissatisfied [adj] unzufrieden ['ʊntsufriːdn̩] ◊ *unzufriedene Kunden* ♦ *Sie ist sehr unzufrieden mit
ihrem Leben.*

dissolve [verb] *(melt, break up parliament, a
country)* auflösen ['aɔfløːzn̩] +haben ◊ *Sie löste den
Zucker/die Tablette in etwas Wasser auf.* ♦ *das
Parlament auflösen* sth dissolves etw. löst sich auf
◊ *Salz löst sich in Wasser auf.*; *(a marriage)* scheiden
['ʃaɛdn̩] <scheidet, schied, hat geschieden> ◊ *Die Ehe
wurde geschieden.* **2.** *(courage, hope)* sth dissolves
etw. schwindet ['ʃvɪndət] <schwand, ist geschwun-
den> *(lofty)* ◊ *Nach drei Tagen schwand ihre
Hoffnung, ihn lebend wiederzusehen.* **3.** dissolve into
laughter/tears in Gelächter/Tränen ausbrechen
[ɪn ɡə'lɛçtɐ/'trɛːnən aɔsbrɛçn̩] <bricht aus, brach aus,
ist ausgebrochen>

distance¹ [noun] **1.** *(large space between two people or
things)* Entfernung [ɛnt'fɛrnʊn] die <–, –en> ◊ *Er
hat das Ereignis aus sicherer Entfernung beobachtet.*
♦ *eine Entfernung von 100 Metern/Kilometern* live
some distance away in einiger Entfernung wohnen
be within walking distance zu Fuß zu erreichen
sein [tsuː 'fuːs tsuː ɛ,raɛçn̩ zaɛn]; *(small space, gap)*
Abstand ['apʃtant] der <–(e)s, Abstände> ◊ *Der
Abstand zwischen den Punkten beträgt zehn Zentimeter.* ♦ *Er folgte ihnen in einigem Abstand.* keep your
distance Abstand halten **2.** *(stretch you go or travel)*
Strecke ['ʃtrɛkə] die <–, –n> ◊ *Er ist es gewohnt,
weite Strecken zu fahren.* ♦ *die Strecke Heidelberg–
Karlsruhe* ♦ *Das Rennen geht über eine Strecke von
400 Metern.* **3.** *(far away space or point in time)*
Ferne ['fɛrnə] die <–> *no pl* ◊ *In der Ferne kann
man die Alpen sehen.* ♦ *jdn/etw. aus der Ferne sehen*
be still some distance away noch in weiter Ferne
liegen; *(in retrospect)* from a distance im Rückblick
[ɪm 'rʏkblɪk] **4.** *(emotional, social)* Distanz [dɪs'tants]
die <–, –en> ◊ *Sollten Lehrer zu ihren Schülern eine
gewisse Distanz wahren?* keep sb at a distance jdn
auf Distanz halten keep your distance Distanz

wahren

distance² [verb] distance yourself (from sb/sth) sich
(von jdm/etw.) distanzieren [dɪstan'tsiːrən] <distan-
ziert sich, distanzierte sich, hat sich distanziert> ◊ *Er
hat sich von den Aussagen seines Kollegen distanziert.*

distance learning [noun] Fernstudium ['fɛrnʃtuːdjʊm]
das <–s> *no pl* ◊ *ein Fernstudium absolvieren*

distant [adj] **1.** *(far in space, time)* fern [fɛrn] *only
before ns* ◊ *Sie reist gern in ferne Länder.* ♦ *in nicht
allzu ferner Zukunft*; *(away)* be two weeks/years
distant in zwei Wochen/Jahren sein
[ɪn tsvaɛ 'vɔxn̩/'jaːrən zaɛn] ◊ *Die Hochzeit ist in
zwei Wochen.* **2.** *(relative, similarity, memory)* entfernt
[ɛnt'fɛrnt] *only before ns* ◊ *ein entfernter Verwandter
von mir* ♦ *Du hast eine entfernte Ähnlichkeit mit
Brad Pitt.* **3.** *(not friendly)* distanziert [dɪstan'tsiːɐt]
<distanzierter, am distanziertesten> ◊ *Sie ist kalt und
distanziert.* ♦ *Sie haben ein sehr distanziertes Verhältnis zueinander.* **4.** *(distracted)* abwesend ['apveːzn̩t]
◊ *ein abwesender Blick* ♦ *Ihr Gesichtsausdruck war
abwesend.*

distantly [adv] **1.** *(far away)* in der Ferne
[ɪn deːɐ 'fɛrnə] ◊ *Ich hörte in der Ferne das Läuten
der Glocken.* **2.** *(smile, look)* abwesend ['apveːzn̩t] ◊
Sie lächelte abwesend und antwortete nicht.
3. *(remember, be related)* entfernt [ɛnt'fɛrnt] <entfern-
ter, am entferntesten> ◊ *Er konnte sich noch entfernt
daran erinnern.* ♦ *Ich bin entfernt mit ihm
verwandt.*

distinct [adj] **1.** *(different)* unterschiedlich ['ʊntɐʃiːtlɪç]
◊ *Sie wurden in drei unterschiedliche Gruppen eingeteilt.* ♦ *Die Methoden sind sehr unterschiedlich.* be
distinct from sth sich von etw. unterscheiden
[fɔn ... ʊntɐʃaɛdn̩] <unterscheidet sich, unterschied
sich, hat sich unterschieden> ◊ *Diese Region unterscheidet sich deutlich vom Rest des Landes.* as
distinct from sb/sth im Unterschied zu jdm/etw.
[ɪm 'ʊntɐʃiːt tsuː] ◊ *Im Unterschied zu anderen Her-
stellern bieten wir eine kostenlose Unterstützung.*
2. *(clear, obvious)* deutlich ['dɔɡtlɪç] ◊ *deutliche
Erfolge* ♦ *Der Unterschied war deutlich.* be distinct
against sth sich deutlich von etw. abheben

distinction [noun] **1.** *(making a difference)* Unterscheidung [ʊntɐʃaɛdʊn] die <–, –en> ◊ *die Unterscheidung zwischen Amateuren und Profis* without distinction of sth ohne Unterscheidung nach etw. ◊ *ohne
Unterscheidung nach Hautfarbe, Religion oder
Geschlecht* make a distinction unterscheiden
[ʊntɐʃaɛdn̩] <unterscheidet, unterschied, hat unter-
schieden> ◊ *Hier muss man unterscheiden.* ♦ *Man
unterscheidet zwischen drei Arten.* **2.** *(in an exam)*
Auszeichnung ['aɔstsaɛçnʊn] die <–, –en> get a distinction in sth etw. mit Auszeichnung bestehen ◊ *Sie
hat die Musikprüfung mit Auszeichnung bestanden.*
3. *(unusual feature, quality)* sb/sth has the distinction of being/doing sth jd/etw. zeichnet sich
dadurch aus, dass er/sie etw. ist/tut
[tsaɛçnət ... 'daːdʊrç aɔs das eːɐ/ɛs ... ɪst/tuːt]
<zeichnete sich aus, hat sich ausgezeichnet> ◊ *Sie
zeichnet sich dadurch aus, dass sie absolut zuverlässig ist.* people of (great) distinction ausgezeichnete
Leute

distinctive(ly) [adj, adv] unverwechselbar
[ʊnfɐ'vɛkslbaːɐ] *no comp/superl* ◊ *ein Whisky mit
unverwechselbarem Geschmack* ♦ *Das Logo dieser*

A B C D E F G H I J K L M N O P Q R S T U V W X Y Z

Firma ist unverwechselbar. a distinctively Italian style ein unverwechselbarer italienischer Stil a distinctively French elegance eine unverwechselbare französische Eleganz distinctive feature Eigenheit ['æŋɡhaɛt] die <–, –en>

distinctly (adv) 1. *(clearly, obviously)* deutlich ['dɔŋtlɪç] ◊ *Ich habe ihr das ganz deutlich gesagt.* ♦ *Kannst du bitte deutlicher sprechen?* 2. *(decidedly)* entschieden [ɛnt'ʃiːdn̩] no comp/superl ◊ *Mir war entschieden unbehaglich zumute.*

distinguish (verb) 1. *(differentiate)* unterscheiden [ʊntɐ'ʃaɛdn̩] <unterscheidet, unterschied, hat unterschieden> ◊ *Man unterscheidet mehrere Arten von Kopfschmerzen.* ♦ *Schon Dreijährige können zwischen Gut und Böse unterscheiden.* ♦ *Nichts unterscheidet ihn von den anderen Popstars.* 2. *(recognize)* ausmachen ['aosmaxn̩] +haben ◊ *Ihre Umrisse waren im Nebel kaum auszumachen.* 3. *(do well)* distinguish yourself by sth, be distinguished by sth sich durch etw. auszeichnen [dʊˈⁱ ... ˌaostsaeçnən] <zeichnet sich aus, zeichnete sich aus, hat sich ausgezeichnet> ◊ *Sie zeichnet sich durch ihre Professionalität aus.*

distinguished → distinguish (adj) 1. *(renowned)* (very) distinguished hoch angesehen [ˌhoːx 'anɡəzeːən] no comp/superl ◊ *ein hoch angesehener Maler* ♦ *Sie ist in der Modewelt hoch angesehen.; (brilliant)* beeindruckend [bə'|aɛndrʊkn̩t] ◊ *eine beeindruckende Laufbahn im diplomatischen Dienst* 2. *(elegant)* vornehm ['foː.ɡneːm] ◊ *ein vornehmer älterer Herr* ♦ *Sie ist sehr vornehm.*

distort (verb) 1. *(a voice, face, description, image etc.)* verzerren [fɐ'tsɛrən] <verzerrt, verzerrte, hat verzerrt> mostly in adjectival passive constructions ◊ *Warum verzerrst du das Gesicht so?* ♦ *Das Bild auf der Leinwand ist verzerrt.* 2. *(fig) (the truth, facts)* verdrehen [fɐ'dreːən] <verdreht, verdrehte, hat verdreht> ◊ *die Tatsachen verdrehen*

distortion (noun) 1. *(of the facts, truth)* Verdrehung [fɐ'dreːʊŋ] die <–, –en> ◊ *die Verdrehung der Fakten* 2. *(of sound, an image)* Verzerrung [fɐ'tsɛrʊŋ] die <–, –en> ◊ *eine Verzerrung der Perspektive*

distract (verb) ablenken ['aplɛŋkŋ̩] +haben ◊ *Der Krach hat mich abgelenkt.* ♦ *Durch die Kinder wird er von seinen Problemen abgelenkt.*

distracted(ly) (adj, adv) zerstreut [tsɐ'ʃtrɔøt] <zerstreuter, am zerstreutesten> ◊ *ein zerstreuter Professor* ♦ *Sie ist manchmal etwas zerstreut.* ♦ *Er beantwortete zerstreut meine Frage.*

distress¹ (noun) 1. *(grief)* Kummer ['kʊmɐ] der <–s> no pl ◊ *Ich möchte ihr keinen Kummer machen.; (worried)* in distress besorgt [bə'zɔʳkt] <besorgter, am besorgtesten> ◊ *die besorgte Mutter* ♦ *Er war offensichtlich besorgt.* ♦ *Besorgt rief sie mich an.* 2. *(great pain)* Qualen ['kvaːlən] die <–> pl be in distress Qualen leiden 3. *(difficult situation, poverty, great danger)* Not [noːt] die <–, Nöte> most sing ◊ *Kinder/ein Flugzeug in Not* ♦ *; (of a ship)* Seenot ['zeːnoːt] get into distress in Seenot geraten distress call Notruf ['noːtruːf] der <–(e)s, –e>

distress² (verb) *(make sb unhappy)* distress sb jdm Kummer bereiten ['kʊmɐ bəraɛtn̩] <bereitet, bereitete, hat bereitet> ◊ *Es bereitet ihr großen Kummer, ihre Tochter so unglücklich zu sehen.; (worry)* distress yourself sich (dat) Sorgen machen ['zɔʳɡn̩ maxn̩] +haben

distribute (verb) 1. *(give out, share, spread)* verteilen [fɛ'taɛlən] <verteilt, verteilte, hat verteilt> ◊ *Flugblätter verteilen* ♦ *eine Last gleichmäßig verteilen* ♦ *Wir verteilten Reis und Mehl an die Flüchtlinge.* 2. *(goods)* vertreiben [fɛ'traɛbm̩] <vertreibt, vertrieb, hat vertrieben> ◊ *Der Hersteller vertreibt seine Produkte über den Großhandel.*

distributed → distribute (adj) *(common)* verbreitet [fɛ'braɛtət] ◊ *Eichhörnchen sind hier weit verbreitet.* ♦ *eine in Europa verbreitete Art*

distribution (noun) 1. *(giving out, sharing, spreading sth among people)* Verteilung [fɛ'taɛlʊŋ] die <–, –en> ◊ *die Verteilung der Hilfsgüter* ♦ *eine ungleiche Verteilung von Vermögen* 2. *(spreading sth over an area)* Verbreitung [fɛ'braɛtʊŋ] die <–> no pl ◊ *die Verbreitung von Pollen durch Wind* 3. *(of goods)* Vertrieb [fɛ'triːp] der <–(e)s, –e>

distributor (noun) 1. *(of goods)* Vertreiber [fɛ'traɛbɐ] der <–s, –> 2. *(in a car engine)* Verteiler [fɛ'taɛlɐ] der <–s, –>

district (noun) 1. *(area)* Gegend ['geːɡn̩t] die <–, –en> ◊ *In dieser Gegend ist die Arbeitslosigkeit sehr hoch.; (of a town, city)* Viertel ['fɪʳtl̩] das <–s, –> ◊ *Er wohnt in einem vornehmen Viertel Münchens.* financial district Bankenviertel ['baŋkŋ̩fɪʳtl̩] 2. *(administrative area)* Bezirk [bə'tsɪʳk] der <–(e)s, –e> ◊ *eine Liste aller Schulen im Bezirk*

district court (noun) Amtsgericht ['amtsɡərɪçt] das <–(e)s, –e> most sing

disturb (verb) 1. *(interrupt, affect mentally)* stören ['ʃtøːrən] +haben ◊ *jdn bei der Arbeit stören* ♦ *Kein Windhauch störte die Ruhe am See.* ♦ *Viele Kinder in den Krisengebieten sind stark gestört.* 2. *(worry)* beunruhigen [bə'|ʊnruːɪɡn̩] <beunruhigt, beunruhigte, hat beunruhigt> often in adjectival passive constructions ◊ *Sein Verhalten beunruhigt mich sehr.* ♦ *Über diese Entwicklungen bin ich sehr beunruhigt.* 3. *(move)* bewegen [bə've:ɡn̩] <bewegt, bewegte, hat bewegt> ◊ *Ein Fisch bewegte die Wasseroberfläche.* 4. *(frighten)* aufschrecken ['aofʃrekn̩] +haben ◊ *Das Geräusch schreckte die Vögel auf.* ⊚ do not disturb bitte nicht stören

disturbance (noun) 1. *(social, political)* Unruhe ['ʊnruːə] die <–, –n> most pl ◊ *politische Unruhen* 2. *(disruption, interruption)* Störung ['ʃtøːrʊŋ] die <–, –en> ◊ *Der Chef wird bei jeder Störung gleich wütend.* behavio(u)ral disturbance Verhaltensstörung [fɛ'haltŋ̩sʃtøːrʊŋ]

ditch (noun) Graben ['ɡraːbm̩] der <–s, Gräben>

dive¹ (noun) 1. *(jump)* Sprung ['ʃprʊŋ] der <–(e)s, Sprünge> ◊ *ein Sprung vom Beckenrand; (head first)* Kopfsprung ['kɔpfʃprʊŋ]; *(with outstretched arms)* Hechtsprung ['hɛçtʃprʊŋ] make a dive for sth nach etw. hechten [naːx ... hɛçtn̩] <hechtet, hechtete, ist gehechtet> *(fam)* ◊ *Der Torwart hechtete nach dem Ball.* 2. *(of a plane)* Sturzflug ['ʃtʊʳtsfluːk] der <–(e)s, Sturzflüge> ◊ *Der Pilot setzte zum Sturzflug an.* 3. *(sudden fall in value)* take a dive absacken ['apzakn̩] +sein *(fam)* ◊ *Der Kurs der Aktie sackte um 30 Prozent ab.*

dive² (verb) 1. *(jump with your head first)* einen Kopfsprung machen [aɛnən 'kɔpfʃprʊŋ maxn̩] +haben ◊ *Sie machte einen Kopfsprung vom Zehnmeterbrett.; (jump with outstretched arms)* hechten ['hɛçtn̩] <hechtet, hechtete, ist gehechtet> *(fam)* ◊ *Er hechtete nach dem Ball.* 2. *(swim underwater)* tauchen ['taoxn̩]

+*haben*/with direction +*sein* ◊ *Im Urlaub geben wir gern tauchen.* ♦ *Er ist bis zum Grund des Beckens getaucht.* dive for sth nach etw. tauchen **3.** *(plane)* einen Sturzflug machen [aenən 'ʃtʊ'tsfluːk maxn̩] +*haben* **4.** *(lose value quickly)* einbrechen ['aenbrɛçn̩] <bricht ein, brach ein, ist eingebrochen> ◊ *Der Dollarkurs ist eingebrochen.*

diverse(ly) ⌐adj, adv¬ unterschiedlich ['ʊnteʃiːtlɪç] ◊ *Die Reaktionen auf die Ausstellung waren sehr unterschiedlich.* ♦ *unterschiedliche Meinungen/Ursachen* ♦ *Das kann man unterschiedlich interpretieren.* a diverse range of issues die unterschiedlichsten Themen

diversion ⌐noun¬ **1.** *(of sb's attention)* Ablenkungsmanöver ['aplɛŋkʊŋsmaˌnøːvɐ] das <-s, -> create a diversion ein Ablenkungsmanöver durchführen **2.** *(change of use or purpose)* Zweckentfremdung ['tsvɛkˌɛntfrɛmdʊŋ] die <-, -en> ◊ *die Zweckentfremdung der Gelder* **3.** *(entertainment)* Unterhaltung [ʊntɐ'haltʊŋ] die <-, -en> ◊ *Was wollen wir zur Unterhaltung der Gäste unternehmen?* **4.** *(in the UK: alternative route for traffic)* Umleitung ['ʊmlaetʊŋ] die <-, -en>

diversity ⌐noun¬ Vielfalt ['fiːlfalt] die <-> ◊ *kulturelle Vielfalt*

divert ⌐verb¬ **1.** *(make sb/sth move in a different direction)* umleiten ['ʊmlaetn̩] <leitet um, leitete um, hat umgeleitet> ◊ *den Verkehr/einen Bach umleiten* ♦ *Alle Anrufe werden automatisch zu ihrer Kollegin umgeleitet.* ♦ *Wenn Sie hier klicken, werden Sie auf unsere neue Website umgeleitet.* *(sb's attention)* ablenken ['aplɛŋkn̩] +*haben* ◊ *jds Aufmerksamkeit von etw. ablenken* **3.** *(use for a different purpose)* divert sb/sth from sth jdn/etw. von etw. abziehen [fɔn ... 'aptsiːən] <zieht ab, zog ab, hat abgezogen> ◊ *Das Personal wurde von anderen Arbeiten abgezogen, um auszuhelfen zu können.* divert sth to sth etw. für etw. verwenden [fyːɐ̯ ... fevɛndn̩] <verwendet, verwendete, hat verwendet> ◊ *Das Geld soll für den Bau neuer Kindergärten verwendet werden.*

divide ⌐verb¬ **1.** *(separate, make a calculation)* divide (up) teilen ['taelən] +*haben* ◊ *Teilen Sie den Teig in zwei Hälften.* divide sth by sth etw. durch etw. teilen ◊ *Neun geteilt durch drei ist drei.* sth divides (up) etw. teilt sich ◊ *Die Zelle teilt sich innerhalb von Minuten.; (share, spread)* divide sth (up) eine. aufteilen ['aʊftaelən] ◊ *Sie teilte die Klasse in drei Gruppen auf.* ♦ *Nach seinem Tod teilten seine Kinder das Vermögen unter sich auf.* **2.** *(be in between)* divide sth (from sth) etw. (von etw.) trennen ['trɛnən] +*haben* ◊ *Eine Mauer trennt den Schulhof vom Sportfeld.* **3.** *(cause disagreement)* spalten ['ʃpaltn̩] <spaltet, spaltete, hat gespaltet/gespalten> ◊ *Der Prozess hat das Land gespalten.* **4.** *(road)* sich gabeln ['gaːbl̩n] +*haben* ◊ *Wenn sich die Straße gabelt, halte dich rechts!*
◉ divide and rule teile und herrsche

dividend ⌐noun¬ **1.** FIN, ECON Dividende [diviˈdɛndə] die <-, -n> ◊ *eine Dividende auszahlen* **2.** *(in the UK: pools win)* Totogewinn ['toːtogəvɪn] der <-(e)s, -e>
◉ pay dividends sich auszahlen

divine ⌐adj¬ göttlich ['ɡœtlɪç] ◊ *göttliche Wesen* ♦ *Ihr Gesang ist einfach göttlich.*

diving board ⌐noun¬ Sprungbrett ['ʃprʊŋbrɛt] das <-(e)s, -er>

division ⌐noun¬ **1.** *(separation)* Teilung ['taelʊŋ] die <-, -en> ◊ *die Teilung des Landes* ♦ *die Teilung von Zellen; (sharing, spreading)* Aufteilung ['aʊftaelʊŋ] ◊ *die Aufteilung der Teilnehmer in Gruppen* division of sth between/among sb die Aufteilung von etw. unter jdm ◊ *die Aufteilung der Aufgaben unter den Mitgliedern* **2.** *(of an organization)* Abteilung [ap'taelʊŋ] die <-, -en>; *(in compound ns)* ... division ...abteilung [ap'taelʊŋ] sales division Verkaufsabteilung [fe'kaɔfs|aptaelʊŋ] **3.** MATH, MIL Division [divi'zjoːn] die <-, -en> Als Nächstes lernen wir die Division. armoured division Panzerdivision ['pantsedivi,zjoːn] **4.** SPORT Liga ['liːgaː] die <-, Ligen> ◊ *Der FC Bayern spielt in der höchsten Liga.* **5.** *(disagreement)* Uneinigkeit ['ʊn|aenɪçkaet] die <-, -en> ◊ *die Uneinigkeit in der Partei* **6.** *(gap)* Kluft [klʊft] die <-, Klüfte> ◊ *eine tiefe Kluft zwischen Arm und Reich*

divorce¹ ⌐noun¬ Scheidung ['ʃaedʊŋ] die <-, -en> ◊ *Ich habe bereits eine Scheidung hinter mir.* grounds for divorce Scheidungsgrund ['ʃaedʊŋsɡrʊnt] der <-(e)s, Scheidungsgründe> get a divorce sich scheiden lassen ['ʃaedn̩ lasn̩] <lässt sich, ließ sich, hat sich ... lassen> The marriage ended in divorce. Die Ehe wurde geschieden.

divorce² ⌐verb¬ **1.** *(end your marriage)* divorce, get divorced sich scheiden lassen ['ʃaedn̩ lasn̩] <lässt sich, ließ sich, hat sich ... lassen> ◊ *Ihre Eltern ließen sich scheiden, als sie zwölf Jahre alt war.* divorce sb sich von jdm scheiden lassen ◊ *Sie will sich von ihm scheiden lassen.* **2.** *(separate)* trennen ['trɛnən] +*haben* ◊ *Man kann eine nicht von dem anderen trennen.*

DIY store ⌐noun¬ Baumarkt ['baɔmaʳkt] der <-(e)s, Baumärkte>

do¹ ⌐noun¬ Feier ['faɛɐ̯] die <-, -n> have a bit of a do eine kleine Feier haben
◉ (the) do's and don'ts was man besser tun und lassen sollte

do² ⌐verb¬ **1.** *(as an auxiliary verb: in positive questions)* Do you like music? Magst du/Mögen Sie Musik? [ˌmaːkst duː/ˌmøːgn̩ ziː muˈziːk]; *(in negative sentences and questions)* I do not know him. Ich kenne ihn nicht. Don't you want to come? Möchtest du/Möchten Sie nicht kommen?; *(in question tags)* You are reading, don't you? Du liest gern, oder? [duː 'liːst ˌgɛʳn ˌoːdɐ̯] **2.** *(for emphasis)* Do come! Komm/Kommen Sie doch bitte! ['kɔm/'kɔmən ziː dɔx bɪtə] I do remember her! Und ob ich mich an sie erinnere! [ʊnt 'ɔp ɪç mɪç an ziː ɛ|ˌɪnərə] **3.** *(auxiliary verb replacing verb)* You sing better than I do. Du singst/Sie singen besser als ich. [duː zɪŋst/ziː zɪŋən 'bɛsɐ als ɪç] so do I ich auch [ɪç 'aɔx] ◊ *„Ich mag Pferde.“* — *„Ich auch.“* neither do I ich auch nicht [ɪç 'aɔx nɪçt] ◊ *Er mag keinen Käse und ich auch nicht.* "Do you often go to there?" — "Yes, I do. „Gehst du oft dorthin?“ — „Ja.“ [geːst duː 'ɔft dɔʳtˌhɪn — jaː] "Do you like snakes?" — "No, I don't". „Magst du Schlangen?“ — „Nein.“ [ˌmaːkst duː 'ʃlaŋən — naen] "May I come in?" — "Do!" „Darf ich hereinkommen?“ — „Ja, bitte!“ [daʳf ɪç heˈraenkɔmən — jaː 'bɪtə] "Who made this cake?" —"I did." „Wer hat diesen Kuchen gebacken?“ — „Ich.“

[veːɐ̯ hat diːzn̩ 'kuːxn̩ ɡəˌbakn̩ — ɪç] **4.** *(accomplish, perform, have an effect, work, take action)* tun [tuːn] <tut, tat, hat getan> ◊ *Das hättest du nicht tun sollen.* ♦ *Das habe ich für dich getan.* ♦ *Sie hat nichts zu tun.* ♦ *Steh hier nicht herum! Tu etwas!* ♦ *Er hat sein Bestes getan.* ♦ *Es gibt viel zu tun.* ♦ *Ich kann nicht zwei Dinge gleichzeitig tun.* **do something about sth** etwas gegen etw. tun **do sb good** jdm gut tun ◊ *Die frische Luft wird dir gut tun.; (harm sb)* do sth to sb jdm etw. antun ['antuːn] <tut an, tat an, hat angetan> ◊ *Merkst du nicht, was dieser ganze Stress deiner Familie antut?* **do sb/sth harm** jdm/etw. schaden ['ʃaːdn̩] <schadet, schadete, hat geschadet> ◊ *Die Ölkrise hat unserer Wirtschaft geschadet.; (a song etc.)* spielen ['ʃpiːlən] +haben ◊ *Bei dem Konzert haben sie auch ihren neuen Song gespielt.; (produce, make, keep yourself busy with, cook, manipulate, tidy, clean)* machen ['maxn̩] +haben ◊ *Ich mache zweimal in der Woche Yoga.* ♦ *Was machst du am Wochenende?* ♦ *Mach jetzt deine Hausaufgaben!* ♦ *Sie macht gern Kreuzworträtsel.* ♦ *Wie hast du das denn gemacht?* ♦ *Das lässt sich machen.* ♦ *sein Bett machen* ♦ *Heute Abend mache ich Nudeln.* **do sth to/with sth** etw. mit etw. machen ◊ *Was hast du mit der Fernbedienung gemacht?* **do the dishes** den Abwasch machen **do sth for a living** etw. beruflich machen **do damage** Schaden anrichten ['ʃaːdn̩ anrɪçtn̩] <richtet an, richtete an, hat angerichtet> **5. do your hair** sich frisieren [fri'ziːrən] <frisiert sich, frisierte sich, hat sich frisiert> ◊ *Ich muss mich noch frisieren, bevor wir ausgehen.* **6.** *(fare, get on)* **How are you doing?** Wie geht es dir? [vi: 'ɡeːt ɛs diːɐ̯] <ging, ist gegangen> **sb is doing well** jdm geht es gut ◊ *Meinem Opa geht es nicht gut.; (in an exam)* do well/badly gut/schlecht abschneiden ['ɡuːt/'ʃlɛçt ˌapʃnaedn̩] <schneidet ab, schnitt ab, hat abgeschnitten> ◊ *Sie hat in der Prüfung schlecht abgeschnitten.; (business)* gut/schlecht laufen ['ɡuːt/'ʃlɛçt ˌlaofn̩] <läuft, lief, ist gelaufen> ◊ *Die Firma läuft gut.* **7.** *(provide a service)* We don't do lunches. Wir haben keinen Mittagstisch. [viːɐ̯ haːbm̩ kaenən 'mɪtaˌkstɪʃ] They don't do bookings here. Sie nehmen hier keine Buchungen an. [ziː neːmən hiːɐ̯ kaenə 'buːxʊŋən ˌan] **8.** *(study)* studieren [ʃtu'diːrən] <studiert, studierte, hat studiert> ◊ *Sie hat vier Jahre Französisch studiert.; (learn about)* durchnehmen ['dʊrçneːmən] <nimmt durch, nahm durch, hat durchgenommen> ◊ *Wann nehmt ihr das große Einmaleins durch?* **9.** *(go at a certain speed, travel a certain distance)* fahren ['faːrən] <fährt, fuhr, ist gefahren> ◊ *Der Wagen fährt 200 Kilometer in der Stunde.* ♦ *Wir sind in drei Tagen fast 2000 Kilometer gefahren.* **10.** *(visit)* besuchen [bə'zuːxn̩] <besucht, besuchte, hat besucht> ◊ *Morgen wollen wir noch die Kathedrale besuchen.*
⊚ **That has nothing to do with you!** *(emph)* Das geht Sie/dich gar nichts an! **have sth/nothing to do with sth/sb** etwas/nichts mit jdm/etw. zu tun haben **sth will do (sb)** etw. reicht (jdm) ◊ *Du brauchst nichts zu kochen; mir reicht ein Butterbrot.* ♦ *Ein Pappkarton reicht als Tisch.*
• **do away with** phras v **1.** *(get rid of)* do away with sth etw. abschaffen ['apʃafn̩] +haben ◊ *Überflüssige Vorschriften sollten abgeschafft werden.* **2.** *(murder)* do away with sb jdn beseitigen [bə'zaetɪɡn̩] <beseitigt, beseitigte, hat beseitigt> *(euph)*

◊ *Der Zeuge wurde von der Mafia beseitigt.*
• **do for** phras v **1.** *(be a failure)* be done for erledigt sein [e'leːdɪçt zaen] +sein *(fam)* ◊ *Ohne einen neuen Auftrag ist die Firma erledigt.* **2.** *(charged and sentenced)* do sb for sth jdn für etw. verknacken [fy:ɐ̯ ... fe'knakn̩] <verknackt, verknackte, hat verknackt> *(slang)* ◊ *Er wurde für Betrug verknackt.*
• **do in** phras v **1.** *(kill)* um die Ecke bringen [ʊm diː 'ɛkə brɪŋən] <bringt, brachte, hat gebracht> *(fam)* ◊ *Er soll den Verräter um die Ecke gebracht haben.* **2.** *(exhaust)* fertig machen ['fɛrtɪç maxn̩] +haben *(fam)* ◊ *Die gestrige Bergtour hat mich total fertig gemacht.* be done in fertig sein
• **do up** phras v **1.** *(a building, vehicle etc.)* herrichten ['heːɐ̯rɪçtn̩] <richtet her, richtete her, hat hergerichtet> ◊ *Er hat das alte Fahrrad für sie hergerichtet.* **2.** *(fam)* *(a zip, shoelaces etc.)* zumachen ['tsuːmaxn̩] +haben ◊ *Mach mal deine Jacke zu!* **3.** *(wrap sth)* einwickeln ['aenvɪkl̩n] <wickelt ein, wickelte ein, hat eingewickelt> ◊ *Könnten Sie das in Geschenkpapier einwickeln?* **4.** *(make yourself look pretty)* sich zurechtmachen [tsu'rɛçtmaxn̩] +haben ◊ *Machst du dich noch für die Party zurecht?*
• **do without** phras v do without (sth) ohne (etw.) auskommen [oːnə ... ˌaoskɔmən] <kommt aus, kam aus, ist ausgekommen> ◊ *Ich werde schon ohne seine Hilfe auskommen.*

dock¹ noun **1.** *(for loading, embarkation)* Kai [kae] der <-s, -s>; *(for repairs)* Dock [dɔk] das <-s, -s> **docks** Hafen ['haːfn̩] der <-s, Häfen> **2.** LAW the dock die Anklagebank [diː 'anklaɡəbaŋk] <-, Anklagebänke> most sing ◊ *auf der Anklagebank sitzen*
dock² verb **1.** *(ship)* anlegen ['anleːɡn̩] +haben ◊ *Das Schiff legt morgen im Hafen von Genua an.; (spacecraft)* andocken ['andɔkn̩] +haben ◊ *Die Discovery dockte an die Raumstation an.* **2.** *(sb's pay)* kürzen ['kʏrtsn̩] +haben ◊ *Ihm wurde der Lohn gekürzt, weil er mehrmals zu spät gekommen war.*
doctor¹ noun **1.** *(physician)* Arzt [aʁtst] der <-es, Ärzte> ⊘Ärztin ['ɛɐ̯tstɪn] die <-, -nen> ◊ *Sie ist Ärztin.* ♦ *Du musst einen Arzt holen!* see a doctor zum Arzt gehen ◊ *Du solltest mal zum Arzt gehen, wenn der Husten nicht weggeht.* **2.** *(title)* Doktor ['dɔktoːɐ̯] der <-s, -en> ◊ *Ich habe einen Termin bei Frau Doktor Meier.* ♦ *Er ist Doktor der Theologie.*
⊚ **just what the doctor ordered** genau das Richtige
doctor² verb **1.** *(fiddle)* frisieren [fri'ziːrən] <frisiert, frisierte, hat frisiert> *(fam)* ◊ *Die Statistiken waren frisiert.* **2.** *(lace)* doctor sth with sth einer Sache dat etw. beimischen ['baemɪʃn̩] +haben ◊ *Dem Tierfutter werden Hormone beigemischt.*
doctorate noun Doktortitel ['dɔktoːɐ̯tiːtl̩] der <-s, –>
doctrine noun Lehre ['leːrə] die <-, -n>
document¹ noun *(paper, computer file)* Dokument [doku'mɛnt] das <-(e)s, -e> ◊ *Dokumente des Geheimdienstes* ♦ *ein Dokument speichern/löschen*
document² verb **1.** *(record)* dokumentieren [dokumɛn'tiːrən] <dokumentiert, dokumentierte, hat dokumentiert> ◊ *Der Bericht dokumentiert die Klimaveränderung in den letzten hundert Jahren.* **2.** *(support with evidence)* belegen [bə'leːɡn̩] <belegt, belegte, hat belegt> ◊ *Sämtliche Behauptungen*

wurden ausführlich belegt.

documentation [noun] **1.** *(documents)* Unterlagen ['ʊntela:gị] die <–> pl ◊ *Die Versicherung wollte alle Unterlagen im Original haben.* **2.** IT *(instructions)* Dokumentation [dokumɛntaˈtsjo:n] die <–, –en>

dodgy [adj] **1.** *(dubious)* zwielichtig ['ʦviːlɪçtɪç] ◊ *ein zwielichtiger Geschäftsmann* ♦ *Das kommt mir sehr zwielichtig vor.* get involved in something dodgy sich auf zwielichtige Machenschaften einlassen; *(not reliable)* unzuverlässig ['ʊntsufɛlɛsɪç] ◊ *ein unzuverlässiger Handwerker* ♦ *Der Klempner war unzuverlässig.* **2.** *(not working properly)* mit Macken [mɪt 'makị] *(fam)* ◊ *ein Fernseher mit Macken* be dodgy Macken haben ['makị ha:bm̩] *(fam)* ◊ *Der CD-Spieler hat Macken.; (heart)* schwach [ʃvax] <schwächer, am schwächsten> ◊ *ein schwaches Herz; (knee)* kaputt [ka'pʊt] <kaputter, am kaputtesten> seldom comp/superl *(fam)* ◊ *ein kaputtes Knie* **3.** *(not safe)* unsicher ['ʊnzɪçɐ] ◊ *die unsichere Lage auf dem Arbeitsmarkt* ♦ *Seine Position ist ziemlich unsicher.* **4.** *(bad)* mies [miːs] <mieser, am miesesten> *(fam)* ◊ *ein mieser Haarschnitt* ♦ *Der Witz war ziemlich mies.*

dog [noun] **1.** *(hound)* Hund [hʊnt] der <–(e)s, –e> ◊ *Draußen bellte ein Hund.* **2.** *(male canine)* Rüde ['ry:də] der <–n, –n>
  ☞ dog eat dog knallhart be going to the dogs vor die Hunde gehen ◊ *Dieses Land geht langsam vor die Hunde.* the dogs das Hunderennen

doing
  ☞ be sb's doing jds Schuld sein ◊ *Es ist alles deine Schuld!* take some doing nicht einfach sein

dole [noun] Arbeitslosengeld ['aˈbaetsloːzŋɡelt] das <–(e)s> no pl ◊ *Sie hat Arbeitslosengeld beantragt.* be on the dole arbeitslos sein ['aˈbaetsloːs zaen] +sein

doll [noun] Puppe ['pʊpə] die <–, –n>

dollar [noun] Dollar ['dɔlaˈ] der <–(s), –s> pl *'Dollar'* when used with expressions of quantity ◊ *Der Dollar steht zurzeit sehr schlecht.* ♦ *Das hat 50 Dollar gekostet.*

dolphin [noun] Delphin [dɛl'fiːn] der <–s, –e>

domain [noun] Bereich [bə'raeç] der <–(e)s, –e> ◊ *der Bereich der Politik* security domain Sicherheitsbereich ['zɪçɐhaetsbəraeç]; *(dominated by a particular person/group, IT)* Domäne [do'mɛːnə] die <–, –n> ◊ *Der Garten ist Peters Domäne.* ♦ *die Domäne des Sports* male domain Männerdomäne ['mɛnedo,mɛːnə]

dome [noun] Kuppel ['kʊpl̩] die <–, –n> ◊ *die riesige Kuppel der Kathedrale*

domestic [adj] **1.** *(family)* häuslich ['hɔøslɪç] ◊ *eine häusliche Szene* ♦ *Sie ist nicht sehr häuslich.* domestic chores Hausarbeit ['haos|aˈbaet] die <–> no pl domestic life Familienleben [fa'miːljənleːbm̩] das <–s, –> **2.** *(not foreign)* heimisch ['haemɪʃ] no comp/superl ◊ *der heimische Markt* ♦ *die heimische Wirtschaft* domestic politics Innenpolitik ['ɪnənpoli,tiːk] die <–> no pl domestic flight Inlandsflug ['ɪnlantsfluːk] der <–s, Inlandsflüge> **3.** *(animal)* Haus... [haos] domestic cat Hauskatze ['haoskatsə] die <–, –n>

dominance [noun] Vorherrschaft ['foːɐhɛrʃaft] die <–, –en> ◊ *die Vorherrschaft der Partei im Norden des Landes*

dominant [adj] *(subject, colo(u)r)* vorherrschend

['foːɐhɛrʃn̩t] no comp/superl, mostly before ns ◊ *Die vorherrschende Farbe in ihren Gemälden ist Rot.; (person, animal, gene)* dominant [domi'nant] <dominanter, am dominantesten> seldom comp/superl ◊ *die dominante Wölfin des Rudels* ♦ *Er ist sehr dominant.* dominant position Vormachtstellung ['foːɐmaxtʃtɛlʊŋ] die <–, –en>

dominate [verb] *(control)* dominieren [domi'niːrən] <dominiert, dominierte, hat dominiert> ◊ *Er wird von seiner Mutter dominiert.* ♦ *Das neue Hochhaus dominiert die Innenstadt.*

domination [noun] Vorherrschaft ['foːɐhɛrʃaft] die <–> no pl ◊ *die türkische Vorherrschaft im östlichen Mittelmeer* domination of sb/sth Vorherrschaft ... [gen] ◊ *die Vorherrschaft der CSU in Bayern*

donate [verb] spenden ['ʃpɛndn̩] <spendet, spendete, hat gespendet> ◊ *Knochenmark spenden* ♦ *Sie hat großzügig gespendet.* ♦ *Wer hat der Partei das Geld gespendet?* donate your time to sth seine Zeit für etw. zur Verfügung stellen [zaenə ,ʦaet fyːɐ ... ʦuːɐ fe'fyːɡʊŋ ʃtɛlən] +haben

donation [noun] Spende ['ʃpɛndə] die <–, –n> ◊ *eine Spende zugunsten Not leidender Kinder*

done[1] → **do**[2] [adj] **1.** *(finished)* done (with sth) fertig (mit etw.) ['fɛˈtɪç] no comp/superl ◊ *Ich bin fast fertig.* ♦ *Bist du mit dem Buch fertig?; (job)* erledigt [ɛ'leːdɪçt] no comp/superl ◊ *So, der erste Teil ist erledigt.* ♦ *erledigte Aufgaben* **2.** *(cooked)* gar [gaːˈ] no comp/superl, not before ns ◊ *Das Gemüse ist noch nicht gar.* **3.** *(exhausted)* fertig ['fɛˈtɪç] *(fam)* ◊ *Nach der Bergtour war ich fertig!*
  ☞ be the done thing üblich sein it is not done to do sth es gehört sich nicht, etw. zu tun

done[2] → **do**[2] [interj] abgemacht ['apɡəmaxt]

donor [noun] Spender ['ʃpɛndɐ] der <–s, –> ♀Spenderin ['ʃpɛndərɪn] die <–, –nen> ◊ *Ein anonymer Spender hat eine Million Euro überwiesen.* blood donor Blutspender ['bluːtʃpɛndɐ] Blutspenderin ['bluːtʃpɛndərɪn] donor kidney Spenderniere ['ʃpɛndeniːrə] die <–, –n>

don't → **do**[2]

donut → **doughnut**

door [noun] **1.** *(of a house, room, vehicle)* Tür [tyːɐ] die <–, –en> ◊ *Mach bitte die Tür zu.* knock on the door an die Tür klopfen answer the door die Tür öffnen front door Haustür ['haostyːɐ] **2.** *(of a barn, garage)* Tor [toːɐ] das <–s, –e> ◊ *Das Tor der Garage schließt sich automatisch.*
  ☞ deliver to your door nach Hause liefern open the door to sth einer Sache [dat] Tür und Tor öffnen shut the door on sth einer Sache ein Ende setzen

doorstep [noun] Schwelle ['ʃvɛlə] die <–, –n>
  ☞ on your doorstep gleich vor der Haustür

doorway [noun] *(of a room)* Tür [tyːɐ] die <–, –en> ◊ *Er stand wartend in der Tür.; (of a building, shop)* Eingang ['aengaŋ] der <–(e)s, Eingänge> ◊ *Wo ist denn der Eingang zu dem Geschäft?*

dormitory [noun] Zimmer ['ʦɪme] das <–s, –> ◊ *Meistens teilen sich vier bis sechs Soldaten ein Zimmer.*

dose [noun] Dosis ['doːzɪs] die <–, Dosen> ◊ *eine hohe/niedrige Dosis*

dot [noun] *(small round point)* Punkt [pʊŋkt] der <–(e)s, –e> ◊ *der Punkt auf dem j* ♦ *ein roter Stoff mit schwarzen Punkten* ♦ *Die Adresse lautet: www*

A B C D E F G H I J K L M N O P Q R S T U V W X Y Z

Punkt google Punkt de.

double¹ [noun] **1.** *(twice as much)* double das Doppelte [das 'dɔpltə] <–n> *no pl* ◊ *Sie verdient jetzt das Doppelte.* **2.** *(person)* Doppelgänger ['dɔplgɛŋɛ] der <–s, –> ♀Doppelgängerin ['dɔplgɛŋɛrɪn] die <–, –nen> ◊ *einen Doppelgänger haben; (actor)* Double ['duːbl] das <–s, –s> **3.** *(room)* Doppelzimmer ['dɔpltsɪmɐ] das <–s, –> ◊ *ein Doppelzimmer reservieren* **4.** *(bed)* Doppelbett ['dɔplbɛt] das <–(e)s, –en> ◊ *ein Zimmer mit Doppelbett* **5.** SPORT doubles Doppel ['dɔpl] das <–s, –> ◊ *Spielen wir ein Doppel?*

double² [adj, adv] *(twice the amount, twofold)* doppelt ['dɔplt] ◊ *doppelt seben* ✦ *eine doppelte Portion Eis* [adj] *(expressing that two elements are involved)* Doppel... ['dɔpl] double name Doppelname ['dɔplnaːmə] der <–ns, –n> double wedding Doppelhochzeit ['dɔplhɔxtsaet] die <–, –en>

double³ [verb] double sth etw. verdoppeln [fɛ'dɔpln] <verdoppelt, verdoppelte, hat verdoppelt> ◊ *den Einsatz verdoppeln* sth doubles etw. verdoppelt sich ◊ *Die Miete hat sich verdoppelt.*

double bed [noun] Doppelbett ['dɔplbɛt] das <–(e)s, –en> ◊ *im Doppelbett schlafen*

doubly [adv] doppelt ['dɔplt] ◊ *Hier musst du doppelt aufpassen.*

doubt¹ [noun] Zweifel ['tsvaefl] der <–s, –> ◊ *ernsthafte/erhebliche Zweifel haben* ✦ *Ihm kamen Zweifel an der Echtheit des Gemäldes.* beyond any doubt ohne jeden Zweifel no doubt zweifellos; *(worry)* doubts Bedenken [bə'dɛŋkn] die <–> *only pl* ◊ *Hast du keine Bedenken, ihn allein fortzulassen?* ☻ be in doubt (sich) nicht sicher sein ◊ *Sie ist sich nicht sicher, ob sie fahren soll oder nicht.* ✦ *Es ist nicht sicher, ob er bleibt.* when in doubt im Zweifelsfall

doubt² [verb] bezweifeln [bə'tsvaefln] <bezweifelt, bezweifelte, hat bezweifelt> ◊ *Ich bezweifle, dass er die Wahrheit gesagt hat.* doubt sb/sth an jdm./etw. [dat] zweifeln [an ... 'tsvaefln] +haben ◊ *Zweifelst du immer noch an mir?*

doubtful [adj] **1.** *(unlikely to happen or be true)* zweifelhaft ['tsvaeflhaft] <zweifelhafter, am zweifelhaftesten> ◊ *Es ist zweifelhaft, ob er es schafft.* ✦ *eine Fluggesellschaft von zweifelhaftem Ruf* **2.** *(not sure)* unsicher ['ʊnziçɐ] ◊ *Er ist noch ziemlich unsicher.* ✦ *Es ist unsicher, ob wir einen Kredit bekommen.* ☻ be doubtful about sth an etw. [dat] zweifeln be doubtful about doing sth Bedenken haben, etw. [acc] zu tun be doubtful of sth einer Sache [dat] nicht trauen

doubtless [adv] zweifellos ['tsvaefllloːs] *no comp/superl* ◊ *Du hast zweifellos Recht.*

dough [noun] *(for bread, pastry etc.)* Teig [taek] der <–(e)s, –e> ◊ *die Zutaten zu einem Teig verrühren*

doughnut, donut [noun] ☻Berliner [bɛr'liːnɐ] der <–s, –>

down¹ [noun] **1.** *(feathers)* Daunen ['daonən] die <–> *pl* ◊ *eine mit Daunen gefüllte Decke* **2.** *(hair)* Flaum [flaom] der <–(e)s> *no pl* ◊ *Er hat den ersten Flaum auf dem Kinn.*

down² [adj] **1.** *(person)* niedergeschlagen ['niːdɐgəʃlaːgn] ◊ *einen niedergeschlagenen Eindruck machen* ✦ *Warum bist du denn so niedergeschlagen?* **2.** *(computer)* abgestürzt ['apgəʃtʏrtst] ◊ *Der PC ist abgestürzt.* ✦ *einen abgestürzten Computer neu starten*

down³ [adv] **1.** *(with certain verbs, expressing downward movement: away from the speaker)* hinunter... [hɪ'nʊntɐ] go down hinuntergehen [hɪ'nʊntɐgeːən] <geht hinunter, ging hinunter, ist hinuntergegangen> ◊ *Ich gehe mal kurz zu den Nachbarn hinunter.; (towards the speaker)* herunter... [hɛ'rʊntɐ] come down herunterkommen [hɛ'rʊntɐkɔmən] <kommt herunter, kam herunter, ist heruntergekommen> ◊ *Komm herunter zu uns!* **2.** *(expressing a static position)* unten ['ʊntn] ◊ *Sie wartet unten auf der Straße auf dich.* ✦ *unten im Süden* **3.** *(with certain verbs: onto the floor, ground, table)* hin... [hɪn] put down hinstellen ['hɪnʃtɛlən] +haben ◊ *Sie können die Koffer dort hinstellen.* **4.** *(decreased)* be down (on ...) niedriger (als ...) liegen ['niːdrɪgɐ liːgn] <liegt, lag, hat gelegen> ◊ *Die Zinsen liegen um 1,2 Prozent niedriger als im Vorjahr.* go down sinken ['zɪŋkn] <sinkt, sank, ist gesunken> ◊ *Die Aktienwerte sind gesunken.* ☻ down under in Australien put/have sb down for sth jdn für etw. eintragen/eingetragen haben ◊ *Du kannst mich für das nächste Spiel eintragen.* ✦ *Ich habe dich für den Schwimmkurs eingetragen.* sth is down to sb *(sb's due)* etw. ist jds Aufgabe ◊ *Die Organisation ist deine Aufgabe.* **2.** *(because of sb)* jd ist für etw. verantwortlich ◊ *Wer ist für diese Situation verantwortlich?* sth is down to sth *(because of sth)* etw. liegt an etw. [dat] down with **1.** *(with sb/sth unpleasant)* down with sb/sth nieder mit jdm./etw. ◊ *Nieder mit dem Rassismus!* **2.** *(with a piece of clothing)* runter mit etw. ◊ *Runter mit den Klamotten!*

'Down' often occurs in phrasal verbs like 'get down' or 'put down' which have their own entries in the dictionary.

down⁴ [prep] **1.** *(expressing downward movement away from the speaker)* hinunter [hɪ'nʊntɐ] *postpositive* ◊ *die Treppe in den Keller hinunter; (with certain verbs)* hinunter... [hɪ'nʊntɐ] climb down sth etw. hinunterklettern [hɪ'nʊntɐklɛtɐn] +sein ◊ *Er kletterte vor mir den Baum hinunter.* go down sth etw. hinuntergehen [hɪ'nʊntɐgeːən] <geht hinunter, ging hinunter, ist hinuntergegangen> ◊ *Wenn du die Treppe hinuntergehst, kommst du in den Weinkeller.* **2.** *(expressing downward movement towards the speaker)* herunter [hɛ'rʊntɐ] *postpositive; (with certain verbs)* herunter... [hɛ'rʊntɐ] climb down sth etw. herunterklettern [hɛ'rʊntɐklɛtɐn] +sein ◊ *Er kletterte so schnell wie möglich die Rampe herunter.* fall down sth etw. herunterfallen [hɛ'rʊntɐfalən] <fällt herunter, fiel herunter, ist heruntergefallen> ◊ *Pass auf, dass du nicht die Leiter herunterfällst!* **3.** *(following a particular route away from a starting point)* hinunter [hɪ'nʊntɐ] *mostly postpositive* [acc] ◊ *Der Bahnhof ist ein Stück die Straße hinunter.* ✦ *eine Fahrt den Rhein hinunter* He lives just down the road. Er wohnt hier gleich um die Ecke.; *(with certain verbs)* entlang... [ɛnt'laŋ]; *(walk along a path, street)* go down sth etw. entlanggehen [ɛnt'laŋgeːən] <geht entlang, ging entlang, ist entlanggegangen> ◊ *Ich ging den Weg entlang, bis ich zur Kreuzung kam.*

downhill [adv] bergab [bɛrk'|ap] *no comp/superl* ◊ *Der Weg führt bergab.*

◉ **sb is going downhill** es geht bergab mit jdm

download [verb] herunterladen [hɛˈrʊntɛlaːdn̩] <lädt herunter, lud herunter, hat heruntergeladen> ◊ *Software aus dem Internet herunterladen*

downright [adj] *(failure)* glatt [glat] *no comp/superl, only before ns (fam)* ◊ *Das ist eine glatte Lüge!*

downstairs¹ [adj] im Erdgeschoss [ɪm ˈeːɐ̯tgǝʃɔs] *postpositive* ◊ *die Bar im Erdgeschoss* downstairs flat Parterrewohnung [paˈtɛravoːnʊŋ] die <-, -en>

downstairs² [adv] **1.** *(expressing movement)* nach unten [naːx ˈʊntn̩] go downstairs nach unten gehen ◊ *Geh jetzt bitte nach unten!* come downstairs nach unten kommen ◊ *Kommt nach unten! Das Essen ist fertig.* **2.** *(static location)* unten [ˈʊntn̩] ◊ *Unsere Büros befinden sich unten.*

downtown [noun] Innenstadt [ˈɪnǝnʃtat] die <-, Innenstädte> ◊ *die Fußgängerzone in der Leipziger Innenstadt*

downward [adj] Abwärts... [ˈapvɛˈts] downward trend Abwärtstrend [ˈapvɛˈtstrɛnt] der <-s, -s> downward slope Gefälle [gǝˈfɛlǝ] das <-s, ->

downwards [adv] nach unten [naːx ˈʊntn̩] ◊ *Die Kalkulation muss nach unten korrigiert werden.*

dozen [noun] Dutzend [ˈdʊtsn̩t] das <-s, – or –e> ◊ *Ich kenne ein paar Dutzend solcher Fälle.* dozens Dutzende ◊ *Dutzende von Neugierigen sahen zu.* half a dozen ein halbes Dutzend

Dr Dr. [ˈdɔktoːɐ̯] ◊ *Frau Dr. Müller*

draft¹ [noun] **1.** *(of a plan, letter etc.)* Entwurf [ɛntˈvʊˈf] der <-(e)s, Entwürfe> ◊ *ein Entwurf für eine Rede* **2.** FIN Wechsel [ˈvɛksl̩] der <-s, –> ◊ *jdm einen Wechsel ausstellen* **3.** MIL *(in the US)* Einberufung [ˈaɛnbaruːfʊŋ] die <-, -en> ◊ *die Einberufung zum Militärdienst* **4.** *(current of air)* Luftzug [ˈlʊftsuːk] der <-(e)s, Luftzüge> *most sing*

draft² [verb] **1.** *(a plan, letter etc.)* entwerfen [ɛntˈvɛˈfn̩] <entwirft, entwarf, hat entworfen> ◊ *ein Konzept entwerfen* **2.** MIL *(in the US)* einberufen [ˈaɛnbaruːfn̩] <beruft ein, berief ein, hat einberufen> ◊ *Er hofft, dass er jetzt nicht einberufen wird.*

drag [verb] **1.** *(take along an unwilling person, pull sth along so that it touches the ground)* drag sb/sth schleifen [ˈʃlaɛfn̩] +haben ◊ *Gestern hat sie mich in die Oper geschleift!* ♦ *Sie schleifte ihre schwere Tasche hinter sich her.* ♦ *Das Kleid schleifte über den Boden.* **2.** *(carry a heavy person or object)* schleppen [ˈʃlɛpn̩] +haben ◊ *einen schweren Koffer schleppen* drag yourself somewhere sich irgendwohin schleppen ◊ *Das angeschossene Reh schleppte sich noch einige Meter weit.* **3.** *(pull with force)* ziehen [ˈtsiːǝn] <zieht, zog, hat gezogen> ◊ *Die Strömung zog ihn aufs offene Meer.* ♦ *Er packte sie unsanft am Arm und zog sie hinter sich her.*

◉ **drag sth out of sb** jdm etw. aus der Nase ziehen ◊ *Er erzählt nie etwas von selbst, alles muss man ihm aus der Nase ziehen!*

• **drag along** [phras v] **1.** *(take along an unwilling or unwelcome person)* drag sb along mitschleppen [ˈmɪtʃlɛpm̩] +haben (pej) ◊ *Musst du die Kinder denn überallhin mitschleppen?* **2.** *(pull an object, a lifeless person or animal)* drag sth/sb along etw./jdn hinter sich herschleifen [hɪntɐ ... ˈheːɐ̯ʃlaɛfn̩] +haben ◊ *Er schleift einen Sack hinter sich her.* sth drags along somewhere etw. schleift irgendwo ◊ *Das Kabel schleifte über den Boden.*

• **drag into** [phras v] **1.** *(talk about sb/sth)* drag sb/

sth into it von jdm/etw. anfangen [fɔn ... ˈanfaŋǝn] <fängt an, fing an, hat angefangen> ◊ *Wieso fängst du jetzt plötzlich von deiner Schwester an?* **2.** *(involve sb against their will)* drag sb into sth jd in etw. [acc] hineinziehen [hɪˈnaɛntsiːǝn] <zieht hinein, zog hinein, hat hineingezogen> ◊ *Zieh mich nicht in deine Affären hinein!*

• **drag out** [phras v] drag sth out *(make sth take a long time)* etw. hinauszögern [hɪˈnaʊstsøːɐ̯n] <zieht hinaus, zog hinaus, hat hinausgezogen> ◊ *Der Chef zog die Besprechung über Stunden hinaus.*

drain¹ [noun] **1.** *(for waste water)* Abflussrohr [ˈapflʊsroːɐ̯] das <-(e)s, -e> ◊ *Das Abflussrohr war verstopft.* **2.** *(sewers)* the drains die Kanalisation [di: kanalizaˈtsjoːn] <-> sing ◊ *Regenwasser gelangt in die Kanalisation.* **3.** *(sth that uses up a lot of resources)* Belastung [bǝˈlastʊŋ] die <-, –en> ◊ *eine finanzielle Belastung* be a big drain on sb eine große Belastung für jdn sein be a big drain on sb's time jds Zeit stark beanspruchen [ˌtsaɛt ʃtaʳk bǝˈanʃprʊxn̩] <beansprucht, beanspruchte, hat beansprucht> **4.** *(loss)* drain of Abwanderung von/... [gen] [ˈapvandǝrʊŋ fɔn] die <-, -en> ◊ *die Abwanderung von Firmen ins Ausland* ♦ *die Abwanderung junger Wissenschaftler* **5.** MED Drainage [drɛˈnaːʒǝ] die <-, -n> place a drain eine Drainage anlegen

◉ **sth goes down the drain 1.** *(be in vain)* etw. ist vergebens ◊ *Die ganze Mühe war vergebens.* *(money)* etw. ist futsch (fam) ◊ *Diese Investition ist futsch!* **2.** *(disappear into the drain)* im Abfluss verschwinden

drain² [verb] **1.** *(liquid, slowly)* sth drains etw. läuft ab [lɔɔft ˈap] <läuft ab, lief ab, ist abgelaufen> ◊ *Das Wasser im Becken läuft schlecht ab.* drain sth etw. ablaufen lassen [ˈaplaɔfn̩ lasn̩] <lässt, ließ, hat lassen> **2.** *(quickly and in large quantities)* sth drains etw. fließt ab [fliːst ˈap] <fließt ab, floss ab, ist abgeflossen> ◊ *Das Wasser im Swimmingpool fließt schnell ab.* drain sth etw. abfließen lassen [ˈapfliːsn̩ lasn̩] <lässt, ließ, hat lassen> **3.** *(a lake, pond)* drain sth ablassen [ˈaplasn̩] <lässt ab, ließ ab, hat abgelassen> ◊ *einen See ablassen; (land)* etw. entwässern [ɛntˈvɛsɐn] <entwässert, entwässerte, hat entwässert> ◊ *Das Sumpfgebiet ist entwässert worden.* **4.** *(fat, pasta, vegetables)* drain sth (off) etw. abtropfen lassen [ˈaptropfn̩ lasn̩] <lässt, ließ, hat lassen> ◊ *Die frittierten Pilze auf einen Rost legen und abtropfen lassen.; (by pouring the liquid off)* etw. abgießen [ˈapgiːsn̩] <gießt ab, goss ab, hat abgegossen> ◊ *Gießt du mal bitte die Nudeln ab?* ♦ *überschüssiges Fett abgießen* **5.** *(a glass)* drain sth leeren [ˈleːrǝn] ◊ *Marta leerte das Glas in einem Zug.* **6.** *(use up too much resources)* drain sth/sb eine Sache/jdn belasten [bǝˈlastn̩] ◊ *Zu große Investitionen belasten die Finanzen der Firma.*

◉ **feel drained** sich ausgelaugt fühlen

drainage [noun] **1.** *(for sewage)* Kanalisation [kanalizaˈtsjoːn] die <-, -en> **2.** *(in agriculture)* drains Entwässerungskanäle [ɛntˈvɛsǝrʊŋskanɛːlǝ] die <-> pl; *(process)* Entwässerung [ɛntˈvɛsǝrʊŋ] die <-, -en> ◊ *die Entwässerung eines Feuchtgebiets*

drama [noun] Drama [ˈdraːma] das <-s, Dramen> ◊ *ein Drama in drei Akten* ♦ *Das Drama um die Geiseln geht weiter.*

dramatic(ally) [adj, adv] dramatisch [draˈmaːtɪʃ] ◊

Goethes dramatische Werke ♦ eine Szene, die sehr dramatisch ist ♦ Die Lage spitzte sich dramatisch zu.

drastic(ally) [adj, adv] (action, measures, reduction, deterioration) drastisch ['drastɪʃ] when used as an adj, mostly before ns ◊ drastische Maßnahmen ♦ Die Preise wurden drastisch erhöht.; (change) einschneidend ['aenʃnaednt] ◊ ein einschneidender Wandel ♦ Die notwendigen Veränderungen sind sehr einschneidend. ♦ Diese Technologie wird unser Leben einschneidend verändern.; (improvement) deutlich ['dɔɡtlɪç] ◊ eine deutliche Verbesserung ♦ Die Fortschritte waren deutlich (erkennbar).

draught [noun] 1. (of air) Zug [tsuːk] der <-(e)s> no pl ◊ Die Pflanze verträgt keinen Zug. draught of air Luftzug ['lʊfttsuːk] 2. (mouthful of drink) Schluck [ʃlʊk] der <-(e)s, -e> ◊ ein Schluck Wein
ⓢ **on draught** vom Fass

draw¹ [noun] 1. SPORT Unentschieden ['ʊnʔɛntʃiːdn̩] das <-s, -> ◊ Es reichte nur zu einem Unentschieden. a draw with sb das Unentschieden gegen jdn 2. (lottery) Ziehung ['tsiːʊŋ] die <-, -en> ◊ die Ziehung der Lottozahlen prize draw Gewinnziehung [gə'vɪntsiːʊŋ] 3. (attraction) Attraktion [atrak'tsjoːn] die <-, -en> ◊ Für Kinder ist Madame Tussaud's eine echte Attraktion.

draw² [verb] 1. (with a pencil etc., a picture) zeichnen ['tsaeçnən] <zeichnet, zeichnete, hat gezeichnet> ◊ mit einem Stift ein Bild zeichnen ♦ Ich zeichne gern. draw a line eine Linie ziehen [aenə 'liːnjə tsiːən] <zieht, zog, hat gezogen> draw sth for sb jdm etw. aufzeichnen ['aoftsaeçnən] +haben ◊ Er zeichnete mir die Route auf. 2. (pull: a person, an object, lots, a winning ticket, card, weapon, tooth, also fig: a conclusion, comparison) ziehen ['tsiːən] <zieht, zog, hat gezogen> ◊ Sie zog ihr Kind an sich und küsste es. ♦ Ich zog ein Feuerzeug aus der Tasche. ♦ ein Messer/einen Zahn/den Hauptgewinn ziehen; (the curtains, a bolt etc.) draw sth back etw. zurückziehen [tsu'rʏktsiːən] <zieht zurück, zog zurück, hat zurückgezogen> ◊ Sie zog die Gardinen zurück. 3. (ideas, information, inspiration) bekommen [bə'kɔmən] <bekommt, bekam, hat bekommen> ◊ Woher haben Sie die Idee zu diesem Buch bekommen? draw inspiration from sb/sth von jdm/etw. inspiriert werden [fɔn ... ɪnspi'riːɐt veːɐdn̩] <wird, wurde, ist worden> 4. (a response: praise, an applause) ernten ['ɛɐntn̩] <erntet, erntete, hat geerntet> ◊ Der neue Roman erntete viel Lob.; (sb's wrath, criticism) auf sich ziehen ['aof ... tsiːən] <zieht auf sich, zog auf sich, hat auf sich gezogen> ◊ Ich habe den Zorn meines Vorgesetzten auf mich gezogen. 5. (money) abheben ['aphɛːbm̩] <hebt ab, hob ab, hat abgehoben> ◊ Wir müssen noch Geld abheben. 6. (a salary, pension, benefit) beziehen [bə'tsiːən] <bezieht, bezog, hat bezogen> ◊ Sie bezieht ein hohes Gehalt. 7. (water from a well, strength, confidence) schöpfen ['ʃœpfn̩] +haben ◊ aus einem Brunnen Wasser schöpfen ♦ Woher schöpft er all diese Kraft? 8. (open the curtains) aufziehen ['aoftsiːən] <zieht auf, zog auf, hat aufgezogen> ◊ Zieh mal bitte die Gardinen auf!; (shut the curtains) zuziehen ['tsuːtsiːən] <zieht zu, zog zu, hat zugezogen> 9. SPORT ausgleichen ['aosglaeçn̩] <gleicht aus, glich aus, hat ausgeglichen> ◊ Mit diesem Tor glich die Mannschaft zum 1:1 aus.
• **draw back** [phras v] sb draws back (from sth/sb) (move away) jd weicht (vor etw./jdm) zurück

[vaeçt tsu'rʏk] <weicht zurück, wich zurück, ist zurückgewichen> ◊ Erschrocken wich sie vor mir zurück. → draw² 2.
• **draw in** [phras v] 1. (the air, smoke) draw sth in etw. einatmen ['aenʔaːtmən] <atmet ein, atmete ein, hat eingeatmet> ◊ Ich atmete die kühle Luft ein.; (feelers, claws) etw. einziehen ['aentsiːən] <zieht ein, zog ein, hat eingezogen> ◊ Die Katze hatte die Krallen wieder eingezogen. 2. (train) sth draws in(to sth) etw. fährt in etw. [acc] ein [fɛːɐt ɪn ... ˌaen] <fährt ein, fuhr ein, ist eingefahren> ◊ Der Zug fährt in den Bahnhof ein. 3. (attract sb) draw sb in auf jdn eine große Anziehungskraft ausüben [aof ... aenə groːsə 'antsiːʊŋskraft aosˌyːbm̩] +haben ◊ Die Landschaft übte ein große Anziehungskraft auf mich aus. 4. (involve sb, make sb take part) draw sb in(to sth) jdn (in etw. [acc]) einbeziehen ['aenbətsiːən] <bezieht ein, bezog ein, hat einbezogen> ◊ Er wurde in das Gespräch einbezogen.; (into sth unpleasant) jdn in etw. hineinziehen [ɪn ... hɪˌnaentsiːən] <zieht hinein, zog hinein, hat hineingezogen> ◊ In diese Sache möchte ich nicht hineingezogen werden.
ⓢ **The days draw in.** Die Tage werden kürzer. **The night draws in.** Die Nacht bricht an.
• **draw on** [phras v] 1. (experience, knowledge) draw on sth auf etw. [acc] zurückgreifen [aof ... tsu,rʏkgraefn̩] <greift zurück, griff zurück, hat zurückgegriffen> ◊ Sie kann auf eine reiche Berufserfahrung zurückgreifen. 2. (a cigarette, cigar) draw on sth an etw. [dat] ziehen [an ... ˌtsiːən] <zieht, zog, hat gezogen> ◊ Kann ich mal an deiner Zigarre ziehen?
• **draw out** [phras v] 1. (a conversation, meeting, dispute) draw sth out etw. ausdehnen ['aosdeːnən] +haben ◊ eine Sitzung auf mehrere Stunden ausdehnen 2. (make sb open up) draw sb out jdn aus der Reserve locken [aos deːɐ re'zɛɐvə lɔkn̩] +haben ◊ Ihre Herzlichkeit lockte ihn aus der Reserve. 3. (train) draw out (of the station) aus dem Bahnhof fahren [aos deːm 'baːnhoːf faːrən] <fährt, fuhr, ist gefahren> ◊ Der ICE fuhr aus dem Bahnhof.
ⓢ **The days draw out.** Die Tag werden länger.
• **draw up** [phras v] 1. (concept, plan) entwerfen [ɛnt'vɛɐfn̩] <entwirft, entwarf, hat entworfen> ◊ Ich werde ein neues Konzept entwerfen. 2. (a letter, contract, will) aufsetzen ['aoftsɛtn̩] +haben ◊ Sie setzten einen Kaufvertrag auf. 3. (car: stop) halten ['haltn̩] <hält, hielt, hat gehalten> ◊ Ein silbernes Auto hielt vor dem Hotel. 4. (a chair) heranziehen [hɛ'rantsiːən] <zieht heran, zog heran, hat herangezogen> ◊ Sie zog einen Stuhl für mich heran.; (your knee, leg) anziehen ['antsiːən] <zieht an, zog an, hat angezogen> ◊ die Beine abwechselnd ausstrecken und anziehen 5. (write a list, an invoice, draw a map of sth) anfertigen ['anfɛɐtɪgn̩] +haben ◊ eine Liste anfertigen; (programme) aufstellen ['aoftʃtɛlən] +haben ◊ Was für ein Programm wurde für morgen aufgestellt?; (a horoscope) stellen ['ʃtɛlən] +haben

drawback [noun] Nachteil ['naːxtael] der <-(e)s, -e> ◊ Ein Nachteil sind die hohen Kosten.
drawer [noun] Schublade ['ʃuːplaːdə] die <-, -n>
drawing [noun] Zeichnung ['tsaeçnʊŋ] die <-, -en> ◊ eine Zeichnung anfertigen be good at drawing gut zeichnen können [,guːt 'tsaeçnən kœnən] <kann, konnte, hat können>

dreadful(ly) [adj, adv] schrecklich ['ʃrɛklɪç] ◊ *eine schreckliche Angewohnheit* ♦ *Das tut schrecklich weh!* ♦ *Das ist ja schrecklich!* ♦ *sich schrecklich ärgern*

dream¹ [noun] Traum [traom] der <-(e)s, Träume> ◊ *der Traum vom Fliegen* ♦ *Diese Torte ist ein Traum aus Schokolade.* ♦ *Er ist ein Traum von einem Mann.* in your dream im Traum ◊ *Im Traum sah er seine verstorbene Mutter.*
ⓔ **rich/beautiful etc. beyond sb's wildest dreams** reicher/schöner etc., als jd es in seinen kühnsten Träumen für möglich gehalten hätte **in your dreams** *(fam, emph)* das hättest du wohl gern

dream² [adj] Traum... [traom] *(fam)* **dream job** Traumberuf ['traombəru:f] der <-(e)s, -e>

dream³ [verb] träumen ['trɔømən] +haben ◊ *Hast du schlecht geträumt?* ♦ *Er träumte, er sei durch die Fahrprüfung gefallen.* ♦ *Wir träumen von einem eigenen Haus.* **dream of doing sth** davon träumen, etw. zu tun ◊ *Als Kind träumte er davon, Pilot zu werden.*
ⓔ **dream on** *(fam, emph)* träum weiter **sb wouldn't dream of doing sth** jdm fiele nicht im Traum ein, etw. zu tun

dreary [adj] 1. *(boring)* öde ['ø:də] <öder, am ödesten> ◊ *In der Schule finde ich es sehr öde.* ♦ *ein ödes Leben führen* 2. *(weather)* trüb [try:p] trübe ['try:bə] <trüber, am trübsten> ◊ *ein trüber Novembertag* ♦ *Schon am Morgen war es trüb.*

dress¹ [noun] 1. *(for women)* Kleid [klaet] das <-(e)s, -er> ◊ *Sie trug ein kurzes Kleid.* 2. *(clothing)* Kleidung ['klaedʊŋ] die <-> no pl ◊ *leichte/warme Kleidung*

dress² [verb] 1. *(put on clothes)* dress, get dressed sich anziehen ['antsi:ən] <zieht sich an, zog sich an, hat sich angezogen> ◊ *Er stand auf und zog sich an.* ♦ *Zieh dich warm an!* 2. *(a salad)* anmachen ['anmaxn] +haben ◊ *Ich mache den Salat mit Essig und Öl an.* 3. *(a wound)* verbinden [fɛ'bɪndn] <verbindet, verband, hat verbunden> ◊ *Die Wunde/Hand muss verbunden werden.*
• **dress up** [phras v] 1. *(put on fancy dress)* sich verkleiden [fɛ'klaedn] <verkleidet sich, verkleidete sich, hat sich verkleidet> ◊ *Ich werde mich als Clown verkleiden.* 2. *(put on smart clothes)* sich schick anziehen [ˌʃɪk 'antsi:ən] <zieht sich an, zog sich an, hat sich angezogen> ◊ *Zieh dich schick an, wir gehen ins Theater!; (a bit too noticeably)* sich herausputzen [hɛ'raospʊtsn] +haben **dress sb up** jdn herausputzen ◊ *Das Kind war wie eine Prinzessin herausgeputzt.*

dressing [noun] 1. *(for salad)* Dressing ['drɛsɪŋ] das <-s, -s> 2. *(for a wound)* Verband [fɛ'bant] der <-(e)s, Verbände> ◊ *jdm einen Verband anlegen*

dressing room [noun] *(for customer or actors)* Garderobe [gaɐ'də'ro:bə] die <-, -n>; *(for an athlete)* Umkleidekabine ['ʊmklaedəka,bi:nə] die <-, -n> ◊ *Entschuldigung, wo sind hier die Umkleidekabinen?*

dried [verb] → **dry²** [adj] getrocknet [gə'trɔknət] **dried milk** Trockenmilch ['trɔknmɪlç] die <-> no pl **dried flowers** Trockenblumen ['trɔknblu:mən] die <-> pl

drift¹ [noun] 1. *(snow, sand)* Wehe ['ve:ə] die <-, -n> **snow drift** Schneewehe ['ʃne:ve:ə] 2. *(leaving somewhere)* drift to somewhere Abwanderung irgendwohin ['apvandərʊŋ] die <-> no pl ◊ *die Abwanderung von Wissenschaftlern ins Ausland; (turning away from established concepts, values)* drift

away from sth Abkehr von etw. ['apke:ɐ fɔn] die <-> no pl ◊ *eine Abkehr von traditionellen Werten* 3. *(of water)* Strömung ['ʃtrø:mʊŋ] die <-, -en> ◊ *Das Boot wurde von der Strömung fortgerissen.* **drift** *(of air)* Luftstrom ['lʊftʃtro:m] der <-(e)s, Luftströme>
ⓔ **catch sb's drift** *(fam)* verstehen, worauf jd hinauswill

drift² [verb] 1. *(in the water, air)* treiben ['traebm] <treibt, trieb, hat/ist getrieben> *transitive use +haben/ intransitive use +sein* ◊ *Der Wind hat den Schnee auf die Straße getrieben.* ♦ *Der Rauch war nach Osten getrieben.* **drift out to sea** aufs Meer hinaustreiben [aofs 'me:ɐ hɪ,naostraebm] +sein 2. *(person, without purpose)* sich treiben lassen ['traebm lasn] <lässt sich, ließ sich, hat sich lassen> ◊ *Ohne jedes Ziel ließ ich mich treiben.* **drift into sth** zufällig in etw. [acc] geraten [ˌtsu:fɛlɪç ɪn ... gə,ra:tn] <gerät, geriet, ist geraten> ◊ *Ich bin zufällig in die Politik geraten.*
• **drift apart** [phras v] sich auseinander leben [aos|ae'nandə le:bm] +haben ◊ *Wir haben uns längst auseinander gelebt.*

drill¹ [noun] 1. *(tool)* Bohrer ['bo:rɐ] der <-s, -> 2. *(for an emergency)* Übung ['y:bʊŋ] die <-, -en> ◊ *eine Übung für den Notfall* 3. MIL Drill [drɪl] der <-s> no pl

drill² [verb] 1. *(a hole)* bohren ['bo:rən] +haben ◊ *ein Loch in die Wand bohren* ♦ *nach Öl/Wasser bohren* 2. MIL exerzieren [ɛksɐ'tsi:rən] <exerziert, exerzierte, hat exerziert> ◊ *Die Soldaten mussten stundenlang exerzieren.* **drill sb** jdn exerzieren lassen 3. *(train sb, make sb learn)* drill sb in sth jdn in etw. [dat] drillen [ɪn ... ˌdrɪlən] +haben *(pej)* ◊ *die Schüler in Grammatik drillen*

drily [adv] trocken ['trɔkŋ] ◊ *ein trocken abgefasster Bericht*

drink¹ [noun] Getränk [gə'trɛŋk] das <-(e)s, -e> ◊ *kühle/heiße Getränke* **a drink of water** ein Schluck Wasser [aen ʃlʊk 'vasɐ] <-(e)s, -e> **May I have a drink?** Könnte ich etwas zu trinken haben?
ⓔ **go for a drink** einen trinken gehen **have a drink problem** ein Alkoholproblem haben

drink² [verb] *(take in liquid, person)* trinken ['trɪŋkŋ] <trinkt, trank, hat getrunken> ◊ *eine Tasse Kaffee trinken* ♦ *Du trinkst zu viel.; (animal)* saufen ['zaofn] <säuft, soff, hat gesoffen>

drinking water [noun] Trinkwasser ['trɪŋkvasɐ] das <-s> no pl

drip¹ [noun] 1. *(action of dripping or the sound it produces)* Tropfen ['trɔpfn] das <-s> no pl ◊ *das Tropfen des Wasserhahns* 2. *(drop of liquid)* Tropfen ['trɔpfn] der <-s, -> ◊ *ein paar Tropfen Blut* 3. MED *(dispenser)* Tropf [trɔpf] der <-(e)s, -e> **be on a drip** am Tropf hängen

drip² [verb] tropfen ['trɔpfn] *transitive use +haben/ intransitive use +sein* ◊ *Ich tropfte mir das Medikament ins Auge.* ♦ *Der Honig tropft gleich vom Brötchen!*

drive¹ [noun] 1. *(by car)* Fahrt [fa:ɐt] die <-, -en> ◊ *die Fahrt nach Köln* **go for a drive** eine Spazierfahrt machen [aenə ʃpa'tsi:ɐfa:ɐt maxn] +haben 2. *(of a private property)* Einfahrt ['aenfa:ɐt] die <-, -en> ◊ *Wem gehört das Auto in unserer Einfahrt?* 3. *(organized operation)* Initiative [initsja'ti:və] die <-, -n> ◊ *eine Initiative für gesündere Arbeitsplätze* 4. BIO *(of people, animals)* Trieb [tri:p] der

<-(e)s, -e> ◊ *ein natürlicher Trieb* ♦ *einen Trieb befriedigen* **5.** (enthusiasm, dynamism) Zielstrebigkeit ['tsi:lʃtre:bɪçkaɛt] die <-> no pl ◊ *Deine Zielstrebigkeit wird dich weit bringen.* not have the drive nicht zielstrebig genug sein [nɪçt 'tsi:lʃtre:bɪç gənu:k zaɛn] +haben **6.** ɪᴛ Laufwerk ['laͻfvɛ'k] das <-(e)s, -e> ◊ *Speicherplatz auf dem Laufwerk*

drive² [verb] **1.** (a vehicle) fahren ['fa:rən] <fährt, fuhr, hat/ist gefahren> *transitive use +haben/intransitive use +sein* ◊ *Hast du ihn zum Bahnhof gefahren? ♦ Bist du zu Fuß hier oder bist du gefahren?*; (be at the wheel) lenken ['lɛŋkŋ] +haben ◊ *Wer lenkte den Bus zum Zeitpunkt des Unfalls?* drive back zurückfahren [tsu'rʏkfa:rən] *transitive use +haben/intransitive use +sein* ◊ *Fahr mich bitte wieder zurück.* drive off/away wegfahren ['vɛkfa:rən] *transitive use +haben/intransitive use +sein* ◊ *Fahr bitte das Auto weg. ♦ Sind sie schon weggefahren?* **2.** (induce sb to do sth, cause sb to be in a bad state, make sb/sth move somewhere) treiben ['traɛbm] <treibt, trieb, hat getrieben> ◊ *jdn zur Verzweiflung treiben ♦ Was treibt ihn dazu, Marathon zu laufen? ♦ Der Bauer trieb seine Kühe auf die Weide.* **3.** (make a machine work, motivate a person) antreiben ['antraɛbm] <treibt an, trieb an, hat angetrieben> ◊ *Diese Pumpe wird von einem Motor angetrieben. ♦ Der Trainer trieb mich zu Höchstleistungen an.* **4.** (force sb to leave a place) vertreiben [fɛ'traɛbm] <vertreibt, vertrieb, hat vertrieben> ◊ *jdn aus dem Land vertreiben* drive sb from their home jdn aus seinem Haus/seiner Heimat vertreiben drive sb out of the country jdn aus dem Land vertreiben
◉ **drive sb mad** jdn verrückt machen
• **drive away** [phras v] (keep sb from coming, suppress sth) drive sb/sth away jdn/etw. [acc] vertreiben [fɛ'traɛbm] <vertreibt, vertrieb, hat vertrieben> ◊ *Das schlechte Wetter vertrieb die Zoobesucher. ♦ trübe Gedanken vertreiben* → **drive² 1.**
• **drive back** [phras v] (cause to withdraw) zurückdrängen [tsu'rʏkdrɛŋən] +haben ◊ *Wir wurden von den Flammen zurückgedrängt.* → **drive² 1.**
• **drive down** [phras v] (prices) drücken ['drʏkŋ] +haben ◊ *Das große Angebot drückt die Preise.*
• **drive off** [phras v] (muggers, attackers) in die Flucht schlagen [ɪn di: 'flͻxt ʃla:gŋ] <schlägt, schlug, hat geschlagen> ◊ *Ich konnte die Angreifer in die Flucht schlagen.* → **drive² 1.**

driver [noun] **1.** (of a car, bus) Fahrer ['fa:re] der <-s, -> ♀Fahrerin ['fa:rərɪn] die <-, -nen> ◊ *Der Fahrer wurde leicht verletzt. ♦ Sie arbeitet als Fahrerin bei einem Taxiunternehmen.*; (of a locomotive) Lokomotivführer [lokomo'ti:ffy:re] der <-s, -> ♀Lokomotivführerin [lokomo'ti:ffy:rərɪn] die <-, -nen> ◊ *Als kleiner Junge wollte er Lokomotivführer werden. ♦ Bei dem Unfall erlitt die Lokomotivführerin einen Schock.* **2.** ɪᴛ Treiber ['traɛbe] der <-s, -> ◊ *ein Treiber für den Drucker*

driver's licence, driver's license [noun] Führerschein ['fy:reʃaɛn] der <-(e)s, -e> ◊ *jdm den Führerschein abnehmen*

driveway [noun] Einfahrt ['aɛnfa:'t] die <-, -en> ◊ *Jemand hat sich in die Einfahrt gestellt.*

driving → **drive²** [adj] driving force treibende Kraft [,traɛbmdə 'kraft] die <-, Kräfte> driving rain peitschender Regen [,paɛtʃndə 're:gŋ] der <-s> no pl driving snow Schneetreiben ['ʃne:traɛbm] das <-s>

no pl

driving licence → **driver's licence**
driving test [noun] Fahrprüfung ['fa:'pry:fʊŋ] die <-, -en>

drop¹ [noun] **1.** (of liquid) Tropfen ['trͻpfn] der <-s, -> ◊ *einige Tropfen Zitronensaft* **2.** ᴍᴇᴅ ear drops Ohrentropfen ['o:rəntrͻpfn] die <-> only pl eye drops Augentropfen ['aͻgŋtrͻpfn] die <-> only pl nose drops Nasentropfen ['na:zŋtrͻpfn] die <-> only pl **3.** (distance to the ground, fall in the amount of sth) Abfall ['apfal] der <-(e)s, Abfälle> ◊ *ein steiler Abfall von 700 Metern* drop in sth ...abfall drop in performance Leistungsabfall ['laɛstʊŋsˌapfal] **4.** ꜰɪɴ (of a currency) Fall [fal] der <-(e)s, Fälle> ◊ *der plötzliche Fall des Euro*
◉ **a drop in the ocean** ein Tropfen auf den heißen Stein

drop² [verb] **1.** (let sth fall) drop sth etw. fallen lassen ['falən lasŋ] <lässt, ließ, hat lassen> ◊ *Vor Schreck ließ sie ihre Tasche fallen.*; (from an aircraft) etw. abwerfen ['apvɛ'fn] <wirft ab, warf ab, hat abgeworfen> sb drops into sth sich in etw. [acc] fallen lassen [ɪn ... ˌfalən lasŋ] ◊ *Ich ließ mich erschöpft in den Sessel fallen.* **2.** (a topic, an arguement, your studys, a subject, project, passtime) mit etw. aufhören [mɪt ... ˌaͻfhø:rən] +haben ◊ *Hören Sie doch endlich mit diesem Thema auf!* **3.** (ground, slope, mountain etc.) drop (away/off) abfallen ['apfalən] <fällt ab, fiel ab, ist abgefallen> ◊ *Der Boden fiel steil ab.* **4.** ᴇᴄᴏɴ (shares, rates, prices etc.) sth drops etw. fällt [fɛlt] <fällt, fiel, ist gefallen> ◊ *Die Immobilienpreise fallen weiterhin.* drop the prices die Preise senken [di: 'praɛzə ˌzɛŋkŋ] +haben **5.** (temperatures, level of substances, water level) sinken ['zɪŋkŋ] <sinkt, sank, ist gesunken> ◊ *Sinkt der Blutzuckerspiegel wieder?*; (drastically and rapidly) abfallen ['apfalən] <fällt ab, fiel ab, ist abgefallen> ◊ *Die Temperaturen fielen in der Nacht stark ab.* **6.** drop sth (off) somewhere etw. irgendwohin bringen ['brɪŋən] <bringt, brachte, hat gebracht> ◊ *Kannst du meine Schuhe zum Schuster bringen?* drop sth (off) at sb's house etw. bei jdm vorbeibringen [baɛ ... fo:ɐ̯ˌbaɛbrɪŋən] <bringt vorbei, brachte vorbei, hat vorbeigebracht> ◊ *Bitte bring die Unterlagen noch bei Nora vorbei.* **7.** drop sb (off) somewhere jdn irgendwo absetzen ['apzɛtsn] +haben ◊ *Setzt du mich bitte an der Haltestelle ab?* **8.** drop your voice die Stimme senken [di: 'ʃtɪmə ˌzɛŋkŋ] +haben sb's voice drops jds Stimme senkt sich
◉ **let sth drop** etw. auf sich beruhen lassen drop sb in it jdn in eine schwierige Situation bringen
• **drop in** [phras v] vorbeikommen [fo:ɐ̯ˈbaɛkͻmən] <kommt vorbei, kam vorbei, ist vorbeigekommen> ◊ *Komm doch auf einen Kaffee vorbei!*
• **drop off** [phras v] **1.** (fall asleep) einnicken ['aɛnnɪkŋ] +sein ◊ *Er nickte während der Vorlesung ein.* **2.** (interest, sales etc.) zurückgehen [tsu'rʏkge:ən] <geht zurück, ging zurück, ist zurückgegangen> ◊ *Ihr Interesse an Tennis ging deutlich zurück.* → **drop² 6., drop² 7.**
• **drop out** [phras v] **1.** (no longer take part in or be part of sth) aussteigen ['aͻsʃtaɛgŋ] <steigt aus, stieg aus, ist ausgestiegen> ◊ *Warum sind Sie aus der Politik ausgestiegen?* **2.** (of school, university) drop out of sth etw. abbrechen ['apbrɛçn] <bricht ab, brach ab, hat abgebrochen> ◊ *Ich brach die Schule*

ab. **3.** *(of a competition etc.)* ausscheiden ['aɔsʃaedn̩] <scheidet aus, schied aus, ist ausgeschieden> ◊ *Er musste vorzeitig aus dem Rennen ausscheiden.*

drought [noun] Dürre ['dʏrə] die <–, –n>

drown [verb] **1.** *(die in the water)* sb/an animal drowns jd/ein Tier ertrinkt [e'trɪŋkt] <ertrank, ist ertrunken> ◊ *beim Baden im Meer ertrinken* drown sb/an animal jdn/ein Tier ertränken [e'trɛŋkn̩] <ertränkte, hat ertränkt> ◊ *Er wollte die Kätzchen im Fluss ertränken.* **2.** *(flood the land)* überschwemmen [ybɐ'ʃvɛmən] <überschwemmt, überschwemmte, hat überschwemmt> ◊ *Der Fluss überschwemmt jeden Herbst das Land.* **3.** *(a voice, noise)* übertönen [ybɐ'tøːnən] <übertönt, übertönte, hat übertönt> ◊ *Sie drehte das Radio lauter, um den Streit zu übertönen.*

drug¹ **1.** *(illegal substance)* Droge ['droːɡə] die <–, –n> ◊ *mit Drogen handeln* drug addict Drogenabhängige ['droːɡn̩|aphɛŋɪɡə] der/die <–n, die Drogenabhängigen> *but: ein Drogenabhängiger/eine Drogenabhängige* **2.** MED *(tablets, drops etc.)* Medikament [medika'mɛnt] das <–(e)s, –e> ◊ *ein Medikament verschreiben*

drug² [verb] **1.** *(a person, an animal)* unter Drogen setzen [ʊntɐ 'droːɡn̩ zɛtsn̩] *mostly passive* ◊ *Ich wurde von den Entführern unter Drogen gesetzt.* **2.** *(food, drink)* drug sth ein Betäubungsmittel in etw. [acc] tun [aen bə'tɔøbʊŋsmɪtl̩ ɪn ... tuːn] <tut, tat, hat getan> ◊ *Man hatte ihr ein Betäubungsmittel in den Wein getan.*

drugstore [noun] Drogerie [droɡə'riː] die <–, –n> ◊ *Diese Tabletten bekommt man in der Drogerie.*

drum¹ [noun] **1.** MUS, TECHN Trommel ['trɔml̩] die <–, –n> ◊ *die Trommel schlagen* **2.** *(large container)* Tonne ['tɔnə] die <–, –n> ◊ *eine Tonne Öl/Chemikalien*

drum² [verb] trommeln ['trɔml̩n] +haben ◊ *Sie trommelte nervös mit den Fingern auf den Tisch.* ♦ *Der Regen trommelte an die Fensterscheibe.*

drunk → drink [adj] betrunken [bə'trʊŋkn̩] ◊ *ein betrunkener Gast* ♦ *Du bist ja völlig betrunken!*

dry¹ [adj] trocken ['trɔkn̩] ◊ *trockene Kleider/Haut* ♦ *Laut Wettervorhersage soll es trocken bleiben.* ♦ *ein trockener Rotwein* ♦ *Sein Humor ist ziemlich trocken.*

dry² [verb] *(remove water, become dry)* trocknen ['trɔknən] <trocknet, trocknete, hat/ist getrocknet> *transitive use +haben/intransitive use +sein* ◊ *Der Wind hat die Wäsche schnell getrocknet.* ♦ *Die Farbe ist schon getrocknet.; (dishes)* dry (up) abtrocknen ['aptrɔknən] ◊ *Er trocknete das Geschirr ab.* ♦ *Trocknest du bitte ab?* dry your hands sich [dat] die Hände abtrocknen ◊ *Sie trocknete sich die Hände an einem Handtuch ab.*

• **dry out** [phras v] *(become/make very dry)* austrocknen ['aɔstrɔknən] <trocknet aus, trocknete aus, hat/ist ausgetrocknet> *transitive use +haben/intransitive use +sein* ◊ *Der Wind hat meine Haut ausgetrocknet.* ♦ *Das Flussbett ist ausgetrocknet.*

• **dry up** [phras v] **1.** *(land, stream)* austrocknen ['aɔstrɔknən] <trocknet aus, trocknete aus, hat/ist ausgetrocknet> *transitive use +haben/intransitive use +sein* ◊ *Das Land ist ausgetrocknet.* ♦ *Die Dürre hat das Land ausgetrocknet.* **2.** *(source of income etc.)* versiegen [fɛ'ziːɡn̩] <versiegt, versiegte, ist versiegt> *(lofty)* ◊ *Was machen wir, wenn die Geldströme versiegen?* **3.** *(speaker)* den Faden verlieren

[deːn 'faːdn̩ fɛliːrən] <verliert, verlor, hat verloren> ◊ *Mitten in seiner Rede verlor er plötzlich den Faden.* → dry²

dry cleaner's [noun] Reinigung ['raenɪɡʊŋ] die <–, –en> ◊ *Ich habe deinen Anzug in die Reinigung gebracht.*

dryer [noun] **1.** *(for clothes)* Wäschetrockner ['vɛʃətrɔknɐ] der <–s, –> **2.** *(for hair)* Föhn [føːn] der <–(e)s, –e> ◊ *sich* [dat] *mit dem Föhn die Haare trocknen*

dual [adj] doppelt ['dɔpl̩t] *no comp/superl* ◊ *die doppelte Staatsbürgerschaft* ♦ *einen doppelten Zweck erfüllen*

dubious [adj] **1.** *(uncertain, questionable)* zweifelhaft ['tsvaefl̩haft] <zweifelhafter, am zweifelhaftesten> ◊ *ein Mann von zweifelhaftem Ruf* ♦ *Diese Methode erscheint mir zweifelhaft.* **2.** *(in doubt)* be dubious about sth an etw. [dat] zweifeln [an ... 'tsvaefl̩n] +haben ◊ *an jds Fähigkeiten zweifeln* be dubious about doing sth nicht sicher sein, ob man etw. tun soll [nɪçt 'zɪçɐ zaen zo man ... zɔl] +haben ◊ *Ich bin nicht sicher, ob ich das Angebot annehmen soll.*

duck¹ [noun] Ente ['ɛntə] die <–, –n> ◊ *Im Teich schwamm eine Ente.* ♦ *Sie isst gern Ente.*

duck² [verb] **1.** *(lower yourself, move quickly somewhere)* sb ducks jd duckt sich [dʊkt] +haben ◊ *Er duckte sich zu spät und lief gegen den Ast.* ♦ *Sie duckte sich hinter eine Parkbank, damit er sie nicht sah.* duck sth sich vor etw. [dat] ducken ◊ *Der Boxer duckte sich vor dem Schlag.* **2.** *(submerge)* duck sb jdn untertauchen ['ʊntɐtaoxn̩] +haben ◊ *Die badenden Kinder versuchten, einander unterzutauchen.* **3.** *(evade)* duck sth einer Sache [dat] ausweichen ['aɔsvaeçn̩] <weicht aus, wich aus, ist ausgewichen> ◊ *einer Frage ausweichen*

due¹ [noun] **1.** *(what sb has the right to get)* sb's due (das), *what* jdm zusteht [(,das) vas ... 'tsuːʃteːt] <steht zu, stand zu, hat zugestanden> ◊ *Er bekam, was ihm zustand.* ♦ *Ich verlange nur das, was mir zusteht.* **2.** *(fee)* dues Beitrag ['baetraːk] der <–(e)s, Beiträge> ◊ *einen Beitrag für die Mitgliedschaft in einem Verein zahlen*

◉ **(to) give sb their due** das muss man jdm lassen ◊ *Das muss man ihr lassen: Sie hat sich wirklich Mühe gegeben.*

due² [adj] **1.** *(expected, scheduled)* be due to do sth etw. tun sollen ['zɔlən] <soll, sollte, hat sollen> ◊ *Ihr neues Album soll nächsten Monat erscheinen.* When is the baby due? Wann soll das Baby kommen? be due somewhere irgendwo sein müssen ['zaen mʏsn̩] +haben ◊ *Ich muss in zehn Minuten im Büro sein.* sb is due for sth jds etw. steht an [ʃteːt 'an] <steht an, stand an, hat angestanden> ◊ *Meine Versetzung/Beförderung steht bald an.* I am due for a visit to the dentist. Ich muss mal wieder zum Zahnarzt. **2.** *(to be paid)* fällig ['fɛlɪç] *no comp/superl* ◊ *fällige Zinsen* ♦ *Die Zahlung ist am 15. Mai fällig.* **3.** *(proper)* gebührend [ɡə'byːrənt] *no comp/superl, only before ns* ◊ *mit der gebührenden Vorsicht vorgehen* ♦ *mit der gebührenden Ehrfurcht sprechen* **4.** *(owed)* due to sb jdm zustehend ['tsuːʃteːənt] *no comp/superl, only before ns* ◊ *der Ihnen zustehende Betrag* be due to sb jdm zustehen ['tsuːʃteːən] <steht zu, stand zu, hat zugestanden> ◊ *jdm steht eine Entschädigung zu*

due to [prep] aufgrund [aɔf'ɡrʊnt] [+gen] ◊ *Sie ist*

aufgrund eines Unfalls gelähmt. ✦ Aufgrund der
hohen Nachfrage steigen die Preise. sth is due to sth
etw. ist auf etw. [acc] zurückzuführen
[ɪst aɔf ... tsu.ˈrʏktsufyːrən] ◊ Der hohe Ölpreis ist auf
den Krieg zurückzuführen.

duke [noun] Herzog [ˈhɛʳtsoːk] der
<–s, Herzöge or seldom –e>

dull¹ [adj] 1. (boring) langweilig [ˈlaŋvaɛlɪç] ◊ In der
Schule ist es immer so langweilig. ✦ Er führt ein
langweiliges Leben ohne Abwechslung. 2. (not shiny,
not sharp) stumpf [ʃtʊmpf] <stumpfer, am
stumpf(e)sten> ◊ Ihr Haar ist stumpf und trocken. ✦
ein stumpfes Messer 3. (slow-witted) langsam
[ˈlaŋzaːm] ◊ Sie ist manchmal ein wenig langsam. ✦
Der Lehrer kümmert sich um die langsamen Schüler.
4. (subdued, sound, pain) dumpf [dʊmpf] <dumpfer,
am dumpf(e)sten> mostly before ns ◊ ein dumpfes
Grollen in der Ferne ✦ Der Schmerz ist dumpf und
schlecht lokalisierbar. 5. (overcast) trübe [ˈtryːbə]
<trüber, am trübsten> ◊ trübes Wetter ✦ Der Himmel
war trübe.

dull² [verb] 1. (the mind, senses) trüben [ˈtryːbm̩]
+haben ◊ ein getrübter Verstand ✦ Ihre Sinne waren
vom Alkohol getrübt. 2. (a sound, pain) dämpfen
[ˈdɛmpfn̩] +haben ◊ Der weiche Teppich dämpfte
unsere Schritte. ✦ Das Medikament dämpft den
Schmerz.

duly [adv] 1. (suitably) gebührend [gəˈbyːrənt] no
comp/superl ◊ Der Sieg wurde gebührend gefeiert.
2. (as was to be expected) erwartungsgemäß
[ɛˈvaʳtʊŋsɡəmɛːs] no comp/superl ◊ Nach dem
Skandal verlor die Partei erwartungsgemäß die Wahl.
3. (in time) rechtzeitig [ˈrɛçtsaɛtɪç] no comp/superl ◊
Wir haben die Arbeit rechtzeitig erledigt.

dumb [adj] (stupid) dumm [dʊm] <dümmer, am
dümmsten> ◊ Das war sehr dumm von dir. ✦ ein
dummer Scherz play dumb sich dumm stellen
⊘ be struck dumb sprachlos sein

dummy [noun] 1. (in the UK: pacifier) Schnuller [ˈʃnʊlɐ]
der <–s, –> 2. (for clothes) Schaufensterpuppe
[ˈʃaɔfɛnstɐpʊpə] die <–, –n> 3. (imitation) Attrappe
[aˈtrapə] die <–, –n> ◊ die Attrappe eines Autos
4. (stupid person) Dummkopf [ˈdʊmkɔpf] der
<–(e)s, Dummköpfe> (fam, pej) ◊ Pass doch auf, du
Dummkopf!

dump¹ [noun] 1. (tip) Deponie [depoˈniː] die <–, –n> ◊
Müll auf Deponien lagern 2. MIL (for weapons) Lager
[ˈlaːgɐ] das <–s, –> ammunition dump Munitionsla-
ger [muniˈtsjoːnslaːgɐ] 3. (flat, room) Loch [lɔx] das
<–(e)s, Löcher> (fam, pej) ◊ Er haust in einem
dunklen, feuchten Loch.
⊘ (down) in the dumps deprimiert

dump² [verb] 1. (waste) abladen [ˈapflaːdn̩] <lädt ab,
lud ab, hat abgeladen> ◊ Müll abladen 2. (a bag)
fallen lassen [ˈfalən lasn̩] <lässt, ließ, hat lassen> ◊
Sie ließ ihren Rucksack auf den Boden fallen. 3. (a
partner) dump sb jdm den Laufpass geben
[deːn ˈlaɔfpas geːbm̩] <gibt, gab, hat gegeben> (fam)
◊ Sie hat ihrem Freund den Laufpass gegeben. 4. (a
dependant) abschieben [ˈapʃiːbm̩] <schiebt ab, schob
ab, hat abgeschoben> ◊ Viele ältere Menschen werden
in Heime abgeschoben. dump sb with sb jdn bei
jdm abladen [baɛ ... ˈapflaːdn̩] <lädt ab, lud ab, hat
abgeladen> ◊ Sie laden die Kinder am Wochenende
bei der Oma ab. 5. (sell at a low price) dump sth
etw. zu Dumpingpreisen verkaufen

[tsuː ˈdampɪŋpraɛtsn̩ fɛkaɔfn̩] <verkauft, verkaufte, hat
verkauft> ◊ Waren, die zu Dumpingpreisen verkauft
werden

dumpling [noun] Kloß [kloːs] der <–es, Klöße> ◊ Es
gab Schweinebraten mit Klößen.

dung [noun] Mist [mɪst] der <–(e)s> no pl

durable [adj] 1. (material) haltbar [ˈhaltbaːʳ] ◊ eine
haltbare Beschichtung ✦ Wie haltbar ist dieses
Material? 2. (solution, friendship) dauerhaft
[ˈdaɔɐhaft] <dauerhafter, am dauerhaftesten> ◊ eine
dauerhafte Lösung ✦ Hoffentlich ist der Friede
dauerhaft.

duration [noun] Dauer [ˈdaɔɐ] die <–> no pl ◊ ein
Aufenthalt von kurzer/langer Dauer ✦ die Dauer
eines Films ✦ Für die Dauer der Konferenz tragen
alle Teilnehmer ein Namensschild. be one hour etc.
in duration eine Stunde etc. dauern
[aɛnə ˈʃtʊndə daɔɐn] +haben ◊ Die Sitzung dauerte
eine Stunde.

during [prep] während [ˈvɛːrənt] +gen ◊ Während der
Schwangerschaft war ihr oft schlecht.

dust¹ [noun] Staub [ʃtaɔp] der <–(e)s> no pl ◊ Auf
den Regalen lag Staub. ✦ Die Ringe des Saturns
bestehen aus Staub und Eis.

dust² [verb] 1. (clean) abstauben [ˈapʃtaɔbm̩] +haben ◊
Staubst du bitte die Möbel ab? ✦ Ich muss mal
wieder gründlich abstauben. 2. (cover in sth) dust
sth with sth etw. mit etw. bestäuben
[mɪt ... bəˈʃtɔɔbm̩] <bestäubt, bestäubte, hat bestäubt>
◊ die fertigen Waffeln mit Puderzucker bestäuben

dustbin [noun] Mülltonne [ˈmʏltɔnə] die <–, –n> ◊
Abfall in die Mülltonne werfen

duster [noun] Staubtuch [ˈʃtaɔptuːx] das
<–(e)s, Staubtücher> ◊ die Regale mit einem
Staubtuch abwischen

dustman [noun] Müllmann [ˈmʏlman] der
<–(e)s, Müllmänner> ◊ Fred ist Müllmann. ✦ Haben
die Müllmänner die Tonnen schon geleert? the
dustmen die Müllabfuhr [ˈmʏlapfuːɐ] <–> sing ◊
Morgen kommt die Müllabfuhr.

dusty [adj] staubig [ˈʃtaɔbɪç] ◊ Im Archiv war es
staubig. ✦ ein staubiger Pfad

Dutch¹ [noun] 1. (inhabitant) Niederländer
[ˈniːdɐlɛndɐ] der <–s, –> ♀Niederländerin
[ˈniːdɐlɛndɐrɪn] die <–, –nen> → German¹ 1.
2. (language, subject) Niederländisch [ˈniːdɐlɛndɪʃ]
das <–(s)> no pl → German¹ 1.

Dutch² [adj] niederländisch [ˈniːdɐlɛndɪʃ] → German²

Dutchman [noun] Niederländer [ˈniːdɐlɛndə] der
<–s, –> → German¹ 1.

Dutchwoman [noun] Niederländerin [ˈniːdɐlɛndərɪn]
die <–, –nen> → German¹ 1.

duty [noun] 1. (obligation, task) Pflicht [pflɪçt] die
<–, –en> ◊ seine Pflicht tun ✦ die Ausübung einer
Pflicht ✦ Zu seinen Pflichten gehört es, die Baustelle
zu kontrollieren. have a duty to sb eine Pflicht
gegenüber jdm haben 2. (work, shift) Dienst [diːnst]
der <–(e)s, –e> be off duty keinen Dienst haben
be on duty Dienst haben ◊ Am Wochenende kann
ich nicht, da habe ich Dienst. 3. (when importing
goods) (customs) duty Zoll [tsɔl] der <–(e)s, Zölle>
◊ Zoll auf Produkte aus China erheben pay duty on
sth auf etw. zahlen ◊ Muss ich für diese Zigaretten Zoll zahlen?; (when buying sth) Steuer [ˈʃtɔɔɐ] die
<–, –n> duty on alcohol Alkoholsteuer
[ˈalkohoːlʃtɔɔɐ]

duty-free [adj, adv] zollfrei ['tsɔlfraɛ] *no comp/superl* ◊ *zollfreie Waren* ♦ *Ist die Ausfuhr von Zigaretten zollfrei?* ♦ *etw. zollfrei in die EU einführen*

duvet [noun] Federbett ['feːdɛbɛt] das <-(e)s, -en> ◊ *Sie schüttelte das Federbett aus.*

duvet cover [noun] Bettbezug ['bɛtbatsuːk] der <-(e)s, Bettbezüge> ◊ *die Bettbezüge wechseln*

DVD DVD [deːfaoˈdeː] die <-, -s>

dwelling [noun] *(form)* Wohnung ['voːnʊŋ] die <-, -en> ◊ *Er hat zurzeit keine Wohnung.*

dwindle [verb] *(strength, resources, interest, chances)* schwinden ['ʃvɪndn̩] <schwindet, schwand, ist geschwunden> ◊ *Ihre Kräfte schwanden.* ♦ *Die Vorräte schwinden zusehends.; (profit, number)* sinken ['zɪŋkn̩] <sinkt, sank, ist gesunken> ◊ *Die Zuschauerzahlen sinken.* dwindle to sth **auf** etw. [acc] sinken ◊ *Die Umsätze sind auf ein Rekordtief gesunken.*

dye [verb] färben ['fɛrbm̩] +*haben* ◊ *Ich möchte diese Bluse blau färben.* dye your hair sich [dat] die Haare färben

dynamic [adj] dynamisch [dyˈnaːmɪʃ] ◊ *ein dynamischer Geschäftsmann* ♦ *Dieser Marktbereich ist sehr dynamisch.*

dynasty [noun] Dynastie [dynasˈtiː] die <-, -n> ◊ *die Dynastie der Kennedys*

dyslexia [noun] Legasthenie [legasteˈniː] die <-> *no pl* ◊ *Legasthenie kann man nicht heilen.*

A
B
C
D
E
F
G
H
I
J
K
L
M
N
O
P
Q
R
S
T
U
V
W
X
Y
Z

E

e, E [noun] 1. *(letter)* e, E [e:] das <–(s), –(s)> ◊ *Dieses Wort wird mit einem kleinen e/großen E geschrieben.* ♦ *E wie Emil* 2. mus E e, E [e:] das <–(s), –(s)> ◊ *Spiel mal ein E!* E minor e-Moll ['e:mɔl] E major E-Dur ['e:du:ɐ̯]

E [noun] *(grade)* Fünf [fynf] die <–, –en> ◊ *eine Fünf in Mathe box@ Note*

each¹ [det] jeder ['je:dɐ] jede ['je:də] jedes ['je:dəs] ◊ *Jeder Schüler hielt ein Referat.* ♦ *Jede Mitarbeiterin muss Schichtdienst leisten.* ♦ *Jedes Zimmer hat ein eigenes Bad.*

each² [pron] 1. *(all the people or things in a group)* jeder ['je:dɐ] jede ['je:də] jedes ['je:dəs] ◊ *Wir haben zwölf Mitarbeiter; jeder hat seine eigene Aufgabe.* ♦ *Es gibt verschiedene Methoden; jede hat ihre Vorteile.* ♦ *Wir haben vier Kinder, und jedes ist anders.* 2. *(per item)* jeweils ['je:vaɪ̯ls] ◊ *Die Gläser kosten jeweils drei Euro.* ♦ *zwei Gruppen mit jeweils 15 Kindern*

each other [pron] *(one person or thing to the other:* 1st pers pl) uns [ʊns] ◊ *Wir hatten uns sehr lieb.;* (2nd pers pl) euch [ɔɥç] ◊ *Hört auf, euch zu schlagen!;* (3rd pers and polite address pl) sich [zɪç] ◊ *Die Brüder schenken sich zu Weihnachten nie etwas.* ♦ *Sie und ihre Frau lieben sich noch immer, nicht wahr?* for each other füreinander [fy:ɐ̯|aɪ̯'nandɐ] ◊ *Wir haben nie genug Zeit füreinander.* ♦ *Sie empfinden Respekt füreinander.* our/their relationship with each other unser/ihr Verhältnis zueinander [ʊnze:/i:ɐ̯ fɛ'hɛltnɪs tsu|aɪ̯'nandɐ]; *(static)* close to each other beieinander [,baɪ̯|aɪ̯'nandɐ] ◊ *Wir standen nah beieinander.; (with sense of movement)* close to each other nah aneinander [,na: an|aɪ̯'nandɐ] ◊ *Die beiden Kinder drängten sich nah aneinander.* next to each other nebeneinander [ne:bm̩|aɪ̯'nandɐ] ◊ *Sie saßen nebeneinander.* on top of each other aufeinander [aɔf|aɪ̯'nandɐ] ◊ *Kisten aufeinander stapeln* be nice to each other nett zueinander sein ['nɛt tsu|aɪ̯,nandɐ zaɪ̯n] +sein ◊ *Seid doch ein bisschen nett zueinander!* get used to each other sich aneinander gewöhnen [an|aɪ̯,nandɐ gə'vøːnən] <gewöhnt sich, gewöhnte sich, hat sich gewöhnt> ◊ *Die beiden Tiere müssen sich erst aneinander gewöhnen.* talk to each other miteinander reden [mɪt|aɪ̯,nandɐ 're:dn̩] +haben ◊ *Sie sollten mehr miteinander reden.*

eager [adj] eifrig ['aɪ̯frɪç] ◊ *ein eifriger Arbeiter* ♦ *Sie ist immer sehr eifrig.* be eager to please sb eifrig bedacht sein, jdn zufrieden zu stellen ◊ *Er war stets eifrig bedacht, seine Lehrerin zufrieden zu stellen.* eager to learn lernbegierig ['lɛʁnbəgi:rɪç] ◊ *Diese Hunde sind intelligent und lernbegierig.* be eager to do sth etw. unbedingt tun wollen [,ʊnbədɪŋt ... vɔlən] <will, wollte, hat wollen> ◊ *Er wollte uns unbedingt helfen.*

eagerly [adv] *(accept)* bereitwillig [bə'raɪ̯tvɪlɪç] ◊ *einen Vorschlag bereitwillig annehmen; (await)* mit Spannung [mɪt 'ʃpanʊŋ] ◊ *Sein neuer Roman wurde mit Spannung erwartet.*

eagerness [noun] Eifer ['aɪ̯fɐ] der <–s> no pl ◊ *In seinem Eifer hatte er vergessen, die Tür zu schließen.* eagerness for knowledge Wissbegierde ['vɪsbəgi:ɐ̯də] die <–> no pl ◊ *ein Kind voller Wissbegierde*

eagle [noun] Adler ['a:dlɐ] der <–s, –>

ear [noun] 1. anat, med Ohr [o:ɐ̯] das <–(e)s, –en> ◊ *jdm etw. ins Ohr flüstern* ♦ *Sie hielt den Telefonhörer ans Ohr.* ♦ *Er ist auf dem rechten Ohr taub.* ♦ *ein Ohr für Musik haben* 2. bot Ähre ['ɛ:rə] die <–, –n> ◊ *reife Ähren*
◉ be all ears ganz Ohr sein auf taube Ohren stoßen have sb's ear bei jdm Gehör finden lend sb an ear jdm Gehör schenken

earl [noun] Graf [gra:f] der <–en, –en>

earlier [adj, adv] früher ['fry:ɐ] when used as an adj, only before ns ◊ *Frühere Ausgaben der Zeitschrift kann man im Internet bestellen.* ♦ *Kannst du nicht etwas früher kommen?*

early [adj, adv] früh [fry:] <früher, am früh(e)sten> ◊ *in den frühen Morgenstunden* ♦ *Als sie aufwachte, war es noch früh.* ♦ *Er steht immer sehr früh auf.* She's in her early forties. *(sooner than expected)* zu früh [tsu: 'fry:] ◊ *Der Zug kam zehn Minuten zu früh an.*

earn [verb] 1. *(in return for work or effort)* verdienen [fɛ'di:nən] <verdient, verdiente, hat verdient> ◊ *Wie viel verdienst du im Monat?* ♦ *seinen Lebensunterhalt mit Klavierunterricht verdienen* have earned sth sich [dat] etw. verdient haben ◊ *Er hat sich den Respekt seiner Kollegen verdient.* 2. *(from an investment)* einbringen ['aɪ̯nbrɪŋən] <bringt ein, brachte ein, hat eingebracht> ◊ *Die Wertpapiere bringen hohe Zinsen ein.* sth has earned sb sth etw. hat jdm etw. eingebracht ◊ *Dieses Buch hat ihr den Nobelpreis eingebracht.*

earnings [noun] *(of an individual)* Einkommen ['aɪ̯nkɔmən] das <–s, –> ◊ *Wie hoch ist das durchschnittliche Einkommen in Thüringen?; (of a business)* Ertrag [ɛ'tra:k] der <–(e)s, Erträge> ◊ *Der Ertrag des Unternehmens ist gestiegen.*

earring [noun] Ohrring ['o:ɐ̯rɪŋ] der <–(e)s, –e> ◊ *Ohrringe tragen*

earth [noun] 1. *(world, ground, soil, of electrical equipment)* Erde ['e:ɐ̯də] die <–> no pl ◊ *Die Astronauten umrundeten die Erde.* ♦ *Die Erde bebte.* ♦ *Erde aufschütten* ♦ *Der Verstärker hat keine Erde.* on earth auf der Erde 2. *(of a fox etc.)* Bau [baɔ̯] der <–(e)s, –e> ◊ *einen Fuchs aus seinem Bau locken*

earthquake [noun] Erdbeben ['e:ɐ̯tbe:bm̩] das <–s, –> ◊ *Ein schweres Erdbeben erschütterte die Türkei.*

ease¹ [noun] 1. *(effortlessness)* Leichtigkeit ['laɪ̯çtɪçkaɪ̯t] die <–> no pl ◊ *Mit Leichtigkeit kletterte die Junge auf die Mauer.* ease of use leichte Handhabung [,laɪ̯çtə 'hanthabʊŋ] die <–> no pl ◊ *Das Gerät überzeugt durch seine leichte Handhabung.* 2. *(calmness)* Ruhe ['ru:ə] die <–> no

pl ◊ Er strahlt eine natürliche Ruhe aus.
◉ be ill at ease sich unwohl fühlen be at ease
sich wohl fühlen put sb at (their) ease jdm die
Befangenheit nehmen
ease² [verb] **1.** *(pain etc.)* ease sth etw. lindern
['lɪndən] +haben ◊ *Die Salbe lindert die Schmerzen.*
♦ *Das hat meinen Kummer gelindert.; (a situation)*
ease sth etw. entspannen [ɛnt'ʃpanən] <entspannt,
entspannte, hat entspannt> ◊ *Die Maßnahmen haben
die Lage entspannt.; (pressure)* ease sth etw. verringern [fɛ'rɪŋən] <verringert, verringerte, hat verringert>
◊ *den Druck auf jdn/etw. verringern* **2.** *(pain,
pressure, wind, rain)* sth eases etw. lässt nach
[lɛst 'na:x] <ließ nach, hat nachgelassen> ◊ *Die
Schmerzen ließen nach.* ♦ *Der Wind lässt langsam
nach.; (situation)* sth eases etw. entspannt sich
[ɛnt'ʃpant zɪç] <entspannte sich, hat sich entspannt> ◊
Die Lage hat sich entspannt. **3.** *(move with care)*
ease (yourself) somewhere sich behutsam irgendwo
[dat]/irgendwohin [acc] niederlassen
[bə,hu:tza:m ... ,ni:dəlasn] <lässt sich nieder, ließ sich
nieder, hat sich niedergelassen> ◊ *Er lässt sich
behutsam auf dem Sofa nieder.* ♦ *Sie ließ sich
behutsam auf den Boden nieder.; (a cork etc.)* ease
sth out of sth etw. behutsam aus etw. ziehen
[bə,hu:tza:m aʊs ... tsi:ən] <zieht, zog, hat gezogen> ◊
Ich zog behutsam den Korken aus der Flasche.
4. *(tensions, your grip, sanctions)* ease sth lockern
['lɔkən] +haben ◊ *Eine Massage lockert die Verspannungen.* ♦ *den Griff um etw. lockern* sth eases etw.
lockert sich ◊ *Sein Griff lockerte sich.* **5.** *(make
easier)* erleichtern [ɛ'laɪçtən] <erleichtert, erleichterte, hat erleichtert> ◊ *den Übergang zu einem
neuen System erleichtern*
● **ease off** [phras v] **1.** *(rain, pain etc.)* nachlassen
['na:xlasn] <lässt nach, ließ nach, hat nachgelassen> ◊
Der Regen ließ allmählich nach. ♦ *Hoffentlich lässt
der Schmerz bald nach.* **2.** *(when driving)* langsamer
fahren ['laŋza:me fa:rən] <fährt, fuhr, ist gefahren> ◊
Du solltest bei Regen etwas langsamer fahren.
● **ease up** [phras v] **1.** *(wind, rain)* sth eases up etw.
lässt nach [lɛst 'na:x] <ließ nach, hat nachgelassen>
◊ *Wir sollten warten, bis der Sturm nachlässt.*
2. *(treat with less severity)* ease up on sb jdn nicht
so hart angehen [nɪçt zo: 'ha:rt ,ange:ən] <geht an,
ging an, ist angegangen> ◊ *Sie sollten ihr Kind nicht
so hart angehen.* **3.** *(reduce sth)* ease up on sth etw.
einschränken ['aɪnʃrɛŋkn] ◊ *Schränken Sie Ihren
Alkoholkonsum ein!*
easily [adv] **1.** *(without difficulty, possibly, quickly)*
leicht [laɪçt] <leichter, am leichtesten> ◊ *Dieser
Effekt ist relativ leicht zu erreichen.* ♦ *So etwas
kann leicht schief gehen!* ♦ *leicht verdauliche Speisen*
all too easily nur allzu leicht ◊ *In den Bergen kann
das Wetter nur allzu leicht umschlagen.* **2.** *(definitely)*
sicher ['zɪçe] ◊ *Das ist sicher ihr bester Film.* **3.** *(in
a relaxed manner)* ungezwungen ['ʊngətsvʊŋən] ◊ *Sie
unterhielten sich ungezwungen.*
east¹ [noun] **1.** *(location)* Osten ['ɔstn] der <-s> with
the article when specifying a place, no pl ◊ *Der Wind
kam von Osten.* ♦ *im Osten von Paris* **2.** *(countries
of Eastern Europe and Asia)* the East der Osten
[de:ɐ 'ɔstn] <-s> no pl
east² [adj] Ost... [ɔst] east coast Ostküste ['ɔstkʏstə]
die <-, -n> most sing east side Ostseite ['ɔstzaɪtə]
die <-, -n> east wind Ostwind ['ɔstvɪnt] der

<-(e)s, -e>
east³ [adv] *(towards the east)* nach Osten [na:x 'ɔstn]
◊ *Wir fuhren nach Osten.* east of östlich ['œstlɪç]
[+gen] ◊ *östlich der Grenze; (when followed by a word
without the article)* east of östlich von ['œstlɪç fɔn] ◊
Der Fluss liegt östlich von hier. ♦ *östlich von Berlin*
Easter [noun] Ostern ['o:sten] seldom with definite
article 'das' ◊ *Er wünschte uns frohe Ostern.* ♦ *Über
Ostern waren wir bei meinen Eltern.*
easterly [adj] östlich ['œstlɪç] only before ns ◊ *Sie
fuhren in östliche Richtung.* easterly wind Ostwind
['ɔstvɪnt] der <-(e)s, -e>
eastern [adj] östlich ['œstlɪç] only before ns ◊ *das
östliche Mittelmeer; (in geographical names)* Eastern
... Ost... [ɔst] Eastern Europe Osteuropa
['ɔstɔø,ro:pa:] das <-s> article only in combination
with attribute, no pl
East German [noun] *(inhabitant)* Ostdeutsche
['ɔstdɔøtʃə] der/die <-n, die Ostdeutschen> but: ein
Ostdeutscher/eine Ostdeutsche → German¹ 1.
East Germany [noun] Ostdeutschland ['ɔstdɔøtʃlant]
das <-s> article only in combination with attribute,
no pl → Germany
easy¹ [adj] **1.** *(simple)* leicht [laɪçt] <leichter, am leich-
testen> ◊ *Diese Aufgabe ist nicht leicht.* ♦ *kein
leichtes Leben haben ◊ etw. ist leicht zu leben* have
an easy time (of it) es leicht haben ◊ *Mit zwei
kleinen Kindern hat sie es nicht leicht.* make sth
easier (for sb) (jdm) etw. erleichtern [ɛ'laɪçtən]
<erleichtert, erleichterte, hat erleichtert> ◊ *Das neue
Computersystem soll Ihnen die Arbeit erleichtern.*
2. *(relaxed)* ungezwungen ['ʊngətsvʊŋən] ◊ *Die Atmosphäre war recht ungezwungen.* ♦ *Sie mochte seine
ungezwungene Art.*
◉ I'm easy mir ist es egal
easy²
◉ sth comes easy to sb etw. fällt jdm leicht easy
come, easy go wie gewonnen so zerronnen go
easy on sb nachsichtig mit jdm sein not rest easy
keine Ruhe geben easier said than done leichter
gesagt als getan take it easy **1.** *(rest)* sich schonen
2. *(calm down)* sich beruhigen
easy-going [adj] gelassen [gə'lasn] ◊ *ein gelassener
Mensch* ♦ *Sie ist gelassen und gutmütig.*
eat [verb] *(person)* essen ['ɛsn] <isst, aß, hat gegessen>
◊ *Ich esse morgens nie etwas.* ♦ *Er hat seine Suppe
nicht gegessen.* ♦ *Du isst nicht besonders gesund.* ♦
in einem teuren Restaurant essen; (animal) fressen
['frɛsn] <frisst, fraß, hat gefressen> ◊ *Kühe fressen
Gras.* ♦ *Das Pony fraß ihr aus der Hand.*
● **eat away** [phras v] **1.** *(destroy)* eat sth away etw.
zerstören [tsɛ'ʃtø:rən] <zerstört, zerstörte, hat
zerstört> +haben ◊ *Erosion zerstört langsam die
Felsen.; (metal)* etw. zerfressen [tsɛ'frɛsn] <zerfrisst,
zerfraß, hat zerfressen> ◊ *Die Säure hat das Metall
zerfressen.* **2.** *(worry)* eat away at sb an jdm nagen
[an ... 'na:gn] +haben ◊ *Die Eifersucht nagt an ihm.*
● **eat in** [phras v] zu Hause essen ['tsu: 'haozə ɛsn]
<isst, aß, hat gegessen> ◊ *Gehen wir heute Abend ins
Restaurant oder essen wir zu Hause?*
● **eat out** [phras v] essen gehen ['ɛsn ge:ən] <geht,
ging, ist gegangen> ◊ *Wollen wir am Wochenende
mal wieder essen gehen?*
● **eat up** [phras v] **1.** *(finish your meal)* aufessen
['aʊfɛsn] <isst auf, aß auf, hat aufgegessen> ◊ *Hast
du schon aufgegessen?* ♦ *Iss bitte deinen Spinat auf.*

A
B
C
D
E
F
G
H
I
J
K
L
M
N
O
P
Q
R
S
T
U
V
W
X
Y
Z

2. *(use up)* kosten ['kɔstn̩] <kostet, kostete, hat gekostet> ◊ *Dieses Hobby kostet viel Zeit.*

eavesdrop [verb] lauschen ['laoʃn̩] +haben ◊ *Jetzt lauscht er wieder an der Tür.* eavesdrop on sb/sth jdn/etw. belauschen [bə'laoʃn̩] <belauscht, belauschte, hat belauscht> ◊ *Sie hatte das Gespräch belauscht.*

ebb tide [noun] Ebbe ['ɛbə] die <-, -n> *most sing* ◊ *Ebbe und Flut* ✦ *Es ist Ebbe.* ✦ *Bei Ebbe suchen wir Muscheln.*

echo¹ [noun] **1.** *(sound)* Echo ['ɛço:] das <-s, -s> ◊ *In den Bergen hört man oft ein Echo.* **2.** *(similarity, agreement)* Anklang ['anklaŋ] der <-(e)s, Anklänge> ◊ *In seinen frühen Bildern findet man noch Anklänge an die Malerei van Goghs.* find an echo Anklang finden ◊ *Sein neues Stück fand großen Anklang beim Publikum.*

echo² [verb] **1.** *(sound)* hallen ['halən] +haben ◊ *Ihre Stimme hallte durch den Saal.* ✦ *Sie liefen durch hallende Flure.* echo with sth von etw. widerhallen [fɔn ... ˌviːdehalən] +haben ◊ *Das Foyer hallte von den Stimmen der Besucher wider.* **2.** *(repeat sb's words, a quality etc.)* wiederholen [viːde'hoːlən] <wiederholt, wiederholte, hat wiederholt> ◊ *In seiner Aussage wiederholte er die Worte des Premierministers.* ✦ *„Er ist tot?", wiederholte sie ungläubig.* sth is echoed etw. wiederholt sich ◊ *Das Muster wiederholt sich in den verschiedenen Zimmern.*

eclipse [noun] **1.** ASTRON Finsternis ['fɪnstenɪs] die <-, -se> lunar eclipse Mondfinsternis ['moːntfɪnstenɪs] solar eclipse Sonnenfinsternis ['zɔnənfɪnstenɪs] ◊ *eine Sonnenfinsternis beobachten* **2.** *(fig) (of people)* Niedergang ['niːdegaŋ] der <-(e)s, Niedergänge> *most sing* ◊ *der Niedergang einer Dynastie*

eco-friendly [adj] umweltfreundlich ['ʊmvɛltfrɔøntlɪç] ◊ *ein umweltfreundliches Verfahren* ✦ *Pappbecher sind umweltfreundlicher als Kunststoffbecher.*

ecological [adj] ökologisch [øko'loːgɪʃ] ◊ *das ökologische Gleichgewicht*

ecology [noun] Ökologie [økolo'giː] die <-> *no pl* ◊ *Ökologie studieren* ✦ *eine Einführung in die Ökologie*

economic [adj] wirtschaftlich ['vɪʁtʃaftlɪç] ◊ *Wie ist die derzeitige wirtschaftliche Situation?*; Wirtschafts... ['vɪʁtʃafts] economic growth Wirtschaftswachstum ['vɪʁtʃaftsvakstuːm] das <-s> *no pl* economic policy Wirtschaftspolitik ['vɪʁtʃaftspoliˌtiːk] die <-> *no pl*

economical [adj] *(saving money, energy etc.)* wirtschaftlich ['vɪʁtʃaftlɪç] ◊ *ein wirtschaftliches Auto* ✦ *Diese Methode ist wirtschaftlicher.*; *(not wasting anything, subdued)* sparsam ['ʃpaːˈzaːm] ◊ *sparsam mit etw. sein* ✦ *Dieses Spülmittel ist besonders sparsam.* ✦ *eine sparsame Geste*

economically [adv] wirtschaftlich ['vɪʁtʃaftlɪç] ◊ *Wir sollten mit den Ressourcen wirtschaftlicher umgehen.*

economics [noun] **1.** UNI *(subject)* Wirtschaftswissenschaft ['vɪʁtʃaftsvɪsnʃaft] die <-, -en> *most pl* ◊ *eine Studentin der Wirtschaftswissenschaften* **2.** *(aspect)* the economics der wirtschaftliche Aspekt [deːɐ̯ ˌvɪʁtʃaftlɪçə as'pɛkt] <-(e)s, -e> ◊ *der wirtschaftliche Aspekt der Bildung*

economist [noun] Wirtschaftswissenschaftler ['vɪʁtʃafts̩vɪsnʃaftle] der <-s, -> ♀Wirtschaftswissen-

schaftlerin ['vɪʁtʃafts̩vɪsnʃaftlərɪn] die <-, -nen> ◊ *Er ist Wirtschaftswissenschaftler.* ✦ *Eine Wirtschaftswissenschaftlerin soll die Situation der Firma analysieren.*

economize [verb] sparen ['ʃpaːʁən] +haben ◊ *Meine Frau kann nicht sparen.* economize on sth an etw. [dat] sparen ◊ *Am Gemüse sollte man beim Kochen nicht sparen.*

economy [noun] **1.** *(system, industry and commerce as a whole)* Wirtschaft ['vɪʁtʃaft] die <-, -en> ◊ *Die deutsche Wirtschaft ist stark exportabhängig.*; *(economic activity of an area or country)* Konjunktur [kɔnjʊŋk'tuːɐ̯] die <-, -en> ◊ *Maßnahmen, um die Konjunktur zu beleben* **2.** *(careful use of sth)* Sparsamkeit ['ʃpaː'zaːmkaet] die <-> *no pl* ◊ *Sparsamkeit bei Nebenausgaben* ✦ *die Sparsamkeit der Mittel*; *(way of saving money)* economies Einsparungen ['aɛnʃpaːrʊŋən] die <-> *pl* ◊ *bei Geschäftsreisen Einsparungen machen*

edge [noun] **1.** *(outer limit)* Rand [rant] der <-(e)s, Ränder> ◊ *der Rand eines Kraters* ✦ *am Rand der Stadt* ✦ *am Rande des Untergangs stehen*; *(where two sides of sth meet)* Kante ['kantə] die <-, -n> ◊ *Pass auf, der Tisch hat eine scharfe Kante.* edge of the bed Bettkante ['bɛtkantə] ◊ *Sie setzte sich auf die Bettkante.* **2.** *(of a blade)* Schneide ['ʃnaedə] die <-, -n> ◊ *ein Messer mit scharfer/stumpfer Schneide* **3.** *(advantage)* Vorteil ['foːɐ̯taɛl] der <-(e)s, -e> have an edge over sb jdm gegenüber einen Vorteil haben ◊ *Er hat den anderen Jungen gegenüber einen Vorteil.* give sb/sth the edge over sb/sth jdm/etw. einen Vorteil gegenüber jdm/etw. verschaffen ℗ be on edge *(about sth)* *(wegen etw.)* nervös sein take the edge off sth etw. abschwächen

edit [verb] **1.** *(revise, modify, amend)* bearbeiten [bə'aˈbaetn̩] <bearbeitet, bearbeitete, hat bearbeitet> ◊ *einen Artikel/eine Datei bearbeiten*; *(a film, tape)* schneiden ['ʃnaedn̩] <schneidet, schnitt, hat geschnitten> ◊ *Den Film hat ein begabter Cutter geschnitten.* **2.** *(publish a paper, book etc.)* herausgeben [hɛ'raosgeːbm̩] <gibt heraus, gab heraus, hat herausgegeben> ◊ *eine Anthologie herausgeben*

edition [noun] Ausgabe ['aosgaːbə] die <-, -n> ◊ *die aktuelle Ausgabe einer Zeitschrift*

editor [noun] **1.** *(publisher)* Herausgeber [hɛ'raosgeːbe] der <-s, -> ♀Herausgeberin [hɛ'raosgeːbərɪn] die <-, -nen> ◊ *die Herausgeberin einer Zeitung* **2.** *(sb who selects and amends contributions for a newspaper etc.)* Redakteur [redak'tøːɐ̯] der <-s, -e> ♀Redakteurin [redak'tøːrɪn] die <-, -nen> ◊ *der leitende politische Redakteur der Süddeutschen Zeitung* ✦ *Sie ist Redakteurin beim Rundfunk/Fernsehen.* FILM Cutter ['katɐ] der <-s, -> ♀Cutterin ['katərɪn] die <-, -nen> ◊ *eine gesuchte Cutterin* ✦ *die Zusammenarbeit von Regisseur und Cutter*

educate [verb] **1.** *(teach)* unterrichten [ʊntɐ'rɪçtn̩] <unterrichtet, unterrichtete, hat unterrichtet> ◊ *jdn in Mathematik unterrichten* be educated at a school/university eine Schule/Universität besuchen [aenə 'ʃuːlə/univɐˈzʁiːtɛːt bəzuːxn̩] <besucht, besuchte, hat besucht> ◊ *Er besucht eine Privatschule.* **2.** *(inform)* informieren [ɪnfɔʁˈmiːrən] <informiert, informierte, hat informiert> ◊ *jdn über Umweltfragen informieren* ✦ *Das Buch will auf unterhaltsame*

Weise informieren.

educated → **educate** [adj] gebildet [gə'bɪldət] ◊ *Er war ein vielseitig gebildeter Mann.* ♦ *Sie ist sehr gebildet.* well educated gebildet

education [noun] 1. *(process of educating)* Erziehung [e'tsi:ʊŋ] die <–> no pl ◊ *die Erziehung unserer Kinder* 2. *(knowledge, culture)* Bildung ['bɪldʊŋ] die <–> no pl ◊ *das Recht auf Bildung* ♦ *Sie hat eine höhere Bildung genossen.* 3. *(classes)* Unterricht ['ʊntərɪçt] der <–(e)s, –e> most sing ◊ *Unterricht in Fremdsprachen* physical education Sportunterricht ['ʃpɔ'ʳt|ʊntərɪçt] 4. university education Hochschulausbildung ['ho:xʃu:l|aʊsbɪldʊŋ] adult education Erwachsenenbildung [e'vaksənənbɪldʊŋ] die <–> no pl 5. *(information)* Aufklärung ['aʊfklɛ:rʊŋ] die <–, –en> most sing ◊ *die Aufklärung Jugendlicher über die Gefahren des Rauchens* health education gesundheitliche Aufklärung

educational [adj] 1. *(relating to teaching)* pädagogisch [pɛda'go:gɪʃ] no comp/superl ◊ *pädagogische Fähigkeiten* ♦ *aus pädagogischen Gründen* educational method Erziehungsmethode [e'tsi:ʊŋsme,to:də] die <–, –n> ◊ *neue Erziehungsmethoden anwenden* 2. *(relating to education)* educational ... Bildungs... ['bɪldʊŋs] educational opportunities Bildungschancen ['bɪldʊŋsʃaŋsn] die <–> pl educational qualification Bildungsabschluss ['bɪldʊŋs|apʃlʊs] der <–es, Bildungsabschlüsse> ◊ *Welchen Bildungsabschluss haben Sie?* 3. *(informative)* lehrreich ['le:grae̯ç] ◊ *ein lehrreiches Buch* ♦ *Der Film war sehr lehrreich.*

education system [noun] Bildungswesen ['bɪldʊŋsve:zn] das <–s> no pl ◊ *eine umfassende Reform des Bildungswesens*

eerie(-ily) [adj, adv] unheimlich ['ʊnhae̯mlɪç] ◊ *Nachts ist es im Wald noch unheimlicher als tagsüber.* ♦ *ein unheimliches Geräusch* ♦ *Der Wind heulte unheimlich.*

effect¹ [noun] 1. *(consequence)* Wirkung ['vɪrkʊŋ] die <–, –en> ◊ *die Wirkung einer Säure auf Metall* ♦ *Die erhoffte Wirkung blieb aus.* have the effect of sth etw. bewirken [bə'vɪrkɳ̍] <bewirkt, bewirkte, hat bewirkt>; *(repercussion)* Auswirkung ['aʊsvɪrkʊŋ] die <–, –en> ◊ *negative/positive Auswirkungen haben* ♦ *die Auswirkung einer Handlung auf die Umwelt* 2. *(impression, in science)* Effekt [ɛ'fɛkt] der <–(e)s, –e> produce an effect einen Effekt erzielen ◊ *Mit der Goldpatina erzielen Sie einen schönen Effekt.* special effects Spezialeffekte [ʃpe'tsja:l|ɛ,fɛktə] die <–> pl 3. *(form) (belongings)* (personal) effects Eigentum ['ae̯gn̩tu:m] der <–s> no pl ◊ *das Eigentum des Verstorbenen* ⊙ put sth into effect etw. einführen take effect 1. *(drug)* wirken 2. *(measure, reforms)* greifen 3. *(law)* in Kraft treten in effect 1. *(in reality)* in Wirklichkeit 2. *(law)* gültig to the effect that mit dem Inhalt, dass ◊ *Sie schickte ihm einen Brief mit dem Inhalt, dass sie ihn verlassen werde.* to that effect in diesem Sinne with effect from *(form)* mit Wirkung vom *(form)*

effect² [verb] *(form) (bring about)* herbeiführen [he'baefy:rən] +haben ◊ *Die Verhandlungen sollen eine Einigung der Parteien herbeiführen.; (a purchase, sale etc.)* tätigen ['tɛ:tɪgn̩] +haben ◊ *wichtige Einkäufe tätigen*

effective(ly) [adj, adv] 1. *(achieving a result)* wirksam ['vɪ'ᵏkza:m] ◊ *Das Verfahren ist teuer, aber wirksam.* ♦ *ein wirksames Medikament* ♦ *sich wirksam vor einer Krankheit schützen; (law)* become effective in Kraft treten [ɪn 'kraft tre:tn̩] <tritt, trat, ist getreten> 2. *(impressive)* wirkungsvoll ['vɪrkʊŋsfɔl] ◊ *ein wirkungsvolles Arrangement verschiedener Blüten* ♦ *Der Künstler setzt die Farben wirkungsvoll ein.* 3. *(real)* effektiv [ɛfɛk'ti:f] no comp/superl; when used as an adj, only before ns ◊ *den effektiven Gewinn ermitteln* ♦ *Durch die Inflation ist mein Einkommen effektiv zurückgegangen.*

effectiveness [noun] 1. *(result)* Wirksamkeit ['vɪ'ᵏkza:mkae̯t] die <–> no pl ◊ *die Wirksamkeit eines Medikaments* 2. *(impression)* Wirkung ['vɪrkʊŋ] die <–, –en> ◊ *Die Wirkung des dunkelroten Hintergrunds ist enorm.*

efficiency [noun] *(of a worker, machine, factory)* Leistungsfähigkeit ['lae̯stʊŋsfɛ:ɪçkae̯t] die <–> no pl ◊ *Haben Sie Zweifel an meiner Leistungsfähigkeit? ♦ die Leistungsfähigkeit einer Maschine erhöhen; (of a system, method)* Effizienz [ɛfi'tsi̯ɛnts] die <–> no pl *(lofty)* ◊ *ein System mit hoher Effizienz*

efficient [adj] *(productive)* leistungsfähig ['lae̯stʊŋsfɛ:ɪç] ◊ *leistungsfähige Mitarbeiter* ♦ *Leider bin ich im Moment nicht besonders leistungsfähig.; (system, method)* effizient [ɛfi'tsi̯ɛnt] <effizienter, am effizientesten> ◊ *effizientere Arbeitsmethoden einführen; (capable)* tüchtig ['tʏçtɪç] ◊ *eine tüchtige Sekretärin* ♦ *Der Kellner war tüchtig und zuvorkommend.* make efficient use of sth etw. gut nutzen [,gu:t 'nʊtsn̩] +haben

efficiently [adv] effizient [ɛfi'tsi̯ɛnt] <effizienter, am effizientesten> ◊ *Wir müssen effizienter arbeiten.*

effort [noun] 1. *(attempt)* Versuch [fe'zu:x] der <–(e)s, –e> ◊ *Das war ihr erster Versuch, einen Roman zu schreiben.* make an effort to do sth versuchen, etw. zu tun [fe'zu:xn̩ ... tsu:] <versucht, versuchte, hat versucht> make no effort to do sth sich [dat] nicht die Mühe machen, etw. zu tun [nɪçt di: 'my:ə maxn̩ ... tsu:] +haben despite sb's efforts trotz jds Bemühungen [trɔts ... bə'my:ʊŋən] 2. *(hard work, activity to reach an aim)* Anstrengung ['anʃtrɛŋʊŋ] die <–, –en> ◊ *Er hob den schweren Sack scheinbar ohne Anstrengung hoch.* ♦ *Ihre Anstrengungen waren vergebens.* with an effort mühsam ['my:za:m] ◊ *Sie kam im Schnee nur mühsam vorwärts.* be an effort Mühe kosten ['my:ə kɔstn̩] <kostet, kostete, hat gekostet> ◊ *Nach dem Urlaub kostet es Mühe, wieder mit der Arbeit anzufangen.* make an effort sich anstrengen ['anʃtrɛŋən] +haben ◊ *Nun komm schon, streng dich an!* 3. *(fam) (product)* Unternehmen [ʊnte'ne:mən] das <–s, –> ◊ *Dieses Unternehmen wird der Finanzierung scheitern.* a pretty poor effort eine ziemlich schwache Leistung [ae̯nə tsi:mlɪç ʃvaxə 'lae̯stʊŋ]

e.g. z. B. [tsʊm 'bae̯ʃpi:l] ◊ *Er hat verschiedene Haustiere, z. B. zwei Hunde und eine Katze.*

egg [noun] Ei [ae̯] das <–(e)s, –er> ◊ *ein Brötchen mit Schinken und Ei* ♦ *Das Küken schlüpft aus dem Ei.*

⊙ put all your eggs in one basket alles auf eine Karte setzen get egg on your face dumm dastehen

egg cup [noun] Eierbecher ['ae̯ebɛçɐ] der <–s, –>

egg white [noun] Eiweiß ['ae̯vae̯s] das <–es, –e> pl 'Eiweiß' when used with expressions of quantity, most

A
B
C
D
E
F
G
H
I
J
K
L
M
N
O
P
Q
R
S
T
U
V
W
X
Y
Z

sing ◊ *Er brauchte für den Eischnee vier Eiweiß.*

egg yolk ⌐noun⌐ Eigelb ['æɡɛlp] das <-s, -e> pl *'Eigelb' when used with expressions of quantity* ◊ *zwei Eigelb in den Teig geben*

ego ⌐noun⌐ **1.** *(opinion about yourself)* Ego ['e:ɡo:] das <-, -s> ◊ *Das Lob schmeichelte ihrem Ego.* boost sb's ego jds Selbstbewusstsein stärken ['zɛlpstbəvʊstzaɛn ʃtɛ'kɪʃ] +haben ◊ *Diese Beförderung wird sein Selbstbewusstsein stärken.* bruised ego angeknackstes Selbstbewusstsein [ˌanɡəknakstəs 'zɛlpstbəvʊstzaɛn] <-s> no pl *(fam)* **2.** *(in psychology)* Ich [ɪç] das <-(s), -s>

egoistic(ally) ⌐adj, adv⌐ egoistisch [eɡo'ɪstɪʃ] ◊ *Sei nicht so egoistisch!* ◆ *egoistische Motive* ◆ *ein egoistisch denkender Mensch*

Egypt ⌐noun⌐ Ägypten [ɛ'ɡyptn̩] das <-s> *article only in combination with attribute, no pl* → **Germany**

Egyptian¹ ⌐noun⌐ **1.** *(inhabitant)* Ägypter [ɛ'ɡyptɐ] der <-s, -> ♀Ägypterin [ɛ'ɡyptərɪn] die <-, -nen> → **German¹**1 **2.** *(language)* Ägyptisch [ɛ'ɡyptɪʃ] das <-(s)> no pl → **German¹**2

Egyptian² ⌐adj⌐ ägyptisch [ɛ'ɡyptɪʃ] → **German²**

eight¹ ⌐noun⌐ Acht [axt] die <-, -en> → **four¹**

eight² ⌐nmrl⌐ acht [axt] → **four²**

eighteen ⌐nmrl⌐ achtzehn ['axtse:n] → **four²**

eightfold ⌐adj, adv⌐ achtfach ['axtfax] → **fourfold**

eighth¹ ⌐noun⌐ **1.** *(fraction)* Achtel ['axtl̩] das <-s, -> → **fourth¹** 1. **2.** *(in a sequence)* Achte ['axtə] der *or* die *or* das <-n, -n> *most sing* → **fourth¹** 2.

eighth² ⌐adj⌐ achte ['axtə] <ein achter …, eine achte …, ein achtes …> → **fourth²**

eighthly ⌐adv⌐ achtens ['axtn̩s] → **fourthly**

eighty ⌐nmrl⌐ achtzig ['axtsɪç] → **four²**

Eire ⌐noun⌐ Irland ['ɪrlant] das <-s> *article only in combination with attribute, no pl* → **Germany**

either¹ ⌐adv⌐ auch nicht ['aox nɪçt] ◊ *Ben war auch nicht gekommen.* ◆ *Anna kann nicht singen und ihre Schwester auch nicht.*

either² ⌐det⌐ *(both)* beide ['baɛdə] ◊ *Das Auto hat auf beiden Seiten Kratzer.* not like either beides nicht mögen ['baɛdəs nɪçt mø:ɡn̩] <mag, mochte, hat gemocht> ◊ *Es gibt Zitronen- und Nusseis, aber ich mag beides nicht.* either way in jedem Fall [ɪn ˌje:dəm 'fal] ◊ *Ob es ein Versehen war oder Absicht, in jedem Fall musst du dich entschuldigen.* of either sex beiderlei Geschlechts [ˌbaɛdəlaɛ ɡə'ʃlɛçts] ◊ *Bewerber beiderlei Geschlechts sind willkommen.*

either³ ⌐pron⌐ *(any one of two objects)* beides ['baɛdəs] ◊ *Bier oder Wein — ich mag beides.;* *(one or the other)* either (of) einer/eine/eines von beiden ['aɛnɐ/'aɛnə/'aɛnəs fɔn ˌbaɛdn̩] ◊ *Urlaub oder Auto — das Geld reicht nur für eines von beiden!* ◆ *Weiß einer von euch beiden, wie spät es ist?*

either⁴ ⌐conjunc⌐ either … or entweder … oder [ɛntveːdə … oːdə] ◊ *Entweder du kommst jetzt sofort nach Hause, oder es gibt Ärger!*

elaborate ⌐verb⌐ **1.** sb elaborates jd äußert sich ausführlicher [ˌɔøsət … aus'fy:ɡlɪçɐ] +haben ◊ *Sie haben also einen Plan — könnten Sie sich ausführlicher äußern?* sb elaborates on sth jd führt etw. näher aus [fy:ɡt … 'nɛ:ɐ ˌaos] +haben ◊ *Ein interessantes Konzept — könnten Sie das näher ausführen?* **2.** *(work on the details, a proposal)* elaborate sth etw. ausarbeiten ['aos|aˌbaɛtn̩] <arbeitet aus, arbeitete aus, hat ausgearbeitet> ◊ *einen Vorschlag*

ausarbeiten

elaborate(ly) ⌐adj, adv⌐ *(design, pattern, drawing, style)* kunstvoll ['kʊnstfɔl] ◊ *ein kunstvolles Design* ◆ *Diese Schnitzerei ist äußerst kunstvoll.* ◆ *kunstvoll gestaltet;* *(plan, system)* ausgeklügelt ['aosɡəkly:ɡlt]

elastic ⌐adj⌐ *(flexible)* elastisch [e'lastɪʃ] ◊ *Der Bund dieser Hose ist sehr elastisch.* ◆ *eine elastische Währung;* *(made of elastic)* Gummi… ['ɡʊmi:] elastic stockings Stützstrümpfe ['ʃtytsˌʃtrʏmpfə] die <-> pl

elbow ⌐noun⌐ Ellbogen ['ɛlbo:ɡn̩] der <-s, -> ◊ *sich auf die Ellbogen stützen*
 ⊚ give sb the elbow jdm den Laufpass geben

elder ⌐noun⌐ **1.** *(older person)* respect your elders die Älteren respektieren [di: 'ɛltərən rɛspɛk'ti:rən] +haben; *(of a Church, tribe)* Älteste ['ɛltəstə] der/die <-n, die Ältesten> *but: ein Ältester/eine Älteste* ◊ *die Ältesten des Stammes* **2.** *(with names)* the Elder der/die Ältere [de:ɐ̯/di: 'ɛltərə] <-n> no pl ◊ *Plinius der Ältere* **3.** ʙᴏᴛ Holunder [ho'lʊndɐ] der <-s, ->
 ⊚ be five/ten etc. years sb's elder fünf/zehn etc. Jahre älter als jd sein

elderly ⌐adj⌐ *(people)* älter ['ɛltɐ] no comp/superl ◊ *ein bunter Nachmittag für ältere Mitbürger* the elderly ältere Menschen

elect ⌐verb⌐ *(a politician etc.)* wählen ['vɛ:lən] +haben ◊ *ein neues Parlament wählen* elect sb to sth jdn in etw. ⌐acc⌐ wählen ◊ *Sie wurde in den Bundestag gewählt.* elect sb president etc. jdn zum Präsidenten etc. wählen

elected → **elect** ⌐adj⌐ gewählt [ɡə've:lt] no comp/ superl ◊ *eine demokratisch gewählte Regierung*

election ⌐noun⌐ Wahl [va:l] die <-, -en> ◊ *die Wahl gewinnen/verlieren* ◆ *Nehmen Sie die Wahl an?* fight an election zur Wahl antreten preliminary election Vorwahl ['fo:ɐ̯va:l] election result Wahlergebnis ['va:lˌɡe:pnɪs] das <-ses, -se> election campaign Wahlkampf ['va:lkampf] der <-(e)s, Wahlkämpfe>

electoral ⌐adj⌐ Wahl… [va:l] electoral system Wahlsystem ['va:lzʏsˌte:m] das <-s, -e> electoral district Wahlbezirk ['va:lbətsɪrk] der <-(e)s, -e>

electorate ⌐noun⌐ Wähler ['vɛ:lɐ] die <-> pl ◊ *ein Parteiprogramm, das alle Wähler anspricht*

electric ⌐adj⌐ elektrisch [e'lɛktrɪʃ] no comp/superl, mostly before ns ◊ *elektrisches Licht;* Elektro… [e'lɛktro:] electric cooker Elektroherd [e'lɛktrohe:ɡt] der <-(e)s, -e> electric fence Elektrozaun [e'lɛktrotsaon] der <-(e)s, Elektrozäune>

electrical ⌐adj⌐ elektrisch [e'lɛktrɪʃ] no comp/superl, mostly before ns ◊ *elektrische Geräte;* Elektro… [e'lɛktro:] electric cooker Elektroherd [e'lɛktrohe:ɡt] der <-(e)s, -e> electrical engineering Elektrotechnik [e'lɛktroteçnɪk] die <-> no pl electrical engineer Elektrotechniker [e'lɛktroteçnɪkɐ] der <-s, -> ♀Elektrotechnikerin [e'lɛktroˌteçnɪkərɪn] die <-, -nen>

electrically ⌐adv⌐ elektrisch [e'lɛktrɪʃ] no comp/superl ◊ *elektrisch geladene Teilchen*

electrician ⌐noun⌐ Elektriker [e'lɛktrɪkɐ] der <-s, -> ♀Elektrikerin [e'lɛktrɪkərɪn] die <-, -nen> ◊ *Sie arbeitet als Elektrikerin.* ◆ *Der Elektriker hat den Ofen repariert.*

electricity ⌐noun⌐ Strom [ʃtro:m] der <-(e)s, Ströme> most sing ◊ *Strom verbrauchen/sparen* ◆ *Strom erzeugen* ◆ *den Strom ausschalten*

electron ⌐noun⌐ Elektron ['e:lɛktrɔn] das <-s, -en> ◊

Die Elektronen bewegen sich um den Atomkern.
electronic [adj] elektronisch [elɛk'trɔːnɪʃ] *no comp/ superl* ◊ *ein elektronischer Taschenrechner*
electronics [noun] Elektronik [elɛk'trɔːnɪk] die <-> *no pl* ◊ *Er interessiert sich sehr für Elektronik.* ♦ *die Elektronik eines Flugzeugs*
elegance [noun] Eleganz [elə'ganʦ] die <-> *no pl* ◊ *sportliche Eleganz*
elegant(ly) [adj, adv] elegant [elə'gant] <eleganter, am elegantesten> ◊ *ein elegant gekleideter Herr* ♦ *ein eleganter Wagen* ♦ *Diese Lösung des Problems ist überaus elegant.*
element [noun] *(basic component, in chemistry, small amount, weather, earth/air/fire/water)* Element [elə'mɛnt] das <-(e)s, -e> ◊ *Welches sind die wesentlichen Elemente des Plans?* ♦ *Diese Musik enthält einige Elemente des Irish Folk.* ♦ *Sauerstoff ist ein chemisches Element.; (of a subject)* the elements of sth die Grundbegriffe ... [gen] [diː 'grʊntbəgrɪfə] die <-> *pl* ◊ *die Grundbegriffe der Mathematik; (weather)* the elements die Elemente [diː elə'mɛntə] *pl*
◉ be in your element in seinem Element sein
elementary school [noun] Grundschule ['grʊntʃuːlə] die <-, -n>
elephant [noun] Elefant [elə'fant] der <-en, -en> ◊ *der indische/afrikanische Elefant*
elevation [noun] **1.** *(altitude)* Höhe ['høːə] die <-, -n> ◊ *Die Hütte liegt auf einer Höhe von 2589 m.* **2.** *(elevated place)* Anhöhe ['anhøːə] die <-, -n> ◊ *Das Haus steht auf einer kleinen Anhöhe.* **3.** ARCH Aufriss ['aʊfrɪs] der <-es, -e> ◊ *Hier ist das Gemeindezentrum im Aufriss dargestellt.* front elevation Frontansicht ['frɔnt|anzɪçt] die <-, -en> **4.** *(rise in the level)* Erhöhung [ɛ'høːʊŋ] die <-, -en> ◊ *eine Erhöhung des Blutdrucks* **5.** *(promoting)* Erhebung [ɛ'heːbʊŋ] die <-, -en> ◊ *jds Erhebung in den Adelsstand*
elevator [noun] Aufzug ['aʊfʦuːk] der <-(e)s, Aufzüge> ◊ *mit dem Aufzug in den 10. Stock fahren*
eleven [nmrl] elf [ɛlf] → four²
eligible [adj] berechtigt [bə'rɛçtɪçt] *no comp/superl* ◊ *Alle berechtigten Bürger melden sich bitte bei der Stadtverwaltung.* eligible for sth zu etw. berechtigt ◊ *Kinder sind nicht zur Teilnahme berechtigt.* eligible to do sth berechtigt, etw. zu tun; *(for a job)* be eligible for sth für etw. infrage kommen [fyː ... ɪn'fraːgə kɔmən] ◊ *kommt, kam, ist gekommen>* eligible bachelor begehrter Junggeselle [bə,geːɐ̯tə 'jʊŋgəzɛlə] <-n, -n>
eliminate [verb] **1.** *(get rid of, kill)* ausschalten ['aʊsʃaltn̩] <schaltet aus, schaltete aus, hat ausgeschaltet> ◊ *Wie können wir die Konkurrenz ausschalten?* ♦ *ungünstige Einflüsse ausschalten* **2.** *(exclude)* ausschließen ['aʊsʃliːsn̩] <schließt aus, schloss aus, hat ausgeschlossen> ◊ *Er schloss ein Versehen als Unfallursache aus.* **3.** *(from a competition)* be eliminated ausscheiden ['aʊsʃaedn̩] <scheidet aus, schied aus, ist ausgeschieden> ◊ *In der dritten Runde des Rennens schied er aus.*
elimination [noun] **1.** *(getting rid of, killing)* Ausschaltung ['aʊsʃaltʊŋ] die <-> *no pl* ◊ *die Ausschaltung der Konkurrenz/eines Gegners* process of elimination Ausschlussverfahren ['aʊsʃlʊsfɛfaːrən] das <-s> *no pl* **2.** *(defeat)* Ausscheiden ['aʊsʃaedn̩] das <-s> *no*

pl ◊ *das Ausscheiden der Mannschaft aus dem Turnier*
elite [noun] Elite [e'liːtə] die <-, -n> ◊ *ein Mitglied der gesellschaftlichen Elite sein*
else [adv] **1.** *(apart from)* (somebody/something etc.) else andere ['andərə] ◊ *Alles andere war richtig.* ♦ *Fragen Sie doch jemand anderen.* ♦ *Jeder andere hätte das genauso gemacht.* ♦ *Kannst du nichts anderes tun?* **2.** *(in addition)* (nobody/nothing etc.) else sonst (keiner/nichts etc.) [zɔnst ('kaenɐ/nɪçts)] ◊ *Paul und Anton waren da, aber sonst keiner.* ♦ *In das Bier dürfen nur diese Zutaten und sonst nichts.* (what/who etc.) else sonst noch ['zɔnst nɔx] ◊ *Wer war sonst noch Zeuge des Unfalls?* ♦ *Was hast du sonst noch zum Geburtstag bekommen?*
◉ somewhere else **1.** *(position)* woanders ◊ *Sie wohnt woanders.* ♦ *Könnten Sie bitte woanders rauchen?* **2.** *(direction)* woandershin ◊ *Wir ziehen nächstes Jahr woandershin.* or else **1.** *(explaining second possibility)* oder aber ◊ *Ihr könnt den Zug nehmen oder aber mit dem Auto fahren.* **2.** *(threatening)* sonst ◊ *Wir müssen uns beeilen, sonst verpassen wir den Zug.*
elsewhere [adv] *(position)* anderswo ['andəsvoː] *(fam)* ◊ *Das Benzin ist hier billiger als anderswo in Deutschland.* ♦ *Sie arbeitet jetzt anderswo.; (direction)* anderswohin ['andəsvoːhɪn] *(fam)* ◊ *Sie möchte anderswohin versetzt werden.* from elsewhere anderswoher ['andəsvoːheːɐ̯] *(fam)* ◊ *Er kommt nicht aus München, sondern anderswoher.*
e-mail¹ [noun] E-Mail ['iːmeːl] die <-, -s> ◊ *Haben Sie E-Mail?* ♦ *Sie bekam eine E-Mail mit einem Anhang.* ♦ *jdm eine E-Mail schicken*
e-mail² [verb] mailen ['meːlən] +haben ◊ *Ich mailte ihr die Übersetzung.* ♦ *Er mailt mir fast täglich.*
embark [verb] embark sb/sth jdn/etw. einschiffen ['aenʃɪfn̩] +haben ◊ *Passagiere/Waren einschiffen* sb embarks jd geht an Bord [geːt an 'bɔʀt] <geht, ging, ist gegangen> ◊ *Wir gingen in Hamburg an Bord.*
• **embark on** [phras v] embark on sth etw. beginnen [bə'gɪnən] <beginnt, begann, hat begonnen> ◊ *ein Studium beginnen*
embarrass [verb] in Verlegenheit bringen [ɪn fɛ'leːgn̩haet brɪŋən] <bringt, brachte, hat gebracht> ◊ *Sein peinlicher Auftritt auf der Party brachte alle in Verlegenheit.*
embarrassed → **embarrass** [adj] verlegen [fɛ'leːgn̩] ◊ *Diese Frage machte ihn noch verlegener.* ♦ *verlegenes Schweigen* ♦ *Verlegen sah sie ihn an.* sb feels/is embarrassed about sth etw. ist jdm peinlich [ɪst ... 'paenlɪç] +sein ◊ *Die ganze Angelegenheit war ihr furchtbar peinlich.* I was so embarrassed! Das war mir so peinlich!
embarrassing → **embarrass** [adj] peinlich ['paenlɪç] ◊ *Seine Antwort war eher peinlich als witzig.* ♦ *peinliches Benehmen*
embarrassment [noun] **1.** *(feeling of shame)* Verlegenheit [fɛ'leːgn̩haet] die <-> *no pl* ◊ *Er errötete vor Verlegenheit.* be an embarrassment to sb, cause embarrassment to sb jdn in Verlegenheit bringen ◊ *Die Frage brachte den Politiker in Verlegenheit.* **2.** *(sth/sb you are ashamed of)* Blamage [bla'maːʒə] die <-, -n> ◊ *Sie ist eine Blamage für die ganze Familie.*
embassy [noun] Botschaft ['boːtʃaft] die <-, -en> ◊ *Sie hat bei der deutschen Botschaft um Asyl gebeten.*

embers [noun] Glut [glu:t] die <-> sing ◊ *Er legte die Kartoffeln in die Glut.*

embezzle [verb] veruntreuen [fɛ|'ʊntrɔɡən] <veruntreut, veruntreute, hat veruntreut> *mostly written* ◊ *Der Geschäftsführer hat große Summen veruntreut.*

embezzlement [noun] Untreue ['ʊntrɔɡə] die <-> *no pl* ◊ *gegen einen Bankmanager Strafanzeige wegen Untreue erstatten*

emblem [noun] Emblem [ɛm'ble:m] das <-s, -e *or also* –ata> ◊ *Die weiße Taube ist das Emblem des Friedens.*

embody [verb] 1. *(stand for)* verkörpern [fɛ'kœ'pen] <verkörpert, verkörperte, hat verkörpert> ◊ *Dieser Star verkörpert den amerikanischen Traum.* 2. *(form) (comprise)* enthalten [ɛnt'haltn] <enthält, enthielt, hat enthalten> ◊ *Das Gerät enthält einige technische Neuerungen.*

embrace [verb] 1. *(lit) (hug)* umarmen [ʊm|'a'man] <umarmt, umarmte, hat umarmt> ◊ *Er umarmte sie und küsste sie zärtlich.* They embrace. Sie umarmen sich. 2. *(form) (accept)* annehmen ['anne:mən] <nimmt an, nahm an, hat angenommen> ◊ *Die Kunden haben das neue Konzept gut angenommen.* ♦ *die katholische Religion annehmen* 3. *(form) (include)* umfassen [ʊm'fasn] <umfasst, umfasste, hat umfasst> ◊ *Der Lehrgang umfasst drei Themenschwerpunkte.*

embroider [verb] 1. *(a cloth)* sticken ['ʃtɪkn] +haben ◊ *Die Prinzessin saß am Fenster und stickte.* ♦ *ein Monogramm auf etw.* [acc] *sticken* 2. *(a story)* ausschmücken ['aʊsʃmykn] +haben ◊ *eine Geschichte ausschmücken*

embryo [noun] Embryo ['ɛmbryo:] der <-s, -nen *or* –s> ◊ *Man kann den Embryo auf dem Ultraschallbild bereits gut erkennen.* in embryo im Anfangsstadium [ɪm 'anfaŋsʃta:djʊm] ◊ *Er befand sich mit seinem Projekt noch im Anfangsstadium.*

emerge [verb] 1. *(appear)* emerge from sth aus etw. auftauchen [aʊs ... aʊftaʊxn] +sein ◊ *Eine dunkle Gestalt tauchte aus dem Nebel auf.* emerge into sth irgendwohin herauskommen [hɛ'raʊskomən] <kommt heraus, kam heraus, ist herausgekommen> ◊ *Die Tür öffnete sich, und die Leute kamen heraus auf die Straße.* 2. *(from a difficult situation)* emerge from sth aus etw. herauskommen [aʊs ... hɛ,raʊskomən] <kommt heraus, kam heraus, ist herausgekommen> ◊ *Die Firma ist nach Jahren endlich aus der Krise herausgekommen.* emerge the winner/a stronger person als Sieger/gestärkt hervorgehen [als 'zi:ɡe/ɡə'ʃtɛ'kt hɛ,fo:gɡe:ən] <geht hervor, ging hervor, ist hervorgegangen> ◊ *Er ging aus dem Kampf als Sieger hervor.* ♦ *Aus dieser Krise ging sie gestärkt hervor.* 3. *(become known)* aufkommen ['aʊfkomən] <kommt auf, kam auf, ist aufgekommen> ◊ *Es kamen beunruhigende Gerüchte auf.* ♦ *Eine neue Mode kommt auf.; (develop)* entstehen [ɛnt'ʃte:ən] <entsteht, entstand, ist entstanden> ◊ *Und so entstand eine neue Tierart.; (truth, fact: come out)* sich herausstellen [zɪç hɛ'raʊsʃtelən] +haben ◊ *Schließlich stellte sich die Wahrheit heraus.; (be a result)* emerge from sth sich aus etw. ergeben [zɪç aʊs ... e'ge:bm] <ergibt sich, ergab sich, hat sich ergeben> ◊ *Aus unserer Diskussion ergab sich, dass wir besser zusammenarbeiten müssen.*

emergence [noun] *(development)* Entstehung [ɛnt'ʃte:ʊŋ] die <-, –en> *most sing* ◊ *die Entstehung*

der modernen Nationalstaaten; *(sudden appearance)* Auftauchen ['aʊftaʊxn] das <-s> *no pl* ◊ *Mit dem Auftauchen eines solchen Problems hatte niemand gerechnet.; (of a theory, political movement, protest group)* Aufkommen ['aʊfkomən] das <-s> *no pl* ◊ *Seit dem Aufkommen dieser Theorie wird vehement diskutiert.*

emergency [noun] Notfall ['no:tfal] der <-(e)s, Notfälle> ◊ *Sind Sie auf den Notfall vorbereitet?* ♦ *Der Arzt ist zu einem Notfall gerufen worden.* in an emergency, in case of emergency im Notfall

emergency brake [noun] 1. *(in a train etc.)* Notbremse ['no:tbrɛmzə] die <-, –n> ◊ *bei Gefahr die Notbremse ziehen/betätigen* 2. *(in the US: of a car)* Handbremse ['hantbrɛmzə] die <-, –n> pull/release the emergency brake die Handbremse anziehen/lösen

emergency call [noun] Notruf ['no:tru:f] der <-(e)s, -e> ◊ *Bei der Feuerwehr gingen an Silvester zahlreiche Notrufe ein.*

emergency doctor [noun] Notarzt ['no:t|a'ʦt] der <-es, Notärzte> ♀Notärztin ['no:t|ɛ'ʦtɪn] die <-, –nen> ◊ *Sie mussten den Notarzt kommen lassen.* ♦ *Als Notärztin ist sie ständig unterwegs.*

emergency exit [noun] Notausgang ['no:t|aʊsɡaŋ] der <-(e)s, Notausgänge>

emergency number [noun] Notruf ['no:tru:f] der <-(e)s, -e> ◊ *die Polizei/Feuerwehr über Notruf alarmieren*

emergency service [noun] Notdienst ['no:tdi:nst] der <-(e)s, -e> ◊ *der Notdienst des Roten Kreuzes*

emigrant [noun] Auswanderer ['aʊsvandərə] der <-s, –> ♀Auswanderin ['aʊsvandərɪn] die <-, –nen> ◊ *Auswanderer aus Indien*

emigrate [verb] auswandern ['aʊsvanden] <wandert aus, wanderte aus, ist ausgewandert> ◊ *Er möchte nach Australien/in die USA auswandern.*

émigré [noun] Emigrant [emi'grant] der <-en, –en> ♀Emigrantin [emi'grantɪn] die <-, –nen> ◊ *Neben uns wohnt ein russischer Emigrant.*

emissary [noun] Abgesandte ['apɡəzantə] der/die <-n, die Abgesandten> *but: ein Abgesandter/eine Abgesandte* ◊ *der Abgesandte des Königs*

emission [noun] *(of gas, smoke)* Emission [emɪ'sjo:n] die <-, –en> ◊ *eine Vorschrift zur Verringerung schädlicher Emissionen; (of liquid)* Austritt ['aʊstrɪt] der <-s> *no pl* ◊ *der Austritt von Wasser/des Wassers*

emit [verb] 1. *(heat, vapo(u)r)* abgeben ['apge:bm] <gibt ab, gab ab, hat abgegeben> ◊ *Der Heizkörper gibt zu wenig Wärme ab.; (light)* ausstrahlen ['aʊsʃtra:lən] +haben ◊ *Der Leuchtturm strahlt ein helles Licht aus.* 2. *(form) (sound)* von sich geben ['fɔn ... ge:bm] <gibt, gab, hat gegeben> ◊ *Sie gab einen tiefen Seufzer von sich.*

emotion [noun] 1. *(feeling)* Gefühl [ɡə'fy:l] das <-s, -e> ◊ *Sie tut sich schwer, ihre Gefühle zu zeigen.* 2. *(state of being moved)* Bewegtheit [bə've:kthaet] die <-> *no pl* ◊ *Mit Bewegtheit dachte er bei diesem Lied an seine Großmutter.* in a voice full of emotion mit bewegter Stimme [mɪt bə,ve:kte 'ʃtɪmə] ◊ *„Das ist furchtbar lieb von euch", sagte die alte Dame mit bewegter Stimme.*

emotional [adj] 1. *(relating to feelings)* emotional [emotsjo'na:l] *no comp/superl, mostly before n* ◊ *Sie braucht jetzt emotionale Unterstützung.* ♦ *der emotionale Zustand einer Person; (illness, shock etc.)*

seelisch ['ze:lɪʃ] *no comp/superl* ◊ *Diese Krankheit hat seelische Ursachen.* ✦ *seelische Qualen ausstehen* **2.** *(expressing feelings)* gefühlsbetont [gə'fy:lsbəto:nt] <gefühlsbetonter, am gefühlsbetontesten> ◊ *Sie ist sehr gefühlsbetont.* ✦ *ein gefühlsbetonter Film; (upset)* erregt [e're:kt] <erregter, am erregtesten> ◊ *Als er das sagte, wurde sie sehr erregt.* ✦ *eine erregte Diskussion; (exciting)* erregend [e're:gn̩t] ◊ *eine erregende Erfahrung*

emotionally adv *(led by your emotions)* gefühlsmäßig [gə'fy:lsmɛ:sɪç] ◊ *gefühlsmäßig reagieren* get emotionally involved *(with sb/sth)* sich (bei jdm/etw.) gefühlsmäßig engagieren [gə,fy:lsmɛ:sɪç aŋga'ʒi:rən] <engagiert sich, engagierte sich, hat sich engagiert> ◊ *Du solltest dich bei deinen Patienten gefühlsmäßig nicht so stark engagieren.; (sympathetic)* gefühlvoll [gə'fy:lfɔl] ◊ *„Ich verstehe dich sehr gut", sagte er gefühlvoll.; (showing excitement)* erregt [e're:kt] <erregter, am erregtesten> ◊ *„Du liebst eine andere!", rief sie erregt.* emotionally disturbed psychisch gestört [,psy:çɪʃ gə'ʃtø:gt] <gestörter, am gestörtesten>

emperor noun Kaiser ['kaɛze] der <-s, -> ◊ *der römische Kaiser Augustus*

emphasis noun Betonung [bə'to:nʊŋ] die <-, -en> ◊ *die Betonung der eigenen Meinung* ✦ *Die Betonung liegt auf der ersten Silbe.* place emphasis on sth etw. betonen [bə'to:nən] <betont, betonte, hat betont> ◊ *Er möchte den Aspekt der Kundenfreundlichkeit mehr betonen.* with emphasis mit Nachdruck [mɪt 'na:xdrʊk] ◊ *„Ich werde das nicht tun", sagte er mit Nachdruck.* main emphasis Schwerpunkt ['ʃve:gpʊŋkt] der <-(e)s, -e>

emphasize verb betonen [bə'to:nən] <betont, betonte, hat betont> ◊ *Diesen Punkt möchte ich besonders betonen.* ✦ *Dieser Lidschatten betont Ihre dunklen Augen.*

empire noun **1.** *(of one ruler)* Reich [raɛç] das <-(e)s, -e> ◊ *der Zerfall des Römischen Reiches* **2.** ECON Imperium [ɪm'pe:rjʊm] das <-s, Imperien> ◊ *das Imperium eines Konzerns*

empirical(ly) adj, adv empirisch [ɛm'pi:rɪʃ] *no comp/superl* ◊ *empirische Untersuchungen* ✦ *etw. empirisch nachweisen*

employ verb **1.** *(take on)* anstellen ['anʃtɛlən] +haben ◊ *Nach dem Praktikum wurde er von der Firma angestellt.* employ sb as sth jdn als etw. anstellen ◊ *Wir würden Sie gern als Haushaltshilfe anstellen.* Over 250 000 people are employed in this industry. In dieser Branche sind über 250 000 Leute beschäftigt. **2.** *(form) (apply)* anwenden ['anvɛndn̩] <wendet an, wandte/wendete an, hat angewandt/angewendet> ◊ *Wir müssen hier eine andere Methode anwenden.* ⊛ be employed to do sth **1.** *(person)* damit beauftragt sein, etw. zu tun **2.** *(tool, method)* eingesetzt werden, um etw. zu tun

employed → employ adj *(working for)* angestellt ['angəʃtɛlt] *no comp/superl* ◊ *Sie ist bei einer Sprachenschule angestellt.*

employee noun *(sb working for a company or person)* Angestellte ['angəʃtɛltə] der/die <-n, die Angestellten> but: ein Angestellter/eine Angestellte ◊ *Sie ist Angestellte bei einer Versicherung.* ✦ *ein Unternehmen mit 45 Angestellten* ✦ *ein leitender Angestellter* employees and employers Arbeitnehmer und Arbeitgeber [aʀbaet,ne:me ʊnt aʀbaet'ge:be] ◊

Arbeitnehmer und Arbeitgeber müssen neu verhandeln.; (in your company) Mitarbeiter ['mɪt|a'baetɐ] der <-s, -> ♀Mitarbeiterin ['mɪt|a'baetərɪn] die <-, -nen>

employer noun Arbeitgeber ['aʀbaetge:be] der <-s, -> ♀Arbeitgeberin ['aʀbaetge:bərɪn] die <-, -nen> ◊ *Als Arbeitgeber hat er viel Verantwortung.*

employment noun **1.** *(job)* Arbeit ['aʀbaet] die <-> *no pl* ◊ *Sie hat ihre Arbeit verloren.* ✦ *Viele Akademiker finden nach dem Studium keine Arbeit.* contract of employment Arbeitsvertrag ['aʀbaetsfetra:k] der <-(e)s, Arbeitsverträge> in employment erwerbstätig [e'vɛrpstɛ:tɪç] *no comp/superl* ◊ *Er ist derzeit nicht erwerbstätig.* ✦ *erwerbstätige Mütter* Employment has risen. Die Zahl der Erwerbstätigen ist gestiegen. **2.** *(taking on)* Einstellung ['aenʃtɛlʊŋ] die <-, -en> ◊ *Sie entschied sich für die Einstellung des Bewerbers.* **3.** *(form) (use)* Anwendung ['anvɛndʊŋ] die <-, -en> ◊ *Wir empfehlen die Anwendung eines anderen Verfahrens.*

empty¹ adj leer [le:ɐ] ◊ *Der Tank ist leer.* ✦ *Am Sonntag sind die Straßen fast leer.* ✦ *Sie fühlte sich innerlich leer und ohne Hoffnung.* ✦ *leere Versprechungen* stand empty leer stehen ◊ *Das Haus steht seit vielen Jahren leer.* empty space freier Platz [,fraee 'plats] <-es, Plätze> ◊ *Haben wir genug freien Platz für einen neuen Schrank?*

empty² verb **1.** *(a container etc.)* empty sth etw. leeren ['le:rən] +haben ◊ *Er leerte sein Glas mit einem Zug.* ✦ *Wann wird der Briefkasten geleert?* sth empties etw. leert sich ◊ *Nach dem Konzert leerte sich die Halle schnell.* empty sth of its contents etw. ausleeren ['aosle:rən] +haben ◊ *Er leerte die Schublade aus.* empty sth into sth etw. irgendwohin schütten ['ʃytn̩] +haben ◊ *Sie schüttete den Müll in den Container.* **2.** *(river)* empty into sth etw. mündet in etw. acc ['mʏndət ɪn] +haben/sein ◊ *Der Fluss mündet ins Meer.*

enable verb ermöglichen [e'mø:klɪçn̩] <ermöglicht, ermöglichte, hat ermöglicht> ◊ *Dieses System soll die schnelle Identifizierung von Verbrechern ermöglichen.* enable sb to do sth es jdm ermöglichen, etw. zu tun ◊ *Das neue Programm ermöglicht es Ihnen, Informationen noch schneller auszutauschen.*

enchant verb verzaubern [fe'tsaobən] <verzaubert, verzauberte, hat verzaubert> ◊ *Ihre Stimme hat alle verzaubert.* ✦ *Die böse Fee verzauberte den Prinzen.*

enclose verb **1.** *(surround)* umgeben [ʊm'ge:bm̩] <umgibt, umgab, hat umgeben> ◊ *Eine hohe Mauer umgibt das Grundstück.; (embrace)* umschließen [ʊm'ʃli:sn̩] <umschließt, umschloss, hat umschlossen> ◊ *Seine Arme umschlossen sie fest.* **2.** *(in an envelope)* beilegen ['baele:gn̩] +haben ◊ *Seine Tante legte der Geburtstagskarte einen Geldschein bei.*

enclosed → enclose adj **1.** *(in an envelope)* beiliegend ['baeli:gn̩t] *no comp/superl, only before ns* ◊ *Bitte unterschreiben Sie beiliegendes Formular.* be enclosed beiliegen ['baeli:gn̩] <liegt bei, lag bei, ist beigelegen> ◊ *Ein Scheck liegt bei* please find enclosed anbei [an'bae] ◊ *Anbei die gewünschten Unterlagen.* **2.** *(isolated, fenced in)* abgeschlossen ['apgəʃlɔsn̩] ◊ *eine abgeschlossene Gemeinde* ✦ *Der Garten ist völlig abgeschlossen.*

enclosure noun **1.** *(fenced area)* eingezäuntes Grundstück [,aengətsɔøntəs 'grʊntʃtyk] <-(e)s, -e> ◊ *Das*

eingezäunte Grundstück hinter dem Haus darf man nicht betreten.; *(for animals)* Gehege [gə'he:gə] das <–s, –> ◊ *Im Zoo gibt es ein neues Gehege für die Raubtiere.* **2.** *(form)* *(in letters)* Anlage ['anla:gə] die <–, –n> *(form)* ◊ *Die Kopien sind als Anlage beigefügt.*

encompass [verb] umfassen [ʊm'fasn̩] <umfasst, umfasste, hat umfasst> ◊ *Die Studie umfasst ein breites Themenspektrum.* ◆ *Seine Ländereien umfassen über 1000 Hektar.*

encounter¹ [noun] *(meeting)* Begegnung [bə'ge:gnʊŋ] die <–, –en> ◊ *Gestern hatte ich eine seltsame Begegnung.* ◆ *Seit unserer letzten Begegnung sind Jahre vergangen.*; *(clash)* Zusammenstoß [tsu'zamənʃto:s] der <–es, Zusammenstöße> ◊ *Es kam zu einem Zusammenstoß zwischen Demonstranten und der Polizei.* a close encounter with Aug in Auge mit [aɛg ɪn aogə mɪt] <–, –en>

encounter² [verb] **1.** *(be confronted with)* encounter sth auf etw. [acc] stoßen [aof ... ʃto:sn̩] <stößt, stieß, ist gestoßen> ◊ *Bei der Überprüfung sind wir auf ein Problem gestoßen.* ◆ *Die Angreifer stießen auf heftigen Widerstand.* **2.** *(lit)* *(meet)* encounter sb jdm begegnen [bə'ge:gnən] <begegnet, begegnete, ist begegnet> ◊ *Sie war die schönste Frau, der er jemals begegnet war.*

encourage [verb] **1.** *(motivate)* ermuntern [ɛ'mʊntɐn] <ermuntert, ermunterte, hat ermuntert> ◊ *Der erste Erfolg hat sie zum Weitermachen ermuntert.* encourage sb to do sth jdn dazu ermuntern, etw. zu tun **2.** *(promote, favo(u)r)* fördern ['fœɐdɐn] +haben ◊ *Solche Bedingungen fördern die Verbreitung der Krankheit.* **3.** *(reassure)* ermutigen [ɛ'mu:tɪgn̩] <ermutigt, ermutigte, hat ermutigt> ◊ *Meine Eltern haben mich zu diesem Schritt ermutigt.* encourage sb to do sth jdn dazu ermutigen, etw. zu tun

encouragement [noun] **1.** *(reassurance)* Ermutigung [ɛ'mu:tɪgʊŋ] die <–, –en> ◊ *Manchmal braucht er ein wenig Ermutigung.* words of encouragement ermutigende Worte [ɛ,mu:tɪgəndə 'vɔ'tə] <–> *pl* **2.** *(support)* Förderung ['fœɐdərʊŋ] die <–, –en> ◊ *die Förderung von Umweltschutzprojekten*

encouraging → encourage [adj] ermutigend [ɛ'mu:tɪgn̩t] ◊ *ermutigende Worte* ◆ *Die Nachrichten sind nicht gerade ermutigend.*

encyclopaedia [noun] Lexikon ['lɛksikɔn] das <–s, Lexika> ◊ *ein Lexikon der Literatur* ◆ *etw. im Lexikon nachschlagen*
🟢 a walking encyclopaedia ein wandelndes Lexikon

end¹ [noun] **1.** *(of a period of time, an object, a connection, life)* Ende ['ɛndə] das <–s, –n> *most sing* ◊ *Das Buch hat ein völlig überraschendes Ende.* ◆ *Das bedeutete das Ende seiner Karriere.* ◆ *das Ende der Welt* ◆ *Er fühlte sein Ende nahen.* at the end of sth am Ende ... [gen] ◊ *am Ende des Jahres* ◆ *am Ende des Gangs* at the very end ganz am Ende at the far end am anderen Ende ◊ *Der Notausgang befindet sich am anderen Ende des Saals.* put an end to sth etw. beenden [bə'ɛndn̩] <beendet, beendete, hat beendet> bring sth to an end etw. abschließen ['apʃli:sn̩] <schließt ab, schloss ab, hat abgeschlossen> ◊ *eine Lektion abschließen* end of work Feierabend ['faɛɐla:bm̩t] der <–s, –e> **2.** *(form)* *(aim)* Ziel [tsi:l] das <–(e)s, –e> ◊ *Sie hat ihre Ziele nicht erreicht.*;

(purpose) Zweck [tsvɛk] der <–(e)s, –e> ◊ *für medizinische Zwecke* to what end zu welchem Zweck
🟢 fulfill your end of the bargain seinen Teil der Abmachung erfüllen at the end of the day letztlich ◊ *Der Streit beruht letztlich auf einem Missverständnis.* the end justifies the means der Zweck heiligt die Mittel be the end of the road for sb/sth das Aus für jdn/etw. bedeuten until the end of time bis in alle Ewigkeit be the thin end of the wedge erst der Anfang sein not be the end of the world kein Weltuntergang sein make ends meet über die Runden kommen at your end bei Ihnen/dir in the end zuletzt ◊ *Zuletzt verlor sie das Match dann doch.*

end² [verb] **1.** *(come to an end)* enden ['ɛndn̩] +haben ◊ *Der Weg endete in einer Sackgasse.* ◆ *Das Spiel endet um 17 Uhr.* ◆ *Der Film endete tragisch.* **2.** *(bring to an end)* beenden [bə'ɛndn̩] <beendet, beendete, hat beendet> ◊ *den Krieg beenden* ◆ *Lassen Sie uns das Gespräch an dieser Stelle beenden.*
🟢 end it all Schluss machen ◊ *Sie hat schon einmal versucht, Schluss zu machen.* the ... to end all ... der/die/das beste/größte/schlechteste etc. ... aller Zeiten ◊ *der beste Film aller Zeiten*
• **end up** [phras v] landen ['landn̩] +sein *(fam)* ◊ *in einer Sackgasse landen* ◆ *Er wird noch im Gefängnis landen!* sb ends up in trouble jd bekommt Ärger [bəkɔmt 'ɛ'gɐ] <bekommt, bekam, hat bekommen> end up doing sth schließlich etw. tun ['ʃli:slɪç] ◊ *Schließlich verbrachte er die Nacht auf einer Parkbank.*

endanger [verb] gefährden [gə'fɛ:gdn̩] <gefährdet, gefährdete, hat gefährdet> ◊ *Die Anschläge gefährden die Friedensverhandlungen.*

ending [noun] **1.** *(of a story, an event)* Ende ['ɛndə] das <–s> *no pl* ◊ *das tragische Ende einer Geschichte* ◆ *Dieses Ereignis markiert das Ende einer Ära.* **2.** GRAM Endung ['ɛndʊŋ] die <–, –en> ◊ *Die Endung „-ung" wird an den Verbstamm angehängt.*

endless(ly) [adj, adv] endlos ['ɛntlo:s] *no comp/superl* ◊ *eine schier endlose Liste* ◆ *Die Fahrt war endlos.* ◆ *sich endlos in die Länge ziehen*

endorse [verb] **1.** *(approve)* befürworten [bə'fy:gvɔ'tn̩] <befürwortet, befürwortete, hat befürwortet> ◊ *Ich befürworte dieses Vorgehen.* **2.** *(a cheque etc.)* auf der Rückseite unterzeichnen [aof de:ɐ 'rʏkzaɛtə ʊntɐ,tsaɛçnən] <unterzeichnet, unterzeichnete, hat unterzeichnet> ◊ *Sie unterzeichnete den Scheck auf der Rückseite.*

endurance [noun] Ausdauer ['aosdaoɐ] die <–> *no pl* ◊ *Er betreibt dieses Hobby mit großer Ausdauer.* beyond endurance auf unerträgliche Weise [aof ,ʊnlɛtrɛːklɪçə 'vaɛzə]

endure [verb] **1.** *(suffer)* ertragen [ɛ'tra:gn̩] <erträgt, ertrug, hat ertragen> ◊ *Er hat die lange Wartezeit geduldig ertragen.* **2.** *(last)* fortbestehen ['fɔ'bəʃte:ən] <besteht fort, bestand fort, hat fortbestanden> ◊ *Diese Traditionen werden fortbestehen.*

enduring → endure [adj] anhaltend ['anhaltn̩t] *no comp/superl, only before ns* die anhaltende Beliebtheit ihrer Musik

enemy¹ [noun] Feind [faɛnt] der <–(e)s, –e> ♀Feindin ['faɛndɪn] die <–, –nen> ◊ *Sie war meine ärgste Feindin.* ◆ *Sie ein erbitterte Feinde.* ◆ *Der Feind ging zum Angriff über.* ◆ *Die Maus hat viele natürliche Feinde.* ◆ *Die Zeit ist jetzt unser größter*

Feind. make an enemy of sb sich (dat) jdn zum
Feind machen make enemies sich (dat) Feinde
machen enemy of the state Staatsfeind ['ʃtaːtsfaɛnt]
mortal enemy Todfeind ['toːtfaɛnt]
◉ be your own worst enemy sich selbst am
meisten schaden

enemy² (adj) feindlich ['faɛntlɪç] *no comp/superl* ◊
*feindliche Soldaten ♦ ein feindlicher Angriff ♦ ein
feindliches Flugzeug*

energetic(ally) (adj, adv) **1.** *(with a lot of energy)* energiegeladen [enɛrˈgiːgəlaːdn̩] ◊ *eine energiegeladene
80-Jährige ♦ Bist du immer so energiegeladen? ♦
Energiegeladen fing sie sofort mit der Arbeit an.;*
(movement) schwungvoll ['ʃvʊŋfɔl] ◊ *schwungvolle
Bewegungen ♦ Die Aufführung war sehr schwungvoll.*
♦ *Schwungvoll setzte er sich ans Steuer.* **2.** *(active)*
tatkräftig ['taːtkrɛftɪç] ◊ *eine tatkräftige Frau ♦ Die
freiwilligen Helfer waren sehr tatkräftig. ♦ Er wurde
dabei von zahlreichen Helfern tatkräftig unterstützt.*

energy (noun) Energie [enɛrˈgiː] die <-, -n> ◊ *Es hat
mich viel Energie gekostet, ihr all das zu erklären. ♦
Energie sparen/verschwenden* put your energies into
sth seine Energie für etw. einsetzen ◊ *Nun kann er
seine Energie für etwas anderes einsetzen.*

enforce (verb) *(the law, a treaty)* enforce sth dafür
sorgen, dass etw. eingehalten wird
[dafyːɐ̯ 'zɔrgn̩] das ... 'aɛngəhaltn̩ vɪrt] +haben ◊ *Die
Polizei muss dafür sorgen, dass die Gesetze eingehalten werden.; (a reform)* durchsetzen ['dʊrçzɛtsn̩]
+haben ◊ *Die Regierung hatte nicht die Macht,
Reformen durchzusetzen.; (sb's cooperation)*
erzwingen [ɛˈtsvɪŋən] <erzwingt, erzwang, hat
erzwungen>

enforcement (noun) Durchsetzung ['dʊrçzɛtsʊŋ] die
<-> *no pl* ◊ *Die Durchsetzung der neuen Vorschrif-
ten ist schwierig.* law enforcement Strafverfolgung
['ʃtraːffɛɐ̯fɔlgʊŋ] die <->

engage (verb) **1.** *(a reader, listener)* fesseln ['fɛsl̩n]
+haben ◊ *Das Buch hat ihn so gefesselt, dass er es
an einem Tag gelesen hat.* **2.** *(employ)* engagieren
[aŋgaˈʒiːrən] <engagiert, engagierte, hat engagiert> ◊
*Sie haben einen Clown engagiert, der für die Unter-
haltung der Kinder sorgen soll.*
• **engage in** (phras v) **1.** engage in sth etw.
betreiben [bəˈtraɛbm̩] <betreibt, betrieb, hat
betrieben> ◊ *investigativen Journalismus betreiben;
(in illegal practices, a conflict, dispute)* in etw. (acc)
verwickelt werden [ɪn ... fɛˌvɪklt zaɛn] +sein ◊ *Er ist in
eine Auseinandersetzung mit seinem Vermieter verwickelt.* engage in sex Sex haben ['zɛks haːbm̩] +haben
engage in dialogue einen Dialog führen
[aɛnən diaˈloːk fyːrən] +haben **2.** engage sb in sth
jdn in etw. (acc) verwickeln [ɪn ... fɛˌvɪkl̩n] <verwi-
ckelt, verwickelte, hat verwickelt> ◊ *Er verwickelte
mich in ein Gespräch über Politik.*
• **engage with** (phras v) engage with sb/sth sich
mit etw./jdm auseinander setzen
[mɪt ... aɔsˌlaɛˌnandə zɛtsn̩] +haben ◊ *sich mit einem
Thema auseinander setzen*

engaged → engage (adj) **1.** *(busy)* be otherwise
engaged anderweitig beschäftigt sein
['andəvaɛtɪç bəˌʃɛftɪçt zaɛn] ◊ *Er ist gerade anderweitig beschäftigt und nicht zu sprechen.* **2.** *(due to
marry)* engaged *(to sb)* (mit jdm) verlobt [fɛɐ̯ˈloːpt]
no comp/superl ◊ *Die beiden sind schon seit drei
Jahren verlobt. ♦ Sie ist mit Peter verlobt.* get

engaged sich verloben [fɛˈloːbm̩] <verlobt sich,
verlobte sich, hat sich verlobt> ◊ *Sie haben sich im
Mai verlobt.* **3.** *(telephone line, toilet)* besetzt
[bəˈzɛtst] *no comp/superl* ◊ *Bei euch war immer
besetzt, als ich angerufen habe. ♦ Alle Toiletten
waren besetzt.*

engagement (noun) **1.** *(to marry)* Verlobung [fɛˈloːbʊŋ]
die <-, -en> break off an engagement eine
Verlobung lösen; *(period before marriage)* Verlo-
bungszeit [fɛˈloːbʊŋstsaɛt] die <-, -en> ◊ *Eine Verlo-
bungszeit von fünf Jahren war damals ganz normal.*
2. *(official meeting or function)* Verpflichtung
[fɛˈpflɪçtʊŋ] die <-, -en> ◊ *Heute hat die Königin
keine offiziellen Verpflichtungen.; (less formal)* Verabredung [fɛˈapreːdʊŋ] die <-, -en> have a previous
engagement schon eine Verabredung haben
3. *(battle)* Kampfhandlung ['kampfhandlʊŋ] die
<-, -en> ◊ *schwere Kampfhandlungen* **4.** *(employ-
ment)* Anstellung ['anʃtɛlʊŋ] die <-, -en> ◊ *die
Anstellung eines neuen Intendanten*

engine (noun) **1.** *(of a vehicle)* Motor ['moːtoːɐ̯] der
<-s, -en> ◊ *Der Motor springt nicht an.* diesel
engine Dieselmotor ['diːzl̩moːtoːɐ̯] jet engine Düsen-
triebwerk ['dyːzn̩triːpvɛrk] das <-(e)s, -e> **2.** *(of a
train)* Lok [lɔk] die <-, -s>

engineer (noun) **1.** *(of roads, railways, bridges etc.)*
Ingenieur [ɪnʒeˈnjøːɐ̯] der <-s, -e> ♀Ingenieurin
[ɪnʒeˈnjøːrɪn] die <-, -nen> ◊ *Sie will Ingenieurin
werden. ♦ die Ausbildung zum Ingenieur* **2.** *(on a
ship)* Maschinist [maʃiˈnɪst] der <-en, -en> ♀Maschi-
nistin [maʃiˈnɪstɪn] die <-, -nen>; *(on an aircraft)*
Bordingenieur ['bɔrtˌɪnʒeˌnjøːɐ̯] der <-s, -e> ♀Bord-
ingenieurin ['bɔrtˌɪnʒeˌnjøːrɪn] die <-, -nen> **3.** *(in
the UK: technician)* Techniker ['tɛçnɪke] der <-s, ->
♀Technikerin ['tɛçnɪkərɪn] die <-, -nen> **4.** *(for
computer programs)* (software) engineer Programmie-
rer [progra'miːre] der <-s, -> ♀Programmiererin
[progra'miːrərɪn] die <-, -nen> **5.** *(in the US: engine
driver)* Lokführer ['lɔkfyːre] der <-s, -> ♀Lokführe-
rin ['lɔkfyːrərɪn] die <-, -nen>
◉ the engineer *(of sth)* *(person responsible)* die
treibende Kraft (hinter etw. (dat)) ◊ *Wer war die
treibende Kraft hinter dieser Revolution?*

engineering (noun) Ingenieurwesen [ɪnʒeˈnjøːɐ̯veːzn̩]
das <-s> *no pl*

England (noun) England ['ɛŋlant] das <-s> *article only
in combination with attribute, no pl* → Germany

English¹ (noun) **1.** the English die Engländer
[di: 'ɛŋlɛndə] <-> *pl* → German¹ **1. 2.** *(language,
subject)* Englisch ['ɛŋlɪʃ] das <-(s)> *no pl* →
German¹ **2.**

English² (adj) englisch ['ɛŋlɪʃ] be English Engländer
sein [ˈɛŋlɛndə zaɛn] Engländerin sein
['ɛŋlɛndərɪn zaɛn] ◊ *Meine Mutter war Engländerin.*
→ German²

Englishman (noun) Engländer ['ɛŋlɛndə] der <-s, ->
→ German¹ **1.**

Englishwoman (noun) Engländerin ['ɛŋlɛndərɪn] die
<-, -nen> → German¹ **1.**

engraving (noun) **1.** *(process)* Gravieren [graˈviːrən] das
<-s> *no pl* **2.** *(picture)* Stich [ʃtɪç] der <-(e)s, -e>

enhance (verb) verbessern [fɛˈbɛsən] <verbessert, verbesserte, hat verbessert> ◊ *die Lebensqualität verbessern*

enjoy (verb) *(get pleasure from, have)* genießen
[gəˈniːsn̩] <genießt, genoss, hat genossen> ◊ *sein*

Leben/ein Glas Wein genießen ♦ Er genießt bei uns hobes Ansehen. **enjoy yourself** sich amüsieren [əmy'zi:rən] <amüsiert sich, amüsierte sich, hat sich amüsiert> ◊ *Sie haben sich auf der Party wirklich gut amüsiert.* Enjoy yourself! Viel Spaß! **enjoy doing sth** etw. gern tun [gɛ͡rn] I enjoy playing the piano. Ich spiele gern Klavier.; *(have an advantage)* sth enjoys sth etw. hat etw. [hat] +haben ◊ *Die Insel hat ein mildes Klima.* enjoy a quiet etc. location sich in ruhiger etc. Lage befinden [ɪn ˌru:ɪgə bəfɪndn̩] <befindet sich, befand sich, hat sich befunden>

enjoyable [adj] *(pleasant)* angenehm ['aŋgəne:m] ◊ *Die Atmosphäre des Hotels war sehr angenehm. ♦ Ich wünsche Ihnen einen angenehmen Aufenthalt.; (day, experience)* schön [ʃø:n] ◊ *Wir haben einen schönen Tag in den Bergen verbracht.* sb finds sth enjoyable etw. macht jdm Spaß [maxt ... 'ʃpa:s] +haben ◊ *Malen macht ihm Spaß.*

enjoyably [adv] angenehm ['aŋgəne:m] ◊ *Das Restaurant ist angenehm altmodisch.*

enjoyment [noun] Vergnügen [fɛ'gny:gn̩] das <–s, –> ◊ *Sie sah sich mit großem Vergnügen das Urlaubsvideo an. ♦ Ins Kino zu gehen ist unser einziges Vergnügen.* enjoyment of sth Freude an etw. [dat] ['frɔɡdə an] die <–, –n> ◊ *ihre Freude am Leben* get enjoyment from sth Spaß an etw. [dat] haben ['ʃpa:s an ... habm̩] +haben ◊ *Kinder haben oft an kleinen Dingen Spaß.*

enlarge [verb] vergrößern [fɛ'grø:sən] <vergrößert, vergrößerte, hat vergrößert> ◊ *ein Foto/eine Firma vergrößern*

enlist [verb] **1.** *(join the armed forces)* sb enlists (in the army) jd tritt in die Armee ein [trɪt ɪn di: a͡r'me: aen] <tritt ein, trat ein, ist eingetreten> **2.** *(helper, partner etc.)* gewinnen [gə'vɪnən] <gewinnt, gewann, hat gewonnen> ◊ *Gewinnen Sie Ihre Mitarbeiter für die Projektarbeit.* enlist sb in a cause jdn für eine Sache gewinnen enlist sb's help jdn um Hilfe bitten [ʊm 'hɪlfə bɪtn̩] <bittet, bat, hat gebeten> enlist the services of a lawyer sich [dat] einen Anwalt nehmen [aenən 'anvalt ne:mən] <nimmt sich, nahm sich, hat sich genommen>

enmity [noun] Feindschaft ['faentʃaft] die <–, –en> ◊ *Zwischen den beiden besteht erbitterte Feindschaft. ♦ Die Nachbarn lebten in Feindschaft.*

enormous [adj] *(very large)* riesig ['ri:zɪç] ◊ *riesige Wellen ♦ riesige Mengen an Kuchen ♦ Seine Freude war riesig.; (pressure, stress)* enorm [e'nɔ͡rm] no comp/superl ◊ *eine enorme Belastung ♦ Der Druck an der Uni ist enorm.* an enormous amount of eine Unmenge von/an etw. [dat] [aenə 'ʊnmɛŋə] <–, –n> *(fam)* ◊ *Das hat mich eine Unmenge von Zeit gekostet.* an enormous number of ... eine Unzahl von ... [aenə 'ʊntsa:l fɔn] ◊ *Eine Unzahl von Besuchern strömten auf den Platz.*

enormously [adv] ungeheuer ['ʊŋgəhɔɡ̯ə] no comp/superl ◊ *sich ungeheuer über ein Geschenk freuen ♦ Die Firma hat sich ungeheuer vergrößert.*

enough¹ [adv] **1.** genug [gə'nu:k] ◊ *Ich habe genug gespart für ein neues Auto. ♦ alt genug für den Führerschein sein ♦ Nimmt er die Lage ernst genug?* as if that wasn't bad enough zu allem Überfluss [ʦu: aləm 'y:bɐflʊs] **2.** *(emph)* ... enough ziemlich ... ['ʦi:mlɪç] ◊ *Sie ist ziemlich nett. ♦ That's doch ziemlich normal.* strangely enough merkwürdigerweise ['mɛ͡rkvy͡rdɪgɐ'vaezə]

enough² [det] genug [gə'nu:k] *invariable* ◊ *Haben wir genug Becher für alle? ♦ Sie kennt genug Leute, die helfen könnten.*

enough³ [pron] **1.** be enough (for sb) (jdm) reichen ['raeçn̩] +haben ◊ *Wir haben nur 100 Euro. Reicht das? ♦ Den Kindern reicht zum Abendessen ein Butterbrot. ♦ Ich habe ihn nur einmal erlebt, und das hat mir gereicht.* That's enough!, Enough is enough! Jetzt reicht's! **2.** enough (of sth) genug (von etw.) [gə'nu:k] ◊ *Die Kinder haben davon nicht genug bekommen. ♦ Ich habe genug von dem Film gesehen, um zu wissen, dass er mir nicht gefällt.* not nearly enough längst nicht genug there aren't enough of us wir sind nicht genug Leute

⊛ have had enough (of sth) die Nase voll (von etw.) haben

enquire [verb] *(ask)* enquire (about sth/after sb) sich (nach etw./jdm) erkundigen [e'kʊndɪgn̩] <erkundigt sich, erkundigte sich, hat sich erkundigt> ◊ *Ruf doch mal an und erkundige dich nach den Zugverbindungen. ♦ Meine Oma hat sich nach dir erkundigt.* enquire why ... fragen, warum ... ['fra:gn̩ va'rom] +haben ◊ *Darf ich fragen, warum Sie den Termin verlegen möchten?*

• **enquire into** [phras v] enquire into sth etw. untersuchen [ʊntɐ'zu:xn̩] <untersucht, untersuchte, hat untersucht> ◊ *Ein Ausschuss soll die Spendenaffäre untersuchen.*

enquiry [noun] **1.** *(request for information)* Anfrage ['anfra:gə] die <–, –n> ◊ *Wir haben schon viele Anfragen bekommen.; (by the police)* enquiry (about sth) Nachforschung (nach etw.) ['na:xfɔ͡rʃʊŋ] die <–, –en> ◊ *diskrete Nachforschungen nach ihren Geschäften* make enquiries Nachforschungen anstellen **2.** *(official investigation)* enquiry (into sth) Untersuchung (... [gen]) [ʊntɐ'zu:xʊŋ] die <–, –en> ◊ *Die Opposition verlangte eine Untersuchung der Affäre. ♦ die Untersuchung der Unfallursache* hold an enquiry eine Untersuchung durchführen line of enquiry Spur [ʃpu:ɐ] die <–, –en> ◊ *Die Polizei verfolgt eine neue Spur.* be helping the police with their enquiries von der Polizei vernommen werden [fɔn de:ɐ poli,ʦae fɛ'nɔmən ve:ɐdn̩] <wird, wurde, ist worden>

enrolment, enrollment [noun] Anmeldung ['anmɛldʊŋ] die <–, –en> ◊ *Für diesen Kurs ist eine Anmeldung erforderlich.*

ensure [verb] sicherstellen ['zɪçɐʃtɛlən] +haben ◊ *Die Qualität der Produkte muss sichergestellt werden.* ensure that dafür sorgen, dass [dafy:ɐ 'zɔ͡rgn̩ das] +haben ◊ *Unsere Mitarbeiter sorgen dafür, dass alles reibungslos abläuft.*

entail [verb] sth entail sth mit etw. verbunden sein [mɪt ... fɛ,bʊndn̩ zaen] +sein ◊ *Der Verkauf ist mit einem Verlust verbunden.* sth entails doing sth etw. bedeutet, dass etw. getan werden muss [bə'dɔɡ̯tət das ... ve:ɐdn̩ mʊs] <bedeutet, bedeutete, hat bedeutet> sth job entails sth etw. gehört zu jds Aufgaben [gəhø:ɐt ʦu: ... 'aofga:bm̩] <gehört, gehörte, hat gehört>

enter [verb] **1.** *(come in)* hineinkommen [hɪ'naenkɔmən] <kommt hinein, kam hinein, ist hineingekommen> ◊ *Der Einbrecher ist durch die Terrassentür hineingekommen.; (towards the speaker)* hereinkommen [hɛ'raenkɔmən] <kommt herein, kam herein, ist hereingekommen> ◊ *Als er hereinkam, lächelte er*

mir zu. **2.** *(a room, an area)* enter sth etw. betreten [bə'treːtn̩] <betritt, betrat, hat betreten> ◊ *Bepackt mit Einkäufen betrat er die Küche.; (a vehicle)* in etw. ⓐⓒⓒ einsteigen ['aenʃtaeɡn̩] <steigt ein, stieg ein, ist eingestiegen> ◊ *in ein Auto einsteigen* **3.** *(bullet)* enter the body in den Körper eindringen [ɪn deːn ˌkœʳpe 'aendrɪŋən] <dringt ein, drang ein, ist eingedrungen> ◊ *An welcher Stelle ist die Kugel in den Körper eingedrungen?* **4.** *(a country)* enter sth in etw. ⓐⓒⓒ einreisen [ɪn ... ˌaenraezn̩] +sein ◊ *Wann sind Sie in die USA eingereist?* enter the country einreisen ◊ *Die fünf Männer waren illegal eingereist.* **5.** *(a phase, period)* enter sth in etw. ⓐⓒⓒ eintreten [ɪn ... ˌaentreːtn̩] <tritt ein, trat ein, ist eingetreten> ◊ *Die Krankheit ist in eine kritische Phase eingetreten.* **6.** *(be noticeable)* A enters B B lässt A erkennen [lɛst ... eˌkɛnən] <ließ, hat lassen> ◊ *Sein Gesichtsausdruck ließ keine Gefühle erkennen.* **7.** enter the legal profession eine juristische Laufbahn einschlagen [aena juˌrɪstɪʃə 'laofbaːn aenʃlaːɡŋ̩] <schlägt ein, schlug ein, hat eingeschlagen> ◊ *Er möchte später einmal eine juristische Laufbahn einschlagen.* **8.** *(a market, area of activity)* enter sth in etw. ⓐⓒⓒ einsteigen [ɪn ... ˌaenʃtaeɡŋ̩] <steigt ein, stieg ein, ist eingestiegen> ◊ *Die Firma will jetzt auch in den deutschen Mobilfunkmarkt einsteigen.* **9.** *(a race, competition)* enter (sth) (an etw. ⓓⓐⓣ) teilnehmen ['taelneːmən] <nimmt teil, nahm teil, hat teilgenommen> ◊ *Meine Tochter nimmt an einem Malwettbewerb teil.; (for an exam, a competition)* enter sb (for sth) jdn anmelden ['anmɛldn̩] <meldet an, meldete an, hat angemeldet> ◊ *Sie haben ihre Tochter für die Aufnahmeprüfung angemeldet.* **10.** *(write down, record)* enter sth etw. eintragen ['aentraːɡŋ̩] <trägt ein, trug ein, hat eingetragen> ◊ *Bitte tragen Sie hier Ihre Telefonnummer ein.; (into a computer)* enter sth etw. eingeben ['aenɡeːbm̩] <gibt ein, gab ein, hat eingegeben> ◊ *Zuerst musste ich mein Passwort eingeben.* **11.** *(a complaint, protest)* enter sth etw. einlegen ['aenleːɡŋ̩] +haben ◊ *Mehrere Mitglieder haben Protest eingelegt.* enter a plea of guilty/not guilty sich schuldig/nicht schuldig bekennen [ˈʃʊldɪç/ˈnɪçt ʃʊldɪç bəˌkɛnən] <bekennt sich, bekannte sich, hat sich bekannt>

• **enter into** ⓟⓗⓡⓐⓢ ⓥ **1.** *(a discussion, negotiations)* aufnehmen ['aofneːmən] <nimmt auf, nahm auf, hat aufgenommen> ◊ *Gespräche mit jdm aufnehmen* **2.** *(an agreement, a contract)* abschließen ['apʃliːsn̩] <schließt ab, schloss ab, hat abgeschlossen> ◊ *Wir haben jetzt einen Vertrag mit einer Softwarefirma abgeschlossen.* **3.** *(be important to sth)* enter into sth bei etw. eine Rolle spielen [bae ... aena 'rɔlə ʃpiːlən] +haben ◊ *Geld spielt dabei keine Rolle.*

enterprise ⓝⓞⓤⓝ **1.** *(project)* Projekt [pro'jɛkt] das <-(e)s, -e> ◊ *Er erzählt mir immer von neuen Projekten.* **2.** *(readiness to think of sth and act on it)* Initiative [initsja'tiːvə] die <-, -n> ◊ *Initiative zeigen* **3.** *(organization)* Unternehmen [ʊntɐ'neːmən] das <-s, -> ◊ *ein großes Unternehmen in der Mobilfunkbranche* **4.** *(creating and managing businesses)* Unternehmertum [ʊntɐ'neːmetuːm] das <-s> no pl ◊ *das private Unternehmertum fördern*

entertain ⓥⓔⓡⓑ **1.** *(amuse)* unterhalten [ʊntɐ'haltn̩] <unterhält, unterhielt, hat unterhalten> ◊ *Sie hatten einen Clown engagiert, der die Kinder unterhalten*

sollte. **2.** *(have guests)* Gäste haben ['ɡɛstə haːbm̩] +haben ◊ *Sie haben fast jeden Abend Gäste.; (give sb food)* entertain sb jdn bewirten [bə'vɪʳtn̩] <bewirtet, bewirtete, hat bewirtet> ◊ *Sie schafft es ohne Schwierigkeiten, 20 Personen zu bewirten.* **3.** *(hopes, fears)* hegen ['heːɡn̩] +haben ◊ *Insgeheim hegte er die Hoffnung, sie könnte seine Liebe erwidern.*

entertainer ⓝⓞⓤⓝ Entertainer ['ɛntɛteːne] der <-s, -> ♀Entertainerin ['ɛntɛteːnərɪn] die <-, -nen> ◊ *Er arbeitet als Entertainer in einem Nachtclub.* ◆ *Die Entertainerin erzählte langweilige Witze.*

entertaining(ly) ⓐⓓⓙ, ⓐⓓⓥ unterhaltsam [ʊntɐ'haltzaːm] ◊ *eine unterhaltsame Geschichte* ◆ *Die Sendung war unterhaltsam und informativ.* ◆ *Das Buch ist unterhaltsam geschrieben.*

entertainment ⓝⓞⓤⓝ Unterhaltung [ʊntɐ'haltʊŋ] die <-, -en> ◊ *für die musikalische Unterhaltung der Gäste sorgen* entertainment business Unterhaltungsindustrie [ʊntɐ'haltʊŋsɪndʊsˌtriː] die <-> no pl

enthusiasm ⓝⓞⓤⓝ **1.** *(interest)* Begeisterung [bə'ɡaestərʊŋ] die <-> ◊ *ihre Begeisterung für Bücher/Fußball* ◆ *die Begeisterung für Kunst und Kultur wecken* dampen sb's enthusiasm jds Begeisterung dämpfen **2.** *(favo(u)rite activity, subject)* Leidenschaft ['laednʃaft] die <-, -en> ◊ *Angeln ist eine Leidenschaft von mir.*

enthusiast ⓝⓞⓤⓝ jd, der sich für etw. begeistert; *(of things modern)* computer enthusiast Computerfan [kɔm'pjuːtefɛn] der <-s, -s>; *(of things traditional)* wine enthusiast Weinliebhaber ['vaenliːphaːbe] der <-s, -> ♀Weinliebhaberin ['vaenliːphaːbərɪn] die <-, -nen> an enthusiast for sth ein Anhänger/eine Anhängerin ... ⓖⓔⓝ [aen 'anhɛŋe/aena 'anhɛŋərɪn] ◊ *Sie ist eine Anhängerin der regionalen Unabhängigkeit.*

enthusiastic(ally) ⓐⓓⓙ, ⓐⓓⓥ begeistert [bə'ɡaestet] ◊ *Das Publikum war begeistert.* ◆ *Die begeisterten Zuschauer klatschten und jubelten.* ◆ *Die Kinder sangen begeistert mit.* enthusiastic about sth begeistert von etw. ◊ *Sie waren von dem neuen Entwurf begeistert.*

entice ⓥⓔⓡⓑ locken ['lɔkn̩] +haben ◊ *Die Konkurrenz lockte sie mit einem höheren Gehalt.; (persuade sb to do sth)* entice sb to do sth jdn dazu bewegen, etw. zu tun [datsu: bə'veːɡŋ̩ ... tsuː] <bewegt, bewegte, hat bewegt> ◊ *Die vielen Vorteile bewegten ihn dazu, in London zu studieren.; (make sb do sth they might regret)* entice sb jdn dazu verleiten, etw. zu tun [datsu: fe'laetn̩ ... tsuː] <verleitet, verleitete, hat verleitet> ◊ *Die Aussicht auf einen schnellen Erfolg verleitete ihn dazu, sein Studium abzubrechen.*

entire ⓐⓓⓙ ganze ['ɡantsə] no comp/superl, only before ns ◊ *eine ganze ... ; eine ganze ...; ein ganzes ...* ◊ *Sie ist im ganzen Bundesgebiet tätig.* ◆ *Die Kinder haben ein ganzes Brot aufgegessen.*

entirely ⓐⓓⓥ **1.** *(completely)* völlig ['fœlɪç] no comp/superl ◊ *Mit dem Bart sieht er völlig anders aus.; (throughout)* durchgehend ['dʊʳçɡeːənt] no comp/superl ◊ *Die Straße ist wieder durchgehend befahrbar.* **2.** *(used for emphasis)* durchaus [dʊʳçˈʔaos] ◊ *Das ist durchaus möglich.* not entirely nicht ganz [ˌnɪçt 'ɡants] ◊ *Er war sich nicht ganz sicher, ob die Drohung ernst gemeint war.*

entitle ⓥⓔⓡⓑ **1.** entitle sb to sth jdn zu etw. berechtigen [tsu: ... bəˌrɛçtɪɡŋ̩] <berechtigt, berechtigte, hat

berechtigt> ◊ *Die Jahreskarte berechtigt den Inhaber auch zum Besuch des Freibads.* be entitled to vote wahlberechtigt sein ['va:lbərɛçtɪçt zaͅen] +*sein* **2.** *(give a title to)* entitle sth ... einer Sache dat den Titel ... geben [de:n ˌti:tl̩ ... ˈge:bm̩] <gibt, gab, hat gegeben> ◊ *Er hat dem Bild den Titel ‚Abschied‘ gegeben.* entitled ... mit dem Titel ... [mɪt de:m ˈti:tl̩] ◊ *Er hat ein neues Buch mit dem Titel ‚Europa‘ geschrieben.*

entitlement noun entitlement (to sth) Anspruch (auf etw. acc) ['anʃprʊx] der <-(e)s, Ansprüche> ◊ *der Anspruch auf Schadenersatz* entitlement to do sth Anspruch darauf, etw. zu tun sb's full entitlement alles, worauf jd Anspruch hat

entity noun **1.** *(independent unit)* Einheit ['aͅenhaͅet] die <-, -en> ◊ *Körper und Seele als getrennte Einheiten betrachten* economic entity Wirtschaftseinheit ['vɪ'tʃafts|aͅenhaͅet] the legal entity die juristische Person [di: ju,rɪstɪʃə pɛr'zoːn] <-, -en> character entity Zeichen ['tsaͅeçn̩] das <-s, -> **2.** *(creature, being)* Wesen ['ve:zn̩] das <-s, -> ◊ *ein außerirdisches Wesen*

entourage noun Gefolge [gə'fɔlgə] das <-, ->

entrance noun **1.** *(door, opening)* Eingang ['aͅengaŋ] der <-(e)s, Eingänge> ◊ *getrennte Eingänge für Kunden und Personal* main entrance Haupteingang ['haͅopt|aͅengaŋ] entrance to the harbo(u)r Hafeneinfahrt ['ha:fn̩|aͅenfa:'t] die <-, -en> **2.** *(right or possibility to enter a place)* Zutritt ['tsu:trɪt] der <-(e)s> *no pl* ◊ *Zutritt verboten!* gain entrance (to sth) sich dat Zutritt (zu etw.) verschaffen **3.** *(admission, right to visit)* Eintritt ['aͅentrɪt] der <-(e)s, -e> ◊ *Der Eintritt in die Kathedrale kostet nichts.* entrance charge/fee Eintrittspreis ['aͅentrɪtspraͅes] der <-es, -e> **4.** *(to an organization)* Beitritt ['baͅetrɪt] der <-(e)s, -e> ◊ *die Kriterien für den Beitritt in die EU erfüllen;* *(to university)* Zulassung ['tsu:lasʊŋ] die <-, -en> **5.** *(on stage)* Auftritt ['aͅoftrɪt] der <-(e)s, -e> make an entrance auftreten ['aͅoftre:tn̩] <tritt auf, trat auf, ist aufgetreten>; *(into a room)* make an entrance eintreten ['aͅentre:tn̩] <tritt ein, trat ein, ist eingetreten>

entrance exam, entrance examination noun Aufnahmeprüfung ['aͅofna:məpry:fʊŋ] die <-, -en>

entry noun **1.** *(ability to go into a place)* Zutritt ['tsu:trɪt] der <-(e)s> *no pl* gain entry sich dat Zutritt verschaffen refuse entry (to sb) (jdm) den Zutritt verweigern No entry. Zutritt verboten! **2.** *(to a museum, exhibition etc.)* Eintritt ['aͅentrɪt] der <-(e)s, -e> ◊ *Der Eintritt ins Museum kostet zwei Euro.* **3.** *(into a country)* Einreise ['aͅenraͅezə] die <-, -n> ◊ *Bestimmungen für die Einreise nach Deutschland* ♦ *Ihm wurde die Einreise in die USA verweigert.* **4.** *(door, opening etc.)* Eingang ['aͅengaŋ] der <-(e)s, Eingänge> ◊ *Wo ist der Eingang?* **5.** *(into a war)* Eintritt ['aͅentrɪt] der <-(e)s, -e> ◊ *der Eintritt Japans in den 2. Weltkrieg* **6.** *(to an organization)* Beitritt ['baͅetrɪt] der <-(e)s, -e> ◊ *der Beitritt Polens zur EU;* *(to university)* Zulassung ['tsu:lasʊŋ] die <-, -en> ◊ *die Zulassung zur Universität erhalten* **7.** *(in a book, diary, dictionary)* Eintrag ['aͅentra:k] der <-(e)s, Einträge> ◊ *ein Eintrag im Kalender/Wörterbuch* ♦ *die Einträge in ihrem Tagebuch waren kaum leserlich.* **8.** *(for a race)* Anmeldung ['anmɛldʊŋ] die <-, -en> ◊ *Für das Rennen haben wir schon 15 Anmeldungen.;* *(for a*

competition) Einsendung ['aͅenzɛndʊŋ] die <-, -en> ◊ *Der Gewinner wird unter den richtigen Einsendungen ausgelost.; (person taking part in a competition)* Teilnehmer ['taͅelne:me] der <-s, -> ♀Teilnehmerin ['taͅelne:mərɪn] die <-, -nen> ◊ *Alle Teilnehmer des Malwettbewerbs bekommen einen Preis.*

enumerate verb aufzählen ['aͅoftsɛ:lən] +*haben* ◊ *Sie zählte auf, was sie sich zu Weihnachten wünscht.*

envelope noun *(for letters)* Briefumschlag ['bri:f|ʊmʃla:k] der <-(e)s, Briefumschläge> ◊ *einen Briefumschlag zukleben; (larger, for documents)* Umschlag ['ʊmʃla:k] der <-(e)s, Umschläge> stuff envelopes Sendungen kuvertieren [ˌzɛndʊŋən kuvɛr'ti:rən] <kuvertiert, kuvertierte, hat kuvertiert> *(tech)* ⊛ on the back of an envelope *(quickly)* auf die Schnelle push the envelope an die Grenzen gehen

envious adj envious (of sb/sth) neidisch (auf jdn/etw.) ['naͅedɪʃ] ◊ *Sie warf neidische Blicke auf unser neues Auto.* ♦ *Er ist neidisch auf mich/auf meinen Erfolg.*

environment noun **1.** *(physical surroundings, computer system)* Umgebung [ʊm'ge:bʊŋ] die <-, -en> ◊ *Kinder brauchen ihre vertraute Umgebung.* ♦ *sich an eine neue Umgebung gewöhnen* ♦ *Tiere in ihrer natürlichen Umgebung beobachten* working environment Arbeitsumgebung ['a'baͅets|ʊmge:bʊŋ] die **2.** *(social, political etc. influences)* Umfeld ['ʊmfɛlt] das <-(e)s, -er> most sing ◊ *Ein stabiles Umfeld ist wichtig für die Erziehung eines Kindes.; (atmosphere)* Klima ['kli:ma:] das <-s, -s> ◊ *ein feindliches Klima* ♦ *ein Klima der Angst* **3.** *(natural world)* the environment die Umwelt [di: 'ʊmvɛlt] <-> *no pl* ◊ *Abgase und Abwässer belasten die Umwelt.*

environmental adj **1.** *(relating to the natural world)* Umwelt... ['ʊmvɛlt] environmental damage Umweltschäden ['ʊmvɛltʃɛ:dn̩] die <-> pl **2.** *(protecting the natural world)* Umweltschutz... ['ʊmvɛltʃʊts] environmental group Umweltschutzorganisation ['ʊmvɛltʃʊts|o'ganiza'tsjoːn] die <-, -en>

environmentally friendly adj umweltfreundlich ['ʊmvɛltfrɔͅøntlɪç] ◊ *Ich benutze ein umweltfreundliches Waschmittel.* ♦ *Diese Verpackung ist umweltfreundlich.*

envisage verb **1.** *(take into consideration)* vorsehen ['fo:ze:ən] <sieht vor, sah vor, hat vorgesehen> ◊ *Ein neuer Plan sieht den Bau einer vierspurigen Straße vor.* ♦ *Es ist vorgesehen, dass ...; (intend)* vorhaben ['fo:'gha:bm̩] <hat vor, hatte vor, hat vorgehabt> ◊ *Wir haben vor, einen Kräutergarten anzulegen.* **2.** *(imagine)* sich dat vorstellen ['fo:ʃtɛlən] +*haben* ◊ *Damals konnte sie sich nicht vorstellen, dass sie einmal Kinder haben würde.* it is hard to envisage es ist kaum vorstellbar [ɛs ɪst ˌkaͅom 'fo:ʃtɛlba:']

envy¹ noun Neid [naͅet] der <-(e)s> *no pl* ◊ *Der Neid auf ihre Schwester nagte an ihr.* envy neidisch ['naͅedɪʃ]

envy² verb envy sb (sth) jdn (um etw.) beneiden [bə'naͅedn̩] <beneidet, beneidete, hat beneidet> ◊ *Ich beneide dich um deine Geduld.* I don't envy sb jd ist nicht zu beneiden ◊ *Er ist nicht zu beneiden bei dem Stress, den er hat.*

enzyme noun Enzym [ɛn'tsy:m] das <-s, -e>

epidemic noun Epidemie [epide'mi:] die <-, -n> ◊ *Scheidungen sind in diesem Land schon fast zur*

Epidemie geworden. flu epidemic Grippeepidemie ['grɪpəlepideˌmiː]

episode [noun] **1.** *(event, incident)* Vorfall ['foːɐ̯fal] der <-(e)s, Vorfälle> ◊ *Nach diesem Vorfall hat sie nie wieder mit mir gesprochen.* **2.** *(part of a series)* Folge ['fɔlɡə] die <-, -n> ◊ *Gleich kommt eine neue Folge von „Star Trek".*

equal[1] [adj] **1.** *(the same)* gleich [ɡlaɛç] no comp/superl ◊ *Alle Kinder haben den gleichen Anteil an der Erbschaft.* ♦ *Sie forderten gleiche Rechte für alle.* of equal importance gleich wichtig equal in size gleich groß equal access to education gleiche Bildungschancen equal opportunities Chancengleichheit ['ʃansnɡlaɛçhaɛt] die <-> no pl **2.** *(having the same rights)* gleichberechtigt ['ɡlaɛçbərɛçtɪçt] no comp/superl ◊ *gleichberechtigte Mitglieder* ♦ *Männer und Frauen sind gleichberechtigt.* **3.** *(equivalent)* sth is equal to sth etw. entspricht einer Sache [dat] [ɛntˈʃprɪçt] <entsprach, hat entsprochen> ◊ *eine Summe, die drei Monatsgehältern entspricht* **4.** *(match, competition)* ausgeglichen ['aʊsɡəɡlɪçn̩] ◊ *Es war eine ausgeglichene Partie.* ♦ *In der ersten Halbzeit war das Spiel ziemlich ausgeglichen.* ⊛ equal to sth einer Sache [dat] gewachsen ◊ *Ob er wohl dieser Herausforderung gewachsen ist?*

equal[2] [verb] **1.** MATH *(in calculations)* sth equals sth etw. ist gleich etw. [ɪst ˈɡlaɛç] ◊ *Vier plus vier ist gleich acht.* **2.** *(result in, entail)* bedeuten [bəˈdɔɪtn̩] <bedeutet, bedeutete, hat bedeutet> ◊ *Höhere Kosten bedeuten höhere Preise.* **3.** *(achieve the same quality or level as)* erreichen [eˈraɛçn̩] <erreicht, erreichte, hat erreicht> ◊ *Unser Design wurde oft kopiert, aber nie erreicht. Her patience was equalled by her skill.* Sie besaß ebenso viel Geduld wie Geschick.; *(a record)* equal sth etw. einstellen ['aɛnʃtɛlən] +haben ◊ *Mit dieser Zeit hat er den Weltrekord eingestellt.*

equality [noun] *(having the same rights)* Gleichberechtigung ['ɡlaɛçbəˌrɛçtɪɡʊŋ] die <-, -en> most sing ◊ *die Gleichberechtigung von Mann und Frau* equality before the law Gleichheit vor dem Gesetz [ˌɡlaɛçhaɛt foːɐ̯ deːm ɡəˈzɛts] die <-> no pl; *(having the same opportunities)* social equality die soziale Gerechtigkeit [diː zoˌtsi̯aːlə ɡəˈrɛçtɪçkaɛt] <-> no pl

equally [adv] **1.** *(the same)* gleich [ɡlaɛç] no comp/superl ◊ *Die beiden Kinder sind gleich groß.* ♦ *Sie bemüht sich, alle ihre Schüler gleich zu behandeln.* The money was divided equally. Das Geld wurde zu gleichen Teilen verteilt. **2.** *(just as)* genauso [ɡəˈnaʊzoː] ◊ *Das Spiel kann man genauso gut zu viert spielen.* **3.** *(also)* ebenso ['eːbm̩zoː] ◊ *Das Einkommen ist wichtig, aber ebenso die Lebensqualität.*

equation [noun] **1.** MATH Gleichung ['ɡlaɛçʊŋ] die <-, -en> ◊ *eine lineare Gleichung* **2.** *(thinking of two things as the same)* Gleichsetzung ['ɡlaɛçzɛtsʊŋ] die <-, -en> ◊ *die Gleichsetzung von Staat und Nation* **3.** come into the equation zu bedenken sein [tsuː bəˈdɛŋkn̩ zaɛn] +sein ◊ *Dabei sind auch die Kosten zu bedenken.*

equilibrium [noun] Gleichgewicht ['ɡlaɛçɡəvɪçt] das <-(e)s> no pl

equip [verb] **1.** *(with equipment)* equip sth etw. einrichten ['aɛnrɪçtn̩] <richtet ein, richtete ein, hat eingerichtet> ◊ *eine Arztpraxis/Werkstatt einrichten* equip sth with sth etw. mit etw. ausstatten ['aʊsʃtatn̩] <stattet aus, stattete aus, hat ausgestattet> ◊ *Alle Klassenzim-*

mer wurden mit PCs ausgestattet. equip sb (with sth) jdn (mit etw.) ausrüsten ['aʊsrʏstn̩] <rüstet aus, rüstete aus, hat ausgerüstet> ◊ *Die Soldaten waren schlecht ausgerüstet.* **2.** *(provide the necessary knowledge or skill)* equip sb for sth jdn auf etw. [acc] vorbereiten [aʊf ... ˈfoːɐ̯bəraɛtn̩] <bereitet vor, bereitete vor, hat vorbereitet> ◊ *Die Schule hat sie nicht gut auf das Arbeitsleben vorbereitet.* equip sb to do sth jdn darauf vorbereiten, etw. zu tun be better equipped to do sth etw. besser tun können ['bɛsɐ ... kœnən] <kann, konnte, hat gekonnt> ◊ *Er kann das besser erklären als ich.*

equipment [noun] **1.** *(for a particular activity)* Ausrüstung ['aʊsrʏstʊŋ] die <-, -en> ◊ *die richtige Ausrüstung für etw. haben* camping equipment Campingausrüstung ['kɛmpɪŋlaʊsrʏstʊŋ] diving equipment Taucherausrüstung ['taʊxɐlaʊsrʏstʊŋ] piece of equipment Gerät [ɡəˈrɛːt] das <-(e)s, -e> ◊ *Wie funktioniert dieses Gerät?* **2.** *(knowledge, ability)* Rüstzeug ['rʏstsɔɪk] das <-(e)s> no pl ◊ *das geistige Rüstzeug für den Berufsleben vermitteln*

equity [noun] **1.** *(fair treatment)* Gerechtigkeit [ɡəˈrɛçtɪçkaɛt] die <-> no pl pay equity gerechte Bezahlung [ɡəˌrɛçtə bəˈtsaːlʊŋ] die <-> no pl **2.** *(of a property)* Eigenanteil ['aɛɡn̩lantaɛl] der <-(e)s, -e> negative equity *Überschuldung, wenn die Hypothekenbelastung den Wert einer Immobilie übersteigt.* **3.** *(value of a company's shares)* Aktienkapital ['aktsi̯ənkapiˌtaːl] das <-s> no pl **4.** *(shares)* equities Stammaktien ['ʃtamlaktsi̯ən] die <-> pl

equivalent[1] [noun] Äquivalent [ɛkviˈva'lɛnt] das <-(e)s, -e> be the equivalent of sth einer Sache [dat] entsprechen [ɛntˈʃprɛçn̩] <entspricht, entsprach, hat entsprochen> ◊ *Zwei Esslöffel Zucker entsprechen ungefähr 20 Gramm.*

equivalent[2] [adj] **1.** *(of the same size, meaning)* entsprechend [ɛntˈʃprɛçnt] no comp/superl, only before ns ◊ *Wie heißt das entsprechende englische Wort?* be equivalent to sth einer Sache [dat] entsprechen [ɛntˈʃprɛçn̩] <entspricht, entsprach, hat entsprochen> ◊ *1 Zoll entspricht etwa 2,5 cm.* **2.** *(of equal value)* gleichwertig ['ɡlaɛçveːɐ̯tɪç] no comp/superl ◊ *ein Diplom oder ein gleichwertiger Abschluss* ♦ *Die beiden Kurse sind gleichwertig.*

era [noun] **1.** *(period of time)* Ära ['ɛːraː] die <-, Ären> most sing ◊ *Eine neue Ära beginnt.; (historical period)* Zeit [tsaɛt] die <-, -en> the Roman era die Römerzeit **2.** *(geological)* Erdzeitalter ['eːɐ̯tsaɛtlaltɐ] das <-s, ->

erase [verb] **1.** *(from a tape, from the mind)* löschen ['lœʃn̩] +haben ◊ *eine Datei löschen* ♦ *eine Erinnerung aus dem Gedächtnis löschen* **2.** *(with a rubber)* ausradieren ['aʊsradiːrən] <radiert aus, radierte aus, hat ausradiert> ◊ *einen Fehler ausradieren*

eraser [noun] *(rubber)* Radiergummi [ra'diːɡɡumiː] der <-s, -s>; *(for a blackboard or whiteboard)* Schwamm [ʃvam] der <-s, Schwämme>

erect[1] [adj] **1.** *(posture)* aufrecht ['aʊfrɛçt] no comp/superl ◊ *eine aufrechte Haltung* ♦ *Ihr Gang war aufrecht.* **2.** *(penis, nipple)* erigiert [eri'ɡiːɡt] no comp/superl

erect[2] [verb] *(a bridge)* bauen ['baʊən] +haben ◊ *eine Brücke über die Themse bauen; (a statue, fence, stage etc.)* errichten [eˈrɪçtn̩] <errichtet, errichtete, hat errichtet> ◊ *eine Bühne errichten* erect a

memorial to sb jdm ein Denkmal errichten; *(a tent)* aufstellen ['aͻfʃtɛlən] +*haben* ◊ *Sie stellten ihr Zelt am Fluss auf.*

erection [noun] **1.** *(of the penis)* Erektion [erɛk'tsjo:n] die <–, –en> **2.** *(of a building)* Bau [bao] der <–(e)s, –ten> ◊ *der Bau einer Kirche* **3.** *(structure, building, in compound ns)* ...konstruktion [kͻnstrͻk'tsjo:n] die <–, –en> steel erection Stahlkonstruktion ['ʃta:lkͻnstrͻk,tsjo:n]

erosion [noun] **1.** *(of land, rock)* Erosion [ero'zjo:n] die <–> *no pl* soil erosion Bodenerosion ['bo:dn̩ero,zjo:n] **2.** *(fig) (undermining)* Aushöhlung ['aoshø:lʊŋ] die <–> *no pl* ◊ *die Aushöhlung des Datenschutzes; (gradual loss)* Verlust [fɛ'lʊst] der <–(e)s> *no pl* erosion of confidence Vertrauensverlust [fɛ'traoənsfɛlʊst]

erotic [adj] erotisch [e'ro:tɪʃ] ◊ *ein erotischer Film* ♦ *Sie findet seine Stimme erotisch.*

erratic [adj] *(person)* sprunghaft ['ʃprͻŋhaft] <sprunghafter, am sprunghaftesten> ◊ *ein sprunghaftes Wesen haben* ♦ *Er ist sprunghaft und unberechenbar.; (performance)* schwankend ['ʃvaŋkn̩t] ◊ *Der Lehrer beklagt sich über meine schwankenden Leistungen.* She's erratic in her work. Ihre Leistungen schwanken stark.

error [noun] Fehler ['fe:lɐ] der <–s, –> ◊ *Fehler korrigieren* ♦ *Der Computer meldete einen Fehler.* driver error ein Fehler des Fahrers grammatical error Grammatikfehler [gra'matɪkfe:lɐ] human error menschliches Versagen [,mɛnʃlɪçəs fe'za:gn̩] <–s> *no pl* error of judgement Fehleinschätzung ['fe:llaͤɛnʃɛtsʊŋ] die <–, –en>

ⓔ **in error** *(by mistake)* aus Versehen ◊ *Die Krankenschwester hatte ihr aus Versehen die falschen Tabletten gegeben.* be in error im Irrtum sein ◊ *Geben Sie doch zu, dass Sie im Irrtum sind!*

erupt [verb] *(spit lava, suddenly start)* ausbrechen ['aosbrɛçn̩] <bricht aus, brach aus, ist ausgebrochen> ◊ *Der Ätna ist erneut ausgebrochen.* ♦ *Ein Bürgerkrieg brach aus.* erupt in laughter/cheers etc. in Gelächter/Jubel etc. ausbrechen The streets erupted in riots. Auf den Straßen brachen Unruhen aus.; *(person)* erupt with anger einen Wutausbruch bekommen [aͤɛnən 'vu:tlaosbrʊx bəkͻmən] <bekommt, bekam, hat bekommen>

eruption [noun] Ausbruch ['aosbrʊx] der <–(e)s, Ausbrüche> ◊ *der Ausbruch eines Bürgerkriegs/Vulkans* ♦ *Weißt du, was zu diesem plötzlichen Ausbruch geführt hat?*

escalation [noun] *(in violence)* Eskalation [ɛskala'tsjo:n] die <–, –en> ◊ *Sie befürchten eine Eskalation der Unruhen.; (of prices etc.)* der sprunghafte Anstieg [de:ɐ ʃprͻŋhaftə 'anʃti:k] der <–(e)s, –e> ◊ *ein sprunghafter Anstieg der Immobilienpreise*

escalator [noun] Rolltreppe ['rͻltrɛpə] die <–, –n>

escape¹ [noun] **1.** *(avoiding, getting away)* Flucht [flʊxt] die <–, –en> ◊ *die Flucht aus dem Gefängnis* ♦ *die Flucht vor der Verantwortung* ♦ *die Flucht in eine Traumwelt* escape route Fluchtweg ['flʊxtve:k] der <–(e)s, –e> make your escape entkommen [ɛnt'kͻmən] <entkommt, entkam, ist entkommen> **2.** *(of gas, oil etc.)* Austritt ['aostrɪt] der <–(e)s, –e> there is an escape of sth etw. tritt aus [trɪt 'aos] <trat aus, ist ausgetreten> ◊ *Aufgrund eines Motorschadens ist Öl ausgetreten.* **3.** escape (key) Escape-

Taste [ɛs'ke:ptastə] die <–, –n>

ⓔ **have a lucky escape** mit einem blauen Auge davonkommen have a narrow escape gerade noch davonkommen

escape² [verb] **1.** *(from danger, prison)* fliehen ['fli:ən] <flieht, floh, ist geflohen> ◊ *vor einem Gewitter/aus dem Gefängnis fliehen* **2.** *(from an unpleasant situation or person)* escape (sb/sth), escape (from sb/sth) (jdm/etw.) entkommen [ɛnt'kͻmən] <entkommt, entkam, ist entkommen> ◊ *Er ist den Entführern entkommen.* ♦ *Diesmal wird er seiner Strafe nicht entkommen.* escape sb's clutches jdm entkommen **3.** *(avoid being killed or harmed)* davonkommen [da'fͻnkͻmən] <kommt davon, kam davon, ist davongekommen> ◊ *mit leichten Verletzungen/mit dem Leben davonkommen* narrowly escape gerade noch davonkommen escape injury unverletzt davonkommen **4.** *(sb fails to notice sth)* sth escapes sb etw. entgeht jdm [ɛnt'ge:t] <entging, ist entgangen> ◊ *Es ist ihm wohl entgangen, dass er den Job nur mir zu verdanken hat.* sth escapes sb's attention etw. entgeht jds Aufmerksamkeit **5.** *(sb forgets sth)* sth escapes sb etw. fällt jdm nicht ein [fɛlt ... nɪçt 'aͤɛn] <fiel ein, ist eingefallen> ◊ *Der Name fällt mir gerade nicht ein.* **6.** *(gas, oil etc.)* austreten ['aostre:tn̩] <tritt aus, trat aus, ist ausgetreten> ◊ *Aus der Pipeline ist Öl ausgetreten.*

ⓔ **there's no escaping the fact that** es lässt sich nicht leugnen, dass

escort¹ [noun] **1.** *(for company, protection)* Begleitung [bə'glaͤɛtʊŋ] die <–, –en> ◊ *In das Viertel sollten Sie nur mit Begleitung gehen.* **2.** *(by the police)* Geleitschutz [gə'laͤɛtʃʊts] der <–es> *no pl* under escort unter Bewachung [ʊntɐ bə'vaxʊŋ]

escort² [verb] begleiten [bə'glaͤɛtn̩] <begleitet, hat begleitet> ◊ *Die Transporte werden von der Polizei begleitet.* escort a bride to the altar eine Braut zum Altar geleiten [aͤɛnə ,braot tsʊm al'ta:ɐ gəlaͤɛtn̩] <geleitet, geleitete, hat geleitet> *(lofty)*

especially [adv] **1.** *(particularly)* besonders [bə'zͻndɐs] ◊ *Das war besonders teuer.* ♦ *Er interessiert sich nicht besonders für Kunst.* ♦ *Dort ist immer viel los, besonders am Wochenende.* ♦ *Ruf mich an, besonders wenn du Hilfe brauchst.* especially because vor allem weil [fo:ɐ 'alɛm vaͤɛl] especially not sb/sth vor allem jdn/etw. nicht [fo:ɐ ,alɛm ... nɪçt] ◊ *Ich will niemanden sehen, vor allem ihn nicht!* **2.** *(for a particular person, reason)* extra ['ɛkstra:] ◊ *Ich habe den Kuchen extra für dich gebacken!* ♦ *Wir sind extra vorbeigekommen, um dir ein paar Blumen zu bringen.*

essay [noun] *(by a pupil, student)* Aufsatz ['aofzats] der <–es, Aufsätze> ◊ *einen Aufsatz über etw.* schreiben; *(by a professional writer)* Essay ['ɛse:] der or das <–s, –s> ◊ *ein Essay über Siegfried Lenz*

essence [noun] **1.** *(most important part)* Kern [kɛɐn] der <–(e)s> ◊ *der Kern des Problems; (the nature of sth)* Wesen ['ve:zn̩] das <–s> ◊ *das Wesen der Zeit/Freiheit* the very essence of sth das grundlegende Wesen ... [gen] **2.** *(liquid)* Essenz [ɛ'sɛnts] die <–, –en> vanilla essence Vanilleessenz [va'nɪljəlɛ,sɛnts]

ⓔ **in essence** im Wesentlichen of the essence das Wichtigste

essential [adj] **1.** *(absolutely necessary)* unerlässlich

['ʊn|ɛlɛslɪç] ◊ *Äußerste Sorgfalt ist bei dieser Arbeit unerlässlich.* ♦ *eine unerlässliche Voraussetzung für die Prüfung* sth is essential reading man muss etw. gelesen haben [man ˌmʊs ... gəˈleːzn haːbm̩] +haben play an essential part in sth bei etw. eine wesentliche Rolle spielen [baɛ ... aɛnə ˌveːzntlɪçə ˈroːlə ʃpiːlən] +haben 2. *(fundamental)* grundlegend [ˈgrʊntleːgn̩t] ◊ *Das ist ein grundlegender Unterschied zwischen dem britischen und dem US-amerikanischen System.* 3. *(basic)* Grund... [grʊnt] essential needs Grundbedürfnisse [ˈgrʊntbədʏˈfnɪsə] <–> pl 4. *(vitamins, minerals)* lebensnotwendig [ˈleːbm̩snoːtvɛndɪç] ◊ *Frisches Obst liefert lebensnotwendige Vitamine.*

essentially [adv] im Wesentlichen [ɪm ˈveːzntlɪçn̩] ◊ *Das ist im Wesentlichen richtig.*

establish [verb] 1. *(introduce)* einführen [ˈaɛnfyːrən] +haben ◊ *ein neues Verfahren einführen; (a relationship)* aufbauen [ˈaɔfbaɔən] +haben ◊ *gute Beziehungen zu den Nachbarländern aufbauen; (a connection)* herstellen [ˈheːɐ̯ʃtɛlən] +haben ◊ *eine Verbindung mit dem Internet herstellen* 2. *(a company, organization)* gründen [ˈgrʏndn̩] +haben ◊ *Wann wurde die Firma gegründet?* 3. *(discover, determine)* feststellen [ˈfɛstʃtɛlən] +haben ◊ *jds Tod feststellen* ♦ feststellen, ob jd ein Alibi für die Tatzeit hat; *(prove)* nachweisen [ˈnaːxvaɛzn̩] <weist nach, wies nach, hat nachgewiesen> ◊ *Eine Studie hat angeblich nachgewiesen, dass Rotwein vor Herzinfarkt schützt.* 4. *(achieve success)* establish a reputation sich [dat] einen Namen machen [aɛnən ˈnaːmən maxn̩] +haben ◊ *Er hat sich als Reporter schnell einen Namen gemacht.* establish sb/yourself (as sth) jdn/sich (als etw. [nom]) etablieren [etaˈbliːrən] <etabliert, etablierte, hat etabliert> ◊ *Mit diesem Film hat sie sich als Schauspielerin etabliert.*

establishment [noun] 1. *(organization, institution)* Einrichtung [ˈaɛnrɪçtʊŋ] die <–, –en> ◊ *eine Einrichtung für behinderte Kinder* research establishment Forschungseinrichtung 2. *(social)* the Establishment das Establishment [das ɪsˈtɛblɪʃmɛnt] <–s> 3. *(of an organization, a company)* establishment (of ...) Gründung (... [gen]) [ˈgrʏndʊŋ] die <–> ◊ *die Gründung eines Ausschusses*

estate [noun] 1. *(in the UK: housing)* Siedlung [ˈziːdlʊŋ] die <–, –en> ◊ *Sie wohnen in einer Siedlung am Stadtrand.; (in the UK: location where industry concentrates)* Gewerbegebiet [gəˈvɛˈbəgəbiːt] das <–s, –e> ◊ *Hier soll ein neues Gewerbegebiet entstehen.* 2. *(agricultural)* Gut [guːt] das <–(e)s, Güter> ◊ *auf einem Gut leben* 3. *(property, money)* Besitz [bəˈzɪts] der <–es, –e> ◊ *Sein Besitz wird auf etwa 3 Millionen Dollar geschätzt.; (after death)* Nachlass [ˈnaːxlas] der <–es, Nachlässe> ◊ *Zum Nachlass gehören auch drei Häuser.* 4. *(in the UK: car)* Kombi [ˈkɔmbiː] der <–s, –s>

estate agent [noun] Immobilienmakler [ɪmoˈbiːljənmaːklɐ] der <–s, –> ♀Immobilienmaklerin [ɪmoˈbiːljənmaːklərɪn] die <–, –nen>

estimate¹ [noun] 1. *(guess)* Schätzung [ˈʃɛtsʊŋ] die <–, –en> ◊ *Laut einer Schätzung waren heute 20 000 Demonstranten auf der Straße.* a rough estimate eine ungefähre Schätzung 2. *(of costs)* Kostenvoranschlag [kɔstn̩ˈfoːɐ̯anʃlaːk] der <–(e)s, Kostenvoranschläge> ◊ *Wir haben sechs Kostenvoranschläge eingeholt.*

estimate² [verb] estimate (sth) (at sth) (etw.) (auf etw. [acc]) schätzen [ˈʃɛtsn̩] +haben ◊ *Versuch mal, sein Gewicht zu schätzen.* ♦ *Die Kosten wurden auf 12 Millionen Euro geschätzt.* ♦ *Er schätzt, dass wir in sechs Monaten fertig sind.* sth is estimated to do sth man schätzt, dass etw. etw. tut ◊ *Man schätzt, dass die Ölreserven noch 100 Jahre reichen.* An estimated 10 000 people came to the concert. Die Zahl der Konzertbesucher wurde auf 10 000 geschätzt.

Estonia [noun] Estland [ˈeːstlant] das <–s> *article only in combination with attribute, no pl* → Germany

Estonian¹ [noun] 1. *(inhabitant)* Este [ˈeːstə] der <–n, –n> ♀Estin [ˈeːstɪn] die <–, –nen> → German¹ 1. 2. *(language)* Estnisch [ˈeːstnɪʃ] das <–(s)> → German¹ 2.

Estonian² [adj] estnisch [ˈeːstnɪʃ] → German²

etc. usw. [ʊnt zoː ˈvaɛtɐ] ◊ *Wir verkaufen Bücher, Zeitungen, Postkarten usw.*

eternal(ly) [adj, adv] ewig [ˈeːvɪç] *no comp/superl* ◊ *die ewige Ruhe* ♦ *Sein Schweigen kam mir ewig vor.* ♦ *Ich werde dir ewig dankbar sein.*

eternity [noun] Ewigkeit [ˈeːvɪçkaɛt] die <–, –en> ◊ *Es dauerte eine Ewigkeit, bis jemand ans Telefon ging.* for all eternity bis in alle Ewigkeit

ethic [noun] 1. *(set of moral principles)* ethics Ethos [ˈeːtɔs] das <–> *no pl* professional ethics Berufsethos [bəˈruːfsˌeːtɔs] the ethics of doing sth die Frage, ob es richtig ist, etw. zu tun [diː ˈfraːgə ɔp ɛs ˈrɪçtɪç ɪst ... tsuː] 2. *(philosophy, general principle)* ethic(s) Ethik [ˈeːtɪk] die <–> *no pl* ◊ *die christliche Ethik*

ethical [adj] 1. *(concerning ethics)* ethisch [ˈeːtɪʃ] *no comp/superl* ◊ *ethische Fragen/Einwände* 2. *(morally right)* ethisch vertretbar [ˌeːtɪʃ fɐˈtreːtbaːɐ̯] ◊ *Sind diese Tests ethisch vertretbar?; (behavio(u)r)* ethisch einwandfrei [ˌeːtɪʃ ˈaɛnvantfraɛ] ◊ *ethisch einwandfreies Verhalten*

ethnic [adj] ethnisch [ˈeːtnɪʃ] *no comp/superl, only before ns* ◊ *ethnische Minderheiten* ethnic Albanians living in Kosovo die albanische Bevölkerung im Kosovo [diː alˌbaːnɪʃə bəˌfœlkərʊŋ ɪm ˈkɔsɔvɔ] ethnic group Volksgruppe [ˈfɔlksgrʊpə] die <–, –n>

etiquette [noun] Etikette [etiˈkɛtə] die <–, –n> *most sing* ◊ *die diplomatische Etikette*

EU EU [eːˈʔuː] die

euro [noun] Euro [ˈɔɐ̯oː] der <–(s), –s> *pl 'Euro' when used with figures* ◊ *Kann man hier mit Euros zahlen?* ♦ *Das kostet 20 Euro.*

Europe [noun] GEOG Europa [ɔɐ̯ˈroːpaː] das <–s> *article only in combination with attribute, no pl* ◊ *Die Popgruppe tourt derzeit durch Europa.*

European¹ [noun] GEOG Europäer [ɔɐ̯roˈpɛːɐ̯] der <–s, –> ♀Europäerin [ɔɐ̯roˈpɛːərɪn] die <–, –nen> → German¹ 1.

European² [adj] GEOG, POL europäisch [ɔɐ̯roˈpɛːɪʃ] *mostly before ns* ◊ *ein europäisches Land*

evacuate [verb] 1. *(leave)* räumen [ˈrɔɐ̯mən] +haben ◊ *Die Angestellten wurden aufgefordert, das Gebäude zu räumen.* 2. *(clear sth, make sb leave)* evakuieren [evakuˈiːrən] <evakuiert, evakuierte, hat evakuiert> ◊ *ein Gebäude/Viertel evakuieren* evacuate sb from sth jdn aus etw. evakuieren ◊ *Menschen aus einem Gebäud evakuieren* 3. *(your bowels)* entleeren [ɛntˈleːrən] <entleert, entleerte, hat entleert> ◊ *den Darm entleeren*

evade [verb] **1.** *(responsibility, prosecution, capture)* evade sth sich einer Sache [dat] entziehen [ɛntˈʦiːən] <entzieht sich, entzog sich, hat sich entzogen> ◊ *sich der Verantwortung entziehen* **2.** *(a law, regulation etc.)* umgehen [ʊmˈgeːən] <umging, hat umgangen> ◊ *Kann man dieses Verbot umgehen?* **3.** *(a question, subject)* evade sth einer Sache [dat] ausweichen [ˈaʊsvaɪçn̩] <weicht aus, wich aus, ist ausgewichen> ◊ *Weichen Sie meiner Frage nicht aus!* **4.** *(taxes)* hinterziehen [hɪntɐˈʦiːən] <hinterzieht, hinterzog, hat hinterzogen> ◊ *Hat sie Steuern hinterzogen?* **5.** *(a pursuer)* evade sb jdm entkommen [ɛntˈkɔmən] <entkommt, entkam, ist entkommen> ◊ *der Polizei entkommen*

evaluate [verb] **1.** *(data, results)* auswerten [ˈaʊsveːɐtn̩] <wertet aus, wertete aus, hat ausgewertet> ◊ *die Ergebnisse einer Studie auswerten* **2.** *(in an appraisal)* bewerten [bəˈveːɐtn̩] <bewertet, bewertete, hat bewertet> ◊ *einen Mitarbeiter bewerten*

evaluation [noun] **1.** *(analysis of data)* Auswertung [ˈaʊsveːɐtʊŋ] die <-, -en> ◊ *die Auswertung einer Umfrage/Studie/von Daten* **2.** *(assessment)* Bewertung [bəˈveːɐtʊŋ] die <-, -en> ◊ *Mein Professor schreibt mir eine Bewertung, wenn ich mich um das Stipendium bewerbe.* ♦ *eine politische Bewertung der Situation abgeben*

even¹ [adj] **1.** *(flat, level)* eben [ˈeːbm̩] ◊ *Die Fahrbahn ist nicht ganz eben.* ♦ *ebenes Gelände* **2.** *(regular, similar in size)* regelmäßig [ˈreːgl̩mɛːsɪç] ◊ *regelmäßige Zähne* ♦ *Seine Schrift ist klein und regelmäßig.* **3.** *(distribution)* gleichmäßig [ˈglaɪçmɛːsɪç] ◊ *eine gleichmäßige Verteilung der Ressourcen* **4.** *(number)* gerade [gəˈraːdə] ◊ *20 ist eine gerade Zahl, 21 eine ungerade.* ♦ *Ihre Anzahl muss gerade sein.* **5.** *(sports)* ausgeglichen [ˈaʊsgəglɪçn̩] ◊ *Die Begegnung war ausgeglichen und offen bis zum Schluss.* ♦ *ein ausgeglichenes Spiel*
◉ be even (with sb) (mit jdm) quitt sein *(fam)* get even with sb es jdm heimzahlen

even² [adv] **1.** *(expressing that sth is unusual)* sogar [zoˈgaːɐ] ◊ *Das macht Spaß und wird sogar noch gut bezahlt.* ♦ *Sie arbeitet sogar am Wochenende.* ♦ *Sogar der sonst so kritische Peter war zufrieden.* not even nicht einmal [ˈnɪçt aɛnmaːl] ◊ *Nicht einmal der Hund wollte fressen, was sie gekocht hatte.* even though obwohl [ɔpˈvoːl] ◊ *Obwohl er eine gute Ausbildung hat, findet er keine Stelle.* **2.** *(emphasizing a comparative)* even [nɔx] ◊ *In Deutschland war es im Juli noch heißer als in Spanien.* **3.** *(qualifying, expressing that sth happens despite sth)* even (if) auch (wenn) [aɔx (vɛn)] ◊ *Ich mache das jetzt so, auch wenn er meckert.* ♦ *Die Arbeit war sehr gut, wenn auch noch nicht perfekt.* even so trotzdem [ˈtrɔtsdeːm] ◊ *Das Haus sah baufällig aus; trotzdem haben wir es gekauft.*

evening [noun] Abend [ˈaːbm̩t] der <-s, -e> ◊ *Gegen Abend kam es zu Gewittern.* ♦ *Er ist keinen Abend zu Hause.* ♦ *ein literarischer Abend* evening after evening Abend für Abend in the evening abends [ˈaːbm̩ts] ◊ *Ich komme abends immer gegen sechs nach Hause.* ♦ *In den USA ist es jetzt 9 Uhr abends.*

evenly [adv] *(equally, breathing)* gleichmäßig [ˈglaɪçmɛːsɪç] ◊ *eine Creme gleichmäßig auftragen* ♦ *gleichmäßig geformte Objekte* ♦ *Er atmetete gleichmäßig.*
◉ be evenly matched einander ebenbürtig sein ◊

Die beiden Mannschaften sind einander ebenbürtig.

even out [verb] **1.** *(also fig) (make even, balance)* ausgleichen [ˈaʊsglaɪçn̩] <gleicht aus, glich aus, hat ausgeglichen> ◊ *alte Dielen mit Holzfaserplatten ausgleichen* ♦ *Defizite und Überschüsse ausgleichen* sth evens out etw. gleicht sich aus ◊ *Er hat wenig Talent, aber ist sehr fleißig. Das gleicht sich dann aus.* All evens out. Alles kommt ins Lot. **2.** *(spread, distribute evenly)* streuen [ˈʃtrɔɪən] +haben ◊ *Zahlungen gleich über einen Zeitraum streuen*

event [noun] **1.** *(occurrence)* Ereignis [eˈɪˈʔaɛɡnɪs] das <-ses, -se> ◊ *ein tragisches Ereignis* ♦ *eine Reihe/Kette von Ereignissen* events surrounding sth Ereignisse um etw. ◊ *die Ereignisse um seinen Tod; (a combination of incidents)* events Geschehen [gəˈʃeːən] das <-s> no pl *(lofty)* ◊ *Wir wohnten nur ein paar Kilometer vom Ort des Geschehens entfernt.* **2.** *(organized programme)* Veranstaltung [fɛˈʔanʃtaltʊŋ] die <-, -en> ◊ *eine dreitägige/festliche Veranstaltung*
◉ in any event auf jeden Fall after the event im Nachhinein in the event in the event of sth im Falle … [dat] ◊ *im Falle eines Unfalls* in the event that im Falle, dass

eventual [adj] schliesslich [ˈʃliːslɪç] *often not translated or translated with an adverbial construction* the eventual demise of the Roman economy der Untergang der römischen Wirtschaft His eventual victory came unexpected. Sein Sieg kam unerwartet. the eventual decision die schließlich getroffene Entscheidung This could lead to the eventual loss of freedom of movement. Das könnte schließlich zum Verlust der Bewegungsfreiheit führen. Her eventual return was a big surprise. Es war eine große Überraschung, als sie schließlich zurückkehrte.

eventuality [noun] Eventualität [evɛntualiˈtɛːt] die <-, -en> ◊ *auf alle Eventualitäten vorbereitet sein* in the eventuality that für den Fall, dass [fyːɐ deːn ˈfal das]

eventually [adv] **1.** *(in the end)* schließlich [ˈʃliːslɪç] ◊ *Schließlich haben wir unser Geld doch bekommen.* **2.** *(some time in the future)* irgendwann [ˈɪrɡn̩tˈˈvan] ◊ *Irgendwann wird er es schon verstehen.*

ever [adv] **1.** *(at any time)* jemals [ˈjeːmaːls] ◊ *Warst du jemals in Amerika?* ♦ *Funktioniert das denn jemals?* ♦ *Wird er jemals wiederkommen?* bigger/better etc. than ever größer/besser etc. denn je [ˌɡrøːsɐ/ˌbɛsɐ dɛn ˈjeː] ◊ *Ihr Zustand ist schlimmer denn je.* than ever before als jemals zuvor not ever, never ever nie [niː] ◊ *Tu das nie wieder!* hardly ever fast nie [fast ˈniː] ◊ *In London schneit es fast nie.* ever since seither [zaɛˈheːɐ] ◊ *Sie ist letztes Jahr nach Dresden gezogen; seither habe ich nichts mehr von ihr gehört.* if ever wenn überhaupt [vɛn ybɐˈhaɔpt] ◊ *Er ruft nur selten an, wenn überhaupt.* **2.** *(expressing a superlative: of all)* überhaupt [ybɐˈhaɔpt] ◊ *das beste Buch überhaupt* ♦ *Das war sein größter Erfolg überhaupt.* **3.** *(always, continuously)* immer [ˈɪmɛ] as ever wie immer ◊ *Wie immer hat er sich danebenbenommen.* ever more/further etc. immer mehr/weiter etc.
◉ for ever **1.** *(definitely)* für immer ◊ *Die alten Zeiten sind für immer vorbei.* **2.** *(for a very long time)* ewig *(fam)* ◊ *Wir haben ewig im Stau gestanden.* ever so überhaupt What/Why etc. ever

... ? Was/Warum etc. ... nur ...? ◊ *Was hat dich nur dazu veranlasst?*

everlasting [adj] ewig ['eːvɪç] *no comp/superl* ◊ *Er hat die ewige Ruhe gefunden.* ✦ *Das Wort Gottes ist ewig.*

every [det] 1. *(each)* jeder ['jeːdɐ] jede ['jeːdə] jedes ['jeːdəs] ◊ *Ich gehe jeden Tag ins Büro.* ✦ *Jedes Buch von ihr ist spannend.* ✦ *jede Gelegenheit nutzen* 2. *(used to describe sth that happens repeatedly)* alle ['alə] ◊ *alle drei Stunden* ✦ *Alle paar Kilometer musste ich anhalten.* ✦ *Wir treffen uns alle zwei Monate.* every other week jede zweite Woche ⊚ one in every einer/eine von ◊ *Einer von zehn Schweden ist schwerhörig.* ✦ *Eine von 100 Patientinnen braucht dieses Medikament.* every so often, every now and again hin und wieder

everybody [pron] 1. *(all (the) people)* alle ['alə] ◊ *Ich habe es noch nicht allen gesagt.* ✦ *Alle wollten mit ihr sprechen.* everybody else alle anderen; *(every person)* jeder ['jeːdɐ] jede ['jeːdə] ◊ *Jeder macht mal einen Fehler.* 2. *(form of address)* zusammen [tsu'zamən] ◊ *Guten Tag zusammen!*

everyday [adj] alltäglich [al'tɛːklɪç] ◊ *eine alltägliche Begebenheit* ✦ *der alltägliche Papierkrieg* everyday life der Alltag ['altaːk] <−(e)s> *only with the definite article, no pl*

everyone [pron] 1. *(all (the) people)* alle ['alə] ◊ *Man kann es nie allen recht machen.* ✦ *Alle standen um mich herum.* everyone else alle anderen; *(every person)* jeder ['jeːdɐ] jede ['jeːdə] jedes ['jeːdəs] ◊ *Jeder sollte das wissen.* ✦ *Jede bekam von ihm eine rote Rose.* ✦ *Schick mir mal die Kinder her; jedes bekommt noch etwas Schokolade.* 2. *(form of address)* zusammen [tsu'zamən] ◊ *Hallo alle zusammen!* ✦ *Guten Tag zusammen!*

everything [pron] alles ['aləs] ◊ *Man kann nicht alles haben.* ✦ *Alles in Ordnung?* ✦ *Schönheit ist nicht alles.* everything else alles andere

everywhere [adv] *(in every place)* überall [ybɐ|'al] ◊ *überall erhältlich sein* ✦ *Hier ist es überall schmutzig.* ✦ *Überall lauern Gefahren.* everywhere else sonst überall; *(to every place)* überallhin [ybɐ|al'hɪn] ◊ *Der Hund folgt seinem Herrchen überallhin.*

evidence [noun] 1. *(indication)* Anzeichen ['antsaeçn] das <−s, −> evidence of sth Anzeichen für etw. evidence, that Anzeichen dafür, dass ◊ *Es gibt keinerlei Anzeichen dafür, dass Fremdverschulden vorliegt.* 2. LAW *(proof)* Beweis [bə'vaes] der <−(e)s, −e> ◊ *Die Beweise reichten für eine Verurteilung nicht aus.; (object)* Beweismittel [bə'vaesmɪtl] das <−s, −> ◊ *neue Beweismittel vorlegen* 3. LAW *(statement)* Aussage ['aoszaːgə] die <−, −n> ◊ *Die Aussage des Zeugen belastete den Angeklagten schwer.* give evidence aussagen ['aoszaːgŋ] +haben ◊ *Er sagte vor Gericht gegen sie aus.*

evident(ly) [adj, adv] offensichtlich ['ɔfnzɪçtlɪç] ◊ *ein offensichtlicher Betrug/Fehler* ✦ *Es ist offensichtlich, dass sie schwanger ist.* ✦ *Sie ist offensichtlich nicht an ihm interessiert.*

evil¹ [noun] 1. *(concept, act)* Böse ['bøːzə] das <−n> *but: Böses, no pl* ◊ *Er verkörpert das Böse schlechthin.* do evil Böses tun 2. *(phenomenon)* Übel ['yːbl] das <−s, −> ◊ *das kleinere Übel* ✦ *das Übel des Rauchens*

evil² [adj] böse ['bøːzə] <böser, am bösesten> ◊ *Es geschah nicht in böser Absicht.* ✦ *Die Hexe war sehr böse.*

evoke [verb] heraufbeschwören [hɛ'raofbəʃvøːrən] <beschwört herauf, beschwor herauf, hat heraufbeschworen> ◊ *Sein Duft beschwor Erinnerungen herauf.*

evolution [noun] 1. BIO Evolution [evolu'tsɪoːn] die <−, −en> ◊ *die Evolution des Menschen* 2. *(cultural, technical)* Entwicklung [ɛnt'vɪklʊŋ] die <−, −en> ◊ *die Entwicklung des Rap/Computers*

evolutionary [adj] BIO evolutionär [evolutsɪo'nɛːɐ] *no comp/superl, mostly before ns* ◊ *evolutionäre Anthropologie*; Evolutions... [evolu'tsɪoːns] evolutionary theory Evolutionstheorie [evolu'tsɪoːnsteoˌriː] die <−, −n>

evolve [verb] entwickeln [ɛnt'vɪkln] <entwickelte, entwickelt, hat entwickelt> ◊ *Wale haben für das Leben im Wasser Flossen entwickelt.* ✦ *Sie hat ihren eigenen Stil entwickelt.* sth evolves etw. entwickelt sich sth evolves into sth etw. entwickelt sich zu etw. ◊ *Winzige Lebewesen haben sich zu Mehrzellern entwickelt.* sth/sb evolves from sth/sb etw./sb entwickelt sich aus etw./jdm ◊ *Aus dieser einfachen Lebensform entwickelten sich die ersten Amphibien.*

exact [adj] 1. *(accurate)* genau [gə'nao] <genauer, am genau(e)sten> ◊ *Genaue Zahlen liegen noch nicht vor.* ✦ *Diese Beschreibung ist nicht sehr genau.* 2. *(specific)* genau der/die/das [gənao 'deːɐ/'diː/'das] ◊ *Das ist genau der Punkt, an dem ich nicht weiterweiß.* ✦ *Das ist genau die Stelle, an der er stand.* ✦ *Genau das Fenster war schon mal kaputt.*

exactly [adv] 1. *(precisely)* genau [gə'nao] <genauer, am genau(e)sten> ◊ *Das ist genau das Richtige für mich!* ✦ *auf den Tag genau heute vor 100 Jahren* 2. *(used for emphasis, agreement)* eben ['eːbm] *no comp/superl* ◊ *„Dann fahren wir halt mit dem Auto."* — *„Eben!"* ✦ *Eben, das sage ich auch immer!* ✦ *Er ist nicht eben intelligent.* 3. *(expressing anger)* eigentlich ['aegŋtlɪç] *no comp/superl* ◊ *Was hast du dir eigentlich dabei gedacht?*

exaggerate [verb] übertreiben [ybɐ'traebm] <übertreibt, übertrieb, hat übertrieben> ◊ *maßlos übertreiben* ✦ *Sie übertreibt nicht, wenn sie sagt, dass es um Leben und Tod geht.*

exam → examination

examination [noun] 1. *(of a student)* Prüfung ['pryːfʊŋ] die <−, −en>; *(esp at university, medical school)* Examen [ɛ'ksaːmən] das <−s, − or Examina> ◊ *ein Examen als Krankenschwester* fail an examination durch eine Prüfung/ein Examen fallen pass an exam eine Prüfung/ein Examen bestehen take an exam eine Prüfung/ein Examen ablegen 2. *(control, inspection)* Untersuchung [ʊntɐ'zuːxʊŋ] die <−, −en> ◊ *sich einer medizinischen Untersuchung unterziehen* ✦ *eine technische Untersuchung* be under examination untersucht werden [ʊntɐ'zuːxt veˈɐdŋ] <wird, wurde, ist worden> ⊚ on closer examination bei genauerer Betrachtung

examine [verb] 1. *(carefully, medically, scientifically)* untersuchen [ʊntɐ'zuːxŋ] <untersucht, untersuchte, hat untersucht> ◊ *Sie untersuchte den Inhalt ihrer Handtasche.* ✦ *zum Arzt gehen und sich gründlich untersuchen lassen* ✦ *den Klimawandel untersuchen* 2. *(in court)* verhören [fɛ'høːrən] <verhört, verhörte,

A B C D E F G H I J K L M N O P Q R S T U V W X Y Z

hat verhört> ◊ *Der Richter verbörte den Angeklagten.*
3. *(a student)* prüfen ['pry:fn̩] +haben ◊ *Welcher Professor prüft diese Woche?* ⬥ examine sb on a subject jdn in einem Fach prüfen

example [noun] Beispiel ['baɛʃpi:l] das <-(e)s, -e> ◊ *ein klassisches Beispiel* ⬥ *Er war für mich immer ein Beispiel des treu sorgenden Vaters.* ⬥ *Sein Verhalten sollte uns allen ein Beispiel sein.* an example of sth ein Beispiel für etw. ◊ *Ein Beispiel für ein trennbares Verb ist „ansehen".* set an example mit gutem Beispiel vorangehen for example zum Beispiel follow sb's example sich [dat] ein Beispiel an jdm nehmen

◉ be an example to all allen ein Vorbild sein
make an example of sb an jdm ein Exempel statuieren

excavation [noun] **1.** *(archaeological)* Grabung ['gra:bʊŋ] die <-, -en> **2.** *(on a building site etc.)* Ausschachtung ['aɔsʃaxtʊŋ] die <-, -en>

excavator [noun] Bagger ['bage] der <-s, -> ◊ *mit einem Bagger eine Grube ausheben*

exceed [verb] *(a limit)* überschreiten [ybe'ʃraetn̩] <überschreitet, überschritt, hat überschritten> ◊ *die tägliche Arbeitszeit von neun Stunden überschreiten* ⬥ *die Höchstgeschwindigkeit deutlich überschreiten; (expectations)* übertreffen [ybe'trɛfn̩] <übertrifft, übertraf, hat übertroffen> ◊ *Der Umsatz übertraf all unsere Erwartungen.; (capacity)* übersteigen [ybe'ʃtaegn̩] <übersteigt, überstieg, hat überstiegen> ◊ *Die Nachfrage überstieg das Angebot.*

exceedingly [adv] überaus ['y:belaɔs] *(lofty)* ◊ *eine überaus erfolgreiche Ausstellung* ⬥ *Ich bin ihm überaus dankbar.*

excel [verb] **1.** *(be very good)* glänzen ['glɛntsn̩] +haben ◊ *Er glänzte mit hervorragenden Leistungen.* excel in/at sth in/bei etw. glänzen **2.** *(also iron) (be better than usual)* excel yourself sich selbst übertreffen ['zɛlpst ybe,trɛfn̩] <übertrifft sich, übertraf sich, hat sich übertroffen> ◊ *Mit dieser Leistung hast du dich selbst übertroffen.*

excellence [noun] **1.** *(quality)* hervorragende Qualität [he,fo:gra'gn̩də kvali'tɛ:t] die <-, -en> ◊ *die hervorragende Qualität unserer Produkte* **2.** *(performance)* hervorragende Leistung [he,fo:gra'gn̩də 'laestʊŋ] die <-, -en> ◊ *die hervorragende Leistung des Teams*

excellent(ly) [adj, adv] hervorragend [he'fo:gra:gn̩t] ◊ *hervorragende Ergebnisse erzielen* ⬥ *Das letzte Geschäftsjahr war hervorragend.* ⬥ *Unsere Mannschaft hat heute hervorragend gespielt.*

except[1] [prep] except (for) außer ['aɔse] [+dat] ◊ *Außer meiner Mutter waren alle Verwandten gekommen.* ⬥ *Felix hat in allen Fächern außer in Französisch gute Noten.* ⬥ *Ich arbeite jeden Tag außer sonntags.*

except[2] [conjunc] außer [aɔse] ◊ *Ich verrate dir nichts, außer dass es eine Überraschung ist.* ⬥ *Ich gehe täglich spazieren, außer wenn ich krank bin.*

exception [noun] Ausnahme ['aɔsna:mə] die <-, -n> ◊ *Dieser Fall ist eine Ausnahme.* ⬥ *Ausnahmen bestätigen die Regel.* ⬥ *Wir machen auch für Sie keine Ausnahme.* ⬥ *Das gilt für alle ohne Ausnahme.* an exception to sth eine Ausnahme von etw. with the exception of sth/sb mit Ausnahme ... [gen], mit Ausnahme von etw./jdm

◉ take exception to sth an etw. [dat] Anstoß nehmen

exceptional(ly) [adj, adv] **1.** *(excellent, extreme)* außer-

ordentlich ['aɔse|'ɔʳdn̩tlɪç] no comp/superl ◊ *etw. mit außerordentlicher Vorsicht tun* ⬥ *Ihre Leistung war außerordentlich.* ⬥ *Das war ein außerordentlich komischer Anblick.* **2.** *(extraordinary)* außergewöhnlich ['aɔsegəvø:nlɪç] ◊ *außergewöhnliche Umstände* ⬥ *Seine Frau ist außergewöhnlich.* ⬥ *ein außergewöhnlich heißer Sommer*

excerpt [noun] *(of a text)* Auszug ['aɔstsu:k] der <-(e)s, Auszüge>; *(of music)* Stück [ʃtʏk] das <-(e)s, -e>

excess[1] [noun] **1.** *(too much)* Übermaß ['y:bema:s] das <-es> no pl an excess of sth ein Übermaß an etw. [dat] ◊ *ein Übermaß an Liebe; (of violence, debauchery, dangerous behavio(u)r)* Exzess [ɛks'tsɛs] der <-es, -e> ◊ *die schlimmsten Exzesse des Diktators* ⬥ *Seine Karriere war von Exzessen begleitet.* a life of excess ein Leben im Exzess bis zum Exzess **2.** *(more than)* sth in excess of sth etw. von über etw. [dat] [fɔn y:be] ◊ *ein Betrag von über einer Million Dollar* ⬥ *ein Tempo von über 200 Stundenkilometer*

excess[2] [adj] **1.** *(more than desired)* überflüssig ['y:beflʏsɪç] ◊ *überflüssige Pfunde abnehmen* **2.** *(more than allowed)* Über... ['y:be] excess weight Übergewicht ['y:begəvɪçt] das <-(e)s> no pl

excessive(ly) [adj, adv] *(extent, scope)* übermäßig ['y:bemɛ:sɪç] no comp/superl, when used as an adj, mostly before n ◊ *übermäßige Schuppenbildung* ⬥ *eine übermäßig hohe Belastung mit Nitrat; (demand, generosity, praise)* übertrieben [ybe'tri:bn̩] ◊ *übertriebene Ansprüche* ⬥ *Eine solche Forderung ist völlig übertrieben.* ⬥ *übertrieben großzügig sein*

exchange[1] [noun] **1.** *(swapping)* Austausch ['aɔstaɔʃ] der <-(e)s, -e> most sing ◊ *der Austausch von Gefangenen/Schülern* in exchange for sth im Austausch gegen etw. ◊ *in exchange dafür* ['da:fy:ɐ̯] ◊ *Sie bringt mir Englisch bei, dafür unterrichte ich sie in Deutsch.* exchange of views Meinungsaustausch ['maenʊŋs|aɔstaɔʃ] exchange of letters Briefwechsel ['bri:fvɛksl̩] der <-s, -> exchange of fire Schusswechsel ['ʃʊsvɛksl̩] **2.** FIN *(of currencies)* Umtausch ['ʊmtaɔʃ] der <-(e)s> no pl ◊ *der Umtausch von Dollar in Euro* **3.** FIN stock exchange Börse ['bœʳzə] die <-, -n> ◊ *die Londoner Börse*

exchange[2] [verb] **1.** *(swap)* austauschen ['aɔstaɔʃn̩] +haben ◊ *Gefangene/Daten/Informationen austauschen* ⬥ *Sie tauschten heimlich Blicke aus.* ⬥ *Gedanken/Küsse/Schläge austauschen* austausch sb/ sth for sth jdn/etw. gegen jdn/etw. austauschen; *(currencies, words)* wechseln ['vɛksl̩n] +haben ◊ *Geld wechseln* ⬥ *Sie wechselten ein paar freundliche Worte.* ⬥ *(a purchase)* umtauschen ['ʊmtaɔʃn̩] +haben ◊ *Ich ging zum Fotoladen, um den defekten Fotoapparat umzutauschen.*

exchange rate [noun] Wechselkurs ['vɛksl̩kʊʳs] der <-es, -e> ◊ *Der Wechselkurs ist im Augenblick 1:1,27.*

excite [verb] **1.** *(thrill)* begeistern [bə'gaestɐn] <begeistert, begeisterte, hat begeistert> ◊ *Die Aussicht auf die Reise begeisterte ihn.* ⬥ *von etw. begeistert sein* **2.** *(agitate)* aufregen ['aɔfre:gn̩] +haben ◊ *Die Nachricht hat ihn sehr aufgeregt.* sb gets excited about sth jd regt sich über etw. [acc] auf **3.** *(arouse, provoke)* erregen [ɛ're:gn̩] <erregt, erregte, hat erregt> ◊ *Sein Anblick erregte sie.* ⬥ *Mitleid erregen*

excited → excite [adj] aufgeregt ['aɔfgə're:kt] <aufge-

regter, am aufgeregtesten> ◊ *Morgen habe ich Geburtstag und bin schon ganz aufgeregt!* be excited about sth sich auf etw. ⟨acc⟩ freuen [aof … ˌfrɔ:ɡən] ◊ *Sie freut sich sehr auf die Reise.* become excited about sth, be excited by sth sich über etw. ⟨acc⟩ freuen

excitement ⟨noun⟩ 1. *(agitation, thrill)* Aufregung ['aofre:ɡʊn] die <–, –en> ◊ *Vor lauter/In der Aufregung habe ich meine Schlüssel vergessen.* ♦ *Es herrschte allgemeine/beträchtliche Aufregung wegen seines Rücktritts.* 2. *(suspense)* Spannung ['ʃpanʊn] die <–, –en> ◊ *Die Spannung stieg/wurde unerträglich.*

exciting(ly) ⟨adj, adv⟩ aufregend ['aofre:ɡn̩t] ◊ *Das war ein aufregender Tag!* ♦ *Ein Gruselfilm kann mir gar nicht aufregend genug sein.* ♦ *aufregend schön/sexy*

exclaim ⟨verb⟩ 1. *(shout sth)* ausrufen ['aosru:fn̩] <ruft aus, rief aus, hat ausgerufen> ◊ *Er rief aus: „Wie schön!"* 2. *(scream)* aufschreien ['aofraeən] <schreit auf, schrie auf, hat aufgeschrien> ◊ *Vor Entsetzen schrie er auf.*

exclude ⟨verb⟩ 1. *(people, a possibility)* ausschließen ['aosʃli:sn̩] <schließt aus, schloss aus, hat ausgeschlossen> ◊ *Ich fühlte mich ausgeschlossen.* ♦ *eine Möglichkeit ausschließen* exclude sb from sth jdn von etw. ausschließen ◊ *ein Kind vom Unterricht ausschließen* exclude draughts/light from sth etw. vor Zugluft/Licht schützen [fo:ɐ 'bu:kloft/'lɪçt ʃʏtsn̩] +haben 2. *(in a calculation)* nicht berücksichtigen [nɪçt bə'rʏkzɪçtɪɡn̩] <berücksichtigt, berücksichtigte, hat berücksichtigt> exclude sth from sth etw. bei etw. nicht berücksichtigen

excluding ⟨prep⟩ exklusive [ɛksklu'zi:və] *sing nouns without article or attribute are not declined when following this prep, otherwise* +gen ◊ *Die Reise kostet 750 Euro exklusive der Tagesausflüge.*

exclusion ⟨noun⟩ *(keeping out)* Ausschluss ['aosʃlʊs] der <–es, Ausschlüsse> ◊ *der Ausschluss von einer Veranstaltung* ♦ *vertraglicher Ausschluss*

exclusive ⟨adj⟩ 1. *(elegant, expensive)* exklusiv [ɛksklu'zi:f] ◊ *Die Gegend ist sehr exklusiv.* ♦ *ein exklusives Restaurant* 2. *(limited to a person or group)* Exklusiv... [ɛksklu'zi:f] exclusive rights Exklusivrechte [ɛksklu'zi:frɛçtə] die <–> pl 3. *(not including)* exclusive of ausschließlich ['aosʃli:slɪç] *sing nouns without article or attribute are declined when following this prep, otherwise* +gen ◊ *Die Arbeitszeit beträgt ausschließlich der Pausen 38 Stunden.* exclusive of VAT exklusive Mehrwertsteuer [ɛksklu,zi:və 'me:ɐve:ɐtʃtɔɐə]

exclusively ⟨adv⟩ ausschließlich ['aosʃli:slɪç] *no comp/superl* ◊ *Diese Regelung trifft fast ausschließlich Beamte.* ♦ *Dafür ist ausschließlich der Bund zuständig.*

excursion ⟨noun⟩ *(also fig)* Ausflug ['aosflu:k] der <–(e)s, Ausflüge> ◊ *Morgen machen wir mit der Schule einen Ausflug.* ♦ *ein Ausflug in die Berge oder ans Meer* ♦ *Der berühmte Sopran macht einen Ausflug in die Popmusik.*

excuse[1] ⟨noun⟩ 1. *(explanation, justification)* Entschuldigung [ɛnt'ʃʊldɪɡʊn] die <–, –en> ◊ *eine ausreichende Entschuldigung* ♦ *Dafür gibt es keine Entschuldigung.; (dishonest)* Ausrede ['aosre:də] die <–, –n> ◊ *Ich will keine Ausreden hören!* ♦ *Das ist doch nur eine faule Ausrede.* 2. *(reason for doing sth)* Anlass ['anlas] der <–es, Anlässe> ◊ *ein willkommener Anlass für eine Party*

⊛ make your excuses sich entschuldigen

excuse[2] ⟨verb⟩ 1. *(forgive, justify, give permission to leave)* entschuldigen [ɛnt'ʃʊldɪɡn̩] <entschuldigt, entschuldigte, hat entschuldigt> ◊ *Dieser Umstand entschuldigt nichts.* ♦ *Wenn Sie mich bitte entschuldigen würden — ich hab's eilig.* ♦ *Bitte entschuldigen Sie meine schlechte Handschrift.* excuse yourself sich entschuldigen excuse sb for doing sth entschuldigen, dass jd etw. tut ◊ *Entschuldige, dass ich zu spät komme.* 2. *(exempt)* excuse sb from sth jdn von etw. befreien [fɔn … bə,fraeən] <befreit, befreite, hat befreit> ◊ *Weil sie sich den Arm gebrochen hatte, wurde sie vom Sportunterricht befreit.*

⊛ excuse me Entschuldigung

excuse note ⟨noun⟩ Entschuldigung [ɛnt'ʃʊldɪɡʊn] die <–, –en> ◊ *Er schrieb seinem Sohn eine Entschuldigung für die Schule.*

execute ⟨verb⟩ 1. *(carry out, perform)* ausführen ['aosfy:rən] +haben ◊ *Die Arbeit wurde ordnungsgemäß ausgeführt.* ♦ *eine Bewegung ausführen* 2. *(kill)* hinrichten ['hɪnrɪçtn̩] <richtet hin, richtete hin, hat hingerichtet> ◊ *Der Gefangene wurde um sechs Uhr morgens hingerichtet.* execute sb for sth jdn wegen etw. hinrichten 3. *(a will)* vollstrecken [fɔl'ʃtrɛkn̩] <vollstreckt, vollstreckte, hat vollstreckt> ◊ *ein Testament vollstrecken*

execution ⟨noun⟩ 1. *(carrying out, performance)* Ausführung ['aosfy:rʊn] die <–, –en> ◊ *die Ausführung einer Arbeit/Bewegung* ♦ *die Ausführung eines Befehls durch ein Computerprogramm* 2. *(killing)* Hinrichtung ['hɪnrɪçtʊn] die <–, –en> ◊ *die Hinrichtung des Todeskandidaten* 3. *(of a will)* Vollstreckung [fɔl'ʃtrɛkʊn] die <–> no pl

executive[1] ⟨noun⟩ 1. ECON *(manager)* Manager ['mɛnɪdʒɐ] der <–s, –> ♀Managerin ['mɛnɪdʒərɪn] die <–, –nen> ◊ *Die Regierung beriet sich mit führenden Managern der Industrie.* 2. POL *(of a political party)* Präsidium [prɛ'zi:djʊm] das <–s, Präsidien> ◊ *Das Präsidium hat folgenden Beschluss gefasst: …* 3. POL *(of a state)* Exekutive [ɛksekuti:və] die <–, –n> ◊ *Die Exekutive ist eine der drei Staatsgewalten.*

executive[2] ⟨adj⟩ 1. *(in an organization)* geschäftsführend [gə'ʃɛftsfy:rənt] *no comp/superl, only before ns* ◊ *der geschäftsführende Direktor* executive committee Vorstand ['fo:ɐʃtant] der <–(e)s, Vorstände> 2. *(luxury)* Luxus... ['lʊksʊs] luxury suite Luxussuite ['lʊksʊs,svi:tə] die <–, –n>

exemplary ⟨adj⟩ *(impeccable)* vorbildlich ['fo:ɐbɪltlɪç] *seldom comp/superl* ◊ *ein vorbildlicher Einsatz der Rettungskräfte* ♦ *Die Zusammenarbeit in unserem Team ist vorbildlich.* 2. *(deterring)* abschreckend ['apʃrɛkn̩t] ◊ *eine abschreckende Strafe*

exemption ⟨noun⟩ Befreiung [bə'fraeʊn] die <–, –en> ◊ *die Befreiung vom Wehrdienst/von den Rundfunkgebühren* tax exemption Steuerbefreiung ['ʃtɔɐbəfraeʊn] grant sb exemption from sth jdn von etw. befreien [fɔn … bə,fraeən] <befreit, befreite, hat befreit>

exercise[1] ⟨noun⟩ 1. *(physical activity)* Bewegung [bə've:ɡʊn] die <–, –en> ◊ *Du brauchst mehr Bewegung.* take exercise sich bewegen [bə've:ɡn̩] <bewegt sich, bewegte sich, hat sich bewegt> ◊ *Ich bewege mich einfach nicht genug.* 2. *(practice, sequence of movements in gymnastics, military training, action with a particular purpose)* Übung

['y:bʊŋ] die <–, –en> ◊ *eine schwierige Übung am Barren* ✦ *Diese Übung stärkt die Muskeln.* ✦ *Die Truppen nehmen an einer Übung teil.* ✦ *Was ist der Zweck der Übung?* **3.** school *(learning task)* Aufgabe ['aʊfgaːbə] die <–, –n> ◊ *jdm eine Aufgabe stellen* ✦ *Was ist das Ergebnis bei der dritten Aufgabe?* **4.** *(execution)* Ausübung ['aʊs|yːbʊŋ] die <–, –en> ◊ *die Ausübung von Pflichten*

exercise² verb **1.** *(physically)* Sport treiben ['ʃpoːrt traɛbm̩] <treibt, trieb, hat getrieben> ◊ *Man sollte regelmäßig Sport treiben.*; *(a part of your body)* trainieren [trɛ'niːrən] <trainiert, trainierte, hat trainiert> ◊ *seine Muskeln trainieren* **2.** *(a right, power)* ausüben ['aʊs|yːbm̩] +haben ◊ *Ich habe bei der letzten Wahl mein Wahlrecht nicht ausgeübt.* **3.** *(a virtue)* üben ['yːbm̩] +haben ◊ *Zurückhaltung/Toleranz üben*

exercise book noun school Heft [hɛft] das <–(e)s, –e> ◊ *die Hefte einsammeln/austeilen*

exert verb **1.** *(influence, force etc.)* ausüben ['aʊs|yːbm̩] +haben ◊ *Einfluss auf jdn/etw. ausüben* ✦ *Druck auf jdn/etw. ausüben* **2.** *(tax yourself)* exert yourself sich anstrengen ['anʃtrɛŋən] +haben ◊ *Streng dich in der Hitze nicht so an!*

exertion noun Anstrengung ['anʃtrɛŋʊŋ] die <–, –en> ◊ *Nach körperlicher Anstrengung sollte man sich entspannen.* ✦ *Die Anstrengungen der Reise waren ihr zu viel.*

exhaust verb erschöpfen [e'ʃœpfn̩] <erschöpft, erschöpfte, hat erschöpft> ◊ *Die lange Reise hatte sie erschöpft.* ✦ *Das Thema war bald erschöpft.* ✦ *Die Ölvorkommen werden bald erschöpft sein.*; *(possibilities)* ausschöpfen ['aʊsʃœpfn̩] +haben ◊ *Wir haben bereits alle Möglichkeiten ausgeschöpft.*

exhaustion noun Erschöpfung [e'ʃœpfʊŋ] die <–, –en> most sing ◊ *Im Zug schlief sie vor Erschöpfung ein.* ✦ *die Erschöpfung der Erdölreserven*

exhibit verb *(in a public place)* ausstellen ['aʊsʃtɛlən] +haben ◊ *etw. auf einer Messe ausstellen* ✦ *Die Fundstücke werden jetzt im Museum ausgestellt.*; *(a symptom, quality etc.)* aufweisen ['aʊfvaɛzn̩] <weist auf, wies auf, hat aufgewiesen> ◊ *Der Patient weist starke Symptome einer allergischen Reaktion auf.* ✦ *besondere Merkmale aufweisen*

exhibition noun **1.** *(public display)* Ausstellung ['aʊsʃtɛlʊŋ] die <–, –en> ◊ *eine Ausstellung moderner Kunst in der Staatsgalerie* ✦ *die Ausstellung über Heimwerkerbedarf in der Messehalle* be on exhibition ausgestellt werden ['aʊsɡəʃtɛlt veːɐ̯dn̩] <wird, wurde, ist worden> **2.** *(of abilities, skills)* Demonstration [demonstra'tsjoːn] die <–, –en> ◊ *Die Vorführung war eine Demonstration besonderer Schauspielkunst.*

Ⓔ make an exhibition of yourself sich danebenbenehmen

exile noun **1.** *(place, situation)* Exil [ɛ'ksiːl] das <–s, –e> most sing ◊ *im Exil leben* ✦ *Während seines Exils schrieb er viele Bücher.* **2.** *(person)* Exilant [ɛksi'lant] der <–en, –en> ♀Exilantin [ɛksi'lantɪn] die <–, –nen> ◊ *Viele deutsche Exilanten lebten in Paris.*

exist verb **1.** *(be)* existieren [ɛksɪs'tiːrən] <existiert, existierte, hat existiert> ◊ *Die Firma existiert bereits seit 1954.* ✦ *Existiert Leben auf anderen Planeten?* sth has ceased to exist etw. existiert nicht mehr **2.** *(live)* leben ['leːbm̩] +haben ◊ *Wie soll ich ohne*

dich leben? exist on sth von etw. leben ◊ *Von so wenig Geld kann ich nicht leben.*

existence noun Existenz [ɛksɪs'tɛnts] die <–, –en> ◊ *Er glaubt an die Existenz von Ufos.* ✦ *Jeder Mensch hat Anspruch auf eine würdige Existenz.* in existence existierend [ɛksɪs'tiːrənt] no comp/superl, only before ns ◊ *Der Film zeigt die einzigen existierenden Aufnahmen des Beutelwolfs.* come into existence entstehen [ɛnt'ʃteːən] <entsteht, entstand, ist entstanden> go out of existence verschwinden [fɛ'ʃvɪndn̩] <verschwindet, verschwand, ist verschwunden>

Ⓔ eke out an existence mühsam seinen Lebensunterhalt verdienen

existing → **exist** adj bestehend [bə'ʃteːənt] no comp/superl, only before ns ◊ *bestehende Gebäude abreißen* ✦ *Das bestehende System muss total erneuert werden.*

exit¹ noun **1.** *(way out, door)* Ausgang ['aʊsɡaŋ] der <–(e)s, Ausgänge> ◊ *Wo ist der Ausgang?* ✦ *Das Messegelände hat fünf Ausgänge.* emergency exit Notausgang ['noːt|aʊsɡaŋ] **2.** *(of a motorway, freeway, driveway)* Ausfahrt ['aʊsfaːɐ̯t] die <–, –en> ◊ *Ausfahrt bitte freihalten!* ✦ *Ein- und Ausfahrt der Baustelle* ✦ *Wir müssen bei der nächsten Ausfahrt von der Autobahn herunter.* **3.** *(action)* Hinausgehen [hɪ'naʊsɡeːən] das <–s> no pl make an exit hinausgehen [hɪ'naʊsɡeːən] <geht hinaus, ging hinaus, ist hinausgegangen>; *(from a stage)* Abgang ['apɡaŋ] der <–s, Abgänge> ◊ *Nach dem Abgang der Band von der Bühne gab es Zugabe-Rufe.*

exit² verb **1.** *(a building, aircraft)* exit (from) sth etw. verlassen [fɛ'lasn̩] <verlässt, verließ, hat verlassen> ◊ *Bei Feuer das Gebäude durch die Notausgänge verlassen!*; *(from a stage)* abgehen ['apɡeːən] <geht ab, ging ab, ist abgegangen> ◊ *Hamlet geht nach links/rechts ab.* **2.** it beenden [bə'ɛndn̩] <beendet, beendete, hat beendet> ◊ *ein Computerprogramm beenden*

exorbitant adj stark überhöht [ʃtaːɐ̯k ybɐ'høːt] no comp/superl ◊ *Der Preis war stark überhöht.* ✦ *ein stark überhöhter Zinssatz*

exotic adj exotisch [ɛ'ksoːtɪʃ] ◊ *exotische Früchte* ✦ *Diese Blume sieht irgendwie exotisch aus.*

expand verb **1.** *(make bigger, materials)* ausdehnen ['aʊsdeːnən] +haben sth expands etw. dehnt sich aus ◊ *Wasser dehnt sich aus, wenn es gefriert.*; *(an organization, a body, company)* erweitern [ɛ'vaɛtn̩] <erweitert, erweiterte, hat erweitert> ◊ *Die EU soll erweitert werden.* **2.** *(business, market)* expandieren [ɛkspan'diːrən] <expandiert, expandierte, hat expandiert> ◊ *Das Unternehmen will in ganz Europa expandieren.* ✦ *Die Firma will ihr Geschäft weltweit expandieren.* **3.** *(talk or write more about sth)* expand on ausführen ['aʊsfyːrən] +haben ◊ *Könnten Sie diese Theorie näher ausführen?*

expanse noun Weite ['vaɛtə] die <–, –n> ◊ *die endlose Weite des Meeres/der Steppe*

expansion noun **1.** *(of material)* Ausdehnung ['aʊsdeːnʊŋ] die <–, –en> most sing ◊ *die Ausdehnung von Metall/Keramik durch Wärmeentwicklung* **2.** *(of business)* Expansion [ɛkspan'zjoːn] die <–, –en> ◊ *die Expansion eines Geschäfts* **3.** *(giving more information)* Ausführung ['aʊsfyːrʊŋ] die <–, –en> ◊ *die Ausführung eines Themas*

expect verb erwarten [e'vaːtn̩] <erwartet, erwartete, hat erwartet> ◊ *Erwartest du Gäste?* ✦ *ein Kind*

erwarten ♦ *Ich erwarte eine Nachricht von ihm.* ♦
Du erwartest zu viel von deinen Kindern. ♦ *Wie
erwartet hat er sich beklagt.* expect sb/sth to do sth
erwarten, dass jd/etw. etw. tut expect sb back jdn
zurückerwarten [ʦuˈrʏkˌevaˈrtn̩] +haben
ⓔ **be too much to expect** wohl zu viel erwartet
sein be expecting schwanger sein I expect so. Ich
nehme es an. I expect that ich nehme an, dass
expectant(ly) ⓐⓓⓙ, ⓐⓓⓥ gespannt [ɡəˈʃpant] <gespann-
ter, am gespanntesten> ◊ *gespannte Zuschauer* ♦ *Sie
waren gespannt, ohne genau zu wissen, warum.* ♦
Gespannt blickten die Kinder zur Tür.
expectation ⓝⓞⓤⓝ Erwartung [eˈvaˈtʊŋ] die <-, -en>
◊ *Der neue Mitarbeiter hat unsere Erwartungen
nicht erfüllt.* in expectation of sth in Erwartung
einer Sache be in line with expectations den Erwartungen entsprechen have high expectations of sb
große Erwartungen in jdn setzen
[groˈsə eˈvaˈtʊŋən ɪn ... zɛʦn̩] +haben
ⓔ **contrary to all expectations** wider Erwarten
expected → expect ⓐⓓⓙ voraussichtlich
[foˈraosˌzɪçtlɪç] no comp/superl, only before ns ◊ *Die
voraussichtliche Dauer des Downloads beträgt 20
Sekunden.*
expedition ⓝⓞⓤⓝ 1. *(journey, party of travellers)* Expedition [ɛkspediˈʦi̯oːn] die <-, -en> ◊ *Die Expedition
erreichte ihr Ziel unbeschadet.* ♦ *eine Expedition
zum Nordpol machen* 2. ⓂⒾⓁ *(campaign)* Feldzug
[ˈfɛltʦuːk] der <-(e)s, Feldzüge> 3. *(excursion)*
Ausflug [ˈaosfluːk] der <-(e)s, Ausflüge>
ⓔ **go on a shopping expedition** einen Einkaufsbummel machen
expel ⓥⒺⓇⒷ 1. *(from a country)* ausweisen [ˈaosvaezn̩]
<weist aus, wies aus, hat ausgewiesen> ◊ *Nachdem ihr
Asylantrag abgelehnt worden war, wurde sie ausgewiesen.* 2. *(from a politcal party etc.)* expel sb (from
sth) jdn (aus etw.) ausschließen [(aos ...) ˈaosʃliːsn̩]
<schließt aus, schloss aus, hat ausgeschlossen> ◊ *Er
wurde aus der Partei ausgeschlossen.* 3. *(from school,
an institution)* expel sb from sth jdn von der Schule
etc. weisen [fon deːʁ ˈʃuːlə vaezn̩] <weist, wies, hat
gewiesen> mostly passive, always with indication of
the place ◊ *Der Schüler wurde von der Schule
gewiesen.* ♦ *Ich bin vom Gymnasium verwiesen
worden.*
expenditure ⓝⓞⓤⓝ 1. *(money spent)* Ausgabe
[ˈaosgaːbə] die <-, -n> most pl ◊ *die Ausgaben für
Material* 2. *(use)* Aufwand [ˈaofvant] der <-(e)s> no
pl ◊ *der Aufwand an Mühe und Zeit*
expense ⓝⓞⓤⓝ *(money spent)* Kosten [ˈkɔstn̩] die <->
only pl ◊ *die Kosten decken* ♦ *für die anfallenden/ent-
stehenden Kosten aufkommen* incur an expense
Kosten haben go to great expense hohe Kosten auf
sich ⓐⓒⒸ nehmen; *(business expense)* Geschäftskos-
ten [ɡəˈʃɛftskɔstn̩] operating expenses Betriebskosten [bəˈtriːpskɔstn̩]; *(of an employee)* expenses
Spesen [ˈʃpeːzn̩] die <-> only pl ◊ *Ihre Spesen
werden Ihnen bezahlt.*
ⓔ **at sb's expense** auf jds Kosten at the expense
of sth auf Kosten ... ⓖⒺⓃ
expensive ⓐⓓⓙ teuer [ˈtɔɡə] <teurer, am teuersten>
<der/die/das teure ...> ◊ *Er fährt ein sündhaft
teures Auto.* ♦ *Das Benzin ist schon wieder teurer
geworden.*
experience¹ ⓝⓞⓤⓝ 1. *(sth you learned)* Erfahrung
[eˈfaːrʊŋ] die <-, -en> ◊ *viel Erfahrung auf einem*

Gebiet haben ♦ *Das weiß ich aus persönlicher
Erfahrung.* ♦ *Erfahrungen mit etw.* in sb's experience nach jds Erfahrung have an experience eine
Erfahrung machen [aenə eˈfaːrʊŋ maxn̩] +haben gain
experience Erfahrung sammeln [eˈfaːrʊŋ zamln̩]
+haben 2. *(event you lived through)* Erlebnis
[eˈleːpnɪs] das <-ses, -se> ◊ *Sie hat uns von ihren
Erlebnissen in Japan erzählt.* ♦ *ein traumatisches
Erlebnis haben*
experience² ⓥⒺⓇⒷ 1. *(undergo)* erleben [eˈleːbm̩]
<erlebt, erlebte, hat erlebt> ◊ *Die Wirtschaft erlebt
zurzeit einen Aufschwung.* ♦ *eine herbe Enttäuschung erleben; (feel the effects of sth yourself)*
erfahren [eˈfaːrən] <erfährt, erfuhr, hat erfahren> ◊
Selten habe ich so viel Undank erfahren.; (a problem)
haben [ˈhaːbm̩] <hat ...> ◊ *Schwierigkeiten haben* ♦
Ich habe ein Problem mit Ihrer Software. 2. *(feel)*
empfinden [ɛmˈpfɪndn̩] <empfindet, empfand, hat
empfunden> ◊ *Schmerz/Freude empfinden*
experienced → experience ⓐⓓⓙ erfahren [eˈfaːrən] ◊
ein erfahrener Lehrer ♦ *erfahren im Umgang mit
etw. sein*
experiment¹ ⓝⓞⓤⓝ Experiment [ɛksperiˈmɛnt] das
<-(e)s, -e> ◊ *ein Experiment durchführen* ♦ *Experi-
mente an Tieren*
experiment² ⓥⒺⓇⒷ experimentieren
[ɛksperimɛnˈtiːrən] <experimentiert, experimentierte,
hat experimentiert> ◊ *mit Drogen experimentieren* ♦
an Tieren experimentieren
experimental ⓐⓓⓙ 1. *(consisting of an experiment)*
experimentell [ɛksperimɛnˈtɛl] ◊ *experimentelle
Musik* ♦ *Die Methode gilt nach wie vor als experimentell.* 2. *(referring to or based on experiments)*
Versuchs... [fɛˈzuːxs] experimental result Versuchs-
ergebnis [fɛˈzuːxsˌɡeˌgeːpnɪs] das <-ses, -se>
expert ⓝⓞⓤⓝ Experte [ɛksˈpɛrtə] der <-n, -n>
♀Expertin [ɛksˈpɛrtɪn] die <-, -nen> ◊ *eine anerkannte Expertin für Quantenphysik* ♦ *Er ist ein
Experte im Kochen/in der deutschen Grammatik.*
computer expert Computerexperte
[kɔmˈpjuːteˌɛksˌpɛrtə]; Computerexpertin
[kɔmˈpjuːteˌɛksˌpɛrtɪn]
expert(ly) ⓐⓓⓙ, ⓐⓓⓥ 1. *(very good)* ausgezeichnet
[ˈaosgəˌtsaeçnət] no comp/superl ◊ *eine ausgezeichnete Köchin* be expert at sth etw. ausgezeichnet
können ◊ *Du kannst ausgezeichnet malen.* 2. *(by an
expert)* fachmännisch [ˈfaxmɛnɪʃ] ◊ *eine fachmänni-
sche Arbeit* ♦ *etw. fachmännisch erledigen*
expertise ⓝⓞⓤⓝ 1. *(skill)* Können [ˈkœnən] das <-s>
no pl ◊ *sein Können beweisen* 2. *(knowledge of a particular field)* Sachkenntnis [ˈzaxkɛntnɪs] die <-, -se>
most pl ◊ *jd mit Sachkenntnissen und einer
positiven Ausstrahlung; (knowledge of a particular
subject)* Fachkenntnis [ˈfaxkɛntnɪs] die <-, -se>
most pl ◊ *medizinische Fachkenntnisse*
expire ⓥⒺⓇⒷ *(deadline, contract, membership)* ablaufen
[ˈaplaofn̩] <läuft ab, lief ab, ist abgelaufen> ◊ *den
Pass verlängern lassen, bevor er abgelaufen ist;
(ticket, voucher)* verfallen [fɛˈfalən] <verfällt, verfiel,
ist verfallen> ◊ *Der Fahrschein verfällt nach Ablauf
eines Jahres.* ♦ *Ein Gutschein verfällt.; (entitlement)*
erlöschen [eˈlœʃn̩] <erlischt, erlosch, ist erloschen> ◊
*Mit seinem Tod sind sämtliche Ansprüche an ihn
erloschen.*
expiry ⓝⓞⓤⓝ *(of a deadline, contract)* Ablauf [ˈaplaof]
der <-(e)s, Abläufe> ◊ *nach Ablauf der Frist*

A B C D E F G H I J K L M N O P Q R S T U V W X Y Z

explain [verb] erklären [ɛˈklɛːrən] <erklärt, erklärte, hat erklärt> ◊ *Unsere Lehrerin erklärt die neuen Vokabeln.* ✦ *Kannst du mir erklären, wie das Handy funktioniert?* ✦ *Seine lange Krankheit erklärt die Lücken in seinem Wissen.* ✦ *Ich kann alles erklären!* explain sth to sb jdm etw. erklären You have to explain yourself more clearly. Das musst du/müssen Sie schon genauer erklären.

• **explain away** [phras v] explain sth away eine Erklärung für etw. finden [aenə eˈklɛːrʊŋ fyːɐ̯ ... fɪndn̩] <findet, fand, hat gefunden> ◊ *Sie hat verzweifelt versucht, eine Erklärung für den Vorfall zu finden.*

explanation [noun] Erklärung [eˈklɛːrʊŋ] die <-, -en> ◊ *Die Erklärungen in diesem Wörterbuch sind leicht verständlich.* ✦ *Wir haben noch keine Erklärung für ihr Verschwinden.* an explanation (of/about) how to do sth eine Erklärung, wie man etw. tut

explicit(ly) [adj, adv] 1. (clear) deutlich [ˈdɔɡtlɪç] ◊ *eine deutliche Warnung* ✦ *Die Anweisungen waren deutlich genug.* ✦ *etw. deutlich machen* ✦ *Das habe ich doch deutlich gesagt.* 2. (detailed) ausführlich [ˈaosfyːɐ̯lɪç] ◊ *ein ausführlicher Bericht* ✦ *Die Gebrauchsanweisung war nicht ausführlich genug.* ✦ *Sie hat mir ausführlich beschrieben, was sie erlebt hat.*

explode [verb] 1. (also fig) (be blown up, get angry, increase quickly) explodieren [ɛksploˈdiːrən] <explodiert, explodierte, ist explodiert> ◊ *Eine Bombe ist explodiert.* ✦ *Als sie das hörte, explodierte sie.* ✦ *Die Erdbevölkerung ist in den letzten 100 Jahren förmlich explodiert.* 2. (blow up) explodieren lassen, zünden [ˈtsʏndn̩] <zündet, zündete, hat gezündet> ◊ *Die Terroristen haben eine Bombe gezündet.*

exploit [verb] 1. (a person, resources) ausbeuten [ˈaosbɔɡtn̩] <beutet aus, beutete aus, hat ausgebeutet> ◊ *Kinder in Fabriken ausbeuten* ✦ *Bodenschätze ausbeuten* 2. (benefit from) ausnutzen [ˈaosnʊtsn̩] +haben ◊ *Er nutzte jede Gelegenheit aus, um neue Kunden zu gewinnen.* ✦ *eine Gesetzeslücke ausnutzen*

exploitation [noun] Ausbeutung [ˈaosbɔɡtʊŋ] die <-, -en> most sing ◊ *die Ausbeutung von Arbeitern/ Bodenschätzen*

exploration [noun] Erforschung [eˈfɔrʃʊŋ] die <-, -en> ◊ *die Erforschung des Weltraums* voyage of exploration Entdeckungsreise [ɛntˈdɛkʊŋsraezə] die <-, -n> ◊ *auf Entdeckungsreise gehen*

explore [verb] erforschen [eˈfɔrʃn̩] <erforscht, erforschte, hat erforscht> ◊ *Diesen Dschungel hat bislang noch niemand erforscht.* ✦ *die Hintergründe eines Vorfalls erforschen* go exploring auf Entdeckungsreise gehen [aof ɛntˈdɛkʊŋsraezə geːən] <geht, ging, ist gegangen> ◊

explosion [noun] 1. (of a bomb, rapid growth of sth) Explosion [ɛksploˈzjoːn] die <-, -en> ◊ *Fachleute brachten den Sprengsatz zur Explosion.* ✦ *eine Explosion der Benzinpreise* 2. (fit of anger) Wutausbruch [ˈvuːtˌaosbrʊx] der <-(e)s, Wutausbrüche>

explosive [adj] 1. (exploding easily, growing rapidly) explosiv [ɛksploˈziːf] ◊ *Dieses Gasgemisch ist sehr explosiv.* ✦ *ein explosives Bevölkerungswachstum* explosive device Sprengkörper [ˈʃprɛŋkœɐ̯pe] der <-s, -> 2. (showing strong emotions) aufbrausend [ˈaofbraoznt] ◊ *ein aufbrausendes Temperament haben* 3. (dangerous) brisant [briˈzant] <brisanter, am

brisantesten> ◊ *Die Lage im Krisengebiet ist nach wie vor brisant.* ✦ *eine höchst brisante Angelegenheit*

export¹ [noun] Export [ɛksˈpɔrt] der <-(e)s, -e> ◊ *Der Export boomt.* ✦ *Die Exporte stiegen um 11 Prozent.* ban on exports Exportverbot [ɛksˈpɔrtfɛboːt] das <-(e)s, -e> ◊ *ein Exportverbot verhängen*

export² [verb] exportieren [ɛkspɔrˈtiːrən] <exportiert, exportierte, hat exportiert> ◊ *Autos aus Deutschland exportieren* ✦ *Die Firma exportiert auch nach Indonesien.* ✦ *Daten in ein anderes Programm exportieren*

expose [verb] 1. (uncover) freilegen [ˈfraeleːgn̩] +haben ◊ *Der verschüttete Stollen wurde wieder freigelegt.;* (part of your body) entblößen [ɛntˈbløːsn̩] <entblößt, entblößte, hat entblößt> ◊ *mit entblößtem Oberkörper* expose yourself sich entblößen 2. expose sb/sth/ yourself to sth jdn/etw./sich einer Sache [dat] aussetzen [ˈaosʦɛtsn̩] +haben ◊ *jdn/sich einer Gefahr aussetzen* ✦ *Das Gerät darf keinem direkten Sonnenlicht ausgesetzt werden.* 3. (a scandal, abuse etc.) aufdecken [ˈaofdɛkn̩] +haben ◊ *Ein Reporter deckte den Skandal auf.;* (a person) entlarven [ɛntˈlaˀfn̩] <entlarvt, entlarvte, hat entlarvt> ◊ *jdn als Lügner entlarven* 4. (in photography) belichten [bəˈlɪçtn̩] <belichtet, belichtete, hat belichtet>

exposure [noun] 1. (to substances, radiation etc.) exposure to sth Kontakt mit etw. [kɔnˈtakt mɪt] der <-(e)s, -e> ◊ *den Kontakt mit Allergenen vermeiden* What are the behavio(u)ral effects of exposure to violence in media? Wie wirkt sich Gewalt in den Medien auf das Verhalten aus? Exposure to violence harms children's health. Kinder Gewalt ausgesetzt sind, leidet ihre Gesundheit. exposure to radiation Strahlenbelastung [ˈʃtraːlənbəlastʊŋ] die <-, -en> noise exposure Lärmbelastung [ˈlɛrmbəlastʊŋ] die <-, -en> 2. (of a scandal, crime) Aufdeckung [ˈaofdɛkʊŋ] die <-, -en> ◊ *Die Aufdeckung des Betrugs verdanken wir einem Zufall.;* (of a person) Entlarvung [ɛntˈlaˀfʊŋ] die <-, -en> ◊ *die Entlarvung eines Betrügers* 3. (public attention) Aufmerksamkeit [ˈaofmɛˀkzaːmkaet] die <-> no pl ◊ *viel öffentliche Aufmerksamkeit bekommen* 4. (to low temperatures) Unterkühlung [ʊntɐˈkyːlʊŋ] die <-, -en> ◊ *an Unterkühlung sterben* 5. (position of a building) Lage [ˈlaːgə] die <-, -n> ◊ *Das Gebäude hat eine ausgezeichnete Lage.* southern exposure Südlage [ˈzyːtlaːgə] die <-, -n> 6. (in photography) Belichtung [bəˈlɪçtʊŋ] die

express¹ [adj] 1. (clear) ausdrücklich [ˈaosdrʏklɪç] no comp/superl, only before ns ◊ *Ohne seine ausdrückliche Erlaubnis darfst du nicht gehen.* ✦ *auf ihren ausdrücklichen Wunsch* 2. (quick) Eil... [ael] express letter Eilbrief [ˈaelbriːf] der <-(e)s, -e> ◊ *etw. per/ als Eilbrief schicken* express train Schnellzug [ˈʃnɛltsuːk] der <-(e)s, Schnellzüge>

express² [verb] 1. (say, show your feelings) ausdrücken [ˈaosdrʏkn̩] +haben ◊ *Er drückte ihr sein Mitgefühl aus.* ✦ *Seine Haltung drückt Müdigkeit aus.* express yourself sich ausdrücken ◊ *Er kann sich in mehreren Sprachen fließend ausdrücken.* 2. (criticism, interest, an opinion etc.) äußern [ˈɔysen] +haben ◊ *seine Bedenken äußern* 3. (represent) wiedergeben [ˈviːdegeːbm̩] <gibt wieder, gab wieder, hat wiedergegeben> ◊ *das Ergebnis in Prozent wiedergeben* 4. (in the US: send) per Express schicken [pɛˀ ɛksˈprɛs ʃɪkn̩] +haben

expression [noun] **1.** *(word, look, manifestation)* Ausdruck ['aʊsdrʊk] der <-(e)s, Ausdrücke> ◊ *Sein Gesicht hatte einen mürrischen Ausdruck.* ♦ *Dieser Ausdruck ist zu umgangssprachlich.* ♦ *mit viel Ausdruck sprechen* ♦ *Sein aggressives Verhalten ist Ausdruck seiner Unsicherheit.* give expression to sth einer Sache [dat] Ausdruck verleihen **2.** *(voicing)* Äußerung ['ɔʏsərʊŋ] die <-, -en> ◊ *Er vermeidet die Äußerung von Gefühlen.*

expropriate [verb] **1.** *(take and use for public purposes)* enteignen [ɛnt|'aeɡnən] <enteignet, enteignete, hat enteignet> ◊ *Die Bauern wurden ohne Entschädigung enteignet.* **2.** *(steal)* unterschlagen [ʊntɐ'ʃlaːɡn̩] <unterschlägt, unterschlug, hat unterschlagen> ◊ *Ein Teil der Hilfsgüter wurde unterschlagen.*

expulsion [noun] **1.** *(from an organization, activity)* Ausschluss ['aʊsʃlʊs] der <-es, Ausschlüsse> ◊ *Man diskutiert über seinen Ausschluss aus der Partei.* expulsion from school Schulverweis ['ʃuːlfɛvaes] der <-es, -e> **2.** *(from a country)* Ausweisung ['aʊsvaezʊŋ] die <-, -en> **3.** *(from a container, your body)* Herauspressen [hɛ'aʊspresn̩] das <-s> no pl ◊ *das Herauspressen von Luft aus der Lunge*

exquisitely [adv] **1.** *(perfectly, beautifully)* herrlich ['hɛʁlɪç] ◊ *Angorawolle ist herrlich weich.* ♦ *Sie haben herrlich gesungen.; (very well)* ausgezeichnet ['aʊsɡətsaeçnat] no comp/superl ◊ *Sie hat ganz ausgezeichnet gekocht.* **2.** *(extremely)* äußerst ['ɔʏsest] no comp/superl ◊ *ein äußerst schönes Kleid*

extend [verb] **1.** *(wall, area etc.)* sich erstrecken [ɛ'ʃtrɛkn̩] <erstreckt sich, erstreckte sich, hat sich erstreckt> ◊ *Der Wald erstreckt sich bis zum Stadtrand.; (last)* extend over dauern ['daʊen] +haben ◊ *Das Fest dauert mehrere Tage.* **2.** *(make bigger)* vergrößern [fɛ'ɡrøːsen] <vergrößert, vergrößerte, hat vergrößert> ◊ *ein Haus durch einen Anbau vergrößern* ♦ *Er konnte seinen Vorsprung vergrößern.; (expand a choice of sth)* erweitern [ɛ'vaeten] <erweitert, erweiterte, hat erweitert> ◊ *das Angebot an Waren erweitern; (make last longer, renew)* verlängern [fɛ'lɛŋen] <verlängert, verlängerte, hat verlängert> ◊ *seinen Urlaub/eine Frist verlängern* ♦ *einen Reisepass verlängern lassen; (a ladder, table)* ausziehen ['aʊstsiːən] <zieht aus, zog aus, hat ausgezogen> ◊ *den Tisch ausziehen, wenn Besuch kommt* Does this table extend? Lässt sich der Tisch ausziehen? **3.** *(your arms, wings)* ausbreiten ['aʊsbraetn̩] <breitet aus, breitete aus, hat ausgebreitet> ◊ *Sie breitete die Arme aus, um mich zu umarmen.; (your hand)* ausstrecken ['aʊsʃtrɛkn̩] +haben **4.** *(a friendship etc.)* vertiefen [fɛ'tiːfn̩] <vertieft, vertiefte, hat vertieft> ◊ *Wollen wir unsere Bekanntschaft nicht vertiefen?* **5.** *(form) (offer)* extend sth to sb jdm etw. aussprechen ['aʊsʃprɛçn̩] <spricht aus, sprach aus, hat ausgesprochen> ◊ *jdm seine Glückwünsche/seinen Dank aussprechen* **6.** *(form) (lend)* extend sth to sb jdm etw. gewähren [ɡə'vɛːrən] <gewährt, gewährte, hat gewährt> ◊ *Hat Ihnen die Bank den Kredit gewährt?* **7.** *(relate to)* extend to betreffen [bə'trɛfn̩] <betrifft, betraf, hat betroffen> ◊ *Diese Vorschrift betrifft auch Minderjährige.*

extension [noun] **1.** *(of a building)* Anbau ['anbaʊ] der <-(e)s, -ten> ◊ *Wir planen einen Anbau auf der Südseite unseres Hauses.* **2.** *(telephone line)* Nebenanschluss ['neːbn̩|anʃlʊs] der <-es, Nebenanschlüsse>

3. *(in length or duration)* Verlängerung [fɛ'lɛŋərʊŋ] die <-, -en> ◊ *Ist eine Verlängerung der Frist möglich?* extension cable/cord/lead Verlängerungsschnur [fɛ'lɛŋərʊŋsʃnuːɐ̯] die <-, Verlängerungsschnüre> **4.** *(continuation)* Fortsetzung ['fɔʁtzɛtsʊŋ] die <-, -en> ◊ *Sie betrachtet ihren Beruf als Tierpflegerin als eine Fortsetzung ihres Hobbys.* **5.** *(arm, leg)* at full extension ganz gestreckt [ˌɡants ɡə'ʃtrɛkt] **6.** *(of powers, abilities)* Erweiterung [ɛ'vaetərʊŋ] die <-, -en> most sing ◊ *Er bemüht sich um die Erweiterung seiner Kompetenzen.* ♦ *eine Erweiterung der Grenzkontrollen* **7.** π Dateikennung [da'taekənʊŋ] die <-, -en> ◊ *Für welches Format steht die Dateikennung „XML"?*

⊚ by extension folglich ◊ *Er mag keine Haustiere und folglich auch keine Katzen.*

extensive(ly) [adj, adv] **1.** *(very large, detailed)* umfangreich ['ʊmfanraeç] ◊ *umfangreiche Nachforschungen anstellen* ♦ *Die Bibliothek ist sehr umfangreich.* ♦ *Das Gebäude wird zurzeit umfangreich renoviert.; (damage)* beträchtlich [ba'trɛçtlɪç] ◊ *beträchtlichen Schaden anrichten* ♦ *Das Gebäude wurde beträchtlich beschädigt.; (use)* häufig ['hɔʏfɪç] ◊ *der häufige Gebrauch von Fremdwörtern* make extensive use of sth etw. häufig benutzen ◊ *Auf Reisen benutze ich mein Handy sehr häufig.* **2.** *(area, space)* weit [vaet] <weiter, am weitesten> ◊ *weite Wälder* sth spreads extensively etw. breitet sich aus ['braetət zɪç aʊs] <breitete sich aus, hat sich ausgebreitet>

extent [noun] **1.** *(of knowledge, power)* Umfang ['ʊmfaŋ] der <-(e)s, Umfänge> to a limited/the full extent in begrenztem/vollem Umfang; *(of sth negative)* Ausmaß ['aʊsmaːs] das <-es, -e> ◊ *Ausmaß der Katastrophe* We had losses to the extent of two million euro. Wir hatten Verluste in Höhe von zwei Millionen Euro. **2.** *(part)* Teil [tael] der <-(e)s, -e> ◊ *Ein großer Teil der Meldungen war falsch.* ♦ *Große Teile des Gebiets sind sumpfig.* to some extent zum Teil **3.** *(degree)* Maß [maːs] das <-es> no pl to some/a large extent in gewissem/hohem Maße ◊ *Der Erfolg hängt in hohem Maße vom Glück ab.* **4.** *(of an area)* Ausdehnung ['aʊsdeːnʊŋ] die <-, -en> the full extent of the lake der See in seiner gesamten Ausdehnung

⊚ to such an extent derart to what extent inwieweit

exterior [adj] **1.** *(on or from the outside)* Außen... ['aʊsn̩] exterior mirror Außenspiegel ['aʊsn̩ʃpiːɡl̩] der <-s, -> exterior view Außenansicht ['aʊsn̩|anzɪçt] die <-, -en> **2.** *(outer)* äußere ['ɔʏsərə] no comp, only before ns ◊ *die äußeren Häute der Zwiebel entfernen*

external [adj] **1.** *(on or from the outside, involving or concerning foreign countries)* Außen... ['aʊsn̩] external door Außentür ['aʊsn̩tyːɐ̯] die <-, -en> external trade Außenhandel ['aʊsn̩handl̩] der <-s> no pl; *(appearance, circumstances, security)* äußere ['ɔʏsərə] no comp/superl, only before ns ◊ *Sie achtet sehr auf ihre äußere Erscheinung.* ♦ *die äußere Sicherheit des Staates; (affairs)* auswärtig ['aʊsvɛ'tɪç] no comp/superl, only before ns ◊ *der Minister für auswärtige Angelegenheiten* external account Auslandskonto ['aʊslands,kɔntoː] das <-s, -s> external loan Auslandsanleihe ['aʊslants|anlaeə] die <-, -n> **2.** *(from a third party, help)* fremd [frɛmt] no comp/superl ◊ *Wir sind auf fremde Hilfe angewiesen.;*

A B C D E F G H I J K L M N O P Q R S T U V W X Y Z

A
B
C
D
E
F
G
H
I
J
K
L
M
N
O
P
Q
R
S
T
U
V
W
X
Y
Z

(pressure) von außen [fən 'aʊsn̩] ◊ *Es gab großen Druck von außen, ihn zu entlassen.* external funds Fremdmittel ['frɛmtmɪtl̩] die <-> *only pl* **3.** for external use zur äußerlichen Anwendung [tsuːɐ̯ 'ɔøsəlɪçn̩ ˌanvɛndʊŋ] **4.** *(student, examiner)* extern [ɛks'tɛrn] *no comp/superl* ◊ *eine externe Schülerin*

externally adv **1.** *(on the outside)* äußerlich ['ɔøsəlɪç] *no comp/superl* ◊ *etw. äußerlich anwenden* ♦ *Sie blieb äußerlich ruhig, obwohl sie innerlich vor Wut kochte.* **2.** *(by or to another institution, organization etc.)* extern [ɛks'tɛrn] *no comp/superl* ◊ *einen Auftrag extern vergeben* ♦ *etw. extern überwachen lassen* externally financed/funded fremdfinanziert ['frɛmtfinantsiːɐ̯t]

extinct adj **1.** *(species, custom)* ausgestorben ['aʊsgəʃtɔrbm̩] *no comp/superl* ◊ *Diese Tierart galt lange als ausgestorben.* ♦ *ein ausgestorbener Brauch* become extinct aussterben ['aʊsʃtɛrbm̩] <stirbt aus, starb aus, ist ausgestorben> ◊ *Sterben die Tiger bald aus?* **2.** *(volcano)* erloschen [ɛ'lɔʃn̩] *no comp/superl* ◊ *Ist der Kilimandscharo erloschen?* become extinct erlöschen [ɛ'lœʃn̩] <erlischt, erlosch, ist erloschen>

extinction noun **1.** *(of a species, custom)* Aussterben ['aʊsʃtɛrbm̩] das <-s> *no pl* ◊ *das Aussterben alter Traditionen* in danger of extinction vom Aussterben bedroht **2.** *(destruction)* Vernichtung [fɛ'nɪçtʊŋ] die <-, -en> *most sing* ◊ *die drohende Vernichtung zahlreicher Arbeitsplätze*

extinguish verb **1.** *(a fire, light)* löschen ['lœʃn̩] +haben ◊ *einen Brand löschen* ♦ *Er löschte das Licht und ging zu Bett.* **2.** *(lit) (an idea, hope)* zerstören [tsɛ'ʃtøːrən] <zerstört, zerstörte, hat zerstört> ◊ *Diese Nachricht zerstörte alle seine Hoffnungen.*

extortionate adj überhöht [ybe'høːt] *no comp/superl* ◊ *Der Preis war überhöht.* ♦ *überhöhte Mieten*

extra¹ noun **1.** *(special feature)* Extra ['ɛkstra] das <-s, -s> ◊ *ein Wagen mit zahlreichen Extras* **2.** FILM, THEAT Statist [ʃta'tɪst] der <-en, -en> ♀Statistin [ʃta'tɪstɪn] die <-, -nen> ◊ *als Statist in einem Film mitwirken* **3.** *(issue of a newspaper)* Sonderausgabe ['zɔndɐˌaʊsgaːbə] die <-, -n>

extra² adj zusätzlich ['tsuːzɛtslɪç] *no comp/superl, only before ns* ◊ *Wir brauchen noch einen zusätzlichen Teller.* ♦ *zusätzliche Arbeit* extra charge Zuschlag ['tsuːʃlaːk] der <-(e)s, Zuschläge> extra pay Zulage ['tsuːlaːgə] die <-, -n>

extra³ adv **1.** *(more)* extra ['ɛkstra] *(fam)* ◊ *Dieser Service kostet extra.* be extra extra berechnet werden ◊ *Getränke werden extra berechnet.* pay extra extra zuzahlen ['tsuːˌtsaːlən] +haben ◊ *Muss ich für diesen Zug zuzahlen?* ♦ *Pro Fahrt müssen fünf Euro zugezahlt werden.* work extra länger arbeiten ['lɛŋɐ ˌarbaɛtn̩] <arbeitet, arbeitete, hat gearbeitet> ◊ *Ich muss nächste Woche schon wieder länger arbeiten.* **2.** *(especially)* besonders [bə'zɔndɐs] ◊ *eine besonders große Portion*

extract¹ noun **1.** *(from a text, speech etc.)* Auszug ['aʊsuːk] der <-(e)s, Auszüge> ◊ *Auszüge aus einer Rede* **2.** *(from plants, meat)* Extrakt [ɛks'trakt] der <-(e)s, -e> ◊ *ein Extrakt aus wilden Kräutern* beef extract Fleischextrakt ['flaɛʃɛksˌtrakt]

extract² verb **1.** *(form) (take out)* entnehmen [ɛnt'neːman] <entnimmt, entnahm, hat entnommen> ◊ extract sth from sth einer Sache dat etw. entnehmen ◊ *Diese Zahlen habe ich Ihrem Bericht*

entnommen.; *(juice, natural resources)* gewinnen [gə'vɪnən] <gewinnt, gewann, hat gewonnen> ◊ *Erdöl gewinnen* extract sth from sth etw. aus etw. gewinnen ◊ *Aus den Früchten dieser Pflanze kann man Saft gewinnen.* **2.** *(a tooth)* ziehen ['tsiːən] <zieht, zog, hat gezogen> ◊ *Der Zahnarzt will mir zwei Zähne ziehen.* **3.** *(fig) (obtain even though the other person is initially unwilling)* extract sth from sb jdm etw. abringen ['apriŋən] <ringt ab, rang ab, hat abgerungen> ◊ *Sie rang ihm das Versprechen ab, vorsichtig zu sein.*; *(by tricking sb)* entlocken [ɛnt'lɔkn̩] <entlockt, entlockte, hat entlockt> ◊ *jdm intime Bekenntnisse entlocken* **4.** *(derive sth from a body of information/data/text)* extract sth from sth etw. aus etw. herausziehen [aʊs ... hɛˌraʊsʦiːən] <zieht heraus, zog heraus, hat herausgezogen> ◊ *eine Namensliste aus einer Adresssammlung herausziehen*; *(rules, maxims, generalizations)* ableiten ['aplaɛtn̩] <leitet ab, leitete ab, hat abgeleitet> ◊ *aus den Daten Regeln ableiten*

extraction noun **1.** *(of juice, mineral resources)* Gewinnung [gə'vɪnʊŋ] die <-> *no pl* ◊ *die Gewinnung von Bodenschätzen*; *(of petroleum)* Förderung ['fœrdərʊŋ] die <-> *no pl*; *(of coal)* Abbau ['apbaʊ] der <-(e)s> *no pl* **2.** *(of a tooth)* Ziehen ['tsiːən] das <-s> *no pl* ◊ *Das Ziehen von Zähnen erfolgt mit örtlicher Betäubung.* **3.** *(origin)* Herkunft ['heːɐ̯kʊnft] die <-, Herkünfte> *most sing* ◊ *Ich bin jüdischer/türkischer Herkunft.*

extraordinarily adv außerordentlich ['aʊsəlˈʔɔrdn̩tlɪç] *no comp/superl* ◊ *ein außerordentlich heißer Sommer* ♦ *Sie haben außerordentlich gute Arbeit geleistet.* How extraordinarily odd! Wie überaus seltsam!

extraordinary adj **1.** *(not usual)* außergewöhnlich ['aʊsəgəvøːnlɪç] ◊ *eine außergewöhnliche Leistung* ♦ *Ist das denn außergewöhnlich?*; *(peculiar)* seltsam ['zɛltzaːm] ◊ *ein seltsamer Mensch* ♦ *Ist das nicht seltsam?* **2.** *(with a special purpose)* außerordentlich ['aʊsəlˈʔɔrdn̩tlɪç] *no comp/superl, only before ns* ◊ *eine außerordentliche Sitzung einberufen* ♦ *außerordentliche Maßnahmen ergreifen*

extreme¹ noun Extrem [ɛks'treːm] das <-s, -e> go from one extreme to the other von einem Extrem ins andere fallen in the extreme im höchsten Grade [ɪm ˌhøːçstn̩ 'graːdə] ◊ *Diese Äußerung ist im höchsten Grade verwirrend.* go to extremes es übertreiben [ɛs ybe'traɛbm̩] <übertreibt, übertrieb, hat übertrieben> ◊ *Er übertreibt es mit der Sauberkeit.* extremes of temperature extreme Temperaturen [ɛks,treːmə tɛmpəra'tuːrən] <-> *pl*

extreme² adj **1.** *(maximum, furthest away)* äußerste ['ɔøsəstə] *no comp/superl, only before ns* ♦ *mit äußerster Zurückhaltung reagieren* ♦ *im äußersten Notfall* ♦ *am äußersten Rand des Bildes* **2.** *(exaggerated)* übertrieben [ybe'triːbm̩] ◊ *Ich finde das ein wenig übertrieben.* ♦ *Übertriebenes Lob wirkt nicht ehrlich.* **3.** *(radical)* extrem [ɛks'treːm] ◊ *Ihre Ansichten zur Kindererziehung sind etwas extrem.* ♦ *extreme Parteien* extreme case Extremfall [ɛks'treːmfal] der <-(e)s, Extremfälle> ◊ *Im Extremfall kann die Krankheit tödlich verlaufen.* extreme example krasses Beispiel [ˌkrasəs 'baɛʃpiːl] <-s, -e>

extremely adv äußerst ['ɔøsest] *no comp/superl* ◊ *eine äußerst schwierige Frage*

exuberant(ly) adj, adv *(enthusiastic)* überschwäng-

lich ['y:beʃvɛŋlɪç] ◊ *Er ist immer so überschwänglich!*
♦ *überschwängliche Freude* ♦ *jdn überschwänglich*
feiern; (imagination) übersprudelnd ['y:beʃpruːdn̩t] ◊
Sie hat eine übersprudelnde Fantasie.; (style)
lebendig [le'bɛndɪç]

eye [noun] **1.** (of a human being, an animal, a storm)
Auge ['aʊɡə] das <–s, –n> ◊ *Sie hat blaue/gute*
Augen. ♦ *Mein Opa ist auf einem Auge blind.* ♦ *die*
Augen öffnen/schließen ♦ *Bakterien sind für das*
menschliche Auge unsichtbar. ♦ *Im Auge des Sturms*
herrscht Windstille. to the naked eye mit dem
bloßen Auge **2.** (discrimination, ability to see sth)
Blick [blɪk] der <–(e)s, –e> ◊ *Er hat einen Blick für*
wertvolle Stücke/für das Wesentliche. ♦ *ein geschulter*
Blick **3.** (of a needle) Öhr [øːɐ̯] das <–(e)s, –e>
4. (for a hook) Öse ['øːzə] die <–, –n> ◊ *Haken und*
Öse
ⓔ catch sb's eye jds Aufmerksamkeit erregen
close your eyes to sth die Augen vor etw. verschließen only have eyes for sb/sth nur Augen für
jdn/etw. haben keep your eye on sb/sth jdn/etw.
im Auge behalten in sb's eyes in jds Augen in
front of sb's eyes vor jds Augen through sb's
eyes aus jds Sicht ◊ *Die Geschichte ist aus der Sicht*
eines Hundes erzählt.

eyebrow [noun] Augenbraue ['aʊɡn̩braʊə] die <–, –n>
◊ *Sie zupft sich die Augenbrauen.* raise your
eyebrows die Augenbrauen hochziehen

eyelash [noun] Wimper ['vɪmpɐ] die <–, –n> *most pl*
◊ *lange Wimpern* bat your eyelashes mit den
Wimpern klimpern

eyelid [noun] Augenlid ['aʊɡn̩liːt] das <–(e)s, –er> ◊
das obere/untere Augenlid ♦ *die Augenlider senken*

eye test [noun] Sehtest ['zeːtɛst] der <–(e)s, –s> ◊
für den Führerschein einen Sehtest machen

eyewitness [noun] Augenzeuge ['aʊɡn̩tsɔʏɡə] der
<–n, –n> ♀Augenzeugin ['aʊɡn̩tsɔʏɡɪn] die
<–, –nen> ◊ *Er wurde Augenzeuge eines Unfalls.* ♦
Eine Augenzeugin konnte den Täter genau beschrei-
ben.

A
B
C
D
E
F
G
H
I
J
K
L
M
N
O
P
Q
R
S
T
U
V
W
X
Y
Z

F

f, F [noun] **1.** *(letter)* f, F [ɛf] das <–(s), –(s)> ◊ *ein kleines f/großes F* ♦ *F wie Friedrich* **2.** MUS F f, F [ɛf] das <–(s), –(s)> ◊ *auf der Flöte ein F spielen* F minor f-Moll ['ɛfmɔl] F major F-Dur ['ɛfduːɐ̯] **F** [noun] *(grade)* Sechs [zɛks] die <–, –en> ◊ *Er hat eine Sechs in Mathe.* box@ **Note**

fabric [noun] **1.** *(textile)* Stoff [ʃtɔf] der <–(e)s, –e> ◊ *Sie haben Puppen aus Holz und Stoff gebastelt.* ♦ *Sie hat fünf Meter Stoff für ihr Kleid gekauft.* **2.** *(structure)* Struktur [ʃtrʊk'tuːɐ̯] die <–, –en> ◊ *eine komplizierte Struktur* ♦ *die Struktur der Gesellschaft* **3.** the fabric of a building ein Gebäude als solches [aɛn gə‚bɔø̯də als 'zɔlçəs] das <–s, –> ◊ *Das Gebäude als solches ist noch recht stabil.*

fabulous [adj] **1.** *(great)* sagenhaft ['zaːgn̩haft] <sagenhafter, am sagenhaftesten> *seldom comp/superl (fam)* ◊ *Der Urlaub war sagenhaft.* ♦ *es zu sagenhaftem Reichtum bringen* **2.** fabulous creature Fabelwesen ['faːblveːzn̩] das <–s, –> ◊ *Riesen, Vampire und andere Fabelwesen*

facade [noun] Fassade [fa'saːdə] die <–, –n> ◊ *Die Fassaden der Häuser werden neu gestrichen.* ♦ *Ihre Selbstsicherheit ist nur Fassade.*

face¹ [noun] **1.** *(front of your head, expression, appearance)* Gesicht [gə'zɪçt] das <–(e)s, –er> ◊ *Sie hatte ein hübsches Gesicht.* ♦ *Er machte ein ernstes Gesicht.* ♦ *Auf der Party waren viele unbekannte Gesichter.* ♦ *Das neue Viertel hat das Gesicht der Stadt stark verändert.* to sb's face jdm ins Gesicht ◊ *Ich werde ihm ins Gesicht sagen, was ich von ihm halte.* **2.** *(of a mountain, cliff)* Steilwand ['ʃtaɛ̯lvant] die <–, Steilwände> north face Nordwand ['nɔʁtvant] **3.** *(of a dice, coin, object)* Seite ['zaɛ̯tə] die <–, –n> ◊ *Ein Würfel hat sechs Seiten.* **4.** *(of a clock)* Zifferblatt ['tsɪfɐblat] das <–(e)s, Zifferblätter> ☻ until you are blue in the face bis zum Gehtnichtmehr *(fam)* fall flat on your face auf die Nase fallen sth is written all over sb's face etw. steht jdm ins Gesicht geschrieben lose face das Gesicht verlieren stuff your face reinhauen *(fam)* ◊ *Heute haue ich noch mal richtig rein.* in the face of sth angesichts einer Sache [gen] ◊ *Was muss angesichts dieser Lage getan werden?*

face² [verb] **1.** *(with your face towards, sitting)* face sb/sth jdm/etw.gegenübersitzen [ge:gn̩ˈʔyːbɐzɪtsn̩] <sitzt gegenüber, saß gegenüber, hat gegenübergesessen> ◊ *Sie saß ihm am Tisch gegenüber.*; *(standing)* jdm/etw. gegenüberstehen [ge:gn̩ˈʔyːbɐʃteːən] <steht gegenüber, stand gegenüber, hat gegenübergestanden> ◊ *Die beiden Ringkämpfer stehen sich gegenüber.* **2.** *(with its front towards)* face sb/sth jdm/etw. gegenüber sein [ge:gn̩ˈʔyːbɐ zaɛ̯n] +sein ◊ *Das Gebäude ist gegenüber der Kirche.*; *(room, window etc.)* liegen zu ['liːgn̩ tsuː] <liegt, lag, hat gelegen> ◊ *Das Schlafzimmer liegt zum Innenhof.* face south etc. nach Süden etc. liegen **3.** *(fig) (a person, danger)* ins Auge sehen [ɪn diː ˈʔaɔ̯ɡn̩ zeːən] <sieht, sah, hat gesehen> ◊ *Nach dieser Blamage*

kann ich ihm nie wieder in die Augen sehen!; *(a responsibility, fact)* face sth sich einer Sache [dat] stellen ['ʃtɛlən] ◊ *sich der Verantwortung stellen müssen* Let's face it: it's not easy. Machen wir uns nichts vor: Leicht ist es nicht. He couldn't face killing the fish. Er brachte es nicht über sich, den Fisch zu töten. be faced with sth sich einer Sache [dat] gegenübersehen [ge:gn̩ˈʔyːbɐzeːən] <sieht sich gegenüber, sah sich gegenüber, hat sich gegenübergesehen> ◊ *Die Stadt sieht sich einer finanziellen Krise gegenüber.* sth faces sb jd sieht sich einer Sache [dat] gegenüber ◊ *Wir sehen uns großen Problemen gegenüber.*

● **face up to** [phras v] face up to sth sich einer Sache [dat] stellen ['ʃtɛlən] ◊ *sich der Verantwortung/ einer Gefahr stellen* She won't face up to the fact that she's ill. Sie will nicht wahrhaben, dass sie krank ist.

facecloth [noun] Waschlappen ['vaʃlapm̩] der <–s, –>

facilitate [verb] *(make easier)* erleichtern [ɛˈlaɛ̯çtɐn] <erleichtert, erleichterte, hat erleichtert> ◊ *Ihre Hilfe würde die ganze Sache erheblich erleichtern.*; *(make possible)* ermöglichen [ɛˈmøːklɪçn̩] <ermöglicht, ermöglichte, hat ermöglicht> ◊ *Dieses Verfahren ermöglicht eine schnelle Datenübertragung.*

facility [noun] **1.** *(rooms and equipment, institutions)* Einrichtung ['aɛ̯nrɪçtʊŋ] die <–, –en> ◊ *Kindergärten und andere Einrichtungen zur Kinderbetreuung* ♦ *Einrichtungen zum Brandschutz* Are there any swimming facilities in town? Gibt es in dieser Stadt ein Schwimmbad?; *(technical, sanitary, for sports)* Anlage ['anlaːgə] die <–, –n> ◊ *sanitäre Anlagen* ♦ *Die Wartung der Anlage ist sehr teuer.* **2.** *(offered, available)* Möglichkeit ['møːklɪçkaɛ̯t] die <–, –en> ◊ *Hast du die Möglichkeit, das Bild zu scannen?* shopping facilities Einkaufsmöglichkeiten ['aɛ̯nkaɔ̯fs‚møːklɪçkaɛ̯tn̩] cooking facilities eine Kochgelegenheit [aɛ̯nə 'kɔxgə‚leːgn̩haɛ̯t] <–> sing ◊ *Das Zimmer bietet keine Kochgelegenheit.* credit facility Kreditfazilität [kre'diːtfatsili‚tɛːt] der <–s, –> leisure facilities Freizeitangebot ['fraɛ̯tsaɛ̯t‚aŋgəboːt] das <–(e)s> sing **3.** *(feature)* Funktion [fʊŋk'tsi̯oːn] die <–, –en> ◊ *Das Gerät hat einige praktische Funktionen.* Has your computer the facility to play DVDs? Kann dein Computer DVDs abspielen? **4.** *(in the US: building for a particular activity)* Anlage ['anlaːgə] die <–, –n> ◊ *In dieser Anlage wird Wasser gereinigt.* industrial facilities Industrieanlagen [ɪndʊs'triː|anlaːgn̩] **5.** *(skill, natural talent)* Begabung [bə'gaːbʊŋ] die <–, –en> ◊ *Er hat eine erstaunliche musikalische Begabung.*

fact [noun] Tatsache ['taːtzaxə] die <–, –n> ◊ *Entspricht es den Tatsachen, dass …?* ♦ *Der Film beruht auf Tatsachen.* hard facts nackte Tatsachen stick to the facts sich an die Tatsachen halten ☻ the facts of life wo die kleinen Kinder herkommen it is a fact of life es ist die raue Wirklichkeit know sth for a fact etw. sicher wissen

after the fact nachträglich **in fact 1.** *(in truth)* in Wirklichkeit ◊ *In Wirklichkeit war alles ganz anders.* **2.** *(really)* tatsächlich ◊ *„Das tust du bestimmt nicht." — „Doch, das würde ich tatsächlich tun."* **3.** *(actually)* eigentlich ◊ *Eigentlich kenne ich ihn nicht sehr gut.* **4.** *(after all)* dann doch ◊ *Ich wollte kommen, hatte dann aber doch keine Zeit.*

faction [noun] **1.** *(group)* Gruppe ['grʊpə] die <–, –n> ◊ *Die Gruppe der Wehrdienstverweigerer wird immer kleiner.* **2.** *(of a party etc.)* Splittergruppe ['ʃplɪtɐgrʊpə] die <–, –n> **3.** *(quarrel)* Unstimmigkeiten ['ʊnʃtɪmɪçkaetn̩] die <–> pl ◊ *In der Partei herrschen Unstimmigkeiten über das neue Programm.* **4.** FILM, LIT *(mix of facts and fiction)* Mischung aus Realität und Fiktion

factor [noun] Faktor ['fakto:ɐ] der <–s, –en> ◊ *Das Wachstum wird von unterschiedlichen Faktoren beeinflusst.* ♦ *einen Bruch mit dem Faktor drei multiplizieren* **risk factor** Risikofaktor ['ri:ziko,fakto:ɐ] **protection factor** Schutzfaktor ['ʃʊts,fakto:ɐ] ◊ *eine Sonnencreme mit hohem Schutzfaktor*

factory [noun] Fabrik [fa'bri:k] die <–, –en> ◊ *In dieser Fabrik arbeiten 1500 Menschen.* **factory worker** Fabrikarbeiter [fa'bri:k|a'baetɐ] der <–s, –> ♀Fabrikarbeiterin [fa'bri:k|a'ɐ,baetərɪn] die <–, –nen>

factual(ly) [adj, adv] sachlich ['zaxlɪç] ◊ *ein sachlicher Bericht* ♦ *eine sachlich falsche Darstellung*

faculty [noun] **1.** *(of a university)* Fakultät [fakʊl'tɛ:t] die <–, –en> ◊ *die medizinische Fakultät* **2.** *(in the US: teaching staff)* Lehrkörper ['le:ɐkœ'pe] der <–s, –> *most sing* ◊ *eine Versammlung von Studenten und Lehrkörper* **3.** **faculty of speech** Sprechvermögen ['ʃpreçfɛmø:gn̩] das <–s> *no pl* **faculty of sight** Sehvermögen ['ze:fɛmø:gn̩] ◊ *Durch eine Operation bekam sie ihr Sehvermögen zurück.* **faculty of reason** Vernunft [fɛ'nʊnft] die <–> *no pl* **in full possession of your faculties** im Vollbesitz seiner geistigen Kräfte [ɪm ,fɔlbəzɪts zaenə ,gaestɪgn̩ 'krɛftə]

fade [verb] **1.** *(colo(u)rs, memory, fame, beauty)* fade (away) verblassen [fɛ'blasn̩] <verblasst, verblasste, ist verblasst> ◊ *Die Fotos sind bereits ziemlich verblasst.* ♦ *Die Erinnerung an seine Großmutter verblasst allmählich.* **sth fades sth** etw. bleicht etw. aus [blaeçt ... ,aos] +haben ◊ *Die Sonne hat die Farben ausgebleicht.* **2.** *(light, sick person)* fade (away) schwächer werden ['ʃvɛçɐ ve:gdn̩] +sein ◊ *Der Kranke wird zusehends schwächer.; (feeling, strength)* nachlassen ['na:xlasn̩] <lässt nach, ließ nach, hat nachgelassen> ◊ *Die Verzweiflung/Der Schmerz ließ allmählich nach.* ♦ *Er fühlte seine Kräfte nachlassen.; (hope, trust etc.)* schwinden ['ʃvɪndn̩] <schwindet, schwand, ist geschwunden> ◊ *Ihr Vertrauen in die Zukunft schwand.; (sound)* verhallen [fɛ'halən] <verhallt, verhallte, ist verhallt> ◊ *Die Schritte verhallten im Nebel.* **3.** *(team, in a competition)* nachlassen ['na:xlasn̩] <lässt nach, ließ nach, hat nachgelassen> ◊ *Im zweiten Drittel ließ die Mannschaft nach.* **4.** *(disappear)* fade (away) verschwinden [fɛ'ʃvɪndn̩] <verschwindet, verschwand, ist verschwunden> ◊ *Das Lächeln verschwand aus ihrem Gesicht.*

fail [verb] **1.** *(be unsuccessful)* scheitern ['ʃaetn̩] +sein ◊ *Ein Versuch, das Tier zu retten, scheiterte.* ♦ *Ich bin mit meiner Diät wieder mal gescheitert.* **2.** **fail to do sth** etw. nicht tun [nɪçt] He failed to turn up

on time. Er ist nicht pünktlich gekommen. **never fail to do sth** etw. immer wieder tun [ɪmɐ 'vi:dɐ] She never fails to surprise me. Sie erstaunt mich immer wieder. **3.** **fail in your duty** seine Pflicht versäumen [zaenə 'pflɪçt fe,zɔymən] <versäumt, versäumte, hat versäumt> ◊ *Er hat seine Pflicht den Vorgesetzten gegenüber versäumt.* **fail sb** jdn im Stich lassen [ɪm 'ʃtɪç lasn̩] <lässt, ließ, hat gelassen> ◊ *Er hat seine Kameraden im Stich gelassen.* ♦ *Manchmal lässt ihn sein Gedächtnis im Stich.* **4.** *(a test, an exam)* **fail sth** bei etw. durchfallen [baʊ ... 'dʊɐçfalən] <fällt durch, fiel durch, ist durchgefallen> ◊ *bei der Abschlussprüfung durchfallen* ♦ *Das Produkt wird beim Sicherheitstest wahrscheinlich durchfallen.; (examiner)* **fail sb** jdn durchfallen lassen ['dʊɐçfalən lasn̩] <lässt, ließ, hat lassen> **5.** *(engine, brakes, heart)* versagen [fe'za:gn̩] <versagt, versagte, hat versagt> ◊ *Sein Herz hat ganz plötzlich versagt.; (machine, power, crops)* ausfallen ['aosfalən] <fällt aus, fiel aus, ist ausgefallen> ◊ *Der Strom ist ausgefallen.; (health)* sich verschlechtern [fe'ʃlɛçtɐn] <verschlechtert sich, verschlechterte sich, hat sich verschlechtert> ◊ *Ihr Gesundheitszustand hat sich verschlechtert.; (rain)* ausbleiben ['aosblaebm̩] <bleibt aus, blieb aus, ist ausgeblieben> ◊ *Leider blieb der dringend nötige Regen aus.* ⊙ **if all else fails** wenn alle Stricke reißen

failing [noun] Schwäche ['ʃvɛçə] die <–, –n>

failure [noun] **1.** *(lack of success, sth unsuccessful)* Misserfolg ['mɪs|ɛfɔlk] der <–(e)s, –e> ◊ *Sein erster Roman war ein Misserfolg.; (unsuccessful person)* Versager [fe'za:gɐ] der <–s, –> ♀Versagerin [fe'za:gərɪn] die <–, –nen> **2.** *(of a machine, equipment etc.)* Ausfall ['aosfal] der <–(e)s, Ausfälle> ◊ *der Ausfall eines Triebwerks* **power failure** Stromausfall ['ʃtro:m|aosfal] **heart failure** Herzversagen ['hɛɐtsfeza:gn̩] das <–s> *no pl; (of health, hearing etc.)* Verschlechterung [fe'ʃlɛçtərʊŋ] die <–, –en> ◊ *die Verschlechterung seines Gesundheitszustandes* **3.** *(omission)* Versäumnis [fe'zɔymnɪs] das <–ses, –se> ◊ *Es ist mein Versäumnis, dass er nicht informiert wurde.* He has been criticized because of his failure to compromise. Er wurde kritisiert, weil er keine Kompromisse eingeht.

faint [verb] ohnmächtig werden ['o:nmɛçtɪç ve:gdn̩] +sein

faint(ly) [adj, adv] schwach [ʃvax] <schwächer, am schwächsten> ◊ *eine schwache Hoffnung* ♦ *Der Duft war schwach, aber wahrnehmbar.* ♦ *Der Wind wehte nur schwach.* **sth grows faint** etw. wird schwächer; *(idea, notion, sound)* leise ['laezə] <leiser, am leisesten> ◊ *Ich habe nicht die leiseste Ahnung, wozu das gut ist.* ♦ *Der Ventilator surrte leise.* ⊙ **sb feels faint** jdm ist schwindelig

faintness [noun] Schwäche ['ʃvɛçə] die <–, –n> ◊ *Er konnte sich vor Schwäche kaum noch auf den Beinen halten.* Such was the faintness of her voice that it was barely audible. Ihre Stimme war so schwach, dass sie kaum zu hören war.

fair[1] [noun] **1.** ECON *(trade)* fair Messe ['mɛsə] die <–, –n> **book fair** Buchmesse ['bu:xmɛsə] **2.** (fun)fair Jahrmarkt ['ja:ɐ'ma'kt] der <–(e)s, Jahrmärkte> ◊ *auf den Jahrmarkt gehen* **3.** *(for a charity)* Wohltätigkeitsveranstaltung ['vo:ltɛ:tɪçkaetsfɛɐ,anʃtaltʊŋ] das <–, –en>

fair[2] [adj] **1.** *(just)* gerecht [gə'rɛçt] <gerechter, am

A
B
C
D
E
F·
G
H
I
J
K
L
M
N
O
P
Q
R
S
T
U
V
W
X
Y
Z

gerechtesten> ◊ *eine gerechte Lösung* ♦ *Mein Chef ist streng, aber gerecht.* **2.** *(trial, price, competition etc.)* fair [fɛːɐ̯] ◊ *Es wäre fair gewesen, mich vorher zu warnen.* ♦ *ein fairer Sportler* **3.** *(considerable)* ziemlich ['tsiːmlɪç] *no comp/superl, only before ns (fam)* ◊ *Das wird noch ein ziemliches Stück Arbeit.* have a fair idea of sth sich [dat] etw. ziemlich gut vorstellen können; *(average, moderate)* ganz ordentlich [gants 'ɔrdn̩tlɪç] *no comp/superl* ◊ *Das war eine ganz ordentliche Leistung.* **4.** *(hair, skin)* hell [hɛl] **5.** *(weather)* schön [ʃøːn]
◉ fair enough na schön *(fam)*

fair³ [adv] play fair fair spielen ['fɛːɐ̯ ˌʃpiːlən] +*haben*
◉ fair and square offen und ehrlich

fair-haired [adj] blond [blɔnt] <blonder, am blondesten> *seldom comp/superl* ◊ *Mein Mann ist blond.* ♦ *ein blondes Mädchen*

fairly [adv] **1.** *(rather)* ziemlich ['tsiːmlɪç] *no comp/superl* ◊ *Er besucht uns ziemlich oft.* **2.** *(justly)* gerecht [gə'rɛçt] <gerechter, am gerechtesten> ◊ *Er hat seine Kinder immer gerecht behandelt.* **3.** *(oldf) (positively)* richtiggehend ['rɪçtɪçɡəˌənt] *no comp/ superl* ◊ *Er hat sie richtiggehend angebrüllt.*

fairness [noun] Gerechtigkeit [gə'rɛçtɪçkaɛ̯t] die <-> *no pl* ◊ *für soziale Gerechtigkeit kämpfen* in all fairness fairerweise ['fɛːɐ̯ə'vaɛ̯zə]

fairy [noun] **1.** *(with magic powers)* Fee [feː] die <-, -n> **2.** *(homosexual)* Schwuchtel ['ʃvʊxtl̩] die <-, -n> *(fam, pej)*

fairy tale [noun] Märchen ['mɛːɐ̯çən] das <-s, -> *(also fig)*

faith [noun] **1.** *(trust)* Vertrauen [fɛ'traʊ̯ən] das <-s> *no pl* ◊ *Blindes Vertrauen kann gefährlich sein.* ♦ *das Vertrauen in jdn/etw. verlieren* have faith in sb jdm vertrauen [fɛ'traʊ̯ən] <vertraut, vertraute, hat vertraut> **2.** *(belief)* Glaube ['glaʊ̯bə] der <-ns> *no pl* ◊ *der Glaube an Gott* ♦ *der christliche/jüdische/muslimische Glaube*
◉ break faith with sb jdm untreu werden keep faith with sb jdm treu bleiben

faithful(ly) [adj, adv] **1.** *(person, dog)* treu [trɔɪ̯] <treuer, am treu(e)sten> ◊ *Sie blieb ihren Prinzipien stets treu.* ♦ *Er kann einfach nicht treu sein.* ♦ *Der Hund hat ihn sein Leben lang treu begleitet.; (of a party, musician, sports team)* the faithful die treuen Anhänger [diː trɔɪ̯ən 'anhɛŋɐ] <-> *pl; (of a religion)* the faithful die Gläubigen [diː 'glɔɪ̯bɪɡn̩] <-> *pl* **2.** *(accurate)* genau [gə'naʊ̯] <genauer, am genauesten> ◊ *eine genaue Übersetzung* ♦ *Die Darstellung war sehr genau.* ♦ *einen Text genau übersetzen*
◉ yours faithfully mit freundlichen Grüßen

faithfulness [noun] **1.** *(loyalty)* Treue ['trɔɪ̯ə] die <-> *no pl* ◊ *Er hat Zweifel an ihrer Treue.* **2.** *(of a translation etc.)* Genauigkeit [gə'naʊ̯ɪçkaɛ̯t] die <-> *no pl* ◊ *sich um Genauigkeit bemühen*

fake¹ [adj] *(as if genuine)* falsch [falʃ] *no comp/superl* ◊ *falsche Wimpern* ♦ *Der Ausweis war falsch.; (not genuine)* unecht ['ʊnʔɛçt] *no comp/superl* ◊ *ein unechter Pelz* ♦ *Ihr Lächeln wirkte unecht.*

fake² [verb] **1.** *(pretend)* vortäuschen ['foːɐ̯tɔɪ̯ʃn̩] +*haben* ◊ *Er täuschte einen Unfall vor.* **2.** *(a signature, money)* fälschen ['fɛlʃn̩] +*haben* ◊ *Sie hat die Unterschrift gefälscht.* **3.** *(an illness)* simulieren [zimu'liːrən] <simuliert, simulierte, hat simuliert> ◊ *Kopfschmerzen simulieren*

fall¹ [noun] **1.** *(downwards movement)* Sturz [ʃtʊrts] der

<-(e)s, Stürze> ◊ *ein Sturz vom Pferd* ♦ *ein überraschender Sturz der Börsenkurse* break sb's fall jds Sturz abfangen have a fall stürzen ['ʃtʏrtsn̩] +*sein* ◊ *Sie ist mit dem Rad schwer gestürzt.* fall of snow Schneefall ['ʃneːfal] der <-(e)s, Schneefälle> *most pl* ◊ *heftige Schneefälle* fall of rock Steinschlag ['ʃtaɛ̯nʃlaːk] der <-(e)s, Steinschläge> **2.** *(of numbers, prices, in temperature)* Rückgang ['rʏkɡaŋ] der <-(e)s> *no pl* a fall in/of sth ein Rückgang ...
[gen] ◊ *einen leichten Rückgang der Arbeitslosenzahlen verzeichnen* **3.** *(collapse, defeat)* Fall [fal] der <-(e)s, Fälle> *most sing* ◊ *der Fall der Berliner Mauer* ♦ *Belagerung und Fall der Festung La Rochelle; (of an empire, culture etc.)* Untergang ['ʊntɐɡaŋ] der <-(e)s, Untergänge> *most sing* ◊ *Aufstieg und Untergang des Römischen Reiches; (of a government)* Sturz [ʃtʊrts] der <-(e)s, Stürze> ◊ *der Sturz des Königs* **4.** *(waterfall)* falls Wasserfall ['vasɐfal] der <-(e)s, Wasserfälle> the Niagara Falls die Niagarafälle [diː nia'gaːrafɛlə] die <-> *pl* **5.** *(in the US: autumn)* Herbst [hɛrpst] der <-(e)s, -e> *most sing*
◉ at the fall of the night bei Einbruch der Nacht the Fall *(biblical)* der Sündenfall

fall² [verb] **1.** *(move downwards, decrease, occur, be killed or conquered, strike)* fallen ['falən] <fällt, fiel, ist gefallen> ◊ *Gib Acht, dass du nicht fällst!* ♦ *ins Wasser fallen* ♦ *vom Fahrrad fallen* ♦ *Dort ist seit Monaten kein Regen gefallen.* ♦ *Ich bin über den Eimer gefallen.* ♦ *Das fällt in eine andere Kategorie.* ♦ *Weihnachten fällt dieses Jahr auf einen Sonntag.* ♦ *Ihr Großvater ist im Krieg gefallen.* ♦ *Ein Schatten/ Ihr Blick fiel auf sein Gesicht.* fall to the ground zu Boden fallen; *(person)* fall down hinfallen ['hɪnfalən] <fällt hin, fiel hin, ist hingefallen> ◊ *Er stolperte und fiel hin.; (tree)* fall down umfallen ['ʊmfalən] <fällt um, fiel um, ist umgefallen>; *(vase etc.)* fall down herunterfallen [hɛ'rʊntɐfalən] <fällt herunter, fiel herunter, ist heruntergefallen>; *(building, structure)* fall down einstürzen ['aɛ̯nʃtʏrtsn̩] +*sein* ◊ *Die alte Brücke stürzte ein.* fall to your death in den Tod stürzen [ɪn deːn 'toːt ʃtʏrtsn̩] +*sein; (prices, interest, temperatures)* fall (away) sinken ['zɪŋkn̩] <sinkt, sank, ist gesunken> ◊ *Die Temperaturen sanken auf den Nullpunkt.* **2.** *(come off)* fall away/off abfallen ['apfalən] <fällt ab, fiel ab, ist abgefallen> ◊ *Die Fesseln fielen von ihm ab.; (in bits and pieces)* abbröckeln ['apbrœkl̩n] <bröckelt ab, bröckelte ab, ist abgebröckelt> ◊ *Hier ist ein Stück der Mauer abgebröckelt.* **3.** *(slope)* fall (away) abfallen ['apfalən] <fällt ab, fiel ab, ist abgefallen> ◊ *Das Gelände fällt zum Fluss hin sanft/steil ab.* **4.** *(darkness, dusk, night)* hereinbrechen [hɛ'raɛ̯nbrɛçn̩] <bricht herein, brach herein, ist hereingebrochen> ◊ *Die Nacht bracher herein* Silence falls. Schweigen tritt ein. **5.** *(government, ruler)* fall (from power) gestürzt werden [gə'ʃtʏrtst veːɐ̯dn̩] <wird, wurde, ist worden> ◊ *Der Diktator wurde von der Armee gestürzt.* **6.** *(in various idioms)* fall asleep einschlafen ['aɛ̯nʃlaːfn̩] <schläft ein, schlief ein, ist eingeschlafen> fall ill krank werden ['kraŋk veːɐ̯dn̩] +*sein* fall in love [with sb] sich [in jdn] verlieben [fɛ'liːbm̩] <verliebt sich, verliebte sich, hat sich verliebt> fall into decay/ruins etc. verfallen [fɛ'falən] <verfällt, verfiel, ist verfallen>
◉ fall to doing sth anfangen, etw. zu tun fall over yourself to do sth sich fast vor Eifer überschlagen,

etw. zu tun

• **fall apart** [phras v] **1.** *(break up)* auseinander fallen [ɑʊsˌæˈnandɐ falən] <fällt auseinander, fiel auseinander, ist auseinander gefallen> ◊ *Mein Rad ist so alt, dass es bald auseinander fällt.* **2.** *(go very wrong)* aus den Fugen geraten [ɑʊs deːn ˈfuːgn̩ gəˈraːtn̩] <gerät, geriet, ist geraten> ◊ *Ihr ganzes Leben schien aus den Fugen zu geraten.*

• **fall away** [phras v] **1.** *(lit) (hope, trust etc.)* schwinden [ˈʃvɪndn̩] <schwindet, schwand, ist geschwunden> ◊ *Ihr Vertrauen in die Zukunft schwand.; (sound)* verhallen [fɛˈhalən] <verhallt, verhallte, ist verhallt> ◊ *Die Schritte verhallten im Nebel.* **2.** *(person)* fall away from sb sich von jdm abwenden [fɔn ... ˈapvɛndn̩] <wendet sich ab, wendete/wandte sich ab, hat sich abgewendet/abgewandt> ◊ *Sie wandte sich von mir ab und schwieg.* ✦ *Seine Freunde wandten sich von ihm ab, als das bekannt wurde.* → fall² 1., fall² 2., fall² 3.

• **fall back** [phras v] *(move backwards)* zurückweichen [ʦuˈrʏkvaɛçn̩] <weicht zurück, wich zurück, ist zurückgewichen> ◊ *Entsetzt wichen sie zurück.*

• **fall back on** [phras v] fall back on sth zurückgreifen auf etw. [acc] [ʦuˈrʏkgraɛfn̩ aʊf] <greift zurück, griff zurück, hat zurückgegriffen> ◊ *auf seine Ersparnisse zurückgreifen*

• **fall behind** [phras v] **1.** *(in school, a race etc.)* zurückbleiben [ʦuˈrʏkblaɛbm̩] <bleibt zurück, blieb zurück, ist zurückgeblieben> ◊ *Er blieb allmählich hinter den anderen zurück.* ✦ *Ihr Sohn droht im Rechnen zurückzubleiben.* **2.** fall behind with sth mit etw. in Verzug geraten [mɪt ... ɪn fɛˈʦuːk gəˈraːtn̩] <gerät, geriet, ist geraten> ◊ *Sie sind mit der Miete in Verzug geraten.*

• **fall down** [phras v] *(theory, argument)* versagen [fɛˈzaːgn̩] <versagt, versagte, hat versagt>

• **fall for** [phras v] **1.** *(fall in love)* fall for sb sich in jdn verlieben [ɪn ... fɛˌliːbm̩] <verliebt sich, verliebte sich, hat sich verliebt> **2.** *(be deceived)* fall for sb/sth auf jdn/etw. hereinfallen [aʊf ... hɛˈraɛnfalən] <fällt herein, fiel herein, ist hereingefallen> ◊ *Wie konntest du nur auf so einen Betrüger/billigen Trick hereinfallen?*

• **fall in** [phras v] MIL antreten [ˈantreːtn̩] <tritt an, trat an, ist angetreten> ◊ *Die Soldaten erhielten den Befehl anzutreten.*

• **fall into** [phras v] fall into doing sth mit etw. anfangen [ˈʦuːfɛlɪç mɪt ... ˌanfaŋən] <fängt an, fing an, hat angefangen> +nominalized verb ◊ *Eigentlich habe ich eher zufällig mit dem Reiten angefangen.*

• **fall in with** [phras v] fall in with sb/sth sich jdm/etw. anschließen [ˈanʃliːsn̩] <schließt sich an, schloss sich an, hat sich angeschlossen> ◊ *Er schloss sich einer Gruppe junger Musiker an, die durch das Land reisten.*

• **fall off** [phras v] *(decrease)* sinken [ˈzɪŋkn̩] <sinkt, sank, ist gesunken> ◊ *Die Nachfrage nach diesem Produkt ist stark gesunken.* → fall² 2.

• **fall on** [phras v] **1.** *(on food)* fall on sth über etw. [acc] herfallen [yːbɐ ... ˌheːɐfalən] <fällt her, fiel her, ist hergefallen> ◊ *Die Kinder fielen wie hungrige Wölfe über den Kuchen her.* **2.** *(hug)* fall on sb jdm um den Hals fallen [ʊm deːn ˈhals falən] <fällt, fiel, ist gefallen> ◊ *Jubelnd fiel sie ihrem Vater um den Hals.* **3.** *(duty, responsibility)* fall on sb jdm zufallen [ˈʦuːfalən] <fällt zu, fiel zu, ist zugefallen> ◊ *Die Ver-*

antwortung für die Kinder fällt meist den Frauen zu.

• **fall out** [phras v] **1.** *(quarrel)* fall out (with sb) sich (mit jdm) streiten [ˈʃtraɛtn̩] <streitet sich, stritt sich, hat sich gestritten> ◊ *Habt ihr zwei euch gestritten?* ✦ *Sie hat sich mit ihrer Schwester gestritten.* **2.** *(hair, teeth, feathers)* jdm/einem Tier ausfallen [ˈaʊsfalən] <fällt aus, fiel aus, ist ausgefallen> ◊ *Mir fallen die Haare aus.*

• **fall over** [phras v] **1.** *(object)* umfallen [ˈʊmfalən] <fällt um, fiel um, ist umgefallen> ◊ *Pass auf, dass die Vase nicht umfällt.* ✦ *Sie ist mit ihrem Stuhl umgefallen.* **2.** *(person)* hinfallen [ˈhɪnfalən] <fällt hin, fiel hin, ist hingefallen> ◊ *Sie stolperte und fiel hin.*

• **fall through** [phras v] fehlschlagen [ˈfeːlʃlaːgn̩] <schlägt fehl, schlug fehl, ist fehlgeschlagen> ◊ *Der Plan schlug fehl.*

• **fall to** [phras v] fall to sb jdm zufallen [ˈʦuːfalən] <fällt zu, fiel zu, ist zugefallen> ◊ *Diese schwere Pflicht fiel ihm zu.* it falls to sb to do sth jdm fällt die Aufgabe zu, etw. zu tun

falling → fall² [adj] rückläufig [ˈrʏklɔɔfɪç] no comp/ superl ◊ *Die Einwohnerzahl ist rückläufig.* ✦ *eine rückläufige Tendenz*

fallow [adj] brach [braːx] no comp/superl, only before ns ◊ *ein bracher Acker* be/lie fallow brachliegen [ˈbraːxliːgn̩] <liegt brach, lag brach, hat brachgelegen> ◊ *Das Feld liegt im Winter brach.*

false [adj] falsch [falʃ] <falscher, am falschesten> seldom comp/superl ◊ *eine falsche Behauptung* ✦ *ein falscher Pass* ✦ *Sein Lächeln wirkte falsch.*

fame [noun] Ruhm [ruːm] der <-(e)s> no pl ◊ *großen Ruhm erlangen*

familiar [adj] **1.** *(known, usual)* vertraut [fɛˈtraʊt] <vertrauter, am vertrautesten> ◊ *ein vertrautes Gesicht in der Menge* ✦ *Bist du mit der Vorgeschichte vertraut?; (phrase, saying)* geläufig [gəˈlɔɔfɪç] ◊ *Dieses Sprichwort ist mir nicht geläufig.* **2.** *(frequent)* häufig [ˈhɔɔfɪç] ◊ *Das ist leider ein häufiges Problem.* **3.** *(not distant, friendly)* ungezwungen [ˈʊngəʦvʊŋən] ◊ *ein ungezwungener Umgangston* ✦ *Die Atmosphäre war ungezwungen.; (overly)* aufdringlich [ˈaʊfdrɪŋlɪç] ◊ *Die neue Kollegin ist mir zu aufdringlich.*

⊚ be on familiar terms with sb mit jdm freundschaftlich verkehren

familiarize [verb] familiarize sb/yourself with sth jdn/ sich mit etw. vertraut machen [mɪt ... fɛˌtraʊt maxn̩] +haben ◊ *Ich muss mich mit dem neuen Computerprogramm erst vertraut machen.*

familiarly [adv] vertraulich [fɛˈtraʊlɪç] ◊ *vertraulich miteinander umgehen* ✦ *Er legte ihr vertraulich die Hand um den Arm.*

⊚ familiarly known as besser bekannt als ◊ *der Karlsplatz in München, besser bekannt als „Stachus"*

family¹ [noun] Familie [faˈmiːljə] die <-, -n> ◊ *An Weihnachten trifft sich die ganze Familie bei Oma.* ✦ *Haben Sie Familie?* ✦ *Das Zebra gehört zur Familie der Pferde.* start a family eine Familie gründen He's like one of the family. Er gehört praktisch zur Familie. a family of four eine vierköpfige Familie

family² [adj] family ... Familien... [faˈmiːljən] family life Familienleben [faˈmiːljənleːbm̩] das <-s> no pl family film Familienfilm [faˈmiːljənfɪlm] der <-(e)s, -e>

family name [noun] Familienname [faˈmiːljənnaːmə] der <-ns, -n> ◊ *Wie ist Ihr Familienname?*

family planning [noun] Familienplanung [fa'mɪːlɪənplaːnʊŋ] die <-> no pl

famous [adj] berühmt [bə'ryːmt] <berühmter, am berühmtesten> ◊ *Sting ist ein berühmter Musiker.* **famous for** berühmt für ◊ *Nürnberg ist berühmt für seine Lebkuchen.*

fan¹ [noun] **1.** (*supporter*) Fan [fɛn] der <-s, -s> ◊ *Der Sänger hat treue Fans.* ♦ *Sie ist ein Fan des VfB.* **2.** (*mechanical device for cooling*) Ventilator [vɛntɪˈlaːtoːɐ̯] der <-s, -en>; (*to hold in your hands*) Fächer ['fɛçɐ] der <-s, ->

fan² [verb] **1.** (*a person*) fan sb/yourself jdm/sich Luft zufächeln ['lʊft ˌtsuːfɛçl̩n] <fächelt zu, fächelte zu, hat zugefächelt> ◊ *einem Ohnmächtigen Luft zufächeln* **2.** (*a fire, feeling*) anfachen ['anfaxn̩] +haben ◊ *Der Wind fachte das Feuer weiter an.* ♦ *Ihre Bemerkung fachte seinen Zorn noch zusätzlich an.*

fancy¹ [adj] **1.** (*fashionable*) schick [ʃɪk] ◊ *ein schickes Restaurant* ♦ *Ich finde dein Kleid schick.* **2.** (*elaborate*) kunstvoll ['kʊnstfɔl] ◊ *eine kunstvolle Frisur* nothing fancy etwas ganz Einfaches [ɛtvas gants 'aɛnfaxəs] ◊ *etwas ganz Einfaches kochen* fancy goods Geschenkartikel [gə'ʃɛŋkˌaɐ̯ˌtɪkl̩] die <-> pl **3.** (*complicated*) kompliziert [kɔmpliˈtsiːɐ̯t] <komplizierter, am kompliziertesten> ◊ *Das Computerprogramm ist ziemlich kompliziert.* **4.** (*unusual*) ausgefallen ['aʊsɡəfalən] ◊ *Er hat immer wieder mal so ausgefallene Ideen.* **5.** (*price*) stolz [ʃtɔlts] <stolzer, am stolzesten> ◊ *In diesem Geschäft haben sie wirklich stolze Preise!* **6.** (*in the US*) fancy food Delikatessen [delikaˈtɛsn̩] die <-> pl

fancy² [verb] **1.** (*like, be attracted to*) mögen ['møːɡn̩] <mag, mochte, hat gemocht> ◊ *Ich glaube, Christian mag dich.* **2.** (*feel like*) fancy sth auf etw. [acc] Lust haben [aʊf ... ˌlʊst haːbm̩] +haben ◊ *Ich hätte jetzt Lust auf ein Eis.* fancy doing sth Lust (darauf) haben, etw. zu tun ◊ *Hast du Lust (darauf), mit mir schwimmen zu gehen?* **3.** (*in the UK*) fancy sb for sth glauben, dass jd etw. gewinnen wird ['ɡlaʊbm̩ das ... ɡə'vɪnən vɪɐ̯t] +haben ◊ *Glaubst du, dass die Mannschaft den Pokal gewinnen wird?* fancy your chances (for sth) glauben, dass man (bei etw.) Chancen hat **4.** (*lit*) (*believe*) glauben ['ɡlaʊbm̩] +haben ◊ *Sie glaubte, sie hätte die Stimme ihrer Tochter gehört.* **5.** fancy yourself as sth sich für etw. halten [fyː ... haltn̩] <hält sich, hielt sich, hat sich gehalten> ◊ *Sie hält sich für eine begabte Sängerin.* fancy yourself sich für Wunder was halten ◊ *Schau dir den an — der hält sich wohl für Wunder was!* ⊚ fancy sb doing that nicht zu fassen, dass jd das tut fancy that nein so was ◊ *Nein so was! Du hier?*

fantasize [verb] (*think unreal things*) fantasieren [fantaˈziːrən] <fantasiert, fantasierte, hat fantasiert> ◊ *Ist das wahr oder fantasierst du wieder mal?* fantasize about fantasieren von ◊ *Sie fantasierte schon als Kind von einem Leben in Reichtum.*; (*imagine sex*) sexuelle Fantasien haben [zɛksuˌɛlə fantaˈziːən haːbm̩] +haben

fantastic [adj] fantastisch [fanˈtastɪʃ] ◊ *fantastisches Wetter* ♦ *Diese Idee erscheint mir doch zu fantastisch.*

fantastically [adv] **1.** (*incredibly*) unglaublich [ʊnˈɡlaʊplɪç] no comp/superl ◊ *ein unglaublich komischer Film* **2.** (*very well*) fantastisch [fanˈtastɪʃ] ◊ *Der Hauptdarsteller hat fantastisch gespielt.*

3. (*unusually, eccentrically*) skurril [skʊˈriːl] ◊ *Die Frau war skurril gekleidet.*

fantasy [noun] **1.** (*imagined thing*) Fantasie [fantaˈziː] die <-, -n> ◊ *sexuelle Fantasien haben* ♦ *Nichts davon stimmt, das ist alles reine Fantasie.* **2.** LIT Fantasy ['fɛntəzi:] die <-> no pl ◊ *Ich lese gern Fantasy und Science Fiction.*

far¹ [adj] **1.** (*further away from the speaker*) andere ['andərə] no comp/superl, only before ns ◊ *Auf der anderen Seite des Flusses ist ein Hotel.* the far window das Fenster am anderen Ende des Zimmers "Which is your car?" — "The far one." „Welches ist dein Auto?" — „Das weiter hinten." **2.** (*remote*) fern [fɛ'n] ◊ *Waren aus fernen Ländern*

far² [adv] **1.** (*in distance, progress, degree, time*) weit [vaɛt] <weiter, am weitesten> ◊ *Geht nicht zu weit weg!* ♦ *Ich möchte so weit vorn wie möglich sitzen.* ♦ *Wie weit ist er denn schon mit seinem Buch?* ♦ *Es ist nicht mehr weit; wir sind gleich da.* ♦ sich so weit wie möglich an die Vorlage halten far away (from) weit entfernt (von) go too far zu weit gehen ◊ *Jetzt ist er aber wirklich zu weit gegangen!* go as far as to do sth so weit gehen, etw. zu tun ◊ *Er ging sogar so weit, sie aus dem Haus zu werfen.* as far as bis zu [bɪs tsuː] ◊ *Sie musste bis zum nächsten Dorf laufen, ehe sie einen Arzt fand.* since as far back as 1500 schon seit 1500 [ʃoːn tsaɛt ˌfʏnftseːn'hʊndɐt] **2.** (*for emphasis*) bigger/better etc. weitaus größer/besser etc. [ˌvaɛtˌaʊs 'ɡrøːsɐ/'bɛsɐ] ◊ *Sie ist weitaus schneller als er.* far too viel zu [fiːl tsuː] ◊ *Er ist viel zu alt für solche Dummheiten.* by far bei weitem [baɛ 'vaɛtm̩] ◊ *Das sind bei weitem meine bequemsten Schuhe.* ⊚ so far, so good so weit, so gut from far and wide von nah und fern as far as I know/remember etc. soweit ich weiß/mich erinnere etc. far from all das andere als ◊ *Diese Leistung ist alles andere als gut.* so far bis jetzt ◊ *Bis jetzt hat man erst drei der zehn Vermissten gefunden.*

fare [noun] **1.** (*charge*) Fahrpreis ['faː'praɛs] der <-es, -e> ◊ *den Fahrpreis bezahlen*; (*money*) Fahrgeld ['faː'ɡɛlt] das <-(e)s, -er> ◊ *Seine Mutter gab ihm das Fahrgeld für den Bus mit.* **2.** (*passenger in a taxi*) Fahrgast ['faː'ɡast] der <-(e)s, Fahrgäste> **3.** (*form*) (*food*) Kost [kɔst] die <-> no pl ◊ *landestypische Kost*

farewell [noun] Lebewohl [leːbəˈvoːl] das <-s, -e or -s> (*lofty*) bid sb farewell jdm Lebewohl sagen make/say your farewells sich verabschieden [fɛ'ˈap̮ʃiːdn̩] <verabschiedet sich, verabschiedete sich, hat sich verabschiedet>

farm [noun] **1.** (*smaller agricultural holding*) Bauernhof ['baʊɐnhoːf] der <-(e)s, Bauernhöfe> ◊ *Sie leben auf einem Bauernhof.*; (*larger agricultural business*) Farm ['faː'm] die <-, -en> ◊ *eine Farm bewirtschaften* chicken farm Hühnerfarm ['hyːnɐfaː'm] fish farm Fischzucht ['fɪʃtsʊxt] die <-, -en> **2.** (*house*) Bauernhaus ['baʊɐnhaʊs] das <-es, Bauernhäuser> ◊ *ein altes Bauernhaus besichtigen*

farmer [noun] Bauer ['baʊɐ] der <-n, -n> ♀Bäuerin ['bɔɪ̯ərɪn] die <-, -nen> ◊ *Der Bauer arbeitet auf dem Feld.*; (*of a larger agricultural business*) Farmer ['faː'mɐ] der <-s, -> ♀Farmerin ['faː'mərɪn] die <-, -nen> ◊ *Sie ist Farmerin und züchtet Rinder.*

farming [noun] (*growing crops*) Landwirtschaft ['lantvɪ'tʃaft] die <-> no pl ◊ *die Förderung der Land-*

wirtschaft dairy farming Milchwirtschaft
['mɪlçvɪ'tʃaft]; *(breeding animals)* Viehzucht ['fiːtsʊxt]
die <–> *no pl* ◊ *von der Viehzucht leben* sheep
farming Schafzucht ['ʃaːftsʊxt]

far-off adj fern [fɛˈn] ◊ *Sie reist gern in ferne
Länder.*

far-sighted adj weitsichtig ['vaetzɪçtɪç] ◊ *ein weitsichtiger Politiker* ✦ *Sie ist weitsichtig und braucht
daher zum Lesen eine Brille.*

fart verb furzen ['fʊˈtsn̩] +haben *(rude)*

farther adv weiter ['vaete] ◊ *Er kam nicht weiter als
bis hierher.* ✦ *weiter nördlich*

fascinate verb faszinieren [fastsi'niːrən] <fasziniert,
faszinierte, hat fasziniert> ◊ *Dieser Mann fasziniert
mich.* be fascinated by sth von etw. fasziniert sein
◊ *Das Publikum war fasziniert von seiner
Geschichte.*

fascinating adj faszinierend [fastsi'niːrənt] ◊ *Ich
fand die Erzählung faszinierend.* ✦ *ein faszinierender Künstler*

fashion noun fashion(s) Mode ['moːdə] die <–, –n>
◊ *sich nach der neuesten Mode kleiden* ✦ *jede Mode
mitmachen* go out of fashion aus der Mode
kommen men's fashions Herrenmode
['hɛrənmoːdə]
⊚ after a fashion mehr schlecht als recht after
the fashion of im Stil ... gen in a ... fashion auf
... Weise ◊ *Konflikte auf friedliche Weise lösen*

fashionable adj 1. *(up-to-date)* modern [moˈdɛˈn] ◊
ein modernes Kleid ✦ *Es ist wieder modern, Hüte zu
tragen.* 2. *(expensive, elegant)* vornehm ['foːɡneːm] ◊
ein vornehmer Badeort ✦ *Diese Wohngegend ist sehr
vornehm.*

fashionably adv modern [moˈdɛˈn] ◊ *sich modern
kleiden*

fast¹ adj 1. *(quick)* schnell [ʃnɛl] ◊ *Er kam mit
schnellen Schritten auf mich zu.* ✦ *Ihre Bewegungen
waren schnell und präzise.* ✦ *Sein neuer Computer
ist sehr schnell.; (speed)* hoch [hoːx] <höher, am
höchsten> <der/die/das hohe ...> ◊ *mit hoher
Geschwindigkeit fahren* 2. *(clock, watch)* be fast
vorgehen ['foːɡeːən] <geht vor, ging vor, ist vorgegan-
gen> ◊ *Meine Uhr geht zehn Minuten vor.* 3. FOTO
hoch empfindlich [hoːx ɛm'pfɪntlɪç] *no comp/superl*
◊ *einen hoch empfindlichen Film benutzen*
4. *(colo(u)r)* waschecht ['vaʃlɛçt] *no comp/superl* ◊
waschechte Farbe ✦ *Der Ausdruck ist waschecht.*
5. *(firm, secure)* fest [fɛst] <fester, am festesten> ◊ *Ist
das Seil fest?* make sth fast etw. festmachen
['fɛstmaxn̩] +haben ◊ *Wir erreichten das Ufer und
machten das Boot fest.*

fast² adv 1. *(quickly)* schnell [ʃnɛl] ◊ *Er fuhr viel zu
schnell.* ✦ *Sie rannte, so schnell sie konnte.*
2. *(firmly, securely, soundly)* fest [fɛst] <fester, am
festesten> be fast asleep fest schlafen hold fast to
sth sich an etw. dat festhalten [an ... ˌfɛsthaltn̩]
<hält sich fest, hielt sich fest, hat sich festgehalten> ◊
Halt dich gut am Seil fest! stand fast by sb/sth zu
jdm/etw. stehen [tsuː ... 'ʃteːən] <steht, stand, hat
gestanden> ◊ *Er steht zu seiner Entscheidung/zu
seinem Sohn.*

fasten verb 1. *(your clothes, shoes, buttons etc.)*
fasten sth etw. zumachen ['tsuːmaxn̩] +haben *(fam)* ◊
Sie machte ihre Skischuhe zu. sth fastens etw. wird
zugemacht ◊ *Der Rock wird hinten zugemacht.*
2. *(fix)* fasten sth (to sth) etw. (an etw. dat) festma-

chen ['fɛstmaxn̩] +haben ◊ *ein Boot festmachen* ✦
Sie machten das Seil an einem Baum fest. fasten
your/sb's seatbelt sich/jdn anschnallen ['anʃnalən]
+haben ◊ *Bitte schnallen Sie sich an!* 3. *(lock)* fasten
sth etw. schließen ['ʃliːsn̩] <schließt, schloss, hat
geschlossen> ◊ *Fenster und Türen schließen* sth
fastens etw. schließt ◊ *Das Tor schließt nicht
richtig.*

fastener noun Verschluss [fɛ'ʃlʊs] der
<–es, Verschlüsse>

fat¹ noun Fett [fɛt] das <–(e)s, –e> ◊ *Jede Portion
enthält fünf Gramm Fett.* ✦ *zu viel Fett ansetzen*

fat² adj *(thick, heavy, large)* dick [dɪk] ◊ *Du bist zu
dick.* ✦ *ein dickes Gehalt bekommen* get fat dick
werden; *(extremely plump, containing fat)* fett [fɛt]
<fetter, am fettesten> *(also pej)* ◊ *Der Kater ist
ziemlich fett.* ✦ *fettes Fleisch*
⊚ grow fat on sth durch etw. reich werden

fatal(ly) adj, adv 1. *(deadly)* tödlich ['tøːtlɪç] *no
comp/superl* ◊ *tödliche Verletzungen erleiden* ✦ *Die
Krankheit war tödlich.* ✦ *tödlich verletzt* 2. *(having
negative consequences)* fatal [faˈtaːl] ◊ *ein fataler
Fehler* ✦ *Die Auswirkungen waren fatal.* ✦ *Er hat
seinen Gegner fatal unterschätzt.* prove fatal sich als
fatal erweisen

fatality noun 1. *(victim)* Todesopfer ['toːdəsɔpfe] das
<–s, –> ◊ *Unter den Todesopfern sind auch Kinder.*
2. *(inevitability)* Schicksalhaftigkeit
['ʃɪkzaːlhaftɪçkaet] die <–> *no pl* I had a sense of
fatality. Ich hatte das Gefühl, dass alles vom
Schicksal vorherbestimmt sei. 3. *(mortality)* Sterblichkeit ['ʃteˈplɪçkaet] die <–> *no pl* ◊ *die hohe Sterblichkeit bei Kindern*

fate noun Schicksal ['ʃɪkzaːl] das <–s, –e> ◊ *über jds
Schicksal entscheiden* ✦ *Das Schicksal nahm seinen
Lauf.* ✦ *jds seinem Schicksal überlassen*

father¹ noun 1. *(also fig) (parent, ancestor, God)*
Vater ['faːte] der <–s, Väter> ◊ *ein allein erziehender Vater* ✦ *Er gilt als der Vater des Computers.* ✦ *der
Gott seiner Väter* a father of two/three etc. ein zwei-
facher/dreifacher etc. Vater Heavenly Father himmli-
scher Vater 2. REL *(monk)* Father Pater ['paːte] der
<–s, – or Patres> ◊ *Pater Johannes liest heute die
Messe.; (priest)* Herr Pfarrer [hɛˈ 'pfaːe] der
<Herrn Pfarrers, Herren Pfarrer>
⊚ like father, like son der Apfel fällt nicht weit
vom Stamm

father² verb zeugen ['tsɔɡn̩] +haben ◊ *Mit 65 zeugte
er noch ein Kind.*

Father Christmas noun Weihnachtsmann
['vaenaxtsman] der <–(e)s, Weihnachtsmänner> ◊
Morgen kommt der Weihnachtsmann!

father-in-law noun Schwiegervater ['ʃviːɡefaːte] der
<–s, Schwiegerväter>

fatigue noun 1. *(tiredness)* Erschöpfung [eˈʃœpfʊŋ]
die <–> *no pl* ◊ *Viele Patienten klagen über Erschöpfung.* 2. *(of material)* Ermüdung [ɛˈmyːdʊŋ] die <–>
no pl ◊ *die Ermüdung von Stahlträgern*

faucet noun Wasserhahn ['vasehaːn] der
<–(e)s, Wasserhähne>

fault noun 1. *(responsibility)* Schuld [ʃɔlt] die <–> *no
pl* ◊ *Es ist alles meine Schuld!* ✦ *Es ist deine Schuld,
dass wir das Flugzeug verpasst haben.* the fault lies
with sb die Schuld liegt bei jdm through no fault of
your own ohne eigenes Verschulden
[oːnə ˌaeɡənəs feˈʃʊldn̩] 2. *(lack of functionality, short-*

coming, in tennis) Fehler ['fe:lɐ] der <-s, -> ◊ *Kann man den Fehler beheben?* ✦ *Ihr größter Fehler ist ihr Hang zum Perfektionismus.* ✦ *ein Fehler beim Aufschlag; (lack of quality)* Mangel ['maŋl] der <-s, Mängel> ◊ *Die Reform wies in mehreren Punkten Mängel auf.* **3.** GEOL Verwerfung [fe'vɛɐfʊŋ] die <-, -en>

🅑 **be at fault** schuld sein **find fault with sb/sth** an jdm/etw. etwas auszusetzen haben ◊ *Sie hat ständig etwas an meiner Arbeit auszusetzen.*

favor → favour
favorable → favourable
favorite → favourite

favour¹, favor [noun] **1.** *(act of kindness)* Gefallen [gə'falən] der <-s, -> ◊ *Kannst du mir einen Gefallen tun?* ✦ *sich* [dat] *keinen Gefallen mit etw. tun* ask a favour of sb jdn um einen Gefallen bitten **2.** **find favour with sb** bei jdm Anklang finden [bae ... 'anklaŋ fɪndn̩] <findet, fand, hat gefunden> ◊ *Meine Idee fand keinen Anklang bei ihm.* **3.** **show favour to sb** jdn bevorzugen [bə'fo:ɐtsu:gŋ̍] <bevorzugt, bevorzugte, hat bevorzugt>

🅑 **fall out of favour (with sb)** *(person etc.)* (bei jdm) in Ungnade fallen *(practice)* (bei jdm) aus der Mode kommen **in favour of sb, in sb's favour** zu jds Gunsten ◊ *Es wurde zu ihren Gunsten entschieden.* **in favour of sth** für etw. ◊ *für etw. sein/ stimmen* **out of favour (with sb)** (bei jdm) unbeliebt ◊ *Der Präsident ist bei seinem Volk unbeliebt.*

favour², favor [verb] **1.** *(be in favour of)* befürworten [bə'fy:ɐvɔɐtn̩] <befürwortet, befürwortete, hat befürwortet> ◊ *Er befürwortet diese Idee.; (prefer, treat better)* bevorzugen [bə'fo:ɐtsu:gŋ̍] <bevorzugt, bevorzugte, hat bevorzugt> ◊ *Wir bevorzugen diese Lösung.* ✦ *einen Schüler bevorzugen* favour sb/sth over sth jdn/ etw. jdm/einer Sache vorziehen ['fo:ɐtsi:ən] <zieht vor, zog vor, hat vorgezogen> ◊ *Ich ziehe deinen Vorschlag den anderen vor.* **2.** *(give an advantage to)* begünstigen [bə'gʏnstɪgŋ̍] <begünstigt, begünstigte, hat begünstigt> ◊ *Die neue Regelung begünstigt Selbstständige.*

favourable, favorable [adj] **1.** *(approving)* positiv ['po:ziti:f] ◊ *eine positive Entscheidung* ✦ *Die meisten Kommentare waren positiv.* be favourable to sth etw. befürworten [bə'fy:ɐvɔɐtn̩] <befürwortet, befürwortete, hat befürwortet> **2.** *(advantageous, reasonable)* günstig ['gʏnstɪç] ◊ *in einem günstigen Licht erscheinen* ✦ *ein günstiger Preis* ✦ *Die Aussichten waren günstig.* be favourable to sb/sth jdm/etw. begünstigen [bə'gʏnstɪgŋ̍] <begünstigt, begünstigte, hat begünstigt>

favourite¹, favorite [noun] **1.** *(translation depends on what or who it refers to: food)* Lieblingsessen ['li:plɪŋs|ɛsn̩] das <-s, -> ◊ *Lasagne ist sein Lieblingsessen.; (actor)* Lieblingsschauspieler ['li:plɪŋsʃao̯ʃpi:lɐ] der <-s, -> ♀Lieblingsschauspielerin ['li:plɪŋsʃao̯ʃpi:lərɪn] die <-, -nen> ◊ *Cheryl Ladd ist meine Lieblingsschauspielerin.; (darling)* Liebling ['li:plɪŋ] der <-s, -e> ◊ *Felix ist Muttis Liebling.* be a favourite with sb bei jdm beliebt sein [bae ... bə,li:pt zaen] +sein ◊ *Der Star ist vor allem bei den Frauen beliebt.* **2.** SPORT Favorit [favo'ri:t] der <-en, -en> ♀Favoritin [favo'ri:tɪn] die <-, -nen> ◊ *Der Favorit liegt vorn.*

favourite², favorite [adj] Lieblings... ['li:plɪŋs]

favourite song Lieblingslied ['li:plɪŋsli:t] das <-(e)s, -er> **favourite restaurant** Lieblingsrestaurant ['li:plɪŋsrɛsto,raŋ] das <-s, -s>

fax [noun] Fax [faks] das <-, -e> ◊ *Habt ihr ein Fax zu Hause?* ✦ *Gerade ist dieses Fax angekommen.* by fax per Fax

fax machine [noun] Faxgerät ['faksgərɛ:t] das <-(e)s, -e> ◊ *Das Faxgerät ist defekt.*

fear¹ [noun] Angst [aŋst] die <-, Ängste> ◊ *Ich zitterte vor Angst.* ✦ *jds Ängste ernst nehmen* fear of sb/sth Angst vor jdm/etw. fear for sb/sth Angst um jdn/ etw. for fear of doing sth aus Angst, etw. zu tun for fear that aus Angst, dass fear about sth Befürchtung hinsichtlich einer Sache [gen] [bə'fʏɐçtʊŋ hɪnzɪçtlɪç] die <-, -en> ◊ *Es gab Befürchtungen hinsichtlich der Sicherheit des Kernreaktors.* fears that ... Befürchtungen, dass ...

🅑 **there's no fear ...** There's no fear of that. Diese Gefahr besteht nicht. There's no fear that ... Es besteht keine Gefahr, dass ...

fear² [verb] **1.** *(be worried)* fear sth etw. befürchten [bə'fʏɐçtn̩] <befürchtet, befürchtete, hat befürchtet> ◊ *das Schlimmste befürchten* ✦ *Er befürchtet, schwer krank zu sein.* **2.** *(be afraid of)* fear sb/sth vor jdm/ etw. Angst haben [fo:ɐ ... 'aŋst ha:bm̩] +haben ◊ *Alle hatten Angst vor diesem Lehrer.* ✦ *Hast du Angst, allein dorthin zu gehen?*

🅑 **I fear ...** Ich fürchte ... ◊ *Ich fürchte, man hat dich betrogen.* I fear so. Ich fürchte, ja. I fear not. Ich fürchte, nein.

• **fear for** [phras v] fear for sb/sth um jdn/etw. bangen [ʊm ... ,baŋən] +haben ◊ *um jds Leben/die Geiseln bangen*

fearful [adj] *(easily scared)* ängstlich ['ɛŋstlɪç] ◊ *Er war von Natur aus ängstlich.* ✦ *ein ängstliches Kind* be fearful (of sth) (vor etw.) Angst haben ['aŋst ha:bm̩] +haben ◊ *Sie hatten Angst vor weiteren Bombenanschlägen.*

feasible [adj] *(solution, route)* möglich ['mø:klɪç] no comp/superl ◊ *die einzig mögliche Lösung* it is feasible to do sth es is zu tun; *(plan, action, idea)* durchführbar ['dʊɐçfy:ɐba:ɐ] no comp/ superl ◊ *Dieser Plan ist praktisch nicht durchführbar.* ✦ *ein kaum durchführbarer Vorschlag*

feast [noun] **1.** *(banquet)* Festessen ['fɛst|ɛsn̩] das <-s, -> ◊ *an einem Festessen teilnehmen* **2.** REL Fest [fɛst] das <-(e)s, -e> ◊ *das Fest des heiligen Johannes*

🅑 **a feast for the ears** ein Ohrenschmaus **a feast for the eyes** eine Augenweide

feather [noun] Feder ['fe:dɐ] die <-, -n> ◊ *Der Vogel plusterte die Federn auf.*

feature¹ [noun] **1.** *(characteristic)* Merkmal ['mɛɐkma:l] das <-(e)s, -e> ◊ *ein besonderes Merkmal dieses Autos* ✦ *Im Pass werden besondere Merkmale angeführt.; (of sb's face)* Zug [tsu:k] der <-(e)s, Züge> ◊ *Sein Gesicht hatte harte Züge.* **2.** MEDIA Beitrag ['baetra:k] der <-(e)s, Beiträge> ◊ *Hast du seinen Beitrag in der Zeitung gelesen?* ✦ *ein Beitrag im Fernsehen*

feature² [verb] **1.** *(product)* feature sth mit etw. ausgestattet sein [mɪt ... ,aosgəʃtatət zaen] +sein ◊ *Der Wagen ist mit Airbags ausgestattet.* **2.** *(paper, magazine)* bringen ['brɪŋən] <bringt, brachte, hat gebracht> ◊ *Die Zeitung bringt heute ein Foto von Prinz Charles auf der Titelseite.* **3.** *(in an exhibition,*

concert) an exhibition that features expressionist paintings eine Austellung expressionistischer Bilder [aɛnə ‚aosʃtɛlʊŋ ɛkspresɪo‚nɪstɪʃe 'bɪldɐ] a concert featuring African music ein Konzert mit afrikanischer Musik [aɛn kɔn‚tsɛˤt mɪt afri‚kaːnɪʃe mu'ziːk] **4.** *(in a film, play)* sth features sb, sb features in sth jd spielt in etw. ⌈dat⌉ mit [ʃpiːlt ɪn … mɪt] +haben ◊ *In dem Film spielen viele berühmte Schauspieler mit.* sth features sb as sth jd spielt etw. in etw. ⌈dat⌉ ◊ *Sie spielt in dem Film eine begabte Malerin.*

feature film ⌈noun⌉ Spielfilm ['ʃpiːlfɪlm] der <-(e)s, -e>

February ⌈noun⌉ Februar ['feːbruaːˤ] der <-(s), -e> *most sing* → **January**

federal ⌈adj⌉ *(system etc.)* föderalistisch [fødera'lɪstɪʃ] *no comp/superl* ◊ *ein föderalistisches System; (government, state, minister etc.)* Bundes… ['bʊndəs] federal government Bundesregierung ['bʊndəsre‚giːrʊŋ] die <-, -en> federal state Bundesstaat ['bʊndəsʃtaːt] der <-(e)s, -en>

federal republic ⌈noun⌉ Bundesrepublik ['bʊndəsrepu‚bliːk] die <-> *no pl* ◊ *die Bundesrepublik Deutschland/Österreich*

federation ⌈noun⌉ **1.** *(of states)* Föderation [fødera'tsɪoːn] die <-, -en> ◊ *die Russische Föderation* **2.** *(organization)* Verband [fe'bant] der <-(e)s, Verbände> ◊ *der Verband der Arzneimittelhersteller* tennis federation Tennisverband ['tɛnɪsfebant]

fed up ⌈adj⌉ be/get fed up with sb/sth jdn/etw. satt haben ['zat ha:bm̩] +haben ◊ *Ich habe seine dummen Witze wirklich satt!* be fed up (with) doing sth es satt haben, etw. zu tun ◊ *Ich habe es satt, dich ständig zu bedienen!*

fee ⌈noun⌉ **1.** *(paid to an organization)* Gebühr [gə'byːɐ̯] die <-, -en> ◊ *Wie hoch ist die Gebühr für die Ummeldung?* charge a fee eine Gebühr erheben entrance fee Eintrittsgebühr ['aɛntrɪtsgəby:ɐ̯] legal fees Gerichtskosten [gə'rɪçtskɔstn̩] die <-> *only pl* **2.** *(paid to a professional)* Honorar [hono'ra:ˤ] das <-s, -e> ◊ *ein Honorar für etw. bekommen* charge a fee ein Honorar verlangen

feeble ⌈adj⌉ **1.** *(person, light, voice, argument, effort, attempt)* schwach [ʃvax] <schwächer, am schwächsten> ◊ *Sie ist jetzt 94 und sehr schwach.* ◆ schwaches Licht ◆ eine schwache Leistung **2.** *(excuse)* lahm [la:m] *(fam, pej)* ◊ *eine lahme Entschuldigung* ◆ *Seine Ausrede war eher lahm.*

feed¹ ⌈noun⌉ **1.** *(for a baby)* Mahlzeit ['ma:ltsaɛt] die <-, -en> ◊ *Wann hat der Kleine seine letzte Mahlzeit bekommen?* give a baby a feed ein Baby füttern [aɛn 'beːbi: ‚fʏtɐn] +haben ◊ *Würdest du bitte das Baby füttern?* **2.** *(for animals)* Futter ['fʊte] das <-s> *no pl* ◊ *Futter für die Tiere kaufen* **3.** *(fertilizer)* Dünger ['dʏŋe] der <-s, -> ◊ *Dünger auf die Pflanzen geben* **4.** TECHN *(of a machine)* Zuführung ['tsu:fy:rʊŋ] die <-, -en> ◊ *Die Zuführung ist verstopft.*

feed² ⌈verb⌉ **1.** *(a person, an animal)* füttern [‚fʏtɐn] +haben ◊ *einen Kranken füttern* feed sb/an animal on sth, feed sth to sb/an animal jdn/ein Tier mit etw. füttern ◊ *Sie fütterte den kranken Igel mit Hundefutter.; (sustain)* ernähren [ɛ'nɛːrən] <ernährt, ernährte, hat ernährt> ◊ *Von meinem Gehalt kann ich meine Familie nicht mehr ernähren.* ◆ *Das Land kann seine Bevölkerung nicht ernähren.* **2.** *(baby)* sb

feeds jd trinkt [trɪŋkt] <trinkt, trank, hat getrunken> ◊ *Das Baby trinkt auch nachts alle drei Stunden.; (animal)* fressen ['frɛsn̩] <frisst, fraß, hat gefressen> ◊ *Die Tiere kommen erst nachts aus dem Wald, um zu fressen.* **3.** *(a plant)* düngen ['dʏŋən] +haben ◊ *die Rosen mit Pferdemist düngen* **4.** *(provide a supply)* feed sb/sth with sth, feed sth to sb/sth jdn/etw. mit etw. versorgen [mɪt … fe‚zɔˤgŋ̩] <versorgt, versorgte, hat versorgt> ◊ *jdn mit Informationen versorgen* ◆ *die Blutgefäße, die das Gehirn mit Sauerstoff versorgen* feed sth into a computer etw. in einen Computer eingeben [ɪn aɛnən kɔm'pjuːte ‚aɛnge:bm̩] <gibt ein, gab ein, hat eingegeben> ◊ *Daten in den Computer eingeben* **5.** *(push into a machine)* feed sth into sth etw. in etw. ⌈acc⌉ stecken [ɪn … ʃtɛkŋ̩] +haben ◊ *Geld in einen Automaten stecken* **6.** *(hope, imagination)* feed sth einer Sache ⌈dat⌉ Nahrung geben ['na:rʊŋ ge:bm̩] <gibt, gab, hat gegeben> ◊ *durch Lesen der Fantasie Nahrung geben; (sb's anxiety, hate)* schüren ['ʃy:rən] +haben ◊ *die Ängste der Menschen schüren* **7.** *(an addiction)* finanzieren [finan'tsiːrən] <finanzierte, hat finanziert> ◊ *Wie finanziert er seine Heroinsucht?*

• **feed off** ⌈phras v⌉ **1.** *(eat)* feed off sth sich von etw. ernähren [fɔn … ɐ‚nɛːrən] <ernährt sich, ernährte sich, hat sich ernährt> ◊ *Kühe ernähren sich von Gras.* **2.** *(fig) (exist on, survive on)* feed off sth von etw. leben [fɔn … ‚le:bm̩] +haben ◊ *Das Unternehmen lebt vom Misserfolg anderer Firmen.* ◆ *Die Zeitung lebt von Klatschgeschichten.*

• **feed on** ⌈phras v⌉ → **feed off**

feedback ⌈noun⌉ **1.** *(comments, reaction)* Rückmeldung ['rʏkmɛldʊŋ] die <-, -en> ◊ *eine positive/negative Rückmeldung bekommen* ◆ *jdm Rückmeldung zu etw. geben* **2.** TECHN *(loud noise)* Rückkopplung ['rʏkkɔpəlʊŋ] die <-, -en> ◊ *wegen der Rückkoppelung das Mikrofon ausschalten*

feel¹ ⌈noun⌉ **1.** *(sensation, understanding)* Gefühl [gə'fy:l] das <-(e)s, -e> ◊ *das Gefühl von Wind und Sand auf der Haut* ◆ *ein Gefühl für etw. haben/bekommen; (of an object, a touch)* like the feel of sth mögen, wie sich etw. anfühlt ['mø:gŋ̩ vi: zɪç … 'anfy:lt] +haben ◊ *Ich mag, wie sich der Stoff anfühlt.* **2.** *(atmosphere)* Atmosphäre [atmo'sfɛːrə] die <-, -n> ◊ *Das Hotel hat eine freundliche Atmosphäre.*

feel² ⌈verb⌉ **1.** *(be in a particular physical or emotional state)* sich fühlen ['fy:lən] +haben ◊ *sich elend fühlen* ◆ *Wie fühlst du dich?* feel a failure sich wie ein Versager fühlen feel a fool sich ⌈dat⌉ dumm vorkommen ['dʊm fo:ɐ̯kɔmən] <kommt vor, kam vor, ist vorgekommen> ◊ *Er kam sich wegen seines Fehlers ziemlich dumm vor.* **2.** *(experience a feeling)* feel sth etw. empfinden [ɛm'pfɪndn̩] <empfindet, empfand, hat empfunden> ◊ *Was empfinden Sie, wenn Sie diese Bilder sehen?* ◆ *Sie empfand große Angst.* **3.** *(cause an emotion, sensation)* it feels … es ist ein … Gefühl [ɛs ɪst aɛn … gə'fy:l] das <-(e)s, -e> ◊ *Es ist ein seltsames Gefühl, so weit weg von zu Hause zu sein.* It feels like home. Es ist wie zu Hause. **4.** *(examining)* feel sth etw. fühlen ['fy:lən] +haben ◊ *Fühl mal meine Stirn. Ich glaube, ich habe Fieber.; (to the touch)* sth feels … etw. fühlt sich … an [fy:lt zɪç … an] +haben ◊ *sich weich/hart anfühlen* ◆ *Der Pullover fühlt sich wie Kaschmir an.*

5. *(sense, be affected by)* spüren ['ʃpyːrən] +haben ◊ *den Fahrtwind im Gesicht spüren* ♦ *Sie spürte sofort, dass sie ihm vertrauen konnte.* ♦ *Der Bürger spürt die Auswirkungen der Steuerreform deutlich.* feel sb/sth do sth spüren, wie jd/etw. etw. tut ◊ *Er spürte, wie sie ihm übers Haar strich.* **6.** *(think)* denken ['dɛŋkn̩] <denkt, dachte, hat gedacht> ◊ *Ich denke, wir hätten mehr tun können.* ♦ *Wie denkst du darüber?* feel sth (to be) sth etw. für etw. halten [fyːɐ̯ ... haltn̩] <hält, hielt, hat gehalten> ◊ *etw. für die richtige Entscheidung halten* feel it appropriate to do sth es für angebracht halten, etw. zu tun **7.** *(search)* feel (around) for sth nach etw. [dat] tasten [naːx ... tastn̩] <tastet, tastete, hat getastet> ◊ *Sie tastete in ihrer Tasche nach Kleingeld.* **8.** *(want)* feel like sth auf etw. [acc] Lust haben [aʊf ... ˌlʊst haːbm̩] +haben ◊ *Ich habe Lust auf ein Glas Wein.* feel like doing sth Lust haben, etw. zu tun

• **feel for** [phras v] feel for sb mit jdm mitfühlen [mɪt ... 'mɪtfyːlən] +haben ◊ *Ich kann gut mit Ihnen mitfühlen.*

feeling [noun] **1.** *(physical, emotional, impression)* Gefühl [gə'fyːl] das <-(e)s, -e> ◊ *Er hatte kein Gefühl mehr in den Zehen.* ♦ *Sie tut sich schwer, ihre Gefühle zu zeigen.* ♦ *Ich habe ein gutes Gefühl dabei.* hurt sb's feelings jdn verletzen [fɛ'lɛtsn̩] <verletzt, verletzte, hat verletzt> **2.** *(opinion)* Ansicht ['anzɪçt] die <-, -en> ◊ *Was ist denn deine Ansicht dazu?* sb's feeling is that jd ist der Ansicht, dass the feeling is that man ist allgemein der Ansicht, dass ◊ *Man war allgemein der Ansicht, dass diese Straße gebaut werden muss.* public feeling (on sth) die öffentliche Meinung (zu etw.) [diː ˌœfntlɪçə 'maɛnʊŋ] <-> no pl ◊ *die öffentliche Meinung zum Thema Genforschung* feeling against sth Ablehnung ... [gen] ['aplɛːnʊŋ] die <-> no pl ◊ *die starke Ablehnung der Regierungspolitik* ◉ bad/ill feeling böses Blut mixed feelings gemischte Gefühle feelings are running high die Emotionen kochen hoch

feign [verb] vortäuschen ['foːɐ̯tɔɪʃn̩] +haben ◊ *Kopfschmerzen vortäuschen* ♦ *Er täuschte Betroffenheit vor.*

fellow¹ [noun] **1.** *(guy)* Bursche ['bʊrʃə] der <-n, -n> ◊ *ein toller Bursche* **2.** *(member)* Fellow ['fɛloː] der <-s, -s> ◊ *Er ist Fellow der British Academy.*

fellow² [adj] fellow ... Mit... [mɪt] fellow citizen Mitbürger ['mɪtbyːɐ̯gɐ] der <-s, -> ♀Mitbürgerin ['mɪtbyːɐ̯gərɪn] die <-, -nen> fellow pupil Mitschüler ['mɪtʃyːlɐ] der <-s, -> ♀Mitschülerin ['mɪtʃyːlərɪn] die <-, -nen> fellow countryman Landsmann ['lantsman] der <-(e)s, Landsleute> *(at university)* fellow student Kommilitone [kɔmiliˈtoːnə] der <-n, -n> ♀Kommilitonin [kɔmiliˈtoːnɪn] die <-, -nen>

fellowship [noun] **1.** *(friendship)* Kameradschaft [kaməˈraːtʃaft] die <-> no pl ◊ *Die Kameradschaft in der Mannschaft war vorbildlich.* **2.** *(scholarship)* Forschungsstipendium ['fɔrʃʊŋsʃtiˌpɛndiʊm] das <-s, Forschungsstipendien> ◊ *Ich habe ein Forschungsstipendium für klinische Pharmakologie bekommen.*

felt-tip, felt-tipped pen [noun] Filzstift ['fɪltsʃtɪft] der <-(e)s, -e> ◊ *mit Filzstiften malen*

female¹ [noun] *(woman)* Frau [fraʊ] die <-, -en> ◊ *Er*

schaut gern den Frauen nach.*; *(child)* Mädchen ['mɛːtçən] das <-s, ->; *(animal)* Weibchen ['vaɛpçən] das <-s, -> ◊ *Bei den meisten Tieren kümmert sich das Weibchen um die Jungen.*

female² [adj] weiblich ['vaɛplɪç] no comp/superl ◊ *Fünf der jungen Hunde sind weiblich, zwei männlich.* ♦ *Es meldete sich eine weibliche Stimme.*

feminine [adj] weiblich ['vaɛplɪç] no comp/superl ◊ *Welche Eigenschaften gelten als typisch weiblich?* ♦ *weibliche Substantive*

feminist [noun] Feminist [femiˈnɪst] der <-en, -en> ♀Feministin [femiˈnɪstɪn] die <-, -nen> ◊ *Sie ist eine überzeugte Feministin.*

fence¹ [noun] **1.** *(around an area)* Zaun [tsaʊn] der <-(e)s, Zäune> ◊ *einen Zaun um etw. errichten* **2.** sport Hindernis ['hɪndɛrnɪs] das <-ses, -se> ◊ *über ein Hindernis springen*

fence² [verb] sport fechten ['fɛçtn̩] <ficht, focht, hat gefochten> ◊ *Sie geht jeden Freitag fechten.*

• **fence in** [phras v] **1.** *(an area)* einzäunen ['aɛntsɔɪnən] +haben ◊ *Die Wiese wurde eingezäunt.* **2.** *(a person)* fence sb in jdn in seiner Freiheit einschränken [ɪn ... 'fraɛhaɛt ˌaɛnʃrɛŋkn̩] +haben ◊ *Er fühlte sich durch die Regeln in seiner Freiheit eingeschränkt.*

• **fence off** [phras v] abzäunen ['aptsɔɪnən] +haben ◊ *Das Gelände wurde abgezäunt.*

ferocious(ly) [adj, adv] **1.** *(very intense or strong)* heftig ['hɛftɪç] ◊ *eine heftige Debatte* ♦ *Der Sturm wurde immer heftiger.* ♦ *jdn heftig kritisieren* **2.** *(aggressive)* angriffslustig [ˈaŋrɪfslʊstɪç] ◊ *ein angriffslustiges Tier* ♦ *Sind Kobras angriffslustig?* ferociously killed brutal ermordet [bruˌtaːl ɛˈmɔˀdət]

ferocity [noun] **1.** *(intensitiy)* Heftigkeit ['hɛftɪçkaɛt] die <-> no pl ◊ *die Heftigkeit des Sturms* **2.** *(aggression)* Angriffslust ['aŋrɪfslʊst] die <-> no pl ◊ *die Angriffslust eines Löwen*

ferry¹ [noun] Fähre ['fɛːrə] die <-, -n> ◊ *mit der Fähre übersetzen*

ferry² [verb] übersetzen ['yːbɐzɛtsn̩] +haben ◊ *Er setzte mich mit einem Boot ans andere Ufer über.*

fertile [adj] fruchtbar ['frʊxtbaːˀ] ◊ *fruchtbare Tiere* ♦ *Dieses Ackerland ist sehr fruchtbar.* ♦ *Die Idee fiel auf fruchtbaren Boden.*

fertility [noun] Fruchtbarkeit ['frʊxtbaːˀkaɛt] die <-> no pl ◊ *die Fruchtbarkeit des Bodens* ♦ *die Göttin der Fruchtbarkeit*

festival [noun] **1.** *(cultural)* Festival ['fɛstɪvl] das <-s, -s> ◊ *das Festival des deutschen Schlagers* film festival Filmfestival ['fɪlmfɛstɪvl] music festival Musikfestival [muˈziːkfɛstɪvl] **2.** REL Fest [fɛst] das <-(e)s, -e> ◊ *religiöse Feste*

festive(ly) [adj, adv] festlich ['fɛstlɪç] ◊ *festliche Kleidung* ♦ *Die Stimmung war sehr festlich.* ♦ *Die Straßen waren festlich beleuchtet.*

fetch [verb] **1.** *(get, bring)* holen ['hoːlən] +haben ◊ *Hilfe/einen Arzt holen* ♦ *Ich gehe schnell zum Bäcker, ein Brot holen.* fetch sb sth, fetch sth for sb jdm etw. holen ◊ *Würdest du mir bitte ein Glas Wasser holen?*; *(collect, pick up)* abholen ['apho:lən] +haben ◊ *die Kinder von der Schule abholen* ♦ *Er kam mit dem Lieferwagen, um die Waren abzuholen.* **2.** *(be sold for)* einbringen ['aɛnbrɪŋən] <bringt ein, brachte ein, hat eingebracht> ◊ *Das Bild brachte 30.000 Dollar ein.*

fever [noun] Fieber ['fiːbɐ] das <-s> no pl ◊ *hohes/*

leichtes Fieber have a fever Fieber haben ◊ *Der Junge hat Fieber.* in a fever of excitement in fieberhafter Erregung [ɪn ˌfiːbəhafte eˈreːgʊŋ]

few¹ [adj] a few ein paar [aⓔn 'paːˈ] ◊ *Ich war mit ein paar Freunden essen.* the ... few die ... paar [diː ... paːˈ] ◊ *die ersten/letzten paar Seiten* ♦ *die nächsten paar Tage* every few alle paar ◊ *alle paar Stunden/Wochen* quite a few etliche ['ɛtlɪçə] ◊ *Vor etlichen Monaten war ich in Rom.*
⊛ be few (and far between) selten sein ◊ *Es gibt Ausnahmen, aber die sind selten.* as few as nicht mehr als no fewer than nicht weniger als

few² [det] wenige ['veːnɪgə] <weniger, am wenigsten> ◊ *mit wenigen Ausnahmen* ♦ *Er hat mit weniger als 3000 Stimmen die Wahl gewonnen.* ♦ *Sie macht mir die wenigsten Probleme.*

few³ [indef pron] (not many) wenige ['veːnɪgə] ◊ *Nur wenige sind zu seiner Party gekommen.* ♦ *Wenige ihrer Romane sind wirklich gut.* a few einige ['aɪnɪgə] ◊ *Als wir ankamen, waren einige schon gegangen.* quite a few etliche ['ɛtlɪçə] ◊ *Etliche glaubten ihm.*
⊛ the lucky/rich etc. few die wenigen Glücklichen/Reichen etc.

fiancé [noun] Verlobte [feˈloːptə] der <-n, die Verlobten> *but: ein Verlobter* ◊ *Sie ist mit ihrem Verlobten verreist.*

fiancée [noun] Verlobte [feˈloːptə] die <-n, die Verlobten> ◊ *Darf ich Ihnen meine Verlobte vorstellen?*

fibre, fiber [noun] **1.** (dietary) fibre Ballaststoffe ['balastʃtɔfə] die <-> pl ◊ *Haferflocken enthalten viele Ballaststoffe.* **2.** (in the body, textiles) Faser ['faːze] die <-, -n> ◊ *die Fasern eines Muskels* ♦ *eine synthetische Faser*

fickle [adj] launisch ['laɔnɪʃ] ◊ *launisches Wetter* ♦ *Er ist sehr launisch.*

fiction [noun] **1.** (novels, short stories etc.) erzählende Literatur [e.tsɛːləndə lɪtəraˈtuːɐ̯] die <-> no pl romantic fiction Liebesromane ['liːbəsroˌmaːnə] die <-> pl ◊ *Ich lese gern Liebesromane.* crime fiction Kriminalromane [krɪmiˈnaːlroˌmaːnə] die <-> pl **2.** (invention) Erfindung [eˈfɪndʊŋ] die <-, -en> ◊ *Das halte ich für eine reine Erfindung.*

fictional [adj] erfunden [eˈfʊndn̩] no comp/superl ◊ *Alle Personen in dem Roman sind frei erfunden.* ♦ *eine erfundene Begebenheit*

fiddle [verb] **1.** (play with sth) fiddle (about/around) with sth mit etw. herumspielen [mɪt ... hɛˌrɔmʃpiːlən] +haben ◊ *Sie spielte nervös mit einem Stift herum.; (in order to improve sth)* an etw. [dat] herumfummeln [an ... hɛˌrɔmfʊmln̩] +haben (fam) ◊ *Er fummelt den ganzen Tag an seinem Wagen herum.* **2.** (falsify) frisieren [friˈziːrən] <frisiert, frisierte, hat frisiert> (fam) ◊ *die Bücher frisieren*
• **fiddle about, fiddle around** [phras v] → fiddle 1.

fidelity [noun] Treue ['trɔɡə] die <-> no pl ◊ *Er hatte Zweifel an ihrer Treue.* ♦ *die Treue zum Original*

field [noun] **1.** (area of land, box, group in competition, in physics) Feld [fɛlt] das <-(e)s, -er> ◊ *Die Felder wurden abgeerntet.* ♦ *Tragen Sie Ihren Namen in das Feld ein.* ♦ *Noch war ihr an der Spitze, doch das Feld holte auf.* ♦ *elektromagnetische Felder* battle field Schlachtfeld ['ʃlaxtfɛlt] corn field Getreidefeld

[gəˈtraɛdəfɛlt] **2.** (for sport) Platz [plats] der <-es, Plätze> take the field auf den Platz kommen football field Fußballplatz ['fuːsbalplats] **3.** (for grazing) Weide ['vaɛdə] die <-, -n> ◊ *Die Kühe stehen auf der Weide.* **4.** (subject area) Gebiet [gəˈbiːt] das <-(e)s, -e> ◊ *das Gebiet der Gentechnologie* in a field auf einem Gebiet ◊ *Sie ist eine Expertin auf diesem Gebiet.*

fierce(ly) [adj, adv] **1.** (debate, criticism, competition, storm) heftig ['hɛftɪç] ◊ *eine heftige Diskussion* ♦ *Der Sturm wurde heftiger.* ♦ *jdn heftig kritisieren; (dog)* aggressiv [agrɛˈsiːf]; (lion, warrior) wild [vɪlt] <wilder, am wildesten>; (fight, enemy) erbittert [eˈbɪtet] ◊ *erbitterte Feinde* ♦ *Die gestrigen Kämpfe waren besonders erbittert.* ♦ *erbittert kämpfen* **2.** (in appearance) grimmig ['grɪmɪç] ◊ *jdm einen grimmigen Blick zuwerfen* ♦ *Er sah äußerst grimmig aus.* ♦ *jdn grimmig ansehen*

fifteen [nmrl] fünfzehn ['fʏnftseːn] → **four²**

fifth¹ [noun] **1.** (fraction) Fünftel ['fʏnftl̩] das <-s, -> → **fourth¹** 1. **2.** (in a sequence) Fünfte ['fʏnftə] der or die or das <-n, -n> most sing → **fourth¹** 2.

fifth² [adj] fünfte ['fʏnftə] <ein fünfter ..., eine fünfte ..., ein fünftes ...> → **fourth¹**

fifthly [adv] fünftens ['fʏnftn̩s] → **fourthly**

fifty [nmrl] fünfzig ['fʏnftsɪç] → **four²**

fig [noun] Feige ['faɛgə] die <-, -n>

fight¹ [noun] **1.** (brawl) Schlägerei [ʃlɛːgəˈraɛ] die <-, -en> ◊ *in eine Schlägerei geraten* have a fight (with sb) sich (mit jdm) prügeln ['pryːgln̩] +haben **2.** (boxing, struggle, competition) Kampf [kampf] der <-(e)s, Kämpfe> ◊ *einen Kampf gewinnen/verlieren* ♦ *Der Ringrichter brach den Kampf ab.* ♦ *sein Kampf gegen den Krebs* fight for sth Kampf um etw. ◊ *der Kampf um die Macht* **3.** mil (battle) Schlacht [ʃlaxt] die <-, -en> ◊ *eine blutige Schlacht* **4.** (argument) Streit [ʃtraɛt] der <-(e)s, Streite> most sing ◊ *Würdet ihr euren lächerlichen Streit endlich mal beenden!* have a fight (with sb) Streit (mit jdm) haben

fight² [verb] **1.** (in a war, a struggle, boxing match, competition) kämpfen ['kɛmpfn̩] +haben ◊ *Die Soldaten haben tapfer gekämpft.* fight (against) sb gegen jdn kämpfen ◊ *Er hat gegen Evander Holyfield gekämpft.* fight for sth um etw. kämpfen ◊ *um sein Leben kämpfen* ♦ *um Gerechtigkeit kämpfen; (an evil, a disaster etc.)* fight (against) etw. bekämpfen [bəˈkɛmpfn̩] <bekämpft, bekämpfte, hat bekämpft> ◊ *den Terrorismus bekämpfen* fight a fire einen Brand bekämpfen fight a war einen Krieg führen [aⓔnən 'kriːk fyːrən] +haben fight for breath nach Atem ringen [naːx 'aːtəm rɪŋən] <ringt, rang, hat gerungen> **2.** (brawl) sich prügeln ['pryːgln̩] +haben ◊ *sich mit jdm prügeln* fight over sth sich um etw. prügeln ◊ *Die beiden Männer prügelten sich um Geld.* **3.** (argue) sich streiten ['ʃtraɛtn̩] <streitet sich, stritt sich, hat sich gestritten> fight over sth sich um etw. streiten ◊ *Die Kinder streiten sich dauernd um ihre Spielsachen.*
• **fight back** [phras v] **1.** (hit back, defend yourself) sich wehren ['veːrən] +haben ◊ *sich gegen einen Angreifer wehren* ♦ *Er wehrte sich gegen die Kritik.* **2.** (an emotion) hold back gegen etw. ankämpfen [ge:gn̩ ... ˌankɛmpfn̩] +haben ◊ *Sie kämpfte gegen die Tränen an.*
• **fight off** [phras v] abwehren ['apveːrən] +haben ◊

einen Angreifer abwehren ♦ *eine Krankheit abwehren*

fighter ⸤noun⸥ **1.** MIL Jagdflugzeug [ˈjaːktfluːktsɔɡk] das <-(e)s, -e> **2.** SPORT Kämpfer [ˈkɛmpfɐ] der <-s, -> ♀Kämpferin [ˈkɛmpfərɪn] die <-, -nen> ◊ *Die beiden Kämpfer standen sich gegenüber.* **3.** *(sb who never gives up)* Kämpfernatur [ˈkɛmpfɐnaˌtuːɐ̯] die <-, -en> ◊ *Er war schon immer eine Kämpfernatur.*

figurative(ly) ⸤adj, adv⸥ **1.** *(language)* bildlich [ˈbɪltlɪç] *no comp/superl* ◊ *ein bildlicher Ausdruck* ♦ *Sie ist, bildlich gesprochen, die gute Fee in unserer Abteilung.* use sth in a figurative sense etw. im übertragenen Sinn gebrauchen [ɪm ybɐˈtraːgənən ˌzɪn gəbraʊ̯xn̩] <gebraucht, gebrauchte, hat gebraucht> **2.** ARTS figurative art gegenständliche Kunst [ˌgeːgn̩ʃtɛntlɪçə ˈkʊnst] die <-> *no pl*

figure¹ ⸤noun⸥ **1.** *(number)* Zahl [tsaːl] die <-, -en> ◊ *ein gutes Gedächtnis für Zahlen* sales figures Verkaufszahlen [fɛɐ̯ˈkaʊ̯fstsaːlən] die <-> *pl* three-figure/four-figure etc. number dreistellige/vierstellige etc. Zahl [ˌdraɪ̯ʃtɛlɪgə/ˌfiːɐ̯ʃtɛlɪgə ˈtsaːl]; *(sum)* Summe [ˈzʊmə] die <-, -n> ◊ *Welche Summe werden wir für dieses Projekt benötigen?* **2.** *(personality)* Persönlichkeit [pɛɐ̯ˈzøːnlɪçkaɛ̯t] die <-, -en> ◊ *eine herausragende Persönlichkeit* figure of fun Witzfigur [ˈvɪtsfiˌguːɐ̯] die <-, -en> **3.** *(human form)* Gestalt [gəˈʃtalt] die <-, -en> ◊ *Seine gedrungene Gestalt stach ihr sofort ins Auge.* ♦ *Am Bahnhof trieben sich dunkle Gestalten herum.*; *(shape of body, statuette)* Figur [fiˈguːɐ̯] die <-, -en> ◊ *eine gute/sportliche Figur haben* ♦ *eine Weihnachtskrippe mit Figuren aus Holz* watch your figure auf seine Figur achten [aʊ̯f zaɛ̯nə fiˈguːɐ̯ ˌaxtn̩] <achtet, achtete, hat geachtet> **4.** *(in dancing, geometry)* Figur [fiˈguːɐ̯] die <-, -en> ◊ *Kreis und Dreieck sind geometrische Figuren.* ♦ *Das Tanzpaar zeigte einige beeindruckende Figuren.* **5.** *(illustration)* Abbildung [ˈapbɪldʊŋ] die <-, -en>

figure² ⸤verb⸥ **1.** *(appear)* vorkommen [ˈfoːɐ̯kɔmən] <kommt vor, kam vor, ist vorgekommen> ◊ *Kinder kommen in seiner Lebensplanung anscheinend nicht vor.* figure in a play in einem Stück mitspielen [ɪn aɛ̯nəm ˈʃtʏk ˌmɪtʃpiːlən] +haben ◊ *Mein Sohn spielt auch in dem Stück mit.* figure prominently eine wichtige Rolle spielen [aɛ̯nə ˌvɪçtɪgə ˈrɔlə ʃpiːlən] +haben **2.** *(fam)* *(reckon)* figure sth sich ⸤dat⸥ etw. denken [ˈdɛŋkn̩] <denkt sich, dachte sich, hat sich gedacht> ◊ *Ich hatte mir gedacht, dass ihr Silvester mit uns feiern könntet.* ⊛ it doesn't figure das passt nicht zusammen it figures that typisch, dass ◊ *Typisch, dass er als Lehrer zum Ferienbeginn krank wird!*

• **figure out** ⸤phras v⸥ **1.** *(find)* herausbekommen [hɛˈraʊ̯sbəkɔmən] <bekommt heraus, bekam heraus, hat herausbekommen> ◊ *Ich bekomme nicht heraus, wie dieses Schloss aufgeht.* **2.** *(understand)* schlau werden aus [ˈʃlaʊ̯ veːɐ̯dn̩ aʊ̯s] +sein ◊ *Ich werde aus ihm einfach nicht schlau.*

file¹ ⸤noun⸥ **1.** *(information)* Akte [ˈaktə] die <-, -n> ◊ *eine Akte anlegen* on file bei den Akten ◊ *Das muss irgendwo bei den Akten sein.* keep a file on sth eine Akte über etw. ⸤acc⸥ führen [aɛ̯nə ˌaktə yːbɐ ... fyːrən] +haben ◊ *Wir führen Akten über alle unsere Kunden.*; *(on computer)* Datei [daˈtaɛ̯] die <-, -en> ◊ *eine Datei abspeichern/löschen/kopieren/öffnen* **2.** *(tool)* Feile [ˈfaɛ̯lə] die <-, -n> ◊ *Kanten mit*

einer Feile abschleifen/glätten **3.** *(row)* Reihe [ˈraɛ̯ə] die <-, -n> ◊ *Die Menschen standen in einer Reihe vor der Kasse an.*

file² ⸤verb⸥ **1.** *(move one after the other)* file past sb/ sth an jdm/etw. vorbeimarschieren [an ... foːɐ̯ˌbaɛ̯maˈʃiːrən] <marschiert vorbei, marschierte vorbei, ist vorbeimarschiert> ◊ *Die Soldaten marschierten an dem Präsidenten vorbei.* file in nacheinander hereinkommen [naːxˈaɛ̯aͅe̯ˌnandə hɛˈraɛ̯nkɔmən] <kommt herein, kam herein, ist hereingekommen> ◊ *Die Schüler kamen nacheinander herein.* file out of sth nacheinander aus etw. herauskommen [naːxˈaɛ̯aͅe̯ˌnandə aʊ̯s ... hɛˈraʊ̯skɔmən] <kommt heraus, kam heraus, ist herausgekommen> **2.** *(a dossier, letter)* ablegen [ˈapleːgn̩] +haben ◊ *Beschwerden werden unter „B" abgelegt.* **3.** *(with a tool)* feilen [ˈfaɛ̯lən] +haben file your fingernails sich ⸤dat⸥ die Fingernägel feilen **4.** LAW einreichen [ˈaɛ̯nraɛ̯çn̩] +haben ◊ *Sie reichte Klage gegen die Firma ein.* file for divorce die Scheidung einreichen

fill ⸤verb⸥ **1.** *(make full, become full)* fill sth etw. füllen [ˈfʏlən] +haben ◊ *Er füllte den Eimer mit kaltem Wasser.* sth fills etw. füllt sich ◊ *Ihre Augen füllten sich mit Tränen.* ♦ *Langsam füllte sich die Halle.*; *(a gap, void)* ausfüllen [ˈaʊ̯sfʏlən] +haben **2.** *(scent, sound, feeling)* erfüllen [ɛˈfʏlən] <erfüllt, erfüllte, hat erfüllt> ◊ *Ein süßer Duft erfüllte den Raum.* ♦ *Diese Worte erfüllten ihn mit Zorn.* **3.** *(work in a position)* innehaben [ˈɪnəhaːbm̩] <hat inne, hatte inne, hat innegehabt> ◊ *Frau Schneider hat bei uns den Posten der Marketingleiterin inne.*; *(give to an employee)* besetzen [bəˈzɛtsn̩] <besetzt, besetzte, hat besetzt> ◊ *eine Stelle mit einem geeigneten Bewerber besetzen* **4.** *(a period of time)* verbringen [fɛˈbrɪŋən] <verbringt, verbrachte, hat verbracht> ◊ *Er weiß oft nicht, wie er seine freie Zeit verbringen soll.* **5.** *(a tooth)* plombieren [plɔmˈbiːrən] <plombiert, plombierte, hat plombiert> ◊ *Der Zahnarzt hat mir mehrere Zähne plombiert.*

• **fill in** ⸤phras v⸥ **1.** *(a form)* ausfüllen [ˈaʊ̯sfʏlən] <füllt aus, füllte aus, hat ausgefüllt> ◊ *einen Antrag/Fragebogen ausfüllen; (a missing word, an address)* eintragen [ˈaɛ̯ntraːgn̩] <trägt ein, trug ein, hat eingetragen> ◊ *Hier musst du noch dein Geburtsdatum eintragen.* **2.** *(a hole etc.)* zustopfen [ˈtsuːʃtɔpfn̩] +haben ◊ *Sie stopften das Loch mit Stroh zu.; (a door etc.)* zumauern [ˈtsuːmaʊ̯ɐn] <mauert zu, mauerte zu, hat zugemauert> **3.** *(fam)* *(provide information)* fill sb in (on sth) jdn (über etw. ⸤acc⸥) aufklären [ˈaʊ̯fklɛːrən] +haben ◊ *Hat Herr Krause Sie über die Details aufgeklärt?* **4.** *(deputize for)* fill in for sb jdn vertreten [fɛˈtreːtn̩] <vertritt, vertrat, hat vertreten> ◊ *Er vertritt den Hausmeister, der gerade in Urlaub ist.*

• **fill out** ⸤phras v⸥ **1.** *(a form etc.)* ausfüllen [ˈaʊ̯sfʏlən] +haben ◊ *Füllen Sie bitte diesen Antrag aus.* **2.** *(fam)* *(become fatter)* fülliger werden [ˈfʏlɪgɐ veːɐ̯dn̩] +sein ◊ *Michael ist im Urlaub fülliger geworden, findest du nicht?*

• **fill up** ⸤phras v⸥ **1.** *(make full, become full)* fill up sth etw. füllen [ˈfʏlən] +haben ◊ *Er füllte ihr Glas noch einmal mit Wasser.* sth fills up etw. füllt sich ◊ *Allmählich füllte sich der Saal.* **2.** *(eat)* fill up on sth sich an etw. satt essen [an ... ˈzat ɛsn̩] <isst sich, aß sich, hat sich ... gegessen> ◊ *Wir aßen uns an*

Kuchen und Keksen satt. I need something to fill me up. *Ich brauche etwas, was satt macht.* **3.** *(a car etc.)* tanken ['taŋkn̩] +haben ◊ *Wir müssen bei nächster Gelegenheit tanken.*

filling [noun] Füllung ['fʏlʊŋ] die <-, –en>

film¹ [noun] Film [fɪlm] der <-(e)s, –e> ◊ *Hast du den neuen Film mit Bruce Willis gesehen?* ✦ *Sie möchte zum Film.* ✦ *Ich muss den Film wechseln.* ✦ *Das Öl bildet einen Film auf dem Wasser.* shoot a film einen Film drehen [aenən 'fɪlm dreːən] +haben ◊ *Der Film wurde in Neuseeland gedreht.*

film² [verb] filmen ['fɪlmən] +haben ◊ *Löwen in freier Wildbahn filmen* ✦ *Im Gerichtssaal darf nicht gefilmt werden.*

filter¹ [noun] **1.** *(for liquids, a camera, cigarette)* Filter ['fɪltɐ] der <-s, –> ◊ *Flüssigkeit durch einen Filter gießen* ✦ *Zigaretten mit/ohne Filter* **2.** *(in the UK: traffic signal)* grüner Pfeil [gryːnɐ 'p͡faɛl] <-(e)s, –e> ◊ *der grüne Pfeil für Rechtsabbieger* filter lane Abbiegespur ['apbiːgəʃpuːɐ̯] die <-, –en>

filter² [verb] **1.** *(light)* sth filters through sth etw. schimmern durch etw. [ʃɪmɐt 'dʊrç] +haben ◊ *Das Sonnenlicht schimmerte durch die Vorhänge.; (information)* etw. sickert durch [zɪkɐt 'dʊrç] +sein ◊ *Irgendwie ist diese Information zur Presse durchgesickert.; (sound)* etw. dringt durch etw. [drɪŋt 'dʊrç] <dringt, drang, ist gedrungen> ◊ *Seine Worte drangen durch die Stille in mein Bewusstsein.* **2.** *(a liquid, air, data)* filtern ['fɪltɐn] +haben ◊ *Das Wasser sollte vor dem Trinken gefiltert werden.* ✦ *Der Katalysator filtert die Abgase.* **3.** *(in the UK: prepare to turn left or right)* sich einordnen ['aɛn|ʔɔr̩dnən] <ordnet sich ein, ordnete sich ein, hat sich eingeordnet> filter to the left/right sich links/rechts einordnen **4.** *(people)* filter somewhere langsam irgendwohin gehen [laŋzaːm 'geːən] <geht, ging, ist gegangen> ◊ *Langsam gingen die Besucher aus dem Saal.*

filth [noun] **1.** *(pornography)* Schweinerei [ʃvaenəˈrae] die <-, –en> *(fam, pej)* ◊ *Keine Schweinereien, bitte!* **2.** *(dirt)* Schmutz [ʃmʊts] der <-es> no pl ◊ *Die Küche war voller Schmutz.*

filthy [adj] **1.** *(dirty, obscene)* schmutzig ['ʃmʊtsɪç] ◊ *Das Haus war unglaublich schmutzig.* ✦ *schmutzige Witze erzählen* **2.** *(fam) (in the UK)* filthy weather Sauwetter ['zaovɛtɐ] das <-s> no pl *(slang)*

fin [noun] **1.** *(of a fish, an aircraft)* Flosse ['flɔsə] die <-, –n> **2.** *(of a radiator)* Rippe ['rɪpə] die <-, –n>

final¹ [noun] **1.** *(in a competition)* Finale [fiˈnaːlə] das <-s, –> ◊ *Das große Finale findet im August statt.* finals Finale ◊ *Leider hat es die Mannschaft nicht ins Finale geschafft.* **2.** UNI finals Abschlussprüfung ['apʃlʊspryːfʊŋ] die <-, –en> ◊ *Sie hat nächsten Monat Abschlussprüfung.* ✦ *durch die Abschlussprüfung fallen*

final² [adj] **1.** *(being a result of sth)* End... [ɛnt] final score Endstand ['ɛntʃtant] der <-(e)s, Endstände> ◊ final product Endprodukt ['ɛntproˌdʊkt] das <-(e)s, –e> ◊ final result Endergebnis ['ɛntlˌeɡeːpnɪs] das <-ses, –se> **2.** *(last)* letzte ['lɛtstə] no comp/ superl, only before ns <ein letzter …, eine letzte …, ein letztes …> ◊ *Das ist mein letztes Angebot.* ✦ *Ich hätte noch eine letzte Frage.* final whistle Schlusspfiff ['ʃlʊspfɪf] der <-(e)s, –e> final examination Abschlussprüfung ['apʃlʊspryːfʊŋ] die <-, –en> **3.** *(definite)* endgültig ['ɛntɡʏltɪç] no comp/superl ◊ *Ist diese Entscheidung endgültig?* ✦ *das endgültige*

Wahlergebnis

finally [adv] **1.** *(eventually, lastly)* schließlich ['ʃliːslɪç] no comp/superl ◊ *Der Täter konnte schließlich doch noch gefasst werden.* ✦ *Es gab Suppe, Hauptspeise, Nachspeise und schließlich noch einen Kaffee.* **2.** *(definitely)* endgültig ['ɛntɡʏltɪç] no comp/superl ◊ *über etw.* [acc] *endgültig entscheiden*

finance¹ [noun] **1.** *(dealing with money)* Finanzwesen [fiˈnantsveːzn̩] das <-s> no pl finance department Finanzabteilung [fiˈnantslaptaɛlʊŋ] die <-, –en> study finance Finanzwissenschaft [fiˈnantsvɪsn̩ʃaft ʃtuˌdiːrən] <studiert, studierte, hat studiert> **2.** *(money)* Geld [ɡɛlt] das <-(e)s, –er> ◊ *Das ist alles eine Frage des Geldes.* finances Finanzen [fiˈnantsn̩] die <–> pl ◊ *Seine Finanzen stehen nicht gut.*

finance² [verb] finanzieren [finanˈtsiːrən] <finanziert, finanzierte, hat finanziert> ◊ *Das Vorhaben wird von einem ausländischen Unternehmen finanziert.*

financial(ly) [adj, adv] *(relating to money)* finanziell [finanˈtsɪɛl] no comp/superl ◊ *Kann er sich das denn finanziell leisten?* ✦ *finanzielle Sorgen haben;* Finanz... [fiˈnants] financial services Finanzdienstleistungen [fiˈnantsdiːnst,laɛstʊŋən] die <–> pl ◊ *Eine Bank bietet verschiedene Finanzdienstleistungen an.* financial adviser Finanzberater [fiˈnantsbəraːtɐ] der <-s, –> ♀Finanzberaterin [fiˈnantsbə,raːtərɪn] die <-, –nen>

ⓔ **financially sound 1.** *(having a lot of money)* potent ◊ *Wir suchen noch potente Anleger/Investoren/Sponsoren.* **2.** *(safe)* solide

find¹ [noun] Fund [fʊnt] der <-(e)s, –e> ◊ *archäologische Funde* ✦ *einen erstaunlichen Fund machen*

find² [verb] **1.** *(discover, get, consider to be, have)* finden ['fɪndn̩] <findet, fand, hat gefunden> ◊ *Ich kann meine Handschuhe nicht finden!* ✦ *eine Lösung finden* ✦ *Er hat immer noch keine Arbeit gefunden.* ✦ *Ich finde Spanien als Urlaubsland zu heiß.* ✦ *Endlich fand er einmal Zeit, ein Buch zu lesen.* **2.** LAW find sb guilty jdn schuldig sprechen ['ʃʊldɪç ʃprɛçn̩] <spricht, sprach, hat gesprochen> How do you find the accused? Wie lautet Ihr Urteil?

ⓔ **find yourself somewhere** sich irgendwo wiederfinden

• **find out** [phras v] **1.** *(discover)* herausfinden [hɛˈraosfɪndn̩] <findet heraus, fand heraus, hat herausgefunden> ◊ *Forscher haben herausgefunden, dass …* ✦ *die Wahrheit über jdn/etw. herausfinden* **2.** find sb out jdm auf die Schliche kommen [aof diː 'ʃlɪçə kɔmən] <kommt, kam, ist gekommen> *(fam)*

findings [noun] Ergebnis [ɛɐ̯ˈɡeːpnɪs] das <-ses, –se> ◊ *Der Ausschuss kam zu folgendem Ergebnis: …* ✦ *das Ergebnis der Untersuchung*

fine¹ [noun] Geldstrafe ['ɡɛltʃtraːfə] die <-, –n> ◊ *Die Firma muss eine hohe Geldstrafe zahlen.; (for minor offences also)* Bußgeld ['buːsɡɛlt] das <-(e)s, –er>

fine² [adj] **1.** *(okay)* in Ordnung [ɪn 'ɔrdnʊŋ] ◊ „*Sind Sie mit dem Zimmer zufrieden?*" — „*Ja, danke, alles in Ordnung!*" ✦ *In Ordnung, machen wir so.* 'More tea?' — 'No thanks, I'm fine!' „*Noch etwas Tee?*" — „*Nein danke, ich habe genug.*" That's fine by me. *Ich habe nichts dagegen.* **2.** *(of very good quality, valuable)* edel ['eːdl̩] <edler, am edelsten> <der/die/das edle …> ◊ *Ihr Brautkleid ist*

wirklich edel. ♦ *Dieser Wein ist ein edler Tropfen.;* *(clothes, manners)* vornehm ['foːɐ̯neːm] ◊ *Er trug einen vornehmen Anzug.; (man, character)* gut [guːt] <besser, am besten> ◊ *Mein Großvater war ein guter Mann.; (artist, painting, novel, view, voice, meal)* großartig ['groːsʔaːɐ̯tɪç] ◊ *Sie hat eine großartige Stimme.* ♦ *Der Nachtisch war wirklich großartig!* sb is/feels fine jdm geht es gut [geːt ɛs 'guːt] <ging, ist gegangen> ◊ *Mir geht es gut, danke!; (weather)* schön [ʃøːn] ◊ *ein schöner Frühlingstag* ♦ *Hoffentlich wird das Wetter morgen schön.* 3. *(hair, sand, features, distinction)* fein [faɛ̯n] ◊ *Ihr Haar war sehr fein.* ♦ *ein feiner Unterschied*

fine³ adv 1. *(fam) (well)* gut [guːt] <besser, am besten> ◊ *Das machst du gut!* do sb fine jdm reichen ['raɛ̯çn̩] +haben ◊ *Danke, eine Tasse Tee reicht mir.* 2. *(cut, chop)* fein [faɛ̯n] ◊ *Petersilie fein hacken*

fine⁴ verb jdn mit einer Geldstrafe belegen [mɪt aɛ̯nɐ 'gɛltʃtraːfə bəleːɡn̩] <belegt, belegte, hat belegt> ◊ *Er wurde mit einer Geldstrafe von 50 Euro belegt. He was fined for speeding. Er bekam einen Strafzettel für zu schnelles Fahren.*

finely adv 1. *(in small pieces, with details)* fein [faɛ̯n] ◊ *Kräuter fein hacken* ♦ *fein gemahlener Kaffee* ♦ *fein geschnittene Gesichtszüge* 2. *(skilfully)* schön [ʃøːn] ◊ *eine schön gearbeitete Skulptur*

finger noun Finger ['fɪŋɐ] der <-s, -> ◊ *einen Ring am Finger tragen* ♦ *Ein Finger an meinem linken Handschuh hat ein Loch.*

⦿ work your fingers to the bone sich die Finger wund arbeiten have a finger in every pie überall die Finger drin haben *(fam)* give sb the finger jdm den Stinkefinger zeigen *(fam)* keep your fingers crossed jdm die Daumen halten *(fam)* snap your fingers mit den Fingern schnippen

fingernail noun Fingernagel ['fɪŋɐnaːɡl̩] der <-s, Fingernägel>

fingerprint noun Fingerabdruck ['fɪŋɐʔapdrʊk] der <-(e)s, Fingerabdrücke> ◊ *am Tatort Fingerabdrücke hinterlassen* ♦ *einem Verdächtigen die Fingerabdrücke abnehmen*

finish¹ noun 1. *(end)* Ende ['ɛndə] das <-s> no pl ◊ *Hast du das Ende des Spiels gesehen?* ♦ *Sie hat bis zum Ende durchgehalten.* from start to finish von Anfang bis Ende 2. *(surface)* Oberfläche ['oːbɐflɛçə] die <-, -n> ◊ *eine raue/glatte Oberfläche* 3. *(perfection)* sth lacks finish einer Sache dat fehlt der letzte Schliff [feːlt deːɐ̯ lɛtstə 'ʃlɪf] +haben ◊ *Seinem Stil fehlt der letzte Schliff.*

finish² verb 1. *(end, complete)* finish sth (off) etw. beenden [bə'ɛndn̩] <beendet, beendete, hat beendet> ◊ *das Spiel/Programm beenden* ♦ *Im Sommer beendet er sein Studium.* have finished doing sth mit etw. fertig sein [mɪt ... 'fɛrtɪç zaɛ̯n] ◊ *Bist du schon mit dem Kochen fertig?* sth finishes etw. endet ['ɛndət] +haben ◊ *Der Kurs endet um 20 Uhr.* 2. *(food)* finish sth (off) etw. aufessen ['aɔf|ɛsn̩] <isst auf, aß auf, hat aufgegessen> ◊ *Du bekommst nur Nachtisch, wenn du dein Gemüse aufisst.; (a drink)* etw. austrinken ['aɔstrɪŋkn̩] <trinkt aus, trank aus, hat ausgetrunken>; *(a cigarette)* etw. zu Ende rauchen [tsuː 'ɛndə raɔxn̩] +haben 3. *(in a race etc.)* finish first etc. als Erster/Erste etc. durchs Ziel gehen [als 'eːɐ̯stɐ/'eːɐ̯stə dʊⁱçs ,tsiːl geːən] <geht, ging, ist gegangen> ◊ *Sie ging bei dem Rennen als*

Zweite durchs Ziel. 4. *(a surface)* sth is well finished etw. hat eine schöne Oberfläche [hat aɛ̯nə ʃøːnə 'oːbɐflɛçə] ◊ *Der Tisch hat eine schöne Oberfläche.* add the finishing touches to sth einer Sache dat den letzten Schliff geben [deːn lɛtstn̩ 'ʃlɪf geːbm̩] <gibt, gab, hat gegeben> ◊ *Der Lack gibt dem Modell den letzten Schliff.*

• **finish off** phras v 1. *(kill)* finish sb off jdn erledigen [ɛ'leːdɪɡn̩] <erledigt, erledigte, hat erledigt> *(fam)* ◊ *Den hat die Mafia erledigt.* 2. *(fam) (exhaust)* fertig machen ['fɛrtɪç maxn̩] +haben ◊ *Der lange Marsch hat ihn ziemlich fertig gemacht.* → finish² 1., finish² 2.

• **finish up** phras v finish up ill/last etc. am Ende krank/Letzter etc. werden [am ɛndə 'kraŋk/'lɛtstə e:ɐ̯dn̩] +sein *I'll always finish up doing all the work. Am Ende muss doch ich wieder alles machen.*

• **finish with** phras v 1. *(no longer need)* finish with sth etw. nicht mehr brauchen [nɪçt meːⁱç 'braɔxn̩] +haben ◊ *Wenn du den Lappen nicht mehr brauchst, häng ihn bitte über die Heizung. Have you finished with the scissors? Brauchst du die Schere noch?* 2. *(separate)* finish with sb mit jdm Schluss machen [mɪt ... 'ʃlʊs maxn̩] +haben

finished adj fertig ['fɛrtɪç] no comp/superl ◊ *Der Rohbau war schon fertig.* ♦ *Kannst du die fertigen Briefe bitte abschicken?*

⦿ be finished 1. *(have completed)* fertig sein 2. *(be exhausted, done for)* erledigt sein

Finland noun Finnland ['fɪnlant] das <-s> article only in combination with attribute, no pl → Germany

Finn noun Finne ['fɪnə] der <-n, -n> ♀Finnin ['fɪnɪn] die <-, -nen> → German¹ 1.

Finnish¹ noun Finnisch ['fɪnɪʃ] das <-(s)> no pl → German¹ 1.

Finnish² adj finnisch ['fɪnɪʃ] → German²

fir noun Tanne ['tanə] die <-, -n> ◊ *Im Wald stehen viele Tannen.* fir cone Tannenzapfen ['tanⁿtsapfn̩] der <-s, ->

fire¹ noun 1. *(sth burning, passion)* Feuer ['fɔɐ̯ɐ] das <-s> no pl ◊ *Er machte Feuer im Kamin.* ♦ *In der Wohnung ist gestern Abend ein Feuer ausgebrochen.* ♦ *In ihren Augen brannte ein leidenschaftliches Feuer.* be on fire brennen ['brɛnən] <brennt, brannte, hat gebrannt> catch fire Feuer fangen ['fɔɐ̯ɐ faŋən] <fängt, fing, hat gefangen> ◊ *Das Auto fing sofort Feuer und brannte vollständig aus.* set fire to sth etw. anzünden ['antsvndn̩] <zündet an, zündete an, hat angezündet> ◊ *Jemand hat den alten Schuppen angezündet.* forest fire Waldbrand ['valtbrant] der <-(e)s, Waldbrände> 2. *(open fireplace)* Kamin [ka'miːn] der <-s, -e>; *(with a gas or electric fire inside)* Kaminfeuer [ka'miːnfɔɐ̯ɐ] das <-s, -> 3. MIL Feuer ['fɔɐ̯ɐ] das <-s> no pl ◊ *das Feuer auf jdn eröffnen* come under fire unter Beschuss geraten [ʊntɐ bə'ʃʊs ɡəraːtn̩] <gerät, geriet, ist geraten> machine gun fire Maschinengewehrfeuer [ma'ʃiːnəngəveːɐ̯fɔɐ̯ɐ]

⦿ fight fire with fire 1. mit den gleichen Waffen kämpfen 2. you cannot fight fire with fire man kann nicht mit dem Teufel den Beelzebub austreiben

fire² verb 1. *(with a weapon)* sb fires somewhere jd feuert irgendwohin ['fɔɐ̯ɐt] +haben ◊ *zur Warnung*

in die Luft feuern fire sth (at sb) *etw.* (auf jdn) **abfeuern** ['apfɔɐ̯ən] <feuert ab, feuerte ab, hat abgefeuert> ◊ *Der Gangster feuerte mehrere Schüsse auf Passanten ab.* ♦ *eine Rakete abfeuern* fire questions at sb jdn mit Fragen **bombardieren** [mɪt ˌfraːgn̩ bɔmbarˈdiːrən] <bombardiert, bombardierte, hat bombardiert> **2.** fire sb jdn **feuern** ['fɔɐ̯ən] +haben (fam) ◊ *Sie sind gefeuert!* **3.** (engine) **zünden** ['tsʏndn̩] <zündet, zündete, hat gezündet> +haben ◊ *Der Motor zündet nicht.* **4.** (clay, tiles etc.) **brennen** ['brɛnən] <brennt, brannte, hat gebrannt> +haben

• **fire away** [phras v] (start asking questions) **losschießen** ['loːsʃiːsn̩] <schießt los, schoss los, hat losgeschossen> (fam) ◊ *Ich habe jetzt Zeit für Sie; schießen Sie los!*

• **fire off** [phras v] **abfeuern** ['apfɔɐ̯ən] <feuert ab, feuerte ab, hat abgefeuert> ◊ *Der Polizist feuerte einen Warnschuss ab.* ♦ *ein Gewehr abfeuern*

fire alarm [noun] **1.** (signal) Feueralarm ['fɔɐ̯əˌlaˈm] der <–(e)s, –e> ◊ *Feueralarm geben* **2.** (device) Feuermelder ['fɔɐ̯əmɛldɐ] der <–s, –>

firearm [noun] Schusswaffe ['ʃʊsvafə] die <–, –n>

fire brigade, fire department [noun] Feuerwehr ['fɔɐ̯veːɐ̯] die <–, –en> ◊ *Er ist bei der freiwilligen Feuerwehr.*

fire extinguisher [noun] Feuerlöscher ['fɔɐ̯əlœʃɐ] der <–s, –>

fireplace [noun] Kamin [kaˈmiːn] der <–s, –e> ◊ *Wir saßen am Kamin.*

firework [noun] **1.** (small combustible device) Feuerwerkskörper ['fɔɐ̯vɛˈkskœˈpe] der <–s, –> ◊ *Feuerwerkskörper für Silvester kaufen* **2.** (display) fireworks Feuerwerk ['fɔɐ̯vɛˈk] das <–(e)s, –e> ◊ *das neue Jahr mit einem Feuerwerk begrüßen*

firm¹ [noun] Firma ['fɪˈmaː] die <–, Firmen> ◊ *eine eigene Firma gründen* firm of ... ...büro [byˈroː] das <–s, –s> firm of architects Architektenbüro [aˈçiˈtɛktn̩byˌroː] firm of solicitors Rechtsanwaltsbüro ['rɛçtsͺanvaltsbyˌroː]

firm² [adj] (solid, steady, definite, strong) fest [fɛst] <fester, am festesten> ◊ *auf festem Boden stehen* ♦ *Er antwortete mit fester Stimme.* ♦ *eine feste Zusage erhalten* ♦ *Ihr Händedruck war sehr fest.* be firm with sb jdm gegenüber bestimmt auftreten [geːˈgn̩yːbe bəˈʃtɪmt ͺaͻftreːtn̩] <tritt auf, trat auf, ist aufgetreten> hold firm to sth an etw. [dat] festhalten [an ... ˈfɛsthaltn̩] <hält fest, hielt fest, hat festgehalten> ◊ *Die Regierung will an ihren Sparplänen festhalten.* firm evidence zuverlässige Beweise [ͺtsuːfɛlɛsɪgə bəˈvaɛzə] <–, pl>
◉ **a firm hand** eine feste Hand

firmly [adv] **1.** (steadily, definitely) fest [fɛst] <fester, am festesten> ◊ *Das Seil ist fest verankert.* ♦ *Er glaubte fest an ihre Unschuld.* **2.** (self-confidently, resolutely) bestimmt [bəˈʃtɪmt] <bestimmter, am bestimmtesten> ◊ *Sie tritt sehr bestimmt auf.* ♦ *„Nein", sagte er bestimmt.*

first¹ [noun] **1.** (before everything or everybody else, the best) Erste ['eːɐ̯stə] der/die <–n, –n> ◊ *Wer von euch ist die Erste?* ♦ *Er war schon immer der Erste in der Klasse.* be the first to do sth etw. als Erster/ Erste tun [als ˈeːɐ̯stəˈeːɐ̯stə] ◊ *Sie war als Erste fertig.* be a first for sb für jdn das erste Mal sein [fyːɡ ... das ͺeːɐ̯stə ˈmaːl tsaɛn] **2.** (the first day of the month) the first der Erste [deːɡ ˈeːɐ̯stə] <–n> no pl

◊ *Die Miete ist jeweils am Ersten fällig.* **3.** UNI (in the UK: grade) Eins [aɛns] die <–, –en> ◊ *Er bestand das Examen mit einer Eins.*
◉ **at first** zuerst ◊ *Zuerst dachte ich, sie meint das gar nicht ernst.* from the first von Anfang an

first² [adj] erste ['eːɐ̯stə] <ein erster ..., eine erste ..., ein erstes ...> ◊ *Heute ist ihr erster Schultag.* ♦ *Biegen Sie an der ersten Kreuzung links ab.* ♦ *Er hat den ersten Preis gewonnen.* the first thing das Erste ◊ *Das Erste, was ich tue, ist zu duschen.* for the first time zum ersten Mal [tsʊm ͺeːɐ̯stn̩ ˈmaːl] at first sight auf den ersten Blick [aɔf deːn ͺeːɐ̯stn̩ ˈblɪk]

first³ [adv] **1.** (before doing anything else, before the others) zuerst [tsuˈeːɐ̯st] ◊ *Geh du zuerst!* ♦ *Du solltest zuerst versuchen, den Fehler zu finden.* **2.** (in a listing) erstens ['eːɐ̯stn̩s] ◊ *Ich habe keine Lust — erstens ist es schon spät, zweitens kalt und drittens regnet es.*
◉ **first come, first served** wer zuerst kommt, mahlt zuerst first of all als Erstes ◊ *nach der Katastrophe als Erstes für sauberes Trinkwasser sorgen*

first-aid kit [noun] Erste-Hilfe-Kasten [eːɐ̯stə'hɪlfəkastn̩] der <–s, Erste-Hilfe-Kästen>

first floor [noun] **1.** (in the UK) erster Stock [ͺeːɐ̯stə ˈʃtɔk] <–(e)s> no pl ◊ *Mein Büro befindet sich im ersten Stock.* **2.** (in the US) Erdgeschoss ['eːɐ̯tgəʃɔs] das <–es, –e>

firstly [adv] **1.** (to start with) zunächst [tsuˈnɛːçst] ◊ *Wir wollen uns zunächst mit der Geschichte der Stadt befassen.* **2.** (first in an enumeration) erstens ['eːɐ̯stn̩s] ◊ *Klettern ist nichts für mich — erstens habe ich Höhenangst und zweitens keine Kraft in den Armen.*

first name [noun] Vorname ['foːɐ̯naːmə] der <–ns, –n> ◊ *Sie heißt mit Vornamen Maria.* be on first name terms with sb jdn mit Vornamen anreden [mɪt ˈfoːɐ̯naːmən ͺanreːdn̩] <redet an, redete an, hat angeredet>

fiscal [adj] Finanz... [fiˈnants] fiscal policies Finanzpolitik [fiˈnantspoliͺtiːk] die <–> no pl fiscal crisis Finanzkrise [fiˈnantskriːzə] die <–, –n> fiscal measures finanzpolitische Maßnahmen [fiͺnantspoͺliːtɪʃə ˈmaːsnaːmən] die <–> pl fiscal year Steuerjahr ['ʃtɔɐ̯jaːɐ̯] das <–(e)s, –e>

fish¹ [noun] (animal, food) Fisch [fɪʃ] der <–(e)s, –e> ◊ *Fische fangen/angeln* ♦ *Am Freitag gibt es bei uns Fisch.*
◉ **neither fish nor fowl** weder Fisch noch Fleisch like a fish out of water wie ein Fisch auf dem Trockenen drink like a fish (fam) wie ein Loch saufen (fam)

fish² [verb] fischen ['fɪʃn̩] +haben ◊ *Hier darf man nicht fischen.* fish a river in einem Fluss fischen go fishing fischen gehen ['fɪʃn̩ geːən] <geht, ging, ist gegangen>

• **fish for** [phras v] fish for sth (be out for) auf etw. [acc] aus sein [aɔf ... ˈaɔs tsaɛn] ◊ *Du bist doch nur auf Komplimente aus!*

• **fish out** [phras v] fish sth/sb out etw./jdn herausfischen [hɛˈraɔsfɪʃn̩] +haben ◊ *Sie öffnete ihren Rucksack und fischte ein Taschenmesser heraus.* fish sb/sth out of sth jdn/etw. aus etw. fischen ◊ *Ein Passant fischte das Kind aus dem Wasser.*

fisherman [noun] Fischer ['fɪʃe] der <–s, –> ◊ *Bereits sein Großvater war Fischer.* ♦ *Der Fischer warf die Netze aus.*

A
B
C
D
E
F
G
H
I
J
K
L
M
N
O
P
Q
R
S
T
U
V
W
X
Y
Z

fisherwoman [noun] Fischerin ['fɪʃərɪn] die <–, –nen> ◊ *Sie war Fischerin von Beruf.* ♦ *Auf dem See zog eine Fischerin die Netze ein.*

fishing [noun] *(activity)* Fischen ['fɪʃn] das <–s> no pl ◊ *beim Fischen sein; (business)* Fischerei [fɪʃə'raɪ] die <–> no pl ◊ *Er lebt von der Fischerei.*

fishing rod [noun] Angelrute ['aŋlruːtə] die <–, –n>

fist [noun] Faust [faʊst] die <–, Fäuste> ◊ *eine Faust machen* ♦ *Er schlug ihm mit der Faust ins Gesicht.* **clench your fist** die Faust ballen [diː 'faʊst balən] +haben

fit¹ [noun] **1.** *(of emotion, coughing, epilepsy etc.)* Anfall ['anfal] der <–(e)s, Anfälle> ◊ *Er bekam einen epileptischen Anfall.* ♦ *ein plötzlicher Anfall von Panik* **fit of laughter** Lachanfall ['laxanfal] **fit of rage** Wutanfall ['vuːtanfal] **coughing fit** Hustenanfall ['huːstn̩anfal] **2.** *(clothes)* **sth is a good/bad fit** etw. passt gut/schlecht [,past 'guːt/'ʃlɛçt] +haben **sth is a tight fit** etw. ist eng [ɪst 'ɛŋ] **to ensure a tight fit** damit alles fest sitzt [damɪt aləs 'fɛst ,zɪtst]

fit² [adj] **1.** *(healthy)* fit [fɪt] <fitter, am fittesten> seldom before ns ◊ *Er ist körperlich und geistig sehr fit.* ♦ *Sport macht/hält fit.* **2.** **not in a fit state to do sth** nicht imstande, etw. zu tun [,nɪçt ɪm'ʃtandə ... tsuː] ◊ *Sie ist noch nicht imstande, die lange Reise anzutreten.* **fit to stand trial** verhandlungsfähig [fɛ'handlʊŋsfɛːɪç] no comp/ superl **3.** *(suitable)* geeignet [gə'laɪɡnət] ◊ *Sie sind für den Job geeignet.* I don't think he's **fit to lead** the department. Er scheint mir nicht zur Leitung der Abteilung geeignet zu sein. **fit to eat** essbar ['ɛsbaːr] no comp/superl ◊ *Ist dieser Kuchen denn noch essbar?* **fit to drink** trinkbar ['trɪŋkbaːr] no comp/superl ◊ *Das Wasser hier ist nicht trinkbar.* **fit for habitation** bewohnbar [bə'voːnbaːr] no comp/ superl ◊ *Das alte Gemäuer ist nicht bewohnbar.* ⊛ **see/think fit to do sth** es für angebracht halten, etw. zu tun ◊ *Ich handle, wie ich es für angebracht halte.*

fit³ [verb] **1.** *(be the right size)* passen ['pasn̩] +haben ◊ *Der Schrank passt nicht in die Lücke.* ♦ *Das Bild sollte auf eine Seite passen.* ♦ *Passen wir alle an den Tisch?* ♦ *Der Anzug passt gut/nicht.* **fit like a glove** wie angegossen passen **2.** *(be compatible with, belong to a group)* **fit (with) sth** zu etw. passen [tsuː ... ,pasn̩] +haben ◊ *Die Vorhänge passen nicht zu den Möbeln.* **fit into sth** in etw. [acc] passen ◊ *Sein Stil passt in keine der bekannten Kategorien.* **fit sth into/with sth** etw. einer Sache [dat] zuordnen ['tsuːlɔrdnən] <ordnet zu, ordnete zu, hat zugeordnet> ◊ *Ich kann diese Symptome keinem bekannten Krankheitsbild zuordnen.* **3.** *(correspond)* zusammenpassen ['tsuːzamənpasn̩] +haben ◊ *Etwas in seiner Geschichte passte nicht zusammen.; (match)* entsprechen [ɛnt'ʃprɛçn̩] <entspricht, entsprach, hat entsprochen> ◊ *Nur ein Bewerber entspricht unseren Kriterien.* **4.** *(try clothes on sb)* **fit sb for sth** jdm etw. anprobieren ['anproːbiːrən] <probiert an, probierte an, hat anprobiert> ◊ *jdm Schuhe anprobieren* **fit sb with sth** jdm etw. anpassen ['anpasn̩] +haben ◊ *Man passte ihm ein Hörgerät an.* **5.** *(install)* montieren [mɔn'tiːrən] <montiert, montierte, hat montiert> ◊ *einen Kindersitz in ein Auto montieren* **fit sth with sth** mit etw. ausstatten [mɪt ... ,aʊsʃtatn̩] <stattet aus, stattete aus, hat ausgestattet> ◊ *Alle unsere Büros sollen mit Klimaanlage*

ausgestattet werden.

• **fit in** [phras v] **1.** *(go into a place)* hineinpassen [hɪ'naɛnpasn̩] +haben ◊ *Passt der Ordner da hinein?* **2.** *(be accepted by a group)* sich einfügen ['aɛnfyːɡn̩] +haben ◊ *Es gelang ihr nur langsam, sich einzufügen.* **3.** *(find space or time for)* unterbringen ['ʊntɐbrɪŋən] <bringt unter, brachte unter, hat untergebracht> ◊ *Wo sollen wir denn diesen riesigen Sessel noch unterbringen?* ♦ *Die Besprechung kann ich in meinem Terminplan nicht mehr unterbringen.* I could fit you in at ten o'clock. Ich hätte um zehn Uhr Zeit für Sie.

• **fit in with** [phras v] **1.** *(with plans, ideas)* hineinpassen in [acc] [hɪ'naɛnpasn̩ ɪn] +haben ◊ *Das passt überhaupt nicht in meine Pläne hinein.* **2.** *(with a group)* sich einfügen in [acc] ['aɛnfyːɡn̩ ɪn] +haben ◊ *Der neue Kollege hat sich schnell ins Team eingefügt.* **3.** *(correspond, harmonize)* **fit in with sb/sth** zu jdm/ etw. passen [tsuː ... ,pasn̩] +haben ◊ *Tom passt nicht zu den anderen Kindern.* ♦ *Diese Geschichte passt nicht zu dem, was ich gebört habe.*

• **fit out** [phras v] **fit sb/sth out with sth** jdn/etw. mit etw. ausstatten [mɪt ... ,aʊsʃtatn̩] <stattet aus, stattete aus, hat ausgestattet> ◊ *Alle Büros werden mit automatischen Rollläden ausgestattet.* ♦ *einen Taucher mit einem Gummianzug ausstatten*

• **fit together** [phras v] **sth fits together** etw. passt zusammen [,past tsu'zamən] +haben ◊ *Die beiden Puzzleteile passen nicht zusammen.* ♦ *Wie passen diese Informationen zusammen?* **fit sth together** etw. zusammenfügen [tsu'zamənfyːɡn̩] +haben ◊ *Er fügte die beiden Bauteile zusammen.*

• **fit up** [phras v] **1.** *(a room etc.)* einrichten ['aɛnrɪçtn̩] <richtet ein, richtete ein, hat eingerichtet> ◊ *Er hat in seinem Schlafzimmer eine Funkstation eingerichtet.* ♦ *Der Keller soll als Büro eingerichtet werden.* **2.** *(fam) (incriminate falsely)* **fit sb up for sth** jdm etw. anhängen ['anhɛŋən] +haben ◊ *Jemand hatte versucht, ihr einen Diebstahl anzuhängen.*

fitness [noun] **1.** *(health, condition)* Kondition [kɔndi'tsjoːn] die <–> no pl ◊ *Seine Kondition ist erstaunlich.* **2.** *(suitability)* Eignung ['aɛɡnʊŋ] die <–, –en> no pl ◊ *jds Eignung für eine Aufgabe überprüfen*

fitter [noun] *(for machines)* Schlosser ['ʃlɔsɐ] der <–s, –> ♀Schlosserin ['ʃlɔsərɪn] die <–, –nen> ◊ *Er ist Schlosser von Beruf.; (for pipes)* Installateur [ɪnstala'tøːɐ] der <–s, –e> ♀Installateurin [ɪnstala'tøːrɪn] die <–, –nen> ◊ *Wir müssen einen Installateur kommen lassen.*

fitting¹ [noun] **1.** *(part)* Zubehörteil ['tsuːbəhøːɐtaɛl] das <–(e)s> sg **fittings** Zubehör ['tsuːbəhøːɐ] das <–(e)s> sg ◊ *ein Zubehörteil bestellen* ♦ *Zubehör für Bad und WC* **2.** *(furniture etc.)* **fittings** Ausstattung ['aʊsʃtatʊŋ] die <–, –en> ◊ *ein Zimmer mit moderner Ausstattung* **3.** *(of clothes)* Anprobe ['anproːbə] die <–, –n> ◊ *Sie muss wegen ihres Brautkleids noch zur Anprobe.*

fitting² [adj] passend ['pasn̩t] ◊ *Das war ein passender Auftakt für das Festival.* **it is not fitting that** es schickt sich nicht, dass [ɛs 'ʃɪkt zɪç nɪçt das] +haben ◊ *Es schickt sich nicht, in Shorts zu einem Begräbnis zu gehen.*

five¹ [noun] Fünf [fʏnf] die <–, –en> → **four¹**
five² [nmrl] fünf [fʏnf] → **four²**
fivefold [adj, adv] fünffach ['fʏnffax] → **fourfold**

fix [verb] **1.** *(make firm)* befestigen [bəˈfɛstɪɡn̩] <befestigt, befestigte, hat befestigt> ◊ *ein Regal mit Schrauben an der Wand befestigen; (install)* anbringen [ˈanbrɪŋən] <bringt an, brachte an, hat angebracht> ◊ *neue Vorhangstangen anbringen lassen* **2.** *(determine a date, price)* festsetzen [ˈfɛstzɛtsn̩] +haben ◊ *Setzen wir doch gleich einen Zeitpunkt für unser nächstes Treffen fest.* fix sth at sth etw. auf etw. [acc] festsetzen ◊ *Der Eintrittspreis ist auf 12 Euro festgesetzt worden.* **3.** *(organize)* arrangieren [araŋˈʒiːrən] <arrangiert, arrangierte, hat arrangiert> ◊ *Ich würde gern mit dem Geschäftsführer sprechen. Könnten Sie das für mich arrangieren?* fix sth (up) for sb etw. für jdn organisieren **4.** fix sth in your mind sich [dat] etw. gut einprägen [guːt ˈaɛnprɛːɡn̩] +haben ◊ *Prägen Sie sich die Notrufnummer gut ein.* **5.** *(a fight, race)* manipulieren [manipuˈliːrən] <manipuliert, manipulierte, hat manipuliert> ◊ *Jemand muss das Rennen manipuliert haben.* **6.** *(a meal etc.)* machen [ˈmaxn̩] +haben ◊ *Machst du mir ein Sandwich?* **7.** *(repair)* in Ordnung bringen [ɪn ˈɔrdnʊŋ brɪŋən] <bringt, brachte, hat gebracht> ◊ *Fabian hat den kaputten Wecker wieder in Ordnung gebracht.* ◆ *seine Ehe in Ordnung bringen* have sth fixed etw. reparieren lassen [repaˈriːrən lasn̩] <lässt, ließ, hat lassen> ◊ *Ich habe den kaputten Stuhl reparieren lassen.* **8.** fix your hair sich frisieren [friˈziːrən] <frisiert sich, frisierte sich, hat sich frisiert> **9.** *(in photography)* fixieren [fɪˈksiːrən] <fixiert, fixierte, hat fixiert> ◊ *einen Film fixieren* **10.** *(in the US: render a dog or cat infertile)* kastrieren [kasˈtriːrən] <kastriert, kastrierte, hat kastriert> ◊ *Ich möchte unseren Hund kastrieren lassen.*

☞ **I'll fix him/her!** Den/Die werde ich mir verknöpfen!

• **fix on** [phras v] **1.** *(decide)* sich entscheiden für [ɛntˈʃaɛdn̩ fyːɐ̯] <entscheidet sich, entschied sich, hat sich entschieden> ◊ *Wir haben uns für Norwegen als Urlaubsziel entschieden.* **2.** *(eyes, attention)* fix sth on sth etw. auf etw. [acc] richten [aɔf ... rɪçtn̩] +haben ◊ *Richten Sie Ihre Aufmerksamkeit auf diese kleine Kugel.* **3.** *(have one aim)* be fixed on doing sth darauf fixiert sein, etw. zu tun [daraɔf fɪˈksiːɐ̯t tsaɛn ... tsuː] ◊ *Sie ist darauf fixiert, nächstes Jahr nach Peru zu fliegen.*

• **fix up** [phras v] **1.** *(procure)* fix sb up with sth jdm etw. besorgen [bəˈzɔrɡn̩] <besorgt, besorgte, hat besorgt> ◊ *Er kann dir alles besorgen, was du brauchst.* **2.** *(repair, clean etc.)* in Ordnung bringen [ɪn ˈɔrdnʊŋ brɪŋən] <bringt, brachte, hat gebracht> ◊ *alte Möbel wieder in Ordnung bringen* ◆ *das Haus in Ordnung bringen* **3.** *(pair off)* fix sb up with sb jdn mit jdm verkuppeln [mɪt ... fɛˌkʊpl̩n] <verkuppelt, verkuppelte, hat verkuppelt> ◊ *Sie wollen ihn mit Petra verkuppeln.* → fix 3.

fixed → fix [adj] *(rules, prices)* fest [fɛst] <fester, am festesten> ◊ *Gibt es schon einen festen Termin?* ◆ *Die Preise sind fest.* ◆ *ein fester Bestandteil/Anteil; (smile)* starr [ʃtaʳ] ◊ *ein starres Lächeln; (expression)* unbeweglich [ˈʊnbəveːklɪç] ◊ *Sein Gesicht blieb völlig unbeweglich.; (idea)* fix [fɪks] no comp/superl ◊ *Das ist nur eine fixe Idee von ihr.*

☞ **how are you fixed for time/money etc.?** wie sieht's bei dir mit der Zeit/dem Geld etc. aus?

fixedly [adv] starr [ʃtaʳ] ◊ *starr geradeaus blicken*

fixture [noun] **1.** *(of a building etc.)* fixtures Ausstattung [ˈaɔsʃtatʊŋ] die <-, –en> ◊ *Zimmer mit moderner Ausstattung* lighting fixtures elektrische Anschlüsse [eˌlɛktrɪʃə ˈanʃlʏsə] <-> pl ◊ *Die elektrischen Anschlüsse müssen erst noch gelegt werden.* fixtures and fittings Austattung [ˈaɔsʃtatʊŋ] die <-> sg be a fixture zum Inventar gehören [tsʊm ɪnvɛnˈtaːʳ ɡəhøːrən] <gehört, gehörte, hat gehört> **2.** SPORT *(in the UK: game or contest)* Spiel [ʃpiːl] das <-(e)s, –e> ◊ *Die Mannschaft hat bis jetzt alle Spiele gewonnen.*

fizzy drink [noun] *alkoholfreies, kohlensäurehaltiges Getränk*

flag [noun] **1.** *(of a nation, an organization)* Fahne [ˈfaːnə] die <-, –n> ◊ *die Fahne Österreichs* ◆ *die tschechische Fahne; (of a ship, as a signal)* Flagge [ˈflaɡə] die <-, –n> ◊ *Das Schiff fährt unter deutscher Flagge.* ◆ *Die rote Flagge bedeutet Badeverbot.* **2.** *(small, for charity)* Fähnchen [ˈfɛːnçən] das <-s, –> ◊ *Fähnchen verkaufen*

flair [noun] **1.** *(stylishness)* Flair [flɛːɐ̯] das or seldom der <-s> no pl ◊ *Diesem Restaurant fehlt es an Flair.; (something special)* das gewisse Etwas [das ɡəˈvɪsə ˈɛtvas] ◊ *Das Essen ist nicht schlecht, aber es fehlt irgendwie das gewisse Etwas.* **2.** *(for selecting good things)* Gespür [ɡəˈʃpyːɐ̯] das <-s> no pl ◊ *Er hat ein Gespür für lukrative Geschäfte.; (aptitude)* Talent [taˈlɛnt] das <-(e)s, –e> ◊ *ein natürliches Talent für Musik*

flake [noun] **1.** *(of snow, cereals)* Flocke [ˈflɔkə] die <-, –n> ◊ *Flocken aus Hafer/Roggen/Gerste* ◆ *Der Schnee fiel in dicken Flocken.* snow flake Schneeflocke [ˈʃneːflɔkə] **2.** *(small by-product, of wood, metal)* Span [ʃpaːn] der <-(e)s, Späne>; *(of skin)* Schuppe [ˈʃʊpə] die <-, –n> ◊ *Die erkrankte Haut war mit juckenden Schuppen bedeckt.*

flame [noun] Flamme [ˈflamə] die <-, –n> ◊ *Sie versuchte, die Flammen mit einer Decke zu ersticken.* ◆ *die Flammen der Leidenschaft* go up in flames in Flammen aufgehen [ɪn ˈflamən aɔfɡeːən] <geht auf, ging auf, ist aufgegangen>

flannel [noun] **1.** *(cloth)* Flanell [flaˈnɛl] der <-s, –e> ◊ *ein Hemd aus Flanell; (in the UK, for washing)* Waschlappen [ˈvaʃlapm̩] der <-s, –> flannels Flanellhose [flaˈnɛlhoːzə] die <-, –n> ◊ *Er trägt zum Arbeiten eine alte Flanellhose.* **2.** *(fam) (in the UK, waffle)* Geschwafel [ɡəˈʃvaːfl̩] das <-s> no pl

flap¹ [noun] **1.** *(of a pocket, letterbox, tent)* Klappe [ˈklapə] die <-, –n> ◊ *Er hob die Klappe des Briefkastens.* flap of skin Hautfetzen [ˈhaɔtfɛtsn̩] der <-s, –> ◊ *einen Hautfetzen vorsichtig wegschneiden* **2.** *(fam) (excitement)* helle Aufregung [hɛlə ˈaɔfreːɡʊŋ] die <-> no pl ◊ *Alle waren wegen der Bombendrohung in heller Aufregung.* **3.** *(sound)* Flattern [ˈflatən] das <-s> no pl ◊ *Man hörte das Flattern großer Flügel.* ◆ *das Flattern der Segel im Wind* **4.** AVIAT Landeklappe [ˈlandəklapə] die <-, –n> ◊ *die Landeklappen ausfahren*

flap² [verb] **1.** *(flag, sail, coat)* flattern [ˈflatən] +haben ◊ *Die Fahne flattert im Wind.* flap its wings mit den Flügeln flattern ◊ *Der gefangene Vogel flatterte wild mit den Flügeln.* flap your arms mit den Armen rudern [mɪt den ˈaʳmən ruːdən] +haben ◊ *Er ruderte beim Laufen heftig mit den Armen.* **2.** *(fam) (get nervous)* sich aufregen [ˈaɔfreːɡn̩] +haben ◊ *Reg dich nicht auf!*

flare[1] [noun] 1. *(short flame)* Auflodern ['aoflo:dɐn] das <–s> no pl ◊ *das Auflodern des Feuers; (signal)* Leuchtrakete ['lɔɣçtra‚ke:tə] die <–, –n> ◊ *sich durch Leuchtraketen bemerkbar machen* 2. *(fashion)* ausgestellter Schnitt [‚aosgəʃtɛltə 'ʃnɪt] <–(e)s, –e> ◊ *Der ausgestellte Schnitt ist durchaus modern.* skirt with a flare ausgestellter Rock [‚aosgəʃtɛltə 'rɔk] <–(e)s, Röcke> flares Schlaghose ['ʃla:kho:zə] die <–, –n>

flare[2] [verb] 1. *(flame, anger, fighting)* auflodern ['aoflo:dɐn] +sein ◊ *Die Flammen loderten noch einmal auf, bevor sie erloschen.* ♦ *Die Kämpfe in der Krisenregion sind wieder aufgelodert.* 2. *(nostrils)* sich blähen ['blɛ:ən] +haben ◊ *Die Nüstern des Hengstes blähten sich.*

flash[1] [noun] 1. *(intense light, for photography)* Blitz [blɪts] der <–es, –e> ◊ *mit Blitz fotografieren* flash of lightning Blitz [blɪts] der <–es, –e> ◊ *Hast du den Blitz gesehen?* 2. flash of wit/inspiration Geistesblitz ['gaestəsblɪts] der <–es, –e> 3. *(of emotion)* flash of sth Anfall von etw. ['anfal fɔn] der <–(e)s, Anfälle> ◊ *In einem Anfall von Wut verbrannte er den Brief.* 4. *(emergence)* Aufblitzen ['aofblɪtsn̩] das <–s> no pl ◊ *das Aufblitzen eines Messers*
● a flash in the pan ein Strohfeuer in a flash wie der Blitz

flash[2] [verb] 1. *(shine very brightly, show an emotion)* blitzen ['blɪtsn̩] +haben ◊ *Die Diamanten blitzen und funkeln.* ♦ *Ihre Augen blitzten vor Wut.; (repeatedly)* blinken ['blɪŋkn̩] +haben ◊ *Die Kontrollleuchte blinkte rot.* flash your headlights at sb jdn anblinken ['anblɪŋkn̩] +haben ◊ *Warum blinkt mich der Fahrer hinter mir an?* 2. *(appear for a very short time)* huschen ['hoʃn̩] +sein ◊ *Ein Lächeln huschte über ihr Gesicht.; (a smile, glance)* flash sb sth jdm etw. zuwerfen ['tsu:vɛrfn̩] <wirft zu, warf zu, hat zugeworfen> ◊ *jdm einen Blick/ein Lächeln zuwerfen; (thought)* flash across your mind jdm durch den Kopf schießen [dʊrç de:n 'kɔpf ʃi:sn̩] <schießt, schoss, ist geschossen> ◊ *Ihm schoss der Gedanke durch den Kopf, dass ihr etwas passiert sein könnte.* 3. *(vehicle)* flash past vorbeisausen [fo:ɐ̯'baezaozn̩] +sein ◊ *Die Autos auf der Autobahn sausten vorbei.*
• **flash around** [phras v] protzen mit ['prɔtsn̩ mɪt] +haben ◊ *Er protzte mit seinem teuren Siegelring.*

flat[1] [noun] 1. *(appartment)* Wohnung ['vo:nʊŋ] die <–, –en> ◊ *eine Wohnung mit zwei Zimmern, Küche und Bad* ♦ *eine Wohnung mieten/suchen* 2. the flat of the/your hand die Handfläche ['hantflɛçə] <–, –n>; *(of a knife, blade)* flache Seite [‚flaxə 'zaetə] die <–, –n> ◊ *die flache Seite einer Klinge* 3. MUS in B, B [be:] das <–(s), –(s)> ◊ *En b vor einer Note erniedrigt diese um einen Halbton.* 4. GEOG flats Ebene ['e:bənə] die <–, –n> sing ◊ *Die Ebene dehnte sich bis zum Horizont aus.* 5. *(fam) (in the US: puncture)* Reifenpanne ['raefn̩panə] die <–, –en> 6. *(in the US: shoes)* flats flache Schuhe [‚flaxə 'ʃu:ə] <–> pl

flat[2] [adj] 1. *(even, smooth, outstretched, shoes, line, hierarchy)* flach [flax] ◊ *Das Land dort ist sehr flach.* ♦ *Sie trug flache Schuhe.* ♦ *ein Unternehmen mit flacher Hierarchie* 2. *(fixed)* pauschal [pao'ʃa:l] no comp/superl ◊ *eine pauschale Gebühr von fünf Euro im Monat* 3. *(voice)* ausdruckslos ['aosdrʊkslo:s] <ausdrucksloser, am ausdruckslosesten> ◊ *„Unser Hund wurde überfahren", sagte er mit seltsam aus-*

druckloser Stimme. 4. *(refusal, denial)* deutlich ['dɔɣtlɪç] ◊ *Sie erteilte ihm eine deutliche Absage.* 5. *(tyre)* platt [plat] <platter, am plattesten> ◊ *Das linke Vorderrad ist platt.* 6. *(battery)* leer [le:ɐ̯] ◊ *Ich glaube, die Batterien sind leer.* 7. *(drink)* schal [ʃa:l] ◊ *schales Bier* ♦ *Der Champagner ist/schmeckt schal.* 8. MUS *(voice, instrument)* um einen halben Ton erniedrigt [ʊm aenən ‚halbm to:n e'ni:drɪçt] C flat/D flat/E flat Ces/Des/Es [tsɛs/dɛs/ɛs] das <–, –> B flat B [be:] das <–s, –> ◊ *Das B ist einen halben Ton tiefer als das H.* 9. *(trade, business, market)* schwach [ʃvax] <schwächer, am schwächsten> ◊ *Im Vorjahr war der Markt schwächer.; (trade, business)* be flat eine Flaute haben [aenə 'flaotə ha:bm̩]

flat[3] [adv] 1. *(onto sth)* sich flach auf den Boden legen/werfen 2. MUS zu tief [tsu: 'ti:f] ◊ *zu tief singen/spielen* 3. *(fam)* in ten seconds/five minutes etc. flat in sage und schreibe zehn Sekunden/fünf Minuten etc. [ɪn ‚za:gə ʊnt ʃraebə ‚tse:n ze'kʊndn̩/fʏnf mi'nu:tn̩] *(fam)* ◊ *Er hat den Teller in sage und schreibe zwei Minuten leer gegessen.* 4. *(refuse etc.)* rundweg ['rʊntvɛk] no comp/superl ◊ *Man hat meinen Vorschlag rundweg abgelehnt.* flat broke total pleite [to‚ta:l 'plaetə] ◊ *Er ist wieder mal total pleite.* go flat against sb's advice jds Rat völlig ignorieren [‚ra:t fœlɪç ɪgno'ri:rən] <ignoriert, ignorierte, hat ignoriert> ◊ *Warum fragst du mich überhaupt, wenn du meinen Rat dann doch wieder völlig ignorierst?*
● fall flat scheitern

flatmate [noun] Mitbewohner ['mɪtbəvo:nɐ] der <–s, –> ◊ ♀Mitbewohnerin ['mɪtbəvo:nərɪn] die <–, –nen> ◊ *Mein Mitbewohner ist zurzeit in Urlaub.* ♦ *Sie hat eine neue Mitbewohnerin.*

flat rate [noun] Pauschale [pao'ʃa:lə] die <–, –n> ◊ *eine wöchentliche Pauschale von 20 Euro zahlen*

flavour, flavor [noun] 1. *(taste)* Geschmack [gə'ʃmak] der <–(e)s, Geschmäcke o fam hum Geschmäcker> ◊ *Beim Trocknen verliert Petersilie stark an Geschmack.* ♦ *ein milder/schaler/komischer Geschmack* 2. *(impression)* give the flavour of sth die Atmosphäre ... [gen]/von etw. vermitteln [di: atmo‚sfe:rə fɔn ... fɛmɪtl̩n] <vermittelt, vermittelte, hat vermittelt> ◊ *Der Film vermittelt die Atmosphäre des mittelalterlichen Paris.* 3. *(character)* Charakter [ka'rakte] der <–s, –> most sing ◊ *Seine Gedichte haben stark regionalen Charakter.*

flaw [noun] Fehler [fe:le] der <–s, –> ◊ *Jeder hat seine Fehler.* ♦ *Das Glas hat einen kleinen Fehler.* fatal flaw entscheidender Fehler [ɛnt‚ʃaednde 'fe:le]

flawless(ly) [adj, adv] *(performance, behavio(u)r, machine etc.)* einwandfrei ['aenvantfrae] <einwandfreier, am einwandfrei(e)sten> ◊ *Sein Verhalten war wie immer einwandfrei.* ♦ *Wir bieten Ihnen einwandfreie Ware.* ♦ *Der neue Computer funktioniert einwandfrei.; (skin)* makellos ['ma:kl̩lo:s] <makelloser, am makellosesten> ◊ *Sie hat einen makellosen Teint.; (diamond)* lupenrein ['lu:pm̩raen] no comp/superl ◊ *ein lupenreiner Diamant*

flea [noun] Floh [flo:] der <–(e)s, Flöhe> ◊ *von einem Floh gebissen werden*
● send sb off with a flea in his/her ear *(fam)* jdn wie einen begossenen Pudel abziehen lassen

flea market [noun] Flohmarkt ['flo:ma˞kt] der <–(e)s, Flohmärkte>

flee [verb] fliehen ['fli:ən] <flieht, floh, ist geflohen> ◊

Zwei der Diebe wurden gefasst; der dritte konnte fliehen. ♦ *Er floh über die Grenze nach Mexiko.* flee sth aus etw. fliehen ◊ *Sie war aus ihrem Heimatland geflohen.* flee your home von zu Hause fliehen

fleet [noun] **1.** *(specific group of ships, aircrafts, trains)* Flotte ['flotə] die <–, –n> ◊ *eine Flotte von Kriegsschiffen* ♦ *die Flotte der Lufthansa* fishing fleet Fischereiflotte [fɪʃ'raeflotə] **2.** *(sum of all vehicles owned by one organization)* Fuhrpark ['fu:ɐparⁿk] der <–s, –s>

flesh [noun] **1.** *(muscle tissue, fruit pulp)* Fleisch [flaeʃ] das <–(e)s> no pl ◊ *das Fleisch einer Avocado* **2.** *(skin)* Haut [haot] die <–> no pl ◊ *die sanfte Haut ihrer Wange*

ⓔ make sb's flesh creep jdm eine Gänsehaut über den Rücken jagen *(fam)* in the flesh in natura

flex [verb] **1.** *(a muscle)* anspannen ['anʃpanən] +haben ◊ *Er spannte seine Muskeln an.* **2.** *(your knee, arm)* beugen ['bɔɡŋ] +haben ◊ *die Knie beugen*

flexibility [noun] **1.** *(adaptability)* Flexibilität [flɛksibili'tɛːt] die <–> no pl ◊ *sich durch Kundennähe und Flexibilität auszeichnen* **2.** *(of the body)* Beweglichkeit [bə've:klɪçkaet] die <–> no pl ◊ *Diese Übung trainiert die Beweglichkeit des Körpers.; (of an object)* Biegsamkeit ['bi:kza:mkaet] die <–> no pl ◊ *die Biegsamkeit des Materials*

flexible [adj] **1.** *(able to change)* flexibel [flɛ'ksi:bl̩] <flexibler, am flexibelsten> <der/die/das flexible …> ◊ *eine flexible Mitarbeiterin* ♦ *Die Arbeitszeiten sind flexibel.* **2.** *(body)* beweglich [bə've:klɪç] ◊ *Gymnastik macht beweglich.* ♦ *ein beweglicher Körper; (object)* biegsam ['bi:kza:m] ◊ *Das Material ist sehr biegsam.* ♦ *ein biegsamer Schlauch*

flick [verb] **1.** *(move sth quickly with your hand)* schnippen ['ʃnɪpm̩] +haben ◊ *Er schnippte den Staub von seinem Ärmel.* flick back zurückwerfen [tsu'rʏkvɛˑfn] <wirft zurück, warf zurück, hat zurückgeworfen> ◊ *Sie warf ihre langen Haare zurück.* flick open aufschlagen ['aofʃlaːɡŋ] <schlägt auf, schlug auf, hat aufgeschlagen> ◊ *Er schlug das Buch auf.* **2.** *(hit sharply and quickly)* schlagen ['ʃlaːɡŋ] <schlägt, schlug, ist geschlagen> ◊ *A branch flicked across his face.* Ein Ast schlug ihm ins Gesicht. **3.** *(turn on)* flick on anknipsen ['anknɪpsn̩] +haben *(fam)* ◊ *Die Kinder knipsen das Licht an.; (turn off)* flick off ausknipsen ['aosknɪpsn̩] +haben *(fam)* ◊ *Sie knipste den Fernseher aus.* **4.** *(look quickly at sth)* sb's eyes flick across sth jd überfliegt etw. [ybɐ'fli:kt] <überflog, hat überflogen> ◊ *Sie überflog den Fahrplan.* flick a glance at sb/sth einen Blick auf jdn/etw. werfen [aenən ,blɪk aof … vɛˑfn] <wirft, warf, hat geworfen>

• **flick through** [phras v] **1.** *(a newspaper, book)* durchblättern ['dʊɐçblɛtɐn] +haben ◊ *Sie blättert den Katalog durch.* **2.** *(TV channels)* flick through sth durch etw. zappen [dʊ'ɐç … tsapm̩] +haben *(fam)* ◊ *durch die Programme/Sender zappen*

flicker [verb] **1.** *(light)* flackern ['flakɐn] +haben ◊ *Die Kerze flackerte und ging dann aus.; (TV)* flimmern ['flɪmɐn] +haben ◊ *Bunte Bilder flimmern über den Bildschirm.* **2.** *(eyelid)* flattern ['flatɐn] +haben **3.** a smile flickers across/on sb's lips ein Lächeln umspielt jds Lippen [aen 'lɛçln̩ ʊmʃpiːlt … ,lɪpm̩] <umspielte, hat umspielt>

flight [noun] **1.** *(journey through air or space, movement in air)* Flug [flu:k] der <–(e)s, Flüge> ◊ *Wir haben einen Flug nach Athen gebucht.* in flight im Flug ◊

Schwalben fangen ihre Beute im Flug. scheduled flight Linienflug ['li:njənflu:k] flight schedule Flugplan ['flu:kplaːn] der <–(e)s, Flugpläne> **2.** *(ability to fly)* Flugfähigkeit ['flu:kfɛːɪçkaet] die <–> no pl ◊ *die Entwicklung der Flugfähigkeit von Vögeln* **3.** *(escape)* Flucht [flʊxt] die <–, –en> most sing take flight die Flucht ergreifen put sb to flight jdn in die Flucht schlagen **4.** flight (of stairs/steps) Treppe ['trɛpə] die <–, –n> ◊ *Ihre Wohnung liegt zwei Treppen höher.*

ⓔ flight of fancy Hirngespinst

fling¹ [noun] **1.** *(affair)* Affäre [a'fɛːrə] die <–, –n> ◊ *eine Affäre mit jdm haben* **2.** *(time when you have fun)* Spaß [ʃpaːs] der <–es> no pl ◊ *seinen Spaß haben* have a final fling noch einmal Spaß haben

fling² [verb] **1.** *(throw)* werfen ['vɛˑfn] <wirft, warf, hat geworfen> ◊ *Sie warf ihre Tasche in die Ecke.* ♦ *sich aufs Bett/auf den Boden werfen* ♦ *Das Kind warf seine Arme um ihren Hals.* fling yourself into sth sich in etw. [acc] stürzen [ɪn … ʃtʏ'tsn̩] +haben ◊ *sich in die Arbeit stürzen* **2.** *(say sth hurtful)* fling sth at sb jdm etw. entgegenschleudern [ɛnt'ge:ɡŋʃlɔøden] <schleudert entgegen, schleuderte entgegen, hat entgegengeschleudert> ◊ *Sie schleuderte ihm Beleidigungen entgegen.* **3.** *(quickly open)* fling sth open etw. aufreißen ['aofraesn̩] <reißt auf, riss auf, hat aufgerissen> ◊ *Er riss plötzlich die Tür auf.*

• **fling off** [phras v] fling sth off *(your clothes)* sich [dat] etw. vom Leib reißen [fɔm 'laep raesn̩] <reißt sich, riss sich, hat sich gerissen> ◊ *Ich riss mir das nasse Kleid vom Leib.* fling off your hat den Hut vom Kopf reißen

• **fling on** [phras v] fling sth on *(your clothes)* in etw. [acc] schlüpfen [ɪn … ʃlʏpfn̩] +sein ◊ *Sie schlüpfte in die Jacke und rannte zur Tür hinaus.*

• **fling out** [phras v] fling sb out jdn rauswerfen ['raosvɛˑfn] <wirft raus, warf raus, hat rausgeworfen> *(fam)* ◊ *Wirf ihn doch raus!*

flirt¹ [noun] *Person, die gern flirtet* be a flirt flirten ['flɪˑtn̩] <flirtet, flirtete, hat geflirtet>

flirt² [verb] **1.** *(with a person)* flirten ['flɪˑtn̩] <flirtet, flirtete, hat geflirtet> ◊ *Er hat den ganzen Abend mit ihr geflirtet.* **2.** *(with an idea)* spielen ['ʃpiːlən] +haben ◊ *Ich spiele mit dem Gedanken, mir ein Auto zu kaufen.*

flirtation [noun] Flirt [flɪˑt] der <–s, –s> ◊ *Er ist zu schüchtern für einen Flirt.* ♦ *ein Flirt mit der Macht*

float [verb] **1.** *(not sink)* schwimmen ['ʃvɪmən] <schwimmt, schwamm, ist geschwommen> ◊ *Holz schwimmt.* **2.** *(drift)* treiben ['traebm̩] <treibt, trieb, ist getrieben> ◊ *Sieh mal, da treibt ein Fass im Fluss!* float by vorbeitreiben [foˑɡ'baetraebm̩] <treibt vorbei, trieb vorbei, ist vorbeigetrieben> ◊ *Ein Eisberg trieb vorbei.; (person)* sich treiben lassen ['traebm̩ lasn̩] <lässt sich, ließ sich, hat sich … lassen> ◊ *sich im Wasser/durchs Leben treiben lassen* **3.** *(let sth drift)* schwimmen lassen ['ʃvɪmən lasn̩] <lässt, ließ, hat lassen> ◊ *Er ließ ein Papierschiffchen auf dem Teich schwimmen.* **4.** *(move through the air, move gracefully)* schweben ['ʃve:bm̩] +sein ◊ *Seifenblasen schwebten in der Luft.* ♦ *Sie schwebte durch den Tanzsaal.* **5.** *(music)* float from sth aus etw. dringen [aos … drɪŋən] <dringt, drang, ist gedrungen> ◊ *Leise Musik drang aus der Bar.* Music floated through the air. Musik lag in der Luft. **6.** ECON, FIN float a company ein Unternehmen an die

Börse bringen [a̯en ʊnte,ne:mən an di: 'bœʳzə brɪŋən] <bringt, brachte, hat gebracht> **7.** *(a proposal, scheme, an idea)* in den Raum stellen [ɪn de:n 'ra̯ɔm ʃtɛlən] *+haben ◊ Ich möchte gern einen Vorschlag in den Raum stellen.* float sth to sb jdm etw. unterbreiten [ʊnte'bra̯etn̩] <unterbreitet, unterbreitete, hat unterbreitet> **8.** FIN *(a currency)* freigeben ['fra̯ege:bn̩] <gibt frei, gab frei, hat freigegeben>

• **float around** phras v **1.** *(lie around)* herumliegen [hɛ'rʊmli:gn̩] <liegt herum, lag herum, hat herumgelegen> *◊ Hier liegt irgendwo ein Kuli herum.* **2.** *(circulate)* im Umlauf sein [ɪm 'ʊmla̯ɔf za̯en] *+sein ◊ Die Idee ist schon lange im Umlauf.*

floating adj schwankend ['ʃvaŋkn̩t] *no comp/superl, mostly before ns ◊ ein schwankender Wechselkurs* be floating schwanken ['ʃvaŋkn̩] *+haben ◊ Die Produktionsmenge schwankt.*

flock noun *(of sheep, goats)* Herde ['he:ɐ̯də] die <–, –n> *◊ ein Schäfer mit seiner Herde* flock of sheep Schafherde ['ʃa:fhe:ɐ̯də]*; (of flying birds)* Schwarm [ʃvaʳm] der <–(e)s, Schwärme> *◊ ein Schwarm Krähen; (of farm birds, people)* Schar [ʃa:ʳ] die <–, –en> *◊ eine Schar Gänse ♦ Scharen von Menschen*

flog verb **1.** *(with a whip)* auspeitschen ['a̯ɔspa̯etʃn̩] *+haben ◊ Er peitschte den Gefangenen aus.; (with a stick)* mit einem Stock schlagen [mɪt a̯enəm 'ʃtɔk ʃla:gn̩] <schlägt, schlug, hat geschlagen> **2.** *(sell)* verscherbeln [fɛ'ʃɛʳbl̩n] <verscherbelt, verscherbelte, hat verscherbelt> *(fam) ◊ Ich habe mein altes Auto verscherbelt.*

flood¹ noun **1.** *(large amount of water)* Hochwasser ['ho:xvase] das <–s, –> *most sing ◊ Starke Regenfälle führten zu Hochwasser.* be in flood Hochwasser führen **2.** *(large amount of sth or of people)* Flut [flu:t] die <–, –en> *◊ eine wahre Flut von Briefen/Erinnerungen*

◉ **in floods of tears** tränenüberströmt **in full flood** in vollem Gang

flood² verb **1.** *(cover or fill with water, letters, complaints etc.)* flood sth etw. überschwemmen [ybe'ʃvɛmən] <überschwemmt, überschwemmte, hat überschwemmt> *◊ Der Fluss überschwemmte die Straße. ♦ den Markt mit Billigware überschwemmen* sth is flooding etw. wird überschwemmt*; (river)* über die Ufer treten [y:be di: 'u:fe tre:tn̩] <tritt, trat, ist getreten> *◊ Der Rhein ist über die Ufer getreten.; (water)* flood in eindringen ['a̯endrɪŋən] <dringt ein, drang ein, ist eingedrungen> *◊ Das Wasser drang durch ein Leck in das Schiff ein.* **2.** *(light)* flood (into) sth etw. durchfluten [dʊʳç'flu:tn̩] <durchflutet, durchflutete, hat durchflutet> *◊ Sonnenlicht durchflutete das Zimmer.* **3.** *(people)* strömen ['ʃtrø:mən] *+sein ◊ Massen von Flüchtlingen strömen ins Nachbarland.* flood back zurückströmen [tsurʏk'ʃtrø:mən] *+haben* **4.** *(engine)* absaufen ['apza̯ɔfn̩] <säuft ab, soff ab, ist abgesoffen> *(fam) ◊ Der Motor ist mir abgesoffen.* **5.** *(emotions)* durchströmen [dʊʳç'ʃtrø:mən] <durchströmt, durchströmte, hat durchströmt> *◊ Ein wohliges Gefühl durchströmte sie.*

floodlight noun Scheinwerfer ['ʃa̯envɛʳfe] der <–s, –> *◊ Der Kirchturm wird nachts von Scheinwerfern beleuchtet.*

floor noun **1.** *(ground)* Boden ['bo:dn̩] der <–s, Böden> *◊ Er hob das Papier vom Boden auf. ♦ den Boden putzen* ocean/sea floor Meeresboden ['me:rəsbo:dn̩] valley floor Talsohle ['ta:lzo:lə] die <–, –n> (dance) floor Tanzfläche ['tantsflɛçə] die <–, –n> **2.** *(storey)* Stockwerk ['ʃtɔkvɛʳk] das <–(e)s, –e> *◊ Das Haus hat drei Stockwerke.; (in the UK)* first floor erster Stock [,e:ɐ̯ste 'ʃtɔk] <–(e)s, Stöcke> *◊ Der erste Stock ist völlig ausgebrannt.; (in the US)* first floor Erdgeschoss ['e:ɐ̯tgəʃɔs] das <–es, –e>*; (in the UK)* ground floor Erdgeschoss ['e:ɐ̯tgəʃɔs] **3.** *(for debates)* Saal [za:l] der <–(e)s, Säle> **4.** *(lowest level)* Untergrenze ['ʊntegrɛntsə] die <–, –n>

◉ **go through the floor** in den Keller fallen *(fam)* **have the floor** das Wort haben **take the floor** **1.** *(start talking)* das Wort ergreifen **2.** *(start dancing)* sich aufs Parkett begeben

floorboard noun **1.** *(wooden)* Diele ['di:lə] die <–, –n> *◊ Die Dielen knarrten.* **2.** *(in the US: of a car)* Boden ['bo:dn̩] der <–s, Böden> *◊ Der Boden ist durchgerostet.*

flop¹ noun **1.** *(failure, disappointment)* Flop [flɔp] der <–s, –s> *(fam) ◊ Ihr neues Album erwies sich als totaler Flop.* **2.** *(fall of sth soft)* Plumps [plʊmps] der <–es, –e> *(fam) ◊ Sie sank mit einem Plumps in den Sessel.*

flop² verb **1.** *(sit, lie down)* sich fallen lassen ['falən lasn̩] <lässt sich, ließ sich, hat sich … lassen> *◊ Müde ließ er sich aufs Sofa fallen.* **2.** *(hang loosely)* hängen ['hɛŋən] <hängt, hing, hat gehangen> sb's hair flops over their face jds Haar hängt ihm im Gesicht*; (fall)* fallen ['falən] <fällt, fiel, ist gefallen> sb's hair flops over their face jds Haar fällt ihm ins Gesicht **3.** *(be a failure or disappointment)* durchfallen ['dʊʳçfalən] <fällt durch, fiel durch, ist durchgefallen> *(fam)* flop with sb bei jdm durchfallen *◊ Sein neues Stück ist beim Publikum durchgefallen.*

floppy disk noun Diskette [dɪs'kɛtə] die <–, –n> *◊ etw. auf Diskette speichern*

flour noun Mehl [me:l] das <–(e)s, –e> *most sing ◊ ein Päckchen Mehl* wheat flour Weizenmehl ['va̯etsn̩me:l]

flourish verb **1.** *(thrive, be healthy)* gedeihen [gə'da̯eən] <gedeiht, gedieh, ist gediehen> *◊ Die Pflanze gedeiht besonders in sonnigen Lagen.; (business, economy)* florieren [flo'ri:rən] <floriert, florierte, hat floriert> *◊ Die Wirtschaft floriert.* **2.** *(wave sth in the air)* flourish sth etw. schwenken ['ʃvɛŋkn̩] *+haben ◊ Er schwenkte drohend seinen Stock.*

flow¹ noun **1.** *(continuous movement, supply, activity)* Strom [ʃtro:m] der <–(e)s, Ströme> *◊ ein Strom von Menschen in Eile* blood flow Blutstrom ['blu:tʃtro:m] flow of water Wasserstrom ['vaseʃtro:m] traffic flow Verkehrsfluss [fɛ'ke:ɐ̯sflʊs] der <–es, Verkehrsflüsse> *most sing* flow of information Informationsfluss [ɪnfoʳma'tsi̯o:nsflʊs] flow of thoughts Gedankenfluss [gə'daŋkn̩flʊs] work flow Arbeitsablauf ['aʳba̯etsǀapla̯ɔf] der <–(e)s, Arbeitsabläufe> **2.** *(rising tide)* Flut [flu:t] die <–, –en> *◊ Ebbe und Flut*

◉ **go with the flow** mit dem Strom schwimmen

flow² verb **1.** *(liquid, electricity, traffic, money, words, information)* fließen ['fli:sn̩] <fließt, floss, ist geflossen> *◊ Der Rhein fließt ins Meer. ♦ Die Worte flossen ihr leicht und schnell aus der Feder.* Beer flowed freely. Das Bier floss in Strömen.*; (ideas)*

sprudeln ['ʃpruːdln̩] +sein ◊ *Jetzt sprudeln die Ideen wieder.* **2.** *(people)* strömen ['ʃtrøːmən] +sein ◊ *Menschenmassen strömten ins Stadion.* **3.** *(conversation)* verlaufen [fɛ'laofn̩] <verläuft, verlief, ist verlaufen> ◊ *Das Gespräch verlief locker und heiter.* **4.** *(feeling)* flow through sb jdn überkommen [ybɐ'kɔmən] <überkommt, überkam, hat überkommen> ◊ *Ein Gefühl tiefer Zuneigung überkam sie.* **5.** *(dress, hair)* fallen ['falən] <fällt, fiel, ist gefallen> ◊ *Das Kleid fällt sehr schön.*

flower [noun] *(blossom)* Blüte ['blyːtə] die <-, -n> ◊ *Der Baum hatte rosa Blüten.; (plant on a stalk)* Blume ['bluːmə] die <-, -n> ◊ *Wir haben der Gastgeberin Blumen mitgebracht.* be in flower blühen ['blyːən] +haben ◊ *Die Kirschbäume blühen.*
⊛ in the flower of his/her youth/years in der Blüte seiner/ihrer Jugend/Jahre

flu [noun] Grippe ['grɪpə] die <-, -n> most sing ◊ *sich gegen Grippe impfen lassen*

fluctuate [verb] schwanken ['ʃvaŋkn̩] +haben ◊ *Die Preise schwanken zwischen 15 und 20 Euro.*

fluctuation [noun] Schwankung ['ʃvaŋkʊŋ] die <-, -en> ◊ *Die Besucherzahlen unterliegen starken Schwankungen.*

fluent(ly) [adj, adv] **1.** *(language, movements)* fließend ['fliːsn̩t] no comp/superl ◊ *ein Vortrag in fließendem Englisch* ◊ *Seine Bewegungen sind fließend.* ◆ *eine Sprache fließend sprechen* be fluent in German fließend Deutsch sprechen **2.** *(eloquent)* gewandt [gə'vant] <gewandter, am gewandtesten> seldom comp/superl ◊ *eine gewandte Rednerin* ◆ *Er ist sehr gewandt im Umgang mit Worten.* ◆ *sich gewandt ausdrücken*

fluid [noun] Flüssigkeit ['flʏsɪçkaet] die <-, -en> ◊ *große Mengen Flüssigkeit zu sich nehmen* brake fluid Bremsflüssigkeit ['brɛmsflʏsɪçkaet]

flush [verb] **1.** *(turn red)* rot werden ['roːt veːɐdn̩] +sein ◊ *Als sie ihn sah, wurde sie rot.* flush with sth vor etw. [dat] rot werden ◊ *vor Scham rot werden* ◆ *Seine Wangen wurden rot vor Anstrengung.* **2.** *(the toilet, a pipe etc.)* spülen ['ʃpyːlən] +haben ◊ *Vergiss nicht zu spülen, wenn du fertig bist.* ◆ *die Toilette/Rohre spülen* flush sth down sth etw. etw. hinunterspülen [hɪ'nʊntɐʃpyːlən] +haben ◊ *Spül bitte keine Essensreste die Toilette hinunter!; (clean with water)* flush sth out etw. ausspülen [aos'ʃpyːlən] +haben ◊ *Rohre spülen; (remove with water)* herausspülen [hɛ'raosʃpyːlən] +haben ◊ *Der Tee spült Giftstoffe heraus.* **3.** *(an animal, a person)* aufscheuchen ['aofʃɔøçn̩] +haben ◊ *Die Jäger scheuchten das Reh aus seinem Versteck auf.*
• **flush out** [phras v] *(force to leave a hiding place)* aufscheuchen ['aofʃɔøçn̩] +haben ◊ *Die Hunde scheuchten den Fuchs aus seinem Versteck auf.* → flush 2.

flute [noun] Flöte ['fløːtə] die <-, -n> ◊ *ein Lied auf der Flöte spielen*

flutter [verb] *(move, flap)* flattern ['flatən] +haben/with indication of direction +sein ◊ *Der Schmetterling ist von Blüte zu Blüte geflattert.* ◆ *Seine Hände flatterten nervös.* flutter your hands mit den Händen flattern The bird fluttered its wings. Der Vogel flatterte mit den Flügeln.; *(a flag)* schwenken ['ʃvɛŋkn̩] +haben ◊ *Die Fans schwenkten Fahnen.*

fly¹ [noun] *(insect, fish hook)* Fliege ['fliːgə] die <-, -n> ◊ *Ein paar Fliegen schwirrten in der Küche*

berum. plague of flies Fliegenplage ['fliːgn̩plaːgə] die <-, -n>
⊛ the (only) fly in the ointment der (einzige) Haken bei der Sache *(fam)* be a fly on the wall Mäuschen spielen *(fam)* drop like flies umfallen wie die Fliegen *(fam)* sb wouldn't hurt a fly jd kann keiner Fliege etw. zuleide tun *(fam)* on the fly auf die Schnelle *(fam)*

fly² [verb] **1.** *(move through the air or space)* fliegen ['fliːgn̩] <fliegt, flog, hat/ist geflogen> transitive use +haben/intransitive use +sein ◊ *Der Vogel ist auf einen Baum geflogen.* ◆ *Welcher Pilot hat die Maschine geflogen?* ◆ *Der Ball flog ins Tor.* ◆ *Ich fliege mit der Lufthansa.* fly (sb/sth) to London/Berlin (jdn/etw.) nach London/Berlin fliegen fly into Tegel/Heathrow etc. nach Tegel/Heathrow etc. fliegen fly (sb/sth) to an area/country (jdn/etw.) in ein Gebiet/Land fliegen ◊ *Hilfsgüter ins Krisengebiet fliegen* fly the Atlantic über den Atlantik fliegen fly sb/sth in jdn/etw. einfliegen ['aenfliːgn̩] <fliegt ein, flog ein, hat eingeflogen> ◊ *Truppen fliegen Lebensmittel ein.* fly sb/sth out jdn/etw. ausfliegen ['aosfliːgn̩] <fliegt aus, flog aus, hat ausgeflogen> ◊ *Die Rettungsmannschaft fliegt Verletzte aus.* fly past vorbeifliegen [foːɐ'baefliːgn̩] <fliegt vorbei, flog vorbei, ist vorbeigeflogen> ◊ *Ein Vogel flog vorbei.* **2.** *(door, window)* fly open auffliegen ['aoffliːgn̩] <fliegt auf, flog auf, ist aufgeflogen> ◊ *Plötzlich flog die Tür auf.* **3.** *(move quickly)* fly into a room in ein Zimmer stürzen [ɪn aen 'tsɪmə ʃtʏrtsn̩] +sein fly along a hallway einen Flur entlangeilen [aenən 'fluːɐ ɛnt,laŋ|aelən] +sein fly into sb's arms jdm um den Hals fallen [ʊm deːn 'hals falən] <fällt, fiel, ist gefallen> fly into each other's arms sich [dat] um den Hals fallen **4.** *(be moved by the wind)* wehen ['veːən] +haben ◊ *Vor dem Gebäude wehte eine Fahne.* fly a flag eine Flagge hissen [aenə 'flagə gɪhɪst haːbm̩] +haben ◊ *Das Rathaus hat die Europaflagge gehisst.* fly a kite einen Drachen steigen lassen [aenən 'draxn̩ ʃtaegn̩ lasn̩] <lässt, ließ, hat lassen> **5.** *(time)* fly (by/past) wie im Flug vergehen [viː ɪm 'fluːk fɛgeːən] <vergeht, verging, ist vergangen> ◊ *Die Zeit verging wie im Flug.* **6.** *(rumo(u)r, idea etc.)* fly (around/about) die Runde machen [diː 'rɔndə maxn̩] +haben ◊ *Wilde Gerüchte machen die Runde.* **7.** *(flee)* fly sth aus etw. fliehen [aos ... ˌfliːən] <flieht, floh, ist geflohen> ◊ *Als der Krieg ausbrach, flohen viele Menschen aus dem Land.*
⊛ I must fly ich muss los *(fam)*
• **fly at** [phras v] fly at sb sich auf jdn stürzen [aof ... ʃtʏrtsn̩] +haben ◊ *Sie stürzte sich wütend auf ihn.*

flyer [noun] **1.** *(advertisement)* Handzettel ['hanttsɛtl̩] der <-s, -> ◊ *Handzettel verteilen* **2.** *(pilot)* Flieger ['fliːgə] der <-s, -> ♀Fliegerin ['fliːgərɪn] die <-, -nen> ◊ *Er ist Flieger bei der Luftwaffe.; (passenger)* frequent flyer Vielflieger ['fiːlfliːgə] Vielfliegerin ['fiːlfliːgərɪn] **3.** *(object or animal that can fly)* Flieger ['fliːgə] der <-s, -> ◊ *Wellensittiche sind gute Flieger.*

foam [noun] **1.** *(bubbles on liquid)* Schaum [ʃaom] der <-(e)s, Schäume> most sing ◊ *Auf dem Wasser hat sich Schaum gebildet.* insulating foam Isolierschaum [izo'liːɐʃaom] **2.** *(rubber or plastic substance)* Schaumstoff ['ʃaomʃtɔf] der <-(e)s, -e> most sing ◊ *einen*

A
B
C
D
E
F
G
H
I
J
K
L
M
N
O
P
Q
R
S
T
U
V
W
X
Y
Z

Stubl mit Schaumstoff polstern foam mattress Schaumstoffmatratze ['ʃaomʃtɔfma,tratsə] die <-, -n>

focal point [noun] **1.** *(centre of attention)* Mittelpunkt ['mɪtl̩pʊŋkt] der <-(e)s, -e> ◊ *Das Kind ist Mittelpunkt der Familie.* **2.** PHYSICS Brennpunkt ['brɛnpʊŋkt] der <-(e)s, -e> ◊ *Lichtstrahlen, die in einem Brennpunkt zusammentreffen*

focus¹ [noun] **1.** *(main point)* (main/major) focus Schwerpunkt ['ʃveːɡpʊŋkt] der <-(e)s, -e> ◊ *der Schwerpunkt unserer Arbeit* focus of concern zentrales Problem [tsɛn,traːləs proˈbleːm] <-s, -e> ◊ *Dies ist das zentrale Problem bei der Sache.* be the focus of attention im Mittelpunkt des Interesses stehen [ɪm ˈmɪtl̩pʊŋkt dɛs ɪntəˌrɛsəs ʃteːən] <steht, stand, hat gestanden> **2.** *(attention, consideration)* Beachtung [bəˈʔaxtʊŋ] die <-> no pl more/greater focus on sth stärkere Beachtung ... [gen] ◊ *eine stärkere Beachtung der Menschenrechte* put a strong focus on sth einer Sache [dat] besondere Beachtung schenken shift the focus towards sth, bring sth into focus die Aufmerksamkeit auf etw. [acc] lenken [diː ˌaofmɛrˈkzaːmkaet aof ... lɛŋkn̩] +haben **3.** *(aim, purpose)* Ziel [tsiːl] das <-(e)s, -e> ◊ *Unsere Arbeit hat ein klares Ziel.* lose your focus sein Ziel aus den Augen verlieren lack focus ziellos sein ['tsiːlloːs zaen] +sein **4.** FOTO, FILM Schärfe ['ʃɛrfə] die <-> no pl ◊ *Du musst beim Fotografieren immer auf die Schärfe achten.* be in focus scharf sein ['ʃarf zaen] +sein be out of focus unscharf sein **5.** PHYSICS Brennpunkt ['brɛnpʊŋkt] der <-(e)s, -e>

focus² [verb] **1.** *(concentrate)* focus (your mind) (on sth) sich (auf etw. [acc]) konzentrieren [kɔntsɛnˈtriːrən] <konzentriert sich, konzentrierte sich, hat sich konzentriert> ◊ *sich auf eine Aufgabe konzentrieren* ♦ *Bitte versuch dich zu konzentrieren.* focus your attention on sth seine Aufmerksamkeit auf etw. [acc] richten [zaenə ˌaofmɛrˈkzaːmkaet aof ... rɪçtn̩] focus your efforts on sth seine Anstrengungen auf etw. [acc] richten **2.** *(camera)* scharf stellen ['ʃarf ʃtɛlən] +haben ◊ *seine Kamera scharf stellen; (not see clearly)* sb/sb's eyes can't focus jd sieht alles verschwommen [ziːt aləs fɛʃˈvɔmən] <sah, hat gesehen>; *(point your camera at, look at)* focus sth on sb/sth etw. auf jdn/etw. richten [aof ... rɪçtn̩] <richtet, richtete, hat gerichtet> ◊ *seine Kamera/Augen auf jdn/etw. richten* sth focuses on sb/sth etw. ist auf jdn/etw. gerichtet **3.** *(lens, mirror)* bündeln ['byndl̩n] +haben ◊ *Die Linse bündelt die Strahlen.* The rays of light focus on the retina. Die Lichtstrahlen werden auf der Netzhaut gebündelt.

fog [noun] *(dense mist)* Nebel ['neːbl̩] der <-s, -> ◊ *dichter Nebel* There are patches of fog. Es gibt stellenweise Nebel. blanket of fog Nebeldecke ['neːbl̩dɛkə] die <-, -n> fog of smoke Rauchschwaden ['raoxʃvaːdn̩] der <-> pl
● fog of sleep Schlaftrunkenheit be in a fog verwirrt sein

foggy [adj] **1.** *(weather)* neblig ['neːblɪç] seldom comp/superl ◊ *ein nebliger Novembertag* ♦ *Heute ist es neblig.* **2.** foggy with sleep schlaftrunken ['ʃlaːftrʊŋkn̩] ◊ *Sie war noch schlaftrunken, als sie sich an den Frühstückstisch setzte.* **3.** *(not clear, confused)* nebelhaft ['neːbl̩haft] no comp/superl, mostly before ns ◊ *eine nebelhafte Erinnerung* not

have the foggiest idea keinen blassen Schimmer haben [kaenən blasn̩ ˈʃɪmɐ haːbm̩] +haben *(fam)*

foil [noun] **1.** *(thin sheet of metal)* Folie ['foːliə] die <-, -n> ◊ *Kartoffel in Folie garen* **2.** *(point of contrast)* foil (for sth/sb) Kontrast (zu etw./jdm) [kɔnˈtrast] der <-(e)s, -e> ◊ *Der schlichte Rock bildet einen schönen Kontrast zur Pelzjacke.*

fold¹ [noun] **1.** *(in paper, fabric etc.)* Falte ['faltə] die <-, -n> ◊ *die Falten eines Vorhangs* fold of fat Fettwulst ['fɛtvʊlst] der <-(e)s, Fettwülste> **2.** *(for sheep)* Pferch [pfɛrç] der <-(e)s, -e> **3.** *(group)* Lager ['laːgɐ] das <-s, -> ◊ *das konservative/kommunistische Lager* family fold Schoß der Familie [ˌʃoːs deːɡ faˈmiːliə] der <-es> no pl *(lit)*

fold² [verb] **1.** *(a piece of paper, fabric, your hands etc.)* falten ['faltn̩] <faltet, faltete, hat gefaltet> ◊ *Er faltete den Brief und steckte ihn in den Umschlag.* ♦ *die Hände falten* fold sth in half etw. in der Mitte falten; *(a piece of paper, your clothes)* fold sth up etw. zusammenfalten [tsuˈzamn̩faltn̩] <faltet zusammen, faltete zusammen, hat zusammengefaltet> ◊ *Er faltete sein Hemd zusammen.* fold your arms die Arme verschränken [diː ˈarmə fɛʃˈrɛŋkn̩] <verschränkt, verschränkte, hat verschränkt>; *(a chair, knife etc.)* fold sth etw. zusammenklappen [tsuˈzamn̩klapm̩] +haben ◊ *Er klappte das Taschenmesser zusammen.* sth folds etw. lässt sich zusammenklappen ◊ *Der Tisch lässt sich zusammenklappen.* fold down herunterklappen [hɛˈrʊntɐklapm̩] +haben ◊ *Er klappte die Armlehne herunter.* fold up hochklappen ['hoːxklapm̩] +haben ◊ *Sie klappte die Tischplatte hoch.* **2.** *(wrap)* fold sth in sth, fold sth around sth etw. in etw. [acc] einschlagen [ɪn ... aenʃlaːgn̩] <schlägt ein, schlug ein, hat eingeschlagen> ◊ *Er schlug das Geschenk in Papier ein.* **3.** *(legs)* fold (under you) (unter jdm) nachgeben ['naːxgeːbm̩] <gibt nach, gab nach, hat nachgegeben> ◊ *Meine Beine gaben unter mir nach.*

folder [noun] **1.** *(for documents, sheets)* Mappe ['mapə] die <-, -n> ◊ *etw. in eine Mappe legen* **2.** IT Ordner ['ɔrdnɐ] der <-s, -> ◊ *einen Ordner anlegen*

folk [noun] **1.** *(people in general, group of people)* folk(s) Leute ['lɔøtə] die <-> only pl *(also fam)* ◊ *junge Leute* ♦ *Ich muss jetzt gehen, Leute.* **2.** *(in the US: parents)* folks Eltern ['ɛltɐn] die <-> pl ◊ *Seine Eltern kommen morgen zu Besuch.* **3.** MUS *(traditional music)* Volksmusik ['fɔlksmuˌziːk] die <-> no pl ◊ *deutsche Volksmusik; (from North America or the British Isles)* Folk [foːk] der <-s> no pl

follow [verb] **1.** *(pursue, come after, go somewhere, understand)* folgen ['fɔlgn̩] +sein ◊ *Sie ist vorausgefahren und ich bin gefolgt.* follow sb/sth jdm/etw. folgen ◊ *Ist dir jemand gefolgt?* ♦ *Folgen Sie den Schildern!* ♦ *Ich hoffe, Sie konnten meinen Ausführungen folgen.* ♦ *Wir gehen wie folgt vor: ...* sth is followed by sth etw. folgt auf etw. [acc] ◊ *Auf den Vortrag folgt eine Diskussion.* the days/years that followed die folgenden Tage/Jahre there followed ... es folgte/folgten ... ◊ *Es folgten lange Jahre der Entbehrung.* follow sth with sth einer Sache [dat] etw. folgen lassen ◊ *Ihrem ersten Erfolg ließ sie weitere Bestseller folgen.* sth is easy/difficult to follow man kann einer Sache [dat] leicht/kaum folgen sth follows from sth etw. folgt aus etw. ◊ *Aus diesem Bericht folgt, dass es dem Unternehmen wieder besser geht.* it follows that ... daraus folgt, dass ...

follow suit das Gleiche tun [das ˈglaeçə tuːn] <tut, tat, hat getan> 2. *(watch, listen closely to)* verfolgen [fɛˈfɔlgn̩] <verfolgt, verfolgte, hat verfolgt> ◊ *Sie verfolgte jede seiner Bewegungen.* ♦ *Er verfolgte aufmerksam jedes Wort.*; *(tell a story)* erzählen [ɛˈtsɛːlən] <erzählt, erzählte, hat erzählt> ◊ *Der Roman erzählt die Geschichte der Scarlett O'Hara.*; *(as a fan)* follow sth Anhänger ... ⟨gen⟩ sein [ˈanhɛŋə zaen] +sein ◊ *Er ist seit Jahren Anhänger dieses Fußballvereins.* 3. *(an advice, order, instruction etc.)* befolgen [bəˈfɔlgn̩] <befolgt, befolgte, hat befolgt> ◊ *einen Befehl befolgen* 4. *(a profession)* ausüben [ˈaosˌyːbm̩] +haben ◊ *Er übt den Beruf des Anwalts seit 20 Jahren aus.* 5. *(a particular faith)* praktizieren [praktiˈtsiːrən] <praktiziert, praktizierte, hat praktiziert> ◊ *Die Familie praktiziert den islamischen Glauben.*

• **follow about** ⟨phras v⟩ follow sb about jdm hinterherlaufen [hɪntɐheːˈglaofn̩] <läuft hinterher, lief hinterher, ist hinterhergelaufen> ◊ *Er läuft ihr ständig hinterher.*

• **follow through** ⟨phras v⟩ follow sth through, follow through with sth etw. zu Ende bringen [tsuː ˈɛndə brɪŋən] <bringt, brachte, hat gebracht> ◊ *Er bringt nie etwas zu Ende.*

• **follow up** ⟨phras v⟩ follow sth up 1. *(investigate further)* einer Sache ⟨dat⟩ nachgehen [ˈnaːxgeːən] <geht nach, ging nach, ist nachgegangen> ◊ *Die Polizei geht weiteren Hinweisen nach.* 2. follow sth up with a letter etw. schriftlich bestätigen [ˈʃrɪftlɪç bəˈʃtɛːtɪgn̩] <bestätigt, bestätigte, hat bestätigt> follow up accusations with threats auf Vorwürfe Drohungen folgen lassen [aof ˌfoːɐˈvvrfə ˈdroːʊŋən fɔlgn̩ lasn̩] <lässt, ließ, hat lassen>

follower ⟨noun⟩ Anhänger [ˈanhɛŋə] der <-s, -> ♀Anhängerin [ˈanhɛŋərɪn] die <-, -nen> ◊ *eine Anhängerin des Buddhismus*

following¹ ⟨noun⟩ 1. Anhängerschaft [ˈanhɛŋəʃaft] die <-, -en> most sing ◊ *eine Religion mit einer Anhängerschaft von 20 Millionen Menschen* 2. *(what follows)* Folgendes [ˈfɔlgn̩dəs] ◊ *Folgendes ist zu beachten: ...* in the following im Folgenden ◊ *Im Folgenden werde ich meine Position erklären.*

following² → follow ⟨adj⟩ folgend [ˈfɔlgn̩t] no comp/superl, only before ns ◊ *die folgenden Tage/Jahre*

following³ ⟨prep⟩ nach [naːx] ⟨+dat⟩ ◊ *Nach Stunden harter Arbeit hatten wir endlich Erfolg.*

fond ⟨adj⟩ 1. *(like sb/sth)* be fond of sb/sth jdn/etw. gern mögen [gɛⁿn møːgn̩] <mag, mochte, hat gemocht> ◊ *Ich mag ihn sehr gern.* be fond of doing sth etw. gern tun [gɛⁿn] He's fond of gardening. Er arbeitet gern im Garten. 2. *(memory)* lieb [liːp] ◊ *eine liebe Erinnerung* 3. *(loving)* liebevoll [ˈliːbəfɔl] ◊ *Er ist ein liebevoller Vater.*

food ⟨noun⟩ 1. *(what people eat)* Essen [ˈɛsn̩] das <-s> no pl ◊ *chinesisches/italienisches Essen* ♦ *Er verträgt kein scharfes Essen.*; *(what animals eat)* Futter [ˈfʊtɐ] das <-s> no pl ◊ *Futter für den Hund kaufen* cat food Katzenfutter [ˈkatsn̩fʊtɐ] 2. *(particular diet, foodstuff)* Nahrung [ˈnaːrʊŋ] die <-> no pl ◊ *feste/leichte Nahrung* baby food Babynahrung [ˈbeːbinaːrʊŋ] 3. *(edibles as merchandise)* Lebensmittel [ˈleːbm̩smɪtl̩] die <-> pl ◊ *Lebensmittel einkaufen* prices of food Lebensmittelpreise [ˈleːbm̩smɪtl̩praezə] die <-> pl frozen food Tiefkühlkost [ˈtiːfkyːlkɔst] die

<-> no pl tinned food Konserven [kɔnˈzɛⁿvn̩] die <-> pl 4. *(meals)* Mahlzeiten [ˈmaːltsaetn̩] die <-> pl ◊ *Alle Mahlzeiten werden von unserem Koch zubereitet.*

⊚ **food for thought** Stoff zum Nachdenken be off your food keinen Appetit haben

fool¹ ⟨noun⟩ 1. *(stupid person)* Dummkopf [ˈdʊmkɔpf] der <-(e)s, Dummköpfe> *(fam, pej)* ◊ *Du Dummkopf!* be a fool dumm sein [ˈdʊm zaen] +sein be fool enough to do sth dumm genug sein, etw. zu tun How could you be such a fool? Wie konntest du nur so dumm sein? feel a fool sich ⟨dat⟩ dumm vorkommen [ˈdʊm foːɐkɔmən] <kommt sich vor, kam sich vor, ist sich vorgekommen> make a fool of sb jdn dumm aussehen lassen [ˈdʊm aoszeːən lasn̩] <lässt, ließ, hat lassen> make sb look like a fool jdn lächerlich machen [ˈlɛçɐlɪç maxn̩] +haben make a fool of yourself sich lächerlich machen [ˈlɛçɐlɪç maxn̩] +haben 2. HIST *(jester)* Narr [narʰ] der <-en, -en> ♀Närrin [ˈnɛrɪn] die <-, -nen> ◊ *Der Narr wurde zum König gerufen, um ihn aufzuheitern.* 3. *(sweet food)* Creme [kreːm] die <-, -s> raspberry fool Himbeercreme [ˈhɪmbeːɐkreːm]

⊚ **be nobody's fool** nicht auf den Kopf gefallen sein *(fam)*

fool² ⟨verb⟩ *(trick)* täuschen [ˈtɔøʃn̩] +haben ◊ *Es gelang ihr, die Polizei zu täuschen.* fool yourself sich etwas vormachen [ˈfoːɐmaxn̩] +haben Don't fool yourself! Mach dir nichts vor! fool sb into doing sth jdn dazu bringen, etw. zu tun [datsu: ˈbrɪŋən ... tsuː] <bringt, brachte, hat gebracht>

⊚ **you could have fooled me** was du nicht sagst, was Sie nicht sagen sb was only fooling jd hat nur Spaß gemacht

• **fool about** ⟨phras v⟩ → **fool around**

• **fool around** ⟨phras v⟩ 1. *(act in a silly way)* herumalbern [hɛˈrʊm|albɐn] +haben *(fam)* ◊ *Während des Unterrichts alberten wir oft herum.* 2. *(sexually)* rummachen [ˈrʊmmaxn̩] +haben *(fam)* ◊ *Sie macht mit einem Kollegen rum.* 3. *(fiddle with)* fool around with sth an etw. ⟨dat⟩ herumspielen [hɛˈrʊmʃpiːlən] +haben *(fam)* ◊ *Spiel nicht an den Knöpfen der Stereoanlage herum!*

foolish(ly) ⟨adj, adv⟩ 1. *(stupid)* dumm [dʊm] <dümmer, am dümmsten> ◊ *eine dumme Frage* ♦ *Es wäre dumm, ihm das Geld zu leihen.* ♦ *Er stand nur dumm herum und tat nichts.* That was a foolish thing to do. Das war ziemlich dumm. foolish things Dummheiten [ˈdʊmhaetn̩] die <-> pl 2. *(silly, ridiculous)* lächerlich [ˈlɛçɐlɪç] ◊ *eine lächerliche Idee* ♦ *Das ist doch lächerlich!* ♦ *sich lächerlich benehmen* make sb/sth look foolish jdn/sich lächerlich machen

foot ⟨noun⟩ 1. *(part of the body, of a sock, bottom of sth)* Fuß [fuːs] der <-es, Füße> ◊ *kalte Füße bekommen* ♦ *am Fuß des Berges* on foot zu Fuß stamp your feet mit den Füßen aufstampfen shuffle your feet von einem Fuß auf den anderen treten wipe your feet sich ⟨dat⟩ die Füße abputzen feet first mit den Füßen zuerst 2. *(unit of measurement)* Fuß [fuːs] der <-es, -> *(outd)* ◊ *Die Säule ist zehn Fuß hoch.* 3. *(far end of a bed)* Fußende [ˈfuːsˌɛndə] das <-s, -n> ◊ *Die Katze schläft am Fußende des Bettes.* the foot of the table das hintere Ende des Tisches [das ˌhɪntərə ˈɛndə dɛs ˌtɪʃəs] 4. LIT

(metrical) Versfuß ['fɛrsfuːs] der <–es, Versfüße>
☺ have a foot in both camps auf zwei Hochzeiten tanzen *(fam)* be on your feet all day den ganzen Tag auf den Beinen sein have one foot in the grave mit einem Bein im Grab stehen keep your feet on the ground auf dem Boden bleiben start off on the right/wrong foot (with sb) (bei jdm) von Anfang an einen guten/schlechten Stand haben be unsteady on your feet wackelig auf den Beinen sein be back on your/its feet wieder auf den Beinen sein get sb/sth back on their/its feet jdn/etw. wieder auf die Beine bringen find your feet sich zurechtfinden put your foot in it ins Fettnäpfchen treten *(fam, hum)*

football ⟨noun⟩ **1.** *(ball, game)* Fußball ['fuːsbal] der <–(e)s, Fußbälle> *when referring to the sport: no pl and article only in combination with attribute* ◊ *ein Fußball aus Leder* ♦ *Fußball spielen* ♦ *der europäische Fußball* **2.** *(in the US)* Football ['fʊtbɔːl] der <–s> *no pl and article only in combination with attribute*

footnote ⟨noun⟩ Fußnote ['fuːsnoːtə] die <–, –n> ◊ *eine Fußnote machen/setzen*

footstep ⟨noun⟩ Schritt [ʃrɪt] der <–(e)s, –e> ◊ *Sie hörte Schritte im Korridor.*
☺ follow in sb's footsteps in jds Fußstapfen treten

for¹ ⟨prep⟩ **1.** *(at a rate of, on behalf of, for a period of, in favo(u)r of, expressing that sth suits sb/sth)* für [fyːɐ] +acc ◊ *eine Pizza für fünf Euro* ♦ *Sie arbeitet für zehn Euro die Stunde.* ♦ *Was kann ich für Sie tun?* ♦ *ein Tisch für die Küche* ♦ *Für wen ist dieses Geschenk?* ♦ *Wir fahren im Sommer für zwei Wochen in den Urlaub.* ♦ *Sie arbeitet für einen Verlag.* ♦ *eine Entscheidung für oder gegen etw.* ♦ *für jdn beten* ♦ *Zuneigung für jdn empfinden* ♦ *jdn für etw. bestrafen* ♦ *Ich spreche hier für alle Mitarbeiter.* ♦ *Es wird Zeit für mich zu gehen.* ♦ *„Download" ist das englische Wort für „herunterladen".* ♦ *Für heute hast du genug gearbeitet.* for now, for the time being fürs Erste not for anything für nichts auf der Welt for that/it dafür [daˈfyːɐ] ◊ *Nature gibst du mir dafür?* for this hierfür ['hiːɐˈfyːɐ] ◊ *Hierfür gibt es keine Entschuldigung.; (with certain verbs)* um [ʊm] +acc ask sb for sth jdn um etw. bitten fight for sth um etw. kämpfen*; (in certain idioms)* mit [mɪt] +dat feel sorry for sb Mitleid mit jdm haben sth is for doing sth mit etw. tut man etw. ◊ *Mit diesem Knopf schaltet man den Fernseher aus.* **2.** *(referring to a period of time)* lang [laŋ] *postpositive* ◊ *Ich war eine Woche lang in Deutschland.; (including the present time)* seit [zaet] +dat ◊ *Wir wohnen seit einem Jahr in diesem Haus.* for the last two etc. years die letzten zwei etc. Jahre [diː ˌlɛt͡stn̩ t͡svae ˈjaːrə] **3.** *(referring to a distance)* weit [vaet] *postpositive* ◊ *zehn Kilometer weit laufen; (referring to an expanse)* über ['yːbɐ] +acc ◊ *Die Küste erstreckt sich über 100 Kilometer.; (referring to a place)* nach [naːx] +dat ◊ *das Flugzeug nach London nehmen* **4.** *(as a consequence of, out of)* aus [aos] +dat ◊ *Aus Angst vor Bestrafung ist sie nicht nach Hause gegangen.* ♦ *Aus welchem Grund hat er wohl gelogen?* for doing sth weil jd etw. getan hat [vael ... hat] He was sacked for always being late. Er wurde entlassen, weil er immer zu spät kam. If it were not for your support I wouldn't have made it. Ohne deine Unterstützung hätte ich es

nicht geschafft.; *(used when giving a reason, describing the frequency of sth, referring to a special occasion)* zu [t͡suː] +dat ◊ *ein Grund zur Sorge* ♦ *Er nahm Baldrian zur Beruhigung.* ♦ *Ich sage das nur zu deiner Information.* ♦ *zum ersten/zweiten/letzten Mal* ♦ *Was wünschst du dir zu Weihnachten?* for one thing erstens ['eːɐstn̩s] ◊ *„Warum bist du nicht gekommen?" — „Erstens war ich müde und zweitens hatte ich keine Zeit."*

for² ⟨conjunc⟩ denn [dɛn] ◊ *Ich schenkte mir ein Glas Wasser ein, denn ich hatte Durst.*

forbid ⟨verb⟩ verbieten [fɛˈbiːtn̩] <verbietet, verbot, hat verboten> ◊ *Das Gericht verbot den Verkauf der Ware.* ♦ *Das verbietet der Anstand.* forbid sb to do sth, forbid sb from doing sth jdm verbieten, etw. zu tun ◊ *Ihre Eltern verbieten ihr, abends allein auszugehen.* sb is forbidden to do sth jdm ist verboten, etw. zu tun

force¹ ⟨noun⟩ **1.** *(physical strength, energy)* Kraft [kraft] die <–, Kräfte> ◊ *Er verfügt über sehr viel Kraft.* ♦ *Diese Partei ist die stärkste Kraft im Parlament.* a force for stability eine stabilisierende Kraft force of gravity Schwerkraft ['ʃveːɐkraft] **2.** *(forcefulness)* Stärke ['ʃtɛrkə] die <–> *no pl* ◊ *die Stärke seiner Persönlichkeit* ♦ *die Stärke ihrer Argumente* **3.** *(violence)* Gewalt [ɡəˈvalt] die <–> *no pl* ◊ *rohe Gewalt* by force mit Gewalt use force Gewalt anwenden **4.** *(of an impact, explosion etc.)* Wucht [vʊxt] die <–> *no pl* ◊ *die Wucht eines Schlages/Aufpralls* **5.** *(of the wind)* Windstärke ['vɪntʃtɛrkə] die <–, –n> a force 12 gale ein Sturm der Windstärke 12 **6.** *(group of people)* Truppe ['trʊpə] die <–, –n> ◊ *Die UNO hat ihre Truppen abgezogen.; (of people working together)* sales force Verkaufsteam [fɛˈkaofstiːm] das <–s, –s> join forces sich zusammentun [t͡suˈt͡saməntuːn] <tut sich zusammen, tat sich zusammen, hat sich zusammengetan> **7.** *(in the UK)* the Forces die Streitkräfte [diː ˈʃtraetkrɛftə] <–> *pl*
☺ by force of circumstances umstandshalber the forces of darkness die Mächte der Finsternis through force of habit durch die Macht der Gewohnheit the forces of nature die Naturgewalten come into force in Kraft treten sb/sth is a force to be reckoned with jd/etw. ist nicht zu unterschätzen in force **1.** *(operational)* in Kraft **2.** *(in crowds)* in Massen

force² ⟨verb⟩ **1.** *(make sb do sth)* zwingen ['t͡svɪŋən] <zwingt, zwang, hat gezwungen> ◊ *Sie zwangen ihn, seinen Namen zu nennen.* ♦ *Du musst dich zwingen, etwas zu essen.* force sb into marriage jdn zur Heirat zwingen force sb into a car jdn zwingen, in ein Auto zu steigen be forced out of business gezwungen sein, sein Geschäft aufzugeben force a smile sich zu einem Lächeln zwingen; *(make sth happen)* erzwingen [ɛˈt͡svɪŋən] <erzwingt, erzwang, hat erzwungen> ◊ *Die Regierung erzwang ein Ende des Streiks.* **2.** *(push)* sth into sth etw. in etw. acc zwängen [ɪn ... t͡svɛŋən] +haben ◊ *Sie zwängte ihre Kleider in den Koffer.* force sth through sth etw. durch etw. drücken [dʊrç ... drʏkn̩] +haben force sth out of sth etw. aus etw. drücken **3.** *(open sth by breaking it)* force sth open etw. aufbrechen ['aofbrɛçn̩] <bricht auf, brach auf, hat aufgebrochen> ◊ *Er brach die Tür auf.* **4.** *force your way sth* [dat] einen Weg bahnen [aenən ˈveːk baːnən] +haben ◊ *sich einen Weg durch die Menge bahnen*

• **force back** [phras v] zurückdrängen [tsu:'rykdrɛŋən] +haben ◊ *Er drängte die Tränen zurück.*

• **force down** [phras v] force sth down **1.** *(prices)* etw. drücken ['drykɳ] +haben ◊ *die Preise drücken* **2.** *(food)* etw. herunterwürgen [hɛ'rʊntevy'gɳ] +haben *(fam)* ◊ *Er würgte sein Mittagessen herunter.* **3.** *(an aircraft)* etw. zur Landung zwingen [tsu:ɐ̯ 'landʊŋ ,tsvɪŋən] <zwingt, zwang, hat gezwungen> ◊ *ein Flugzeug zur Landung zwingen*

• **force on** [phras v] force sth on sb jdm etw. aufzwingen ['aoftsvɪŋən] <zwingt auf, zwang auf, hat aufgezwungen> ◊ *jdm seine Meinung aufzwingen wollen*

• **force up** [phras v] force sth up *(prices, costs)* etw. hochtreiben ['ho:xtraɛbɳ] <treibt hoch, trieb hoch, hat hochgetrieben> ◊ *Die Knappheit der Rohstoffe hat die Preise hochgetrieben.*

forced → force² [adj] Zwangs... [tsvaŋs] forced labo(u)r Zwangsarbeit ['tsvaŋs|a'baɛt] die <-> *no pl* forced resettlement Zwangsumsiedlung ['tsvaŋs|ʊmzi:dlʊŋ] die <-, -en>

foreboding [noun] Vorahnung ['fo:ɐ̯|a:nʊŋ] die <-, -en> ◊ *Düstere Vorahnungen quälten sie.*

forecast¹ [noun] *(relating to the future)* Prognose [pro'gno:zə] die <-, -n> ◊ *Wie ist die Prognose für die Zukunft?; (weather)* Vorhersage [fo:ɐ̯'he:ɐ̯za:gə] die <-, -n> ◊ *Laut Vorhersage regnet es morgen.*

forecast² [verb] vorhersagen [fo:ɐ̯'he:ɐ̯za:gɳ] +haben ◊ *das Wetter vorhersagen* forecast inflation at 3% eine Inflation von 3% vorhersagen

forefinger [noun] Zeigefinger ['tsaɛgəfɪŋɐ] der <-s, ->

foreground [noun] Vordergrund ['fɔ'dɐgrʊnt] der <-(e)s, Vordergründe> ◊ *Was ist im Vordergrund des Bildes zu sehen?*

forehead [noun] Stirn [ʃtɪrn] die <-, -en> *most sing* wrinkle your forehead die Stirn runzeln

foreign [adj] **1.** *(alien, unfamiliar)* fremd [frɛmt] *no comp/superl* ◊ *ein fremdes Land* sth is foreign to sb etw. ist jdm fremd; Fremd... [frɛmt] foreign body Fremdkörper ['frɛmtkœ'pɐ] der <-s, -> foreign language Fremdsprache ['frɛmtʃpra:xə] die <-, -n> **2.** *(from or in another country)* ausländisch ['aoslɛndɪʃ] *no comp/superl, mostly before ns* ◊ *ausländische Mitbürger* foreign holiday Auslandsurlaub ['aoslants|u:glaop] der <-(e)s, -e> foreign policy/affairs Außenpolitik ['aosnpoli,ti:k] die <-> *no pl*

foreigner [noun] Ausländer ['aoslɛndɐ] der <-s, -> ♀Ausländerin ['aoslɛndərɪn] die <-, -nen> ◊ *Er hat eine Ausländerin geheiratet.* ♦ *Als Ausländer hat man es nicht immer leicht.*

Foreign Office [noun] Außenministerium ['aosnmɪns,te:rjʊm] das <-s, Außenministerien>

Foreign Secretary [noun] Außenminister ['aosnmi,nɪstɐ] der <-s, -> ♀Außenministerin ['aosnmi,nɪstərɪn] die <-, -nen> ◊ *der neue Außenminister im Kabinett* ♦ *Sie hat ihr Amt als Außenministerin angetreten.*

foresee [verb] voraussehen [fo'raosze:ən] <sieht voraus, sah voraus, hat vorausgesehen> ◊ *Wir können nicht voraussehen, was in 20 Jahren sein wird.*

foreseeable [adj] absehbar ['apze:ba:'] *no comp/superl* ◊ *Die Konsequenzen sind nicht absehbar.* in the foreseeable future in absehbarer Zeit

forest [noun] Wald [valt] der <-(e)s, Wälder> ◊ *ein dichter Wald* ♦ *Sie hatten sich im Wald verirrt.*

primeval forest Urwald ['u:ɐ̯valt]

forestry [noun] Forstwirtschaft ['fɔ'stvɪ'tʃaft] die <-, -en> ◊ *in der Forstwirtschaft arbeiten* ♦ *Forstwirtschaft studieren*

forever [adv] ewig ['e:vɪç] ◊ *sich ewig lieben* forever and ever für immer und ewig

foreword [noun] Vorwort ['fo:gvʊ't] das <-(e)s, -e>

forge [verb] **1.** *(an alliance, peace, friendship)* schließen ['ʃli:sɳ] <schließt, schloss, hat geschlossen> ◊ *ein Bündnis schließen; (a link)* knüpfen ['knypfɳ] +haben forge a link with sb/etw eine Verbindung zu jdm/etw. knüpfen; *(a career, life etc.)* forge sth sich [dat] etw. aufbauen ['aofbaoən] +haben ◊ *Sie hat sich eine Karriere in der Computerbranche aufgebaut.* **2.** *(counterfeit)* fälschen ['fɛlʃɳ] +haben ◊ *Du hast die Unterschrift gefälscht.* **3.** *(metal)* schmieden ['ʃmi:dɳ] <schmiedet, schmiedete, hat geschmiedet> ◊ *Eisen schmieden* **4.** *(move with difficulty)* forge through sth sich durch etw. kämpfen [dʊ'ç ... ,kɛmpfɳ] +haben ◊ *Sie kämpften sich durch den Sumpf.* forge on sich vorkämpfen ['fo:ɐ̯kɛmpfɳ] +haben ◊ *Sie kämpften sich zur Front vor.*

• **forge ahead** [phras v] gut vorankommen [,gu:t fo'raŋkɔmən] <kommt voran, kam voran, ist vorangekommen> ◊ *Wir kamen gut voran und erreichten am Abend die Herberge.*

forget [verb] vergessen [fɛ'gɛsn] <vergisst, vergaß, hat vergessen> ◊ *Jetzt habe ich vergessen, was ich sagen wollte.* ♦ *Ich habe vergessen, den Herd auszumachen.* ♦ *Oh nein, ich habe die Schlüssel vergessen!* forget about sb/sth jdn/etw. vergessen ◊ *Den Urlaub kannst du vergessen.* sth is best forgotten etw. vergisst man besser forget yourself sich vergessen Forget it! Vergiss es! Don't you forget it! Vergiss das ja nicht! not forgetting nicht zu vergessen ◊ *Sie hat einen harten Job und, nicht zu vergessen, zwei kleine Kinder.*

forgetful [adj] vergesslich [fɛ'gɛslɪç] ◊ *Opa wird immer vergesslicher.* ♦ *ein vergesslicher Mensch*

forgive [verb] **1.** *(no longer be angry)* verzeihen [fɛ'tsaɛən] <verzeiht, verzieh, hat verziehen> ◊ *Verzeihst du mir noch einmal?* ♦ *jdm eine Lüge verzeihen* forgive sb for doing sth jdm verzeihen, dass er/sie etw. getan hat **2.** *(a debt)* erlassen [ɛ'lasn] <erlässt, erließ, hat erlassen> ◊ *jdm seine Schulden erlassen*

ⓔ sb could be forgiven for doing sth jd könnte leicht etw. tun ◊ *Man könnte leicht glauben, dass Ehrlichkeit nicht mehr zählt.* forgive me Verzeihung ◊ *Verzeihung, aber ich muss jetzt gehen.* forgive me for asking, ... Verzeih/Verzeihen Sie die Frage, ...

fork [noun] **1.** *(piece of cutlery, garden tool)* Gabel ['ga:bl] die <-, -n> ◊ *mit Messer und Gabel essen* **2.** *(of a road)* Gabelung ['ga:bəlʊŋ] die <-, -en> ◊ *An der Gabelung folgen Sie bitte der B 14.*

form¹ [noun] **1.** *(type, shape, structure)* Form [fɔ'm] die <-, -en> ◊ *unterschiedliche Formen des Zusammenlebens* ♦ *Bausteine nach Farben und Formen sortieren* ♦ *Der Hut hat eine schöne Form.* ♦ *die unregelmäßigen Formen eines Verbs* ♦ *Dieses Medikament gibt es in Form von Tropfen und Tabletten.* take the form of sth die Form ... [gen] annehmen ◊ *Die Krankheit kann die Form einer psychischen Störung annehmen.* in form im Form ◊ *Ich bin zurzeit nicht/gut in Form.* **2.** *(figure)* Gestalt [gə'ʃtalt] die <-, -en> ◊ *Im Nebel tauchte eine Gestalt auf.*

A B C D E F G H I J K L M N O P Q R S T U V W X Y Z

3. *(document)* Formular [fɔrmuˈlaːr] das <-s, –e> ◊ *ein Formular ausfüllen* **4.** school Klasse [ˈklasə] die <-, –n> ◊ *Sie kommt nächstes Jahr in die sechste Klasse.*

◉ in a clear form übersichtlich ◊ *ein übersichtlich gestalteter Text* in tabular form tabellarisch ◊ *ein tabellarischer Lebenslauf*

form² verb **1.** *(take shape)* sth forms etw. bildet sich [ˈbɪldət zɪç] <bildete sich, hat sich gebildet> ◊ *Im Tal bildete sich Nebel.*; *(idea)* nimmt Gestalt an [nɪmt gəˈʃtalt an] <nahm an, hat angenommen> ◊ *In seinen Gedanken nahm eine Idee Gestalt an.*
2. *(produce)* form sth etw. formen [ˈfɔrmən] +haben ◊ *Seine Lippen formten ein O.* ♦ *ein Hörnchen aus Teig formen* turn sth into sth etw. zu etw. formen ◊ *Schnee zu einer Kugel formen*; *(a plan)* etw. entwerfen [ɛntˈvɛrfn] <entwirft, entwarf, hat entworfen> ◊ *einen Plan zur Lösung des Problems entwerfen*; *(a liking)* etw. entwickeln [ɛntˈvɪkln] <entwickelt, entwickelte, hat entwickelt> ◊ *Sie hatte eine tiefe Zuneigung zu ihm entwickelt.*; *(a company)* etw. gründen [ˈgrʏndn] <gründet, gründete, hat gegründet> ◊ *Die Firma wurde vor 35 Jahren gegründet.*
3. *(represent, constitute)* form sth etw. bilden [ˈbɪldn] <bildet, bildete, hat gebildet> ◊ *Der Fluss bildet eine natürliche Grenze zwischen den beiden Staaten.* ♦ *Die Kinder bildeten einen Kreis um die Lehrerin.* ♦ *Im Englischen bildet man den Plural meist durch Anhängen eines s.* sth is formed by sth etw. besteht aus etw. [bəˈʃteːt aos] <besteht, bestand, hat bestanden> ◊ *Der Ausschuss besteht aus zwei Expertenteams.* **4.** *(influence)* form sth/sth jdn/etw. prägen [ˈprɛːgn] +haben ◊ *Diese frühen Erfahrungen haben ihn geprägt.* ♦ *jds Charakter prägen*

formal(ly) adj, adv **1.** *(complaint, decision, apology)* offiziell [ɔfiˈtsjel] no comp/superl ◊ *Es ist noch keine offizielle Entscheidung gefallen.* ♦ *Der Minister hat sich offiziell entschuldigt.*; *(education)* regulär [reguˈlɛːr] no comp/superl ◊ *Er verfügt über keine reguläre Ausbildung in diesem Beruf.* ♦ *Sind Sie dafür regulär ausgebildet?* **2.** *(person, language, occasion)* förmlich [ˈfœrmlɪç] ◊ *Er ist immer sehr förmlich.* ♦ *eine förmliche Begrüßung* ♦ *Finden Sie diesen Brief nicht etwas zu förmlich formuliert?*; *(reception)* feierlich [ˈfaeɐlɪç] ◊ *ein feierlicher Empfang* ♦ *Der hohe Gast wurde feierlich begrüßt.* **3.** *(structural(ly))* formal [fɔrˈmaːl] no comp/superl ◊ *formale Änderungen an einem Vertrag vornehmen* ♦ *Wie ist das Gedicht formal gegliedert?*

formality noun **1.** *(official rule, matter of form)* Formalität [fɔrmaliˈtɛːt] die <-, –en> ◊ *die Formalitäten erledigen* ♦ *Die Erteilung der Genehmigung ist nur eine Formalität.* **2.** *(of behavio(u)r, style)* Förmlichkeit [ˈfœrmlɪçkaet] die <-, –en> ◊ *Die Förmlichkeit des Stils ist dem Inhalt des Textes nicht angemessen.*

format¹ noun Format [fɔrˈmaːt] das <-(e)s, –e> ◊ *ein neues Format für eine Fernsehsendung entwickeln* ♦ *Fotos im Format 10×15cm* ♦ *Das Format dieser Datei ist mir unbekannt.*

format² verb formatieren [fɔrmaˈtiːrən] <formatiert, formatierte, hat formatiert> ◊ *einen Text/eine Diskette formatieren*

formation noun **1.** *(act of forming)* Bildung [ˈbɪldʊŋ] die <-, –en> ◊ *die Bildung von Nierensteinen/ von Rost/einer Kommission/des Konjunktivs*; *(of a company, an organization)* Gründung [ˈgrʏndʊŋ] die

<-, –en> ◊ *seit der Gründung der Firma*; *(of a habit, idea)* Entstehung [ɛntˈʃteːʊŋ] die <-, –en> ◊ *Seit der Entstehung dieser Idee sind Jahre vergangen.*
2. *(pattern)* Formation [fɔrmaˈtsjoːn] die <-, –en> ◊ *in einer bestimmten Formation marschieren* ♦ *eine interessante Formation von steilen Felsen* in formation in Formation ◊ *in Formation fliegen*

former¹ adj ehemalig [ˈeːəmaːlɪç] no comp/superl, only before ns ◊ *Trainer ist jetzt ein ehemaliger Spieler.* ♦ *auf dem Gebiet der ehemaligen Sowjetunion* in former times früher [ˈfryːɐ] ◊ *Früher arbeiteten die Menschen vorwiegend im Freien.* from former times von früher [fɔn ˈfryːɐ] ◊ *Gebrauchsgegenstände von früher*

former² pron der/die/das Erstere [deːɐ/diː/das ˈeːɐstərə] ◊ *Herr Schneider und Herr Koch stehen zur Wahl; ich werde den Ersteren wählen.*

formerly adv früher [ˈfryːɐ] ◊ *Wo früher Felder waren, ist jetzt ein Einkaufszentrum.* ♦ *Istanbul, früher bekannt als Konstantinopel*

formidable adj *(task, size, achievement etc.)* gewaltig [gəˈvaltɪç] ◊ *Die Aufgabe ist gewaltig.* ♦ *ein Gebäude von gewaltiger Größe* ♦ *Alle Achtung — das war eine gewaltige Leistung!*; *(person)* furchterregend [ˈfʊrçtʔɛɐreːgnt] ◊ *Er sah sich einem furchterregenden Gegner gegenüber.* ♦ *Ich fand ihn schon damals furchterregend.*

formula noun **1.** *(method)* Rezept [reˈtsɛpt] das <-(e)s, –e> ◊ *Gibt es ein Rezept für eine glückliche Ehe?* ♦ *Bei uns lernen Sie das Programmieren nach bewährtem Rezept.* magic formula Zauberformel [ˈtsaobɐfɔrməl] die <-, –n> **2.** math, chem Formel [ˈfɔrməl] die <-, –n> ◊ *eine mathematische Formel anwenden* **3.** *(set of ingredients)* Rezeptur [retsɛpˈtuːr] die <-, –en> ◊ *Sie verrät die Rezeptur der Hautecreme.*

formulate verb formulieren [fɔrmuˈliːrən] <formuliert, formulierte, hat formuliert> ◊ *Die Partei hat ihre Ziele formuliert.* ♦ *Er versuchte, eine passende Antwort zu formulieren.*

formulation noun Formulierung [fɔrmuˈliːrʊŋ] die <-, –en> ◊ *Er suchte nach einer passenden Formulierung.* ♦ *Die Formulierung der Ziele ist oft schwierig.*

forth adv **1.** go forth hingehen [ˈhɪngeːən] <geht hin, ging hin, ist hingegangen>; *(lit)* Gebt hin und verkündet diese Botschaft allen Menschen! **2.** stretch forth ausstrecken [ˈaosʃtrɛkn] +haben ◊ *Sie streckte die Hand aus.* **3.** draw forth hervorziehen [hɛˈfoːɐtsiːən] <zieht hervor, zog hervor, hat hervorgezogen> ◊ *Er zog ein Messer hervor.*
◉ from that day/moment forth von diesem Tag/ Augenblick an and so forth und so weiter

forthcoming adj **1.** *(event)* bevorstehend [bəˈfoːɐʃteːənt] no comp/superl, only before ns ◊ *die Proben für das bevorstehende Konzert*; *(book, album)* in Kürze erscheinend [ɪn ˈkʏrtsə ɛɐˈʃaenənt] ◊ *ein Auszug aus meinem in Kürze erscheinenden Roman* **2.** *(help, money)* be forthcoming kommen [ˈkɔmən] <kommt, kam, ist gekommen> ◊ *Von der Regierung kam keine Hilfe.* ♦ *Als keine Antwort kam, schrieb sie einen zweiten Brief.* **3.** *(person)* mitteilsam [ˈmɪttaelzaːm] ◊ *In Bezug auf ihr Privatleben ist sie nicht besonders mitteilsam.*

forthright adj offen [ˈɔfn] ◊ *Ich schätze seine offene*

Art. ♦ *Das war eine offene Antwort.*

fortify [verb] 1. *(a place)* befestigen [bəˈfestɪgɪ̩] <befestigt, befestigte, hat befestigt> ◊ *eine Stadt befestigen* 2. *(make stronger)* stärken [ˈʃtɛ'kn̩] +haben ◊ *jds Position stärken* ♦ *Sie stärkten sich mit einem guten Frühstück.* 3. *(food)* fortify sth with sth etw. mit etw. anreichern [mɪt ...ˈanraeçen] +haben ◊ *Säuglingsnahrung mit Vitaminen und Eisen anreichern*

fortnight [noun] a fortnight zwei Wochen [ˌtsvae 'vɔxn̩] die <-> pl ◊ *Zwei Wochen sind nicht lang.* a fortnight's holiday zwei Wochen Urlaub once a fortnight alle zwei Wochen ◊ *Sie passt alle zwei Wochen auf unseren Hund auf.*

fortunate [adj] glücklich [ˈglʏklɪç] only before ns ◊ *der glückliche Gewinner* ♦ *Das war ein glücklicher Zufall.* less fortunate people Menschen, die weniger Glück haben [ˈmɛnʃn̩ diː 'veːnɪgə ˌglʏk haːbm̩] die <-> pl; *(be lucky)* be fortunate Glück haben [ˈglʏk haːbm̩] +haben ◊ *Nicht jeder hat so viel Glück wie du.* ♦ *Ich hatte das Glück, in einem liebevollen Elternhaus aufzuwachsen.* it was fortunate that es war ein Glück, dass [ɛs vaːr aen 'glʏk das]

fortunately [adv] zum Glück [tsʊm 'glʏk] ◊ *Zum Glück hat er sich bei dem Sturz nicht wehgetan.* ♦ *Der Brand konnte zum Glück bald gelöscht werden.*

fortune [noun] 1. *(a lot of money)* Vermögen [fɛˈmøːgn̩] das <-s, -> ◊ *Sie hat von ihrer Tante ein Vermögen geerbt.* ♦ *Der Wagen hat ein Vermögen gekostet.* spend a fortune on sth ein Vermögen für etw. ausgeben seek your fortune sein Glück versuchen [zaen 'glʏk fɛzuːxn̩] <versucht, versuchte, hat versucht> ◊ *Ich ging in die Stadt, um mein Glück zu versuchen.* 2. *(fate)* fortunes Geschicke [gəˈʃɪkə] die <-> pl ◊ *die Geschicke eines Landes/ Unternehmens* 3. *good fortune* Glück [glʏk] das <-(e)s> no pl ◊ *Es war ihr Glück, dass sie den späteren Zug nahm.* ♦ *Er hat das Glück, gesund zu sein.*
ⓔ **fortune smiles on sb** jdm lacht das Glück **tell sb's fortune** jdm die Zukunft voraussagen

forty [nmrl] vierzig [ˈfɪˈtsɪç] → **four²**

forum [noun] Forum [ˈfoːrʊm] das <-s, Foren> ◊ *Diese Homepage soll als Forum für Betroffene dienen.* ♦ *das Forum in Rom*

forward¹ [adj] 1. *(at the front)* vordere [ˈfɔˈdəʁə] no comp, only before ns <ein vorderer ..., eine vordere ..., ein vorderes ...> ◊ *Unser Waggon befindet sich im vorderen Teil des Zuges.* **be too far forward** zu weit vorn sein [tsu: vaet 'foˈn zaen] +sein 2. *(advance)* Voraus... [foˈraos] **forward planning** Vorausplanung [foˈraosplaːnʊŋ] die <-, -en> **forward thinking** Vorausdenken [foˈraosdɛŋkn̩] das <-s> no pl 3. *(presumptuous)* dreist [draest] <dreister, am dreistesten> ◊ *Es war schon ein wenig dreist von ihr, mich um Geld zu bitten.*

forward², **forwards** [adv] 1. *(ahead)* vorwärts [ˈfoːɐ̯vɛˈts] ◊ *Sie machte ein paar Schritte vorwärts.* ♦ *eine vorwärts weisende Entwicklung* **from that day/ time forward** von diesem Tag/Zeitpunkt an [fɔn ˌdiːzm̩ 'taːk/'tsaetpʊŋkt an] ◊ *Von diesem Tag an trank er keinen Tropfen Alkohol mehr.* 2. *(to the front)* nach vorn [naːx 'foˈn] ◊ *sich weiter nach vorn setzen* ♦ *Das ist für ihn ein gewaltiger Schritt nach vorn.* 3. look forward to sth sich auf etw. [acc]

freuen [aof ... ˌfrɔ͜øən] +haben ◊ *Ich freue mich auf die Ferien.* ♦ *Wir freuen uns darauf, Sie persönlich kennen zu lernen.* 4. put a clock forward eine Uhr vorstellen [aena uːɐ̯ ˈfoːɐ̯ʃtɛlən] +haben

forwards → **forward²**

fossil [noun] Fossil [fɔˈsiːl] das <-s, -ien> ◊ *Fossilien aus dem Oligozän*

foster [verb] 1. *(encourage)* fördern [ˈfœˈdn̩] +haben ◊ *die Integration ausländischer Kinder fördern* 2. *(a child)* in Pflege nehmen [ɪn 'pfleːgə neːmən] <nimmt, nahm, hat genommen> ◊ *Sie haben einen kleinen Jungen in Pflege genommen.*

foul [adj] 1. *(smell, air, food)* schlecht [ʃlɛçt] <schlechter, am schlechtesten> ◊ *Die Luft hier ist wirklich schlecht.* ♦ *ein schlechter Geruch; (water)* faul [faol] ◊ *Das Wasser riecht faul.* 2. sport unerlaubt [ˈʊn|ɛlaopt] no comp/superl ◊ *Das war ein unerlaubter Zug!* 3. *(mood, behavio(u)r, weather)* mies [miːs] <mieser, am miesesten> *(fam)* ◊ *Sie ist heute in sehr mieser Stimmung.* ♦ *mieses Wetter* 4. *(language)* unflätig [ˈʊnflɛːtɪç] ◊ *unflätige Worte*
ⓔ **fall foul of sth** mit etw. in Konflikt geraten ◊ *Er ist mit dem Gesetz in Konflikt geraten.*

found → **find** [verb] 1. *(set up, establish)* gründen [ˈgʁʏndn̩] <gründet, gründete, hat gegründet> ◊ *Augsburg wurde im Jahre 15 vor Christus von den Römern gegründet.* ♦ *ein Kloster/eine Schule gründen* 2. *(rest on sth)* be founded on sth auf etw. [dat] beruhen [aof ... bə,ʁuːən] <beruht, beruhte, hat beruht> ◊ *Ihre Liebe beruht auf Respekt und gegenseitigem Vertrauen.*

foundation [noun] 1. *(part of a building, basis of sth)* Fundament [fʊndaˈmɛnt] das <-(e)s, -e> ◊ *Das Fundament des Hauses ist bereits gelegt.* ♦ *das Fundament für die eigene Karriere legen* **shake sth to its foundations** etw. in seinen Grundfesten erschüttern [ɪn zaenən ˌgʁʊntfɛstn̩ ɐ'ʃʏtɐn] <erschüttert, erschütterte, hat erschüttert> 2. *(institution, organization)* Stiftung [ˈʃtɪftʊŋ] die <-, -en> ◊ *eine Stiftung einrichten/gründen* ♦ *eine private/gemeinnützige Stiftung* 3. *(act of setting up sth)* Gründung [ˈgʁʏndʊŋ] die <-, -en> ◊ *Seit der Gründung des Unternehmens sind viele Jahre vergangen.* 4. *(for your face)* Make-up [meːkˈ|ap] das <-s, -s> ◊ *Make-up auftragen*

founder [noun] Gründer [ˈgʁʏndɐ] der <-s, -> ♀Gründerin [ˈgʁʏndəʁɪn] die <-, -nen> ◊ *Sie ist die Gründerin dieses Verlages.* ♦ *der Gründer einer Stadt*

fountain [noun] 1. *(with upward jets of water)* Springbrunnen [ˈʃpʁɪŋbʁʊnən] der <-s, -> ◊ *Im Park gibt es einen Springbrunnen.; (without upward jets)* Brunnen [ˈbʁʊnən] der <-s, -> ◊ *ein gotischer Brunnen* 2. *(jet of liquid)* Fontäne [fɔn'tɛːnə] die <-, -n> ◊ *Das Wasser spritzte in einer Fontäne nach oben.* 3. *(fig) (source)* Quelle [ˈkvɛlə] die <-, -n> ◊ *Seine Tiere waren für ihn immer eine Quelle der Freude.* **fountain of youth** Jungbrunnen [ˈjʊŋbʁʊnən] der <-s, ->

fountain pen [noun] Füller [ˈfʏlɐ] der <-s, -> ◊ *mit Füller schreiben*

four¹ [noun] 1. *(number)* Vier [fiːɐ̯] die <-, -en> ◊ *Ist das eine Vier oder eine Neun?* ♦ *Er hat eine Vier gewürfelt.* ♦ *Die Vier hat gewonnen!* ♦ *Am besten fahren Sie mit der Vier bis zum Nordbahnhof.* 2. sport *(in rowing)* Vierer [ˈfiːʁɐ] der <-s, -> ◊ *der Vierer mit/ohne Steuermann*

ⓔ **on all fours** auf allen vieren

four² ⟨nmrl⟩ vier [fiːɐ] ◊ *Zwei plus zwei ist vier.* ♦ *Ich hätte gern vier Brötchen.* ♦ *vier Millionen Euro* ♦ *Meine kleine Tochter ist vier Jahre alt.* ♦ *Wann wird er vier?* ♦ *Es ist schon Viertel nach vier.* **four times** **viermal** ['fiːɐmaːl] ◊ *Sie hat schon viermal angerufen.*

fourfold ⟨adj, adv⟩ vierfach ['fiːɐfax] ◊ *die vierfache Menge Wasser* ♦ *der vierfache Weltmeister* ♦ *Der Benzinverbrauch ist in diesem Fall vierfach.* ♦ *Diese Abbildung ist vierfach vergrößert.* ♦ *etw. vierfach kopieren lassen*

four-star ⟨noun⟩ (petrol) Super ['zuːpɐ] das <-s> *mostly used without the article, no pl* ◊ *Er tankt stets Super.*

fourteen ⟨nmrl⟩ vierzehn ['fɪrˌtseːn] → **four²**

fourth¹ ⟨noun⟩ **1.** (fraction) Viertel ['fiːɐtəl] das <-s, -> ◊ *ein Viertel der Summe/Weltbevölkerung* ♦ *Ein Viertel der Strecke liegt hinter uns.* ♦ *Der Umsatz stieg um ein Viertel.* ♦ *Im letzten Viertel des 19. Jahrhunderts.* **2.** (in a sequence) Vierte ['fiːɐtə] der or die or das <-n, -n> *most sing* ◊ *Jeder Vierte hat Angst vor Arbeitslosigkeit.* ♦ *Sie wurde bei dem Rennen Vierte.* ♦ *Er kam als Vierter ins Ziel* ♦ *Ich brauche ein neues Rad. Das ist schon das Vierte dieses Jahr.*

fourth² ⟨adj⟩ vierte ['fiːɐtə] <ein vierter …, eine vierte …, ein viertes> ◊ *Heute ist Freitag, der vierte Juni.* ♦ *Am vierten März habe ich Geburtstag.* ♦ *Er kann die vierte Frage nicht beantworten.* ♦ *das vierte Mal* ♦ *im vierten Stock* ♦ *auf dem vierten Platz sein* ♦ *das vierte Kapitel des Romans*

fourthly ⟨adv⟩ viertens ['fiːɐtn̩s] ◊ *… und viertens haben wir kein Geld für solche Sachen.*

fox ⟨noun⟩ **1.** (animal) Fuchs [fʊks] der <-es, Füchse> ◊ *Der Fuchs schlich in den Hühnerstall.* ♦ *Er ist schlau wie ein Fuchs!* **2.** (fur) Fuchspelz ['fʊkspɛlts] der <-es> *no pl* ◊ *ein Kragen aus Fuchspelz*

fraction ⟨noun⟩ **1.** (very small part) Bruchteil ['brʊxtaɛl] der <-(e)s, -e> ◊ *Die Aktie ist nur noch den Bruchteil ihres ursprünglichen Preises wert.* ♦ *Er reagierte um den Bruchteil einer Sekunde zu spät.* **open the door a fraction** die Tür einen Spalt öffnen [diː ˌtyːɐ̯ aɛnən ˈʃpalt ˈœfnən] +haben **miss sb by a fraction of an inch** jdn um Haaresbreite verfehlen [ʊm ˌhaːrəsbraɛtə fɛˈfeːlən] <verfehlt, verfehlte, hat verfehlt> **2.** MATH Bruch [brʊx] der <-(e)s, Brüche> ◊ *Null Komma fünf kann man auch als Bruch darstellen:* ½ ♦ *einen Bruch kürzen oder erweitern*

fracture ⟨noun⟩ (of a bone) Bruch [brʊx] der <-(e)s, Brüche> ◊ *mit schweren Brüchen ins Krankenhaus eingeliefert werden;* (of other hard substances) Riss [rɪs] der <-es, -e> ◊ *einen Betonpfeiler auf Risse überprüfen*

fragile ⟨adj⟩ **1.** (delicate, easy to break) zerbrechlich [tseˈbrɛçlɪç] ◊ *zerbrechliche Knochen haben* ♦ *Sie sieht so zerbrechlich aus.;* (agreement, peace) brüchig ['brʏçɪç] ◊ *In diesem Land herrscht jetzt ein brüchiger Frieden.* ♦ *Die Einheit der Gewerkschaften war brüchig geworden.;* (confidence, economy, balance) labil [la'biːl] ◊ *Ihr Selbstbewusstsein ist immer noch sehr labil.* ♦ *eine labile Konjunktur* **2.** (not healthy) angeschlagen ['angəʃlaːgŋ̍] ◊ *Ich fühle mich ein wenig angeschlagen.* ♦ *eine angeschlagene Gesundheit haben*

fragment ⟨noun⟩ **1.** (small part of sth) Bruchstück ['brʊxʃtʏk] das <-(e)s, -e> ◊ *Sie bekam nur Bruch-*

stücke der Unterhaltung mit.; (of glass, porcelain etc.) Scherbe ['ʃɛrbə] die <-, -n> ◊ *Die Vase zerbrach in tausend Scherben.* **fragment of paper** Papierschnipsel [pa'piːɐ̯ʃnɪpsl̩] der or das <-s, -> ◊ *Überall lagen Papierschnipsel herum.* **2.** (part of sth which remains) Fragment [frag'mɛnt] das <-(e)s, -e> ◊ *Von dem Text sind nur Fragmente erhalten.*

fragrance ⟨noun⟩ Duft [dʊft] der <-(e)s, Düfte> ◊ *der Duft von frisch gebackenem Kuchen* ♦ *Testen Sie unsere neuen Düfte!*

frail ⟨adj⟩ **1.** (feeble, usually because of age) gebrechlich [gə'brɛçlɪç] ◊ *alte und gebrechliche Menschen* ♦ *Sie war schwach und gebrechlich.* **2.** (delicate, fragile) zerbrechlich [tse'brɛçlɪç] ◊ *die zerbrechlichen Flügel des Schmetterlings.* ♦ *Obwohl Claire zerbrechlich wirkt, hat sie doch einen eisernen Willen.;* (hopes, economy) schwach [ʃvax] <schwächer, am schwächsten> ◊ *Seine Hoffnung auf Rettung war nur noch schwach.* ♦ *Maßnahmen zur Ankurbelung der schwachen Wirtschaft*

frame¹ ⟨noun⟩ **1.** (of a picture, window, bicycle) Rahmen ['raːmən] der <-, -> ◊ *Der Dieb hat das Gemälde aus dem Rahmen geschnitten.* **2.** (support, part of your glasses) Gestell [gə'ʃtɛl] das <-(e)s, -e> ◊ *Das Gerät kann auf ein fahrbares Gestell montiert werden.* **3.** FILM Einzelbild ['aɛntsl̩bɪlt] das <-(e)s, -er> ◊ *24 Einzelbilder pro Sekunde erzeugen den Eindruck von Bewegung.* **4.** (shape of sb's body) Gestalt [gə'ʃtalt] die <-, -en> ◊ *Sie war von schmächtiger Gestalt.* **5. frame of mind** Verfassung [fɛ'fasʊŋ] die <-> *no pl* ◊ *Seit dem Unfall ist er in keiner guten Verfassung.* **6.** IT Frame [freːm] das or der <-s, -s> ◊ *Die Homepage ist mit Frames aufgebaut.* **7.** (for young plants) Frühbeet ['fryːbeːt] das <-(e)s, -e> ◊ *Gurken im Frühbeet ziehen*

frame² ⟨verb⟩ **1.** (a picture) rahmen ['raːmən] +haben ◊ *Ich möchte dieses Bild gern rahmen lassen.* **2.** (surround) umrahmen [ʊm'raːmən] <umrahmt, umrahmte, hat umrahmt> ◊ *Ihr Gesicht wird von blonden Locken umrahmt.* **3.** (devise, conceive) entwerfen [ɛnt'vɛrfn̩] <entwirft, entwarf, hat entworfen> ◊ *Wer hat diese Theorie ursprünglich entworfen?* ♦ *Wir müssen einen Plan entwerfen.* **4.** (fam) (incriminate) frame sb jdm etw. anhängen ['anhɛŋən] +haben (fam) ◊ *Er behauptet, man habe ihm den Mord angehängt.* **5.** (express, formulate) formulieren [fɔmu'liːrən] <formuliert, formulierte, hat formuliert> ◊ *Formulieren Sie die Frage bitte anders.*

framework ⟨noun⟩ (supporting structure, model) Grundgerüst ['grʊntgərʏst] das <-(e)s, -e> ◊ *Das Gebäude hat ein Grundgerüst aus Stahl.* ♦ *das theoretische Grundgerüst der Hypothese* **within the framework of sth im Rahmen …** [ɪm 'raːmən] ◊ *Im Rahmen dieser Sparmaßnahmen wurden auch die Gehälter gekürzt.*

France ⟨noun⟩ Frankreich ['frankraɛç] das <-s> *article only in combination with attribute, no pl* → **Germany**

franchise ⟨noun⟩ **1.** ECON (permission) Lizenz [li'tsɛnts] die <-, -en> ◊ *eine Lizenz erteilen/entziehen;* (business) Franchiseunternehmen ['frɛntʃaɛzˌʊntene,meːn] das <-s, -> **2.** POL Wahlrecht ['vaːlrɛçt] das <-(e)s> *no pl* ◊ *das Prinzip des allgemeinen Wahlrechts*

frank ⟨adj⟩ offen ['ɔfn̩] ◊ *ein offenes Wesen haben* ♦ *ein offenes Gespräch führen* **be frank with sth offen zu jdm sein be frank about sth sich offen über etw.**

[acc] äußern ◊ *Er äußerte sich offen über seine familiären Probleme.* to be frank ehrlich gesagt ['eːglɪç gəzaːkt] ◊ *Ehrlich gesagt habe ich daran kein Interesse.*

frankly [adv] **1.** *(openly)* offen ['ɔfn̩] ◊ *jdm offen die Meinung sagen* ♦ *Wir sprachen ganz offen miteinander.* **2.** *(to be honest)* ehrlich gesagt ['eːglɪç gəzaːkt] ◊ *Ehrlich gesagt hat mir die Torte überhaupt nicht geschmeckt.*

fraud [noun] **1.** *(deceit)* Betrug [bəˈtruːk] der <-(e)s> no pl ◊ *einen Betrug begehen* ♦ *Das ist Betrug!* insurance fraud Versicherungsbetrug [fɛˈzɪçərʊŋsbətruːk] tax fraud Steuerbetrug ['ʃtɔɡəbətruːk] **2.** *(person)* Betrüger [bəˈtryːɡɐ] der <-s, -> ♀Betrügerin [bəˈtryːɡarɪn] die <-, -nen> ◊ *auf einen Betrüger/eine Betrügerin hereinfallen;* *(thing)* Schwindel ['ʃvɪndl̩] der <-s> no pl ◊ *Der Schwindel kam am Ende doch heraus.*

free¹ [adj] **1.** *(costing nothing)* kostenlos ['kɔstn̩loːs] no comp/superl ◊ *kostenlose Beratung/Parkplätze* ♦ *Die Benutzung der Sauna ist für Kurgäste kostenlos.* **2.** *(at liberty, unrestricted, without sth, available)* frei [fraɪ] <freier, am frei(e)sten> ◊ *Nach zwei Jahren Haft ist er wieder frei.* ♦ *Mit der freien Hand griff er nach dem Telefon.* ♦ *Sie haben freien Zugang zu allen Büros.* ♦ *freie Wahlen* ♦ *Sie ist frei von Schuld.* ♦ *In diesem Kurs sind noch Plätze frei.* ♦ *Er fühlte sich herrlich frei und unbeschwert.* I'll be free tomorrow. Morgen habe ich Zeit. sb is free to do sth es steht jdm frei, etw. zu tun free from pain schmerzfrei ['ʃmɛɐˈtsfraɪ] no comp/superl **3.** *(not in prison or a cage)* frei [fraɪ] no comp/superl ◊ *Er wird bald wieder ein freier Mann sein/wieder frei sein.* set sb free jdn freilassen ['fraɪlasn̩] <lässt frei, ließ frei, hat freigelassen> ◊ *Man hat ihn gegen Kaution freigelassen.* ♦ *den eingefangenen Vogel wieder freilassen; (escape)* get/struggle free sich befreien [bəˈfraɪən] ◊ *Das Tier versuchte, sich aus der Falle zu befreien.* **4.** be free with your opinions seine Meinung offen sagen [zaɪnə ˌmaɪnʊŋ 'ɔfn̩ zaːgŋ̍] +haben ◊ *Sie sagt ihre Meinung immer ziemlich offen.* be free with your money großzügig mit seinem Geld umgehen ['groːstsyːgɪç mɪt zaɪnəm ˌgɛlt ˌʊmgeːən] <geht um, ging um, ist umgegangen> ◊ *Sven geht mit seinem Geld großzügig um.*

◉ free and easy ungezwungen make free with sth sich einer Sache [gen] bedienen ◊ *sich bestimmter Informationen bedienen*

free² [verb] **1.** *(release from imprisonment)* freilassen ['fraɪlasn̩] <lässt frei, ließ frei, hat freigelassen> ◊ *Schließlich wurden alle Geiseln freigelassen.; (help escape)* befreien [bəˈfraɪən] <befreit, befreite, hat befreit> ◊ *Alle Gefangenen konnten befreit werden.* ♦ *ein unterdrücktes Volk befreien* free sb/sth from sth jdn/etw. aus etw. befreien ◊ *ein Tier aus einem Käfig befreien* **2.** *(remove a burden: debts, anxieties, remove)* free sb/sth of/from sth jdn/etw. von etw. befreien [fɔn ... bə̍fraɪən] <befreit, befreite, hat befreit> ◊ *ein Land von seinen Schulden befreien* ♦ *Die Therapie hat sie endlich von ihren Ängsten befreit.* **3.** *(make available)* zur Verfügung stellen [tsuːɐ feˈfyːgʊŋ ʃtɛlən] +haben ◊ *Wie viel Geld wird für das Projekt zur Verfügung gestellt?*

free³ [adv] **1.** *(without paying)* kostenlos ['kɔstn̩loːs] no comp/superl get sth for free etw. umsonst

bekommen [ʊmˈzɔnst bəkɔmən] <bekommt, bekam, hat bekommen> ◊ *Hast du die Karten umsonst bekommen?* **2.** *(out of sth)* break free sich losmachen ['loːsmaxn̩] +haben ◊ *Er wollte mich festhalten, aber ich konnte mich losmachen.* pull your hand free seine Hand befreien [zaɪnə 'hant bəˌfraɪən] <befreit, befreite, hat befreit> ◊ *Sie befreite ihre Hand aus seinem Griff.* **3.** *(unrestricted)* frei [fraɪ] <freier, am frei(e)sten> ◊ *Die Hunde rannten frei herum.* go/walk free straffrei davonkommen [ˈʃtraːfraɪ daˈfɔnkɔmən] <kommt davon, kam davon, ist davongekommen>

freedom [noun] Freiheit ['fraɪhaɪt] die <-, -en> ◊ *Ich hatte als Kind die Freiheit, zu tun, was ich wollte.* ♦ *Er genießt seine neue Freiheit.* ♦ *Sie hat dem Vogel die Freiheit geschenkt.* freedom of the press Pressefreiheit ['prɛsəfraɪhaɪt] freedom of speech Redefreiheit ['reːdəfraɪhaɪt] freedom of movement Freizügigkeit ['fraɪtsyːgɪçkaɪt] die <-> no pl

freelance [adj, adv] freiberuflich ['fraɪbaruːflɪç] no comp/superl; when used as an adj, only before ns ◊ *Sie ist freiberufliche Journalistin.* ♦ *Seit 1990 ist er freiberuflich tätig.*

freely [adv] **1.** *(unrestricted, not exactly)* frei [fraɪ] <freier, am frei(e)sten> ◊ *Die Gänse laufen frei herum.* ♦ *sich frei entscheiden können* ♦ *Das ist ziemlich frei übersetzt.* **2.** *(lavishly)* großzügig ['groːstsyːgɪç] ◊ *großzügig für die Opfer der Flutkatastrophe spenden*

freeway [noun] Autobahn ['aʊtobaːn] die <-, -en> ◊ *die Autobahn München–Stuttgart*

freeze¹ [noun] **1.** *(on investments)* Stopp [ʃtɔp] der <-s, -s> ◊ *Umweltschützer fordern den Stopp der Atommülltransporte.* freeze on wages Lohnstopp ['loːnʃtɔp] **2.** *(low temperatures)* Frost [frɔst] der <-(e)s, Fröste> ◊ *extremer Frost*

freeze² [verb] **1.** *(water, ground)* gefrieren [gəˈfriːrən] <gefriert, gefror, ist gefroren> ◊ *Das Wasser gefror zu Eis.* ♦ *Wasser gefriert bei 0° Celsius.* ♦ *Der Boden war gefroren.; (lake, river)* zufrieren ['tsuːfriːrən] <friert zu, fror zu, ist zugefroren> ◊ *Der Fluss ist zugefroren.; (pipes)* freeze (up) einfrieren ['aɪnfriːrən] <friert ein, fror ein, ist eingefroren> ◊ *Das Wasser ist in der Leitung eingefroren.* frozen solid gefroren [gəˈfroːrən] no comp/superl ◊ *Das Wasser in der Pfütze ist gefroren.* **2.** *(food or drink, money)* einfrieren ['aɪnfriːrən] <friert ein, fror ein, hat eingefroren> ◊ *Bohnen kochen und einfrieren* sth freezes well etw. lässt sich gut einfrieren **3.** *(feel very cold)* frieren ['friːrən] <friert, fror, hat gefroren> ◊ *Frierst du an den dünnen Mantel nicht?* I'm freezing. Mir ist eiskalt. freeze to death erfrieren [ɛˈfriːrən] <erfriert, erfror, ist erfroren> **4.** it freezes es friert [ɛs ˈfriːgt] <friert, fror, hat gefroren> ◊ *Letzte Nacht hat es gefroren.* **5.** *(stop moving)* erstarren [ɛˈʃtarən] <erstarrt, erstarrte, ist erstarrt> ◊ *Sie erstarrte vor Schreck, als sie den Mann im Wohnzimmer sah.* Freeze! Keine Bewegung! make sb's blood freeze jdm das Blut in den Adern gefrieren lassen [das 'bluːt ɪn deːn ˌaːden gəˌfriːrən lasn̩] <lässt, ließ, hat lassen> frozen to the spot wie angewurzelt [viː 'angəvʊˈtsl̩t] ◊ *Er stand wie angewurzelt da und starrte auf das viele Blut.* **6.** *(time)* stehen bleiben ['ʃteːən blaɪbm̩] <bleibt, blieb, ist geblieben> ◊ *Die Zeit schien stehen geblieben zu sein.* **7.** *(computer)* freeze (up) einfrieren ['aɪnfriːrən] <friert ein, fror

ein, hat eingefroren> 8. *(a film)* anhalten ['anhaltn̩]
<hält an, hielt an, hat angehalten> ◊ *Er hielt den Film
an, um die Szene genau zu betrachten.*

• **freeze out** (phras v) freeze sb out of sth jdn von
etw. ausschließen [fɔn ... ˌaʊsʃliːsn̩] <schließt aus,
schloss aus, hat ausgeschlossen> ◊ *Man schloss ihn
von allen wichtigen Entscheidungen aus.*

• **freeze over** (phras v) *(lake, river)* zufrieren
['ʦuːfriːrən] <friert zu, fror zu, ist zugefroren> ◊ *Der
See wird bald zufrieren.; (road surface)* überfrieren
[ybɐ'friːrən] <überfriert, überfror, ist überfroren> ◊
Vorsicht, die Fahrbahn ist überfroren!

freezer compartment (noun) Gefrierfach [gə'friːɡfax]
das <-(e)s, Gefrierfächer> ◊ *ein Kühlschrank mit
Gefrierfach*

freezer (noun) Tiefkühltruhe ['tiːfkyːltruːə] die <-, -n>

freezing (adj) eiskalt ['aɛs'kalt] *no comp/superl* ◊ *Hier
drin ist es ja eiskalt.*

freight (noun) Fracht [fraxt] die <-, -en> ◊ *eine
kostbare Fracht an Bord haben* by air freight per
Luftfracht [peɐ 'lʊftfraxt] ◊ *Die Waren werden per
Luftfracht versandt.* freight charges Frachtkosten
['fraxtkɔstn̩] die <-> *pl* freight train Güterzug
['gyːtɐʦuːk] der <-(e)s, Güterzüge>

French¹ (noun) 1. *(inhabitants)* the French die
Franzosen [diː fran'ʦoːzn̩] <-> *pl* → **German¹** 1.
2. *(language)* Französisch [fran'ʦøːzɪʃ] das <-(s)>
no pl → **German¹** 2.

French² (adj) französisch [fran'ʦøːzɪʃ] be French
Franzose/Französin sein
[fran'ʦoːzə/fran'ʦøːzɪn zaɛn] +*sein* → **German²**

Frenchman (noun) Franzose [fran'ʦoːzə] der <-n, -n>
→ **German¹** 1.

Frenchwoman (noun) Französin [fran'ʦøːzɪn] die
<-, -nen> → **German¹** 1.

frequency (noun) 1. *(number of times)* Häufigkeit
['hɔɡfɪçkaɛt] die <-, -en> *most sing* ◊ *An dieser
Kreuzung ereignen sich mit zunehmender Häufigkeit
Unfälle.* ♦ *Die Häufigkeit dieser Erkrankung macht
uns Sorgen.* 2. PHYSICS, RADIO Frequenz [fre'kvɛnts] die
<-, -en> ◊ *Dieser Radiosender sendet ab sofort auf
einer anderen Frequenz.*

frequent (adj) *(happening often)* häufig ['hɔɡfɪç]
häufige Wiederholungen ♦ *Das ist bei uns ein
häufiges Problem.* ♦ *Die Krankheit ist bei Kindern
ziemlich häufig.; (criticism)* häufig geäußert
[ˌhɔɡfɪç gə'ʔɔɡsət] ◊ *eine häufig geäußerte Kritik;
(visit)* regelmäßig ['reːglmɛːsɪç] *no comp/superl* ◊
regelmäßige Ausflüge/Theaterbesuche be a frequent
visitor oft zu Gast sein [ˌɔft zuː 'gast zaɛn] +*sein*

frequently (adv) häufig ['hɔɡfɪç] ◊ *ein häufig vorkommender Fehler* ♦ *Diese Meinung findet man häufig
unter jungen Leuten.*

fresh (adj) 1. *(new, clean, bright, cold)* frisch [frɪʃ]
<frischer, am frischesten> ◊ *frisches Gemüse/Obst* ♦
Sind diese Brötchen auch frisch? ♦ *frische Blumen* ♦
frische Fußspuren im Schnee ♦ *frische Unterwäsche*
♦ *Die Luft im Wald riecht herrlich frisch.* ♦ *Sie hat
eine frische Gesichtsfarbe.* ♦ *Abends wurde es dann
doch ziemlich frisch.* ♦ *Nach der Pause fühlte sie
sich frisch und erholt.* sth is fresh in sb's mind etw.
ist jdm noch frisch in Erinnerung sb is fresh from
sth jd kommt frisch von etw. 2. *(new, different)* neu
[nɔɡ] <neuer, am neu(e)sten> ◊ *Er nahm ein neues
Blatt Papier.* ♦ *Wir brauchen neue Ideen!* ♦ *einen
neuen Anfang machen* 3. fresh water Süßwasser

['ʦyːsvasə] das <-s> *no pl*

freshly (adv) frisch [frɪʃ] <frischer, am frischesten> ◊
Er war frisch rasiert. ♦ *ein Glas frisch gepresster
Orangensaft*

freshness (noun) Frische ['frɪʃə] die <-> *no pl* ◊ *Das
Gelingen des Gerichts hängt von der Frische der
Zutaten ab.* ♦ *Die Frische des Windes ließ sie
frösteln.*

FRG BRD [beː|ɛɐ'deː] die ◊ *die Menschen in der BRD*

Friday (noun) Freitag ['fraɛtaːk] der <-(e)s, -e> →
Monday

fridge (noun) Kühlschrank ['kyːlʃraŋk] der
<-(e)s, Kühlschränke> ◊ *etw. im Kühlschrank aufbe-
wahren* ♦ *den Kühlschrank abtauen*

fried → fry (adj) gebraten [gə'braːtn̩] *no comp/superl* ◊
gebratene Zwiebeln fried potatoes Bratkartoffeln
['braːtkaˌtɔfln̩] die <-> *pl* fried egg Spiegelei
['ʃpiːglaɛ] das <-(e)s, -er>

friend (noun) Freund [frɔɡnt] der <-(e)s, -e>
♀Freundin ['frɔɡndɪn] die <-, -nen> ◊ *Chris ist ein
guter Freund von ihm.* ♦ *Ute ist ihre beste Freundin.*
♦ *ein alter Freund der Familie* ♦ *Auch nach ihrer
Trennung blieben sie Freunde.* ♦ *Er galt als ein
Freund der Armen.* be friends (with sb) (mit jdm)
befreundet sein [bə'frɔɡndət zaɛn] +*sein* ◊ *Sie ist
seit Jahren mit ihm befreundet.* circle of friends
Freundeskreis ['frɔɡndəskraɛs] der <-es, -e> *most
sing* ◊ *Sie hat einen großen Freundeskreis.*
ⓔ be no friend of sth kein Freund von etw./...
(gen) sein ◊ *Ich bin kein Freund von vielen Worten.*
♦ *Er ist kein Freund langer Erklärungen.* make
friends Freunde finden make friends with sb sich
mit jdm anfreunden

friendly (adj) 1. *(kind, welcoming)* freundlich
['frɔɡntlɪç] ◊ *Sie war sehr freundlich zu ihm.* ♦ *ein
freundliches Lächeln* 2. friendly with sb mit jdm
befreundet [mɪt ... bə'frɔɡndət] *no comp/superl* ◊
Wir waren früher befreundet. ♦ *Sind Sie mit dem
Angeklagten befreundet?* 3. SPORT friendly match
Freundschaftsspiel ['frɔɡntʃaftsˌʃpiːl] das <-(e)s, -e>
4. *(nations)* befreundet [bə'frɔɡndət] *no comp/superl*
◊ *befreundete Staaten; (relations between nations)*
freundschaftlich ['frɔɡntʃaftlɪç] ◊ *Zwischen Deutschland und Frankreich herrschen freundschaftliche
Beziehungen.*

friendship (noun) Freundschaft ['frɔɡntʃaft] die
<-, -en> ◊ *Die beiden verbindet eine tiefe Freund-
schaft.* ♦ *Zwischen den beiden Staaten besteht eine
enge Freundschaft.* strike up a friendship Freundschaft schließen

fries (noun) *(French)* fries Pommes frites [pɔm'frɪt(s)]
die <-> *pl* ◊ *eine Portion Pommes frites mit
Ketchup*

fright (noun) *(scare)* Schreck [ʃrɛk] der <-(e)s, -e>
most sing ◊ *Vor Schreck ließ er das Glas fallen.* ♦ *Sie
bekam einen furchtbaren Schreck, als sie das sah.*
give sb a fright jdn erschrecken [e'ʃrɛkn̩]
<erschreckt, erschreckte, hat erschreckt>
ⓔ take fright es mit der Angst zu tun bekommen
◊ *Da bekam er es plötzlich mit der Angst zu tun
und rannte weg.*

frighten (verb) *(make sb scared)* frighten sb jdm Angst
machen ['aŋst maxn̩] +*haben* ◊ *den Kindern mit Gru-
selgeschichten Angst machen* ♦ *Der Gedanke daran
macht mir Angst.; (give sb a shock)* jdn erschrecken
[e'ʃrɛkn̩] <erschreckt, erschreckte, hat erschreckt> ◊

Ich hoffe, ich habe dich nicht erschreckt. frighten sb into doing sth jdn so verunsichern, dass jd etw. tut ['zo: fɛl,ʊnzɪçən das] <verunsichert, verunsicherte, hat verunsichert> ◊ *Der Vertreter verunsicherte die alte Dame so, dass sie den Kaufvertrag unterschrieb.*

• **frighten away** [phras v] *(drive away)* verscheuchen [fɛˈʃɔ̯ɔçn̩] <verscheucht, verscheuchte, hat verscheucht> ◊ *Der laute Knall hat die Tiere verscheucht.*; *(deter)* abschrecken ['apʃrɛkn̩] <schreckt ab, schreckte ab, hat abgeschreckt> ◊ *Der hohe Preis wird viele Käufer abschrecken.*

• **frighten off** [phras v] → **frighten away**

frightened [adj] ängstlich ['ɛŋstlɪç] ◊ *Die Kinder sahen ängstlich aus.* ♦ *„Was ist das?", fragte sie mit ängstlicher Stimme.* be frightened of sb/sth vor jdm/etw. Angst haben [fo:ɐ̯ ... 'aŋst ha:bm̩] +haben ◊ *Ich habe Angst vor großen Hunden.* be frightened to do sth, be frightened of doing sth Angst davor haben, etw. zu tun ◊ *Sie hat Angst davor, abends allein nach Hause zu gehen.* Don't be frightened. Hab keine Angst. be frightened by sth/sb vor jdm/etw. erschrecken [fo:ɐ̯ ... eˈʃrɛkn̩] <erschrickt, erschrak, ist erschrocken> ◊ *Das Baby ist vor dem Hund erschrocken.*

frightening(ly) [adj, adv] beängstigend [bəˈʔɛŋstɪɡn̩t] ◊ *ein beängstigender Gedanke* ♦ *Der Anstieg der Arbeitslosigkeit ist beängstigend.* ♦ *Das Kind ist beängstigend blass.*

frightful(ly) [adj, adv] furchtbar ['fʊrçtbaːr] ◊ *ein furchtbarer Unfall* ♦ *Hier herrscht ja eine furchtbare Unordnung!* ♦ *furchtbar schlecht Englisch sprechen*

fringe [noun] **1.** *(hair)* Pony ['pɔniː] der <-s, -s> ◊ *Sie trug einen Pony.* ♦ *sich* [dat] *den Pony schneiden lassen; (on a shawl etc.)* Franse ['franzə] die <-, -n> most pl ◊ *ein Schal mit langen Fransen* **2.** *(periphery)* Rand [rant] der <-(e)s, Ränder> ◊ *Am Rand der Stadt werden neue Siedlungen gebaut.* ♦ *am Rande der Gesellschaft leben* ♦ *Am Rande der Konferenz wurden wichtige Themen angesprochen.* fringe group Randgruppe ['rantɡrʊpə] die <-, -n>

frog [noun] Frosch [frɔʃ] der <-(e)s, Frösche> ◊ *Man hörte Frösche quaken.*

◉ have a frog in your throat einen Frosch im Hals haben

from [prep] **1.** *(indicating who sends sth/sb or gives sth)* von [fɔn] +dat ◊ *Helfer von Unicef sind bereits vor Ort.* ♦ *Das ist ein Geschenk von meiner Tante.* ♦ *sich von jdm Geld leihen* **2.** *(indicating the origins of sb/sth)* aus [aʊs] +dat ◊ *Sie kommt aus Berlin/ Deutschland.* ♦ *Käse aus Frankreich* ♦ *aus der Flasche trinken* ♦ *aus guter Familie stammen* ♦ *Geschichten aus meiner Jugend* ♦ *Fotos aus der Zeit vor dem Krieg* ♦ *ein Gesetz aus dem Jahr 1910* Where are you from? Woher kommen Sie/kommst du? from all over the world aus aller Welt from it/ that daraus [da'raʊs] ◊ *Das ist mein Glas. Wer hat daraus getrunken?* ♦ *Was können wir daraus lernen?* **3.** *(indicating where or when sth starts)* von [fɔn] +dat ◊ *ein Zug von Augsburg nach Hamburg* ♦ *Sie arbeitet von 9 bis 17 Uhr.* ♦ *Der Preis ist von 35 auf 45 Euro gestiegen.; (from a certain place or time in the future onwards)* ab [ap] +dat ◊ *Ab hier sind es noch 25 Meter.* from ... onwards ab ... ◊ *Ab nächster Woche habe ich Urlaub.* ♦ *Ab 20 Uhr spielt hier eine Band.* ♦ *Ab sofort kann man auch mit Kreditkarte zahlen.* ♦ *ab Mitte Juli* from now on ab jetzt;

(describing past time) from the age of 20 etc. seit jd 20 etc. ist [zaɐ̯t ... 'tsvantsɪç ɪst] ◊ *Sie wohnt hier, seit sie 12 ist.* **4.** *(indicating the removal of sth)* aus [aʊs] +dat ◊ *Er riss ein Blatt aus dem Heft.* ♦ *eine Arie aus Verdis Oper „Aida"* ♦ *Sie nahm mir das Tablett aus der Hand.* ♦ *Sie nahm einen Schraubenzieher aus der Kiste.* ♦ *Drei Gefangene sind aus dem Gefängnis entkommen.* 21 from 40 is 19. 40 weniger 21 ist 19. **5.** *(indicating distance)* from sth von etw. entfernt [fɔn ... ɛntˈfɛɐ̯nt] ◊ *Das Schloss ist mehrere Kilometer von der Küste entfernt.* from it/ there davon entfernt [daˈfɔn ɛntˈfɛɐ̯nt] ◊ *Kennst du die Hirsch-Apotheke? Ich wohne nur 100 Meter davon entfernt.* **6.** *(indicating the cause of sth)* an [an] +dat ◊ *Sie starben an Erschöpfung.* ♦ *Er leidet an einer seltenen Krankheit.* ♦ *Ich sah an seinen Augen, dass er sehr traurig war.* from what I hear soviel ich gehört habe ◊ *Soviel ich gehört habe, soll er morgen zurückkommen.; (because of a particular activity)* vom [fɔm] contraction of 'von' + 'dem' ◊ *vom Arbeiten müde sein* **7.** *(indicating range)* von [fɔn] +dat ◊ *Hier können Sie alles kaufen, vom Spülmittel bis zur Pelzmütze.* **8.** *(indicating a return from sth)* aus [aʊs] +dat ◊ *Erst nach Jahren kam er aus der Kriegsgefangenschaft zurück.* **9.** *(indicating sb's position while they are doing sth)* von [fɔn] +dat ◊ *Von oben gesehen sieht alles so winzig aus.* ♦ *Von hier kann man das ganze Tal überblicken.* **10.** *(indicating the material out of which sth is made)* aus [aʊs] +dat ◊ *Diese Stühle werden aus Kunststoff gemacht.*

front¹ [noun] **1.** *(forward side of sth)* Vorderseite ['fɔrdɛzaɐ̯tə] die <-, -n> ◊ *Der Eingang befindet sich auf der Vorderseite des Gebäudes.* ♦ *Das Hemd hat auf der Vorderseite einen Fleck.* north front Nordseite ['nɔrtzaɐ̯tə] die <-, -n> **2.** *(of a row, train etc.)* Spitze ['ʃpɪtsə] die <-, -n> ◊ *der Wagen an der Spitze der Kolonne* ♦ *Er ging an der Spitze und zeigte uns den Weg.* at the front vorn [fɔrn] ◊ *Wenn du gut sehen willst, setz dich vorn hin.* ♦ *Sie stand ganz vorn in der Schlange.* **3.** on the job etc. front was die Arbeit etc. betrifft [vas diː a'baɐ̯t bətrɪft] ◊ *Was die Arbeit betrifft, so gibt es leider keine guten Nachrichten.* **4.** *(cover for illegal activity, outward appearance)* Fassade [fa'saːdə] die <-, -n> ◊ *Der Obstladen dient nur als Fassade für seine Drogengeschäfte.* ♦ *Das ist alles nur Fassade.* **5.** POL, METEO, MIL Front [frɔnt] die <-, -en> ◊ *Es war Krieg und die meisten Männer waren an der Front.* ♦ *Die Front verlief entlang dem Fluss.* ♦ *an allen Fronten angegriffen werden* ♦ *Eine Front kalter Luftmassen zieht herüber.* ♦ *die Front der Kriegsgegner* warm front Warmfront ['vaɐ̯mfrɔnt] cold front Kaltfront ['kaltfrɔnt] **6.** *(at the seaside)* Strandpromenade ['ʃtrantproməˌnaːdə] die <-, -n> ◊ *die Strandpromenade entlanggehen*

◉ in front of vor ... [dat] ◊ *Sie sitzen vor dem Fernseher.* ♦ *Sie ging vor mir durchs Ziel.* in front (of it/that/them etc.) davor ◊ *Die Jungen standen in der zweiten Reihe, die Mädchen davor.* ♦ *ein Haus mit einem hohen Zaun davor*

front² [adj] **1.** *(forward)* vordere ['fɔrdərə] no comp, only before ns <ein vorderer ..., eine vordere ..., ein vorderes ...> ◊ *der vordere Teil des Zuges* ♦ *Im Theater saßen wir in einer der vorderen Reihen.* front seat Vordersitz ['fɔrdɛzɪts] der <-es, -e> front

wheel Vorderrad ['fɔ'deːraːt] das
<-(e)s, Vorderräder> front paw Vorderpfote
['fɔ'depfoːtə] die <-, -n> front garden Vorgarten
['foːggaʳtn̩] der <-s, Vorgärten> 2. *(covering illegal
activities)* front ... Tarn... Tarn... [taʳn] front organization
Tarnorganisation ['taʳn|ɔʳganizaˌtsjoːn] die <-, -en>
◊ *Der Verein ist eine Tarnorganisation für rechtsextreme Gruppen.*

front door [noun] Haustür ['haostyːɐ̯] die <-, -en> ◊
Vor der Haustür stand ein fremder Mann.

frontier [noun] *(border)* Grenze ['grɛntsə] die <-, -n>
◊ *die Grenze zwischen Deutschland und Frankreich*
♦ *Deutschlands Grenze zu Österreich* ♦ *Die Wissenschaft stößt immer wieder an ihre Grenzen.; (peripheral area)* Grenzgebiet ['grɛntsgəbiːt] das <-(e)s, -e>
◊ *Siedlungen im Grenzgebiet* push back the frontiers
of science wissenschaftliches Neuland betreten
[ˌvɪsn̩ʃaftlɪçəs ˈnɔɪ̯lant bətreːtn̩] <betritt, betrat, hat
betreten> frontier controls Grenzkontrollen
['grɛntskɔnˌtrɔlən] die <-> *pl* ◊ *Grenzkontrollen
durchführen* frontier post Grenzposten ['grɛntspɔstn̩]
der <-s, -> ◊ *Sie erreichten einen bewachten Grenzposten.*

front page [noun] Titelseite ['tiːtl̩zaetə] die <-, -n>

frost [noun] **1.** *(layer of ice)* Raureif ['raoraɛf] der
<-(e)s> *no pl* ◊ *von Raureif bedeckte Bäume*
2. *(cold weather)* Frost [frɔst] der <-(e)s, Fröste> ◊
Es herrscht strenger Frost. ♦ *Diese Pflanzen vertragen
keinen Frost.*

frostily [adv] *(unfriendly)* kühl [kyːl] ◊ *jdn kühl
empfangen*

frosty [adj] **1.** *(very cold)* frostig ['frɔstɪç] ◊ *ein
frostiger Morgen* ♦ *Die Luft war frostig.* **2.** *(fig)*
(unfriendly) kühl [kyːl] ◊ *eine kühle Reaktion* ♦ *Die
Atmosphäre war kühl und reserviert.*

frown¹ [noun] Stirnrunzeln ['ʃtɪʳnrʊntsl̩n] das <-s> *no
pl*

frown² [verb] frown (at sth) die Stirn (über etw. [acc])
runzeln [di: 'ʃtɪʳn rʊntsl̩n] +haben ◊ *Sie sah von
seinem Buch auf und runzelte die Stirn.* ♦ *Worüber
runzelst du denn jetzt schon wieder die Stirn?*

frozen [adj] **1.** *(food)* tiefgefroren
['tiːfgəfroːrən] *no comp/superl* ◊ *Die Pizza ist tiefgefroren.* ♦ *tiefgefrorenes Fleisch* **2.** *(water, ground)*
gefroren [gə'froːrən] *no comp/superl* ◊ *gefrorenes
Wasser* ♦ *Der Boden ist hier das ganze Jahr über
gefroren.* **3.** *sb is frozen* jdm ist eiskalt
[ɪst 'aes'kalt] +sein ◊ *Mir ist eiskalt. Können wir
nach Hause gehen?* frozen stiff steif gefroren
['ʃtaef gə,froːrən] ◊ *Meine Finger sind schon ganz
steif gefroren.*
◉ **frozen with fear/terror** etc. starr vor Angst/
Schreck ein.

fruit [noun] *(collective noun)* Obst [oːpst] das <-(e)s>
no pl ◊ *Du solltest mehr Obst essen.; (of a plant,
tree, of sb's labo(u)rs)* Frucht [frʊxt] die
<-, Früchte> ◊ *kandierte/tropische Früchte* ♦ *Die
Frucht der Buche heißt Buchecker.* ♦ *Mein Buch ist
die Frucht jahrelanger Arbeit.* fruit juice Fruchtsaft
['frʊxtzaft] der <-(e)s, Fruchtsäfte> ◊
◉ **bear fruit** Früchte tragen

fruitful [adj] fruchtbar ['frʊxtbaːʳ] *(also fig)* ◊ *Die
Zusammenarbeit erwies sich als besonders fruchtbar.*
♦ *fruchtbares Ackerland*

frustrate [verb] *(a person)* frustrieren [frʊs'triːrən]
<frustriert, frustrierte, hat frustriert> ◊ *Die negative*

Antwort seines Chefs frustrierte ihn.*; (plans, hopes
etc.)* zunichte machen [tsu'nɪçtə maxn̩] +haben ◊
*Diese Entscheidung macht alle unsere Pläne
zunichte.*

frustrated → frustrate [adj] frustriert [frʊs'triːɐ̯t]
<frustrierter, am frustriertesten> ◊ *Die meisten
Wähler sind angesichts der politischen Lage frustriert.*
♦ *eine frustrierte Ehefrau*

frustrating [adj] frustrierend [frʊs'triːrənt] ◊ *eine
frustrierende Erfahrung* ♦ *Ach, das ist alles so frustrierend!*

frustration [noun] *(of a person)* Frustration
[frʊstra'tsjoːn] die <-, -en> ◊ *die wachsende Frustration der Arbeitslosen* ♦ *Ich esse nur aus Frustration.*
♦ *sexuelle Frustration* in frustration frustriert
[frʊs'triːɐ̯t] <frustrierter, am frustriertesten> ◊ „*Warum
hast du denn schon wieder keine Zeit?"*, fragte sie
frustriert.; *(of plans, hopes etc.)* Zerstörung
[tsɛ'ʃtøːrʊŋ] die <-, -en> most sing ◊ *Diese Entscheidung bedeutete die Zerstörung all unserer Hoffnungen.*

fry [verb] *(in a frying pan, in the sun)* braten ['braːtn̩]
<brät, briet, hat gebraten> ◊ *Kartoffeln in Öl braten*
♦ *In der Pfanne brieten Zwiebeln.* ♦ *Ich mag nicht
stundenlang in der Sonne braten.*

frying pan [noun] Pfanne ['pfanə] die <-, -n> ◊ *ein
Steak in der Pfanne braten*
◉ **jump out of the frying pan into the fire** vom
Regen in die Traufe kommen

fuck [verb] ficken ['fɪkn̩] +haben *(taboo)*
◉ **fuck him/her** etc. der/die etc.soll mich doch
am Arsch lecken *(rude)* **fuck you** leck mich am
Arsch *(rude)*
● **fuck off** [phras v] **1.** *(go away)* sich verpissen
[fɛ'pɪsn̩] <verpisst sich, verpisste sich, hat sich
verpisst> *(rude)* ◊ *Verpiss dich!* **2.** fuck sb off jdn
ankotzen ['ankɔtsn̩] +haben *(rude)* ◊ *Du kotzt mich
echt an mit deinem ewigen Genörgel!*

fucking [adj, adv] verdammt [fɛ'damt] *no comp/superl;
when used as a adj, only before ns (fam)* ◊ *Wo
bleibt der verdammte Mechaniker?* ♦ *Du verdammter
Idiot!* ♦ *Er ist ein verdammt guter Tennisspieler.* It's
fucking raining again! Verdammte Scheiße, es
regnet schon wieder!

fuel [noun] **1.** *(coal, oil, wood etc.)* Brennstoff
['brɛnʃtɔf] der <-(e)s, -e> ◊ *Steinkohle, Erdöl und
Erdgas sind Brennstoffe.; (for a motor vehicle)* Kraftstoff ['kraftʃtɔf] der <-(e)s, -e> ◊ *zu viel Kraftstoff
verbrauchen; (for aircraft, rockets)* Treibstoff
['traepʃtɔf] der <-(e)s, -e> ◊ *Treibstoff sparen*
2. *(fig) (encouragement)* Nahrung ['naːrʊŋ] die <->
no pl ◊ *Durch diese Entdeckung fand ihr Misstrauen
neue Nahrung.* add fuel to sth neue Nahrung geben [dat]
◊ *Seine Äußerung gab den Spekulationen neue Nahrung.*

fulfil, fulfill [verb] **1.** *(a condition, duty, promise etc.)*
erfüllen [e'fʏlən] <erfüllt, erfüllte, hat erfüllt> ◊ *die
erforderlichen Voraussetzungen erfüllen* ♦ *Diese Voraussetzung erfüllt ihren Zweck nicht.* ♦ *Er hat seine
Pflicht immer erfüllt.* ♦ *einen Wunsch erfüllen* ♦
Damit hast du dein Versprechen erfüllt. **2.** *(satisfy)*
ausfüllen ['aosfʏlən] +haben ◊ *ein Beruf, der einen
ganz und gar ausfüllt* ♦ *Diese Tätigkeit füllt sie
nicht aus.* fulfil yourself sich selbst verwirklichen
['zɛlpst fɛˌvɪʳklɪçn̩] <verwirklicht sich, verwirklichte
sich, hat sich verwirklicht> ◊ *Sie wünscht sich einen*

Beruf, in dem sie sich selbst verwirklichen kann.
full [adj] voll [fɔl] ◊ *Du hast meine volle Unterstüt-zung!* ♦ *Ich warte seit einer vollen Stunde auf dich!* ♦ *Dein Glas ist ja noch halb voll!* full of voller ['fɔlə] invariable, only before ns ◊ *Sie war voller Taten-drang.* ♦ *Das Programm war voller störender Fehler.* to the/in full vollständig ['fɔlʃtɛndɪç]
ⓔ **enjoy to the full** in vollen Zügen genießen
full moon [noun] Vollmond ['fɔlmoːnt] der <-(e)s> no pl ◊ *Bei Vollmond schlafe ich schlecht.*
full stop [noun] Punkt [pʊŋkt] der <-(e)s, -e> ◊ *einen Punkt machen/setzen*
ⓔ **come to a full stop** zum Stillstand kommen
full-time¹ [adj] Vollzeit... ['fɔltsaet] full-time job Voll-zeitbeschäftigung ['fɔltsaetbəʃɛftɪɡʊŋ] die <-, -en> full-time mother Vollzeitmutter ['fɔltsaetmʊtə] die <-, Vollzeitmütter>
full-time² [adv] ganztags ['gantstaːks] no comp/superl ◊ *Wird Ihre Tochter ganztags betreut?* work full-time Vollzeit arbeiten ['fɔltsaet a'rbaetn] <arbeitet, arbeitete, hat gearbeitet>
fully [adv] **1.** *(completely)* völlig ['fœlɪç] no comp/superl ◊ *Sie ist mit dem Ergebnis völlig zufrieden.* ♦ *Er hat das Problem noch nicht völlig verstanden.* **2.** *(to the utmost)* voll [fɔl] no comp/superl ◊ *ein voll besetzter Bus* ♦ *Das Gerät ist alt, aber noch voll funk-tionsfähig.* ♦ *Sie ist körperlich schon voll entwickelt.* **3.** *(before expressions of quantity)* ganze ['gantsə] invariable, only before ns ◊ *Er kann ganze 5,80 m weit springen.* ♦ *Sie ist ganze 1,90 m groß.*
fumes [noun] *(from cigarettes)* Dunst [dʊnst] der <-es> sing ◊ *In der Kneipe hing der Dunst von Zigaretten.; (from traffic)* Abgase ['apgaːzə] die <-> pl; *(from a fire)* Rauch [raox] der <-(e)s> no pl; *(toxic)* Dämpfe ['dɛmpfə] die <-> pl
fun¹ [noun] Spaß [ʃpaːs] der <-es> no pl ◊ *Die Gäste hatten auf der Feier viel Spaß.* ♦ *jdm den Spaß verderben* for fun zum Spaß be good fun viel Spaß machen
ⓔ **make fun of sb** sich über jdn lustig machen
sound like fun prima klingen
fun² [adj] vergnüglich [fɛ'gnyːklɪç] ◊ *eine vergnügliche Beschäftigung* ♦ *Der Tag war sehr vergnüglich.* He is a fun person. Mit ihm kann man viel Spaß haben. It's a fun thing to do. Es macht viel Spaß.
function¹ [noun] **1.** *(job, task, purpose, process in your body, variable quantity)* Funktion [fʊŋk'tsjoːn] die <-, -en> ◊ *Welche Funktion hat der Künstler in der Gesellschaft?* perform a function eine Funktion erfüllen bodily functions Körperfunktionen ['kœrpɐfʊŋk,tsjoːnən] die <-> pl **2.** *(social event)* Ver-anstaltung [fɛɐ'anʃtaltʊŋ] die <-, -en> ◊ *Die Veran-staltung beginnt um 20 Uhr.*
function² [verb] funktionieren [fʊŋktsjo'niːrən] <funk-tioniert, funktionierte, hat funktioniert> ◊ *Jetzt funktio-niert die Heizung wieder.* ♦ *Das transplantierte Herz funktionierte perfekt.* function as sth als etw. fungieren [als ... fʊŋ,giːrən] <fungiert, fungierte, hat fungiert> ◊ *Er fungierte als Haushälter.*
functional [adj] **1.** *(fulfilling a job)* funktional [fʊŋktsjoːna'l] ◊ *funktionale Küchengeräte* ♦ *Dieses Möbelstück ist sehr funktional.* **2.** *(working correctly)* funktionstüchtig [fʊŋk'tsjoːnstyçtɪç] ◊ *ein funktions-tüchtiger Ofen* ♦ *voll funktionstüchtig sein*
fund¹ [noun] **1.** *(collected, invested etc.)* Fonds [fɔŋ] der <-, -> ◊ *ein Fonds für die Opfer der Flutkata-*

strophe contribute towards a fund Geld spenden; *(available)* funds Mittel ['mɪtl] die <-> pl ◊ *öffentli-che Mittel* raise the funds for sth die Mittel für etw. aufbringen be in funds über (ausreichende) Mittel verfügen I ran out of funds. Mir ging das Geld aus. **2.** *(supply)* fund of sth Fundus [ˈfʊndʊs an] der <-, -> most sing ◊ *Sie besitzt einen reichen Fundus an Wissen.*
fund² [verb] fördern ['fœɐdən] +haben ◊ *Die Stiftung fördert junge Musiker.*
fundamental [adj] fundamental [fʊndamɛn'taːl] ◊ *ein fundamentaler Fehler/Unterschied* ♦ *Diese Frage ist fundamental.* be fundamental to sth das Fundament für etw. bilden [das fʊndaˈmɛnt fyːɐ ... bɪldn] ◊ *Das Studium bildete das Fundament für meine Karriere.*
fundamentally [adv] grundsätzlich ['grʊntzɛtslɪç] ◊ *Grundsätzlich ist sie auf der Seite der Schwachen.* ♦ *sein Leben grundsätzlich verändern*
funding [noun] **1.** *(financing)* Finanzierung [finan'tsiːrʊŋ] die <-, -en> **2.** *(financial support)* Förderung ['fœɐdərʊŋ] die <-, -en> ◊ *die staatliche Förderung von Privatschulen*
funeral [noun] Beerdigung [bə'eːɐdɪgʊŋ] die <-, -en> ◊ *Die Beerdigung fand gestern im engsten Familien-kreis statt.; (in compounds)* funeral ... Trauer... ['traoɐ] funeral procession Trauerzug ['traoɐtsuːk] der <-s, Trauerzüge> funeral service Trauergottesdienst ['traoɐgɔtəsdiːnst] der <-(e)s, -e> funeral director Bestatter [bə'ʃtatɐ] der <-s, -> ♀Bestatterin [bə'ʃtatərɪn] die <-, -nen>
funnel [noun] **1.** *(in the kitchen)* Trichter ['trɪçtɐ] der <-s, -> ◊ *etw. in einen Trichter schütten* **2.** *(on a boat)* Schornstein ['ʃɔrnʃtaen] der <-(e)s, -e>
funny [adj] **1.** *(amusing)* lustig ['lʊstɪç] ◊ *eine lustige Geschichte* ♦ *Ich finde seine Witze überhaupt nicht lustig.* **2.** *(strange)* komisch ['koːmɪʃ] ◊ *Gestern ist mir eine komische Sache passiert.* ♦ *Dieser Zufall ist wirklich komisch.*
fur [noun] **1.** *(of an animal)* Fell [fɛl] das <-(e)s, -e> mostly with the article ◊ *Die Katze hatte ein schwarzes Fell.* ♦ *Sie strich dem Hund übers Fell.* made of fur aus Pelz hergestellt **2.** *(coat etc.)* Pelz [pɛlts] der <-es, -e> ◊ *Sie zog ihren Pelz aus.* **3.** *(on the tongue)* Belag [bə'laːk] der <-(e)s, Beläge>
furious(ly) [adj, adv] wütend ['vyːtnt] ◊ *Er ist wütend, weil sie gelogen hat.* ♦ *wütende Proteste* ♦ *„Du Schuft!", schrie sie ihn wütend an.*
furnish [verb] **1.** *(with furniture)* einrichten ['aenrɪçtn] <richtet ein, richtete ein, hat eingerichtet> ◊ *Ihr Haus ist sehr geschmackvoll eingerichtet.* ♦ *einen Raum als Kinderzimmer einrichten* **2.** *(with information)* furnish sb with sth jdm etw. verschaffen [fe'ʃafn] <verschafft, verschaffte, hat verschafft> ◊ *Sie hat ihm Informationen verschafft.*
furnished → **furnish** [adj] *(with furniture)* möbliert [mø'bliːɐt] no comp/superl ◊ *Alle Zimmer sind komplett möbliert.* ♦ *in eine möblierte Wohnung ziehen*
furnishings [noun] Einrichtung ['aenrɪçtʊŋ] die <-, -en>
furniture [noun] Möbel ['møːbl] die <-> pl
ⓔ **be part of the furniture** zum Inventar gehören
furry [adj] pelzig ['pɛltsɪç] ◊ *ein pelziger Belag* ♦ *Meine Zunge fühlt sich pelzig an.* furry animal Plüschtier ['plʏʃtiːɐ] das <-s, -e> a furry cat eine Katze mit kuscheligem Fell [aenə ˌkatsə mɪt ˌkʊʃəlɪgəm 'fɛl]

A
B
C
D
E
F
G
H
I
J
K
L
M
N
O
P
Q
R
S
T
U
V
W
X
Y
Z

further¹ [adj] **1.** *(more exact)* nähere ['nɛːərə] *no comp/superl, only before ns* ◊ *Nähere Einzelheiten sind nicht bekannt.* **2.** *(additional)* weitere ['vaɛtərə] *no comp/superl, only before ns* ◊ *Haben Sie noch weitere Fragen?*

further² [adv] weiter ['vaɛtə] ◊ *Halt, nicht weiter!* ♦ *Müssen wir noch viel weiter gehen?* further and further **immer weiter**
⊙ **further back** früher **further on** später

furthermore [adv] zudem [tsu'deːm] *(lofty)* ◊ *Er ist reich und sieht zudem gut aus.*

furthest [superl] **1.** *(the longest distance)* am weitesten [am 'vaɛtəstn̩] ◊ *Er kann von uns allen am weitesten springen.* be furthest (away) from sth **am weitesten entfernt von etw. sein 2.** *(most distant)* entfernteste [ɛnt'fɛɐ̯ntəstə] ◊ *die entferntesten Galaxien im Universum*

fury [noun] **1.** *(emotion)* Wut [vuːt] die <-> *no pl* ◊ *in Wut geraten* ♦ *Ich musste in ohnmächtiger Wut zusehen.* with fury vor Wut ◊ *Er konnte vor Wut nicht sprechen.* fury at sth/sb **Wut auf etw./jdn 2.** *(intensity)* Heftigkeit ['hɛftɪçkaɛt] die <-> *no pl* ◊ *Die Heftigkeit des Windes nahm noch zu.*
⊙ **fly into a fury** sich fürchterlich aufregen

fuse¹ [noun] **1.** *(in plugs, electrical appliances)* Sicherung ['zɪçərʊŋ] die <-, -en> ◊ *eine Sicherung auswechseln* ♦ *eine durchgebrannte Sicherung* A fuse blew. **Eine Sicherung brannte durch.** It blew a fuse. **Es verursachte einen Kurzschluss. 2.** *(of a bomb, fireworks)* Zünder ['tsʏndɐ] der <-s, ->; *(string)* Zündschnur ['tsʏntʃnuːɐ̯] die <-, Zündschnüre>
⊙ **blow a fuse** ausrasten sb has a short fuse jd rastet leicht aus

fuse² [verb] **1.** *(substances)* verschmelzen [fɐ'ʃmɛltsn̩] <verschmilzt, verschmolz, hat/ist verschmolzen> *transitive use +haben/intransitive use +sein* ◊ *Form und Inhalt verschmelzen zu einem gelungenen Gedicht.* ♦ *Die Band verschmilzt Pop mit Klassik. 2. (electrical device)* durchbrennen ['dʊɐ̯çbrɛnən] <brennt durch, brannte durch, ist durchgebrannt> ◊ *Alle Sicherungen*

sind durchgebrannt. fuse sth einen Kurzschluss in etw. [dat] verursachen [aɛnən 'kʊɐ̯tsʃlʊs ɪn ... feːˌuːɡzaxn̩] <verursacht, verursachte, hat verursacht>

fusion [noun] **1.** *(of different styles, ideas)* Verschmelzung [fɐ'ʃmɛltsʊŋ] die <-, -en> ◊ *eine Verschmelzung von Musikstilen* **2.** *(of atoms, companies)* Fusion [fu'zjoːn] die <-, -en> ◊ *die Fusion von Atomkernen* ♦ *die Fusion zweier Unternehmen*

fuss [noun] Theater [te'aːtɐ] das <-s> *no pl (fam, pej)* ◊ *Jetzt mach nicht so ein Theater wegen dem bisschen Arbeit!*
⊙ **kick up a fuss** Krach schlagen

futile [adj] **1.** *(without success)* vergeblich [fɛ'geːplɪç] *no comp/superl* ◊ *Mein Versuch, sie zu beruhigen, war vergeblich.* ♦ *unsere vergeblichen Bemühungen um eine Aussöhnung* **2.** *(making no sense)* zwecklos ['tsvɛkloːs] *no comp/superl* ◊ *Widerstand ist zwecklos.* ♦ *eine zwecklose Maßnahme*

future¹ [noun] **1.** *(time ahead)* Zukunft ['tsuːkʊnft] die <-> *no pl* ◊ *Wie stellt er sich seine Zukunft vor?* ♦ *Ihr steht eine großartige Zukunft bevor.* in the near future **in nächster Zukunft** in future **künftig** ['kʏnftɪç] ◊ *Künftig will sie sich stärker auf ihre Karriere konzentrieren.* **2.** GRAM future (tense) Futur [fu'tuːɐ̯] das <-s, -e> *most sing* ◊ *das Futur eines Verbs bilden* future perfect **Futur II**

future² [adj] zukünftig ['tsuːkʏnftɪç] *no comp/superl, only before ns* ◊ *Das ist seine zukünftige Frau.* ♦ *zukünftige Ereignisse*

fuzzy [adj] **1.** *(picture, image)* unscharf ['ʊnʃaˑf] <unschärfer, am unschärfsten> ◊ *ein unscharfes Fernsehbild* ♦ *Alle Fotos waren leider unscharf.* **2.** *(hair, fur)* kraus [kraʊs] <krauser, am krausesten> ◊ *Sein Haar war kraus und lockig.* ♦ *eine Katze mit krausem Fell* **3.** *(memory, details, explanation)* vage ['vaːgə] <vager, am vag(e)sten> ◊ *ein vage Vorstellung von etw. haben* ♦ *Dein Konzept ist eher vage.* **4.** *(feeling)* a warm fuzzy feeling **ein warmes Gefühl** [aɛn vaˑmas gə'fyːl] ◊ *ein warmes Gefühl im Bauch haben*

G

g, G noun **1.** *(letter)* g, G [ge:] das <–(s), –(s)> ◊ *ein kleines g/großes G* ♦ *G wie Gustav* **2.** MUS G g, G [ge:] das <–(s), –(s)> ◊ *auf der Flöte ein G spielen* G minor g-Moll ['ge:mɔl] G major G-Dur ['ge:du:ɐ̯]

gadget noun Gerät [gə'rɛ:t] das <–(e)s, –e> ◊ *Ein Dosenöffner ist ein nützliches Gerät.*

gain¹ noun **1.** *(increase)* Zunahme ['tsu:na:mə] die <–, –n> a gain in sth eine Zunahme ... gen ◊ *eine Zunahme des Umsatzes* a gain of sth eine Zunahme um etw. ◊ *eine Zunahme der Arbeitslosigkeit um 10%* gain in weight Gewichtszunahme [gə'vɪçtstsu:na:mə]; *(increase in profits, productivity, votes)* Zuwachs ['tsu:vaks] der <–es> no pl The party made gains in the last election. **Die Partei konnte bei der letzten Wahl einen Stimmenzuwachs verzeichnen.** gain in profits Gewinnzuwachs [gə'vɪntsu:vaks] gain in productivity Produktivitätszuwachs [prɔdʊktivi'tɛ:tstsu:vaks] **2.** *(advantage, benefit)* Gewinn [gə'vɪn] der <–(e)s, –e> ◊ *Die neue Schauspielerin ist ein echter Gewinn für das Ensemble.* ♦ *Die Firma machte dieses Jahr große Gewinne.; (progress)* Fortschritt ['fɔ'tʃrɪt] der <–(e)s, –e> ◊ *Er hat in Mathe Fortschritte gemacht.* ♦ *im Kampf gegen den Krebs Fortschritte erzielen*

⊚ for financial gain des Geldes wegen for personal gain in eigennütziger Absicht

gain² verb **1.** *(achieve)* erlangen [ɛ'laŋən] <erlangt, erlangte, hat erlangt> +haben ◊ *Die Konservativen konnten nur 35 Prozent der Stimmen erlangen.* ♦ *Mit diesem Roman erlangte sie Weltruhm.* gain sth from sth etw. durch etw. erlangen; *(confidence, influence, insight, time)* gewinnen [gə'vɪnən] <gewinnt, gewann, hat gewonnen> ◊ *Erkenntnisse gewinnen* gain in self-confidence an Selbstvertrauen gewinnen There is nothing to be gained from waiting/being impatient. **Mit Warten/Ungeduld ist nichts gewonnen.**; *(a degree, diploma)* erwerben [ɛ'vɛrbm̩] <erwirbt, erwarb, hat erworben>; *(experience)* sammeln ['zaml̩n] +haben ◊ *Erfahrungen sammeln; (access, admission, entry)* erhalten [ɛ'haltn̩] <erhält, erhielt, hat erhalten> ◊ *Zugang zu Unterlagen erhalten* ♦ *Zutritt zu einem Gebäude erhalten* gain speed/momentum schneller werden ['ʃnɛlɐ veːɐ̯dn̩] +sein **2.** *(weight, in value)* zulegen ['tsu:le:gŋ̩] +haben ◊ *Bis zum Börsenschluss legten die Aktien deutlich zu.* ♦ *zwei Kilo zugelegt haben* **3.** *(clock)* gain sth (um) etw. vorgehen ['fo:ɐ̯ge:ən] <geht vor, ging vor, ist vorgegangen> ◊ *Deine Uhr geht (um) zehn Minuten vor.* **4.** *(make up)* gutmachen ['gu:tmaxn̩] +haben ◊ *Er machte zwei Sekunden auf den führenden Läufer gut.*

galaxy noun ASTRON Galaxie [gala'ksi:] die <–, –n> the Galaxy die Milchstraße [di: 'mɪlçʃtra:sə] <–> no pl

⊚ a galaxy of eine Unzahl von ◊ *eine Unzahl von Sternen*

gale noun Sturm [ʃtʊ'm] der <–(e)s, Stürme>

⊚ gales of laughter Lachsalven

gall bladder noun Galle ['galə] die <–, –n> ◊ *jdn*

an der Galle operieren

gallery noun **1.** *(for art)* Galerie [galə'ri:] die <–, –n> **2.** *(in church)* Empore [ɛm'po:rə] die <–, –n> ◊ *Wir saßen auf der Empore.; (in a cinema, theatre)* Rang [raŋ] der <–(e)s, Ränge> ◊ *Plätze im dritten Rang* **3.** *(underground)* Stollen ['ʃtɔlən] der <–s, –> ◊ *Der Stollen stürzte ein.*

gallon noun Gallone [ga'lo:nə] die <–, –n>

gallop verb galoppieren [galo'pi:rən] <galoppiert, galoppierte, hat/ist galoppiert> +haben/with indication of direction +sein ◊ *Drei Reiter galoppierten die Straße entlang.* ♦ *galoppierende Inflation/Schwindsucht* Time gallops by. **Die Zeit vergeht rasend schnell.** I galloped through the book. **Ich las das Buch in Windeseile.** Prices gallop ahead. **Die Preise ziehen stark an.**

gamble verb spielen ['ʃpi:lən] +haben ◊ *Er spielte den ganzen Abend im Kasino.* ♦ *Roulette spielen* gamble on sth auf etw. acc setzen [aɔf ... zɛtsn̩] +haben ◊ *Er setzte auf Rot.* ♦ *Sie setzten auf Kursgewinne.* gamble that darauf setzen, dass

• **gamble away** phras v gamble sth away etw. verspielen [fɐ'ʃpi:lən] <verspielt, verspielte, hat verspielt> ◊ *Ich habe mein Glück verspielt.*

game noun **1.** *(of play, sport, competition)* Spiel [ʃpi:l] das <–(e)s, –e> ◊ *ein Spiel gewinnen/verlieren* ♦ *Für ihn ist die Liebe nur ein Spiel.* ♦ *Das ist ein riskantes Spiel.* The game is up. **Das Spiel ist aus.** **2.** *(single event)* Partie [par'ti:] die <–, –n> ◊ *eine Partie Billard/Bridge/Schach spielen* **3.** *(section of tennis, table tennis, badminton)* Satz [zats] der <–es, Sätze> **4.** *(official competition)* the games die Spiele [di: 'ʃpi:lə] <–> pl ◊ *Die Spiele finden jedes Jahr statt.* **5.** *(fam) (line of work)* Branche ['brãʃə] die <–, –n> ◊ *Sie arbeitet schon lange in dieser Branche.* **6.** *(wild animal)* Wild [vɪlt] das <–(e)s> no pl ◊ *Diese Wälder sind reich an Wild.* ♦ *Sie isst kein Wild.*

⊚ be ahead of the game die Nase vorn haben be on the game auf den Strich gehen beat sb at their own game jdn mit den eigenen Mitteln schlagen give the game away alles verraten play games **1.** spielen ◊ *In unserer Familie wird viel gespielt.* **2.** play games with sb mit jdm sein Spielchen treiben ◊ *Du liebst ihn nicht, sondern du treibst nur dein Spielchen mit ihm!* what's sb's game etw. führt jd im Schilde ◊ *Du bist auf einmal so freundlich. Was führst du im Schilde?* ♦ *Er lächelt so komisch. Wer weiß, was er im Schilde führt.*

gang noun **1.** *(of criminals, children)* Bande ['bandə] die <–, –n> ◊ *Ist er ein Mitglied ihrer Bande?; (of friends)* Clique ['klɪkə] die <–, –n> ◊ *Die ganze Clique traf sich im Freibad.* **2.** *(of workmen)* Trupp [trʊp] der <–s, –s> ◊ *ein Trupp Bauarbeiter*

gap noun **1.** *(where sth is missing)* Lücke ['lʏkə] die <–, –n> ◊ *eine Lücke im Zaun* ♦ *Sprachkenntnisse mit großen Lücken* gap in the market Marktlücke ['ma'ktlʏkə] **2.** *(opening, cleft)* Spalt [ʃpalt] der

<-(e)s, -e> ◊ *ein Spalt im Felsen* **3.** *(difference)*
Kluft [klɔft] die <-, Klüfte> ◊ *Eine tiefe Kluft*
zwischen Theorie und Praxis tat sich auf. **4.** *(in*
time) Pause ['paozə] die <-, -n> ◊ *Nach einer Pause*
von zwei Monaten wurde die Serie fortgeführt.

garage [noun] **1.** *(for keeping cars)* Garage [ga'ra:ʒə]
die <-, -n> ◊ *das Auto in die Garage fahren*
2. *(repairing cars)* Werkstatt ['ve'kʃtat] die
<-, Werkstätten> ◊ *Das Auto muss dringend in die*
Werkstatt.; (selling cars) Autohändler ['aotohɛndlɐ]
der <-s, -> **3.** *(selling petrol)* Tankstelle ['taŋkʃtɛlə]
die <-, -n> ◊ *zur Tankstelle müssen*

garbage [noun] Müll [mʏl] der <-s> *no pl* ◊ *etw. in*
den Müll werfen ♦ *Red keinen Müll!*

garbage can [noun] Mülltonne ['mʏltɔnə] die <-, -n>

garbage collector [noun] Müllmann ['mʏlman] der
<-es, Müllmänner> the garbage collectors die Müll-
abfuhr [di: 'mʏlapfu:ɐ] <-> *sing* ◊ *Am Montag*
kommt die Müllabfuhr.

garden¹ [noun] **1.** *(private)* Garten ['ga'tn̩] der
<-s, Gärten> ◊ *Gemüse aus dem eigenen Garten* ♦
Er fand sie im Garten hinter dem Haus. **2.** *(public)*
gardens Park [pa'k] der <-s, -s>

garden² [verb] gärtnern ['gɛ'tnɐn] +haben ◊ *Er*
gärtnert gern.

gardener [noun] Gärtner ['gɛ'tnɐ] der <-s, -> ♀Gärt-
nerin ['gɛ'tnərɪn] die <-, -nen> ◊ *Er arbeitet als*
Gärtner bei der Stadt. ♦ *Die Gärtnerin schneidet die*
Rosen.

gargle [verb] gurgeln ['gʊ'gl̩n] +haben ◊ *Bei Hals-*
schmerzen hilft es, mit Salzwasser zu gurgeln.

garish(ly) [adj, adv] grell [grɛl] ◊ *grelle Farben* ♦ *Ich*
finde das Rot zu grell. ♦ *grell leuchten*

garlic [noun] Knoblauch ['kno:plaox] der <-(e)s> *no pl*

garment [noun] Kleidungsstück ['klaɛdʊŋsʃtʏk] das
<-(e)s, -e> ◊ *das passende Kleidungsstück suchen*
garments Kleidung ['klaɛdʊŋ] die <-> *sing* ◊ *Ihre*
Kleidung war nass geworden.; (in compound ns)
garment ... Bekleidungs... [bə'klaɛdʊŋs] garment
industry Bekleidungsindustrie
[bə'klaɛdʊŋsɪndʊs,tri:] die <-, -n>

gas [noun] **1.** Gas [ga:s] das <-es, -e> ◊ *Bei dem*
Unfall wurden giftige Gase frei. ♦ *Heizt ihr mit Gas*
oder mit Öl? **2.** *(in the US: petrol)* Benzin [bɛn'tsi:n]
das <-s> *no pl* ◊ *bleifreies Benzin* ♦ *Fährt das Auto*
mit Benzin oder mit Diesel?

gasoline [noun] Benzin [bɛn'tsi:n] das <-s> *no pl* ◊
bleifreies Benzin

gasp [verb] *(breathe in suddenly)* nach Luft schnappen
[na:x 'lʊft ʃnapm̩] +haben; *(be speechless)* sb gasps
at sth etw. verschlägt jdm den Atem
[fɛʃlɛ:kt ... de:n 'a:təm] <verschlägt, verschlug, hat ver-
schlagen> ◊ *Ihre Schönheit verschlug mir den Atem.*

gastric [adj] Magen... ['ma:gn̩] gastric ulcer Magenge-
schwür ['ma:gn̩gəʃvy:ɐ] das <-s, -e>

gate [noun] **1.** *(large)* Tor [to:ɐ] das <-(e)s, -e> ◊ *Die*
Tore des Zoos schließen um 18 Uhr.; (small) Pforte
['pfɔ'tə] die <-, -n> ◊ *Ein eiserne Pforte führte in*
das Kloster. **2.** *(at the airport)* Flugsteig ['flu:kʃtaɛk]
der <-(e)s, -e> ◊ *Bitte begeben Sie sich zum*
Flugsteig 12. **3.** the gate die Besucherzahlen
[di: bə'zu:xɐtsa:lən] <-> *pl* ◊ *Die Besucherzahlen bei*
Tennisturnieren sind stark zurückgegangen.

gateau [noun] Torte ['tɔ'tə] die <-, -n>

gather [verb] **1.** *(people)* versammeln [fɛ'zaml̩n] <ver-
sammelt, versammelte, hat versammelt> ◊ *Sie versam-*

melte ihre Kinder um sich. They gather. Sie versammeln sich. ◊ *Wir haben uns versammelt, um gegen*
die Reform zu protestieren. **2.** *(clouds, storm)*
aufziehen ['aoftsi:ən] <zieht auf, zog auf, ist aufgezo-
gen> ◊ *Ein Gewitter zog auf.* **3.** *(collect, accumulate)*
sammeln [zaml̩n] +haben ◊ *Die Polizei sammelt*
Beweise. ♦ *Beeren sammeln* ♦ *Ich habe mit Mitarbei-*
tern so meine Erfahrungen gesammelt.; (pick up)
gather sth up etw. aufheben ['aofhe:bm̩] <hebt auf,
hob auf, hat aufgehoben> ◊ *Er hob die Karten vom*
Boden auf. **4.** *(yourself, your courage, strength, wits)*
zusammennehmen [tsu'zamənne:mən] <nimmt
zusammen, nahm zusammen, hat zusammengenom-
men> ◊ *Nimm dich zusammen und streng dich an!*
♦ *Er nahm all seinen Mut/Verstand zusammen.*
5. gather sb in your arms jdn in den Arm nehmen
[ɪn de:n 'a'm ne:mən] <nimmt, nahm, hat genommen>
6. gather force/strength stärker werden
['ʃtɛ'kɐ ve:ɐdn̩] +sein gather momentum in Schwung
kommen [ɪn 'ʃvʊŋ kɔmən] <kommt, kam, ist
gekommen> gather speed schneller werden
['ʃnɛlɐ ve:ɐdn̩] +sein **7.** gather dust verstauben
[fɛ'ʃtaobm̩] <verstaubt, verstaubte, ist verstaubt> **8.** *(a*
curtain, fabric) raffen ['rafn̩] +haben ◊ *Die Bluse ist*
am Bund gerafft. **9.** *(infer)* gather (from sth) that
(aus etw.) schließen, dass ['ʃli:sn̩ das] <schließt,
schloss, hat geschlossen> ◊ *Ich schließe aus deinem*
Brief, dass du nicht kommst. She's ill, I gather. Sie
scheint krank zu sein. You're not coming, I gather?
Du kommst also nicht?

gathering [noun] **1.** *(meeting)* Treffen ['trɛfn̩] das
<-s, -> ◊ *Das Treffen findet morgen statt.* family
gathering Familientreffen [fa'mi:ljəntrɛfn̩]; *(formal)*
Versammlung [fɛ'zamlʊŋ] die <-, -en> ◊ *eine Ver-*
sammlung einberufen/abhalten ♦ *sich mit einer Rede*
an die Versammlung wenden **2.** *(of information,*
evidence, things) Sammeln ['zaml̩n] das <-s> *no pl* ◊
Das Sammeln von Information erwies sich schwerer
als gedacht.

gauge [noun] **1.** *(for measuring)* Messgerät ['mɛsgərɛːt]
das <-(e)s, -e> ◊ *Das Messgerät muss man regelmä-*
ßig eichen lassen. **2.** *(thickness of plastic, wire,*
needles) Dicke ['dɪkə] die <-, -n> *most sing; (of a*
gun) Kaliber [ka'li:bɐ] das <-s, -> **3.** *(between rails,*
wheels) Spurbreite ['ʃpu:ɐbraɛtə] die <-, -n>

gay [adj] *(homosexual)* schwul [ʃvu:l] *(fam)* ◊ *Wusstest*
du, dass er schwul ist? ♦ *ein schwules Pärchen*

gaze¹ [noun] Blick [blɪk] der <-(e)s, -e> ◊ *Sie konnte*
seinen Blick nicht vergessen. hold/meet sb's gaze
jdm in die Augen schauen [ɪn di: 'aogn̩ ʃaoən]
+haben

⊙ the public gaze die Augen der Öffentlichkeit

gaze² [verb] *(look)* schauen ['ʃaoən] +haben ◊ *zum*
Himmel schauen ♦ *jdm in die Augen schauen;*
(stare) starren ['ʃtarən] +haben ◊ *Er starrte geistesab-*
wesend aus dem Fenster. gaze at sb/sth jdn/etw.
anstarren ['anʃtarən] +haben ◊ *Sie wurden ange-*
starrt.

GDR DDR [de:de:|'ɛ'] die

gear¹ [noun] **1.** *(of a car, bicycle etc.)* Gang [gaŋ] der
<-(e)s, Gänge> ◊ *in den ersten/zweiten etc. Gang*
schalten ♦ *einen Gang zurückschalten* Are you in
gear? Hast du einen Gang eingelegt? the gears die
Schaltung [di: 'ʃaltʊŋ] <-> ◊ *Bei meinem*
Wagen ist die Schaltung kaputt. out of gear im
Leerlauf [ɪm 'le:ɐlaof] take sth out of gear in den

Leerlauf schalten **2.** *(clothes, equipment)* Ausrüstung ['aɔsrʏstʊŋ] die <–, –en> ◊ *die richtige Ausrüstung für eine Bergtour* **3.** *(fashionable clothes)* Klamotten [kla'mɔtn̩] die <–> *pl (fam)* ◊ *ihre coolen Klamotten* ⊛ **in top gear 1.** *(driving)* im höchsten Gang **2.** *(figurative)* auf Hochtouren ◊ *Die Vorbereitungen laufen auf Hochtouren.* **get into gear** in Schwung kommen **put/throw sth out of gear** etw. durcheinander bringen

gear² [verb] gear toward sb/sth sich auf jdn/etw. einstellen [aɔf … ˌaɛnʃtɛlən] +haben ◊ *Sie stellten sich auf viele Besucher ein.* **gear sb for sth** jdn auf etw. [acc] gut vorbereiten [aɔf … guːt ˌfoːɐ̯bəraɛtn̩] <bereitet vor, bereitete vor, hat vorbereitet> ◊ *Der Kurs hat sie gut auf die Arbeit vorbereitet.*; *(make sure sth is in tune with sth)* gear sth for sth etw. auf etw. [acc] abstimmen [aɔf … ˌapʃtɪmən] +haben ◊ *das Angebot besser auf die Bedürfnisse der Kunden abstimmen*

• **gear up** [phras v] sich vorbereiten ['foːɐ̯bəraɛtn̩] <bereitet sich vor, bereitete sich vor, hat sich vorbereitet> ◊ *Sie haben sich auf dieses Ereignis gut vorbereitet.*

gem [noun] **1.** *(stone)* Edelstein ['eːdl̩ʃtaɛn] der <–(e)s, –e> **2.** *(person)* Perle ['pɛˈlə] die <–, –n> ◊ *Sie ist eine wahre Perle.*

Gemini [noun] *(star sign)* Zwillinge ['ʦvɪlɪŋə] <–> *pl*; *(a member of the star sign)* Zwilling ['ʦvɪlɪŋ] der <–s, –e>

gender [noun] **1.** *(of people, animals)* Geschlecht [gə'ʃlɛçt] das <–(e)s, –er> ◊ *Welches Geschlecht hat euer Papagei?* **2.** *(of words)* Genus ['geːnʊs] das <–, Genera> ◊ *Im Deutschen gibt es drei Genera: männlich, weiblich und sächlich.*

gene [noun] Gen ['geːn] das <–s, –e>

general¹ [noun] General [genə'raːl] der <–s, Generäle> ♀Generalin [genə'raːlɪn] die <–, –nen>

general² [adj] **1.** *(usual, not limited or specialised)* allgemein [algə'maɛn] *seldom comp/superl, mostly before ns* ◊ *von allgemeinem Interesse sein* ♦ *eine allgemeine Vorstellung vermitteln* be the general practice/rule allgemein üblich sein in general terms allgemein ausgedrückt as a general rule im Allgemeinen [ɪm algə'maɛnən] general education Allgemeinbildung [algə'maɛnbɪldʊŋ] die <–> *no pl* **2.** *(widespread)* weit verbreitet [ˌvaet fɐ'braetət] <weiter verbreitet, am weitesten verbreitet> ◊ *ein weit verbreitetes Vorurteil/Leiden* **3.** *(vague, roughly)* ungefähr ['ʊngəfɛːɐ̯] *no comp/superl* ◊ *jdm eine ungefähre Vorstellung davon vermitteln, was geplant ist* ♦ *die ungefähre Richtung/Lage* That was the general idea. So war das in etwa gedacht. The general idea/plan is … Gedacht/Geplant ist Folgendes:… **4.** *(average)* Durchschnitts… ['dʊɐ̯çʃnɪts] the general reader der Durchschnittsleser [deːɐ̯ 'dʊɐ̯çʃnɪtsleːze] <–s> **5.** *(along basic lines)* grundsätzlich ['grʊntzɛtslɪç] ◊ *eine grundsätzliche Entscheidung treffen* ♦ *eine grundsätzliche Einigung erzielen* **6.** *(chief)* General… [genə'raːl] general agency Generalagentur [genə'raːlˌagɛnˌtuːɐ̯] die <–, –en> general manager Generaldirektor [genə'raːldiˌrɛktoːɐ̯] der <–s, –en> ♀Generaldirektorin [genə'raːldirɛkˌtoːrɪn] die <–, –nen> ⊛ **in general** im Allgemeinen

generalize [verb] verallgemeinern [fɛˌalgə'maɛnen] <verallgemeinert, verallgemeinerte, hat verallgemei-

nert> ◊ *eine Erfahrung, die man nicht verallgemeinern kann*

generally [adv] **1.** *(mostly, usually)* im Allgemeinen [ɪm algə'maɛnən] ◊ *Das wird im Allgemeinen anders gehandhabt.* **2.** *(by most people)* allgemein [algə'maɛn] ◊ *allgemein anerkannt/bekannt sein* **3.** *(as a whole)* im Großen und Ganzen [ɪm ˌgroːsn̩ ʊnt 'gantsn̩] ◊ *Das ist im Großen und Ganzen zutreffend.*

general public [noun] Allgemeinheit [algə'maɛnhaet] die <–> *no pl* ◊ *etw. für die Allgemeinheit tun*

generate [verb] **1.** *(produce, create)* erzeugen [e'tsɔøgn̩] <erzeugt, erzeugte, hat erzeugt> ◊ *Druck erzeugt Gegendruck.* ♦ *Das Kraftwerk erzeugt Strom für die ganze Stadt.*; *(a reaction, response)* bewirken [bə'vɪɐ̯kn̩] <bewirkt, bewirkte, hat bewirkt> ◊ *Damit wirst du die gegenteilige Reaktion bewirken.* **2.** *(develop)* entwickeln [ɛnt'vɪkl̩n] <entwickelt, entwickelte, hat entwickelt> ◊ *einen neuen Impfstoff entwickeln* ♦ *Ehrgeiz entwickeln*

generation [noun] Generation [genəra'tsio:n] die <–, –en>

generator [noun] Generator [genə'raːtoːɐ̯] der <–s, –en>

generic [adj] **1.** *(category)* übergeordnet ['yːbəgəˌɔrdnət] generic name Gattungsbezeichnung ['gatʊŋsbətsaeçnʊn] die <–, –en> generic term/word Oberbegriff ['oːbəbɡrɪf] der <–(e)s, –e> **2.** *(not specialized)* allgemein [algə'maɛn] ◊ *allgemeine und spezifische Eigenschaften* **3.** generic drug Generikum [ge'neːrikʊm] das <–s, Generika>

generically [adv] **1.** LING *(sth that comes under a certain category)* generisch [ge'neːrɪʃ] *no comp/superl* *(tech)* ◊ *ein generisch verwendeter Begriff* **2.** BIO *(referring to a species)* in einer Gattung [ɪn aene 'gatʊn] *(tech)* Big cats are generically called Panthera. Die Großkatzen werden in der Gattung Panthera zusammengefasst. **3.** *(generally, across the board)* allgemein [algə'maɛn] *no comp/superl* be generically called sth allgemein etw. [nom] genannt werden

generous(ly) [adj, adv] **1.** großzügig ['groːstsyːgɪç] ◊ *ein großzügiger Gastgeber* ♦ *Sie war so großzügig, ihm zu verzeihen.* ♦ *Er hat sie überaus großzügig unterstützt.* **2.** *(amount of sth)* reichlich ['raeçlɪç] ◊ *eine reichliche Auswahl an Salaten* ♦ *Die Mahlzeit war reichlich.* ♦ *Wir wurden reichlich beschenkt.*

genetic(ally) [adj, adv] genetisch [ge'neːtɪʃ] *no comp/superl*

genitive case [noun] Genitiv ['geːnitiːf] der <–s, –e> ◊ *Welches Nomen steht im Genitiv?*

genius [noun] Genie [ʒe'niː] das <–s, –s> ◊ *Mozart, das musikalische Genie* ♦ *Du bist ein Genie!* ⊛ **have a genius for sth** in etw. [dat] sehr begabt sein

genre [noun] Gattung ['gatʊŋ] die <–, –en> ◊ *literarische Gattungen*

gentle [adj] **1.** *(person, voice, slope, action etc.)* sanft [zanft] <sanfter, am sanftesten> ◊ *Sie sprach mit sanfter Stimme.* ♦ *Diese Creme ist besonders sanft zur Haut.* **2.** *(fragrance, sound, colo(u)r etc.)* zart [tsaːɐ̯t] <zarter, am zartesten> ◊ *zarte Klänge* ♦ *ein zartes Blau*; *(rain, touch)* leicht [laeçt] <leichter, am leichtesten>; *(heat, wind)* schwach [ʃvax] <schwächer, am schwächsten>; *(hill, slope)* sanft [zanft] <sanfter, am sanftesten> ◊ *eine sanfte Steigung*

gentleman [noun] **1.** *(man)* Herr [hɛʳ] der <–n, –en> ◊ *Wer war der Herr neben ihr?* **2.** *(with perfect manners)* Gentleman ['dʒɛntl̩mɛn] der <–s, Gentlemen> ◊ *Er ist ein echter Gentleman.* ◉ **gentlemen** *(polite address)* meine Herren ◊ *Meine Herren, lassen Sie uns anfangen!*

gently [adv] **1.** *(tenderly)* sanft [zanft] <sanfter, am sanftesten> ◊ *Sie sprach ganz sanft zu dem Kind.* ✦ *Er streichelte sie sanft.; (carefully)* behutsam [bə'huːtzaːm] ◊ *mit jdm behutsam umgeben; (softly)* zart [tsaːʳt] <zarter, am zartesten> ◊ *Sie küsste ihn zart auf die Wange.* ✦ *Er geht manchmal nicht gerade zart mit ihr um.* **2.** *(slightly, just a bit)* leicht [laɛçt] <leichter, am leichtesten> ◊ *Es regnete leicht.* ✦ *leicht schwanken* **3.** *(gradually)* sanft [zanft] <sanfter, am sanftesten> ◊ *ein sanft ansteigender Hügel*

genuine [adj] echt [ɛçt] *no comp/superl* ◊ *ein echter Brillant* ✦ *Ihre Wut war echt.*

genuinely [adv] **1.** *(seriously)* wirklich ['vɪʳklɪç] *no comp/superl* ◊ *Das tut mir wirklich Leid.* **2.** *(authentically)* echt [ɛçt] *no comp/superl* ◊ *echt vergoldet*

geographical(ly) [adj] geografisch [geo'graːfɪʃ] *no comp/superl* ◊ *die geografische Lage eines Ortes* ✦ *Geografisch gesehen ist diese Insel eher uninteressant.*

geography [noun] Geografie [geogra'fiː] die <–, –n> ◊ *sich mit Geografie beschäftigen* ✦ *die Geografie Schottlands; (in school)* Erdkunde ['eːʳtkʊndə] die <–> *no pl* ◊ *In der ersten Stunde haben wir Erdkunde.*

geological(ly) [adj] geologisch [geo'loːgɪʃ] *no comp/superl* ◊ *geologische Funde* ✦ *Geologisch betrachtet ist hier viel passiert.*

geology [noun] Geologie [geolo'giː] die <–> *no pl*

geometry [noun] Geometrie [geome'triː] die <–> *no pl*

German¹ [noun] **1.** *(person)* Deutsche ['dɔøtʃə] der/die <–n, die Deutschen> *but: ein Deutscher/eine Deutsche* ◊ *Er ist mit einer Deutschen verheiratet.* ✦ *Die Deutschen sind Weltmeister im Reisen.* ✦ *Deutsche haben oft Probleme mit der Aussprache des englischen „th".* ✦ *Als Deutscher braucht man für dieses Land ein Visum.* **2.** *(language, subject)* Deutsch [dɔøtʃ] das <–(s)> *article only in combination with attribute, no pl* ◊ *fließend/perfekt Deutsch sprechen* ✦ *ein holpriges Deutsch sprechen* ✦ *Sein Deutsch ist gut.* ✦ *Er lernt seit zwei Jahren Deutsch.* ✦ *Verstehen/Sprechen Sie Deutsch?* ✦ *Deutsch ist mein Lieblingsfach.* ✦ *Deutsch studieren* ✦ *eine Eins in Deutsch* in German auf/in Deutsch ◊ *Was heißt das auf Deutsch?* ✦ *ein Brief auf/in Deutsch; (language, esp. in translations)* Deutsche ['dɔøtʃə] das <–n> *always with the definite article, no pl* ◊ *einen Text ins Deutsche übersetzen* ✦ *etw. aus dem/vom Deutschen ins Englische übertragen* standard/High German Hochdeutsch ['hoːxdɔøtʃ] das <–(s)> *no pl* ◊ *Sie spricht ein gepflegtes Hochdeutsch.* ✦ *Wie heißt das auf Hochdeutsch?*

German² [adj] deutsch [dɔøtʃ] ◊ *die deutsche Nationalmannschaft* ✦ *ein Buch in deutscher Übersetzung* ✦ *Zu Hause sprechen sie deutsch miteinander.* standard German, High German hochdeutsch ['hoːxdɔøtʃ] ◊ *die hochdeutsche Aussprache*

Germany [noun] Deutschland ['dɔøtʃlant] das <–s> *article only in combination with attribute, no pl* ◊ *Deutschland ist ein wichtiger Handelspartner Frank-* reichs. ✦ *die Bevölkerung Deutschlands* ✦ *die Wiedervereinigung des geteilten Deutschlands* ✦ *Er lebt in Deutschland.* ✦ *Ich komme aus Deutschland.* ✦ *Sie fliegt morgen nach Deutschland.*

gesture [noun] Geste ['geːstə] die <–, –n> ◊ *Er machte mit dem Arm eine einladende Geste.* ✦ *Sein Geschenk war eine nette Geste.* ✦ *eine drohende Geste*

get [verb] **1.** *(receive, obtain)* bekommen [bə'kɔmən] <bekommt, bekam, hat bekommen> ◊ *Was hast du zu Weihnachten bekommen?* ✦ *Ben hat in der Englischarbeit eine Zwei bekommen.* ✦ *Sozialhilfe bekommen* ✦ *Sie bekamen den Befehl, das Haus zu räumen.* ✦ *Er hat für den Mord „lebenslänglich" bekommen.* ✦ *Für diesen Tisch bekommst du höchstens noch 20 Euro.* ✦ *Hoffentlich bekomme ich keine Erkältung.; (permission, advice, an offer)* einholen ['aɛnhoːlən] +haben ◊ *Ich holte den Rat eines Fachmanns ein.* ✦ *Angebote einholen; (get hold of)* get sth (for sb) (jdm) etw. besorgen [bə'zɔʳgn̩] <besorgt, besorgte, hat besorgt> ◊ *Du musst noch Brot besorgen.* ✦ *Ich kann dir eine günstige Wohnung besorgen.; (fetch)* get sth for sb jdm etw. holen ['hoːlən] +haben ◊ *Kannst du mir ein Glas Wasser holen?* **2.** *(change into a certain state)* werden ['veːʳdn̩] <wird, wurde, ist geworden> ◊ *Wenn der Ausschlag schlimmer wird, sollten Sie zum Arzt gehen.* ✦ *Sie sind im Regen nass geworden.* ✦ *Da wurde er richtig wütend auf sie.* get sth finished/clean etc. etw. fertig/sauber etc. bekommen ['fɛʳtɪç/'zaʊbɐ bəkɔmən] <bekommt, bekam, hat bekommen> ◊ *Hoffentlich bekomme ich den Brief heute noch fertig.* get sth dirty/wet etc. etw. schmutzig/nass etc. machen ['ʃmʊtsɪç/'nas maxn̩] +haben ◊ *Du hast ja dein Hemd schmutzig gemacht!* get sth to work etw. zum Laufen bringen [tsʊm 'laʊfn̩ brɪŋən] <bringt, brachte, hat gebracht> ◊ *Ich bringe die Maschine einfach nicht zum Laufen.* get to sleep einschlafen ['aɛnʃlaːfn̩] <schläft ein, schlief ein, ist eingeschlafen> ◊ *Sie hat manchmal Probleme damit, abends einzuschlafen.* get dressed sich anziehen ['antsiːən] <zieht sich an, zog sich an, hat sich angezogen> ◊ *Los, zieh dich an. Wir sind spät dran!* get sb dressed jdn anziehen ['antsiːən] <zieht an, zog an, hat angezogen> ◊ *Könntest du bitte die Kinder anziehen?* **3.** *(have sth done to you)* get beaten/laughed at etc. geschlagen/ausgelacht etc. werden [gə'ʃlaːgn̩/'aʊsgəlaxt veːʳdn̩] <wird, wurde, ist worden> ◊ *Ich wurde heute wegen meines Haarschnitts ausgelacht.* **4.** *(arrange for sth to be done)* get sth done etw. tun lassen ['lasn̩] <lässt, ließ, hat lassen> ◊ *Du solltest dir mal wieder die Haare schneiden lassen.* ✦ *Er hat sein Auto reparieren lassen.* get sb to do sth jdn etw. tun lassen ['lasn̩] <lässt, ließ, hat lassen> ◊ *Ich werde Schmidt das erledigen lassen.; (by means of persuasion)* jdn dazu bringen, etw. zu tun [daːtsuː 'brɪŋən ... tuːn] <bringt, brachte, hat gebracht> ◊ *Wie bringe ich sie dazu, mir zu glauben?* **5.** *(reach a place)* sb/sth gets somewhere jd/etw. kommt irgendwohin [kɔmt] <kommt, kam, ist gekommen> ◊ *Weißt du, wie man zum Museum kommt?* ✦ *Er kommt morgens meist um 8 Uhr zur Arbeit.* ✦ *Wie kommst dieser Stein in meinen Rucksack?* ✦ *Sie sind in einer Stunde nicht sehr weit gekommen.* sb gets home jd kommt nach

Hause; (climb onto) sb gets on sth jd steigt auf etw. acc [ˈʃtaekt ˈa͜of] <stieg, ist gestiegen> ◊ *Er stieg auf einen Felsen und hielt nach seinen Freunden Ausschau.*; (enter a bus or train) get on jd steigt ein [ˈʃtaekt ˈaen] <stieg ein, ist eingestiegen> get on the bus/train jd steigt in den Bus/Zug; (enter a car) sb gets in jd steigt ein [ˈʃtaekt ɪn ... ˌaen] ◊ *Er öffnete die Tür des Wagens und stieg ein.* sb gets into the car jd steigt in das Auto; (be able to enter) sb gets in(to sth) jd kommt (in etw. acc) hinein [ˈkɔmt hɪˈnaen] <kam hinein, ist hineingekommen> ◊ *Der Einbrecher muss durch das Kellerfenster hineingekommen sein.* **6.** (leave a place) sb gets out jd kommt heraus [ˈkɔmt hɛˈra͜os] <kam heraus, ist herausgekommen> ◊ *Er ist im Labyrinth. Weiß er wie man herauskommt?* sb gets out of sth jd kommt aus etw. heraus ◊ *Wie komme ich aus dem Labyrinth wieder heraus?*; (exit a vehicle) sb gets out jd steigt aus [ˈʃtaekt ˈa͜os] <stieg aus, ist ausgestiegen> ◊ *Bitte halt an; ich möchte hier aussteigen.* sb gets out of sth jd steigt aus etw. ◊ *Er stieg aus dem Auto.* sb gets off jd kommt herunter [ˈkɔmt hɛˈrʊnte] <kam herunter, ist heruntergekommen> ◊ *Komm sofort herunter!* sb gets sth off jd kommt von etw. herunter ◊ *Die Kinder sollten von der Straße herunterkommen.*; (exit a bus or train) sb gets off jd steigt aus [ˈʃtaekt ˈa͜os] ◊ *An der nächsten Haltestelle steigen wir aus.* **7.** (move or transport sb or sth, manage to lift sth somewhere) get sth on sth etw. auf etw. acc bekommen [a͜of ... bəˈkɔmən] <bekam, hat bekommen> ◊ *Ich bekomme den Fernseher allein nicht auf das Sideboard.*; (take down) get sth off etw. von etw. bekommen [fɔn ... bəˈkɔmən] ◊ *Und wie bekomme ich den Koffer vom Schrank?*; (take away, remove) get sth off sth etw. von etw. nehmen [fɔn ... neːmən] <nimmt, nahm, hat genommen> ◊ *Würden Sie bitte ihre Tasche vom Tisch nehmen?*; (manage to extract or remove) get sth out of sth etw. aus etw. bekommen [a͜os ... bəˈkɔmən] <bekommt, bekam, hat bekommen> ◊ *Ich bekomme den Nagel nicht aus der Wand.*; (fetch, take out) holen [a͜os ... hoːlən] +haben ◊ *Sie holte einen Taschenrechner aus der Schublade.*; (find room for) get sth/sb into sth etw./jdn in etw. hineinbekommen [ɪn ... hɪˌnaenbəkɔmən] <bekommt hinein, bekam hinein, hat hineinbekommen> ◊ *Wie viele Personen bekommt man in diesen Wagen hinein?* **8.** (send or mail sth) get sth to sb jdm etw. schicken [ˈʃɪkɪ̩] +haben ◊ *Wir schicken Ihnen die Preisliste, sobald sie erschienen ist.* **9.** (progress in an activity) kommen [ˈkɔmən] <kommt, kam, ist gekommen> ◊ *Ich bin in dem Roman nur bis Seite 14 gekommen.*; (start an activity) get working/cleaning etc. anfangen zu arbeiten/putzen etc. [ˌanfaŋən tsuː aˈbaetn̩/ˈpʊtsn̩] <fängt an, fing an, hat angefangen> ◊ *Los, Leute, fangt an zu arbeiten!* get to work sich an die Arbeit machen [an diː ˈaˈbaet maxn̩] +haben ◊ *Anstatt zu reden, sollten wir uns lieber an die Arbeit machen.* not get sb anywhere jdn nicht weiterbringen [nɪçt ˈvaetebrɪŋən] <bringt weiter, brachte weiter, hat weitergebracht> ◊ *Heucheleien werden dich bei ihm auch nicht weiterbringen.* not get anywhere with sth mit etw. nicht weiterkommen [mɪt ... nɪçt ˈvaetekɔmən] <kommt weiter, kam weiter, ist weitergekommen> ◊ *Ich komme mit meiner Dok-*

torarbeit nicht weiter. **10.** (understand) kapieren [kaˈpiːrən] <kapiert, kapierte, hat kapiert> (fam) ◊ *Ich kapiere nicht, was sie von mir will.* ✦ *In Mathe habe ich heute wieder gar nichts kapiert.* get sb wrong jdn falsch verstehen [ˈfalʃ fɛˈʃteːən] <versteht, verstand, hat verstanden> **11.** (have the opportunity) get to do sth es schaffen, etw. zu tun [ɛs ˈʃafn̩ ... tsuː] +haben ◊ *Ich habe es heute nicht einmal geschafft, dich anzurufen.* **12.** (take a taxi, train etc.) nehmen [ˈneːmən] <nimmt, nahm, hat genommen> ◊ *Er nahm den nächsten Zug nach Hause.* **13.** (be able to receive a TV or radio channel) bekommen [bəˈkɔmən] <bekommt, bekam, hat bekommen> (fam) ◊ *Diesen Sender bekommen wir nicht.*; (a newspaper, information) beziehen [bəˈtsiːən] <bezieht, bezog, hat bezogen> ◊ *Wir beziehen eine Tageszeitung.* ✦ *Er bezieht sein ganzes Wissen aus Büchern.* **14.** get to know sb jdn kennen lernen [ˈkɛnən lɛˈnən] +haben

• **get across** phras v (communicate) get sth across etw. verständlich machen [fɛˈʃtɛntlɪç maxn̩] +haben ◊ *Wie kann ich meine Position besser verständlich machen?* get sth across to sb jdm etw. übermitteln [ybeˈmɪtl̩n] <übermittelt, übermittelte, hat übermittelt> ◊ *Welche Botschaft will er seinen Zuschauern übermitteln?*; (be understood) sth gets across etw. wird verständlich [wɪɐt fɛˈʃtɛntlɪç] +sein ◊ *Die Bedeutung der Äußerung wird nicht verständlich.*

• **get ahead** phras v vorankommen [foˈrankɔmən] <kommt voran, kam voran, ist vorangekommen> ◊ *Ich komme mit meiner Arbeit nicht voran.*

• **get along** phras v **1.** (be on good terms) get along with sb mit jdm auskommen [mɪt ... ˈa͜oskɔmən] <kommt aus, kam aus, ist ausgekommen> ◊ *Er kommt gut mit seiner Schwiegermutter aus.* How do they get along? Wie kommen sie miteinander aus? **2.** (cope) get along (with sth) (mit etw.) zurechtkommen [tsuˈrɛçtkɔmən] <kommt zurecht, kam zurecht, ist zurechtgekommen> ◊ *Kommen Sie mit Ihrer Aufgabe gut zurecht?* ✦ *Ohne seine Frau kommt er im Alltag nicht zurecht.* **3.** (leave) gehen [ˈgeːən] <geht, ging, ist gegangen> ◊ *Es tut mir Leid, aber ich muss jetzt gehen.*

• **get around** phras v **1.** (visit different places) herumkommen [hɛˈrʊmkɔmən] <kommt herum, kam herum, ist herumgekommen> ◊ *Ich bin im Leben viel herumgekommen.* **2.** (a rumo(u)r) sich verbreiten [fɛˈbraetn̩] <verbreitet sich, verbreitete sich, hat sich verbreitet> ◊ *Das Gerücht verbreitete sich schnell.*; (news) sich herumsprechen [hɛˈrʊmʃprɛçn̩] <spricht sich herum, sprach sich herum, hat sich herumgesprochen> ◊ *Haben sich die Neuigkeiten schon herumgesprochen?* **3.** (a law, rule, problem) umgehen [ʊmˈgeːən] <umgeht, umging, hat umgangen> ◊ *eine Möglichkeit, strenge Bestimmungen zu umgehen* **4.** get around to doing sth dazu kommen, etw. zu tun [daˈtsuː ˈkɔmən ... tsuː] <kommt, kam, ist gekommen> ◊ *Ich bin noch nicht einmal dazu gekommen, die Zeitung zu lesen.*

• **get at** phras v **1.** (mean) get at sth auf etw. acc hinauswollen [a͜of ... hɪˌna͜osvɔln̩] <will hinaus, wollte hinaus, hat hinausgewollt> ◊ *Worauf wollen Sie hinaus?* **2.** (discover) herausfinden [hɛˈra͜osfɪndn̩] <findet heraus, fand heraus, hat herausgefunden> ◊ *Niemand darf die Wahrheit herausfinden!* **3.** (criticize) get at sb an jdm herumnörgeln

[an ... hɛˈrʊmnœˈgln] +haben (fam) ◊ *Du nörgelst
ständig an mir herum.*
• **get away** [phras v] **1.** *(escape)* get away (from sb)
(jdm) **entkommen** [ɛntˈkɔmən] <entkommt, entkam,
ist entkommen> ◊ *Drei der Gefangenen konnten
entkommen.* **2.** *(from an idea, opinion etc.)* get away
from sth von etw. **wegkommen** [fɔn ... ˌvɛkkɔmən]
<kommt weg, kam weg, ist weggekommen> ◊ *Wie
müssen von der Vorstellung wegkommen, dass
Frauen allein für die Kindererziehung verantwortlich
sind.* **3.** *(deviate from a topic)* get away from sth
sich von etw. **entfernen** [fɔn ... ɛntˌfɛˈnən] <entfernt
sich, entfernte sich, hat sich entfernt> ◊ *Ich glaube,
wir entfernen uns zu weit vom Thema.* **4.** *(avoid punishment)* get away with sth mit etw. **durchkommen**
[mɪt ... ˈdʊˈçkɔmən] <kommt durch, kam durch, ist
durchgekommen> ◊ *Damit kommt er nicht durch.*
5. *(ordering sb to disappear)* **verschwinden**
[fɛˈʃvɪndn̩] <verschwindet, verschwand, ist verschwun-
den> ◊ *Verschwinden Sie von meinem Grundstück!*
⊙ get away from it all alles hinter sich lassen
• **get back** [phras v] **1.** *(return)* **zurückkommen**
[tsuˈrʏkkɔmən] <kommt zurück, kam zurück, ist
zurückgekommen> ◊ *Leo kommt morgen aus dem
Urlaub zurück.; (walk back)* **zurückgehen**
[tsuˈrʏkgeːbm̩] <geht zurück, ging zurück, ist zurückge-
gangen> ◊ *Es wird bald dunkel; wir sollten zur Hütte
zurückgehen.* **2.** *(recover, be handed back)* get sth
back etw. **zurückbekommen** [tsuˈrʏkbəkɔmən]
<bekommt zurück, bekam zurück, hat zurückbekom-
men> ◊ *Heute bekommen wir die Klassenarbeit
zurück.* ♦ *Sie bekommen einen anderen Artikel oder
Ihr Geld zurück.* **3.** *(resume an activity: return to your
job)* get back to/into sth in etw. [acc] **zurückkehren**
[ɪn ... tsuˌrʏkkeːrən] +sein ◊ *Nach der Babypause
kehrte sie wieder ins Berufsleben zurück.* get back
to sleep wieder **einschlafen** [viːdɐ ˈaɛnʃlaːfn̩]
<schläft ein, schlief ein, ist eingeschlafen> ◊ *Ich
wachte auf und konnte nicht wieder einschlafen.* get
back to watching the telly wieder **fernsehen**
[viːdɐ ˈfɛˈnzeːən] <sieht fern, sah fern, hat ferngese-
hen> **4.** get back at sb sich an jdm **rächen**
[an ... ˈrɛçn̩] +haben ◊ *Du willst dich doch bloß an
mir rächen!* **5.** get back to sb sich wieder mit jdm
in Verbindung setzen
[viːdɐ mɪt ... ɪn fɛˈbɪndʊŋ zɛtsn̩] +haben ◊ *Ich werde
mich wieder mit Ihnen in Verbindung setzen, sobald
ich mehr darüber weiß.* I'll get back to you on that.
Ich werde darauf zurückkommen.
• **get behind** [phras v] **1.** *(with payments, work)* get
behind (with sth) (mit etw.) in **Rückstand kommen**
[ɪn ˈrʏkʃtant kɔmən] <kommt, kam, ist gekommen> ◊
Wir sind mit der Arbeit in Rückstand gekommen.
2. *(support sb/sth)* get behind sb/sth sich hinter
jdn/etw. **stellen** [ˈhɪntɐ ... ʃtɛlən] +haben ◊ *Zum
Glück hat sich der Chef hinter uns gestellt.*
• **get by** [phras v] *(muddle through, manage)* sich
durchschlagen [ˈdʊˈçʃlaːgn̩] <schlägt sich durch,
schlug sich durch, hat sich durchgeschlagen> ◊ *Ich
habe gerade genug Deutschkenntnisse, um mich
durchzuschlagen.* get by with sth mit etw.
auskommen [mɪt ... ˈaɔskɔmən] <kommt aus, kam
aus, ist ausgekommen> ◊ *Ich komme auch mit einem
kleineren Auto aus.* ♦ *Mit 1000 Euro im Monat kann
komme ich gerade noch aus.*
• **get down** [phras v] **1.** get sb down jdn **deprimie-**

ren [depriˈmiːrən] <deprimiert, deprimierte, hat depri-
miert> ◊ *Die Kündigung hat ihn ziemlich deprimiert.*
sb gets down jd ist deprimiert ◊ *In letzter Zeit ist
sie öfters deprimiert.* Don't let it get you down. Lass
dich davon nicht unterkriegen! **2.** *(make a note)*
notieren [noˈtiːrən] <notiert, notierte, hat notiert> ◊
*Einen Moment, ich notiere nur rasch die Telefon-
nummer.* **3.** *(start doing)* get down to sth sich an
etw. [acc] **machen** [an ... maxn̩] +haben ◊ *sich an die
Arbeit machen* get down to doing sth sich daran
machen, etw. zu tun **4.** *(swallow)* get sth down etw.
hinunterbringen [hɪˈnʊntɐbrɪŋən] <bringt hinunter,
brachte hinunter, hat hinuntergebracht> ◊ *Ich bringe
das zähe Fleisch nicht hinunter.*
• **get in** [phras v] **1.** *(arrive home)* nach Hause
kommen [naːx ˈhaɔzə kɔmən] <kommt, kam, ist
gekommen> ◊ *Wir sind gestern sehr spät nach Hause
gekommen.; (arrive at work)* **kommen** [ˈkɔmən] ◊ *Der
Chef kommt nie vor 9 Uhr.; (train, plane)* **ankommen**
[ˈankɔmən] ◊ *Wann kommt der Zug an?* **2.** *(be
admitted to a school, team etc.)* **aufgenommen**
werden [ˈaɔfgənɔmən veːɐdn̩] <wird, wurde, ist
worden> ◊ *Er musste eine Prüfung ablegen, um aufgenommen zu werden.* **3.** *(be elected)* **gewählt**
werden [gəˈvɛːlt veːɐdn̩] <wird, wurde, ist worden> ◊
Er wurde nicht wieder gewählt. **4.** *(in the UK: send
for)* kommen **lassen** [ˈkɔmən lasn̩] <lässt kommen,
ließ kommen, hat kommen lassen> ◊ *Ich glaube, wir
sollten lieber einen Arzt kommen lassen.* **5.** *(join)* get
in on sth sich an etw. [dat] **beteiligen**
[an ... bəˌtaelɪgn̩] <beteiligt sich, beteiligte sich, hat
sich beteiligt> ◊ *Er zögerte nicht lange, sich an dem
Geschäft zu beteiligen.* → **get 5.**
• **get into** [phras v] **1.** *(start to like sth)* sb gets into
sth etw. fängt an, jdm Spaß zu machen
[fɛŋt ˈan ... ˈʃpaːs tsuː maxn̩] <fing an, hat angefan-
gen> ◊ *Das Fotografieren fängt an, ihm Spaß zu
machen.* **2.** *(a subject)* get into sth auf etw. [acc]
eingehen [aɔf ... ˌaengeːən] <geht ein, ging ein, ist
eingegangen> ◊ *Auf dieses Thema möchte ich jetzt
nicht eingehen.* **3.** *(arrive somewhere)* get into
somewhere in etw. [dat] **ankommen** [ɪn ... ˌankɔmən]
<kommt an, kam an, ist angekommen> ◊ *Wann
kommt das Flugzeug in München an?* **4.** *(be
admitted)* get into sth in etw. [acc] **aufgenommen**
werden [ɪn ... ˌaɔfgənɔmən veːɐdn̩] <wird, wurde, ist
worden> ◊ *Leider ist er nicht in die Mannschaft aufgenommen worden.* **5.** *(a situation, an emotional
state)* get into sth in etw. [acc] **geraten**
[ɪn ... gəraːtn̩] <gerät, geriet, ist geraten> ◊ *in Wut/
Panik geraten* ♦ *mit jdm in Streit geraten* get into a
bad mood schlechte **Laune bekommen**
[ˌʃlɛçtə ˈlaɔnə bəkɔmən] <bekommt, bekam, hat
bekommen> ◊ *Als er den Brief las, bekam er
schlechte Laune.* **6.** *(start to do)* get into the habit of
doing sth sich [dat] **angewöhnen**, etw. zu tun
[ˈangəvøːnən ... tsuː] <gewöhnt sich an, gewöhnte sich
an, hat sich angewöhnt> ◊ *Du solltest dir angewöhnen, dir nach dem Essen die Zähne zu putzen.*
⊙ what's got into sb was ist bloß in jdn gefahren
• **get off** [phras v] **1.** *(let go of)* get off sb jdn
loslassen [ˈloːslasn̩] <lässt los, ließ los, hat losgelas-
sen> ◊ *Lass mich los!* **2.** get time off Urlaub
bekommen [ˈuːɐlaɔp bəkɔmən] <bekommt, bekam,
hat bekommen> get a day/week off einen Tag/eine
Woche **freibekommen**

[ˈaenən ˌtaːk/aenə ˌvɔxə ˈfraebəkɔmən] +*haben* ◊ *Wenn Sie wollen, bekommen Sie ein paar Tage frei.* **3.** *(be able to leave)* wegkommen [ˈvɛkkɔmən] <kommt weg, kam weg, ist weggekommen> *(fam)* ◊ *Ich weiß noch nicht, wann ich heute wegkomme.* **4.** *(send away)* get sth off etw. wegschicken [ˈvɛkʃɪkn̩] +*haben* ◊ *Schickst du den Brief heute noch weg?* **5.** *(save from punishment)* get sb off jdn freibekommen [ˈfraebəkɔmən] <bekommt frei, bekam frei, hat freibekommen> ◊ *Sein Anwalt hat ihn doch tatsächlich freibekommen.* get off with sth mit etw. davonkommen [mɪt ... daˌfɔnkɔmən] <kommt davon, kam davon, ist davongekommen> ◊ *Er ist mit einer Geldstrafe davongekommen.* **6.** *(obtain, borrow)* get sth off sb etw. von jdm bekommen [fɔn ... bəkɔmən] <bekommt, bekam, hat bekommen> ◊ *Ich habe diesen Stift von Sabine bekommen.* **7.** *(in the UK)* get off to sleep einschlafen [ˈaenʃlaːfn̩] <schläft ein, schlief ein, ist eingeschlafen> ◊ *Ich konnte nicht einschlafen, weil ich so aufgeregt war.* ◉ **Get off!** Verschwinde! → **get 6.**, **get 7.**
- **get on** ⸢phras v⸣ **1.** *(continue)* get on (with sth) (mit etw.) weitermachen [ˈvaetemaxn̩] +*haben* ◊ *Lass uns weitermachen, damit wir heute noch fertig werden.; (manage to make progress)* (mit etw.) weiterkommen [ˈvaetekɔmən] <kommt weiter, kam weiter, ist weitergekommen> ◊ *Ich komme mit meiner Arbeit heute einfach nicht weiter.* **2.** *(join a team, appear on TV)* get on sth in etw. ⸢acc⸣ kommen [ɪn ... kɔmən] <kommt, kam, ist gekommen> ◊ *Er ist in die Mannschaft gekommen.* get sb on sth jdn in etw. ⸢acc⸣ bringen [ɪn ... brɪŋən] <bringt, brachte, hat gebracht> ◊ *Sein Manager brachte ihn ins Fernsehen.* **3.** *(be successful)* Erfolg haben [eˈfɔlk haːbm̩] +*haben* **4.** *(be on good terms)* get on with sb mit jdm auskommen [mɪt ... ˌaoskɔmən] <kommt aus, kam aus, ist ausgekommen> ◊ *Er kommt gut mit seiner Schwiegermutter aus.* They get on. Sie kommen miteinander aus. **5.** *(manage, cope)* get on with sth mit etw. zurechtkommen [mɪt ... tsuˌrɛçtkɔmən] <kommt zurecht, kam zurecht, ist zurechtgekommen> ◊ *Ich komme mit der Aufgabe nicht zurecht.* → **get 6.**
- **get out** ⸢phras v⸣ **1.** *(ordering sb to disappear)* verschwinden [feˈʃvɪndn̩] <verschwindet, verschwand, ist verschwunden> ◊ *Verschwinde endlich!; (remove sb unwanted)* get sb out of somewhere dafür sorgen, dass jd irgendwo verschwindet [dafyːɐ̯ ˈzɔˈgn̩ das ... feˈʃvɪndət] +*haben* **2.** *(get around an obligation or punishment)* get out of sth um etw. herumkommen [ʊm ... hɛˈrʊmkɔmən] <kommt herum, kam herum, ist herumgekommen> ◊ *Er wird um eine saftige Strafe nicht herumkommen.* get out of doing sth darum herumkommen, etw. zu tun; *(a difficulty)* get out of sth aus etw. herauskommen [aos ... hɛˈraoskɔmən] <kommt heraus, kam heraus, ist herausgekommen> ◊ *Sie weiß nicht, wie sie aus diesen Schwierigkeiten wieder herauskommen soll.* **3.** *(gain, benefit)* get sth out of etw. von etw. haben [fɔn ... ˌhaːbm̩] +*haben* ◊ *Was hast du eigentlich davon, wenn du sie ärgerst?; (happiness, fulfilment)* get sth out of sth etw. in etw. ⸢dat⸣ finden [ɪn ... fɪndn̩] <findet, fand, hat gefunden> ◊ *Sie findet in ihrem Beruf die Erfüllung, die sie gesucht hat.* → **get 6.**, **get 7.**
- **get over** ⸢phras v⸣ **1.** *(an illness, a shock)* get over

sth sich von etw. erholen [fɔn ... eˌhoːlən] <erholt sich, erholte sich, hat sich erholt> ◊ *Ich habe mich nun von der Grippe erholt.; (a loss, disappointment)* get over sth über etw. ⸢acc⸣ hinwegkommen [yːbɐ ... hɪnˌvɛkɔmən] <kommt hinweg, kam hinweg, ist hinweggekommen> ◊ *Sie kam nicht über den Verlust ihres Kindes hinweg.* get over sb über die Trennung von jdm hinwegkommen **2.** *(a problem, an obstacle)* get over sth etw. überwinden [ybeˈvɪndn̩] <überwindet, überwand, hat überwunden> ◊ *Wir konnten alle Probleme erfolgreich überwinden.* **3.** *(finish, bring to an end)* get sth over (with) etw. hinter sich ⸢acc⸣ bringen [ˈhɪntɐ ... brɪŋən] <bringt, brachte, hat gebracht> ◊ *Ich möchte zuerst die Prüfungen hinter mich bringen.*
- **get round** ⸢phras v⸣ → **get around**
- **get through** ⸢phras v⸣ **1.** *(cope with a difficult situation)* get through sth etw. überstehen [ybeˈʃteːən] <übersteht, überstand, hat überstanden> ◊ *eine schwierige Zeit überstehen; (help sb/sth master a difficult situation)* get sb/sth through sth jdn/etw. durch etw. bekommen [dʊˈç ... bəkɔmən] <bekommt, bekam, hat bekommen> ◊ *einen Schüler durch die Abschlussprüfung bekommen* ♦ *ein Gesetz durchs Parlament bekommen* He needs a lot of coffee to get him through the day. Er schafft es nur mit jeder Menge Kaffee durch den Tag. **2.** *(by telephone)* durchkommen [ˈdʊˈçkɔmən] <kommt durch, kam durch, ist durchgekommen> ◊ *Ich wollte ihn anrufen, komme aber nicht durch.; (be able to contact, be understood)* get through to sb jdn erreichen [eˈraeçn̩] <erreicht, erreichte, hat erreicht> ◊ *Endlich gelang es ihm, sie auf dem Handy zu erreichen.* **3.** *(do, complete)* erledigen [eˈleːdɪgn̩] <erledigt, erledigte, hat erledigt> ◊ *Sie hat heute noch einiges zu erledigen.* **4.** *(in the UK: use up)* aufbrauchen [ˈaofbraoxn̩] +*haben* ◊ *Brauch nicht wieder die ganze Butter auf!* **5.** *(get through to the final in de)* Endrunde kommen [ɪn diː ˈɛntrʊndə kɔmən] <kommt, kam, ist gekommen>
- **get to** ⸢phras v⸣ **1.** *(annoy)* get to sb jdn aufregen [ˈaofreːgn̩] +*haben* ◊ *Ihr ewiges Gejammer regt mich allmählich auf.* **2.** get to thinking that ... zu der Überzeugung gelangen, dass ... [tsuː deːɐ̯ ybeˈtsɔɡʊŋ ɡalaŋən das] <gelangt, gelangte, ist gelangt> ◊ *Er gelangte zu der Überzeugung, dass sie ihn nicht mehr liebte.*
- **get together** ⸢phras v⸣ **1.** *(meet)* get together (with sb) sich (mit jdm) treffen [ˈtrɛfn̩] <trifft sich, traf sich, hat sich getroffen> ◊ *An Weihnachten trifft sich die ganze Familie.* ♦ *Sie traf sich mit ein paar Freundinnen.* get sb together jdn zusammenrufen [tsuˈzamənruːfn̩] <ruft zusammen, rief zusammen, hat zusammengerufen> ◊ *alle Nachbarn zusammenrufen* **2.** *(reach a consensus)* sich einigen [ˈaenɪɡn̩] <einigt sich, einigte sich, hat sich geeinigt> ◊ *Sie konnten sich über dieses Thema nicht einigen.* **3.** *(organize, collect money)* zusammenbekommen [tsuˈzamənbəkɔmən] <bekommt zusammen, bekam zusammen, hat zusammenbekommen> ◊ *Ich muss die Unterlagen bis nächsten Dienstag zusammenbekommen.; (compile)* zusammenstellen [tsuˈzamənʃtɛlən] +*haben* ◊ *Er hat eine Liste mit den wichtigsten Kunden zusammengestellt.* **4.** get yourself together sich zusammenreißen [tsuˈzamənraesn̩] <reißt sich zusammen, riss sich zusammen, hat sich zusammenge-

rissen> *(fam)* ◊ *Reiß dich jetzt endlich zusammen!*
• **get up** [phras v] **1.** *(from your bed)* aufstehen
['aʊfʃteːən] <steht auf, stand auf, ist aufgestanden> ◊
Sie steht jeden Morgen um sieben Uhr auf. get sb up
jdn aufwecken ['aʊfvɛkŋ] +haben ◊ *Weckst du mich
morgen bitte um acht Uhr auf?* **2.** *(in the UK:
organize)* organisieren [ɔrɡani'ziːrən] <organisiert,
organisierte, hat organisiert> ◊ *Jemand hat eine Unter-
schriftensammlung gegen den Straßenbau organisiert.* **3.** *(in the UK: dress)* get sb/yourself up in/as
sth jdn/sich als etw. verkleiden [als ... fɛ̩ˈklaɛdŋ]
<verkleidet, verkleidete, hat verkleidet> ◊ *sich als
Cowboy verkleiden* **4.** *(wind)* aufkommen ['aʊfkɔmən]
<kommt auf, kam auf, ist aufgekommen> ◊ *Plötzlich
kam starker Wind auf.* **5.** get up to sth etw.
anstellen ['anʃtɛlən] +haben ◊ *Wenn sie nicht zu
Hause ist, stellen die Kinder allerhand Unsinn an.*
gherkin [noun] Essiggurke ['ɛsɪçɡʊrkə] die <–, –n> ◊
ein Glas Essiggurken
ghost [noun] Geist [ɡaɛst] der <–(e)s, –er> ◊ *Geister
beschwören* ♦ *In der Burg geht ein Geist um/spuken
Geister.*
🔘 not have the ghost of a chance nicht die
geringste Chance haben the ghost of a smile der
Anflug eines Lächelns give up the ghost seinen
Geist aufgeben
giant¹ [noun] **1.** *(company, successful person)* Gigant
[ɡi'ɡant] der <–en, –en> ◊ *die Giganten des Fußballs*
2. *(in fairy tales, very tall person)* Riese ['riːzə] der
<–n, –n>
giant² [adj] riesig ['riːzɪç] ◊ *Er arbeitet in einem
riesigen Unternehmen.* ♦ *Die Zuschauer konnten das
Spiel auf einem riesigen Bildschirm verfolgen.; (esp
in names of animals, plants)* Riesen... ['riːzŋ] giant
tortoise Riesenschildkröte ['riːzŋʃɪltkrɔtə] die
<–, –n> giant step Riesenschritt ['riːzŋʃrɪt] der
<–(e)s, –e>
Gibraltar [noun] Gibraltar [ɡi'braltar] das <–s> *article
only in combination with attribute, no pl* → **Germany**
gift [noun] **1.** *(thing given, sth to be grateful for)*
Geschenk [ɡə'ʃɛŋk] das <–(e)s, –e> ◊ *Sie kaufte
Geschenke für Freunde und Verwandte.* ♦ *Wahre
Liebe ist ein Geschenk.; (to charity)* Spende ['ʃpɛndə]
die <–, –n> ◊ *eine großzügige Spende machen*
2. *(talent)* Gabe ['ɡaːbə] die <–, –n> ◊ *Er hat die
Gabe, mit allen gut auszukommen.* a gift for sth ein
Talent für etw. [aɛn 'talɛnt fyːɐ] das <–(e)s, –e> ◊
Ihr Talent für Musik hat sie von ihrem Vater.
🔘 sth is in the gift of sb jd kann etw. vergeben
gifted [adj] begabt [bə'ɡaːpt] <begabter, am begabtes-
ten> ◊ *praktisch/handwerklich/mathematisch begabt
sein* ♦ *ein begabtes Kind*
gig [noun] **1.** MUS Konzert [kɔn'tsɛrt] das <–(e)s, –e> ◊
Die letzten beiden Konzerte sind toll gelaufen. do a
gig auftreten ['aʊftreːtŋ] <tritt auf, trat auf, ist aufge-
treten> ◊ *Am 25. Oktober tritt die Gruppe in der
Stadthalle auf.* **2.** *(in the US: temporary job)* Job
[dʒɔp] der <–s, –s> ◊ *Er hat zurzeit einen Job als
Gärtner.*
giggle [verb] kichern ['kɪçen] +haben ◊ *Hört endlich
auf zu kichern!*
ginger [noun] Ingwer ['ɪŋvɐ] der <–s> *no pl*
giraffe [noun] Giraffe [ɡi'rafə] die <–, –n>
girl [noun] Mädchen ['mɛːtçən] das <–s, –> ◊ *In der
Klasse sind 17 Mädchen und 12 Jungen.* ♦ *Er ist mit
einem tollen Mädchen zusammen.*

girlfriend [noun] Freundin ['frɔøndɪn] die <–, –nen> ◊
Seine neue Freundin scheint sehr nett zu sein. ♦ *Sie
trifft sich jeden Samstag mit ihren Freundinnen.*
give [verb] **1.** *(hand over, grant, allow, pay money)*
geben ['ɡeːbm̩] <gibt, gab, hat gegeben> ◊ *Gib mir
bitte mal den Kugelschreiber.* ♦ *Du solltest dir eine
Quittung geben lassen.* ♦ *Er gab ihr 20 Euro als
Belohnung.* ♦ *Bitte geben Sie mir noch ein wenig
Zeit.* ♦ *Wir werden dieser Angelegenheit Vorrang
geben.; (as a present)* schenken ['ʃɛŋkŋ] +haben ◊
*Was schenkst du deinem Mann zu Weihnachten?;
(donate)* spenden ['ʃpɛndn̩] <spendet, spendete, hat
gespendet> ◊ *Sie hat großzügig gespendet.* ♦ *Wir
spenden jedes Jahr eine Summe an Unicef.; (a loan)*
gewähren [ɡə've:rən] <gewährt, gewährte, hat
gewährt> ◊ *Zum Glück hat uns die Bank einen
Kredit gewährt.* **2.** *(make sb the owner of sth)* give sb
sth, give sth to sb jdm etw. übergeben [ybɐ'ɡeːbm̩]
<übergibt, übergab, hat übergeben> ◊ *Er hat das
Geschäft seinem Sohn übergeben.* **3.** *(a medicine)* verabreichen [fɛ'ʔapraɛçn̩] <verabreicht, verabreichte, hat
verabreicht> ◊ *jdm etwas gegen die Schmerzen verabreichen* ♦ *Dieses Medikament kann man oral oder
als Injektion verabreichen.* **4.** *(cause a feeling or
problem)* bereiten [bə'raɛtn̩] <bereitet, bereitete, hat
bereitet> ◊ *Dein Geschenk hat mir große Freude
bereitet.* ♦ *Seit wir den Wagen haben, bereitet er uns
nur Probleme; (a fright, courage)* machen ['maxn̩]
+haben ◊ *Sein Geschrei machte ihr Angst.* ♦ *Ihre
Worte machten ihm Mut.* **5.** *(communicate, atriculate)*
geben ['ɡeːbm̩] <gibt, gab, hat gegeben> ◊ *Er gab ihr
am Telefon genaue Anweisungen.* ♦ *Kannst du mir
vielleicht einen Rat geben?; (a comment, an opinion
etc.)* abgeben ['apɡeːbm̩] ◊ *Willst du einen
Kommentar/Tipp abgeben?* ♦ *Er gab eine schriftliche
Erklärung ab.; (a performance)* bieten ['biːtn̩] <bietet,
bot, hat geboten> ◊ *Er gab ihnen eine tolle Vorstellung
geboten.; (a speech)* halten ['haltn̩] <hält, hielt, hat
gehalten> ◊ *eine Abschiedsrede halten; (a sense or
feeling of sth)* vermitteln [fɛ'mɪtln̩] <vermittelt, vermittelte, hat vermittelt> ◊ *Er versuchte, den Betroffenen
Sicherheit zu vermitteln.* give sb the impression that
jdm den Eindruck vermitteln, dass ◊ *Sein Verhalten
vermittelte ihr den Eindruck, dass er sich unwohl
fühlt.* give sb a hug jdn umarmen [ʊm|'aˈmən]
<umarmt, umarmte, hat umarmt> give sb a call jdn
anrufen ['anruːfn̩] <ruft an, rief an, hat angerufen>
give sth a try etw. versuchen [fɛ'zuːxn̩] <versucht,
versuchte, hat versucht> give sb thought/consider-
ation über etw. [acc] nachdenken
[yːbɐ ... ,naxdɛŋkŋ] <denkt nach, dachte nach, hat
nachgedacht> ◊ *Wir werden über Ihren Vorschlag
nachdenken.* give a laugh auflachen ['aʊflaxŋ]
+haben ◊ *Als sie das sagte, lachte er auf und schüttelte den Kopf.* give a sigh aufseufzen ['aʊftsɔɡftsn̩]
+haben ◊ *Sie seufzte auf und ging zurück an ihre
Arbeit.* give sb a smile jdn anlächeln ['anlɛçln̩]
+haben ◊ *Er lächelte sie an und nahm ihre Hand.*
6. *(an illness)* give sth to sb jdm mit etw. anstecken
[mɪt ... ,anʃtɛkn̩] +haben ◊ *Sie hat mehrere Kollegen
mit der Grippe angesteckt.* **7.** *(bend, stretch)*
nachgeben ['naːxɡeːbm̩] <gibt nach, gab nach, hat
nachgegeben> ◊ *Der Boden gab unter der Last ein
wenig nach.* **8.** give yourself to sth sich einer Sache
[dat] widmen ['vɪtmən] <widmet sich, widmete sich,
hat sich gewidmet> ◊ *Sie widmete sich ganz ihrer*

Familie.

Ⓢ **give or take** plus/minus ◊ *Sie haben eine Stunde Zeit, plus/minus fünf Minuten.* I give you sb auf jdn ◊ *Auf Michael!* I'll give you that das gebe ich zu ◊ *Sie ist ganz attraktiv, das gebe ich ja zu, aber …* what she's was gibt's

• **give away** ⟨phras v⟩ 1. *(a secret, an emotion)* verraten [fɛˈraːtn̩] <verrät, verriet, hat verraten> ◊ *Ihr Gesicht verriet keinerlei Neugier.* ♦ *Er wollte das Geheimnis nicht verraten.* 2. *(give without charge)* verschenken [fɛˈʃɛŋkn̩] <verschenkt, verschenkte, hat verschenkt> ◊ *Ich habe die alten Kindersachen verschenkt.* 3. *(a bride)* zum Altar führen [tsʊm alˈtaːʳ fyːrən] +haben

• **give back** ⟨phras v⟩ give (sb) sth back (jdm) etw. zurückgeben [tsʊˈrʏkɡeːbn̩] <gibt zurück, gab zurück, hat zurückgegeben> ◊ *Hast du Carola das Buch schon zurückgegeben?* ♦ *Dieser Triumph gab ihm sein Selbstvertrauen zurück.*

• **give in** ⟨phras v⟩ 1. *(stop fighting)* aufgeben [ˈaʊfɡeːbn̩] <gibt auf, gab auf, hat aufgegeben> ◊ *Sein Gegner gab schließlich auf.; (stop arguing)* nachgeben [ˈnaːxɡeːbn̩] <gibt nach, gab nach, hat nachgegeben> ◊ *Als sie sah, dass die Diskussion zu nichts führte, gab sie nach.* give in to sth einer Sache ⟨dat⟩ nachgeben ◊ *Sie weigert sich, seiner Bitte nachzugeben.* 2. *(a document, essay)* give sth in etw. einreichen [ˈaɛnraɛçn̩] +haben ◊ *Sie reichte den Antrag pünktlich ein.*

• **give off** ⟨phras v⟩ give sth off *(heat, gas)* etw. abgeben [ˈapɡeːbn̩] <gibt ab, gab ab, hat abgegeben> ◊ *Der Ofen gibt zu wenig Wärme ab.; (a smell)* verbreiten [fɛˈbraɛtn̩] <verbreitet, verbreitete, hat verbreitet> ◊ *Diese Rosen verbreiten einen wunderbaren Duft.*

• **give out** ⟨phras v⟩ 1. *(distribute)* give sth out etw. verteilen [fɛˈtaɛlən] <verteilt, verteilte, hat verteilt> ◊ *Studenten verteilten auf der Straße Flugblätter.; (announce)* etw. bekannt geben [bəˈkant ɡeːbn̩] <gibt, gab, hat gegeben> ◊ *Näheres zu dem Vorfall werden wir später bekannt geben.* 2. *(fail)* versagen [fɛˈzaːɡŋ̍] <versagt, versagte, hat versagt> ◊ *Plötzlich versagte der Motor.* 3. *(supplies, strength)* zu Ende gehen [tsuː ˈɛndə ɡeːən] <geht, ging, ist gegangen> ◊ *Ihre Kräfte gehen allmählich zu Ende.* 4. *(a sound)* von sich geben [ˈfɔn … ɡeːbn̩] <gibt, gab, hat gegeben> ◊ *Das Gerät gibt ein seltsames Geräusch von sich.; (a light)* ausstrahlen [ˈaʊsʃtraːlən] +haben ◊ *Die Kerze strahlte ein warmes Licht aus.*

• **give up** ⟨phras v⟩ 1. *(stop doing sth, relinquish)* give sth up etw. aufgeben [ˈaʊfɡeːbn̩] <gibt auf, gab auf, hat aufgegeben> ◊ *Sie versucht seit Jahren, das Rauchen aufzugeben.* ♦ *Du darfst die Hoffnung nicht aufgeben!* ♦ *Ich habe es aufgegeben, ihn davon überzeugen zu wollen.* 2. *(let sb use sth)* give sth up to sb jdm etw. überlassen [ybɐˈlasn̩] <überlässt, überließ, hat überlassen> ◊ *Er überließ seinen Sitzplatz einer älteren Dame.* 3. *(admit to a crime)* give yourself up sich stellen [ˈʃtɛlən] +haben 4. give sb up for dead jdn für tot halten [fyːɐ ˈtoːt haltn̩] <hält, hielt, hat gehalten>

given → **give** ⟨adj⟩ 1. *(particular)* bestimmt [bəˈʃtɪmt] *no comp/superl, only before ns* ◊ *Die Uhr piepst zu bestimmten Zeiten.* at any given point etc. an jedem beliebigen Punkt etc. [an ˌjeːdəm bəˌliːbɪɡŋ̍ ˈpʊŋkt] 2. *(inclined)* be given to sth zu etw. neigen

[tsuː … ˌnaɛɡŋ̍] +haben ◊ *Sie neigt zu Übertreibungen.*

glad ⟨adj⟩ froh [froː] <froher, am froh(e)sten> ◊ *ein frohes Lachen* ♦ *Sie war froh, dass er wieder zu Hause war.* be glad about sth sich über etw. ⟨acc⟩ freuen [yːbɐ … ˌfrɔɐən] +haben ◊ *Sie freut sich über seine Ankunft.* be glad for sb sich für jdn freuen

Ⓢ I'd be glad to aber gern

gladly ⟨adv⟩ gern [ɡɛʳn] <lieber, am liebsten> ◊ *Ich beantworte gern Ihre Fragen.*

glance¹ ⟨noun⟩ Blick [blɪk] der <−(e)s, −e> ◊ *Die beiden Mädchen tauschten Blicke aus und kicherten.* ♦ *Ohne einen Blick zurück rannte er davon.* cast a glance at sb jdm einen Blick zuwerfen have/take a glance at sth einen Blick auf etw. ⟨acc⟩ werfen

Ⓢ at a glance mit einem Blick

glance² ⟨verb⟩ 1. *(look at)* blicken [ˈblɪkn̩] +haben ◊ *Er blickte auf seine Uhr und stand auf.* ♦ *Sie blickte nervös über die Schulter.* glance up aufblicken [ˈaʊfblɪkn̩] +haben ◊ *Der Mann blickte nur kurz auf und vertiefte sich wieder in seine Zeitung.* glance around sich umblicken [ˈʊmblɪkn̩] +haben ◊ *Die Frau blickte sich suchend um.* 2. *(read quickly)* glance at sth einen kurzen Blick auf etw. ⟨acc⟩ werfen [aɛnən kʊʳtsn̩ ˈblɪk aɔf … vɛʳfn̩] <wirft, warf, hat geworfen>

glare ⟨verb⟩ 1. *(look angrily)* glare at sb jdn zornig anstarren [ˌtsɔʳnɪç ˈanʃtarən] +haben ◊ *Zornig starrte er seinen Widersacher an.* 2. *(sun, light)* grell scheinen [ˌɡrɛl ˈʃaɛnən] <scheint, schien, hat geschienen> ◊ *Die Sonne schien grell auf sie herunter.*

glaring → **glare** ⟨adj⟩ 1. *(colo(u)r, light)* grell [ɡrɛl] ◊ *Die Sonne ist grell.* ♦ *grelle Farben* 2. *(fig) (obvious)* eklatant [eklaˈtant] <eklatanter, am eklatantesten> ◊ *ein eklatanter Fehler/Widerspruch* ♦ *Hier ist der Unterschied besonders eklatant.*

glass ⟨noun⟩ Glas [ɡlaːs] das <−es, Gläser> ◊ *Die Wände sind aus Glas.* ♦ *Er hat eines meiner guten Gläser zerbrochen.* ♦ *Möchten Sie ein Glas Wein?* sliver of glass Glassplitter [ˈɡlaːsʃplɪtɐ] der <−s, −>

glasses ⟨noun⟩ Brille [ˈbrɪlə] die <−, −n> ◊ *Er setzte seine Brille auf.* wear glasses eine Brille tragen

gleam ⟨verb⟩ glänzen [ˈɡlɛntsn̩] +haben ◊ *Der Helm glänzte in der Sonne.* ♦ *Sie lachte und ihre Augen glänzten.*

glide ⟨verb⟩ gleiten [ˈɡlaɛtn̩] <gleitet, glitt, ist geglitten> ◊ *Die Tänzer glitten über die Tanzfläche.* ♦ *Ein Adler/Segelflugzeug gleitet durch die Luft.*

glimmer ⟨verb⟩ *(light, water)* schimmern [ˈʃɪmen] +haben ◊ *Das Wasser schimmerte im Sonnenlicht.; (fire, feeling)* glimmen [ˈɡlɪmən] <glimmt, glomm/glimmte, hat geglommen/geglimmt> ◊ *Zigaretten glommen in der Dunkelheit.* ♦ *In ihren Augen glomm noch eine letzte Hoffnung.*

glimpse ⟨noun⟩ 1. *(short look)* Blick [blɪk] der <−(e)s, −e> ♦ *Werfen wir einen kurzen Blick auf das, was hinter den Kulissen geschieht.* catch/get a glimpse of sb/sth einen flüchtigen Blick auf jdn/etw. erhaschen [ˈaɛnblɪk] 2. *(idea)* Einblick [ˈaɛnblɪk] der <−(e)s, −e> ◊ *ein faszinierender Einblick in das Leben der Wale* catch/get a glimpse of sth eine Ahnung von etw. bekommen [aɛnə ˌaːnʊŋ fɔn … bəkɔmən] <bekommt, bekam, hat bekommen>

global(ly) ⟨adj, adv⟩ global [ɡloˈbaːl] *no comp/superl; when used as an adj, only before ns* ◊ *ein globaler*

Konflikt ♦ *global wettbewerbsfähig bleiben* ♦ *ein globales Wissen haben* taking a global view of the matter global gesehen ◊ *Global gesehen ist das alles kein Problem.* global economy Weltwirtschaft ['vɛltvɪrtʃaft] die <-> *no pl* global warming Erwärmung der Erdatmosphäre [ɛ,vɛɐ'mʊŋ deːɐ 'eːɐtʔatmo,sfɛːrə] die <-> *no pl*

gloom [noun] **1.** *(sadness, depression)* (atmosphere of) gloom düstere Stimmung [,dyːstərə 'ʃtɪmʊŋ] die <-> *no pl* ◊ *Im Land herrschte eine düstere Stimmung.* **2.** *(darkness)* Düsterkeit ['dyːstɐkaet] die <-> *no pl* ◊ *In der Düsterkeit des Zimmers konnte sie nichts erkennen.*

gloomy(-ily) [adj, adv] düster ['dyːstɐ] ◊ *In der Kirche war es düster.* ♦ *düstere Farben* ♦ *düstere Gedanken*

glorious(ly) [adj, adv] **1.** *(marvel(l)ous)* herrlich ['hɛɐlɪç] ◊ *Das Wetter war herrlich.* ♦ *Wir hatten eine herrliche Sicht auf das Meer.* ♦ *Die Blumen dufteten herrlich.* **2.** *(deed, victory)* glorreich ['gloːɐraeç] *when used as an adj, mostly before ns* ◊ *einen glorreichen Sieg erringen* ♦ *Sie haben glorreich gewonnen.*

glory [noun] **1.** *(fame)* Ruhm [ruːm] der <-(e)s> *no pl* ◊ *von Ruhm und Ansehen träumen* ♦ *weltweiten Ruhm erlangen* **2.** *(beauty)* Pracht [praxt] die <-> *no pl* ◊ *die Orchidee in ihrer ganzen Pracht* **3.** REL *(praise)* Ehre ['eːrə] die <-> *no pl* ◊ *Ehre sei Gott in der Höhe!*

glossy [adj] glänzend ['glɛntsn̩t] ◊ *Die Katze hat glänzendes Fell.* ♦ *Möchten Sie die Abzüge matt oder glänzend?* glossy paper Glanzpapier ['glantspa,piːɐ] das <-s, -e> glossy magazine Illustrierte [ɪlʊs'triːɡtə] die <-n, -n>

glove [noun] Handschuh ['hantʃuː] der <-(e)s, -e> ⊚ the gloves are off die Schonzeit ist vorbei

glow¹ [noun] **1.** *(of a candle, lamp etc.)* Schein [ʃaen] der <-(e)s, -e> *most sing* ◊ *Sie saßen im Schein des Feuers beisammen.;* *(of a colo(u)r, screen)* Leuchten ['lɔøçtn̩] das <-s> *no pl* ◊ *das schwache Leuchten des Bildschirms* **2.** *(of skin)* Schimmer ['ʃɪmɐ] der <-s> *no pl* ◊ *Ein rosiger Schimmer lag auf ihrem Gesicht.* **3.** *(feeling)* a glow of sth ein angenehmes Gefühl ... [gen] [aen ,angəˈneːməs ɡəˈfyːl] <-s, -e> ◊ *Das angenehme Gefühl der Zufriedenheit war immer noch da.*

glow² [verb] **1.** *(burn without flame, flush)* glühen ['ɡlyːən] +haben ◊ *Das Feuer glühte rot.* ♦ *Ihr Gesicht glühte vor Aufregung.;* *(lamp, colo(u)rs etc.)* leuchten ['lɔøçtn̩] <leuchtet, leuchtete, hat geleuchtet> ◊ *Die Farben des Kirchenfensters leuchteten in der Sonne.* ♦ *Das Zifferblatt leuchtet in der Dunkelheit.* **2.** *(with pride, joy)* strahlen ['ʃtraːlən] +haben ◊ *Die Augen der Kinder strahlten.* ♦ *Er strahlte vor Freude/Stolz.*

glue¹ [noun] Klebstoff ['kleːpʃtɔf] der <-(e)s, -e> ◊ *eine Tube Klebstoff*

glue² [verb] kleben ['kleːbn̩] +haben ◊ *Die Tasse kann man wieder kleben.* ♦ *einen Zettel an die Wand kleben* glue sth together etw. zusammenkleben [tsuˈzamənkleːbn̩] +haben ◊ *Glaubst du, die Teile können wieder zusammengeklebt werden?* ⊚ sb's eyes are glued to sth jds Augen hängen an etw. [dat] ◊ *Die Augen der Kinder hingen am Bildschirm.*

gnaw [verb] *(bite)* gnaw (at) sth an etw. [dat] nagen [an ... naːɡŋ̩] +haben ◊ *Der Hund nagt an einem Knochen.* gnaw holes in sth Löcher in etw. [acc] nagen gnaw at your fingernails an den Fingernägeln

kauen [an deːn 'fɪŋənɛːɡl̩n kaoən] +haben • **gnaw at** [phras v] gnaw at sb *(fig)* jdn quälen ['kvɛːlən] +haben ◊ *Die Sorge um ihren Sohn quälte sie.*

go¹ [noun] **1.** *(attempt)* have a go at sth etw. versuchen [fɛ'zuːxn̩] <versucht, versuchte, hat versucht> have a go at doing sth versuchen, etw. zu tun ◊ *Sie versuchte, das Klavierspielen zu lernen, gab es aber bald wieder auf.* Have a go! Versuch's mal! Can I have a go? Darf ich mal? it's sb's go jd ist dran [ɪst 'dran] +sein ◊ *Du bist dran!* at/in one go auf einmal [aof 'aenmaːl] **2.** *(energy)* Schwung [ʃvʊŋ] der <-(e)s> *no pl* ◊ *Voller Schwung ging er an die Arbeit.* ⊚ have a go at sb jdn herunterputzen *(fam)* have sth on the go etw. laufen haben it's all go es ist immer was los

go² [verb] **1.** *(walk, proceed, move, visit, leave, attend, lead, be directed or aimed at, function or work, sum of money: exceed)* gehen ['geːən] <geht, ging, ist gegangen> ◊ *auf die Toilette gehen* ♦ *Wir gehen heute ins Kino.* ♦ *Ich glaube, du solltest jetzt besser gehen.* ♦ *Gehst du schon in die Schule?* ♦ *Wohin geht diese Straße?* ♦ *Dieses Schreiben geht an alle unsere Kunden.* ♦ *Meine Uhr geht nicht mehr.* ♦ *Höher als 150 Euro kann ich nicht gehen.* go shopping/fishing etc. einkaufen/angeln etc. gehen ◊ *Meine Mutter ist einkaufen gegangen.;* *(descend)* go down hinuntergehen [hɪ'nʊnteɡeːən] ◊ *Sie ging die Treppe hinunter.;* *(ascend)* go up hinaufgehen [hɪ'naofɡeːən] ◊ *Er ging die Treppe hinauf.* go there hingehen ['hɪnɡeːən] ◊ *Morgen gibts dort eine Party; ich würde gern hingehen.* go and see nachsehen [naˈxzeːən] <sieht nach, sah nach, hat nachgesehen> ◊ *Sieh mal nach, ob das Wasser schon kocht.* **2.** *(vehicle: move, get somewhere using a vehicle)* fahren ['faːrən] <fährt, fuhr, ist gefahren> ◊ *Dieser Bus fährt direkt ins Zentrum.* ♦ *Sie wollen nächsten Sommer nach Frankreich fahren.* go by car/train mit dem Auto/Zug fahren go there hinfahren ['hɪnfaːrən] ◊ *Wir können gleich mit dem Fahrrad hinfahren.;* *(drive around an obstacle etc.)* go around sth etw. umfahren [ʊm'faːrən] <umfährt, umfuhr, hat umfahren> ◊ *eine große Stadt umfahren* **3.** *(aircraft: fly, go somewhere by aircraft)* fliegen ['fliːɡn̩] <fliegt, flog, ist geflogen> ◊ *Dieses Flugzeug fliegt nach Rom.* ♦ *Mein Sohn fliegt nächste Woche nach Australien.* **4.** *(happen, turn out)* laufen ['laofn̩] <läuft, lief, ist gelaufen> ◊ *Die Gespräche liefen gut.* ♦ *Na, wie läuft's in der Arbeit?* go all right, go ok gut laufen **5.** *(become, change into a particular state)* werden ['veːɐdn̩] <wird, wurde, ist geworden> ◊ *blind/taub/verrückt werden* ◊ *Die Milch ist sauer geworden.;* *(remain in a particular state)* go unnoticed/unpunished unbemerkt/ungestraft bleiben ['ʊnbəmɛˈkt/'ʊnɡəʃtraˈft blaebm̩] <bleibt, blieb, ist geblieben> ◊ *Sein Verschwinden blieb nicht unbemerkt.* **6.** *(fail, wear out)* kaputtgehen [ka'pʊtɡeːən] <geht kaput, ging kaputt, ist kaputtgegangen> ◊ *Diese Uhr geht allmählich kaputt.* **7.** *(belong)* go somewhere irgendwohin gehören [ɡə'høːrən] <gehört, gehörte, hat gehört> ◊ *Die Töpfe gehören ins linke Fach.;* *(fit, match)* passen ['pasn̩] +haben ◊ *Dieser Schrank passt gut ins Wohnzimmer.* **8.** *(time)* vergehen [fɛˈɡeːən] <vergeht, verging, ist vergangen> ◊ *Unglaublich, wie schnell die Zeit vergeht!* **9.** *(be used up: money)* go on sth für etw.

ausgegeben werden [fy:ɐ̯ ... ˌaɔsɡəɡeːbm̩ veːɐ̯dn̩] <wird, wurde, ist worden> ◊ *Das Geld wurde für Nahrungsmittel ausgegeben.* I don't know where all the money goes. Ich weiß nicht, wo das ganze Geld bleibt. **10.** *(use up: provisions etc.)* aufgebraucht werden [ˈaɔfɡəbraɔxt veːɐ̯dn̩] +*sein* be gone aufgebraucht sein ◊ *Mehl und Zucker sind schon aufgebraucht.* **11.** *(disappear, be no longer there)* verschwinden [fɛˈʃvɪndn̩] <verschwindet, verschwand, ist verschwunden> ◊ *Eben waren die Schlüssel noch hier; jetzt sind sie verschwunden.* **12.** *(make a certain sound)* machen [ˈmaxn̩] +*haben* ◊ *Die Katze macht miau.* ✦ *Die Uhr macht ticktack.* There goes the bell. Es klingelt. **13.** *(consist of particular notes, words etc.)* gehen [ˈɡeːən] <geht, ging, ist gegangen> ◊ *Wie geht die zweite Strophe des Liedes noch einmal?* the story goes that man erzählt sich, dass [man ɛˈtsɛːlt zɪç das] <erzählt sich, erzählte sich, hat sich erzählt> ◊ *Man erzählt sich, dass es hier spukt.* **14.** *(be sold)* gehen [ˈɡeːən] <geht, ging, ist gegangen> ◊ *Im Winter geht Eis nicht so gut.* be going cheap billig sein [ˈbɪlɪç zaɛn] +*sein* ◊ *Im Moment sind die Trauben billig.* **15.** *(as an auxiliary)* be going to do sth etw. tun werden [ˈveːɐ̯dn̩] We're going to have a party on Saturday. Wir werden am Samstag eine Party geben. I think it's going to rain. Ich glaube, es wird bald regnen.
◉ **going, going, gone** zum Ersten, zum Zweiten, und zum Dritten **to go 1.** *(remaining)* noch ◊ *Noch zwei Seiten, dann habe ich das Manuskript fertig.* ✦ *Noch zwei Wochen, dann sind endlich Ferien!* **2.** *(food: to take away)* zum Mitnehmen ◊ *eine Pizza zum Mitnehmen*

• **go about** (phras v) **1.** *(an activity)* go about sth einer Sache (dat) nachgehen [ˈnaːxɡeːən] <geht nach, ging nach, ist nachgegangen> ◊ *Die Menschen gehen ihrer täglichen Arbeit nach.* **2.** *(a problem, task)* anpacken [ˈanpakn̩] +*haben* ◊ *Wie hast du die Aufgabe angepackt?* go about doing sth es anstellen, etw. zu tun [ɛs ˈanʃtɛlən ... tsuː] +*haben* ◊ *Wie hast du es angestellt, diesen Auftrag zu bekommen?* **3.** *(in the UK: wear particular clothes)* go about in in etw. (dat) herumlaufen [hɛˈʁʊmlaɔfn̩] <läuft herum, lief herum, ist herumgelaufen> *(fam)* ◊ *Du kannst doch nicht den ganzen Tag im Pyjama herumlaufen!* **4.** *(in the UK: circulate)* umgehen [ˈʊmɡeːən] <geht um, ging um, ist umgegangen> ◊ *Es geht das Gerücht um, dass ...* **5.** go about with sb mit jdm herumziehen [mɪt ... hɛˌʁʊmtsiːən] <zieht herum, zog herum, ist herumgezogen> ◊ *Er zieht jeden Tag mit seinen Freunden herum.*

• **go after** (phras v) **1.** *(follow)* go after sb jdm nachgehen [ˈnaːxɡeːən] <geht nach, ging nach, ist nachgegangen> ◊ *Du solltest ihm nachgehen, um zu sehen, ob er tatsächlich in die Sauna will.; (in a vehicle)* jdm nachfahren [ˈnaːxfaːrən] <fährt nach, fuhr nach, ist nachgefahren> ◊ *Sie fuhr dem Wagen nach.* **2.** *(pursue)* jdn verfolgen [fɛˈfɔlɡn̩] <verfolgt, verfolgte, hat verfolgt> ◊ *Die Polizei verfolgte den Täter.* **2.** *(a girl, job)* go after sb/sth sich um jdn/etw. bemühen [ʊm ... bəˌmyːən] <bemüht sich, bemühte sich, hat sich bemüht> ◊ *Er bemüht sich um eine Stelle bei Siemens.*

• **go against** (phras v) **1.** *(oppose)* go against sth einer Sache (dat) widersprechen [viːdɐˈʃpʁɛçn̩] <widerspricht, widersprach, hat widersprochen> ◊

Diese Forderung widerspricht allem, woran sie glaubt. go against sb/sth sich jdm/einer Sache widersetzen [viːdeˈzɛtsn̩] <widersetzt sich, widersetzte sich, hat sich widersetzt> ◊ *Sie hat sich den Anordnungen ihres Vorgesetzten widersetzt.* **2.** *(take an unfavo(u)rable course)* go against sb ungünstig für jdn verlaufen [ˈʊnɡʏnstɪç fyːɐ̯ ... fɐlaɔfn̩] <verläuft, verlief, ist verlaufen> ◊ *Der Prozess verlief ungünstig für ihn.; (verdict)* go against sb zu jds Ungunsten ausfallen [tsuː ... ˈʊnɡʊnstn̩ aɔsfalən] <fällt aus, fiel aus, ist ausgefallen>

• **go ahead** (phras v) **1.** *(proceed)* go ahead with sth etw. durchführen [ˈdʊɐ̯çfyːrən] <führt durch, führte durch, hat durchgeführt> ◊ *Wir werden den Umbau erst im nächsten Jahr durchführen.* **2.** *(go before, first)* vorausgehen [foˈraɔsɡeːən] <geht voraus, ging voraus, ist vorausgegangen> ◊ *Geh schon mal voraus; ich komme nach, wenn ich fertig bin.* ✦ *Ich gehe voraus und zeige euch den Weg.* **3.** *(take place)* stattfinden [ˈʃtatfɪndn̩] <findet statt, fand statt, hat stattgefunden> ◊ *Das Fest fand wie geplant statt.*
◉ **go ahead!** nur zu!

• **go along** (phras v) **1.** *(happen)* laufen [ˈlaɔfn̩] <läuft, lief, ist gelaufen> ◊ *Alles ist prima gelaufen, bis er kam.* **2.** *(accompany)* mitkommen [ˈmɪtkɔmən] <kommt mit, kam mit, ist mitgekommen> ◊ *Mein Mann geht morgen auf Geschäftsreise, und ich komme vielleicht auch mit.* **3.** *(agree)* go along with sb/sth jdm/einer Sache zustimmen [ˈtsuːʃtɪmən] +*haben* ◊ *Ich stimme dem zu, was du gesagt hast.*
◉ **do sth as you go along** She thought up the rules as she went along. Sie dachte sich Regeln aus, wie es ihr gerade passte. He made up the story as he went along. Seine Geschichte ergab sich beim Erzählen.

• **go around** (phras v) **1.** *(visit)* go around (to sb) (bei jdm) vorbeischauen [foːɐ̯ˈbaeʃaɔən] +*haben* ◊ *Schaust du nach der Arbeit noch bei Peter vorbei?* **2.** *(wear particular clothes)* herumlaufen [hɛˈʁʊmlaɔfn̩] <läuft herum, lief herum, ist herumgelaufen> ◊ *Das ist eine Kirche! Mit Minirock kannst du da nicht herumlaufen!* **3.** *(illness, rumo(u)r)* umgehen [ˈʊmɡeːən] <geht um, ging um, ist umgegangen> ◊ *Im Kindergarten gehen die Masern um.* **4.** go around with sb mit jdm herumziehen [mɪt ... hɛˌʁʊmtsiːən] <zieht herum, zog herum, ist herumgezogen> ◊ *Sie zieht jedes Wochenende mit ihrer Clique herum.* **5.** be enough to go around (sb) (für jdn) reichen [ˈraɛçn̩] +*haben* ◊ *Die Würstchen reichen für alle Kinder.* **6.** *(turn)* sich drehen [ˈdreːən] +*haben* ◊ *Die Kinder drehten sich fröhlich im Kreis.*

• **go at** (phras v) **1.** *(attack)* go at sb/sth auf jdn/etw. losgehen [aɔf ... ˌloːsɡeːən] <geht los, ging los, ist losgegangen> ◊ *Knurrend ging der Hund auf den Eindringling los.* **2.** *(a task)* go at sth sich an etw. (acc) machen [an ... maxn̩] +*haben* ◊ *Sie machte sich mit Feuereifer an die Aufgaben.*

• **go away** (phras v) **1.** *(leave, disappear)* weggehen [ˈvɛkɡeːən] <geht weg, ging weg, ist weggegangen> ◊ *Geh mal bitte da weg, du stehst mir im Weg.* ✦ *Die Schmerzen sind durch das Medikament nicht weggegangen.; (on holiday)* wegfahren [ˈvɛkfaːrən] <fährt weg, fuhr weg, ist weggefahren> ◊ *Fahrt ihr in den Ferien weg?*

• **go back** (phras v) **1.** *(return to a place, person)* go back to sb/sth zu jdm/etw. zurückgehen

[tsuː: ... ˌtsuˌrʏkgeːən] <geht zurück, ging zurück, ist zurückgegangen> ◊ *Sollen wir zum Hotel zurückgehen?; (in a vehicle)* zurückfahren [tsuːˈrʏkfaːrən] <fährt zurück, fuhr zurück, ist zurückgefahren> ◊ *nach Hause zurückfahren; (return to a subject)* go back to sth **auf** etw. [acc] zurückkommen [aof ... tsuˌrʏkkɔmən] <kommt zurück, kam zurück, ist zurückgekommen> ◊ *Ich möchte später darauf zurückkommen.* **2.** *(date back)* go back to sth **aus** etw. stammen [aos ... ʃtamən] +haben ◊ *Dieser Brauch stammt aus dem Mittelalter.* We go back a long time. *Wir kennen uns schon lange.*

• **go beyond** [phras v] go beyond sth **über** etw. [acc] hinausgehen [yːbɐ ... hɪˌnaosgeːən] <geht hinaus, ging hinaus, ist hinausgegangen> ◊ *Die Kosten sollten nicht über 15 000 Euro hinausgehen.* ♦ *Das geht über seine Forderungen hinaus.*

• **go by** [phras v] **1.** *(time)* vergehen [fɐˈgeːən] <vergeht, verging, ist vergangen> ◊ *Jahre vergingen und es änderte sich nichts.* **2.** *(be guided by)* go by sth sich nach etw. richten [naːx ... rɪçtn̩] <richtet sich, richtete sich, hat sich gerichtet> ◊ *Sollen wir uns danach richten, was er sagt?; (base a decision on)* nach etw. gehen [naːx ... geːən] <geht, ging, ist gegangen> ◊ *nicht nach dem Äußeren gehen; (stick to rules etc.)* **an** etw. [acc] halten [an ... haltn̩] <hält sich, hielt sich, hat sich gehalten> ◊ *Wir müssen uns genau an die Anweisungen halten.* **3.** go by the name of ... sich ... nennen [ˈnɛnən] <nennt sich, nannte sich, hat sich genannt> ◊ *Als ich sie kennen lernte, nannte sie sich Carmen.*

• **go down** [phras v] **1.** *(sink)* untergehen [ˈʊntɐgeːən] <geht unter, ging unter, ist untergegangen> ◊ *Sie ertrank, als das Schiff unterging.* ♦ *Die Sonne geht bald unter.* **2.** *(decrease)* fallen [ˈfalən] <fällt, fiel, ist gefallen> ◊ *Der Pegel des Flusses ist wieder gefallen.* ♦ *Die Preise sind stark gefallen.; (flood, swelling, number)* zurückgehen [tsuːˈrʏkgeːən] <geht zurück, ging zurück, ist zurückgegangen> ◊ *Das Hochwasser geht langsam zurück.* ♦ *Der Umsatz/Die Kriminalität ist zurückgegangen.* **3.** *(be noted)* sb will go down as ... man wird sich an jdn als ... erinnern [man vɪrt zɪç an ... als ... eˈ|ɪnɐn] ◊ *Man wird sich an ihn als strengen, aber gerechten Lehrer erinnern.* go down in history in die Geschichte eingehen [ɪn diː gəˈʃɪçtə aengeːən] <geht ein, ging ein, ist eingegangen> **4.** *(be received)* go down (well/badly) (with sb) (gut/schlecht) (bei jdm) ankommen [(ˌguːt/ʃlɛçt) ˈankɔmən] <kommt an, kam an, ist angekommen> ◊ *Wie ist dein Vortrag beim Publikum angekommen?* **5.** *(pill)* rutschen [ˈrʊtʃn̩] +sein ◊ *Trink etwas Wasser zu den Tabletten, dann rutschen sie besser.* **6.** *(go south)* hinunterfahren [hɪˈnʊntɐfaːrən] <fährt hinunter, fuhr hinunter, ist hinuntergefahren> ◊ *Wir fahren übers Wochenende nach München hinunter.* **7.** SPORT *(be defeated)* geschlagen werden [gəˈʃlaːgn̩ veːɐdn̩] <wird, wurde, ist worden> ◊ *Die Mannschaft wurde 3:5 geschlagen.; (in the UK: in league)* absteigen [ˈapʃtaegn̩] <steigt ab, stieg ab, ist abgestiegen> ◊ *in die zweite Liga absteigen* **8.** *((computer) system)* zusammenbrechen [tsuːˈzamənbrɛçn̩] <bricht zusammen, brach zusammen, ist zusammengebrochen> ◊ *Das System ist wegen Überlastung zusammengebrochen.* **9.** *(light)* langsam ausgehen [ˌlaŋzaːm ˈaosgeːən] <geht aus, ging aus, ist ausgegangen> ◊ *Langsam gingen die Lichter im Saal*

aus und der Vorhang hob sich. **10.** *(quality, standard)* sich verschlechtern [fɐˈʃlɛçtɐn] <verschlechtert sich, verschlechterte sich, hat sich verschlechtert> ◊ *Die Qualität der Waren hat sich merklich verschlechtert.* **11.** *(go to prison)* eingelocht werden [ˈaengəlɔxt veːɐdn̩] <wird, wurde, ist worden> *(fam)* **12.** *(become ill)* go down with sth etw. bekommen [bəˈkɔmən] <bekommt, bekam, hat bekommen> ◊ *Sie hat eine Erkältung bekommen.*

• **go for** [phras v] **1.** *(aim at)* go for sth **auf** etw. [acc] aus sein [aof ... aos zaen] +sein ◊ *Sie ist auf die Goldmedaille aus.* **2.** *(like)* go for sth **auf** etw. [acc] stehen [aof ... ʃteːən] <steht, stand, hat gestanden> *(fam)* ◊ *Ich steh nicht so auf Horrorfilme.* **3.** *(choose)* nehmen [ˈneːmən] <nimmt, nahm, hat genommen> ◊ *Ich nehme einen Salatteller. Und du?* **4.** *(attack, criticize)* angreifen [ˈangraefn̩] <greift an, griff an, hat angegriffen> ◊ *Der Hund hat ihn ohne jeden Grund angegriffen.* **5.** *(be sold at a certain price)* go for ... **für** ... weggehen [fyːɐ ... vɛkgeːən] <geht weg, ging weg, ist weggegangen> ◊ *Das antike Sofa ist für 2 500 Euro weggegangen.* **6.** *(fetch)* go for sb/sth jdn/etw. holen gehen [ˈhoːlən geːən] <geht, ging, ist gegangen> ◊ *Gehst du bitte mal meinen Mann holen?* **7.** *(be true of, apply to)* go for sb/sth für jdn/etw. gelten [fyːɐ ... gɛltn̩] <gilt, galt, hat gegolten> ◊ *Michael, ich möchte, dass du ordentlich isst — und dasselbe gilt für dich, Sandra!* ☞ go for it nichts wie ran go for nothing völlig umsonst sein

• **go in for** [phras v] go in for sth **1.** *(like, enjoy)* etw. mögen [ˈmøːgn̩] <mag, mochte, hat gemocht> ◊ *Skifahren mag ich nicht so gern.* **2.** *(in the UK: enter)* **an** etw. [dat] teilnehmen [an ... ˌtaelneːmən] <nimmt teil, nahm teil, hat teilgenommen> ◊ *Nimmst du an der Aufnahmeprüfung teil?* **3.** *(choose as a career)* sich **für** etw. entscheiden [fyːɐ ... ɛntʃaedn̩] <entscheidet sich, entschied sich, hat sich entschieden> ◊ *Sie hat sich für eine Karriere als Journalistin entschieden.*

• **go into** [phras v] go into sth **1.** *(a particular trade)* **in** etw. [acc] gehen [ɪn ... geːən] <geht, ging, ist gegangen> ◊ *in die Politik gehen* go into the army zum Militär gehen **2.** *(enter a different state)* **in** etw. [acc] geraten [ɪn ... gəraːtn̩] <gerät, geriet, ist geraten> ◊ *Der Wagen geriet plötzlich ins Schleudern.; (a coma, trance)* **in** etw. [acc] fallen [ɪn ... falən] <fällt, fiel, ist gefallen> ◊ *ins Koma fallen; (a fit)* etw. bekommen [bəˈkɔmən] <bekommt, bekam, hat bekommen> ◊ *Plötzlich bekam sie einen heftigen Anfall.* **3.** *(investigate, look at)* sich mit etw. befassen [mɪt ... bəˌfasn̩] <befasst sich, befasste sich, hat sich befasst> ◊ *sich mit einem Thema befassen* go into detail ins Detail gehen [ɪns deˈtae geːən] <geht, ging, ist gegangen> **4.** *(be spent on)* **für** etw. verwendet werden [fyːɐ ... fɐˌvɛndət veːɐdn̩] <wird, wurde, ist worden> ◊ *Mehr als die Hälfte des Geldes wird für die Verwaltung verwendet.* **5.** *(an explanation, description)* etw. von sich [dat] geben [ˈfɔn ... geːbm̩] <gibt, gab, hat gegeben> ◊ *Er gab eine lange Erklärung von sich, warum er nicht kommen konnte.* **6.** *(in sums)* **in** etw. [acc] gehen [ɪn ... geːən] <geht, ging, ist gegangen> ◊ *Wie oft geht 5 in 25?* **7.** *(crash into)* gegen etw. fahren [geːgn̩ ... faːrən] <fährt, fuhr, ist gefahren> ◊ *Der Wagen fuhr gegen den Baum.*

• **go off** [phras v] **1.** *(alarm, gun)* losgehen ['lɔ:sɡeːən] <geht los, ging los, ist losgegangen> ◊ *Plötzlich ging der Alarm los.; (bomb)* hochgehen ['ho:xɡeːən] <geht hoch, ging hoch, ist hochgegangen> **2.** *(light)* ausgehen ['aʊsɡeːən] <geht aus, ging aus, ist ausgegangen> ◊ *Alle Lichter im Saal gingen aus.* **3.** *(not like any more)* nicht mehr mögen [,nɪçt meːɐ 'møːɡn̩] <mag, mochte, hat gemocht> ◊ *Diese Musik mag ich seit Jahren nicht mehr.* go off meat kein Fleisch mehr mögen **4.** *(leave for a short time)* fortgehen ['fɔrtɡeːən] <geht fort, ging fort, ist fortgegangen> ◊ *Sie ging fort und kam nach kurzer Zeit wieder.; (in a vehicle)* fortfahren ['fɔrtfaːrən] <fährt fort, fuhr fort, ist fortgefahren> ◊ *Mein Mann ist fortgefahren, um Wein zu kaufen.* go off to a place irgendwohin fahren ['faːrən] <fährt, fuhr, ist gefahren> ◊ *Sie ist nach Österreich gefahren.* **5.** *(in the UK: food)* schlecht werden ['ʃlɛçt veːɐdn̩] +sein ◊ *Das Fleisch ist schlecht geworden.* **6.** *(in the UK: performance, work)* sich verschlechtern [fɛ'ʃlɛçtɐn] <verschlechtert sich, verschlechterte sich, hat sich verschlechtert> ◊ *Ihre Arbeit hat sich in den letzten Monaten deutlich verschlechtert.* **7.** *(take place, pass in a certain way)* verlaufen [fɛ'laʊfn̩] <verläuft, verlief, ist verlaufen> ◊ *Die Demonstration verlief friedlich.* **8.** go off to sleep einschlafen ['aɛnʃlaːfn̩] <schläft ein, schlief ein, ist eingeschlafen> **9.** *(with a new partner, sth that belongs to sb else)* go off with sb/ sth mit jdm/etw. auf und davon laufen [mɪt ... ,aʊf ʊnt da'fɔn laʊfn̩] <läuft, lief, ist gelaufen> ◊ *Er packte die Handtasche und lief damit auf und davon.*

• **go on** [phras v] **1.** *(continue)* weitergehen ['vaɛtəɡeːən] <geht weiter, ging weiter, ist weitergegangen> ◊ *Die Diskussion ging noch stundenlang weiter.* ♦ *Die Kämpfe gehen weiter.; (person)* weitermachen ['vaɛtəmaxn̩] +haben ◊ *So können wir nicht weitermachen.* ♦ *Sie sah kurz auf und machte dann mit ihrer Arbeit weiter.* go on working weiterarbeiten ['vaɛtəˈʔaɛbatn̩] <arbeitet weiter, arbeitete weiter, hat weitergearbeitet> **2.** *(happen)* vor sich gehen ['foːɐ zɪç ɡeːən] <geht, ging, ist gegangen> ◊ *Niemand weiß, was hinter diesen Türen vor sich geht.* **3.** *(start sth)* go on holiday in Urlaub fahren [ɪn 'uːɐlaʊp faːrən] <fährt, fuhr, ist gefahren> go on a trip to ... eine Reise nach ... machen [aɛnə ,raɛzə naːx ... maxn̩] +haben ◊ *Er möchte eine Reise nach Nepal machen.* go on a diet eine Diät machen [aɛnə diˈɛːt maxn̩] +haben; *(medicine)* go on sth etw. nehmen ['neːmən] <nimmt, nahm, hat genommen> **4.** *(light, TV etc.)* angehen ['anɡeːən] <geht an, ging an, ist angegangen> ◊ *Plötzlich gingen die Scheinwerfer an.* **5.** *(talk incessantly)* go on about sb/sth stundenlang von jdm/etw. erzählen [,ʃtʊndn̩laŋ fɔn ... ɛ,tsɛːlən] <erzählt, erzählte, hat erzählt> ◊ *Sie hat wieder stundenlang von ihrem Pferd erzählt.; (resume talking)* go on fortfahren ['fɔrtfaːrən] <fährt fort, fuhr fort, ist fortgefahren> ◊ *Die Moderatorin fuhr mit dem Interview fort.* ♦ *Entschuldigen Sie die Unterbrechung! Bitte fahren Sie fort.* **6.** *(begin a new topic)* go on to sth mit etw. weitermachen [mɪt ... ,vaɛtəmaxn̩] +haben ◊ *Lassen Sie uns mit dem nächsten Punkt weitermachen.* **7.** *(continue moving after a stop)* weitergehen ['vaɛtəɡeːən] <geht weiter, ging weiter, ist weitergegangen> ◊ *Nach einer kurzen Rast gingen sie weiter.; (in*

a vehicle) weiterfahren ['vaɛtəfaːrən] <fährt weiter, fuhr weiter, ist weitergefahren> **8.** *(time)* vergehen [fɛ'ɡeːən] <vergeht, verging, ist vergangen> ◊ *Die Zeit vergeht, und wir werden alle nicht jünger.* **9.** *(evidence)* go on sth sich auf etw. [acc] stützen [aʊf ... ʃtʏtsn̩] +haben ◊ *Worauf stützt du dich bei deiner Behauptung?* **10.** *(criticize)* go on at sb an jdm herumnörgeln [an ... hɛ,rʊmnœrɡl̩n] +haben ◊ *Ständig nörgelt sie an ihm herum.*
☞ **go on** komm ◊ *Komm, versuch's einfach mal!* ♦ *Ach komm, das glaube ich dir nicht!*

• **go out** [phras v] **1.** *(leave the house)* hinausgehen [hɪ'naʊsɡeːən] <geht hinaus, ging hinaus, ist hinausgegangen> ◊ *Geh doch hinaus und spiel mit deinen Freunden!; (meet friends and enjoy yourself)* ausgehen ['aʊsɡeːən] <geht aus, ging aus, ist ausgegangen> ◊ *Wollen wir am Samstag ausgehen?* go out to eat essen gehen ['ɛsn̩ ɡeːən] **2.** *(tide)* zurückgehen [tsu'rʏkɡeːən] <geht zurück, ging zurück, ist zurückgegangen> ◊ *Das Wasser geht wieder zurück.* **3.** *(have a relationship)* be going out with sb mit jdm gehen [mɪt ... ,ɡeːən] <gehen, ging, ist gegangen> ◊ *Mark geht seit fünf Monaten mit Andrea.* two people are going out (together) zwei Personen gehen miteinander **4.** *(light, fire, appliance)* ausgehen ['aʊsɡeːən] <geht aus, ging aus, ist ausgegangen> ◊ *Wenn du diese Taste drückst, geht der Computer aus.* **5.** *(be broadcast on TV or radio)* ausgestrahlt werden ['aʊsɡəʃtraːlt veːɐdn̩] <wird, wurde, ist worden> ◊ *Die Sendung wird erst nach 22 Uhr ausgestrahlt.; (be sent by post)* rausgehen ['raʊsɡeːən] <geht raus, ging raus, ist rausgegangen> *(fam)* ◊ *Der Brief geht heute noch an Sie raus.* **6.** *(of a competition)* ausscheiden ['aʊsʃaɛdn̩] <scheidet aus, schied aus, ist ausgeschieden> ◊ *Er ist in der dritten Runde ausgeschieden.* ♦ *aus einem Wettkampf ausscheiden* **7.** go out of fashion aus der Mode kommen [aʊs deːɐ 'moːdə kɔmən] <kommt, kam, ist gekommen> **8.** *(no longer possess)* sth goes out of sb/sth jd/etw. verliert etw. [fɛ'liːɐt] <verliert, verlor, hat verloren> ◊ *Das Leben in der Stadt hat seinen Reiz verloren.*

• **go over** [phras v] **1.** *(examine, look through, rehearse, review)* durchgehen ['dʊrçɡeːən] <geht durch, ging durch, ist durchgegangen> ◊ *Bist du deine Rolle noch mal durchgegangen?* go over sth in your mind etw. noch einmal durchdenken [nɔx aɛnmaːl dʊrç'dɛŋkn̩] <durchdenkt, durchdachte, hat durchdacht> **2.** *(search)* durchsuchen [dʊrç'zuːxn̩] <durchsucht, durchsuchte, hat durchsucht> ◊ *ein Gelände/jds Gepäck durchsuchen* **3.** *(move towards sb/sth)* go over to sb/sth zu jdm/etw. hinübergehen [tsu: ... hɪ,nyːbeɡeːən] <geht hinüber, ging hinüber, ist hinübergegangen> ◊ *Ich gehe mal zu den Nachbarn hinüber.* ♦ *Er ging zum Fenster hinüber und sah hinaus.* **4.** *(in the US: be received)* go over (with sb) (bei jdm) ankommen ['ankɔmən] <kommt an, kam an, ist angekommen> ◊ *Wie ist der Vorschlag bei deinen Eltern angekommen?* **5.** *(quickly wash, dust etc.)* schnell sauber machen [ʃnɛl 'zaʊbe maxn̩] +haben ◊ *Ich habe den Tisch schnell mit einem Lappen sauber gemacht.* **6.** *(change your behavio(u)r)* go over to (doing) sth zu etw. übergehen [tsu: ... ,yːbeɡeːən] <geht über, ging über, ist übergegangen> ◊ *Ich bin dazu übergegangen, abends nur noch Salat zu essen.* **7.** *(to the enemy, opposition)* go

A
B
C
D
E
F
G
H
I
J
K
L
M
N
O
P
Q
R
S
T
U
V
W
X
Y
Z

over to sb/sth zu jdm/etw. **überlaufen**
[ˈtʊː ... ˌyːbɐlaofn̩] <läuft über, lief über, ist übergelaufen> ◊ *Er ist zum Feind übergelaufen.*
• **go round** ⸢phras v⸣ → **go around**
• **go through** ⸢phras v⸣ **1.** *(search)* go through sth etw. **durchsuchen** [dʊˈdʒˈzuːxn̩] <durchsucht, durchsuchte, hat durchsucht> ◊ *Sie durchsuchte alle Akten, konnte aber nichts finden.* **2.** *(law)* **durchkommen** [ˈdʊˈçkɔmən] <kommt durch, kam durch, ist durchgekommen> ◊ *Das Gesetz wird so nicht durchkommen.*; *(deal, contract)* **abgeschlossen werden** [ˈapɡəʃlɔsn̩ veːɐdn̩] <wird, wurde, ist worden> ◊ *Ist der Vertrag bereits abgeschlossen worden?* **3.** *(suffer, endure)* **durchmachen** [ˈdʊˈçmaxn̩] +haben ◊ *Er hat in seinem Leben Schreckliches/viel durchgemacht.* **4.** *(use up, spend)* go through sth etw. **aufbrauchen** [ˈaofbraoxn̩] +haben ◊ *Sie braucht die Vorräte innerhalb kurzer Zeit auf.* **5.** *(rehearse, look over)* go through sth etw. **durchgehen** [ˈdʊˈçɡeːən] <geht durch, ging durch, ist durchgegangen> ◊ *Er ging seine Ansprache noch einmal durch.* **6.** *(carry out)* go through with sth etw. **durchziehen** [ˈdʊˈçtsiːən] <zieht durch, zog durch, hat durchgezogen> *(fam)* ◊ *Er hat das Projekt trotzdem durchgezogen.* **7.** *(successfully complete)* go through sth etw. **durchlaufen** [dʊˈçˈlaofn̩] <durchläuft, durchlief, hat durchlaufen> *(lofty)* ◊ *Er durchlief seine Ausbildung sehr schnell.*
• **go to** ⸢phras v⸣ **1.** *(begin to do sth)* go to sleep **einschlafen** [ˈaenʃlaːfn̩] <schläft ein, schlief ein, ist eingeschlafen> ◊ *Das Baby ist endlich eingeschlafen.* go to work **sich an die Arbeit machen** [an diː ˈaˈbaet maxn̩] +haben ◊ *Er nahm sein Werkzeug und machte sich an die Arbeit.* **2.** *(money, donations etc.)* go to sb/sth an jdn/etw. **gehen** [an ... ɡeːən] <geht, ging, ist gegangen> ◊ *Der Erlös geht an das Tierheim.* ♦ *Unser Dank geht an alle Mitarbeiter.*
ⓔ **go to it** auf geht's ◊ *Auf geht's! Wir müssen in zwei Stunden fertig sein!*
• **go together** ⸢phras v⸣ **1.** *(exist together)* **Hand in Hand gehen** [ˌhant ɪn ˈhant ɡeːən] <geht, ging, ist gegangen> ◊ *Macht und Korruption gehen leider oft Hand in Hand.* **2.** *(harmonize)* **zusammenpassen** [tsuˈzamənpasn̩] +haben ◊ *Rot und Orange passen nicht gut zusammen.* **3.** *(have a relationship)* **miteinander gehen** [mɪtʔaeˌnandɐ ˈɡeːən] <gehen, gingen, sind gegangen> *(fam)* ◊ *Kirsten und Tim gehen seit Mai miteinander.*
• **go towards** ⸢phras v⸣ go towards sth einer Sache ⸢dat⸣ **zugute kommen** [tsuˈɡuːtə kɔmən] <kommt, kam, ist gekommen> ◊ *Der Erlös kommt dem Altenheim zugute.*
• **go under** ⸢phras v⸣ **1.** *(ship)* **untergehen** [ˈʊntɐɡeːən] <geht unter, ging unter, ist untergegangen> ◊ *Langsam ging das Schiff unter.* **2.** *(business, businessman)* **scheitern** [ˈʃaetɐn] +sein ◊ *Er ist mit seinem Projekt gescheitert.* ♦ *Die Firma ist endgültig gescheitert.* **3.** *(poster, sign)* **aufgehängt werden** [ˈaofɡəhɛŋt veːɐdn̩] <wird, wurde, ist worden> ◊

• **go up** ⸢phras v⸣ **1.** *(rise)* **steigen** [ˈʃtaeɡn̩] <steigt, stieg, ist gestiegen> ◊ *Die Preise/Kosten/Zinsen steigen.* ♦ *Die Temperaturen steigen im Laufe des Tages auf 25 Grad.* **2.** *(be built)* **gebaut werden** [ɡəˈbaot veːɐdn̩] <wird, wurde, ist worden> ◊ *Am Stadtrand werden neue Wohnungen gebaut.*

4. *(explode)* **in die Luft gehen** [ɪn diː ˈlʊft ɡeːən] <geht, ging, ist gegangen> ◊ *Schließlich ging das ganze Gebäude in die Luft.* go up in flames **in Flammen aufgehen** [ɪn ˈflamən aofɡeːən] <geht auf, ging auf, ist aufgegangen> **5.** *(in the UK: travel northwards)* **hinauffahren** [hɪˈnaoffaːrən] <fährt hinauf, fuhr hinauf, ist hinaufgefahren> ◊ *Kai fährt übers Wochenende nach Kiel hinauf.* **6.** *(in the UK)* go up (to university) auf die Universität **gehen** [aof diː univeˈziˈtɛːt ɡeːən] <geht, ging, ist gegangen> **7.** sport *(in the UK)* **aufsteigen** [ˈaofʃtaeɡn̩] <steigt auf, stieg auf, ist aufgestiegen> ◊ *in die Bundesliga aufsteigen* **8.** *(lights)* langsam **angehen** [ˌlaŋzaːm ˈangeːən] <geht an, ging an, ist angegangen> ◊ *Langsam gingen im Theater die Lichter an.* **9.** *(move upwards)* **hochgehen** [ˈhoːxɡeːən] <geht hoch, ging hoch, ist hochgegangen> ◊ *Der Vorhang/Die Schranke ging hoch.*
• **go with** ⸢phras v⸣ **1.** *(accompany sth)* go with sth zu etw. **gehören** [tsuː ... ɡəhøːrən] <gehört, gehörte, hat gehört> ◊ *Zu diesem Beruf gehört viel Verantwortung.* **2.** *(match sth)* go with sth zu etw. **passen** [tsuː ... pasn̩] +haben ◊ *Passt das Hemd zu dem Anzug?* **3.** *(fam) (date sb)* go with sb mit jdm **gehen** [mɪt ... ɡeːən] <geht, ging, ist gegangen> ◊ *Sie geht jetzt mit Horst.*
• **go without** ⸢phras v⸣ go without sth etw. **nicht haben** [ˌnɪçt ˈhaːbm̩] +haben ◊ *Wir hatten die ganze Nacht keinen Strom.* go without doing sth etw. **nicht tun** [ˌnɪçt ˈtuːn] I've gone without sleeping for the last two days. Ich habe zwei Tage nicht geschlafen.
ⓔ **go without saying** sich von selbst verstehen

goal ⸢noun⸣ **1.** *(aim)* **Ziel** [tsiːl] das <-(e)s, -e> ◊ *Was hatte diese Aktion zum Ziel?* ♦ *sein Ziel erreichen* **2.** sport **Tor** [toːɐ] das <-(e)s, -e> ◊ *Wer steht bei euch heute im Tor?* ♦ *Das erste Tor fiel in der 32. Minute.* score a goal **ein Tor schießen**

goalkeeper ⸢noun⸣ **Torwart** [ˈtoːɐvaˈt] der <-(e)s, -e> ♀**Torwartin** [ˈtoːɐvaˈtɪn] die <-, -nen> ◊ *Er ist seit Jahren Torwart der Nationalmannschaft.* ♦ *Die Torwartin hat gut gehalten.*

goat ⸢noun⸣ **1.** zoo **Ziege** [ˈtsiːɡə] die <-, -n> ◊ *Die Ziege meckerte.* **2.** *(lecher)* **Bock** [bɔk] der <-(e)s, Böcke> ◊ *Er ist ein sturer alter Bock.*
ⓔ **act the goat** **herumalbern** ◊ *Sie albert gerne mit ihren Kindern herum.*

gob ⸢noun⸣ **1.** *(in the UK: mouth)* **Schnauze** [ˈʃnaotsə] die <-, -n> *(fam, pej)* ◊ *Halt die Schnauze!* **2.** *(of sticky liquid)* **Klumpen** [ˈklʊmpm̩] der <-s, -> ◊ *Klumpen von Rohöl*

god ⸢noun⸣ *(deity)* god **Gott** [ɡɔt] der <-es, Götter> ◊ *die römischen Götter Jupiter und Minerva* ♦ *Er sieht aus wie ein junger Gott.* Good God ◊ *Glaubst du an Gott?*
ⓔ **how/what/where etc. in God's name** wie/was/wo in Gottes Namen ◊ *Wo in Gottes Namen hast du dieses Video her?* for God's sake um Himmels willen **dear God** du lieber Gott

gold¹ ⸢noun⸣ **Gold** [ɡɔlt] das <-(e)s> no pl ◊ *ein Ring aus purem Gold* ♦ *24-karätiges Gold* ♦ *das Gold der Sonne*
ⓔ **win gold** **Gold holen**

gold² ⸢adj⸣ **golden** [ˈɡɔldn̩] no comp/superl ◊ *eine goldene Uhr*; **Gold...** [ɡɔlt] gold coin **Goldmünze** [ˈɡɔltmʏntsə] die <-, -n> gold jewellery **Gold-**

schmuck ['gɔltʃmʊk] der <-(e)s> no pl

golden [adj] golden ['gɔldn̩] no comp/superl ◊ *Ihr Haar schimmerte golden.* ◆ *ein goldener Ring* ◆ *goldene Jahre* golden brown goldbraun ['gɔltbraʊn] no comp/superl

golf [noun] Golf [gɔlf] das <-s> article only in combination with attribute, no pl ◊ *Spielen Sie Golf?*

good¹ [noun] **1.** (benefit) do sb good jdm gut tun ['guːt tuːn] <tut, tat, hat getan> ◊ *Ein warmes Bad wird ihm jetzt gut tun.* be for sb's own good zu jds Besten sein [tsuː ... 'bɛstn̩ zaɛn] +sein do more harm than good mehr schaden als nutzen [meːɐ̯ 'ʃaːdn̩ als ˌnʊtsn̩] +haben the common good das Allgemeinwohl [das algə'maɛnvoːl] das <-(e)s> no pl ◊ *dem Allgemeinwohl dienen* **2.** (sth that is morally right, pleasant part of sth) Gute ['guːtə] das <-n> but: ein Gutes, no pl ◊ *Er hat in seinem Leben viel Gutes getan.* ◆ *das Gute an der Sache* good and evil Gut und Böse [ˌguːt ʊnt 'bøːzə]; (people who are morally right) the good die Guten [diː 'guːtn̩] <-> pl ◊ *Gehört er zu den Guten?*
  ℗ **be no good 1.** (be of low quality, unable to do sth) nicht gut sein ◊ *Das Essen war nicht gut.* ◆ *Er ist in Mathematik nicht gut.* **2.** (be unable to deal with) be no good with sb/sth mit jdm/etw. nicht umgehen können ◊ *Sie kann mit Tieren nicht umgehen.* **3.** (be useless) be no good for sth zu etw. ungeeignet sein ◊ *Diese Hose ist zum Radfahren ungeeignet* **4.** (not be convenient) be no good nicht passen ◊ *Freitag passt leider nicht, wie wäre es am Montag?* be up to no good nichts Gutes im Schilde führen do (some) good (etwas) nutzen it's no good doing sth es nutzt nichts, etw. zu tun for good für immer

good² [adj] **1.** (decent, acceptable, kind, pleasant) gut [guːt] <besser, am besten> ◊ *Er hat seinen besten Anzug an.* ◆ *Ihr Englisch ist sehr gut.* ◆ *Er ist ein guter Läufer.* ◆ *Es ist nicht gut, wenn er so viel allein ist.* ◆ *Sie war ein guter Mensch.* ◆ *Ihre Eltern waren immer gut zu ihr.* ◆ *Ist die Milch noch gut?* ◆ *Gut, dann treffen wir uns um acht am Bahnhof.* ◆ *Wir waren eine gute Stunde unterwegs.* ◆ *Guten Abend/Morgen!* a good deal viel [fiːl] ◊ *Das Grundstück kostet viel mehr, als wir dachten.*; (be valid) be good for two weeks etc. zwei Wochen etc. gelten [tsvaɛ 'vɔxn̩ gɛltn̩] <gilt, galt, hat gegolten> ◊ *Der Fahrschein gilt zwei Wochen.* **2.** (child, pet) brav [braːf] ◊ *ein braver Hund* ◆ *Seid brav, wenn ich weg bin!*
  ℗ **as good as new** so gut wie neu **that's as good as it gets** besser geht's nicht **would you be so good as ...** könntest du/könnten Sie bitte ... ◊ *Könnten Sie mir bitte sagen, wie spät es ist?*

goodbye¹ [noun] Abschiedsgruß ['apʃiːtsgruːs] der <-es, Abschiedsgrüße> ◊ *Er ging ohne einen Abschiedsgruß.* say your goodbyes sich verabschieden [fɛl'apʃiːdn̩] <verabschiedet sich, verabschiedete sich, hat sich verabschiedet> say goodbye to sb sich von jdm verabschieden wave goodbye (to sb) (jdm) zum Abschied winken [tsʊm ˌapʃiːt 'vɪŋkn̩] +haben

goodbye² [interj] (general) auf Wiedersehen [aof 'viːdezeːən]; (on the phone) auf Wiederhören [aof 'viːdəhøːrən]

Good Friday [noun] Karfreitag [kaːˈfraɛtaːk] der <-(e)s, -e> most sing

good-natured(ly) [adj, adv] gutmütig ['guːtmyːtɪç] ◊ *ein gutmütiger Mensch* ◆ *Sie ist sehr gutmütig.* ◆ *Gutmütig lächelnd schüttelte er den Kopf.*

goodness [noun] **1.** (kindness, decency) Güte ['gyːtə] die <-> no pl ◊ *eine Frau voller Weisheit und Güte* ◆ *die Güte Gottes* **2.** (of food) wichtige Nährstoffe [ˌvɪçtɪgə 'nɛːɐ̯ʃtofə] die <-> pl ◊ *Gemüse enthält wichtige Nährstoffe.*

goods [noun] **1.** (merchandise) Ware ['vaːrə] die <-, -n> zollfreie/importierte/abgepackte/verderbliche Waren ◊ *Wann wird die Ware geliefert?* leather goods Lederwaren ['leːdevaːrən] stolen goods Diebesgut ['diːbəsguːt] das <-(e)s> no pl goods train Güterzug ['gyːtetsuːk] der <-(e)s, Güterzüge> **2.** (possessions) Habe ['haːbə] die <-> no pl ◊ *jds bewegliche Habe*

goodwill [noun] **1.** (benevolence) Wohlwollen ['voːlvɔlən] das <-s> no pl ◊ *Meine Beförderung hängt von seinem Wohlwollen ab.* as a gesture of goodwill als Zeichen seines/ihres etc. guten Willens [als ˌtsaɛçn̩ zaɛnəs/iːrəs guːtn̩ 'vɪləns] **2.** ECON Geschäftswert [gə'ʃɛftsveːɐ̯t] der <-(e)s> no pl ◊ *Wie hoch ist der Geschäftswert der Firma?*

goose [noun] Gans [gans] die <-, Gänse> ◊ *Gänse halten/hüten* ◆ *Es gibt Gans mit Kartoffeln.* ◆ *Du dumme Gans!*

gorgeous [adj] (person, smile) hinreißend ['hɪnraɛsn̩t] ◊ *Du siehst heute Abend wieder hinreißend aus!* ◆ *ein hinreißender Mann;* (weather) herrlich ['hɛʁlɪç] ◊ *Das Wetter war herrlich.*

gospel [noun] **1.** MUS Gospelmusik ['gɔspl̩muˌziːk] die <-> no pl ◊ *gospel choir* Gospelchor ['gɔspl̩koːɐ̯] der <-(e)s, Gospelchöre> **2.** REL Gospel Evangelium [evan'geːljʊm] das <-s, Evangelien> preach the Gospel das Evangelium verkünden **3.** (doctrine) Prinzipien [prɪn'tsiːpiən] die <-> pl ◊ *für die Prinzipien der freien Marktwirtschaft eintreten*
  ℗ **take sth as gospel** etw. für bare Münze nehmen

gossip¹ [noun] **1.** (talk, conversation) Klatsch [klatʃ] der <-es> no pl (fam, also pej) ◊ *Hör bloß nicht auf den Klatsch der Nachbarn!* **2.** (person) Klatschbase ['klatʃbaːzə] die <-, -n> (fam, pej) ◊ *Frau Hutmacher ist eine alte Klatschbase.*

gossip² [verb] klatschen ['klatʃn̩] +haben ◊ *Die Leute klatschen schon über uns.*

gourmet [noun] Feinschmecker ['faɛnʃmɛkɐ] der <-s, -> ♀Feinschmeckerin ['faɛnʃmɛkərɪn] die <-, -nen>

govern [verb] **1.** POL (rule a state) regieren [re'giːrən] <regiert, regierte, hat regiert> ◊ *Das Land wird von einer Koalition regiert.* ◆ *Die Partei regiert seit 20 Jahren.*; (a colony) verwalten [fɛ'valtn̩] <verwaltet, verwaltete, hat verwaltet> ◊ *Indien wurde damals von der East India Company verwaltet.* **2.** (regulate) regeln ['reːgl̩n] +haben ◊ *Strenge Vorschriften regeln das Verfahren.* **3.** (an organization) leiten ['laɛtn̩] +haben ◊ *Der Vorstand leitet das Unternehmen verantwortungsvoll.* **4.** (dominate) bestimmen [bə'ʃtɪmən] <bestimmt, bestimmte, hat bestimmt> ◊ *Angst und Schrecken bestimmen das Leben der Bevölkerung.*

government [noun] **1.** POL (administration) Regierung [re'giːrʊŋ] die <-, -en> ◊ *eine Regierung bilden* ◆ *unter der Regierung Kohl* ◆ *Das Militär hat die Regierung des Landes übernommen.* central government Zentralregierung [tsɛn'traːlreˌgiːrʊŋ] local government Kommunalverwaltung [kɔmu'naːlfɛvaltʊŋ]

die <–, –en> 2. *(state)* Staat [ʃtaːt] der <–(e)s, –en> ◊ *vom Staat finanziert/gefördert* ✦ *beim Staat angestellt sein*

governor [noun] 1. POL *(of a state, province, colony)* Gouverneur [guvɛrˈnøːɐ̯] der <–s, –e> ♀Gouverneurin [guvɛrˈnøːrɪn] die <–, –nen> ◊ *Sie ist Gouverneurin von Massachusetts.* ✦ *der Gouverneur von Indien/ der Provinz Buenos Aires* 2. *(of a bank, company)* Direktor [diˈrɛktoːɐ̯] der <–s, –en> ♀Direktorin [dɪrɛkˈtoːrɪn] die <–, –nen> ◊ *der Direktor der Zentralbank* ✦ *Als Direktorin trägt sie viel Verantwortung.* 3. SCHOOL *(parents' representative)* Elternvertreter [ˈɛltɐnfɛtʀeːtɐ] der <–s, –> ♀Elternvertreterin [ˈɛltɐnfɛˌtʀeːtɐrɪn] die <–, –nen> 4. *(fam) (form of address)* Chef [ʃɛf] der <–s, –s> ◊ „*Alles klar, Chef?*"

gown [noun] 1. *(fine dress)* Kleid [klaɛ̯t] das <–(e)s, –er> wedding gown Hochzeitskleid [ˈhɔxtsaɛ̯tsklaɛ̯t] 2. *(worn by a judge, professor)* Talar [taˈlaːr] der <–s, –e> 3. *(worn by a surgeon)* Kittel [ˈkɪtl̩] der <–s, –>

grab [verb] 1. *(also fig) (seize)* grab (hold of) packen [ˈpakn̩] +haben ◊ *Der Mann packte ihn und zerrte ihn ins Auto.* ✦ *Das Buch hat mich gepackt.* grab sb by sth jdn an etw. [dat] packen ◊ *Er packte sie an den Schultern und schüttelte sie.* 2. *(get, obtain)* ergattern [ɛˈɡatɐn] <ergattert, ergatterte, hat ergattert> ◊ *gute Plätze im Theater ergattern; (an opportunity)* ergreifen [ɛˈɡʀaɛ̯fn̩] <ergreift, ergriff, hat ergriffen> ◊ *die Gelegenheit ergreifen* grab sb's attention jds Aufmerksamkeit erregen [ˈaofmɛrkzaːmkaɛ̯t eʀeːɡn̩] <erregt, erregte, hat erregt>

grace [noun] 1. *(elegance)* Anmut [ˈanmuːt] die <–> no pl *(lofty)* ◊ *Er war von ihrer Anmut überwältigt.* 2. *(decency, manners)* Anstand [ˈanʃtant] der <–(e)s> no pl ◊ *mit Würde und Anstand* have the grace to do sth so anständig sein, etw. zu tun [zoː ˈanʃtɛndɪç zaɛ̯n … tsuː] +sein social graces Umgangsformen [ˈʊmɡaɲsfɔrmən] die <–> pl 3. REL *(prayer)* Tischgebet [ˈtɪʃɡəbeːt] das <–(e)s, –e> say grace das Tischgebet sprechen 4. REL *(God's mercy)* Gnade [ˈɡnaːdə] die <–, –n> ◊ *durch Gottes Gnade* 5. *(reprieve)* Aufschub [ˈaofʃuːp] der <–(e)s, Aufschübe> give sb a day's grace jdm einen Tag Aufschub gewähren ◉ with bad grace widerwillig with good grace bereitwillig fall from grace in Ungnade fallen

graceful(ly) [adj, adv] *(delicate and elegant)* anmutig [ˈanmuːtɪç] ◊ *eine anmutige Gestalt* ✦ *Ihre Bewegungen sind anmutig.* ✦ *Sie tanzten sehr anmutig.*

grade¹ [noun] 1. SCHOOL *(mark)* Note [ˈnoːtə] die <–, –n> ◊ *Sie hat für den Aufsatz eine gute Note bekommen.* ✦ *mündliche/schriftliche Noten* 2. SCHOOL *(year)* Klasse [ˈklasə] die <–, –n> ◊ *Er ist in der 12. Klasse.* 3. *(of a product)* Güteklasse [ˈɡyːtəklasə] die <–, –n> ◊ *ein Produkt der Güteklasse A; (of textiles)* Qualität [kvaliˈtɛːt] die <–, –en> ◊ *Stoffe von feinerer Qualität* 4. *(rank)* Rang [ʀaŋ] der <–(e)s, Ränge> ◊ *Beamte höheren Ranges*

grade² [verb] 1. *(goods)* sortieren [zɔrˈtiːrən] <sortiert, sortierte, hat sortiert> ◊ *Eier nach der Größe sortieren* 2. *(give a mark to)* benoten [bəˈnoːtn̩] <benotet, benotete, hat benotet> ◊ *Wird die Mitarbeit in diesem Kurs auch benotet?*

gradient [noun] *(ascent)* Steigung [ˈʃtaɛ̯ɡʊŋ] die <–, –en> ◊ *eine Straße mit einer leichten Steigung; (descent)* Gefälle [ɡəˈfɛlə] das <–, –> most sing ◊

ein Gefälle von 14%

gradual(ly) [adj, adv] 1. *(slow(ly))* allmählich [alˈmɛːlɪç] no comp/superl, mostly before ns ◊ *ein allmählicher Ausstieg aus der Atomwirtschaft* ✦ *Allmählich kam er wieder zu sich.* 2. *(not steep(ly))* sanft [zanft] <sanfter, am sanftesten> ◊ *ein sanftes Gefälle* ✦ *Die Steigung war ganz sanft.* ✦ *sanft ansteigen*

graduate¹ [noun] 1. UNI *(sb with a university degree)* Hochschulabsolvent [ˈhoːxʃuːlʔapzɔlˌvɛnt] der <–en, –en> ♀Hochschulabsolventin [ˈhoːxʃuːlʔapzɔlˌvɛntɪn] die <–, –nen> Oxford graduate Absolvent der Universität Oxford [apzɔlˌvɛnt deːɐ̯ univɛrˈziˌtɛːt ˈɔksfɔrt] history graduate Historiker [hɪsˈtoːrɪkɐ] der <–s, –> ♀Historikerin [hɪsˈtoːrɪkərɪn] die <–, –nen> science graduate Naturwissenschaftler [naˈtuːɐ̯vɪsn̩ˌʃaftlɐ] der <–s, –> ♀Naturwissenschaftlerin [naˈtuːɐ̯vɪsn̩ˌʃaftlərɪn] die <–, –nen> 2. SCHOOL *(in the US)* high school graduate Schulabgänger [ˈʃuːlʔapɡɛŋɐ] der <–s, –> ♀Schulabgängerin [ˈʃuːlʔapˌɡɛŋərɪn] die <–, –nen>

graduate² [verb] UNI *(obtain a degree)* sein Studium abschließen [zaɛ̯n ˈʃtuːdi̯ʊm ˌapʃliːsn̩] <schließt ab, schloss ab, hat abgeschlossen> ◊ *Er hat 1995 sein Studium an der Leipziger Universität abgeschlossen.* graduate in history sein Geschichtsstudium abschließen ◉ graduate (from sth) to sth (von etw.) zu etw. aufsteigen

grain [noun] 1. *(crop)* Getreide [ɡəˈtraɛ̯də] das <–s> no pl ◊ *Getreide anbauen* 2. *(seed, individual piece of sth)* Korn [kɔrn] das <–(e)s, Körner> ◊ *Die Hühner pickten die Körner auf.* grain of salt Salzkorn [ˈzaltskɔrn] 3. *(in wood)* Maserung [ˈmaːzərʊŋ] die <–, –en> ◊ *Das Holz hat eine schöne Maserung.* ◉ a grain of truth ein Körnchen Wahrheit go against the grain with sb jdm gegen den Strich gehen

gram [noun] Gramm [ɡram] das <–s, –> ◊ *200 Gramm Schinken kaufen*

grammar² [noun] Grammatik [ɡraˈmatɪk] die <–, –en> ◊ *die deutsche Grammatik beherrschen* ✦ *Hast du eine lateinische Grammatik?*

grammar school [noun] ⊕Gymnasium [ɡymˈnaːzi̯ʊm] das <–s, Gymnasien> ◊ *Sie kommt nächstes Jahr aufs Gymnasium.*

grammatical(ly) [adj, adv] 1. *(error, rules etc.)* grammatikalisch [ɡramatiˈkaːlɪʃ] no comp/superl, mostly before ns ◊ *grammatikalische und inhaltliche Fehler* ✦ *grammatikalisch falsch* 2. *(following the rules of a language)* grammatikalisch richtig [ɡramatiˌkaːlɪʃ ˈrɪçtɪç] no comp/superl ◊ *ein grammatikalisch richtiger Satz* ✦ *Ist das grammatikalisch richtig?*

grand [adj] 1. *(impressive)* eindrucksvoll [ˈaɛ̯ndrʊksfɔl] ◊ *ein ziemlich eindrucksvolles Gebäude* ✦ *Das Fest war einfach eindrucksvoll.* 2. *(ambitious)* groß [ɡroːs] <größer, am größten> mostly before ns ◊ *große Pläne schmieden* 3. *(distinguished)* vornehm [ˈfoːgneːm] ◊ *ein vornehmer alter Herr* ✦ *Dafür bist du dir wohl zu vornehm.* 4. *(great)* großartig [ˈɡroːsʔaːrtɪç] ◊ *Das ist einfach großartig!* ✦ *Es war eine großartige Party.* 5. *(in titles)* Groß... [ɡroːs] grand duke Großherzog [ˈɡroːshɛrtsoːk] der <–s, –e> grand grandad [noun] Opa [ˈoːpa(ː)] der <–s, –s> *(kidsp, also pej)* ◊ *Mein Opa hat mir ein Fahrrad geschenkt.* ✦ *Mensch, Opa, das ist nichts für dich!*

grandchild [noun] Enkelkind ['ɛŋk|kɪnt] der
<-(e)s, -er>

granddaughter [noun] Enkelin ['ɛŋkəlɪn] die
<-, -nen>

grandfather [noun] Großvater ['groːsfaːtɐ] der
<-s, Großväter>

grandly [adv] **1.** *(pompously)* hochtrabend
['hoːxtraːbm̩t] <hochtrabender, am hochtrabendsten>
(pej) ◊ *Ihr Wohnzimmer nannte sie hochtrabend
„den Salon".* **2.** *(emph)* *(extremely, to a large extent)*
ausgesprochen ['aʊsɡəʃprɔxn̩] *no comp/superl* ◊ *ein
ausgesprochen unterhaltsamer Film*

grandma [noun] Oma ['oːma(ː)] die <-, -s> *(kidsp,
also pej)*

grandmother [noun] Großmutter ['groːsmʊtɐ] die
<-, Großmütter>

grandparent [noun] *(male)* Großvater ['groːsfaːtɐ] der
<-, Großväter>; *(female)* Großmutter ['groːsmʊtɐ]
die <-, Großmütter> grandparents Großeltern
['groːs|ɛltɐn] die <-> *only pl* ◊ *die Großeltern mütter-
licherseits/väterlicherseits*

grandson [noun] Enkel ['ɛŋk|] der <-s, ->

grandstand [noun] Tribüne [tri'byːnə] die <-, -n> ◊
*Beim Endspiel saßen viele prominente Gäste auf der
Tribüne.*

grant¹ [noun] **1.** *(subsidy)* Zuschuss ['tsuːʃʊs] der
<-es, Zuschüsse> ◊ *Die Stadt gewährt Zuschüsse zur
Anschaffung von Sportgeräten.* **2.** *(scholarship,
bursary)* Stipendium [ʃti'pɛndjʊm] das
<-s, Stipendien> ◊ *sich um ein Stipendium
bewerben* ✦ *ein Stipendium vergeben/bekommen*

grant² [verb] *(allow)* gewähren [ɡə'vɛːrən] <gewährt,
gewährte, hat gewährt> *(lofty)* ◊ *den Flüchtlingen Asyl
gewähren* ✦ *jdm ein Darlehen/eine Audienz gewähren*
grant (sb) permission (to do sth) (jdm) die Erlaubnis
erteilen (,etw. zu tun) [diː ɛ'laʊpnɪs ɛtaɛlən (tsu …)]
<erteilt, erteilte, hat erteilt> grant a request einen
Antrag genehmigen [aɛnən 'antraːk ɡə,neːmɪɡn̩]
<genehmigt, genehmigte, hat genehmigt>
⊛ **take sb for granted** sich jds allzu sicher sein
take sth for granted etw. als selbstverständlich
hinnehmen **I grant you** das gebe ich zu **I grant you
that** ich gebe zu, dass ◊ *Ich gebe zu, dass diese
Lösung nicht immer die beste ist.*

grape [noun] Traube ['traʊbə] die <-, -n>

graph [noun] Diagramm [diaˈɡram] das <-s, -e> ◊ *ein
Diagramm zeichnen*

graphic(ally) [adj, adv] **1.** *(vivid)* anschaulich
['anʃaʊlɪç] ◊ *Der Bericht ist sehr anschaulich.* ✦ *eine
anschauliche Darstellung* ✦ *etw. anschaulich
schildern* **in graphic detail** in allen Einzelheiten
[ɪn ,alən 'aɛntsl̩haɛtn̩] **2.** *(in drawing)* grafisch
['ɡraːfɪʃ] *when used as adj, only before ns* ◊ *eine
grafische Darstellung* ✦ *etw. grafisch darstellen*
graphic arts Grafik ['ɡraːfɪk] die <-> *no pl* **graphic
artist** Grafiker ['ɡraːfɪkɐ] der <-s, -> ♀Grafikerin
['ɡraːfɪkərɪn] die <-, -nen>

graphics [noun] Grafik ['ɡraːfɪk] die <-, -en> ◊ *Unser
Angebot umfasst Layout, Grafik, und Satz.*

grasp¹ [noun] **1.** *(grip)* Griff [ɡrɪf] der <-(e)s, -e> ◊
seinen Griff lockern **2.** *(understanding)* Auffassungsgabe ['aʊffasʊŋsɡaːbə] die <-> *no pl* **be beyond
sb's grasp** jds Auffassungsgabe übersteigen; *(begin
to understand sth)* have/get a grasp of sth etw.
begreifen [bə'ɡraɛfn̩] <begreift, begriff, hat begriffen>;
(understand sth (well)) have a (good) grasp of sth

etw. (gut) beherrschen [(,ɡuːt) bə'hɛrʃn̩] <beherrscht,
beherrschte, hat beherrscht> **3.** **be within/beyond
sb's grasp** in/außer jds Reichweite sein
[ɪn/aʊsɐ … 'raɛçvaɛtə zaɛn] +sein

grasp² [verb] **1.** *(also fig) (seize)* ergreifen [ɐ'ɡraɛfn̩]
<ergreift, ergriff, hat ergriffen> ◊ *Er ergriff das
Lenkrad.* ✦ *eine Gelegenheit ergreifen* **grasp sb by
the shoulders** jdn bei den Schultern packen
[baɛ deːn 'ʃʊltɐn pakn̩] +haben **2.** *(understand)*
begreifen [bə'ɡraɛfn̩] <begreift, begriff, hat begriffen>
◊ *Begreifst du, was das für mich bedeutet?* ✦ *einen
mathematischen Zusammenhang begreifen*

grass [noun] **1.** *(plant, species, cannabis)* Gras [ɡraːs]
das <-es, Gräser> ◊ *im Gras liegen* ✦ *verschiedene
Gräser* ✦ *Gras rauchen* **2.** *(lawn)* Rasen ['raːzn̩] der
<-s, -> **most sing** ✦ *(den) Rasen mähen*

grate¹ [noun] Rost [rɔst] der <-es, -e>

grate² [verb] **1.** *(cheese, vegetables etc.)* reiben
['raɛbm̩] <reibt, rieb, hat gerieben> **2.** *(produce an
unpleasant noise)* knarren ['knarən] +haben ◊ *Das
Tor knarrte.* **grate against sth** an etw. kratzen
[an … 'kratsn̩] +haben ◊ *Die Schaufel kratzte am
Boden.* **3.** *(fig) (annoy)* **grate sb** jdn krank machen
['kraŋk maxn̩] +haben ◊ *Dein ewiges Gejammer
macht mich ganz krank.* **grate on sb's nerves** jdm
auf die Nerven gehen [aʊf diː 'nɛrfn̩ ɡeːən] <geht,
ging, ist gegangen>

grateful(ly) [adj, adv] dankbar ['daŋkbaːr] ◊ *Ich bin
ihr unendlich dankbar.* ✦ *dankbare Blicke* ✦ *Er
nahm ihre Hilfe dankbar an.*

grater [noun] Reibe ['raɛbə] die <-, -n>

grave¹ [noun] Grab [ɡraːp] das <-(e)s, Gräber>
⊛ **turn in your grave** sich im Grab umdrehen

grave² [adj] **1.** *(mistake, crime etc.)* schwerwiegend
['ʃveːɡviːɡn̩t] <schwerwiegender, am schwerwiegends-
ten> ◊ *Sein Fehler war schwerwiegend.* ✦ *ein schwerwiegender Vorwurf* **2.** *(face, expression)* ernst [ɛrnst]
<ernster, am ernstesten> ◊ *Ihr Gesicht war ernst.* ✦
ein ernster Gesichtsausdruck

gravel [noun] Kies [kiːs] der <-es> *no pl*

gravestone [noun] Grabstein ['ɡraːpʃtaɛn] der
<-(e)s, -e>

graveyard [noun] Friedhof ['friːthoːf] der
<-(e)s, Friedhöfe>

gravity [noun] **1.** PHYSICS, ASTRON Schwerkraft ['ʃveːɡkraft]
die <-> *no pl* ◊ *Die Schwerkraft der Erde ist größer
als die des Mondes.* **2.** *(seriousness of sth)* Ernst
[ɛrnst] der <-es> *no pl* ◊ *der Ernst der Lage; (of a
crime)* Schwere ['ʃveːrə] die <-> *no pl* ◊ *die Schwere
eines Verbrechens*

gravy [noun] Soße ['zoːsə] die <-, -n>

gray → grey

graze¹ [noun] Schürfwunde ['ʃʏrfvʊndə] die <-, -n>

graze² [verb] **1.** *(eat grass)* an animal grazes ein Tier
weidet [aɛn … 'vaɛdət] <weidete, hat geweidet> **graze
an animal** ein Tier weiden lassen ['vaɛdn̩ lasn̩]
<lässt, ließ, hat lassen> **2.** *(injure)* aufschürfen
['aʊffʏrfn̩] +haben **graze your sth** sich [dat] etw. aufschürfen ◊ *Bei dem Sturz schürfte ich mir die Hand
auf.* **3.** *(touch slightly)* streifen ['ʃtraɛfn̩] +haben ◊
*Der Hubschrauber streifte einen Hochspannungsmast
und stürzte ab.*

greasy [adj] **1.** *(oily)* fettig ['fɛtɪç] ◊ *Der Herd war ganz
fettig.* ✦ *ein Shampoo für fettiges Haar* **2.** *(pej)*
(overly friendly) schmierig ['ʃmiːrɪç] *(fam, pej)* ◊ *ein
schmieriger Typ* ✦ *Der Verkäufer war unglaublich*

schmierig.

great[1] (adj) **1.** *(considerable, significant)* groß [gro:s]
<größer, am größten> ◊ *Die Überraschung war groß.*
♦ *Er ist kein großer Tänzer.* ♦ *die große Mehrheit;*
(age, speed) hoch [ho:x] <höher, am höchsten>
mostly before ns <der/die/das hohe ...> ◊ *in hohem*
Alter ♦ *bei hoher Geschwindigkeit* **2.** *(very good)*
großartig ['gro:s|a:'tɪç] *(fam)* ◊ *Die Stimmung war*
großartig. ♦ *Sie ist eine großartige Schauspielerin.*
be great at sth großartig in etw. (dat) sein ◊ *Sie ist*
in Mathe großartig. be great with sb/sth großartig
mit jdm./etw. umgehen können ◊ *Er kann großartig*
mit Tieren umgehen.
ⓔ the Great der/die Große ◊ *Katharina die Große*
♦ *Friedrich der Große*

great[2] (adv) großartig ['gro:s|a:'tɪç] ◊ *Unser Geschäft*
läuft großartig.

Great Britain (noun) Großbritannien [gro:sbri'tanjən]
das <-s> *article only in combination with attribute,*
no pl → **Germany**

greatly (adv) *(very much)* stark [ʃta'k] <stärker, am
stärksten> ◊ *stark reduzierte Preise* ♦ *stark*
schwanken; (praise, appreciate) hoch [ho:x] <höher,
am höchsten> ◊ *jdn hoch achten* ♦ *hoch gelobt*
werden

Greece (noun) Griechenland ['gri:çn̩lant] das <-s>
article only in combination with attribute, no pl →
Germany

greed (noun) **1.** *(for money)* Habgier ['ha:pgi:ɐ̯] die
<-> *no pl* greed for power Machtgier ['maxtgi:ɐ̯] die
2. *(for food)* Gefräßigkeit [gə'frɛ:sɪçkae̯t] die <-> *no*
pl

greedy(-ily) (adj, adv) gierig ['gi:rɪç] ◊ *Die Katze*
starrte mit gierigem Blick auf das Aquarium. ♦ *Sei*
nicht so gierig! ♦ *Sie stürzten sich gierig auf das*
Büffet. greedy for sth gierig nach etw.

Greek[1] (noun) **1.** *(inhabitant)* Grieche ['gri:çə] der
<-n, -n> ♀Griechin ['gri:çɪn] die <-, -nen> →
German[1] **1. 2.** *(language, subject)* Griechisch
['gri:çɪʃ] das <-(s)> *no pl* → **German**[1] **2.**

Greek[2] (adj) griechisch ['gri:çɪʃ] → **German**[2]

green[1] (noun) **1.** Grün [gry:n] das <-s> *no pl* ◊ *ein*
leuchtendes Grün ♦ *ein Kleid in Grün* **2.** *(member of*
the Green Party) Green Grüne ['gry:nə] der/die
<-n, die Grünen> *but: ein Grüner/eine Grüne* **3.** *(vege-*
tables) greens *(grünes) Blattgemüse*

green[2] (adj) **1.** *(colo(u)r, full of plants or trees, environ-*
mentally friendly) grün [gry:n] ◊ *Fahr los, die Ampel*
ist grün. ♦ *grüner Salat* ♦ *grüne Energie* **2.** POL
(referring to the Green Party) Green grün [gry:n] ◊ *ein*
grüner Abgeordneter ♦ *grün wählen*

greenery (noun) Grün [gry:n] das <-s> *no pl* ◊ *In*
meiner Straße gibt es viel Grün. ♦ *ein bisschen*
Grün für die Wohnung

greenhouse (noun) Gewächshaus [gə'vɛkshao̯s] das
<-es, Gewächshäuser>

greet (verb) *(acknowledge, receive)* begrüßen
[ba'gry:sn̩] <begrüßt, begrüßte, hat begrüßt> ◊ *Sie*
begrüßten einander mit einem Kopfnicken. ♦ *Sie*
begrüßten die Nachricht mit Freudentränen.; (meet
with a negative reaction) be greeted with sth auf
etw. (acc) stoßen [aof ... ʃto:sn̩] <stößt, stieß, ist
gestoßen> ◊ *Der Vorschlag stieß auf Skepsis.*

greeting (noun) Gruß [gru:s] der <-es, Grüße> ◊ *jds*
Gruß erwidern

grey, gray (adj) grau [grao̯] <grauer, am grau(e)sten>

◊ *Der Himmel ist ganz grau.*

grid (noun) **1.** *(pattern)* Raster ['raste] das <-s, -> ◊
das Raster einer Tabelle **2.** *(for electricity)* Netz [nɛts]
das <-es, -e> ◊ *etw. ans Netz anschließen* **3.** *(metal*
bars) Gitter ['gɪte] das <-s, -> ◊ *ein eisernes Gitter*

grief (noun) Trauer ['trao̯ɐ] die <-> *no pl* ◊ *die Trauer*
über den Tod eines geliebten Menschen
ⓔ come to grief **1.** *(fail)* scheitern **2.** *(have an*
accident) verunglücken give sb grief jdm Ärger
machen

grill[1] (noun) **1.** *(for cooking)* Grill [grɪl] der <-s, -s> ◊
Er legte die Steaks auf den Grill. **2.** *(type of restau-*
rant) Grillrestaurant ['grɪlrɛsto̯raŋ] das <-s, -s>

grill[2] (verb) **1.** *(cook)* grillen ['grɪlən] +haben ◊
Würstchen grillen **2.** *(fam) (interrogate)* in die
Mangel nehmen [ɪn di: 'maŋl̩ ne:mən] <nimmt,
nahm, hat genommen> *(fam)* ◊ *Der Staatsanwalt*
nahm den Zeugen in die Mangel.

grim (adj) **1.** *(unpleasant, hopeless)* trostlos ['tro:stlo:s]
<trostloser, am trostlosesten> ◊ *eine trostlose*
Existenz ♦ *Die Wohnung wirkte trostlos.* **2.** *(gloomy)*
düster ['dy:ste] ◊ *düsteres Wetter* ♦ *Es sieht düster*
für uns aus. **3.** *(stern)* grimmig ['grɪmɪç] ◊ *Sein*
Blick war grimmig. ♦ *grimmige Entschlossenheit*

grin[1] (noun) Grinsen ['grɪnzn̩] das <-s> *no pl* ◊ *mit*
einem breiten Grinsen

grin[2] (verb) grinsen ['grɪnzn̩] +haben ◊ *hämisch/*
verlegen grinsen grin at sb jdn angrinsen ['angrɪnzn̩]
+haben
ⓔ grin and bear it gute Miene zum bösen Spiel
machen

grind (verb) **1.** *(crush)* mahlen ['ma:lən] <mahlt, mahlte,
hat gemahlen> ◊ *Kaffee/Getreide mahlen* ♦ *den*
Pfeffer fein/grob mahlen **2.** *(sharpen)* schleifen
['ʃlae̯fn̩] <schleift, schliff, hat geschliffen> ◊ *Messer*
schleifen **3.** *(rub noisily against sth)* knirschen
['knɪʁʃn̩] +haben grind your teeth mit den Zähnen
knirschen **4.** grind a cigarette into the ground eine
Zigarette austreten [ae̯nə tsiga'rɛtə ,ao̯stre:tn̩] <tritt
aus, trat aus, hat ausgetreten>

grip[1] (noun) **1.** *(also fig) (grasp, hold, handle)* Griff
[grɪf] der <-(e)s, -e> ◊ *Sie hielt das Tier mit*
eisernem Griff fest. ♦ *Der Griff nach der Macht*
loosen your grip on sth den Griff um etw.
lockern [de:n ,grɪf ʊm ... 'lɔkɐn] +haben **2.** *(adhesion*
of tyres, shoes) Griffigkeit ['grɪfɪçkae̯t] die <-> *no pl*
◊ *die Griffigkeit von Winterreifen* **3.** *(in the UK, for*
hair) Haarklammer ['ha:'klamɐ] die <-, -n>
ⓔ be in the grip of sth von etw. beherrscht
werden get a grip (on yourself) sich zusammenreißen get a grip on sth, come to grips with sth etw.
in den Griff bekommen

grip[2] (verb) **1.** *(grab)* ergreifen [ɛ'grae̯fn̩] <ergreift,
ergriff, hat ergriffen> ◊ *jds Hand ergreifen* grip sb by
the shoulders jdn bei den Schultern packen
[bae̯ de:n 'ʃʊltɐn pakn̩] +haben **2.** *(clasp)* umklammern [ʊm'klamɐn] <umklammert, umklammerte, hat
umklammert> ◊ *Er umklammerte das Lenkrad.*
3. *(tyre)* greifen ['grae̯fn̩] <greift, griff, hat gegriffen> ◊
Die Reifen greifen sehr gut. **4.** *(overcome)* erfassen
[ɛ'fasn̩] <erfasst, erfasste, hat erfasst> ◊ *Angst erfasste*
die Menschen. **5.** *(fascinate)* fesseln ['fɛsl̩n] +haben ◊
Das Buch hat mich gefesselt.

groan (verb) **1.** *(moan)* stöhnen ['ʃtø:nən] +haben ◊ *Sie*
stöhnt über die viele Arbeit. groan with sth vor etw.
(dat) stöhnen ◊ *vor Schmerz/Lust stöhnen* **2.** *(also*

fig) (creak) ächzen [ˈɛçtsn̩] +*haben* ◊ *Der Stuhl ächzte unter seinem Gewicht.* ✦ *Die Wirtschaft ächzt unter dem hohen Ölpreis.*

groom¹ [noun] **1.** *(bridegroom)* Bräutigam [ˈbrɔɪtɪɡam] der <-s, -e> **2.** *(for horses)* Pferdepfleger [ˈpfeːɐ̯dəpfleːɡə] der <-s, -> ♀Pferdepflegerin [ˈpfeːɐ̯dəpfleːɡərɪn] die <-, -nen>

groom² [verb] **1.** *(a horse)* striegeln [ˈʃtriːɡl̩n] <striegelte, hat gestriegelt> +*haben* **2.** *(person: look after yourself)* groom sth etw. pflegen [ˈpfleːɡn̩] +*haben* ◊ *Du musst dein Haar besser pflegen.* groom yourself sich pflegen **3.** *(animal: clean)* groom an animal ein Tier putzen [ˈpʊtsn̩] +*haben* ◊ *Der Papagei putzte seine Jungen.* The cat groomed itself. Die Katze putzte sich. **4.** *(prepare)* vorbereiten [ˈfoːɐ̯bəraɪtn̩] <bereitet vor, bereitete vor, hat vorbereitet> groom sb for sth jdn auf etw. [acc] vorbereiten ◊ *jdn auf eine Aufgabe vorbereiten*

groove [noun] **1.** *(ridge, cut)* Rille [ˈrɪlə] die <-, -n> ◊ *die Rillen einer Schallplatte* **2.** *(fam) (rhythm)* Groove [ɡruːf] der <-s> *no pl* ◊ *Das Stück hat einen tollen Groove.*

gross¹ [adj] **1.** *(before tax)* brutto [ˈbrʊtoː] *no comp/ superl, postpositive* ◊ *Sein Einkommen beträgt 30.000 Euro brutto.;* Brutto... [ˈbrʊtoː] gross income Bruttoeinkommen [ˈbrʊtoˌaɪnkɔmən] das <-s, -> **2.** *(serious)* grob [ɡroːp] <gröber, am gröbsten> *only before ns* ◊ *Es war ein grober Fehler, ihm zu vertrauen.* ✦ *grobe Fahrlässigkeit* **3.** *(disgusting)* ekelhaft [ˈeːkl̩haft] <ekelhafter, am ekelhaftesten> ◊ *Das ist ja ekelhaft!* ✦ *eine ekelhafte Angewohnheit*

gross² [adv] brutto [ˈbrʊtoː] ◊ *Wie viel verdienen Sie brutto?*

grossly [adv] grob [ɡroːp] <gröber, am gröbsten> ◊ *grob fahrlässig handeln*

ground¹ [noun] **1.** *(earth)* Boden [ˈboːdn̩] der <-s, Böden> *most sing* ◊ *Sie fiel zu Boden.* ✦ *einen Pfosten in den Boden rammen* ✦ *Der Ballon schwebte fünf Meter über dem Boden.* below ground unter der Erde [ˌʊntə deːɐ̯ ˈeːɐ̯də] **2.** *(land)* Land [lant] das <-(e)s *no pl* ◊ *ein Hektar Land* **3.** *(land surrounding sth or used for a specific purpose)* ground(s) Gelände [ɡəˈlɛndə] das <-s, -> ◊ *offenes Gelände* ✦ *auf dem Gelände des Krankenhauses* parade ground Exerzierplatz [ɛksɛrˈtsiːɐ̯plats] der <-es, Exerzierplätze> nesting ground Nistplatz [ˈnɪstplats] fishing ground Fischgrund [ˈfɪʃɡrʊnt] der <-(e)s, Fischgründe> *most pl;* (*land surrounding a castle, stately home etc.*) Anlage [ˈanlaːɡə] die <-, -n> *most pl* ◊ *in den Anlagen des Schlosses spazieren gehen* **4.** *(reason)* ground(s) Grund [ɡrʊnt] der <-(e)s, Gründe> ◊ *ein Grund für etw.* on religious/health grounds aus religiösen/gesundheitlichen Gründen on (the) grounds of aufgrund [aɔfˈɡrʊnt] [+gen] ◊ *Diskriminierung aufgrund des Geschlechts* on the grounds that mit der Begründung, dass [mɪt deːɐ̯ bəˈɡrʏndʊŋ das] ◊ *Das Gesetz wurde mit der Begründung abgelehnt, dass es gegen die Verfassung verstoße.* **5.** *(of coffee)* grounds Kaffeesatz [ˈkafəzats] der <-es> *no pl* **6.** *(first layer of paint)* Grundierung [ɡrʊnˈdiːrʊŋ] die <-, -en> ⊙ **fall on fertile ground** auf fruchtbaren Boden fallen **cover much ground** weit vorankommen **gain/lose ground** an Boden gewinnen/verlieren **get off the ground** Gestalt annehmen **get sth off the ground** etw. in die Tat umsetzen **hold your ground**

nicht nachgeben

ground² [verb] **1.** *(be based on sth)* be grounded on sth auf etw. [dat] basieren [aɔf ... baˈziːrən] <basiert, basierte, hat basiert> ◊ *Diese Idee basiert auf gesundem Menschenverstand.* **2.** *(a child)* ground sb jdm Hausarrest erteilen [haɔsˌarɛst ɛtaelən] <erteilt, erteilte, hat erteilt> **3.** ground a plane einem Flugzeug die Starterlaubnis verweigern [aɛnəm ˌfluːktsɔɪɡə ˈʃtaˈtlɛlaɔpnɪs feˌvaɛɡən] <verweigert, verweigerte, hat verweigert> **4.** *(boat, sth grounds)* etw. läuft auf Grund [lɔɔft aɔf ˈɡrʊnt] <lief, ist gelaufen> ground sth etw. auf Grund setzen [aɔf ˈɡrʊnt zɛtsn̩] +*haben* ◊ *Der Kapitän hat den Frachter auf Grund gesetzt.*

ground floor [noun] Erdgeschoss [ˈeːɐ̯tɡəʃɔs] das <-es, -e> ◊ *eine Wohnung im Erdgeschoss*

groundless [adj] unbegründet [ˈʊnbəɡrʏndət] *no comp/superl* ◊ *Der Verdacht erwies sich als unbegründet.* ✦ *unbegründete Eifersucht*

group¹ [noun] Gruppe [ˈɡrʊpə] die <-, -n> ◊ *eine Gruppe von Menschen/Wörtern/Bäumen* ✦ *einer Gruppe beitreten/angehören* ✦ *Delfine gehören zur Gruppe der Wale.* ✦ *in Gruppen arbeiten;* *(of companies)* Unternehmensgruppe [ʊntəˈneːmənsɡrʊpə] drama group Theatergruppe [teˈaːtɐɡrʊpə] ethnic group Volksgruppe [ˈfɔlksɡrʊpə]

group² [verb] **1.** *(categorize)* ordnen [ˈɔˈdnən] <ordnet, ordnete, hat geordnet> group sth according to sth etw. nach etw. ordnen ◊ *Bücher nach Autoren ordnen* group sb/sth into sth jdn/etw. einer Sache [dat] zuordnen [ˈtsuːˌɔˈdnən] <ordnet zu, ordnete zu, hat zugeordnet> ◊ *Themen verschiedenen Kategorien zuordnen* group sth together etw. zusammenfassen [tsuˈzamənfasn̩] +*haben* **2.** *(arrange)* gruppieren [ɡrʊˈpiːrən] <gruppiert, gruppierte, hat gruppiert> ◊ *Sessel um einen Tisch gruppieren*

grouping [noun] Gruppe [ˈɡrʊpə] die <-, -n> ◊ *Unter unseren Patienten stellen die Senioren die größte Gruppe dar.*

grow [verb] **1.** *(increase in size, become stronger)* wachsen [ˈvaksn̩] <wächst, wuchs, ist gewachsen> ◊ *Du bist aber gewachsen!* ✦ *Die Pflanze wächst bis zu (einer Höhe von) 3m.* ✦ *Seine Angst wuchs immer mehr.* ✦ *wachsende Nachfrage* grow by sth um etw. wachsen ◊ *Die Wirtschaft ist um ein Prozent gewachsen.* fully grown ausgewachsen [ˈaɔsɡəvaksn̩] *no comp/superl* ◊ *ein ausgewachsener Hund* ✦ *Das Tier ist ausgewachsen.* grow in importance wichtiger werden [ˈvɪçtɪɡə veːɐ̯dn̩] +*sein* grow in popularity beliebter werden [bəˈliːptə veːɐ̯dn̩] +*sein* **2.** *(cultivate)* anbauen [ˈanbaɔən] <baut an, baute an, hat angebaut> ◊ *Ich baue im Garten Tomaten an.;* *(plants, bacteria, cells)* züchten [ˈtsʏçtn̩] <züchtet, züchtete, hat gezüchtet> ◊ *Rosen/Tomaten züchten* grow sth from seed etw. aus Samen ziehen [aɔs ˈtsaːmən tsiːən] <zieht, zog, hat gezogen> **3.** grow your hair sich [dat] die Haare wachsen lassen [diː ˈhaːrə ˌvaksn̩ lasn̩] <lässt, ließ, hat lassen> grow a beard sich [dat] einen Bart wachsen lassen

• **grow apart** [phras v] sich auseinander leben [aɔsˌae̯ˈnandə leːbm̩] +*haben* ◊ *Das Paar hat sich auseinander gelebt.*

• **grow into** [phras v] **1.** *(become)* sb/sth grows into sb/sth aus jdm/etw. wird jd/etw. [aɔs ... vɪˈt] +*sein* ◊ *Aus dem kleinen Jungen ist ein stattlicher Mann*

geworden. **2.** *(also fig) (become the right size, adapt)* grow into sth in etw. `acc` hineinwachsen [ɪn ... hɪˌnaɛnvaksn̩] <wächst hinein, wuchs hinein, ist hineingewachsen> ◊ *in einen Anzug hineinwachsen* ♦ *in eine neue Rolle hineinwachsen*

• **grow on** `phras v` grow on sb sb grows on sb jd lernt jdn schätzen [lɛˈnt ... ˈʃɛtsn̩] +haben ◊ *Ich habe ihn mit der Zeit schätzen gelernt.* sth grows on sb jd findet Gefallen an etw. `dat` [fɪndət gəˈfalən an] <fand, hat gefunden>

• **grow out** `phras v` **1.** *(hair colo(u)r, perm)* herauswachsen [hɛˈraosvaksn̩] <wächst heraus, wuchs heraus, ist herausgewachsen> ◊ *Die Farbe ist schon wieder herausgewachsen.* **2.** *(person: get too big for your clothes)* grow out of sth aus etw. herauswachsen [aos ... hɛˌraosvaksn̩] <wächst heraus, wuchs heraus, ist herausgewachsen> ◊ *Mein Sohn wächst so schnell aus seinen Kleidern heraus.* **3.** *(person: stop a bad habit)* grow out of sth etw. ablegen [ˈaple:gn̩] +haben ◊ *schlechte Gewohnheiten ablegen* **4.** *(sth new: be created by sth)* grow out of sth aus etw. erwachsen [aos ... ɐˌvaksn̩] <erwächst, erwuchs, ist erwachsen> ◊ *Aus dieser Situation erwachsen neue Probleme.*

• **grow up** `phras v` **1.** *(become more mature)* erwachsen werden [ɐˈvaksn̩ veːɐdn̩] +sein ◊ *Sie wird langsam erwachsen.* ♦ *Werd endlich erwachsen!* **2.** *(spend your childhood)* aufwachsen [ˈaofvaksn̩] <wächst auf, wuchs auf, ist aufgewachsen> ◊ *zweisprachig aufwachsen* ♦ *bei den Großeltern/in einfachen Verhältnissen aufwachsen*

growl `verb` *(dog, person)* knurren [ˈknʊrən] +haben ◊ *Der Hund knurrte laut.* ♦ *„Lass mich in Ruhe", knurrte er.*; *(bear)* brummen [ˈbrʊmən] +haben; *(thunder)* grollen [ˈɡrɔlən] +haben

grown-up¹ `noun` Erwachsene [ɐˈvaksənə] der/die <-n, die Erwachsenen> *but: ein Erwachsener/eine Erwachsene*

grown-up² `adj` erwachsen [ɐˈvaksn̩] *no comp/superl* ◊ *Wenn er erwachsen ist, will er Pilot werden.* ♦ *Sie hat zwei erwachsene Töchter.*

growth `noun` **1.** *(increase in size)* Wachstum [ˈvakstuːm] das <-s> *no pl* ◊ *das Wachstum hemmen* ♦ *ein Wachstum der Wirtschaft um 2%* **2.** *(increase in occurence)* Zunahme [ˈtsuːnaːmə] die <-> *no pl* ◊ *die Zunahme von Verbrechen* **3.** *(plants)* Vegetation [vegetaˈtsjoːn] die <-, -en> ◊ *Langsam entwickelte sich eine neue Vegetation.* **4.** MED *(tumo(u)r)* Geschwür [gəˈʃvyːɐ̯] das <-s, -e> ◊ *ein gutartiges Geschwür*

grumble `verb` **1.** *(complain)* murren [ˈmʊrən] +haben ◊ *Hör auf zu murren.* ♦ *Ständig murrt sie über ihre Arbeit* grumble at sth sich bei jdm beklagen [bæ ... bəˈklaːgn̩] <beklagt sich, beklagte sich, hat sich beklagt> **2.** *(rumble)* rumpeln [ˈrʊmpl̩n] +haben/ with indication of direction +sein ◊ *Das Auto hat ziemlich laut gerumpelt.* ♦ *Der Zug war aus dem Bahnhof gerumpelt.*; *(stomach)* knurren [ˈknʊrən] +haben ◊ *Vor Hunger knurrte ihm der Magen.*; *(thunder)* grollen [ˈɡrɔlən] +haben ◊ *Hörst du den Donner grollen?*

grunt `verb` *(person)* brummen [ˈbrʊmən] +haben ◊ *Brumm doch nicht!* ♦ *Er brummte nur: „Schon gut.";* *(pig)* grunzen [ˈɡrʊntsn̩] +haben

guarantee¹ `noun` *(warranty, promise)* Garantie [garanˈtiː] die <-, -n> ◊ *jdm eine Garantie geben* ♦

unter Garantie ♦ *Die Garantie ist abgelaufen.* a guarantee of sth eine Garantie für etw. ◊ *eine Garantie für Qualität* a guarantee of one year ein Jahr Garantie sth carries a guarantee auf etw. `acc` gibt es Garantie; *(for a loan)* Bürgschaft [ˈbyːɐ̯kʃaft] die <-, -en> ◊ *für jdn eine Bürgschaft übernehmen*

guarantee² `verb` garantieren [garanˈtiːrən] <garantiert, garantierte, hat garantiert> ◊ *Erfolg garantieren* ♦ *Er garantiert dir, dass das klappt.* ♦ *durch die Verfassung garantiert sein* be guaranteed to do sth garantiert etw. tun ◊ *Bei uns finden Sie garantiert, was Sie suchen.*; *(product)* be guaranteed for three years drei Jahre Garantie haben [draɛ ˌjaːrə garanˈtiː haːbn̩] +haben; *(a loan)* guarantee sth für etw. bürgen [fyːgn̩ ... ˌbyːɐ̯gn̩] +haben

guard¹ `noun` **1.** *(general, military)* Wache [ˈvaxə] die <-, -n> ◊ *Vor dem Tor standen zwei Wachen.* ♦ *Wachen an den Eingängen des Gebäudes postieren* The guards are changed. Die Wache wird abgelöst.; *(at a gate, in a museum etc.)* Wächter [ˈvɛçtɐ] der <-s, -> ♀Wächterin [ˈvɛçtərɪn] die <-, -nen> ◊ *Die Wächter machten ihren Rundgang.* ♦ *Sie arbeitet als Wächterin im Museum.*; *(in a prison)* Wärter [ˈvɛrtɐ] der <-s, -> ♀Wärterin [ˈvɛrtərɪn] die <-, -nen> ◊ *Die Gefangenen überwältigten einen Wärter und brachen aus.* security guard Sicherheitsbeamte [ˈzɪçɐhaɛtsbəˌamtə] der <-n, die Sicherheitsbeamten> ♀Sicherheitsbeamtin [ˈzɪçɐhaɛtsbəˌamtɪn] die <-, -nen> *but: ein Sicherheitsbeamter* ◊ *Zwei bewaffnete Sicherheitsbeamte standen vor dem Eingang.* **2.** *(unit of soldiers or police officers)* Garde [ˈɡaːdə] die <-, -n> ◊ *die königliche Garde* National Guard Nationalgarde [natsjoˈnaːlɡaːdə] Guards Garderegiment [ˈɡaːdəreɡiˌmɛnt] das <-(e)s, -e or -er> **3.** *(protection)* Schutz [ʃʊts] der <-es> *no pl* ◊ *Der Zaun dient als Schutz gegen Eindringlinge.* mouth guard Mundschutz [ˈmʊntʃʊts]; *(in fencing, boxing)* Deckung [ˈdɛkʊŋ] die <-, -en> ◊ *jds Deckung durchbrechen* **4.** *(on a train)* Schaffner [ˈʃafnɐ] der <-s, -> ♀Schaffnerin [ˈʃafnərɪn] die <-, -nen> ◊ *Er fragte die Schaffnerin, wie lange die Fahrt noch dauere.* **5.** SPORT *(in basketball)* Verteidigungsspieler [fɛˈtaɛdɪɡʊŋsʃpiːlɐ] der <-s, -> ♀Verteidigungsspielerin [fɛˈtaɛdɪɡʊŋsʃpiːlərɪn] die <-, -nen> ◊ *Er ist Verteidigungsspieler.*

ⓔ be on your guard auf der Hut sein off your guard catch sb off their guard jdn überrumpeln put sb off their guard jdn in Sicherheit wiegen be off your guard sich in Sicherheit wiegen

guard² `verb` **1.** *(watch carefully)* bewachen [bəˈvaxn̩] <bewacht, bewachte, hat bewacht> ◊ *ein bewachter Parkplatz* ♦ *Unser Hund bewacht das Baby.* guard sb/sth from jdn/etw. vor etw. `dat` schützen [foːɐ̯ ... ˈʃʏtsn̩] +haben ◊ *Die Deiche schützen das Dorf vor der Flut.*; *(a secret, treasure, your tongue)* hüten [ˈhyːtn̩] <hütet, hütete, hat gehütet> ◊ *Hüte deine Zunge!* **2.** SPORT decken [ˈdɛkn̩] +haben ◊ *einen Spieler decken*

• **guard against** `phras v` einer Sache `dat` vorbeugen [ˈfoːɐ̯bɔygn̩] +haben ◊ *einer Erkältung vorbeugen* ♦ *Um Missverständnissen vorzubeugen, erkläre ich das jetzt noch einmal.* guard against doing sth sich davor in Acht nehmen, etw. zu tun [dafoːɐ̯ ɪn ˈaxt neːmən ... tuː] <nimmt sich, nahm sich, hat sich genommen> ◊ *Sie sollten sich davor in*

Acht nehmen, ihnen zu sehr zu vertrauen.

guardian [noun] **1.** *(protector of sth)* Hüter ['hy:tɐ] der <-s, -> ♀Hüterin ['hy:tərɪn] die <-, -nen> ◊ *ein Hüter der Moral/des Gesetzes* guardian angel Schutzengel ['ʃʊts|ɛŋl] der <-s, -> **2.** LAW *(of a child)* Vormund ['fo:ɡmʊnt] der <-(e)s, -e or Vormünder> ◊ *Ihr Onkel wurde als ihr Vormund eingesetzt.*

guerrilla [noun] Guerillakämpfer [ɡe'rɪljakɛmpfɐ] der <-s, -> ♀Guerillakämpferin [ɡe'rɪljakɛmpfərɪn] die <-, -nen> guerilla warfare Guerillakrieg [ɡe'rɪljakriːk] der <-(e)s, -e>

guess¹ [noun] **1.** *(speculation)* Vermutung [fɛ'muːtʊŋ] die <-, -en> ◊ *Wie lautet Ihre Vermutung?* have a guess raten ['raːtn̩] <rät, riet, hat geraten> ◊ *Rate mal, was ich in der Tasche habe!* It was just a good guess. Ich habe nur geraten. **2.** *(estimation)* Schätzung ['ʃɛtsʊŋ] die <-, -en> ◊ *Sie lag mit ihrer Schätzung gar nicht so falsch.* ◆ *eine grobe Schätzung* have a guess schätzen ['ʃɛtsn̩] +haben ◊ *Schätzen Sie, wie viele Ameisen in einem Haufen leben.*

⊛ your guess is as good as mine da kann ich auch nur raten I'll give you three guesses dreimal darfst du raten

guess² [verb] *(surmise)* raten ['raːtn̩] <rät, riet, hat geraten> ◊ *Rate mal, wen ich vorhin getroffen habe!* ◆ *Richtig geraten!*; *(a number, weight, the time)* schätzen ['ʃɛtsn̩] +haben ◊ *die Anzahl der Besucher schätzen* ◆ *Ich schätze, dass es ungefähr Mitternacht ist.* guess sb to be 30 etc. years old jdn auf 30 etc. schätzen; *(correctly)* erraten [ɛ'raːtn̩] <errät, erriet, hat erraten> ◊ *Wie hast du das bloß erraten?* guess sth from sth etw. aufgrund einer Sache [gen] vermuten [aofɡrʊnt ... fɛ'muːtn̩] <vermutet, vermutete, hat vermutet> ◊ *Aufgrund des Lärms vermutete sie, dass sie Besuch hatten.*

⊛ keep sb guessing jdn im Ungewissen lassen I guess *(fam)* ich schätze ◊ *„Glaubst du, er kommt auch?" — „Ich schätze nicht."*

guest [noun] Gast [ɡast] der <-(e)s, Gäste> ◊ *ein geladener/ungebetener Gast* ◆ *Gäste erwarten/haben* hotel guest Hotelgast [ho'tɛlɡast] guest appearance Gastauftritt ['ɡast|aoftrɪt] der <-(e)s, -e>

⊛ be my guest *(fam)* nur zu ◊ *„Darf ich mich setzen?" — „Nur zu!"*

guest house [noun] **1.** *(small hotel)* Pension [paŋ'zjoːn] die <-, -en> ◊ *Zimmer in einer Pension buchen* **2.** *(house where guests can stay)* Gästehaus ['ɡɛstəhaos] das <-es, Gästehäuser> ◊ *Sie können gern im Gästehaus der Universität übernachten.*

guidance [noun] **1.** *(advice)* Beratung [bə'raːtʊŋ] die <-, -en> ◊ *Wünschen Sie eine Beratung?* marriage guidance Eheberatung ['eːəbəraːtʊŋ]; *(from an official source)* Anleitung ['anlaetʊŋ] die <-, -en> ◊ *die Anleitung genau befolgen* **2.** *(for aircraft, space vehicles)* guidance system Steuerungssystem ['ʃtɔøərʊŋszʏs,teːm] das <-s, -e>

guide¹ [noun] **1.** *(book)* (travel) guide Reiseführer ['raezəfyːrɐ] der <-s, -> ◊ *ein Reiseführer über die Philippinen; (manual)* Ratgeber ['raːtɡeːbɐ] der <-s, -> ◊ *ein Ratgeber mit Tipps für den Hauskauf* **2.** *(indication)* Anhaltspunkt ['anhaltspʊŋkt] der <-(e)s, -e> ◊ *Das Verhalten der Tiere ist ein zuverlässiger Anhaltspunkt dafür, wie streng der Winter wird.* **3.** *(person)* Führer ['fyːrɐ] der <-s, -> ♀Führerin ['fyːrərɪn] die <-, -nen> ◊ *Ich würde*

diese Expedition niemals ohne einen erfahrenen Führer machen. ◆ *Sie kam als Führerin mit.* ◆ *der spirituelle Führer des Gikuyu-Stammes* mountain guide Bergführer ['bɛʳkfyːrɐ] Bergführerin ['bɛʳkfyːrərɪn] **4.** *(model)* Leitbild ['laetbɪlt] das <-(e)s, -er> ◊ *Sie war schon in seiner Jugend sein Leitbild.*

guide² [verb] **1.** *(show the way, lead)* führen ['fyːrən] +haben ◊ *Sie führte uns durch das Moor.* ◆ *Er führte die alte Dame über die Straße.*; *(serve as an orientation point)* leiten ['laetn̩] <leitet, leitete, hat geleitet> ◊ *Nur die Sterne leiteten ihn auf seinem Weg.*; *(a vehicle, missile)* lenken ['lɛŋkn̩] +haben ◊ *Vorsichtig lenkte er das Boot durch den Kanal.* **2.** *(support, advise)* begleiten [bə'ɡlaetn̩] <begleitet, begleitete, hat begleitet> ◊ *Der Tutor begleitet die Studenten durch den Kurs.* be guided by sb/sth sich von jdm/etw. leiten lassen [fɔn ... ˌlaetn̩ lasn̩] <lässt sich, ließ sich, hat sich ... lassen> ◊ *Sie lässt sich von ihrem Glauben an Gott leiten.* **3.** *(influence)* lenken ['lɛŋkn̩] +haben ◊ *die Kinder lenken* ◆ *die Diskussion auf ein anderes Thema lenken*

guidebook [noun] Reiseführer ['raezəfyːrɐ] der <-s, ->

guidelines [noun] Richtlinien ['rɪçtliːnjən] die <-> pl lay down guidelines Richtlinien erlassen

guild [noun] **1.** *(of people having the same job)* Zunft [tsʊnft] die <-, Zünfte> *(oldf)* ◊ *die Zunft der Bäcker* **2.** *(of people having the same interests)* Verein [fɛ'|aen] der <-(e)s, -e> ◊ *der Verein der Heimatfreunde*

guilt [noun] Schuld [ʃʊlt] die <-> no pl ◊ *Die Schuld des Angeklagten gilt als erwiesen.* ◆ *Die Schuld liegt in diesem Fall bei den Eltern.* feeling of guilt Schuldgefühl ['ʃʊltɡəfyːl] das <-(e)s, -e>

guilty [adj] **1.** *(person)* schuldig ['ʃʊldɪç] ◊ *Glauben Sie, dass der Mann schuldig ist?* ◆ *sich (wegen etw.) schuldig fühlen; (conscience, thought)* schlecht [ʃlɛçt] <schlechter, am schlechtesten> ◊ *Sie hatte ein schlechtes Gewissen.; (voice, look)* schuldbewusst ['ʃʊltbəvʊst] <schuldbewusster, am schuldbewusstesten> ◊ *Seine Stimme klang schuldbewusst.* **2.** LAW find sb guilty/not guilty of sth jdn einer Sache [gen] für schuldig/nicht schuldig befinden [fyːɐ̯ 'ʃʊldɪç/nɪçt ʃʊldɪç bəfɪndn̩] <befindet, befand, hat befunden> ◊ *Man hat ihn des Mordes für schuldig befunden.* plead guilty to sth sich einer Sache [gen] schuldig bekennen ['ʃʊldɪç bəkɛnən] <bekennt sich, bekannte sich, hat sich bekannt>

guinea pig [noun] **1.** *(animal)* Meerschweinchen ['meːɐ̯ʃvaençən] das <-s, -> **2.** *(person used in an experiment)* Versuchskaninchen [fɛ'zuːkska.nɪnçən] das <-s, ->

guitar [noun] Gitarre [ɡi'tarə] die <-, -n> ◊ *eine akustische/elektrische Gitarre* play the guitar Gitarre spielen

gulf [noun] **1.** *(gap, divide)* Kluft [klʊft] die <-, Klüfte> ◊ *Eine tiefe Kluft tat sich plötzlich vor ihnen auf.* ◆ *die Kluft zwischen Arm und Reich* **2.** GEOG *(area of sea)* Golf [ɡɔlf] der <-(e)s, -e> ◊ *der Golf von Mexiko*

gulp¹ [noun] Schluck [ʃlʊk] der <-(e)s, -e> ◊ *einen Schluck aus der Flasche nehmen* in one gulp auf einen Zug [aof aenən 'tsuːk]

gulp² [verb] **1.** *(a drink)* runterstürzen ['rʊntɐʃtʏʳtsn̩] +haben ◊ *Sie stürzte hastig ihren Kaffee runter.*;

(food) runterschlingen ['rʊntəʃlɪŋən] <schlingt runter, schlang runter, hat runtergeschlungen> **2.** *(air)* hastig einatmen ['hastɪç aen|a:tmən] <atmet ein, atmete ein, hat eingeatmet> +*haben* ◊ *Hastig atmete sie die frische Luft in ihre Lungen ein.* gulp for air/breath nach Luft ringen [na:x 'lʊft rɪŋən] <ringt, rang, hat gerungen> **3.** *(because you are surprised, shocked etc.)* schlucken ['ʃlʊkn̩] +*haben* ◊ *Sie schluckte, als sie die Rechnung sah.*

gum ⸤noun⸥ **1.** ANAT gum(s) Zahnfleisch ['tsa:nflaeʃ] das <–(e)s> *no pl* **2.** *(chewing)* gum Kaugummi ['kaogʊmi:] *der or also das* <–s, –s> ◊ *Sie kaut gern Kaugummi.* **3.** *(glue)* Klebstoff ['kle:pʃtɔf] *der* <–(e)s, –e> ◊ *Ich brauche Schere und Klebstoff.*

gun ⸤noun⸥ **1.** *(weapon)* Waffe ['vafə] die <–, –n> ◊ *mit vorgehaltener Waffe* ♦ *Er bedrohte die Geiseln mit einer Waffe.* point a gun at sb/sth eine Waffe auf jdn/etw. richten; *(pistol)* Pistole [pɪs'to:lə] die <–, –n>; *(rifle)* Gewehr [gə've:ɐ] das <–(e)s, –e>; *(cannon)* Kanone [ka'no:nə] die <–, –n> ◊ *eine Kanone abfeuern* **2.** *(fam) (person)* Schütze ['ʃʏtsə] der <–n, –n> ♀Schützin ['ʃʏtsɪn] die <–, –nen> **3.** SPORT *(used to start a race)* Startpistole ['sta'tpɪs,to:lə] die <–, –n> **4.** *(tool)* Presse ['prɛsə] die <–, –n> grease gun Fettpresse ['fɛtprɛsə]

gun down ⸤verb⸥ niederschießen ['ni:dəʃi:sn̩] <schießt nieder, schoss nieder, hat niedergeschossen> ◊ *Der Mann schoss wahllos einige Passanten nieder.*

gunman ⸤noun⸥ Bewaffnete [bə'vafnətə] der/die <–n, die Bewaffneten> but: *ein Bewaffneter/eine Bewaffnete* ◊ *Der Bewaffnete bedrohte die Angestellten.*

gurgle ⸤verb⸥ gurgeln ['gʊrgl̩n] +*haben* ◊ *Das Baby gurgelte zufrieden vor sich hin.* ♦ *Mein Bauch gurgelte laut.*

gut ⸤noun⸥ **1.** *(intestine)* Darm [da'm] der <–(e)s, Därme> ◊ *Saiten aus Darm* guts Eingeweide ['aengəvaedə] die <–> *pl* **2.** *(belly)* Bauch [baox] der <–(e)s, Bäuche> ◊ *Er hat einen dicken Bauch bekommen.* **3.** gut feeling Gefühl im Bauch [gə'fy:l ɪm baox] das <–s> *no pl* ◊ *Ich habe so ein Gefühl im Bauch, dass das nicht richtig ist.* gut reaction rein gefühlsmäßige Reaktion [raen gə,fy:lsmɛ:sɪgə reak'tsjo:n] die <–, –en> **4.** *(courage)* guts Mumm [mʊm] der <–s> *no pl (fam)* ◊ *Er hat nicht den/genug Mumm, sich zu beschweren.*

ⓔ have sb's guts for garters jdn zur Minna machen *(fam)* hate sb's guts jdn auf den Tod nicht ausstehen können *(fam)*

gutter ⸤noun⸥ **1.** *(also fig) (in the street)* Gosse ['gɔsə] die <–, –n> ◊ *Wasser in die Gosse gießen* ♦ *Er wird noch in der Gosse landen.* **2.** *(on a roof)* Dachrinne ['daxrɪnə] die <–, –n>

guy ⸤noun⸥ **1.** *(man)* Typ [ty:p] der <–s or also –en, –en> *(fam)* ◊ *Hat der Typ dich belästigt?* ♦ *ein cooler Typ* **2.** guys Leute ['lɔøtə] die <–> *only pl (fam)* ◊ *He, Leute, darf ich mitmachen?* **3.** *(for Guy Fawkes' Night)* Guy-Fawkes-Puppe [gae'fɔ:kspʊpə] die <–, –n> **4.** guy rope Halteseil ['haltəzael] das <–(e)s, –e>

gym ⸤noun⸥ **1.** *(hall or room)* Turnhalle ['tʊ'nhalə] die <–, –n> ◊ *in der Turnhalle Basketball spielen* **2.** *(gymnastics)* Turnen ['tʊ'nən] das <–s> *no pl* ◊ *nicht am Turnen teilnehmen können* gym shoes Turnschuhe ['tʊ'nʃu:ə] die <–> *pl*

gynaecologist, gynecologist ⸤noun⸥ Frauenarzt ['fraoən|a'tst] der <–es, Frauenärzte> ♀Frauenärztin ['fraoən|ɛ'tstɪn] die <–, –nen> ◊ *Sie ist Frauenärztin.* ♦ *Ich muss nächste Woche zum Frauenarzt.*

H

h, H [noun] h, H [haː] das <-(s), -(s)> ◊ *Dieses Wort wird mit einem kleinen h/großen H geschrieben.* ♦ *ein stummes h* ♦ *H wie Heinrich*

ha [interj] ha [ha(ː)] ◊ *Ha! Ich habe das Fotoalbum doch noch gefunden!*

habit [noun] 1. *(sth you often do)* Gewohnheit [gəˈvoːnhaet] die <-, -en> ◊ *Es ist ihm zur Gewohnheit geworden, täglich zu duschen.* ♦ *eine Gewohnheit annehmen/ablegen* get into the habit of doing sth sich angewöhnen, etw. zu tun [ˈangəvøːnən ... tsuː] <gewöhnt sich an, gewöhnte sich an, hat sich angewöhnt> ◊ *Ich habe mir angewöhnt, früh ins Bett zu gehen.* get out of the habit of doing sth sich abgewöhnen, etw. zu tun [ˈapgəvøːnən ... tsuː] <gewöhnt sich ab, gewöhnte sich ab, hat sich abgewöhnt> 2. *(sth bad that you often do)* Angewohnheit [ˈangəvoːnhaet] die <-, -en> ◊ *Das ist eine schlechte Angewohnheit von ihm.*; *(addiction)* Abhängigkeit [ˈaphɛnɪçkaet] die <-, -en> most sing ◊ *seine Abhängigkeit durch Prostitution finanzieren* heroin habit Heroinabhängigkeit [heroˈiːnˌapˌhɛnɪçkaet] 3. *(religious clothes)* Habit [haˈbiːt] der <-s, -e> ◊ *ein Mann im Habit der Kapuziner*

⊛ *old habits die hard* der Mensch ist ein Gewohnheitstier *kick the habit* aufhören ◊ *Vielen Rauchern gelingt es nicht, aufzuhören*

habitat [noun] Lebensraum [ˈleːbmsraom] der <-(e)s, Lebensräume>

hack [verb] 1. *(cut)* hacken [ˈhakn̩] +haben ♦ *Fleisch hacken* I hacked a path through the undergrowth. Ich habe mir einen Weg durch das Gestrüpp gehackt. hack sth off etw. abhacken [ˈaphakn̩] +haben ◊ *Er hackte mit der Axt mehrere Äste ab.* 2. *(destroy sth, esp sth written)* hack sth to pieces etw. zerstückeln [tsɛˈʃtʏkl̩n] <zerstückelt, zerstückelte, hat zerstückelt> ◊ *Der Lektor hat meinen Artikel völlig zerstückelt.* 3. *(fam)* *(cope with)* packen [ˈpakn̩] +haben *(fam)* ◊ *Glaubst du, du packst den Kurs dieses Semester?* 4. IT *(into a computer)* einbrechen [ˈaenbrɛçn̩] <bricht ein, brach ein, ist eingebrochen> ◊ *in das Computersystem des Verteidigungsministeriums einbrechen* 5. *(cough loudly)* laut husten [laot ˈhuːstn̩] +haben

hadn't → **had**

haemorrhage [noun] Blutung [ˈbluːtʊŋ] die <-, -en> ◊ *eine Blutung stillen/stoppen* ♦ *innere Blutungen haben*

haggard [adj] *(thin)* ausgezehrt [ˈaosgətseːɐt] <ausgezehrter, am ausgezehrtesten> ◊ *ausgezehrte Gestalten* ♦ *Er wirkte ausgezehrt und kraftlos.*; *(tired)* abgespannt [ˈapgəʃpant] <abgespannter, am abgespanntesten> ◊ *Ihr Gesicht sah müde und abgespannt aus.*

haggle [verb] 1. *(argue over prices)* haggle (with sb) (about sth) (mit jdm) (um etw.) feilschen [ˈfaelʃn̩] +haben ◊ *Auf dem Basar wurde eifrig gefeilscht.* ♦ *Er hat mit dem Händler um jeden Cent gefeilscht.* haggle sth down etw. herunterhandeln [hɛˈrʊntɐhandln̩] <handelt herunter, handelte herunter, hat heruntergehandelt> ◊ *Wir haben den Preis um fast 40 Prozent heruntergehandelt.* 2. *(argue over details)* haggle about sth sich wegen etw. herumstreiten [veːgn̩] ... hɛˈrʊmʃtraetn̩] <streitet sich herum, stritt sich herum, hat sich herumgestritten> ◊ *Wir sollten aufhören, uns wegen der Vetragsklauseln herumzustreiten.*

hail¹ [noun] Hagel [ˈhaːgl̩] der <-s, -> most sing ◊ *Sturm und Hagel hatten die Ernte verwüstet.* ♦ *Ein Hagel von Fragen/Flüchen prasselte auf sie herab.* in a hail of bullets im Kugelhagel [ɪm ˈkuːglˌhaːgl̩]

hail² [verb] 1. *(celebrate)* hail sb/sth as sth jdn/etw. als etw. [acc] feiern [als ... faeɐn] +haben ◊ *Man feierte ihn als neuen Star.* ♦ *Die Entscheidung wurde als Sieg für die Gerechtigkeit gefeiert.* 2. *(call loudly)* rufen [ˈruːfn̩] <ruft, rief, hat gerufen> ◊ *Plötzlich rief ihn eine vertraute Stimme.*; *(a taxi)* anhalten [ˈanhaltn̩] <hält an, hielt an, hat angehalten> ◊ *Könnten Sie mir bitte ein Taxi anhalten?* 3. METEO hageln [ˈhaːgl̩n] +haben ◊ *Gestern hat es gehagelt.*

hair [noun] Haar [haːɐ] das <-(e)s, -e> ◊ *blonde/ glatte/lockige Haare haben* ♦ *blondes/glattes/lockiges Haar haben* ♦ *jdn an den Haaren ziehen* ♦ *Männer mit Haaren auf der Brust* a fine head of hair schönes volles Haar have your hair cut sich [dat] die Haare schneiden lassen body hair Körperbehaarung [ˈkœɐpəbaːarʊŋ] die <-, -en>

⊛ *by a hair's breadth* um Haaresbreite *make sb's hair stand on end* jdm die Haare zu Berge stehen lassen *not touch a hair on sb's head* jdm kein Haar krümmen *let your hair down* aus sich herausgehen *keep your hair on* ruhig Blut ◊ *Nur ruhig Blut! Das wird schon wieder.*

haircut [noun] 1. *(process of cutting sb's hair)* go for/ have a haircut zum Friseur gehen [tsʊm friˈzøːɐ geːən] <geht, ging, ist gegangen> ◊ *Ich muss mal wieder zum Freuseur gehen.* 2. *(hairstyle)* Haarschnitt [ˈhaːɐʃnɪt] der <-(e)s, -e> ◊ *Dein neuer Haarschnitt gefällt mir.*

hairdo [noun] Frisur [friˈzuːɐ] die <-, -en> ◊ *Diese Frisur steht ihr gut.*

hairdresser [noun] *(person)* Friseur [friˈzøːɐ] der <-s, -e> ♀Friseurin [friˈzøːrɪn] die <-, -nen> ◊ *Der Friseur fragte sie nach ihren Wünschen.* ♦ *Sie ist Friseurin.*; *(place)* hairdresser's Friseur [friˈzøːɐ] der <-s, -e>

hairdryer [noun] Föhn [føːn] der <-(e)s, -e>

hairstyle [noun] Frisur [friˈzuːɐ] die <-, -en> ◊ *Sie wollte eine modernere Frisur.*

hairy [adj] 1. *(having a lot of hair)* behaart [bəˈhaːɐt] <behaarter, am behaartesten> ◊ *behaarte Arme und Beine haben* ♦ *Die Blätter der Pflanze sind stark behaart.* 2. *(frightening, risky)* gefährlich [gəˈfɛːɐlɪç] ◊ *eine gefährliche Kurve* ♦ *Allmählich wird's wirklich gefährlich.*

half¹ [noun] 1. *(50%)* Hälfte [ˈhɛlftə] die <-, -n> ◊ *Die Hälfte der Insel ist von Wald bedeckt.* ♦ *Durch die*

Impfungen konnte die Zahl der Erkrankungen um die Hälfte verringert werden. cut sth in half etw. halbieren [hal'bi:rən] <halbiert, halbierte, hat halbiert> ◊ *Sie halbierte das Brot.* one and a half **eineinhalb** ['aen|aen'halp] ◊ *Er hat eineinhalb Scheiben Brot gegessen.* two and a half **zweieinhalb** ['tsae|aen'halp] half an hour eine halbe Stunde [aenə ,halbə 'ʃtʊndə] half a year ein halbes Jahr [aen ,halbəs 'jaːɐ] **2.** SPORT **Halbzeit** ['halptsaet] die <-, -en> ◊ *In der zweiten Halbzeit wurde der Torwart ausgewechselt.* **3.** (of beer) kleines Bier [,klaenəs 'biːɐ] <-(e)s, - or -e> pl *'Bier' when used with expressions of quantity* ◊ *Zwei kleine Bier, bitte.* ♦ *Haben Sie auch kleine Biere?* **4.** (child's ticket) **Kinderkarte** ['kɪndeka'tə] die <-, -n> ◊ *eine Kinderkarte kaufen* Two adults and one half, please. Zwei Erwachsene und ein Kind, bitte.

half² [adj] halb [halp] *no comp/superl, only before ns* ◊ *eine halbe Flasche Wein* ♦ *In der ersten halben Stunde kam fast niemand.*

half³ [adv] halb [halp] ◊ *Ich war schon halb betrunken.* ♦ *nur halb zuhören* ♦ *Ich bin halb krank vor Angst um dich!* ♦ *Sie verdient nur halb so viel wie er.* half sth (and) half sth halb etw. (und) halb etw. ◊ *ein Fabelwesen, das halb Mensch, halb Tier ist* I was half sad and half glad. Ich war teils traurig und teils froh. sb is half afraid that jd befürchtet fast, dass [bə'fʏɐçtət ,fast das] <befürchtet, befürchtete, hat befürchtet> ◊ *Ich befürchte fast, dass er nicht mehr kommt.* I half think that Ich habe beinahe den Eindruck, dass [ɪç haːbə ,baenaːə deːn 'aendrʊk das] +*haben*

half⁴ [pron] die Hälfte [di: 'hɛlftə] <-> *no pl* ◊ *Ich habe genug Geld — ich gebe dir die Hälfte.*

half-... [prefix] **1.** (with adjectives) halb... [halp] half-hearted **halbherzig** ['halphɛɐ'tsɪç] half-hourly **halbstündlich** ['halpʃtʏntlɪç] *no comp/superl* **2.** (in compound ns) Halb... [halp] half-moon **Halbmond** ['halpmoːnt] der <-(e)s> *no pl* half-sister **Halbschwester** ['halpʃvɛstɐ] die <-, -n>

half board [noun] **Halbpension** ['halppã,zjoːn] die <-> *no pl* ◊ *eine Woche Halbpension*

half time [noun] **Halbzeit** ['halptsaet] die <-, -en> ◊ *Zur Halbzeit stand es 4:2.*

halfway [adv] **1.** halfway to auf halbem Weg nach [aof ,halbəm 'veːk naːx] ◊ *Auf halbem Weg nach Berlin versagte der Motor.* halfway between auf halbem Weg zwischen [dat] ◊ *Sie wohnt auf halbem Weg zwischen Bahnhof und Stadtzentrum.* They drove halfway to Munich. Sie fuhren die halbe Strecke nach München. She lives halfway up the mountain. Sie wohnt auf halber Höhe des Berges. They left halfway through the film. Sie gingen mitten im Film. **2.** (fam) (reasonably) **halbwegs** ['halpveːks] ◊ *Jeder halbwegs gebildete Mensch weiß das.* ♦ *ein halbwegs anständiges Hotel* ⊚ be halfway there es fast geschafft haben meet sb halfway (also fig) jdm auf halbem Weg entgegenkommen

hall [noun] **1.** (large building) Halle ['halə] die <-, -n> ◊ *Besuchen Sie unseren Stand in Halle 9.* sports hall **Sporthalle** ['ʃpɔɐ'thalə] concert hall **Konzerthalle** [kɔn'tsɛɐ'thalə] **2.** (large room) Saal [zaːl] der <-(e)s, Säle> ◊ *ein festlich geschmückter Saal* dining hall **Speisesaal** ['ʃpaezəzaːl] lecture hall **Hörsaal** ['hø:ɐzaːl] village hall **Gemeindesaal**

[gə'maendə,zaːl] **3.** (in a house) Flur [fluːɐ] der <-(e)s, -e> ◊ *Die Garderobe ist im Flur.* **4.** (in the UK) hall (of residence) **Studentenwohnheim** [ʃtu'dɛntnvo:nhaem] das <-(e)s, -e> **5.** (mansion) **Herrenhaus** ['hɛrənhaos] das <-es, Herrenhäuser>

hallway [noun] Flur [fluːɐ] der <-(e)s, -e>

halt¹ [noun] (pause) Pause ['paozə] die <-, -n> ◊ *Er bat um eine kurze Pause.* ♦ *fünf Minuten Pause;* (stop) **Stillstand** ['ʃtɪlʃtant] der <-(e)s, Stillstände> ◊ *den Verkehr/einen Zug zum Stillstand bringen* ♦ *zum Stillstand kommen* call a halt to sth einer Sache [dat] ein Ende bereiten [aen 'ɛndə bəraetn̩] <bereitet, bereitete, hat bereitet> ◊ *der Gewalt ein Ende bereiten* halt sign **Stoppschild** ['ʃtɔpʃɪlt] das <-(e)s, -er>

halt² [verb] **1.** (a development, process) halt sth etw. zum Stillstand bringen [tsʊm 'ʃtɪlʃtant brɪŋən] <bringt, brachte, hat gebracht> ◊ *Die Streiks haben das öffentliche Leben zum Stillstand gebracht.* sth halts etw. kommt zum Stillstand [kɔmt tsʊm 'ʃtɪlʃtant] <kommt, kam, ist gekommen> **2.** (movement) anhalten ['anhaltn̩] <hält an, hielt an, hat angehalten> ◊ *Sie hielt kurz an, um auf die Uhr zu sehen.* ♦ *Polizisten hielten den Wagen an.*

halve [verb] halve sth etw. halbieren [hal'bi:rən] <halbiert, halbierte, hat halbiert> ◊ *eine Tafel Schokolade halbieren* sth halves etw. halbiert sich ◊ *Die Zahl der Unfälle hat sich halbiert.*

ham [noun] **1.** (meat) Schinken ['ʃɪŋkn̩] der <-s, -> ◊ *ein Brot mit Schinken* **2.** RADIO **Funkamateur** ['fʊŋk|ama,tøːɐ] der <-s, -e> ♀**Funkamateurin** ['fʊŋk|ama,tø:rɪn] der <-s, -> ◊ *Er ist Funkamateur.* ♦ *Eine Funkamateurin fing den Notruf auf.* **3.** FILM, THEAT ham (actor) **Schmierenkomödiant** ['ʃmi:rənkomø,djant] der <-en, -en> ♀**Schmierenkomödiantin** ['ʃmi:rənkomø,djantn̩] die <-, -nen> (pej) ◊ *Was für ein grauenvoller Schmierenkomödiant!*

hammer¹ [noun] **1.** (tool, used in sports, part of a piano) Hammer ['hamɐ] der <-s, Hämmer> ◊ *mit dem Hammer Nägel in die Wand schlagen* ♦ *den Hammer werfen;* (sports event) the hammer das **Hammerwerfen** [das 'hamevɐfn̩] <-s> *no pl* ◊ *Weltmeister im Hammerwerfen* **2.** (part of a gun) Hahn [haːn] der <-(e)s, Hähne> ◊ *Er spannte den Hahn und drückte ab.* ⊚ come under the hammer unter den Hammer kommen

hammer² [verb] **1.** (hit or beat hard) hämmern ['hɛmɐn] +*haben* ◊ *Wir hörten sie im Keller hämmern.* ♦ *Er hämmerte mit den Fäusten an die Tür.* ♦ *Mein Herz hämmerte bis zum Hals.* hammer a nail into a wall einen Nagel in die Wand schlagen [aenən 'naːgl̩ ɪn diː ,vant ʃlaːgn̩] <schlägt, schlug, hat geschlagen> **2.** (defeat) vernichtend schlagen [fɛɐ,nɪçtn̩t 'ʃlaːgn̩] <schlägt, schlug, hat geschlagen> **3.** (criticize) scharf kritisieren [ʃaɐf kriti'zi:rən] <kritisiert, kritisierte, hat kritisiert> **4.** (rain) hammer down herunterprasseln [hɛ'rʊntɐprasl̩n] <prasselt herunter, prasselte herunter, ist heruntergeprasselt> ● hammer out [phras v] aushandeln ['aoshandl̩n] ◊ *Sie handelten einen Kompromiss aus.*

hand¹ [noun] **1.** ANAT Hand [hant] die <-, Hände> ◊ *Was hast du denn da in der Hand?* ♦ *Der Junge nahm mich bei der Hand und führte mich hinaus.* by hand von Hand ◊ *von Hand gefertigt* ♦ *ein Tier von Hand aufziehen* shake hands sich [dat] die

Hände schütteln 2. *(worker)* Arbeiter ['aˈbae̯tɐ] der
<–s, –> ♀Arbeiterin ['aˈbae̯tərɪn] die <–, –nen> ◊
*Die Landwirtschaft braucht in der Hauptsaison
Arbeiter.; (on a ship)* Besatzungsmitglied
[bəˈzaʦʊŋsmɪtˌɡliːt] das <–(e)s, –er> ◊ *neue Besat-
zungsmitglieder anheuern* All hands on deck! *Alle
Mann an Deck!* 3. *(help, assistance)* give sb a hand
jdm helfen [ˈhɛlfn̩] <hilft, half, hat geholfen> need a
hand with sth bei etw. Hilfe brauchen
[bae̯ … ˈhɪlfə brao̯xn̩] +haben 4. *(applause)* Applaus
[apˈlao̯s] der <–es, –e> *most sing* 5. *(set of cards)*
Blatt [blat] das <–(e)s, Blätter *or* –> ◊ *Ich hatte ein
gutes Blatt.* 6. *(of a clock)* Zeiger [ˈʦae̯ɡɐ] der
<–s, –> ◊ *Wenn der große Zeiger auf der Zwölf und
der kleine auf der Sechs steht, ist es sechs Uhr.*
7. *(esp lit) (handwriting)* Handschrift [ˈhantʃrɪft] die
<–, –en> ◊ *eine saubere/leserliche Handschrift
haben*

⊙ **on the one hand …, on the other hand …** einerseits …, andererseits … ◊ *Einerseits hätte sie sehr
gern ein Haustier, andererseits fehlt ihr aber das
Geld dafür.* **fall into sb's hands** jdm in die Hände
fallen **get out of hand** außer Kontrolle geraten **go
hand in hand** Hand in Hand gehen **join hands**
einander die Hände reichen **show your hand** sich
⟨dat⟩ in die Karten sehen lassen **sb's hands are tied**
jdm sind die Hände gebunden **hands off (sth)**
Hände weg (von etw.) ◊ *Hände weg von meinem
Wagen!* **hands up** Hände hoch

hand² ⟨verb⟩ hand sb sth, hand sth to sb jdm etw.
reichen [ˈrae̯çn̩] +haben ◊ *Er reichte ihr einen ver-
schlossenen Umschlag.*

⊙ **you have to hand it to him/her** etc. das muss
man ihm/ihr etc. lassen
• **hand back** ⟨phras v⟩ hand sb sth back, hand sth
back to sb jdm etw. zurückgeben [ʦuˈrʏkɡeːbm̩]
<gibt zurück, gab zurück, hat zurückgegeben> ◊ *Die
Kassiererin gab ihm seine Kreditkarte zurück.*
• **hand down** ⟨phras v⟩ 1. *(traditions, clothes)* weitergeben [ˈvae̯tɐɡeːbm̩] <gibt weiter, gab weiter, hat wei-
tergegeben> ◊ *Bräuche von Generation zu Generation weitergeben* ♦ *Kleidung an jüngere Geschwister
weitergeben* 2. *(a sentence, judgement)* fällen [ˈfɛlən]
+haben ◊ *Welches Urteil hat der Richter gefällt?*
• **hand in** ⟨phras v⟩ abgeben [ˈapɡeːbm̩] <gibt ab, gab
ab, hat abgegeben> ◊ *die Schlüssel an der Rezeption
abgeben* ♦ *Wann gibst du die Diplomarbeit ab?*
• **hand on** ⟨phras v⟩ hand sth on to sb etw. an jdn
weitergeben [an … ˌvae̯tɐɡeːbm̩] <gibt weiter, gab
weiter, hat weitergegeben> ◊ *eine Beschwerde an den
zuständigen Mitarbeiter weitergeben* ♦ *seinen Besitz
an seine Kinder weitergeben*
• **hand out** ⟨phras v⟩ hand sth out (to sb) etw. (an
jdn) verteilen [fɛˈtae̯lən] <verteilt, verteile, hat
verteilt> ◊ *Der Lehrer verteilt die Klassenarbeit an
die Schüler.*
• **hand over** ⟨phras v⟩ hand (sth/sb) over (to sb)
(jdm) (etw./jdn) übergeben [ybɐˈɡeːbm̩] <übergibt,
übergab, hat übergeben> ◊ *Sie hat das Geschenk persönlich übergeben.* ♦ *den Täter der Polizei übergeben*
♦ *Ich übergebe nun an meinen Kollegen, Stefan
Kraus.*

handbag ⟨noun⟩ Handtasche [ˈhantˌtaʃə] die <–, –n>
handcuff ⟨noun⟩ Handschelle [ˈhantˌʃɛlə] die <–, –n>
most pl ◊ *Der Angeklagte wurde in Handschellen vorgeführt.*

handful ⟨noun⟩ a handful of sth eine Hand voll …
⟨nom⟩ [ˈænə ˈhant fɔl] ◊ *nur eine Hand voll Reis zu
essen haben* ♦ *eine Hand voll Leute*

⊙ **sb is a (real) handful** jd kann einen ganz schön
auf Trab halten
handicap¹ ⟨noun⟩ 1. *(disability)* Behinderung
[bəˈhɪndərʊŋ] die <–, –en> ◊ *Menschen mit
geistiger/körperlicher Behinderung* 2. *(disadvantage)*
Nachteil [ˈnaːxtae̯l] der <–(e)s, –e> ◊ *Seine
fehlenden Sprachkenntnisse sind für ihn ein großer
Nachteil.* 3. GOLF Vorgabe [ˈfoːɐ̯ɡaːbə] die <–, –n> ◊
Trotz der Vorgabe konnte er sie nicht schlagen.
handicap² ⟨verb⟩ beeinträchtigen [bəˈʔae̯ntrɛçtɪɡn̩]
<beeinträchtigt, beeinträchtigte, hat beeinträchtigt> ◊
*Ihre Nachtblindheit beeinträchtigt sie beim Autofah-
ren.*

handkerchief ⟨noun⟩ Taschentuch [ˈtaʃn̩tuːx] das
<–(e)s, Taschentücher>
handle¹ ⟨noun⟩ 1. *(of a cup, basket, bucket)* Henkel
[ˈhɛŋkl̩] der <–s, –> ◊ *einen Eimer am Henkel
tragen; (of a knife, window, drawer)* Griff [ɡrɪf] der
<–(e)s, –e>; *(of a saucepan, broom)* Stiel [ʃtiːl] der
<–(e)s, –e> ◊ *ein Besen mit einem langen Stiel; (of
a door)* Klinke [ˈklɪŋkə] die <–, –n> ◊ *Er drückte vorsichtig die Klinke herunter und öffnete die Tür.*
2. *(fam) (sb's name)* Name [ˈnaːmə] der <–ns, –n> ◊
*Er ist als Amateurfunker unter dem Namen „Nachtvo-
gel" bekannt.*
handle² ⟨verb⟩ 1. *(deal with)* umgehen mit
[ˈʊmɡeːən mɪt] <geht um, ging um, ist umgegangen> ◊
*Sie weiß, wie man mit schwierigen Kunden/
Problemen umgeht.* ♦ *Kannst du mit einer Kettensäge
umgehen?; (a case, complaint, area of responsibility)*
bearbeiten [bəˈʔaɐ̯bae̯tn̩] <bearbeitet, bearbeitete, hat
bearbeitet> ◊ *Briefe/Kundenanfragen/Beschwerden
bearbeiten; (material, information)* verarbeiten
[fɛˈʔaɐ̯bae̯tn̩] <verarbeitet, verarbeitete, hat verarbeitet>
◊ *Dieser Rechner kann ungeheure Datenmengen verarbeiten.; (people, goods in an airport etc.)* abferti-
gen [ˈapfɛɐ̯tɪɡn̩] +haben ◊ *Im neuen Terminal werden
täglich Tausende von Fluggästen abgefertigt.;
(difficult people or things)* fertig werden mit
[ˈfɛɐ̯tɪç veːɐ̯dn̩ mɪt] +sein ◊ *Sie wird mit den Kindern
nicht mehr fertig.* 2. *(touch, treat)* behandeln
[bəˈhandl̩n] <behandelt, behandelte, hat behandelt> ◊
Diese Maschine muss sorgfältig behandelt werden. ♦
Häftlinge unsanft behandeln Handle with care!
Vorsicht — zerbrechlich! 3. *(control with your
hands)* lenken [ˈlɛŋkn̩] +haben ◊ *Er lenkte das Boot
sehr geschickt.* sth handles well/badly etw. lässt sich
gut/schlecht lenken [lɛst … ˈɡuːt/ˈʃlɛçt ˌlɛŋkn̩] <lässt
sich, ließ sich, hat sich … lassen> ◊ *Der Wagen lässt
sich sehr schlecht lenken.* 4. *(buy and sell)* handeln
mit [ˈhandl̩n mɪt] +haben ◊ *Er handelt mit gestohlener Ware.*

handlebars ⟨noun⟩ Lenker [ˈlɛŋkɐ] der <–s, –>
handling ⟨noun⟩ 1. *(of a person, food, drugs)*
handling of sth Umgang mit etw. [ˈʊmɡaŋ mɪt] der
<–(e)s, Umgänge> *most sing* ◊ *der richtige Umgang
mit Lebensmitteln/Medikamenten* ♦ *Er ist erfahren
im Umgang mit Kindern.; (of an animal, a particular
matter)* Behandlung [bəˈhandlʊŋ] die <–, –en> ◊ *Die
Behandlung dieser Angelegenheit erfordert Fingerspit-
zengefühl.* sb's handling of a problem die Art und
Weise, wie jd mit einem Problem umgeht
[di: ˌaːɐ̯t ʊnt ˈvae̯zə vi: … mɪt ae̯nəm proˌbleːm ˈʊmɡeːt]

<geht um, ging um, ist umgegangen> 2. *(of a machine, vehicle, tool)* Handhabung ['hantha:bʊŋ] die <–, –en> ◊ *Die Handhabung der Maschine ist denkbar einfach.* 3. *(of data, information)* Verarbeitung [fɛl'aꞋbaɛtʊŋ] die <–, –en> ◊ *Bei der Verarbeitung der Daten ist ein Fehler aufgetreten.*

hand luggage [noun] Handgepäck ['hantgəpɛk] das <–(e)s> no pl ◊ *Kann ich diese Tasche als Handgepäck mitnehmen?*

handmade [adj] handgearbeitet ['hantgəlaꞋbaɛtət] no comp/superl ◊ *Diese Spitzendeckchen sind handgearbeitet.* ♦ *ein handgearbeiteter Teppich aus Persien*

handshake [noun] Händedruck ['hɛndədrʊk] der <–(e)s> no pl ◊ *Er verabschiedete ihn mit einem Händedruck.*

handsome [adj] 1. *(man)* gut aussehend ['guːt aɔszeːənt] <besser aussehend, am besten aussehend> ◊ *ein gut aussehender junger Mann;* *(woman, building, object)* schön [ʃøːn] ◊ *Sie ist jung, schön und erfolgreich.* ♦ *Was für eine schöne, gepflegte Villa!* 2. *(profit, sum)* beträchtlich [bə'trɛçtlɪç] ◊ *Die Summe war beträchtlich.* ♦ *beträchtliche Gewinne machen; (price)* stolz [ʃtɔlts] <stolzer, am stolzesten>; *(gift, donation)* großzügig ['groːstsyːgɪç] ◊ *eine großzügige Spende* ♦ *Das Geschenk war wirklich großzügig.*

handsomely [adv] 1. *(attractively)* elegant [elə'gant] <eleganter, am elegantesten> ◊ *Sie war sehr elegant angezogen.* 2. *(generously)* großzügig ['groːstsyːgɪç] ◊ *Er hat großzügig gespendet.* be handsomely rewarded for sth für etw. reichlich belohnt werden [fyːɐ̯ ... ˌraɛçlɪç bə'loːnt veːɐ̯dn̩] <wird, wurde, ist worden>

handwriting [noun] Handschrift ['hantʃrɪft] die <–, –en> ◊ *eine schöne Handschrift haben* ♦ *Ist das nicht Karins Handschrift?*

handy [adj] 1. *(convenient)* praktisch ['praktɪʃ] ◊ *Dieser Camcorder ist klein und praktisch.* ♦ *praktische Tipps für Heimwerker* 2. *(close at hand)* keep sth handy etw. griffbereit haben ['grɪfbəraɛt haːbm̩] +haben ◊ *Asthmakranke sollten ihre Medikamente stets griffbereit haben.* Our house is handy for the shops. Wir haben es nicht weit zum Einkaufen. 3. *(skilful)* be handy with sth gut mit etw. umgehen können [ˌguːt mɪt ... ˌʊmgeːən kœnən] <kann, konnte, hat können> ◊ *Er kann geschickt mit dem Pinsel umgehen.* be handy at doing sth Geschick für etw. haben [gə'ʃɪk fyːɐ̯ ... haːbm̩] +haben ◊ *Sie hat Geschick fürs Basteln.*

ⓢ sth comes in handy The money comes in handy for my holidays. Das Geld kann ich für meinen Urlaub gut gebrauchen. My language skills came in handy when I applied for a post. Meine Sprachkenntnisse kamen mir zugute, als ich mich um eine Stelle bewarb. This feature comes in handy when you want to retrieve deleted files. Diese Funktion ist praktisch, wenn man gelöschte Dateien wiederherstellen möchte.

hang¹

ⓔ get/have the hang of sth den richtigen Dreh bei etw. herausbekommen/heraushaben

hang² [verb] 1. *(suspend)* hang sth somewhere etw. irgendwohin hängen ['hɛŋən] +haben ◊ *einen Mantel an den Haken hängen* ♦ *Er hängte seine Jacke über den Stuhl.* sth hangs somewhere etw. hängt irgendwo ['hɛŋt] <hängt, hing, hat gehangen> ◊ *Die*

Lampe hängt an der Decke. ♦ *Die Haare hingen ihm wirr ins Gesicht.; (clothes)* fallen ['falən] <fällt, fiel, ist gefallen> ◊ *Dieses Kleid fällt schön.* 2. *(fix onto a wall)* aufhängen ['aɔfhɛŋən] +haben ◊ *Hängst du bitte den Spiegel im Bad auf?; (be fixed onto a wall)* sth hangs somewhere etw. hängt irgendwo ['hɛŋt] <hängt, hing, hat gehangen> ◊ *Ein Porträt seines Großvaters hängt an der Wand.* 3. *(kill)* aufhängen ['aɔfhɛŋən] +haben ◊ *Sie hängten ihn an einem Baum auf.* hang yourself sich aufhängen sb hangs jd hängt ['hɛŋt] <hing, hat gehangen> ◊ *Wenn sie ihn schuldig sprechen, wird er hängen.* 4. *(a door)* einhängen ['aɛnhɛŋən] +haben ◊ *Sie hängte eine neue Tür ein.* 5. *(smoke, smell)* hängen ['hɛŋən] <hängt, hing, hat gehangen> ◊ *Ein Geruch nach Orangen hing in der Luft.; (fog)* liegen ['liːgn̩] <liegt, lag, hat gelegen> ◊ *Nebel lag über den Wäldern.; (moon)* stehen ['ʃteːən] <steht, stand, hat gestanden> ◊ *Der Mond stand hoch am Himmel.* 6. *(fam) (spend time somewhere)* hang (with sb) (mit jdm) herumhängen [hɛ'rʊmhɛŋən] <hängt herum, hing herum, hat herumgehangen> *(fam)* ◊ *Abends hängt er meist mit seinen Freunden in Kneipen herum.*

ⓐ hang sth pfeif auf etw. [acc] *Pfeif doch auf den Abwasch und komm mit!*

• **hang around** [phras v] 1. *(spend time)* herumhängen [hɛ'rʊmhɛŋən] <hängt herum, hing herum, hat herumgehangen> *(fam)* ◊ *mit Freunden im Schwimmbad herumhängen* 2. *(wait)* warten ['vaꞋtn̩] <wartet, wartete, hat gewartet> ◊ *Du kannst ihn doch nicht so lange warten lassen.*

• **hang on** [phras v] 1. *(hold)* hang on to sth sich an etw. [dat] festhalten [an ... ˌfɛsthaltn̩] <hält sich fest, hielt sich fest, hat sich festgehalten> ◊ *Er hielt sich am Geländer fest.* 2. *(hold out, endure)* durchhalten ['dʊꞋçhaltn̩] <hält durch, hielt durch, hat durchgehalten> ◊ *Halten Sie durch! Ich hole Hilfe.* 3. *(fam) (wait)* warten ['vaꞋtn̩] <wartet, wartete, hat gewartet> ◊ *Warte mal eine Minute; ich sehe nach.* 4. *(depend on sth)* hang on sth von etw. abhängen [fɔn ... ˌaphɛŋən] <hängt ab, hing ab, hat abgehangen> ◊ *Alles hängt jetzt vom Ergebnis des letzten Spiels ab.*

• **hang out** [phras v] 1. *(fam) (spend time somewhere)* zu finden sein [tsuː 'fɪndn̩ zaɛn] +sein ◊ *Sie weiß, wo ihre Freunde am Abend meist zu finden sind.* 2. *(the washing)* raushängen ['raɔshɛŋən] +haben ◊ *Ich habe die Wäsche rausgehängt, damit sie schneller trocknet.* 3. hang out of the window sich aus dem Fenster lehnen [aɔs deːm 'fɛnstɐ leːnən] +haben

• **hang over** [phras v] hang over sb/sth drohend über jdm/etw. hängen [ˌdroːənt yːbɐ ... 'hɛŋən] <hängt, hing, hat gehangen> ◊ *Ein Gefühl der Bedrohung hing über der Stadt.*

• **hang up** [phras v] 1. *(a receiver, coat etc.)* aufhängen ['aɔfhɛŋən] +haben ◊ *Als sie seine Stimme hörte, hängte sie (den Hörer) sofort auf.* ♦ *seine Jacke an der Garderobe aufhängen* She hung up on me. Sie hat einfach aufgehängt. 2. *(fam) (stop using sth)* hang sth up etw. an den Nagel hängen [an deːn 'naːgl̩ hɛŋən] +haben ◊ *Er beschloss, die Wanderstiefel an den Nagel zu hängen und künftig öfter zu Hause zu bleiben.*

hanger [noun] Kleiderbügel ['klaɛdebyːgl̩] der <–s, –>

hangover [noun] 1. *(from drinking alcohol)* Kater

['kaːtɐ] der <–s, –> *(fam)* **2.** *(sth left over)* Überbleibsel ['yːbɐblaepsl̩] das <–s, –> ◊ *Dieser Aberglaube ist ein Überbleibsel aus dem Mittelalter.*

hanky [noun] Taschentuch ['taʃn̩tuːx] das <–(e)s, Taschentücher>

happen [verb] **1.** *(take place)* passieren [pa'siːrən] <passiert, passierte, ist passiert> ◊ *Wann ist der Unfall passiert?* ✦ *Ich halte zu dir, was auch immer passiert.* sth happens to sb etw. passiert jdm ◊ *Hoffentlich ist ihm nichts passiert!* ✦ *Das ist das Beste, was mir je passiert ist.* **2.** happen to know/need/do etc. sth etw. zufällig kennen/brauchen/tun etc. [ˌtsuːfɛlɪç 'kɛnən/'braoxn̩/'tuːn] ◊ *Ich kam zufällig vorbei, als der Unfall geschah.* ✦ *Zufällig brauche ich auch ein wenig Schlaf. Also sei bitte etwas leiser!* How do you happen to know? Woher weißt du das?
✪ as it happens zufälligerweise

happily [adv] **1.** *(fortunately)* glücklicherweise ['ɡlʏklɪçɐ'vaezə] ◊ *Glücklicherweise ist nichts passiert.* **2.** *(full of joy)* glücklich ['ɡlʏklɪç] ◊ *Glücklich lächelnd schauten sie ihr Baby an.* ✦ *glücklich verheiratet sein* **3.** *(willingly)* gern [ɡɛʳn] <lieber, am liebsten> ◊ *Ich kann das gern für dich erledigen.*
✪ they lived happily ever after und wenn sie nicht gestorben sind, dann leben sie noch heute

happiness [noun] Glück [ɡlʏk] das <–(e)s> no pl ◊ *Sie weinte vor Glück.* ✦ *Mit ihr hat er endlich sein Glück gefunden.*

happy [adj] *(contented, full of joy)* glücklich ['ɡlʏklɪç] ◊ *Sie führen eine glückliche Ehe.* ✦ *Wir sind sehr glücklich miteinander.* ✦ *Geld allein macht nicht glücklich.* ✦ *Ich bin über diese Entwicklung nicht sehr glücklich.* ✦ *Sie feierten die glückliche Geburt eines Sohnes.; (cheerful also)* fröhlich ['frøːlɪç] ◊ *Nach der guten Nachricht waren alle fröhlich.* be happy for sb sich für jdn freuen [fyːɡ ... 'frɔøən] +haben be happy to do sth sich freuen, etw. tun zu können ◊ *Ich freue mich, helfen zu können.*

harass [verb] **1.** *(bother, upset)* schikanieren [ʃika'niːrən] <schikaniert, schikanierte, hat schikaniert> ◊ *Die Gefangenen wurden von den Aufsehern schikaniert.; (sexually, with complaints)* belästigen [bə'lɛstɪɡn̩] <belästigt, belästigte, hat belästigt> ◊ *Sie wurde an ihrem Arbeitsplatz sexuell belästigt.* **2.** MIL *(enemy)* harass sb/sth Anschläge verüben auf jdn/etw. ['anʃlɛːɡə fɛˌɡyːbm̩ aof] <verübt, verübte, hat verübt> ◊ *Terroristen verübten Anschläge auf Hotels.*

harbour, harbor [noun] Hafen ['haːfn̩] der <–s, Häfen>

hard¹ [adj] **1.** *(not soft, with a lot of minerals)* hart [haʳt] <härter, am härtesten> ◊ *Kristallglas ist besonders hart.* ✦ *harte Muskeln* ✦ *hartes Wasser; (book cover, knot)* fest [fɛst] <fester, am festesten> ◊ *ein Buch mit festem Einband* ✦ *eine feste Schleife binden* **2.** *(unpleasant, difficult)* schwer [ʃveːɡ] ◊ *Sie hat ein schweres Leben.* ✦ *Seine Arbeit ist sehr schwer.* hard to believe schwer zu glauben hard to imagine schwer vorstellbar It is hard for me to believe/imagine this. Es fällt mir schwer, das zu glauben/mir das vorzustellen. give sb a hard time jdm das Leben schwer machen; *(situation, problem)* schwierig ['ʃviːrɪç] ◊ *Ich befinde mich in einer schwierigen Situation.* **3.** *(cruel, severe)* hart [haʳt] <härter, am härtesten> ◊ *Der letzte Winter war sehr*

hart. **4.** *(full of force etc.)* heftig ['hɛftɪç] ◊ *Sie versetzte mir einen heftigen Stoß/Schlag.; (rain, frost, drinker)* stark [ʃtaʳk] <stärker, am stärksten> A hard rain fell last night. In der Nacht regnete es stark. **5.** *(penis)* steif [ʃtaef] *(fam)* ◊ *Sein Glied wollte nicht steif werden.*
✪ hard on sb **1.** *(person)* hart zu jdm ◊ *Sei nicht so hart zu ihr, das hat sie nicht verdient.* **2.** *(situation)* hart für jdn ◊ *Es ist hart für ihn, dass er keine Arbeit hat.* hard on sth/sb *(harmful)* schlecht für jdn/etw. ◊ *Rauchen ist schlecht für die Gesundheit.*

hard² [adv] **1.** *(with great effort and discipline, with great force)* hart [haʳt] <härter, am härtesten> ◊ *Ich arbeite hart für mein Geld.* ✦ *hart trainieren/zuschlagen* hit sb hard jdm einen harten Schlag versetzen **2.** *(rain, snow)* stark [ʃtaʳk] <stärker, am stärksten> ◊ *Es regnete so stark, dass man kaum etwas sah.* drink hard ein starker Trinker sein; *(press, push etc.)* fest [fɛst] <fester, am festesten> ◊ *fest aufs Gaspedal treten* **3.** *(with a lot of concentration)* genau [ɡə'nao] <genauer, am genau(e)sten> ◊ *genau hinsehen/nachdenken*
✪ be hard done by ungerecht behandelt werden feel hard done by sich ungerecht behandelt fühlen be hard pressed/pushed to do sth große Mühe haben, etw. zu tun take sth hard etw. schwer nehmen try hard sich große Mühe geben

hard disk [noun] Festplatte ['fɛstplatə] die <–, –n>

harden [verb] **1.** *(also fig) (become hard or firm)* hart werden ['haʳt veːɡdn̩] +sein ◊ *Der Boden trocknete aus und wurde hart.* ✦ *Durch diese Enttäuschung ist er hart geworden.; (glue)* trocknen ['trɔknən] +sein ◊ *warten, bis der Klebstoff/Kleister getrocknet ist; (cement)* binden ['bɪndn̩] <bindet, band, hat gebunden> **2.** *(sb's attitude)* sich verhärten [fɛ'hɛʳtn̩] <verhärtet, verhärtete, hat verhärtet> ◊ *Seine Position verhärtete sich zunehmend.* The government hardened its attitude to terrorists. Die Haltung der Regierung zu Terroristen verhärtete sich. **3.** *(make firm or hard)* hart werden lassen ['haʳt veːɡdn̩ lasn̩] <lässt, ließ, hat lassen> ◊ *Das Alter lässt das Material hart und spröde werden.; (steel)* härten ['hɛʳtn̩] <härtet, härtete, hat gehärtet> ◊ *Stahl wird durch Wärmebehandlung gehärtet.* **4.** *(make or become insensible)* abstumpfen ['apʃtʊmpfn̩] transitive use +haben/ intransitive use +sein ◊ *Die gewalttätigen Computerspiele haben ihn abgestumpft.* ✦ *Sie stumpfte durch die schlimmen Erlebnisse ab.*

hardly [adv] kaum [kaom] no comp/superl ◊ *Mehr Gewinn ist kaum noch möglich.* ✦ *Sie kann es kaum erwarten, in Urlaub zu fahren.* ✦ *Kaum jemand interessiert sich dafür.* hardly any kaum ◊ *Damals gab es kaum Frauen in der Politik.*

hard of hearing [adj] schwerhörig ['ʃveːɡhøːrɪç] ◊ *Ich bin schwerhörig.* ✦ *ein schwerhöriger alter Mann*

hardship [noun] Not [noːt] die <–, Nöte> most sing ◊ *Sie litten finanzielle Not.*
✪ be no hardship nicht schwer sein

hard shoulder [noun] Seitenstreifen ['zaetn̩ʃtraefn̩] der <–s, –> ◊ *auf dem Seitenstreifen halten*

hardware [noun] **1.** *(computer)* Hardware ['haːʳtveːɡ] die <–, –s> most sing **2.** *(military)* Ausrüstung ['aosrʏstʊŋ] die <–, –en> **3.** *(kitchen)* Küchengerät ['kʏçŋɡərɛːt] das <–(e)s, –e> ◊ *Er hat viele Küchengeräte.; (garden)* Gartengerät ['ɡaʳtn̩ɡərɛːt] das <–(e)s, –e>

hard-wearing [adj] strapazierfähig [ʃtrapa'tsiːɐ̯fɛːɪç] ◊ *strapazierfähige Kleidung*

hard-working [adj] fleißig ['flaɛ̯sɪç] ◊ *Er bedankte sich bei den fleißigen Helfern.*

hardy [adj] 1. *(person, with a lot of stamina)* zäh [tsɛː] <zäher, am zäh(e)sten> ◊ *Esel sind zähe Tiere.* ♦ *Marathonläufer müssen zäh sein.; (able to stand cold/pain etc.)* abgehärtet ['apɡəhɛ'tət] ◊ *Nur abgehärtete Schwimmer baden in diesem Bergsee.* 2. *(plant)* winterhart ['vɪntɐhaʁt] *no comp/superl* ◊ *Efeu ist winterhart.*

hare [noun] Hase ['haːzə] der <-n, -n>

harm¹ [noun] Schaden ['ʃaːdn̩] der <-s, Schäden> do harm Schaden anrichten cause sb/sth harm jdm/einer Sache Schaden zufügen ⓟ out of harm's way in Sicherheit do sb harm/no harm 1. *(have a/no bad effect)* jdm schaden/nicht schaden ◊ *Ein bisschen mehr Fleiß würde dir auch nicht schaden.* 2. *(hurt/not hurt)* jdm etwas/nichts tun ◊ *Keine Angst, ich tu dir nichts.* there's no harm in doing sth es kann nicht schaden, etw. zu tun no harm done nichts passiert

harm² [verb] 1. *(damage, have a bad effect)* schaden ['ʃaːdn̩] <schadet, schadete, hat geschadet> ◊ *Sein Verhalten schadet seiner Karriere.* 2. *(injure)* verletzen [fɛ'lɛtsn̩] <verletzt, verletzte, hat verletzt> ◊ *Mehrere Kinder wurden verletzt.* I wouldn't harm a fly. Ich könnte keiner Fliege etwas zuleide tun. No animals were harmed in the making of this picture. Bei den Dreharbeiten zu diesem Film kamen keine Tiere zu Schaden.

harmful [adj] schädlich ['ʃɛːtlɪç] ◊ *schädlichen Einflüssen ausgesetzt sein* ♦ *Diese Substanzen sind schädlich.*

harmless [adj] harmlos ['haʁmloːs] <harmloser, am harmlosesten> ◊ *ein harmloses Insekt* ♦ *Der Ausschlag ist zwar lästig, aber harmlos.*

harmony [noun] 1. *(relationship between people)* Frieden ['friːdn̩] der <-s> *no pl* ◊ *Der häusliche Frieden war gestört.* ♦ *Es herrschte Frieden zwischen den Fraktionen.* in harmony with im Einklang mit [ɪm 'aɛ̯nklaŋ mɪt] ◊ *Wir leben im Einklang mit der Natur.* 2. *(of music, emotions, decorations)* Harmonie [haʁmo'niː] die <-, -n> ◊ *Sie bewegen sich in perfekter Harmonie zur Musik.; (study of music)* Harmonielehre [haʁmo'niːleːrə] die <-> *no pl*

harsh(ly) [adj, adv] 1. *(manner, custom, tone, climate)* rau [ʁaɔ̯] <rauer, am rauesten> ◊ *raue Sitten* ♦ *Sie sind rau mit ihm umgegangen.* ♦ *Dort herrscht ein raues Klima.* 2. *(punishment, living conditions, words, winter)* hart [haʁt] <härter, am härtesten> ◊ *jdn hart bestrafen* ♦ *ein harter Gegner* ♦ *Das Leben in Sibirien ist hart.; (frost)* streng [ʃtʁɛŋ] <strenger Frost 3. *(criticism)* scharf [ʃaʁf] <schärfer, am schärfsten> ◊ *jdn scharf kritisieren/zurechtweisen* ♦ *Er musste scharfe Kritik einstecken.*

harvest¹ [noun] Ernte ['ɛʁntə] die <-, -n> ◊ *Die Ernte ist dieses Jahr schlecht ausgefallen.*

harvest² [verb] 1. *(fruit, crop, potatoes)* ernten ['ɛʁntn̩] <erntet, erntete, hat geerntet> ◊ *Trauben werden im Herbst geerntet.; (pick wild fruit/herbs etc.)* sammeln ['zamln̩] +haben ◊ *Sie hat viele Kräuter gesammelt.* 2. *(timber)* schlagen ['ʃlaːɡn̩] <schlägt, schlug, hat geschlagen> ◊ *Holz schlagen* 3. *(flowers)* schneiden ['ʃnaɛ̯dn̩] <schneidet, schnitt, hat geschnitten>

hassle [noun] Ärger ['ɛʁɡɐ] der <-s> *no pl* ◊ *Ich habe*

schon wieder Ärger mit meinem Chef.

haste [noun] Eile ['aɛ̯lə] die <-> *no pl* ◊ *In großer Eile packte er seine Sachen.* In her haste she forgot her key. In der Eile vergass sie ihren Schlüssel. in haste übereilt [y:bə'aɛ̯lt] ◊ *Diese Entscheidung solltest du nicht übereilt treffen.*

hasty(-ily) [adj, adv] hastig ['hastɪç] ◊ *hastige Bewegungen* ♦ *Sie packte hastig ihren Koffer.* ♦ *ein hastig ausgefüllter Antrag*

hat [noun] 1. *(for wearing on your head, with rim)* Hut [huːt] der <-(e)s, Hüte> ◊ *einen Hut aufsetzen/tragen* ♦ *Nimm bitte den Hut ab.; (made of wool)* Mütze ['mʏtsə] die <-, -n>; *(with peak, for riding)* Kappe ['kapə] die <-, -n> 2. *(fig) (function, role)* Rolle ['ʁɔlə] die <-, -n> When you are starting a business, you are wearing several hats. Wenn Sie ein Unternehmen gründen, übernehmen Sie mehrere Rollen auf einmal. Would you mind me putting my counselling hat on when I answer? Würde es Ihnen etwas ausmachen, wenn ich in meiner Rolle als Berater antworte? ⓟ be old that ausgedient haben keep sth under your hat etw. geheim halten hats off to sb Hut ab ◊ *Hut ab! Das hast du wirklich gut gemacht.*

hate¹ [noun] Hass [has] der <-es> *no pl* ◊ *Sie sah ihn voller Hass an.*

hate² [verb] hassen ['hasn̩] +haben ◊ *Die beiden hassen einander.* ♦ *Sie hasst Knoblauch wie die Pest.* ♦ *Er hasst es, zu spät zu kommen.* hate sb/sth doing sth es gar nicht mögen, wenn jd/etw. etw. tut [ɛs 'gaːr nɪçt møːɡn̩ vɛn] <mag, mochte, hat gemocht> ◊ *Ich mag es gar nicht, wenn du nach 22 Uhr anrufst.*

hatred [noun] Hass [has] der <-es> *no pl* ◊ *Sie empfand ihm gegenüber nur Hass.*

haughty(-ily) [adj, adv] hochmütig ['hoːxmyːtɪç] ◊ *Er warf mir einen hochmütigen Blick zu.* ♦ *Sei doch nicht so hochmütig!* ♦ *Sie wies seine Hilfe hochmütig zurück.*

haul¹ [noun] 1. *(of criminals, fish)* Fang [faŋ] der <-(e)s, Fänge> ◊ *Den Drogenfahndern gelang ein großer Fang.; (of illegal/stolen objects)* Beute ['bɔɛ̯tə] die <-> *no pl* ◊ *Die Diebe mussten ihre Beute zurücklassen.* 2. *(sth you get as result)* Ausbeute ['aɔ̯sbɔɛ̯tə] die <-> *no pl* ◊ *eine magere/reiche Ausbeute*

haul² [verb] 1. *(pull)* ziehen ['tsiːən] <zieht, zog, hat gezogen> ◊ *Er zog den Eimer aus dem Brunnen.; (carry, move with effort)* schleppen ['ʃlɛpm̩] +haben ◊ *Ich schleppte meine Einkäufe nach Hause.* ♦ *Müde schleppte sie sich ins Bad.; (a net)* haul sth in etw. einholen ['aɛ̯nhoːln̩] +haben ◊ *Morgens holen die Fischer die Netze ein.* 2. *(a vehicle)* abschleppen ['apʃlɛpm̩] +haben ◊ *Wir schleppen das Auto bis zur nächsten Werkstatt ab.* 3. *(transport goods)* befördern [bə'fœʁdɐn] <befördert, beförderte, hat befördert> ◊ *Die Waren wurden mit der Bahn befördert.* 4. *(before a court)* haul sb before sth jdn vor etw. [acc] zerren [foːɡ ... tsɛʁən] +haben *(fam)* ◊ *Sie wurde vor Gericht gezerrt.*

• **haul in** [phras v] *(money)* einbringen ['aɛ̯nbʁɪŋən] <bringt ein, brachte ein, hat eingebracht> ◊ *Der neue Verkäufer brachte viel Geld ein.*

• **haul off** [phras v] verfrachten [fɛ'fʁaxtn̩] <verfrachtet, verfrachtete, hat verfrachtet> ◊ *die Kinder ins Bett verfrachten* ♦ *jdn ins Gefängnis verfrachten*

• **haul up** [phras v] → **haul²** 3.

haunt [verb] 1. *(ghosts)* haunt sb jdn heimsuchen ['haɛmzuːxn̩] +haben sth is haunted in etw. [dat] spukt es [ɪn ... 'ʃpuːkt ɛs] +haben ◊ *In dem Haus spukte es.* 2. *(images, fear)* verfolgen [fɛ'fɔlgn̩] <verfolgt, verfolgte, hat verfolgt> ◊ *Die Bilder verfolgten sie lange Zeit.*

have [verb] 1. *(auxilliary verb: with the majority of German verbs)* haben ['haːbm̩] <hat, hatte, hat gehabt> +past p ◊ *Du hattest geschlafen.* ♦ *Wir hätten uns gern noch ein bisschen ausgeruht.* haven't nicht haben ◊ *Sie hat den Film noch nicht gesehen.; (with some German verbs)* sein [zaɛn] <ist, war, ist gewesen> ◊ *Ich bin noch nie richtig krank gewesen.* ♦ *Die Pakete sind heute angekommen.* ♦ *Er war zum Bäcker gegangen.* ♦ *Wir wären heute gern früher gegangen.* haven't nicht sein ◊ *Er ist noch nicht gekommen.* 2. *(used for describing sb or sth, stating a relationship, possess, feel, suffer from sth, experience, contain or include, learn sth, be able to do sth, think of sth, result in or cause sth)* haben ['haːbm̩] <hat, hatte, hat gehabt> *no passive* ◊ *lange Beine/viel Verstand haben* ♦ *Sie haben zwei Kinder/gerade Besuch.* ♦ *ein eigenes Haus haben* ♦ *Zeit für jdn/etw. haben* ♦ *viel Verständnis für etw. haben* ♦ *Kopfweh haben* ♦ *ein aufregendes Erlebnis haben* ♦ *einen langen Arbeitstag vor sich haben* ♦ *Die Wohnung hat 100 Quadratmeter.* ♦ *die Erlaubnis/Macht/Gelegenheit haben, etw. zu tun* ♦ *eine Idee/einen Vorschlag haben* ♦ *schlimme Folgen haben* have sth on you etw. bei sich haben ◊ *Ich habe kein Geld bei mir.* not have sth keinen/keine/kein ... haben [kaɛnən/kaɛnə/kaɛn ... haːbm̩] ◊ *Er hat keinen Unfall gehabt.* ♦ *keine Geduld mit jdm haben* have a shower duschen ['duːʃn̩] +haben ◊ *Ich dusche jeden Morgen.* have a bath baden ['baːdn̩] +haben 3. *(expressing that sth is being done to sb)* sb has sth done jdm wird etw. getan [vɪˈt] <wird, wurde, ist worden> He had his driving licence taken away. Ihm wurde der Führerschein weggenommen.; *(see to it that sth is done)* have sth done etw. tun lassen ['lasn̩] <lässt, ließ, hat lassen> He had his car washed. Er ließ sein Auto waschen. You should have your hair cut. Du solltest dir die Haare schneiden lassen.; *(get sb to do sth)* have sb do(ing) sth jdn etw. tun lassen ['lasn̩] The teacher had us translate the story. Der Lehrer ließ uns die Geschichte übersetzen.; *(cause sb to feel or do sth)* have sb doing sth jdn zu etw. bringen [tsuː ... brɪŋən] He had me laughing/thinking. Er brachte mich zum Lachen/Nachdenken. He had me in tears. Er brachte mich zum Weinen. She had me yelling at her. Sie brachte mich dazu, dass ich sie anschrie. have sb worried jdm Sorgen machen ['zɔʁɡn̩ maxn̩] +haben She had me ready to go there with her. Sie hatte mich schon so weit, dass ich mit ihr hingehen wollte. This prospect had me anxious to return home. Diese Aussicht erfüllte mich mit dem dringenden Wunsch, heimzufahren. 4. *(receive, give birth to)* bekommen [bəˈkɔmən] <bekommt, bekam, hat bekommen> ◊ *einen Anruf/Brief bekommen* ♦ *Wir bekamen viele Beschwerden.* ♦ *Mein Hund hat Junge bekommen.* She's having a baby. Sie bekommt ein Kind. 5. *(drink)* trinken ['trɪŋkn̩] <trinkt, trank, hat getrunken> ◊ *Welchen Cocktail trinkst du?; (eat)* essen ['ɛsn̩] <isst, aß, hat

gegessen> ◊ *Ich habe heute mittag eine Pizza gegessen.; (when choosing food)* nehmen ['neːmən] <nimmt, nahm, hat genommen> ◊ *Ich nehme eine Pizza.* ♦ *Warum nimmst du keine Sahne?* have breakfast frühstücken ['fryːʃtʏkn̩] +haben ◊ *Haben Sie schon gefrühstückt?* 6. *(modal: must)* have to do sth etw. tun müssen ['mʏsn̩] <muss, musste, hat müssen> ◊ *Sie musste dringend einkaufen gehen.* ♦ *Das Wetter muss ja auch einmal wieder besser werden!* ♦ *Du musst dir das unbedingt ansehen!* 7. *(a conversation, negotiations)* führen ['fyːʁən] +haben ◊ *ein Telefongespräch führen* 8. *(a party)* machen ['maxn̩] +haben ◊ *Er macht am Samstag eine Party.* 9. *(as a question tag)* haven't you/hasn't he etc.? oder? ['oːdɐ] ◊ *Das hast du doch schon erledigt, oder?* ♦ *Er ist doch gekommen, oder?*

• **have got in** [phras v] → **have in**

• **have in** [phras v] *(a doctor, plumber etc.)* have sb in jdn kommen lassen ['kɔmən lasn̩] <lässt, ließ, hat lassen> ◊ *Wir mussten einen Installateur kommen lassen.; (friends)* jdn zu Besuch haben [tsuː bəˈzuːx haːbm̩] +haben ◊ *Gestern hatten sie Freunde zu Besuch.*

☞ **have it in for sb** jdn auf dem Kieker haben *(fam)*

• **have off** [phras v] have it off (with sb) es (mit jdm) treiben [ɛs 'tʁaɛbm̩] <treibt, trieb, hat getrieben> *(fam)* ◊ *Er hat es mit ihr im Auto getrieben.*

• **have on** [phras v] 1. *(clothes, radio, TV)* have sth on etw. anhaben ['anhaːbm̩] <hat an, hatte an, hat angehabt> *(fam)* ◊ *Er hat einen schicken Anzug an.* ♦ *Sie hatten das Radio an.* 2. *(possess information)* have sth on sb etw. gegen jdn in der Hand haben [geːɡn̩ ... ɪn deːɐ̯ 'hant haːbm̩] +haben ◊ *Hat die Polizei etwas gegen ihn in der Hand?* 3. *(plans, projects)* have sth on etw. vorhaben ['foːɐ̯haːbm̩] <hat vor, hatte vor, hat vorgehabt> ◊ *Hast du morgen etwas vor?* 4. *(dupe, tease)* have sb on jdn auf den Arm nehmen [aɔf deːn 'aʁm neːmən] <nimmt, nahm, hat genommen> ◊ *Du willst mich wohl auf den Arm nehmen?*

• **have out** [phras v] have sth out sb has sth out jdm wird etw. entfernt [vɪˈt ... ɛntˌfɛʁnt] <wird, wurde, ist worden> ◊ *Sein Blinddarm wurde schon vor Jahren entfernt.* sb has a tooth out jdm wird ein Zahn gezogen [vɪˈt aɪn 'tsaːn gəˈtsoːɡn̩] ◊ *Ihr wurde ein Zahn gezogen.*

• **have over** [phras v] have sb over jdn zu Gast haben [tsuː 'gast haːbm̩] +haben ◊ *Gestern hatten wir ein paar Nachbarn zu Gast.*

• **have round** [phras v] → **have over**

hay [noun] Heu [hɔɡ] das <-(e)s> *no pl*

hay fever [noun] Heuschnupfen ['hɔɡʃnʊpfn̩] der <-s> *no pl* ◊ *Heuschnupfen haben*

hazard [noun] Gefahr [gəˈfaːɐ̯] die <-, -en> ◊ *Wie groß ist die Gefahr eines Erdbebens/, dass es ein Erdbeben gibt?* ♦ *die Gefahr für das Geflügel durch die Vogelgrippe* fire hazard Brandgefahr ['bʁantgəˌfaːɐ̯] health hazard Gesundheitsrisiko [gəˈzʊnthaɛtsˌʁiziko:] das <-s, Gesundheitsrisiken>

hazard light [noun] Warnblinklicht ['vaʁnblɪŋklɪçt] das <-(e)s, -er> *most sing* hazard lights Warnblinkanlage ['vaʁnblɪŋklanlaːɡə] die <-> *sing* ◊ *ein Pkw mit eingeschalteter Warnblinkanlage*

hazardous [adj] gefährlich [gəˈfɛːɐ̯lɪç] ◊ *gefährliche Substanzen* ♦ *Übergewicht ist gefährlich für die*

Gesundheit.
haze [noun] Dunst [dʊnst] der <-(e)s, Dünste> ◊ *Feiner Dunst lag über dem Fluss.* ♦ *In der Kneipe hing der Dunst von Zigaretten.* ⊙ in a haze of sth benebelt von etw.
hazelnut [noun] Haselnuss ['haːzl̩nʊs] die <-, Haselnüsse>
hazy [adj] **1.** (weather conditions) diesig ['diːzɪç] ◊ *ein diesiger Tag* ♦ *Es war den ganzen Nachmittag diesig.* **2.** (lacking clarity) unklar ['ʊnklaːʳ] ◊ *eine unklare Vorstellung von etw.* haben; (photo) unscharf ['ʊnʃaʳf] <unschärfer, am unschärfsten> ◊ *ein unscharfes Bild* ♦ *Das Foto ist unscharf.*; (memory) vage ['vaːgə] <vager, am vag(e)sten> be hazy about sth nur eine vage Vorstellung von etw. haben
he [pers pron] er [eːɐ̯] ◊ *Das ist mein Bruder; er heißt Hannes.* ♦ *Der Hund bellt. Sieh mal nach, was er hat.* → er
head¹ [noun] **1.** (body part, manager, top of a list, top of an object) Kopf [kɔpf] der <-(e)s, Köpfe> ◊ *meine Frage schüttelte er nur den Kopf.* ♦ *der Kopf eines Dokuments/einer Organisation/eines Nagels* hang your head den Kopf hängen lassen a/per head pro Kopf from head to toe von Kopf bis Fuß **2.** (leader: of a community, family) Oberhaupt ['oːbɐhaɔpt] das <-(e)s, Oberhäupter> ◊ *das Oberhaupt der Familie* ♦ *Der Papst ist das Oberhaupt der katholischen Kirche.*; (of a company, department) Chef [ʃɛf] der <-s, -s> ♀Chefin ['ʃɛfɪn] die <-, -nen> ◊ *Sie ist Uwes Chefin.* ♦ *Wir bekommen einen neuen Chef.* head of government Regierungschef [reˈgiːrʊŋsʃɛf] **3.** (leader in education : of a research institute, museum) Direktor [diˈrɛktoːɐ̯] der <-s, -en> ♀Direktorin [dirɛkˈtoːrɪn] die <-, -nen> ◊ *Er ist als Direktor eines Forschungsinstituts tätig.* ♦ *die neue Direktorin des Museums; (university)* Rektor ['rɛktoːɐ̯] der <-s, -en> ♀Rektorin [rɛkˈtoːrɪn] die <-, -nen> ◊ *die neue Rektorin der TU; (of a school)* Schulleiter ['ʃuːllaɪtɐ] der <-s, -> ♀Schulleiterin ['ʃuːllaɪtərɪn] die <-, -nen> **4.** (of a row, train etc.) Spitze ['ʃpɪtsə] die <-, -n> ◊ *der Wagen an der Spitze der Kolonne des Zuges* ♦ *sich an die Spitze stellen* **5.** (of beer) Blume ['bluːmə] die <-, -n> **6.** (of cattle) Stück [ʃtʏk] das <-(e)s, -> ◊ *50 Stück Vieh* ⊙ head over heels Hals über Kopf heads or tails Kopf oder Zahl enter your head jdm in den Sinn kommen get it into your head (that) es in den Schädel kriegen, dass (fam) get sb/sth out of your head sich [dat] jdn/etw. aus dem Kopf schlagen go to your head jdm zu Kopf steigen laugh your head off sich vor Lachen ausschütten (fam)
head² [verb] **1.** (in a direction, walk) head somewhere irgendwohin gehen ['geːən] <geht, ging, ist gegangen> ◊ *Wohin gehst du?* ♦ *nach Hause gehen* ♦ *Er geht zum Supermarkt.*; (drive) irgendwohin fahren ['faːrən] <fährt, fuhr, ist gefahren>; (move) sich auf jdn/etw. zubewegen [aɔf ... ˌtsuːbəveːgŋ̩] <bewegt sich zu, bewegte sich zu, hat sich zubewegt> ◊ *Der Demonstrationszug bewegte sich auf das Rathaus zu.* **2.** (a discussion, meeting etc.) leiten ['laɪtn̩] <leitet, leitete, hat geleitet> **3.** (a list, a procession etc.) anführen ['anfyːrən] +haben ◊ *die Liste der besten Restaurants anführen* ♦ *Die engsten Angehörigen führen den Trauerzug an.* **4.** (paper) be headed einen Titel tragen [aɛnən 'tiːtl̩ traːgŋ̩] <trägt, trug, hat

getragen> ◊ *eine Arbeit mit folgendem Titel: ...* **5.** (the ball) köpfen ['kœpfn̩] +haben ◊ *den Ball ins Tor köpfen*
• **head for** [phras v] steuern ['ʃtɔʏɐn] +sein ◊ *in eine Finanzkrise/in den Ruin steuern* ♦ *Die Firma steuert auf Erfolgskurs.* She is heading for a nervous breakdown. Sie steuert auf einen Nervenzusammenbruch zu.
• **head off** [phras v] **1.** (avert) abwenden ['apvɛndn̩] <wendet ab, wendete ab, hat abgewendet> ◊ *Die Gefahr wurde in letzter Sekunde abgewendet.* **2.** (depart) gehen ['geːən] <geht, ging, ist gegangen> ◊ *Sie mussten schon früh gehen.* **3.** (obstruct) head sb off sich jdm in den Weg stellen [ɪn deːn 'veːk ʃtɛlən] +haben
• **head up** [phras v] leiten ['laɪtn̩] <leitet, leitete, hat geleitet> ◊ *Sie leitete die Besprechung.* ♦ *Er leitet jetzt die Abteilung.*
headache [noun] Kopfschmerz ['kɔpfʃmɛʳts] der <-es, -en> most pl ◊ *starke Kopfschmerzen haben*
heading [noun] Überschrift ['yːbɐʃrɪft] die <-, -en>
headlight [noun] Scheinwerfer ['ʃaɪnvɛʳfɐ] der <-s, -> dip your headlights die Scheinwerfer abblenden
headline [noun] Schlagzeile ['ʃlaːktsaɛlə] die <-, -n> ⊙ make the headlines in die Schlagzeilen kommen
headmaster [noun] Direktor [diˈrɛktoːɐ̯] der <-s, -en> ◊ *Er war als Direktor eines Gymnasiums tätig.* ♦ *Kann ich den Direktor sprechen?*
headmistress [noun] Direktorin [dirɛkˈtoːrɪn] die <-, -nen> ◊ *einen Schüler zur Direktorin schicken*
head office [noun] Zentrale [tsɛnˈtraːlə] die <-, -n> ◊ *die Zentrale einer Bank/Partei*
head-on [adj, adv] **1.** frontal [frɔnˈtaːl] no comp/superl; when used as an adj, only before ns ◊ *ein frontaler Angriff* ♦ *frontal zusammenstoßen* **2.** (fig) direkt [diˈrɛkt] <direkter, am direktesten> ◊ *eine direkte Art haben* ♦ *ein Problem direkt angehen*
headquarters [noun] (of an institution, a company) Hauptsitz ['haɔptzɪts] der <-es, -e> ◊ *Unsere Firma hat ihren Hauptsitz in Bonn.*; (military) Hauptquartier ['haɔptkvaʳˌtiːɐ̯] das <-s, -e> ◊ *Das Hauptquartier wurde in den Süden verlegt.*
headteacher [noun] Schulleiter ['ʃuːllaɪtɐ] der <-s, -> ♀Schulleiterin ['ʃuːllaɪtərɪn] die <-, -nen>
headword [noun] Stichwort ['ʃtɪçvɔʳt] das <-(e)s, Stichwörter> ◊ *Wie viele Stichwörter enthält dieses Wörterbuch?*
heal [verb] heilen ['haɛlən] transitive use +haben/intransitive use +sein ◊ *Die Verbrennungen heilten schnell.* ♦ *Diese Krankheit kann man heute gut heilen.*
• **heal up** [phras v] verheilen [fɛ'haɛlən] <verheilt, verheilte, ist verheilt> ◊ *Die Wunde ist gut verheilt.*
health [noun] Gesundheit [gəˈzʊnthaɛt] die <-s no pl ◊ *Rauchen gefährdet Ihre Gesundheit!* be in good/poor health bei guter/schlechter Gesundheit sein
health care [noun] Gesundheitswesen [gəˈzʊnthaɛtsveːzn̩] das <-s> no pl
health food [noun] Naturkost [naˈtuːɐ̯kɔst] die <-> no pl
healthy(-ily) [adj, adv] gesund [gəˈzʊnt] <gesünder/gesunder, am gesündesten/gesundesten> ◊ *ein gesundes Kind* ♦ *Er ist sehr gesund.* ♦ *Die Wirtschaft ist gesund.*
heap¹ [noun] Haufen ['haɔfn̩] der <-s, -> ◊ *den

Schmutz zu einem Haufen zusammenkehren ♦ *ein Haufen Kleider* in heaps haufenweise ['haʊfnvaezə] *no comp/superl* ◊ *Ich fand haufenweise Fehler.*

heap² verb **1.** (objects) häufen ['hɔɡfn] +haben ◊ *sich* dat *Essen auf den Teller häufen* ♦ *ein gehäufter Teelöffel Zucker* **2.** (praise, criticism) heap sth on sb *jdn mit etw. überhäufen* [mɪt ... ybɛ,hɔɡfn] <überhäuft, überhäufte, hat überhäuft> ◊ *Er wurde mit Lob überhäuft.*

hear verb **1.** (sounds, information) hören ['hø:rən] +haben ◊ *Unter Wasser kann man nicht hören.* ♦ *Ich hörte sie staubsaugen.* ♦ *Über sie hört man nur Gutes.* ♦ *Sei vorsichtig, hörst du?* ♦ *Wie ich höre, soll er krank sein.* ♦ *Die Zeugen sind noch nicht gehört worden.* Hear! Hear! Hört, hört! **2.** (a court case) verhandeln [fɛ'hand|n] <verhandelt, verhandelte, hat verhandelt> ◊ *Sein Fall wird in der ersten Instanz verhandelt.*
- **hear from** phras v hear from sb von jdm hören [fɔn ... ,hø:rən] +haben ◊ *Wir haben nie wieder von den beiden gehört.*
- **hear of** phras v hear of sb/sth hear of sb/sth von jdm/etw. hören [fɔn ... ,hø:rən] +haben ◊ *Ich habe von seiner Beförderung gehört.*
- **hear out** phras v hear sb out jdn ausreden lassen ['aʊsre:dn lasn] <lässt, ließ, hat lassen> ◊ *Lass mich doch mal ausreden!*

hearing noun **1.** (faculty, opportunity to speak up) Gehör [gə'hø:ɐ] das <-s> *no pl* ◊ *ein ausgezeichnetes/feines Gehör haben* ♦ *bei jdm mit einem Anliegen Gehör finden* I request a fair hearing! *Ich verlange, dass man mir zuhört!* She got a fair hearing. *Sie bekam die Chance, ihr Anliegen vorzutragen.* **2.** (in court) Anhörung ['anhø:rʊŋ] die <-, -en> ◊ *Morgen findet die Anhörung im Fall Schmid statt.*
- out of/within hearing außer/in Hörweite

hearing aid noun Hörgerät ['hø:ɡɐɛːt] das <-(e)s, -e> ◊ *Er trägt ein Hörgerät.*

heart noun **1.** (organ, shape, emotions, central part) Herz [hɛ'ts] das <-ens, -en> ◊ *ein schwaches Herz haben* ♦ *Paraguay liegt im Herzen Südamerikas.* with all your heart von ganzem Herzen break sb's heart jdm das Herz brechen take sth to heart sich dat etw. zu Herzen nehmen **2.** (most important part) Kern [kɛ'n] der <-(e)s> *no pl* ◊ *der Kern des Problems/Konfliktes* **3.** (playing card, suit) heart(s) Herz [hɛ'ts] das <-, -> ◊ *Wie viele Herz hast du?* Hearts are trumps. Herz ist Trumpf.
- be dear to sb's heart jdm am Herzen liegen cross your heart Hand aufs Herz harden your heart (against sb/sth) sein Herz (vor jdm/etw.) verschließen have the heart to do sth **1.** (sth unkind) es übers Herz bringen, etw. zu tun ◊ *Sie brachte es nicht übers Herz, das Tier zu töten.* **2.** (sth dangerous) sich trauen, etw. zu tun ◊ *Er traute sich nicht, sie anzusprechen.* lose heart den Mut verlieren take heart **1.** (pluck up your courage) sich dat ein Herz fassen ◊ *Fass dir ein Herz und frag sie einfach!* **2.** (comfort yourself) take heart (from sth) sich (mit etw.) trösten ◊ *Er tröstete sich mit dem Gedanken, dass es nur besser werden könne.* Take heart! Kopf hoch! at heart im Grunde by heart auswendig ◊ *ein Gedicht auswendig lernen*

heart attack noun Herzinfarkt ['hɛ'ts|ɪn,fa'kt] der <-(e)s, -e>

hearth noun Kamin [ka'mi:n] der <-s, -e> ◊ *Wir saßen am Kamin.* ♦ *Im Kamin prasselte ein gemütliches Feuer.*

heart-throb noun Schwarm [ʃva'm] der <-(e)s, Schwärme> most sing ◊ *der Schwarm aller jungen Mädchen*

hearty(-ily) adj, adv herzhaft ['hɛ'tshaft] <herzhafter, am herzhaftesten> ◊ *Ihr Lachen ist herzhaft.* ♦ *eine herzhafte Mahlzeit* ♦ *Er biss herzhaft in das Brötchen.*

heat¹ noun **1.** (high temperature) Hitze ['hɪtsə] die <-> *no pl* ◊ *Es herrschte eine unerträgliche Hitze.* bake sth at a medium heat etw. bei mittlerer Hitze backen; (less intense, physical energy) Wärme ['vɛ'mə] die <-> *no pl* ◊ *die Wärme ihres Körpers* ♦ *Dieses Material leitet Wärme sehr gut.* **2.** (in the US: heating) Heizung ['haetsʊŋ] die <-, -en> ◊ *Es gab keine Heizung.*
- in the heat of the day in der größten Mittagshitze in the heat of the moment im Eifer des Gefechts the heat is on die Hölle ist los (fam) take the heat out of sth einer Sache dat die Schärfe nehmen

heat² verb **1.** (water, oil etc.) erhitzen [e'hɪtsn] <erhitzt, erhitzte, hat erhitzt> ◊ *Öl in einer Pfanne erhitzen; (a meal) aufwärmen* ['aʊfvɛ'mən] +haben ◊ *Ich wärme dir das Essen auf.* **2.** (become hot) heiß werden ['haes ve:ɡdn] +sein **3.** (a room) heat heizen ['haetsn] +haben ◊ *Das Schlafzimmer heizen wir nicht.*
- **heat up** phras v **1.** (water, oil etc.) erhitzen [e'hɪtsn] <erhitzt, erhitzte, hat erhitzt> ◊ *Öl in einer Pfanne erhitzen; (a meal) aufwärmen* ['aʊfvɛ'mən] +haben ◊ *Ich wärme dir die Suppe auf.* **2.** (become (too) hot) (sehr) heiß werden [(ze:ɡ) 'haes ve:ɡdn] +sein ◊ *Dieser Raum wird im Sommer sehr heiß.* The food is heating up. Das Essen ist gleich warm. **3.** (argument, debate) sich zuspitzen ['tsu:ʃpɪtsn] +haben ◊ *Der Streit spitzte sich zu.*

heated → heat² adj **1.** (room, house) beheizt [bə'haetst] *no comp/superl* ◊ *ein beheizter Raum* ♦ *Der Keller ist nicht beheizt.* **2.** (debate, discussion etc.) hitzig ['hɪtsɪç] ◊ *Sie lieferten sich hitzige Debatten.* ♦ *Die Stimmung auf der Versammlung war hitzig.*

heater noun (appliance that generates heat, with a fan) Heizlüfter ['haetslvfte] der <-s, -> ◊ *Der Heizlüfter läuft noch.; (using gas/oil/wood etc.) Ofen* ['o:fn] der <-s, Öfen> ◊ *den Ofen anstellen* water heater Boiler ['bɔglɐ] der <-s, ->

heath noun Heide ['haedə] die <-, -n> ◊ *die Lüneburger Heide*

heating noun (system) Heizung ['haetsʊŋ] die <-, -en> ◊ *die Heizung anstellen/abstellen*

heave verb **1.** (by pushing or pulling) heave sth somewhere etw. mühsam irgendwohin rücken [,my:za:m 'rʏkń] +haben ◊ *Mühsam rückte sie den Schrank vor die Tür.; (by lifting it up) etw. irgendwohin hieven* ['hi:fn] +haben ◊ *Sie hievten das Klavier auf den Lastwagen.* heave yourself from/out of sth sich mühsam von/aus etw. dat erheben [,my:za:m fɔn/aʊs ... ɛ,he:bm] <erhebt sich, erhob sich, hat sich erhoben> ◊ *Der alte Mann erhob sich mühsam von seinem Platz.* **2.** (breast) sich heben und senken [,he:bm ʊnt 'zɛŋkń] <hebt und senkt sich, hob und senkte sich, hat sich gehoben und

A B C D E F G H I J K L M N O P Q R S T U V W X Y Z

gesenkt> **3.** *(fam) (be sick)* brechen ['brɛçn̩] <bricht, brach, hat gebrochen> ◊ *Er hatte zu viel gegessen und musste brechen.*

heaven [noun] Himmel ['hɪml̩] der <-s, -> *most sing* ◊ *Er betete zu Gott im Himmel.*

◉ in heaven's name in Gottes Namen for heaven's sake, good heavens, heavens above um Himmels willen the heavens open die Schleusen des Himmels öffnen sich

heavenly [adj] himmlisch ['hɪmlɪʃ] ◊ *eine himmlische Eingebung ◊ Das Essen schmeckte einfach himmlisch.*

heavily [adv] **1.** *(armed, guarded, loaded, wounded, breathe, fall)* schwer [ʃveːɐ̯] ◊ *ein schwer beladenes Auto ◆ Er stürzte schwer.* **2.** *(bleed, depend, influence, rain, snow)* stark [ʃtaʳk] <stärker, am stärksten> drink heavily ein starker Trinker/eine starke Trinkerin sein smoke heavily ein starker Raucher/eine starke Raucherin sein **3.** *(lose, in debt, taxed)* hoch [hoːx] <höher, am höchsten> ◊ *hoch verlieren/verschuldet* heavily pregnant hochschwanger ['hoːxˈʃvaŋɐ] *no comp/superl* **4.** *(populated)* dicht [dɪçt] <dichter, am dichtesten> ◊ *dicht besiedelte Gegenden*

heavy [adj] **1.** *(load, food and drink, losses, fragrance, blow, fighting, responsibility, storm etc.)* schwer [ʃveːɐ̯] ◊ *Mein Koffer ist schwer. ◆ ein schweres Parfüm ◆ schwere Verluste erleiden ◆ ein schweres Gewitter* **2.** *(rainfall, clouds, traffic, smoker, drinker, cold)* stark [ʃtaʳk] <stärker, am stärksten> ◊ *starke Regenfälle ◆ Der Verkehr auf den Straßen war ziemlich stark. ◆ ein starker Raucher ◆ einen starken Schnupfen haben* **3.** *(fine, casualties, price)* hoch [hoːx] <höher, am höchsten> <der/die/das hohe ...> ◊ *einen hohen Preis für etw. zahlen ◆ Die Strafe war hoch.* **4.** *(air, silence)* drückend ['drʏkn̩t] ◊ *Die Luft war drückend und schwül. ◆ Im Saal herrschte eine drückende Stille.* **5.** *(features)* grob [groːp] <gröber, am gröbsten> ◊ *Ihre Gesichtszüge waren grob. ◆ ein grobes Gesicht*

heavy-handed(ly) [adj, adv] plump [plʊmp] <plumper, am plump(e)sten> *(pej)* ◊ *eine plumpe Anmache ◆ Kann man das sagen oder ist das zu plump? ◆ plump vorgehen*

Hebrew¹ [noun] Hebräisch [heˈbrɛːɪʃ] das <-(s)> *no pl* → **German¹** 2.

Hebrew² [adj] hebräisch [heˈbrɛːɪʃ] → **German²**

hectare [noun] Hektar ['hɛktaːʳ] der <-s, -e>

hedge [noun] Hecke ['hɛkə] die <-, -n>

hedgehog [noun] Igel ['iːgl̩] der <-s, ->

heel [noun] **1.** *(of a foot, sock)* Ferse ['fɛʳzə] die <-, -n> ◊ *Er hatte Blasen an den Fersen. ◆ Sie hatte ein Loch in der Ferse der linken Socke.* **2.** *(of a shoe)* Absatz ['apzats] der <-es, Absätze> ◊ *Schube mit flachen/hohen Absätzen* **3.** *(of a hand)* Handballen ['hantbalən] der <-s, ->

hefty [adj] **1.** *(person, kick)* kräftig ['krɛftɪç] ◊ *ein kräftiger Mann ◆ Der Schlag war kräftig.* **2.** *(fine, bill)* saftig ['zaftɪç] *(fam)* ◊ *eine saftige Strafe zahlen müssen ◆ Die Rechnung war saftig.*

height [noun] **1.** *(of a body)* Größe ['grøːsə] die <-, -n>; *(of objects, from the ground)* Höhe ['høːə] die <-, -n> ◊ *Der Monitor hat eine Höhe von 42 cm.* lose height an Höhe verlieren ◊ *Das Flugzeug verlor plötzlich an Höhe.* fear of heights Höhenangst ['høːənaŋst] die <-> *no pl* **2.** *(unsurpassable maximum)* the heigt of sth der Gipfel ... [gen]

[deːɐ̯ ˈgɪpfl̩] <-s, -> ◊ *der Gipfel der Dummheit; (of sb's career)* Höhepunkt ['høːəpʊŋkt] der <-(e)s, -e> be the height of fashion der letzte Schrei sein [deːɐ̯ lɛtstə ˈʃraɪ zaɪn]

heir [noun] Erbe ['ɛʳbə] der <-n, -n> ♀Erbin ['ɛʳbɪn] die <-, -nen> ◊ *Er hat sie als alleinige Erbin eingesetzt.*

helicopter [noun] Hubschrauber ['huːpʃraʊbɐ] der <-s, ->

helix [noun] Spirale [ʃpiˈraːlə] die <-, -n>

hell [noun] Hölle ['hœlə] die <-> *no pl* ◊ *Meine Ehe war die Hölle. ◆ durch die Hölle geben*

◉ come hell or high water komme, was wolle absolute hell die wahre Hölle bloody hell verdammt noch mal put sb through hell jdm das Leben zur Hölle machen

hello [interj] hallo ['halo:] *(fam)* ◊ *Hallo, Peter! ◆ Hallo, Sie da! ◆ Hallo, ist da jemand?*

helmet [noun] Helm [hɛlm] der <-(e)s, -e> ◊ *einen Helm aufsetzen/tragen ◆ den Helm abnehmen*

help¹ [noun] Hilfe ['hɪlfə] die <-, -n> ◊ *Er bat sie um Hilfe. ◆ Hilfe! Ich ertrinke! ◆ Ich brauche eine Hilfe für den Haushalt. ◆ Ist dir dieses Buch bei den Hausaufgaben eine Hilfe? ◆ humanitäre Hilfe*

help² [verb] **1.** *(offer assistance)* helfen ['hɛlfn̩] <hilft, half, hat geholfen> ◊ *Er hilft ihr regelmäßig bei den Hausaufgaben.* **2.** *(food and drink)* help sb to sth jdm etw. anbieten ['anbiːtn̩] <bietet an, bot an, hat angeboten> ◊ *Sie bot ihnen noch eine weitere Portion an.* help yourself zugreifen ['tsuːgraɪfn̩] <greift zu, griff zu, hat zugegriffen> ◊ *Greifen Sie zu — es ist noch Kuchen da!* help yourself to sth sich [dat] etw. nehmen ['neːmən] <nimmt, nahm, hat genommen> ◊ *Nimm dir doch ein Stück Kuchen!*

◉ sth can't be helped etw. lässt sich nicht vermeiden not if I can help it **1.** *(only if absolutely necessary)* nur, wenn es sich nicht vermeiden lässt **2.** *(expressing that sb will do everything to stop sth)* das werde ich verhindern ◊ *Du wirst sie nicht heiraten; das werde ich verhindern!*

helpful [adj] **1.** *(useful)* hilfreich ['hɪlfraɪç] ◊ *ein hilfreicher Vorschlag ◆ War der Tipp hilfreich?* **2.** *(willing to help)* hilfsbereit ['hɪlfsbəraɪt] ◊ *hilfsbereite Freunde ◆ Sie ist ihren Kollegen gegenüber immer hilfsbereit.*

helpfully [adv] freundlicherweise ['frɔʏntlɪçɐvaɪzə] ◊ *Sie hat uns freundlicherweise den Weg gezeigt.*

helping [noun] Portion [pɔʳˈtsjoːn] die <-, -en> second helping Nachschlag ['naːxʃlaːk] der <-(e)s, Nachschläge>

helpless(ly) [adj, adv] **1.** *(not able to help)* hilflos ['hɪlfloːs] <hilfloser, am hilflosesten> ◊ *ein hilfloses Opfer ◆ Die Regierung sieht der Inflation hilflos zu.* **2.** *(knowing no advice)* ratlos ['raːtloːs] <ratloser, am ratlosesten> ◊ *Die Ärzte sind in seinem Fall völlig ratlos. ◆ Er warf mir einen ratlosen Blick zu. ◆ Der Schüler saß ratlos vor seinen Aufgaben.*

hem [noun] Saum [zaʊm] der <-(e)s, Säume> ◊ *der Saum eines Kleides*

hemisphere [noun] Hemisphäre [hemiˈsfɛːrə] die <-, -n> ◊ *die nördliche Hemisphäre*

hen [noun] **1.** *(female chicken)* Henne ['hɛnə] die <-, -n> **2.** *(female bird)* Weibchen ['vaɪpçən] das <-s, ->

hence [adv] **1.** *(for this reason)* daher auch

['da:heːɐ̯ ao̯x] ◊ *Er ist Allergiker und daher auch oft krank.* ✦ *Sie ist in England aufgewachsen; daher auch ihr exzellentes Englisch.* **2.** *(from now)* in [ɪn] ⟨+dat⟩ two weeks/years etc. hence in zwei Wochen/Jahren etc.

her¹ ⟨det⟩ *(belonging to a female person or animal)* ihr [iːɐ̯] ihre ['iːrə] ◊ *Ihr Mann arbeitet an der Universität.* ✦ *Ihre Brille ist kaputt.* ✦ *Während ihrer Krankheit konnte sie nicht arbeiten.*; *(with a German neuter noun)* sein [zaɛn] seine ['zaɛnə] the au pair and her boy-friend das Au-pair-Mädchen und sein Freund → **ihr²**, **sein²**

her² ⟨pers pron⟩ *(acc)* sie [ziː] ◊ *Britta ist krank. Ich rufe sie morgen an.*; *(dat)* ihr [iːɐ̯] ◊ *Warum schreibst du ihr nicht?* → **sie¹**

herb ⟨noun⟩ Kraut [krao̯t] das <−(e)s, Kräuter>

herd ⟨noun⟩ Herde ['heːɐ̯də] die <−, −n> ◊ *ein Schäfer mit seiner Herde* a herd of sheep/cows eine Herde Schafe/Kühe

⊕ follow the herd mit dem Strom schwimmen

here ⟨adv⟩ **1.** *(in this place, at this point, when proffering sth to sb)* hier [hiːɐ̯] ◊ *Hier können wir nicht bleiben.* ✦ *Das hier ist mein Auto.* ✦ *Dein Schlüssel ist hier unten.* ✦ *Hier bin ich!* ✦ *Hier, nimm meinen Mantel!* ✦ *Ab hier ist der Film langweilig.* **2.** *(to this place)* her… [heːɐ̯] come here herkommen ['heːɐ̯kɔmən] <kommt her, kam her, ist hergekommen> ◊ *Komm mal her!* look here hersehen ['heːɐ̯zeːən] <sieht her, sah her, hat hergesehen> ◊ *Sieh her, was ich gefunden habe!*; *(with emphasis on the destination)* hierher ['hiːɐ̯'heːɐ̯] ◊ *Kommt er hierher oder zu dir?*

⊕ here we go again geht das schon wieder los here, there, and everywhere überall here today, gone tomorrow *was heute noch da ist, kann morgen schon vergangen sein* be here to stay uns lange erhalten bleiben ◊ *Es sieht so aus, als würde uns das schlechte Wetter lange erhalten bleiben.* here we go aber was solls ◊ *Ich kann nicht tanzen, aber was solls — ich probiers mal.* here's to sb auf jdn ◊ *Auf unsere fleißigen Helfer, Peter und Max!*

hereby ⟨adv⟩ hiermit ['hiːɐ̯mɪt] ◊ *Hiermit bestätige ich meine Teilnahme am Kurs.*

hereditary ⟨adj⟩ erblich ['ɛrplɪç] no comp/superl ◊ *Die Veranlagung zu Brustkrebs ist erblich.* ✦ *ein erblicher Titel* hereditary monarchy Erbmonarchie ['ɛrpmonarˌçiː] die <−, −n> a hereditary peer *eine Person, die von einem Elternteil das Recht geerbt hat, Mitglied des britischen Oberhauses zu sein*

herewith ⟨adv⟩ hiermit ['hiːɐ̯mɪt] *(form)* ◊ *Ich erkläre die Diskussion hiermit für eröffnet.*

heritage ⟨noun⟩ Erbe ['ɛrbə] das <−s> no pl ◊ *sein kulturelles Erbe pflegen*

hero ⟨noun⟩ Held [hɛlt] der <−en, −en> ♀Heldin ['hɛldɪn] die <−, −nen> ◊ *ein wahrer Held* ✦ *Bitte spiel jetzt nicht die Heldin.* ✦ *Der Held des Films stirbt am Schluss.* unsung hero unbesungener Held, unbesungene Heldin

⊕ the local hero die Lokalgröße

heroin ⟨noun⟩ Heroin [hero|'iːn] das <−s> no pl ◊ *sich* ⟨dat⟩ *Heroin spritzen*

heroine ⟨noun⟩ Heldin ['hɛldɪn] die <−, −nen>

hers ⟨poss pron⟩ **1.** *(belonging to a female person or animal)* ihrer ['iːrɐ] ihre ['iːrə] ihrs [iːɐ̯s] ◊ *Der Fehler war nicht ihrer.* ✦ *Diese Handschrift ist ihre.* ✦ *Das Problem ist einzig und allein ihrs.* ✦ *Sind die Kinder ihre?* **2.** *(with a German neuter noun)* seiner ['zaɛnɐ] seine ['zaɛnə] seins ['zaɛns] ◊ *Da liegt eine Tasche. Das Mädchen behauptet, es sei seine.* ✦ *ihrer* ⊕ of hers von ihr ◊ *Das war nur eine Idee von ihr.*

herself ⟨ref pron⟩ **1.** *(referring to a female person or animal)* sich [zɪç] ◊ *Sie schützt sich mit einem Hut vor der Sonne.* ✦ *Sie erzählte mir alles über sich und ihre Familie.* Tonight she is not quite herself. Heute Abend ist sie nicht ganz sie selbst. After the accident she has never been herself again. Von dem Unfall hat sie sich nie wieder ganz erholt. a shadow of herself ein Schatten ihrer selbst After a good meal she feels more herself again. Nach einer anständigen Mahlzeit geht es ihr wieder besser.; *(emphatic)* the headmistress/queen herself … die Direktorin/Königin … persönlich [di: dɪrɛkˌtoːrɪn/ˌkøːnɪgɪn … pɛrˈzøːnlɪç] ◊ *Die Direktorin kam persönlich zur Begrüßung der Schüler.* **2.** *(without anybody's help)* selbst [zɛlpst] ◊ *Hat sie das Auto selbst repariert?*

⊕ (all) by herself (ganz) allein ◊ *Anna kann sich schon allein anziehen.* ✦ *Was macht sie denn hier so ganz allein?* (all) to herself *(referring to time)* für sich ◊ *Nach der Arbeit hatte sie den Abend (ganz) für sich.* *(referring to a place)* (ganz) für sich allein ◊ *Sie hatte die Sauna für sich allein.*

hesitate ⟨verb⟩ zögern ['tsøːgɐn] +haben ◊ *Sie zögerte kurz, willigte dann aber ein.* ✦ *Du solltest nicht zögern, dieses Angebot anzunehmen.*

hesitation ⟨noun⟩ Zögern ['tsøːgɐn] das <−s> no pl ◊ *Nach kurzem Zögern stimmte ich zu.* have no hesitation in doing sth nicht zögern, etw. zu tun [nɪçt 'tsøːgɐn … tsuː] +haben ◊ *Zögern Sie nicht, die Polizei anzurufen.*

hey ⟨interj⟩ **1.** *(attracting attention, expressing surprise, annoyance)* he [heː] *(fam)* ◊ *He, du da! Komm mal her!* ✦ *He, was ist denn das?* ✦ *He, lass das gefälligst!* **2.** *(in the US)* hallo ['halo] ◊ *Hallo, Anja! Wie gehts dir denn so?*

⊕ but hey zwar …, aber … ◊ *Es ist zwar anstrengend, aber es macht Spaß.*

hi ⟨interj⟩ hallo ['halo] ◊ *Hallo, Lisa! Wie gehts?* ✦ *Hallo, da bin ich wieder.*

hidden → **hide²** ⟨adj⟩ hidden reserves stille Reserven [ˈʃtɪlə reˈzɛrvn̩] <−> pl

hide¹ ⟨noun⟩ **1.** *(of an animal)* Haut [hao̯t] die <−, Häute> ◊ *Häute von Rindern und Schweinen* **2.** *(for watching animals or birds)* Beobachtungsstand [bə|'oːbaxtʊŋsʃtant] der <−(e)s, Beobachtungsstände>

⊕ have the hide of an elephant/rhinoceros ein dickes Fell haben not see hide nor hair of sb/sth keine Spur von jdm/etw. entdecken können save your/sb's hide seine/jds Haut retten have the hide to do sth den Mumm haben, etw. zu tun

hide² ⟨verb⟩ **1.** *(from sight)* verstecken [fɛˈʃtɛkŋ] <versteckt, versteckte, hat versteckt> ◊ *Versteck das Geld gut!* sb hides (from sb/sth) jd versteckt sich (vor jdm/etw.) ◊ *Er versteckte sich unter dem Bett.* ✦ *Du kannst dich nicht ewig vor der Wahrheit verstecken.* hide sth/sb from sb/sth etw./jdn vor jdm/etw. verstecken ◊ *Sie versteckte die Pistole/ihn vor der Polizei.* hide sth away etw. verstecken ◊ *Er muss noch irgendwo Geld versteckt haben.* **2.** *(an intention,*

A
B
C
D
E
F
G
H
I
J
K
L
M
N
O
P
Q
R
S
T
U
V
W
X
Y
Z

action, the truth) verheimlichen [fɛˈhaɛmlɪçn̩] <verheimlicht, verheimlichte, hat verheimlicht> hide sth from sb jdm etw. verheimlichen ◊ *Er verheimlichte ihr, dass er beim Pokern Geld verloren hatte.*; *(emotions, sth illegal, immoral)* verbergen [fɛˈbɛʳgn̩] <verbirgt, verbarg, hat verborgen> ◊ *Ich konnte meine Gefühle nicht verbergen.* ✦ *Ich glaube, sie hat etwas zu verbergen.* hide a smile sich [dat] das Lachen verkneifen [das ˈlaxn̩ fɛˌknaɛfn̩] <verkneift, verkniff, hat verkniffen> ◊ *Bei diesem Anblick musste ich mir das Lachen verkneifen.* **3.** *(a face, the sun through clouds)* verdecken [fɛˈdɛkn̩] <verdeckt, verdeckte, hat verdeckt> ◊ *Der große Hut verdeckte ihr Gesicht.* hide sth from sight/view etw. verdecken

hierarchy [noun] **1.** *(system)* Hierarchie [hiraˈçiː] die <-, -n> ◊ *Sie steht in der Hierarchie weit oben.* ✦ *die Hierarchie der Begriffe bei Suchmaschinen* **2.** *(people at the top)* Führungsspitze [ˈfyːrʊŋsʃpɪtsə] die <-, -n> ◊ *Solche Entscheidungen liegen allein bei der Führungsspitze.*

high¹ [adj] **1.** *(from bottom to top, above ground, in amount, level)* hoch [hoːx] <höher, am höchsten> <der/die/das hohe ...> ◊ *ein hoher Berg* ✦ *Das Regal ist 1,80 m hoch.* ✦ *Die Arbeiter forderten höhere Löhne.* ✦ *ein hohes Risiko eingehen* ✦ *ein hohes Maß an Konzentration* ✦ *hohe Töne* the river is high der Wasserstand ist hoch; *(hopes, praise, proportion, volume)* groß [groːs] <größer, am größten> ◊ *Ein großer Teil der Menschheit lebt in Armut.* be high fashion groß in Mode sein Casualties were high. Die Zahl der Todesopfer war groß.; *(passion, wind)* stark [ʃtaʳk] <stärker, am stärksten> ◊ *Der Wind war so stark, dass unser Zelt umfiel.* a high incidence of sth ein häufiges Auftreten von etw. [aɛn ˌhɔʏfɪɡəs ˈaͻftreːtn̩ fͻn] ◊ *ein häufige Auftreten von Erkältungen in der kalten Jahreszeit* high in sth reich an etw. [dat] [raͼç an] ◊ *Frisches Obst ist reich an Vitaminen.* high in alcohol alkoholreich [ˈalkohoːlraɛç] high in calories kalorienreich [kaloˈriːənraɛç]; *(a list)* high on weit oben [vaɛt ˈoːbm̩] **2.** *(euphoric)* aufgedreht [ˈaͻfgədreːt] <aufgedrehter, am aufgedrehtesten> ◊ *Auf der Feier war sie völlig aufgedreht.* **3.** *(on drugs)* high [haɛ] no comp/superl, not before ns ◊ *Nach einem Joint war er high.* high on cocaine im Kokainrausch [ɪm kokaˈiːnraͻʃ] **4.** *(temperatures)* in the high twenties/thirties etc. von fast dreißig/vierzig etc. Grad [fͻn fast ˌdraɛsɪç/ˌfɪrˈtsɪç ˈgraːt] Temperatures were in the high 30s. Die Temperaturen lagen bei fast 40 Grad. **5.** *(the height of)* Hoch... [hoːx] high summer Hochsommer [ˈhoːxzͻmɐ] der <-s, -> high middle ages Hochmittelalter [ˈhoːxmɪtl̩ˌʔaltɐ] das <-s> no pl **6.** *(cheese)* überreif [ˈyːbɐraͼf] no comp/superl; *(meat)* be high streng riechen [ˌʃtrɛŋ ˈriːçn̩] <riecht, roch, hat gerochen>

high² [adv] *(from bottom to top, above ground, in amount, level)* hoch [hoːx] <höher, am höchsten> ◊ *Das Haus liegt hoch auf dem Berg.* ✦ *Der Ball flog hoch in die Luft.* ✦ *Er ist in der Partei hoch aufgestiegen.* ✦ *hoch singen* Emotions ran high. Die Gemüter erhitzten sich.

☞ look/search high and low for sth/sb überall nach etw./jdm suchen

higher → **high¹**, **high²** [adj] höhere [ˈhøːərə] no superl, only before ns <ein höherer ..., eine höhere ..., ein höheres ...> ◊ *Die höheren Klassen müssen sich auf*

das Abitur vorbereiten. ✦ *sich mit höheren Dingen beschäftigen* ✦ *die höhere Mathematik* ✦ *höhere Tiere* higher education Hochschulbildung [ˈhoːxʃuːlbɪldʊŋ] die <-> no pl

highlight¹ [noun] **1.** *(of a party etc.)* Höhepunkt [ˈhøːəpͻŋkt] der <-(e)s, -e> ◊ *die Höhepunkte des Spiels* ✦ *Der Höhepunkt der Reise war, als unser Auto kaputtging.* **2.** *(in hair)* highlights Strähnchen [ˈʃtrɛːnçən] die <-> pl ◊ *Ich lasse mir blonde Strähnchen färben.*

highlight² [verb] **1.** *(facts)* verdeutlichen [fɛˈdͻʏtlɪçn̩] <verdeutlicht, verdeutlichte, hat verdeutlicht> ◊ *Der Vorfall verdeutlicht den Ernst der Lage.* **2.** *(optically)* betonen [bəˈtoːnən] <betont, betonte, hat betont> ◊ *Das enge Kleid betont ihre gute Figur.* **3.** *(on paper, in a computer file)* markieren [maʳˈkiːrən] <markiert, markierte, hat markiert> ◊ *wichtige Textpassagen markieren*

☞ to highlight your/sb's hair sich/jdm Strähnchen färben

highly [adv] *(mainly with participles)* hoch [hoːx] <höher, am höchsten> ◊ *ein hoch begabtes Kind* ✦ *hoch bezahlte/qualifizierte Fachleute* ✦ *hoch angesehen/geschätzt sein*; *(mainly with adjectives)* höchst [høːçst] ◊ *höchst erfreulich/effektiv/erfolgreich* ✦ *Es ist höchst unwahrscheinlich, dass er noch kommt.* it is highly likely that ... höchstwahrscheinlich ... [ˈhøːçstvaʳˈʃaɛnlɪç] ◊ *Höchstwahrscheinlich kennst du es schon.* value sb/sth highly jdn/etw. sehr schätzen [zeːɐ ˈʃɛtsn̩] +haben

☞ speak/think highly of sb/sth große Stücke auf jdn/etw. halten

high-pressure area [noun] Hoch [hoːx] das <-s, -s> ◊ *Ein Hoch lag über Nordeuropa.*

high-rise building [noun] Hochhaus [ˈhoːxhaͻs] das <-es, Hochhäuser>

high season [noun] Hochsaison [ˈhoːxzɛˌzͻŋ] die <-> no pl

high school [noun] High School [ˈhaɛ skuːl] die <-, -s>

Children in Germany only receive a four-year standardized form of education in the *Grundschule*, roughly equivalent to the British junior school. Some federal states offer an additional two-year period known as the *Orientierungsstufe*, during which time pupils are assessed for the most appropriate type of secondary school.
The following schools, each with their own final examinations, correspond to the British secondary school, or the American high school: the *Hauptschule* providing pupils with nine years of general education culminating in the *Hauptschulabschluss*, a qualification allowing pupils to embark on a course of vocational training, the *Realschule* providing pupils with ten years of education, culminating in the *Mittlere Reife*, a qualification which offers a choice of on-the-job vocational training or continued secondary education, and the *Gymnasium*, roughly equivalent to the British grammar school, which provides pupils with 12 or 13 years of secondary education culminating in the *Abitur*, a university entrance exam.

high street [noun] **1.** *(main street with shops)* Hauptstraße [ˈhaͻptʃtraːsə] die <-, -n> ◊ *ein Geschäft in der Hauptstraße* **2.** *(retail trade)* Einzelhandel

['aents|handl] der <–s> no pl ◊ *Der Einzelhandel war mit dem Weihnachtsgeschäft zufrieden.* ✦ *Was kostet das im Einzelhandel?*

high-tech [adj] Hightech... ['haɛtɛk] high-tech device Hightechgerät ['haɛtɛkgərɛːt] das <–(e)s, –es> high-tech industry Hightechindustrie ['haɛtɛk|ɪndʊs,triː] die <–, –n>

highway [noun] (*out of town*) Landstraße ['lantʃtraːsə] die <–, –n> ◊ *der Verkehr auf Landstraßen und Autobahnen;* (*for long-distance travel also*) Fernstraße ['fɛʳnʃtraːsə] die <–, –n>; (*for long-distance travel in Germany*) Bundesstraße ['bʊndəsʃtraːsə] die <–, –n> ◊ *die Bundestraße B 12* public highway öffentliche Straße ['œfntlɪçə ʃtraːsə] die <–, –n> ◊ *Das gilt nur für öffentliche Straßen.;* (*in compound ns*) highway ... Straßen... ['ʃtraːsn̩] Highway Code Straßenverkehrsordnung ['ʃtraːsn̩fɛɐ̯keːɐ̯s|ɔʳdnʊŋ] die <–, –en> highway robbery Straßenraub ['ʃtraːsn̩raop] der <–(e)s> no pl ◉ highways and byways 1. (*streets*) Wege und Straßen 2. (*of a subject area*) die verschlungenen Wege ◊ *die verschlungenen Wege der Alchemie*

hijack [verb] entführen [ɛnt'fyːrən] <entführt, entführte, hat entführt> ◊ *Das Flugzeug wurde entführt.*

hike¹ [noun] 1. (*for recreation*) Wanderung ['vandərʊŋ] die <–, –en> ◊ *Sie unternahmen/machten eine Wanderung.* 2. (*walking distance, time spent walking*) Marsch [maʳʃ] der <–(e)s, Märsche> ◊ *Zur Hütte ist es ein zweistündiger Marsch.* 3. (*increase*) hike in costs Kostenexplosion ['kɔstn̩|ɛksplo,zjoːn] die <–, –en> hike in prices Preisexplosion ['praes|ɛksplo,zjoːn] die <–, –en>

hike² [verb] 1. (*ramble*) wandern ['vanden] +*sein* ◊ *Sie wandern sehr viel.* ✦ *Morgen wollen wir wandern gehen.* 2. (*prices etc.*) hike (up) drastisch anheben [,drastɪʃ 'anheːbm̩] <hebt an, hob an, hat angehoben> ◊ *Die Regierung hat die Tabaksteuer drastisch angehoben.*

hill [noun] Hügel ['hyːgl̩] der <–s, –> ◊ *die sanften Hügel des Thüringer Waldes* ◉ not amount to a hill of beans (*not be decisive*) keinen (großen) Unterschied machen ◊ *Die paar Stimmen machen keinen großen Unterschied.* (*not be of interest*) nicht weltbewegend sein ◊ *Deine Probleme sind nicht gerade weltbewegend.* over the hill jenseits von Gut und Böse

him [pers pron] (*acc*) ihn [iːn] ◊ *Ich habe das für ihn gemacht.;* (*dat*) ihm [iːm] ◊ *Hast du es ihm schon gesagt?*

himself [ref pron] 1. (*referring to a male person or animal, reflexive and personal pron*) sich [zɪç] ◊ *Frank trocknete sich ab.* ✦ *Er hatte sich unbeliebt gemacht.* ✦ *Er erzählte mir alles über sich und seine Familie.* After a good rest he feels more himself again. Nach einer guten Pause geht es ihm wieder besser. After the accident he has never been himself again. Von dem Unfall hat er sich nie wieder ganz erholt. Today he is not quite himself. Heute ist er nicht ganz er selbst.; (*emphatic*) the headmaster/president himself ... der Direktor/ Präsident ... persönlich [deːɐ̯ di,rɛktoːɐ̯/prɛsi,dɛnt ... pɛʳ'zøːnlɪç] ◊ *Der Präsident beantwortete den Brief persönlich.* 2. (*without anybody's help*) selbst [zɛlpst] ◊ *Hat er den Kuchen selbst gebacken?* ◉ (all) by himself (*ganz*) allein ◊ *Das kann er*

schon allein! ✦ *Was macht er denn hier so ganz allein?* (all) to himself (*referring to time*) für sich ◊ *Den nächsten Tag hatte er ganz für sich.* (*referring to a place*) für sich allein ◊ *Er hatte das ganze Abteil für sich allein.*

hinder [verb] 1. (*obstruct*) behindern [bə'hɪndən] <behindert, behinderte, hat behindert> ◊ *Behindern dich die langen Fingernägel nicht beim Tippen?* ✦ *Starker Nebel behinderte die Sicht.;* (*slow down*) hemmen ['hɛmən] +*haben* ◊ *den Fortschritt/das Wirtschaftswachstum hemmen* 2. (*prevent*) hinder sb from doing sth jdn davon abhalten, etw. zu tun [dafɔn 'aphaltn̩ ... tsuː] <hält ab, hielt ab, hat abgehalten> ◊ *Der Regen hat ihn nicht davon abgehalten, schwimmen zu gehen.*

Hindi [noun] Hindi ['hɪndiː] das <–> no pl → German¹ 2.

hindrance [noun] 1. (*obstacle*) Hindernis ['hɪndɛnɪs] das <–ses, –se> a hindrance to sth ein Hindernis für etw. ◊ *Diese Ungerechtigkeit ist ein Hindernis für den Frieden.;* (*have a negative effect*) be a hindrance schaden ['ʃaːdn̩] <schadet, schadete, hat geschadet> ◊ *Manchmal kann zu viel Hilfe auch schaden.;* (*be a disadvantage*) be a hindrance for sb für jdn ein Nachteil sein [fyːɐ̯ ... aen 'naːxtael zaen] +*sein* ◊ *Ist ein hoher IQ für Frauen ein Nachteil?* 2. (*impairment*) Behinderung [bə'hɪndərʊŋ] die <–, –en> ◊ *eine Behinderung der freien Entwicklung der Persönlichkeit* be a hindrance to sth eine Behinderung für etw. darstellen without hindrance ungehindert ['ʊngəhɪndət] no comp/superl

Hindu [noun] Hindu ['hɪndu] der <–(s), –(s)> ♀Hindu ['hɪnduː] die <–, –(s)> ◊ *Rinder sind einem Hindu heilig.* ✦ *Meine Frau ist Hindu.*

hinge [noun] 1. (*bolt on which a door or window rests*) Angel ['aŋl̩] die <–, –n> ◊ *eine Tür aus den Angeln heben* 2. (*on the lid of a container*) Scharnier [ʃaʳ'niːɐ̯] das <–s, –e> ◊ *Die Scharniere quietschen beim Öffnen.* 3. (*joint that makes parts of a device or appliance adjustable*) Gelenk [gə'lɛŋk] das <–(e)s, –e> ◊ *eine Schreibtischlampe mit zwei Gelenken*

hint¹ [noun] 1. (*to sb personally*) Wink [vɪŋk] der <–(e)s, –e> ◊ *Sie hatte von ihm einen Wink bekommen.* a broad/heavy hint ein Wink mit dem Zaunpfahl take a/the hint einen/den Wink verstehen 2. (*indication*) Andeutung ['andɔøtʊŋ] die <–, –en> ◊ *Er machte vage Andeutungen, dass er andere Pläne habe.* ✦ *die Andeutung eines Lächelns;* (*of amusement, impatience etc.*) Anflug ['anfluːk] der <–(e)s, Anflüge> most sing ◊ *Er antwortete mit mehr als nur einem Anflug von Heiterkeit.;* (*of sth to come, going on*) Anzeichen ['antsaeçn̩] das <–s, –> ◊ *Es gab keine Anzeichen für eine Wetterbesserung.* sth/sb gives no hint of sth etw./jd lässt nichts von etw. erkennen [lɛst ,nɪçts fɔn ... ɛ,kɛnən] <ließ, hat lassen> ◊ *Ihre Stimme ließ nichts von ihrem wahren Alter erkennen.* 3. (*small amount*) Hauch [haox] der <–(e)s, –e> most sing ◊ *ein Hauch von Luxus* 4. (*piece of useful information*) Tipp [tɪp] der <–s, –s> ◊ *Er gab ihr ein paar nützliche Tipps.* hints on sth Tipps für etw. ◊ *Tipps für das Beschneiden von Obstbäumen*

hint² [verb] andeuten ['andɔøtn̩] <deutet an, deutete an, hat angedeutet> She hinted that she would give up her job., She hinted at giving up her job. Sie deutete

an, dass sie ihre Arbeit aufgeben würde.

hip[1] [noun] Hüfte ['hʏftə] die <-, -n>

hip[2] [adj] angesagt ['angəzaːkt] <angesagter, am angesagtesten> *(fam)* ◊ *Er hat ein Gespür für angesagte Trends.* ♦ *Welche Farben sind diesen Winter angesagt?*

hire[1] [noun] *(fee for using cars, rooms etc.)* Miete ['miːtə] die <-, -n> ◊ *Was kostet die Miete für den Saal pro Abend?*; *(for boats, books, equipment)* Leihgebühr ['laegəbyːɐ̯] die <-, -en> ◊ *Die Leihgebühren für Ruderboote sind recht günstig.* hire car Mietwagen ['miːtvaːgn̩] der <-s, ->

ⓔ **for hire** *(car etc.)* zu vermieten *(taxi, person)* frei ◊ *Klavierlehrer frei, Anfragen Tel. ... on hire* 1. *(not your own, car etc.)* gemietet ◊ *Diese Versicherung zahlt nicht für Schäden an gemieteten oder geliehenen Sachen. (book etc.)* geliehen 2. *(not available any more)* vergeben ◊ *Alle Boote waren bereits vergeben.*

hire[2] [verb] 1. *(in the UK: rent a car or room etc.)* mieten ['miːtn̩] <mietet, mietete, hat gemietet> ◊ *ein Auto mieten* ♦ *einen Saal für eine Hochzeitsfeier mieten; (a boat, book, equipment)* ausleihen ['aoslaeən] <leiht aus, lieh aus, hat ausgeliehen> ◊ *Sollen wir uns heute Abend ein Video ausleihen?* 2. *(employ long-term)* einstellen ['aenʃtɛlən] +haben ◊ *Wir stellen ein: 11 Mechaniker, 15 Lagerarbeiter.* 3. *(employ short-term: a builder, babysitter etc.)* kommen lassen ['kɔmən lasn̩] <lässt, ließ, hat lassen> ◊ *Lass doch jemanden kommen, der auf die Kinder aufpasst!; (a nanny, musician etc.)* engagieren [anga'ʒiːrən] <engagiert, engagierte, hat engagiert> ◊ *für das Kinderfest einen Clown engagieren* 4. *(in the UK: lend sb a car or room etc.)* hire (out) vermieten [fe'miːtn̩] <vermietet, vermietete, hat vermietet> ◊ *Autos vermieten; (a boat, books, equipment, staff)* verleihen [fe'laeən] <verleiht, verlieh, hat verliehen> ◊ *Boote stundenweise verleihen*

• **hire out** [phras v] *(a car, room)* vermieten [fe'miːtn̩] <vermietet, vermietete, hat vermietet> ◊ *eine Limousine vermieten; (a boat, books, equipment, staff)* verleihen [fe'laeən] <verleiht, verlieh, hat verliehen> ◊ *Boote stundenweise verleihen* hire yourself out Gelegenheitsarbeiten annehmen [gə'leːgn̩haets|aˈbaetn̩ anneˈmən] <nimmt an, nahm an, hat angenommen>

hire company [noun] Verleih [fe'lae] der <-(e)s, -e> ◊ *ein Verleih für Ruder- und Tretboote* boat hire company Bootsverleih ['boːtsfelae] car hire company Autoverleih ['aotofelae]

his[1] [det] sein [zaen] seine ['zaenə] ◊ *Das ist Leo. Sein Bruder kommt auch.* ♦ *Er hat wieder seine Brille vergessen.* ♦ *Gib ihm sein Buch zurück.* ♦ *Das sind seine Schwestern.* ♦ *Während seiner Krankheit konnte er nicht arbeiten.* → **sein**[2]

his[2] [poss pron] *(belonging to a male person or animal)* seiner ['zaenɐ] seine ['zaenə] seins [zaens] ◊ *„Wem gehört dieser Schlüssel?" — „Das ist seiner."* ♦ *Die Frau da drüben ist seine.* ♦ *Das ist nicht sein Buch, das ist seins.* ♦ *Diese Kinder sind seine.* ♦ *Mein Stift ist kaputt; ich nehme seinen zum Schreiben.* → **seiner**

ⓔ **of his** von ihm ◊ *Ist das ein Freund von ihm?*

hiss [verb] 1. *(make an angry or snake-like sound)* zischen ['tsɪʃn̩] +haben ◊ *„Lass mich in Ruhe!", zischte sie.* ♦ *Es zischte laut, als sie die Dose öffnete.*

♦ *Die Kobra zischte bedrohlich.* 2. *(audience, to show disagreement)* ⓔpfeifen ['pfaefn̩] <pfeift, pfiff, hat gepfiffen> ◊ *Die Zuschauer pfiffen empört.* 3. *(cat)* fauchen ['faoxn̩] +haben hiss at an animal/sb ein Tier/jdn anfauchen ['anfaoxn̩] +haben

historian [noun] Historiker [hɪsˈtoːrɪke] der <-s, -> ♀Historikerin [hɪsˈtoːrɪkərɪn] die <-, -nen> ◊ *Der bekannte Historiker lehrt an der Universität Freiburg.* ♦ *Sie ist als Historikerin für das Museum tätig.*

historic [adj] historisch [hɪsˈtoːrɪʃ] no comp/superl ◊ *ein historisches Bauwerk/Ereignis*

historical [adj] historisch [hɪsˈtoːrɪʃ] no comp/superl ◊ *ein historischer Roman* ♦ *Ist Hamlet eine historische oder eine erfundene Gestalt?*

historically [adv] historisch [hɪsˈtoːrɪʃ] no comp/superl ◊ *historisch wichtige Funde*; *(introducing a sentence)* geschichtlich gesehen [gə'ʃɪçtlɪç gə'zeːən] ◊ *Geschichtlich gesehen kommen Revolutionen eher selten vor.*

history [noun] Geschichte [gə'ʃɪçtə] die <-, -n> most sing ◊ *die Geschichte Italiens/der USA* ♦ *Sie studiert Geschichte.* ♦ *In ihrer 200-jährigen Geschichte ist die Kirche zweimal abgebrannt.* a checkered history, quite a history eine bewegte Geschichte medical history Krankengeschichte ['kraŋkŋ̍gəʃɪçtə] contemporary history Zeitgeschichte ['tsaetgəʃɪçtə] in recorded history seit Beginn der Aufzeichnungen [zaet bəˌgɪn deːɐ̯ 'aoftsaeçnʊŋən]

ⓔ **be history** längst vorbei sein **go down in history** in die Geschichte eingehen **have a history** *(event, conflict etc.)* eine Vorgeschichte haben *(object, person)* eine lange Vergangenheit haben My family has a history of cancer. In meiner Familie hat es schon viele Fälle von Krebs gegeben. **make history** Geschichte schreiben **history will show** das wird die Zukunft zeigen

hit[1] [noun] 1. *(success)* Hit [hɪt] der <-s, -s> *(fam)* ◊ *Der Film wurde ein Hit.* ♦ *die größten Hits der Beatles* a hit with sb ein Hit bei jdm 2. *(with force)* Schlag [ʃlaːk] der <-(e)s, Schläge> ◊ *Er bekam einen Schlag auf den Kopf.* 3. *(of a bomb, bullet, an internet search)* Treffer ['trɛfe] der <-s, -> ◊ *Wie viele Treffer hatte deine Suchanfrage?* direct hit Volltreffer ['fɔltrɛfe] 4. *(visit to a website)* Besucher [bə'zuːxe] der <-s, -> ◊ *Ihre Webseite hat täglich über 100 Besucher.* 5. *(murder)* Auftragsmord ['aoftraːksmɔ't] der <-(e)s, -e> 6. *(amount of a drug)* Schuss [ʃʊs] der <-es, Schüsse> *(slang)* ◊ *Er brauchte einen Schuss.*

ⓔ **score a hit** treffen **take a hit** betroffen sein ◊ *Vom Unwetter am schlimmsten betroffen waren die Küstenstädte.*

hit[2] [verb] 1. *(a target)* treffen ['trɛfn̩] <trifft, traf, hat getroffen> ◊ *Der Ball flog über ihn hinweg und traf die Wand.* ♦ *Er schoss auf sie, traf aber nicht.* ♦ *Wen trifft diese Preiserhöhung am schwersten?* 2. *(touch with force, falling)* hit sth auf etw. [dat/acc] aufschlagen [aof ... ˌaofʃlaːgn̩] <schlägt auf, schlug auf, ist aufgeschlagen> ◊ *Er schlug mit dem Kopf auf dem/den Boden auf.*; *(moving horizontally)* hit sth gegen etw. prallen [ge:gn̩ ... ˌpralən] +sein ◊ *Ich prallte gegen die Wand.; (hurting yourself)* hit sth on/against sth etw. stoßen ['ʃtoːsn̩] <stößt sich, stieß sich, hat sich gestoßen> ◊ *Ich habe mir den Kopf am Schrank gestoßen.* 3. *(deliberately, with your fist, hand, an*

object) schlagen ['ʃlaːgn̩] <schlägt, schlug, hat geschlagen> ◊ *Meine Eltern haben mich nie geschlagen.* ♦ *jdm/jdn ins Gesicht schlagen* ♦ *einen Nagel in die Wand schlagen* ♦ *den Ball ins Aus schlagen* to hit at sb/sth auf jdn/etw. einschlagen [aof ... ˌaɛnˈʃlaːgn̩] <schlägt ein, schlug ein, hat eingeschlagen> ◊ *Sie schlug verzweifelt auf die verschlossene Tür ein.*
4. (*in an accident*) rammen ['ramən] +*haben* ◊ *Der Bus rammte ein entgegenkommendes Auto.*; (*injure sb*) anfahren ['anfaːrən] <fährt an, fuhr an, hat angefahren> ◊ *Er wurde von einem Auto angefahren.*
5. (*reach a place, find a solution, get into the papers or the rush hour*) sth irgendwohin kommen ['kɔmən] <kommt, kam, ist gekommen> ◊ *Wenn ihr zum Fluss kommt, folgt ihm bis zum Wald.* ♦ *auf die richtige Lösung/in die Zeitung/in den Berufsverkehr kommen* hit the right road die richtige Straße finden [diː ˌrɪçtɪgə ˈʃtraːsə ˌfɪndn̩] <findet, fand, hat gefunden>; (*a problem, oil etc.*) hit sth auf etw. [acc] stoßen [aof ... ˈʃtoːsn̩] <stößt, stieß, ist gestoßen> ◊ *auf eine Goldader/Widerstand stoßen*; (*an age*) hit 30 etc. 30 etc. werden ['draɛsɪç veːɐdn̩] +*sein*; (*a certain level, speed etc.*) erreichen [ɛ'raɛçn̩] <erreicht, erreichte, hat erreicht> ◊ *Die Temperaturen erreichen heute 30 Grad.* **6.** (*a score etc.*) erzielen [ɛ'tsiːlən] <erzielt, erzielte, hat erzielt> ◊ *ein Tor/20 Punkte erzielen* **7.** (*with your foot*) treten ['treːtn̩] <tritt, trat, hat getreten> ◊ (*auf*) *die Bremse/das Gaspedal/die Kupplung treten*; (*with your hand*) drücken ['drʏkn̩] ◊ (*auf*) *den Knopf/Schalter/Türöffner drücken* ♦ (*occur to sb: thought, truth etc.*) sth sb etw. geht jdm auf [geːt aof] <ging auf, ist aufgegangen> ◊ *Plötzlich ging ihr auf, dass er Recht hatte.* **9.** (*kill*) hit sb jdn umlegen ['ʊmleːgn̩] +*haben* (*fam*)

• **hit back** [phras v] **1.** (*physically, improve performance*) zurückschlagen [tsu'rʏkʃlaːgn̩] <schlägt zurück, schlug zurück, hat zurückgeschlagen> ◊ *Er schlug mich und ich schlug zurück.* ♦ *In der zweiten Halbzeit schlugen die Gäste zurück und erzielten drei Tore.* **2.** (*verbally*) hit back (at sb) (jdm) Kontra geben ['kɔntra: geːbm̩] <gibt, gab, hat gegeben> ◊ *Sie ließ das nicht gefallen und gab ordentlich Kontra.*

• **hit on** [phras v] hit on sth auf etw. [acc] kommen [aof ... ˌkɔmən] <kommt, kam, ist gekommen> ◊ *Wie kommst du auf diese Idee?* ♦ *auf die richtige Lösung kommen*

• **hit out** [phras v] hit out at sb jdn angreifen ['angraɛfn̩] <greift an, griff an, hat angegriffen> ◊ *Sie hat ihn in der Diskussion heftig angegriffen.*

hitherto [adv] bislang [bɪs'laŋ] ◊ *Das war mir bislang unbekannt.*

hoarse(ly) [adj, adv] heiser ['haɛze] ◊ *Er hatte Halsschmerzen und war heiser.* ♦ *Sie konnte nur noch heiser flüstern.* ♦ *eine heisere Stimme*

hobby [noun] Hobby ['hɔbi] das <-s, -s>

hockey [noun] Hockey ['hɔkɛ] das <-s> *only pl*

hold¹ [noun] **1.** (*with your hand, wrestling etc.*) Griff [grɪf] der <-(e)s, -e> ◊ *Ich kann Judo. Soll ich dir ein paar Griffe zeigen?* ♦ *Er lockerte seinen Griff und ließ los.* grab hold of packen ['pakn̩] +*haben* ◊ *Ich packte sie am Arm und zerrte sie mit mir.* **2.** (*grip, stability*) Halt [halt] der <-(e)s, -e> *most sing* ◊ *Sie verlor den Halt und stürzte ab.* ♦ *Dieses Gel verleiht dem Haar Halt.* **3.** (*possession*) Gewalt

[gə'valt] die <-> *no pl* ◊ *Die Armee hatte das Gebiet fest in ihrer Gewalt.* seize hold of sb jdn in seine Gewalt bringen ◊ *Die Bankräuber hatten zwei Geiseln in ihre Gewalt gebracht.* have a hold over sb Macht über jdn [acc] haben ['maxt yːbe ... haːbm̩] +*haben*; (*influence*) hold on/over sth Einfluss auf etw. [acc] ['aɛnflʊs aof] ◊ *Ich habe keinen Einfluss auf seine Entscheidungen.* **4.** (*in a plane, ship*) Laderaum ['laːdəraom] der <-(e)s, Laderäume>
◉ **get hold of sth 1.** (*grab*) etw. halten ◊ *Kannst du das mal halten?* **2.** (*get*) etw. bekommen ◊ *Hast du Karten für das Spiel bekommen?* get hold of sb jdn erwischen put a hold on sth etw. stoppen put on hold (*a project, plans*) auf Eis legen (*an account, payments, wages*) einfrieren (*a person*) warten lassen take hold **1.** (*person*) take hold of ergreifen ◊ *Sie ergriff den Ast und zog daran.* **2.** (*fire, disease*) sich ausbreiten ◊ *Das Feuer breitete sich aus.* on hold (*on the phone*) in der Warteschleife

hold² [verb] **1.** (*carry, clasp, contain, place*) halten ['haltn̩] <hält, hielt, hat gehalten> ◊ *ein Buch in der Hand halten* ♦ *Er hielt schützend den Arm vor das Gesicht.* ♦ *sich sehr gerade halten* ♦ *Dieser Reifen hält die Luft nicht mehr.* ♦ *Anteile einer Firma halten* hold sth open etw. aufhalten ['aofhaltn̩] +*haben* ◊ *Halt mal bitte die Tüte auf!* ♦ *jdm die Tür aufhalten* hold sth shut etw. zuhalten ['tsuːhaltn̩] +*haben* hold your ears/nose sich [dat] die Ohren/Nase zuhalten; (*up high*) hold sth up etw. hochhalten ['hoːxhaltn̩] <hält hoch, hielt hoch, hat hochgehalten> ◊ *Sie hielt ihr Glas hoch gegen das Licht.* **2.** (*not let go*) festhalten ['fɛsthaltn̩] <hält fest, hielt fest, hat festgehalten> ◊ *Halt den Hund fest, damit er nicht wegläuft!* ♦ *Sie wurden am Flughafen/von der Polizei festgehalten.* hold sb captive jdn gefangen halten [gə'faŋən haltn̩]. **3.** (*hold sb close*)) jdn an sich [acc] drücken ['drʏkn̩] +*haben* ◊ *Ich drückte mein Kind an mich.* **4.** (*contain, incorporate*) sth holds sth/sb in etw. [dat] ist etw./jd [ɪn ... ɪst] +*sein* ◊ *In jedem Krankenzimmer sind drei Patienten.* ♦ *In ihren Augen war Furcht.* **5.** (*have room for*) fassen ['fasn̩] +*haben* ◊ *Der Heizöltank fasst 8000 Liter. Dieses Stadion fasst 60 000 Zuschauer.*; (*vehicle, ship*) aufnehmen ['aofneːmən] <nimmt auf, nahm auf, hat aufgenommen> ◊ *Das Schiff kann 200 Passagiere aufnehmen.* **6.** (*an election, a meeting etc.*) abhalten ['aphaltn̩] <hält ab, hielt ab, hat abgehalten> ◊ *Der Chef hält gleich eine Besprechung ab.*; (*a concert, fair etc.*) veranstalten [fɛ'anʃtaltn̩] <veranstaltet, veranstaltete, hat veranstaltet> ◊ *eine Ausstellung/einen Flohmarkt veranstalten*; (*a match, competition*) austragen ['aostraːgn̩] <trägt aus, trug aus, hat ausgetragen> ◊ *die Olympischen Spiele/Meisterschaften austragen*; (*a party, church service*) feiern ['faɛen] +*haben* hold a trial verhandeln [fɛ'handln̩] <verhandelt, verhandelte, hat verhandelt> ◊ *Gegen ihn wird wegen Steuerhinterziehung verhandelt.* **7.** (*a job, passport, quality etc.*) haben ['haːbm̩] +*haben* ◊ *Sie hat einen gut bezahlten Posten.* ♦ *Er hat einen deutschen Pass.* ♦ *Du hast keine Macht über mich.* ♦ *eine starke Anziehungskraft haben*; (*an office*) innehaben ['ɪnəhaːbm̩] <hat inne, hatte inne, hat innegehabt> (*lofty*) ◊ *Er hat das Amt des Vorsitzenden inne.* **8.** (*a table, seat etc.*) reservieren [rezɛɐ'viːrən] <reserviert, reservierte, hat reserviert> ◊ *Ich kann Ihnen die Plätze für den Flug nach Berlin bis*

morgen reservieren. **9.** *(stop from leaving etc.)* aufhalten ['aofhaltn̩] <hält auf, hielt auf, hat aufgehalten> ◊ *Ich konnte sie nicht mehr länger aufhalten.* ♦ *Halten Sie bitte das Taxi auf!* **10.** *(stay or keep undamaged, unchanged)* halten ['haltn̩] <hält, hielt, hat gehalten> ◊ *Meinst du, das Dach/der Knoten/das Wetter wird halten?* ♦ *Wir konnten den Preis von 1,20 Euro halten.; (offer, promise etc.)* noch gelten [nɔx 'gɛltn̩] <gilt, galt, hat gegolten> ◊ *Gilt das noch, was du gestern gesagt hast?* **11.** *(a point of view, an opinion)* vertreten [fɛ'treːtn̩] <vertritt, vertrat, hat vertreten> ◊ *einen Standpunkt vertreten* hold that ... die Ansicht vertreten, dass ...; *(court etc.)* befinden [bə'fɪndn̩] <befindet, befand, hat befunden> *(form)* ◊ *Das Gericht befand ihn für schuldig.* hold sb liable/responsible jdn haftbar/verantwortlich machen ['haftbaːʳ/fɛ|'antvɔʳtlɪç maxn̩] +haben
Ⓢ **hold it 1.** *(wait)* Moment mal **2.** *(stop it)* aufhören ◊ *Sofort aufhören, ihr zwei!* **3.** *(when taking pictures)* gut so hold your own *(against sb/sth)* (neben jdm/etw.) bestehen können
• **hold against** [phras v] hold sth against sb jdm etw. vorwerfen ['foːɐ̯vɛʳfn̩] <wirft vor, warf vor, hat vorgeworfen> ◊ *Wirst du mir das später einmal vorwerfen?*
• **hold back** [phras v] *(prevent from moving)* zurückhalten [tsu'rʏkhaltn̩] <hält zurück, hielt zurück, hat zurückgehalten> ◊ *Wir mussten ihn zurückhalten, sonst hätte er ihn geschlagen.* ♦ *Ich konnte mich kaum zurückhalten.* ♦ *die Tränen zurückhalten* ♦ *Sie hielten die Zahlung noch zurück.; (slow down)* bremsen ['brɛmzn̩] +haben ◊ *Wenn sie erst mal loslegt, dann kann sie keiner bremsen.*
• **hold down** [phras v] **1.** hold sb down jdn niederhalten ['niːdɐhaltn̩] <hält nieder, hielt nieder, hat niedergehalten> ◊ *Die Schwestern mussten ihn niederhalten.* ♦ *Sie wurde ihr Leben lang von ihrer Familie niedergehalten.* **2.** *(prices, wages, pressure etc.)* niedrig halten ['niːdrɪç haltn̩] <hält, hielt, hat gehalten> ◊ *Seit Jahren werden die Löhne niedrig gehalten.* **3.** *(a job)* halten ['haltn̩] <hält, hielt, hat gehalten> ◊ *Du kannst keinen Job länger als drei Monate halten.*
• **hold in** [phras v] *(keep back, contain)* zurückhalten [tsu'rʏkhaltn̩] <hält zurück, hielt zurück, hat zurückgehalten> ◊ *Er hielt seinen Ärger zurück.; (hide)* verbergen [fɛ'bɛʳgn̩] <verbirgt, verbarg, hat verborgen> ◊ *Ich konnte meine Gefühle nicht verbergen.*
• **hold off** [phras v] **1.** *(an action, a task)* hold off *(on sth)* (mit etw.) warten ['vaʳtn̩] <wartet, wartete, hat gewartet> ◊ *Er will nicht länger warten.* ♦ *Wie lange können wir mit der Reparatur noch warten?* hold off doing sth etw. hinauszögern [hɪ'naɔstsøːgɐn] <zögert hinaus, zögerte hinaus, hat hinausgezögert> ◊ *eine Entscheidung hinauszögern* **2.** *(attackers, an attack)* hold sb/sth off jdn/etw. abwehren ['apveːrən] +haben ◊ *einen Angreifer/Angriff abwehren; (protect against rain, wind etc.)* abhalten ['aphaltn̩] <hält ab, hielt ab, hat abgehalten> ◊ *Das Dach hält den Regen ab.* **3.** *(rain or storm: not come)* ausbleiben ['aɔsblaɛbm̩] <bleibt aus, blieb aus, ist ausgeblieben> ◊ *Das angekündigte Gewitter blieb aus.*
• **hold on** [phras v] **1.** *(with your hands, so you don't loose balance)* sich festhalten ['fɛsthaltn̩] <hält

sich fest, hielt sich fest, hat sich festgehalten> ◊ *Haltet euch gut fest, Kinder!* hold on to sth sich an etw. [dat] festhalten ◊ *sich am Geländer festhalten; (so that sth doesn't fall down)* etw. festhalten ['fɛsthaltn̩] ◊ *Halt das Seil fest!* **2.** *(fig) (to an idea, memory, emotion)* hold on to sth an etw. [dat] festhalten [an ... ‚fɛsthaltn̩] <hält fest, hielt fest, hat festgehalten> ◊ *an einer Hoffnung/Vorstellung festhalten* **3.** *(not lose or give away)* hold on to sth auf etw. [acc] gut aufpassen [aof ... ‚guːt ‚aofpasn̩] +haben ◊ *Pass gut auf die Schrauben auf, die brauchen wir nachher noch.* **4.** *(wait)* warten ['vaʳtn̩] <wartet, wartete, hat gewartet> ◊ *Warte mal kurz; ich bin gleich wieder da.* ♦ *Warte mal! Nein, das kann nicht stimmen.* **5.** *(not give up)* durchhalten ['dʊʳçhaltn̩] <hält durch, hielt durch, hat durchgehalten> ◊ *Halte durch, es dauert nicht mehr lange.*
• **hold out** [phras v] **1.** *(so that the person addressed can reach the object held out)* hinhalten ['hɪnhaltn̩] <hält hin, hielt hin, hat hingehalten> ◊ *jdm sein Glas hinhalten; (so the speaker can reach it)* herhalten ['heːɐhaltn̩] <hält her, hielt her, hat hergehalten> ◊ *Kannst du bitte mal deine Tasse herhalten?* hold out your hand die Hand ausstrecken [diː 'hant ‚aɔsʃtrɛkn̩] +haben ◊ *Ich streckte die Hand aus und sie gab mir das Geld.; (cup your hand)* die Hand aufhalten [diː 'hant ‚aofhaltn̩] <hält auf, hielt auf, hat aufgehalten> ◊ *Halt mal die Hand auf — ich hab was für dich.* **2.** *(not give up, survive)* durchhalten ['dʊʳçhaltn̩] <hält durch, hielt durch, hat durchgehalten> ◊ *Wenn du langsamer läufst, hältst du länger durch.* ♦ *Wie lange kann man ohne Wasser durchhalten?* hold up for another quarter of an hour noch eine Viertelstunde durchhalten können hold up for a competition etc. einen Wettkampf etc. durchstehen [aenən ‚vɛtkampf 'dʊʳçʃteːən] <steht durch, stand durch, hat durchgestanden> ◊ *Ob ihr Arm den Wettkampf durchstehen wird?* **3.** *(wait for sth better)* hold out for sth etw. abwarten ['apvaʳtn̩] <wartet ab, wartete ab, hat abgewartet> ◊ *ein besseres Angebot/einen günstigeren Kurs abwarten* **4.** *(not reveal)* hold out on sth etw. für sich behalten [fyːɐ̯ ... bəhaltn̩] <behält, behielt, hat behalten> ◊ *Ich behielt meine Meinung für mich.* hold out on sb Geheimnisse vor jdm haben [gə'haemnɪsə foːɐ̯ ... haːbm̩] +haben
• **hold over** [phras v] **1.** *(postpone)* hold sth over etw. verschieben [fɛ'ʃiːbm̩] <verschiebt, verschob, hat verschoben> ◊ *Die Sitzung wurde auf den nächsten Tag verschoben.* **2.** *(blackmail)* hold sth over sb jdn mit etw. erpressen [mɪt ... ɐ‚prɛsn̩] <erpresst, erpresste, hat erpresst>
• **hold to** [phras v] **1.** *(maintain sth)* hold to sth bei etw. bleiben [bae ... 'blaebm̩] <bleibt, blieb, ist geblieben> ◊ *Bleibst du bei deinem Plan/deiner Ansicht?* **2.** *(insist sb does sth)* hold sb to their promise/word darauf bestehen, dass jd sein Versprechen/Wort hält [daraof 'bəʃteːən das ... zaen fɛʃprɛçn̩/vɔʳt 'hɛlt] <besteht, bestand, hat bestanden> be held to sth an etw. [acc] gebunden sein [an ... gə‚bʊndn̩ zaen] +sein ◊ *Ich bin an die Vorschriften gebunden.* I'll hold you to that. Ich werde darauf zurückkommen.
• **hold together** [phras v] zusammenhalten [tsu'tsamn̩haltn̩] <hält zusammen, hielt zusammen, hat zusammengehalten> ◊ *das Haar mit einem Band zusammenhalten* ♦ *Wie halten die einzelnen Teile*

zusammen?

● **hold up** [phras v] **1.** *(support)* halten ['hαltn] <hält, hielt, hat gehalten> ◊ *Kannst du den Sack noch halten, oder ist er zu schwer?* **2.** *(delay, put off)* aufhalten ['aͻfhaltn] <hält auf, hielt auf, hat aufgehalten> ◊ *Solche Probleme können mich nicht aufhalten.* ♦ *Geb ruhig, lass dich nicht aufhalten.; (stop)* stoppen ['ʃtͻpm] +haben ◊ *Das Projekt wurde wegen Geldmangels gestoppt.* sth is held up etw. verzögert sich [fɛ'tsøːget] <verzögert sich, verzögerte sich, hat sich verzögert> **3.** *(rob)* überfallen [ybɐ'falən] <überfällt, überfiel, hat überfallen> ◊ *eine Bank/eine Tankstelle überfallen* **4.** *(as an example etc.)* hold sb/sth up as sth jdn/etw. als etw. hinstellen [als ... hɪnʃtɛlən] +haben ◊ *Sie stellt mir meine Schwester immer als leuchtendes Vorbild hin.* → **hold²** 1.

holder [noun] **1.** *(of shares, a licence etc.)* Inhaber ['ɪnhaːbɐ] der <-s, -> ♀Inhaberin ['ɪnhaːbərɪn] die <-, -nen> ◊ *Inhaber eines gültigen Passes sein* ♦ *der Inhaber eines eingetragenen Warenzeichens* **2.** *(of a distinction)* Träger ['trɛːgə] der <-s, -> ♀Trägerin ['trɛːgərɪn] die <-, -nen> ◊ *die Trägerin des Friedensnobelpreises* **3.** *(support, container for sth)* Halter ['haltɐ] der <-s, -> ◊ *ein Halter für Räucherstäbchen* candle holder Kerzenhalter ['kɛ'tsnhaltɐ]

holding [noun] **1.** *(of shares)* Aktien ['aktsi̯ən] die <-> pl ◊ *seine Aktien verkaufen* holding company Holdinggesellschaft ['hoːldɪŋgəzɛlʃaft] die <-, -en> **2.** *(land with buildings)* Anwesen ['anveːzn] das <-s, -> ◊ *ein herrschaftliches/landwirtschaftliches Anwesen*

hold-up [noun] **1.** *(of people, things)* Stau [ʃtao] der <-(e)s, -s or seldom -e> ◊ *Bitte rechtzeitig kommen, sonst gibt es wieder Stau an den Kassen!* **2.** *(at a bank, garage etc.)* Überfall ['yːbɐfal] der <-(e)s, Überfälle> ◊ *ein bewaffneter Überfall auf die Sparkasse*

hole [noun] **1.** *(aperture, damaged area, sunken target, lack of sth, filthy place)* Loch [lͻx] das <-(e)s, Löcher> ◊ *ein Loch graben/buddeln* ♦ *ein Loch im Knie/in der Hose haben* ♦ *ein Golfplatz mit 18 Löchern* ♦ *ein Loch im Etat* ♦ *Er haust in einem dunklen, feuchten Loch.* **2.** *(dug by sb)* Grube ['gruːbə] die <-, -n> ◊ *eine Grube ausheben/graben* **3.** *(village)* Nest [nɛst] das <-(e)s, -er> *(fam, pej)* ◊ *Sie wohnt in irgendeinem Nest in der Eifel.* **4.** *(predicament)* Klemme ['klɛmə] die <-, -n> *most sing (fam)* ◊ *in einer/der Klemme sein* ♦ *jdm aus der Klemme helfen* **5.** *(of rabbits)* Bau [bao] der <-(e)s, -e> mouse hole Mauseloch ['maozəlͻx] ⊚ *riddled with holes* völlig durchlöchert blow a hole in sth *(in arguments, a theory etc.)* etw. widerlegen make a hole in sth *(in supplies etc.)* ein Loch in etw. [acc] reißen

holiday [noun] **1.** *(in the UK: time off work)* Urlaub ['ʊɐlaop] der <-(e)s, -e> ◊ *Ich brauche ein paar Tage Urlaub.* ♦ *zu Hause/in Spanien Urlaub machen* ♦ *in Urlaub fahren* ♦ *Wie viel Urlaub steht mir jährlich zu?* **2.** *(in the UK: time off school)* Ferien ['feːri̯ən] die <-> only pl ◊ *Im Sommer haben wir sechs Wochen Ferien.* ♦ *Die Ferien an der Nordsee waren wirklich toll!* **3.** *(statutory holiday)* (bank/public) holiday (gesetzlicher) Feiertag [(gə,zɛtslɪçɐ) 'faɐetaːk] <-(e)s, -e> ◊ *Der 1. Mai ist*

ein Feiertag.

holidaymaker [noun] Urlauber ['ʊːɐlaobɐ] der <-s, -> ♀Urlauberin ['ʊːɐlaobərɪn] die <-, -nen>

Holland [noun] Niederlande ['niːdɐlandə] die <-> *article only in combination with attribute, only pl* ◊ *Ich komme aus den Niederlanden.*

hollow [adj] **1.** *(cavity, voice)* hohl [hoːl] ◊ *Der alte Baum war hohl.* ♦ *ein hohler Zahn* **2.** *(cheeks)* eingefallen ['aɛngəfalən] ◊ *eingefallene Wangen haben* ♦ *Ihr Gesicht war eingefallen.*

holly [noun] *(plant)* Stechpalme ['ʃtɛçpalmə] die <-, -n>; *(decoration)* Stechpalmzweig ['ʃtɛçpalmtsvaɛk] der <-(e)s, -e>

holy [adj] heilig ['haɛlɪç] ◊ *die heilige Messe* ♦ *Diese Stätte ist heilig.* ♦ *ein heiliger Mann*

home¹ [noun] **1.** *(place of residence)* Zuhause [tsu'haozə] das <-s> no pl ◊ *einem Hund ein neues Zuhause geben* ♦ *kein Zuhause haben* ♦ *ihr neues Berliner Zuhause* at home zu Hause [tsu: 'haozə] ◊ *zu Hause sein/bleiben/arbeiten* be/feel at home sich wie zu Hause fühlen be away from home nicht zu Hause sein to work from home von zu Hause aus arbeiten leave home das Haus verlassen [das 'haos fɛ,lasn] <verlässt, verließ, hat verlassen> **2.** *(nice and cosy, institution)* Heim [haɛm] das <-(e)s, -e> ◊ *sich ein gemütliches Heim schaffen* ♦ *in ein Heim eingewiesen werden* **3.** *(country)* Heimat ['haɛmaːt] die <-> no pl ◊ *in die (alte) Heimat zurückkehren* ♦ *Die Heimat der Eisbären ist die Arktis.* make sth your home sich irgendwo niederlassen ['niːdɐlasn] <lässt sich nieder, ließ sich nieder, hat sich niedergelassen> **4.** *(within your country)* at home im Inland [ɪm 'ɪnlant] ◊ *Der Umsatz im Inland stieg um 5%.* home affairs Innenpolitik ['ɪnənpoli,tiːk] die <-> no pl home market Inlandsmarkt ['ɪnlantsma'kt] der <-(e)s, Inlandsmärkte> ⊚ *make yourself at home* es sich bequem machen *(as an invitation)* fühl dich/fühlen Sie sich wie zu Hause

home² [adv] nach Hause [naːx 'haozə] ◊ *nach Hause fahren/gehen/kommen* ♦ *Der Flug nach Hause war angenehm.* ⊚ *drive/hammer/hit sth home (so you understand)* jdm etw. klarmachen *(so you act like you should)* jdm etw. einbläuen ◊ *Sie bläute ihren Kindern ein, vorsichtig zu sein.* hit/strike sth home bei jdm ankommen take sth home etw. heimbringen ◊ *Sie bringt im Monat 1500 Euro heim.* nothing to write home about nichts Besonderes

homeless [adj] obdachlos ['ͻpdaxloːs] no comp/superl ◊ *ein obdachloser Bettler* ♦ *Er ist obdachlos geworden.*

home page [noun] Homepage ['hoːmpeːtʃ] die <-, -s>

homesick [adj] heimwehkrank ['haɛmveːkraŋk] no comp/superl, only before ns ◊ *ein heimwehkrankes Kind* be homesick Heimweh haben ['haɛmveː: haːbm] +haben

home town [noun] Wohnort ['voːnlͻ'rt] der <-(e)s, -e>

homework [noun] Hausaufgabe ['haoslaofgaːbə] die <-, -n> ◊ *Was habt ihr in Deutsch als Hausaufgabe auf?* ♦ *Hast du deine Hausaufgaben schon gemacht?*

homosexual [adj] homosexuell [homozɛksu'ɛl] no comp/superl ◊ *homosexuelle Männer* ♦ *Er ist homosexuell.*

honest(ly) [adj, adv] ehrlich ['eːɐlɪç] ◊ *Sei doch mal*

ebrlich — stimmt das wirklich? ✦ *Geben Sie mir eine ebrliche Antwort!* ✦ *Das muss ich offen und ebrlich zugeben.* be honest with sb ehrlich zu jdm sein to be honest um ehrlich zu sein ◊ *Um ehrlich zu sein: Das Essen war schrecklich.* be honest about sth ehrlich in Bezug auf etw. [acc] sein

honesty [noun] Ehrlichkeit ['eːɡlɪtʃkəet] die <–> no pl ◊ *Seine Ehrlichkeit steht außer Zweifel.*

⊙ in all honesty ganz ehrlich

honey [noun] Honig ['hoːnɪç] der <–s, –e> ◊ *eine Scheibe Brot mit Honig*

honor → honour¹, honour²

honorary [adj] **1.** *(as an hono(u)r)* honorary ... Ehren... ['eːrən] honorary citizen Ehrenbürger ['eːrənbyˈɡɐ] der <–s, –> ♀Ehrenbürgerin ['eːrənbyˈɡɐrɪn] die <–, –nen> **2.** *(without pay)* ehrenamtlich ['eːrənˌamtlɪç] no comp/superl ◊ *Ihre Tätigkeit ist ehrenamtlich.* ✦ *ehrenamtliches Engagement*

honour¹, honor [noun] **1.** *(respect, integrity, sth to be proud of)* Ehre ['eːrə] die <–, –> ◊ *Die Ehre des Vaterlandes ging ihm über alles.* ✦ *jd hat die Ehre, etw. zu tun* on my honour bei meiner Ehre it is an honour to do sth es ist jdm eine Ehre, etw. zu tun do sb the honour of doing sth jdm die Ehre erweisen, etw. zu tun **2.** *(award)* honour(s) Auszeichnung ['aostsaeçnʊŋ] die <–, –en> ◊ *Der Oscar ist die höchste Auszeichnung für Filmschaffende.* honours degree Hochschulabschluss mit Auszeichnung [ˌhoːxʃuːlˈapʃlʊs mɪt 'aostsaeçnʊŋ] der <–es, Hochschulabschlüsse>

honour², honor [verb] **1.** *(show your respect for)* würdigen ['vʏˈdɪɡn̩] +haben ◊ *jdn/etw. mit einem Preis würdigen* **2.** *(fulfil)* honour sth sich an etw. [acc] halten [an ... ˌhaltn̩] <hält sich, hielt sich, hat sich gehalten> ◊ *sich an ein Versprechen halten; (a contract)* einhalten ['aenhaltn̩] +haben ◊ *Der Vertrag wurde nicht eingehalten.* **3.** *(a cheque)* einlösen ['aenløːzn̩] +haben ◊ *Die Bank weigerte sich, den Scheck einzulösen.*

honourable, honorable [adj] **1.** *(deserving respect)* ehrenwert ['eːrənveːɡt] <ehrenwerter, am ehrenwertesten> ◊ *ein ehrenwerter Mann* ✦ *Seine Ziele sind ehrenwert.* **2.** *(honest)* ehrlich ['eːɡlɪç] ◊ *Seine Absichten sind ehrlich.* ✦ *ehrliche Geschäftspraktiken*

⊙ the right honourable ... *(in the UK: formal address)* formelle Anrede von Richtern und Parlamentsmitgliedern

honourably, honorably [adv] ehrenhaft ['eːrənhaft] <ehrenhafter, am ehrenhaftesten> ◊ *ehrenhaft handeln*

hood [noun] Kapuze [kaˈpuːtsə] die <–, –n> ◊ *die Kapuze aufsetzen*

hoof [noun] Huf [huːf] der <–(e)s, –e>

hook¹ [noun] **1.** *(piece of metal, hit in boxing)* Haken ['haːkn̩] der <–s, –> ◊ *Sie zog ihre Jacke aus und hängte sie an den Haken.* ✦ *einen Fisch am Haken haben* **2.** *(for a telephone)* Gabel ['ɡaːbl̩] die <–, –n>

⊙ off the hook **1.** The telephone is off the hook. Der Hörer ist nicht aufgelegt. **2.** let sb off the hook jdn davonkommen lassen

hook² [verb] **1.** *(also fig) (a fish, customer)* angeln ['aŋl̩n] +haben ◊ *einen Fisch/Kunden angeln* **2.** *(fasten)* hook sth onto sth etw. an etw. [dat]

festhaken [an ... ˌfɛsthaːkn̩] +haben ◊ *Er bakte die Leiter sorgfältig am Dach fest.*

• **hook up** [phras v] **1.** TECHN, IT *(connect)* verbinden [fe'bɪndn̩] <verbindet, verband, hat verbunden> ◊ *zwei Computer verbinden* hook sth up to sth etw. an etw. [acc] anschließen [an ... ˌanʃliːsn̩] <schließt an, schloss an, hat angeschlossen> ◊ *einen Computer ans Internet anschließen* **2.** IT *(access)* hook up to sth auf etw. [acc] zugreifen [aof ... ˌtsuːɡraefn̩] <greift zu, griff zu, hat zugegriffen> ◊ *auf einen Computer/ein Netz zugreifen* **3.** *(hang up)* hook sth up etw. an den Haken hängen [an deːn 'haːkŋ hɛŋən] +haben ◊ *Sie bängte den Mantel an den Haken.* **4.** *(people)* sich zusammentun [tsu'tsaməntuːn] <tut sich zusammen, tat sich zusammen, hat sich zusammengetan> ◊ *sich mit jdm zusammentun* ✦ *Die beiden haben sich zusammengetan, um mehr zu erreichen.*

hoop [noun] Reifen ['raefn̩] der <–s, –> ◊ *Er jonglierte mit fünf Reifen.*

Hoover™ [noun] Staubsauger ['ʃtaopzaoɡə] der <–s, –>

hoover [verb] staubsaugen ['ʃtaopzaoɡŋ] +haben ◊ *das/ im Wohnzimmer staubsaugen*

hop [verb] **1.** *(jump)* hüpfen ['hʏpfn̩] +sein ◊ *Kannst du auf einem Bein hüpfen?* **2.** *(into a vehicle)* hop in(to sth) in (etw. [acc]) einsteigen ['aenʃtaeɡn̩] <steigt ein, stieg ein, ist eingestiegen> ◊ *in ein Auto einsteigen* ✦ *Steig ein! Ich nehm dich ein Stück mit.* hop onto a train/plane in einen Zug/ein Flugzeug einsteigen

hope¹ [noun] Hoffnung ['hɔfnʊŋ] die <–, –en> ◊ *jds einzige/letzte Hoffnung* die Hoffnung aufgeben hope of sth Hoffnung auf etw. [acc] hope of doing sth Hoffnung, etw. zu tun the brightest/best hope die größte Hoffnung give sb hope, raise sb's hopes jdm Hoffnung machen

⊙ beyond (all) hope hoffnungslos

hope² [verb] hoffen ['hɔfn̩] +haben ◊ *Ich boffte, dass er Präsident werden würde.* ✦ *Jetzt können wir nur noch boffen.* hope for sth auf etw. [acc] hoffen ◊ *Er bofft auf eine Gehaltserhöhung.*

⊙ I should hope so das will ich doch hoffen I hope not hoffentlich nicht I hope so hoffentlich

hopeful [adj] **1.** *(confident)* zuversichtlich ['tsuːfezɪçtlɪç] ◊ *ein zuversichtlicher Kandidat* ✦ *zuversichtlich sein, dass etw. passiert* be hopeful of doing sth zuversichtlich sein, dass man etw. tut **2.** *(promising)* vielversprechend ['fiːlfɛʃprɛçnt] ◊ *eine vielversprechende Entwicklung* ✦ *Die Aussichten sind vielversprechend.* **3.** *(full of hope)* hoffnungsvoll ['hɔfnʊŋsfɔl] ◊ *ein hoffnungsvoller Blick* be hopeful that sth will happen hoffen, dass etw. passiert ['hɔfn̩ das ... paˌsiːɡt] +haben

hopefully [adv] **1.** *(expressing hope that sth will happen)* hoffentlich ['hɔfn̩tlɪç] no comp/superl ◊ *Hoffentlich kommt er bald.* **2.** *(full of hope)* hoffnungsvoll ['hɔfnʊŋsfɔl] ◊ *Er sah sie hoffnungsvoll an.*

hopeless [adj] **1.** *(without hope, awful)* hoffnungslos ['hɔfnʊŋsloːs] <hoffnungsloser, am hoffnungslosesten> ◊ *Dieser Fall ist absolut hoffnungslos.* ✦ *ein hoffnungsloses Durcheinander* **2.** *(incompetent)* unfähig ['ʊnfɛːɪç] ◊ *ein unfähiger Lehrer* ✦ *Als Managerin ist sie einfach unfähig.* be hopeless at (doing) sth etw. überhaupt nicht können [ybeˈhaopt nɪçt ˌkœnən] <kann, konnte, hat können> ◊ I'm hopeless at dancing. Ich kann überhaupt nicht tanzen.

hopelessly [adv] hoffnungslos ['hɔfnʊŋsloːs] <hoffnungsloser, am hoffnungslosesten> ◊ *hoffnungslos verliebt sein*

horizon [noun] Horizont [hori'tsɔnt] der <-(e)s, -e> ◊ *Damit haben sich uns neue Horizonte aufgetan.* on the horizon am Horizont ◊ *Die Sonne versank am Horizont.* broaden your horizons seinen Horizont erweitern

horizontal(ly) [adj, adv] waagerecht ['vaːgərɛçt] *no comp/superl* ◊ *Die waagerechte Achse wird x-Achse genannt.* ♦ *Der Wasserspiegel ist immer waagerecht.* ♦ *die Arme waagerecht ausstrecken*

horn [noun] **1.** *(on an animal, musical instrument)* Horn [hɔʳn] das <-(e)s, Hörner> ◊ *ein Stier mit spitzen Hörnern* ♦ *ein Schublöffel aus Horn* play the horn Horn spielen forest horn Waldhorn ['valthɔʳn] **2.** *(of a vehicle)* Hupe ['huːpə] die <-, -n> sound your horn hupen ['huːpm̩] +haben

horny [adj] **1.** *(sexually excited, attractive)* geil [gael] *(rude, esp pej)* ◊ *jdn geil machen* ♦ *ein geiler Typ* **2.** *(skin)* verhornt [fɛ'hɔʳnt] <verhornter, am verhorntesten> ◊ *verbornte Haut; (hands)* schwielig ['ʃviːlɪç]

horrible(-ibly) [adj, adv] scheußlich ['ʃɔøslɪç] ◊ *Das Wetter ist wirklich scheußlich.* ♦ *ein scheußlicher Anblick/Gestank* ♦ *Das tut scheußlich web!*

horrify [verb] mit Schrecken erfüllen [mɪt 'ʃrɛkn̩ ɛ,fylən] <erfüllt, erfüllte, hat erfüllt> ◊ *Der Anblick erfüllte mich mit Schrecken.* be horrified entsetzt sein [ɛnt'zɛtst zaen] +sein ◊ *Ich war entsetzt, als ich von dem Unglück erfuhr.*

horror [noun] **1.** *(feeling)* Entsetzen [ɛnt'zɛtsn̩] das <-s> *no pl* ◊ *Es herrschten Trauer und Entsetzen.* in horror entsetzt [ɛnt'zɛtst] *no superl* ◊ *Entsetzt saben sie die Bilder im Fernseben.* have a horror of sth einen Horror vor etw. haben [aenən 'hɔroː̯ɡ foː̯ɡ ... haːbm̩] +haben *(fam)* have a horror of doing sth einen Horror davor haben, etw. zu tun **2.** *(experience)* Schrecken ['ʃrɛkn̩] der <-s, -> ◊ *die Schrecken des Krieges* **3.** *(person)* Scheusal ['ʃɔøzaːl] das <-s, -e> ◊ *Sie ist ein kleines Scheusal.* **4.** horror film Horrorfilm ['hɔroːgfɪlm] der <-(e)s, -e> horror novel Horrorroman ['hɔroːgroˌmaːn] der <-s, -e>

hors d'oeuvre [noun] *(starter)* Vorspeise ['foː̯ɡʃpaezə] die <-, -n> ◊ *Als Vorspeise nehme ich gefüllte Pilze.; (canapé)* Häppchen ['hɛpçən] das <-s, -> ◊ *appetitliche Häppchen berumreichen*

horse [noun] Pferd [pfeːgt] das <-(e)s, -e> ◊ *auf einem Pferd reiten* ♦ *am Pferd turnen* ⊚ from the horse's mouth aus erster Hand back the wrong horse aufs falsche Pferd setzen *(fam)* hold your horses immer sachte *(fam)*

horsepower [noun] Pferdestärke ['pfeːgdəʃtɛʳkə] die <-, -n>

hose, hosepipe [noun] Schlauch [ʃlaox] der <-(e)s, Schläuche> ◊ *den Rasen mit dem Schlauch sprengen* garden hose Gartenschlauch ['gaʳtn̩ʃlaox] fire hose Feuerwehrschlauch ['fɔøveːgʃlaox]

hospital [noun] Krankenhaus ['kraŋkn̩haos] das <-es, Krankenhäuser> ◊ *aus dem Krankenhaus entlassen werden* in hospital im Krankenhaus admit sb to hospital jdn ins Krankenhaus einliefern

hospitality [noun] Gastfreundschaft ['gastfrɔøntʃaft] die <-> *no pl* ◊ *Ich möchte mich für eure Gastfreundschaft bedanken.*

host¹ [noun] **1.** *(person, institution, city, country inviting*

sb) Gastgeber ['gastgeːbɐ] der <-s, -> ♀Gastgeberin ['gastgeːbərɪn] die <-, -nen> ◊ *Er ist ein perfekter Gastgeber.* be/play host to sth Gastgeber ... [gen] sein ◊ *Japan ist Gastgeber des nächsten Weltwirtschaftsgipfels.* **2.** TV Showmaster ['ʃoːmaːstɐ] der <-s, -> ♀Showmasterin ['ʃoːmaːstərɪn] die <-, -nen> ◊ *Er ist Showmaster bei einem bekannten Fernsebsender.* ♦ *eine sympathische Showmasterin* **3.** *(a lot)* a host of eine Reihe von etw. [aenə 'raeə fɔn] ◊ *Er batte eine ganze Reihe von Fragen.* **4.** BOT, ZOO, MED *(to a parasite)* Wirt [vɪʳt] der <-(e)s, -e> ◊ *Der Erreger benutzt Rinder als Wirt.* **5.** IT Hauptrechner ['haoptrɛçnɐ] der <-s, -> **6.** REL Host Hostie ['hɔstiə] die <-, -n>

host² [verb] **1.** *(a special event)* ausrichten ['aosrɪçtn̩] <richtet aus, richtete aus, hat ausgerichtet> ◊ *ein Fest ausrichten* **2.** TV moderieren [modeˈriːrən] <moderiert, moderierte, hat moderiert> ◊ *eine Fernsebsendung moderieren* **3.** IT *(a website)* verwalten [fɐ'valtn̩] <verwaltet, verwaltete, hat verwaltet> ◊ *Wir verwalten Webseiten für Firmen.*

hostage [noun] Geisel ['gaezl̩] die <-, -n> hold sb hostage jdn als Geisel festhalten take sb hostage jdn als Geisel nehmen

hostel [noun] **1.** *(for the homeless, refugees)* Wohnheim ['voːnhaem] das <-(e)s, -e> ◊ *ein Wohnheim für Flüchtlinge* **2.** *(for tourists)* (youth) hostel Jugendherberge ['juːɡn̩thɛʳbɛʳɡə] die <-, -n> ◊ *in einer Jugendherberge übernachten*

hostile [adj] **1.** *(threatening, bleak)* feindselig ['faentzeːlɪç] ◊ *Sie war ibm gegenüber offen feindselig.* ♦ *eine feindselige Umgebung* **2.** *(enemy, country)* feindlich ['faentlɪç] *no comp/superl, mostly before ns* ◊ *eine feindliche Übernahme* **3.** *(attitude, stance)* ablehnend ['apleːnənt] ◊ *eine ablehnende Haltung* be hostile to(wards) sth etw. ablehnen ['apleːnən] +haben ◊ *Der Großteil der Bevölkerung lehnt Kernenergie ab.*

hostility [noun] **1.** *(opposition)* Ablehnung ['apleːnʊŋ] die <-, -en> *most sing* hostility to/towards sth Ablehnung ... [gen] ◊ *die Ablehnung neuer Technologien* **2.** *(aggressive behavio(u)r)* Feindseligkeit ['faentzeːlɪçkaet] die <-, -en> ◊ *die Feindseligkeit zwischen den Verhandlungspartnern* hostility to(wards) sb Feindseligkeit gegenüber jdm **3.** *(fighting)* hostilities Kampfhandlungen ['kampfhandlʊŋən] die <-> *pl* ◊ *Ein Ende der Kampfhandlungen ist nicht abzuseben.*

hot [adj] **1.** *(high in temperature, exciting, passionate, stolen, dangerous)* heiß [haes] <heißer, am heißesten> ◊ *Das Wasser war kochend heiß.* ♦ *ein heißer Tipp* ♦ *heiße Ware* ♦ *Einige Szenen des Films sind echt heiß.* ♦ *Die Sache ist mir zu heiß.* sb is *(feeling)* hot jdm ist heiß ◊ *Kannst du das Fenster aufmachen? Mir ist heiß.* be hot for sb/sth heiß auf jdn/etw. sein; *(cooked)* warm [vaʳm] ◊ *eine warme Mahlzeit; (temper)* hitzig ['hɪtsɪç] ◊ *Sie bat ein hitziges Temperament.* **2.** *(spicy)* scharf [ʃaʳf] <schärfer, am schärfsten> ◊ *ein scharfes Gewürz* ♦ *Die Chilisoße ist sehr scharf!* **3.** *(good at sth)* toll [tɔl] *(fam)* ◊ *ein toller Sänger* ♦ *Dieser Spieler ist wirklich toll.* be hot at sth gut in etw. [dat] sein [gʊt ɪn ... zaen] +sein ◊ *Er ist ziemlich gut in Mathe.* **4.** *(news)* aktuell [aktuˈɛl] ◊ *aktuelle Nachrichten* ♦ *Die Meldung ist ganz aktuell.*

hot chocolate [noun] Kakao [ka'kao] der <-s, -s> *pl*

'*Kakao*' when used with expressions of quantity ◊ *Sie schenkte dem Kind einen Becher Kakao ein.*

hot dog [noun] Hotdog ['hɔtdɔk] das *or also* der <-s, -s> ◊ *Ein Hotdog, bitte!*

hotel [noun] Hotel [ho'tɛl] das <-s, -s> ◊ *in einem Hotel übernachten* hotel room Hotelzimmer [ho'tɛltsɪmɐ] das <-s, ->

hot-headed [adj] hitzköpfig ['hɪtskœpfɪç] ◊ *Sie ist ziemlich hitzköpfig.* ◆ *ein hitzköpfiger Mensch*

hotplate [noun] Herdplatte ['heːɐtplatə] die <-, -n> ◊ *Er zog den Topf von der Herdplatte.*

hot-water bottle [noun] Wärmflasche ['vɛrmflaʃə] die <-, -n>

hour [noun] **1.** *(60 minutes, particular time)* Stunde ['ʃtʊndə] die <-, -n> ◊ *Die Fahrt dauerte vier Stunden.* ◆ *In zwei Stunden kommen die Gäste.* ◆ *Hamburg ist eine Stunde entfernt.* half an hour eine halbe Stunde on the hour zur vollen Stunde every hour on the hour zu jeder vollen Stunde sb's darkest hour jds schwerste Stunde sb's finest hour jds größte Stunde it is hours until sth es dauert noch Stunden bis zu etw. earn 20 pounds an hour 20 Pfund pro Stunde verdienen pay sb by the hour jdn pro Stunde bezahlen a quarter of an hour eine Viertelstunde [aenə ˌfɪrtl̩'ʃtʊndə] three-quarters of an hour eine Dreiviertelstunde [aenə ˌdraefɪrtl̩'ʃtʊndə] for hours stundenlang ['ʃtʊndn̩laŋ] no comp/superl ◊ *Ich habe stundenlang gewartet.* **2.** *(time at work)* hours Arbeitszeit ['arbaetstsaet] die <-, -en> ◊ *Ich kann mir meine Arbeitszeit frei einteilen.* **3.** business hours Geschäftszeiten [gə'ʃɛftstsaetn̩] die <-> only pl ◊ *Unsere Geschäftszeiten sind werktags von 8 bis 18 Uhr.* **4.** *(measured time)* 13/14 etc. hundred hours 13/14 etc. Uhr [ˌdraetseːn/ˌfɪrtseːn 'uːɐ] ◊ *Wir treffen uns um 13 Uhr.*

🅡 for hours on end stundenlang ununterbrochen after hours *(in a shop, office)* außerhalb der Geschäftszeit *(in a bar, pub etc.)* nach der Sperrstunde at all hours zu jeder Zeit

hourly [adj, adv] stündlich ['ʃtʏntlɪç] no comp/superl; when used as an adj, only before ns ◊ *im stündlichen Wechsel* ◆ *Der Zug verkehrt stündlich.*

house¹ [noun] Haus [haos] das <-es, Häuser> ◊ *die Häuser in unserer Straße* ◆ *Sie geht kaum noch aus dem Haus.* ◆ *Er war so laut, dass er das ganze Haus geweckt hat.* ◆ *Spezialitäten des Hauses* ◆ *Sie haben vor vollem Haus gespielt.* in house im Haus ◊ *Diese Arbeiten erledigen wir im Haus.* out of house außer Haus the House of Habsburg das Haus Habsburg auction house Auktionshaus [aok'tsjoːnshaos] publishing house Verlag [fɛ'laːk] der <-(e)s, -e> house wine Hauswein ['haosvaen] der <-(e)s, -e> move house umziehen ['ʊmtsiːən] <zieht um, zog um, ist umgezogen>

🅡 get on like a house on fire sich prächtig verstehen keep house (for sb) (jdm) den Haushalt führen

house² [verb] **1.** *(give a place to live or stay)* unterbringen ['ʊntebrɪŋən] <bringt unter, brachte unter, hat untergebracht> ◊ *Die Familien werden in Sozialwohnungen untergebracht.* **2.** *(contain, hold)* beherbergen [bə'hɛrbɐgn̩] <beherbergt, beherbergte, hat beherbergt> ◊ *Das Museum beherbergt eine großartige Sammlung.*

household [noun] Haushalt ['haoshalt] der

<-(e)s, -e> ◊ *Wie viele Personen leben in ihrem Haushalt?* one-person household Einpersonenhaushalt ['aenpɛrzoːnən̩haoshalt]

house husband [noun] Hausmann ['haosman] der <-(e)s, Hausmänner> ◊ *Ich bin Hausmann und kümmre mich um die Kinder.*

housekeeper [noun] Haushälter ['haoshɛltɐ] der <-s, -> ♀Haushälterin ['haoshɛltərɪn] die <-, -nen> ◊ *Sie ist Haushälterin bei einer kinderreichen Familie.* ◆ *einen neuen Haushälter einstellen*

House of Commons [noun] Unterhaus ['ʊntehaos] das <-es, Unterhäuser> most sing ◊ *das britische Unterhaus*

House of Lords [noun] Oberhaus ['oːbehaos] das <-es, Oberhäuser> most sing ◊ *das britische Oberhaus*

House of Representatives [noun] Repräsentantenhaus [reprɛzɛn'tantn̩haos] das <-es> no pl

house-share [noun] Wohngemeinschaft ['voːngəmaenʃaft] die <-, -en> ◊ *eine Wohngemeinschaft gründen/aufmachen*

Houses of Parliament [noun] the Houses of Parliament das Parlament [das pa'la'mɛnt] <-(e)s>

house-trained [adj] stubenrein ['ʃtuːbn̩raen] no comp/superl ◊ *Zum Glück ist unser Hund endlich stubenrein.* ◆ *eine stubenreine Katze*

housewife [noun] Hausfrau ['haosfrao] die <-, -en> ◊ *Sie ist gern Hausfrau.* ◆ *Die Hausfrau empfing die Gäste.*

housework [noun] Hausarbeit ['haosarbaet] die <-, -en> ◊ *Sie hilft ihrer Mutter bei der Hausarbeit.*

housing [noun] **1.** *(dwellings)* Wohnungen ['voːnʊŋən] die <-> pl ◊ *erschwingliche Wohnungen* housing market Wohnungsmarkt ['voːnʊŋsmarkt] der <-(e)s, Wohnungsmärkte> housing office Wohnungsamt ['voːnʊŋsamt] das <-(e)s, Wohnungsämter> most sing housing benefit Wohngeld ['voːngɛlt] das <-(e)s, -er> council housing Sozialwohnungen [zo'tsjaːlvoːnʊŋən] **2.** *(cover, protection)* Gehäuse [gə'hɔøzə] das <-s, -> ◊ *das Gehäuse einer Maschine*

hover [verb] **1.** *(in the air, between two states)* schweben ['ʃveːbn̩] +haben/with indication of direction +sein ◊ *zwischen Leben und Tod schweben* ◆ *Der Ballon war lange durch die Luft geschwebt.* **2.** *(remain hesitantly)* verharren [fɛ'haran] <verharrt, verharrte, hat verharrt> ◊ *Seine Hand verharrte über dem Telefonhörer.*

how¹ [adv] wie [viː] ◊ *Wie geht es dir?* ◆ *Wie macht er das nur?* ◆ *Wie alt bist du?* ◆ *Wie schnell fährt das Auto?* ◆ *Wie dumm von dir!* ◆ *Wie kommt es, dass du schon wieder zu spät bist?* ◆ *Wie funktioniert das?*

🅡 how about **1.** *(in an invitation, proposal)* wie wär's mit ◊ *Wie wär's mit einer Partie Schach?* how about doing sth wie wär's (damit), wenn jd etw. täte ◊ *Wie wär's (damit), wenn wir ins Kino gingen?* **2.** *(when asking after sb/sth)* was ist mit ◊ *Was ist mit Susanne? Kommt sie auch mit?* **3.** *(when asking about an aspect of sth discussed)* wie steht es mit ◊ *Wie steht es mit Ihren Englischkenntnissen?* **4.** *(when referring to sth very exciting or annoying)* How about that? Was sagst du dazu?, Was sagen Sie dazu?

how² [conjunc] wie [viː] ◊ *Ich verstehe nicht, wie das funktioniert.* ◆ *Das kannst du machen, wie du willst.*

however [adv] **1.** (used to express a difference, an opposite) jedoch [je'dɔx] ◊ Er ist von der Idee begeistert. Ich jedoch habe Bedenken. ♦ Das muss jedoch nicht immer ein Nachteil sein. **2.** (when saying that sth makes no difference) egal wie… [e'ga:l vi:] ◊ Ich schaffe es nicht, egal wie hart ich arbeite. ♦ Egal wie man es betrachtet, es bleibt ein Problem. however much so viel (zo: fi:l] ◊ So viel er auch arbeitet, er schafft sein Pensum nie. However much you want it, he won't allow it. Er wird es nicht erlauben, so sehr du es auch wünscht. **3.** (expressing surprise) however … wie … nur [vi: … nu:ɐ̯] ◊ Wie konnte das nur passieren?

howl [verb] **1.** (animal) heulen ['hɔɡlən] +haben ◊ Hörst du die Wölfe heulen? **2.** (person: shout angrily) schreien ['ʃraɛən] <schreit, schrie, hat geschrien> ◊ Sie schrie wütend.; (cry) heulen ['hɔɡlən] +haben (fam) ◊ Das Kind fing an zu heulen.

h.p. PS [pe:|'ɛs] das ◊ Wie viel PS hat dein neuer Wagen?

hug[1] [noun] Umarmung [ʊm|'a'mʊŋ] die <-, -en> give sb a hug jdn umarmen [ʊm|'a'mən] <umarmt, umarmte, hat umarmt>

hug[2] [verb] **1.** (put your arms around) umarmen [ʊm|'a'mən] <umarmt, umarmte, hat umarmt> ◊ Sie umarmte ihn fest. They hug. Sie umarmen sich.; (your knees) umfassen [ʊm'fasn̩] <umfasst, umfasste, hat umfasst> ◊ Sie saß auf dem Boden und umfasste ihre Knie. **2.** (put sth around) hug sth round yourself/sb sich/jdn in etw. [acc] wickeln [ɪn … vɪkl̩n] +haben ◊ sich in seinen Mantel wickeln **3.** (lie close to) hug sth sich an etw. [acc] schmiegen [an … ʃmi:gṅ] +haben ◊ Das Dorf schmiegt sich an eine Felswand. **4.** (move closely along) hug sth sich dicht an etw. [acc] halten [dɪçt an … haltn̩] <hält sich, hielt sich, hat sich gehalten> ◊ sich dicht an die Mauer/Küste halten

huge [adj] **1.** (very big) riesig ['ri:zɪç] ◊ riesige Wellen ♦ Seine Freude war riesig. **2.** (very successful) ungeheuer erfolgreich [ˌʊŋɡəhɔɡ̯ə ɛ'fɔlkraɛç] no comp/superl ◊ Die Band soll in Japan ungeheuer erfolgreich sein.

hugely [adv] ungeheuer ['ʊŋɡəhɔɡ̯ə] no comp/superl ◊ ungeheuer enttäuscht/erfolgreich

hum [verb] **1.** (person, animal) summen ['zʊmən] +haben ◊ Die Bienen summten. ♦ Er summte eine Melodie.; (machine, appliance) brummen ['brʊmən] +haben ◊ Der Kühlschrank brummt so laut! **2.** (a place) sth is humming with activity irgendwo geht es zu wie in einem Bienenstock [ge:t ɛs ˌtsu: vi: ɪn aɛnəm 'bi:nənʃtɔk] <geht zu, ging zu, ist zugegangen>

human[1], **human being** [noun] Mensch [mɛnʃ] der <-en, -en> ◊ Menschen vertragen solche extremen Temperaturen schlecht.

human[2] [adj] menschlich ['mɛnʃlɪç] ◊ menschliche Überreste ♦ Dieses Verhalten ist doch menschlich. ◉ sb is only human jd ist auch nur ein Mensch

humane(ly) [adj, adv] human [hu'ma:n] ◊ Es gibt keinen humanen Krieg. ♦ Diese Praxis ist alles andere als human. ♦ Laut Genfer Konvention müssen Gefangene human behandelt werden.

humanity [noun] **1.** (human race) Menschheit ['mɛnʃhaɛt] die <-> no pl ◊ die Geschichte der Menschheit **2.** (human decency) Menschlichkeit ['mɛnʃlɪçkaɛt] die <-> no pl ◊ Dem Staatschef fehlt

es an Menschlichkeit. **3.** (state of being human) Menschsein ['mɛnʃzaɛn] das <-s> no pl ◊ Was uns verbindet, ist unser Menschsein.

humanly [adv] humanly possible menschenmöglich ['mɛnʃn̩'møklɪç] no comp/superl ◊ Sie leistet mehr, als menschenmöglich ist. ◉ do everything humanly possible alles Menschenmögliche tun

humble [adj] (modest) bescheiden [bə'ʃaɛdn̩] ◊ Er ist sehr bescheiden. ♦ aus bescheidenen Verhältnissen kommen

humid [adj] feucht [fɔɡçt] <feuchter, am feuchtesten> ◊ Die Luft war sehr feucht. ♦ feuchtes Wetter

humiliate [verb] demütigen ['de:my:tɪgṅ] +haben ◊ Ständig muss sie ihn demütigen.

humor → humour

humorous(ly) [adj, adv] humorvoll [hu'mo:ɡfɔl] ◊ Der Film ist humorvoll. ♦ ein humorvoller Mensch ♦ Das Buch ist humorvoll geschrieben.

humour, humor [noun] **1.** (being funny, ability to find sth funny) Humor [hu'mo:ɡ] der <-s> no pl ◊ der Humor der Situation ♦ Humor haben have a sense of humour Sinn für Humor haben **2.** (mood) Laune ['lɑɡnə] die <-, -n> ◊ gute/schlechte Laune be in a good humour guter Laune sein

hundred[1] [noun] **1.** (number) Hundert ['hʊndɛt] die <-, -en> → **four**[1] **2.** MATH (third digit before decimal point) hundreds Hunderter ['hʊndɛtɐ] die <-> pl ◊ Einer, Zehner und Hunderter addieren ◉ hundreds (a lot of people, money) Hunderte, hunderte ◊ Bei dem Absturz starben Hunderte. ♦ Hunderte von Zuschauern

hundred[2] [nmrl] hundert ['hʊndɛt] two hundred zweihundert → **four**[2]

Hungarian[1] [noun] **1.** (inhabitant) Ungar ['ʊŋɡaɐ̯] der <-n, -n> ♀Ungarin ['ʊŋɡarɪn] die <-, -nen> → German[1] **1.** **2.** (language, subject) Ungarisch ['ʊŋɡarɪʃ] das <-(s)> no pl → German[1] **2.**

Hungarian[2] [adj] ungarisch ['ʊŋɡarɪʃ] → **German**[2]

Hungary [noun] Ungarn ['ʊŋɡa'n] das <-s> article only in combination with attribute, no pl → **Germany**

hunger [noun] (also fig) Hunger ['hʊŋɐ] der <-s> no pl ◊ Hunger und Armut ♦ der Hunger nach Macht

hungry [adj] **1.** (feeling hunger) hungrig ['hʊŋrɪç] ◊ hungrige Gäste ♦ Ich werde allmählich hungrig. be hungry Hunger haben ['hʊŋə ha:bm̩] +haben **2.** (starving) hungernd ['hʊŋɐnt] no comp/superl, only before ns ◊ hungernde Kinder the hungry Hungernde ◊ Hungernde in Afrika bread for the hungry Brot für die Hungernden go hungry hungern ['hʊŋɐn] +haben **3.** (keen) gierig ['gi:rɪç] mostly after ns be hungry for sth gierig nach etw. sein

hungrily [adv] hungrig ['hʊŋrɪç] ◊ Hungrig stürzten wir uns auf das Essen.

hung up → hang up [adj] gehemmt [gə'hɛmt] <gehemmter, am gehemmtesten> ◊ ein gehemmter Mensch ♦ So bist du gehemmt.

hunt[1] [noun] **1.** (search) Suche ['zu:xə] die <-, -n> most sing hunt for sb/sth Suche nach jdm/etw. ◊ die Suche nach einem verschwundenen Kind **2.** (for animals) Jagd [ja:kt] die <-, -en> hunt for sth Jagd auf etw. [acc] ◊ die Jagd auf Rehe **3.** (people) Jagdgesellschaft ['ja:ktɡəzɛlʃaft] die <-, -en> ◊ Die Jagdgesellschaft verfolgte den Fuchs.

hunt[2] [verb] (an animal, a criminal) hunt (for) jagen ['ja:gṅ] +haben ◊ Wildschweine jagen; (an object,

information etc.) hunt for sth nach etw. suchen [na:x ... ˌzu:xn̩] +*haben* ◊ *nach Informationen suchen* hunt through sth (for sth) etw. (nach etw.) durchsuchen [dʊrç'zu:xn̩] <durchsucht, durchsuchte, hat durchsucht> ◊ *seine Taschen nach einem Schlüssel durchsuchen*

• **hunt down** phras v aufspüren ['aofʃpy:rən] +*haben* ◊ *einen Verbrecher/ein Buch aufspüren*

hunter noun Jäger ['jɛ:gɐ] der <−s, −> ♀Jägerin ['jɛ:gərɪn] die <−, −nen> ◊ *Achim ist begeisterter Jäger.* autograph hunter Autogrammjäger [aoto'gramjɛ:gɐ] Autogrammjägerin [aoto'gramjɛ:gərɪn]

hunting noun 1. *(for an animal etc.)* Jagd [ja:kt] die <−, −en> ◊ *die Jagd auf Rotwild/nach Ruhm* go hunting auf die Jagd gehen fox hunting Fuchsjagd ['fʊksja:kt] bargain hunting Schnäppchenjagd ['ʃnɛpçənja:kt] hunting dog Jagdhund ['ja:kthʊnt] der <−(e)s, −e> hunting lodge Jagdhütte ['ja:kthʏtə] die <−, −n> 2. *(for a flat, treasure etc.)* Suche ['zu:xə] die <−, −n> most sing ◊ *die Suche nach einem Schatz*

hurdle noun 1. *(obstacle)* Hürde ['hʏrdə] die <−, −n> ◊ *Der Läufer hat eine Hürde gerissen.* ◆ *finanzielle Hürden nehmen/überwinden* 2. *(race)* Hürdenlauf ['hʏrdn̩laof] der <−(e)s, Hürdenläufe>; *(in horsejumping)* Hindernisrennen ['hɪndɐnɪsrɛnən] das <−s, −>

⊛ clear a hurdle ein Hindernis bewältigen

hurl verb 1. *(throw)* schleudern ['ʃlɔødɐn] +*haben* ◊ *voller Wut eine Flasche an/gegen die Wand schleudern* hurl yourself over sth sich über etw. acc schwingen [y:bɐ ... ʃvɪŋən] <schwingt sich, schwang sich, hat sich geschwungen> ◊ *sich über einen Zaun schwingen* 2. *(shout)* hurl sth at sb jdm etw. entgegenschleudern [ɛnt'geːgŋ̩ʃlɔødɐn] +*haben* ◊ *jdm Beleidigungen entgegenschleudern*

hurricane noun Orkan [ɔr'ka:n] der <−(e)s, −e>

hurried → **hurry²** adj eilig ['aelɪç] ◊ *eine Zusammenfassung für den eiligen Leser* ◆ *Unser Abschied war sehr eilig.*

hurry¹ noun Eile ['aelə] die <−> no pl ◊ *Er drängte/mahnte zur Eile.* ◆ *In der Eile habe ich viele Fehler gemacht.* in a hurry in Eile ◊ *in großer Eile sein* ◆ *etw. in Eile tun*

⊛ sb will not be doing sth again in a hurry jd wird etw. so schnell nicht wieder tun no hurry es eilt nicht

hurry² verb 1. *(move quickly)* eilen ['aelən] +*sein* ◊ *jdm zu Hilfe eilen* ◆ *Er eilte zur Tür.* hurry to do sth etw. schnell tun [ʃnɛl] When the phone rang, she hurried to pick it up. Als das Telefon klingelte, hob sie schnell ab. 2. *(make sb rush)* hurry sb jdn drängen ['drɛŋən] +*haben* ◊ *Er drängte sie zur Tür.* hurry sb into doing sth jdn drängen, etw. zu tun 3. *(rush sth)* hurry sth etw. überstürzen [ybɐ'ʃtʏrtsn̩] <überstürzt, überstürzte, hat überstürzt> ◊ *Wir sollten die Sache nicht überstürzen.*

• **hurry up** phras v sich beeilen [bə'aelən] <beeilt sich, beeilte sich, hat sich beeilt> ◊ *Nun beeil dich doch ein bisschen!*

hurt verb 1. *(cause physical or emotional pain, injure)* wehtun ['ve:tu:n] <tut weh, tat weh, hat wehgetan> ◊

Mir tut das Knie weh. hurt sb/yourself jdm/sich wehtun ◊ *Du hast mir sehr wehgetan.* hurt your/sb's head/arm etc. sich/jdm am Kopf/Arm etc. wehtun; *(sb's feelings)* verletzen [fe'lɛtsn̩] <verletzt, verletzte, hat verletzt> ◊ *jds Gefühle verletzen* 2. *(damage)* schaden ['ʃa:dn̩] <schadet, schadete, hat geschadet> hurt sb/sth jdm/einer Sache schaden ◊ *Der schwache Dollar schadet der Konjunktur.* 3. *(person)* be hurting leiden ['laedn̩] <leidet, litt, hat gelitten> ◉ sth cannot hurt etw. kann nicht schaden it never hurts to do sth es kann nie schaden, etw. zu tun

hurtful adj verletzend [fe'lɛtsn̩t] ◊ *Sie machte eine verletzende Bemerkung.* ◆ *Das war sehr verletzend für ihn.*

husband noun Ehemann ['e:əman] der <−(e)s, Ehemänner>; *(informal)* Mann [man] der <−(e)s, Männer> ◊ *Ihr Mann heißt Christian.* ◆ *Er ist bereits ihr dritter Mann.* ◉ husband and wife Mann und Frau

husbandry noun Haltung ['haltʊŋ] die <−, −en> ◊ *die Haltung von Rindern und Schafen*

husky(-ily) adj, adv heiser ['haezɐ] ◊ *Sein Markenzeichen ist seine heisere Stimme.* ◆ *Meine Stimme ist heiser.* ◆ *Sie flüsterte heiser.*

hut noun Hütte ['hʏtə] die <−, −n> ◊ *eine Hütte aus Wellblech*

hybrid noun Kreuzung ['krɔøtsʊŋ] die <−, −en> ◊ *eine Kreuzung aus verschiedenen Apfelsorten*

hydrogen noun Wasserstoff ['vasɐʃtɔf] der <−(e)s> no pl

hyphen noun Bindestrich ['bɪndəʃtrɪç] der <−(e)s, −e>

hygiene noun Hygiene [hy'gje:nə] die <−> no pl ◊ *Die Hygiene in diesem Krankenhaus lässt zu wünschen übrig.* personal hygiene Körperpflege ['kœrpɐpfle:gə] die <−> no pl ◊ *Artikel für die Körperpflege*

hygienic adj hygienisch [hy'gje:nɪʃ] ◊ *schlechte hygienische Verhältnisse in Elendsvierteln* ◆ *Ich finde es nicht sehr hygienisch, den Hund im Bett schlafen zu lassen.*

hypocritical adj scheinheilig ['ʃaenhaelɪç] ◊ *Sie ist berechnend und scheinheilig.* ◆ *Sie kritisierte seine scheinheilige Haltung.*

hypothesis noun Hypothese [hypo'te:zə] die <−, −n> ◊ *eine Hypothese aufstellen/widerlegen* ◆ *Die Ergebnisse des Experiments stützen unsere Hypothese.* working hypothesis Arbeitshypothese ['arbaetshypo,te:zə]

hypothetical(ly) adj, adv hypothetisch [hypo'te:tɪʃ] no comp/superl ◊ *Das ist rein hypothetisch.* ◆ *einen hypothetischen Fall diskutieren* ◆ *Die Frage war nur hypothetisch gemeint.*

hysterical(ly) adj, adv 1. *(upset, unreasonable, suffering from hysteria)* hysterisch [hʏs'te:rɪʃ] ◊ *Sie wird nicht so leicht hysterisch.* ◆ *hysterisch auf etw.* acc *reagieren* ◆ *einen hysterischen Anfall bekommen* 2. *(very amusing)* hysterical, hysterically funny wahnsinnig komisch [ˌva:nzɪnɪç 'ko:mɪʃ] no comp/superl ◊ *Ich fand den Auftritt wahnsinnig komisch.* ◆ *ein wahnsinnig komischer Film*

I

i, I [noun] i, I [iː] das <–(s), –(s)> ◊ *Dieses Wort wird mit einem kleinen i/großen I geschrieben.* ♦ *I wie Ida*

I [pers pron] ich [ɪç] ◊ *Ich bin traurig.* ♦ *Immerhin muss ich das alles bezahlen.* → **ich**

ice [noun] Eis [aes] das <–es> no pl ◊ *Das Eis trägt noch nicht.* ♦ *Straßenglätte infolge von Eis und Schnee* ♦ *Er trank Cola mit viel Eis.* ice age Eiszeit ['aestsaet] die <–, –en> ice cube Eiswürfel ['aesvʏ'fl] der <–s, –>
◉ **keep sth on ice** etw. auf Eis legen

ice compartment [noun] Gefrierfach [gə'friːɐfax] das <–(e)s, Gefrierfächer> ◊ *ein Kühlschrank mit Gefrierfach*

ice cream [noun] Eis [aes] das <–es> no pl ◊ *Wollen wir Eis essen gehen?* ♦ *Möchtest du ein Eis?*

ice cream parlour, ice cream parlor [noun] Eisdiele ['aesdiːlə] die <–, –n>

Iceland [noun] Island ['iːslant] das <–s> article only in combination with attribute, no pl → **Germany**

Icelander [noun] Isländer ['iːslɛndɐ] der <–s, –> ♀Isländerin ['iːslɛndərɪn] die <–, –nen> → **German¹ 1.**

Icelandic¹ [noun] Isländisch ['iːslɛndɪʃ] das <–(s)> no pl → **German¹ 2.**

Icelandic² [adj] isländisch ['iːslɛndɪʃ] → **German²**

ice rink [noun] *(building)* Eisstadion ['aesʃtaːdjon] das <–s, Eisstadien> ◊ *ins Eisstadion gehen; (area of ice)* Eisfläche ['aesflɛçə] die <–, –n> ◊ *Sie drehte auf der Eisfläche ihre Pirouetten.*

ice skate [noun] Schlittschuh ['ʃlɪtʃuː] der <–(e)s, –e>

icon [noun] **1.** IT Icon ['aekən] das <–s, –s> ◊ *auf ein Icon klicken* **2.** *(famous person, religious painting)* Ikone [i'koːnə] die <–, –n> ◊ *sie gilt als eine Ikone des französischen Chansons.* ♦ *eine russische Ikone*

icy [adj] **1.** *(chilly, unfriendly)* eisig ['aezɪç] ◊ *Der Wind war eisig.* ♦ *Sie begrüßte mich mit eisiger Miene.* **2.** METEO *(covered with ice)* vereist [fɛl'aest] no comp/ superl ◊ *auf der vereisten Fahrbahn ins Schleudern kommen* ♦ *Vorsicht, die Straßen sind vereist!* icy conditions Glätte ['glɛtə] die <–> no pl ◊ *Bei Glätte müssen Radfahrer besonders vorsichtig sein.*

ID [noun] Ausweis ['aosvaes] der <–es, –e> ◊ *Der Polizist zeigte uns seinen Ausweis.* ♦ *Der Mann hatte keinen Ausweis bei sich.* Do you have any ID? Können Sie sich ausweisen? ID card Personalausweis [pe'zo'naːl|aosvaes]

idea [noun] **1.** *(thought)* Idee [i'deː] die <–, –n> ◊ *Ich habe eine Idee, was ich ihm schenken könnten.* ♦ *Wie kommst du denn auf die Idee?* ◊ *Ich hoffe, er kommt nicht auf dumme Ideen!* ♦ *Die Idee zu dem Roman kam ihm auf seiner Italienreise.* **2.** *(concept)* Vorstellung ['foːɐʃtɛlʊŋ] die <–, –en> ◊ *Er hat eine merkwürdige Vorstellung davon, was eine gute Ehe auszeichnet.* ♦ *Das entspricht meiner Vorstellung von einem Leben im Paradies!; (opinion)* Meinung ['maenʊŋ] die <–, –en> ◊ *Ich stimme mit seiner Meinung nicht überein.* **3.** *(knowledge)* Ahnung

['aːnʊŋ] die <–, –en> ◊ *Er hatte nur eine ungefähre Ahnung davon, wie das Ergebnis aussehen sollte.* not have the slightest/faintest idea nicht die leiseste/ geringste Ahnung haben **4.** *(purpose)* Absicht ['apzɪçt] die <–, –en> ◊ *Welche Absicht steckt hinter diesem Plan?* ♦ *Sie wollte, dass er Karriere machte, aber er hatte andere Absichten.* the idea is to do sth damit soll etw. [nom] getan werden [,daːmɪt zɔl ... ve:ɐdn] <soll, sollte, hat sollen> ◊ *Damit sollen Familien mit Kindern entlastet werden.* **5.** *(principle)* Prinzip [prɪn'tsiːp] das <–s, –ien> ◊ *das Prinzip der Gleichheit aller Menschen*
◉ **that's the idea** genau

ideal¹ [noun] Ideal [ide'aːl] das <–s, –e> ◊ *Sie ist ihren Idealen treu geblieben.* ♦ *das Ideal der Chancengleichheit* ♦ *Er sah in ihr sein Ideal.* ♦ *mein Ideal von Männlichkeit*

ideal² [adj] ideal [ide'aːl] ◊ *Dieses Hotel ist ideal für Kongresse.* ♦ *Die ideale Familie gibt es nicht.*

ideally [adv] **1.** *(under the best conditions)* im Idealfall [ɪm ide'aːlfal] ◊ *Im Idealfall arbeiten beide Eltern halbtags.* **2.** *(very well)* ideal [ide'aːl] be ideally suited for sth ideal für etw. geeignet sein

identical [adj] gleich [glaeç] no comp/superl ◊ *Alle Experimente wurden unter gleichen Bedingungen durchgeführt.* ♦ *vier gleiche Hunde* sth is identical to sth das ist der/die/das gleiche etw. wie etw. [das ɪst deːɐ/diː/das 'glaeçə ... viː] ◊ *Das ist fast der gleiche Teddy wie der, den ich als Kind hatte.* identical twins eineiige Zwillinge [,aen|aeɪɡə 'tsvɪlɪŋə] <–> pl

identification [noun] **1.** *(document)* Ausweispapiere ['aosvaespaˌpiːrə] die <–> pl ◊ *Haben Sie irgendwelche Ausweispapiere bei sich?* proof of identification Identitätsnachweis [idɛnti'tɛːtsnaːxvaes] der <–es, –e> ◊ *Wir benötigen einen Identitätsnachweis von Ihnen.* **2.** *(recognizing sb)* Identifizierung [idɛntifi'tsiːrʊŋ] die <–, –en> ◊ *die Identifizierung eines Verdächtigen; (realizing sth)* Erkennen [e'kɛnən] das <–s> no pl ◊ *das Erkennen eines Missstandes* **3.** *(considering yourself equal)* Identifizierung [idɛntifi'tsiːrʊŋ] die <–, –en> ◊ *Seine Identifizierung mit dem Nationalhelden ist geradezu krankhaft.*

identify [verb] **1.** *(recognize, pinpoint, identify sth)* etw./ jdn erkennen [e'kɛnən] <erkennt, erkannte, hat erkannt> ◊ *Wir haben das Problem bereits erkannt.* identify sb by sth jdn an etw. [dat] erkennen sth identifies sb as sb man kann jdn an etw. [dat] als jdn erkennen; *(a corpse, criminal)* identify sb jdn identifizieren [idɛntifi'tsiːrən] <identifiziert, identifizierte, hat identifiziert> ◊ *Zeugen konnten den Täter später identifizieren.* **2.** *(a species)* bestimmen [bə'ʃtɪmən] <bestimmt, bestimmte, hat bestimmt> ◊ *Mithilfe welcher Merkmale kann man diese Pflanze bestimmen?* **3.** *(perceive yourself to be equal to sb)* identify with sb sich mit jdm identifizieren [mɪt ... idɛntifiˌtsiːrən] <identifiziert sich, identifizierte sich, hat sich identifiziert> ◊ *Sie identifiziert sich*

stark mit der Hauptfigur des Films.

identity ⌜noun⌝ Identität [ɪdɛnti'tɛ:t] die <–, –en> ◊ *Die Identität des Opfers konnte noch nicht festgestellt werden.* ♦ *eine falsche Identität annehmen* identity crisis Identitätskrise [ɪdɛnti'tɛ:tskriːzə] die <–, –n> case of mistaken identity Verwechslung [fɛ'vɛkslʊŋ] die <–, –en> ◊ *Hier muss eine Verwechslung vorliegen.*

identity card ⌜noun⌝ *(general)* Ausweis ['aʊsvaɪs] der <–es, –e> ◊ *Kann ich Ihren Ausweis sehen?*; *(state-issued)* Personalausweis [pɛ'zoːna:l|aʊsvaɪs] ◊ *den Personalausweis vorzeigen*

ideological(ly) ⌜adj, adv⌝ ideologisch [ideo'loːgɪʃ] no comp/superl, when used as an adj, mostly before ns ◊ *ein ideologisches Problem* ♦ *ideologisch geschult sein*

ideology ⌜noun⌝ Ideologie [ideolo'giː] die <–, –n>

idiom ⌜noun⌝ **1.** *(special phrase)* Redewendung ['reːdəvɛndʊŋ] die <–, –en> ◊ *eine gebräuchliche Redewendung* **2.** *(language)* Sprache ['ʃpraːxə] die <–, –n> ◊ *Ich finde die Sprache dieses Autors recht ungewöhnlich.*

idiot ⌜noun⌝ Idiot [i'djoːt] der <–en, –en> *(pej)*

idle ⌜adj⌝ **1.** *(machine)* stillstehend ['ʃtɪlʃteːənt] no comp/superl, only before ns ◊ *eine stillstehende Produktionsanlage* lie/stand idle stillstehen ['ʃtɪlʃteːən] <steht still, stand still, hat stillgestanden> ◊ *Die Fließbänder stehen vorübergehend still.* Don't let the money lie idle. Du solltest das Geld arbeiten lassen.; *(person)* unbeschäftigt ['ʊnbəʃɛftɪçt] no comp/superl ◊ *Die Arbeiter sind seit Tagen unbeschäftigt.* be made idle die Arbeit einstellen müssen [di: ˌaˈbaɪt 'aɪnʃtɛlən mʏsn] <muss, musste, hat müssen> ◊ *Aufgrund des Streiks mussten 250 Mitarbeiter ihre Arbeit einstellen.* **2.** *(lazy)* faul [faʊl] ◊ *ein fauler Schüler* ♦ *Der Kater ist faul und träge.; (not doing anything)* untätig ['ʊntɛːtɪç] no comp/superl ◊ *Ich war während deiner Abwesenheit nicht untätig.* ♦ *Er hasst untätiges Warten.* **3.** *(without a good reason or purpose)* from idle curiosity aus purer Neugier [aʊs puːrɐ 'nɔɡiːɐ]; *(fear)* unbegründet ['ʊnbəɡrʏndət] no comp/superl ◊ *unbegründete Angst; (promise, threat, words)* leer [leːɐ] no comp/superl ◊ *leere Versprechungen machen*

idly ⌜adv⌝ **1.** *(without any good reason or purpose)* müßig ['myːsɪç] ◊ *Er blätterte müßig in einer Zeitung.* **2.** *(lazily)* faul [faʊl] ◊ *Wir lagen faul am Strand.; (without doing anything)* untätig ['ʊntɛːtɪç] ◊ *untätig herumsitzen*

⊛ sit/stand idly by tatenlos zusehen

i.e. d. h. [das 'haɪst] ◊ *ein Euro von hundert, d. h. ein Prozent*

if ⌜conjunc⌝ **1.** *(in case, when, expressing surprise)* wenn [vɛn] ◊ *Wenn es regnet, essen wir drinnen.* ♦ *Wenn du magst, kannst du bei uns übernachten.* ♦ *Es tut mir Leid, wenn ich unhöflich war.* ♦ *Wäre es nicht toll, wenn wir nächstes Jahr nach Norwegen fahren könnten?* ♦ *Wenn Sie nichts dagegen haben, öffne ich kurz das Fenster.; (although perhaps)* wenn auch [vɛn aʊx] ◊ *Das Buch ist sehr spannend, wenn auch manchmal ein wenig brutal.* if so wenn ja [vɛn 'jaː] ◊ *Bleibst du zum Essen, und wenn ja, magst du Fisch?* if not wenn nicht [vɛn 'nɪçt] ◊ *Stimmt das, und wenn nicht, warum nicht?* ♦ *Hunderte, wenn nicht Tausende von Menschen sind obdachlos geworden.* even if auch wenn [aʊx vɛn] ◊ *Ich mag*

ihn, auch wenn er nur selten Zeit für mich hat. What if ...? Was wäre, wenn ...? [vas 'vɛːrə vɛn] ◊ *Was wäre, wenn dein Mann uns jetzt sehen könnte?* if only wenn nur [vɛn nuːɐ] ◊ *Wenn ich nur wüsste, wie ich ihm helfen kann!* if it had not been for sb/ sth wenn jd/etw. nicht gewesen wäre [vɛn ... nɪçt ɡəˌveːzn veːrə] ◊ *Wenn sie nicht gewesen wäre, hätte er die Krise niemals überwunden.* if I were you an deiner/Ihrer Stelle [an 'daɪnɐ/'iːrə ʃtɛlə] ◊ *An deiner Stelle würde ich dieses Angebot annehmen.* **2.** *(whether)* ob [ɔp] ◊ *Weißt du, ob sie zu Hause ist?*

ignorance ⌜noun⌝ *(general lack of knowledge)* Unwissenheit ['ʊnvɪsnhaɪt] die <–> no pl ◊ *Sie hat aus Unwissenheit falsch gehandelt.* ♦ *Seine Unwissenheit überraschte mich.; (of a particular thing)* Unkenntnis ['ʊnkɛntnɪs] die <–> no pl ◊ *Unkenntnis des Gesetzes schützt nicht vor Strafe.*

ignorant ⌜adj⌝ **1.** *(uneducated)* ungebildet ['ʊnɡəbɪldət] ◊ *ein ungebildeter Mensch; (not know about a special case)* be ignorant of sth über etw. ⌜acc⌝ nicht informiert sein [yːbɐ ... nɪçt ɪnfɔr'miːɐt zaɪn]; *(not know about a field of knowledge)* sich in etw. ⌜dat⌝ nicht auskennen [ɪn ... nɪçt 'aʊskɛnən] <kennt sich aus, kannte sich aus, hat sich ausgekannt> ◊ *Ich kenne mich in Astronomie nicht aus.* **2.** *(in the UK: impolite)* unhöflich ['ʊnhøːflɪç] ◊ *Er ist so ein unhöflicher Trottel!*

ignore ⌜verb⌝ ignorieren [ɪɡno'riːrən] <ignoriert, ignorierte, hat ignoriert> ◊ *eine Frage ignorieren* ♦ *Du hast mich ganz einfach ignoriert.*

ill¹ ⌜adj⌝ **1.** *(sick)* krank [kraŋk] <kränker, am kränksten> ◊ *unheilbar krank sein* ♦ *Er war zu krank, um aufzustehen.* ♦ *Sie ist krank vor Angst.* the ill die Kranken fall ill krank werden ['kraŋk veːɐdn] +sein be ill with a fever Fieber haben ['fiːbɐ haːbm] +haben **2.** *(bad)* schlecht [ʃlɛçt] <schlechter, am schlechtesten> ◊ *schlechte Laune* ♦ *über schlechte Behandlung klagen; (effects)* schlimm [ʃlɪm] ◊ *Eine Lebensmittelvergiftung kann schlimme Auswirkungen haben.* ill feeling/will böses Blut [bøːzəs 'bluːt] ◊ *So ein Testament kann böses Blut schaffen.*

ill² ⌜adv⌝ schlecht [ʃlɛçt] <schlechter, am schlechtesten> ◊ *Sie war schlecht vorbereitet.* ♦ *Man soll nie schlecht über andere Menschen sprechen.* sb can ill afford to do sth jd kann es sich ⌜dat⌝ schlecht leisten, etw. zu tun ◊ *Sie kann es sich schlecht leisten, das Angebot abzulehnen.*

illegal(ly) ⌜adj, adv⌝ *(immigration, possession, trade etc.)* illegal ['ɪleɡaːl] no comp/superl ◊ *illegale Einwanderer* ♦ *Dieser Steuertrick ist illegal.* ♦ *Das Geld hat er illegal verdient.; (against a specific law)* rechtswidrig ['rɛçtsviːdrɪç] seldom comp/superl ◊ *eine rechtswidrige Kündigung* ♦ *Dieses Verhalten ist rechtswidrig.* ♦ *rechtswidrig handeln*

illegible(-ibly) ⌜adj, adv⌝ unleserlich ['ʊnleːzɐlɪç] ◊ *eine unleserliche Unterschrift* ♦ *Die Schrift war völlig unleserlich.* ♦ *unleserlich schreiben*

illegitimate ⌜adj⌝ **1.** *(contrary to law)* illegitim ['ɪleɡitiːm] no comp/superl ◊ *War dieser Krieg nicht illegitim?* ♦ *illegitimes Vorgehen* **2.** *(child)* unehelich ['ʊnʔeːəlɪç] no comp/superl ◊ *eine uneheliche Tochter*

illicit(ly) ⌜adj, adv⌝ illegal ['ɪleɡaːl] no comp/superl ◊ *illegale Geschäfte* ♦ *illegal Elfenbein importieren* ♦ *Der Handel mit Waffen ist hier illegal.* illicit work

Schwarzarbeit [ˈʃvaʳts|aʳbaet] die <-> *no pl*

illiterate [adj] **1.** *(incapable of reading or writing)* be illiterate Analphabet sein [anǀalfaˈbeːt zaen] Analphabetin sein [anǀalfaˈbeːtɪn zaen] ◊ *Sie ist Analphabetin.* illiterate person Analphabet [anǀalfaˈbeːt] der <-en, -en> ♀Analphabetin [anǀalfaˈbeːtɪn] die <-, -nen> the illiterate (die) Analphabeten ◊ *die Analphabeten eines Landes* ♦ *Analphabeten brauchen viel Ermutigung.* **2.** *(ignorant)* unbedarft [ˈʊnbədaʳft] <unbedarfter, am unbedarftesten> ◊ *politisch unbedarft* be computer illiterate keine Computerkenntnisse haben [ˌkaenə kɔmˈpjuːtɛkɛntnɪsə haːbm̩] scientifically illiterate wissenschaftlich ungebildet [ˌvɪsn̩ʃaftlɪç ˈʊngəbɪldət] *no comp/superl*

illness [noun] Krankheit [ˈkraŋkhaet] die <-, -en> ◊ *eine ansteckende Krankheit haben* ♦ *Er leidet an einer unheilbaren Krankheit.* ♦ *sich von einer Krankheit erholen*

illuminate [verb] **1.** *(light up, decorate)* beleuchten [bəˈlɔøçtn̩] <beleuchtet, beleuchtete, hat beleuchtet> ◊ *Nachts wird die Kathedrale festlich beleuchtet.* **2.** *(a subject)* erläutern [ɛˈlɔøtɐn] <erläutert, erläuterte, hat erläutert> ◊ *Lassen Sie mich an anhand von Beispielen erläutern.*

illusion [noun] Illusion [ɪluˈzjoːn] die <-, -en> ◊ *Lass ihr doch ihre Illusionen!* ♦ *Ein Spiegel schafft die Illusion räumlicher Größe.* be under no illusions sich [dat] keine Illusionen machen be under the illusion that sich [dat] einbilden, dass [ˈaenbɪldn̩ das] <bildet sich ein, bildete sich ein, hat sich eingebildet>

illustrate [verb] **1.** *(illuminate)* veranschaulichen [fɛ|ˈanʃaølɪçn̩] <veranschaulicht, veranschaulichte, hat veranschaulicht> ◊ *Lassen Sie mich an einem Beispiel veranschaulichen, was ich meine.* **2.** *(a book)* illustrieren [ɪlʊsˈtriːrən] <illustriert, illustrierte, hat illustriert> ◊ *Der Autor hat das Buch selbst illustriert.*

illustration [noun] **1.** *(picture, art of illustrating)* Illustration [ɪlʊstraˈtsjoːn] die <-, -en> ◊ *die Illustrationen in einem Bilderbuch* **2.** *(example)* Beispiel [ˈbaeʃpiːl] das <-s, -e> give an illustration of sth ein Beispiel für etw. sein ◊ *Dieses Gedicht ist ein gutes Beispiel für den damaligen Stil.* by way of illustration als Beispiel

image [noun] **1.** *(opinion, idea)* Vorstellung [ˈfoːɐʃtɛlʊŋ] die <-, -en> ◊ *Unsere Vorstellung vom Leben in Armut ist oft unzutreffend.* **2.** *(public perception)* Image [ˈɪmɪtʃ] das <-(s), -s> ◊ *Der Konzern hat kein gutes Image.* ♦ *sein Image pflegen* **3.** *(work of art, description, picture: on screen, in your mind, a mirror)* Bild [bɪlt] das <-(e)s, -er> ◊ *Das Bild zeigt ein seltsames Tier.* ♦ *Er spricht gern in Bildern.* ♦ *Sie betrachtete ihr Bild im Spiegel.* conjure up an image ein Bild heraufbeschwören

⊛ be the (spitting) image of sb jdm wie aus dem Gesicht geschnitten sein

imaginary [adj] imaginär [imagiˈnɛːɐ̯] *no comp/superl* ◊ *imaginäre Zahlen* ♦ *Kinder haben oft imaginäre Spielkameraden.*

imagination [noun] **1.** *(creative power)* Fantasie [fantaˈziː] die <-> *no pl* ◊ *Dieses Buch regt die Fantasie an.* ♦ *Das Kind hat eine lebhafte Fantasie.* leave sth to sb's imagination etw. jds Fantasie überlassen use your imagination seine Fantasie spielen lassen lack of imagination Fantasielosigkeit

[fantaˈziːloːzɪçkaet] die <-> *no pl* **2.** *(believing or seeing sth that is not rue)* Einbildung [ˈaenbɪldʊŋ] die <-> *no pl* ◊ *Dieser Freund existiert nur in ihrer Einbildung.* **3.** catch sb's imagination jdn begeistern [bəˈgaesten] <begeistert, begeisterte, hat begeistert> ◊ *Die Musik der Beatles hat Generationen von Menschen begeistert.*

imaginative(ly) [adj, adv] fantasievoll [fantaˈziːfɔl] ◊ *Das Kind ist sehr fantasievoll.* ♦ *der fantasievolle Umgang mit Sprache* ♦ *ein fantasievoll geschriebenes Buch*

imagine [verb] **1.** *(visualize, have an idea of, think of)* sich [dat] vorstellen [ˈfoːɐ̯ʃtɛlən] +haben ◊ *Stell dir vor, du würdest eine Million Euro gewinnen.* ♦ *Du kannst dir vorstellen, was sie dazu gesagt hat.* imagine doing sth sich vorstellen, wie man etw. tut imagine sb doing sth sich vorstellen, wie jd etw. tut **2.** *(be under the illusion that)* sich einbilden [ˈaenbɪldn̩] <bildet sich ein, bildete sich ein, hat sich eingebildet> ◊ *Manchmal bildete er sich ein, alle anderen starrten ihn an.* **3.** *(assume)* annehmen [ˈanneːmən] <nimmt an, nahm an, hat angenommen> ◊ *Ich nehme an, sie möchte auch gern dabei sein.* I would never have imagined she would have done that. Ich hätte nie gedacht, dass sie das tun würde.

imitate [verb] nachmachen [ˈnaːxmaxn̩] ◊ *ein Verfahren nachmachen* ♦ *Sie machte ihre jammernde Mutter nach.*

imitation [noun] **1.** *(process)* Imitation [imitaˈtsjoːn] die <-, -en> ◊ *Sie beherrscht die Imitation von Vogelstimmen.* ♦ *Kleine Kinder lernen vieles durch Imitation.* do an imitation of sb jdn nachmachen [ˈnaːxmaxn̩] +haben **2.** *(object)* Kopie [koˈpiː] die <-, -n> ◊ *eine Kopie von etw. anfertigen* poor imitation billige Kopie [ˌbɪlɪgə koˈpiː] die <-, -n> imitation fur Webpelz [ˈveːppɛlts] der <-es, -e> imitation leather Kunstleder [ˈkʊnstleːdɐ] das <-s, ->

immediate [adj] *(effect, danger, superior, vicinity)* unmittelbar [ˈʊnmɪtlbaːʳ] *only before ns* ◊ *Es besteht keine unmittelbare Gefahr.* ♦ *ein Einkaufszentrum in unmittelbarer Nähe* My immediate plan is to go to Berlin. Ich fahre zuerst einmal nach Berlin.; *(execution, completion, reply)* sofortig [zoˈfɔʳtɪç] *only before ns* ◊ *Wir bitten um sofortige Erledigung.* take immediate action sofort handeln [zoˌfoʳt ˈhandl̩n] +haben

immediately¹ [adv] **1.** *(at once)* sofort [zoˈfoʳt] ◊ *Ruf sofort zu Hause an!* ♦ *Er war sofort tot.* **2.** *(directly)* unmittelbar [ˈʊnmɪtlbaːʳ] ◊ *Die Straße wurde unmittelbar nach dem Unfall gesperrt.* ♦ *Schusters wohnen unmittelbar unter uns.*

immediately² [conjunc] sobald [zoˈbalt] ◊ *Ich rufe dich an, sobald ich nach Hause komme.*

immense(ly) [adj, adv] enorm [eˈnoʳm] ◊ *ein enormes Vermögen* ♦ *Die Fortschritte in der heutigen Medizin sind enorm.* ♦ *ein enorm begabter Musiker* enjoy yourself immensely sich köstlich amüsieren [kœstlɪç amyˈziːrən] <amüsiert sich, amüsierte sich, hat sich amüsiert>

immigrant [noun] Einwanderer [ˈaenvandərə] der <-s, -> ♀Einwanderin [ˈaenvandərɪn] die <-, -nen> ◊ *illegale Einwanderer* ♦ *Einwanderer aus vielen Ländern*

immigrate [verb] einwandern [ˈaenvandɐn] +sein ◊ *in*

die USA/nach Australien einwandern
immigration [noun] **1.** *(coming into a country)* Einwanderung ['æɪnvandərʊŋ] die <–, –en> *most sing* immigration authorities Einwanderungsbehörde ['æɪnvandərʊŋsbəhøːɐdə] die <–, –n> immigration policy Einwanderungspolitik ['æɪnvandərʊŋspoli,tiːk] die <–, –en> *most sing* **2.** *(passport control)* Passkontrolle ['paskɔn,trɔlə] die <–, –n> ◊ *durch die Passkontrolle gehen*

imminent [adj] bevorstehend [bə'foːɡʃteːənt] *no comp/ superl, only before ns* ◊ *Sie bereitete sich auf ihre bevorstehende Rückkehr nach Rom vor.* be imminent bevorstehen [bə'foːɡʃteːən] <steht bevor, stand bevor, hat bevorgestanden> ◊ *Die Katastrophe steht unmittelbar bevor.* be in imminent danger of sth unmittelbar von etw. bedroht sein [,ʊnmɪtlbaːʳ fɔn ... bə,droːt zaɛn]

immoral(ly) [adj, adv] unmoralisch ['ʊnmoraːlɪʃ] ◊ *ein unmoralischer Lebenswandel* ♦ *Ist so ein Verhalten unmoralisch?* ♦ *sich unmoralisch verhalten*

immovable [adj] **1.** *(steadfast)* unbeirrbar ['ʊnbəɪ'baːʳ] ◊ *In Bezug auf Ihren Entschluss ist sie unbeirrbar.; (hostility, obstacle etc.)* unüberwindlich ['ʊnlybevɪntlɪç] ◊ *ein unüberwindliches Hindernis* **2.** LAW unbeweglich ['ʊnbəve:klɪç] *no comp/superl, only before ns* ◊ *Immobilien sind unbewegliche Güter.*

immune [adj] **1.** *(not affected by)* be immune from/to sth vor etw. [dat] sicher sein [foːɡ ... 'zɪçə zaɛn] ◊ *Kein Politiker ist vor Kritik sicher.* be immune to sb's charms jds Charme nicht erliegen [ʃaʳm nɪçt e'liːɡɪi] <erliegt, erlag, ist erlegen> **2.** MED, LAW immun [ɪ'muːn] *no comp/superl* ◊ *immune Patienten* ♦ *Abgeordnete sind immun.* be immune from sth gegen etw. immun sein ◊ *Durch die Impfung bin ich gegen Hepatitis immun.* be immune from prosecution vor Strafverfolgung geschützt sein [foːɡ 'ʃtraːffefɔlɡʊŋ gə,ʃʏtst zaɛn]

impact [noun] **1.** *(effect)* Auswirkungen ['aʊsvɪʳkʊŋən] die <–> *pl* ◊ *die Auswirkungen der Kolonisation auf Afrika* ♦ *Die Auswirkungen der Flutkatastrophe waren verheerend.* **2.** *(collision, crash)* Aufprall ['aʊfpral] der <–(e)s, –e> *most sing* ◊ *Sie wurde durch den Aufprall zu Boden geschleudert.* on impact beim Aufprall ◊ *Das Flugzeug explodierte beim Aufprall.*

impair [verb] beeinträchtigen [bə'aɛntrɛçtɪɡɪi] <beeinträchtigt, beeinträchtigte, hat beeinträchtigt> ◊ *Die Verletzung scheint das Tier nicht zu beeinträchtigen.* ♦ *Zu starkes Erhitzen kann den Geschmack des Produkts beeinträchtigen.*

impartial(ly) [adj, adv] unparteiisch ['ʊnpaʳtaɛɪʃ] *no comp/superl* ◊ *ein unparteiischer Beobachter* ♦ *Ein Schiedsrichter muss unparteiisch sein.* ♦ *unparteiisch urteilen*

impatient(ly) [adj, adv] ungeduldig ['ʊngəduldɪç] ◊ *Wo bleibt er nur? Langsam werde ich ungeduldig!* ♦ *ein ungeduldiger Kunde* ♦ *ungeduldig auf jdn/etw. warten.* be impatient to do sth es kaum erwarten können, etw. zu tun [ɛs kaom e'vaʳtn kœnən ... tsuː] <kann, konnte, hat können> ◊ *Sie kann es kaum erwarten, ihn endlich wiederzusehen.*

impeccable(-ably) [adj, adv] einwandfrei ['æɪnvantfreɪ] *no comp/superl* ◊ *einwandfreie Ware* ♦ *Der Zustand des Wagens ist einwandfrei.* ♦ *einwandfrei funktionieren*

impede [verb] behindern [bə'hɪndɐn] <behindert, behinderte, hat behindert> ◊ *Der Verkehr wurde durch falsch geparkte Fahrzeuge behindert.* ♦ *den Fortschritt behindern*

imperfect, imperfect tense [noun] Präteritum [prɛ'teːritʊm] das <–s, Präterita> ◊ *Das Verb steht im Präteritum.*

imperial [adj] **1.** *(of an empire)* des Reiches [dɛs 'raɛçəs] ◊ *die Ausdehnung des Reiches;* Reichs... [raɛçs] imperial borders Reichsgrenzen ['raɛçsgrɛntsn] die <–> *pl; (of the British Empire)* des Empire [dɛs 'ɛmpaɛɐ] ◊ *die Expansion des Empire unter Elisabeth I.* **2.** *(of an emperor or empress)* kaiserlich ['kaɛzelɪç] *no comp/superl* ◊ *am kaiserlichen Hof* imperial era Kaiserzeit ['kaɛzetsaɛt] die <–> *no pl* **3.** *(measures, weights)* britisch ['brɪtɪʃ] *no comp/ superl* ◊ *Pfund, Fuß und Pint sind britische Maßeinheiten.*

impersonal(ly) [adj, adv] unpersönlich ['ʊnpɛʳzøːnlɪç] ◊ *Geldgeschenke finde ich sehr unpersönlich.* ♦ *Das Zimmer ist unpersönlich eingerichtet.* ♦ *„Blitzen" und „donnern" sind unpersönliche Verben.*

impertinent(ly) [adj, adv] unverschämt ['ʊnfeʃɛːmt] <unverschämter, am unverschämtesten> ◊ *Was für eine unverschämte Frage!* ♦ *Ich wollte nicht unverschämt sein.* ♦ *unverschämt grinsen/lügen*

impetus [noun] **1.** *(momentum)* Schwung [ʃvʊŋ] der <–(e)s> *no pl* ◊ *an Schwung gewinnen/verlieren* **2.** *(stimulus, spur, in science)* Impuls [ɪm'pʊls] der <–es, –e> ◊ *Von dem neuen Gesetz gehen entscheidende Impulse aus.* ♦ *Impuls ist das Produkt aus der Kraft und der Dauer eines Stoßes.* the impetus behind sth die treibende Kraft hinter etw. [dat] [di: ,traebmdə 'kraft hɪntɐ]

implant [verb] **1.** MED implant sb/sth with sth, implant sth in sb/sth jdm/etw. etw. einpflanzen ['æɪnpflantsn] +haben ◊ *Dem Tier wurde ein Chip eingepflanzt.* **2.** *(an idea)* implant sth in sb jdm etw. einimpfen ['æɪn|ɪmpfn] +haben ◊ *Diese Überzeugung hat man ihm von klein auf eingeimpft.*

implausible [adj] unglaubwürdig ['ʊnglaopvʏʳdɪç] ◊ *Deine Entschuldigung klingt unglaubwürdig.* ♦ *eine ziemlich unglaubwürdige Geschichte*

implement [verb] **1.** *(a plan, changes)* durchführen ['dʊʳçfyːrən] +haben ◊ *Der Aktionsplan wurde in zwei Phasen durchgeführt.; (an agreement)* erfüllen [e'fʏlən] <erfüllt, erfüllte, hat erfüllt> ◊ *ein internationales Abkommen erfüllen* **2.** *(a law)* einführen ['æɪnfyːrən] +haben ◊ *Die Regierung hat ein neues Gesetz gegen Schwarzarbeit eingeführt.*

implementation [noun] **1.** *(of a plan, changes)* Durchführung ['dʊʳçfyːrʊŋ] die <–, –en> ◊ *Was steht der Durchführung des Plans im Weg?; (of an agreement)* Erfüllung [e'fʏlʊŋ] die <–, –en> ◊ *die Erfüllung des Kioto-Abkommens* **2.** *(of a law)* Einführung ['æɪnfyːrʊŋ] die <–, –en> ◊ *die Einführung eines Gesetzes zur Informationsfreiheit*

implication [noun] **1.** *(possible consequence)* Auswirkung ['aʊsvɪʳkʊŋ] die <–, –en> ◊ *die rechtlichen Auswirkungen einer neue Richtlinie* implication for sth Auswirkung auf etw. [acc] **2.** *(hint, suggest)* die implication of sth ist etw. legt nahe, dass [leːkt 'naːə das] +haben ◊ *Ihre Äußerung legt nahe, dass er von dem Vorfall wusste.* by implication implizit [ɪmpli'tsiːt] *no comp/superl* ◊ *Der Autor kritisiert das System und damit implizit den Diktator*

selbst. **3.** _(in a crime)_ Verwicklung [fɛˈvɪklʊŋ] die <–, –en> ◊ _die Verwicklung hoher Beamter in illegale Geschäfte_
implicit [adj] **1.** _(expressed covertly)_ implizit [ɪmpliˈtsiːt] _no comp/superl_ ◊ _eine implizite Drohung_ be implicit in sth einer Sache [dat] implizit zugrunde liegen [ɪmpliˌtsiːt tsuˈɡrʊndə liːɡn̩] <liegt, lag, hat gelegen> ◊ _Diesem Ansatz liegen folgende Annahmen implizit zugrunde: ..._ **2.** _(being an important part of sth)_ A is implicit in B B bringt A mit sich [brɪŋt ... mɪt zɪç] <brachte, hat gebracht> ◊ _Die Elternrolle bringt ein großes Maß an Verantwortung mit sich._ **3.** _(absolute)_ bedingungslos [bəˈdɪŋʊŋsloːs] _no comp/superl, mostly before ns_ ◊ _bedingungsloses Vertrauen in jdn haben_
imply [verb] **1.** _(indicate)_ imply sth auf etw. [acc] schließen lassen [aɔf ... ʃliːsn̩ lasn̩] <lässt, ließ, hat lassen> ◊ _Die Zahlen lassen auf ein Wachstum von zwei Prozent schließen._ ♦ _Ihre Blutwerte lassen darauf schließen, dass Sie zu fett essen._ as the name implies wie der Name schon sagt [viː deːɐ̯ ˌnaːmə ʃoːn ˈzaːkt] **2.** _(suggest, mean)_ sth implies sth etw. kommt einer Sache [dat] gleich [kɔmt ... ɡlaɛç] <kam gleich, ist gleichgekommen> ◊ _Diese Stellungnahme kommt einer Kritik an meinem Vorgehen gleich._ sb implies that jd will sagen, dass [vɪl ˈzaːɡn̩ das] <wollte, hat wollen> ◊ _Wollen Sie etwa sagen, dass ich zu langsam arbeite?_ an implied threat eine unterschwellige Drohung [aenə ˌʊntɐʃvɛlɪɡə ˈdroːʊŋ]
impolite(ly) [adj, adv] unhöflich [ˈʊnhøːflɪç] ◊ _Es wäre unhöflich, das Geschenk nicht anzunehmen._ ♦ _So ein unhöflicher Kerl!_ ♦ _sich unhöflich benehmen_
import¹ [noun] **1.** _(of goods)_ Import [ɪmˈpɔʁt] der <–(e)s, –e> ◊ _die Nachfrage durch zusätzliche Importe decken_ ♦ _Dieser Wein ist ein Import aus Südafrika._ import duties Importzoll [ɪmˈpɔʁtsɔl] der <–(e)s, Importzölle> import license Importerlaubnis [ɪmˈpɔʁtʔɛlaɔpnɪs] die <–> _no pl_ **2.** _(importance)_ Bedeutung [bəˈdɔɪtʊŋ] die <–> _no pl_ ◊ _eine Angelegenheit von großer Bedeutung_
import² [verb] importieren [ɪmpɔʁˈtiːrən] <importiert, importierte, hat importiert> ◊ _Fleisch aus den USA nach Deutschland importieren_ ♦ _Daten in ein Programm importieren_
importance [noun] Bedeutung [bəˈdɔɪtʊŋ] die <–> _no pl_ ◊ _eine Entscheidung von großer Bedeutung_ importance to sb/sth Bedeutung für jdn/etw. attach importance to sth einer Sache [dat] Bedeutung beimessen decline in importance an Bedeutung verlieren be of importance (to sb/sth) (für jdn/ etw.) wichtig sein [ˈvɪçtɪç zaen] +sein be great/ no importance sehr/nicht wichtig sein be of little importance nicht besonders wichtig sein of secondary importance zweitrangig [ˈtsvaetranɪç] _no comp/superl_ ◊ _Quantität ist zweitrangig — auf die Qualität kommt es an!_ ♦ _zweitrangige Themen_
important [adj] wichtig [ˈvɪçtɪç] ◊ _eine wichtige Frage_ ♦ _Tägliche Bewegung ist wichtig._ ♦ _Wichtig ist, dass du es verstanden hast._ important for/to sb/sth wichtig für jdn/etw. sth is important in doing sth etw. ist wichtig, um etw. zu tun
importantly [adv] **1.** more importantly was noch wichtiger ist [vas nɔx ˈvɪçtɪɡɐ ɪst] most importantly was am wichtigsten ist [vas am ˈvɪçtɪçstn̩ ɪst] **2.** _(thinking you are important)_ wichtigtuerisch

[ˈvɪçtɪçtuːərɪʃ] ◊ _Wichtigtuerisch drängte sie sich vor._ ♦ _„Also, ich mache das immer ganz anders", sagte er wichtigtuerisch._
impose [verb] **1.** _(a task, condition)_ impose sth on sb jdm etw. aufzwingen [ˈaɔftsvɪŋən] <zwingt auf, zwang auf, hat aufgezwungen> ◊ _Ich möchte meine Meinung niemandem aufzwingen._ **2.** _(a fine, ban, sentence, restrictions)_ verhängen [fɛˈhɛŋən] <verhängt, verhängte, hat verhängt> ◊ _Der Richter hat die Höchststrafe verhängt._ ♦ _Sanktionen gegen ein Land verhängen_ **3.** _(cause inconvenience)_ impose on sb jdm zur Last fallen [tsuːɐ̯ ˈlast falən] <fällt, fiel, ist gefallen> ◊ _Sie haben mich eingeladen, aber ich wollte ihnen nicht zur Last fallen._ I don't like to impose. Ich möchte Ihnen nicht zur Last fallen. impose yourself (on sb) sich (jdm) aufdrängen [ˈaɔfdrɛŋən] +haben
impossible(-ibly) [adj, adv] unmöglich [ˈʊnmøːklɪç] _seldom comp/superl_ ◊ _eine technisch unmögliche Reparatur_ ♦ _Es ist unmöglich, diesen Film anzusehen, ohne zu weinen._ ♦ _Hör auf, so zu schreien! Du bist unmöglich!_ ♦ _sich unmöglich benehmen/aufführen_
◉ do the impossible das Unmögliche tun
impound [verb] beschlagnahmen [bəˈʃlaːknaːmən] <beschlagnahmt, beschlagnahmte, hat beschlagnahmt> ◊ _gestohlene Waren beschlagnahmen_
imprecise(ly) [adj, adv] ungenau [ˈʊŋɡənaɔ] <ungenauer, am ungenauesten> ◊ _Wetterprognosen sind oft ungenau._ ♦ _ungenaue Informationen_ ♦ _ein Thermometer, das die Werte nur ungenau anzeigt_
impress [verb] **1.** _(fascinate)_ beeindrucken [bəˈʔaendrʊkn̩] <beeindruckt, beeindruckte, hat beeindruckt> ◊ _Dieses Buch hat mich sehr beeindruckt._ ♦ _Er lässt sich nicht so leicht beeindrucken._ **2.** _(make a mark)_ einprägen [ˈaenprɛːɡn̩] +haben ◊ _Sie ließ ihre Initialen in das Schmuckstück einprägen._ **3.** _(fix in sb's mind)_ impress sth on sb jdm etw. einschärfen [ˈaenʃɛʁfn̩] +haben ◊ _Sein Vater schärfte ihm ein, gut auf seine kleine Schwester aufzupassen._
impression [noun] **1.** _(effect, idea, feeling)_ Eindruck [ˈaendrʊk] der <–(e)s, Eindrücke> ◊ _einen guten Eindruck bei jdm hinterlassen_ ♦ _Was hast du für einen Eindruck von ihr?_ ♦ _von der Reise vielfältige Eindrücke mitbringen_ ♦ _Deine Worte scheinen Eindruck gemacht zu haben._ first impressions der erste Eindruck ◊ _Der erste Eindruck täuscht oft._ be under the impression that den Eindruck haben, dass give the impression den Eindruck machen **2.** _(impersonation)_ Imitation [imitaˈtsi̯oːn] die <–, –en> ◊ _Wie findest du meine Imitation von Michael Jackson?_ do an impression of sb jdn nachmachen [ˈnaːxmaxn̩] +haben **3.** _(imprint)_ Abdruck [ˈapdrʊk] der <–(e)s, Abdrücke> ◊ _Die Reifen haben tiefe Abdrücke in der Erde hinterlassen._ ♦ _Er hat einen Abdruck seiner Hand gießen lassen._ **4.** _(of a book)_ Nachdruck [ˈnaːxdrʊk] der <–(e)s, –e> ◊ _ein durchgesehener Nachdruck_
impressive(ly) [adj, adv] eindrucksvoll [ˈaendrʊksfɔl] ◊ _Seine Darstellung war sehr eindrucksvoll._ ♦ _ein eindrucksvolles Gebäude_ ♦ _Sie hat sehr eindrucksvoll gesprochen._
imprint [noun] **1.** _(on a surface etc.)_ Abdruck [ˈapdrʊk] der <–(e)s, Abdrücke> ◊ _Der Polizist nahm einen Abdruck des rechten Daumens._ ♦ _Abdrücke im Schnee_ **2.** _(influence)_ leave an imprint (on sb/sth)

A
B
C
D
E
F
G
H
I
J
K
L
M
N
O
P
Q
R
S
T
U
V
W
X
Y
Z

(bei jdm/in etw. [dat]) Spuren hinterlassen ['ʃpuːrən hɪntə‚lasn̩] <hinterlässt, hinterließ, hat hinterlassen> ◊ *Das Erlebnis hat bei ihm bleibende Spuren hinterlassen.* ♦ *Ein schwierige Kindheit hinterließ tiefe Spuren in seinem Werk.* **3.** *(in a book)* Impressum [ɪm'prɛsʊm] das <-s, Impressen> ◊ *Das Buch erscheint mit dem Impressum eines anderen Verlags.*

imprison [verb] einsperren ['aɛnʃpɛrən] +haben ◊ *Die Täter wurden verhaftet und eingesperrt.* ♦ *Manchmal fühle ich mich in dieser engen Wohnung wie eingesperrt.*

imprisonment [noun] *(punishment)* Haft [haft] die <-> ◊ *Ich wurde zu drei Monaten Haft verurteilt.* life imprisonment lebenslange Haft; *(being locked up)* Gefangenschaft [gə'faŋənʃaft] die <-, -en> most sing ◊ *die Dauer seiner Gefangenschaft*

improper(ly) [adj, adv] **1.** *(not quite right in its extent or intensity)* unangemessen ['ʊn|aŋəmɛsn̩] ◊ *eine unangemessene Reaktion* ♦ *unangemessen hohe Kosten*; *(wrong)* unangebracht ['ʊn|aŋəbraxt] ◊ *Es wäre höchst unangebracht gewesen, das Geschenk anzunehmen.*; *(indecent)* unanständig ['ʊn|anʃtɛndɪç] ◊ *Was für ein unanständiges Angebot!* **2.** *(not allowed, illegal)* unzulässig ['ʊntsuːlɛsɪç] no comp/superl ◊ *eine unzulässige Einmischung in etw.* [acc] ♦ *Der Polizeieinsatz war unzulässig.* ♦ *Staatliche Mittel wurden unzulässig verwendet.* **3.** *(incorrect)* unsachgemäß ['ʊnzaxɡəmɛːs] no comp/superl *(form)* ◊ *der unsachgemäße Gebrauch eines Geräts* ♦ *eine Aussage, die unsachgemäß und irreführend ist* ♦ *eine Maschine unsachgemäß bedienen*

improve [verb] improve sth etw. verbessern [fɛ'bɛsɐn] <verbessert, verbesserte, hat verbessert> ◊ *Das Niveau der Zeitschrift könnte noch verbessert werden.* ♦ *Ich möchte meine Französischkenntnisse verbessern.* sb/sth improves jd/etw. verbessert sich ◊ *Er will versuchen, sich in Physik und Chemie zu verbessern.* Things are improving. Es sieht schon besser aus. improve yourself an sich [dat] arbeiten [an ... 'aˈbaetn̩] +haben ◊ *Ich will versuchen, an mir zu arbeiten.*; *(ill person)* sb is improving jdm geht es allmählich besser [ɡeːt ɛs al'mɛːlɪç ‚besɐ] <ging, ist gegangen>
• **improve on** [phras v] improve on sth etw. übertreffen [ybɐ'trɛfn̩] <übertrifft, übertraf, hat übertroffen> ◊ *Er hofft, seine Leistung von letzter Woche zu übertreffen.*

improved → improve [adj] besser ['bɛsɐ] ◊ *Gegen diese Krankheit gibt es jetzt bessere Medikamente.*

improvement [noun] Verbesserung [fɛ'bɛsərʊŋ] die <-, -en> ◊ *Vorschriften zur Verbesserung der Luftqualität* ◊ *Wir müssen noch einige Verbesserungen vornehmen.*; *(of sb's health, morals, behavio(u)r)* Besserung ['bɛsərʊŋ] die <-> no pl ◊ *Der Patient befindet sich auf dem Wege der Besserung.* ♦ *eine Besserung in jds Verhalten* personal improvement persönlicher Fortschritt [pɛʁ‚zøːnlɪçɐ 'foʁtʃrɪt] <-(e)s, -e>

impudent(ly) [adj, adv] unverschämt ['ʊnfɛʃɛːmt] <unverschämter, am unverschämtesten> ◊ *Der Junge war unverschämt.* ♦ *eine unverschämte Bemerkung* ♦ *unverschämt grinsen*

impulse [noun] Impuls [ɪm'pʊls] der <-es, -e> ◊ *Er unterdrückte den Impuls loszubrüllen.* ♦ *ein elektrischer Impuls* You are ruled by your impulses. Du

lässt dich zu sehr von spontanen Regungen leiten. impulse buy Impulsivkauf [ɪmpʊl'ziːfkaͦf] der <-(e)s, Impulsivkäufe>

in¹ [adv] **1.** *(into an enclosed space; towards the speaker or narrator)* herein... [hɛ'raen] come in hereinkommen [hɛ'raenkɔmən] <kommt herein, kam herein, ist hereingekommen> ◊ *Warum kommst du nicht kurz zu uns herein?*; *(away from the speaker or narrator)* hinein... [hɪ'naen] fall in hineinfallen [hɪ'naenfalən] <fällt hinein, fiel hinein, ist hineingefallen> ◊ *Das Wasser ist tief; fall nicht hinein!* **2.** *(train or bus etc.; arrive)* come in, pull in ankommen ['ankɔmən] <kommt an, kam an, ist angekommen> ◊ *Wann kommt der Zug an?* come in late sich verspäten [fɛ'ʃpɛːtn̩] <verspätet sich, verspätete sich, hat sich verspätet> ◊ *Der Reisebus hatte sich um zwei Stunden verspätet.* **3.** *(person; arrived at home)* da [daː] *(fam)* ◊ *Ist Karin schon da?* come in late spät nach Hause kommen [‚ʃpɛːt naːx 'haͦzə kɔmən] <kommt, kam, ist gekommen>

in² [prep] **1.** *(expressing the position or direction of sth, during, within, having, wearing, containing)* in [ɪn] with acc when expressing motion towards a place, with dat when there is no or undirected motion ◊ *Er wohnt in Köln.* ♦ *Sie ist bestimmt in ihrem Zimmer.* ♦ *in die Luft schießen* ♦ *Schau mal in die linke Schublade.* ♦ *Im Winter wird es hier sehr kalt.* ♦ *Im letzten Jahr sind die Zinsen deutlich gestiegen.* ♦ *Er hat in fünf Wochen Examen.* ♦ *Sie hat in einer Woche viel geschafft.* ♦ *100 Dollar — wie viel ist das in Euro?* ♦ *Er arbeitet in der Computerbranche.* ♦ *In der Genetik werden fast täglich neue Erkenntnisse gewonnen.* ♦ *Er hat eine Eins in Erdkunde.* ♦ *In deinem Anzug siehst du toll aus.* ♦ *Ich musste eine Stunde im Regen warten.* ♦ *In diesem Film spielt Brad Pitt mit.* ♦ *Hast du das in der Zeitung gelesen?* ♦ *In seiner Wut zerschlug er einen Teller.* ♦ *Nehmen Sie Zucker in Ihren Kaffee?* ♦ *Haben Sie diesen Pullover auch in Grün?* ♦ *in jdn verliebt sein* He was born in 1973. Er ist 1973 geboren. There are 1000 kilograms to a tonne. Eine Tonne hat 1000 Kilogramm. in it/that darin [da'rɪn] ◊ *eine Kiste mit Sand darin* in the country auf dem Land [aͦf deːm 'lant] ◊ *Sie wohnt auf dem Land.* in the morning am Morgen [am 'mɔʁɡn̩] in the afternoon am Nachmittag [am 'naːxmɪtaːk] in the evening am Abend [am 'aːbm̩t] four o'clock in the afternoon vier Uhr nachmittags [‚fiːɐ̯ uːɐ̯ 'naːxmɪtaːks] in their hundreds etc. zu Hunderten etc. [‚tsuː 'hʊndɐtn̩] ◊ *Die Menschen demonstrierten zu Tausenden gegen die Reformen.* in ten etc. einer von zehn etc. [‚aenɐ fɔn 'tseːn] ◊ *Einer von zehn wird im Laufe seines Lebens von dieser Krankheit befallen.* sth is 20 metres/meters in length etw. ist 20 Meter lang [ɪst ‚tsvantsɪç 'meːtɐ laŋ] in your twenties etc. in den Zwanzigern etc. [ɪn deːn 'tsvantsɪɡɐn] ◊ *eine Frau in den Dreißigern* **2.** *(over a certain period of time)* seit [zaet] [+dat] ◊ *Das war das erste Mal seit fünf Jahren, dass mir das wieder passiert ist.* ♦ *Ich habe seit Jahren nicht mehr so gelacht.* **3.** *(when talking about a change of state)* change in sth Änderung ... [gen] ['ɛndərʊŋ] die <-, -en> ◊ *eine Änderung des Klimas* rise in sth Anstieg ... [gen] ['anʃtiːk] der <-(e)s, -e> ◊ *ein Anstieg der Ölpreise* **4.** *(expressing the manner in which sth is done)* in [ɪn] [+dat] ◊ *Diese Häuser sind alle im selben Stil gebaut.* in a ... way auf ... Art

[a͜of ... aːʳt] ◊ *Ich möchte das Problem gern auf andere Art lösen.* ♦ *Sie versuchte es zuerst auf die elegante Art.* in cash bar [baːʳ] ◊ *Kann ich hier bar bezahlen?* in a loud etc. voice mit lauter etc. Stimme [mɪt la͜ote ˈʃtɪmə] ◊ *Er rief sie mit lauter Stimme.* in silence schweigend [ˈʃva͜egŋ̩t] ◊ *Schweigend saßen die Männer am Tisch.* be in tears weinen [ˈva͜enən] +haben ◊ *Der kleine Junge weinte und klammerte sich an seinen Vater.* in German etc. auf Deutsch etc. [a͜of ˈdɔøtʃ] ◊ *Er sagte irgendetwas auf Russisch und ging.* **5.** *(using a particular pen, colo(u)r etc.)* mit [mɪt] ⌈+dat⌉ ◊ *etw. mit Kreide an die Tafel schreiben* ♦ *Dieses Bild ist mit Wasserfarben gemalt.*; *(using a particular style of type)* in [ɪn] ⌈+dat⌉ ◊ *Er schrieb in Druckbuchstaben.* in bold fett [fɛt] ◊ *Der Titel war fett gedruckt.* in italics kursiv [kʊʳˈziːf] ◊ *Die Fremdwörter waren kursiv gesetzt.* **6.** *(when describing what sb/sth is part of, what sb's position or attitude is)* in [ɪn] ⌈+dat⌉ ◊ *Sie ist in mehreren Vereinen.* ♦ *Haben Sie diese Briefmarke in Ihrer Sammlung?* ♦ *Die Kinder stellten sich im Kreis auf.* ♦ *Die Partei hat in ihr eine ausgezeichnete Vorsitzende.* ♦ *in alphabetischer Reihenfolge* ♦ *In seiner Haltung den Angestellten gegenüber ist er eisern.* **7.** *(when referring to the cause of sth, the event during which sth happened)* bei [ba͜e] ⌈+dat⌉ ◊ *Er ist bei einem Unfall ums Leben gekommen.* ♦ *Bei dem Vulkanausbruch wurden mehrere Dörfer zerstört.* **8.** *(when describing a set of circumstances)* unter [ˈʊntɐ] ⌈+dat⌉ ◊ *Sie verschwand unter mysteriösen Umständen.* ♦ *Er gestand unter Tränen, was er getan hatte.*

‘In’ often occurs in phrasal verbs like ‘get in’ or ‘put in’ which have their own entries in the dictionary.

inability ⌈noun⌉ Unfähigkeit [ˈʊnfeːɪçkaɛt] die <-> no pl ◊ *Sie klagte über ihre Unfähigkeit, Kinder und Beruf zu vereinbaren.*

inaccessible ⌈adj⌉ *(impossible to access)* unzugänglich [ˈʊntsugɛnlɪç] ◊ *Das Tal ist für Fahrzeuge unzugänglich.* ♦ *ein für Privatleute unzugängliches Archiv;* *(difficult to access)* schwer zugänglich [ˌʃveːɐ ˈtsuːgɛnlɪç] <schwerer zugänglich, am schwersten zugänglich> ◊ *schwer zugängliche Stellen/Bereiche* ♦ *„Das Kapital" von Karl Marx ist ein schwer zugängliches Buch.*; *(remote)* abgelegen [ˈapgəleːgŋ̩] ◊ *eine abgelegene Insel/Gegend*

inaccurate(ly) ⌈adj, adv⌉ ungenau [ˈʊngəna͜o] <ungenauer, am ungenauesten> ◊ *Wetterprognosen sind oft ungenau.* ♦ *ungenaue Informationen* ♦ *ein Thermometer, das die Werte nur ungenau anzeigt*

inadequate(ly) ⌈adj, adv⌉ **1.** *(with abstract ns)* unzureichend [ˈʊntsuraɛçn̩t] ◊ *Bei dem Nebel ist die Sicht unzureichend.* ♦ *unzureichende Kenntnisse/Verpflegung* ♦ *Seine Arbeit wird unzureichend bezahlt.* **2.** *(person)* inadequate (to sth) *(mit etw.)* überfordert [ybɐˈfɔʳdɐt] ◊ *Sie fühlte sich mit der Aufgabe überfordert.* be inadequate to do sth etw. nicht tun können [ˌnɪçt ... kœnən] <kann, konnte, hat können> ◊ *Seine Argumente können mich nicht überzeugen.*

inappropriate(ly) ⌈adj, adv⌉ *(not suitable)* unangemessen [ˈʊnlaɴɡəmɛsn̩] ◊ *Der Preis war hoch, aber nicht unangemessen.* ♦ *unangemessenes Verhalten* ♦ *unangemessen reagieren; (comment, clothing)* unpassend [ˈʊnpasn̩t] ◊ *Diese Bemerkung war jetzt völlig unpassend.* ♦ *unpassend gekleidet; (wrong(ly))* falsch

[falʃ] <falscher, am falschesten> *seldom comp/superl* ◊ *eine falsche Entscheidung* ♦ *ein falsch übersetzter Begriff* ♦ *Es ist nie falsch, sich zu entschuldigen.* ♦ *Es war falsch von dir, ihm zu helfen.*

inaudible(-ibly) ⌈adj, adv⌉ unhörbar [ˈʊnhøːɡbaːʳ] *no comp/superl* ◊ *Seine Schritte waren fast unhörbar.* ♦ *ein fast unhörbares Flüstern* ♦ *unhörbar leise*

inbox ⌈noun⌉ Postfach [ˈpɔstfax] das <-(e)s, Postfächer>

Inc. *(abbr of Incorporated)* AG [aːˈgeː] die ◊ *die Lufthansa AG*

incapable ⌈adj⌉ **1.** *(unable)* incapable of sth zu etw. nicht fähig [ˈtsuː ... ˌnɪçt ˈfeːɪç] ◊ *Er ist zu einem solchen Verbrechen nicht fähig.* be incapable of doing sth etw. nicht tun können [ˌnɪçt ... kœnən] <kann, konnte, hat können> ◊ *Ich konnte nicht reagieren.* **2.** *(incompetent)* unfähig [ˈʊnfɛːɪç] ◊ *Als Chef ist er völlig unfähig.*

incentive ⌈noun⌉ Anreiz [ˈanra͜ets] der <-es, -e> ◊ *möglichen Kunden zusätzliche Anreize zum Kauf bieten* tax incentives steuerliche Anreize

incessant(ly) ⌈adj, adv⌉ unaufhörlich [ˈʊnla͜ofhøːɐlɪç] *no comp/superl; when used as an adj, mostly before ns* ◊ *ein unaufhörlicher Kreislauf* ♦ *Das Baby schrie unaufhörlich.*

inch ⌈noun⌉ Zoll [tsɔl] der <-(e)s, -> ◊ *Die Größe von Computerbildschirmen wird in Zoll gemessen.* ⊚ not give/budge an inch keinen Zoll nachgeben

Zoll is only used figuratively, or in cases where a conversion into centimetres would be inadequate.

incidence ⌈noun⌉ Häufigkeit [ˈhɔøfɪçkaɛt] die <-> no pl ◊ *Die Häufigkeit von Krebs/Infektionen/Fehlern hat zugenommen.* ♦ *die Häufigkeit der Unfälle reduzieren* a high/low incidence of sth ein häufiges/seltenes Auftreten ... ⌈gen⌉/von etw. [aen ˌhɔøfɪgəs/zɛltənəs ˈa͜oftreːtn̩ fɔn] <-s> no pl ◊ *das häufige Auftreten von Allergien* there is a high/low incidence of sth somewhere etw. tritt irgendwo häufig/selten auf [trɪt ... ˈhɔøfɪç/ˈzɛltn̩ a͜of] <trat auf, ist aufgetreten> ◊ *In der frühen Schwangerschaft tritt häufig Übelkeit auf.*

incident ⌈noun⌉ **1.** *(disruption)* Zwischenfall [ˈtsvɪʃn̩fal] der <-(e)s, Zwischenfälle> ◊ *Die Party/Demonstration verlief ohne Zwischenfälle.* a major/minor incident ein schwerer/harmloser Zwischenfall **2.** *(unusual occurrence)* Vorfall [ˈfoːɐfal] der <-(e)s, Vorfälle> ◊ *ein bedauerlicher/peinlicher Vorfall* ♦ *ungewöhnliche Vorfälle melden*

incidentally ⌈adv⌉ **1.** *(introducing additional information)* übrigens [ˈyːbrɪgŋ̩s] ◊ *Er heißt übrigens auch Christian.* ♦ *Übrigens hat unsere Mannschaft gestern gewonnen.* **2.** *(in passing)* nebenbei [neːbm̩ˈba͜e] ◊ *etw. nebenbei erwähnen*

inclination ⌈noun⌉ **1.** *(interest)* Interesse [ɪntəˈrɛsə] das <-s, -n> ◊ *weder Zeit noch Interesse für etw. haben* ♦ *kein Interesse daran haben/zeigen, etw. zu tun* **2.** *(tendency, angle of a slope)* Neigung [ˈnaɛgʊŋ] die <-, -en> ◊ *Dieser Beruf entspricht seinen Neigungen.* ♦ *Sie zeigte wenig Neigung, ihm zu glauben.* ♦ *ein Abhang mit starker Neigung* ♦ *Er hat die Neigung, sich häufig zu wiederholen.*

incline ⌈noun⌉ **1.** *(slope)* Abhang [ˈaphaŋ] der <-(e)s, Abhänge> ◊ *Der Ball rollte den Abhang hinunter.* **2.** *(angle upwards)* Steigung [ˈʃta͜egʊŋ] die <-, -en> ◊ *An einer starken Steigung blieb der*

A
B
C
D
E
F
G
H
I
J
K
L
M
N
O
P
Q
R
S
T
U
V
W
X
Y
Z

A
B
C
D
E
F
G
H
I
J
K
L
M
N
O
P
Q
R
S
T
U
V
W
X
Y
Z

Lastwagen hängen. ✦ *eine Strecke mit zehnprozentiger Steigung* **3.** *(angle downwards)* Gefälle [gə'fɛlə] das <-s, -> *most sing* ◊ *eine Straße mit starkem Gefälle*

inclined adj **1.** *(wishing to do sth)* be/feel inclined to do sth Lust haben, etw. zu tun ['lʊst haːbm̩ ... tsuː] +haben ◊ *Ich hatte wenig Lust, mich einzumischen.* if sb is so inclined wenn jd will [vɛn ... 'vɪl] ◊ *Tu es doch, wenn du willst.* **2.** *(having a tendency to do sth)* be inclined to do sth dazu neigen, etw. zu tun [datsu: 'naɛgn̩ ... tsuː] +haben ◊ *Er neigt dazu, alles zu glauben, was man ihm erzählt.* be inclined to be sth zu etw. neigen ◊ *Ältere Menschen neigen mehr/eher zur Vorsicht als junge.* be inclined to agree (with sb) geneigt sein(, jdm) zuzustimmen [gə,naɛkt zaɛn 'tsuː:tsuːʃtɪmən] be inclined to believe/think sth geneigt sein, etw. zu glauben/denken

include verb **1.** *(contain)* enthalten [ɛnt'haltn̩] <enthält, enthielt, hat enthalten> ◊ *Das Buch enthält zahlreiche Abbildungen.* ✦ *Die Nebenkosten sind im Mietpreis enthalten.* **2.** *(consist of)* umfassen [ʊm'fasn̩] <umfasst, umfasste, hat umfasst> ◊ *Unser Service umfasst folgende Angebote: ...* **3.** *(make a part of sth)* aufnehmen ['aɔfneːmən] <nimmt auf, nahm auf, hat aufgenommen> ◊ *etw. ins Programm aufnehmen; (a document etc.)* include sth (with sth) etw. (einer Sache dat) beifügen ['baɛfyːgn̩] +haben ◊ *Bitte fügen Sie dem Bewerbungsschreiben Ihren Lebenslauf bei.*

including prep **1.** *(containing sb/sth)* einschließlich ['aɛnʃliːslɪç] *sing nouns without article or attribute are not declined when following this prep, otherwise* +gen ◊ *die ganze Klasse einschließlich des Lehrers* ✦ *der Preis für eine Übernachtung einschließlich Frühstück* not including ausschließlich ['aɔsʃliːslɪç] *sing nouns without article or attribute are not declined when following this prep, otherwise* +gen ◊ *der Preis ausschließlich der Transportkosten* not including VAT ohne Mehrwertsteuer [,oːnə 'meːɐvɛɐtʃtɔɪɐ] **2.** *(relating to a previously specified noun or section of sentence)* darunter [da'rʊntɐ] ◊ *Er besitzt viele Bücher, darunter einige wertvolle Erstausgaben.*

inclusion noun **1.** *(act of including)* Aufnahme ['aɔfnaːmə] die <-> *no pl* ◊ *die Aufnahme von 200 neuen Einträgen in das Wörterbuch; (new additions)* Neuaufnahme ['nɔɪ|aɔfnaːmə] die <-, –n> with the inclusion of einschließlich ... gen/*fam* dat ['aɛnʃliːslɪç] *sing ns without article or attribute are not declined when following this prep* ◊ *Einschließlich der drei Kinder waren wir zehn Personen.* **2.** *(in a community, group)* Integration [ɪntegra'tsjoːn] die <-> *no pl* ◊ *die Integration behinderter Kinder in normale Schulen*

inclusive adj inclusive of einschließlich ['aɛnʃliːslɪç] *sing nouns without article or attribute are not declined when following this prep, otherwise* +gen ◊ *Übernachtung inklusive Frühstück (from) ... to ...* inclusive von ... bis einschließlich [fɔn ... bɪs 'aɛnʃliːslɪç] ◊ *Die Jugendherberge ist von Mai bis einschließlich September geöffnet.*

incoherent(ly) adj, adv wirr [vɪr] ◊ *wirre Gedanken* ✦ *Die Gliederung wirkt wirr und unübersichtlich.* ✦ *wirr daherreden*

income noun Einkommen ['aɛnkɔmən] das <-s, -> *most sing* ◊ *ein gutes/schlechtes Einkommen haben* ✦ *Familien mit geringem Einkommen*

income support noun Sozialhilfe [zo'tsjaːlhɪlfə] die <-> *no pl* ◊ *Sozialhilfe beantragen/bekommen* ✦ *von der Sozialhilfe leben*

incomparable adj einzigartig ['aɛntsɪçla:'tɪç] *no comp/superl* ◊ *ein einzigartiger Blick auf die Berge* ✦ *Die Aussicht war einzigartig.*

incompetent adj unfähig ['ʊnfɛːɪç] ◊ *ein unfähiger Mitarbeiter* ✦ *Der neue Lehrer ist völlig unfähig.*

incomprehensible(-ibly) adj, adv *(hard to understand)* unverständlich ['ʊnfɛʃtɛntlɪç] ◊ *ein unverständlicher Satz* ✦ *unverständlich formulieren* sb finds sth incomprehensible etw. ist jdm unbegreiflich [ɪst ... 'ʊnbəgraɛflɪç] ◊ *Seine Reaktion war mir unbegreiflich.* sb finds it incomprehensible that jd findet es unbegreiflich, dass

inconsiderate(ly) adj, adv **1.** *(not caring)* rücksichtslos ['rʏkzɪçtslo:s] <rücksichtsloser, am rücksichtslosesten> ◊ *Das war ziemlich rücksichtslos von dir!* ✦ *die rücksichtslose Abholzung der Wälder* ✦ *rücksichtslos rasen* **2.** *(not thinking)* gedankenlos [gə'daŋkn̩lo:s] <gedankenloser, am gedankenlosesten> ◊ *der gedankenlose Umgang mit Trinkwasser* ✦ *Wie kann man nur so gedankenlos sein!* ✦ *Er handelte völlig gedankenlos.*

inconsistent adj **1.** *(not homogeneous)* uneinheitlich ['ʊn|aɛnhaɛtlɪç] ◊ *Insgesamt ergibt sich ein uneinheitliches Bild.* ✦ *Die Tendenz war uneinheitlich.* **2.** *(contradictory)* be inconsistent with sth im Widerspruch zu etw. stehen [ɪm 'viːdɐʃprɔx tsu: ... ʃteːən] <steht, stand, hat gestanden> ◊ *Die Entwicklung steht im Widerspruch zur ursprünglichen Prognose.* **3.** *(not reliable or constant)* unbeständig ['ʊnbəʃtɛndɪç] ◊ *unbeständiges Wetter* ✦ *Seine Leistungen sind recht unbeständig.; (punishment, discipline etc.)* inkonsequent ['ɪnkɔnzekvɛnt] <inkonsequenter, am inkonsequentesten> ◊ *inkonsequente Erziehung* ✦ *Kinder werden verunsichert, wenn Eltern inkonsequent sind.*

inconsistently adv uneinheitlich ['ʊn|aɛnhaɛtlɪç] ◊ *Diese Fälle sind uneinheitlich geregelt.*

inconspicuous(ly) adj, adv unauffällig ['ʊn|aɔffɛlɪç] ◊ *Die Weinrebe hat unauffällige Blüten.* ✦ *Ihre Erscheinung ist eher unauffällig.* ✦ *Folgen Sie mir bitte unauffällig.*

inconvenient adj *(causing problems)* ungünstig ['ʊngʏnstɪç] ◊ *ein ungünstiger Moment* ✦ *Die Lage des Hotels ist ungünstig.* come at an inconvenient time ungelegen kommen ['ʊngəleːgn̩ kɔmən] <kommt, kam, ist gekommen>; *(not easy)* it is inconvenient to do sth es ist umständlich, etw. zu tun [ɛs ɪst 'ʊmʃtɛntlɪç ... tsuː]

incorporate verb **1.** *(include)* incorporate sth in(to) sth etw. in etw. acc aufnehmen [ɪn ... ,aɔfneːmən] <nimmt auf, nahm auf, hat aufgenommen> ◊ *Diese Klausel wurde nachträglich in das Gesetz aufgenommen.; (use)* incorporate sth in(to) sth etw. irgendwo verwenden [fɛˈvɛndn̩] <verwendet, verwendete, hat verwendet> ◊ *Grafiken auf einer Webseite verwenden;* *(work in)* incorporate sth in(to) sth etw. irgendwo einarbeiten ['aɛn|aˈbaɛtn̩] <arbeitet ein, arbeitete ein, hat eingearbeitet> ◊ *Die Korrekturen sind bereits in die neue Ausgabe eingearbeitet.* **2.** *(a company)* gründen ['grʏndn̩] <gründet, gründete, hat gegründet> ◊ *eine Aktiengesellschaft gründen* When a company incorporates ... Wenn aus einer Firma eine Aktiengesellschaft wird, ... incorporated

company Aktiengesellschaft ['aktsɪəngəzɛlʃaft] die <–, –en> **3.** BIO *(nutrients)* aufnehmen ['aʊfneːmən] <nimmt auf, nahm auf, hat aufgenommen> ◊ *Die meisten Pflanzen nehmen Nährstoffe mit den Wurzeln auf.* **4.** *(into a community)* eingemeinden ['aɛngəmaɛndn̩] <gemeindet ein, gemeindete ein, hat eingemeindet> ◊ *Das kleine Dorf wurde 1970 in unseren Ort eingemeindet.*

incorrect [adj] **1.** *(not right or true)* falsch [falʃ] <falscher, am falschesten> *seldom comp/superl* ◊ *Die Diagnose war falsch.* ♦ *Das war die falsche Antwort!* **2.** *(not suitable)* politically incorrect politisch nicht korrekt [poˌliːtɪʃ nɪçt kɔˈrɛkt] *no comp/superl*

increase¹ [noun] *(growth)* Zunahme ['tsuːnaːmə] die <–> *no pl* increase in sth Zunahme … [gen]/von etw. ◊ *die dramatische Zunahme von Allergien bei Kindern* ♦ *Eine deutliche Zunahme des Verkehrs wird erwartet.*; *(in turnover, efficiency)* Steigerung ['ʃtaɛgərʊŋ] die <–, –en> ◊ *Das bedeutet eine erhebliche Steigerung gegenüber dem Vorjahr.* increase in sth Steigerung … [gen] ◊ *Eine weitere Steigerung der Leistungsfähigkeit gelang nicht.*

increase² [verb] **1.** *(prices, costs, numbers etc.)* sth increases etw. steigt [ʃtaɛkt] <stieg, ist gestiegen> ◊ *Die Nachfrage nach Gas ist gestiegen.* increase by/to sth um/auf etw. [acc] steigen ◊ *Die Zahl der Arbeitslosen ist um 0,2% auf 12,7% gestiegen.*; *(pressure, risk, traffic, population, interest in sth)* sth increases etw. nimmt zu [nɪmt ˈtsuː] <nahm zu, hat zugenommen> ◊ *Die Weltbevölkerung nimmt immer mehr zu.* ♦ *Das Interesse an diesem Thema hat stark zugenommen.*; *(market, fear)* etw. wächst [vɛkst] <wuchs, ist gewachsen> ◊ *Ihre Angst wuchs.* an increasing number eine wachsende Zahl ◊ *Eine wachsende Zahl von Menschen nutzt das Internet.* an increasing proportion ein wachsender Anteil **2.** *(prices, production, temperatures, a risk, the volume of sound)* increase sth etw. erhöhen [ɛ'høːən] <erhöht, erhöhte, hat erhöht> ◊ *Rauchen erhöht das Risiko, an Krebs zu erkranken.* ♦ *mit erhöhter Konzentration arbeiten* increase sth by/to sth etw. um/auf etw. [acc] erhöhen ◊ *die Benzinpreise um zwei Cent auf 1,15 Euro erhöhen;* *(your efficiency, turnover)* etw. steigern ['ʃtaɛgɐn] +haben ◊ *seinen Marktanteil auf/um 20% steigern* ♦ *das Arbeitstempo steigern* **3.** *(pressure, efforts, an effect)* increase sth etw. verstärken [fɛ'ʃtɛrkn̩] <verstärkt, verstärkte, hat verstärkt> ◊ *seine Anstrengungen/Bemühungen verstärken* ♦ *Methan verstärkt den Treibhauseffekt.* sth increases etw. verstärkt sich ◊ *Der Druck auf mich verstärkte sich.* **4.** *(the pulse, heart rate)* increase sth etw. beschleunigen [bə'ʃlɔɪnɪgn̩] <beschleunigt, beschleunigte, hat beschleunigt> ◊ *Anstrengung beschleunigt den Herzschlag.* sth increases etw. beschleunigt sich

increasingly [adv] zusehends ['tsuːzeːənts] ◊ *Dieses Thema gewinnt zusehends an Bedeutung.*

incredible(-ibly) [adj, adv] **1.** *(hard to believe)* unbegreiflich ['ʊnbəgraɛflɪç] ◊ *Sie ging mit unbegreiflicher Naivität vor.* ♦ *Sie reagierte unbegreiflich heftig.* sb finds sth incredible etw. ist jdm unbegreiflich ◊ *Seine Reaktion war mir völlig unbegreiflich.* **2.** *(expressing surprise or annoyance)* unglaublich [ʊn'glaʊplɪç] ◊ *Die Geschichte ist unglaublich, aber wahr.* ♦ *Das ist ja eine unglaubliche Frechheit/ Zumutung!* ♦ *Sie hat sich unglaublich verändert.* **3.** *(extreme(ly))* unheimlich ['ʊnhaɛmlɪç] when used

as an adj, only before ns *(fam)* ◊ *unheimliches Glück/Pech haben* ◊ *Das Ganze tut mir wirklich unheimlich Leid!* ♦ *unheimlich glücklich/wichtig sein;* *(extremely good)* sagenhaft ['zaːgn̩haft] <sagenhafter, sagenhafteste> *(fam)* ◊ *sagenhafte Gewinne/ Preise* ♦ *Ich finde ihn einfach sagenhaft!* ♦ *sagenhaft billig/gut;* *(misfortune, ill luck etc.)* unfassbar ['ʊnfasbaːʳ] ◊ *Es ist unfassbar, wie sie leiden.* ♦ *ein unfassbares Unglück* ♦ *Diese Leute sind unfassbar arm.*

incur [verb] **1.** *(costs, damages, expenses)* sb incurs sth etw. entsteht jdm [ɛnt'ʃteːt] <entsteht, entstand, ist entstanden> ◊ *Welche Kosten entstehen mir, wenn ich das mache?;* *(debts, losses)* incur sth etw. machen ['maxn̩] +haben ◊ *hohe Schulden machen;* *(a fine)* incur sth etw. bekommen [bə'kɔmən] <bekommt, bekam, hat bekommen> **2.** incur sb's wrath sich [dat] jds Unwillen zuziehen ['ʊnvɪlən ˌtsuːtsiːən] <zieht sich zu, zog sich zu, hat sich zugezogen> *(lofty)* ◊ *Durch seine Verspätung zog er sich den Unwillen seiner Eltern zu.* incur a penalty einen Platzverweis bekommen [aɛnən 'platsfɛvaɛs bəkɔmən] <bekommt, bekam, hat bekommen> incur danger sich in Gefahr bringen [ɪn gə'faːʳ brɪŋən] <bringt, brachte, hat gebracht> ◊ *Sie brachte sich durch ihren Leichtsinn in Gefahr.* incur a risk ein Risiko eingehen [aɛn 'riːzikoː ˌaɛngeːən] <geht ein, ging ein, ist eingegangen>

incurable(-ably) [adj, adv] unheilbar ['ʊnhaɛlbaːʳ] *no comp/superl* ◊ *Aids gilt noch immer als unheilbar.* ♦ *an einer unheilbaren Krankheit leiden/sterben* ♦ *unheilbar krank sein*

indecent(ly) [adj, adv] **1.** *(offensive(ly))* anstößig ['anʃtøːsɪç] ◊ *anstößige Bilder* ♦ *Sie fand sein Verhalten anstößig.* ♦ *sich anstößig benehmen/ aufführen* be dressed indecently anstößige Kleidung tragen; *(in a sexual way)* unsittlich [ˌʊnzɪtlɪç] ◊ *jdn unsittlich berühren* **2.** LAW an indecent assault ein sexueller Übergriff [aɛn zɛksuˌɛlɐ 'yːbɐgrɪf] <–(e)s, –e> assault sb indecently einen sexuellen Übergriff auf jdn begehen indecent exposure Erregung öffentlichen Ärgernisses [ɛˌreːgʊŋ œfntlɪçn̩ 'ɛʳgɐnɪsəs] die <–> *no pl* expose yourself indecently *(to sb)* sich *(vor jdm)* entblößen [ɛnt'bløːsn̩] <entblößt sich, entblößte sich, hat sich entblößt>

indeed [adv] **1.** *(used to add emphasis to a statement)* wirklich ['vɪʳklɪç] ◊ *Das Fest war wirklich sehr schön.* ♦ *Doch, das hat er wirklich gesagt.;* *(used in short answers or responses)* in der Tat [ɪn deːɐ 'taːt] ◊ *„Kennst du ihn?"* — *„In der Tat!"* Thank you very much indeed! Vielen herzlichen Dank! Yes, indeed! Aber ja! **2.** *(in fact)* sogar [zo'gaːʳ] ◊ *Er war nicht gekränkt, er war sogar erleichtert.* and indeed ja sogar [ja: zo'gaːʳ] ◊ *in ganz Europa, ja sogar in der ganzen Welt* **3.** *(expressing doubt, suprise, annoyance)* tatsächlich [ta:t'zɛçlɪç] ◊ *Wenn das tatsächlich geschehen sollte, bin ich vorbereitet.* ♦ *„Ich bin viel stärker als du!"* — *„Ach, tatsächlich?"*

indefinite [adj] **1.** *(article, time)* unbestimmt ['ʊnbəʃtɪmt] ◊ *die Deklination des Adjektivs nach unbestimmtem Artikel* for the indefinite future auf unbestimmte Zeit have indefinite leave auf unbestimmte Zeit beurlaubt sein **2.** *(vague)* unklar ['ʊnklaːʳ] ◊ *Unsere Vorstellungen sind noch unklar.*

indefinitely [adv] *(without time limit)* unbegrenzt ['ʊnbəgrɛnʦt] *no comp/superl* ◊ *Mineralwasser ist so gut wie unbegrenzt haltbar.*; *(without a definite time limit)* auf unbestimmte Zeit [aof ˌʊnbəʃtɪmtə 'ʦaet] ◊ *jdn auf unbestimmte Zeit suspendieren*

independence [noun] Unabhängigkeit ['ʊn|aphɛnɪçkaet] die <-> *no pl* ◊ *Kolonien in die Unabhängigkeit entlassen* ♦ *die Unabhängigkeit erlangen*

independent(ly) [adj, adv] **1.** *(in political, financial etc. terms)* unabhängig ['ʊn|aphɛnɪç] *no comp/superl* ◊ *ein unabhängiger Kandidat* ♦ *Mit eigenem Einkommen ist sie finanziell unabhängig.* ♦ *Brasilien wurde 1822 von Portugal unabhängig.* ♦ *Sie entschlossen sich unabhängig voneinander, in diesem Bereich zu forschen.* be of independent means eigenes Vermögen haben [ˌaegənəs fɛˈmøːgn̩ haːbm̩] +haben **2.** *(capable of acting alone, without help)* selbstständig ['zɛlpstʃtɛndɪç] ◊ *selbstständiges Lernen* ♦ *Meine neunjährige Tochter ist schon sehr selbstständig.* ♦ *mit einer Behinderung selbstständig leben*; *(author, school etc.)* frei [fraɪ] *when used as an adj, only before ns* ◊ *eine freie Schule* ♦ *ein frei finanziertes Projekt* independent traveller Individualtourist [ɪndividuˈaːltuˌrɪst] der <-en, -en> ♀Individualtouristin [ɪndividuˈaːltuˌrɪstɪn] die <-, -nen>

in-depth [adj] eingehend ['aengeːənt] ◊ *eine eingehende Analyse/Untersuchung*

indescribable(-ably) [adj, adv] unbeschreiblich ['ʊnbəʃraeplɪç] *no comp/superl* ◊ *eine unbeschreibliche Aussicht* ♦ *Deine Naivität ist wirklich unbeschreiblich.* ♦ *unbeschreiblich kompliziert*

index [noun] **1.** *(list)* Verzeichnis [fɛˈʦaeçnɪs] das <-ses, -se> ◊ *Legen Sie ein Verzeichnis aller Teilnehmer an.* ♦ *etw. in Verzeichnis aufnehmen*; *(alphabetical, in a book)* Register [reˈgɪstɐ] das <-s, -> ◊ *etw. im Register nachschlagen* **2.** ECON Index ['ɪndɛks] der <-es, Indizes> ◊ *der Nasdaq, der Index der US-amerikanischen Technologiebörse*

index card [noun] Karteikarte [karˈtaekaʁtə] die <-, -n>

index finger [noun] Zeigefinger ['ʦaegəfɪŋ] der <-s, ->

India [noun] Indien ['ɪndjən] das <-s> *article only in combination with attribute, no pl* → **Germany**

Indian¹ [noun] **1.** *(person from India)* Inder ['ɪndɐ] der <-s, -> ♀Inderin ['ɪndərɪn] die <-, -nen> **2.** *(pej) (native American)* Indianer [ɪnˈdjaːnɐ] der <-s, -> ♀Indianerin [ɪnˈdjaːnərɪn] die <-, -nen> → **German¹ 1.**

Indian² [adj] **1.** *(relating to India)* indisch ['ɪndɪʃ] *mostly before ns* ◊ *ein indischer Autor* ♦ *Chutney ist typisch indisch.* **2.** *(pej) (relating to native Americans)* indianisch [ɪnˈdjaːnɪʃ] ◊ *ein indianischer Pueblo*

indicate [verb] **1.** *(show)* zeigen ['ʦaegn̩] +haben ◊ *Die Analyse wird zeigen, ob wir mit unserer Vermutung richtig liegen.* ♦ *Ihre Körperhaltung zeigt, dass sie sehr verspannt ist.*; *(instrument, piece of equipment)* anzeigen ['anʦaegn̩] +haben ◊ *Das Thermometer zeigt 39 Grad an.* ♦ *Das Display zeigte drei Anrufe an.*; *(signal)* indicate sth etw. signalisieren [zɪgnaliˈziːrən] +haben ◊ *Er signalisierte Bereitschaft zur Zusammenarbeit.*; *(indirectly)* sth indicates sth etw. deutet auf etw. [acc] hin [ˈdɔøtət aof ... ˌhɪn] <deutet hin, deutete

hin, hat hingedeutet> ◊ *Alle Anzeichen deuten stark auf eine baldige Katastrophe hin.* ♦ *Sein Verhalten deutet darauf hin, dass er einsam ist.* **2.** *(be necessary)* be indicated angezeigt sein ['angəˌzaekt zaen] ◊ *Eine Operation ist jetzt noch nicht angezeigt.* **3.** *(direct sb's attention somewhere)* indicate sth irgendwohin deuten ['dɔøtn̩] <deutet, deutete, hat gedeutet> ◊ *Er deutete zur Tür.* ♦ *Sie deutete auf meinen Begleiter.* **4.** *(car)* blinken ['blɪŋkn̩] +haben ◊ *Sie bog ab, ohne zu blinken.* ♦ *links/rechts blinken*

indication [noun] **1.** *(sign)* indication of sth Hinweis auf etw. [acc] ['hɪnvaes aof] der <-es, -e> ◊ *Es gibt keinen Hinweis auf einen Mittäter.* indication that ... Hinweis darauf, dass ... ◊ *Gibt es Hinweise darauf, dass sich die Lage verbessern wird?* the indications are that ... alles weist darauf hin, dass ... [ˌaləs vaest daːraof 'hɪn das] <weist hin, wies hin, hat hingewiesen> **2.** *(information)* give an indication of sth Angaben zu etw. machen [ˌanga:bm̩ ʦuː ... maxn̩] +haben ◊ *Können Sie bitte Angaben zu Ihren Computerkenntnissen machen?* give an indication of how/why etc. Angaben dazu machen, wie/warum ... etc.

indicative [noun] Indikativ ['ɪndikatiːf] der <-s, -e> *most sing* ◊ *Bei der indirekten Rede wird oft der Indikativ statt des Konjunktivs verwendet.*

indicator [noun] **1.** *(on a piece of equipment)* Zeiger ['ʦaegɐ] der <-s, -> ◊ *Der Zeiger des Seismographen schlägt aus.*; *(display)* Anzeige ['anʦaegə] die <-, -n> ◊ *Die Anzeige des Anrufbeantworters blinkt.* **2.** *(on a car)* Blinker ['blɪŋkɐ] der <-s, -> **3.** *(sign)* Indikator [ɪndiˈkaːtoːɐ] der <-s, -en> *(lofty)* ◊ *Hohe Blutzuckerwerte sind ein Indikator für Diabetes.*

indifference [noun] Gleichgültigkeit ['glaeçgʏltɪçkaet] die <-> *no pl*

indifferent(ly) [adj, adv] **1.** *(unconcerned)* gleichgültig ['glaeçgʏltɪç] ◊ *ein gleichgültiges Achselzucken* ♦ *Solches Leid lässt mich nicht gleichgültig.* ♦ *Diesem Thema darf man nicht gleichgültig gegenüberstehen.* sb is indifferent to sb/sth jd/etw. ist jdm gleichgültig ◊ *Die Probleme seines Bruders sind ihm gleichgültig.* **2.** *(mediocre)* mittelmäßig ['mɪtlmɛːsɪç] ◊ *Er ist ein mittelmäßiger Schüler.* ♦ *Die Qualität war mittelmäßig.* ♦ *Er schnitt bei der Prüfung nur mittelmäßig ab.*

indigenous [adj] einheimisch ['aenhaemɪʃ] *no comp/superl, mostly before ns* ◊ *einheimische Tierarten*

indignant(ly) [adj, adv] empört [ɛmˈpøːɐt] <empörter, am empörtesten> ◊ *Das Urteil löste empörte Reaktionen aus.* ♦ *Er schilderte empört, was ihm passiert war.* indignant at sth empört über etw. [acc] ◊ *Er war über ihr Verhalten empört.*

indignation [noun] Empörung [ɛmˈpøːrʊŋ] die <-> *no pl*

indirect(ly) [adj, adv] indirekt ['ɪndirɛkt] *when used as an adj, mostly before ns* ◊ *indirekte Rede* ♦ *auf indirektem Wege* ♦ *Er war indirekt für den Unfall mit verantwortlich.*

indiscriminate(ly) [adj, adv] wahllos ['vaːllos] *no comp/superl* ◊ *Die Anordnung war völlig wahllos.* ♦ *eine wahllose Aneinanderreihung* ♦ *Sie schossen wahllos in die Menge.*

indisputable(-ably) [adj, adv] unbestreitbar ['ʊnbəʃtraetbaːʁ] *no comp/superl* ◊ *Das ist ein unbestreitbarer Vorteil.* ♦ *Ihre Erfolge sind unbestreitbar.*

♦ *Er ist unbestreitbar im Recht.*
indistinct(ly) [adj, adv] undeutlich ['ʊndəʒtlɪç] ◊
undeutliche Konturen ♦ *Die Umrisse der Gestalt
waren undeutlich.* ♦ *Ich konnte die Spuren nur
undeutlich ausmachen.*
individual [noun] *(one single person)* Einzelne
['aɛnts|nə] der/die <–n, die Einzelnen> *but: ein
Einzelner/eine Einzelne* ◊ *Jeder Einzelne kann etwas
tun.* ♦ *Die Arbeit ist zu viel für einen Einzelnen.;
(person considered as distinct from others)* Individuum [ɪndi'viːduʊm] das <–s, Individuen> ◊ *jdn als
Individuum behandeln/wahrnehmen; (person with
particular characteristics)* Person [pɛr'zoːn] die
<–, –en> ◊ *Personen mit Führungsqualitäten* ♦
begabte Personen
individual(ly) [adj, adv] 1. *((as) one among several)*
einzeln ['aɛntsln] *no comp/superl; when used as an
adj, only before ns* ◊ *Die einzelnen Teilnehmer
trugen sich in Listen ein.* ♦ *Sie betraten den Raum
einzeln.* ♦ *Die Gläser waren einzeln verpackt.* individ-
ual part Einzelteil ['aɛnts|taɛl] das <–(e)s, –e> indi-
vidual liberty/rights die Freiheit/Rechte des
Einzelnen [diː ˌfraɛhaɛt/ˌrɛçtə dɛs 'aɛnts|nən]
2. *(relating to a particular person)* persönlich
[pɛr'zøːnlɪç] *when used as an adj, only before ns; no
comp/superl* ◊ *jds persönliche Wünsche* ♦ *Jeder
wurde persönlich begrüßt.* 3. *(unusual or special)*
individuell [ɪndivuʊ|'ɛl] ◊ *Die Einrichtung der
Wohnung war sehr individuell.* ♦ *ein individuelles
Geschenk* ♦ *individuell gestaltet*
Indonesia [noun] Indonesien [ɪndo'neːzjən] das <–s>
article only in combination with attribute, no pl →
Germany
Indonesian¹ [noun] 1. *(inhabitant)* Indonesier
[ɪndo'neːzjɐ] der <–s, –> ♀Indonesierin
[ɪndo'neːzjərɪn] die <–, –nen> → **German¹** 1.
2. *(language)* Indonesisch [ɪndo'neːzɪʃ] das <–(s)>
no pl → **German¹** 2.
Indonesian² [adj] indonesisch [ɪndo'neːzɪʃ] →
German²
indoor [adj] 1. *(inside a hall)* indoor ... Hallen...
['haɫən] indoor (swimming) pool Hallenbad
['haɫənbaːt] das <–(e)s, Hallenbäder> indoor
handball Hallenhandball ['haɫənhantbaɫ] das <–(e)s>
no pl 2. *(inside a room)* indoor ... Zimmer... ['tsɪmɐ]
indoor antenna Zimmerantenne ['tsɪmɐ|antɛnə] die
<–, –n> indoor plant Zimmerpflanze ['tsɪmɐpflantsə]
die <–, –n> indoor air Raumluft ['raʊmlʊft] die <–>
no pl 3. *(not outside)* indoor activities/games etc.
Tätigkeiten/Spiele etc. im Haus
[ˌtɛːtɪçkaɛtn/ˌʃpiːlə ɪm 'haʊs]
indoors [adv] drinnen ['drɪnən] ◊ *Wenn es regnet,
bleibe ich lieber drinnen.* ♦ *Das Spiel fand drinnen
statt.* go indoors reingehen ['raɛngeːən] <geht rein,
ging rein, ist reingegangen> *(fam)* ◊ *Als es anfing
zuregnen, gingen sie rein.*
induce [verb] 1. *(cause, trigger)* bewirken [bə'vɪrkn]
<bewirkt, bewirkte, hat bewirkt> ◊ *Veränderungen
bewirken* ♦ *Wie wurde dieser Effekt bewirkt?; (not
deliberately)* induce labo(u)r/birth Wehen/die Geburt
auslösen ['veːən/diː gə'buːɐt ˌaʊsløːzn] +haben ◊ *Der
Unfall hatte vorzeitige Wehen ausgelöst.; (deliberately)* induce birth die Geburt einleiten
[diː gə'buːɐt ˌaɛnlaɛtn] <leitet ein, leitete ein, hat einge-
leitet> ◊ *Der Arzt beschloss, die Geburt einzuleiten.*
2. *(make sb do sth)* induce sb to do sth jdn dazu

bewegen, etw. zu tun [daːtsuː bə'veːgŋ ... tsuː]
<bewegt, bewog, hat bewogen> ◊ *Ich konnte sie nicht
dazu bewegen aufzugeben.*
indulge [verb] 1. *(be good to sb or yourself)* indulge
sb/yourself jdn/sich verwöhnen [fɛ'vøːnən]
<verwöhnt, verwöhnte, hat verwöhnt> ◊ *seine Kinder
verwöhnen* ♦ *Ich verwöhnte mich selbst mit einem
Restaurantbesuch.* indulge sb's every whim jdm
absolut jeden Wunsch erfüllen
[apzoluːt ˌjeːdn̩ 'vʊnʃ ɛˌfʏlən] <erfüllt, erfüllte, hat
erfüllt> 2. *(a passion, pastime)* indulge (in) sth einer
Sache [dat] frönen ['frøːnən] +haben ◊ *seinen
Gelüsten/dem Nichtstun/seinem Hobby frönen; (your
dreams, emotions etc.)* sich einer Sache [dat]
hingeben ['hɪngeːbm̩] <gibt sich hin, gab sich hin, hat
sich hingegeben> ◊ *Gib dich nicht der Illusion/
Hoffnung hin, dass sich das noch einmal ändert.;
(sth bad or wicked)* sich zu etw. hinreißen lassen
[tsuː ... ˌhɪnraɛsn̩ lasn̩] <lässt, ließ, hat lassen> ◊ *sich
zu Gewalt/Beschimpfungen hinreißen lassen*
indulgent(ly) [adj, adv] nachsichtig ['naːxzɪçtɪç] ◊ *ein
nachsichtiges Verhalten* ♦ *Er lächelte nachsichtig.*
indulgent with/towards sb nachsichtig mit jdm ◊
Meine Mutter war nachsichtig mit uns.
indulgent towards sth einer Sache [dat] gegenüber
nachsichtig ◊ *Er ist ihren Schwächen gegenüber
recht nachsichtig*
industrial(ly) [adj, adv] 1. *(related to manufacturing)*
industriell [ɪndʊstri'ɛl] *no comp/superl; when used as
an adj, only before ns* ◊ *die industrielle Revolution* ♦
industriell gefertigte Güter industrial age Industrie-
zeitalter [ɪndʊs'triːˌtsaɛt|altɐ] das <–s> *no pl* indus-
trial espionage Industriespionage
[ɪndʊs'triːʃpioˌnaːʒə] die <–> *no pl* 2. *(relating to the
relationship between employers and employees)*
Arbeits... ['aˈbaɛts] industrial dispute Arbeitskampf
['aˈbaɛtskampf] der <–(e)s, Arbeitskämpfe>
industrial estate [noun] Gewerbegebiet
[gə've'bəgəbiːt] das <–(e)s, –e>
industrious [adj] fleißig ['flaɛsɪç] ◊ *fleißiges Üben/
Trainieren* ♦ *Sie ist sehr fleißig.*
industry [noun] 1. *(in general)* Industrie [ɪndʊs'triː] die
<–, –n> der ◊ *Er will in die Industrie gehen.*
♦ *die Metall/Kunststoff/Holz/Papier verarbeitende
Industrie* car industry Autoindustrie ['aɔto|ɪndʊsˌtriː]
heavy industry Schwerindustrie ['ʃveːg|ɪndʊsˌtriː]
industry standard Industrienorm [ɪndʊs'triːnɔ'm] die
<–, –en> 2. *(business, trade etc.)* Branche ['branʃə]
die <–, –n> ◊ *In welcher Branche sind Sie tätig?* ♦
Die Branche der Telekommunikation boomt. industry
... Branchen... ['branʃn̩] industry expert Branchen-
kenner ['branʃnkɛnɐ] der <–s, –> industry leader
Branchenführer ['branʃnfyːre] der <–s, –> 3. *(hard
work)* Fleiß [flaɛs] der <–es> *no pl* ◊ *mit Fleiß zum
Ziel gelangen*
ineffective(ly) [adj, adv] erfolglos [ɛ'fɔlkloːs] ◊ *erfolglose Versuche* ♦ *Die Maßnahmen blieben erfolglos.* ♦
Sie bemühte sich erfolglos, zu helfen.
inequality [noun] Ungleichheit ['ʊnɡlaɛçhaɛt] die
<–, –en> ◊ *soziale/wirtschaftliche Ungleichheit* ♦
eine krasse Ungleichheit zwischen Nord und Süd
inequality of opportunities Chancenungleichheit
['ʃansn̩|ʊnɡlaɛçhaɛt]
inevitable [adj] unausweichlich ['ʊn|aɔsvaɛçlɪç] *no
comp/superl* ◊ *Der Konkurs des Unternehmens
scheint unausweichlich.* ♦ *unausweichliche Folgen*

A
B
C
D
E
F
G
H
I
J
K
L
M
N
O
P
Q
R
S
T
U
V
W
X
Y
Z

haben

inevitably [adv] zwangsläufig [ˈtsvaŋslɔ̯øfɪç] *no comp/ superl* ◊ *In diesem Labyrinth verirrt man sich zwangsläufig.*

inexact [adj] ungenau [ˈʊŋɡənau̯] <ungenauer, am ungenauesten> ◊ *Wetterprognosen sind oft ungenau.* ◆ *ungenaue Informationen*

inexhaustible [adj] unerschöpflich [ˈʊn|ɛʃœpflɪç] *no comp/superl* ◊ *Ihre Energie/Geduld ist unerschöpflich.* ◆ *ein unerschöpfliches Thema*

inexorable(-ably) [adj, adv] unaufhaltsam [ˈʊn|a̯ofhaltsa:m] *no comp/superl* ◊ *Die Entwicklung schien unaufhaltsam zu sein.* ◆ *der unaufhaltsame Fortschritt der Technologie* ◆ *Der Verfall schreitet unaufhaltsam voran.*

inexpensive(ly) [adj, adv] preiswert [ˈpra̯esve:ɡt] <preiswerter, am preiswertesten> ◊ *Das Angebot war sehr preiswert.* ◆ *ein preiswertes Hotel* ◆ *etw. preiswert einkaufen*

infant [noun] **1.** *(baby)* Säugling [ˈzɔ̯øklɪŋ] der <-s, -e> ◊ *ein neugeborener Säugling* infant care Säuglingspflege [ˈzɔ̯øklɪŋspfle:ɡə] die <-> *no pl* infant mortality Säuglingssterblichkeit [ˈzɔ̯øklɪŋsʃtɛˈplɪçkae̯t] die <-> *no pl* infant daughter kleine Tochter [klae̯nə ˈtɔxtə] <-, Töchter> the infant son kleiner Sohn [ˌklae̯nə ˈzo:n] <-(e)s, Söhne> **2.** *(in the UK: school children between the ages of four and seven)* Schulkinder im Alter zwischen vier und sieben

infect [verb] **1.** *(person)* anstecken [ˈanʃtɛkn̩] +haben ◊ *Er hat seine Schwester mit Windpocken angesteckt.* be infected (with sth) (by sb) sich (mit etw.) *(bei jdm)* anstecken [ˈanʃtɛkn̩] +haben ◊ *Steck dich nicht bei ihm an.* **2.** *(germ, virus)* infizieren [ɪnfiˈtsi:rən] <infiziert, infizierte, hat infiziert> *often in adjectival passive constructions* ◊ *Das Virus infiziert hauptsächlich Vögel.* ◆ *von einem Virus infizierte Dateien* ◆ *Er weiß nicht, wie lange er schon infiziert ist.* **3.** *(spread germs to sth)* infect sth with sth etw. mit etw. verseuchen [mɪt ... fɛˌzɔ̯øçn̩] <verseucht, verseuchte, hat verseucht> ◊ *das Trinkwasser mit Bakterien verseuchen*

infection [noun] Infektion [ɪnfɛkˈtsi̯o:n] die <-, -en> ◊ *eine Infektion mit HIV* ◆ *sich vor Infektionen schützen*

infectious [adj] ansteckend [ˈanʃtɛkn̩t] ◊ *ansteckende Meningitis* ◆ *Der Patient ist jetzt nicht mehr ansteckend.* ◆ *Ihr Lachen ist sehr ansteckend.*

infer [verb] infer sth from sth aus etw. auf etw. [dat] schließen [a̯os ... a̯of ... ʃli:sn̩] <schließt, schloss, hat geschlossen> infer from sth that ... aus etw. schließen, dass ... ◊ *Aus seinem Verhalten schloss ich, dass er müde war.*

inference [noun] Schluss [ʃlʊs] der <-es, Schlüsse> ◊ *Welche Schlüsse kann man aus diesem Ergebnis ziehen?*

inferior [adj] **1.** *(product, person)* minderwertig [ˈmɪndɐve:gtɪç] ◊ *minderwertige Qualität* ◆ *In seiner Anwesenheit fühle ich mich oft minderwertig.* inferior to sth schlechter als etw. [ˈʃlɛçtɐ als] ◊ *Dieses Material ist schlechter als das andere.* inferior to sb jdm unterlegen [ʊntɐˈle:ɡn̩] ◊ *Er fühlte sich ihr unterlegen.* **2.** *(in a hierarchy)* untergeordnet [ˈʊntɐɡə|ɔˈdnət] ◊ *in untergeordneter Stellung tätig sein*

infidelity [noun] **1.** *(trait)* Untreue [ˈʊntrɔ̯øə] die <->

no pl ◊ *Untreue ist eine seiner schlechtesten Eigenschaften.* **2.** *(short affair)* Seitensprung [ˈzae̯tnʃprʊŋ] der <-(e)s, Seitensprünge> ◊ *jdm einen Seitensprung gestehen/verzeihen*

infinite(ly) [adj, adv] unendlich [ʊnˈɛntlɪç] *no comp/ superl* ◊ *eine unendliche Zahlenreihe/Zahl* ◆ *Meine Liebe zu dir ist unendlich!* ◆ *Ich war unendlich froh darüber.*

infinitive [noun] Infinitiv [ˈɪnfiniti:f] der <-s, -e> ◊ *der Infinitiv mit „zu‘* ◆ *Das Verb steht im Infinitiv.*

infirm [adj] gebrechlich [ɡəˈbrɛçlɪç] ◊ *alte und gebrechliche Menschen* ◆ *Sie war schon ziemlich gebrechlich.*

inflame [verb] entzünden [ɛntˈtsʏndn̩] <entzündet, entzündete, hat entzündet> ◊ *jds Hass/die Gemüter entzünden* become inflamed sich entzünden ◊ *Die Wunde hat sich entzündet.*

inflation [noun] Inflation [ɪnflaˈtsi̯o:n] die <-, -en> *most sing*

inflect [verb] GRAM flektiert werden [flɛkˈti:gt ve:ɡdn̩] <wird, wurde, ist worden> ◊ *Adverbien werden nicht flektiert.*

inflexible [adj] **1.** *(slow to think, move or change)* unbeweglich [ˈʊnbəve:klɪç] ◊ *ein unbewegliches System* ◆ *Er ist geistig ziemlich unbeweglich.;* *(stiff)* steif [ʃtae̯f] ◊ *Ich bin so steif, ich muss mehr Gymnastik machen.* **2.** *(uncompromising)* unnachgiebig [ˈʊnna:xgi:bɪç] ◊ *eine unnachgiebige Haltung einnehmen* ◆ *Der Richter war unnachgiebig.*

inflict [verb] inflict sth (up)on sb/sth jdm/etw. etw. zufügen [ˈtsu:fy:ɡn̩] +haben ◊ *jdm ein Leid/Stichwunden zufügen* ◆ *Sie fügten dem Gegner schwere Verluste zu.*

influence¹ [noun] Einfluss [ˈae̯nflʊs] der <-es, Einflüsse> ◊ *an Einfluss gewinnen/verlieren* ◊ *Sie machte all ihren Einfluss geltend, um ihm zu helfen.* ◆ *Er steht unter Petras Einfluss.* ◆ *unter dem Einfluss von Alkohol* influence on/over sb/sth Einfluss auf jdn/etw. ◊ *Seine Freunde üben einen positiven Einfluss auf ihn aus.*

influence² [verb] **1.** *(affect)* beeinflussen [bəˈae̯nflʊsn̩] <beeinflusst, beeinflusste, hat beeinflusst> ◊ *Du lässt dich so leicht beeinflussen.* ◆ *Seine Werke stark von Picasso beeinflusst.* ◆ *Das Erlebnis hat meine Entscheidung nicht beeinflusst.* **2.** influence sb to do sth jdn (dazu) bewegen, etw. zu tun [bəˈve:ɡn̩ ... ˈtsu:] <bewegt, bewegte, hat bewegt> ◊ *Wie kann ich dich dazu bewegen, deine Entscheidung zu überdenken?*

influential [adj] einflussreich [ˈae̯nflʊsrae̯ç] ◊ *einen einflussreichen Posten haben* ◆ *Sie ist sehr einflussreich.* be highly influential in sth eine einflussreiche Rolle bei etw. spielen

influenza [noun] Grippe [ˈgrɪpə] die <-> *no pl*

info [noun] Info [ˈɪnfo:] die <-, -s> *(fam)*

inform [verb] informieren [ɪnfɔrˈmi:rən] <informiert, informierte, hat informiert> ◊ *Habt ihr die Polizei informiert?* ◆ *Ich wurde informiert, dass die Lieferung unterwegs ist.* inform sb of/about/as to sth jdn über etw. [acc] informieren ◊ *Bist du über die Terminänderung informiert worden?* inform sb as to how/why/what etc. ... jdn darüber informieren, wie/warum/was etc. ...

informal(ly) [adj, adv] **1.** *(relaxed)* familiär [famiˈli:ɡ] ◊ *Der Rahmen der Feier war familiär.* ◆ *ein familiäres Ambiente* ◆ *ein familiär geführter Gasthof;*

(clothes) leger [le'ʒe:ɐ̯] ◊ *legere Kleidung* ♦ *Sie kleidet sich eher leger.* **2.** *(not official)* informell ['ɪnfɔ'mɛl] *when used as an adj, mostly before ns* ◊ *informelle Gespräche* meet informally sich informell treffen discuss sth informally etw. in einem informellen Gespräch diskutieren

information [noun] **1.** *(facts, knowledge)* Information [ɪnfɔ'maːtsi̯oːn] die <-, -en> ◊ *Informationen aus erster Hand* ♦ *Ich brauche noch nähere Informationen.* ♦ *Nur zu deiner Information: Ich mache nicht mehr mit!* **2.** *(official statement)* Angaben ['angaːbm̩] die <-> pl ◊ *Die Partei hat nach eigenen Angaben 12 000 Mitglieder.* give information Angaben machen ◊ *Er konnte keine Angaben zum Unfallhergang machen.* **3.** *(advice, enlightenment)* Aufklärung ['aɔfklɛːrʊŋ] die <-, -en> ◊ *die gesundheitliche/politische Aufklärung stärker betreiben* ♦ *um Aufklärung bitten*

information centre, information center [noun] Beratungsstelle [bə'raːtʊŋsʃtɛlə] die <-, -n>

information desk [noun] Auskunft ['aɔskʊnft] die <-, Auskünfte>

information technology [noun] Informatik [ɪnfɔr'maːtɪk] die <-> *no pl* ◊ *Informatik studieren*

informative [adj] informativ [ɪnfɔr'maːtiːf] ◊ *ein informativer Text* ♦ *Ich fand seinen Beitrag recht informativ.*

infrastructure [noun] Infrastruktur ['ɪnfraʃtrʊk,tuːɐ̯] die <-, -en>

infringe [verb] *(a law etc.)* infringe (on) sth gegen etw. verstoßen [ge:ɐ̯ŋ ... fɛˌʃtoːsn̩] <verstößt, verstieß, hat verstoßen> ◊ *gegen ein Gesetz/eine Regel/Vereinbarung verstoßen* infringe on sb's privacy jds Privatsphäre verletzen [pri'vaːtsfɛːrə fɛˌlɛtsn̩] <verletzt, verletzte, hat verletzt>

ingenious [adj] genial [ge'ni̯aːl] ◊ *Deine Erfindung/Lösung ist einfach genial!* ♦ *eine geniale Idee haben*

ingredient [noun] **1.** *(for cooking)* Zutat ['tsuːtaːt] die <-, -en> ◊ *die Zutaten gut vermischen* ♦ *Hast du alle Zutaten?; (component of a product)* Inhaltsstoff ['ɪnhaltsʃtɔf] der <-(e)s, -e> ◊ *gefährliche Inhaltsstoffe; (of a drug)* active ingredient Wirkstoff ['vɪrkʃtɔf] **2.** *(prerequisite)* Voraussetzung [fo'raɔszɛtsʊŋ] die <-, -en> ◊ *Kreativität ist eine wichtige Voraussetzung für Erfolg.*

inhabit [verb] *(live in a place)* bewohnen [bə'voːnən] <bewohnt, bewohnte, hat bewohnt> ◊ *Seit wann ist diese Gegend bewohnt?* ♦ *Die Küste wird von unzähligen Vögeln und Robben bewohnt.; (plant)* besiedeln [bə'ziːdl̩n] <besiedelt, besiedelte, hat besiedelt> ◊ *Fleischfressende Pflanzen besiedeln karge Böden.*

inhabitant [noun] Einwohner ['aɛnvoːnɐ] der <-s, -> ♀Einwohnerin ['aɛnvoːnərɪn] die <-, -nen> ◊ *Hamburg hat 1,69 Millionen Einwohner.* ♦ *die Einwohner Frankreichs*

inhale [verb] **1.** *(breathe in)* einatmen ['aɛn|aːtmən] <atmet ein, atmete ein, hat eingeatmet> ◊ *Sie atmete tief ein.* ♦ *Ich atmete die würzige Meeresluft ein.* **2.** *(smoke, fumes etc.)* inhalieren [ɪnha'liːrən] <inhaliert, inhalierte, hat inhaliert> ◊ *Er inhalierte gierig den Rauch seiner Zigarette.* ♦ *bei Erkältungen mehrmals täglich inhalieren*

inherent [adj] immanent [ɪma'nɛnt] *no comp/superl, mostly before ns (lofty)* ◊ *Diese Methode hat immanente Schwächen.* inherent to sb/sth jdm/einer Sache eigen ['aɛɡn̩] ◊ *Er ging mit der ihm*

eigenen Beharrlichkeit vor. have an inherent appeal seinen eigenen Reiz haben

inherit [verb] erben ['ɛrbm̩] +haben ◊ *Der älteste Sohn erbte den Bauernhof.* inherit sth from sb etw. von jdm erben ◊ *Das musikalische Talent hat er von seinem Großvater geerbt.*

inheritance [noun] Erbe ['ɛrbə] das <-s> *no pl* ◊ *das kulturelle Erbe eines Volkes*

inhibit [verb] hemmen ['hɛmən] +haben ◊ *Er fühlte sich durch die fremden Leute gehemmt.* ♦ *den Fortschritt hemmen* inhibit sb from doing sth jdn daran hindern, etw. zu tun [daran 'hɪndɐn ... tsu:] +haben ◊ *Seine Unfreundlichkeit hinderte mich daran, ihn um Hilfe zu bitten.*

inhibition [noun] Hemmung ['hɛmʊŋ] die <-, -en> ◊ *ein Medikament zur Hemmung des Tumorwachstums* ♦ *Als Kind war sie voller Hemmungen.*

inhospitable [adj] **1.** *(region)* unwirtlich ['ʊnvɪrtlɪç] *mostly before ns* ◊ *Sie lebten in einer unwirtlichen Gegend.* **2.** *(person)* unfreundlich ['ʊnfrɔɛntlɪç] ◊ *Er war zu seinen Gästen sehr unfreundlich.* ♦ *ein unfreundlicher Empfang*

initial¹ [noun] Initiale [ini'tsi̯aːlə] die <-, -n> *most pl* ◊ *Er signierte das Bild mit seinen Initialen.*

initial² [adj] anfänglich ['anfɛŋlɪç] *no comp/superl, only before ns* ◊ *Seine anfängliche Scheu war bald verflogen.* initial stage Anfangsphase ['anfaŋsfaːzə] die <-, -n>

initial³ [verb] abzeichnen ['aptsaɛçnən] <zeichnet ab, zeichnete ab, hat abgezeichnet> ◊ *Können Sie mir diese Rechnung abzeichnen?*

initially [adv] anfangs ['anfaŋs] ◊ *Anfangs war ich etwas nervös.*

initiate [verb] **1.** *(start)* beginnen [bə'ɡɪnən] <beginnt, begann, hat begonnen> ◊ *ein Gespräch beginnen; (take the first steps)* in die Wege leiten [ɪn diː 'veːɡə laɛtn̩] +haben ◊ *Reformen in die Wege leiten; (cause/encourage to start)* den Anstoß geben zu [deːn 'anʃtoːs ɡeːbm̩ tsu:] <gibt, gab, hat gegeben> ◊ *Was hat den Anstoß zu diesem Kurswechsel gegeben?* **2.** LAW *(legal proceedings)* anstrengen ['anʃtrɛŋən] +haben ◊ *Er strengte eine Klage gegen das Unternehmen an.* **3.** *(familiarize with, introduce)* initiate sb into sth jdn in etw. [acc] einführen [ɪn ... ˌaɛnfyːrən] +haben ◊ *Seine Eltern führten ihn in die Gesellschaft ein.*

initiative [noun] Initiative [inits̩i̯aˈtiːvə] die <-, -n> on your own initiative aus eigene Initiative heraus take the initiative die Initiative ergreifen; *(legislative)* Gesetzesinitiative [ɡə'zɛtsəsinits̩i̯aˌtiːvə]

inject [verb] **1.** *(a drug)* spritzen ['ʃprɪtsn̩] +haben ◊ *Das Insulin wird unter die Haut gespritzt.* inject sb with sth, inject sth into sb jdm etw. spritzen ◊ *Ihm wurde ein Mittel zur Blutgerinnung gespritzt.* inject yourself with sth sich [dat] etw. spritzen ◊ *Ich muss mir Insulin spritzen.* inject sth into sb's sth jdm etw. in etw. [acc] spritzen ◊ *Er spritzte ihr den Impfstoff in den Arm.* **2.** *(fig) (new life)* inject sth into etw. in etw. [acc] bringen [ɪn ... brɪŋən] <bringt, brachte, hat gebracht> ◊ *Sie brachten neuen Schwung in die Firma.; (money)* etw. in etw. [acc] pumpen [ɪn ... pʊmpm̩] +haben ◊ *In dieses Projekt ist schon viel Geld gepumpt worden.*

injection [noun] **1.** *(of a drug)* Spritze ['ʃprɪtsə] die <-, -n> ◊ *jdm eine schmerzstillende Spritze geben* ♦

A
B
C
D
E
F
G
H
I
J
K
L
M
N
O
P
Q
R
S
T
U
V
W
X
Y
Z

eine Spritze in den Arm bekommen **2.** *(of money)* Finanzspritze [fi'nantsʃprɪtsə] *die* <-, -n> **3.** TECHN *(of fuel)* Einspritzung ['aɛnʃprɪtsʊŋ] *die* <-, -en>

injunction (noun) Verfügung [fɛ'fyːgʊŋ] *die* <-, -en> ◊ *Der Richter hat folgende Verfügung erlassen: ...*

injure (verb) verletzen [fɛ'lɛtsn̩] <verletzt, verletzte, hat verletzt> ◊ *Bei dem Unfall wurde sie am Kopf verletzt.* **be severely injured** schwer verletzt sein

injury (noun) Verletzung [fɛ'lɛtsʊŋ] *die* <-, -en> ◊ *Er hatte eine kleine Verletzung am Knie.* ♦ *eine Verletzung der Menschenrechte* do yourself an injury, suffer/sustain an injury **sich verletzen** [fɛ'lɛtsn̩] <verletzt sich, verletzte sich, hat sich verletzt>

ink (noun) Tinte ['tɪntə] *die* <-, -n>

inland (adj) *(in compound ns)* inland ... Binnen... ['bɪnən] inland sea Binnenmeer ['bɪnənmeːɐ̯] *das* <-(e)s, -e> inland water/waterways Binnengewässer ['bɪnəngəvɛsɐ] *die* <-> *pl*

in-law (noun) angeheiratete Verwandte [ˌangəhaɛraːtətə fɛ'vantə] *der/die* <-n, die angeheirateten Verwandten> but: ein angeheirateter Verwandter/eine angeheiratete Verwandte; *(parents of husband/wife)* the/sb's in-laws **die/jds Schwiegereltern** [diː/... 'ʃviːgɐ|ɛltɐn] <-> *only pl*

inmate (noun) Insasse ['ɪnzasə] *der* <-n, -n> ♀Insassin ['ɪnzasɪn] *die* <-, -nen> *most pl (form)*

inn (noun) Gasthaus ['gasthaʊs] *das* <-es, Gasthäuser>

innate (adj) angeboren ['angəboːrən] *no comp/superl* ◊ *Sein Herzfehler ist angeboren.* ♦ *ein angeborenes Talent*

inner (adj) innere ['ɪnərə] *no comp, only before ns* ◊ *die innere Struktur eines Textes* ♦ *mein inneres Gleichgewicht* inner ear Innenohr ['ɪnən|oːɐ̯] *das* <-(e)s, -en> inner pocket Innentasche ['ɪnəntaʃə] *die* <-, -n> inner London/Munich etc. **die Londoner/Münchner Innenstadt** [diː ˌlɒndənə/ˌmʏnçnɐ 'ɪnənʃtat] *die* <-, Innenstädte> most sth/sing inner Birmingham **die Innenstadt von Birmingham**

inner city (noun) Innenstadt ['ɪnənʃtat] *die* <-, Innenstädte>

innermost (adj) *(carefully hidden from others)* innerste ['ɪnɐstə] *no comp/superl, only before ns* ◊ *jds innerste Wünsche/Sehnsüchte* ♦ *der innerste Kreis*

innocence (noun) Unschuld ['ʊnʃʊlt] *die* <-> *no pl* ◊ *Er konnte seine Unschuld beweisen.* protest your innocence **seine Unschuld beteuern** in all innocence **in aller Unschuld**

innocent (adj) *(not guilty, naive)* unschuldig ['ʊnʃʊldɪç] ◊ *Sie war unschuldig und wurde freigesprochen.* ♦ *ein unschuldiges Kind*

innovation (noun) Neuerung ['nɔøərʊŋ] *die* <-, -en>

innovative (adj) innovativ [inova'tiːf] ◊ *Dieser Designer ist sehr innovativ.* ♦ *innovative Ideen*

inpatient (noun) stationäre Patient [ʃtatsjoˌnɛːrə pa'tsjɛnt] *der* <-en, -en> ♀stationäre Patientin [ʃtatsjoˌnɛːrə pa'tsjɛntɪn] *die* <-, -nen> but: ein stationärer Patient/eine stationäre Patientin

input¹ (noun) **1.** *(of ideas, knowledge)* Beitrag ['baɛtraːk] *der* <-(e)s, Beiträge> ◊ *Beiträge von Experten aus der ganzen Welt* **2.** IT *(information)* Eingabe ['aɛngaːbə] *die* <-, -n> ◊ *die Eingabe mittels Tastatur, Maus oder Joystick* **3.** *(connection)* Eingang ['aɛngaŋ] *der* <-(e)s, Eingänge> ◊ *analoge/digitale Eingänge* **4.** BIO *(by receptors)* Information [ɪnfɔrˈmaˈtsjoːn] *die* <-, -en> ◊ *Die Information wird*

vom Auge an das Gehirn weitergeleitet.

input² (verb) eingeben ['aɛngeːbm̩] <gibt ein, gab ein, hat eingegeben> ◊ *Sie gibt Adressdaten in den Computer ein.*

inquest (noun) gerichtliche Untersuchung [gəˌrɪçtlɪçə ʊntɐˈtsuːxʊŋ] *die* <-, -en>

inquire (verb) → **enquire**

inquiry (noun) → **enquiry**

inquisitve(ly) (adj, adv) neugierig ['nɔøgiːrɪç] ◊ *ein neugieriges Kind* ♦ *Meine Mutter ist schrecklich neugierig.* ♦ *Er schaute mich neugierig an.*

insane (adj) **1.** *(fam) (very stupid)* wahnsinnig ['vaːnzɪnɪç] *(also fam)* ◊ *eine wahnsinnige Idee* ♦ *Sie wurde fast wahnsinnig vor Schmerzen.* drive sb insane **jdn wahnsinnig machen 2.** *(mentally ill)* geisteskrank ['gaɛstəskraŋk] *no comp/superl* ◊ *eine geisteskranke Patientin*

insanity (noun) **1.** *(fam) (stupid behaviour)* Wahnsinn ['vaːnzɪn] *der* <-s> *no pl* ◊ *Es ist Wahnsinn, so etwas zu tun!* **2.** MED Geisteskrankheit ['gaɛstəskraŋkhaɛt] *die* <-, -en>; *(before a court)* Unzurechnungsfähigkeit ['ʊntsurɛçnʊŋsfɛːɪçkaɛt] *die* <-> *no pl* suffer from insanity **geisteskrank sein** ['gaɛstəskraŋk zaɛn]

inscription (noun) Inschrift ['ɪnʃrɪft] *die* <-, -en>

insect (noun) Insekt [ɪn'zɛkt] *das* <-s, -en>

insecure (adj) **1.** *(person)* unsicher ['ʊnzɪçɐ] ◊ *Er fühlt sich in ihrer Gegenwart sehr unsicher.* ♦ *ein unsicherer junger Mitarbeiter* **2.** *(door, window)* ungesichert ['ʊngəzɪçɐt] *no comp/superl* ◊ *Der Täter ist durch ein ungesichertes Fenster eingestiegen.* ♦ *Die Türen waren völlig ungesichert.*

insert¹ (noun) Beilage ['baɛlaːgə] *die* <-, -n> ◊ *Die Zeitschrift hat eine CD als Beilage.*

insert² (verb) **1.** *(into a narrow opening)* insert sth into/in sth etw. in etw. (acc) **stecken** [ɪn ... ʃtɛkn̩] +haben ◊ *Er steckte sich Stöpsel in die Ohren.* **2.** *(into a document, text)* insert sth (into/in sth) etw. (in etw. (acc)) **einfügen** [ɪn ... aɛnfyːgn̩] +haben ◊ *Er fügte ein Bild in das Dokument ein.*

inside¹ (noun) **1.** *(of a building, an object)* Innere ['ɪnərə] *das* <Inner(e)n> *no pl* ◊ *der Druck im Inneren der Kammer* **2.** *(areas facing inwards)* Innenseite ['ɪnənzaɛtə] *die* <-, -n> ◊ *Die Innenseiten meiner Arme waren wund gerieben.*

inside² (adj) **1.** *(facing inwards, inner part)* innere ['ɪnərə] *no comp, only before ns* ◊ *Er läuft auf einer inneren Bahnen.* inner side Innenseite ['ɪnənzaɛtə] *die* <-, -n> ◊ *die Innenseite des Fußes* inner pages Innenteil ['ɪnəntaɛl] *der* <-(e)s, -e> ◊ *Die Titelgeschichte wird im Innenteil fortgesetzt.* **2.** *(from within an organization)* Insider... ['ɪnsaɛdɐ] inside knowledge/information Insiderwissen ['ɪnsaɛdɐvɪsn̩] *das* <-s> *no pl*

inside³ (adv) **1.** *(a room, house)* drinnen ['drɪnən] ◊ *Das Tennisturnier wurde nach drinnen verlegt.* ♦ *Von drinnen drang kein Ton nach draußen.* **2.** *(on the inside of an object etc.)* innen ['ɪnən] ◊ *Der Baum war innen ganz hohl.* **3.** *(towards the interior: from the point of view of a person outside)* hinein... [hɪ'naɛn] look inside **hineinsehen** [hɪ'naɛnzeːən] <sieht hinein, sah hinein, hat hineingesehen> ◊ *Er konnte in ihr Zimmer hineinsehen.; (from the point of view of a person inside)* herein... [hɛ'raɛn] get inside **hereinkommen** [hɛ'raɛnkɔmən] <kommt herein, kam herein, ist hereingekommen> ◊ *Komm*

berein! Es regnet gleich.

inside⁴ [prep] **1.** in [ɪn] *with acc when expressing motion towards a place, with dat when there is no or undirected motion* ◊ *Ich gehe gleich ins Haus.* ♦ *In ihrem Haus waren sie sicher.* **2.** *(within a specified period of time)* innerhalb ['ɪnehalp] [+gen] ◊ *innerhalb eines Monats*

inside out [adv] verkehrt herum [fe'keːɡt hɛrʊm] *no comp/superl* ◊ *einen Pulli verkehrt herum tragen* ⊙ **know sb/sth inside out** etw./jdn in- und auswendig kennen **turn sth inside out 1.** *(a bag, coat)* etw. umdrehen **2.** *(a room, flat)* etw. auf den Kopf stellen

insider [noun] Insider ['ɪnsaɛde] der <-s, -> ♀Insiderin ['ɪnsaɛdərɪn] die <-, -nen>

insidious(ly) [adj, adv] heimtückisch ['haɛmtvkɪʃ] ◊ *ein heimtückischer Anschlag* ♦ *Darmkrebs gilt als besonders heimtückisch.* ♦ *heimtückisch handeln*

insight [noun] **1.** *(knowledge)* Einblick ['aɛnblɪk] der <-(e)s, -e> ◊ *Er hat einen Einblick in die Finanzierung der Forschung gewonnen.* provide an insight into sth einen Einblick in etw. [acc] geben **2.** *(ability to grasp sth)* Verständnis [fe'ʃtɛntnɪs] das <-ses> *no pl* ◊ *ein überraschend großes Verständnis für komplexe Vorgänge*

insignificant [adj] unbedeutend ['ʊnbədəɡtnt] ◊ *Sie spielt eine unbedeutende Nebenrolle.* ♦ *Diese Unterschiede sind völlig unbedeutend.*

insignificantly [adv] geringfügig [gə'rɪŋfyːgɪç] ◊ *Die Kosten sind nur geringfügig gestiegen.*

insipid [adj] **1.** *(food)* fade ['faːdə] ◊ *fade Hausmannskost* ♦ *Ich finde die Soße etwas fade.* **2.** *(colo(u)rs, people)* langweilig ['laŋvaɛlɪç] ◊ *Ist Grau eine langweilige Farbe?* ♦ *Der Typ ist so langweilig!*

insist [verb] darauf bestehen [daraof bə'ʃteːən] <besteht, bestand, hat bestanden> ◊ *Hier, nimm das Geld — ich bestehe darauf!* ♦ *Sie besteht darauf, dass ich mich entschuldige.*

• **insist on** [phras v] **1.** *(be determined to do sth)* insist on doing sth darauf bestehen, etw. zu tun [daraof bə'ʃteːən ... tsuː] <besteht, bestand, hat bestanden> ◊ *Er besteht darauf, alles selbst zu überprüfen.* insist on sth auf etw. [dat] bestehen ◊ *Ich bestand auf einer Pause.* **2.** *(pej)* insist on doing sth etw. immer wieder tun [,ɪmɐ 'viːdɐ tuːn] <tut, tat, hat getan> ◊ *Sie lässt immer wieder ihre Schuhe im Weg stehen.*

insistence [noun] insistence on sth Beharren auf etw. [dat] [bə'harən aof] das <-s> *no pl* ◊ *Sein Beharren auf diesem Punkt blockierte die Verhandlungen.* insistence that Beharren darauf, dass ◊ *das Beharren darauf, dass Mann und Frau gleichberechtigt sind* at sb's insistence auf jds Drängen [aof ... 'drɛŋən] ◊ *Auf ihr Drängen ging ich zum Arzt.*

insolvency [noun] Konkurs [kɔn'kʊrs] der <-es, -e> ◊ *Die Firma steht kurz vor dem Konkurs.*

inspect [verb] **1.** *(control, monitor)* kontrollieren [kɔntrɔ'liːrən] <kontrolliert, kontrollierte, hat kontrolliert> ◊ *Sie kontrollieren alle Waren vorschriftsmäßig.* **2.** *(look closely, examine with an eye to details)* inspizieren [ɪnspi'tsiːrən] <inspiziert, inspizierte, hat inspiziert> ◊ *Sie inspizierte das Bild genau.* ♦ *die Truppe inspizieren* inspect sth for sth etw. auf etw. [acc] inspizieren inspect sth for sth etw. auf etw. [acc] untersuchen [aof ... ʊnte,zuːxn] <untersucht,

untersuchte, hat untersucht> ◊ *Das Programm wurde auf Fehler untersucht.*

inspection [noun] **1.** *(of documents)* Überprüfung [ybe'pryːfʊŋ] die <-, -en> ◊ *Bei der Überprüfung Ihrer Unterlagen wurde ein Fehler gefunden.* The records are available for public inspection. Die Aufzeichnungen können öffentlich eingesehen werden. **2.** TECHN, MIL Inspektion [ɪnspɛk'tsjoːn] die <-, -en> ◊ *die Inspektion der Truppe/von Atomanlagen* ⊙ **on closer inspection** bei näherer Betrachtung

inspector [noun] **1.** *(official overseer)* Inspektor [ɪn'spɛktoːɐ] der <-s, -en> ♀Inspektorin [ɪnspɛk'toːrɪn] die <-, -nen> ◊ *Er ist Inspektor beim Tierschutzverein.* ♦ *Die Inspektorin der Gesundheitsbehörde hat den Betrieb geschlossen.* **2.** *(in the UK: person who examines train or bus tickets)* Kontrolleur [kɔntrɔ'løːɐ] der <-s, -e> ♀Kontrolleurin [kɔntrɔ'løːrɪn] die <-, -nen> ◊ *Sie arbeitet als Kontrolleurin bei der Bahn.* ♦ *Auf dieser Strecke kommt selten ein Kontrolleur.* **3.** *(of police)* Kommissar [kɔmɪ,saː'] der <-s, -e> ♀Kommissarin [kɔmɪ,saːrɪn] die <-, -nen> ◊ *Sie ist Kommissarin.* ♦ *Der Kommissar hat den Fall gelöst.*

inspiration [noun] Inspiration [ɪnspira'tsjoːn] die <-, -en> ◊ *Die Inspiration zu dem Bild kam ihr auf einer Reise.* be an inspiration to sb eine Inspiration für jdn sein draw inspiration from sth/sb sich von etw./jdm inspirieren lassen [fɔn ... ɪnspi'riːrən lasn̩] <lässt sich, ließ sich, hat sich lassen>

inspire [verb] **1.** *(touch the imagination of)* inspirieren [ɪnspi'riːrən] <inspiriert, inspirierte, hat inspiriert> ◊ *Diese Dichterin hat mich inspiriert.* ♦ *Der Kurs inspirierte mich dazu, mit dem Malen wieder anzufangen.* **2.** *(evoke feelings: envy)* hervorrufen [he'foːɡruːfn̩] <ruft hervor, rief hervor, hat hervorgerufen> ◊ *Seine Vorstellung hat Neid hervorgerufen.* inspire sth in sb etw. bei jdm hervorrufen ◊ *Sein Erfolg ruft bei seinen Konkurrenten Neid hervor.; (affection, distrust, hope)* erwecken [e'vɛkn̩] <erweckt, erweckte, hat erweckt> inspire sth in sb etw. bei/in jdm erwecken ◊ *Zuneigung in jdm erwecken* ♦ *Ihr Verhalten erweckt bei mir Misstrauen.; (fear, respect, confidence)* einflößen ['aɛnfløːsn̩] +haben inspire sth in sb jdm etw. einflößen ◊ *Der Direktor flößte uns Respekt ein.; (enthusiasm, a reaction)* auslösen ['aʊsløːzn̩] +haben inspire sth in sb etw. bei jdm auslösen ◊ *Seine Ankündigung löste wahre Begeisterungsstürme aus.*

inspired → inspire [adj] genial [ge'njaːl] ◊ *Deine Lösung ist einfach genial!* ♦ *eine geniale Künstlerin*

install [verb] **1.** *(as part of the house/a machine)* einbauen ['aɛnbaʊən] +haben ◊ *eine neue Heizung/ Dusche einbauen* have sth installed etw. einbauen lassen; *(a telephone, cooker etc.)* anschließen ['anʃliːsn̩] <schließt an, schloss an, hat angeschlossen> ◊ *Der Herd ist noch nicht angeschlossen.; (an electrical one)* legen ['leːgn̩] +haben ◊ *neue Leitungen legen lassen; (a computer program, electrical eqipment)* installieren [ɪnsta'liːrən] <installiert, installierte, hat installiert> ◊ *ein neues Programm/Überwachungskameras installieren* **2.** *(a person)* install sb as sth jdn als etw. einsetzen [als ... aɛntsɛtsn̩] +haben ◊ *Sie wurde als neue Abteilungsleiterin eingesetzt.* install sb in office jdn an die Macht bringen [an diː 'maxt brɪŋən] +haben ◊ *die Entwicklung, die*

den Diktator an die Macht brachte **3.** *(take a seat)*
install yourself sich niederlassen ['ni:dɐlasn̩] <lässt
sich nieder, ließ sich nieder, hat sich niedergelassen>
◊ *Er hat sich am Tisch niedergelassen.*

installation [noun] **1.** *(of a machine, furniture)*
Montage [mɔn'taːʒə] die <-, –n> ◊ *Wir übernehmen
die Montage von PCs.* ♦ *die Montage einer neuen
Heizung; (of a computer programme, work of art)*
Installation [ɪnstala'tsjoːn] die <-, –en>; *(of furniture
in a room)* Aufstellung ['aʊfʃtɛlʊŋ] die <-> no pl ◊
*Wir übernehmen die Lieferung und Aufstellung der
Möbel.* **2.** *(system, structure)* Anlage ['anlaːgə] die
<-, –n> ◊ *sanitäre Anlagen* ♦ *Die Wartung der
Anlage ist sehr teuer.* **3.** *(in a job)* Amtseinführung
['amts|aɛnfyːrʊŋ] die <-, –en> ◊ *die Amtseinführung
des neuen Präsidenten*

instalment, installment [noun] Rate ['raːtə] die
<-, –n> ◊ *Die erste Rate wird beim Kauf fällig.* ♦
Die Rückzahlung erfolgt in Raten.

instance [noun] Fall [fal] der <-(e)s, Fälle> ◊ *Das ist
ein typischer Fall von Selbstbetrug.* ♦ *Was ist in
diesem Fall zu tun?*
⊛ **for instance** zum Beispiel

instant[1] [noun] Moment [mo'mɛnt] der <-s, –e> ◊
Einen Moment lang habe ich geglaubt, er fällt um. ♦
in diesem Moment in an instant im Nu [ɪm 'nuː] ◊
Es regnete so stark, dass ich im Nu nass war.
⊛ **this instant** sofort ◊ *Komm sofort hierher!*

instant[2] [adj] **1.** *(immediate)* unmittelbar ['ʊnmɪt|baːr]
only before ns ◊ *Eine unmittelbare Lösung ist nicht
in Sicht.* She took an instant liking to him. Sie
mochte ihn sofort. He became an instant hero. Er
wurde über Nacht zum Helden. **2.** instant coffee
Pulverkaffee ['pʊlfekafeː] der <-s> no pl instant
meal Fertiggericht ['fɛrtɪçgərɪçt] das <-(e)s, –e>
instant soup Tütensuppe ['tyːtn̩zʊpə] die <-, –n>

instantly [adv] augenblicklich [aʊgn̩'blɪklɪç] ◊ *Wenn
du nicht augenblicklich hörst, gibt es Ärger!* ♦ *Ein
Fehler stoppt das System augenblicklich.*

instead [adv] **1.** *(as an alternative)* stattdessen ˙
[ʃtat'dɛsn̩] ◊ *Wenn du keine Lust zum Tanzen hast,
könnten wir stattdessen ins Kino gehen.* **2.** *(in preference to)* instead of anstatt [an'ʃtat] ◊ *Warum
versöhnen sie sich nicht, anstatt ständig zu streiten?*
3. *(as a substitute for sth/sb)* instead of anstelle ...
[gen], anstelle von [an'ʃtɛlə fɔn] ◊ *Er erschien
anstelle seiner Schwester zur der Feier.* ♦ *Anstelle von
Äpfeln kann man auch Birnen verwenden.*

instinct [noun] Instinkt [ɪn'stɪŋkt] der <-(e)s, –e>
follow your instincts seinem Instinkt folgen instinct
for survival Überlebensinstinkt [ybɐ'leːbm̩s|ɪn,stɪŋkt]

institute[1] [noun] Institut [ɪnsti'tuːt] das <-(e)s, –e> ◊
das Institut für Kunstgeschichte

institute[2] [verb] einführen ['aɛnfyːrən] +haben ◊ *Sie
führten neue Regeln ein.*

institution [noun] **1.** *(organization, fundamental
tradition)* Institution [ɪnstitu'tsjoːn] die <-, –en> ◊
die Institution der Ehe ♦ *Eine unabhängige Institution soll dies überprüfen.* **2.** *(process)* Einführung
['aɛnfyːrʊŋ] die <-, –en> ◊ *die Einführung neuer
Qualitätsstandards*

institutional [adj] **1.** *(of an organization)* institutionell
[ɪnstitutsjo'nɛl] ◊ *die institutionelle Förderung der
Wohlfahrtsverbände* **2.** *(of a hospital etc.)* Anstalts...
['anʃtalts] institutional food Anstaltsessen
['anʃtalts|ɛsn̩] das <-s, ->

instruct [verb] **1.** *(explain, order)* anweisen ['anvaezn̩]
<weist an, wies an, hat angewiesen> ◊ *Ich wies ihn
an, wie das Regal zusammenzubauen sei.* ♦ *Er wies
seine Mitarbeiter an, schneller zu arbeiten.; (teach
sb)* instruct sb in sth jdn in etw. [dat] unterrichten
[ɪn ... ʊntɐ,rɪçtn̩] <unterrichtet, unterrichtete, hat
unterrichtet> ◊ *Er hat seine Schüler in Latein unterrichtet.* **2.** LAW *(a lawyer)* beauftragen [bə'aʊftraːgn̩]
<beauftragt, beauftragte, hat beauftragt> ◊ *Sie hat
einen Rechtsanwalt mit dem Fall beauftragt.*

instruction [noun] **1.** *(explanation, order)* Anweisung
['anvaezʊŋ] die <-, –en> ◊ *Bitte befolgen Sie die
Anweisungen zur Benutzung des Geräts.* ♦ *klare
Anweisungen geben* **2.** *(of a product, printed)* instruc-
tions Gebrauchsanweisung [gə'braʊxs|anvaezʊŋ] die
<-, –en> ◊ *Lesen Sie bitte die Gebrauchsanweisung!*
3. *(teaching)* Unterricht ['ʊntɐrɪçt] der <-(e)s, –e>
most sing ◊ *Ich nehme Unterricht in Mathematik.*

instructor [noun] **1.** *(in a course)* Kursleiter
['kʊrslaetɐ] der <-s, -> ♀Kursleiterin ['kʊrslaetərɪn]
die <-, –nen>; *(in compound ns)* ...lehrer ['leːrɐ]
der <-s, -> ◊ ...lehrerin ['leːrərɪn] die <-, –nen>
driving instructor Fahrlehrer ['faːɡleːrɐ] Fahrlehrerin
['faːɡleːrərɪn] yoga instructor Yogalehrer ['joːɡaleːrɐ]
Yogalehrerin ['joːɡaleːrərɪn] **2.** *(in a company, the
army etc.)* Ausbilder ['aʊsbɪldɐ] der <-s, -> ♀Ausbil-
derin ['aʊsbɪldərɪn] die <-, –nen> **3.** *(in the US, at
school)* Lehrer ['leːrɐ] der <-s, -> ♀Lehrerin
['leːrərɪn] die <-, –nen> ◊ *Er ist Lehrer an einer
Grundschule.* ♦ *Sie ist eine gute Lehrerin.; (at university)* Dozent [do'tsɛnt] der <-en, –en> ♀Dozentin
[do'tsɛntɪn] die <-, –nen>

instrument [noun] Instrument [ɪnstru'mɛnt] das
<-(e)s, –e> ◊ *Spielst du ein Instrument?* ♦ *Die
Instrumente eines Chirurgen müssen steril sein.* ♦
Geld — das Instrument der Macht.

instrumental [adj] **1.** *(important)* zentral [tsɛn'traːl] ◊
ein zentrales Problem be instrumental in sth eine
zentrale Rolle bei etw. spielen **2.** MUS instrumental
[ɪnstrumɛn'taːl] no comp/superl ◊ *ein instrumentales
Stück*

insufficient(ly) [adj, adv] ungenügend ['ʊngənyːgn̩t] ◊
Bei diesem Nebel ist die Sicht ungenügend. ♦ *unge-
nügende Kenntnisse* ♦ *Seine Arbeit wird ungenügend
bezahlt.*

insulate [verb] isolieren [izo'liːrən] <isoliert, isolierte,
hat isoliert> ◊ *Das Kabel ist schlecht isoliert.*

insult[1] [noun] Beleidigung [bə'laedɪgʊŋ] die <-, –en>
throw insults at sb jdm Beleidigungen an den Kopf
werfen be an insult to sb jdn beleidigen
[bə'laedɪgn̩] <beleidigt, beleidigte, hat beleidigt>
⊛ **add insult to injury** alles noch schlimmer
machen trade insults sich gegenseitig beleidigen

insult[2] [verb] beleidigen [bə'laedɪgn̩] <beleidigt, beleidigte, hat beleidigt> ◊ *Mit dieser Äußerung hat sie
ihn schwer beleidigt.*

insurance [noun] **1.** *(cover)* Versicherung [fɛ'zɪçərʊŋ]
die <-, –en> ◊ *eine Versicherung gegen Diebstahl*
take out an insurance eine Versicherung abschließen claim sth on your insurance etw. bei der Versicherung geltend machen **2.** *(security)* Sicherheit
['zɪçɐhaet] die <-, –en> ◊ *Als Sicherheit hatten wir
ein Haus.*

insure [verb] versichern [fɛ'zɪçɐn] <versichert, versicherte, hat versichert> ◊ *War er/das Gepäck versichert?* ♦ *Sie haben das Bild versichert.* insure sb

against sth jdn gegen etw. versichern ◊ *Wir sind gegen Diebstahl versichert.*

intact [adj] intakt [ɪn'takt] <intakter, am intaktesten> ◊ *Sein Ruf ist intakt.* ✦ *eine intakte Beziehung*

intake [noun] **1.** *(of food, drink)* Aufnahme ['aʊfnaːmə] die <-, -n> ◊ *die Aufnahme von Schadstoffen über die Nahrung* **2.** *(of people)* Anzahl der Neuzugänge [,antsaːl deːɐ 'nɔʏtsuːgɛŋə] die <-> *no pl* ◊ *Die Anzahl der Neuzugänge belief sich auf 2000.*

integral [adj] **1.** *(essential)* wesentlich ['veːzntlɪç] ◊ *Grammatik ist ein wesentlicher Teil des Sprachunterrichts.* be integral to sth ein wesentlicher Bestandteil ... [gen] sein ◊ *Vertrauen ist ein wesentlicher Bestandteil jeder Beziehung.* be integral in sth eine wichtige Rolle in etw. [dat] spielen [aɛnə ,vɪçtɪgə 'rɔlə ɪn ... ʃpiːlən] +haben **2.** *(part of)* eingebaut ['aɛngəbaʊt] *no comp/superl* ◊ *ein Haus mit eingebautem Swimmingpool*

integrate [verb] integrieren [ɪntɛ'griːrən] <integriert, integrierte, hat integriert> ◊ *Nach einem Jahr war sie völlig integriert.* ✦ *Kann dieses Seminar noch in das Programm integriert werden?* integrate with sth sich in etw. [dat] integrieren integrate sth with sth etw. auf etw. [acc] abstimmen [aʊf ... ,apʃtɪmən] +haben ◊ *Alle Entscheidungen sollten auf die Gesamtstrategie abgestimmt werden.*

integration [noun] Integration [ɪntɛgra'tsjoːn] die <-, -en> ◊ *die Integration in die Gesellschaft/ein Betriebssystem*

integrity [noun] **1.** *(personal, professional)* Integrität [ɪntɛgri'tɛːt] die <-> *no pl* ◊ *Seine professionelle Integrität ist ihm wichtig.* ✦ *Ich möchte meine Integrität bewahren.* **2.** *(without any damage etc.)* Unversehrtheit ['ʊnfɛzeːɐthaɛt] die <-> *no pl* ◊ *körperliche/territoriale Unversehrtheit; (without anything missing)* Vollständigkeit ['fɔlʃtɛndɪçkaɛt] die <-> *no pl* ◊ *die Vollständigkeit der Daten*

intellectual [noun] Intellektuelle [ɪntɛlɛktu'ɛlə] der/die <-n, die Intellektuellen> *but: ein Intellektueller/eine Intellektuelle* ◊ *ein Buch für Intellektuelle*

intellectual(ly) [adj, adv] intellektuell [ɪntɛlɛktu'ɛl] ◊ *intellektuelle Fähigkeiten* ✦ *Du bist mir zu intellektuell.* ✦ *ein intellektuell befriedigendes Buch*

intelligence [noun] **1.** *(mental ability)* Intelligenz [ɪntɛli'gɛnts] die <-, -en> ◊ *Er besaß enorme Intelligenz.* **2.** *(information)* Informationen [ɪnfɔ'ma'tsjoːnən] die <-> *pl* ◊ *Er sammelte Informationen über den Vorfall.; (organization)* Nachrichtendienst ['naːxrɪçtndiːnst] der <-(e)s, -e>

intelligent(ly) [adj, adv] intelligent [ɪntɛli'gɛnt] <intelligenter, am intelligentesten> ◊ *Ist er intelligent?* ✦ *eine intelligente Frage* ✦ *ein Problem intelligent lösen*

intelligible(-ibly) [adj, adv] verständlich [fɛ'ʃtɛntlɪç] ◊ *eine verständliche Aussprache* ✦ *etw. verständlich formulieren* intelligible to sb verständlich für jdn ◊ *Diese Technik ist für jedermann verständlich.*

intend [verb] beabsichtigen [bə'ʔapzɪçtɪgŋ] <beabsichtigt, beabsichtigte, hat beabsichtigt> ◊ *Ich hatte das nicht beabsichtigt.* ✦ *Ich beabsichtige, nach Polen zu fahren.* intend to do sth etw. mit etw. beabsichtigen ◊ *Ich möchte wissen, was er mit dieser Bemerkung beabsichtigte.* intend sb/sth to do sth wollen, dass etw./jd tut ['vɔlən das] <will, wollte, hat gewollt> ◊ *Ich habe nicht gewollt, dass das passiert.*

◉ be intended for bestimmt sein für

intense [adj] **1.** *(heat, cold)* groß [groːs] <größer, am größten> ◊ *Draußen herrscht große Kälte.* ✦ *Die Hitze war sehr groß.; (pain, pressure, increase)* stark [ʃtaʳk] <stärker, am stärksten> ◊ *Sind die Schmerzen sehr stark?* ✦ *ein starkes Wachstum der Umsätze* **2.** *(colo(u)rs, light)* grell [grɛl] ◊ *ein Bild in grellen Farben* ✦ *Ohne Sonnenbrille ist mir das Licht zu grell.* **3.** *(pej) (person)* anstrengend ['anʃtrɛŋənt] ◊ *eine anstrengende Persönlichkeit* ✦ *Er konnte sehr anstrengend sein.*

intensely [adv] äußerst ['ɔʏsɛst] ◊ *eine äußerst anstrengende Frau* dislike sb intensely jdn nicht ausstehen können [nɪçt 'aʊsʃteːən kœnən] <kann, konnte, hat können>

intensify [verb] **1.** *(increase)* verstärken [fɛ'ʃtɛʳkŋ] <verstärkt, verstärkte, hat verstärkt> ◊ *Hörgeräte verstärken den Ton.* ✦ *seine Anstrengungen verstärken den Druck auf jdn verstärken* **2.** *(a situation, conflict)* verschärfen [fɛ'ʃɛʳfŋ] <verschärft, verschärfte, hat verschärft> ◊ *Mehrere Attentate verschärften die politische Lage.*

intensity [noun] **1.** *(an increase of temperature, weather)* Stärke ['ʃtɛʳkə] die <-, -n> *most sing* ◊ *Die Stärke des Sturms lässt schon wieder nach.* **2.** *(of colo(u)rs, feelings)* Intensität [ɪntɛnzi'tɛːt] die <-, -en> *most sing* ◊ *Die Intensität seiner Gefühle überraschte sie.*

intensive(ly) [adj, adv] intensiv [ɪntɛn'ziːf] ◊ *intensive Verhandlungen* ✦ *Ihre Gefühle waren sehr intensiv.* ✦ *Wir werden intensiv zusammenarbeiten.*

intensive care unit [noun] Intensivstation [ɪntɛn'ziːfʃta,tsjoːn] die <-, -en> ◊ *Sie liegt auf der Intensivstation.*

intent [noun] Absicht ['apzɪçt] die <-, -en> ◊ *Es war nie meine Absicht, Sie zu beleidigen.* ✦ *kriminelle Absichten* statement of intent Absichtserklärung ['apzɪçts|ɛklɛːrʊŋ] die <-, -en> with intent to do sth mit dem Vorsatz, etw. zu tun [mɪt deːm 'foːgzats ... tsuː] with intent mit Vorsatz ◊ *Hat sie mit Vorsatz gehandelt?*

intent(ly) [adj, adv] *(focused on)* konzentriert [kɔntsɛn'triːgt] <konzentrierter, am konzentriertesten> ◊ *ihr konzentrierte Arbeitsweise* ✦ *konzentriert arbeiten*

◉ be intent on sth **1.** *(be concentrated)* sich auf etw. [acc] konzentrieren ◊ *Sie konzentrierte sich so auf ihr Buch, dass sie die Milch anbrennen ließ.* **2.** *(be determined)* auf etw. [acc] aus sein ◊ *auf Streit aus sein*

intention [noun] Absicht ['apzɪçt] die <-, -en> ◊ *Es war nie meine Absicht, Sie zu beleidigen.* ✦ *Sie hat in der besten Absicht gehandelt.* ✦ *kriminelle Absichten* have no intention of doing sth nicht die Absicht haben, etw. zu tun

intentional(ly) [adj, adv] absichtlich ['apzɪçtlɪç] *no comp/superl* ◊ *Das war ein absichtlicher Verstoß gegen die Spielregeln!* ✦ *War das absichtlich?* ✦ *jdn absichtlich treten*

interact [verb] interagieren [ɪntɐ|a'giːrən] <interagiert, interagierte, hat interagiert> ◊ *Beobachten Sie, wie die Kinder (miteinander) interagieren!*

interaction [noun] Interaktion [ɪntɐ|ak'tsjoːn] die <-, -en>

interactive(ly) [adj, adv] interaktiv [ɪntɐ|ak'tiːf] *no comp/superl* ◊ *interaktive Computerprogramme* ✦ *Diese Übung ist interaktiv.* ✦ *interaktiv lernen*

A
B
C
D
E
F
G
H
I
J
K
L
M
N
O
P
Q
R
S
T
U
V
W
X
Y
Z

intercourse ⟨noun⟩ Geschlechtsverkehr [ɡəˈfleçtsfɛkeːɐ̯] der <-(e)s> *no pl*

interest[1] ⟨noun⟩ **1.** *(focused attention)* Interesse [ˈɪntəˈrɛsə] das <-s, -n> ◊ *Dieser Beruf entspricht genau meinen Interessen.* ♦ *Die Gewerkschaften vertreten die Interessen der Arbeitnehmer.* ♦ *für jdn von Interesse sein* have an interest in sth/sb Interesse an etw. ⟨dat⟩ haben declare an interest in sth sein Interesse an etw. ⟨dat⟩ bekunden take an interest in sth/sb an etw./jdm interessiert sein [an … ɪntərɛˈsiːɐ̯t za̯ɛn] +sein place of interest Sehenswürdigkeit [ˈzeːənsvʏˈdɪçkaɛt] die <-, -en> **2.** FIN *(charge for lending money)* Zinsen [ˈtsɪnzn̩] die <-> *pl* ◊ *hohe/niedrige Zinsen bringen* ♦ *die Zinsen anheben/senken* ♦ *Jdm den Kredit werden monatlich 10,9 % Zinsen fällig.* pay interest on sth etw. verzinsen [fɛˈtsɪnzn̩] <verzinst, verzinste, hat verzinst> ◊ *Die Bank verzinst das Kapital mit 3%.* **3.** *(investment, stake)* Beteiligung [bəˈtaɛlɪɡʊŋ] die <-, -en> ◊ *Er besitzt eine Beteiligung an einer Firma.* ⊛ *pay sb back with interest* jdm etw. gründlich heimzahlen just out of interest nur so aus Neugierde

interest[2] ⟨verb⟩ interessieren [ɪntərɛˈsiːrən] <interessiert, interessierte, hat interessiert> ◊ *Ich konnte ihn leider nicht für meinen Vorschlag interessieren.* It might interest you to know that … Vielleicht interessiert es dich/Sie, dass … could I interest you in sth wärst du/wären Sie an etw. ⟨dat⟩ interessiert ◊ *Wären Sie an einem Katalog interessiert?* be interested in sth/sb sich für etw./jdn interessieren ◊ *Sie interessierten sich überhaupt nicht für Musik.*

interesting ⟨adj⟩ interessant [ɪntərɛˈsant] ◊ *Sie hat ein sehr interessantes Leben geführt.* ♦ *Ich halte Ihre Idee für sehr interessant.*

interface ⟨noun⟩ Schnittstelle [ˈfnɪtftɛlə] die <-, -n> ◊ *Über welche Schnittstellen kann ich auf andere Datenbanken zugreifen?*

interfere ⟨verb⟩ sich einmischen [ˈaɛnmɪfn̩] +haben ◊ *Er mischt sich überall ein.* interfere in sth sich in etw. ⟨acc⟩ einmischen ◊ *sich in einen Streit einmischen*
• **interfere with** ⟨phras v⟩ **1.** *(have an adverse effect)* beeinträchtigen [bəˈaɛntrɛçtɪɡn̩] <beeinträchtigt, beeinträchtigte, hat beeinträchtigt> ◊ *Ihre Arbeit beeinträchtigte ihr Privatleben.* **2.** *(without authorization)* interfere with sth an etw. ⟨dat⟩ zu schaffen machen [an … tsuː fafn̩ maxn̩] +haben ◊ *Er machte sich am Tresor zu schaffen.* **3.** *(sexually)* interfere with sb jdn sexuell missbrauchen [zɛksuˌɛl mɪsˈbraɔxn̩] <missbraucht, missbrauchte, hat missbraucht> ◊ *Er wurde als Kind sexuell missbraucht.*

interference ⟨noun⟩ **1.** *(meddling)* Einmischung [ˈaɛnmɪfʊŋ] die <-, -en> ◊ *Ohne seine Einmischung wäre der Streit nicht so eskaliert.* **2.** *(on the telephone, television etc.)* Störung [ˈftøːrʊŋ] die <-, -en>

interim ⟨adj⟩ vorläufig [ˈfoːlɔɔfɪç] ◊ *eine vorläufige Arbeitserlaubnis* interim period Zwischenzeit [ˈtsvɪfn̩tsaɛt] die <-, -en> *most sing* interim payment Abschlagszahlung [ˈapflaːkstsaːlʊŋ] die <-, -en> interim government Übergangsregierung [ˈyːbegaŋsreˌɡiːrʊŋ] die <-, -en>

interior[1] ⟨noun⟩ Innere [ˈɪnərə] das <-n> *no pl* ◊ *das Innere des Hauses*; *(of a country)* Landesinnere

[ˈlandəsˌɪnərə] ◊ *Auch im Landesinneren gibt es viel zu sehen.*

interior[2] ⟨adj⟩ innere [ˈɪnərə] *no comp/superl, only before ns* ◊ *der innere Aufbau der Erdkugel*

interjection ⟨noun⟩ **1.** GRAM Interjektion [ɪntɛjɛkˈtsjoːn] die <-, -en> **2.** *(in a conversation)* Einwurf [ˈaɛnvʊf] der <-(e)s, Einwürfe> ◊ *Ihr Einwurf war berechtigt.*

intermediate ⟨adj⟩ mittlere [ˈmɪtlərə] *no comp/superl, only before ns* ◊ *eine Übung von mittlerem Schwierigkeitsgrad* intermediate examination Zwischenprüfung [ˈtsvɪfnprʏːfʊŋ] die <-, -en>

intern ⟨noun⟩ **1.** *(person who gains work experience)* Praktikant [praktiˈkant] der <-en, -en> ♀Praktikantin [praktiˈkantɪn] die <-, -nen> ◊ *Sie ist Praktikantin in einem Verlag.* ♦ *Morgen kommt ein neuer Praktikant.* **2.** *(in the US: newly qualified doctor who is being trained in a hospital)* ⊕Arzt im praktischen Jahr [ˌaːtst ɪm praktɪfn̩ ˈjaːɐ̯] der <-es, Ärzte> ♀Ärztin im praktischen Jahr [ˌɛɐ̯tstɪn ɪm praktɪfn̩ ˈjaːɐ̯] die <-, -nen> ◊ *Er ist Arzt im praktischen Jahr in einem Katharinenhospital.* ♦ *Ich wurde von einer Ärztin im praktischen Jahr behandelt.*

internal ⟨adj⟩ **1.** *(within a country, inside your body or mind)* innere [ˈɪnərə] *no comp/superl, only before ns* ◊ *die inneren Angelegenheiten eines Staates* ♦ *innere Blutungen/Verletzungen haben* internal flight Inlandsflug [ˈɪnlantsfluːk] der <-(e)s, Inlandsflüge> **2.** *(inside a house or an object)* internal … Innen… [ˈɪnən] internal wall Innenwand [ˈɪnənvant] die <-, Innenwände> **3.** *(in a company etc.)* intern [ɪnˈtɛrn] *no comp/superl* ◊ *interne Angelegenheiten*

international(ly) ⟨adj, adv⟩ international [ɪntɛnatsjoˈnaːl] *no comp/superl; when used as an adj, mostly before ns* ◊ *internationaler Protest gegen etw.* ♦ *Diese Firma operiert international.*

Internet ⟨noun⟩ Internet [ˈɪntɛnɛt] das <-s> *no pl* ◊ *im Internet surfen*

internship ⟨noun⟩ Praktikum [ˈpraktikʊm] das <-s, Praktika> ◊ *Damals war er noch Arzt im Praktikum.* ♦ *mehrere Praktika absolvieren/machen*

interpret ⟨verb⟩ **1.** *(translate)* dolmetschen [ˈdɔlmɛtfn̩] +haben ◊ *Könnten Sie bitte für uns dolmetschen?* **2.** *(understand)* deuten [ˈdɔɔtn̩] <deutet, deutete, hat gedeutet> ◊ *einen Traum/eine Geste/ein Zeichen deuten* **3.** *(a text, piece of music etc.)* interpretieren [ɪntəpreˈtiːrən] <interpretiert, interpretierte, hat interpretiert> ◊ *einen Text interpretieren* interpret a role eine Rolle spielen [aɛnə ˈrɔlə fpiːlən] +haben

interpretation ⟨noun⟩ **1.** *(performance, explanation)* Interpretation [ɪntəpretaˈtsjoːn] die <-, -en> ◊ *die Interpretation eines Gedichts/einer Bibelstelle; (of a part in a play)* Darstellung [ˈdaːftɛlʊŋ] die <-, -en> **2.** *(of dreams, signs etc.)* Deutung [ˈdɔɔtʊŋ] die <-, -en> ◊ *die Deutung von Traumsymbolen* put an interpretation on sth etw. interpretieren [ɪntəpreˈtiːrən] <interpretiert, interpretierte, hat interpretiert>

interpreter ⟨noun⟩ **1.** *(translator)* Dolmetscher [ˈdɔlmɛtfə] der <-s, -> ♀Dolmetscherin [ˈdɔlmɛtfərɪn] die <-, -nen> ◊ *Sie ist Dolmetscherin von Beruf.* ♦ *Wir brauchen einen Dolmetscher.* **2.** *(musician, singer)* Interpret [ɪntɛˈpreːt] der <-en, -en> ♀Interpretin [ɪntɛˈpreːtɪn] die <-, -nen>

interrogate ⟨verb⟩ verhören [fɛˈhøːrən] <verhört,

verhörte, hat verhört> ◊ *einen Zeugen verhören*
interrupt [verb] unterbrechen [ʊntɐ'breçn̩] <unterbricht, unterbrach, hat unterbrochen> ◊ *die Fahrt mehrmals unterbrechen müssen* ♦ *einen Stromkreis unterbrechen*
interruption [noun] **1.** *(pause, period of time)* Unterbrechung [ʊntɐ'breçʊŋ] die <-, -en> ◊ *eine kurze Unterbrechung der Arbeit* **2.** *(disruption)* Störung ['ʃtøːrʊŋ] die <-, -en> ◊ *Störungen bei der Arbeit*
intersect [verb] **1.** *(path, road)* kreuzen ['krɔøtsn̩] +haben ◊ *Der Radweg kreuzt die Straße.* The roads intersect. Die Straßen kreuzen sich.; *(lines, routes)* schneiden ['ʃnaedn̩] <schneidet, schnitt, hat geschnitten> ◊ *Strecke A schneidet Strecke B in Punkt C.* The lines intersect. Die Linien schneiden sich. **2.** *(divide)* durchziehen [dʊ'çʼtsiːən] <durchzieht, durchzog, hat durchzogen> ◊ *Zahlreiche Flüsse durchziehen die Landschaft.* be intersected by sth von etw. durchzogen sein
intersection [noun] **1.** *(junction)* Kreuzung ['krɔøtsʊŋ] die <-, -en> ◊ *an der Kreuzung links/rechts abbiegen; (of motorways)* Kreuz [krɔøts] das <-es, -e> ◊ *Stau auf der Autobahn am Mannheimer Kreuz* **2.** *(of lines)* Schnittpunkt ['ʃnɪtpʊŋkt] der <-(e)s, -e> ◊ *der Schnittpunkt zweier Linien*
interval [noun] **1.** *(in time, space)* Abstand ['apʃtant] der <-(e)s, Abstände> at … intervals in Abständen von …, in … Abständen ◊ *in Abständen von drei Metern/zehn Minuten* ♦ *in regelmäßigen Abständen* **2.** *(pause, break)* Pause ['paozə] die <-, -n> ◊ *eine 20-minütige Pause während der Opernaufführung* ◉ at intervals hin und wieder
intervene [verb] **1.** *(get involved)* eingreifen ['aengraefn̩] <greift ein, griff ein, hat eingegriffen> ◊ *Die Polizei musste eingreifen.* ♦ *in etw.* [acc] eingreifen; *(military)* intervenieren [ɪntɐve'niːrən] <interveniert, intervenierte, hat interveniert> ◊ *in etw.* [dat] intervenieren **2.** *(prevent sth)* dazwischenkommen [da'tsvɪʃn̩kɔmən] <kommt dazwischen, kam dazwischen, ist dazwischengekommen> ◊ *Er wollte studieren, aber der Krieg kam dazwischen.* **3.** *(time)* verstreichen [fe'ʃtraecn̩] <verstreicht, verstrich, ist verstrichen>
intervention [noun] **1.** *(involvement)* Eingreifen ['aengraefn̩] das <-s> no pl ◊ *das Eingreifen der Polizei; (military)* Intervention [ɪntɐven'tsjoːn] die <-, -en> ◊ *militärische Interventionen* **2.** *(medical)* Eingriff ['aengrɪf] der <-(e)s, -e> ◊ *ein chirurgischer Eingriff*
interview¹ [noun] *(for the media, for research)* Interview ['ɪntɐvjuː] das <-s, -s> ◊ *Sie gibt keine Interviews.; (for a job)* Vorstellungsgespräch ['foːʃtɛlʊŋsɡəʃprɛːç] das <-(e)s, -e> ◊ *jdn zu einem Vorstellungsgespräch einladen; (by the police)* Vernehmung [fe'neːmʊŋ] die <-, -en> ◊ *die Vernehmung eines Zeugen*
interview² [verb] *(for the media)* interviewen [ɪntɐ'vjuːən] <interviewt, interviewte, hat interviewt> ◊ *einen Schauspieler interviewen; (for research)* befragen [bə'fraːɡn̩] <befragt, befragte, hat befragt> ◊ *Kunden befragen; (for a job)* interview sb mit jdm ein Vorstellungsgespräch führen [mɪt … aen 'foːʃtɛlʊŋsɡəʃprɛːç fyːrən] +haben; *(suspects, witnesses)* vernehmen [fe'neːmən] <vernimmt, vernahm, hat vernommen> ◊ *einen Angeklagten/Zeugen vernehmen*
intestine [noun] intestine(s) Darm [daʳm] der

<-(e)s, Därme>
intimacy [noun] **1.** *(close relationship)* Vertrautheit [fe'traothaet] die <-> most sing ◊ *die Vertrautheit zwischen Eheleuten* **2.** *(private matter, sexual act)* Intimität [ɪntimi'tɛːt] die <-, -en> *(also euph)* ◊ *Es kam zu Intimitäten zwischen ihnen.*
intimate¹ [adj] **1.** *(close)* eng [ɛŋ] ◊ *Sie sind enge Freunde* ♦ *Unser Verhältnis ist sehr eng.* **2.** *(private, sexual)* intim [ɪn'tiːm] ◊ *intime Details aus jds Leben* ♦ *Die Atmosphäre des Hotels ist sehr intim.* ♦ *mit jdm intim sein*
intimate² [verb] andeuten ['andɔøtn̩] <deutet an, deutete an, hat angedeutet> ◊ *Er deutete an, dass er aus der Wohnung ausziehen wolle.*
into [prep] **1.** *(expressing movement, direction)* in [ɪn] [+acc] ◊ *Sie legte die Wäsche in den Koffer.* ♦ *Alle Straßen, die in die Stadt führen, sind verstopft.* ♦ *etw. ins Englische übersetzen* ♦ *Zucker in die Sahne rühren* ♦ *sich in die Arbeit stürzen* ♦ *das Essen in Portionen aufteilen* turn into sth zu etw. werden [tsuː … veːɐdn̩] +sein ◊ *Sie kann zur Furie werden.* into each other/one another ineinander [ɪn|ae'nandɐ] ◊ *Die Zahnräder greifen ineinander.* **2.** *(describing an impact)* gegen ['geːɡn̩] [+acc] ◊ *Der Wagen fuhr gegen einen Baum.* ◉ be into sth auf etw. [acc] stehen

> 'Into' often occurs in phrasal verbs like 'get into' or 'come into' which have their own entries in the dictionary.

intolerable [adj] unerträglich ['ʊn|ɛtrɛːklɪç] ◊ *unerträgliche Schmerzen* ♦ *Der Krach hier ist unerträglich.*
intonation [noun] Intonation [ɪntɔna'tsjoːn] die <-, -en> ◊ *Fragen haben im Deutschen eine andere Intonation als im Englischen.*
intoxication [noun] Rausch [raoʃ] der <-(e)s, Räusche>
intransitive(ly) [adj, adv] intransitiv ['ɪntranzitiːf] no comp/superl ◊ *transitive und intransitive Verben* ♦ *„Liegen" ist intransitiv.* ♦ *Bestimmte Verben werden nur intransitiv gebraucht.*
intricate [adj] kompliziert [kɔmpli'tsiːɐt] <komplizierter, am kompliziertesten> ◊ *ein kompliziertes Muster* ♦ *Die Rechenaufgabe war kompliziert.*
introduce [verb] **1.** *(a person)* vorstellen ['foːɐʃtɛlən] +haben introduce sb to sb jdm jdn vorstellen ◊ *Darf ich dir meinen Mann vorstellen?* introduce yourself sich vorstellen ◊ *Du stellst dich am besten selbst vor.* **2.** *(sth new)* einführen ['aenfyːrən] +haben ◊ *Studiengebühren/eine neue Steuer einführen* introduce sth (in)to sth etw. in etw. [dat] einführen ◊ *Die Venezianer haben den Kaffee in Europa eingeführt.* introduce sb to sth jdn in etw. [acc] einführen ◊ *Als Kind wurde sie von ihrem Onkel in die Mathematik eingeführt.; (a new species)* einbürgern ['aenbʏʳgɐn] +haben ◊ *Im 12. Jahrhundert wurden Kaninchen in England eingebürgert.* **3.** *(a subject, talk, book)* einleiten ['aenlaetn̩] <leitet ein, leitete ein, hat eingeleitet> ◊ *Ein kurzer Überblick über das Thema leitet den Vortrag ein.* **4.** *(present to an audience)* ankündigen ['ankʏndɪɡn̩] +haben ◊ *einen Künstler ankündigen*
introduction [noun] **1.** *(of sth new)* Einführung ['aenfyːrʊŋ] die <-, -en> ◊ *die Einführung neuer Gesetze/Medikamente* introduction to/into sth Einfüh-

A
B
C
D
E
F
G
H

I

J
K
L
M
N
O
P
Q
R
S
T
U
V
W
X
Y
Z

rung in etw. acc ◊ *eine Einführung in die Philoso-*
phie; *(of a new species)* Einbürgerung ['aɛnbʏˈgərʊn]
die <–, –en> ◊ *die Einbürgerung neuer Tierarten*
2. *(to a book, report etc.)* Einleitung ['aɛnlaɛtʊn] die
<–, –en> ◊ *die Einleitung eines Buches* **3.** *(of a
person)* Vorstellung ['foːɐ̯ʃtɛlʊn] die <–, –en> ◊ *die
Vorstellung der Gäste/eines neuen Kollegen* take over
the introductions jdn vorstellen

> In German, phrases around the term 'introduction'
> are often rendered with a verb construction in which
> you have to specify whom you are introducing: 'do
> the introductions' — *die Gäste/die Anwesenden etc.*
> *vorstellen* (introduce the guests/those present etc.).
> 'Introductions are unnecessary since you all know
> each other.' — *Ich brauche euch einander nicht*
> *vorzustellen, da ihr euch alle kennt.* (I don't need
> to introduce you to each other, since you all know
> each other.)

intruder noun Eindringling ['aɛndrɪnlɪn] der
<–s, –e> ◊ *Als die Polizei kam, waren die Eindring-*
linge schon geflohen.
intrusion noun *(of a peaceful situation)* Störung
['ʃtøːrʊn] die <–, –en> ◊ *eine Störung der Ruhe; (on*
sb's privacy) Eingriff ['aɛngrɪf] der <–(e)s, –e> ◊ *ein*
schwerwiegender Eingriff in jds Privatsphäre
invade verb *(enter)* invade sth in etw. acc eindringen [ɪn ... ˌaɛndrɪnən] <dringt ein, drang ein, ist ein-
gedrungen> ◊ *Scharen von Touristen dringen in die*
Stadt ein. ✦ *in jds Privatsphäre eindringen; (army)*
invade (sth) (in etw. dat acc) einmarschieren
['aɛnmaɐ̯ʃiːrən] <marschiert ein, marschierte ein, ist
einmarschiert> ◊ *Truppen sind (in dem/das Land)*
einmarschiert.; (occupy) invade sth etw. besetzen
[bəˈzɛtsn̩] <besetzt, besetzte, hat besetzt> ◊ *eine Stadt*
besetzen
invalid[1] noun Invalide [ɪnvaˈliːdə] der <–n, –n> ♀In-
validin [ɪnvaˈliːdɪn] die <–, –nen>
invalid[2] adj **1.** *(not accepted)* ungültig ['ʊngʏltɪç] *no*
comp/superl ◊ *ein ungültiger Ausweis* ✦ *Der Vertrag*
ist ohne Unterschrift ungültig. **2.** *(unconvincing)*
nicht schlüssig [nɪçt 'ʃlʏsɪç] *no comp/superl* ◊ *Diese*
Folgerung ist nicht schlüssig. ✦ *ein nicht schlüssiges*
Argument.
invaluable adj von unschätzbarem Wert
[fɔn ˌʊnʃɛtsbaːrəm 'veːɐ̯t] ◊ *Diese Erfahrungen sind*
von unschätzbarem Wert.
invariably adv immer ['ɪmɐ] ◊ *Sie kommt immer zu*
spät.
invasion noun *(entry into a place)* Eindringen
['aɛndrɪnən] das <–s> *no pl* invasion of sth Eindringen in etw. acc ◊ *das Eindringen eines Erregers in*
die Blutbahn; (of an army, large numbers of people,
pests) Invasion [ɪnvaˈzjoːn] die <–, –en> ◊ *die*
Invasion eines Landes durch feindliche Truppen
invent verb erfinden [ɛˈfɪndn̩] <erfindet, erfand, hat
erfunden> ◊ *Edison erfand die elektrische*
Glühlampe.
invention noun **1.** *(creation of sth new, story or*
excuse) Erfindung [ɛˈfɪndʊn] die <–, –en> ◊ *die*
Erfindung neuer Produkte ✦ *Er ließ sich seine*
Erfindung patentieren. **2.** *(inventiveness)* Erfindungsgabe [ɛˈfɪndʊnsgaːbə] die <–> *no pl* ◊ *Ihm mangelt*
es nicht an Erfindungsgabe.
inventor noun Erfinder [ɛˈfɪndɐ] der <–s, –> ♀Erfin-
derin [ɛˈfɪndərɪn] die <–, –nen> ◊ *Er ist Erfinder.* ✦

Valerie Wilson Wesley ist die Erfinderin der ersten
schwarzen Privatdetektivin.
inventory noun Inventar [ɪnvɛnˈtaːɐ̯] das <–s, –e>
(tech) ◊ *Er führt ein Inventar all seiner Kunst-*
schätze.
inverted comma noun Anführungszeichen
['anfyːrʊnstsaɛçn̩] das <–s, –> *most pl* ◊ *in Anfüh-*
rungszeichen stehen put sth in inverted commas
etw. in Anführungszeichen setzen
invest verb investieren [ɪnvɛsˈtiːrən] <investiert, investierte, hat investiert> ◊ *Er investierte 20 000 Euro in*
Wertpapiere. ✦ *Das Unternehmen will jetzt in China*
investieren.
• **invest in** phras v invest (sth) in sth (etw.) in
etw. acc investieren [ɪn ... vɛsˈtiːrən] <investiert,
investierte, hat investiert> ◊ *viel Zeit/Kraft in eine*
Aufgabe investieren ✦ *(Geld) in einen neuen*
Computer investieren invest sth in doing sth etw.
darin investieren, etw. zu tun
investigate verb *(examine)* untersuchen [ʊnteˈzuːxn̩]
<untersucht, untersuchte, hat untersucht> ◊ *Schadens-*
ursachen untersuchen; (police) ermitteln [ɛˈmɪtl̩n]
<ermittelt, ermittelte, hat ermittelt> investigate a case
in einem Fall ermitteln investigate sb gegen jdn
ermitteln
investigation noun *(examination)* Untersuchung
[ʊnteˈzuːxʊn] die <–, –en> ◊ *Die Untersuchung ergab*
menschliches Versagen als Unfallursache. investigation of/into sth Untersuchung ... gen sth is under
investigation etw. wird untersucht [vɪˈt ʊnteˈzuːxt]
<wurde, ist worden>; *(by the police)* Ermittlung
[ɛˈmɪtl ʊn] die <–, –en> ◊ *Die Ermittlungen der*
Polizei sind noch nicht abgeschlossen. sb is under
investigation gegen jdn wird ermittelt
[geːgn̩ ... vɪˈt ɛˈmɪtl̩t] <wurde, ist worden>
investigator noun *(government official)* Untersu-
chungsbeamte [ʊnteˈzuːxʊnsbəˈamtə] der
<–n, die Untersuchungsbeamten> ♀Untersuchungs-
beamtin [ʊnteˈzuːxʊnsbəˌamtɪn] die <–, –nen> *but:*
ein Untersuchungsbeamter/eine Untersuchungsbeam-
tin; (police) Ermittler [ɛˈmɪtlɐ] der <–s, –> ♀Ermittle-
rin [ɛˈmɪtlərɪn] die <–, –nen> ◊ *Sie arbeitet als*
Ermittlerin bei der Polizei. private investigator Privatdetektiv [priˈvaːtdetɛkˌtiːf] der <–s, –e> ♀Privatdetek-
tivin [priˈvaːtdetɛkˌtiːvɪn] die <–, –nen> ◊ *der*
berühmte Privatdetektiv Sherlock Holmes
investment noun Investition [ɪnvɛstiˈtsjoːn] die
<–, –en> ◊ *eine Investition von 5000 Euro* ✦ *Investi-*
tionen in die Bildung
investor noun Investor [ɪnˈvɛstoːɐ̯] der <–s, –en>
♀Investorin [ɪnvɛsˈtoːrɪn] die <–, –nen> ◊ *ausländi-*
sche Investoren anlocken
invigilate verb die Aufsicht führen
[diː ˈaofzɪçt fyːrən] +*haben* invigilate sb/sth die
Aufsicht über jdn/etw. führen
invigilation noun Aufsicht ['aofzɪçt] die <–, –en>
invigilator noun Aufseher ['aofzeːɐ̯] der <–s, –>
invisible adj unsichtbar ['ʊnzɪçtbaːɐ̯] *no comp/superl*
◊ *Elfen sind unsichtbar.* ✦ *für das menschliche Auge*
unsichtbare Kleinstlebewesen
invitation noun Einladung ['aɛnlaːdʊn] die <–, –en>
◊ *eine Einladung zu einer Party bekommen* at sb's
invitation auf jds Einladung by invitation only nur
mit Einladung
ⓔ **an (open) invitation** an (open) invitation to sth
eine Aufforderung zu etw. ◊ *Offene Fenster sind*

eine Aufforderung zum Diebstahl. an (open) invitation to do sth *eine Aufforderung, etw. zu tun*

invite [verb] 1. *(ask sb to come somewhere)* einladen ['aenla:dn] <lädt ein, lud ein, hat eingeladen> ◊ *Gäste einladen* invite sb to/for sth *jdn zu etw. einladen.* invite sb to do sth *jdn dazu einladen, etw. zu tun* invite sb over *jdn zu sich einladen* 2. *(ask sb to do or provide sth)* invite sb to do sth *jdn bitten, etw. zu tun* ['bɪtn ... tsu:] <bitten, bat, hat gebeten> ◊ *Er wurde gebeten, an den Gesprächen teilzunehmen.* invite sth (from sb) *etw. (von jdm) erbitten* [ɐ'bɪtn] <erbittet, erbat, hat erbeten> 3. *(attract sth negative)* invite sth *sich [dat] etw. zuziehen* ['tsu:tsi:ən] <zieht sich zu, zog sich zu, hat sich zugezogen> ◊ *Er zog sich meine Kritik zu.*

• **invite back** [phras v] invite sb back 1. *(invite sb to your house after you have been to theirs)* jds *Einladung erwidern* [,aenla:dʊŋ ɐ'vi:den] <erwidert, erwiderte, hat erwidert> 2. *(invite sb in after you have been out together)* jdn *noch zu sich einladen* [nɔx tsu: ... 'aenla:dn] <lädt ein, lud ein, hat eingeladen>

• **invite round** [phras v] invite sb round *jdn zu sich einladen* [tsu: ... 'aenla:dn] <lädt ein, lud ein, hat eingeladen> ◊ *Sie hat mich zum Abendessen zu sich eingeladen.*

invoice [noun] Rechnung ['rɛçnʊŋ] die <–, –en> ◊ *eine Rechnung über 100 Euro*

invoke [verb] 1. *(claim support from)* invoke sb/sth *sich auf jdn/etw. berufen* [aof ... bə,ru:fn] <beruft sich, berief sich, hat sich berufen> ◊ *sich auf einen Experten/ein Gesetz berufen* 2. *(evoke)* heraufbeschwören [hɛ'raofbəʃvøːrən] <beschwört herauf, beschwor herauf, hat heraufbeschworen> ◊ *Bilder/Ängste heraufbeschwören* 3. *(ask for help, make appear)* beschwören [bə'ʃvøːrən] <beschwört, beschwor, hat beschworen> ◊ *Gott/einen Geist beschwören*

involuntary(-ily) [adj, adv] unwillkürlich ['ʊnvɪlkyːɐlɪç] no comp/superl; when used as an adj, only before ns ◊ *eine unwillkürliche Bewegung* ♦ *unwillkürlich schaudern*

involve [verb] 1. *(include, contain)* mit sich bringen ['mɪt zɪç brɪŋən] <bringt, brachte, hat gebracht> ◊ *Die Arbeit bringt ein gewisses Risiko mit sich.* sth involves doing sth *es gehört zu etw., etw. zu tun* [ɛs gə'høːɐt tsu: ... tsu:] <gehörte, hat gehört> ◊ *Zu meinen Aufgaben gehört es, Texte zu korrigieren.* 2. *(let sb take part in sth, draw sb into sth)* beteiligen [bə'taelɪgn] <beteiligt, beteiligte, hat beteiligt> involve sb/yourself in sth *jdn/sich an etw.* [dat] *beteiligen* ◊ *jdn/sich an einem Projekt beteiligen* be involved in sth *an etw.* [dat] *beteiligt sein* ◊ *an einem Unfall beteiligt sein*

involved → involve [adj] kompliziert [kɔmpli'tsiːɐt] <komplizierter, am kompliziertesten> ◊ *Diese Erklärung ist mir viel zu kompliziert.* ♦ *eine komplizierte Methode*

involvement [noun] 1. *(taking part)* Beteiligung [bə'taelɪgʊŋ] die <–, –en> ◊ *die Beteiligung aller Mitarbeiter* involvement in/with sth *Beteiligung an etw.* [dat] ◊ *die Beteiligung an einem Forschungsprojekt/Verbrechen* 2. *(interest)* Interesse [ɪntə'rɛsə] das <–s> no pl ◊ *das Interesse des Zuschauers* involvement in/with sth *Interesse an etw.* [dat] ◊ *das*

Interesse an einer Geschichte/Figur 3. *(affair)* Affäre [a'fɛːrə] die <–, –n> ◊ *eine Affäre mit jdm haben*

iodine [noun] Jod [joːt] das <–(e)s> no pl ◊ *eine Wunde mit Jod desinfizieren*

ion [noun] Ion [joːn] das <–s, –en>

Ireland [noun] Irland ['ɪrlant] das <–s> article only in combination with attribute, no pl → Germany

Irish¹ [noun] Irisch ['iːrɪʃ] das <–(s)> no pl → German¹ 2.

Irish² [adj] irisch ['iːrɪʃ] → German²

Irishman [noun] Ire ['iːrə] der <–n, –n> → German¹ 2.

Irishwoman [noun] Irin ['iːrɪn] die <–, –nen> → German¹ 1.

iron¹ [noun] 1. *(metal)* Eisen ['aezn] das <–s> no pl ◊ *Brokkoli enthält viel Eisen.* ♦ *eine Brücke aus Eisen* 2. *(household appliance)* Bügeleisen ['byːgḷaezn] das <–s, –> ◊ *das Bügeleisen einschalten/ausschalten* ⊚ have several irons in the fire *mehrere Eisen im Feuer haben*

iron² [adj] eisern ['aezn] no comp/superl, only before ns ◊ *ein eisernes Tor* ♦ *Sie hat einen eisernen Willen.*

iron³ [verb] bügeln ['byːgḷn] +haben ◊ *Hemden/Wäsche bügeln*

ironic, ironical [adj] ironisch [i'roːnɪʃ] ◊ *eine ironische Bemerkung* ♦ *Sie ist immer so ironisch.*

ironically [adv] 1. *(in an ironic way)* ironisch [i'roːnɪʃ] ◊ *„Sind wir nicht eine glückliche Familie?", fragte er ironisch.* 2. *(paradoxically)* ironischerweise [i'roːnɪʃɐvaezə] no comp/superl ◊ *Ironischerweise machte ihn sein Buch über die Vorteile der Armut zum reichen Mann.*

irony [noun] Ironie [iro'niː] die <–> no pl ◊ *etw. mit Ironie sagen*

irregular(ly) [adj, adv] unregelmäßig ['ʊnreːgḷmɛːsɪç] ◊ *unregelmäßige Arbeitszeiten/Verben* ♦ *Die Form der Blätter ist unregelmäßig.* ♦ *Sein Herz schlägt unregelmäßig.*

irrelevant [adj] belanglos [bə'laŋloːs] no comp/superl ◊ *eine belanglose Bemerkung* ♦ *Das ist doch völlig belanglos!* be irrelevant to sth *ohne Belang für etw. sein* [oːnə bə'laŋ fyːɐ ... zaen] +sein

irreparable [adj] nicht wieder gutzumachende [,nɪçt viːdɐ 'guːttsumaxndə] no comp/superl, only before ns <ein nicht wieder gutzumachender ..., eine nicht wieder gutzumachende ..., ein nicht wieder gutzumachendes ...> ◊ *ein nicht wieder gutzumachender Verlust* sth is irreparable *etw. ist nicht wieder gutzumachen* [ɪst ,nɪçt viːdɐ 'guːttsumaxn] +sein ◊ *Der Schaden ist nicht wieder gutzumachen.*

irreplaceable [adj] unersetzlich ['ʊn|ezɛtslɪç] no comp/superl ◊ *von unersetzlichem Wert sein* ♦ *Der Teddy ist für die Kleine unersetzlich.*

irrespective [adj] irrespective of sth *unabhängig von etw.* ['ʊn|aphɛŋɪç fɔn] no comp/superl ◊ *Unser Kindergarten steht allen offen, unabhängig von Religion oder Nationalität.*

irresponsible(-ibly) [adj, adv] unverantwortlich ['ʊnfɛ|antvɔˈtlɪç] ◊ *eine unverantwortliche Bemerkung* ♦ *Weitere Schulden zu machen wäre unverantwortlich.* ♦ *unverantwortlich handeln*

irritable [adj] *(as a characteristic)* reizbar ['raetsbaːˈ] ◊ *Wenn er schlecht geschlafen hat, ist er leicht/sehr reizbar.* ♦ *ein reizbarer Mensch*; *(on a special occasion)* gereizt [gə'raetst] <gereizter, am gereiztes-

A
B
C
D
E
F
G
H
I
J
K
L
M
N
O
P
Q
R
S
T
U
V
W
X
Y
Z

ten> ◊ *Sie ist in gereizter Stimmung.* ✦ *Sein Tonfall war gereizt.*

irritate ⟨verb⟩ **1.** *(annoy)* ärgern [ˈɛʳgen] +haben ◊ *Die ständigen Unterbrechungen ärgerten ihn.* **2.** *(make sth sore)* reizen [ˈraɛtsn̩] +haben ◊ *Trockene Luft reizt die Atemwege.*

irritated → irritate ⟨adj⟩ gereizt [gəˈraɛtst] <gereizter, am gereiztesten> ◊ *Sie wirkte sehr gereizt.* ✦ *gereizte Augen*

irritating → irritate ⟨adj⟩ nervend [ˈnɛʳfn̩t] *(fam)* ◊ *eine nervende Angewohnheit* ✦ *Das Geräusch ist ziemlich nervend.*

irritation ⟨noun⟩ **1.** *(feeling of annoyance)* Ärger [ˈɛʳgɐ] der <–s> no pl ◊ *Ich fühlte Ärger in mir aufsteigen.* irritation at sb/sth Ärger über jdn/etw. **2.** *(sth annoying)* Ärgernis [ˈɛʳgenɪs] das <–ses, –se> ◊ *die Ärgernisse des Alltags* **3.** *(soreness)* Reizung [ˈraɛtsʊŋ] die <–, –en> ◊ *eine Reizung des Magens*

Islam ⟨noun⟩ der Islam [ɪsˈlaːm] <–(s)> no pl ◊ *Der Islam verbietet den Konsum von Alkohol.*

island ⟨noun⟩ Insel [ˈɪnzl̩] die <–, –n>

isolate ⟨verb⟩ isolieren [izoˈliːrən] <isoliert, isolierte, hat isoliert> ◊ *einen Stoff isolieren* ✦ *Der Patient muss isoliert werden.*

isolated → isolate ⟨adj⟩ **1.** *(remote)* abgelegen [ˈapgəleːgn̩] ◊ *eine abgelegene Insel* ✦ *Die Gegend war ziemlich abgelegen.* **2.** *(infrequent)* einzelne [ˈaɛntsl̩nə] no comp/superl, only before ns <ein einzelner …, eine einzelne …, ein einzelnes …> ◊ *Morgen kann es einzelne Regenschauer geben.* isolated case Einzelfall [ˈaɛntsl̩fal] der <–(e)s, Einzelfälle> ◊ *Solche Vorkommnisse sind leider keine Einzelfälle.*

isolation ⟨noun⟩ Isolation [izolaˈtsjoːn] die <–> no pl ◊ *ein Gefühl der Isolation (von anderen); (in compound ns)* isolation … Isolier… [izoˈliːɐ] isolation ward Isolierstation [izoˈliːɐ̯ʃtaˌtsjoːn] die <–, –en> in isolation isoliert [izoˈliːɐ̯t] no comp/superl ◊ *etw. isoliert betrachten*

Israel ⟨noun⟩ Israel [ˈɪsraeːl] das <–s> article only in combination with attribute, no pl → **Germany**

Israeli¹ ⟨noun⟩ Israeli [ɪsraˈeːliː] der <–(s), –s> ♀Israeli [ɪsraˈeːliː] die <–, –s> → **German¹ 1.**

Israeli² ⟨adj⟩ israelisch [ɪsraˈeːlɪʃ] → **German²**

issue¹ ⟨noun⟩ **1.** *(subject)* Thema [ˈteːmaː] das <–s, Themen> ◊ *ein umstrittenes/wichtiges Thema; (problem)* Problem [proˈbleːm] das <–s, –e> ◊ *ein großes Problem* an issue about/with sth ein Problem mit etw. make an issue of sth ein Problem aus etw. machen **2.** *(of a magazine, shares)* Ausgabe [ˈaɒsgaːbə] die <–, –n> ◊ *die Ausgabe von Banknoten/Aktien* ✦ *Das Interview erscheint in der nächsten Ausgabe.* **3.** *(of a document)* Ausstellung [ˈaɒsʃtɛlʊŋ] die <–, –en> ◊ *um die Ausstellung eines Führungszeugnisses bitten*

⊛ take issue with sb/sth jdm/einer Sache nicht zustimmen

issue² ⟨verb⟩ **1.** *(give, announce)* geben [ˈgeːbm̩] <gibt, gab, hat gegeben> ◊ *einen Befehl geben* issue a warning (to sb) (jdn) warnen [ˈvaʳnən] +haben issue a warrant for sb's arrest einen Haftbefehl gegen jdn erlassen [aɐnən ˈhaftbəfeːl geːgn̩ … ɛlasn̩] <erlässt, erließ, hat erlassen> **2.** *(make available)* herausgeben [hɛˈraɒsgeːbm̩] <gibt heraus, gab heraus, hat herausgegeben> ◊ *eine neue Briefmarke herausgeben* **3.** issue sb with sth jdn mit etw. ausstatten [mɪt … ˌaɒsʃtatn̩]

<stattet aus, stattete aus, hat ausgestattet> ◊ *jdn mit einer Uniform ausstatten; (a passport, certificate, licence etc.)* issue sth (for sb) (jdm) etw. ausstellen [ˈaɒsʃtɛlən] +haben ◊ *einen Führerschein ausstellen*

it ⟨pers pron⟩ **1.** *(referring to a masculine noun)* er [eːɐ] ihn [iːn] ihm [iːm] ◊ „*Wo ist der Besen?*" — „*Er steht da drüben in der Ecke.*" ✦ *Der Roman ist spannend. Hast du ihn schon gelesen?* ✦ *Der Teller liegt auf dem Boden, weil du ihm einen Stoß versetzt hast.; (referring to a feminine noun)* sie [ziː] ihr [iːɐ] ◊ „*Hast du meine Tasche gesehen?*" — „*Sie liegt auf dem Tisch.*" ✦ *Die Schokolade war so lecker, dass ich sie ganz aufgegessen habe.* ✦ *Unsere Beziehung ist wichtig. Wir sollten ihr mehr Zeit widmen.; (referring to a neuter noun)* es [ɛs] ihm [iːm] ◊ *Wir waren im Konzert. Es war sehr schön.* ✦ *Wenn dir das Bild gefällt, schenke ich es dir.* ✦ *Das Baby schläft; ich habe ihm schon die Milch gegeben.* → er, sie¹, es **1.** **2.** *(impersonal use)* es [ɛs] ◊ *Hier ist es gemütlich.* ✦ *Es regnet.* ✦ *Es ist noch früh.* ✦ *Hat es ihm in Frankreich gefallen?* ✦ *Es sind 10 km bis Bonn.* ✦ „*Was ist das für ein Film?*" — „*Es ist ein Krimi.*"

⊛ of it davon ◊ *Die Suppe schmeckt gut. Kann ich mehr davon haben.*

IT (abbr of Information Technology) IT [aeˈtiː] die ◊ *Kenntnisse im Bereich IT*

Italian¹ ⟨noun⟩ **1.** *(inhabitant)* Italiener [itaˈlie̯ːne] der <–s, –> ♀Italienerin [itaˈlie̯ːnərɪn] die <–, –nen> → **German¹ 1.** **2.** *(language, subject)* Italienisch [itaˈlie̯ːnɪʃ] das <–(s)> no pl → **German¹ 2.**

Italian² ⟨adj⟩ italienisch [itaˈlie̯ːnɪʃ] → **German²**

italics ⟨noun⟩ Kursivschrift [kʊrˈziːfʃrɪft] die <–> no pl

Italy ⟨noun⟩ Italien [iˈtaːliən] das <–s> article only in combination with attribute, no pl → **Germany**

itch ⟨verb⟩ jucken [ˈjʊkŋ̩] +haben ◊ *Ich trage keine Wollpullis — die jucken so.* ✦ *Meine Augen jucken.* ✦ *Ihn juckt die Haut.*

⊛ be itching for sth auf etw. ⟨acc⟩ brennen be itching to do sth darauf brennen, etw. zu tun

item ⟨noun⟩ **1.** *(object)* Gegenstand [ˈgeːgn̩ʃtant] der <–(e)s, Gegenstände> ◊ *Gegenstände des täglichen Bedarfs* item of equipment Ausrüstungsgegenstand [ˈaɒsrystʊŋsgeˌgn̩ʃtant]; *(product)* Artikel [aʳˈtɪkl̩] der <–s, –> luxury item Luxusartikel [ˈlʊksʊsaʳˌtɪkl̩] **2.** *(subject on a list)* Punkt [pʊŋkt] der <–(e)s, –e> ◊ *der nächste Punkt auf der Tagesordnung* **3.** *(in the media)* Bericht [bəˈrɪçt] der <–(e)s, –e> ◊ *ein Bericht über jdn/etw.* news item Nachricht [ˈnaːxrɪçt] die <–, –en>

its ⟨det⟩ *(referring to a masculine or neuter noun)* sein [zaen] seine [ˈzaenə] ◊ *Das Baby schreit. Seine Windel ist voll.* ✦ *Der Winter hat auch seine schönen Seiten.* ✦ *das Leben und seine Tücken; (referring to a feminine noun)* ihr [iːɐ] ihre [ˈiːrə] ◊ *die Gentechnologie und ihre Möglichkeiten* ✦ *Die Pflanze hat all ihre Blätter verloren.* → sein², ihr²

itself ⟨pron⟩ **1.** *(referring to sth/sb you have already mentioned)* sich [zɪç] ◊ *Die Katze verteidigte sich gegen den Hund.* **2.** *(used directly after the noun)* selbst [zɛlpst] ◊ *Das Problem liegt am Computer selbst, nicht an der Software.*

⊛ by itself **1.** *(alone)* allein ◊ *Der Baum stand ganz allein auf der Wiese.* **2.** *(without help)* von allein ◊ *Die Tür ist von allein aufgegangen.* in/of itself an sich ◊ *Haschischkonsum an sich ist straffrei.* to

itself **1.** *(used when describing sth unique)* a ... all to itself ein ganz eigener ..., eine ganz eigene ..., ein ganz eigenes ... ◊ *Jazz ist eine ganz eigene Form der Musik.* **2.** *(of its own)* a ... to itself ein

eigener ..., eine eigene ..., ein eigenes ... ◊ *Das Thema verdient ein eigenes Kapitel.*

ivory [noun] Elfenbein ['ɛlfn̩baɛn] das <-(e)s> *no pl*

A
B
C
D
E
F
G
H
I
J
K
L
M
N
O
P
Q
R
S
T
U
V
W
X
Y
Z

J

j, J [noun] j, J [jɔt] das <–(s), –(s)> ◊ *Dieses Wort wird mit einem kleinen j/großen J geschrieben.* ♦ *J wie Julius*

jack [noun] **1.** *(for cars)* Wagenheber ['vaːɡn̩heːbɐ] der <–s, –> **2.** *(in a deck of cards)* Bube ['buːbə] der <–n, –n> jack of hearts Herzbube ['hɛrtsbuːbə] **3.** TECHN *(plug)* Stecker ['ʃtɛkɐ] der <–s, –> **4.** TECHN *(socket)* Buchse ['bʊksə] die <–, –n>

jacket [noun] **1.** *(item of clothing)* Jacke ['jakə] die <–, –n> ◊ *Er trug eine graue Jacke.* denim jacket Jeansjacke ['dʒiːnsjakə] leather jacket Lederjacke ['leːdɐjakə] **2.** *(of a book)* Umschlag ['ʊmʃlaːk] der <–(e)s, Umschläge>

jail¹ [noun] Gefängnis [gəˈfɛŋnɪs] das <–ses or –se> in jail im Gefängnis go/be sent to jail ins Gefängnis kommen get out of jail aus dem Gefängnis kommen

jail² [verb] einsperren ['aɛnʃpɛrən] +haben jail sb for sth jdn wegen etw. einsperren ◊ *Er wurde wegen Drogenhandels eingesperrt.*

jam¹ [noun] **1.** *(food)* Marmelade [marməˈlaːdə] die <–, –n> ◊ *ein Glas Marmelade* strawberry jam Erdbeermarmelade ['eːɐtbeːɐmarməˌlaːdə] **2.** *(blockage, congestion)* Stau [ʃtaʊ] der <–(e)s, –s or seldom –e> traffic jam Verkehrsstau [fɛˈkeːɐsʃtaʊ] paper jam Papierstau [paˈpiːɐʃtaʊ]
⊛ be in a jam in der Klemme stecken *(fam)*

jam² [verb] **1.** *(squeeze)* stopfen ['ʃtɔpfn̩] +haben ◊ *etw. in seine Tasche stopfen; (push)* drücken ['drʏkn̩] +haben ◊ *jdm etw. in die Hand drücken* **2.** *(block)* verstopfen [fɛˈʃtɔpfn̩] <verstopft, verstopfte, hat verstopft> ◊ *Die Straßen waren mit Autos verstopft.; (crowd of people)* jam a place sich irgendwo drängen ['drɛŋən] +haben ◊ *Tausende drängten sich auf dem Markusplatz.* **3.** *(wheels, brakes)* blockieren [blɔˈkiːrən] <blockiert, blockierte, hat blockiert> ◊ *Der Wagen kam ins Schleudern, weil die Bremse blockierte.; (door, window, zip)* klemmen ['klɛmən] +haben ◊ *Die Tür/Der Reißverschluss klemmt.* **4.** *(get a part of your body stuck somewhere)* einklemmen ['aɛnklɛmən] +haben jam your finger in the door sich [dat] den Finger in der Tür einklemmen **5.** *(a radio signal)* stören ['ʃtøːrən] +haben ◊ *den Radioempfang stören*

janitor [noun] Hausmeister ['haʊsmaɛstɐ] der <–s, –> ♀Hausmeisterin ['haʊsmaɛstərɪn] die <–, –nen> ◊ *Er arbeitet als Hausmeister.* ♦ *Wir haben eine neue Hausmeisterin.*

January [noun] Januar ['januaːɐ] der <–(s), –e> most sing ◊ *Leo ist im Januar geboren.* ♦ *Heute ist der 10. Januar.* ♦ *Das war am 15. Januar 1999.* ♦ *Köln, den 4. Januar 2005* ♦ *Er ist am Mittwoch, den 4. Januar abgereist.* ♦ *Die Januare verbringt sie immer auf Hawaii.* ♦ *Nächsten Januar ziehen wir um.* ♦ *Letzten Januar waren wir in Indien.* ♦ *Thema des Monats Januar:* ... in early January Anfang Januar in late January Ende Januar

Japan [noun] Japan ['jaːpan] das <–s> article only in combination with attribute, no pl → **Germany**

Japanese¹ [noun] **1.** *(inhabitant)* Japaner [jaˈpaːnɐ] der <–s, –> ♀Japanerin [jaˈpaːnərɪn] die <–, –nen> → **German¹** **1.** **2.** *(language, subject)* Japanisch [jaˈpaːnɪʃ] das <–(s)> no pl → **German¹** **2.**

Japanese² [adj] japanisch [jaˈpaːnɪʃ] → **German²**

jar [noun] *(made of glass)* Glas [glaːs] das <–es, Gläser> ◊ *ein halbes Glas Marmelade; (made of clay)* Topf [tɔpf] der <–(e)s, Töpfe> ◊ *ein Topf (voll/mit) Honig/Schmalz/Senf etc.; (with a handle)* Krug [kruːk] der <–(e)s, Krüge> ◊ *ein Krug Wein*

jargon [noun] Jargon [ʒaˈɡɔŋ] der <–s, –s> ◊ *wissenschaftlicher Jargon*

jaw [noun] Kiefer ['kiːfɐ] der <–s, –> upper jaw Oberkiefer ['oːbɐkiːfɐ] lower jaw Unterkiefer ['ʊntɐkiːfɐ]

jazz [noun] Jazz [dʒɛs] der <–> no pl ◊ *Er spielt Jazz und Klassik.*

jealous [adj] **1.** *(envious)* neidisch ['naɛdɪʃ] jealous of sb/sth auf jdn/etw. neidisch ◊ *Er warf neidische Blicke auf unser neues Auto.* ♦ *Du bist neidisch auf meinen Erfolg.* **2.** *(in relationships)* eifersüchtig ['aɛfɐzʏçtɪç] ◊ *jdn eifersüchtig machen* ♦ *eine eifersüchtige Ehefrau* jealous of sb eifersüchtig auf jdn

jealousy [noun] **1.** *(envy)* Neid [naɛt] der <–(e)s> no pl ◊ *Nur kein Neid! Gönn ihm doch den Erfolg!* **2.** *(a relationship)* Eifersucht ['aɛfɐzʊxt] die <–> no pl ◊ *krankhafte/unbegründete Eifersucht*

jeans [noun] Jeans [dʒiːns] die <–, –> a pair of jeans ein Paar Jeans

> In German the plural or the singular can be used to refer to a pair of jeans: *Er trägt eine Jeans./Er trägt Jeans.*

jelly [noun] Gelee [ʒeˈleː] das or der <–s, –s> ◊ *Brötchen mit mehreren Sorten Gelee und Marmelade* ♦ *Hering in Gelee*

jerk¹ [noun] **1.** *(movement)* Ruck [rʊk] der <–(e)s, –e> ◊ *Es gab einen Ruck und der Wagen blieb stecken.* **2.** *(idiot)* Blödmann ['bløːtman] der <–(e)s, Blödmänner> *(fam)*

jerk² [verb] **1.** *(move suddenly)* sth jerks etw. ruckt [rʊkt] +haben ◊ *Das Auto ruckte und blieb stehen.* **2.** *(move sth suddenly)* jerk sth etw. reißen ['raɛsn̩] <reißt, riss, hat gerissen> ◊ *Er riss das Lenkrad nach rechts.* jerk sth up etw. hochreißen ['hoːxraɛsn̩] ◊ *Sie riss den Kopf hoch und starrte mich an.*

jerky(-ily) [adj, adv] ruckartig ['rʊkaˈtɪç] ◊ *ruckartige Bewegungen* ♦ *sich ruckartig bewegen*

jerrycan [noun] Kanister [kaˈnɪstɐ] der <–s, –> ◊ *ein Kanister Benzin*

jersey [noun] **1.** *(sweater)* Pullover [pʊˈloːvɐ] der <–s, –> ◊ *einen Pullover anziehen; (in sports)* Trikot [triˈkoː] das <–s, –s> **2.** *(fabric)* Jersey ['dʒœrziː] der <–(s), –s> ◊ *Bettwäsche aus Jersey*

jet [noun] **1.** *(plane)* Jet [dʒɛt] der <–(s), –s> ◊ *mit einem Jet fliegen* **2.** *(of a liquid, air)* Strahl [ʃtraːl] der <–(e)s, –en> most sing ◊ *ein dünner Strahl Wasser* **3.** *(stone)* Jett [dʒɛt] der or das <–(e)s> no pl ◊ *Per-*

lenschmuck aus Jett

jetty (noun) Steg [ʃteːk] der <-(e)s, -e> ◊ *das Boot am Steg festmachen*

Jew (noun) Jude ['juːdə] der <-n, -n> ♀Jüdin ['jyːdɪn] die <-, -nen> ◊ *be a Jew Jude/Jüdin sein*

jewel (noun) *(treasure, precious thing)* Juwel [ju'veːl] das <-s, -en> ◊ *Juwelen rauben; (precious stone)* Edelstein ['eːdlʃtaen] der <-(e)s, -e> ◊ *ein Ring mit einem großen Edelstein*

jeweller (noun) Juwelier [juve'liːɐ] der <-s, -e> ♀Juwelierin [juve'liːrɪn] die <-, -nen> ◊ *Sie ist Juwelierin von Beruf.* ♦ *ein erfolgreicher Juwelier aus Amsterdam*

jewellery, jewelry (noun) Schmuck [ʃmʊk] der <-(e)s> *no pl* ◊ *Schmuck anlegen*

Jewish (adj) jüdisch ['jyːdɪʃ] *no comp/superl, mostly before ns* ◊ *ein jüdisches Fest* He is Jewish. Er ist Jude.

jiggle (verb) 1. *(move)* wackeln ['vakl̩n] +haben 2. *(move sth)* jiggle sth an etw. (dat) rütteln [an ... ,rytl̩n] +haben ◊ *an einer Türklinke rütteln*

jigsaw (noun) 1. *(game)* jigsaw (puzzle) Puzzle ['pʊzl̩] das <-s, -s> 2. *(tool)* Stichsäge ['ʃtɪçzɛːgə] die <-, -n>

job (noun) 1. *(employment)* Stelle ['ʃtɛlə] die <-, -n> ◊ *eine Stelle suchen/finden* ♦ *eine Stelle als leitender Arzt antreten* ♦ *Man hat ihm eine Stelle als Koch angeboten.* part-time job Teilzeitstelle ['taeltsaetʃtɛlə] full-time job Vollzeitstelle ['foltsaetʃtɛlə]; *(short-term employment)* Job [dʒɔp] der <-s, -s> ◊ *Er hat für die Ferien einen Job gefunden.* create jobs Arbeitsplätze schaffen ['aʁbaetsplɛtsə ʃafn̩] <schafft, schuf, hat geschaffen> job losses der Verlust von Arbeitsplätzen [fɐ,lʊst fɔn 'aʁbaetsplɛtsn̩] <-(e)s> *sing* job interview Vorstellungsgespräch ['foːɐʃtɛlʊŋsɡəʃprɛːç] das <-(e)s, -e> out of a job arbeitslos ['aʁbaetsloːs] *no comp/superl* ◊ *Sie ist seit zwei Monaten arbeitslos.* 2. *(piece of work)* Arbeit ['aʁbaet] die <-, -en> ◊ *Es war eine ganz schöne Arbeit, das Bad zu renovieren.* do a good etc. job gute etc. Arbeit leisten do a great job of doing sth es meisterhaft verstehen, etw. zu tun [ɛs 'maestɐhaft fɐ'ʃteːən] <versteht es, verstand es, hat es verstanden> have several jobs to do Verschiedenes zu erledigen haben [fɐ,ʃiːdənəs tsuː eːˈleːdɪɡn̩ haːbm̩] +haben know your job sein Handwerk verstehen [zaen ,hantvɛʁk fɐ'ʃteːən] <versteht, verstand, hat verstanden> ◊ *Ich muss sagen, der Mann versteht sein Handwerk.* 3. *(task)* Aufgabe ['aofɡaːbə] die <-, -n> ◊ *Es ist Ihre Aufgabe, für einen reibungslosen Ablauf der Konferenz zu sorgen.* ♦ *Er fühlte sich dieser Aufgabe nicht gewachsen.* be only doing your job nur seine Pflicht tun [nuːɐ zaenə 'pflɪçt tuːn] ◊ *Sei mir nicht böse; ich tue nur meine Pflicht.* 4. *(crime)* Ding [dɪŋ] das <-(e)s, -er> *(slang)* do a job ein Ding drehen

◉ it's a good job that was für ein Glück, dass *sb* has a job doing sth/to do sth *(find doing sth difficult)* jd hat Schwierigkeiten, etw. zu tun

jobcentre (noun) *(official name)* JobCenter ['dʒɔptsɛntɐ] das <-s, -> ◊ *auf Stellensuche im JobCenter; (colloquial)* Arbeitsamt ['aʁbaetsʔamt] das <-(e)s, Arbeitsämter> ◊ *Stellen, die im Arbeitsamt vermittelt werden*

jobless (adj) arbeitslos ['aʁbaetsloːs] *no comp/superl* ◊ *Er ist seit vier Monaten arbeitslos.* ♦ *arbeitslos*

werden ♦ *ein arbeitsloser Maurer*

jockey (noun) Jockey ['dʒɔkiː] der <-s, -s> ◊ *Sie ist Jockey.* ♦ *Der Jockey hat das Pferd gut im Griff.*

jogging (noun) Jogging ['dʒɔɡɪŋ] das <-s> *no pl* ◊ *Jogging ist ihr Hobby.* jogging suit Jogginganzug ['dʒɔɡɪŋʔantsuːk] der <-(e)s, Jogginganzüge> go jogging joggen gehen ['dʒɔɡn̩ geːən] <geht, ging, ist gegangen>

join (verb) 1. *(a club, organization, party)* join sth in etw. (acc) eintreten [ɪn ... ,aentreːtn̩] <tritt ein, trat ein, ist eingetreten> ◊ *Sie ist vor fünf Jahren in die Partei eingetreten.* join the army zur Armee gehen [tsuːɐ ar'meː geːən] <geht, ging, ist gegangen>; *(a company)* join sb/sth bei jdm/etw. anfangen [bae ... ,anfaŋən] <fängt an, fing an, hat angefangen> ◊ *Wann haben Sie bei uns angefangen?* 2. *(connect)* join sth to sth etw. mit etw. verbinden [mɪt ... fɐˌbɪndn̩] <verbindet, verband, hat verbunden> ◊ *Die Brücke verbindet die Insel mit dem Festland.* join things (together) Dinge miteinander verbinden ◊ *zwei Kabel miteinander verbinden* two things join zwei Dinge fügen sich aneinander [fyːgn̩ zɪç anˌaenandɐ] +haben ◊ *der Punkt, an dem die Rohre sich aneinander fügen; (street, river)* join sth in etw. (acc) münden [ɪn ... mʏndn̩] +haben ◊ *Die Mosel mündet bei Koblenz in den Rhein.* 3. join a road auf eine Straße fahren [aof aenə 'ʃtraːsə faːrən] <fährt, fuhr, ist gefahren> ◊ *Nach einigen Kilometern fuhren wir auf die Autobahn.* 4. *(walk over to or follow sb, help with sth)* join sb/sth sich jdm/einer Sache anschließen ['anʃliːsn̩] <schließt sich an, schloss sich an, hat sich angeschlossen> ◊ *Viele Freiwillige schlossen sich der Suche/Suchmannschaft an.; (sit with sb)* join sb sich zu jdm setzen [,tsuː ... zɛtsn̩] +haben ◊ *Darf ich mich zu Ihnen setzen?; (follow sb)* nachkommen ['naːxkɔmən] <kommt nach, kam nach, ist nachgekommen> ◊ *Ich komme in fünf Minuten nach.; (in a game)* mitmachen ['mɪtmaxn̩] +haben ◊ *Darf ich mitmachen?; (meet sb somewhere)* zu jdm stoßen [,tsuː ... ʃtoːsn̩] <stößt, stieß, ist gestoßen> ◊ *Herr Martens wird in Hamburg zu uns stoßen.* join together, join forces sich zusammentun [tsu'zaməntuːn] <tut sich zusammen, tat sich zusammen, hat sich zusammengetan>

• **join in** (phras v) join in (sth) (bei etw.) mitmachen ['mɪtmaxn̩] +haben ◊ *Wir wollen Fußball spielen, machst du mit?* ♦ *Willst du bei unserem Spiel mitmachen?* She laughed and he joined in. Sie lachte und er lachte mit.

• **join up** (phras v) 1. *(become a soldier)* zum Militär gehen [tsʊm mili'tɛːɐ geːən] <geht, ging, ist gegangen> 2. *(meet)* aufeinander treffen [aofˌaenandɐ trɛfn̩] <treffen, trafen, sind getroffen> ◊ *Wo treffen die beiden Straßen aufeinander?* 3. *(join forces)* sich zusammenschließen [tsu'zamənʃliːsn̩] <schließt sich zusammen, schloss sich zusammen, hat sich zusammengeschlossen> → join¹ 2.

joiner (noun) Schreiner ['ʃraenɐ] der <-s, -> ♀Schreinerin ['ʃraenərɪn] die <-, -nen> ◊ *Er ist Schreiner von Beruf.* ♦ *Die Schreinerin baut die Küche ein.*

joint (noun) 1. ANAT, TECHN Gelenk [gə'lɛŋk] das <-(e)s, -e> ◊ *Schmerzen in den Gelenken haben* ♦ *eine Schreibtischlampe mit zwei Gelenken; (in a pipe)* Verbindungsstelle [fɛ'bɪndʊŋsʃtɛlə] die <-, -n> ◊ *eine undichte Verbindungsstelle abdichten; (in*

woodwork) Fuge ['fuːgə] die <-, -n> **2.** *(meat)* Braten ['braːtn̩] der <-s, -> ◊ *den Braten in den Ofen schieben* joint of beef Rinderbraten ['rɪndebraːtn̩] **3.** *(bar etc.)* Laden ['laːdn̩] der <-s, Läden> *(fam)* ◊ *Ein mieser Laden ist das hier!* **4.** *(of cannabis)* Joint [dʒɔønt] der <-s, -s> *(slang)* ◊ *einen Joint rauchen*

joint(ly) (adj, adv) gemeinsam [gə'maɛnzaːm] *no comp/ superl; when used as adj, only before ns* ◊ *ein gemeinsames Konto* ◆ *Wir nutzen den Computer gemeinsam.* ◆ *gemeinsam für etw. verantwortlich sein* It was a joint effort. Das ist in Gemeinschafts-arbeit entstanden.

joke¹ (noun) *(funny story, something silly)* Witz [vɪts] der <-es, -e> ◊ *Diese Geldsumme ist doch ein Witz!* ◆ *einen Witz erzählen; (prank)* Streich [ʃtraɛç] der <-(e)s, -e> ◊ *Das war ein dummer Streich.* play a joke on sb jdm einen Streich spielen
◉ crack a joke einen Witz zum Besten geben

joke² (verb) Witze machen ['vɪtsə maxn̩] +haben ◊ *Über so etwas macht man keine Witze.* You're joking! Mach keine Witze! not be joking es ernst meinen [ɛs 'ɛːrnst maɛnən] +haben ◊ *Ich meine es ernst.*

jolly (adj) fröhlich ['frøːlɪç] ◊ *Ich mag ihre fröhliche Art.* ◆ *An dem Abend waren wir alle fröhlich.*

jolt (noun) **1.** *(sudden emotion)* with a jolt mit einem Schlag [mɪt 'aɛnəm ʃlaːk] ◊ *Mit einem Schlag wurde ihr klar, was das bedeutete.* **2.** *(shock)* Schock [ʃɔk] der <-(e)s, -s> ◊ *Diese Nachricht wird ein Schock für ihn sein.* **3.** *(jerk)* Ruck [rʊk] der <-(e)s, -e> ◊ *Es gab einen Ruck, und der Wagen blieb stecken.*

jostle (verb) **1.** *(compete)* jostle for sth um etw. wetteifern [ʊm ... ˌvɛtʲaɛfən] +haben ◊ *Die beiden Teilneh-mer wetteiferten um den ersten Platz.* **2.** *(push)* sb jostles jd drängelt ['drɛŋlt] +haben ◊ *Der Typ hinter mir drängelt schon die ganze Zeit.* jostle your way somewhere sich irgendwohin drängeln ◊ *Es gelang ihr, sich bis zur Bühne zu drängeln.* jostle sb jdn schubsen ['ʃʊpsn̩] +haben

journal (noun) **1.** *(magazine)* Zeitschrift ['tsaɛtʃrɪft] die <-, -en> ◊ *Im Wartezimmer liegen immer Zeitschrif-ten aus.; (newspaper)* Zeitung ['tsaɛtʊŋ] die <-, -en> **2.** *(diary)* Tagebuch ['taːgəbuːx] das <-(e)s, Tagebücher> ◊ *Sie führt seit Jahren Tagebuch.*

journalism (noun) Journalismus [ʒʊr'aˈlɪsmʊs] der <-> *no pl*

journalist (noun) Journalist [ʒʊr'naˈlɪst] der <-en, -en> ♀Journalistin [ʒʊr'naˈlɪstɪn] die <-, -nen> ◊ *Sie ist freie Journalistin.* ◆ *Was wollte der Journalist von dir?*

journey (noun) Reise ['raɛzə] die <-, -n> ◊ *mit dem Bus eine Reise durch Skandinavien machen* ◆ *Auf der Reise wurde sie krank.* set out on a journey eine Reise antreten outward journey Hinreise ['hɪnraɛzə] return journey Rückreise ['rʏkraɛzə]

joy (noun) **1.** *(happiness, thing that makes you happy)* Freude ['frɔødə] die <-, -n> ◊ *Er weinte/strahlte vor Freude.* ◆ *die Freuden des Lebens/Urlaubs genießen* jump for joy einen Freudensprung machen [aɛnən 'frɔødnʃprʊŋ maxn̩] +haben ◊ *Sie hat nicht gerade einen Freudensprung gemacht, als sie das Geschenk sah.* **2.** *(success)* Erfolg [e'fɔlk] der <-(e)s, -e> ◊ *Hatten Sie bei Ihrer Suche Erfolg?* Any joy? Hat es geklappt?

joyful (adj) froh [froː] <froher, am froh(e)sten> ◊ *Ihre*

Geburt war ein frohes Ereignis. ◆ *Ihr Lachen war richtig froh.*

jubilee (noun) Jubiläum [jubi'lɛːʊm] das <-s, Jubiläen> ◊ *Die Firma feiert ihr Jubiläum mit einem großen Fest.*

Judaism (noun) Judentum ['juːdn̩tuːm] das <-s> *no pl* ◊ *Im Judentum ist der Samstag heilig.*

judge¹ (noun) **1.** LAW Richter ['rɪçte] der <-, -> ♀Richterin ['rɪçtərɪn] die <-, -nen> ◊ *Wie hat der Richter entschieden?* ◆ *Sie ist Richterin.* I will be the judge of it. Das müssen Sie mich schon selbst beur-teilen lassen. **2.** *(in a competition)* Preisrichter ['praɛsrɪçte] der <-, -> ♀Preisrichterin ['praɛsrɪçtərɪn] die <-, -nen> ◊ *Zu welcher Entschei-dung sind die Preisrichter gelangt?*
◉ be a good/no judge of wine etc. ein guter/kein Weinkenner etc. sein ◊ *Er ist ein guter Weinkenner.*

judge² (verb) **1.** *(assess a competition)* judge sb/sth (on sth) jdn/etw. (nach etw.) beurteilen [bə'lʊˈtaɛlən] <beurteilt, beurteilte, hat beurteilt> ◊ *Ich kann nicht beurteilen, ob das richtig ist.* ◆ *Die Hunde werden nach Aussehen und Gehorsam beurteilt.* judge sth from sth etw. aus etw. schließen [aʊs ... ʃliːsn̩] <schließt, schloss, hat geschlossen> ◊ *Er schloss aus ihrem Verhalten, dass sie wütend war.* judge it right/necessary etc. to do sth es für richtig/notwendig etc. halten, etw. zu tun [ɛs fyːɐ 'rɪçtɪç/'noːtvɛndɪç haltn̩ ... tuː] <hält, hielt, hat gehalten> ◊ *Er hielt es für richtig, den Chef darüber zu informieren.; (estimate)* einschätzen ['aɛnʃɛtsn̩] +haben ◊ *Sie schätzte die Geschwindigkeit des Zuges falsch ein.* **2.** *(pass a judgement on)* (über jdn/etw.) urteilen ['ʊˈtaɛlən] +haben ◊ *Du solltest nicht über Menschen urteilen, die du nicht kennst.* **3.** LAW judge sb (not) guilty jdn für (nicht) schuldig befinden [fyːɐ (nɪçt) 'ʃʊldɪç bəfɪndn̩] <befindet, befand, hat befunden> judge a case einen Fall ver-handeln [aɛnən 'faːl fɛˈhandl̩n] <verhandelt, verhan-delte, hat verhandelt> ◊ *Richter Bartl wird Ihren Fall verhandeln.*
◉ judging by/from sth einer Sache (dat) nach zu urteilen ◊ *Dem Glanz nach zu urteilen ist das Hemd aus Seide.*

judgement (noun) **1.** *(opinion, verdict)* Urteil ['ʊˈtaɛl] das <-s, -e> ◊ *ein negatives Urteil über ein Buch fällen* ◆ *Die Richter gelangten zu folgendem Urteil: … make a judgement about sb/sth sich (dat) über jdn/etw. ein Urteil bilden in sb's judgement jds Meinung nach ['maɛnʊŋ naːx] ◊ *Was ist deiner Meinung nach zu tun?* **2.** *(discernment)* Urteilsvermö-gen ['ʊˈtaɛlsfɛmøːgn̩] das <-s> *no pl* ◊ *Sie hat ein gutes Urteilsvermögen bewiesen.* **3.** *(punishment from God)* Strafe Gottes [ʃtraːfə 'gɔtəs] das <-> *no pl* ◊ *Das Unwetter war eine Strafe Gottes!*
◉ sit in judgement on/over sb über jdn zu Gericht sitzen

judicial (adj) **1.** LAW *(relating to courts and judges)* Justiz... [jʊs'tiːts] judicial system Justizwesen [jʊs'tiːtsveːzn̩] das <-s> *no pl; (done by a judge)* rich-terlich ['rɪçtelɪç] *no comp/superl* ◊ *eine richterliche Entscheidung* **2.** *(critical)* kritisch ['kriːtɪʃ] ◊ *eine kritische Betrachtung* after judicial consideration nach reiflicher Überlegung [naːx ˌraɛflɪçe ybe'leːgʊŋ] ◊ *Wir sind nach reiflicher Überlegung zu diesem Schluss gelangt.*

jug (noun) *(without a lid: made of glass)* Kanne ['kanə]

die <-, –n> ◊ *eine Kanne Saft; (made of clay)* Krug [kruːk] der <-(e)s, Krüge> ◊ *ein Krug Wein* *measuring jug* Messbecher ['mɛsbɛçɐ] der <-s, –> ◊ *Zucker in einem Messbecher abmessen* milk jug Milchkännchen ['mɪlçkɛnçən] das <-s, –>

juice ⌐noun⌐ Saft [zaft] der <-(e)s, Säfte> ◊ *Saft von frisch gepressten Orangen* ◆ *Das Fleisch soll im eigenen Saft garen.* ◆ *Die Batterie hat keinen Saft mehr.* apple juice Apfelsaft ['apfl̩zaft] digestive juices Verdauungssäfte [fɛ'daʊ̯ŋszɛftə]

juicy ⌐adj⌐ 1. *(food, profit)* saftig ['zaftɪç] ◊ *Das Fruchtfleisch der Aprikose ist saftig.* ◆ *ein saftiges Steak* ◆ *saftige Gewinne erzielen* 2. *(story)* pikant [pi'kant] <pikanter, am pikantesten> ◊ *eine pikante Geschichte veröffentlichen* 3. *(sexy)* geil [ɡaɛ̯l] *(rude)* ◊ *Die Kleine auf dem Plakat ist ziemlich geil.* ◆ *ein geiler Typ*

July ⌐noun⌐ Juli ['juːliː] der <-(s), –s> *most sing* → January

jump¹ ⌐noun⌐ 1. *(leap, distance, difference)* Sprung [ʃprʊŋ] der <-(e)s, Sprünge> ◊ *Der Sprung war über sechs Meter weit!* ◆ *ein Sprung aus zehn Metern Höhe* ◆ *Von der Grundschule zum Gymnasium ist es ein großer Sprung.* 2. *(start)* give sb a jump jdn erschrecken [ɛ'ʃrɛkn̩] <erschreckt, erschreckte, hat erschreckt> 3. *(on a race-course, race-track)* Hindernis ['hɪndɐnɪs] das <-ses, -se> ◊ *Das Pferd scheiterte am zweiten Hindernis.* 4. *(of prices, profit)* sprunghafter Anstieg [ˌʃprʊŋhaftə 'anʃtiːk] <-(e)s, -e> ◊ *Der sprunghafte Anstieg der Preise bereitet uns Sorgen.*

⊛ be one jump ahead of sb jdm einen Schritt voraus sein ◊ *Sie sind uns immer einen Schritt voraus!*

jump² ⌐verb⌐ 1. *(leap, move over, let yourself drop, move quickly, react quickly)* springen ['ʃprɪŋən] <springt, sprang, ist gesprungen> ◊ *aus dem Stand/ mit Anlauf drei Meter weit springen* ◆ *vor Freude in die Luft springen* ◆ *über ein Hindernis springen* ◆ *Der Mann sprang vom Dach.* ◆ *Du musst nicht immer gleich springen, wenn er etwas will.* jump to your feet aufspringen ['aʊ̯fʃprɪŋən] <springt auf, sprang auf, ist aufgesprungen> ◊ *Er sprang auf und bot ihr seinen Platz an.* 2. *(start)* zusammenzucken [tsu'zamən̩tsʊkn̩] +sein ◊ *Er zuckte vor Schreck zusammen.* make sb jump jdn erschrecken [ɛ'ʃrɛkn̩] <erschreckt, erschreckte, hat erschreckt> sb's heart jumps jds Herz macht einen Satz [ˌhɛɐ̯ts maxt aɛ̯nən 'zats] +haben 3. *(prices)* sprunghaft ansteigen [ˌʃprʊŋhaft 'anʃtaɛ̯gn̩] <steigt an, stieg an, ist angestiegen> ◊ *Die Preise sind sprunghaft angestiegen.* 4. *(in a sequence)* springen ['ʃprɪŋən] <springt, sprang, ist gesprungen> ◊ *Er sprang beim Lesen vom vierten direkt zum sechsten Kapitel.* jump to conclusions voreilige Schlüsse ziehen [ˌfoːɐ̯aɛ̯lɪgə 'ʃlʏsə tsiːən] <zieht, zog, hat gezogen>; *(leave out)* jump sth etw. überspringen [ybɐ'ʃprɪŋən] <überspringt, übersprang, hat übersprungen> ◊ *Ich glaube, Sie haben eine Zeile übersprungen.* 5. *(attack)* jump (on) überfallen [ybɐ'falən] <überfällt, überfiel, hat überfallen> ◊ *Er wurde auf der Straße von Jugendlichen überfallen.*

• jump up ⌐phras v⌐ aufspringen ['aʊ̯fʃprɪŋən] <springt auf, sprang auf, ist aufgesprungen> ◊ *Als sie gehen wollte, sprang er auf, um ihr den Mantel zu holen.*

jumper ⌐noun⌐ 1. *(garment)* Pullover [pʊ'loːvɐ] der <-s, –> ◊ *einen Pullover anziehen* ◆ *Er trug einen braunen Pullover.; (in the US: dress)* Trägerkleid ['trɛːgɐklaɛ̯t] das <-(e)s, -er> 2. *(person, animal)* Springer ['ʃprɪŋɐ] der <-s, –> ♀Springerin ['ʃprɪŋərɪn] die <-, -nen> ◊ *Unser Hund ist ein guter Springer.* ◆ *Eine der Springerinnen wurde leicht verletzt.*

junction ⌐noun⌐ *(of roads)* Kreuzung ['krɔɛ̯tsʊŋ] die <-, -en> ◊ *an der Kreuzung links/rechts abbiegen* ◆ *die Kreuzung Goethestraße/Schillerstraße; (for leaving a motorway)* Ausfahrt ['aʊ̯sfaːt] die <-, -en> ◊ *Verlassen Sie die Autobahn an der nächsten Ausfahrt.; (of railway lines)* (railway) junction Eisenbahnknotenpunkt ['aɛ̯zn̩baːn̩ˌknoːtn̩pʊŋkt] der <-(e)s, -e>

June ⌐noun⌐ Juni ['juːniː] der <-(s), –s> *most sing* → January

jungle ⌐noun⌐ Dschungel ['dʒʊŋl̩] der <-s, –> ◊ *der afrikanische Dschungel* ◆ *Euer Garten ist ja ein richtiger Dschungel.* ◆ *im Dschungel der Großstadt*

junior ⌐adj⌐ 1. *(subordinate)* untergeordnet ['ʊntɐgəʔɔɐ̯dnət] no comp/superl ◊ *ein untergeordneter Mitarbeiter* be junior to sb jdm untergeordnet sein ◊ *Ihr sind drei Angestellte untergeordnet.* junior clerk Bürogehilfe [by'roːgəhɪlfə] der <-n, -n> ♀Bürogehilfin [by'roːgəhɪlfɪn] die <-, -nen> junior minister Staatssekretär ['ʃtaːtszekreˌtɛːɐ̯] der <-s, -e> ♀Staatssekretärin ['ʃtaːtszekreˌtɛːrɪn] die <-, -nen> ◊ *Sie ist seit zwei Jahren Staatssekretärin.* ◆ *eine Presseerklärung des Staatssekretärs* 2. *(for young people)* junior team Juniorenmannschaft [ju'nioːrənmanʃaft] die <-, -en> junior school Grundschule ['grʊntʃuːlə] die <-, -n> junior high school Realschule [re['aːlʃuːlə] die <-, -n> ◊ *auf eine Realschule gehen*

junk ⌐noun⌐ 1. *(discarded objects)* Gerümpel [gə'rʏmpl̩] das <-s> no pl ◊ *Wohin mit dem ganzen Gerümpel im Keller?* 2. *(sth worthless)* Schund [ʃʊnt] der <-(e)s> no pl ◊ *Im Fernsehen läuft fast nur noch Schund.* 3. *(drug)* Stoff [ʃtɔf] der <-(e)s> no pl *(slang)* ◊ *sich Stoff besorgen* 4. SHIP Dschunke ['dʒʊŋkə] die <-, -n>

jurisdiction ⌐noun⌐ Gerichtsbarkeit [gə'rɪçtsbaːˌkaɛ̯t] die <-> no pl have jurisdiction over sb/sth für jdn/ etw. zuständig sein [fyːɐ̯ ... 'tsuːʃtɛndɪç zaɛ̯n] +sein ◊ *Das Gericht ist für diesen Fall nicht zuständig.* be within sb's jurisdiction in jds Zuständigkeitsbereich fallen [ɪn ... 'tsuːʃtɛndɪçkaɛ̯tsbəraɛ̯ç falən] be outside sb's jurisdiction nicht in jds Zuständigkeitsbereich fallen

jury ⌐noun⌐ 1. LAW the jury die Geschworenen [di: gə'ʃvoːrənən] <-n> pl ◊ *Die Geschworenen beraten sich noch.* 2. *(in a competition)* Jury ['ʒyːriː] die <-, -s> ◊ *Eine unabhängige Jury wird den Sieger bestimmen.*

just¹ ⌐adj⌐ gerecht [gə'rɛçt] <gerechter, am gerechtesten> ◊ *eine gerechte Entscheidung* ◆ *für eine gerechte Sache kämpfen* ◆ *Er gilt als streng, aber gerecht.*

just² ⌐adv⌐ 1. *(at this moment, shortly before)* gerade [gə'raːdə] ◊ *Der Film hat gerade begonnen.* ◆ *Ich wollte gerade gehen.* ◆ *Er duscht gerade.* only just gerade erst ◊ *Wir haben gerade erst angefangen.* just after gleich nach [glaɛ̯ç naːx] <+dat> ◊ *Ich bin gleich nach dem Essen mit ihr verabredet.* just

before direkt vor [dɪrɛkt foːɐ̯] +dat ◊ *Geben Sie mir die Dokumente direkt vor der Sitzung.* **2.** *(only)* nur [nuːɐ̯] ◊ *nur zehn Euro* ♦ *nach nur fünf Minuten* ♦ *Er ist nicht wirklich krank, er hat nur keine Lust!* ♦ *Ich wollte nur mal fragen, wie es dir so geht.* Just because he's old, doesn't mean he's wise. Nur weil er alt ist, ist er noch lange nicht weise.*; (referring to age or time)* erst [eːɐ̯st] ◊ *Es ist erst zehn Uhr.* ♦ *Sie ist erst neun Jahre alt.; (a little more than)* just over gut [guːt] ◊ *Das dauert gut zwei Stunden.; (a little less than)* just under knapp [knap] ◊ *Es dauerte knapp fünf Minuten.; (a short distance away)* gleich [glaɛç] ◊ *Ich wohne hier gleich um die Ecke.* **3.** *(precisely)* genau [ɡəˈnaʊ̯] ◊ *Es ist genau 17 Minuten nach acht.* ♦ *Das ist genau das, was ich wollte.* just as/like genauso [ɡəˈnaʊ̯zoː] ◊ *Er kam zu spät, genauso wie ich es erwartet hatte.* ♦ *Er ist genauso groß wie seine Schwester.* just a minute/moment einen Moment [aɛnan moˈmɛnt] ◊ *Einen Moment, ich komme sofort!* **4.** *(for emphasis)* einfach [ˈaɛnfax] ◊ *Es war einfach schrecklich!* ♦ *Ich habe es einfach vergessen.* ♦ *Versuch es doch einfach mal!; (encouraging, warning, threatening)* nur [nuːɐ̯] ◊ *Geb nur zu dem Hund, er tut dir nichts!* ♦ *Werd jetzt nur nicht unverschämt!* Just listen to that. Hör dir das mal an. Just shut up! Sei bloß still! **5.** *(almost not)* gerade noch [ɡəraːdə nɔx] ◊ *Wir haben das Flugzeug gerade noch erwischt.* **6.** *(in polite requests)* eben [ˈeːbm̩] ◊ *Darf ich das eben noch fertig machen?*

◉ just like that einfach so just think stell dir bloß vor not just any ... nicht irgendein ..., nicht irgendeine ... ◊ *Ich will nicht irgendein Auto, sondern dieses!*

justice noun **1.** *(fairness)* Gerechtigkeit [ɡəˈrɛçtɪçkaɛt] die <-> no pl ◊ *Wir wollen soziale Gerechtigkeit!; (of a claim)* Rechtmäßigkeit [ˈrɛçtmɛːsɪçkaɛt] die <-> no pl ◊ *die Rechtmäßigkeit eines Anspruchs* **2.** LAW *(system)* Justiz [jʊsˈtiːts] die <-> no pl ◊ *jdn der Justiz übergeben* miscarriage of justice Justizirrtum [jʊsˈtiːts|ɪ̯rˈtuːm] der <-s, Justizirrtümer> bring sb to justice jdn vor Gericht bringen [foːɐ̯ ɡəˈrɪçt brɪŋən] <bringt, brachte, hat gebracht> **3.** LAW *(in the US: judge)* Richter [ˈrɪçtɐ] der <-s, -> ♀Richterin [ˈrɪçtərɪn] die <-, -nen> ◊ *Wie hat die Richterin entschieden?* ♦ *Er ist Richter.*

◉ do sb/sth justice jdm/einer Sache gerecht werden ◊ *Diese Beurteilung wird ihr nicht gerecht.* do yourself justice zeigen, was man kann ◊ *Sie haben in der Prüfung nicht gezeigt, was Sie können.* with justice mit Recht

justification noun **1.** *(reason)* Rechtfertigung [ˈrɛçtfɛˈtɪɡʊŋ] die <-> no pl ◊ *Für so eine Tat gibt es keine Rechtfertigung.* **2.** TECHN, IT Blocksatz [ˈblɔkzaʦ] der <-es> no pl

justified → justify adj **1.** be justified in doing sth etw. zu Recht tun [ʦuː ˈrɛçt] ◊ *Hat sie in diesem Fall zu Recht gelogen?* **2.** TECHN, IT left justified linksbündig [ˈlɪŋksbʏndɪç] right justified rechtsbündig [ˈrɛçtsbʏndɪç] ◊ *ein rechtsbündiger Text*

justify verb **1.** *(give reasons for sth, be a good reason for sth)* rechtfertigen [ˈrɛçtfɛˈtɪɡn̩] +haben; often in adjectival passive constructions ◊ *So eine Tat lässt sich kaum rechtfertigen.* ♦ *Ihre Sorge ist nicht gerechtfertigt.* justify yourself (to sb) sich (jdm gegenüber) rechtfertigen ◊ *Sie werden sich dem Chef gegenüber rechtfertigen müssen.* **2.** TECHN, IT ausrichten [ˈaʊ̯srɪçtn̩] <richtet aus, richtete aus, hat ausgerichtet> ◊ *Bitte richten Sie den Text zentriert aus.*

juvenile noun Jugendliche [ˈjuːɡn̩tlɪçə] der/die <-n, die Jugendlichen> but: *ein Jugendlicher/eine Jugendliche* ◊ *Mehrere Jugendliche wurden von der Polizei festgenommen.*

K

k, K [noun] k, K [kaː] das <–(s), –(s)> ◊ *Dieses Wort wird mit einem kleinen k/großen K geschrieben.* ♦ *K wie Kaufmann*

kangaroo [noun] Känguru [ˈkɛŋɡuruː] das <–s, –s>

karate [noun] Karate [kaˈraːtə] das <–(s)> *no pl*

kebab [noun] Kebab [keˈbap] der <–(s), –s> ◊ *Zu Mittag haben wir Kebab gegessen.*

keen [adj] **1.** *(want)* be keen on doing sth/to do sth etw. gern tun wollen [gɛᵊn … vɔlən] <will, wollte, hat wollen> ◊ *Sie wollte ihn nicht gern in ihrer Abteilung haben.* ♦ *Die Firma will ihr Image gern verbessern.* be keen for sb to do sth gern wollen, dass jd etw. tut **2.** *(enthusiastic)* begeistert [bəˈɡaestet] ◊ *Er ist ein begeisterter Tänzer.* ♦ *Die Mannschaft ist unerfahren, aber begeistert.; (hardworking)* eifrig [ˈaefrɪç] ◊ *Dieser Schüler ist besonders eifrig.* ♦ *ein eifriger Anhänger einer Theorie; (like very much)* be keen on sth etw. sehr mögen [zeːɐ̯ ˈmøːɡn̩] <mag, mochte, hat gemocht> ◊ *Sie mag amerikanische Countrysongs sehr.; (consider attractive)* be keen on sb scharf auf jdn sein [ˈʃaᵊf aof … zaen] +sein *(fam)* ◊ *Ich glaube, er ist scharf auf dich!* **3.** *(interest, feeling, desire, pain)* stark [ʃtaᵊk] <stärker, am stärksten> ◊ *Die Schmerzen waren sehr stark.* ♦ *Sie hatte den starken Wunsch, ihm nahe zu sein.* **4.** *(wind, blade, eye, mind, wit, competition)* scharf [ʃaᵊf] <schärfer, am schärfsten> ◊ *Sie hat einen scharfen Verstand.* ♦ *Die Augen des Adlers sind scharf.; (instinct, hearing, nose, sense)* fein [faen] ◊ *Er hat ein feines Gespür dafür, was seine Kunden wollen.* ♦ *Die Nase von Hunden ist viel feiner als unsere.* have a keen eye for sth ein gutes Auge für etw. haben [aen ˌɡuːtəs ˈaoɡə fyːɐ̯ … haːbm̩] +haben ◊ *Sie hat ein gutes Auge für schlechte Texte.*

keenly [adv] **1.** *(strongly)* sehr [zeːɐ̯] ◊ *sehr an etw. interessiert sein* ♦ *sich etw. sehr wünschen* **2.** *(closely)* genau [ɡəˈnao] <genauer, am genau(e)sten> ◊ *Sie beobachtete ihn genau.*

keep¹ [noun] **1.** *(livelihood, food)* Unterhalt [ˈʊntehalt] der <–(e)s> *no pl* ◊ *seinen Unterhalt verdienen* He got 80 euros a week and his keep. Er bekam 80 Euro pro Woche sowie freie Kost und Logis. **2.** ARCH *(in a castle)* Bergfried [ˈbɛᵊkfriːt] der <–(e)s, –e> ♦ **for keeps** für immer

keep² [verb] **1.** *(remain in a state)* bleiben [ˈblaebm̩] <bleibt, blieb, ist geblieben> ◊ *fit bleiben* ♦ *Sie blieb drei Tage im Haus.* keep still stillhalten [ˈʃtɪlhaltn̩] <hält still, hielt still, hat stillgehalten> ◊ *Halt endlich mal still!* keep quiet sich ruhig verhalten [ˈruːɪç fehaltn̩] <verhält sich, verhielt sich, hat sich verhalten> ◊ *Verhaltet euch ganz ruhig, damit uns niemand hört.; (maintain in a state)* halten [ˈhaltn̩] <hält, hielt, hat gehalten> ◊ *Er versuchte, sie warm zu halten.* ♦ *die Kosten innerhalb bestimmter Grenzen halten* keep sb alive jdn am Leben halten keep sth under control die Kontrolle über etw. [acc] behalten [diː kɔnˈtrɔlə yːbɐ … bəhaltn̩] <behält,

behielt, hat behalten> keep things apart Dinge voneinander trennen [fɔnˈ|aenandɐ ˈtrɛnən] +haben ◊ *Sie versucht, Arbeit und Privatleben voneinander zu trennen.* **2.** *(continue, not stop)* keep doing sth etw. weiter tun [ˈvaetə] ◊ *Ich werde dich weiter lieben, auch wenn du mich verlässt.; (with certain verbs)* weiter… [ˈvaetə] keep walking weitergehen [ˈvaeteɡeːən] <geht weiter, ging weiter, ist weitergegangen>; *(repeatedly)* keep doing sth etw. immer wieder tun [ɪmɐ ˈviːdɐ] ◊ *Er hat sie immer wieder belogen.; (constantly)* keep doing sth etw. dauernd tun [ˈdaoɐnt] ◊ *Sie spricht dauernd von ihm.* keep sb waiting jdn warten lassen [ˈvaᵊtn̩ lasn̩] <lässt, ließ, hat lassen> keep left/right sich links/rechts halten [ˈlɪŋks/ˈrɛçts haltn̩] <hält sich, hielt sich, hat sich gehalten>; *(not change)* beibehalten [ˈbaebəhaltn̩] <behält bei, behielt bei, hat beibehalten> ◊ *Es empfiehlt sich, diese Einstellung beizubehalten.; (save)* bewahren [bəˈvaːrən] <bewahrt, bewahrte, hat bewahrt> ◊ *Sie hat sich ihr jugendliches Aussehen bewahrt.* **3.** *(retain)* behalten [bəˈhaltn̩] <behält, behielt, hat behalten> ◊ *Darf ich das behalten?* ♦ *Sie hofft, ihren Arbeitsplatz zu behalten.* ♦ *jdn im Krankenhaus/in Haft behalten* ♦ *Er hat seinen Humor/die Ruhe behalten.* keep your temper sich beherrschen [bəˈhɛᵊʃn̩] <beherrscht sich, beherrschte sich, hat sich beherrscht> keep sb/sth in mind an jdn/etw. denken [an … ˌdɛŋkn̩] <denkt, dachte, hat gedacht> ◊ *Ich werde immer an die schöne Zeit mit ihm denken.* **4.** *(in a certain place, store)* aufbewahren [ˈaofbəvaːrən] <bewahrt auf, bewahrte auf, hat aufbewahrt> ◊ *Milch muss kühl aufbewahrt werden.; (not throw away)* aufheben [ˈaofheːbm̩] <hebt auf, hob auf, hat aufgehoben> ◊ *Ich habe alle ihre Briefe aufgehoben.* **5.** *(a list, diary, accounts, minutes)* führen [ˈfyːrən] +haben ◊ *über alle Einnahmen und Ausgaben Buch führen* **6.** *(fulfil, a promise, vow)* halten [ˈhaltn̩] <hält, hielt, hat gehalten> ◊ *Sie hat ihr Wort gehalten und ihm geholfen.; (observe, a law, treaty, an appointment)* einhalten [ˈaenhaltn̩] <hält ein, hielt ein, hat eingehalten> ◊ *Leider kann ich den Termin nicht einhalten.* **7.** *(support, pay for)* unterhalten [ʊntɐˈhaltn̩] <unterhält, unterhielt, hat unterhalten> ◊ *Mit diesem Gehalt kann man keine Familie unterhalten.* keep sb in food/clothing etc. für jds Essen/Kleidung etc. sorgen [fyːɐ̯ … ˈɛsn̩/ˈklaedʊŋ zɔᵊɡn̩] +haben **8.** *(a pet, farm animal)* halten [ˈhaltn̩] <hält, hielt, hat gehalten> ◊ *eine Katze als Haustier halten* **9.** *(food etc.)* sich halten [ˈhaltn̩] <hält sich, hielt sich, hat sich gehalten> ◊ *Das Fleisch hält sich im Kühlschrank etwa eine Woche.* **10.** *(delay)* aufhalten [ˈaofhaltn̩] <hält auf, hielt auf, hat aufgehalten> ◊ *Was hat Sie aufgehalten?* ♦ *Ich werde Sie nicht lange aufhalten.* **11.** *(sell goods)* führen [ˈfyːrən] +haben ◊ *Führen Sie auch Tapeten?* ⊛ **keep sth to yourself** etw. für sich behalten **How are you keeping?** Wie geht es Ihnen denn so?

• **keep away** [phras v] *(remain at a distance)* keep sb/sth away (from sb/sth) jdn/etw. (von jdm/etw.) fernhalten ['fɛʳnhaltn̩] <hält fern, hielt fern, hat ferngehalten> ◊ *Ein Gitter hält die Fliegen fern.* ♦ *Halten Sie die Kinder vom Feuer fern.* sb keeps away from sb/sth jd hält sich von jdm/etw. fern; *(avoid)* sb keeps away from sth jd meidet etw. ['maedət] <meidet, mied, hat gemieden> ◊ *Sie sollten Alkohol meiden.*

• **keep back** [phras v] **1.** *(a piece of information)* keep sth back (from sb) (jdm) etw. verschweigen [fɛ'ʃvaegn̩] <verschweigt, verschwieg, hat verschwiegen> ◊ *Sie verschweigt doch irgendetwas.; (a feeling)* keep sth back (from sb) (jdm) etw. verheimlichen [fɛ'haemlɪçn̩] <verheimlicht, verheimlichte, hat verheimlicht> ◊ *Er verheimlichte ihr seine wahren Gefühle.* **2.** *(money)* einbehalten ['aenbəhaltn̩] <behält ein, behielt ein, hat einbehalten> ◊ *Sie behielt einen Teil der Summe für sich selbst ein.* **3.** *(for later use)* zurückbehalten [ʦu'rʏkbəhaltn̩] <behält zurück, behielt zurück, hat zurückbehalten> ◊ *Er behielt den Ring als Pfand zurück.* **4.** *(hold back a person, tears etc.)* zurückhalten [ʦu'rʏkhaltn̩] <hält zurück, hielt zurück, hat zurückgehalten> ◊ *aggressive Demonstranten zurückhalten*

• **keep down** [phras v] **1.** *(taxes, costs, prices)* niedrig halten ['niːdrɪç ˌhaltn̩] <hält, hielt, hat gehalten> ◊ *die Ausgaben niedrig halten* **2.** *(in your stomach)* bei sich [dat] behalten [bae ... bəˌhaltn̩] <behält, behielt, hat behalten> ◊ *Sie kann im Moment nichts bei sich behalten.*

• **keep from** [phras v] **1.** *(prevent)* keep sb from doing sth jdn von etw. abhalten [fɔn ... ˌaphaltn̩] <hält ab, hielt ab, hat abgehalten> ◊ *Der Lärm hielt ihn vom Schlafen ab.* keep sth from doing sth verhindern, dass etw. tut [fɛ'hɪndɐn das] <verhindert, verhinderte, hat verhindert> ◊ *Wir müssen verhindern, dass die Waren nass werden.* **2.** *(not tell)* keep sth from sb jdm etw. verschweigen [fɛ'ʃvaegn̩] <verschweigt, verschwieg, hat verschwiegen> ◊ *Sie verschwieg ihm die unangenehme Nachricht.*

• **keep in** [phras v] dabehalten ['daːbəhaltn̩] <behält da, behielt da, hat dabehalten> ◊ *Man hat sie im Krankenhaus gleich dabehalten.; (a pupil)* nachsitzen lassen ['naːxzɪtsn̩ lasn̩] <lässt, ließ, hat lassen> ◊ *Der Lehrer ließ ihn nachsitzen.*

• **keep off** [phras v] **1.** *(prevent from touching or coming in)* abhalten ['aphaltn̩] <hält ab, hielt ab, hat abgehalten> ◊ *Der Geruch hält Insekten ab.* ♦ *Das Vordach hält den Regen ab.* Keep your hands off! Hände weg! **2.** *(not go somewhere)* keep off sth von etw. wegbleiben [fɔn ... ˌvɛkblaebn̩] <bleibt weg, blieb weg, ist weggeblieben> ◊ *Bleib von der Stromleitung weg!* Keep off! Betreten verboten! **3.** *(a subject, food)* vermeiden [fɛ'maedn̩] <vermeidet, vermied, hat vermieden> ◊ *Wenn du mit ihr sprichst, solltest du das Thema Urlaub vermeiden.*

• **keep on** [phras v] **1.** *(an employee)* weiterbeschäftigen ['vaetəbəʃɛftɪgn̩] <beschäftigt weiter, beschäftigte weiter, hat weiterbeschäftigt> ◊ *Wir können Sie leider nicht weiterbeschäftigen.* **2.** *(talk incessantly)* keep on about sth dauernd über etw. [acc] reden [ˌdaoɐnt yːbɐ ... ˌreːdn̩] +haben ◊ *Sie redet dauernd über ihre Schmerzen.* **3.** *(your clothes)* anbehalten ['anbəhaltn̩] <behält an, behielt an, hat anbehalten> ◊ *Sie behielt ihren Mantel an.* → keep² 2.

• **keep out** [phras v] **1.** *(not let in)* keep sb/sth out jdn/etw. abhalten ['aphaltn̩] <hält ab, hielt ab, hat abgehalten> ◊ *Diese Mauer sollte früher Feinde abhalten.; (not enter)* keep out of sth etw. nicht betreten [ˌnɪçt bə'treːtn̩] <betritt, betrat, hat betreten> ◊ *Er hat die Baustelle nicht betreten.* Keep out of my room! Komm nicht in mein Zimmer! Keep out! Zutritt verboten! **2.** *(not become involved)* keep out of sth sich aus etw. heraushalten [aos ... hɛ'raoshaltn̩] <hält sich heraus, hielt sich heraus, hat sich herausgehalten> ◊ *Halte dich bitte aus unserem Streit heraus!*

• **keep to** [phras v] **1.** *(restrict)* keep sth to sth etw. auf etw. [acc] beschränken [aof ... bə'ʃrɛŋkn̩] <beschränkt, beschränkte, hat beschränkt> ◊ *Sie sollten Ihren Fettkonsum auf ein Minimum beschränken.* **2.** *(follow)* keep to sth sich an etw. [acc] halten [an ... ˌhaltn̩] <hält sich, hielt sich, hat sich gehalten> ◊ *Halten Sie sich an den Plan/die Vorschriften.* **3.** *(not leave)* keep to sth auf etw. [dat] bleiben [aof ... ˌblaebm̩] <bleibt, blieb, ist geblieben> ◊ *Bleiben Sie auf der Hauptstraße.* keep to the point beim Thema bleiben

• **keep up** [phras v] **1.** *(be as fast as)* keep up with sb/sth mit jdm/etw. Schritt halten [mɪt ... 'ʃrɪt haltn̩] <hält, hielt, hat gehalten> keep up with the news sich auf dem Laufenden halten; *(understand)* keep up with sb/sth jdm/einer Sache folgen ['fɔlgn̩] +sein ◊ *Nur mit Mühe konnte er der Vorlesung folgen.* **2.** *(continue to do, maintain)* aufrechterhalten ['aofrɛçtɐhaltn̩] <erhält aufrecht, erhielt aufrecht, hat aufrechterhalten> ◊ *den Betrieb/den Kontakt/die Ordnung aufrechterhalten* ♦ *seine Behauptung/Forderung aufrechterhalten* **3.** *(not let go to bed)* keep sb up am Schlafen(gehen) hindern [am 'ʃlaːfn̩(geːən) ˌhɪndɐn] +haben ◊ *Das Geschrei hinderte ihn die ganze Nacht am Schlafen.*

keeper [noun] *(guard, in a park)* Wächter ['vɛçtɐ] der <-s, -> ♀Wächterin ['vɛçtərɪn] die <-, -nen> ◊ *Der Wächter sah nach, woher der Lärm kam.* ♦ *Sie verdient ihr Geld als Wächterin in einem großen Park.; (in an asylum, a zoo, lighthouse)* Wärter ['vɛʳtɐ] der <-s, -> ♀Wärterin ['vɛʳtərɪn] die <-, -nen> ◊ *Als Wärter muss er auch die Löwen füttern.* ♦ *Eine der Wärterinnen wurde angegriffen.; (of a museum)* Kustos ['kʊstɔs] der <-, Kustoden> ◊ *der Kustos der Kunstsammlung des Museums*

Kenya [noun] Kenia ['keːnja] das <-s> *article only in combination with attribute, no pl* → Germany

Kenyan¹ [noun] Kenianer [ke'njaːnɐ] der <-s, -> ♀Kenianerin [ke'njaːnərɪn] die <-, -nen> → German¹ 1.

Kenyan² [adj] kenianisch [ke'njaːnɪʃ] *mostly before ns* ◊ *das kenianische Hinterland*

kernel [noun] Kern [kɛʳn] der <-(e)s, -e>

kettle [noun] Kessel ['kɛsl] der <-s, -> ◊ *Das Fleisch in einem Kessel garen lassen.* put the kettle on Wasser aufsetzen ['vasɐ ˌaofzɛtsn̩] +haben ⊚ be a different kettle of fish etw. ganz anderes sein

key¹ [noun] **1.** *(to lock, achieve sth)* Schlüssel ['ʃlʏsl] der <-s, -> ◊ *den Schlüssel abziehen/(im Schloss/in der Tür) stecken lassen* ♦ *Fleiß ist der Schlüssel zum Erfolg.* car key Autoschlüssel ['aotoʃlʏsl] **2.** *(of a computer, piano etc.)* Taste ['tastə] die <-, -n> ◊ *Drücken Sie eine beliebige Taste.* **3.** MUS Tonart

['tɔːn|aːrt] die <–, –en> ◊ *In welcher Tonart steht das Stück?* in the key of D sharp/D minor in D-Dur/ d-Moll [ɪn 'deːduːɐ̯/'deːmɔl] **4.** *(for maps etc.)* Zeichenerklärung ['tsaeçn̩|ɛklɛːrʊŋ] die <–, –en> ◊ *Sieh in der Zeichenerklärung nach, was dieses Symbol bedeutet.*; *(for answers)* Lösungsschlüssel ['løːzʊŋsʃlʏsl̩] der <–s, –>

key² [adj] Schlüssel… ['ʃlʏsl̩] key figure Schlüsselfigur ['ʃlʏslˌfiˌguːɐ̯] die <–, –en> key role Schlüsselrolle ['ʃlʏslˌrɔlə] die <–> *no pl* key point springender Punkt [ʃprɪŋənde 'pʊŋkt] <–(e)s> *no pl* ◊ *Genau das ist der springende Punkt.* key (to sth) äußerst wichtig (für etw.) [ɔøsest 'vɪçtɪç] ◊ *Qualifizierte Mitarbeiter sind äußerst wichtig für unsere Firma.* ♦ *Ein äußerst wichtiger Spieler fällt wegen Krankheit aus.*

key³ [verb] key (in) eingeben ['aengeːbm̩] <gibt ein, gab ein, hat eingegeben> ◊ *Daten eingeben*

keyboard [noun] **1.** *(of a computer, typewriter, piano)* Tastatur [tastaˈtuːɐ̯] die <–, –en> ◊ *etw. über die Tastatur in den Computer eingeben* **2.** *(musical instrument)* Keyboard ['kiːbɔːt] das <–s, –s> ◊ *Keyboard spielen/lernen*

keyword [noun] Stichwort ['ʃtɪçvɔʳt] das <–(e)s, –e *or* Stichwörter> ◊ *Geben Sie ein Stichwort ein und klicken Sie auf 'Suchen'.* ♦ *Was fällt euch zum Stichwort 'Gesundheit' ein?*

kg kg ['kiːlogram] ◊ *Er wog damals 75 kg.*

kick¹ [noun] **1.** *(with your foot)* Tritt [trɪt] der <–(e)s, –e> ◊ *Sie versetzte ihm einen kräftigen Tritt.*; *(in a game)* Schuss [ʃʊs] der <–es, Schüsse> ◊ *Das war ein toller Schuss!* **2.** *(excitement)* sb gets a kick out of sth etw. macht jdm einen Riesenspaß [maxt … aenən riːzn̩ˈʃpaːs] +haben for kicks zum Spaß [tsʊm 'ʃpaːs]

kick² [verb] **1.** *(hit sb, an animal)* treten ['treːtn̩] <tritt, trat, hat getreten> ◊ *Sie trat und schlug um sich.* ♦ *Er hat den Hund getreten.* kick a door/ball gegen eine Tür/einen Ball treten; *(open with your foot)* kick sth open etw. auftreten ['aoftreːtn̩] +haben ◊ *Sie trat die Tür auf.*; *(an object)* kick sth einer Sache [dat] einen Tritt versetzen [aenən 'trɪt fezɛtsn̩] <versetzt, versetzte, hat versetzt> ◊ *Er versetzte der Dose einen Tritt, sodass sie auf die Straße rollte.*; *(move a ball with your foot)* schießen ['ʃiːsn̩] <schießt, schoss, hat geschossen> ◊ *einen Ball ins Tor schießen* **2.** *(baby)* strampeln ['ʃtrampl̩n] +haben ◊ *Das Baby strampelt fröhlich auf der Decke.* **3.** *(stop)* kick sth sich [dat] etw. abgewöhnen ['apgəvøːnən] <gewöhnt sich ab, gewöhnte sich ab, hat sich abgewöhnt> ◊ *Sie will sich das Rauchen abgewöhnen.* kick the habit es sich [dat] abgewöhnen ◊ *Er raucht drei Schachteln am Tag, aber er will es sich abgewöhnen.*

  ⊛ kick yourself sich ohrfeigen

• **kick around** [phras v] **1.** *(an idea etc.)* durchdiskutieren ['dʊʳçdɪskutiˈrən] <diskutiert durch, diskutierte durch, hat durchdiskutiert> ◊ *Wir haben ein paar Vorschläge durchdiskutiert.* **2.** *(treat badly)* kick sb around jdn herumschubsen [hɛˈrʊmʃʊpsn̩] +haben *(fam)* ◊ *Früher wurde ich von allen nur herumgeschubst.* **3.** *(object)* be kicking around somewhere irgendwo rumliegen ['rʊmliːgn̩] <liegt rum, lag rum, hat rumgelegen> *(fam)* ◊ *Liegt hier irgendwo mein Schlüssel rum?* **4.** *(person)* be kicking around somewhere irgendwo rumfahren ['rʊmfaːrən] <fährt

rum, fuhr rum, ist rumgefahren> *(fam)* ◊ *Er ist drei Monate in Australien rumgefahren.*

• **kick in** [phras v] **1.** *(effect)* eintreten ['aentreːtn̩] <tritt ein, trat ein, ist eingetreten> ◊ *Die Wirkung tritt erst nach ein paar Tagen ein.*; *(drug)* zu wirken beginnen [tsu: 'vɪʳkn̩ bəginən] <beginnt, begann, hat begonnen> ◊ *Das Schmerzmittel begann schon zu wirken.*; *(law, rule)* in Kraft treten [ɪn 'kraft treːtn̩] <tritt, trat, ist getreten> **2.** *(in the US: give money)* beisteuern ['baeʃtɔøən] <steuert bei, steuerte bei, hat beigesteuert> ◊ *Wir kaufen ein Geschenk für sie, möchtest du auch etwas beisteuern?* **3.** *(a door)* eintreten ['aentreːtn̩] <tritt ein, trat ein, hat eingetreten> ◊ *Die Polizei trat die Tür ein.* kick sb's teeth in jdm die Zähne einschlagen [di: 'tsɛːnə aenʃlaːgn̩] <schlägt ein, schlug ein, hat eingeschlagen>

• **kick off** [phras v] **1.** *(start)* beginnen [bəˈgɪnən] <beginnt, begann, hat begonnen> ◊ *Wann beginnt das Spiel?* kick off with sth mit etw. beginnen **2.** *(your shoes)* von sich [dat] schleudern ['fɔn … ʃlɔødən] +haben **3.** *(make leave)* kick sb off sth jdn aus etw. werfen [aos … veˈʳfn̩] <wirft, warf, hat geworfen> *(fam)* ◊ *Man hat ihn aus der Universität geworfen.*

• **kick out** [phras v] kick sb out jdn rauswerfen ['raosveˈʳfn̩] <wirft raus, warf raus, hat rausgeworfen> *(fam)* ◊ *Seine Frau hat ihn rausgeworfen.* kick sb out of sth jdn aus etw. rauswerfen ◊ *Sie wurde aus dem Verein rausgeworfen.*

• **kick up** [phras v] aufwirbeln ['aofvɪʳbl̩n] +haben ◊ *Unsere Schritte wirbelten Staub auf.*

kick-off [noun] Anstoß ['anʃtoːs] der <–es, Anstöße> ◊ *Welcher Spieler führt den Anstoß aus?*

kid¹ [noun] **1.** *(child)* Kind [kɪnt] das <–(e)s, –er> ◊ *Die Kinder spielen auf der Straße.* ♦ *Haben Sie Kinder?*; *(young person)* Jugendliche ['juːgn̩tlɪçə] der/ die <–n, die Jugendlichen> *but: ein Jugendlicher/eine Jugendliche* **2.** *(young goat)* Kitz [kɪts] das <–es, –e> ◊ *Die Ziege hat zwei Kitze.*; *(leather)* Ziegenleder ['tsiːgn̩leːde] das <–s> *no pl*

  ⊛ kid's stuff Kinderkram

kid² [verb] *(tease)* kid sb (about sth) jdn (wegen etw.) aufziehen ['aoftsiːən] <zieht auf, zog auf, hat aufgezogen> ◊ *Du willst mich wohl aufziehen!* ♦ *Sie ziehen ihn immer wegen seiner großen Füße auf.* Just kidding. Das war nicht ernst gemeint. no kidding im Ernst ◊ *Im Ernst, er ist in Jeans in die Oper gegangen!* Are you kidding? Machst du Witze?; *(deceive)* kid sb/yourself jdm/sich etw. vormachen ['foːʳmaxn̩] +haben ◊ *Mir kannst du nichts vormachen.* ♦ *Machen Sie sich nichts vor. Ihre Arbeit ist einfach nicht gut genug.*

kidnap [verb] entführen [ɛntˈfyːrən] <entführt, entführte, hat entführt> ◊ *Im Irak wurden wieder drei Journalisten entführt.*

kidney [noun] Niere ['niːrə] die <–, –n> ◊ *Ihre Nieren arbeiten nicht richtig.* ♦ *saure Nieren mit Bratkartoffeln* kidney transplant Nierentransplantation ['niːrəntransplantaˌtsjoːn] die <–, –en>

kill [verb] **1.** *(extinguish life)* töten ['tøːtn̩] <tötet, tötete, hat getötet> ◊ *Er tötete das Reh mit einem Schuss.* ♦ *Sie wurde bei einem Unfall getötet.* ♦ *Wenn Blicke töten könnten, hätte ich das Gespräch nicht überlebt.*; *(intentionally)* kill sb/yourself jdn/sich umbringen ['ʊmbrɪŋən] ◊ *Man sagt, er habe seine Frau umgebracht.* ♦ *Nach dem Tod ihres Kindes brachte sie sich um.* ♦ *Die Kälte wird dich schon*

nicht umbringen. **2.** *(hurt)* sth is killing sb etw. tut jdm unheimlich weh [tu:t ... ʊnhaemlɪç 'veː] <tat weh, hat wehgetan> *(fam)* ◊ *Meine Füße taten mir unheimlich weh.*; *(exhaust)* jdn fertig machen ['fɛʳtɪç maxn̩] *+haben (fam)* **3.** kill time sich dat die Zeit vertreiben [diː 'tsaet fɛtraebm̩] <vertreibt sich, vertrieb sich, hat sich vertrieben> kill a few hours sich für ein paar Stunden die Zeit vertreiben **4.** *(work too hard)* kill yourself sich schinden ['ʃɪndn̩] <schindet sich, schindete sich, hat sich geschunden> ◊ *Er schindet sich, um seine Familie zu ernähren.* **5.** *(stop speculation, a conversation)* beenden [bə|'ɛndn̩] <beendet, beendete, hat beendet> ◊ *ein Gespräch abrupt beenden*; *(pain)* stillen ['ʃtɪlən] *+haben* ◊ *Nichts konnte ihre Schmerzen stillen.*; *(a light)* ausmachen ['aosmaxn̩] *+haben* ◊ *Machst du bitte die Lichter aus?*

• **kill off** phras v vernichten [fɛ'nɪçtn̩] <vernichtet, vernichtete, hat vernichtet> ◊ *Das Gift hat alles Leben im See vernichtet.*

killer noun *(sb who kills sb)* Mörder ['mœʳdɐ] der <–s, –> ♀Mörderin ['mœʳdərɪn] die <–, –nen> ◊ *Ihr Mörder wurde noch nicht gefunden.* ♦ *ein bezahlter Mörder*; *(illness etc.)* be a killer tödlich sein ['tøːtlɪç zaen] *+sein* ◊ *Die Krankheit ist tödlich.* Cancer is the second largest killer in the US. Krebs ist die zweithäufigste Todesursache in den USA. weed killer Unkrautvernichtungsmittel ['ʊnkraotfɛˌnɪçtʊŋsmɪtl̩] das <–s, –>

◉ **be a killer** *(be extremely difficult)* glatter Mord sein

killing noun *(act of making die)* Tötung ['tøːtʊŋ] die <–, –en> *most sing* ◊ *Aufgrund der Seuchengefahr wurde die Tötung der Schweine angeordnet.*; *(murder)* Mord [mɔʳt] der <–(e)s, –e> ◊ *drei weitere Morde in Bagdad*

◉ **make a killing** einen Riesengewinn machen

kilo noun Kilo ['kiːloː] das <–s, –s> *pl 'Kilo' when used with expressions of quantity* ◊ *zwei Kilo Tomaten* ♦ *der Kampf gegen die Kilos*

kilogram noun Kilogramm ['kiːlogram] das <–s, –e> *pl 'Kilogramm' when used with expressions of quantity* ◊ *fünf Kilogramm Kartoffeln* ♦ *Zwei Pfund sind ein Kilogramm.*

kilometer → **kilometre**

kilometre, kilometer noun Kilometer [kilo'meːtɐ] der <–s, –> ◊ *Wir sind im Urlaub 5000 Kilometer gefahren.* ♦ *Die Entfernung beträgt etwa 100 Kilometer.* kilometers an/per hour Stundenkilometer ['ʃtʊndn̩kiloˌmeːtɐ] ◊ *mit 120 Stundenkilometern fahren* ♦ *eine Geschwindigkeit von 150 Stundenkilometern*

kilt noun Kilt [kɪlt] der <–(e)s, –s> ◊ *einen Kilt tragen*

kind[1] noun Art [aːʳt] die <–, –en> ◊ *Was für eine Art von Drucker brauchst du?* ♦ *Gefällt dir diese Art Buch?* ♦ *Kennst du noch mehr Gedichte dieser Art?*; *(of a food product, drink etc.)* Sorte ['zɔʳtə] die <–, –n> ◊ *Wir haben mehrere Sorten Käse.* what kind of ... was für ein/eine … ['vas fyːɐ̯ aen/aenə] ◊ *Was für ein Mensch ist er?* ♦ *Was für eine Mutter bist du eigentlich?* She's not that kind of person. So ist sie nicht. ...of all kinds alle möglichen … [alə 'møːklɪçn̩] ◊ *Sie haben alle möglichen Spielsachen.* the biggest/best etc. ... of its/their kind der/die/das größte/beste etc. … dieser Art [deːɐ̯/diː/das ˌgrøːstə/ˌbɛstə ... diːzə 'aːʳt] ◊ *Das ist der höchste Turm dieser Art.* be the kind of person to do sth der Typ sein, der etw. tut [deːɐ̯ 'tyːp zaen deːɐ̯] *+sein* ◊ *Er ist nicht der Typ, der viele Worte macht.* not be sb's kind of thing nicht jds Fall sein [ˌnɪçt ... 'fal zaen] *+sein* ◊ *Diese Party ist nicht mein Fall.*

◉ **nothing of the kind** nichts dergleichen **something of the kind** so etwas **two/three etc. of a kind** vom gleichen Schlag ◊ *Die beiden sind vom gleichen Schlag.* **in kind** **1.** *(with goods)* in Naturalien ◊ *in Naturalien bezahlen* **2.** respond in kind es jdm mit gleicher Münze heimzahlen **kind of** irgendwie ◊ *Sie war gestern irgendwie seltsam.*

kind[2] adj *(of pleasant disposition, obliging)* freundlich ['frɔ̯ntlɪç] ◊ *Wären Sie so freundlich, das Fenster zu schließen?* ♦ *ein freundliches Gesicht* ♦ *Danke für Ihr freundliches Angebot.*; *(treat sb well)* be kind to sb gut zu jdm sein ['guːt tsuː ... zaen] *+sein* ◊ *Sie ist gut zu Tieren.*

kindergarten noun Kindergarten ['kɪndɐgaʳtn̩] der <–s, Kindergärten>

kindly adv **1.** *(in a kind way)* freundlich ['frɔ̯ntlɪç] ◊ *Sie lächelte das Mädchen freundlich an.* ♦ *„Möchtest du ein Eis?", fragte sie freundlich.* **2.** *(in a slightly annoyed request, showing gratefulness)* freundlicherweise ['frɔ̯ntlɪçɐ'vaezə] ◊ *Könntest du freundlicherweise etwas weniger Lärm machen?* ♦ *Sie haben mir freundlicherweise angeboten, über Nacht zu bleiben.*

◉ **not take kindly to sth** sich über etw. acc ärgern ◊ *Sie ärgert sich über seine Unpünktlichkeit.*

king noun König ['køːnɪç] der <–s, –e>

◉ **a king's ransom** ein Vermögen

kingdom noun *(of a king)* Königreich ['køːnɪçraeç] das <–(e)s, –e> the United Kingdom das Vereinigte Königreich the kingdom of heaven das Himmelreich [das 'hɪml̩raeç]; *(of plants, animals)* Reich [raeç] das <–(e)s, –e> ◊ *im Reich der wilden Tiere* animal kingdom Tierreich ['tiːɐ̯raeç] plant kingdom Pflanzenreich ['pflantsn̩raeç]

kiosk noun Kiosk ['kiːɔsk] der <–(e)s, –e>

kiss[1] noun Kuss [kʊs] der <–es, Küsse> ◊ *Sie gab ihm zum Abschied einen Kuss.* ♦ *Er drückte ihr einen Kuss auf die Stirn.*

◉ **blow sb a kiss** jdm eine Kusshand zuwerfen

kiss[2] verb küssen ['kʏsn̩] *+haben* ◊ *Er küsste sie zum Abschied.* ♦ *Er küsst leidenschaftlich gern.* kiss sb's cheek jdn auf die Wange küssen kiss sb's hand jdm die Hand küssen They kiss. Sie küssen sich. kiss sb goodbye/goodnight jdm einen Abschiedskuss/Gutenachtkuss geben [aenən 'apʃiːtskʊs/guːtə'naxtkʊs geːbm̩] <gibt, gab, hat gegeben>

kit noun **1.** *(set of items, tools)* Werkzeug ['vɛʳktsɔ̯k] das <–(e)s> *no pl* ◊ *Dafür braucht man besonderes Werkzeug.*; *(in a box)* Werkzeugkasten ['vɛʳktsɔ̯kkastn̩] der <–s, Werkzeugkästen> ◊ *Der Werkzeugkasten ist im Keller.* puncture repair kit Flickzeug ['flɪktsɔ̯k] das <–(e)s, –e> sewing kit Nähzeug ['nɛːtsɔ̯k] das <–(e)s, –e> **2.** *(clothes for sport, things for photography, of a soldier)* Ausrüstung ['aosrʏstʊŋ] die <–, –en> ◊ *seine Ausrüstung in Ordnung halten* gym kit Sportsachen ['ʃpɔʳtzaxn̩] die <–> *pl* **3.** *(for making a model etc.)* Bausatz ['baozats] der <–es, Bausätze> ◊ *ein Bausatz für ein Modellflugzeug*

kitchen [noun] Küche ['kʏçə] die <-, -n> ◊ *eine Drei-zimmerwohnung mit Küche und Bad* ♦ *Er ist in der Küche.*; *(in compound ns)* kitchen ... Küchen... ['kʏçn̩] kitchen cupboard Küchenschrank ['kʏçn̩ʃraŋk] der <-(e)s, Küchenschränke> ◊ *das Geschirr in den Küchenschrank stellen*

kitchen paper [noun] Küchenkrepp ['kʏçn̩krɛp] der <-s> *no pl*

kite [noun] 1. *(toy)* Drachen ['draxn̩] der <-s, -> ◊ *Sie ließen ihre Drachen steigen.* 2. *(bird)* Milan [mi'laːn] der <-s, -e>

kitten [noun] Kätzchen ['kɛtsçən] das <-s, ->
⊛ have kittens *(be very nervous)* Zustände kriegen

km km [kilo'meːtə]

knead [verb] kneten ['kneːtn̩] <knetet, knetete, hat geknetet> ◊ *Teig kneten* ♦ *Der Masseur knetete ihre verkrampften Muskeln.*

knee [noun] Knie [kniː] das <-s, -> ◊ *Ich habe mir das Knie gestoßen/verletzt.* ♦ *Bei seiner Jeans waren die Knie durchgescheuert.* ♦ *Sie fiel vor ihm auf die Knie.* go down on your knees sich hinknien ['hɪnkniː(ə)n] <kniet sich hin, kniete sich hin, hat sich hingekniet> ◊ *Er kniete sich vor ihr hin und nahm ihre Hand.*
⊛ on bended knee auf Knien bring sb to their knees jdn in die Knie zwingen

kneel [verb] *(be on your knees)* knien [kniːn] <kniet, kniete, hat gekniet> ◊ *Er kniete auf dem Boden/vor dem Altar.*; *(get down on your knees)* kneel (down) sich hinknien ['hɪnkniː(ə)n] +haben ◊ *Sie kniete sich vor das Baby hin und lächelte es an.*

knickers [noun] Unterhose ['ʊntehoːzə] die <-, -n> *can be used in the pl or sing* ♦ *eine frische Unterhose anziehen* ♦ *Er zog die Unterhosen aus.* a pair of knickers eine Unterhose
⊛ get your knickers in a twist sich [dat] ins Hemd machen

knife [noun] Messer ['mɛsɐ] das <-s, -> ◊ *etw. mit dem Messer klein schneiden* ♦ *mit Messer und Gabel essen* ♦ *ein scharfes Messer*
⊛ twist the knife in the wound Salz in die Wunde streuen unter the knife unters Messer ◊ *Sie kommt nächste Woche unters Messer.*

knight [noun] 1. *(in armour, title)* Ritter ['rɪtɐ] der <-s, -> ◊ *jdn zum Ritter schlagen* 2. CHESS Springer ['ʃprɪŋɐ] der <-s, -> ◊ *mit dem Springer einen Läufer schlagen*

knit [verb] 1. *(with wool)* stricken ['ʃtrɪkn̩] +haben ◊ *Socken stricken* 2. *(join)* knit together miteinander verwachsen [mɪt|aɛnandɐ fɛ'vaksn̩] <verwachsen, verwuchsen, sind verwachsen> ◊ *Regionen, die im Laufe der Zeit miteinander verwuchsen* knit into sth sich zu etw. verbinden [tsuː ... fɛ'bɪndn̩] <verbindet sich, verbanden sich, haben sich verbunden> ◊ *kleinere Initiativen, die sich zu einer Organisation verbanden* 3. *(bones)* zusammenwachsen [tsu'zamənvaksn̩] <wächst zusammen, wuchs zusammen, ist zusammenge-wachsen> ◊ *Der Knochen ist nicht mehr richtig zusammengewachsen.*; *(fracture)* verheilen [fɛ'haɛlən] <verheilt, verheilte, ist verheilt> ◊ *ein Knochenbruch, der nur langsam verheilt*

knitting [noun] 1. *(activity)* Stricken ['ʃtrɪkŋ] das <-s> *no pl* knitting needle Stricknadel ['ʃtrɪknaːdl̩] die <-, -n> 2. *(sth you are knitting)* Strickzeug ['ʃtrɪktsɔɡk] das <-(e)s> *no pl*

knob [noun] 1. *(on a door, radio etc.)* Knopf [knɔpf] der

<-(e)s, Knöpfe> 2. *(in the UK: small piece of sth)* Stückchen ['ʃtʏkçən] das <-s, -> ◊ *ein Stückchen Butter in der Pfanne schmelzen*

knock¹ [noun] 1. *(sound of sb knocking)* Klopfen ['klɔpfn̩] das <-s> *no pl* ◊ *Ich hörte ein Klopfen an der Tür.*; *(of a machine)* Klappern ['klapɐn] das <-s> *no pl* 2. *(blow)* Schlag [ʃlaːk] der <-(e)s, Schläge> ◊ *einen Schlag auf den Kopf bekommen; (less forceful)* Stoß [ʃtoːs] der <-es, Stöße> 3. *(misfortune)* Schicksalsschlag ['ʃɪksaːlʃlaːk] der <-(e)s, Schicksalsschläge> ◊ *eine Kindheit voller Schicksalsschläge*

knock² [verb] 1. *(hit with force)* schlagen ['ʃlaːɡn̩] <schlägt, schlug, hat geschlagen> ◊ *jdn zu Boden/bewusstlos schlagen* ♦ *einen Nagel in die Wand schlagen*; *(hurt yourself)* knock your sth against sth sich [dat] etw. an etw. [dat] stoßen [an ... ʃtoːsn̩] <stößt sich, stieß sich, hat sich gestoßen> ◊ *Ich habe mir das Knie am Tisch gestoßen.* 2. *(hit noisily, motor)* klopfen ['klɔpfn̩] +haben ◊ *Er klopfte an die Tür.* ♦ *Der Motor klopft so seltsam.*; *(machine)* klappern ['klapɐn] +haben 3. *(criticize)* heruntermachen [hɛ'rʊntəmaxn̩] +haben ◊ *Mach mich nicht immer so herunter!*

• **knock around** [phras v] 1. *(beat up)* verprügeln [fɛ'pryːɡl̩n] <verprügelt, verprügelte, hat verprügelt> ◊ *Er ist sie oft verprügelt.* 2. *(spend time)* sich herumtreiben [hɛ'rʊmtraɛbm̩] <treibt sich herum, trieb sich herum, hat sich herumgetrieben> ◊ *sich mit jdm herumtreiben* knock around a place sich irgendwo herumtreiben 3. *(object)* herumliegen [hɛ'rʊmliːɡŋ] <liegt herum, lag herum, hat herumgelegen> ◊ *Hier liegt irgendwo ein Korkenzieher herum.*

• **knock back** [phras v] 1. *(drink)* saufen ['zaɔfn̩] <säuft, soff, hat gesoffen> (fam) ◊ *Er soff ein Bier nach dem anderen.* 2. *(in the UK: impede)* zurückwerfen [tsu'rʏkvɛrfn̩] <wirft zurück, warf zurück, hat zurückgeworfen> ◊ *Probleme haben uns immer wieder zurückgeworfen.*

• **knock down** [phras v] 1. *(a building)* abreißen ['apraɛsn̩] <reißt ab, riss ab, hat abgerissen> ◊ *ein Haus abreißen; (a wall)* einreißen ['aɛnraɛsn̩] <reißt ein, riss ein, hat eingerissen> 2. *(in the UK: run over)* umfahren ['ʊmfaːrən] <fährt um, fuhr um, hat umgefahren> ◊ *ein Verkehrsschild umfahren* 3. *(a price)* heruntersetzen [hɛ'rʊntɛzɛtsn̩] +haben ◊ *Könnten Sie den Preis etwas heruntersetzen?* knock sb down to sth jdn auf etw. [acc] herunterhandeln [aɔf ... hɛ,rʊntəhandl̩n] +haben ◊ *Ich konnte ihn auf 500 Euro herunterhandeln.*

• **knock off** [phras v] 1. *(of a price)* knock sth off sth etw. um etw. reduzieren [ʊm ... redu,tsiːrən] <reduziert, reduzierte, hat reduziert> ◊ *etw. um 20 Euro reduzieren* knock off jdm etw. vom Preis nachlassen [fɔm ,praɛs 'naːxlasn̩] <lässt nach, ließ nach, hat nachgelassen> I like the coat. Could you knock off 20 pounds? **Der Mantel gefällt mir. Könnten Sie mir 20 Pfund nachlassen?** 2. *(off a time span)* knock sth off sth etw. um etw. verbessern [ʊm ... fɛ,bɛsɐn] <verbessert, verbesserte, hat verbessert> ◊ *Die Läuferin hat ihre Bestzeit um eine halbe Sekunde verbessert.* 3. *(stop working)* Feierabend machen ['faɛɐ|aːbmt maxn̩] +haben (fam) knock off sth mit etw. aufhören [mɪt ... ,aɔfhøːrən] +haben 4. *(kill)* um die Ecke bringen [ʊm diː 'ɛkə brɪŋən] <bringt, brachte, hat gebracht>

(fam)
• **knock out** [phras v] **1.** *(make unconscious)* bewusstlos machen [bəˈvʊstloːs maxn̩] +*haben* ◊ *Der Sturz auf den Hinterkopf hatte sie kurzzeitig bewusstlos gemacht.; (in boxing)* k. o. schlagen [kaːˈʔoː ʃlaːɡn̩] <schlägt, schlug, hat geschlagen> ◊ *Er schlug ihn in der ersten Runde k. o.* **2.** *(from a competition)* knock sb out of sth jdn aus etw. werfen [aʊs ... vɛˈɐ̯fn̩] <wirft, warf, hat geworfen> ◊ *Die Mannschaft wurde schon bald aus dem Rennen geworfen.* **3.** *(destroy)* zerstören [tsɛˈʃtøːrən] <zerstört, zerstörte, hat zerstört> +*haben* ◊ *Bei einem Angriff wurden die Telefonleitungen zerstört.* **4.** *(impress, upset)* umhauen [ˈʊmhaʊ̯ən] <haut um, haute um, hat umgehauen> *(fam)* ◊ *Die Nachricht hat ihn umgehauen.*
• **knock up** [phras v] *(in the UK: produce quickly)* zusammenschustern [tsuˈzamənʃuːstɐn] +*haben* *(fam)* ◊ *eine Website zusammenschustern; (a meal)* zaubern [ˈtsaʊ̯bɐn] +*haben* ◊ *eine Mahlzeit zaubern*
knot¹ [noun] *(tied string, lump, hairstyle, speed unit)* Knoten [ˈknoːtn̩] der <-s, -> ◊ *In der Schnur/ihrem Haar waren Knoten.* ♦ *Sie machte einen doppelten Knoten.*
knot² [verb] **1.** *(tie)* knot sth einen Knoten in etw. [acc] machen [aɪnən ˈknoːtn̩ ɪn ... maxn̩] +*haben* ◊ *Sie machte einen Knoten in die Schnur.* **2.** *(become tangled)* sich verheddern [fɛˈhɛdɐn] <verheddert sich, verhedderte sich, hat sich verheddert> ◊ *Die Schnur hat sich verheddert.*
know [verb] **1.** *(be aware, certain of sth)* wissen [ˈvɪsn̩] <weiß, wusste, hat gewusst> *no passive* ◊ *Sie weiß recht viel.* ♦ *„Margit ist schwanger.“ — „Ich weiß.“* know sth for sure etw. ganz sicher wissen know sth from experience etw. aus Erfahrung wissen **2.** *(be familiar with, have knowledge of)* kennen [ˈkɛnən] <kennt, kannte, hat gekannt> *no passive* ◊ *Sie kennt ein gutes Lokal in der Altstadt.* ♦ *Kennst du diesen Autor? ♦ Der Täter kannte keine Gnade.; (experience)* know sb (to) do sth erleben, dass jd etw. tut [ɛˈleːbm̩ das] <erlebt, erlebte, hat erlebt> I've never known her tell a joke. Ich habe noch nie erlebt, dass sie einen Witz erzählt. **3.** *(master, be able to do sth)* können [ˈkœnən] <kann, konnte, hat gekonnt> ◊ *Kannst du Karate? ♦ Sie kann das Gedicht schon auswendig.* **4.** *(recognize)* erkennen

[ɛˈkɛnən] <erkennt, erkannte, hat erkannt> ◊ *Ich hätte ihn überall erkannt.* know sb by their voice jdn an der Stimme erkennen
knowing → **know** [adj] vielsagend [ˈfiːlzaːɡn̩t] ◊ *ein vielsagender Blick ♦ Sein Gesichtsausdruck war vielsagend.*
knowingly [adv] **1.** *(consciously)* wissentlich [ˈvɪsn̩tlɪç] *no comp/superl* ◊ *Er hat wissentlich gegen das Gesetz verstoßen.* **2.** *(in a way that shows you have knowledge of sth)* vielsagend [ˈfiːlzaːɡn̩t] ◊ *Sie lächelte vielsagend.*
knowledge [noun] **1.** *(about a particular subject)* Kenntnis [ˈkɛntnɪs] die <-, -se> *most pl* knowledge of/about sth Kenntnisse ... [gen] ◊ *Kenntnisse der Mathematik* knowledge of a field Kenntnisse auf einem Gebiet knowledge of a language/languages Sprachkenntnisse [ˈʃpraːxkɛntnɪsə] die <-> *pl* **2.** *(awareness)* Wissen [ˈvɪsn̩] das <-s> *no pl* ◊ *jedes Wissen von etw. abstreiten* to my knowledge meines Wissens have no knowledge of sth von etw. nichts wissen [fɔn ... nɪçts ˈvɪsn̩] <weiß, wusste, hat gewusst> have no knowledge that nicht wissen, dass not to my knowledge nicht dass ich wüsste ◉ to the best of your knowledge nach bestem Wissen und Gewissen
knowledgeable [adj] gebildet [ɡəˈbɪldət] ◊ *ein gebildeter Mensch ♦ Sie ist sehr gebildet.* be knowledgeable about sth viel über etw. [acc] wissen [ˌfiːl yːbɐ ... ˌvɪsn̩] <weiß, wusste, hat gewusst>
known → **know** [adj] bekannt [bəˈkant] <bekannter, am bekanntesten> ◊ *die bekannten Tatsachen ♦ Er ist vor allem als Maler bekannt.* be known to be sth als etw. bekannt sein ◊ *Diese Firma ist als sehr zuverlässig bekannt.* sth is known to do sth es ist bekannt, dass etw. tut ◊ *Es ist bekannt, dass das Medikament starke Nebenwirkungen hat.* sb is known to do sth jd ist bekannt dafür, dass er etw. tut
knuckle [noun] **1.** *(of the finger)* Fingerknöchel [ˈfɪŋknœçl̩] der <-s, -> ◊ *Er klopfte mit dem Fingerknöchel gegen das Holz.* **2.** *(meat)* Hachse [ˈhaksə] die <-, -n> knuckle of pork Schweinshachse [ˈʃvaɪnshaksə]
Koran [noun] Koran [koˈraːn] der <-s> *no pl* ◊ *im Koran lesen*
kph km/h [kaːˈʔɛmˈhaː] ◊ *Er fuhr 53 km/h.*

L

l, L (noun) l, L [ɛl] das <–(s), –(s)> ◊ *Dieses Wort wird mit einem kleinen l/großen L geschrieben.* ♦ *L wie Ludwig*

lab (noun) Labor [la'boːɐ̯] das <–s, –s or –e> ◊ *Experimente im Labor machen*

label[1] (noun) **1.** *(small piece of paper or fabric, description of sb)* Etikett [eti'kɛt] das <–(e)s, –e(n)> ◊ *Waren mit einem Etikett versehen* ♦ *Er wehrt sich gegen das Etikett des Intellektuellen.; (on luggage)* Anhänger ['anhɛŋɐ] der <–s, –> **2.** *(record company)* Label ['leːbl̩] das <–s, –> **3.** *(fashion company)* Modefirma ['moːdəˌfɪrmaː] die <–, Modefirmen> ◊ *die Modefirma Chanel; (clothing)* designer labels Designermode [di'zaɛ̯nemoːdə] die <–, –n> *most sing*

label[2] (verb) etikettieren [etikɛ'tiːrən] <etikettiert, etikettierte, hat etikettiert> ◊ *Waren etikettieren* label sb/sth (as) sth jdm/etw. als etw. etikettieren

labor → labour[1], labour[2]

laboratory (noun) Labor [la'boːɐ̯] das <–s, –s or –e> ◊ *Der Fund wird im Labor eingehend untersucht.*

Labor Day (noun) Tag der Arbeit [ˌtaːk deːɐ̯ 'arbaɛ̯t] der <–(e)s> *no pl*

laborious(ly) (adj, adv) **1.** *(arduous(ly))* mühsam ['myːzaːm] ◊ *Diese Arbeit ist sehr mühsam.* ♦ *ein mühsamer Prozess* ♦ *Mühsam rückte er den Sessel an den Kamin.* **2.** *(slow(ly))* umständlich ['ʊmʃtɛntlɪç] ◊ *umständliche Vorbereitungen* ♦ *Die Methode ist umständlich und langsam.* ♦ *Umständlich erklärte er mir den Weg zum Bahnhof.*

labor union (noun) Gewerkschaft [gə'vɛrkʃaft] die <–, –en>

labour[1], labor (noun) **1.** *(workers)* Arbeitskräfte ['arbaɛ̯tskrɛftə] die <–> *pl* ◊ *billige/ungelernte Arbeitskräfte; (union of workers)* Arbeitnehmervertretung ['arbaɛ̯tnemefetreˌtʊŋ] die <–, –en> **2.** *(work)* Arbeit ['arbaɛ̯t] die <–, –en> cost of labour Arbeitskosten ['arbaɛ̯tskɔstn̩] das <–> *only pl* **3.** *(when giving birth)* Wehen ['veːən] die <–> *pl* be in labour in den Wehen liegen go into labour Wehen bekommen

labour[2], labor (verb) Schwerarbeit verrichten ['ʃveːɐ̯ˌarbaɛ̯t fɛrɪçtn̩] <verrichtet, verichtete, hat verrichtet> ◊ *Sie haben in den Kohlebergwerken Schwerarbeit verrichtet.*

• **labour under** (phras v) labour under sth **1.** *(struggle with)* mit etw. zu kämpfen haben [mɪt ... tsuː ˌkɛmpfn̩ haːbm̩] +haben ◊ *Wir hatten oft mit Schwierigkeiten zu kämpfen.* **2.** *(a wrong idea)* sich einer Sache [dat] hingeben ['hɪŋɡeːbm̩] <gibt sich hin, gab sich hin, hat sich hingegeben> ◊ *Du gibst dich einer Illusion hin.*

Labour[1] (noun) die Labour Party [diː 'leːbɐ ˌpaːrtiː] <–> *no pl* ◊ *Welche Politik befolgt die Labour Party?*

Labour[2] (noun) Labour-... ['leːbɐ] Labour government Labour-Regierung ['leːbɐɡiˌriːrʊŋ] die <–, –en> Labour voter Labour-Wähler ['leːbɐˌvɛːlɐ] der <–s, –> ♀Labour-Wählerin ['leːbɐˌvɛːlərɪn] die

labourer (noun) Hilfsarbeiter ['hɪlfsˌarbaɛ̯tɐ] der <–s, –> ♀Hilfsarbeiterin ['hɪlfsˌarˌbaɛ̯tərɪn] die <–, –nen>

lace[1] (noun) Spitze ['ʃpɪtsə] die <–, –n> ◊ *eine mit Spitzen besetzte Tischdecke*

lace[2] (verb) **1.** *(tie up)* schnüren ['ʃnyːrən] +haben ◊ *Er schnürte sich* [dat] *die Schuhe.* **2.** *(a drink)* lace sth with sth etw. mit etw. versetzen [mɪt ... fɛtsɛtsn̩] <versetzt, versetzte, hat versetzt> ◊ *ein Getränk mit Whisky/Drogen versetzen*

lack[1] (noun) Mangel ['maŋl̩] der <–s> *no pl* ◊ *der Mangel an qualifiziertem Personal* ♦ *Er wurde aus Mangel an Beweisen freigesprochen.*

lack[2] (verb) sb/sth lacks sth jdm/etw. fehlt es an etw. [dat] ['feːlt ɛs an] +haben ◊ *Ihnen fehlt es am nötigen Ernst.*

lacking (adj) **1.** *(absent)* be lacking fehlen ['feːlən] +haben ◊ *Die Sicherheitshinweise fehlen.* lacking in sth arm an etw. [dat] ['arm an] <ärmer, am ärmsten> ◊ *ein an echten Höhepunkten armes Finale* ♦ *Seine Ernährung ist arm an Vitaminen.* **2.** *(inadequate)* be found lacking sich als ungeeignet erweisen [als 'ʊŋɡəˌaɛ̯ɡnət ɛvaɛ̯zn̩] <erweist sich, erwies sich, hat sich erwiesen> ◊ *Der Kandidat erwies sich als ungeeignet.*

lacquer[1] (noun) Lack [lak] der <–(e)s, –e> ◊ *Lack auf etw.* [acc] *auftragen*

lacquer[2] (verb) lackieren [la'kiːrən] <lackiert, lackierte, hat lackiert> ◊ *einen Tisch lackieren*

lad (noun) Bursche ['bʊrʃə] der <–n, –n> *(also oldf)*

ladder (noun) **1.** *(for climbing)* Leiter ['laɛ̯tɐ] die <–, –n> ◊ *auf eine Leiter steigen* ladder of success Erfolgsleiter [e'fɔlksˌlaɛ̯tɐ] **2.** *(in the UK: in stockings)* Laufmasche ['laɛ̯fmaʃə] die <–, –n>

Ladies (noun) Damentoilette ['daːməntɔaˌlɛta] die <–, –n> ◊ *Wo ist bitte die Damentoilette?*

ladies room → Ladies

ladle (noun) Kelle ['kɛlə] die <–, –n> ◊ *ein Kelle Suppe*

lady (noun) Dame ['daːmə] die <–, –n> ◊ *Kennst du diese Dame?* ♦ *Sehr geehrte Damen und Herren!*

Lady (noun) Lady ['leːdiː] die <–, –s> ◊ *Lady Windermere*

lag (verb) **1.** *(be less successful)* zurückliegen [tsu'rʏkliːɡn̩] <liegt zurück, lag zurück, hat zurückgelegen> ◊ *Die Partei liegt weit hinter den anderen zurück.* **2.** *(walk more slowly)* lag behind zurückbleiben [tsu'rʏkblaɛ̯bm̩] <bleibt zurück, blieb zurück, ist zurückgeblieben> ◊ *Er blieb hinter den anderen zurück.*

lager (noun) Lagerbier ['laːɡebiːɐ̯] das <–(e)s, –e> Two pints of lager, please! Zwei Helle, bitte!

laid-back (adj) gelassen [gə'lasn̩] ◊ *eine gelassene Art haben* ♦ *Er ist ziemlich gelassen.*

lair (noun) Unterschlupf ['ʊntɐʃlʊpf] der <–(e)s, –e> *most sing* ◊ *der Unterschlupf eines Verbrechers/Tieres* wolf's lair Wolfshöhle ['vɔlfshøːlə] die <–, –n>

lake (noun) See [zeː] der <–s, –n> ◊ *im See baden*

lamb [noun] Lamm [lam] das <-(e)s, Lämmer>
lame [adj] lahm [laːm] *(also pej)* ◊ *Das Pferd ist lahm.*
♦ *eine lahme Entschuldigung*

lament[1] [noun] *(expression of sadness)* Klage ['klaːgə] die <-, -n> ◊ *die Klage einer Mutter über den Tod ihres Kindes; (song, poem)* Klagelied ['klaːgəliːt] das <-(e)s, Klagelieder>

lament[2] [verb] *(express sadness)* klagen ['klaːgn̩] +haben *(lofty)* ◊ *Sie weinte und klagte.; (mourn, complain)* lament sth etw. beklagen [bəˈklaːgn̩] <beklagt, beklagte, hat beklagt> *(lofty)* ◊ *Er beklagte den Tod seiner Eltern.*

lamp [noun] Lampe ['lampə] die <-, -n> ◊ *die Lampe einschalten/ausschalten* oil lamp Öllampe ['øːllampə] infrared lamp Infrarotlampe [ɪnfraˈroːtlampə]

land[1] [noun] **1.** *(for agriculture, region, opposite of sea)* Land [lant] das <-(e)s, Länder> ◊ *ein Stück Land* ♦ *fruchtbares Land* ♦ *Das Land hier ist ziemlich flach.* ♦ *Meeresschildkröten legen ihre Eier an Land ab.; (property)* lands Ländereien [lɛndəˈraɛən] die <-> pl **2.** *(federal state in Germany or Austria)* Land Bundesland ['bʊndəslant] das <-(e)s, Bundesländer> ◊ *die neuen/alten Bundesländer* ♦ *das Bundesland Salzburg* ⊛ find out how the land lies herausfinden, wie die Dinge liegen

land[2] [verb] **1.** *(arrive, come down, end up)* landen ['landn̩] <landet, landete, hat/ist gelandet> *transitive use +haben/intransitive use +sein* ◊ *Der Pilot hat das Flugzeug sicher gelandet.* ♦ *Sie müssten jetzt schon in London gelandet sein.* ♦ *Sie stolperte und landete im Schnee.; (go ashore)* an Land gehen [an 'lant geːən] <geht, ging, ist gegangen> **2.** *(also fig) (bring sb/sth somewhere)* land sb/sth in sth jdn/etw. irgendwohin bringen ['brɪŋən] <bringt, brachte, hat gebracht> ◊ *Die Fähre hat uns sicher nach Calais gebracht.* land sb in trouble jdn in Schwierigkeiten bringen **3.** *(esp fig) (get, catch)* an Land ziehen [an 'lant tsiːən] <zieht, zog, hat gezogen> *(also fam)* ◊ *einen Fisch/tollen Job an Land ziehen* **4.** land a punch on sb's sth jdm eins auf etw. [acc] geben [aɛns aof ... geːbm̩] <gibt, gab, hat gegeben> *(fam)* ◊ *jdm eins auf die Nase geben* ⊛ land sb in it jdn reinreißen *(fam)* • **land with** [phras v] land sb with sth jdm etw. aufhalsen ['aofhalzn̩] +haben *(fam)* ◊ *Immer wird mir die unangenehme Arbeit aufgehalst!*

landfill [noun] landfill (site) Deponie [depoˈniː] die <-, -n> ◊ *Müll auf Deponien lagern*

landing [noun] **1.** *(of a plane, troops)* Landung ['landʊŋ] die <-, -en> ◊ *während der Landung angeschnallt bleiben* ♦ *die Landung der Alliierten* emergency landing Notlandung ['noːtlandʊŋ] **2.** *(of stairs)* Absatz ['apzats] der <-es, Absätze> ◊ *Ich stand auf dem untersten Absatz der Treppe.* **3.** *(place to disembark)* Anlegestelle ['anleːgəʃtɛlə] die <-, -n> ◊ *ein Boot an der Anlegestelle festmachen*

landlady [noun] **1.** *(of a rented accommodation)* Vermieterin [fɛˈmiːtərɪn] die <-, -nen> **2.** *(in the UK: of a pub)* Wirtin ['vɪrtɪn] die <-, -nen>

landline [noun] **1.** *(system)* Festnetz ['fɛstnɛts] das <-es, -e> most sing ◊ *aus dem Festnetz telefonieren* **2.** *(telephone set)* Festnetztelefon ['fɛstnɛtsˌteːləfoːn] das <-s, -e>

landlord [noun] **1.** *(of a rented accommodation)* Vermieter [fɛˈmiːtɐ] der <-s, -> **2.** *(in the UK: of a*

pub) Wirt [vɪrt] der <-(e)s, -e> ◊ *Der Wirt brachte das Bier.*

landmark [noun] **1.** *(striking building or object)* Wahrzeichen ['vaːɐ̯tsaɛçn̩] das <-s, -> ◊ *Das Wahrzeichen Kölns ist der berühmte Dom.* **2.** *(influential event, work of art)* Meilenstein ['maɛlənʃtaɛn] der <-(e)s, -e> ◊ *ein Meilenstein der Kunstgeschichte*

landowner [noun] Grundbesitzer ['grʊntbəzɪtsɐ] der <-s, -> ♀Grundbesitzerin ['grʊntbəzɪtsərɪn] die <-, -nen>; *(owning a great deal of land)* Großgrundbesitzer ['groːsgrʊntbəˌzɪtsɐ]

land registry [noun] Grundbuchamt ['grʊntbuːxˌamt] das <-(e)s> no pl

landscape [noun] **1.** *(area, situation, painting)* Landschaft ['lantʃaft] die <-, -en> ◊ *Der Ackerbau veränderte die Landschaft.* ♦ *die politische Landschaft Deutschlands* **2.** *(way of describing a piece of paper)* Querformat ['kveːɐ̯foˌmaːt] das <-(e)s> no pl ◊ *eine Seite im Querformat ausdrucken*

landslide [noun] Erdrutsch ['eːɐ̯trʊtʃ] der <-(e)s, -e> ◊ *ein Erdrutsch in den Anden*

lane [noun] **1.** *(narrow road)* (country) lane Landstraße ['lantʃtraːsə] die <-, -n>; *(in a town)* Gasse ['gasə] die <-, -n> **2.** *(part of a road)* Spur [ʃpuːɐ̯] die <-, -en> ◊ *von der linken auf die rechte Spur wechseln* bus lane Busspur ['bʊsʃpuːɐ̯] fast lane Überholspur [ybɐˈhoːlʃpuːɐ̯] **3.** SPORT *(of a race track, swimming pool)* Bahn [baːn] die <-, -en> ◊ *Der deutsche Läufer läuft auf Bahn drei.* **4.** *(route)* shipping lane Schifffahrtsweg ['ʃɪfaːɐ̯tsveːk] der <-(e)s, -e> air lane Luftverkehrsstraße ['lʊftfɛɐ̯keːɐ̯sʃtraːsə]

language [noun] Sprache ['ʃpraːxə] die <-, -n> ◊ *Wie viele Sprachen sprichst du?* ♦ *die Sprache der Musik* ♦ *ein Text in einfacher/gehobener Sprache* body language Körpersprache ['kœrpɐʃpraːxə] foreign language Fremdsprache ['frɛmtʃpraːxə] native/first language Muttersprache ['mʊtɐʃpraːxə] written language Schriftsprache ['ʃrɪftʃpraːxə] strong language Kraftausdrücke ['kraftˌaosdrʏkə] die <-> pl; *(in compound ns)* language ... Sprach... [ʃpraːx] language barrier Sprachbarriere ['ʃpraːxbaˌrɪɛːrə] die <-, -n> language skills Sprachkenntnisse ['ʃpraːxkɛntnɪsə] die <-> pl

lap [noun] **1.** *(part of your body)* Schoß [ʃoːs] der <-es, Schöße> most sing ◊ *Sie nahm das Kind auf den Schoß.* **2.** *(part of a course, circuit)* Runde ['rʊndə] die <-, -n> ◊ *ein paar Runden mit dem Testauto fahren*

lapse[1] [noun] **1.** *(slip, temporary failure)* Versehen [fɛˈzeːən] das <-s, -> ◊ *sich für ein Versehen entschuldigen* lapse of control Kontrollverlust [kɔnˈtrɔlfɛlʊst] der <-(e)s, -e> lapse in concentration Konzentrationsmangel [kɔntsɛntraˈtsjoːnsmaŋl̩] der <-s> no pl memory lapse Gedächtnislücke [gəˈdɛçtnɪslʏkə] die <-, -n> security lapse Sicherheitslücke ['zɪçɐhaɛtslʏkə] a lapse into strong language peinliche sprachliche Entgleisung [aɛnə ʃpraːxlɪçə ɛntˈglaɛzʊŋ] die <-, -en> ◊ *eine peinliche sprachliche Entgleisung* **2.** *(of time)* Zeitraum ['tsaɛtraom] der <-(e)s, Zeiträume> ◊ *ein Zeitraum von zehn Jahren* There was a lapse of one year before ... Ein Jahr verging, bevor ... lapse in the conversation Gesprächspause [gəˈʃprɛːçspaozə] die <-, -n>

lapse[2] [verb] **1.** *(conversation)* verstummen [fɛˈʃtʊmən]

<verstummt, verstummte, ist verstummt> ◊ *Plötzlich verstummte unser Gespräch.* **2.** *(entitlement, contract, treaty)* verfallen [fɛ'falən] <verfällt, verfiel, ist verfallen> ◊ *Der Anspruch verfällt nach 2 Jahren.*
• **lapse into** [phras v] lapse into sth in etw. [acc] verfallen [ɪn ... fɛfalən] <verfällt, verfiel, ist verfallen> ◊ *in Dialekt/seine alten Gewohnheiten verfallen* lapse into a trance in Trance fallen [ɪn trɑːs falən] <fällt, fiel, ist gefallen>

lap up [verb] lap sth up **1.** *(with your tongue)* etw. auflecken ['aoflɛkn̩] +haben ◊ *Die Katze leckte die Milch auf.* **2.** lap up sb's words/stories/teachings an jds Lippen hängen [an ... 'lɪpm̩ hɛŋən] <hängt, hing, hat gehangen> ◊ *Sie hingen an den Lippen ihres Gurus.*

larder [noun] Speisekammer ['ʃpaezəkameə] die <–, –n>

large [adj] *(big)* groß [groːs] <größer, am größten> ◊ *ein großes Haus* ♦ *Die Schuhe sind mir zu groß.*; *(person)* kräftig ['krɛftɪç] ◊ *Sie ist ziemlich kräftig.* ♦ *ein kräftiger Mann*
⊛ **at large 1.** *(as a whole)* insgesamt the public at large die breite Öffentlichkeit **2.** *(roaming free)* in Freiheit

largely [adv] größtenteils ['grøːstn̩taels] no comp/superl ◊ *Die Umstellung erfolgte größtenteils reibungslos.*

large-scale [adj] **1.** *(in large numbers)* massenhaft ['masn̩haft] no comp/superl, mostly before ns ◊ *der massenhafte Abbau von Arbeitsplätzen; (over a large area)* großflächig ['groːsflɛçɪç] ◊ *großflächige Bebauung* **2.** *(map)* in großem Maßstab [ɪn ˌgroːsəm 'maːsʃtaːp] ◊ *eine Landkarte in großem Maßstab*

laser [noun] Laser ['leːze] der <–s, –> ◊ *mit (einem) Laser operieren* laser beam Laserstrahl ['leːzeʃtraːl] der <–(e)s, –en>

lash [verb] **1.** *(hit, strike)* schlagen ['ʃlaːgn̩] <schlägt, schlug, hat geschlagen> ◊ *einen Gefangenen (mit einem Stock) schlagen* sth lashes sth etw. schlägt gegen etw. ◊ *Die Äste schlugen gegen die Fensterläden.* sth lashes at sb's face etw. schlägt jdm ins Gesicht; *(with a whip)* auspeitschen ['aospaetʃn̩] +haben ◊ *Die Verbrecher wurden öffentlich ausgepeitscht.; (rain, tail)* peitschen ['paetʃn̩] +haben/with a word expressing direction of movement +sein lash against sth gegen etw. peitschen ◊ *Der Regen ist gegen das Fenster gepeitscht.* lash its tail mit dem Schwanz peitschen The lion's tail lashed. Der Schwanz des Löwen peitschte hin und her. **2.** *(tie, secure)* festbinden ['fɛstbɪndn̩] <bindet fest, band fest, hat festgebunden> lash sth to sth etw. an etw. [dat] festbinden ◊ *ein Boot an einem Steg festbinden* lash together zusammenbinden [tsu'zamənbɪndn̩] <bindet zusammen, band zusammen, hat zusammengebunden> **3.** *(criticize)* abkanzeln ['apkantsln̩] +haben **4.** *(stir up emotion)* lash sb into sth jdn zu etw. anstacheln [tsu: ...ˌanʃtaxln̩] +haben ◊ *jdn zum Hass anstacheln*
• **lash out** [phras v] **1.** *(attack)* lash out at sb/sth jdn/etw. attackieren [ata'kiːrən] <attackiert, attackierte, hat attackiert> ◊ *Plötzlich attackierte er sie.* **2.** *(in the UK: spend a lot)* tief in die Tasche greifen [ˌtiːf ɪn diː 'tafə graefn̩] <greift, griff, hat gegriffen>; *(spend a certain amount)* lash out sth etw. lockermachen ['lokəmaxn̩] +haben *(fam)* ◊ *Ich machte 100 Euro für die Party locker.*

lass [noun] Mädchen ['mɛːtçən] das <–s, –> ◊ *Sie ist ein nettes Mädchen.*

last¹ [noun] the last of ... der/die/das letzte ... [deːɐ/diː/das 'lɛtstə] no comp/superl, only before ns ◊ *der letzte Mohikaner* ♦ *Der letzte Gast ist gegangen.*

> In German, 'the last of' is followed by singular not plural nouns. Thus 'the last of the Mohicans' is simply 'the last Mohican' — *der letzte Mohikaner.*

last² [adj] letzte ['lɛtstə] no comp/superl, only before ns <ein letzter ..., eine letzte ..., ein letztes ...> ◊ *im letzten Augenblick* ♦ *Während der letzten Monate war er krank.* last but one vorletzte ['foːɐlɛtstə] no comp/superl, only before ns ◊ *ihr vorletzter Auftritt in Deutschland* ... before last vorletzten/vorletzte/ vorletztes ... ◊ *Vorletztes Jahr waren wir in Spanien.*
⊛ **the last one 1.** *(last person)* der/die Letzte ◊ *Sie war die Letzte, die ging.* **2.** *(the previous one)* der/die/das letzte ◊ *Die heutige Sendung war so gut wie die letzte.*

last³ [adv] zuletzt [tsu'lɛtst] ◊ *Das Bad putze ich zuletzt.* ♦ *Wann warst du zuletzt im Urlaub?* next to last als Vorletzter [als 'foːɐlɛtste] als Vorletzte [als 'foːɐlɛtstə] als Vorletztes [als 'foːɐlɛtstəs] ◊ *Sie ging als Vorletzte durchs Ziel.*
⊛ **last but not least** nicht zuletzt ◊ *Nicht zuletzt möchte ich mich bei meinen Fans bedanken.*

last⁴ [verb] **1.** *(go on)* dauern ['daoen] +haben ◊ *Der Film dauert fast drei Stunden.* **2.** *(continue to be available, be enough)* reichen ['raeçn̩] +haben ◊ *Wie lange reichen die Vorräte noch?* sth lasts sb ... jd kommt ... mit etw. aus [komt ... mɪt ... aos] <kam aus, ist ausgekommen> ◊ *Mit dem Geld komme ich höchstens eine Woche aus.* **3.** *(survive)* durchhalten ['dʊɐçhaltn̩] <hält durch, hielt durch, hat durchgehalten> ◊ *Wie lange kann man ohne Wasser durchhalten?; (appliance, plant)* halten ['haltn̩] <hält, hielt, hat gehalten> ◊ *Die Waschmaschine wird nicht mehr lange halten.* ♦ *Schnittblumen halten oft nicht lange.*

last⁵ [det] letzten ['lɛtstn̩] letzte ['lɛtstə] letztes ['lɛtstəs] only acc ◊ *Letzte Nacht war es sehr kalt.* ♦ *Letztes Mal es mir besser gefallen.*

last⁶ [pron] the last **1.** *(referring to a noun)* der/die/das letzte [deːɐ/diː/das 'lɛtstə] ◊ *Dieser Wein ist besser als der letzte.* be the last to do sth etw. als Letzter tun [als 'lɛtste] She was the last to leave. Sie ist als Letzte gegangen. **2.** *(referring to sth that has been said or done before)* das Letzte [das 'lɛtstə] <–n> no pl ◊ *Das war das Letzte, was ich je von ihr gehört habe.*

last name [noun] Nachname ['naːxnaːmə] der <–ns, –n>

latch [noun] Riegel ['riːgl̩] der <–s, –>

latch on [verb] schalten ['ʃaltn̩] <schaltet, schaltete, hat geschaltet> *(fam)* ◊ *Er hat sofort geschaltet und eine gute Antwort gegeben.*

latch onto [verb] **1.** *(become very interested)* latch onto sth sich auf etw. [acc] stürzen [aof ... ʃtʏɐtsn̩] +haben *(fam)* ◊ *Die Medien haben sich gleich auf die Story gestürzt.* **2.** *(go somewhere with sb)* latch onto sb sich an jdn hängen [an ... hɛŋən] +haben *(fam)* ◊ *Sie haben sich einfach an uns gehängt.*

late¹ [adj] **1.** *(not on time)* zu spät [tsu: 'ʃpɛːt] be (too) late zu spät kommen He was even later than you. Er kam noch später als du. be late for sth zu etw.

zu spät kommen ◊ *Er kommt immer zu spät zur Arbeit.* be late with sth mit etw. zu spät dran sein ◊ *Ich bin schon wieder mit der Miete zu spät dran.*; *(payments, trains)* verspätet [fɛ'ʃpɛːtət] *no comp/ superl, mostly before ns* ◊ *verspätete Zahlungen/Züge* **2.** *(near the end of sth)* spät [ʃpɛːt] <später, am spätesten> ◊ *Es ist schon ziemlich spät.* ♦ *seine späten Werke* ♦ *Das ist der späteste Abgabetermin, den ich Ihnen anbieten kann.* **3.** *(dead)* verstorben [fɛ'ʃtɔ'bm̩] *no comp/superl* ◊ *mein verstorbener Vater* **4.** *(very recent)* aktuell [aktu'ɛl] ◊ *eine aktuelle Meldung*

late² [adv] *(after the usual time, near the end of sth)* spät [ʃpɛːt] <später, am spätesten> ◊ *So spät kannst du ihn nicht mehr anrufen.* ♦ *Das mache ich später.* not do sth until late etw. erst sehr spät tun We won't be arriving until very late. Wir kommen erst sehr spät an. late in July Ende Juli [ˌɛndə 'juːliː] late in the year Ende des Jahres run late sich verspäten [fɛ'ʃpɛːtn̩] <verspätet sich, verspätete sich, hat sich verspätet>

⊛ as late as noch ◊ *Noch 1920 gab es dort 70 Prozent Analphabeten.* of late in letzter Zeit

latecomer [noun] Nachzügler ['naːxtsyːglɐ] der <-s, -> ♀Nachzüglerin ['naːxtsyːglərɪn] die <-, -nen> ◊ *Wir müssen noch auf ein paar Nachzügler warten.*

lately [adv] **1.** *(recently)* kürzlich ['kʏɐ̯tslɪç] *no comp/ superl* ◊ *eine kürzlich erschienene Studie* ♦ *Ich habe ihn erst kürzlich getroffen.* **2.** *(nowadays)* neuerdings ['nɔɡə'dɪŋs] *no comp/superl* ◊ *Diese Frage ist neuerdings wieder ganz aktuell.*

later¹ [adj] **1.** *(future)* spätere ['ʃpɛːtərə] *only before ns* <ein späterer …, eine spätere …, ein späteres …> ◊ *der spätere Besitzer* ♦ *in späteren Jahren* ♦ *zu einem späteren Zeitpunkt* **2.** *(newer, more recent)* neuere ['nɔɡərə] *only before ns* <ein neuerer …, eine neuere …, ein neueres …> ◊ *Die neuere Ausgabe des Lexikons ist viel besser.* ♦ *eine neuere Version der Software*

later² [adv] **1.** *(after sth)* danach [da'naːx] ◊ *Er ist verschwunden und zwei Tage danach wieder aufgetaucht.* **2.** *(in the future, not now)* later (on) nachher [naːx'heːɐ̯] ◊ *„Machst du das bitte?"* — *„Jetzt nicht, vielleicht nachher."*

⊛ no/not later than spätestens

latest *superl* of late¹ [adj] neuste ['nɔɡstə] neueste ['nɔɡəstə] *only before ns* ◊ *sein neuster Roman* ♦ *die neuesten Arbeitslosenzahlen* the latest das Neueste ◊ *das Neueste auf dem Markt*

⊛ at the latest spätestens

lather [noun] Schaum [ʃaɔm] der <-(e)s, Schäume> *most sing* ◊ *Auf dem Wasser hat sich Schaum gebildet.*

Latin¹ [noun] **1.** *(person)* Romane [ro'maːnə] der <-n, -n> ♀Romanin [ro'maːnɪn] die <-, -nen> → **German¹** 1. **2.** *(language)* Latein [la'taen] das <-(s)> *no pl* → **German¹** 2.

Latin² [adj] **1.** *(referring to the language of the Romans)* lateinisch [la'taenɪʃ] *mostly before ns* ◊ *lateinische Schrift* → **German²** 2. **2.** *(southern, Mediterranean)* südländisch ['zyːtlɛndɪʃ] *mostly before ns* ◊ *ein südländischer Typ*

Latin America [noun] Lateinamerika [la'taen|a,me:rika:] das <-s> *article only in combination with attribute, no pl* → **Germany**

Latin American¹ [noun] Lateinamerikaner [la'taen|ameri,ka:nɐ] der <-s, -> ♀Lateinamerikanerin [la'taen|ameri,ka:nərɪn] die <-, -nen> → **German¹** 1.

Latin American² [adj] lateinamerikanisch [la'taen|ameri,ka:nɪʃ] *mostly before ns* → **German²**

latitude [noun] Breite ['braetə] die <-, -n> ◊ *In unseren Breiten scheint nicht oft die Sonne.*

latter¹ [adj] letztere ['lɛtstərə] *no comp/superl, only before ns* ◊ *Wir können geben oder bleiben; die letztere Möglichkeit wäre mir lieber.*

latter² [demonstr pron] the latter Letzterer ['lɛtstərɐ] Letztere ['lɛtstərə] Letzteres ['lɛtstərəs] <Letzteren, die Letzteren> ◊ *Da sind Peter und Paul; mit Letzterem gebe ich heute aus.*

Latvia [noun] Lettland ['lɛtlant] das <-s> *article only in combination with attribute, no pl* → **Germany**

Latvian¹ [noun] **1.** *(inhabitant)* Lette ['lɛtə] der <-n, -n> ♀Lettin ['lɛtɪn] die <-, -nen> → **German¹** 1. **2.** *(language)* Lettisch ['lɛtɪʃ] das <-(s)> *no pl* → **German¹** 2.

Latvian² [adj] lettisch ['lɛtɪʃ] *mostly before ns* → **German²**

laugh¹ [noun] **1.** *(laughter)* Lachen ['laxn̩] das <-s> *no pl* ◊ *ein lautes Lachen* **2.** *(fun)* Spaß [ʃpaːs] der <-es, Späße> have a good laugh viel Spaß haben for a laugh zum Spaß sth is good for a laugh, sth is a good laugh etw. macht Spaß sb is good for a laugh, sb is a good laugh mit jdm hat man Spaß

⊛ have the last laugh als Letzter lachen

laugh² [verb] lachen ['laxn̩] +*haben* ◊ *Die Kinder lachten vor Freude.* laugh at/about sth über etw. [acc] lachen ◊ *über einen Witz/sich selbst lachen* • **laugh at** [phras v] laugh at sb/sth jdn/etw. belächeln [bə'lɛçln̩] <belächelt, belächelte, hat belächelt> ◊ *einen Vorschlag als naiv belächeln*

laughter [noun] Lachen ['laxn̩] das <-s> *no pl* ◊ *ein schadenfrohes Lachen* scream with laughter schreien vor Lachen

launch¹ [noun] Start [ʃtaʁt] der <-(e)s, -s> ◊ *der Start einer Rakete/Werbekampagne*

launch² [verb] **1.** *(a missile, satellite etc.)* abschießen ['apʃiːsn̩] <schießt ab, schoss ab, hat abgeschossen> ◊ *eine Rakete abschießen* launch sth somewhere etw. irgendwohin schießen ['ʃiːsn̩] <schießt, schoss, hat geschossen> ◊ *einen Satelliten in die Umlaufbahn schießen* **2.** *(a boat)* zu Wasser lassen [tsu: 'vasə lasn̩] <lässt, ließ, hat gelassen> **3.** *(an activity)* einleiten ['aenlaetn̩] <leitet ein, leitete ein, hat eingeleitet> ◊ *eine Untersuchung/einen Angriff einleiten; (help a person)* launch sb on sth jdm zu etw. verhelfen [su... fehɛlfn̩] <verhilft, verhalf, hat verholfen> ◊ *Er hat ihm zu einer Karriere im Showgeschäft verholfen.* **4.** *(a product)* herausbringen [hɛ'ʁaosbʁɪŋən] <bringt heraus, brachte heraus, hat herausgebracht> ◊ *Die Post hat neue Sondermarken herausgebracht.*

laundry [noun] **1.** *(clothing)* Wäsche ['vɛʃə] die <-> *no pl* ◊ *Er hängte die Wäsche auf.* **2.** *(place where clothes are washed)* Wäscherei [vɛʃə'ʁae] die <-, -en> ◊ *Hemden in die Wäscherei geben*

lavatory [noun] Toilette [tɔa'lɛtə] die <-, -n> ◊ *auf die Toilette gehen* ◊ *ein Bad mit Toilette*

lavish(ly) [adj, adv] **1.** *(involving a lot of effort or money)* aufwändig ['aofvɛndɪç] ◊ *ein aufwändiges Design* ♦ *ein aufwändig saniertes Gebäude*

2. *(decoration)* reich [ʀae̯ç] ◊ *eine Fassade mit reichen Verzierungen* ♦ *Der Weihnachtsbaum war reich geschmückt.*

law [noun] **1.** *(official rule)* Gesetz [gə'zɛts] das <-es, -e> ◊ *ein neues Gesetz verabschieden* ♦ *Er hat gegen das Gesetz verstoßen.* ♦ *physikalische Gesetze* **2.** *(legal system)* Recht [ʀɛçt] das <-(e)s, -e> ◊ *Das Recht war auf ihrer Seite.* ♦ *das Recht brechen* **3.** *(subject studied at university)* Jura ['juːʀaː] *without the article* ◊ *Ich studiere Jura in Paris.* **4.** practise law als Anwalt/Anwältin arbeiten [als 'anvalt/'anvɛltɪn a'baetn] <arbeitet, arbeitete, hat gearbeitet> **5.** *(the police)* the law die Polizei [di: poli'tsae̯] <-> *no pl*

law court [noun] Gericht [gə'ʀɪçt] das <-(e)s, -e> ◊ *Ich muss morgen früh aufs Gericht.*

lawful(ly) [adj, adv] rechtmäßig ['ʀɛçtmɛːsɪç] *seldom comp/superl* ◊ *Die Verordnung ist rechtmäßig.* ♦ *eine rechtmäßige Kündigung* ♦ *etw. rechtmäßig erwerben*

law-making [adj] gesetzgebend [gə'zɛtsgeːbm̩t] *no comp/superl* ◊ *die gesetzgebende Gewalt*

lawn [noun] Rasen ['ʀaːzn̩] der <-s, -> *most sing* ◊ *den Rasen mähen*

lawnmower [noun] Rasenmäher ['ʀaːznmɛːɐ] der <-s, ->

lawsuit [noun] Prozess [pʀo'tsɛs] der <-es, -e> ◊ *Er hat den Prozess verloren.* file a lawsuit against sb einen Prozess gegen jdn anstrengen

lawyer [noun] **1.** *(person trained in legal matters)* Jurist [ju'ʀɪst] der <-en, -en> ♀Juristin [ju'ʀɪstɪn] die <-, -nen> ◊ *Er arbeitet als Jurist.* ♦ *die erfolgreiche Juristin* **2.** *(who represents people in court)* Rechtsanwalt ['ʀɛçtsʔanvalt] der <-(e)s, Rechtsanwälte> ♀Rechtsanwältin ['ʀɛçtsʔanvɛltɪn] die <-, -nen> ◊ *Er ist Rechtsanwalt.* ♦ *Sie arbeitet als Rechtsanwältin in einer Kanzlei.*

laxative [noun] Abführmittel ['apfyːɐmɪtl̩] das <-s, ->

lay¹ [adj] Laien... ['laen] lay preacher Laienprediger ['laenpʀeːdɪɡɐ] der <-s, -> ♀Laienpredigerin ['laenpʀeːdɪɡəʀɪn] die <-, -nen>

lay² [verb] **1.** *(place)* legen ['leːɡn̩] +haben ◊ *Er legte die Hemden in den Schrank.* ♦ *Sie legte mir die Hand auf die Schulter.* lay eggs Eier legen lay the table den Tisch decken [deːn 'tɪʃ dɛkn̩] +haben **2.** *(a carpet, pipes, tiles)* verlegen [fɛ'leːɡn̩] <verlegt, verlegte, hat verlegt> ◊ *Rohre verlegen*
🐦 get laid flachgelegt werden *(fam)*

• **lay aside** [phras v] **1.** *(money, objects)* beiseite legen [bae'zaetə leːɡn̩] +haben ◊ *Geld für den Urlaub beiseite legen* ♦ *Sie legte ihre Zeitung beiseite.* **2.** *(differences)* beilegen ['baeleːɡn̩] +haben ◊ *Sie haben ihren Streit endlich beigelegt.*

• **lay down** [phras v] **1.** *(put down)* lay down hinlegen ['hɪnleːɡn̩] +haben ◊ *Er legte sein Buch hin.* lay down your arms die Waffen niederlegen [di: 'vafn̩ ˌniːdeləˈɡn̩] +haben **2.** *(establish, determine)* festlegen ['fɛstleːɡn̩] +haben ◊ *Die Richtlinien wurden von der Behörde festgelegt.*

• **lay off** [phras v] **1.** *(make temporarily redundant)* vorübergehend entlassen [fo,ʀyːbegeːənt ɛnt'lasn̩] <entlässt, entließ, hat entlassen> ◊ *Er wurde vorübergehend entlassen.*; *(permanently)* entlassen [ɛnt'lasn̩] ◊ *Man hat mich entlassen.* **2.** lay off sth mit etw. aufhören [mɪt ... ˌaofhøːʀən] +haben ◊ *Hör doch mit diesem dummen Gerede auf!* lay off doing sth

aufhören, etw. zu tun ◊ *Sie sollten endlich aufhören, sich zu beklagen.*

• **lay on** [phras v] *(an event)* organisieren [ɔʀɡaniˈziːʀən] <organisiert, organisierte, hat organisiert> ◊ *Sie organisierten ein großes Fest.*

• **lay out** [phras v] **1.** *(spread out)* ausbreiten ['aosbʀaetn̩] <breitet aus, breitete aus, hat ausgebreitet> ◊ *den Stadtplan auf dem Tisch ausbreiten*; *(clothes to wear)* lay out sth etw. herauslegen [hɛ'ʀaoslɛːɡn̩] <legt heraus, legte heraus, hat herausgelegt> ◊ *Ich habe deinen Anzug für morgen herausgelegt.* **2.** *(explain)* verdeutlichen [fɛ'dɔɡtlɪçn̩] <verdeutlicht, verdeutlichte, hat verdeutlicht> ◊ *Er verdeutlichte dies mit einem Diagramm.* **3.** *(arrange)* anordnen ['anʔɔʀdnən] <ordnet an, ordnete an, hat angeordnet> ◊ *Wir sollten die Icons neu anordnen.* **4.** *(a body)* aufbahren ['aofbaːʀən] +haben ◊ *Sie wurde in der Leichenhalle aufgebahrt.*

layer [noun] Schicht [ʃɪçt] die <-, -en> ◊ *Auf dem Schrank liegt eine dicke Schicht Staub.* ♦ *eine Schicht Schlagsahne*

layout [noun] **1.** *(of objects)* Anordnung ['anʔɔʀdnʊŋ] die <-, -en> ◊ *die Anordnung der Tasten.* *(of a document)* Layout [leːˈlaot] das <-s, -s> ◊ *Das Layout der Bewerbung war miserabel.* **3.** *(of a flat, house)* Schnitt [ʃnɪt] der <-(e)s, -e> ◊ *Größe und Schnitt der Wohnung waren perfekt.*

layperson [noun] Laie ['laeə] der <-n, -n> ◊ *Auf diesem Gebiet ist meine Anwältin Laie.*

lazy(-ily) [adj, adv] faul [faol] ◊ *ein fauler Schüler* ♦ *Der Kater ist faul und träge.* ♦ *Wir lagen faul am Strand.*

lead¹ [noun] **1.** *(in a competition)* Führung ['fyːʀʊŋ] die <-, -en>; *(distance)* Vorsprung ['foːɐ̯ʃpʀʊŋ] der <-(e)s, Vorsprünge> ◊ *Sie hatte einen komfortablen Vorsprung.* **2.** FILM, THEAT, TV Hauptrolle ['haoptʀɔlə] die <-, -n> ◊ *Er bekam eine Hauptrolle.*; *(actor)* Hauptdarsteller ['haoptdaːɐ̯ʃtɛlɐ] der <-s, -> ♀Hauptdarstellerin ['haoptdaːɐ̯ˌʃtɛləʀɪn] die <-, -nen> ◊ *Die Hauptdarstellerin des Films bekommt einen Oskar.* **3.** *(piece of information)* Hinweis ['hɪnvae̯s] der <-es, -e> ◊ *Die Polizei erhielt viele Hinweise.* **4.** *(example)* Beispiel ['bae̯ʃpiːl] das <-s, -e> give a lead ein Beispiel geben [aen 'bae̯ʃpiːl ɡeːbm̩] <gibt, gab, hat gegeben> follow sb's lead jds Beispiel folgen ['bae̯ʃpiːl ˌfɔlɡn̩] +haben **5.** *(in a paper, news programme)* Aufmacher ['aofmaxɐ] der <-s, -> ◊ *der heutige Aufmacher der Tageszeitung.* **6.** *(for dogs)* Leine ['lae̯nə] die <-, -n> ◊ *einen Hund an die Leine legen/nehmen* **7.** *(for electricity)* Kabel ['kaːbl̩] das <-s, ->

lead² [noun] **1.** *(metal)* Blei [blae̯] das <-s> *no pl* ◊ *Wasserrohre aus Blei* **2.** *(of a pencil)* Mine ['miːnə] die <-, -n> ◊ *ein Bleistift mit weicher Mine*

lead³ [verb] führen ['fyːʀən] +haben ◊ *ein glückliches/ interessantes Leben führen* ♦ *Die Straße führt nach Köln.* ♦ *„Wer führt?" — „Die Bochumer, mit 3:1."* lead sb by ... gegen jdn mit ... führen ◊ *Arsenal führt gegen United mit 2:1.*

• **lead into** [phras v] → lead to 1.

• **lead on** [phras v] lead sb on jdn täuschen ['tɔɡʃn̩] +haben ◊ *Sie wurden getäuscht.*

• **lead on to, lead onto** [phras v] → lead to 1.

• **lead to** [phras v] **1.** *(result in)* lead to sth zu etw. führen [tsuː ... fyːʀən] +haben ◊ *Seine Bemerkung führte zu einer heftigen Debatte.* **2.** *(make sb think*

of sth) lead sb to sth jdn auf etw. acc bringen [aof ... brɪŋən] <bringen, brachte, hat gebracht> ◊ *Das bringt mich auf ein anderes Thema.* → lead³
• **lead up** phras v **1.** *(come before and result in sth)* lead up to sth einer Sache dat vorausgehen [fo'raosge:ən] <geht voraus, ging voraus, ist vorausgegangen> ◊ *Der Einigung waren schwierige Verhandlungen vorausgegangen.* The days leading up to the exam were very hard. Die Tage vor der Prüfung waren sehr hart. **2.** *(in a conversation etc.)* sb leads up to sth jd will auf etw. acc hinaus [vɪl aof ... hɪˌnaos] <will hinaus, wollte hinaus, hat hinausgewollt> ◊ *Ich hatte keine Ahnung, worauf er hinauswollte.*

leader noun **1.** *(person in charge)* Führer ['fy:rɐ] der <-s, -> ♀Führerin ['fy:rərɪn] die <-, -nen> ◊ *ein politischer Führer;* *(of a department, an organisation, a delegation)* Leiter ['laetɐ] der <-s, -> ♀Leiterin ['laetərɪn] die <-, -nen> **2.** *(in a paper)* Leitartikel ['laet|aˌtɪkl̩] der <-s, -> ◊ *Wer hat den Leitartikel geschrieben?* **3.** mus *(conductor)* Dirigent [diri'gɛnt] der <-en, -en> ♀Dirigentin [diri'gɛntɪn] die <-, -nen>

leadership noun **1.** *(leaders, position)* Führung ['fy:rʊŋ] die <-, -en> ◊ *die politische Führung* ♦ *Unter seiner Führung expandierte das Unternehmen.* **2.** *(quality)* Führungsqualität ['fy:rʊŋskvaliˌtɛːt] die <-, -en> ◊ *Ihre Führungsqualität ist unbestritten.*

leading → lead adj führend ['fy:rənt] ◊ *der führende Läufer* ♦ *Die Firma ist weltweit führend auf dem Gebiet der Internetsicherheit.* leading cause Hauptursache ['haopt|uːɡzaxə] die <-, -n> ◊ *Abgase sind die Hauptursache für den Anstieg der Ozonwerte.* leading part Hauptrolle ['haoptrɔlə] die <-, -n> ◊ *Wer spielt die Hauptrolle?*

leaf noun **1.** *(of a plant)* Blatt [blat] das <-(e)s, Blätter> ◊ *Im Herbst verlieren die Bäume ihre Blätter.* be in leaf grün sein ['gry:n zaen] +sein come into leaf ausschlagen ['aosʃlaːɡn̩] <schlägt aus, schlug aus, hat ausschlagen> **2.** *(of paper)* Blatt [blat] das <-(e)s, Blätter *or* -> *with expressions of quantity* pl *'Blatt'* a leaf of paper ein Blatt Papier ◊ *zehn Blatt Papier;* *(of a book)* Seite ['zaetə] die <-, -n> **3.** *(of a table)* Ausziehplatte ['aostsi:platə] die <-, -n> **4.** gold leaf Blattgold ['blatgɔlt] das <-(e)s> *no pl* silver leaf Blattsilber ['blatzɪlbɐ] das <-s> *no pl*

leaflet noun Broschüre [brɔ'ʃy:rə] die <-, -n> ◊ *eine Broschüre über das Museum*

league noun **1.** sport Liga ['li:ɡa] die <-, Ligen> ◊ *Mein Fußballverein ist in eine höhere Liga aufgestiegen.* not be in the same league as sb/sth nicht in der gleichen Liga wie jd/etw. spielen **2.** *(organization)* Bündnis ['bʏntnɪs] das <-ses, -se> ◊ *das Bündnis der arabischen Staaten*
◉ not be in the same league as sb/sth sich nicht mit jdm/etw. messen können be out of sb's league für jdn eine Klasse zu hoch sein *(fam)*

leak¹ noun **1.** *(hole)* Leck [lɛk] das <-(e)s, -s> ◊ *Der Tank hatte ein Leck.* **2.** *(information)* leaks to sb jdm zugespielte Informationen [ˌtsu:ɡəʃpiːltə ɪnfɔrmaˈtsi̯oːnən] <-> pl
◉ take a leak pinkeln gehen *(fam)*

leak² verb **1.** *(container)* lecken ['lɛkn̩] +haben ◊ *Der Eimer leckte.;* *(roof, pipe)* sth is leaking etw. ist undicht [ɪst 'ʊndɪçt] ◊ *Das Dach ist undicht, es*

regnet herein.; *(liquid, gas)* austreten ['aostre:tn̩] <tritt aus, trat aus, ist ausgetreten> ◊ *Gas tritt aus dem Tank aus.* **2.** *(a piece of information)* leak sth to sb jdm etw. zuspielen ['tsu:ʃpi:lən] +haben ◊ *Die Informationen wurden ihm zugespielt.* leak sth durchsickern lassen ['dʊrçzɪkɐn lasn̩] <lässt, ließ, hat gelassen> ◊ *Wer hat die Identität des Agenten durchsickern lassen?*

lean¹ adj **1.** *(slim, economical)* schlank [ʃlaŋk] <schlanker, schlank(e)ste> ◊ *Der Mann war schlank.* ♦ *eine schlanke Verwaltung* **2.** *(meat, crop, period)* mager ['ma:ɡɐ] ◊ *Das Fleisch ist sehr mager.* ♦ *eine magere Ernte*

lean² verb **1.** lean forward sich vorbeugen ['fo:ɐbɔøɡn̩] +haben ◊ *Sie beugte sich vor, um ihn besser zu verstehen.* lean back sich nach hinten beugen [na:x 'hɪntn̩ bɔøɡn̩] +haben lean over sth/sb sich über etw./jdn beugen [y:bɐ ... bɔøɡn̩] +haben ◊ *Sie beugte sich über ihn, damit er den Brief auch lesen konnte.* **2.** *(place against)* lehnen ['le:nən] +haben ◊ *Er lehnte seinen Kopf an ihre Schulter.* ♦ *Die Leiter lehnt am Apfelbaum.* lean back sich zurücklehnen ['tsu:rʏklenən] +haben ◊ *Lehnen Sie sich zurück und entspannen Sie sich!* **3.** *(be inclined to do sth)* be leaning towards sth zu etw. tendieren [tsu: ... tɛnˌdi:rən] <tendiert, tendierte, hat tendiert> ◊ *Sie tendierte dazu, ihm zu glauben.*

leap¹ noun **1.** *(jump, progress)* Sprung [ʃprʊŋ] der <-(e)s, Sprünge> ◊ *Das Reh flüchtete mit großen Sprüngen.* ♦ *Dieser Erfolg ist für uns ein gewaltiger Sprung vorwärts.* **2.** *(increase)* (big) leap in sth sprunghafter Anstieg ... gen [ʃprʊŋhafte 'anʃtiːk] <-(e)s, -e> ◊ *die sprunghafte Anstieg der Energiepreise*

leap² verb springen ['ʃprɪŋən] <springt, sprang, ist gesprungen> ◊ *Der Hund sprang bellend über den Platz.* ♦ *Der Zeiger der Uhr sprang auf die Zwölf.* leap up aufspringen ['aofʃprɪŋən] <springt auf, sprang auf, ist aufgesprungen>

learn verb **1.** *(study, gain knowledge of)* lernen ['lɛrnən] +haben ◊ *sprechen lernen* ♦ *Sie muss noch lernen, höflicher zu sein.* ♦ *seine Lektion lernen* learn sth by heart etw. auswendig lernen **2.** *(information)* erfahren [ɛˈfaːrən] <erfährt, erfuhr, hat erfahren> ◊ *Ich habe das aus der Zeitung erfahren.* learn about/of sth von etw. erfahren ◊ *Warum erfahre ich erst jetzt davon?*

learner noun Lernende ['lɛrnəndə] der/die <-n, die Lernenden> but: ein Lernender/eine Lernende ◊ *Wie motiviert man die Lernenden am besten?;* *(of a language)* Lerner ['lɛrnɐ] der <-s, -> ♀Lernerin ['lɛrnərɪn] die <-, -nen>; *(sb learning to drive)* Fahrschüler ['faːˈʃyːlɐ] der <-s, -> ♀Fahrschülerin ['faːˈʃyːlərɪn] die <-, -nen>

learning noun **1.** *(process)* Lernen ['lɛrnən] das <-s> *no pl* ◊ *Das Lernen fällt mir leicht.* **2.** *(knowledge)* Wissen ['vɪsn̩] das <-s> *no pl* ◊ *Sie hat sehr viel Wissen angehäuft.*

lease noun *(contract)* Pachtvertrag ['paxtfɛtraːk] der <-(e)s, Pachtverträge>; *(on a flat, apartment)* Mietvertrag ['miːtfɛtraːk]
◉ a new lease of life neuer Auftrieb

leaseholder noun *(owner of a leasehold: on a house)* Pächter ['pɛçtɐ] der <-s, -> ♀Pächterin ['pɛçtərɪn] die <-, -nen> ◊ *der Pächter des Gasthauses;* *(on a flat, apartment)* Mieter ['miːtɐ] der <-s, ->

♀**Mieterin** ['miːtərɪn] die <-, –nen> ◊ *Die Mieterin hat gekündigt.*

leash [noun] Leine ['laɛnə] die <-, –n> ◊ *einen Hund an die Leine nehmen*

least¹ [adj] geringste [gə'rɪŋstə] *no comp/superl, only before ns* <der/die/das geringste ...> ◊ *Beim geringsten Anzeichen von Problemen gibt sie gleich auf.*

least² [adv] am wenigsten [am 've:nɪçstn̩] ◊ *Ich wurde befördert, als ich es am wenigsten verdiente.* ◆ *die am wenigsten entwickelten Länder der Welt*

least³ [det] der/die/das geringste [deːɡ/diː/das gə'rɪŋstə] ◊ *den Weg des geringsten Widerstands wählen*

least⁴ [pron] the least am wenigsten [am 've:nɪçstn̩] ◊ *Du arbeitest am wenigsten von uns.* be the least of sb's problems noch das kleinste Problem sein [nɔx das 'klaɛnstə pro͜ble:m zaɛn] ◊ *Unsere finanziellen Sorgen sind noch das kleinste Problem.*

leather [noun] Leder ['le:dɐ] das <-s> *no pl* ◊ *eine Handtasche aus feinstem Leder*

leave¹ [noun] **1.** *(time off work)* Urlaub ['u:ɡlaɔp] der <-(e)s, -e> on leave im Urlaub be on sick leave krankgeschrieben sein ['kraŋkgəʃriːbm̩ zaɛn] *+sein* maternity leave Mutterschaftsurlaub ['mʊtɐʃafts|uːɡlaɔp] **2.** *(permission)* leave to do sth die Erlaubnis, etw. zu tun [di: e'laɔpnɪs ... tsuː] die <-, -se> *most sing* ◊ *Er erhielt die Erlaubnis, das Land zu verlassen.* sb is granted leave to appeal jds Berufung wird stattgegeben [bə,ruːfʊŋ vɪˈ't ˈʃtatgəgeːbm̩] <wird, wurde, ist worden> *(form)*

leave² [verb] **1.** *(go away from sb/sth)* verlassen [fɛ'lasn̩] <verlässt, verließ, hat verlassen> ◊ *Eilig verließ ich den Raum.* ◆ *Sie hat ihren Mann verlassen.* ◆ *Er verließ wegen der Streitigkeiten die Firma.* leave sb/sth behind jdn/etw. zurücklassen [tsu'rʏklasn̩] <lässt zurück, ließ zurück, hat zurückgelassen> ◊ *Er musst seine Liebsten in der Heimat zurücklassen.; (your job)* aufhören ['aɔfhøːrən] *+haben* ◊ *Nächsten Monat höre ich auf.; (without a diploma)* leave school von der Schule abgehen [fɔn deːɡ 'ʃuːlə ˌapgeːən] <geht ab, ging ab, ist abgegangen>; *(move out)* leave home von zu Hause ausziehen [fɔn tsu: ˌhaɔzə 'aɔstsiːən] <zieht aus, zog aus, ist ausgezogen> **2.** *(depart: train, plane etc.)* gehen ['geːən] <geht, ging, ist gegangen> ◊ *Wann geht der nächste Zug nach Köln?* **3.** *(start a journey)* losfahren ['loːsfaːrən] <fährt los, fuhr los, ist losgefahren> ◊ *Wir sind vor drei Stunden losgefahren.* **4.** *(let sth remain in a particular place or state, not do sth)* leave sth etw. lassen ['lasn̩] <lässt, ließ, hat gelassen> ◊ *Ich habe den schweren Koffer unten gelassen.* ◆ *Lass mich in Ruhe!* ◆ *Lass doch die Arbeit und geh mit mir aus!* leave sb sth jdm etw. lassen ◊ *Lass den Kindern bitte noch etwas von dem Kuchen!* leave sb with sb jdn bei jdm lassen; *(an appliance, a light, clothes)* leave sth on etw. anlassen ['anlasn̩] *+haben* ◊ *Mir ist kalt; ich lasse die Jacke lieber an.* leave sth open etw. auflassen ['aɔflasn̩] *+haben (fam)* ◊ *das Fenster auflassen* ◆ *Er ließ das Geschäft über Mittag auf.; (a door)* leave sth ajar etw. anlehnen ['anleːnən] *+haben* ◊ *Er lehnte die Tür an.* ◆ *Das Fenster war nur angelehnt.* **5.** *(forget)* leave sth somwhere etw. irgendwo vergessen [fɛ'gesn̩] <vergisst, vergaß, hat vergessen> ◊ *Ich habe mein Handy im Büro vergessen.* **6.** *(let sb do sth)* leave

sth to sb jdm etw. überlassen [ybe'lasn̩] <überlässt, überließ, hat überlassen> ◊ *Überlass das ruhig mir.* leave sb to sth jdn einer Sache [dat] überlassen ◊ *Ich überlasse dich deinem Buch.* leave sb to it jdn machen lassen ['maxn̩ lasn̩] <lässt, ließ, hat lassen> *(fam)* ◊ *Hast du alles verstanden? Dann lass ihn dich mal machen.* **7.** *(not use sth)* übrig lassen ['y:brɪç lasn̩] <lässt übrig, ließ übrig, hat übrig gelassen> ◊ *Lass mir noch etwas Saft übrig!* have sth left etw. übrig haben ['y:brɪç ha:bm̩] *+haben* ◊ *Er hat noch etwas Geld übrig.* How much time have we left? Wie viel Zeit haben wir noch? be left übrig sein ['y:brɪç zaɛn] *+sein* ◊ *Ist noch was vom Abendessen übrig?; (time)* bleiben ['blaɛbm̩] <bleiben, blieb, ist geblieben> There isn't much time left. Es bleibt nicht mehr viel Zeit. How much time is there left? Wie viel Zeit bleibt noch? leave a space Platz lassen ['plats lasn̩] *+haben* **8.** *(a message, legacy, inheritance, close relatives etc.)* hinterlassen [hɪntɐ'lasn̩] <hinterlässt, hinterließ, hat hinterlassen> ◊ *Er hinterließ viele Schulden.* ◆ *auf dem Anrufbeantworter eine Nachricht hinterlassen* ◆ *Die Erfahrung hat bei ihr Spuren hinterlassen.* ◆ *Er hinterlässt eine Frau und drei Kinder.* leave sb sth, leave sth to sb jdm etw. hinterlassen ◊ *Sie hat ihm ihr ganzes Geld hinterlassen.* **9.** *(make sb feel or think sth)* leave sb with the impression that bei jdm den Eindruck hinterlassen, dass [bae ... deːn 'aɛndrʊk hɪntɐlasn̩ das] <hinterlässt, hinterließ, hat hinterlassen> this leaves me wondering ... deshalb frage ich mich, ... [dɛshalp 'fra:gə ɪç mɪç]

⊛ **leave it** at that es dabei bewenden lassen **leave it out** so ein Quatsch *(fam)*

• **leave aside** [phras v] leave sb/sth aside von jdm/etw. absehen [fɔn ... ˌapzeːən] <sieht ab, sah ab, hat abgesehen> ◊ *Der Wagen ist toll, wenn man von der Farbe mal absieht.* leaving sb/sth aside abgesehen von jdm/etw.

• **leave behind** [phras v] leave sth/sb behind *(get away from, be better than)* etw./ jdn hinter sich [dat] lassen ['hɪntɐ ... lasn̩] <lässt, ließ, hat gelassen> ◊ *die Konkurrenz hinter sich lassen* → **leave²** 1.

• **leave off** [phras v] aufhören ['aɔfhøːrən] *+haben* ◊ *Hoffentlich hört er bald auf.* leave off doing sth aufhören, etw. zu tun

• **leave out** [phras v] **1.** *(omit)* weglassen ['vɛklasn̩] <lässt weg, ließ weg, hat weggelassen> ◊ *Wir haben die brutalen Stellen weggelassen.* **2.** *(a person)* übergehen [ybe'geːən] <übergeht, überging, hat übergangen> ◊ *Sie wurde bewusst übergangen.* feel left out sich übergangen fühlen

lecture¹ [noun] **1.** *(talk)* Vortrag ['foːɡtraːk] der <-(e)s, Vorträge> ◊ *einen Vortrag über etw.* [acc] halten; *(at university)* Vorlesung ['foːɡleːzʊŋ] die <-, -en> ◊ *eine Vorlesung über etw.* [acc] halten **2.** *(criticism)* Predigt ['preːdɪçt] die <-, -en> *(fam)* ◊ *Ich kann deine ewigen Predigten nicht mehr hören!*

lecture² [verb] **1.** *(give lectures at a university)* lecture (on sth) (etw.) lesen ['leːzn̩] <liest, las, hat gelesen> ◊ *Er liest Physik an der Technischen Universität.* **2.** *(criticize sb)* lecture (sb) (jdm) eine Predigt halten [aɛnə 'preːdɪçt haltn̩] <hält, hielt, hat gehalten> *(fam)* lecture on sth eine Predigt über etw. [acc] halten

lecturer [noun] Dozent [do'tsɛnt] der <-s, –en> ♀**Dozentin** [do'tsɛntɪn] die <-, –nen> ◊ *Er ist*

Dozent für Soziologie. ✦ *die neue Dozentin für Linguistik*

lecture theatre, lecture theater [noun] Hörsaal ['hø:ɡza:l] der <-(e)s, Hörsäle> ◊ *Die Vorlesung findet im Hörsaal 127 statt.*

ledge [noun] **1.** *(of a window, wall)* Sims [zɪms] der <-es, -e> ◊ *Auf dem Sims steht ein Blumentopf.* **2.** *(of rock)* Vorsprung ['fo:ɐ̯ʃprʊŋ] der <-(e)s, Vorsprünge> ◊ *Er stand auf dem schmalen Vorsprung über der Schlucht.*

leek [noun] leek(s) Lauch [laox] der <-(e)s> *no pl* a leek eine Stange Lauch

leeway [noun] Spielraum ['ʃpi:lraom] der <-(e)s, Spielräume> ◊ *wenig Spielraum für höhere Gebühren*

left¹ [noun] **1.** *(not the right)* linke Seite [ˌlɪŋkə 'zaɛtə] die <-, -n> on the left of sth auf der linken Seite ... [gen] ◊ *Auf der linken Seite des Zimmers steht ein Schrank.* on/to your left, on the left links [lɪŋ̯ks] ◊ *Links sehen Sie jetzt das Rathaus.* to the left nach links ◊ *Rutsch mal bitte nach links!* make/take a left links abbiegen **2.** POL the Left die Linke [di: 'lɪŋkə] die <-, -n> *most sing; (of a party)* the left der linke Flügel [de:ɐ̯ ˌlɪŋkə 'fly:gl̩] <-s, -> ◊ *Sie ist dem linken Flügel der Partei zuzurechnen.* **3.** *(punch)* Linke ['lɪŋkə] die <-n, -n> ◊ *Er schlug seinen Gegner mit einer Linken zu Boden.*

left² [adj] linke ['lɪŋkə] *no comp/superl, only before ns* <ein linker ..., eine linke ..., ein linkes ...> ◊ *Sein linkes Bein war verletzt.*

left³ [adv] links [lɪŋ̯ks] ◊ *links abbiegen*

left-handed [adj] be left-handed Linkshänder/Linkshänderin sein ['lɪŋkshɛndə/'lɪŋkshɛndərɪn zaɛn] +sein a left-handed guitar eine Gitarre für Linkshänder

leftovers [noun] Rest [rɛst] der <-(e)s, -e> ◊ *Reste essen*

left-wing [adj] linke ['lɪŋkə] <linker, am linkesten> *only before ns* <ein linker ..., eine linke ..., ein linkes ...> ◊ *Er gehört zum linken Flügel der Partei.* be left-wing links sein ['lɪŋ̯ks zaɛn] ◊ *Er ist links.*

leg [noun] **1.** *(of a person, an animal, of furniture, trousers)* Bein [baɛn] das <-(e)s, -e> ◊ *Er hat sich ein Bein gebrochen.* ✦ *Hosen mit weiten Beinen* **2.** *(meat)* Keule ['kɔɶlə] die <-, -n> chicken leg Hähnchenkeule ['hɛ:nçankɔɶlə] leg of lamb Lammkeule ['lamkɔɶlə] **3.** *(of a journey, race)* Etappe [e'tapə] die <-, -n> ◊ *Wir haben Polen in mehreren Etappen bereist.* ⊛ not have a leg to stand on nichts in der Hand haben

legacy [noun] Erbe ['ɛrbə] das <-s> *no pl* ◊ *Der neue Trainer trat ein schweres Erbe an.*

legal [adj] **1.** *(relating to the law)* rechtlich ['rɛçtlɪç] *no comp/superl* ◊ *Wir haben keine rechtliche Handhabe gegen ihn.* legal system Rechtssystem ['rɛçtszʏsˌte:m] das <-s, -e>; *(relating to lawyers)* seek legal advice einen Anwalt zurate ziehen [aɛnən 'anvalt tsuˌra:tə 'tsi:ən] <zieht, zog, hat gezogen> legal fees Anwaltskosten ['anvaltskɔstn̩] die <-> *pl; (compulsory)* sth is a legal requirement etw. ist gesetzlich vorgeschrieben [ɪst gəˌzɛtslɪç 'fo:ɐ̯gəʃri:bm̩] +sein **2.** *(allowed by the law)* rechtmäßig ['rɛçtmɛ:sɪç] ◊ *Die Verordnung ist rechtmäßig.* ✦ *eine rechtmäßige Kündigung; (drugs)* legal [le'ga:l] *no comp/superl* ◊ *legale Drogen*

legal action [noun] Prozess [pro'tsɛs] der <-es, -e> ◊

einen Prozess führen take legal action vor Gericht gehen [fo:ɐ̯ gə'rɪçt ge:ən] <geht, ging, ist gegangen> ◊ *Mit diesem Fall gehen sie vor Gericht.*

legally [adv] dem Gesetz nach [de:m gə'zɛts na:x] ◊ *Wir sind dem Gesetz nach verpflichtet, Ihnen Folgendes mitzuteilen:* ... legally binding rechtsverbindlich ['rɛçtsfɛbɪntlɪç] ◊ *Der Vertrag ist rechtsverbindlich.*

legend [noun] **1.** *(story)* Sage ['za:gə] die <-, -n> ◊ *die Sage von König Artus* ✦ *Der Sage nach wurden Romulus und Remus von einer Wölfin aufgezogen.* **2.** *(very famous person)* Legende [le'gɛndə] die <-, -n> ◊ *Marilyn Monroe ist längst eine Legende.* **3.** *(writing on a coin)* Inschrift ['ɪnʃrɪft] die <-, -en> ⊛ sth is legend *(well known)* etw. ist legendär

legendary [adj] legendär [legɛn'dɛ:ɐ̯] ◊ *der legendäre König Midas* ✦ *Der Fall Schneider ist legendär geworden.*

legible(-ibly) [adj, adv] *(handwriting)* leserlich ['le:zɐlɪç] ◊ *eine leserliche Schrift* ✦ *leserlich schreiben; (inscription etc.)* lesbar ['le:sba:ʳ] ◊ *Die Inschrift der Wandtafel war kaum noch lesbar.*

legislation [noun] **1.** *(laws)* Gesetze [gə'zɛtsə] die <-> *pl* ◊ *Gesetze zum Umweltschutz* **2.** *(making of laws)* Gesetzgebung [gə'zɛtsge:bʊŋ] die <-, -en> ◊ *Die Gesetzgebung ist ein komplizierter Prozess.*

legislative [adj] gesetzgebend [gə'zɛtsge:bm̩t] *no comp/superl, only before ns* ◊ *die gesetzgebende Gewalt*

legislature [noun] Legislative [legɪsla'ti:və] die <-, -n>

legitimate [adj] **1.** *(justified)* berechtigt [bə'rɛçtɪçt] ◊ *Dieser Einwand ist durchaus berechtigt.; (reason, excuse)* triftig ['trɪftɪç] ◊ *einen triftigen Grund für etw. haben* **2.** *(according to law)* rechtmäßig ['rɛçtmɛ:sɪç] ◊ *Die Verordnung ist rechtmäßig.* ✦ *eine rechtmäßige Kündigung; (child)* ehelich ['e:əlɪç] *no comp/superl* ◊ *ein eheliches Kind*

legitimately [adv] **1.** *(with justification)* zu Recht [tsu: 'rɛçt] *no comp/superl* ◊ *Er war zu Recht verärgert über diesen Vorschlag.* **2.** *(according to law)* rechtmäßig ['rɛçtmɛ:sɪç] ◊ *rechtmäßig hergestellte Kopien* **3.** *(of married parents)* ehelich ['e:əlɪç] *no comp/superl* ◊ *ehelich geboren sein*

leisure [noun] *(free time)* leisure (time) Freizeit ['fraɛzaɛt] die <-, -en> ◊ *In meiner Freizeit laufe ich Ski.* leisure activities Freizeitaktivitäten ['fraɛzaɛtaktivi̩tɛ:tn̩] die <-> *pl* have the leisure to do sth die Muße haben, etw. zu tun [di: 'mu:sə ha:bm̩ ... tsu:] +haben ⊛ at leisure **1.** *(as you like)* nach Belieben **2.** *(in your own time)* in Ruhe

leisurely [adj, adv] gemütlich [gə'my:tlɪç] ◊ *ein gemütlicher Spaziergang* ✦ *Die Fahrt nach Hause war gemütlich.* ✦ *Am Nachmittag radelten wir ganz gemütlich zurück.*

lemon [noun] **1.** *(fruit)* Zitrone [tsi'tro:nə] die <-, -n> ◊ *eine Zitrone auspressen* **2.** *(colo(u)r)* Zitronengelb [tsi'tro:nəngɛlp] das <-s> *no pl* **3.** *(bad purchase)* Gurke ['gʊʳkə] die <-, -n> *(fam)* ◊ *Wo hast du denn diese Gurke her?* **4.** *(in the UK: fool)* Idiot [i'djo:t] der <-en, -en> *(fam)* ◊ *So ein Idiot!*

lemonade [noun] Zitronenlimonade [tsi'tro:nənlimoˌna:də] die <-, -n>

lend [verb] **1.** *(an object)* lend sth to sb, lend sb sth

jdm etw. **leihen** ['laɛən] <leiht, lieh, hat geliehen> ◊ *Er leiht ihr sein Auto nicht.* **2.** *(give sth a certain quality)* lend sth to sth, lend sth sth einer Sache `dat` etw. **verleihen** [fɛ'laɛən] <verleiht, verlieh, hat verliehen> ◊ *Sie versuchte, ihren Worten Nachdruck zu verleihen.* **3.** lend (your) support to sth etw. **unterstützen** [ʊntɐ'ʃtʏtsn̩] <unterstützt, unterstützte, hat unterstützt> lend a hand **helfen** ['hɛlfn̩] <hilft, half, hat geholfen> **4.** *(be suitable)* lend itself to sth sich **für** etw. **eignen** [fy:ɐ̯ ... ,aɛɡnən] ◊ *Der Film eignet sich gut für den Einsatz im Unterricht.*

lender `noun` **Kreditgeber** [kre'di:tɡe:bɐ] der <–s, –> ♀**Kreditgeberin** [kre'di:tɡe:bərɪn] die <–, –nen>

length `noun` **1.** *(measurement, distance)* **Länge** ['lɛŋə] die <–, –n> ◊ *Die Länge der Mauer beträgt fünf Meter.* ◆ *Wie viele Längen Vorsprung hat er?* The road is paved along its entire length. Die Straße ist durchgehend gepflastert. be 12 m etc. in length 12 m etc. **lang sein** [tsvœlf 'me:tɐ ,laŋ zaɛn] +*sein* be twice the length of sth **doppelt so lang wie** etw. **sein**; *(path, road)* run the length of sth an etw. `dat` **entlangführen** [an ... ɛnt,laŋfy:rən] <führt entlang, führte entlang, hat entlanggeführt> ◊ *Ein Radweg führt am Kanal entlang.*; *(in a swimming pool)* **Bahn** [ba:n] die <–, –en> ◊ *Ich bin heute 20 Bahnen geschwommen.* **2.** *(of how long sth lasts)* length (of time) **Dauer** ['daʊə] die <–> *no pl* length of stay **Aufenthaltsdauer** ['aʊfn̩thaltsdaʊə] for any length of time **eine Zeit lang** [aɛnə 'tsaɛt laŋ] **3.** *(piece)* **Stück** [ʃtʏk] das <–(e)s, –e> a length of rope **ein Stück Seil** ◉ **the length and breadth of sth** der/die/das ganze ... ◊ *Wir sind durch das ganze Land gereist.* go to great lengths **alles Erdenkliche tun** at (great) length **(sehr) ausführlich**

lengthen `verb` **1.** *(make longer)* **verlängern** [fɛ'lɛŋɐn] <verlängert, verlängerte, hat verlängert> ◊ *Er hat das Kabel um 3 m verlängert.* ◆ **den Aufenthalt verlängern 2.** *(become longer)* **länger werden** ['lɛŋɐ ve:ɐ̯dn̩] +*sein* ◊ *Abends wurden die Schatten länger.*

lengthwise `adv` **längs** [lɛŋs] ◊ *Soll ich die Melone längs aufschneiden?*

lengthy `adj` **sehr lang** [,ze:ɐ̯ 'laŋ] <noch länger, am längsten> ◊ *Der Abend wurde sehr lang.* ◆ *eine sehr lange Liste*

lenient(ly) `adj, adv` **mild** [mɪlt] <milder, am mildesten> ◊ *Das Urteil war mild.* ◆ *eine milde Strafe* ◆ *Der Richter hat sehr mild geurteilt.*

lens `noun` **1.** *(of or for the eye)* **Linse** ['lɪnzə] die <–, –n> ◊ *Im Alter hatten sich seine Linsen getrübt.* contact lense **Kontaktlinse** [kɔn'taktlɪnzə] **2.** *(of glasses)* **Glas** [gla:s] das <–es, Gläser> ◊ *eine Brille mit dünnen Gläsern*; *(of a camera)* **Objektiv** [ɔpjɛk'ti:f] das <–(e)s, –e> ◊ *ein Objektiv für Nahaufnahmen*

Lent `noun` **Fastenzeit** ['fastn̩tsaɛt] die <–, –en>

lentil `noun` **Linse** ['lɪnzə] die <–, –n> ◊ *Heute gibt es Linsen mit Speck.*

Leo `noun` **Löwe** ['lø:və] der <–n, –n>

leotard `noun` **Trikot** [tri'ko:] das <–s, –s> ◊ *ein Akrobat in einem roten Trikot*

lesbian `adj` **lesbisch** ['lɛsbɪʃ] *no comp/superl* ◊ *lesbische Paare*

less¹ `adv` **weniger** ['ve:nɪɡɐ] ◊ *Dieser Käse ist weniger fett.* less than **weniger als** ◊ *Die Behandlung dauerte weniger als ein Jahr.*

less² `det` **weniger** ['ve:nɪɡɐ] ◊ *weniger Zeit haben*

less³ `indef pron` less of sb's time **weniger Zeit** [,ve:nɪɡɐ 'tsaɛt] ◊ *Ich will in Zukunft weniger Zeit mit ihm verbringen.* be less of a problem **weniger problematisch sein** ['ve:nɪɡə proble,ma:tɪʃ zaɛn] +*sein*

less⁴ `prep` **abzüglich** ['aptsy:klɪç] `+gen` ◊ *Sie bekommen die Summe abzüglich der Anmeldegebühr zurück.*

lesser `adj` **geringere** [ɡə'rɪŋərə] <ein geringerer ..., eine geringere ..., ein geringeres ...> ◊ *das geringere Übel*

lesson `noun` **1.** *(period of time in which sth is taught)* **Stunde** ['ʃtʊndə] die <–, –n> ◊ *In der ersten Stunde haben wir Mathe.* lessons **Unterricht** ['ʊntɐrɪçt] der <–(e)s> *no pl* ◊ *Unterricht geben* ◆ *Sie nimmt Unterricht in Geige und Klavier.* **2.** *(chapter, bad experience)* **Lektion** [lɛk'tsjo:n] die <–, –en> ◊ *Wir sind bei Lektion 12.* ◆ *Die Niederlage war eine bittere Lektion für sie.*

let `verb` **1.** *(allow, permit)* **lassen** ['lasn̩] <lässt, ließ, hat gelassen> ◊ *die Luft aus dem Reifen lassen* ◆ *Lass die Katze nicht ins Schlafzimmer!* let sb/sth do sth jdn/etw. etw. **tun lassen** ['lasn̩] <lässt, ließ, hat lassen> ◊ *Lass sie doch schlafen!* ◆ *Lässt du mich dein Auto benutzen?* ◆ *Lasst uns gehen!* let sb help you sich `dat` von jdm **helfen lassen** let yourself be persuaded sich **überreden lassen**; *(allow inside)* let sb/sth in jdn/etw. **hereinlassen** [hɛ'raɛnlasn̩] <lässt herein, ließ herein, hat hereingelassen> ◊ *Lass niemanden herein!* ◆ *frische Luft hereinlassen* let through **durchlassen** ['dʊrçlasn̩] <lässt durch, ließ durch, hat durchgelassen> ◊ *Lassen Sie den Arzt durch!*; *(allow to get off a vehicle)* let sb off jdn **aussteigen lassen** ['aʊsʃtaɛɡn̩ lasn̩] <lässt, ließ, hat lassen> ◊ *Lassen Sie mich bitte an der Ecke aussteigen.* **2.** *(rent out)* **vermieten** [fɛ'mi:tn̩] <vermietet, vermietete, hat vermietet> let a room to sb jdm ein Zimmer **an jdn vermieten** ◉ **let it be known that** **bekanntgeben, dass** let sb be jdn **in Ruhe lassen** let go **1.** *(not hold up)* let sb go jdn **gehen lassen 2.** *(sack)* let sb go jdn **entlassen 3.** *(loosen your grip)* let go (of sb/sth) (jdn/etw.) **loslassen** ◊ *He, lass mich los!* let sth pass auf etw. `acc` **nicht reagieren** ◊ *Ich reagierte nicht auf ihre Bemerkung.* sb lets slip that jdm **rutscht es heraus, dass**

• **let down** `phras v` **1.** *(lower from a height)* let sth/yourself down etw./sich **herablassen** [hɛ'raplasn̩] <lässt herab, ließ herab, hat herabgelassen> *(lofty)* **den Vorhang herablassen** ◆ *Ich ließ mich an einem Seil vom Gipfel herab.* **2.** *(not help sb)* let sb down jdn **im Stich lassen** [ɪm 'ʃtɪç lasn̩] <lässt, ließ, hat gelassen> ◊ *Ich fühle mich von dir im Stich gelassen.* **3.** *(spoil)* let sth down etw. **beeinträchtigen** [bə'|aɛntrɛçtɪɡn̩] <beeinträchtigt, beeinträchtigte, hat beeinträchtigt> ◊ *Der Film wird durch die schlechte Musik beeinträchtigt.*

• **let in** `phras v` *(confide in sb)* let sb in on sth jdn **in** etw. `acc` **einweihen** [ɪn ... ,aɛnvaɛən] +*haben* ◊ *Sie weihte mich in ihr Geheimnis ein.* → **let 1.**

• **let off** `phras v` **1.** *(with no/little punishment)* let sb off jdn **davonkommen lassen** [da'fɔnkɔmən lasn̩] <lässt, ließ, hat lassen> ◊ *jdn mit einer Verwarnung davonkommen lassen* **2.** *(spare sb sth)* let sb off sth jdm etw. **erlassen** [ɛ'lasn̩] <erlässt, erließ, hat erlassen> ◊ *jdm eine Arbeit erlassen* **3.** *(explosives)*

let sth off etw. zünden ['tsʏndn̩] <zündet, zündete, hat gezündet> ◊ *einen Kracher zünden* → **let 1**.
• **let on** phras v **1.** *(reveal)* not want to let on sich [dat] nichts anmerken lassen wollen [nɪçts 'anmɛ'kn̩ lasn̩ vɔlən] <will, wollte, hat wollen> ◊ *Ich war nervös, wollte mir aber nichts anmerken lassen.* sb does not want to let on to sb how/what etc. jd will nicht, dass jd erfährt wie/was etc. ['vɪl nɪçt das ... ɛ'fɛːɐ̯t viː/vas] <will, wollte, hat gewollt> ◊ *Ich will nicht, dass die Presse erfährt, wo ich die Nacht verbringe.* **2.** *(admit)* let on sth etw. zugeben ['tsuːgeːbm̩] <gibt zu, gab zu, hat zugegeben> ◊ *Er hat seinen Fehler nicht zugegeben.*
• **let out** phras v **1.** *(allow to get out)* let sb/sth out etw./jdn hinauslassen [hɪ'naʊslasn̩] <lässt hinaus, ließ hinaus, hat hinausgelassen> ◊ *Lass den Hund nicht hinaus!* **2.** *(a sound)* ausstoßen ['aʊsʃtoːsn̩] <stößt aus, stieß aus, hat ausgestoßen> ◊ *einen Schrei/Seufzer ausstoßen* **3.** *(a piece of clothing)* let sth out etw. auslassen ['aʊslasn̩] <lässt aus, ließ aus, hat ausgelassen> ◊ *den Saum/einen Rock auslassen*
• **let up** phras v nachlassen ['naːxlasn̩] <lässt nach, ließ nach, hat nachgelassen> ◊ *Der Wind lässt nach.*
let-down noun Pleite ['plaɛtə] die <-, -n> *(fam)* ◊ *Die Reform war eine Pleite.*
lethal adj tödlich ['tøːtlɪç] no comp/superl ◊ *Der Biss dieser Schlange ist tödlich.* ♦ *eine tödliche Dosis Gift*
lethargic(ally) adj, adv träge ['trɛːgə] <träger, am trägsten> ◊ *Er ist viel zu träge für Tennis.* ♦ *Sie macht einen trägen Eindruck.*
letter noun **1.** *(written message)* Brief [briːf] der <-(e)s, -e> ◊ *(jdm) einen Brief schreiben* ♦ *Er hat nicht auf meinen Brief geantwortet.; (official)* Schreiben ['ʃraɛbm̩] das <-s, -> ◊ *Er verfasste ein Schreiben an das Finanzamt.* letter of thanks Dankschreiben ['daŋkʃraɛbm̩] letter of confirmation Bestätigung [bə'ʃtɛːtɪgʊŋ] die <-, -en> **2.** *(symbol used in writing)* Buchstabe ['buːxʃtaːbə] der <-ns, -n> ◊ *Wie viele Buchstaben hat das deutsche Alphabet?*
ⓔ follow sth to the letter etw. genauestens befolgen
letter box noun Briefkasten ['briːfkastn̩] der <-s, Briefkästen> ◊ *Der Briefkasten wird zweimal am Tag geleert.*
lettering noun Schrift [ʃrɪft] die <-, -en> ◊ *ein gelbes Nummernschild mit schwarzer Schrift*
lettuce noun Salat [za'laːt] der <-(e)s, -e> most sing ◊ *Salat anpflanzen/säen*
level¹ noun **1.** *(amount, value or extent that is reached at a specific point in time)* Stand [ʃtant] der <-(e)s, Stände> ◊ *Um acht Uhr erreichte das Hochwasser seinen höchsten Stand.* ♦ *Die Aktien sind auf dem niedrigsten Stand seit Jahren.* water level Wasserstand ['vaseʃtant] **2.** *(physical height, level of income, tax etc.)* Höhe ['høːə] die <-, -n> ◊ *Alle Fenster liegen auf gleicher Höhe.* ♦ *Die Steuern richten sich nach der Höhe des Einkommens.* shoulder level Schulterhöhe ['ʃʊltehøːə] **3.** *(setting)* Stufe ['ʃtuːfə] die <-, -n> ◊ *den Mixer eine Stufe höher stellen* **4.** *(in a hierarchy, within society, in a relationship)* Ebene ['eːbənə] die <-, -n> on/at a level auf einer Ebene ◊ *auf internationaler/persönlicher Ebene* **5.** *(of sb's ability)* Niveau [ni'voː] das <-s, -s> ◊ *Welches Niveau hat er in diesem Fach erreicht?* university level Hochschulniveau ['hoːxʃuːlniˌvoː] for advanced level für Fortgeschrit-

tene [fyːɐ̯ 'fɔ'tgəʃrɪtənə] ◊ *Englisch für Fortgeschrittene* **6.** *(frequency)* level of ... ...rate ['raːtə] die <-, -n> level of crime Kriminalitätsrate [krɪminaliˈtɛːtsraːtə] level of inflation Inflationsrate [ɪnflaˈtsjoːnsraːtə] **7.** *(of radiation, harmful substances)* Belastung [bə'lastʊŋ] die <-, -en> ◊ *eine hohe Belastung mit Cadmium* the level of sth in sth die Belastung ... gen mit etw. ◊ *die Belastung des Trinkwassers mit Nitraten* radiation level radioaktive Belastung **8.** *(of a building)* Geschoss [gə'ʃɔs] das <-es, -e> ◊ *im zweiten Geschoss* ground level Erdgeschoss ['eːɐ̯tgəʃɔs] **9.** MED *(of a substance in the blood)* ...spiegel ['ʃpiːgl̩] der <-s, -> blood sugar level Blutzuckerspiegel ['bluːttsʊkeʃpiːgl̩] alcohol level Alkoholspiegel ['alkohoːlʃpiːgl̩] **10.** *(of stress, noise, pain)* Pegel ['peːgl̩] der <-s, -> ◊ *Der Lärm hat einen unerträglichen Pegel erreicht.* level of stress Stresspegel ['ʃtrɛspeːgl̩]
ⓔ descend to sb's level sich auf jds Niveau herablassen
level² adj **1.** *(flat)* eben ['eːbm̩] ◊ *Die Fahrbahn ist nicht ganz eben.* ♦ *ein ebenes Gelände; (spoonful)* gestrichen [gə'ʃtrɪçn̩] no comp/superl, only before ns ◊ *ein gestrichener Teelöffel Zucker/Salz* **2.** *(of the same height)* gleich hoch ['glaɛç ˌhoːx] level (with sth) (mit etw.) auf gleicher Höhe [gçɔf ˌglaɛçe 'høːə] +sein ◊ *Shanghai liegt etwa auf gleicher Höhe mit dem südlichen Ende von Japan* **3.** *(be the same as, equal)* be level miteinander abschließen [mɪtlaɛˌnande 'apʃliːsn̩] <schließt ab, schloss ab, hat abgeschlossen> ◊ *Die Ränder sollen miteinander abschließen.* be level with sth etw. abschließen; (in a competition) be level with sb mit jdm auf gleicher Höhe sein [mɪt ... aɔf ˌglaɛçe 'høːə zaɛn] +sein draw level with sb mit jdm gleichziehen [mɪt ... 'glaɛçtsiːən] <zieht gleich, zog gleich, hat gleichgezogen> **4.** *(stay the same)* remain level gleich bleiben ['glaɛç blaɛbm̩] <bleibt, blieb, ist geblieben> ◊ *Die Preise sind gleich geblieben.* **5.** *(calm)* ruhig ['ruːɪç] ◊ *mit ruhiger Stimme* ♦ *Sein Blick war ruhig.*
level³ verb **1.** *(make flat)* ebnen ['eːbnən] <ebnet, ebnete, hat geebnet> ◊ *den Boden ebnen* **2.** *(destroy)* dem Erdboden gleichmachen [deːm 'eːɐ̯tboːdn̩ ˌglaɛçmaxn̩] +haben ◊ *Das Stadtviertel wurde im Krieg dem Erdboden gleichgemacht.* **3.** *(make equal)* ausgleichen ['aʊsglaɛçn̩] <gleicht aus, glich aus, hat ausgeglichen> ◊ *Sein Tor hat den Spielstand ausgeglichen.*
• **level off** phras v **1.** *(a surface)* ebnen ['eːbnən] <ebnet, ebnete, hat geebnet> ◊ *den Untergrund ebnen* **2.** *(prices)* sich stabilisieren [ʃtabiliˈziːrən] <stabilisiert sich, stabilisierte sich, hat sich stabilisiert> ◊ *Der Ölpreis hat sich stabilisiert.; (road)* eben werden ['eːbm̩ veːɐ̯dn̩] +sein ◊ *Die Straße wird eben.; (plane)* die Flughöhe beibehalten [diː 'fluːkhøːə ˌbaɛbəhaltn̩] <behält bei, behielt bei, hat beibehalten>
• **level with** phras v level with sb ehrlich mit jdm sein ['eːɐ̯lɪç mɪt ... zaɛn] +sein ◊ *Warum bist du nicht ehrlich mit mir und sagst einfach, dass du Geld brauchst?*
lever noun **1.** *(handle)* Hebel ['heːbl̩] der <-s, -> ◊ *einen Hebel betätigen* ♦ *etw. mit einem Hebel hochstemmen* **2.** *(fig)* lever (against/for sth) Druckmittel [gegen/fyːɐ̯] ['drʊkmɪtl̩] das <-s, -> ◊ *etw. als Druckmittel einsetzen*
levy verb erheben [ɛ'heːbm̩] <erhebt, erhob, hat

erhoben> *(form)* ◊ *Steuern/Gebühren erheben*
liability ⌈noun⌉ **1.** *(legal responsibility)* Haftung
['haftʊŋ] die <-, –en> most sing accept liability (for
sth) die Haftung (für etw.) übernehmen
[di: 'haftʊŋ ybɐˌneːmən] <übernimmt, übernahm, hat
übernommen> **2.** *(debts)* liabilities Schulden ['ʃʊldn̩]
die <-> *pl* have liabilities worth several million
dollars Schulden in der Höhe von mehreren
Millionen Dollar haben **3.** *(problem)* Belastung
[bə'lastʊŋ] die <-, –en> a liability to sb/sth eine
Belastung für jdn/etw. ◊ *Die Politikerin ist zu einer
Belastung für ihre Partei geworden.*
liable ⌈adj⌉ **1.** *(legally responsible)* haftbar ['haftbaːʳ] *no
comp/superl, mostly after ns* be liable for sth für
etw. haftbar sein hold sb liable for sth für etw.
haftbar machen liable for tax steuerpflichtig
['ʃtɔøɐpflɪçtɪç] *no comp/superl* ◊ *eine steuerpflichtige
Person* ♦ *Mieteinnahmen sind steuerpflichtig.; (a punishment)* be liable to sth mit etw. rechnen müssen
[mɪt ... ˌrɛçnən mʏsn̩] <muss, musste, hat müssen> ◊
*Wer gegen diese Verordnung verstößt, muss mit einer
Geldstrafe rechnen.* be liable to prosecution strafrechtlich verfolgt werden
[ˌʃtraːfrɛçtlɪç fɐ'fɔlkt veːɐdn̩] <wird, wurde, ist
worden> **2.** *(prone to be affected by sth, exposed to
sth)* be liable to sth anfällig für etw. sein
[ˌanfɛlɪç fyːɐ ... zaɛn] *+sein* ◊ *Jungpflanzen sind
anfällig für Frostschäden.* liable to flooding flutge-
fährdet ['fluːtgəfɛːɐdət] liable to draught dürregefähr-
det ['dʏrəgəfɛːɐdət] **3.** *(likely)* be liable to do sth
sicher etw. tun ['zɪçɐ] The handle is liable to break.
Der Griff bricht sicher ab.
liaise ⌈verb⌉ zusammenarbeiten [ʦuˈzamən|aˈbaɛtn̩]
<arbeitet zusammen, arbeitete zusammen, hat zusam-
mengearbeitet> ◊ *Die beiden Behörden arbeiten
zusammen.* ♦ *Ich arbeite eng mit meiner Kollegin
zusammen.*
liaison ⌈noun⌉ **1.** *(cooperation)* Zusammenarbeit
[ʦuˈzamən|aˈbaɛt] die <-> *no pl* ◊ *die Zusammenar-
beit mit jdm* ♦ *die Zusammenarbeit zwischen den
Abteilungen* **2.** *(contact)* Kontakt [kɔn'takt] der
<-(e)s, –e> ◊ *Kontakt mit dem Kunden* be in close
liaison with sb in engem Kontakt mit jdm stehen
[ɪn ˌɛŋəm kɔnˌtakt mɪt ... ʃteːən] <steht, stand, hat
gestanden> **3.** *(romantic affair)* Verhältnis [fɛ'hɛltnɪs]
das <-ses, –se> ◊ *Sie hat ein Verhältnis mit einem
verheirateten Mann.*
liar ⌈noun⌉ Lügner ['lyːgnɐ] der <-s, –> ♀Lügnerin
['lyːgnərɪn] die <-, –nen> *(pej)* ◊ *Du bist ein Lügner!*
liberal¹ ⌈noun⌉ **1.** *(person believing in tolerance and
freedom)* Liberale [libe'raːlə] der/die
<-n, die Liberalen> *but: ein Liberaler/eine Liberale*
2. *(pej)* POL *(person believing leftist principles)* Linke
['lɪŋkə] der/die <-n, die Linken> *but: ein Linker/eine
Linke* **3.** POL *(esp in the UK: connected to the Liberal
Democratic Party)* Liberal Liberaldemokrat
[libe'raːldemoˌkraːt] der <-en, –en> ♀Liberaldemo-
kratin [libe'raːldemoˌkraːtɪn] die <-, –nen>
liberal² ⌈adj⌉ **1.** *(prepared to be tolerant, promoting
freedom)* liberal [libe'raːl] ◊ *eine liberale Haltung
einnehmen* ♦ *Ihre Erziehungsmethoden waren sehr
liberal.* **2.** *(pej)* POL *(leftist)* links [lɪŋks] <ein linker
..., eine linke ..., ein linkes ...> ◊ *Ist er eher konservativ oder eher links?* ♦ *ein linker Politiker*
3. *(generous, not strict)* be liberal with sth
großzügig mit etw. umgehen

[ˌgroːsˈsyːgɪç mɪt ... ˌʊmgeːən] ◊ *Er geht mit Lob nie
großzügig um.* **4.** POL *(esp in the UK: connected with
the Liberal Democratic Party)* Liberal liberaldemokra-
tisch [libe'raːldemoˌkraːtɪʃ] ◊ *eine liberaldemokrati-
sche Politik*
liberally ⌈adv⌉ großzügig [ˈgroːsˈsyːgɪç] ◊ *großzügig
mit jdm teilen*
liberate ⌈verb⌉ befreien [bə'fraɛən] <befreit, befreite,
hat befreit> liberate sb from prison jdn aus dem
Gefängnis befreien
liberation ⌈noun⌉ Befreiung [bə'fraɛʊŋ] die <-, –en>
most sing ◊ *die Befreiung der Frau*
liberty ⌈noun⌉ Freiheit ['fraɛhaɛt] die <-, –en> ◊ *das
Recht auf persönliche Freiheit* be at liberty auf
freiem Fuß sein [aɔf fraɛəm 'fuːs zaɛn] *+sein* sb is
at liberty to do sth jdm steht es frei, etw. zu tun
[ʃteːt ɛs 'fraɛ ... 'tuː] <stand frei, hat freigestanden> ◊
*Es steht dir frei, nach Hause zu gehen oder länger
zu bleiben.*
⊙ take the liberty of doing sth sich ⌈dat⌉ erlauben,
etw. zu tun take liberties with sth großzügig mit
etw. umgehen
Libra ⌈noun⌉ Waage ['vaːgə] die <-, –n>
librarian ⌈noun⌉ Bibliothekar [bibliote'kaːʳ] der
<-s, –e> ♀Bibliothekarin [bibliote'kaːrɪn] die
<-, –nen> ◊ *Sie ist Bibliothekarin.* ♦ *der neue Bib-
liothekar der Stadtbücherei*
library ⌈noun⌉ Bibliothek [biblio'teːk] die <-, –en> ◊
Mein Onkel hat eine umfangreiche Bibliothek. ♦ *sich
⌈dat⌉ ein Buch aus der Bibliothek ausleihen*
licence, license ⌈noun⌉ **1.** *(permission)* Genehmigung
[gə'neːmɪgʊŋ] die <-, –en> ◊ *ohne schriftliche
Genehmigung; (more formal)* Lizenz [li'tsɛnts] die
<-, –en> ◊ *Dem Trainer wurde die Lizenz entzogen.*
♦ *etw. unter Lizenz herstellen* a licence to print
money eine Lizenz zum Gelddrucken licence
agreement Lizenzvertrag [li'tsɛntsfɛtraːk] der
<-(e)s, Lizenzverträge>; *(for a pub, taxi)* Konzession
[kɔntsɛˈsjoːn] die <-, –en> ◊ *jdm eine Konzession
erteilen* TV licence (fee) Rundfunkgebühren
['rʊntfʊŋgəbyːrən] die <-> *pl* **2.** *(document, in
compound nfs)* ... licence ...schein [ʃaɛn] der
<-(e)s, –e> driving licence Führerschein ['fyːrəʃaɛn]
(rod) fishing licence Angelschein ['aŋlʃaɛn]
3. *(freedom)* Handlungsfreiheit ['handlʊŋsfraɛhaɛt]
die <-> *no pl* ◊ *Handlungsfreiheit haben* give sb
licence to do sth jdm erlauben, etw. zu tun
[ɛ'laɔbm̩ ... ʦuː] <erlaubt, erlaubte, hat erlaubt>;
(artistic) Freiheit ['fraɛhaɛt] die <-> *no pl* ◊ *künstle-
rische/dichterische Freiheit* **4.** *(pej)* *(permission to do
sth wrong)* Freibrief ['fraɛbriːf] der <-(e)s, –e> a
licence to steal/be lazy ein Freibrief zum Stehlen/
Faulenzen
license¹ → licence
license² ⌈verb⌉ **1.** *(give permission to do sth)* license
sb to do sth jdm die Lizenz erteilen, etw. zu tun
[di: li'tsɛnts ɛtaɛlən ... 'tuː] <erteilt, erteilte, hat
erteilt> be licensed to do sth die Lizenz haben, etw.
zu tun [di: li'tsɛnts ha:bm̩ ... 'tuː] *+haben* **2.** *(drugs,
medicines)* zulassen ['tsuːlasn̩] <lässt zu, ließ zu, hat
zugelassen> ◊ *ein Medikament zulassen*
license plate ⌈noun⌉ Nummernschild ['nʊmɐnʃɪlt] das
<-(e)s, –er>
lick ⌈verb⌉ **1.** *(with your tongue)* lecken ['lɛkn̩] *+haben* ◊
einen Teller sauber lecken The dog licked my/at my
hand. Der Hund leckte mir die/an meiner Hand.

lick sth from/off sth etw. von etw. ablecken [fɔn ... ˌaplɛkn̩] +haben ◊ *Er leckte die Marmelade vom Löffel ab.* **2.** *(fire)* lick sth an etw. ⟨dat⟩ emporzüngeln [an ... ɛmˌpoːɐ̯tsʏŋln̩] +sein ◊ *Flammen züngelten an den Wänden empor.* **3.** *(water)* lick sb's feet jdm über die Füße schwappen [yːbɐ diː ˈfyːsə ʃvapm̩] +haben
⊛ have sb licked jdn in die Tasche stecken *(fam)* have sth licked etw. in der Tasche haben *(fam)*

lid ⟨noun⟩ **1.** *(of a container)* Deckel [ˈdɛkl̩] der <-s, -> ◊ *der Deckel einer Schachtel/eines Marmeladenglases* **2.** *(of the eye)* Lid [liːt] das <-(e)s, -er> ⊛ take the lid off sth etw. aufdecken

lido ⟨noun⟩ Freibad [ˈfraɛbaːt] das <-(e)s, Freibäder>

lie¹ ⟨noun⟩ Lüge [ˈlyːgə] die <-, -n> ◊ *Erzähl mir keine Lügen.* ⊛ the lie of the land die Lage der Dinge give the lie to sth etw. Lügen strafen sb lives a lie jds Leben ist eine einzige Lüge

lie² ⟨verb⟩ **1.** *(be in a horizontal position, be somewhere in space or time)* liegen [ˈliːgn̩] <liegt, lag, hat gelegen> ◊ *Er liegt im Bett.* ♦ *Der Patient muss liegen.* ♦ *Die Betonung liegt auf der ersten Silbe.* ♦ *Das Dorf liegt in einem Tal.* ♦ *Sie liegt auf dem ersten Platz.* lie on your back/stomach auf dem Rücken/Bauch liegen **2.** *(tell a lie)* lügen [ˈlyːgn̩] <lügt, log, hat gelogen> ◊ *Du lügst doch!* ♦ *Können Statistiken lügen?* lie to sb jdn belügen [bəˈlyːgn̩] <belügt, belog, hat belogen>
• **lie ahead** ⟨phras v⟩ lie ahead (of sb) (jdm) bevorstehen [bəˈfoːɐ̯ʃteːən] <steht bevor, stand bevor, hat bevorgestanden> ◊ *Laut Wetterbericht steht ein Unwetter bevor.* ♦ *Ihm steht eine große Zukunft bevor.*
• **lie around** ⟨phras v⟩ herumliegen [hɛˈrʊmliːgn̩] <liegt herum, lag herum, hat herumgelegen> ◊ *Warum liegen deine Klamotten überall herum?*
• **lie back** ⟨phras v⟩ *(relax)* sich zurücklehnen [tsuˈrʏkleːgn̩] +haben ◊ *Es wird Zeit sich ein wenig zurückzulehnen und sich zu erholen*
• **lie behind** ⟨phras v⟩ lie behind sth hinter etw. stecken [ˈhɪntɐ ... ʃtɛkn̩] +haben ◊ *Was steckt wohl hinter dieser Entscheidung?*
• **lie down** ⟨phras v⟩ sich hinlegen [ˈhɪnleːgn̩] +haben ◊ *Er legt sich nach dem Essen immer eine halbe Stunde hin.* lie down on sth sich auf etw. ⟨acc⟩ legen [aʊf ... leːgn̩] ◊ *sich aufs Bett legen*
• **lie with** ⟨phras v⟩ lie with sb bei jdm liegen [baɛ ... liːgn̩] <liegt, lag, hat gelegen> ◊ *Die Schuld/Entscheidung liegt bei ihr.*
lie-in ⟨noun⟩ have a lie in sich ausschlafen [ˈaʊsʃlaːfn̩] <schläft sich aus, schlief sich aus, hat sich ausgeschlafen> ◊ *Ich muss mich dringend mal wieder ausschlafen.*

life ⟨noun⟩ Leben [ˈleːbm̩] das <-s, -> most sing ◊ *ein gesundes Leben führen* ♦ *Auf dem Marktplatz herrschte reges Leben.* ♦ *Gibt es Leben auf anderen Planeten?* ♦ *sein Leben verlieren* village life Dorfleben [ˈdɔrfleːbm̩] married life Eheleben [ˈeːələbm̩] plant life Pflanzenwelt [ˈpflantsn̩vɛlt] die <-> no pl way of life Lebensart [ˈleːbm̩saːɐ̯t] die <-> no pl sb's early life jds Jugend [ˈjuːgn̩t] in later life in späteren Jahren [ɪn ˈʃpɛːtərən jaːrən] ⊛ late in life erst im fortgeschrittenen Alter life is not a bed of roses im Leben ist man nicht auf Rosen gebettet breathe new life into sth frischen

Wind in etw. ⟨acc⟩ bringen claim lives Menschenleben fordern get life lebenslänglich bekommen not for the life of me *(fam)* nicht um alles in der Welt **lifeguard** ⟨noun⟩ Rettungsschwimmer [ˈrɛtʊŋsʃvɪmɐ] der <-s, -> ⚺Rettungsschwimmerin [ˈrɛtʊŋsʃvɪmərɪn] die <-, -nen> ◊ *eine Ausbildung als Rettungsschwimmer* ♦ *ein Rettungsschwimmer der Wasserwacht*
life jacket ⟨noun⟩ Schwimmweste [ˈʃvɪmvɛstə] die <-, -n> ◊ *Legen Sie eine Schwimmweste an!*
lifeless ⟨adj⟩ leblos [ˈleːploːs] <lebloser, am leblosesten> ◊ *ein lebloser Gesichtsausdruck* ♦ *Das Kind trieb leblos auf der Wasseroberfläche.*
lifespan ⟨noun⟩ **1.** *(of people, animals)* Lebenserwartung [ˈleːbm̩sʲlɛvaˈtʊŋ] die <-, -en> most sing ◊ *Wie hoch ist die Lebenserwartung eines Elefanten?* **2.** *(of objects)* Lebensdauer [ˈleːbm̩sdaʊɐ] die <-> no pl ◊ *die Lebensdauer eines Fernsehers*
lifestyle ⟨noun⟩ Lebensstil [ˈleːbm̩sʃtiːl] der <-(e)s, -e> ◊ *einen gesunden Lebensstil haben*
lifetime ⟨noun⟩ **1.** *(of a person)* Leben [ˈleːbm̩] das <-s, -> ◊ *während meines Lebens* **2.** *(of an object)* Lebensdauer [ˈleːbm̩sdaʊɐ] die <-> no pl ◊ *die Lebensdauer eines Produkts*
lift¹ ⟨noun⟩ **1.** *(in the UK: elevator)* Aufzug [ˈaʊftsuːk] der <-(e)s, Aufzüge> ◊ *den Aufzug nehmen* ♦ *mit dem Aufzug in den 6. Stock fahren* **2.** *(ride in a vehicle)* Mitfahrgelegenheit [ˈmɪtfaːɐ̯gəˌleːgn̩haɛt] die <-, -en> give sb a lift jdn mitnehmen [ˈmɪtneːmən] <nimmt mit, nahm mit, hat mitgenommen> get a lift (from sb) (von jdm) mitgenommen werden **3.** PHYSICS *(force)* Auftrieb [ˈaʊftriːp] der <-(e)s> no pl **4.** *(movement upwards)* Hochziehen [ˈhoːxtsiːən] das <-s> no pl ◊ *ein leichtes Hochziehen der Schultern/Augenbrauen*
lift² ⟨verb⟩ **1.** *(raise)* lift (up) heben [ˈheːbm̩] <hebt, hob, hat gehoben> ◊ *den Arm/die Hand heben* ♦ *Lasten mit einem Kran heben* lift your eyes den Blick heben; *(slightly)* anheben [ˈanheːbm̩] ◊ *Ich hebe den Tisch an, und du schiebst ein Brett unter das Bein.*; *(higher)* hochheben [ˈhoːxheːbm̩]; *(a telephone receiver)* abnehmen [ˈapneːmən] <nimmt ab, nahm ab, hat abgenommen> ◊ *den Hörer abnehmen* **2.** *(rise)* sich erheben [ɐˈheːbm̩] <erhebt sich, erhob sich, hat sich erhoben> *(lofty)* ◊ *Der Ballon erhob sich in die Luft.* **3.** *(end, remove)* aufheben [ˈaʊfheːbm̩] <hebt auf, hob auf, hat aufgehoben> ◊ *ein Embargo aufheben* **4.** *(fog, clouds)* sich verziehen [fɛˈtsiːən] <verzieht sich, verzog sich, hat sich verzogen> ◊ *Ob die Wolken sich heute noch verziehen?*
• **lift off** ⟨phras v⟩ abheben [ˈapheːbm̩] <hebt ab, hob ab, hat abgehoben> ◊ *Das Flugzeug hebt ab.*
• **lift up** ⟨phras v⟩ → **lift²** 1.
ligament ⟨noun⟩ Band [bant] das <-(e)s, Bänder> have a torn ligament einen Bänderriss haben [aɛnən ˈbɛndərɪs haːbm̩]
light¹ ⟨noun⟩ **1.** *(brightness or source thereof)* Licht [lɪçt] das <-(e)s, -er> ◊ *Setz dich ans Fenster, da hast du mehr Licht.* ♦ *das Licht einschalten/ausschalten* by the light of sth beim Schein ... ⟨gen⟩ [baɛm ˈʃaɛn] ◊ *beim Schein des Feuers/Mondes* **2.** *(lamp)* Lampe [ˈlampə] die <-, -n> ◊ *eine Lampe einschalten/ausschalten* ♦ *Im Cockpit leuchtete eine rote Lampe auf.* street light Laterne [laˈtɛrnə] die <-, -n> car light Scheinwerfer [ˈʃaɛnvɛrfɐ] der

<--s, --> traffic lights Ampel ['ampḷ] die <--, --n>
3. *(for a cigarette)* Feuer ['fɔøe] das <--s, --> ◊
Haben Sie mal Feuer?
◉ in a bad/different light in einem schlechten/
anderen Licht bring sth to light etw. ans Licht
bringen set light to sth etw. anzünden shed light
on sth Licht in etw. acc bringen
light² adj **1.** *(not heavy, not serious)* leicht [laeçt]
<leichter, am leichtesten> ◊ *leichte Lektüre/Verletzun-*
gen ♦ *leichter Regen* ♦ *leichte Kleidung tragen* ♦ *Der*
Koffer ist ganz leicht. ♦ *eine leichte Mahlzeit/Strafe*
be a light sleeper einen leichten Schlaf haben;
(kiss, touch, sound) sanft [zanft] <sanfter, am sanftes-
ten> ◊ *Seine Berührung war ganz sanft.* ♦ *ein*
sanfter Kuss **2.** *(bright, pale)* hell [hɛl] ◊ *helle Augen*
haben ♦ *Um sechs Uhr wird es hell.; (with colo(u)rs)*
light ... hell... [hɛl] light blue hellblau light red
hellrot **3.** *(easy to break up)* locker ['lɔke] ◊ *Pulver-*
schnee ist schön locker. ♦ *ein lockerer Kuchenteig*
light³ verb **1.** *(set alight)* light sth etw. anzünden
['antsyndn̩]; *(fireworks)* etw. zünden ['tsyndn̩] <zündet,
zündete, hat gezündet> +haben ◊ *ein Feuerwerk*
zünden **2.** *(start to burn)* sth will not light etw.
brennt nicht ['brɛnt nɪçt] <brannte, hat gebrannt> ◊
Die Kerze brennt nicht, weil der Docht nass ist.
• **light up** phras v **1.** *(make bright)* beleuchten
[bə'lɔøçtn̩] <beleuchtet, beleuchtete, hat beleuchtet> ◊
Das Licht der Kerze beleuchtete ihr Gesicht. ♦ *eine*
Bühne mit Scheinwerfern beleuchten **2.** *(also fig)*
(become bright, look happier) aufleuchten ['aoflɔøçtn̩]
<leuchtet auf, leuchtete auf, hat aufgeleuchtet> ◊ *Ein*
Warnlicht hat aufgeleuchtet. ♦ *Ihre Augen leuchteten*
auf.; (sb's face) sich aufhellen [zɪç 'aofhɛlən]
+haben ◊ *Als sie ihn kommen sah, hellte sich ihr*
Gesicht auf.

light bulb noun Glühbirne ['glyːbɪrnə] die <--, --n>
lighter noun Feuerzeug ['fɔøetsɔøk] das <--(e)s, --e>;
(in a car) Zigarettenanzünder [tsiga'rɛtn̩antsynde] der
<--s, -->
lighting noun Beleuchtung [bə'lɔøçtuŋ] die <--, --en>
most sing
lightly adv **1.** *(not heavily, not severely)* leicht [laeçt]
<leichter, am leichtesten> ◊ *Ich war nur leicht*
verletzt. ♦ *die Kuchenform leicht einfetten; (touch,*
kiss etc.) sanft [zanft] <sanfter, am sanftesten> ◊ *Er*
berührte sie sanft am Arm. **2.** *(without much consider-*
ation) leichtfertig ['laeçtfɛˈtɪç] ◊ *etw. leichtfertig*
sagen ♦ *eine Entscheidung leichtfertig treffen*
◉ get off lightly glimpflich davonkommen
lightning noun *(flash of)* lightning Blitz [blɪts] der
<--es, --e> ◊ *Blitz und Donner* ♦ *vom Blitz getroffen*
werden like lightning wie ein Blitz
like¹ noun **1.** the likes of sb Leute wie jd ['lɔøtə viː]
<--> pl ◊ *Leute wie du und ich* ♦ *Leute wie euch*
können wir hier nicht brauchen! **2.** and the like und
dergleichen [ʊnt deːˈɡ'glaeçn̩] invariable *(lofty)* ◊
Diebstahl, Mord und dergleichen
◉ sb's likes and dislikes jds Vorlieben und Abneigungen compare like with like *Vergleichbares*
gegenüberstellen
like² adj gleich [glaeç] no comp/superl ◊ *von gleicher*
Qualität/Art be of like mind (on sth) (über etw.
acc) gleich denken ['glaeç dɛŋkn̩] <denkt, dachte,
hat gedacht> ◊ *Wir denken über diese Sache gleich.*
like³ verb **1.** *(be fond of)* mögen ['møːɡn̩] <mag,
mochte, hat gemocht> ◊ *Sie mag keine Schokolade.* ♦

Ich mag ihn nicht. like sth about sb/sth etw. an
jdm/etw. mögen like sth best etw. am liebsten
mögen ◊ *sb would like sth* jd möchte etw. ◊ *Möchtest*
du ein Stück Kuchen? sb would like sb to do sth jd
möchte, dass jd etw. tut like doing/to do sth etw.
gern tun [gɛˈn̩] I like sleeping in. Ich schlafe gern
lange. Would you like to go out for a meal? Würdest
du gern essen gehen? sb likes sb to do sth jd hat
es gern , wenn jd etw. tut [hat ɛs 'gɛˈn vɛn] +haben
◊ *Ich habe es gern, wenn du für mich kochst.*
2. *(find pleasant)* sb likes sth jdm gefällt etw.
[gə'fɛlt] <gefällt, gefiel, hat gefallen> ◊ *Gefällt dir*
mein neues Kleid?
◉ how do you like that was sagst du dazu, was
sagen Sie dazu, was sagt ihr dazu if you like
1. *(when suggesting sth)* wenn du willst, wenn Sie
wollen, wenn ihr wollt ◊ *Wenn du willst,*
übernehme ich das. ♦ *Wir gehen jetzt nach Hause,*
wenn ihr wollt. **2.** *(expressing indifference)* meinetwegen ◊ *„Gehen wir ins Kino?" — „Meinetwegen."*
3. *(qualifying)* wenn man so will ◊ *Wenn man so*
will, ist das Leben eine Kette von Problemen. like it
or not auch wenn es jdm nicht passt ◊ *Ich bin*
jetzt Ihr Chef, auch wenn es Ihnen nicht passt!
like⁴ prep wie [viː] ◊ *Sie sieht aus wie du.* ♦ *Wir*
machen es, wie wir es immer gemacht haben.
◉ sth is just like sb etw. sieht jdm ähnlich it's
not like sb to do sth es ist gar nicht jds Art, etw.
zu tun ◊ *Es ist doch gar nicht deine Art, andere zu*
belügen.
like⁵ conjunc als ob [als ɔp] ◊ *Es sieht aus, als ob es*
gleich regnen würde. ♦ *Sie feiern, als ob es kein*
Morgen gäbe.

> In German, the conjunction 'like' is often followed by
> a subjunctive construction because it usually intro-
> duces a clause describing sth that is not certain or
> definite.

likeable adj sympathisch [zym'paːtɪʃ] ◊ *Ich finde sie*
nicht besonders sympathisch. ♦ *eine sympathische*
Stimme
likelihood noun Wahrscheinlichkeit [vaːˈʃaenlɪçkaet]
die <--, --en> most sing ◊ *die Wahrscheinlichkeit,*
dass etw. geschieht ♦ *Die Wahrscheinlichkeit einer*
Epidemie ist gering. in all likelihood wahrscheinlich
[vaːˈʃaenlɪç]
likely adj wahrscheinlich [vaːˈʃaenlɪç] ◊ *Es ist nicht*
sehr wahrscheinlich, dass er noch einmal heiratet. ♦
Du musst die wahrscheinlichste Antwort ankreuzen.
sb is more likely to do sth jd tut etw. häufiger
['hɔøfɪɡe] People who are overweight are more likely
to suffer from diabetes. Leute mit Übergewicht
leiden häufiger an Diabetes.
likewise adv ebenso ['eːbn̩zoː] ◊ *Der zweite Versuch*
ist ebenso gescheitert. Cats don't like dogs, and
likewise, dogs don't like cats. Katzen mögen keine
Hunde, und umgekehrt mögen Hunde auch keine
Katzen.
liking noun *(fondness)* Vorliebe ['foːgliːbə] die
<--, --n> ◊ *Seine Vorliebe für schnelle Autos wurde*
ihm zum Verhängnis. take a liking to sb/sth an
jdm/etw. Gefallen finden [an ... gə'falən fɪndn̩]
<findet, fand, hat gefunden> for sb's liking für jds
Geschmack [fyːɡ ... gə'ʃmak] sth is to sb's liking
etw. ist nach jds Geschmack ◊ *Dieses Haus ist ganz*
nach meinem Geschmack.

lilac [adj] lila ['liːlaː] *invariable* ◊ *Sie trug einen lila Pullover.* ✦ *Sein neues Auto ist lila.*

limb [noun] *(part of the body)* Glied [gliːt] das <-(e)s, -er> ◊ *Alle meine Glieder taten mir weh.*

⊚ go out on a limb sich exponieren

limber up [verb] sich lockern ['lɔken] +haben ◊ *Vor dem Wettkampf wollen wir uns lockern.*

lime [noun] 1. *(tree)* Linde ['lɪndə] die <-, -n> ◊ *die Linde vor dem Haus* 2. *(wood)* Lindenholz ['lɪndn̩hɔlts] das <-es> *no pl* ◊ *eine aus Lindenholz geschnitzte Figur* 3. *(fruit)* Limone [li'moːnə] die <-, -n> ◊ *ein Cocktail mit einem Stück Limone* 4. *(white substance)* Kalk [kalk] der <-(e)s> *no pl* ◊ *Azaleen vertragen keinen Kalk.*

limestone [noun] Kalkstein ['kalkʃtaen] der <-(e)s, -e> *most sing* ◊ *ein Plateau aus Kalkstein*

limit[1] [noun] Grenze ['grɛntsə] die <-, -n> ◊ *die Grenzen seiner Macht* there is a limit to sth etw. hat seine Grenzen ◊ *Meine Geduld hat ihre Grenzen.* set a limit eine Grenze setzen within limits innerhalb gewisser Grenzen; *(with figures)* Höchstgrenze ['høːçstɡrɛntsə] ◊ *Die Inflation darf die Höchstgrenze von drei Prozent nicht überschreiten.* city limit Stadtgrenze ['ʃtatɡrɛntsə] speed limit Geschwindigkeitsbegrenzung [ɡə'ʃvɪndɪçkaetsbəɡrɛntsʊŋ] die <-, -en> time limit Frist [frɪst] die <-, -en>

⊚ off limits verboten be over the limit zu viel Alkohol im Blut haben

limit[2] [verb] begrenzen [bə'ɡrɛntsn̩] <begrenzt, begrenzte, hat begrenzt> ◊ *den Stromverbrauch begrenzen* limit sth to sth etw. auf etw. [acc] begrenzen ◊ *Die Dauer wurde auf zwei Jahre begrenzt.* limit yourself to sth sich auf etw. [acc] beschränken [aof ... bə'ʃrɛŋkn̩] <beschränkt sich, beschränkte sich, hat sich beschränkt> ◊ *Ich beschränke mich auf wenige Kunden.* sth is limited to sb/sth etw. beschränkt sich auf jdn/etw. sth limits sb to sth jd muss sich wegen etw. auf etw. [acc] beschränken ◊ *Er muss sich wegen seiner Verletzung auf zwei Wettkämpfe beschränken.* sb is limited by sth jdm sind durch etw. Grenzen gesetzt [zɪnt dʊʳç ... 'ɡrɛntsn̩ ɡəzɛtst]; *(freedom, intake of sth, ability to do sth)* etw. einschränken ['aenʃrɛŋkn̩] +haben ◊ *Die Pressefreiheit wurde dadurch eingeschränkt.*

limitation [noun] 1. *(limiting of sth)* Begrenzung [bə'ɡrɛntsʊŋ] die <-, -en> ◊ *die Begrenzung der Zuwanderung* 2. *(deficiency, weakness)* limitation(s) Mangel ['maŋl̩] der <-s, Mängel-> ◊ *Die neue Technologie hat ihre Mängel.* space limitations Platzmangel ['platsmaŋl̩]

limp [verb] hinken ['hɪŋkn̩] +haben/with indication of direction +sein ◊ *Er hinkte ein bisschen.* ✦ *Sie ist zum Auto gehinkt.*

limp(ly) [adj, adv] schlaff [ʃlaf] ◊ *ein schlaffer Händedruck* ✦ *Mein Haar ist schlaff.* ✦ *Seine Arme hingen schlaff herunter.*

line[1] [noun] 1. *(long thin mark)* Linie ['liːnjə] die <-, -n> ◊ *Der Ball war über der Linie!* ✦ *die durchgezogene Linie auf der Straße; (short written mark)* Strich [ʃtrɪç] der <-(e)s, -e> ◊ *einen Strich ziehen* 2. *(way of thinking, of soldiers, air line)* Linie ['liːnjə] die <-, -n> ◊ *Unser Chef versucht, immer nur seine Linie durchzusetzen.* ✦ *hinter den feindlichen Linien* ✦ *Mit dieser Linie fliege ich nie wieder!* 3. *(row)* Reihe ['raeə] die <-, -n> ◊ *Die Bäume sind in einer*

Reihe gepflanzt. 4. *(string)* Leine ['laenə] die <-, -n> ◊ *die Wäsche auf die Leine hängen* 5. *(supply cable)* Leitung ['laetʊŋ] die <-, -en> ◊ *Leitungen für Strom/Telefon* 6. *(telephone)* Anschluss ['anʃlʊs] der <-es, Anschlüsse> ◊ *Ihr Anschluss ist ständig besetzt.* direct line Durchwahl ['dʊʳçvaːl] die <-, -en> 7. *(stretch of railway)* Strecke ['ʃtrɛkə] die <-, -n> ◊ *die Strecke von Bonn nach Koblenz; (track)* Gleis [ɡlaes] das <-es, -e> ◊ *Arbeiten an den Gleisen* 8. *(wrinkle)* Falte ['faltə] die <-, -n> ◊ *kleine Falten um den Mund* 9. *(boundary)* Grenze ['ɡrɛntsə] die <-, -n> ◊ *Es gibt eine feine Grenze zwischen Leidenschaft und Besessenheit.* 10. *(direction, strategy)* Kurs [kʊʳs] der <-es, -e> ◊ *der liberale Kurs der Regierung* line of argument Argumentation [aʳɡumɛnta'tsioːn] die <-, -en> bring sth in(to) line (with sth) etw. (einer Sache [dat]) anpassen ['anpasn̩] +haben ◊ *Er passte die Texte dem Zeitgeist an.* 11. *(of text)* Zeile ['tsaelə] die <-, -n> ◊ *Die Beschreibung ist nur wenige Zeilen lang.*

⊚ along similar lines auf ähnliche Art along the lines of sb/sth vergleichbar mit jdm/etw. all down the line *(constantly)* die ganze Zeit further down the line *(later)* zu einem späteren Zeitpunkt be in line for sth Aussicht auf etw. [acc] haben sth is on the line *(at risk)* etw. steht auf dem Spiel

line[2] [verb] 1. *(cover the inside with fabric)* füttern ['fʏten] +haben ◊ *Die Stiefel sind mit Schaffell gefüttert.; (with paper)* auslegen ['aosleːɡn̩] +haben ◊ *Legen Sie die Form mit Backpapier aus.* 2. *(form rows along sth)* säumen ['zɔømən] +haben ◊ *Menschen/Bäume säumten die Straße.*

• **line up** [phras v] 1. *(place next to each other)* aufstellen ['aofʃtɛlən] +haben ◊ *Flaschen nebeneinander/hintereinander aufstellen* sb lines up jd stellt sich auf ◊ *Bitte stellt euch hintereinander auf.* 2. *(plan, prepare)* organisieren [ɔʳɡani'ziːrən] <organisiert, organisierte, hat organisiert> ◊ *ein Unterhaltungsprogramm organisieren*

linear [adj] linear [line'aːʳ] *no comp/superl, mostly before ns (lofty)* ◊ *eine lineare Erzählweise*

linen [noun] 1. *(fabric)* Leinen ['laenən] das <-s> *no pl* ◊ *ein Hemd aus feinstem Leinen* 2. *(sheets, clothing etc.)* Wäsche ['vɛʃə] die <-> *no pl* ◊ *ein Schrank voll Wäsche*

line-up [noun] 1. *(of a sports team)* Mannschaftszusammenstellung ['manʃaftsʊ saˌmənʃtɛlʊŋ] die <-, -en> ◊ *die Mannschaftszusammenstellung für das Spiel gegen Bayern München* 2. *(people who perform together)* Ensemble [ãː'sãːbl̩] das <-s, -s> ◊ *Zum Schluss trat das gesamte Ensemble noch einmal auf die Bühne.* 3. *(TV programmes)* Programm [pro'ɡram] das <-s, -e> ◊ *das Programm zu Weihnachten* 4. *(in the US: identity parade)* Gegenüberstellung [ɡeːɡn̩'yːbeʃtɛlʊŋ] die <-, -en>

linger [verb] noch bleiben [nɔx 'blaebm̩] <bleibt, blieb, ist geblieben> ◊ *Nach der Arbeit blieben sie noch im Büro und schwatzten.; (smell)* noch hängen [nɔx 'hɛŋən] <hängt, hing, hat gehangen> ◊ *Der Fischgeruch hing noch in der Küche.* linger over a meal gemächlich essen [ɡə'mɛːçlɪç ˌɛsn̩] <isst, aß, hat gegessen>

linguist [noun] 1. *(sb who is good at languages)* Sprachler ['ʃpraːxle] der <-s, -> ♀Sprachlerin ['ʃpraːxlərɪn] die <-, -nen> *(fam)* 2. *(sb who has studied linguistics)* Linguist [lɪŋ'ɡʊɪst] der

<–en, –en> ♀Linguistin [lɪŋˈgʊɪstɪn] die <–, –nen>

linguistic [adj] sprachlich [ˈʃpraːxlɪç] *no comp/superl; when used as an adj, mostly before ns* ◊ *eine sprachliche Minderheit/Begabung*

lining [noun] Futter [ˈfʊtɐ] das <–s, –>

link¹ [noun] **1.** *(connection)* Verbindung [fɛˈbɪndʊŋ] die <–, –en> ◊ *eine Verbindung vom Computer zum Telefonnetz* ♦ *eine Verbindung schaffen* rail link Zugverbindung [ˈtsuːkfɛbɪndʊŋ]; *(causal relationship)* link between Zusammenhang zwischen [tsuˈzamənhaŋ tsvɪʃn̩] der <–(e)s, Zusammenhänge> ◊ *der Zusammenhang zwischen Rauchen und Lungenkrebs* **2.** *(connecting part)* Bindeglied [ˈbɪndəgliːt] das <–es, –er> a vital link between ein wichtiges Bindeglied zwischen **3.** *(to a web site)* Link [lɪŋk] der <–(s), –s> **4.** *(of a chain)* Glied [gliːt] das <–(e)s, –er>
🖝 the missing link das fehlende Glied the weakest link das schwächste Glied

link² [verb] **1.** *(connect)* verbinden [fɛˈbɪndn̩] <verbindet, verband, hat verbunden> ◊ *zwei Bretter mit einem Scharnier verbinden* ♦ *eng mit etw.* verbunden sein link sth to sth etw. mit etw. verbinden link arms sich einhaken [ˈaɛnhaːkn̩] +haben link arms with sb sich bei jdm einhaken ◊ *Ich hakte mich bei meiner Freundin ein.* **2.** *(show a relationship)* link sb/sth to sth jdn/etw. mit etw. in Verbindung bringen [mɪt ... ɪn fɛˌbɪndʊŋ brɪŋən] <bringt, brachte, hat gebracht> ◊ *Die Polizei bringt ihn mit dem Verbrechen in Verbindung.*

lion [noun] Löwe [ˈløːvə] der <–n, –n> ◊ *Der Löwe brüllte.*

lioness [noun] Löwin [ˈløːvɪn] die <–, –nen> ◊ *eine Löwin mit ihren Jungen*

lip [noun] **1.** *(part of the mouth)* Lippe [ˈlɪpə] die <–, –n> ◊ *Sie hatte sich die Lippen geschminkt.* **2.** *(of a cup)* Rand [rant] der <–(e)s, Ränder>
🖝 read my lips hören Sie gut zu, hör gut zu my lips are sealed ich schweige wie ein Grab

lipstick [noun] Lippenstift [ˈlɪpm̩ʃtɪft] der <–(e)s, –e> ◊ *Lippenstift auftragen*

liqueur [noun] Likör [liˈkøːɐ] der <–s, –e> ◊ *Ich trinke nicht gern Likör.*

liquid¹ [noun] Flüssigkeit [ˈflʏsɪçkaɛt] die <–, –en> ◊ *große Mengen an Flüssigkeit zu sich nehmen*

liquid² [adj] **1.** *(like water)* flüssig [ˈflʏsɪç] ◊ *ein flüssiges Waschmittel* ◊ *Wenn man Blei erhitzt, wird es flüssig.* **2.** FIN liquid [liˈkviːt] ◊ *liquide Aktien*

list¹ [noun] Liste [ˈlɪstə] die <–, –n> ◊ *eine Liste von/ der Aufgaben* ♦ *ganz oben/unten auf der Liste stehen* ♦ *eine Liste machen/schreiben* shopping list Einkaufsliste [ˈaɛnkaɔfslɪstə] bestseller list Bestsellerliste [ˈbɛstsɛlɐlɪstə]

list² [verb] *(enumerate, mention)* aufführen [ˈaɔffyːrən] +haben ◊ *Welche Gründe für ihre Entscheidung hat sie aufgeführt?* ♦ *Einige Produkte sind im Katalog nicht aufgeführt.; (phone number)* be listed im Telefonbuch stehen [ɪm teleˈfoːnbuːx ʃteːən] <steht, stand, hat gestanden>; *(verbally)* aufzählen [ˈaɔftsɛːlən] +haben ◊ *Sie zählte auf, was sie sich zu Weihnachten wünscht.*

listen [verb] *(hear attentively)* zuhören [ˈtsuːhøːrən] +haben ◊ *Hör gut zu!* listen to sb jdm zuhören; *(to music, the radio, sb's advice)* hören [ˈhøːrən] +haben ◊ *Musik hören* ♦ *Er hört einfach nicht.* listen to sb's advice auf jds Rat hören listen for sth auf etw. [acc]

horchen [aɔf ... ˌhɔˈrçn̩] +haben
• **listen in** [phras v] mithören [ˈmɪthøːrən] +haben ◊ *Vorsicht, Feind hört mit!* listen in on sth etw.
mithören ◊ *Kann jemand unser Gespräch mithören?*
• **listen up** [phras v] zuhören [ˈtsuːhøːrən] +haben ◊ *Hört mal alle zu!*

listener [noun] Hörer [ˈhøːrɐ] der <–s, –> ♀Hörerin [ˈhøːrərɪn] die <–, –nen> ◊ *Guten Abend, liebe Hörerinnen und Hörer.*

listless(ly) [adj, adv] lustlos [ˈlʊstloːs] <lustloser, am lustlosesten> ◊ *ein lustloser Versuch* ♦ *Er ist so lustlos.* ♦ *Sie bewegte sich lustlos.*

liter → litre

literacy [noun] Schreib- und Lesekundigkeit [ˌʃraɛp ʊnt ˈleːzəkʊndɪçkaɛt] die <–> *no pl*

literal [adj] wörtlich [ˈvœˈtlɪç] *no comp/superl, only before ns* ◊ *eine wörtliche Übersetzung*

literally [adv] **1.** *(truly)* buchstäblich [ˈbuːxʃtɛːplɪç] *no comp/superl* ◊ *Wir werden buchstäblich mit Werbung überschwemmt.* **2.** *(in the true sense of the word)* wörtlich [ˈvœˈtlɪç] *no comp/superl* ◊ *Ein „Tool" ist wörtlich übersetzt ein „Werkzeug".* ♦ *etw. wörtlich nehmen*

literary [adj] literarisch [lɪtəˈraːrɪʃ] ◊ *eine literarische Begabung* literary critic Literaturkritiker [lɪtəraˈtuːɐkriːtɪkɐ] der <–s, –> ♀Literaturkritikerin [lɪtəraˈtuːɐˌkriːtɪkərɪn] die <–, –nen>

literature [noun] Literatur [lɪtəraˈtuːɐ] die <–, –en> ◊ *die Literatur des 19. Jahrhunderts* ♦ *Literatur zum Thema Gentechnik*

Lithuania [noun] Litauen [ˈlɪtaɔən] das <–s> *article only in combination with attribute, no pl* → **Germany**

Lithuanian¹ [noun] **1.** Litauer [ˈlɪtaɔɐ] der <–s, –> ♀Litauerin [ˈlɪtaɔərɪn] die <–, –nen> → **German¹** **1. 2.** Litauisch [ˈlɪtaɔɪʃ] das <–(s)> *no pl* → **German¹ 2.**

Lithuanian² [adj] litauisch [ˈlɪtaɔɪʃ] → **German²**

litigation [noun] Rechtsstreit [ˈrɛçtsʃtraɛt] der <–(e)s, –e> be in litigation with sb mit jdm im Rechtsstreit liegen

litre, liter [noun] Liter [ˈliːtɐ] der <–s, –> ◊ *fünf Liter Wein* ♦ *ein halber Liter Milch*

litter [noun] **1.** *(rubbish)* Abfall [ˈapfal] der <–(e)s, Abfälle> ◊ *Die Straßen sind voller Abfall.* **2.** *(baby animals)* Wurf [vʊˈf] der <–(e)s, Würfe> ◊ *ein Wurf von sieben Kätzchen* **3.** *(for cats)* Streu [ʃtrɔɪ] die <–, –en> *most sing* ◊ *Streu fürs Katzenklo*

little¹ [adj] **1.** *(young, small)* klein [klaɛn] ◊ *Er ist noch zu klein, um das zu verstehen.* ♦ *Wir haben hier ein kleines Problem.* **2.** *(a short time)* a little while ago vor kurzem [foːɐ ˈkʊˈtsəm] ◊ *Er hat sie vor kurzem in der Stadt getroffen.* in a little while bald [balt] ◊ *Ich bin bald wieder da.* **3.** *(smile, laugh etc.)* kurz [kʊˈts] <kürzer, am kürzesten> ◊ *Er verabschiedete sich mit einem kurzen Lächeln.*
🖝 a little something eine Kleinigkeit

little² [adv] wenig [ˈveːnɪç] ◊ *In den letzten Wochen habe ich ihn wenig gesehen.* ♦ *Sie hat sich wenig verändert.* ♦ *wenig bekannt sein* as little as possible so wenig wie möglich as little as nicht mehr als [nɪçt meːɐ als]
🖝 do little to solve/stop etc. sth wenig tun, um etw. zu lösen/aufzuhalten etc. little does sb know/ realize that jd ahnt nicht, dass little by little allmählich

little³ [det] wenig ['veːnɪç] *indefinite and invariable* ◊ *Ich habe wenig Gutes gehört.* ◆ *wenig Zeit haben* ◆ *Sie haben meist wenig oder gar kein Geld.* too little zu wenig ◊ *Die Blumen bekommen hier zu wenig Sonne.* a little ein wenig ◊ *Mit ein wenig Glück schaffst du das bestimmt.*
little⁴ [indef pron] **1.** *(not much)* wenig ['veːnɪç] ◊ *Ich habe heute wenig gemacht.* ◆ *Man sah im Nebel sehr wenig von dem Haus.* **2.** the little das bisschen [das 'bɪsçən] ◊ *Das bisschen, was ich verdiene, reicht kaum aus.*
live¹ [adj] **1.** *(alive)* lebend ['leːbm̩t] *no comp/superl* ◊ *der Transport lebender Tiere* ◆ *Dieses Tier bringt lebende Junge zur Welt.* **2.** RADIO, TV live [laɛf] *no comp/superl, not before ns* ◊ *Die Sendung ist live.*; Live... [laɛf] live music Livemusik ['laɛfmuˌziːk] die <-> *no pl* live programme Livesendung ['laɛfzɛndʊŋ] die <-, –en> **3.** *(with electricity)* unter Strom stehend [ʊntɐ 'ʃtroːm ʃteːənt] *no comp/superl, only before ns* ◊ *ein unter Strom stehender Zaun* sth is live etw. steht unter Strom ◊ *Das Kabel steht unter Strom.* Danger, live wires! Vorsicht, Hochspannung! **4.** *(ammunition, bomb)* scharf [ʃaʁf] *no comp/superl* ◊ *scharfe Munition* ◆ *Ist die Bombe scharf?*; *(match)* ungebraucht ['ʊngəbraʊxt] *no comp/superl* ◊ *ein ungebrauchtes Zündholz* **5.** *(question, issue etc.)* aktuell [aktuˈɛl] ◊ *Das Waldsterben ist immer noch ein aktuelles Thema.*
⊚ real live waschecht ◊ *Sie ist mit einem waschechten Grafen verheiratet.*
live² [adv] live [laɛf] ◊ *Das Spiel wird live übertragen.* ◆ *Singt der Sänger live?*
live³ [verb] **1.** *(reside)* wohnen ['voːnən] +haben ◊ *Er wohnt in der Liebigstr. 11.* ◆ *Sie wohnen im zweiten Stock.* ◆ *auf dem Land wohnen* ◆ *Wohnst du noch bei deinen Eltern?* **2.** *(be alive, experience a particular way of life, exist on sth, enjoy your life)* leben ['leːbm̩] +haben ◊ *Lebt er noch?* ◆ *Wann hat Goethe gelebt?* ◆ *In diesem Land kann man billig leben.*; *(a life)* führen ['fyːrən] +haben ◊ *ein ruhiges Leben/ein Leben in Armut führen* live to be 80/90 etc. 80/90 etc. Jahre alt werden [ˌaxtsɪç/ˌnɔøntsɪç 'jaːrə alt veːɐdn̩] +sein live to see erleben [ɛˈleːbm̩] <erlebt, erlebte, hat erlebt> ◊ *Meine Oma hat die Geburt meiner Tochter leider nicht mehr erlebt.* **3.** *(still have influence)* weiterleben ['vaɛtɐleːbm̩] +haben ◊ *Sein Ruhm aber lebte ewig weiter.* **4.** *(fig) (belong)* live somewhere irgendwohin gehören [gəˈhøːrən] <gehört, gehörte, hat gehört> ◊ *Wohin gehört die Schere?*
⊚ sb can live with sth jd kann mit etw. leben live and let live leben und leben lassen
• **live by** [phras v] **1.** live by sth nach etw. leben [naːx ... leːbm̩] +haben ◊ *nach strengen Regeln leben* **2.** live by doing sth von etw. leben [fɔn ... leːbm̩] live by hunting von der Jagd leben
• **live for** [phras v] live for sb/sth für jdn/etw. leben [fyːɐ ... leːbm̩] +haben ◊ *nur für die Arbeit/Familie leben* He had nothing to live for. Er hatte nichts, wofür es sich zu leben lohnte.
• **live in** [phras v] im Haus wohnen [ɪm 'haʊs voːnən] +haben ◊ *Die Angestellten wohnen im Haus.*
• **live off** [phras v] live off sth von etw. leben [fɔn ... leːbm̩] +haben ◊ *Er lebt von seiner Erbschaft.* live off sb auf jds Kosten leben ◊ *Sie lebt immer*

noch auf Kosten ihrer Eltern.
• **live on** [phras v] **1.** *(not die)* weiterleben ['vaɛtəleːbm̩] +haben ◊ *Großvater lebt in unseren Herzen weiter.* **2.** *(on money, food)* live on sth von etw. leben [fɔn ... leːbm̩] +haben ◊ *Sie lebt von einer kleinen Rente.* ◆ *Viele Wale leben von winzigen Krebsen.*
• **live out** [phras v] **1.** *(a fantasy)* ausleben ['aʊsleːbm̩] +haben ◊ *Er träumt davon, seine Fantasien endlich einmal auszuleben.* **2.** *(not live where you work or study)* außerhalb wohnen ['aʊsehalp voːnən] +haben ◊ *Viele Studenten wohnen außerhalb.* **3.** *(your life, a period of time etc.)* verbringen [fɛˈbrɪŋən] <verbringt, verbrachte, hat verbracht> ◊ *Er wollte die letzten Tage seines Lebens bei seiner Familie verbringen.*
• **live through** [phras v] live through sth etw. miterleben ['mɪtˌele leːbm̩] <erlebt mit, erlebte mit, hat miterlebt> ◊ *Er hat zwei Weltkriege miterlebt.*
• **live together** [phras v] zusammenleben [tsuˈzamənleːbm̩] +haben ◊ *Sie leben seit drei Jahren zusammen.*
• **live up to** [phras v] live up to sth *(an expectation, promise)* einer Sache [dat] entsprechen [ɛntˈʃpreçn̩] <entspricht, entsprach, hat entsprochen> ◊ *Das Zimmer entspricht ihren Erwartungen.* ◆ *Das Essen entspricht nicht dem, was man uns versprochen hat.*; *(a standard, reputation)* einer Sache [dat] gerecht werden [gəˈrɛçt veːɐdn̩] +sein ◊ *den Anforderungen gerecht werden* ◆ *Sie wurde ihrem Ruf nicht gerecht.*
livelihood [noun] Existenz [ɛksɪsˈtɛnts] die <-, –en> ◊ *Die Existenz vieler Bauern ist bedroht.* sth is sb's livelihood jd verdient sich [dat] seinen Lebensunterhalt mit etw. [fɛˌdiːnt ... zaːnən 'leːbm̩sˌʊntəhalt mɪt] <verdiente sich, hat sich verdient> ◊ *Sie verdient sich ihren Lebensunterhalt mit Schneidern.*
lively [adj] *(person, imagination, discussion, interest)* lebhaft ['leːphaft] <lebhafter, am lebhaftesten> ◊ *ein lebhaftes Kind* ◆ *Deine Fantasie ist sehr lebhaft.* ◆ *lebhaftes Interesse für etw. zeigen*; *(account, scene)* lebendig [leˈbɛndɪç] <-> ◊ *Sein Aufsatz war sehr lebendig.*; *(mind)* wach [vax] ◊ *Er hat einen wachen Verstand.*
liver [noun] Leber ['leːbɐ] die <-, –n> ◊ *Alkohol schadet der Leber.* ◆ *gebratene Leber*
livestock [noun] Vieh [fiː] das <-(e)s> *no pl* ◊ *Vieh füttern/versorgen*
living¹ [noun] **1.** *(livelihood)* Lebensunterhalt ['leːbm̩sˌʊntəhalt] der <-(e)s> *no pl* earn/make a living sich [dat] seinen Lebensunterhalt verdienen ◊ *Sie verdient sich ihren Lebensunterhalt als Tänzerin.* do sth for a living etw. beruflich machen [bəˈruːflɪç maxn̩] +haben ◊ *Was machen Sie beruflich?* **2.** *(way of life)* Leben ['leːbm̩] das <-s> *no pl* ◊ *das moderne Leben* ◆ *das Leben in der Großstadt*
⊚ scratch a living über die Runden kommen
living² [adj] **1.** *(not dead)* lebend ['leːbm̩t] *no comp/superl* ◊ *ein lebender Frosch* ◆ *Er hat keine lebenden Verwandten.* ◆ *lebende Sprachen* ◆ *ein lebendes Beispiel für etw.* the living die Lebenden living creature/thing Lebewesen ['leːbəˌveːzn̩] das <-s, -> **2.** living conditions Wohnverhältnisse ['voːnfɛˌhɛltnɪsə] die <-> *pl*
living room [noun] Wohnzimmer ['voːntsɪmɐ] das

<--s, -->

lizard [noun] Eidechse ['aɛdɛksə] die <-, –n>

load¹ [noun] **1.** *(weight, burden)* Last [last] die <-, –en> *(also fig)* ◊ *Lasten bis zu 200 Kilo* ♦ *die Last gleichmäßig verteilen* ♦ *Das Geheimnis war eine schwere Last.*; *(cargo, quantity)* Ladung ['la:dʊŋ] die <-, –en> ◊ *Er kam mit einer Ladung Holz/Steine zurück.* **2.** *(workload)* Pensum ['pɛnzʊm] das <-s, Pensen or Pensa> *most sing* ◊ *Er konnte das Pensum nicht mehr bewältigen.* **3.** *(amount of washing)* Maschine [ma'ʃi:nə] die <-, –n> *(fam)* ◊ *Sie hat heute drei Maschinen Wäsche gewaschen.*
Ⓔ **a load of, loads of** eine Menge ◊ *eine Menge Probleme/Geld*

load² [verb] **1.** *(goods onto/into sth)* einladen ['aɛnla:dn̩] <lädt ein, lud ein, hat eingeladen> ◊ *Wir laden gerade ein.* **load sth onto/into sth** etw. auf/in [acc] etw. laden [aʊf/ɪn ... la:dn̩] <lädt, lud, hat geladen> ◊ *Sie luden die Güter auf den Lastwagen.*; *(a lorry, plate etc.)* load sth (with sth) etw. (mit etw.) beladen [bə'la:dn̩] <belädt, belud, hat beladen> ◊ *Sie belud seinen Teller mit Fleisch und Gemüse.* ♦ *Der Lastwagen war mit Fässern beladen.* **2.** *(a camera, DVD player etc.)* load sth into sth etw. in etw. [acc] einlegen ['aɛnle:gn̩] +haben ◊ *Sie legte eine Kassette in den Rekorder ein und drückte auf „Start".* **load a camera with a film** einen Film in eine Kamera einlegen; *(a gun, data)* laden ['la:dn̩] <lädt, lud, hat geladen> ◊ *Er lud sein Gewehr.* ♦ *ein Programm aus dem Internet auf die Festplatte laden*

loaded → **load** [adj] **1.** *(having very much of sth)* loaded with sth voller etw. [gen] ['fɔlɐ] *invariable*; *when followed by a noun attribute, the noun remains uninflected* ◊ *ein Baum voller Kerzen und Weihnachtsschmuck* **2.** **loaded question** Fangfrage ['faŋfra:gə] die <-, –n> **3.** *(very rich)* stinkreich ['ʃtɪŋk'raɛç] *no comp/superl* *(fam)* ◊ *Diese Familie ist stinkreich.* ♦ *Er hat eine stinkreiche Frau geheiratet.*

loaf [noun] Laib [laɛp] der <-(e)s, –e> *pl 'Laib' when used with expressions of quantity* ◊ *zwei Laib Brot vom Bäcker holen* ♦ *die Laibe in den Ofen schieben*

loaf about [verb] faulenzen ['faʊlɛntsn̩] +haben *(esp pej)* ◊ *Er faulenzt den ganzen Tag.*

loan [noun] **1.** *(money borrowed)* Darlehen ['da:ʳle:ən] das <-s, –> ◊ *Er hat zum Kauf eines Grundstücks ein Darlehen über 180 000 Euro aufgenommen.*; *(by a business or government)* Anleihe ['anlaɛə] die <-, –n> ◊ *öffentliche Anleihen* **2.** *(lend sb sth)* give sb a/the loan of sth jdm etw. leihen ['laɛən] <leiht, lieh, hat geliehen> ◊ *Sie hat mir ihr Auto geliehen.*; *(borrowed, not belonging to you)* on loan geliehen [gə'li:ən] *no comp/superl* ◊ *Der Koffer gehört mir nicht, er ist nur geliehen.*; *(out on loan)* on loan ausgeliehen ['aʊsgəli:ən] *no comp/superl* ◊ *Leider ist das Buch gerade ausgeliehen.*

lobby [noun] **1.** POL *(group of supporters, place in the Houses of Parliament)* Lobby ['lɔbi] die <-, –s> ◊ *Die Bauern haben in Deutschland eine starke Lobby.* ♦ *jdn in der Lobby treffen* **2.** *(entrance hall)* Eingangshalle ['aɛngaŋshalə] die <-, –n>

lobe [noun] **1.** *(of the brain, lungs)* Lappen ['lapn̩] der <-s, –> **2.** *(of the ear)* Ohrläppchen ['o:ɐlɛpçən] das <-s, –>

local¹ [noun] **1.** *(person)* Einheimische ['aɛnhaɛmɪʃə] der/die <-n, die Einheimischen> *but: ein Einheimischer/eine Einheimische* ◊ *Die Einheimischen waren*

sehr hilfsbereit. **2.** *(in the UK: pub)* Stammlokal ['ʃtamlo,ka:l] das <-s, –e> ◊ *Er geht jeden Samstag in sein Stammlokal.*

local² [adj] **1.** *(in or from a particular area, anaesthetic)* örtlich ['œʳtlɪç] *no comp/superl, only before ns* ◊ *die örtliche Bevölkerung/Tageszeitung* ♦ *eine örtliche Betäubung erhalten*; *(in this area)* hiesig ['hi:zɪç] *no comp/superl, only before ns* ◊ *die hiesigen Firmen* **2.** *(community)* Kommunal... [kɔmu'na:l] *local election* Kommunalwahl [kɔmu'na:lva:l] die <-, –en> *most pl* *local politician* Kommunalpolitiker [kɔmu'na:lpo,li:tɪkɐ] der <-s, –> ♀Kommunalpolitikerin [kɔmu'na:lpo,li:tɪkərɪn] die <-, –nen>

local council [noun] Gemeindeverwaltung [gə'maɛndəfɛvaltʊŋ] die <-, –en>

local court [noun] Amtsgericht ['amtsgərɪçt] das <-(e)s, –e> *most sing*

locality [noun] Gegend ['ge:gn̩t] die <-, –en> ◊ *eine andere Gegend ziehen* ♦ *Gibt es hier in der Gegend ein Kino?*

locally [adv] **1.** *(in a particular place)* vor Ort [fo:ɐ 'ɔʳt] ◊ *Ich kaufe lieber vor Ort ein.* **2.** *(in some places)* örtlich ['œʳtlɪç] *no comp/superl* ◊ *Örtlich kann es zu schweren Unwettern kommen.*

local resident [noun] Anwohner ['anvo:nɐ] der <-s, –> ♀Anwohnerin ['anvo:nərɪn] die <-, –nen> ◊ *Die Anwohner hatten sich über den Lärm beschwert.*

locate [verb] **1.** *(find)* ausfindig machen ['aʊsfɪndɪç maxn̩] +haben ◊ *Man versucht, den Fehler ausfindig zu machen.*; *(a ship, plane)* orten ['ɔʳtn̩] <ortet, ortete, hat geortet> ◊ *ein gesunkenes Schiff orten* **2.** *(build)* errichten [ɛ'rɪçtn̩] <errichtet, errichtete, hat errichtet> ◊ *Am Stadtrand soll eine Fabrik errichtet werden.*

located → **locate** [adj] gelegen [gə'le:gn̩] *no comp/superl* ◊ *Das Restaurant ist in der Nähe des Bahnhofs gelegen.* ♦ *ein günstig/zentral gelegenes Hotel*

location [noun] **1.** *(site, position)* Lage ['la:gə] die <-, –n> ◊ *Die Jugendherberge befindet sich in ruhiger Lage.*; *(place)* Ort [ɔʳt] der <-(e)s, –e> ◊ *erste Eindrücke vom Ort des Geschehens* ♦ *Sie hält sich an einem geheimen/sicheren Ort auf.*; *(for a building, firm)* Standort ['ʃtant|ɔʳt] der <-(e)s, –e> ◊ *Unsere Stadt ist ein attraktiver Standort für große Unternehmen.* **2.** *(act of finding)* Auffinden ['aʊffɪndn̩] das <-s> *no pl* ◊ *Das Auffinden der Verirrten war nicht einfach.* **3.** FILM Drehort ['dre:|ɔʳt] der <-(e)s, –e> ◊ *Der Film wurde an verschiedenen Drehorten in Deutschland und Frankreich gedreht.* **be somewhere on location** irgendwo bei Außenaufnahmen sein
[baɛ 'aʊsn̩|aʊfna:mən tsaɛn] +sein ◊ *Sie ist zurzeit bei Außenaufnahmen in Südfrankreich.*

lock¹ [noun] **1.** *(to prevent opening)* Schloss [ʃlɔs] das <-es, Schlösser> ◊ *Der Schlüssel drehte sich im Schloss.* **2.** *(on a river, canal)* Schleuse ['ʃlɔɡzə] die <-, –n> ◊ *Das Schiff passierte die Schleuse.* **3.** *(in a fight)* Schwitzkasten ['ʃvɪtskastn̩] der <-s> *no pl* ◊ *jdn in den Schwitzkasten nehmen* **4.** IT Sperre ['ʃpɛrə] die <-, –n> ◊ *Der Zugang zum Internet war mit einer Sperre versehen.* **5.** *(steering wheel)* on full lock mit voll eingeschlagener Lenkung
[mɪt ˌfɔl aɛngəʃla:gənɐ 'lɛŋkʊŋ] ◊ *Auch mit voll eingeschlagener Lenkung konnte sie auf der schmalen*

Straße nicht wenden. **6.** *(of hair)* Locke ['lɔkə] die <–, –n> ◊ *ein Kind mit blonden Locken* ⚫ **keep sth under lock and key** etw. unter Verschluss halten **put sb under lock and key** jdn hinter Schloss und Riegel bringen

lock² [verb] **1.** *(a door, house, car etc.)* abschließen ['apʃliːsn̩] <schließt ab, schloss ab, hat abgeschlossen> ◊ *Hast du das Auto abgeschlossen?* **lock sb/sth in sth** jdn/etw. in etw. [acc]/[dat] einschließen [ɪn ... 'aɛnʃliːsn̩] <schließt ein, schloss ein, hat eingeschlossen> ◊ *Schließ das Geld besser in den Safe ein.* ♦ *Er schloss den Jungen in sein/seinem Zimmer ein.* **sth locks etw.** schließt [ʃliːst] <schloss, hat geschlossen> ◊ *Die Tür schließt nicht richtig.*; *(have a lock)* **sth locks etw.** lässt sich abschließen [lɛst zɪç 'apʃliːsn̩] <ließ sich, hat sich lassen> ◊ *ein Koffer, der sich abschließen lässt* **2.** *(stick in one position)* blockieren [blɔ'kiːrən] <blockiert, blockierte, hat blockiert> ◊ *Plötzlich blockierten die Räder.*; *(hold sb/sth tightly)* **lock sth around sb/sth** jdn/etw. mit etw. umschließen [mɪt ... ʊmʃliːsn̩] <umschließt, umschloss, hat umschlossen> ◊ *Sie umschloss seinen Hals mit beiden Armen.* **3.** *(data etc.)* sperren ['ʃpɛrən] +haben ◊ *Die Daten sind gesperrt und können somit nicht verändert werden.* **4.** **sb's eyes lock** jds Blicke treffen sich [ˌblɪkə 'trɛfn̩ zɪç] <trafen sich, haben sich getroffen> ◊ *Ihre Blicke trafen sich.* **5.** **be locked in each other's arms/an embrace** sich fest umschlungen halten [ˌfɛst ʊm'ʃlʊŋən haltn̩] <hält sich, hielt sich, hat sich gehalten> ◊ *Die Liebenden hielten sich fest umschlungen.*

• **lock away** [phras v] **1.** *(an object)* wegschließen ['vɛkʃliːsn̩] <schließt weg, schloss weg, hat weggeschlossen> ◊ *Wertsachen/Schmuck/Waffen wegschließen* **2.** *(a criminal)* einsperren ['aɛnʃpɛrən] +haben *(fam)* ◊ *Solche Verbrecher sollten für den Rest ihres Lebens eingesperrt werden!*

• **lock in** [phras v] **lock sb/yourself in** jdn/sich einsperren ['aɛnʃpɛrən] +haben ◊ *Du kannst doch das Kind nicht einsperren!* ♦ *Sie ging ins Bad und sperrte sich ein.*

• **lock into** [phras v] **lock sb/sth into sth** jdn/etw. an etw. [acc] binden [an ... ˌbɪndn̩] <bindet, band, hat gebunden> ◊ *Wir sind an diesen Lieferanten/Vertrag gebunden.*

• **lock out** [phras v] **lock sb/yourself out** *(of sth)* jdn/sich (aus etw.) aussperren ['aɔsʃpɛrən] +haben ◊ *Sie sperrte ihn aus der Wohnung aus.* ♦ *Ich habe mich aus Versehen ausgesperrt.*

• **lock up** [phras v] **1.** *(a house, bicycle etc.)* abschließen ['apʃliːsn̩] <schließt ab, schloss ab, hat abgeschlossen> ◊ *Vergiss nicht, abzuschließen, wenn du gehst.* ♦ *Er schloss das Fahrrad ab.* **2.** *(valuable or dangerous objects)* wegschließen ['vɛkʃliːsn̩] <schließt weg, schloss weg, hat weggeschlossen> ◊ *Wertsachen/Waffen wegschließen* **3.** *(a criminal)* einsperren ['aɛnʃpɛrən] +haben *(fam)* ◊ *Ich hoffe, sie sperren ihn dafür ein!*

locker [noun] Schließfach ['ʃliːsfax] das <–(e)s, Schließfächer> ◊ *das Gepäck in einem Schließfach aufbewahren*; *(for clothes)* Spind [ʃpɪnt] der or das <–(e)s, –e> **locker room** Umkleideraum ['ʊmklaɛdəraɔm] der <–(e)s, Umkleideräume>

locksmith [noun] Schlosser ['ʃlɔsɐ] der <–s, –> ♀Schlosserin ['ʃlɔsərɪn] die <–, –nen> ◊ *einen Schlosser kommen lassen* ♦ *Sie ist Schlosserin.*

locomotive [noun] Lokomotive [lokomo'tiːvə] die <–, –n>

lodge¹ [noun] **1.** *(for shooting, skiing etc.)* Hütte ['hʏtə] die <–, –n> ◊ *Sie verbrachten die Ferien in einer kleinen Hütte in den Bergen.*; *(in the grounds of a large property)* Pförtnerhaus ['pfœrtnehaɔs] das <–es, Pförtnerhäuser> **2.** *(room at the entrance to a building)* Pförtnerloge ['pfœrtnelo:ʒə] die <–, –n> ◊ *Sie versuchte, unbemerkt an der Pförtnerloge vorbeizukommen.* **3.** *(of a beaver)* Bau [baɔ] der <–(e)s, –e>

lodge² [verb] **1.** *(a complaint)* einlegen ['aɛnle:gn̩] +haben ◊ *Bitte legen Sie bei der zuständigen Behörde Beschwerde ein.*; *(a claim)* einreichen ['aɛnraɛçn̩] +haben ◊ *ein Gesuch einreichen* **2.** *(be stuck)* be lodged somewhere irgendwo stecken ['ʃtɛkn̩] +haben ◊ *Eine Gräte steckt ihm im Hals.* **3.** *(live)* wohnen ['vo:nən] +haben ◊ *Er wohnt im Moment bei seiner Tante.* **lodge sb** jdn unterbringen ['ʊntebrɪŋən] <bringt unter, brachte unter, hat untergebracht> ◊ *Wer kann einen französischen Gastschüler unterbringen?* **4.** *(deposit)* deponieren [depo'niːrən] <deponiert, deponierte, hat deponiert> ◊ *Sie deponierten den Schmuck im Safe.* **lodge sth with sb/a bank** etw. bei jdm/einer Bank deponieren

lodger [noun] Untermieter ['ʊntemiːtɐ] der <–s, –> ♀Untermieterin ['ʊntemiːtərɪn] die <–, –nen> ◊ *Frau Schneider nimmt Untermieter auf.* **be a lodger somewhere** irgendwo zur Untermiete wohnen [tsuːɐ 'ʊntemiːtə vo:nən] +haben

loft [noun] **1.** *(attic, for hay)* Speicher ['ʃpaɛçɐ] der <–s, –> ◊ *Wir haben die alten Möbel auf den Speicher gebracht.* ♦ *Heu in einem Speicher lagern*; *(in a church)* Empore [ɛm'po:rə] die <–, –n> ◊ *Der Chor stand auf der Empore.*; *(flat)* Loft [lɔft] der <–(s), –s> ◊ *Sie haben ein Loft in Berlin.* **2.** *(for pigeons)* Taubenschlag ['taɔbmʃla:k] der <–(e)s, Taubenschläge>

lofty [adj] **1.** *(high)* hoch [ho:x] <höher, am höchsten> ◊ *Das Gebäude ist sehr hoch.* ♦ *hohe Ansprüche haben*; *(style of writing)* gehoben [gə'ho:bm] ◊ *ein Text in gehobenem Stil* **2.** *(haughty)* hochmütig ['ho:xmy:tɪç] ◊ *Ihre hochmütige Art kommt nicht gut an.*

log¹ [noun] **1.** *(of wood)* Klotz [klɔts] der <–es, Klötze>; *(for a fire)* Scheit [ʃaɛt] das <–es, –e or also –er> ◊ *ein paar Scheite nachlegen* **2.** *(record)* Aufzeichnungen ['aɔftsaɛçnʊŋən] die <–> pl ◊ *Er hat genaue Aufzeichnungen hinterlassen.* **keep a log of sth** über etw. [acc] Buch führen [y:bɐ ... 'bu:x fy:rən] +haben ◊ *Sie hat über ihre Fahrten immer Buch geführt.*; *(ship's record)* Logbuch ['lɔkbu:x] das <–(e)s, Logbücher> ◊ *etw. ins Logbuch eintragen*

log² [verb] **1.** *(write down)* log sth über etw. [acc] Buch führen [y:bɐ ... 'bu:x fy:rən] +haben ◊ *Er führt über alle Ereignisse genau Buch.* **2.** *(travel)* zurücklegen [tsu'rʏkle:gn̩] +haben ◊ *Sie hatten bereits über 3 000 Kilometer zurückgelegt.* **3.** *(cut down trees)* log *(trees)* Bäume fällen ['bɔɡmə fɛlən] +haben ◊ *Die Arbeiter fällen Bäume für Bauholz.*

• **log off** [phras v] → **log out**

• **log in** [phras v] sich anmelden ['anmɛldn̩] +haben ◊ *Melden Sie sich mit Ihrem Passwort an!*

• **log on** [phras v] → **log in**

• **log out** [phras v] sich abmelden ['apmɛldn̩] +haben ◊ *Vergessen Sie nicht, sich am Schluss abzumelden!*

logic [noun] Logik ['lɔːgɪk] die <–> *no pl* ◊ *Ich sehe die Logik Ihrer Schlussfolgerung nicht.* **defy logic** gegen die Logik verstoßen ◊ *Das verstößt gegen jede Logik.*

logical(ly) [adj, adv] logisch ['lɔːgɪʃ] ◊ *das logische Denken fördern* ♦ *Diese Folgerung ist nicht logisch.* ♦ *logisch denken können*

lollipop [noun] Lutscher ['lʊtʃe] der <–s, –> ◊ *an einem Lutscher lecken*

lone [adj] **1.** *(solitary)* einzeln ['aentsļn] *no comp/superl* ◊ *Sie konnte in der Ferne eine einzelne Gestalt ausmachen.* **2.** *(just one)* einzig ['aentsɪç] *no comp/ superl* ◊ *Wie kann ein einziger Mensch so großes Unheil anrichten?* **3.** *(in the UK: bringing up children as a single parent)* allein erziehend [a'laen e,tsiːənt] *no comp/superl* ◊ *eine allein erziehende Mutter*

lonely [adj] einsam ['aenzaːm] ◊ *Sie fühlte sich einsam und allein.* ♦ *Sie wohnen in einer einsamen Gegend.*

loner [noun] Einzelgänger ['aentsļgɛŋe] der <–s, –> ♀Einzelgängerin ['aentsļgɛŋerɪn] die <–, –nen> ◊ *Er war schon immer ein Einzelgänger.* ♦ *Als Einzelgängerin unternimmt sie viel allein.*

long¹ [adj] **1.** *(in time, size, distance)* lang [laŋ] <länger, am längsten> ◊ *für eine lange Zeit* ♦ *Der Rock ist mir zu lang.* ♦ *Das Brett ist drei Meter lang.* ♦ *eine lange Geschichte* ♦ *Das erste „e" in „beten" ist lang.* **sth is a long way** etw. ist weit [ɪst 'vaet] ◊ *Von hier nach Australien ist es weit.*; *(temporal)* sth is ... long etw. dauert ... ['daoet] ◊ *Der Film dauert 90 Minuten.* ♦ **long memory** ein gutes Gedächtnis haben [aen ,guːtəs gə'dɛçtnɪs haːbm̩] *+haben* **2. long drink** Longdrink ['lɔndrɪŋk] der <–(s), –s> ⊛ **at long last** endlich

long² [adv] lang(e) [laŋ, 'laŋə] <länger, am längsten> ◊ *Hast du lange gewartet?* ♦ *Wie lange möchtet ihr bleiben?* ♦ *schon lange bevor ...* ♦ *erst lange nachdem ...* ♦ *Lang lebe die Königin!* **all day/week etc.** long den ganzen Tag/die ganze Woche etc. lang ⊛ **long ago 1.** *(much earlier)* schon längst ◊ *Ich hätte ihn schon längst verlassen sollen* **2.** *(way back in the past)* vor langer Zeit ◊ *Vor langer Zeit lebte einmal ein Bauer.* **sb won't be long** jd braucht nicht lange ◊ *Ich brauche nicht lange; warte einen Augenblick.* **it won't be long** es wird nicht lange dauern ◊ *Es wird nicht lange dauern, bis das neue Handy kaputtgeht.* **as long as** solange ◊ *Wie viel ich verdiene, ist mir egal, solange die Arbeit Spaß macht.* **no longer** nicht mehr **so long** bis dann *(fam)*

long³ [verb] long for sth/sb sich nach etw./jdm sehnen [naːx ... ,zeːnən] *+haben* ◊ *Nach dem langen Winter sehnte sie sich nach dem Sommer.* ♦ *Ich sehne mich so nach ihm!* **long to do sth** sich danach sehnen, etw. zu tun **long for sb/sth to do sth** es kaum erwarten können, dass jd/etw. etw. tut [ɛs kaom e'va'tn̩ kœnən das] <kann, konnte, hat können> ◊ *Die Kinder konnten es kaum erwarten, dass ihr Vater nach Hause kam.*

longing [noun] Sehnsucht ['zeːnzʊxt] die <–, Sehnsüchte> ◊ *die Sehnsucht nach Liebe*

longing(ly) [adj, adv] sehnsüchtig ['zeːnzʏçtɪç] ◊ *sehnsüchtige Blicke* ♦ *Sie wartete sehnsüchtig auf seine Rückkehr.*

longitude [noun] Länge ['lɛŋə] die <–, –n> ◊ *Die Insel liegt auf 20° östlicher Länge.*

long-life [adj] *(food)* haltbar ['haltbaːʳ] ◊ *haltbare Nahrungsmittel* **long-life milk** H-Milch ['haːmɪlç] die <–> *no pl*; *(battery)* mit langer Lebensdauer [mɪt ,laŋe 'leːbm̩sdaoe] ◊ *Batterien mit langer Lebensdauer kaufen*

long-sighted [adj] weitsichtig ['vaetzɪçtɪç] *(also fig)* ◊ *Sie ist weitsichtig und braucht daher zum Lesen eine Brille.* ♦ *Wir brauchen weitsichtige Politiker.*

long-term [adj] **1.** *(investment, plan etc.)* langfristig ['laŋfrɪstɪç] ◊ *eine langfristige Investition/Strategie* **2.** *(memory, effect)* Langzeit... ['laŋtsaet] **long-term effect** Langzeitwirkung ['laŋtsaetvɪrkʊŋ] die <–, –en> **long-term memory** Langzeitgedächtnis ['laŋtsaetgədɛçtnɪs] das <–ses, –se> **long-term unemployed** Langzeitarbeitslose ['laŋtsaetļ,aʳbaetsloːzə] der/die <–n, die Langzeitarbeitslosen> *but: ein Langzeitarbeitsloser/eine Langzeitarbeitslose*

loo [noun] *(in the UK)* Klo [kloː] das <–s, –s> *(fam)* ◊ *need to go to the loo* aufs Klo müssen

look¹ [noun] **1.** *(glance, expression)* Blick [blɪk] der <–(e)s, –e> ◊ *Sie erkannte mit einem Blick, wo der Fehler lag.* ♦ *Mit verzweifeltem Blick öffnete sie die Tür.* **give sb a dirty look** jdm einen bösen Blick zuwerfen **have/take a look at sb/sth sich** [dat] jdn/etw. ansehen ['anzeːən] <sieht sich an, sah sich an, hat sich angesehen> ◊ *Sehen Sie sich bitte mal den Bericht an.* **the look of surprise/horror etc. (on sb's face)** jds überraschter/entsetzter etc. Gesichtsausdruck [ybe,raʃte/ɛnt,zɛtste gə'zɪçts|aosdrʊk] der <–(e)s, Gesichtsausdrücke> **put on a serious etc. look** ein ernstes etc. Gesicht machen [aen ,ɛ'rnstəs gə'zɪçt maxn̩] *+haben* **2.** *(appearance)* Gesicht [gə'zɪçt] das <–(e)s, –er> ◊ *Die Internetseite der Firma hat ein neues Gesicht bekommen.* **sth has a ... look about it** etw. sieht ... aus [ziːt ... aos] <sah aus, hat ausgesehen> ◊ *Dieses Viertel sieht sehr heruntergekommen aus.* **by the look of sb/sth** so wie jd/etw. aussieht [,zoː viː ... 'aosziːt] ◊ *So wie er aussieht, hat er letzte Nacht nicht viel geschlafen.* **sb doesn't like the look of sb/sth** jd/etw. gefällt jdm nicht [gə'fɛlt ... ,nɪçt] <gefiel, hat gefallen> ◊ *Diese Wunde gefällt mir nicht.*; *(appearance of a person)* (good) looks gutes Aussehen [,guːtəs 'aoszeːən] <–s> *no pl* ◊ *Ihr gutes Aussehen wird sie viele Vorteile bringen.* ♦ *Sie legt viel Wert auf gutes Aussehen.*; *(style, fashion)* Look [lʊk] der <–s, –s> ◊ *im Look der achtziger Jahre* **3.** *(search for)* **have a look for sb/sth** jdn/etw. suchen ['zuːxn̩] *+haben* ◊ *Könntest du mal die alten Fotos suchen?*

look² [verb] **1.** *(in a certain direction)* schauen ['ʃaoən] *+haben* ◊ *Schau mal aus dem Fenster!* ♦ *Alle Schüler schauten zur Lehrerin.* ♦ *Ich will auch mal durchs Fernglas schauen.* ♦ *Schau mal, was ich hier habe!* **look at your watch** auf die Uhr schauen **look into sb's eyes** jdm in die Augen schauen **look closely** genau hinsehen [gə,nao 'hɪnzeːən] <sieht hin, sah hin, hat hingesehen> ◊ *Man bemerkt den Fleck nur, wenn man genau hinsieht.* **look at sb/sth** jdn/etw. ansehen ['anzeːən] <sieht an, sah an, hat angesehen> ◊ *Er sah sie traurig an.* **look away** wegsehen ['vɛkzeːən] <sieht weg, sah weg, hat weggesehen> ◊ *Verlegen sah er weg.* **2.** *(search)* nachsehen ['naːxzeːən] <sieht nach, sah nach, hat nachgesehen> ◊ *Sieh mal im Keller nach, ob die Tasche dort ist.*

3. *(have a certain appearance)* aussehen ['aʊsze:ən] <sieht aus, sah aus, hat ausgesehen> ◊ *Er sieht gut/ krank aus.* ♦ *Die Lage am Arbeitsmarkt sieht nicht gut aus.* ♦ *Sie sah aus, als ob sie gleich einschlafen würde.* What does ... look like? Wie sieht ... aus? ◊ *Wie sieht dein neues Auto aus?* not look yourself ganz verändert aussehen sb looks their best jd sieht sehr vorteilhaft aus sb looks his/her age man sieht jdm sein Alter an [man zi:t ... zaɛn alte 'an] <sah an, hat angesehen> ◊ *Man sieht ihm sein Alter nicht an.* **4.** *(seem)* sth looks good/all right etc. to sb etw. scheint jdm gut/in Ordnung etc. zu sein [ʃaɛnt ... 'gu:t/ɪn 'ɔ'dnʊŋ tsu: zaɛn] <schien, hat geschienen> ◊ *Der Wagen scheint mir in Ordnung zu sein.* look a fool etc. wie ein Idiot etc. dastehen [vi: aɛn i'djo:t ,da:ʃte:ən] <steht da, stand da, hat dagestanden> ◊ *Musstest du das erzählen? Jetzt stehe ich wie ein Idiot da!* sb looks certain/unlikely to do sth es sieht (nicht) so aus, als ob jd etw. tun würde [ɛs zi:t ('nɪçt) zo: 'aʊs als ɔp ... vv'də] <sah aus, hat ausgesehen> ◊ *Es sieht so aus, als ob er gewinnen würde.* it looks as if ... es sieht so aus, als ob ... ◊ *Es sieht so aus, als ob er den Urlaub tatsächlich bekommt.* **5.** *(room, window)* look north/south etc. nach Norden/Süden etc. gehen [na:x 'nɔ'dn̩/'zy:dn̩ ge:ən] <geht, ging, ist gegangen> ◊ *Dieses Zimmer geht nach Süden.* a house that looks south/north ein Haus in Südlage/Nordlage [aɛn haʊs ɪn 'zy:tla:gə/'nɔ'tla:gə] ◉ be just looking sich nur ein wenig umsehen „Kann ich Ihnen helfen?" — „Danke, ich sehe mich nur ein wenig um." look sb up and down jdn von Kopf bis Fuß mustern

• **look after** [phras v] **1.** *(take care of)* look after sb/ sth sich um jdn/etw. kümmern [ʊm ... ,kymen] <kümmert sich, kümmerte sich, hat sich gekümmert> ◊ *sich um einen Kranken kümmern* ♦ *Wer kümmert sich um die Pflanzen, während du im Urlaub bist?*; *(watch temporarily)* auf jdn/etw. aufpassen [aʊf ... ,aʊfpasn̩] +haben ◊ *Passt du bitte auf Timmi auf, während ich einkaufen gehe?* ♦ *Würden Sie bitte kurz für mich auf meine Tasche aufpassen?* look after yourself auf sich aufpassen ◊ *Ich bin alt genug, um auf mich selbst aufzupassen.* ♦ *Mach's gut und pass auf dich auf!* **2.** *(sb's rights, interests)* wahrnehmen ['va:'ne:mən] <nimmt wahr, nahm wahr, hat wahrgenommen> *(form)* ◊ *die Interessen eines Kindes/Kranken wahrnehmen*

• **look down** [phras v] look down on sb/sth auf jdn/ etw. herabsehen [aʊf ... hɛ'rapze:ən] <sieht herab, sah herab, hat herabgesehen> ◊ *Du solltest nicht immer auf andere herabsehen.*

• **look for** [phras v] look for sb/sth jdn/etw. suchen ['zu:xn̩] +haben ◊ *Ich suche meinen Schlüssel.* ♦ *Wir suchen neue Mitarbeiter.*

• **look forward to** [phras v] look forward to sth sich auf etw. [acc] freuen [aʊf ... ,frɔɡən] +haben ◊ *Die Kinder freuen sich auf die Ferien.* look forward to doing sth sich darauf freuen, etw. zu tun ◊ *Er freute sich darauf, sie wiederzusehen.*

• **look in** [phras v] look in (on sb) (bei jdm) vorbeischauen [fo:'baɛʃaʊən] +haben ◊ *Ich schaue auf dem Rückweg kurz bei Oma vorbei.*

• **look into** [phras v] look into sth etw. prüfen ['pry:fn̩] +haben ◊ *Die Polizei prüfte zahlreiche Hinweise.*

• **look on** [phras v] **1.** *(watch)* zusehen ['tsu:ze:ən] <sieht zu, sah zu, hat zugesehen> ◊ *Der Junge sah interessiert zu, wie sein Vater den Reifen wechselte.* **2.** *(regard)* look on sb/sth as sth jdn/etw. als etw. betrachten [als ... bətraxtn̩] <betrachtet, betrachtete, hat betrachtet> ◊ *Ich betrachte sie als meine beste Freundin.* look on sb/sth with sth etw. für jdn/etw. empfinden [fy:ɐ̯ ... ɛm,pfɪndn̩] <empfindet, empfand, hat empfunden> ◊ *Seit dieser Tat empfand sie nur noch Verachtung für ihn.*

• **look out** [phras v] **1.** *(keep watch for)* look out for sb/sth nach jdm/etw. Ausschau halten [na:x ... 'aʊsʃaʊ haltn̩] <hält, hielt, hat gehalten> ◊ *Halte einfach nach einem roten Wagen Ausschau!* **2.** *(take care of)* look out (for sb) (auf jdn) aufpassen ['aʊfpasn̩] +haben ◊ *Er passt oft auf seinen kleinen Bruder auf.* ♦ *Pass auf! Da kommt ein Zug!* look out for yourself nur auf seinen Vorteil bedacht sein [nu:ɐ̯ aʊf zaɛnən ,fo:ɐ̯taɛl bə,daxt zaɛn] +sein

• **look over** [phras v] look sth over **1.** *(read through)* etw. durchsehen ['dʊ'çze:ən] <sieht durch, sah durch, hat durchgesehen> ◊ *ein Dokument genau durchsehen* **2.** *(a property, location)* sich [dat] etw. ansehen ['anze:ən] <sieht sich an, sah sich an, hat sich angesehen> ◊ *Am besten fahren wir hin und sehen uns das Gebäude einmal an.*

• **look round** [phras v] look round (sth) sich (irgendwo) umsehen ['ʊmze:ən] <sieht sich um, sah sich um, hat sich umgesehen> ◊ *Möchten Sie sich im Haus ein wenig umsehen?* look round for sth nach etw. umsehen ◊ *Mark und Susi sehen sich nach einer größeren Wohnung um.*

• **look through** [phras v] **1.** *(read quickly, examine)* look through sth etw. durchsehen ['dʊ'çze:ən] <sieht durch, sah durch, hat durchgesehen> ◊ *Sieh bitte noch die Post durch — ich erwarte eine Rechnung.* ♦ *Ich habe den ganzen Stapel durchgesehen, aber den Vertrag nicht gefunden.* **2.** *(ignore)* look straight through sb durch jdn hindurchsehen [dʊ'ç ... hɪn'dʊ'çze:ən] +haben ◊ *Seit dem Streit sieht sie einfach durch mich hindurch.*

• **look to** [phras v] **1.** *(expect)* look to sb for sth etw. von jdm erwarten [fɔn ... ɛ'va:'tn̩] <erwartet, erwartete, hat erwartet> ◊ *Von ihm können wir keine Hilfe erwarten.* look to sb to do sth sich darauf verlassen, dass jd etw. tut [daraʊf fɛ'lasn̩ das] <verlässt sich, verließ sich, hat sich verlassen> ◊ *Sie verlassen sich darauf, dass er das Problem lösen kann.* **2.** *(concentrate on)* look to sth sich auf etw. [acc] konzentrieren [aʊf ... kɔntsɛn,tri:rən] <konzentriert sich, konzentrierte sich, hat sich konzentriert> ◊ *Wir müssen uns auf neue Methoden konzentrieren.* look to sb to do sth dafür zu sorgen, dass ['tsu:ze:ən das] ◊ *Sieh zu, dass du das bis Freitag fertig bekommst!*

• **look up** [phras v] **1.** *(find out)* nachschlagen ['na:xʃla:gn̩] <schlägt nach, schlug nach, hat nachgeschlagen> ◊ *ein Wort im Wörterbuch nachschlagen* **2.** *(prospects, prices)* steigen ['ʃtaɛgn̩] <steigt, stieg, ist gestiegen> ◊ *Seine Erfolgsaussichten steigen.* Things are looking up. Es geht bergauf. **3.** *(visit)* look sb up bei jdm vorbeischauen [baɛ ... fo:ɐ̯,baɛʃaʊən] +haben **4.** *(respect)* look up to sb zu jdm aufsehen [tsu: ... 'aʊfze:ən] <sieht auf, sah auf, hat aufgesehen>

loop [noun] **1.** *(curved shape or object)* Schlaufe

['ʃlaʊfə] die <–, –n> ◊ *Er steckte den Gürtel durch die Schlaufen.*; *(of wire, rope)* Schlinge ['ʃlɪŋə] die <–, –n> ◊ *die Schlinge eines Lassos; (of a river)* Schleife ['ʃlaɪfə] die <–, –n> ◊ *Der Fluss machte eine Schleife.* 2. IT, FILM, MUS, TECHN Schleife ['ʃlaɪfə] die <–, –n> 3. *(made by a plane)* Looping ['luːpɪŋ] der *or also das* <–s, –s> ◊ *Der Pilot drehte mehrere Loopings.*

loo paper [noun] Klopapier ['kloːpaˌpiːɐ̯] das <–s> *no pl (fam)* ◊ *eine Rolle Klopapier*

loophole [noun] Lücke ['lʏkə] die <–, –n> ◊ *eine Lücke im Gesetz ausnutzen* ♦ *eine Lücke in etw.* [dat] *schließen*

loose [adj] 1. *(not tight or fixed)* lose ['loːzə] *no comp/superl* ◊ *Vorsicht, das Brett ist lose.* ♦ *ein loser Knopf; (screw, soil, tooth, knot)* locker ['lɔkə] ◊ *ein lockerer Zahn* ♦ *Der Knoten ist zu locker.* come loose *sich lösen* ['løːzn̩] *+haben* ◊ *Eine der Schrauben hatte sich gelöst.* 2. *(free, unconfined)* be loose *frei herumlaufen* [fraɛ hɛˈʁʊmlaʊfn̩] ◊ *läuft herum, lief herum, ist herumgelaufen*> ◊ *Ein Wolf läuft in der Gegend frei herum.* break loose *sich losreißen* ['loːsʁaɛsn̩] <reißt sich los, riss sich los, hat sich losgerissen> ◊ *Es gelang ihr, sich von dem Angreifer loszureißen.* let loose *freilassen* ['fʁaɛlasn̩] <lässt frei, ließ frei, hat freigelassen> ◊ *Die Entführer ließen den Jungen im Wald frei.* 3. *(not kept or sold together)* lose ['loːzə] *no comp/superl* ◊ *Hier kann man lose Briefumschläge kaufen.* ♦ *Möchten Sie den Tee lose oder in Beuteln?* 4. *(clothing)* weit [vaɛt] <weiter, am weitesten> ◊ *Ist dir diese Hose nicht etwas zu weit?* 5. *(not exact)* frei [fraɛ] <freier, am frei(e)sten> ◊ *eine freie Übersetzung* 6. *(not strictly organized)* locker ['lɔkə] ◊ *ein lockeres Bündnis* ♦ *sich in lockerer Ordnung aufstellen* 7. have loose bowels Durchfall haben ['dʊʁçfal haːbm̩] *+haben*

loosely [adv] 1. *(not tightly, not strictly)* locker ['lɔkə] ◊ *Er hielt die Waffe locker in der Hand.* ♦ *Vorschriften locker handhaben* 2. *(not exactly)* frei [fraɛ] ◊ *Das ist frei übersetzt.*

loosen [verb] *(make less tight)* lösen ['løːzn̩] *+haben* ◊ *Lösen Sie zuerst die beiden Schrauben.* loosen your grip on sth *den Griff um etw. lösen* ◊ *Er löste den Griff um ihren Arm.; (a tie, belt, regulations)* lockern ['lɔkɐn] *+haben* ◊ *Er lockerte seine Krawatte/seinen Gürtel.* ♦ *Bestimmungen/Vorschriften lockern*
• **loosen up** [phras v] 1. SPORT lockern ['lɔkɐn] *+haben* ◊ *vor dem Sport seine Muskeln lockern* sb loosens up *jd lockert sich* 2. *(relax)* sich entspannen [ɛntˈʃpanən] <entspannt sich, entspannte sich, hat sich entspannt> ◊ *Komm, versuch dich ein wenig zu entspannen!*

loot¹ [noun] 1. *(stolen goods)* Beute ['bɔɪtə] die <–> *no pl* 2. *(money)* Zaster ['tsastɐ] der <–s> *no pl (fam)* ◊ *Wo ist der Zaster?*

loot² [verb] plündern ['plʏndɐn] *+haben* ◊ *Die Soldaten plünderten die eroberte Stadt.* ♦ *Wer plündert, macht sich strafbar.*

lopsided(ly) [adj, adv] 1. *(biased)* einseitig ['aɛnzaɛtɪç] *seldom comp/superl* ◊ *Seine Sicht der Dinge ist sehr einseitig.* ♦ *eine einseitige Darstellung* lopsidedly *liberal/conservative etc.* mehrheitlich liberal/konservativ etc. ['meːɐ̯haɛtlɪç libeˈʁaːl/kɔnzɛʁvaˈtiːf] *no comp/superl* 2. *(not straight)* schief [ʃiːf] ◊ *Ist das schief oder gerade?* ♦ *ein schiefes Grinsen* ♦ *Deine Krawatte sitzt schief.*

lord [noun] 1. REL the Lord der Herr [deːɐ̯ ˈhɛʳ] der <–n> *no pl* ◊ *Der Herr sei mit dir.* 2. *(master, ruler)* Herr [hɛʳ] der <–n, –en> *(lofty, oldf)* ◊ *Was wünscht Ihr, mein Herr und Meister?* 3. *(in the UK: nobleman, member of the House of Lords)* Lord Lord [lɔʳt] der <–s, –s> ◊ *Lord und Lady Chester; (in official titles)* Lord Chancellor Lordkanzler ['lɔʳtkantslɐ] der <–s, –> Lord Mayor Oberbürgermeister ['oːbeˌbʏʳ'gemaɛstɐ] der <–s, –>

lordship
⊚ **Your/His Lordship** 1. *(talking to/about a Lord)* Eure/Seine Lordschaft ◊ *Was wünschen Eure Lordschaft?* 2. *(talking to/about a bishop)* Eure/Seine Exzellenz ◊ *Seine Exzellenz fühlt sich heute nicht gut.* 3. *(talking to/about a judge)* Euer/Seine Gnaden

lorry [noun] Lastwagen ['lastvaːgn̩] der <–s, –>

lose [verb] 1. *(no longer possess, fail to win)* verlieren [fɛˈliːʁən] <verliert, verlor, hat verloren> ◊ *Er hat seinen Job/sein Handy verloren.* ♦ *Sie verlor 400 Euro im Spielkasino.* ♦ *Der Reifen verliert Luft.* ♦ *Sie hat im sechsten Monat ihr Baby verloren.* ♦ *Durch einen Unfall verlor er das Augenlicht.* ♦ *Die Schüler verloren schon bald das Interesse.* ♦ *Die Mannschaft hat 2:4 verloren.* lose height an Höhe verlieren lose consciousness das Bewusstsein verlieren lose your mind den Verstand verlieren lose your nerve die Nerven verlieren lose sth to sb etw. an jdn verlieren ◊ *Er verlor den Auftrag an seinen Konkurrenten.* lose weight abnehmen ['apneːmən] <nimmt ab, nahm ab, hat abgenommen> ◊ *Hast du abgenommen?* ♦ *Ich habe fünf Kilo abgenommen.; (waste)* lose sb sth jdn etw. kosten ['kɔstn̩] *+haben* ◊ *Dieser Fehler kostete ihn zwei Tage Zeit.* 2. *(fail to catch or make use of)* verpassen [fɛˈpasn̩] <verpasst, verpasste, hat verpasst> ◊ *Sie verpassten den Zug.* ♦ *So eine Gelegenheit darfst du nicht verpassen!; (time)* verlieren [fɛˈliːʁən] <verliert, verlor, hat verloren> 3. a watch has lost two/three etc. hours eine Uhr geht zwei/drei etc. Stunden nach [aɛnə ˌuːɐ̯ geːt ˌtsvaɛ/draɛ ʃtʊndn̩ 'naːx] <geht nach, ging nach, ist nachgegangen>
⊚ have nothing to lose nichts zu verlieren haben lose yourself in sth ganz in etw. [dat] aufgehen ◊ *Sie geht ganz in ihrer Arbeit auf.* you've lost me (there) da komme ich nicht mehr mit

loser [noun] 1. *(sb who loses, sb who suffers negative consequences)* Verlierer [fɛˈliːʁə] der <–s, –> ♀Verliererin [fɛˈliːʁərɪn] die <–, –nen> ◊ *Er war ein guter/schlechter Verlierer.* 2. *(sb who has no success in life)* Versager [fɛˈzaːgɐ] der <–s, –> ♀Versagerin [fɛˈzaːgərɪn] die <–, –nen> ◊ *sich als Versager fühlen*

loss [noun] 1. *(state of no longer having sth or losing sth)* Verlust [fɛˈlʊst] der <–(e)s, –e> ◊ *Bei Verlust des Gepäcks bekommt man 500 Euro erstattet.* ♦ *Der Verlust ihres Bruders hat sie schwer getroffen.* ♦ *Das Unternehmen hat letztes Jahr große/hohe Verluste gemacht.* ♦ *Trotz schwerer Verluste kämpfte die Truppe weiter.* ♦ *Chemotherapie führt oft zum Verlust der Haare.* at a loss mit Verlust loss of confidence Vertrauensverlust [fɛˈtraʊənsfɛlʊst] loss of time Zeitverlust ['tsaɛtfɛlʊst] weight loss Gewichtsverlust [gəˈvɪçtsfɛlʊst] 2. *(defeat)* Niederlage ['niːdɐlaːgə] die <–, –n> ◊ *Die jüngste Niederlage gegen Bielefeld macht der Mannschaft zu schaffen.*
⊚ a dead loss 1. *(thing)* ein totaler Reinfall 2. *(person)* ein hoffnungsloser Fall be at a loss

A B C D E F G H I J K L´ M N O P Q R S T U V W X Y Z

nicht mehr weiterwissen be at a loss to do sth etw. nicht tun können ◊ *Ich kann nicht erklären, warum das passiert ist.* be at a loss for words nicht wissen, was man sagen soll

lost → **lose** [adj] **1.** *(lose your way: on foot)* get lost sich verlaufen [fɐˈlaͻfn̩] <verläuft sich, verlief sich, hat sich verlaufen> ◊ *Die Kinder haben sich im Wald verlaufen.* be lost sich verlaufen haben; *(by car etc.)* sich verfahren [fɐˈfaːrən] <verfährt sich, verfuhr sich, hat sich verfahren> be lost sich verfahren haben **2.** *(be nowhere to be found)* be lost verschwunden sein [fɐˈʃvʊndn̩ zaͻn̩] +sein ◊ *Meine goldene Kette ist verschwunden.* **3.** *(no longer existing, helpless, unable to survive)* verloren [fɐˈloːrən] ◊ *die verlorene Unschuld* ◆ *Sie wirkte ein wenig verloren zwischen all den Menschen.* ◆ *Die Verschütteten waren verloren.* **4.** *(opportunity)* verpasst [fɐˈpast] *no comp/ superl* ◊ *eine verpasste Chance/Gelegenheit* **5.** *(dead)* be lost at sea auf See geblieben sein [aͻf ˈzeː ɡəˌbliːbm̩ zaͻn̩] be lost in battle im Kampf gefallen sein [ɪm ˈkampf ɡəˌfalən zaͻn̩] **6.** *(occupied)* be lost in sth in etw. [dat] verloren sein [ɪn ... fɐˌloːrən zaͻn̩] +sein lost in thought gedankenverloren [ɡəˈdaŋkŋ̩feloːrən] *no comp/superl* ◊ *Gedankenverloren starrte er in den Himmel.* **7.** *(not understanding)* be lost überhaupt nichts mehr verstehen [yːbɐˈhaͻpt nɪçts meːɐ fɐˈʃteːən] <versteht, verstand, hat verstanden> ◊ *Ich verstehe überhaupt nichts mehr nichts mehr! Wie hängt das alles zusammen?* ◉ get lost verschwinde ◊ *Verschwinde! Ich möchte niemanden sehen!* all is not lost es ist noch nicht alles verloren sth is lost on sb jd hat keinen Sinn für etw. ◊ *Er hat keinen Sinn für klassische Musik.*

lost-and-found [noun] Fundbüro [ˈfʊntbyˌroː] das <-s, -s>

lost property [noun] **1.** *(objects)* Fundsachen [ˈfʊntzaxn̩] die <-> *pl* ◊ *Fundsachen können beim Hausmeister abgegeben werden.* **2.** *(place)* Fundbüro [ˈfʊntbyˌroː] das <-s, -s> ◊ *Sie brachten die Handtasche zum Fundbüro.*

lot¹ [noun] **1.** *(group of things)* this/that lot das hier/ dort [ˈdas hiːɐ̯/dɔɐ̯t] ◊ *Wo soll ich das hier hinstellen?* ◆ *Kannst du das dort auch noch durchsehen?;* *(group of people)* Haufen [ˈhaͻfn̩] der <-s, -> ◊ *Sie hat wirklich den ganzen Haufen zum Essen eingeladen!* you lot ihr (alle) [iːɐ̯ (alə)] ◊ *Kommt ihr (alle) mit ins Kino?* **2.** FILM *(setting)* Filmgelände [ˈfɪlmɡəlɛndə] das <-s, -> ◊ *Zuschauer dürfen das Filmgelände nicht betreten.* **3.** *(at an auction)* Posten [ˈpɔstn̩] der <-s, -> **4.** *(the whole of sth)* the lot alles [ˈaləs] ◊ *Das ist alles.* ◆ *Hat sie etwa alles gegessen?* **5.** *(plot of land)* Stück Land [ʃtʏk ˈlant] das <-(e)s> *no pl* **6.** *(destiny)* sb's lot *(in life)* jds Los [loːs] das <-es, -e>

◉ throw in your lot with sb sich mit jdm zusammentun

lot² [adj] a lot of, lots of viel [fiːl] *invariable when used before uncountable ns* ◊ *viel Arbeit/Mühe* ◆ *viele Fragen* ◆ *Sie hat viele Freunde.* lots and lots of ... eine Unmenge ... [gen] [aͻnə ˈʊnmɛŋə] ◊ *Sie hat eine Unmenge Fehler gemacht.*

lot³ [adv] a lot/lots **1.** *(very much)* viel [zeːɐ̯] ◊ *Sie mag dich sehr.* ◆ *Er hat sich in der Schule sehr verbessert.* a lot better/longer etc. *(than)* viel besser/ länger etc. *(als)* [fiːl ˈbɛsɐ/ˈlɛŋɐ (als)] ◊ *Ich kann das viel besser als du.* **2.** *(often)* oft [ɔft] <öfter, am

öftesten> ◊ *Sie gehen oft ins Theater.* **3.** *(a large amount)* viel [fiːl] <mehr, am meisten> ◊ *Der Wagen hat viel gekostet.* ◆ *In Paris gibt es viel zu sehen.* an awful lot furchtbar viel ◊ *Ich habe furchtbar viel zu tun.*

lot⁴ [indef pron] a lot, lots viel [fiːl] ◊ *Ich habe viel verdient, aber viel gelernt.*

lotion [noun] Lotion [loˈtsjoːn] die <-, -en>

lottery [noun] **1.** GAME Lotterie [lɔtəˈriː] die <-, -n> ◊ *Lotterie spielen* **2.** *(fig)* Glücksspiel [ˈɡlʏksʃpiːl] das <-(e)s, -e> ◊ *Das Leben ist manchmal ein Glücksspiel.*

loud(ly) [adj, adv] **1.** *(sound, person)* laut [laͻt] <lauter, am lautesten> ◊ *Sie hat eine laute Stimme.* ◆ *Die Musik war schrecklich laut.* ◆ *Schrei doch nicht so laut!* in a loud voice mit lauter Stimme **2.** *(colo(u)r)* grell [ɡrɛl] ◊ *ein grelles Muster* ◆ *Ich finde die Farbe zu grell.* ◆ *ein grell gemustertes Kleid* **3.** be loud in your support of sth etw. nachdrücklich unterstützen [naːxdrʏklɪç ʊntɐˈʃtʏtsn̩] <unterstützt, unterstützte, hat unterstützt> be loud in your opposition to sth etw. nachdrücklich ablehnen [naːxdrʏklɪç ˈapleːnən] +haben

loudspeaker [noun] Lautsprecher [ˈlaͻtʃprɛçɐ] der <-s, ->

lounge [noun] **1.** *(in the UK: front room)* Wohnzimmer [ˈvoːntsɪmɐ] das <-s, -> **2.** *(at an airport)* Warteraum [ˈvaʁtəraͻm] der <-(e)s, Warteräume> ◊ *Der Warteraum war fast leer.;* *(at a hotel, hospital)* Aufenthaltsraum [ˈaͻfn̩thaltsraͻm] der <-(e)s, Aufenthaltsräume> **3.** *(in the UK: bar)* lounge (bar) Bar [baːˀ] die <-, -s>

louse [noun] **1.** ZOO Laus [laͻs] die <-, Läuse> **2.** *(person)* Ratte [ˈratə] die <-, -en> *(fam, pej)*

lousy [adj] *(bad or insignificant)* lausig [ˈlaͻzɪç] *(fam)* ◊ *Sie ist eine lausige Sängerin.* ◆ *ein paar lausige Cent;* *(mean, nasty)* mies [miːs] <mieser, am miesesten> ◊ *Er ist ein ganz mieser Betrüger!*

◉ be lousy with sth *(in the US)* voll von etw. sein ◊ *Flegel* [ˈfleːɡl̩] der <-s, ->

love¹ [noun] **1.** *(feeling of strong affection)* Liebe [ˈliːbə] die <-> *no pl* ◊ *Die beiden verbindet eine große Liebe.* ◆ *Er hat sie aus Liebe geheiratet.* ◆ *Die erste Liebe vergisst man nie.* love for sb Liebe zu jdm love of/for sth Liebe zu etw. ◊ *aus Liebe zum Leben* in love *(with sb)* verliebt *(in jdn)* [fɐˈliːpt] <verliebter, am verliebtesten> ◊ *Sie ist sehr (in ihn) verliebt.* ◆ *ein verliebtes Paar* madly in love wahnsinnig verliebt fall in love *(with sb)* sich *(in jdn)* verlieben [fɐˈliːbm̩] <verliebt sich, verliebte sich, hat sich verliebt> **2.** *(in the UK: form of address)* Liebling [ˈliːplɪŋ] der <-s, -e> ◊ *Kommst du, (mein) Liebling?;* *(in the UK: in a shop etc.)* my love meine Liebe [maͻnə ˈliːbə] ◊ *Was darf's denn sein, meine Liebe?* **3.** *(in the UK: sb kind)* Schatz [ʃats] der <-es> *no pl* ◊ *Sie ist ein richtiger Schatz.* be a love and ... sei so lieb und ... [zaͻ zoː ˌliːp ʊnt] **4.** *(in letters)* (lots of) love *(from ...)* alles Liebe(, dein/deine ...) [aləs ˈliːbə (daͻn/daͻnə)] ◊ *Bis bald. Alles Liebe, deine Susi* all my love in Liebe [ɪn ˈliːbə] **5.** *(in tennis)* null [nʊl] ◊ *Es steht vierzig zu null.*

◉ for the love of God um Himmels willen not for love nor money nicht für Geld und gute Worte give my/our love to sb grüße jdn von mir/uns there is no love lost between sb and sb jd und jd

können sich nicht ausstehen make love miteinander schlafen make love to sb mit jdm schlafen send your love to sb jdn grüßen lassen ◊ *Mutter lässt dich schön grüßen.*

love² [verb] *(care for, enjoy)* lieben ['liːbm̩] +haben ◊ *Ich liebe dich, Andi.* ♦ *Kerstin liebt Pizza über alles.* ♦ *Sie liebt nichts mehr als tanzen zu gehen.; (wish)* love sth (liebend) gern etw. haben [(liːbm̩t) ˌgɛʳn ... haːbm̩] ◊ *Ich hätte gern eine Tasse Tee.* love to do sth (liebend) gern etw. tun ◊ *Ich würde liebend gern tanzen gehen.*
ⓔ you're going to love this: ... du wirst dich freuen zu hören, dass ... I'd love to mit Vergnügen I love it klasse

love life [noun] Liebesleben ['liːbəsleːbm̩] das <–s> no pl

lovely [adj] 1. *(enjoyable)* schön [ʃøːn] ◊ *ein schönes Geschenk* ♦ *Das Wetter war schön.* ♦ *Schön, dass du kommen konntest.; (thanking sb)* (that's) lovely danke schön ['daŋkə ʃøːn] lovely and ... schön ... [ʃøːn] ◊ *Der Tee war schön süß/heiß/stark.* 2. *(person, behavio(u)r)* lieb [liːp] ◊ *Wie lieb von dir!* ♦ *Er ist so ein lieber Kerl!*

lover [noun] 1. *(sb you love)* Geliebte [gə'liːptə] der/die <–n, die Geliebten> *but: ein Geliebter/eine Geliebte* ◊ *Sie wurde seine Geliebte.* ♦ *Sie hat einen Geliebten.; (two who love each other)* lovers Liebespaar ['liːbəspaːʳ] das <–(e)s, –e> ◊ *Sie waren ein Liebespaar.; (sb who loves you)* Liebhaber ['liːphaːbe] der <–s, –> ♀Liebhaberin ['liːphaːbərɪn] die <–, –nen> be a good/bad lover ein guter/schlechter Liebhaber sein 2. *(sb who is fond of certain objects)* Liebhaber ['liːphaːbe] der <–s, –> ♀Liebhaberin ['liːphaːbərɪn] die <–, –nen> ◊ *ein Liebhaber alter Autos*

lovesick [adj] liebeskrank ['liːbəskraŋk] no comp/superl ◊ *ein liebeskranker Narr* he lovesick Liebeskummer haben ['liːbəskʊme haːbm̩]

loving(ly) [adj, adv] *(affectionate)* liebevoll ['liːbəfɔl] ◊ *Seine Mutter war immer sehr liebevoll.* ♦ *Katze in liebevolle Hände abzugeben* ♦ *sich liebevoll um jdn kümmern*

low¹ [noun] 1. *(lowest)* Tiefstand ['tiːfʃtant] der <–(e)s, Tiefstände> ◊ *Die Wirtschaft ist auf einem neuen Tiefstand.; (of temperatures)* Tiefstwert ['tiːfʃtveːɐt] der <–(e)s, –e> ◊ *Tiefstwerte in der Nacht um 2 Grad.* 2. *(air pressure etc., bad time)* Tief [tiːf] das <–s, –s> ◊ *Das Tief über Norddeutschland bringt Regen.* ♦ *Die Mannschaft hat gerade ein Tief.* ♦ *die Höhen und Tiefen meines Lebens*
ⓔ the lowest of the low das Letzte vom Letzten

low² [adj] 1. *(height, level, cost)* niedrig ['niːdrɪç] ◊ *Die Brücke ist zu niedrig.* ♦ *eine niedrige Mauer* ♦ *die Kosten niedrig halten* the river is low der Wasserstand ist niedrig; *(sound, valley etc.)* tief [tiːf] ◊ *Das Kleid hat einen tiefen Ausschnitt.* ♦ *In tieferen Lagen schmilzt jetzt schon der Schnee.* ♦ *Die Schuhabteilung ist zwei Etagen tiefer.* the sun is low die Sonne steht tief low on a list weit unten auf einer Liste [vaet 'ʊntn̩ aof aene ˌlɪstə]; *(shoes)* flach [flax] ◊ *flache Schuhe tragen* 2. *(priority, proportion, speed, stocks, volume, substance in food)* gering [gə'rɪŋ] ◊ *geringe Intensität* ♦ *Der Verbrauch/Fettgehalt war gering.* Casualties were low. Die Anzahl der Todesopfer war gering.; *(food)* low in sth arm an etw. [dat] [aʳm an] <ärmer, am ärmsten> ◊ *arm an Fett/Kalorien; (incidence etc.)* selten ['zɛltn̩] ◊ *das seltene*

Vorkommen einer Tierart ♦ *Das Auftreten von Nebenwirkungen ist eher selten.* 3. *(temperatures)* in the low twenties/thirties etc. über zwanzig/dreißig etc. Grad [yːbe ˌtsvantsɪç/draesɪç 'graːt] 4. *(not loud)* leise ['laezə] <leiser, am leisesten> ◊ *mit leiser Stimme* ♦ *Das Geräusch war sehr leise.* 5. *(morale, opinion etc.)* schlecht [ʃlɛçt] <schlechter, am schlechtesten> ◊ *Die Stimmung in der Mannschaft war schlecht.* 6. *(trick)* gemein [gə'maen]
ⓔ get/run low *(stocks etc.)* zur Neige gehen *(battery)* leer werden sb gets/runs low on sth jdm geht bald etw. aus ◊ *Mir geht bald die Geduld aus.* be low *(sad)* niedergeschlagen sein feel low 1. *(physically)* wie erschlagen sein 2. *(feel mean)* sich gemein vorkommen

low³ [adv] *(aim, hang)* niedrig ['niːdrɪç] ◊ *Du hast die Kosten zu niedrig angesetzt.* ♦ *ein niedrig dosiertes Medikament; (fly, sing, sink etc.)* tief [tiːf] ◊ *tief fliegen* ♦ *Die Temperaturen sind tief gesunken.*
ⓔ sink/stoop so low as to do sth so tief sinken, dass man etw. tut

lower¹ → low [adj] 1. *(storey, social stratum)* untere ['ʊntərə] no comp, only before ns <ein unterer ..., eine untere ..., ein unteres ...> ◊ *die unteren Stockwerke* ♦ *die untere Schicht der Gesellschaft* ♦ *die untere Donau; (clergy, nobility, plant etc.)* nieder ['niːdɐ] no comp/superl ◊ *der niedere Adel/Klerus* ♦ *niedere Lebewesen* lower ... Unter... ['ʊntɐ] lower lip Unterlippe ['ʊntɐlɪpə] die <–, –n> lower leg Unterschenkel ['ʊntɐʃɛŋkl̩] der <–s, –> 2. *(turnout, temperature)* lower than unter ['ʊntɐ] ◊ *Die Wahlbeteiligung fiel unter 40 Prozent.*

lower² [verb] 1. *(spatial, quantitative)* senken ['zɛŋkn̩] +haben ◊ *Verlegen senkte er den Kopf/Blick.* ♦ *den Wasserspiegel/die Kosten senken* ♦ *Sie senkte ihre Stimme und flüsterte mir etwas zu.; (on a rope, towards the speaker)* herablassen [hɛ'raplasn̩] <lässt herab, ließ herab, hat herabgelassen> ◊ *Er ließ sich an einem Seil zu mir herab.; (away from speaker)* hinablassen [hɪ'naplasn̩] <lässt hinab, ließ hinab, hat hinabgelassen> ◊ *Ich ließ den Eimer an einer Kette in den Brunnen hinab.; (sit down)* lower yourself onto sth sich auf etw. [dat] niederlassen [aof ... ˌniːdɐlasn̩] <lässt sich nieder, ließ sich nieder, hat sich niedergelassen> ◊ *sich auf einem Sessel niederlassen* 2. *(a flag, sail)* einholen ['aenhoːlən] +haben ◊ *Wir holten das Segel ein.*

lower case [noun] lower case letter Kleinbuchstabe ['klaenbuːxʃtaːbə] der <–ns, –n> in lower case in Kleinbuchstaben

lowest → low [superl] unterste ['ʊntɐstə] <der/die/das unterste ...> ◊ *die unterste Schublade* ♦ *die unterste gerichtliche Instanz*

low-fat [adj] fettarm ['fɛtaʳm] <fettärmer, am fettärmsten> ◊ *fettarme Milch* ♦ *fettarmer Joghurt* low-fat margarine Halbfettmargarine ['halpfɛtmaʳgaˌriːnə] die <–, –n>

lowly [adj] nieder ['niːdɐ] ◊ *von niederer Geburt/Herkunft*

low tide [noun] Ebbe ['ɛbə] die <–, –n> most sing ◊ *Bei Ebbe suchen wir Muscheln.*

loyal(ly) [adj, adv] treu [trɔy] <treuer, am treu(e)sten> ◊ *ein treuer Freund/Kunde* ♦ *Er tut immer treu seine Pflicht.* loyal to sb/sth jdm/etw. treu ◊ *Sie blieb ihren Überzeugungen treu.*

loyalty [noun] Treue ['trɔyə] die <–> no pl ◊ *Er hat*

seinem Verein immer die Treue gehalten. ♦ Wir
bedanken uns bei unseren Kunden für ihre Treue.
loyalty to sb/sth Treue zu jdm/etw. He inspires
loyalty among his friends. Seine Freunde sind ihm
treu ergeben. loyalties Loyalität [lo̯ajali'tɛːt] die <->
no pl ◊ die Loyalität innerhalb der Gruppe sb's
loyalties are with sb/sth jds Loyalität gilt jdm/etw.
divided loyalties Loyalitätskonflikt
[lo̯ajali'tɛːtskɔn,flɪkt] der <-(e)s, -e>

Ltd GmbH [ge:|ɛmbe:'ha:] die

lubricate [verb] (with grease etc.) schmieren ['ʃmiːrən]
+haben (also fig) ◊ eine Fahrradkette reinigen und
schmieren ♦ die Räder der Bürokratie schmieren;
(with oil) ölen ['øːlən] +haben ◊ ein Schloss ölen lubri-
cated condoms feuchte Kondome [,fɔ̯çtə kɔn'doːmə]

lucid [adj] klar [klaːꞏ] ◊ eine klare Beschreibung ♦ bei
klarem Verstand sein; (explanation) einleuchtend
['a̯enlɔ̯çtn̩t]; (moments) licht [lɪçt] <lichter, am lich-
testen>; (dream, dreaming) luzide [lu'tsiːdə] no comp/
superl (tech)

luck [noun] 1. (good fortune) (good) luck Glück [glʏk]
das <-(e)s no pl ◊ Das war aber Glück! ♦ Du hast
mir Glück gebracht. ♦ jdm viel Glück wünschen be
in luck Glück haben push your luck sein Glück strapazieren sb's luck changes jds Glück wendet sich
sb's luck holds/lasts jdm ist das Glück treu sb's
luck runs out jdn verlässt das Glück better luck
mehr Glück ◊ Das nächste Mal hast du mehr Glück!
Any luck? Glück gehabt? piece/stroke of (good) luck
Glücksfall ['glʏksfal] der <-(e)s, Glücksfälle>
2. (chance) Zufall ['tsuːfal] der <-(e)s, Zufälle> ◊
Wie es der Zufall wollte, war Martin auch dort. ♦ Bei
dem Erfolg hat der Zufall mitgespielt. 3. (ill-fortune,
single stroke) bad/hard/tough luck Pech [pɛç] das
<-(e)s no pl ◊ So ein Pech!; (longer lasting) bad
luck Unglück ['ʊnglʏk] das <-(e)s no pl ◊ Eine
schwarze Katze soll Unglück bringen.
◉ be down on your luck vom Pech verfolgt sein
just my luck so etwas passiert auch nur mir worse
luck leider no such luck ich/er etc. hatte kein
Glück sth for luck etw. als Glücksbringer do sth
for luck etw. tun, weil es Glück bringen soll

luckily [adv] zum Glück [tsʊm 'glʏk] ◊ Zum Glück
passierte nichts. luckily for sb zu jds Glück ◊ Zu
meinem Glück erkannte er mich nicht.

lucky [adj] 1. (person) be/get lucky Glück haben
['glʏk ha:bm̩] ◊ Du hast Glück, dass du gesund bist/
das überlebt hast. ♦ Ich hatte das Glück, zur rechten
Zeit dort zu sein. ♦ Er hat kein Glück bei den
Frauen.; (winner) glücklich ['glʏklɪç] lucky fellow/
man etc. Glückspilz ['glʏkspɪlts] der <-es, -e> (fam)
2. (object, action etc.) sth is lucky etw. bringt Glück
[brɪŋt 'glʏk] ◊ Dieser Talisman soll Glück bringen. it
is lucky that es ist ein Glück, dass
[ɛs ɪst a̯en 'glʏk das] ◊ Es ist ein Glück, dass ich
dich hier treffe.; (circumstance, coincidence)
glücklich ['glʏklɪç] ◊ Glückliche Umstände verhinder-
ten eine Katastrophe. lucky break glücklicher Zufall;
(in compound ns) lucky ... Glücks... [glʏks] lucky
charm Glücksbringer ['glʏksbrɪŋə] der <-s, -> lucky
day Glückstag ['glʏkstaːk] der <-(e)s, -e> lucky
goal Glückstreffer ['glʏkstrɛfɐ] der <-s, ->
◉ consider/count yourself lucky sich glücklich
schätzen you'll be lucky na dann viel Glück ◊ Du
willst ihn davon abhalten? Na dann viel Glück! sb'll
be lucky to jd kann von Glück sagen, dass ♦ Er

kann von Glück sagen, dass ihm nichts passiert ist.
lucky (old) me/you etc. ich/du etc. Glückliche/
Glücklicher

lucrative [adj] lukrativ [lukra'tiːf] ◊ ein lukratives
Angebot ♦ Der Job war recht lukrativ.

ludicrous(ly) [adj, adv] lächerlich ['lɛçɐlɪç] (pej) ◊ Sie
trug einen lächerlichen Hut. ♦ Die Situation war
einfach lächerlich. ♦ Er verdient lächerlich wenig.

lug [verb] schleppen ['ʃlɛpm̩] +haben ◊ Eimer/Kisten/
Sandsäcke schleppen

luggage [noun] Gepäck [gə'pɛk] das <-(e)s> no pl ◊
mit leichtem/kleinem/wenig Gepäck reisen

lukewarm [adj] 1. (liquid) lauwarm ['la̯ova'm] no
comp/superl ◊ Das Wasser war lauwarm. ♦
lauwarmer Tee 2. (applause, support) mäßig
['mɛːsɪç] ◊ Er erntete nur mäßigen Beifall.;
(response) zurückhaltend [tsu'rʏkhaltn̩t] ◊ Ihre
Reaktion war eher zurückhaltend.

lump [noun] 1. (of butter, gold etc.) Klumpen ['klʊmpm̩]
der <-s, -> ◊ aus einem Klumpen Ton eine Vase
formen ♦ Im Pudding sind Klumpen.; (of meat,
stone) Brocken ['brɔkn̩] der <-s, -> ◊ Brocken aus
einem Steinbruch schlagen; (of sugar) Stück [ʃtʏk]
das <-es, -> ◊ zwei Stück Zucker in den Tee tun a
lump of coal ein Stück Kohle [a̯en ʃtʏk 'koːlə] a few
lumps of coal ein paar Kohlen [a̯en paːꞏ 'koːlən]
2. (big person) Brocken ['brɔkn̩] der <-s, ->; (stupid
person) Trampel ['trampl̩] der <-s, -> (pej) 3. MED
(swelling) Schwellung ['ʃvɛlʊŋ] die <-, -en> ◊ eine
Schwellung am Hals; (in the breast) Knoten ['knoːtn̩]
der <-s, ->
◉ have a lump in your throat einen Kloß im Hals
haben

lump sum [noun] Pauschale [pa̯o'ʃaːlə] die <-, -n>

lunatic [noun] Verrückte [fɛ'rʏktə] der/die
<-n, die Verrückten> der: ein Verrückter/eine
Verrückte ◊ Nur ein Verrückter würde so etwas tun.

lunch [noun] Mittagessen ['mɪtaːk|ɛsn̩] das <-s, -> ◊
Wann gibt es Mittagessen? ♦ Willst du nicht zum Mittagessen bleiben? have lunch zu Mittag essen
[tsuː 'mɪtaːk ɛsn̩] <isst, aß, hat gegessen> be at lunch
Mittagspause ['mɪtaːkspa̯ozə maxn̩] +haben

lunch break [noun] Mittagspause ['mɪtaːkspa̯ozə] die
<-, -n>

lunchtime [noun] Mittag ['mɪtaːk] der <-s, -e> ◊ Es
ist schon fast Mittag. at lunchtime mittags ['mɪtaːks]

lung [noun] (single) Lungenflügel ['lʊŋənflyːgl̩] der
<-s, -> ◊ der linke/rechte Lungenflügel; (both)
lungs Lunge ['lʊŋə] die <-, -n> ◊ Rauchen schadet
vor allem der Lunge.

lurk [verb] lauern ['la̯oɐn] +haben ◊ Der Tiger lauerte
im Gebüsch. ♦ Überall lauern Gefahren.

lush [adj] 1. (plant, grass) saftig ['zaftɪç] ◊ saftige
Weiden/Wiesen ♦ Das Gras war grün und saftig.;
(garden, vegetation) üppig ['ʏpɪç] ◊ üppiger Pflanzen-
wuchs 2. (hotel, pool area etc.) luxuriös ausgestattet
[lʊksu'rjøːs ,a̯osgəʃtatət] <luxuriöser, am luxuriöses-
ten> lush car Luxusauto ['lʊksʊsa̯oto:] das <-s, -s>
3. (sexually attractive) sexy ['sɛksi:] invariable, mostly
after ns (fam) ◊ Seine Lippen sind echt sexy. ♦ Sie
hat einen sexy Mund.

lust [noun] 1. (sexual) Begierde [ba'gi:gdə] die <-, -n>
◊ Ist es Liebe oder Begierde? lust after/for sb
Begierde nach jdm 2. (craving) Gier [gi:ɐ] die <->
no pl lust after/for sth Gier nach etw. ◊ die Gier
nach Macht/Geld

Luxembourg[1] [noun] Luxemburg ['lʊksm̩bʊˈk] das <-s> *article only in combination with attribute, no pl* → **Germany**

Luxembourg[2] [adj] Luxemburger ['lʊksm̩bʊˈgɐ] *invariable, only before ns* ◊ *Geld auf einem Luxemburger Konto*

Luxembourger [noun] Luxemburger ['lʊksm̩bʊˈgɐ] der <-s, -> ♀Luxemburgerin ['lʊksm̩bʊˈgərɪn] die <-, -nen> → **German**[1] **1.**

Luxemburgish[1] [noun] Luxemburgisch ['lʊksm̩bʊˈgɪʃ] das <-(s)> *no pl* → **German**[1] **2.**

Luxemburgish[2] [adj] luxemburgisch ['lʊksm̩bʊˈgɪʃ] → **German**[2]

luxurious(ly) [adj, adv] edel ['eːdl̩] <edler, am edelsten> <der/die/das edle …> ◊ *Das Brautkleid ist echt edel.* ✦ *Dieser Wein ist ein edler Tropfen.* ✦ *ein edel ausgestattetes Auto*

luxury[1] [noun] Luxus ['lʊksʊs] der <-> *no pl* ◊ *im Luxus leben* ✦ *Das ist der reinste Luxus.*

luxury[2] [adj] luxury … Luxus… ['lʊksʊs] luxury goods Luxusgüter ['lʊksʊsgyːtɐ] die <-> *only pl* luxury hotel Luxushotel ['lʊksʊshoˌtel] das <-s, -s>

lyrics [noun] **1.** *(of a song)* Text [tɛkst] der <-(e)s, -e> ◊ *Sie kannte den Text nicht, summte aber mit.* **2.** *(poems)* Lyrik ['lyːrɪk] die <-> *no pl*

M

m, M [noun] m, M [ɛm] das <–(s), –(s)> ◊ *Dieses Wort wird mit einem kleinen m/großen M geschrieben.* ✦ *M wie Martha*

m. Mio. [mɪˈljoːn(ən)] die ◊ *2 Mio. Menschen*

M *(on signs, street maps)* A [aː] die ◊ *die A8 Karlsruhe–Salzburg*

MA Magister [maˈgɪstɐ] der <–s, –> ◊ *Sie hat ihren Magister in Politologie gemacht.*

machine [noun] **1.** *(mechanical device, vehicle)* Maschine [maˈʃiːnə] die <–, –n> ◊ *eine Maschine anstellen/bedienen/abstellen* ✦ *die Wäsche in die Maschine tun* ✦ *Ich funktionierte nur noch wie eine Maschine.* ✦ *Er fährt eine schwere japanische Maschine.* washing machine Waschmaschine [ˈvaʃmaˌʃiːnə]; *(cash or vending machine)* Automat [aoˈtoˈmaːt] der <–en, –en> ◊ *Getränke aus dem Automaten* ✦ *Geld am Automaten holen* cash machine Geldautomat [ˈgɛltʔaoˌtoˌmaːt] by machine maschinell [maʃiˈnɛl] ◊ *etw. maschinell herstellen* answering machine Anrufbeantworter [ˈanruːfbəʔantvɔɐ̯tɐ] der <–s, –> **2.** IT Rechner [ˈrɛçnɐ] der <–s, –> ◊ *den Rechner hochfahren* **3.** *(group, system)* Maschinerie [maʃinəˈriː] die <–, –n> ◊ *eine gut geölte Maschinerie* ✦ *die bürokratische Maschinerie in Gang setzen*

machinery [noun] **1.** *(machines)* Maschinen [maˈʃiːnən] die <–> only pl ◊ *die Maschinen eines Betriebs warten* **2.** *(system)* Maschinerie [maʃinəˈriː] die <–, –n> ◊ *die komplizierte Maschinerie im Innern einer Uhr* ✦ *Die juristische Maschinerie ist angelaufen.*

mad [adj] **1.** *(insane, silly, irritating)* verrückt [fɛˈrʏkt] *(fam)* ◊ *ein verrückter Wissenschaftler* ✦ *Sie haben sie für verrückt erklärt.* ✦ *Was ihr da vorhabt, ist doch völlig verrückt!* ✦ *verrückt vor Angst/Schmerzen/Zorn* ✦ *Der Stich juckte wie verrückt.* **2.** *(angry)* sauer [ˈzaoɐ] *not before ns (fam)* ◊ *Ich bin total sauer!* mad at/with sb sauer auf jdn mad about sth sauer wegen etw. hopping mad stinksauer [ˈʃtɪŋkˈzaoɐ] *not before ns (fam)*
ⓔ be mad about sth/sb, be mad (keen) on sth/sb (ganz) verrückt nach etw./jdm sein drive sb mad **1.** *(bored, nervous)* jdn verrückt machen **2.** *(angry)* jdn sauer machen go mad **1.** *(bored, nervous)* verrückt werden **2.** *(angry)* sauer werden

madam [noun] **1.** *(address)* gnädige Frau [ˌgnɛːdɪgə ˈfrao] *(oldf)* Can I help you, madam? Kann ich Ihnen helfen? [kan ɪç iːnən ˈhɛlfn̩] Yes, madam? Ja bitte? [jaː ˈbɪtə] Dear Sir/Madam Sehr geehrte Damen und Herren [zeːɐ̯ gəʔeːɐ̯tə ˌdaːmən ʊnt ˈhɛran] Madam Chairwoman/Secretary etc. Frau Vorsitzende/Ministerin etc. [frao ˈfoːɐ̯zɪtsn̩də/miˈnɪstərɪn] **2.** *(in a brothel)* Puffmutter [ˈpʊfmʊtɐ] die <–, Puffmütter> *(slang)*
ⓔ a proper/right little madam eine richtige kleine Dame

As *gnädige Frau* is considered to be old-fashioned, and a more up-to-date version does not exist, people generally avoid using a personal form of address when meeting a woman for the first time. *Gnädige Frau* is, however, still used today in polite society or when the intention is to create an ironic undertone.

made → make [adj] **1.** *(consisting of)* made of aus [aos] [+dat] ◊ *Aus welchem Holz ist der Tisch?* ✦ *ein Herz aus Stein haben* **2.** *(well suited to)* made for wie geschaffen für [viː gəˈʃafn̩ fyːɐ̯] ◊ *wie geschaffen für eine Aufgabe/Arbeit sein* not be made for nicht geschaffen für ◊ *Ich bin fürs Tanzen einfach nicht geschaffen.* be made for each other füreinander geschaffen sein
ⓔ be made (for life), have (got) it made es geschafft haben a made man ein gemachter Mann what sb is made of was in jdm steckt

madman [noun] Irre [ˈɪrə] der <–n, die Irren> *but: ein Irrer (fam, pej)* ◊ *Diesem Irren glaube ich kein Wort.*

madness [noun] Wahnsinn [ˈvaːnzɪn] der <–s> no pl ◊ *Sie war den Wahnsinn nahe.* ✦ *Der Gedanke grenzt ja an Wahnsinn!* ✦ *Es wäre Wahnsinn, das zu tun.*

madwoman [noun] Irre [ˈɪrə] die <–n, die Irren> *(fam, pej)* ◊ *Sie fährt wie eine Irre.*

magazine [noun] **1.** *(published regularly)* Zeitschrift [ˈtsaetʃrɪft] die <–, –en> ◊ *Er hat mehrere Zeitschriften abonniert.* ✦ *in einer Zeitschrift blättern; (copy)* Heft [hɛft] das <–(e)s, –e> ◊ *Leihst du mir das Heft, wenn du es gelesen hast?* **2.** *(programme, storeroom, part of a gun)* Magazin [magaˈtsiːn] das <–s, –e> ◊ *ein politisches Magazin* ✦ *Er hat das ganze Magazin leer geschossen.* ✦ *Waffen aus dem Magazin holen*

maggot [noun] Made [ˈmaːdə] die <–, –n> ◊ *Maden im Fleisch/Käse; (in fruit, mushrooms, nuts)* Wurm [vʊrm] der <–(e)s, Würmer> *(fam)* ◊ *Der Apfel hat einen Wurm.*

magic[1] [noun] **1.** *(faculty of wizards etc.)* Magie [maˈgiː] die <–> no pl ◊ *weiße/schwarze Magie; (activity)* Zauberei [tsaobaˈrae] die <–, –en> ◊ *Wie durch Zauberei wurde er wieder gesund.; (a magician's tricks)* Zauberkunst [ˈtsaobɐkʊnst] die <–, Zauberkünste> ◊ *Er führte seine Zauberkunst vor.* do/perform/work magic zaubern [ˈtsaobɐn] [+haben] ◊ *Hexen können zaubern.* **2.** *(fascination)* Zauber [ˈtsaobɐ] der <–s> no pl ◊ *der Zauber des verschneiten Waldes* ✦ *Er ist ihrem Zauber erlegen.*
ⓔ work your magic on **1.** *(transform through magic)* work your magic on sb/sth jdn/etw. verzaubern **2.** *(enchant with personal attractiveness)* work your magic on sb jdn bezaubern **3.** *(persuade against will)* work your magic on sb jdn herumkriegen work like magic Wunder wirken

magic[2] [adj] **1.** Zauber… [ˈtsaobɐ] magic potion Zaubertrank [ˈtsaobɐtraŋk] der <–(e)s, Zaubertränke> magic wand Zauberstab [ˈtsaobɐʃtaːp] der <–(e)s, Zauberstäbe>; *(number, square)* magisch [ˈmaːgɪʃ] ◊ *Drei ist eine magische Zahl.* **2.** *(very good*

or nice) traumhaft ['traʊmhaft] ◊ *Die Atmosphäre war einfach traumhaft.* ✦ *ein traumhafter Urlaub*

magical [adj] **1.** *(wizard etc., in compound ns)* Zauber… ['tsaʊbə] magical power Zauberkraft ['tsaʊbekraft] die <-, Zauberkräfte> **2.** *(like magic, very good or nice)* wunderbar ['vʊndeba:ɐ̯] ◊ *wunderbare Heilkräfte haben* ✦ *Der Abend war einfach wunderbar.*

magistrate [noun] Richter ['rɪçtɐ] der <-s, -> ♀Richterin ['rɪçtərɪn] die <-, -nen> ◊ *eine strenge Richterin* ✦ *Er möchte Richter werden.*

magnetic [adj] magnetisch [maˈɡneːtɪʃ] ◊ *ein magnetisches Feld* ✦ *Aluminium ist nicht magnetisch.* ✦ *Die Stadt hat eine magnetische Anziehungskraft auf Touristen.*; Magnet… [maˈɡneːt] magnetic card Magnetkarte [maˈɡneːtkaʁtə] die <-, -n> magnetic tape Magnetband [maˈɡneːtbant] das <-(e)s, Magnetbänder>

magnificence [noun] *(impressiveness)* Großartigkeit ['ɡroːsartɪçkaɪt] die <-> no pl ◊ *die Großartigkeit des Universums/der Alpen; (lavishness, beauty)* Pracht [praxt] die <-> no pl ◊ *die Pracht eines Palastes/Sonnenuntergangs*

magnificent(ly) [adj, adv] **1.** *(very impressive, very good)* großartig ['ɡroːsˌartɪç] ◊ *Die Vorführung war großartig.* ✦ *eine großartige Idee* ✦ *Wir haben uns großartig amüsiert.; (very agreeable)* herrlich ['hɛʁlɪç] ◊ *Das Wetter war herrlich.* ✦ *Wir hatten eine herrliche Sicht auf das Meer.* ✦ *Sie war herrlich unverkrampft.* **2.** *(luxurious)* prächtig ['prɛçtɪç] ◊ *Sie wohnten in einer prächtigen Villa.* ✦ *prächtig ausgestattet*

magnify [verb] **1.** *(enlarge)* vergrößern [fɛɐ̯ˈɡrøːsen] <vergrößert, vergrößerte, hat vergrößert> ◊ *Diese Lupe vergrößert alles um 20 Prozent.* ✦ *Damit wird das Problem ja noch vergrößert.* **2.** *(fig) (exaggerate)* aufbauschen ['aʊfbaʊʃn̩] +haben ◊ *Er bauschte die Angelegenheit auch noch auf.*

magnifying glass [noun] Lupe ['luːpə] die <-, -n>

magnitude [noun] Größe ['ɡrøːsə] die <-, -n> ◊ *die unvorstellbare Größe des Weltalls* ✦ *ein Problem von beachtlicher Größe* ✦ *ein Stern erster Größe; (earthquake)* Stärke ['ʃtɛɐ̯kə] die <-, -n> ◊ *Das Beben hatte die Stärke 7 auf der Richterskala.*

maid [noun] *(household help)* Mädchen ['mɛːtçən] das <-s, -> ◊ *Sie haben zwei Mädchen für die Küche.; (in a hotel)* Zimmermädchen ['tsɪmɐmɛːtçən] ⊚ old maid alte Jungfer *(pej)*

maiden name [noun] Mädchenname ['mɛːtçənnaːmə] der <-ns, -n>

mail [noun] **1.** *(post)* Post [pɔst] die <-> no pl ◊ *Hast du deine Post schon gelesen?* ✦ *Die Rechnung war gestern in der Post.* by/through the mail mit der/per Post ◊ *etw. mit der Post bekommen/schicken* **2.** *(e-mail)* Mail [meːl] die <-, -s> **3.** *(for knights etc.)* Rüstung ['rʏstʊŋ] die <-, -en> chain mail Kettenpanzer ['kɛtn̩pantsɐ] der <-s, ->

mailbox [noun] **1.** *(for e-mail)* Postfach ['pɔstfax] das <-(e)s, Postfächer> ◊ *Mein Postfach quillt über von E-Mails.* **2.** *(in the US)* Briefkasten ['briːfkastn̩] der <-s, Briefkästen> ◊ *Der Briefkasten wird zweimal am Tag geleert.*

mailman [noun] Briefträger ['briːftrɛːɡɐ] der <-s, -> ◊ *War der Briefträger heute schon da?* ✦ *Er ist seit drei Jahren Briefträger bei der Post.*

mailwoman [noun] Briefträgerin ['briːftrɛːɡərɪn] die

<-, -nen> ◊ *Sie arbeitet als Briefträgerin.* ✦ *Die Briefträgerin kommt um elf.*

main¹ [noun] **1.** *(water/gas pipe, electricity line)* Leitung ['laɪtʊŋ] die <-, -en> **2.** *(in the UK: electricity supply)* the mains der Stromanschluss [deːɐ̯ ˈʃtroːmlanʃlʊs] <-es> sing; *(gas supply)* der Gasanschluss [deːɐ̯ ˈɡaːslanʃlʊs]; *(water supply)* der Wasseranschluss [deːɐ̯ ˈvaselanʃlʊs] **3.** *(in the UK: point where the gas or water supply enters)* the mains der Haupthahn [deːɐ̯ ˈhaʊptaːn] <-(e)s> sing; *(where the electricity supply enters)* der Hauptschalter [deːɐ̯ ˈhaʊptʃaltɐ] <-s, ->

main² [adj] Haupt… [haʊpt] main course Hauptgericht ['haʊptɡərɪçt] das <-(e)s, -e> main thing Hauptsache ['haʊptzaxə] die <-, -n> most sing

mainland [noun] Festland ['fɛstlant] das <-(e)s> ◊ *Die Insel liegt etwa 150 km vom Festland entfernt.*

mainly [adv] **1.** *(for the most part)* hauptsächlich ['haʊptzɛçlɪç] ◊ *Der menschliche Körper besteht hauptsächlich aus Wasser.* ✦ *Er hat das hauptsächlich deswegen gesagt, weil er mich ärgern wollte.* **2.** *(mostly)* vorwiegend ['foːɐ̯viːɡn̩t] ◊ *vorwiegend im Winter/Süden auftreten* ✦ *Das Wetter: vorwiegend heiter.*

main road [noun] Hauptstraße ['haʊptʃtraːsə] die <-, -n>

main station [noun] Hauptbahnhof ['haʊptbaːnhoːf] der <-s, Hauptbahnhöfe>

mainstream [noun] the political mainstream die politische Mitte [di: poˌliːtɪʃə ˈmɪtə] die <-> no pl; *(music, literature etc.)* Mainstream ['meːnstriːm] der <-s> no pl outside the mainstream of society am Rande der Gesellschaft [am ˌrandə deːɐ̯ ɡəˈzɛlʃaft] enter the mainstream (of sth) sich (irgendwo) etablieren [etaˈbliːrən] <etabliert sich, etablierte sich, hat sich etabliert>

maintain [verb] **1.** *(cause to continue)* aufrechterhalten ['aʊfrɛçtlɛhaltn̩] <erhält aufrecht, erhielt aufrecht, hat aufrechterhalten> ◊ *den Betrieb/die Ordnung aufrechterhalten* ✦ *seine Behauptung aufrechterhalten; (a relationship, an institution)* unterhalten [ʊntɐˈhaltn̩] <unterhält, unterhielt, hat unterhalten> ◊ *Geschäftsziehungen unterhalten* ✦ *Der Kindergarten wird von der Kirche unterhalten.; (protect)* bewahren [bəˈvaːrən] <bewahrt, bewahrte, hat bewahrt> ◊ *Traditionen bewahren* ✦ *die Lebensräume seltener Tiere bewahren; (a position)* behaupten [bəˈhaʊptn̩] <behauptet, behauptete, hat behauptet> ◊ *Er konnte den ersten Platz behaupten.* maintain your position sich behaupten ◊ *sich gegen die Konkurrenz behaupten* **2.** *(in good condition, a building)* instand halten [ɪnˈʃtant haltn̩] <hält, hielt, hat gehalten>; *(a vehicle, relationship, interests, contacts)* pflegen ['pfleːɡn̩] +haben ◊ *die Karosserie mit Wachs pflegen* ✦ *Als Journalistin muss sie ihre Kontakte pflegen.; (mechanic etc.)* warten ['vaʁtn̩] <wartet, wartete, hat gewartet> ◊ *Flugzeuge müssen regelmäßig gewartet werden.* **3.** *(statement)* behaupten [bəˈhaʊptn̩] <behauptet, behauptete, hat behauptet> ◊ *Er behauptet, er habe keinen Fehler gemacht.* maintain your innocence seine Unschuld beteuern [zaɛnə ˈʊnʃʊlt bəˌtɔɪɐn] <beteuert, beteuerte, hat beteuert>

maintenance [noun] **1.** *(of machines etc.)* Pflege ['pfleːɡə] die <-> no pl ◊ *Die Lebensdauer eines Autos steigt bei guter Pflege.; (by mechanics etc.)*

Wartung ['va^rtʊŋ] die <–> *no pl* ◊ *die Wartung eines Flugzeugs; (of buildings)* Instandhaltung [ɪn'ʃtanthaltʊŋ] die <–> *no pl* **2.** *(of good relations, discipline)* Aufrechterhaltung ['aʊfrɛçt|ɛhaltʊŋ] die <–> *no pl* ◊ *die Aufrechterhaltung freundschaftlicher Beziehungen* **3.** *(payment)* Unterhalt ['ʊntehalt] der <–(e)s *no pl* ◊ *seiner geschiedenen Frau/für seine Kinder Unterhalt zahlen* ◆ *Der Unterhalt eines Schwimmbads ist sehr teuer.*

maize [noun] Mais [maes] der <–es> *no pl*

majesty [noun] Majestät [majɛs'tɛːt] die <–, –en> ◊ *die Majestät der schneebedeckten Berge* Your/His/Her Majesty Eure/Seine/Ihre Majestät

major¹ [noun] **1.** *(in the army)* Major [ma'joːɐ] der <–s, –e> **2.** *(in the US: subject at college)* Hauptfach ['haʊptfax] das <–(e)s, Hauptfächer> ◊ *Welches Hauptfach hast du belegt?* a biology/maths major ein Student/eine Studentin mit Biologie/Mathematik als Hauptfach

major² [adj] **1.** *(large, great)* größer ['grøːsɐ] *mostly before ns* ◊ *Es gab keine größeren Probleme.* ◆ *Größere Veränderungen werden nötig sein.; (important)* wichtig ['vɪçtɪç] ◊ *wichtige Faktoren; (serious)* schwerwiegend ['ʃveːɐviːgn̩t] ◊ *schwerwiegende Mängel/Bedenken haben* major part Großteil ['groːstael] der <–s> *no pl* ◊ *Den Großteil ihrer Freizeit verbringt sie mit Sport.* **2.** *(largest, greatest)* größte ['grøːstə] ◊ *Unser größtes Problem ist im Moment …* ◆ *die größten Künstler unserer Zeit; (most important)* wichtigste ['vɪçtɪçstə] ◊ *Was ist euer wichtigstes Ziel?; (most serious)* schlimmste ['ʃlɪmstə] ◊ *Die schlimmsten Schäden wurden behoben.* **3.** *(in the US)* major subject Hauptfach ['hɔʊptfax] das <–(e)s, Hauptfächer> ◊ *Welches Hauptfach hast du belegt?* ◆ *Sie studiert Germanistik im Hauptfach.* **4.** mus C etc. major C-Dur etc. ['tseːduːɐ] das <–> *no pl* major key Durtonart ['duːɐtoːn|aːt] die <–, –en>

majority [noun] **1.** *(most)* Mehrzahl ['meːɐtsaːl] die <–> *no pl* the majority of sb/sth die Mehrzahl … [gen] ◊ *Die Mehrzahl der Fehler war harmlos.* the vast majority die große Mehrzahl be in the majority in der Überzahl sein [ɪn deːɐ 'yːbɐtsaːl tsaen] +*sein* ◊ *Frauen waren auf dem Fest in der Überzahl.* **2.** *(of votes, voters etc.)* Mehrheit ['meːɐhaet] die <–, –en> ◊ *Die Mehrheit der Bürger ist für Reformen.* ◆ *Ihr Vorschlag fand eine Mehrheit.* be in the majority die Mehrheit haben ◊ *Welche Partei hat dort die Mehrheit?* the majority opinion is that die Mehrheit ist der Ansicht, dass majority decision/vote Mehrheitsbeschluss ['meːɐhaetsbəʃlʊs] der <–es, Mehrheitsbeschlüsse> **3.** *(age)* Volljährigkeit ['fɔljɛːrɪçkaet] die <–> *no pl* reach your majority volljährig werden ['fɔljɛːrɪç veːɐdn̩]

make¹ [noun] **1.** *(manufacturer, trade name)* Marke ['maʳkə] die <–, –n> ◊ *ein Pkw der Marke Volkswagen* make of car Automarke ['aʊtomaʳkə] **2.** *(product)* Fabrikat [fabri'kaːt] das <–(e)s, –e> ◊ *Der Fernseher ist ein älteres Fabrikat.* **3.** *(style etc.)* Machart ['max|aːt] die <–, –en> ◊ *Produkte ähnlicher Machart*

◉ on the make **1.** *(up and coming)* auf dem Weg nach oben ◊ *Berlin: eine Stadt auf dem Weg nach oben.* **2.** *(get money/advantages)* auf Geld/seinen Vorteil aus **3.** *(sexually)* auf Abenteuer aus

make² [verb] **1.** *(create, cause, prepare)* machen ['maxn̩] +*haben* ◊ *Die Kacheln werden von Hand gemacht.* ◆ *einen Film über Hexen machen* ◆ *Musik/Lärm/Fehler machen* ◆ *ein Feuer machen* ◆ *Kaffee/Tee/Frühstück/einen Salat machen* ◆ *mit dem Bohrer ein Loch in die Wand machen* make sth from/(out) of sth etw. aus etw. machen ◊ *Wein wird aus Trauben gemacht.* make sb sth jdm etw. machen ◊ *Sie hat mir zum Geburtstag einen Kuchen gemacht.; (handicraft)* basteln ['bastl̩n] +*haben* ◊ *Schau mal, ich habe eine Fingerpuppe gebastelt!* **2.** *(build)* bauen ['baʊən] +*haben* ◊ *eine Sandburg bauen* ◆ *Diese Firma baut Orgeln.; (manufacture, bring about)* herstellen ['heːɐʃtɛlən] +*haben* ◊ *Viele Autoteile werden im Ausland hergestellt.* ◆ *maschinell hergestellt* ◆ *eine Verbindung mit dem Internet herstellen; (produce)* produzieren [produ'tsiːrən] <produziert, produzierte, hat produziert> ◊ *Strom produzieren* ◆ *Die Drüse produziert Gift.* **3.** *(say or do sth, an attempt, a suggestion)* machen ['maxn̩] +*haben* ◊ *Ich machte mehrmals den Versuch, mich zu entschuldigen.; (a comment, declaration, judgement)* abgeben ['apgeːbm̩] <gibt ab, gab ab, hat abgegeben> ◊ *Dazu kann ich kein Urteil abgeben.; (a confession)* ablegen ['apleːgn̩] +*haben* ◊ *Sie legte die Beichte/ein Geständnis ab.; (a speech etc.)* halten ['haltn̩] <hält, hielt, hat gehalten> ◊ *eine Rede/Vorlesung/einen Vortrag halten; (prognosis, demand, diagnosis)* stellen ['ʃtɛlən] +*haben* ◊ *eine Prognose stellen* ◆ *Ansprüche/Bedingungen stellen; (rules)* aufstellen ['aʊfʃtɛlən] +*haben* ◊ *Er stellte eine neue Regel auf.; (assumptions, comparisons, enquiries)* anstellen ['anʃtɛlən] +*haben* ◊ *Recherchen/Nachforschungen anstellen; (a decision, resolution)* fassen ['fasn̩] +*haben* ◊ *Sie fasste den Vorsatz, 20 Kilo abzunehmen.; (preparations)* treffen ['trɛfn̩] <trifft, traf, hat getroffen> ◊ *Vorbereitungen für eine Reise treffen; (an adjustment, a change)* vornehmen ['foːɐneːmən] <nimmt vor, nahm vor, hat vorgenommen> ◊ *Änderungen an einem Text vornehmen* **4.** *(achieve a certain state)* machen ['maxn̩] +*haben* ◊ *Gewinne/Verluste/Fortschritte/einen Unterschied machen* ◆ *jdn glücklich/traurig machen* ◆ *Ich kann mich ihm nicht verständlich machen.* ◆ *Die Blumen machen den Raum freundlicher.* make sb look … jdn … machen ◊ *Die Frisur macht dich jünger.* make sb sth jdn zu etw. machen ◊ *Sie machten ihn zum Anführer.* make sb your wife jdn zur Frau nehmen [tsuːɐ fraʊ neːmən] <nimmt, nahm, hat genommen> **5.** *(require or cause sb to do sth)* make sb do sth jdn etw. tun lassen ['lasn̩] <lässt, ließ, hat lassen> ◊ *Sie ließ die Schüler das Gedicht auswendig lernen.* ◆ *jdn warten lassen; (force sb)* jdn zu etw. zwingen [tsuː …, 'tsvɪŋən] <zwingt, zwang, hat gezwungen> ◊ *Zwing mich nicht, etw. zu versprechen, was ich nicht halten kann.* **6.** *(earn money)* verdienen [fɛ'diːnən] <verdient, verdiente, hat verdient> ◊ *Wie viel verdienst du im Monat?* ◆ *Er hat an der Börse viel Geld verdient.* ◆ *sich* [dat] *seinen Lebensunterhalt verdienen* **7.** *(have as a result)* ergeben [ɛ'geːbm̩] <ergibt, ergab, hat ergeben> ◊ *Fünf mal zehn ergibt fünfzig.* ◆ *Der Bratensaft ergibt eine gute Soße.* **8.** *(be right for sth)* abgeben ['apgeːbm̩] <gibt ab, gab ab, hat abgegeben> ◊ *Du würdest einen guten Musiker abgeben.* **9.** *(reach)* schaffen ['ʃafn̩] +*haben* (fam) ◊ *Schaffen wir es noch rechtzeitig nach Hause?* **10.** *(a scene, fuss)* machen ['maxn̩] +*haben* ◊ *Mach jetzt bloß*

keine Szene! make a fuss einen Wirbel machen
ⓔ **make it through sth** etw. überleben make
believe that so tun, als ◊ *Sie taten so, als hätten
sie einen Schatz gefunden .* make do with/without
sth mit/ohne etw. auskommen **I make it ...** *(time)*
bei mir ist es ... ◊ *Bei mir ist es fünf Uhr.* I make
that ... **1.** *(result)* das macht bei mir ... ◊ *2 und 2
macht bei mir 4.* **2.** *(estimate)* ich schätze das auf
...
• **make away with** [phras v] make away with sth
sich mit etw. davonmachen [mɪt ... daˈfɔnmaxn̩]
+haben *(fam)* ◊ *Er machte sich mit den Einnahmen
davon.*
• **make for** [phras v] make for sth **1.** *(head towards)*
auf etw. zugehen [aʊf ... ˈtsuːɡeːən] <geht zu, ging zu,
ist zugegangen> ◊ *Sie ging auf das Fenster zu.*
2. *(make possible)* zu etw. beitragen
[tsuː ... ˌbaɪtraːɡn̩] <trägt bei, trug bei, hat beigetra-
gen> ◊ *Trägt diese Alarmanlage zu mehr Sicherheit
bei?*
• **make into** [phras v] make sb/sth into sth etw. aus
jdm/etw. machen [aʊs ... maxn̩] +haben ◊ *Mach
keinen Helden aus mir!*; *(a book, story)* make sth
into a film etw. verfilmen [fɛˈfɪlmən] <verfilmt,
verfilmte, hat verfilmt> ◊ *Ihre Lebensgeschichte wurde
verfilmt.*
• **make of** [phras v] make sth of sb/sth **1.** *(bring
about a condition)* etw. aus jdm/etw. machen
[aʊs ... maxn̩] +haben ◊ *Sie hat aus dem kleinen
Laden ein blühendes Geschäft gemacht.* make a
success of sth etw. zum Erfolg führen
[tsʊm ɛˈfɔlk fyːrən] +haben ◊ *Mit diesem Motto führte
er die Firma zum Erfolg.* **2.** *(view in a certain way)*
etw. von jdm/etw. halten [fɔn ... haltn̩] ◊ *Was hältst
du von dem neuen Lehrer?*
• **make off** [phras v] verschwinden [fɛˈʃvɪndn̩] <ver-
schwindet, verschwand, ist verschwunden> ◊ *Er ist mit
meinem Geld verschwunden.*
• **make out** [phras v] **1.** *(see)* erkennen [ɛˈkɛnən]
<erkennt, erkannte, hat erkannt> ◊ *Ich konnte im
Dunkeln kaum etwas erkennen.*; *(read)* entziffern
[ɛntˈtsɪfɐn] <entziffert, entzifferte, hat entziffert>;
(hear) hören [ˈhøːrən] +haben; *(understand)*
verstehen [fɛˈʃteːən] <versteht, verstand, hat verstan-
den> ◊ *Sie sprach so leise, dass ich sie kaum
verstand.* **2.** *(a cheque)* ausstellen [ˈaʊsʃtɛlən] +haben
3. *(get on, fare)* sich machen [ˈmaxn̩] +haben ◊ *Wie
macht er sich bei der Arbeit?* **4.** *(understand)* make
sb out aus jdm schlau werden [aʊs ... ˈʃlaʊ veːɐdn̩]
+sein *(fam)* ◊ *Ich werde aus ihr einfach nicht schlau.*
5. *(pretend)* make out that ... so tun, als ...
[zo: ˈtuːn als] <tut, tat, hat getan> +subj ◊ *Er tat so,
als wäre er krank.* **6.** make sb out to be sth jdn als
etw. hinstellen [als ... hɪnʃtɛlən] +haben ◊ *Sie ist
nicht so dumm, wie ihr sie immer hinstellt.* **7.** *(in
the US)* make out (with sb) (mit jdm) rummachen
[ˈrʊmmaxn̩] +haben *(fam)* ◊ *Du bist noch zu jung,
um mit Mädchen rumzumachen.*
• **make over** [phras v] make sth over (to sb) etw.
(auf jdn) überschreiben [ybɐˈʃraɪbn̩] <überschreibt,
überschrieb, hat überschrieben> ◊ *Er überschrieb das
Geschäft auf seine Tochter.*
• **make up** [phras v] **1.** *(an excuse, a story etc.)*
make sth up sich [dat] etw. ausdenken [ˈaʊsdɛŋkn̩]
<denkt sich aus, dachte sich aus, hat sich ausgedacht> ◊
◊ *Ich habe mir das nur/selbst ausgedacht.* **2.** *(a*

person, face) schminken [ˈʃmɪŋkn̩] +haben ◊ *sich
zum Ausgehen schminken* ♦ *einen Schauspieler
schminken* **3.** *(clothing, a list, report etc.)* anfertigen
[ˈanfɛʁtɪɡn̩] +haben ◊ *Sie fertigt die Kostüme für den
Ball an.* **4.** *(catch up on)* nachholen [ˈnaːxhoːlən]
+haben ◊ *Ich mache heute frei und hole das
Versäumte morgen nach.* make up for lost time
verlorene Zeit (wieder) reinholen
[fɛˌloːrənə ˌtsaɪt (viːdɐ) ˈraɪnhoːlən] +haben *(fam)*
5. *(reconcile differences)* make up (with sb) sich (mit
jdm) wieder vertragen [viːdɐ fɛˈtraːɡn̩] <verträgt
sich, vertrug sich, hat sich vertragen> ◊ *Kommt,
vertragt euch wieder!* **6.** *(form sth)* bilden [ˈbɪldn̩]
<bildet, bildete, hat gebildet> ◊ *Das Kniegelenk wird
von drei Knochen gebildet.*; *(complete sth)* voll
machen [ˈfɔl maxn̩] +haben ◊ *Diese zwei Kisten
machen das Dutzend/die 50 voll.* **7.** *(compensate for)*
make up for sth jdn für etw. entschädigen
[fyːɐ ... ɛntˈʃɛːdɪɡn̩] <entschädigt, entschädigte, hat ent-
schädigt> ◊ *Das gute Essen entschädigte uns für die
lange Wartezeit.* make up for the loss of sth/sb etw./
jdn ersetzen [eˈzɛtsn̩] <ersetzt, ersetzte, hat ersetzt>
8. *(curry favo(u)r with)* make up to sb sich bei jdm
einschmeicheln [baɛ ... ˈaɛnʃmaɛçln̩] <schmeichelt
sich ein, schmeichelte sich ein, hat sich eingeschmei-
chelt>
ⓔ **make it up to sb** es wieder gutmachen
maker [noun] **1.** *(manufacturer)* Hersteller [ˈheːɐʃtɛlɐ]
der <-s, -> ♀Herstellerin [ˈheːɐʃtɛlərɪn] die
<-, -nen> ◊ *ein Hersteller elektronischer Geräte*
2. *(machine)* coffee maker Kaffeemaschine
[ˈkafeːmaˌʃiːnə] die <-, -n>
ⓔ **meet your maker** vor seinen Schöpfer treten
makeshift [adj] notdürftig [ˈnoːtdʏʁftɪç] *only before ns*
◊ *Kerzen als notdürftige Beleuchtung*
make-up [noun] **1.** *(cosmetic)* Make-up [meːkˈlʲap] das
<-s, -s> ◊ *Make-up tragen/auflegen* **2.** *(composition)*
Zusammensetzung [tsuˈzamənzɛtsʊŋ] die <-, -en> ◊
die Zusammensetzung des Bundestags ♦ *die
chemische Zusammensetzung der DNS* **3.** *(of a page)*
Umbruch [ˈʊmbrʊx] der <-(e)s> *no pl*
making [noun] **1.** *(with machines)* Herstellung
[ˈheːɐʃtɛlʊŋ] die <-> *no pl* ◊ *die Herstellung von
Computern*; *(creation)* Schaffung [ˈʃafʊŋ] die <-> *no
pl* ◊ *die Schaffung eines Kunstwerks* **2.** *(development,
emergence)* Entstehung [ɛntˈʃteːʊŋ] die <-> *no pl* ◊
die Entstehung eines Mythos ♦ *Der Plan ist noch in
der Entstehung.*
ⓔ **have the makings of sth** das Zeug zu etw.
haben **of your own making 1.** selbst gemacht ◊ *ein
selbst gemachtes Gedicht* **2.** *(sth negative)* selbst verschuldet ◊ *eine selbst verschuldete Krise*
male¹ [noun] **1.** *(animal)* Männchen [ˈmɛnçən] das
<-s, -> ◊ *das Männchen der Eule* **2.** *(human)* Mann
[man] der <-(e)s, Männer> ◊ *eine Gesprächsgruppe
für Männer*
male² [adj] männlich [ˈmɛnlɪç] ◊ *War der Täter
männlich oder weiblich?* ♦ *Eine männliche Gans
heißt Ganter.*
malice [noun] Tücke [ˈtʏkə] die <-> *no pl* ◊ *Seine
Augen waren voller Tücke.*
malicious [adj] boshaft [ˈbɔshaft] <boshafter, am bos-
haftesten> ◊ *Ich finde ihn richtig boshaft.* ♦ *eine
boshafte Unterstellung*
malignant [adj] *(tumor)* bösartig [ˈbøːsˌaːɐtɪç] ◊ *Ist die
Geschwulst bösartig oder gutartig?*

Malta [noun] Malta ['maltɐ] das <–s> *article only in combination with attribute, no pl* I live in Malta. Ich lebe auf Malta.

Maltese¹ [noun] **1.** *(inhabitant)* Malteser [mal'te:zɐ] der <–s, –> ♀Malteserin [mal'te:zərɪn] die <–, –nen> → **German¹** 1. **2.** *(language)* Maltesisch [mal'te:zɪʃ] das <–(s)> *no pl* → **German¹** 2.

Maltese² [adj] maltesisch [mal'te:zɪʃ] → **German²**

mammal [noun] Säugetier ['zɔɡɐtiːɐ̯] das <–(e)s, –e>

man¹ [noun] **1.** *(male)* Mann [man] der <–(e)s, Männer> *pl* 'Mann' *when used in the sense of 'person'* ◊ *Er ist ein gut aussehender Mann.* ♦ *ein Schiff mit 50 Mann Besatzung* ♦ *Er führte seine Männer in den Kampf.* ♦ *Mann, mach doch endlich!* a Dublin etc. man ein Mann aus Dublin etc. the right man der Richtige [de:ɐ̯ 'rɪçtɪɡə] <–n, –n> her new man ihr Neuer [iːɐ̯ 'nɔʏ̯ɐ] <Neuen, Neuen> **2.** *(human)* Mensch [mɛnʃ] der <–en, –en> ◊ *Menschen können grausam sein.* every man jeder ['jeːdɐ] no man niemand ['niːmant] many men viele ['fiːlə] few men nur wenige [nuːɐ̯ 've:nɪɡə] **3.** *(chess etc.)* Spielfigur ['ʃpiːlfiˌɡuːɐ̯] die <–, –en> ➏ man and boy von Kindesbeinen an a man of the world ein Mann von Welt be man enough for sth Manns genug für etw. sein be man enough to do sth Manns genug sein, etw. zu tun every man for himself jeder für sich sein be your own man sein eigener Herr sein

man² [verb] *(a post, counter etc.)* besetzen [bə'zɛtsn̩] <besetzt, besetzte, hat besetzt> ◊ *Unsere Schalter werden 90 Minuten vor Abflug besetzt.; (a ship etc.)* bemannen [bə'manən] <bemannt, bemannte, hat bemannt>

manage [verb] **1.** *(succeed in, be able to eat or drink)* schaffen ['ʃafn̩] +haben ◊ *Er hat die Prüfung erst beim dritten Mal geschafft.* ♦ *Ein Stück Kuchen schaffe ich noch.* manage to do sth es schaffen, etw. zu tun ◊ *Die Sängerin schaffte es, das Publikum zu begeistern.; (when forcing yourself)* zustande bringen [tsu'ʃtandə brɪŋən] <bringt, brachte, hat gebracht> ◊ *Sie brachte nur ein müdes Lächeln zustande.* **2.** *(deal successfully with a problem, be able to live on)* zurechtkommen [tsu'rɛçtkɔmən] <kommt zurecht, kam zurecht, ist zurechtgekommen> ◊ *Keine Angst, ich komme schon zurecht.* ♦ *mit der Arbeit zurechtkommen* ♦ *ohne Job zurechtkommen* manage on sth mit etw. zurechtkommen ◊ *Mit so wenig Geld komme ich nicht zurecht.* manage sb/sth mit jdm/etw. umgehen [mɪt ... ˌɔmɡeːən] <geht um, ging um, ist umgegangen> ◊ *mit einem Problem/schwierigen Kunden umgehen* **3.** *(an organization, a business)* leiten ['laɪ̯tn̩] <leitet, leitete, hat geleitet> ◊ *Sie leitet ein Übersetzungsbüro.; (a hotel, restaurant)* führen ['fyːrən] +haben ◊ *ein Hotel, dass von einer Familie geführt wird; (your/sb's money etc.)* verwalten [fɛ'valtn̩] <verwaltet, verwaltete, hat verwaltet> ◊ *ein Vermögen verwalten; (your time)* einteilen ['aɪ̯ntaɪ̯lən] +haben; *(an area of land)* pflegen ['pfleːɡn̩] ◊ *ein Waldstück pflegen*

manageable [adj] **1.** *(amount, size)* überschaubar [ˌybɐ'ʃaʊ̯baːɐ̯] ◊ *eine überschaubare Menge an Lernstoff* ♦ *Die Größe der Gruppe ist überschaubar.* **2.** *(hair)* leicht kämmbar [laɪ̯çt 'kɛmbaːɐ̯] <leichter, am leichtesten> ◊ *leicht kämmbares Haar*

management [noun] **1.** *(control of a company)* Leitung ['laɪ̯tʊŋ] die <–, –en> ◊ *die Leitung einer Firma* be

under new management unter neuer Leitung stehen; *(of a building, public institution)* Verwaltung [fɛ'valtʊŋ] die <–, –en> ◊ *die Verwaltung eines Wohnhauses/einer Schule; (people who control a company)* Geschäftsleitung [ɡə'ʃɛftslaɪ̯tʊŋ] ◊ *die Mitglieder der Geschäftsleitung* **2.** *(dealing with a problem)* Bewältigung [bə'vɛltɪɡʊŋ] die <–, –en> most sing ◊ *die Bewältigung von Stress*

manager [noun] **1.** *(of a company, organization)* Geschäftsführer [ɡə'ʃɛftsfyːre] der <–s, –> ♀Geschäftsführerin [ɡə'ʃɛftsfyːrərɪn] die <–, –nen>; *(in compound ns)* ... manager ...leiter ['laɪ̯tɐ] der <–s, –> ♀...leiterin ['laɪ̯tərɪn] die <–, –nen> branch manager Filialleiter [fi'lia:laɪ̯tɐ] Filialleiterin [fi'lia:llaɪ̯tərɪn] sales manager Verkaufsleiter [fɛ'kaʊ̯fslaɪ̯tɐ] Verkaufsleiterin [fɛ'kaʊ̯fslaɪ̯tərɪn] **2.** *(of a sports team, artists)* Manager ['mɛnɪdʒɐ] der <–s, –> ♀Managerin ['mɛnɪdʒərɪn] die <–, –nen> ◊ *der Manager der Nationalelf*

managerial [adj] leitend ['laɪ̯tn̩t] *no comp/superl, mostly before ns* ◊ *eine leitende Position;* Führungs... ['fyːrʊŋs] managerial experience Führungserfahrung ['fyːrʊŋsʔɛfaːrʊŋ] die <–, –en>

managing [adj] geschäftsführend [ɡə'ʃɛftsfyːrənt] *no comp/superl, only before ns* ◊ *der geschäftsführende Vorstand* managing editor Chefredakteur ['ʃɛfredakˌtøːɐ̯] der <–s, –e> ♀Chefredakteurin ['ʃɛfredakˌtøːrɪn] die <–, –nen>

managing director [noun] Geschäftsführer [ɡə'ʃɛftsfyːre] der <–s, –> ♀Geschäftsführerin [ɡə'ʃɛftsfyːrərɪn] die <–, –nen> ◊ *Der Geschäftsführer möchte Sie sprechen.* ♦ *Sie ist Geschäftsführerin eines Reisebüros.*

mandate [noun] *(task)* Auftrag ['aʊ̯ftraːk] der <–(e)s, Aufträge> have the mandate to do sth den Auftrag haben, etw. zu tun; *(of a government)* Regierungsauftrag [re'ɡiːrʊŋsˌaʊ̯ftraːk]; *(of an organization controlling a country)* Mandat [man'daːt] das <–(e)s, –e> *(lofty)* ◊ *das Mandat der UN-Mission im Kongo; (period)* Mandatszeit [man'daːtstsaɪ̯t] die <–, –en>

mandatory [adj] obligatorisch [ɔbliɡa'toːrɪʃ] *no comp/superl (lofty)* ◊ *obligatorische Ruhezeiten für Lkw-Fahrer* sth is mandatory etw. ist Pflicht [ɪst 'pflɪçt] +sein it is mandatory to do sth es ist Pflicht, etw. zu tun

maneuver → **manoeuvre**

mangle [noun] Mangel ['maŋl̩] die <–, –n>

manhole [noun] Kanaleinstieg [ka'naːlʔaɪ̯nʃtiːk] der <–(e)s, –e>

maniac [noun] **1.** *(lunatic)* Irre ['ɪrə] der/die <–n, die Irren> *but: ein Irrer/eine Irre (fam, pej)* ◊ *Er fährt wie ein Irrer.* **2.** *(fanatic)* Fanatiker [fa'naːtɪke] der <–s, –> ♀Fanatikerin [fa'naːtɪkərɪn] die <–, –nen> ◊ *eine religiöse Fanatikerin*

manifest(ly) [adj, adv] offenkundig ['ɔfn̩kʊndɪç] *(lofty)* ◊ *ein offenkundiger Betrug/Fehler* ♦ *Es ist jetzt offenkundig, dass sie die Stelle bekommt.* ♦ *Sie ist offenkundig nicht an ihm interessiert.*

manifest [verb] zeigen ['tsaɪ̯ɡn̩] +haben ◊ *Sie zeigte deutlich ihr mangelndes Interesse.* sth manifests itself etw. zeigt sich ◊ *Musikalisches Talent zeigt sich schon in früher Kindheit.*

manifestation [noun] **1.** *(evidence)* Anzeichen ['antsaɪ̯çn̩] das <–s, –> manifestation of sth Anzeichen für etw. ◊ *Gewalt ist ein Anzeichen unge-*

löster Konflikte. ◆ *Mundgeruch kann ein Anzeichen für eine Krankheit sein.* **2.** manifestation of a spirit Geistererscheinung ['gaestə|eʃaenʊn] die <-, –en>

manipulate [verb] **1.** *(influence, alter)* manipulieren [manipu'li:rən] <manipuliert, manipulierte, hat manipuliert> ◊ *Menschen/Zahlen manipulieren* genetically manipulated genmanipuliert ['ge:nmanipu,li:gt] *no comp/superl* ◊ *genmanipulierter Mais* ◆ *Diese Tomaten sind genmanipuliert.* **2.** *(operate)* handhaben ['hantha:bm̩] +haben ◊ *Er hat das Gerät geschickt gehandhabt.*

manipulation [noun] *(influencing, alteration)* Manipulation [manipula'tsjo:n] die <-, –en> ◊ *die Manipulation der Massen/von Preisen* genetic manipulation Genmanipulation ['ge:nmanipula,tsjo:n]

mankind [noun] Menschheit ['mɛnʃhaet] die <-> *no pl* ◊ *die Geschichte der Menschheit*

man-made [adj] **1.** *(not natural)* künstlich ['kʏnstlɪç] *no comp/superl* ◊ *ein künstlicher See* ◆ *Diese Blumen sind künstlich.* **2.** *(caused by humans)* von Menschen verursacht [fɔn 'mɛnʃn̩ fɛ|,u:ʁgzaxt] *no comp/no superl* ◊ *eine von Menschen verursachte Katastrophe* ◆ *Die Klimaveränderung ist von Menschen verursacht.*

manner [noun] **1.** *(way of doing sth, way sth happens)* Art [a:ʳt] die <-, –en> ◊ *Es gibt verschiedene Arten, damit umzugehen.* sb's manner of doing sth die Art, wie jd etw. tut sb's manner of work jds Arbeitsweise ['a:ʳbaetsvaezə] die <-, –n> in a lively manner lebendig [le'bɛndɪç] ◊ *Sie schreibt sehr lebendig.* in a friendly manner freundlich ['frɔɪntlɪç] sth in the manner of sb etw. im Stil ... [gen] [ɪm ʃti:l] ◊ *ein Gedicht im Stil Shakespeares* **2.** *(behavio(u)r)* Art [a:ʳt] die <-> *no pl* ◊ *Sie hat so eine aggressive Art.; (socially accepted)* manners Manieren [ma'ni:rən] die <-> *only pl* ◊ *gute/schlechte/keine Manieren haben* ⓢ in a manner of speaking gewissermaßen

manoeuvre¹, maneuver [noun] Manöver [ma'nø:ve] das <-s, -> ◊ *Ich wendete mit einem riskanten Manöver.* ◆ *ein taktisches Manöver* be on manoeuvres beim Manöver sein

manoeuvre², maneuver [verb] **1.** *(steer)* manövrieren [manø'vri:rən] <manövriert, manövrierte, hat manövriert> ◊ *einen Wagen geschickt (durch dichten Verkehr) manövrieren* **2.** *(influence skillfully)* manoeuvre yourself somewhere sich [dat] etw. erobern [e]'o:ben] <erobert sich, eroberte sich, hat sich erobert> ◊ *Ich eroberte mir einen Platz an der Spitze des Konzerns* manoeuvre sb into doing sth jdn dazu bringen, etw. zu tun [datsu: 'brɪŋən ... tsu:] <bringt, brachte, hat gebracht> ◊ *Ich brachte sie dazu, ein Geständnis abzulegen.*

manor [noun] *(house)* Herrenhaus ['hɛrənhaʊs] das <-es, Herrenhäuser>; *(estate)* Landgut ['lantgu:t] das <-(e)s, Landgüter>

manpower [noun] Personal [pɛʳzo'na:l] das <-s> *no pl*

mansion [noun] *(old)* Herrenhaus ['hɛrənhaʊs] das <-es, Herrenhäuser>; *(modern)* Villa ['vɪla:] die <-, Villen>

manual¹ [noun] Handbuch ['hantbu:x] das <-(e)s, Handbücher>

manual² [adj] *(with your hands, physical, non-automatic)* manuell [manu'ɛl] *no comp/superl, mostly before ns* ◊ *eine manuelle Tätigkeit* ◆ *auf manuellen Betrieb umschalten* manual worker Arbeiter ['a:ʳbaete] der <-s, -> ♀Arbeiterin

['a:ʳbaetərɪn] die <-, –nen>

manufacture¹ [noun] **1.** *(production)* Herstellung ['he:ɐ̯ʃtɛlʊn] die <-> *no pl* ◊ *die Herstellung von Autos* **2.** *(goods)* manufactures Erzeugnisse [e'tsɔøknɪsə] die <-> *pl* ◊ *Erzeugnisse für die Automobilindustrie*

manufacture² [verb] herstellen ['he:ɐ̯ʃtɛlən] +haben ◊ *Autoteile herstellen* ◆ *Die Tische sind aus Tropenholz hergestellt.*

manufacturer [noun] Hersteller ['he:ɐ̯ʃtɛle] der <-s, -> ♀Herstellerin ['he:ɐ̯ʃtɛlərɪn] die <-, –nen> *mostly masculine* ◊ *Hersteller von Turbinen* car manufacturer Automobilhersteller [aɔtomo'bi:lhe:ɐ̯ʃtɛle] der

manufacturing [noun] **1.** *(production)* Herstellung ['he:ɐ̯ʃtɛlʊn] die <-> *no pl* ◊ *die Herstellung von Stahlrohren* **2.** *(sector)* Industrie [ɪndʊs'tri:] die <-> *no pl* ◊ *Arbeitsplätze in der Industrie*

manuscript [noun] **1.** *(writer's original of a book)* Manuskript [manu'skrɪpt] das <-(e)s, -e> ◊ *einem Verlag ein Manuskript zuschicken* **2.** *(old handwritten document)* Handschrift ['hantʃrɪft] die <-, –en> ◊ *eine mittelalterliche Handschrift*

many¹ [adj] viele ['fi:lə] ◊ *die vielen Gesichter der Großstadt* ◆ *Seine vielen Freunde nahmen Abschied von ihm.*

many² [det] viele ['fi:lə] *before pl ns* ◊ *viele Menschen* ◆ *Der Raum ist mit vielen hundert Blumen geschmückt.* ◆ *Weißt du, wie viele Gäste erwartet werden?* ◆ *zu viele Fehler* ◆ *viele Male* many different vielerlei ['fi:le'lae] *invariable* ◊ *Es gibt hier vielerlei Arten von Insekten.* many things vieles ['fi:ləs] ◊ *Vieles ging von Anfang an schief.* many a manch (ein/eine) [manç (aen/aenə)] *(lofty)* ◊ *Sie besaß manch gute Eigenschaft.* ◆ *Manch ein Kritiker spottete über diesen Autor.* as many as nicht weniger als [nɪçt 've:nɪgə als] ◊ *nicht weniger als eine Million Kunden* ⓢ a good/great many sb/sth eine ganze Reihe von jdm/etw. ◊ *eine ganze Reihe von Jahren/Leuten*

many³ [indef pron] viele ['fi:lə] ◊ *Viele haben das noch nicht begriffen.* ◆ *Viele der besten Ärzte wurden hier ausgebildet.*

map¹ [noun] *(of a greater area)* Landkarte ['lantka:ʳtə] die <-, –n> ◊ *Sie suchte die Stadt auf der Landkarte.; (of a smaller area, an object)* Plan [pla:n] der <-(e)s, Pläne> ◊ *Die Haltestellen sind im Plan eingezeichnet.; (of a city, town)* Stadtplan ['ʃtatpla:n] der

map² [verb] **1.** *(chart)* kartografieren [kaʳtogra'fi:rən] <kartografiert, kartografierte, hat kartografiert> *(tech)* ◊ *ein Gebiet kartografieren* **2.** *(analyze)* erforschen [e'fɔ'ʃn̩] <erforscht, erforschte, hat erforscht> ◊ *Freud erforschte die menschliche Psyche.* mapping of sth Erforschung ... [gen] [e'fɔ'ʃʊn] die <-, –en> ◊ *die Erforschung des Y-Chromosoms* mapping of the election results Analyse der Wahlergebnisse [ana,ly:zə de:ɐ̯ 'va:l|e,ge:pnɪsə] die <-, –n>

• **map out** [phras v] festlegen ['fɛstle:gn̩] +haben ◊ *einen Plan festlegen*

marathon [noun] Marathon ['ma(:)raton] der <-s, -s> ◊ *einen Marathon laufen* chess marathon Schachmarathon ['ʃax,ma(:)raton] marathon negotiation(s) Verhandlungsmarathon [fɛɐ̯'hantlʊns,ma(:)raton]

marble [noun] **1.** *(stone)* Marmor ['maʳmoːɐ̯] der <-s> *no pl* ◊ *Säulen/ein Fußboden aus Marmor* **2.** *(ball)* Murmel ['mʊʳml̩] die <-, –n> ◊ *(mit) Murmeln spielen*

A B C D E F G H I J K L M N O P Q R S T U V W X Y Z

⊙ lose your marbles verrückt werden *(fam)*

march¹ [noun] Marsch [maʳʃ] der <-(e)s, Märsche> ◊ *ein Marsch durch die Wüste* ♦ *einen Marsch spielen/komponieren* protest march Protestmarsch [proˈtɛstmaʳʃ] a day's march ein Tagesmarsch [aɛn ˈtaːgəsmaʳʃ]

⊙ the march of time/history der Lauf der Zeit/Geschichte **be on the march** auf dem Vormarsch sein

march² [verb] 1. *(walk in a group, walk somewhere quickly)* marschieren [maʳˈʃiːrən] <marschiert, marschierte, ist marschiert> ◊ *Soldaten marschierten durch die Straßen.* ♦ *Sie marschierte sofort aufs Revier und erstattete Anzeige.* march on sth auf etw. [acc] zumarschieren [aʊf ... ˌtsuːmaʳˈʃiːrən] <marschiert zu, marschierte zu, ist zumarschiert> ◊ *Die Demonstranten marschierten auf das Rathaus zu.* 2. *(force to walk)* geleiten [gəˈlaɛtn] <geleitet, geleitete, hat geleitet> *(euph)* ◊ *Der Betrunkene wurde von Sicherheitsbeamten aus dem Saal geleitet.*

March [noun] März [mɛʳts] der <-(es), -e> most sing → January

margarine [noun] Margarine [maʳgaˈriːnə] die <-> no pl ◊ *sich* [dat] *Margarine aufs Brot schmieren*

margin [noun] 1. *(edge)* Rand [rant] der <-(e)s, Ränder> ◊ *Bitte lassen Sie 5 cm Rand.* in/on the margin am Rand ◊ *Die Korrekturzeichen müssen am Rand wiederholt werden.* ♦ *am westlichen Rand des Gebirges* ♦ *am Rand des politischen Spektrums* 2. *(in a competition, an election)* Vorsprung [ˈfoːɐʃprʊŋ] der <-(e)s, Vorsprünge> most sing ◊ *ein Vorsprung von 5%* win by a narrow margin mit knappem Vorsprung gewinnen 3. *(additional amount of time or space)* Spielraum [ˈʃpiːlraɔm] der <-(e)s, Spielräume> ◊ *Es gibt keinen Spielraum für Fehler.* 4. ECON *(profit)* Gewinnspanne [gəˈvɪnʃpanə] die <-, -n>

marginal [adj] 1. *(very small, irrelevant)* geringfügig [gəˈrɪŋfyːgɪç] ◊ *Die Veränderungen sind geringfügig.* ♦ *geringfügige Probleme* 2. POL *(in the UK)* a marginal seat/constituency *ein mit knapper Mehrheit gewonnener Sitz im Parlament/Wahlbezirk* 3. *(written in the margin)* marginal note Randnotiz [ˈrantnoˌtiːts] die <-, -en>

marginally [adv] geringfügig [gəˈrɪŋfyːgɪç] no comp/superl ◊ *Die Ergebnisse waren geringfügig besser als erwartet.*

marine [adj] 1. *(relating to or living in the sea)* Meeres... [ˈmeːrəs] marine animal Meerestier [ˈmeːrəstiːɐ] das <-(e)s, -e> marine biologist Meeresbiologe [ˈmeːrəsbioˌloːgə] der <-n, -n> ♀Meeresbiologin [ˈmeːrəsbioˌloːgɪn] die <-, -nen> 2. *(nautical)* Schiffs... [ʃɪfs] marine equipment Schiffszubehör [ˈʃɪfstsuːbəhøːɐ] das <-s> no pl marine industry Schiffsbau [ˈʃɪfsbaɔ] der <-s> no pl

marital status [noun] Familienstand [faˈmiːljənʃtant] der <-(e)s> no pl *(form)*

mark¹ [noun] 1. *(small area of dirt, different colour)* Fleck [flɛk] der <-(e)s, -e> ◊ *Da ist ein Fleck auf deinem Hemd.* ♦ *Der Kater hat einen weißen Fleck auf der Brust.*; *(of damage)* scratch mark Kratzer [ˈkratsɐ] der <-s, -> ◊ *ein Kratzer auf einer CD* 2. SCHOOL, SPORT *(grade)* Note [ˈnoːtə] die <-, -n> ◊ *jdm eine schlechte Note geben* ♦ *eine gute Note bekommen* 3. *(threshold)* Marke [ˈmaʳkə] die <-, -n> ◊ *Der Euro hat die Marke von 1,30 US-*

Dollar überschritten. 4. *(old German currency)* Mark [maʳk] die <-, -> ◊ *Ein Euro entspricht 1,95583 Mark.* 5. *(symbol, sign)* Zeichen [ˈtsaɛçn] das <-s, -> ◊ *ein Zeichen des Respekts* ♦ *Was bedeutet das Zeichen auf dem Schild?* the mark of sth/sb is sth etw./jd zeichnet sich durch etw. aus [ˈtsaɛçnət ... dʊʳç ... aɔs] <zeichnet sich aus, zeichnete sich aus, hat sich ausgezeichnet> ◊ *Ein guter Lehrer zeichnet sich durch die Fähigkeit, zuhören zu können, aus.* 6. *(evidence, effect)* Spur [ʃpuːɐ] die <-, -en> ◊ *Spuren der Verwüstung* leave a/your mark Spuren hinterlassen 7. *(spot you want to hit)* Markierung [maʳˈkiːrʊŋ] die <-, -en> ◊ *Du musst die Markierung treffen.*

⊙ sb is wide of the mark jd liegt falsch **sth is wide of the mark** etw. ist falsch **be on the mark** sb is on the mark jd liegt richtig **sth is on the mark** etw. ist korrekt **hit the mark** ins Schwarze treffen

mark² [verb] 1. *(soil)* schmutzig machen [ˈʃmʊtsɪç maxn̩] +haben ◊ *seine Kleidung schmutzig machen* sth marks easily etw. wird leicht schmutzig mark sth with sth etw. mit etw. beflecken [mɪt ... bəˈflɛkn̩] <befleckt, befleckte, hat befleckt> ◊ *Das Hemd war mit Blut befleckt.* 2. *(scratch)* verkratzen [fɛˈkratsn̩] <verkratzt, verkratzte, hat verkratzt> ◊ *einen Tisch verkratzen* sth marks easily etw. verkratzt leicht. 3. SCHOOL, UNI *(grade)* benoten [bəˈnoːtn̩] <benotet, benotete, hat benotet> ◊ *Wird die Mitarbeit in diesem Kurs auch benotet?* 4. *(write, draw sth on sth)* kennzeichnen [ˈkɛntsaɛçnən] +haben ◊ *Die Wanderwege sind gekennzeichnet.* ♦ *etw. mit einem Kreuz kennzeichnen* 5. *(symbolize, point out, make visible)* markieren [maʳˈkiːrən] <markiert, markierte, hat markiert> ◊ *eine Textstelle markieren* ♦ *Dieser alte Stacheldrahtzaun markiert die Grenze.* ♦ *Der Roman markierte den Beginn der Moderne.* 6. SPORT *(a player)* decken [ˈdɛkn̩] +haben

● mark down [phras v] 1. *(write down)* aufschreiben [ˈaɔfʃraɛbm̩] <schreibt auf, schrieb auf, hat aufgeschrieben> ◊ *eine Adresse aufschreiben* 2. *(decide that you think)* mark sb/sth down as sb/sth jdn/etw. als jdn/etw. einschätzen [als ... aɛnʃɛtsn̩] +haben ◊ *Man schätzte mich leider sofort als unzuverlässig ein.* 3. *(reduce the price)* mark sth down herabsetzen [hɛˈrapzɛtsn̩] +haben ◊ *Die Hosen sind heruntergesetzt worden*

● mark off [phras v] 1. *(fence off)* abgrenzen [ˈapgrɛntsn̩] +haben ◊ *Das Areal wurde mit einem Zaun abgegrenzt.* 2. *(tick off)* abhaken [ˈaphaːkn̩] +haben ◊ *Sie hakte die Namen auf ihrer Liste ab.*

● mark out [phras v] 1. *(show that sb/sth is special)* auszeichnen [ˈaɔstsaɛçnən] <zeichnet aus, zeichnete aus, hat ausgezeichnet> ◊ *Das Gütezeichen soll Ware von hoher Qualität auszeichnen.* ♦ *Dein Verhalten zeichnet dich als Ehrenmann aus.* 2. *(for a certain destiny, future)* mark sb/sth out for sth jdn/etw. für etw. bestimmen [fyːɐ ... bəʃtɪmən] +haben <bestimmt, bestimmte, hat bestimmt> ◊ *Sein Talent bestimmt ihn für eine glänzende Karriere.* 3. *(draw the outline)* markieren [maʳˈkiːrən] <markiert, markierte, hat markiert> ◊ *Zuerst müssen die Umrisse der Baugrube markiert werden.*

● mark up [phras v] mark sth up den Preis ... [gen] erhöhen [aɔf deːn ˌpraɛs ɛˈhøːən] <erhöht, erhöhte, hat erhöht> mark sth up by sth etw. auf den Preis ... [gen] aufschlagen [aɔf deːn ˌpraɛs ˈaɔflaːgn̩] <schlägt

auf, schlug auf, hat aufgeschlagen> ◊ *Das Geschäft schlägt 100% auf den Einkaufspreis der Ware auf.*
marked(ly) [adj, adv] deutlich ['dɔːtlɪç] ◊ *ein deutlicher Widerspruch* ✦ *Hier ist der Unterschied besonders deutlich.* ✦ *sich deutlich unterscheiden*
marker [noun] 1. *(pen)* Marker ['maʳkɐ] der <–s, –> 2. *(object showing where sth is)* Markierung [maˈkiːrʊŋ] die <–, –en>
market¹ [noun] Markt [maʳkt] der <–(e)s, Märkte> ◊ *Er verkauft Obst auf dem Markt.* ✦ *Im Herbst kommt ein neuer PC auf den Markt.* ✦ *neue Märkte erschließen*
market² [verb] vermarkten [fɛˈmaʳktn̩] <vermarktet, vermarktete, hat vermarktet> ◊ *ein Produkt vermarkten*
marketing [noun] Marketing ['maʳkɐtɪŋ] das <–(s)> *no pl* ◊ *das Marketing eines Produkts*
marketplace [noun] 1. Marktplatz ['maʳktplats] der <–es, Marktplätze> ◊ *Das Fest findet auf dem Marktplatz statt.* 2. ECON Markt [maʳkt] der <–(e)s, Märkte> ◊ *auf dem Markt Erfolg haben*
marking [noun] 1. *(pattern of marks)* Markierung [maˈkiːrʊŋ] die <–, –en> ◊ *eine Markierung auf der Straße* 2. *(on an animal)* markings Zeichnung ['tsaeçnʊŋ] die <–, –en> ◊ *Der Tiger hat eine auffallende Zeichnung.* 3. SCHOOL, UNI *(grading)* Benotung [bəˈnoːtʊŋ] die <–, –en> ◊ *der Schlüssel für die Benotung der Klausur*
marksman [noun] Schütze ['ʃʏtsə] der <–n, –n>
markswoman [noun] Schützin ['ʃʏtsɪn] die <–, –nen>
marmalade [noun] Marmelade [maʳməˈlaːdə] die <–, –n> ◊ *Er strich sich Marmelade auf das Brot.*
marriage [noun] 1. *(relationship between two married people)* Ehe ['eːə] die <–, –n> ◊ *ihre Kinder aus erster Ehe* ✦ *Die Ehe wurde nach fünf Jahren geschieden.* 2. *(wedding)* Heirat ['haera:t] die <–, –en> *most sing* ◊ *eine Heirat aus Liebe*
married → marry [adj] no comp/superl ◊ *Er ist nicht verheiratet.* ✦ *eine Affäre mit einem verheirateten Mann* be married to sb mit jdm verheiratet sein get married heiraten ['haera:tn̩] +*haben* married couple Ehepaar ['eːəpaːʳ] das <–(e)s, –e>
marrow [noun] 1. *(vegetable)* Kürbis ['kʏʳbɪs] der <–ses, –se> 2. *(of bone)* Mark [maʳk] das <–(e)s> *no pl* ✎ to the marrow bis ins Mark
marry [verb] 1. *(get married)* heiraten ['haera:tn̩] <heiratet, heiratete, hat geheiratet> ✦ *standesamtlich/ kirchlich heiraten* ✦ *Willst du mich heiraten?* 2. *(make sb get married to sb)* verheiraten [fɛˈhaera:tn̩] <verheiratet, verheiratete, hat verheiratet> ◊ *Der Sultan wollte seine älteste Tochter verheiraten.* marry sb to sb jdn mit jdm verheiraten ◊ *Ihre Eltern verheirateten sie mit einem respektablen Mann.*; *(priest)* trauen ['traɔən] +*haben;mostly passive* ◊ *Sie wurden in der Kirche getraut.*
marsh [noun] Sumpf [zʊmpf] der <–(e)s, Sümpfe> ◊ *im Sumpf stecken bleiben*
marvel [verb] staunen ['ʃtaɔnən] +*haben* ◊ *Ich staunte, dass alles so schnell ging.* marvel at sth etw. bestaunen [bəˈʃtaɔnən] <bestaunt, bestaunte, hat bestaunt> ◊ *Das Kunstwerk wurde von den Besuchern bestaunt.*
marvellous(ly), marvelous(ly) [adj, adv] wunderbar ['vʊndebaːʳ] ◊ *Das Wetter war wunderbar.* ✦ *eine wunderbare Reise* ✦ *Sie hat wunderbar gesungen.*

mascara [noun] Wimperntusche ['vɪmpɐntʊʃə] die <–, –n>
masculine [adj] männlich ['mɛnlɪç] ◊ *Seine Stimme ist sehr männlich.* ✦ *ein männliches Substantiv* ✦ *der männliche Artikel* ✦ *männliche Tugenden*
mash [verb] zerdrücken [tsɛˈdrʏkn̩] <zerdrückt, zerdrückte, hat zerdrückt> ◊ *Die Kartoffeln zerdrücken und mit Butter und Milch verrühren.*
mask¹ [noun] Maske ['maskə] die <–, –n> ◊ *eine Maske mit pflegenden Substanzen* wear a mask eine Maske tragen gas mask Gasmaske ['gaːsmaskə] cleansing mask Reinigungsmaske ['raenɪgʊŋsmaskə]
mask² [verb] *(cover, hide)* verdecken [fɛˈdɛkn̩] <verdeckt, verdeckte, hat verdeckt> ◊ *Eine schwarze Sonnenbrille verdeckte seine Augen.*; *(a taste, smell)* überdecken [ybɐˈdɛkn̩] <überdeckt, überdeckte, hat überdeckt> ◊ *Der Koriander überdeckt den Geschmack der anderen Gewürze.*; *(a sound)* übertönen [ybɐˈtøːnən] <übertönt, übertönte, hat übertönt> ◊ *Sein Schrei wurde von der lauten Musik übertönt.*; *(your feelings, thoughts)* verbergen [fɛˈbɛʳgn̩] <verbirgt, verbarg, hat verborgen> ◊ *seine Gefühle/Gedanken verbergen*
mass¹ [noun] 1. *(a lot, crowd, paste, matter)* Masse ['masə] die <–, –n> ◊ *Teer ist eine klebrige schwarze Masse.* ✦ *Sie erhielt eine ganze Masse Leserbriefe.* ✦ *Die Masse der Bevölkerung war dafür.* ✦ *Sie konnte die Massen begeistern.* ✦ *Der Stein hat eine Masse von 714g.* 2. *(church service, music)* Messe ['mɛsə] die <–, –n> ◊ *eine Messe lesen* ✦ *zur Messe gehen* ✦ *Mozarts Messe in c-Moll*
mass² [adj] Massen… ['masn̩] mass unemployment Massenarbeitslosigkeit ['masn̩ˌaʳbaetsloːzɪçkaet] die <–> *no pl*
massacre [noun] Massaker [maˈsaːkɐ] das <–s, –> ◊ *ein Massaker anrichten*
massage [verb] 1. *(sb's body)* massieren [maˈsiːrən] <massiert, massierte, hat massiert> ◊ *Er massierte ihren Nacken.* 2. *(figures)* manipulieren [manipuˈliːrən] <manipuliert, manipulierte, hat manipuliert> ◊ *Zahlen manipulieren*
massive [adj] enorm [eˈnɔʳm] no comp/superl ◊ *eine enorme Überraschung* ✦ *Die Gewinne waren enorm.*; *(tree)* mächtig ['mɛçtɪç] ◊ *eine mächtige, alte Eiche*
master¹ [noun] 1. *(man who is in control: of servants)* Herr [hɛʳ] der <–n, –en> ◊ *Wer ist der Herr des Hauses?*; *(of a dog)* Herrchen ['hɛʳçən] das <–s, –>; *(of a college)* Rektor ['rɛktoːʳ] der <–s, –en> 2. *(person who's very good at sth)* Meister ['maestɐ] der <–s, –> ♀Meisterin ['maestərɪn] die <–, –nen> ◊ *die niederländischen Meister* ✦ *Sie ist eine Meisterin der Verwandlung.* be a master at sth ein Meister in etw. [dat] sein 3. UNI master's degree Magister [maˈgɪstɐ] der <–s, –> ◊ *einen Magister in Psychologie haben* 4. *(original)* Vorlage ['foːɐlaːgə] die <–, –n> ✎ be the master of your own fate sein Schicksal selbst bestimmen be your own master sein eigener Herr sein serve two masters Diener zweier Herren sein show sb who's master jdm zeigen, wer hier den Ton angibt
master² [verb] 1. *(know well)* beherrschen [bəˈhɛʳʃn̩] <beherrscht, beherrschte, hat beherrscht> ◊ *eine Sprache beherrschen* ✦ *die Kunst beherrschen, etw. zu tun* 2. *(get under control)* in den Griff bekommen [ɪn deːn ˈɡrɪf bəˈkɔmən] <bekommt,

bekam, hat bekommen> +haben ◊ *Hast du deine Gefühle nun in den Griff bekommen?* master your fear seine Angst meistern [zaɐnə ˌaŋst ˈmaestən] +haben

mat (noun) **1.** *(of rubber, straw etc.)* Matte [ˈmatə] die <-, -n> ◊ *auf einer Matte turnen/schlafen* **2.** *(on a table, bar etc.)* Unterlage [ˈʊntɐlaːgə] die <-, -n> ◊ *eine hitzebeständige/rutschfeste Unterlage* place mat Set [sɛt] das <-(s), -s> beer mat Bierdeckel [ˈbiːɐdɛkl̩] der <-s, ->

match¹ (noun) **1.** SPORT *(game)* Spiel [ʃpiːl] das <-(e)s, -e> ◊ *Das Spiel endete unentschieden.* ♦ *ein Spiel gegen den Tabellenführer* **2.** *(stick for lighting sth)* Streichholz [ˈʃtraeçhɔlts] das <-es, Streichhölzer> ◊ *ein Streichholz anzünden* **3.** *(expressing that sth goes well with sth else)* be a match for sth einer Sache (dat) entsprechen [ɛntˈʃprɛçn̩] <entspricht, entsprach, hat entsprochen> ◊ *Ich finde keine Farbe, die diesem Rot genau entspricht.*; *(go together well)* be a good match for sth gut zu etw. passen [ˌguːt ˈtsuː: ... ˌpasn̩] +haben ◊ *Die Couch passt gut zum Teppich.* **4.** *(expressing equality)* be a/no match for sb jdm gewachsen/nicht gewachsen sein [gəˈvaksn̩/ˌnɪçt gəˈvaksn̩ zaen] +sein ◊ *Trotz des langen Trainings war ich dem Gegner nicht gewachsen.* **5.** *(marriage)* Heirat [ˈhaeraːt] die <-, -en> ◊ *eine Heirat vermitteln* make a good match eine gute Partie machen [aenə guːtə paˈtiː: maxn̩] +haben ◊ *Sie hat eine gute Partie gemacht.*

● meet your match seinen Meister finden

match² (verb) **1.** *(be the same, similar, suitable for)* match sth einer Sache (dat) entsprechen [ɛntˈʃprɛçn̩] <entspricht, entsprach, hat entsprochen> ◊ *Die Umsätze entsprechen nicht unseren Erwartungen.* Two things match. Zwei Dinge stimmen überein. be matched by sth eine Entsprechung in etw. (dat) finden [aenə ɛntˈʃprɛçʊŋ ɪn ... fɪndn̩] <findet, fand, hat gefunden> **2.** *(go together well)* match sth zu etw. passen [tsuː: ... ˌpasn̩] +haben ◊ *Die Couch passt gut zum Teppich.* **3.** *(find that sth is the same)* match sth to sth etw. einer Sache (dat) zuordnen [ˈtsuː|ɔˈɐdnən] <ordnet zu, ordnete zu, hat zugeordnet> ◊ *Dieses Mineral konnte den Quarzen zugeordnet werden.* **4.** *(harmonize)* match sth with sth etw. auf etw. (acc) abstimmen [aof ... ˌapʃtɪmən] <stimmt ab, stimmte ab, hat abgestimmt>

• **match up** (phras v) **1.** *(be the same, similar)* sth matches up etw. stimmt überein [ʃtɪmt ybɐˈ|aen] +haben ◊ *Die Aussagen stimmen nicht überein.* **2.** *(harmonize)* match sth up with sth etw. auf etw. (acc) abstimmen [aof ... ˌapʃtɪmən] +haben **3.** *(be as good as)* match up to sth/sb mit etw./jdm. aufnehmen können [ɛs mɪt ... ˈaofneːmən kœnən] <kann, konnte, hat können>

mate (noun) **1.** *(in the UK: friend, form of address)* Kumpel [ˈkʊmpl̩] der <-s, -(s)> *(fam)* ◊ *Er ging mit seinen Kumpels einen trinken.* ♦ *He, Kumpel, hast du mal Feuer?* **2.** *(an animal's sexual partner)* Männchen [ˈmɛnçən] das <-s, -> ♀Weibchen [ˈvaepçən] das <-s, -> ◊ *Er hilft seinem Weibchen beim Nestbau.*; *(in the US: sb's sexual partner)* Partner [ˈpaˈtnɐ] der <-s, -> ♀Partnerin [ˈpaˈtnərɪn] die <-, -nen> **3.** CHESS Matt [mat] das <-s, -> most sing

material¹ (noun) *(matter, fabric, documents, ideas)*

Material [mateˈrjaːl] das <-s, -ien> ◊ *ein robustes/temperaturbeständiges Material* ♦ *die Materialien für den Sprachkurs kaufen* in compound ns, ... material ...material [mateˈrjaːl] teaching material Lehrmaterial [ˈleːɐ̯mateˌrjaːl]; *(for a book, film etc.)* Stoff [ʃtɔf] der <-(e)s, -e> ◊ *Stoff für einen Film/Roman sammeln*

material² (adj) **1.** *(financial, physical)* materiell [mateˈrjɛl] seldom comp/superl ◊ *materielle Sorgen* ♦ *Nicht jede Not ist materiell.* ♦ *die materielle Welt* **2.** *(important)* wesentlich [ˈveːzn̩tlɪç] ◊ *wesentliche Veränderungen* ♦ *Der Unterschied ist nicht wesentlich.* be material to sth wesentlich für etw. sein

materialistic (adj) materialistisch [materjaˈlɪstɪʃ] seldom comp/superl *(esp pej)* ◊ *Ist unsere Gesellschaft zu materialistisch?* ♦ *ein materialistischer Mensch*

maternal (adj) **1.** *(relating to being a mother)* mütterlich [ˈmʏtɐlɪç] ◊ *Sie ist sehr mütterlich.* ♦ *mütterliche Pflichten* **2.** *(related to you through your mother)* mütterlicherseits [ˈmʏtɐlɪçɐzaets] invariable, postpositive ◊ *ein Onkel mütterlicherseits*

maternity (noun) Mutterschaft [ˈmʊtɐʃaft] die <-> no pl

maternity leave (noun) Mutterschaftsurlaub [ˈmʊtɐʃafts|uːɐ̯laop] der <-(e)s, -e> ◊ *Sie ist im Mutterschaftsurlaub.*

math → **maths**

mathematical(ly) (adj, adv) mathematisch [mateˈmaːtɪʃ] no comp/superl; when used as an adjective, mostly before ns ◊ *ein mathematisches Problem* ♦ *Sie ist mathematisch sehr begabt.*

mathematics (noun) Mathematik [matemaˈtiːk] die <-> no pl ◊ *die höhere Mathematik* ♦ *Mathematik studieren*

maths, math (noun) Mathe [ˈmatə] die <-> *mostly used without the article, no pl (fam)* ◊ *Was haben wir in Mathe auf?*

matrix (noun) Matrix [ˈmaːtrɪks] die <-, Matrizes>

matter¹ (noun) **1.** *(problem, business)* Angelegenheit [ˈangəleːgn̩haet] die <-, -en> ◊ *Für diese Angelegenheit ist mein Kollege zuständig.* there is something the matter with sb/sth es gibt ein Problem mit jdm/etw. [ɛs giːpt aen proˈbleːm mɪt] <gibt, gab, hat gegeben> What's the matter with you? Was ist mit dir los? **2.** *(substance)* Materie [maˈteːrjə] die <-, -n> ◊ *feste/flüssige/gasförmige Materie*; *(material)* Material [mateˈrjaːl] das <-s, -ien> ◊ *organisches Material*

● in a matter of days/weeks innerhalb weniger Tage/Wochen to make matters worse zu allem Überfluss be a matter of sth eine Frage ... (gen) sein ◊ *Das ist eine Frage des Geschmacks/des Prinzips.* as a matter of ... **1.** as a matter of fact um genau zu sein **2.** as a matter of routine routinemäßig **3.** as a matter of urgency dringend no matter how/what/where egal wie/was/wo

matter² (verb) *(be important)* wichtig sein [ˈvɪçtɪç zaen] +sein ◊ *Das ist doch nicht wichtig.* matter to sb jdm wichtig sein; *(make a difference)* sth doesn't matter etw. macht nichts [ˈmaxt nɪçts] +haben Does it matter ...? Macht es etwas aus, ...? [maxt ɛs etwas ˈaos] +haben ◊ *Macht es etwas aus, dass der Film keinen richtigen Schluss hat?* What does it matter? Was macht es schon aus?

● it doesn't matter how/what/where egal wie/

was/wo

mattress noun Matratze [ma'tratsə] die <-, -n>
mature¹ adj reif [raef] ◊ *Sie ist sehr reif für ihr Alter.* ✦ *reifer Käse*
mature² verb reifen ['raefn] +sein ◊ *Der Wein reift in Eichenfässern.* mature into sb/sth zu jdm/etw. reifen ◊ *Sie war zu einer Persönlichkeit gereift.*
maturity noun 1. (being mature) Reife ['raefə] die <-> no pl ◊ *Ihm fehlt die nötige körperliche/geistige Reife.* 2. FIN Fälligkeit ['fɛlɪçkaet] die <-, -en> ◊ *Fälligkeiten von Wertpapieren mit fester Laufzeit*
maximum¹ noun Maximum ['maksimʊm] das <-s, Maxima> ◊ *ein Maximum von 20kg Gepäck*
maximum² adj maximal [maksi'ma:l] no comp/superl, mostly before ns ◊ *maximalen Nutzen aus etw. ziehen*; Höchst... [høːçst] maximum penalty Höchststrafe ['høːçstʃtra:fə] die <-, -n> maximum speed Höchstgeschwindigkeit ['høːçstgəʃvɪndɪçkaet] die <-, -en> most sing
may verb 1. (expressing possibility) sb/sth may do sth jd/etw. kann etw. tun [kan] <kann, konnte, hat können> often in subjunctive II ◊ *Er könnte sich verletzt haben.* ✦ *Diese Pflanzen können drei Meter hoch werden.* ✦ *Es könnte regnen.* sb may (not) be able to do sth jd kann vielleicht etw. (nicht) tun ◊ *Ich kann morgen vielleicht nicht kommen.* sb may as well do sth jd kann ebenso gut etw. tun ◊ *Wir sind viel zu spät dran und können ebenso gut zu Hause bleiben.* sth may be sth etw. könnte etw. sein ◊ *Was du sagst, könnte wahr sein.* it may well be that es könnte sein, dass ◊ *Es könnte sein, dass es nicht klappt.* 2. (expressing or requesting permission in a polite way) dürfen ['dʏrfn] <darf, durfte, hat dürfen> ◊ *Darf ich hier rauchen?* ✦ *Darf ich Ihnen nachschenken?* ✦ *Darf ich mich vorstellen?* I may not play with you. Ich darf nicht mit dir spielen.
⊛ may sb win May he/she win. Möge er/sie gewinnen. May they win. Mögen sie gewinnen.
May noun Mai [mae] der <- or -(e)s, -e> most sing
→ January
maybe adv vielleicht [fi'laeçt] ◊ *Vielleicht hat er ja Recht.* ✦ *"Gehst du heute Abend noch weg?" — "Vielleicht."* ✦ *ein Mann von vielleicht 70 Jahren*
mayor noun Bürgermeister ['bʏ'gemaestə] der <-s, -> ⚥Bürgermeisterin ['bʏ'gemaestərɪn] die <-, -nen> ◊ *Er ist zweiter Bürgermeister von Leipzig.* ✦ *Sie war 15 Jahre lang unsere Bürgermeisterin.*
me pers pron (nom) ich [ɪç] ◊ *Immer ich!* ✦ *"Wer ist da?" — "Ich bin's!";* (acc) mich [mɪç] ◊ *Rufst du mich an?;* (dat) mir [miːɐ] ◊ *Gib mir mal das Messer!* ✦ *Er ist mit mir zum Zahnarzt gegangen.*
meadow noun Wiese ['viːzə] die <-, -n> in the meadow auf der Wiese ◊ *Die Kinder spielten auf der Wiese.*
meagre, meager adj bescheiden [bə'ʃaedn] ◊ *Die Bezahlung war eher bescheiden.* ✦ *bescheidene Vorräte*
meagrely, meagerly adv knapp [knap] ◊ *Die Nudeln waren zu knapp bemessen.*
meal noun 1. (lunch etc.) Mahlzeit ['ma:ltsaet] die <-, -en> ◊ *eine Mahlzeit zu sich nehmen* main meal Hauptmahlzeit ['haoptma:ltsaet] die go out for a meal essen gehen ['ɛsn ge:ən] <geht, ging, ist gegangen> 2. (flour) Mehl [me:l] das <-(e)s, -e> most sing

⊛ **make a meal of sth** eine große Sache aus etw. machen (fam)
mean¹ noun Durchschnitt ['dʊ'çʃnɪt] der <-(e)s, -e> most sing ◊ *Der Durchschnitt der Klassenarbeit lag bei 2,5.*
mean² adj 1. (cruel) gemein [gə'maen] ◊ *ein gemeiner Trick* ✦ *Ich finde es gemein, was ihr da tut!* 2. (not generous) geizig ['gaetsɪç] ◊ *ein geiziger Mann* ✦ *Seine Eltern sind sehr geizig.* 3. (average) mittlere ['mɪtlərə] no comp/superl, only before ns <ein mittlerer ..., eine mittlere ..., ein mittleres ...> ◊ *ein mittlerer Wert*
mean³ verb 1. (signify, have as a consequence, be important) bedeuten [bə'dɔøtn] <bedeutet, bedeutete, hat bedeutet> ◊ *Was bedeutet dieses Wort?* ✦ *Du weißt gar nicht, was es bedeutet, allein zu sein!* ✦ *Sein Schweigen bedeutet nichts Gutes.* ✦ *Staatsschulden bedeuten meist eine Steuererhöhung.* sth means that sb/sth does sth, sth means doing sth etw. bedeutet, dass jd/etw. etw. tut ◊ *Der neue Vertrag bedeutet, dass wir für weniger Geld arbeiten.* man sth to sb jdm etw. bedeuten ◊ *Seine Liebe bedeutet mir alles.* 2. (intend) wollen ['vɔlən] <will, wollte, hat wollen> ◊ *Ich wollte dir nicht wehtun.* mean sb to do sth wollen, dass jd etw. tut ◊ *Ich wollte nicht, dass er deswegen seine Stelle verliert.;* (intend to say) meinen ['maenən] ◊ *Ich meine, du solltest dich nicht so aufregen.* ✦ *Ich weiß, was du meinst.* mean sth by sth etw. mit etw. meinen What do you mean (by that)?, How do you mean? Was meinst du/meinen Sie damit? mean sth as sth etw. als etw. meinen ◊ *Ich meine das als Kompliment.*
⊛ **mean business** es ernst meinen mean well es gut meinen ◊ *Er meint es gut.* be meant for sb/sth für jdn/etw. bestimmt sein be meant for each other füreinander bestimmt sein be meant to be/do sth etw. sein/tun sollen it was not meant to be es sollte nicht sein Does sth mean anything to sb? Hat jd schon mal etw. gehört? ◊ *Hast du den Namen schon mal gehört?*
meaning noun Bedeutung [bə'dɔøtʊn] die <-, -en> ◊ *die Bedeutung eines Fremdworts/Zeichens kennen* ✦ *seine Bedeutung verlieren;* (more profound) Sinn [zɪn] der <-(e)s> no pl ◊ *der Sinn des Lebens*
meaningful(ly) adj, adv 1. (making sense) sinnvoll ['zɪnfɔl] ◊ *eine sinnvolle Debatte* ✦ *Ist diese Arbeit sinnvoll?* ✦ *Kann man darüber sinnvoll diskutieren?* 2. (expressing sth without words) vielsagend ['fi:lza:gn̩t] ◊ *ein vielsagender Blick* ✦ *Sein Gesichtsausdruck war vielsagend.* ✦ *Sie lächelte vielsagend.*
meaningless adj sinnlos ['zɪnloːs] <sinnloser, am sinnlosesten> ◊ *sinnlose Worte* ✦ *Mein Leben war nicht mehr sinnlos.* be meaningless to sb für jdn bedeutungslos sein [fy:ɐ ... bə'dɔøtʊnsloːs zaen] +sein ◊ *Ist der Begriff der Ehre für uns bedeutungslos geworden?*
means noun Mittel ['mɪtl] das <-s, -> ◊ *Das Auto ist für mich ein Mittel, um von A nach B zu kommen.* ✦ *begrenzte (finanzielle) Mittel* means of transport Verkehrsmittel [fe'ke:ɐsmɪtl] means of payment Zahlungsmittel ['tsa:lʊnsmɪtl] by means of mittels ['mɪtls] sing nouns without article or attribute are not declined when following this prep, otherwise +gen (form) ◊ *etw. mittels eines Schraubenziehers öffnen*
⊛ **by all means** natürlich by fair means or foul ohne Rücksicht auf Verluste by no means keines-

A
B
C
D
E
F
G
H
I
J
K
L
M
N
O
P
Q
R
S
T
U
V
W
X
Y
Z

wegs ◊ *Er nimmt die Kritik keineswegs übel.* ♦ *Die Gefahr sollte keineswegs unterschätzt werden.*

meantime [noun] **1.** *(for the time being)* for the meantime vorläufig ['foːɐ̯ɡlɔøfɪç] *no comp/superl* ◊ *Das Treffen wird vorläufig verschoben.* **2.** *(during sth)* in the meantime in der Zwischenzeit [ɪn deːɐ̯ 'tsvɪʃn̩tsaet] ◊ *Koch du bitte das Essen, ich spüle in der Zwischenzeit.*

meanwhile [adv] **1.** *(in the meantime)* inzwischen [ɪn'tsvɪʃn̩] ◊ *Du hättest inzwischen ruhig anfangen können!* **2.** *(emph) (expressing a contrast)* während ['vɛːrənt] ◊ *Ich spare jeden Cent, während du ständig neue Kleider kaufst.*

measure¹ [noun] **1.** *(action)* Maßnahme ['maːsnaːmə] die <-, -n> ◊ *Auch Unschuldige sind von diesen Maßnahmen betroffen.* measures to fight unemployment Maßnahmen zur Bekämpfung der Arbeitslosigkeit take measures (against sb/sth) Maßnahmen (gegen jdn/etw.) ergreifen half measures halbherzige Maßnahmen **2.** *(unit, measurement, degree)* Maß [maːs] das <-es, -e> ◊ *das englische Maß „inch"* ♦ *Maße und Gewichte* in large measure in hohem Maß a measure of security/responsibility etc. ein gewisses Maß an Sicherheit/Verantwortung etc. **3.** *(way of judging sth)* Maßstab ['maːsʃtaːp] der <-(e)s, Maßstäbe> measure of sth Maßstab für etw. ◊ *Schulnoten sind nicht unbedingt ein Maßstab für die Intelligenz.* **4.** mus Takt [takt] der <-(e)s, -e> ⊚ the full measure of sth das ganze Ausmaß ... [gen] ◊ *Plötzlich wurde ihm das ganze Ausmaß seiner Misere klar.* for good measure sicherheitshalber get the measure of sb/sth jdn/etw. verstehen beyond measure über alle Maßen

measure² [verb] *(find the exact amount or size, judge, be a certain size)* messen ['mɛsn̩] <misst, maß, hat gemessen> ◊ *den Abstand messen* ♦ *Der Satellit misst das Ozon in der Erdatmosphäre.* ◊ *Die Wohnung misst etwa 80 Quadratmeter.* measure sb/sth by/ against sth jdn/etw. an etw. [dat] messen ◊ *Unser Erfolg lässt sich an der Reaktion unserer Kunden messen.; (an object, room etc.)* vermessen [fɛ'mɛsn̩] <vermisst, vermaß, hat vermessen> ◊ *Ich habe die Wohnung vermessen.* measure sb for sth bei jdm für etw. Maß nehmen [baɐ̯ ... fyːɐ̯ ... 'maːs neːmən] <nimmt, nahm, hat genommen> ◊ *Der Schneider nimmt bei ihm für einen Anzug Maß.*

• **measure out** [phras v] measure sth out etw. abmessen ['apmɛsn̩] <misst ab, maß ab, hat abgemessen> ◊ *Sie hat zehn Zentimeter vom Stoff abgemessen.*

• **measure up** [phras v] **1.** *(meet expectations)* den Erwartungen entsprechen [deːn e'vaʁtʊŋən ɛnt.ʃprɛçn̩] <entspricht, entsprach, hat entsprochen> ◊ *Dieser CD-Player entspricht überhaupt nicht meinen Erwartungen.; (challenges)* measure up to sth einer Sache [dat] gewachsen sein [gə'vaksn̩ zaen] +sein ◊ *Wird er der Herausforderung gewachsen sein, die eine neue Arbeitsstelle mit sich bringt?* **2.** *(find the exact measurement)* abmessen ['apmɛsn̩] <misst ab, maß ab, hat abgemessen> ◊ *die Tapeten abmessen*

measurement [noun] **1.** *(size)* Maß [maːs] das <-es, -e> ◊ *Die Maße des Schranks stimmen nicht.* ♦ *Welche Maße hat dieses Fotomodell?* take sb's measurements bei jdm Maß nehmen ◊ *Für das Brautkleid wurde bei ihr Maß genommen.; (of an*

amount of sth) take measurements of sth etw. messen ['mɛsn̩] <misst, maß, hat gemessen> ◊ *den Lärm/die Luftverschmutzung messen; (of an object, room etc.)* take measurements of sth etw. vermessen [fɛ'mɛsn̩] <vermisst, vermaß, hat vermessen> ◊ *Der Optiker vermisst die Hornhaut.* **2.** *(process of measuring)* Messen ['mɛsn̩] das <-s> *no pl* ◊ *das Messen der Wandhöhe*

meat [noun] **1.** *(food)* Fleisch [flaeʃ] das <-(e)s> *no pl* ◊ *robes/gekochtes/gebratenes Fleisch* ♦ *Vegetarier essen kein Fleisch.; (in the US)* ground meat Hackfleisch ['hakflaeʃ] ◊ *Hackfleisch vom Rind/Schwein* meats Fleischsorten ['flaeʃzɔˀtn̩] die <-> *pl* **2.** *(content)* Substanz [zʊps'tants] die <-> *no pl* ◊ *Der Film war völlig ohne Substanz.*

mechanic [noun] **1.** Mechaniker [me'çaːnɪkɐ] der <-s, -> ♀Mechanikerin [me'çaːnɪkərɪn] die <-, -nen> ◊ *Sie ist Mechanikerin.* ♦ *Er ist ein schlechter Mechaniker.* **2.** *(way of doing sth)* mechanic(s) Technik ['tɛçnɪk] die <-, -en> ◊ *eine Technik beherrschen* **3.** physics mechanics Mechanik [me'çaːnɪk] die <-, -en> *most sing*

mechanical [adj] **1.** *(operated by moving parts, relating to physical forces)* mechanisch [me'çaːnɪʃ] *no comp/superl, mostly before ns* ◊ *ein mechanischer Webstuhl* ♦ *die mechanischen Eigenschaften eines Stoffes; (problems)* technisch ['tɛçnɪʃ] *no comp/ superl, mostly before ns* ◊ *Es gab technische Probleme.* **2.** *(reply, gesture)* automatisch [aɔto'maːtɪʃ] *no comp/superl, mostly before ns* ◊ *eine automatische Antwort geben* **3.** *(person)* technisch begabt [ˌtɛçnɪʃ bə'gaːpt] <begabter, am begabtesten> ◊ *Er ist technisch sehr begabt.* ♦ *ein technisch begabter Mensch*

mechanism [noun] Mechanismus [meça'nɪsmʊs] der <-, Mechanismen> ◊ *Der Mechanismus der Spieluhr musste repariert werden.* ♦ *Mechanismen, die im Gehirn ablaufen* defence mechanism Abwehrmechanismus ['apveːɐ̯meça.nɪsmʊs] locking mechanism Schließmechanismus ['ʃliːsmeça.nɪsmʊs]

medal [noun] Medaille [me'daljə] die <-, -n> ◊ *bei den Olympischen Spielen eine Medaille gewinnen* bronze medal Bronzemedaille [brɔ̃ːsəme.daljə] gold medal Goldmedaille ['ɡɔltme.daljə] silver medal Silbermedaille ['zɪlbeme.daljə]

media → **medium**

mediate [verb] vermitteln [fɛ'mɪtl̩n] <vermittelt, vermittelte, hat vermittelt> mediate a dispute in einem Streit vermitteln mediate an agreement ein Abkommen vermitteln mediate between sb zwischen jdm vermitteln ◊ *Er vermittelte zwischen Eltern und Kind.* ♦ *Es gelang ihr, zwischen den Streithähnen zu vermitteln.*

mediation [noun] Vermittlung [fɛ'mɪtlʊŋ] die <-, -en> ◊ *Durch Vermittlung des Papstes wurde Frieden geschlossen.*

mediator [noun] Vermittler [fɛ'mɪtlɐ] der <-s, -> ♀Vermittlerin [fɛ'mɪtlərɪn] die <-, -nen> ◊ *Russland fungierte als Vermittler.* ♦ *In diesem Streit tritt sie als Vermittlerin auf.*

medical(ly) [adj, adv] medizinisch [medi'tsiːnɪʃ] *no comp/superl; when used as an adj, only before ns* ◊ *medizinische Einrichtungen* ◊ *die medizinische Versorgung* ♦ *ein medizinisch notwendiger Eingriff*

medication [noun] Medikament [medika'mɛnt] das <-(e)s, -e> ◊ *ein Medikament verschreiben* ♦

Dieses Medikament ist apothekenpflichtig. be on medication Medikamente nehmen
medicine noun **1.** *(substance)* Medikament [medika'mɛnt] das <–(e)s, –e> ◊ *jdm ein Medikament verschreiben* ◆ *Dieses Medikament ist nicht für Kinder geeignet.* take the medicine das Medikament einnehmen **2.** *(study, practice)* Medizin [medi'tsi:n] die <–> no pl ◊ *die ganzheitliche Medizin* ◆ *Medizin studieren*
medieval adj mittelalterlich ['mɪt|altɛlɪç] mostly before ns ◊ *eine mittelalterliche Burg* ◆ *Ihre Ansichten waren geradezu mittelalterlich.*
mediocre adj mittelmäßig ['mɪt|mɛːsɪç] ◊ *Er ist ein mittelmäßiger Schüler.* ◆ *Die Qualität war mittelmäßig.*
medium¹ noun **1.** *(means of communication, of artistic expression, spiritualist)* Medium ['me:djʊm] das <–s, Medien> ◊ *in den Medien über etwas* acc *berichten* ◆ *Fotografie als künstlerisches Medium* ◆ *Sie war ein Medium.* broadcast media Rundfunkmedien ['rʊntfʊŋkme:djən] print media Printmedien ['prɪntme:djən] **2.** BIO, BOT Substrat [zʊps'tra:t] das <–(e)s, –e> ◊ *ein Substrat für die Vermehrung von Bakterien* **3.** *(artist's material)* Material [mate'rjaːl] das <–s, –ien> ◊ *Die Künstlerin arbeitet mit traditionellen Materialien wie Ölfarbe und Leinwand.* **4.** IT Speichermedium ['ʃpaeçeme:djʊm] das <–, Speichermedien> ◊ *Speichermedien wie CD-ROM und Memorystick* **5.** *(size)* mittlere Größe [,mɪtlərə 'grøːsə] die <–, –n> ◊ *Gibt es diesen Rock noch in einer mittleren Größe?*
medium² adj mittlere ['mɪtlərə] no comp/superl, only before ns <ein mittlerer ..., eine mittlere ..., ein mittleres ...> ◊ *ein mittleres Unternehmen* medium blond hair mittelblondes Haar ['mɪt|blɔndəs ˌhaːɐ] <–(e)s> no pl
medium-sized adj mittelgroß ['mɪt|groːs] no comp/superl ◊ *Die Frucht dieser Apfelsorte ist mittelgroß.* ◆ *Ich hätte gern eine mittelgroße Packung.*
meet verb **1.** *(come together intentionally, look at each other)* meet (sb) sich (mit jdm) treffen ['trɛfn̩] <trifft, traf sich, hat sich getroffen> ◊ *Wir haben uns getroffen.* ◆ *Der Kanzler trifft sich mit dem französischen Präsidenten.* meet for sth sich zu etw. treffen ◊ *Wir treffen uns zum Kaffee.* meet to do sth sich treffen, um etw. zu tun I'd like to meet. Ich würde mich gern mit dir/Ihnen/euch treffen. Their eyes met. Ihre Blicke trafen sich.*; (come together unintentionally)* treffen ['trɛfn̩] +haben ◊ *Ich habe Klaus auf der Straße getroffen.* **2.** *(get to know)* kennen lernen ['kɛnən lɛ'nən] +haben ◊ *Wir haben uns im Zug kennen gelernt.* Have you met my husband? Kennen Sie meinen Mann schon? **3.** *(pick up)* abholen ['aphoːlən] +haben ◊ *Wir holen dich am Bahnhof ab.* **4.** *(play against)* meet sb auf jdn treffen [aof ... trɛfn̩] <trifft, traf, ist getroffen> ◊ *Bayern trifft im Endspiel auf Liverpool.* **5.** *(a negative reaction)* meet (with) sth auf etw. acc stoßen [aof ... ʃtoːsn̩] <stößt, stieß, ist gestoßen> ◊ *Unser Plan stieß auf Ablehnung/Widerstand.* meet with (sb's) approval (jds) Zustimmung finden ['tsuːʃtɪmʊŋ fɪndn̩] <findet, fand, hat gefunden> ◊ *Der Vorschlag fand die Zustimmung der Mitarbeiter.* **6.** *(roads, rivers)* aufeinander treffen [aof|aeˈnandɐ trɛfn̩] <treffen, trafen, sind getroffen> ◊ *Die beiden Straßen treffen nach zwei Kilometern auf-*

einander. **7.** *(a challenge, need)* meet sth einer Sache dat gerecht werden [gə'rɛçt veːɐdn̩] +sein ◊ *Wir müssen den Bedürfnissen unserer Kunden gerecht werden.* ◆ *Werden wir dieser Herausforderung gerecht?; (a condition)* erfüllen [ɛ'fʏlən] <erfüllt, erfüllte, hat erfüllt> ◊ *die erforderlichen Voraussetzungen erfüllen; (a target)* erreichen [ɛ'raeçn̩] <erreicht, erreichte, hat erreicht> ◊ *Wir müssen unser Geschäftsziel erreichen.* **8.** *(your expenses)* decken ['dɛkn̩] +haben ◊ *Unsere Kosten werden gerade so gedeckt.* **9.** *(touch)* berühren [bə'ryːrən] <berührt, berührte, hat berührt> ◊ *Seine Hand berührte meine.* Their lips met. Ihre Lippen berührten sich.
meeting noun **1.** *(coming together)* Treffen ['trɛfn̩] das <–s, –> ◊ *Das hat er mir bei unserem letzten Treffen erzählt.; (conference, people attending it)* Konferenz [kɔnfe'rɛnts] die <–, –en> ◊ *In Florenz fand eine Konferenz der EU-Umweltminister statt.* ◆ *Die Konferenz hat beschlossen, ihre Arbeit besser zu koordinieren.* a meeting on sth eine Konferenz über etw. acc hold a meeting eine Konferenz abhalten attend a meeting an einer Konferenz teilnehmen **2.** SPORT Begegnung [bə'geːgnʊŋ] die <–, –en> ◊ *die Begegnung zwischen dem 1. FC Köln und Bayern München*
◉ meeting of minds Übereinstimmung
meeting place noun Treffpunkt ['trɛfpʊŋkt] der <–(e)s, –e> ◊ *Diese Kneipe ist ein beliebter Treffpunkt für Studenten.* ◆ *Er kam nicht zu dem vereinbarten Treffpunkt.*
melody noun Melodie [melo'di:] die <–, –n> ◊ *eine Melodie singen*
melon noun Melone [me'loːnə] die <–, –n> ◊ *Parmaschinken mit Melone*
melt verb **1.** *(ice, snow)* schmelzen ['ʃmɛltsn̩] <schmilzt, schmolz, hat/ist geschmolzen> transitive use +haben/intransitive use +sein ◊ *Die Sonne hat den Schnee geschmolzen.* ◆ *Das Eis ist geschmolzen.; (a piece of fat)* zerlassen [tse'lasn̩] <zerlässt, zerließ, hat zerlassen> ◊ *Für den Kuchen hat er Butter zerlassen.* **2.** *(feeling)* verfliegen [fe'fli:gŋ̍] <verfliegt, verflog, ist verflogen> ◊ *Meine anfänglichen Zweifel waren schnell verflogen.* **3.** *(become invisible)* melt into sth von etw. verschluckt werden [fɔn ... fe'ʃlʊkt veːɐdn̩] <wird, wurde, ist worden> ◊ *Dann wurde er von der Dunkelheit verschluckt.* **4.** *(become kinder)* weich werden ['vaeç veːɐdn̩] +sein ◊ *Wenn ihr Sohn sie anlächelt, wird sie weich.* melt sb's heart jds Herz erweichen ['hɛɐts ɐ,vaeçn̩] <erweicht, erweichte, hat erweicht> **5.** *(blend)* melt into sth mit etw. verschmelzen [mɪt ... fe,ʃmɛltsn̩] <verschmilzt, verschmolz, ist verschmolzen> (jdt) ◊ *Am Horizont verschmolz der Himmel mit dem Meer.*
• **melt away** phras v **1.** *(feeling)* verfliegen [fe'fli:gŋ̍] <verfliegt, verflog, ist verflogen> ◊ *Meine Angst verflog allmählich.* **2.** *(become invisible)* melt away into sth von etw. verschluckt werden [fɔn ... fe,ʃlʊkt veːɐdn̩] <wird, wurde, ist worden> ◊ *Ein Wagen fuhr vorbei und wurde von der Dunkelheit verschluckt.*
member noun **1.** *(sb or sth belonging to a group or an organization)* Mitglied ['mɪtgliːt] das <–(e)s, –er> ◊ *Bist du Mitglied eines Sportvereins?* ◆ *Bist du Mitglied der NATO* ◆ *Der Wolf ist Mitglied der Familie der Hunde.* family member Familienmitglied [fa'miːljənmɪtgliːt] member state Mitgliedsstaat

['mɪtgliːtsʃtaːt] der <-(e)s, -en> 2. *(penis)* Glied
[gliːt] das <-(e)s, -er> ◊ *ein steifes Glied*
Member of Parliament (noun) Abgeordnete
['apgə|ɔ'dnətə] der/die <-n, die Abgeordneten> *but:*
ein Abgeordneter/eine Abgeordnete ◊ *eine Abgeord-*
nete der Grünen ♦ *Er ist Abgeordneter im*
Bundestag.

membership (noun) 1. *(being part of a group or an*
organization) Mitgliedschaft ['mɪtgliːtʃaft] die
<-, -en> membership of sth Mitgliedschaft in etw.
(dat) ◊ *Die Mitgliedschaft im Sportverein kostet*
monatlich 40 Euro. 2. *(members)* Mitglieder
['mɪtgliːdɐ] die <-> *pl* ◊ *Die Mitglieder wählen den*
Vorstand.; (number of members) Mitgliederzahl
['mɪtgliːdetsaːl] die <-, -en> ◊ *Die Mitgliederzahl*
geht seit Jahren zurück.

membership card (noun) Mitgliedsausweis
['mɪtgliːts|aosvaes] der <-es, -e>

membrane (noun) Membran [mɛm'braːn] die <-, -en>

memento (noun) Andenken ['andɛŋkn̩] das <-s, -> ◊
Ich schenkte ihr als Andenken ein Bild.

memorable (adj) unvergesslich ['ʊnfɛgɛslɪç] ◊ *ein*
unvergesslicher Augenblick ♦ *Die Party war unver-*
gesslich.

memorandum (noun) 1. *(letter, note)* Mitteilung
['mɪttaelʊŋ] die <-, -en> ◊ *Er schrieb seinen Mitar-*
beitern kurze Mitteilungen. 2. LAW, ECON Dokument
[doku'mɛnt] das <-(e)s, -e> memorandum of associ-
ation Gründungsurkunde ['grʏndʊŋs|uːgkʊndə] die
<-, -n>

memorial (noun) 1. *(monument)* Denkmal ['dɛŋkmaːl]
das <-s, Denkmäler> ◊ *ein Denkmal errichten/*
enthüllen war memorial Kriegerdenkmal
['kriːgɛdɛŋkmaːl] 2. *(obituary)* Nachruf ['naːxruːf] der
<-(e)s, -e> memorial to sb Nachruf auf jdn ◊ *Er*
schrieb einen Nachruf auf die Dichterin.

memorize (verb) auswendig lernen ['aosvɛndɪç lɛ'rnən]
+haben ◊ *Ich musste ein ganzes Gedicht auswendig*
lernen.

memory (noun) 1. *(sth you remember)* Erinnerung
[ɛ|'ɪnərʊŋ] die <-, -en> ◊ *mit alten Freunden Erin-*
nerungen austauschen ♦ *Schreckliche Erinnerungen*
werden oft verdrängt. memory of sb/sth Erinnerung
an jdn/etw. ◊ *Die Erinnerung an meine Kindheit ist*
verblasst. 2. *(ability to remember)* Gedächtnis
[gə'dɛçtnɪs] das <-ses, -se> ◊ *Nach dem Unfall hatte*
er sein Gedächtnis verloren. ♦ *Sie hat ein ausgezeich-*
netes Gedächtnis. have a good memory for sth ein
gutes Gedächtnis für etw. haben ◊ *Er hatte ein*
gutes Gedächtnis für Namen. long-term memory
Langzeitgedächtnis ['laŋsaetgədɛçtnɪs] short-term
memory Kurzzeitgedächtnis ['kʊˈtssaetgədɛçtnɪs]
3. *(of the deceased)* Andenken ['andɛŋkn̩] das <-s>
no pl sb's memory das Andenken an jdn to sb's
memory, in memory of sb zum Andenken an jdn ◊
Es wurde ein Denkmal zum Andenken an die Opfer
der Gewaltherrschaft errichtet. 4. IT Speicher
['ʃpaeçɐ] der <-s, -> ◊ *den Speicher erweitern* ♦
Der Computer hat für meine Zwecke zu wenig
Speicher.

◉ in living memory seit Menschengedenken if my
memory serves me well wenn ich mich recht
erinnere

mend (verb) 1. *(in the UK: repair)* reparieren
[repa'riːrən] <repariert, reparierte, hat repariert> ◊ *Ich*
muss diese Schuhe reparieren lassen.; (a hole in a

piece of clothing) stopfen ['ʃtɔpfn̩] +haben ◊ *Sie*
stopfte ihre Strümpfe. 2. *(a relationship)* wieder verbessern [viːdɐ fɛ'bɛsən] <verbessert, verbesserte, hat
verbessert> ◊ *die Beziehungen zum Nachbarland*
wieder verbessern 3. *(heal)* heilen ['haelən] transitive
use +haben/intransitive use +sein ◊ *Der Arzt hat den*
Knochenbruch geheilt. ♦ *Der Arm ist sehr gut geheilt.*

mental (adj) 1. *(relating to the mind)* geistig ['gaestɪç]
no comp/superl, mostly before ns ◊ *Seine geistigen*
Fähigkeiten lagen weit über dem Durchschnitt.
mental state Geisteszustand ['gaestəstsuːʃtant] der
<-(e)s> *no pl* mental illness Geisteskrankheit
['gaestəskraŋkhaet] die <-, -en> mental image Vorstellung ['foːɐʃtɛlʊŋ] die <-, -en> 2. *(crazy)* verrückt
[fɛ'rʏkt] <verrückter, am verrücktesten> *(fam)* ◊ *Bist*
du verrückt? ♦ *ein verrückter Mensch*

mentally (adv) geistig ['gaestɪç] *no comp/superl* ◊ *Er*
war geistig nicht mehr fit. mentally ill geisteskrank
['gaestəskraŋk] *no comp/superl*

mention[1] (noun) Erwähnung [ɛ'vɛːnʊŋ] die <-, -en>
◊ *keinerlei Erwähnung seines Namens* make mention
of sb/sth jdn/etw. erwähnen [ɛ'vɛːnən] <erwähnt,
erwähnte, hat erwähnt> ◊ *Er erwähnte sie mit*
keinem Wort. get a mention erwähnt werden ◊ *Sie*
wurde nicht erwähnt. there is no mention of sth
etw. wird nicht erwähnt

mention[2] (verb) erwähnen [ɛ'vɛːnən] <erwähnt,
erwähnte, hat erwähnt> ◊ *Dein Name wurde in*
diesem Zusammenhang auch erwähnt. ♦ *Sie hat nur*
kurz erwähnt, dass sie das vorhat. ♦ *das oben*
erwähnte Buch mention sth to sb jdn auf etw.
ansprechen [aof … ,anʃprɛçn̩] <spricht an, sprach an,
hat angesprochen> worth mentioning erwähnenswert
[ɛ'vɛːnənsveːɐt] *no comp/superl* ◊ *eine erwähnens-*
werte Tatsache ♦ *Es ist erwähnenswert, dass …*
◉ don't mention it gern geschehen now you
mention it … jetzt, wo du es sagst, …; jetzt, wo
Sie es sagen, … not to mention … ganz zu
schweigen von …

menu (noun) 1. *(list of food)* Speisekarte ['ʃpaezəkaˈtə]
die <-, -n> ◊ *ein Restaurant mit umfangreicher*
Speisekarte 2. IT Menü [me'nyː] das <-s, -s> ◊
Klicken Sie im Menü auf Datei und Öffnen. drop-
down menu Drop-down-Menü [drɔp'daonme,nyː]

merchant (noun) Händler ['hɛndlɐ] der <-s, ->
♀Händlerin ['hɛndlərɪn] die <-, -nen> ◊ *Wie viel*
verdient der Händler an diesem Produkt? ♦ *Sie ist*
Händlerin in Obst und Gemüse. wine merchant Wein-
händler ['vaenhɛndlɐ] Weinhändlerin
['vaenhɛndlərɪn] merchant bank Handelsbank
['hand̩lsbaŋk] die <-, -en> merchant ship Handels-
schiff ['hand̩lsʃɪf] das <-(e)s, -e>

merciful (adj) *(person, god, death)* gnädig ['gnɛːdɪç] ◊
ein gnädiges Ende finden ♦ *Gott ist gnädig.; (relief)*
groß [groːs] <größer, am größten> ◊ *Es war eine*
große Erleichterung.

mercifully (adv) 1. *(luckily)* glücklicherweise
['glʏklɪçɐ'vaezə] *no comp/superl* ◊ *Glücklicherweise*
ist ihr bei dem Unfall nichts passiert. 2. *(sympatheti-
cally)* gnädig ['gnɛːdɪç] ◊ *jdn gnädig behandeln*

merciless(ly) (adj, adv) gnadenlos ['gnaːdn̩loːs] <gna-
denloser, am gnadenlosesten> ◊ *ein gnadenloser*
Richter ♦ *Seine Kritik war gnadenlos.* ♦ *Früher*
wurden Tiger gnadenlos gejagt.

mercy (noun) 1. *(sympathy)* Gnade ['gnaːdə] die
<-, -n> most sing ◊ *Die Behörden kennen keine*

Gnade. beg for mercy um Gnade flehen ◊ *Der zum Tode Verurteilte flehte um Gnade.* show sb mercy sich jdm gegenüber gnädig zeigen [ge:gᴈɪly:be 'gnɛ:dɪç ʦaegᴈɪ] +*haben* ◊ *Der Richter zeigte sich dem Angeklagten gegenüber gnädig.* have mercy (on sb) (jdm gegenüber) gnädig sein ['gnɛ:dɪç zaen] +*sein* mercy mission Hilfsmission ['hɪlfsmɪ‚sjo:n] die <-, –en> 2. *(in the UK: luck)* Glück [glʏk] das <–(e)s> *no pl* what a mercy it is that ... welch ein Glück, dass ... ◊ *Welch ein Glück, dass er überlebt hat!*

⊛ be grateful for small mercies nicht zu viel verlangen be at the mercy of sb/sth jdm/einer Sache ausgeliefert sein

mere [adj] 1. *(not more than)* bloß [blo:s] *no comp/ superl, only before ns* ◊ *Das sind doch bloße Spekulationen!* ◆ *Der bloße Gedanke daran macht mir schon Angst.*; *(amount)* a mere ... ganze ... ['gantsə] *no comp/superl, only before ns* ◊ *Ich habe ganze 50 Euro verdient.* 2. *(smallest)* merest geringste [gə'rɪŋstə] ◊ *Er hat nicht die geringste Chance.*

merely [adv] lediglich ['le:dɪklɪç] *no comp/superl* ◊ *Ich tue lediglich meine Pflicht.*

merge [verb] 1. *(companies)* fusionieren [fuzjo'ni:rən] <fusioniert, fusionierte, hat fusioniert> ◊ *Die beiden Autohersteller fusionieren.* ◆ *Die Firma fusioniert mit einem Konkurrenzunternehmen.* merge sth (with sth) etw. (mit etw.) zusammenschließen [ʦu'zamənʃli:sn̩] <schließt zusammen, schloss zusammen, hat zusammengeschlossen> ◊ *Die beiden Unternehmen werden zusammengeschlossen.* 2. *(blend, become indistinguishable)* merge into/with sth in etw. [acc] übergehen [ɪn ... y:bege:ən] <geht über, ging über, ist übergegangen> ◊ *Das Meer scheint in den Himmel überzugehen.* merge into one another ineinander übergehen ◊ *Bei mir gehen Beruf und Privatleben ineinander über.*

merger [noun] Fusion [fu'zjo:n] die <-, –en> ◊ *die Fusion von Daimler und/mit Chrysler*

merit [noun] 1. *(advantage)* Vorzug ['fo:ʦu:k] der <–(e)s, Vorzüge> ◊ *Die Vorzüge einer eigenen Wohnung liegen auf der Hand.* be of merit Vorzüge haben; *(quality)* Qualität [kvali'tɛ:t] die <-, –en> choose sb/sth on their/its merit jdn/etw. nach seinen Qualitäten auswählen judge sb/sth on their/ its own merits jdn/etw. nach seinen eigenen Qualitäten beurteilen 2. *(recognition of outstanding performance)* Auszeichnung ['aosʦaeçnʊŋ] die <-, –en> ◊ *Ich habe das Examen mit Auszeichnung bestanden.*

merrily [adv] fröhlich ['frø:lɪç] ◊ *Er lachte fröhlich.*

merry [adj] 1. *(in the UK: tipsy)* angeheitert ['angəhaetet] *no comp/superl* ◊ *angeheiterte Gäste* ◆ *Sie war bereits angeheitert, als sie auf die Party ging.* 2. *(cheerful)* fröhlich ['frø:lɪç] ◊ *Überall sah man fröhliche Gesichter.* ◆ *Das Fest wurde noch richtig fröhlich.*

mesh [noun] Geflecht [gə'fleçt] das <–(e)s, –e> ◊ *ein Geflecht von Kabeln* wire mesh Maschendraht ['maʃn̩dra:t] der <–(e)s> *no pl*

mess [noun] 1. *(dirt)* Dreck [drɛk] der <–(e)s> *no pl* *(fam)* ◊ *Mach bloß keinen Dreck!* ◆ *Was für ein Dreck!* be a mess dreckig sein ['drɛkɪç zaen] +*sein* *(fam)* ◊ *Deine Bluse ist ganz dreckig!* make a mess of sth etw. dreckig machen ['drɛkɪç maxn̩] +*haben* *(fam)* 2. *(muddle, untidiness)* Durcheinander [dʊʳçlae'nande] das <–s> *no pl* make a mess ein

Durcheinander anrichten be in a mess durcheinander sein [dʊʳçlae'nande zaen] +*sein* ◊ *Nach dem Einbruch war alles durcheinander.* make a mess of sth etw. durcheinander bringen [dʊʳçlae'nande brɪŋən] <bringt, brachte, hat gebracht> ◊ *Bring meine Sachen nicht durcheinander!* 3. *(state of mind, health)* sb is a mess jdm geht es sehr schlecht [ge:t ɛs ze:ɐ̯ 'ʃlɛçt] <geht, ging, ist gegangen> ◊ *Mir ging es damals sehr schlecht.* look a mess sehr schlecht aussehen [ze:ɐ̯ 'ʃlɛçt ‚aosze:ən] <sieht aus, sah aus, hat ausgesehen> ◊ *Er sah sehr schlecht aus.* 4. *(difficult situation)* Schwierigkeiten ['ʃvi:rɪçkaetn̩] die <-> *pl* ◊ *Die Schwierigkeiten schienen nahezu unüberwindbar.* be in a mess in Schwierigkeiten sein get into a mess in Schwierigkeiten geraten get sb into a mess jdn in Schwierigkeiten bringen make a mess of sth etw. vermasseln [fe'masl̩n] <vermasselt, vermasselte, hat vermasselt> *(fam)* ◊ *Er hat seine Arbeit vermasselt.* 5. *(dining room)* Messe ['mɛsə] die <-, –n> 6. *(animal's faeces)* Kot [ko:t] der <–(e)s, –e> *most sing*

mess about [verb] 1. *(being silly)* herumalbern [hɛ'rʊmlalben] +*haben* ◊ *Musst du jetzt herumalbern?* 2. *(being lazy)* gammeln ['gamln̩] +*haben* *(fam)* ◊ *Wir haben den ganzen Sonntag nur gegammelt.* 3. *(in the UK: treat sb badly)* mess sb about jdm übel mitspielen [‚y:bl̩ 'mɪtʃpi:lən] +*haben* ◊ *Er hat ihr übel mitgespielt.* 4. *(waste time)* Zeit vergeuden ['ʦaet fe‚gᴐydn̩] <vergeudet, vergeudete, hat vergeudet> 5. *(try to repair)* mess about with sth an etw. [dat] herumbasteln [an ... hɛ‚rʊmbastl̩n] <bastelt herum, bastelte herum, hat herumgebastelt> *(fam)* ◊ *Ich habe drei Tage lang an meinem Staubsauger herumgebastelt.* 6. *(have sex with)* mess about with sb etwas mit jdm haben [ɛtvas mɪt ... ha:bm] +*haben* *(fam)* ◊ *Er hatte etwas mit seiner Sekretärin.*

message [noun] 1. *(personal information)* Nachricht ['na:xrɪçt] die <-, –en> ◊ *eine Nachricht auf dem Anrufbeantworter für Kerstin von Susi* leave a message eine Nachricht hinterlassen take a message etwas ausrichten ['aosrɪçtn̩] <richtet aus, richtete aus, hat ausgerichtet> ◊ *Kann ich etwas ausrichten?* 2. *(email)* E-Mail ['i:me:l] die <-, –s> ◊ *Während meines Urlaubs haben sich viele E-Mails angesammelt.* error message Fehlermeldung ['fe:lemeldʊŋ] die <-, –en> 3. *(of a speech, book, action, advertisement etc.)* Botschaft ['bo:tʃaft] die <-, –en> ◊ *Hat der Film eine Botschaft?* ◆ *Die schwache Wahlbeteiligung ist eine klare Botschaft an die Politiker.* get the message across die Botschaft vermitteln bring home the message that ... deutlich machen, dass ... ['dᴐʏtlɪç maxn̩ das] +*haben* ⊛ get the message kapieren

messenger [noun] Bote ['bo:tə] der <–n, –n> ♀Botin ['bo:tɪn] die <-, –nen> ◊ *Der König schickte einen Boten ins Dorf.* ◆ *Der Bote überbrachte ein Telegramm.*

messily [adv] 1. *(untidily)* unordentlich ['ʊnlɔʳdntlɪç] ◊ *unordentlich schreiben* 2. eat messily sich beim Essen bekleckern [baem ‚ɛsn̩ bə'klɛkᴇn] <bekleckert sich, bekleckerte sich, hat sich bekleckert>

mess up [verb] 1. *(not succeed)* vermasseln [fe'masl̩n] <vermasselt, vermasselte, hat vermasselt> *(fam)* I messed up. Ich habe es vermasselt.; *(your life)* verpfuschen [fe'pfʊʃn̩] <verpfuscht, verpfuschte, hat verpfuscht> *(fam)* ◊ *Sie hat ihr Leben verpfuscht.*

A
B
C
D
E
F
G
H
I
J
K
L
M
N
O
P
Q
R
S
T
U
V
W
X
Y
Z

2. *(make untidy)* durcheinander bringen [dʊˈrçl̩aeˈnandɐ brɪŋən] <bringt, brachte, hat gebracht> ◊ *Sie hat die Papiere durcheinander gebracht.* **3.** *(make dirty)* dreckig machen [ˈdrɛkɪç maxn̩] +haben *(fam)* ◊ *Er hat den Teppich dreckig gemacht.* **4.** *(cause problems)* mitnehmen [ˈmɪtneːmən] <nimmt mit, nahm mit, hat mitgenommen> ◊ *Die Grippe hat mich ganz schön mitgenommen.*

messy [adj] **1.** *(untidy)* unordentlich [ˈʊnl̩ɔˈrdn̩tlɪç] ◊ *eine unordentliche Wohnung* ♦ *Dein Büro ist aber unordentlich.* **2.** *(dirty)* dreckig [ˈdrɛkɪç] *(fam)* ◊ *Das Bad ist dreckig.* ♦ *eine dreckige Küche* **3.** *(difficult, unpleasant)* schwierig [ˈʃviːrɪç] ◊ *eine schwierige Trennung* ♦ *Ihre Beziehung ist schwierig.*

metal [noun] Metall [meˈtal] das <-s, -e> ◊ *eine Skulptur aus Metall* heavy metal Schwermetall [ˈʃveːɐ̯mɛˌtal] precious metal Edelmetall [ˈeːdl̩mɛˌtal]

metaphor [noun] Metapher [meˈtafɐ] die <-, -n>

metaphorical(ly) [adj, adv] metaphorisch [metaˈfoːrɪʃ] no comp/superl ◊ *ein metaphorischer Ausdruck* ♦ *Die Sprache in diesem Text ist stark metaphorisch.* ♦ *Sie ist, metaphorisch gesprochen, die gute Fee in unserer Abteilung.*

meter → **metre**

method [noun] Methode [meˈtoːdə] die <-, -n> ◊ *Behandlung mit traditionellen Methoden* a method of/for sth eine Methode zu etw. ◊ *eine neue Methode zur Qualitätskontrolle* a method of/for doing sth eine Methode, um etw. zu tun ☻ there's method in sb's madness jds Wahnsinn hat Methode

methodology [noun] Methodik [meˈtoːdɪk] die <-, -en>

meticulous(ly) [adj, adv] sorgfältig [ˈzɔˈrkfɛltɪç] ◊ *Als sorgfältiger Mensch überprüfe ich das lieber noch einmal.* ♦ *Franz ist sehr sorgfältig.* ♦ *etw. sorgfältig aufschreiben*

metre, meter [noun] **1.** *(unit of measurement)* Meter [ˈmeːtɐ] der <-s, -> ◊ *Das Zimmer ist fünf mal zehn Meter groß.* ♦ *Ein Kilometer hat 1000 Meter.* **2.** LIT Versmaß [ˈfɛˈsmaːs] das <-es, -e>

metropolitan [adj] großstädtisch [ˈgroːsʃtɛ(ː)tɪʃ] mostly before ns ◊ *großstädtische Kultur*

microphone [noun] Mikrofon [mikroˈfoːn] das <-s, -e> ◊ *Während seines Auftritts fiel das Mikrofon aus.* ♦ *das Mikrofon einschalten*

microscope [noun] Mikroskop [mikroˈskoːp] das <-s, -e> ◊ *Sie betrachteten den Krankheitserreger unter dem Mikroskop.*

microwave [noun] Mikrowelle [ˈmiːkrovɛlə] die <-, -n> ◊ *Essen in der Mikrowelle aufwärmen* ♦ *Wie entstehen Mikrowellen?*

mid- [prefix] Mitte [ˈmɪtə] in mid-August Mitte August ◊ *Die Truppen sollen Mitte August abgezogen werden.* a woman in her mid-fourties ein Frau Mitte vierzig in mid-air in der Luft [ɪn deːɐ̯ ˈlʊft]

midday [noun] Mittag [ˈmɪtaːk] der <-s, -e> ◊ *Vor Mittag steht sie nie auf.* ♦ *Ich komme gegen Mittag an.*

middle¹ [noun] **1.** *(centre, halfway in a period of time)* Mitte [ˈmɪtə] die <-, -n> most sing ◊ *die Mitte des Zimmers* ♦ *die Mitte des 20. Jahrhunderts* ♦ *In der Mitte stand ein großer Tisch.* in the middle of sth mitten in etw. [dat] [ˈmɪtn̩ ɪn] ◊ *mitten in der Nacht/Stadt* ♦ *mitten im Zimmer* in the middle of the road mitten auf der Straße into the middle of sth mitten

in etw. [acc] ◊ *Ich habe das Sofa mitten ins Zimmer gestellt.* **2.** *(waist)* Taille [ˈtaljə] die <-, -n> ◊ *Sie hatte sich ein Handtuch um die Taille gebunden.* ☻ be caught in the middle zwischen den Stühlen sitzen be in the middle of doing sth gerade dabei sein, etw. zu tun divide/split sth down the middle **1.** *(into two opposing parts)* etw. spalten ◊ *Diese Frage droht die Kirche zu spalten.* **2.** *(into two equal shares)* teilen ◊ *Wir sollten die Kosten teilen.* in the middle of nowhere am Ende der Welt

middle² [adj] **1.** *(central)* mittlere [ˈmɪtlərə] no comp/superl, only before ns <ein mittlerer …, eine mittlere …, ein mittleres …> ◊ *im mittleren Fach* **2.** *(halfway in a period of time)* Mitte [ˈmɪtə] die <-> no pl the middle 1950s etc. die Mitte der 50er Jahre etc. by/in the middle 1980s etc. Mitte der achtziger Jahre etc. a man in his middle 30s etc. ein Mann Mitte dreißig etc.

Middle Ages [noun] Mittelalter [ˈmɪtl̩ˌaltɐ] das <-s> no pl ◊ *im Mittelalter* ♦ *das frühe/späte Mittelalter*

middle class [noun] Mittelschicht [ˈmɪtl̩ʃɪçt] die <-, -en>

middle-class [adj] bürgerlich [ˈbʏˈɡɐlɪç] ◊ *eine bürgerliche Familie* ♦ *Sein familiärer Hintergrund ist bürgerlich.*

Middle East [noun] the Middle East der Nahe Osten [deːɡ ˌnaːə ˈɔstn̩] der <-s> no pl ◊ *die Länder des Nahen Ostens*

middle finger [noun] Mittelfinger [ˈmɪtl̩fɪŋɐ] der <-, ->

middle way [noun] Mittelweg [ˈmɪtl̩veːk] der <-(e)s, -e> ◊ *einen Mittelweg finden*

midfield [noun] Mittelfeld [ˈmɪtl̩fɛlt] das <-(e)s> no pl in midfield im Mittelfeld

midge [noun] Mücke [ˈmʏkə] die <-, -n>

midnight [noun] Mitternacht [ˈmɪtɐnaxt] die <-> no pl at midnight um Mitternacht

midst [noun] **1.** *(among)* in sb's midst in jds Mitte [ɪn … ˈmɪtə] ◊ *ein Verräter in unserer Mitte* **2.** *(while sth is taking place)* in the midst of sth mitten in etw. [dat] [ˈmɪtn̩ ɪn] ◊ *Mitten im Gespräch stand er auf und ging.* ♦ *Das Land befindet sich mitten in einer Wirtschaftskrise.*

midsummer [noun] *(hottest season)* Hochsommer [ˈhoːxzɔmɐ] der <-s, -> most sing ◊ *ein Tag im Hochsommer; (exact middle of summer)* Mittsommer [ˈmɪtzɔmɐ]

midwife [noun] Hebamme [ˈheːpˌlamə] die <-, -n> ◊ *Meine Mutter ist Hebamme.* ♦ *Welchen Rat hat dir die Hebamme gegeben?*

might [verb] **1.** *(expressing possibility, likelihood, criticism, making a suggestion)* sb/sth might do sth jd/etw. könnte etw. tun [kœntə] subjunctive II ◊ *Es könnte anfangen zu regnen.* ♦ *Ich dachte, wir könnten einen Spaziergang machen.* sb/sth might just do sth jd/etw. könnte etw. gerade noch tun ◊ *Wenn wir uns beeilen, könnten wir den Zug gerade noch erwischen.* sb/sth might easily do sth jd/etw. könnte leicht etw. tun ◊ *Die Krise könnte leicht in eine Rezession führen.* sb might like to do sth jd würde vielleicht gern etw. tun [ˈvʊˈdə fɪlaeçt ɡɛˈrn] ◊ *Vielleicht würden Sie gern zum Essen bleiben.; (expressing a possibility that sth could have happened)* sb/sth might have done sth jd/etw. hätte etw. tun können [hɛtə … kœnən] ◊ *Du hättest dich verletzen können.* ♦ *Du hättest mir auch Bescheid sagen*

können.; *(expressing a small possibility, presumption that sth may have happened)* sb/sth might have done sth jd/etw. könnte etw. getan haben [kœntə ... haːbm̩] ◊ *Könnte er sich schon gemeldet haben?* ♦ *Sie ist noch nicht zu Hause – sie könnte einen Unfall gehabt haben.*; *(when imagining different circumstances)* sb/sth might not/never have done sth jd/etw. hätte etw. vielleicht nicht/nie getan [hɛtə ... filaɛçt ˈnɪçt/niː] ◊ *Wenn er das gewusst hätte, wäre er vielleicht nicht gekommen.* ♦ *Ohne Hilfe hätten wir es vielleicht nie geschafft.* **2.** *(asking for or giving permission)* sb might do sth jd darf etw. tun [daˈf] <darf, durfte, hat dürfen> ◊ *Darf ich Ihnen eine Frage stellen?* ♦ *Er sagte, wir dürften seinen Swimmingpool benutzen.* **3.** *(expressing a purpose)* ... so that sb might do sth ..., damit jd etw. tun kann [damɪt ... kan] ◊ *Ich erledige das jetzt, damit wir später zusammen ausgehen können.* **4.** *(expressing how sth seems)* it might have been yesterday als wäre es gestern gewesen [als vɛːrə ɛs ˈɡɛstɐn ɡəveːzn̩] ◊ *Ich erinnere mich noch so deutlich, als wäre es gestern gewesen.* **5.** *(expressing that sth doesn't make much difference)* sb might (just) as well do sth jd kann genauso gut etw. tun [kan ɡəˈnaozoː ɡuːt] ◊ *Wir können genauso gut zu Hause bleiben.* sb might as well have done sth jd. hätte genauso gut etw. tun können **6.** *(as a question tag)* mightn't you/he etc?, might you/he etc? oder? [ˈoːdɐ] ◊ *Sie könnten uns morgen besuchen, oder?* ♦ *Er würde vielleicht gern kommen, oder?*
◉ as you might expect wie zu erwarten war as you might imagine wie man sich vorstellen kann I might have known/guessed ... ich hätte mir ja denken können, ...

mightily [adv] mächtig [ˈmeçtɪç] *no comp/superl (fam)* ◊ *Ich bin mächtig stolz auf dich.*

mightn't → might

mighty [adj] *(powerful)* mächtig [ˈmeçtɪç] ◊ *ein mächtiger Mann* ♦ *Die Firma ist sehr mächtig.*; *(blow, kick)* kräftig [ˈkrɛftɪç] ◊ *ein kräftiger Schlag*

migrate [verb] **1.** *(birds)* ziehen [ˈtsiːən] <zieht, zog, ist gezogen> ◊ *Die Vögel ziehen nach Süden.*; *(fish)* wandern [ˈvandɐn] +sein **2.** *(people)* auswandern [ˈaosvandɐn] +sein ◊ *Er ist nach Kanada ausgewandert.*

migration [noun] **1.** *(of birds)* Zug [tsuːk] der <–(e)s, Züge> ◊ *der Zug der Störche;* *(of fish)* Wanderung [ˈvandərʊŋ] die <–, –en> ◊ *die Wanderung der Lachse* **2.** *(leaving your home country)* Auswanderung [ˈaosvandərʊŋ] die <–, –en> *most sing* ◊ *die Auswanderung der Iren;* *(settling in a new country)* Einwanderung [ˈaenvandərʊŋ] die <–, –en>; *(movement between cultures)* Migration [migraˈtsjoːn] die <–, –en> ◊ *soziale Probleme durch Migration*

mild [adj] **1.** *(illness, crisis, amusement, surprise)* leicht [laeçt] <leichter, am leichtesten> *mostly before ns* ◊ *eine leichte Grippe* ♦ *Die Nachricht hat leichtes Erstaunen ausgelöst.* **2.** *(weather, temperature, food, expression, criticism)* mild [mɪlt] <milder, am mildesten> ◊ *Der letzte Winter war mild.* ♦ *ein milder Käse* **3.** *(person, voice)* sanft [zanft] <sanfter, am sanftesten> ◊ *ein sanfter Mensch* ♦ *Sie ist sehr sanft.*

mildly [adv] **1.** *(slightly)* halbwegs [ˈhalpveːks] *no comp/superl* ◊ *Seine Geschichten sind nur halbwegs*

amüsant. **2.** *(in a restrained way)* verhalten [fɐˈhaltn̩] ◊ *Er sagte verhalten: „Das geht in Ordnung."*

mile [noun] Meile [ˈmaelə] die <–, –n> ◊ *Das Haus liegt zwei Meilen von hier entfernt.* ♦ *Die Insel ist nur zwei Meilen lang.* miles per hour Meilen pro Stunde for miles meilenweit [ˈmaelənvaet] *no comp/superl* ◊ *meilenweit laufen*
◉ a mile a minute rasend schnell be miles away mit den Gedanken woanders sein go the extra mile besondere Anstrengungen unternehmen stick out a mile unübersehbar sein recognize sb/sth a mile off jdn/etw. schon von weitem erkennen

military¹ [noun] Militär [miliˈtɛːɐ] das <–s> *no pl* in the military beim Militär ◊ *Daniel ist zurzeit beim Militär.*; Militär... [miliˈtɛːɐ] military action Militäreinsatz [miliˈtɛːɐˌaenzats] der <–es, Militäreinsätze>

military² [adj] militärisch [miliˈtɛːrɪʃ] *no comp/superl, only before ns* ◊ *militärische Überlegenheit* military action Militäreinsatz [miliˈtɛːɐˌaenzats] der <–es, Militäreinsätze>

military service [noun] Wehrdienst [ˈveːɐdiːnst] der <–(e)s> *no pl* ◊ *Er ist zum Wehrdienst einberufen/eingezogen worden.* do military service Wehrdienst leisten

milk [noun] Milch [mɪlç] die <–> *no pl* ◊ *ein Glas Milch* ♦ *die Milch der Kokosnuss* UHT milk H-Milch [ˈhaːmɪlç]

mill [noun] **1.** *(for grain, coffee, pepper)* Mühle [ˈmyːlə] die <–, –n> ◊ *Am Bach steht eine alte Mühle.* ♦ *Pfefferkörner in die Mühle füllen* **2.** *(factory)* Fabrik [faˈbriːk] die <–, –en>

milligram [noun] Milligramm [ˈmɪligram] das <–s, –e> *pl 'Milligramm' when used with expressions of quantity* ◊ *zehn Milligramm*

millilitre, milliliter [noun] Milliliter [ˈmɪliliːtɐ] der <–s, –> ◊ *250 Milliliter Milch*

millimetre, millimeter [noun] Millimeter [ˈmɪlimeːtɐ] der <–s, –> ◊ *eine Öffnung von zehn Millimeter Durchmesser*

million [noun] Million [mɪˈljoːn] die <–, –en> ◊ *Sie hat Millionen verdient.*
◉ be one in a million ein absoluter Glücksstreffer sein

millionaire [noun] Millionär [mɪljoˈnɛːɐ] der <–s, –e> ♀Millionärin [mɪljoˈnɛːrɪn] die <–, –nen>

mince [noun] Hackfleisch [ˈhakflaeʃ] das <–(e)s> *no pl* ◊ *Hackfleisch von Rind/Schwein*

mind¹ [noun] **1.** *(brain, intelligent person)* Kopf [kɔpf] der <–(e)s, Köpfe> ◊ *Er ist ein kluger Kopf.* sb's mind is full of sth jd hat den Kopf voll mit etw. sth goes on in sb's mind etw. geht in jds Kopf vor ◊ *Was geht nur in ihrem Kopf vor?* set your mind on doing sth sich [dat] in den Kopf setzen, etw. zu tun; *(thoughts)* Gedanken [ɡəˈdaŋkn̩] die <–> *pl* ◊ *jds Gedanken lesen* sb's mind is on something else jd ist mit den Gedanken woanders keep your mind on sth seine Gedanken auf etw. [acc] konzentrieren turn your mind to sth seine Gedanken einer Sache [dat] zuwenden with sb/sth in mind mit dem Gedanken an jdn/etw. take sb's mind off sth jdn von etw. ablenken [fɔn ... ˌaplɛŋkn̩] +haben bear/keep sth in mind an etw. [acc] denken [an ... dɛŋkn̩] <denkt, dachte, hat gedacht> ◊ *an die gesundheitlichen Folgen denken* speak your mind sagen, was man denkt; *(worries)* sb has sth on their mind jdn beschäftigt etw. [bəˈʃɛftɪçt] <beschäftigt, beschäftigte,

A
B
C
D
E
F
G
H
I
J
K
L
M
N
O
P
Q
R
S
T
U
V
W
X
Y
Z

hat beschäftigt> **2.** *(way of thinking)* have a suspicious mind **ein misstrauischer Mensch sein** [aen ˌmɪstrao̯ɪʃe 'mɛnʃ zaen] +sein; *(feeling)* state of mind **Zustand** ['tsuːʃtant] der <-(e)s, Zustände> *most sing* ◊ *In diesem Zustand solltest du nicht mit ihm sprechen.* **3.** *(intelligence, ability to think)* **Verstand** [fɛ'ʃtant] der <-(e)s> *no pl* ◊ *ein scharfer Verstand* be in your right mind **bei Verstand sein** be of sound mind **bei klarem Verstand sein**
◉ **be/go out of your mind wahnsinnig sein/werden** be/go out of your mind with jealousy/worry **vor Eifersucht/Sorge wahnsinnig sein/werden** cross sb's mind **jdm einfallen** ◊ *Es fiel mir ein, dass er früher Pferde gezüchtet hatte.* sb's mind is at rest **jd ist beruhigt** put sb's mind at rest **jdn beruhigen** to my mind **meiner Meinung nach**
mind² [verb] **1.** *(not tolerate, mostly in questions or negations)* sb minds sth **etw. macht jdm etwas aus** [maxt ... ɛtvas 'ao̯s] +haben sb doesn't mind sth **etw. macht jdm nichts aus** ◊ *Die Kälte macht mir nichts aus.* sb doesn't mind doing sth **es macht jdm nichts aus, etw. zu tun** ◊ *Es macht mir nichts aus, den Müll hinauszubringen.* sb minds/doesn't mind sb doing sth, sb minds/doesn't mind if sb does sth **jdm macht es etwas/nichts aus, wenn jd etw. tut** ◊ *Macht es dir etwas aus, wenn ich das Fenster öffne?*
♦ *Wenn es Ihnen nichts ausmacht, gehe ich jetzt.*
2. *(be careful)* mind (that) ... **aufpassen, dass ...** ['ao̯fpasn̩ das] +haben ◊ *Pass auf, dass du den Rotwein nicht verschüttest.* Mind the step! **Vorsicht, Stufe! 3.** *(in the UK: look after)* mind sb/sth **auf jdn/ etw. aufpassen** [ao̯f ... ˌao̯fpasn̩] +haben ◊ *Kannst du kurz auf den Laden aufpassen?*
◉ **never mind 1.** *(for saying that sth isn't important)* **macht nichts 2.** *(for saying that sth is more true for sth else)* never mind ... **ganz zu schweigen von ... 3.** *(for saying that sb should ignore sth)* **schon gut** don't mind sb **kümmere dich nicht um jdn, kümmern Sie sich nicht um jdn, kümmert euch nicht um jdn** I don't mind if I do. **Ich hätte nichts dagegen.** I wouldn't mind ... **ich hätte nichts gegen ...** ◊ *Ich hätte jetzt nichts gegen ein kühles Bier.* mind (you) **allerdings**
mindless [adj] **hirnlos** ['hɪ'nloːs] <hirnloser, am hirnlosesten> *(pej)* ◊ *Sie grölten hirnlose Parolen.* ♦ *Diese Sendung ist doch völlig hirnlos.*; *(violence, vandalism)* **sinnlos** ['zɪnloːs] <sinnloser, am sinnlosesten> ◊ *sinnlose Zerstörungswut*
mine¹ [noun] *(explosive, area where minerals can be found)* **Mine** ['miːnə] die <-, -n> ◊ *Der Panzer fuhr auf eine Mine.* gold mine **Goldmine** ['gɔltmiːnə]; *(industrial site)* **Bergwerk** ['bɛ'kvɛ'k] das <-(e)s, -e> coal mine **Kohlebergwerk** ['koːləbɛ'kvɛ'k]
mine² [verb] **1.** *(for minerals)* mine (for) sth **etw. abbauen** ['apbao̯ən] +haben ◊ *Erz/Braunkohle abbauen* **2.** *(with explosives)* **verminen** [fɛ'miːnən] <vermint, verminte, hat vermint> ◊ *Die Straße war vermint.*
mine³ [poss pron] **meiner** ['maenɐ] **meine** ['maenə] **mein(e)s** [mae(ə)ns] ◊ *Das hier ist dein Mantel, aber wo ist meiner?* ♦ *Deine Mutter ist schon da, nur meine kommt zu spät.* ♦ *Ihre Noten sind schlechter als meine.* ♦ *Da steht sein Auto. Wo hab ich nur meins geparkt?* → **meiner**
◉ **of mine von mir** ◊ *ein Freund von mir*
miner [noun] **Bergmann** ['bɛ'kman] der

<-(e)s, Bergleute> ◊ *Er war lange als Bergmann beschäftigt.* ♦ *die Bergleute der hiesigen Kohlebergwerke*
mineral [noun] **1.** *(substance)* **Mineral** [mine'raːl] das <-s, -ien> ◊ *Mineralien zur Nahrungsergänzung* ♦ *Mineralien wie Eisen und Zink* **2.** *(soft drink)* **Erfrischungsgetränk** [ɛ'frɪʃʊŋsɡətrɛŋk] das <-(e)s, -e>
mineral water [noun] **Mineralwasser** [mineˈraːlvasɐ] das <-s, Mineralwässer>
mingle [verb] **1.** **vermischen** [fɛ'mɪʃn̩] <vermischt, vermischte, hat vermischt> mingle sth with sth **etw. mit etw. vermischen** sth mingles with sth **etw. vermischt sich mit etw.** ◊ *Entsetzen vermischte sich mit Freude.* **2.** *(people)* mingle with sb **sich unter jdn mischen** [ʊntɐ ... mɪʃn̩] +haben ◊ *Bei der Party haben sie sich unter die Gäste gemischt.*
minimal [adj] **minimal** [mini'maːl] ◊ *nur eine minimale Chance haben* ♦ *Der Aufwand war minimal.*
minimize [verb] **1.** *(reduce)* **minimieren** [mini'miːrən] <minimiert, minimierte, hat minimiert> ◊ *mögliche Risiken minimieren* ♦ *ein Fenster minimieren* **2.** *(play down sth negative)* **bagatellisieren** [bagatɛli'ziːrən] <bagatellisiert, bagatellisierte, hat bagatellisiert> *(sth positive)* **herabwürdigen** [hɛ'rapvʏ'dɪɡn̩] +haben ◊ *jds Leistung herabwürdigen*
minimum¹ [noun] **Mindestmaß** ['mɪndəstmaːs] das <-es, -e> ◊ *etw. auf ein Mindestmaß reduzieren* ♦ *ein Mindestmaß an Aufwand* as a minimum **mindestens** ['mɪndəstn̩s]
minimum² [adj] **minimum ... Mindest...** ['mɪndəst] minimum age **Mindestalter** ['mɪndəstˌaltɐ] das <-s, -> minimum wage **Mindestlohn** ['mɪndəstloːn] der <-(e)s, Mindestlöhne>
mining [noun] **1.** *(activity)* **Abbau** ['apbao̯] der <-(e)s> *no pl* ◊ *der Abbau von Braunkohle* gold mining **Goldgewinnung** ['ɡɔltɡəvɪnʊŋ] **2.** *(industry)* **Bergbau** ['bɛ'kbao̯] der <-(e)s> *no pl* mining village **Bergbausiedlung** ['bɛ'kbao̯ziːdlʊŋ] die <-, -en>
minister [noun] **1.** *(government)* **Minister** [mi'nɪstɐ] der <-s, ->; **♀Ministerin** [mi'nɪstərɪn] die <-, -nen> ◊ *Er war Minister unter Bundeskanzler Helmut Schmidt.* ♦ *Sie wurde zur Ministerin ernannt.* minister of defence **Verteidigungsminister** [fɛ'tae̯dɪɡʊŋsmiˌnɪstɐ] **Verteidigungsministerin** [fɛ'tae̯dɪɡʊŋsmiˌnɪstərɪn] minister of education **Kultusminister** ['kʊltʊsmiˌnɪstɐ] **Kultusministerin** ['kʊltʊsmiˌnɪstərɪn] minister of state **Staatssekretär** ['ʃtaːtszekreˌtɛːɐ̯] der <-s, -e>; **♀Staatssekretärin** ['ʃtaːtszekreˌtɛːrɪn] die <-, -nen> **2.** *(representative abroad)* **Gesandte** [ɡə'zantə] der/die <-n, die Gesandten> *but:* ein Gesandter/eine Gesandte ◊ *Der König empfing die ausländischen Gesandten.* **3.** REL *(priest)* **Geistliche** ['ɡae̯stlɪçə] der/die <-n, die Geistlichen> *but:* ein Geistlicher/eine Geistliche ◊ *Er will Geistlicher werden.* ♦ *Im Radio sprach eine Geistliche.*
ministerial [adj] **ministeriell** [mɪnɪste'riɛl] *mostly before ns* ◊ *ein ministerieller Erlass*
ministry [noun] **1.** **Ministerium** [mɪnɪs'teːri̯ʊm] das <-s, Ministerien> ◊ *das Ministerium für Umwelt und Naturschutz* ministry of defence **Verteidigungsministerium** [fɛ'tae̯dɪɡʊŋsminɪsˌteːri̯ʊm] ministry of education **Kultusministerium** ['kʊltʊsminɪsˌteːri̯ʊm] **2.** REL *(profession or term of office of a priest)*

Pfarramt ['pfaˈ|amt] das <–(e)s, Pfarrämter> *most sing* ◊ *das Pfarramt anstreben* sb's ministry jds Tätigkeit als Geistlicher [ˌtɛːtɪçkaet als ˈgaestlɪçə]; *(clergy)* Geistlichkeit [ˈgaestlɪçkaet] die <–, –en> *most sing* ◊ *die gesamte Geistlichkeit*

minor[1] [noun] **1.** *(sb who is not yet an adult)* Minderjährige [ˈmɪndejɛːrɪgə] der/die <–n, die Minderjährigen> *but: ein Minderjähriger/eine Minderjährige* ◊ *Bei Minderjährigen ist die Unterschrift der Eltern erforderlich.* be a minor minderjährig sein [ˈmɪndejɛːrɪç zaen] +*sein* **2.** *(in the US: subsidiary subject)* Nebenfach [ˈneːbɱfax] das <–(e)s, Nebenfächer> ◊ *Sie studiert Germanistik als Nebenfach.*

minor[2] [adj] **1.** *(small, insignificant)* klein [klaen] ◊ *Geschirr mit kleinen Fehlern* ♦ *ein kleiner chirurgischer Eingriff* ♦ *Die Unterschiede sind klein.*; *(injury)* leicht [laeçt] <leichter, am leichtesten> ◊ *Der Beifahrer erlitt leichte Verletzungen.*; *(damage)* gering [gəˈrɪŋ] ◊ *Der Schaden an meinem Auto ist gering.* **2.** MUS A/B etc. minor a/b-Moll etc. [ˈaːmɔl, ˈbeːmɔl] das <–> *no pl* minor key Molltonart [ˈmɔltoːn|aːˈt] die <–, –en>

minority [noun] **1.** *(smaller part of sth)* Minderheit [ˈmɪndehaet] die <–, –en> ◊ *in der Minderheit sein* ♦ *einer verfolgten Minderheit angehören* ♦ *Nur in einer Minderheit der Fälle kam es zu Komplikationen.* **2.** *(state of not yet being an adult)* Minderjährigkeit [ˈmɪndejɛːrɪçkaet] die <–> *no pl* ◊ *Wegen seiner Minderjährigkeit bekam er eine milde Strafe.*

minus[1] [adj] **1.** *(below zero)* minus [ˈmiːnʊs] ◊ *Temperaturen zwischen minus 15 und plus 10 Grad* **2.** *(negative)* negativ [ˈneːgatiːf] ◊ *a minus quantity eine negative Zahl* minus point Minuspunkt [ˈmiːnʊspʊnkt] der <–(e)s, –e>
⊙ A/B etc. minus ⊙*Eins/Zwei etc. minus*

minus[2] [prep] **1.** *(with sth deducted)* abzüglich [ˈaptsyːklɪç] +*gen* ◊ *Sie bekommen die Summe abzüglich der Anmeldegebühr zurück.* **2.** *(without)* ohne [ˈoːnə] +*acc* ◊ *Das Foto zeigt die ganze Familie ohne meine Schwester.*

minus[3] [conjunc] MATH minus [ˈmiːnʊs] ◊ *Fünf minus drei ist gleich zwei.*

minute[1] [noun] **1.** *(unit of time, part of a degree)* Minute [miˈnuːtə] die <–, –n> ◊ *Die Straßenbahn fährt alle 10 Minuten.* ♦ *Es ist 10 Minuten vor 3.* ♦ *ein Winkel von 18 Grad und 10 Minuten* at the last minute in letzter Minute by the minute mit jeder Minute ◊ *Sie wurde mit jeder Minute nervöser.* within minutes nach wenigen Minuten **2.** *(short time)* Augenblick [aogŋˈblɪk] der <–(e)s, –e> for a minute einen Augenblick lang ◊ *Ich dachte schon einen Augenblick lang, er sei tot.* Just a minute! Einen Augenblick, bitte! Wait a minute, ... Augenblick mal, ... **3.** *(record of a meeting)* minutes Protokoll [protoˈkɔl] das <–s> *sing* ◊ *Nehmen Sie das bitte ins Protokoll auf.* take the minutes das Protokoll führen
⊚ not for one minute absolut nicht the minute you do sth sobald man etw. tut in a minute gleich ◊ *Ich bin gleich wieder da.* this minute (jetzt) sofort ◊ *Komm sofort wieder her!*

minute[2] [adj] **1.** *(very small)* winzig [ˈvɪntsɪç] ◊ *winzige Unterschiede* ♦ *Das Handy war winzig.* in minute detail bis ins kleinste Detail [bɪs ɪns ˌklaenstə deˈtae] **2.** *(very detailed)* minutiös

[minuˈtsjøːs] <minutiöser, am minutiösesten> ◊ *ein minutiöser Bericht* ♦ *Die Beschreibung war minutiös.*

miracle [noun] Wunder [ˈvʊndə] das <–s, –> ◊ *Es ist ein Wunder, dass sie noch lebt.* ♦ *Ich glaube nicht an Wunder.* work miracles Wunder wirken a miracle of sth ein Wunder ... [gen] ◊ *ein Wunder der Natur* economic miracle Wirtschaftswunder [ˈvɪrtʃaftsvʊndə] (fam) miracle cure Wunderheilung [ˈvʊndehaelʊŋ] die <–, –en>

miraculous [adj] *(surprising)* erstaunlich [eˈʃtaonlɪç] ◊ *eine erstaunliche Leistung* ♦ *Es ist erstaunlich, dass sie das geschafft haben.*; *(like a miracle)* wunderbar [ˈvʊndebaːˈ] ◊ *eine wunderbare Rettung* ♦ *Der Erfolg war geradezu wunderbar.*

mirror [noun] Spiegel [ˈʃpiːgl] der <–s, –> ◊ *Sie betrachtete sich prüfend im Spiegel.* ♦ *jdm einen Spiegel vorhalten*
⊚ a mirror of sth ein Spiegelbild ... [gen] ◊ *Unsere Schulen sind ein Spiegelbild unserer Gesellschaft.*

misappropriate [verb] **1.** *(money)* unterschlagen [ʊnteˈʃlaːgŋ] <unterschlägt, unterschlug, hat unterschlagen> ◊ *öffentliche Gelder unterschlagen* **2.** *(property)* misappropriate sth sich [dat] etw. unrechtmäßig aneignen [ˈʊnrɛçtmɛːsɪç ˌanlaegnən] <eignet sich an, eignete sich an, hat sich angeeignet> ◊ *sich unrechtmäßig Land aneignen*

miscarriage [noun] Fehlgeburt [ˈfeːlgəbuːgt] die <–, –en> ◊ *Sie hatte eine Fehlgeburt.*

mischief [noun] **1.** *(silly behavio(u)r)* Dummheiten [ˈdʊmhaetn] die <–> *pl* ◊ *Lass diese Dummheiten!* be up to mischief Dummheiten im Kopf haben get into mischief Dummheiten machen keep out of mischief keine Dummheiten machen **2.** *(wish to cause trouble)* Übermut [ˈyːbemuːt] der <–(e)s> *no pl* ◊ *jugendlicher Übermut* **3.** *(trouble)* Unfrieden [ˈʊnfriːdn] der <–s> *no pl* make mischief Unfrieden stiften

miserable [adj] **1.** *(sad)* traurig [ˈtraorɪç] ◊ *Ich war sehr traurig.* ♦ *ein trauriger Anblick*; *(wretched)* elend [ˈeːlɛnt] ◊ *Er fühlte sich elend.* ♦ *Das Tier war in einem elenden Zustand.* **2.** *(very bad)* erbärmlich [eˈbɛˈmlɪç] ◊ *eine erbärmliche Leistung* ♦ *Die Luftqualität war erbärmlich.*; *(weather)* trist [trɪst] <trister, am tristesten> ◊ *ein trister Tag im November* ♦ *Das Wetter ist seit einer Woche richtig trist.* **3.** *(person)* verdrießlich [feˈdriːslɪç] ◊ *ein verdrießlicher alter Mann* ♦ *Sei nicht so verdrießlich!* **4.** *(amount, number)* armselig [ˈaˈmzeːlɪç] ◊ *Ich habe nur noch armselige zwei Euro.* ♦ *Nur drei Teilnehmer? Das ist ja armselig.*

miserably [adv] **1.** *(sadly)* traurig [ˈtraorɪç] ◊ *er lächelte traurig* **2.** *(very badly)* erbärmlich [eˈbɛˈmlɪç] ◊ *Er hat bei der Prüfung erbärmlich abgeschnitten.* **3.** *(painfully, dreadfully)* elend [ˈeːlɛnt] ◊ *Sie sind elend zugrunde gegangen.* **4.** *(pitifully)* kläglich [ˈklɛːklɪç] ◊ *Wir sind kläglich gescheitert.*

miserly [adj] geizig [ˈgaetsɪç] ◊ *Dazu ist sie zu geizig.* ♦ *Er ist ein geiziger Mensch.*

misery [noun] Elend [ˈeːlɛnt] das <–s> *no pl* ◊ *in Armut und Elend leben*
⊚ make sb's life a misery jdm das Leben zur Hölle machen put sb/an animal out of their/its misery jdn/ein Tier von seinen Qualen erlösen

misfortune [noun] **1.** *(bad luck)* Pech [pɛç] das <–(e)s> *no pl* ◊ *Sie hatte das Pech, den Zug zu*

verpassen. **2.** *(ill fortune, disaster)* Unglück ['ʊnglʏk] das <-(e)s, -e> ◊ *Das war ein großes Unglück für sie.*

misleading [adj] irreführend ['ɪrəfyːrənt] ◊ *irreführende Angabe machen* ♦ *Der Eindruck ist irreführend.*

miss¹ [noun] **1.** *(form of address)* Miss, miss Frau [fraọ] die <-, -en> ◊ *Darf ich Ihnen Frau Sterff vorstellen?; (addressing the teacher)* Frau Lehrerin [fraọ 'leːrərɪn] ◊ *Darf ich mal zur Toilette, Frau Lehrerin?* **2.** *(winner of a beauty competition)* Miss Miss [mɪs] die <-, -es> ◊ *die aktuelle Miss Germany* **3.** *(in shooting, football)* Fehlschuss ['feːlʃʊs] der <-es, Fehlschüsse>; *(in other ball games)* Fehlwurf ['feːlvʊrf] der <-(e)s, Fehlwürfe> **4.** *(financial flop)* Pleite ['plaẹtə] die <-, -n> ◊ *Der Film war eine totale Pleite.* **5.** *(almost an accident)* near miss Beinahezusammenstoß [baẹ'naːətsu,zamənʃtoːs] der <-es, Beinahezusammenstöße> ⓖ give sth a miss etw. auslassen

In modern German, the old-fashioned form of address *Fräulein* is rarely used, and is considered rather patronizing. In fact, Germans tend not to use polite forms of address such as 'miss' or 'madam' at all: 'Can I help you, miss?' is thus translated as *Kann ich Ihnen helfen?*.

miss² [verb] **1.** *(not reach)* miss sb/sth jdn/etw. verfehlen [fe'feːlən] <verfehlt, verfehlte, hat verfehlt> ◊ *Der Ball hat das Tor knapp verfehlt.* ♦ *Haben die Grünen ihr Wahlziel verfehlt?; (when catching)* miss sth etw. nicht erwischen [,nɪçt e'vɪʃn] <erwischt, erwischte, hat erwischt> *(fam)* ◊ *Ich konnte den Ball nicht erwischen.; (when aiming)* miss (sb/sth) (jdn/etw.) nicht treffen [,nɪçt 'trefn] <trifft, traf, hat getroffen> ◊ *Er schoss auf mich, traf (mich) aber nicht.; (when shooting)* sth misses etw. geht daneben [geːt da'neːbm] <ging daneben, ist danebengegangen> ◊ *Der Schuss ging daneben.* **2.** *(not attend, not use)* versäumen [fe'zɔɡmən] <versäumt, versäumte, hat versäumt> ◊ *wegen Krankheit den Unterricht versäumen* ♦ *Er versäumt keine Gelegenheit, sie zu besuchen.; (be too late for sth, fail to get sth)* verpassen [fe'pasn] <verpasst, verpasste, hat verpasst> ◊ *Er hat seinen Zug verpasst.* ♦ *Jetzt hast du deine letzte Chance verpasst.* She missed a period. Ihre Periode blieb aus. [iːrə pe,rịoːdə bliːp 'aọs] **3.** *(not see)* übersehen [ybɐ'zeːən] <übersieht, übersah, hat übersehen> ◊ *ein paar Fehler übersehen* You can't miss the café. Das Café ist nicht zu übersehen.; *(not understand)* nicht verstehen [,nɪçt fe'ʃteːən] <versteht, verstand, hat verstanden> ◊ *Den letzten Satz habe ich nicht verstanden.* miss the point nicht verstehen, was jd meint ◊ *Du verstehst nicht, was ich meine.; (notice)* sb doesn't miss much jdm entgeht nichts [ɛnt,geːt 'nɪçts] <entging, ist entgangen> ◊ *Sie ist zwar schon 80, aber ihr entgeht nichts.* **4.** *(sth unpleasant)* miss sth um etw. herumkommen [ʊm ... hɛ,rʊmkɔmən] <kommt herum, kam herum, ist herumgekommen> *(fam)* ◊ *um eine Strafe herumkommen* **5.** *(a person, activity, sth you have lost)* vermissen [fe'mɪsn] <vermisst, vermisste, hat vermisst> ◊ *Sie vermisst ihre Schwester sehr.* ♦ *Ich vermisse unsere gemeinsamen Ausflüge.* miss doing

sth es vermissen, etw. zu tun

missile [noun] *(weapon)* Rakete [ra'keːtə] die <-, -n> ◊ *Raketen auf den Feind abschießen; (object thrown or fired)* Geschoss [ɡə'ʃɔs] das <-es, -e> ◊ *von einem Geschoss getroffen werden*

missing [adj] **1.** *(not there)* fehlend ['feːlənt] *only before ns* ◊ *Die fehlende Summe soll durch Spenden aufgebracht werden.* the missing link das fehlende Bindeglied be missing fehlen ['feːlən] +haben ◊ *Wer fehlt?* ♦ *Sieh mal nach, ob etwas fehlt.* The knife is missing from the drawer. Das Messer fehlt aus der Schublade. Your name is missing from the list. Dein Name fehlt auf der Liste. He has a finger missing. Ihm fehlt ein Finger. **2.** *(not to be found)* verschwunden [fe'ʃvʊndn] ◊ *die verschwundenen Schlüssel suchen* ♦ *Immer wenn ich sie brauche, ist sie spurlos verschwunden.; (after a battle, crime, an accident)* vermisst [fe'mɪst] ◊ *Ihr Vater ist im Krieg vermisst.* ♦ *Das vermisste Kind wurde bald gefunden.* ♦ *Nach dem Erdbeben werden noch 200 Personen vermisst.* missing in action vermisst report sb missing jdn vermisst melden; *(not recoverable)* verschollen [fe'ʃɔlən] ◊ *Das Gemälde galt lange als verschollen.* ♦ *ein verschollenes Schiff* go missing verschwinden [fe'ʃvɪndn] <verschwindet, verschwand, ist verschwunden> ◊ *Mein Schlüssel/Bruder ist verschwunden.*

mission [noun] **1.** *(task)* Auftrag ['aọftraːk] der <-(e)s, Aufträge> ◊ *Seine Einheit hat den Auftrag, die Insel zu erobern.* ♦ *Melde: Auftrag ausgeführt!* special mission Sonderauftrag ['zɔndɐ,aọftraːk]; *(diplomatic, ethical)* Mission [mɪ'sịoːn] die <-, -en> ◊ *Der Gesandte ist auf einer wichtigen Mission im Ausland.* ♦ *in geheimer Mission* **2.** *(operation)* Einsatz ['aẹnzats] der <-(e)s, Einsätze> ◊ *ein Einsatz der Polizei* ♦ *Er musste einen gefährlichen Einsatz fliegen.* mercy mission Hilfsaktion ['hɪlfs|ak,tsịoːn] rescue mission Rettungsaktion ['rɛtʊŋs|ak,tsịoːn] **3.** *(goal)* Ziel [tsiːl] das <-(e)s, -e> ◊ *Unser Ziel ist es, armen Kindern zu helfen.* mission in life Lebensaufgabe ['leːbms|aọfgaːbə] die <-, -n> **4.** *(religious)* Mission [mɪ'sịoːn] die <-, -en> ◊ *die katholische Mission in China*

miss out [verb] **1.** *(lose your chance)* miss out (on sth) etw. verpassen [fe'pasn] <verpasst, verpasste, hat verpasst> ◊ *Habe ich etwas verpasst?* ♦ *Diese Chance hat sie verpasst.* **2.** *(not include)* weglassen ['vɛklasn] <lässt weg, ließ weg, hat weggelassen> ◊ *Unwichtiges weglassen*

mist [noun] *(in the air)* Dunst [dʊnst] der <-(e)s, Dünste> ◊ *Dunst hing über dem Fluss.; (thicker)* Nebel ['neːbl̩] der <-s, -> ◊ *Die Berge waren in Nebel gehüllt.* mist of perfume Parfümwolke [par'fyːmvɔlkə] die <-, -n> mist of tears Tränenschleier ['trɛːnənʃlaẹ] der <-s, ->

mistake¹ [noun] *(error)* Fehler ['feːlɐ] der <-s, -> ◊ *Fehler korrigieren* ♦ *einen großen Fehler machen* ♦ *aus seinen Fehlern lernen* spelling mistake Rechtschreibfehler ['rɛçtʃraẹpfeːlɐ] ⓖ there must be some mistake das muss ein Irrtum sein by mistake aus Versehen

mistake² [verb] verkennen [fe'kɛnən] <verkennt, verkannte, hat verkannt> ◊ *Er verkannte die Gefahr.* there is no mistaking sth etw. ist nicht zu verkennen

• **mistake for** [phras v] mistake sb/sth for sb/sth

jdn/etw. mit jdm/etw. verwechseln [mɪt ... fɛˌvɛksl̩n] <verwechselt, verwechselte, hat verwechselt> ◊ *Ich habe sie mit ihrer Schwester verwechselt.*

mistreat [verb] *(treat badly)* schlecht behandeln [ˌʃlɛçt bəˈhandl̩n] <behandelt, behandelte, hat behandelt> ◊ *Er fühlte sich von ihr schlecht behandelt.*; *(treat cruelly)* misshandeln [mɪsˈhandl̩n] <misshandelt, misshandelte, hat misshandelt> ◊ *Wer Tiere misshandelt, macht sich strafbar.*

mistress [noun] **1.** *(lover)* Geliebte [gəˈliːptə] die <–n, –n> ◊ *Er hat eine Geliebte.* **2.** *(in charge or control)* Herrin [ˈhɛrɪn] die <–, –nen> ◊ *die Herrin des Hauses*

misunderstand [verb] missverstehen [ˈmɪsfɛʃteːən] <missversteht, missverstand, hat missverstanden> ◊ *Da habe ich Sie wohl missverstanden.*

misunderstanding [noun] Missverständnis [ˈmɪsfɛʃtɛntnɪs] das <–ses, –se> ◊ *Das muss ein Missverständnis sein.*

misuse [verb] missbrauchen [mɪsˈbraʊxn̩] <missbraucht, missbrauchte, hat missbraucht> ◊ *Er hat sein Amt dazu missbraucht, sich persönlich zu bereichern.*

mitten [noun] Fausthandschuh [ˈfaʊsthantʃuː] der <–s, –e>

mix¹ [noun] Mischung [ˈmɪʃʊŋ] die <–, –en> ◊ *Das Programm war eine interessante Mischung.* a mix of sth and sth eine Mischung aus etw. [dat] und etw. [dat] cake mix Backmischung [ˈbakmɪʃʊŋ] give sth a mix mischen [ˈmɪʃn̩] +haben

mix² [verb] **1.** *(substances)* mix sth etw. mischen [ˈmɪʃn̩] +haben ◊ *Apfelsaft mit Mineralwasser mischen* ◆ *Beton mischen; (a cocktail)* mixen [ˈmɪksn̩] +haben ◊ *jdm einen Drink mixen* mix sth and sth together etw. mit etw. vermischen [mɪt ... fɛˌmɪʃn̩] <vermischt, vermischte, hat vermischt> ◊ *das Pulver mit dem Wasser vermischen* sth mixes etw. vermischt sich ◊ *Öl und Wasser vermischen sich nicht.* **2.** *(activities, features etc.)* mix sth with sth etw. mit etw. verbinden [mɪt ... fɛˌbɪndn̩] <verbindet, verband, hat verbunden> mix business with pleasure das Angenehme mit dem Nützlichen verbinden sth mixes with sth etw. verbindet sich mit etw. **3.** *(have regular contact)* mix with sb mit jdm verkehren [mɪt ... fɛˌkeːrən] <verkehrt, verkehrte, hat verkehrt> ◊ *Seine Eltern wollen nicht, dass er mit uns verkehrt.; (get to know better)* mix with sb jdn (näher) kennen lernen [(ˌnɛːɐ) ˈkɛnən lɛˈnən] +haben ◊ *Beim Betriebsausflug konnte ich meine Kollegen besser kennen lernen.; (have social contacts)* mix (with other people) unter Leute kommen [ʊntə ˈlɔɡtə kɔmən] <kommt, kam, ist gekommen> ◊ *Du solltest mehr unter Leute kommen.*

◉ **mix and match sth** etw. kombinieren **not mix** nicht zusammenpassen

• **mix up** [phras v] **1.** *(mistake for)* mix sb/sth up (with sb/sth) jdn (mit jdm/etw.) verwechseln [fɛˈvɛksl̩n] <verwechselt, verwechselte, hat verwechselt> ◊ *Er hat die beiden (miteinander) verwechselt.* **2.** *(mess up)* mix sth up etw. durcheinander bringen [dʊˈçˌlaɛˈnandə brɪŋən] <bringt, brachte, hat gebracht> ◊ *Sie hat die Rechnungen ganz durcheinander gebracht.*

mixed → **mix²** [adj] gemischt [gəˈmɪʃt] *no comp/superl* ◊ *ein gemischter Salat* ◆ *gemischte Gefühle haben* ◆

Das Publikum war bunt gemischt.

mixed-up [adj] **1.** *(confused)* durcheinander [dʊˈçˌlaeˈnandə] *no comp/superl, not before ns (fam)* ◊ *Die Zahlen sind alle durcheinander.* ◆ *Nach dem Streit war ich ganz durcheinander.* **2.** *(emotionally unstable)* labil [laˈbiːl] ◊ *eine labile junge Frau* ◆ *Ihr neuer Freund ist ziemlich labil.*

◉ **be mixed up in sth** in etw. [acc] verwickelt sein **get mixed up with sb** sich mit jdm einlassen

mixture [noun] Mischung [ˈmɪʃʊŋ] die <–, –en> ◊ *Die Musik ist eine Mischung aus Jazz und Hip-Hop.*

moan [verb] **1.** *(make a low sound)* stöhnen [ˈʃtøːnən] +haben ◊ *Sie stöhnte lustvoll.* ◆ *„Ich schaffe das nicht",* stöhnte er.; *(in pain, irritation)* jammern [ˈjamɐn] +haben ◊ *„Das tut so web",* jammerte das Kind. ◆ *Sie jammert ständig über die viele Arbeit.*

mob [noun] **1.** *(crowd)* Pöbel [ˈpøːbl̩] der <–s, –> ◊ *Der Pöbel stürmte das Rathaus.* ◆ *der Pöbel auf der Straße* mob rule die Herrschaft des Pöbels mob law Lynchjustiz [ˈlʏnçjustiːts] die <–> *no pl* ◊ *ein Opfer der Lynchjustiz* **2.** *(group of criminals)* Mafia [ˈmafiaː] die <–, –s> ◊ *die sizilianische/russische Mafia* **3.** *(group of people)* Bande [ˈbandə] die <–, –n> ◊ *Ihr seid schon eine undankbare Bande.*

mobile¹ [noun] **1.** *(phone)* Handy [ˈhɛndiː] das <–s, –s> ◊ *mit dem Handy telefonieren* **2.** *(for decoration)* Mobile [ˈmoːbilə] das <–s, –s> ◊ *ein Mobile über dem Kinderbett*

mobile² [adj] **1.** *(able to move or be moved)* beweglich [bəˈveːklɪç] ◊ *ein bewegliches Regal auf Rollen* ◆ *Mit dem Gipsbein bin ich nicht sehr beweglich.* **2.** *(able to travel)* mobil [moˈbiːl] ◊ *ein mobiles Einsatzkommando* ◆ *Mein Auto ist repariert — jetzt bin ich wieder mobil!* ◆ *Moderne Arbeitnehmer müssen mobil sein.* **3.** *(library, clinic etc.)* fahrbar [ˈfaːʁbaːʁ] *no comp/superl, mostly before ns* ◊ *ein fahrbares Labor* ◆ *eine fahrbare Würstchenbude*

mobile phone [noun] Handy [ˈhɛndiː] das <–s, –s>

mobility [noun] **1.** *(physical)* Beweglichkeit [bəˈveːklɪçkaɛt] die <–> *no pl* ◊ *eingeschränkte Beweglichkeit aufgrund von Schmerzen* **2.** *(ability to move or travel)* Mobilität [mobiliˈtɛːt] die <–> *no pl* ◊ *die Mobilität in der modernen Gesellschaft*

mobilize [verb] mobilisieren [mobiliˈziːrən] <mobilisiert, mobilisierte, hat mobilisiert> ◊ *Truppen/die Wähler/die letzten Kräfte mobilisieren*

mock¹ [adj] **1.** *(fake)* mock knife/gun etc. Attrappe [aˈtrapə] die <–, –n> ◊ *Die Kamera war nur eine Attrappe.* **2.** *(feigned, pretend)* gespielt [gəˈʃpiːlt] *no comp/superl* ◊ *mit gespielter Entrüstung; (not real)* mock ... Schein... [ʃaen] mock attack Scheinangriff [ˈʃaenˌaŋrɪf] der <–(e)s, –e> mock battle Scheingefecht [ˈʃaengəfɛçt] das <–(e)s, –e> **3.** *(for practice)* zur Übung [tsuːɐ ˈyːbʊŋ] do a mock interview/presentation ein Vorstellungsgespräch/eine Präsentation zur Übung durchspielen mock exam Übungsarbeit [ˈyːbʊŋsˌarbaet] die <–, –en>

mock² [verb] *(with words)* spotten [ˈʃpɔtn̩] <spottet, spottete, hat gespottet> ◊ *„Sehr beldenhaft!",* spottete er. mock sb/sth sich über jdn/etw. lustig machen [yːbɐ ... ˈlʊstɪç maxn̩] +haben ◊ *Machst du dich über mich lustig?*

mockery [noun] Hohn [hoːn] der <–(e)s> *no pl* ◊ *Dieses Gerichtsurteil ist blanker Hohn!*

◉ **make a mockery of sth** etw. zur Farce machen

mocking(ly) [adj, adv] höhnisch [ˈhøːnɪʃ] ◊ *Seine höhni-*

A

schen Worte verletzten mich. ◆ *Sein Lachen war höhnisch.* ◆ *Sie grinste höhnisch.*

modal verb [noun] Modalverb [mo'da:lvɛ'p] das <-s, –en>

mode [noun] **1.** *(form, type)* Form [fɔ'm] die <-, –en> ◊ *verschiedene Formen der Kommunikation; (way of doing sth)* Weise ['vaezə] die <-, –n> mode of payment Zahlungsweise ['ʦa:lʊŋsvaezə] 2. TECHN, TECHN *(of a machine)* Betriebsart [bə'tri:psǀa:'t] die <-, –en>; *(of a computer)* Modus ['mo:dʊs] der <-, Modi> automatic mode Automatikbetrieb [aoto'ma:tɪkbətri:p] manual mode Handbetrieb ['hantbətri:p] **3.** *(emotional state)* be in … mode auf etw. eingestellt sein [aof … ˌaengəʃtɛlt zaen] ◊ *Ich war ganz auf Urlaub eingestellt.* in happy mode glücklich ['glʏklɪç] **4.** *(style)* Stil [ʃti:l] der <-(e)s, –e> ◊ *ein Text in ironischem Stil*

model¹ [noun] **1.** *(small copy, ideal example, type)* Modell [mo'dɛl] das <-s, –e> ◊ *ein maßstabsgetreues Modell des Tadsch Mahal* ◆ *Sie war das bevorzugte Modell des Künstlers.* ◆ *Dieses Auto ist das neueste Modell.* model railway Modelleisenbahn [mo'dɛlǀaeznba:n] die <-, –en> **2.** *(to be admired or imitated)* Vorbild ['fo:ɐbɪlt] das <-(e)s, –er> ◊ *Du bist deiner Schwester kein gutes Vorbild.* a model of … ein Muster an … [dat] [aen 'mʊstɐ an] das <-s, –> ◊ *Er ist ein Muster an Geduld.* model farm Musterfarm ['mʊstɐfa'm] die <-, –en> model husband Mustergatte ['mʊstɐgatə] der <-n, –n> **3.** *(for a work of literature or art)* Vorlage ['fo:ɐla:gə] die <-, –n> ◊ *die historische Vorlage für meinen Roman; (for formal documents)* Muster ['mʊstɐ] das <-s, –> ◊ *ein Muster für einen Lebenslauf* **4.** *(fashion)* model Model ['mɔdl] das <-s, –s> ◊ *Sie möchte Model werden.* ◆ *ein gefragtes Model*

model² [verb] **1.** *(work as a model)* als Model arbeiten [als 'mɔdl a'baetn] <arbeitet, arbeitete, hat gearbeitet>; *(wear a particular piece of clothing)* model sth etw. vorführen ['fo:ɐfy:rən] +haben ◊ *Sie führte ein Kleid von Gucci vor.* **2.** *(allow yourself to be painted or photographed: in a standing position)* model for sb/sth jdm/für etw. Modell stehen [fy:ɐ … mo'dɛl ʃte:ən] <steht, stand, hat gestanden>; *(in a sitting position)* jdm/für etw. Modell sitzen [fy:ɐ … mo'dɛl zɪtsn] <sitzt, saß, hat gesessen> **3.** *(copy)* model sth on sth etw. nach dem Vorbild … [gen] gestalten [na:x de:m ˌfo:ɐbɪlt … gəʃtaltn] <gestaltet, gestaltete, hat gestaltet> ◊ *Die Schulen sind nach dem Vorbild des amerikanischen Systems gestaltet.* model yourself on sb sich [dat] jdn zum Vorbild nehmen [tsʊm 'fo:ɐbɪlt ne:mən] <nimmt, nahm, hat genommen> **4.** *(plan, design)* model sth ein Modell einer Sache [gen] entwerfen [aen mo'dɛl … ɛnt,vɛ'fn] <entwirft, entwarf, hat entworfen> ◊ *am Computer ein Modell des Gebäudes entwerfen* **5.** *(in clay, wax etc.)* model sth into sth etw. aus etw. modellieren [aos … mɔdɛˌli:rən] <modelliert, modellierte, hat modelliert> ◊ *Figuren aus Wachs modellieren*

moderate¹ [adj] **1.** *(not high or low, large or small)* mäßig ['mɛ:sɪç] ◊ *bei mäßiger Hitze garen* ◆ *Der Preisanstieg war mäßig.* **2.** *(reasonable)* gemäßigt [gə'mɛ:sɪçt] ◊ *gemäßigte Ansichten* ◆ *Der Ton des Schreibens ist gemäßigt.* **3.** *(not excessive in your consumption)* maßvoll ['ma:sfɔl] ◊ *ein maßvoller Raucher*

moderate² [verb] **1.** *(make less extreme)* mäßigen ['mɛ:sɪgn] +haben ◊ *Du solltest deinen Ton ihm gegenüber mäßigen.* **2.** *(a debate)* leiten ['laetn] <leitet, leitete, hat geleitet> ◊ *eine Podiumsdiskussion leiten* **3.** *(exam papers)* nachkorrigieren ['na:xkɔrigi:rən] <korrigiert nach, korrigierte nach, hat nachkorrigiert> ◊ *Wer wird die Arbeiten nachkorrigieren?*

moderately [adv] mäßig ['mɛ:sɪç] ◊ *Sie trinkt nur mäßig.* ◆ *Das Match war nur mäßig spannend.*

modern [adj] modern [mo'dɛ'n] ◊ *die Möglichkeiten der modernen Medizin* ◆ *Sein Stil ist modern.*

modest(ly) [adj, adv] **1.** *(moderate, humble)* bescheiden [bə'ʃaedn] ◊ *Trotz ihres Erfolges ist sie bescheiden geblieben.* ◆ *nur bescheidene Ansprüche stellen* ◆ *bescheidene Fortschritte machen* ◆ *Sein Einkommen ist eher bescheiden.* ◆ *einfach und bescheiden leben* **2.** *(shy)* schüchtern ['ʃʏçtɐn] ◊ *Sie war zu schüchtern, um in die Sauna zu gehen.* ◆ *Sie bedeckte schüchtern ihre Blöße.; (clothing)* dezent [de'tsɛnt] <dezenter, am dezentesten> ◊ *ein dezentes knielanges Kleid* ◆ *sich dezent kleiden*

modification [noun] Änderung ['ɛndərʊŋ] die <-, –en> ◊ *eine kleine Änderung des Plans* ◆ *Bitte nehmen Sie die nötigen Änderungen am Programm vor.*

modify [verb] **1.** ändern ['ɛndɐn] +haben ◊ *eine Liste ändern* ◆ *sein Verhalten ändern* a modified version eine leicht geänderte Version **2.** GRAM *(a word, phrase)* näher bestimmen [ˌnɛ:ɐ bə'ʃtɪmən] <bestimmt, bestimmte, hat bestimmt> ◊ *Adjektive können durch Adverbien näher bestimmt werden.* ◉ genetically modified gentechnisch verändert

module [noun] Modul [mo'du:l] das <-s, –e> *(tech)*

moisture [noun] Feuchtigkeit ['fɔyçtɪçkaet] die <-> no pl

mold → mould

mole [noun] **1.** *(also fig)* ZOO Maulwurf ['maolvʊ'f] der <-(e)s, Maulwürfe> ◊ *Maulwürfe im Garten haben* ◆ *Er war als Maulwurf für die Konkurrenz tätig.* **2.** ANAT Muttermal ['mʊtɐma:l] das <-(e)s, –e> ◊ *ein Muttermal wegen Krebsverdachts entfernen* **3.** ARCH Mole ['mo:lə] die <-, –n> ◊ *Das Boot machte an der Mole fest.* **4.** CHEM Mol [mo:l] das <-s, –e>

molecular [adj] molekular [moleku'la:'] no comp/ superl, only before n ◊ *auf molekularer Ebene*

molecule [noun] Molekül [mole'ky:l] das <-s, –e> water molecule Wassermolekül ['vasemole,ky:l]

mom [noun] Mama ['mama(:)] die <-, –s> *(fam)* ◊ *„Ich will zu meiner Mama!", rief das Kind.*

moment [noun] **1.** *(short period of time)* Augenblick [aogn'blɪk] der <-(e)s, –e> ◊ *den richtigen Augenblick abwarten* any moment jeden Augenblick ◆ *Er muss jeden Augenblick kommen.* for a moment einen Augenblick lang a moment einen Augenblick brauchen take a moment einen Augenblick dauern just a moment einen Augenblick, bitte for the moment fürs Erste [fy:ɐs 'e:ɐstə] in a moment gleich [glaeç] ◊ *Ich bin gleich fertig.* **2.** *(important time)* Stunde ['ʃtʊndə] die <-, –n> ◊ *Das war die schwerste Stunde seines Lebens.* ◆ *Ihre große Stunde war endlich gekommen.* of the moment der Stunde ◊ *Er ist der Mann für diese Stunde!* the moment of truth die Stunde der Wahrheit ◉ at this moment in time zum gegenwärtigen Zeitpunkt every spare moment jede freie Minute

seize the moment die Gelegenheit ergreifen **at the moment** im Moment **not for one moment** absolut nicht

momentarily [adv] **1.** *(briefly)* einen Moment lang [ˈeɪnən moˈmɛnt laŋ] ◊ *Sie zögerte einen Moment lang.* **2.** *(in the US: soon)* gleich [glaɪç] ◊ *Wir werden das Ergebnis gleich erfahren.*

momentary [adj] vorübergehend [foˈrɪːbeɡeːənt] ◊ *eine vorübergehende Besserung* ◆ *Die Freude war nur vorübergehend.*

momentum [noun] **1.** *(speed, movement)* Schwung [ʃvʊŋ] der <–es> no pl ◊ *einer Entwicklung neuen Schwung verleihen* ◆ *Schwung verlieren* gain **momentum** in Schwung kommen maintain the **momentum** of sth etw. in Schwung halten **2.** PHYSICS Impuls [ɪmˈpʊls] der <–(e)s, –e>

mommy → mom

monarch [noun] Monarch [moˈnaʳç] der <–en, –en> ♀Monarchin [moˈnaʳçɪn] die <–, –nen>

monarchy [noun] **1.** *(system, state)* Monarchie [monaˈʳçiː] die <–, –n> ◊ *Großbritannien ist eine konstitutionelle Monarchie.* **2.** *(ruling person or family)* Krone [ˈkroːnə] die <–, –n> ◊ *die schwedische Krone*

monastery [noun] Kloster [ˈkloːstɐ] das <–s, Klöster> ◊ *ins Kloster gehen*

Monday [noun] Montag [ˈmoːntaːk] der <–(e)s, –e> ◊ *Die Ware wird am Montag geliefert.* ◆ *von Montag bis Freitag arbeiten* ◆ *ein regnerischer Montag* ◆ *Nächsten Montag ist Feiertag.* ◆ *Heute ist Montag, der 12. April.* **on Monday** (am) Montag ◊ *Hast du (am) Montag Zeit?* **on Mondays** montags [ˈmoːntaːks] **Monday evening** Montagabend [ˌmoːntaːkˈʔaːbm̩t] der <–s, –e> **on Monday evening** (am) Montagabend ◊ *Hast du Montagabend schon was vor?* **Monday morning** Montagmorgen [ˌmoːntaːkˈmoʳɡn̩] der <–s, –> most sing

monetary [adj] **1.** *(relating to a particular currency)* monetary ... Währungs... [ˈvɛːrʊŋs] monetary policy Währungspolitik [ˈvɛːrʊŋspoliˌtiːk] die <–, –en> monetary union Währungsunion [ˈvɛːrʊŋsʔuˌnioːn] die <–, –en> **2.** *(relating to state finances)* monetary ... Finanz... [fiˈnants] monetary authority Finanzbehörde [fiˈnantsbəhøːɐ̯də] die <–, –n> **3.** *(relating to money in general)* monetary ... Geld... [ɡɛlt] monetary fine Geldbuße [ˈɡɛltbuːsə] die <–, –n> monetary value Geldwert [ˈɡɛltveːɐ̯t] der <–(e)s, –e> most sing ◊ *Der Schmuck hat keinen besonderen Geldwert.*

money [noun] Geld [ɡɛlt] das <–(e)s, –er> ◊ *viel/wenig Geld haben* ◆ *Geld sparen/verdienen* ◆ *Die Neuerung kostet den Staat viel Geld.* ◆ *öffentliche Gelder* ◆ *Hast du schweizerisches Geld?* **make money** Geld verdienen spend money (on sth) Geld (für etw.) ausgeben be out of money kein Geld haben ⊕ **get your money's worth** etwas für sein Geld bekommen **have money to burn** Geld wie Heu haben *(fam)* **not be made of money** kein Krösus sein *(fam)*

monitor¹ [noun] **1.** *(screen, device)* Monitor [ˈmoːnitoːɐ̯] der <–s, –en or –e> ◊ *Mein Monitor flimmert.* ◆ *von einem Monitor überwachte Räume* **2.** *(person)* Aufsicht [ˈaʊfzɪçt] die <–, –en> ◊ *Die Aufsicht kontrollierte seine Tasche.; (in school)* ein Schüler oder eine Schülerin, der/die dem Lehrer assistiert

monitor² [verb] überwachen [ybɐˈvaxn̩] <überwacht, überwachte, hat überwacht> ◊ *den Verkehr überwachen*

monitoring [noun] Überwachung [ybɐˈvaxʊŋ] die <–> no pl

monk [noun] Mönch [mœnç] der <–(e)s, –e> ◊ *Ihr Sohn ist Mönch geworden.* ◆ *Die Mönche beten in der Kirche.*

monkey [noun] **1.** ZOO Affe [ˈafə] der <–n, –n> **2.** *(naughty child)* Schlingel [ˈʃlɪŋl̩] der <–s, –> *(hum)* ◊ *Na, du kleiner Schlingel?* cheeky monkey Frechdachs [ˈfrɛçdaks] der <–es, –e> *(fam)* ⊕ **sb couldn't give a monkey's for sth** etw. kümmert jdn nicht who gives a monkey's wen kümmert es

monolingual(ly) [adj, adv] einsprachig [ˈaɪnʃpraːxɪç] no comp/superl ◊ *ein einsprachiges Wörterbuch* ◆ *Die wenigsten Länder sind einsprachig.* ◆ *einsprachig aufwachsen*

monopoly [noun] Monopol [monoˈpoːl] das <–s, –e> ◊ *ein Monopol missbrauchen* ◆ *das staatliche Monopol auf Sportwetten*

monotonous(ly) [adj, adv] eintönig [ˈaɪntøːnɪç] ◊ *eine eintönige Stimme* ◆ *Ihr Leben ist recht eintönig.* ◆ *Er sprach so eintönig, dass ich fast einschlief.*

monster [noun] **1.** *(horrible creature, person)* Ungeheuer [ˈʊŋɡəhɔɪ̯ɐ] das <–s, –> ◊ *das Ungeheuer von Loch Ness* ◆ *Was ist er doch für ein Ungeheuer!* **2.** *(huge organization or structure)* Koloss [koˈlɔs] der <–es, –e> ◊ *Das Schiff/Die Firma ist ein riesiger Koloss.*

month [noun] Monat [ˈmoːnat] der <–(e)s, –e> ◊ *die Veranstaltungen des kommenden Monats* ◆ *im vergangenen Monat* ◆ *Der Termin ist Anfang/Mitte/Ende des Monats.* ◆ *ein fünf Monate altes Kind* ◆ *Das kann ja noch Monate dauern!* per month pro Monat in the month of January/February etc. im Januar/ Februar etc.

monthly [adj, adv] monatlich [ˈmoːnatlɪç] when used as an adj, only before ns ◊ *Der monatliche Beitrag beträgt 20 Euro.* ◆ *Was verdienst du monatlich?*

monument [noun] Denkmal [ˈdɛŋkmaːl] das <–s, Denkmäler> ◊ *ein Denkmal enthüllen*

mood [noun] **1.** *(specific state of mind)* Laune [ˈlaʊnə] die <–, –n> ◊ *jdm die Laune verderben* ◆ *Ich habe sehr unter deinen Launen zu leiden.* in a bad/good mood guter/schlechter Laune be in a good/bad mood schlechte Laune haben be in a mood schlechte Laune haben be in an angry/a relaxed mood ärgerlich/entspannt sein [ˈɛʳɡeltɪç/ɛntˈʃpant zaɛn] **2.** *(atmosphere that prevails somewhere, emotional state for doing sth)* Stimmung [ˈʃtɪmʊŋ] die <–, –en> ◊ *Das Foto kann die Stimmung nicht ganz wiedergeben.* ◆ *Die Stimmung im Land ist angespannt.* be in no mood to do sth nicht in der Stimmung sein, etw. zu tun ◊ *Ich bin jetzt nicht in der Stimmung, mit dir zu spielen.* sb is in no mood for sth jdm ist nicht nach etw. zumute [ɪst ˌnɪçt naːx ... ʦuˌmuːtə] ◊ *Mir ist jetzt nicht nach Witzen zumute.* be in the mood for sth auf etw. [acc] Lust haben [aʊf ... ˌlʊst haːbm̩] +haben ◊ *Ich hätte jetzt Lust auf ein Glas Wein.* be in the mood to do sth Lust dazu haben, etw. zu tun ◊ *Hast du Lust dazu, mit mir zu tanzen?* ⊕ **when the mood takes sb** wenn jd in Stimmung ist

A
B
C
D
E
F
G
H
I
J
K
L
M
N
O
P
Q
R
S
T
U
V
W
X
Y
Z

moon [noun] Mond [moːnt] der <-(e)s, -e> ◊ *Der Mond geht auf.* ♦ *die Monde des Saturn* ⊙ *once in a blue moon* alle Jubeljahre (einmal) (fam, hum) *be over the moon (about sth)* überglücklich (über etw. [acc]) sein

moor[1] [noun] **1.** *(bog)* Moor [moːɐ] das <-(e)s, -e> ◊ *eine Wanderung durchs Moor machen* **2.** *(heath)* Heide ['haedə] die <-, -n>

moor[2] [verb] festmachen ['fɛstmaxn̩] <macht fest, machte fest, hat festgemacht> ◊ *Sie hat das Kanu am Steg festgemacht.* ♦ *Das Schiff machte im Hafen von Genua fest.*

mop up [verb] *(a liquid)* aufwischen ['aʊfvɪʃn̩] +haben ◊ *Er wischte das Wasser vom Boden auf.*

moral[1] [noun] **1.** morals Moral [moˈraːl] die <-> no pl ◊ *die christliche Moral* have *no morals* unmoralisch sein ['ʊnmoraːlɪʃ zaɛn] +sein **2.** *(of a tale)* Moral [moˈraːl] die <-> no pl ◊ *Und was ist die Moral von der Geschichte?*

moral[2] [adj] moralisch [moˈraːlɪʃ] ◊ *Du hast die moralische Verpflichtung, ihr zu helfen.* ♦ *Politik ist nicht moralisch.*

morale [noun] Stimmung ['ʃtɪmʊŋ] die <-, -en> ◊ *Die Stimmung unter den Mitarbeitern war schlecht.*

morality [noun] Moral [moˈraːl] die <-> no pl ◊ *Anstand und Moral*

more[1] [adv] **1.** *(before adj or adv)* more ... (than sb/sth) ...er (als jd/etw.) [...e (als ...)] more complicated komplizierter [kɔmpliˈtsiːɐtə] more often öfter ['œftɐ] more reasonable vernünftiger [fɛˈnʏnftɪgɐ] **2.** *(closer to being)* more ... than ever ... als [eːɐ ... als] ◊ *Er ist eher schlank als dick.* **3.** *(modifying verbs)* mehr [meːɐ] ◊ *Du solltest mehr lernen.* ♦ *In diesem Sommer regnet es mehr als sonst.* the more ..., the more ... je mehr ..., umso ... ◊ *Je mehr sie sich anstrengte, umso mehr Fehler machte sie.* **4.** *(with quantities, numbers)* noch [nɔx] ◊ *noch ein paar Tage* ♦ *Noch drei Aufgaben, dann haben wir es geschafft.* **5.** no more, not any more nicht mehr [nɪçt meːɐ] ◊ *Sie lebt nicht mehr.* ♦ *Ich kann nicht mehr hier bleiben.* **6.** more and more zusehends ['tsuːzeːənts] ◊ *Dieses Thema gewinnt zusehends an Bedeutung.* **7.** more than über ['yːbɐ] ◊ *ein Film von über drei Stunden Länge* ♦ *Diese Bluse hat über 100 Euro gekostet.* more than ever mehr denn je [meːɐ dɛn 'jeː] more than happy/likely etc. sehr glücklich/wahrscheinlich etc. [zeːɐ 'glʏklɪç/vaːˈʃaenlɪç] no more than nur [nuːɐ] ◊ *Sie hatten nur noch zwei Minuten Zeit.* not much more than kaum mehr als [kaom meːɐ als] ◊ *Wir hatten kaum mehr als die Hälfte geschafft.* It took not much more than a minute. *Es dauerte kaum länger als eine Minute.*

more[2] [det] mehr [meːɐ] indefinite and invariable ◊ *Ich bekomme mehr Geld und Unterstützung.* ♦ *Wir haben noch viel mehr Zeit.* more and more immer mehr ◊ *Immer mehr junge Paare entscheiden sich zur Heirat.* no more ... keine ... mehr ◊ *Ich will keine Ausreden mehr hören.*

more[3] [indef pron] mehr [meːɐ] ◊ *Das ist mehr, als ich erwartet habe.* ⊙ *the more the merrier* je mehr umso besser *no more can/do/will etc.* I ich auch nicht

moreover [adv] außerdem ['aosedeːm] ◊ *Außerdem müssen wir bedenken, dass ...* ♦ *Er ist reich und sieht außerdem gut aus.*

morning [noun] **1.** *(until after breakfast time)* Morgen ['mɔrgn̩] der <-s, -> ◊ *früh am Morgen aufstehen* ♦ *heute Morgen* tomorrow morning morgen früh [ˌmɔrgn̩ 'fryː] in the morning(s) morgens ['mɔrgn̩s] ◊ *Die Kinder möchten morgens länger schlafen.* ♦ *um sechs Uhr morgens* **2.** *(time before lunch)* Vormittag ['foːɐmɪtaːk] der <-s, -e> ◊ *gestern Vormittag* ♦ *Am Vormittag scheint die Sonne in dieses Zimmer.* ♦ *im Laufe des Vormittags* in the morning(s) vormittags ['foːɐmɪtaːks] ◊ *Vormittags sind die Kinder in der Schule.* ⊙ *morning, noon and night* Tag und Nacht

mortal [adj] **1.** *(human, not eternal)* sterblich ['ʃtɛrplɪç] no comp/superl ◊ *Alle Menschen sind sterblich.* ♦ *Zeus hatte zwei Kinder von sterblichen Müttern.* mortal remains sterbliche Überreste **2.** *(deadly, fatal)* tödlich ['tøːtlɪç] ◊ *jdm tödliche Verletzungen zufügen* ♦ *Der Stich war nicht tödlich.* mortal danger Lebensgefahr ['leːbm̩sɡəfaːɐ] die <-> no pl *be in mortal danger* in Lebensgefahr schweben mortal enemy Todfeind ['toːtfaent] der <-(e)s, -e> mortal fear Todesangst ['toːdəsˌaŋst] die <-> no pl ⊙ *strike a mortal blow to sb/sth* jdm/etw. den Todesstoß versetzen

mortality [noun] Sterblichkeit ['ʃtɛrplɪçkaet] die <-> no pl

mortgage [noun] Hypothek [hypoˈteːk] die <-, -en> ◊ *Er hat auf sein Haus eine Hypothek aufgenommen.* ♦ *Das Haus ist mit einer Hypothek belastet.*

mosaic [noun] Mosaik [mozaˈiːk] das <-s, -e>

mosque [noun] Moschee [mɔˈʃeː] die <-, -n>

mosquito [noun] Mücke ['mʏkə] die <-, -n>

moss [noun] Moos [moːs] das <-es, -e>

most[1] [adv] **1.** *(before adj)* the most ... der/die/das ...ste [deːɐ/diː/das ...stə] the most complicated task die komplizierteste Aufgabe the most important question die wichtigste Frage according to the most recent findings nach jüngsten Erkenntnissen [naːx ˌjʏŋstn̩ ɛˈkɛntnɪsn̩] sb's most ... jds ...ster/...ste/...stes [...stɐ/...stə/...stəs] my most private wish mein geheimster Wunsch; *(before adv)* most ... am ...sten [am ...stn̩] most frequently am häufigsten [am 'hɔyfçstn̩] most likely am wahrscheinlichsten [am vaːˈʃaenlɪçstn̩]; *(predicative)* ... is/are the most ... ist/sind am ...sten [ɪst/zɪnt am ...stn̩] This painting is the most beautiful. *Dieses Bild ist am schönsten.* Of all my friends he is the most reliable. *Von allen meinen Freunden ist er am zuverlässigsten.* **2.** *(extremely)* höchst [høːçst] ◊ *Es ist höchst unwahrscheinlich, dass er noch kommt.; (very)* sehr [zeːɐ] ◊ *Sie ist eigentlich immer sehr pünktlich.* **3.** *(modifying verbs)* the most am meisten [am 'maestn̩] ◊ *Weißt du, wovor ich mich am meisten fürchte?* ♦ *Am meisten habe ich mich über dich geärgert.* most of all am allermeisten [am 'aleˈmaestn̩]

most[2] [det] meiste ['maestə] der/die/das meiste ... ◊ *Sie verdient das meiste Geld von uns.* ♦ *Die meisten Menschen glauben nicht an Wunder.*

most[3] [pron] **1.** *(most people)* die meisten [di: 'maestn̩] ◊ *Die meisten ekeln sich vor Spinnen.* **2.** *(the largest part of sth)* (the) most das meiste [das 'maestə] ◊ *Das meiste, wie er sagt, ist richtig.* ♦ *Ich habe das meiste schon fertig.; (the largest amount possible)* the most das Äußerste [das 'ɔysestə] <-n> no pl ◊ *Das ist das Äußerste, was ich tun kann.*

⊛ **at (the very) most** höchstens

mostly [adv] **1.** *(usually)* meistens ['maəstn̩s] ◊
Meistens esse ich Müsli zum Frühstück. **2.** *(for the
largest part)* zumeist [ʦu'maəst] ◊ *Die zumeist weiblichen Fans waren begeistert.*

MOT ⊖*TÜV* [tʏf] der ◊ *Mein Auto ist nicht durch den
TÜV gekommen.*

mother [noun] Mutter ['mʊtɐ] die <-, Mütter> ◊
meine Mutter und mein Vater ♦ *Sie ist jetzt Mutter.*
⊛ **the mother of ...** *(the very first)* die Wiege ...
[gen] ◊ *Griechenland gilt als die Wiege der Demokratie.*

mother-in-law [noun] Schwiegermutter ['ʃviːgɐmʊtɐ]
die <-, Schwiegermütter>

mother tongue [noun] Muttersprache ['mʊtɐʃpraːxə]
die <-, -n>

motif [noun] **1.** *(shape, pattern)* Muster ['mʊstɐ] das
<-s, -> ◊ *eine Krawatte mit dezentem Muster* **2.** *(in
art, literature, music)* Motiv [mo'tiːf] das <-s, -e> ◊
Dieses Motiv zieht sich durch alle seine Romane.

motion [noun] **1.** *(movement)* Bewegung [bə've:gʊŋ] die
<-, -en> ◊ *die Bewegung der Erde um die Sonne* ♦
eine plötzliche Bewegung mit der Hand machen ♦ **be
in motion** sich bewegen [bə've:gn̩] <bewegt sich,
bewegte sich, hat sich bewegt> **2.** *(in a parliament,
meeting)* Antrag ['antraːk] der <-(e)s, Anträge> ◊
einen Antrag stellen/annehmen **3.** *(bowel movement)*
Stuhlgang ['ʃtuːlɡaŋ] der <-(e)s> *no pl; (solid body
waste)* Stuhl [ʃtuːl] der <-(e)s> *no pl*
⊛ **go through the motions of doing sth 1.** *(perform
sth without enthusiasm)* etw. der Form halber tun
2. *(simulate sth)* etw. durchspielen **set sth in
motion** etw. in Gang bringen

motionless [adj] unbeweglich ['ʊnbəve:klɪç] ◊ *ein
unbewegliches Ziel* ♦ *Sein Gesicht blieb völlig unbeweglich.*

motivate [verb] motivieren [moti'vi:rən] <motiviert,
motivierte, hat motiviert> ◊ *Wie kann man Kinder
dazu motivieren, mehr zu lesen?* The crime was
motivated by jealousy. Das Motiv der Tat war Eifersucht.

motivation [noun] Motivation [motiva'ʦjo:n] die
<-, -en> ◊ *Ihr fehlt die Motivation zum Arbeiten.* ♦
Die Mitarbeiter haben ihre Motivation verloren.

motive [noun] **1.** *(for an action, a crime)* Motiv [mo'ti:f]
das <-s, -e> ◊ *Was war das Motiv für den Mord?* ♦
Sein Motiv ist, anderen zu helfen. **2.** *(real reason)*
Grund [ɡrʊnt] der <-(e)s, Gründe> ◊ *Der eigentliche
Grund für seinen Anruf war Neugier.* ulterior motive
Hintergedanke ['hɪntɐɡədaŋkə] der <-n, -n>
question sb's motive sich fragen, warum jd das tut
['fra:gŋ̩ va'rʊm ... das ˌtuːt] +haben

motor [noun] *(part of a machine)* Motor ['mo:to:ɐ̯] der
<-s, -en> ◊ *den Motor anlassen/abstellen*

motorcycle [noun] Motorrad ['mo:to:ɐ̯at] das
<-(e)s, Motorräder> ◊ *Motorrad fahren*

motorist [noun] Autofahrer ['aʊtofa:rɐ] der <-s, ->
♀Autofahrerin ['aʊtofa:rərɪn] die <-, -nen>

motorway [noun] Autobahn ['aʊtoba:n] die <-, -en>
◊ *Auf der Autobahn München–Stuttgart gibt es oft
Stau.*

motto [noun] Motto ['mɔto:] das <-s, -s> ◊ *Unser
Motto ist: „Geht nicht, gibts nicht!"*

mould¹, mold [noun] **1.** *(fungus)* Schimmel ['ʃɪml̩] der
<-s, -> ◊ *Die Marmelade hat Schimmel angesetzt.* ♦
Schimmel an den Wänden **2.** *(shaped container)*

Form [fɔrm] die <-, -en> ◊ *Die Bronze wird in eine
Form gegossen.*
⊛ **break the mould** mit der Tradition brechen fit
the mould aus dem gleichen Holz geschnitzt sein

mould², mold [verb] **1.** *(shape)* mould sth (into sth)
etw. (zu etw.) formen ['fɔrmən] +haben ◊ *Sie hat
den Ton zu einem Igel geformt.* **2.** *(make)* mould sb/
sth into sth etw. aus jdm/etw. machen
[aʊs ... maxn̩] +haben ◊ *Er machte aus der Firma ein
Millionenunternehmen.*

mound [noun] **1.** *(small hill)* Hügel ['hy:gl̩] der <-s, ->
◊ *Die Kapelle steht auf einem Hügel.; (with a tomb)*
Grabhügel ['gra:phy:gl̩] **2.** *(heap)* Haufen ['haofn̩] der
<-s, -> ◊ *ein Haufen Sand/Zeitungsausschnitte*

mount [verb] **1.** *(increase)* steigen ['ʃtaegŋ̩] <steigt,
stieg, ist gestiegen> ◊ *Die Spannung stieg mit jeder
Minute.* **2.** *(prepare, begin)* organisieren
[ɔrgani'zi:rən] <organisiert, organisierte, hat organi-
siert> ◊ *eine Spendenaktion zur Rettung des Regen-
waldes organisieren* **3.** *(fix an object in position)*
montieren [mɔn'ti:rən] <montiert, montierte, hat
montiert> ◊ *Die Antenne ist auf dem Dach montiert.;
(a tyre, picture)* aufziehen ['aoftsi:ən] <zieht auf, zog
auf, hat aufgezogen> ◊ *Ich ziehe heute die Winterreifen auf.* **4.** *(get on a horse)* aufsteigen ['aofʃtaegŋ̩]
<steigt auf, stieg auf, ist aufgestiegen> ◊ *Steigen Sie
auf, wir reiten los.* mount a horse auf ein Pferd
steigen [aof aen 'pfe:ɐ̯t ʃtaegŋ̩] <steigt, stieg, ist
gestiegen> mounted beritten [bə'rɪtn̩] ◊ *berittene Polizisten* be mounted on sth auf etw. [dat] reiten
[aof ... raetn̩] <reitet, ritt, ist geritten> ◊ *Er ritt auf
einem Mustang.* **5.** mount the stairs die Treppe
hochsteigen [di: 'trɛpə ˌho:xʃtaegŋ̩] <steigt hoch, stieg
hoch, ist hochgestiegen> ◊ *Sie stieg langsam die
Treppe hoch.*

mountain [noun] Berg [bɛrk] der <-(e)s, -e> ◊ *Wir
fahren im Sommer in die Berge.* ♦ *einen Berg
besteigen* ♦ *Berge von Müll/Arbeit*
⊛ **make a mountain out of a molehill** aus einer
Mücke einen Elefanten machen move mountains
Berge versetzen

mountainous [adj] *(with mountains)* bergig ['bɛrgɪç] ◊
90 Prozent der Fläche Kalabriens sind bergig. ♦ *eine
bergige Landschaft*

mourn [verb] *(a loss, death)* beklagen [bə'kla:gŋ̩]
<beklagt, beklagte, hat beklagt> *(lofty)* ◊ *Er beklagte
den Tod seiner Eltern sehr.* mourn (for) sb um jdn
trauern [ʊm ... ˌtraoən] +haben ◊ *Sie trauert um
ihren Vater.*

mourning [noun] Trauer ['traoɐ] die <-> *no pl* ◊ *Nach
dem Unglück wurde eine dreitägige Trauer angeordnet.* wear mourning dress Trauer tragen be in
mourning for sb um jdn trauern [ʊm ... ˌtraoən]
+haben

mouse [noun] Maus [maos] die <-, Mäuse> ◊ *Die
Katze hat eine Maus gefangen.* ♦ *mit der Maus auf
etw.* [acc] klicken
⊛ **quiet as a mouse** mucksmäuschenstill *(fam)*

moustache, mustache [noun] Schnurrbart
['ʃnʊrbaːɐ̯t] der <-(e)s, Schnurrbärte> ◊ *Er trug/hatte
einen Schnurrbart.*

mouth [noun] **1.** *(of a person)* Mund [mʊnt] der
<-(e)s, Münder> ◊ *den Mund aufmachen/zumachen*
♦ *jdn auf den Mund küssen* sb's mouth waters jdm
läuft das Wasser im Mund zusammen a mouth to
feed ein hungriger Mund zu stopfen **2.** *(of a cave,*

tunnel, container) Öffnung ['œfnʊŋ] die <-, -en> ◊ *die Öffnung der Flasche luftdicht verschließen* **3.** *(of a river)* Mündung ['mʏndʊŋ] die <-, -en> ◊ *die Mündung des Nils*

ⓘ **me and my big mouth** ich und meine große Klappe *(fam)* **keep your mouth shut** den Mund halten *(fam)* **be all mouth** eine große Klappe haben *(fam)*

movable ⓐⓓⓙ beweglich [bə'veːklɪç] *no comp/superl* ◊ *Die Puppe hat bewegliche Arme und Beine.* ♦ *Die Rückenlehne ist beweglich.*

move¹ ⓝⓞⓤⓝ **1.** *(action)* Schritt [ʃrɪt] der <-(e), -e> ◊ *Das ist ein Schritt in die richtige Richtung.* **a move towards sth** ein Schritt zu etw. ◊ *ein wichtiger Schritt zum Schutz der Verbraucher* **2.** *(change)* Bewegung [bə'veːgʊŋ] die <-, -en> ◊ *eine unerwartete Bewegung der Aktienkurse* **move into sth** Wechsel in etw. ⓐⓒⓒ ['vɛksl̩ ɪn] der <-s, -> ◊ *Einige Akademiker planen einen Wechsel in die Wirtschaft.* **3.** *(to a new place)* Umzug ['ʊmtsuːk] der <-(e)s, Umzüge> ◊ *jdm beim Umzug helfen* ♦ *ein Umzug von Cardiff nach Leeds* **4.** *(in board games)* Zug [tsuːk] der <-(e)s, Züge> ◊ *jdn in fünf Zügen matt setzen* **it's sb's move** jd ist am Zug ◊ *Weiß ist am Zug.* ♦ *Du bist am Zug!*

ⓘ **follow sb's every move** jdn nicht aus den Augen lassen **get a move on** sich beeilen ◊ *Beeil dich, sonst kommen wir noch zu spät!* **make a move 1.** *(move)* sich rühren ◊ *Wir rührten uns nicht.* **2.** *(leave)* gehen ◊ *Ich muss jetzt aber wirklich gehen.* **make a move for sth** nach etw. greifen **make a move to do sth** Anstalten machen, etw. zu tun ◊ *Niemand machte Anstalten, den Streit zu beenden.* **make no move to do sth** keine Anstalten machen, etw. zu tun **on the move 1.** *(travelling)* unterwegs **2.** *(active)* in Bewegung **3.** *(progressing quickly)* aufstrebend ◊ *ein aufstrebender Markt*

move² ⓥⓔⓡⓑ **1.** *(also fig) (change the position of sth)* **move sth** etw. bewegen [bə'veːgn̩] <bewegt, bewegte, hat bewegt> ◊ *Ich kann meinen Arm nicht bewegen.* **sb/sth moves** jd/etw. bewegt sich ◊ *Der Zug bewegte sich ganz langsam.* ♦ *Ich konnte mich nicht bewegen.* ♦ *Die Verhandlungen bewegen sich in die falsche Richtung.; (furniture)* **move sth** etw. rücken ['rʏkn̩] +haben ◊ *Sie versuchten, den Schrank von der Wand zu rücken.* **Things are moving.** Die Dinge kommen in Bewegung. **2.** *(in board games)* ziehen ['tsiːən] <zieht, zog, hat gezogen> ◊ *Beim Schach kann man den Bauern nur nach vorne ziehen.* ♦ *Hast du schon gezogen?* **3.** *(in a specific social environment)* **sb moves somewhere** jd/etw. bewegt sich irgendwo [bə'veːkt] <bewegt sich, bewegte sich, hat sich bewegt> ◊ *Sie bewegen sich in den besten Kreisen.* **4.** *(to a different place)* **move to ...** nach ... ziehen [naːx ... 'tsiːən] <zieht, zog, ist gezogen> ◊ *Wann sind sie nach Deutschland gezogen?* **move (house)** umziehen ['ʊmtsiːən] +sein ◊ *Am 1. März ziehen wir um.; (move away)* wegziehen ['vɛktsiːən] +sein ◊ *Sie sind letztes Jahr weggezogen.* **move into sth** in etw. ⓐⓒⓒ einziehen [ɪn ... ˌaɛntsiːən] <zieht ein, zog ein, ist eingezogen> ◊ *Wann zieht ihr in euer neues Haus ein?* **5.** *(take action)* handeln ['handl̩n] +haben ◊ *Der Schulleiter handelte sofort, um die Situation in den Griff zu bekommen.* **6.** *(change)* **move (from sth) to/towards sth** (von etw.) zu etw. übergehen [tsuː ... yːbəgeːən] <geht über, ging über,

ist übergegangen> ◊ *zum nächsten Tagesordnungspunkt übergehen* ♦ *von der sozialistischen Wirtschaft zur freien Marktwirtschaft übergehen; (change your school, course)* **move (from sth) to sth** (von etw.) zu etw. wechseln [tsuː: ... ˌvɛksl̩n] +haben ◊ *Er wechselte vom Gymnasium zur Realschule.* **7.** *(an appointment, a meeting)* verlegen [fɛ'leːgn̩] <verlegt, verlegte, hat verlegt> ◊ *eine Besprechung verlegen* ♦ *Der Arzttermin wurde auf Donnerstag verlegt.* **8.** *(persuade)* **move sb** jdn umstimmen ['ʊmʃtɪmən] +haben ◊ *Du kannst mich nicht umstimmen!; (be persuaded)* **sb moves (on sth)** jd ändert seine Meinung (zu etw.) [ˌɛndɐt ˈzaɛnə ˈmaɛnʊŋ] +haben ◊ *Hat sie ihre Meinung zu diesem Thema inzwischen geändert?* **9.** *(influence)* **move sb to do sth** jdn dazu veranlassen, etw. zu tun [datsu: fɛ|'anlasn̩ ... tsuː] <veranlasst, veranlasste, hat veranlasst> ◊ *Was hat ihn wohl dazu veranlasst, sein Testament zu ändern?* **10.** *(affect emotionally)* **move sb** jdn bewegen [bə'veːgn̩] <bewegt, bewegte, hat bewegt> ◊ *Das Schicksal dieser Kinder bewegt mich sehr.* **move sb to tears** jdn zu Tränen rühren [tsuː: 'trɛːnən ryːrən] +haben; *(music, sb's death)* jdn ergreifen [e'graɛfn̩] <ergreift, ergriff, hat ergriffen> ◊ *Ihr Tod hat uns zutiefst ergriffen.* ♦ *von der Musik ergriffen* **11.** LAW *(make a formal request)* **move (for) sth** etw. beantragen [bə|'antraːgn̩] <beantragt, beantragte, hat beantragt> ◊ *Er beantragte eine Neuwahl.* **12.** *(mostly spoken: leave)* gehen ['geːən] <geht, ging, ist gegangen> ◊ *Komm, es ist Zeit zu gehen!*

ⓘ **move it** schnell machen *(fam)* ◊ *Mach schnell, wir kommen zu spät!*

• **move along** ⓟⓗⓡⓐⓢⓥ **1.** *(walk on)* **sb moves along** jd geht weiter [geːt 'vaɛtɐ] <geht weiter, ging weiter, ist weitergegangen> ◊ *Man sagte uns, wir sollten weitergehen.* **move sb along** jdn zum Weitergehen auffordern [tsʊm 'vaɛtəgeːən ˌaoffoːdɐn] +haben ◊ *Der Polizist forderte die Demonstranten zum Weitergehen auf.* **2.** *(process)* **sth moves along** etw. geht weiter [geːt 'vaɛtɐ] <ging weiter, ist weitergegangen> ◊ *Die Friedensverhandlungen gingen weiter.* **move sth along etw.** vorantreiben [fo'rantraɛbm̩] <treibt voran, trieb voran, hat vorangetrieben> ◊ *ein energischer Vorsitzender, der die Verhandlungen vorantreiben kann*

• **move in** ⓟⓗⓡⓐⓢⓥ **1.** *(move into a new home)* **move in (with sb)** (bei jdm) einziehen ['aɛntsiːən] <zieht ein, zog ein, ist eingezogen> ◊ *Wann ziehen die neuen Mieter ein?* ♦ *Ihr Freund ist bei ihr eingezogen.* **2.** *(army)* **move in (on sb)** (gegen jdn) vorrücken ['foːrʏkn̩] +sein ◊ *Die Regierungstruppen rückten gegen die Rebellen vor.*

• **move into** ⓟⓗⓡⓐⓢⓥ **move into sth** (gain market share) irgendwohin ⓐⓒⓒ vordringen ['foːgdrɪŋən] <dringt vor, drang vor, ist vorgedrungen> ◊ *Die Firma ist mit diesem Produkt auf den japanischen Markt vorgedrungen.* → **move² 4.**

• **move off** ⓟⓗⓡⓐⓢⓥ *(leave)* sich in Bewegung setzen [ɪn bə'veːgʊŋ zɛtsn̩] +haben ◊ *Der Zug setzte sich langsam in Bewegung.*

• **move on** ⓟⓗⓡⓐⓢⓥ **1.** *(travel on)* weiterfahren ['vaɛtəfaːrən] <fährt weiter, fuhr weiter, ist weitergefahren> ◊ *Nach zwei Tagen fuhren wir weiter.* **2.** *(do sth new)* etwas Neues anfangen [ɛtvas 'nɔøəs ˌanfaŋən] <fängt an, fing an, hat angefangen> ◊ *Ich habe zehn Jahre als Lehrer gearbeitet. Ich würde gern etwas Neues anfangen.* **3.** *(to a different

topic etc.) move on to sth zu etw. übergehen [ˈtsuː: ... ˌyːˈbeːgeːən] <geht über, ging über, ist übergegangen> ◊ *Sie gingen zum nächsten Tagesordnungspunkt über.* **4.** *(change in the course of time)* sich ändern [ˈɛndɐn] *+haben* ◊ *Seitdem haben sich die Dinge geändert.*

• **move out** ‹phras v› ausziehen [ˈaʊstsiːən] <zieht aus, zog aus, ist ausgezogen> ◊ *Unsere Nachbarn sind ausgezogen.* move out of sth aus etw. ausziehen

• **move over** ‹phras v› zur Seite rücken [ˈtsuːɐ̯ ˈtsaɛtə ʁʏkn̩] *+sein* ◊ *Er rückte zur Seite und ließ mich vorbei.*

• **move up** ‹phras v› **1.** *(to make room)* sb moves up jd rückt auf [ʁʏkt ˈaʊf] *+sein* ◊ *Alle rückten auf, damit wir einsteigen konnten.* **2.** *(to a better position)* sb moves up jd steigt auf [ˈʃtaɛkt ˈaʊf] <steigt auf, stieg auf, ist aufgestiegen> ◊ *Sie ist zur Abteilungsleiterin aufgestiegen.* move sb up jdn befördern [bəˈfœ̯rdn̩] <befördert, beförderte, hat befördert> ◊ *Er wurde zum Abteilungsleiter befördert.* **3.** *(interest rates etc.)* sth moves up etw. steigt [ʃtaɛkt] <stieg, ist gestiegen> ◊ *Die Preise steigen wieder.*

movement ‹noun› **1.** *(way of moving, change of position, organization, progress)* Bewegung [bəˈveːɡʊŋ] die <-, -en> ◊ *Jede Bewegung ist schmerzhaft für sie.* ♦ *die Bewegung der Aktienkurse* ♦ *eine Bewegung für den Frieden* The movement in his arm is restricted. Er kann den Arm nicht richtig bewegen. get movement in sth etw. in Bewegung bringen **2.** *(of goods)* Beförderung [bəˈfœ̯rdəʁʊŋ] die <-, -en> ◊ *die Beförderung gefährlicher Güter* **3.** *(trend)* movement towards sth/away from sth Trend zu etw./weg von etw. [tʁɛnt ˈtsuː/vɛk fɔn] der <-s, -e> ◊ *ein Trend zu strengeren Qualitätsstandards* ♦ *der Trend weg von der Ehe* **4.** *(activities)* movements of soldiers Truppenbewegungen [ˈtʁʊpm̩bəˌveːɡʊŋən] die <-> *pl* movements of terrorists Aktivitäten von Terroristen [aktiviˌtɛːtn̩ fɔn tɛʁoˈʁɪstn̩] die <-> *pl* **5.** *(in a piece of music)* Satz [zats] der <-es, Sätze> ◊ *das Tempo des zweiten Satzes* **6.** *(of a clock, watch)* Uhrwerk [ˈuːɐ̯vɛʁk] das <-(e)s, -e>

movie ‹noun› **1.** *(film)* Film [fɪlm] der <-(e)s, -e> ◊ *Der Film wurde in Neuseeland gedreht.* **2.** the movies die Filmindustrie [diː ˈfɪlmˌɪndʊsˌtʁiː] <-, -n> ◊ *Sie arbeitet in der Filmindustrie.* **3.** *(cinema)* the movies das Kino [das ˈkiːnoː] <-s, -s> ◊ *Sie geht jeden Sonntag ins Kino.* ♦ *Er ist ein Star des deutschen Kinos.*

movie theater ‹noun› Kino [ˈkiːnoː] das <-s, -s> ◊ *Wir treffen uns um acht vor dem Kino.*

moving ‹verb› → **move²** ‹adj› ergreifend [ɛˈɡʁaɛfn̩t] ◊ *eine ergreifende Geschichte* ♦ *Die Bilder waren wirklich ergreifend.*

mow ‹verb› mähen [ˈmɛːən] *+haben* ◊ *den Rasen mähen*

MP ‹noun› Abgeordnete [ˈapɡəˌʔɔʁdnətə] der/die <-n, die Abgeordneten> *but: ein Abgeordneter/eine Abgeordnete* ◊ *ein Abgeordneter der Labour-Partei* ♦ *Sie ist seit acht Jahren als Abgeordnete tätig.*

Mr ‹noun› Herr [hɛʁ] der <-n, -en> ◊ *Guten Morgen, Herr Fritze!*

Mrs ‹noun› Frau [fʁaʊ] die <-, -en> ◊ *Darf ich Ihnen Frau Billes vorstellen?*

Ms ‹noun› Frau [fʁaʊ] die <-, -en> ◊ *Frau Müller ist*

für die Finanzen zuständig.

much¹ ‹adv› **1.** *(with a verb or past participle, before a comparative)* viel [fiːl] ◊ *Hier hat sich nicht viel verändert.* ♦ *Du isst zu viel.* ♦ *Sie ist viel jünger als ich.* ♦ *Der Artikel ist viel zu kompliziert.* much the same so ziemlich das Gleiche [zoː ˈtsiːmlɪç das ˈɡlaɛçə] much like sth ganz ähnlich wie etw. [ɡants ˈɛːnlɪç viː] ◊ *Dieses Getränk schmeckt ganz ähnlich wie Kaffee.* be much as so wie [zoː viː] The house was much as I had imagined. Das Haus war so, wie ich es mir vorgestellt hatte.; *(before a superlative)* much the biggest bei weitem der/die/das Größte [bae ˈvaɛtəm deːɡ/diː/das ˈɡʁøːstə] **2.** *(expressing that you feel strongly about sth)* (very) much sehr [zeːɐ̯] ◊ *Er war sehr besorgt.* ♦ *Der Song gefällt mir sehr gut.* ♦ *Sie lieben sich sehr.* ♦ *Ich hoffe sehr, dass du mir schreibst.* ♦ *Das stört mich nicht allzu sehr.*

ⓔ for much of the day/night fast den ganzen Tag/die ganze Nacht be very much sth/sb wirklich etw./jd sein ◊ *Die Informationsflut ist wirklich ein Produkt der modernen Technologie.* ♦ *Dieser Erfinder war wirklich ein Genie.* as much as sb likes sb sosehr jd jdn mag ◊ *Sosehr ich sie auch mag, kann ich doch nicht verstehen, warum sie so viel raucht.* thank you very much vielen Dank

much² ‹det› *(amount)* viel [fiːl] *before uncountable ns, indefinite and invariable* ◊ *Wie viel Zeit haben wir noch?* ♦ *nicht viel Mühe machen* ♦ *viel Geld kosten;* *(intensity)* groß [ɡʁoːs] ◊ *größer, am größten> ◊ Es gab großen Ärger wegen ihr.* ♦ *mit großer Begeisterung*

much³ ‹pron› viel [fiːl] *invariable, indefinite* ◊ *Wie viel möchtest du?* ♦ *Er erzählt nie viel von der Schule.* ♦ *Du redest zu viel.* ♦ *Das kostet genauso viel.* ♦ *Wir brauchen doppelt so viel.* ♦ *Er isst nicht so viel wie sonst.* not see much of sb jdn nicht oft sehen [ˌnɪçt ˌɔft ˈzeːən] <sieht, sah, hat gesehen>

ⓔ nothing much nichts Besonderes not much of a ... kein besonders guter .../ keine besonders gute .../ kein besonders gutes ... ◊ *kein besonders guter Fahrer* ♦ *keine besonders gute Köchin* ♦ *kein besonders gutes Auto* not so much ... as ... weniger ... als ... ◊ *Es war weniger die Kälte als der Regen, der uns störte.* too much of a ... ein zu großer .../ eine zu große .../ ein zu großes ... ◊ *Er ist ein zu großer Egoist, um auch mal an andere zu denken.* ♦ *eine zu große Versuchung, als dass man ihr widerstehen könnte* ♦ *ein zu großes Problem für jdn*

mud ‹noun› **1.** *(wet earth)* Schlamm [ʃlam] der <-(e)s, Schlämme> ◊ *im Schlamm stecken bleiben* **2.** *(as a building material)* Lehm [leːm] der <-(e)s, -e> ◊ *Hütten aus Lehm*

ⓔ as clear as mud alles andere als klar fling mud at sb jdn mit Dreck bewerfen *(fam)* mud sticks etwas bleibt immer hängen

muddle ‹verb› muddle sth/sb (up) jdn/etw. durcheinander bringen [dʊʁçlaɛˈnandɐ bʁɪŋən] <bringt, brachte, hat gebracht> ◊ *Du hast mich völlig durcheinander gebracht.* ♦ *Wer hat die Papiere durcheinander gebracht?* ♦ *zwei Konzepte durcheinander bringen* muddle sth (up) with sth etw. und etw. nicht voneinander trennen [ʊnt ...nɪçt fɔnlaɛˈnandɐ ˈtʁɛnən] *+haben* ◊ *Hast du private und geschäftliche Ausgaben nicht voneinan-*

A
B
C
D
E
F
G
H
I
J
K
L
M
N
O
P
Q
R
S
T
U
V
W
X
Y
Z

der getrennt?
• **muddle up** phras v → muddle
muddled verb → muddle adj wirr [vɪrʳ] ◊ *wirre Gedanken* ♦ *Die Handlung ist wirr und manchmal komisch.*
muddy adj 1. *(full of mud)* schlammig ['ʃlamɪç] ◊ *Deine Schuhe sind ganz schlammig.* ♦ *schlammige Wege* 2. *(dull in colo(u)r)* trübe ['try:bə] <trüber, am trübsten> ◊ *eine trübe Flüssigkeit* ♦ *Nach dem Regen war das Wasser im Teich ganz trübe.*
muffle verb *(a sound)* dämpfen ['dɛmpfn̩] +haben ◊ *Die Isolierung dämpft den Lärm.*
mug noun 1. *(for coffee etc.)* Becher ['bɛçɐ] der <–s, –> ◊ *ein Becher heiße Milch* 2. *(for beer)* Krug [kru:k] der <–(e)s, Krüge> ◊ *Das Bier wird in Krügen serviert.*
multimedia noun 1. *(in computers)* Multimedia… [mʊlti'me:dia:] multimedia product Multimediaprodukt [mʊlti'me:diapro,dʊkt] das <–(e)s, –e> 2. *(in art, education)* multimedial [mʊltime'dia:l] ◊ *eine multimediale Ausstellung* ♦ *Das Lernprogramm ist multimedial und interaktiv.*
multiple adj 1. *(tech)* MED, IT multipel [mʊl'ti:pl̩] no comp/superl, only before ns <der/die/das multiple> ◊ *eine multiple Persönlichkeit* ♦ *ein multipler Input* multiple birth Mehrlingsgeburt ['me:ɡlɪŋsɡəbuːɡt] die <–, –en> 2. *(various, several: before countable ns)* mehrere ['me:rərə] no comp/superl, only before ns ◊ *ein Text, der mehrere Interpretationen erlaubt;* *(before uncountable ns)* mehrfache ['me:ɡfaxə] no comp/superl, only before ns ♦ *mehrfache Diskriminierung* multiple pile-up Massenkarambolage ['masn̩karambo,la:ʒə] die <–, –n> multiple injuries zahlreiche Verletzungen [,tsa:lraeçə fɛ'lɛtsʊŋən] die <–> pl
multiply verb 1. *(increase in value)* multiply sth etw. vervielfachen [fɛ'fi:lfaxn̩] <vervielfacht, vervielfachte, hat vervielfacht> ◊ *Durch geschickte Geldanlagen hat sie ihr Vermögen vervielfacht.* sth multiplies etw. vervielfacht sich ◊ *Der Wert dieser Aktie hat sich vervielfacht.* 2. *(increase in numbers)* sth multiplies etw. vermehrt sich [fɛ'me:ɡt] <vermehrt sich, vermehrte sich, hat sich vermehrt> ◊ *Die Bakterien vermehren sich bei Zimmertemperatur.* 3. MATH multiply sth by sth etw. mit etw. multiplizieren [mɪt … mʊltipli,tsi:rən] <multipliziert, multiplizierte, hat multipliziert> ◊ *zwei Zahlen miteinander multiplizieren*
multi-storey car park noun Parkhaus ['paʳkhaos] das <–es, Parkhäuser>
multitude noun 1. *(crowd)* Menge ['mɛŋə] die <–, –n> ◊ *Die Menge auf dem Petersplatz wartete auf den Papst.* the multitudes die Massen [di: 'masn̩] <–> pl ◊ *der Aufstand der Massen* 2. *(large number)* a multitude of … eine Vielzahl von etw. dat/… gen [aenə 'fi:ltsa:l fɔn] die <–> no pl ◊ *eine Vielzahl von Möglichkeiten* ♦ *eine Vielzahl möglicher Motive* Ⓔ hide a multitude of sins vieles verbergen
mum verb → mummy
mumble verb murmeln ['mʊʳmln̩] +haben ◊ *Sie murmelte ein paar unverständliche Worte.* ♦ *„Ich weiss nicht!", murmelte er.*
mummy noun 1. *(mother)* Mama ['mama(:)] die <–, –s> *(fam)* ◊ *„Ich will zu meiner Mama!", rief das Kind.* 2. *(mummified body)* Mumie ['mu:miə] die <–, –n> ◊ *ägyptische Mumien*

municipal adj 1. *(local)* kommunal [kɔmu'na:l] no comp/superl, only before ns ◊ *Die kommunalen Abgaben wurden erhöht.* municipal elections Kommunalwahlen [kɔmu'na:lva:lən] die <–> pl 2. *(of a town)* städtisch ['ʃtɛ(:)tɪʃ] no comp/superl ◊ *Ist der Kindergarten städtisch oder kirchlich?* ♦ *eine städtische Einrichtung*
municipality noun 1. *(local area, administration)* Gemeinde [ɡə'maendə] die <–, –n> ◊ *die Gemeinde Neudorf* ♦ *bei der Gemeinde arbeiten* 2. *(town, administration)* Stadt [ʃtat] die <–, Städte> ◊ *als Gärtner bei der Stadt arbeiten*
municipally adv 1. *(locally)* kommunal [kɔmu'na:l] no comp/superl ◊ *Die Müllabfuhr ist kommunal geregelt.* 2. *(by the town administration)* städtisch ['ʃtɛ(:)tɪʃ] no comp/superl ◊ *eine städtisch geführte Schule*
murder[1] noun Mord [mɔʳt] der <–(e)s, –e> ◊ *einen Mord begehen* ♦ *ein Mord aus Eifersucht* attempted murder Mordversuch ['mɔʳtfezuːx] der <–(e)s, –e> Ⓔ be murder tödlich sein *(fam)* get away with murder sich *(dat)* alles erlauben können
murder[2] verb *(kill)* ermorden [ɐ'mɔʳdn̩] <ermordet, ermordete, hat ermordet>
murderer noun Mörder ['mœʳdɐ] der <–s, –> ♀Mörderin ['mœʳdərɪn] die <–, –nen>
murmur verb 1. *(say)* murmeln ['mʊʳmln̩] +haben ◊ *Sie murmelte etwas Unverständliches und ging.* murmur in sb's ear jdm etwas ins Ohr murmeln 2. *(stream, wind, leaves)* rauschen ['raoʃn̩] +haben ◊ *Der Wind rauscht in den Bäumen.* 3. *(complain)* murren ['mʊrən] +haben ◊ *Die Angestellten begannen, über die schlechte Bezahlung zu murren.*
muscle noun 1. *(in your body)* Muskel ['mʊskl̩] der <–s, –n> ◊ *die Muskeln anspannen* ♦ *Leo zeigte stolz seine Muskeln.* 2. *(physical strength)* Kraft [kraft] die <–, Kräfte> ◊ *Das Sofa zu tragen, braucht man viel Kraft.* 3. *(influence)* Einfluss ['aenflʊs] der <–es, Einflüsse> ◊ *Er hat seinen politischen Einfluss spielen lassen.* Ⓔ not move a muscle sich nicht rühren put some muscle into it sich mehr anstrengen
museum noun Museum [mu'ze:ʊm] das <–s, Museen> ◊ *ins Museum gehen*
mush noun *(soft mass)* Brei [brae] der <–(e)s, –e> ◊ *Kartoffeln zu einem Brei zerstampfen*
mushroom noun Pilz [pɪlts] der <–(e)s, –e> ◊ *im Wald Pilze sammeln* ♦ *Reis mit Pilzen* mushroom soup Pilzsuppe ['pɪltszʊpə] die <–, –n>
music noun 1. *(sounds, art, activity)* Musik [mu'zi:k] die <–, –en> ◊ *klassische Musik* ♦ *Musik studieren* piece of music Musikstück [mu'zi:kʃtʏk] das <–(e)s, –e> 2. *(symbols, sheet)* Noten ['no:tn̩] das <–> pl ◊ *Kannst du Noten lesen?* ♦ *Hast du deine Noten dabei?* Ⓔ music to your ears Musik in jds Ohren
musical adj 1. *(relating to music)* Musik… [mu'zi:k] musical instrument Musikinstrument [mu'zi:k|ɪnstru,mɛnt] das <–s, –e> 2. *(good at music, consisting of music)* musikalisch [muzi'ka:lɪʃ] ◊ *Das Kind ist musikalisch.* ♦ *die musikalische Untermalung einer Filmszene* 3. *(voice, sound)* melodisch [me'lo:dɪʃ] ◊ *eine melodische Stimme* ♦ *Ihr Lachen war sehr melodisch.*
musician noun Musiker ['mu:zɪkɐ] der <–s, –> ♀Musikerin ['mu:zɪkərɪn] die <–, –nen> ◊ *eine begabte*

junge Musikerin ♦ *Er ist Musiker.*

Muslim[1] [noun] Moslem ['mɔslɛm] der <–s, –s>
♀Moslemin [mɔs'le:mɪn] die <–, –nen> be a Muslim
Moslem/Moslemin sein
Muslim[2] [adj] muslimisch [mʊs'li:mɪʃ] *no comp/superl*
◊ *die muslimische Welt* ♦ *Ein großer Teil der Bevölke-*
rung ist muslimisch.
mussel [noun] Muschel ['mʊʃl] die <–, –n>
must [verb] **1.** sb/sth must do sth jd/etw. muss etw.
tun [mʊs] <muss, musste, hat müssen> ◊ *Die Straße*
ist nass; es muss geregnet haben. ♦ *Er muss ein*
Formular ausfüllen. ♦ *Du musst unbedingt dieses*
Buch lesen. **2.** *(negative form)* must not, mustn't
nicht dürfen [nɪçt 'dʏ'fn] <darf, durfte, hat dürfen> ◊
Du darfst nicht dorthin geben. ♦ *Man darf hier nicht*
rauchen. **3.** *(as a question tag)* mustn't you/he
etc.?, must you/he etc.? oder? ['o:de] ◊ *Wir müssen*
um 9 Uhr dort sein, oder? ♦ *Du willst doch noch*
einkaufen, oder?
Ⓔ if you must wenn es sein muss must you musst
du unbedingt ◊ *Musst du unbedingt jetzt staubsau-*
gen?
mustache → **moustache**
mustard [noun] Senf [zɛnf] der <–(e)s, –e> ◊
Bockwurst mit Senf
Ⓔ be able to cut the mustard es auf die Reihe
bringen *(fam)*
mustn't → **must**
mutation [noun] Mutation [muta'tsjo:n] die <–, –en> ◊
die Mutation eines Gens
mutter [verb] **1.** *(speak indistinctly, annoyed)* brummen
['brʊmən] +haben ◊ *„Lass mich in Ruhe!", brummte*
er.; (embarrassed) murmeln ['mʊrmln] +haben ◊ *Sie*
murmelte ein paar unverständliche Worte. mutter
(sth) about sb/sth etwas von jdm/etw. murmeln ◊
Er murmelte etwas davon, dass er noch arbeiten
müsse, und ging. mutter to yourself Selbstgespräche
führen ['zɛlpstgəʃprɛ:çə fy:rən] +haben **2.** *(complain)*
murren ['mʊrən] +haben ◊ *Sie murren über das*
schlechte Essen in der Kantine.
mutton [noun] Hammelfleisch ['haml̩flaeʃ] das <–s>
no pl
mutual [adj] **1.** *(reciprocal)* gegenseitig ['ge:gn̩zaetɪç]
no comp/superl ◊ *Gegenseitiges Vertrauen ist wichtig.*
♦ *Die Abneigung war gegenseitig.* in mutual
agreement im gegenseitigen Einvernehmen The
feeling is mutual. Das beruht auf Gegenseitigkeit.
2. *(in common, shared)* gemeinsam [gə'maenza:m] *no*
comp/superl, only before ns ◊ *gemeinsame Interessen*
be to our mutual benefit für uns beide von Vorteil
sein [fy:ɐ̯ ʊns ˌbaedə fɔn 'fo:ɐ̯taɛl zaen]
muzzle [noun] **1.** *(of a dog, horse)* Schnauze ['ʃnaotsə]

die <–, –n> ◊ *Das Pony stupste mich mit der*
Schnauze an. **2.** *(to stop a dog from biting)*
Maulkorb ['maolkɔ'p] der <–(e)s, Maulkörbe> ◊
Mein Hund muss einen Maulkorb tragen. **3.** *(of a*
weapon) Mündung ['mʏndʊŋ] die <–, –en> ◊ *die*
Mündung einer Pistole
my [det] mein [maen] meine ['maenə] ◊ *Mein Mann*
arbeitet an der Universität. ♦ *Meine Brille ist kaputt.*
♦ *Gib mir mein Buch zurück.* ♦ *Das sind meine*
beiden Schwestern.
myself [ref pron] **1.** *(acc)* mich [mɪç] ◊ *Ich frage mich,*
ob ich das machen soll.; (dat) mir [mi:ɐ̯] ◊ *Ich goss*
mir noch einen Kognak ein. of myself von mir ◊ *ein*
Foto von mir mit meiner Mutter **2.** *(emph) (for my*
own person, on my own) selbst [zɛlpst] *invariable* ◊
Das kann ich selbst. ♦ *Ich selbst war nicht betroffen.*
♦ *Ich war selbst einmal in dieser Situation.* ♦ *Das*
hab ich für mich selbst gekauft, nicht für dich.
Ⓔ be myself mich wohl fühlen ◊ *Ich fühle mich*
heute nicht ganz wohl. all by myself ganz allein all
to myself ganz für mich allein ◊ *Ich hatte das Büro*
ganz für mich allein.
mysterious [adj] **1.** *(not explained, not understood)* rätselhaft ['rɛːtsl̩haft] <rätselhafter, am rätselhaftesten> ◊
Ihr Tod war rätselhaft. ♦ *unter einer rätselhaften*
Krankheit leiden **2.** *(secretive, full of secrets)* geheim-
nisvoll [gə'haemnɪsfɔl] ◊ *ein geheimnisvoller Unbe-*
kannter ♦ *Die Sache wird immer geheimnisvoller.*
mystery [noun] **1.** *(riddle, puzzle)* Rätsel ['rɛːtsl̩] das
<–s, –> ◊ *Seine Herkunft ist ein Rätsel.* ♦ *Sie war*
mir schon immer ein Rätsel. ♦ *Es ist mir ein Rätsel,*
warum sie geben will. **2.** *(secret)* Geheimnis
[gə'haemnɪs] das <–ses, –se> ◊ *Sie weihte uns in*
die Geheimnisse der Trigonometrie ein. shrouded in
mystery geheimnisumwittert [gə'haemnɪsʊmvɪtet]
air of mystery geheimnisvolle Ausstrahlung
[gə,haemnɪsfɔlə 'aosʃtra:lʊŋ] der <–, –en> ◊ *eine*
Frau mit geheimnisvoller Ausstrahlung **3.** *(story, film,*
play) Krimi ['krɪmi:] der <–s, –s> *(fam)* ◊ *Ich lese*
gern Krimis. ♦ *ein Krimi von Agatha Christie*
myth [noun] **1.** *(ancient, traditional)* Mythos ['my:tɔs]
der <–, Mythen> ◊ *griechische Mythen* ♦ *Sind das*
nur Mythen oder wahre Geschichten? **2.** *(wrongly*
believed to be true) Gerücht [gə'rʏçt] das <–
<–(e)s, –e> dispel a myth ein Gerücht aus der
Welt schaffen perpetuate a myth die Unwahrheit
verbreiten [aena 'ʊnvaːɐ̯haet febra:ẽtn] <verbreitet, verbreitete, ht verbreitet> **3.** *(superstition)* Aberglaube
['a:bɐglaobə] der <–s no pl (pej)* ◊ *der Aberglaube,*
dass eine schwarze Katze Unglück bringe
Ⓔ contrary to popular myth im Gegensatz zur herrschenden Meinung

A B C D E F G H I J K L **M** N O P Q R S T U V W X Y Z

N

n, N [noun] n, N [ɛn] das <–(s), –(s)> ◊ *ein kleines n/ großes N* ♦ *N wie Nordpol*

nag [verb] **1.** *(complain)* meckern ['mɛken] +haben ◊ *Hör doch endlich auf zu meckern!* **2.** *(criticize)* nag sb (about sth) an jdm (wegen etw.) herumnörgeln [an ... hɛ,rʊmnœ^rgln] +haben *(pej)* ◊ *Du nörgelst immerzu an mir herum.* **3.** nag sb to do sth jdm damit in den Ohren liegen, dass er etw. tun soll [damɪt ɪn deːn 'oːrən liːgn̩] das ... zɔl] <liegt, lag, hat gelegen> ◊ *Meine Mutter liegt mir ständig damit in den Ohren, dass ich zum Friseur gehen soll.* **4.** *(doubt, fear)* nag at sb jdm keine Ruhe lassen [kaenə 'ruːə lasn̩] <lässt, ließ, hat gelassen> ◊ *Die Sorge um die Kinder ließ ihr keine Ruhe.*

nail¹ [noun] Nagel ['naːgl] der <–s, Nägel> ◊ *einen Nagel in die Wand schlagen* ♦ *jdm/sich die Nägel schneiden/lackieren*

⊙ a nail in the coffin ein Nagel zu jds Sarg/im Sarg ... [gen] ◊ *Dieser Skandal ist ein weiterer Nagel im Sarg der Monarchie.* hard as nails eiskalt

nail² [verb] *(fix with nails)* nageln ['naːgln] +haben ◊ *Sie nagelte ein Schild an den Zaun.* nail sth shut etw. zunageln ['tsuːnaːgln] +haben ◊ *Die Fenster waren zugenagelt.*

• **nail down** [phras v] **1.** *(fix with nails)* festnageln ['fɛstnaːgln] +haben ◊ *ein loses Brett wieder festnageln* **2.** *(decide, arrange)* nail sth down etw. festmachen ['fɛstmaxn̩] +haben ◊ *Heute machen wir endlich den Vertrag/einen Termin fest.* **3.** *(get sb to agree)* nail sb down jdn festnageln ['fɛstnaːgln] +haben *(fam)* ◊ *Ich habe es geschafft, die Handwerker auf ein Datum festzunageln.*

nail file [noun] Nagelfeile ['naːglfaelə] die <–, –n>

naive(ly) [adj, adv] naiv [naˈiːf] ◊ *ein naives junges Mädchen vom Lande* ♦ *Wie kann man nur so naiv sein?* ♦ *naiv handeln*

naked [adj] **1.** *(also fig) (without clothes, undisguised)* nackt [nakt] no comp/superl *(fam)* ◊ *Die Kinder waren nackt.* ♦ *nackte Haut* ♦ *die nackte Angst* strip naked sich nackt ausziehen naked to the waist mit nacktem Oberkörper stark naked splitternackt ['ʃplɪtɐˈnakt] no comp/superl half-naked halbnackt ['halp'nakt] no comp/superl **2.** *(flame, light)* offen ['ɔfn̩] no comp/superl, only before ns open flame offenes Feuer; *(bulb)* nackt [nakt] no comp/superl, only before ns ◊ *Von der Decke hing eine nackte Glühbirne.; (blade, sword)* blank [blaŋk] no comp/ superl, only before ns ◊ *Der Ritter stand mit dem blanken Schwert vor ihm.* visible to the naked eye mit bloßem Auge erkennbar [mɪt bloːsəm 'aogə e,kɛnbaːr]

name¹ [noun] **1.** *(term of reference)* Name ['naːmə] der <–ns, –n> ◊ *Bitte geben Sie Ihren Namen und Ihre Adresse an.* my name is ... ich heiße ... [ɪç 'haesə] <heißt, hieß, hat geheißen> What is your name? Wie heißt du?, Wie heißen Sie? What is the name of this village? Wie heißt dieses Dorf? **2.** *(insult)* call sb names jdn beschimpfen [bəˈʃɪmpfn̩] <beschimpft,

beschimpfte, hat beschimpft> ◊ *Die anderen Kinder haben mich immer beschimpft.* **3.** *(reputation)* Ruf [ruːf] der <–s, –e> ◊ *Diese Universität hat einen guten/schlechten Ruf.* make a name for yourself sich [dat] einen Namen machen [aenən 'naːmən maxn̩] +haben have a name for sth für etw. bekannt sein [fyːɐ̯ ... bəˈkant zaen] +sein ◊ *Diese Firma ist für ihren guten Service bekannt.* **4.** *(famous person)* Persönlichkeit [pɛrˈzøːnlɪçkaet] die <–, –en> ◊ *bekannte Persönlichkeiten aus Film und Fernsehen* a household name ein Begriff [aen bəˈgrɪf] <–(e)s, –e> ◊ *Dieses Museum ist international zu einem Begriff geworden.*

⊙ put a name to a face sich daran erinnern, wie jd heißt the name of the game is ... ohne ... geht nichts ◊ *Ohne Beziehungen geht nichts.* clear sb's name jds Unschuld beweisen name names Namen nennen put a name to sth etw. beschreiben in all but name praktisch in name only nur dem Namen nach under the name of unter dem Namen by name **1.** *(mention sb)* namentlich ◊ *Alle Mitarbeiter werden namentlich erwähnt.* **2.** *(know sb)* dem Namen nach ◊ *Ich kenne ihn nur dem Namen nach.* by the name of namens in the name of ... im Namen ... [gen] ◊ *im Namen des Volkes*

name² [verb] **1.** *(give a name, identify by name, decide on)* name sb/sth (after sb/sth) jdn/etw. (nach jdm/ etw.) nennen [naːx ... nɛnən] <nennt, nannte, hat genannt> ◊ *Wie wollt ihr euer Kind nennen?* ♦ *Ich habe meine Tochter nach dir genannt.* ♦ *Nennt mir drei deutsche Großstädte!* ♦ *Nennen Sie mir Ihren Preis!* be aptly named den richtigen Namen haben [deːn ˌrɪçtɪgn̩ 'naːmən haːbm̩] +haben name the day den Hochzeitstermin festsetzen [deːn 'hɔxtsaetstɛrˌmiːn ˌfɛstzɛtsn̩] +haben **2.** *(choose)* name sb (as/for the post of) sth jdn zu etw. wählen [tsuː ... vɛːlən] +haben ◊ *Man hat ihn zum Sportler des Jahres gewählt.* ♦ *Ich wurde in den Vorstand gewählt.*

⊙ name and shame anprangern

namely [adv] nämlich ['nɛːmlɪç] ◊ *Sie liebten beide dasselbe Mädchen, nämlich Marie.*

nap [noun] Nickerchen ['nɪkeçən] das <–s, –> *(fam)* take a nap ein Nickerchen machen

nape [noun] Nacken ['nakn̩] der <–s, –> the nape of sb's neck jds Nacken

napkin [noun] Serviette [zɛrˈvjɛtə] die <–, –n> ◊ *Ich wischte mir den Mund mit der Serviette ab.*

nappy [noun] Windel ['vɪndl̩] die <–, –n> ◊ *Sie wechselte die Windel des Babys.*

narcotic [noun] **1.** *(illegal drug)* Rauschgift ['raoʃgɪft] das <–(e)s, –e> ◊ *Opium ist ein Rauschgift.* narcotics abuse Drogenmissbrauch ['droːgn̩mɪsbraox] der <–(e)s> no pl **2.** *(in medicine)* Betäubungsmittel [bəˈtɔøbʊŋsmɪtl̩] das <–s, –>

narrative [noun] **1.** *(story)* Geschichte [gəˈʃɪçtə] die <–, –n> ◊ *die Geschichte eines Films/Romans* ♦ *mit seiner Geschichte fortfahren* **2.** *(way of telling a*

story) Erzählform [e'tsɛːlfoʳm] die <–, –en> ◊ *die Erzählform des Tagebuchs*
narrator ⟨noun⟩ **1.** *(of a novel, film)* Erzähler [e'tsɛːlɐ] der <–s, –> ♀Erzählerin [e'tsɛːlərɪn] die <–, –nen> **2.** *(of a TV programme)* Kommentator [kɔmɛn'taːtoːɐ̯] der <–s, –en> ♀Kommentatorin [kɔmɛnta'toːrɪn] die <–, –nen> ◊ *die Kommentatorin eines Tierfilms*
narrow[1] ⟨adj⟩ **1.** *(street, definition)* eng [ɛŋ] ◊ *Die Gasse ist sehr eng.* ◆ *die enge Auslegung eines Gesetzes; (view, range)* beschränkt [bə'ʃrɛŋkt] <beschränkter, am beschränktesten> ◊ *seine beschränkten Ansichten* ◆ *Die Auswahl ist ziemlich beschränkt.* **2.** *(opening, strip)* schmal [ʃmaːl] ◊ *Papier in schmale Streifen schneiden* ◆ *Der Spalt war sehr lang und schmal.* **3.** *(win, result)* knapp [knap] ◊ *ein knappes Ergebnis* ◆ *Der Sieg war knapp.*
narrow[2] ⟨verb⟩ verengen [fɛ|'ɛŋən] <verengt, verengte, hat verengt> ◊ *eine Straße verengen* sth narrows etw. verengt sich ◊ *Die Schlucht verengte sich stark.*
narrow the gap between people/things den Abstand zwischen Personen/Dingen ⟨dat⟩ verringern [dɛːn ˌapʃtant tsvɪʃn̩... fɛ'rɪŋən] <verringert, verringerte, hat verringert>
narrowly ⟨adv⟩ **1.** *(strictly)* eng [ɛŋ] ◊ *eine Regel eng auslegen* **2.** *(only just)* knapp [knap] ◊ *Die Mannschaft verlor nur knapp.*
narrow-minded ⟨adj⟩ engstirnig ['ɛnʃtɪʳnɪç] *(pej)* ◊ *engstirnige Ansichten haben* ◆ *Er ist so engstirnig.*
nasty(-ily) ⟨adj, adv⟩ **1.** *(mood, situation, smell, taste)* übel ['yːbl̩] <übler, übelste> <der/die/das üble ...> ◊ *Seine Laune ist heute besonders übel.* ◆ *Wir befinden uns in einer üblen Lage.* ◆ *übel riechen/aussehen* **2.** *(disease, injury, surprise)* böse ['bøːzə] <böser, am bösesten> ◊ *Ich habe eine böse Erkältung.* ◆ *Die Wunde sieht böse aus.* ◆ *Der Finger hatte sich böse entzündet.* a nasty shock eine böse Überraschung **3.** *(behaviour, person)* gemein [gə'maɪn] ◊ *Es ist gemein, wie ihr euch über ihn lustig macht!* ◆ *sich gemein verhalten* ◆ *eine gemeine Tat* turn nasty unangenehm werden ['ʊn|aŋɡəneːm veːɐ̯dn̩] +sein
nation ⟨noun⟩ **1.** *(country)* Nation [na'tsi̯oːn] die <–, –en> ◊ *die chinesische Nation* industrial nation Industrienation [ɪndʊs'triːna,tsi̯oːn] **2.** *(people)* Volk [fɔlk] das <–(e)s, Völker> ◊ *das deutsche/französische/jüdische Volk* ◆ *die Völker Afrikas/Europas*
national[1] ⟨noun⟩ Staatsbürger ['ʃtaːtsbyʳɡɐ] der <–s, –> ♀Staatsbürgerin ['ʃtaːtsbyʳɡərɪn] die <–, –nen> ◊ *ein britischer/deutscher Staatsbürger* foreign national Ausländer ['aʊslɛndɐ] der <–s, –> ♀Ausländerin ['aʊslɛndərɪn] die <–, –nen>
national[2] ⟨adj⟩ **1.** *(relating to a country)* national [natsi̯o'naːl] *no comp/superl, mostly before ns* ◊ *nationale Interessen* ◆ *europäische und nationale Regelungen* national ... National... [natsi̯o'naːl] national park Nationalpark [natsi̯o'naːlpaʳk] der <–s, –s> national language Landessprache ['landəsʃpraːxə] die <–, –n> national average Landesdurchschnitt ['landəsdʊʳçʃnɪt] der <–(e)s, –e> **2.** *(television, newspaper)* überregional ['yːbɐreɡi̯oˌnaːl] *no comp/superl* ◊ *ein überregionaler Fernsehsender* ◆ *Unsere Zeitung ist überregional.*
national insurance ⟨noun⟩ Sozialversicherung [zo'tsi̯aːlfɛɐ̯ˌzɪçərʊŋ] die <–, –en> ◊ *Die Sozialversicherung ist ein vom Staat geschaffenes Vorsorgesystem.*
national insurance card ⟨noun⟩ Sozialversicherungsausweis [zo'tsi̯aːlfɛɐ̯ˌzɪçərʊŋs|aͭosvaes] der <–es, –e>

nationalism ⟨noun⟩ Nationalismus [natsi̯ona'lɪsmʊs] der <–> *no pl*
nationalist ⟨noun⟩ Nationalist [natsi̯ona'lɪst] der <–en, –en> ♀Nationalistin [natsi̯ona'lɪstɪn] die <–, –nen>
nationality ⟨noun⟩ **1.** *(being the citizen of a country)* Staatsangehörigkeit ['ʃtaːts|aŋɡə,høːrɪçkaet] die <–, –en> ◊ *die britische Staatsangehörigkeit beantragen/bekommen* ◆ *die doppelte Staatsangehörigkeit* **2.** *(ethnic group)* Nationalität [natsi̯onali'tɛːt] die <–, –en> ◊ *In unserer Klasse gibt es neun verschiedene Nationalitäten.*
nationally ⟨adv⟩ landesweit ['landəsvaet] *no comp/superl* ◊ *die Sendung wird landesweit übertragen* ◆ *ein landesweit anerkannter Experte*
nationwide ⟨adj, adv⟩ landesweit ['landəsvaet] *when used as an adj, only before ns* ◊ *eine landesweite Kampagne* ◆ *Die Partei errang landesweit über 50 Prozent.*
native[1] ⟨noun⟩ **1.** *(person born in a place)* a native of Germany etc. ein gebürtiger Deutscher etc. [aͭen ɡəˌbyʳtɪɡe 'dɔ͜ɔtʃe]; eine gebürtige Deutsche etc. [aͭenə ɡəˌbyʳtɪɡə 'dɔ͜ɔtʃə] **2.** *(local)* Einheimische ['aͭenhaemɪʃə] der/die <–n, die Einheimischen> *but:* ein Einheimischer/eine Einheimische ◊ *mit den Einheimischen Kontakt bekommen*
native[2] ⟨adj⟩ **1.** *(being born somewhere)* gebürtig [ɡə'byʳtɪç] *no comp/superl* ◊ *ein gebürtiger Londoner* **2.** Heimat... ['haematː]; *(used when talking about where you were born)* native land Heimatland ['haematlant] das <–(e)s, Heimatländer> ◆ *her native Germany* ihr Heimat Deutschland [iːrə ˌhaematː 'dɔ͜ɔtʃlant] **3.** *(used when referring to the language sb speaks)* native language Muttersprache ['mʊtɐʃpraːxə] die <–, –n> native speaker Muttersprachler ['mʊtɐʃpraːxlɐ] der <–s, –> ♀Muttersprachlerin ['mʊtɐʃpraːxlərɪn] die <–, –nen> **4.** *(local)* einheimisch ['aͭenhaemɪʃ] *no comp/superl* ◊ *die einheimische Bevölkerung; (plants, animals etc.)* heimisch ['haemɪʃ] *no comp/superl* ◊ *die heimische Flora* ◆ *eine heimische Art* ◆ to a place an einem Ort heimisch sein **5.** *(indigenous)* native people Ureinwohner ['uːɐ̯|aͭenvoːnɐ] die <–> *pl* native American amerikanische Ureinwohner [ameriˌkaːnɪʃə 'uːɐ̯|aͭenvoːnɐ] der <–s, –> ♀amerikanische Ureinwohnerin [ameriˌkaːnɪʃə 'uːɐ̯|aͭenvoːnərɪn] die <–, –nen> **6.** *(innate)* angeboren ['angəboːrən] *no comp/superl* ◊ *angeborene Fähigkeiten*
nativity ⟨noun⟩ **1.** *(Jesus Christ's birth)* Nativity Geburt Christi [ɡə,buːɐ̯t 'krɪstiː] die <–> *no pl* **2.** *(crib)* nativity (scene) Krippe ['krɪpə] die <–, –n> ◊ *Unter dem Weihnachtsbaum war eine Krippe aufgebaut.*
natural[1] ⟨noun⟩ **1.** *(sb who is naturally good at sth)* Naturtalent [na'tuːɐ̯ta,lɛnt] das <–(e)s, –e> ◊ *Sie ist einfach ein Naturtalent.* **2.** MUS *(note that is not sharp or flat)* Stammton ['ʃtamtoːn] der <–(e)s, Stammtöne>
natural[2] ⟨adj⟩ **1.** *(normal, not artificial, innate)* natürlich [na'tyːɐ̯lɪç] ◊ *eine natürliche Begabung für Sprachen* ◆ *Es ist doch nur natürlich, dass du dir Sorgen machst.* ◆ *Sie hat eine natürliche Art.* die from natural causes eines natürlichen Todes sterben **2.** *(caused or determined by the natural world)* natural ... Natur... [na'tuːɐ̯] natural disaster Naturkatastrophe [na'tuːɐ̯katas,troːfə] die <–, –n> natural law Naturgesetz [na'tuːɐ̯ɡəzɛts] das

<-es, -e> **3.** *(when referring to an innate skill)* geboren [gə'bo:rən] *no comp/superl, only before ns* ◊ *Er ist ein geborener Anführer.* ♦ *Sie ist eine geborene Schauspielerin.* **4.** *(biological)* leiblich ['laɛplɪç] *no comp/superl, only before ns* ◊ *Er ist mein leiblicher Vater.*

naturalize [verb] einbürgern ['aɛnbyˈgɐn] <bürgert ein, bürgerte ein, hat eingebürgert> ◊ *einen Menschen/eine Pflanze einbürgern*

naturally [adv] **1.** *(as you would expect, of course, in a frank and unaffected manner)* natürlich [naˈtyːɐ̯lɪç] ◊ *„Kommst du mit?" — „Natürlich!"* ♦ *Karin ist natürlich wieder zu spät gekommen.* ♦ *Sie gab sich ganz natürlich.* **2.** *(by nature)* von Natur aus [fɔn naˈtuːɐ̯ aɔs] ◊ *Kinder sind von Natur aus neugierig.* ♦ *Die Substanz kommt von Natur aus im Körper vor.*

nature [noun] **1.** *(the natural world)* die Natur [diː naˈtuːɐ̯] <-> *no pl* ◊ *die Wunder der Natur* ♦ *ungestört die Natur genießen* let nature take its course *der Natur ihren Lauf lassen* **2.** *(personality, characteristic features)* Wesen ['veːzn̩] das <-s, -> ◊ *ein ernstes Wesen haben* ♦ *das wahre Wesen des Menschen* by nature *von Natur aus* [fɔn naˈtuːɐ̯ aɔs] ◊ *Ist der Mensch von Natur aus gut?* it is in the nature of things *es liegt in der Natur der Dinge* [ɛs liːkt ɪn deːɐ̯ naˌtuːɐ̯ deːɐ̯ ˈdɪŋə] **3.** *(kind, sort)* Art [aːɐ̯t] die <-, -en> ◊ *ein Erlebnis besonderer Art* ♦ *Verletzungen dieser Art hatte der Arzt noch nie gesehen.*

naught → nought

naughty(-ily) [adj, adv] unartig ['ʊn|aˌtɪç] ◊ *Lukas war unartig; deshalb habe ich ihn ins Bett geschickt.* ♦ *ein unartiges Kind* ♦ *sich unartig benehmen*

nausea [noun] Übelkeit ['yːblˌkaɛt] die <-, -en> *most sing* ◊ *unter Übelkeit leiden*

naval [adj] *(referring to the navy)* Marine... [maˈriːnə] naval officer Marineoffizier [maˈriːnəˌɔfiˌtsiːɐ̯] der <-s, -e>; *(at sea)* See... [zeː] naval battle Seeschlacht ['zeːʃlaxt] die <-, -en>

navel [noun] Nabel ['naːbl̩] der <-s, -> ◊ *sich* [dat] *den Nabel piercen lassen*

navigate [verb] **1.** *(steer)* steuern ['ʃtɔøen] +haben ◊ *Er steuerte das Schiff sicher in den Hafen.* **2.** *(show sb the way)* Lotse spielen ['loːtsə ʃpiːlən] +haben *(fam)* ◊ *Du fährst, und ich spiele Lotse.* **3.** *(find your way through)* navigate with sth in/auf etw. [dat] zurechtfinden [ɪn/aɔf ... tsuˌrɛçtˈfɪndn̩] <findet sich zurecht, fand sich zurecht, hat sich zurechtgefunden> ◊ *sich auf einer Bergstraße/im Internet/in einer Situation zurechtfinden*

navy [noun] Marine [maˈriːnə] die <-, -n> ◊ *Sie ist Offizierin bei der Marine.* navy ship Marineschiff [maˈriːnəʃɪf] das <-(e)s, -e>

Nazi¹ [noun] Nazi ['naːtsiː] der <-s, -s> ◊ *Er/Sie war ein Nazi.* ♦ *Die Nazis kamen 1933 an die Macht.*

Nazi² [adj] nazistisch [naˈtsɪstɪʃ] *no comp/superl* ◊ *seine nazistische Vergangenheit* Nazi propaganda Nazipropaganda ['naːtsiːpropaˌgandaː] die <-> *no pl*

near¹ [adj] nah [naː] nahe ['naːə] <näher, am nächsten> ◊ *ein naher Verwandter* ♦ *Das nächste Geschäft ist 5 Kilometer entfernt.* ♦ *Die beiden Punkte liegen nahe beieinander.*

near² [adv] nah [naː] nahe ['naːə] <näher, am nächsten> ◊ *Komm doch näher!* draw near näher rücken ['nɛːɐ̯ rʏkn̩] +sein ◊ *Der Termin rückt näher.*

near³ [verb] near (sth) sich (einer Sache [dat]) nähern ['nɛːɐn] +haben ◊ *sich dem Ende nähern* ♦ *Der Zug näherte sich dem Bahnhof.*; *(an age, a period of your life)* near sth auf etw. [acc] zugehen [aɔf ... ˌtsuːˈgeːən] <geht zu, ging zu, ist zugegangen> ◊ *Er geht auf die 50/Rente zu.*; *(date)* sth nears etw. rückt näher [rʏkt 'nɛːɐ̯] +sein ◊ *Der Termin rückt näher.*

near⁴ [prep] **1.** *(spatial, close to)* nahe bei ['naːə baɛ] [+dat] ◊ *Ludwigsburg liegt nahe bei Stuttgart.* ♦ *Er stand nahe bei mir, als es passierte.* **2.** *(approaching a situation, an emotion)* near to nahe ['naːə] *mostly postpositive* [+dat] be near to sb/sth jdm/einer Sache nahe sein ◊ *Das Land ist einer Katastrophe nahe.* ♦ *Ich wollte dir nahe sein.* be near to doing sth nahe daran sein, etw. zu tun; *(be similar)* be near to sth einer Sache [dat] nahe kommen ['naːə kɔmən] <kommt, kam, ist gekommen> ◊ *Das Leben dort kommt der Hölle ziemlich nahe.* **3.** *(almost)* beinahe [baɛˈnaːə] ◊ *Die Temperatur betrug beinahe 40 Grad.*

nearby [adj, adv] in der Nähe [ɪn deːɐ̯ 'nɛːə] *postpositive when used with a noun* ◊ *Das habe ich in einem Geschäft in der Nähe gekauft.* ♦ *Meine Eltern wohnen in der Nähe.*

nearly [adv] fast [fast] ◊ *Ich bin fast fertig.* ♦ *Es ist schon fast fünf Uhr.* ♦ *Fast 100 Leute kamen auf das Fest.* ♦ *Ich wäre fast gestorben vor Angst.*

neat [adj] **1.** *(tidy)* ordentlich ['ɔ'dn̩tlɪç] ◊ *Er führt ein sehr ordentliches Heft.* ♦ *Ihre Arbeitsweise ist ordentlich.* **2.** *(clever)* geschickt [gəˈʃɪkt] <geschickter, am geschicktesten> ◊ *eine geschickte Lösung* ♦ *Es war wirklich geschickt, wie er das gemacht hat.* **3.** *(pure)* pur [puːɐ̯] *no comp/superl, postpositive* ◊ *Ich nehme einen Whisky pur.* **4.** *(in the US: nice)* nett [nɛt] <netter, am nettesten> ◊ *eine nette kleine Stadt* ♦ *Sie ist wirklich ganz nett.*

neatly [adv] ordentlich ['ɔ'dn̩tlɪç] ◊ *die Wäsche ordentlich zusammenlegen*

necessarily [adv] zwangsläufig ['tsvaŋsˌlɔøfɪç] *no comp/superl* ◊ *Die schlechte wirtschaftliche Lage wirkt sich zwangsläufig auf die Nachfrage aus.* not necessarily nicht unbedingt [nɪçt 'ʊnbədɪŋt] *no comp/superl* ◊ *Das muss nicht unbedingt stimmen.* ♦ *„Verläuft die Krankheit immer tödlich?" — „Nicht unbedingt."*

necessary [adj] nötig ['nø:tɪç] ◊ *Sie hält es für nötig, mehr Sport zu treiben.* ♦ *Falls nötig, helfe ich gern.* ♦ *über die nötigen Kenntnisse für etw. verfügen*

necessity [noun] Notwendigkeit ['noːtvɛndɪçkaɛt] die <-> *no pl* ◊ *Viele zweifeln an der Notwendigkeit dieses Krieges.* ♦ *Ein Auto ist auf dem Land eine Notwendigkeit.* the bare necessities das Notwendigste [das 'noːtvɛndɪçstə] <-> *no pl*; *(adverbial)* notwendigerweise ['noːtvɛndɪgɐˌvaɛzə] *no comp/superl* ◊ *Das Gesetz wird notwendigerweise geändert.*
ⓔ necessity is the mother of invention Not macht erfinderisch

neck [noun] **1.** *(of a person, animal, bottle, musical instrument)* Hals [hals] der <-es, Hälse> ◊ *eine Creme für Hals und Gesicht* ♦ *eine Flasche mit engem Hals* ♦ *Der Hals des Cellos ist aus Ahornholz.*; *(back of sb's/an animal's neck)* Nacken ['nakn̩] der <-s, -> ◊ *einen steifen/verspannten Nacken haben* **2.** *(of a piece of clothing)* Ausschnitt ['aɔʃnɪt] der <-(e)s, -e>
ⓔ put your neck on the line seinen Hals riskieren

be up to your neck in sth bis zum Hals in etw.
[dat] stecken breathe down sb's neck jdm auf der
Pelle hocken *(fam)* get it in the neck eins drauf
kriegen *(fam)* by a neck mit einer Nasenlänge
Vorsprung
necklace [noun] Kette ['kɛtə] die <–, –n> ◊ *Sie trug*
eine goldene Kette mit Anhänger. pearl necklace Perlenkette ['pɛ'lɛnkɛtə]
neckline [noun] Ausschnitt ['aosʃnɪt] der <–(e)s, –e>
◊ *der Ausschnitt eines Kleides/Pullovers*
need¹ [noun] **1.** *(situation when sth is needed)* Bedarf
[bə'daʳf] der <–(e)s> *no pl* need for/of sth Bedarf
an etw. [dat] ◊ *Es gibt dringenden Bedarf an Hilfsgü-*
tern. need for action Handlungsbedarf
['handlʊŋsbəda'f] if need be nötigenfalls
['nø:tɪgŋfals] ◊ *Das könnte man nötigenfalls*
versuchen. there is no need for sth etw. ist nicht
nötig [ɪst nɪçt 'nø:tɪç] there is a/no need to do sth
es ist nötig/nicht nötig, etw. zu tun **2.** *(sth that sb*
needs) Bedürfnis [bə'dyʳfnɪs] das <–ses, –se> ◊ *die*
Bedürfnisse unserer Kunden ♦ *ein Bedürfnis befriedi-*
gen ♦ *die besonderen Bedürfnisse seelisch Kranker*
be in need of sth etw. brauchen ['braoxn̩] *+haben* ◊
Ich brauche dringend eine heiße Dusche. **3.** *(lack of*
food, money etc.) Not [no:t] die <–, Nöte> ◊ *Nach*
der Dürre herrschte dort große Not. ♦ *Kinder in Not*
need² [verb] **1.** need sth etw. brauchen ['braoxn̩]
+haben ◊ *Wir brauchen mehr Geld.* ♦ *Ich brauchte*
dringend Ruhe. ♦ *Wenn Sie mich brauchen, sagen*
Sie Bescheid. need sb to do sth jdn brauchen, der
etw. tut ◊ *Ich brauche jemanden, der die Gartenar-*
beit macht. **2.** need to do sth. tun müssen
['mʏsn̩] <muss, musste, hat müssen> ◊ *Sie müssen*
die Prüfung wiederholen. ♦ *Muss ich noch mehr*
sagen? needn't do sth etw. nicht tun müssen ◊ *Wir*
müssen heute die Blumen nicht gießen. need to be
sth etw. sein müssen ◊ *Sie müssen Mitglied sein,*
um in der Jugendherberge zu übernachten. The
house needs painting. Das Haus muss gestrichen
werden.
needle [noun] Nadel ['na:dl̩] die <–, –n> ♦ *eine Nadel*
einfädeln ♦ *Die Nadel am Kompass zeigt stets nach*
Norden. ♦ *Die Lärche wirft ihre Nadeln im Winter*
ab. knitting needle Stricknadel ['ʃtrɪkna:dl̩]
needless(ly) [adj, adv] sinnlos ['zɪnlo:s] <sinnloser, am
sinnlosesten> ◊ *sinnlose Verschwendung* ♦ *Der Krieg*
war sinnlos. ♦ *sinnlos Geld ausgeben*
needlework [noun] Handarbeit ['hantla'baet] die
<–, –en>
needn't → **need²**
negation [noun] **1.** LING Verneinung [fɛ'naenʊŋ] die
<–, –en> ◊ *die Verneinung des Verbs* **2.** PHILOS
Negation [nega'tsjo:n] die <–, –en> ◊ *Ist die*
Republik die Negation der Monarchie?
negative [noun] **1.** FOTO, FILM Negativ ['ne:gati:f] das
<–s, –e> ◊ *Negative entwickeln* **2.** LING Verneinung
[fɛ'naenʊŋ] die <–, –en> ◊ *Kommt in dem Satz eine*
Verneinung vor? answer in the negative mit Nein
antworten [mɪt 'naen antvɔ'tn̩] ◊ *Auf diese Frage ant-*
wortete er mit Nein.
negative(ly) [adj, adv] negativ ['ne:gati:f] ◊ *Sie hat*
eine negative Einstellung zum Leben. ♦ *der negative*
Pol ♦ *Der Test fiel negativ aus.* ♦ *sich negativ über*
jdn äußern ♦ *negative Zahlen*
neglect¹ [noun] Vernachlässigung [fɛ'na:xlɛsɪgʊŋ] die
<–, –en> *most sing* ◊ *die Vernachlässigung von*

Kindern ♦ *Nach langen Jahren der Vernachlässigung*
wird das Gebäude jetzt renoviert. neglect of duty
Pflichtverletzung ['pflɪçtfɛlɛtsʊŋ] die <–, –en>
neglect² [verb] vernachlässigen [fɛ'na:xlɛsɪgŋ] <ver-
nachlässigt, vernachlässigte, hat vernachlässigt> ◊ *seine*
Kinder/sein Haus vernachlässigen ♦ *seine Pflichten*
vernachlässigen neglect to do sth es versäumen,
etw. zu tun [ɛs fɛ'zɔømən ... tsu:] <versäumt,
versäumte, hat versäumt> ◊ *Er hat es versäumt, mich*
zu benachrichtigen.
negligence [noun] Fahrlässigkeit ['fa:'lɛsɪçkaet] die
<–> *no pl* ◊ *Die Fahrlässigkeit des Arztes hatte dra-*
matische Folgen.
negligent(ly) [adj, adv] fahrlässig ['fa:'lɛsɪç] ◊ *fahrlässi-*
ges Verhalten ♦ *Das Vorgehen des Arztes war fahrläs-*
sig. ♦ *sich fahrlässig verhalten*
negotiate [verb] **1.** *(have formal discussions)* verhandeln [fɛ'handl̩n] <verhandelt, verhandelte, hat verhan-
delt> ◊ *Ich bin bereit, mit ihnen zu verhandeln.*
negotiate sth etw. aushandeln ['aoshandl̩n] <handelt
aus, handelte aus, hat ausgehandelt> ◊ *einen Vertrag*
mit jdm aushandeln ♦ *einen Waffenstillstand aushan-*
deln **2.** *(find your way through)* negotiate a road auf
einer Straße fahren [aof aene 'ʃtra:sə fa:rən] <fährt,
fuhr, ist gefahren> negotiate the traffic durch den
Verkehr fahren negotiate a bend eine Kurve
nehmen [aenə 'kʊʳvə ne:mən] <nimmt, nahm, hat
genommen>
negotiation [noun] Verhandlung [fɛ'handlʊŋ] die
<–, –en> ◊ *zu Verhandlungen nach Washington*
reisen sth is open to negotiation über etw. [acc]
kann verhandelt werden
[y:bɐ ... kan fɛ'handl̩t ve:ɐdn̩] sth is under negotiation über etw. [acc] wird verhandelt
[y:bɐ ... vɪʳt fɛ'handl̩t]
neighbor → **neighbour**
neighborhood → **neighbourhood**
neighboring → **neighbouring**
neighbour, neighbor [noun] *(living next to you)*
Nachbar ['naxba:'] der <–n, –n> ♀Nachbarin
['naxba:rɪn] die <–, –nen> ◊ *mein Nachbar von*
gegenüber/nebenan ♦ *Deutschland und seine*
Nachbarn; (sitting next to you) Sitznachbar
['zɪtsnaxba:'] Sitznachbarin ['zɪtsnaxba:rɪn]
neighbourhood, neighborhood [noun] **1.** *(area*
where you live, people who live there) Nachbarschaft
['naxba:'ʃaft] die <–, –en> ◊ *in der Nachbarschaft*
wohnen ♦ *Die ganze Nachbarschaft war bei dem*
Fest. from the neighbourhood aus der Nachbarschaft
2. *(part of town)* Viertel ['fɪʳtl̩] das <–s, –> ◊ *ein*
schönes Viertel poor neighbourhood Armenviertel
['a'mənfɪʳtl̩] Chinese neighbourhood Chinesenviertel
[çi'ne:znfɪʳtl̩]
neighbouring, neighboring [adj] Nachbar...
['naxba:'] neighbouring village Nachbardorf
['naxba:'do'f] das <–(e)s, Nachbardörfer>
neither¹ [adv] auch nicht ['aox nɪçt] ◊ *„Ich will den*
Film nicht sehen.“—„Ich auch nicht.“ ♦ *Sie ist nicht*
gekommen, und ihre Mutter auch nicht.
neither² [det] keiner/keine/keins der beiden
['kaenɐ/'kaenə/'kaens ...] ◊ *Keiner der*
beiden Männer hatte etwas gesehen.
neither³ [pron] keiner ['kaenɐ] keine ['kaenə] keins
[kaens] ◊ *Nur drei Schüler kamen, und keiner hatte*
die Hausaufgaben gemacht. ♦ *Keins der Bücher*
gefällt mir.

neither[4] [conjunc] neither ... nor ... weder ... noch ... [ˈveːðə ... nɔx] ◊ *Dafür habe ich weder Zeit noch Geld.*

nephew [noun] Neffe [ˈnɛfə] der <-n, -n>

nerve [noun] Nerv [nɛrf] der <-s, -en> ◊ *Der Zahnarzt hat den Nerv betäubt.* ♦ *Meine Nerven sind etwas angespannt.* it takes a lot of nerve to do sth man braucht starke Nerven, um etw. zu tun lose your nerve die Nerven verlieren sb's got a lot of nerve, the nerve of sb jd hat vielleicht Nerven get on sb's nerves jdm auf die Nerven gehen [ɑof diː ˈnɛrfn̩ geːən] <geht, ging, ist gegangen> war of nerves Nervenkrieg [ˈnɛrfn̩kriːk] der <-(e)s, -e> ⊛ nerves of steel Nerven wie Drahtseile have the nerve to do sth die Frechheit besitzen, etw. zu tun

nervous [adj] 1. *(anxious)* nervös [nɛrˈvøːs] <nervöser, am nervösesten> ◊ *Du machst mich ganz nervös.* ♦ *ein nervöser Mensch* be nervous about/of sth Angst vor etw. [dat] haben [ˈaŋst foːɐ̯ ... haːbm̩] be nervous about/of doing sth Angst davor haben, etw. zu tun 2. *(relating to your nerves)* Nerven... [ˈnɛrfn̩] nervous breakdown Nervenzusammenbruch [ˈnɛrfn̩tsuˌzamənbrʊx] der <-s, Nervenzusammenbrüche> nervous system Nervensystem [ˈnɛrfn̩zʏsˌteːm] das <-s, -e>

nervously [adv] nervös [nɛrˈvøːs] <nervöser, am nervösesten> ◊ *Er lief nervös auf und ab.*

nest [noun] Nest [nɛst] das <-(e)s, -er> ◊ *(sich) ein Nest bauen* ♦ *ein Nest von Terroristen ausheben* nest of criminals Verbrechernest [fɛˈbrɛçɐnɛst]

net[1] [noun] Netz [nɛts] das <-es, -e> ◊ *Die Fischer werfen ihre Netze aus.* ♦ *den Ball übers Netz schlagen* ◊ *Das Lied habe ich aus dem Netz runtergeladen.*

net[2] [adj] 1. *(after deducting taxes or costs, without packaging)* netto [ˈnɛto:] *not before ns* ◊ *Ist dieser Preis brutto oder netto?*; Netto... [ˈnɛto:] net earnings Nettoeinkommen [ˈnɛtoˌaɛnkɔmən] das <-s, -> net weight Nettogewicht [ˈnɛtogəvɪçt] das <-s, -e> 2. *(final)* net effect Endresultat [ˈɛntrezʊlˌtaːt] das <-s, -e>

net[3] [adv] netto [ˈnɛto:] ◊ *Netto kostet das 100 Euro, also mit Mehrwertsteuer 116.*

net[4] [verb] 1. *(an animal)* fangen [ˈfaŋən] <fängt, fing, hat gefangen> ◊ *Fische fangen* 2. *(a job, information)* ergattern [ɛˈgatɐn] <ergattert, ergatterte, hat ergattert> *(fam)* ◊ *Ich habe eine gute Stelle ergattert.; (a client)* angeln [ˈaŋln̩] +haben ◊ *Wie können wir neue Kunden angeln?* 3. *(earn after tax)* netto verdienen [ˈnɛto: fɛdiːnən] <verdient, verdiente, hat verdient> ◊ *1250 Euro netto verdienen* 4. *(protect with a net)* mit einem Netz schützen [mɪt ˈaɛnəm ˈnɛts ʃʏtsn̩] +haben ◊ *die Blaubeeren mit einem Netz schützen* 5. SPORT *(in ball games)* ins Netz schlagen [ɪns ˈnɛts ʃlaːgn̩] <schlägt, schlug, hat geschlagen> ◊ *Sie schlug den Ball ins Netz.; (football)* ins Tor schießen [ɪns ˈtoːɐ̯ ʃiːsn̩] <schießt, schoss, hat geschossen> ◊ *Er schoss den Ball ins Tor.*

net curtain [noun] Gardine [gaˈrdiːnə] die <-, -n>

Netherlands [noun] Niederlande [ˈniːdɐlandə] die <-> *only pl*

network[1] [noun] Netz [nɛts] das <-es, -e> ◊ *ein weltweites Netz*

network[2] [verb] 1. *(meet people)* Kontakte knüpfen [kɔnˈtaktə knʏpfn̩] +haben ◊ *Sie besuchte die Konferenz, um Kontakte zu knüpfen.* 2. *(connect)*

vernetzen [fɛˈnɛtsn̩] <vernetzt, vernetzte, hat vernetzt> ◊ *zwei Computer vernetzen* They network. Sie vernetzen sich.

neurotic(ally) [adj, adv] neurotisch [nɔɡˈroːtɪʃ] ◊ *ein neurotischer Mensch* ♦ *Er ist schwer neurotisch.* ♦ *neurotisch handeln*

neuter [noun] Neutrum [ˈnɔɡtrʊm] das <-s, Neutren> *most sing* ◊ *Das Neutrum hat den bestimmten Artikel „das".* ♦ *Das Wort „Mädchen" ist ein Neutrum.*

neutral[1] [noun] Leerlauf [ˈleːɡlaɡf] der <-(e)s> *no pl* in neutral im Leerlauf ◊ *Er ließ das Auto im Leerlauf den Berg hinunterrollen.*

neutral[2] [adj] neutral [nɔɡˈtraːl] *seldom comp/superl* ◊ *ein neutrales Land/Gebiet* ♦ *eine neutrale Stimme/Farbe* ♦ *neutral bleiben*

neutralize [verb] 1. *(a conflict)* entschärfen [ɛntˈʃɛrfn̩] <entschärft, entschärfte, hat entschärft> 2. *(a chemical)* neutralisieren [nɔɡtraliˈziːrən] <neutralisiert, neutralisierte, hat neutralisiert> ◊ *eine Säure neutralisieren*

never [adv] nie [niː] ◊ *Er darf das nie erfahren.* ♦ *Er lügt nie.* ♦ *Sie war noch nie in Italien.* ♦ *Tu das nie wieder!* ♦ „*Ob das wohl stimmt?"* — „*Nie!"; (more emphatic)* never (ever) niemals [ˈniːmaːls] ◊ *Das wird er dir niemals verzeihen.*

never-ending [adj] endlos [ˈɛntloːs] *no comp/superl* ◊ *Deine endlose Nörgelei geht mir auf die Nerven.* ♦ *Die Liste war endlos.*

nevertheless [adv] trotzdem [ˈtrɔtsdeːm] ◊ *Wir sind sehr unterschiedlich, verstehen uns aber trotzdem gut.* ♦ *Der Film ist angeblich langweilig; ich will ihn aber trotzdem sehen.*

new(ly) [adj, adv] neu [nɔɡ] <neuer, neu(e)ste/am neu(e)sten> ◊ *in eine neue Wohnung ziehen* ♦ *Morgen fange ich ein neues Leben an.* ♦ *Ich bin neu hier.* ♦ *Jetzt sieht das Auto aus wie neu.* ♦ *Der Laden ist neu eröffnet.* ♦ *neu geschaffene Stellen*

newborn [noun] Neugeborene [ˈnɔɡgəboːrənə] das <-n, -n> *but: ein Neugeborenes*

newcomer [noun] 1. *(sb who has just arrived)* Neuankömmling [ˈnɔɡlankœmlɪŋ] der <-s, -e> ◊ *Die Neuankömmlinge wurden herzlich begrüßt.* 2. *(sb who has just started sth)* Neuling [ˈnɔɡlɪŋ] der <-s, -e> ◊ *Ich bin ein Neuling auf diesem Gebiet.*

news [noun] 1. *(item/piece of) news* Nachricht [ˈnaːxrɪçt] die <-, -en> ◊ *Er überraschte uns mit der Nachricht, dass er gekündigt habe.* ♦ *Die Nachricht von ihrem Tod kam überraschend.* break the news to sb jdm die schlechte Nachricht beibringen 2. TV, RADIO *the news* die Nachrichten [diː ˈnaːxrɪçtn̩] *pl* ◊ *Hast du heute die Nachrichten gesehen/gehört?* on the news im Fernsehen

newspaper [noun] 1. *(paper, organization)* Zeitung [ˈtsaɛtʊŋ] die <-, -en> ◊ *eine überregionale Zeitung* ♦ *Er liest Zeitung.* ♦ *Was steht heute in der Zeitung?* ♦ *Sie arbeitet bei einer Zeitung.* 2. *(sheets)* Zeitungspapier [ˈtsaɛtʊŋspaˌpiːɐ̯] das <-s> *no pl* ◊ *Es war in Zeitungspapier eingewickelt.*

newsreader [noun] Nachrichtensprecher [ˈnaːxrɪçtn̩ʃprɛçɐ] der <-s, -, ⚥Nachrichtensprecherin [ˈnaːxrɪçtn̩ʃprɛçɐrɪn] die <-, -nen> ◊ *als Nachrichtensprecherin bei der ARD arbeiten* ♦ *ein bekannter Nachrichtensprecher*

New Year('s Day) [noun] Neujahr [ˈnɔɡjaːɐ̯] das <-s> *seldom with definite article 'das', no pl*

New Year's Eve [noun] Silvester [zɪl'vɛstɐ] das <–s> *seldom with definite article 'das', no pl*

next¹ [adj] *(following)* nächste ['nɛːçstɐ] *no comp/ superl* <ein nächster …, eine nächste …, ein nächstes …> ◊ *Die nächste Runde gewinne ich!* ✦ *Am nächste Tag regnete es.* ✦ *Ein nächstes Mal wird es nicht geben.* ✦ *Bis zur nächsten Tankstelle sind es etwa zehn Kilometer.*; *(closest)* the next room das Zimmer nebenan [das ˌtsɪmɐ neːbm̩'an] *postpositive*; *(person)* next (one) Nächste ['nɛːçstɐ] der/die <–n, die Nächsten> *only with the definite article* ◊ *Wer ist der Nächste?* ✦ *„Kommst du bald dran?"* — *„Ja, ich bin die Nächste."*

next² [adv] **1.** *(used with a verb)* als Nächstes [als 'nɛːçstəs] ◊ *Was tun wir als Nächstes?* ✦ *Als Nächstes musst du das Mehl hinzugeben.* **2.** *(used with an adj)* nächst… [nɛːçst] next possible nächst-möglich ['nɛːçstmøːklɪç] *no comp/superl* ◊ *Wann wäre denn der nächstmögliche Termin?*

next³ [det] nächsten ['nɛːçstn̩] nächste ['nɛːçstɐ] nächstes ['nɛːçstəs] *only acc* ◊ *Nächsten Monat fahren wir in Urlaub.* ✦ *Sehen wir uns nächste Woche?* ✦ *Wir ziehen nächstes Jahr um.* next time das nächste Mal

next to [prep] **1.** *(beside)* neben ['neːbm̩] *with acc when expressing motion towards a place, with dat when there is no or undirected motion* ◊ *Unser Haus ist neben der Kirche.* ✦ *Sie stand neben mir.* next to each other nebeneinander [neːbm̩ǀaeˈnandɐ] ◊ *Stühle nebeneinander stellen* ✦ *Sie saßen im Konzert nebeneinander.* next to it/that daneben [daˈneːbm̩] ◊ *Hier ist das Museum und dicht daneben befindet sich die Kapelle.* **2.** *(with the exception of)* außer ['aosɐ] [+dat] ◊ *Außer dir ist Frank mein bester Freund.* **3.** *(compared to)* verglichen mit [fɐ'glɪçn̩ mɪt] ◊ *Verglichen mit ihm bist du ein Genie.* **4.** next to nothing fast nichts [fast 'nɪçts] ◊ *Ich habe mit diesem Job fast nichts verdient.*

nibble [verb] knabbern ['knabɐn] +haben ◊ *Erdnüsse/ Salzstangen knabbern* nibble on/at sth an etw. [dat] knabbern ◊ *Das Kaninchen knabberte an einer Karotte.*

nice [adj] **1.** *(friendly, kind)* nett [nɛt] <netter, am nettesten> ◊ *ein netter junger Mann* ✦ *Er sagte mir ein paar nette Worte.* ✦ *Es war nicht nett von dir, mich anzulügen.* ✦ *Wärst du so nett und würdest das Fenster öffnen? ✦ Nett habt ihr's hier!* ✦ *Sei bitte nett zu ihr!*; *(attractive, enjoyable)* schön [ʃøːn] ◊ *ein schöner Blick auf den See* ✦ *Das Wetter soll morgen schön werden.* ✦ *Schön, dich zu sehen.* ✦ *Das wäre ja eine schöne Überraschung gewesen!* Nice to meet you. Angenehm! **2.** *(used for emphasis)* nice and … schön … [ʃøːn] ◊ *Es ist schön warm hier.* ✦ *Der Test war schön einfach.*

nicely [adv] **1.** *(very well)* sehr gut ['zeːɐ ˌguːt] *no comp/superl* ◊ *sich sehr gut an eine neue Umgebung anpassen* ✦ *Die Theorie wird in diesem Artikel sehr gut erklärt.* **2.** *(in a pleasant or friendly way)* nett [nɛt] <netter, am nettesten> ◊ *Sie hat sich nett bedankt.* ✦ *Das Haus ist nett eingerichtet.*

niche [noun] Nische ['niːʃə] die <–, –n> ◊ *Sie saß in der hintersten Nische des Cafés.* ✦ *eine ökologische Nische*

nickname [noun] Spitzname ['ʃpɪtsnaːmə] der <–ns, –n> ◊ *Kinder geben sich untereinander oft Spitznamen.*

niece [noun] Nichte ['nɪçtə] die <–, –n>

night¹ [noun] **1.** *(time when it's dark, when most people sleep)* Nacht [naxt] die <–, Nächte> ◊ *Sie feierten die ganze Nacht.* ✦ *bis tief/weit in die Nacht hinein* ✦ *eine schlaflose Nacht haben* ✦ *Gute Nacht!* at/by night, nights nachts [naxts] ◊ *samstags nachts* ✦ *zwei Uhr nachts* ✦ *Sie arbeitet nachts.* **2.** *(evening)* Abend ['aːbm̩t] der <–s, –e> ◊ *Sie ist keinen Abend zu Hause.* ✦ *Abend für Abend stand er auf der Bühne.* last night gestern Abend the other night neulich abends ['nɔølɪç 'aːbm̩ts] have a night out abends ausgehen [ˌaːbm̩ts 'aosgeːən] <geht aus, ging aus, ist ausgegangen>
ⓔ have an early night früh ins Bett gehen a late night eine lange Nacht have a late night spät ins Bett gehen

night² [adj] Nacht… [naxt] night shift Nachtschicht ['naxtʃɪçt] die <–, –en>

nightmare [noun] Albtraum ['alptraom] der <–(e)s, Albträume> ◊ *Er hatte einen Albtraum.* ✦ *Bungeejumping ist ein Albtraum für mich.*

nil [noun] null [nʊl] be nil gleich null sein ◊ *Deine Gewinnchance ist gleich null.* → four¹

nine [nmrl] neun [nɔøn] → four²

nineteen [nmrl] neunzehn ['nɔøntseːn] → four²

ninety [nmrl] neunzig ['nɔøntsɪç] → four²

nipple [noun] **1.** ANAT Brustwarze ['brʊstvaˈtsə] die <–, –n> **2.** *(of a bottle)* Sauger ['zaogɐ] der <–s, –>

nitrogen [noun] Stickstoff ['ʃtɪkʃtɔf] der <–(e)s no pl

no¹ [noun] *(answer)* Nein [naen] das <–(s)> no pl ◊ *Das war ein klares Nein.*; *(vote)* Gegenstimme ['geːgn̩ʃtɪmə] die <–, –n> ◊ *Wie viele Gegenstimmen gab es?*

no² [adv] **1.** *(the opposite of yes)* nein [naen] ◊ *„Möchtest du noch ein Stück Kuchen?"* — *„Nein, danke."* ✦ *Nein, ich will das nicht!* ✦ *Das wird Hunderte, nein Tausende kosten.* **2.** *(before an adjective)* nicht [nɪçt] ◊ *Ich spiele gern Fußball, aber ich bin nicht gut.* ✦ *Der zweite Versuch war nicht besser als der erste.*

no³ [det] kein [kaen] keine ['kaenə] ◊ *Keine Frau würde sich das gefallen lassen.* ✦ *Kein Auto ist ihm schnell genug.* ✦ *Ich habe leider keine Ideen.* ✦ *„Für Unbefugte kein Zutritt!"* no … at all keinerlei ['kaenɐˈlae] *invariable* ◊ *Wir übernehmen keinerlei Verantwortung.* ✦ *Es gibt keinerlei Einwände.*

No. Nr. ['nʊmɐ] ◊ *Wir sitzen in Reihe Nr. 9.*

nobility [noun] Adel ['aːdl̩] der <–s> no pl ◊ *der deutsche/englische Adel* ✦ *dem Adel angehören*

noble [adj] **1.** *(person, thought, act)* nobel ['noːbl̩] <nobler, am nobelsten> <der/die/das noble …> *(lofty)* ◊ *Was für ein nobler Mensch!* ✦ *Das Geschenk war sehr nobel.*; *(selfless)* edel ['eːdl̩] <edler, am edelsten> <der/die/das edle …> ◊ *Es war sehr edel von ihm, ihr zu verzeihen.* **2.** *(aristocratic)* ad(e)lig ['aːd(ə)lɪç] *no comp/superl* ◊ *ein Mann von adeliger Herkunft* ✦ *Alle seine Gäste waren adelig.* **3.** *(monument)* prächtig ['prɛçtɪç] ◊ *Was für ein prächtiges Schloss!*

nobly [adv] **1.** *(finely, aristocratically)* vornehm ['foːɐneːm] ◊ *Er hielt sich vornehm zurück.* nobly born von edler Geburt [fɔn ˌeːdlɐ gə'buːɐt] ◊ *ein junger Mann von edler Geburt*; *(selflessly)* edel ['eːdl̩] <edler, am edelsten> ◊ *edel handeln* **2.** *(impressively)* prächtig ['prɛçtɪç] ◊ *prächtig geformte Blüten*

nobody¹ [noun] Niemand ['niːmant] der <–s> no pl ◊

Damals war er noch ein Niemand.

nobody² [indef pron] niemand ['ni:mant] ◊ *Das darf niemand wissen.* ◆ *Ich lasse mich von niemandem ärgern.* nobody else sonst (…) niemand ◊ *Sonst wollte ihr niemand helfen.*

nod¹ [noun] Nicken ['nɪkŋ̍] das <-s> no pl ◊ *Er signalisierte seine Zustimmung mit einem Nicken.* give a (quick) nod (kurz) nicken [(kʊˈts) 'nɪkŋ̍] +haben ◊ *Sie nickte kurz und wandte sich wieder ihrer Arbeit zu.*

nod² [verb] 1. (move your head) nicken ['nɪkŋ̍] +haben ◊ *„Ja, das geht", sagte er und nickte.* nod in agreement zustimmend nicken nod your head mit dem Kopf nicken nod at sb jdm zunicken ['tsu:nɪkŋ̍] +haben ◊ *Der Lehrer nickte den Schülern freundlich zu.* nod a greeting etc. to sb jdm zur Begrüßung etc. zunicken 2. SPORT (a ball) köpfen ['kœpfn̩] +haben ◊ *Der Spieler köpfte den Ball ins Tor.* 3. (lit) (plant) sich wiegen ['vi:gŋ̍] +haben ◊ *Die langen Gräser wiegten sich im Wind.*
◆ **nod off** [phras v] einnicken ['aɛnnɪkŋ̍] +sein ◊ *Er war beim Lernen kurz eingenickt.*

node [noun] Knoten ['kno:tŋ̍] der <-s, -> ◊ *einen Knoten in der Brust entdecken*

noise [noun] (loud, irritating sound) Lärm [lɛˈm] der <-(e)s> no pl ◊ *Der Lärm der Maschinen war kaum auszuhalten.* make a noise (einen) Lärm machen ◊ *Macht doch nicht so viel Lärm!* ◆ *Die Kinder machten einen fürchterlichen Lärm.; (sth you hear)* Geräusch [gəˈrɔɣʃ] das <-(e)s, -e> ◊ *ein leises/lautes Geräusch* ◆ *Sie hörten das Geräusch von zerbrechendem Glas.*
☞ make all the right noises Interesse signalisieren

noisy [adj] laut [laɔt] <lauter, am lautesten> ◊ *Sie wohnt an einer lauten Straße.* ◆ *Hier ist es mir zu laut.*

nominal [adj] 1. (small, in name) nominell [nomi'nɛl] no comp/superl, mostly before ns ◊ *der nominelle Vorsitzende des Vereins* This sum's only nominal. Das ist nur eine nominelle Summe. nominal value Nennwert ['nɛnveːɐt] der <-(e)s, -e> 2. GRAM nominal [nomi'na:l] no comp/superl, only before ns ◊ *ein nominaler Stil* This adjective's use is nominal. Dies ist ein nominaler Gebrauch des Adjektivs.

nominate [verb] 1. (suggest) nominate sb (as sth) (for sth) jdn (als etw.) (für etw.) nominieren [nomi'ni:rən] <nominiert, nominierte, hat nominiert> ◊ *Sie wurde als Kandidatin für den Vorstand nominiert.* 2. (appoint) nominate sb sth jdn zu etw. ernennen [tsu: … ɛnɛnən] <ernennt, ernannte, hat ernannt> ◊ *Sie wurde zur Vorsitzenden ernannt.* 3. (select a day, time) vorgeben ['fo:geːbm̩] <gibt vor, gab vor, hat vorgegeben> ◊ *Bitte geben Sie das Datum der Abreise vor.*

nomination [noun] 1. (suggestion) Nominierung [nomi'ni:rʊŋ] die <-, -en> ◊ *jds Nominierung als Kandidat* Oscar nomination Oscarnominierung ['ɔskaˈnomiˌniːrʊŋ] 2. (appointment) Ernennung [ɛɐ'nɛnʊŋ] die <-, -en> ◊ *Ihre Ernennung zur Nachfolgerin des Chefs überraschte alle.*

nominative [noun] Nominativ ['no:minatiːf] der <-s> no pl ◊ *ein Pronomen, das im Nominativ steht*

non-committal [adj] unverbindlich ['ʊnfɛbɪntlɪç] no comp/superl ◊ *eine unverbindliche Antwort* ◆ *Diese Auskunft ist unverbindlich.* be non-committal about sth sich in Bezug auf etw. [acc] nicht festlegen

[ɪn bətsu:k aɔf … nɪçt 'fɛstleːgŋ̩] +haben ◊ *Sie legte sich in Bezug auf ihre Urlaubspläne nicht fest.*

none¹ [adv] none too durchaus nicht [dʊˈɛˈaɔs nɪçt] ◊ *Das ist durchaus nicht einfach.* be none the wiser auch nicht schlauer sein ['aɔx nɪçt ʃlaɔe zaɛn] +sein

none² [indef pron] keiner ['kaɛne] keine ['kaɛnə] kein(e)s [kaɛn(ə)s] ◊ *Keiner konnte ihr helfen.* ◆ *Er wollte noch etwas Milch, aber es war keine mehr da.* ◆ *Ein kleines Haus ist besser als keins.* none of sb keiner/keine … [gen] ◊ *Keiner der Passagiere wurde verletzt.* none of sth nichts von etw. [nɪçts fɔn] ◊ *Es ist nichts von dem Kuchen übrig.*
☞ have none of sth nichts von etw. hören wollen ◊ *Ich will nichts von diesen verrückten Plänen hören!* none but nur ◊ *Nur ihre Mutter konnte sie verstehen.*

nonetheless [adv] trotzdem ['trɔtsdeːm] ◊ *Wir sind sehr unterschiedlich, verstehen uns aber trotzdem gut.*

non-existent [adj] nicht vorhanden [ˌnɪçt foːɐ'handn̩] no comp/superl ◊ *nicht vorhandene Ware* sth is (virtually) non-existent etw. gibt es (fast) nicht ['giːpt ɛs (fast) nɪçt] <gab, hat gegeben>

non-profit [adj] gemeinnützig [gəˈmaɛnnʏtsɪç] no comp/superl ◊ *eine gemeinnützige Organisation* ◆ *Unsere Stiftung ist gemeinnützig.*

nonsense [noun] (sth wrong or unreasonable) Unsinn ['ʊnzɪn] der <-(e)s> no pl ◊ *Wer hat dir denn diesen Unsinn erzählt?* ◆ *Ich hielt den Aufsatz für Unsinn.* complete nonsense blanker Unsinn talk nonsense Unsinn reden make (a) nonsense of sth etw. sinnlos machen ['zɪnloːs maxn̩] +haben; (silly behavio(u)r) Dummheiten ['dʊmhaɛtn̩] die <-> pl not put up with any nonsense keine Dummheiten dulden nonsense poem Unsinnsgedicht ['ʊnzɪnsgədɪçt] das <-(e)s, -e>

nonsensical(ly) [adj, adv] unsinnig ['ʊnzɪnɪç] ◊ *unsinnige Vorschriften* ◆ *Was du da redest, ist doch völlig unsinnig.* ◆ *Die Fragen waren unsinnig formuliert.*

non-smoker [noun] Nichtraucher ['nɪçtraɔxe] der <-s, -> ♀Nichtraucherin ['nɪçtraɔxərɪn] die <-, -nen> ◊ *Sie ist Nichtraucherin.*

non-smoking [adj] Nichtraucher… ['nɪçtraɔxe] non-smoking area Nichtraucherbereich ['nɪçtraɔxebəraɛç] der <-(e)s, -e> non-smoking compartment Nichtraucherabteil ['nɪçtraɔxeˌaptaɛl] das <-(e)s, -e>

non-stop¹ [adj] (entertainment, flight) Nonstop… [nɔn'ʃtɔp] non-stop entertainment Nonstopunterhaltung [nɔn'ʃtɔpˌʊnteˌhaltʊŋ] die <-> no pl non-stop flight Nonstopflug [nɔn'ʃtɔpfluːk] der <-(e)s, Nonstopflüge>; (train) durchgehend ['dʊˈçgeːənt] no comp/superl, only before ns ◊ *ein durchgehender Zug nach Hamburg*

non-stop² [adv] (discuss, talk) ununterbrochen ['ʊnɪʊntebrɔxn̩] no comp/superl ◊ *Sie redete ununterbrochen über ihren Mann.; (journey)* ohne Unterbrechung [oːnə ʊnteˈbrɛçʊŋ] ◊ *Der Zug fährt ohne Unterbrechung bis Aachen.*

noodle [noun] Nudel ['nu:dl̩] die <-, -n> most pl ◊ *Nudeln mit Soße*

noon [noun] Mittag ['mɪtaːk] der <-s, -e> ◊ *Vor Mittag steht er nie auf.* ◆ *Ich komme gegen Mittag an.* at noon um 12 Uhr mittags

no one [indef pron] niemand ['ni:mant] ◊ *Niemand zweifelte an seinen Worten.* no one else sonst niemand ◊ *Sonst wurde niemand verletzt.*

noose [noun] Schlinge ['ʃlɪŋə] die <-, -n> ◊ *eine Schlinge machen* tighten the noose around sb's neck die Schlinge um jds Hals enger ziehen

nor [conjunc] und ... auch nicht [ʊnt ... 'aʊx nɪçt] ◊ *Ich werde nicht kommen und Sabine auch nicht.* neither ... nor weder ... noch [ve:de ... nɔx] ◊ *Weder Claudia noch Fabian haben Lust zu spielen.*

Nordic [adj] nordisch ['nɔrdɪʃ] no comp/superl, only before ns ◊ *nordische Länder/Sprachen*

norm [noun] Norm [nɔrm] die <-, -en> ◊ *von der Norm abweichen* ♦ *sich an die gesellschaftlichen Normen halten*

normal [adj] normal [nɔrˈmaːl] no comp/superl ◊ *Ist es normal, dass er so ruhig ist?* ♦ *Sie ist ein ganz normaler Mensch.* perfectly normal völlig normal get back to normal sich normalisieren [zɪç nɔrmaliˈziːrən] <normalisiert sich, normalisierte sich, hat sich normalisiert> ◊ *Nach dem Unglück dauerte es eine Weile, bis sich alles wieder normalisiert hatte.*

◉ be your normal self ganz der/die Alte sein

normally [adv] **1.** *(usually)* normalerweise [nɔrˈmaːləˈvaɛzə] ◊ *Normalerweise geht sie um elf Uhr ins Bett.* ♦ *Diese Krankheit tritt normalerweise nur bei Katzen auf.* **2.** *(in a normal way)* normal [nɔrˈmaːl] no comp/superl ◊ *Er ist ein normal begabter Schüler.*

north¹ [noun] Norden ['nɔrdn̩] der <-s> with the article when specifying a place, no pl ◊ *von Norden nach Süden fahren* ♦ *Sie wohnen im Norden Frankreichs.*

north² [adj] Nord... [nɔrt] north coast Nordküste ['nɔrtkʏstə] die <-, -n> north side Nordseite ['nɔrtzaɛtə] die <-, -n> north wind Nordwind ['nɔrtvɪnt] der <-(e)s, -e>

north³ [adv] *(towards the north)* nach Norden [naːx 'nɔrdn̩] ◊ *Sie marschierten weiter nach Norden.* north of nördlich ['nœrtlɪç] [+gen] ◊ *nördlich der Stadt;* *(when followed by a word without the article)* north of nördlich von ['nœrtlɪç fɔn] ◊ *Unsere Freunde wohnen nördlich von Hamburg/hier.* up north im Norden [ɪm 'nɔrdn̩] ◊ *Er wohnt jetzt im Norden.*

northerly [adj] nördlich ['nœrtlɪç] only before ns ◊ *in nördliche Richtung reisen* northerly wind Nordwind ['nɔrtvɪnt] der <-(e)s, -e>

northern [adj] *(location, accent)* nördlich ['nœrtlɪç] only before ns ◊ *der nördliche Teil des Landes;* *(in geographical names)* Northern ... Nord... [nɔrt] Northern Europe Nordeuropa ['nɔrtʔɔɪˌroːpaː] das <-s> article only in combination with attribute, no pl Northern Ireland Nordirland ['nɔrtʔɪrlant] das <-s> article only in combination with attribute, no pl

North Sea [noun] Nordsee ['nɔrtzeː] die <-> no pl ◊ *Urlaub an der Nordsee machen*

Norway [noun] Norwegen ['nɔrveːgn̩] das <-s> article only in combination with attribute, no pl → **Germany**

Norwegian¹ [noun] **1.** *(inhabitant)* Norweger ['nɔrveːgɐ] der <-s, -> ♀Norwegerin ['nɔrveːgərɪn] die <-, -nen> → **German¹** 1. **2.** *(language, subject)* Norwegisch ['nɔrveːgɪʃ] das <-(s)> no pl → **German¹** 2.

Norwegian² [adj] norwegisch ['nɔrveːgɪʃ] → **German²**

nose [noun] Nase ['naːzə] die <-, -n> ◊ *Er hat eine große Nase.* hold your nose sich [dat] die Nase zuhalten sb's nose is running jdm läuft die Nase blow your nose sich [dat] die Nase putzen ◊ *Sie putzte sich die Nase.* pick your nose in der Nase bohren

◉ look down your nose/turn your nose up at sb/sth die Nase über jdn/etw. rümpfen cut off your nose to spite your face sich [dat] ins eigene Fleisch schneiden put sb's nose out of joint jdn vor den Kopf stoßen have a (good) nose for sth einen guten Riecher für etw. haben keep your nose out of sth sich aus etw. heraushalten poke your nose into sth seine Nase in etw. [acc] stecken rub sb's nose in sth jdm etw. unter die Nase reiben under your nose vor jds Augen

nostril [noun] Nasenloch ['naːznlɔx] das <-(e)s, Nasenlöcher>

nosy(-ily) [adj, adv] neugierig ['nɔɡiːrɪç] ◊ *Die Kinder schauten neugierig durchs Schlüsselloch.* ♦ *Sei nicht so neugierig!* ♦ *neugierige Nachbarn*

not [adv] nicht [nɪçt] ◊ *Er hat sich nicht gefreut.* ♦ *Gehst du jetzt hin oder nicht?* ♦ *„Will noch jemand Sahne?" — „Ich nicht."* ♦ *Ist das nicht schön?* not even nicht einmal ◊ *Sie hat sich nicht einmal bedankt.* It's nice, isn't it? Es ist hübsch, nicht wahr?; *(less than)* not five minutes keine fünf Minuten [kaɛnə fʏnf miˈnuːtn̩] ◊ *Keine fünf Minuten, bevor es zu regnen begann, kamen wir im Hotel an.*

◉ not at all **1.** *(emphasizing a negative statement)* überhaupt nicht ◊ *Diese Idee gefällt mir überhaupt nicht.* **2.** *(answer to 'thank you')* keine Ursache ◊ *„Vielen herzlichen Dank!" — „Keine Ursache!"* not only ..., but (also) nicht nur ..., sondern (auch)

notable [adj] bemerkenswert [bəˈmɛrkn̩sveːɐt] <bemerkenswerter, am bemerkenswertesten> ◊ *eine bemerkenswerte Person* ♦ *Es ist bemerkenswert, dass niemand gegen die Reformen protestiert.* be notable for sth wegen etw. [gen] bemerkenswert sein ◊ *Der Film ist vor allem wegen der Kostüme bemerkenswert.*

notably [adv] **1.** *(in particular)* vor allem [foːɐ 'aləm] ◊ *Einige Leute, vor allem Umweltschützer, sind gegen den Bau der Autobahn.* **2.** *(strikingly)* beträchtlich [bəˈtrɛçtlɪç] ◊ *Die Benzinpreise sind beträchtlich gestiegen.*

notary [noun] Notar [noˈtaːɐ] der <-s, -e> ♀Notarin [noˈtaːrɪn] die <-, -nen> ◊ *Sie ist Notarin.* ♦ *Am besten gehen wir mit dem Vertrag zu einem Notar.*

note¹ [noun] **1.** *(short letter, reminder)* Notiz [noˈtiːts] die <-, -en> ◊ *Ich habe die Notiz in meinem Kalender übersehen.;* *(piece of paper)* Zettel ['tsɛtl] der <-s, -> ◊ *einen Zettel ans schwarze Brett hängen* leave sb a note jdm einen Zettel hinterlassen ◊ *Er hatte ihr einen Zettel mit seiner Telefonnummer hinterlassen.* make a note of sth sich [dat] etw. notieren [noˈtiːrən] <notiert sich, notierte sich, hat sich notiert>; *(short pieces of information in a book)* Anmerkung ['anmɛrkʊŋ] die <-, -en> ◊ *Vergleichen Sie hierzu die Anmerkungen auf Seite 45.* **2.** *(summary, draft)* notes Aufzeichnungen ['aʊftsaɛçnʊŋən] die <-> pl ◊ *Ich war letzte Woche nicht im Unterricht. Kann ich mir deine Aufzeichnungen ausleihen?* study notes Lernhilfe ['lɛrnhɪlfə] die <-, -n> sing take notes Notizen machen

[no'ti:tsn maxn] +haben ◊ *Sie hat viele Notizen gemacht.* speak without notes **frei sprechen** ['fraɪ ʃprɛçn] <spricht, sprach, hat gesprochen> **3.** *(money)* Schein [ʃaɛn] der <-(e)s, -e> ◊ *Der Automat nimmt Münzen und Scheine.* five-pound note **Fünfpfundschein** [fʏnf'pfʊntʃaɛn] **4.** *(official document)* delivery note **Lieferschein** ['li:feʃaɛn] der <-(e)s, -e> sick note **Krankmeldung** ['kraŋkmɛldʊŋ] die <-, -en> **5.** MUS *(musical sign)* Note ['no:tə] die <-, -n> ◊ *eine punktierte/halbe/ganze Note; (sound)* Ton [to:n] der <-(e)s, Töne> ◊ *Sie spielte einige Töne auf dem Klavier.* **6.** *(in sb's voice)* Klang [klaŋ] der <-(e)s, Klänge> There is a desperate note in her voice. **Ihre Stimme klingt verzweifelt.**; *(quality, characteristic of an object)* Note ['no:tə] die <-> no pl ◊ *Das Briefpapier hat eine nostalgische Note.* sound a note of caution **zur Vorsicht mahnen** [tsu:ɐ 'fo:ɐzɪçt ma:nən] +haben ◊ *In diesem Fall kann ich nur zur Vorsicht mahnen.* sound a positive note **sich optimistisch äußern** [ɔpti'mɪstɪʃ ɔøsen] +haben ⊛ make a mental note of sth **sich** [dat] etw. **merken** worthy of note **erwähnenswert** compare notes **Erfahrungen austauschen** take note of sth **einer Sache** [dat] **Beachtung schenken** of note **von Bedeutung**

note² [verb] **1.** *(realize)* bemerken [bə'mɛʳkn] <bemerkt, bemerkte, hat bemerkt> ◊ *Sie bemerkte, wie er plötzlich blass wurde.; (pay attention)* beachten [bə'axtn] <beachtet, beachtete, hat beachtet> ◊ *Bitte beachten Sie, dass das Parken nur im Hof erlaubt ist.* **2.** *(mention)* erwähnen [ɛ'vɛ:nən] <erwähnt, erwähnte, hat erwähnt> ◊ *Diese Tatsache wurde bereits zu Beginn des Buches erwähnt.* **3.** *(write down)* note (down) notieren [no'ti:rən] <notiert, notierte, hat notiert> ◊ *Bitte notieren Sie alle Beobachtungen in diesem Heft.* ⊛ be noted for sth **für etw. bekannt sein**

notebook [noun] **1.** *(for writing down sth)* Notizbuch [no'ti:sbu:x] das <-(e)s, Notizbücher> ◊ *Er schrieb etwas in sein Notizbuch.* **2.** IT Notebook ['no:tbʊk] das <-s, -s>

nothing [indef pron] nichts [nɪçts] ◊ *Nichts geschah.* ♦ *Ich habe nichts zu tun.* ♦ *Ich finde daran nichts Komisches.* ♦ *Der Wagen ist nichts mehr wert.* ♦ *„Was hat er gesagt?" — „Nichts!"* nothing at all **überhaupt nichts** nothing else **sonst nichts** She is nothing if not patient. **Sie ist äußerst geduldig.** ⊛ nothing but **lauter** ◊ *Der Text hatte lauter Fehler.* nothing doing *(describing a negative experience, answer)* Fehlanzeige *(fam)* ◊ *Ich hoffte auf gutes Wetter. Aber Fehlanzeige!* *(describing a situation in which nothing is happening)* nichts los *(fam)* ◊ *In der Kneipe war nichts los.* for nothing **umsonst** ♦ *Umsonst mache ich das aber nicht.* ♦ *Nun ist er umsonst den langen Weg hierher gefahren.* there's nothing in/to sth an etw. [dat] ist nichts dran *(fam)* ◊ *An den Gerüchten über seinen Rücktritt ist nichts dran.* there's nothing to it etw. ist kinderleicht

no through road [noun] Sackgasse ['zakgasə] die <-, -n>

notice¹ [noun] **1.** *(sign)* Schild [ʃɪlt] das <-(e)s, -er> ◊ *Sie hängte ein Schild an die Ladentür, auf dem „Geschlossen" stand.; (information on a noticeboard)* Anschlag ['anʃla:k] der <-(e)s, Anschläge> ◊ *ein Anschlag am schwarzen Brett; (notification of a wedding, birth)* Anzeige ['antsaɛgə] die <-, -n> ◊

Hast du die Anzeige in der Zeitung gesehen? obituary notice **Todesanzeige** ['to:dəsantsaɛgə] **2.** *(beforehand warning)* give notice of sth etw. **ankündigen** ['ankʏndɪgn] +haben at short notice **kurzfristig** ['kʊʳtsfrɪstɪç] ◊ *Sie können die Wohnung auch kurzfristig kündigen.* at a moment's notice **jederzeit** ['je:de'tsaɛt] ◊ *Der Wagen steht Ihnen jederzeit zur Verfügung.* at three days' notice **innerhalb von drei Tagen** [ˌɪnehalp fɔn draɛ 'ta:gn] ◊ *Wir können innerhalb von drei Tagen Ersatz besorgen.* without notice **fristlos** ['frɪstlo:s] no comp/superl; when used as an adj, mostly before ns ◊ *eine fristlose Kündigung* ♦ *Er wurde fristlos entlassen.* **3.** *(official document)* Hinweis ['hɪnvaɛs] der <-es, -e> ◊ *Hier steht noch ein Hinweis zum Copyright.* **4.** *(review)* Kritik [kri'ti:k] die <-, -en> ◊ *Das Buch bekam hervorragende Kritiken.* ⊛ until further notice **bis auf weiteres** bring sth to sb's notice **jdn auf etw.** [acc] **aufmerksam machen** give sb notice **jdm kündigen** hand in your notice **kündigen** take notice of sb/sth **jdn/etw. beachten**

notice² [verb] bemerken [bə'mɛʳkn] <bemerkt, bemerkte, hat bemerkt> ◊ *Bemerkt er denn nicht, dass sie ihn belügt?* ♦ *Sie bemerkt das Chaos gar nicht mehr.* ⊛ get noticed **Aufmerksamkeit erregen**

noticeable(-ably) [adj, adv] deutlich ['dɔøtlɪç] when used as an adj, only before ns ◊ *eine deutliche Zunahme/Abnahme* ♦ *Unsere Situation ist deutlich besser als vor einem Jahr.* be (very) noticeable (deutlich) auffallen [(dɔøtlɪç) 'aoffalən] <fällt auf, fiel auf, ist aufgefallen> ◊ *Seine Unfähigkeit fällt deutlich auf.*

noticeboard [noun] schwarzes Brett [ˌʃvaʳtsəs 'brɛt] <-(e)s, -er> ◊ *einen Zettel ans schwarze Brett hängen*

notification [noun] Benachrichtigung [bə'na:xrɪçtɪgʊŋ] die <-, -en> ◊ *die Benachrichtigung der Angehörigen/Behörden* the notification of sth **die Mitteilung** ... [gen] ◊ *die Mitteilung der Prüfungsergebnisse*

notify [verb] notify sb (of sth) jdn (von etw.) benachrichtigen [bə'na:xrɪçtɪgn] <benachrichtigt, hat benachrichtigt> ◊ *Hat man Sie schon von der Sache benachrichtigt?* notify sth to sb jdm etw. mitteilen ['mɪttaɛlən] +haben ◊ *Wir teilen Ihnen eventuelle Änderungen umgehend mit.*

notion [noun] **1.** *(idea)* Vorstellung ['fo:ɐʃtɛlʊŋ] die <-, -en> ◊ *Ihre Vorstellung von Familienleben ist recht altmodisch.* give sb the notion of doing sth jdn auf den Gedanken bringen, etw. zu tun [aof de:n gə'daŋkn̩ brɪŋən ... tsu:] <bringt, brachte, hat gebracht> ◊ *Das brachte mich auf den Gedanken, sie mal wieder einzuladen.* **2.** *(whim)* a notion to do sth Lust, etw. zu tun [lʊst ... tsu:] die <-> no pl ◊ *Plötzlich bekam sie Lust, einen Kuchen zu backen.*

notorious [adj] berüchtigt [bə'rʏçtɪçt] ◊ *eine berüchtigte Gegend* ♦ *Er ist berüchtigt für seinen Jähzorn.*

notwithstanding [prep] trotz [trɔts] sing nouns without article or attribute are not declined when following this prep, otherwise [+gen] ◊ *Er will trotz seiner Krankheit kommen.*

nought, naught [noun] *(number)* Null [nʊl] die <-, -en> ♦ four¹ ⊛ come to nought **sich zerschlagen** ◊ *Alle unsere*

Hoffnungen hatten sich zerschlagen.

noun [noun] Nomen ['noːmən] das <–s, – or Nomina> ◊ „*Wut" ist ein Nomen ohne Pluralform.* **proper noun** Eigenname ['aeɡŋnaːmə] der <–ns, –n> **noun phrase** [noun] Nominalphrase [nomi'naːlfraːzə] die <–, –n>

novel¹ [noun] Roman [ro'maːn] der <–s, –e> ◊ *einen Roman lesen/schreiben*

novel² [adj] *(new, unusual)* neu [nɔɠ] <neuer, am neu(e)sten> ◊ *eine neue Methode* ◆ *Dieses Verfahren ist völlig neu.*

novelist [noun] Romanschriftsteller [ro'maːnʃrɪftʃtɛlɐ] der <–s, –> ♀Romanschriftstellerin [ro'maːnʃrɪftʃtɛlərɪn] die <–, –nen> ◊ *Konsalik ist ein bekannter Romanschriftsteller.* ◆ *Sie ist Romanschriftstellerin.*

novelty [noun] 1. *(sth new, innovative, original)* Neuheit ['nɔɠhaet] die <–, –en> ◊ *Damals war die Waschmaschine noch eine Neuheit.* 2. *(excitement)* Reiz des Neuen [,raets dɛs 'nɔɠən] der <–(e)s> *no pl* ◊ *Der Reiz des Neuen faszinierte ihn.* The novelty wears off. Der Reiz des Neuen lässt nach. 3. *(cheap object)* Krimskrams ['krɪmskrams] der <–(es)> *no pl* ◊ *eine Kiste voller Krimskrams*

November [noun] November [no'vɛmbɐ] der <–(s), –> *most sing →* January

now¹ [adv] 1. *(at the moment, immediately, next, up to the present, as a result of sth, for emphasis)* jetzt [jɛtst] ◊ *Wir müssen jetzt handeln.* ◆ *Muss das jetzt sein?* ◆ *Ich gehe jetzt ins Bett.* ◆ *Ich bin mit allem fertig. Was jetzt?* ◆ *Jetzt wird alles besser werden!* ◆ *Jetzt komm schon und sag mir, was los ist!* What is it now? Was ist denn jetzt schon wieder? from now on von jetzt an up to now bis jetzt right now jetzt gleich by now inzwischen [ɪn'tsvɪʃn] ◊ *Inzwischen habe ich gelernt, mit Computern umzugehen.* as of now mit sofortiger Wirkung [mɪt zo,fɔɐ'tɪɡɐ 'vɪɾkʊŋ] for now erst einmal ['eːɐst aen,maːl] ◊ *Danke erst einmal.* 2. *(introducing an explanation)* nun [nuːn] ◊ „*Warum hat er das gemacht?" — „Nun, eigentlich hatte ich es ihm aufgetragen."* now then also ['alzoː] ◊ *Also, gibt es noch Fragen?*

◉ it's now or never jetzt oder nie now and then ab und zu now, now na, na ◊ *Na, na, nun beruhige dich erst mal wieder.* now … now bald …, bald ◊ *Bald lachte sie, bald weinte sie vor Freude.*

now² [conjunc] now (that) jetzt, wo ['jɛtst voː] ◊ *Jetzt, wo er wieder zu Hause ist, fühlt sie sich nicht mehr einsam.*

nowadays [adv] heutzutage ['hɔɠtsuːtaːɡə] ◊ *Heutzutage helfen viele Männer im Haushalt.*

nowhere [adv] 1. *(in no place)* nirgends ['nɪɾɡŋts] ◊ *Ich kann meine Hausschuhe nirgends finden.* 2. *(direction, to no place)* nirgendwohin ['nɪɾɡŋtvoːhɪn] ◊ *Diese Straße führt nirgendwohin.*

nuance [noun] Nuance [ny'ãsə] die <–, –n> ◊ *kleinste/feinste Nuancen erkennen*

nuclear [adj] 1. *(energy, weapons)* Atom… [a'toːm] nuclear physics Atomphysik [a'toːmfy,ziːk] die <–> *no pl* nuclear waste Atommüll [a'toːmmʏl] der <–s> *no pl* nuclear weapons Atomwaffen [a'toːmvafŋ] die <–> *pl* 2. *(relating to a nucleus)* Kern… [kɛɾn] nuclear fission Kernspaltung ['kɛɾnʃpaltʊŋ] die <–, –en>

nuclear energy [noun] Kernenergie ['kɛɾn|enɛɐˌɡiː] die <–> *no pl* ◊ *die friedliche Nutzung der Kernenergie*

nuclear power [noun] 1. *(energy)* Atomkraft [a'toːmkraft] die <–> *no pl* 2. *(country with nuclear weapons)* Atommacht [a'toːmmaxt] die <–, Atommächte>

nuclear power station [noun] Atomkraftwerk [a'toːmkraftvɛɾk] das <–(e)s, –e>

nucleus [noun] Kern [kɛɾn] der <–(e)s, –e> ◊ *Im Kern der Zelle befinden sich die Chromosomen.* ◆ *Vater, Mutter und Kinder bilden den Kern der Familie.*

nude [adj] nackt [nakt] *no comp/superl* ◊ *Alle Menschen auf dem Bild sind nackt.* nude scene Nacktszene ['naktstseːnə] die <–, –n> nude portrait Akt [akt] der <–(e)s, –e> ◊ *einen Akt malen*

nuisance [noun] 1. *(sb/sth annoying)* Plage ['plaːɡə] die <–, –n> ◊ *Zu dieser Jahreszeit sind die Wespen eine echte Plage.* be a nuisance to sb jdm auf die Nerven gehen [aof diː 'nɛɾfŋ ɡeːən] <geht, ging, ist gegangen> *(fam)* ◊ *Dein Hund kann einem manchmal auf die Nerven gehen!* make a nuisance of yourself lästig werden ['lɛstɪç veːɐdŋ] +sein ◊ *Ich hoffe, die Kinder sind nicht lästig geworden.* 2. LAW Ärgernis ['ɛɾɡɛnɪs] das <–ses> *no pl* cause a public nuisance öffentliches Ärgernis erregen

numb¹ [adj] 1. *(having no feeling)* taub [taɔp] *seldom comp/superl* ◊ *Er hatte schon ganz taube Finger vor Kälte.* ◆ *Nach der Operation blieb sein Bein noch lange taub.* 2. *(unable to react)* numb with grief/fear starr vor Schmerz/Angst ['ʃtar foːɐ ʃmɛɾts/,aŋst] *no comp/superl*

numb² [verb] betäuben [bə'tɔɠbm̩] <betäubt, betäubte, hat betäubt> ◊ *Die Wunde wurde vor dem Nähen betäubt.* numbed with grief/fear wie betäubt vor Schmerz/Angst

number¹ [noun] 1. MATH Zahl [tsaːl] die <–, –en> ◊ *die Zahlen 1 bis 10* ◆ *mit großen Zahlen rechnen* a round/an even/odd number eine runde/gerade/ ungerade Zahl 2. *(of a phone, house, for defining position, marking sth, song)* Nummer ['nʊmɐ] die <–, –n> ◊ *eine Nummer wählen* ◆ *Sie wohnt im Haus Nummer 16.* ◆ *Bitte ziehen Sie eine Nummer.* dial the wrong number sich verwählen [fɐ'vɛːlən] <verwählt sich, verwählte sich, hat sich verwählt> account number Kontonummer ['kɔntonʊmɐ] Social Security number Sozialversicherungsnummer [zo'tsjaːlfɛˌzɪçərʊŋsnʊmɐ] 3. *(quantity, amount of people or things)* Anzahl ['antsaːl] die <–> *no pl* ◊ *Die Anzahl der Verletzten stieg ständig.* a (large) number of eine (große) Anzahl von ◊ *Wir haben eine große Anzahl von Bewerbern.* in small/large numbers in kleiner/großer Zahl [ɪn klaenɐ/ɡroːsɐ 'tsaːl] ◊ *Man findet diese Tiere dort noch in großer Zahl.* on a number of occasions des Öfteren [dɛs 'œftərən] ◊ *Wir sind uns des Öfteren begegnet.* 4. *(of a magazine, periodical)* Ausgabe ['aosɡaːbə] die <–, –n> ◊ *Sie las eine alte Ausgabe der Tageszeitung.* 5. *(piece of clothing)* Outfit ['aotfɪt] das <–(s), –s> *(fam)* ◊ *Auf der Party trug sie ein schwarzes Outfit.* 6. GRAM Numerus ['nuːmerʊs] der <–, Numeri> ◊ *In welchem Numerus steht das Wort?*

◉ sb's number is up jd ist dran *(fam)* any number of 1. *(many)* sehr viele ◊ *Er hat sehr viele erfolgreiche Bücher geschrieben.* 2. *(when choosing sth)* beliebig viele ◊ *Ziehen Sie beliebig viele Karten.* beyond numbers unzählig ◊ *Unzählige Ameisen*

liefen über den Boden. by the numbers nach Schema F *(pej)*

number² ⟨verb⟩ **1.** *(put numbers on sth)* nummerieren [nʊmə'riːrən] <nummeriert, nummerierte, hat nummeriert> ◊ *die Seiten eines Dokuments nummerieren* **2.** *(amount to)* zählen ['tsɛːlən] +haben ◊ *Die Stadt zählt 25 000 Einwohner.* ⊙ **number sb among sth** jdn zu etw. zählen ◊ *Ich zähle sie zu meinen besten Freundinnen.*

number one ⟨noun⟩ *(person, team, record)* Nummer eins [nʊmə 'aɛns] die <−> no pl ◊ *Das Album ist seit Wochen die Nummer eins.* ⊙ **do number one** klein machen *(kidsp)* ◊ *Musst du klein oder groß machen?* **look out for number one** an sich ⟨acc⟩ selbst denken ◊ *Er denkt immer nur an sich selbst.*

number plate ⟨noun⟩ Nummernschild ['nʊmənʃɪlt] das <−(e)s, −er>

numeral ⟨noun⟩ Ziffer ['tsɪfe] die <−, −n> ◊ *arabische und römische Ziffern*

numerous ⟨adj⟩ zahlreich ['tsaːlraɛç] ◊ *Zahlreiche Kunden haben sich beschwert.* ♦ *Solche Fälle sind zum Glück nicht sehr zahlreich.*

nun ⟨noun⟩ Nonne ['nɔnə] die <−, −n> ◊ *Seine Tochter ist Nonne geworden.* ♦ *Die Nonnen beten in der Kirche.*

nurse¹ ⟨noun⟩ *(in a hospital: female)* Krankenschwester ['kraŋkŋʃvestɐ] die <−, −n> ◊ *Sie möchte Krankenschwester werden.*; *(male)* Krankenpfleger ['kraŋkŋpfleːge] der <−s, −> ◊ *Der Krankenpfleger kommt gleich.*

nurse² ⟨verb⟩ **1.** *(look after a sick person)* pflegen ['pfleːgŋ] +haben ◊ *Seine Frau hat ihn während seiner Krankheit liebevoll gepflegt.* nurse sb back to health jdn gesund pflegen **2.** *(a cold)* auskurieren ['aʊskuriːrən] <kuriert aus, kurierte aus, hat auskuriert> ◊ *Sie liegt im Bett und kuriert eine Erkältung aus.*; *(an injury)* schonen ['ʃoːnən] +haben ◊ *Sie sollten den Arm schonen.* **3.** *(a feeling, plan)* hegen ['heːgŋ] +haben ◊ *Misstrauen gegen jdn hegen* ♦ *Sie*

begen den Plan, heimlich zu heiraten. **4.** *(a drink)* nurse sth an etw. ⟨dat⟩ nippen [an ... nɪpm̩] +haben ◊ *Ich nippte an meinem Sektglas.* **5.** nurse a baby ein Baby stillen [aɛn 'beːbi: ʃtɪlən] +haben ◊ *Sie saß im Sessel und stillte ihr Baby.* a baby nurses ein Baby trinkt an der Brust [aɛn ˌbeːbi: trɪŋkt an deːɐ 'brʊst] <trank, hat getrunken>

nursery ⟨noun⟩ **1.** *(institution)* nursery *(school)* Kindergarten ['kɪndegaˈtn̩] der <−s, Kindergärten> ◊ *in den Kindergarten gehen/kommen* **2.** *(room at home, in a hospital)* Kinderzimmer ['kɪndetsɪmɐ] das <−s, −> ◊ *Die Jungen spielten im Kinderzimmer.* **3.** *(for plants)* Gärtnerei [gɛˈtnəˈraɛ] die <−, −en> ◊ *Pflanzen in der Gärtnerei bestellen/abholen;* *(for trees)* Baumschule ['baʊmʃuːlə] die <−, −n>

nursing ⟨noun⟩ Krankenpflege ['kraŋkŋpfleːgə] die <−> no pl ◊ *eine Schule für Krankenpflege*

nursing home ⟨noun⟩ Pflegeheim ['pfleːgəhaɛm] das <−(e)s, −e> ◊ *in einem Pflegeheim untergebracht sein*

nut ⟨noun⟩ **1.** BOT Nuss [nʊs] die <−, Nüsse> ◊ *Nüsse knacken* **2.** TECHN Mutter ['mʊtɐ] die <−, −n> ◊ *die Muttern nachziehen* **3.** *(crazy person)* Spinner ['ʃpɪnɐ] der <−s, −> ♀Spinnerin ['ʃpɪnərɪn] die <−, −nen> *(fam, pej)* ◊ *Hör nicht auf das, was dieser alte Spinner sagt.* **4.** *(fam) (enthusiastic fan)* a ... nut ein großer Fan von jd, ein großer Fan ... ⟨gen⟩ [aɛn ˌgroːsɐ 'fɛn] with pl nouns +gen ◊ *Sie ist ein großer Fan von Elvis Presley.* ♦ *Ich bin ein großer Fan der Beatles.* **5.** *(fam) (head)* Rübe ['ryːbə] die <−, −n> *(fam)* ◊ *eins auf die Rübe kriegen* **6.** *(rude) (testicles)* nuts Eier ['aɛɐ] die <−> pl *(rude)* ◊ *jdm in die Eier treten* ⊙ **the nuts and bolts of sth** das Einmaleins ... ⟨gen⟩ ◊ *das Einmaleins der Hautpflege* off your nut nicht ganz bei Trost *(fam)*

nutrient ⟨noun⟩ Nährstoff ['nɛːɐʃtɔf] der <−(e)s, −e> most pl ◊ *Obst und Gemüse enthalten viele Nährstoffe.*

O

o, O [noun] o, O [oː] das <–(s), –(s)> ◊ *Dieses Wort wird mit einem kleinen o/großen O geschrieben.* ♦ *O wie Otto*

oak [noun] Eiche ['æçə] die <–, –n> ◊ *Am Waldrand steht eine Eiche.* ♦ *Der Tisch ist aus Eiche.*

oar [noun] Ruder ['ruːdɐ] das <–s, –> ◊ *Er nahm die Ruder in die Hand.*
ⓖ **stick your oar in** sich einmischen

oath [noun] **1.** *(official promise)* Eid [aɛt] der <–(e)s, –e> ◊ *einen Eid brechen* take/swear an oath einen Eid ablegen/schwören be under oath unter Eid stehen take the oath vereidigt werden [fɐ'aɛdɪçt veːɐɡdn̩] <wird, wurde, ist worden> ◊ *Der Angeklagte wird jetzt vereidigt.* **2.** *(curse)* Fluch [fluːx] der <–(e)s, Flüche> ◊ *Seine Flüche waren im ganzen Haus zu hören.*

oats [noun] Hafer ['haːfɐ] der <–s> no pl ◊ *Das Pferd frisst Hafer.* rolled oats Haferflocken ['haːfɐflɔkn̩] die <–> pl

obedient(ly) [adj, adv] gehorsam [ɡə'hoːɐzaːm] ◊ *Ihre Kinder sind nicht sehr gehorsam.* ♦ *ein gehorsamer Hund* ♦ *Die Kinder wuschen sich gehorsam die Hände.*

obey [verb] *(do what is expected, what sb tells you)* obey (sb) (jdm) gehorchen [ɡə'hɔrçn̩] <gehorcht, gehorchte, hat gehorcht> ◊ *Der Hund gehorcht mir nicht.* ♦ *Das gehorcht bestimmten physikalischen Gesetzen.; (an order, instruction, a law)* obey sth etw. befolgen [bə'fɔlɡn̩] <befolgt, befolgte, hat befolgt> ◊ *Der Soldat weigerte sich, den Befehl zu befolgen.*

obituary [noun] Nachruf ['naːxruːf] der <–(e)s, –e> ◊ *In der Zeitung erschien ein Nachruf über ihn.* obituary notice Todesanzeige ['toːdəsˌantsaeɡə] die <–, –n>

object¹ [noun] **1.** *(thing, target of a feeling or action)* Gegenstand ['ɡeːɡn̩ʃtant] der <–(e)s, Gegenstände> ◊ *Mit einem spitzen Gegenstand bohrte er ein Loch in den Deckel.* ♦ *Der Gegenstand seiner Forschungen sind Spinnen.* **2.** *(aim, purpose)* Ziel [tsiːl] das <–(e)s, –e> ◊ *Du scheinst kein Ziel im Leben zu haben.* with the object of doing sth mit dem Ziel, etw. zu tun ◊ *Sie rief ihn an, mit dem Ziel, ihn zu überzeugen.* **3.** GRAM Objekt [ɔp'jɛkt] das <–(e)s, –e> ◊ *direktes und indirektes Objekt*
ⓖ **be no object** nebensächlich sein

object² [verb] *(disagree, disapprove)* object (to sb doing sth) etwas dagegen haben (wenn jd etw. tut) [ɛtvas daˈɡeːɡn̩ haːbm̩] +haben ◊ *Haben Sie etwas dagegen, wenn ich rauche?; (protest)* object to sth gegen etw. protestieren [ɡeːɡn̩ ... proˌtɛsˌtiːrən] <protestiert, protestierte, hat protestiert> ◊ *Ich protestiere gegen diese Behauptung!; (raise an objection, argue)* object that einwenden, dass ['aɛnvɛndn̩ das] <wendet ein, wendete/wandte ein, hat eingewendet/eingewandt> ◊ *Sie wendete ein, dass das alles sehr teuer sei.; (reject)* object to sth etw. ablehnen ['apleːnən] +haben ◊ *Einige Staaten lehnten das Abkommen ab.*

objection [noun] **1.** *(argument against)* Einwand ['aɛnvant] der <–(e)s, Einwände> ◊ *Ich habe keine Einwände.* raise an objection einen Einwand erheben **2.** LAW Einspruch ['aɛnʃprʊx] der <–(e)s, Einsprüche> ◊ *Einspruch! Das ist Hörensagen!*

objective [noun] Ziel [tsiːl] das <–(e)s, –e> ◊ *Das Ziel unserer Politik ist die Schaffung von Arbeitsplätzen.* achieve an objective ein Ziel erreichen main objective Hauptziel ['haoptˌtsiːl]

objective(ly) [adj, adv] **1.** objektiv [ɔpjɛk'tiːf] no comp/ superl ◊ *Sie versuchte, objektiv zu bleiben.* ♦ *etw. objektiv beurteilen* ♦ *eine objektive Meinung* **2.** GRAM be objective, be in the objective case als Objekt verwendet werden [als ɔp'jɛkt fɐvɛndət veːɐɡdn̩] <wird, wurde, ist worden>

obligation [noun] Verpflichtung [fɐ'pflɪçtʊŋ] die <–, –en> ◊ *eine moralische Verpflichtung* ♦ *eine Verpflichtung auf sich nehmen* fulfil an obligation eine Verpflichtung erfüllen be under an obligation to do sth dazu verpflichtet sein, etw. zu tun [daːtsu: fɐ'pflɪçtət tsaːn ... tsuː] +sein ◊ *Ich bin nicht dazu verpflichtet, Ihnen darüber Auskunft zu geben.* feel an obligation to sb sich jdm verpflichtet fühlen [fɐ'pflɪçtət fyːlən] +haben ◊ *Sie fühlte sich ihm verpflichtet, weil er ihr geholfen hatte.* without obligation unverbindlich ['ʊnfɛbɪntlɪç] ◊ *jdm Informationsmaterial kostenlos und unverbindlich zuschicken*

obligatory [adj] obligatorisch [ɔbliga'toːrɪʃ] no comp/ superl ◊ *eine Fremdsprache ist im dritten Jahr ist obligatorisch.* ♦ *eine obligatorische Vorlesung*

oblige [verb] **1.** *(be forced)* be obliged to do sth verpflichtet sein, etw. zu tun [fɐ'pflɪçtət tsaːn ... tsuː] +sein ◊ *Sie sind gesetzlich verpflichtet, uns dies mitzuteilen.* feel obliged to do sth sich verpflichtet fühlen, etw. zu tun [fɐ'pflɪçtət fyːlən ... tsuː] +haben ◊ *Er fühlte sich verpflichtet, für sie zu sorgen.* **2.** *(do a favo(u)r)* oblige (sb) jdm einen Gefallen tun [aɛnən ɡə'falən tuːn] <tut, tat, hat getan> Please oblige me by closing the window. Würden Sie mir bitte den Gefallen tun und das Fenster schließen? She asked him to come home earlier and he obliged. Sie bat ihn, früher nach Hause zu kommen, und er tat ihr den Gefallen. be happy to oblige gern zur Verfügung stehen [ɡɛrn tsuːɐ fe'fyːɡʊŋ ʃteːən] <steht, stand, hat gestanden> ◊ *Wenn Sie noch etwas brauchen, stehe ich gern zur Verfügung.*
ⓖ **much obliged** herzlichen Dank be much obliged to sb jdm für etw. sehr verbunden sein

obliging(ly) [adj, adv] entgegenkommend [ɛntˈgeːɡn̩kɔmənt] ◊ *Der Prüfer war sehr entgegenkommend.* ♦ *Ich habe einen entgegenkommenden Chef.* ♦ *Sie wurde äußerst entgegenkommend behandelt.*

oblivious [adj] be oblivious of/to sth etw. nicht wahrnehmen [nɪçt 'vaːrneːmən] <nimmt wahr, nahm wahr, hat wahrgenommen> ◊ *Er schien den Lärm ringsum nicht wahrzunehmen.*

obscene(ly) [adj, adv] **1.** *(sexually offensive)* obszön [ɔps'tsɔːn] ◊ *Der Witz war obszön.* ✦ *Sie erhielt obszöne Anrufe.* ✦ *Rede nicht so obszön daher!* **2.** *(demand, price)* unverschämt ['ʊnfɛʃɛːmt] <unverschämter, am unverschämtesten> ◊ *eine unverschämte Forderung* ✦ *Diese Preise sind unverschämt.* ✦ *Der neue Supermarkt ist unverschämt teuer.*

obscure¹ [adj] **1.** *(little known)* unbekannt ['ʊnbəkant] <unbekannter, am unbekanntesten> ◊ *Die genaue Herkunft dieses Dokuments bleibt unbekannt.* ✦ *ein unbekannter Dichter.* **2.** *(hard to understand)* verworren [fɛ'vɔrən] ◊ *Seine Sprache ist ziemlich verworren.* ✦ *Was für eine verworrene Geschichte!* for some obscure reason aus einem unerfindlichen Grund [aʊs ˌaɛnəm ˌʊnǀɛfɪntlɪçn 'grʊnt]

obscure² [verb] **1.** *(hide)* verdecken [fɛ'dɛkŋ] <verdeckt, verdeckte, hat verdeckt> ◊ *Wolken verdecken die Sonne.* **2.** *(confuse)* obscure sth von etw. ablenken [fɔn ... ˌaplɛŋkŋ] +haben ◊ *Der Zwischenfall darf nicht von der Tatsache ablenken, dass dieser Wagen zu den sichersten der Welt gehört.*

observance [noun] **1.** *(of a rule)* Beachtung [bə'axtʊŋ] die <-> no pl ◊ *eine strenge Beachtung der Gesetze/Regeln/Vorschriften; (of a tradition)* in observance of sth anlässlich ... [gen] ['anlɛslɪç] ◊ *anlässlich des Nationalfeiertags* **2.** observances Feierlichkeiten ['faɛɐlɪçkaɛtŋ] die <-> pl

observation [noun] **1.** *(act of watching)* Beobachtung [bə'oːbaxtʊŋ] die <-, -en> ◊ *die Beobachtung eines Verdächtigen* be under observation unter Beobachtung stehen be in hospital under observation zur Beobachtung im Krankenhaus sein keep sb/sth under observation jdn/etw. beobachten [bə'oːbaxtŋ] <beobachtet, beobachtete, hat beobachtet> remain under observation weiter beobachtet werden **2.** *(remark)* Bemerkung [bə'mɛʳkʊŋ] die <-, -en> ◊ *eine unpassende Bemerkung über jdn/etw. machen* **3.** powers of observation Beobachtungsgabe [bə'oːbaxtʊŋsgaːbə] die <-> no pl ◊ *eine gute/schlechte Beobachtungsgabe haben*

observe [verb] **1.** *(notice, watch)* beobachten [bə'oːbaxtŋ] <beobachtet, beobachtete, hat beobachtet> ◊ *Wir konnten keine Verbesserung beobachten.* ✦ *Hast du beobachtet, wie er das gemacht hat?* ✦ *Die Polizei lässt ihn beobachten.* observe sb/sth doing sth jdn/etw. dabei beobachten, wie er etw. tut ◊ *Er beobachtete sie dabei, wie sie das Geld stahl.* **2.** *(a rule)* beachten [bə'axtŋ] <beachtet, beachtete, hat beachtet> ◊ *Gesetze/Konventionen beachten* ✦ *Er hatte die Vorfahrt nicht beachtet.* **3.** *(a custom, festival, an agreement)* einhalten ['aɛnhaltŋ] <hält ein, hielt ein, hat eingehalten> ◊ *Er und die Ramadan auch fern der Heimat ein.* ✦ *den Waffenstillstand einhalten* a nationally observed holiday ein nationaler Feiertag [aɛn natsio̯ˌnaːle 'faɛeta̩k] observe a minute's silence eine Schweigeminute einlegen [aɛnə 'ʃvaɛgəmiˌnuːtə ˌaɛnleːgŋ] +haben **4.** *(remark)* bemerken [bə'mɛʳkŋ] <bemerkt, bemerkte, hat bemerkt> ◊ *Wie der Kanzler sehr richtig bemerkte, ... ✦ Sie bemerkte spitz, dass sie sich das schon gedacht habe.*

observer [noun] Beobachter [bə'oːbaxtɐ] der <-s, -> ♀Beobachterin [bə'oːbaxtərɪn] die <-, -nen> ◊ *ein aufmerksamer/unabhängiger Beobachter*

obsessed [adj] obsessed (with sb/sth) (von jdm/etw.) besessen [bə'zɛsn] ◊ *ein besessener Sammler* ✦ *Sie war von der Idee völlig besessen.*

obsession [noun] **1.** *(mental state)* Besessenheit [bə'zɛsŋhaɛt] die <-> no pl ◊ *Seine Besessenheit nimmt immer schlimmere Ausmaße an.* **2.** *(idea, object)* Obsession [ɔpzɛ'sjoːn] die <-, -en> ◊ *Der Gedanke wurde zur Obsession.*

obstacle [noun] Hindernis ['hɪndenɪs] das <-ses, -se> ◊ *ein Hindernis überwinden* put obstacles in sb's way jdm Hindernisse in den Weg legen ⊛ be an obstacle to sb/sth jdm/etw. im Weg stehen

obstinate(ly) [adj, adv] **1.** *(stubborn)* eigensinnig ['aɛgŋzɪnɪç] ◊ *ein eigensinniges Kind* ✦ *Leo blieb eigensinnig und wollte sich durchsetzen.* ✦ *eigensinnig auf etw. bestehen* **2.** *(unchanging)* hartnäckig ['haʳtnɛkɪç] ◊ *hartnäckige Flecken* ✦ *Sein Husten war sehr hartnäckig.* ✦ *etw. hartnäckig leugnen*

obstruct [verb] **1.** *(a passage, road)* blockieren [blɔ'kiːrən] <blockiert, blockierte, hat blockiert> ◊ *Die Stühle versperren den Notausgang.; (a view)* versperren [fɛ'ʃpɛrən] <versperrt, versperrte, hat versperrt> ◊ *Er versperrt mir die Sicht.; (a blood vessel, tube, pipe)* verstopfen [fɛ'ʃtɔpfŋ] <verstopft, verstopfte, hat verstopft> ◊ *Seine Arterien sind verstopft.* **2.** *(make difficult)* behindern [bə'hɪndɐn] <behindert, behinderte, hat behindert> ◊ *Behindern dich die langen Fingernägel nicht beim Tippen?* ✦ *Ihr Fahrzeug behindert den Verkehr.*

obtain [verb] **1.** *(get)* beschaffen [bə'ʃafŋ] <beschafft, beschaffte, hat beschafft> ◊ *Dieses Buch ist schwer zu beschaffen.* ✦ *sich* [dat] *Informationen beschaffen; (permission, advice)* einholen ['aɛnhoːlən] +haben ◊ *bei jdm eine Erlaubnis einholen* ✦ *den Rat eines Fachmanns einholen* **2.** *(be given)* erhalten [ɛ'haltŋ] <erhält, erhielt, hat erhalten> ◊ *Er erhielt die Genehmigung für den Bau.* ✦ *Ich habe keinen Zugang zu den Akten erhalten.* sth can be obtained from sb/etw. erhältlich [ɪst bae ... e̩,hɛltɪç]

obvious [adj] **1.** *(easy to see)* offensichtlich ['ɔfnzɪçtlɪç] ◊ *Es ist doch ganz offensichtlich, dass er lügt.* ✦ *ein offensichtlicher Fall von Betrug* be obvious to sb jdm klar sein ['klaːʳ zaen] ◊ *Es war uns allen klar, dass das nicht gut gehen konnte.* be obvious from sth aus etw. deutlich werden [aʊs ... 'dɔgtlɪç veːɐdn] ◊ *Aus seinem Zögern wurde deutlich, dass er sich nicht sicher war.* **2.** *(explanation)* einfach ['aɛnfax] ◊ *Dafür gibt es eine ganz einfache Erklärung.* ✦ *(solution, excuse)* nahe liegend ['naːə liːgn̩t] <näher liegend, am nächsten liegend> only before ns ◊ *Seinen Namen wollte sie aus nahe liegenden Gründen nicht nennen.* sth is the obvious thing to do es liegt nahe, etw. zu tun [ɛs liːkt 'naːə ... tuː] <liegt, lag, hat gelegen>

obviously [adv] **1.** *(clearly)* offensichtlich ['ɔfnzɪçtlɪç] ◊ *Sie hat offensichtlich keine Lust mitzukommen.* **2.** *(of course)* natürlich [na'tyːɡlɪç] ◊ *Natürlich freue ich mich sehr über Ihr Angebot.*

occasion [noun] **1.** *(instance)* Gelegenheit [gə'leːgŋhaɛt] die <-, -en> ◊ *Bei welcher Gelegenheit habt ihr euch kennen gelernt?* on one occasion einmal ['aɛnmaːl] ◊ *Einmal kam sie erst um elf zur Arbeit.* on this occasion dieses Mal ['diːzəs maːl] ◊ *Dieses Mal hat er Glück gehabt.* on occasion gelegentlich [gə'leːgŋtlɪç] **2.** *(special event, cause)* Anlass ['anlas] der <-es, Anlässe> ◊ *die passende Kleidung zum festlichen Anlass* ✦ *ein Anlass zum Feiern* ✦ *Es*

gab keinen Anlass zur Freude. on the occasion of aus Anlass ... [gen] ◊ *Aus Anlass seiner Beförderung wollen wir heute feiern.* to mark the occasion aus diesem Anlass not the occasion for sth nicht der richtige Zeitpunkt für etw. [ˌnɪçt deːɐ̯ ˌrɪçtɪɡə ˈt͡saɛ̯tpʊŋkt fyːɐ̯] ⊙ rise to the occasion sich der Situation gewachsen zeigen

occasional(ly) [adj, adv] **1.** *(not often)* gelegentlich [ɡəˈleːɡn̩tlɪç] *no comp/superl; when used as an adj, only before ns* ◊ *gelegentliche Zwischenrufe* ♦ *Sie besucht mich gelegentlich.* only (very) occasionally nur selten [nuːɡ ˈzɛltn̩] **2.** *(not many)* vereinzelt [fɛlˈaɛ̯nt͡sl̩t] ◊ *nur vereinzelte Fehler finden* ♦ *Im Neckar gibt es vereinzelt sogar Forellen.*

Occident [noun] *(culturally, literary)* Abendland [ˈaːbm̩tlant] das <-(e)s> *no pl; (politically)* Westen [ˈvɛstn̩] der <-s> *no pl*

occupant [noun] **1.** *(of a house, an area)* Bewohner [bəˈvoːnɐ] der <-s, -> ♀Bewohnerin [bəˈvoːnərɪn] die <-, -nen> ◊ *die Evakuierung der Bewohner; (of a car)* Insasse [ˈɪnzasə] der <-n, -n> ♀Insassin [ˈɪnzasɪn] die <-, -nen> *most pl* ◊ *Die Insassen des Wagens wurden nicht verletzt.* **2.** *(of a post)* Inhaber [ˈɪnhaːbɐ] der <-s, -> ♀Inhaberin [ˈɪnhaːbərɪn] die <-, -nen> ◊ *der Inhaber eines Lehrstuhls*

occupation [noun] **1.** *(job)* Beruf [bəˈruːf] der <-(e)s, -e> ◊ *Er ist Bäcker von Beruf.* **2.** *(activity)* Beschäftigung [bəˈʃɛftɪɡʊŋ] die <-, -en> ◊ *Wenn dir langweilig ist, such dir eine Beschäftigung!* **3.** MIL Besetzung [bəˈzɛtsʊŋ] die <-, -en> ♦ *Polen unter sowjetischer Besetzung* ♦ *die gewaltsame Besetzung eines Gebiets; (in compound ns)* occupation ... Besatzungs... [bəˈzat͡sʊŋs] occupation troops Besatzungstruppen [bəˈzat͡sʊŋstrʊpm̩] die <-> *pl* **4.** *(of a house, flat)* ready for occupation bezugsfertig [bəˈt͡suːksfɛrˈtɪç] *no comp/superl* ◊ *Die Wohnungen sind jetzt bezugsfertig.* property in owner occupation Hausbesitz, der vom Eigentümer bewohnt wird

occupational [adj] **1.** *(relating to work in general)* Arbeits... [ˈarbaɛ̯ts] occupational accident Arbeitsunfall [ˈarbaɛ̯tsʊnfal] der <-(e)s, Arbeitsunfälle> [ˈarbaɛ̯tsʊnfɛlə] occupational medicine Arbeitsmedizin [ˈarbaɛ̯tsmediˌt͡siːn] die <-> *no pl* **2.** *(relating to sb's job)* Berufs... [bəˈruːfs] occupational hazard Berufsrisiko [bəˈruːfsˌriːziko] das <-s, -s> occupational outlook Berufsaussichten [bəˈruːfslaɔ̯st͡sɪçtn̩] die <-> *pl* **3.** *(relating to sb's workplace)* occupational ... ... am Arbeitsplatz [am ˈaˈbaɛ̯tsplats] ◊ *Psychologie/ Sicherheit am Arbeitsplatz* **4.** ECON occupational pension Betriebsrente [bəˈtriːpsrɛntə] die <-, -n> **5.** MED occupational therapy Beschäftigungstherapie [bəˈʃɛftɪɡʊŋsteraˌpiː] die <-, -n>

occupy [verb] **1.** *(a seat, bed, place)* belegen [bəˈleːɡn̩] <belegt, belegte, hat belegt> ◊ *Zurzeit sind leider alle Zimmer belegt.* ♦ *Platz 1 belegte die russische Läuferin.; (a house, an area)* bewohnen [bəˈvoːnən] <bewohnt, bewohnte, hat bewohnt> ◊ *Diese Höhle wurde einmal von Menschen bewohnt.* **2.** *(sb's time, a space)* einnehmen [ˈaɛ̯nneːmən] <nimmt ein, nahm ein, hat eingenommen> ◊ *Diese Aufgabe nimmt einen großen Teil meiner Zeit ein.* ♦ *Die Tabellen nehmen zu viel Platz ein.* **3.** *(take control of)* besetzen [bəˈzɛtsn̩] <besetzt, besetzte, hat besetzt> ◊ *Aus Protest gegen die Studiengebühren besetzten Studenten die Universität.* ♦ *Die Truppen besetzten das feindliche*

Gebiet. **4.** *(a post)* bekleiden [bəˈklaɛ̯dn̩] <bekleidet, bekleidete, hat bekleidet> *(lofty)* ◊ *das Amt des Vorsitzenden bekleiden* **5.** *(keep busy)* beschäftigen [bəˈʃɛftɪɡn̩] <beschäftigt, beschäftigte, hat beschäftigt> ◊ *Sie war mit der Buchführung beschäftigt.* ♦ *Mit Basteln kann man die Kinder stundenlang beschäftigen.* keep sb occupied jdn beschäftigen occupy yourself (with sth) sich (mit etw.) beschäftigen

occur [verb] *(exist, arise)* vorkommen [ˈfoːɐ̯kɔmən] <kommt vor, kam vor, ist vorgekommen> ◊ *Wie oft kommt dieses Wort im Text vor?* ♦ *Koalas kommen nur in Australien vor.; (happen)* geschehen [ɡəˈʃeːən] <geschieht, geschah, ist geschehen> ◊ *Wann geschah der Unfall?; (problem, mistake)* auftreten [ˈaɔ̯ftreːtn̩] <tritt auf, trat auf, ist aufgetreten> ◊ *Ist dieser Fehler schon oft aufgetreten?*

• **occur to** [phras v] occur to sb *(come to mind)* jdm einfallen [ˈaɛ̯nfalən] <fällt ein, fiel ein, ist eingefallen> ◊ *Plötzlich fiel ihm ein, dass er die Tür nicht abgeschlossen hatte.; (strike)* jdm auffallen [ˈaɔ̯ffalən] <fällt auf, fiel auf, ist aufgefallen> ◊ *Das ist mir noch nie aufgefallen.*

occurrence [noun] **1.** *(event)* Ereignis [ɛlˈaɛ̯ɡnɪs] das <-ses, -se> ◊ *ein seltenes/alltägliches Ereignis; (noteworthy)* Begebenheit [bəˈɡeːbm̩haɛ̯t] die <-, -en> ◊ *eine amüsante Begebenheit aus seinem Leben* schildern be a ... occurrence ... vorkommen [ˈfoːɐ̯kɔmən] <kommt vor, kam vor, ist vorgekommen> ◊ *So etwas kommt oft/regelmäßig/täglich vor.* **2.** *(presence)* Auftreten [ˈaɔ̯ftreːtn̩] das <-s> *no pl* ◊ *das häufige Auftreten von Erkältungskrankheiten im Winter; (of a species, mineral)* Vorkommen [ˈfoːɐ̯kɔmən] das <-s> *no pl* ◊ *das Vorkommen von Wölfen in Mitteleuropa*

ocean [noun] Ozean [ˈoːt͡seaːn] der <-s, -e> ◊ *der Atlantische Ozean*

◉ oceans of ... massenhaft ... *(fam)* ◊ *massenhaft Zeit haben*

October [noun] Oktober [ɔkˈtoːbɐ] der <-(s), -> *most sing* → **January**

odd [adj] **1.** *(strange)* seltsam [ˈzɛltzaːm] ◊ *ein seltsamer Zufall* ♦ *Es ist seltsam, dass er noch nicht angerufen hat.* strike sb as odd jdm seltsam vorkommen the odd thing (about it) is ... das Seltsame (daran) ist ... **2.** *(a few, one separated from a pair)* einzeln [ˈaɛ̯nt͡sl̩n] *no comp/superl* ◊ *Es gab nur einzelne Wolken am Himmel.* ♦ *von einzelnen Fehlern abgesehen* ♦ *eine einzelne Socke* **3.** *(not often or regular)* gelegentlich [ɡəˈleːɡn̩tlɪç] *no comp/superl, only before ns* the odd drink ein gelegentliches Gläschen at odd times gelegentlich **4.** *(all sorts of, various)* alle möglichen [alə ˈmøːklɪçn̩] *no comp/superl, only before pl ns* ◊ *In der Kiste waren alle möglichen Dinge.* **5.** *(number)* ungerade [ˈʊnɡaradə] *no comp/superl* ◊ *1, 3 und 5 sind ungerade Zahlen.* **6.** *(approximately)* 10/20/30 odd etwa 10/20/30 [ɛtva: ˈt͡seːn/ˈt͡svant͡sɪç/ˈdraɛ̯sɪç] ◊ *Es waren etwa 30 Tiere.* ♦ *Sie ist etwa 20.; (a bit more than 10/20/30)* etwas über 10/20/30 [ɛtvas yːbɐ ˈt͡seːn/ˈt͡svant͡sɪç/ˈdraɛ̯sɪç] ◊ *Er spielt Tennis seit etwas über 10 Jahren.*

◉ the odd man/one out ein Außenseiter be the odd one out *(on a list)* nicht dazugehören

oddity [noun] **1.** *(person, object)* Exot [ɛˈksoːt] der <-en, -en> ♀Exotin [ɛˈksoːtɪn] die <-, -nen> ◊ *Unter den Eisläuferinnen ist die Kubanerin eine*

echte *Exotin.* ♦ *Das Elektroauto wird noch heute als Exot bestaunt.* **2.** *(quality)* the oddity of sth das Merkwürdige an etw. [dat] [das ˈmɛˑkvʏˈdɪɡə an] <-n> no pl ◊ *das Merkwürdige an der Situation/an ihrem Verhalten*

oddly [adv] seltsam [ˈzɛltzaːm] ◊ *ein seltsam geformter Baum* ♦ *Du bist heute so seltsam still.* oddly (enough) seltsamerweise [ˈzɛltzaːmɐˈvaɪzə]

odds [noun] **1.** *(chances)* Chancen [ˈʃaŋsn̩] die <-> pl long/short odds gute/schlechte Chancen the odds are in favour/against sth/sb die Chancen für etw./ jdn stehen gut/schlecht What are the odds? Wie stehen die Chancen? The odds are two to one. Die Chancen stehen zwei zu eins. **2.** *(likelihood)* Wahrscheinlichkeit [vaˑˈʃaɪnlɪçkaɪt] die <-> no pl the odds of ... die Wahrscheinlichkeit, dass ... ◊ *Die Wahrscheinlichkeit, dass er die Wahl gewinnt, ist gering.* the odds are that ... aller Wahrscheinlichkeit nach ... ◊ *Aller Wahrscheinlichkeit nach wird sie kommen.* it's odds that ... wahrscheinlich ... [vaˑˈʃaɪnlɪç] against all odds entgegen allen Erwartungen [ɛntˌgeːɡn̩ alən ɛˈvaˑtʊŋən] ◊ *Entgegen allen Erwartungen haben sie es doch geschafft.* **3.** *(at betting)* Quote [ˈkvoːtə] die <-, -n> ◊ *Das Pferd ist ein Außenseiter; da sind die Quoten sehr gut.* ♦ *Auf die Nr. 5 gab es eine Quote von 6 :1.*
☉ odds and ends Krimskrams ◊ *Wem gehört der Krimskrams hier?* be at odds with sb mit jdm uneins sein be at odds with sth zu etw. im Widerspruch stehen

odour, odor [noun] Geruch [ɡəˈrɔx] der <-(e)s, Gerüche> ◊ *ein schlechter Geruch*

of [prep] **1.** *(expressing possession or relation, in names of the nobility, without determiner)* von [fɔn] [+dat] ◊ *der Verkauf von Waren* ♦ *das Auto von Herrn Meier* ♦ *das Gewicht von Holz* ♦ *ein Freund von mir* ♦ *ein Foto von ihr* ♦ *Das war gemein von ihm.* ♦ *Exbundespräsident Richard von Weizsäcker* a feeling of joy ein Gefühl der Freude the history of Japan die Geschichte Japans; *(followed by a determiner)* expressed with the genitive the colo(u)r of my/ the/this book die Farbe meines/des/dieses Buches [di: ˌfaˑbə maɪnəs/dɛs/diːzəs ˈbuːxəs] in case of an accident im Falle eines Unfalls [ɪm falə aɪnəs ˈʊnfals]; *(not translated in appositions)* the province of Ontario die Provinz Ontario [di: proˌvɪnts ɔnˈtaːrjo:] in the month of May im Monat Mai [ɪm moːnat ˈmaɪ] the 1st of April der 1. April [deːˈɡ ˌeːˈɡstə aˈprɪl] **2.** *(in expressions of a defined quantity, indicating an age)* von [fɔn] [+dat] ◊ *ein Stundenlohn von 20 Euro* ♦ *zehn Prozent vom Umsatz* ♦ *Tausende von Zuschauern* ♦ *Sie lernte im Alter von sechs Jahren schwimmen.; (not translated in expressions of quantity with kilo, pound, litre/liter, gallon, pair, piece etc.)* a pound of coffee ein Pfund Kaffee [aɛn pfʊnt ˈkafeː] five litres of water fünf Liter Wasser a pair of socks ein Paar Socken a cup of tea eine Tasse Tee a bottle of milk eine Flasche Milch a herd of cattle eine Herde Kühe a group of children eine Gruppe Kinder **3.** *(in expressions of an undefined quantity)* an [an] [+dat] ◊ *ein Defizit an Magnesium* ♦ *eine große Menge an Informationen; (with sums, quantities)* a loan/an order of ... ein Kredit/eine Bestellung über ... [aɛn kreˈdiːt/aɛnə bəˈʃtɛlʊŋ yːbɐ] [+acc] ◊ *Er hat einen Kredit über 10 000 Euro aufgenommen.* ♦ *eine Bestel-*

lung über drei Exemplare **4.** *(consisting of a material)* aus [aʊs] [+dat] ◊ *Die Tasse ist aus Porzellan.* ♦ *eine Bluse aus weißer Seide* **5.** *(smell, taste)* nach [naːx] [+dat] ◊ *Die Suppe schmeckt nach Knoblauch.* ♦ *Hier stinkt es nach Abgasen!* ♦ *Dein Haar duftet nach Rosen.*

of course [adv] natürlich [naˈtyːɡlɪç] ◊ *„Kommst du mit?" — „Natürlich!"* ♦ *Karin ist natürlich wieder zu spät gekommen.* ♦ *Natürlich kannst du das tun, aber klug ist es nicht.*

off¹ [adj] **1.** *(not at your workplace or school)* a day/ week off ein freier Tag/eine freie Woche [aɛn ˌfraɛə ˈtaːk/aɛnə ˌfraɛə ˈvɔxə] ◊ *Heute ist sein freier Tag.* **2.** *(bad)* schlecht [ʃlɛçt] ◊ *Die Milch/Wurst ist schlecht.* ♦ *Er hat heute einen schlechten Tag.*

off² [adv] **1.** *(away)* weg [vɛk] ◊ *Wie lange ist sie schon weg?* He's off to school. Er ist auf dem Weg zur Schule. She's off to Italy tomorrow. Sie fährt morgen nach Italien. I'll be off. Ich gehe jetzt. [ɪç ˈgeːə jɛtst] Be off! Verschwinde! [feˈfvɪndə]; *(with certain verbs)* weg... [vɛk] run off weglaufen [ˈvɛklaʊfn̩] ◊ *läuft weg, lief weg, ist weggelaufen>* **2.** *(not in operation, not on the menu)* aus [aʊs] ◊ *Der Fernseher/Die Heizung ist aus.* ♦ *Ich bedaure, aber der Schweinebraten ist aus.; (with certain verbs)* aus... [aʊs] switch off ausschalten [ˈaʊsʃaltn̩] <schaltet aus, schaltete aus, hat ausgeschaltet> ◊ *das Handy/Radio ausschalten* **3.** *(with certain verbs, expressing downward direction)* herunter... [hɛˈrʊntɐ] fall off herunterfallen [hɛˈrʊntɐfalən] <fällt herunter, fiel herunter, ist heruntergefallen> **4.** *(with certain verbs, starting off)* los... [loːs] drive off losfahren [ˈloːsfaːrən] <fährt los, fuhr los, ist losgefahren> **5.** *(with certain verbs: separated, removed)* ab... [ap] take sth off etw. abnehmen [ˈapneːmən] <nimmt ab, nahm ab, hat abgenommen> ◊ *Fürs Schwimmen nehme ich die Brille ab.* call off absagen [ˈapzaːgn̩] +haben ◊ *eine Hochzeit ist abgesagt sein [ˈapgəzaːkt zaɛn] ◊ Die Hochzeit ist abgesagt.* **6.** take time off sich [dat] freinehmen [ˈfraɛneːmən] <nimmt sich frei, nahm sich frei, hat sich freigenommen> ◊ *Sie nimmt sich nie frei.*
☉ off and on, on and off immer mal wieder

'Off' often occurs in phrasal verbs like 'get off' or 'put off' which have their own entries in the dictionary.

off³ [prep] **1.** *(away or down from sth)* von [fɔn] [+dat] ◊ *vom Fahrrad steigen* ♦ *den Schnee vom Auto fegen* ♦ *Er nahm die Jacke vom Haken und zog sie an.* **2.** *(away from a route etc.)* abseits [ˈapzaɛts] [+gen] ◊ *Der Wasserfall liegt etwas abseits des Weges.; (on the sea)* vor [foːɐ] [+dat] ◊ *Das Schiff lag/ankerte vor Madagaskar.* ♦ *eine halbe Meile vor der Küste*

offence [noun] *(infringement against a rule)* Vergehen [fɛˈgeːən] das <-s, -> ◊ *Ist das ein Vergehen?* ♦ *jedes noch so kleine Vergehen ahnden* an offence against sth ein Verstoß gegen etw. [aɛn fɛˈʃtoːs geːɡn̩] ◊ *ein Verstoß gegen die Spielregeln/ das Tierschutzgesetz; (criminal offence)* Delikt [deˈlɪkt] das <-(e)s, -e> (tech) ◊ *das Delikt der Steuerhinterziehung/Körperverletzung* commit an offence sich strafbar machen [ˈʃtraːfbaːˑ maxn̩]
☉ cause offence (to sb) (bei jdm) Anstoß erregen mean no offence es nicht böse meinen take offence (at sth) (with good reason) (wegen etw.)

gekränkt sein **no offence** nichts für ungut *(fam)*
offend [verb] **1.** *(upset, hurt)* verletzen [fe'letsn̩]
<verletzt, verletzte, hat verletzt> ◊ *Ich wollte dich*
nicht verletzen. ◆ *Ich fühlte mich/war ein bisschen*
verletzt.; (cause offence) offend (sb) *(bei jdm)*
Anstoß erregen ['anʃtoːs ere:gn̩] <erregt, erregte, hat
erregt> ◊ *Diese Bilder könnten bei manchen Leuten*
Anstoß erregen. **2.** LAW *(commit an offence)* straffällig
werden ['ʃtraːffɛlɪç veːɐdn̩] +sein ◊ *erstmals/wieder-*
holt straffällig werden offend **against** sth **gegen** etw.
verstoßen [geːgn̩] ... feˌʃtoːsn̩] <verstößt, verstieß, hat
verstoßen> ◊ *gegen ein Gesetz/den guten Geschmack*
verstoßen
offender [noun] **1.** LAW *(criminal)* Straftäter ['ʃtraːftɛːtɐ]
der <-s, -> ♀Straftäterin ['ʃtraːftɛːtərɪn] die
<-, -nen> ◊ *Der Straftäter wurde verurteilt.*
2. *(culprit)* Übeltäter ['yːbl̩tɛːtɐ] der <-s, -> ♀Übeltä-
terin ['yːbl̩tɛːtərɪn] die <-, -nen> ◊ *Dieser Dorn war*
der Übeltäter. ◆ *Hat der Lehrer die Übeltäterin*
erwischt?
offensive [adj] **1.** *(causing offence)* anstößig
['anʃtøːsɪç] ◊ *anstößige Sprache* ◆ *Die Bilder waren*
anstößig.; (insulting) beleidigend [bə'laedɪgn̩t] ◊
beleidigende Äußerungen ◆ *Ich finde seine Kommen-*
tare beleidigend. **2.** *(not defensive)* offensiv [ɔfɛn'ziːv]
◊ *ein offensiver Kampf* ◆ *Sein Fußballspiel war*
offensiv. offensive war Angriffskrieg ['angrɪfskriːk]
der <-(e)s, -e>
offensively [adv] **1.** *(insultingly)* auf beleidigende
Weise [aof bə,laedɪɡn̩də 'vaezə] ◊ *jdn/etw. auf beleidi-*
gende Weise kritisieren **2.** *(not defensively)* offensiv
[ɔfɛn'ziːv] ◊ *offensiv kämpfen/spielen*
offer¹ [noun] Angebot ['angəboːt] das <-(e)s, -e> ◊
ein Angebot annehmen/ablehnen ◆ *jdm ein Angebot*
für etw. machen ◆ *Er erhöhte sein Angebot auf 200*
Euro. **on offer** im Angebot ◊ *eine große Auswahl im*
Angebot haben This flat is under offer. Jemand hat
für diese Wohnung ein Angebot gemacht.
offer² [verb] **1.** *(show your willingness to give, do, or*
sell sth) anbieten ['anbiːtn̩] <bietet an, bot an, hat
angeboten> ◊ *Er bot ihr an, sie mitzunehmen.* ◆ *Sie*
bot ihm ihre Hilfe an. ◆ *Darf ich Ihnen etwas zum*
Trinken anbieten? ◆ *etw. zum Verkauf anbieten* ◆
Welche Kurse werden angeboten?; (show your willing-
ness to pay a price) bieten ['biːtn̩] <bietet, bot, hat
geboten> ◊ *Ich biete 100 Euro für die Vase.* ◆ *Wer*
bietet mehr?; (a reward) aussetzen ['aoszɛtsn̩] +haben
◊ *Auf seine Ergreifung sind 5000 Euro ausgesetzt.*
2. *(present, provide)* bieten ['biːtn̩] <bietet, bot, hat
geboten> ◊ *jede Gelegenheit nutzen, die sich einem*
bietet ◆ *Mein Auto bietet wenig Komfort.* ◆ *viel zu*
bieten haben **3.** *(give)* geben ['geːbn̩] <gibt, gab, hat
gegeben> ◊ *jdm einen Rat geben* ◆ *Er hat mir keine*
Erklärung gegeben. **4.** *(express)* aussprechen
['aosʃprɛçn̩] <spricht aus, sprach aus, hat ausgespro-
chen> ◊ *jdm sein Mitgefühl/seinen Dank ausspre-*
chen
ⓢ **offer sb your hand** jdm die Hand reichen
offering [noun] **1.** *(product)* Produkt [proˈdʊkt] das
<-(e)s, -e> ◊ *das neueste Produkt von Apple/*
Microsoft; (work) Werk [vɛʳk] das <-(e)s, -e> ◊ *Ihr*
jüngstes Werk trägt den Titel „Sehnsucht".
2. *(sacrifice)* Opfer ['ɔpfɐ] das <-s, -> ◊ *ein Tier als*
Opfer darbringen; (money) Opfergabe ['ɔpfɡaːbə] die
<-, -n>
office [noun] **1.** *(building, room, people who work there)*

Büro [byˈroː] das <-s, -s> ◊ *Sie ist in ihrem Büro.* ◆
Das Büro in New York wurde geschlossen. ◆ *Die*
restliche Arbeit erledigt unser Büro. at/out of the
office im/außer Haus [ɪm/aose 'haos]; *(of an institu-*
tion) Geschäftsstelle [gəˈʃɛftsʃtɛlə] die <-, -n> ◊
Einen Katalog können Sie bei unserer Geschäftsstelle
anfordern. head office Hauptgeschäftsstelle
['haoptgəˌʃɛftsʃtɛlə] **2.** *(government ministry, depart-*
ment) Office Ministerium [mɪnɪsˈteːrɪʊm] das
<-s, Ministerien> Foreign Office Außenministerium
['aosn̩mɪnɪsˌteːrɪʊm] **3.** *(official public or political*
post, government authority) Amt [amt] das
<-(e)s, Ämter> ◊ *das Amt des Bundespräsidenten* ◆
Wird sie weiterhin im Amt bleiben? ◆ *sein Amt nie-*
derlegen ◆ *Er arbeitet im Amt für Umweltschutz.* run
for office für ein Amt kandidieren take office sein
Amt antreten tax office Finanzamt [fiˈnantsˌamt]
officer [noun] **1.** MIL Offizier [ɔfiˈtsiːɐ] der <-s, -e>
♀Offizierin [ɔfiˈtsiːrɪn] die <-, -nen> ◊ *Er wurde mit*
25 schon Offizier. **2.** *(in an organization)* Funktionär
[fʊŋktsjoˈnɛːɐ] der <-s, -e> ♀Funktionärin
[fʊŋktsjoˈnɛːrɪn] die <-, -nen> ◊ *Als Funktionärin*
hat sie großen Einfluss. **3.** *(police)* officer Beamte
[bəˈamtə] der <-n, die Beamten> ♀Beamtin
[bəˈamtɪn] die <-, -nen> but: *ein Beamter/eine*
Beamtin ◆ *ein Beamter in Uniform/Zivil*
official [noun] **1.** *(in an organization)* Funktionär
[fʊŋktsjoˈnɛːɐ] der <-s, -e> ♀Funktionärin
[fʊŋktsjoˈnɛːrɪn] die <-, -nen> ◊ *die Funktionäre der*
SPD **2.** *(in the government administration)* Beamte
[bəˈamtə] der <-n, die Beamten> ♀Beamtin
[bəˈamtɪn] die <-, -nen> but: *ein Beamter/eine*
Beamtin ◆ *Als Beamter hat er eine sichere Stelle.*
official(ly) [adj, adv] *(relating to sb's job or office)*
dienstlich ['diːnstlɪç] no comp/superl ◊ *jds dienstli-*
che Pflichten ◆ *Das Gespräch war nicht privat,*
sondern dienstlich. ◆ *dienstlich unterwegs sein; (for*
sb's job or office) official ... Dienst... [diːnst] official
car Dienstwagen ['diːnstvaːgn̩] der <-s, ->
offline [adj, adv] offline ['ɔflaen] no comp/superl; *when*
used as an adj, not before ns ◊ *offline sein/gehen/*
arbeiten; (before ns) offline ... Offline... ['ɔflaen]
offline function Offlinefunktion ['ɔflaenfʊŋkˌtsjoːn]
die <-, -en>
offset [verb] ausgleichen ['aosglaeçn̩] <gleicht aus,
glich aus, hat ausgeglichen> ◊ *Die Verluste wurden*
durch Gewinne in gleicher Höhe ausgeglichen. offset
sth für etw. von der Steuer absetzen
[fɔn deːɐ 'ʃtɔøɐ ˌapzɛtsn̩] +haben ◊ *Die Fahrtkosten*
setze ich von der Steuer ab.
offspring [noun] **1.** *(child)* Kind [kɪnt] das <-es, -er>;
(young animal) Junge ['jʊŋə] das <-n, die Jungen>
aber: *ein Junges* ◊ *Die Löwin beschützt ihr Junges/*
ihre Jungen. **2.** *(result, consequence)* Ergebnis
[ɛʳˈgeːpnɪs] das <-ses, -se> ◊ *Diese Erfindung ist ein*
Ergebnis jahrelanger Forschung.
often [adv] oft [ɔft] <öfter, am öftesten> seldom superl
◊ *Ich denke oft an ihn.* ◆ *Das hat sie dir doch schon*
oft genug gesagt! ◆ *Wie oft besuchst du deine*
Eltern?
ⓢ **as often as not, more often than not** meistens
every so often hin und wieder
oil [noun] **1.** *(liquid)* Öl [øːl] das <-(e)s, -e> ◊ *nach Öl*
bohren ◆ *mit Öl heizen* ◆ *beim Auto das Öl wechseln*
◆ *eine Salatsoße aus Essig und Öl* ◆ *eine Massage*
mit ätherischen Ölen crude oil Rohöl ['roːˌøːl]

suntan oil Sonnenöl ['zɔnən|øːl] *2. (paint)* oils
Ölfarben ['øːlfaˈbm̩] die <–> *pl* paint in oils mit
Ölfarben malen *3. (painting)* Ölgemälde
['øːlgəmeːldə] das <–s, –>

oily [adj] *1. (fish, sauce)* fett [fɛt] <fetter, am fettesten>
◊ *Aal ist sehr fett.* ♦ *eine fette Soße 2. (skin, hair)*
fettig ['fɛtɪç] ◊ *eine Creme für fettige Haut* ♦ *Mein
Haar ist sehr fettig.* **3.** *(person)* schmierig ['ʃmiːrɪç]
(pej) ◊ *ein schmieriger Kerl*

ointment [noun] Salbe ['zalbə] die <–, –n> ◊ *eine
Salbe gegen Rheumaschmerzen*

OK¹ [noun] Zustimmung ['tsuːʃtɪmʊŋ] die <–, –en> ◊
seine Zustimmung zu etw. geben ♦ *Wir warten noch
auf die Zustimmung vom Chef.*

OK² [adj] **1.** *(acceptable)* in Ordnung [ɪn 'ɔ'dnʊŋ] ◊ *Ist
das in Ordnung, wenn Petra mitkommt?* ♦ *Ich habe
nichts gegen Simon, er ist schon in Ordnung.*
2. *(well)* sb is OK jdm geht es gut [geːt ɛs 'guːt] ◊
*Sie hat zwar einen Schrecken bekommen, aber es
geht ihr gut.* Are you/Is he OK? Ist dir/ihm was
passiert? [ɪst ˌdiːɐ̯/ˌiːm vas paˈsiːɐ̯t]
♠ be OK by sb jdm recht sein it's OK for sb to do
sth jd kann ruhig etw. tun that's OK ist schon gut
turn out OK gut ausgehen

OK³ [adv] ganz gut [gants 'guːt] *(fam)* ◊ *Es hat alles
ganz gut geklappt.* ♦ *Das Radio funktioniert noch
ganz gut.* be doing OK ganz gut zurechtkommen

OK⁴ [interj] gut [guːt] ◊ *Gut, dann fangen wir an.* ♦ *Na
gut, wenn du darauf bestehst.*; *(check if sb agrees
with you or understands you)* ja [jaː] ◊ *Dann geben
wir also um sechs, ja?*
♠ OK, OK ist ja schon gut

old [adj] alt [alt] <älter, am ältesten> ◊ *Wie alt bist du?*
♦ *Sie ist neun Jahre älter als er.* ♦ *eine alte Freundschaft* ♦ *Deine alte Frisur hat mir besser gefallen.* ♦
Wie geht's, alter Freund? get/grow old alt werden
old town Altstadt ['altʃtat] die <–, Altstädte> ◊ *die
engen Straßen der Altstadt* Old English Altenglisch
['alt|ɛŋlɪʃ] das <–(s)> *no pl*

old age [noun] Alter ['altɐ] das <–s> *no pl* ◊ *Sie war
bis ins hohe Alter geistig rege.* ♦ *für das Alter
vorsorgen* in sb's old age im Alter ◊ *Wer soll sich
im Alter um ihn kümmern?*

old-fashioned [adj] altmodisch ['altmoːdɪʃ] ◊ *altmodische Kleider* ♦ *Deine Ansichten sind hoffnungslos altmodisch.*

old people's home [noun] Altenheim ['altn̩haem] das
<–(e)s, –e> ◊ *Meine Mutter lebt im Altenheim.*

olive [noun] **1.** *(fruit)* Olive [oˈliːvə] die <–, –n> ◊
Möchten Sie grüne oder schwarze Oliven?
2. *(colo(u)r)* Oliv [oˈliːf] das <–s, –> ◊ *Er trug einen
Anzug in Oliv.*

Olympics [noun] Olympiade [olʏmˈpjaːdə] die <–, –n>
◊ *an der Olympiade teilnehmen*

omission [noun] Auslassung ['aʊslasʊŋ] die <–, –en>
◊ *Die Auslassung von Wörtern wird mit drei Punkten
gekennzeichnet.* omission of payment Nichtzahlung
['nɪçtsaːlʊŋ] die <–, –en> *most pl*

omit [verb] **1.** *(leave out)* auslassen ['aʊslasn̩] <lässt
aus, ließ aus, hat ausgelassen> ◊ *beim Abschreiben
ein Wort auslassen* **2.** *(fail to do)* omit to do sth es
unterlassen, etw. zu tun [ɛs ʊntɐˈlasn̩ ... tsuː] <unter-
lässt, unterließ, hat unterlassen> ◊ *Er hatte es unterlassen, sie ausreichend zu informieren.*

on¹ [adv] **1.** *(describing a position)* auf [aʊf] ◊ *Helm
auf! Brille auf beim Lesen!* be on drauf sein

['draʊf zaen] *(fam)* ◊ *Schau mal, da ist ein Bild von
einem Eisbären drauf.*; *(in phrasal verbs)* auf... [aʊf]
leave on auflassen ['aʊflasn̩] <lässt auf, ließ auf, hat
aufgelassen> ◊ *Er ließ seinen Hut/seine Brille auf.*
2. *(continuing with an activity)* weiter ['vaetɐ] ◊ *Und
nun weiter im Programm!*; *(in phrasal verbs)*
weiter... ['vaetɐ] play on weiterspielen
['vaetɐʃpiːlən] +haben ◊ *Kannst du weiterspielen oder
müssen wir aufhören?* **3.** *(in operation, wearing sth)*
an [an] ◊ *In ihrem Zimmer war das Licht an.* ♦ *Jacke
an!* with your shoes/hat on mit Schuhen/Hut
[mɪt 'ʃuːən/'huːt] ◊ *Man darf eine Moschee nicht mit
Schuhen betreten.*; *(in phrasal verbs)* an... [an] leave
on anlassen ['anlasn̩] <lässt an, ließ an, hat angelas-
sen> ◊ *das Radio/den Mantel anlassen*
♠ go on about sth/sb ständig von etw./jdm reden
go on at sb jdm ständig in den Ohren liegen *(fam)*
on and off von Zeit zu Zeit on and on immer
weiter sth is on es gibt etw. ◊ *Ich gehe ins Kino;
heute gibt's einen guten Film.* you're on abgemacht
(fam)

on² [prep] **1.** *(onto or on a horizontal surface, a list)* auf
[aʊf] with *acc* when expressing motion towards a
place, with *dat* when there is no or undirected motion
◊ *sich auf das Bett legen* ♦ *ein Glas auf den Tisch
stellen* ♦ *Sie legte mir die Hand auf den Bauch.* ♦
Schreib mich bitte auch auf die Liste. ♦ *auf dem
Bett liegen* ♦ *Er hat Haare auf der Brust.* ♦ *auf
einem Bein stehen* ♦ *auf der Tagesordnung stehen*
2. *(on or moving towards a vertical surface, at the
side of a river)* an [an] with *acc* when expressing
motion towards a place, with *dat* when there is no or
undirected motion ◊ *Ich hängte den Kalender an die
Wand.* ♦ *Er stieß mit dem Kopf an den Türrahmen.* ♦
Das Bild hing an der Wand. ♦ *Regensburg liegt an
der Donau.* wear a ring on your finger einen Ring
am Finger tragen **3.** *(indicating the side)* zu [tsuː]
<+dat> on the left/right zu Linken/Rechten on both
sides zu beiden Seiten **4.** *(into or in a vehicle, group)*
in [ɪn] with *acc* when expressing motion towards a
place, with *dat* when there is no or undirected motion
◊ *in den Bus einsteigen* ♦ *in die Jury kommen* ♦
Wird dir im Flugzeug schlecht? ♦ *Sie ist schon lange
im Vorstand.* **5.** *(at a time, on a day or date)* an [an]
<+dat> ◊ *an einem sonnigen Nachmittag* ♦ *am 1. April*
♦ *am Montag*; *(when sth happens)* bei [bae] <+dat> ◊
bei der Ankunft/Abfahrt ♦ *Beim Signalton ist es acht
Uhr.* **6.** *(during a journey, on the way)* auf [aʊf] <+dat>
◊ *Auf der Rückfahrt wurde ihm übel.* ♦ *auf dem Weg
von Rom nach Dubai* **7.** *(dealing with a topic)* über
['yːbɐ] <+acc> ◊ *ein Buch über die Alpen* ♦ *ein Bericht
über den Krieg* **8.** *(on the radio, TV)* in [ɪn] <+dat> ◊
*Was kommt heute im 1. Programm? ♦ *Es kam gerade
in den Nachrichten: ...* **9.** *(onto or on a disc, tape
etc.)* auf [aʊf] with *acc* when expressing motion
towards a place, with *dat* when there is no or undirected motion <+acc> or <+dat> ◊ *Kannst du mir das Spiel
auf diese CD-ROM brennen?* ♦ *Was ist auf dem
Video?* **10.** *(using sth to eat, support yourself)* von
[fɔn] <+dat> ◊ *Frösche ernähren sich von Insekten.* ♦
Ich lebe von einer kleinen Rente. **11.** *(running on a
particular fuel, type of energy)* mit [mɪt] <+dat> ◊ *Fährt
dein Auto mit Benzin oder mit Diesel?* ♦ *mit
Atomkraft/Strom betrieben werden* **12.** *(by dialling a
particular phone number)* unter ['ʊntɐ] <+dat> ◊ *Sie
erreichen mich unter der Nummer 257434.* **13.** *(in*

comparisons) gegenüber [ge:gn̩|'y:bɐ] +dat ◊ *Der Umsatz ist gegenüber dem Vorjahr um zwei Prozent gestiegen.* **14.** *(taking a particular medication, drug)* be on sth etw. nehmen ['ne:mən] <nimmt, nahm, hat genommen> ◊ *Ich nehme keine Schmerzmittel mehr.*

once¹ noun the once einmal ['aɛnmaːl] ◊ *Sie hat nur einmal mit mir gesprochen.* this once dieses eine Mal [,diːzəs ,aɛnə 'maːl] ◊ *Nur dieses eine Mal noch, bitte!* for once ausnahmsweise ['aʊsnaːmsvaɛzə] ◊ *Kannst du nicht mal ausnahmsweise den Mund halten?*

⊛ every once in a while von Zeit zu Zeit all at once **1.** *(suddenly)* urplötzlich *(fam)* ◊ *Urplötzlich war er sauer.* **2.** *(everybody at the same time)* alle auf einmal ◊ *Wir waren alle auf einmal fertig. (everything at the same time)* alles auf einmal ◊ *Man kann nicht alles auf einmal tun.* at once **1.** *(immediately)* sofort ◊ *Mach das bitte sofort, nicht erst später.* **2.** *(at the same time)* zugleich ◊ *Er ist klug und einfühlsam zugleich.*

once² adv **1.** *(a single time)* einmal ['aɛnmaːl] ◊ *Er war erst einmal in den USA.* ♦ *Diesen Fehler macht man nur einmal.* once before schon einmal once a week/month etc. einmal in der Woche/im Monat etc.; *(recurrent)* once every … alle … ['alə] ◊ *Sie schaut alle zehn Minuten nach ihm.* **2.** *(in the past)* (früher) einmal [('fryːɐ) 'aɛnmaːl] ◊ *Hier lebten früher einmal Dinosaurier.* ♦ *Weißt du, dass sie einmal miteinander verheiratet waren?*

⊛ once again/more **1.** *(one more time)* noch einmal ◊ *Können Sie das bitte noch einmal sagen? (again)* wieder ◊ *Der Termin wurde wieder verschoben.* **2.** *(as it used to be)* wieder ◊ *Bald wird hier wieder Ruhe einkehren.* once or twice einige Male ◊ *Ich habe ihn nur einige Male getroffen.* once and for all ein für alle Mal

once³ conjunc wenn … erst [vɛn … eːɐst] once sb does sth wenn jd erst einmal etw. tut ◊ *Wenn du sie erst einmal richtig kennen lernst, wirst du sie mögen.* once sth is done wenn etw. erst einmal getan ist ◊ *Wenn das erst einmal geschafft ist, wird es leichter.*

one¹ noun Eins [aɛns] die <–, –en> → four¹

one² det **1.** *(one single)* ein [aɛn] eine ['aɛnə] ◊ *Ein Fehler ist schon zu viel.* ♦ *Die Beschwerde nur einer Kundin hat keine Wirkung.* ♦ *Ich habe heute die Post einer ganzen Woche erledigt.* one and a half eineinhalb ['aɛn|aɛn'halp] ◊ *in den letzten eineinhalb Jahren* ♦ *eine eineinhalb Meter breite Mauer* one hundred einhundert ['aɛn'hʊndɐt] one thousand eintausend ['aɛn'taʊznt] **2.** the one (and only) … der/die/das einzige … [deːɐ/diː/das 'aɛntsɪgə] no comp/superl, only before ns ◊ *Der einzige Nachteil ist der hohe Preis.* sb's one (and only) … jds einziger/einzige/einziges … ◊ *Das war meine einzige Hoffnung.* **3.** *(with names)* ein (gewisser) [aɛn (gəvɪsɐ)] eine (gewisse) [aɛnə (gəvɪsə)] ◊ *Ein Herr Kügel hat angerufen.* ♦ *Kennst du eine gewisse Klara Brock?*

one³ pron **1.** *(a single person or thing)* einer ['aɛnɐ] eine ['aɛnə] eins [aɛns] ◊ *Einer von uns sollte es tun.* ♦ *Hast du zwei Töchter oder nur eine?* ♦ *Ich habe zwei Stück Kuchen. Möchtest du eins?* one by one einer nach dem anderen one after another nacheinander [naːx|aɛ'nandɐ] ◊ *nacheinander das Zimmer betreten* **2.** the one der [deːɐ] die [diː] das

[das] ◊ *Kennst du den mit der Brille?* ♦ *Wer ist die mit den blonden Haaren?* ♦ *Ich hätte gern das dort drüben.* the ones die [diː] ◊ *Ich mag die mit den dicken Autos nicht.* just the one nur der/die/das eine [nuːɐ deːɐ/diː/das 'aɛnə] ◊ *Sei vorsichtig mit der Uhr, ich habe nur die eine.* **3.** the best one der/die/das Beste [deːɐ/diː/das 'bɛstə] <–n, –n> ◊ *Das erste Lied ist das Beste auf der CD.* ♦ *Sie ist eine der Besten in der Klasse.* the only one der/die/das Einzige [deːɐ/diː/das 'aɛntsɪgə] <–n, –n> ◊ *Ted war der Einzige, der fehlte.* ♦ *Ihr Kind war das Einzige, das krank wurde.* Your car? Which one is it — this one or that one? Dein Auto? Welches ist es — dieses oder jenes? **4.** *(lofty) (you)* man [man] ◊ *Wie macht man das am besten?* ♦ *Man spricht nicht mit vollem Mund!*

⊛ be one up on sb jdm voraus sein be at one with sb sich dat mit jdm einig sein be at one with sth/yourself eins mit etw./sich sein get one up on sb jdn überholen as one geschlossen ◊ *Wir verließen geschlossen den Saal.* for one zum Beispiel

one⁴ nmrl eins [aɛns] → four²

⊛ one and the same ein und derselbe/dieselbe/dasselbe in ones and twos grüppchenweise

one another pron einander [aɛ'nandɐ] ◊ *Sie sind einander nie begegnet.* ♦ *Die Methoden ähneln einander sehr.* play with one another miteinander spielen [mɪt|aɛnandɐ 'ʃpiːlən] be nice to one another nett zueinander sein ['nɛt tsu|aɛnandɐ zaɛn] respect one another's privacy die Privatsphäre des anderen achten [diː pri,vaːtsfɛːrə dɛs ,andəran 'axtn̩]

oneself pron **1.** *(referring to the pronoun 'one')* sich [zɪç] ◊ *Vorsicht! Damit kann man sich leicht verletzen!; (more emphatic)* sich selbst [zɪç 'zɛlpst] ◊ *Um andere lieben zu können, muss man zuerst sich selbst lieben.* **2.** *(alone, without help)* selbst [zɛlpst] ◊ *Wichtig ist, dass man das Formular selbst ausfüllt.*

⊛ (all) by oneself (ganz) allein (all) to oneself für sich (ganz) allein

one-sided adj einseitig ['aɛnzaɛtɪç] ◊ *eine einseitige Berichterstattung* ♦ *Diese Darstellung ist zu einseitig.*

onion noun Zwiebel ['tsviːbl̩] die <–, –n>

online adj, adv online ['ɒnlaɛn] no comp/superl; when used as an adj, not before ns ◊ *online sein/gehen/arbeiten/spielen; (before ns)* online … Online… ['ɒnlaɛn] online function Onlinefunktion ['ɒnlaɛnfʊŋk,tsi̯oːn] die <–, –en>

onlooker noun Zuschauer ['tsuːʃaʊɐ] der <–s, –> ♀Zuschauerin ['tsuːʃaʊərɪn] die <–, –nen>

only¹ adj einzig ['aɛntsɪç] no comp/superl, only before ns ◊ *Er war ihr einziges Kind.* ♦ *Das war sicher nicht der einzige Grund dafür.* the only person der/die Einzige [deːɐ/diː: 'aɛntsɪgə] <–n> the only people die Einzigen [diː 'aɛntsɪgn̩] <–> pl the only thing das Einzige [das 'aɛntsɪgə] <–n>

only² adv **1.** *(just, solely)* nur [nuːɐ] ◊ *Ich habe leider nur wenig Zeit.* ♦ *Er trinkt nur morgens Kaffee, abends gar nicht.* ♦ *Ich wollte nur sagen, dass …* ♦ *Das hat er nur gesagt, weil er dich ärgern wollte.* **2.** *(temporal, no more than, no earlier than, contrary to expectations)* erst [eːɐst] ◊ *Er ist erst drei Jahre alt.* ♦ *Es ist erst 11 Uhr.* ♦ *Ich habe erst die Hälfte des Buches gelesen.* ♦ *Erst gestern hast du noch etwas anderes gesagt.* only now erst jetzt **3.** *(one and only)* einzig ['aɛntsɪç] ◊ *Das ist der einzig richtige*

Weg.

◉ **only just 1.** *(by a very small margin)* knapp **2.** *(a very short time ago)* gerade erst only too nur allzu if only *(+subjunctive II)* nur ◊ *Hätte er doch nur auf meinen Rat gehört!* ♦ *Wäre doch nur schon Sommer!*

only³ conjunc nur [nuː̯ɡ] ◊ *Ich wollte schon kommen; mir kam nur etwas dazwischen.*

only child noun Einzelkind ['aɛnts|kɪnt] das <–(e)s, Einzelkinder> ◊ *Sie war (ein) Einzelkind.*

onset noun Ausbruch ['aɔsbrʊx] der <–(e)s, Ausbrüche> ◊ *bei Ausbruch einer Grippe* onset of winter Wintereinbruch ['vɪntɛ|aɛnbrʊx]

onto prep **1.** *(onto a flat surface, list)* auf [aɔf] +acc ◊ *Sie legte das Buch auf den Tisch.* ♦ *auf die Straße laufen* ♦ *Schreib mich bitte auch auf die Liste.* **2.** *(onto an upright surface)* an [an] +acc ◊ *Ich hängte das Bild an die Wand.* slip a ring onto your finger sich dat einen Ring an den Finger stecken **3.** *(into a vehicle)* in [ɪn] +acc ◊ *in den Bus einsteigen*

◉ be/get onto sb *(talk to sb)* sich mit jdm in Verbindung setzen be onto sb *(catch a criminal)* jdm auf der Spur sein be onto something auf etwas Wichtiges gestoßen sein

onwards adv **1.** *(starting from a point)* from ...onwards von ... an [fɔn ... an] ◊ *Von da an waren sie Freunde.* ♦ *Von hier an wird der Weg steil.; (with a particular time)* from ...onwards ab ... [ap] ◊ *ab 16 Uhr geöffnet* **2.** *(forward)* weiter... ['vaɛtɛ] travel onwards weiterreisen ['vaɛtɛraɛzn̩] +sein

open¹

◉ **in the open 1.** *(outside)* im Freien ◊ *Ich bin gern im Freien.* **2.** *(public)* an der Öffentlichkeit ◊ *Sind diese Zahlen schon an der Öffentlichkeit?* into the open **1.** *(outside)* ins Freie ◊ *Gehen wir ein bisschen ins Freie?* **2.** *(public)* an die Öffentlichkeit ◊ *Wenn das an die Öffentlichkeit kommt, ist er erledigt.* come into the open *(with sth)* (mit etw.) an die Öffentlichkeit treten

open² adj **1.** *(not closed, not secret, honest)* offen ['ɔfn̩] seldom comp/superl ◊ *Die Tür war offen.* ♦ *Das Schiff fährt auf das offene Meer hinaus.* ♦ *eine offene Wunde* ♦ *Ich bin für vernünftige Vorschläge offen.* ♦ *offener Widerstand* ♦ *eine offene Beziehung* be open to sb jdm offen stehen ◊ *Ihr stehen jetzt zahlreiche Möglichkeiten offen.; (in phrasal verbs)* auf... [aɔf] keep open aufhalten ['aɔfhaltn̩] <hält auf, hielt auf, hat aufgehalten> ◊ *Sie konnte vor Müdigkeit kaum noch die Augen aufhalten.* rip open, throw open aufreißen ['aɔfraɛsn̩] <reißt auf, riss auf, hat aufgerissen> ◊ *Er riss den Umschlag auf.* ♦ *eine Tür aufreißen* **2.** *(shop, museum etc.)* open *(for business)* geöffnet [gə'|œfnət] no comp/superl ◊ *Manche Geschäfte sind abends bis 20 Uhr geöffnet.* open to the public für die Öffentlichkeit zugänglich [fyːɡ diː 'œfn̩tlɪçkaɛt ‚tsuːɡɛnlɪç] **3.** *(competition, road, space)* frei [fraɛ] <freier, am frei(e)sten> ◊ *freier Wettbewerb* ♦ *Die Leitung ist jetzt frei; du kannst telefonieren.* ♦ *auf freiem Feld*

◉ **wide open 1.** *(door, eyes)* weit offen **2.** *(outcome)* völlig offen

open³ verb **1.** *(sth that was closed)* open sth etw. öffnen ['œfnən] <öffnet, öffnete, hat geöffnet> ◊ *Das Land hat seine Grenzen geöffnet.* ♦ *Das neue Museum öffnet im Juni seine Pforten.* ♦ *eine Datei öffnen* ♦ *Hast du meine Post geöffnet?* ♦ *den Mund/*

die Augen öffnen ♦ *das Fenster/die Flasche öffnen; (a book)* aufschlagen ['aɔfʃlaːgn̩] <schlägt auf, schlug auf, hat aufgeschlagen> ◊ *Schlag das Buch auf Seite 14 auf!* ♦ *Welche Seite soll ich aufschlagen?* sth opens etw. öffnet sich ['œfnət] +haben ◊ *Die Tür öffnete sich.* ♦ *Der Fallschirm hat sich nicht geöffnet.* ♦ *Der Markt hat sich dem Wettbewerb geöffnet.; (shop etc)* etw. öffnet ['œfnət] +haben ◊ *Die Bank öffnet um neun.* **2.** *(an account, a new business, meeting, trial, round of shooting)* eröffnen [ɛ|'œfnən] <eröffnet, eröffnete, hat eröffnet> ◊ *ein Konto eröffnen* ♦ *Er will ein Internetcafé eröffnen.* ♦ *Hiermit eröffne ich die heutige Sitzung.* sth opens etw. wird eröffnet ◊ *Morgen wird hier eine neue Boutique eröffnet.; (a hotline)* einrichten ['aɛnrɪçtn̩] <richtet ein, richtete ein, hat eingerichtet> **3.** *(begin)* beginnen [bə'gɪnən] <beginnt, begann, hat begonnen> ◊ *Sie begann ihre Rede mit den Worten: „Liebe Freunde!"* ♦ *Die Jagdsaison hat jetzt begonnen.* **4.** *(spread)* ausbreiten ['aɔsbraɛtn̩] <breitet aus, breitete aus, hat ausgebreitet> ◊ *Ich breitete meine Arme aus.* ♦ *Der Vogel breitete die Flügel aus und flog davon.; (your legs)* spreizen ['ʃpraɛtsn̩] +haben **5.** *(be on a particular side of a building)* open into/onto sth auf etw. acc gehen [aɔf ... geːən] <geht, ging, ist gegangen> ◊ *Das Fenster geht auf den Hof.* **6.** *(film, play)* anlaufen ['anlaɔfn̩] <läuft an, lief an, ist angelaufen> ◊ *Wann läuft sein neuester Film an?*

● **open out** phras v **1.** *(tunnel, street)* open out (into sth) sich (zu etw.) verbreitern [fɛ'braɛtɐn] <verbreitert sich, verbreiterte sich, hat sich verbreitert> ◊ *Schließlich verbreiterte sich der Gang zu einer Höhle.* **2.** *(buds, flowers)* sich öffnen ['œfnən] <öffnet sich, öffnete sich, hat sich geöffnet> ◊ *Schon bald öffneten sich die Knospen.* **3.** *(a map, cloth)* ausbreiten ['aɔsbraɛtn̩] <breitet aus, breitete aus, hat ausgebreitet> ◊ *Er breitete den Stadtplan auf dem Boden aus.* **4.** *(a discussion)* ausweiten ['aɔsvaɛtn̩] <weitet aus, weitete aus, hat ausgeweitet> ◊ *die Gespräche ausweiten* sth opens out etw. weitet sich aus [vaɛtət tsɪç 'aɔs] +hat ◊ *Die Debatte weitete sich aus.*

● **open up** phras v **1.** *(a door, container, shop)* aufmachen ['aɔfmaxn̩] <macht auf, machte auf, hat aufgemacht> ◊ *Sie machte das Tor auf.* ♦ *Aufmachen!* **2.** *(an area, a market)* erschließen [ɛ'ʃliːsn̩] <erschließt, erschloss, hat erschlossen> ◊ *Die Forscher erschlossen das Landesinnere.* sth opens up etw. erschließt sich ◊ *Im Osten erschließen sich neue Absatzmärkte.* **3.** *(a prospect, opportunity)* open up sth (to sb) jdm etw. eröffnen [ɛ|'œfnən] <eröffnet, eröffnete, hat eröffnet> ◊ *Das Studium eröffnet mir neue Möglichkeiten.* sth opens up (to sb) bietet sich (jdm) ['biːtət tsɪç] <bietet sich, bot sich, hat sich geboten> ◊ *Mir haben sich viele Chancen geboten.* **4.** *(a difference, division)* open up sth zu etw. führen [tsuː ... fyːrən] ◊ *zu Streitigkeiten innerhalb einer Gruppe führen* **5.** *(encourage business links)* open up sth to sb sich einer Sache dat öffnen ['œfnən] ◊ *Das Land hat sich dem Westen geöffnet.; (become less withdrawn)* open up (to sb) (jdm) sein Herz erschließen [fɔn ... ɛ'tsɛːlən] <erzählt, erzählte, hat erzählt> ◊ *Erst war sie sehr schüchtern, aber jetzt erzählt sie von sich.* **6.** *(in an operation)* open sb up jdn aufschneiden ['aɔfʃnaɛdn̩] <schneidet auf, schnitt auf, hat aufgeschnitten> *(fam)*

open-air swimming pool (noun) Freibad ['fraːbaːt] das <-(e)s, Freibäder> ◊ *Kommst du mit ins Freibad?*

opener (noun) **1.** *(tool)* Öffner ['œfnɐ] der <-s, -> letter opener Brieföffner ['briːf|œfnɐ] tin opener Dosenöffner ['doːzn̩|œfnɐ] **2.** *(of a competition)* Eröffnungsspiel [ɐ|'œfnʊŋsʃpiːl] das <-(e)s, -e>; *(of the season)* Auftaktspiel ['aʊftaktʃpiːl] das <-(e)s, -e> ⊛ **for openers** zunächst einmal

opening (noun) **1.** *(of a new shop, an exhibition)* Eröffnung [ɐ|'œfnʊŋ] die <-, -en> ◊ *die Eröffnung eines Restaurants planen* ♦ *Wann wird die Eröffnung stattfinden?*; *(official ceremony)* Einweihung ['aɛnvaɛʊŋ] die <-, -en> ◊ *die feierliche Einweihung eines Denkmals* **2.** *(aperture, process)* Öffnung ['œfnʊŋ] die <-, -en> ◊ *eine Öffnung in einer Mauer* ♦ *die Öffnung der Grenzen innerhalb der EU* ♦ *die Öffnung der Geschäfte am Marktsonntag* **3.** *(opportunity)* opening (for sth) Möglichkeit (für etw.) ['møːklɪçkaɛt] die <-, -en> ◊ *Möglichkeiten für Geschäfte im Fernen Osten* **4.** *(available job)* Stelle [ˌɔfənə 'ʃtɛlə] die <-, -n> ◊ *In dieser Abteilung gibt es jetzt eine offene Stelle.* **5.** *(start)* Beginn [bə'gɪn] der <-s> no pl ◊ *zu Beginn der Saison*

opening hours (noun) Öffnungszeiten ['œfnʊŋstsaɛtn̩] die <-> pl ◊ *außerhalb der normalen Öffnungszeiten*

openly (adv) offen ['ɔfn̩] ◊ *etw. offen und ehrlich zugeben* ♦ *offen seine Meinung sagen*

open-minded (adj) aufgeschlossen ['aʊfgəʃlɔsn̩] ◊ *ein aufgeschlossener Mensch* ♦ *Neuen Ideen gegenüber war er sehr aufgeschlossen.*

Open University (noun) *britische Fernuniversität*

opera (noun) Oper ['oːpɐ] die <-, -n> ◊ *Gehst du gern in die Oper?* ♦ *eine Oper von Mozart*

operate (verb) **1.** *(machine, company, organization)* sth operates etw. arbeitet ['aʳbaɛtət] <arbeitet, arbeitete, hat gearbeitet> ◊ *Die Kühlung arbeitete fehlerfrei/ununterbrochen.* ♦ *mit Verlust/Gewinn arbeiten* operate at high speeds auf Hochtouren arbeiten sb operates somewhere jd ist irgendwo tätig [ɪst ... tɛːtɪç] +sein ◊ *Die Firma ist auch im Ausland tätig.* **2.** *(a machine)* operate sth etw. bedienen [bə'diːnən] <bedient, bediente, hat bedient> ◊ *Meine Oma kann keinen Computer bedienen.; (a switch, lever, indicator)* etw. betätigen [bə'tɛːtɪgŋ̩] <betätigt, betätigte, hat betätigt> *(lofty)* ◊ *beim Abbiegen den Blinker betätigen; (a tool etc.)* etw. handhaben ['hanthaːbm̩] +haben ◊ *Weißt du, wie man diesen Bohrer handhaben muss?* **3.** *(a company, an organization)* führen ['fyːrən] +haben ◊ *Die Firma wird als selbstständiges Unternehmen geführt.* **4.** *(a service)* betreiben [bə'traɛbm̩] <betreibt, betrieb, hat betrieben> +haben ◊ *ein Kraftwerk betreiben* ♦ *Der Kindergarten wird von der Kirche betrieben.* **5.** *(bus etc.)* verkehren [fɐ'keːrən] <verkehrt, verkehrte, ist verkehrt> ◊ *Der Zug verkehrt stündlich.* **6.** MED operate (on sb/sth) (jdn/etw.) operieren [opə'riːrən] <operiert, operierte, hat operiert> ◊ *Die Ärzte müssen noch einmal operieren.* ♦ *Der Bruch muss operiert werden.* ♦ *jdn am Gehirn operieren* **7.** *(factor, rule)* sich auswirken ['aʊsvɪʳkŋ̩] <wirkt sich aus, wirkte sich aus, hat sich ausgewirkt> ◊ *Die neue Regelung wirkt sich zum Nachteil von Kleinbetrieben aus.* **8.** *(act)* vorgehen ['foːɐgeːən] <geht vor,

ging vor, ist vorgegangen> ◊ *Wir müssen uns überlegen, wie wir in Zukunft vorgehen wollen.*

operating room (noun) Operationssaal [opəra'tsjoːnszaːl] der <-(e)s, Operationssäle>

operating system (noun) Betriebssystem [bə'triːpszʏsˌteːm] das <-s, -e>

operating theatre (noun) Operationssaal [opəra'tsjoːnszaːl] der <-(e)s, Operationssäle>

operation (noun) **1.** *(medical, military, technical, mathematical)* Operation [opəra'tsjoːn] die <-, -en> ◊ *Wer wird die Operation durchführen?* ♦ *eine komplizierte mathematische Operation* have an operation operiert werden [opə'riːɐt veːɐdn̩] <wird, wurde, ist worden> **2.** *(organized activity or campaign)* Aktion [ak'tsjoːn] die <-, -en> ◊ *eine groß angelegte Aktion* zur Befreiung der Geiseln relief operation Hilfsaktion ['hɪlfs|ak,tsjoːn] rescue operation Rettungsaktion ['rɛtʊŋs|ak,tsjoːn]; *(of the police, emergency services)* Einsatz ['aɛnzats] der <-(e)s, Einsätze> ◊ *Bei dem Einsatz wurde ein Polizist verletzt.* ♦ *ein Einsatz der Feuerwehr* **3.** *(company, of machinery)* Betrieb [bə'triːp] der <-(e)s, -e> ◊ *Der Betrieb in Köln soll geschlossen werden.* ♦ *Während des Betriebs kam es immer wieder zu Störungen.* ♦ *Das neue Werk wird nächsten Monat den Betrieb aufnehmen.* **4.** *(handling, of machines or tools etc.)* Bedienung [bə'diːnʊŋ] die <-, -en> ◊ *Die Bedienung dieser Waschmaschine ist kinderleicht.; (of rules, laws)* Anwendung ['anvɛndʊŋ] die <-, -en> ◊ *Die Anwendung der Regel auf diesen Fall ist nicht möglich.* ⊛ **be in operation 1.** *(machines)* in Betrieb sein **2.** *(company)* tätig sein **3.** *(law)* in Kraft sein bring sth into operation **1.** *(a machine, factory)* in Betrieb nehmen **2.** *(a law)* in Kraft setzen come into operation **1.** *(factory)* in Betrieb gehen **2.** *(law)* in Kraft treten

operational (adj) betriebsbereit [bə'triːpsbəraɛt] no comp/superl ◊ *Das Telefon ist frühestens morgen wieder betriebsbereit.* fully operational voll funktionsfähig [fɔl fʊŋk'tsjoːnsfɛːɪç] no comp/superl ◊ *ein voll funktionsfähiges System*

operator (noun) **1.** *(of a telephone switchboard)* Vermittlung [fɐ'mɪtlʊŋ] die <-, -en> ◊ *die Vermittlung anrufen* **2.** *(of a machine)* Maschinenarbeiter [ma'ʃiːnən|aʳbaɛtɐ] der <-s, -> ♀Maschinenarbeiterin [ma'ʃiːnən|ˌaʳbaɛtərɪn] die <-, -nen> Who is the operator of this machine? Wer bedient diese Maschine? crane operator Kranführer ['kraːnfyːrɐ] der <-s, -> ♀Kranführerin ['kraːnfyːrərɪn] die <-, -nen> computer operator Computerfachkraft [kɔm'pjuːtɐfakkraft] die <-, Computerfachkräfte> ◊ *Ich bewerbe mich um eine Stelle als Computerfachkraft.* **3.** *(company)* Unternehmen [ʊntɐ'neːmən] das <-s, -> coach operator Reisebusunternehmen ['raɛzəbʊsˌʊntɐneːmən] das <-s, -> ⊛ **be a smooth operator** raffiniert vorgehen

ophthalmologist (noun) Augenarzt ['aʊgŋ̩|aʳtst] der <-es, Augenärzte> ♀Augenärztin ['aʊgŋ̩|ɛʳtstɪn] die <-, -nen> ◊ *Du solltest einen Augenarzt aufsuchen.* ♦ *Sie ist Augenärztin von Beruf.*

opinion (noun) Meinung ['maɛnʊŋ] die <-, -en> ◊ *Sie hat keine eigene Meinung.* ♦ *eine weit verbreitete Meinung* in sb's opinion jds Meinung nach ◊ *Was soll ich deiner Meinung nach tun?* be of the opinion that der Meinung sein, dass ◊ *Ich bin der Meinung,*

A B C D E F G H I J K L M N O P Q R S T U V W X Y Z

A

B

C

D

E

F

G

H

I

J

K

L

M

N

O

P

Q

R

S

T

U

V

W

X

Y

Z

dass du den Job annehmen solltest. form an opinion (on sth) sich ⟨dat⟩ eine Meinung (über etw. ⟨acc⟩) bilden ◇ *Am Informationsabend konnte ich mir eine Meinung über die Schule bilden.* have a good/high opinion of sb/sth eine hohe Meinung von jdm/etw. haben have a low opinion of sb/sth eine schlechte Meinung von jdm/etw. haben give an opinion seine Meinung sagen be of the same opinion gleicher Meinung sein public opinion die öffentliche Meinung sb's political/religious opinions jds politische/religiöse Ansichten [pə͵liːtɪʃə/reli͵giøːzə 'anzɪçtn̩] be a matter of opinion Ansichtssache sein ['anzɪçtszaxə zaɛn]

opinion poll ⟨noun⟩ *(political)* Meinungsumfrage ['maɛnʊŋs|ʊmfraːgə] die <–, –n>

opponent ⟨noun⟩ Gegner ['geːgnɐ] der <–s, –> ♀Gegnerin ['geːgnərɪn] die <–, –nen> ◇ *Wer wird sein Gegner im Halbfinale sein?* ♦ *Sie ist eine Gegnerin der EU-Erweiterung.*

opportunity ⟨noun⟩ 1. *(chance)* Gelegenheit [gə'leːgn̩haɛt] die <–, –en> ◇ *eine günstige/verpasste Gelegenheit* ♦ *Hattest du schon Gelegenheit, dir den Film anzusehen?* ♦ *Das wiederholt er bei jeder Gelegenheit.* a golden opportunity eine einmalige Gelegenheit take the opportunity to do sth die Gelegenheit nutzen, etw. zu tun ◇ *Wir möchten diese Gelegenheit nutzen, uns bei Ihnen zu bedanken.* given the opportunity wenn er/sie etc. die Gelegenheit dazu hätte ◇ *Wenn sie die Gelegenheit dazu hätte, wäre sie bestimmt eine gute Managerin.* 2. *(possibility)* Möglichkeit ['møːklɪçkaɛt] die <–, –en> ◇ *gute berufliche Möglichkeiten haben* 3. *(on the job market)* freie Stelle [͵fraɛə 'ʃtɛlə] die <–, –n> ◇ *Es gibt zurzeit viele freie Stellen in unserer Marketingabteilung.* ♦ *Ich suche eine freie Stelle als Modedesigner.*

⑨ at the earliest opportunity so bald wie möglich

oppose ⟨verb⟩ 1. *(be against)* oppose sth etw. ablehnen ['apleːnən] +haben ◇ *Die Partei lehnt diese Pläne ab.* 2. *(prevent from succeeding)* oppose sb/sth sich gegen jdn/etw. stellen [geːgn̩ ... ʃtɛlən] +haben ◇ *Niemand wagte es, sich gegen ihn zu stellen.* 3. *(fight)* oppose sb/sth gegen jdn/etw. kämpfen [geːgn̩ ... ͵kɛmpfn̩] +haben ◇ *Sie kämpften erbittert gegen die Schließung des Werks.*

opposed → oppose ⟨adj⟩ 1. be opposed to sth gegen etw. sein ['geːgn̩ ... zaɛn] +sein ◇ *Bist du gegen den Bau der neuen Straße?* be opposed to doing sth dagegen sein, dass etw. getan wird ◇ *Ich bin dagegen, dass die Gelder gekürzt werden.* 2. *(very different)* gegensätzlich ['geːgn̩zɛtslɪç] ◇ *völlig gegensätzliche Charaktere sein* ♦ *Ihre Ansichten könnten kaum gegensätzlicher sein.*

⑨ as opposed to im Gegensatz zu

opposite¹ ⟨noun⟩ Gegenteil ['geːgn̩taɛl] das <–(e)s, –e> most sing ◇ *Dein Bruder behauptet das Gegenteil.* ♦ *Das Gegenteil von „hell" ist „dunkel".* ♦ *Wenn man diesem Kind etwas sagt, tut es genau das Gegenteil.*

⑨ opposites attract Gegensätze ziehen sich an

opposite² ⟨adj⟩ 1. *(side)* gegenüberliegend [geːgn̩'|yːbeːliːgn̩t] no comp/superl, only before ns ◇ *Ihr Haus ist auf der gegenüberliegenden Straßenseite.* 2. *(direction, end)* entgegengesetzt [ɛnt'geːgn̩gəzɛtst] no comp/superl, only before ns ◇ *in die entgegengesetzte Richtung fahren* ♦ *am entgegen-*

gesetzten Ende der Stadt wohnen 3. *(very different)* gegensätzlich ['geːgn̩zɛtslɪç] ◇ *gegensätzliche Reaktionen auf etw.* ⟨acc⟩; *(effect)* gegenteilig ['geːgn̩taɛlɪç] no comp/superl, only before ns It had the opposite effect. Es bewirkte genau das Gegenteil.

opposite³ ⟨adv⟩ gegenüber [geːgn̩'|yːbɐ] ◇ *Wir wohnen hier gleich gegenüber.*

opposite⁴ ⟨prep⟩ gegenüber [geːgn̩'|yːbɐ] +dat ◇ *Gegenüber der Bank steht ein Brunnen.* ♦ *Er stand mir gegenüber.*

opposition ⟨noun⟩ 1. *(resistance)* opposition (to sth) Widerstand (gegen etw.) ['viːdɐʃtant] der <–(e)s, Widerstände> ◇ *Du gibst beim geringsten Widerstand auf.* come out in opposition to sth Widerstand gegen etw. leisten face strong opposition auf starken Widerstand stoßen 2. POL Opposition [ɔpozi'tsjoːn] die <–, –en> most sing ◇ *Die Opposition ist gegen diesen Vorschlag.* in opposition in der Opposition 3. SPORT Gegenseite ['geːgn̩zaɛtə] die <–> no pl ◇ *ein Tor für die Gegenseite* 4. *(great difference)* Gegensatz ['geːgn̩zats] der <–es, Gegensätze> ◇ *der Gegensatz zwischen jung und alt*

oppress ⟨verb⟩ 1. *(treat very badly)* unterdrücken [ʊntɐ'drʏkn̩] <unterdrückt, unterdrückte, hat unterdrückt> ◇ *eine Minderheit unterdrücken* 2. *(sadden)* bedrücken [bə'drʏkn̩] <bedrückt, bedrückte, hat bedrückt> ◇ *Was bedrückt dich denn?*

oppression ⟨noun⟩ 1. *(of a people)* Unterdrückung [ʊntɐ'drʏkʊŋ] die <–> no pl ◇ *die Unterdrückung Andersdenkender* 2. *(sadness)* Bedrücktheit [bə'drʏkthaɛt] die <–> no pl ◇ *Ihre Bedrücktheit nahm noch zu.*

opt ⟨verb⟩ opt for sth sich für etw. entscheiden [fyːɐ ... ɛnt͵ʃaɛdn̩] <entscheidet sich, entschied sich, hat entschieden> ◇ *Sie entschied sich für die Wohnung in der Stadtmitte.* opt to do sth sich entscheiden, etw. zu tun ◇ *Er entschied sich schließlich, bei seiner alten Firma zu bleiben.*

• **opt out** ⟨phras v⟩ *(not take part)* nicht mitmachen [nɪçt 'mɪtmaxn̩] +haben ◇ *Die Firma macht nicht mit.* opt out of sth bei etw. nicht mitmachen; *(stop taking part)* aussteigen ['aʊsʃtaɛgn̩] <steigt aus, stieg aus, ist ausgestiegen> opt out of sth aus etw. aussteigen ◇ *Einer der Partner will aus dem Geschäft aussteigen.*

optical(ly) ⟨adj, adv⟩ optisch ['ɔptɪʃ] no comp/superl, only before ns ◇ *eine optische Täuschung* ♦ *optisch lesbar*

optician ⟨noun⟩ Optiker ['ɔptɪkɐ] der <–s, –> ♀Optikerin ['ɔptɪkərɪn] die <–, –nen> ◇ *Er arbeitet als Optiker.* ♦ *Die Optikerin hat ihr eine neue Brille angepasst.*

optimism ⟨noun⟩ Optimismus [ɔpti'mɪsmʊs] der <–> no pl ◇ *Optimismus ausstrahlen*

optimistic(ally) ⟨adj, adv⟩ optimistisch [ɔpti'mɪstɪʃ] ◇ *eine optimistische Einstellung* ♦ *Meine Grundhaltung ist optimistisch.* ♦ *Wir blicken optimistisch in die Zukunft.* be optimistic about sth optimistisch sein, was etw. angeht be optimistic that zuversichtlich sein, dass ['tsuːfɛɐzɪçtlɪç zaɛn das] +sein

option ⟨noun⟩ 1. *(choice)* Möglichkeit ['møːklɪçkaɛt] die <–, –en> ◇ *Zur Lösung des Problems gibt es verschiedene Möglichkeiten.* have the option of doing sth die Möglichkeit haben, etw. zu tun be a viable option eine Möglichkeit sein sb has no option but to do sth jdm bleibt nichts anderes übrig, als etw. zu tun

[blæpt nɪʧts andərəs 'yːbrɪç als ... tsuː] <blieb, ist geblieben> ◊ *Mir blieb nichts anderes übrig, als ihn zu entlassen.* **2.** IT, FIN, ECON Option [ɔpˈtsjoːn] die <-, –en> ◊ *die Option „Speichern" wählen* ♦ *eine Option auf etw.* ⟨acc⟩ haben stock option Aktienoption ['aktsjən|ɔp,tsjoːn] (preset) options Voreinstellungen ['foːɐ̯|aɛnʃtɛlʊŋən] die <-> pl **3.** *(additional feature)* Extra ['ɛkstraː] das <-s, –s> ◊ *ein Wagen mit vielen Extras* **4.** SCHOOL, UNI *(in the UK)* Wahlfach ['vaːlfax] das <-(e)s, Wahlfächer> ◉ **take the easy option** es sich ⟨dat⟩ einfach machen

optional ⟨adj⟩ **1.** *(if required)* auf Wunsch [aɔf 'vʊnʃ] ◊ *Extras auf Wunsch* sth is optional auf Wunsch gibt es etw. ◊ *Auf Wunsch gibt es auch andere Farben.* with optional ... auf Wunsch mit ... ◊ *Zimmer auf Wunsch mit Frühstück; (in recipes)* nach Belieben [naːx bəˈliːbm̩] ◊ *Salz, Pfeffer und etwas Knoblauch nach Belieben* **2.** *(not compulsory)* freiwillig ['fraɛvɪlɪç] no comp/superl ◊ *Der Französischkurs ist freiwillig.* ♦ *ein freiwilliges Praktikum*

or ⟨conjunc⟩ **1.** *(expresses that there is an alternative)* oder ['oːdɐ] ◊ *Kommst du mit oder bleibst du da?* ♦ *Willst du Kaffee oder Tee?* ♦ *die Europäische Zentralbank oder kurz EZB* **2.** *(otherwise)* or (else) sonst [zɔnst] ◊ *Es ist bestimmt etwas dazwischengekommen, sonst wäre er schon hier.*

oral ⟨adj⟩ **1.** *(spoken)* mündlich ['mʏntlɪç] no comp/superl ◊ *Die Prüfung ist mündlich.* ♦ *eine mündliche Überlieferung* **2.** *(through or for the mouth)* oral [oˈraːl] no comp/superl, only before ns ◊ *orale Medikamente* oral sex Oralverkehr [oˈraːlfekeːɐ̯] der <-s> no pl; *(of the mouth)* Mund... [mʊnt] oral hygiene Mundhygiene ['mʊnthyˌgieːnə] die <-> no pl

orally ⟨adv⟩ **1.** *(by speech)* mündlich ['mʏntlɪç] no comp/superl ◊ *etw. mündlich vereinbaren* **2.** *(through the mouth)* oral [oˈraːl] no comp/superl ◊ *ein Medikament oral einnehmen*

orange¹ ⟨noun⟩ **1.** *(fruit)* Orange [oˈraŋʒə] die <-, –n> ◊ *eine Orange auspressen* **2.** *(juice)* Orangensaft [oˈraŋʒn̩zaft] der <-(e)s, Orangensäfte> most sing ◊ *Ich trinke (ein) Orangensaft.* **3.** *(colo(u)r)* Orange [oˈraŋʃ] das <-> no pl ◊ *Orange ist meine Lieblingsfarbe.*

orange² ⟨adj⟩ orange [oˈraŋʃ] <oranger, am orangesten> ◊ *ein oranges Hemd* ♦ *Die Kücheneinrichtung ist orange.*

orbit¹ ⟨noun⟩ **1.** *(path around a planet)* Umlaufbahn ['ʊmlaɔfbaːn] die <-, –en> ◊ *die Umlaufbahnen der Planeten* be in orbit in der Umlaufbahn sein **2.** *(sphere of influence)* Einflussbereich ['aɛnflʊsbəraɛç] der <-(e)s, –e> ◊ *im Einflussbereich des Islam*

orbit² ⟨verb⟩ umkreisen [ʊmˈkraɛzn̩] <umkreist, umkreiste, hat umkreist> ◊ *Der Mond umkreist die Erde.*

orchestra ⟨noun⟩ Orchester [ɔrˈkɛstɐ] das <-s, –> ◊ *in einem Orchester spielen*

ordeal ⟨noun⟩ Tortur [tɔrˈtuːɐ̯] die <-, –en> ◊ *Der Zahnarztbesuch war eine schreckliche Tortur.*

order¹ ⟨noun⟩ **1.** *(sequence)* Reihenfolge ['raɛənfɔlgə] die <-, –n> ◊ *in alphabetischer Reihenfolge* in order in der richtigen Reihenfolge out of order durcheinander [dʊrçlaɛˈnandɐ] no comp/superl **2.** *(for services)* Auftrag ['aɔftraːk] der <-(e)s, Aufträge> ◊ *den Auftrag für eine Übersetzung bekommen* place

an order einen Auftrag erteilen; *(for goods, in a restaurant, sth you ordered)* Bestellung [bəˈʃtɛlʊŋ] die <-, –en> place an order eine Bestellung aufgeben take sb's order jds Bestellung aufnehmen on order bestellt [bəˈʃtɛlt] no comp/superl ◊ *Die Waren sind bestellt.* made to order speziell angefertigt [ʃpeˌtsjɛl ˈaŋəfɐˌtɪçt] no comp/superl **3.** *(instruction, legal document)* Befehl [bəˈfeːl] der <-(e)s, –e> ◊ *einen Befehl geben* take orders from sb Befehle von jdm entgegennehmen have orders to do sth den Befehl haben, etw. zu tun by order of sb auf jds Befehl eviction order Räumungsbefehl ['rɔɶmʊŋsbəfeːl] **4.** *(state in which everything is well organized, system, group of species)* Ordnung ['ɔrdnʊŋ] die <-, –en> ◊ *die öffentliche Ordnung* ♦ *Ordnung halten* ◊ *die Ordnung der Primaten* get sth in order etw. in Ordnung bringen social order Gesellschaftsordnung [gəˈzɛlʃafts|ɔrdnʊŋ] **5.** *(of monks, nuns)* Orden ['ɔrdn̩] der <-s, –> ◊ *ein buddhistischer Orden* ◉ of the highest order hochgradig

order² ⟨verb⟩ **1.** *(tell sb to do sth)* anordnen ['anlɔrdnən] <ordnet an, ordnete an, hat angeordnet> ◊ *Eine Obduktion der Leiche wurde angeordnet.* order sb to do sth jdn anweisen, etw. zu tun ['anvaɛzn ... tsuː] <weist an, wies an, hat angewiesen>; *(more authoritarian)* befehlen [bəˈfeːlən] <befiehlt, befahl, hat befohlen> ◊ *Der König befahl die Freilassung der Rebellen.* ♦ *Cäsar befahl den Soldaten, eine Brücke zu bauen.* order sb back jdn zurückbeordern [tsuˈrʏkbəˈɔrdən] <beordert zurück, beordere zurück, hat zurückbeordert> order sb out of sth jdn auffordern, etw. zu verlassen ['aɔffɔrdɐn ... tsuː fɐˈlasn̩] +haben ◊ *Die Polizisten forderten ihn auf, die Wohnung zu verlassen.* **2.** *(ask for sth)* bestellen [bəˈʃtɛlən] <bestellt, bestellte, hat bestellt> ◊ *Ich habe dir noch ein Bier bestellt.* ♦ *Tut mir Leid, dass ich so spät komme. Hast du schon bestellt?* **3.** *(arrange, organize)* ordnen ['ɔrdnən] <ordnet, ordnete, hat geordnet> ◊ *etw. alphabetisch ordnen*

orderly ⟨adj⟩ *(tidy)* ordentlich ['ɔrdntlɪç] ◊ *eine ordentliche Küche* ♦ *Die Wohnung war sauber und ordentlich.; (disciplined)* diszipliniert [dɪstsipliˈniːɐ̯t] <disziplinierter, am diszipliniertesten> ◊ *diszipliniertes Verhalten* ♦ *die Schüler waren diszipliniert.; (life)* geregelt [gəˈreːgl̩t] no comp/superl, only before ns ◊ *ein geregeltes Leben*

ordinarily ⟨adv⟩ **1.** *(in an ordinary way)* einfach ['aɛnfax] ◊ *einfach gekleidet sein* **2.** *(normally)* normalerweise [nɔrˈmaːlɐvaɛzə] no comp/superl ◊ *Normalerweise ist er immer ein ruhiger Typ.*

ordinary ⟨adj⟩ **1.** *(average, not unusual)* normal [nɔrˈmaːl] ◊ *ein Vorfall, der völlig normal ist* ♦ *ein ganz normales Kind* no ordinary ... kein gewöhnlicher ... [kaɛn gəˈvøːnlɪçɐ] keine gewöhnliche ... [kaɛnə gəˈvøːnlɪçə] ◊ *Sie war keine gewöhnliche Frau.* **2.** *(plain, simple)* einfach ['aɛnfax] ◊ *einfache Leute* ♦ *Das Haus ist recht einfach, aber preisgünstig.*

organ ⟨noun⟩ **1.** *(of the body, vehicle for sth)* Organ [ɔrˈgaːn] das <-s, –e> ◊ *das offizielle Organ des Verbandes* ♦ *Die Leber ist ein lebenswichtiges Organ.* digestive organ Verdauungsorgan [fɛrˈdaɔʊŋs|ɔrˌgaːn] organ donor Organspender [ɔrˈgaːnʃpɛndə] der

A

<-s, -> ♀Organspenderin [ɔrˈgaːnʃpɛndərɪn] die <-, -nen> 2. *(musical instrument)* Orgel [ˈɔrgl̩] die <-, -n> ◊ *(an/auf der) Orgel spielen* 3. *(penis)* Glied [gliːt] das <-(e)s, -er>

B

organic [adj] 1. *(without chemicals)* biologisch [bioˈloːgɪʃ] *no comp/superl* ◊ *biologische Landwirtschaft* ✦ *Unser Fleisch ist biologisch.; Bio...* [ˈbiːoː]

C

organic products Bioerzeugnisse [ˈbiːoˌle̩tsɔøknɪsə] die <-> *pl* organic vegetables Biogemüse [ˈbiːoɡəmyːzə] das <-s, -> *most sing* 2. *(of living*

D

things, systems, relating to the body's organs) organisch [ɔrˈgaːnɪʃ] *no comp/superl* ◊ *organische Chemie* ✦ *ein organisches Leiden*

E

organically [adv] biologisch [bioˈloːgɪʃ] *no comp/superl* ✦ *biologisch angebaute Lebensmittel*

F

organism [noun] Organismus [ɔrˈgaːnɪsmʊs] der <-, Organismen>

G

organization [noun] 1. *(society, planning of sth)* Organisation [ɔrˈganizaˈtsi̯oːn] die <-, -en> ◊ *sich einer Organisation anschließen* ✦ *mit der Organisation einer Hochzeit beschäftigt sein* aid organization Hilfsorganisation [ˈhɪlfsɔrˌganizaˌtsi̯oːn] terrorist organization Terrororganisation [ˈtɛroːɡəˌlɔrˌganizaˌtsi̯oːn] 2. *(structure)* Aufbau [ˈaofbao] der <-(e)s> *no pl* ◊ *der Aufbau des menschlichen Auges*

H

I

J

K

L

organizational [adj] organisatorisch [ɔrˈganizaˈtoːrɪʃ] *no comp/superl, only before ns* ◊ *organisatorische Fähigkeiten*

M

N

organize [verb] 1. *(plan, obtain, synchronize)* organisieren [ɔrˈganiˈziːrən] <organisiert, organisierte, hat organisiert> ◊ *eine Konferenz organisieren* ✦ *Getränke für eine Party organisieren* They organize. Sie organisieren sich. 2. *(divide up, establish an order)* einteilen [ˈaentaelən] +haben ◊ *Ich habe mir die Arbeit gut eingeteilt.*

O

P

organizer [noun] 1. *(person)* Organisator [ɔrˈganiˈzaːtoːg] der <-s, -en> ♀Organisatorin [ɔrˈganizaˈtoːrɪn] die <-, -nen> ◊ *der Organisator einer Konferenz* 2. *(diary)* Terminkalender [tɛrˈmiːnˌkalɛndɐ] der <-s, ->; *(hand-held computer)* Organizer [ˈɔrɡənaeze] der <-s, ->

Q

R

orgasm [noun] Orgasmus [ɔrˈgasmʊs] der <-, Orgasmen>

S

Orient [noun] Ferne Osten [ˌfɛrnə ˈɔstn̩] der <Fernen Ostens> *only with the definite article, no pl*

T

U

orientation [noun] 1. *(inclination, information)* Orientierung [orjɛnˈtiːrʊŋ] die <-, -en> ◊ *die sexuelle Orientierung* orientation to/towards sth Orientierung in Richtung ... [gen] ◊ *Die osteuropäische Wirtschaft hat eine starke Orientierung in Richtung EU.* client orientation Kundenorientierung [ˈkʊndn̩ˌorjɛnˌtiːrʊŋ] orientation course Orientierungskurs [orjɛnˈtiːrʊŋskuːrs] der <-es, -e> 2. *(position of an object)* Lage [ˈlaːɡə] die <-, -n> ◊ *die Lage des Hauses; (direction)* Ausrichtung [ˈaosrɪçtʊŋ] die <-> *no pl* ◊ *die Ausrichtung des Gebäudes nach Südwesten*

V

W

X

Y

Z

origin [noun] 1. *(source)* origin(s) Ursprung [ˈuːɐ̯ʃprʊŋ] der <-(e)s, Ursprünge> ◊ *Diese Rebsorte hat ihren Ursprung in Griechenland.* ✦ *der Ursprung des Lebens* place of origin Ursprungsort [ˈuːɐ̯ʃprʊŋsˌɔrt] der <-(e)s, -e>; *(coming into existence)* Entstehung [ɛntˈʃteːʊŋ] die <-, -en> *most sing* ◊ *etw. verdankt jdm/etw. seine Entstehung* of recent origin erst kürzlich entstanden [eːɐ̯st ˌkʏrtslɪç ɛntˈʃtandn̩] *no comp/superl* ◊ *ein erst kürzlich entstandener Begriff*

2. *(sb's background)* origin(s) Herkunft [ˈheːɐ̯kʊnft] die <-> sing ◊ *Sie war jüdischer/türkischer/bürgerlicher Herkunft.* humble origins einfache Herkunft country of origin Herkunftsland [ˈheːɐ̯kʊnftslant] das <-(e)s, Herkunftsländer> ethnic origin Volkszugehörigkeit [ˈfɔlkstsuːɡəˌhøːrɪçkaet] die <-> *no pl*

original[1] [noun] Original [origiˈnaːl] das <-s, -e> ◊ *Dieses Gemälde ist ein Original.*

original[2] [adj] 1. *(existing in or from the beginning)* ursprünglich [ˈuːɐ̯ʃprʏŋlɪç] *no comp/superl, only before ns* ◊ *Die ursprüngliche Idee wurde fallen gelassen.* 2. *(new, special)* originell [origiˈnɛl] ◊ *ein originelles Geschenk* ✦ *Der Vorschlag ist nicht sehr originell.* 3. *(not copied, genuine)* original [origiˈnaːl] *no comp/superl, mostly before ns* ◊ *originale Werke berühmter Künstler; Original...* [origiˈnaːl] original manuscript Originalhandschrift [origiˈnaːlhantʃrɪft] die <-, -en>

originally [adv] ursprünglich [ˈuːɐ̯ʃprʏŋlɪç] *no comp/superl* ◊ *Die Konferenz war ursprünglich für April geplant, sie findet jetzt aber erst im Juni statt.*

originate [verb] 1. *(begin to exist)* entstehen [ɛntˈʃteːən] <entsteht, entstand, ist entstanden> ◊ *Diese Technologie ist in Großbritannien entstanden.* 2. *(come from)* originate from a place irgendwoher stammen [ˈʃtaman] +haben ◊ *Diese Kräuter stammen aus dem Mittelmeerraum.* originate with sb von jdm stammen 3. *(create)* erfinden [ɛˈfɪndn̩] <erfindet, erfand, hat erfunden> ◊ *eine Figur/einen Begriff erfinden; (an idea, rumo(u)r)* sb originates sth etw. stammt von jdm [ʃtamt fɔn] +haben ◊ *Von wem stammt dieses Gerücht?*

orphan [noun] Waise [ˈvaezə] die <-, -n> ◊ *Das Kind war Waise.* ✦ *Sie nahmen eine arme Waise bei sich auf.*

orthodox [adj] 1. *(upholding a traditional doctrine)* orthodox [ɔrˈtoːdɔks] *no comp/superl* ◊ *Sein Glauben ist orthodox.* ✦ *orthodoxer Marxismus* the Orthodox Church die orthodoxe Kirche 2. *(conventional)* konventionell [kɔnvɛntsi̯oˈnɛl] ◊ *konventionelle Medizin* ✦ *Die Handlung der Geschichte ist eher konventionell.*

other[1] [adj] andere [ˈandərə] ◊ *Das andere Kleid gefällt mir besser.* ✦ *Hör nicht auf andere Leute!* in other words mit anderen Worten some other time ein anderes Mal the other one der/die/das andere [deːɡ/diː/das ˈandərə] ◊ *Eine Socke habe ich gefunden, die andere suche ich noch.* the other way round andersherum [ˈandeshɛrʊm] ◊ *In Wirklichkeit war es andersherum.*

other[2] [indef pron] the other der/die/das andere [deːɡ/diː/das ˈandərə] ◊ *Der Wein ist schlecht, aber der andere schmeckt mir besser.* others andere [ˈandərə] ◊ *Warum kannst du das nicht? Andere können es doch auch!*

otherwise [adv] 1. *(if not, apart from that)* sonst [zɔnst] ◊ *Beeil dich, sonst kommen wir zu spät!* ◊ *Das Wetter war scheußlich, aber sonst war es ein toller Urlaub.* 2. *(differently)* think otherwise anderer Meinung sein [ˈandərə ˌmaenʊŋ zaen] +sein tell sb otherwise jdm etwas anderes sagen [ˈandərəs zaːɡn̩] +haben sth cannot be otherwise etw. kann nicht anders sein [kan nɪçt ˈandes ˌzaen] <konnte, hat gekonnt> otherwise known as auch bekannt als [aox bəˈkant als]

ought to [verb] 1. *(expressing obligation)* sb/sth ought to do sth jd/etw. sollte etw. tun [ˈzɔltə] *subjunctive*

II ◊ *Er sollte schon längst zurück sein.* ♦ *Du solltest dich schämen!* ♦ *Die Adresse sollte jetzt stimmen.* ♦ *Wir sollten ihr etwas schenken.* sb ought to be here jd sollte hier sein sb/sth ought not to do sth jd/ etw. sollte etw. nicht tun ◊ *Wir sollten nicht so spät nach Hause kommen.* sb/sth ought to have done sth jd/etw. hätte etw. tun sollen ◊ *Du hättest nicht hingeben sollen.* **2.** *(expressing a presumption, probability)* sb/sth ought to do sth jd/etw. müsste etw. tun ['mʏstə] *subjunctive II* ◊ *Das Paket müsste morgen ankommen.* ♦ *Ihr müsstet den Brief eigentlich schon bekommen haben.* ♦ *Zehn Minuten müssten reichen.* That ought not to cause any problems. Das soll keine Probleme verursachen. sb ought to be somewhere jd müsste irgendwo sein

o umlaut, O umlaut ⟨noun⟩ ö, Ö [ø:] das <–(s), –(s)> ◊ *Dieses Wort wird mit einem kleinen ö/großen Ö geschrieben.* ♦ *Ö wie Österreich*

our ⟨det⟩ unser ['ʊnzɐ] unsere ['ʊnzərə] ◊ *Unser Vater geht mit uns in Kino.* ♦ *unsere neue Lehrerin* ♦ *Unser Auto ist kaputt.* → **unser**

ours ⟨poss pron⟩ unserer ['ʊnzərɐ] unsere ['ʊnzərə] unseres ['ʊnzərəs] ◊ *Das ist euer Raum und dieser ist unserer.* ♦ *Sind diese Schlüssel unsere?* ♦ *Das rote Auto ist unseres.* → **unserer**
ⓔ of ours von uns ◊ *Freunde von uns*

ourselves ⟨ref pron⟩ **1.** *(referring to a group the speaker belongs to)* uns [ʊns] ◊ *Wir haben uns nur verteidigt.; (more emphatic)* uns selbst [ʊns 'zɛlpst] ◊ *Der Kurs hilft uns, uns selbst besser kennen zu lernen.* **2.** *(instead of sb else)* selbst [zɛlpst] ◊ *Wenn der Elektriker nicht kommt, reparieren wir es eben selbst.*
ⓔ (all) by ourselves (ganz) allein (all) to ourselves *(referring to time)* (ganz) für uns allein ◊ *Wir haben den Abend für uns allein. (referring to a place)* (ganz) für uns ◊ *Endlich hatten wir das Wohnzimmer für uns.*

oust ⟨verb⟩ **1.** *(remove)* absetzen ['apzɛtsn̩] +haben ◊ *Der Minister wurde abgesetzt.; (a government, ruler)* stürzen ['ʃtʏ'tsn̩] +haben ◊ *einen Diktator stürzen* oust sb from office jdn aus seinem Amt drängen [aʊs ... 'amt drɛŋən] +haben **2.** *(replace)* verdrängen [fɛ'drɛŋən] <verdrängt, verdrängte, hat verdrängt> ◊ *Der Tennisstar wurde vom ersten Platz verdrängt.*

out¹ ⟨adj⟩ *(male)* offen schwul [ɔfn̩ 'ʃvuːl] no comp/ superl ◊ *Er ist offen schwul.* ♦ *ein offen schwuler Fernsehmoderator; (female)* offen lesbisch [ɔfn̩ 'lɛsbɪʃ] no comp/superl

out² ⟨adv⟩ **1.** *(not at home, outside sth, not burning or shining, not available in a shop)* aus [aʊs] ◊ *Ich habe gestern angerufen, aber du warst wohl aus.* ♦ *Der Ball war aus.* ♦ *Alle Lichter waren aus.* ♦ *Brötchen sind aus.; (with certain verbs)* aus... [aʊs] go out ausgehen ['aʊsgeːən] <geht aus, ging aus, ist ausgegangen> ◊ *abends ausgehen* ♦ *Das Feuer ist ausgegangen.* wash out auswaschen ['aʊsvaʃn̩] <wäscht aus, wusch aus, hat ausgewaschen> ◊ *Flecken aus einer Bluse auswaschen* **2.** *(expressing movement away from a place)* hinaus [hɪ'naʊs] ◊ *Lass uns allein! Hinaus!* ♦ *Ich will hinaus an die frische Luft.; (with certain verbs)* hinaus... [hɪ'naʊs] see sb out jdn hinausbegleiten [hɪ'naʊsbəɡlaɪtn̩] <begleitet hinaus, hat hinausbegleitet> ◊ *Soll ich dich noch hinausbegleiten?* slip out sich hinausschleichen [hɪ'naʊsʃlaɛçn̩] <schleicht sich hinaus, schlich

sich hinaus, hat sich hinausgeschlichen> ◊ *Wir schlichen uns zur Hintertür hinaus.; (used to express that sth is removed, available, visible)* heraus... [hɛ'raʊs] come out herauskommen [hɛ'raʊskɔmən] <kommt heraus, kam heraus, ist herausgekommen> ◊ *Nach dem Regen kam die Sonne heraus.* **3.** *(not inside, no longer in prison, far away)* draußen ['draʊsn̩] ◊ *Die Kinder sind draußen im Garten.* ♦ *Er ist wieder draußen.* out there da draußen The tide is out. Es ist Ebbe. **4.** *(unconscious)* bewusstlos [bə'vʊstloːs] no comp/superl ◊ *Er war 20 Minuten lang bewusstlos.* **5.** *(not fashionable)* out [aʊt] no comp/superl (fam) ◊ *Lila ist doch total out.* **6.** *(not possible)* nicht drin [nɪçt 'drɪn] (fam) ◊ *Ich hab Rückenschmerzen — Sport ist im Moment nicht drin.* **7.** *(publicly known)* raus [raʊs] (fam) ◊ *Die Ergebnisse sind noch nicht raus.*
ⓔ be out **1.** *(in your calculations)* danebenliegen (fam) ◊ *Du liegst mit deiner Rechnung um 100 Euro daneben.* **2.** *(pursuing sth)* be out for sth auf etw. ⟨acc⟩ aus sein ◊ *Sie sind auf Rache aus.* be out to do sth darauf aus sein, etw. zu tun out and about unterwegs out with it raus damit (fam) ◊ *Sag mir endlich, was los ist — raus damit!*

'Out' often occurs in phrasal verbs like 'get out' or 'come out' which have their own entries in the dictionary.

out³ ⟨verb⟩ outen ['aʊtn̩] <outet, outete, hat geoutet> (fam) ◊ *Sie hat ihn als skrupellosen Geschäftemacher geoutet.* out yourself sich outen

outbreak ⟨noun⟩ Ausbruch ['aʊsbrʊx] der <–(e)s, Ausbrüche> ◊ *bei Ausbruch des Krieges* ♦ *Seit Ausbruch der Epidemie sind 200 Personen umgekommen.*

outcome ⟨noun⟩ Ergebnis [ɛ'geːpnɪs] das <–es, –se> ◊ *ein positives Ergebnis erzielen*

outcry ⟨noun⟩ Aufschrei ['aʊfʃraɛ] der <–(e)s, –e> ◊ *Ein Aufschrei (der Empörung) ging durchs Land.* outcry against sb/sth Empörung über jdn/etw. [ɛm'pøːrʊŋ yːbɐ] die <–> no pl

outdated ⟨adj⟩ überholt [ybeˈhoːlt] no comp/superl ◊ *überholte Anschauungen/Theorien* ♦ *Einige Kapitel des Buches sind überholt.*

outdo ⟨verb⟩ übertreffen [ybe'trɛfn̩] <übertrifft, übertraf, hat übertroffen> ◊ *Sie versuchten, einander zu übertreffen.*
ⓔ not to be outdone um nicht zurückzustehen

outdoor ⟨adj⟩ *(done outside)* im Freien [ɪm 'fraɛ̯ən] ◊ *Aktivitäten im Freien; (used outside)* wetterfest ['vɛtɐfɛst] no comp/superl ◊ *die wetterfeste Kleidung/ Ausrüstung; (situated outside)* outdoor swimming pool Freibad ['fraɛbaːt] das <–(e)s, Freibäder>

outer ⟨adj⟩ *(on the outside, furthest away)* äußere ['ɔɡsərə] no comp, only before ns <ein äußerer ..., eine äußere ..., ein äußeres ...> ◊ *die äußere Erscheinung eines Menschen* ♦ *die äußere Grenze unseres Universums;* Außen... ['aʊsn̩] outer wall Außenmauer ['aʊsn̩maʊɐ] die <–, –n>; *(layer)* obere ['oːbərə] no comp, only before ns <ein oberer ..., eine obere ..., ein oberes ...> ◊ *Die Creme versorgt die oberen Hautschichten mit Feuchtigkeit.;* Ober... ['oːbɐ] outer clothing Oberbekleidung ['oːbɐbəklaɛdʊŋ] die <–, –en>

outfit ⟨noun⟩ **1.** *(clothes)* Kleider ['klaɛdɐ] die <–> pl; *(clothes that match)* Ensemble [aŋ'sambl̩] das

<-s, -s> *(lofty)* **2.** *(organization, enterprise)* Laden ['laːdn̩] der <-s, Läden> *(fam)*

outlet [noun] **1.** *(shop)* Verkaufsstelle [feˈkaʊfsʃtɛlə] die <-, -n> **2.** *(for emotions, energy)* Ventil [vɛnˈtiːl] das <-s, -e> ◊ *ein Ventil für seinen Frust suchen* **3.** *(for liquids)* Abfluss ['apflʊs] der <-es, Abflüsse>; *(for gas)* Abzug ['apt͡suːk] der <-(e)s, Abzüge>

outline[1] [noun] **1.** *(summary)* Abriss ['aprɪs] der <-es, -e> ◊ *ein Abriss der ägyptischen Kunst;* *(draft)* Entwurf [ɛntˈvʊrf] der <-(e)s, Entwürfe> **2.** *(contours, shape)* Umriss ['ʊmrɪs] der <-es, -e> ◊ *Im Dunkeln zeichneten sich die Umrisse eines Hauses ab.*

outline[2] [verb] **1.** *(sum up)* umreißen [ʊmˈraɛsn̩] <umreißt, umriss, hat umrissen> ◊ *Er umriss kurz das Thema des Buches.* **2.** *(draw a line around)* umranden [ʊmˈrandn̩] <umrandet, umrandete, hat umrandet> ◊ *seine Augen schwarz umranden;* *(be silhouetted)* be outlined against sth sich gegen etw. abzeichnen [ɡeːɡn̩ ... ˌapt͡saɛçnən] <zeichnet sich ab, zeichnete sich ab, hat sich abgezeichnet> ◊ *Das weiße Segel zeichnet sich gegen den blauen Himmel ab.*

outlive [verb] überleben [ybɐˈleːbm̩] <überlebt, überlebte, hat überlebt> ◊ *Sie hat ihren Mann um viele Jahre überlebt.*

outlook [noun] **1.** *(prospect)* Aussichten ['aʊszɪçtn̩] die <-> pl ◊ *Die Aussichten für die Wirtschaft sind gut.* **2.** *(attitude)* Einstellung ['aɛnʃtɛlʊŋ] die <-, -en> outlook on sth Einstellung zu etw. ◊ *jds Einstellung zum Leben*

out of [prep] **1.** *(expressing movement away from sth, giving a reason for sth)* aus [aʊs] [+dat] ◊ *Er sah aus dem Fenster.* ♦ *Er riss ein Blatt aus dem Heft.* ♦ *Sie haben aus Liebe geheiratet.* ♦ *etw. aus Holz herstellen* out of it daraus [daˈraʊs] ◊ *Das ist mein Glas. Wer hat daraus getrunken?* Let's make the best out of it! Machen wir das Beste daraus! **2.** *(no longer in a situation, not within a certain distance)* außer ['aʊsɐ] [+dat] ◊ *Der Patient ist außer Lebensgefahr.* ♦ *Die Inflation ist außer Kontrolle geraten.* ♦ *außer Sichtweite sein;* *(have sth behind you)* be out of it es hinter sich [dat] haben [ɛs ˈhɪntɐ ... haːbm̩] +haben ◊ *Das war die schlimme Zeit. Ich bin froh, dass ich es hinter mir habe.* **3.** *(outside, not during)* außerhalb ['aʊsɐhalp] [+gen] ◊ *außerhalb der Geschäftszeiten/Saison* ♦ *außerhalb der Stadt* **4.** *(have used up)* be out of bread/milk etc. kein Brot/keine Milch etc. mehr haben [kaɛn ˈbroːt/kaɛnə ˈmɪlç meːɐ haːbm̩] +haben **5.** *(no longer taking part)* be out of sth mit etw. nichts mehr zu tun haben [mɪt ... ˌnɪçt͡s meːɐ t͡suː ˈtuːn haːbm̩] +haben ◊ *Ich habe mit diesen Geschäften nichts mehr zu tun.;* *(no longer in a competition)* nicht mehr in etw. [dat] sein [ˌnɪçt meːɐ ɪn ... t͡saɛn] +sein ◊ *Drei weitere Deutsche sind nicht mehr im Wettbewerb.* **6.** *(from among a certain number)* von [fɔn] [+dat] ◊ *Neun von zehn Teilzeitkräften in Deutschland sind Frauen.*

ⓔ be out of it zu sein *(fam)* ◊ *Der Typ war total zu.*

outpatient [noun] ambulanter Patient [ambuˌlantɐ paˈt͡siɛnt] <-en, -en> ♀ambulante Patientin [ambuˌlantə paˈt͡siɛntɪn] die <-, -nen> ◊ *Der ambulante Patient wird meist durch den Hausarzt überwiesen.*

output [noun] **1.** *(amount produced)* Produktion

[prodʊkˈt͡sjoːn] die <-, -en> ◊ *die literarische Produktion österreichischer Autoren* industrial output Industrieproduktion [ɪndʊsˈtriːprodʊkˌt͡sjoːn]; *(power)* Leistung ['laɛstʊŋ] die <-, -en> ◊ *die Leistung eines Generators* **2.** π *(on a screen, from a printer)* Ausgabe ['aʊsɡaːbə] die <-, -n> ◊ *eine Ausgabe am Bildschirm*

outrage [noun] **1.** *(anger, indignation)* Empörung [ɛmˈpøːrʊŋ] die <-> no pl ◊ *Die Nachricht löste Empörung aus.* outrage at/about sth Empörung über etw. [acc] **2.** *(sth shocking)* Skandal [skanˈdaːl] der <-s, -e> ◊ *Das Urteil ist ein Skandal.;* *(more serious)* Verbrechen [fɛˈbrɛçn̩] das <-s, -> ◊ *Dieser Krieg ist ein Verbrechen (gegen die Menschlichkeit).*

outraged [adj] empört [ɛmˈpøːɐt] <empörter, am empörtesten> ◊ *Das Urteil löste empörte Reaktionen aus.* outraged by sth über etw. [acc] empört ◊ *Er war über ihr Verhalten mächtig empört.*

outrageous [adj] **1.** *(shocking)* empörend [ɛmˈpøːrənt] ◊ *Es ist empörend, was er für Lügen erzählt!* ♦ empörende Unterstellungen/Vorwürfe **2.** *(excessive)* unverschämt ['ʊnfɛʃɛːmt] <unverschämter, am unverschämtesten> ◊ *unverschämte Forderungen stellen* ♦ *Die Preise in diesem Restaurant sind unverschämt.* **3.** *(clothes)* schrill [ʃrɪl] ◊ *Ihre Aufmachung war schrill.* ♦ schrille Kleidung

outrageously [adv] unverschämt ['ʊnfɛʃɛːmt] <unverschämter, am unverschämtesten> ◊ *sich unverschämt verhalten* ♦ *unverschämt teure Schuhe*

outright[1] [adj] **1.** *(not hidden)* offen ['ɔfn̩] ◊ *offene Feindseligkeit* ♦ *Seine Kritik war offen, aber gut gemeint.* **2.** *(victory, defeat, majority)* eindeutig ['aɛndɔʏtɪç] ◊ *Das Spiel endete mit einer eindeutigen Niederlage für uns.;* *(lie)* glatt [glat] no comp/superl, only before ns *(fam)* ◊ *eine glatte Lüge*

outright[2] [adv] freiheraus [fraɛhɛˈraʊs] no comp/superl ◊ *Sie sagte ihm freiheraus, er solle gehen.* ♦ *freiheraus lachen*

ⓔ buy sth outright etw. sofort bezahlen be killed outright auf der Stelle tot sein

outset [noun] Anfang ['anfaŋ] der <-(e)s, -e> most sing at the outset zu Anfang from the outset von Anfang an

outside[1] [noun] Außenseite ['aʊsnzaɛtə] die <-, -n> ◊ *die Außenseite des Hauses* from the outside von außen [fɔn ˈaʊsn̩] ◊ *Von außen sah das Haus ziemlich heruntergekommen aus.* to the outside nach außen

ⓔ on the outside **1.** *(on the outer surface)* außen ◊ *Außen war mein Steak verbrannt und innen roh.* **2.** *(outwardly, externally)* äußerlich ◊ *Äußerlich lässt er sich nichts anmerken.* **3.** *(not involved)* people on the outside Außenstehende **4.** *(not in prison etc.)* draußen

outside[2] [adj] **1.** *(not inside, from sb else)* äußere ['ɔʏsərə] no comp, only before ns <ein äußerer ..., eine äußere ... in äußere ...> ◊ *äußere Einflüsse;* *(not involved)* Außen... ['aʊsn̩] ◊ *outside wall* Außenmauer ['aʊsn̩maʊɐ] die <-, -n> ◊ *(not part of an organization)* unabhängig ['ʊn|aphɛŋɪç] ◊ *ein unabhängiger Experte/Auftragnehmer*

outside[3] [adv] **1.** *(not inside a house or room)* draußen ['draʊsn̩] ◊ *Ich warte draußen auf dich.* ♦ *Er stand draußen vor der Haustür.;* *(expressing movement)* nach draußen [naːx ˈdraʊsn̩] ◊ *nach draußen gehen/sehen* **2.** *(from an external position)*

from outside von außen [fɔn ˈaʊsn̩] ◊ *etw. von außen betrachten*

outside⁴ [prep] outside (of) **1.** *(not inside, not during, not within the limits of)* außerhalb [ˈaʊsɐhalp] ◊ *Der Hof liegt außerhalb des Dorfes.* ♦ *außerhalb der Geschäftszeiten/Saison* **2.** *(not inside a building)* vor [foːɐ̯] [+dat] ◊ *Vor dem Haus stand ein Auto.*; *(expressing movement from inside a building)* vor [foːɐ̯] [+acc] ◊ *vor die Tür gehen* **3.** *(apart from)* außer [ˈaʊsɐ] [+dat] ◊ *Hast du noch andere Hobbys außer Literatur?*

outsider [noun] **1.** *(sb not belonging to a group or an organization)* Außenstehende [ˈaʊsnʃteːəndə] der/die <–, die Außenstehenden> *but:* *ein Außenstehender/ eine Außenstehende* ◊ *Wir brauchen Hilfe von einem Außenstehenden.* **2.** *(competitor not likely to win, sb not accepted by a group)* Außenseiter [ˈaʊsnzaetɐ] der <–s, –> ♀Außenseiterin [ˈaʊsnzaetərɪn] die <–, –nen> ◊ *Er gilt in der Schule als Außenseiter.*

outskirts [noun] outskirts (of a town/city) Stadtrand [ˈʃtatrant] der <–(e)s, Stadtränder> *most* sing on the outskirts of ... am Stadtrand ... [gen] ◊ *am Stadtrand Berlins*

outstanding [adj] **1.** *(excellent)* hervorragend [hɛˈfoːɐ̯gra:gn̩t] ◊ *hervorragende Ergebnisse erzielen* ♦ *Das letzte Geschäftsjahr war hervorragend.*; *(exceptional)* außergewöhnlich [ˈaʊsɡəvøːnlɪç] ◊ *außergewöhnlicher Mut* ♦ *Ihre Schönheit war außergewöhnlich.* **2.** *(not yet paid)* offen [ˈɔfn̩] no comp/superl ◊ *Ich muss noch eine offene Rechnung bezahlen.* ♦ *Die Zahlung ist noch offen.* **3.** *(not yet done)* unerledigt [ˈʊn|ele:dɪçt] no comp/superl ◊ *unerledigte Aufgaben* ♦ *Zu viele Probleme sind unerledigt.*

outstandingly [adv] *(very well)* hervorragend [hɛˈfoːɐ̯gra:gn̩t] ◊ *Unsere Mannschaft hat heute hervorragend gespielt.*; *(exceptionally)* außergewöhnlich [ˈaʊsɡəvøːnlɪç] no comp/superl ◊ *ein außergewöhnlich gutes Buch*

outward [adj] **1.** *(visible, obvious)* äußere [ˈɔʏsərə] no comp/superl, only before ns <ein äußerer ..., eine äußere ..., ein äußeres> ◊ *die äußere Erscheinung eines Menschen*; *(only on the surface)* äußerlich [ˈɔʏsəlɪç] ◊ *äußerliche Gelassenheit/Ruhe* **2.** *(journey)* Hin... [hɪn] outward journey Hinreise [ˈhɪnraezə] die <–, –n> outward flight Hinflug [ˈhɪnfluːk] der <–(e)s, Hinflüge>

outwardly [adv] äußerlich [ˈɔʏsəlɪç] no comp/superl ◊ *äußerlich gelassen*

oven [noun] Ofen [ˈoːfn̩] der <–s, Öfen> ◊ *den Braten/ Kuchen in den Ofen schieben*

over¹ [adv] **1.** *(more than)* über [ˈyːbɐ] ◊ *Diese Bluse hat über 100 Euro gekostet.* 65 years and over 65 Jahre und älter [ˌfʏnfʊntˌzɛçtsɪç ˌjaːrə ʊnt ˈɛltɐ] **2.** *(in a different place)* drüben [ˈdryːbm̩] ◊ *Die Kinder sind drüben bei den Nachbarn.* **3.** um... [ʊm]; *(with certain verbs: down, around)* knock over umwerfen [ˈʊmvɛˈfn̩] <wirft um, warf um, hat umgeworfen> run over umfahren [ˈʊmfaːrən] <fährt um, fuhr um, hat umgefahren> **4.** *(with certain verbs, expressing that sth is covered)* zu... [tsuː] freeze over zufrieren [ˈtsuːfriːrən] <friert zu, fror zu, ist zugefroren> ◊ *Der See ist zugefroren.* **5.** *(with certain verbs: to the side, towards sb/sth)* herüber... [hɛˈryːbɐ] come over herüberkommen [hɛˈryːbɐkɔmən] <kommt herüber, kam herüber, ist herübergekommen> ◊ *Komm hier herüber.* lean over sich herüberlehnen [hɛˈryːbɐleːnən] +haben **6.** *(with*

certain verbs, expressing a change) über... [ˈyːbɐ] go over to sth zu etw. übergehen [tsuː: ... ˌyːbegeːən] <geht über, ging über, ist übergegangen> **7.** *(again)* noch einmal [ˌnɔx ˈaɛnmaːl] ◊ *noch einmal anfangen* over and over immer wieder [ɪmɐ ˈviːdɐ]

over² [prep] **1.** *(above, across, during)* über [ˈyːbɐ] with acc when expressing motion towards a place, with dat when there is no or undirected motion ◊ *Das Bild hängt über dem Sofa.* ♦ *Sie hat das Bild über das Sofa gehängt.* ♦ *eine Brücke über den Fluss bauen* ◊ *Das Wasser schwappte über den Rand des Eimers.* ♦ *eine Fahrt über den Bodensee* ♦ *Wir waren übers Wochenende in Berlin.* ♦ *Über Nacht hat es geregnet.* ♦ *Kontrolle über die Situation haben* over the road auf der anderen Straßenseite [aʊf deːɐ̯ ˌandərən ˈʃtraːsnzaetə] over it/that darüber [daˈryːbɐ] ◊ *ein Tisch mit einer Lampe darüber* **2.** *(with certain verbs: past sb/sth)* ... over sb/sth über jdn/etw. hinweg... [yːbɐ ... hɪnˈvɛk] +verb jump over sb/sth über jdn/etw. hinwegspringen [yːbɐ ... hɪnˈvɛkʃprɪŋən] <springt hinweg, sprang hinweg, ist hinweggesprungen> **3.** *(while having a meal or a drink)* bei [baɛ] [+dat] ◊ *beim Mittagessen/ Kaffee*

ⓢ be over **1.** *(be past)* vorbei sein **2.** *(have dealt with sth)* be over sth über etw. [acc] hinweg sein over and above sth über etw. [acc] hinaus be over and above sth über etw. [acc] hinausgehen

'Over' often occurs in phrasal verbs like 'get over' or 'take over' which have their own entries in the dictionary.

over... [prefix] **1.** *(excessively, expresses that sth is covered)* über... [ˈyːbɐ] with verbs unstressed and inseparable overexert yourself sich überanstrengen [ybɐˈʔanʃtrɛŋən] <überanstrengt sich, überanstrengte sich, hat sich überanstrengt> overgrow überwuchern [ybɐˈvuːxɐn] <überwuchert, überwucherte, hat überwuchert> ◊ *Der Garten wurde von Gestrüpp überwuchert.*; *(in nouns)* Über... [ˈyːbɐ] overproduction Überproduktion [ˈyːbɐprodʊkˌtsjoːn] die <–, –en> most sing overreaction Überreaktion [ˈyːbɐreakˌtsjoːn] die <–, –en> **2.** *(more than)* over-... über ... [ˈyːbɐ] the over-seventies etc. die über Siebzigjährigen etc.

overall¹ [noun] *(protective clothing)* Arbeitskittel [ˈaˈbaɛtskɪtl̩] der <–s, –>; *(including trousers)* overall(s) Overall [ˈoːvəral] der <–s, –s>; *(in the US: dungarees)* overalls Latzhose [ˈlatshoːzə] die <–, –n> can be used in the pl or sing ◊ *Er trug Latzhosen/ eine Latzhose.*

overall² [adj] allgemein [alɡəˈmaɛn] no comp/superl, only before ns ◊ *die allgemeine Verantwortung tragen*; Gesamt... [ɡəˈzamt] overall winner Gesamtsieger [ɡəˈzamtziːɡɐ] der <–s, –> ♀Gesamtsiegerin [ɡəˈzamtziːɡərɪn] die <–, –nen>

overall³ [adv] insgesamt [ɪnsɡəˈzamt] ◊ *Insgesamt hat sich die Lage verbessert.* finish second overall Zweiter der Gesamtwertung werden [ˌtsvaetɐ deːɐ̯ ɡəˈzamtveːɐ̯tʊŋ veːɐ̯dn̩] +sein

overcast [adj] bedeckt [bəˈdɛkt] <bedeckter, am bedecktesten> seldom comp/superl ◊ *Der Himmel ist heute bedeckt.* ♦ *ein bedeckter Tag*

overcome [verb] **1.** *(deal with, master)* überwinden [ybɐˈvɪndn̩] <überwindet, überwand, hat überwunden> ◊ *eine Gefahr/Krise überwinden* **2.** *(have a very strong effect on)* übermannen [ybɐˈmanən]

A
B
C
D
E
F
G
H
I
J
K
L
M
N
O
P
Q
R
S
T
U
V
W
X
Y
Z

<übermannt, übermannte, hat übermannt> ◊ *Die Müdigkeit übermannte sie.*; *(emotionally)* überwältigen [ybɐˈvɛltɪɡn̩] <überwältigt, überwältigte, hat überwältigt> *mostly passive* be overcome with sth *von etw.* überwältigt werden ◊ *von Liebe überwältigt werden* **3.** *(make unconscious)* betäuben [bəˈtɔɪbm̩] <betäubt, betäubte, hat betäubt>

overcrowded [adj] überfüllt [ybɐˈfʏlt] <überfüllter, am überfülltesten> ◊ *Der Zug war völlig überfüllt.* ♦ *überfüllte Schulen*

overdo [verb] overdo sth, overdo it with sth es mit etw. übertreiben [ɛs mɪt ... ybɐˈtraɪbm̩] <übertreibt, übertrieb, hat übertrieben> ◊ *Übertreib es nicht mit dem Sport!*; *(work too hard)* overdo it sich übernehmen [ybɐˈneːmən] <übernimmt sich, übernahm sich, hat sich übernommen>; *(take or use too much of)* overdo ... zu viel ... nehmen [tsuː fiːl ... neːmən] <nimmt, nahm, hat genommen> ◊ *Nimm nicht zu viel Pfeffer, sonst wird es zu scharf.*

overdose [noun] Überdosis [ˈyːbedoːzɪs] die <–, Überdosen> ◊ *eine Überdosis Schlaftabletten*

overdraft [noun] **1.** *(agreed loan)* Überziehungskredit [ybɐˈtsiːʊŋskreˌdiːt] der <–(e)s, –e> **2.** *(missing amount of money)* Minus [ˈmiːnʊs] das <–> *no pl* ◊ *ein Minus von 1000 Euro haben*

overdue [adj] überfällig [ˈyːbefɛlɪç] *no comp/superl* ◊ *ein überfälliger Zug* ♦ *Ein neuer Anstrich ist schon lange überfällig.* be overdue for sth etw. schon längst brauchen [ʃoːn lɛŋst ˈbraʊxn̩] +haben

overestimate [verb] überschätzen [ybɐˈʃɛtsn̩] <überschätzt, überschätzte, hat überschätzt> ◊ *ein Problem überschätzen*

overflow [verb] **1.** *(with liquids)* überlaufen [ˈyːbelaʊfn̩] <läuft über, lief über, ist übergelaufen> ◊ *Die Badewanne ist übergelaufen.*; *(with emotion)* overflow with sth vor etw. überquellen [foːɐ ... ˈyːbekvɛlən] <quillt über, quoll über, ist übergequollen> ◊ *Ihr Herz quoll über vor Freude.* sth overflows with people/sth etw. quillt über von Menschen/etw. ◊ *Die Schublade quoll über von Socken.* **2.** *(river, lake)* overflow *(its banks)* über die Ufer treten [yːbe diː ˈuːfe treːtn̩] <tritt, trat, ist getreten>; *(flood sth)* overflow into sth etw. überschwemmen [ybɐˈʃvɛmən] <überschwemmt, überschwemmte, hat überschwemmt> ◊ *Der Fluss hat die Felder überschwemmt.*

overlap [verb] **1.** *(objects)* überlappen [ybɐˈlapm̩] <überlappt, überlappte, hat überlappt> ◊ *Die obere Folie überlappt die untere.* They overlap. Sie überlappen sich. **2.** *(responsibilities, engagements)* overlap sth sich mit etw. überschneiden [zɪç mɪt ... ybɐˈʃnaɪdn̩] <überschneidet sich, überschnitt sich, hat sich überschnitten> ◊ *Mein Aufgabenbereich überschneidet sich mit Ihrem.* They overlap. Sie überschneiden sich.; *(ideas)* overlap sth sich teilweise mit etw. decken [zɪç taɪlvaɪzə mɪt ... ˈdɛkn̩] +haben They overlap. Sie decken sich teilweise.

overload [verb] *(with people, objects)* überladen [ybɐˈlaːdn̩] <überlädt, überlud, hat überladen> *often in adjectival passive constructions* ◊ *Die Fähre ist überladen.* ♦ *einen Lkw überladen*; *(with work, information)* überlasten [ybɐˈlastn̩] <überlastet, überlastete, hat überlastet> *often in adjectival passive constructions* ◊ *Er war vollkommen überlastet.* ♦ *Stromleitungen überlasten*

overlook [verb] **1.** *(not see, ignore)* übersehen [ybɐˈzeːən] <übersieht, übersah, hat übersehen> ◊ *ein paar Tippfehler übersehen* **2.** *(leave unpunished)* overlook sth über etw. [acc] hinwegsehen [yːbe ... hɪnˈvɛkzeːən] <sieht hinweg, sah hinweg, hat hinweggesehen> ◊ *Über Ihr Fehlverhalten will ich noch einmal hinwegsehen.* **3.** *(offer a view of)* sth overlooks sth von etw. aus hat man einen Blick auf etw. [acc] [fɔn ... aʊs hat man aɛnən ˌblɪk aʊf] +haben ◊ *Vom Balkon aus hatte man einen Blick auf den Park.*

overnight [adv] über Nacht [yːbe ˈnaxt] ◊ *über Nacht bleiben*

overpower [verb] **1.** *(defeat, overwhelm)* überwältigen [ybɐˈvɛltɪɡn̩] <überwältigt, überwältigte, hat überwältigt> ◊ *Die Polizei konnte den Geiselnehmer überwältigen.* ♦ *von Schmerz überwältigt werden* **2.** *(cover up, conceal)* überdecken [ybɐˈdɛkn̩] <überdeckt, überdeckte, hat überdeckt> ◊ *Der Chili überdeckt die anderen Aromen sicht.*

overrate [verb] überbewerten [ˈyːbebəveːɐtn̩] <überbewertet, überbewertete, hat überbewertet> ◊ *Diese Ergebnisse dürfen nicht überbewertet werden.*

overrated → **overrate** [adj] überschätzt [ybɐˈʃɛtst] *seldom comp/no superl* ◊ *ein überschätzter Autor* ♦ *Sie wird als Schauspielerin völlig überschätzt.*

overrun [verb] **1.** *(use more time or money than is available)* überziehen [ybɐˈtsiːən] <überzieht, überzog, hat überzogen> ◊ *Der Moderator überzog seine Sendezeit.* ♦ *sein Budget überziehen* overrun by ... um ... überziehen ◊ *Er hat um 15 Minuten überzogen.*; *(take longer)* zu lange dauern [tsuː ˈlaŋə daʊen] +haben sth overruns by an hour etw. dauert eine Stunde zu lange **2.** *(invade and occupy)* einnehmen [ˈaɛnneːmən] <nimmt ein, nahm ein, hat eingenommen> ◊ *Regierungstruppen haben das Gebiet eingenommen.* **3.** *(crowded)* be overrun by sb von jdm überlaufen sein [fɔn ... ybɐˌlaʊfn̩ zaɛn] +sein ◊ *Die ganze Stadt war von Touristen überlaufen.*

overseas¹ [adj] ausländisch [ˈaɔslɛndɪʃ] *no comp/superl* ◊ *ausländische Touristen; Auslands...* [ˈaɔslants] overseas trip Auslandsreise [ˈaɔslantsraɛzə] die <–, –n>

overseas² [adv] *(in a foreign country)* im Ausland [ɪm ˈaɔslant] ◊ *im Ausland studieren*; *(to a foreign country)* ins Ausland [ɪns ˈaɔslant] ◊ *ins Ausland reisen*

overshadow [verb] **1.** *(cast a shadow over)* überschatten [ybɐˈʃatn̩] <überschattet, überschattete, hat überschattet> ◊ *Ein Baum überschattete das Ufer.* **2.** *(be less successful)* be overshadowed by sb in jds Schatten stehen [ɪn ... ˈʃatn̩ ʃteːən] <steht, stand, hat gestanden> ◊ *Er stand im Schatten seines berühmten Bruders.*

oversleep [verb] verschlafen [fɛˈʃlaːfn̩] <verschläft, verschlief, hat verschlafen> ◊ *zu spät zum Unterricht kommen, man hat verschlafen hat*

overtake [verb] **1.** *(go past, be better than)* überholen [ybɐˈhoːlən] <überholt, überholte, hat überholt> ◊ *einen Lkw überholen* ♦ *Als alles frei war, überholte sie.* **2.** *(feeling)* sth overtakes sb etw. überkommt jdn [ybɐˈkɔmt] <überkam, ist überkommen> *(lofty)* ◊ *Wut überkam ihn.*

overthrow [verb] stürzen [ˈʃtʏɐtsn̩] +haben ◊ *Die Rebellen wollen den Präsidenten/die Regierung*

stürzen.

overtime [noun] *(extra work)* Überstunden ['y:beʃtʊndn̩] die <-> pl ◊ *Überstunden abbauen* work overtime Überstunden machen; *(money)* Überstundengeld ['y:beʃtʊndn̩gɛlt] das <-(e)s, -er>

overturn [verb] **1.** *(knock over, fall over, capsize)* umkippen ['ʊmkɪpm̩] *transitive use +haben/intransitive use +sein ◊ Ich habe die Flasche versehentlich mit dem Arm umgekippt.* ✦ *Das Boot ist umgekippt.* **2.** *(a ruling, law etc.)* aufheben ['aɔfhe:bm̩] <hebt auf, hob auf, hat aufgehoben> ◊ *Die nächste Instanz hat das Urteil aufgehoben.*

overview [noun] Überblick ['y:beblɪk] der <-(e)s, -e> ◊ *eine Liste mit allen Tarifen im Überblick* overview of sth Überblick über etw. [acc] ◊ *Das Buch gibt einen Überblick über die Geschichte des 20. Jahrhunderts.*

overwhelm [verb] **1.** *(have a strong effect on)* überwältigen [ybe'vɛltɪɡn̩] <überwältigt, überwältigte, hat überwältigt> ◊ *Von Müdigkeit überwältigt, schlief er ein.* **2.** *(be too much for)* erdrücken [ɛ'drʏkn̩] <erdrückt, erdrückte, hat erdrückt> ◊ *Mich erdrücken die Schulden.*

overwhelming [adj] *(very strong or large)* überwältigend [ybe'vɛltɪɡn̩t] ◊ *eine überwältigende Mehrheit; (desire, urge)* unbändig ['ʊnbɛndɪç] ◊ *Ich verspürte das unbändige Verlangen, eine Zigarette zu rauchen.*

overwhelmingly [adv] **1.** *(very, extremely)* ungeheuer ['ʊngəhɔɔə] *no comp/superl ◊ Ihre Bücher sind ungeheuer beliebt.* **2.** *(with a huge majority)* mit überwältigender Mehrheit [mɪt ybe,vɛltɪɡn̩de 'me:ɐhaet] ◊ *Sie stimmten mit überwältigender Mehrheit für den EU-Beitritt.*

overworked [adj] **1.** *(person)* überlastet [ybe'lastət] *seldom comp/superl ◊ Die Mitarbeiter waren völlig überlastet.* ✦ *Es gibt viele überlastete Lehrer.* **2.** *(used too often)* überstrapaziert ['y:beʃtrapatsi:ɐt] *no comp/superl ◊ ein überstrapazierter Begriff* ✦ *Das Thema ist mittlerweile überstrapaziert.*

overwrite [verb] überschreiben [ybe'ʃraebm̩] <überschreibt, überschrieb, hat überschrieben> ◊ *gespeicherte Daten versehentlich überschreiben*

owe [verb] **1.** *(money)* schulden ['ʃʊldn̩] <schuldet, schuldete, hat geschuldet> owe sb sth jdm etw. schulden ◊ *Du schuldest mir noch Geld.* **2.** *(be obliged to do sth)* owe sb sth jdm etw. schuldig sein ['ʃʊldɪç zaen] +sein ◊ *Du bist mir noch eine Antwort auf meine Frage schuldig.* owe it to sb to do sth es jdm schuldig sein, etw. zu tun **3.** *(have achieved sth thanks to sb)* owe sb sth jdm etw. verdanken [fɐ'daŋkn̩] <verdankt, verdankte, hat verdankt> ◊ *Wir*

verdanken unseren Erfolg nicht zuletzt unseren freien Mitarbeitern.

owing to [prep] aufgrund [aɔf'ɡrʊnt] [+gen] ◊ *Aufgrund der hohen Benzinpreise nehmen immer mehr Leute öffentliche Verkehrsmittel.*

owl [noun] Eule ['ɔɡlə] die <-, -n>

own¹ [adj] eigene ['aeɡənə] *no comp/superl, only before ns <ein eigener …, eine eigene …, ein eigenes …>* ◊ *Das ist ihre eigene Schuld!* have your (very) own room ein eigenes Zimmer haben at your own expense/risk auf eigene Kosten/Gefahr do your own washing seine Wäsche selbst waschen [zaenə ,vɛʃə 'zɛlpst vaʃn̩] <wäscht, wusch, hat gewaschen>

own² [verb] besitzen [bə'zɪtsn̩] <besitzt, besaß, hat besessen> ◊ *alles, was sie besaß* ✦ *Ich besitze nichts Wertvolles.* Who owns this house? Wem gehört dieses Haus? They behaved as if they owned the place. Sie benahmen sich, als ob das Haus/Hotel etc. ihnen gehörte.

own³ [pron] eigener ['aeɡənə] eigene ['aeɡənə] eigenes ['aeɡənəs] ◊ *Ihre Wohnung gefällt mir besser als meine eigene.* ✦ *Warum willst du immer mein Lineal ausleihen? Nimm doch dein eigenes!* a … of your own ein eigener …/eine eigene … ◊ *Die Schule hat eine eigene Turnhalle.* ✦ *Ich hätte so gern ein eigenes Zimmer.* have children of your own selbst Kinder haben ['zɛlpst ,kɪndɐ ha:bm̩] +haben ◊ *Ich habe selbst Kinder; ich weiß genau, wie anstrengend das ist.* sth is sb's own etw. gehört jdm [ɡə'høːɐt] <gehört, gehörte, hat gehört> ◊ *„Hast du dir das Ballkleid ausgeliehen?" — „Nein, es gehört mir."*

ⓔ **(all) on your own** (ganz) allein ◊ *Das habe ich ganz allein gemacht!*

owner [noun] *(of an object, animal)* Besitzer [bə'zɪtsɐ] der <-s, -> ♀Besitzerin [bə'zɪtsərɪn] die <-, -nen> ◊ *Sie ist nicht die Besitzerin dieses Hauses.; (of a company, shop, account)* Inhaber ['ɪnha:bɐ] der <-s, -> ♀Inhaberin ['ɪnha:bərɪn] die <-, -nen> ◊ *Er ist Inhaber eines Softwareunternehmens.*

ownership [noun] Besitz [bə'zɪts] der <-es> *no pl ◊ Zu meinem Besitz gehören mehrere Häuser und Grundstücke.* ✦ *Das Haus ist in den Besitz der Bank übergegangen.* This country has a high level of home ownership. In diesem Land gibt es viele Eigenheimbesitzer.

oxygen [noun] Sauerstoff ['zaɔeʃtɔf] der <-(e)s> *seldom with the article, no pl*

ozone [noun] Ozon [o'tso:n] das <-s> *no pl*

A B C D E F G H I J K L M N **O** P Q R S T U V W X Y Z

P

p, P [noun] p, P [pe:] das <– or –(s), –(s)> ◊ *ein kleines p/großes P ♦ P wie Paula*

pace [noun] **1.** *(speed)* Tempo ['tɛmpo:] das <–s, –s> ◊ *das enorme Tempo, mit dem sich die Gentechnik entwickelt hat ♦ sein Tempo beschleunigen* set the pace *das Tempo vorgeben* The pace of life in the village is leisurely. *Das Leben im Dorf ist geruhsam.* The pace of life is increasing. *Das Leben wird immer hektischer.; (film, novel)* lack pace Längen haben ['lɛŋən haːbm̩] +haben ◊ *Sein neuer Film hat einige Längen.* **2.** *(step)* Schritt [ʃrɪt] der <–(e)s, –e> ◊ *Mit wenigen Schritten war sie bei dem Verletzten.* take a pace *einen Schritt machen* **3.** *(of a horse)* Gangart ['ɡaŋaːɐt] die <–, –en>
    ℗ **gather pace 1.** *(campaign)* in Schwung kommen **2.** *(vehicle)* in Fahrt kommen keep pace (with sb/ sth) (mit jdm/etw.) Schritt halten put sb/sth through their/its paces jdn/etw. testen stand the pace *mithalten können*

pacifier [noun] **1.** *(person)* Friedensstifter ['friːdn̩sʃtɪftɐ] der <–s, –> ♀Friedensstifterin ['friːdn̩sʃtɪftərɪn] die <–, –nen> **2.** *(in the US: dummy)* Schnuller ['ʃnʊlɐ] der <–s, –> ◊ *Sie steckte dem Baby einen Schnuller in den Mund.*

pack¹ [noun] **1.** *(of a particular product)* Packung ['pakʊŋ] die <–, –en> ◊ *eine Packung Nudeln ♦ zwei Packungen Papiertaschentücher; (in the US: packet of cigarettes)* Schachtel ['ʃaxtl̩] die <–, –n> ◊ *eine Schachtel Zigaretten* **2.** *(of documents)* Mappe ['mapə] die <–, –n> ◊ *Die Mappe enthält alle Informationen, die Sie benötigen.* **3.** GAME pack of cards Kartenspiel ['kaˈtn̩ʃpiːl] das <–(e)s, –e> **4.** *(backpack)* Rucksack ['rʊkzak] der <–(e)s, Rucksäcke> **5.** *(of wild animals)* Rudel ['ruːdl̩] das <–s, –> Wolves are pack hunters. *Wölfe jagen im Rudel.; (of hounds)* Meute ['mɔɪtə] die <–, –n> **6.** *(in a race)* Feld [fɛlt] das <–(e)s no pl ◊ *Welcher Fahrer führt jetzt das Feld an?* **7.** *(of people)* Horde ['hɔːdə] die <–, –n> *(pej)* ◊ *eine Horde von Touristen* **8.** *(for wounds)* Kompresse [kɔmˈprɛsə] die <–, –n> ◊ *eine sterile Kompresse*
    ℗ **a pack of lies** ein Haufen Lügen **lead the pack** der Konkurrenz voraus sein

pack² [verb] **1.** *(for a journey)* packen ['pakn̩] +haben ◊ *Hast du schon für den Urlaub gepackt? ♦ einen Koffer packen* pack sb sth jdm etw. einpacken ['aɛnpakn̩] +haben ◊ *Er packte den Kindern etwas zu essen ein.* **2.** *(for protection, sale)* verpacken [fɛˈpakn̩] <verpackt, verpackte, hat verpackt> ◊ *Die Bluse war in Seidenpapier verpackt.; (into separate containers)* abpacken ['appakn̩] +haben ◊ *Das Obst wird noch am selben Tag abgepackt.* **3.** *(fill a place)* pack a place sich irgendwo drängen ['drɛŋən] +haben ◊ *Die Zuschauer drängten sich im Stadion.* **4.** *(snow, soil)* festdrücken ['fɛstdrʏkn̩] +haben ◊ *Nach dem Einpflanzen drückte sie die Erde fest.*
    • **pack away** [phras v] pack sth away etw. wegpacken ['vɛkpakn̩] +haben ◊ *Kann ich die Bücher*

wieder wegpacken? sth packs away sich wegpacken lassen
    • **pack in** [phras v] **1.** *(spectators)* in Scharen anziehen [ɪn ˈʃaːrən ˈantsiːən] <zieht an, zog an, hat angezogen> ◊ *Sein neuer Film zieht die Zuschauer in Scharen an.* **2.** *(your job)* aufgeben ['aɔfɡeːbm̩] <gibt auf, gab auf, hat aufgegeben> **3.** *(many people)* unterbringen ['ʊntebrɪŋən] <bringt unter, brachte unter, hat untergebracht> ◊ *So viele Leute kann man hier nicht unterbringen!; (many things)* hineinstopfen [hɪˈnaɛnʃtɔpfn̩] +haben ◊ *Er nahm die Tasche und stopfte seine Sachen hinein.* **4.** *(many activities)* pack sth in sth etw. in etw. [acc] packen [ɪn ... pakn̩] +haben ◊ *Wir haben viele Programmpunkte in die kurze Zeit gepackt.*
    ℗ **pack it in** hör auf damit
    • **pack off** [phras v] pack sb off to somewhere jdn irgendwohin schicken ['ʃɪkn̩] +haben ◊ *Sie haben die Kinder ins Internat geschickt.*
    • **pack up** [phras v] **1.** *(your belongings)* packen ['pakn̩] +haben ◊ *die Schultasche packen ♦ Er packte und ging.* **2.** *(in the UK: stop working)* seinen Geist aufgeben [zaɛnən ˈɡaɛst aɔfɡeːbm̩] <gibt auf, gab auf, hat aufgegeben> *(fam, hum)* ◊ *Der Fernseher hat seinen Geist aufgegeben.*

package¹ [noun] Paket [paˈkeːt] das <–(e)s, –e> ◊ *ein Paket bei der Post aufgeben ♦ ein Paket von Sparmaßnahmen; (from your employer)* Leistungspaket ['laɛstʊŋspaˌkeːt] die <> ◊ *Führungskräfte erhalten ein umfangreiches Leistungspaket.* aid package Hilfspaket ['hɪlfspaˌkeːt] software package Softwarepaket ['sɔftveːɐpaˌkeːt]

package² [verb] **1.** *(for sale)* abpacken ['appakn̩] +haben ◊ *Jeweils zehn Tabletten werden zusammen abgepackt.* **2.** *(sell together with)* package sth with sth etw. mit etw. verkaufen [mɪt ... fekaɔfn̩] <verkauft, verkaufte, hat verkauft> ◊ *Das neue Modell wird mit vielen Extras verkauft.* **3.** *(a product, an idea)* präsentieren [prɛzɛnˈtiːrən] <präsentiert, präsentierte, hat präsentiert> ◊ *Wie präsentiere ich diese Idee am besten?*

packaging [noun] **1.** *(material)* Verpackung [feˈpakʊŋ] die <–, –en> ◊ *Porto und Verpackung kosten sechs Euro.* **2.** *(process of packing goods)* Abpacken ['appakn̩] das <–s> no pl ◊ *das Abpacken von Waren*

packed → **pack²** [adj] **1.** *(crowded)* überfüllt [ybeˈfʏlt] <überfüllter, am überfülltesten> seldom comp/superl ◊ *Der Zug war völlig überfüllt. ♦ überfüllte Schulen* **2.** *(full up)* randvoll ['rantfɔl] no comp/superl *(fam)* ◊ *Wir haben ein randvolles Programm vor uns.; (full of)* packed with voller ['fɔlɐ] invariable, only before ns ◊ *Tomaten sind voller Vitamine.* **3.** sb is packed (up) jd hat alles gepackt [hat aləs ɡəˈpakt] +haben ◊ *Na, bist du alles gepackt?*

packet [noun] **1.** *(of a particular product)* Packung ['pakʊŋ] die <–, –en> ◊ *eine Packung Spaghetti; (smaller)* Päckchen ['pɛkçən] das <–s, –> ◊ *ein Päckchen Taschentücher; (larger)* Paket [paˈkeːt] das

<-(e)s, -e> ◊ *ein Paket Windeln; (bag)* Tüte ['ty:tə]
die <-, -n> ◊ *eine Tüte Kartoffelchips; (box)*
Schachtel ['ʃaxtl̩] die <-, -n> ◊ *eine Schachtel Ziga-*
retten **2.** *(packaging)* Verpackung [fɛ'pakʊŋ] die
<-, -en> ◊ *Das Gewicht steht auf der Verpackung.*
3. *(in the US: set of documents)* Mappe ['mapə] die
<-, -n> ◊ *eine Mappe mit Informationen*

packing [noun] **1.** *(of suitcases, bags)* Packen ['pakŋ̍]
das <-s> no pl ◊ *Das Packen dauert bei mir nur*
zehn Minuten. do the packing packen ['pakŋ̍]
+haben ◊ *Hast du schon gepackt?* **2.** *(of goods)* Verpackung [fɛ'pakʊŋ] die <-> no pl packing industry
Verpackungsindustrie [fɛ'pakʊŋs|ɪndʊs,tri:] die
<-, -n>

pact [noun] Pakt [pakt] der <-(e)s, -e> ◊ *einen Pakt*
schließen

pad¹ [noun] **1.** *(for protection)* Schützer ['ʃʏtsɐ] der
<-s, -> knee pads Knieschützer ['kni:ʃʏtsɐ] pl **2.** *(for*
comfort, enlarging, padding) Polster ['pɔlstɐ] das
<-s, -> **3.** *(for cleaning, sponging sth up)* Schwamm
[ʃvam] der <-(e)s, Schwämme> pad of cotton wool
Wattebausch ['vatəbaʊʃ] der <-(e)s, Wattebäusche> ◊
die Wunde mit einem Wattebausch abtupfen **4.** *(of*
paper) Block [blɔk] der <-(e)s, Blöcke or Blocks> ◊
Die Sekretärin zückte ihren Block, um das Diktat
aufzunehmen. **5.** *(for helicopters)* Landeplatz
['landəplats] der <-es, Landeplätze>; *(for rockets)*
Abschussrampe ['apfʊsrampə] die <-, -n> **6.** *(where*
sb lives) Bude ['bu:də] die <-, -n> *(fam)* ◊ *zu jdm*
mit auf die Bude gehen

pad² [verb] **1.** *(walk)* tappen ['tapŋ̍] +sein ◊ *Sie tappte*
ins Bad. **2.** *(with a soft substance)* polstern ['pɔlstɐn]
+haben ◊ *Der Helm ist gut gepolstert.* ◆ *eine*
Sitzbank polstern; (for changing a shape) auspols-
tern ['aʊspɔlstɐn] ◊ *Ich polsterte mir den Bauch mit*
einem Kissen aus.

page [noun] **1.** *((one side of) a sheet of paper in a book*
etc., on a computer screen) Seite ['zaɛtə] die <-, -n>
◊ *Schlagen Sie bitte Seite 23 auf.* ◆ *eine Seite heraus-*
reißen ◆ *Schreib deinen Namen oben auf die Seite.*
the front/back page die erste/letzte Seite the facing
page die gegenüberliegende Seite the sports page
die Sportseite [di: 'ʃpɔrtzaɛtə] over the page auf der
Rückseite [aɔf de:ɐ 'rʏkzaɛtə] turn a/the page
umblättern ['ʊmblɛtɐn] <blättert um, blätterte um, hat
umgeblättert> **2.** *(boy)* Page ['pa:ʒə] der <-n, -n>

paid → **pay**² [adj] bezahlt [bə'tsa:lt] no comp/superl ◊ *eine*
bezahlter Urlaub ◆ *Ist die Arbeit gut bezahlt?* ◆ *eine*
schlecht bezahlte Mitarbeiterin

pain [noun] Schmerz [ʃmɛʳts] der <-es, -en> ◊ *ein ste-*
chender Schmerz in der Brust ◆ *die Schmerzen*
lindern ◆ *bei jds Tod tiefen Schmerz empfinden* in
pain Schmerzen haben do sth in pain etw. vor
Schmerzen tun ◊ *vor Schmerzen weinen* back pain
Rückenschmerzen ['rʏkŋ̍ʃmɛʳtsn̩] pl cause (sb) pain
(jdn) schmerzen ['ʃmɛʳtsn̩] +haben ◊ *Das verletzte*
Knie schmerzte ihn sehr.
● be a pain (in the neck) nerven ◊ *Hör auf, du*
nervst! take great pains sich [dat] große Mühe
geben for sb's pains als Dank für jds Mühe under
pain of sth unter Androhung ... [gen], unter
Androhung von etw.

painful [adj] **1.** *(memory, experience)* schmerzlich
['ʃmɛʳtslɪç] ◊ *eine schmerzliche Erinnerung* ◆ *Dieser*
Prozess kann schmerzlich sein. unbearably painful
unerträglich ['ʊn|ɛtrɛ:klɪç] **2.** *(feet, back, joints etc.)*

schmerzend ['ʃmɛʳtsn̩t] no comp/superl, only before
ns ◊ *Sie klagte über ihre schmerzenden Knie.* be
painful wehtun ['ve:tu:n] <tut weh, tat weh, hat
wehgetan> ◊ *Die Behandlung hat ziemlich wehgetan.*
3. *(very bad, embarrassing)* peinlich ['paɛnlɪç] ◊ *eine*
peinliche Vorführung ◆ *Es war richtig peinlich, wie*
er herumstotterte.

painfully [adv] **1.** *(emotionally)* schmerzlich ['ʃmɛʳtslɪç]
◊ *sich* [dat] *seiner Fehler schmerzlich bewusst sein*
2. *(physically)* schmerzhaft ['ʃmɛʳtshaft] no comp/
superl ◊ *Der Knöchel war schmerzhaft geschwollen.*
3. *(very)* schrecklich ['ʃrɛklɪç] ◊ *Er war schrecklich*
schüchtern.

paint¹ [noun] Farbe ['faʳbə] die <-, -n> ◊ *ein Eimer*
rote Farbe ◆ *Die Farbe blättert schon ab.* ◆ wet
Malblock und Farben; (shiny, for cars etc.) Lack [lak]
der <-(e)s, -e> coat of paint Anstrich ['anʃtrɪç] der
<-(e)s, -e> ◊ *Nach dem ersten Anstrich sollte man*
die Farbe gut trocknen lassen. box of paints
Malkasten ['ma:kastn̩] der <-s, Malkästen>

paint² [verb] **1.** *(create a picture)* malen ['ma:lən]
+haben ◊ *gut malen können* ◆ *Wer hat diese Bilder*
gemalt? ◆ *die Zukunft in rosigen Farben malen* paint
an accurate picture of sth ein genaues Bild von
etw. zeichnen [aɛn gə,naʊɐs 'bɪlt fɔn ... tsaɛçnən]
+haben **2.** *(a house, door, walls etc.)* streichen
['ʃtraɛçn̩] <streicht, strich, hat gestrichen> ◊ *Sie haben*
das Haus frisch streichen lassen. ◆ *Diese Wand will*
ich blau streichen. **3.** *(nails, a car etc.)* lackieren
[la'ki:rən] <lackiert, lackierte, hat lackiert> ◊ *sich/jdm*
die Fingernägel lackieren

painter [noun] *(artist, decorator)* Maler ['ma:lɐ] der
<-s, -> ♀Malerin ['ma:lərɪn] die <-, -nen> ◊ *Sie ist*
eine bekannte Malerin. ◆ *Der Maler streicht das Kin-*
derzimmer.

painting [noun] **1.** *(picture)* Gemälde [gə'mɛ:ldə] das
<-s, -> ◊ *eine Ausstellung mit Gemälden von Monet*
2. *(art)* Malen ['ma:lən] das <-s> no pl ◊ *Zu ihren*
Hobbys gehören Malen und Stricken. **3.** *(decorating)*
Anstreichen ['anʃtraɛçn̩] das <-s> no pl ◊ *Das*
Anstreichen solltest du einem Fachmann überlassen.

pair [noun] **1.** *(two people, things)* Paar [pa:ʳ] der
<-(e)s, -e> ◊ *ein junges Paar* a pair of shoes ein
Paar Schuhe a pair of lovers ein Liebespaar
[aɛn 'li:bəspa:ʳ] a pair of twins ein Zwillingspaar
[aɛn 'tsvɪlɪŋspa:ʳ] a pair of blue eyes zwei blaue
Augen [tsvaɛ blaʊə 'aɔgn̩] the pair die beiden
[di: 'baɛdn̩] ◊ *Die beiden sind gestern nach Frank-*
reich gefahren. **2.** *(the other one)* the pair for/to ...
der/die/das andere ... [de:ɐ/di:/das 'andərə] no
comp/superl, only before ns ◊ *Wo ist der andere*
Strumpf? **3.** *(pair of scissors* Schere ['ʃe:rə] die
<-, -n> sing two pairs of scissors zwei Scheren
of trousers Hose ['ho:zə] die <-, -n> sing **4.** *(male*
and female animal) Pärchen ['pɛ:ɐçən] das <-s, -> ◊
Ich habe zwei Meerschweinchen, ein Pärchen. a pair
of magpies ein Elsternpärchen [aɛn 'ɛlstɐnpɛ:ɐçən]
● an extra pair of hands ein zusätzlicher Helfer,
eine zusätzliche Helferin a safe pair of hands ein
zuverlässiger Mensch in pairs paarweise

When 'pair of' is used to indicate a single piece of
clothing or an object consisting of two parts it is not
translated: 'a pair of jeans/tongs' —*eine Jeans/*
Zange.

A
B
C
D
E
F
G
H
I
J
K
L
M
N
O
P
Q
R
S
T
U
V
W
X
Y
Z

palace (noun) **1.** *(building)* Palast [pa'last] der
<–(e)s, Paläste> ◊ *der prunkvolle Palast der Königin*
2. *(people)* the Palace das Königshaus
[das 'kø:nɪçshaos] <–es, Königshäuser>

palate (noun) Gaumen ['gaomən] der <–s, –> ◊ *Das
Essen war ein Fest für Auge und Gaumen.*

pale (adj) **1.** *(skin)* blass [blas] <blasser, am blassesten>
◊ *ein blasses Gesicht* ♦ *Du bist so blass, bist du
krank?* turn pale blass werden **2.** *(colo(u)r, beer)* hell
[hɛl] ◊ *ein helles Bier* ♦ *Dieses Rosa ist ziemlich hell.*
pale blue hellblau ['hɛlblao] *no comp/superl*

palm (noun) **1.** *(of a hand)* Handfläche ['hantflɛçə] die
<–, –n> **2.** *(tree)* Palme ['palmə] die <–, –n>

pan (noun) **1.** *(for cooking)* Topf [tɔpf] der
<–(e)s, Töpfe> ◊ *Auf dem Herd stand ein Topf mit
Suppe.; (for frying)* Pfanne ['pfanə] die <–, –n> ◊ *das
Fett in einer Pfanne erhitzen; (in the US: for baking)*
Backform ['bakfɔ'm] die <–, –en> pots and pans
Kochtöpfe ['kɔxtœpfə] die <–> pl **2.** *(in the UK: of a
toilet)* Toilettenschüssel [tɔa'lɛtn̩fʏsl] die <–, –n>
3. *(of scales)* Waagschale ['va:kfa:lə] die <–, –n>
🅟 go down the pan den Bach runtergehen *(fam)*

pancake (noun) Pfannkuchen ['pfanku:xn̩] der <–s, –>

panel (noun) **1.** *(of experts)* Gremium ['gre:mjom] das
<–s, Gremien> panel of judges Jury ['ʒy:ri:] die
<–, –s> **2.** *(on TV, radio)* Diskussionsrunde
[dɪskʊ'sjo:nsrʊndə] die <–, –n>; *(in a quiz show)*
Rateteam ['ra:təti:m] das <–s, –s> **3.** *(of wood)*
Paneel [pa'ne:l] das <–s, –e>; *(of other materials)*
Platte ['platə] die <–, –n> fence panel Zaunbrett
['t͡saonbrɛt] das <–(e)s, –er> glass panel Glas-
scheibe ['gla:sfaebə] die <–, –n> **4.** *(of the body of
a car)* Karosserieteil [karɔsə'ri:tael] das <–(e)s, –e>
5. *(control)* panel Schalttafel ['faltta:fl̩] die <–, –n>
instrument panel Armaturenbrett [a'rma:tu:rənbrɛt]
das <–(e)s, –er>

panelling (noun) Täfelung ['tɛ:fəloŋ] die <–, –en>

panic (noun) Panik ['pa:nɪk] die <–, –en> *most sing* ◊
Sie wurde von Panik erfasst. ♦ *Auf dem Schiff brach
eine Panik aus.* in panic voller Panik get into a
panic in Panik geraten

panic-stricken (adj) von Panik ergriffen
[fɔn 'pa:nɪk ɛɡrɪfn̩] ◊ *Sie waren von Panik ergriffen.*
♦ *Die von Panik ergriffenen Dorfbewohner flüchteten.*

pants (noun) **1.** *(in the UK: underpants)* Unterhose
['ʊnteho:zə] die <–, –n> *can be used in the pl or
sing* ◊ *Zieh jeden Tag eine frische Unterhose an!* ♦
Beim Skifahren trage ich lange Unterhosen. a pair of
pants eine Unterhose **2.** *(in the US: trousers)* Hose
['ho:zə] die <–, –n> *can be used in the pl or sing* ◊
Er trug eine graue Hose. ♦ *Sie hatte lange Hosen an.*
a pair of pants eine Hose
🅟 bore the pants off sb jdn zu Tode langweilen
catch sb with their pants down jdn auf frischer
Tat ertappen

paper (noun) **1.** *(material)* Papier [pa'pi:ɐ] das
<–s, –e> ◊ *Weihnachtssterne aus Papier* ♦ *Das
Geschenk war in buntes Papier eingepackt.* a piece/
sheet of paper ein Stück/Blatt Papier
2. *(documents)* papers Papiere [pa'pi:rə] die <–> pl
◊ *Darf ich mal Ihre Papiere sehen?* ♦ *einen Stapel
Papiere durchsehen* **3.** *(newspaper)* Zeitung ['t͡saetoŋ]
die <–, –en> ◊ *Es stand in der Zeitung.* **4.** *(examination, at university)* Klausur [klao'zu:ɐ] die <–, –en> ◊
Morgen schreibt sie eine Klausur.; (at school) Arbeit

['a'baet] die <–, –en> ◊ *Wir haben heute in Mathe
eine Arbeit geschrieben.* **5.** *(academic)* Referat
[refe'ra:t] das <–(e)s, –e> ◊ *ein Referat über Kafka*
present a paper ein Referat halten; *(mainly in the
US: essay for school)* Aufsatz ['aofsats] der
<–es, Aufsätze> ◊ *einen Aufsatz zum Thema
„Umweltschutz" schreiben* **6.** *(wallpaper)* Tapete
[ta'pe:tə] die <–, –n>
🅟 on paper **1.** *(in writing)* schriftlich **2.** *(in theory)*
theoretisch put sth on paper etw. aufschreiben

paperback (noun) Taschenbuch ['taʃn̩bu:x] das
<–(e)s, Taschenbücher>

paper clip (noun) Büroklammer [by'ro:klame] die
<–, –n>

paperwork (noun) **1.** *(work)* Papierkram [pa'pi:ɡkra:m]
der <–s> *no pl (fam, esp pej)* ◊ *Ich muss noch jede
Menge Papierkram erledigen.* **2.** *(documents)* Papiere
[pa'pi:rə] die <–> pl ◊ *Darf ich bitte die Papiere für
diese Lieferung sehen?*

paprika (noun) Paprika ['paprika:] der <–s> *no pl*

par (noun) **1.** *(expected standard)* Niveau [ni'vo:] das
<–s, –s> ◊ *Ihre Leistungen sind unter Niveau.* not
up to par nicht gut genug [nɪçt 'gu:t gənu:k] ◊ *Er ist
einfach nicht gut genug.* **2.** *(of shares)* par *(value)*
Nennwert ['nɛnve:ɐt] der <–(e)s, –e>
🅟 par for the course ist erwarten on a par with
vergleichbar mit

parachute (noun) Fallschirm ['falʃɪ'm] der
<–(e)s, –e> ◊ *Sein Fallschirm öffnete sich zu spät.*

parade (noun) **1.** *(procession)* Umzug ['ʊmtsu:k] der
<–(e)s, Umzüge> ◊ *Zu Karneval gibt es in vielen
Städten am Rhein große Umzüge.; (military)* Parade
[pa'ra:də] die <–, –n> military parade Militärparade
[mili'tɛ:ɡpa,ra:də] **2.** *(line, series)* Reihe ['raeə] die
<–, –n> ◊ *Eine Reihe von Freiwilligen füllte
Sandsäcke auf.* a *(shopping)* parade eine Reihe von
Läden **3.** *(proud showing)* Zurschaustellung
[t͡su:ɐ'ʃaoʃtɛloŋ] die <–, –en> ◊ *eine Zurschaustellung der militärischen Macht des Landes*
🅟 be on parade **1.** *(soldiers)* eine Parade abhalten
2. *(products)* ausgestellt werden

paradise (noun) Paradies [para'di:s] das <–es, –e> an
art lover's paradise ein Paradies für Kunstliebhaber

paragraph (noun) *(section of a text etc.)* Absatz
['apzats] der <–es, Absätze> ◊ *Ich habe erst zwei
Absätze gelesen.* ♦ *Du solltest da einen Absatz
machen.; (numbered, of a law etc.)* Paragraph
[para'gra:f] der <–en, –en>

parallel[1] (noun) **1.** *(similarity, similar thing, line in the
same direction)* Parallele [para'le:lə] die <–, –n> ◊ *Es
gibt interessante Parallelen zwischen den Fällen.* ♦
Parallelen zeichnen without parallel unvergleichlich
['ʊnfeglaeçlɪç] *no comp/superl* ◊ *ein unvergleichli-
cher Fußballspieler* ♦ *Ihre Leistung ist wirklich unvergleichlich.* **2.** *(comparison)* Vergleich [fe'glaeç] der
<–(e)s, –e> ◊ *einen Vergleich zwischen den Römern
und den Germanen ziehen* **3.** GEOG Breitengrad
['braetngra:t] der <–(e)s, –e> ◊ *der 33. Breitengrad*
🅟 in parallel (with) parallel (zu)

parallel[2] (adj) **1.** parallel parallel [para'le:l] *no comp/
superl* ◊ *zwei parallele Linien* ♦ *Die Linien verlaufen
parallel.* parallel to parallel zu ◊ *Die Breitengrade
verlaufen parallel zum Äquator.* **2.** *(at the same time)*
gleichzeitig stattfindend ['glaeçt͡saetɪç ʃtatfɪndn̩t] *only
before ns* ◊ *zwei gleichzeitig stattfindende Veranstaltungen; (in the same way)* vergleichbar [fe'glaeçba:']

no comp/superl ◊ *Wir brauchen mehrere vergleichbare Untersuchungen.*
paralyse [verb] lähmen ['lɛːmən] +haben ◊ *Der Strom-
ausfall lähmte die ganze Stadt.* paralysed with fear/
fright vor Schreck wie gelähmt
paramedic [noun] Sanitäter [zani'tɛːtɐ] der <-s, ->
♀Sanitäterin [zani'tɛːtərɪn] die <-, -nen> ◊ *eine Ausbildung als Sanitäter* ♦ *eine Sanitäterin des Roten
Kreuzes*
parameter [noun] Parameter [pa'raːmetɐ] der <-s, ->
set parameters (for sth) den Rahmen (für etw.)
festsetzen [deːn 'raːmən ˌfɛstzetsn̩] +haben
paraphrase [verb] umschreiben [ʊm'ʃraebm̩]
<umschreibt, umschrieb, hat umschrieben> ◊ *Er
versuchte, den Begriff zu umschreiben.*
parcel [noun] *(smaller)* Päckchen ['pɛkçən] das
<-s, -> ◊ *ein Päckchen an jdn schicken; (larger)*
Paket [pa'keːt] das <-(e)s, -e> ◊ *ein Paket bei der
Post aufgeben*
pardon¹ [noun] Begnadigung [bə'gnaːdɪgʊŋ] die
<-, -en>
🔊 I beg your pardon Verzeihung
pardon² [interj] **1.** *(request to repeat sth)* wie bitte
['viː bɪtə] ◊ *Wie bitte? Was hast du gesagt?*
2. *(apology)* Verzeihung [fɐ'tsaeʊŋ] ◊ *Verzeihung, ich
habe Schluckauf.*
parent [noun] Elternteil ['ɛltəntael] der <-(e)s, -e> ◊
*Familien, bei denen ein Elternteil aus England
kommt* ♦ *Beide Elternteile sprechen türkisch.*
parents Eltern ['ɛltɐn] die <-> only pl

> If possible, the singular ist avoided in German by
> using mother/father ('your responsibility as a
> parent' — *Ihre Verantwortung als Mutter/Vater*),
> the plural ('So what is a parent to do?' — *Was
> sollen Eltern also tun?*), or no noun at all ('Are you
> a single parent?' — *Sind Sie allein erziehend?*).

parental [adj] elterlich ['ɛltɐlɪç] no comp/superl, only
before ns ◊ *elterliche Pflichten*
parenthesis [noun] **1.** *(added information)* Einschub
['aenʃuːp] der <-(e)s, Einschübe> **2.** *(mainly in the
US: bracket)* Klammer ['klamɐ] die <-, -n> ◊ *etw. in
Klammern setzen* open/close parentheses Klammer
auf/zu
parents-in-law [noun] Schwiegereltern ['ʃviːgɐˌɛltɐn]
die <-> only pl
parish [noun] Gemeinde [gə'maendə] die <-, -n> ◊
*Die ganze Gemeinde kam zum Weihnachtsgottes-
dienst.* ♦ *Zur Gemeinde St. Johannes gehören
mehrere Dörfer.*
park¹ [noun] **1.** *(area with grass and trees)* Park [park]
der <-s, -s> ◊ *im Park spazieren gehen* national
park Nationalpark [natsio'naːlpark] country park
Naturpark [na'tuːɐpark] **2.** *(in the UK: location for
football)* the park der Fußballplatz
[deːɐ 'fuːsbalplats] <-es, Fußballplätze>; *(in the US:
location for baseball)* Baseballplatz ['beːsbɔːlplats]
der <-es, Baseballplätze>
park² [verb] **1.** *(a vehicle)* parken ['parkn̩] +haben ◊ *Wo
hast du (dein Auto) geparkt?* **2.** *(for storage)*
abstellen ['apʃtɛlən] +haben ◊ *etw. im Keller
abstellen*
parking [noun] **1.** *(putting your vehicle into a place)*
Einparken ['aenparkn̩] das <-s> no pl ◊ *Das
Einparken müssen wir noch üben.; (leaving your
vehicle somewhere)* Parken ['parkn̩] das <-s> no pl ◊

Parken verboten **2.** parking (space) Parkplatz
['parkplats] der <-es, Parkplätze> ◊ *In der Innenstadt findet man nie einen Parkplatz.*
parking lot [noun] Parkplatz ['parkplats] der
<-es, Parkplätze> ◊ *ein bewachter Parkplatz*
parking meter [noun] Parkuhr ['parkluːɐ] die
<-, -en> ◊ *Münzen in die Parkuhr werfen*
parliament [noun] **1.** *(institution)* Parlament
[parla'mɛnt] das <-(e)s, -e> ◊ *das finnische
Parlament* Parliament das Parlament enter Parliament ins Parlament gewählt werden **2.** *(period of
time)* Legislaturperiode [legɪslaˈtuːɐperioːdə] die
<-, -n> ◊ *Das Gesetz soll noch in dieser Legislatur-
periode verabschiedet werden.*
parliamentary [adj] Parlaments... [parla'mɛnts] parliamentary elections Parlamentswahlen
[parla'mɛntsvaːlən] die <-> pl
parrot [noun] Papagei [papa'gae] der <-en *or* -s, -en>
parsley [noun] Petersilie [peteˈziːliə] die <-, -n>
part¹ [noun] **1.** *(of a whole)* Teil [tael] der <-(e)s, -e>
◊ *Das Schlafzimmer liegt im hinteren Teil des
Hauses.* ♦ *der erste Teil der Unterrichtsstunde* ♦ *Ein
beträchtlicher Teil der Bevölkerung glaubt daran.* ♦
ein Teil Saft zu zwei Teilen Wasser part of ein Teil
... [gen] ◊ *Wir sind einen Teil des Weges gelaufen.*
part of the body Körperteil ['kœɐpɐtael] the early
part of the 20th century das frühe 20. Jahrhundert
[das ˌfryːə ˌtsvantsɪçstə jaːˈhʊndɐt] be part of sth zu
etw. dazugehören [tsuː: ... daˈtsuːgəhøːrən] <gehört
dazu, gehörte dazu, hat dazugehört> ◊ *Liebeskummer
gehört zum Erwachsenwerden dazu.* as part of sth
im Rahmen ... [gen 'im 'raːmən] ◊ *ein Konzert im
Rahmen der Sommerfestspiele* be only part of the
story nur ein Aspekt sein [nuːɐ 'aen asˌpɛkt zaen]
+sein ◊ *Die schlechte Versorgungslage ist nur ein
Aspekt.* in parts teilweise ['taelvaezə] ◊ *Der Film ist
teilweise ganz unterhaltsam.* **2.** *(of a machine,
vehicle)* Teil [tael] das <-(e)s, -e> ◊ *Dieses Teil
muss ausgetauscht werden.* spare part Ersatzteil
[ɐ'zatstael] **3.** *(of a country, town)* Gegend ['geːgn̩t]
die <-, -en> ◊ *Sie wohnen in einer ruhigen Gegend.*
♦ *In manchen Gegenden Südenglands hat es heute
geschneit.* in these parts in dieser Gegend **4.** *(of a
group, team)* be part of sth zu etw. gehören
[tsuː: ... gəhøːrən] <gehört, gehörte, hat gehört> ◊
Peter gehört bei uns schon zur Familie. **5.** THEAT, FILM
(in a play, film, situation) Rolle ['rɔlə] die <-, -n> ◊
Ich musste die Rolle in einer Woche lernen. ♦ *Welche
Rolle hat er in dem Skandal gespielt?* ♦ *Glück spielt
dabei keine Rolle.* the part of ... die Rolle des/der
... ◊ *Sie spielt die Rolle der Ophelia.* **6.** *(of a series)*
Folge ['fɔlgə] die <-, -n> ◊ *eine Fernsehserie mit 36
Folgen* **7.** *(of an instrument, singer)* Part [part] der
<-s, -s> *(voice)* part Stimme ['ʃtɪmə] die <-, -n> ◊
die erste/zweite Stimme singen **8.** *(in the US: in your
hair)* Scheitel ['ʃaetl̩] der <-s, ->
🔊 the best part of ... fast einen ganzen/eine
ganze/ein ganzes ... ◊ *Die Fahrt dauert fast einen
ganzen Tag.* for the most part zum größten Teil
have a part to play in sth zu etw. beitragen
können take part (in sth) (an etw. [dat]) teilnehmen for sb's part for my part meinerseits ◊ *Ich
meinerseits würde lieber hier bleiben.* for their part
ihrerseits ◊ *Sie würden ihrerseits lieber geben.* in
part teilweise
part² [verb] **1.** *(move apart)* part sth etw. teilen

A
B
C
D
E
F
G
H
I
J
K
L
M
N
O
P
Q
R
S
T
U
V
W
X
Y
Z

['taelən] +haben ◊ *Sie teilte den Vorhang und schaute hinaus.* sth parts etw. teilt sich ◊ *Die Menge teilte sich.* **2.** *(people, couple)* sich trennen ['trɛnən] +haben ◊ *Wir trennten uns an der Ecke.* ♦ *Sie haben sich schon wieder getrennt.* **3.** *(your hair)* scheiteln ['ʃaetl̩n] +haben ◊ *Sie hatte ihr Haar in der Mitte gescheitelt.*

◉ be parted (from sb) (von jdm) getrennt sein
• **part with** phras v part with sth sich von etw. trennen [fɔn ... ˌtrɛnən] +haben ◊ *Sie kann sich nicht von ihren alten Stofftieren trennen.*

partial adj **1.** *(in part)* partiell [par'tsi̯ɛl] no comp/superl, only before ns ◊ *eine partielle Sonnenfinsternis* **2.** *(biased)* voreingenommen ['fo:gˌaengənɔmən] ◊ *Richter dürfen nicht voreingenommen sein.* be partial towards sb/sth jdn/etw. bevorteilen [bə'fo:gˌtaelən] <bevorteilt, bevorteilte, hat bevorteilt> ◊ *Der Schiedsrichter bevorteilte die Dortmunder.*

◉ be partial to sb/sth eine Schwäche für jdn/etw. haben

partially adv *(in part)* teilweise ['taelvaezə] ◊ *Die Wunde ist teilweise verheilt.* ♦ *eine teilweise bekleidete Leiche* partially sighted sehbehindert ['ze:bəhɪndet] no comp/superl

participant noun *(participant (in sth))* Teilnehmer (an etw. dat) ['taelne:me] der <-s, -> ♀Teilnehmerin ['taelne:mərɪn] die <-, -nen>

participate verb participate (in sth) (an etw. dat) teilnehmen ['taelne:mən] <nimmt teil, nahm teil, hat teilgenommen> ◊ *die teilnehmenden Kinder* ♦ *Sie weigern sich, an den Verhandlungen teilzunehmen.*

participation noun **1.** *(taking an active part)* participation (in sth) Beteiligung (an etw. dat) [bə'taelɪgʊŋ] die <-, -en> ◊ *Die Beteiligung an der Umfrage war nur gering.* **2.** *(being among the participants)* participation (in sth) Teilnahme (an etw. dat) ['taelna:mə] die <-, -n> ◊ *Seine Teilnahme an der Konferenz/am Rennen steht noch nicht fest.*

participle noun Partizip [par'ti'tsi:p] das <-s, -ien>
particle noun **1.** PHYSICS Teilchen ['taelçən] das <-s, -> ◊ *positiv geladene Teilchen* **2.** *(of dust, truth)* Körnchen ['kœrnçən] das <-s, -> ◊ *Auf den Möbeln war nicht ein Körnchen Staub zu sehen.* ♦ *ein Körnchen Wahrheit* **3.** GRAM *(with reference to German)* Partikel [par'ti:kl̩] die <-, -n> ◊ *„Schon"* *wird oft als Partikel verwendet.; (to English)* Bestandteil eines *„phrasal verbs"*

particular¹ noun **1.** particulars Einzelheiten ['aentsl̩haetn̩] die <-> pl ◊ *Ich kenne die Einzelheiten nicht.* **2.** sb's particulars jds Personalien [pɛr'zo'na:li̯ən] die <-> pl ◊ *seine Personalien angeben*

particular² adj **1.** *(specific)* bestimmt [bə'ʃtɪmt] no comp/superl, only before ns ◊ *Ich suche ein ganz bestimmtes Buch.* **2.** *(special, distinctive)* besondere [bə'zɔndərə] no comp/superl, only before ns <ein besonderer ..., eine besondere ..., ein besonderes ...> ◊ *Sie hat ein ganz besonderes Talent.* ♦ *besondere Umstände* **3.** *(about food)* heikel ['haekl̩] <heikler, am heikelsten> <der/die/das heikle ...> ◊ *Er ist ziemlich heikel.* ♦ *eine sehr heikle junge Dame* be particular about your food beim Essen heikel sein; *(about your choices)* wählerisch ['vɛ:lərɪʃ] ◊ *Bei Männern bin ich wählerisch.* ♦ *Was die Methode angeht, bin ich nicht wählerisch.* This plant is not particular about soil type. Diese Pflanze stellt keine

besonderen Ansprüche an den Boden.; *(about getting or doing sth etc.)* be particular about sth auf etw. acc Wert legen [aof ... ˌve:gt le:gn̩] +haben I am very particular about detail. Ich lege großen Wert auf die Details. He is very particular about his work. Er nimmt es mit seiner Arbeit sehr genau. I'm not particular. Es ist mir egal.

◉ in particular ganz besonders anything in particular etwas Bestimmtes ◊ *Haben Sie fürs Wochenende etwas Bestimmtes geplant?* nothing in particular nichts Besonderes ◊ *„Was hast du gekauft?" —* *„Nichts Besonderes."*

particularly adv besonders [bə'zɔndes] ◊ *Sie ist besonders begabt.* ♦ *Das war nicht besonders lustig.* ♦ *Er hat gestern besonders viel getrunken.* ♦ *Das ist wichtig, besonders für dich.*

parting noun **1.** *(act of leaving)* Abschied ['apʃi:t] der <-(e)s, -e> on parting beim Abschied; *(end of a relationship)* Trennung ['trɛnʊŋ] die <-, -en> **2.** *(in the UK: in your hair)* Scheitel ['ʃaetl̩] der <-s, -> ◊ *den Scheitel auf der rechten Seite haben*

◉ come to a parting of the ways getrennte Wege gehen

partition off verb abtrennen ['aptrɛnən] +haben ◊ *Die Kochnische war mit einem Vorhang abgetrennt.*

partly adv zum Teil [tsʊm 'tael] ◊ *Es war zum Teil seine eigene Schuld.*

partner noun **1.** *(in a relationship, an activity)* Partner ['pa'tne] der <-s, -> ♀Partnerin ['pa'tnərɪn] die <-, -nen> ◊ *Ich suche eine Partnerin zum Tennisspielen.* ♦ *eine Ehe, in der beide Partner erwerbstätig sind* trading partner Handelspartner ['handl̩spa'tne] business partner Geschäftspartner [gə'ʃɛftspa'tne] **2.** *(in a company)* partner (in sth) Teilhaber (... gen) ['taelha:be] der <-s, -> ♀Teilhaberin ['taelha:bərɪn] die <-, -nen> ◊ *Er war geschäftsführender Teilhaber des Verlags.*

partnership noun **1.** *(company)* Personengesellschaft [pɛr'zo:nəngəzɛlʃaft] die <-, -en> go into partnership (with sb) (mit jdm) eine Personengesellschaft gründen take sb into partnership jdn zu seinem Teilhaber machen [tsu: zaenəm 'taelha:be maxn̩] +haben **2.** *(co-operation)* Partnerschaft ['pa'tneʃaft] die <-, -en> ◊ *eine Partnerschaft eingehen* ◊ *Das Festival wurde in Partnerschaft mit dem Musikverein organisiert.*

part of speech noun Wortart ['vɔrtˌla:'t] die <-, -en>

part-time¹ adj Teilzeit... ['taeltsaet] part-time work Teilzeitarbeit ['taeltsaetˌla'baet] die <-> no pl part-time worker Teilzeitkraft ['taeltsaetkraft] die <-, Teilzeitkräfte>

part-time² adv halbtags ['halpta:ks] ◊ *Er arbeitet halbtags.*

party¹ noun **1.** *(social event, among friends)* Party ['pa:'ti:] die <-, -s> ◊ *Am Samstag gehe ich auf eine Party.* ♦ *Sie feiert gern Partys.* have a party eine Party geben; *(larger, more formal)* Feier ['faee] die <-, -n> ◊ *Warst du auf der Feier?* have a party (for sb/sth) eine Feier (für jdn/anlässlich einer Sache gen) veranstalten ◊ *eine Feier anlässlich des 50-jährigen Bestehens des Vereins* farewell party Abschiedsfeier ['apʃi:tsfaee] **2.** *(political)* party Partei [par'tae] die <-, -en> ◊ *die stärkste Partei im Bundestag* ♦ *einer Partei angehören* the party faithful die treuen Anhänger der Partei opposition

party Oppositionspartei [ɔpozi'tsio:nspaʳ,tae] ruling party Regierungspartei [re'gi:rʊŋspaʳ,tae] **3.** *(group)* Gruppe ['grʊpə] die <-, -n> ◊ *eine Gruppe von Schulkindern* coach party Reisegruppe ['raezəgrʊpə] rescue party Rettungsmannschaft ['rɛtʊŋsmanʃaft] die <-, -en> **4.** *(in contracts, legal cases)* Partei [paʳ'tae] die <-, -en> ◊ *Bei der Scheidung konnten sich beide Parteien schnell einigen.* the guilty party der/die Schuldige [dɛ:ɡ/di: 'ʃʊldɪɡə] <-n, -n> the interested parties die Beteiligten [di: bə'taelɪçtn̩] <-> pl

◉ **be a party to sth** an etw. ⟨dat⟩ beteiligt sein

party² ⟨verb⟩ feiern ['faeɐn] +haben ◊ *Habt ihr gestern Abend noch lange gefeiert?*

pass¹ ⟨noun⟩ **1.** *(identification)* Ausweis ['aosvaes] der <-es, -e> ◊ *Ohne deinen Ausweis kommst du nicht hinein.; (card)* Karte ['kaʳtə] die <-, -n> ◊ *Jedes Mitglied bekommt eine Karte.* boarding pass Bordkarte ['bɔʳtkaʳtə] weekly pass Wochenkarte ['vɔxŋ̍kaʳtə] security pass Passierschein [pa'si:ɐʃaen] der <-(e)s, -e> **2.** *(in an exam)* get a pass in ... die ...Prüfung bestehen [di: ...pry:fʊŋ bəˌʃte:ən] <besteht, bestand, hat bestanden> get a pass in Spanish die Spanischprüfung bestehen [di: 'ʃpa:nɪʃpry:fʊŋ bəˌʃte:ən] **3.** *(in the mountains)* Pass [pas] der <-es, Pässe> ◊ *Der Pass ist für Lkw gesperrt.* **4.** *(stage in a process)* Durchgang ['dʊʳçɡaŋ] der <-(e)s, Durchgänge> ◊ *Beim ersten Durchgang prüfe ich den Inhalt, beim zweiten die Rechtschreibung.* **5.** *(of the ball)* Pass [pas] der <-es, Pässe> ◊ *Bei dem Pass von Scholl stand Elber im Abseits.*

◉ **make a pass at sb** jdn anmachen *(fam)*

pass² ⟨verb⟩ **1.** *(move past sb/sth, vehicle)* pass (sb/sth) (an jdm/etw.) vorbeifahren [fo:ɡ'baefa:rən] <fährt vorbei, fuhr vorbei, ist vorbeigefahren> ◊ *Ein Auto fuhr an uns vorbei.; (pedestrian)* (an jdm/etw.) vorbeigehen [fo:ɡ'baege:ən] <geht vorbei, ging vorbei, ist vorbeigegangen>; *(procession)* (an jdm/etw.) vorbeiziehen [fo:ɡ'baetsi:ən] <zieht vorbei, zog vorbei, ist vorbeigezogen> **2.** *(in the US: overtake)* überholen [ybɐ'ho:lən] <überholt, überholte, hat überholt> ◊ *Hier darf man nicht überholen.* ◆ *Wir haben einen Lastwagen überholt.* **3.** *(move in a certain direction, person, object, thought)* gehen ['ge:ən] <geht, ging, ist gegangen> ◊ *über eine Brücke gehen* ◆ *Der Brief ging von Hand zu Hand.* ◆ *Wenn ich sterbe, geht alles an meine Kinder.* All these thoughts passed through his head. All dies ging ihm durch den Kopf. Are we going to pass through Bonn? Kommen wir auch durch Bonn? Secret looks passed between them. Sie tauschten heimlich Blicke aus. No words passed between them. Sie wechselten kein Wort. Hard words passed between us. Es fielen harte Worte.; *(vehicle, your hand)* fahren ['fa:rən] <fährt, fuhr, ist gefahren> ◊ *in einen Tunnel fahren* ◆ *sich* ⟨dat⟩ *mit der Hand über die Stirn fahren* The car passed under the railway. Das Auto fuhr unter der Bahnlinie durch.; *(plane, bird)* pass over sb/sth über jdn/etw. hinwegfliegen [y:be ... hɪn,vɛkfli:gn̩] <fliegt hinweg, flog hinweg, ist hinweggeflogen> pass out of sth aus etw. verschwinden [aos ... fe'ʃvɪndn̩] <verschwindet, verschwand, ist verschwunden> **4.** *(river)* pass through sth durch etw. fließen [dʊʳç ... fli:sn̩] <fließt, floss, ist geflossen> ◊ *Der Rhein fließt durch Düsseldorf.;*

(road) pass through sth durch etw. führen [dʊʳç ... fy:rən] +haben **5.** *(an exam)* pass sth etw. bestehen [bə'ʃte:ən] <besteht, bestand, hat bestanden> ◊ *Hast du bestanden?* ◆ *Sie hat die Prüfung erst beim zweiten Mal bestanden.; (examiner)* pass sb jdn bestehen lassen [bə'ʃte:ən lasn̩] <lässt, ließ, hat lassen> ◊ *Die Prüfer haben alle bestehen lassen.* **6.** *(give)* pass (sb) sth, pass sth to sb jdm etw. geben ['ge:bm̩] <gibt, gab, hat gegeben> ◊ *Würdest du mir bitte die Butter geben?; (a secret, information)* pass sth to sb etw. an jdn weitergeben [an ... ,vaetege:bm̩] <gibt weiter, gab weiter, hat weitergegeben> **7.** *(a law)* erlassen [ɛ'lasn̩] <erlässt, erließ, hat erlassen> sth passes (sth/sb) etw. wird (von etw./jdm) verabschiedet [vɪʳt fɛʳ'apʃi:dət] <wird, wurde, ist worden> ◊ *Wann wurde dieses Gesetz verabschiedet?* ◆ *Das Gesetz muss erst noch vom Bundesrat verabschiedet werden.* Will the law pass? Wird das Gesetz durchkommen? **8.** *(time)* vergehen [fɛʳ'ge:ən] <vergeht, verging, ist vergangen> ◊ *Der Vormittag ist aber schnell vergangen!* with every day that passes mit jedem Tag [mɪt je:dm̩ 'ta:k] ◊ *Mit jedem Tag fehlt sie mir mehr.; (spend, the day, some time)* verbringen [fɛʳ'brɪŋən] <verbringt, verbrachte, hat verbracht> ◊ *Sie verbrachten den Tag im Hotel.* pass the time sich ⟨dat⟩ die Zeit vertreiben [di: 'tsaet fɛtraebm̩] <vertreibt sich, vertrieb sich, hat sich vertrieben> ◊ *Sie sahen fern, um sich die Zeit zu vertreiben.* **9.** *(come to an end)* vorbeigehen [fo:ɡ'baege:ən] <geht vorbei, ging vorbei, ist vorbeigegangen> ◊ *Die Schmerzen gehen schnell vorbei.* **10.** *(a ball)* pass sth to sb etw. zu jdm spielen [tsu: ... ʃpi:lən] +haben ◊ *Er spielte den Ball zu Klose.* **11.** *(happen)* vorfallen ['fo:ɐfalən] <fällt vor, fiel vor, ist vorgefallen> ◊ *Was ist denn nur zwischen den beiden vorgefallen?* **12.** *(not make a bid, not play a card, be unable to answer)* passen ['pasn̩] +haben *(also fam)* ◊ *Bei dieser Frage muss ich passen.* **13.** *(exceed)* überschreiten [ybɐ'ʃraetn̩] <überschreitet, überschritt, hat überschritten> ◊ *Sie hat die fünfzig schon weit überschritten.* **14.** pass unnoticed unbemerkt bleiben ['ʊnbəmɛʳkt blaebm̩] <bleibt, blieb, ist geblieben> ◊ *Der kleine Fehler in seiner Arbeit blieb unbemerkt.* let sth pass etw. durchgehen lassen ['dʊʳçge:ən lasn̩] <lässt, ließ, hat lassen> ◊ *Das kann ich so nicht durchgehen lassen.* **15.** *(from your body)* ausscheiden ['aosʃaedn̩] <scheidet aus, schied aus, hat ausgeschieden> ◊ *Der Kranke scheidet Blut im Urin aus.* pass urine/water Wasser lassen ['vasɐ lasn̩] <lässt, ließ, hat gelassen> ◊ **16.** *(ownership, property)* pass to sb auf jdn übergehen [aof ... ,y:bege:ən] <geht über, ging über, ist übergegangen> ◊ *Das Geschäft ist von der Mutter auf die Tochter übergegangen.*

• **pass around** ⟨phras v⟩ pass sth around etw. herumgehen lassen [hɛ'rʊmge:ən ,lasn̩] <lässt, ließ, hat ... lassen> ◊ *Sie ließ eine Tüte Bonbons herumgehen.*

• **pass as** ⟨phras v⟩ *(be thought to be)* als etw. gelten [als ... gɛltn̩] <gilt, galt, hat gegolten> ◊ *Das galt damals als schick.; (wrongly)* sb/sth passes as sb/sth jd hält jdn/etw. für jdn/etw. [hɛlt ... fy:ɡ] <hält, hielt, hat gehalten> ◊ *Es ist verrückt, was man heute alles für normal hält.; (could be thought to be)* als etw. durchgehen [als ... ,dʊʳçge:ən] <geht durch, ging durch, ist durchgegangen> ◊ *Sie ist erst 14, geht aber*

leicht als 18 durch.

• **pass away** (phras v) einschlafen ['æɲʃlaːfn̩] <schläft ein, schlief ein, ist eingeschlafen> *(euph)* ◊ *Nach langer, schwerer Krankheit ist er nun sanft eingeschlafen.*

• **pass by** (phras v) **1.** *(car, bus)* pass by (sb/sth) (an jdm/etw.) vorbeifahren [foːɐ̯'baefaːrən] <fährt vorbei, fuhr vorbei, ist vorbeigefahren> ◊ *Ein Bus fuhr vorbei, aber er hielt nicht.* ♦ *Ein Auto fuhr an uns vorbei.;* *(person)* pass by (sb/sth) (an jdm/etw.) vorbeigehen [foːɐ̯'baegeːən] <geht vorbei, ging vorbei, ist vorbeigegangen> ◊ *Er ging wortlos an uns vorbei.* **2.** sth passes sb by etw. geht an jdm vorüber [geːt an ... fo'ryːbɐ] <geht vorüber, ging vorüber, ist vorübergegangen> ◊ *Das ist ganz an mir vorübergegangen!* ♦ *Das Leben ist an ihr vorübergegangen.*

• **pass down** (phras v) weitergeben ['vaetegeːbm̩] <gibt weiter, gab weiter, hat weitergegeben>

• **pass for** (phras v) → pass as

• **pass off** (phras v) **1.** pass yourself/sb/sth off as sth sich/jdn/etw. als etw. ausgeben [als ... aosgeːbm̩] <gibt aus, gab aus, hat ausgegeben> ◊ *Die Einbrecher gaben sich als Handwerker aus.* **2.** *(event)* verlaufen [fe'laofn̩] <verläuft, verlief, ist verlaufen> ◊ *Die Kundgebung verlief ohne Zwischenfälle.* **3.** *(the ball)* abgeben ['apgeːbm̩] <gibt ab, gab ab, hat abgegeben> ◊ *Er gab den Ball an Elber ab.*

• **pass on** (phras v) pass sth on (to sb) etw. (an jdn) weitergeben ['vaetegeːbm̩] <gibt weiter, gab weiter, hat weitergegeben> ♦ *eine Nachricht weitergeben* ♦ *die Kosten an den Verbraucher weitergeben; (a disease)* pass sth on (to sb) etw. (auf jdn) übertragen [ybe'traːgn̩] <überträgt, übertrug, hat übertragen> ◊ *Kann die Krankheit auf den Menschen übertragen werden?* ♦ *Die Tsetsefliege überträgt die Schlafkrankheit.; (a cold etc.)* pass sth on to sb jdn mit etw. anstecken [mɪt ... ˌanʃtɛkn̩] +haben ◊ *Er hat uns mit seinem Schnupfen angesteckt.*

• **pass out** (phras v) **1.** *(faint)* ohnmächtig werden ['oːnmɛçtɪç veːɐ̯dn̩] +sein ◊ *Beim Anblick des Blutes wurde ich ohnmächtig.* **2.** *(give out)* austeilen ['aostaelən] +haben ◊ *Der Lehrer teilte die Klassenarbeiten aus.*

• **pass over** (phras v) übergehen [ybe'geːən] <übergeht, überging, hat übergangen> ◊ *Meine Frage/Mich haben sie einfach übergangen.*

• **pass round** (phras v) → pass around

• **pass through** (phras v) pass through sth durch etw. fahren [dʊrç ... faːrən] <fährt, fuhr, ist gefahren> ◊ *Auf unserer Reise nach Schweden fuhren wir durch Dänemark.* I'm only passing through. Ich bin nur auf der Durchreise.

• **pass up** (phras v) pass sth up sich (dat) etw. entgehen lassen [ɛnt'geːən lasn̩] <lässt sich, ließ sich, hat sich ... lassen> ◊ *Was? Du hast dir diese einmalige Gelegenheit entgehen lassen!*

passage (noun) **1.** *(passageway)* Durchgang ['dʊrçgaŋ] der <-(e)s, Durchgänge> ◊ *Durch diesen Durchgang gelangt man in den Innenhof.* **2.** *(of a book, article, piece of music)* Passage [pa'saːʒə] die <-, -n> ◊ *Er zitierte die entsprechende Passage.* ♦ *Diese Passage gefällt mir besonders gut.* **3.** *(way through)* Weg [veːk] der <-(e)s, -e> ◊ *Der Weg durchs Gebirge war mit großen Gefahren verbunden.; (through a country)* Durchreise ['dʊrçraezə] die <-, -n> most

sing ◊ *An der Grenze wurde ihm die Durchreise verweigert.* safe passage sicheres Geleit [zɪçərəs gə'laet] <-(e)s, -e> most sing ◊ *jdm sicheres Geleit geben* **4.** *(of a law)* Verabschiedung [fe̯|'apʃiːdʊŋ] die <-> no pl **5.** *(in your body)* air passages Atemwege ['aːtəmveːgə] die <-> pl nasal passages obere Atemwege ear passages Gehörgang [gə'høːɐ̯gaŋ] der <-(e)s> sing **6.** *(sea journey)* Überfahrt ['yːbɐfaːɐ̯t] die <-, -en> ◊ *Die Überfahrt nach Amerika dauerte fünf Wochen.* work your passage seine Überfahrt abarbeiten ⊚ with the passage of time im Laufe der Zeit

passageway (noun) Durchgang ['dʊrçgaŋ] der <-(e)s, Durchgänge> ◊ *Der Durchgang führt in einen Innenhof.*

passenger (noun) *(in a ship, plane)* Passagier [pasa'ʒiːɐ̯] der <-s, -e> ♀Passagierin [pasa'ʒiːrɪn] die <-, -nen> ◊ *40 Passagiere erlitten Verletzungen.; (in a car)* Insasse ['ɪnzasə] der <-n, -n> ♀Insassin ['ɪnzasɪn] die <-, -nen>

passer-by (noun) Passant [pa'sant] der <-en, -en> ♀Passantin [pa'santɪn] die <-, -nen>

passing[1] (noun) **1.** *(disappearance)* passing (of ...) Verschwinden (... (gen)) [fe'ʃvɪndn̩] das <-s> no pl ◊ *das Verschwinden der alten Traditionen* **2.** *(of time)* Vergehen [fe'geːən] das <-s> no pl ◊ with the passing of time im Laufe der Zeit [ɪm laofə deːɐ̯ 'tsaet] ⊚ in passing beiläufig ◊ *etw. beiläufig erwähnen*

passing[2] (adj) **1.** *(moving past)* vorbeikommend [foːɐ̯'baekɔmənt] no comp/superl, only before ns ◊ *Ein vorbeikommender Autofahrer hat sie gerettet.* **2.** *(short)* vorübergehend [foːry:bege:ənt] no comp/superl ◊ *eine vorübergehende Schwäche* ♦ *Diese Phase ist nur vorübergehend.* **3.** *(resemblance, glance, knowledge)* flüchtig ['flʏçtɪç] ◊ *Er hat eine flüchtige Ähnlichkeit mit meinem Vater.* ♦ *Ihr Blick war nur flüchtig.*

passion (noun) **1.** *(love, enthusiasm)* Leidenschaft ['laedn̩ʃaft] die <-, -en> ◊ *Seine Leidenschaft für sie ließ nie nach.* ♦ *Ihre große Leidenschaft gilt der Kunst.* ♦ *Meine Leidenschaft ist Fußball/Kochen.* **2.** *(anger)* Erregung die <-, -en> Passions were running high. Die Erregung schlug hohe Wellen. work yourself up into a passion sich furchtbar aufregen [ˌfʊ̯'çtbaːɐ̯ 'aofreːgn̩] +haben ⊚ the Passion die Passion

passionate(ly) (adj, adv) leidenschaftlich ['laedn̩ʃaftlɪç] ◊ *eine leidenschaftliche Affäre* ♦ *Italiener gelten als sehr leidenschaftlich.* ♦ *Sie küssten sich leidenschaftlich.* be passionate about sth sich leidenschaftlich für etw. interessieren

passive[1] (noun) Passiv ['pasiːf] das <-s, -e> most sing

passive[2] (adj) **1.** *(not active)* passiv ['pasiːf] ◊ *zum passiven Widerstand aufrufen* ♦ *Krebse sind eher passiv und zurückhaltend.* **2.** GRAM im Passiv [ɪm 'pasiːf] a passive sentence ein Satz im Passiv

passively (adv) passiv ['pasiːf] ◊ *passiv herumstehen und nichts tun*

passport (noun) **1.** *(document)* Pass [pas] der <-es, Pässe> ◊ *seinen Pass verlängern lassen* ♦ *Der Beamte überprüfte unsere Pässe.* **2.** *(fig) (key)* Schlüssel ['ʃlʏsl̩] der <-s, -> ◊ *Eine gute Ausbildung ist der Schlüssel zum Erfolg.*

password (noun) Passwort ['pasvɔ̯t] das <-(e)s, Passwörter> ◊ *ein Passwort eingeben*

past¹ [noun] **1.** *(time before now)* Vergangenheit [fɐˈɡaŋənhaɛt] die <–> *no pl* ◊ *Mein Großvater lebt in der Vergangenheit.* ♦ *Über meine Vergangenheit möchte ich nicht sprechen.* in the past früher [ˈfryːɐ] ◊ *War früher tatsächlich alles besser?* **2.** LING Vergangenheitsform [fɐˈɡaŋənhaɛtsfɔˈm] die <–, –en>
⊚ **put the past behind you** Vergangenes ruhen lassen

past² [adj] **1.** *(right before the present time, no longer existing)* vergangen [fɐˈɡaŋən] *no comp/superl* ◊ *Im vergangenen Jahr waren die Zahlen besser.* ♦ *Was haben Sie in den vergangenen 24 Stunden gemacht?*; *(at any earlier time)* früher [ˈfryːɐ] *no comp/superl, only before ns* <ein früherer …, eine frühere…, ein früheres …> ◊ *Die frühere Vorsitzende wird auch anwesend sein.* ♦ *In früheren Zeiten hatten die meisten Haushalte kein Telefon.* **2.** *(over)* be past vorüber sein [foˈryːbɐ zaɛn] ◊ *Der Winter ist vorüber.*

past³ [adv] vorbei… [foːɐˈbaɛ] walk past vorbeigehen [foːɐˈbaɛɡeːən] <geht vorbei, ging vorbei, ist vorbeigegangen> ◊ *Der Polizist ging einfach vorbei.* run past vorbeirennen [foːɐˈbaɛrɛnən] <rennt vorbei, rannte vorbei, ist vorbeigerannt> ◊ *Zwei Jungen rannten vorbei.*

past⁴ [prep] **1.** *(temporal: after)* nach [naːx] [+dat] ◊ *Es ist zehn Minuten nach drei.* ♦ *Es war schon nach Mitternacht, als ich nach Hause kam.* half past four halb fünf [ˌhalp ˈfvnf] **2.** *(spatial: expressing you are passing sth, with certain verbs)* … past sb/sth an jdm/etw. vorbei… [an … foːɐˈbaɛ] walk past sth an etw. [dat] vorbeigehen [an … foːɐˈbaɛɡeːən] <geht vorbei, ging vorbei, ist vorbeigegangen> drive past sth an etw. [dat] vorbeifahren [an … foːɐ ˌbaɛfaːrən] <fährt vorbei, fuhr vorbei, ist vorbeigefahren> **3.** *(spatial: beyond, on the other side of)* hinter [ˈhɪntɐ] [+dat] ◊ *Fahren Sie geradeaus; der Supermarkt ist gleich hinter der Kirche.* ♦ *Wir wohnen in dem Haus direkt hinter der Kreuzung.* **4.** *(beyond a certain stage or point)* past sth über etw. [acc] hinaus [yːbɐ … hɪˌnaʊs] ◊ *Bist du über dieses Alter nicht schon hinaus?* get past sth über etw. [acc] hinauskommen [yːbɐ … hɪˌnaʊskɔmən] <kommt hinaus, kam hinaus, ist hinausgekommen> ◊ *Sie kam nicht über die sechste Klasse hinaus.* sb is past caring es kümmert jdn nicht mehr [ɛs ˈkʏmɐt … ˌnɪçt meːɐ] +haben ◊ *Früher machte sie sich Sorgen, wenn er unpünktlich war, aber jetzt kümmert es sie nicht mehr.*
⊚ **not put sth past sb** jdm etw. zutrauen ◊ *Diese Gemeinheit würde ich dir schon zutrauen!* past it zu alt

pasta [noun] Nudeln [ˈnuːdl̩n] die <–> *pl* ◊ *Ich mache heute Nudeln mit Soße.*

paste [noun] **1.** *(for sticking)* Kleister [ˈklaɛstɐ] der <–s> *no pl* ◊ *Sie rührte in einem Eimer Kleister an.* wallpaper paste Tapetenkleister [taˈpeːtŋklaɛstɐ] **2.** *(mash, food)* Brei [braɛ] der <–(e)s, –e> ◊ *Bananen zu einem Brei zerdrücken* ♦ *aus Gipspulver und Wasser einen zähen Brei anrühren; (spread)* Brotaufstrich [ˈbroːtlaʊfʃtrɪç] der <–(e)s, –e> ◊ *ein Brotaufstrich mit Gurken und Zwiebeln* tomato paste Tomatenmark [toˈmaːtŋmaˈk] das <–(e)s> *no pl* **3.** *(jewellery)* Strass [ʃtras] der <– *or* –es> *no pl* ◊ *Knöpfe aus Strass*

past perfect [noun] Plusquamperfekt

[ˈplʊskvampɐˈfɛkt] das <–s, –e> ◊ *Das Verb steht im Plusquamperfekt.*

pastry [noun] **1.** *(raw mixture)* Teig [taɛk] der <–(e)s, –e> ◊ *den Teig für eine Pastete zubereiten* **2.** *(cake)* Teilchen [ˈtaɛlçən] das <–s, –> *(regional)* ◊ *Holst du zum Tee noch ein paar Teilchen vom Bäcker?* Danish pastry Plunderteilchen [ˈplʊndɐtaɛlçən] cake and pastries Kuchen und Gebäck [ˌkuːxŋ ʊnt ɡəˈbɛk]

pasture [noun] *(field)* Weide [ˈvaɛdə] die <–, –n> ◊ *Die Schafe laufen auf der Weide herum.* put out to pasture auf die Weide treiben ◊ *Die Kühe wurden auf die Weide getrieben.* pasture (land) Weideland [ˈvaɛdəlant] das <–(e)s> *no pl* ◊ *Sein Besitz umfasst mehrere Hektar Weideland.*
⊚ **move on to pastures new** zu neuen Ufern aufbrechen

pat [verb] *(reassure, touch lightly)* tätscheln [ˈtɛtʃl̩n] +haben ◊ *Sie tätschelte beruhigend seine Hand.* ♦ *Er tätschelte dem Pferd den Hals.; (touch your face)* abtupfen [ˈaptʊpfn̩] +haben ◊ *Er tupfte sich das Gesicht vorsichtig ab.; (draw attention to sth)* pat sth auf etw. [acc] klopfen [aʊf … ˌklɔpfn̩] +haben ◊ *Sie klopfte auf den Platz neben sich und forderte ihn auf, sich zu setzen.*
⊚ **pat sb/yourself on the back** jdm/sich auf die Schulter klopfen

patch [noun] **1.** *(stain, small area)* Stelle [ˈʃtɛlə] die <–, –n> ◊ *Der Hund hat eine weiße Stelle auf der Brust.* ♦ *nasse Stellen auf dem Teppich* in patches stellenweise [ˈʃtɛlənvaɛzə] ◊ *Die Straßen sind stellenweise vereist.* **2.** *(for growing fruit, vegetables)* Beet [beːt] das <–(e)s, –e> ◊ *Was hast du in dem Beet dort gepflanzt?* vegetable patch Gemüsebeet [ɡəˈmyːzəbeːt]; *(of land, road)* Stück [ʃtʏk] das <–(e)s, –e> ◊ *Dieses Stück Straße war sehr schlecht.; (turf, home ground)* sb's patch jds Revier [reˈviːɐ] das <–s, –e> ◊ *Er weiß über alles Bescheid, was in seinem Revier vorgeht.* **3.** *(for mending)* Flicken [ˈflɪkŋ] der <–s, –> ◊ *eine alte Jacke mit bunten Flicken; (for covering your eye)* eye patch Augenklappe [ˈaʊɡŋklapə] die <–, –n> ◊ *Nach der Operation musste er eine Augenklappe tragen.* **4.** IT Patch [pɛtʃ] der <–(s), –s> ◊ *einen Patch aus dem Internet herunterladen* **5.** *(nicotine)* patch Nikotinpflaster [nikoˈtiːnpflastɐ] das <–s, –>
⊚ **go through a difficult patch** eine schwierige Phase durchmachen

patch together [verb] zusammenbasteln [tsuˈzamənbastl̩n] +haben *(fam)* ◊ *Wir haben schnell einen neuen Plan zusammengebastelt.*

patch up [verb] **1.** *(a relationship)* wieder ins Lot bringen [viːdɐ ɪns ˈloːt brɪŋən] <bringt, brachte, hat gebracht> ◊ *Ich möchte unsere Beziehung gerne wieder ins Lot bringen.; (your differences)* beilegen [ˈbaɛleːɡn̩] +haben ◊ *Habt ihr eure Meinungsverschiedenheiten endlich beigelegt?* patch things up with sb sich mit jdm wieder versöhnen [mɪt … viːdɐ fɛˈzøːnən] <versöhnt sich, versöhnte sich, hat sich versöhnt> ◊ *Habt ihr euch nun wieder versöhnt?* **2.** *(repair)* flicken [ˈflɪkŋ] +haben ◊ *das Dach flicken lassen* ♦ *eine Hose flicken* **3.** *(an injured person)* zusammenflicken [tsuˈzamənflɪkŋ] +haben *(fam)* ◊ *Nach seinem Unfall flickten ihn die Ärzte wieder zusammen.*

patchy [adj] **1.** *(fog, rain)* örtlich [ˈœˈtlɪç] *no comp/*

superl, only before ns ◊ örtlicher Nebel; (clouds) patchy clouds leichte Bewölkung [la͜eçtə bə'vœlkʊŋ]; (colo(u)r) fleckig ['flɛkɪç] ◊ Der Stoff hatte eine fleckige Färbung. **2.** (knowledge, memory) lückenhaft ['lʏkŋ̍haft] <lückenhafter, am lückenhaftesten> ◊ Meine Italienischkenntnisse sind ziemlich lückenhaft. ✦ ein lückenhaftes Gedächtnis **3.** (performance) durchwachsen [dʊʳç'vaksn̩] ◊ „Wie ist ihre Arbeit?" — „Durchwachsen." ✦ durchwachsene Leistungen zeigen ✦ Die Filme waren von durchwachsener Qualität.

pâté [noun] Pastete [pas'teːtə] die <-, -n> ◊ ein Brötchen mit Pastete bestreichen

patent [noun] Patent [pa'tɛnt] das <-(e)s, -e> ◊ ein Patent auf eine Erfindung erhalten

path [noun] **1.** (on a field, pavement, in sb's life, towards an achievement) Weg [veːk] der <-(e)s, -e> ◊ Ein schmaler Weg führte durch den Wald. ✦ Der Weg zum Gipfel war ziemlich steil. ✦ Zwei Polizisten versperrten ihr den Weg. ✦ Hier trennen sich unsere Wege. ✦ Der Weg zum Erfolg ist nicht einfach. **2.** (trajectory) Bahn [baːn] die <-, -en> ◊ die Bahn der Planeten

◉ **two people's paths cross** jds Wege kreuzen sich ◊ Damals kreuzten sich unsere Wege zum ersten Mal.

pathetic(ally) [adj, adv] **1.** (very bad) erbärmlich [e'bɛʳmlɪç] ◊ Das ist die erbärmlichste Ausrede, die ich je gehört habe. ✦ Das ist doch einfach erbärmlich! ✦ Er hat bei der Prüfung erbärmlich abgeschnitten. **2.** (pitiful) mitleiderregend ['mɪtla͜et|ere:gŋ̍t] ◊ ein mitleiderregender Anblick ✦ Diese Geschichte ist mitleiderregend.

pathological(ly) [adj, adv] **1.** (not based on reason, uncontrollable) krankhaft ['kraŋkhaft] <krankhafter, am krankhaftesten> seldom comp/superl ◊ ein krankhafter Lügner ✦ Sie ist krankhaft eifersüchtig. ✦ Deine Ordnungsliebe ist krankhaft! **2.** (connected with pathology, caused by a disease) pathologisch [pato'loːɡɪʃ] no comp/superl ◊ einen Tierkörper pathologisch untersuchen ✦ ein pathologischer Prozess ✦ Ihre Blutwerte sind pathologisch.

patience [noun] **1.** (endurance, self-control) Geduld [ɡə'dʊlt] die <-> no pl ◊ Sie ertragen Ihre Krankheit mit viel Geduld. ✦ Für das Basteln von Modellen braucht man Geduld. ✦ Mit Kindern hat sie wenig Geduld. **run out of patience** die Geduld verlieren try sb's patience jds Geduld auf die Probe stellen **2.** GAME Patience [pa'siã s] die <-, -n> play patience Patiencen legen

patient [noun] Patient [pa'ts͜iɛnt] der <-en, -en> ♀Patientin [pa'ts͜iɛntɪn] die <-, -nen> ◊ Der Patient wurde gestern aus dem Krankenhaus entlassen. ✦ Die Patientin wird morgen operiert. cancer patient Krebspatient ['kreːpspa,ts͜iɛnt] Krebspatientin ['kreːpspa,ts͜iɛntɪn]

patient(ly) [adj, adv] geduldig [ɡə'dʊldɪç] ◊ Er ist mit kleinen Kindern sehr geduldig. ✦ Sie ist eine geduldige Zuhörerin. ✦ Ich wartet geduldig, bis wir nach Hause kam.

patio [noun] Terrasse [tɛ'rasə] die <-, -n> ◊ Wollen wir heute auf der Terrasse essen?

patrol [noun] ((by) police) Streife ['ʃtra͜efə] die <-, -n> ◊ Während der Streife fanden die Polizisten ein gestohlenes Auto. ✦ Die Streife folgte dem Fliehenden mit Blaulicht. on patrol auf Streife ◊ auf Streife sein/gehen; ((by) soldiers) Patrouille [pa'trʊljə] die

<-, -n> ◊ Patrouillen durchführen on patrol auf Patrouille make patrols of an area in einem Gebiet patrouillieren [ɪn a͜enəm ɡə,bi:t patrʊ'li:rən] <patrouilliert, patrouillierte, hat patrouilliert> patrol boat Patrouillenboot [pa'trʊljənboːt] das <-(e)s, -e>

patron [noun] **1.** (in a hotel, restaurant) Gast [ɡast] der <-(e)s, Gäste> ◊ Parkplatz nur für Gäste **2.** (of an event) Schirmherr ['ʃɪʳmhɛʳ] der <-n, -en> ♀Schirmherrin ['ʃɪʳmhɛrɪn] die <-, -nen> ◊ Wer ist der Schirmherr dieser Veranstaltung?; (of an artist) Mäzen [mɛ'tseːn] der <-s, -e> ♀Mäzenin [mɛ'tseːnɪn] die <-, -nen> ◊ Der junge Maler hat einen einflussreichen Mäzen.

pattern [noun] **1.** (design, model, system of events, behavio(u)r) Muster ['mʊstɐ] das <-s, -> ◊ ein Muster für eine Tapete entwerfen ✦ eine Demokratie nach westlichem Muster ✦ Der Unterricht läuft immer nach demselben Muster ab. make a pattern ein Muster bilden ◊ Die Kreise bilden ein Muster. set a pattern for sth ein Muster für etw. sein ◊ Ihr Verhalten war ein Muster für die Schüler. behaviour pattern Verhaltensmuster [fɛ'haltns̩mʊstɐ] **2.** (template for sewing) Schnitt [ʃnɪt] der <-(e)s, -e> ◊ Sie kaufte einen Schnitt für ein Kleid.; (for knitting) Strickanleitung ['ʃtrɪk|anla͜etʊŋ] die <-, -nen> ◊ Hast du die Strickanleitung genau beachtet?

pause¹ [noun] **1.** (brief interruption, hesitation) Pause ['pa͜ozə] die <-, -n> ◊ Nach ihrer Rede trat eine Pause. ✦ Es entstand eine Pause, während er nach seinem Manuskript suchte. have a pause eine Pause machen ◊ Er machte eine kurze Pause, bevor er weitersprach. **2.** TECHN (on a CD player) Pausentaste ['pa͜ozn̩tastə] die <-, -n> ◊ die Pausentaste drücken

◉ **give sb pause for thought** jdm zu denken geben

pause² [verb] **1.** (when walking) stehen bleiben ['ʃteːən bla͜ebm̩] <bleibt, blieb, ist geblieben> ◊ Sie blieben stehen, um die herrliche Aussicht zu genießen.; (when speaking, exercising, working) eine Pause machen [a͜enə 'pa͜ozə maxn̩] +haben ◊ Er redete eine Stunde, ohne eine Pause zu machen. pause for breath eine Pause machen, um Luft zu holen **2.** TECHN (a video, CD) kurz anhalten [kʊʳts 'anhaltn̩] <hält an, hielt an, hat angehalten> ◊ Könntest du das Band/die CD kurz anhalten?

pavement [noun] **1.** (in the UK: path for pedestrians) Gehsteig ['ɡeːʃta͜ek] der <-(e)s, -e> ◊ Die Kinder spielten auf dem Gehsteig. **2.** (in the US: road surface) Straßenbelag ['ʃtraːsn̩bəlaːk] der <-(e)s, Straßenbeläge> ◊ Der Straßenbelag hatte Risse bekommen.

paw [noun] Pfote ['pfoːtə] die <-, -n> (also pej) ◊ Der Hund leckte sich die Pfoten sauber. ✦ Nimm deine dreckigen Pfoten da weg!

pawn¹ [noun] **1.** CHESS Bauer ['ba͜oɐ] der <-n, -n> ◊ Er hat meinen Bauern geschlagen. **2.** (fig) Schachfigur ['ʃaxfi,ɡuːɐ] die <-, -en> ◊ Wir sind doch alle nur Schachfiguren für ihn.

pawn² [verb] **1.** (at a pawnshop) versetzen [fɛ'zɛtsn̩] <versetzt, versetzte, hat versetzt> ◊ seinen Schmuck versetzen ✦ um Geld zu beschaffen **2.** (passed as) pawn sb/sth off as sb/sth jdn/etw. als jdn/etw. ausgeben [als ... a͜osge:bm̩] <gibt aus, gab aus, hat ausgegeben> ◊ Ich gab meinen Freund als meinen

Mann aus. ♦ *Du willst diese Geschichte doch wohl nicht als Wahrheit ausgeben, oder?*

pay¹ [noun] *(wages)* Lohn [loːn] der <-(e)s, Löhne> ◊ *einen höheren Lohn fordern; (salary)* Gehalt [gəˈhalt] das <-(e)s, Gehälter> ◊ *jdm etw. vom Gehalt abziehen* ♦ *die Gehälter kürzen/erhöhen* pay rise/increase Gehaltserhöhung [gəˈhalts|ɛhøːʊŋ] die <-, -en> basic pay Grundgehalt [ˈɡrʊntgəhalt] additional/extra pay Zulage [ˈtsuːlaːɡə] die <-, -n> ◊ *Zulagen für Sonn- und Feiertagsarbeit; (received for a particular period, in compound ns)* ... pay ...geld [gɛlt] das <-(e)s> *no pl* sick pay Krankengeld [ˈkraŋkŋɡɛlt] maternity pay Mutterschaftsgeld [ˈmʊtəʃaftsgɛlt]
ⓔ **be in the pay of sb** für jdn arbeiten

pay² [verb] **1.** *(for sth you buy, a service, a salary, debts)* bezahlen [bəˈtsaːlən] <bezahlt, bezahlte, hat bezahlt> ◊ *Wir müssen noch bezahlen, bevor wir gehen.* ♦ *Steuern bezahlen* ♦ *eine Rechnung bezahlen* ♦ *Die Versicherung bezahlt in so einem Fall nicht.* ♦ *Er bezahlt seine Angestellten gut.* ♦ *Die Arbeiter sind seit Wochen nicht bezahlt worden.* ♦ *in Euro bezahlen* pay (for) sth etw. bezahlen ◊ *Wer bezahlt die Pizza?* ♦ *Sie hat mir 25 Euro für den alten Schrank bezahlt.* pay by cash/cheque bar/mit Scheck bezahlen **2.** *(bring in, earn)* sth pays sth etw. bringt etw. [brɪŋt] <bringt, brachte, hat gebracht> ◊ *ein Konto, das 4 Prozent Zinsen im Jahr bringt; (work)* sth pays well etw. ist gut bezahlt [ɪst ˌɡuːt bəˈtsaːlt] +sein ◊ *Meine neue Arbeit ist gut bezahlt.; (be profitable)* sth pays sich lohnen [zɪç ˈloːnən] +haben ◊ *Lohnt sich das Geschäft?* it pays (sb) to do sth es lohnt sich (für jdn), etw. zu tun ◊ *Es lohnt sich nicht, Überstunden zu machen.* pay for itself sich rentieren [zɪç rɛnˈtiːrən] <rentiert sich, rentierte sich, hat sich rentiert> ◊ *Der Kauf wird sich innerhalb eines Jahres rentieren.* **3.** *(be of advantage, benefit)* sth pays etw. zahlt sich aus [tsaːlt zɪç ˈaʊs] +haben ◊ *Am Ende zahlte sich die Mühe aus.* **4.** *(suffer)* pay for sth für etw. büßen [fyːɡ ... ˈbyːsṇ] +haben ◊ *Dafür wirst du büßen!* make sb pay for sth jdn für etw. büßen lassen I'll make you pay for this! Das wirst du mir büßen! pay dearly for sth teuer für etw. bezahlen [tɔɡə fyːɡ ... bəˈtsaːlən] <bezahlt, bezahlte, hat bezahlt> ◊ *Sie hat für ihre Eitelkeit teuer bezahlt.*
• **pay back** [phras v] **1.** *(money)* pay (sb) sth back (jdm) etw. zurückzahlen [tsuˈrʏktsaːlən] +haben ◊ *Ich zahle Ihnen die Summe nächste Woche zurück.* **2.** *(take revenge)* pay sb back for sth jdm etw. heimzahlen [ˈhaɛmtsaːlən] +haben ◊ *Diese Gemeinheit werde ich ihr heimzahlen!*
• **pay in, pay into** [phras v] pay sth in(to sth) etw. (in etw. [acc]) einzahlen [ˈaɛntsaːlən] +haben ◊ *Kann ich den Betrag am Schalter einzahlen?*
• **pay off** [phras v] **1.** *(a hire purchase, debts)* abzahlen [ˈaptsaːlən] +haben ◊ *Mein Auto ist noch nicht abgezahlt.* ♦ *etw. in Raten abzahlen* **2.** *(a worker)* auszahlen [ˈaʊstsaːlən] +haben ◊ *Die Arbeiter wurden von der Firma ausgezahlt.* **3.** *(bribe)* bestechen [bəˈʃtɛçṇ] <besticht, bestach, hat bestochen> ◊ *Angeblich wurden bei der Sache zwei Beamte bestochen.; (incentive to keep a secret)* pay sb off jdm Schweigegeld zahlen [ˈʃvaɛgəgɛlt tsaːlən] +haben
• **pay out** [phras v] **1.** *(spend money)* ausgeben

[ˈaʊsgeːbm̩] <gibt aus, gab aus, hat ausgegeben> ◊ *Für den PC muss ich eine große Summe ausgeben.* **2.** TECHN *(a rope)* ablaufen lassen [ˈaplaʊfṇ lasn̩] <lässt, ließ, hat lassen> ◊ *Langsam ließen sie das Seil ablaufen.*
• **pay up** [phras v] zahlen [ˈtsaːlən] +haben ◊ *Die Versicherung weigerte sich, zu zahlen.*

payable [adj] zahlbar [ˈtsaːlbaːr] *no comp/superl, not before ns* ◊ *Rechnung zahlbar in drei Monatsraten* ♦ zahlbar innerhalb von 14 Tagen make a cheque payable to sb einen Scheck auf jdn ausstellen [aɛnən ʃɛk aɔf ... aɔsʃtɛlən] +haben ◊ *Bitte stellen Sie den Scheck auf meine Frau aus.*

payment [noun] **1.** *(sum, process)* Bezahlung [bəˈtsaːlʊŋ] die <-, -en> *most sing* ◊ *Er arbeitet nur gegen Bezahlung.* ♦ *Wir bieten Ihnen für Ihre Dienste eine gute Bezahlung an.* ♦ *Wir bitten um Bezahlung der Rechnung bis zum 15. August.* on payment of sth bei Bezahlung ... [gen] ◊ *Übergabe bei Bezahlung der Ware* withhold payment die Bezahlung verweigern settle payments bezahlen [bəˈtsaːlən] <bezahlt, bezahlte, hat bezahlt> make a payment of sth etw. bezahlen ◊ *Ich muss jeden Monat 60 Euro für die Garage bezahlen.* payment in kind Sachleistung [ˈzaxlaɛstʊŋ] die <-, -en> **2.** *(fig) (reward)* Belohnung [bəˈloːnʊŋ] die <-, -en> ◊ *Betrachten Sie die Beförderung als Belohnung für Ihren Einsatz.; (punishment)* Strafe [ˈʃtraːfə] die <-, -n> ◊ *Das ist die gerechte Strafe für ihr unfaires Verhalten.*

PC 1. IT PC [peːˈtseː] ◊ *am PC arbeiten* **2.** *(member of the police)* Polizist [poliˈtsɪst] der <-en, -en> ♀Polizistin [poliˈtsɪstɪn] die <-, -nen> ◊ *Sie ist Polizistin von Beruf.* ♦ *Ein Polizist regelte den Verkehr.*

PE Sport [ʃpɔˈt] der <-(e)s> *no pl* ◊ *Er unterrichtet Sport am Gymnasium.* ♦ *In Sport haben wir gestern Volleyball gespielt.*

pea [noun] Erbse [ˈɛrpsə] die <-, -n> *most pl* ◊ *im Garten Erbsen pflanzen* ♦ *Erbsen und Karotten als Beilage*
ⓔ **be like two peas in a pod** sich gleichen wie ein Ei dem anderen

peace [noun] **1.** *(harmony, freedom from war)* Frieden [ˈfriːdṇ] der <-s> *no pl* ◊ *Der häusliche Frieden war gestört.* ♦ *Wie kann der Frieden gesichert werden?* a lasting peace ein dauerhafter Frieden be at peace with sb mit jdm in Frieden leben ◊ *Wir leben in Frieden mit unseren Nachbarn.* make peace sich mit jdm versöhnen [mɪt ... feˈzøːnən] <versöhnt sich, versöhnte sich, hat sich versöhnt> peace conference Friedenskonferenz [ˈfriːdṇskɔnfeˌrɛnts] die <-, -en> ◊ *eine Friedenskonferenz einberufen* peace negotiations Friedensverhandlungen [ˈfriːdṇsfeˌhandlʊŋən] die <-> *pl* **2.** *(tranquillity)* peace and quiet Ruhe [ˈruːə] die <-> *no pl* ◊ *Beim Lernen brauche ich viel Ruhe.* peace of mind innere Ruhe ◊ *durch Meditation innere Ruhe finden* in peace in Ruhe ◊ *sich in Ruhe unterhalten* leave sb in peace jdn in Ruhe lassen
ⓔ **be at peace** *(euph) (be dead)* in Frieden ruhen *(euph)* **disturb the peace** LAW die öffentliche Ordnung stören **hold your peace** sich zurückhalten

peaceable(-ably) [adj, adv] friedlich [ˈfriːtlɪç] ◊ *eine friedliche Demonstration* ♦ *Die Atmosphäre war sehr friedlich.* ♦ *Die Stämme leben friedlich miteinander.*

peaceful(ly) [adj, adv] *(non-violent, at peace, calm)*

A
B
C
D
E
F
G
H
I
J
K
L
M
N
O
P
Q
R
S
T
U
V
W
X
Y
Z

friedlich ['fri:tlɪç] ◊ *ein friedlicher Mensch* ♦ *Auf der Versammlung war die Stimmung nicht sehr friedlich.* ♦ *Die Demonstration verlief weitgehend friedlich.* ♦ *friedlich schlafen; (moment, place)* ruhig ['ru:ɪç] ◊ *ein rubiger Augenblick* ♦ *Es ist so herrlich ruhig hier!*

peach [noun] Pfirsich ['pfɪ'zɪç] der <–s, –e> ◊ *Sie isst gern Pfirsiche.*

peak [noun] 1. *(of a career, performance, period)* Höhepunkt ['hø:əpʊŋkt] der <–(e)s, –e> ◊ *Sie befand sich auf dem Höhepunkt ihrer Laufbahn.* ♦ *Um diese Zeit erreicht der Besucherandrang seinen Höhepunkt.; (on a graph)* Scheitelpunkt ['ʃaɛtlpʊŋkt] der <–(e)s, –e> 2. *(of a mountain)* Gipfel ['gɪpfl] der <–s, –> ◊ *der Gipfel des Matterhorns* ♦ *auf einen Gipfel steigen* ♦ *Welches ist der höchste Gipfel Deutschlands?; (sharp point)* Spitze ['ʃpɪtsə] die <–, –n> ◊ *Die Spitze des Felsens ragte aus dem Nebel.* 3. *(of a cap)* Schirm [ʃɪ'm] der <–(e)s, –e>

peanut [noun] Erdnuss ['e:gtnʊs] die <–, Erdnüsse> ◊ *geröstete Erdnüsse* peanut butter Erdnussbutter ['e:gtnʊsbʊtɐ] die <–> no pl

pear [noun] Birne ['bɪ'nə] die <–, –n> ◊ *ein Kilo Birnen*

pearl [noun] 1. *(jewel, sb/sth considered excellent)* Perle ['pɛ'lə] die <–, –n> ◊ *ein Ring mit einer echten Perle* ♦ *Sie ist eine Perle von einer Köchin.* pearl necklace Perlenkette ['pɛ'lɛnkətə] die <–, –n> 2. *(mother-of-pearl)* Perlmutt ['pɛ'lmʊt] das <–s> no pl ◊ *Der Griff des Messers ist aus Perlmutt.* ℗ cast pearls before swine Perlen vor die Säue werfen ♦ a pearl of wisdom ein kluger Spruch

peasant [noun] Bauer ['baʊɐ] der <–n, –n> *(also pej)* ◊ *Seine Eltern waren arme Bauern.* ♦ *So ein Bauer, er hat sich nicht einmal bedankt!* peasant woman Bäuerin ['bɔøərɪn] die <–, –nen>

pebble [noun] Kieselstein ['ki:zlʃtaɛn] der <–(e)s, –e>

peculiar [adj] 1. *(strange)* seltsam ['zɛltza:m] ◊ *Er ist ein seltsamer Typ.* ♦ *Ich finde ihr Benehmen seltsam.; (nauseous)* sb feels peculiar jdm ist etwas übel [ɪst ɛtvas 'y:bl] 2. *(special)* besondere [bə'zɔndərə] no comp/superl, only before ns <ein besonderer …, eine besondere …, ein besonderes …> ◊ *eine besondere Faszination auf jdn ausüben; (typical)* peculiar to sb/sth charakteristisch für jdn/ etw. [karakte'rɪstɪʃ fy:ɐ] ◊ *Dieses Verhalten ist charakteristisch für Wölfe.*

peculiarity [noun] 1. *(special feature or characteristic)* Besonderheit [bə'zɔndɐhaɛt] die <–, –en> ◊ *die Besonderheiten der Quantenphysik; (of behaviour, character)* Eigenheit ['aɛghaɛt] die <–, –en> ◊ *Eine seiner Eigenheiten war seine Sammelleidenschaft.* ♦ *die liebenswerten Eigenheiten der Italiener* 2. *(strangeness)* Eigentümlichkeit ['aɛgnty:mlɪçkaɛt] die <–, –en> ◊ *die Eigentümlichkeit eines Kunstwerks*

peculiarly [adv] 1. *(in a strange way)* seltsam ['zɛltza:m] ◊ *ein seltsam geformter Baum* 2. *(typically)* typisch ['ty:pɪʃ] ◊ *Diese Haltung gilt als typisch amerikanisch.* 3. *(extremely)* besonders [bə'zɔndɐs] no comp/superl ◊ *ein besonders schwieriges Problem*

pedal [noun] Pedal [pe'da:l] das <–s, –e> ◊ *in die Pedale treten* ♦ *ein Musikstück mit Pedal spielen* gas pedal Gaspedal ['ga:spe,da:l]

pedantic [adj] pedantisch [pe'dantɪʃ] ◊ *Sei nicht so*

pedantisch! ♦ *ein pedantischer Mensch*

pedestal [noun] Sockel ['zɔkl] der <–s, –> ◊ *Das Monument steht auf einem Sockel aus Marmor.* ℗ knock sb off their pedestal jdn von seinem Podest stürzen put sb on a pedestal jdn in den Himmel heben

pedestrian [noun] Fußgänger ['fu:sgɛŋɐ] der <–s, –> ℗Fußgängerin ['fu:sgɛŋərɪn] die <–, –nen> ◊ *Dieser Weg ist nur für Fußgänger und Radfahrer.*

pedestrian crossing [noun] Fußgängerüberweg ['fu:sgɛŋəly:beve:k] der <–(e)s, –e> ◊ *den Fußgängerüberweg benutzen*

pedestrian precinct [noun] Fußgängerzone ['fu:sgɛnɛtso:nə] die <–, –n> ◊ *Das Kaufhaus ist in der Fußgängerzone.*

pedigree [noun] 1. *(ancestors or a list thereof)* Stammbaum ['ʃtambaom] der <–(e)s, Stammbäume> ◊ *Ihr Stammbaum reicht bis ins 16. Jahrhundert zurück.* ♦ *einen Stammbaum erstellen; (animal)* be a pedigree reinrassig sein ['raenrasɪç zaen] +sein ◊ *Dieser Hund ist reinrassig.* 2. *(fig) (past achievements, distinction)* Tradition [tradi'tsjo:n] die <–, –en> no pl ◊ *eine Firma mit langer Tradition im Maschinenbau*

peel¹ [noun] Schale ['ʃa:lə] die <–, –n> take the peel off die Schale entfernen orange peel Orangenschale [o'ranʒnʃa:lə]

peel² [verb] 1. *(a fruit, vegetable)* schälen ['ʃɛ:lən] +haben ◊ *Kartoffeln/eine Orange schälen* 2. *(remove by pulling)* peel sth from sth etw. von etw. abziehen [fon …, aptsi:ən] <zieht ab, zog ab, hat abgezogen> ◊ *die Tapete vorsichtig von der Wand abziehen* peel sth off (sth) etw. (von etw.) abziehen ◊ *einen Aufkleber abziehen* 3. *(wallpaper)* sth peels off etw. löst sich ['lø:st zɪç] +haben ◊ *In den Ecken beginnt sich die Tapete zu lösen.; (paint)* etw. blättert ab [blɛtɐt 'ap] +haben ◊ *Die Farbe blättert langsam ab.; (dead skin)* etw. schält sich ['ʃɛ:lt zɪç] +haben ◊ *Seine Nase schält sich.*

• **peel off** [phras v] 1. *(a dress, glove)* abstreifen ['apʃtraefn] +haben ◊ *Sie streifte das enge Kleid ab.* 2. *(move in a different direction)* ausscheren ['aosʃe:rən] +sein ◊ *Ein Läufer/Fahrzeug scherte aus.*

peer¹ [noun] 1. *(of the same age, social group; referring to masculine or neuter nouns)* sb's peers seinesgleichen ['zaenəs'glaeçn] invariable He is very popular with his peers. Er ist bei seinesgleichen sehr beliebt. have/know no peers seinesgleichen suchen ◊ *Als Künstler sucht er seinesgleichen.; (referring to a woman or feminine noun)* ihresgleichen ['i:rəs'glaeçn] invariable ◊ *Sie verbringt ihre Zeit lieber mit ihresgleichen.* have/know no peers ihresgleichen suchen ◊ *Als Musikerin sucht sie ihresgleichen.* 2. *(noble)* dem hohen Adel Großbritanniens angehörende Person

peer² [verb] spähen ['ʃpɛ:ən] +haben ◊ *Er spähte aus dem Fenster.* ♦ *Sie spähte auf die Uhr.*

peg¹ [noun] 1. *(for wet clothing) (clothes)* peg Wäscheklammer ['vɛʃəklamɐ] die <–s, –> ◊ *Strümpfe mit Wäscheklammern an der Leine befestigen* 2. *(hook)* Haken ['ha:kŋ] der <–s, –> ◊ *eine Jacke an den Haken hängen* 3. *(for joining pieces of wood, in games)* Stift [ʃtɪft] der <–(e)s, –e> ◊ *den Stift in das gebohrte Loch stecken* 4. *(for tents)* Hering ['he:rɪŋ] der <–s, –e> ◊ *Heringe in den Boden schlagen*

⊛ bring sb down a peg or two jdm einen Dämpfer geben *(fam)* a peg on which to hang sth ein guter Aufhänger für etw.

peg² [verb] 1. *(washing on a line)* mit Klammern aufhängen [mɪt ˈklamən ˌaʊfhɛŋən] <hängt auf, hängte auf, hat aufgehängt> ◊ *Die Wäsche muss bei Wind mit Klammern aufgehängt werden.; (a tent)* im Boden verankern [ɪm ˈboːdn̩ fɛlˌaŋkən] <verankert, verankerte, hat verankert> peg sb to the ground jdn am Boden festhalten [am ˈboːdn̩ ˌfɛsthaltn̩] <hält fest, hielt fest, hat festgehalten> 2. *(make a value dependent on sth else)* peg sth to sth etw. an etw. [acc] binden [an ... ˌbɪndn̩] <bindet, band, hat gebunden> ◊ *eine Währung an eine andere binden;* (fix the level of wages, prices) peg sth at sth etw. auf etw. [acc] festsetzen [aʊf ... ˌfɛstzɛtsn̩] +haben ◊ *Jedes Jahr werden die Löhne neu festgesetzt.* ♦ *Der Preis wurde auf 149 Euro festgesetzt.* 3. *(consider, categorize)* peg sb as sth jdn für etw. halten [fy:ɐ̯ ... haltn̩] <hält, hielt, hat gehalten> ◊ *Wir haben ihn von Anfang an für einen Betrüger gehalten.*

pelvis [noun] Becken [ˈbɛkn̩] das <-s, ->

pen [noun] 1. *(generic)* Stift [ʃtɪft] der <-(e)s, -e> ◊ *Ich habe keinen Stift dabei.* ♦ *Haben Sie Papier und Stift zur Hand?* red pen Rotstift [ˈroːtʃtɪft] ◊ *einen Text mit Rotstift korrigieren* fountain pen Füller [ˈfʏlɐ] der <-s, -> ◊ *mit Füller schreiben* ballpoint pen Kugelschreiber [ˈkuːɡl̩ʃraɛbɐ] der <-s, ->; *(ink)* Tinte [ˈtɪntə] die <-, -n> ◊ *Der Brief war mit schwarzer Tinte geschrieben.* 2. *(for farm animals)* Pferch [pfɛrç] der <-(e)s, -e> ◊ *die Schafe in den Pferch treiben* 3. *(in the US: prison)* Knast [knast] der <-(e)s, Knäste or also Knaste> *(fam)* ◊ *Ihr Mann sitzt im Knast.*

⊛ put pen to paper zur Feder greifen the pen is mightier than the sword die Feder ist mächtiger als das Schwert

penalty [noun] 1. *(punishment)* Strafe [ˈʃtraːfə] die <-, -n> ◊ *eine schwere/strenge Strafe über jdn verhängen* sth carries a penalty auf etw. [acc] steht eine Strafe ◊ *Auf dieses Verbrechen steht eine schwere Strafe.* death penalty Todesstrafe [ˈtoːdəsˌʃtraːfə] 2. *(in football)* Elfmeter [ɛlfˈmeːtɐ] der <-s, -> ◊ *einen Elfmeter bekommen/verwandeln* ⊛ pay the penalty for sth *(deal with unpleasant consequences)* für etw. büßen müssen ◊ *Wir mussten schon bald für die schlechte Planung büßen.* that's the penalty your pay for das ist die Strafe dafür, dass ◊ *Das ist die Strafe dafür, dass du nicht auf mich gehört hast.*

pencil [noun] Bleistift [ˈblaɛʃtɪft] der <-(e)s, -e> ◊ *Er nahm einen Bleistift und begann zu zeichnen.* ♦ *einen Bleistift anspitzen* in pencil mit Bleistift ◊ *Jemand hatte mit Bleistift seinen Namen in das Buch geschrieben.* colo(u)red pencil Buntstift [ˈbʊntʃtɪft]

pencil case [noun] Federmäppchen [ˈfeːdɐmɛpçən] das <-s, ->

pencil sharpener [noun] Spitzer [ˈʃpɪtsɐ] der <-s, ->

pendant [noun] Anhänger [ˈanhɛŋɐ] der <-s, -> ◊ *Sie trug einen goldenen Anhänger an ihrer Kette.*

pendulum [noun] Pendel [ˈpɛndl̩] das <-s, -> ◊ *Das Pendel der Uhr schwingt hin und her.*

⊛ the pendulum has swung back in favo(u)r of sth die Tendenz geht wieder in Richtung ... [gen] ◊ *Die Tendenz geht wieder in Richtung Ehe und Familie.*

penetrate [verb] 1. *(enter into)* penetrate (into) sth in etw. [acc] eindringen [ɪn ... ˌaɛndrɪŋən] <dringt ein, drang ein, ist eingedrungen> ◊ *Ein Splitter war in die Haut eingedrungen.* ♦ *in feindliches Gebiet eindringen* 2. *(be heard, felt, noticed)* sth penetrates sth etw. dringt durch etw. [drɪŋt ˈdʊrç] <dringt, drang, ist gedrungen> ◊ *Kein Geräusch drang durch die schweren Türen.* 3. *(be understood)* verstanden werden [fɛˈʃtandn̩ veːɐ̯dn̩] <wird, wurde, ist worden> Has that penetrated? Hast du das verstanden? penetrate sb's consciousness zu jdm durchdringen [tsu: ... ˌdʊrçdrɪŋən] <dringt durch, drang durch, ist durchgedrungen> 4. *(infiltrate)* infiltrieren [ɪnfɪlˈtriːrən] <infiltriert, infiltrierte, hat infiltriert> ◊ *eine Partei infiltrieren* 5. *(during intercourse)* penetrate sb in jdn eindringen [ɪn ... ˌaɛndrɪŋən] <dringt ein, drang ein, ist eingedrungen>

penis [noun] Penis [ˈpeːnɪs] der <-, -se>

penny [noun] Penny [ˈpɛniː] der <-s, -s or Pence> ◊ *Das kostet doch nur ein paar Pence.* ♦ *Er fand einen Penny auf dem Boden.*

⊛ not have a penny to your name keinen Pfennig haben in for a penny, in for a pound wennschon, dennschon not a penny the wiser genauso klug wie zuvor the penny dropped der Groschen ist gefallen *(fam)* spend a penny mal müssen *(fam)*

pension [noun] Rente [ˈrɛntə] die <-, -n> ◊ *die gesetzliche Rente* ♦ *Anspruch auf Rente haben* draw a pension eine Rente beziehen; *(of a civil servant)* Pension [paŋˈzjoːn] die <-, -en> ◊ *Von meiner Pension kann ich gut leben.* occupational pension Betriebsrente [bəˈtriːpsˌrɛntə] pension contribution Rentenbeitrag [ˈrɛntn̩baɛtraːk] der <-(e)s, Rentenbeiträge>

pensioner [noun] Rentner [ˈrɛntnɐ] der <-s, -> ♀Rentnerin [ˈrɛntnərɪn] die <-, -nen> ◊ *eine rüstige Rentnerin*; *(former civil servant)* Pensionär [paŋzjoːˈnɛːɐ̯] der <-s, -e> ♀Pensionärin [paŋzjoːˈnɛːrɪn] die <-, -nen> ◊ *Er ist seit drei Jahren Pensionär.*

pension scheme [noun] Rentenversicherung [ˈrɛntn̩fɛˌzɪçərʊŋ] die <-, -en> ◊ *in die gesetzliche Rentenversicherung einzahlen*

penultimate [adj] vorletzte [ˈfoːɐ̯lɛtstə] no comp/superl, only before ns ◊ *Erst im vorletzten Kapitel erfährt man, wer sie ist.*

people [noun] 1. *(pl of person, human beings, men or women sharing the same qualities)* Menschen [ˈmɛnʃn̩] die <-> pl ◊ *Bei dem Unfall wurden drei Menschen verletzt.* ♦ *Alle Menschen auf der Welt wünschen sich Frieden.* ♦ *Menschen mit Behinderung; (in informal context, for addressing sb)* Leute [ˈlɔɔtə] die <-> only pl ◊ *Manche Leute wollen das nicht glauben.* ♦ *Solche Musik gefällt den jungen Leuten.* ♦ *Auf der Party waren etwa 50 Leute.* ♦ *Also, Leute, was machen wir jetzt?* ♦ *Was werden bloß die Leute sagen?* ♦ *Du bezahlst deine Leute gut.;* (in general, one, they) man [man] ◊ *Man sagt, er habe eine Tochter aus erster Ehe.* ♦ *Man ist in diesen Sachen heutzutage toleranter.* 2. *(nation, masses)* Volk [fɔlk] das <-(e)s, Völker> ◊ *das deutsche/französische/jüdische Volk* ♦ *die Völker Afrikas* ♦ *das einfache Volk* the people das Volk ◊ *Der Bundestag wird vom Volk gewählt.* ♦ *ein Mann aus dem Volk*

⊛ sb of all people ausgerechnet jd ◊ *Warum muss*

das ausgerechnet mir passieren?

pepper [noun] **1.** *(spice)* Pfeffer ['pfɛfɐ] der <–s> no pl ◊ *grüner/schwarzer/weißer Pfeffer* ♦ *ein Gericht mit Pfeffer und Salz würzen* **2.** *(vegetable)* Paprika ['paprika:] die <–, –(s)> ◊ *die Paprika in Streifen schneiden* ♦ *Zu Mittag gibt es gefüllte Paprika.*

per [prep] pro [pro:] [+acc] ◊ *Sie verdient 20 Euro pro Stunde.* ♦ *Der Eintritt kostet zehn Euro pro Person.*

as per gemäß [gə'mɛ:s] *sing nouns without article or attribute are not declined when following this prep,* otherwise [+dat] ◊ *Wir werden das gemäß unserer Vereinbarung regeln.*

perceive [verb] **1.** *(understand, notice using your senses)* wahrnehmen ['va:ˈneːmən] <nimmt wahr, nahm war, hat wahrgenommen> ◊ *Kinder nehmen ihre Eltern auf unterschiedliche Weise wahr.* ♦ *Wir nehmen unsere Umwelt primär mit den Augen wahr.* ♦ *jdn/etw. als Bedrohung wahrnehmen* perceive sb/sth to be sth jdn/etw. für etw. halten [fy:ɐ̯ ... haltn̩] <hält, hielt, hat gehalten> **2.** *(realize)* erkennen [ɛ'kɛnən] <erkennt, erkannte, hat erkannt> ◊ *Sie erkannte die Wahrheit viel zu spät.* ♦ *Er erkannte sofort, wo das Problem war.*

per cent [noun] Prozent [pro'tsɛnt] das <–(e)s, –e or –> pl 'Prozent' *when used with figures* ◊ *20 Prozent von 100 sind 20.* ♦ *Der Artikel ist um 20 Prozent reduziert.* ♦ *Bruchteile als Prozente darstellen*

percentage [noun] **1.** *(rate)* Prozentsatz [pro'tsɛntzats] der <–(e)s, Prozentsätze> highest/lowest percentage of sth/people höchster/niedrigster Prozentsatz an etw. [dat]/Menschen ◊ *Welches Land hat den niedrigsten Prozentsatz an Internetnutzern?*; *(proportion, part)* Teil [taɛl] der <–(e)s, –e> ◊ *ein großer Teil der Bevölkerung* ♦ *Einen großen Teil meines Gehalts gebe ich für die Miete aus.* **2.** *(commission, payment)* Anteil ['antaɛl] der <–(e)s, –e> ◊ *Wann bekomme ich denn nun meinen Anteil?* ♦ *seinen Anteil fordern*

ⓔ there is no percentage in doing sth es bringt nichts, etw. zu tun

perception [noun] **1.** *(conception)* Auffassung ['aoffasʊŋ] die <–, –en> ◊ *unterschiedliche Auffassungen von Wahrheit* ♦ *eine weit verbreitete Auffassung* **2.** *(ability to see, hear, feel)* Wahrnehmung ['va:ˈneːmʊŋ] die <–, –en> ◊ *die Wahrnehmung von Farben* ♦ *Diese Drogen verändern die Wahrnehmung.* **3.** *(sharpness, awareness)* Auffassungsgabe ['aoffasʊŋsga:bə] die <–> no pl ◊ *Du besitzt eine erstaunliche Auffassungsgabe.*

perfect¹ [noun] GRAM Perfekt ['pɛʁfɛkt] das <–s, –e> most sing ◊ *ein Verb im Perfekt*

perfect² [adj] **1.** *(faultless, excellent)* perfekt [pɛʁ'fɛkt] <perfekter, am perfektesten> ◊ *Sein Französisch ist perfekt.* ♦ *Den perfekten Partner gibt es nicht.* ♦ *Der Wagen ist in perfektem Zustand.*; *(completely suitable)* ideal [ide'a:l] ◊ *Dieses Hotel ist ideal für Kongresse.* ♦ *ein idealer Wein zum Fisch* **2.** *(absolute, complete)* völlig ['fœlɪç] no comp/superl, only before ns ◊ *völliger Unsinn* **3.** GRAM perfect tense Perfekt ['pɛʁfɛkt] das <–s, –e> most sing ◊ *ein Verb im Perfekt*

perfection [noun] **1.** *(state)* Vollkommenheit [fɔl'kɔmənhaɛt] die <–, –en> ◊ *moralische Vollkommenheit*; *(of sb's beauty, skin, figure)* Makellosigkeit ['ma:kl̩lo:zɪçkaɛt] die <–> no pl **2.** *(striving to make*

sth perfect) Perfektion [pɛʁfɛk'tsio:n] die <–> no pl ◊ *die Perfektion der Technik* to perfection bis zur Perfektion

perfectly [adv] **1.** *(flawlessly, in the best possible way)* perfekt [pɛʁ'fɛkt] <perfekter, am perfektesten> ◊ *die perfekte Lösung* ♦ *Das Bild passt perfekt zur Einrichtung des Wohnzimmers.* ♦ *Sie spricht perfekt Englisch.* **2.** *(absolutely, completely)* völlig ['fœlɪç] no comp/superl ◊ *Es ist völlig normal, wenn Kinder so reagieren.* ♦ *Ich bin damit völlig zufrieden.* know perfectly well ganz genau wissen [gants gə'nao ˌvɪsn̩] <weiß, wusste, hat gewusst> ◊ *Du weißt ganz genau, dass ich diese Musik nicht mag.*

perform [verb] **1.** *(an experiment, operation, check)* durchführen ['dʊʁçfyːrən] +haben ◊ *Das Experiment wurde erfolgreich durchgeführt.* ♦ *einen Test durchführen*; *(a task, duty, function)* erfüllen [ɛ'fʏlən] <erfüllt, erfüllte, hat erfüllt> ◊ *Sie hat ihre Aufgaben stets gut erfüllt.* ♦ *eine Kontrollfunktion erfüllen*; *(a ceremony, ritual)* vollziehen [fɔl'tsi:ən] <vollzieht, vollzog, hat vollzogen> ◊ *Wer wird die Trauung vollziehen?*; *(a miracle)* vollbringen [fɔl'brɪŋən] <vollbringt, vollbrachte, hat vollbracht> ◊ *Ich kann leider keine Wunder vollbringen.* **2.** MUS, THEAT *(a play, an opera)* aufführen ['aoffyːrən] +haben ◊ *eine Oper aufführen*; *(a piece of music, song)* vortragen ['fo:ɐ̯tra:gn̩] <trägt vor, hat vorgetragen> ◊ *Eine Sängerin trug Lieder von Schubert vor.* ♦ *Das Ensemble trug mehrere mittelalterliche Tänze vor.*; *(play a part)* spielen ['ʃpiːlən] +haben ◊ *Sie spielt die Rolle der Linda.* ♦ *Spielst du auch in diesem Stück?* **3.** *(in a test, an exam, election)* perform well/badly gut/schlecht abschneiden ['gu:t/'ʃlɛçt ˌapʃnaɛdn̩] <schneidet ab, schnitt ab, hat abgeschnitten> ◊ *Das Auto hat im Test gut abgeschnitten.* ♦ *Die Partei schnitt bei den Wahlen schlecht ab.*

performance [noun] **1.** *(effectiveness, level to which sth was achieved)* Leistung ['laɛstʊŋ] die <–, –en> ◊ *die Leistungen der Studenten vergleichen* ♦ *eine bessere Leistung bringen* ♦ *jdn nach Leistung bezahlen* ♦ *ein Wagen mit ausgezeichneter Leistung* ♦ *Dich zu einem Zahnarztbesuch zu überreden war eine echte Leistung!* **2.** *(of a play, an opera)* Aufführung ['aoffyːrʊŋ] die <–, –en> ◊ *Die Aufführung von „Hamlet" beginnt um 19 Uhr.*; *(in a cinema)* Vorstellung ['fo:ɐ̯ʃtɛlʊŋ] die <–, –en> ◊ *Wann ist die letzte Vorstellung?* give a performance of sth etw. aufführen ['aoffyːrən] +haben ◊ *Die Kinder führten das Stück „Hänsel und Gretel" auf.*; *(of a particular role)* Darstellung ['da:ʁʃtɛlʊŋ] die <–, –en> ◊ *Die Kritiker lobten ihre Darstellung der Maria Stuart.* **3.** *(fulfillment of a duty, task)* Erfüllung [ɛ'fʏlʊŋ] die <–> no pl ◊ *jdn an der Erfüllung seiner Pflichten hindern* ♦ *die Erfüllung einer Aufgabe*

performer [noun] **1.** *(artist)* Künstler ['kʏnstlɐ] der <–s, –> ♀Künstlerin ['kʏnstlərɪn] die <–, –nen> ◊ *Heute Abend treten verschiedene Künstler auf.* **2.** *(at school)* poor/good performer schwacher/guter Schüler [ʃvaxɐ/ˌguːtɐ 'ʃyːlɐ] <–s, –> ♀schwache/gute Schülerin [ˌʃvaxə/ˌguːtɐ 'ʃyːlərɪn] die <–, –nen> ◊ *In Deutsch ist er ein schwacher Schüler.* ♦ *Sie war immer eine gute Schülerin.* top performer Spitzenschüler ['ʃpɪtsn̩ʃyːlɐ] Spitzenschülerin ['ʃpɪtsn̩ʃyːlərɪn]

perfume [noun] **1.** *(substance)* Parfüm [pa'fyːm] das <–s, –e or –s> ◊ *ein Parfüm mit herber Note* **2.** *(smell)* Duft [dʊft] der <–(e)s, Düfte> ◊ *der Duft*

von Rosen ♦ *Der Duft der Blüten war intensiv.*

perhaps [adv] vielleicht [fi'laeçt] ◊ *Vielleicht solltest du mal zum Arzt gehen.* ♦ *„Gehst du heute Abend noch weg?" — „ Vielleicht."* ♦ *Der Mann war vielleicht 70 Jahre alt.*

period [noun] **1.** *(length of time)* period *(of time)* Zeitraum ['tsaetraom] der <–(e)s, Zeiträume> ◊ *etw. über einen langen Zeitraum hinweg tun* ♦ *etw. umfasst einen Zeitraum von fünf Tagen/Wochen* ♦ *für den Zeitraum von einem Jahr* for a three-month period drei Monate lang [drae 'mo:natə laŋ] ◊ *Sie war drei Monate lang im Krankenhaus.* for an unlimited period unbegrenzt ['ʊnbəgrɛntst] *no comp/ superl* ◊ *Ist Mineralwasser unbegrenzt haltbar?* within a three-month period innerhalb von drei Monaten [ɪnehalp fɔn drae 'mo:natn] within the period stipulated fristgerecht ['frɪstgərɛçt] *no comp/superl* ◊ *die fristgerechte Erledigung der Aufgaben* ♦ *die Steuererklärung fristgerecht einreichen; (in sb's life)* Zeit [tsaet] die <–, –en> ◊ *Zu dieser Zeit ging es mir nicht besonders gut.; (in an artist's career)* Periode [pe'rjo:də] die <–, –n> ◊ *Picassos blaue Periode* **2.** *(age, epoch)* Zeitalter ['tsaet|alte] das <–s, –> ◊ *das Zeitalter der Römer* **3.** SCHOOL Stunde ['ʃtʊndə] die <–, –n> ◊ *Du hast heute zwei Stunden Chemie.* ♦ *In der ersten Stunde haben wir Mathe.* **4.** MED Periode [pe'rjo:də] die <–, –n> ◊ *Sie hat ihre Periode.* **5.** LING *(in the US: full stop)* Punkt [pʊŋkt] der <–(e)s, –e> ◊ *Am Ende eines Aussagesatzes macht man einen Punkt.*

   ◉ **period** *(and that's that)* und damit basta ◊ *Du bleibst heute zu Hause und damit basta!*

periodical [noun] Zeitschrift ['tsaetʃrɪft] die <–, –en> ◊ *Im Wartezimmer liegen immer Zeitschriften aus.* ♦ *Sie hat mehrere Zeitschriften abonniert.*

permanent(ly) [adj, adv] *(solution, relationship, damage)* dauerhaft ['daoehaft] *no comp/superl* ◊ *eine dauerhafte Lösung finden* ♦ *Wie dauerhaft wird der Frieden sein?* ♦ *Die Arbeitsplätze müssen dauerhaft gesichert werden.; (address, job, arrangement)* fest [fɛst] *no comp/superl* ◊ *ein fester Wohnsitz in London* ♦ *Sie war fest angestellt.; (agreement, permission)* unbefristet ['ʊnbəfrɪstət] *no comp/superl* ◊ *eine unbefristete Aufenthaltserlaubnis* ♦ *Die Lizenz wurde unbefristet verlängert.* permanent employee Festangestellte ['fɛst|angəʃtɛltə] der/die <–n, –n, die Festangestellten> *but: eine Festangestellter/ eine Festangestellte* ◊ *In der Firma sind überwiegend Festangestellte beschäftigt.*

permeable [adj] durchlässig ['dʊ'çlɛsɪç] ◊ *Das Material ist für Wasser nicht durchlässig.*

permissible [adj] zulässig ['tsu:lɛsɪç] *no comp/superl* ◊ *Diese Methode ist zulässig.* ♦ *zulässige Hilfsmittel*

permission [noun] Erlaubnis [e'laopnɪs] die <–, –se> *most sing* ◊ *Franz bat um die Erlaubnis, früher gehen zu dürfen.* ♦ *jdm die Erlaubnis für etw. geben* ask sb's permission jdn um Erlaubnis fragen

permit¹ [noun] Genehmigung [gə'ne:mɪgʊŋ] die <–, –en> ◊ *jdm eine Genehmigung erteilen* ♦ *ohne schriftliche Genehmigung* export permit Ausfuhrgenehmigung ['aosfu:egə,ne:mɪgʊŋ] work permit Arbeitserlaubnis ['a'baets|elaopnɪs] die <–, –se>

permit² [verb] erlauben [e'laobm] <erlaubt, erlaubte, hat erlaubt> ◊ *Meine Eltern erlauben mir nicht, so spät noch wegzugehen.* ♦ *Es ist nicht erlaubt zu*

rauchen. permit me to do sth erlauben Sie, dass ich etw. tue ◊ *Erlauben Sie, dass ich mich vorstelle.* permit of sth etw. zulassen ['tsu:lasn] <lässt zu, ließ zu, hat zugelassen> ◊ *Ihr Verhalten lässt nur eine Schlussfolgerung zu.* weather permitting wenn das Wetter es zulässt

perpendicular(ly) [adj, adv] *(vertical)* senkrecht ['zɛŋkrɛçt] <senkrechter, am senkrechtesten> *seldom comp/superl* ◊ *eine senkrechte Kletterwand* ♦ *Der Berg fiel fast senkrecht ab.* be perpendicular to sth senkrecht zu etw. stehen

perpetrator [noun] Täter ['tɛ:te] der <–s, –> ♀Täterin ['tɛ:tərɪn] die <–, –nen> ◊ *Die Täter konnten unerkannt entkommen.* perpetrators of domestic violence Täter, die häusliche Gewalt ausüben/ ausgeübt haben

perpetual(ly) [adj, adv] **1.** *(continuous)* anhaltend ['anhaltnt] *no comp/superl, only before ns* ◊ *eine anhaltende Identitätskrise* in a perpetual condition of insecurity/fear in ständiger Unsicherheit/Angst [ɪn ʃtɛndɪgɛ 'ʊnzɪçehaet/'aŋst]; *(eternal)* ewig ['e:vɪç] *no comp/superl* ◊ *Hier herrscht ewiger Winter.* **2.** LAW *(of lasting validity)* unbegrenzt gültig [,ʊnbəgrɛntst 'gʏltɪç] *no comp/superl* ◊ *Das Abkommen ist unbegrenzt gültig.* ♦ *eine unbegrenzt gültige Lizenz*

persecute [verb] **1.** *(treat badly because of different religion, race etc.)* verfolgen [fe'fɔlgn] <verfolgt, verfolgte, hat verfolgt> ◊ *eine Minderheit verfolgen* **2.** *(harrass)* belästigen [bə'lɛstɪgn] <belästigt, belästigte, hat belästigt> ◊ *Sie wurde immer wieder von ihrem Exmann belästigt.*

persevere [verb] durchhalten ['dʊ'çhaltn] <hält durch, hielt durch, hat durchgehalten> ◊ *Die Arbeit war schwer, aber ich habe durchgehalten.* persevere in/ with sth etw. unbeirrt fortsetzen [,ʊnba|ɪ'rt 'fɔ'tzetsn] +haben ◊ *Sie setzte ihr Studium unbeirrt fort.*

persist [verb] **1.** *(person: be tenacious)* beharren [bə'haren] <beharrt, beharrte, hat beharrt> ◊ *„Ich will das aber nicht tun", beharrte er.* persist in sth auf etw. [dat] beharren ◊ *auf seinem Standpunkt beharren* persist in doing sth darauf beharren, etw. weiterhin zu tun persist with sth mit etw. nicht aufhören [mɪt ... nɪçt 'aofhø:rən] +haben **2.** *(condition: last, continue)* andauern ['andaoen] <dauert an, dauerte an, hat angedauert> ◊ *Das Fieber kann noch einige Tage andauern.*

persistent(ly) [adj, adv] hartnäckig ['ha'tnɛkɪç] ◊ *Er war sehr hartnäckig und setzte sich schließlich durch.* ♦ *eine hartnäckige Erkältung* ♦ *etw. hartnäckig verweigern*

person [noun] **1.** *(in official contexts, with numbers, grammatical category)* Person [pɛ'zo:n] die <–, –en> ◊ *Drei Personen werden noch vermisst.* ♦ *Der Eintritt beträgt fünf Euro pro Person.* ♦ *Die erste Person Singular ist „ich".; (human being)* Mensch [mɛnʃ] der <–en, –en> ◊ *Er ist ein netter Mensch.* ♦ *ältere Menschen* ◊ *per also* als Mensch **2.** *(person with a liking for sth particular)* ... person ...-Typ [ty:p] der <–s, –en> football person Fußball-Typ ['fu:sbalty:p]

   ◉ **do sth in person** etw. persönlich tun **have sth on your person** etw. dabeihaben

personal [adj] persönlich [pɛ'zø:nlɪç] ◊ *über seine persönlichen Erfahrungen sprechen* ♦ *Werden Sie nicht gleich persönlich!* for personal reasons aus

persönlichen Gründen sb's personal life jds Privatleben [pri'va:tle:bm̩] das <–s> no pl
personality ⸢noun⸣ Persönlichkeit [pɛrˈzø:nlɪçkae̯t] die <–, –en> ◊ die Wohnung eines Menschen als Spiegelbild seiner Persönlichkeit ♦ Sie besitzt viel Persönlichkeit. ♦ eine berühmte Persönlichkeit personality traits Persönlichkeitsmerkmale [pɛrˈzø:nlɪçkae̯tsmɛrkma:lə] die <–> pl
personally ⸢adv⸣ persönlich [pɛrˈzø:nlɪç] ◊ Kennen Sie ihn persönlich? ♦ Ich persönlich halte davon nichts. ♦ etw. persönlich nehmen
personal pronoun ⸢noun⸣ Personalpronomen [pɛrˈzo:naːlpro,no:mən] das <–s, – or Personalpronomina> ◊ „Ich" und „du" sind Personalpronomen.
personnel ⸢noun⸣ 1. (in a company etc.) Personal [pɛrˈzo:naːl] das <–s> no pl ◊ weniger Personal beschäftigen; (on a plane, ship) Besatzung [bəˈzatsʊn] die <–, –en> 2. (department) Personalabteilung [pɛrˈzo:naːllaptae̯lʊn] die <–, –en> ◊ Er arbeitet in der Personalabteilung.
perspective ⸢noun⸣ Perspektive [pɛrˈspɛkˈti:və] die <–, –n> ◊ Auf diesem Bild stimmt die Perspektive nicht. ♦ aus der Perspektive einer allein erziehenden Mutter from a historical perspective aus historischer Perspektive get sth in perspective etw. aus der richtigen Perspektive betrachten
persuade ⸢verb⸣ 1. (talk into) überreden [ybeˈre:dn̩] <überredet, überredete, hat überredet> ◊ Der Makler hat sie zum Kauf des Hauses überredet. ♦ Sie wollte ihn überreden, mit ihr ins Kino zu gehen. 2. (convince) überzeugen [ybeˈtsɔø̯gn̩] <überzeugt, überzeugte, hat überzeugt> ◊ Sie konnte ihn überzeugen, den neuen Job anzunehmen. ♦ Er konnte sie von seiner Unschuld überzeugen.
persuasion ⸢noun⸣ 1. (persuading) Überredung [ybeˈre:dʊn] die <–, –en> most sing ◊ Durch Überredung konnten wir sie dazu bringen, ins Flugzeug zu steigen. powers of persuasion Überredungskünste [ybeˈre:dʊnskynstə] die <–> pl 2. (belief) Überzeugung [ybeˈtsɔø̯gʊn] die <–, –en> ◊ einer bestimmten Überzeugung anhängen
persuasive(ly) ⸢adj, adv⸣ überzeugend [ybeˈtsɔø̯gn̩t] ◊ ein überzeugendes Argument ♦ Das ist sehr überzeugend. ♦ überzeugend argumentieren
pervert ⸢verb⸣ 1. (deprave) verderben [feˈdɛrbm̩] <verdirbt, verdarb, hat verdorben> ◊ Der Reichtum hat ihn verdorben. ♦ die Jugend verderben 2. (distort) verzerren [feˈtsɛrən] <verzerrt, verzerrte, hat verzerrt> ◊ die Wahrheit verzerren
perverted → **pervert** ⸢adj⸣ pervers [pɛrˈvɛrs] <perverser, am perversesten> ◊ eine perverse Sexualität ♦ Diese Ansichten sind pervers!
pessimistic(ally) ⸢adj⸣ pessimistisch [pɛsiˈmɪstɪʃ] ◊ eine pessimistische Einstellung ♦ Die Experten sind sehr pessimistisch. ♦ etw. pessimistisch sehen
pest ⸢noun⸣ 1. zoo (parasites) Ungeziefer [ˈʊngətsi:fe] das <–s> no pl ◊ Die Pflanze ist voller Ungeziefer. 2. (person) Nervensäge [ˈnɛrfn:zɛ:gə] die <–, –n> (fam) ◊ die kleinen Nervensägen; (thing) Plage [ˈpla:gə] die <–, –n> ◊ Die Arbeit ist eine Plage.
pester ⸢verb⸣ nerven [ˈnɛrfn̩] +haben ◊ Hör auf mich zu nerven! pester sb for sth jdn wegen etw. nerven
pet¹ ⸢noun⸣ 1. (animal) Haustier [ˈhao̯sti:g] das <–(e)s, –e> ◊ Haustiere halten 2. (favo(u)rite) Liebling [ˈli:plɪŋ] der <–s, –e> ◊ Er war der Liebling

des Dozenten. 3. (fam) (loveable person) Schatz [ʃats] der <–es, Schätze> ◊ Danke, du Schatz! ♦ Er ist wirklich ein Schatz.
pet² ⸢verb⸣ 1. (touch gently) streicheln [ˈʃtrae̯çln̩] +haben ◊ Er streichelte das Kaninchen. ♦ Sie streichelte ihn sanft. 2. (sexually) fummeln [ˈfʊml̩n] +haben (fam)
petition ⸢noun⸣ 1. (list of signatures) Unterschriftenliste [ˈʊnteʃrɪftn̩lɪstə] die <–, –n> ◊ eine Unterschriftenliste unterzeichnen; (request) Petition [petiˈtsjo:n] die <–, –en> ◊ Sie reichten eine Petition ein. 2. LAW Antrag [ˈantra:k] der <–(e)s, Anträge> file a petition einen Antrag einreichen petition for divorce Scheidungsantrag [ˈʃae̯dʊŋslantra:k]
pet name ⸢noun⸣ Kosename [ˈko:zəna:mə] der <–ns, –n>
petrol ⸢noun⸣ Benzin [bɛnˈtsi:n] das <–s, –e> most sing ◊ Wir tanken bleifreies Benzin. ♦ Fährt das Auto mit Benzin oder mit Diesel? I need some petrol. Ich muss noch tanken.
petroleum ⸢noun⸣ Erdöl [ˈe:gtˈlø:l] das <–(e)s, –e> most sing ◊ Erdöl fördern
petrol station ⸢noun⸣ Tankstelle [ˈtaŋkʃtɛlə] die <–, –n>
petticoat ⸢noun⸣ Unterrock [ˈʊnterɔk] der <–(e)s, Unterröcke>
petty ⸢adj⸣ 1. (not important, trivial) belanglos [bəˈlaŋlo:s] <belangloser, am belanglosesten> ◊ eine belanglose Unterhaltung ♦ Der Streit war belanglos. 2. (small-minded) kleinlich [ˈklae̯nlɪç] ◊ Musst du immer so kleinlich sein! ♦ ein kleinlicher Mensch 3. (minor) klein [klae̯n] ◊ ein kleiner Beamter petty criminal Kleinkriminelle [ˈklae̯nkrimi,nɛlə] der/die <–n, die Kleinkriminellen> but: ein Kleinkrimineller/ eine Kleinkriminelle
phantom ⸢noun⸣ 1. (sb's ghost) Geist [gae̯st] der <–(e)s, –er> ◊ In dem alten Haus spukt ein Geist. 2. (sth unreal) Phantom [fanˈto:m] das <–s, –e> ◊ Sie jagten einem Phantom hinterher.
pharmacist ⸢noun⸣ Apotheker [apoˈte:ke] der <–s, –> ♀Apothekerin [apoˈte:kərɪn] die <–, –nen> ◊ Sie ist den Rat des Apothekers befolgen
pharmacy ⸢noun⸣ 1. (shop) Apotheke [apoˈte:kə] die <–, –n> ◊ Dieses Medikament gibt es nur in der Apotheke. 2. (science) Pharmazie [farˈma:tsi:] die <–> no pl ◊ Sie hat Pharmazie studiert.
phase ⸢noun⸣ Phase [ˈfa:zə] die <–, –n> ◊ eine wichtige Phase in meinem Leben ♦ der Mond in der abnehmenden Phase
PhD ⸢noun⸣ Dr. [ˈdɔkto:g] Adrian Stevens PhD Dr. Adrian Stevens do a PhD promovieren [promoˈvi:rən] <promoviert, promovierte, hat promoviert> ◊ phenomenon ⸢noun⸣ Phänomen [fɛnoˈme:n] das <–s, –e> ◊ Dieses Phänomen muss untersucht werden. ♦ Er ist ein echtes Phänomen.
philosopher ⸢noun⸣ Philosoph [filoˈzo:f] der <–en, –en> ♀Philosophin [filoˈzo:fɪn] die <–, –nen> ◊ Sie ist weniger Dichterin als Philosophin. ♦ ein berühmter Philosoph hat einmal gesagt: …
philosophical ⸢adj⸣ philosophisch [filoˈzo:fɪʃ] no comp/superl, mostly before ns ◊ ein philosophisches Weltbild
ⓔ be philosophical about sth (accept without getting annoyed) sich mit etw. abfinden
philosophy ⸢noun⸣ Philosophie [filozoˈfi:] die <–, –n> ◊ Philosophie studieren ♦ Wie lautet deine Philoso-

phie?

phone¹ [noun] **1.** *(telephone)* Telefon ['teːləfoːn] das <–s, –e> ◊ *Bestellen Sie per Telefon, Fax oder E-Mail.* answer the phone ans Telefon gehen on the phone am Telefon by phone telefonisch [teleˈfoːnɪʃ] no comp/superl ◊ *Termine nur nach telefonischer Voranmeldung.* ♦ *Sie haben mir telefonisch zugesagt.* **2.** *(receiver)* Hörer ['høːrɐ] der <–s, –> ◊ *den Hörer abheben/auflegen*

phone² [verb] phone (in/up) anrufen ['anruːfn̩] <ruft an, rief an, hat angerufen> ◊ *Sie hat ihn in der Arbeit angerufen.* ♦ *Hat jemand für mich angerufen?* ♦ *Er hat mehrmals angerufen.* phone in sick sich telefonisch krankmelden [tele,foːnɪʃ ˈkraŋkmɛldn̩] <meldet sich krank, meldete sich krank, hat sich krankgemeldet>; *(a message)* phone sth in etw. telefonisch übermitteln [tele,foːnɪʃ ybɐˈmɪtl̩n] <übermittelt, übermittelte, hat übermittelt> ◊ *Er hat seinen Bericht telefonisch übermittelt.*

phone call [noun] Anruf ['anruːf] der <–(e)s, –e> ◊ *Ich muss noch einen Anruf erledigen.* ♦ *einen Anruf erwarten*

phonecard [noun] Telefonkarte [tele'foːnkaˈtə] die <–, –n>

phonetic alphabet [noun] Lautschrift ['laʊtʃrɪft] die <–, –en> most sing ◊ *die internationale Lautschrift*

photo [noun] Foto ['foːtoː] das <–s, –s> ◊ *Machst du mal ein Foto von mir?*

photocopier [noun] Kopierer [ko'piːrɐ] der <–s, –>

photocopy¹ [noun] Fotokopie [fotoko'piː] die <–, –n>

photocopy² [verb] fotokopieren [fotoko'piːrən] <kopiert, kopierte, hat kopiert> ◊ *einen Artikel fotokopieren*

photograph¹ [noun] Foto ['foːto] das <–s, –s> take a photograph ein Foto machen

photograph² [verb] fotografieren [fotogra'fiːrən] <fotografiert, fotografierte, hat fotografiert> ◊ *Fotografierst du uns bitte?* ♦ *Sie fotografiert gern.*

photographer [noun] Fotograf [foto'graːf] der <–en, –en> ♀Fotografin [foto'graːfɪn] die <–, –nen> ◊ *Sie ist Fotografin von Beruf.* ♦ *Hochzeitsfotos vom Fotografen*

photographic [adj] fotografisch [foto'graːfɪʃ] no comp/superl ◊ *eine fotografische Aufnahme* photographic equipment Fotoausrüstung ['foːtoˌaʊsrʏstʊŋ] die <–, –en>

photography [noun] Fotografie [fotogra'fiː] die <–> no pl ◊ *die Fotografie im 20. Jahrhundert*

phrase [noun] **1.** *(mode of expression)* Ausdruck ['aʊsdrʊk] der <–(e)s, Ausdrücke> ◊ *Der Ausdruck „jdm geht ein Licht auf" wird häufig verwendet.;* *(complete sentence by a famous person)* Ausspruch ['aʊsprʊx] der <–(e)s, Aussprüche> ◊ *ein Ausspruch von Winston Churchill* **2.** GRAM Satzglied ['zatsgliːt] das <–(e)s, –er>

phrase book [noun] Sprachführer ['ʃpraːxfyːrɐ] der <–s, –> ◊ *etw. im Sprachführer nachschlagen*

physical [adj] **1.** *(of the body)* körperlich ['kœrpɐlɪç] no comp/superl, mostly before ns ◊ *verbale und körperliche Attacken* ♦ *körperliche Betätigung* sb's physical appearance jds Äußeres ['ɔøsərəs] <Äußeren> no pl; *(opposite of psychological)* psychisch ['fyːzɪʃ] no comp/superl, mostly before ns ◊ *die psychische und physische Gesundheit eines Patienten* **2.** *(tangible)* wirklich ['vɪrklɪç] no comp/superl ◊ *wirkliche Beweise* sth is physical etw. ist

nicht greifbar [ɪst nɪçt 'graɪfbaːʔ] **3.** SPORT körperbetont ['kœrpɐbətoːnt] <körperbetonter, am körperbetontesten> ◊ *Football ist ein körperbetonter Sport.* ♦ *Das Spiel ist mir zu körperbetont.* physical contact Körperkontakt ['kœrpɐkɔnˌtakt] der <–(e)s, –e> **4.** PHYSICS physikalisch [fyzi'kaːlɪʃ] no comp/superl ◊ *physikalische Gesetze* ♦ *Ist dieser Vorgang chemisch oder physikalisch?*

physical education [noun] Sport [ʃpɔʁt] der <–(e)s> no pl ◊ *Er unterrichtet Sport und Mathematik.*

physically [adv] **1.** *(relating to the body)* körperlich ['kœrpɐlɪç] no comp/superl ◊ *eine körperlich anstrengende Tätigkeit* **2.** PHYSICS physikalisch [fyzi'kaːlɪʃ] no comp/superl ◊ *Es ist physikalisch unmöglich, dass Wasser bergauf fließt.*

physician [noun] Arzt [aˈtst] der <–es, Ärzte> ♀Ärztin ['ɛːɐtstɪn] die <–, –nen> ◊ *Du musst einen Arzt holen!* ♦ *Sie ist Ärztin.*

physicist [noun] Physiker ['fyːzɪkɐ] der <–s, –> ♀Physikerin ['fyːzɪkərɪn] die <–, –nen> ◊ *Newton war ein berühmter Physiker.* ♦ *Sie möchte später Physikerin werden.*

physics [noun] Physik [fy'ziːk] die <–> no pl ◊ *die experimentelle Physik* ♦ *Physik studieren* ♦ *Er hat in Physik eine Drei.*

pianist [noun] Pianist [pia'nɪst] der <–en, –en> ♀Pianistin [pia'nɪstɪn] die <–, –nen> ◊ *Meine Tochter ist Pianistin.* ♦ *Der Pianist hat ausgezeichnet gespielt.*

piano [noun] Klavier [kla'viːɐ] das <–s, –e> ◊ *Ich spiele Klavier.*

pick [verb] **1.** *(choose)* aussuchen ['aʊszuːxn̩] +haben ◊ *Du kannst dir dein Geschenk selbst aussuchen.* ♦ *Er kann es sich aussuchen, was er tun will.; (select from a group for a special purpose)* pick (out) auswählen ['aʊsvɛːlən] +haben ◊ *Unter allen Kandidaten haben sie mich ausgewählt.* ♦ *Für die Party wählte ich ein elegantes Kleid aus.* **2.** *(remove small bits)* entfernen [ɛnt'fɛrnən] <entfernt, entfernte, hat entfernt> ◊ *Krümel vom Teppich entfernen; (try to remove by pulling)* pick at sth etw. zupfen [an ... ˈtsʊpfn̩] +haben ◊ *Hör auf, an dem Faden zu zupfen!* **3.** *(flowers)* pflücken ['pflʏkn̩] +haben ◊ *Ich habe dir einen Blumenstrauß gepflückt.* **4.** *(pull at the strings of a musical instrument)* zupfen ['tsʊpfn̩] +haben ◊ *die E-Saite zupfen*

• **pick at** [phras v] pick at sth *(eat very little)* in etw. [dat] herumstochern [ɪn ... hɛˌrʊmʃtɔxən] <stochert herum, stocherte herum, hat herumgestochert> ◊ *Sie stochert in ihrem Essen herum.* → pick 2.

• **pick on** [phras v] pick on sb auf jdm herumhacken [aʊf ... hɛˌrʊmhakŋ̩] ◊ *Der Lehrer hackt ständig auf mir herum.*

• **pick out** [phras v] **1.** *(distinguish)* erkennen [ɐ'kɛnən] <erkennt, erkannte, hat erkannt> ◊ *Kannst du mich auf dem Klassenfoto erkennen?* **2.** *(make sb/sth visible by using a light)* sb/sth is picked out by sth jd/etw. wird von etw. erfasst [vɪˈt fɔn ... efast] +sein ◊ *Plötzlich wurde er von einem Scheinwerfer erfasst.* **3.** *(highlight, emphasize)* sth is picked out by sth etw. wird durch etw. hervorgehoben [vɪˈt dʊʁç ... hɛˌfoːɐgəhoːbm̩] +sein ◊ *Die Aufschrift wird durch das helle Rot gut hervorgehoben.*

• **pick over** [phras v] pick sth over *(search through sth: facts, issues etc.)* durchgehen ['dʊʁçgeːən] <geht

durch, ging durch, ist durchgegangen> ◊ *Ich ging noch einmal alle Einzelheiten durch.; (sort pulses)* verlesen [fɛˈleːzn̩] <verliest, verlas, hat verlesen>

• **pick up** [phras v] pick sth up **1.** *(take up, the receiver)* abnehmen [ˈapneːmən] <nimmt ab, nahm ab, hat abgenommen> ◊ *den Telefonhörer abnehmen; (things, a baby)* aufheben [ˈaʊfheːbm̩] <hebt auf, hob auf, hat aufgehoben> ◊ *etw. vom Boden aufheben* **2.** *(collect: a leaflet, hitchhiker)* mitnehmen [ˈmɪtneːmən] <nimmt mit, nahm mit, hat mitgenommen> ◊ *Sie hat eine Broschüre mitgenommen.* ♦ *Er nahm einen Anhalter mit.; (sb/sth waiting for you)* abholen [ˈaphoːlən] +haben ◊ *Holst du ihn vom Bahnhof ab?* ♦ *Kleidung aus der Reinigung abholen* **3.** *(a new skill, word, news, gossip)* aufschnappen [ˈaʊfʃnapm̩] +haben ◊ *Im Urlaub hat er ein bisschen Deutsch aufgeschnappt.; (an illness)* pick sth up sich [dat] etw. einfangen [ˈaɛnfaŋən] <fängt sich ein, fing sich ein, hat sich eingefangen> ◊ *Ich habe mir eine Grippe eingefangen.; (a bargain)* finden [ˈfɪndn̩] <findet, fand, hat gefunden> ◊ *Ich habe auf dem Flohmarkt tolle Schnäppchen gefunden.; (radio waves)* empfangen [ɛmˈpfaŋən] <empfängt, empfing, hat empfangen> ◊ *einen Radiosender empfangen* **4.** *(a smell)* aufnehmen [ˈaʊfneːmən] <nimmt auf, nahm auf, hat aufgenommen> ◊ *Der Hund nahm die Fährte auf.; (a conversation)* wieder aufnehmen [viːdɐ ˈaʊfneːmən] ◊ *Sie haben die Unterhaltung wieder aufgenommen.* **5.** *(improve)* besser werden [ˈbɛsɐ veːɐdn̩] +sein ◊ *Ihr Zustand ist besser geworden.; (wind)* stärker werden [ˈʃtɛʳkə veːɐdn̩] pick up speed schneller werden [ˈʃnɛlə veːɐdn̩]

pickpocket [noun] Taschendieb [ˈtaʃndiːp] der <–(e)s, –e> ♀Taschendiebin [ˈtaʃndiːbɪn] die <–, –nen>

picnic [noun] Picknick [ˈpɪknɪk] das <–s, –e or –s> ◊ *Wir machten ein Picknick auf der Wiese.*

picnic area [noun] Rastplatz [ˈrastplats] der <–es, Rastplätze>

picture[1] [noun] **1.** *(painting, drawing, photo, mental image, idea)* Bild [bɪlt] das <–(e)s, –er> ◊ *Bilder von Rubens* ♦ *ein Bild malen/zeichnen* ♦ *Du hast ein falsches Bild von mir.* take a picture ein Bild machen **2.** FILM Film [fɪlm] der <–(e)s, –e> ◊ *ein künstlerisch wertvoller Film* **3.** *(state of affairs)* the picture die Situation [diː zitʊaˈtsi̯oːn] die <–, –en> ◊ *Letztes Jahr sah die Situation besser aus.*

⊕ be the picture of health vor Gesundheit strotzen get the big picture den Überblick haben get the picture *(fam)* etw. verstehen

picture[2] [verb] **1.** *(imagine)* picture sth sich [dat] etw. vorstellen [ˈfoːɐʃtɛlən] +haben ◊ *Stell dir meine Überraschung vor, als ich das erfuhr!* picture sb/sth as sb/sth sich jdn/etw. als jdn/etw. vorstellen ◊ *Kannst du ihn dir als Vater vorstellen?* picture sb/yourself doing sth sich [dat] jdn/sich bei etw. vorstellen ◊ *Ich stelle ihn mir beim Tanzen vor.* **2.** *(show on a photo etc.)* abbilden [ˈapbɪldn̩] <bildet ab, bildete ab, hat abgebildet> ◊ *Er ist auf allen Titelblättern abgebildet.*

picturesque [adj] **1.** *(beautiful)* malerisch [ˈmaːlərɪʃ] ◊ *ein malerisches Dorf* ♦ *Die Lage der Burg ist malerisch.* **2.** *(language, description)* bildhaft [ˈbɪlthaft] <bildhafter, am bildhaftesten> ◊ *eine bildhafte Sprache*

pie [noun] *(of meat)* Pastete [pasˈteːtə] die <–, –n> ◊

eine Pastete im Ofen backen; *(of fruit)* Obstkuchen [ˈoːpstkuːxn̩] der <–s, –> apple pie Apfelkuchen [ˈapflkuːxn̩] der <–s, –>

⊕ pie in the sky Luftschloss

piece [noun] **1.** *(part of a whole, countable unit, musical composition)* Stück [ʃtyk] das <–(e)s, –e> ◊ *etw. in Stücke schneiden* a piece of cake/paper ein Stück Kuchen/Papier; *(furniture)* take sth to pieces etw. zerlegen [tsɛˈleːgn̩] <zerlegt, zerlegte, hat zerlegt> ◊ *Er zerlegte den Schrank in seine Einzelteile.* piece of news Neuigkeit [ˈnɔyɪçkaɛt] die <–, –en> piece of information Information [ɪnfɔʳmaˈtsi̯oːn] die <–, –en> piece of string Schnur [ʃnuːɐ̯] die <–, Schnüre> **2.** *(newspaper article)* Artikel [aʳˈtɪkl̩] der <–s, –> write a piece on/about sth einen Artikel über etw. [acc] schreiben **3.** *(coin of a specific value)* Münze [ˈmʏntsə] die <–, –n> 50p piece 50-Pence-Münze [ˌfʏnftsɪçˈpɛnsmʏntsə]

⊕ piece of advice Rat ◊ *jdm einen Rat geben* give sb a piece of your mind jdm die Meinung sagen piece of paper Zettel go to pieces zusammenbrechen pull sb/sth to pieces jdn/etw. verreißen

pier [noun] **1.** SHIP Pier [piːɐ̯] der <–s, –e or –s> ◊ *Das Schiff legte am Pier an.* **2.** *(of a bridge etc.)* Pfeiler [ˈpfaɛlɐ] der <–s, –> ◊ *von einem Pfeiler gestützt*

pierce [verb] **1.** *(knife, bullet)* durchbohren [dʊʳçˈboːrən] <durchbohrt, durchbohrte, hat durchbohrt> ◊ *Die Klinge durchbohrte die Lunge.* **2.** *(make small holes for jewellery)* piercen [ˈpiːɐ̯sn̩] +haben ◊ *Er will sich piercen lassen.* have your ears pierced sich [dat] Ohrlöcher stechen lassen [ˈoːɐ̯lœçə ʃtɛçn̩ lasn̩] <lässt sich, ließ sich, hat sich lassen> **3.** *(sound, light)* durchdringen [dʊʳçˈdrɪŋən] <durchdringt, durchdrang, hat durchdrungen> ◊ *Ein Schrei durchdrang die Nacht.*

pig [noun] *(animal, insult)* Schwein [ʃvaɛn] das <–(e)s, –e> ◊ *Er züchtet Schweine.* ♦ *Isst du lieber Schwein oder Rind?* ♦ *Du bist ein Schwein!*

⊕ and pigs might fly wers glaubt wird selig *(fam)*

pigeon [noun] Taube [ˈtaʊbə] die <–, –n>

pile[1] [noun] **1.** *(stacked)* Stapel [ˈʃtaːpl̩] der <–s, –> a pile of books ein Stapel Bücher; *(unordered)* Haufen [ˈhaʊfn̩] der <–s, –> ◊ *ein Haufen Müll* in piles stapelweise [ˈʃtaːplvaɛzə] haufenweise [ˈhaʊfn̩vaɛzə] ◊ *Auf dem Weg lagen haufenweise Blätter.* **2.** *(large amount)* a pile of time eine Menge [aɛnə ˈmɛŋə] <–> ◊ *Ich muss noch eine Menge Briefe schreiben.* piles of work jede Menge Arbeit **3.** *(support of a building or bridge)* Pfeiler [ˈpfaɛlə] der <–s, –> **4.** *(fam) (haemorrhoids)* piles Hämorriden [hɛmɔˈriːdn̩] die <–> pl ◊ *unter Hämorriden leiden*

pile[2] [verb] **1.** *(stack in orderly fashion)* pile sth (up) etw. aufstapeln [ˈaʊfʃtaːpln̩] <stapelt auf, stapelte auf, hat aufgestapelt> ◊ *Schubkartons aufstapeln* sth piles (up) etw. stapelt sich [ˈʃtaːplt] <stapelt sich, stapelte sich, hat sich gestapelt> ◊ *Die Akten stapeln sich auf meinem Schreibtisch.* **2.** *(arrange large quantities in heaps)* pile sth somewhere etw. irgendwo anhäufen [ˈanhɔyfn̩] +haben ◊ *Kohle im Keller anhäufen* pile your/sb's plate with sth sich/jdm etw. auf den Teller häufen ◊ *Er häufte sich Reis auf den Teller.; (food on a plate)* pile your/sb's plate with sth sich/jdm etw. auf den Teller häufen [aɔf deːn ˈtɛlə hɔyfn̩] +haben ◊ *Er häuft sich eine große Portion Reis auf den Teller.* **3.** pile your hair up sich [dat] das Haar hochstecken [das ˈhaːʳ ˌhoːxʃtɛkn̩] +haben

• **pile in** ⟨phras v⟩ hereindrängen [hɛˈraɛndrɛŋən] +haben ◊ *Eine große Menschenmenge drängte berein.* pile into sth in etw. ⟨acc⟩ drängen [ɪn ... drɛŋən] +haben; *(into a car, lift)* sich in etw. ⟨acc⟩ zwängen [ɪn ... ˌtsvɛŋən] +haben ◊ *Sie zwängten sich in den Aufzug.*

• **pile on** ⟨phras v⟩ **1.** *(intensify sth)* pile on the pressure den Druck verstärken [deːn ˈdrɔk fɛˌʃtɛˀkŋ] <verstärkt, verstärkte, hat verstärkt> pile on the guilt jdm ein schlechtes Gewissen machen [aɛn ʃlɛçtəs ɡəˈvɪsŋ maxŋ] +haben **2.** sport *(gain a lot)* pile on the points massiv punkten [maˌsiːf ˈpʊŋktŋ] +haben pile on the pounds einige Pfunde zulegen [aɛnɪɡə ˌpfʊndə ˈtsuːleːɡŋ] +haben **☞** pile it on dick auftragen *(fam)*

• **pile out** ⟨phras v⟩ sich hinausdrängen [hɪˈnaosdrɛŋən] +haben ◊ *Zahlreiche unzufriedene Besucher drängten sich hinaus.*

pill ⟨noun⟩ Pille [ˈpɪlə] die <–, –n> ◊ *Pillen schlucken* ♦ *mit der Pille verbüten* a pill for sth eine Pille gegen etw. ◊ *eine Pille gegen Haarausfall* go on the pill die Pille nehmen go off the pill die Pille absetzen

pillar ⟨noun⟩ Säule [ˈzɔɪlə] die <–, –n> ◊ *eine korinthische Säule* ♦ *Er gehört zu den Säulen unserer Gesellschaft.* pillar of strength Stütze [ˈʃtʏtsə] die <–, –n> ◊ *Sie war ihm in schweren Zeiten eine Stütze.*

pillow ⟨noun⟩ Kopfkissen [ˈkɔpfkɪsŋ] das <–s, –>

pillowcase, pillowslip ⟨noun⟩ Kissenbezug [ˈkɪsŋbətsuːk] der <–(e)s, Kissenbezüge> ◊ *die Kissenbezüge wechseln*

pilot¹ ⟨noun⟩ **1.** aviat Pilot [piˈloːt] der <–en, –en> ♀Pilotin [piˈloːtɪn] die <–, –nen> ◊ *Sie ist Pilotin aus Leidenschaft.* ♦ *Der Pilot konnte die Maschine sicher landen.* **2.** ship Lotse [ˈloːtsə] der <–n, –n> ♀Lotsin [ˈloːtsɪn] die <–, –nen> ◊ *Der Lotse ging von Bord.* ♦ *als Lotsin auf einem Schiff arbeiten*

pilot² ⟨verb⟩ **1.** aviat fliegen [ˈfliːɡŋ] <fliegt, flog, hat geflogen> ◊ *Er fliegt diese Maschine zum ersten Mal.* **2.** ship lotsen [ˈloːtsŋ] +haben ◊ *ein Schiff lotsen* **3.** *(try)* testen [ˈtɛstŋ] +haben ◊ *ein neues Programm testen*

pin¹ ⟨noun⟩ **1.** *(for sewing)* Stecknadel [ˈʃtɛknaːdl̩] die <–, –n> ◊ *etw. mit Stecknadeln befestigen* **2.** *(brooch)* Brosche [ˈbrɔʃə] die <–, –n> ◊ *Sie trug eine bübsche Brosche.; (on a tie, hat)* Anstecknadel [ˈanʃtɛknaːdl̩] die <–, –n> **3.** *(to hold pieces together, of grenade, small nail, in medicine)* Stift [ʃtɪft] der <–(e)s, –e> ◊ *den Stift in das gebohrte Loch stecken* **4.** *(on a plug)* Kontakt [kɔnˈtakt] der <–(e)s, –e> ◊ *die Kontakte eines Steckers* **5.** game *(in bowling)* Kegel [ˈkeːɡl̩] der <–s, –> ◊ *Mit nur einer Kugel warf er alle Kegel um.*

pin² ⟨verb⟩ **1.** *(fasten: with a needle)* pin sth onto sth etw. an etw. ⟨acc⟩ stecken [an ... ʃtɛkŋ] +haben ◊ *Sie steckte sich eine Brosche an die Bluse.* pin up your hair sich ⟨dat⟩ das Haar hochstecken [das ˈhaːˀ ˌhoːxʃtɛkŋ] +haben; *(with a pin)* pin sth onto sth etw. an etw. ⟨acc⟩ heften [an ... ˈhɛftŋ] <heftet, heftete, hat geheftet> ◊ *Er beftete die Stellenanzeige an das schwarze Brett.* pin sth together etw. zusammenheften [tsuˈzamŋhɛftŋ] ◊ *Heften Sie vor dem Nähen die Einzelteile zusammen.* **2.** pin sb against/on sth jdn gegen/auf etw. drücken [ɡɛːɡŋ/aof ... drʏkŋ] +haben ◊ *Er drückte ihn gegen die Wand/auf den Boden.* pin sb down jdn zu Boden drücken [tsuː ˈboːdn̩ drʏkŋ] +haben ◊ *Er wurde von vier Männern zu Boden gedrückt.*

• **pin down** ⟨phras v⟩ **1.** *(find out)* pin sth down etw. feststellen [ˈfɛstʃtɛlən] +haben ◊ *Konnten Sie die Ursache des Unfalls feststellen?* **2.** *(force to decide)* pin sb down jdn festnageln [ˈfɛstnaːɡl̩n] <nagelt fest, nagelte fest, hat festgenagelt> ◊ *Sie versuchten ibn festzunageln.* → pin³

PIN ⟨noun⟩ PIN [pɪn] die <–, –s> ◊ *Bitte geben Sie Ihre PIN ein.*

pinch¹ ⟨noun⟩ **1.** *(small amount)* Prise [ˈpriːzə] die <–, –n> ◊ *eine Prise Pfeffer zugeben* **2.** give sb a pinch jdn kneifen [ˈknaɛfŋ] <kneift, kniff, hat gekniffen> ◊ *Er kniff sie in den Arm.* feel a pinch somewhere spüren, wie einen etwas kneift ◊ *Plötzlich spürte ich, wie mich etwas am Bein kniff.*

pinch² ⟨verb⟩ **1.** *(squeeze with fingers)* kneifen [ˈknaɛfŋ] <kneift, kniff, hat gekniffen> ◊ *Er kniff sich in den Arm.* ♦ *Au, er hat mich gekniffen!* **2.** *(shoes)* drücken [ˈdrʏkŋ] +haben ◊ *Meine neuen Schuhe drücken.* shoes that pinch your feet Schuhe, die an den Zehen drücken **3.** *(fam) (steal)* klauen [ˈklaoən] +haben *(fam)* ◊ *Jemand hat mir das Handy geklaut.*

pine ⟨noun⟩ Kiefer [ˈkiːfɐ] die <–, –n> ◊ *Vor dem Haus steht eine Kiefer.* ♦ *ein Tisch aus massiver Kiefer*

pineapple ⟨noun⟩ Ananas [ˈananas] die <–, –> ◊ *drei Scheiben Ananas aus der Dose*

pink ⟨adj⟩ rosa [ˈroːza] invariable ◊ *ein rosa Lippenstift* ♦ *Das T-Shirt ist rosa.* bright/shocking pink pink [pɪŋk] invariable

pint ⟨noun⟩ **1.** *(unit)* 0,57 Liter **2.** *(in the UK: large glass of beer)* Bier [biːɐ] das <–(e)s, –> ◊ *in der Kneipe ein paar Bier trinken*

pioneer ⟨noun⟩ Pionier [pioˈniːɐ] der <–s, –e> ♀Pionierin [pioˈniːrɪn] die <–, –nen> ◊ *Die Pioniere zogen nach Westen.* ♦ *Diese Firma ist ein Pionier auf dem Gebiet der Mikroprozessoren.*

pip ⟨noun⟩ **1.** *(seed)* Kern [kɛˀn] der <–(e)s, –e> **2.** *(sound)* Piepston [ˈpiːpstoːn] der <–(e)s, Piepstöne>; *(in the UK: sound signal on the radio)* pips Zeitzeichen [ˈtsaɛttsaɛçn̩] das <–s, –> **3.** mil *(on a uniform)* Stern [ʃtɛˀn] der <–(e)s, –e> ◊ *Sterne auf einer Uniform*

pipe¹ ⟨noun⟩ **1.** *(hard tube)* Rohr [roːɐ] das <–(e)s, –e> lay a pipe ein Rohr verlegen; *(connected to a system)* Leitung [ˈlaɛtʊŋ] die <–, –en> gas pipe Gasleitung [ˈɡaːslaɛtʊŋ] die <–, –en> **2.** *(for smoking)* Pfeife [ˈpfaɛfə] die <–, –n> ◊ *sich ⟨dat⟩ eine Pfeife stopfen/anzünden* **3.** mus Flöte [ˈfløːtə] die <–, –n>; *(of an organ)* Orgelpfeife [ˈɔrɡl̩pfaɛfə] die <–(e)s, –e> ◊ *(Scottish)* pipes Dudelsack [ˈduːdl̩zak] der <–(e)s, –e> pan pipes Panflöte [ˈpaːnfløːtə]

pipe² ⟨verb⟩ **1.** *(channel, direct)* leiten [ˈlaɛtŋ] <leitet, leitete, hat geleitet> ◊ *Abwässer in einen Fluss leiten* **2.** *(make a high-pitched sound, speak in a high-pitched voice)* piepsen [ˈpiːpsŋ] +haben ◊ *Da piepst ein kleiner Vogel vor dem Fenster.* ♦ *Der Junge piepste: „Mami, wo bist du?"* **3.** *(sth onto a cake etc.)* spritzen [ˈʃprɪtsŋ] +haben ◊ *Sahne auf eine Torte spritzen*

• **pipe down** ⟨phras v⟩ leise sein [ˈlaɛzə zaɛn] +sein ◊ *Sei doch mal leise!*

• **pipe up** ⟨phras v⟩ sich zu Wort melden [tsuː ˈvɔˀt mɛldn̩] <meldet sich, meldete sich, hat sich gemeldet> ◊ *Eine junge Frau meldete sich zu Wort und sagte: …*

Pisces [noun] *(star sign)* Fische ['fɪʃə] <-> *pl; (a member of the star sign)* Fisch [fɪʃ] der <-es, -e>

piss [verb] pissen ['pɪsn̩] +*haben (rude)* ◊ *pissen müssen*

pit [noun] **1.** *(hole in the ground, mine, quarry)* Grube ['gruːbə] die <-, -n> ◊ *In dieser Grube wird Eisenerz abgebaut.* ♦ *eine Grube ausheben/graben* gravel pit Kiesgrube ['kiːsgruːbə]; *(in a coal mine)* down the pit unter Tage [ʊntə 'taːgə] **2.** mus *(orchestra)* pit Orchestergraben [ɔrˈkɛstəgraːbm̩] der <-s, Orchestergräben> **3.** *(in the stock exchange)* Börsensaal ['bœrznzaːl] der <-(e)s, Börsensäle> **4.** *(scar)* Narbe ['narbə] die <-, -n> ◊ *Narben im Gesicht haben* **5.** sport *(for racing cars)* pits Box [bɔks] die <-, -en> *most sing* ◊ *Der Rennwagen musste in die Box.* **6.** *(in the US: hard core in fruit)* Kern [kɛrn] der <-(e)s, -e>
● the pit of your stomach die Magengrube be the pits ätzend sein *(fam)*

pitch¹ [noun] **1.** sport *(playing field)* Platz [plats] der <-es, Plätze> ◊ *Hooligans stürmten den Platz.* football pitch Fußballplatz ['fuːsbalplats] **2.** *(high level)* (high) pitch Höhepunkt ['høːəpʊŋkt] der <-(e)s, -e> ◊ *Die Debatte hat einen neuen Höhepunkt erreicht.* be at a high pitch auf dem Höhepunkt sein **3.** *(of a sound, voice)* Höhe ['høːə] die <-, -n> ◊ *die Höhe eines Tons/seiner Stimme; (ability to hit the right musical note)* Gehör [gəˈhøːɐ̯] das <-s> *no pl* have perfect pitch das absolute Gehör haben **4.** sales pitch Verkaufspräsentation [fɛˈkaɔfsprɛzɛnta̯ˌtsjoːn] die <-, -en> make a pitch *(for sth)* Argumente (für etw.) vorbringen [aˈguːmɛnta ˌfoːɡbrɪŋən] <bringt vor, brachte vor, hat vorgebracht> **5.** *(in the UK: place)* Platz [plats] der <-es, Plätze> ◊ *Der Blumenverkäufer war an seinem üblichen Platz.* **6.** *(black substance)* Pech [pɛç] das <-(e)s, -e> *most sing* ◊ *Fugen mit Pech abdichten* **7.** *(slope)* Neigung ['naegʊŋ] die <-, -en> ◊ *die Neigung eines Dachs*

pitch² [verb] **1.** *(aim, direct)* pitch sth at sb/sth etw. auf jdn/etw. zuschneiden [aɔf ... ˌtsuːʃnaedn̩] <schneidet zu, schnitt zu, hat zugeschnitten> ◊ *Die Firma hat das Produkt auf den deutschen Markt zugeschnitten.* **2.** pitch your voice high/low in hoher/tiefer Stimmlage sprechen/singen [ɪn ˌhoːɐ̯/ˌtiːfɐ 'ʃtɪmlaːgə ʃprɛçn̩/zɪŋən] with my/his etc. voice pitched high/low in hoher/tiefer Stimmlage **3.** *(fling, throw)* schleudern ['ʃlɔøden] +*haben* ◊ *Er schleuderte die leere Flasche über den Zaun.* **4.** *(fall)* stürzen ['ʃtʏrtsn̩] +*sein* ◊ *Sie stürzte in die Tiefe.* **5.** *(try to sell)* präsentieren [prɛznˈtiːrən] <präsentiert, präsentierte, hat präsentiert> pitch sth to sb jdm etw. präsentieren; *(try to get)* pitch for sth sich um etw. bemühen [ʊm ... bəˌmyːən] <bemüht sich, bemühte sich, hat sich bemüht> ◊ *sich um einen Geschäftsabschluss bemühen* **6.** *(ship, plane)* schaukeln ['ʃaɔkln̩] +*haben* **7.** *(a tent)* aufschlagen ['aɔfʃlaːgŋ̩] <schlägt auf, schlug auf, hat aufgeschlagen> ◊ *Sie brauchten nur fünf Minuten, um ihr Zelt aufzuschlagen.* pitch camp Lager aufschlagen
● **pitch against** [phras v] pitch sb against sb jdn gegen jdn aufstellen [ˈaɔfʃtɛlən] +*haben* ◊ *Seine Partei stellt ihn als Kandidaten gegen den Präsidenten auf.* be pitched against sb gegen jdn antreten [geˈtreːtŋ̩] ... [ˌantreːtn̩] <tritt an, trat an, ist angetreten>

● **pitch in** [phras v] **1.** *(help)* mithelfen ['mɪthɛlfn̩] <hilft mit, half mit, hat mitgeholfen> ◊ *Wenn alle mithelfen, geht's schneller.* **2.** *(say sth)* pitch in with sth etw. einwerfen ['aenvɛrfn̩] <wirft ein, warf ein, hat eingeworfen> ◊ *eine Frage einwerfen*
● **pitch into** [phras v] **1.** *(bring into a situation, mood)* pitch sb into sth jdn in etw. [acc] stürzen [ɪn ... ʃtʏrtsn̩] +*haben* ◊ *Der Selbstmord seines Freundes hat ihn in Depressionen gestürzt.* **2.** *(criticize, attack)* pitch into sb über jdn herfallen [yːbe ... ˌheːɐ̯falən] <fällt her, fiel her, ist hergefallen> ◊ *Die Medien fielen über den neuen Minister her.*

pitch-black [adj] **1.** *(with no light)* stockdunkel ['ʃtɔkdʊŋkl̩] *no comp/superl* <der/die/das stockdunkle ...> ◊ *ein stockdunkler Keller* ♦ *Bei Neumond ist es nachts stockdunkel.* **2.** *(colo(u)r)* pechschwarz ['pɛçˈʃvaʁts] *no comp/superl* ◊ *Ihr Haar war pechschwarz.* ♦ *ein pechschwarzes Pferd*

pitfall [noun] Tücke ['tʏkə] die <-, -n> ◊ *Diese Aufgabe ist nicht ohne Tücken.*

pitiful(ly) [adj, adv] erbärmlich [ɛˈbɛrmlɪç] ◊ *Sie lebten in erbärmlichen Verhältnissen.* ♦ *Ihre Leistung war erbärmlich.* ♦ *Der Hund jaulte erbärmlich.*

pity¹ [noun] **1.** *(sympathy)* Mitleid ['mɪtlaet] das <-(e)s> *no pl* feel pity for sb Mitleid mit jdm empfinden **2.** *(mercy)* Erbarmen [ɛˈbarmən] das <-s> *no pl* ◊ *Erbarmen zeigen* take pity on sb Erbarmen mit jdm haben
● (it's a) pity (es ist) schade ◊ *Schade, dass du nicht dabei warst!* ♦ *Es ist schade, dass du das nicht gesehen hast.* more's the pity leider what a pity wie schade

pity² [verb] bemitleiden [bəˈmɪtlaedn̩] <bemitleidet, bemitleidete, hat bemitleidet> ◊ *Als Behinderter wird man oft bemitleidet.*

place¹ [noun] **1.** *(position)* Platz [plats] der <-es, Plätze> ◊ *Seiner Meinung nach war ihr Platz am Herd.* ♦ *ein Platz im Kindergarten* take second place den zweiten Platz belegen; *(on a train, in a theatre etc.)* Sitzplatz ['zɪtsplats] place at university Studienplatz ['ʃtuːdjənplats] place of work Arbeitsplatz [ˈarbaetsplats] **2.** *(area, location)* Ort [ɔrt] der <-(e)s, -e> ◊ *etw. an einem sicheren Ort aufbewahren* ♦ *Sie wohnen in einem kleinen Ort an der Grenze.* place of birth Geburtsort [gəˈbuːɐ̯tsˌɔrt] hiding place Versteck [fɛˈʃtɛk] das <-(e)s, -e> ◊ *Polizisten stürmten das Versteck der Terroristen.* store sth in a cool place etw. kühl aufbewahren [ˌkyːl ˈaɔfbeːvaːrən] somewhere is a great place to do sth irgendwo gut tun [ɛs lɛst zɪç ... guːt] <lässt, ließ, hat lassen> ◊ *In Frankreich lässt es sich gut leben.* sth is a great place for sth ist ideal für etw. [ɪst ideˈaːl fyːɡ] +*sein* ◊ *Irland ist ideal für einen Aktivurlaub.* place of business Firmensitz ['fɪrmənzɪts] der <-es, -e> place of residence Wohnsitz ['voːnzɪts] der <-es, -e> ◊ *Sie hat ihren Wohnsitz nach Frankreich verlegt.* **3.** *(house)* Haus [haɔs] das <-es, Häuser> ◊ *ein Haus kaufen; (flat)* Wohnung ['voːnʊŋ] die <-, -en> ◊ *eine Wohnung mieten* place to stay Unterkunft ['ʊntɐkʊnft] die <-, Unterkünfte> at sb's place bei jdm [bae] ◊ *Wir haben uns bei ihm getroffen.* to sb's place zu jdm [tsuː] ◊ *Gehen wir doch zu mir!* **4.** *(particular spot in a book, after the decimal point)* Stelle ['ʃtɛlə] die <-, -n> ◊ *An dieser Stelle stand früher ein Tempel.* ♦ *eine Stelle im Buch markieren*

◆ *eine Stelle hinter dem Komma* **5.** *(on a committee, in an organization etc.)* Sitz [zɪts] der <–es, –e> have a place on sth einen Sitz in etw. ⟨dat⟩ haben ◊ *einen Sitz im Aufsichtsrat haben; (in a sports team)* win a place in a team in eine Mannschaft aufgenommen werden [ɪn ˈaɛnə ˈmanʃaft ˌaofgənɔmən veːɐdn̩] <wird, wurde, ist worden> **6.** *(importance, significance)* Rolle [ˈrɔlə] die <–, –n> ◊ *jds Rolle in der Geschichte* sb has a place in sth jd spielt eine Rolle in etw. ⟨dat⟩ **7.** *(at a meal)* Gedeck [gəˈdɛk] das <–s, –e> ◊ *schnell zwei Gedecke mehr auflegen*
⊛ **all over the place 1.** *(everywhere)* überall **2.** *(not in order)* durcheinander have a place in sb's heart einen Platz in jds Herzen haben in the first place erstens ◊ *Ich habe keine Lust auszugehen; erstens ist es schon spät, und zweitens ist es zu kalt.* take place stattfinden ◊ *Wo/Wann soll denn das Fest stattfinden?* trade places tauschen in places stellenweise in place of ... statt ... ⟨gen⟩ ◊ *Statt der Äpfel kann man auch Birnen für den Kuchen verwenden.* in sb's place in jds Lage put yourself in sb's place sich in jds Lage versetzen out of place **1.** *(not in the right spot)* falsch platziert **2.** *(inappropriate, uncomfortable)* fehl am Platz

place² ⟨verb⟩ **1.** *(put)* stellen [ˈʃtɛlən] +haben ◊ *die Milch in den Kühlschrank stellen* ◆ *Teller auf den Tisch stellen; (lay sth somewhere)* legen [ˈleːgn̩] +haben ◊ *Er legte die Hemden in den Schrank.* ◆ *Sie legte mir ihre Hand auf die Schulter.; (lay sth alongside sth)* anlegen [ˈanleːgn̩] +haben ◊ *ein Lineal genau anlegen* place sth next to sth etw. an etw. ⟨acc⟩ anlegen ◊ *eine Karte an eine andere anlegen; (put sth into a container)* geben [ˈgeːbm̩] <gibt, gab, hat gegeben> ◊ *die Zutaten in den Mixer geben und pürieren* **2.** *(fix sth somewhere)* anbringen [ˈanbrɪŋən] <bringt an, brachte an, hat angebracht> ◊ *Steckdosen an einer Wand anbringen* **3.** *(be situated)* be placed somewhere irgendwo liegen [ˈliːgn̩] <liegt, lag, hat gelegen> ◊ *Die Jugendherberge liegt günstig im Zentrum von St. Petersburg.* **4.** *(bring sb into a situation)* bringen [ˈbrɪŋən] <bringt, brachte, hat gebracht> ◊ *jdn in eine unangenehme Lage bringen; (under arrest, sb's control)* stellen [ˈʃtɛlən] +haben ◊ *jdn unter Hausarrest stellen* ◆ *Das Gebiet wurde unter UN-Aufsicht gestellt.* place sb under pressure jdn unter Druck setzen [ˈʊntɐ ˈdrʊk zɛtsn̩] +haben be well placed to do sth in einer guten Position sein, um etw. zu tun [ɪn ˈaɛnə guːtn̩ poziˈtsioːn zaɛn ʊm ... ˈtuː] +sein ◊ *Das Unternehmen ist in einer guten Position, um vom Wirtschaftswachstum zu profitieren.* **5.** *(impose)* place limits on sth etw. begrenzen [bəˈgrɛntsn̩] <begrenzt, begrenzte, hat begrenzt> place burdens/strain on sb/sth jdn/etw. belasten [bəˈlastn̩] <belastet, belastete, hat belastet> **6.** *(have a particular attitude towards)* place the blame on sb jdm die Schuld geben [diː ˈʃʊlt geːbm̩] <gibt, gab, hat gegeben> place hope in jdn Hoffnung in jdn setzen [ˈhɔfnʊŋ ɪn ... zɛtsn̩] +haben **7.** *(an advertisement, order)* aufgeben [ˈaofgeːbm̩] <gibt auf, gab auf, hat aufgegeben> ◊ *bei der Zeitung eine Annonce aufgeben* ◆ *Sie hat die Bestellung telefonisch aufgegeben.* **8.** place a bet setzen [ˈzɛtsn̩] +haben ◊ *auf ein Pferd setzen*
⊛ **sb can't place sb** jd weiß nicht, wo er jdn hintun soll

placement ⟨noun⟩ **1.** *(internship)* Praktikum [ˈpraktikʊm] das <–s, Praktika> a placement with a company ein Praktikum bei einer Firma **2.** *(finding a place for sb)* Vermittlung [fɛˈmɪtlʊŋ] die <–, –en> job placement Arbeitsvermittlung [ˈaˈbaɛtsfɛˌmɪtlʊŋ] placement for adoption Adoptionsvermittlung [adɔpˈtsioːnsfɛˌmɪtlʊŋ] **3.** *(home)* Zuhause [tsuˈhaozə] das <–s> no pl ◊ *ein Zuhause für misshandelte Kinder finden*

plague¹ ⟨noun⟩ **1.** *(epidemic)* Seuche [ˈzɔɡçə] die <–, –n> ◊ *Die Stadt wurde von einer Seuche heimgesucht.* **2.** *(black death)* the plague die Pest [diː pɛst] <–> no pl ◊ *Die Pest raffte viele Menschen dahin.* **3.** *(evil)* Übel [ˈyːbl̩] das <–s, –> ◊ *gegen das Übel der Korruption vorgehen* **4.** *(of insects, vermin etc.)* Plage [ˈplaːgə] die <–, –n> plague of rats Rattenplage [ˈratnplaːgə]

plague² ⟨verb⟩ **1.** *(torment, cause trouble to)* heimsuchen [ˈhaɛmzuːxn̩] +haben, mostly passive ◊ *Vor der Prüfung wurde ich oft von Albträumen heimgesucht.* ◆ *Neuseeland wird häufig von Erdbeben heimgesucht.; (disease, pain)* sth plagues sb, sb is plagued by sth jd leidet unter etw. ⟨dat⟩ [ˈlaɛdət ʊntɐ] <leidet, litt, hat gelitten> ◊ *unter Migräneanfällen leiden* **2.** *(annoy, irritate)* belästigen [bəˈlɛstɪɡn̩] <belästigt, belästigte, hat belästigt> ◊ *von Journalisten belästigt werden*

plain¹ ⟨noun⟩ **1.** *(flat area)* plain(s) Ebene [ˈeːbənə] die <–, –n> ◊ *eine karge, sandige Ebene* **2.** *(in the UK: in knitting)* rechte Masche [ˌrɛçtə ˈmaʃə] die <–, –n>

plain² ⟨adj⟩ **1.** *(unambiguous, easy to understand)* klar [klaːɐ] ◊ *Was er meinte, war ziemlich klar.* ◆ *eine klare Sprache* it is plain to sb that jdm ist klar, dass ◊ *Mir ist klar, dass es so nicht weitergehen kann.* make sth plain etw. klar machen [ˈklaːɐ maxn̩] +haben; *(obvious)* plain (to see) offensichtlich [ˈɔfnzɪçtlɪç] ◊ *Es war offensichtlich, dass sie Recht hatte.* **2.** *(design, truth)* schlicht [ʃlɪçt] <schlichter, am schlichtesten> ◊ *Ihr Kleid war sehr schlicht.* ◆ *Die schlichte Wahrheit ist: Ich habe es vergessen.; (food)* einfach [ˈaɛnfax] ◊ *ein einfaches Abendessen aus Brot und Käse* ◆ *Das Essen war einfach, aber gut.* **3.** *(unattractive)* unattraktiv [ˈʊn|atraktiːf] ◊ *ein unattraktives Mädchen* ◆ *Ich finde sie eher unattraktiv.* **4.** *(honest)* offen [ˈɔfn̩] ◊ *offene Worte* be plain about sth etw. offen sagen **5.** *(sheer, pure)* rein [raɛn] only before sb ◊ *reines Glück* ◆ *reine Dummheit*
⊛ **plain and simple** schlicht und einfach

plainly ⟨adv⟩ **1.** *(clearly)* deutlich [ˈdɔɡtlɪç] ◊ *Ich sah deutlich, dass etwas nicht stimmte.* **2.** *(honestly)* offen [ˈɔfn̩] ◊ *Du kannst ruhig offen sprechen.* **3.** *(obviously)* offensichtlich [ˈɔfnzɪçtlɪç] ◊ *Er glaubte mir offensichtlich nicht.* **4.** *(without decoration)* schlicht [ʃlɪçt] <schlichter, am schlichtesten> ◊ *Er war meistens schlicht gekleidet.*

plaintiff ⟨noun⟩ Kläger [ˈklɛːgɐ] der <–s, –> ♀Klägerin [ˈklɛːgərɪn] die <–, –nen> ◊ *Klägerin in dieser Sache ist die Stadt Bayern*

plait¹ ⟨noun⟩ Zopf [tsɔpf] der <–(e)s, Zöpfe> ◊ *Ina trägt heute einen Zopf.*

plait² ⟨verb⟩ flechten [ˈflɛçtn̩] <flicht, flocht, hat geflochten> plait sb's hair jdm die Haare flechten

plan¹ ⟨noun⟩ Plan [plaːn] der <–(e)s, Pläne> ◊ *Das war wirklich ein raffinierter Plan.* ◆ *Hast du schon Pläne fürs Wochenende?* ◆ *Er legte die Pläne zum Umbau des Gebäudes vor.* go according to plan nach

Plan laufen

plan² [verb] **1.** *(organize, arrange)* planen ['plaːnən] +haben ◊ *alles bis ins letzte Detail planen* ♦ *Die Feier ist für den 15. Mai geplant.* ♦ *Er hat wie geplant im Mai seine Prüfungen abgelegt.* plan ahead vorausplanen [fo'rɔøsplaːnən] +haben; *(your work)* einteilen ['aentaelən] +haben ◊ *Ich habe mir die Arbeit gut eingeteilt.* **2.** *(intend)* vorhaben ['foːɡhaːbm̩] <hat vor, hatte vor, hat vorgehabt> ◊ *Hast du am Wochenende schon etwas vor?* ♦ *Ich hatte vor, früh ins Bett zu gehen, aber daraus wurde nichts.*

plane [noun] **1.** *(aircraft)* Flugzeug ['fluːktsɔøk] das <-(e)s, -e> by plane mit dem Flugzeug catch a plane ein Flugzeug nehmen plane crash Flugzeugabsturz ['fluːktsɔøk|apʃtuˀts] der <-es, Flugzeugabstürze> **2.** *(flat surface, level)* Ebene ['eːbənə] die <-, -n> ◊ *die Geometrie der Ebene* ♦ *auf einer höheren Ebene* **3.** *(tool)* Hobel ['hoːbl̩] der <-s, -> **4.** *(tree)* Platane [pla'taːnə] die <-, -n>

planet [noun] Planet [pla'neːt] der <-en, -en>

plank [noun] **1.** *(of wood)* Brett [brɛt] das <-(e)s, -er> ◊ *aus Brettern ein Regal bauen* **2.** *(important point)* Punkt [pʊŋkt] der <-(e)s, -e> ◊ *Der zentrale Punkt dieses Programms ist die Verbesserung der Qualität.* main plank Schwerpunkt ['ʃveːɡpʊŋkt]

planner [noun] **1.** *(person who creates plans)* Planer ['plaːnɐ] der <-s, -> ♀Planerin ['plaːnərɪn] die <-, -nen> ◊ *die Planer des Projekts* city planner Stadtplaner ['ʃtatplaːnɐ] Stadtplanerin ['ʃtatplaːnərɪn] ◊ *Sie ist Stadtplanerin von Beruf.* **2.** *(thing that helps with planning and organizing)* year planner Jahresplaner ['jaːrəsplaːnɐ] wedding planner Hochzeitsplaner ['hɔxtsaetsplaːnɐ] route planner Routenplaner ['ruːtn̩plaːnɐ] **3.** *(in the US: diary)* Terminkalender [tɛrˈmiːnkaˌlɛndɐ] der <-s, ->

planning [noun] **1.** *(organization)* Planung ['plaːnʊŋ] die <-, -en> ◊ *Welche Faktoren müssen bei der Planung berücksichtigt werden?* **2.** *(of area development)* Stadtplanung ['ʃtatplaːnʊŋ] die <-, -en> planning application Bauantrag ['bao|antraːk] der <-(e)s, Bauanträge> planning department Bauamt ['bao|amt] das <-(e)s, Bauämter> planning permission Baugenehmigung ['baoɡəneːmɪɡʊŋ] die <-, -en>

plant¹ [noun] **1.** *(growing)* Pflanze ['pflantsə] die <-, -n> ◊ *eine Pflanze gießen/umtopfen* house plant Zimmerpflanze ['tsɪmɐpflantsə] lettuce plant Salatpflanze [za'laːtpflantsə] **2.** *(factory)* Werk [vɛˀk] das <-(e)s, -e> ◊ *Unser Werk in München stellt neue Mitarbeiter ein.* chemical plant Chemiewerk [çe'miːvɛˀk] assembly plant Montagewerk [mɔn'taːʒəvɛˀk]; *(power station)* Kraftwerk ['kraftvɛˀk] nuclear plant Kernkraftwerk ['kɛˀnkraftvɛˀk] **3.** *(large machines)* Maschinen [ma'ʃiːnən] die <-> pl ◊ *in Maschinen investieren*

plant² [verb] **1.** *(put into the soil)* pflanzen ['pflantsn̩] +haben ◊ *einen Baum pflanzen; (seeds)* aussäen ['aosˌzɛːən] +haben plant sth with sth etw. mit etw. bepflanzen [mɪt ... bə,pflantsn̩] <bepflanzt, bepflanzte, hat bepflanzt> ◊ *ein mit Rosen bepflanztes Beet* **2.** *(press)* plant a kiss on sb's sth jdm einen Kuss auf etw. [acc] drücken [aenən ˌkʊs aof ... drʏkn̩] +haben ◊ *Sie drückte ihm einen Kuss auf die Backe.* **3.** *(sit down)* plant yourself somewhere sich irgendwohin pflanzen ['pflantsn̩] +haben *(fam)* ◊ *sich aufs Sofa pflanzen; (stand)* sich irgendwo aufpflanzen

['aofpflantsn̩] +haben *(fam)* ◊ *Er pflanzte sich drohend vor mir auf.* **4.** *(a spy, an informer)* einschleusen ['aenʃlɔøzn̩] +haben ◊ *einen Spion in eine Organisation einschleusen* **5.** *(a bomb)* legen ['leːgn̩] +haben **6.** *(a thought, an idea)* verbreiten [fɛ'braetn̩] <verbreitet, verbreitete, hat verbreitet> ◊ *Misstrauen/ eine Idee verbreiten* plant an idea in sb's mind jdn auf eine Idee bringen [aof aenə i'deː brɪŋən] <bringt, brachte, hat gebracht> plant (a) doubt in sb's mind jdn zweifeln lassen ['tsvaefl̩n lasn̩] <lässt, ließ, hat lassen> plant suspicion in sb's mind jdn misstrauisch machen ['mɪstraoɪʃ maxn̩] +haben

plaque [noun] **1.** *(memorial)* Gedenktafel [gə'dɛŋktaːfl̩] die <-, -n> **2.** *(on the teeth)* Zahnbelag ['tsaːnbəlaːk] der <-(e)s, Zahnbeläge>

plasma [noun] Plasma ['plasmaː] das <-s, Plasmen> most sing plasma screen Plasmabildschirm ['plasmabɪltʃɪˀm] der <-(e)s, -e>

plaster [noun] **1.** *(for walls)* Putz [pʊts] der <-es> no pl ◊ *Der Putz bröckelt.* **2.** *(for casts)* plaster (of Paris) Gips [gɪps] der <-es, -e> ◊ *eine Plastik aus Gips* ♦ *ein Bein in Gips haben* **3.** *(for wounds)* Pflaster ['pflastɐ] das <-s, -> ◊ *ein Pflaster auf eine Wunde kleben*

plaster cast [noun] MED *(for broken limbs)* Gipsverband ['gɪpsfəbant] der <-(e)s, Gipsverbände> ◊ *jdm einen Gipsverband anlegen* **2.** *(model)* Gipsabdruck ['gɪps|apdrʊk] der <-(e)s, Gipsabdrücke>

plastic¹ [noun] **1.** *(material)* Kunststoff ['kʊnstʃtɔf] der <-(e)s, -e> ◊ *Tragetaschen aus Kunststoff* **2.** *(credit card payments)* Plastikgeld ['plastɪkgɛlt] das <-(e)s> no pl *(fam)* ◊ *mit Plastikgeld bezahlen*

plastic² [adj] **1.** *(synthetic)* Plastik... ['plastɪk] plastic bag Plastiktüte ['plastɪkyːtə] die <-, -n> plastic packaging Plastikverpackung ['plastɪkfəpakʊŋ] die <-, -en> **2.** MED plastisch ['plastɪʃ] no comp/superl, only before ns ◊ *die plastische Chirurgie* **3.** *(artificial)* künstlich ['kʏnstlɪç] ◊ *ein künstliches Lächeln* **4.** *(malleable)* modellierbar [mɔdɛ'liːɡbaːˀ] ◊ *eine modellierbare Masse* ♦ *Diese Substanz ist modellierbar.*

plate [noun] **1.** *(for food)* Teller ['tɛlɐ] der <-s, -> ◊ *Sie häufte sich Kartoffeln auf den Teller.* ♦ *Muss ich meinen Teller leer essen?* a plate of ... ein Teller ... ◊ *ein Teller Spaghetti* **2.** *(flat piece of metal or other hard material, part of the earth's surface)* Platte ['platə] die <-, -n> ◊ *die Verschiebung der Platten an der Erdoberfläche* steel plate Stahlplatte ['ʃtaːlplatə]; *(for printing)* Druckplatte ['drʊkplatə] **3.** *(small metallic sign)* Metallschild [me'talʃɪlt] das <-(e)s, -er>; *(made from tin)* Blechschild ['blɛçʃɪlt] ◊ *Was steht auf dem Blechschild?* **4.** *(thin layer of precious metal)* Auflage ['aoflaːgə] die <-, -n> etw. mit einer Auflage aus Silber/Gold versehen gold plate Goldauflage ['gɔlt|aoflaːgə]; *(objects covered with silver or gold)* versilbertes/vergoldetes Besteck und Geschirr

platform [noun] **1.** *(raised structure, computer system, forum)* Plattform [platfɔˀm] die <-, -en> ◊ *Der Arbeitskreis bietet eine Plattform für den Erfahrungsaustausch.* election platform Wahlplattform ['vaːlplatfɔˀm] oil platform Ölplattform ['øːlplatfɔˀm] viewing platform Aussichtsplattform ['aoszɪçtsplatfɔˀm] **2.** *(in a train station)* Bahnsteig ['baːnʃtaek] der <-(e)s, -e> ◊ *Sie stand auf dem Bahnsteig und winkte dem Zug nach.; (track)* Gleis

[glæs] das <–es, –e> ◊ *Der Zug fährt von Gleis 13 ab.* **3.** *(stage)* Podium ['po:djʊm] das <–s, Podien> ◊ *Die Diskussionsteilnehmer saßen auf dem Podium.*

platter (noun) Platte ['platə] die <–, –n> ◊ *eine Platte mit Häppchen*

plausible (adj) *(convincing)* plausibel [plao̯'zi:bl̩] <plausibler, am plausibelsten> <der/die/das plausible …> ◊ *eine plausible Erklärung* ♦ *Seine Geschichte ist nicht plausibel.*; *(person)* be plausible glaubwürdig wirken ['glao̯pvʏ'dɪç vɪ'ʁkn̩] +haben

play¹ (noun) **1.** *(drama)* Stück [ʃtʏk] das <–(e)s, –e> ◊ *Das Stück kommt im Juni auf die Bühne.* radio play Hörspiel ['hø:ɐ̯ʃpi:l] das <–(e)s, –e> television play Fernsehspiel ['fɛɐ̯nze:ʃpi:l] das <–(e)s, –e> **2.** *(game)* Spiel [ʃpi:l] das <–(e)s, –e> ◊ *Spaß am/beim Spiel.* foul play Foulspiel ['fao̯lʃpi:l] play on words Wortspiel ['vɔɐ̯tʃpi:l] **3.** *(ability to move)* Spielraum ['ʃpi:lrao̯m] der <–(e)s, Spielräume> ◊ *etwas Spielraum lassen*

⊛ **bring into play 1.** bring sb into play jdn ins Spiel bringen **2.** bring sth into play etw. anwenden **come into play 1.** *(become part of sth)* ins Spiel kommen **2.** *(become active)* wirksam werden make a play for sb/sth sich um jdn/etw. bemühen

play² (verb) spielen ['ʃpi:lən] +haben ◊ *eine wichtige Rolle spielen* ♦ *Er spielt mit seiner Eisenbahn.* ♦ *Sie spielen in der Bundesliga.* ♦ *Sie spielt in dem Film die Hauptrolle/eine Kommissarin.* ♦ *Spiel das Lied bitte noch mal.* ♦ *Fangen/Verstecken spielen* ♦ *Schach/Tennis/Fußball spielen* ♦ *Das Licht spielte auf den Wellen.* play the guitar/piano Gitarre/Klavier spielen play sb gegen jdn spielen ◊ *Sonntag spielt er gegen Agassi.*

• **play around** (phras v) **1.** *(sexually)* herummachen [hɛ'rʊmmaxn̩] +haben *(fam)* ◊ *Sie hat mit anderen Männern herumgemacht.* **2.** *(consider)* play around with sth etw. durchspielen ['dʊɐ̯çʃpi:lən] +haben ◊ *verschiedene Möglichkeiten durchspielen* **3.** *(have fun)* spielen ['ʃpi:lən] +haben ◊ *Die Kinder spielten im Garten.*

• **play at** (phras v) spielen ['ʃpi:lən] +haben ◊ *Er spielt gern den harten Geschäftsmann.* play at families Familie spielen

• **play back** (phras v) abspielen ['apʃpi:lən] +haben ◊ *eine Aufnahme/Videodatei abspielen*

• **play down** (phras v) herunterspielen [hɛ'rʊntɐʃpi:lən] +haben ◊ *eine Gefahr/einen Vorfall herunterspielen*

play-acting (noun) Theater [te'ʔa:tɐ] das <–s, –> *(fam, pej)* ◊ *Sie hat nicht wirklich geweint — das war nur Theater.*

playback (noun) Wiedergabe ['vi:dega:bə] die <–, –n> ◊ *Software für die Wiedergabe von Videos*

player (noun) **1.** *(sb who plays a game, athlete)* Spieler ['ʃpi:lɐ] der <–s, –> ♀Spielerin ['ʃpi:lərɪn] die <–, –nen> ◊ *die beste Spielerin der Mannschaft* ♦ *Jeder Spieler erhält 13 Karten.* football player Fußballspieler ['fu:sbalʃpi:lɐ] Fußballspielerin ['fu:sbalʃpi:lərɪn]; *(musician, only in compound ns)* piano player Klavierspieler [kla'vi:ɐ̯ʃpi:lɐ] Klavierspielerin [kla'vi:ɐ̯ʃpi:lərɪn] **2.** *(sb/sth involved in sth)* Akteur [ak'tø:ɐ̯] der <–s, –e> ♀Akteurin [ak'tø:rɪn] die <–, –nen> ◊ *die wichtigsten Akteure im Entscheidungsprozess* major player Hauptakteur ['hao̯ptʔak,tø:ɐ̯] Hauptakteurin ['hao̯ptʔak,tø:rɪn]

playground (noun) Spielplatz ['ʃpi:lplats] der

<–es, Spielplätze> ◊ *Die Kinder spielen auf dem Spielplatz.* ♦ *Las Vegas, der Spielplatz der Reichen*

playing field (noun) Sportplatz ['ʃpɔɐ̯tplats] der <–es, Sportplätze> ◊ *zum Fußballspielen/Training auf den Sportplatz gehen*

plc AG [a:'ge:] die

plea (noun) **1.** *(urgent request)* inständige Bitte [,ɪnʃtɛndɪgə 'bɪtə] die <–, –n> a plea for mercy eine inständige Bitte um Gnade make a plea for sth inständig um etw. bitten [,ɪnʃtɛndɪç ʊm ... bɪtn̩] <bittet, bat, hat gebeten> **2.** LAW guilty plea Schuldbekenntnis ['ʃʊltbəkɛntnɪs] das <–ses, –se> not guilty plea Unschuldserklärung ['ʊnʃʊlts|ɛklɛ:rʊŋ] die <–, –en>

plead (verb) **1.** *(request urgently)* flehen ['fle:ən] +haben ◊ *„Nein, bitte nicht!", flehte sie.* plead for sth um etw. flehen plead with sb jdn anflehen ['anfle:ən] +haben ◊ *jdn anflehen, etw. zu tun* **2.** LAW sich bekennen [bə'kɛnən] <bekennt sich, bekannte sich, hat sich bekannt> plead guilty sich schuldig bekennen plead not guilty sich nicht schuldig bekennen **3.** plead the case for sb/sth sich für jdn/etw. einsetzen [fy:ɐ̯ ... ,aɛnt͡sɛtsn̩] +haben ◊ *sich für Reformen einsetzen*

pleasant(ly) (adj, adv) **1.** *(enjoyable)* angenehm ['angəne:m] ◊ *Der Stoff ist sehr angenehm auf der Haut.* ♦ *Ich wünsche Ihnen einen angenehmen Aufenthalt.* ♦ *angenehm überrascht sein* **2.** *(friendly)* freundlich ['frɔɪ̯ntlɪç] ◊ *Er ist ein freundlicher Junge.* ♦ *Sie war freundlich, aber bestimmt.* ♦ *freundlich lächeln*

please¹ (verb) *(satisfy)* sth pleases sb etw. macht jdm Freude [maxt ... 'frɔɪ̯də] +haben ◊ *Es macht mir Freude, anderen zu helfen.* do anything to please sb alles für jdn tun ['aləs fy:ɐ̯ ... ,tu:n] <tut, tat, hat getan> be hard to please schwer zufrieden zu stellen sein [,ʃve:ɐ̯ tsu'fri:dn̩ tsu: ʃtɛlən zaːn] +sein

⊛ **you can't please everyone** man kann es nicht jedem recht machen ... as/whenever sb pleases ... wie/wann es jdm passt ◊ *Er kommt und geht, wie es ihm passt.* if you please bitte schön whatever sb pleases was jd will ◊ *Tu, was du willst!*

please² (interj) bitte ['bɪtə] ◊ *Könntest du bitte das Fenster zumachen?* ♦ *Bitte, darf ich jetzt gehen?*

⊛ **oh, please!** ich bitte dich/euch/Sie!

pleased ▸ **please¹** (adj) *(satisfied)* zufrieden [tsu'fri:dn̩] ◊ *zufriedene Kunden* ♦ *Ich bin mit dem Ergebnis sehr zufrieden.*; *(happy)* be pleased about sth sich über etw. (acc) freuen [y:bɐ ... ,frɔɪ̯ən] +haben ◊ *Ich freue mich über seinen Erfolg.* be pleased to do sth sich freuen, etw. zu tun ◊ *Ich freue mich, Sie begrüßen zu dürfen.* not too pleased nicht sehr erfreut ['nɪçt ze:ɐ̯ ɛ,frɔɪ̯t] mostly after ns ◊ *Er war nicht sehr erfreut über den unverhofften Besuch.* pleased with yourself selbstzufrieden ['zɛlpstsufri:dn̩] ◊ *Sie sah sehr selbstzufrieden aus.*

⊛ **pleased to meet you** sehr erfreut

pleasure (noun) **1.** *(joy, pleasant thing)* Freude ['frɔɪ̯də] die <–, –n> ◊ *die Freuden des Lebens* genießen beam/cry with pleasure vor Freude strahlen/weinen sb gets pleasure from sth, sth gives pleasure to sb etw. takes pleasure in sth bereitet jdm Freude sb takes pleasure in doing sth es bereitet jdm Freude, etw. zu tun **2.** *(delight or source thereof)* Vergnügen [fɛ'gny:gn̩] das <–s, –> ◊

etw. nur zum Vergnügen tun have the pleasure of doing sth das Vergnügen haben, etw. zu tun it's a pleasure to do sth es ist jdm ein Vergnügen, etw. zu tun ◊ *Es ist mir ein Vergnügen, Ihnen zu helfen.* ☺ my pleasure gern geschehen with pleasure mit Vergnügen

pleat [noun] Falte ['faltə] die <-, -n>

pledge¹ [noun] **1.** *(promise)* Versprechen [fɛ'ʃprɛçn̩] das <-s, -> ◊ *ein Versprechen brechen* make a pledge ein Versprechen geben election pledge Wahlversprechen ['va:lfɛʃprɛçn̩] **2.** *(promised money)* zugesagte Summe [ˌtsu:gəza:ktə 'zʊmə] die <-, -n> **3.** *(given as security)* Pfand [pfant] das <-(e)s, Pfänder>

pledge² [verb] **1.** *(promise)* versprechen [fɛ'ʃprɛçn̩] <verspricht, versprach, hat versprochen> ◊ *(jdm/sich) versprechen, etw. zu tun; (money, support)* zusagen ['tsu:za:gn̩] +haben ◊ *jdm seine Unterstützung zusagen* **2.** *(as security)* verpfänden [fɛ'pfɛndn̩] <verpfändet, verpfändete, hat verpfändet> ◊ *sein Haus verpfänden*

plenty [pron] **1.** *(a lot)* plenty (of) eine Menge [aenə 'mɛŋə] ◊ *Es gibt noch eine Menge zu tun.* ♦ *Wir haben noch eine Menge Zeit.* ♦ *eine Menge Bier* **2.** *(enough)* genug [gə'nu:k] ◊ *Es gibt genug für uns alle.* ♦ *Ein Kilo Muscheln ist genug für zwei Personen.*

plight [noun] Notlage ['no:tla:gə] die <-, -n> ◊ *die Notlage der Flüchtlinge*

plot¹ [noun] **1.** *(of a novel, film)* Handlung ['handlʊŋ] die <-, -en> ◊ *Der Film hat keine durchgehende Handlung.* **2.** *(conspiracy)* Verschwörung [fɛ'ʃvø:rʊŋ] die <-, -en> ◊ *eine Verschwörung gegen den König* a plot to do sth eine Verschwörung, um etw. zu tun ◊ *eine Verschwörung, um Richelieu zu stürzen* hatch a plot eine Verschwörung planen **3.** plot *(of land)* Grundstück ['grʊntʃtʏk] das <-(e)s, -e> ◊ *ein 500 Quadratmeter großes Grundstück kaufen; (for a grave)* Grab [gra:p] das <-(e)s, Gräber> ☺ lose the plot **1.** *(no longer understand sth)* nicht mehr mitkommen *(fam)* **2.** *(not be able to cope any more)* nicht mehr klarkommen *(fam)* **3.** *(go crazy)* anfangen zu spinnen *(fam)* the plot thickens die Sache wird kompliziert

plot² [verb] **1.** *(secretly plan)* planen ['pla:nən] +haben ◊ *eine Party planen* ♦ *Sie planen, den Präsidenten zu stürzen.* **2.** *(mark up, draw)* einzeichnen ['aentsaeçnən] <zeichnet ein, zeichnete ein, hat eingezeichnet> ◊ *eine Route auf einer Seekarte einzeichnen* ♦ *Punkte in ein Diagramm einzeichnen* **3.** *(a story)* plot sth die Handlung einer Sache [gen] entwerfen [di: 'handlʊŋ ... ɛnt,vɛ'rfn̩] <entwirft, entwarf, hat entworfen> ◊ *die Handlung eines Films entwerfen* ♦ *a densely plotted story* eine Geschichte mit verwickelter Handlung

pluck [verb] **1.** *(a bird)* rupfen ['rʊpfn̩] +haben ◊ *ein Huhn rupfen; (a hair)* auszupfen ['aostsʊpfn̩] +haben pluck a hair from your chest sich [dat] ein Brusthaar auszupfen; *(a guitar string, a piece of hair etc. from sth)* zupfen ['tsʊpfn̩] +haben ◊ *die Saiten einer Gitarre zupfen* ♦ *Sie zupfte sich einen Fussel von der Bluse.* pluck your eyebrows sich [dat] die Augenbrauen zupfen; *(a piece of fruit)* pflücken ['pflʏkn̩] +haben ◊ *einen Apfel pflücken* **2.** *(save sb from somewhere)* holen ['ho:lən] +haben ◊ *Ein Rettungsteam holte ihn aus dem Meer.* pluck sb to safety jdn

in Sicherheit bringen [ɪn 'zɪçehaet brɪŋən] <bringt, brachte, hat gebracht>

plug¹ [noun] **1.** *(for electrical equipment)* Stecker ['ʃtɛkɐ] der <-s, -> ◊ *den Stecker herausziehen/einstecken* **2.** *(for a book, album, film)* Werbung ['vɛrbʊŋ] die <-, -en> most sing get in a plug for sth für etw. Werbung machen **3.** *(for a hole, for your ears)* Stöpsel ['ʃtœpsl̩] der <-s, -> ◊ *den Stöpsel aus der Flasche/Badewanne ziehen; (for screws)* Dübel ['dy:bl̩] der <-s, -> ◊ *einen Dübel in die Wand drücken* ☺ pull the plug **1.** *(stop sth)* pull the plug on sth etw. stoppen **2.** *(withhold money)* pull the plug (on sb/sth) (jdm/etw.) den Hahn zudrehen

plug² [verb] **1.** *(also fig) (fill)* stopfen ['ʃtɔpfn̩] +haben ◊ *das Loch im Staatshaushalt stopfen* plug sth up with sth etw. mit etw. zustopfen [mɪt ... ,tsu:ʃtɔpfn̩] +haben ◊ *Das Loch in der Wand war mit Papier zugestopft.* **2.** *(promote)* plug sth Werbung für etw. machen [,vɛ'rbʊŋ fy:ɐ̯ ... maxn̩] +haben ◊ *In dem Artikel machte sie geschickt Werbung für ihr neues Buch.*

• **plug away** [phras v] sich abschuften ['apʃʊftn̩] <schuftet sich ab, schuftete sich ab, hat sich abgeschuftet> *(fam)*

• **plug in** [phras v] plug sth in einstecken ['aenʃtɛkn̩] +haben ◊ *die Lampe/den Videorecorder einstecken* sth plugs in somewhere etw. wird irgendwo eingesteckt

• **plug into** [phras v] **1.** *(connect to a piece of equipment)* plug sth into etw. an etw. [acc] anschließen [an ... ,anʃli:sn̩] <schließt an, schloss an, hat angeschlossen> ◊ *den Drucker an den Computer anschließen* sth plugs into sth etw. wird irgendwo angeschlossen **2.** *(take part in sth)* plug into sth Anschluss an etw. [acc] finden ['anʃlʊs an ... fɪndn̩] <findet, fand, hat gefunden> ◊ *Anschluss an den Weltmarkt finden*

plum [noun] **1.** *(fruit)* Pflaume ['pflaomə] die <-, -n> **2.** *(tree)* plum (tree) Pflaumenbaum ['pflaomənbaom] der <-(e)s, Pflaumenbäume>

plumber [noun] Installateur [ɪnstala'tø:ɐ̯] der <-s, -e> ♀Installateurin [ɪnstala'tø:rɪn] die <-, -nen> ◊ *Ich bin Installateurin von Beruf.* ♦ *Der Installateur hat die Heizung repariert.*

plump [adj] *(person)* rundlich ['rʊntlɪç] ◊ *Er ist recht rundlich.* ♦ *eine rundliche Frau; (object)* prall [pral] ◊ *Sie pflückten die prallen Beeren.* ♦ *Die Tomaten sind schön prall.*

plunder [verb] plündern ['plʏndɐn] +haben ◊ *Die Soldaten plünderten die eroberte Stadt.* ♦ *Sie plünderten und brandschatzten.*

plunge [verb] **1.** *(fall, throw, run)* stürzen ['ʃtʏ'tsn̩] +haben ◊ *Das Flugzeug stürzte ins Meer.* ♦ *Die Temperatur stürzte auf minus acht Grad.* ♦ *jdn von einem Felsen stürzen* ♦ *Wütend stürzte er sich auf sie.* **2.** *(fall away steeply)* steil abfallen [ʃtael 'apfalən] <fällt ab, fiel ab, ist abgefallen> ◊ *Die Felsen fallen steil ins Meer ab.*

• **plunge into** [phras v] **1.** *(start doing sth energetically)* plunge sth into sich in etw. [acc] stürzen [ɪn ... ʃtʏ'tsn̩] +haben ◊ *sich in die Arbeit stürzen* **2.** *(put sth deep into sth)* plunge sth into sth etw. in etw. [acc] tauchen [ɪn ... taoxn̩] +haben ◊ *Sie tauchte ihr erhitztes Gesicht in kühlendes Wasser.* plunge a knife into etw. ein Messer in etw. [acc] stechen

[aen 'mɛsə ɪn ... ʃtɛçn̩] <sticht, stach, hat gestochen>
3. *(bring or get into a situation)* plunge into sth in
etw. ⓐⓒⓒ stürzen [ɪn ... ʃtʏrʦn̩] *transitive use +haben;*
intransitive use +sein ◊ *Die Trennung stürzte ihn in*
tiefe Depressionen. ◆ *Das Land stürzte ins Chaos.*
4. *(jump, dive)* plunge into sth in etw. ⓐⓒⓒ springen
[ɪn ... ʃprɪŋən] <springt, sprang, ist gesprungen> ◊
ins Wasser springen
pluperfect ⓝⓞⓤⓝ Plusquamperfekt ['plʊskvampɛ'fɛkt]
das <-s, -e>
plural ⓝⓞⓤⓝ Plural ['plu:ra:l] der <-s, -e>
plus¹ ⓐⓓⓙ **1.** *(above zero)* plus [plʊs] ◊ *Temperaturen*
zwischen minus 20 und plus 40 Grad **2.** *(positive)*
Plus... [plʊs] plus point Pluspunkt ['plʊspʊŋkt] der
<-(e)s, -e> **3.** *(more than)* ... plus über ... ['y:bɐ]
◊ *Bei der Veranstaltung waren über 100 Studenten.*
◊ A/B etc. plus ⊖*Eins/Zwei etc. minus*
plus² ⓟⓡⓔⓟ *(adding an amount of money or tax)*
zuzüglich ['ʦu:ʦy:klɪç] *sing nouns without article or*
attribute are not declined when following this prep,
otherwise ⓖ⁺ⓖⓔⓝ ◊ *Das Gerät kostet 250 Euro*
zuzüglich der Mehrwertsteuer.
plus³ ⓒⓞⓝⓙⓤⓝⓒ **1.** *(besides)* außerdem ['aosedə:m] ◊
Ich habe keine Lust mitzukommen; außerdem habe
ich zu viel zu tun. **2.** ⓜⓐⓣⓗ plus [plʊs] ◊ *Fünf plus*
drei ist acht.
p.m. *(from around 1 p.m. to 6 p.m.)* nachmittags
['na:xmɪta:ks] ◊ *Ich habe um 4 Uhr nachmittags*
einen Termin bei einem Kunden.; (from around 6
p.m.) abends ['a:bm̩ts] ◊ *Sie kommt jeden Tag um 7*
Uhr abends nach Hause. We are meeting at 8 p.m.
Wir treffen uns um 20 Uhr.

> In German it is common to use the 24-hour clock to
> differentiate between a.m. and p.m.

PO box ⓝⓞⓤⓝ Postfach ['pɔstfax] das
<-(e)s, Postfächer>
pocket¹ ⓝⓞⓤⓝ **1.** *(in clothing)* Tasche ['taʃə] die
<-, -n> ◊ *eine Hose mit zwei Taschen* ◆ *Er steckte*
die Hand in die Tasche. in a bag Fach [fax] das
<-(e)s, Fächer> ◊ *In der Handtasche ist auch ein*
Fach für ein Handy. **2.** *(on a billiard or snooker table)*
Loch [lɔx] das <-(e)s, Löcher> **3.** *(small area where*
sth exists) there are small pockets of sth etw. gibt
es nur an wenigen Stellen
[gi:pt ɛs nu:ɐ̯ an ˌve:nɪgn̩ 'ʃtɛlən] <gibt, gab, hat
gegeben> ◊ *Diese Pflanze gibt es nur an wenigen*
Stellen im Gebirge. small pockets of deprivation
Armenviertel ['a'mənfɪ'tl̩] die <-> *pl* small pockets
of resistance kleine Widerstandsgruppen
[klaenə 'vi:deʃtantsgrʊpm̩] die <-> *pl*
◉ dig deep into your pocket tief in die Tasche
greifen out of your own pocket aus eigener Tasche
line your own pockets Geld in die eigene Tasche
stecken be in pocket Geld verdient haben be out
of pocket ein Verlustgeschäft gemacht haben pick
sb's pocket jdn bestehlen sth to suit every pocket
etw. für jeden Geldbeutel
pocket² ⓥⓔⓡⓑ **1.** *(put into your pocket, steal)* einstecken ['aenʃtɛkn̩] +haben *(fam)* ◊ *Hast du die Auto-*
schlüssel eingesteckt? ◆ *im Geschäft ein Buch einste-*
cken **2.** *(embezzle)* in die eigene Tasche stecken
[ɪn di: ˌaegənə 'taʃə ʃtɛkn̩] +haben **3.** *(win, receive)*
einsacken ['aenzakn̩] +haben *(fam)* ◊ *einen Gewinn*
einsacken **4.** *(in pool or billiards)* versenken
[fɛ'zɛŋkn̩] <versenkt, versenkte, hat versenkt> *(fam)* ◊

eine Kugel versenken
pocket money ⓝⓞⓤⓝ Taschengeld ['taʃŋgɛlt] das
<-(e)s, -er> *most sing* ◊ *Sie bekommt von ihren*
Eltern fünf Euro Taschengeld in der Woche. ◆ *Der*
Lohn war kaum mehr als ein Taschengeld.
podium ⓝⓞⓤⓝ Podium ['po:dium] das <-s, Podien> ◊
Der Dirigent stieg aufs Podium.
poem ⓝⓞⓤⓝ Gedicht [gə'dɪçt] das <-(e)s, -e>
poet ⓝⓞⓤⓝ Dichter ['dɪçtɐ] der <-s, -> ♀Dichterin
['dɪçtərɪn] die <-, -nen> ◊ *eine bekannte deutsche*
Dichterin ◆ *Er war Dichter und Musiker.*
poetry ⓝⓞⓤⓝ *(poems)* Gedichte [gə'dɪçtə] die <-> *pl* ◊
Magst du ihre Gedichte?; (as a subject) Dichtung
['dɪçtʊŋ] die <-, -en> ◊ *die höfische Dichtung des*
Mittelalters
◉ sth is pure poetry etw. ist ein Gedicht
point¹ ⓝⓞⓤⓝ **1.** *(topic, place, spot, in games, at the*
stock exchange) Punkt [pʊŋkt] der <-(e)s, -e> ◊ *ein*
strittiger/wichtiger Punkt ◆ *Die Gerade schneidet den*
Kreis im Punkt S. ◆ *einen kritischen Punkt*
erreichen/überschreiten ◆ *An diesem Punkt der*
Handlung betritt der Vater die Bühne. ◆ *einen Punkt*
gewinnen/verlieren ◆ *Der DAX verlor fast 20 Punkte.*
point by point Punkt für Punkt weak point Schwachpunkt ['ʃvaxpʊŋkt] strong point Stärke ['ʃtɛ'kə] die
<-, -n> freezing point Gefrierpunkt [gə'fri:gpʊŋkt]
2. *(meaning, significance)* Sinn [zɪn] der <-(e)s, -e>
◊ *Das war nicht Sinn der Sache.* there is a/no point
in doing sth es hat Sinn/keinen Sinn, etw. zu tun
see no point in doing sth keinen Sinn darin sehen,
etw. zu tun my point is ... ich meine ... [ɪç 'maenə]
3. *(sharp end)* Spitze ['ʃpɪtsə] die <-, -n> ◊ *Die*
Spitze der Nadel/des Bleistifts ist abgebrochen.
4. *(decimal point)* Komma ['kɔma:] das <-s, -s> ◊
zwei Komma fünf
◉ be beside the point irrelevant sein a sore point
ein wunder Punkt be to the point treffend sein get
to the point auf den Punkt kommen sb has got a
point da hat jd gar nicht so Unrecht miss the
point nicht verstehen, wie gemeint ist I take your
point ich verstehe, was du meinst/Sie meinen
point² ⓥⓔⓡⓑ **1.** *(hold your finger towards, be directed*
towards) zeigen ['ʦaegń̩] +haben point at/to sb/sth
auf jdn/etw. zeigen ◊ *Er zeigte ungeduldig auf die*
Uhr. ◆ *Der kleine Zeiger zeigt auf drei.* point sth at
sb/sth mit etw. auf jdn/etw. zeigen ◊ *mit dem*
Finger auf einen Mann zeigen point somewhere
irgendwohin zeigen point left/right/north nach
links/rechts/Norden zeigen ◊ *Die Nadel des*
Kompasses zeigt nach Norden. point sb in the
direction of sb/sth jdm den Weg zu etw. zeigen
2. *(aim)* point at sb/sth mit etw. auf jdn/etw. zeigen
[aof ... rɪçtn̩] richten auf jdn/etw. ◊ *ein Fotoapparat/eine Pistole*
auf jdn richten **3.** *(indicate, hint at)* point towards
sth etw. aufzeigen ['aofsaegń̩] +haben ◊ *Die Studie*
zeigt Problemlösungen auf.
● **point out** ⓟⓗⓡⓐⓢ ⓥ **1.** *(direct attention towards)*
point sb/sth out auf jdn/etw. zeigen [aof ... ʦaegń̩]
+haben ◊ *Er zeigte auf ein Schiff im Hafen.* **2.** *(tell*
sb sth) point sth out auf etw. ⓐⓒⓒ hinweisen
[aof ... ˌhɪnvaezn̩] <weist hin, wies hin, hat hingewie-
sen> ◊ *Sie wies auf die Vorzüge der neuen Technolo-*
gie hin. point out that darauf hinweisen
● **point to** ⓟⓗⓡⓐⓢ ⓥ point to sth auf etw. ⓐⓒⓒ
schließen lassen [aof ... ʃli:sn̩ lasn̩] <lässt, ließ, hat
lassen> ◊ *Neue archäologische Funde lassen auf eine*

A B C D E F G H I J K L M N O P Q R S T U V W X Y Z

Hochkultur schließen.

pointed [adj] spitz [[pɪts] <spitzer, am spitzesten> ◊ *Seine Nase war lang und spitz.* ♦ *eine spitze Bemerkung machen*

pointless(ly) [adj, adv] sinnlos ['zɪnloːs] <sinnloser, am sinnlosesten> ◊ *sinnlose Gewalt* ♦ *Sie hatte das Gefühl, dass ihr Leben sinnlos geworden war.* ♦ *Du solltest aufhören, sinnlos Geld auszugeben.*

point of view [noun] 1. *(perspective)* Gesichtspunkt [gə'zɪçtspʊŋkt] der <-(e)s, -e> from a historic/ religious etc. point of view unter historischem/religiösem Gesichtspunkt 2. *(opinion)* Standpunkt ['ʃtantpʊŋkt] der <-(e)s, -e> ◊ *unterschiedliche Standpunkte haben* from sb's point of view von jds Standpunkt aus

poison¹ [noun] Gift [ɡɪft] das <-(e)s, -e> ◊ *ein tödliches Gift* ♦ *Die neue Steuer ist Gift für die Wirtschaft.*

poison² [verb] vergiften [fɛ'ɡɪftn] <vergiftet, vergiftete, hat vergiftet> ◊ *Ungeziefer/die Umwelt vergiften* ♦ *jds Essen vergiften* ♦ *Der Streit hat die Atmosphäre vergiftet.*

poisonous [adj] giftig ['ɡɪftɪç] ◊ *giftige Gase/Beeren* ♦ *giftige Worte* ♦ *Diese Substanz wird als leicht giftig eingestuft.*

Poland [noun] Polen ['poːlən] das <-s> article only in combination with attribute, no pl → Germany

pole [noun] 1. *(stick)* Stange ['ʃtaŋə] die <-, -n> ◊ *Die Bohnen ranken sich an den Stangen hoch.* 2. *(one of two things that are opposites)* Pol [poːl] der <-s, -e> ◊ *die geografischen/magnetischen Pole* ♦ *die Pole der Gesellschaft*

Pole [noun] Pole ['poːlə] der <-n, -n> ♀Polin ['poːlɪn] die <-, -nen> → German¹ 1.

police [noun] *(organization)* Polizei [poli'tsae] die <-, -en> most sing ◊ *Er ist bei der Polizei.* ♦ *Sie rief die Polizei.; (as a group of individuals)* Polizisten [poli'tsɪstn] die <-> pl ◊ *Über 200 Polizisten waren bei der Demonstration im Einsatz.*

policeman [noun] Polizist [poli'tsɪst] der <-en, -en> ◊ *Er ist Polizist.* ♦ *ein junger Polizist*

police officer [noun] Polizist [poli'tsɪst] der <-en, -en> ♀Polizistin [poli'tsɪstɪn] die <-, -nen> ◊ *Er ist Polizist.* ♦ *Die Polizistin nahm seine Daten auf.*

police station [noun] Polizeirevier [poli'tsaere,viːɐ] das <-s, -e> ◊ *Sie musste sich auf dem Polizeirevier melden.*

policewoman [noun] Polizistin [poli'tsɪstɪn] die <-, -nen> ◊ *Er wurde von zwei Polizistinnen abgeführt.* ♦ *eine junge Polizistin*

policy [noun] 1. *(of a government, party, group)* Politik [poli'tiːk] die <-, -en> most sing ◊ *eine neue Politik zur Familienförderung* ♦ *die Politik der USA gegenüber dem Nahen Osten* policy of sth Politik ... [gen] ◊ *Das Land verfolgt eine Politik der Abrüstung/ Neutralität.* It is not our policy to talk to the press. Wir geben prinzipiell keine Interviews. foreign policy Außenpolitik ['aosnpoli,tiːk] policy on immigration Einwanderungspolitik ['aenvandərʊŋspoli,tiːk] 2. *(set of ideas)* Linie ['liːnjə] die <-, -n> ◊ *Meine Linie ist, immer direkt und ehrlich zu sein.* ♦ *Unser Chef versucht, immer nur seine Linie durchzusetzen.* 3. *(insurance)* Police [po'liːsə] die <-, -n> ◊ *Bewahren Sie die Police in einem Safe auf.* insurance policy Versicherungspolice

[fɛ'zɪçərʊŋspo,liːsə]

polish [verb] 1. *(rub)* polieren [po'liːrən] <poliert, polierte, hat poliert> ◊ *Sie polierte die Schuhe mit einem Lappen.* 2. *(improve)* polish (up) verbessern [fɛ'bɛsɛn] <verbessert, verbesserte, hat verbessert> ◊ *Wie kann ich mein Französisch verbessern?* • **polish off** [phras v] 1. *(eat, drink)* wegputzen ['vɛkpʊtsn] +haben *(fam)* ◊ *Die Jungen haben das ganze Essen weggeputzt.* 2. *(defeat)* erledigen [ɛ'leːdɪɡn] <erledigt, erledigte, hat erledigt> *(fam)* ◊ *Die Bayern haben ihren Gegner mit 6:0 erledigt.; (kill)* umbringen ['ʊmbrɪŋən] <bringt um, brachte um, hat umgebracht> *(fam)* ◊ *Die letzte Übung hat mich fast umgebracht!*

Polish¹ [noun] *(language, subject)* Polnisch ['pɔlnɪʃ] das <-(s)> no pl → German¹ 1.

Polish² [adj] polnisch ['pɔlnɪʃ] → German²

polished → polish [adj] glänzend ['ɡlɛntsn̩t] mostly before ns ◊ *Er ist ein glänzender Unterhalter.; (speech)* geschliffen [ɡə'ʃlɪfn̩] ◊ *die geschliffene Sprache der Autorin* ♦ *Seine Rhetorik war geschliffen.*

polite(ly) [adj, adv] höflich ['høːflɪç] ◊ *Ich wollte nur höflich zu ihm sein.* ♦ *eine höfliche Frage* ♦ *Sie grüßte ihn höflich.* He was just being polite. Er hat das nur aus Höflichkeit gesagt. polite conversation Konversation [kɔnvɛɐ'za'tsjoːn] die <-, -en> most sing ◊ *Sie machten Konversation.* to put it politely gelinde gesagt [ɡə'lɪndə ɡəzaːkt] ◊ *Dieser Politiker war, gelinde gesagt, nicht ganz ehrlich.*

political [adj] 1. *(relating to politics)* politisch [po'liːtɪʃ] ◊ *das politische System in Peru* ♦ *jdn wegen seiner politischen Überzeugung verfolgen* ♦ *Die Entscheidung war rein politisch.* 2. *(involved in politics)* politisch engagiert [po,liːtɪʃ aŋa'ʒiːɡt] ◊ *a political animal* ein politisch engagierter Mensch ➌ **it's very political somewhere** irgendwo spielen sich ständig Machtkämpfe ab

politically [adv] politisch [po'liːtɪʃ] ◊ *Er war politisch sehr aktiv.* ♦ *Die Entführung war politisch motiviert.*

politician [noun] Politiker [po'liːtɪkɐ] der <-s, -> ♀Politikerin [po'liːtɪkərɪn] die <-, -nen> ◊ *eine einflussreiche Politikerin* ♦ *Als Politiker ist er viel unterwegs.*

politics [noun] 1. *(political life)* Politik [po'liːtiːk] die <-> no pl ◊ *Sie redeten über Politik.* go into politics in die Politik gehen ◊ *Sie will in die Politik gehen.* local politics Kommunalpolitik [kɔmu'naːlpoli,tiːk] play politics politische Spiele treiben [po,liːtɪʃə 'ʃpiːlə traebm̩] 2. *(corporate intrigue)* office politics Machtkämpfe im Büro [,maxtkɛmpfə ɪm by'roː] die <-> pl 3. *(political views)* sb's politics jds politische Ansichten [po,liːtɪʃə 'anzɪçtn̩] <-> pl ◊ *Ich kann mich mit ihren politischen Ansichten nicht anfreunden.* 4. UNI *(subject)* Politikwissenschaft [po'liːtiːkvɪsn̩ʃaft] die <-, -en> ◊ *Er studiert Politikwissenschaft.*

poll [noun] 1. *(survey)* Umfrage ['ʊmfraːɡə] die <-, -n> ◊ *eine Umfrage durchführen* opinion poll Meinungsumfrage ['maenʊŋs|ʊmfraːɡə] conduct a poll eine Umfrage durchführen 2. *(election)* Wahl [vaːl] die <-, -en> ◊ *Bei der Wahl haben die Sozialisten gewonnen.* 3. *(votes)* the poll die Stimmen [di: 'ʃtɪmən] <-> pl ◊ *Sie bekam 75% der Stimmen.* 4. *(polling station)* the polls die Wahllokale [di: 'vaːl,loːka:lə] <-> pl ◊ *Die Wahllokale sind bis 20 Uhr geöffnet.*

Ⓟ **go to the polls** wählen

pollute ⟨verb⟩ **1.** *(the environment)* verschmutzen [fə'ʃmuːtṇ] <verschmutzt, verschmutzte, hat verschmutzt> ◊ *Das Öl hat die Strände verschmutzt.* **2.** *(spoil)* verderben [fɛ'dɛ'bm] <verdirbt, verdarb, hat verdorben> ◊ *Diese Videospiele verderben den Charakter unserer Kinder.*

pollution ⟨noun⟩ Verschmutzung [fɛ'ʃmuːtsʊŋ] die <–, –en> ◊ *die Verschmutzung der Meere* air pollution Luftverschmutzung ['lʊftfɛʃmuːtsʊŋ]

polytechnic ⟨noun⟩ Fachhochschule ['faxhoːxʃuːlə] die <–, –n> ◊ *ein Studium an einer Fachhochschule*

pond ⟨noun⟩ Teich [taɛç] der <–(e)s, –e> ◊ *Sie fütterten die Enten im Teich.*

pony ⟨noun⟩ Pony ['pɔniː] das <–s, –s> ◊ *Das Kind ritt auf einem Pony.*

ponytail ⟨noun⟩ Pferdeschwanz ['pfeːɐdəʃvants] der <–es, Pferdeschwänze> ◊ *Ihr blondes Haar ist zu einem Pferdeschwanz gebunden.*

poo ⟨noun⟩ Aa [aˈʔaː] das <–> *no pl (kidsp)* do a poo Aa machen

pool ⟨noun⟩ **1.** *(small area of liquid)* Pfütze ['pfʏtsə] die <–, –n> ◊ *Das Wasser sammelte sich in einer Pfütze.* pool of blood Blutlache ['bluːtlaxə] die <–, –n> **2.** *(artificial)* Bassin [ba'sɛŋ] das <–s, –s> ◊ *Die Pinguine schwimmen in ihrem Bassin.* **3.** *(for swimming)* Becken ['bɛkṇ] das <–s, –> ◊ kopfüber ins Becken springen → swimming pool **4.** *(game)* Poolbillard ['puːlbɪljaˈt] das <–s> *no pl* **5.** *(area)* pool of light Lichtfleck ['lɪçtflɛk] der <–(e)s, –en> **6.** *(competition)* the pools Fußballtoto ['fuːsbalˌtoːtoː] das *or also der* <–s, –s> ◊ *Er hat im Fußballtoto viel Geld gewonnen.* **7.** *(available people or things)* Pool [puːl] der <–s, –s> ◊ *Unser Team besteht aus 15 Festangestellten und einem Pool von Freiberuflern.* car pool Fahrgemeinschaft ['faːʳgəmaɛnʃaft] die <–, –en>

poor ⟨adj⟩ **1.** *(not rich, unfortunate)* arm [aˈm] <ärmer, am ärmsten> ◊ *Die Familie war ziemlich arm.* ♦ *Der arme Junge! Er hat keine Mutter mehr.* Poor old Tom! Der arme Tom! poor in sth arm an etw. ⟨dat⟩ ◊ *Die Region ist arm an Bodenschätzen.* the Armen ◊ *Die Armen brauchen unsere Unterstützung.* **2.** *(not good)* schlecht [ʃlɛçt] <schlechter, am schlechtesten> ◊ *Bei dem schlechten Licht kannst du doch nicht lesen!* ♦ *Die Arbeitsbedingungen sind sehr schlecht.* ♦ *Sein schlechter Gesundheitszustand gibt Anlass zur Sorge.* ♦ *ein schlechter Verlierer;* (achievement, performance etc.) schwach [ʃvax] <schwächer, am schwächsten> ◊ *schwache schulische Leistungen* ♦ *In Mathematik war ich schon immer schwach.*

poorly ⟨adv⟩ *(paid, organized)* schlecht [ʃlɛçt] <schlechter, am schlechtesten> ◊ *ein schlecht bezahlter Job;* (represented, attended) schwach [ʃvax] <schwächer, am schwächsten> ◊ *Das Konzert war schwach besucht.* ♦ *Frauen sind in diesem Beruf sehr schwach vertreten.*
Ⓟ **be poorly off** schlecht gestellt sein

pop¹ ⟨noun⟩ **1.** MUS Pop [pɔp] der <–(s)> *no pl* **2.** *(sound)* Knall [knal] der <–(e)s, –e>

pop² ⟨verb⟩ **1.** *(cork)* sth pops etw. knallt [knalt] +haben ◊ *Um Mitternacht knallten die Sektkorken.;* (balloon, corn) etw. platzt [platst] +sein ◊ *Der Luftballon ist geplatzt.* pop sth etw. platzen lassen ['platsṇ lasṇ] <lässt, ließ, hat lassen> ◊ *Ich lasse den Luftballon jetzt platzen.* **2.** *(go)* sb pops somewhere

jd geht schnell irgendwohin [geːt ʃnɛl] <ging, ist gegangen> ◊ *Ich gebe schnell mal nach unten.* pop out rausgehen ['raʊsgeːən] *(fam)* ◊ *Ich gebe kurz raus und hole Brötchen.;* (go for a visit) pop round rübergehen ['ryːbeːgeːən] *(fam)* ◊ *Ich gebe kurz zu Tina rüber. In einer Stunde bin ich wieder da.* pop in reinkommen ['raɛnkɔmən] <kommt rein, kam rein, ist reingekommen> *(fam)* ◊ *Sie kam rein und brachte mir die Zeitung.;* (come for a visit) pop round rüberkommen ['ryːbeːkɔmən] *(fam)* ◊ *Du kannst jederzeit auf einen Kaffee rüberkommen.* **3.** *(put)* pop sth in sth etw. in etw. ⟨acc⟩ tun [tuːn ... tuːn] <tut, tat, hat getan> *(fam)* ◊ *Er tat die leere Packung in den Müll.* ♦ *Tu schnell die Blumen ins Wasser!* **4.** *(due to air pressure)* sb's ears pop jdm knacken die Ohren [knakŋ diː 'oːrən] +haben ◊ *Beim Start und bei der Landung haben mir die Ohren geknackt.* **5.** *(due to amazement)* sb's eyes pop jdm fallen die Augen fast aus dem Kopf [falən diː ˌaʊgŋ fast aʊs deːm 'kɔpf] <fielen, sind gefallen> ◊ *Als er uns zusammen sah, fielen ihm die Augen fast aus dem Kopf.* **6.** *(a pill)* schlucken ['ʃlʊkŋ] +haben ◊ *Sie schluckt am Tag bestimmt zehn verschiedene Tabletten.*

• **pop out** ⟨phras v⟩ sth pops out etw. rutscht jdm raus [rʊtʃt ... 'raʊs] +sein *(fam)* ◊ *Entschuldige, ich wollte dich nicht beleidigen — das ist mir nur so rausgerutscht.*

• **pop up** ⟨phras v⟩ auftauchen ['aʊftaʊxŋ] +sein ◊ *Ständig tauchen neue Computerviren auf.*

Pope ⟨noun⟩ Papst [paːpst] der <–(e)s, Päpste>

pop music ⟨noun⟩ Popmusik ['pɔpmuˌziːk] die <–, –en>

popular ⟨adj⟩ **1.** *(liked)* popular (with sb) (bei jdm) beliebt [bə'liːpt] <beliebter, am beliebtesten> ◊ *beliebte Melodien* ♦ *Dieser Lehrer ist bei den Schülern sehr beliebt.;* (with the public) populär [popu'lɛːɐ] ◊ *eine populäre Bürgermeisterin* ♦ *Die Reform ist bei den Wählern nicht sehr populär.* **2.** *(wanted by many people)* gefragt [gə'fraːkt] <gefragter, am gefragtesten> ◊ *Sie ist ein gefragtes Fotomodell.* have popular appeal sehr gefragt sein ◊ *Sein neues Buch ist im Augenblick sehr gefragt.* due to popular demand wegen der großen Nachfrage [veːgŋ deːɐ groːsṇ 'naːxfraːgə] **3.** *(widespread)* weit verbreitet [vaɛt fɛ'braɛtət] a popular misconception ein weit verbreiteter Irrtum contrary to popular belief im Gegensatz zur vorherrschenden Meinung [ɪm ˌgeːgŋzats tsuːɐ ˌfoːɐhɛʳʃṇdən 'maɛnʊŋ] **4.** *(for ordinary people)* Populär... [popu'lɛːɐ] popular science Populärwissenschaft [popu'lɛːɐvɪsṇʃaft] die <–, –en> **5.** *(discontent, support)* there is little popular support for sth etw. findet in der Öffentlichkeit wenig Anklang [fɪndət ɪn deːɐ ˌœfṇtlɪçkaɛt ˌveːnɪç 'anklaŋ] not before ns popular uprising Volksaufstand ['fɔlksˌaʊfʃtant] der <–s, Volksaufstände>

popularity ⟨noun⟩ Beliebtheit [bə'liːptˌhaɛt] die <–> *no pl* at the height of sb's popularity auf dem Höhepunkt seiner/ihrer Beliebtheit ◊ *Er zog sich auf dem Höhepunkt seiner Beliebtheit ins Privatleben zurück.* gain in popularity immer beliebter werden [ɪmə bə'liːptə veːɐdņ] +sein

populate ⟨verb⟩ populate sth **1.** *(establish settlements)* etw. besiedeln [bə'ziːdḷn] <besiedelt, besiedelte, hat besiedelt> ◊ *Die eroberten Gebiet wurden schon bald besiedelt.* densely/sparsely populated dicht/dünn

besiedelt 2. *(live somewhere)* irgendwo leben ['le:bm̩] +haben ◊ *Eine seltene Lemurenart lebt auf der Insel.* sth is populated by people/animals irgendwo leben Menschen/Tiere ◊ *In dieser Region leben nur 3000 Menschen.* **3.** *(fig) (a film, novel etc.)* irgendwo vorkommen ['fo:ɐkɔmən] <kommt vor, kam vor, ist vorgekommen> ◊ *die Menschen, die in Thomas Manns Romanen vorkommen*

population [noun] **1.** *(inhabitants, group of people)* Bevölkerung [bə'fœlkərʊŋ] die <-, -en> most sing ◊ *die Bevölkerung Kanadas* ♦ *Das Land hat eine Bevölkerung von 60 Millionen.* ♦ *die arbeitende/kurdische Bevölkerung* population growth Bevölkerungswachstum [bə'fœlkərʊŋsvakstu:m] das <-s> no pl population explosion Bevölkerungsexplosion [bə'fœlkərʊŋsɛksplo͜ozio:n] die <-, -en> **2.** *(of wild animals)* Bestand [bə'ʃtant] der <-(e)s, Bestände> ◊ *Das Füttern von Wildtieren kann deren Bestände verringern.* tiger population Tigerbestand ['ti:gəbəʃtant]

porcelain [noun] Porzellan [pɔr'tsɛ'la:n] das <-s, -e> ◊ *Geschirr/eine Figur aus Porzellan*

pore [noun] Pore ['po:rə] die <-, -n> most pl ◊ *Der Schweiß brach ihm aus allen Poren.*

pore over [verb] pore over sth etw. studieren [ʃtu'di:rən] <studiert, studierte, hat studiert>

pork [noun] Schweinefleisch ['ʃvaenəflaeʃ] das <-(e)s> no pl ◊ *Er isst kein Schweinefleisch.* pork chop Schweinekotelett ['ʃvaenəkɔt.lɛt] das <-s, -s>

porridge [noun] Haferbrei ['ha:fəbrae] der <-(e)s, -e>

port [noun] **1.** *(area for ships)* Hafen ['ha:fn̩] der <-s, Häfen> ◊ *Ein Schiff ist in den Hafen eingelaufen.* in port im Hafen; *(city)* Hafenstadt ['ha:fn̩ʃtat] die <-, Hafenstädte> ◊ *die größte Hafenstadt Frankreichs* **2.** IT Anschluss ['anʃlʊs] der <-es, Anschlüsse> ◊ *ein Anschluss für den Drucker* **3.** *(wine)* Portwein ['pɔrtvaen] der <-(e)s, -e> **4.** *(left side)* Backbord ['bakbɔrt] das <-(e)s> no pl

portable [adj] **1.** *(easy to carry)* tragbar ['tra:kba:r] no comp/superl ◊ *ein tragbarer Fernseher* ♦ *Das Gerät ist tragbar.* **2.** *(skill, insurance, software)* übertragbar [ybe'tra:kba:r] no comp/superl ◊ *übertragbare Software* ♦ *Die Versicherung ist nicht übertragbar.*

porter [noun] **1.** *(in a station, airport)* Gepäckträger [gə'pɛktrɛːgɐ] der <-s, -> ♀Gepäckträgerin [gə'pɛktrɛːgərɪn] die <-, -nen> ◊ *Sie rief einen Gepäckträger herbei.* **2.** *(in a hotel)* Portier [pɔr'tje:] der <-s, -s> ◊ *Wir gaben den Zimmerschlüssel beim Portier ab.* **3.** *(in a hospital)* Hilfspfleger ['hɪlfspfle:gɐ] der <-s, -> ♀Hilfspflegerin ['hɪlfspfle:gərɪn] die <-, -nen>

portfolio [noun] **1.** *(case for pictures)* Mappe ['mapə] die <-, -n> ◊ *Er zeigte eine Mappe mit seinen Entwürfen.* **2.** *(of products etc.)* Kollektion [kɔlɛk'tsio:n] die <-, -en> portfolio of customers Kundenbasis ['kʊndnba:zɪs] die <-, Kundenbasen> ◊ *Die Firma weitete ihre Kundenbasis aus.* **3.** *(investments)* Portefeuille [pɔrtə'fœːj] das <-s, -s> **4.** POL Geschäftsbereich [gə'ʃɛftsbəraeç] der <-(e)s, -e> ◊ *ein Minister ohne Geschäftsbereich*

portion [noun] **1.** *(part)* Teil [tael] der <-(e)s, -e> ◊ *ein großer Teil der Bevölkerung* ♦ *Das Museum zeigt nur einen kleinen Teil seiner Sammlung.* **2.** *(of food)* Portion [pɔr'tsio:n] die <-, -en> ◊ *Er aß eine riesige Portion Nudeln.* ♦ *den Nachtisch in acht Portionen aufteilen*

portrait [noun] **1.** *(painting, photo, description)* portrait

(of) Porträt (... [gen]) [pɔr'trɛ:] das <-s, -s> ◊ *ein Porträt malen* ♦ *das Porträt der Königin* ♦ *ein literarisches Porträt Londons* **2.** *(page layout)* Hochformat ['ho:xfɔr,ma:t] das <-(e)s, -e> ◊ *eine Seite im Hochformat*

portray [verb] *(show, play)* portray sb (as sth) jdn (als etw.) darstellen ['da:ʃtɛlən] +haben ◊ *Dieses Gemälde stellt die Schwester des Künstlers dar.* ♦ *Der Staatsanwalt stellte den Zeugen als unglaubwürdig dar.* ♦ *Er stellt in dem Stück den Butler dar.* ♦ *etw.* in einem guten/schlechten Licht darstellen; *(film, book)* zeigen ['tsaegn̩] +haben ◊ *Der Film zeigt das Leben in Ostberlin nach der Wende.*

Portugal [noun] Portugal ['pɔrtugal] das <-s> article only in combination with attribute, no pl → **Germany**

Portuguese¹ [noun] **1.** *(inhabitant)* Portugiese [pɔrtu'gi:zə] der <-n, -n> ♀Portugiesin [pɔrtu'gi:zɪn] die <-, -nen> the Portuguese die Portugiesen → **German¹** **1. 2.** *(language, subject)* Portugiesisch [pɔrtu'gi:zɪʃ] das <-(s)> no pl → **German¹** **2.**

Portuguese² [adj] portugiesisch [pɔrtu'gi:zɪʃ] → **German²**

pose [verb] **1.** *(a threat, risk, challenge)* darstellen ['da:ʃtɛlən] +haben ◊ *Er stellt ein Sicherheitsrisiko dar.; (a problem, difficulty)* aufwerfen ['aofvɛrfn̩] <wirft auf, warf auf, hat aufgeworfen> ◊ *Das wirft ein neues Problem auf.* **2.** *(for a photograph)* posieren [po'zi:rən] <posiert, posierte, hat posiert> ◊ *Der Star posierte für die Presse.; (for a painting)* Modell stehen [mo'dɛl ʃte:ən] <steht, stand, hat gestanden> ◊ *Wer hat wohl für das Bild Modell gestanden?* **3.** pose as sb/sth sich als jd/etw. ausgeben [als ...,aosge:bm̩] <gibt aus, gab aus, hat ausgegeben> ◊ *Er hat sich als Polizist ausgegeben.*

posh [adj] **1.** *(expensive)* nobel ['no:bl̩] <nobler, am nobelsten> <ein nobler ..., eine noble ..., ein nobles ...> ◊ *eine noble Gegend* ♦ *Die Einrichtung des Hotels ist sehr nobel.* **2.** *(upper-class)* vornehm ['fo:gne:m] ◊ *ein vornehmer Herr* ♦ *Seine neue Freundin ist sehr vornehm.*

position¹ [noun] **1.** *(way your body/sth is placed)* Stellung ['ʃtɛlʊŋ] die <-, -en> ◊ *Diese Stellung ist sehr unbequem.* ♦ *etw. in eine aufrechte Stellung bringen* **2.** *(situation)* Lage ['la:gə] die <-, -n> ◊ *in einer unangenehmen Lage sein* ♦ *Im Moment ist die Lage ziemlich unklar.* ♦ *In ihrer Lage können sie sich keine Fehler mehr leisten.* improve sb's *(financial)* position jds finanzielle Lage verbessern be in a position to do sth in der Lage sein, etw. zu tun ◊ *Er war nicht in der Lage, uns zu helfen.* If I were in your position, I wouldn't do it. Ich würde es an deiner Stelle nicht tun. **3.** *(place in relation to other things)* Standort ['ʃtant|ɔrt] der <-(e)s, -e> ◊ *Diese Pflanze braucht einen warmen Standort.* ♦ *In den Karten ist der aktuelle Standort der Planeten eingezeichnet.; (in team sports)* Position [pozi'tsio:n] die <-, -en> ◊ *„Auf welcher Position spielt er?"* — *„Rechtsaußen."* **4.** *(opinion)* Standpunkt ['ʃtantpʊŋkt] der <-(e)s, -e> ◊ *Was ist denn dein Standpunkt zu diesem Thema?* take a position einen Standpunkt beziehen take the position that auf den Standpunkt stehen, dass **5.** *(job in a company)* Stelle ['ʃtɛlə] die <-, -n> ◊ *sich um eine Stelle bewerben; (more senior)* Position [pozi'tsio:n] die <-, -en> ◊ *Sie hat eine leitende Position in der Firma.* **6.** *(rank, status)*

Position [pozi'ts̮jo:n] die <-, -en> ◊ *Er hat seine Position als Arzt/Lehrer missbraucht.* a position of responsibility eine verantwortungsvolle Position position of power **Machtposition** ['maxtpozi,ts̮jo:n] **7.** *(on a list, in a competition)* Stelle ['ʃtɛlə] die <-, -n> ◊ *Er liegt im Moment an fünfter Stelle.* ♦ *An erster Stelle auf ihrer Wunschliste steht ein Auto.* ◉ in position an der richtigen Stelle into position an die richtige Stelle out of position an der falschen Stelle

position² [verb] **1.** *(place)* platzieren [pla'ts̮i:rən] <platziert, platzierte, hat platziert> ◊ *Sie platzierte einen Link ganz unten auf der Seite.* ♦ *Überleg dir, wo du die Regale platzieren willst.* **2.** ECON *(a product)* positionieren [pozits̮jo'ni:rən] <positioniert, positionierte, hat positioniert> ◊ *Die Produktreihe konnte erfolgreich am Markt positioniert werden.* ◉ be well positioned sich in einer guten Ausgangsposition befinden

positive [adj] **1.** *(sure)* sicher ['zɪçɐ] ◊ *Sind Sie sicher, dass er es war?* be positive about sth sich [dat] einer Sache [gen] sicher sein ◊ *Sie wird kommen, dessen bin ich mir sicher.* **2.** *(not negative)* positiv ['po:ziti:f] ◊ *Positives Denken ist wichtig.* ♦ *Die Resonanz auf das Angebot war durchweg positiv.* ♦ *Das Testergebnis war positiv.* ♦ *Sie hat die Blutgruppe A positiv.* ♦ *eine positive Zahl* be positive about sth eine positive Einstellung zu etw. haben sb tests positive jds Test fällt positiv aus She tested positive for HIV. Ihr HIV-Test fiel positiv aus. **3.** *(for emphasis)* total [to'ta:l] *no comp/superl, only before ns (fam)* ◊ *Das Fest war der totale Reinfall.* **4.** *(constructive)* konstruktiv [kɔnstrʊk'ti:f] ◊ *Der Vorschlag ist sehr konstruktiv.* ♦ *einen konstruktiven Beitrag zu etw. leisten*

positively [adv] **1.** *(for emphasis)* total [to'ta:l] *no comp/superl (fam)* ◊ *Sie wurde total sauer.* **2.** *(not in a negative way)* positiv ['po:ziti:f] ◊ *positiv denken* ♦ *Der Film wurde vom Publikum positiv aufgenommen.*

possess [verb] **1.** *(own)* besitzen [bə'zɪts̮n̩] <besitzt, besaß, hat besessen> **2.** *(have)* haben ['ha:bm̩] +haben ◊ *Der neue Mitarbeiter sollte viel Humor haben.* ♦ *Ich habe keinerlei Vorkenntnisse.*

possessed → possess [adj] besessen [bə'zɛsn̩] ◊ *Er ist von einem bösen Geist besessen.* ♦ *In dem Film geht es um ein vom Teufel besessenes Kind.* like sb is possessed wie besessen ◊ *Sie schrie wie besessen.*

possession [noun] Besitz [bə'zɪts] der <-es> *no pl* ◊ *unerlaubter Besitz von Schusswaffen* be in possession of sth im Besitz ... [gen] *Sie waren im Besitz gestohlener Waffen/außerordentlicher Fähigkeiten.* all sb's possessions jds ganzer Besitz ◊ *In diesem Möbelwagen befindet sich mein ganzer Besitz.* take possession of sth etw. in Besitz nehmen possession of drugs Drogenbesitz ['dro:gm̩bəzɪts] ◉ in full possession of your faculties im Vollbesitz seiner geistigen Kräfte

possibility [noun] **1.** *(opportunity, chance, choice)* Möglichkeit ['mø:klɪçkaet] die <-, -en> ◊ *eine Möglichkeit, Geld zu verdienen* ♦ *Gibt es noch eine andere Möglichkeit?* ♦ *Diese Möglichkeit lässt sich nicht ausschließen.* ♦ the possibility of injury die Möglichkeit,

dass jd sich verletzt there is a strong possibility that es besteht durchaus die Möglichkeit, dass be a real possibility sehr wahrscheinlich sein [ze:ɐ̯ va:r'ʃaenlɪç ze:n] +sein ◊ *Entlassungen sind jetzt sehr wahrscheinlich.* be a possibility for sth für etw. in Frage kommen [fy:ɐ̯ ... ɪn 'fra:gə kɔmən] ◊ *Frau Meier kommt für die frei gewordene Stelle in Frage.* **2.** *(potential)* possibilities Potenzial [potɛn'ts̮ja:l] das <-s, -e> *(lofty)* ◊ *Die deutsche Frauenfußballmannschaft hat Potenzial.*

possible [adj] **1.** *(sth is feasible, may happen, be true)* möglich ['mø:klɪç] *no comp/superl* ◊ *Es ist möglich, dass sie heute noch kommt.* ♦ *mögliche Gründe für das Scheitern des Projekts* ♦ *Das Internet macht diese Art der Zusammenarbeit möglich.* it is possible to do sth man kann etw. tun [man kan] <kann, konnte, hat können> ◊ *Von hier aus kann man bei gutem Wetter das Festland sehen.* if (at all) possible möglichst ['mø:klɪçst] ◊ *Fehler sollten möglichst verbessert werden.* do everything humanly possible alles Menschenmögliche tun [aləs ˌmɛnʃn̩'mø:klɪçə tu:n] <tut, tat, hat getan> ◊ *Wir werden alles Menschenmögliche tun, um euch zu helfen.* it's just possible (that) es könnte sein(, dass) [ɛs kœntə 'zaen (das)] ◊ *Es könnte sein, dass sie sie vergessen hat.* **2.** *(with a superlative)* at the worst possible time zum schlechtesten Zeitpunkt [ts̮ʊm ʃlɛçtəstn̩ 'ts̮aetpʊŋkt] the highest score possible die bestmögliche Punktzahl [di: ˌbɛstmø:klɪçə 'pʊŋktts̮a:l] ◉ would it be possible to do sth könnte jd etw. tun ◊ *Könnte ich mal dein Fahrrad leihen?* ♦ *Könnten Sie bitte das Fenster öffnen?* as soon as possible so bald wie möglich whenever possible immer wenn es möglich ist

possibly [adv] **1.** *(likely to happen)* möglicherweise ['mø:klɪçɐ'vaezə] ◊ *Morgen gibt es Regen und möglicherweise Schnee.* quite possibly höchstwahrscheinlich [va:r'ʃaenlɪç] very possibly höchstwahrscheinlich ['hø:çstva:r'ʃaenlɪç] **2.** *(shocked, surprised)* nur [nu:ɐ̯] Where can she possibly be? Wo kann sie nur sein? What can he possibly have thought? Was hat er sich nur dabei gedacht? How can anybody possibly ...? Wie kann man nur ...? ◊ *Wie kann man sich nur so dumm anstellen?* **3.** *(in polite requests)* vielleicht [fi'laeçt] *(fam)* ◊ *Könnten Sie mir vielleicht sagen, wie spät es ist?* ◉ sb can't possibly jd kann nun wirklich nicht ◊ *Da kannst du wirklich nicht Nein sagen.* everything sb can possibly think of alles Menschenmögliche

post¹ [noun] **1.** *(mail)* Post [pɔst] die <-> *no pl* ◊ *Ist die Post schon gekommen?* ♦ *Ist Post für mich da?* ♦ *Die Rechnung war gestern in der Post.* send sth through the post etw. mit der Post schicken be in the post (mit der Post) unterwegs sein be mit der Post **2.** *(in the UK: collection)* catch the post rechtzeitig zur Leerung des Briefkastens [ˌrɛçts̮aets̮ɪç ts̮u:ɐ̯ ˌle:rʊŋ dɛs 'bri:fkastn̩s kɔmən] What time does the next post go? Wann wird der Briefkasten das nächste Mal geleert? **3.** *(pole)* Pfahl [pfa:l] der <-(e)s, Pfähle> ◊ *einen Pfahl in den Boden treiben* fence post Zaunpfahl ['ts̮aonpfa:l] **4.** *(in football, horse racing)* Pfosten ['pfɔstn̩] der <-s, -> ◊ *Der Schuss ging gegen den Pfosten.* winning post Zielpfosten ['ts̮i:lpfɔstn̩] **5.** *(job)* Stelle ['ʃtɛlə] die <-, -n> ◊ *Er hat eine sichere Stelle in*

der Firma seines Vaters. a teaching post eine Stelle als Lehrer take up a post eine Stelle antreten fill a post eine Stelle besetzen; (more senior) Position [pozi'tsjo:n] die <-, -en> ◊ _eine gehobene Position_ ◉ first past the post Mehrheitswahlsystem

post² [verb] **1.** (a letter, a parcel) abschicken ['apʃɪkn̩] +haben ◊ _Hast du den Brief abgeschickt?_ **2.** (information) post (up) aushängen ['aoshɛnən] +haben ◊ _Die Ergebnisse werden am schwarzen Brett ausgehängt._ post sth on a web site etw. auf eine Website stellen [aof æenə 'vɛpsaet ʃtɛlən] +haben **3.** (a guard) aufstellen ['aofʃtɛlən] +haben **4.** (to another place of work) versetzen [fɛ'zɛtsn̩] <versetzt, versetzte, hat versetzt> ◊ _Sie wurde nach London versetzt._

◉ keep sb posted jdn auf dem Laufenden halten

postage [noun] Porto ['pɔ'to:] das <-s, -s or Porti> ◊ _das Porto für eine Postkarte_ ♦ _Wie viel Porto kostet ein Brief nach Irland?_ postage and packing Porto und Verpackung

postbox [noun] Briefkasten ['bri:fkastn̩] der <-s, Briefkästen> ◊ _einen Brief in den Briefkasten werfen_ ♦ _Der Briefkasten wird zweimal am Tag geleert._

postcard [noun] Postkarte ['pɔstka'tə] die <-, -n> ◊ _jdm eine Postkarte schicken_

postcode [noun] Postleitzahl ['pɔstlaettsa:l] die <-, -en>

poster [noun] (with advertising) Plakat [pla'ka:t] das <-(e)s, -e> ◊ _ein Plakat ankleben/aufhängen; (for decoration)_ Poster ['po:stɐ] das <-s, -> ◊ _In seinem Zimmer hingen viele Poster._

postman [noun] Briefträger ['bri:ftrɛ:gɐ] der <-s, -> ◊ _War der Briefträger heute schon da?_ ♦ _Er ist seit drei Jahren Briefträger._

post office [noun] Post [pɔst] die <-> no pl ◊ _Sie arbeitet bei der Post._ ♦ _Bringst du bitte die Briefe zur Post?_

> Post has no plural form, but for the building or postal outlet the plural of the less frequent _Postfiliale – Postfilialen –_ can be used.

postpone [verb] verschieben [fɛ'ʃi:bn̩] <verschiebt, verschob, hat verschoben> postpone sth until sth etw. auf etw. [acc] verschieben ◊ _Der Vortrag/Das Spiel wird auf nächsten Samstag verschoben._ postpone sth for three weeks etw. um drei Wochen verschieben

posture [noun] Haltung ['haltʊŋ] die <-, -en> ◊ _Sie hat eine schlechte Haltung._ ♦ _Ich verstehe seine ablehnende Haltung nicht._

post-war [adj] Nachkriegs... ['na:xkri:ks] the post-war years die Nachkriegszeit [di: 'na:xkri:kstsaet] <-> no pl the post-war division of the country die Teilung des Landes in der Nachkriegszeit

postwoman [noun] Briefträgerin ['bri:ftrɛ:gərɪn] die <-, -nen> ◊ _Sie arbeitet als Briefträgerin._ ♦ _Die Briefträgerin war gerade da._

pot [noun] **1.** (for cooking, plants) Topf [tɔpf] der <-(e)s, Töpfe> ◊ _ein Topf Suppe_ ♦ _Wir ziehen Küchenkräuter in Töpfen auf der Fensterbank._ **2.** (for coffee, tea) Kanne ['kanə] die <-, -n> ◊ _Tee koche ich immer in der blauen Kanne._ ♦ _Sie hat eine ganze Kanne Kaffee getrunken._ **3.** (container) Becher ['bɛçɐ] der <-s, -> ◊ _drei Becher Joghurt; (made of glass)_ Glas [gla:s] das <-es, Gläser> ◊ _ein Glas Marmelade_

◉ a pot of gold ein Goldschatz go to pot herunterkommen ◊ _Dieses Stadtviertel ist in den letzten Jahren ziemlich heruntergekommen._ pots of jede Menge ◊ _Seine Eltern haben jede Menge Geld._

potato [noun] Kartoffel [ka'tɔfl] die <-, -n> ◊ _Kartoffeln schälen_ baked potatoes in der Schale gebackene Kartoffeln potato salad Kartoffelsalat [ka'tɔflza,la:t] der <-s, -e>

potato chip [noun] Chip [tʃɪp] der <-s, -s> most pl ◊ _Sie aßen Chips und tranken Cola._

potency [noun] **1.** (strength) Wirksamkeit ['vɪ'kza:mkaet] die <-> no pl ◊ _die Wirksamkeit eines Medikaments_ **2.** (sexual) Potenz [po'tɛns] die <-> no pl ◊ _Viagra ist ein Mittel, das die Potenz steigert._

potent [adj] **1.** (powerful) wirkungsvoll ['vɪ'kʊŋsfɔl] ◊ _Diese Bilder sind eine wirkungsvolle Abschreckung._ sth is still potent etw. hat seine Wirkung nicht eingebüßt [hat zæenə ,vɪ'kʊŋ nɪçt 'æeŋgəby:st] **2.** (strong) stark [ʃta'k] <stärker, am stärksten> ◊ _Pass auf, dieses Bier ist ziemlich stark._ ♦ _starke Medikamente_ **3.** (sexually) potent [po'tɛnt] <potenter, am potentesten> ◊ _Es stimmt nicht, dass Männer mit Glatze potenter sind._ ♦ _ein potenter Liebhaber_

potential¹ [noun] Potenzial [potɛn'tsja:l] das <-s, -e> (lofty) ◊ _Die Aktie besitzt noch viel Potenzial._ realize your full potential sein Potenzial ausschöpfen

potential² [adj] potenziell [potɛn'tsjɛl] no comp/superl, only before ns (lofty) ◊ _die potenziellen Risiken abwägen_ ♦ _potenzielle Kunden ansprechen_

potentially [adv] potenziell [potɛn'tsjɛl] no comp/superl (lofty) ◊ _eine potenziell lebensgefährliche Erkrankung_ potentially harmful bedenklich [bə'dɛŋklɪç] ◊ _Schon fünf Zigaretten pro Tag sind bedenklich._

pottery [noun] **1.** (objects) Töpferwaren ['tœpfəva:rən] die <-s> pl **2.** (activity) Töpfern ['tœpfɐn] das <-s> no pl pottery class Töpferkurs ['tœpfekʊ's] der <-es, -e>

potty [noun] Töpfchen ['tœpfçən] das <-s, -> ◊ _aufs Töpfchen gehen_

pouch [noun] Beutel ['bɔøtl] der <-s, -> ◊ _ein Beutel aus Leder_ ◊ _Kängurus transportieren ihre Jungen in einem Beutel._

poultry [noun] Geflügel [gə'fly:gl] das <-s> no pl ◊ _Sie isst nur Geflügel und Fisch._

pound¹ [noun] **1.** (money) Pfund [pfʊnt] das <-(e)s, -e> pl 'Pfund' when used with figures ◊ _Das kostet vier Pfund._ **2.** (weight) ⊜Pfund [pfʊnt] das <-(e)s, -e> pl 'Pfund' when used with figures ◊ _ein halbes/zwei Pfund Butter_ **3.** (for animals) Tierheim ['ti:ghaem] das <-(e)s, -e> **4.** (in the US: site for towed-away cars, for cars) Abschlepphof ['apʃlɛpho:f] der <-(e)s, Abschlepphöfe>

◉ demand your pound of flesh verlangen, was einem zusteht

pound² [verb] **1.** (hit) pound (on) sth gegen etw. hämmern [ge:gn̩ ...,hɛmɐn] +haben ◊ _Er hämmerte gegen die Tür, aber niemand kam._ **2.** (break up) pound sth (into sth) etw. (zu etw.) zerstoßen [tsɐ'ʃto:sn̩] <zerstößt, zerstieß, hat zerstoßen> ◊ _die Gewürze zu einem Pulver zerstoßen_ **3.** (beat) sth pounds etw. pocht [pɔxt] +haben ◊ _Er war so aufgeregt, dass sein Herz heftig pochte._ sb's head pounds jd hat pochende Kopfschmerzen **4.** (walk) stapfen ['ʃtapfn̩] ◊ _Wir stapften durch den Wald._

5. MIL *(with bombs, shells)* pound sth etw. ununterbrochen beschießen [ˌʊn|ʊntebrɔxn̩ bəˈʃiːsn̩] <beschießt, beschoss, hat beschossen> ◊ *Die Stadt wurde wochenlang ununterbrochen beschossen.*

pour [verb] **1.** *(transfer liquid)* pour sth (into sth) etw. (in etw. [acc]) gießen [ˈgiːsn̩] <gießt, goss, hat gegossen> ◊ *Gießen Sie die Mischung in eine Auflaufform.* ✦ *Sie goss den Rest in die Spüle.* **2.** *(provide a drink)* pour (sb) sth (jdm) etw. einschenken [ˈaɛnʃɛŋkn̩] +haben ◊ *Sie schenkte ihm ein Glas Wein ein.* ✦ *Er schenkte noch mehr Tee ein.* **3.** *(come, go, flow)* strömen [ˈʃtrøːmən] +sein ◊ *Durch das Fenster strömte Tageslicht ins Zimmer.* ✦ *Nach der Vorstellung strömten die Zuschauer aus dem Theater.* Tears were pouring down her face. Tränen strömten ihr übers Gesicht. The results are pouring in. Die Ergebnisse kommen alle auf einmal herein. **4.** *(rain)* it pours (down) es gießt (in Strömen) [ɛs ˈgiːst (ɪn ˈʃtrøːmən)] <goss, hat gegossen> ◊ *Es hat den ganzen Tag in Strömen gegossen.*

• **pour into** [phras v] pour sth into sth etw. in etw. [acc] stecken [ɪn ... ʃtɛkn̩] +haben ◊ *Sie haben viel Geld in dieses Projekt gesteckt.*

• **pour out** [phras v] **1.** *(a drink)* pour sth out etw. ausschenken [ˈaɔsʃɛŋkn̩] +haben ◊ *Sie schenkte Wein aus.* pour sth out for sb jdm etw. einschenken [ˈaɛnʃɛŋkn̩] +haben ◊ *Schenkst du mir bitte noch mehr Tee ein?* **2.** *(your feelings)* pour out sth sich [dat] etw. von der Seele reden [ʃɔn deːɐ ˈzeːlə reːdn̩] <redet, redete, hat geredet> ◊ *Sie ging zu ihrer besten Freundin, um sich ihren Kummer von der Seele zu reden.*

poverty [noun] Armut [ˈaʳmuːt] die <–> no pl ◊ *Sie lebten in Armut.* ✦ *In diesem Land herrscht große Armut.* ✦ *geistige Armut* poverty of ideas Einfallslosigkeit [ˈaɛnfalsloːzɪçkaɛt] die <–> no pl

powder [noun] **1.** *(for washing, for firearms, drug)* Pulver [ˈpʊlfe] das <–s, –> ◊ *etw. zu Pulver zermahlen/zerreiben* **2.** *(for your skin)* Puder [ˈpuːde] der <–s, –> ◊ *Puder auftragen*

power[1] [noun] **1.** *(ability to influence or control, political or legal power, country)* Macht [maxt] die <–, Mächte> ◊ *die Macht der Liebe* ✦ *Er hat keine Macht über mich.* ✦ *eine feindliche Macht* ✦ *Sie sollte ihre Macht nicht missbrauchen.* be in power an der Macht sein ◊ *Diese Partei ist schon seit vielen Jahren an der Macht.* do everything in your power alles tun, was in seiner Macht steht ◊ *Ich werde alles tun, was in meiner Macht steht, um Ihnen zu helfen.* seize power die Macht ergreifen exercise your power Macht ausüben power struggle Machtkampf [ˈmaxtkampf] der <–(e)s, Machtkämpfe> bargaining power Verhandlungsmacht [fɛˈhandlʊŋsmaxt] **2.** *(strength)* Kraft [kraft] die <–, Kräfte> purchasing power Kaufkraft [ˈkaɔfkraft] **3.** *(ability)* Fähigkeit [ˈfɛːɪçkaɛt] die <–, –en> ◊ *Er hat die Fähigkeit, andere in seinen Bann zu ziehen.* be beyond sb's power über jds Fähigkeiten gehen **4.** *(energy)* Energie [enɛʳˈgiː] die <–, –n> solar power Sonnenenergie [ˈzɔnənˌenɛʳˌgiː] **5.** *(electricity)* Strom [ʃtroːm] der <–(e)s, Ströme> ◊ *Der Strom ist ausgefallen.* **6.** *(force)* Stärke [ˈʃtɛʳkə] die <–, –n> ◊ *die Stärke der Explosion* **7.** *(of a machine, vehicle)* Leistung [ˈlaɛstʊŋ] die <–, –en> ◊ *die Leistung eines Rechners* ✦ *ein Motor mit 80 PS Leistung* **8.** MATH Potenz [poˈtɛnts] die <–, –en> ◊ *das Rechnen mit*

Potenzen und Wurzeln to the power of ... hoch ... [hoːx] ◊ *fünf hoch drei* ⊙ the powers that be die da oben *(fam)*

power[2] [verb] antreiben [ˈantraɛbm̩] <treibt an, trieb an, hat angetrieben> mostly passive ◊ *Das Fahrzeug wird von einer Batterie angetrieben.*

powerful [adj] **1.** *(having a lot of control over others)* mächtig [ˈmɛçtɪç] ◊ *China ist ein mächtiges Land.* ✦ *Der amerikanische Präsident ist sehr mächtig.; (with influence)* einflussreich [ˈaɛnflʊsraɛç] ◊ *ein einflussreicher Politiker* ✦ *Die Kommission ist sehr einflussreich.; (argument)* überzeugend [ybeˈtsɔɡn̩t] **2.** *(physically strong, intense, effective)* stark [ʃtaʳk] <stärker, am stärksten> ◊ *Die Gewichtheberin ist sehr stark.* ✦ *ein starkes Mittel gegen Kopfschmerzen* ✦ *ein starker Geruch; (blow etc.)* kräftig [ˈkrɛftɪç] ◊ *ein kräftiger Tritt gegen das Schienbein; (weapon)* effektiv [ɛfɛkˈtiːf] ◊ *Der Langbogen war im Mittelalter eine sehr effektive Waffe.; (explosion)* gewaltig [gəˈvaltɪç] ◊ *Eine gewaltige Explosion erschütterte die Stadt.; (computer, car)* leistungsstark [ˈlaɛstʊŋsʃtaʳk] <leistungsstärker, am leistungsstärks­ten> ◊ *Dieses Auto braucht eigentlich einen leistungsstärkeren Motor.; (light)* hell [hɛl] ◊ *ein heller Scheinwerfer*

powerfully [adv] kräftig [ˈkrɛftɪç] ◊ *ein kräftig gebauter junger Mann*

power station [noun] Kraftwerk [ˈkraftvɛʳk] das <–(e)s, –e>

practicable [adj] durchführbar [ˈdʊʳçfyːɐbaːʳ] no comp/superl ◊ *ein kaum durchführbares Projekt* ✦ *Dieser Plan ist nicht durchführbar.*

practical [adj] **1.** *(not theoretical, useful, successful)* praktisch [ˈpraktɪʃ] ◊ *Ihm fehlt die praktische Erfahrung.* ✦ *Der kurze Haarschnitt ist wirklich praktisch.* **2.** *(sensible)* vernünftig [fɛˈnʏnftɪç] ◊ *eine vernünftige Einstellung* ✦ *Diese Einteilung ist vernünftig.* be practical about sth vernünftig mit etw. umgehen ◊ *Die Kinder müssen lernen, vernünftig mit Geld umzugehen.* **3.** *(handy, skilful)* praktisch veranlagt [ˈpraktɪç fɛˌanlaːkt] <praktischer veranlagt, am praktischsten veranlagt> ◊ *Mein Bruder ist sehr praktisch veranlagt.* ✦ *Sie ist eine äußerst praktisch veranlagte Frau.*

practically [adv] praktisch [ˈpraktɪʃ] no comp/superl ◊ *Er kommt praktisch jeden Tag.* ✦ *Vollkommene Gerechtigkeit ist praktisch unmöglich.* ✦ *Das kommt praktisch nie vor.* everything practically consisting of alles, was machbar ist [ˈaləs was ˈmaxbaːʳ ɪst]

practice [noun] **1.** *(to improve skills, for an emergency)* Übung [ˈyːbʊŋ] die <–, –en> ◊ *Mit ein bisschen Übung kannst du bald ein Rad schlagen.* ✦ *Zeichnen erfordert viel Übung.* ✦ *Es brennt nicht wirklich; das ist nur eine Übung.* **2.** *(for sports)* Training [ˈtrɛːnɪŋ] das <–s, –s> ◊ *Sie hat sich beim Training verletzt.; (for orchestras, choirs)* Probe [ˈproːbə] die <–, –n> ◊ *Das Orchester hat jeden Mittwoch Probe.* do piano practice Klavier üben [klaˈviːɐ yːbm̩] +haben ◊ *Sie übt jeden Tag eine Stunde Klavier.* **3.** *(real situation)* Praxis [ˈpraksɪs] die <–, –> no pl ◊ *der Unterschied zwischen Theorie und Praxis* put sth into practice etw. in die Praxis umsetzen **4.** *(way of doing sth)* Praxis [ˈpraksɪs] die <–> no pl ◊ *the practice of sth* die Praxis, etw. zu tun ◊ *die Praxis, behinderte Kinder in eigenen Schulen zu unterrichten* common practice gängige Praxis ◊ *Folter ist dort gängige*

Praxis.; *(dubious)* Praktik ['praktɪk] die <–, –en> most pl ◊ *die zweifelhaften Praktiken dieser Geschäftsleute*; *(habit)* Angewohnheit ['angavo:nhaet] die <–, –en> ◊ *Es ist eine gute Angewohnheit, Texte wörtlich zu zitieren.*; *(custom)* Brauch [braox] der <–(e)s, Bräuche> ◊ *In den Niederlanden ist es Brauch, die Kinder zum Nikolaustag zu beschenken.* **5.** *(of a doctor, lawyer)* Praxis ['praksɪs] die <–, Praxen> ◊ *eine Praxis für Krankengymnastik* ♦ *Die Praxis ist mittwochs geschlossen.*; *(of a professional)* Büro [by'ro:] das <–s, –s> ◊ *Der Architekt hat ein Büro mit fünf Angestellten.*

⊘ **practice makes perfect** Übung macht den Meister **be in practice** in Übung sein **be out of practice** aus der Übung sein

practise, practice (verb) **1.** *(to improve)* üben ['y:bm̩] +haben ◊ *Er will Pianist werden und übt deshalb täglich mehrere Stunden.* ♦ *Der Trainer ließ die Spieler Elfmeter üben.* ♦ *für den Ernstfall üben* **practise doing sth** üben, wie man etw. tut ◊ *Üben Sie schon vor der Geburt, wie man Windeln wechselt.* **practise sth on sb** etw. an jdm ausprobieren [an ... ,aosprobi:rən] <probiert aus, probierte aus, hat ausprobiert> ◊ *Sie probierte ihre Spanischkenntnisse an den Besuchern aus.* **2.** *(choir, orchestra)* proben ['pro:bm̩] +haben ◊ *Das Orchester probt täglich von 10 bis 12 Uhr.* ♦ *Der Chor probt für das Konzert am Sonntag.* **3.** *(an activity)* betreiben [bə'traebm̩] <betreibt, betrieb, hat betrieben> ◊ *Die frühen Siedler betrieben Landwirtschaft.*; *(a job, religion)* ausüben ['aos|y:bm̩] +haben ◊ *Welchen Beruf üben Sie aus?* ♦ *seine Religion ausüben*; *(a custom, tradition)* practise sth einer Sache (dat) nachgehen ['na:xge:ən] <geht nach, ging nach, ist nachgegangen> **4.** *(a profession)* practice (as sth) (als etw.) praktizieren [prakti'tsi:rən] <praktiziert, praktizierte, hat praktiziert> ◊ *In dieser Klinik praktizieren 50 Ärzte.* **practise law** als Anwalt praktizieren

practitioner (noun) **medical practitioner** Arzt [a:ˀtst] der <–(e)s, Ärzte> ♀Ärztin ['ɛˀtstɪn] die <–, –nen> **legal practitioner** Anwalt ['anvalt] der <–(e)s, Anwälte> ♀Anwältin ['anvɛltɪn] die <–, –nen>

pragmatic(ally) (adj, adv) pragmatisch [prag'ma:tɪʃ] ◊ *eine pragmatische Lösung für ein Problem finden* ♦ *Das muss man pragmatisch sehen.* ♦ *Wir haben das Problem ganz pragmatisch gelöst.*

praise¹ (noun) Lob [lo:p] das <–(e)s> no pl ◊ *Er verlor kein Wort des Lobes.* ♦ *Sie verdienen das höchste Lob.* **be full of praise for sb/sth** jdn/etw. sehr loben [ze:ɐ̯ 'lo:bm̩] +haben **win the praise of sb** von jdm gelobt werden [fɔn ... gə'lo:pt ve:ɐ̯dn̩] <wird, wurde, ist worden> ◊ *Sie ist vom Schulleiter für ihren Einsatz gelobt worden.*

praise² (verb) loben ['lo:bm̩] +haben ◊ *Der Polizist lobte ihn für seinen Mut.* ♦ *Der Entwurf wurde sehr gelobt.* **praise sb for doing sth** jdn dafür loben, dass er etw. getan hat ◊ *Sie lobte die Kinder dafür, dass sie ihre Zimmer aufgeräumt hatten.*

pram (noun) Kinderwagen ['kɪndeva:gn̩] der <–s, –>

prank (noun) Streich [ʃtraeç] der <–(e)s, –e> **play a prank on sb** jdm einen Streich spielen

prat (noun) Idiot [i'djo:t] der <–en, –en> *(fam)* ◊ *Du Idiot!*

pray (verb) **1.** *(to God)* pray (for sth) (um etw.) beten ['be:tn̩] ◊ *betet, betete, hat gebetet* ◊ *Wir beten um*

Frieden in der Welt. ♦ *Sie betete zu Gott/zum heiligen Antonius.* ♦ *Er betete, dass er heil nach Hause kommen möge.* **2.** *(hope)* pray (for sth) (auf etw. (acc)) hoffen ['hɔfn̩] +haben ◊ *Alle hoffen, dass der Plan gelingen wird.* ♦ *Sie hofften auf eine schnelle Lösung des Konflikts.*

prayer (noun) **1.** *(communication with God)* prayer (for sth) Gebet (um etw.) [gə'be:t] das <–(e)s, –e> ◊ *ein Gebet für den Frieden in der Welt* ♦ *Ein Gebet, das fast jeder kennt, ist das Vaterunser.* **say a prayer, say your prayers** beten ['be:tn̩] <betet, betete, hat gebetet> ◊ *Jeden Abend beten wir.* **2.** *(ceremony)* prayers Andacht ['andaxt] die <–, –en> ◊ *Die Mönche treffen sich zur Andacht in der Kapelle.*

preach (verb) **1.** *(in church)* preach (the sermon) predigen ['pre:dɪgn̩] +haben ◊ *Heute predigt Pastorin Schulze.* **preach to sb** vor jdm predigen ◊ *Er predigte vor Tausenden von Menschen.* **preach about sth über etw. (acc) predigen** ◊ *Sie predigt heute über die Auferstehung.* **2.** *(lecture)* eine Moralpredigt halten [aena mo'ra:lpre:dɪçt haltn̩] <hält, hielt, hat gehalten> ◊ *Oma hat wieder eine Moralpredigt gehalten.* **3.** *(virtues)* propagieren [propa'gi:rən] <propagiert, propagierte, hat propagiert> ◊ *Sie propagieren vegetarische Kost.*

⊘ **preach to the converted** offene Türen einrennen *(fam)*

precaution (noun) **1.** *(protection)* Vorsichtsmaßnahme ['fo:ɐ̯zɪçtsma:sna:mə] die <–, –n> ◊ *Keine Angst, das ist nur eine Vorsichtsmaßnahme.* **take precautions** Vorsichtsmaßnahmen ergreifen **as a precaution** vorsichtshalber ['fo:ɐ̯zɪçtshalbe] **2.** *(use contraceptives)* take precautions verhüten [fe'hy:tn̩] <verhütet, verhütete, hat verhütet> ◊ *Habt ihr auch verhütet?*

precede (verb) **1.** *(come before in time, order)* precede sth einer Sache vorausgehen [fo'raosge:ən] <geht voraus, ging voraus, ist vorausgegangen> ◊ *Dem Frühling war ein harter Winter vorausgegangen.* ♦ *Dem Streit ging eine Beschwerde voraus.*; *(in writing)* vor etw. (dat) stehen [fo:ɐ̯ ... ʃte:ən] <steht, stand, hat gestanden> ◊ *Auf Autonummern stehen vor den Zahlen Buchstaben.* **2.** *(be sb's predecessor)* precede sb jds Vorgänger/in sein ['fo:ɐ̯gɛŋe/'fo:ɐ̯gɛŋərɪn zaen] +sein ◊ *Sie sind kompetenter als der Lehrer, der Ihr Vorgänger war.* **3.** *(introduce sth)* precede sth with sth einer Sache (dat) etw. vorausschicken [fo'raosʃɪkŋ̩] +haben ◊ *Er schickte seiner Rede einen Witz voraus.*

precedent (noun) Präzedenzfall [prɛtse'dɛntsfal] der <–(e)s, Präzedenzfälle> ◊ *Gibt es dafür einen Präzedenzfall?* **create a precedent** einen Präzedenzfall schaffen **without precedent** noch nie da gewesen [nɔx ,ni: 'da: gəve:zn̩] ◊ *Ein solcher Fall ist noch nie da gewesen.*

precept (noun) Grundsatz ['grʊntsats] der <–es, Grundsätze> ◊ *moralische Grundsätze*

precinct (noun) **1.** *(in the UK)* shopping precinct Einkaufsviertel ['aenkaofsfɪˀtl] das <–s, –> ◊ *Sie wohnt in der Nähe des Einkaufsviertels.* **pedestrian precinct** Fußgängerzone ['fu:sgɛŋetso:nə] die <–, –n> ◊ *durch die Fußgängerzone bummeln* **2.** *(around a building)* precincts Gelände [gə'lɛndə] das <–s, –> in **the precincts** auf dem Gelände **the precincts of the university** das Universitätsgelände [das univeˀzi'tɛ:tsgəlɛndə] **3.** *(in the US: district)* Bezirk [bə'tsɪˀk] der <–(e)s, –e> ◊ *Wie wurde in*

A B C D E F G H I J K L M N O P Q R S T U V W X Y Z

diesem Bezirk gewählt? **4.** *(in the US: police station)* Revier [re'viːɐ̯] das <–s, –e> ◊ *sich auf dem Revier melden* ♦ *einen Verdächtigen aufs Revier bringen*

precious [adj] **1.** *(costly, treasured)* wertvoll ['veːɐ̯tfəl] ◊ *ein wertvolles Schmuckstück* ♦ *wertvolle Zeit verschwenden* ♦ *Die Erinnerungen an diese Zeit sind mir sehr wertvoll.* **2.** *(iron) (expressing annoyance)* heiß geliebt [haes gə'liːpt] <heißer geliebt, am heißesten geliebt> *seldom comp/superl* ◊ *Deine heiß geliebte Karriere scheint dir wichtiger zu sein als deine Familie!* **3.** *(language, behavio(u)r)* gekünstelt [gə'kʏnstl̩t] ◊ *ein gekünstelter Stil* ♦ *Sein Auftritt wirkte sehr gekünstelt.*

precious stone [noun] Edelstein ['eːdl̩ʃtaen] der <–(e)s, –e>

precipitation [noun] **1.** METEO, CHEM Niederschlag ['niːdɐʃlaːk] der <–(e)s, Niederschläge> ◊ *Starke Niederschläge haben zu Hochwasser geführt.* ♦ *der Niederschlag der Kristalle am Boden des Glases* **2.** *(overhastiness)* Voreiligkeit ['foːɐ̯ʔaelɪçkaet] die <–> *no pl* ◊ *Später bereute er seine Voreiligkeit.*

precise(ly) [adj, adv] genau [gə'nao] <genauer, am genau(e)sten> ◊ *genaue Angaben machen* ♦ *Das genaue Datum ist noch nicht bekannt.* ♦ *Sie weiß genau, was sie will.* ♦ *Der Zeitplan wurde genau eingehalten.* ♦ *Was genau wollen Sie eigentlich von mir?* ♦ *„Du meinst, er will sie wirklich heiraten?"* — *„Genau!"* ♦ *Er ist bei solchen Sachen immer sehr genau.* at that precise moment genau in dem Augenblick ◊ *Genau in dem Augenblick klingelte das Telefon.* at precisely 7 o'clock genau um 7 Uhr be more precise sich genauer ausdrücken ⓟ to be precise nämlich ◊ *Sie liebten beide dasselbe Mädchen, nämlich Marie.*

precision [noun] Präzision [prɛtsi'zjoːn] die <–> *no pl* ◊ *eine Arbeit mit äußerster Präzision erledigen*

precocious [adj] frühreif ['fryːraef] ◊ *Das Mädchen ist frühreif.* ♦ *ein frühreifes Kind*

predator [noun] **1.** *(mammal)* Raubtier ['raoptiːɐ̯] das <–(e)s, –e>; *(fish or bird)* Räuber ['rɔøbɐ] der <–s, –> **2.** *(pej, fig)* ECON Person oder Firma, die Personal oder andere Organisationen rücksichtslos ausbeutet

predecessor [noun] Vorgänger ['foːɐ̯gɛŋɐ] der <–s, –> ♀Vorgängerin ['foːɐ̯gɛŋərɪn] die <–, –nen> ◊ *Ihre Vorgängerin im Amt ist vor kurzem verstorben.* ♦ *Anders als sein Vorgänger hat dieses Modell vier Airbags.*

> The feminine form only applies to persons. For objects always use the masculine form.

predicative(ly) [adj, adv] prädikativ [prɛdika'tiːf] *no comp/superl* ◊ *ein prädikativ gebrauchtes Adjektiv* ♦ *die prädikative Verwendung von Adjektiven*

predict [verb] vorhersagen [foːɐ̯'heːɐ̯gaːzgŋ̩] +haben ◊ *Für morgen wurden heftige Schneefälle vorhergesagt.* ♦ *Er hatte vorhergesagt, dass es so kommt.*

predictable [adj] *(development, result)* vorhersehbar [foːɐ̯'heːɐ̯zeːbaːɐ̯] ◊ *Das Ende des Films war vorhersehbar.* ♦ *eine vorhersehbare Entwicklung; (person)* berechenbar [bə'rɛçn̩baːɐ̯] ◊ *Gut, dass er so berechenbar ist.*

prediction [noun] Vorhersage [foːɐ̯'heːɐ̯gaːgə] die <–, –n> ◊ *Die Vorhersage von Naturkatastrophen ist nur selten möglich.* ♦ *eine Vorhersage machen*

predisposition [noun] Veranlagung [fɛl'anlaːgʊŋ] die

<–, –en> ◊ *Sie hat die Veranlagung zu dieser Krankheit von ihrer Mutter geerbt.*

predominant [adj] **1.** *(opinion, view, condition)* vorherrschend ['foːɐ̯hɛʁʃn̩t] *no comp/superl* ◊ *Die Demokratie ist das vorherrschende politische System des Westens.* be predominant vorherrschen ['foːɐ̯hɛʁʃn̩] +haben ◊ *Diese Ansicht herrscht weiterhin vor.* **2.** sb's predominent feeling is sth jd verspürt vor allem etw. [fɛʃpyːɐ̯t foːɐ̯ aləm] <verspürt, verspürte, hat verspürt> ◊ *Ich verspürte vor allem Angst.*

predominantly [adv] überwiegend ['yːbɐviːgŋ̩t] *seldom comp/superl* ◊ *Die Bevölkerung des Landes ist überwiegend katholisch.* ♦ *Sie hat bislang überwiegend für Verlage gearbeitet.*

predominate [verb] *(have more influence, be greater in amount)* überwiegen [ybɐ'viːgŋ̩] <überwiegt, überwog, hat überwogen> ◊ *Die Nachteile überwiegen.* ♦ *In unseren Wäldern überwiegen Fichten.; (be stronger than)* predominate over sth über etw. [acc] siegen [yːbɐ ... ziːgŋ̩] +haben ◊ *Schließlich siegte sein Interesse über seine Angst.*

pre-eminence [noun] überragende Bedeutung [ybɐ'raːgn̩də bə'dɔøtʊŋ] die <–> *no pl* ◊ *die überragende Bedeutung seines künstlerischen Werks* challenge sb's pre-eminence/the pre-eminence of sth jdm/einer Sache den Vorrang streitig machen [deːn 'foːɐ̯ʁaŋ ʃtʁaetɪç maxn̩] +haben ◊ *Sie wollte ihm den Vorrang in der Gruppe streitig machen.*

preface [noun] Vorwort ['foːɐ̯vɔʁ't] das <–(e)s, –e> ◊ *Im Vorwort dankt der Autor seiner Familie.* ♦ *ein Buch mit einem Vorwort des Herausgebers*

prefer [verb] *(food, music, a person)* lieber mögen ['liːbɐ møːgŋ̩] <mag, mochte, hat gemocht> ◊ *Was magst du lieber, Kaffee oder Tee?* ♦ *Welchen Lehrer magst du lieber, Herrn Karl oder Frau Friese?* prefer sb/sth to sb/sth jdn/etw. lieber mögen als jdn/etw. ◊ *Sie mag Gelb lieber als Blau.* prefer sth (to be) ... etw. lieber ... mögen ◊ *Ich mag mein Frühstücksei lieber weich.* sb much prefers sb/sth jdm gefällt jd/ etw. viel besser [gəfɛlt ... fiːl 'bɛsɐ] <gefällt, gefiel, hat gefallen> ◊ *So gefällt mir euer Wohnzimmer viel besser.* prefer to do sth, prefer doing sth. lieber tun ['liːbə] ◊ *Gehst du lieber ins Schwimmbad oder an den See?* ♦ *Sie arbeitet lieber allein.* sb would prefer that.../prefer it if ... jdm wäre es lieber, wenn ... [vɛːɐ̯ə ɛs 'liːbə vɛn] ◊ *Mir wäre es lieber, dass heute noch erledigt würde.* ♦ *Wäre es dir lieber, wenn wir einen Arzt rufen?; (a solution, an applicant)* vorziehen ['foːɐ̯tsiːən] <zieht vor, zog vor, hat vorgezogen> ◊ *Ich ziehe die zweite Lösung vor.* sth is to be preferred to sth etw. ist einer Sache [dat] vorzuziehen ◊ *Diese Arbeit ist deinem alten Job mit Sicherheit vorzuziehen.*

preferable [adj] sth is preferable to sth, a Sache [dat] vorzuziehen [ɪst ... 'foːɐ̯tsutsiːən] +sein ◊ *Herrn Schulzes Vorschlag ist Ihrer Idee vorzuziehen.* it would be preferable to do sth es wäre besser, etw. zu tun [ɛs vɛːɐ̯ə 'bɛsɐ ... tsuː] ◊ *Es wäre besser, die Arbeit gleich zu erledigen.*

preferably [adv] am liebsten [am 'liːpstn̩] ◊ *Er hätte gern einen Hund, am liebsten einen Dackel.* preferably wenn möglich nicht [vɛn 'møːklɪç ˌnɪçt] ◊ *Ich bräuchte noch einen Termin, aber wenn möglich nicht am Freitag.*

preference [noun] Vorliebe ['foːɐ̯liːbə] die <–, –n> ◊ *Seine Vorliebe für schnelle Autos wurde ihm zum Ver-*

A
B
C
D
E
F
G
H
I
J
K
L
M
N
O
P
Q
R
S
T
U
V
W
X
Y
Z

hängnis. sb's preference is for sth jd zieht etw. vor [tsi:t ... ,fo:ɐ̯] <zieht vor, zog vor, hat vorgezogen> ◊ *Wir ziehen eine diplomatische Lösung des Konflikts vor.* What is your preference? Was wäre dir/Ihnen am liebsten? I have no preference. Das ist mir gleich. give preference to sb/sth etw./jdn bevorzugen [bə'fo:ɐ̯tsu:gn̩] <bevorzugt, bevorzugte, hat bevorzugt> ◊ *Ein Lehrer sollte niemanden im Unterricht bevorzugen.* in preference to lieber als ['li:bɐ als] ◊ *Ich trinke lieber Wein als Bier.*

preferred → prefer [adj] bevorrechtigt [bə'fo:ɐ̯rɛçtɪçt] no comp/superl ◊ *bevorrechtigte Gläubiger* preferred stock Vorzugsaktien ['fo:ɐ̯tsu:ks|ˌaktsi̯ən] die <–> pl ◊ *Vorzugsaktien ausgeben*

prefix [noun] Präfix ['prɛ:fɪks] das <–es, –e> ◊ *betonte und unbetonte Präfixe*

pregnancy [noun] Schwangerschaft ['ʃvaŋɐʃaft] die <–, –en> ◊ *Während der Schwangerschaft sollten Sie keinen Alkohol trinken.*

pregnant [adj] **1.** *(expecting a child)* schwanger ['ʃvaŋɐ] no comp/superl ◊ *eine schwangere Frau* ♦ *Als sie mit Florian schwanger war, war ihr oft übel.* five etc. months pregnant im fünften etc. Monat schwanger get pregnant schwanger werden heavily pregnant hochschwanger ['ho:x'ʃvaŋɐ] no comp/superl **2.** *(pause, remark, silence)* bedeutungsvoll [bə'dɔɪtʊŋsfɔl] ◊ *Nach einer bedeutungsvollen Pause sprach er weiter.*

prejudice [noun] Vorurteil ['fo:ɐ̯ʊ'tai̯l] das <–s, –e> ◊ *Haben Sie etwa Vorurteile gegen Familien mit Kindern?*

preliminary [adj] *(taking place before sth else)* Vor... [fo:ɐ̯] preliminary investigation Voruntersuchung ['fo:ɐ̯|ʊntəˌzu:xʊn] die <–, –en> preliminary negotiations Vorverhandlungen ['fo:ɐ̯fɛˌhandlʊŋən] die <–> pl; *(preparatory)* vorbereitend ['fo:ɐ̯bəraetn̩t] no comp/superl, before ns ◊ *vorbereitende Maßnahmen ergreifen* ♦ *vorbereitende Schritte*

premature(ly) [adj, adv] **1.** *(too early)* verfrüht [fɛ'fry:t] no comp/superl ◊ *Es wäre verfrüht, jetzt schon ein Urteil abzugeben.* ♦ *eine Maßnahme verfrüht einleiten; (death, arrival etc.)* vorzeitig ['fo:ɐ̯tsae̯tɪç] no comp/superl ◊ *eine vorzeitige Pensionierung* ♦ *ein vorzeitiger Wintereinbruch* ♦ *vorzeitig abreisen/ altern* premature birth Frühgeburt ['fry:gəbu:ɐ̯t] die <–, –en> be born prematurely eine Frühgeburt sein ◊ *Ihre Tochter war eine Frühgeburt.* be six etc. weeks premature sechs etc. Wochen zu früh geboren werden [ˌzɛks ˌvɔxn̩ tsu: 'fry: gəbo:rən ve:ɐ̯dn̩] <wird, wurde, ist worden> **2.** *(overhasty)* voreilig ['fo:ɐ̯|ae̯lɪç] ◊ *Da waren Sie wohl ein wenig voreilig.* ♦ *eine voreilige Entscheidung treffen* ♦ *etw. voreilig behaupten*

premier¹ [noun] Premierminister [pre'mi̯e:miˌnɪstɐ] der <–s, –> ♀Premierministerin [pre'mi̯e:miˌnɪstərɪn] die <–, –nen> ◊ *der britische Premierminister* ♦ *Sie ist seit drei Jahren Premierministerin.*

premier² [adj] führend ['fy:rant] no comp/superl ◊ *Wir sind eines der führenden Hotels in Berlin.*

premise [noun] Voraussetzung [fo'rao̯szɛtsʊn] die <–, –en> ◊ *von einer falschen Voraussetzung ausgehen*

premises [noun] *(of a factory, school etc.)* Gelände [gə'lɛndə] das <–s, –> ◊ *ein Gelände für eine Fabrik erwerben* ♦ *Nur Schüler, Eltern und Lehrer dürfen das Gelände betreten.* school premises Schulgelände

['ʃu:|ɡəlɛndə]; *(particular building)* Gebäude [gə'bɔɪ̯də] das <–s, –> ◊ *Das Rauchen ist im gesamten Gebäude verboten.*; *(rooms)* business premises Geschäftsräume [gə'ʃɛftsrɔɪ̯mə] die <–> pl

premium [noun] *(payment or amount of money)* Prämie ['prɛ:mi̯ə] die <–, –n> ◊ *Die Prämie richtet sich nach der Versicherungssumme.* ♦ *eine Prämie für etw. aussetzen; (surcharge)* Zuschlag ['tsu:ʃla:k] der <–(e)s, Zuschläge> ◊ *Für diese Leistung müssen Sie einen Zuschlag bezahlen.* ☞ put a premium on sth auf etw. [acc] Wert legen

premonition [noun] Vorahnung ['fo:ɐ̯|a:nʊn] die <–, –en> ◊ *Ich hatte so eine Vorahnung, dass das passiert.* ♦ *Düstere Vorahnungen quälten sie.*

preoccupation [noun] sb's preoccupation with sth jds ständige Sorge um etw. [ˌʃtɛndɪɡə 'zɔ'ɡə ʊm] <–> no pl ◊ *Ihre ständige Sorge um ihre Gesundheit ist nicht mehr normal.* main preoccupation Hauptanliegen ['hao̯pt|anliːɡn̩] das <–s, –> ◊ *Zurzeit ist das Abbezahlen der Schulden sein Hauptanliegen.*

prepaid card [noun] Karte ['ka'tə] die <–, –n> ◊ *ein Handy mit Karte*

preparation [noun] **1.** *(act of preparing, measures taken)* Vorbereitung ['fo:ɐ̯bəraetʊn] die <–, –en> ◊ *eine gute Vorbereitung auf das Berufsleben* ♦ *Er steckt mitten in den Vorbereitungen auf der Prüfung.* ♦ *Sie ist mit der Vorbereitung des Nachtischs beschäftigt.* ♦ *Weitere Titel sind in Vorbereitung.* make preparations for sth Vorbereitungen für etw. treffen **2.** MED Präparat [prɛpa'ra:t] das <–(e)s, –e> ◊ *ein Präparat zur Reinigung der Haut*

prepare [verb] *(arrange, make ready)* vorbereiten ['fo:ɐ̯bəraetn̩] <bereitet vor, bereitete vor, hat vorbereitet> ◊ *So ein Fest muss man gut vorbereiten.* ♦ *Sie bereitete das Zimmer für die Gäste vor.* prepare sb/yourself for sth jdn/sich auf etw. [acc] vorbereiten ◊ *Dieser Kurs bereitet die Schüler auf die Prüfung vor.* ♦ *Bereite dich auf eine Überraschung vor!* prepare (yourself) to do sth sich darauf vorbereiten, etw. zu tun ◊ *Er bereitete sich darauf vor, in das Krisengebiet zu fliegen.*; *(food, medicine)* zubereiten ['tsu:bəraetn̩] <bereitet zu, bereitete zu, hat zubereitet> ◊ *ein Mahlzeit zubereiten* ♦ *Wie wird der Fisch zubereitet?* prepare sth from sth etw. aus etw. zubereiten ◊ *Diese Medizin wird aus Kräutern zubereitet.*

prepared → prepare [adj] **1.** *(ready)* prepared (for sth) (auf etw. [acc]) vorbereitet ['fo:ɐ̯bəraetət] no comp/superl ◊ *Auf so etwas war ich nicht vorbereitet.* ♦ *Er schien gut vorbereitet zu sein.* **2.** *(willing)* be prepared to do sth bereit sein, etw. zu tun [bə'rai̯t zaen ... tsu:] ◊ *Ich bin nicht bereit, noch länger zu warten.*

preposition [noun] Präposition [prɛpozi'tsi̯o:n] die <–, –en> ◊ *„In" und „an" sind Präpositionen.*

prerequisite [noun] Voraussetzung [fo'rao̯szɛtsʊn] die <–, –en> ◊ *Gute Sprachkenntnisse gehören zu den Voraussetzungen für diese Stelle.*

prescribe [verb] **1.** MED prescribe (sb) sth (jdm) etw. verschreiben [fɛ'ʃrai̯bm̩] <verschreibt, verschrieb, hat verschrieben> ◊ *jdm zehn Massagen/ein Medikament verschreiben* ♦ *Sie bekam Antibiotika verschrieben.* prescribe sth for sth etw. gegen etw. verschreiben ◊ *Soll ich Ihnen etwas gegen die Schmerzen verschreiben?* **2.** *(form) (order, dictate)* vorschreiben ['fo:ɐ̯ ʃraebm̩] <schreibt vor, schrieb vor, hat vorgeschrieben> ◊ *Das Gesetz schreibt vor, dass ...*

prescription [noun] **1.** *(given by a doctor, suggestion for achieving sth)* Rezept [re'tsɛpt] das <–(e)s, –e> ◊ *ein Rezept ausstellen ♦ ein Rezept für ein Schmerzmittel ♦ Unser Rezept gegen Arbeitslosigkeit lautet: Steuersenkung.* on prescription auf Rezept ◊ *Diese Tabletten gibt es nur auf Rezept.* prescription charge Rezeptgebühr [re'tsɛptgəbyːɡ] die <–, –en> **2.** *(act of prescribing)* Verschreibung [fɛ'ʃraebʊŋ] die <–> no pl ◊ *die Verschreibung von Medikamenten*

presence [noun] **1.** *(being somewhere: of a person)* Anwesenheit ['anveːznhaet] die <–> no pl ◊ *Man bemerkte seine Anwesenheit nicht einmal. ♦ in Anwesenheit eines Zeugen; (of a thing, substance or state)* Vorhandensein [foːɡ'handnzaen] das <–s> no pl ◊ *das Vorhandensein einer Krankheit/von Bakterien* make your presence felt sich bemerkbar machen [bə'mɛɐ̯kbaːɐ̯ maxn̩] +haben **2.** *(of soldiers, police)* Präsenz [prɛ'zɛnts] die <–> no pl ◊ *eine starke militärische Präsenz* police presence Polizeipräsenz [poli'tsaeprɛˌzɛnts] **3.** *(dignity)* Auftreten ['aoftreːtn̩] das <–s> no pl ◊ *ein Mann von eindrucksvollem Auftreten*

present¹ [noun] **1.** *(gift)* Geschenk [gə'ʃɛŋk] das <–(e)s, –e> ◊ *die Geschenke unterm Weihnachtsbaum ♦ ein Geschenk bekommen ♦ Geschenke einpacken/auspacken* birthday present Geburtstagsgeschenk [gə'buːɐ̯tstaːksgəʃɛŋk] Christmas present Weihnachtsgeschenk ['vaenaxtsgəʃɛŋk] get sth as a present etw. geschenkt bekommen [gə'ʃɛŋkt bəkɔmən] <bekommt, bekam, hat bekommen> ◊ *Den Hut hat sie geschenkt bekommen.* **2.** *(time)* Gegenwart ['geːɡn̩vaʁt] die <–> no pl ◊ *Seine Kunstsammlung reicht bis zur Gegenwart. ♦ in der Gegenwart leben* at present, for the present zurzeit [tsuːɐ̯'tsaet] ◊ *Zurzeit ist die Lage auf dem Arbeitsmarkt nicht sehr gut. ♦ Er möchte zurzeit nicht darüber reden.* **3.** LING Präsens ['prɛːzɛns] das <–> no pl ◊ *Das Verb steht im Präsens.*

present² [adj] **1.** *(current)* gegenwärtig ['geːɡn̩vɛʁtɪç] no comp/superl, only before ns ◊ *Die gegenwärtige Situation ist eher schlecht. ♦ Der gegenwärtige Besitzer möchte das Haus nicht verkaufen.; (being considered at the moment)* vorliegend ['foːɡliːɡn̩t] no comp/superl, only before ns ◊ *Im vorliegenden Fall müssen wir anders entscheiden.* **2.** *(in attendance)* anwesend ['anveːzn̩t] no comp/superl ◊ *Sie war bei der Besprechung nicht anwesend. ♦ Die Königin war persönlich anwesend.* those present die Anwesenden; *(existing)* vorhanden [foːɡ'handn̩] no comp/superl ◊ *in der Atmosphäre vorhandene Gase ♦ Das Medikament tötet alle vorhandenen Viren.*

present³ [verb] **1.** *(a prize, medal)* present sth to sb, present sb with sth jdm etw. überreichen [ybe'raeçn̩] <überreicht, überreichte, hat überreicht> ◊ *Der Bürgermeister überreichte den Gewinnern der Preise.; (as a gift)* present sth to sb, present sb with sth jdm etw. schenken ['ʃɛŋkn̩] +haben ◊ *Er schenkte ihr einen teuren Wagen.* **2.** *(cause, generate)* present sth (to/for sb) (für jdn) darstellen ['daːɐ̯ʃtɛlən] +haben ◊ *Für jemanden mit Ihrer Erfahrung dürfte das doch kein Problem darstellen. ♦ eine Gefahr darstellen; (confront)* present sb with sth jdn vor etw. stellen [foːɡ ... ʃtɛlən] +haben ◊ *Diese Entscheidung stellt uns vor ein Problem.* **3.** *(put forward, submit)* present sth (to sb) (jdm) etw. vorlegen ['foːɡleːɡn̩] +haben ◊ *Wir werden den Fall*

einem Richter vorlegen. ♦ *Sie legte ein Attest vor.; (show sb)* (jdm) etw. vorzeigen ['foːɡtsaegn̩] +haben ◊ *Ergebnisse vorzeigen können ♦ Ich zeigte an der Grenze meinen Ausweis vor.* **4.** *(show, depict)* zeigen ['tsaegn̩] +haben ◊ *Die Reportage zeigt ein erschütterndes Bild der Zustände in diesem Land. ♦ Sein Bericht zeigt die Angelegenheit in einem anderen Licht.* present sb/sth as sth jdn/etw. als etw. darstellen [als ... 'daːɐ̯ʃtɛlən] +haben ◊ *Stellen Sie doch diese Vermutungen nicht als Tatsache dar!* **5.** RADIO, TV moderieren [mode'riːrən] <moderiert, moderierte, hat moderiert> ◊ *Die Sendung wird von Michael Marwitz moderiert.* **6.** *(a play)* aufführen ['aoffyːrən] +haben ◊ *Nächste Woche führt das Theater Shakespeares „Hamlet" auf.; (an exhibition)* präsentieren [prɛzɛn'tiːrən] <präsentiert, präsentierte, hat präsentiert> ◊ *Das Werk des Malers wird in einer Ausstellung präsentiert.* **7.** *(introduce)* present sb (to sb) (jdm) jdn vorstellen ['foːɡʃtɛlən] +haben ◊ *Darf ich Ihnen meine Frau vorstellen? ♦ Er hoffte, dem Botschafter vorgestellt zu werden.* **8.** *(sb's apologies, greetings)* übermitteln [ybe'mɪtl̩n] übermittelte, hat übermittelt> *(form)* ◊ *Bitte übermitteln Sie Ihrer Mutter meine herzlichsten Grüße.* **9.** *(a bill)* vorlegen ['foːɡleːɡn̩] +haben ◊ *Sie legte mir ihre Rechnung vor.; (a cheque at your bank)* einreichen ['aenraeçn̩] +haben ◊ *einen Scheck einreichen* **10.** *(arise)* sich ergeben [e'geːbm̩] <ergibt sich, ergab sich, hat sich ergeben> ◊ *Wenn sich die Gelegenheit ergibt, werde ich ihn besuchen.*

presentation [noun] **1.** *(act or way of presenting sth)* Präsentation [prɛzɛnta'tsjoːn] die <–, –en> ◊ *Die Präsentation unseres Produkts war sehr gut.* **2.** *(of a prize)* Preisverleihung ['praesfɛlaeʊŋ] die <–, –en> ◊ *Bei der Preisverleihung waren viele Ehrengäste anwesend.; (of a medal)* Ordensverleihung ['ɔɐ̯dnsfɛlaeʊŋ]; *(of a gift)* Überreichung [ybe'raeçʊŋ] die <–, –en> ◊ *Wir übernimmt die Überreichung des Geschenks?* **3.** *(talk)* Referat [refe'raːt] das <–(e)s, –e> ◊ *Ihr Referat hat mir gut gefallen.* give a presentation ein Referat halten ◊ *Alle Seminarteilnehmer müssen ein einstündiges Referat halten.* **4.** *(of a case, state of affairs)* Darlegung ['daːɐ̯leːɡʊŋ] die <–, –en> ◊ *die Darlegung eines Falles/Sachverhalts* **5.** *(of a report, document etc.)* Vorlage ['foːɡlaːɡə] die <–, –n> ◊ *Gegen Vorlage dieses Gutscheins erhalten Sie ein Gratisgetränk.* **6.** THEAT, MUS Darbietung ['daːɐ̯biːtʊŋ] die <–, –en> ◊ *Die Darbietung des Stücks war gelungen.*

presenter [noun] Moderator [mode'raːtoːɡ] der <–s, –en> ♀Moderatorin [modera'toːrɪn] die <–, –nen> ◊ *Der Moderator führt durch die Sendung. ♦ Sie ist Moderatorin beim ZDF.*

presently [adv] *(now)* im Augenblick [ɪm aoɡn̩'blɪk] ◊ *Warte ein bisschen. Im Augenblick habe ich keine Zeit!; (currently)* derzeit ['deːɡtsaet] ◊ *Die Gebühr liegt derzeit bei 103,74 Euro.*

present tense [noun] Präsens ['prɛːzɛns] das <–> no pl ◊ *Der Roman ist im Präsens geschrieben. ♦ Dieses Verb steht im Präsens.*

preservation [noun] **1.** *(keeping intact)* Erhaltung [e'haltʊŋ] die <–> no pl ◊ *Geld für die Erhaltung eines Gebäudes/Denkmals spenden ♦ sich für die Erhaltung des Friedens einsetzen* state of preservation Zustand ['tsuːʃtant] der <–(e)s, Zustände> most sing be in a good state of preservation gut erhalten

sein [ˌguːt ɛ'haltn̩ zaͤɪn] +sein ◊ *Die alte Windmühle ist sehr gut erhalten.* **2.** *(of sb's reputation, the public order)* Aufrechterhaltung ['aᶷfrɛçt|ehaltʊn] die <–> no pl ◊ *die Aufrechterhaltung der öffentlichen Ordnung sichern* **3.** *(of food)* Konservierung [kɔnzɐ'viːrʊŋ] die <–, –en> ◊ *die Konservierung von Fleisch/Gemüse*

preserve ⟨verb⟩ **1.** *(keep intact)* erhalten [ɛ'haltn̩] <erhält, erhielt, hat erhalten> ◊ *Gebäude unter Denkmalschutz müssen erhalten werden.* ♦ *Maßnahmen, die den Frieden erhalten sollen; (a memory, your reputation, dignity)* wahren ['vaːrən] +haben ◊ *versuchen, seinen guten Ruf zu wahren* ♦ *das Andenken an jdn wahren; (your looks)* preserve sth sich ⟨dat⟩ etw. bewahren [bə'vaːrən] <bewahrt sich, bewahrte sich, hat sich bewahrt> ◊ *Sie hat sich ihre Schönheit bewahrt.* **2.** *(food)* konservieren [kɔnzɐ'viːrən] <konserviert, konservierte, hat konserviert> ◊ *Mit Salz oder Zucker lassen sich Lebensmittel konservieren.; (by cooking)* einmachen ['aͤɪnmaxn̩] +haben ◊ *Obst/ Gemüse einmachen*

presidency ⟨noun⟩ Präsidentschaft [prɛzi'dɛntʃaft] die <–, –en> most sing ◊ *die Präsidentschaft anstreben* ♦ *Während seiner Präsidentschaft haben sich die Staatsschulden stark erhöht.*

president ⟨noun⟩ **1.** *(of a state, organization, company etc.)* Präsident [prɛzi'dɛnt] der <–en, –en> ♀Präsidentin [prɛzi'dɛntɪn] die <–, –nen> ◊ *Sie ist seit drei Jahren Präsidentin des Verbands.* ♦ *der Präsident der Vereinigten Staaten* ♦ *der französische/russische Präsident; (in Germany, Austria)* Federal President Bundespräsident ['bʊndəsprɛziˌdɛnt] der <–en, –en> ♀Bundespräsidentin ['bʊndəsprɛziˌdɛntɪn] die <–, –nen> **2.** *(of a university)* Rektor ['rɛktoːɐ] der <–s, –en> ♀Rektorin [rɛk'toːrɪn] die <–, –nen> ◊ *Er wurde zum Rektor der TU gewählt.* ♦ *Sie wird demnächst Rektorin.*

presidential ⟨adj⟩ *(relating to the president)* Präsidenten... [prɛzi'dɛntn̩] presidential palace Präsidentenpalast [prɛzi'dɛntn̩paˌlast] der <–(e)s> no pl; *(relating to elections)* Präsidentschafts... [prɛzi'dɛntʃafts] presidential election Präsidentschaftswahl [prɛzi'dɛntʃaftsvaːl] die <–, –en> presidential candidate Präsidentschaftskandidat [prɛzi'dɛntʃaftskandiˌdaːt] der <–en, –en> ♀Präsidentschaftskandidatin [prɛzi'dɛntʃaftskandiˌdaːtɪn] die <–, –nen>

press¹ ⟨noun⟩ **1.** *(newspapers, journalists)* Presse ['prɛsə] die <–> no pl ◊ *Wie die internationale/ lokale Presse berichtete, hat ...* ♦ *In der Presse stand, dass er heiraten will.* ♦ *Sie hat eine gute Presse bekommen.* press agency Presseagentur ['prɛsəaˌgɛnˌtuːɐ] die <–, –en> press conference Pressekonferenz ['prɛsəkɔnfeˌrɛns] die <–, –en> **2.** *(for printing)* Druckmaschine ['drʊkmaˌʃiːnə] die <–, –n> ◊ *eine Druckmaschine für Zeitungen* go to press in Druck gehen [ɪn 'drʊk geːən] <geht, ging, ist gegangen> **3.** *(publishing house)* Verlag [fɛ'laːk] der <–(e)s, –e> ◊ *Der Verlag ist auf Reiseführer spezialisiert.* **4.** *(for making sth smooth, for squeezing sth)* Presse ['prɛsə] die <–, –n> ◊ *eine hydraulische/ mechanische Presse* garlic press Knoblauchpresse ['knoːplaͦxˌprɛsə] **5.** *(act of pushing, squeezing)* Druck [drʊk] der <–(e)s> no pl ◊ *Bei einem leichten Druck auf den Knopf geht das Licht an.* give sth a press etw. drücken ['drʏkn̩] +haben ◊ *Drücken*

Sie die rote Taste. **6.** *(iron)* give sth a press etw. bügeln ['byːgl̩n] +haben ◊ *Könntest du schnell noch meine Hose bügeln?* **7.** *(crowd)* press (of people) Gedränge [gə'drɛŋə] das <–s> no pl ◊ *Sie bahnte sich einen Weg durch das Gedränge.* **8.** *(in the US and Scotland: cupboard)* Wandschrank ['vantʃraŋk] der <–(e)s, Wandschränke>

press² ⟨verb⟩ **1.** drücken ['drʏkn̩] +haben ◊ *Drücken Sie die rechte Maustaste.* press sb's hand jdm die Hand drücken ◊ *Er drückte ihr dankbar die Hand.* press sth into sb's hand jdm etw. in die Hand drücken ◊ *Sie drückte ihm den Schlüssel in die Hand.* press sb/sth/yourself against sth jdn/etw./ sich gegen etw. drücken ◊ *Das Kind drückte die Nase gegen die Scheibe.* ♦ *Er drückte sich gegen die Felswand, um nicht abzustürzen.* press down on sb/ sth schwer auf jdn/etw. lasten [ˌʃveːɐ̯ aͦf ... ˌlastn̩] <lastet, lastete, hat gelastet> ◊ *Das Gewicht lastete schwer auf seinen Schultern.* ♦ *Die Sorgen/Schulden lasten schwer auf uns.* **2.** *(move forwards while pushing)* sich drängen ['drɛŋən] +haben ◊ *Zahlreiche Fans drängten sich um den Star.* ♦ *Sie drängte sich zum Ausgang.* **3.** *(urge)* press sb to do sth jdn drängen, etw. zu tun ['drɛŋən ... tsuː] +haben ◊ *Sie drängte ihn, noch ein wenig zu bleiben.* press sb about/on sth jd mit Fragen zu etw. bedrängen [mɪt ˌfraːgn̩ tsuː: ... bə'drɛŋən] <bedrängt, bedrängte, hat bedrängt> ◊ *Sie bedrängten ihn mit Fragen zu seiner politischen Einstellung.* press the point darauf herumreiten [daˌraͦf hɛ'rʊmraͤɪtn̩] <reitet herum, ritt herum, ist herumgeritten> *(fam)* ◊ *Er hat nichts dazu gesagt; also bin ich nicht darauf herumgeritten.* **4.** *(iron)* bügeln ['byːgl̩n] +haben ◊ *Könntest du schnell noch mein Hemd bügeln?* **5.** *(fruit)* auspressen ['aͦsprɛsn̩] +haben ◊ *eine Zitrone auspressen* **6.** *(a CD, record)* pressen ['prɛsn̩] +haben ◊ *eine Platte/CD pressen lassen*

• **press ahead** ⟨phras v⟩ press ahead (with sth) (mit etw.) weitermachen ['vaͤɪtɐmaxn̩] +haben ◊ *Sie wollen trotz aller Einwände mit dem Projekt weitermachen.*

• **press for** ⟨phras v⟩ press for sth auf etw. ⟨acc⟩ drängen [aͦf ... ˌdrɛŋən] +haben ◊ *Die Opposition drängt auf Reformen.* press sb for an answer/a decision etc. auf jds Antwort/Entscheidung etc. drängen ◊ *Alle drängten auf eine Entscheidung des Chefs.*

• **press on** ⟨phras v⟩ **1.** *(continue)* weitermachen ['vaͤɪtɐmaxn̩] +haben ◊ *Wollen Sie tatsächlich trotz der hohen Kosten weitermachen?* **2.** *(try to make sb accept sth)* press sth on sb jdm etw. aufdrängen ['aͦfdrɛŋən] +haben ◊ *Versuch nicht immer, mir deine Meinung aufzudrängen!* ♦ *Er wollte mir wieder Alkohol aufdrängen.*

pressing ⟨adj⟩ **1.** *(urgent)* dringend ['drɪŋənt] ◊ *Die Sache ist dringend.* ♦ *Ich hätte eine dringende Bitte an Sie.* **2.** *(insistent)* nachdrücklich ['naːxdrʏklɪç] ◊ *eine nachdrückliche Aufforderung*

pressure ⟨noun⟩ Druck [drʊk] der <–(e)s, selten od seltener –e> most sing ◊ *der atmosphärische Druck* ♦ *Auf ihm lastet ein enormer Druck.* ♦ *Der Druck des Wassers bewegt das Rad.* come under pressure unter Druck geraten give in to pressure dem Druck nachgeben exert/put pressure on sb Druck auf jdn ausüben exert/put pressure on sb to do sth jdn drängen, etw. zu tun

['drɛŋən ... ʦuː] +*haben* ◊ *Ihre Eltern drängten sie, endlich zu heiraten.* the pressures of modern life der Stress des modernen Lebens [deːɐ̯ ʃtrɛs dɛs moˌdɛʳnən 'leːbm̩s] der <–es> *no pl* ◊ *Viele Menschen sind dem Stress des modernen Lebens nicht gewachsen.* social pressures gesellschaftliche Zwänge [gəˌzɛlʃaftlɪçə 'ʦvɛŋə] die <–> *pl* ◊ *Den gesellschaftlichen Zwängen kann man sich nicht immer entziehen.* area of high pressure Hochdruckgebiet ['hoːxdrʊkɡəbiːt] das <–(e)s, –e> ◊ *Süddeutschland gerät unter den Einfluss eines Hochdruckgebiets.* area of low pressure Tiefdruckgebiet ['tiːfdrʊkɡəbiːt]

prestige [noun] Prestige [prɛs'tiːʃ] das <–s> *no pl* ◊ *Der Konzern hat an Prestige gewonnen/verloren.*

presumably [adv] vermutlich [fɐ'muːtlɪç] *no comp/ superl* ◊ *Er kommt vermutlich erst morgen.* ♦ *Sie haben vermutlich schon gegessen, nicht wahr?*

presume [verb] 1. *(suppose)* annehmen ['anneːmən] <nimmt an, nahm an, hat angenommen> ◊ *Ich nehme an, Sie möchten zuerst Ihr Zimmer sehen.* be presumed innocent als unschuldig gelten [als 'ʊnʃʊldɪç gɛltn̩] <gilt, galt, hat gegolten> ◊ *Ein Angeklagter gilt so lange als unschuldig, bis seine Schuld bewiesen ist.* be presumed dead vermutlich tot sein [fɐˌmuːtlɪç 'toːt zaɛ̯n] +*sein* ◊ *Etwa 20 Bergleute werden vermisst und sind vermutlich tot.; (presuppose)* voraussetzen [fo'raʊ̯szɛtsn̩] +*haben* ◊ *Diese Vorlesung setzt Grundkenntnisse des Italienischen voraus.* 2. *(dare)* presume to do sth sich [dat] erlauben, etw. zu tun [ɐ'laʊ̯bm̩ ... ʦuː] <erlaubt sich, erlaubte sich, hat sich erlaubt> ◊ *Sie würde sich niemals erlauben, ihm Vorschriften zu machen.*

• **presume on** [phras v] überbeanspruchen ['yːbəbəanʃprʊxn̩] <überbeansprucht, überbeanspruchte, hat überbeansprucht> ◊ *Du solltest ihre Gastfreundschaft nicht überbeanspruchen.*

presumed → **presume** [adj] mutmaßlich ['muːtmaːslɪç] *no comp/superl, only before ns* ◊ *Die mutmaßliche Todesursache war Herzversagen.* ♦ *Der mutmaßliche Täter wurde gestern verhaftet.*

presumptuous [adj] überheblich [yːbe'heːplɪç] ◊ *So ein überheblicher Kerl!* ♦ *Es wäre überheblich, das zu behaupten.*

pretence [noun] Heuchelei [hɔ̯ɣçə'laɛ̯] die <–, –en> ◊ *Seine Begeisterung ist nur Heuchelei.* sb's pretence of friendship/innocence etc. jds gespielte Freundschaft /Unschuld etc. [gaˌʃpiːltə 'frɔɡ̩ntʃaft/'ʊnʃʊlt] ◊ *Sie durchschaut seine gespielte Freundlichkeit nicht.* keep up the pretence of sth den Anschein ... [gen] wahren [deːn 'anʃaɛ̯n vaːrən] +*haben* ◊ *Sie versuchen, den Anschein einer harmonischen Beziehung zu wahren.* make a pretence of doing sth vorgeben, etw. zu tun ['foːɡ̩geːbm̩ ... ʦuː] <gibt vor, gab vor, hat vorgegeben> ◊ *Er gab vor, überrascht zu sein.*

ⓟ **under false pretences** unter Vorspiegelung falscher Tatsachen

pretend [verb] 1. *(make believe)* pretend that, pretend to do sth tun, als (ob) ['tuːn als ɔp] <tut, tat, hat getan> ◊ *Er lag mit geschlossenen Augen da und tat, als schliefe er.* ♦ *Wir können doch nicht einfach so tun, als ob nichts passiert wäre!* pretend innocence/deafness etc. so tun, als ob man unschuldig/taub etc. wäre 2. *(claim)* behaupten [bə'haɔ̯ptn̩] <behauptet, behauptete, hat behauptet> ◊ *Willst du*

etwa behaupten, dass du damit erfolgreich warst? ♦ *Ich behaupte nicht, dass ich für alles eine Lösung habe.* pretend to sth behaupten, dass man etw. hat ◊ *Ich habe nie behauptet, dass ich gute Kenntnisse auf diesem Gebiet habe.*

preterite [noun] Präteritum [prɛ'teːritʊm] das <–s, Präterita> ◊ *Hier steht das Verb im Präteritum.*

pretext [noun] Vorwand ['foːɐ̯vant] der <–(e)s, Vorwände> ◊ *Das Wetter war ihr ein willkommener Vorwand, nicht im Garten zu arbeiten.* ♦ *Sein Gesundheitszustand dient ihm als Vorwand für seine Faulheit.* on/under the pretext of doing sth unter dem Vorwand, etw. zu tun ◊ *Er blieb der Feier unter dem Vorwand fern, sein Auto reparieren zu müssen.*

prettily [adv] hübsch [hʏpʃ] <hübscher, am hübschesten> ◊ *Sie war hübsch gekleidet.*

pretty¹ [adj] 1. *(child, woman)* hübsch [hʏpʃ] <hübscher, am hübschesten> ◊ *Sie hat ein hübsches Gesicht.* ♦ *All ihre Kinder sind hübsch.; (building, dress etc.)* nett [nɛt] <netter, am nettesten> ◊ *Was für ein nettes Kleid!* ♦ *Das Haus sieht nett aus.* not a pretty sight kein schöner Anblick ['kaɛ̯n ˌʃøːne ˌanblɪk] ◊ *Der Verletzte war kein schöner Anblick.* 2. *(iron) (price, sum)* hübsch [hʏpʃ] *no comp/superl* ◊ *Für das Auto hast du sicher eine hübsche Summe bezahlt.* cost a pretty penny etw. hübsche Stange Geld kosten

pretty² [adv] 1. *(rather)* ziemlich ['ʦiːmlɪç] ◊ *Heute ist es ziemlich kalt draußen.* ♦ *Du siehst ziemlich müde aus.* ♦ *Ich bin mir ziemlich sicher, dass er kommt.* 2. *(very)* sehr [zeːɐ̯] ◊ *Es ist sehr schwer, die zukünftigen Entwicklungen abzuschätzen.*

ⓟ **pretty much/nearly/well** fast ◊ *Sie sind mit dem Dach fast fertig.* ♦ *Die beiden sehen fast gleich aus.*

prevail [verb] 1. *(conditions, atmosphere, weather etc.)* herrschen ['hɛʳʃn̩] +*haben* ◊ *Im Büro herrscht gedämpfte Stimmung.* ♦ *Unter den Bedingungen, die dort herrschen, ist das Leben nicht einfach.* 2. *(overrule)* prevail (over/against sth) sich (gegenüber einer Sache [dat]) durchsetzen ['dʊʳçzɛtsn̩] +*haben* ◊ *Die Meinung der Mehrheit setzte sich durch.* ♦ *Seine Idee setzte sich gegenüber den anderen Vorschlägen durch.* 3. *(win)* siegen ['ziːɡn̩] +*haben* ◊ *Am Ende wird die Gerechtigkeit siegen.* prevail in sth etw. gewinnen [gə'vɪnən] <gewinnt, gewann, hat gewonnen> ◊ *Die Partei hofft, die nächsten Wahlen zu gewinnen.* prevail over sb jdn besiegen ['bəˈziːɡn̩] <besiegt, besiegte, hat besiegt> ◊ *Die englische Mannschaft besiegte die deutsche.*

prevalence [noun] weite Verbreitung [ˌvaɛ̯tə fɐ'braɛ̯tʊŋ] die <–> *no pl* ◊ *Die weite Verbreitung der Krankheit unter jungen Leuten ist erschreckend.*

prevent [verb] verhindern [fɐ'hɪndɐn] <verhindert, verhinderte, hat verhindert> ◊ *einen Unfall/eine Ansteckung verhindern* ♦ *Wir konnten das Schlimmste verhindern.* prevent sth (from) happening verhindern, dass etw. geschieht ◊ *Wie kann man verhindern, dass die Masse zu fest wird?* prevent sb (from) doing sth jdn daran hindern, etw. zu tun [daran 'hɪndɐn ... ʦuː] +*haben* ◊ *Der Lärm hinderte ihn daran, sich auf seine Arbeit zu konzentrieren.*

prevention [noun] Verhütung [fɐ'hyːtʊŋ] die <–, –en> *no pl* ◊ *Maßnahmen zur Verhütung von Unfällen*

Krankheiten

previous [adj] *(earlier, preceding)* vorherige ['fo:g'he:rɪgə] *no comp/superl, only before ns* <ein vorheriger ... eine vorherige ..., ein vorheriges ...> ◊ *In der vorherigen Nacht/Woche war es sehr kalt gewesen.* ♦ *Findest du seinen neuen Roman besser als den vorherigen?; (before a certain point in time)* previous to vor [fo:g] [+dat] ◊ *Vor 1975 hatten meine Eltern keinen Fernseher.; (at some time before now)* frühere ['fry:ərə] *no comp/superl, only before ns* <ein früherer ..., eine frühere ..., ein früheres ...> ◊ *Ist das der frühere Besitzer des Ladens?* ♦ *In früheren Jahren konnte sie sich noch alleine versorgen.* ♦ *Er hat zwei Kinder aus einer früheren Ehe.* previous knowledge Vorkenntnisse ['fo:gkɛntnɪsə] die <–> pl

previously [adv] vorher ['fo:gheːg] ◊ *Sie war vorher bei einer amerikanischen Firma beschäftigt.* three days/two years etc. previously drei Tage/zwei Jahre etc. zuvor [,drae ,ta:gə/,tsvae ,ja:rə tsu'fo:g]

prey [noun] **1.** *(animal)* Beute ['bɔɡtə] die <–> no pl ◊ *Der Tiger schleicht sich an seine Beute heran.* easy prey leichte Beute bird of prey Greifvogel ['graeffoːgḷ] der <–s, Greifvögel> **2.** *(victim)* Opfer ['ɔpfe] das <–s, –> ◊ *Der Täter suchte sich seine Opfer in der U-Bahn aus.* fall prey to sb/sth Opfer ... [gen]/von jdm/etw. werden. ◊ *Die alte Dame wurde Opfer eines Gewaltverbrechens/von Trickbetrügern.*

price¹ [noun] Preis [praes] der <–es, –e> ◊ *Welchen Preis verlangen Sie für das Schmuckstück?* ♦ *Die Preise sind gestiegen/gefallen.* ♦ *die Preise erhöhen* ♦ *Heute gibt es alle Lampen zum halben Preis.* pay the price for sth den Preis für etw. zahlen ◊ *Er hat einen hohen Preis für seine Unabhängigkeit gezahlt.* at a price zum entsprechenden Preis ◊ *Sie übernehmen die Renovierung des Hauses — zum entsprechenden Preis.* at what price um welchen Preis ◊ *Er hat sein Ziel erreicht. Aber um welchen Preis!* at any price um jeden Preis not at any price um keinen Preis

⊙ put a price on sb's head eine Belohnung auf jds Kopf aussetzen ◊ *Auf seinen Kopf ist eine hohe Belohnung ausgesetzt.*

price² [verb] **1.** *(put a label on a product)* auszeichnen ['aɔstsaeçnən] <zeichnet aus, zeichnete aus, hat ausgezeichnet> ◊ *Der Verkäufer zeichnet die Waren aus.* be priced at sth mit etw. ausgezeichnet sein ◊ *Die Ware ist mit 15 Euro ausgezeichnet.* **2.** *(cost)* be priced (at) £5 etc. fünf Pfund etc. kosten [fynf 'pfʊnt kɔstṇ] <kostet, kostete, hat gekostet> ◊ *Die Tickets kosten 17 Euro.* reasonably priced im Preis angemessen [ɪm ,praes 'angəmɛsṇ] ◊ *Die Wohnung ist im Preis angemessen.* priced too high zu teuer [tsu: 'tɔɡe] ◊ *Der Wagen ist zu teuer.* **3.** *(compare)* price sth die Preise ... [gen] vergleichen [di: 'praeza fe,glaeçṇ] <vergleicht, verglich, hat verglichen> ◊ *Sie verglichen die Preise verschiedener Waschmaschinen.*

priceless [adj] **1.** *(very valuable, useful)* unbezahlbar ['ʊnbɛtsaːlbaːɡ] *no comp/superl* ◊ *unbezahlbare Gemälde* ♦ *Diese Erfahrung war einfach unbezahlbar!* **2.** *(very amusing)* köstlich ['kœstlɪç] ◊ *Ich fand die Komödie köstlich.* ♦ *Sein Gesichtsausdruck war einfach köstlich!*

prick¹ [noun] **1.** *(with a needle, sensation)* Stich [ʃtɪç] der <–(e)s, –e> ◊ *Er fühlte plötzlich einen Stich im*

Rücken. give sb a prick jdn stechen ['ʃtɛçṇ] <sticht, stach, hat gestochen> ◊ *jdn mit einer Nadel stechen* **2.** *(penis)* Schwanz [ʃvants] der <–es, Schwänze> *(rude)* **3.** *(unpleasant man)* Arsch [aʳʃ] der <–(e)s, Ärsche> *(rude)* ◊ *Hau ab, du Arsch!* **4.** pricks of conscience Gewissensbisse [gə'vɪsṇsbɪsə] die <–> pl

prick² [verb] **1.** *(make a small hole)* stechen ['ʃtɛçṇ] <sticht, stach, hat gestochen> ◊ *Etwas hat mich gestochen.* prick yourself sich stechen ◊ *Hast du dich an dem Kaktus gestochen?* prick your finger with/on sth sich [dat] mit etw. in den Finger stechen ◊ *Ich habe mir mit der Nadel in den Finger gestochen.* **2.** *(cause a stinging feeling)* prick sth auf etw. [dat] brennen [aɔf ... 'brɛnən] <brennt, brannte, hat gebrannt> ◊ *Das Salz brannte auf ihrem Körper.* sth pricks sb's eyes etw. brennt jdm in den Augen ◊ *Der Rauch brennt mir in den Augen.* **3.** sb's conscience pricks them jd hat Gewissensbisse [hat gə'vɪsṇsbɪsə] +haben

• **prick up** [phras v] prick up your ears die Ohren spitzen [di: 'o:rən ʃpɪtsṇ] +haben ◊ *Nun spitzt mal schön die Ohren!* sb's ears prick up jd spitzt die Ohren

prickle [noun] **1.** *(sensation)* Stechen ['ʃtɛçṇ] das <–s> no pl ◊ *Er spürte das Stechen der Nadel kaum.; (from sb's beard, wool etc.)* Kratzen ['kratsṇ] das <–s> no pl ◊ *Das Kratzen der Wolle war ihr unangenehm.; (tingling sensation)* Prickeln ['prɪkḷn] das <–s> no pl ◊ *Er fühlte ein Prickeln auf der Haut.* **2.** *(part of a plant)* Stachel ['ʃtaxḷ] der <–s, –n> ◊ *Der Busch war voller Stacheln.*

pride [noun] Stolz [ʃtɔlts] der <–es> no pl ◊ *Seine lobenden Worte erfüllten sie mit Stolz.* ♦ *Es verletzt ihn in seinem Stolz, wenn man ihm Geld schenken will.* take pride in sth auf etw. [acc] stolz sein [aɔf ... 'ʃtɔlts tsaeṇ] ◊ *Sie ist stolz auf ihre Arbeit.*

⊙ sb's pride and joy jds ganzer Stolz ◊ *Die CD-Sammlung ist sein ganzer Stolz.*

priest [noun] Priester ['pri:stɐ] der <–s, –> ♀Priesterin ['pri:stərɪn] die <–, –nen> ◊ *Sie möchte Priesterin werden.* ◊ *Der Priester brachte ein Opfer dar.*

priestess [noun] Priesterin ['pri:stərɪn] die <–, –nen>

primarily [adv] hauptsächlich ['haɔptzɛçlɪç] ◊ *Sie lernt hauptsächlich abends.* ♦ *Er macht das hauptsächlich wegen der guten Bezahlung.*

primary [adj] **1.** *(main)* Haupt... [haɔpt] primary problem Hauptproblem ['haɔptpro,ble:m] das <–s, –e> ◊ *Das Hauptproblem scheinen nicht die illegalen Drogen zu sein.* primary concern Hauptanliegen ['haɔpt|anli:gṇ] das <–s, –> ◊ *Unser Hauptanliegen ist die Versorgung der Kinder.* of primary importance von äußerster Wichtigkeit [fɔn ,ɔɡseste 'vɪçtɪçkaet] ◊ SCHOOL. Grundschul... ['grʊntʃuːl] primary education Grundschulbildung ['grʊntʃuːl|bɪldʊŋ] die <–, –en> primary teacher Grundschullehrer ['grʊntʃuːlleːrɐ] der <–s, –> ♀Grundschullehrerin ['grʊntʃuːlleːrərɪn] die <–, –nen> **3.** *(happening before sth else)* primary election Vorwahl ['fo:gvaːl] die <–, –en> ◊ *Nächste Woche finden die Vorwahlen statt.* primary tumour Tumor im Anfangsstadium [,tu:moːg ɪm 'anfaŋs‚ʃta:dɪʊm] ◊ *Es wurde ein Tumor im Anfangsstadium diagnostiziert.*

primary school [noun] Grundschule ['grʊntʃuːlə] die

<‒, ‒n> ◊ *Sie geht noch in die Grundschule.*

prime¹ (noun) in the prime of life/youth in der Blüte
seiner/ihrer Jahre/Jugend
[ɪn deːɡ ˌblyːtə zˌaene/iːre ˈjaːrə/ˈjuːɡn̩t] ◊ *Er war in
der Blüte seiner Jugend.*; *(in terms of age)* be in your
prime in den besten Jahren sein
[ɪn deːn ˌbestn̩ ˈjaːrən zˌaen] ◊ *Mit 35 ist eine Frau
doch in den besten Jahren!*; *(in terms of ability)* be in
your prime an seinem Höhepunkt angelangt sein
[an zˌaenəm ˈhøːapʊŋkt ˌanɡəlaŋt zˌaen] ◊ *Der Sänger
ist an seinem Höhepunkt angelangt.* be past your/its
prime schon bessere Zeiten gesehen haben
[ʃoːn ˈbesərə ˌtsaetn̩ ɡəzˌeːən haːbm̩]

prime² (adj) **1.** *(main, central)* Haupt... [hˌaopt] prime
cause Hauptursache [ˈhaoptlˌuːɐzaxə] die <‒, ‒n> ◊
Rauchen ist die Hauptursache für Lungenkrebs.
prime concern Hauptanliegen [ˈhaoptˌanliːɡn̩] das
<‒s, ‒> ◊ *Unser Hauptanliegen ist die Sicherheit
unserer Gäste.* prime suspect Hauptverdächtige
[ˈhaoptfɛˌdɛçtɪɡə] der/die
<‒n, die Hauptverdächtigen> but: *ein Hauptverdächti-
ger/eine Hauptverdächtige* ◊ *Sie ist in dem Fall die
Hauptverdächtige.* of prime importance von
äußerster Wichtigkeit [fɔn ˌɔøseste ˈvɪçtɪçkaet] ◊
Diese Angelegenheit ist von äußerster Wichtigkeit.
2. *(excellent, perfect)* erstklassig [ˈeːɐstklasɪç] *no
comp/superl* ◊ *ein Hotel in erstklassiger Lage* ♦ *Das
ist ein erstklassiges Beispiel für den damaligen Stil.*;
(foodstuffs) von hervorragender Qualität
[fɔn heˌfoːɡraːɡn̩də kvaliˈtɛːt] ◊ *Wir verkaufen nur
Fleisch von hervorragender Qualität.*

prime minister (noun) Premierminister
[preˈmjeːmiˌnɪstɐ] der <‒s, ‒> ♀Premierministerin
[preˈmjeːmiˌnɪstərɪn] die <‒, ‒nen> ◊ *ein Besuch des
britischen Premierministers.*

primitive (adj) **1.** *(very simple, not very developed)*
primitiv [primiˈtiːf] *(also pej)* ◊ *unter primitivsten
Bedingungen leben* ♦ *primitive Werkzeuge benutzen*
♦ *Diese Methode ist ziemlich primitiv.*; *(organism)*
einfach [ˈaenfax] ◊ *einfache Lebewesen wie
Bakterien* primitive people Naturvolk [naˈtuːɡfɔlk] das
<‒(e)s, Naturvölker> **2.** *(prehistoric)* primitive man
Urmensch [ˈuːɐmɛnʃ] der <‒en, ‒en>

prince (noun) *(son of a king or queen)* Prinz [prɪnts]
der <‒en, ‒en> ◊ *Der Frosch war ein verzauberter
Prinz.* ♦ *Prinz Charles;* *(ruler)* Fürst [fyˈst]
<‒en, ‒en> ◊ *Fürst Rainier von Monaco*

princess (noun) *(daughter of a king or queen)* Prinzessin [prɪnˈtsɛsɪn] die <‒, ‒nen> ◊ *Prinzessin Diana;*
(wife of a ruler) Fürstin [ˈfyˈstɪn] die <‒, ‒nen> ◊
Fürstin Gracia von Monaco

principal¹ (noun) **1.** THEAT Hauptdarsteller
[ˈhaoptdaːˌʃtɛlɐ] der <‒s, ‒> ♀Hauptdarstellerin
[ˈhaoptdaːˌʃtɛlərɪn] die <‒, ‒nen> ◊ *Wer ist die
Hauptdarstellerin in dem Stück?* **2.** UNI, SCHOOL Rektor
[ˈrɛktoːɐ] der <‒s, ‒en> ♀Rektorin [rɛkˈtoːrɪn] die
<‒, ‒nen> ◊ *Er soll demnächst Rektor werden.* ♦ *die
neue Rektorin der Schule* **3.** FIN Kreditsumme
[kreˈdiːtzʊmə] die <‒, ‒n> ◊ *Wie hoch ist die Kreditsumme?* **4.** LAW Mandant [manˈdant] der <‒en, ‒en>
♀Mandantin [manˈdantɪn] die <‒, ‒nen> ◊ *einen
Mandanten vor Gericht vertreten* ♦ *Meine Mandantin
möchte sich nicht zu den Vorwürfen äußern.*

principal² (adj) Haupt... [hˌaopt] principal aim
Hauptziel [ˈhaoptˌtsiːl] das <‒(e)s, ‒e> ◊ *Die
Erhaltung der Arbeitsplätze ist unser Hauptziel.*

principal concern Hauptanliegen [ˈhaoptlˌanliːɡn̩] das
<‒s, ‒> ◊ *Mein Hauptanliegen ist das Überleben der
Firma.* principal character Hauptfigur [ˈhaoptfiˌɡuːɐ]
die <‒, ‒en> ◊ *die Hauptfiguren des Buches*

principally (adv) hauptsächlich [ˈhaoptzɛçlɪç] *no
comp/superl* ◊ *Der Film ist hauptsächlich für Kinder
gedacht.* ♦ *Ich arbeite hauptsächlich zu Hause.*

principle (noun) Prinzip [prɪnˈtsiːp] das <‒s, ‒ien> ◊
Qualität ist unser oberstes Prinzip! ♦ *Hast du denn
keine Prinzipien?* ◊ *Die Maschinen funktionieren
alle nach demselben Prinzip.* stick to your principles
seinen Prinzipien treu bleiben a man/woman of
principle ein Mann/eine Frau mit Prinzipien sth is
a matter of principle bei etw. geht es ums Prinzip
basic principle Grundprinzip [ˈɡrʊntprɪnˌtsiːp] ◊
*Gleiches Recht für alle ist ein Grundprinzip unserer
Verfassung.*
⊚ in principle prinzipiell

print¹ (noun) **1.** *(of a foot, finger etc.)* Abdruck
[ˈapdrʊk] der <‒(e)s, Abdrücke> ◊ *Der Polizist nahm
einen Abdruck des rechten Daumens.* ♦ *Ich sehe
fand man die Abdrücke großer Schuhe.* **2.** *(typeface)*
Schrift [ʃrɪft] die <‒, ‒en> ◊ *Die Schrift ist so klein,
dass man sie kaum lesen kann.* in bold print fett
gedruckt [fɛt ɡədrʊkt] *no comp/superl* ◊ *eine fett
gedruckte Überschrift* **3.** ARTS *(picture)* Druck [drʊk]
der <‒(e)s, ‒e> ◊ *Der Druck ist in Holz gerahmt.*
4. FOTO Abzug [ˈaptsuːk] der <‒(e)s, Abzüge> ◊ *Ich
hätte von diesem Negativ gern drei Abzüge im
Format 10 mal 15.* **5.** *(fabric)* bedruckter Stoff
[bəˌdrʊkte ˈʃtɔf] <‒(e)s, ‒e> ◊ *Der bedruckte Stoff
ist reine Baumwolle.* print dress Druckkleid
[ˈdrʊkklˌaet] das <‒(e)s, ‒er> **6.** FILM Kopie [koˈpiː]
die <‒, ‒n> ◊ *Von diesem Film existieren keine
Kopien mehr.*
⊚ in print **1.** *(published)* gedruckt ◊ *Es war ein
seltsames Gefühl, seinen Namen gedruckt zu sehen.*
2. *(available)* erhältlich ◊ *Das Buch ist noch erhältlich.* out of print vergriffen ◊ *Leider ist dieses Buch
bereits vergriffen.*

print² (verb) **1.** *(a book, page, design)* drucken [ˈdrʊkŋ]
+haben ◊ *Die Überschrift war fett/kursiv gedruckt.* ♦
*Wir haben 400 Einladungskarten/Plakate drucken
lassen.*; *(publish)* veröffentlichen [fɛˈlˈœfntlɪçn] <veröf-
fentlicht, veröffentlichte, hat veröffentlicht> ◊ *Ihr Leserbrief wurde tatsächlich veröffentlicht.* **2.** *(write in
block letters)* in Druckschrift schreiben
[ɪn ˈdrʊkʃrɪft ʃrˌaebm̩] <schreibt, schrieb, hat geschrie-
ben> ◊ *Bitte schreiben Sie Ihren Namen in Druckschrift auf das Formular.* **3.** FOTO abziehen [ˈaptsiːən]
<zieht ab, zog ab, hat abgezogen> ◊ *Im Labor wurde
das falsche Negativ abgezogen.*

printer (noun) **1.** IT Drucker [ˈdrʊkɐ] der <‒s, ‒> ◊
Im Drucker ist kein Papier mehr. **2.** *(person)*
Drucker [ˈdrʊkɐ] der <‒s, ‒> ♀Druckerin
[ˈdrʊkərɪn] die <‒, ‒nen> ◊ *Er ist gelernter Drucker,
doch jetzt macht er etwas anderes.* ♦ *Die Druckerin
erklärte ihm, wie die Maschinen funktionieren.*

printing (noun) **1.** *(process)* Druck [drʊk] der
<‒(e)s, ‒e> ◊ *den Druck eines Buches überwachen*
♦ *Haben Sie den Artikel schon in Druck gegeben?*
printing error Druckfehler [ˈdrʊkfeːlɐ] der <‒s, ‒>
printing press Druckerpresse [ˈdrʊkɐprɛsə] die
<‒, ‒n> **2.** *(quantity printed)* Auflage [ˈaoflaːɡə] die
<‒, ‒n> ◊ *Wie hoch war die erste Auflage?* ♦ *in
einer Auflage von 300 000 Exemplaren erscheinen*

3. *(writing)* Druckschrift ['drʊkʃrɪft] die <-, –en>
printout ⟨noun⟩ Ausdruck ['aͻsdrʊk] der <-(e)s, –e>
◊ *Ich habe einen Ausdruck von der Liste gemacht.*

prior ⟨adj⟩ vorherig [foːɐ̯'heːrɪç] *no comp/superl, only
before ns* ◊ *Ohne vorherige Vereinbarung können Sie
Herrn Gruber nicht sprechen.* prior ... Vor... [foːɐ̯]
prior knowledge Vorwissen ['foːɐ̯vɪsn̩] das <–s> *no
pl* ◊ *Diese Vorlesung war ohne Vorwissen nicht zu
verstehen.* prior warning Vorwarnung ['foːɐ̯va'nʊŋ]
die <-, –en> ◊ *Ohne Vorwarnung schoss der Mann
plötzlich auf den Verkäufer.* prior to vor [foːɐ̯] +dat ◊
*Die Entscheidung wurde bereits vor meiner Ankunft
getroffen.*

priority ⟨noun⟩ Priorität [priori'tɛːt] die <-, –en> ◊
Diese Sache hat Priorität. ♦ *Sie müssen Ihre Prioritäten richtig setzen.* ♦ *Bitte geben Sie diesem Projekt
höchste Priorität.* take priority over sth Vorrang vor
etw. ⟨dat⟩ haben ['foːɐ̯raŋ foːɐ̯ ... haˈbm̩] +haben ◊
*Sicherheit hat Vorrang vor Kostenersparnis.; (on the
road)* take priority (over sth) Vorfahrt (vor etw.
⟨dat⟩) haben ['foːɐ̯faːɐ̯t haˈbm̩] +haben ◊ *Krankenwagen haben Vorfahrt vor allen anderen Fahrzeugen.*

prison ⟨noun⟩ Gefängnis [gə'fɛŋnɪs] das <–ses, –se> ◊
Er wurde gestern aus dem Gefängnis entlassen. in
prison im Gefängnis ◊ *Sie sitzt im Gefängnis.* go to
prison ins Gefängnis kommen

prisoner ⟨noun⟩ Gefangene [gə'faŋənə] der/die
<–n, die Gefangenen> *but: ein Gefangener/eine
Gefangene (also fig)* ◊ *Mehrere Gefangene konnten
fliehen.* ♦ *ein politischer Gefangener*

prisoner of war ⟨noun⟩ Kriegsgefangene
['kriːksɡə,faŋənə] der/die <–n, die Kriegsgefangenen>
but: ein Kriegsgefangener/eine Kriegsgefangene

prison sentence ⟨noun⟩ Freiheitsstrafe
['fraɪhaͻtsʃtraːfə] die <-, –n> ◊ *Er wurde zu einer
dreijährigen Freiheitsstrafe verurteilt.* ♦ *eine Freiheitsstrafe verbüßen*

privacy ⟨noun⟩ Privatsphäre [pri'vaːtsfɛːrə] die <–> *no
pl* ◊ *In diesem Großraumbüro hat man überhaupt
keine Privatsphäre.* ♦ *in jds Privatsphäre eindringen*

private ⟨adj⟩ **1.** *(opposite of public)* privat [pri'vaːt] *no
comp/superl* ◊ *Diese Angelegenheit ist rein privat.* ♦
die privaten Fernsehsender; Privat... [pri'vaːt] private
life Privatleben [pri'vaːtleːbm̩] das <–s> *no pl* private
property Privateigentum [pri'vaːt|aͻeͻntuːm] das <–s>
no pl; (place) ungestört ['ʊnɡəˌʃtøːɐ̯t] <ungestörter, am
ungestörtesten> ◊ *Sie suchten einen ungestörten Ort
zum Reden.; (information)* vertraulich [fe'traͻlɪç] ◊
Diese Details sind vertraulich. private joke Insider-
witz ['ɪnsaͻdevɪts] der <–es, –e> **2.** *(personality)* int-
rovertiert [ɪntrovɛˈtiːɐ̯t] <introvertierter, am introver-
tiertesten> ◊ *ein introvertierter Mensch*

privately ⟨adv⟩ **1.** *(in private)* speak privately to sb
unter vier Augen mit jdm sprechen
[ʊntɐ fiːɐ̯ 'aͻɡn̩ mɪt ... ʃprɛçn̩] <spricht, sprach, hat
gesprochen> ◊ *Könnte ich kurz unter vier Augen mit
Ihnen sprechen?; (secretly)* insgeheim ['ɪnsɡəhaͻm]
no comp/superl ◊ *Insgeheim hoffte sie, dass er zu ihr
zurückkehren würde.* ♦ *Er hält das Projekt
insgeheim für Zeitverschwendung.* **2.** *(not publicly)*
privat [pri'vaːt] ◊ *Ein Teil der Kosten soll künftig
privat finanziert werden.* privately owned in Privat-
besitz [ɪn pri'vaːtbəzɪts]

privatization ⟨noun⟩ Privatisierung [privati'ziːrʊŋ] die
<-, –en> ◊ *die Privatisierung der Bahn*

privilege ⟨noun⟩ **1.** *(advantage, right)* Privileg

[privi'leːk] das <-(e)s, –ien> ◊ *Privilegien besitzen* a
life of privilege ein privilegiertes Leben
[aͻn privileˌɡiːɐ̯təs 'leːbm̩] <–s> **2.** *(hono(u)r)* Ehre
['eːrə] die <-, –n> *most sing* ◊ *Es war eine große
Ehre für ihn, dass er die Rede halten durfte.* ♦ *Es ist
mir eine große Ehre, Sie willkommen zu heißen.;
(pleasure)* Vergnügen [fe'ɡnyːɡn̩] das <–s, –> *most
sing* ◊ *Es ist ein Vergnügen, mit so talentierten
Leuten zu arbeiten.* **3.** *(of doctors, lawyers)* Schweigepflicht ['ʃvaͻɡəpflɪçt] die <–> *no pl* ◊ *die ärztliche
Schweigepflicht*

privileged ⟨adj⟩ **1.** *(having advantages)* privilegiert
[privi'ɡiːɐ̯t] <privilegierter, am privilegiertesten> ◊ *ein
privilegiertes Leben führen* ♦ *Sie ist privilegiert.* be
privileged to do sth das Privileg haben, etw. zu tun
[das privi'leːk haˈbm̩ ... tsuː] +haben **2.** *(information)*
vertraulich [fe'traͻlɪç] ◊ *Diese Information ist vertraulich.*

prize ⟨noun⟩ Preis [praͻs] der <–es, –e> ◊ *Sie
erhielten einen Preis für den schönsten Blumenstrauß.* ♦ *den ersten/zweiten etc. Preis gewinnen*
award a prize einen Preis verleihen ◊ *Ihm wurde
ein Preis für den besten Film verliehen.* prize money
Preisgeld ['praͻsɡɛlt] das <-(e)s, –er>

prize-winning ⟨adj⟩ preisgekrönt ['praͻsɡəkrøːnt] *no
comp/superl* ◊ *ein preisgekrönter Zuchtstier*

probability ⟨noun⟩ Wahrscheinlichkeit
[vaːˈʃaͻnlɪçkaͻt] die <-, –en> ◊ *mit 50-prozentiger
Wahrscheinlichkeit* there is a strong probability that
höchstwahrscheinlich ['høːçstvaːˈʃaͻnlɪç] ◊ *Höchstwahrscheinlich wird der Vorschlag abgelehnt.* in all
probability vermutlich [fe'muːtlɪç] ◊ *Die Entscheidung fällt vermutlich am Dienstag.*

probable(-ably) ⟨adj, adv⟩ wahrscheinlich [va:ˈʃaͻnlɪç]
◊ *Sie gilt als wahrscheinliche Nachfolgerin.* ♦ *Es ist
nicht wahrscheinlich, dass wir eine bessere
Lösung finden.* ◊ *it is probable that, probably* wahrscheinlich ◊ *Wahrscheinlich kommt sie zu Fuß.* ♦
*Man wird wahrscheinlich keinen Unterschied feststel-
len können.* very probably höchstwahrscheinlich
['høːçstvaːˈʃaͻnlɪç]

probation ⟨noun⟩ **1.** LAW Bewährung [bə'vɛːrʊŋ] die
<-, –en> ◊ *Er bekam drei Jahre auf Bewährung.*
place sb on probation jdm Bewährung geben **2.** *(in
a new job)* Probezeit ['proːbətsaͻt] die <-, –en> ◊ *Er
hatte drei Monate Probezeit.*

probe¹ ⟨noun⟩ **1.** *(inquiry)* probe into sth Untersuchung
... ⟨gen⟩ [ʊntə'zuːxʊŋ] die <-, –en> ◊ *die Untersuchung der Schwarzgeldaffäre* **2.** *(medical instrument,
piece of equipment)* Sonde ['zͻndə] die <-, –n> ◊
*Bei der Untersuchung wird eine Sonde in den Magen
eingeführt.* ♦ *eine Sonde in den Weltraum schicken*

probe² ⟨verb⟩ **1.** *(try to find out)* untersuchen
[ʊntə'zuːxn̩] <untersucht, untersuchte, hat untersucht>
◊ *Der Vorfall wurde genau untersucht.* probe sth
in etw. ⟨dat⟩ herumschnüffeln [ɪn ... hɛˌrͻmʃnʏfl̩n]
+haben *(fam)* ◊ *Warum schnüffelst du in meinem
Privatleben herum?* probe deep (into sth) gründliche
Nachforschungen (über etw. ⟨acc⟩) anstellen
[ɡrʏntlɪçə 'naːxfͻʃͻŋən anʃtɛln̩] +haben **2.** MED
sondieren [zͻn'diːrən] <sondiert, sondierte, hat
sondiert> **3.** *(with a finger, stick)* probe in etw.
⟨dat⟩ stochern [ɪn ... ʃtͻxɐn] +haben ◊ *Der Schim-
panse stocherte in dem Loch, um das Futter zu
kommen.* **4.** *(search)* durchsuchen [dͻˈç'tsuːxn̩]
<durchsucht, durchsuchte, hat durchsucht> ◊ *Sie*

haben das Gebiet genauestens durchsucht.
problem [noun] **1.** *(difficulty)* Problem [pro'bleːm] das
<–s, –e> ◊ *Das Problem besteht darin, dass* … ♦
*Wir haben ziemliche Probleme mit unseren
Nachbarn.* **cause sb a problem** jdm Probleme
bereiten **pose a problem (for sb/sth)** (für jdn/etw.)
ein Problem darstellen **drug problem** Drogenprob-
lem ['droːgŋproˌbleːm] **problem child** Problemkind
[pro'bleːmkɪnt] das <–(e)s, –er> **2.** MATH Aufgabe
['aofgaːbə] die <–, –n> ◊ *Lösen Sie folgende
Aufgabe:* …
⊙ **have a problem with sb/sth** *(dislike)* ein
Problem mit jdm/etw. **haben no problem** kein
Problem ◊ *„Schaffst du das bis morgen?"* — *„Ja,
sicher. Kein Problem!"*
problematic [adj] problematisch [proble'maːtɪʃ] ◊ *Das
ist eine höchst problematische Situation.* ♦ *Das wird
problematisch.*
procedure [noun] **1.** *(way of proceeding)* Verfahren
[fe'faːrən] das <–s, –> ◊ *Das Verfahren ist ganz
einfach.* **follow a procedure** ein Verfahren
anwenden **2.** *(surgery)* Operation [opəra'tsioːn] die
<–, –en> ◊ *eine Operation am offenen Herzen*
proceed [verb] **1.** *(go on)* weitergehen ['vaetegeːən]
<geht weiter, ging weiter, ist weitergegangen> ◊ *Die
Arbeiten gingen die ganze Nacht über weiter.*
2. *(continue to do sth)* proceed (with sth) (mit etw.)
fortfahren ['fɔ'tfaːrən] <fährt fort, fuhr fort, hat/ist fort-
gefahren> ◊ *mit der Arbeit fortfahren* **proceed with a
plan** einen Plan umsetzen [aenən ˌplaːn 'ʊmtsɛtsn̩]
+haben **3.** *(go somewhere)* gehen ['geːən] <geht, ging,
ist gegangen> ◊ *Bitte gehen Sie zum Ausgang.; (road)*
weiterführen ['vaetefyːrən] +haben ◊ *Die Straße führt
weiter nach Westen.* **4.** *(start)* proceed to do sth
anfangen, etw. zu tun ['anfaŋən … tsuː] <fängt an,
fing an, hat angefangen> ◊ *Dann fing sie an, über
ihre Beziehung zu reden.* **5.** *(to the next stage)*
proceed to sth etw. erreichen [e'raeçn̩] <erreicht,
erreichte, hat erreicht> ◊ *Die Mannschaft hat das
Finale erreicht.; (to the next item)* proceed to sth zu
etw. übergehen [tsuː … ˌyːbegeːən] <geht über, ging
über, ist übergegangen> ◊ *Gehen wir zum nächsten
Punkt auf der Tagesordnung über.*
● **proceed against** [phras v] proceed against sb
einen Prozess gegen jdn führen
[aenən pro'tsɛs geːgŋ … fyːrən] +haben ◊ *Er führte
einen Prozess gegen seinen Nachbarn.*
● **proceed from** [phras v] proceed from sth/sb
irgendwoher/von jdm kommen [fɔn … kɔmən]
<kommt, kam, ist gekommen> ◊ *Die eigenartigen
Geräusche kamen aus dem Keller* ♦ *Diese Information hätte nur von mir kommen können.*
proceedings [noun] **1.** LAW Verfahren [fe'faːrən] das
<–s, –> ◊ *Die Staatsanwaltschaft wird gegen ihn ein
Verfahren einleiten.* ♦ *Morgen wird das Verfahren in
Sachen Schmid eröffnet.* **2.** *(events)* Ereignisse
[e'aegnɪsə] die <–> pl **3.** *(of a meeting)* Protokoll
[proto'kɔl] das <–s, –e> ◊ *Sie schrieb das Protokoll.*
proceeds [noun] proceeds (from sth) Erlös (… [gen])
[e'løːs] der <–es, –e> ◊ *Der Erlös geht an ein Kin-
derhilfsprojekt.*
process[1] [noun] **1.** *(development)* Prozess [pro'tsɛs] der
<–es, –e> ◊ *ein kontinuierlicher Prozess* **process of**
ageing Alterungsprozess ['altərʊŋsproˌtsɛs] **peace
process** Friedensprozess ['friːdn̩sproˌtsɛs] **2.** *(method,
way of doing sth)* Verfahren [fe'faːrən] das <–s, –> ◊

umweltschonende Verfahren ♦ *ein technisches
Verfahren* **3.** LAW Vorladung ['foːɐ̯laːdʊŋ] die
<–, –en> ◊ *Er erhielt eine gerichtliche Vorladung.*
⊙ **in the process of doing sth** *(while doing sth)* bei
etw. ◊ *Beim Sortieren der Post fiel mir der Brief
sofort auf.* **be in the process of doing sth** gerade
dabei sein, etw. zu tun ◊ *Ich war gerade dabei, die
Liste zu überprüfen.*
process[2] [verb] **1.** *(deal with)* bearbeiten [bə'a'baetn̩]
<bearbeitet, bearbeitete, hat bearbeitet> ◊ *Briefe/Kun-
denanfragen/Beschwerden bearbeiten* **2.** *(data)* verarbeiten [fe'a'baetn̩] <verarbeitet, verarbeitete, hat verar-
beitet> ◊ *Die Daten werden im Computer verarbei-
tet.* **3.** *(a substance)* aufbereiten ['aofbəˌraetn̩]
<bereitet auf, bereitete auf, hat aufbereitet> ◊ *Erdöl
aufbereiten; (food)* verarbeiten [fe'a'baetn̩] <verar-
beitet, verarbeitete, hat verarbeitet> **processed cheese**
Schmelzkäse ['ʃmɛltskɛːzə] der <–s> **no pl processed
food** Fertigprodukte ['fɛ'tɪçproˌdʊktə] die <–> pl
4. FOTO, FILM entwickeln [ɛnt'vɪkln̩] <entwickelt, entwickelte, hat entwickelt> ◊ *Kann man hier Fotos entwickeln lassen?* ♦ *einen Film zum Entwickeln wegbringen*
procession [noun] **1.** *(parade)* Umzug ['ʊmtsuːk] der
<–(e)s, Umzüge> ◊ *ein festlicher Umzug der Schüt-
zenvereine* ♦ *einen Umzug machen/veranstalten;
(religious)* Prozession [protsɛ'sioːn] die <–, –en> in
procession in einer Reihe [ɪn aenə 'raeə] **2.** *(fig)
(series)* Reihe ['raeə] die <–, –> ◊ *Er hatte eine
Reihe von Freundinnen.*
processor [noun] **1.** IT Prozessor [pro'tsɛsoːɐ̯] der
<–s, –en> **2.** *(kitchen equipment)* (food) processor
Küchenmaschine ['kʏçnmaˌʃiːnə] die <–, –n> ◊ *die
Zutaten in der Küchenmaschine zu einem Teig verarbeiten* **3.** *(food company)* Verarbeitungsbetrieb
[fe'a'baetʊŋsbətriːp] der <–(e)s, –e> **meat
processor** Fleischverarbeitungsbetrieb
['flaeʃfe'a'baetʊŋsbətriːp] **4.** FOTO, FILM processor's
Fotolabor ['foːtolaˌboːɐ̯] das <–s, –>
proclaim [verb] **1.** *(say officially)* verkünden [fe'kʏndn̩]
<verkündet, verkündete, hat verkündet> ◊ *den Zusam-
menschluss der Firmen verkünden* ♦ *Sie hat offiziell
verkündet, dass sie ins Ausland geht.* proclaim sb/
sth (to be) sth jdn/etw. zu etw. erklären
[tsuː … ɛklɛːrən] <erklärt, erklärte, hat erklärt> ◊ *Er
wurde zum Gewinner erklärt.* **2.** *(give away, indicate)*
verraten [fe'raːtn̩] <verrät, verriet, hat verraten> ◊ *Das
Auto in der Garage verriet, dass er zu Hause war.*
produce[1] [noun] Produkte [pro'dʊktə] die <–> pl ◊
landwirtschaftliche Produkte
produce[2] [verb] **1.** *(make, grow)* produzieren
[produ'tsiːrən] <produziert, produzierte, hat produ-
ziert> ◊ *Wir produzieren große Mengen von
Tomaten.* ◊ *Das Kraftwerk produziert günstigen
Strom.* ♦ *einen Film produzieren* **2.** *(bring forth)* hervorbringen [he'foːɐ̯brɪŋən] <bringt hervor, brachte
hervor, hat hervorgebracht> ◊ *Dieses Land hat viele
Komponisten hervorgebracht.* **3.** *(reach, achieve)*
erzielen [e'tsiːlən] <erzielt, erzielte, hat erzielt> ◊ *Er
erzielte ein besseres Ergebnis als gedacht.* produce
the opposite result genau das Gegenteil erreichen
[gənao das ˌgeːgn̩tael erˌaeçn̩] <erreicht, erreichte, hat
erreicht> sth produces results etw. führt zu Ergeb-
nissen [fyːɐ̯t tsuː erˈgeːbnɪsn̩] +haben **4.** *(show)*
vorweisen ['foːɐ̯vaezn̩] <weist vor, wies vor, hat vorge-
wiesen> ◊ *Er musste an der Grenze seinen Pass*

vorweisen. produce sth from sth etw. aus etw. holen [aʊs ... hoːlən] +haben ◊ *Er holte einen Spiegel aus seiner Tasche.* **5.** *(a newborn)* bekommen [bəˈkɔmən] <bekommt, bekam, hat bekommen> ◊ *Die Löwin hat zwei Junge bekommen.*

producer [noun] Produzent [produˈtsɛnt] der <-en, -en> ♀Produzentin [produˈtsɛntɪn] die <-, -nen> ◊ *George Lucas, der Regisseur und Produzent von „Star Wars"* ♦ *Deutschland ist einer der größten Produzenten von Gerste.*

product [noun] **1.** *(thing or person produced, sum of a multiplication)* Produkt [proˈdʊkt] das <-(e)s, -e> ◊ *ein neues Produkt entwickeln/auf den Markt bringen* ♦ *Sie ist ein typisches Produkt ihrer Zeit.* ♦ *Das Produkt aus 11 und 12 beträgt 132.* **2.** *(result)* Ergebnis [ɛˈɡeːpnɪs] das <-ses, -se> ◊ *das Ergebnis jahrelanger Verhandlungen*

production [noun] **1.** *(process of making, film or TV programme, manufacturing department)* Produktion [prodʊkˈtsi̯oːn] die <-, -en> ◊ *die Produktion von Fernsehgeräten* ♦ *die Produktion von Insulin in der Bauchspeicheldrüse* ♦ *Die Serie/Show ist eine Produktion des Westdeutschen Rundfunks.* ♦ *In der Produktion sind 100 Mitarbeiter beschäftigt.* ♦ *Das neue Modell ist bereits in Produktion (gegangen).* **2.** *(showing)* on production of sth auf Vorzeigen ... [gen] [aʊf ˈfoːɐ̯tsaeɡn̩] das <-s> *no pl* ◊ *Einlass nur auf Vorzeigen des Mitgliedsausweises* ⊛ make a production out of sth *(complicate sth)* ein Drama aus etw. machen

production line [noun] Fließband [ˈfliːsbant] das <-s, Fließbänder>

productive(ly) [adj, adv] produktiv [prodʊkˈtiːf] ◊ *produktive Arbeit leisten* ♦ *Morgens bin ich am produktivsten.* ♦ *produktiv arbeiten*

productivity [noun] Produktivität [prodʊktiviˈtɛːt] die <-> *no pl* ◊ *die Produktivität steigern*

Prof. Prof. [proˈfɛsoːɐ̯] ◊ *Frau Prof. Dr. Berger*

profession [noun] **1.** *(job requiring a special skill or qualification)* Beruf [bəˈruːf] der <-(e)s, -e> ◊ *Ich liebe meinen Beruf.* by profession von Beruf ◊ *Er ist Krankenpfleger von Beruf.* enter the teaching profession den Beruf des Lehrers ergreifen enter the legal profession Jurist/in werden [juˈrɪst/juˈrɪstɪn veːɐ̯dn̩] +sein **2.** *(all the people who work in a particular area)* the medical profession die Ärzteschaft [diː ˈɛˤtstəˌʃaft] <-> the teaching/legal profession die Lehrer/Juristen [diː ˈleːrɐ/juˈrɪstn̩] <-> *pl* **3.** *(admission)* Bekenntnis [bəˈkɛntnɪs] das <-ses, -se> ◊ *ein Bekenntnis seiner Liebe* ⊛ the oldest profession (in the world) das älteste Gewerbe (der Welt)

professional[1] [noun] **1.** *(highly qualified person)* IT professional Informatiker [ɪnfɔˈmaːtɪkɐ] der <-s, -> ♀Informatikerin [ɪnfɔˤˈmaːtɪkərɪn] die <-, -nen> health professionals qualifizierte Kräfte im Gesundheitswesen [kvalifiˌtsiːɐ̯tə ˌkrɛftə ɪm ɡəˈzʊnthaetsveːzn̩] <-> *pl* **2.** *(not an amateur)* Profi [ˈproːfi] der <-s, -s> *(fam)* ◊ *die hoch bezahlten Profis der Bundesliga*

professional[2] [adj] **1.** *(requiring specific knowledge)* qualifiziert [kvalifiˈtsiːɐ̯t] <qualifizierter, am qualifiziertesten> ◊ *eine qualifizierte Tätigkeit ausüben* ♦ *qualifizierte Teilzeitarbeit* ♦ *ein qualifiziertes Urteil abgeben* **2.** *(behavio(u)r)* professionell [profɛsi̯oˈnɛl] ◊ *eine professionelle Vorgehensweise* ♦ *So ein Verhalten*

ist wenig professionell. **3.** *(relating to sb's work)* beruflich [bəˈruːflɪç] *no comp/superl* ◊ *jds berufliche Laufbahn* ♦ *Mein Interesse an der Sache ist rein beruflich.* **4.** *(doing sth as a job)* Profi... [ˈproːfiː] professional footballer Profifußballer [ˈproːfifuːsbalɐ] der <-s, -> ♀Profifußballerin [ˈproːfifuːsbalərɪn] die <-, -nen> professional photographer Profifotograf [ˈproːfifotoˌɡraːf] der <-en, -en> ♀Profifotografin [ˈproːfifotoˌɡraːfɪn] die <-, -nen> go professional Profi werden [ˈproːfiː veːɐ̯dn̩] +sein

professionally [adv] **1.** professionally trained ausgebildet [ˈaʊsɡəbɪldət] ◊ *eine ausgebildete Bibliothekarin* **2.** *(behaviour, skill)* professionell [profɛsi̯oˈnɛl] ◊ *Sie arbeiten dort sehr professionell und zuverlässig.* **3.** *(in your job)* beruflich [bəˈruːflɪç] *no comp/superl* ◊ *Ich habe beruflich viel mit Menschen zu tun.* **4.** *(as a job)* berufsmäßig [bəˈruːfsmɛːsɪç] *no comp/superl* ◊ *Sie übt den Reitsport nicht mehr berufsmäßig aus.*

professor [noun] Professor [proˈfɛsoːɐ̯] der <-s, -en> ♀Professorin [profɛˈsoːrɪn] die <-, -nen> ◊ *Unser Professor für Physik lehrte früher in Marburg.*

profile [noun] **1.** *(image, public appearance)* Image [ˈɪmɪtʃ] das <-(s), -s> ◊ *Das Image der Firma muss verbessert werden.* raise sb's profile jds Image verbessern **2.** *(attention)* enjoy a high profile große Beachtung finden [ɡroːsə baˈʔaxtʊŋ fɪndn̩] <findet, fand, hat gefunden> maintain a high pofile Präsenz zeigen [preˈzɛnts tsaeɡn̩] +haben keep a low profile sich zurückhalten [tsuˈrʏkhaltn̩] <hält sich zurück, hielt sich zurück, hat sich zurückgehalten> ◊ *Sie haben sich eher zurückgehalten.* **3.** *(description of sb/sth, shape of sb's face)* Profil [proˈfiːl] das <-s, -e> ◊ *Die Polizei hat das Verdächtigen erstellt.* ♦ *Ihr Profil passte genau zu der Stellenausschreibung.* ♦ *Auf dem Foto ist sie im Profil zu sehen.*

profit[1] [noun] **1.** *(financial gain)* Gewinn [ɡəˈvɪn] der <-(e)s, -e> ◊ *hohe Gewinne bringen* ♦ *einen Gewinn machen* at a profit mit Gewinn **2.** *(advantage)* Nutzen [ˈnʊtsn̩] der <-s> *no pl* ◊ *Die Beziehung hatte für ihn keinen Nutzen.*

profit[2] [verb] profit sb/sth profit sb/sth jdm/einer Sache. nutzen [ˈnʊtsn̩] +haben ◊ *Das Übereinkommen nutzte beiden Parteien.* profit from sth von etw. profitieren [fɔn ... profiˌtiːrən] <profitiert, profitierte, hat profitiert> ◊ *Wer profitiert am meisten von den Neuerungen?*

profitability [noun] Rentabilität [rɛntabiliˈtɛːt] die <-> *no pl* ◊ *die Rentabilität erhöhen*

profitable(-ably) [adj, adv] **1.** *(bringing financial gain)* rentabel [rɛnˈtaːbl̩] <rentabler, am rentabelsten> <der/die/das rentable ...> ◊ *eine rentable Kapitalanlage* ♦ *Die Investitionen müssen rentabler gemacht werden.* ♦ *Das Unternehmen arbeitet rentabel.* **2.** *(useful, valuable)* nützlich [ˈnʏtslɪç] ◊ *eine nützliche Erfahrung* spend your time profitably seine Zeit sinnvoll nutzen [zaenə ˌtsaet ˈzɪnfɔl ˌnʊtsn̩] +haben

profound [adj] **1.** *(extreme)* tief greifend [ˈtiːf ɡraefn̩t] <tiefer greifend, am tiefsten greifend> *mostly before ns* ◊ *tief greifende Veränderungen* ♦ *ein tief greifender Einfluss;* *(difference)* gravierend [ɡraˈviːrənt] ◊ *ein gravierender Unterschied;* *(significance)* groß [ɡroːs] <größer, am größten> ◊ *von großer Wichtigkeit* ♦ *Das Ereignis hatte eine große Bedeutung für*

sie. **2.** *(deep)* tiefgründig ['tiːfgrʏndɪç] ◇ *tiefgründige Ideen/Fragen* **3.** *(complete)* völlig ['fœlɪç] *no comp/ superl* ◇ *völlige Blindheit*

program¹ → **programme¹** [noun] ɪᴛ Programm [proˈgram] *das* <-(e)s, -e> ◇ *Welches Programm benutzt du zur Textverarbeitung?* ♦ *ein Programm installieren/deinstallieren*

program² → **programme²** [verb] programmieren [progra'miːrən] <programmiert, programmierte, hat programmiert> ◇ *Software programmieren*

programme¹, program [noun] **1.** *(plan, brochure)* Programm [proˈgram] *das* <-(e)s, -e> ◇ *im Theater ein Programm kaufen* a programme for sth ein Programm zu etw. ◇ *ein Programm zur Bekämpfung der Arbeitslosigkeit* **2.** *(radio, TV)* Sendung ['zɛndʊŋ] *die* <-, -en> ◇ *die Sendung mit der Maus* ♦ *Diese Sendung kommt jeden Montag um 20 Uhr.*

programme², program [verb] **1.** *(make sb/sth behave in a certain way)* programmieren [progra'miːrən] <programmiert, programmierte, hat programmiert> ◇ *Sie wurde auf Freundlichkeit programmiert.* **2.** *(plan)* planen ['plaːnən] +haben

progress¹ [noun] **1.** *(development)* Fortschritt ['fɔˀtʃrɪt] *der* <-(e)s, -e> ◇ *Fortschritte erzielen* ♦ *Der Fortschritt ist unaufhaltsam.* progress on sth Fortschritte bei etw. progress towards sth Fortschritte in Richtung ... [gen] ◇ *Sie machten Fortschritte in Richtung einer Einigung.* make progress Fortschritte machen monitor progress Fortschritte beobachten ◇ *Er beobachtet die Fortschritte seiner Schüler ganz genau.* progress report Zwischenbericht ['tsvɪʃnbərɪçt] *der* <-(e)s, -e> **2.** *(movement)* Vorwärtskommen ['foːɐvɛˀtskɔmən] *das* <-s> *no pl* ⊙ in progress im Gange

progress² [verb] **1.** *(make progress)* vorankommen [foˈrankɔmən] <kommt voran, kam voran, ist vorangekommen> progress beyond sth über etw. [acc] hinausgehen [yːbe ... hɪˌnaʊsɡeːən] <geht hinaus, ging hinaus, ist hinausgegangen> ◇ *Die Friedensgespräche gingen nicht über vorsichtige Kompromisse hinaus.* progress towards sth einer Sache [dat] näher kommen ['nɛːɐ kɔmən] <kommt, kam, ist gekommen> ◇ *Wir sind einer Lösung noch nicht näher gekommen.* progress (from sth) to sth (von etw.) in etw. [acc] aufsteigen [ɪn ... ˌaʊftʃtaɪɡn̩] <steigt auf, stieg auf, ist aufgestiegen> ◇ *Sie sind in die erste Liga aufgestiegen.* **2.** *(disease)* fortschreiten ['fɔˀtʃraɪtn̩] <schreitet fort, schritt fort, ist fortgeschritten> ◇ *Die Infektion ist schon weit fortgeschritten.* **3.** *(move slowly)* sich (langsam) bewegen [(ˌlaŋzaːm) bəˈveːɡn̩] <bewegt sich, bewegte sich, hat sich bewegt> ◇ *Sie bewegten sich langsam auf das Haus zu.* **4.** *(time)* as time progesses im Laufe der Zeit [ɪm laʊfə deːɐ 'tsaet] ◇ *Im Laufe der Zeit wurde aus dem Dorf eine Stadt.* as the 21st century progresses im Laufe des 21. Jahrhunderts **5.** *(make sth develop faster)* progress sth etw. vorantreiben [foˈrantraɪbm̩] <treibt voran, trieb voran, hat vorangetrieben> ◇ *ein Projekt vorantreiben*

progression [noun] **1.** *(development)* Aufstieg ['aʊfʃtiːk] *der* <-(e)s, -e> most sing ◇ *ein beruflicher Aufstieg; (of a disease)* Fortschreiten ['fɔˀtʃraɪtn̩] *das* <-s> *no pl* ◇ *Das Fortschreiten der Krankheit muss aufgehalten werden.* **2.** *(series of things)* Reihenfolge ['raeənfɔlɡə] *die* <-, -n> ◇ *in die richtige Reihenfolge bringen*

progressive [adj] **1.** *(forward-looking)* fortschrittlich ['fɔˀtʃrɪtlɪç] ◇ *ein fortschrittlicher Politiker* ♦ *Seine Ansichten sind fortschrittlich.* **2.** *(disease)* fortschreitend ['fɔˀtʃraɛtn̩t] *no comp/superl* ◇ *eine langsam fortschreitende Krankheit* **3.** ʟɪɴɢ progressive form/mode Verlaufsform [fɛˈlaʊfsfɔˀm] ◇ *die Verlaufsform des englischen Verbs* **4.** *(music)* progressiv [progrɛˈsiːf] ◇ *progressiver Jazz*

prohibit [verb] **1.** *(not allow)* verbieten [fɛˈbiːtn̩] <verbietet, verbot, hat verboten> ◇ *Baden verboten!* prohibit sb from doing sth jdm verbieten, etw. zu tun **2.** *(prevent from happening)* verhindern [fɛˈhɪndɐn] <verhindert, verhinderte, hat verhindert> ◇ *Ein hoher Zaun verhindert das unerlaubte Betreten des Grundstücks.*

project¹ [noun] Projekt [proˈjɛkt] *das* <-(e)s, -e> ◇ *ein Projekt zuverlässig abwickeln* ♦ *Das Projekt ließ sich leider nicht realisieren.* embark on a project ein Projekt in Angriff nehmen research project Forschungsprojekt ['fɔˀʃʊŋsproˌjɛkt] sb's pet project jds Lieblingsprojekt ['liːplɪŋsproˌjɛkt]

project² [verb] **1.** *(predict)* voraussagen [foˈraʊszaːɡŋ̩] +haben ◇ *Sie sagten hohe Gewinne voraus.* **2.** *(stick out)* herausragen [hɛˈraʊsraːɡŋ̩] +haben ◇ *Aus der Wand ragt ein Balken heraus.* project outwards/ forwards/up nach außen/vorne/oben ragen [naːx 'aʊsn̩/'foˀnə/'oːbm̩ raːɡŋ̩] +haben **3.** *(an image)* projizieren [projiˈtsiːrən] <projiziert, projizierte, hat projiziert> ◇ *Sie projizierten das Bild an die Wand.* **4.** *(propel, throw)* schleudern ['ʃlɔɪdɐn] +haben ◇ *Einige Teile des Flugzeugs wurden hunderte Meter weit geschleudert.* **5.** *(give an impression of)* vermitteln [fɛˈmɪtl̩n] <vermittelt, vermittelte, hat vermittelt> ◇ *Sie vermittelten ein Bild der Eintracht.* **6.** project yourself sich als etw. darstellen [als ... ˌdaːˀʃtɛlən] +haben ◇ *Er hat sich als der perfekte Vater dargestellt.* **7.** project sth onto sb etw. auf jdn übertragen [aʊf ... ybeˌtraːɡŋ̩] <überträgt, übertrug, hat übertragen> ◇ *Sie hat ihre Minderwertigkeitsgefühle auf ihn übertragen.* **8.** *(plan)* planen ['plaːnən] +haben ◇ *Die ansässige Bevölkerung protestiert gegen den geplanten Staudamm.*

projection [noun] **1.** *(prediction)* Prognose [proˈgnoːzə] *die* <-, -n> ◇ *Die Prognosen für das kommende Jahr sind positiv.* **2.** *(of images, psychological)* Projektion [projɛkˈtsjoːn] *die* <-, -en> ◇ *die Projektion von Bildern auf eine Leinwand* ♦ *eine Projektion der eigenen Gefühle auf eine andere Person* **3.** *(self-presentation)* projection (of yourself) Selbstdarstellung ['zɛlpstdaːˀʃtɛlʊŋ] *die* <-, -en> ◇ *die Selbstdarstellung der Partei als Moralwächter*

projector [noun] Projektor [proˈjɛktoːɐ] *der* <-s, -en> ◇ *Dias/Folien mit dem Projektor an die Wand werfen*

prolific [adj] **1.** *(writer, artist etc.)* produktiv [produkˈtiːf] ◇ *eine äußerst produktive Autorin* ♦ *Als Künstler ist er momentan nicht sehr produktiv.* **2.** *(producing many babies)* fruchtbar ['frʊxtbaːˀ] ◇ *Ratten sind sehr fruchtbare Tiere.* **3.** *(exist in large numbers)* be prolific zahlreich sein ['tsaːlraɛç zaɛn] +sein ◇ *Diese Vögel sind an der Küste recht zahlreich.*

prolong [verb] verlängern [fɛˈlɛŋɐn] <verlängert, verlängerte, hat verlängert> ◇ *Das Medikament verlängerte sein Leben um einige Jahre.; (take longer)* be prolonged länger dauern ['lɛŋɐ daʊɐn] +haben

prolonged → **prolong** [adj] lang andauernd

['laŋ ˌandaọɛnt] <länger andauernd, am längsten andauernd> only before ns ◊ ein lang andauerndes Gespräch

prominent [adj] **1.** (famous) prominent [promiˈnɛnt] <prominenter, am prominentesten> ◊ eine Talkshow mit prominenten Gästen ◆ Der Chirurg ist hier sehr prominent. prominent in sth bedeutend für etw. [bəˈdɔːtn̩t fyːg̊] ◊ Er war recht bedeutend für die Modebranche. **2.** (easy to see) deutlich erkennbar [ˌdɔːtlɪç ɛˈkɛnbaːɾ] <deutlicher erkennbar, am deutlichsten erkennbar> ◊ Der Mond war in der Dämmerung bereits deutlich erkennbar. **3.** (cheek bones) ausgeprägt [ˈaọsɡəprɛːkt] <ausgeprägter, am ausgeprägtesten> ◊ Er hatte ausgeprägte Wangenknochen.

prominently [adv] **1.** (easy to spot) deutlich sichtbar [ˌdɔːtlɪç ˈzɪçtbaːɾ] <deutlicher sichtbar, am deutlichsten sichtbar> ◊ Das Schild ist deutlich sichtbar über dem Eingang angebracht. **2.** (be important) figure prominently somewhere irgendwo eine bedeutende Rolle spielen [aẹnə bəˌdɔːtn̩də ˈrɔlə ʃpiːlən] +haben

promise¹ [noun] **1.** (pledge) Versprechen [fɛˈʃprɛçn̩] das <-s, -> ◊ ein Versprechen abgeben/brechen/halten ◆ jdm sein Versprechen geben, dass man etw. tun wird make a promise to sb jdm ein Versprechen geben show promise viel versprechend sein [ˈfiːl fɛʃprɛçn̩t zaẹn] +sein ◊ Seine Karriere ist viel versprechend. **2.** (sign of sth) promise of sth Hoffnung auf etw. [acc] [ˈhɔfnʊŋ aọf] die <-, -en> ◊ die Hoffnung auf eine Wetterbesserung

promise² [verb] versprechen [fɛˈʃprɛçn̩] <verspricht, versprach, hat versprochen> ◊ Es verspricht ein schöner Tag zu werden. ◆ Ich verspreche, dort gleich anzurufen. ◆ Er hat ihr versprochen, dass er sich darum kümmert. promise sth to sb jdm etw. versprechen ◊ Sie haben uns das Geld versprochen. as promised wie versprochen

promising [adj] vielversprechend [ˈfiːlfɛʃprɛçn̩t] ◊ Es wurde ein vielversprechender Abend. ◆ Das sieht vielversprechend aus.

promote [verb] **1.** (support) fördern [ˈfœɐdn̩] +haben ◊ begabte Schüler fördern ◆ Diese Vitamine fördern die Sehkraft. **2.** (move to a better position) befördern [bəˈfœɐdn̩] <befördert, beförderte, hat befördert> ◊ Er wurde zum Gruppenleiter befördert.; (sports team) be promoted to sth in etw. [acc] aufsteigen [ɪn ... ˌaọfʃtaẹgn̩] <steigt auf, stieg auf, ist aufgestiegen> ◊ Sie sind in die erste Liga aufgestiegen.; (in the US: move a student to a different year) versetzen [fɛˈzɛtsn̩] <versetzt, versetzte, hat versetzt> ◊ Er wurde in die dritte Klasse versetzt. **3.** (advertise) promote sth für etw. Werbung machen [fyːg̊ ...ˌvɛɾbʊŋ maxn̩] +haben ◊ Sie machen Werbung für Seife.

promoter [noun] **1.** (sb organizing concerts, sports events) Veranstalter [fɛˈʔanʃtaltɐ] der <-s, -> ♀Veranstalterin [fɛˈʔanʃtaltərɪn] die <-, -nen> **2.** (sb promoting ideas or projects) Förderer [ˈfœɐdərɐ] der <-s, -> ♀Förderin [ˈfœɐdərɪn] die <-, -nen> ◊ ein großer Förderer der Kunst

promotion [noun] **1.** (in your job) Beförderung [bəˈfœɐdərʊŋ] die <-, -en> ◊ eine Beförderung zum Abteilungsleiter gain promotion befördert werden [bəˈfœɐdɛt veːɐdn̩] <wird, wurde, ist worden>; (of a sports team) Aufstieg [ˈaọfʃtiːk] der <-(e)s, -e> ◊ der Aufstieg in die nächste Liga **2.** (support) Unterstützung [ʊntɐˈʃtʏtsʊŋ] die <-, -en> ◊ die Unterstüt-

zung seiner Pläne **3.** (advertisement) Werbung [ˈvɛɾbʊŋ] die <-, -en> promotion of sth Werbung für etw. ◊ Werbung für Fernsehgeräte

prompt¹ [adj] **1.** (without delay) prompt [prɔmpt] no comp/superl ◊ Er erhielt eine prompte Reaktion. ◆ Die Antwort war prompt. be prompt in doing sth etw. umgehend tun [ˈʊmɡeːənt] **2.** (punctual) pünktlich [ˈpʏŋktlɪç] ◊ Bei einem pünktlichen Ende der Veranstaltung erreichen sie den Bus.

prompt² [verb] **1.** (cause) prompt sth der Auslöser für etw. sein [deːɐ ˌaọsløːzɐ fyːg̊ ... zaẹn] +sein ◊ Dieses Ereignis war der Auslöser für einschneidende Veränderungen. prompt sb to do sth jdn dazu veranlassen, etw. zu tun [datsuː fɛ|ˈanlasn̩ ... tsuː] <veranlasst, veranlasste, hat veranlasst> ◊ Seine Worte veranlassten mich dazu, mein Verhalten zu überdenken. **2.** (make sb say sth) fragen [ˈfraːgn̩] +haben ◊ „Was jetzt?“, fragte er. without being prompted aus freien Stücken [aọs ˌfraẹən ˈʃtʏkn̩] ◊ Sie sagt nie etwas aus freien Stücken. **3.** THEAT (an actor) soufflieren [zuˈfliːrən] <soufflliert, soufflierte, hat soufffliert> ◊ den Schauspielern soufflieren

promptly [adv] **1.** (immediately) prompt [prɔmpt] no comp/superl ◊ Er reagierte prompt. **2.** (punctually) pünktlich [ˈpʏŋktlɪç] ◊ Pünktlich um drei Uhr fuhren sie ab.

prone [adj] **1.** (susceptible to disease, errors, disaster) prone to sth anfällig für etw. [ˈanfɛlɪç fyːg̊] ◊ anfällig für Infektionskankheiten sein sb is prone to injury jd verletzt sich häufig [fɛˈlɛtst ... ˌhoɔfɪç] <verletzt sich, verletzte sich, hat sich verletzt> **2.** (have a particular tendency) be prone to sth zu etw. neigen [tsuː ... naẹɡn̩] +haben ◊ Sie neigt zu/zur Eifersucht. be prone to do sth dazu neigen, etw. zu tun ◊ Er neigt dazu, sich ständig Sorgen zu machen.

pronoun [noun] Pronomen [proˈnoːmən] das <-s, - or Pronomina> ◊ die unbestimmten Pronomen ‚man‘ und ‚es‘

pronounce [verb] **1.** LING aussprechen [ˈaọsʃprɛçn̩] <spricht aus, sprach aus, hat ausgesprochen> ◊ Ich weiß nicht, wie man das Wort ausspricht. **2.** (declare) pronounce sb/sth jdn/etw. für etw. erklären [fyːg̊ ... ɛklɛːrən] <erklärt, erklärte, hat erklärt> ◊ Nach ein paar Jahren wurde er für tot erklärt. pronounce yourself satisfied with sth sich mit etw. zufrieden erklären

pronunciation [noun] Aussprache [ˈaọsʃpraːxe] die <-, -n>

proof [noun] **1.** (evidence) Beweis [bəˈvaẹs] der <-(e)s, -e> ◊ der Beweis eines mathematischen Satzes proof of sth Beweis für etw./... [gen] ◊ Das ist der Beweis für eure Unschuld. ◆ als Beweis meiner Treue **2.** (of an article or a book) Korrekturfahne [kɔrɛkˈtuːɡfaːnə] die <-, -n> ◊ Sie muss die Korrekturfahnen lesen. **3.** (alcohol content) Maßeinheit zur Angabe des Alkoholgehalts

In Germany, as in many other European countries, the content of alcohol in a beverage is measured as a percentage by volume at 20°C.

prop¹ [noun] **1.** (also fig) (support) Stütze [ˈʃtʏtsə] die <-, -n> ◊ Sie benutzte das Wörterbuch als Stütze für ihre anderen Bücher. ◆ Stützen aus Stahl ◆ Ihr Mann war ihr in der schweren Zeit eine wichtige Stütze. **2.** THEAT, FILM Requisite [rekviˈziːtə] die <-, -n>

prop² [verb] *(lean against)* prop sth against sth etw.
an etw. [acc] lehnen [an ... le:nən] +haben ◊ *Er
lehnte die Leiter an die Wand.; (lean on)* prop sth on
sth etw. auf etw. [acc] stützen [aof ... ʃtʏtsn̩] +haben
◊ *Ich stützte meinen Kopf auf die Hände.* prop sth
open etw. offen halten ['ɔfn̩ haltn̩] <hält offen, hielt
offen, hat offen gehalten> ◊ *Er klemmte ein Buch ins
Fenster, um es offen zu halten.*
• **prop up** [phras v] stützen ['ʃtʏtsn̩] +haben ◊ *Die
Decke wird von mehreren Balken gestützt.* ◆ *den
Dollar/die Wirtschaft stützen* prop yourself up with
sth sich auf etw. [acc] stützen prop yourself up with
pillows sich [dat] Kissen in den Rücken legen
[ˌkɪsn̩ ɪn de:n 'rʏkn̩ le:gn̩] +haben

propaganda [noun] Propaganda [propa'ganda:] die
<-> *no pl*

propagate [verb] **1.** *(spread: ideas, beliefs etc.)* verbreiten [fe'braɛtn̩] <verbreitet, verbreitete, hat verbreitet>
◊ *Seine Ideen wurden von seinen Anhängern schnell
verbreitet.* **2.** *(a plant, cells, animals)* vermehren
[fe'me:rən] <vermehrt, vermehrte, hat vermehrt> They
propagate. Sie vermehren sich. ◊ *Mäuse vermehren
sich ungeheuer schnell.* propagate sth from seed
etw. aus Samen ziehen [aos 'za:mən tsi:ən] <zieht,
zog, hat gezogen> ◊ *Er hat viele Tomatenpflanzen
aus dem Samen gezogen.*

proper [adj] **1.** *(right, real)* richtig ['rɪçtɪç] ◊ *Sie hatte
die richtigen Argumente.* ◆ *Es ist nicht richtig, was
er da tut.* ◆ *eine richtige kleine Dame* proper procedures ordnungsgemäßes Verfahren
[ˌɔ'dnʊŋsgəmɛ:səs fe'fa:rən] das <-> *sing* right and
proper recht und billig [ˌreçt ʊnt 'bɪlɪç] ◊ *Es ist nur
recht und billig, dass du dich entschuldigst.*
2. *(upright, decent)* anständig ['anʃtɛndɪç] ◊ *zwei
anständige junge Frauen* ◆ *Er ist sehr anständig und
zuverlässig.* **3.** *(typical)* proper to sb/sth für jdn/etw.
typisch [ty:g ... 'ty:pɪʃ] ◊ *Die grellen Farben sind
typisch für seine Gemälde.*

properly [adv] **1.** *(rightly, correctly)* richtig ['rɪçtɪç] ◊
Das kann ich nicht richtig beurteilen. **2.** *(suitably)*
ordentlich ['ɔ'dn̩tlɪç] *(fam)* ◊ *Er hat seine Sache ganz
ordentlich gemacht.*
ⓟ **properly speaking** genau genommen

proper name [noun] → **proper noun**

proper noun [noun] Eigenname ['aɛgn̩na:mə] der
<-ns, -n>

property [noun] **1.** *(things owned)* Eigentum
['aɛgn̩tu:m] das <-s> ◊ *öffentliches und
privates Eigentum* ◆ *mein rechtmäßiges Eigentum*
2. *(land)* Grundstück ['grʊntʃtʏk] das <-(e)s, -e>;
(house) Immobilie [ɪmo'bi:liə] die <-, -n> most pl
property prices Immobilienpreise [ɪmo'bi:liənpraɛzə]
die <-> pl **3.** *(quality)* Eigenschaft ['aɛgn̩ʃaft] die
<-, -en> ◊ *die physikalischen/chemischen Eigen-
schaften eines Stoffes*

prophecy [noun] Prophezeiung [profe'tsaɛʊŋ] die
<-, -en> ◊ *Seine Prophezeiung hat sich nicht
erfüllt.*

proportion [noun] **1.** *(part)* proportion of sb/sth Teil
... [gen] [taɛl] der <-s, -e> ◊ *Ein kleiner Teil der
Schüler fällt im Test durch.; (relationship, ratio)* Verhältnis [fe'hɛltnɪs] das <-ses, -se> ◊ *Farbe im Verhältnis zwei zu eins mischen* the proportion of sth
to sth das Verhältnis von etw. und etw. ◊ *Das Verhältnis von Einsatz und Bezahlung muss stimmen.*
2. *(correct relationship)* Proportion [propɔ'tsio:n] die

<-, -en> ◊ *Er hatte perfekte Proportionen.* be out
of proportion (to sth) die Proportionen stimmen
nicht (mit etw. überein) sense of proportion ein
Sinn für Proportionen keep a sense of proportion
die Proportionen wahren **3.** *(size)* proportions
Ausmaße ['aosma:sə] die <-> pl ◊ *Die Ausmaße des
Parks waren beeindruckend.*
ⓟ **blow sth out of all proportion** etw. maßlos aufbauschen be out of all proportion (to sth) in
keinem Verhältnis (zu etw.) stehen keep sth in proportion etw. nicht zu wichtig nehmen

proportional [adj] **1.** *(suitable)* angemessen
['angəmɛsn̩] ◊ *ein angemessenes Verhalten* be porpor-
tional to sth einer Sache [dat] angemessen sein ◊
War meine Reaktion der Situation angemessen?
2. *(in the same relationship)* proportional
[propɔ'tsio'na:l] no comp/superl ◊ *proportionale
Kosten*

proposal [noun] **1.** *(suggestion)* Vorschlag ['fo:gʃla:k]
der <-(e)s, Vorschläge> ◊ *Sie machte (uns) den
Vorschlag, eine Pause einzulegen.* ◆ *Er griff ihren
Vorschlag, das Angebot zu erweitern, dankbar auf.*
2. *(of marriage)* Heiratsantrag ['haɛra:tsǀantra:k] der
<-(e)s, Heiratsanträge> ◊ *Sie machte ihm einen Hei-
ratsantrag.*

propose [verb] **1.** *(suggest)* vorschlagen ['fo:gʃla:gn̩]
<schlägt vor, schlug vor, hat vorgeschlagen> ◊ *Er hat
vorgeschlagen, dass sie in den Urlaub fliegen.*
propose sb for sth jdn als etw. vorschlagen ◊ *Sie
haben ihn als Trainer vorgeschlagen.* propose doing
sth vorschlagen, etw. zu tun ◊ *Sie haben vorgeschlagen, neue Bücher anzuschaffen.* propose a motion
einen Antrag stellen [aɛnən 'antra:k ʃtɛlən] +haben
2. propose (marriage) (to sb) (jdm) einen Heiratsantrag machen [aɛnən 'haɛra:tsǀantra:k maxn̩]
+haben ◊ *Er machte ihr einen Heiratsantrag.*

proposition [noun] **1.** *(statement)* Aussage ['aosza:gə]
die <-, -n> ◊ *die Aussage, dass Gerechtigkeit vor
Recht gehen sollte* **2.** *(suggestion)* Vorschlag
['fo:gʃla:k] der <-(e)s, Vorschläge> ◊ *Der Vorsitzende
machte einige Vorschläge.* put a proposition to sb
jdm einen Vorschlag unterbreiten ◊ *Darf ich Ihnen
einen Vorschlag unterbreiten?* **3.** *(sexual)* Anmache
['anmaxə] die <-> *(fam, pej)* **4.** math Lehrsatz
['le:gzats] der <-es, Lehrsätze> ◊ *Sie mussten den
Lehrsatz beweisen.* **5.** law *(in the US)* Gesetzesvor-
schlag, über den die Bürger abstimmen
ⓟ **not be a very attractive proposition** keine
angenehme Aussicht sein

proprietor [noun] Eigentümer ['aɛgrity:mə] der
<-s, -> ♀Eigentümerin ['aɛgrity:mərɪn] die
<-, -nen>

prose [noun] Prosa ['pro:za:] die <-> *no pl* ◊
schlichte/einfache Prosa

prosecute [verb] **1.** *(start court proceedings)* sb prose-
cutes jd leitet ein Verfahren ein
[laɛtət aɛn fe'fa:rən aɛn] <leitet ein, leitete ein, hat
eingeleitet> ◊ *Die Staatsanwältin entschied, ein
Verfahren einzuleiten.* prosecute sb (for sth) jdn
(wegen einer Sache [gen]) anklagen ['ankla:gn̩]
+haben ◊ *Er wurde wegen Betrugs angeklagt.* **2.** *(officially accuse sb)* die Anklage vertreten
[di: 'ankla:gə fetre:tn̩] <vertritt, vertrat, hat vertreten>
prosecute a case in einem Fall die Anklage
vertreten **3.** *(a war)* weiterführen ['vaɛtəfy:rən]
+haben ◊ *Der Krieg wurde weitergeführt.*

A
B
C
D
E
F
G
H
I
J
K
L
M
N
O
P
Q
R
S
T
U
V
W
X
Y
Z

prosecution ⟨noun⟩ **1.** LAW *(bringing to justice)* Verfolgung [fɛˈfɔlɡʊŋ] die <-> no pl ◊ *die Verfolgung von Kriegsverbrechen; (charge, prosecutor)* Anklage [ˈanklaːɡə] die <-, -n> ◊ *Die Anklage warf ihm Betrug vor.* ✦ *Die erste Zeugin der Anklage wurde vernommen.* prosecution for sth Anklage wegen einer Sache ⟨gen⟩ ◊ *eine Anklage wegen Körperverletzung* **2.** *(of war)* Fortführung [ˈfɔʁtfyːʁʊŋ] die <-, -en> ◊ *die Fortführung des Krieges*

prospect ⟨noun⟩ **1.** *(chance, view)* Aussicht [ˈaʊszɪçt] die <-, -en> ◊ *Wie sind meine Aussichten, die Stelle zu bekommen?* ✦ *Wie stehen die Aussichten auf einen Studienplatz?* in prospect in Aussicht a prospect of sth eine Aussicht auf etw. ⟨acc⟩ ◊ *ein wunderbare Aussicht aufs Meer* **2.** *(person likely to succeed)* a prospect ein vielversprechender Kandidat [aen ˈfiːlfɛʃpʁɛçn̩də kandiˈdaːt] <-en, -en> ♀eine vielversprechende Kandidatin [aenə ˈfiːlfɛʃpʁɛçn̩də kandiˈdaːtɪn] <-, -nen> **3.** *(likely customer)* a prospect ein potenzieller Kunde [aen protɛnˌtsjɛlɐ ˈkʊndə] <-n, -n> ♀eine potenzielle Kundin [aenə protɛnˌtsjɛlə ˈkʊndɪn] <-, -nen>

prospective ⟨adj⟩ **1.** *(potential)* potenziell [potɛnˈtsjɛl] no comp/superl ◊ *ein potenzieller Kunde* **2.** *(likely)* voraussichtlich [foˈʁaʊszɪçtlɪç] no comp/superl ◊ *ein voraussichtliches Wachstum von zehn Prozent*

prosperity ⟨noun⟩ Wohlstand [ˈvoːlʃtant] der <-(e)s> no pl ◊ *Er kam relativ schnell zu Wohlstand.* ✦ *Sie lebten in Wohlstand.*

prosthesis ⟨noun⟩ Prothese [proˈteːzə] die <-, -n> ◊ *eine Prothese tragen*

prostitute ⟨noun⟩ Prostituierte [prɔstituˈiːɐtə] der/die <-n, die Prostituierten> *but: ein Prostituierter/eine Prostituierte*

prostitution ⟨noun⟩ Prostitution [prɔstituˈtsjoːn] die <-> no pl

protect ⟨verb⟩ **1.** *(keep safe)* schützen [ˈʃʏtsn̩] +haben ◊ *geschützte Tierarten* ✦ *Der Text ist urheberrechtlich geschützt.* protect from/against vor etw. schützen ◊ *sich mit einem Schirm vor dem Regen schützen* ✦ *Das dicke Fell schützt den Wolf vor Kälte.* **2.** *(insure)* versichern [fɛˈzɪçɐn] <versichert, versicherte, hat versichert> *mostly in adjectival passive constructions* protect sb/sth against sth jdn/etw. gegen etw. versichern ◊ *Ihr Haus war gegen Sturmschäden versichert.*

protection ⟨noun⟩ **1.** *(keeping sb/sth safe, sth that keeps sb/sth safe)* Schutz [ʃʊts] der <-es> no pl ◊ *der Schutz der Menschenrechte* ✦ *Kein Land wollte ihnen Schutz gewähren.* protection from/against sth/sb Schutz vor etw./jdm ◊ *Er bot ihm Schutz vor seinen Feinden.* **2.** *(insurance cover)* Versicherungsschutz [fɛˈzɪçɐʊŋsʃʊts] der <-es> no pl

protective(ly) ⟨adj, adv⟩ **1.** *(wanting to keep sb/sth safe)* fürsorglich [ˈfyːɐzɔʁklɪç] ◊ *Er war ihr gegenüber sehr fürsorglich.* be protective of sth etw. beschützen [bəˈʃʏtsn̩] <beschützt, beschützte, hat beschützt> protective instinct Beschützerinstinkt [bəˈʃʏtsɐɪnˌstɪŋkt] der <-(e)s, -e> **2.** *(for protection, in compound ns)* Schutz... [ʃʊts] protective clothing Schutzkleidung [ˈʃʊtsklaedʊŋ] die <-, -en> ◊ *Bei der Gletscherüberquerung trug sie Schutzkleidung.*

protein ⟨noun⟩ Eiweiß [ˈaevaes] das <-es, -e> ◊ *Fleisch enthält viel Eiweiß.* ✦ *pflanzliches Eiweiß*

protest¹ ⟨noun⟩ Protest [proˈtɛst] der <-(e)s, -e> ◊ *heftiger/schwacher Protest gegen etw.* ✦ *etw. unter*

lautem Protest tun in protest aus Protest storm of protest Proteststurm [proˈtɛstʃtʊɐm] der <-(e)s, Proteststürme> raise a storm of protest einen Proteststurm hervorrufen

protest² ⟨verb⟩ **1.** *(demonstrate, express disagreement)* protestieren [protɛsˈtiːʁən] <protestiert, protestierte, hat protestiert> ◊ *Sie protestieren gegen die Einführung von Studiengebühren.* protest at/about/over sth gegen etw. protestieren **2.** *(insist)* beteuern [bəˈtɔøɐn] <beteuert, beteuerte, hat beteuert> ◊ *Sie beteuerte ihre Unschuld.* ✦ *Er beteuert, dass er keine Ahnung davon hat.*

Protestant¹ ⟨noun⟩ Protestant [protɛsˈtant] der <-en, -en> ♀Protestantin [protɛsˈtantɪn] die <-, -nen> be a Protestant Protestant/Protestantin sein

Protestant² ⟨adj⟩ evangelisch [evaŋˈɡeːlɪʃ] ◊ *eine evangelische Kirchengemeinde* ✦ *35% der Bevölkerung sind evangelisch.*

protocol ⟨noun⟩ Protokoll [protoˈkɔl] das <-s, -e> ◊ *Das Protokoll verlangt, dass der Gast mit militärischen Ehren begrüßt wird.*

prototype ⟨noun⟩ Prototyp [ˈproːtotyp] der <-s, -en>

proud(ly) ⟨adj, adv⟩ stolz [ʃtɔlts] <stolzer, am stolzesten> ◊ *die stolzen Besitzer eines Hauses* ✦ *Er blickte stolz auf die anderen herab.* ✦ *Bist du zu stolz, um dir helfen zu lassen?* proud of sb stolz auf jdn ◊ *Sie sind stolz auf ihren Sohn.* proud to do sth stolz darauf, etw. zu tun ◊ *Wir sind sehr stolz darauf, ein Haus bauen zu können.* proud (that) stolz darauf, dass ◊ *Ich bin stolz darauf, dass so viele Bücher gelesen habe.* too proud to do sth zu stolz, (um) etw. zu tun ◊ *Ich war zu stolz, meinen Fehler zuzugeben.*

prove ⟨verb⟩ **1.** *(give evidence of)* beweisen [bəˈvaezn̩] <beweist, bewies, hat bewiesen> ◊ *Die Polizei konnte nicht beweisen, dass er der Täter war.* ✦ *jds Unschuld beweisen* prove sth to sb jdm etw. beweisen ◊ *Sie will ihrem Mann beweisen, dass sie es allein schaffen kann.* prove sb right jdm Recht geben [ˈʁɛçt ɡeːbm̩] <gibt, gab, hat gegeben> **2.** *(turn out to be sth)* prove to be sth sich als etw. erweisen [als ... evaezn̩] <erweist sich, erwies sich, hat sich erwiesen> ◊ *Die Entscheidung hat sich als richtig erwiesen.* **3.** *(bread)* gehen [ˈɡeːən] <geht, ging, ist gegangen> ◊ *Der Brotteig muss eine Stunde gehen.*

proven → prove ⟨adj⟩ *(method)* erprobt [ɛˈpʁoːpt] <erprobter, am erprobtesten> ◊ *eine klinisch erprobte Methode; (person)* sb is a proven crook jd ist erwiesenermaßen ein Gauner [ɪst ɐ̯viːzənɐ̩ˈmaːsn̩ aen ˈɡaɔnə] +sein

proverb ⟨noun⟩ Sprichwort [ˈʃpʁɪçvɔɐt] das <-(e)s, Sprichwörter> ◊ *Wie schon das Sprichwort sagt: Wer zuletzt lacht, lacht am besten.*

provide ⟨verb⟩ **1.** *(make available)* bereitstellen [bəˈʁaetʃtɛlən] +haben ◊ *Die Regierung stellt mehrere Millionen Euro für die Opfer bereit.* ✦ *Auf Gleis 2 wird ein Ersatzzug bereitgestellt.* provide sb with sth jdn mit etw. versorgen [mɪt ... fɛˈzɔɐɡn̩] <versorgt, versorgte, hat versorgt> ◊ *Er hat sie mit Nahrung versorgt.* provide sth for sb jdm etw. zur Verfügung stellen [tsuːɐ fɛˈfyːɡʊŋ ʃtɛlən] +haben ◊ *Das Hotel stellte ihnen zusätzliche Decken zur Verfügung.* **2.** *(an opportunity, insight)* bieten [ˈbiːtn̩] <bietet, bot, hat geboten> **3.** LAW festlegen [ˈfɛstleːɡn̩] +haben ◊ *Die einzelnen Schritte wurden genau festgelegt.*

- **provide against** [phras v] provide against sth vor etw. schützen [foːɐ̯ ... ʃʏtsn̩] +haben
- **provide for** [phras v] **1.** provide for sb für jdn sorgen [fyːɐ̯ ... ˌzɔʳɡn̩] +haben ◊ *Sie sorgt allein für ihre drei Kinder.* **2.** provide for sth etw. vorsehen [ˈfoːɐ̯ɡzeːən] <sieht vor, sah vor, hat vorgesehen> ◊ *Ist dieser Fall im Vertrag vorgesehen?*

provided → provide [conjunc] vorausgesetzt [foˈraosɡəzɛtst] ◊ *Du kannst morgen anfangen, vorausgesetzt, du bist einverstanden.* ♦ *Wir schaffen täglich 100 Kilometer, immer vorausgesetzt, dass das Wetter hält.*

providence [noun] Fügung [ˈfyːɡʊŋ] die <-, -en> ◊ *War es Zufall oder Fügung?*

provider [noun] **1.** IT Anbieter [ˈanbiːtɐ] der <-s, -> ♀Anbieterin [ˈanbiːtərɪn] die <-, -nen> ◊ *verschiedene Anbieter für Internetdienste* ♦ *eine neue Firma, die sich als Anbieterin für E-Mail-Dienste vorstellt* **2.** *(of a family)* Ernährer [ɛˈnɛːrɐ] der <-s, -> ♀Ernährerin [ɛˈnɛːrərɪn] die <-, -nen> ◊ *Er war seit Jahren der Ernährer der Familie.*

providing, providing that [conjunc] vorausgesetzt [foˈraosɡəzɛtst] ◊ *Du kannst ausgehen, vorausgesetzt, du bist um 22 Uhr wieder zurück.*

province [noun] **1.** *(administrative, rural area)* Provinz [proˈvɪnts] die <-, -en> ◊ *eine ehemalige römische Provinz* ♦ *Er kam aus der tiefsten Provinz nach New York.* **2.** REL Kirchenprovinz [ˈkɪʳçn̩proˌvɪnts] die <-, -en> **3.** *(responsibility)* Bereich [bəˈraɛç] der <-(e)s, -e> ◊ *Die Kindererziehung ist sein Bereich.*

provincial [adj] **1.** *(in the province)* Provinz... [proˈvɪnts] provincial town Provinzstadt [proˈvɪntsʃtat] die <-, Provinzstädte> ◊ *Das Kulturangebot wirkt ziemlich provinziell.* ♦ *eine provinzielle Atmosphäre*

provision [noun] **1.** *(providing sth)* provision of sth Bereitstellung von etw. [bəˈraɛtʃtɛlʊŋ fɔn] der <-, -en> most sing ◊ *die Bereitstellung von Hilfsgütern* there is provision for sth etw. steht zur Verfügung [ʃteːt tsuːɐ̯ fɛˈfyːɡʊŋ] <stand, hat gestanden> ◊ *Zusätzliche Parkplätze stehen im Hof zur Verfügung.* **2.** *(for the future)* provision for sth Vorkehrungen für etw. [ˈfoːɐ̯keːrʊŋən fyːɐ̯] die <-> pl make provisions for sth Vorkehrungen für etw. treffen there is no provision for sth etw. ist nicht vorgesehen [ɪst nɪçt ˈfoːɐ̯ɡəzeːən] **3.** *(in a contract, constitution)* Bestimmung [bəˈʃtɪmʊŋ] die <-, -en> ◊ *Das Grundgesetz enthält eine Bestimmung über die Bundesflagge* **4.** *(food supplies)* provisions Proviant [proˈvjant] der <-s, -e> most sing ◊ *Habt ihr genug Proviant für die Reise dabei?*

provisional(ly) [adj, adv] provisorisch [proviˈzoːrɪʃ] ◊ *Der Arzt legte einen provisorischen Verband an.* ♦ *Diese Aufstellung ist nur provisorisch.* ♦ *etw. provisorisch reparieren* provisional government Übergangsregierung [ˈyːbɐɡaŋsreɡiːrʊŋ] die <-, -en>

provocation [noun] *(act of)* provocation Provokation [provokaˈtsjoːn] die <-, -en> ◊ *Das ist eine Provokation.* ♦ *etw. als Provokation auffassen*

provocative(ly) [adj, adv] **1.** *(intending to annoy)* provozierend [provoˈtsiːrənt] ◊ *eine provozierende Bemerkung* ♦ *Dieser Artikel ist provozierend.* ♦ *Peter grinste seine Eltern provozierend an.* **2.** *(sexually)* aufreizend [ˈaofraɛtsn̩t] ◊ *Sie trug eine aufreizende Bluse.* ♦ *Das Kleid ist ziemlich aufreizend.* ♦ *sich aufreizend anziehen*

provoke [verb] **1.** *(make angry)* provozieren [provoˈtsiːrən] <provoziert, provozierte, hat provoziert> ◊ *Mit diesem Verhalten wollte sie ihre Mutter nur provozieren.* provoke sb into doing sth jdn dazu provozieren, etw. zu tun **2.** *(cause)* auslösen [ˈaosløːzn̩] +haben ◊ *Die neue Regelung löste Proteste aus.* ♦ *Konservierungsmittel können Allergien auslösen.*

proximity [noun] proximity (to) Nähe (zu) [ˈnɛːə] die <-> no pl ◊ *Sie kritisierten die Nähe der Neubausiedlung zur Autobahn.* in close proximity in nächster Nähe

prudent(ly) [adj, adv] umsichtig [ˈʊmzɪçtɪç] ◊ *Sie ist eine umsichtige Mitarbeiterin.* ♦ *Er war schon immer sehr umsichtig.* ♦ *Sie hat sehr umsichtig gehandelt.* it might be prudent to do sth es wäre klug, etw. zu tun [ɛs vɛːrə ˈkluːk ... tsuː]

prudish [adj] prüde [ˈpryːdə] <prüder, am prüdesten> ◊ *Er gilt als prüde und verklemmt.* ♦ *eine prüde Einstellung haben*

PS PS [peːˈʔɛs] das ◊ *PS: Bitte antworte so schnell wie möglich!*

psyche [noun] Psyche [ˈpsyːçə] die <-, -n> ◊ *Körper und Psyche als Einheit*

psychiatric [adj] **1.** *(hospital, unit)* psychiatrisch [psyˈçjaːtrɪʃ] no comp/superl, only before ns ◊ *Er wurde in eine psychiatrische Klinik verlegt.; (nurse, nursing)* in der Psychiatrie [ɪn deːɐ̯ psyçjaˈtriː] not before ns ◊ *Sie ist Krankenschwester in der Psychiatrie.* **2.** *(illness, problem)* psychisch [ˈpsyːçɪʃ] no comp/superl ◊ *psychische Krankheiten* ♦ *Ihre Probleme sind rein psychisch.*

psychiatrist [noun] Psychiater [psyˈçjaːtɐ] der <-s, -> ♀Psychiaterin [psyˈçjaːtərɪn] die <-, -nen> ◊ *Sie ist Psychiaterin von Beruf.* ♦ *Du solltest zu einem Psychiater gehen.*

psychological(ly) [adj, adv] **1.** *(involving your mind, caused by your mind)* psychisch [ˈpsyːçɪʃ] no comp/superl ◊ *Diese Krankheit hat psychische Ursachen.* ♦ *Seine Abhängigkeit ist rein psychisch.* ♦ *Sie leidet psychisch.* sth is psychological etw. ist psychisch bedingt **2.** *(connected with psychology)* psychologisch [psyçoˈloːɡɪʃ] no comp/superl ◊ *ein psychologisches Gutachten* ♦ *jdn psychologisch behandeln* ♦ *psychologisch geschickt vorgehen*

psychologist [noun] Psychologe [psyçoˈloːɡə] der <-n, -n> ♀Psychologin [psyçoˈloːɡɪn] die <-, -nen> ◊ *Sie ist Psychologin von Beruf.* ♦ *ein bekannter Psychologe und Autor*

psychology [noun] **1.** *(subject, knowledge)* Psychologie [psyçoloˈɡiː] die <-> no pl ◊ *Er hat Psychologie studiert.* ♦ *Mit ein bisschen Psychologie kannst du sie bestimmt dazu bringen.* **2.** *(of a person)* Psyche [ˈpsyːçə] die <-, -n> ◊ *die Psyche von Kindern und Jugendlichen*

pub [noun] Wirtschaft [ˈvɪʳtʃaft] die <-, -en> ◊ *Er ging in die Wirtschaft und trank ein Bier.; (simple, small)* Kneipe [ˈknaɛpə] die <-, -n> *(fam)* ◊ *Nach dem Kino gingen wir noch in die Kneipe.*

puberty [noun] Pubertät [pubɐˈtɛːt] die <-> no pl ◊ *Mein Sohn ist in der Pubertät.* ♦ *in die Pubertät kommen*

public[1] [noun] **1.** *(people)* the public die Öffentlichkeit [diː ˈʔœfn̩tlɪçkaɛt] <-> no pl ◊ *sich an die Öffentlichkeit wenden* ♦ *die britische Öffentlichkeit* the general public die breite Öffentlichkeit the sporting public das sportinteressierte Öffentlichkeit member

of the public Bürger ['bʏʳgə] der <–s, –> ♀Bürgerin ['bʏʳgərɪn] die <–, –nen> 2. *(audience)* Publikum ['puːblɪkʊm] das <–s> no pl ◊ *Wir möchten mit dieser Kampagne ein breites Publikum erreichen.* ♦ *Sein Publikum besteht hauptsächlich aus alten Leuten.*

➲ in public öffentlich

public² [adj] öffentlich ['œfn̩tlɪç] no comp/superl ◊ *Die Veranstaltung ist öffentlich und der Eintritt frei.* ♦ *ein öffentliches Ärgernis* ♦ *mit öffentlichen Mitteln finanziert* public opinion öffentliche Meinung make sth public etw. bekannt machen ◊ *Sie hat ihre Entscheidung am Freitag bekannt gemacht.* Can we go somewhere a little less public? Können wir irgendwo hingehen, wo nicht so viele Leute sind? have a lot of public support von der Öffentlichkeit befürwortet werden [fɒn deːɐ̯ ˌœfn̩tlɪçkaet bəˈfyːɐ̯vɔʳtət veːɐ̯dn̩]

➲ go public 1. *(make sth public)* an die Öffentlichkeit gehen 2. *(become a public company)* an die Börse gehen

publication [noun] 1. *(of a book, magazine)* publication (of …) Veröffentlichung (… [gen]) [fe|'œfn̩tlɪçʊn] die <–, –en> ◊ *Er plädierte für die Veröffentlichung des Romans.* 2. *(book, magazine published)* Publikation [publikaˈtsi̯oːn] die <–, –en> ◊ *Von diesem Autor sind bereits mehrere Publikationen erschienen.* 3. *(of information)* publication (of …) Bekanntgabe (… [gen]) [bəˈkantɡaːbə] die <–, –n> ◊ *die Bekanntgabe der Ergebnisse*

public holiday [noun] gesetzlicher Feiertag [ɡəˌzɛtslɪçə ˈfaeetaːk] <–(e)s, –e> ◊ *Ist der 1. Mai ein gesetzlicher Feiertag?* ♦ *An gesetzlichen Feiertagen ist das Museum geschlossen.*

publicity [noun] 1. *(media attention)* Publicity [paˈblɪsiti] die <–> no pl ◊ *Die Fotos sorgten für Publicity.* 2. *(advertising)* Werbung ['vɛʳbʊŋ] die <–, –en> ◊ *Werbung für jdn/etw. machen* ♦ *in der Werbung arbeiten* publicity materials Werbematerial ['veʳbəmateˌri̯aːl] das <–s, –ien>

publicly [adv] öffentlich ['œfn̩tlɪç] seldom comp/superl ◊ *Er hat den Minister öffentlich kritisiert.* ♦ *Das Hilfsprojekt wird öffentlich unterstützt.* ♦ *sich öffentlich zu etw. äußern*

public prosecutor [noun] Staatsanwalt ['ʃtaːtsˌanvalt] der <–(e)s, Staatsanwälte> ♀Staatsanwältin ['ʃtaːtsˌanvɛltɪn] die <–, –nen> ◊ *Sie ist Staatsanwältin.* ♦ *Der Staatsanwalt erhob Anklage wegen Mordes.*

public school [noun] Privatschule [priˈvaːtʃuːlə] die <–, –n> ◊ *Sie geht in eine Privatschule.*

public transport [noun] öffentliche Verkehrsmittel ['œfn̩tlɪçə feˈkeːɐ̯smɪtl̩] die <–> pl ◊ *Es gibt Leute, die nie öffentliche Verkehrsmittel benutzen.*

publish [verb] 1. *(a book, magazine, newspaper)* verlegen [feˈleːgn̩] <verlegt, verlegte, hat verlegt> ◊ *Die Firma verlegt mehrere Zeitschriften.* 2. *(a letter, an article)* veröffentlichen [fe|'œfn̩tlɪçn̩] <veröffentlicht, veröffentlichte, hat veröffentlicht> ◊ *Die Süddeutsche Zeitung hat seinen Brief veröffentlicht.* He has never been published. Seine Werke sind nicht veröffentlicht worden. 3. *(information)* bekannt geben [bəˈkant geːbn̩] <gibt, gab, hat gegeben> ◊ *Die Ergebnisse wurden letzte Woche bekannt gegeben.*

publisher [noun] 1. *(person)* Verleger [feˈleːge] der <–s, –> ♀Verlegerin [feˈleːgərɪn] die <–, –nen> 2. *(company)* Verlag [feˈlaːk] der <–(e)s, –e> ◊ *Er*

arbeitet in einem Verlag.

publishing [noun] Verlagswesen [feˈlaːksveːzn̩] das <–s> no pl ◊ *Sie arbeitet im Verlagswesen.*

publishing house [noun] Verlag [feˈlaːk] der <–(e)s, –e> ◊ *ein bekannter Verlag*

pudding [noun] 1. *(dessert)* Dessert [dɛˈseːɐ̯] das <–s, –s> ◊ *Was gibt es zum Dessert?* 2. *(cooked sweet dish)* süßer Auflauf mit Biskuit- oder Rührteig; *(blancmange)* Pudding ['pʊdɪŋ] der <–s, –e or –s> ◊ *Soll ich dir einen Pudding kochen?* 3. *(pastry with meat)* Pastete [pasˈteːtə] die <–, –n>

puddle [noun] Pfütze ['pfʏtsə] die <–, –n>

puff¹ [noun] 1. *(from a cigarette)* Zug [tsuːk] der <–(e)s, Züge> ◊ *Er nahm einen Zug aus seiner Zigarette.* ♦ *Nach zwei Zügen musste sie husten.* 2. *(breathing)* Stoß [ʃtoːs] der <–es, Stöße> ◊ *Sein Atem kam in kurzen Stößen.; (sound)* Schnaufen ['ʃnaofn̩] das <–s> no pl ◊ *das Schnaufen der Dampflok* 3. *(enough air)* Puste ['puːstə] die <–> no pl run out of puff aus der Puste kommen 4. *(small amount)* puff of smoke Rauchwolke ['raoxvɔlkə] die <–, –n> puff of wind Windstoß ['vɪntʃtoːs] der <–es, Windstöße> puff of air Luftzug ['lʊftsuːk] der <–(e)s, Luftzüge> 5. *(type of pie)* Blätterteigtasche ['blɛtetaektaʃə] die <–, –n> cream puff Windbeutel ['vɪntbɔɔtl̩] der <–s, –>

puff² [verb] 1. *(on a cigarette)* puff on sth etw. paffen ['pafn̩] +haben *(fam)* 2. *(breathe noisily)* pusten ['puːstn̩] <pustet, pustete, hat gepustet> +haben *(fam)* ◊ *Er muss beim Training immer ordentlich pusten und schwitzen.* huff and puff pusten und schnaufen 3. *(make puffing noises)* schnaufen ['ʃnaofn̩] <schnauft, schnaufte, hat geschnauft> ◊ *Die Dampflok schnaufte den Berg hinauf.*

• **puff out** [phras v] 1. *(your cheeks)* aufblasen ['aofblaːzn̩] <bläst auf, blies auf, hat aufgeblasen> ◊ *Sie blies die Backen auf.; (your chest)* herausstrecken [hɛˈraosʃtrɛk] ◊ *Er streckte stolz die Brust heraus.* 2. *(air, smoke)* puff out sth etw. ausstoßen ['aosʃtoːsn̩] <stößt aus, stieß aus, hat ausgestoßen> ◊ *Er stieß eine kunstvolle Rauchwolke aus.*

• **puff up** [phras v] 1. *(swell)* anschwellen ['anʃvelən] <schwillt an, schwoll an, ist angeschwollen> ◊ *Seine Backe war dick angeschwollen.* 2. *(take in more air)* aufgehen ['aofgeːən] <geht auf, ging auf, ist aufgegangen> ◊ *Der Teig ist aufgegangen.*

pull¹ [noun] 1. *(movement)* Ziehen ['tsiːən] das <–s> no pl give sth a pull an etw. [dat] ziehen [an … ˌtsiːən] <zieht, zog, hat gezogen> ◊ *Sie zog an dem Seil.* 2. *(physical force)* Anziehungskraft ['antsiːʊŋskraft] die <–, Anziehungskräfte> ◊ *die Anziehungskraft der Erde.* 3. *(attraction)* Reiz [raets] der <–es> ◊ *der Reiz fremder Länder* 4. *(influence)* Einfluss ['aenflʊs] der <–es, Einflüsse> ◊ *Er hat großen Einfluss im Ministerium.*

➲ take a pull at sth an etw. [dat] ziehen take a pull on sth einen Schluck von etw. nehmen

pull² [verb] 1. *(move, remove)* ziehen ['tsiːən] <zieht, zog, hat gezogen> +haben ◊ *Er schob und ich zog.* ◊ *Du musst ziehen, nicht drücken.* ♦ *Ich zog mir die Bettdecke über den Kopf.* ♦ *Das Auto wurde aus dem Graben gezogen.* ♦ *Vater zog den Schlitten.* ♦ *Der Zahnarzt musste den Zahn ziehen.* ♦ *die Notbremse ziehen* pull at/on sth an etw. [dat] ziehen ◊ *Das Kind zog an meinem Mantel.* ♦ *Er zog an seiner Zigarette.* pull sth open etw. aufziehen ['aofˌtsiːən] +haben ◊

Sie zog die Tür auf. pull sth shut, pull sth tight etw.
zuziehen ['tsu:tsi:ən] +haben ◊ *Zieb die Tür hinter
dir zu!* ✦ *die Schlinge zuzieben*; (out of the soil) pull
sth up etw. herausziehen [hɛ'raostsi:ən] +haben ◊ *Ich
zog ein paar Möhren heraus.; (your trousers, skirt)*
pull sth up etw. hochziehen ['ho:xtsi:ən] +haben pull
sth from under sth etw. unter etw. hervorziehen
[ʊnte ... hɛ,fo:ɐ̯tsi:ən] +haben ◊ *Sie zog eine Kiste
unter dem Bett hervor.* pull sth off etw. abreißen
['apraesn] <reißt ab, riss ab, hat abgerissen> ◊ *Sie
hat einen Knopf von ihrem Mantel abgerissen.*
2. *(injure)* pull a muscle sich (dat) einen Muskel
zerren [aenən 'mʊskl̩ ,tsɛrən] +haben ◊ *Er hat sich
beim Training einen Muskel gezerrt.* **3.** *(a knife, gun)*
pull sth on sb jdn mit etw. bedrohen
[mɪt ... bə,dro:ən] <bedroht, bedrohte, hat bedroht> ◊
Er hat einen Mitschüler mit einem Messer bedroht.
4. *(a curtain, blind)* pull sth (shut) etw. zuziehen
['tsu:tsi:ən] <zieht zu, zog zu, hat zugezogen> ◊ *Sie
zog die Vorbänge zu.* pull sth down etw. herunterzie-
hen [hɛ'rʊntetsi:ən] <zieht herunter, zog herunter, hat
heruntergezogen> ◊ *Ich zog das Rollo herunter.* **5.** *(an
audience)* pull sb/sth (in) jdn/etw. anziehen
['antsi:ən] <zieht an, zog an, hat angezogen> ◊ *Seine
Konzerte ziehen immer noch Mengen von Fans an.*
6. *(pick up)* pull sb jdn aufreißen ['aofraesn] <reißt
auf, riss auf, hat aufgerissen> (slang) ◊ *in der Disko
Mädchen aufreißen*
⊚ pull yourself together sich zusammenreißen
• **pull ahead** [phras v] in Führung gehen
[ɪn 'fy:rʊŋ ge:ən] <geht, ging, ist gegangen> ◊ *Der
Favorit ging gleich zu Beginn des Rennens in
Führung.*
• **pull apart** [phras v] pull sb apart jdn trennen
['trɛnən] +haben ◊ *Der Lehrer musste die beiden
kämpfenden Jungen trennen.*
• **pull away** [phras v] **1.** *(vehicle, driver)* losfahren
['lo:sfa:rən] <fährt los, fuhr los, ist losgefahren> ◊ *Der
Bus fuhr gerade los, als sie angerannt kam.* **2.** pull
away (from sb) (vor jdm) zurückweichen
[tsu'rʏkvaeçn̩] <weicht zurück, wich zurück, ist zurück-
gewichen> ◊ *Er wollte sie umarmen, aber sie wich
zurück.* **3.** *(in a race, an election)* pull away (from
sb) (vor jdm) in Führung gehen [ɪn 'fy:rʊŋ ge:ən]
<geht, ging, ist gegangen> ◊ *Die Europameisterin
ging gleich zu Beginn des Rennens in Führung.* ✦
*Letzte Woche ging die CDU in den Umfragen in
Führung.*
• **pull back** [phras v] **1.** *(restrain, hold back)* pull sb
back jdn zurückziehen [tsu'rʏktsi:ən] <zieht zurück,
zog zurück, hat zurückgezogen> ◊ *Die USA zogen
daraufhin ihre Streitkräfte zurück.* sb pulls back jd
zieht sich zurück [tsi:t ... tsu'rʏk] <zog sich zurück,
hat sich zurückgezogen> ◊ *Die Truppen haben sich
von der Frontlinie zurückgezogen.* **2.** *(back out)* pull
back from sth sich doch gegen etw. entscheiden
['dɔx ,ge:gn̩ ... ɛntʃaedn̩] <entscheidet sich, entschied
sich, hat sich entschieden> ◊ *Wir haben uns jetzt
doch gegen den Hauskauf entschieden.* **3.** pull back
(from sth) (vor jdm) zurückweichen [tsu'rʏkvaeçn̩]
<weicht zurück, wich zurück, ist zurückgewichen> ◊
Sie wollte ihn umarmen, aber er wich zurück.
• **pull down** [phras v] **1.** *(a building)* abbrechen
['apbrɛçn̩] <bricht ab, brach ab, hat abgebrochen> ◊
Das Gebäude wurde 1930 abgebrochen. **2.** *(in the US:
earn)* verdienen [fɛ'di:nən] <verdient, verdiente, hat

verdient>
• **pull in** [phras v] **1.** *(train)* einfahren ['aenfa:rən]
<fährt ein, fuhr ein, ist eingefahren> ◊ *Als der Zug
einfuhr, babe ich sie gleich am Fenster geseben.*
2. *(vehicle, driver)* anhalten ['anhaltn̩] <hält an, hielt
an, hat angehalten> ◊ *Können Sie hier bitte anhalten?*
3. *(in the US: earn)* verdienen [fɛ'di:nən] <verdient,
verdiente, hat verdient> ◊ *Sie verdient mindestens 50
000 im Jahr* **4.** *(an audience)* anziehen ['antsi:ən]
<zieht an, zog an, hat angezogen> ◊ *Die Sendung
zieht immer noch viele Zuschauer an.*
• **pull into** [phras v] *(train)* sth pulls into sth etw.
fährt in etw. (acc) ein [fɛ:ɐ̯t ɪn ... ,aen] <fuhr ein, ist
eingefahren> ◊ *Der Zug fuhr in den Bahnhof ein.;
(vehicle, driver)* sth/sb pulls into a drive(way) etw./jd
hält in einer Einfahrt [hɛlt ɪn aene 'aenfa:ɐ̯t] <hielt,
hat gehalten> pull (sth) into the side of the road
(mit einem Fahrzeug) am Straßenrand halten pull
(sth) into a parking space/bay (mit einem
Fahrzeug) in einer Parkbucht halten pull (sth) into
a car park/parking lot (mit einem Fahrzeug) auf
dem Parkplatz halten
• **pull off** [phras v] **1.** *(manage successfully)* pull sth
off etw. schaffen ['ʃafn̩] +haben pull it off es
schaffen ◊ *Sie haben es tatsächlich geschafft.*
2. *(vehicle, driver)* pull off von etw. abfahren
[fɔn ... ,apfa:rən] <fährt ab, fuhr ab, ist abgefahren> ◊
Wir fuhren von der Schnellstraße ab. pull sth off sth
mit etw. von etw. abfahren [mɪt ... fɔn ... ,apfa:rən]
<fährt ab, fuhr ab, ist abgefahren> ◊ *Er fuhr mit
seinem Lkw von der Autobahn ab.* **3.** *(your clothes)*
schnell ausziehen [ʃnɛl 'aostsi:ən] <zieht aus, zog
aus, hat ausgezogen> ◊ *Sie zog schnell ihren Mantel
aus.*
• **pull on** [phras v] schnell überziehen
[ʃnɛl 'y:betsi:ən] <zieht über, zog über, hat übergezo-
gen> ◊ *Sie zog schnell einen Bademantel über.*
• **pull out** [phras v] **1.** *(back out)* pull out (of sth)
(aus etw.) aussteigen ['aosʃtaegn̩] <steigt aus, stieg
aus, ist ausgestiegen> ◊ *Der Konzern ist aus dem
Geschäft ausgestiegen.* **2.** *(train)* pull out (of the
station)* den Bahnhof verlassen
[de:n ,ba:nho:f fɛ'lasn̩] <verlässt, verließ, hat
verlassen> ◊ *Der Zug verließ pünktlich den Bahnhof.*
3. *(vehicle, driver)* ausscheren ['aosʃe:rən] +sein ◊
Wir scherten hinter einem Lastwagen aus.
• **pull over** [phras v] *(vehicle, driver)* an den Straßenrand fahren [an de:n 'ʃtra:sn̩rant fa:rən] <fährt, fuhr,
ist gefahren> ◊ *Das Handy klingelte und sie fuhr an
den Straßenrand.; (police)* pull sb over jdn an den
Straßenrand winken [an de:n 'ʃtra:sn̩rant vɪŋkn̩]
+haben ◊ *Ein Polizist winkte mich an den Straßenrand.*
• **pull through** [phras v] **1.** *(stay alive)* durchkommen ['dʊɐ̯çkɔmən] <kommt durch, kam durch, ist
durchgekommen> ◊ *Die Ärzte wussten nicht, ob er
durchkommen würde.* **2.** *(succeed)* es durchstehen
[ɛs 'dʊɐ̯çʃte:ən] <steht durch, stand durch, hat durchge-
standen> ◊ *Es war nicht leicht, aber sie hat es durch-
gestanden.; (help cope with)* pull sb through jdn
durchziehen ['dʊɐ̯çtsi:ən] <zieht durch, zog durch, hat
durchgezogen>
• **pull up** [phras v] **1.** *(vehicle, driver)* anhalten
['anhaltn̩] <hält an, hielt an, hat angehalten> ◊ *Bitte
halten Sie hier an.* **2.** *(a chair)* heranrücken
[hɛ'ranrʏkn̩] +haben ◊ *Rück noch einen Stuhl an den*

Tisch heran. **3.** *(criticize)* pull sb up on sth jdn wegen etw. zurechtweisen [ve:g̊] ... ʦu,reçtvaeʦn] <weist zurecht, wies zurecht, hat zurechtgewiesen> ◊ *Sie weist die Kinder immer wegen ihrer Essmanieren zurecht.* pull sb up on his spelling jds Rechtschreibung korrigieren ['reçtʃraebʊŋ kɔri,giːrən] <korrigiert, korrigierte, hat korrigiert> ◊ *Der Lehrer hat Veras Rechtschreibung korrigiert.*

pulley noun *(piece of equipment)* Flaschenzug ['flaʃnʦuːk] der <-(e)s, Flaschenzüge> ◊ *etw. mit einem Flaschenzug heraufholen; (wheel)* Rolle ['rɔlə] die <-, -n> ◊ *Das Seil wird über vier Rollen geführt.*

pullover noun Pullover [pʊ'loːve] der <-s, -> ◊ *einen Pullover anziehen*

pulse noun **1.** *(movement of blood)* Puls [pʊls] der <-es> *no pl* ◊ *einen beschleunigten/langsamen/ schwachen/unregelmäßigen Puls haben* ◆ *Wie hoch ist sein Puls?* take sb's pulse jdm den Puls messen **2.** *(of energy)* Impuls [ɪm'pʊls] der <-es, -e> **3.** *(of music)* Rhythmus ['rʏtmʊs] der <-, Rhythmen>

pump¹ noun **1.** *(piece of equipment)* Pumpe ['pʊmpə] die <-, -n> ◊ *die Pumpe eines Brunnens* **2.** *(shoe, for PE)* Turnschuh ['tʊʁnʃuː] der <-(e)s, -e>; *(for dancing)* Ballettschuh [ba'lɛtʃuː] der <-(e)s, -e>; *(in the US: woman's shoe)* Pumps [pœmps] der <-, ->

pump² verb **1.** *(use a pump, push up and down)* pumpen ['pʊmpn̩] +haben ◊ *Du musst kräftig pumpen, bis das Wasser läuft.* ◆ *Giftstoffe ins Meer pumpen* pump the accelerator *(am/mit dem Gaspedal)* pumpen ◊ *Der Motor drohte abzusterben und ich musste pumpen.* **2.** *(of a liquid, come out quickly)* schießen ['ʃiːsn̩] <schießt, schoss, ist geschossen> ◊ *Durch den Riss schoss das Wasser ins Boot.* **3.** *(heart)* pochen ['pɔxn̩] +haben ◊ *Mein Herz pochte rasend schnell.* **4.** *(get information)* pump sb jdn aushorchen ['aʊshɔʁçn̩] +haben

◉ pump sb full of sth jdn mit etw. voll pumpen *(fam)*

• **pump into** phras v pump sth into sth etw. in etw. acc hineinpumpen [ɪn ... hɪ,naenpʊmpn̩] +haben ◊ *Sie haben Millionen in das Projekt hineingepumpt.*

• **pump out** phras v *(a liquid, gas)* herauspumpen [hɛ'raʊspʊmpn̩] +haben; *(a boat, cellar, stomach)* auspumpen ['aʊspʊmpn̩] +haben

• **pump up** phras v aufpumpen ['aʊfpʊmpn̩] +haben ◊ *Pumpst du mir bitte den Reifen auf?*

pumpkin noun Kürbis ['kʏʁbɪs] der <-ses, -se>

punch¹ noun **1.** *(with your fist)* Faustschlag ['faʊstʃlaːk] der <-(e)s, Faustschläge> ◊ *jdm einen Faustschlag in die Magengrube versetzen* land a punch einen Faustschlag austeilen **2.** *(drink)* Bowle ['boːlə] die <-, -n> **3.** *(power, force)* Wucht [vʊxt] die <-> *no pl* ◊ *Die Erkenntnis traf ihn mit großer Wucht.; (drive)* Schwung [ʃvʊŋ] der <-(e)s> *no pl* ◊ *Der Geschichte/Wahlkampagne mangelt es an Schwung.* **4.** *(tool)* Locher ['lɔxe] der <-s, ->

◉ be as pleased as punch sich freuen wie ein Schneekönig *(fam)* not pull any punches sich nicht zurückhalten

punch² verb **1.** *(hit)* mit der Faust schlagen [mɪt deːɐ̯ 'faʊst ʃlaːg̊n̩] <schlägt, schlug, hat geschlagen> ◊ *Er schlug mich/mir mit der Faust in den Bauch.* **2.** *(press)* punch sth auf etw. acc drücken [aʊf ... drʏkn̩] +haben ◊ *Ich drückte auf einen Knopf, und das Tor ging auf.* **3.** *(make a hole)* lochen ['lɔxn̩] +haben

◉ punch the air in die Luft boxen

• **punch in** phras v eingeben ['aengeːbm̩] <gibt ein, gab ein, hat eingegeben> ◊ *Er gab seine Geheimnummer ein.*

punchline noun Pointe [po'ɛntə] die <-, -n> ◊ *Er hat die Pointe des Witzes nicht verstanden.*

punch-up noun Schlägerei [ʃlɛːgə'rae] die <-, -en> ◊ *eine Schlägerei anzetteln* ◆ *Die Fußballfans lieferten sich wüste Schlägereien.*

punctual(ly) adj, adv pünktlich ['pʏŋktlɪç] ◊ *Er ist immer sehr pünktlich.* ◆ *Sie erwarten eine pünktliche Ablieferung der Arbeit.* ◆ *Der Zug kommt pünktlich an.*

punctuation noun Zeichensetzung ['ʦaeçnzɛtsʊŋ] die <-> *no pl*

punctuation mark noun Satzzeichen ['zatsʦaeçn̩] das <-s, ->

puncture noun *(hole)* Loch [lɔx] das <-(e)s, Löcher>; *(in your skin)* Einstich ['aenʃtɪç] der <-(e)s, -e>; *(in a tyre)* Reifenpanne ['raefnpanə] die <-, -n> ◊ *Wir hatten eine Reifenpanne und mussten das Rad wechseln.*

pungent(ly) adj, adv scharf [ʃaʁf] <schärfer, am schärfsten> ◊ *ein scharfer Geruch nach Desinfektionsmitteln* ◆ *Die Soße ist sehr scharf.* ◆ *Die scharfe Kritik überraschte mich.* ◆ *Sein Vorgehen wurde scharf kritisiert.*

punish verb bestrafen [bə'ʃtraːfn̩] <bestraft, bestrafte, hat bestraft> ◊ *Ihr Vater bestrafte sie hart für ihre Lüge.* ◆ *Der Besitz von Drogen wird dort bestraft.* punish sb by (doing) sth jdn mit etw. bestrafen

punishment noun **1.** *(punishing sb)* Strafe ['ʃtraːfə] die <-, -n> ◊ *Zur Strafe für ihre Ungezogenheit bekam sie Hausarrest.* ◆ *Als Strafe musste er den ganzen Aufsatz noch einmal abschreiben.* ◆ *Die Strafe für Steuerhinterziehung ist meist eine Geldbuße.* **2.** take a lot of punishment sehr strapaziert werden [zeːɐ̯ ʃtrapa'tsiːɐ̯t veːɐ̯dn̩] <wird, wurde, ist worden> ◊ *In einem Haushalt mit vier Kindern werden die Möbel sehr strapaziert.*

punk noun **1.** *(music)* punk (rock) Punk [paŋk] der <-s> *no pl* ◊ *Sie hört immer Punk.* **2.** *(person)* punk (rocker) Punker ['paŋke] der <-s, -> ♀Punkerin ['paŋkərɪn] die <-, -nen> ◊ *Ihr Freund ist ein Punker.*

pup noun **1.** *(young animal)* Junge ['jʊŋə] das <-n, die Jungen> *but: ein Junges* ◊ *ein Robbe und ihr Junges* ◆ *Das Junge war noch ganz klein.* **2.** *(young dog, wolf)* Welpe ['vɛlpə] der <-n, -n> ◊ *Die Hündin hat sechs Welpen geworfen.*

pupil noun **1.** *(at school)* Schüler ['ʃyːle] der <-s, -> ♀Schülerin ['ʃyːlərɪn] die <-, -nen> ◊ *eine gute/ schlechte Schülerin* **2.** *(part of the eye)* Pupille [pu'pɪlə] die <-, -n> ◊ *Die Pupillen erweitern/ verengen sich.*

puppet noun **1.** *(on a string)* Marionette [mario'nɛtə] die <-, -n> ◊ *Die hölzernen Marionetten wirkten sehr lebensecht.* ◆ *Die Regierung dort ist eine Marionette der USA.* puppet show Puppentheater ['pʊpnteˌaːte] das <-s, -> puppet regime Marionettenregime [mario'nɛtnreˌʒiːm] das <-s, -s> **2.** *(hand puppet)* Handpuppe ['hantpʊpə] die <-, -n> ◊ *Er hat auf jeder Hand eine Handpuppe.*

puppy noun Welpe ['vɛlpə] der <-n, -n> ◊ *Die Hündin hat vier Welpen geworfen.*

purchase¹ noun Anschaffung ['anʃafʊŋ] die <-, -en>

◊ *Die Schule braucht Geld für die Anschaffung neuer Wörterbücher.* ✦ *Der Drucker war eine gute Anschaffung.* make a purchase etwas kaufen [ɛtvas ˈkaofn̩] +haben

◉ get a purchase on sth Halt an etw. [dat] finden

purchase² [verb] kaufen [ˈkaofn̩] +haben ◊ *Aktien/Immobilien kaufen* ✦ *Sie haben letztes Jahr ein Haus gekauft.*

purchaser [noun] Käufer [ˈkɔøfɐ] der <-s, -> ♀Käuferin [ˈkɔøfərɪn] die <-, -nen>

pure [adj] rein [raen] ◊ *reiner Bienenhonig/Alkohol* ✦ *reine Bergluft/Farben/Kunst/Theorie* ✦ *Es war reiner Zufall, dass ich es gemerkt habe.* ✦ *„Ich bin klein, mein Herz ist rein", betete das Kind.* ✦ *die Abteilung für reine Mathematik*

◉ pure and simple schlicht und einfach ◊ *Das ist schlicht und einfach Dummheit.*

purée [noun] Püree [pyˈreː] das <-s, -s> ◊ *ein Püree aus Kartoffeln und Erbsen*

purely [adv] nur [nuːɐ̯] ◊ *Dies ist nur meine eigene Meinung.* ✦ *Sie hat ihn nur wegen seines Geldes geheiratet.*

◉ purely and simply schlicht und einfach

purity [noun] Reinheit [ˈraenhaet] die <-> *no pl*

purple [adj] lila [ˈliːla] *invariable* ◊ *Sie trug einen lila Pullover.* ✦ *Die Wände waren lila.*

purpose [noun] 1. *(goal, intention)* purpose (of ...) Zweck (... [gen]) [ʦvɛk] der <-(e)s, -e> ◊ *Der Zweck seines Besuchs war, das Geld abzuholen.* ✦ *Die Maßnahme hat ihren Zweck nicht erfüllt.* ✦ *Darf ich den Wagen auch für private Zwecke nutzen?* have the purpose of doing sth den Zweck haben, etw. zu tun serve a purpose einen Zweck haben suit sb's purpose jds Zwecken dienen for the purpose of doing sth mit der Absicht, etw. zu tun [mɪt deːɐ̯ ˈapʦɪçt ... ʦuː] sb's purpose in doing sth der Grund, warum jd etw. tut [deːɐ̯ ˈgrʊnt vaˈrʊm] defeat the purpose of sth einer Sache [dat] den Sinn nehmen [deːn ˈzɪn neːmən] 2. *(meaning)* Sinn [zɪn] der <-(e)s, -e> ◊ *Sein Leben hatte keinen Sinn mehr.*; *(aim)* Ziel [ʦiːl] das <-(e)s, -e> sense of purpose Zielbewusstsein [ˈʦiːlbəvʊstʦaen] das <-s> *no pl*

◉ to all intents and purposes praktisch for the purposes of sth zum Zweck einer Sache [gen] to no purpose 1. *(without success)* ohne Erfolg 2. *(without good reason)* grundlos on purpose absichtlich

purse [noun] 1. *(bag for carrying money)* Portmonee [pɔrtmɔˈneː] das <-s, -s> ◊ *Geld im Portmonee haben* 2. *(money available)* Finanzen [fiˈnantsn̩] die <-> *pl* ◊ *Das übersteigt meine Finanzen.* public purse Staatskasse [ˈʃtaːtskasə] die <-, -n> ◊ *etw. wird aus der Staatskasse bezahlt* 3. *(in a sports competition)* Preisgeld [ˈpraesgɛlt] das <-(e)s, -er> 4. *(in the US: handbag, handbag)* Handtasche [ˈhanttaʃə] die <-, -n>

pursue [verb] 1. *(follow, chase, try to achieve)* verfolgen [fɛˈfɔlgn̩] <verfolgt, verfolgte, hat verfolgt> ◊ *Die Polizei verfolgte das Auto/den Mann.* ✦ *ein Star, der von Reportern verfolgt wird* ✦ *eine Politik der Versöhnung verfolgen* ✦ *die Absicht verfolgen, eine Firma zu übernehmen* 2. *(an activity, a career)* pursue sth einer Sache [dat] nachgehen [ˈnaːxgeːən] <geht nach, ging nach, ist nachgegangen> ◊ *Früher war es für Frauen mit Kindern schwierig, einem Beruf nachzugehen.* pursue the matter der Sache

[dat] nachgehen pursue a career in medicine eine medizinische Laufbahn einschlagen [aenə mediˌʦiːnɪʃə ˈlaofbaːn aenʃlaːgn̩] <schlägt ein, schlug ein, hat eingeschlagen> pursue an inquiry eine Untersuchung durchführen [aenə ʊntɐˈzuːxʊŋ ˌdʊrçfyːrən] +haben 3. pursue sb jdm nachstellen [ˈnaːxʃtɛlən] +haben ◊ *Er stellt mir schon seit einiger Zeit nach.*

pursuit [noun] 1. *(search)* pursuit of sth Jagd nach etw. [jaːkt naːx] die <-, -en> ◊ *die Jagd nach dem Glück* 2. *(following, chasing, trying to achieve)* pursuit of ... Verfolgung ... [gen] [fɛˈfɔlgʊŋ] die <-, -en> ◊ *Bei der Verfolgung seiner Ziele kennt er keine Rücksicht.* set off in pursuit die Verfolgung aufnehmen be in pursuit of sb/sth jdn/etw. verfolgen [fɛˈfɔlgn̩] <verfolgt, verfolgte, hat verfolgt> in hot pursuit of sb jdm hinterher [hɪntɐˈheːɐ̯] ◊ *Ich hob ihre Tasche auf und rannte ihr hinterher.* 3. *(activity)* Beschäftigung [bəˈʃɛftɪgʊŋ] die <-, -en>

pus [noun] Eiter [ˈaetɐ] der <-s> *no pl*

push¹ [noun] 1. *(pushing movement)* Stoß [ʃtoːs] der <-es, Stöße> ◊ *ein Stoß mit dem Ellenbogen* give sb/sth a push jdn/etw. schieben [ˈʃiːbm̩] <schiebt, schob, hat geschoben>; *(a car, swing etc.)* anschieben [ˈanʃiːbm̩] <schiebt an, schob an, hat angeschoben> ◊ *Die Nachbarn halfen mir und schoben das Auto an.* 2. *(attempt)* push to do sth Anstrengung, etw. zu tun [ˈanʃtrɛŋʊŋ ... ʦuː] die <-, -en> ◊ *eine letzte Anstrengung, einen Kompromiss zu erzielen* push for reforms Reformbestrebungen [reˈfɔrmbəˌʃtreːbʊŋən] die <-> *pl* 3. *(encouragement)* give sb a push (to do sth) jdm den Anstoß geben(, etw. zu tun) [aenən ˈanʃtoːs geːbm̩] need a push (to do sth) einen Anstoß brauchen(, um etw. zu tun) [aenən ˈanʃtoːs braoxn̩] 4. *(of an army)* push (on sth) Vorstoß (in etw. [acc]) [ˈfoːɐ̯ʃtoːs] der <-es, Vorstöße> ◊ *In der Nacht begann der Vorstoß in die Hauptstadt.* 5. *(drive, determination)* Durchsetzungsvermögen [ˈdʊrçzɛtsʊŋsfɛmøːgn̩] das <-s> *no pl* ◊ *Hat er das nötige Durchsetzungsvermögen für den Job?*

◉ when push comes to shove wenn es hart auf hart kommt give the push entlassen werden give sb the push jdn entlassen at a push wenn es sein muss ◊ *Ich kann es in einer Woche schaffen, wenn es sein muss.*

push² [verb] 1. *(move)* schieben [ˈʃiːbm̩] <schiebt, schob, hat geschoben> ◊ *das Fahrrad schieben* ✦ *Als das Auto nicht ansprang, mussten wir schieben.* ✦ *das Sofa an die Seite/Wand schieben* push sb/sth away jdn/etw. wegschieben [ˈvɛkʃiːbm̩] +haben ◊ *Das Kind wollte ihm auf den Schoß klettern, aber er schob es weg.* push sth shut etw. zuschieben [ˈʦuːʃiːbm̩] +haben ◊ *Sie schob die Schublade zu.* push sth open etw. aufstoßen [ˈaofʃtoːsn̩] <stößt auf, stieß auf, hat aufgestoßen> ◊ *die Tür aufstoßen* push at sth gegen etw. drücken [geːgn̩ ... drʏkn̩] +haben ◊ *Ich drücke gegen die Tür.* 2. *(a button)* push sth auf etw. [acc] drücken [aof ... drʏkn̩] +haben ◊ *Drücken Sie auf diesen Knopf, wenn Sie Hilfe brauchen.* 3. *(through a crowd)* drängen [ˈdrɛŋən] +haben ◊ *Bitte drängen Sie nicht (so)!* ✦ *Die Fans drängten nach vorn.* push your way through the crowd sich durch die Menge drängen push and shove drängen und schubsen ◊ *Die Journalisten drängten und schubsten.* push past sb sich an jdm vorbeidrängen

[an ... foːɐ̯ˌba̯ɛdrɛnən] +*haben* **4.** *(promote)* push sth
für etw. werben [fyːɐ̯ ... ˌvɛrˈbm̩] <wirbt, warb, hat
geworben> ◊ *In der Talkshow hat er geschickt für
sein neues Buch geworben.* **5.** *(illegal drugs)* push
sth mit etw. dealen [mɪt ... diːlən] *... (slang)* ◊ *mit
Heroin dealen* **6.** *(to a particular level)* treiben
[ˈtra̯ɛbm̩] <treibt, trieb, hat getrieben> ◊ *Die Hitzewelle trieb die Temperaturen auf fast 40 Grad.* push
sth up etw. in die Höhe treiben push sth down etw.
nach unten treiben **7.** *(encourage, urge)* drängen
[ˈdrɛŋən] +*haben* push sb to do sth jdn dazu
drängen, etw. zu tun push sb into sth jdn zu etw.
drängen; *(pupil, worker)* antreiben [ˈantra̯ɛbm̩] <treibt
an, trieb an, hat angetrieben> ◊ *Seine Eltern treiben
ihn zu sehr an.* **8.** *(annoy)* reizen [ˈra̯ɛtsn̩] +*haben*
push sb too far bei jdm zu weit gehen
[ba̯ɛ ... ʦuː ˈva̯ɛt ɡeːən] <geht, ging, ist gegangen> ◊
Pass auf, dass du bei ihm nicht zu weit gehst!
9. *(army)* vorstoßen [ˈfoːɐ̯ʃtoːsn̩] <stößt vor, stieß vor,
ist vorgestoßen>
☞ be pushing thirty etc. auf die Dreißig etc.
zugehen push it es übertreiben
• **push ahead** [phras v] push ahead with sth etw.
vorantreiben [foˈrantra̯ɛbm̩] <treibt voran, trieb voran,
hat vorangetrieben>
• **push around** [phras v] push sb around jdn herumkommandieren [hɛˈrʊmkɔmandiːrən] <kommandiert
herum, kommandierte herum, hat herumkommandiert>
• **push aside** [phras v] push sth aside etw. beiseite
schieben [ba̯ɛˈza̯ɛtə ʃiːbm̩] <schiebt, schob, hat
geschoben>
• **push for** [phras v] push for sth auf etw. [acc]
drängen [a̯ɔf ... drɛŋən] +*haben* ◊ *Er drängte auf
eine schnelle Beilegung des Konflikts.* push sb for
sth etw. von jdm verlangen [fɔn ... fɛlaŋən]
<verlangt, verlangte, hat verlangt> ◊ *Sie verlangte eine
sofortige Entscheidung von ihm.*
• **push forward** [phras v] **1.** *(continue, persist)* push
forward with sth etw. vorantreiben [foˈrantra̯ɛbm̩]
<treibt voran, trieb voran, hat vorangetrieben> ◊ *ein
Projekt vorantreiben* **2.** *(get yourself noticed)* push
yourself forward auf sich aufmerksam machen
[a̯ɔf ... ˈa̯ɔfmɛrˈkzaːm maxn̩] +*haben*; *(more aggres-
sively)* sich in den Vordergrund drängen
[ɪn deːn ˈfɔ'deɡrʊnt drɛŋən] +*haben*
• **push in** [phras v] sich vordrängeln [ˈfoːɐ̯drɛŋln̩]
<drängelt sich vor, drängelte sich vor, hat sich vorge-
drängelt> *(fam)* ◊ *Also bitte, drängeln Sie sich nicht
vor! Ich bin zuerst dran.*
• **push off** [phras v] **1.** *(leave)* abhauen [ˈapha̯ɔən]
<haut ab, haute ab, ist abgehauen> *(fam)* ◊ *Er ist
gerade abgehauen.* ◆ *Hau endlich ab und lass uns in
Ruhe!* **2.** *(from the shore)* abstoßen [ˈapʃtoːsn̩] <stößt
ab, stieß ab, hat abgestoßen> ◊ *Das Boot/Der Ruderer
stieß ab.* ◆ *Sie stießen das Boot vom Steg ab und
ruderten davon.*
• **push on** [phras v] **1.** *(continue a journey)* weiterfahren [ˈva̯ɛtefaːrən] <fährt weiter, fuhr weiter, ist weiter-
gefahren> ◊ *Nach einer kurzen Pause fuhren sie
weiter.* **2.** *(continue doing sth)* push on (with sth)
(mit etw.) weitermachen [ˈva̯ɛtemaxn̩] +*haben* ◊ *Sie
musste mit der Arbeit weitermachen, weil sie bis
morgen fertig sein sollte.*
• **push over** [phras v] umstoßen [ˈʊmʃtoːsn̩] <stößt
um, stieß um, hat umgestoßen>
pushchair [noun] Sportwagen [ˈʃpɔrtvaːɡn̩]

<—s, —> ◊ *Das Kind saß in seinem Sportwagen und
schaute sich um.*
pushy [adj] **1.** *(too ambitious)* ehrgeizig [ˈeːɐ̯ɡa̯ɛtsɪç] ◊
ein ehrgeiziger Vater ◆ *Die Eltern des Kinderstars
waren schrecklich ehrgeizig.* **2.** *(too eager, intrusive)*
zudringlich [ˈʦuːdrɪŋlɪç] ◊ *ein zudringlicher Verehrer*
◆ *Ich empfinde seine ständigen Fragen als zudringlich.*
put [verb] **1.** *(lay, place an object)* legen [ˈleːɡn̩] +*haben*
◊ *Sie legte ihre Hand auf meine Schulter.* ◆ *Er legte
das Buch auf den Tisch.* **2.** *(push, insert)* stecken
[ˈʃtɛkn̩] +*haben* ◊ *einen Brief in ein Kuvert stecken* ◆
Der Hund steckte seinen Kopf durch den Zaun.
3. *(place, position)* stellen [ˈʃtɛlən] +*haben* ◊ *Kannst
du die Milch in den Kühlschrank stellen?* ◆ *eine Vase
auf den Tisch stellen* ◆ *die Schuhe in den Flur stellen*
4. *(kick)* schießen [ˈʃiːsn̩] <schießt, schoss, hat
geschossen> ◊ *Ich schoss den Ball ins Tor.* **5.** *(in
danger, a difficult position)* put sb in sth jdn in etw.
[acc] bringen [ɪn ... brɪŋən] <bringt, brachte, hat
gebracht> ◊ *Du bringst mich in eine schwierige
Lage.*; *(out of a job, work)* put sb out of sth jdn um
etw. bringen [ʊm ... brɪŋən] ◊ *Diese Entscheidung
hat 200 Arbeiter um ihre Stelle gebracht.* **6.** *(in sb's
place, a good/bad mood)* put sb in sth jdn in etw.
[acc] versetzen [ɪn ... fɛtsɛtsn̩] <versetzt, versetzte, hat
versetzt> ◊ *Versuch doch mal, dich in meine Lage zu
versetzen!* ◆ *Der Film hat ihn wieder in eine bessere
Laune versetzt.* **7.** *(write)* schreiben [ˈʃra̯ɛbm̩]
<schreibt, schrieb, hat geschrieben> ◊ *Er schrieb
einen kurzen Gruß auf die Karte.*; *(in your diary, a
list)* eintragen [ˈa̯ɛntraːɡn̩] <trägt ein, trug ein, hat ein-
getragen> ◊ *Ich trage es gleich auf dem Kalender
ein.*; *(a tick, comma, signature)* setzen [ˈzɛtsn̩]
+*haben* ◊ *Dort musst du ein Komma setzen.* ◆ *Er
setzte seine Unterschrift unter den Brief.* **8.** *(send sb
somewhere)* put sb to bed jdn ins Bett bringen
[ɪns ˈbɛt brɪŋən] <bringt, brachte, hat gebracht> ◊ *Er
brachte die Kinder um acht Uhr ins Bett.* put sb
in(to) a home jdn in einem Heim unterbringen
[ɪn a̯ɛnəm ˈha̯ɛm ˌʊntebrɪŋən] <bringt unter, brachte
unter, hat untergebracht> ◊ *Sie mussten ihn schließlich in einem Heim unterbringen.* **9.** *(on a train,
bus)* put sb on sth jdn in etw. [acc] setzen
[ɪn ... zɛtsn̩] +*haben* ◊ *Ich habe sie in Frankfurt ins
Flugzeug gesetzt.* **10.** *(say)* sagen [ˈzaːɡn̩] +*haben* as
sb puts it wie jd schon sagte/immer sagt ◊ *wie
schon Goethe sagte/mein Vater immer sagt* let me
put it this way, how shall I put it? sagen wir es mal
so to put it another way/bluntly/mildly anders/
offen/gelinde gesagt ◊ *Er ist offen gesagt ein ziemlicher Träumer.*; *(express)* ausdrücken [ˌa̯ɔsdrʏkn̩]
+*haben* I couldn't have put it better myself. Das
war sehr gut ausgedrückt. put it diplomatically sich
diplomatisch ausdrücken ◊ *Er hat sich sehr diplomatisch ausgedrückt.* put simply einfach ausgedrückt
put sth into words etw. in Worte fassen
[ɪn ˈvɔrtə fasn̩] +*haben* **11.** *(build, construct)* bauen
[ˈba̯ɔən] +*haben* ◊ *Auf dem Grundstück sollen drei
Häuser gebaut werden.*; *(place, situate)* verlegen
[fɛˈleːɡn̩] +*haben* <verlegt, verlegte, hat verlegt> ◊ *Wir wollen
den Hobbyraum in den Keller verlegen.* **12.** *(rank,
include)* put sb/sth among sth jdn/etw. zu etw.
zählen [tsuː ... tsɛːlən] +*haben* ◊ *Ich zähle sie zu den
besten Dichterinnen aller Zeiten.* put sb/sth in sth
jdn/etw. in etw. [acc] einordnen [ɪn ... ˌa̯ɛnˈɔrdnən]

<ordnet ein, ordnete ein, hat eingeordnet> ◊ *Kann man die beiden Maler in die gleiche Kategorie einordnen?* **13.** *(give greater importance to)* put sb/ sth before sth jdn/etw. über etw. [acc] stellen [yːbɐ ... ˈʃtɛlən] +haben ◊ *Er stellt seinen Beruf über seine Familie.* sb puts sb/sth first bei jdm steht jd/ etw. an erster Stelle [baɛ ... ˈʃteːt ... an ˌeːɐstɐ ˈʃtɛlə] <stand, hat gestanden> ◊ *Das Tanzen steht bei mir an erster Stelle.* **14.** put the shot kugelstoßen [ˈkuːɡl̩ʃtoːsn̩] *only inf*

◉ not know where to put yourself sich vor Verlegenheit winden put sth behind you einen Strich unter etw. [acc] ziehen not put it past sb (to do sth) es jdm zutrauen(, etw. zu tun) put sb straight on sth etw. klarstellen

• **put across** [phras v] put sth across (to sb) (jdm) etw. vermitteln [fɛˈmɪtl̩n] <vermittelt, vermittelte, hat vermittelt> ◊ *Informationen/seine Ideen vermitteln* put yourself across den richtigen Eindruck von sich vermitteln

• **put aside** [phras v] **1.** *(forget)* vergessen [fɛˈɡɛsn̩] <vergisst, vergaß, hat vergessen> ◊ *Vergessen Sie Ihre Sorgen und genießen Sie Ihren Urlaub!* put aside your differences seine Differenzen beiseite lassen [zaɛnə dɪfəˌʁɛntsn̩ baɛˈzaɛtə lasn̩] <lässt, ließ, hat gelassen> ◊ *Es ist Zeit, alle Differenzen beiseite zu lassen und für den Frieden zu arbeiten.* **2.** *(money)* zurücklegen [tsuˈʁʏkl̩ˌɡṇ] +haben ◊ *Geld für Notfälle zurücklegen* **3.** *(time)* sich [dat] freihalten [ˈfʁaɛhaltn̩] <hält sich frei, hielt sich frei, hat sich freigehalten> ◊ *Ich halte mir einen Tag in der Woche frei.*

• **put away** [phras v] **1.** *(tidy away)* put sth away etw. wegräumen [ˈvɛkʁɔɡmən] +haben ◊ *Die Kinder räumten ihre Spielsachen weg.* **2.** *(eat)* verdrücken [fɛˈdʁʏkn̩] <verdrückt, verdrückte, hat verdrückt> *(fam)*; *(drink)* schlucken [ˈʃlʊkn̩] +haben *(fam)* ◊ *Er kann ganz schön viel schlucken.* **3.** *(in prison, a mental institution)* put sb away jdn einsperren [ˈaɛnʃpɛʁən] +haben ◊ *Solche Leute müssen eingesperrt werden.* **4.** *(money)* zurücklegen [tsuˈʁʏkl̩ˌɡṇ] +haben ◊ *Jeden Monat legt sie 200 Euro zurück.*

• **put back** [phras v] put sth back **1.** *(an object, a clock)* etw. zurückstellen [tsuˈʁʏkʃtɛlən] +haben ◊ *etw. an seinen Platz zurückstellen* ◆ *Er stellte das Buch ins Regal zurück.* I put my watch back an hour. *Ich habe meine Uhr um eine Stunde zurückgestellt.* **2.** *(an event)* etw. verschieben [fɛˈʃiːbm̩] <verschiebt, verschob, hat verschoben> ◊ *Die Besprechung ist auf 16 Uhr verschoben worden.*

• **put down** [phras v] **1.** *(an object)* abstellen [ˈapʃtɛlən] +haben ◊ *Sie stellte das Tablett auf dem Tisch ab.*; *(a heavy object)* absetzen [ˈapzɛtsn̩] +haben ◊ *Die Tasche ist schwer; etw. muss sie absetzen.* **2.** *(criticize)* herabsetzen [hɛˈʁapzɛtsn̩] +haben ◊ *Ich mag es nicht, wie er sie immer vor anderen herabsetzt.* put yourself down sein Licht unter den Scheffel stellen [zaɛn ˌlɪçt ʊntə deːn ˈʃɛfl̩ ʃtɛlən] +haben **3.** *(an animal)* einschläfern [ˈaɛnʃlɛːfɐn] +haben ◊ *Der Kater musste eingeschläfert werden.* have an animal put down ein Tier einschläfern lassen **4.** *(on a list, in a book)* eintragen [ˈaɛntʁaːɡṇ] <trägt ein, trug ein, hat eingetragen> ◊ *Tragen Sie bitte hier Ihre Telefonnummer ein.* put sb down to do sth eintragen, dass jd etw. tut ◊ *Ich habe eingetragen, dass du den Kuchen mitbringst.* put sb down for sth jdn für etw.

eintragen ◊ *Ich trage dich für 20 Euro ein.*; *(for a school, an activity)* put sb down for sth jdn für etw. anmelden [fyːɐ ... ˌanmɛldn̩] <meldet an, meldete an, hat angemeldet> ◊ *Sie haben ihr Kind jetzt schon für eine Privatschule angemeldet.* **5.** *(a sum of money)* anzahlen [ˈantsaːlən] +haben ◊ *Er hat für das Auto 1000 Euro angezahlt.* put down a deposit eine Anzahlung machen [aɛnə ˈantsaːlʊŋ maxn̩] +haben ◊ *Möchten Sie jetzt eine Anzahlung machen?* **6.** *(a passenger)* put sb down jdn absetzen [ˈapzɛtsn̩] +haben ◊ *Setzt du mich bitte am Bahnhof ab?* **7.** *(a baby)* put sb down jdn hinlegen [ˈhɪnleːɡṇ] +haben ◊ *Sei leise! Ich habe das Baby gerade hingelegt.* **8.** *(an uprising)* niederschlagen [ˈniːdɐʃlaːɡṇ] <schlägt nieder, schlug nieder, hat niedergeschlagen> ◊ *Die Armee hat den Aufstand blutig niedergeschlagen.* **9.** *(consider, believe to be)* put sb down as sth jdn für etw. halten [fyːɐ ... haltṇ] <hält, hielt, hat gehalten> ◊ *Ich hatte sie immer für eine Karrierefrau gehalten.* **10.** *(attribute to)* put sth down to etw. auf etw. [acc] zurückführen [aɔf ... tsuˌʁʏkfyːʁən] +haben ◊ *Der Trainer führte die Niederlage auf die vielen Verletzungen zurück.*

◉ put the phone down auflegen put the phone down on sb jdn nicht ausreden lassen und einfach auflegen sb can't put sth down jd kann etw. nicht aus der Hand legen

• **put forward** [phras v] **1.** *(suggest)* vorschlagen [ˈfoːɐʃlaːɡṇ] <schlägt vor, schlug vor, hat vorgeschlagen> ◊ *einen Plan/eine Lösung vorschlagen* ◆ *jdn für einen Job/eine Beförderung vorschlagen* put yourself forward to do sth sich anbieten, etw. zu tun [ˈanbiːtn̩ ... tsuː] <bietet sich an, bot sich an, hat sich angeboten> **2.** *(an event)* vorverlegen [ˈfoːɐfɛleˑɡṇ] <verlegt vor, verlegte vor, hat vorverlegt> ◊ *Die Besprechung ist auf zehn Uhr vorverlegt worden.* **3.** *(a clock)* vorstellen [ˈfoːɐʃtɛlən] +haben ◊ *die Uhr eine Stunde vorstellen*

• **put in** [phras v] **1.** put in more hours Überstunden machen [ˈyːbɐʃtʊndn̩ maxn̩] +haben put in a lot of work sich [dat] viel Mühe geben [fiːl ˈmyːə geːbm̩] <gibt, gab, hat gegeben> **2.** *(install)* einbauen [ˈaɛnbaɔən] +haben ◊ *Sie haben eine neue Küche einbauen lassen.* **3.** *(a claim)* stellen [ˈʃtɛlən] +haben ◊ *Sie hat Antrag auf Schadensersatz gestellt.*; *(an offer, a request)* machen [ˈmaxn̩] +haben ◊ *Er machte ein sehr niedriges Angebot.* **4.** *(a comment)* einwerfen [ˈaɛnvɛʁfn̩] <wirft ein, warf ein, hat eingeworfen> ◊ *eine dumme Bemerkung einwerfen* **5.** *(money)* hineinstecken [hɪˈnaɛnʃtɛkn̩] +haben **6.** *(apply)* put in for sth etw. beantragen [bəˈantraːɡṇ] <beantragt, beantragte, hat beantragt> **7.** *(ship)* einlaufen [ˈaɛnlaɔfn̩] +haben ◊ *läuft ein, lief ein, ist eingelaufen>*

• **put into** [phras v] **1.** *(work, time, money)* put sth into sth in etw. [acc] hineinstecken [ɪn ... hɪˌnaɛnʃtɛkn̩] +haben ◊ *Ich habe viel Arbeit in das Projekt hineingesteckt.* **2.** *(introduce into your voice)* put sth into sth etw. in etw. [acc] legen [ɪn ... leːɡṇ] +haben ◊ *Er versuchte, mehr Gefühl in seine Stimme zu legen.*; *(into your life)* put sth into sth etw. in etw. [acc] bringen [ɪn ... brɪŋən] <bringt, brachte, hat gebracht> ◊ *Sie wollte etwas Aufregung in ihr Leben bringen.* **3.** *(ship)* put into sth in etw. [acc] einlaufen [ɪn ... ˌaɛnlaɔfn̩] <läuft ein, lief ein, ist eingelaufen>

• **put off** ⟨phras v⟩ **1.** *(deter)* put sb off jdn abschrecken ['apʃrɛkn̩] +haben ◊ *Die hohen Preise haben die Kunden abgeschreckt.* put sb off sb jdm jdn mies machen ['miːs maxn̩] +haben ◊ *Ihre Mutter versuchte, ihr den neuen Freund mies zu machen* put sb off sth jdn von etw. abbringen [fɔn ... 'apbrɪŋən] <bringt ab, brachte ab, hat abgebracht> ◊ *Ich habe ihn von der Idee abgebracht.* put sb off doing sth jdn davon abbringen, etw. zu tun **2.** *(delay)* put sth off etw. aufschieben ['aoffiːbm̩] <schiebt auf, schob auf, hat aufgeschoben> ◊ *eine Entscheidung so lange aufschieben, bis es fast zu spät ist; (change to a later time)* etw. verschieben [fɛ'ʃiːbm̩] <verschiebt, verschob, hat verschoben> ◊ *Die Feier musste verschoben werden.* put off doing sth damit warten, etw. zu tun [damɪt 'vaʁtn̩ ... tsuː] +haben **3.** *(cancel)* put sb off jdm absagen ['apzaːgn̩] +haben ◊ *Ich muss meiner Freundin absagen, weil meine Mutter erkrankt ist.* **4.** *(distract)* put sb off jdn stören ['ʃtøːrən] +haben ◊ *Er hat so viel geredet, dass er mich bei der Arbeit gestört hat.*

• **put on** ⟨phras v⟩ **1.** *(clothes, shoes)* anziehen ['antsiːən] <zieht an, zog an, hat angezogen> ◊ *Er zog ein Hemd an.; (hat, glasses)* aufsetzen ['aofzɛtsn̩] +haben ◊ *Setz eine Mütze auf, wenn du rausgehst.; (jewellery)* anlegen ['anleːgn̩] +haben *(lofty)* ◊ *Sie legte ein Perlencollier an.; (make-up)* auflegen ['aofleːgn̩] +haben ◊ *Sie legte Make-up/Lippenstift auf.* **2.** *(the light, TV, radio)* einschalten ['aenʃaltn̩] <schaltet ein, schaltete ein, hat eingeschaltet> ◊ *Nach dem Essen schaltet er immer den Fernseher ein.* **3.** *(the handbrake)* anziehen ['antsiːən] <zieht an, zog an, hat angezogen> ◊ *Hast du die Handbremse angezogen?* **4.** *(music, a CD, a video)* auflegen ['aofleːgn̩] +haben ◊ *Sie legte mein Lieblingslied auf.* **5.** *(an event, a concert)* veranstalten [fɛ'anʃtaltn̩] +haben ◊ *Sie haben ein interessantes Menü zusammengestellt; eine Ausstellung/einen Wettbewerb veranstalten; (a play)* aufführen ['aoffyːrən] +haben ◊ *Die Klasse führte ein Theaterstück auf.* **6.** *(a voice, an accent)* sprechen mit ['ʃprɛçŋ mɪt] <spricht, sprach, hat gesprochen> ◊ *Der Mann sprach mit einem komischen Akzent.; (an expression)* aufsetzen ['aofzɛtsn̩] +haben ◊ *Sie setzte eine freundliche Miene auf.* be putting it on so tun [zoː 'tuːn] <tut, tat, hat getan> ◊ *Stefan hat sich nicht wehgetan — er tut nur so.* put on an act eine Show abziehen [aenə 'ʃoː aptsiːən] <zieht ab, zog ab, hat abgezogen> *(fam)* ◊ *Er zieht eine Show ab, damit alle Mitleid mit ihm haben.* **7.** *(gain weight)* zunehmen ['tsuːneːmən] <nimmt zu, nahm zu, hat zugenommen> ◊ *Sie hat zehn Kilo zugenommen.* put on weight zunehmen **8.** *(start cooking)* aufsetzen ['aofzɛtsn̩] +haben ◊ *Setzt du bitte Wasser für die Nudeln auf?* **9.** *(on the telephone)* put sb on jdn ans Telefon holen [ans 'teːləfoːn hoːlən] +haben **10.** *(special transport)* einsetzen ['aenzɛtsn̩] +haben ◊ *Sonderzüge für die Fans einsetzen* **11.** *(give, prescribe)* put sb on sth jdm etw. verschreiben [fɛ'ʃraebm̩] <verschreibt, verschrieb, hat verschrieben> ◊ *Der Arzt hat ihm ein Antibiotikum verschrieben.; (give sb a task)* put sb on sth jdn zu etw. einteilen [tsuː ... aentaelən] +haben ◊ *Sie hat mich zum Spülen eingeteilt.* **12.** put sth on the bill etw. auf die Rechnung setzen [aof diː 'rɛçnʊŋ zɛtsn̩] +haben

• **put out** ⟨phras v⟩ **1.** *(a fire)* löschen ['lœʃn̩] +haben ◊ *Die Feuerwehr hat den Brand schnell gelöscht.; (a* cigarette) ausmachen ['aosmaxn̩] +haben ◊ *Mach hier bitte die Zigarette aus!* **2.** *(the light)* ausschalten ['aosʃaltn̩] <schaltet aus, schaltete aus, hat ausgeschaltet> **3.** *(make available)* auslegen ['aosleːgn̩] +haben ◊ *Informationsmaterial auslegen* ◆ *Im Winter legen wir Vogelfutter aus.* **4.** *(cause inconvenience)* put sb out jdm Umstände machen ['ʊmʃtɛndə maxn̩] +haben ◊ *Ich möchte Ihnen wirklich keine Umstände machen.* put yourself out (for sb) sich ⟨dat⟩ *(wegen jdm)* Umstände machen ['ʊmʃtɛndə maxn̩] +haben ◊ *Warum soll ich mir wegen dieser Leute solche Umstände machen?* put yourself out to do sth sich ⟨dat⟩ Umstände machen, um etw. zu tun ['ʊmʃtɛndə maxn̩ ʊm ... tsuː] +haben ◊ *Sie machte sich große Umstände, um uns alle bei sich unterzubringen.* **5.** *(move outside)* hinausbringen [hɪ'naosbrɪŋən] <bringt hinaus, brachte hinaus, hat hinausgebracht> ◊ *Bring bitte den Müll hinaus.; (a* cat) hinauslassen [hɪ'naoslasn̩] <lässt hinaus, ließ hinaus, hat hinausgelassen> ◊ *Lass bitte die Katze hinaus, bevor du ins Bett gehst.* **6.** *(a statement)* herausgeben [hɛ'raosgeːbm̩] <gibt heraus, gab heraus, hat herausgegeben> **7.** *(on TV, radio)* senden ['zɛndn̩] <sendet, sendete, hat gesendet>; *(a book, magazine)* herausbringen [hɛ'raosbrɪŋən] <bringt heraus, brachte heraus, hat herausgebracht>; *(a video, CD)* produzieren [produ'tsiːrən] <produziert, produzierte, hat produziert>

• **put through** ⟨phras v⟩ **1.** *(cause to experience)* put sb through sth jdm etw. zumuten ['tsuːmuːtn̩] <mutet zu, mutete zu, hat zugemutet> ◊ *Einem Kind kann man eine Gerichtsverhandlung nicht zumuten.* **2.** *(a test, trials)* put sb/sth through sth jdn/etw. einer Sache ⟨dat⟩ unterziehen [ʊntɐ'tsiːən] <unterzieht, unterzog, hat unterzogen> ◊ *Er/Es wurde einem langwierigen Test unterzogen.* **3.** *(on the telephone)* durchstellen ['dʊɐ̯çʃtɛlən] +haben ◊ *einen Anruf durchstellen* put sb through to sb jdn mit jdm verbinden [mɪt ... fɛˌbɪndn̩] <verbindet, verband, hat verbunden> ◊ *Verbinden Sie mich bitte mit Herrn Meier.*

• **put to** ⟨phras v⟩ **1.** *(propose)* put sth to sb jdm etw. vorlegen ['foːɐ̯leːgn̩] +haben put a question to sb jdm eine Frage stellen [aenə 'fraːgə ʃtɛlən] +haben put sth to sb jdm zu bedenken geben, dass [tsuː bə'dɛŋkŋ̍ geːbm̩ ... gibt, gab, hat gegeben> **2.** put sb to trouble jdm Umstände machen ['ʊmʃtɛndə maxn̩] +haben ◊ *Ich möchte Ihnen wirklich keine Umstände machen.*

• **put together** ⟨phras v⟩ put sth together **1.** *(organize, coordinate)* etw. zusammenstellen [tsu'zamənʃtɛlən] +haben ◊ *Sie haben ein interessantes Menü zusammengestellt.* **2.** *(make sth from parts)* zusammensetzen [tsu'zamənzɛtsn̩] +haben ◊ *Sie hat das Puzzle zusammengesetzt.; (a piece of* furniture) etw. zusammenbauen [tsu'zamənbaoən] +haben ◊ *Wir haben Stunden gebraucht, um den Schrank zusammenzubauen.*

• **put up** ⟨phras v⟩ **1.** *(wall, fence, building)* errichten [ɛ'rɪçtn̩] <errichtet, errichtete, hat errichtet> ◊ *Hier soll ein neues Museum errichtet werden.; (tent)* aufbauen ['aofbaoən] +haben ◊ *ein Gerüst/Zelt aufbauen; (parasol)* aufstellen ['aofʃtɛlən] +haben ◊ *Im Biergarten wurden bereits die Sonnenschirme aufgestellt.* **2.** *(picture, poster etc.)* aufhängen ['aofhɛŋən] +haben ◊ *ein Poster an der Tür*

aufhängen; (a shelf, cupboard) anbringen ['anbrɪŋən] <bringt an, brachte an, hat angebracht> ◊ *Er brachte den Hängeschrank an der Wand an.* **3.** *(prices, interest rates)* erhöhen [ɛ'høːən] <erhöht, erhöhte, hat erhöht> ◊ *Die Benzinpreise sind schon wieder erhöht worden.* **4.** *(a sum of money)* bereitstellen [bə'raɛtʃtɛlən] +*haben* **5.** *(an umbrella)* aufspannen ['aɔfʃpanən] +*haben; (your hood)* aufsetzen ['aɔfzɛtsn̩] +*haben* ◊ *Setz die Kapuze auf! Der Wind ist so kalt.* **6.** *(a guest)* unterbringen ['ʊntɛbrɪŋən] <bringt unter, brachte unter, hat untergebracht> ◊ *Ich kann bei mir zu Hause zwei Leute unterbringen.* **7.** *(in a hotel, motel etc.)* absteigen ['apʃtaɛgn̩] <steigt ab, stieg ab, ist abgestiegen> *(lofty)* ◊ *Sie stiegen im Hotel zur Post ab.* **8.** *(a candidate)* aufstellen ['aɔfʃtɛlən] +*haben* ◊ *Sie wurde (als Kandidatin) für den Vorstand aufgestellt.* **9.** put up a fight, put up resistance Widerstand leisten ['viːdeʃtant laɛstn̩] <leistet, leistete, hat geleistet> ◊ *Er hat überhaupt keinen Widerstand geleistet.* **10.** *(raise)* hochheben ['hoːxheːbm̩] <hebt hoch, hob hoch, hat hochgehoben> ◊ *Wer dafür ist, hebt jetzt bitte die Hand hoch.; (at school)* put your hand up sich melden ['mɛldn̩] <meldet sich, meldete sich, hat sich gemeldet> ◊ *Bitte meldet euch, wenn ihr etwas sagen wollt.* **11.** *(encourage to do sth bad)* put sb up to sth jdn zu etw. anstiften [tsuː ... ,anʃtɪftn̩] <stiftet an, stiftete an, hat angestiftet> ◊ *Sein großer Bruder*

hat ihn dazu angestiftet. **12.** *(tolerate)* put up with sb jdn ertragen [ɛ'traːgn̩] <erträgt, ertrug, hat ertragen> put up with sth sich ⟨dat⟩ etw. gefallen lassen [gə'falən lasn̩] <lässt sich, ließ sich, hat sich ... lassen> ◊ *Hör auf damit! Das lasse ich mir nicht mehr gefallen!*

puzzle¹ ⟨noun⟩ Rätsel ['rɛːtsl̩] das <-s, -> ◊ *ein Rätsel lösen* ♦ *Die Lösung des Rätsels erfahren Sie im nächsten Heft.* be a puzzle to sb jdm ein Rätsel sein crossword puzzle Kreuzworträtsel ['krɔøtsvoˈtrɛːtsl̩] jigsaw puzzle Puzzle ['pʊzl̩] das <-s, -s>

puzzle² ⟨verb⟩ puzzle sb jdm ein Rätsel sein [aɛn 'rɛːtsl̩ zaɛn] +*sein*
• **puzzle out** ⟨phras v⟩ herausfinden [hɛ'raɔsfɪndn̩] <findet heraus, fand heraus, hat herausgefunden>
• **puzzle over** ⟨phras v⟩ puzzle over sb/sth sich ⟨dat⟩ über jdn/etw. den Kopf zerbrechen [y:bɐ ... deːn 'kɔpf tsɛbrɛçn̩] <zerbricht, zerbrach, hat zerbrochen>

puzzled ⟨adj⟩ verwirrt [fe'vɪrt] <verwirrter, am verwirrtesten>

pyjamas ⟨noun⟩ Schlafanzug ['ʃlaːf|antsuːk] der <-(e)s, Schlafanzüge>

pyramid ⟨noun⟩ Pyramide [pyra'miːdə] die <-, -n> ◊ *Berechnen Sie das Volumen der Pyramide.* ♦ *die berühmten Pyramiden von Gizeh* ♦ *eine Pyramide aus Tomatendosen*

A
B
C
D
E
F
G
H
I
J
K
L
M
N
O
P
Q
R
S
T
U
V
W
X
Y
Z

Q

q, Q [noun] q, Q [ku:] das <–(s), –(s)> ◊ *ein kleines q/großes Q* ♦ *Q wie Quelle*

qualification [noun] **1.** *(educational)* Abschluss ['apʃlʊs] der <–es, Abschlüsse> ◊ *Ich habe einen Abschluss in Psychologie.* ♦ *Sie verließ die Schule ohne Abschluss.* **2.** *(ability, prerequisite, in sport)* Qualifikation [kvalifika'tsjoːn] die <–, –en> ◊ *Sie verlangen als Qualifikation die mittlere Reife.* ♦ *das Rennen um die Qualifikation* **3.** *(limitation)* Einschränkung ['aɛnʃrɛŋkʊŋ] die <–, –en> ◊ *Bei diesem Vertrag gibt es eine wichtige Einschränkung: Er gilt nur innerhalb der EU.* accept sth with/without qualifications etw. unter Vorbehalt/vorbehaltlos akzeptieren [ʊntɐ 'foːɐ̯bəhalt/,foːɐ̯bəhaltloːs aktsɛp'tiːrən] <akzeptiert, akzeptierte, hat akzeptiert> ◊ *Der Vorstand akzeptiert den Vorschlag nur unter Vorbehalt.*

qualified [adj] **1.** *(trained)* ausgebildet ['aʊsɡəbɪldət] no comp/superl ◊ *Sie ist ausgebildete Krankenschwester.* qualified for sth für etw. qualifiziert [fyːɐ̯ ... kvalifiˈtsiːɐ̯t] <qualifizierter, am qualifiziertesten> ◊ *Sind Sie für diese Arbeit qualifiziert?* highly qualified hoch qualifiziert **2.** *(entitled)* berechtigt [bəˈrɛçtɪçt] no comp/superl ◊ *Ich bin nicht berechtigt, das zu entscheiden.* qualified to vote wahlberechtigt **3.** *(limited)* bedingt [bəˈdɪŋt] no comp/superl ◊ *Der Vorschlag fand nur bedingte Zustimmung.*

qualify [verb] **1.** *(for a profession)* qualify as sth seine Ausbildung als etw. abschließen [,aʊsbɪldʊŋ als ... ,apʃliːsn̩] <schließt ab, schloss ab, hat abgeschlossen> ◊ *Letztes Jahr hat sie ihre Ausbildung als Lehrerin/Anwältin abgeschlossen.* qualify sb to do sth jdn für etw. qualifizieren [fyːɐ̯ ... kvalifiˌtsiːrən] <qualifiziert, qualifizierte, hat qualifiziert> ◊ *Dieser Kurs qualifiziert Sie für die Tätigkeit als Sozialarbeiter.* **2.** *(have certain qualities)* qualify for sth die Bedingungen für etw. erfüllen [diː bə,dɪŋʊŋən fyːɐ̯ ... ɐ,fʏlən] <erfüllt, erfüllte, hat erfüllt> ◊ *Er erfüllt die Bedingungen für das Stipendium.* qualify as sth als etw. angesehen werden können [als ... ,aŋɡəzeːən veːɐ̯dn̩ kœnən] <kann, konnte, hat können> ◊ *Sie kann kaum als Künstlerin angesehen werden.; (entitle)* qualify sb to do sth jdn dazu berechtigen, etw. zu tun [datsuː bəˈrɛçtɪɡn̩ ... tsuː] <berechtigt, berechtigte, hat berechtigt> ◊ *Ihr geringes Einkommen berechtigt sie dazu, einen Zuschuss zu beantragen.* **3.** SPORT qualify for sth sich für etw. qualifizieren [fyːɐ̯ ... kvalifiˌtsiːrən] <qualifiziert sich, qualifizierte sich, hat sich qualifiziert> ◊ *Sie hat sich für die Olympischen Spiele qualifiziert.* **4.** GRAM näher bestimmen [,nɛːɐ bəˈʃtɪmən] <bestimmt, bestimmte, hat bestimmt> ◊ *In dem Ausdruck ‚ausgezeichnet spielen' wird das Verb ‚spielen' durch das Adverb ‚ausgezeichnet' näher bestimmt.* **5.** *(limit)* einschränken ['aɛnʃrɛŋkn̩] +haben ◊ *Er schränkte seine Behauptung sofort wieder ein.*

quality [noun] **1.** *(high standards)* Qualität [kvaliˈtɛːt]

die <–, –en> ◊ *Wir legen großen Wert auf Qualität.* ♦ *ein Produkt von guter/schlechter Qualität* **2.** *(characteristic)* Eigenschaft ['aɛɡn̩ʃaft] die <–, –en> ◊ *Welche Eigenschaft ist dir bei deinem Partner besonders wichtig?* ♦ *die chemischen Eigenschaften einer Substanz untersuchen*

quantitative [adj] quantitativ [kvantitaˈtiːf] no comp/superl ◊ *eine quantitative Analyse machen*

quantity [noun] *(amount of sth)* Quantität [kvantiˈtɛːt] die <–> no pl ◊ *Qualität der Arbeit geht vor Quantität.; (proportion)* Menge ['mɛŋə] die <–, –n> ◊ *In ihrem Blut wurde eine winzige Menge Gift gefunden.* ♦ *Lebensmittel in großen Mengen kaufen; (large amount)* quantities of sth Unmengen von etw. ['ʊnmɛŋən fɔn] die <–> pl ◊ *Auf dem Dachboden lagen Unmengen von Büchern herum.*

quarrel¹ [noun] **1.** *(argument)* Streit [ʃtraɛt] der <–(e)s, –e> most sing ◊ *Er hatte Streit mit seiner Frau.* ♦ *Die Kinder gerieten in Streit um ein Spielzeug.* ♦ *Fangt bitte keinen Streit an.* **2.** *(cause for complaint)* have no quarrel with sb/sth nichts gegen jdn/etw. haben [,nɪçts ɡeːgn̩ ... 'haːbm̩] +haben ◊ *Ich habe nichts gegen den neuen Mitarbeiter.*

quarrel² [verb] (sich) streiten ['ʃtraɛtn̩] <streitet (sich), stritt (sich), hat (sich) gestritten> ◊ *Ich mag (mich) nicht schon wieder streiten.* ♦ *Er hat sich mit seiner Frau über den Urlaub gestritten.* ♦ *Ich hasse es, mit ihr zu streiten.* They quarrel. Sie streiten (sich).

quarry¹ [noun] **1.** *(place)* Steinbruch ['ʃtaɛnbrʊx] der <–(e)s, Steinbrüche> ◊ *in einem Steinbruch arbeiten* **2.** *(animal or person chased)* Opfer ['ɔpfɐ] das <–s, –> ◊ *Raubtiere verfolgen ihr Opfer oft kilometerweit.*

quarry² [verb] abbauen ['apbaʊən] +haben ◊ *Erz/ Braunkohle abbauen ... is quarried for sth* etw. wird ... abgebaut ◊ *Früher wurde in dieser Gegend Schiefer abgebaut.*

quarter [noun] **1.** *(fourth part of sth)* Viertel ['fɪrtl̩] das <–s, –> ◊ *Ein Viertel der Zeit ist bereits vorbei.* ♦ *Fast drei Viertel der Bevölkerung sind gegen das neue Gesetz.* quarter past five Viertel nach fünf quarter to eight Viertel vor acht quarter of an hour Viertelstunde [fɪrtl̩'ʃtʊndə] die <–, –n> quarter of a litre/liter Viertelliter [,fɪrtl̩'liːtɐ] der <–s, –> **2.** *(of a year)* Quartal [kvaˈtaːl] das <–s, –e> ◊ *Im ersten Quartal hat die Firma 25 Prozent Gewinn gemacht.* **3.** *(district in a town)* Viertel ['fɪrtl̩] das <–s, –> ◊ *Wir wohnen in einem ruhigen Viertel.* **4.** from all quarters von allen Seiten [fɔn alən 'zaɛtn̩] ◊ *Sie wurde von allen Seiten beglückwünscht.* from this quarter von dieser Seite [fɔn 'diːzɐ zaɛtə] ◊ *Von dieser Seite brauchen Sie keine Unterstützung zu erwarten.* **5.** *(for measuring weight)* unit for measuring weight that corresponds to 0,113 kg **6.** *(US coin)* Vierteldollar [,fɪrtl̩'dɔlaʳ] der <–s> no pl

quarters [noun] Quartier [kvaˈtiːɐ̯] das <–s, –e> ◊ *Sie mussten sich ein neues Quartier suchen.* take up

your quarters sein Quartier beziehen

quay noun Kai [ka͜e] der <–s, –s> ◊ *Sie gingen am Kai spazieren.*

queen noun **1.** *(woman, female bee or ant)* Königin ['kɔːnɪɡɪn] die <–, –nen> ◊ *Königin Elisabeth II.* ♦ *Sie wurde zur Königin gekrönt.* ♦ *Joan Baez wird oft als die Königin des Folk bezeichnet.* ♦ *Alle Bienen versammelten sich um die Königin.* **2.** GAME, CHESS Dame ['daːmə] die <–, –n> ◊ *Sie schlug seine Dame.* **3.** *(homosexual)* Tunte ['tʊntə] die <–, –n> *(rude, pej)* ◊ *Das ganze Lokal war voller Tunten.* drag queen Transvestit [transvɛsˈtiːt] der <–en, –en>

quench verb **1.** *(thirst)* stillen ['ʃtɪlən] +haben ◊ *seinen Durst stillen* ♦ *Nichts kann den Wissensdurst eines kleinen Kindes stillen.* **2.** *(oldf) (a fire)* löschen ['lœʃn̩] +haben ◊ *Zum Glück konnten sie das Feuer rasch löschen.*

query¹ noun Frage ['fraːɡə] die <–, –n> ◊ *Ich habe eine Frage zu den Versandkosten.* ♦ *Haben Sie Fragen, was die Organisation betrifft?*

query² verb **1.** *(express doubt about)* query (whether) bezweifeln (dass) [bəˈtsva͜efl̩n (das)] <bezweifelt, bezweifelte, hat bezweifelt> ◊ *Bezweifeln Sie die Richtigkeit ihrer Entscheidung etwa?* ♦ *Ich bezweifle, dass er dazu in der Lage ist.* **2.** *(ask)* fragen ['fraːɡn̩] +haben ◊ *„Und was machen wir jetzt?", fragte sie.*

quest noun Suche ['zuːxə] die <–, –n> ◊ *die Suche nach dem Glück* ♦ *sich auf die Suche nach etw. machen* ♦ *auf der Suche nach der Wahrheit sein*

question¹ noun Frage ['fraːɡə] die <–, –n> ◊ *eine Frage beantworten* ♦ *Es stehen noch einige Fragen im Raum.* ♦ *Bei Frage vier musste er lange überlegen.* ♦ *Das ist nicht nur eine Frage des Geldes.* ask a question eine Frage stellen raise questions Fragen aufwerfen ⓔ be beyond question außer Zweifel stehen be out of the question nicht infrage kommen call sth into question etw. infrage stellen in question fraglich without question **1.** *(without any doubt)* zweifellos ◊ *Sie ist zweifellos eine sehr schöne Frau.* **2.** *(without asking questions)* bedingungslos ◊ *jdm bedingungslos gehorchen*

question² verb **1.** *(interrogate)* befragen [bəˈfraːɡn̩] <befragt, befragte, hat befragt> ◊ *Zu dem Fall wurden mehrere Zeugen befragt.; (curiously)* ausfragen ['a͜osfraːɡn̩] +haben ◊ *Sie fing an, mich auszufragen, wo ich gestern Abend gewesen sei.* **2.** *(express doubts about)* question (whether) bezweifeln (dass) [bəˈtsva͜efl̩n (das)] <bezweifelt, bezweifelte, hat bezweifelt> ◊ *Bezweifeln Sie seine Aussage?* ♦ *Ich bezweifle, dass sich das Projekt lohnt.; (challenge)* infrage stellen [ɪnˈfraːɡə ʃtɛlən] <stellt, stellte, hat gestellt> ◊ *Ich möchte Ihren Vorschlag nicht infrage stellen, aber …*

questionable adj zweifelhaft ['tsva͜efl̩haft] <zweifelhafter, am zweifelhaftesten> ◊ *Diese Methode finde ich zweifelhaft.* ♦ *Die Ergebnisse der Studie sind äußerst zweifelhaft.* ♦ *ein Mann von zweifelhaftem Ruf* ♦ *zweifelhaftes Verhalten*

question mark noun Fragezeichen ['fraːɡətsa͜eçn̩] das <–s, –> ◊ *Sie machte/setzte auf der Liste ein Fragezeichen neben ihren Namen.*

questionnaire noun Fragebogen ['fraːɡəboːɡn̩] der <–s, –> ◊ *einen Fragebogen ausfüllen*

queue¹ noun Schlange ['ʃlaŋə] die <–, –n> ◊ *Am Eingang bildete sich eine lange Schlange.* ♦ *Er war*

der Letzte in der Schlange. stand in a queue Schlange stehen ◊ *Sie musste in der Bäckerei Schlange stehen.* join the queue sich hinten anstellen ['hɪntn̩ ˌanʃtɛlən] +haben ◊ *Bitte stellen Sie sich hinten an.* jump the queue sich vordrängen ['foːɡdrɛŋən] +haben ◊ *Jemand hat versucht, sich vorzudrängen.*

queue², **queue up** verb queue (up) (for sth) *(für etw.)* anstehen ['anʃteːən] <steht an, stand an, hat angestanden> ◊ *Die Leute standen an der Kasse an.* ♦ *Wir mussten für die Eintrittskarten anstehen.*

quick¹ adj **1.** *(rapid)* schnell [ʃnɛl] ◊ *Er kam mit schnellen Schritten auf mich zu.* ♦ *Seine Bewegungen waren schnell und präzise.* ♦ *Welches ist der schnellste Weg zum Bahnhof?* ♦ *Ich helfe dir. Zu zweit geht's schneller.; (understand easily)* be quick schnell begreifen ['ʃnɛl bəˌɡra͜efn̩] <begreift, begriff, hat begriffen> ◊ *Sie begreift schnell und tut sich leicht beim Lernen.* **2.** *(short)* kurz [kʊɐts] <kürzer, am kürzesten> ◊ *eine kurze Pause machen* ♦ *Er nahm einen kurzen Imbiss zu sich.* ♦ *einen kurzen Blick über die Schulter werfen.* ⓔ be quick schnell machen be quick to do sth etw. sehr schnell tun

quick² adv schnell [ʃnɛl] ◊ *Schnell, mach ein Foto von dem Wagen!* ♦ *Komm schnell her und sieh dir das an!* quick as a flash schnell wie der Blitz

quickly adv **1.** *(fast)* schnell [ʃnɛl] ◊ *so schnell wie möglich* ♦ *Die Geschichte ist schnell erzählt.* ♦ *Sie bemerkte schnell, dass mit ihm etwas nicht stimmte.* ♦ *Schnell, rufen Sie einen Arzt!* go quickly schnell vorbeigehen ◊ *Warum gehen die Ferien immer so schnell vorbei?* **2.** *(briefly)* kurz [kʊɐts] ◊ *Ich muss kurz in die Stadt zum Einkaufen.* ♦ *Lassen Sie mich kurz erklären, was ich meine.*

quick-tempered adj leicht erregbar [ˌla͜eçt ɛɐˈkbaːɐ] <leichter erregbar, am leichtesten erregbar> ◊ *Er ist sehr leicht erregbar.* ♦ *ein leicht erregbarer Mensch*

quid noun Pfund [pfʊnt] das <–(e)s, –e or –> pl *'Pfund' when used with figures* ◊ *Er verdient mindestens 500 Pfund die Woche.*

quiet¹ noun Ruhe ['ruːə] die <–> no pl ◊ *Im Zimmer herrschte absolute Ruhe.* ♦ *Nachts tritt im Haus endlich Ruhe ein.* on the quiet heimlich ['ha͜emlɪç] ◊ *Er hat sich heimlich aus dem Haus geschlichen.*

quiet² adj **1.** *(car, music, voice)* leise ['la͜ezə] <leiser, am leisesten> ◊ *Seid bitte leise, das Baby schläft!* in a quiet voice mit leiser Stimme; *(person, place)* ruhig ['ruːɪç] ◊ *Er ist ein sehr ruhiges Kind* ♦ *sich in eine ruhige Ecke zurückziehen* a room goes quiet im Zimmer wird es ruhig ◊ *Als er hereinkam, wurde es plötzlich ruhig im Zimmer.* **2.** *(not busy, with little activity)* ruhig ['ruːɪç] ◊ *eine ruhige Wohngegend* ♦ *An der Grenze blieb alles ruhig.* **3.** *(not overt)* still [ʃtɪl] ◊ *in stiller Trauer* ♦ *ein stiller Vorwurf* ⓔ keep quiet **1.** *(not say anything)* schweigen ◊ *Wenn ich nichts zu sagen habe, schweige ich.* **2.** *(not argue)* stillhalten ◊ *Sie hat lange stillgehalten, aber jetzt wehrt sie sich.* **3.** *(not tell)* keep quiet about sth, keep sth quiet etw. für sich behalten ◊ *Bitte behalten Sie diese Information für sich.*

quietly adv **1.** *(making little or no noise)* leise ['la͜ezə] <leiser, am leisesten> ◊ *leise lachen* ♦ *Sie schloss leise die Tür.* ♦ *Die beiden unterhielten sich leise.* **2.** *(without being noticed)* in aller Stille [ɪn ale 'ʃtɪlə]

◊ *Sie starb zu Hause in aller Stille.* ♦ *Er hat in aller Stille Geld für das Projekt gesammelt.* quietly confident/optimistic etc. insgeheim zuversichtlich/ optimistisch etc.

[ˌɪnsgəhaɛm ˈtsuːfeːzɪçtlɪç/ɔptiˈmɪstɪʃ] ◊ *Sie ist insgeheim zuversichtlich, dass sie gewinnen wird.*

quietness (noun) **1.** *(silence)* Stille [ˈʃtɪlə] die <–> no pl ◊ *Im Konzertsaal herrschte absolute Stille.* ♦ *eine unheimliche Stille* ♦ *die Stille der Nacht; (noiseless-ness)* Lautlosigkeit [ˈlaʊtloːzɪçkaɛt] die <–> no pl ◊ *Die Lautlosigkeit seiner Schritte war unheimlich.* **2.** *(peacefulness)* Ruhe [ˈruːə] die <–> no pl ◊ *Sie genoss die Ruhe auf dem Land.*

quirk (noun) **1.** *(odd habit)* Marotte [maˈrɔtə] die <–, –n> *(fam)* ◊ *Wir haben alle unsere Marotten.* ♦ *Das ist eine Marotte von ihr.* **2.** *(of fate, nature)* Laune [ˈlaʊnə] die <–, –n> ◊ *Diese Felsformen sind eine Laune der Natur.* ♦ *eine Laune des Schicksals*

quit (verb) **1.** *(a job)* kündigen [ˈkʏndɪgn̩] +haben ◊ *Ich habe genug von diesem Stress. Ich kündige!* ♦ *Sie will ihre Stelle kündigen und nach Australien aus-wandern.; (school)* verlassen [fɛˈlasn̩] <verlässt, verließ, hat verlassen> ◊ *Er verließ mit 17 die Schule und suchte sich eine Arbeit.* **2.** *(stop)* quit (sth) (mit etw.) aufhören [ˈaʊfhøːrən] +haben ◊ *Ich will mit dem Tennisspielen aufhören.* ♦ *Er hört demnächst als Trainer auf.* quit doing sth aufhören, etw. zu tun ◊ *Hör auf, ihn anzuschreien!* ♦ *Sie will aufhören zu rauchen.* **3.** give sb notice to quit jdm kündigen [ˈkʏndɪgn̩] +haben ◊ *Mein Vermieter hat mir letzte Woche gekündigt.*

quite (adv) **1.** *(relatively)* ziemlich [ˈtsiːmlɪç] ◊ *Sie sehen sich ziemlich oft.* ♦ *Er war ziemlich schwer verletzt.* quite a few/lot ziemlich viele/viel for quite a long time ziemlich lange quite a good singer etc. ein ziemlich guter Sänger etc. sb quite likes sth etw. gefällt jdm ganz gut [gəfɛlt … gants ˈguːt] <gefällt, gefiel, hat gefallen> ◊ *Dieses Bild gefällt mir ganz gut.* **2.** *(completely)* ganz [gants] ◊ *Es ist ganz anders, als du denkst.* ♦ *Ich verstehe nicht ganz, was du meinst.* ♦ *„Bist du fertig?" — „Noch nicht ganz."* ♦ *Keine Angst, das geht ganz einfach.; (used for emphasis)* völlig [ˈfœlɪç] ◊ *Es ist völlig unmöglich, bei diesem Wetter in die Berge zu gehen.* ♦ *Ich stimme völlig mit Ihnen überein.* **3.** *(indeed)* quite a, quite some wirklich [ˈvɪrklɪç] ◊ *Das war wirklich eine Überraschung!* ♦ *Sie ist wirklich eine Schönheit.* quite the best wirklich der/die/das beste … ◊ *Das ist wirklich der beste Kuchen, den ich je gegessen habe!* quite a shock/disappointment etc. ein ziemli-cher Schock/eine ziemliche Enttäuschung etc. [aɛn tsiːmlɪçɐ ˈʃɔk/aɛnə tsiːmlɪçə ɛntˈtɔʏʃʊŋ] ◊ *Das war ein ziemlicher Schock für sie.* It was quite a party! Das war vielleicht eine Party! He is quite the gentleman now. Er ist jetzt ganz der feine Herr. quite the opposite ganz im Gegenteil

[gants ɪm ˈgeːgn̩taɛl] ◊ *„Hat sie sich gefreut?" — „Nein, ganz im Gegenteil, sie fing an zu weinen."* **4.** *(not exactly)* not quite nicht genau [ˌnɪçt gəˈnaʊ] ◊ *Ich konnte mich nicht genau erinnern, wo sie wohnt.* **5.** *(expressing agreement)* quite (so) sehr richtig [zeːɐ ˈrɪçtɪç] ◊ *„Sicherheit ist unser oberstes Ziel." — „Sehr richtig."*

ⓔ that's quite all right **1.** *(in response to an apology)* das macht nichts ◊ *„Oh, das tut mir Leid!" — „Das macht nichts."* **2.** *(in response to "thank you")* bitte schön ◊ *„Vielen herzlichen Dank!" — „Bitte schön!"*

quiz (noun) Quiz [kvɪs] das <–, –> ◊ *ein Quiz machen* ♦ *an einem Quiz teilnehmen*

quota (noun) **1.** *(permitted amount)* Quote [ˈkvoːtə] die <–, –n> ◊ *eine Quote für etw. einführen* ♦ *eine Quote erreichen; (usual amount)* Quantum [ˈkvantʊm] das <–s, Quanten> ◊ *Ich habe mein tägliches Quantum Kaffee heute schon gehabt.* **2.** *(of work)* Pensum [ˈpɛnzʊm] das <–s, Pensen or Pensa> ◊ *sein tägliches Pensum erledigen/erfüllen*

quotation (noun) **1.** *(written)* Zitat [tsiˈtaːt] das <–(e)s, –e> ◊ *Bitte geben Sie genau an, woher die Zitate stammen.* ♦ *etw. mit einem Zitat belegen* **2.** *(estimated price)* Kostenvoranschlag [ˌkɔstn̩ˈfoːɐʃlaːk] der <–(e)s, Kostenvoranschläge> ◊ *Bitte machen Sie mir einen Kostenvoranschlag für die Renovierung.*

quotation mark (noun) Anführungszeichen [ˈanfyːrʊŋstsaɛçn̩] das <–s, –> most pl ◊ *„Pop" steht in Anführungszeichen.* put sth in quotation marks etw. in Anführungszeichen setzen

quote¹ (noun) **1.** *(written)* Zitat [tsiˈtaːt] das <–(e)s, –e> ◊ *Woher stammt dieses Zitat?* **2.** *(estimated price)* Kostenvoranschlag [ˌkɔstn̩ˈfoːɐʃlaːk] der <–(e)s, Kostenvoranschläge> ◊ *Bitte machen Sie mir einen Kostenvoranschlag für die Renovierung.* **3.** *(fam)* quotes Anführungszeichen [ˈanfyːrʊŋstsaɛçn̩] die <–> pl ◊ *„Produkt" steht in Anführungszeichen.*

quote² (verb) **1.** *(a text, author etc.)* zitieren [tsiˈtiːrən] <zitiert, zitierte, hat zitiert> ◊ *jdn/etw.* wörtlich/ sinngemäß zitieren ♦ *Ich zitiere aus dem aktuellen Bericht: …* ♦ *einen Satz zitieren* ♦ *Hier zitiere ich den Präsidenten selbst: …* sb is quoted as saying sth jd soll etw. gesagt haben [zɔl … gəˌzaːkt haːbm̩] ◊ *Er soll gesagt haben, dass er zurücktreten will.* **2.** *(cite)* anführen [ˈanfyːrən] +haben ◊ *Er führte das Beispiel einer Frau an, der man aus dem Fahrrad-korb die Handtasche gestohlen hatte.* **3.** *(a price)* verlangen [fɛˈlaŋən] <verlangt, verlangte, hat verlangt> ◊ *Wie viel verlangen Sie für die Reparatur?*

♦ quote … unquote Zitat … Zitatende ◊ *Er sagte, Zitat: „Ich bin dafür nicht verantwortlich.", Zitatende.*

R

r, R [noun] r, R [ɛʳ] das <–(s), –(s)> ◊ *Dieses Wort wird mit einem kleinen r/großen R geschrieben.* ♦ *R wie Richard*

rabbit [noun] Kaninchen [ka'niːnçən] das <–s, –> ◊ *Sie haben drei Kaninchen zu Hause.* ♦ *Es gibt Kaninchen zum Mittagessen.*

rabbit on [verb] quasseln ['kvasl̩n] +haben *(fam, esp pej)* ◊ *Diese Frau quasselt die ganze Zeit!*

race¹ [noun] **1.** *(competition)* Rennen ['rɛnən] das <–s, –> ◊ *ein Rennen gewinnen/verlieren* ♦ *Die beiden lieferten sich ein spannendes Rennen.* race for Rennen um ◊ *das Rennen um die Präsidentschaft; (of horses)* the races Pferderennen ['pfeːɐdərɛnən] ◊ *Sie waren gestern beim Pferderennen.* **2.** *(ethnic group, species)* Rasse ['rasə] die <–, –n> ◊ *Niemand darf aufgrund seiner Rasse diskriminiert werden.* ♦ *ein Pferd von edler Rasse* the human race die menschliche Rasse ⊛ **a race against time** ein Wettlauf mit der Zeit

race² [verb] **1.** *(take part in a race)* laufen ['laʊfn̩] <läuft, lief, ist gelaufen> ◊ *Wie viele Pferde werden am Sonntag laufen?* race against sb gegen jdn laufen race sb mit jdm um die Wette laufen; *(in a vehicle)* mit jdm um die Wette fahren [mɪt ... ʊm diː 'vɛtə faːɐn] <fährt, fuhr, ist gefahren> **2.** *(move very quickly, be very quick)* rasen ['raːzn̩] +sein ◊ *Sie raste zur Tür, als es klingelte.* ♦ *Plötzlich raste ein Wagen um die Ecke.* ♦ *Die Zeit rast nur so.* ♦ *Sein Herz/Puls raste.* race sb somewhere mit jdm irgendwohin rasen

racetrack [noun] Rennbahn ['rɛnbaːn] die <–, –en>

racial [adj] **1.** *(between people of different races)* Rassen... ['rasn̩] racial discrimination Rassendiskriminierung ['rasn̩dɪskrimi,niːrʊŋ] die <–, –en> racial prejudice Rassenvorurteil ['rasn̩foːɐˌʊɐ,taɪl] das <–s, –e> **2.** *(relating to sb's race)* ethnisch ['ɛtnɪʃ] no comp/superl ◊ *einer bestimmten ethnischen Gruppe/Minderheit angehören* ♦ *Kinder unterschiedlicher ethnischer Herkunft*

racing driver [noun] Rennfahrer ['rɛnfaːrɐ] der <–s, –> ♀Rennfahrerin ['rɛnfaːrərɪn] die <–, –nen> ◊ *Michael Schumacher ist der bekannteste Rennfahrer Deutschlands.* ♦ *Sie wäre am liebsten Rennfahrerin.*

racism [noun] Rassismus [ra'sɪsmʊs] der <–> no pl ◊ *ein Opfer von Rassismus werden*

racist [adj] rassistisch [ra'sɪstɪʃ] ◊ *Ihre Anspielung auf seine Hautfarbe war rassistisch.* ♦ *rassistische Propaganda*

rack [noun] **1.** *(stand for clothes, CDs etc.)* Ständer ['ʃtɛndɐ] der <–s, –> ◊ *Sie sah sich die Kleider auf dem Ständer an.* ♦ *eine CD in den Ständer stellen; (shelves)* Regal [re'gaːl] das <–s, –e> ◊ *Sie legte die Zeitschrift zurück ins Regal.* wine rack Weinregal ['vaɪnreˌgaːl] der *(for plates, dishes etc.)* Gestell [gə'ʃtɛl] das <–(e)s, –e>; *(on a bicycle, car)* Gepäckträger [gə'pɛktrɛːgɐ] der <–s, –> ◊ *Das Fahrrad hatte keinen Gepäckträger.; (for luggage)* Gepäcknetz

[gə'pɛknɛts] das <–es, –e> ◊ *Sie legte ihre Tasche ins Gepäcknetz.* **2.** *(instrument of torture)* Folterbank ['fɔltebaŋk] die <–, Folterbänke> ◊ *Er fühlte sich wie auf der Folterbank.* ⊛ **go to rack and ruin** vor die Hunde gehen *(fam)* put sb on the rack jdn auf die Folter spannen

racket [noun] **1.** *(noise)* Krach [krax] der <–(e)s> no pl ◊ *Macht doch nicht so einen Krach!* **2.** SPORT *(for tennis, badminton)* Schläger ['ʃlɛːgɐ] der <–s, –> **3.** *(dishonest business)* ... racket ...geschäft [gə'ʃɛft] das <–(e)s, –e> drugs racket Drogengeschäft ['droːgŋ̩gəˌʃɛft] ◊ *im Drogengeschäft/sein* smuggling racket Schmuggelgeschäft ['ʃmʊglgəˌʃɛft]

radar [noun] Radar [ra'daːʳ] das or der <–s> no pl ◊ *die Verkehrsüberwachung mit Radar* ♦ *Ein unbekanntes Flugobjekt wurde vom Radar erfasst.* radar trap Radarfalle [ra'daːʳfalə] die <–, –n> ◊ *in eine Radarfalle geraten*

radiate [verb] **1.** *(heat, light etc.)* ausstrahlen ['aʊsʃtraːlən] +haben ◊ *Wärme ausstrahlen* ♦ *das helle Licht, das die Sonne ausstrahlt* sth radiates from sb jd strahlt etw. aus ◊ *Sie strahlte Zufriedenheit aus.* **2.** *(lines, roads etc.)* radiate from sth strahlenförmig von etw. ausgehen [,ʃtraːlənfœˈmɪç fɔn ... ,aʊsgeːən] <geht aus, ging aus, ist ausgegangen> ◊ *Von dem Denkmal gehen strahlenförmig mehrere Straßen aus.*

radiation [noun] *(rays, heat, light)* Strahlung ['ʃtraːlʊŋ] die <–, –en> ◊ *einer hohen Strahlung ausgesetzt sein* ◊ *Strahlung in tödlicher Dosis* ♦ *elektromagnetische/ultraviolette Strahlung; (in compound ns)* radiation ... Strahlen... ['ʃtraːlən] radiation injury Strahlenschäden ['ʃtraːlənʃɛːdn̩] die <–> pl ◊ *Einige Arbeiter erlitten Strahlenschäden.* radiation therapy Strahlenbehandlung ['ʃtraːlənbəhandlʊŋ] die <–, –en> ◊ *sich einer Strahlenbehandlung unterziehen*

radiator [noun] **1.** *(for heating)* Heizkörper ['haɪtskœʳpe] der <–s, –> ◊ *die Heizkörper andrehen/ausdrehen/zurückdrehen* ♦ *Der Heizkörper wird nicht warm.* **2.** *(of a car)* Kühler ['kyːle] der <–s, –> ◊ *Der Kühler darf nicht zu heiß werden.*

radical [noun] Radikale [radi'kaːlə] der/die <–(n), Radikalen> but: *ein Radikaler/ein Radikale* ◊ *Eine Gruppe junger Radikaler demonstrierte in der Innenstadt.*

radical(ly) [adj, adv] **1.** *(extreme)* radikal [radi'kaːl] ◊ *Er forderte eine radikale Umkehr in der Wirtschaftspolitik.* ♦ *Ihre Position in der Ausländerfrage ist radikal.* ♦ *Diese Technologie wird unser Leben radikal verändern.* **2.** *(fundamental)* fundamental [fʊndamɛn'taːl] ◊ *ein fundamentaler Unterschied* ♦ *Die beiden Ansätze unterscheiden sich fundamental.*

radio¹ [noun] **1.** *(piece of electronic equipment, activity of broadcasting)* Radio ['raːdio] das <–s, –s> ◊ *ein tragbares Radio* ♦ *Sie schaltete das Radio ein/aus.* ♦ *Ich habe davon im Radio gehört.* ♦ *Die Sendung wird im Radio übertragen.* ♦ *Radio Bremen* **2.** *(system for*

A B C D E F G H I J K L M N O P Q R S T U V W X Y Z

sending and receiving messages) Funk [fʊŋk] der <–s> *seldom with the article, no pl ◊ Haben Sie Funk an Bord?* by radio über Funk ◊ *jdn über Funk erreichen/verständigen; (piece of equipment)* Funkgerät ['fʊŋkɡəreːt] das <–(e)s, –e> ◊ *Der Mann hatte ein Funkgerät bei sich.*

radio² [verb] funken ['fʊŋkn̩] +haben ◊ *SOS/einen Hilferuf funken ♦ Der Pilot funkte, dass alles in Ordnung sei.*

radioactive(ly) [adj, adv] radioaktiv [radio|ak'tiːf] *no comp/superl ◊ Das Wasser, das den Reaktorkern verlässt, ist radioaktiv. ♦ Wohin mit dem radioaktiven Müll? ♦ Die Gegend ist radioaktiv verseucht.*

radish [noun] *(general)* Rettich ['rɛtɪç] der <–s, –e> ◊ *Rettich schneiden und salzen; (smaller)* Radieschen [ra'diːsçən] das <–s, –> ◊ *Sie isst gern Butterbrot mit Radieschen.*

radius [noun] 1. MATH Radius ['raːdiʊs] der <–, Radien> ◊ *Wie berechnet man den Radius eines Kreises?* within a 200 metres/2 miles etc. radius *(of sth)* in einem Umkreis von 200 Metern/zwei Meilen etc. *(von etw.)* [ɪn aɛnəm ˌʊmkraɛs fɔn ˌtsvaehʊndət 'meːtən/tsvaɛ 'maɛlən] ◊ *Die Explosion war in einem Umkreis von 60 Kilometern zu hören.* 2. ANAT Speiche ['ʃpaɛçə] die <–, –n> ◊ *Sie brach sich bei dem Sturz Elle und Speiche des linken Arms.*

rag [noun] 1. *(cloth)* Lumpen ['lʊmpn̩] der <–s, –> ◊ *Nimm einen Lumpen und wisch den Dreck weg.* in rags in Lumpen ◊ *in Lumpen gekleidet sein ♦ Ein Mann in Lumpen saß an der Straße und bettelte.* 2. *(fam) (newspaper)* Käseblatt ['kɛːzəblat] das <–(e)s, Käseblätter> *(fam) ◊ Was in diesem Käseblatt steht, brauchst du nicht zu glauben.* 3. MUS Rag [rɛk] der <–s, –s> ◊ *einen Rag spielen* ℗ **go from rags to riches** vom armen Schlucker zum reichen Mann/zur reichen Frau werden

rage¹ [noun] Wut [vuːt] die <–> *no pl ◊ Tränen der Wut stiegen ihr in die Augen. ♦ Ich musste in ohnmächtiger Wut zusehen. ♦ Außer sich vor Wut/Voller Wut schlug sie die Tür zu.* fly into a rage einen Wutanfall bekommen [aɛnən 'vuːt|anfal bəkɔmən] <bekommt, bekam, hat bekommen> ℗ **all the rage** der letzte Schrei *(fam) ◊ Solche Hosen sind zurzeit der letzte Schrei.*

rage² [verb] toben ['toːbm̩] +haben ◊ *„Der kann was erleben!", tobte sie. ♦ Stundenlang tobte ein Sturm ums Haus. ♦ In der Hauptstadt toben Straßenkämpfe.*

ragged [adj] 1. *(clothing, person)* zerlumpt [tsɛ'lʊmpt] <zerlumpter, am zerlumptesten> ◊ *ein Bettler in zerlumpter Kleidung ♦ ein zerlumpter alter Mann* 2. *(edge)* ausgefranst ['aosɡəfranst] <ausgefranster, am ausgefranstesten> ◊ *ausgefranste Ränder; (coastline)* zerklüftet [tsɛ'klʏftət] ◊ *eine zerklüftete Felsenküste* 3. *(performance)* stümperhaft ['ʃtʏmpɐhaft] <stümperhafter, am stümperhaftesten> ◊ *Das war gestern ein recht stümperhafter Auftritt.* 4. *(breathing)* unregelmäßig ['ʊnreːɡl̩mɛːsɪç] ◊ *unregelmäßige Atemzüge* ℗ **run sb ragged** jdn an den Rand der Erschöpfung bringen

raging [adj] *(pain, fever, storm, emotion)* heftig ['hɛftɪç] ◊ *Sie hatte heftige Schmerzen. ♦ Draußen tobte ein heftiger Sturm.; (thirst)* brennend ['brɛnənt] ◊ *brennenden Durst verspüren; (river, torrent etc.)* reißend ['raɛsn̩t] ◊ *ein reißender Gebirgsbach/Fluss*

raid¹ [noun] 1. MIL raid *(on sb/sth)* Angriff *(auf/gegen jdn/etw.)* ['anɡrɪf] der <–(e)s, –e> ◊ *einen Angriff auf feindliche Stellungen ausführen ♦ Angriffe auf verschiedene Ziele* air raid Luftangriff ['lʊft|anɡrɪf] 2. *(by the police)* Razzia ['ratsiaː] die <–, Razzien or seldom –s> ◊ *In der Diskothek wurde eine Razzia auf Dealer gemacht.* 3. *(by thieves)* raid *(on sb/sth)* Überfall *(auf jdn/etw.)* ['yːbɐfal] der <–(e)s, Überfälle> ◊ *einen Überfall auf eine Bank verüben*

raid² [verb] 1. *(police)* raid sth irgendwo eine Razzia durchführen [aɛnə 'ratsiaː dʊɐ̯çfyːrən] +haben ◊ *In der Disco/Auf der Feier wurde eine Razzia durchgeführt.* 2. *(attack suddenly)* überfallen [ybɐ'falən] <überfällt, überfiel, hat überfallen> ◊ *Das Dorf wird immer wieder von feindlichen Stämmen überfallen.* 3. *(steal)* plündern ['plʏndɐn] +haben ◊ *Jemand hat den Geldschrank geplündert. ♦ Die Gäste plünderten das Büffet.*

rail [noun] 1. *(for clothing)* Stange ['ʃtaŋə] die <–, –n> ◊ *einen Kleiderbügel an die Stange hängen* towel rail Handtuchhalter ['hanttuːxhaltɐ] der <–s, –> ◊ *ein Handtuch zum Trocknen über den Handtuchhalter hängen; (on stairs, a bridge)* Geländer [ɡə'lɛndɐ] das <–s, –> ◊ *sich am Geländer festhalten; (on a ship)* Reling ['reːlɪŋ] die <–, –s or seldom –> most sing ◊ *sich über die Reling beugen; (fence)* rails Umzäunung [ʊm'tsɔɔnʊŋ] die <–, –en> ◊ *Bitte bleiben Sie innerhalb der Umzäunung.* 2. *(track for trains)* Schiene ['ʃiːnə] die <–, –n> ◊ *Schienen verlegen ♦ Ein Zug ist aus den Schienen gesprungen.* 3. *(rail travel, railway)* Bahn [baːn] die <–, –en> ◊ *Die Bahn ist ein umweltfreundliches Verkehrsmittel.* travel by rail mit der Bahn fahren

railing [noun] *(on a bridge, stairs)* Geländer [ɡə'lɛndɐ] das <–s, –> ◊ *sich gegen/über das Geländer lehnen ♦ Er hielt sich am Geländer fest.; (on a ship)* Reling ['reːlɪŋ] die <–, –s or seldom –> most sing ◊ *Sie stand an der Reling und winkte. ♦ sich über die Reling beugen; (fence)* railing(s) Zaun [tsaɔn] der <–(e)s, Zäune> ◊ *über den Zaun klettern*

railroad [noun] Eisenbahn ['aɛzn̩baːn] die <–, –en>

railway [noun] 1. railway *(line)* Eisenbahnlinie ['aɛznbaːnliːniə] die <–, –n> ◊ *Diese Eisenbahnlinie ist schon lange stillgelegt.* railway bridge Eisenbahnbrücke ['aɛznbaːnbrʏkə] die <–, –n> railway carriage Eisenbahnwagen ['aɛznbaːnvaːɡn̩] der <–s, –> 2. *(company, system)* the railway(s) die Eisenbahn [diː 'aɛznbaːn] <–, –en> ◊ *die Züge der Transsibirischen Eisenbahn* travel by railway mit der Eisenbahn fahren

railway station [noun] Bahnhof ['baːnhoːf] der <–(e)s, Bahnhöfe> ◊ *Hält der am nächsten Bahnhof? ♦ Könnten Sie mich zum Bahnhof bringen? ♦ ein Restaurant im Bahnhof*

rain¹ [noun] Regen ['reːɡn̩] der <–s> *no pl ◊ Morgen zeitweise Regen. ♦ Im/Bei Regen mag ich nicht spazieren gehen.* heavy/torrential/light rain heftiger/strömender/leichter Regen ◊ *Ich habe zwei Stunden im strömenden Regen gewartet.* acid rain saurer Regen drop of rain Regentropfen ['reːɡn̩trɔpfn̩] der <–s, –> ◊ *Sie verspürte einen Regentropfen im Gesicht.* the rains die Regenzeit [diː 'reːɡn̩tsaɛt] <–, –en> ◊ *Wann beginnt wieder die Regenzeit?* ℗ **come rain or shine** 1. *(in all weathers)* ob es

regnet oder schneit ◊ *Mit einem Hund muss man täglich raus, ob es regnet oder schneit.* **2.** *(fig) (no matter what happens)* was auch geschieht ◊ *Ich stehe zu dir, was auch geschieht.*

rain² [verb] **1.** METEO regnen ['reːɡnən] <regnet, regnete, hat geregnet> ◊ *Gestern hat es den ganzen Tag geregnet.* ✦ *leicht/stark regnen* **2.** rain (down) on sth auf etw. hageln [aͻf … haːɡln] +sein ◊ *Bomben hagelten auf die Stadt.* rain (down) on sb auf jdn niederhageln [aͻf … ˌniːdehaːɡln] +sein ◊ *Dutzende von Schlägen hagelten auf ihn nieder.*

rainbow [noun] Regenbogen ['reːɡnboːɡn] der <–s, –>
rainforest [noun] Regenwald ['reːɡnvalt] der <–(e)s, Regenwälder> ◊ *die tropischen Regenwälder*

raise [verb] **1.** *(lift)* heben ['heːbm̩] <hebt, hob, hat gehoben> ◊ *den Arm/die Hand heben* ✦ *Er hob das Glas und brachte einen Toast aus.* ✦ *Lasten mit einem Kran heben; (into an upright position)* aufrichten ['aͻfrɪçtn̩] <richtet auf, richtete auf, hat aufgerichtet> ◊ *Es kostete einige Mühe, das Gerüst wieder aufzurichten.; (with effort)* raise yourself sich erheben [ɛ'heːbm̩] <erhebt sich, erhob sich, hat sich erhoben> ◊ *Sie schaffte es kaum, sich vom Boden/Stuhl zu erheben.* **2.** *(increase)* erhöhen [ɛ'høːən] <erhöht, erhöhte, hat erhöht> ◊ *Die Benzinpreise sind schon wieder erhöht worden.* ✦ *Der Beitragssatz wird (um zwei Prozent) erhöht.* ✦ *Die Altersgrenze für den Waffenerwerb wurde erhöht.* ✦ *die Qualität eines Produkts erhöhen* ✦ *Die Produktion kann noch weiter erhöht werden.* **3.** *(money)* zusammenbringen [ʦu'zamənbrɪŋən] <bringt zusammen, brachte zusammen, hat zusammengebracht> ◊ *das Geld für ein neues Auto zusammenbringen* **4.** *(a problem, question)* aufwerfen ['aͻfvɛrfn̩] <wirft auf, warf auf, hat aufgeworfen> ◊ *Dieser Unfall wirft eine Menge Fragen auf.* ✦ *Ihr unkollegiales Verhalten wirft Probleme auf.; (an objection)* erheben [ɛ'heːbm̩] <erhebt, erhob, hat erhoben> ◊ *Niemand erhob einen Einwand.* **5.** *(doubts, fears etc.)* hervorrufen [hɛ'foːɐruːfn̩] <ruft hervor, rief hervor, hat hervorgerufen> ◊ *Der Vorfall rief Zweifel an der Sicherheit des Produkts hervor.* **6.** *(children, animals)* großziehen ['groːsʦiːən] <zieht groß, zog groß, hat großgezogen> ◊ *ein Kind allein großziehen* ✦ *ein Kälbchen mit der Flasche großziehen* raise a family Kinder großziehen; *(crops)* anbauen ['anbaͻən] +haben ◊ *Sie baut seit Jahren Mais an.* **7.** *(form) (a statue, building)* errichten [ɛ'rɪçtn̩] <errichtet, errichtete, hat errichtet> ◊ *ein Gebäude/Denkmal errichten* **8.** *(lit) (wake up)* wecken ['vɛkŋ̍] +haben ◊ *Am Morgen wurde er vom Zwitschern der Vögel geweckt.* **9.** MATH raise a number to the power of 2/3 etc. eine Zahl in die zweite/ dritte etc. Potenz erheben [aͣnə ˌtsaːl ɪn diː ˌtsvaͤtə/ˌdrɪtə po'tɛnts ɛheːbm̩] <erhebt, erhob, hat erhoben> ◊ *Erhebt man 3 in die dritte Potenz, erhält man 27.* **10.** *(an embargo, siege)* aufheben ['aͻfheːbm̩] <hebt auf, hob auf, hat aufgehoben> ◊ *Sanktionen aufheben* **11.** raise your voice laut werden ['laͻt veːɐdn̩] +sein

raised → raise² [adj] **1.** *(area, surface)* erhöht [ɛ'høːt] no comp/superl ◊ *etw. auf einer erhöhten Tafel präsentieren* ✦ *Hier ist der Boden leicht erhöht.; (arm, leg)* angehoben ['angəhoːbm̩] no comp/superl ◊ *leicht angehobene Arme; (tail, finger)* erhoben [ɛ'hoːbm̩] no comp/superl ◊ *mit erhobenem Zeigefinger* **2.** *(temperature, pressure)* erhöht [ɛ'høːt] no comp/superl ◊

Wie reagiert die Substanz auf erhöhte Temperaturen? **3.** *(voice)* laut [laͻt] <lauter, am lautesten> ◊ *Aus dem Flur hörte man laute Stimmen.*

raisin [noun] Rosine [ro'ziːnə] die <–, –n> ◊ *ein Kuchen mit Rosinen*

rake [noun] **1.** *(tool)* Harke ['haͬkə] die <–, –n> ◊ *den Boden mit der Harke glätten* **2.** *(oldf) (hedonistic man)* Lebemann ['leːbəman] der <–(e)s, Lebemänner> *(fam)*

rally¹ [noun] **1.** *(gathering)* Versammlung [fɛ'zamlʊŋ] die <–, –en> ◊ *eine geheime/öffentliche/politische Versammlung von Tierversuchsgegnern* hold a rally eine Versammlung abhalten; *(with a speaker)* Kundgebung ['kʊntgeːbʊŋ] die <–, –en> ◊ *Ich war auf einer Kundgebung.* peace rally Friedenskundgebung ['friːdn̩skʊntgeːbʊŋ] ◊ *an einer Friedenskundgebung teilnehmen* **2.** *(car race)* Rallye ['rɛliː] die <–, –s> ◊ *eine Rallye fahren/gewinnen* **3.** SPORT *(in tennis)* Ballwechsel ['balvɛksl̩] der <–s, –> ◊ *ein spannender Ballwechsel* **4.** *(of prices)* Anstieg ['anʃtiːk] der <–(e)s> no pl ◊ *Wir erwarten einen baldigen Anstieg des Preises.* **5.** *(of health)* Erholung [ɛ'hoːlʊŋ] die <–> no pl ◊ *Alle waren erleichtert über ihre rasche Erholung.*

rally² [verb] **1.** *(people, troops)* rally sb jdn versammeln [fɛ'zamln̩] <versammelt, versammelte, hat versammelt> ◊ *Er versammelt seine Anhänger um sich.* sb rallies jd versammelt sich [fɛ'zamlt] <versammelt sich, versammelte sich, hat sich versammelt> ◊ *Die Menschen versammelten sich um ihren Anführer.* rally to sb's support jdm in Scharen zu Hilfe eilen [ɪn faːrən tsu: 'hɪlfə aͤlən] +sein ◊ *Die Leute eilten ihm in Scharen zu Hilfe.* **2.** FIN *(prices)* sich erholen [ɛ'hoːlən] <erholt sich, erholte sich, hat sich erholt> ◊ *Nach der Krise erholten sich die Preise langsam wieder.* **3.** *(after an illness, setback etc.)* Fortschritte machen ['fͻɐtʃrɪtə maxn̩] +haben ◊ *Die Patientin macht nach dem Eingriff nur langsam Fortschritte.*

ram [noun] **1.** ZOO Widder ['vɪdɐ] der <–s, –> **2.** *(for battering, part of a machine)* Rammbock ['rambͻk] der <–(e)s, Rammböcke> ◊ *eine Tür mit dem Rammbock aufbrechen*

ramp [noun] **1.** *(for access)* Rampe ['rampə] die <–, –n> ◊ *eine Rampe für Behinderte* **2.** *(on a plane)* (boarding) ramp Gangway ['gɛnveː] die <–, –s> ◊ *ein Flugzeug über die Gangway betreten/ verlassen* **3.** *(speed bump)* Bodenschwelle ['boːdn̩ʃvɛlə] die <–, –n> ◊ *Am Anfang der Spielstraße waren mehrere Bodenschwellen.* **4.** Beware ramp! Vorsicht, unebene Fahrbahn! ['foːɐzɪçt ˌʊnˌeːbənə 'faːɐbaːn] **5.** *(for joining a motorway)* Autobahnauffahrt ['aͻtobaːnˌaͻffaːɐt] die <–, –en> ◊ *auf der Autobahnauffahrt stark beschleunigen*

random(ly) [adj, adv] willkürlich ['vɪlkyːɐlɪç] ◊ *eine willkürliche Auswahl/Einteilung* ✦ *Die Reihenfolge der Zahlen ist willkürlich.* ✦ *willkürlich ausgewählte Zuschauer* ☺ **at random** *(speak, walk)* aufs Geratewohl ◊ *Sie lief aufs Geratewohl in den Wald hinein.; (shoot)* ziellos ◊ *Der Mann schoss ziellos in die Menge.; (take)* wahllos ◊ *Sie nahm wahllos einen Zettel aus der Kiste.*

randy [adj] geil [gaͤl] *(rude, pej)* ◊ *Ihn geil machen* ✦ *So ein geiler alter Bock!*

range¹ [noun] **1.** *(selection)* Reihe ['raͤə] die <–, –n>

◊ *jdm eine Reihe von Fragen stellen* ♦ *Wir wollen uns mit einer Reihe interessanter Themen befassen.*; *(of products)* Sortiment [zɔrˈtiˈmɛnt] das <-(e)s, -e> ◊ *Testen Sie unser neues Sortiment an Pflegeprodukten.* ♦ *ein breites/reichhaltiges Sortiment anbieten*; *(of patterns, models)* Auswahl [ˈaosvaːl] die <-> no pl ◊ *Die Auswahl an günstigen Computern ist groß.* ♦ **nur in begrenzter Auswahl erhältlich** a wide range **eine große Auswahl**; *(of colo(u)rs)* Skala [ˈskaːlaː] die <-, Skalen> ◊ *Die Skala der Rottöne reicht von einem blassen Rosa bis zu Tiefrot.* price range **Preisklasse** [ˈprɛsklasə] die <-, -n> ◊ *In dieser Preisklasse haben wir drei Parfums vorrätig.* temperature range **Temperaturbereich** [tɛmpəraˈtuːɡbaraeç] der <-(e)s, -e> ◊ *Diese Pflanze fühlt sich in einem Temperaturbereich von 18 bis 22 Grad wohl.* vocal range **Stimmumfang** [ˈʃtɪmˌʊmfaŋ] der <-(e)s, Stimmumfänge> *most sing* ◊ *Sie hat einen Stimmumfang von fast vier Oktaven.* **2.** *(domain, sphere)* Kompetenz [kɔmpeˈtɛnts] die <-, -en> ◊ *Die Entscheidung liegt außerhalb der Kompetenz dieser Abteilung/dieses Beamten.* **3.** *(of a missile, gun, transmitter)* Reichweite [ˈraeçvaetə] die <-, -n> ◊ *Der Griff ist nicht in meiner Reichweite.* ♦ *eine Rakete mit einer Reichweite von 1300 Kilometern* out of range **außer Reichweite** within shouting range in Hörweite [ɪn ˈhøːɡvaetə] ◊ *Er forderte die Kinder auf, beim Spielen in Hörweite zu bleiben.* at close range **aus der Nähe** [aos deːɡ ˈnɛːə] ◊ *Es war interessant, einen Elefanten mal aus der Nähe zu betrachten.* **4.** *(shooting)* range Schießplatz [ˈʃiːsplats] der <-es, Schießplätze> ◊ *auf dem Schießplatz üben* **5.** *(for cattle)* Weideland [ˈvaedəlant] das <-(e)s> no pl ◊ *Zur Farm gehören mehrere Hektar Weideland.* **6.** *(in the US: cooking stove)* Herd [heːɡt] der <-(e)s, -e> ◊ *Er stand am Herd und kochte für die Familie.* **7.** mountain range Bergkette [ˈbɛrkkɛtə] die <-, -n> ◊ *Hinter dem See erhob sich eine mächtige Bergkette.*

range² [verb] **1.** *(extend)* range from sth to sth **zwischen etw.** [dat] **und etw.** [dat] **liegen** [ˈtsvɪʃn ... ʊnt ... liːɡn] <liegt, lag, hat gelegen> ◊ *Die Preise für diese Hüte liegen zwischen 15 und 150 Euro.*; *(interests, offers)* range from sth to sth **von etw. bis zu etw. reichen** [fɔn ... bɪs tsu: ... raeçn] +haben ◊ *Seine Interessen reichen vom Reiten bis zum Golfspielen.* range over sth **sich über etw.** [acc] **erstrecken** [yːbe ... ɛʃtrɛkŋ] <erstreckt sich, erstreckte sich, hat sich erstreckt> ◊ *Sein Wissen erstreckt sich über ein weites Gebiet.* **2.** *(roam over)* range (over) an area etc. **ein Gebiet durchstreifen** [aen ɡəˈbiːt dʊrçˌʃtraefn] <durchstreift, durchstreifte, hat durchstreift> ◊ *Die Tiere durchstreifen das ganze Gebiet.* ♦ *Er durchstreifte den Wald auf der Suche nach seinem Hund.* **3.** *(place in a row)* aufstellen [ˈaofʃtɛlən] +haben ◊ *Er stellte die Bücher ordentlich im Regal auf.* **4.** *(support)* range yourself with sb **sich auf jds Seite stellen** [aof ... ˈzaetə ʃtɛlən] +haben ◊ *Alle Mitglieder stellten sich auf die Seite des Vorsitzenden.* range yourself against sb **sich gegen jdn stellen**

rank¹ [noun] **1.** *(within a hierarchy)* Rang [raŋ] der <-(e)s, Ränge> ◊ *den Rang eines Generals erlangen* ♦ *einen hohen Rang in der Regierung/Armee haben/einnehmen* ♦ *Die deutschen Teilnehmer belegten die Ränge 10 und 12.*; *(social class)* Schicht [ʃɪçt] die <-, -en> ◊ *Leute aus allen Schichten* people of high rank **hochgestellte Persönlichkeiten** [ˌhoːxɡəʃtɛltə pɛrˈzøːnlɪçkaetn] die <-> pl of the first rank **erstklassig** [ˈeːɡstklasɪç] ◊ *ein erstklassiger Sänger* **2.** *(row)* Reihe [ˈraeə] die <-, -n> ◊ *Sie marschierten in Reihen von jeweils fünf Männern.* ♦ *In dem Internetcafé stehen zwei Reihen von Computern.* taxi rank **Taxistand** [ˈtaksiʃtant] der <-(e)s, Taxistände> ◊ *Gibt es hier in der Nähe einen Taxistand?* **3.** *(members of a group or organization)* ranks Reihen [ˈraeən] die <-> pl ◊ *Sie nahmen sie in ihre Reihen auf.* ♦ *Der Optimismus in den Reihen der Partei ist ungebrochen.*; *(soldiers who are not officers)* ranks Mannschaften und Unteroffiziere [ˌmanʃaftn ʊnt ˈʊnteˌʔofitsiːrə] die <-> pl ◊ *Mannschaften und Unteroffiziere traten zur Ordensverleihung an.* serve in the ranks **gemeiner Soldat sein** [ɡəmaene zɔlˈdaːt zaen] +sein ◊ *Er ist gemeiner Soldat.*

◉ **rise through the ranks** sich hocharbeiten
rank² [verb] **1.** *(figure, feature)* rank high/low **eine wichtige/unwichtige Rolle spielen** [aenə ˌvɪçtɪɡə/ˌʊnvɪçtɪɡə ˈrɔlə ʃpiːlən] +haben ◊ *In unserer Gesellschaft spielt das Geld eine wichtige Rolle.* rank as/among sth **zu etw. zählen** [tsuː ... tsɛːlən] +haben ◊ *Dieser Film zählt zu den besten, die ich je gesehen habe.* ♦ *Er zählt zu den bedeutendsten Autoren seiner Zeit.* **2.** *(count)* be ranked **als etw. eingestuft werden** [als ... ˌaenɡəʃtuːft veːɡdn] <wird, wurde, ist worden> ◊ *Nach ihrem Sieg wurde sie als beste Schwimmerin der Welt eingestuft.* **3.** MIL *(have a higher position)* rank sb **rangmäßig über jdm stehen** [ˌraŋmɛːsɪç ˈyːbe ... ʃteːən] <steht, stand, hat gestanden> ◊ *Sie steht rangmäßig über ihm.* **4.** *(place in rows)* ordentlich nebeneinander stellen [ˈɔrdntlɪç neːbmˌaeˈnande ʃtɛlən] +haben ◊ *Sie hatte die Schuhe im Flur ordentlich nebeneinander gestellt.*

rant [verb] schimpfen [ˈʃɪmpfn] +haben ◊ *Sie schimpfte lautstark über das Wetter.* rant at sb **mit jdm schimpfen** ◊ *Er schimpft schon wieder mit dem Hund.*

◉ **rant and rave** herumschimpfen
rape¹ [noun] **1.** *(crime)* Vergewaltigung [fɛɡəˈvaltɪɡʊŋ] die <-, -en> ◊ *Er wurde wegen Vergewaltigung angezeigt.* ♦ *Sie wurde das Opfer einer Vergewaltigung.* **2.** *(destruction)* Raubbau [ˈraobbao] der <-(e)s> no pl ◊ *den Raubbau am Regenwald stoppen* **3.** BOT Raps [raps] der <-es> no pl ◊ *Raps anbauen/ernten*

rape² [verb] vergewaltigen [fɛɡəˈvaltɪɡn] <vergewaltigt, vergewaltigte, hat vergewaltigt> ◊ *Er soll seine eigene Tochter vergewaltigt haben.* ♦ *Sie wurde auf dem Heimweg vergewaltigt.*

rapid(ly) [adj, adv] schnell [ʃnɛl] ◊ *eine schnelle Verwirklichung der Reform* ♦ *eine schnelle Bewegung machen* ♦ *Sein Puls war sehr schnell.* ♦ *Der Patient hat sich schnell wieder erholt.*

rapt(ly) [adj, adv] **1.** gespannt [ɡəˈʃpant] <gespannter, am gespanntesten> ◊ *gespannte Aufmerksamkeit* ♦ *Im Publikum herrschte gespannte Stille.* ♦ *gespannt lauschende Zuhörer* rapt in thought **in Gedanken versunken** [ɪn ɡəˈdaŋkŋ fɛɡˈzʊŋkŋ] ◊ *In Gedanken versunken blickte sie aufs Meer hinaus.* ♦ *Er war ganz in Gedanken versunken.* **2.** *(smile, look)* verzückt [fɛˈtsʏkt] <verzückter, am verzücktesten> ◊

jdm einen verzückten Blick zuwerfen ♦ *Sie lächelte verzückt.*

rare ⟨adj⟩ **1.** *(not common)* selten ['zɛltn̩] ◊ *eine seltene Gelegenheit* ♦ *Diese Krankheit ist äußerst selten.* **2.** *(steak)* blutig ['bluːtɪç] ◊ *Ich mag mein Steak am liebsten blutig.* **3.** *(air)* dünn [dʏn] ◊ *Hier oben ist die Luft schon recht dünn.*

rarely ⟨adv⟩ selten ['zɛltn̩] ◊ *Er ist selten krank.* ♦ *Diesen Vogel sieht man nur selten.*

rarity ⟨noun⟩ Seltenheit ['zɛltn̩haet] die <-, -en> ◊ *Aufgrund seiner Seltenheit ist der Stein sehr wertvoll.* ♦ *Friedliche Tage sind bei uns eine Seltenheit.*

rascal ⟨noun⟩ **1.** *(naughty child)* Schlingel ['ʃlɪŋl̩] der <-s, -> *(fam)* ◊ *Komm her, du kleiner Schlingel!* **2.** *(oldf)* *(scoundrel)* Schurke ['ʃʊrkə] der <-n, -n> ◊ *Was für ein gemeiner Schurke!*

rash(ly) ⟨adj, adv⟩ voreilig ['foːɐ̯ʔaelɪç] ◊ *Sie ist manchmal ein wenig zu voreilig.* ♦ *voreilige Schlüsse ziehen* ♦ *Es war etwas voreilig, den Urlaub schon zu buchen.* ♦ *Ich will nicht voreilig urteilen.*

raspberry ⟨noun⟩ ʙᴏᴛ Himbeere ['hɪmbeːrə] die <-, -n> ◊ *Himbeeren pflanzen/pflücken*
◉ **blow a raspberry** verächtlich schnauben

rat ⟨noun⟩ **1.** ᴢᴏᴏ Ratte ['ratə] die <-, -n> ◊ *Diese Krankheit wird von Ratten übertragen.* **2.** *(fam)* *(person)* Schwein [ʃvaen] das <-(e)s, -e> *(fam, pej)* ◊ *Er ist ein mieses Schwein.* ♦ *Dieses Schwein hat mich betrogen.*
◉ **smell a rat** Lunte riechen *(fam)*

rate¹ ⟨noun⟩ **1.** *(number, proportion)* Rate ['raːtə] die <-, -n> *mostly in compounds* birth rate Geburtenrate [gə'buːɐ̯tn̩raːtə] ◊ *Die Geburtenrate in den Industrieländern sinkt weiter.* rate of unemployment Arbeitslosenquote ['aʁbaetsloːznkvoːtə] die <-, -n> ◊ *Die Arbeitslosenquote ist gestiegen.* rate of success Erfolgsquote [ɛ'fɔlkskvoːtə] die ◊ *Die Erfolgsquote bei diesem Verfahren ist hoch.* **2.** *(frequency)* Frequenz [fre'kvɛnts] die <-, -en> ◊ *Sein Herz schlägt mit einer Frequenz von 70 Schlägen pro Minute.; (speed)* Geschwindigkeit [gə'ʃvɪndɪçkaet] die <-, -en> ◊ *Die Zahl der Kranken steigt mit erschreckender Geschwindigkeit.* at a rate of ... mit einer Geschwindigkeit von ... **3.** *(money to pay)* Satz [zats] der <-es, Sätze> ◊ *Die Krankenkassen erhöhen ihre Sätze.* ♦ *Für jede zahnärztliche Leistung ist der Satz festgelegt.* rate of interest Zinssatz ['tsɪnszats] hourly rate of pay Stundensatz ['ʃtʊndn̩zats] tax rate Steuersatz ['ʃtɔ̯øezats] **4.** *(in the UK: municipal tax)* rates Gemeindesteuern [gə'maendəʃtɔ̯øen] die <-> pl ◊ *Gemeindesteuern zahlen*

rate² ⟨verb⟩ **1.** *(estimate the value of sth)* einschätzen ['aenʃɛtsn̩] +haben ◊ *Wie schätzen Sie seine Fähigkeiten ein?* rate sb/sth highly jdn/etw. hoch einschätzen; *(count as)* rate sb/sth as sth jdn/etw. für etw. halten [fyː ... haltn̩] <hält, hielt, hat gehalten> ◊ *Ich halte das für ein wichtiges Thema.* sb/sth rates as sth jd/etw. gilt als etw. [gɪlt als] <gilt, galt, hat gegolten> ◊ *Er gilt als einer der größten Künstler der Moderne.* **2.** ꜰɪʟᴍ rate a film 16 etc. einen Film ab 16 etc. Jahren freigeben [aenən ˌfɪlm ap ˌzɛçtseːn jaːɐ̯ən 'fʁaege:bm̩] <gibt frei, gab frei, hat freigegeben> ◊ *Der Film wurde ab 12 Jahren freigegeben.* ♦ *Freigegeben ab 6.* **3.** *(deserve)* verdienen [fɛ'diːnən] ◊ *Verdient dieses Hotel vier Sterne?* ♦ *Das verdient eine Erwähnung im Jahresbericht.* **4.** *(think highly of)* gut finden

['guːt fɪndn̩] <findet, fand, hat gefunden> *(fam)* ◊ *Ich finde die Musik/Lehrerin gut.*

rather ⟨adv⟩ **1.** *(considerably)* ziemlich ['tsiːmlɪç] ◊ *Sie sehen sich ziemlich oft.* ♦ *Ich bin ziemlich müde.* ♦ *Die Geschichte ist ziemlich konfus.* rather more complicated/difficult etc. um einiges komplizierter/schwieriger etc. [ʊm aenɪgəs kɔmpli'tsiːɐ̯te/'ʃviːrɪgə] ◊ *Die Sache ist um einiges komplizierter, als du denkst.* rather too much etwas zu viel [ɛtvas tsuː 'fiːl] ◊ *Sie hat an dem Abend etwas zu viel getrunken.* **2.** *(more accurately)* vielmehr [fiːl'meːɐ̯] ◊ *Das ist kein Scherz, sondern vielmehr eine ernste Angelegenheit.* or rather beziehungsweise [bə'tsiːʊŋsvaezə] ◊ *In England beziehungsweise Großbritannien ist der Euro bislang noch nicht eingeführt worden.* **3.** *(expressing a preference)* lieber ['liːbə] ◊ *Er ging lieber, als dass er wartete.* ♦ *Ich möchte das lieber gestern als heute erledigt haben.* sb would rather do sth (than ...) jd würde lieber etw. tun (als ...) ◊ *Sie würde lieber zu Hause bleiben und lesen.* ♦ *Ich würde lieber nach Schottland als nach Portugal fahren.* sb would rather sb did sth jdm wäre es lieber, wenn jd etw. täte ◊ *Mir wäre es lieber, wenn du es ihm nicht erzähltest.*

rating ⟨noun⟩ **1.** *(assessment)* Einschätzung ['aenʃɛtsʊŋ] die <-, -en> ◊ *eine Einschätzung geben* ♦ *Wie ist Ihre Einschätzung seiner Arbeit?; (in a quality test)* Wertung ['veːɐ̯tʊŋ] die <-, -en> ◊ *Das Shampoo erhielt bei dem Test die Wertung "gut".* **2.** ʀᴀᴅɪᴏ, ᴛᴠ ratings Einschaltquote ['aenʃaltkvoːtə] die <-, -n> ◊ *Maßnahmen zur Erhöhung der Einschaltquote* ♦ *eine hohe/niedrige Einschaltquote erzielen* **3.** *(of a film)* Freigabe ['fʁaegaːbə] die <-, -n> ◊ *Eine Freigabe des Films ab 12 Jahren erscheint mir verantwortungslos.*

ratio ⟨noun⟩ Verhältnis [fɛ'hɛltnɪs] das <-ses, -se> ◊ *Farbe im Verhältnis zwei zu eins mischen* ♦ *Bei unseren Mitgliedern beträgt das Verhältnis von Männern zu Frauen momentan 52 : 48.*

rational(ly) ⟨adj, adv⟩ rational [ratsjo'naːl] ◊ *der Mensch als rationales Wesen* ♦ *Es fiel ihr schwer, rational zu bleiben.* ♦ *rational denken/handeln*

rattle ⟨verb⟩ **1.** *(make a knocking sound)* klappern ['klapen] +haben ◊ *Dein Schutzblech klappert.* rattle sth mit etw. klappern ◊ *Er klapperte mit den Tassen.* **2.** *(go somewhere noisily)* rattern ['raten] +sein ◊ *Der Zug ratterte durch die Gebirgslandschaft.* **3.** *(make angry)* verärgern [fɛ'ʔɛɐ̯gen] ◊ *Ihre Bemerkung hat ihn sehr verärgert.; (make nervous)* verunsichern [fɛ'ʊnzɪçen] <verunsicherte, verunsicherte, hat verunsichert> ◊ *Seine Gegenwart verunsicherte sie völlig.*

rave ⟨verb⟩ **1.** *(angrily)* toben ['toːbm̩] +haben ◊ *Sie hat getobt wie eine Wahnsinnige.* **2.** *(crazily)* fantasieren [fanta'ziːrən] <fantasierte, fantasiert, hat fantasiert> ◊ *Als sie Fieber hatte, fantasierte sie.* **3.** *(enthusiastically)* rave about sth von jdm/etw. schwärmen [fɔn ... 'ʃvɛɐ̯mən] +haben ◊ *Er schwärmte von dem Konzert.*

raw ⟨adj⟩ **1.** *(not cooked)* roh [roː] no comp/superl ◊ *rohes Gemüse* ♦ *Kann man das auch roh essen?; (not processed)* Roh... [roː] raw silk Rohseide ['roːzaedə] die <-, -n> **2.** *(feelings, talent)* rein [raen] ◊ *Aus ihm sprach reine Wut.* **3.** *(data)* nicht aufbereitet [nɪçt 'aofbəraetət] no comp/superl ◊ *Die Daten in der Tabelle waren nicht aufbereitet.* **4.** *(soldier)* uner-

fahren ['ʊn|ɛfaːrən] ◊ *ein unerfahrener Soldat* **5.** *(skin)* wund [vʊnt] <wunder, am wundesten> ◊ *wunde Haut* ♦ *Seine Hände waren ganz wund.* **6.** *(weather, climate)* rau [ra͜o] <rauer, am rauesten> ◊ *Die Winter sind dort sehr rau.* ♦ *ein rauer Wind*

raw material (noun) Rohstoff ['roːʃtɔf] der <–(e)s, –e> ◊ *Erdöl ist einer der wichtigsten Rohstoffe.*

ray (noun) **1.** *(of light, sun)* Strahl [ʃtraːl] der <–(e)s, –en> ◊ *kosmische Strahlen* ♦ *etw. im Strahl einer Lampe erkennen* sun ray Sonnenstrahl ['zɔnənʃtraːl] der <–(e)s, –en> *most pl* **2.** ZOO Rochen ['rɔxn̩] der <–s, –>
⊛ **ray of hope** Hoffnungsschimmer **ray of sunshine** Sonnenschein

razor (noun) Rasierer [ra'ziːrɐ] der <–s, –>

reach¹ (noun) **1.** *(distance)* Reichweite ['raɛçva͜etə] die <–, –n> within reach in Reichweite ◊ *Das Telefon stand in (meiner) Reichweite auf dem Tisch.* out of reach außer Reichweite ◊ *Medikamente außer Reichweite von Kindern aufbewahren; (distance to travel)* within (easy) reach leicht erreichbar [ˌlaɛt ɛ'raɛçbaːʳ] ◊ *Das Dorf war leicht erreichbar.* **2.** *(influence, authority)* sth is within the reach of sb/sth etw. unterliegt jds Einfluss/dem Einfluss … (gen) [ʊntɐ'liːkt … 'aɛnflʊs/deːm 'aɛnflʊs] <unterliegt, unterlag, ist unterlegen> ◊ *Diese Entscheidung unterliegt dem Einflussbereich dieser Institution.*
⊛ **the upper/lower reaches 1.** *(of river)* Oberlauf/Unterlauf der **2.** *(of organization)* höhere/niedere Etagen **out of/beyond sb's reach** außerhalb jds Möglichkeiten ◊ *Die Finanzierung des Hauses lag außerhalb ihrer Möglichkeiten.*

reach² (verb) **1.** *(get there, be heard)* erreichen [ɛ'raɛçn̩] <erreicht, erreichte, hat erreicht> ◊ *Die Insel ist nur mit dem Schiff zu erreichen.* ♦ *In wenigen Minuten erreichen wir Bonn Hauptbahnhof.* ♦ *Die Sendung erreichte sehr viele Hörer.* reach an agreement/a decision eine Übereinkunft/Entscheidung treffen [aɛnə yːbɐ|'aɛnkʊnft/ɛnt'ʃaɛdʊŋ trɛfn̩] <trifft, traf, hat getroffen> **2.** *(hair, clothes, area)* reach to sth, reach as far as sth bis zu etw. reichen [bɪs ʦuː … raɛçn̩] +haben ◊ *Ihre Jacke reicht bis zum Knie.* **3.** *(with hand)* greifen ['graɛfn̩] <greift, griff, hat gegriffen> reach for sth nach etw. greifen ◊ *Er griff nach ihrer Hand.* reach into sth in etw. (acc) greifen ◊ *Er griff in die Tasche, um ein Buch hervorzuholen.; (manage to touch)* sb can reach sth jd kommt an etw. (acc) [kɔmt an] <kam, ist gekommen> ◊ *Ich komme nicht ans Fenster.* reach out die Hand ausstrecken [diː 'hant ˌa͜osʃtrɛkn̩] +haben ◊ *Sie streckte die Hand aus und streichelte den kleinen Hund.*
• **reach out** (phras v) reach out to sb sich jdm zuwenden ['ʦuːvɛndn̩] <wendet zu, wandte/wendete zu, hat zugewandt/zugewendet> ◊ *Wir sollten uns den Armen mehr zuwenden.*

react (verb) **1.** *(to a situation, chemical substances)* reagieren [rea'giːrən] <reagiert, reagierte, hat reagiert> ◊ *Er reagierte prompt/ärgerlich.* react to sth auf etw. (acc) reagieren ◊ *Auf diese Nachricht reagierten sie wütend.* react accordingly entsprechend reagieren react with sth mit etw. reagieren ◊ *Stärke reagiert mit Jod.* **2.** *(become ill)* react badly to sth etw. nicht vertragen [nɪçt fɛ'traːgn̩] <verträgt, vertrug, hat vertragen> ◊ *Das Baby verträgt die Medizin nicht.*

reaction (noun) **1.** *(action, effect, chemical process, conservative political forces)* Reaktion [reak'ʦi͜oːn] die <–, –en> ◊ *Wie war Ihre erste Reaktion, als Sie davon hörten?* ♦ *eine allergische/chemische Reaktion* reaction to sth Reaktion auf etw. (acc) ◊ *Seine Reaktion auf ihr Erscheinen war übertrieben.* suffer a reaction allergisch reagieren [a'lɛʳgɪʃ rea.giːrən] <reagiert, reagierte, hat reagiert> ◊ *Sie reagierte allergisch auf die Hautcreme.* **2.** *(ability to react)* reactions Reaktionsvermögen [reak'ʦi͜oːnsfɛmøːgn̩] das <–s> no pl ◊ *ein gutes Reaktionsvermögen haben* **3.** *(different attitude)* reaction against sth Auflehnung gegen etw. ['a͜oflɛnʊŋ geːgn̩] die <–, –en> ◊ *eine Auflehnung gegen traditionelle Werte*

reactor (noun) Reaktor [re|'aktoːɐ] der <–s, –en> ◊ *Der Reaktor soll demnächst abgeschaltet werden.*

read (verb) **1.** *(a book, newspaper etc.)* lesen ['leːzn̩] <liest, las, hat gelesen> ◊ *Er saß am Frühstückstisch und las die Zeitung.* ♦ *Ich lese gern abends im Bett.* read sb's mind jds Gedanken lesen A reads B like a book B ist für A ein offenes Buch ◊ *Ich weiß genau, was du denkst. Du bist ein offenes Buch für mich.* read through durchlesen ['dʊʳçleːzn̩] +haben ◊ *Lesen Sie den Vertrag genau durch.* **2.** *(aloud)* read (out) vorlesen ['foːɐleːzn̩] <liest vor, las vor, hat vorgelesen> ◊ *Er las die Liste vor.* read (sth) (out) to sb jdm (etw.) vorlesen ◊ *Mama las mir eine Geschichte vor.* read from sth aus etw. vorlesen **3.** *(a gas meter etc.)* ablesen ['apleːzn̩] <liest ab, las ab, hat abgelesen> ◊ *den Ölverbrauch am Zähler ablesen* **4.** *(interpret)* read sth as sth etw. als etw. deuten [als … dɔ͜ytn̩] <deutet, deutete, hat gedeutet> ◊ *Sie deutete sein Schweigen als Zustimmung.* **5.** *(label, sign)* sth reads sth auf etw. (dat) steht etw. [a͜of … ʃteːt] <steht, stand, hat gestanden> ◊ *Auf dem Schild steht: ,Rauchen verboten!'; (measuring equipment)* sth reads sth etw. zeigt etw. an [tsaɛkt … an] +haben ◊ *Der Zähler hat mehr als 300 Liter Öl angezeigt.* **6.** *sth reads well/badly* etw. liest sich gut/schlecht [liːst zɪç 'guːt/'ʃlɛçt] <liest sich, las sich, hat sich gelesen> ◊ *Das Buch liest sich gut.*
• **read into** (phras v) read sth into etw. in etw. hineinlesen [ɪn … hɪ'naɛnleːzn̩] <liest hinein, las hinein, hat hineingelesen> ◊ *Sie hat zu viel in das Gedicht hineingelesen.*
• **read up** (phras v) read up about/on sth sich über etw. (acc) informieren [yːbɐ … ɪnfɔʳˌmiːrən] <informiert sich, informierte sich, hat sich informiert> ◊ *Sie informierte sich genau über das Thema.*

reader (noun) **1.** *(person who reads sth)* Leser ['leːzɐ] der <–s, –> ♀Leserin ['leːzərɪn] die <–, –nen> ◊ *ein tolles Angebot für unsere Leser* **2.** *(machine)* Lesegerät ['leːzəgɛrɛːt] das <–(e)s, –e> **3.** *(book)* Lesebuch ['leːzəbuːx] das <–(e)s, Lesebücher> ◊ *Bitte schlagt die Lesebücher auf Seite 34 auf* **4.** UNI Dozent [do'ʦɛnt] der <–en, –en> ♀Dozentin [do'ʦɛntɪn] die <–, –nen> ◊ *Er ist Dozent an der Uni.* ♦ *Wie findest du die neue Dozentin?*

readily (adv) **1.** *(easily)* leicht [laɛçt] <leichter, am leichtesten> ◊ *Die Anleitung ist nicht leicht zu verstehen.* **2.** *(willingly)* bereitwillig [bə'raɛtvɪlɪç] ◊ *Er ließ sich bereitwillig dazu überreden, bei dem Spiel mitzumachen.*

readiness (noun) Bereitschaft [bə'raɛtʃaft] die <–, –en> ◊ *Vielen Menschen fehlt die Bereitschaft, sich für andere einzusetzen.* ♦ *ihre mangelnde Bereit-*

schaft zur Mitarbeit in readiness for **für** [fyː‿ɐ̯] +acc ◊
Sie stapelten Holz für ein Lagerfeuer. ✦ *eine Mahlzeit*
für jds Ankunft vorbereiten
reading noun **1.** *(ability)* reading (skills) Lesefertigkeit
['leːzəfɛ'tɪçkaet] die <–> *no pl* ◊ *die Lesefertigkeit*
fördern **2.** *(act)* Lesen ['leːzn̩] das <–s> *no pl* ◊ *Sie*
hat Probleme beim Lesen. background reading das
Lesen von Hintergrundmaterial sth makes for interesting reading etw. liest sich interessant
[liːst zɪç ɪntərɛ'sant] <liest sich, las sich, hat sich
gelesen> ◊ *Der Bericht liest sich sehr interessant.*
3. *(reading matter)* Lektüre [lɛk'tyːrə] die <–, –n>
most sing ◊ *eine spannende/leichte Lektüre*
4. *(before an audience, in parliament)* Lesung
['leːzʊŋ] die <–, –en> ◊ *eine Lesung von Gedichten*
✦ *ein Gesetz in zweiter Lesung beschließen* **5.** *(of a*
meter) Anzeige ['antsaegə] die <–, –n> **6.** *(interpret-*
ation) Interpretation [ɪntɛprɛta'tsjoːn] die <–, –en> ◊
Der Text lässt unterschiedliche Interpretationen zu.
ready adj **1.** *(suitable)* fertig ['fɛ'tɪç] *no comp/superl*
◊ *Das Essen ist in zehn Minuten fertig.* get sb ready
jdn fertig machen sb gets ready jd macht sich
fertig **2.** *(prepared, willing)* bereit [bə'raet] *no comp/*
superl, not before ns ◊ *Ich bin bereit. Wir können*
abfahren. be ready to do sth bereit sein, etw. zu
tun; *(be willing to say sth)* be ready with sth etw.
parat haben [pa'raːt haːbm̩] *+haben* ◊ *Er hatte*
immer einen Witz parat. **3.** *(quick)* schnell [ʃnɛl] ◊
schnellen Zugang zum Computer haben
ready meal noun Fertiggericht ['fɛ'tɪçgərɪçt] das
<–(e)s, –e> ◊ *ein Fertiggericht aufwärmen*
real adj **1.** *(existing, genuine)* echt [ɛçt] *no comp/*
superl ◊ *Sind die Gefahren echt, vor denen er warnt?*
✦ *Die Uhr ist aus echtem Gold.* ✦ *Sie ist eine echte*
Freundin. **2.** *(true, not imaginary, important)* wirklich
['vɪ'klɪç] *no comp/superl* ◊ *War er der wirkliche*
Täter? ✦ *Das ist kein wirklicher Verlust.* **3.** *(film*
scene etc.) realistisch [rea'lɪstɪʃ] ◊ *Die Kampfszene*
wirkte sehr realistisch.
real estate noun **1.** *(property)* Immobilien
[ɪmo'biːljən] die <–> *pl* ◊ *Immobilien erwerben*
2. *(dealing with property)* Immobilienhandel
[ɪmo'biːljənhandl̩] der <–s> *no pl* ◊ *Er ist im Immobi-*
lienhandel tätig.
real estate agent noun Makler ['maːklɐ] der
<–s, –> ♀Maklerin ['maːklərɪn] die <–, –nen> ◊ *Die*
Maklerin zeigte ihnen die Wohnung. ✦ *Er ist Makler*
von Beruf.
realism noun Realismus [rea'lɪsmʊs] der <–> *no pl*
◊ *Seine Denkweise ist von Realismus geprägt.* ✦ *der*
Realismus in der Kunst
realistic(ally) adj, adv realistisch [rea'lɪstɪʃ] ◊ *Alle*
anderen Alternativen sind wenig realistisch. ✦ *eine*
Situation realistisch einschätzen ✦ *realistische Bilder*
reality noun Realität [reali'tɛːt] die <–> *no pl* ◊ *Diese*
Theorie widerspricht der Realität. ✦ *Leider sieht die*
Realität anders aus. bear no relation to reality keine
Ähnlichkeit mit der Realität aufweisen
Ⓔ in reality tatsächlich
realization noun **1.** *(recognition)* Erkenntnis
[ɛ'kɛntnɪs] die <–, –se> ◊ *Ich bin zu der Erkenntnis*
gekommen, dass mir dieser Beruf nicht liegt. **2.** *(of*
hope, plan) Verwirklichung [fɛ'vɪ'klɪçʊŋ] die
<–, –en> *most sing* ◊ *die Verwirklichung eines Plans*
realize verb **1.** *(notice)* merken ['mɛ'kn̩] *+haben* ◊ *Ich*
habe die Datei versehentlich gelöscht, ohne es zu

merken. **2.** *(become aware of, come to understand)*
erkennen [ɛ'kɛnən] <erkennt, erkannte, hat erkannt>
◊ *Ich habe meinen Fehler erkannt.* ✦ *Sie erkannte*
seine Absicht und war verstimmt.; (be aware of)
realize that ... sich dat dessen bewusst sein, dass
... [dɛsn̩ bə'vʊst zaen das] *+sein* ◊ *Ich bin mir*
dessen bewusst, dass das nicht einfach für dich ist.
3. *(achieve)* verwirklichen [fɛ'vɪ'klɪçn̩] <verwirklicht,
verwirklichte, hat verwirklicht> ◊ *einen Plan/eine Idee*
verwirklichen realize your *(full)* potential sein
(volles) Potenzial ausschöpfen
[zaen (fɔləs) potɛn'tsjaːl ˌaosʃœpfn̩] *+haben*
really¹ adv **1.** *(very)* sehr [zeːɐ̯] ◊ *Er hat sich sehr*
gefreut. **2.** *(in reality, entirely, for emphasis or*
expressing interest or surprise) wirklich ['vɪ'klɪç] *no*
comp/superl ◊ *Ist das wirklich passiert, oder hat er*
sich das nur ausgedacht? ✦ *Dieser Film ist wirklich*
spannend. ✦ *Musst du wirklich schon gehen?* really
and truly wirklich und wahrhaftig
Ⓔ not really eigentlich nicht ◊ *„Hat dir der Film*
gefallen?" — „Eigentlich nicht."
really² interj **1.** *(expressing surprise, interest, disap-*
proval) wirklich ['vɪ'klɪç] ◊ *„Er geht ins Ausland." —*
„Wirklich? Das hätte ich nicht erwartet." ✦ *Also*
wirklich, das muss doch nicht sein! **2.** *(expressing*
doubt) tatsächlich [taːt'zɛçlɪç] ◊ *Ich bin mir sicher,*
dass ich gewinnen werde." — „Tatsächlich?"
realm noun **1.** *(area of interest)* Bereich [bə'raeç] der
<–(e)s, –e> ◊ *Im wirtschaftlichen Bereich gibt es*
nur wenige Leute, die so gut sind wie sie.
2. *(kingdom)* Reich [raeç] das <–(e)s, –e> ◊ *das*
Reich der Finsternis
reap verb ernten ['ɛ'nt̩n̩] <erntet, erntete, hat
geerntet> ◊ *den Lohn für seine Mühe ernten* ✦
Getreide ernten
Ⓔ reap what you sow ernten, was man gesät hat
rear¹ noun **1.** *(back, of a house, an object)* the rear der
hintere Teil [deːɐ̯ 'hɪntərə ˌtael] der <–(e)s, –e> ◊
Im hinteren Teil des Hauses fand eine Party statt.;
(of a car) Heck [hɛk] das <–(e)s, –s or –e> at the
rear hinten ['hɪntn̩] ◊ *Die Tür ist hinten.* **2.** *(bottom)*
Hintern ['hɪntɐn] der <–s, –> *(fam)* ◊ *auf den*
Hintern fallen
rear² adj hintere ['hɪntərə] *no comp, only before ns*
<ein hinterer ..., eine hintere ..., ein hinteres ...> ◊
die hintere Tür eines Autos ✦ *ein hinterer Reifen*
rear³ verb **1.** *(bring up)* aufziehen ['aoftsiːən] <zieht
auf, zog auf, hat aufgezogen> ◊ *ein Kind allein*
aufziehen ✦ *ein Kälbchen mit der Flasche aufziehen*
2. *(horse)* rear (up) sich aufbäumen ['aofbɔ̯gmən]
+haben ◊ *Das Pferd bäumte sich auf.* **3.** *(lit) (rise up)*
sich erheben [zɪç ɛ'heːbm̩] <erhebt sich, erhob sich, hat
sich erhoben> ◊ *Vor uns erhob sich der majestäti-*
sche Berg.
Ⓔ be reared on sth mit etw. aufwachsen ◊ *Er ist*
mit Computern aufgewachsen.
rearrange verb **1.** *(change position)* umstellen
['ʊmʃtɛlən] *+haben* ◊ *Ich habe im Wohnzimmer die*
Möbel umgestellt. ✦ *Stell diese Sätze ein wenig um.*
2. *(change date)* rearrange sth (for sth) etw. (auf
etw. acc) verlegen [fɛ'leːgn̩] <verlegt, verlegte, hat
verlegt> ◊ *Die Besprechung wurde auf den nächsten*
Tag verlegt.
rear-view mirror noun Rückspiegel ['rʏkʃpiːgl̩] der
<–s, –> ◊ *vor dem Überholen in den Rückspiegel*
sehen

reason¹ [noun] **1.** *(cause, explanation)* Grund [grʊnt] der <-(e)s, Gründe> ◊ *ohne Angabe von Gründen* for a reason aus einem besonderen Grund for a simple reason aus einem einfachen Grund reason for sth Grund zu etw. ◊ *Es gibt Grund zu feiern: Er hat seine Prüfung bestanden.* give a reason einen Grund nennen ◊ *Nenne mir nur einen einzigen guten Grund dafür.* there is every reason to do sth es gibt allen Grund, etw. zu tun for no apparent reason ohne ersichtlichen Grund for reasons of safety aus Sicherheitsgründen [aʊs 'zɪçɐhaɛtsɡrʏndn̩] **2.** *(common sense)* Vernunft [fɛ'nʊnft] die <-> no pl ◊ *Er zeigte Vernunft.* listen to reason auf die Stimme der Vernunft hören within reason innerhalb vernünftiger Grenzen [ɪnɛhalp fɛˌnʏnftɪɡɐ 'ɡrɛntsn̩] **3.** *(mind)* Verstand [fɛ'ʃtant] der <-(e)s> no pl ◊ *den Verstand verlieren*

reason² [verb] **1.** *(combine)* reason from sth that aus etw. folgern, dass [aʊs ... 'fɔlɡɐn das] +haben ◊ *Die Schlange ist grell gefärbt; daraus folgere ich, dass sie giftig ist.* **2.** *(think logically)* logisch denken [ˌloːɡɪʃ 'dɛŋkn̩] <denkt, dachte, hat gedacht> ◊ *Der Mensch hat die Fähigkeit, logisch zu denken.*

reasonable [adj] **1.** *(rational, sensible)* vernünftig [fɛ'nʏnftɪç] ◊ *eine vernünftige Entscheidung* ♦ *Bitte sei vernünftig!* **2.** *(acceptable, fair)* angemessen ['anɡəmɛsn̩] ◊ *eine angemessene Entschädigung zahlen* ♦ *Der Preis war durchaus angemessen.*

reasonably [adv] **1.** *(fairly)* ziemlich ['tsiːmlɪç] ◊ *Es ist ziemlich sicher, dass er die Prüfung nicht bestehen wird.* **2.** *(rationally)* vernünftig [fɛ'nʏnftɪç] ◊ *Er reagierte vernünftig.* **3.** *(with good reason, really)* durchaus [dʊr̩ç|'aʊs] ◊ *Für diesen Einsatz kann man durchaus eine Belohnung erwarten.* not reasonably nicht ernsthaft [nɪçt 'ɛːrnsthaft] ◊ *Sie können nicht ernsthaft erwarten, dass ich allein für den Schaden aufkomme.*

reasoning [noun] Argumentation [aˈrɡumɛntaˈtsjoːn] die <-, -en> ◊ *Ich konnte seiner Argumentation folgen.* line of reasoning Betrachtungsweise [bə'traxtʊŋsvaɛzə] die <-, -n> ◊ *Ihre Betrachtungsweise war sehr interessant.*

reassure [verb] *(calm down)* beruhigen [bə'ruːɪɡn̩] <beruhigt, beruhigte, hat beruhigt> ◊ *Sie beruhigte das Kind.* reassure sb that jdm versichern, dass [fɛ'zɪçɐn das] <versichert, versicherte, hat versichert> ◊ *Er versicherte ihr, dass sie sich keine Sorgen machen müsse.; (make sure)* reassure yourself that sich vergewissern, dass [fɛɡɐ'vɪsɐn das] <vergewissert sich, vergewisserte sich, hat sich vergewissert> ◊ *Er vergewisserte sich, dass die Fenster geschlossen waren.*

rebel [noun] Rebell [re'bɛl] der <-en, -en> ♀Rebellin [re'bɛlɪn] die <-, -nen> ◊ *Robin Hood, der Rebell* ♦ *kurdische/tschetschenische Rebellen* rebel leader Rebellenführer [re'bɛlənfyːrɐ] der <-s, -> ♀Rebellenführerin [re'bɛlənfyːrɐrɪn] die <-, -nen> ◊ *Der Rebellenführer wurde festgenommen.*

rebellion [noun] *(political, against a leader)* Aufstand ['aʊfʃtant] der <-(e)s, Aufstände> ◊ *Das Militär warf den Aufstand nieder.; (of teenagers, against an authority)* Auflehnung ['aʊfleːnʊŋ] die <-, -en> ◊ *die Auflehnung Jugendlicher gegen ihre Eltern*

rebuff [noun] Abfuhr ['apfuːɡ] die <-, -en> ◊ *jdm eine Abfuhr erteilen* ♦ *eine Abfuhr bekommen*

rebuild [verb] wieder aufbauen [viːdɐ 'aʊfbaʊən] +haben ◊ *Das Haus wurde nach dem Erdbeben wieder aufgebaut.* ♦ *ein Land/sein Leben wieder aufbauen*

recall¹ [noun] **1.** *(memory)* recall (of sth) Erinnerung (an etw. [acc]) [e|'ɪnarʊŋ] die <-, -en> ◊ *Ich habe keine Erinnerung mehr an den Abend.* **2.** *(of a product)* Rückruf ['rʏkruːf] der <-(e)s, -e> ◊ *Das Gesundheitsministerium ordnete den Rückruf des Arzneimittels an.* **3.** *(of an ambassador etc.)* Abberufung ['apbaruːfʊŋ] die <-, -en> most sing ◊ *die Abberufung eines Botschafters*

recall² [verb] **1.** *(remember)* recall sth sich an etw. [acc] erinnern [an ... e|,ɪnɐn] <erinnert sich, erinnerte sich, hat sich erinnert> ◊ *Sie konnte sich an ihre erste Schulstunde erinnern.* ♦ *Ich erinnere mich nicht daran, ihn je gesehen zu haben.* **2.** *(an ambassador)* abberufen ['apbaruːfn̩] <beruft ab, berief ab, hat abberufen> ◊ *Die Botschafterin wurde von ihrem Posten abberufen.* **3.** sport *(a player)* wieder einsetzen [viːdɐ 'aɛntsetsn̩] +haben ◊ *Der Spieler wurde wieder eingesetzt.* **4.** *(a product)* zurückrufen [tsu'rʏkruːfn̩] <ruft zurück, rief zurück, hat zurückgerufen> ◊ *Das fehlerhafte Produkt wurde zurückgerufen.*

recede [verb] **1.** *(flood, hairline, chances)* zurückgehen [tsu'rʏkgeːən] <geht zurück, ging zurück, ist zurückgegangen> ◊ *Die Überschwemmung geht zurück.* ♦ *Sein Haaransatz geht jetzt schon zurück.; (disappear)* verschwinden [fɛ'ʃvɪndn̩] <verschwindet, verschwand, ist verschwunden> ◊ *Das Flugzeug ist fast völlig aus unserem Blickfeld verschwunden.* **2.** *(pain)* nachlassen ['naːxlasn̩] <lässt nach, ließ nach, hat nachgelassen> ◊ *Die Schmerzen lassen mit der Zeit nach.*

receipt [noun] **1.** *(document)* Quittung ['kvɪtʊŋ] die <-, -en> ◊ *jdm eine Quittung (über 100 Euro) ausstellen; (at checkout)* Bon [bɔŋ] der <-s, -s> ◊ *Kein Umtausch ohne Bon!* **2.** *(of goods)* Empfang [ɛm'pfaŋ] der <-(e)s> no pl ◊ *Würden Sie mir bitte den Empfang der Ware bestätigen?* on receipt (of sth) bei Empfang (... [gen]) **3.** *(money)* receipts Einnahmen ['aɛnaːmən] die <-> pl ◊ *Einnahmen aus Auslandsgeschäften*

receive [verb] **1.** *(get)* bekommen [bə'kɔmən] <bekommt, bekam, hat bekommen> ◊ *Für diese Frechheit hat er eine Rüge bekommen.* ♦ *Sozialhilfe bekommen* ♦ *Theo bekommt von Frau Schnorr Nachhilfe in Englisch.* **2.** *(sell stolen goods)* Hehlerei treiben [heːlɐ'raɛ traɛbm̩] <treibt, trieb, hat getrieben> **3.** *(a ball)* annehmen ['anneːmən] <nimmt an, nahm an, hat angenommen> **4.** *(welcome, get a radio or TV channel)* empfangen [ɛm'pfaŋən] <empfängt, empfing, hat empfangen> ◊ *Sie wurden herzlich empfangen.* ♦ *Diesen Sender können wir nicht empfangen.; (accept)* aufnehmen ['aʊfneːmən] <nimmt auf, nahm auf, hat aufgenommen> ◊ *Der Vorstand nahm ihren Vorschlag mit Begeisterung auf.* receive sb into sth jdn in etw. [acc] aufnehmen ◊ *Sie wurde in die Gemeinde aufgenommen.*

receiver [noun] **1.** *(of a telephone)* Hörer ['høːrɐ] der <-s, -> ◊ *Sie nahm den Hörer ab und meldete sich.* **2.** radio, tv Empfänger [ɛm'pfɛŋɐ] der <-s, -> **3.** *(manager of a bankrupt company)* Konkursverwalter [kɔn'kʊ'sfevaltɐ] der <-s, -> ♀Konkursverwalterin [kɔn'kʊ'sfe,valtarɪn] die <-, -nen> ◊ *einen Konkursverwalter einsetzen* **4.** *(person who gets sth)* Empfänger [ɛm'pfɛŋɐ] der <-s, -> ♀Empfängerin [ɛm'pfɛŋɐrɪn] die <-, -nen> ◊ *der Empfänger eines*

Briefs

recent [adj] *(discovery, study)* neu [nɔø] <neuer, am neu(e)sten> ◊ *eine neue Studie* ♦ *Diese Entdeckung ist noch ziemlich neu.*; *(past, event)* jüngste ['jʏnstə] *no comp/superl, only before ns* <der/die/das jüngste ...> ◊ *die jüngsten Ereignisse* in recent years in den letzten Jahren [ɪn deːn lɛtstn̩ 'jaːrən]

recently [adv] **1.** *(a short time ago)* kürzlich ['kʏʳtslɪç] *no comp/superl* ◊ *eine kürzlich erschienene Studie* ♦ *Ich habe ihn erst kürzlich getroffen.* **2.** *(during the last few days or weeks)* in letzter Zeit [ɪn lɛtste 'tsaet] ◊ *Du bist in letzter Zeit immer so mürrisch.*

reception [noun] Empfang [ɛm'pfaŋ] der <-(e)s, Empfänge> ◊ *Die Schlüssel sind am Empfang erhältlich.* ♦ *Anschließend findet ein offizieller Empfang statt.* ♦ *Sie hatten ihm einen herzlichen Empfang bereitet.* ♦ *Der Empfang des Senders war gestört.*

receptive [adj] aufgeschlossen ['aofgəʃlɔsn̩] ◊ *ein aufgeschlossener Mensch* receptive to sth einer Sache [dat] gegenüber aufgeschlossen ◊ *Neuen Ideen gegenüber war er immer aufgeschlossen.*

recess [noun] **1.** *(of lawcourts, Parliament)* Ferien ['feːrjən] die <-> pl ◊ *Das Parlament geht in die Ferien.*; *(of school)* Pause ['paozə] die <-, -n> ◊ *In der Pause konnten sie an die frische Luft gehen.* **2.** *(alcove)* Nische ['niːʃə] die <-, -n> ◊ *Er saß in der hintersten Nische des Cafés.*

⊛ the recesses of sth die Tiefen ... [gen] ◊ *Sie suchte in den Tiefen ihrer Tasche nach den Schlüsseln.*

recession [noun] Rezession [retse'sjoːn] die <-, -en> ◊ *Das Land steckte in einer Rezession.*

recharge [verb] aufladen ['aoflaːdn̩] <lädt auf, lud auf, hat aufgeladen> ◊ *Batterien aufladen*

recipe [noun] Rezept [re'tsɛpt] das <-(e)s, -e> ◊ *Sie kocht nur nach Rezept.* ♦ *Gibt es ein Rezept für Erfolgsromane?*

⊛ sth is a recipe for sth bei etw. ist etw. vorprogrammiert ◊ *Bei so viel Fleiß ist der Erfolg vorprogrammiert.*

recipient [noun] Empfänger [ɛm'pfɛŋɐ] der <-s, -> ♀Empfängerin [ɛm'pfɛŋərɪn] die <-, -nen> ◊ *Das Porto zahlt der Empfänger.* ♦ *Empfänger staatlicher Beihilfen*

reciprocate [verb] erwidern [ɛ'viːdɐn] <erwidert, erwiderte, hat erwidert> ◊ *Ihre Liebe wurde nicht erwidert.* ♦ *ein Lächeln erwidern*

recite [verb] vortragen ['foːɐtraːgn̩] <trägt vor, trug vor, hat vorgetragen> ◊ *Er hat die ‚Bürgschaft‘ von Schiller auswendig vorgetragen.*

reckless(ly) [adj, adv] rücksichtslos ['rʏkzɪçtsloːs] <rücksichtsloser, am rücksichtslosesten> ◊ *Das war ziemlich rücksichtslos von dir!* ♦ *die rücksichtslose Abholzung der Wälder* ♦ *rücksichtslos rasen*

reckon [verb] **1.** *(expect)* schätzen ['ʃɛtsn̩] +haben *(fam)* ◊ *Ich schätze, er kommt wieder mal zu spät.* ♦ *Er schätzt, dass sie noch anrufen wird.* be reckoned to be sth als etw. gelten [als ... gɛltn̩] <gilt, galt, hat gegolten> ◊ *Er gilt als der beste Arzt in der Stadt.* What do you reckon? Was meinst du/meinen Sie? What do you reckon to it? Was hältst du/halten Sie davon? **2.** *(calculate)* reckon sth etw. errechnen [ɛ'rɛçnən] <errechnet, errechnete, hat errechnet> ◊ *Wir errechneten Produktionskosten von über einer Million.* reckon sth at sth etw. für etw. veranschlagen [fy:ɐ̯ ... fɛl̩ˌanʃlaːgn̩] <veranschlagt, veranschlagte, hat veranschlagt> ◊ *Für die Produktentwicklung werden zwei Monate veranschlagt.* **3.** *(in the UK: expect)* sb reckons to do sth jd rechnet damit, dass er etw. tut ['rɛçnət damɪt das] <rechnete, hat gerechnet> ◊ *Wir rechnen damit, dass wir bis morgen fertig sind.*

• **reckon on** [phras v] reckon on sth mit etw. rechnen [mɪt ...ˌrɛçnən] <rechnet, rechnete, hat gerechnet> ◊ *Sie müssen mit mindestens zehn Personen rechnen.*

• **reckon with** [phras v] reckon with sb/sth *(take seriously)* mit jdm/etw. rechnen [mɪt ...ˌrɛçnən] <rechnet, rechnete, hat gerechnet> ◊ *eine Mannschaft, mit der man rechnen muss* be a force/power to reckon with eine einflussreiche Kraft/Macht sein [aenə ˌaenflʊsraeçə 'kraft/'maxt zaen] +sein

reckoning [noun] Berechnung [bə'rɛçnʊŋ] die <-, -en> ◊ *Nach meiner Berechnung kostet das zusammen über 250 Euro.*

⊛ be in/out of reckoning (nicht) in Betracht kommen

recognition [noun] **1.** *(identification)* Erkennen [ɛ'kɛnən] das <-s> no pl ◊ *das frühzeitige Erkennen von Krankheitssymptomen* beyond (all) recognition bis zur Unkenntlichkeit [bɪs tsuːg 'ʊnkɛntlɪçkaet] ◊ *Das Opfer war bis zur Unkenntlichkeit verbrannt.* speech recognition Spracherkennung ['ʃpraːxlɛkɛnʊŋ] die <-> no pl **2.** *(acknowledgement)* Anerkennung ['anlɛkɛnʊŋ] die <-, -en> most sing ◊ *Er sucht die Anerkennung der anderen.* ♦ *die Anerkennung des kleinen Inselstaates* in recognition of/ for sth in Anerkennung ... [gen] ◊ *in Anerkennung ihrer Leistung*

recognizable(-ably) [adj, adv] erkennbar [ɛ'kɛnbaːʳ] ◊ *erkennbare Fortschritte* ♦ *Das Gemälde war leicht als Fälschung erkennbar.* ♦ *Seine Leistung hat sich erkennbar verbessert.*

recognize [verb] **1.** *(identify)* erkennen [ɛ'kɛnən] <erkennt, erkannte, hat erkannt> ◊ *Ich habe sie sofort an ihrer Stimme erkannt.* ♦ *Ich hätte ihn fast nicht erkannt, so sehr war er gealtert.* **2.** *(acknowledge, accept, praise)* anerkennen ['anlɛkɛnən] <erkennt, erkannte an, hat anerkannt> ◊ *die Regeln anerkennen* ♦ *jds Bemühungen anerkennen* ♦ *einen Staat diplomatisch anerkennen* be recognized as sth als etw. gelten [als ... gɛltn̩] <gilt, galt, hat gegolten> ◊ *Sie gilt als die beste Fußballerin Europas.*

recommend [verb] empfehlen [ɛm'pfeːlən] <empfiehlt, empfahl, hat empfohlen> recommend (that), recommend doing sth empfehlen, etw. zu tun recommend sb to do sth jdm empfehlen, etw. zu tun ◊ *Er hat ihr empfohlen, das Geld anzulegen.* recommend sb/sth to sb jdm etw./jdn empfehlen ◊ *Können wir hier einen guten Kinderarzt/PC empfehlen?* sb/sth has much/little to recommend them/it es spricht viel/wenig für jdn/etw. [ɛs ʃprɪçt 'fiːl/'veːnɪç fyːɐ̯] <sprach, hat gesprochen> ◊ *Für dieses Restaurant spricht nur wenig.*

recommendation [noun] Empfehlung [ɛm'pfeːlʊŋ] die <-, -en> ◊ *Ich komme auf Empfehlung meines Arztes zu Ihnen.*

recommended → recommend [adj] empfehlenswert [ɛm'pfeːlənsveːɐt] <empfehlenswerter, am empfehlens-

wertesten> ◊ *empfehlenswerte Links zum Thema* ♦ *Wie viel Taschengeld ist empfehlenswert?*

reconcile [verb] **1.** *(conflicting things)* miteinander vereinbaren [mɪt|ae̯nande fe|'ae̯nbaːrən] <bringt, brachte, hat gebracht> ◊ *verschiedene Bedürfnisse miteinander vereinbaren* ♦ *Es fällt ihm schwer, seinen Beruf mit dem Familienleben zu vereinbaren.* reconcile differences Meinungsverschiedenheiten beilegen ['mae̯nʊŋsfeˌʃiːdn̩hae̯tn̩ ˌbae̯leːgn̩] +haben **2.** *(conflicting persons)* versöhnen [feˈzøːnən] <versöhnt, versöhnte, hat versöhnt> ◊ *Ich wollte ihn mit seinem Freund versöhnen.* They reconcile. Sie versöhnen sich. **3.** *(accept)* reconcile yourself to sth sich mit etw. abfinden [mɪt ... 'apfɪndn̩] <findet sich ab, fand sich ab, hat sich abgefunden> ◊ *Sie konnte sich mit dem Verlust nicht abfinden.*

reconnaissance [noun] Aufklärung ['aʊfklɛːrʊŋ] die <–, –en> ◊ *strategische/taktische Aufklärung*

reconstruct [verb] **1.** *(a country, building)* wieder aufbauen [viːdɐ 'aʊfbaʊən] <baut auf, baute auf, hat aufgebaut> ◊ *Nach dem Kriegsende soll das Land wieder aufgebaut werden.* **2.** *(form an idea, copy sth that existed before)* rekonstruieren [rekɔnstruˈiːrən] <rekonstruiert, rekonstruierte, hat rekonstruiert> ◊ *Das abgebrannte Fachwerkhaus wurde originalgetreu rekonstruiert.* ♦ *Es dauerte Monate, bis der genaue Unfallhergang rekonstruiert werden konnte.* **3.** *(organize in a different way)* reorganisieren [reˌɔrganiˈziːrən] <reorganisiert, reorganisierte, hat reorganisiert> ◊ *Die Abteilung wurde von Grund auf reorganisiert.*

reconstruction [noun] **1.** *(of a society, building, country)* Wiederaufbau [viːdɐ|'aʊfbaʊ] der <–s> no pl ◊ *der Wiederaufbau der Gesellschaft* ♦ *der Wiederaufbau der Häuser nach dem Krieg* **2.** *(process of putting together information, copy of sth that existed previously)* Rekonstruktion [rekɔnstrʊkˈtsjoːn] die <–, –en> ◊ *die Rekonstruktion des Tathergangs* ♦ *die Rekonstruktion eines ägyptischen Palastes*

record¹ [noun] **1.** *(of data)* Aufzeichnung ['aʊftsae̯çnʊn] die <–, –en> ◊ *Die Aufzeichnungen sind verloren gegangen.* keep a record of sth) (über etw. [acc]) Buch führen ['buːx fyːrən] +haben ◊ *Ich führe Buch über alle Ausgaben, die ich habe.* **2.** *(reputation)* Ruf [ruːf] der <–(e)s> no pl ◊ *In Bezug auf Pünktlichkeit hast du einen schlechten Ruf.* ♦ *Als Musiker hat er einen sehr guten Ruf.* **3.** SPORT Rekord [reˈkɔʳt] der <–(e)s, –e> ◊ *Das ist neuer olympischer Rekord.* ♦ *einen Rekord brechen/halten/aufstellen* **4.** MUS Platte ['platə] die <–, –n> ◊ *Ich habe viele Platten von Joan Baez.*

⊚ set the record straight etw. berichtigen *just for the record* nur der Vollständigkeit halber off the record inoffiziell

record² [verb] **1.** *(document, register)* aufzeichnen ['aʊftsae̯çnən] <zeichnet auf, zeichnete auf, hat aufgezeichnet> ◊ *seine Gedanken in einem Tagebuch aufzeichnen* ♦ *Das Messgerät zeichnet die Schwankungen auf.* ♦ *Ihre Stimme wurde auf Band aufgezeichnet.* **2.** FILM, MUS aufnehmen ['aʊfneːmən] <nimmt auf, nahm auf, hat aufgenommen> ◊ *Sie haben ein neues Album aufgenommen.* ♦ *einen Film auf Video aufnehmen* **3.** *(achieve)* verzeichnen [feˈtsae̯çnən] <verzeichnet, verzeichnete, hat verzeichnet> ◊ *Sie konnten ihren dritten Heimsieg verzeichnen.*

recorder [noun] **1.** MUS *(musical instrument)* Blockflöte

['blɔkfløːtə] die <–, –n> ◊ *ein Lied auf der Blockflöte spielen* **2.** *(machine for recording sth)* Aufnahmegerät ['aʊfnaːməgərɛːt] das <–(e)s, –e> cassette recorder Kassettenrekorder [kaˈsɛtn̩rekoʳdɐ] der <–s, –> ◊ *den Kassettenrekorder ein-/ausschalten* **3.** LAW *(in the UK: lawyer working as a judge)* ein Anwalt, der nebenberuflich als Richter arbeitet

recording [noun] Aufnahme ['aʊfnaːmə] die <–, –n> ◊ *eine Aufnahme von jdm/etw. machen* ♦ *Das ist eine Aufnahme ihres letzten Konzerts.* recording studio Aufnahmestudio ['aʊfnaːməˌʃtuːdjoː] das <–s, –s>

record player [noun] Plattenspieler ['platn̩ʃpiːlɐ] der <–s, –>

recount [verb] wiedergeben ['viːdeːgebm̩] <gibt wieder, gab wieder, hat wiedergegeben> ◊ *Sie hat den Tathergang genau wiedergegeben.*

recover [verb] **1.** *(become healthy again, get over sth)* recover (from sth) sich (von etw.) erholen [eˈhoːlən] <erholt sich, erholte sich, hat sich erholt> ◊ *sich von einer Operation/einem Schock nur langsam erholen* ♦ *Die Wirtschaft wird sich wieder erholen.* **2.** *(get back, money)* wiederbekommen ['viːdebəkɔmən] <bekommt wieder, bekam wieder, hat wiederbekommen> ◊ *Sie hat ihr Geld vom Finder wiederbekommen.*; *(bodily functions)* wiedererlangen ['viːde|ɛlaŋən] <erlangt wieder, erlangte wieder, hat wiedererlangt> ◊ *seine Gesundheit wiedererlangen* recover consciousness das Bewusstsein wiedererlangen recover your composure seine Fassung wiedererlangen recover the use of sth etw. wieder gebrauchen können [viːde gəˈbraʊxn̩ kœnən] <kann, konnte, hat können> ◊ *Er wird sein linkes Bein wieder gebrauchen können.*

recovery [noun] **1.** *(getting healthy)* Genesung [gəˈneːzʊŋ] die <–, –en> most sing ◊ *Ihre Genesung schreitet gut voran.* make a recovery sich erholen [eˈhoːlən] <erholt sich, erholte sich, hat sich erholt> ◊ *Er hat sich überraschend schnell erholt.* **2.** *(getting better)* Besserung ['bɛsərʊŋ] die <–, –en> ◊ *Eine Besserung auf dem Arbeitsmarkt ist nicht in Sicht.* **3.** *(getting back)* Rückgewinnung ['rʏkɡəvɪnʊŋ] die <–> no pl ◊ *die Rückgewinnung verlorener Gebiete*; *(of a capacity, data)* Wiederherstellung [viːdeˈheːɐ̯ʃtɛlʊŋ] die <–> no pl ◊ *Die Wiederherstellung der Bewegungsfähigkeit nach einem Schlaganfall* ♦ *die Wiederherstellung verlorener Daten*

recreation [noun] Freizeitbeschäftigung ['fraɛ̯tsae̯tbəˌʃɛftɪɡʊŋ] die <–, –en> ◊ *Meine liebste Freizeitbeschäftigung ist Kochen.* do sth for recreation etw. als Freizeitbeschäftigung tun

recruit¹ [noun] **1.** MIL Rekrut [reˈkruːt] der <–en, –en> ♀Rekrutin [reˈkruːtɪn] die <–, –nen> ◊ *Rekruten ausbilden* **2.** *(in a company)* neuer Mitarbeiter [nɔɔ̯e 'mɪt|aʳbae̯te] <–s, –> ♀neue Mitarbeiterin [nɔɔ̯e 'mɪt|aʳbae̯tərɪn] die <–, –nen> ◊ *Der neue Mitarbeiter scheint recht kompetent zu sein.* ♦ *Sie ist für die Einweisung neuer Mitarbeiter zuständig.*

recruit² [verb] **1.** *(staff)* einstellen ['ae̯nʃtɛlən] +haben ◊ *Sie stellen ihres wieder neue Mitarbeiter ein.* **2.** MIL rekrutieren [rekruˈtiːrən] <rekrutiert, rekrutierte, hat rekrutiert> ◊ *Man hat neue Soldaten rekrutiert.*

recruitment [noun] Rekrutierung [rekruˈtiːrʊŋ] die <–, –en> ◊ *die Rekrutierung von Arbeitskräften/Soldaten*

rectangle [noun] Rechteck ['rɛçt| ɛk] das <–(e)s, –e> ◊ *ein Rechteck zeichnen*

rectangular [adj] rechteckig ['rɛçtˌ|ɛkɪç] no comp/

superl ◊ *ein rechteckiger Tisch* ♦ *Das Grundstück ist rechteckig.*

rectify [verb] verbessern [fe'bɛsən] <verbessert, verbesserte, hat verbessert> ◊ *einen Fehler/eine Situation verbessern*

recur [verb] wiederkehren ['viːdeːkeːrən] +sein ◊ *Dieses Problem kehrt immer wieder.*

recycle [verb] *(waste materials)* recyceln [riˈsæɛkļn] <recycelt, recycelte, hat recycelt> ◊ *Wir recyceln Glas.*; *(use again)* wieder verwenden ['viːdeː fevɛndņ] <verwendet, verwendete, hat verwendet> ◊ *Stoffreste wieder verwenden*

red¹ ⊙ be in the red rote Zahlen schreiben

red² [adj] rot [roːt] <röter/roter, am rötesten/rotesten> ◊ *ein roter Pulli* ♦ *Sie wiegen rot vor Verlegenheit.* ♦ *rote Haare* red wine Rotwein ['roːtvaɛn] der <-(e)s, -e>

redecorate [verb] *(wallpaper)* neu tapezieren [nɔø tapeˈtsiːrən] <tapeziert, tapezierte, hat tapeziert> ◊ *ein Zimmer neu tapezieren; (paint)* neu streichen [nɔø ˈʃtraɛçņ] <streicht, strich, hat gestrichen>

red-hot [adj] **1.** *(shining red)* rotglühend ['roːtglyːənt] no comp/superl ◊ *rotglühendes Eisen; (very hot)* glühend heiß [glyːənt ˈhaɛs] no comp/superl ◊ *Pass auf — der Griff ist glühend heiß!* **2.** *(successful)* total angesagt [toˌtaːl ˈaŋgəzaːkt] no comp/superl *(fam)* ◊ *eine total angesagte Band* **3.** *(exciting)* heiß [haɛs] <heißer, am heißesten> *(fam)* ◊ *Der Typ ist heiß.* ♦ *heiße Liebesszenen*

red light [noun] rote Ampel [roːtə 'ampļ] die <-, -n> ◊ *Er hat die rote Ampel überseben.*

red tape [noun] Bürokratie [byrokraˈtiː] die <-> no pl *(pej)* ◊ *über zu viel Bürokratie klagen*

reduce [verb] **1.** *(decrease, make cheaper)* reduzieren [reduˈtsiːrən] <reduziert, reduzierte, hat reduziert> ◊ *Wir konnten unseren Papierverbrauch deutlich reduzieren.* reduce sth to sth. um etw. reduzieren ◊ *Ziel ist es, die Luftverschmutzung deutlich zu reduzieren.* reduce sth (from sth) to sth etw. (von etw.) auf etw. [acc] reduzieren ◊ *Der Preis der Hosen wurde auf fünfzehn Euro reduziert.* reduce sth to the minimum etw. auf ein Minimum reduzieren **2.** *(a sauce)* einkochen ['aɛnkɔxņ] +haben ◊ *Die Soße einkochen und mit Zitronensaft abschmecken.*

reduced → **reduce** [adj] *(circumstances)* ärmlich ['ɛ'rmlɪç] ◊ *ärmliche Lebensumstände*

reduction [noun] **1.** *(of speed, rate, temperature)* Verringerung [fe'rɪŋərʊŋ] die <-, -en> ◊ *eine Verringerung der Geschwindigkeit; (in expenses, wages)* Kürzung ['kʏrtsʊŋ] die <-, -en> ◊ *Viele Arbeitnehmer fürchten eine Kürzung der Löhne.* ♦ *eine Kürzung der Ausgaben planen* **2.** *(of price)* Ermäßigung [e'mɛːsɪgʊŋ] die <-, -en> ◊ *Kinder, Studenten, Rentner und Behinderte bekommen eine Ermäßigung.* ♦ *Es gibt eine Ermäßigung von 20 Prozent auf alle Sommerschube.* **3.** FOTO Verkleinerung [fe'klaɛnərʊŋ] die <-, -en> ◊ *eine Verkleinerung des Bildes*

redundancy [noun] **1.** *(job loss)* Entlassung [ɛnt'lasʊŋ] die <-, -en> ◊ *Es gab sehr viele Entlassungen.* ♦ *200 Arbeiter stehen nun vor der Entlassung.* take redundancy die Entlassung akzeptieren compulsory redundancy Entlassung **2.** *(surplus, what is too much)* Redundanz [redʊn'dants] die <-, -en> *(lofty)* ◊ *funktionelle Redundanz*

---

redundant [adj] **1.** *(jobless)* arbeitslos ['a'baɛtsloːs] no comp/superl ◊ *arbeitslose Fachkräfte* ♦ *Er wurde arbeitslos.* be made redundant entlassen werden [ɛnt'lasņ veːɡdņ] <wird, wurde, ist worden> ◊ *Fast 150 Mitarbeiter wurden entlassen.* **2.** *(superfluous)* überflüssig ['yːbeflʏsɪç] ◊ *ein überflüssiger Gegenstand* ♦ *Das Auto ist völlig überflüssig.* **3.** *(system)* redundant [redʊn'dant] no comp/superl

reef [noun] Riff [rɪf] das <-(e)s, -e> ◊ *Das Boot lief auf ein Riff auf.*

refer [verb] **1.** *(talk about)* refer to sb/sth jdn/etw. erwähnen [e've:nən] <erwähnt, erwähnte, hat erwähnt> ◊ *Er erwähnte sie nur kurz.; (mention again, be about)* refer (back) to sth sich auf etw. [acc] beziehen [aɔf ... bəˌtsiːən] <bezieht sich, bezog sich, hat sich bezogen> ◊ *Er hat sich auf einen früheren Aufsatz bezogen.* ♦ *Worauf bezieht sich diese Bezeichnung?* **2.** *(send to another doctor)* refer sb to sb/sth jdn an jdn/etw. überweisen [an ... ybe,vaɛzņ] <überweist, überwies, hat überwiesen> ◊ *Sein Hausarzt überwies ihn an einen Spezialisten.; (to court)* refer sb/sth to sb/sth jdn/etw. an etw. überweisen [an ... fe,vaɛzņ] <verweist, verwies, hat verwiesen> ◊ *Die Klage wurde an das Amtsgericht verwiesen.* **3.** *(look up)* refer to sth etw. konsultieren [kɔnzʊl'tiːrən] <konsultiert, konsultierte, hat konsultiert> *(lofty)* ◊ *Sie konsultierten ein Wörterbuch.*

referee [noun] **1.** SPORT Schiedsrichter ['ʃiːtsrɪçtə] der <-s, -> ♀Schiedsrichterin ['ʃiːtsrɪçtərɪn] die <-, -nen> ◊ *Der Schiedsrichter zeigte ihm die rote Karte.* **2.** *(person who gives reference)* Referenz [refe'rɛnts] die <-, -en> ◊ *Sie dürfen mich gern als Referenz angeben.*

reference [noun] **1.** *(mention)* reference to sb/sth) Erwähnung (... [gen]) die <-, -en> ◊ *Die Erwähnung ihres Fehlers ärgerte sie.; (allusion)* Anspielung (auf jdn/etw.) ['anʃpiːlʊŋ] die <-, -en> ◊ *Der Titel ist eine Anspielung auf ein Gedicht von Wordsworth.; (mention)* make a reference to sth etw. erwähnen [e've:nən] <erwähnt, erwähnte, hat erwähnt> ◊ *Zum Glück hat sie ihre Vergangenheit nicht erwähnt.; (allude to)* auf etw. [acc] anspielen [aɔf ... ,anʃpiːlən] +haben ◊ *An dieser Stelle spielt der Autor auf die aktuellen politischen Ereignisse an.* **2.** *(testimonial)* Referenz [refe'rɛnts] die <-, -en> ◊ *Er konnte mehrere Referenzen vorweisen.* **3.** *(citation)* Zitat [tsi'taːt] das <-(e)s, -e> ◊ *Die Autorin verwendet viele Zitate.* **4.** *(bibliographical information)* Quellenangabe ['kvɛlən|anga:bə] die <-, -n> ◊ *Sie finden die Quellenangaben am Ende des Buches.* ⊙ with reference to ... was ... anbetrifft

referendum [noun] Referendum [refe'rɛndʊm] das <-s, Referenden> ◊ *ein Referendum abbalten*

referral [noun] **1.** *(sending sb/sth to another person or place)* Verweisung [fe'vaɛzʊŋ] die <-, -en> ◊ *die Verweisung eines Falles an ein anderes Gericht* **2.** MED Überweisung [ybe'vaɛzʊŋ] die <-, -en> ◊ *die Überweisung an einen Spezialisten* **3.** *(of a doctoral thesis)* die Anweisung, seine Doktorarbeit zu überarbeiten und den Prüfern nochmals vorzulegen

refill [noun] **1.** Nachfüllpackung ['naːxfʏlpakʊŋ] die <-s, -en> ◊ *(cartridge)* Ersatzpatrone [e'zatspa,troːnə] die <- or -n> ◊ *Ich brauche eine Ersatzpatrone für*

A B C D E F G H I J K L M N O P Q R S T U V W X Y Z

meinen Drucker.

ⓦ **Would you like a refill?** Darf ich nachschenken?

refined [adj] **1.** *(sugar, oil)* raffiniert [rafi'ni:ɡt] *no comp/superl* ◊ *Weißer Zucker ist raffiniert.* ♦ *zu Treibstoff raffiniertes Rohöl* **2.** *(person)* kultiviert [kʊlti'vi:ɡt] <kultivierter, am kultiviertesten> ◊ *eine kultivierte Dame*

reflect [verb] **1.** *(cast back)* reflektieren [reflɛk'ti:rən] <reflektiert, reflektierte, hat reflektiert> ◊ *Der weiße Sand reflektiert das Sonnenlicht.* ♦ *Ein schmutziger Spiegel reflektiert nicht gut.* **2.** *(illustrate, show)* widerspiegeln ['vi:dɐʃpi:gln̩] <spiegelt wider, spiegelte wider, hat widergespiegelt> ◊ *eine Umfrage, die die Meinung der Bürger widerspiegelt* **3.** *(think about)* nachdenken ['na:xdɛŋkn̩] <denkt nach, dachte nach, hat nachgedacht> ◊ *Sie dachte einen Moment nach und stand dann auf.* reflect on sth über etw. [acc] nachdenken ◊ *Er dachte über seine Zukunft nach.*

reflection [noun] **1.** *(image, illustration)* Spiegelbild ['ʃpi:glbɪlt] das <–(e)s, –er> ◊ *Sie sah ihr Spiegelbild im Fenster.* ♦ *Kultur ist das Spiegelbild einer Gesellschaft.* **2.** *(consideration)* Nachdenken ['na:xdɛŋkn̩] das <–s> *no pl* ◊ *Gründliches Nachdenken führte zu dieser Entscheidung.* upon reflection bei genauem Nachdenken **3.** *(of light, sound)* Reflexion [reflɛ'ksi̯o:n] die <–, –en> ◊ *die Reflexion des Sonnenlichts auf der Meeresoberfläche*

reflex [noun] Reflex [re'flɛks] der <–es, –e> ◊ *ein Reiz, der einen Reflex auslöst* ♦ *Beim Fußball braucht man gute Reflexe.*

reflexive pronoun [noun] Reflexivpronomen [reflɛ'ksi:fpro,no:mən] das <–s, –> ◊ *das Reflexivpronomen „sich"*

reform[1] [noun] Reform [re'fɔrm] die <–, –en> ◊ *nötige Reformen durchsetzen* reform of sth Reform … [gen] ◊ *eine grundlegende Reform der Agrarpolitik*

reform[2] [verb] **1.** *(improve, change)* reformieren [refɔr'mi:rən] <reformiert, reformierte, hat reformiert> ◊ *Luther reformierte die Kirche.* **2.** *(behave better)* sich bessern ['bɛsən] +haben ◊ *Sie versprach, sich zu bessern.; (transform a criminal)* resozialisieren [rezotsi̯ali'zi:rən] <resozialisiert, resozialisierte, hat resozialisiert> ◊ *ein Straftäter, der resozialisiert wurde* reformed gambler ehemaliger Spieler [aen ,e:əma:lɪgə 'ʃpi:lɐ] <–s, –> ♀ehemalige Spielerin [aenə,e:əma:lɪgə 'ʃpi:lərɪn] die <–, –nen> *but: ein ehemaliger Spieler* reformed alcoholic trockener Alkoholiker [,trɔkənɐ alko'ho:lɪkɐ] <–s, –> ♀trockene Alkoholikerin [,trɔkənə alko'ho:lɪkərɪn] die <–, –nen>

reformer [noun] Reformer [re'fɔrmɐ] der <–s, –> ♀Reformerin [re'fɔrmərɪn] die <–, –nen> ◊ *ein Reformer wie Atatürk*

refresh [verb] **1.** erfrischen [e'frɪʃn̩] <erfrischt, erfrischte, hat erfrischt> refresh yourself sich erfrischen refresh your sth sich [dat] etw. kühlen ['ky:lən] +haben ◊ *sich das Gesicht mit Wasser kühlen* refresh your memory sein Gedächtnis auffrischen [zaen gə'dɛçtnɪs ,aoffrɪʃn̩] +haben refresh your skills seine Kenntnisse auffrischen ◊ *Sie sollten Ihre Computerkenntnisse auffrischen!* **2.** IT aktualisieren [aktuali'zi:rən] <aktualisiert, aktualisierte, hat aktualisiert> ◊ *eine Webseite aktualisieren*

refreshed → **refresh** [adj] *(rested)* frisch [frɪʃ] ◊ *Wir waren alle frisch und munter.*

refreshment [noun] *(food)* Stärkung ['ʃtɛrkʊŋ] die <–, –en> ◊ *ein Joghurt als kleine Stärkung zwischendurch; (drink)* Erfrischung [e'frɪʃʊŋ] die <–, –en> ◊ *Im Anschluss an das Konzert werden Erfrischungen serviert.*

refrigerator [noun] Kühlschrank ['ky:lʃraŋk] der <–(e)s, Kühlschränke>

refuel [verb] *(a vehicle, aircraft)* auftanken ['aoftaŋkn̩] +haben sth refuels etw. wird aufgetankt ◊ *Der Lastwagen wurde an der Tankstelle aufgetankt.*

refuge [noun] **1.** *(protection)* Zuflucht ['tsu:flʊxt] die <–> ◊ *Die Asylanten suchten Zuflucht in einer Kirche.* **2.** *(place)* Zufluchtsstätte ['tsu:flʊxtsʃtɛtə] die <–, –n> ◊ *eine Zufluchtsstätte für verwaiste Elefanten*

ⓦ **take/seek refuge in sth** sich in etw. [acc] flüchten

refugee [noun] Flüchtling ['flʏçtlɪŋ] der <–s, –e> ◊ *Flüchtlinge aufnehmen*

refund[1] [noun] Erstattung [e'ʃtatʊŋ] die <–, –en> ◊ *Eine Erstattung der Gebühren ist ausgeschlossen.*

refund[2] [verb] erstatten [e'ʃtatn̩] <erstattet, erstattete, hat erstattet> refund sb an amount jdm einen Betrag erstatten ◊ *Die Fahrtkosten werden Ihnen erstattet.*

refusal [noun] **1.** *(rejection)* Ablehnung ['aple:nʊŋ] die <–> *no pl* refusal of sth die Ablehnung … [gen] die Ablehnung eines Preises/Geschenks refusal of entry Einreiseverweigerung ['aenraezə,vaegərʊŋ] die <–, –en> *most sing* visa refusal Visaverweigerung ['vi:zafe,vaegərʊŋ] die <–, –en> *most sing* **2.** *(unwillingness to do sth)* refusal to do sth Weigerung, etw. zu tun ['vaegərʊŋ … tu:] die <–, –en> ◊ *die Weigerung der Regierung, mit den Entführern zu verhandeln*

ⓦ **give sb first refusal (on sth)** jdm das Vorkaufsrecht (auf etw. [acc])einräumen

refuse[1] [noun] Abfall ['apfal] der <–(e)s, Abfälle> ◊ *radioaktive Abfälle*

refuse[2] [verb] **1.** *(not want to do sth)* sich weigern ['vaegən] +haben ◊ *Ich bat sie um Hilfe, aber sie weigerte sich.* ♦ *Er weigerte sich, sich zu entschuldigen.* flatly refuse sich strikt weigern **2.** *(not accept sth)* ablehnen ['aple:nən] +haben ◊ *Wir lehnen eine weitere Debatte über dieses Thema ab.* ♦ *eine Einladung ablehnen* **3.** *(not allow sth)* verweigern [fe'vaegən] <verweigert, verweigerte, hat verweigert> ◊ *Die Baugenehmigung wurde uns verweigert.*

regain [verb] *(get back)* wiedererlangen ['vi:dɐʔelaŋən] <erlangt wieder, erlangte wieder, hat wiedererlangt> ◊ *sein Selbstvertrauen/das Bewusstsein wiedererlangen* regain control of sth etw. wieder in den Griff bekommen [vi:dɐ ɪn de:n 'grɪf bəkɔmən] <bekommt, bekam, hat bekommen>

regard[1] [noun] **1.** *(giving attention)* have regard for einer Sache [dat] Beachtung schenken [bə'laxtʊŋ ʃɛŋkn̩] +haben ◊ *Wir müssen diesen neuen Entwicklungen mehr Beachtung schenken.* without regard for sb/sth ohne Rücksicht auf jdn/etw. [o:nə 'rʏkzɪçt aof] ◊ *Er handelte ohne Rücksicht auf die Folgen.* with little regard for sb/sth ohne viel Rücksicht auf jdn/etw. **2.** *(showing admiration)* have a high regard for sb/sth, hold sb/sth in high regard jdn/etw. sehr schätzen [ze:ɐ 'ʃɛtsn̩] +haben ◊ *Sein Arbeitgeber schätzt ihn sehr.* **3.** *(greetings)* regards Grüße ['gry:sə] die <–> *pl* give sb sb's regards jdm Grüße von jdm bestellen kind regards herzliche

Grüße 4. in this/that regard in dieser Hinsicht [ɪn 'diːzə ˌhɪnzɪçt] ◊ *In dieser Hinsicht ist noch nichts unternommen worden.* with regard to hinsichtlich ['hɪnzɪçtlɪç] *sing nouns without article or attribute are not declined when following this prep, otherwise* [+gen] *(form)* ◊ *Bedenken hinsichtlich möglicher Mängel* ✦ *Das Programm ist hinsichtlich Datensicherheit verbesserungsbedürftig.*

regard² [verb] ansehen ['anzeːən] <sieht an, sah an, hat angesehen> ◊ *Diese Meinung wird mittlerweile als überholt angesehen.* ✦ *Er wird als einer der ganz großen Komponisten angesehen.* regard sb/sth with suspicion jdm/etw. mit Misstrauen begegnen [mɪt 'mɪstraʊən bəgeːgnən] <begegnet, begegnete, ist begegnet>
◉ as regards sb/sth was jdn/etw. betrifft

regarding [prep] bezüglich [bə'ʦyːklɪç] *sing nouns without article or attribute are not declined when following this prep, otherwise* [+gen] ◊ *Fragen bezüglich des Lehrplans*

regardless [adv] **1.** *(nevertheless)* trotzdem ['trɔʦdeːm] ◊ *Ich war todmüde, aber ich habe trotzdem weitergemacht.; (despite)* regardless of trotz [trɔʦ] *sing nouns without article or attribute are not declined when following this prep, otherwise* [+gen] ◊ *Trotz schrecklicher Kopfschmerzen musste ich arbeiten.* **2.** *(without considering)* regardless of ungeachtet ['ʊngəˌaxtət] [+gen] *(form)* ◊ *Ungeachtet aller Einwände wurde sein Vorschlag angenommen.*

regime [noun] **1.** *(undemocratic government)* Regime [reˈʒiːm] das <-s, -s> *(pej)* ◊ *ein totalitäres Regime* ✦ *das Regime* Pol Pots **2.** *(system)* System [zʏsˈteːm] das <-s, -e> tax regime Steuersystem ['ʃtɔʏɐzʏsˌteːm]

regiment [noun] Regiment [regiˈmɛnt] das <-(e)s, -er>

region [noun] *(area)* Region [reˈgioːn] die <-, -en> ◊ *Kunsthandwerker aus der gesamten Region zeigten ihre Arbeiten.* ✦ *die arktische Region* ✦ *die Region Berlin-Brandenburg; (of your body)* heart region Herzgegend ['hɛɐʦgeːgn̩t] die <-> *no pl*
◉ in the region of etwa ◊ *Die Uhr kostet etwa 200 Euro.*

regional(ly) [adj, adv] regional [regioˈnaːl] *seldom comp/superl, mostly before ns* ◊ *eine beliebte regionale Spezialität* ✦ *ein regional tätiger Verband*

register¹ [noun] **1.** *(book, list)* Verzeichnis [fɛɐˈʦaɛçnɪs] das <-ses, -se> ◊ *das Verzeichnis europäischer Institutionen; (in school)* Klassenbuch ['klasnbuːx] das <-(e)s, Klassenbücher> register of births, deaths, and marriages Personenstandsbuch [pɛɐˈzoːnənʃtantsbuːx] **2.** mus Tonumfang ['toːnʊmfaŋ] der <-(e)s, Tonumfänge> ◊ *Diese Kasse schließt jetzt.* **4.** *(of language)* Stilebene ['ʃtiːlˌleːbənə] die <-, -n> ◊ *in einem Aufsatz verschiedene Stilebenen mischen*

register² [verb] **1.** *(with an authority, organization)* anmelden ['anmɛldn̩] <meldet an, meldete an, hat angemeldet> ◊ *sein Auto anmelden* sb registers (for sth) jd meldet sich (für etw.) an ◊ *Hast du dich für den Musikwettbewerb angemeldet?* sb registers with sth jd meldet sich bei etw. an ◊ *Sie müssen sich beim Einwohnermeldeamt anmelden.* **2.** *(list in a book)* eintragen ['aɛntraːgn̩] <trägt ein, trug ein, hat eingetragen> ◊ *etw. ins Grundbuch eintragen lassen*

register a company eine Firma ins Handelsregister eintragen **3.** *(a measurement)* anzeigen ['anˈʦaɛgn̩] +haben ◊ *Welche Temperatur zeigt das Thermometer an?* sth registers etw. wird angezeigt ◊ *Die Temperatur wird in Celsius angezeigt.* **4.** *(notice)* sb registers sth jd nimmt etw. wahr [nɪmt ... vaːɐ] <nahm wahr, hat wahrgenommen> ◊ *Ich hatte deine Anwesenheit gar nicht wahrgenommen.* sth registers etw. wird registriert [vɪɐˈt regɪsˈtriːɐt] <wurde, ist worden> ◊ *Ihre Bestellung wird erst registriert, wenn der Betrag überwiesen worden ist.* **5.** *(betray your feelings)* verraten [fɛˈraːtn̩] <verrät, verriet, hat verraten> ◊ *Ihre Stimme verriet Angst.* His eyes registered surprise. Sein Blick verriet, dass er überrascht war. **6.** *(make your opinion known)* register a complaint (with sb) sich (bei jdm) beschweren [bəˈʃveːrən] <beschwert sich, beschwerte sich, hat sich beschwert> ◊ *Ich möchte mich bei dem Geschäftsleiter beschweren.* register an objection against sth einen Einwand gegen etw. erheben [aenən 'aɛnvant geːgn̩ ... eheːbm̩] <erhebt, erhob, hat erhoben> **7.** *(a letter)* als Einschreiben verschicken [als 'aɛnʃraɛbm̩ fɛʃɪkń] <verschickt, verschickte, hat verschickt> ◊ *einen Brief als Einschreiben verschicken*

registered → register² [adj] **1.** registered letter/parcel Einschreiben ['aɛnʃraɛbm̩] das <-s, -> **2.** registered nurse examinierter Krankenpfleger [ɛksamiˌniːɐtɐ 'kraŋkŋpfleːgɐ] <-s, -> ♀examinierte Krankenschwester [ɛksamiˌniːɐtə 'kraŋkŋʃvɛstɐ] <-, -n>

registration [noun] *(with an authority, organization)* Anmeldung ['anmɛldʊŋ] die <-, -en> ◊ *Anmeldung eines Gewerbes/Patents*

registration number [noun] Kennzeichen ['kɛnʦaɛçn̩] das <-s, -> ◊ *das Fahrzeug mit dem Kennzeichen S-MJ 1414* ✦ *Wie lautet das amtliche Kennzeichen Ihres Wagens?*

registry office [noun] Standesamt ['ʃtandəsˌamt] das <-(e)s, Standesämter> ◊ *eine Trauung auf dem Standesamt*

regret¹ [noun] **1.** *(feeling of sadness)* Bedauern [bəˈdaʊɐn] das <-s> *no pl* with deep regret mit großem Bedauern express regret sein Bedauern ausdrücken He sends his regrets that he had to cancel. Er lässt ausrichten, dass er leider absagen muss. **2.** *(wish you hadn't done sth)* Reue ['rɔʏə] die <-> *no pl* ◊ *Sie zeigte keine Reue.* have no regrets nichts bereuen [nɪçts bəˈrɔʏən] <bereut, bereute, hat bereut> have no regrets about sth etw. nicht bereuen sb's biggest regret is doing sth jd bereut am meisten, dass er/sie etc. ◊ *Ich bereue am meisten, dass ich nie schwimmen gelernt habe.*

regret² [verb] **1.** *(feel sad or ashamed)* bedauern [bəˈdaʊɐn] <bedauert, bedauerte, hat bedauert> ◊ *Er bedauert seine unbedachten Äußerungen.* ✦ *Sie bedauert, dass sie keine Geschwister hat.* regret to inform/tell sb that jdm leider mitteilen müssen, dass [laɛdɐ 'mɪttaɛlən mʏsn̩ das] müssen> ◊ *Wir müssen Ihnen leider mitteilen, dass die Stelle bereits vergeben wurde.* **2.** *(wish you hadn't done sth)* bereuen [bəˈrɔʏən] <bereut, bereute, hat bereut> ◊ *Ich habe niemals bereut, ihn geheiratet zu haben.* ✦ *Das ist eine Entscheidung, die ich sehr bereue.* sb will live to regret sth jd wird etw. noch bereuen

regrettable [adj] bedauerlich [bəˈdaɵelɪç] ◊ *eine bedauerliche Niederlage* ♦ *Es ist bedauerlich, dass du so wenig liest.*

regular¹ [noun] **1.** *(in a pub, restaurant, hotel)* Stammgast [ˈʃtamgast] der <-(e)s, Stammgäste> ◊ *Ich war Stammgast in diesem Hotel.* ♦ *ein Stammgast aus dem Dorf* **2.** *(soldier)* Berufssoldat [bəˈruːfszɔlˌdaːt] der <-en, -en> ♀Berufssoldatin [bəˈruːfszɔlˌdaːtɪn] die <-, -nen> ◊ *Er ist Berufssoldat bei der Bundeswehr.* ♦ *eine amerikanische Berufssoldatin* **3.** *(petrol, gasoline)* Normal [nɔrˈmaːl] das <-s> *no pl* ◊ *Normal tanken*

regular² [adj] **1.** *(in equal amounts of space or time, following a normal pattern)* regelmäßig [ˈreːglmɛːsɪç] ◊ *in regelmäßigen Abständen* ♦ *Dieses Verb ist regelmäßig.* on a regular basis regelmäßig [ˈreːglmɛːsɪç] ◊ *Wir treffen uns regelmäßig.* **2.** regular customer Stammkunde [ˈʃtamkʊndə] der <-ns, -n> ♀Stammkundin [ˈʃtamkʊndɪn] die <-, -nen> ◊ *Sie ist eine wichtige Stammkundin.* regular guest Stammgast [ˈʃtamgast] der <-(e)s, Stammgäste> ◊ *Er ist schon Stammgast in unserem Hotel.* **3.** *(face)* ebenmäßig [ˈeːbm̩mɛːsɪç] ◊ *Ihr Gesicht ist ebenmäßig.* ♦ *ebenmäßige Gesichtszüge* **4.** *(opening hours, employment)* fest [fɛst] *only before ns* ◊ *feste Öffnungszeiten* **5.** *(ordinary)* normal [nɔrˈmaːl] *mostly before ns* ◊ *ein ganz normaler Kerl* regular petrol Normal [nɔrˈmaːl] das <-s> *no pl* ◊ *Normal tanken* **6.** *(soldier, officer)* Berufs... [bəˈruːfs] regular *(soldier)* Berufssoldat [bəˈruːfszɔlˌdaːt] der <-en, -en> ♀Berufssoldatin [bəˈruːfszɔlˌdaːtɪn] die <-, -nen>

regularly [adv] regelmäßig [ˈreːglmɛːsɪç] ◊ *Ich gehe regelmäßig joggen.*

regulate [verb] **1.** *(by rules, regulations, standards)* regeln [ˈreːgln̩] +haben ◊ *den Verkehr regeln* sth regulates itself etw. regelt sich selbst ◊ *Der Markt regelt sich selbst.* **2.** *(make it possible to set sth to a desired standard or strength)* regulieren [reguˈliːrən] <reguliert, regulierte, hat reguliert> ◊ *ein Medikament, das den Blutdruck reguliert* ♦ *Mit diesem Knopf kann man die Lautstärke regulieren.*

regulation [noun] **1.** *(rule)* Bestimmung [bəˈʃtɪmʊŋ] die <-, -en> ◊ *Dieser Sachverhalt fällt nicht unter die neue Bestimmung.* environmental regulation Umweltschutzbestimmung [ˈʊmvɛltʃʊtsbəʃtɪmʊŋ] safety regulation Sicherheitsbestimmung [ˈzɪçɐhaɛtsbəʃtɪmʊŋ] **2.** *(control)* Regulierung [reguˈliːrʊŋ] die <-, -en> ◊ *eine strengere Regulierung des Marktes*

rehabilitate [verb] **1.** *(a prisoner, ill, disabled person, person in disrepute)* rehabilitieren [rehabiliˈtiːrən] <rehabilitiert, rehabilitierte, hat rehabilitiert> ◊ *Suchtkranke/Haftentlassene/einen Politiker rehabilitieren;* *(sb's image, reputation)* wiederherstellen [viːdɐˈheːɐ̯ʃtɛlən] <stellt wiederher, stellte wiederher, hat wiederhergestellt> ◊ *Es ist oft schwierig, einen guten Ruf wiederherzustellen.* **2.** *(a building, company)* sanieren [zaˈniːrən] <saniert, sanierte, hat saniert> ◊ *Der Wohnblock wird saniert.* ♦ *Die neue Eigentümerin hat es geschafft, die Firma zu sanieren.*

rehabilitation [noun] Rehabilitation [rehabilitaˈtsjoːn] die <-, -en> ◊ *die berufliche Rehabilitation von Langzeitarbeitslosen* rehabilitation centre Rehabilitationszentrum [rehabilitaˈtsjoːnstsɛntrʊm] das <-s, Rehabilitationszentren>

rehearsal [noun] Probe [ˈproːbə] die <-, -n> ◊ *die Probe eines Stücks*

rehearse [verb] **1.** *(for a play, musical performance)* proben [ˈproːbm̩] +haben ◊ *Das Orchester probt täglich.* ♦ *ein Stück proben* **2.** *(what you want to say)* einüben [ˈaɛnˌlyːbm̩] +haben ◊ *Sie hatte ihre Rede nicht eingeübt.*

reign¹ [noun] Herrschaft [ˈhɛrʃaft] die <-, -en> in the reign of sb unter jds Herrschaft ◊ *unter der Herrschaft Königin Viktorias* reign of terror Schreckensherrschaft [ˈʃrɛkŋ̍shɛrʃaft]

reign² [verb] **1.** *(rule, prevail)* reign (over sb/sth) (über etw./jdn) herrschen [ˈhɛrʃn̩] +haben ◊ *Wann herrschte Elizabeth I.?* ♦ *ein Fürst, der über zwei Staaten herrscht* sth reigns es herrscht etw. ◊ *Es herrschte Verwirrung.* **2.** *(be strong, important)* reign (supreme) die Oberhand haben [diː ˈoːbɐhant haːbm̩] +haben ◊ *Michael Schumacher hatte erneut die Oberhand.*

reimburse [verb] *(a person)* entschädigen [ɛntˈʃɛːdɪgn̩] <entschädigt, entschädigte, hat entschädigt> ◊ *Käufer des defekten Geräts werden entschädigt.;* *(an amount)* erstatten [eˈʃtatn̩] <erstattet, erstattete, hat erstattet> reimburse sb for sth jdm etw. erstatten ◊ *Die Fahrtkosten werden Ihnen erstattet.*

reimbursement [noun] Erstattung [eˈʃtatʊŋ] die <-, -en> ◊ *die Erstattung der Mehrwertsteuer*

reinforce [verb] **1.** *(a situation, troops)* verstärken [fɛˈʃtɛrkŋ̍] <verstärkt, verstärkte, hat verstärkt> ◊ *die Truppen verstärken* ♦ *Verstärkt das derzeitige Schulsystem die Ungleichheit?;* *(a point of view, prejudice)* bestätigen [bəˈʃtɛːtɪgn̩] <bestätigt, bestätigte, hat bestätigt> ◊ *eine Ansicht bestätigen* reinforce sb's opinion jdn in seiner Meinung bestärken [ɪn zaɛnə ˈmaɛnʊŋ bəˈʃtɛrkŋ̍] <bestärkt, bestärkte, hat bestärkt> reinforce a message einer Botschaft Nachdruck verleihen [aɛnə ˌboːtʃaft ˈnaːxdrʊk fɛlaɛən] <verleiht, verlieh, hat verliehen> **2.** *(a wall, embankment)* befestigen [bəˈfɛstɪgn̩] <befestigt, befestigte, hat befestigt> ◊ *Die Ufer der Teiche wurden künstlich befestigt.*

reject [verb] **1.** *(an offer, a request, suggestion, candidate)* ablehnen [ˈaplɛːnən] +haben ◊ *Der Antrag/Vorschlag wurde abgelehnt.* ♦ *einen Bewerber/eine Bewerbung ablehnen* reject sth out of hand etw. rundweg ablehnen **2.** *(sth you ordered)* zurückgehen lassen [tsuˈrʏkgeːən lasn̩] <lässt, ließ, hat lassen> ◊ *eine Lieferung zurückgehen lassen* **3.** *(a suitor, sb showing you affection)* zurückweisen [tsuˈrʏkvaɛzn̩] <weist zurück, wies zurück, hat zurückgewiesen> ◊ *Sie wies ihn zurück und heiratete einen anderen.* **4.** MED *(an organ from a donor)* abstoßen [ˈapʃtoːsn̩] <stößt ab, stieß ab, hat abgestoßen> ◊ *ein Spenderherz abstoßen*

rejection [noun] **1.** *(of people, authority, a belief)* Ablehnung [ˈaplɛːnʊŋ] die <-, -en> ◊ *Kinder, die Ablehnung erfahren* ♦ *die Ablehnung eines Antrags;* *(of goods)* Abnahmeverweigerung [ˈapnaːməfɐˌvaɛgərʊŋ] die <-, -en>; *(letter of rejection)* Absage [ˈapzaːgə] die <-, -n> ◊ *Er hat auf seine Bewerbungen lauter Absagen erhalten.* **2.** MED *(of a donated organ)* Abstoßung [ˈapʃtoːsʊŋ] die <-, -en> ◊ *eine Abstoßung eines gespendeten Organs*

rejoice [verb] *(celebrate)* jubeln [ˈjuːbl̩n] +haben ◊ *Er jubelte, als sie die Mannschaft die Meisterschaft gewann.* rejoice in sth sich über etw. [acc] freuen [ˈyːbɐ ... ˌfrɔɥən] ◊ *Sie freuten sich über meinen Miss-*

erfolg.

relate [verb] **1.** *(be connected)* zusammenhängen [ˈtsuˈzamənhɛŋən] <hängt zusammen, hing zusammen, hat zusammengehangen> ◊ *Auf welche Weise hängen die beiden Probleme zusammen?* relate to sth mit etw. zusammenhängen ◊ *Aspekte, die mit diesem Thema zusammenhängen* **2.** *(report)* relate sth von etw. berichten [fɔn ... bəˈrɪçtn̩] <berichtet, berichtete, hat berichtet> *(lofty)* ◊ *Er berichtete von seinen Erfahrungen.* relate sth to sb jdm von etw. berichten
♦ **relate to** [phras v] **1.** *(establish a connection)* relate sth to sth eine Verbindung zwischen etw. und etw. herstellen [aenə feˌbɪndʊŋ tsvɪʃn̩ ... ʊnt ... heːɐ̯ʃtɛlən] +haben ◊ *Dieses Buch stellt eine Verbindung zwischen Theorie und Praxis her.* **2.** *(emotionally, socially)* relate to sb eine Beziehung zu jdm aufbauen [aenə bəˌtsiːʊŋ tsuː ... ˌaofbaoən] +haben ◊ *Es gelingt mir nicht, eine Beziehung zu ihm aufzubauen.* **3.** *(understand)* sb can/cannot relate to sth jd kann etwas/nichts mit etw. anfangen [kan ɛtvas/nɪçts mɪt ... ˌanfaŋən] <kann, konnte, hat gekonnt> ◊ *Mit Zahlen kann ich einfach nichts anfangen.*

related → relate [adj] *(of the same family, group, origins)* verwandt [fɛˈvant] no comp/superl ◊ *verwandte Schmetterlingsarten* be related to sb mit jdm verwandt sein They are related to each other. Sie sind miteinander verwandt.

relation [noun] **1.** *(relationship, connection)* relation(s) Beziehung [bəˈtsiːʊŋ] die <-, -en> ◊ *wirtschaftliche Beziehungen* ♦ *die Beziehung zwischen Rauchen und Lungenkrebs* **2.** *(proportion)* Verhältnis [fɛˈhɛltnɪs] das <-ses, -se> ◊ *Das Verhältnis zwischen Einsatz und Bezahlung muss stimmen.* ♦ *eine Farbe im Verhältnis zwei zu eins mischen* bear no relation to sth in keinem Verhältnis zu etw. stehen **3.** *(relative)* Verwandte [fɛˈvantə] der/die <-n, die Verwandten> *but:* ein Verwandter/eine Verwandte ◊ *Er ist ein naher Verwandter meiner Frau.*
ⓔ **in relation to sth 1.** *(in comparison to sth)* im Verhältnis zu etw. **2.** *(concerning sth)* in Bezug auf etw. [acc]

relationship [noun] *(connection between things, of partners)* Beziehung [bəˈtsiːʊŋ] die <-, -en> ◊ *die Beziehung zwischen Armut und Kriminalität* ♦ *Er will keine feste Beziehung.* a relationship with sb eine Beziehung zu jdm; *(interaction with people, sexual affair)* Verhältnis [fɛˈhɛltnɪs] das <-ses, -se> ◊ *Das Verhältnis zwischen den Mitarbeitern ist gut.* ♦ *Die beiden haben ein Verhältnis.* a relationship with sb ein Verhältnis mit jdm ◊ *ein gutes Verhältnis mit seinen Eltern haben* ♦ *Mit seinem Chef sollte man kein Verhältnis anfangen.*

relative¹ [noun] Verwandte [fɛˈvantə] der/die <-n, die Verwandten> *but:* ein Verwandter/eine Verwandte ◊ *Sie ist eine nahe Verwandte meiner Frau.* ♦ *Freunde und Verwandte einladen* ♦ *Der Barsch ist ein Verwandter des Zanders.*

relative² [adj] *(compared with sth else)* relativ [relaˈtiːf] no comp/superl ◊ *die relative Mehrheit haben* ♦ *Alles ist relativ.; (comparing similar and respective things)* jeweilige [ˈjeːvaelɪgə] no comp/superl, only before ns ◊ *Worin bestehen die jeweiligen Vorteile der beiden Methoden?*
ⓔ **relative to sth 1.** *(compared to)* im Vergleich zu

etw. **2.** *(relating to)* für etw. relevant

relative clause [noun] Relativsatz [relaˈtiːfzats] der <-es, Relativsätze>

relatively [adv] relativ [relaˈtiːf] no comp/superl ◊ *Die Gefahr ist relativ gering.* ♦ *Sie verdient relativ gut.* relatively speaking relativ gesehen

relative pronoun [noun] Relativpronomen [relaˈtiːfproˌnoːmən] das <-s, ->

relax [verb] **1.** *(loosen up your muscles, become calm, less tense)* relax sth etw. entspannen [ɛntˈʃpanən] <entspannt, entspannte, hat entspannt> ◊ *Entspannen Sie die Beinmuskulatur.* sb/sth relaxes jd/etw. entspannt sich ◊ *Ich entspanne mich beim Joggen.* ♦ *Meine Nackenmuskeln entspannten sich.* **2.** *(a rule, control, your grip)* relax sth etw. lockern [ˈlɔkən] +haben ◊ *Die Regierung lockert die Einfuhrbeschränkungen für Rindfleisch.* sth relaxes etw. lockert sich ◊ *Sein Griff lockerte sich und ich konnte mich losreißen.*

relaxation [noun] **1.** *(rest, calming down)* Entspannung [ɛntˈʃpanʊŋ] die <-, -en> most sing ◊ *Ruhe und Entspannung in der Sauna* **2.** *(of rules, conditions, control)* Lockerung [ˈlɔkərʊŋ] die <-, -en> most sing ◊ *die Lockerung der Vorschriften*

relaxed → relax [adj] *(informal, not strict)* locker [ˈlɔkɐ] ◊ *Die Atmosphäre dort ist ziemlich locker.* ♦ *eine lockere Handhabung der Regeln*

release¹ [noun] **1.** *(of a prisoner or an animal)* Freilassung [ˈfraelasʊŋ] die <-, -en> ◊ *die Freilassung der Geisel; (from custody, hospital)* Entlassung [ɛntˈlasʊŋ] die <-, -en> ◊ *release from sth* Entlassung aus etw. ◊ *meine Entlassung aus dem Gefängnis/Krankenhaus* **2.** *(of chemicals, gas)* Freisetzung [ˈfraezɛtsʊŋ] die <-> no pl ◊ *die Freisetzung giftiger Chemikalien* **3.** *(of a book, record)* Veröffentlichung [fɛlˈœfn̩tlɪçʊŋ] die <-, -en>; *(of a film)* Kinostart [ˈkiːnoʃtaʳt] der <-(e)s, -s> go on (general) release in die Kino kommen [ɪns ˈkiːno kɔmən] <kommt, kam, ist gekommen> **4.** TECHN *(button, handle)* Auslöser [ˈaosløːzɐ] der <-s, -> **5.** *(from sth unpleasant, constraints)* Erlösung [eˈløːzʊŋ] die <-> no pl ◊ *Der Urlaub war eine echte Erlösung.* ♦ *Die Tabletten brachten Erlösung von den Schmerzen.*

release² [verb] **1.** *(set free)* freilassen [ˈfraelasn̩] <lässt frei, ließ frei, hat freigelassen> ◊ *Gefangene freilassen* release sb on bail jdn gegen Kaution freilassen release an animal from its cage ein Tier aus dem Käfig lassen [aos deːm ˈkɛːfɪç lasn̩] <lässt, ließ, hat gelassen>; *(from hospital, custody)* entlassen [ɛntˈlasn̩] <entlässt, entließ, hat entlassen> ◊ *Die Patientin wurde heute Morgen entlassen.* release sb from sth jdn aus etw. entlassen ◊ *Er wurde vorzeitig aus dem Vertrag/aus der Haft entlassen.; (sb who is trapped)* release sb [bəˈfraeən] <befreit, befreite, hat befreit> ◊ *jdn aus einem brennenden Auto befreien* **2.** *(let go)* release (your grip on) sth etw. loslassen [ˈloːslasn̩] <lässt los, ließ los, hat losgelassen> ◊ *Er ließ meine Hand los.* **3.** *(a substance, energy)* freisetzen [ˈfraezɛtsn̩] +haben ◊ *Bei einer Verbrennung wird Energie freigesetzt.* release sth into etw. an/in etw. [dat] abgeben [an ... ˌapgeːbm̩] <gibt ab, gab ab, hat abgegeben> ◊ *Kohlenmonoxid in die Atmosphäre abgeben* ♦ *Wärme in die Umgebung abgeben* **4.** *(make publicly available)* herausbringen [hɛˈraosbrɪŋən] <bringt heraus, brachte heraus, hat herausgebracht> ◊ *Die Band hat eine neue CD*

herausgebracht. 5. *(the handbrake)* lösen ['lø:zn̩] +haben **6.** *(a negative feeling)* abbauen ['apbaʊən] +haben ◊ *Sportliche Betätigung baut Spannungen ab.* **7.** *(from a duty)* release sb from sth jdn von etw. entbinden [fɔ ... ɛnt,bɪndn̩] <entbindet, entband, hat entbunden> ◊ *jdn von einer Pflicht entbinden*

relentless(ly) ⟨adj, adv⟩ unerbittlich ['ʊn|ebɪtlɪç] ◊ *mit unerbittlicher Härte vorgehen* ♦ *Seine Kritik war unerbittlich.* ♦ *Sie trieb die Verhandlungen unerbittlich voran.*

relevance ⟨noun⟩ Relevanz [rele'vants] die <-> no pl *(lofty)* ◊ *die gesellschaftliche Relevanz der Religionen* of relevance for sb/sth relevant für jdn/etw. [rele'vant fy:ɐ̯] *(lofty)* ◊ *für unsere Arbeit relevante Informationen* ♦ *Alle Prüfungen sind relevant für die Abschlussnote.*

relevant ⟨adj⟩ relevant [rele'vant] <relevanter, am relevantesten> *(lofty)* ◊ *relevante Informationen* ♦ *Ich halte diesen Gesichtspunkt für relevant.*

reliable(-ly) ⟨adj, adv⟩ zuverlässig ['tsu:fɛlɛsɪç] ◊ *eine zuverlässige Methode* ♦ *Ist diese Kollegin zuverlässig?* ♦ *Das System funktioniert zuverlässig.* be reliably informed that aus zuverlässiger Quelle wissen, dass

reliance ⟨noun⟩ **1.** *(dependence)* Abhängigkeit ['aphɛŋɪçkaet] die <-, -en> reliance on sb/sth Abhängigkeit von jdm/etw. ◊ *die Abhängigkeit der Firma von ihren Geschäftspartnern* ♦ *die Abhängigkeit des Westens vom Erdöl* **2.** *(trust)* Vertrauen [fɛ'traʊən] das <-s> no pl sb's reliance on sb/sth jds Vertrauen in jdn/etw. ◊ *das Vertrauen der Firma in ihre Mitarbeiter* ♦ *mein Vertrauen in diese Technologie* Reliance on this information would be a mistake. Es wäre ein Fehler, sich auf diese Information zu verlassen.

relic ⟨noun⟩ **1.** *(very old object, system, idea)* Relikt [re'lɪkt] das <-(e)s, -e> ◊ *ein Relikt aus der Steinzeit* ♦ *Für mich ist Religion ein überholtes Relikt.* **2.** REL *(object or bone of a holy person)* Reliquie [re'li:kviə] die <-, -n> ◊ *die Reliquien der Heiligen Drei Könige im Kölner Dom*

relief ⟨noun⟩ **1.** *(sth that reduces a strain, costs)* Erleichterung [e'laeçtərʊŋ] die <-, -en> ◊ *Deine Hilfe ist eine große Erleichterung für mich.* ♦ *Zu meiner Erleichterung ist nichts passiert.* tax relief Steuererleichterung ['ʃtɔøəle,laeçtərʊŋ] **2.** *(reduction of pain)* Linderung ['lɪndərʊŋ] die <-> no pl ◊ *Eine Massage verschafft Linderung.* relief from pain Linderung ... ⟨gen⟩ ◊ *eine Linderung der Symptome* pain relief Schmerzlinderung ['ʃmɛʳtslɪndərʊŋ] **3.** *(help)* Hilfe ['hɪlfə] die <-, -n> flood relief Hochwasserhilfe ['hoːxvasɐhɪlfə] relief supplies Hilfsgüter ['hɪlfsgyːtɐ] die <-> pl **4.** ARTS, ARCH Relief [re'liɛf] das <-s, -s> sculptured in relief als Relief dargestellt **5.** *(replacement for sb)* Ablösung ['apløːzʊŋ] die <-, -en> ◊ *In einer Stunde kommt die Ablösung; dann können wir uns ausruhen.* **6.** *(from sth difficult or boring)* Abwechslung ['apvɛkslʊŋ] die <-, -en> ◊ *eine willkommene Abwechslung* light relief eine kleine Abwechslung

◉ throw sth into (sharp) relief etw. (deutlich) hervorheben

relieve ⟨verb⟩ **1.** *(a problem)* verringern [fɛ'rɪŋɐn] <verringert, verringerte, hat verringert> ◊ *Maßnahmen, um Verkehrsstaus zu verringern; (pain)* lindern ['lɪndɐn] +haben ◊ *Die Salbe lindert die Schmerzen.; (boredom)* vertreiben [fɛ'traebm̩] <vertreibt, vertrieb,

hat vertrieben> ◊ *mit einem Spiel die Langeweile vertreiben* **2.** *(take over from sb)* ablösen ['apløːzn̩] +haben ◊ *Um 16 Uhr löse ich meinen Kollegen ab.* **3.** *(of a responsibility, position)* relieve sb of sth jd von etw. entbinden [fɔn ... ɛnt,bɪndn̩] <entbindet, entband, hat entbunden> *(form)* ◊ *jdn von einer Pflicht/einem Amt entbinden* **4.** *(of money)* relieve sb of sth jdn um etw. erleichtern [ʊm ... e,laeçtɐn] <erleichtert, erleichterte, hat erleichtert> *(fam, hum)* ◊ *Der Taschendieb hat mich um 100 Euro erleichtert.*

◉ relieve yourself *(use the toilet)* sich erleichtern

religion ⟨noun⟩ Religion [reli'gioːn] die <-, -en> ◊ *die Religionen Indiens*

◉ get religion fromm werden

religious ⟨adj⟩ religiös [reli'giøːs] <religiöser, am religiösesten> ◊ *eine religiöse Gemeinschaft* ♦ *Sie ist sehr religiös.*

reluctance ⟨noun⟩ Widerwille ['viːdɐvɪlə] der <-ns> no pl ◊ *Sein Widerwille, sich auf ein Gespräch einzulassen, ärgert mich.*

reluctant(ly) ⟨adj, adv⟩ widerwillig ['viːdɐvɪlɪç] seldom comp/superl ◊ *ein widerwilliges Zugeständnis* ♦ *Widerwillig gab er mir das Geld zurück.* be reluctant to do sth etw. nicht tun wollen [nɪçt ... vɔlən] <will, wollte, hat wollen> ◊ *Aus Angst um seine Sicherheit wollte der Zeuge nicht aussagen.*

rely on ⟨verb⟩ **1.** *(trust)* rely on sb/sth sich auf jdn/etw. verlassen [aof ... fɛ,lasn̩] <verlässt sich, verließ sich, hat sich verlassen> ◊ *Auf dich kann ich mich immer verlassen.* ♦ *sich auf sein eigenes Urteil verlassen* **2.** *(be dependent on)* rely on sth auf etw. ⟨acc⟩ angewiesen sein [aof ... ,angaviːzn̩ zaen] +sein ◊ *auf Spenden angewiesen sein*

remain ⟨verb⟩ *(continue to exist, stay as it is, be left over)* bleiben ['blaebm̩] <bleibt, blieb, ist geblieben> ◊ *im Bett bleiben* ♦ *Es bleibt noch viel zu tun.* ♦ *Hoffentlich bleibt das Wetter schön.* ♦ *Lass uns Freunde bleiben.* ♦ *Der Zinssatz bleibt niedrig.* remain in power an der Macht bleiben it only remains for sb to do sth jdm bleibt nur noch, etw. zu tun ◊ *Mir bleibt nur noch, Sie zu beglückwünschen.* it remains to be seen ... es bleibt abzuwarten, ... ◊ *Es bleibt abzuwarten, wie sich die Dinge entwickeln.*

remainder ⟨noun⟩ Rest [rɛst] der <-(e)s, -e> ◊ *20 geteilt durch 3 ist 6, Rest 2.* ♦ *Für den Rest des Jahres fallen keine Zahlungen mehr an.*

> In German *der Rest* is always followed by a singular verb: *Die meisten meiner Freunde leben in London; der Rest lebt in Leeds.* (Most of my friends live in London; the remainder live in Leeds.)

remaining ⟨adj⟩ *(sth left over)* übrig ['yːbrɪç] no comp/superl ◊ *Wo ist das übrige Geld?; (doubt, hope, person)* verblieben [fɛ'bliːbm̩] no comp/superl, only before ns ◊ *jede verbliebene Hoffnung zunichte machen* ♦ *meine in Europa verbliebenen Verwandten*

remains ⟨noun⟩ Überreste ['yːbɐrɛstə] die <-> pl ◊ *die Überreste eines Tempels* ♦ *menschliche Überreste*

remark¹ ⟨noun⟩ *(spontaneous)* Bemerkung [bə'mɛʳkʊŋ] die <-, -en> ◊ *eine unpassende Bemerkung; (carefully considered)* Anmerkung ['anmɛʳkʊŋ] die <-, -en> ◊ *Es gab auch ein paar kritische Anmerkungen.* make a remark about sth eine Bemerkung/Anmerkung zu etw. machen

remark² ⟨verb⟩ bemerken [bə'mɛʳkn̩] <bemerkt, bemerkte, hat bemerkt> *followed by the subjunctive*

when used in reported speech ◊ *„Sehr gut!",*
bemerkte der Lehrer. remark that bemerken, dass ◊
Er bemerkte, dass ich dick geworden sei. remark
(up)on sth eine Bemerkung zu etw. machen
[æˈnə bəˌmɛˈkʊn ˈtsuː … maxn] +haben

remarkable(-ably) [adj, adv] bemerkenswert
[bəˈmɛˈkŋ̩sveːgt] <bemerkenswerter, am bemerkenswer-
testen> ◊ *eine bemerkenswerte Leistung* ♦ *Sein*
Einsatz ist wirklich bemerkenswert. ♦ *Für eine*
Anfängerin spielt sie bemerkenswert gut Klavier.

remedy¹ [noun] Heilmittel [ˈhaelmɪtl̩] das <-s, -> ◊
ein pflanzliches Heilmittel ♦ *Ist die EU ein Heilmittel*
gegen die Globalisierung? remedy for sth Mittel
gegen etw. [ˈmɪtl̩ geːgŋ̩] das <-s, -> ◊ *ein Mittel*
gegen Schnupfen/Arbeitslosigkeit

remedy² [verb] beheben [bəˈheːbm̩] <behebt, behob,
hat behoben> ◊ *einen Fehler/Defekt beheben*

remember [verb] **1.** *(recall)* sich erinnern [ɐˈɪnɐn]
<erinnert sich, erinnerte sich, hat sich erinnert> ◊ *Ich*
kann mich noch erinnern, wie es damals war. ♦
Wenn ich mich recht erinnere, hatten wir eine Verab-
redung. remember sb/sth sich an jdn/etw. erinnern
◊ *Ich erinnere mich noch genau an ihn.* **2.** *(not*
forget an appointment, occasion, errand) remember
sth an etw. [acc] denken [an … ˌdɛŋkŋ̩] <denkt,
dachte, hat gedacht> ◊ *Denk an deinen Termin*
morgen früh! remember to do sth daran denken,
etw. zu tun
⊚ **remember sb to sb** jdn von jdm grüßen ◊
Grüßen Sie Ihren Onkel von mir! **sb is remembered**
as sth jd bleibt als etw. unvergessen **sb is remem-**
bered for sth jds etw. bleibt unvergessen ◊ *Seine*
Verdienste bleiben unvergessen. **you have to**
remember that man darf nicht vergessen, dass

remembrance [noun] Gedenken [gəˈdɛŋkŋ̩] das <-s>
no pl in remembrance of sb/sth zum Gedenken an
jdn/etw. ◊ *ein Gottesdienst zum Gedenken an die*
Flutopfer

remind [verb] erinnern [ɐˈɪnɐn] <erinnert, erinnerte,
hat erinnert> remind sb of/about sb/sth jdn an jdn/
etw. erinnern ◊ *Das Lied erinnerte sie an ihn.* ♦
Erinnere mich bitte an meinen Zahnarzttermin.
remind sb that jdn daran erinnern, dass ◊ *Darf ich*
Sie daran erinnern, dass wir Ihnen damals geholfen
haben? remind sb to do sth jdn daran erinnern,
etw. zu tun ◊ *Sie erinnerte ihn daran, ein Geschenk*
für seine Mutter zu kaufen.
⊚ **Don't remind me!** Erinnere mich bloß nicht
daran! **that reminds me …** dabei fällt mir ein, …

reminder [noun] **1.** *(sth that reminds you of sth)* Erinnerung [ɐˈɪnɐrʊŋ] die <-, -en> ◊ *eine Erinnerung*
an die glorreiche Vergangenheit be a reminder of sth
(to sb) (jdn) an etw. [acc] erinnern [an … ɐˌɪnɐn]
<erinnert, erinnerte, hat erinnert> ◊ *Ihre Gegenwart*
erinnerte mich an alte Zeiten. be a reminder that
daran erinnern, dass ◊ *Die Krankheit erinnert mich*
daran, dass Gesundheit ein Geschenk ist. **2.** *(of*
payment due) Mahnung [ˈmaːnʊŋ] die <-, -en> ◊
eine Mahnung bekommen/schreiben

remnant [noun] Überrest [ˈyːbɐrɛst] der <-(e)s, -e>
most pl ◊ *Überreste antiker Mauern*

remorse [noun] Reue [ˈrɔɐə] die <-> no pl ◊ *Du*
zeigst keine Reue über deine Tat.

remote [adj] **1.** *(isolated)* abgelegen [ˈapgəleːgŋ̩] ◊ *eine*
abgelegene Insel ♦ *Die Gegend war ziemlich*
abgelegen. **2.** *(distant)* fern [fɛˈn] mostly before ns ◊

ferne Länder ♦ *die ferne Zukunft; (in the past)* be
remote weit zurückliegen [vaet ˈtsuˈrvkliːgŋ̩] <liegt
zurück, lag zurück, hat zurückgelegen> ◊ *Unsere letzte*
Begegnung lag so weit zurück, dass ich mich kaum
daran erinnerte. **3.** *(from a distance)* Fern… [ˈfɛˈn]
remote monitoring Fernüberwachung
[ˈfɛˈn|ybɐˌvaxʊŋ] die <-> remote access Fernzugriff
[ˈfɛˈntsuːgrɪf] der <-(e)s, -e> most sing **4.** *(small,*
insignificant) gering [gəˈrɪŋ] ◊ *Diese Gefahr ist recht*
gering. ♦ *nicht die geringste Chance haben*
5. *(person)* distanziert [dɪstanˈtsiːɐt] <distanzierter,
am distanziertesten> ◊ *Er wirkt so distanziert.* ♦ *eine*
distanzierte Person
⊚ **be remote from sth 1.** *(geographically)* fern
einer Sache [gen] liegen ◊ *Die Höhle liegt fern der*
Küste. **2.** *(have little to do with sth)* nicht viel mit
etw. zu tun haben ◊ *Was in diesem Roman steht,*
hat mit der Wirklichkeit nicht viel zu tun.

remote control [noun] Fernbedienung [ˈfɛˈnbədiːnʊŋ]
die <-, -en> ◊ *die rote Taste auf der Fernbedienung*
drücken

removal [noun] **1.** Entfernung [ɛntˈfɛˈnʊŋ] die
<-, -en> *(lofty)* ◊ *seine Entfernung aus dem Amt*
removal of sb/sth Entfernung … [gen] ◊ *die*
operative Entfernung eines Tumors **2.** *(in the UK:*
moving furniture) Umzug [ˈʊmtsuːk] der
<-(e)s, Umzüge> removal firm Umzugsfirma
[ˈʊmtsuːksˌfɪrmaː] die <-, Umzugsfirmen> removal
man Möbelpacker [ˈmøːbl̩pakɐ] der <-s, ->

remove [verb] **1.** *(take away, dismiss, wash out)*
entfernen [ɛntˈfɛˈnən] <entfernt, entfernte, hat
entfernt> ◊ *etw. chirurgisch entfernen* ♦ *jdn aus dem*
Amt entfernen ♦ *Flecken entfernen; (take sth off sth)*
remove sth from the heat etw. vom Feuer nehmen
[fəm ˈfɔɐe neːmən] <nimmt, nahm, hat genommen> ◊
Den Topf vom Feuer nehmen und die Butter
dazugeben. **2.** *(take off clothing)* ausziehen
[ˈaostsiːən] <zieht aus, zog aus, hat ausgezogen> ◊ *Sie*
zog ihre Jacke aus. **3.** *(a problem, traces of sth)*
beseitigen [bəˈzaetɪgŋ̩] <beseitigt, beseitigte, hat
beseitigt> ◊ *ein Hindernis/alle Spuren beseitigen*

remuneration [noun] Bezahlung [bəˈtsaːlʊŋ] die
<-, -en> most sing ◊ *Wir bieten gute*
Bezahlung für Ihre Dienste.

renaissance [noun] **1.** Renaissance [renɛˈsãs] die
<-, -n> *(lofty)* ◊ *eine Renaissance erleben* **2.** ARTS
the Renaissance die Renaissance [diː renɛˈsãs]
<-> no pl renaissance castle Renaissanceschloss
[renɛˈsãsʃlɔs] das <-es, Renaissanceschlösser>

render [verb] **1.** *(help)* leisten [ˈlaestn̩] <leistet, leistete,
hat geleistet> render help to sb jdm Hilfe leisten
render a service to sb jdm einen Dienst erweisen
[æˈnən ˈdiːnst ɐˈvaezn̩] <erweist, erwies, hat erwiesen>
2. *(express)* wiedergeben [ˈviːdegeːbm̩] <gibt wieder,
gab wieder, hat wiedergegeben> ◊ *Deutsche Substan-*
tive werden im Englischen manchmal mit einem
Verb wiedergegeben.; (translate) render sth into
German etw. ins Deutsche übersetzen
[ɪns ˈdɔɐtʃə ybɐˌzɛtsn̩] <übersetzt, übersetzte, hat
übersetzt> **3.** *(cause to become)* machen [ˈmaxn̩]
+haben ◊ *jdn verrückt machen* ♦ *Die Währungsre-*
form hat das alte Geld wertlos gemacht. **4.** *(a verdict)*
abgeben [ˈapgeːbm̩] <gibt ab, gab ab, hat abgegeben> ◊
ein Urteil abgeben

renew [verb] **1.** *(a contract, passport, library book)* verlängern [fɐˈlɛŋɐn] <verlängert, verlängerte, hat verlän-

A
B
C
D
E
F
G
H
I
J
K
L
M
N
O
P
Q
R
S
T
U
V
W
X
Y
Z

gert> ◊ *Die Firma verlängerte seinen Vertrag um weitere drei Jahre.* **2.** *(a relationship, contact)* **wieder beleben** ['viːdə bəˌleːbm̩] <belebt, belebte, hat belebt> ◊ *eine alte Freundschaft wieder beleben* **3.** *(repeat, replace)* **erneuern** [ɛˈnɔøɐn] <erneuert, erneuerte, hat erneuert> ◊ *Der Minister erneuerte seine Forderung.* ♦ *Die Reifen müssen erneuert werden.*

renewal [noun] **1.** *(of a conflict, talks)* **Wiederaufnahme** [viːdəʔˈaofnaːmə] die <-, -n> ◊ *die Wiederaufnahme der Kampfhandlungen* ♦ *die Wiederaufnahme der Verhandlungen* **2.** *(of a contract, passport)* **Verlängerung** [fɛˈlɛŋɐʊŋ] die <-, -en> ◊ *die Verlängerung eines Vertrags* **be up for renewal verlängert werden müssen** [fɛˈlɛŋɐt veːɐdn̩ mʏsn̩] <muss, musste, hat müssen> ◊ *Mein Pass muss bald verlängert werden.* **3.** *(improvement, regeneration)* **Erneuerung** [ɛˈnɔøɐʊŋ] die <-, -en> ◊ *ein Konzept für die wirtschaftliche Erneuerung des Landes* **urban renewal Stadterneuerung** ['ʃtatˌʔeˌnɔøɐʊŋ]

renewed → **renew** [adj] **1.** *(happening again)* **erneut** [ɛˈnɔøt] *no comp/superl, only before ns* ◊ *ein erneuter Versuch* **2.** *(fit, healthy, strong)* **frisch** [frɪʃ] <frischer, am frischesten> ◊ *Er ging mit frischer Energie an die Arbeit.* ♦ *Sie fühlte sich frisch und ausgeruht.*

renovate [verb] **renovieren** [renoˈviːrən] <renoviert, renovierte, hat renoviert> ◊ *Wir mussten die Wohnung von Grund auf renovieren lassen.*

renowned [adj] **renommiert** [renɔˈmiːɐt] <renommierter, am renommiertesten> *(lofty)* ◊ *ein renommierter Wissenschaftler* ♦ *Sie ist für ihre Forschung international renommiert.*

rent¹ [noun] **Miete** ['miːtə] die <-, -n> ◊ *die Miete bezahlen* ♦ *die Miete für ein Auto*

rent² [verb] **1.** *(pay for a house, car, equipment)* **mieten** ['miːtn̩] <mietet, mietete, hat gemietet> ◊ *ein Büro in der Innenstadt mieten* ♦ *ein Auto mieten* **sth rents for sth etw. kann man für etw. mieten** ◊ *Man kann das Fahrrad für 20 Euro am Tag mieten.* **2.** *(offer to others against payment)* **rent (out) vermieten** [fɛˈmiːtn̩] <vermietet, vermietete, hat vermietet> **rent sth out to sb etw. an jdn vermieten** ◊ *Ich vermiete das Zimmer an einen Studenten.*

rental [noun] **Miete** ['miːtə] die <-, -n> ◊ *die Miete einer Wohnung* ♦ *die Miete für ein Auto*

repair¹ [noun] *(of a car, bicycle, machine, roof, shoes)* **Reparatur** [repaʁaˈtuːɐ] die <-, -en> ◊ *eine Reparatur an einem Auto* ♦ *Reparaturen ausführen* **repair of/to sth Reparatur … [gen]** ◊ *Die Reparatur des Daches kostet über 2000 Euro.* **be under repair repariert werden** [repaˈriːɐt veːɐdn̩] <wird, wurde, ist worden> **be in need of repair repariert werden müssen** [repaˈriːɐt veːɐdn̩ mʏsn̩] <muss, musste, hat müssen> **be beyond repair sich nicht mehr reparieren lassen** [nɪçt meːɐ repaˈriːrən lasn̩] <lässt sich, ließ sich, hat sich … lassen> ◊ *Nach dem Unfall ließ sich das Fahrrad nicht mehr reparieren.* **carry out repairs on sth etw. reparieren** [repaˈriːrən] <repariert, reparierte, hat repariert> ◊ *Mein Vater wird morgen unser Auto reparieren.* **repair costs Reparaturkosten** [repaʁaˈtuːɐˌkɔstn̩] die <-> pl ◍ **in bad/good repair in schlechtem/gutem Zustand**

repair² [verb] **1.** *(a car, bicycle, machine, roof, shoes)* **reparieren** [repaˈriːrən] <repariert, reparierte, hat repariert> ◊ *ein Dach/Auto reparieren* ♦ *Ich muss*

diese Schuhe reparieren lassen.; *(a building, bridge)* **instand setzen** [ɪnˈʃtant zɛtsn̩] +haben ◊ *ein Haus instand setzen; (a street, scratch)* **ausbessern** ['aosbɛsɐn] <bessert aus, besserte aus, hat ausgebessert> ◊ *Straßenschäden ausbessern* ♦ *einen Kratzer im Lack ausbessern* **2.** *(undo damage to a relationship)* **beheben** [bəˈheːbm̩] <behebt, behob, hat behoben> *(lofty)* ◊ *Lässt sich der Schaden, den unsere Freundschaft genommen hat, noch beheben?*

repay [verb] **1.** *(give back money)* **repay sth etw. zurückzahlen** [ʦuˈrʏktsaːlən] +haben ◊ *Ich habe den Kredit bereits zurückgezahlt.* **repay sb jdm sein Geld zurückzahlen** **2.** *(reward for kindness, help)* **repay (sb) sich (bei jdm) revanchieren** [revanˈʃiːrən] <revanchiert sich, revanchierte sich, hat sich revanchiert> ◊ *Ich möchte mich bei meinem Nachbarn für seine Hilfe revanchieren.* **3.** *(be worthwhile)* **lohnen** ['loːnən] +haben ◊ *Das Museum lohnt einen Besuch.*

repayment [noun] **Rückzahlung** ['rʏktsaːlʊŋ] die <-, -en> ◊ *die Rückzahlung eines Kredits*

repeal¹ [noun] **Aufhebung** ['aofheːbʊŋ] die <-, -en> *most sing* ◊ *die Aufhebung des Gesetzes*

repeal² [verb] **aufheben** ['aofheːbm̩] <hebt auf, hob auf, hat aufgehoben> ◊ *die Preisbindung für Bücher aufheben*

repeat¹ [noun] **1.** *repeat (performance)* **Wiederholung** [viːdəˈhoːlʊŋ] die <-, -en> ◊ *Im Fernsehen kommen dauernd Wiederholungen.* ♦ *eine Wiederholung der Ereignisse befürchten* **Are you a repeat customer? Sind Sie bereits Kunde?** ['ʦɪnt ziː bəʁaets ˌkʊndə]

repeat² [verb] **1.** *(do or show again)* **wiederholen** [viːdəˈhoːlən] <wiederholt, wiederholte, hat wiederholt> ◊ *Das Konzert wird im Radio wiederholt.* ♦ *Er wiederholte seine Frage.* ♦ *Sie musste die neunte Klasse wiederholen.* **repeat yourself sich wiederholen** ◊ *Du wiederholst dich — das hast du bereits gesagt!* **2.** *(sth you have learnt)* **aufsagen** ['aofzaːgn̩] +haben ◊ *Er sagte ein Gedicht auf.* **repeat sth (after sb) (jdm) etw. nachsprechen** ['naːxʃprɛçn̩] <spricht nach, sprach nach, hat nachgesprochen> ◊ *Bitte sprechen Sie mir jeden Satz einzeln nach.* **3.** *(a secret)* **repeat sth (to sb) (jdm) etw. weitersagen** ['vaeteza:gn̩] +haben ◊ *Sag das bitte niemandem weiter!* • **repeat on** [phras v] **repeat on sb jdm aufstoßen** ['aofˌʃtoːsn̩] <stößt auf, stieß auf, hat aufgestoßen>

repeated(ly) [adj, adv] **wiederholt** [viːdəˈhoːlt] *when used as an adj, only before ns* ◊ *wiederholtes Fehlen in der Schule* ♦ *Sie haben wiederholt Ihr Versprechen gebrochen.*

repercussion [noun] **Auswirkung** ['aosvɪˌkʊŋ] die <-, -en> ◊ *Die politischen Auswirkungen sind noch nicht absehbar.* **have repercussions on sth sich auf etw. [acc] auswirken** [aof …ˌaosvɪˌkn̩] +haben ◊ *Wie wirkt sich der steigende Ölpreis auf die Wirtschaft aus?*

repetition [noun] **Wiederholung** [viːdəˈhoːlʊŋ] die <-, -en>

replace [verb] **1.** *(substitute)* **ersetzen** [ɛˈzɛtsn̩] <ersetzt, ersetzte, hat ersetzt> ◊ *Ich musste die kaputte Vase ersetzen.* **replace sth with sth etw. durch etw. ersetzen** ◊ *Die veraltete Broschüre wurde durch eine neue ersetzt.; (renew)* **austauschen** ['aostaoʃn̩] +haben ◊ *eine Glühbirne austauschen* **2.** *(take sb's/sth's place temporarily)* **replace sb jdn vertreten** [fɛˈtreːtn̩] <vertritt, vertrat, hat vertreten> ◊

Sie hat mich während meiner Krankheit vertreten.; *(permanently)* replace sb jds Stelle einnehmen ['ʃtelə æenneːmən] <nimmt ein, nahm ein, hat eingenommen> ◊ *Wer wird meine Stelle einnehmen, nachdem ich die Firma verlassen habe?*; *(drive out, supersede)* verdrängen [feˈdrɛŋən] <verdrängt, verdrängte, hat verdrängt> ◊ *Der Computer hat die Schreibmaschine völlig verdrängt.* **3.** *(put sth back in its place)* zurückstellen [ʦuˈrʏkʃtelən] +haben ◊ *Sie stellte die Bücher ins Regal zurück.*; *(sth flat)* zurücklegen [ʦuˈrʏkleːgŋ̩] +haben ◊ *Ich legte den Schreibblock auf den Tisch zurück.*; *(a receiver)* auflegen ['aoːfleːgŋ̩] +haben

replacement [noun] Ersatz [eˈzaʦ] der <–es, Ersätze> ◊ *Bernd ist als Ersatz für den verletzten Spieler eingesprungen.*

reply¹ [noun] *(answer, reaction)* Antwort ['antvɔˈt] die <–, –en> ◊ *Sie wartet noch auf eine Antwort von ihm.* ♦ *Als Antwort warf er ihr einen wütenden Blick zu.* reply to sth Antwort auf etw. [acc] ◊ *Ich habe auf meinen Brief keine Antwort bekommen.* make no reply keine Antwort geben in reply to sth in Beantwortung ... [gen] [ɪn bəˈantvɔˈtʊŋ] die <–> no pl *(form)* ◊ *In Beantwortung Ihres Schreibens vom 2. Mai möchte ich Ihnen mitteilen, dass ...*

reply² [verb] *(give an answer)* antworten ['antvɔˈtŋ̩] <antwortet, antwortete, hat geantwortet> ◊ *Ich antwortete: „Das weiss ich nicht."* ♦ *Er antwortete, dass er nicht daran denke nachzugeben.*; *(answer a question, letter, e-mail)* reply to sth etw. beantworten [bəˈantvɔˈtŋ̩] <beantwortet, beantwortete, hat beantwortet> ◊ *einen Brief beantworten* ♦ *Sie beantwortete die Frage der Lehrerin.*; *(react)* reply to sth with sth mit etw. auf etw. [acc] reagieren [mɪt ... aoː ... reaˌgiːrən] <reagiert, reagierte, hat reagiert> ◊ *Der Finanzminister reagierte auf den Protest mit Steuersenkungen.*

report¹ [noun] **1.** *(summary, information)* Bericht [bəˈrɪçt] der <–(e)s, –e> ◊ *Schreib einen Bericht über das Experiment.* ♦ *Nach offiziellen Berichten ist der Aufstand niedergeschlagen.*; *(in mass media)* Reportage [repoˈˈtaːʒə] die <–, –n> ◊ *Das Fernsehen bringt eine Reportage aus China.* **2.** *(at school: certificates with grades)* Zeugnis ['ʦɔɡknɪs] das <–ses, –se> ◊ *gute Noten im Zeugnis haben*

report² [verb] **1.** *(summarize, inform)* berichten [bəˈrɪçtŋ̩] <berichtet, berichtete, hat berichtet> ◊ *Wenn ich wieder da bin, habe ich viel zu berichten.* ♦ *Sie berichteten, dass es Probleme gegeben habe.* report sth von etw. berichten ◊ *Augenzeugen berichteten von dramatischen Szenen.* report on sth/sb über etw./jdn berichten ◊ *Der Reporter berichtete über das Erdbeben.*; *(give an account of)* report sth etw. wiedergeben ['viːdeːgeːbm̩] <gibt wieder, gab wieder, hat wiedergegeben> ◊ *Das Buch gibt die Fakten unrichtig wieder.* **2.** *(an incident)* report sth (to sb) (jdm) etw. melden ['mɛldŋ̩] <meldet, meldete, hat gemeldet> ◊ *Ich finde, du solltest den Schulleitung melden.* report sb missing jdn als vermisst melden; *(a crime, a criminal)* report sb/sth (to the police)) jdn/etw. (bei der Polizei) anzeigen [(bæ deːɛ poliˌʦae) 'anʦaegŋ̩] +haben ◊ *Sie hat ihn wegen Körperverletzung angezeigt.* **3.** *(your presence)* sich melden ['mɛldŋ̩] <meldet sich, meldete sich, hat sich gemeldet> ◊ *sich bei Dienstantritt melden* report to sb sich bei jdm melden ◊ *Er soll sich sofort*

beim Chef melden. report for duty sich zum Dienst melden ♦ **report back** [phras v] sich zurückmelden [ʦuˈrʏkmɛldŋ̩] <meldet sich zurück, meldete sich zurück, hat sich zurückgemeldet> ◊ *sich von einer Patrouille zurückmelden* ♦ *Er meldete sich mit interessanten Forschungsergebnissen zurück.* report back to sb jdm Bericht erstatten [bəˈrɪçt ɛʃtatn̩] <erstattet, erstattete, hat erstattet> ◊ *Sie erstattete dem Ausschuss Bericht über ihre Untersuchung.* ♦ **report to** [phras v] report to sb jdm unterstehen [ʊnteˈʃteːən] <untersteht, unterstand, hat unterstanden> ◊ *Er untersteht direkt dem Präsidenten.*

reportedly [adv] angeblich ['angeːplɪç] no comp/superl ◊ *Angeblich hat er Kontakte zum Geheimdienst.*

reporter [noun] Reporter [reˈpoˈte] der <–s, –> ♀Reporterin [reˈpoˈtərɪn] die <–, –nen> ◊ *Sie arbeitet als freiberufliche Reporterin.* ♦ *Die Zeitung schickte einen Reporter zur Berichterstattung.*

represent [verb] **1.** *(officially)* vertreten [feˈtreːtŋ̩] <vertritt, vertrat, hat vertreten> ◊ *Die Gewerkschaft vertritt die Interessen der Arbeitnehmer.* ♦ *Wer wird unser Land bei dem Wettkampf vertreten?* be well/poorly represented stark/schwach vertreten sein ◊ *Frauen sind im Verein nur schwach vertreten.* **2.** *(constitute, depict, portray)* darstellen ['daːʃtelən] +haben ◊ *Sie stellen in der Bevölkerung eine Minderheit dar.* ♦ *keine Gefahr darstellen* ♦ *ein Problem realistisch darstellen* ♦ *Der Film stellt ihn als Helden dar.* **3.** *(stand for sth)* represent sth für etw. stehen [fyːɛ ... ʃteːən] <steht, stand, hat gestanden> ◊ *Das Symbol des Totenkopfes steht für Gift.*

representation [noun] **1.** *(picture, depiction)* Darstellung ['daːʃtelʊŋ] die <–, –en> ◊ *die grafische Darstellung von Daten* ♦ *eine dreidimensionale Darstellung der Akropolis* **2.** *(official)* Vertretung [feˈtreːtʊŋ] die <–, –en> ◊ *die diplomatische Vertretung eines Landes im Ausland* ◊ *Wer übernimmt seine Vertretung vor Gericht?* **3.** make representations to sb (about sth) bei jdm Einspruch (gegen etw.) erheben [bæ ... 'æɛnʃprox eheːbm̩] <erhebt, erhob, hat erhoben> ◊ *Sie erhoben bei den Behörden Einspruch gegen die Entscheidung.*

representative [noun] Vertreter [feˈtreːte] der <–s, –> ♀Vertreterin [feˈtreːtərɪn] die <–, –nen> ◊ *Die Abgeordneten sind die Vertreter des Volkes.* ♦ *Vertreter aus Wirtschaft und Industrie* ♦ *ein berühmter Vertreter des Expressionismus*; *(in the US: in parliament)* Abgeordnete ['apgəˌɔˈdnətə] der/die <–n, die Abgeordneten> *but: ein Abgeordneter/eine Abgeordnete* ◊ *Die Mehrheit der Abgeordneten stimmte zu.*

representative(ly) [adj, adv] repräsentativ [reprɛzɛntaˈtiːf] ◊ *eine repräsentative Untersuchung* ◊ *2500 repräsentativ ausgewählte Bürger wurden befragt.* representative of sth repräsentativ für etw. ◊ *Die Studie ist repräsentativ für Österreich.* a representative section ein repräsentativer Querschnitt

repress [verb] **1.** *(an expression of emotion, a group, people)* unterdrücken [ʊnteˈdrʏkŋ̩] <unterdrückt, unterdrückte, hat unterdrückt> ◊ *Sie musste ein Kichern unterdrücken.* ♦ *von einem Diktator unterdrückt werden* **2.** *(a feeling, memory)* verdrängen [feˈdrɛŋən] <verdrängt, verdrängte, hat verdrängt> ◊ *Viele Gewaltopfer verdrängen, was ihnen angetan*

A
B
C
D
E
F
G
H
I
J
K
L
M
N
O
P
Q
R
S
T
U
V
W
X
Y
Z

worden ist.

reprimand [noun] Verweis [fɛ'vaɛs] der <–es, –e> ◊ *ein scharfer Verweis*

reprint [noun] Nachdruck ['naːxdrʊk] der <–(e)s, –e>

reproach [verb] reproach sb for sth jdm etw. vorwerfen ['foːɐ̯vɛʁfn̩] <wirft vor, warf vor, hat vorgeworfen> ◊ *Er musste sich mangelnde Sorgfalt vorwerfen lassen.* reproach sb for doing sth jdm vorwerfen, dass er etw. tut ◊ *Der Chef warf ihr vor, dass sie ständig zu spät kommt.* reproach yourself sich [dat] Vorwürfe machen ['foːɐ̯vʏʁfə maxn̩] +haben ◊ *Mach dir keine Vorwürfe!*

reproduce [verb] **1.** *(a sound, an image, data)* wiedergeben ['viːdeːgeːbm̩] <gibt wieder, gab wieder, hat wiedergegeben> ◊ *Dieser Bildschirm kann fast alle Farben wiedergeben.;* *(in a book)* abdrucken ['abdrʊkn̩] +haben ◊ *ein Bild abdrucken; (copy)* vervielfältigen [fɛ'fiːlfɛltɪgn̩] <vervielfältigt, vervielfältigte, hat vervielfältigt> ◊ *ein durch Copyright geschütztes Werk vervielfältigen* **2.** *(repeat)* wiederholen [viːdɐ'hoːlən] <wiederholt, wiederholte, hat wiederholt> ◊ *Wird sie den Erfolg wiederholen können?* **3.** *(people, animals, plants)* sich fortpflanzen ['fɔʁtpflantsn̩] +haben ◊ *Wie pflanzen sich Schnecken fort?*

reproduction [noun] **1.** *(of people, animals, plants)* Fortpflanzung ['fɔʁtpflantsʊŋ] die <–> no pl ◊ *die Fortpflanzung bei Insekten* **2.** *(of sounds, images, data)* Wiedergabe ['viːdegaːbə] die <–, –n> ◊ *eine detailgetreue Wiedergabe; (in a book)* Abdruck ['apdrʊk] der <–(e)s, –e> ◊ *Abdruck ohne Genehmigung des Autors verboten.; (of copies)* Vervielfältigung [fɛ'fiːlfɛltɪgʊŋ] die <–, –en> ◊ *die unerlaubte Vervielfältigung urheberrechtlich geschützter Werke* **3.** *(of a painting)* Reproduktion [reprodʊk'tsjoːn] die <–, –en> ◊ *eine Postkarte mit der Reproduktion eines Gemäldes* reproduction furniture Stilmöbel ['ʃtiːlmøːbl̩] die <–> pl

reptile [noun] Reptil [rɛp'tiːl] das <–s, –ien>

republic [noun] Republik [repu'bliːk] die <–, –en>

republican, Republican [noun] Republikaner [republi'kaːnɐ] der <–s, –> ♀Republikanerin [republi'kaːnɐrɪn] die <–, –nen> ◊ *Er bat im Wahlkampf die Republikaner unterstützt.*

reputation [noun] *(general)* Ruf [ruːf] der <–(e)s, –e> ◊ *Die Firma hat einen guten/schlechten Ruf.; (good)* Ansehen ['anzeːən] das <–s> no pl ◊ *Mein Ansehen hat enorm gelitten.* ♦ *Sie hat in der Firma ein gutes Ansehen.* have a reputation for sth für etw. bekannt sein [fyːɐ̯ ... bə̩kant zaɛn] +sein ◊ *Dieser Richter ist für seine Härte bekannt.* have a reputation as sth als etw. bekannt sein ◊ *Sie ist international als Expertin auf diesem Gebiet bekannt.*

request¹ [noun] **1.** *(polite)* request (for sth) Bitte (um etw.) ['bɪtə] die <–, –n> ◊ *Sie hat meine Bitte erfüllt.* ♦ *Seine Bitte um Unterstützung wurde abgewiesen.* ♦ *jdm eine Bitte abschlagen* **2.** *(formal, to an authority)* request (for sth) Antrag (auf etw. [acc]) ['antraːk] der <–(e)s, Anträge> ◊ *ein Antrag auf ein Stipendium* grant a request einen Antrag annehmen refuse a request einen Antrag ablehnen **3.** *(wish)* Wunsch [vʊnʃ] der <–(e)s, Wünsche> ◊ *Hast du irgendwelche Wünsche, was ich dir aus Paris mitbringen soll?* on request auf Wunsch ◊ *Die Beratung erfolgt auf Wunsch auch anonym.* at sb's request auf jds Wunsch ◊ *Auf Wunsch der Familie wurden*

alle Namen in dem Bericht geändert.; (for music) Musikwunsch [mu'ziːkvʊnʃ] play requests Musikwünsche erfüllen **4.** *(for information)* Anfrage ['anfraːgə] die <–, –n> ◊ *eine Anfrage an jdn richten* ♦ *Broschüre auf Anfrage kostenlos erhältlich.*

request² [verb] **1.** *(politely)* request sth um etw. bitten [ʊm ... bɪtn̩] <bittet, bat, hat gebeten> ◊ *um Auskunft bitten* request that darum bitten, dass ◊ *Er bat darum, dass die Sache vertraulich behandelt wird.* request sb to do sth jdn darum bitten, etw. zu tun ◊ *Die Gäste werden gebeten, in den Zimmern nicht zu rauchen.* **2.** *(formally and in writing)* beantragen [bə'antraːgn̩] <beantragt, beantragte, hat beantragt> ◊ *ein Darlehen beantragen* **3.** *(sth you are entitled to)* anfordern ['anfɔʁdɐn] +haben ◊ *Informationsmaterial anfordern* ♦ *Der Polizist forderte einen Rettungswagen an.* **4.** *(a song)* request sth sich [dat] etw. wünschen ['vʏnʃn̩] +haben ◊ *Welches Lied hast du dir gewünscht?*

require [verb] **1.** *(ability, action)* erfordern [ɛ'fɔʁdɐn] <erfordert, erforderte, hat erfordert> ◊ *Diese Therapie erfordert viel Zeit.* ♦ *Eine solche Aufgabe erfordert einige Erfahrung.* **2.** *(demand)* verlangen [fɛ'laŋən] <verlangt, verlangte, hat verlangt> ◊ *Von Vorgesetzten wird Verantwortungsgefühl verlangt.* require sb to do sth von jdm verlangen, dass jd etw. tut ◊ *Von den Studenten wird verlangt, dass sie ein Semester ins Ausland gehen.* be required to do sth etw. tun müssen ['mʏsn̩] <muss, musste, hat müssen> ◊ *Alle Bewerber müssen einen Eignungstest machen.* **3.** *(as a prerequisite)* voraussetzen [fo'raosztsn̩] +haben ◊ *Wir setzen perfekte Englischkenntnisse voraus.*

required → **require** [adj] erforderlich [ɛ'fɔʁdɐlɪç] ◊ *seldom comp/superl* ◊ *eine Bewerbung mit den erforderlichen Unterlagen* ♦ *Dafür ist eine Genehmigung erforderlich.* required by law gesetzlich vorgeschrieben [gə,zɛtslɪç 'foːɐ̯gəʃriːbm̩] required reading Pflichtlektüre ['pflɪçtlɛk,tyːrə] die <–> no pl required subject Pflichtfach ['pflɪçtfax] das <–(e)s, Pflichtfächer>

requirement [noun] **1.** *(what is expected, what is needed to qualify for sth)* Anforderung ['anfɔʁdərʊŋ] die <–, –en> ◊ *Sie war den Anforderungen nicht gewachsen.* ♦ *Diese Fenster entsprechen nicht mehr den heutigen Anforderungen.* **2.** *(prerequisite)* Voraussetzung [fo'raosztsʊŋ] die <–, –en> ◊ *Gute Sprachkenntnisse sind eine Voraussetzung für die Stelle.* **3.** *(needs)* requirement(s) Bedarf [bə'daʁf] der <–(e)s> no pl ◊ *Der Bedarf der Kunden ist durch Bedarf an neuen Produkten gedeckt.*

rescue¹ [noun] Rettung ['rɛtʊŋ] die <–, –en> ◊ *Die Verschütteten hofften auf Rettung.* ♦ *die Rettung der Verletzten* come to sb's rescue jdm zu Hilfe kommen [tsuː 'hɪlfə kɔmən] <kommt, kam, hat gekommen> ◊ *Die Feuerwehr kam uns zu Hilfe.; in compound* rescue ... Rettungs-. ['rɛtʊŋs] rescue attempt Rettungsversuch ['rɛtʊŋsfɛzuːx] der <–(e)s, –e>

rescue² [verb] rescue sb/sth (from sth) jdn/etw. (vor etw. [dat]) retten ['rɛtn̩] <rettet, rettete, hat gerettet> ◊ *200 Rinder konnten aus der brennenden Scheune gerettet werden.* ♦ *jdn vor dem Ertrinken retten*

research¹ [noun] **1.** *(scientific, academic)* Forschung ['fɔʁʃʊŋ] die <–, –en> ◊ *Nach seinem Universitätsabschluss will er in die Forschung gehen.* ♦ *in der medizinischen Forschung arbeiten* research into sth

Forschung über etw. [acc] carry out research
forschen ['fɔʁʃn̩] +haben ◊ *Sie forscht im Bereich der*
Gentechnologie. carry out research into sth etw.
erforschen [e'fɔʁʃn̩] <erforscht, erforschte, hat
erforscht> +haben ◊ *die Ursachen einer Krankheit*
erforschen; (in compound ns) research ... For-
schungs... ['fɔʁʃʊŋs] research programme For-
schungsprogramm ['fɔʁʃʊŋspro,ɡram] das <-s, -e>
2. *(for a book, on the internet)* Recherche [re'ʃɛʁʃə]
die <-, -n> ◊ *Recherchen für einen Artikel ◆ eine*
Recherche im Internet
research² [verb] **1.** *(for scientific, academic purposes)*
erforschen [e'fɔʁʃn̩] <erforscht, erforschte, hat
erforscht> ◊ *klimatische Veränderungen erforschen*
2. *(for a book, on the internet)* recherchieren
[reʃɛʁ'ʃiːrən] <recherchiert, recherchierte, hat recher-
chiert> *(lofty)* ◊ *Er recherchiert die Hintergründe zu*
aktuellen Themen. ◆ *ein gut recherchierter Artikel*
researcher [noun] **1.** *(scientist, academic)* Forscher
['fɔʁʃɐ] der <-s, -> ♀Forscherin ['fɔʁʃərɪn] die
<-, -nen> ◊ *eine bekannte Forscherin ◆ Forscher*
haben eine neue Saurierart entdeckt. **2.** RADIO, TV
Rechercheur [reʃɛʁ'ʃøːɐ] der <-s, -e> ♀Rechercheu-
rin [reʃɛʁ'ʃøːrɪn] die <-, -nen>
resemblance [noun] Ähnlichkeit ['ɛːnlɪçkaet] die
<-, -en> ◊ *Zwischen den beiden besteht eine auffäl-*
lige Ähnlichkeit. bear a (passing) resemblance to
sb/sth (eine gewisse) Ähnlichkeit mit jdm/etw.
haben
resemble [verb] resemble sb/sth jdm/einer Sache
ähneln ['ɛːnəln] +haben ◊ *Du ähnelst deiner Mutter*
sehr. ◆ *Der Garten ähnelte einer Müllhalde.*
resent [verb] sb resents sth etw. ärgert jdn ['ɛʁɡet]
+haben ◊ *Die Niederlage ärgerte sie sehr.* resent sb
doing sth es ärgert jdn, dass/wenn jd etw. tut/ist ◊
Es ärgert mich, dass er nie pünktlich ist. ◆ *Ärgert es*
Sie, wenn Ihre Schüler faul sind? resent doing sth es
ärgert jdn, dass/wenn er/sie etc. etw. tut/ist
resentment [noun] Unmut ['ʊnmuːt] der <-(e)s> no
pl ◊ *Ihr Unmut über die Missstände wurde immer*
stärker.
reservation [noun] **1.** *(of a room, table, seat)* Reservierung [rezɛʁ'viːrʊŋ] die <-, -en> ◊ *Eine frühzeitige*
Reservierung ist ratsam. make a reservation sich
[dat] etw. reservieren lassen [rezɛʁ'viːrən lasn̩] <lässt,
ließ, hat lassen> ◊ *Ich habe uns einen Tisch/Platz*
reservieren lassen. have a reservation ein Zimmer/
einen Tisch/Platz etc. reserviert haben ◊ *Wir haben*
einen Tisch für vier Personen reserviert. **2.** *(on a*
flight) Buchung ['buːxʊŋ] die <-, -en> ◊ *Wir bitten*
um rechtzeitige Buchung Ihrer Reise. make a reservation on a flight einen Flug buchen
[aenən 'fluːk ,buːxn̩] ◊ *Welchen Flug hast du gebucht?*
3. *(doubts)* reservation(s) Bedenken [bə'dɛŋkn̩] die
<-> only pl ◊ *Sie hatte Bedenken, ihre Tochter*
abends allein weggehen zu lassen. reservations
about sth Bedenken wegen etw. with reservations
(nur) unter Vorbehalt [(nuːɐ) ʊntɐ 'foːɐbəhalt]
without reservation vorbehaltlos ['foːɐbəhaltloːs] no
comp/superl ◊ *jdm/einer Sache vorbehaltlos*
zustimmen **4.** *(for native Americans)* Reservat
[rezɛʁ'vaːt] das <-(e)s, -e> ◊ *Wie viele Indianer*
leben in diesem Reservat? **5.** *(for wildlife)* Naturschutzgebiet [na'tuːɐʃʊtsɡəbiːt] das <-(e)s, -e>
reserve¹ [noun] **1.** *(spare supply)* Reserve [re'zɛʁvə] die
<-, -n> ◊ *auf seine finanziellen Reserven zurück-*

greifen müssen ◆ *Die Reserven an fossilen Brennstof-*
fen gehen zur Neige. keep sth in reserve etw. in
Reserve behalten ◊ *ein bisschen Geld in Reserve*
behalten **2.** SPORT, MIL reserves Reserve [re'zɛʁvə] die
<-> sing ◊ *die Reserve einberufen ◆ in der Reserve*
spielen **3.** *(reticence)* Zurückhaltung [tsu'rʏkhaltʊŋ]
die <-> no pl ◊ *Viele interpretieren seine Zurückhal-*
tung als Arroganz. without reserve vorbehaltlos
['foːɐbəhaltloːs] no comp/superl ◊ *vorbehaltlos*
zustimmen **4.** *(for wildlife)* Naturschutzgebiet
[na'tuːɐʃʊtsɡəbiːt] das <-(e)s, -e> **5.** *(at an auction)*
reserve (price) Mindestgebot ['mɪndəstɡəboːt] das
<-(e)s, -e>
reserve² [verb] **1.** *(for later)* aufheben ['aofheːbm̩]
<hebt auf, hob auf, hat aufgehoben> ◊ *die Eier*
trennen und das Eiweiß aufheben reserve (your)
judgement sich mit seinem Urteil zurückhalten
[mɪt ... ˌʊʁtael tsu'rʏkhaltn̩] <hält sich zurück, hielt
sich zurück, hat sich zurückgehalten> **2.** *(a room,*
table, seat) reservieren [rezɛʁ'viːrən] <reserviert, reservierte, hat reserviert> ◊ *Wir reservieren gern ein*
Hotelzimmer für Sie. ◆ *einen Tisch für zwei*
Personen reservieren ◆ Für diese Züge kann man
einen Sitzplatz reservieren.; (a flight) buchen ['buːxn̩]
+haben **3.** *(exclusively)* vorbehalten ['foːɐbəhaltn̩]
<behält vor, behielt vor, hat vorbehalten> ◊ *Dieses*
Privileg bleibt dem Vorstand vorbehalten. ◆ *Alle*
Rechte vorbehalten! reserve the right to do sth sich
[dat] das Recht vorbehalten, etw. zu tun
reserved(ly) → reserve² [adj, adv] reserviert
[rezɛʁ'viːɐt] <reservierter, reservierteste> ◊ *die reser-*
vierten Karten abholen ◆ Er blieb mir gegenüber
ziemlich reserviert. ◆ *Sie reagierte reserviert auf*
seinen Vorschlag.
reservoir [noun] **1.** *(artificial lake)* Stausee ['ʃtaozeː]
der <-s, -n> **2.** *(container)* Behälter [bə'hɛltɐ] der
<-s, -> ◊ *der Behälter für das Kühlmittel*
3. *(reserves)* reservoir of sth Reservoir an etw. [dat]
[rezɛʁ'voaːʁ an] das <-s, -e> ◊ *ein unerschöpfliches*
Reservoir an Einfällen haben
residence [noun] **1.** *(of an important person)* Residenz
[rezi'dɛnts] die <-, -en> ◊ *die Residenz des*
Schweizer Botschafters in Berlin official residence
Amtssitz ['amtszɪts] der <-es, -e> **2.** *(building)*
private residence Wohnhaus ['voːnhaos] das
<-es, Wohnhäuser>; *(flat)* Privatwohnung
[pri'vaːtvoːnʊŋ] die <-, -en> **3.** *(town, place where*
sb lives) Wohnsitz ['voːnzɪts] der <-es, -e> ◊ *Wo ist*
Ihr ständiger Wohnsitz? take up residence
somewhere irgendwohin ziehen ['tsiːən] <zieht, zog,
ist gezogen> ◊ *Wann seid ihr in die USA gezogen?* be
in residence somewhere irgendwo wohnen ['voːnən]
+haben ◊ *die Schüler, die im Internat wohnen*
4. right of residence Aufenthaltsrecht
['aofn̩thaltsʁɛçt] das <-(e)s> no pl grant residence
to sb jdm eine Aufenthaltserlaubnis erteilen
[aenə ˌaofn̩thalts|ɛʁlaopnɪs ɛtaelən] <erteilt, erteilte,
hat erteilt> **5.** *(lecturing)* scholar in residence Gastdo-
zent ['ɡastdoˌtsɛnt] der <-en, -en> ♀Gastdozentin
['ɡastdoˌtsɛntɪn] die <-, -nen>; *(researching)*
Person, die Gast in einem Institut ist und dort
forscht
residence permit [noun] Aufenthaltserlaubnis
['aofn̩thalts|ɛʁlaopnɪs] die <-, -se> most sing ◊ *eine*
Aufenthaltserlaubnis beantragen
resident¹ [noun] **1.** *(of a town, country)* Einwohner

['æɛnvo:nɐ] der <–s, –> ♀Einwohnerin ['æɛnvo:nərɪn] die <–, –nen> ◊ *Berlin hat etwa 3,45 Millionen Einwohner.* ♦ *die ausländischen Einwohner Frankreichs* ♦ *die Einwohner von Fulda; (of a house, flat, home)* Bewohner [bə'vo:nɐ] der <–s, –> ♀Bewohnerin [bə'vo:nərɪn] die <–, –nen> ◊ *die Bewohner des Hauses evakuieren; (of a street)* Anlieger ['anli:gɐ] der <–s, –> ♀Anliegerin ['anli:gərɪn] die <–, –nen> *(form)* ◊ *Zufahrt nur für Anlieger* 2. *(of a hotel)* Hotelgast [ho'tɛlgast] der <–(e)s, Hotelgäste> ◊ *Strand nur für Hotelgäste!* 3. *(in the US: doctor)* Arzt im Praktikum [,aˑɐ̯t̩st ɪm 'praktikʊm] der <–es, Ärzte> ♀Ärztin im Praktikum [,ɛˑɐ̯tstɪn ɪm 'praktikʊm] die <–, Ärztinnen> ◊ *Sie ist jetzt Ärztin im Praktikum.* ♦ *Auf der Station arbeitet ein Arzt im Praktikum.*

resident² [adj] 1. *(local, living in a certain place)* ortsansässig ['ɔˑɐ̯ts|anzɛsɪç] *no comp/superl, only before ns* ◊ *die ortsansässigen Künstler fördern* resident in sth in etw. [dat] ansässig [ɪn ... ,anzɛsɪç] ◊ *Die Familie ist in Berlin ansässig.* 2. *(in a hotel, an institution)* hauseigen ['haʊs|aɛɡn̩] *no comp/superl, only before ns* ◊ *Das Hotel hat einen hauseigenen Arzt.*

residential [adj] 1. *(for living)* residential ... Wohn... [vo:n] residential area Wohngebiet ['vo:ngəbi:t] das <–(e)s, –e> residential building Wohngebäude ['vo:ngəbɔʏdə] das <–s, –> 2. *(institution)* residential *(nursing)* home Pflegeheim ['pfle:gəhaɛm] das <–(e)s, –e> residential school Internat [ɪnte'na:t] das <–(e)s, –e>

residue [noun] 1. *(substance)* Rückstand ['rʏkʃtant] der <–(e)s, Rückstände> ◊ *Rückstände von Medikamenten im Trinkwasser* 2. LAW *(of an estate)* Nachlass ['na:xlas] der <–es, Nachlässe>

resign [verb] 1. *(from an official position, office)* zurücktreten [ʦu'rʏktre:tn̩] <tritt zurück, trat zurück, ist zurückgetreten> ◊ *Der Präsident ist zurückgetreten.* ♦ *Sie trat als Teamchefin zurück.; (from a job)* kündigen ['kʏndɪɡn̩] +haben ◊ *Er hat gestern gekündigt.* resign *(from)* sth etw. aufgeben ['aʊfge:bm̩] <gibt auf, gab auf, hat aufgegeben> ◊ *ein Amt aufgeben* 2. *(member)* austreten ['aʊstre:tn̩] <tritt aus, trat aus, ist ausgetreten> resign from sth aus etw. austreten ◊ *aus einer Partei austreten* 3. resign yourself to sth sich mit etw. abfinden [mɪt ... ,apfɪndn̩] <findet sich ab, fand sich ab, hat sich abgefunden> ◊ *sich mit seinem Schicksal abfinden* You have to resign yourself to it! Finden Sie sich damit ab!

resignation [noun] 1. *(from an office)* Rücktritt ['rʏktrɪt] der <–(e)s, –e> ◊ *einen Minister zum Rücktritt auffordern; (from a job)* Kündigung ['kʏndɪgʊŋ] die <–, –en> ◊ *Seine Kündigung kam überraschend.* hand in your resignation kündigen ['kʏndɪgn̩] +haben ◊ *Ich habe gestern gekündigt.* resignation from sth Ausscheiden aus etw. ['aʊsʃaɛdn̩ aʊs] das <–s> *no pl* ◊ *Ihr Ausscheiden aus dem Vorstand kam überraschend.; (from politics)* Rückzug ['rʏktsu:k] der <–(e)s, Rückzüge> ◊ *Er kündigte seinen Rückzug aus der Politik an.* 2. *(from a party, an organization)* Austritt ['aʊstrɪt] der <–(e)s, –e> ◊ *der Austritt aus der Partei* 3. *(acceptance)* Resignation [rezɪgna'tsjo:n] die <–> *no pl* ◊ *Resignation machte sich in ihm breit.*

resin [noun] Harz [ha:ɐ̯ts] das <–es, –e>

resist [verb] 1. *(a temptation, pressure)* widerstehen [vi:dɐ'ʃte:ən] <widersteht, widerstand, hat widerstan-

den> ◊ *Ich konnte nicht widerstehen — ich musste einfach probieren.* resist sth einer Sache [dat] widerstehen ◊ *einer Versuchung nicht widerstehen können* ♦ *Die Ministerin widerstand dem Druck der Öffentlichkeit.* 2. *(struggle, fight)* Widerstand leisten ['vi:dɐʃtant laɛstn̩] <leistet, leistete, hat geleistet> ◊ *Er leistete keinen Widerstand, als sie ihn verhaften wollten.* resist sth gegen etw. Widerstand leisten ◊ *gegen Diskriminierung Widerstand leisten; (defend yourself)* sich wehren ['ve:rən] +haben ◊ *Sie hatte keine Kraft mehr, sich zu wehren.* 3. *(infection, chemicals)* resist sth gegen etw. immun sein [ge:ɡn̩ ... ɪ'mu:n zaɛn] +sein ◊ *Die zweite Testgruppe war gegen die Krankheit immun.*

resistance [noun] 1. *(refusal, opposition, power, electricity)* Widerstand ['vi:dɐʃtant] der <–(e)s, Widerstände> ◊ *Er leistete starken Widerstand.* ♦ *passiver Widerstand* ♦ *sich dem Widerstand anschließen* ♦ *Die Uhr so lange aufziehen, bis ein Widerstand spürbar wird.* ♦ *den Widerstand berechnen* meet with resistance auf Widerstand stoßen the path of least resistance der Weg des geringsten Widerstands 2. *(to infections, adverse conditions)* Widerstandsfähigkeit ['vi:dɐʃtantsfɛ:ɪçkaɛt] die <–> *no pl* ◊ *die Widerstandsfähigkeit des Körpers stärken; (to chemicals, heat)* Beständigkeit [bə'ʃtɛndɪçkaɛt] die <–> *no pl* ◊ *die chemische Beständigkeit von Kunststoffen* tear resistance Reißfestigkeit ['raɛsfɛstɪçkaɛt] die <–> *no pl* water resistance Wasserfestigkeit ['vasɐfɛstɪçkaɛt]

resit [verb] *(an exam)* wiederholen [vi:dɐ'ho:lən] <wiederholt, wiederholte, hat wiederholt> ◊ *Die Prüfung kann zweimal wiederholt werden.*

resolute(ly) [adj, adv] entschlossen [ɛnt'ʃlɔsn̩] ◊ *Sie sagte das in einem sehr entschlossenen Ton.* ♦ *Ich bin fest entschlossen, nicht nachzugeben.* ♦ *jdm entschlossen entgegentreten*

resolution [noun] 1. *(formal appeal)* Resolution [rezolu'tsjo:n] die <–, –en> ◊ *eine Resolution der Vereinten Nationen* 2. *(of a conflict, problem)* Lösung ['lø:zʊŋ] die <–, –en> ◊ *eine rasche Lösung des Problems anstreben* ♦ *Eine Lösung der Krise ist nicht in Sicht.* 3. *(decision)* Entschluss [ɛnt'ʃlʊs] der <–es, Entschlüsse> ◊ *Er war zu dem Entschluss gekommen, dass ...; (for the future)* Vorsatz ['fo:ɐ̯zats] der <–es, Vorsätze> ◊ *Hast du gute Vorsätze fürs neue Jahr?* make a resolution to sth den Vorsatz fassen, etw. zu tun; *(of a group, political party)* Beschluss [bə'ʃlʊs] der <–es, Beschlüsse> ◊ *ein einstimmiger Beschluss* 4. *(determination)* Entschlossenheit [ɛnt'ʃlɔsn̩haɛt] die <–> *no pl* ◊ *Ihre Entschlossenheit wurde auf eine harte Probe gestellt.* 5. TECHN Auflösung ['aʊflø:zʊŋ] die <–, –en> *most sing* ◊ *ein Bildschirm mit hoher Auflösung*

resolve [verb] 1. *(a conflict, crisis)* beilegen ['baɛle:ɡn̩] +haben ◊ *Sie haben ihren Streit inzwischen beigelegt.; (a problem, mystery)* lösen ['lø:zn̩] +haben ◊ *Endlich ist das Rätsel gelöst!* 2. *(a crime, misunderstanding)* aufklären ['aʊfklɛ:rən] +haben ◊ *Die Hintergründe der Tat konnten nie aufgeklärt werden.; (a question)* klären ['klɛ:rən] +haben ◊ *Diese Frage muss noch geklärt werden.* 3. *(decide)* resolve to do sth beschließen, etw. zu tun [bə'ʃli:sn̩ ... tu:] <beschließt, beschloss, beschlossen> ◊ *Ich beschloss mitzumachen.* ♦ *Der Vorstand beschloss,*

die Produktion zu erhöhen.
resort [noun] Ferienort ['feːrjən|ɔʳt] der <‑(e)s, ‑e> ◊ *ein beliebter Ferienort in den Bergen* seaside resort Badeort ['baːdə|ɔʳt] health resort Kurort ['kuːɐ̯|ɔʳt] ⊛ **last resort** letzter Ausweg *in the last resort* letzten Endes
resort to [verb] resort to sth zu etw. greifen [tʊː ... ɡɹæfn̩] <greift, griff, hat gegriffen> ◊ *Er griff zu Drohungen.* resort to violence Gewalt anwenden [ɡə'valt anvɛndn̩] +haben
resource [noun] **1.** *(source of information)* Hilfsmittel ['hɪlfsmɪtl̩] das <‑s, ‑> ◊ *Welche Hilfsmittel hast du für dein Referat verwendet?* **2.** *(economical)* Ressource [rɛ'sʊʳsə] die <‑, ‑n> most pl ◊ *jds finanzielle Ressourcen* ♦ *die natürlichen Ressourcen eines Landes* pool your resources seine Ressourcen konzentrieren mineral resource Bodenschatz ['boːdn̩ʃats] der <‑es, die Bodenschätze> most pl **3.** *(ability)* resources Fähigkeiten ['fɛːɪçkaetn̩] die <‑> pl ◊ *Ich musste alle meine Fähigkeiten einsetzen, um dieses Problem zu lösen.*
respect¹ [noun] **1.** *(consideration)* Respekt [rɛs'pɛkt] der <‑(e)s> no pl ◊ *jdn mit Respekt behandeln* respect for sb/sth Respekt vor jdm/etw. ◊ *Respekt vor dem Eigentum anderer haben* **2.** *(admiration)* Achtung ['axtʊŋ] die <‑> no pl ◊ *Seine Verdienste um das Land verdienen hohe Achtung.* respect for sb/sth Achtung vor jdm/etw. ◊ *die Achtung vor jdm verlieren* pay your respects to sb/sth jdm/etw. Achtung erweisen **3.** *(point of view, aspect)* Hinsicht ['hɪnzɪçt] die <‑> no pl ◊ *In dieser Hinsicht versteht er keinen Spaß.* ♦ *Die Vorwürfe waren in jeder Hinsicht unbegründet.* ⊛ **with all (due) respect** bei allem Respekt **pay your last respects to sb** jdm die letzte Ehre erweisen **give sb sb's respects** jdn von jdm grüßen **in respect of**, **with respect to** hinsichtlich ... [gen] ◊ *Was soll hinsichtlich des Problems getan werden?*
respect² [verb] **1.** *(treat with reverence)* achten ['axtn̩] <achtet, achtete, hat geachtet> ◊ *die Eltern achten* **2.** *(show consideration)* respektieren [rɛspɛk'tiːrən] <respektiert, respektierte, hat respektiert> ◊ *andere Meinungen respektieren* **3.** *(accept)* anerkennen ['an|ɛkɛnən] <erkennt an, erkannte an, hat anerkannt> ◊ *gesellschaftlich anerkannt* ♦ *Sie erkennt an, dass er sich bemüht hat.; (a law, rule)* respect sth einer Sache [dat] Folge leisten ['fɔlɡə laestn̩] <leistet, leistete, hat geleistet> *(lofty)* ◊ *einem Gesetz Folge leisten*
respectable [adj] **1.** *(decent)* anständig ['anʃtɛndɪç] ◊ *einen anständigen Beruf erlernen* ♦ *Es war sehr anständig von ihm, dass er sich entschuldigt hat.; (trustworthy)* seriös [zeʳ'rjøːs] <seriöser, am seriösesten> ◊ *eine seriöse Zeitung* ♦ *Er beurteilt die Firma als absolut seriös.; (with a good reputation)* ehrbar ['eːɐ̯baːʳ] ◊ *ein ehrbarer Bürger* **2.** *(quite good)* beachtlich [bə'|axtlɪç] ◊ *eine beachtliche Summe* ♦ *Es ist beachtlich, wie viel Geld zusammengekommen ist.*
respectably [adv] **1.** *(decently)* anständig ['anʃtɛndɪç] ◊ *sich anständig benehmen* **2.** *(inspiring trust)* seriös [zeʳ'rjøːs] <seriöser, am seriösesten> ◊ *ein seriös gekleideter Geschäftsmann*
respected → **respect²** [adj] **1.** *(admired)* geachtet [ɡə'|axtət] ◊ *ein allseits geachteter Mann* ♦ *In der*

Gemeinde ist sie sehr geachtet.; (reputable) angesehen ['anɡəzeːən] ◊ *eine hoch angesehene Forscherin* ♦ *Diese Firma ist für ihre Qualitätsprodukte angesehen.* **2.** *(approved)* anerkannt ['an|ɛkant] <anerkannter, am anerkanntesten> seldom comp/superl ◊ *Sie fühlten sich vor Firmenleitung nicht anerkannt.*
respective [adj] jeweilige ['jeːvaelɪɡə] no comp/superl, only before ns <ein jeweiliger ..., eine jeweilige ..., ein jeweiliges ...> ◊ *Beide Redner sind Experten auf ihrem jeweiligen Gebiet.*
respectively [adv] beziehungsweise [bə'tsiːʊŋsvaezə] ◊ *Ihre Kinder sind acht beziehungsweise elf Jahre alt.*
respond [verb] **1.** *(react)* reagieren [rea'ɡiːrən] <reagiert, reagierte, hat reagiert> ◊ *Er sprach sie an, aber sie reagierte nicht.* respond to sth (by doing sth) auf etw. [acc] (mit etw.) reagieren ◊ *Die Schule reagierte auf die Vorfälle mit einem Appell an die Eltern.; (to medical treatment)* respond to sth auf etw. [acc] ansprechen [aof ... ˌanʃprɛçn̩] <spricht an, sprach an, hat angesprochen> ◊ *Der Kranke spricht auf das Medikament nicht an.; (to music, sb's enthusiasm)* respond to sth mit etw. mitgehen [mɪt ... ˌmɪtɡeːən] <geht mit, ging mit, ist mitgegangen> ◊ *Sie geht mit der Musik mit.* **2.** *(reply)* antworten ['antvɔʳtn̩] <antwortet, antwortete, hat geantwortet> ◊ *Sie antwortete: „Das glaube ich nicht."* respond to sth auf etw. [acc] antworten ◊ *Hat er auf den Brief schon geantwortet?*
respondent [noun] **1.** *(of a questionnaire, an opinion poll)* Befragte [bə'fraːktə] der/die <‑n, die Befragten> but: ein Befragter/eine Befragte ◊ *Zehn Prozent der Befragten waren mit der Situation unzufrieden.* **2.** LAW *(defendant)* Beklagte [bə'klaːktə] der/die <‑n, die Beklagten> but: ein Beklagter/eine Beklagte ◊ *Der Beklagte hat den Prozess verloren.*
response [noun] **1.** *(reaction)* Reaktion [reak'tsjoːn] die <‑, ‑en> ◊ *Ich drückte verschiedene Tasten – keinerlei Reaktion!* response to sth Reaktion auf etw. [acc] ◊ *Als Reaktion auf das Attentat kam es zu schweren Unruhen.* **2.** *(answer)* Antwort ['antvɔʳt] die <‑, ‑en> ◊ *Auf seine Briefe kam keine Antwort.* ♦ *Was ist die richtige Antwort auf Frage 5?* in response to sth als Antwort auf etw. [acc] ◊ *(from many people)* Resonanz [rezo'nants] die <‑, ‑en> *(lofty)* ◊ *Die Resonanz auf die Änderungen war durchweg positiv.* ♦ *Das Konzept ist nur auf schwache Resonanz gestoßen.*
responsibility [noun] Verantwortung [fɛ|'antvɔʳtʊŋ] die <‑, ‑en> ◊ *die Verantwortung für etw. haben* ♦ *Es ist deine Verantwortung, dafür zu sorgen, dass alles klappt.* ♦ *Verantwortung gegenüber der Gesellschaft haben* take responsibility for sth die Verantwortung für die Richtigkeit der Angaben haben Verantwortung übernehmen on your own responsibility auf eigene Verantwortung position of responsibility verantwortungsvoller Posten [aen fɛ|ˌantvɔʳtʊŋsfɔlə 'pɔstn̩] <‑s, ‑> claim responsibility for an attack etc. sich zu einem Anschlag etc. bekennen [tuː ... aenəm ˌanʃtaːk bə'kɛnən] <bekennt sich, bekannte sich, hat sich bekannt>
responsible [adj] **1.** resonsible (for sb/sth) (für jdn/etw.) verantwortlich [fɛ|'antvɔʳtlɪç] no comp/superl ◊ *sich für jdn verantwortlich fühlen* responsible die verantwortliche Person **2.** *(job)* verantwor‑

tungsvoll [fɐ|'antvɔ'tʊŋsfɔl] ◊ *ein sehr verantwor-tungsvoller Beruf* **3.** *(reliable)* verantwortungsbewusst [fɐ|'antvɔ'tʊŋsbəvʊst] <verantwortungsbewusster, am verantwortungsbewusstesten> ◊ *Seine große Schwester ist schon sehr verantwortungsbewusst.*

⊛ **be responsible to sb 1.** *(be answerable to sb)* jdm (gegenüber) verantwortlich sein **2.** *(take orders from sb)* jdm unterstellt sein **find sb responsible** jdn für schuldig befinden **hold sb responsible for sth 1.** *(blame sb)* jdn für etw. verantwortlich machen **2.** *(make sb pay compensation)* jdn für etw. haftbar machen

responsibly ⓐₐdᵥ verantwortungsbewusst [fɐ|'antvɔ'tʊŋsbəvʊst] <verantwortungsbewusster, am verantwortungsbewusstesten> ◊ *verantwortungsbewusst handeln*

rest¹ ⓝₒᵤₙ **1.** *(remaining part)* Rest [rɛst] der <-(e)s, -e> In German 'der Rest' is always followed by a singular verb: 'Der Rest meiner Freunde lebt im Ausland.' (The rest of my friends live abroad.) ◊ *Es blieb nur ein kleiner Rest übrig.* ♦ *Kann ich den Rest vom Kuchen haben?* **the rest of us/them** wir/die Übrigen [viːɐ/diː 'yːbrɪgŋ̩] **2.** *(during an activity, in a piece of music)* Pause ['paozə] die <-, -n> ◊ *Ich brauche mal eine Pause.* ♦ *eine Pause im zweiten Takt* **take a rest** eine Pause machen **give sth a rest** mit etw. eine Pause machen **3.** *(state of relaxation)* Ruhe ['ruːə] die <-> no pl ◊ *Der Kranke braucht jetzt viel Ruhe.* **lay sb to rest** jdn zur letzten Ruhe betten **get some rest** sich ausruhen ['aosruːən] +haben ◊ *Er muss sich jetzt ausruhen.* **4.** *(for the back, arms)* Lehne ['leːnə] die <-, -n> ◊ *die Arme auf die Lehne legen/stützen; (for the feet, head)* Stütze ['ʃtʏtsə] die <-, -n>

⊛ **and the rest is history** und der Rest ist Geschichte **be at rest 1.** *(be dead)* ruhen **2.** *(not move)* in Ruhestellung sein **give it a rest** hör doch mal auf **put sth to rest** etw. beenden **and all the rest (of it)** und so weiter

rest² ⓥₑᵣᵦ **1.** *(be calm, undisturbed, motionless)* ruhen ['ruːən] +haben ◊ *Ich werde nicht eher ruhen, bis das geklärt ist.* ♦ *Die Toten ruhen in Frieden.* ♦ *jds Blick ruht auf jdm/etw.* ♦ *Lassen wir die Sache lieber ruhen.* **2.** *(when tired)* rest (sich) ausruhen ['aosruːən] +haben ◊ *Ruh (dich) doch ein bisschen aus.* **rest your sth** etw. ausruhen ◊ *Ich muss meine Beine ausruhen.* **3.** *(for support)* rest sth onto sth etw. auf etw. ⓐ꜀꜀ legen [aof ... leːgŋ̩] +haben ◊ *den Arm auf die Lehne legen* **sth rests on sth** etw. liegt auf etw. ⓓₐₜ [liːkt aof] <liegt, lag, hat gelegen> ◊ *Ihre Hand lag auf seinem Knie.; (vertically)* rest sth against sth etw. an etw. ⓐ꜀꜀ lehnen [an ... 'leːnən] +haben ◊ *Er lehnte die Leiter an die Wand.* sth rests against sth etw. lehnt an etw. ⓓₐₜ ◊ *Das Fahrrad lehnt am Zaun.*

• **rest on** ⓟₕᵣₐₛ ᵥ rest on sth auf etw. ⓓₐₜ beruhen [aof ... bəruːən] <beruht, beruhte, hat beruht> ◊ *Die Geschichte beruht auf Tatsachen.*

• **rest with** ⓟₕᵣₐₛ ᵥ rest with sb bei jdm liegen [bae ... liːgŋ̩] <liegt, lag, hat gelegen> ◊ *Die Entschei-dung darüber liegt bei dir.* ♦ *Die Schuld lag allein bei mir.*

restaurant ⓝₒᵤₙ Restaurant [rɛsto'raŋ] das <-s, -s> ◊ *Sonntags ist er gern im Restaurant.*

restless(ly) ⓐdⱼ, ₐdᵥ unruhig ['ʊnruːɪç] ◊ *Die Kinder werden schnell unruhig.* ♦ *eine unruhige Nacht* ♦

unruhig auf seinem Stuhl herumrutschen

restoration ⓝₒᵤₙ **1.** *(of old buildings, works of art)* Restaurierung [rɛstao'riːrʊŋ] die <-, -en> ◊ *die Restaurierung des Doms; (after recent damage)* Instand-setzung [ɪn'ʃtantzɛtsʊŋ] die <-, -en> ◊ *die Instand-setzung des Rathauses nach dem Hochwasser* **2.** *(of a situation, data)* Wiederherstellung [viːdɐ'heːɐʃtɛlʊŋ] die <-, -en> ◊ *die Wiederherstellung der Ordnung*

restore ⓥₑᵣᵦ **1.** *(to its original state)* wiederherstellen [viːdɐ'heːɐʃtɛlən] <stellt wieder her, stellte wieder her, hat wiederhergestellt> ◊ *jds Gesundheit wiederherstel-len* ♦ *eine gelöschte Datei wiederherstellen* **2.** *(sth that has been abolished)* wieder einführen [viːdɐ 'aenfyːrən] +haben ◊ *Die Vermögenssteuer soll wieder eingeführt werden.* **3.** *(a historic building, work of art)* restaurieren [rɛstao'riːrən] <restauriert, restaurierte, hat restauriert> ◊ *ein verblasstes Wandge-mälde restaurieren; (a building of no historical value)* instand setzen [ɪn'ʃtant zɛtsŋ̩] +haben ◊ *ein vom Einsturz bedrohtes Gebäude instand setzen* **4.** *(give back)* restore sth to sb jdm etw. zurückgeben [tsu'rʏkgeːbm̩] <gibt zurück, gab zurück, hat zurückge-geben> ◊ *gestohlene Sachen ihrem Besitzer zurückge-ben* **restore sb to power** jdn wieder an die Macht bringen [viːdɐ an diː 'maxt brɪŋən] <bringt, brachte, hat gebracht>

restrain ⓥₑᵣᵦ **1.** *(control, prevent)* restrain yourself sich beherrschen [bə'hɛɐʃn̩] <beherrscht sich, beherrschte sich, hat beherrscht> ◊ *Kannst du dich denn nicht mal beherrschen?* restrain yourself from doing sth sich beherrschen, um etw. nicht zu tun ◊ *Ich musste mich beherrschen, um etw. nicht anzuschreien.* restrain sb jdn zurückhalten [tsu'rʏkhaltn̩] <hält zurück, hielt zurück, hat zurück-halten> ◊ *Wir konnten ihn nicht zurückhalten.* restrain sb from sth jdn von etw. abhalten [fɔn ... ˌaphaltn̩] <hält ab, hielt ab, hat abgehalten> ◊ *Sie versuchten, ihn davon abzuhalten, sich auf den Mann zu stürzen.* **2.** *(physically)* festhalten ['fɛsthaltn̩] <hält fest, hielt fest, hat festgehalten> ◊ *Halten Sie den Hund fest!*

restraint ⓝₒᵤₙ **1.** *(control of emotions)* Zurückhal-tung [tsu'rʏkhaltʊŋ] die <-> no pl ◊ *Etwas mehr Zurückhaltung, bitte!* **2.** *(restriction)* Beschränkung [bə'ʃrɛŋkʊŋ] die <-, -en> ◊ *dem Handel Beschrän-kungen auferlegen* exercise restraint sich etw. beschränken [bə'ʃrɛŋkŋ̩] <beschränkt, beschränkte, hat beschränkt> restrain under Zwang [ʊntɐ 'tsvaŋ] **3.** TECHN head restraint Kopfstütze ['kɔpfʃtʏtsə] die <-, -n> restraint system Rückhalte-system ['rʏkhaltəzʏsˌteːm] das <-s, -e> ◊ *Rückhalte-systeme für Kinder im Auto*

restrict ⓥₑᵣᵦ **1.** *(limit)* beschränken [bə'ʃrɛŋkŋ̩] <beschränkt, beschränkte, hat beschränkt> ◊ *die Pres-sefreiheit beschränken* restrict sth/yourself to sth etw./sich auf etw. ⓐ꜀꜀ beschränken ◊ *Die Höchst-dauer wurde auf zwei Jahre beschränkt.* ♦ *Er muss sich auf zwei Zigaretten am Tag beschränken.* **2.** *(hinder)* beeinträchtigen [bə'aentrɛçtɪgŋ̩] <beein-trächtigt, beeinträchtigte, hat beeinträchtigt> ◊ *Schnee beeinträchtigt den Straßenverkehr.*

restricted → **restrict** ⓐdⱼ *(freedom, rights, movement)* eingeschränkt ['aengəʃrɛŋkt] <eingeschränkter, am eingeschränktesten> ◊ *ein eingeschränkte Bewegungs-freiheit haben* ♦ *Ich fühlte mich in meinen Möglich-keiten eingeschränkt.; (access)* beschränkt

[bəˈʃrɛŋkt] <beschränkter, am beschränktesten> ◊ *nur beschränkten Zugang zu etw. haben* restricted to sth auto etw. [acc] beschränkt ◊ *Die Redezeit ist auf zehn Minuten beschränkt.* restricted to sb nur für jdn zugänglich [nuːɡ fyːɡ … ʦuːɡɛnlɪç] ◊ *Diese Räume sind nur für die Patienten zugänglich.* restricted area Sperrgebiet [ˈʃpɛˈɡabiːt] das <-(e)s, -e>
restriction [noun] Beschränkung [bəˈʃrɛŋkʊŋ] die <-, -en> ◊ *dem Handel Beschränkungen auferlegen* ♦ *eine Beschränkung der Redefreiheit*
restrictive [adj] **1.** *(laws, rules, clause)* einschränkend [ˈaɛnʃrɛŋkŋt] *mostly before ns* ◊ *einschränkende Vorschriften* ♦ *ein einschränkender Relativsatz* **2.** *(clothing)* beengend [bəˈɛŋənt] *mostly before ns* ◊ *beengende Kleidung*
restroom [noun] Toilette [toaˈlɛtə] die <-, -n> ◊ *zur Toilette gehen*
restructure [verb] umstrukturieren [ˈʊmʃtrʊkturiːrən] <strukturiert um, strukturierte um, hat umstrukturiert> ◊ *Der ganze Betrieb wurde umstrukturiert.*
result¹ [noun] **1.** *(consequence)* Folge [ˈfɔlɡə] die <-, -n> ◊ *Der Unfall hatte katastrophale Folgen.* ♦ *Die Schäden waren eine unmittelbare Folge des Sturms.* as a result of sth als Folge … [gen] ◊ *Datenverlust als Folge eines Stromausfalls* **2.** *(of an action, mathematical operation, test, election, game)* Ergebnis [ɛˈɡeːpnɪs] das <-ses, -se> ◊ *das Ergebnis eines Fußballspiels* ♦ *Welches Ergebnis hatten deine Bemühungen?* ♦ *Unser Chef möchte endlich Ergebnisse sehen.* end result Endergebnis [ˈɛntlɛɡeːpnɪs] exam result(s) Prüfungsergebnis [ˈpryːfʊŋslɛɡeːpnɪs] **3.** *(company figures)* results Bilanz [biˈlants] die <-, -en> ◊ *Das Unternehmen wird morgen die Bilanz vorlegen.* **4.** MED result(s) Befund [bəˈfʊnt] der <-(e)s, -e> ◊ *Bei positivem Befund wird der Patient mit Medikamenten behandelt.* **5.** *(summary)* Fazit [ˈfaːtsɪt] das <-s, -s or -e> ◊ *Was war das Fazit der Podiumsdiskussion?*
result² [verb] die Folge sein [diː ˈfɔlɡə zaɛn] +sein ◊ *Zeitdruck ist schlecht; Fehler können die Folge sein.* result from sth sich aus etw. ergeben [aɔs … ɛɡeːpm] <ergibt sich, ergab sich, hat sich ergeben> ◊ *Aus dieser zufälligen Begegnung ergab sich eine langjährige Zusammenarbeit.* • result in [phras v] result in sth zu etw. führen [ʦuː … fyːrən] +haben ◊ *Mangelnde Sprachkenntnisse führten zu Missverständnissen.*
resume [verb] **1.** *(start again)* resume sth etw. fortsetzen [ˈfɔˈtsɛtsn] +haben ◊ *den Friedensprozess fortsetzen* sth resumes etw. wird fortgesetzt ◊ *Die Verhandlungen wurden am nächsten Tag fortgesetzt.; (continue)* sb resumes jd fährt fort [fɛːɡt ˈfɔˈt] <fuhr fort, hat/ist fortgefahren> ◊ *Wir fahren später fort.* **2.** resume your place sich wieder an seinen Platz begeben [viːdə an zaɛnən ˈplats bəɡeːpm] <begibt sich, begab sich, hat sich begeben>
résumé [noun] **1.** *(summary)* Resümee [rezyˈmeː] das <-s, -s> ◊ *ein erstes Resümee ziehen* **2.** *(curriculum vitae)* Lebenslauf [ˈleːbmslaɔf] der <-(e)s, Lebensläufe> ◊ *ein tabellarischer Lebenslauf*
retail¹ [adj] retail outlet Einzelhandelsgeschäft [ˈaɛntslhandlsɡəʃɛft] das <-(e)s, -e> retail price Einzelhandelspreis [ˈaɛntslhandlspraɛs] der <-es, -e> retail sector Einzelhandel [ˈaɛntslhandl] der <-s> no pl
retail² [verb] **1.** *(sell)* retail sth etw. im Einzelhandel

verkaufen [ɪm ˈaɛntslhandl fekaɔfn] <verkauft, hat verkauft> ◊ *Wir verkaufen Fleisch im Einzelhandel.* sth retails at … etw. kostet im Einzelhandel … [kɔstət ɪm ˈaɛntslhandl] +haben ◊ *Diese Eier kosten im Einzelhandel zwei Euro.* **2.** *(a story)* zum Besten geben [tsʊm ˈbɛstn ɡeːbm] <gibt, gab, hat gegeben> ◊ *Auf der nächsten Party gab er die Geschichte zum Besten.; (information)* weitererzählen [ˈvaɛtəlɛtsəːlən] <erzählt weiter, erzählte weiter, hat weitererzählt> ◊ *Sie erzählte die Tratschgeschichte ihren Freunden weiter.*
retailer [noun] Einzelhändler [ˈaɛntslhɛndlɐ] der <-s, -> ♀Einzelhändlerin [ˈaɛntslhɛndlərɪn] die <-, -nen>
retain [verb] **1.** *(keep, remember)* behalten [bəˈhaltn] <behält, behielt, hat behalten> ◊ *Behält Gold seinen Wert?* ♦ *Es ist erstaunlich, wie viele Einzelheiten sie behalten hat.; (staff, customers)* halten [ˈhaltn] <hält, hielt, hat gehalten> ◊ *Mit einer Gehaltserhöhung könnten wir sie vielleicht halten.* **2.** *(your sense of humour, composure, a secret, traditions)* bewahren [bəˈvaːrən] <bewahrt, bewahrte, hat bewahrt> ◊ *seinen Humor/die Fassung bewahren* ♦ *ein Geheimnis/Traditionen bewahren* **3.** *(the heat, water)* speichern [ˈʃpaɛçɐn] +haben ◊ *Das Wasser speichert tagsüber die Wärme und gibt sie nachts wieder ab.* **4.** *(a lawyer)* beauftragen [bəˈaɔftraːɡŋ] <beauftragt, beauftragte, hat beauftragt> ◊ *Wir haben einen bekannten Anwalt mit der Verteidigung beauftragt.*
retake [verb] **1.** *(an exam)* wiederholen [viːdəˈhoːlən] <wiederholt, wiederholte, hat wiederholt> ◊ *Sie musste die Prüfung wiederholen.* **2.** FOTO, FILM retake a picture/photo/film noch eine Aufnahme machen [ˈnɔx aɛnə ˌaɔfnaːmə maxn] +haben ◊ *Das Bild ist unscharf; ich werde noch eine Aufnahme machen.* **3.** MIL *(a town, village)* zurückerobern [tsʊˈrʏklelɔːbɐn] <erobert zurück, eroberte zurück, hat zurückerobert> ◊ *Die Truppen haben heute Morgen die Stadt zurückerobert.*
retention [noun] **1.** *(of customers, staff)* Bindung [ˈbɪndʊŋ] die <-> no pl ◊ *Die Bindung der Mitarbeiter an die Firma ist sehr gut.* **2.** *(of substances)* Speicherung [ˈʃpaɛçərʊŋ] die <-> no pl **3.** MED fluid retention Wasseransammlung [ˈvasəlanzamlʊŋ] die <-, -en> urine retention Harnverhaltung [ˈhaˈnfehaltʊŋ] die <-> no pl **4.** *(memory)* Gedächtnis [ɡəˈdɛçtnɪs] das <-ses> no pl ◊ *ein gutes Gedächtnis für Zahlen und Daten haben*
rethink [verb] umdenken [ˈʊmdɛŋkŋ] <denkt um, dachte um, hat umgedacht> ◊ *Wir müssen radikal umdenken.* ♦ *Es ist an der Zeit umzudenken.* rethink sth etw. überdenken [ybɐˈdɛŋkŋ] <überdenkt, überdachte, hat überdacht> ◊ *Den Plan müssen wir noch einmal überdenken.*
retire [verb] **1.** *(cease to work)* in Rente gehen [ɪn ˈrɛntə ɡeːən] <geht, ging, ist gegangen> ◊ *Mein Vater geht nächstes Jahr in Rente.; (from the civil service, the army)* in den Ruhestand treten [ɪn deːn ˈruːəʃtant ɡeːən] +sein; (from a political or official post)* retire from office aus dem Amt ausscheiden [aɔs deːm ˌamt ˈaɔ ʃaɛdn] <scheidet aus, schied aus, ist ausgeschieden> **2.** *(force sb to leave)* retire sb jdn in den Ruhestand versetzen [ɪn deːn ˈruːəʃtant fezɛtsn] <versetzt, versetzte, hat versetzt> **3.** *(withdraw)* retire (from sth) sich (aus etw.) zurückziehen [tsʊˈrʏktsiːən] <zieht sich zurück,

zog sich zurück, hat sich zurückgezogen> ◊ *Das Gericht zieht sich zur Beratung zurück.* ✦ *sich aus dem aktiven Sport zurückziehen* ✦ *Er wollte allein sein und zog sich in sein Zimmer zurück.; (from a competition)* aufgeben ['ʔaͻfgeːbm̩] <gibt auf, gab auf, hat aufgegeben> ◊ *Er verletzte sich und musste aufgeben.*

retired → retire [adj] pensioniert [panziͻ'niːgt] *no comp/superl* ◊ *eine pensionierte Lehrerin* ✦ *Mein Vater ist jetzt pensioniert.*

retirement [noun] 1. *(from work)* Ruhestand ['ruːͻʃtant] der <-(e)s> *no pl* ◊ *im Ruhestand sein* take retirement in den Ruhestand gehen retirement age Rentenalter ['rɛntn̩|alte] das <-s, -> *most sing* ◊ *Die Regierung will das Rentenalter anheben.* retirement pension Altersruhegeld ['altesruːͻgɛlt] das <-(e)s, -er> 2. *(from an activity, place)* Rückzug ['rʏktsuːk] der <-(e)s, Rückzüge> ◊ *Sie kündigte ihren Rückzug aus der Politik an.*

◉ **come out of retirement** noch einmal antreten

retort [verb] entgegnen [ɛnt'geːgnͻn] <entgegnet, entgegnete, hat entgegnet> +subjunctive I ◊ *Er entgegnete, dass er nicht daran denke nachzugeben.*

retract [verb] 1. *(a statement)* widerrufen [viːdeʹruːfn̩] <widerruft, widerrief, hat widerrufen> ◊ *eine Behauptung widerrufen* 2. *(a vehicle's undercarriage, an animal's claws)* einziehen ['ʔaͻntsiːͻn] <zieht ein, zog ein, hat eingezogen> ◊ *Nach dem Start wird das Fahrwerk eingezogen.*

retreat¹ [noun] 1. *(place)* Refugium [re'fuːgiͻm] das <-s, Refugien> *(lofty)* ◊ *Mein Zimmer ist mein Refugium.* 2. *(of troops, from public life, to a place)* Rückzug ['rʏktsuːk] der <-(e)s, Rückzüge> ◊ *der Rückzug der Truppen* ✦ *jds Rückzug aufs Land* sound the retreat zum Rückzug blasen; *(from an idea, a policy, promise)* Rückzieher ['rʏktsiːe] der <-s, -> *(fam)* ◊ *Der Rückzieher bei den angekündigten Reformen wird Konsequenzen haben.*

◉ **beat a hasty retreat** schnell das Weite suchen

retreat² [verb] 1. *(move away, withdraw)* sich zurückziehen [tsu'rʏktsiːͻn] <zieht sich zurück, zog sich zurück, hat sich zurückgezogen> ◊ *sich aufs Land zurückziehen* ✦ *Bei Ebbe zieht sich das Wasser zurück.* retreat from sth sich aus etw. zurückziehen ◊ *Er hat sich aus der Politik zurückgezogen.* ✦ *Die Truppen mussten sich aus der Stellung zurückziehen.* retreat into sth sich in etw. [acc] flüchten [ɪn ... flʏçtn̩] <flüchtet sich, flüchtete sich, hat sich geflüchtet> ◊ *Sie flüchtete sich in eine Fantasiewelt.* 2. *(from an idea, a decision etc., retreat from sth)* von etw. abgehen [fͻn ... ˌapgeːͻn] <geht ab, ging ab, ist abgegangen> ◊ *Die Regierung musste von ihren Reformplänen abgehen.; (from a position)* etw. aufgeben ['ʔaͻfgeːbm̩] <gibt auf, gab auf, hat aufgegeben> ◊ *Sie haben ihre kritische Haltung endlich aufgegeben.*

retrieval [noun] 1. *(of sth lost)* Wiederbeschaffung ['viːdebͻʃafͻn] die <-> *no pl* ◊ *die Wiederbeschaffung des verlorenen Gepäcks; (from a wreck, an accident)* Bergung ['bɛʹgͻn] die <-> *no pl* ◊ *die Bergung eines Schatzes* 2. ɪт Abfrage ['ʔapfraːgͻ] die <-, -n> ◊ *die Abfrage der gespeicherten Daten*

◉ **beyond retrieval** hoffnungslos

retrieve [verb] 1. *(get)* holen ['hoːlͻn] +haben ◊ *Er holte den Ball, der über den Zaun geflogen war.; (pick up)* aufheben ['ʔaͻfheːbm̩] <hebt auf, hob auf,

hat aufgehoben> ◊ *Sie hob das heruntergefallene Tuch vom Boden auf.; (from a wreck, an accident)* bergen ['bɛʹgn̩] <birgt, barg, hat geborgen> ◊ *die Verletzten aus dem verunglückten Zug bergen* 2. *(information on a computer)* abrufen ['apruːfn̩] <ruft ab, rief ab, hat abgerufen> ◊ *Daten abrufen* 3. *(save)* retten ['rɛtn̩] <rettet, rettete, hat gerettet> ◊ *etw. aus einem sinkenden Schiff retten* ✦ *Es gelang ihr, die Lage zu retten.* 4. *(dog)* apportieren [apͻʹtiːrͻn] <apportiert, apportierte, hat apportiert> ◊ *Der Hund apportierte den Stock.*

retrospect in retrospect im Nachhinein [ɪm 'naːxhɪnaͻn] ◊ *Im Nachhinein betrachtet war das ein großer Fehler.*

retrospective(ly) [adj] 1. *(study, analysis, exhibition)* retrospektiv [retrospɛk'tiːf] *no comp/superl; when used as an adj, mostly before ns* ◊ *eine retrospektive Analyse* ✦ *Die Studie war retrospektiv angelegt.* 2. *(law, payment)* rückwirkend ['rʏkvɪʹkn̩t] *no comp/ superl; when used as an adj, mostly before ns* ◊ *eine rückwirkende Zahlung von Kindergeld* ✦ *Die Gehaltserhöhung gilt rückwirkend ab dem 1. Juli.*

return¹ [noun] 1. *(coming back)* Rückkehr ['rʏkkeːe] die <-> *no pl* ◊ *die Rückkehr nach Berlin/in die Stadt* ✦ *die Angst vor einer Rückkehr der Seuche* ✦ *die Rückkehr zur Demokratie; (coming home)* Heimkehr ['haͻmkeːe] die <-> *no pl* ◊ *die Heimkehr aus dem Exil* ✦ *Wir freuen uns auf seine Heimkehr nach Deutschland.* 2. *(giving back)* Rückgabe ['rʏkgaːbͻ] die <-, -n> ◊ *die Rückgabe der Bücher in der Bibliothek* on return of sth nach Rückgabe ... [gen] ◊ *Nach Rückgabe des Mietwagens bekamen wir die Kaution zurück.* 3. *(profit)* Ertrag [ɛ'traːk] der <-(e)s, Erträge> ◊ *Sein Handel mit Stoffen wirft gute Erträge ab.* return on capital Kapitalertrag [kapi'taːl|ɛtraːk] 4. *(ticket for travel)* Rückfahrkarte ['rʏkfaːʹkaʹtͻ] die <-, -n> ◊ *Er kaufte eine Rückfahrkarte nach München.* 5. *(returned ticket for an event)* zurückgegebene Karte [tsu'rʏkgͻgͻːbͻnͻ ˌkaʹtͻ] die <-, -n> ◊ *an der Abendkasse noch eine zurückgebene Karte bekommen* 6. *(in an election)* returns Wahlergebnisse ['vaːl|ͻˌgeːpnɪsͻ] die <-> *pl* ◊ *Die ersten Wahlergebnisse kommen gegen herein.* 7. *(form)* Formular [fͻʹmuˈlaːʹ] das <-s, -e> tax return Steuererklärung ['ʃtͻͻ|ͻklɛːrͻn] die <-, -en> 8. *(on a keyboard)* return (key) Eingabetaste ['aͻngaːbͻtastͻ] die <-, -n> ◊ *die Eingabetaste drücken*

◉ **by return of post** postwendend many happy returns herzlichen Glückwunsch zum Geburtstag in return for sth als Gegenleistung für etw. on sb's return 1. *(afterwards)* nach jds Rückkehr 2. *(at the point of)* bei jds Rückkehr

return² [verb] 1. *(come back)* zurückkommen [tsu'rʏkkͻmͻn] <kommt zurück, kam zurück, ist zurückgekommen> ◊ *aus Italien/aus dem Urlaub/vom Schwimmen zurückkommen* ✦ *Wann kommen sie nach Deutschland zurück?; (go back)* zurückgehen [tsu'rʏkgeːͻn] <geht zurück, ging zurück, ist zurückgegangen> ◊ *Sollen wir zum Hotel zurückgehen?; (in a vehicle)* zurückfahren [tsu'rʏkfaːrͻn] <fährt zurück, fuhr zurück, ist zurückgefahren> ◊ *ins Hotel zurückfahren* return home nach Hause kommen [naːx 'haͻzͻ kͻmͻn] <kommt, kam, ist gekommen> ◊ *Wird er je wieder nach Hause kommen?* 2. *(feeling, situation)* wiederkommen ['viːdekͻmͻn] <kommt

wieder, kam wieder, ist wiedergekommen> ◊ *Wenn die Schmerzen wiederkommen, geben Sie sofort zum Arzt.* ♦ *Ihre Angst kam wieder, als sie die Geräusche hörte.* return to normal sich wieder normalisieren [viːdɐ nɔˈmaliˈziːrən] <normalisiert sich, normalisierte sich, hat sich normalisiert> ◊ *Die Lage hat sich noch nicht wieder normalisiert.* **3.** *(to a subject)* return to sth auf etw. ⟨acc⟩ zurückkommen [aof … tsuˈrʏkkɔmən] <kommt zurück, kam zurück, ist zurückgekommen> ◊ *Ich möchte noch einmal auf Ihre Frage zurückkommen.* **4.** *(to an activity)* return to sth sich einer Sache ⟨dat⟩ wieder zuwenden [viːdɐ ˈtsuːvɛndn̩] <wendet sich zu, wandte/wendete sich zu, hat sich zugewandt/zugewendet> ◊ *Sie sah kurz auf, dann wandte sie sich wieder ihrem Strickzeug zu.*; *(after a brief interruption)* return to doing sth weiter… [ˈvaɛtə] return to reading sth etw. weiterlesen [ˈvaɛtəleːzn̩] <liest weiter, las weiter, hat weitergelesen> ◊ *Er sagte etwas und las dann seine Zeitung weiter.*; *(after a long interruption)* return to doing sth wieder anfangen, etw. zu tun [viːdɐ ˈanfaŋən … tsuː] <fängt an, fing an, hat angefangen> ◊ *Nach langer Pause hat sie wieder angefangen, Fußball zu spielen.* return to work/school wieder an die Arbeit/in die Schule gehen [viːdɐ an diː ˈaʁbaɛt/ɪn diː ˈʃuːlə geːən] <geht, ging, ist gegangen> **5.** *(send back)* return sth (to sb/sth) etw. (an jdn/etw.) zurückschicken [tsuˈrʏkʃɪkn̩] +haben ◊ *Er hat vergessen, das Formular ans Finanzamt zurückzuschicken.*; *(give back)* return sth (to sb) (jdm) etw. zurückgeben [tsuˈrʏkɡeːbm̩] <gibt zurück, gab zurück, hat zurückgegeben> ◊ *Ich habe ihr das Buch noch nicht zurückgegeben.*; *(goods)* umtauschen [ˈʊmtaoʃn̩] +haben ◊ *Ich habe die Hose umgetauscht, weil sie mir zu kurz war.* **6.** *(a greeting, compliment)* erwidern [ɛˈviːdɐn] <erwidert, erwiderte, hat erwidert> ◊ *Sie hat meinen Gruß mit einem Nicken erwidert.* ♦ *Er sagte, sie sehe gut aus, und sie erwiderte das Kompliment.* return sb's fire das Feuer erwidern return sb's call jdn zurückrufen [tsuˈrʏkruːfn̩] <ruft zurück, rief zurück, hat zurückgerufen> ◊ *Es tut mit Leid, dass ich Sie erst jetzt zurückrufe.* return the favour/favor sich revanchieren [revãˈʃiːrən] <revanchiert sich, revanchierte sich, hat sich revanchiert> ◊ *Danke, ich revanchiere mich gern mal bei Ihnen.* **7.** *(a profit)* abwerfen [ˈapvɛɐfn̩] <wirft ab, warf ab, hat abgeworfen> ◊ *Das angelegte Geld hat einen guten Gewinn abgeworfen.* **8.** *(a ball)* zurückschlagen [tsuˈrʏkʃlaːgn̩] <schlägt zurück, schlug zurück, hat zurückgeschlagen> **9.** *(elect)* return sb to sth jdn wieder in etw. ⟨acc⟩ wählen [viːdɐ ɪn … vɛːlən] +haben ◊ *Sie wurde wieder ins Parlament gewählt.* return sb to office jdn wieder wählen ◊ *Er wurde nicht wieder gewählt.*
return flight ⟨noun⟩ Rückflug [ˈrʏkfluːk] der <-(e)s, Rückflüge>
return game ⟨noun⟩ → return match
return journey ⟨noun⟩ Rückreise [ˈrʏkraɛzə] die <-, -n>
return match ⟨noun⟩ Rückspiel [ˈrʏkʃpiːl] das <-s, -e>
return ticket ⟨noun⟩ Rückfahrkarte [ˈrʏkfaːɐˈkaɐtə] die <-, -n>
reunification ⟨noun⟩ Wiedervereinigung [ˈviːdɐfɛɐˌʔaɛnɪɡʊŋ] die <-, -en>
reunion ⟨noun⟩ **1.** *(social event)* Treffen [ˈtrɛfn̩] das

<-s, -> family reunion Familientreffen [faˈmiːli̯əntrɛfn̩] **2.** *(after a separation)* Wiedersehen [ˈviːdeːzeːən] das <-s> no pl ◊ *Es gab ein freudiges Wiedersehen.* ♦ *Sie konnte das Wiedersehen mit ihrer Tochter kaum erwarten.*
revalue ⟨verb⟩ *(increase the value)* aufwerten [ˈaofveːɡtn̩] <wertet auf, wertete auf, hat aufgewertet> ◊ *Der Dollar wurde um fünf Prozent aufgewertet.*
reveal ⟨verb⟩ **1.** *(a fact)* enthüllen [ɛntˈhylən] <enthüllt, enthüllte, hat enthüllt> ◊ *Die neue Biografie Napoleons enthüllt Erstaunliches.*; *(a secret)* lüften [ˈlʏftn̩] <lüftet, lüftete, hat gelüftet> ◊ *Es gelang ihnen endlich, das Geheimnis des Burggespenstes zu lüften.*; *(your name, identity)* preisgeben [ˈpraɛsɡeːbm̩] <gibt preis, gab preis, hat preisgegeben> *(lofty)* ◊ *Sie wollte seinen Namen/ihre Identität nicht preisgeben.* reveal sth to sb jdm etw. zeigen [ˈtsaɛɡn̩] +haben ◊ *Die Pläne für den Umbau der Fabrik werden morgen den Mitarbeitern gezeigt.* reveal that ergeben, dass [ɛˈgeːbm̩ das] <ergibt, ergab, hat ergeben> ◊ *Die Ermittlungen ergaben, dass er ins Ausland geflohen war.* reveal who verraten, wer [fɛˈraːtn̩ veːɐ] <verrät, verriet, hat verraten> ◊ *Er wollte nicht verraten, wer ihm diese Informationen gegeben hatte.* **2.** *(an object)* zum Vorschein bringen [tsʊm ˈfoːɐʃaɛn brɪŋən] <bringt, brachte, hat gebracht> ◊ *Sie machte ihre Tasche auf und brachte ein Geschenk zum Vorschein.*
revelation ⟨noun⟩ **1.** *(surprising information)* Enthüllung [ɛntˈhylʊŋ] die <-, -en> ◊ *Die Zeitungen brachten immer neue Enthüllungen über sein Privatleben.* **2.** *(great experience, message from God, letting sb in on a secret)* Offenbarung [ˈɔfn̩ˈbaːrʊŋ] die <-, -en> ◊ *eine Offenbarung Gottes* ♦ *die Offenbarung des Geheimnisses* ♦ *Ihr Tanz war eine Offenbarung für die Zuschauer.*
revenge ⟨noun⟩ **1.** *(retaliation)* Rache [ˈraxə] die <-> no pl ◊ *Das ist die Rache für deine Gemeinheiten!* a revenge killing ein Mord aus Rache in revenge for sth aus Rache für etw. take revenge on sb, your revenge on sb sich an jdm rächen [an … ˈrɛːçn̩] +haben ◊ *Ich werde mich eines Tages an ihm rächen.* revenge attack Vergeltungsaktion [fɛˈgɛltʊŋsˌak.tsɪoːn] die <-, -en> **2.** sport Revanche [rəˈvãʃ(ə)] die <-, -n> ◊ *Der Verlierer will Revanche.*
revenue ⟨noun⟩ Einnahmen [ˈaɛnaːmən] die <-> pl ◊ *die Einnahmen aus diesem Geschäft* tax revenues Steueraufkommen [ˈʃtɔøɐˌʔaofkɔmən] das <-s, ->
reverent(ly) ⟨adj, adv⟩ *(respectful)* ehrfürchtig [ˈeːɐfʏɐ̯çtɪç] ◊ *ehrfürchtige Stille* ♦ *Sie hörten ehrfürchtig zu.* be reverent voller Ehrfurcht sein [fɔlɐ ˈeːɐfʊɐ̯çt tsaɛn] +sein
reverse¹ ⟨noun⟩ **1.** *(opposite)* the reverse das Gegenteil [das ˈgeːgn̩taɛl] <-(e)s, -e> ◊ *Du irrst dich; genau das Gegenteil ist der Fall.* **2.** *(of a coin etc.)* the reverse die Rückseite [diː ˈrʏkzaɛtə] <-, -n> ◊ *Auf der Rückseite der Münze ist ein Adler.* **3.** *(gear)* Rückwärtsgang [ˈrʏkvɛɐ̯tsgaŋ] der <-(e)s, Rückwärtsgänge> put the car in reverse den Rückwärtsgang einlegen
reverse² ⟨verb⟩ **1.** *(a development, sequence etc.)* umkehren [ˈʊmkeːrən] +haben ◊ *Diese Entwicklung lässt sich nicht umkehren.* ♦ *Warum kehren wir die Reihenfolge nicht einfach um?* **2.** *(a judgement)* aufheben [ˈaofheːbm̩] <hebt auf, hob auf, hat aufgeho-

ben> ◊ *Das Revisionsgericht hob das Urteil auf.* **3.** *(a decision)* zurücknehmen [ʦuˈrʏkneːmən] <nimmt zurück, nahm zurück, hat zurückgenommen> ◊ *Hoffentlich nimmt sie ihre Entscheidung zurück.; (a policy)* rückgängig machen [ˈrʏkgɛnɪç maxn̩] +haben ◊ *Die neue Regierung machte die Reformen sofort rückgängig.; (in the US)* reverse yourself seine Meinung ändern [zaɛnə ˈmaɛnʊŋ ˌɛndən] +haben **4.** *(a car)* zurücksetzen [ʦuˈrʏkzɛʦn̩] +haben ◊ *Kannst du den Wagen ein bisschen zurücksetzen?* ♦ zwei Meter zurücksetzen reverse into a parking space rückwärts einparken [ˈrʏkvɛˀʦ ˌaɛnpaˀkn̩] +haben **5.** *(a garment)* wenden [ˈvɛndn̩] <wendet, wendete, hat gewendet> ◊ *Man sollte die Jeans vor dem Waschen wenden.* **6.** *(your roles)* vertauschen [fɛˈtaʊʃn̩] <vertauscht, vertauschte, hat vertauscht> ◊ *Sie haben die Rollen vertauscht; jetzt kümmert er sich um die Kinder, und sie geht arbeiten.*

revert to ⟨verb⟩ **1.** *(to a previous state or occupation)* revert to sth zu etw. zurückkehren [ʦuː ... ʦuˌrʏkkeːrən] +sein ◊ *Diese Zeitung ist zu den alten Schreibregeln zurückgekehrt.; (to a habit)* revert to sth in etw. ⟨acc⟩ zurückfallen [ɪn ... ʦuˌrʏkfalən] <fällt zurück, fiel zurück, ist zurückgefallen> ◊ *Sie fiel schnell in ihre alten Gewohnheiten zurück.* **2.** *(to a topic)* revert to sth auf etw. ⟨acc⟩ zurückkommen [aʊf ... ʦuˌrʏkkɔmən] <kommt zurück, kam zurück, ist zurückgekommen> ◊ *Er kam schnell auf sein Lieblingsthema, sein Auto, zurück.* **3.** *(to its previous owner)* revert to sb an jdn zurückfallen [an ... ʦuˌrʏkfalən] <fällt zurück, fiel zurück, ist zurückgefallen> ◊ *Das Haus fiel an seinen früheren Besitzer zurück.*

review[1] ⟨noun⟩ **1.** *(re-examination)* Überprüfung [ybɐˈpryːfʊŋ] die <-, -en> ◊ *Der Minister kündigte eine Überprüfung des Systems an.* conduct a review of sth etw. überprüfen [ybɐˈpryːfn̩] <überprüft, überprüfte, hat überprüft> ◊ *Wir werden die Angaben überprüfen.* be under review überprüft werden ◊ *Diese Regelung wird gerade überprüft.* be subject to review nochmals überprüft werden **2.** *(of all relevant information)* Überblick [ˈyːbɐblɪk] der <-(e)s, -e> ◊ *ein Überblick über die Sekundärliteratur zu diesem Thema* **3.** *(of a book, play etc.)* Kritik [kriˈtiːk] die <-, -en> ◊ *Das Buch bekam gute/schlechte Kritiken.* rave reviews begeisterte Kritiken **4.** MIL Inspektion [ɪnspɛkˈʦjoːn] die <-, -en> **5.** *(in the US: revision for an exam)* Wiederholung [viːdɐˈhoːlʊŋ] die <-, -en> ◊ *die Wiederholung des Lehrstoffs*

review[2] ⟨verb⟩ **1.** *(re-examine)* überprüfen [ybɐˈpryːfn̩] <überprüft, überprüfte, hat überprüft> ◊ *Das muss regelmäßig überprüft werden.* ♦ das Beweismaterial genau überprüfen **2.** *(a book, play etc.)* besprechen [bəˈʃprɛçn̩] <bespricht, besprach, hat besprochen> ◊ *Ihr Roman wurde in der Zeitung besprochen.* **3.** MIL inspizieren [ɪnspiˈʦiːrən] <inspiziert, inspizierte, hat inspiziert> ◊ *Der Verteidigungsminister hat die Truppen inspiziert.* **4.** *(in the US: revise for an exam)* wiederholen [viːdɐˈhoːlən] <wiederholt, wiederholte, hat wiederholt> ◊ *den Lehrstoff wiederholen*

revise ⟨verb⟩ **1.** *(change)* ändern [ˈɛndən] +haben ◊ *Er hat seine Meinung geändert.* ♦ *Die Firma hat die Sicherheitsvorschriften geändert.; (improve, correct)* revidieren [reviˈdiːrən] <revidiert, revidierte, hat

revidiert> ◊ *Die Schätzungen mussten revidiert werden.* ♦ *eine revidierte Fassung/Auflage* **2.** *(for an exam)* wiederholen [viːdeˈhoːlən] <wiederholt, wiederholte, hat wiederholt> ◊ *Wir müssen alle Vokabeln wiederholen.* revise for sth für etw. lernen [fyːɐ ... ˌlɛˀnən] +haben ◊ *Für den Test hat er fleißig gelernt.*

revision ⟨noun⟩ **1.** *(change)* Änderung [ˈɛndərʊŋ] die <-, -en> ◊ *Die neuen Ziele erfordern eine Änderung unserer Strategie.* sth is subject to revision etw. kann geändert werden [kan gəˈʔɛndet veːɐdn̩] <kann, konnte, hat können> ◊ *Die Geschäftsbedingungen können jederzeit geändert werden.; (improvement, correction)* Revision [reviˈzjoːn] die <-, -en> ◊ *die Revision des Gesetzes; (revised version)* Überarbeitung [yːbɐˈʔaɛtʊŋ] die <-, -en> ◊ *Er plant eine Überarbeitung des Stückes.* **2.** *(in the UK: preparation for an exam)* Wiederholung [viːdeˈhoːlʊŋ] die <-, -en> ◊ *Die Wiederholung des Gelernten trainiert das Gedächtnis.* do some revision for sth für etw. lernen [fyːɐ ... ˌlɛˀnən] +haben ◊ *Er muss für die Prüfung lernen.*

revival ⟨noun⟩ **1.** *(becoming active again)* Wiederaufleben [viːdeˈʔaʊfleːbn̩] das <-s> no pl ◊ *das Wiederaufleben des Interesses an klassischer Musik* religious revival Wiederaufleben der Religion the revival in sb's fortunes jds Comeback [kamˈbɛk] das <-s, -s> **2.** THEAT Wiederaufführung [viːdeˈʔaʊffyːrʊŋ] die <-, -en>

revive ⟨verb⟩ **1.** *(make conscious again)* wiederbeleben [ˈviːdəbeleːbm̩] <belebt, belebte, hat belebt> ◊ *Der Notarzt hat ihn wiederbelebt.; (become conscious again)* wieder zu sich kommen [viːde ˈʦuː ... kɔmən] <kommt, kam, ist gekommen> ◊ *Sie kam bald wieder zu sich.* **2.** *(recover)* sich erholen [əˈhoːlən] <erholt sich, erholte sich, hat sich erholt> ◊ *Als ich die Pflanze ins Wasser stellte, erholte sie sich schnell.* ♦ *Nach dem langen Spaziergang erholte er sich bei einer Tasse Kaffee.* **3.** *(make active again)* wieder aufleben lassen [viːde ˈʔaʊfleːbm̩ lasn̩] <lässt, ließ, hat lassen> ◊ *alte Traditionen wieder aufleben lassen; (become active again)* wieder aufleben [viːde ˈʔaʊfleːbm̩] +sein ◊ *Die alten Bräuche leben wieder auf.* **4.** *(memories)* wieder lebendig werden lassen [viːde leˈbɛndɪç veːɐdn̩ lasn̩] <lässt, ließ, hat lassen> ◊ *Die Fotos ließen die Erinnerung an diese schöne Zeit wieder lebendig werden.; (a friendship)* erneuern [ɛˈnɔɛɐn] +haben ◊ *Das Treffen hat unsere alte Freundschaft erneuert.* **5.** THEAT wieder auf die Bühne bringen [viːde aɔf diː ˈbyːnə brɪŋən] <bringt, brachte, hat gebracht> ◊ *ein Stück wieder auf die Bühne bringen* **6.** *(make sb feel better)* munter machen [ˈmʊntɐ maxn̩] +haben ◊ *Eine Tasse Kaffee wird dich wieder munter machen.*

revoke ⟨verb⟩ *(a law)* aufheben [ˈʔaʊfheːbm̩] <hebt auf, hob auf, hat aufgehoben> ◊ *Das Gesetz wurde schnell wieder aufgehoben.; (a decision)* zurücknehmen [ʦuˈrʏkneːmən] <nimmt zurück, nahm zurück, hat zurückgenommen> ◊ *Hoffentlich nimmt sie ihre Entscheidung zurück.* revoke sb's driving license jdm den Führerschein entziehen [deːn ˈfyːreʃaɛn ɛntˌʦiːən] <entzieht, entzog, hat entzogen>

revolt ⟨noun⟩ Aufstand [ˈʔaʊfʃtant] der <-(e)s, Aufstände> ◊ *Das Militär warf den Aufstand nieder.* rise in revolt (against sb/sth) (gegen jdn/

etw.) **revoltieren** [revɔl'tiːrən] <revoltiert, revoltierte, hat revoltiert> ◊ *gegen ein Gesetz revoltieren*

revolting(ly) [adj, adv] ekelhaft ['eːk‖haft] <ekelhafter, am ekelhaftesten> ◊ *ein ekelhafter Anblick* ♦ *Diese Medizin schmeckt ekelhaft!* ♦ *ekelhaft hässlich*

revolution [noun] **1.** *(radical change)* Revolution [revolu'tsjoːn] die <-, -en> ◊ *die Revolution von 1848/49* ♦ *die sexuelle Revolution* **2.** *(complete turn)* Umdrehung [ʊm'dreːʊŋ] die <-, -en> ◊ *Der Motor macht 4000 Umdrehungen pro Minute.*; *(of a planet)* Umlauf ['ʊmlaʊf] der <-s, Umläufe> ◊ *der Umlauf der Venus um die Sonne*

revolutionary [adj] *(party, war, idea)* revolutionär [revolutsjo'nɛːɐ] ◊ *eine revolutionäre Partei* ♦ *Dieses Konzept ist revolutionär.*; *(change)* umwälzend ['ʊmvɛltsnt] ◊ *eine umwälzende Veränderung* ♦ *Die Entwicklung der Technik in den letzten zehn Jahren war umwälzend.*

revolve [verb] *(turn, spin)* revolve (on sth) sich (um etw. [acc]) drehen ['dreːən] +haben ◊ *sich um seine eigene Achse drehen* ♦ *Die Erde dreht sich um die Sonne.*

• **revolve around** [phras v] revolve around sth sich um etw. drehen [ʊm ... dreːən] +haben ◊ *Bei ihnen dreht sich das ganze Leben nur um die Arbeit.*

• **revolve round** [phras v] → revolve around

revolver [noun] Revolver [re'vɔlve] der <-s, ->

reward[1] [noun] **1.** *(for sth you have done, for helping the police)* Belohnung [bə'loːnʊŋ] die <-, -en> ◊ *Als Belohnung für das gute Zeugnis bekam er ein neues Rad.* ♦ *Die Polizei setzte eine Belohnung für Informationen über den Täter aus.* a just reward eine verdiente Belohnung; *(for finding sth)* Finderlohn ['fɪndeloːn] der <-(e)s, Finderlöhne> ◊ *Ich bekam 100 Euro Finderlohn.* **2.** financial reward Vergütung [fɛ'ɡyːtʊŋ] die <-, -en> ◊ *eine Vergütung für besondere Leistungen* reap rewards for sb sich für jdn lohnen [zɪç fyːɐ ... 'loːnən] +haben reap the rewards of sth von etw. profitieren [fɔn ... profi'tiːrən] <profitiert, profitierte, hat profitiert>

reward[2] [verb] belohnen [bə'loːnən] <belohnt, belohnte, hat belohnt> ◊ *Er hat ihn für seine Treue belohnt.* ♦ *Fleiß mit guten Noten belohnen* handsomely rewarded reich belohnt

rewarding [adj] *(work, experience)* lohnend ['loːnənt] ◊ *eine lohnende Aufgabe* ♦ *Ein Besuch im Heimatmuseum ist lohnend.*; *(financially)* einträglich ['aɛntrɛːklɪç] ◊ *eine einträgliche Investition* ♦ *Das Geschäft ist einträglich.*

rework [verb] überarbeiten [ybe‖a'baɛtn] <überarbeitet, überarbeitete, hat überarbeitet> ◊ *eine Internetseite überarbeiten* ♦ *einen Plan/Aufsatz überarbeiten*

rewrite [verb] *(a text, software)* umschreiben ['ʊmʃraɛbm] <schreibt um, schrieb um, hat umgeschrieben> ◊ *Wir müssen das Drehbuch/die Software umschreiben.*; *(a law)* neu fassen ['nɔø fasn] +haben ◊ *Das umstrittene Gesetz soll neu gefasst werden.*

rhetoric [noun] Rhetorik [re'toːrɪk] die <-, -en> most sing ◊ *Sie unterrichtet Rhetorik.* ♦ *Seine Äußerungen erwiesen sich als bloße Rhetorik.*

rhetorical(ly) [adj, adv] rhetorisch [re'toːrɪʃ] no comp/ superl ◊ *Die Frage war rein rhetorisch; er hat keine Antwort erwartet.* ♦ *Er besitzt beachtliche rhetorische Fähigkeiten.* ♦ *ein rhetorisch ausgefeilter Artikel*

rheumatism [noun] Rheuma ['rɔømaː] das <-s> no pl

Rhine [noun] Rhein [raɛn] der <-s> no pl ◊ *Der Rhein mündet in die Nordsee.* ♦ *Köln liegt am Rhein.*

rhyme [noun] Reim [raɛm] der <-(e)s, -e> ◊ *Die Kinder sagten einige Reime auf.* in rhyme in Reimen ◊ *Das Bilderbuch ist in Reimen geschrieben.* be a rhyme for sth sich auf etw. [acc] reimen [aɔf ... ˌraɛmən] +haben ◊ *Was reimt sich auf „Liebe"?*

☺ there is no rhyme or reason for sth etw. hat keinen vernünftigen Grund

rhythm [noun] Rhythmus ['rʏtmʊs] der <-, Rhythmen> ◊ *Sie klatschten zum/im Rhythmus der Trommeln.* ♦ *Kinder haben oft ein gutes Gefühl für Rhythmus.* ♦ *der Rhythmus von Ebbe und Flut*

rhythmic(ally) [adj] rhythmisch ['rʏtmɪʃ] ◊ *rhythmische Sportgymnastik* ♦ *Lateinamerikanische Musik ist sehr rhythmisch.* ♦ *Sie bewegten sich rhythmisch zur Musik.*

rib [noun] **1.** *(bone)* Rippe ['rɪpə] die <-, -n> ◊ *Er brach sich bei dem Unfall mehrere Rippen.* ♦ *Sie stieß ihm in die Rippen.* **2.** *(meat)* Rippchen ['rɪpçən] das <-s, -> ◊ *gegrillte Rippchen*

ribbon [noun] **1.** *(long piece of cloth or paper, strip)* Band [bant] das <-(e)s, Bänder> ◊ *sich* [dat] *die Haare mit einem Band zusammenbinden* ♦ *Aus der Luft sah die Autobahn wie ein graues Band aus.* a ribbon of blue ein blaues Band; *(to show support)* Schleife ['ʃlaɛfə] die <-, -n> ◊ *eine gelbe Schleife als Zeichen des Gedenkens an die im Golfkrieg Gefallenen* **2.** *(torn pieces)* ribbons Fetzen ['fɛtsn] die <-> pl tear sth to ribbons etw. in Fetzen reißen in ribbons zerfetzt [zɛ'fɛtst] ◊ *Sein Mantel war zerfetzt.* **3.** TECHN *(in typewriters)* Farbband ['faɐbant] das <-(e)s, Farbbänder>

rice [noun] Reis [raɛs] der <-es> no pl ◊ *Reis anbauen* ♦ *Als Beilage gab es Reis.*

rich [adj] **1.** *(owning a lot of money, property, heritage)* reich [raɛç] ◊ *ein reiches Land* ♦ *Durch einen Lottogewinn wurde er über Nacht reich.* ♦ *das reiche Kulturerbe dieses Landes* the rich die Reichen ◊ *Die Reichen werden immer reicher.* rich and poor, the rich and the poor Arm und Reich ◊ *Die Kluft zwischen Arm und Reich hat sich vergrößert.* rich in proteins eiweißreich ['aɛvaɛsraɛç] ◊ *Fisch ist sehr eiweißreich.* ♦ *eine eiweißreiche Ernährung* filthy rich steinreich ['ʃtaɛn'raɛç] no comp/superl **2.** *(containing many calories)* schwer [ʃveːɐ] ◊ *ein schwerer Nachtisch* ♦ *Dieses Essen ist mir zu schwer.* rich diet gehaltvolle Nahrung [ɡə,haltfɔlə 'naːrʊŋ] **3.** *(soil)* fruchtbar ['frʊxtbaːr] ◊ *der fruchtbare Boden in der Ebene* ♦ *Hier ist das Land weniger fruchtbar.* **4.** *(fabric)* prachtvoll ['praxtfɔl] ◊ *Kleider aus prachtvoller Seide* ♦ *Die Stoffe sind prachtvoll und teuer.* **5.** *(sound, voice, smell)* voll [fɔl] ◊ *Das Fagott hat einen vollen Ton.* ♦ *das volle Aroma dieser Kaffeesorte* ♦ *Seine Stimme war voll und tief.*; *(colo(u)r)* satt [zat] <satter, am sattesten> ◊ *ein sattes Rot* **6.** *(life)* erfüllt [ɛɐ'fʏlt] <erfüllter, am erfülltesten> ◊ *Er hat ein erfülltes Leben geführt.*

☺ that's rich ausgerechnet ◊ *Er fühlt sich ungerecht behandelt? — Ausgerechnet!* that's rich coming from you ausgerechnet du musst das sagen

riches [noun] Reichtum ['raɛçtuːm] der <-s, Reichtümer> ◊ *Er ist zu plötzlichem Reichtum gelangt.* ♦ *Sie hat unermessliche Reichtümer angehäuft.*

richly (adv) **1.** *(beautifully, expensively)* reich [ɾaɛç] ◊ *reich verzierte Möbel* ♦ *ein Haus mit reich ausgestatteten Zimmern* **2.** *(with strong colo(u)rs)* prächtig ['pɾɛçtɪç] ◊ *prächtig bunte Gewänder;* *(with a strong flavo(u)r, smell)* intensiv [ɪntɛn'ziːf] ◊ *eine intensiv gewürzte Suppe* **3.** *(completely)* richly deserved wohlverdient ['voːlfɛdiːnt] *no comp/superl* ◊ *eine wohlverdiente Belohnung* ♦ *Der Applaus war wohlverdient.* **4.** *(with a lot of money)* reich [ɾaɛç] ◊ *Sie wurden reich belohnt.* **5.** *(extremely)* äußerst ['ɔøsɛst] ◊ *ein äußerst komischer Roman*

rid¹ (adj) **1.** be rid of sb/sth jdn/etw. los sein ['loːs zaɛn] ◊ *Endlich bin ich ihn/den Job los!* be glad to be rid of sb/sth froh sein, dass man jdn/etw. los ist ◊ *Sei froh, dass du die Kinder mal einen Tag los bist.* sb is well rid of sb/sth es ist gut, dass jd jdn/etw. los ist ◊ *Sie ist zwar traurig, aber es ist gut, dass sie ihn los ist.* **2.** get rid of sb/sth jdn/etw. loswerden ['loːsveːɐdn̩] <wird los, wurde los, ist losgeworden>

rid² (verb) rid sb/sth of sb/sth jdn/etw. von jdm/etw. befreien [fɔn ... bə,fɾaɛən] <befreit, befreite, hat befreit> ◊ *die Welt vom Terrorismus befreien;* *(an idea etc.)* rid yourself of sth sich von etw. frei machen [fɔn ... 'fɾaɛ maxn̩] +haben ◊ *Wenn sie sich nur von diesen Vorurteilen frei machen könnte!*

riddle (noun) Rätsel ['ɾɛːtsl̩] das <-s, -> ◊ *ein Rätsel lösen* ♦ *in Rätseln sprechen* ♦ *Die Lösung des Rätsels erfahren Sie im nächsten Heft.* ♦ *das Rätsel ihres Verschwindens*

ride¹ (noun) **1.** *(on a horse)* Ritt [ɾɪt] der <-(e)s, -e> ◊ *ein Ritt auf einem Pferd* have a ride on a horse auf einem Pferd reiten [aof aɛnəm 'pfeːɐt ɾaɛtn̩] <reitet, ritt, ist geritten> **2.** *(on a bicycle, motorbike, in a vehicle)* Fahrt [faːɐt] die <-, -en> ◊ *Die Fahrt in dem alten Auto war sehr unbequem.* bus ride Busfahrt ['bʊsfaːɐt] bicycle ride Fahrradtour ['faːɐatuːɐ] die <-, -en> go for a ride in/on sth, take a ride in sth, have a ride in/on sth mit etw. fahren [mɪt ... faːɾən] <fährt, fuhr, ist gefahren> ◊ *Gestern bin ich zum ersten Mal mit einer Schwebebahn gefahren.* ♦ *Darf ich mal mit deinem Fahrrad fahren?;* *(fly)* go for a ride in a helicopter/balloon mit einem Hubschrauber/Ballon fliegen [mɪt aɛnəm 'huːpʃɾaobɐ/ba'lɔ̃ fliːgn̩] <fliegt, flog, ist geflogen> **3.** *(in the US)* give sb a ride jdn mitnehmen ['mɪtneːmən] <nimmt mit, nahm mit, hat mitgenommen> ◊ *Kannst du mich in die Stadt mitnehmen?* get a ride (with sb) (von jdm) mitgenommen werden hitch a ride per Anhalter fahren [pɛɐ 'anhaltɐ faːɾən] <fährt, fuhr, ist gefahren> ◊ *„Wie kommst du nach Hause?" — „Ich fahre per Anhalter."* **4.** *(machine at an amusement park)* Fahrgeschäft [faːɐgəʃɛft] das <-(e)s, -e>; *(time spent on a ride)* ride (on sth) Fahrt (mit etw.) die <-, -en> ◊ *Eine Fahrt mit dem Riesenrad kostet drei Euro.* have a ride (on sth) (mit etw.) fahren ['faːɾən] <fährt, fuhr, ist gefahren> ◊ *Die Kinder wollten mit der Achterbahn fahren.* ⊛ come along for the ride nur zum Vergnügen mitkommen give sb an easy/rough ride es jdm leicht/schwer machen have an easy/rough ride es leicht/schwer haben take sb for a ride jdn reinlegen

ride² (verb) **1.** *(an animal)* reiten ['ɾaɛtn̩] <reitet, ritt, ist geritten> transitive use +haben/intransitive use

+sein ◊ *Sie hat ein wildes Pferd geritten.* ♦ *Er ist nach Süden geritten.* ride on an animal auf einem Tier reiten ◊ *Im Urlaub sind wir auf Kamelen geritten.* ride away davonreiten [da'fɔnɾaɛtn̩] *(lit)* ◊ *Er ritt schnell davon.* **2.** *(a bicycle, motorbike, train, bus, in a carriage, balloon)* fahren ['faːɾən] <fährt, fuhr, hat/ist gefahren> transitive use +haben/intransitive use +sein ◊ *Kannst du Fahrrad/Motorrad fahren?* ♦ *Sie hat ein schweres Motorrad gefahren.* ♦ *Ich bin zum Park gefahren.* ride on/in sth mit etw. fahren ◊ *Die Kinder sind mit ihren Rädern zur Schule gefahren.* ♦ *mit der Straßenbahn/einem Ballon fahren* ride around herumfahren [hɛ'ɾʊmfaːɾən] +sein ◊ *Sie fuhr mit ihrem neuen Auto herum.* ride away wegfahren ['vɛkfaːɾən] +sein ◊ *Sie fuhr schnell weg.* ride back zurückfahren [tsu'ɾʏkfaːɾən] +sein ◊ *Ich fahre zurück.; (in a helicopter)* ride (in sth) (mit etw.) fliegen ['fliːgn̩] <fliegt, flog, ist geflogen> ◊ *Wir flogen mit einem Hubschrauber über die Stadt.* **3.** *(hover, float)* sich von etw. tragen lassen [fɔn ... tɾaːgn̩ lasn̩] <lässt sich, ließ sich, hat sich ... lassen> ◊ *Die Vögel ließen sich vom Wind tragen.* ⊛ let sth ride etw. ignorieren be riding high oben schwimmen

• **ride on** (phras v) ride on sth von etw. abhängen [fɔn ... ,aphɛŋən] <hängt ab, hing ab, hat abgehangen> ◊ *Seine politische Zukunft hängt von dieser Wahl ab.*

• **ride out** (phras v) überstehen [ybɐ'ʃteːən] <übersteht, überstand, hat überstanden> ◊ *Wir werden auch diese Krise überstehen.*

• **ride up** (phras v) hochrutschen ['hoːxɾʊtʃn̩] +sein ◊ *Dein Rock ist hochgerutscht; zieh ihn wieder herunter.*

rider (noun) **1.** *(on an animal)* Reiter ['ɾaɛtɐ] der <-s, -> ♀Reiterin ['ɾaɛtəɾɪn] die <-, -nen> ◊ *Zwei Reiter kamen uns entgegen.* ♦ *Sie ist eine gute Reiterin.* **2.** *(on a bicycle, motorbike)* Fahrer ['faːɾɐ] der <-s, -> ♀Fahrerin ['faːɾəɾɪn] die <-, -nen> ◊ *Der Fahrer des Motorrads wurde schwer verletzt.*

ridge (noun) **1.** *(of a mountain)* Bergkamm ['bɛɾkkam] der <-(e)s, Bergkämme> ◊ *Wir haben eine Wanderung entlang dem Bergkamm gemacht.* **2.** *(on a surface, fingernail)* Rille ['ɾɪlə] die <-, -n>; *(on cardboard)* Rippe ['ɾɪpə] die <-, -n> **3.** *(of a roof)* Dachfirst ['daxfɪɾst] der <-(e)s, -e> **4.** METEO ridge of high pressure Hochdruckgebiet ['hoːxdɾʊkgəbiːt] das <-(e)s, -e>

ridiculous(ly) (adj, adv) lächerlich ['lɛçɛɾlɪç] *(pej)* ◊ *Sie trug einen lächerlichen Hut.* ♦ *Die Situation war einfach lächerlich.* ♦ *Er verdient lächerlich wenig.* Don't be ridiculous! Das ist doch Unsinn!

rifle (noun) Gewehr [gə've:ɐ] das <-(e)s, -e> ◊ *ein Gewehr abfeuern*

rig (noun) **1.** *(for getting oil or gas)* Bohrinsel ['boːɡlɪnzl̩] die <-, -n> ◊ *auf einer Bohrinsel arbeiten* **2.** *(in the US)* Schwertransporter ['ʃveːɐtɾanspɔɐtɐ] der <-s, -> *einen Schwertransporter fahren* **3.** *(scaffold)* Gerüst [gəˈɾʏst] das <-(e)s, -e> lighting rig Beleuchtungsbrücke [bə'lɔøçtʊŋsbɾʏkə] die <-, -n> **4.** SHIP Takelung ['taːkəlʊŋ] die <-, -en> *(tech)*

right¹ (noun) **1.** *(morally or legally correct)* Recht [ɾɛçt] das <-(e)s, -e> ◊ *Recht auf unserer Seite.* right and wrong Recht und Unrecht right to sth Recht auf etw. (acc) ◊ *das Recht auf Arbeit* sb is in

the right jd ist im Recht have a/no right to do sth
das/kein Recht haben, etw. zu tun ◊ *Du hast das*
Recht, angehört zu werden. ◆ *Er hat kein Recht, dir*
Vorwürfe zu machen. sb has every right to do sth es
ist jds gutes Recht, etw. zu tun be within your
rights to do sth etw. mit Recht tun können human
rights Menschenrechte ['mɛnʃnrɛçtə] die <–> pl
equal rights (for sb) Gleichberechtigung (... ɡᴇ̄n)
['ɡlaeçbərɛçtɪɡʊn] die <–> no pl ◊ *Sie kämpften für*
die Gleichberechtigung der Frau. belong to sb as of/
by right jds rechtmäßiges Eigentum sein
[ˌrɛçtmɛːsɪɡəs 'aeɡ̍tuːm zaen] 2. *(for publication, per-*
formance) rights (to sth) Rechte (an etw. dat)
['rɛçtə] die <–> pl ◊ *Der Verlag hat sich die Rechte*
an dem Roman gesichert. ◆ *Alle Rechte vorbehalten.*
3. *(not the left)* rechte Seite [ˌrɛçtə 'zaetə] die <–>
no pl ◊ *auf der rechten Seite des Raumes* on/to your
right, on the right rechts [rɛçts] ◊ *Rechts sehen Sie*
jetzt den Kölner Dom. ◆ *Es ist das zweite Haus*
rechts. to the right nach rechts ◊ *Machen Sie doch*
bitte einen Schritt nach rechts. make/take a right
rechts abbiegen the first/second etc. right die
erste/zweite etc. Straße rechts 4. ᴘᴏʟ the right, the
Right die Rechte [diː 'rɛçtə] <–n> no pl ◊ *Die*
Rechte ist in ganz Europa wieder im Vormarsch.; *(of*
a party) the right der rechte Flügel
[deːɐ ˌrɛçtə 'flyːɡl̩] <–s, –> ◊ *Er ist dem rechten*
Flügel seiner Partei zuzurechnen. 5. *(punch)* Rechte
['rɛçtə] die <–n, –n> ◊ *Er streckte seinen Gegner*
mit einer Rechten zu Boden.
⊕ the rights and wrongs of sth was an etw. dat
gut oder schlecht ist in **sb's own right** selbst ◊
Camille Claudel war selbst eine große Künstlerin. do
right by sb jdn richtig behandeln put sth to rights
etw. in Ordnung bringen by rights von Rechts
wegen
right² adj **1.** *(correct, normally expected, suitable,*
important) richtig ['rɪçtɪç] ◊ *Für jede richtige Antwort*
bekommt man zehn Punkte. ◆ *Es war nicht richtig*
von dir, sie anzulügen. ◆ *Der Schlüssel liegt nicht*
am richtigen Platz. ◆ *den richtigen Zeitpunkt wählen*
the right way up richtig herum get sth right etw.
richtig verstehen ◊ *Wenn ich das richtig verstehe,*
sollen wir in einer Woche wiederkommen. Let me
get this right. Habe ich das richtig verstanden? He
isn't right for her. Er ist nicht der Richtige für sie.
do the right thing das Richtige tun; *(have the correct*
opinion, explanation) be right Recht haben
['rɛçt haˌbm̩] +haben ◊ *Wer von den beiden hat*
Recht? ◆ *Du hast Recht — er ist wirklich ein Schatz.*
be right in saying sth Recht haben, wenn man etw.
sagt ◊ *Ihre Mutter hat Recht, wenn sie sagt, dass die*
beiden nicht zusammenpassen. sb doesn't feel right
jd fühlt sich nicht wohl [fyːlt ... nɪçt 'voːl]
something isn't right etwas stimmt nicht
[ɛtvas 'ʃtɪmt nɪçt] +haben **2.** *(not left)* rechte ['rɛçtə]
only before ns <ein rechter ..., eine rechte ..., ein
rechtes ...> ◊ *Auf dem rechten Ohr ist er taub.* ◆ *Er*
schoss den Ball in die rechte Ecke.
⊕ put/set sb right jdn aufklären **that's right**
1. *(affirmative)* richtig ◊ *"Warst du letzte Woche im*
Urlaub?" — "Richtig!" **2.** *(expressing indignation)*
also wirklich ◊ *Also wirklich! Sei nur weiter so faul.*
right³ adv **1.** *(exactly)* genau [ɡə'nao] ◊ *Das Loch*
muss genau in der Mitte sein. ◆ *Er kam genau*
pünktlich. right here genau an dieser Stelle right

behind sb/sth direkt hinter jdm/etw. [dɪrɛkt 'hɪntə]
◊ *Sie stand direkt hinter mir.* right in front of sb/sth
direkt vor jdm/etw. [dɪrɛkt 'foːɐ] **2.** *(immediately)*
gleich [ɡlaeç] ◊ *Sie haben sich gleich gut verstanden.*
◆ *Ich bin gleich nach dir dran.* right away sofort
[zoˈfɔˑʳt] ◊ *Komm sofort nach Hause!* ◆ *Sie hat sofort*
begriffen, worum es ging. sb will be right there jd
kommt sofort ◊ *Warten Sie bitte hier; Dr. Meier*
kommt sofort. **3.** *(all the way, completely)* ganz
[ɡants] ◊ *Er ist ganz bis auf den Grund getaucht.* ◆
Sie ist ganz verrückt geworden. ◆ *Das steht ganz*
vorn im Buch. The car went right into a tree. Das
Auto ist frontal gegen einen Baum gefahren.
4. *(correctly, as it should be)* richtig ['rɪçtɪç] no
comp/superl ◊ *Habe ich es richtig gemacht?* go right
gut klappen [ɡuːt 'klapm̩] +haben (fam) ◊ *Alles hat*
gut geklappt. do right das Richtige tun
[das 'rɪçtɪɡə ˌtuːn] <tut, tat, hat getan> **5.** *(not left)*
rechts [rɛçts] ◊ *rechts abbiegen*
⊕ right, left and centre überall ◊ *Überall laufen*
Touristen herum. right now **1.** *(at the present time)*
im Augenblick ◊ *Sie kann im Augenblick nicht ans*
Telefon kommen. **2.** *(immediately)* sofort ◊ *Komm*
sofort her!
right⁴ interj **1.** *(getting attention)* so [zoː] ◊ *So!*
Können wir jetzt losfahren? **2.** *(changing activity)*
also ['alzoː] ◊ *Also, jetzt kommen wir zu unserer*
nächsten Übung. **3.** *(checking if correct)* ... right? ...
oder nicht? [oːdɐ 'nɪçt] ◊ *Sie waren auch dabei,*
oder nicht? **4.** *(saying you agree)* right (you are) in
Ordnung [ɪn 'ɔʳdnʊn] ◊ *"Wir treffen uns*
morgen." — "In Ordnung."
rightful(ly) adj, adv rechtmäßig ['rɪçtmɛːsɪç] no
comp/superl ◊ *etw. seinem rechtmäßigen Besitzer*
zurückgeben ◆ *Das steht uns rechtmäßig zu.*
right-handed adj be right-handed Rechtshänder/
Rechtshänderin sein
['rɛçtshɛndɐ/'rɛçtshɛndərɪn zaen] a right-handed
guitar eine Gitarre für Rechtshänder
rightly adv **1.** *(for a good reason)* (quite) rightly zu
Recht [tsuː 'rɛçt] ◊ *Er macht sich zu Recht Sorgen*
um seinen Sohn. and rightly so und zwar zu Recht
2. *(correctly)* richtig ['rɪçtɪç] as you rightly say wie
Sie ganz richtig sagen if I remember rightly wenn
ich mich recht entsinne [vɛn ɪç mɪç 'rɛçt ɛntˌzɪnə]
⊕ I can't rightly say ich kann es nicht genau
sagen rightly oder wrongly ob das nun richtig ist
oder nicht
right of way noun **1.** *(in front of other vehicles)*
Vorfahrt ['foːɐfaˑʳt] die <–> no pl ◊ *Wer hat hier*
Vorfahrt? **2.** *(over sb's private land)* Wegerecht
['veːɡərɛçt] das <–(e)s, –e> ◊ *Wanderer haben*
Wegerecht auf den offiziellen Wanderwegen.
right-wing adj rechte ['rɛçtə] only before ns <ein
rechter ..., eine rechte ..., ein rechtes ...> ◊
Skinheads und andere rechte Gewalttäter be right-
wing rechts sein ['rɛçts zaen] ◊ *Sie ist rechts.*
rigid adj **1.** *(not easy to change, bend, move)* starr
[ʃtaʳ] ◊ *eine starre Haltung der Regierung in einem*
Konflikt ◆ *Die Glieder der Toten waren bereits starr.*
rigid with fear starr vor Schreck **2.** *(strict)* streng
[ʃtrɛn] ◊ *In der Schule herrscht strenge Disziplin.* ◆
Die Regeln sind sehr streng. **3.** *(not willing to*
change) unflexibel ['ʊnflɛksiːbl̩] <unflexibler, am unfle-
xibelsten> <ein unflexibler ..., eine unflexible ...,
ein unflexibles ...> ◊ *Beide Seiten waren unflexibel.* ◆

A
B
C
D
E
F
G
H
I
J
K
L
M
N
O
P
Q
R
S
T
U
V
W
X
Y
Z

seine unflexible Einstellung

rigorous(ly) (adj, adv) strikt [ʃtrɪkt] <strikter, am strik-testen> ◊ *die strikte Einhaltung der Vorschriften* ✦ *Die Kontrolle am Flughafen war diesmal wirklich ganz strikt.* ✦ *Sie hat die Diät strikt befolgt.*

rim (noun) **1.** *(of spectacles, circular object)* Rand [rant] der <-(e)s, Ränder> ◊ *Das Glas hatte einen goldenen Rand.* ✦ *am Rand eines Kraters stehen* rim of dirt Schmutzrand ['ʃmʊtsrant] **2.** *(of a wheel)* Felge ['fɛlɡə] die <-, -n> ◊ *Das Auto hatte ver-chromte Felgen.*

ring¹ (noun) **1.** *(jewellery, circular object, for boxing, group of people)* Ring [rɪŋ] der <-(e)s, -e> ◊ *Er trug einen Ring am rechten Mittelfinger.* ✦ *Ich hatte dunkle Ringe unter den Augen.* ✦ *Der Boxer stieg in den Ring.* **2.** *(circle)* Kreis [kraɛs] der <-es, -e> ◊ *Die Gruppe bildete einen Kreis um den Tisch.* in a ring im Kreis ◊ *Wir saßen im Kreis um den Lehrer herum.* **3.** *(on a gas cooker)* Brenner ['brɛnɐ] der <-s, ->; *(on an electric cooker)* Herdplatte ['heːɐtplatə] die <-, -n> **4.** *(sound of phone, doorbell, alarm clock)* Klingeln ['klɪŋln̩] das <-s> no pl ◊ *Sie wurde vom Klingeln des Telefons geweckt.* give sb a ring jdn anrufen ['anruːfn̩] <ruft an, rief an, hat angerufen> ◊ *Ich rufe dich nächste Woche an.* give a ring on the doorbell an der Tür klingeln [an deːɐ 'tyːɐ ˌklɪŋln̩] +haben I was interrupted by the ring of the doorbell. Ich wurde unterbrochen, weil es an der Tür klingelte. **5.** *(sound of a bell)* Läuten ['lɔøtn̩] das <-s> no pl ◊ *Er wurde vom Läuten der Kirchenglocken geweckt.; (metallic sound)* Klirren ['klɪrən] das <-s> no pl ◊ *das Klirren der Gläser/Schwerter* **6.** *(at a circus)* Maneġe [ma'neːʒə] die <-, -n> **7.** have a ring of authenticity sich echt anhören [zɪç 'ɛçt anhøːrən] +haben have a familiar ring sich bekannt anhören have a ring of truth glaubhaft klingen ['ɡlaͻphaft klɪŋən] <klingt, klang, hat geklungen>

⊛ **run rings around sb** jdn in die Tasche stecken können

ring² (verb) **1.** *(a bell)* läuten ['lɔøtn̩] <läutet, läutete, hat geläutet> ◊ *Er läutete die Glocken.* ✦ *Die Kirchen-glocken läuten.* ✦ *Bitte läuten Sie, wenn Sie etwas brauchen.* ring for assistance nach der Bedienung läuten; *(telephone, alarm clock, doorbell)* klingeln ['klɪŋln̩] +haben ◊ *Das Telefon/Der Wecker klingelte.* the doorbell rang es klingelte an der Tür ring the doorbell an der Tür klingeln ◊ *Er klingelte an der Haustür.* **2.** *(make a loud high sound, hear a sound, seem)* klingen ['klɪŋən] <klingt, klang, hat geklungen> ◊ *Die Glocken/Gläser klingen.* ✦ *Seine Erklärungen klingen hohl.* ring true glaubhaft klingen My ears are ringing. Mir klingen die Ohren.; *(be loud and clear)* schallen ['ʃalən] +haben ◊ *Ihr Gesang schallte durch den Wald.; (unpleasantly)* sth rings in sb's ears etw. dröhnt jdm in den Ohren [drøːnt ... ɪn deːn 'oːrən] +haben ◊ *Die laute Musik dröhnt mir immer noch in den Ohren.* **3.** *(call)* anrufen ['anruːfn̩] <ruft an, rief an, hat angerufen> ◊ *Sie hat ihn gestern angerufen.* ✦ *Hat jemand für mich angerufen? Bitte rufen Sie erst nach 19 Uhr an.* ✦ *Ich muss mal kurz bei der Bank anrufen.* ring about sth wegen etw. anrufen ring for sth etw. bestellen [bə'ʃtɛlən] <bestellt, bestellte, hat bestellt> ◊ *Wir haben ein Taxi bestellt.* **4.** *(surround)* umringen [ʊm'rɪŋən] <umringt, umringte, hat umringt> ◊ *Die*

Polizei umringte das Gebäude. **5.** *(draw a circle)* ein-kreisen ['aɛnkraɛzn̩] +haben ◊ *Der Tag war in seinem Kalender rot eingekreist.* **6.** *(a bird)* beringen [bə'rɪŋən] <beringt, beringte, hat beringt>

• **ring back** (phras v) zurückrufen [tsu'rʏkruːfn̩] <ruft zurück, rief zurück, hat zurückgerufen> ◊ *Ich rufe morgen zurück.* ✦ *Herr Meier wird Sie morgen zurückrufen.*

• **ring in** (phras v) anrufen ['anruːfn̩] <ruft an, rief an, hat angerufen> ◊ *Viele Zuschauer haben angerufen und sich über die Sendung beschwert.* ring in sick sich krankmelden ['kraŋkmɛldn̩] <meldet sich krank, meldete sich krank, hat sich krankgemeldet> +haben ◊ *Heute Morgen habe ich mich krankgemeldet.*

• **ring off** (phras v) auflegen ['aͻfleːɡn̩] +haben ◊ *Sie legte auf, bevor ich etwas dazu sagen konnte.*

• **ring out** (phras v) ertönen [ɛ'tøːnən] <ertönt, ertönte, ist ertönt> ◊ *Lauter Beifall ertönte, als er die Bühne betrat.*

• **ring round** (phras v) herumtelefonieren [hɛ'rʊmtelefoniːrən] <telefo-niert herum, telefonierte herum, hat herumtelefoniert>

• **ring through** (phras v) anrufen ['anruːfn̩] <ruft an, rief an, hat angerufen>

• **ring up** (phras v) **1.** *(call)* anrufen ['anruːfn̩] <ruft an, rief an, hat angerufen> ◊ *Er hat (mich) gestern angerufen.* **2.** *(on a cash register)* eintippen ['aɛntɪpm̩] +haben ◊ *Die Kassiererin tippte den Preis ein.*

ring binder (noun) Ringbuch ['rɪŋbuːx] das <-(e)s, Ringbücher>

ring road (noun) Ring [rɪŋ] der <-(e)s, -e> *(fam)* ◊ *Sie fuhr nicht durch die Innenstadt, sondern über den Ring.*

rinse (verb) *(clothes)* auswaschen ['aͻsvaʃn̩] <wäscht aus, wusch aus, hat ausgewaschen> ◊ *Ich wusch den Pullover im Becken aus.; (hair)* ausspülen ['aͻsʃpyːlən] +haben ◊ *sich* (dat) *die Haare ausspülen; (dishes)* abspülen ['apʃpyːlən] +haben ◊ *Er spülte die Teller kurz mit kaltem Wasser ab.* rinse your hands sich (dat) die Hände abspülen [diː 'hɛndə ˌapʃpyːlən] +haben rinse your mouth sich (dat) den Mund ausspülen [deːn 'mʊnt ˌaͻsʃpyːlən] +haben

riot (noun) *(uprising)* Aufstand ['aͻfʃtant] der <-(e)s, Aufstände> ◊ *ein Aufstand gegen die Regierung* spark a riot einen Aufstand auslösen quell a riot einen Aufstand niederschlagen; *(at a demonstration, football match)* Krawall [kra'val] der <-s, -e> ◊ *Die Kundgebung war von Krawallen begleitet.* riot gear Schutzausrüstung ['ʃʊtsˌaͻsrʏstʊŋ] die <-, -en> riot shield Schutzschild ['ʃʊtsʃɪlt] der <-(e)s, -e>

⊛ **read sb the riot act** jdm die Leviten lesen a riot of colours/colors ein Farbenmeer a riot of emotions ein Gefühlschaos run riot **1.** *(person)* ran-dalieren **2.** *(imagination)* mit jdm durchgehen **3.** *(virus)* sich ausbreiten

rip (verb) **1.** *(tear)* reißen ['raɛsn̩] <reißt, riss, hat gerissen> ◊ *Der Sturm hatte ein Loch in das Dach gerissen.* rip sth to shreds etw. in Fetzen reißen; *(into pieces)* zerreißen [tsɛ'raɛsn̩] <zerreißt, zerriss, hat zerrissen> ◊ *Seine Jacke war zerrissen.* rip sth open etw. aufreißen ['aͻfraɛsn̩] +haben ◊ *Sie riss den Brief sofort auf.* rip sth on sth sich (dat) etw. an etw. (dat) aufreißen ◊ *Ich habe mir an diesem Nagel die Bluse aufgerissen.* **2.** *(remove)* rip sth etw.

herausreißen [hɛˈraʊsraɛsn̩] <reißt heraus, riss heraus, hat herausgerissen> ◊ *Sie haben die alten Fenster herausgerissen und durch neue ersetzt.* rip sth down etw. **herunterreißen** [hɛˈrʊntɐraɛsn̩] <reißt herunter, riss herunter, hat heruntergerissen> ◊ *Er riss das Poster von der Wand herunter.* rip sth off sich ⌷dat⌷ etw. **vom Leib reißen** [fɔm ˈlaɛp raɛsn̩] <reißt sich, riss sich, hat sich gerissen> ◊ *Er riss sich die Kleider vom Leib und sprang in den Fluss.* ⊙ **let rip 1.** *(get angry)* losschimpfen **2.** *(start to do sth)* loslegen *(fam)*

ripe ⌷adj⌷ **1.** *(fruit, crops, wine, cheese)* reif [raɛf] ◊ *Die Himbeeren sind bald reif.* ♦ *ein reifer Rotwein* **2.** *(pej) (smelly)* miefig [ˈmiːfɪç] *(fam)* ◊ *der miefige Geruch ungewaschener Füße* be ripe miefen [ˈmiːfn̩] +haben *(fam)* ⊙ **be ripe for sth** für etw. reif sein

ripen ⌷verb⌷ reifen [ˈraɛfn̩] +sein ◊ *Der Wein reift in Eichenfässern.* ripen into sth zu etw. reifen ◊ *Sie war zu einer Persönlichkeit gereift.* ripen sth etw. reifen lassen [ˈraɛfn̩ lasn̩] <lässt, ließ, hat lassen> ◊ *Die Sonne lässt die Tomaten reifen.*

ripeness ⌷noun⌷ Reife [ˈraɛfə] die <—> no pl ◊ *die Reife einer Melone prüfen*

rise¹ ⌷noun⌷ **1.** *(increase)* rise (in sth) Anstieg (... ⌷gen⌷) [ˈanʃtiːk] der <—(e)s> no pl ◊ *ein Anstieg der Einwohnerzahl; (in prices, tax, rent)* Erhöhung (... ⌷gen⌷) [ɛˈhøːʊŋ] die <—, —en> ◊ *eine Erhöhung des Stundenlohns* tax rise Steuererhöhung [ˈʃtɔɐ̯ɐ|ɛhøːʊŋ] (pay) rise Gehaltserhöhung [ɡəˈhalts|ɛhøːʊŋ] ◊ *eine Gehaltserhöhung von vier Prozent* be on the rise steigen [ˈʃtaɛɡn̩] <steigt, stieg, ist gestiegen> ◊ *Die Benzinpreise steigen wieder.* ♦ *Die Zahl der Insolvenzen steigt.* the rise and fall of sth das Auf und Ab ... ⌷gen⌷ [das ˌaʊf ʊnt ˈʔap] ◊ *das Auf und Ab der Aktienkurse* **2.** *(in power, influence)* Aufstieg [ˈaʊfʃtiːk] der <—(e)s, —e> ◊ *jds beruflicher/ gesellschaftlicher Aufstieg* ♦ *sein Aufstieg zur Macht* ♦ *ihr kometenhafter Aufstieg an die Spitze* rise and fall of sth/sb Aufstieg und Fall ... ⌷gen⌷ sb's rise to prominence jds wachsende Berühmtheit [valksndə bəˈryːmthaɛt] **3.** *(upward movement)* Heben [ˈheːbm̩] das <—s> ◊ *Beim Heben des Vorhangs war das Lampenfieber weg.* the rise and fall of sth das Heben und Senken ... ⌷gen⌷ **4.** *(slope)* Anhöhe [ˈanhøːə] die <—, —n> ◊ *Hinter dem Haus lag eine kleine Anhöhe.* ⊙ **give rise to sth** zu etw. führen

rise² ⌷verb⌷ **1.** *(aircraft)* rise (up) steigen [ˈʃtaɛɡn̩] <steigt, stieg, ist gestiegen> ◊ *Das Flugzeug stieg auf 1200 Meter.; (smoke)* rise (up) aufsteigen [ˈaʊfʃtaɛɡn̩] +sein ◊ *Rauch stieg aus dem Schornstein auf.* **2.** *(sun, moon, dough)* aufgehen [ˈaʊfɡeːən] <geht auf, ging auf, ist aufgegangen> ◊ *Der Mond ist aufgegangen.* ♦ *warten, bis der Hefeteig aufgegangen ist* **3.** *(ground, water)* ansteigen [ˈanʃtaɛɡn̩] <steigt an, stieg an, ist angestiegen> ◊ *Das Land steigt hier etwas an.* ♦ *Das Wasser der Elbe stieg an.* **4.** *(voice)* höher werden [ˈhøːə veːɐ̯dn̩] +sein ◊ *Ihre Stimme wurde immer höher, je mehr sie sich aufregte.* **5.** *(hair)* sich sträuben [ˈʃtrɔɛbm̩] +haben ◊ *Seine Haare sträubten sich vor Angst.* **6.** *(source of a river)* entspringen [ɛntˈʃprɪŋən] <entspringt, entsprang, ist entsprungen> ◊ *Wo entspringt die Themse?* **7.** *(stand, get up)* rise (up), rise to your feet aufstehen [ˈaʊfʃteːən] <steht auf, stand auf, ist aufgestanden> ◊ *Er stand auf und*

ging hinaus. ♦ *Sie stand vom Tisch auf.* ♦ *Heute bin ich früh aufgestanden.* Rise and shine! Aufstehen! **8.** *(prices, costs, interest)* steigen [ˈʃtaɛɡn̩] <steigt, stieg, ist gestiegen> ◊ *steigende Preise* ♦ *Die Temperaturen steigen heute auf 25 Grad.* ♦ *Die Nachfrage nach Lehrern ist gestiegen.* ♦ *im Wert steigen* the rising tide of sth die steigende Flut ... ⌷gen⌷ ◊ *die steigende Flut der Werbe-Mails* **9.** *(wind)* stärker werden [ˈʃtɛɐ̯kə veːɐ̯dn̩] +sein ◊ *Am Nachmittag wurde der Wind stärker.* **10.** *(feeling)* aufsteigen [ˈaʊfʃtaɛɡn̩] <steigt auf, stieg auf, ist aufgestiegen> ◊ *Zorn/Mitleid stieg in ihr auf.* sb's spirits rise jds Stimmung steigt [ˌʃtɪmʊn ˈʃtaɛkt] <steigt, stieg, ist gestiegen> ◊ *Beim Anblick des Essens stieg unsere Stimmung sofort.* tensions rise es kommt zu stärkeren Spannungen [ɛs kɔmt ʦuː ˈʃtɛɐ̯kərən ˈʃpanʊŋən] <kommt, kam, ist gekommen> **11.** *(revolt)* rise (up) (against sb/sth) sich (gegen jdn/etw.) erheben [ɛˈheːbm̩] <erhebt, erhob, hat erhoben> ◊ *Das Volk erhob sich gegen den Diktator.* **12.** *(achieve success)* aufsteigen [ˈaʊfʃtaɛɡn̩] <steigt auf, stieg auf, ist aufgestiegen> ◊ *Er ist vom Tellerwäscher zum Chef der Firma aufgestiegen.* rise to fame berühmt werden [bəˈryːmt veːɐ̯dn̩] +sein rise to power an die Macht kommen [an diː ˈmaxt kɔmən] <kommt, kam, ist gekommen> ◊ *rise to the top* an die Spitze kommen rise through the ranks sich hocharbeiten [ˈhoːx|aˈbaɛtn̩] <arbeitet sich hoch, arbeitete sich hoch, hat sich hochgearbeitet> **13.** *(building, mountain)* rise up (above sth) sich (über etw. ⌷dat⌷) erheben [ɛˈheːbm̩] <erhebt, erhob, hat erhoben> ◊ *Die Berge erheben sich über der Ebene.* ● **rise above** ⌷phras v⌷ rise above sth **1.** *(cope)* etw. fertig werden [mɪt ... ˈfɛʳtɪç veːɐ̯dn̩] +sein ◊ *mit einem Problem fertig werden* **2.** *(not be tempted)* über etw. ⌷dat⌷ stehen [ˈyːbə ... ʃteːən] <steht, stand, hat gestanden> ◊ *über den Dingen stehen* **3.** *(stand out)* etw. überragen [ybɐˈraːɡn̩] <überragt, überragte, hat überragt> ◊ *Der Film überragt alle anderen Werke des Regisseurs.* ● **rise up** ⌷phras v⌷ *(animal)* sich aufrichten [ˈaʊfrɪçtn̩] <richtet sich auf, richtete sich auf, hat sich aufgerichtet> ◊ *Der Bär richtete sich auf seine Hinterbeine auf.* → **rise²** 1., 3., 7., 13.

risk¹ ⌷noun⌷ *(possible danger or loss)* Risiko [ˈriːziko] das <—s, Risiken> ◊ *Damit ist ein hohes/geringes Risiko verbunden.* ♦ *Das Risiko, den Prozess zu verlieren, ist erheblich.* an element of risk ein gewisses Risiko take a risk ein Risiko eingehen take the risk of doing sth das Risiko eingehen, etw. zu tun sb a good/bad risk bei jdm ein Risiko gering/hoch the risk of sth die Gefahr ... ⌷gen⌷ [diː ɡəˈfaːʳ] <—, —en> ◊ *Man darf die Gefahr einer Ausbreitung der Krankheit nicht unterschätzen.* at your own risk auf eigene Gefahr there is no risk that es besteht keine Gefahr, dass pose a risk to sb/sth Gefahr für jdn/etw. darstellen ◊ *Das ausgelaufene Öl stellt angeblich keine Gefahr für die Umwelt dar.* run the risk of doing sth Gefahr laufen, etw. zu tun ◊ *Du läufst Gefahr, deinen Job zu verlieren.* run the risk of sth auf die Gefahr hin, dass man etw. tut health risk Gesundheitsgefahr [ɡəˈzʊnthaɛtsɡəfaːʳ] fire risk Feuergefahr [ˈfɔɐ̯ɡəfaːʳ] put sb/sth at risk jdn/etw. gefährden [ɡəˈfɛːɐ̯dn̩] <gefährdet, gefährdete, hat gefährdet> ◊ *Du gefährdest mit deinem Verhalten eure Ehe.* be at risk of/from sth durch etw. gefährdet sein ◊ *Auch*

im Mai sind Geranien noch durch Nachtfrost gefährdet.

risk² `verb` **1.** *(do sth risky)* riskieren [rɪs'kiːrən] <riskiert, riskierte, hat riskiert> ◊ *Sie riskieren sehr viel.* ✦ *Er riskiert damit, dass ihm gekündigt wird.* ✦ *Sie riskierte, sich vor allen zu blamieren.* ✦ *Er riskierte einen Blick/ein vorsichtiges Lächeln.* ✦ *sein Leben riskieren* risk sth on sth etw. für etw. riskieren ◊ *Er hat für dieses Projekt sein ganzes Vermögen riskiert.* **2.** *(be exposed to a danger)* risk death vom Tod bedroht sein [fɔm 'toːt bə‚droːt zaɛn] +sein risk doing sth Gefahr laufen, etw. zu tun [gə'faːr laͻfn̩ ... tsuː] <läuft, lief, ist gelaufen> ◊ *Wer ins Krisengebiet reist, läuft Gefahr, überfallen zu werden.*

risky `adj` riskant [rɪs'kant] <riskanter, am riskantesten> ◊ *eine riskante Entscheidung* ✦ *Die Flucht erschien ihm zu riskant.*

ritual `noun` Ritual [ritu'aːl] das <-s, -e> ◊ *ein Ritual vollziehen*

rival¹ `noun` *(in a sports event, competition)* Rivale [ri'vaːlə] der <-n, -n> ♀Rivalin [ri'vaːlɪn] die <-, -nen> ◊ *Er hat seinen schärfsten Rivalen haushoch geschlagen.; (in business)* Konkurrent [kɔnkʊ'rɛnt] der <-en, -en> ♀Konkurrentin [kɔnkʊ'rɛntɪn] die <-, -nen> ◊ *Wer ist unser größter Konkurrent auf dem europäischen Markt?* rival for sth Konkurrent um etw. ◊ *Er hatte nur einen Konkurrenten um die Stelle.*

rival² `adj` rivalisierend [rivali'ziːrənt] *only before ns* ◊ *Streitigkeiten zwischen rivalisierenden Parteien* rival bid Konkurrenzangebot [kɔnkʊ'rɛnts‚aŋɡəboːt] das <-(e)s, -e>

rivalry `noun` *(between people, in sports)* Rivalität [rivali'tɛːt] die <-, -en> ◊ *Zwischen den beiden besteht eine gewisse Rivalität.* sibling rivalry Rivalität zwischen Geschwistern; *(in business)* Konkurrenz [kɔnkʊ'rɛnts] die <-> ◊ *die Konkurrenz zwischen den beiden Firmen*

river `noun` Fluss [flʊs] der <-es, Flüsse> ◊ *im Fluss schwimmen/angeln* ✦ *Der Fluss mündet ins Meer.* ✦ *Auf dem Fluss fährt ein Boot.* up river flussaufwärts [flʊs]'aͻfvɛrts] down river flussabwärts [flʊs]'apvɛrts] rivers of lava Lavaströme ['laːvaʃtrøːmə] die <-> pl the River Thames die Themse [diː 'tɛmzə] <->

rivet `noun` Niete ['niːtə] die <-, -n> ◊ *Jeans/ein Hundehalsband mit Nieten*

road `noun` **1.** *(for traffic)* Straße ['ʃtraːsə] die <-, -n> ◊ *Durch den Ort führt eine enge Straße.* ✦ *eine Straße sperren* ✦ *die nächste Straße links* ✦ *Wie lange wohnen Sie schon in dieser Straße?* a busy road eine stark befahrene Straße up the road ein Stück die Straße entlang road traffic Straßenverkehr ['ʃtraːsn̩feːke‚ɐ] der <-s> no pl road Verkehrsunfall [fɛ'keːɡs‚ʊnfal] der <-s, Verkehrsunfälle> by road mit dem Auto [mɪt deːm 'aͻto‚] ◊ *Es ist ungefähr zwei Stunden mit dem Auto entfernt.* **2.** *(course of action)* Weg [veːk] der <-(e)s, -e> ◊ *Er hat sich einen gefährlichen Weg ausgesucht.* go down that road diesen Weg einschlagen the road to sth der Weg zu etw. ◊ *Die Band war auf dem Weg zum Erfolg.* on the road to recovery auf dem Wege der Besserung. ⊕ **on the road 1.** *(driver)* unterwegs **2.** *(entertainer)* auf Tournee **3.** *(homeless person)* auf der Straße

roadblock `noun` Straßensperre ['ʃtraːsn̩ʃpɛrə] die

<-, -n> ◊ *Straßensperren errichten*

road sign `noun` Verkehrszeichen [fɛ'keːɡsˌtsaͻçn̩] das <-s, -> ◊ *die Verkehrszeichen beachten*

roadworks `noun` Baustelle ['baͻʃtɛlə] die <-, -n> ◊ *Wegen mehrerer Baustellen kommt es auf der Autobahn zu Behinderungen.*

roam `verb` roam sth durch etw. streifen [dʊ'ç ... ʃtraͻfn̩] +sein ◊ *Wir streiften durch die Felder.* roam around sth in etw. `dat` umherstreifen [ɪn ... ʊm‚heːɡʃtraͻfn̩] +sein ◊ *Sie streiften stundenlang im Wald umher.* roam wild in freier Wildbahn leben [ɪn fraͻe 'vɪltbaːn leːbm̩] +haben

roar `verb` **1.** *(crowd, person, lion)* brüllen ['brʏlən] +haben ◊ *Die Zuschauer brüllten vor Begeisterung.* ✦ *„Ruhe!", brüllte er.* roar with laughter vor Lachen brüllen **2.** *(engines)* dröhnen ['drøːnən] +haben ◊ *Der Motor dröhnte immer lauter.*

roast¹ `noun` Braten ['braːtn̩] der <-s, -> ◊ *Am Sonntag gibt es bei uns immer Braten.* ✦ *Den Braten in den Ofen schieben und etwa drei Stunden garen.*

roast² `verb` **1.** *(meat)* im Ofen braten [ɪm 'oːfn̩ ‚braːtn̩] <brät, briet, hat gebraten> ◊ *eine Gans im Ofen braten* ✦ *Der Truthahn sollte mindestens drei Stunden im Ofen braten.; (vegetables, nuts, coffee beans)* rösten ['rœstn̩] <röstet, röstete, hat geröstet> ◊ *geröstete Erdnüsse* **2.** *(criticize)* runtermachen ['rʊntəmaxn̩] +haben *(fam)* ◊ *Er wurde von seinem Chef runtergemacht.*

rob `verb` **1.** *(steal from sb)* rob sb jdn ausrauben ['aͻsraͻbm̩] +haben ◊ *Letzte Woche wurde ich überfallen und ausgeraubt.* rob sb at gunpoint/knifepoint jdn mit vorgehaltener Waffe/vorgehaltenem Messer ausrauben rob a bank eine Bank überfallen [aͻnə 'baŋk ybe‚falən] <überfällt, überfiel, hat überfallen> rob sb of sth jdm etw. stehlen ['ʃteːlən] <stiehlt, stahl, hat gestohlen> ◊ *Einige Jugendliche haben ihr das Handy gestohlen.* **2.** *(of an opportunity, faculty etc.)* rob sth of sth jdm etw. nehmen ['neːmən] <nimmt, nahm, hat genommen> ◊ *Die Verletzung nahm ihr die Möglichkeit, am Wettkampf teilzunehmen. The shock had robbed her of the power of speech. Sie hatte vor Schreck die Sprache verloren.*

robber `noun` Räuber ['rͻbe] der <-s, -> ♀Räuberin ['rͻbərɪn] die <-, -nen> ◊ *Ein Räuber hat ihr die Handtasche gestohlen.*

robbery `noun` Raub [raͻp] der <-(e)s, -> ◊ *einen Raub begehen* ✦ *Er wurde wegen bewaffneten/ schweren Raubes verurteilt.* bank robbery Bankraub ['baŋkraͻp] armed robbery bewaffneter Raubüberfall [bə‚vafnəte 'raͻp‚ybefal] <-(e)s, Raubüberfälle> ◊ *Hier hat sich gestern ein bewaffneter Raubüberfall ereignet.*

robot `noun` Roboter ['rͻbotɐ] der <-s, ->

robust `adj` **1.** *(strong)* robust [ro'bʊst] <robuster, am robustesten> ◊ *Er hatte eine robuste Gesundheit.* ✦ *Dieses Material ist sehr robust.; (stable)* stabil [ʃta'biːl] ◊ *eine stabile Wirtschaft* ✦ *Ist die Konstruktion stabil genug, um diese Belastung standzuhalten?* ✦ *psychisch nicht besonders stabil sein* **2.** *(determined)* entschieden [ɛnt'ʃiːdn̩] ◊ *ihre entschiedene Haltung* ✦ *Seine Vorgehensweise war hart und entschieden.* **3.** *(food, drink)* kräftig ['krɛftɪç] ◊ *Dazu gehört ein kräftiger Rotwein.* ✦ *Die bayerische Küche ist kräftig und herzhaft.*

rock¹ `noun` **1.** *(geological substance, huge stone)*

Felsen ['fɛlzn̩] der <‑s, ‑> ◊ *Das Auto war auf einen Felsen geprallt.* ♦ *Die Stufen waren in den Felsen gehauen.* ♦ *der Felsen von Gibraltar;* (edge of land or sea) rocks Klippe ['klɪpə] die <‑, ‑n> sing ◊ *Das Schiff zerschellte an der Klippe.;* (small stone) Stein [ʃtaɛn] der <‑(e)s, ‑e> ◊ *Die Eidechse sonnte sich auf einem Stein.* ♦ *Steine auf jdn* [acc] *werfen* **2.** MUS Rock [rɔk] der <‑(s)> (fam) ◊ *Er hörte nur Rock.* rock concert Rockkonzert ['rɔkkɔn̩ˌtsɛʳt] das <‑(e)s, ‑e> **3.** (sweet) Zuckerstange ['tsʊkəʃtaŋə] die <‑, ‑n> ◊ *Die Kinder schleckten ihre Zuckerstangen.* **4.** (ostentatious jewel) Klunker ['klʊŋkɐ] der <‑s, ‑> (fam) ◊ *Sie trug bei der Preisverleihung viele Klunker.*
⊚ be caught between a rock and a hard place sich in einer Zwickmühle befinden solid as a rock unerschütterlich on the rocks **1.** (relationship) kaputt **2.** (drink) mit Eis
rock² [verb] **1.** (move gently from side to side) schaukeln ['ʃaok̩l̩n] +haben ◊ *Er schaukelte sanft hin und her.;* (a baby) wiegen ['viːɡŋ̩] +haben ◊ *Sie wiegte das Kind in den Schlaf.* **2.** (news) erschüttern [ɛˈʃʏtɐn] <erschüttert, erschütterte, hat erschüttert> ◊ *Das Verbrechen erschütterte die ganze Stadt.* **3.** (because of an earthquake, explosion) beben ['beːbm̩] +haben ◊ *Die Erde bebt.* ♦ *Die Explosion ließ die Häuser beben.* **4.** (fam) MUS rocken ['rɔkŋ̩] +haben (fam) ◊ *Sie rockten den ganzen Abend* **5.** (fam) (in the US: be great) klasse sein ['klasə zaɛn] +sein ◊ *Die neue CD ist klasse!*
rocket [noun] **1.** (aircraft, weapon, firework) Rakete [raˈkeːtə] die <‑, ‑n> ◊ *Die Astronauten flogen mit einer Rakete ins All.* ♦ *Raketen zur Abwehr einsetzen* ♦ *an Silvester Raketen in die Luft gschießen* **2.** (vegetable) Rucola ['ruːkola:] der <‑> no pl ◊ *Sie isst gern Pizza mit Rucola.*
⊚ give sb a rocket jdm den Marsch blasen (fam)
rocky [adj] **1.** (stony) felsig ['fɛlzɪç] ◊ *ein felsiger Weg* ♦ *Die Küste ist sehr felsig.* **2.** (problematic) schwierig ['ʃviːrɪç] ◊ *eine schwierige Beziehung* ♦ *Die Situation war sehr schwierig.*
rod [noun] (stick) Stange ['ʃtaŋə] die <‑, ‑n> ◊ *Mit einer Stange haben sie versucht, den Korb aus dem Wasser zu ziehen.* (fishing) rod Angel ['aŋl̩] die <‑, ‑n> ◊ *Er warf die Angel aus.*
roe deer [noun] Reh [reː] das <‑(e)s, ‑e> ◊ *im Wald Rehe beobachten*
role [noun] Rolle ['rɔlə] die <‑, ‑n> ◊ *die Rolle der Frau im Mittelalter* ♦ *bei einer Entscheidung eine wichtige Rolle spielen* ♦ *In dieser Rolle erlangte sie unsterblichen Ruhm.* play the role of sb jds Rolle spielen ◊ *Sie spielt die Rolle der Ophelia.* leading role Hauptrolle ['haɔptrɔlə]
role model [noun] Vorbild ['foːɐbɪlt] das <‑(e)s, ‑er> ◊ *Er eiferte seinem großen Vorbild Albert Einstein nach.*
role play [noun] Rollenspiel ['rɔlənʃpiːl] das <‑(e)s, ‑e> ◊ *ein Rollenspiel machen*
roll¹ [noun] **1.** (of paper, carpet etc.) Rolle ['rɔlə] die <‑, ‑n> ◊ *Er hat das Poster in einer Rolle verschickt.* ♦ *Sie kaufte fünf Rollen dieser Tapete.* **2.** (small bread) Brötchen ['brøːtçən] das <‑s, ‑> ◊ *beim Bäcker frische Brötchen kaufen* ♦ *ein Brötchen mit Käse* **3.** SHIP Schlingern ['ʃlɪŋɐn] das <‑s> no pl ◊ *Vom Schlingern des Schiffs wurde ihm übel.* **4.** (of

a dice) roll of dice Würfelwurf ['vvʳflvʊʳf] das <‑(e)s, Würfelwürfe> **5.** (list) Liste ['lɪstə] die <‑, ‑n> **6.** (of thunder) Rollen ['rɔlən] das <‑s> no pl ◊ *Das Rollen des Donners war noch lange zu hören.* **7.** (of fat, skin) Wulst [vʊlst] der <‑(e)s, Wülste>
⊚ be on a roll (fam) eine Glückssträhne haben
roll² [verb] **1.** (move while turning, move on wheels, wrap around itself, thunder) rollen ['rɔlən] transitive use +haben/intransitive use +sein ◊ *Der Zug rollte in den Bahnhof.* ♦ *Der Donner rollte in der Ferne.* ♦ *Er rollte das Fass zur Seite.* roll down hinunterrollen [hɪˈnʊntɐrɔlən] +sein ◊ *Der Ball rollte den Berg hinunter.* **2.** (animals, children) sich wälzen ['vɛltsn̩] +haben ◊ *Sie wälzten sich im Schlamm.* **3.** (change position) roll sb/sth (over) jdn/etw. drehen ['dreːən] +haben ◊ *Sie drehte ihre Puppe auf den Bauch.* sb rolls (over) jd dreht sich ◊ *Er drehte sich auf die Seite.* **4.** (a dice) roll a/the dice würfeln ['vvʳfl̩n] +haben ◊ *Wer ist an der Reihe zu würfeln?* **5.** (pastry, dough) roll (out) ausrollen ['aɔsrɔlən] +haben ◊ *den Teig dünn ausrollen*
• roll back [phras v] **1.** (restrict, reduce the power of sth) zurückdrängen [tsuˈrʏkdrɛŋən] +haben ◊ *Ist es möglich, die Globalisierung zurückzudrängen?* ♦ *den Staat aus dem Privatleben zurückdrängen;* (reforms, changes, rules) rückgängig machen ['rʏkɡɛŋɪç maxn̩] +haben **2.** (prices, costs) senken ['zɛŋkn̩] +haben ◊ *Die Preise für Handys wurden drastisch gesenkt.* **3.** roll back the time die Zeit zurückdrehen [di: ˌtsaɛt tsuˈrʏkdreːən] +haben
• roll down [phras v] **1.** (a car window, automatically) herunterlassen [hɛˈrʊntɐlasn̩] <lässt herunter, ließ herunter, hat heruntergelassen> ◊ *die Fenster herunterlassen* **2.** (sleeves etc.) herunterkrempeln [hɛˈrʊntɐkrɛmpl̩n] +haben ◊ *Er krempelte die Hemdsärmel herunter.*
• roll in [phras v] **1.** (arrive in large numbers) hereinströmen [hɛˈraɛnʃtrøːmən] +sein ◊ *Unmengen von Menschen sind durch die Tore hereingeströmt.* ♦ *Das Geld strömte nur so herein.* **2.** (arrive late) eintrudeln ['aɛntruːdl̩n] +sein ◊ *Um kurz vor neun trudelte er dann endlich ein.*
• roll out [phras v] **1.** (a carpet, dough) ausrollen ['aɔsrɔlən] +haben ◊ *Er musste den Teig ausrollen.* ♦ *Ich rollte den Teppich aus.* **2.** (a new product, service) vorstellen ['foːɐʃtɛlən] +haben ◊ *Die Bank stellte ihren neuen Fonds vor.*
• roll over [phras v] **1.** (change position) sich umdrehen ['ʊmdreːən] +haben ◊ *Sie drehte sich um und sah ihn neben sich liegen.* **2.** FIN (invest money elsewhere) roll sth (over) etw. woanders investieren [voˈandɐs ɪnvɛsˌtiːrən] <investiert, investierte, hat investiert> ◊ *Es ist Zeit, mein Geld woanders zu investieren.* roll over sth into sth etw. in eine andere Sache investieren ◊ *Sie haben ihr Geld in einen anderen Fonds investiert.* FIN (a credit) roll over debts/loans Kredite umschulden [kreˌdiːtə ˈʊmʃʊldn̩] <schuldet um, schuldete um, hat umgeschuldet> ◊ *Sie mussten die Darlehen umschulden.*
• roll up [phras v] **1.** (wrap around itself) aufrollen ['aɔfrɔlən] +haben ◊ *einen Teppich aufrollen* **2.** (a sleeve etc.) hochkrempeln ['hoːxkrɛmpl̩n] +haben ◊ *Er krempelte die Hosenbeine hoch.* **3.** (with button) schließen ['ʃliːsn̩] <schließt, schloss, hat geschlossen> ◊ *Bevor sie in die Waschanlage fuhr, schloss sie das

roller [noun] **1.** *(equipment to flatten sth)* Walze ['valtsə] die <–, –n> ◊ *mit einer Walze die Straßendecke glätten; (to flatten dough)* Nudelholz ['nu:dlhɔlts] das <–es, Nudelhölzer> ◊ *Teig mit einem Nudelholz dünn ausrollen* **2.** *(curler)* Lockenwickler ['lɔkŋvɪklɐ] der <–s, –> ◊ *Lockenwickler ins Haar drehen* **3.** *(for moving heavy objects)* Rolle ['rɔlə] die <–, –n> most pl **4.** *(wave)* Brecher ['brɛçɐ] der <–s, –> ◊ *Große Brecher schlugen an den Strand.*

romance [noun] **1.** *(affair)* Romanze [ro'mantsə] die <–, –n> ◊ *eine heimliche Romanze mit jdm haben* holiday romance Urlaubsromanze ['u:glaopsro,mantsə] **2.** *(feelings, behavio(u)r)* Romantik [ro'mantɪk] die <–> no pl ◊ *Hast du denn gar keinen Sinn für Romantik?* **3.** *(book)* Liebesroman ['li:bəsro,ma:n] der <–s, –e> ◊ *Sie liest gern Liebesromane.; (film)* Liebesfilm ['li:bəsfɪlm] der <–(e)s, –e>

romantic(ally) [adj, adv] romantisch [ro'mantɪʃ] ◊ *Ich fand seinen Heiratsantrag sehr romantisch.* ◆ *romantische Musik* ◆ *ein romantisch gelegenes Dorf*

roof [noun] **1.** ARCH *(of a building, vehicle, tent, cave)* Dach [dax] das <–(e)s, Dächer> ◊ *Das Dach ist undicht.* ◆ *Das Auto blieb auf dem Dach liegen.* **2.** ANAT *(of the mouth)* Gaumen ['gaomən] der <–s, –> ◊ *Die Erdnussbutter bleibt am Gaumen kleben.*

◉ a roof over your head ein Dach über dem Kopf go through the roof **1.** *(go up)* sprunghaft steigen ◊ *Die Preise sind sprunghaft gestiegen.* **2.** *(get angry)* an die Decke gehen ◊ *Deswegen brauchst du dich nicht gleich an die Decke zu gehen!* under the same roof unter einem Dach

roofed [adj] überdacht [ybe'daxt] no comp/superl ◊ *überdachte Parkplätze* ◆ *Die Brücke ist überdacht.*

room [noun] **1.** *(part of a building)* Zimmer ['tsɪmɐ] das <–s, –> ◊ *Geh auf/in dein Zimmer und mach deine Hausaufgaben!* ◆ *ein Zimmer reservieren/buchen* **2.** *(space)* Platz [plats] der <–es, Plätze> ◊ *Es gab nur wenig Platz für ihre Kleidung.* ◆ *Im Auto war nicht genug Platz.* make room Platz schaffen **3.** *(fig) (for possibilities, improvement etc.)* Spielraum ['ʃpi:lraom] der <–(e)s, Spielräume> ◊ *der Fantasie viel/wenig Spielraum lassen*

rooster [noun] Hahn [ha:n] der <–(e)s, Hähne> ◊ *Der Hahn kräht.*

root¹ [noun] **1.** *(of a plant, hair, tooth, problem, in mathematics)* Wurzel ['vʊrtsl] die <–, –n> ◊ *Unkraut mit den Wurzeln ausreißen* ◆ *Die Wurzel des Zahns ist entzündet.* ◆ *die Wurzel allen Übels* ◆ *Die Wurzel aus 49 ist 7.* go back to your roots zu seinen Wurzeln zurückkehren **2.** *(cause)* Grund [grʊnt] der <–(e)s, Gründe> ◊ *Der Grund für seine Unzufriedenheit lag in seiner Arbeitsstelle.* **3.** LING Stamm [ʃtam] der <–(e)s, Stämme> ◊ *„Gestell" und „stellen" haben beide den Stamm „stell".* **4.** MUS Grundton ['grʊntto:n] der <–(e)s, Grundtöne>

◉ blush to the roots of your hair knallrot werden put down roots Wurzeln schlagen

root² [verb] **1.** *(search)* root around in sth (for sth), root through sth etw. (nach etw.) durchwühlen [dʊrç'vy:lən] <durchwühlt, durchwühlte, hat durchwühlt> ◊ *Er durchwühlte seine Taschen nach dem*

Schlüssel.; *(animal)* wühlen ['vy:lən] +haben ◊ *Das Schwein wühlte im Boden nach Futter.* **2.** BOT *(grow roots)* Wurzeln schlagen ['vʊrtsl̩n ʃla:gn̩] <schlägt, schlug, hat geschlagen>

● root for sth *(support sb)* jdm die Daumen drücken [di: 'daomən drʏkŋ] +haben ◊ *Wir werden dir alle die Daumen drücken!; (cheer)* jdn anfeuern ['anfɔøɐn] +haben ◊ *eine Mannschaft anfeuern*

● root out sth einer Sache [dat] ein Ende bereiten [aen 'ɛndə bəraetn̩] <bereitet, bereitete, hat bereitet> ◊ *der Korruption endgültig den Garaus machen*

● root up sth mit der Wurzel herausreißen [mɪt de:ɐ 'vʊrtsl̩ hɛ,raosraesn̩] <reißt heraus, riss heraus, hat herausgerissen> ◊ *Sie hat die Pflanze mit der Wurzel herausgerissen.*

rope [noun] **1.** *(string)* Seil [zael] das <–(e)s, –e> ◊ *Zwischen zwei Pfosten war ein langes Seil befestigt/gespannt.* ◆ *einen Kletterer mit dem Seil sichern* **2.** rope of pearls Perlenkette ['pɛrlənkɛtə] die <–, –n> ◊ *eine Perlenkette tragen*

◉ at the end of your rope am Ende learn the ropes sich einarbeiten show sb the ropes jdn einführen

rose [noun] **1.** BOT Rose ['ro:zə] die <–, –n> ◊ *ein Strauß roter Rosen* **2.** *(colo(u)r)* Rosa ['ro:za:] das <–s, fam –s> ◊ *ein Kleid in zartem Rosa* **3.** *(nozzle)* Brause ['braozə] die <–, –n> ◊ *die Brause auf die Gießkanne aufsetzen*

rosy [adj] rosig ['ro:zɪç] ◊ *rosige Haut* ◆ *Die Zukunft sieht nicht gerade rosig aus.*

rot [verb] **1.** *(food, wood, teeth)* verfaulen [fɛ'faolən] <verfault, verfaulte, ist verfault> ◊ *Die Früchte sind verfault.* **2.** *(in prison)* verrotten [fɛ'rɔtn̩] <verrottet, verrottete, ist verrottet> *(fam)* ◊ *Von mir aus kann er im Gefängnis verrotten!*

rotate [verb] **1.** *(move in a circle)* sth rotates etw. rotiert [ro'ti:ɐt] <rotiert, rotierte, hat rotiert> ◊ *Das Objekt rotierte um die eigene Achse.* rotate sth etw. rotieren lassen **2.** *(chairmanship, duty)* sth rotates etw. wechselt regelmäßig [,vɛksl̩t 're:glmɛ:sɪç] +haben ◊ *sth rotates monthly* etw. wechselt monatlich; *(a team etc.)* rotate sb jdn auswechseln ['aosvɛksl̩n] +haben ◊ *Wir wechseln die Wachmannschaft alle sechs Stunden aus.; (take turns with sth)* rotate sth sich bei etw. abwechseln [bae ... 'apvɛksl̩n] +haben ◊ *Wir wechseln uns bei unangenehmen Arbeiten ab.*

rotation [noun] **1.** *(circular movement, regular replacement)* Rotation [rota'tsjo:n] die <–, –en> ◊ *die Rotation eines Rades* ◆ *etw. in schnelle Rotation versetzen* in rotation abwechselnd ['apvɛksl̩nt] no comp/superl ◊ *Sie führen den Vorstand abwechselnd.* **2.** crop rotation Fruchtfolge ['frʊxtfɔlgə] die <–, –n>

rotten [adj] **1.** *(decayed)* faul [faol] ◊ *faules Obst* ◆ *Das Holz war faul und morsch.* **2.** *(fam) (very bad)* mies [mi:s] <mieser, am miesesten> *(fam)* ◊ *„Wie geht es dir?" — „Ziemlich mies!"* ◆ *Er ist ein mieser Schauspieler.* be rotten to sb jdn mies behandeln be rotten at (doing) sth sehr schlecht in etw. [dat] sein [ze:ɐ ʃlɛçt ɪn ... zaen] +sein ◊ *Er ist sehr schlecht im Rechnen.* **3.** *(for emphasis)* verdammt [fɛ'damt] no comp/superl, only before ns ◊ *Der verdammte Typ kann mir gestohlen bleiben.*

rough [adj] **1.** *(not smooth, not soft, with a lot of*

violence, voice) rau [rao] <rauer, am rauesten> ◊ *Ihre Haut ist rau.* ♦ *die raue See* ♦ *Dort herrschen raue Sitten.* ♦ *eine raue Stimme; (street etc.)* holprig ['hɔlprɪç] ◊ *Die Straße war sehr holprig.* ♦ *ein holpriger Weg* 2. *(difficult)* hart [haʳt] <härter, am härtesten> ◊ *ein harter Tag* ♦ *Die Zeit nach seinem Unfall war sehr hart für ihn.* a rough patch eine harte Zeit 3. *(not gentle, not well finished, not exact)* grob [groːp] <gröber, am gröbsten> ◊ *Sei doch nicht so grob! Du tust mir weh!* ♦ grobe Holzstühle ♦ *ein grober Entwurf* rough draft Skizze ['skɪtsə] die <–, –n> ◊ *eine Skizze von etw. anfertigen* 4. *(fam) (in the UK: be ill)* feel rough sich mies fühlen ['miːs fyːlən] +haben
☻ be rough on sb hart zu jdm sein

roughly [adv] 1. *(approximately)* ungefähr ['ʊngəfɛːɐ] ◊ *Ungefähr 400 Gäste waren auf der Hochzeit.* ♦ *Ihre Zahl hat sich ungefähr verdoppelt.* 2. *(not gently, not exactly)* grob [groːp] <gröber, am gröbsten> ◊ *Sie sind grob mit ihm umgegangen.* ♦ *grob gehackte Kräuter*
☻ roughly speaking grob gesagt

round¹ [noun] 1. *(one of a series of visits, talks, in sports, drinks for everyone)* Runde ['rʊndə] die <–, –n> ◊ *Der Postbote dreht seine Runde.* ♦ *Die Verhandlungen gehen in die nächste Runde.* ♦ *eine Runde Golf spielen* ♦ *in der Kneipe eine Runde ausgeben; (of an election)* Durchgang ['dʊʳçgaŋ] der <–(e)s, Durchgänge> ◊ *Die Wahl entschied sich im zweiten Durchgang.* 2. *(shot)* Schuss [ʃʊs] der <–es, Schüsse> ◊ *Er hat noch drei Schüsse.* 3. *(slice)* Scheibe ['ʃaebə] die <–, –n> ◊ *mehrere Scheiben Wurst; (sandwich)* Sandwich ['sɛntvɪtʃ] das <–(e)s or –, –(e)s or –e> ◊ *Sandwiches mit Schinken und Gurke vorbereiten*
☻ a round of applause eine Runde Applaus do the rounds die Runde machen ◊ *Das Gerücht machte schnell die Runde.*

round² [adj] rund [rʊnt] <runder, am rundesten> seldom comp/superl ◊ *Die Erde ist rund.* ♦ *runde Wangen haben* ♦ *eine runde Summe/Zahl* ♦ *Das kostet runde 200 Euro.* a round dozen ein rundes Dutzend

round³ [adv] 1. *(with certain verbs: expressing circular movement, change of direction, circular order, aimlessness, indecision)* herum… ['hɛˈrʊm] turn sth round etw. herumdrehen [hɛˈrʊmdreːən] +haben ◊ *den Zündschlüssel herumdrehen* sb turns round jd dreht sich herum ◊ *Die Kinder drehten sich im Kreis herum.* pass sth round etw. herumreichen [hɛˈrʊmraeçn] +haben ◊ *Sie reichte ein paar Häppchen herum.* sit round herumsitzen [hɛˈrʊmtsɪtsn] <sitzt herum, saß herum, hat herumgesessen> ◊ *Sitz nicht so faul herum, sondern hilf mir lieber!* 2. *(to sb)* rüber ['ryːbə] *(fam)* come over rüberkommen ['ryːbəkɔmən] <kommt rüber, kam rüber, ist rübergekommen> ◊ *Komm doch mal rüber zu uns!* 3. *(at a place)* da [daː] ◊ *Sie wird auch da sein.*
☻ all round 1. *(everywhere)* ringsherum ◊ *Ringsherum sah man nur fröhliche Gesichter.* 2. *(for everyone)* für alle ◊ *Er bestellte Drinks für alle* round and round 1. *(all over the place)* überall herum ◊ *Er lief überall im Gebäude herum, konnte aber niemanden finden.* 2. *(in circles)* im Kreis ◊ *Wir tanzten im Kreis.*

'Round' often occurs in phrasal verbs like 'go round' or 'have round' which have their own entries in the dictionary.

round⁴ [verb] 1. *(a cape, mountain etc.)* round sth etw. umrunden [ʊmˈrʊndn] <umrundet, umrundete, hat umrundet> ◊ *einen See mit dem Auto umrunden; (a bend, corner)* round sth um etw. biegen [ʊm … biːgn] ◊ *biegt, bog, ist gebogen> ◊ *Sie bog um die Kurve.* ♦ *Ein Auto biegt um die Ecke.* 2. *(your lips)* round sth etw. spitzen ['ʃpɪtsn] +haben ◊ *Sie spitzte die Lippen.; (eyes)* sth rounds etw. weitet sich ['vaetət zɪç] <weitete sich, hat sich geweitet> ◊ *Seine Augen weiteten sich vor Entsetzen.*
• **round off** [phras v] 1. *(finish)* abschließen ['apʃliːsn] <schließt ab, schloss ab, hat abgeschlossen> ◊ *Sie haben ihre Tournee mit einem fantastischen Konzert abgeschlossen.* round sth off by doing sth etw. abschließen, indem man etw. tut ◊ *Sie schloss die Geburtstagsfeier ab, indem sie den Kindern eine Geschichte vorlas.* 2. *(make round)* abrunden ['aprʊndn] <rundet ab, rundete ab, hat abgerundet> ◊ *die Tischecken abrunden* 3. *(a number)* runden ['rʊndn] <rundet, rundete, hat gerundet> ◊ *Die Summe wird gerundet.*
• **round on** [phras v] round on sb jdn anfahren ['anfaːrən] <fährt an, fuhr an, hat angefahren> ◊ *Sie fuhr ihn mit unfreundlicher Stimme an.*
• **round up** [phras v] 1. *(catch, arrest)* round sb up jdn stellen ['ʃtɛlən] +haben ◊ *Die Ausbrecher wurden gestellt und ins Polizeirevier gebracht.* 2. *(animals)* zusammentreiben [tsuˈzaməntraebm] <treibt zusammen, trieb zusammen, hat zusammengetrieben> ◊ *Die Cowboys trieben die Kühe zusammen.* 3. *(a sum, price, cost)* aufrunden ['aofrʊndn] <rundet auf, rundete auf, hat aufgerundet> ◊ *Er rundete den Betrag auf.*

round⁵ [prep] 1. *(around the outer sides of sth, encircling sth)* um [ʊm] +acc ◊ *Die Erde dreht sich um die Sonne.* ♦ *Der Bus bog um die Kurve.* ♦ *Er hatte den Arm um ihre Schulter gelegt.* ♦ *Die Kinder versammelten sich um die Mutter.* somewhere round irgendwo in der Gegend von [ˌɪʳgntˌvoː ɪn deːɐ 'geːgnt fɔn] ◊ *Sie wohnt irgendwo in der Gegend von Bonn.* round that/it darum [daˈrʊm] ◊ *ein Schloss mit einem Park darum; (with certain verbs: encircling sth)* … umher um etw. herum… [ʊm … hɛˈrʊm] sit round um etw. herumsitzen [ʊm … hɛˌrʊmtsɪtsn] <sitzt herum, saß herum, hat herumgesessen> ◊ *Wir saßen alle um das Feuer herum.* walk round um etw. herumgehen [ʊm … hɛˌrʊmgeːən] <geht herum, ging herum, ist herumgegangen> ◊ *Sie gingen um das Auto herum.* go round by sth an etw. [dat] vorbeigehen [an … foːɐˌbaegeːən] <geht vorbei, ging vorbei, ist vorbeigegangen> ◊ *Wir können ja auf dem Heimweg noch an der Eisdiele vorbeigehen.* 2. A is focused/built round B B bildet den Mittelpunkt … [gen]/von A [bɪldət deːn 'mɪtlpʊŋkt] +haben ◊ *Die Feuerstelle bildete den Mittelpunkt des Stammeslebens.* ♦ *Die komischen Dialoge bilden den Mittelpunkt von Peter Sellers' Inszenierung.* 3. *(everywhere within a certain area)* look round the house sich im ganzen Haus umsehen [ɪm gantsn 'haos ˌʊmzeːən] <sieht sich um, sah sich um, hat sich umgesehen> go round the building das ganze Gebäude absuchen

[das ˈgantsə gəˈbɔ̜ɡdə ˌapzuːxn̩] +haben

> 'Round' often occurs in phrasal verbs like 'get round' or 'come round' which have their own entries in the dictionary.

roundabout [noun] 1. *(in traffic)* Kreisverkehr ['kraɛsfekeːɡ] der <–s, –e> ◊ *Beim Verlassen des Kreisverkehrs muss man blinken.* 2. *(in a playground)* Karussell [karʊˈsɛl] das <–s, –s or –e> ◊ *Sie fährt gern Karussell.*

round-trip ticket [noun] Rückfahrkarte ['rʏkfaːˌkaˈtə] die <–, –n> ◊ *Eine Rückfahrkarte nach München, bitte.*

route¹ [noun] 1. *(of a bus, train etc.*, roads from one place to another) Strecke ['ʃtrɛkə] die <–, –n> ◊ *Der Bus fährt immer die gleiche Strecke.* ♦ *Welches ist die kürzeste Strecke?* 2. *(way of doing sth)* Weg [veːk] der <–(e)s, –e> ◊ *der Weg zum Erfolg/Glück* take a route einen Weg einschlagen

route² [verb] leiten ['laɛtn̩] <leitet, leitete, hat geleitet> ◊ *Alle Züge wurden über Hamburg geleitet.* ♦ *Der Verkehr wird durch den Tunnel geleitet.* route sth through sb etc. durch jdn weiterleiten [dʊ'rç ... ˈvaɛtəlaɛtn̩] <leitet weiter, leitete weiter, hat weitergeleitet>

routine [noun] 1. *(usual way, set of instructions)* Routine [ruˈtiːnə] die <–> no pl ◊ *Ihr Eheleben ist zur Routine geworden.* ♦ *Diese Arbeit ist für ihn schon lange Routine.* 2. *(performance)* Nummer ['nʊmə] die <–, –n> ◊ *eine Nummer einstudieren/vorführen* 3. *(annoying behavio(u)r)* alte Geschichte [altə ɡəˈʃɪçtə] die <–, –n> *(fam)* ◊ *Komm mir bloß nicht wieder mit dieser alten Geschichte, dass du pleite bist!*

row¹ [noun] 1. *(line)* Reihe ['raɛə] die <–, –n> ◊ *Die Kinder stellten sich in einer Reihe auf.* ♦ *im Theater in der letzten Reihe sitzen* 2. *(with a boat)* go for a row rudern gehen ['ruːdɐn ɡeːən] <geht, ging, ist gegangen> ◦ **in a row** 1. *(in a line)* in einer Reihe ◊ *Die Kinder warteten in einer Reihe.* 2. *(one after another)* hintereinander ◊ *Sie sah sich den Film zweimal hintereinander an.*

row² [noun] Krach [krax] der <–(e)s, Kräche> most sing ◊ *Er hat wieder mal Krach mit seinem Bruder.* ♦ *Hört auf mit dem Krach!*

row³ [verb] rudern ['ruːdɐn] +haben/with indication of direction +sein ◊ *Du musst schneller rudern.* ♦ *Wir sind über den See gerudert.*

royal [adj] 1. *(related to a king or queen)* königlich ['køːnɪklɪç] no comp/superl ◊ *die königliche Gemäldegalerie besichtigen* ♦ *der königliche Hoflieferant* 2. *(fam) (real, typical)* echt [ɛçt] no comp/superl, only before ns ◊ *Du bist ein echter Bayer!*

royal family [noun] königliche Familie [ˌkøːnɪklɪçə faˈmiːljə] die <–, –n> ◊ *ein Besuch der königlichen Familie*

royalty [noun] 1. *(payment)* Tantieme [tanˈtjeːmə] die <–, –n> most pl ◊ *Er konnte gut von seinen Tantiemen leben.* 2. *(family of a king and queen)* Mitglieder des Königshauses [ˌmɪtɡliːdɐ dɛs ˈkøːnɪçshaɔzəs] die <–> pl

RSPCA [noun] Tierschutzverein ['tiːɐ̯ʃʊtsfəlaɛn] der <–(e)s, –e> ◊ *Das Tierheim wird vom Tierschutzverein betrieben.* ♦ *Mitglied des Tierschutzvereins sein*

rub [verb] 1. *(move sth over sth)* reiben ['raɛbm̩] <reibt,

rieb, hat gerieben> ◊ *Die neuen Schuhe reiben an der Ferse.* ♦ *Schmutz von den Schuhen reiben* ♦ *sich* [dat] *die Hände reiben* rub sth against sth etw. an etw. [dat] reiben ◊ *Das Pferd rieb seinen Kopf an Inas Schulter.* rub sth together etw. aneinander reiben 2. *(massage)* massieren [maˈsiːrən] <massiert, massierte, hat massiert> ◊ *Sie massierte ihm den Rücken.* 3. *(spread liquid)* einreiben ['aɛnraɛbm̩] <reibt ein, rieb ein, hat eingerieben> ◊ *Er hat seiner Freundin den Rücken mit Sonnencreme eingerieben.*

rubber [noun] 1. *(material, condom)* Gummi ['ɡʊmiː] der or das <–s, –(s)> ◊ *Schuhsohlen aus Gummi* ♦ *einen Gummi benutzen* rubber plant Gummibaum ['ɡʊmibaɔm] der <–(e)s, Gummibäume> rubber band Gummi ['ɡʊmiː] das or der <–s, –s> *(fam)* ◊ *die Haare mit einem Gummi zusammenbinden* 2. *(for erasing pencil)* Radiergummi [raˈdiːɡɡʊmiː] der <–s, –s> ◊ *ein Bleistift mit Radiergummi*

rubbish [noun] 1. *(refuse)* Abfall ['apfal] der <–(e)s, Abfälle> ◊ *radioaktive/organische Abfälle* ♦ *Abfall produzieren/entsorgen/vermeiden* 2. *(nonsense)* Blödsinn ['bløːtzɪn] der <–(e)s> no pl *(fam)* ◊ *Er erzählt lauter Blödsinn!* ♦ *Ich hielt den Aufsatz für Blödsinn.* 3. *(sth of low quality)* Schrott [ʃrɔt] der <–(e)s> no pl *(fam, pej)* ◊ *Im Fernsehen kommt unglaublich viel Schrott.*

rubbish bin [noun] Mülleimer ['mʏlˌlaɛmə] der <–s, –> ◊ *etw. in den Mülleimer werfen*

rubble [noun] Schutt [ʃʊt] der <–(e)s> no pl ◊ *Schutt abladen* reduce sth to rubble etw. in Schutt und Asche legen

rucksack [noun] Rucksack ['rʊkzak] der <–(e)s, Rucksäcke> ◊ *einen schweren Rucksack tragen*

rudder [noun] Ruder ['ruːdə] das <–s, –> ◊ *das Ruder führen/herumreißen*

rude [adj] 1. *(impolite)* unhöflich ['ʊnhøːflɪç] ◊ *Es wäre unhöflich, das Geschenk nicht anzunehmen.* ♦ *So ein unhöflicher Kerl!* downright rude absolut unhöflich 2. *(obscene)* unanständig ['ʊnˌanʃtɛndɪç] ◊ *unanständige Witze* 3. *(lit) (unexpected and unpleasant)* böse ['bøːzə] <böser, am bösesten> ◊ *ein böses Erwachen* ♦ *eine böse Überraschung*

rudely [adv] 1. *(impolitely)* unhöflich ['ʊnhøːflɪç] ◊ *sich unhöflich verhalten* 2. *(obscenely)* unanständig ['ʊnˌanʃtɛndɪç] ◊ *sich unanständig benehmen*

ruffle [verb] 1. *(clothes etc.)* ruffle sth (up) etw. zerknittern ['tsɛɐ̯knɪtɐn] <zerknittert, zerknitterte, hat zerknittert> ◊ *Pass auf, dass du das Kleid nicht zerknitterst.* 2. *(sb's hair)* ruffle sth (up) zerzausen [tsɛ'tsaɔzn̩] <zerzaust, zerzauste, hat zerzaust> ◊ *Der Onkel zerzauste dem Kleinen die Haare.* 3. *(bird)* ruffle sth (up) etw. aufplustern ['aɔfplʊstɐn] +haben ◊ *Die kleine Meise plusterte ihr Gefieder auf.* 4. *(a water surface)* ruffle sth kräuseln ['krɔɡzln̩] +haben ◊ *Ein leichter Wind kräuselte die Oberfläche des kleinen Sees.* 5. *(upset)* ruffle sb jdn aus der Ruhe bringen [aɔs deːɐ̯ ruːə brɪŋən] <bringt, brachte, hat gebracht> ◊ *Lass dich von ihm nicht aus der Ruhe bringen.* sb is easily ruffled jd lässt sich leicht aus der Ruhe bringen

rug [noun] 1. *(carpet)* Teppich ['tɛpɪç] der <–s, –e> ◊ *In seinem Wohnzimmer liegen wertvolle Teppiche.* 2. *(blanket)* Decke ['dɛkə] die <–, –n> ◊ *Jeden Abend kuschelte er sich in seine Decke.* ◦ **pull the rug out from under sb** jdm den Boden

unter den Füßen wegziehen

rugby [noun] Rugby ['rakbiː] das <-(s)> no pl ◊ *Rugby spielen*

rugged(ly) [adj, adv] **1.** *(rough, uneven)* zerklüftet [ˈtsɐˈklʏftət] ◊ *eine zerklüftete Landschaft* ♦ *Im Süden ist die Küste besonders zerklüftet.* ruggedly shaped zerklüftet ◊ *eine zerklüftete Insel* **2.** *(sturdy)* robust [roˈbʊst] <robuster, am robustesten> ◊ *ein robustes Kleidungsstück* ♦ *Er ist sehr robust.* ♦ *eine robust konstruierte Brücke* **3.** *(attractive)* markant [maɐˈkant] <markanter, am markantesten> ◊ *markante Züge* ♦ *ein markant geschnittenes Gesicht* **4.** SPORT *(with a lof of muscle power)* hart [haɐt] <härter, am härtesten> ◊ *ein harter Sport* ♦ *hart spielen*

ruin¹ [noun] **1.** *(financial, social, of person)* Ruin [ruˈiːn] der <-s> no pl ◊ *Der Alkohol war sein Ruin.* ♦ *Der Krieg brachte das Land finanziell an den Rand des Ruins.* in ruins ruiniert [ruiˈniːɐt] no comp/superl ◊ *Sein Geschäft war ruiniert.* **2.** *(of a building)* Ruine [ruˈiːnə] die <-, -n> ◊ *Von der Burg ist noch eine Ruine übrig.*

ruin² [verb] **1.** *(destroy)* zerstören [tsɐˈʃtøːrən] <zerstört, zerstörte, hat zerstört> ◊ *Die Gerüchte haben seinen guten Ruf zerstört.* ♦ *Ihre Untreue zerstörte ihre Ehe.* **2.** *(spoil)* verderben [fɛˈdɛɐbm̩] <verdirbt, verdarb, hat verdorben> ◊ *Er hat ihr gründlich den Spaß verdorben.* **3.** *(financially, socially)* ruinieren [ruiˈniːrən] <ruiniert, ruinierte, hat ruiniert> ◊ *jdn finanziell ruinieren*

rule¹ [noun] **1.** *(principles, in grammar)* Regel [ˈreːgl̩] die <-, -n> ◊ *Hier gelten strenge Regeln.* ♦ *die Regeln einhalten/brechen* ♦ *klare Regeln aufstellen* ♦ *die Regeln der deutschen Grammatik* follow a rule ♦ *eine Regel befolgen* **2.** *(government)* Herrschaft [ˈhɛɐʃaft] die <-> no pl ◊ *Macao stand lange Zeit unter portugiesischer Herrschaft.* ☞ rule of thumb Faustregel bend the rules die Regeln nicht so genau nehmen work to rule Dienst nach Vorschrift as a rule in der Regel

rule² [verb] **1.** *(govern)* regieren [reˈgiːrən] <regiert, regierte, hat regiert> ◊ *Er regierte das Land viele Jahre lang.* ♦ *Salomo regierte über Israel.* ◊ *Hier regiert schon lange nicht mehr die Vernunft.* **2.** LAW *(decide)* entscheiden [ɛntˈʃaedn̩] <entscheidet, entschied, hat entschieden> ◊ *Das Gericht hat entschieden, dass das Kind bei seinem Vater bleibt.* rule sb ... jdn für ... erklären [fyːɐ ... ɛkˈlɛːrən] <erklärt, erklärte, hat erklärt> ◊ *Sie wurde für schuldunfähig erklärt.* **3.** *(influence)* beherrschen [bəˈhɛɐʃn̩] <beherrscht, beherrschte, hat beherrscht> ◊ *Die Arbeit beherrschte mein ganzes Leben.* **4.** *(draw a line, margin)* ziehen [ˈtsiːən] <zieht, zog, hat gezogen> ◊ *eine Linie ziehen* • **rule out** [phras v] ausschließen [ˈaʊsʃliːsn̩] <schließt aus, schloss aus, hat ausgeschlossen> ◊ *Die Ärzte schließen eine Ansteckungsgefahr aus.*

ruler [noun] **1.** *(for measuring distances)* Lineal [lineˈaːl] das <-s, -e> ◊ *ein Lineal benutzen/anlegen* **2.** *(sovereign)* Herrscher [ˈhɛɐʃə] der <-s, -> ♀Herrscherin [ˈhɛɐʃərɪn] die <-, -nen> ◊ *der Herrscher des Landes*

ruling¹ [noun] Entscheidung [ɛntˈʃaedʊŋ] die <-, -en> ◊ *Sie haben eine endgültige Entscheidung getroffen.* ♦ *Wann ist die Entscheidung gefallen?*

ruling² [adj] herrschend [ˈhɛɐʃn̩t] no comp/superl, only before ns ◊ *die herrschende Klasse*

rumble [verb] **1.** *(thunder)* grollen [ˈgrɔlən] +haben ◊ *Der Donner grollt.* **2.** *(car)* rumpeln [ˈrʊmpl̩n] +haben/with indication of direction +sein *(fam)* ◊ *Es rumpelte und polterte, als wir über die Brücke fuhren.* ♦ *Der Wagen rumpelte durch einen Wald.* **3.** *(stomach)* knurren [ˈknʊrən] +haben ◊ *Ihm knurrte der Magen.* **4.** *(fam) (a trick, person)* durchschauen [dʊɐçˈʃaʊən] <durchschaut, durchschaute, hat durchschaut> ◊ *Man hatte ihn durchschaut.*

rumour, rumor [noun] Gerücht [gəˈrʏçt] das <-(e)s, -e> ◊ *In der Firma kursieren Gerüchte, er wolle kündigen.* ♦ *Gerüchte verbreiten* rumour has it ... es geht das Gerücht, ... ◊ *Es geht das Gerücht, er habe dafür Geld erhalten.*

run¹ [noun] **1.** *(action of running, of cricket, baseball)* Lauf [laʊf] der <-(e)s, Läufe> ◊ *Er war von dem langen Lauf völlig erschöpft.* go for a run laufen gehen [ˈlaʊf geːən] <geht, ging, ist gegangen> ◊ *Sie geht gern laufen.* **2.** *(series)* Serie [ˈzeːrjə] die <-, -n> ◊ *Eine Serie von Siegen führte zum Aufstieg.; (in theatre)* Spielzeit [ˈʃpiːltsaet] die <-, -en> extend a run die Spielzeit verlängern **3.** *(distance)* Strecke [ˈʃtrɛkə] die <-, -n> ◊ *Er lief die Strecke jeden Morgen.* ♦ *Der Bus fährt die Strecke vom Bahnhof zur Innenstadt.; (pleasure journey)* Spazierfahrt [ʃpaˈtsiːɐfaːɐt] die <-, -en> ◊ *Sie unternahmen eine kleine Spazierfahrt mit dem neuen Auto.* **4.** *(amount produced)* Auflage [ˈaʊflaːgə] die <-, -n> ◊ *Es gibt nur eine kleine Auflage.* **5.** *(for election)* Kandidatur [kandidaˈtuːɐ] die <-, -en> ◊ *Sie entschied sich gegen eine Kandidatur.* **6.** *(enclosure for animals)* Gehege [gəˈheːgə] das <-s, -> ◊ *Im Gehege liefen einige Kaninchen herum, die die Kinder streicheln durften.* **7.** *(for skiing)* Abfahrt [ˈapfaːɐt] die <-, -en> ◊ *Auch für ungeübte Skifahrer ist diese Abfahrt geeignet.* **8.** *(cards)* Sequenz [zeˈkvɛnts] die <-, -en> ◊ *ein Ansturm auf etw.* ☞ have free run of sth etw. zur freien Verfügung haben in the long run langfristig in the short run kurzfristig break into a run losrennen make a run for sth auf etw. [acc] zulaufen on the run **1.** *(from the police)* auf der Flucht **2.** *(in a hurry)* auf die Schnelle *(fam)*

run² [verb] **1.** *(move quickly)* rennen [ˈrɛnən] <rennt, rannte, ist gerannt> ◊ *Er rannte über die Straße.* run like hell so schnell wie möglich rennen; *(a race)* laufen [ˈlaʊfn̩] <läuft, lief, hat gelaufen> +sein ◊ *Er läuft diesen zwölften Mal einen Marathon.; (aimlessly)* round around herumlaufen [hɛˈrʊmlaʊfn̩] <läuft herum, lief herum, ist herumgelaufen> ◊ *Ich bin den ganzen Tag herumgelaufen.* **2.** *(operate)* betreiben [bəˈtraebm̩] <betreibt, betrieb, hat betrieben> ◊ *Die Firma betreibt eine Kantine.; (be responsible for)* leiten [ˈlaetn̩] <leitet, leitete, hat geleitet> ◊ *eine Firma leiten* run a country regieren [reˈgiːrən] <regiert, regierte, hat regiert> ◊ *Welcher König regierte damals das Land?* **3.** *(machine, program, tap, TV show, document, nose, butter, curtains, thoughts)* laufen [ˈlaʊfn̩] <läuft, lief, ist gelaufen> ◊ *Er ließ den Fernseher laufen.* ♦ *Das Programm läuft auf meinem Computer perfekt.* ♦ *Wie lange läuft dein Vertrag noch?* ♦ *Die Schubladen laufen auf Schienen.* ♦ *Meine Gedanken laufen in eine ganz andere Richtung.* run on petrol mit Benzin fahren [mɪt bɛnˈtsiːn faːrən] <fährt, fuhr, ist gefahren> run off the mains mit Strom betrieben werden

[mɪt 'ʃtroːm bə'triːbm̩ okveːɡd̩n] <wird, wurde, ist worden> **4.** *(tap water, tears, river)* fließen ['fliːsn̩] <fließt, floss, ist geflossen> ◊ *Wohin fließt dieser Fluss?*; *(sweat)* rinnen ['rɪnən] <rinnt, rann, ist geronnen> ◊ *Schweiß rann ihm von der Stirn.*; *(a bath)* einlassen ['aɛnlasn̩] <lässt ein, ließ ein, hat eingelassen> ◊ *Er ließ mir ein Bad ein.* **5.** *(bus, tram etc.)* verkehren [fɛ'keːrən] <verkehrt, verkehrte, hat/ist verkehrt> ◊ *Die U-Bahn verkehrt zwischen 5 und 24 Uhr.* ♦ *Dieser Bus verkehrt täglich.* run sb into town jdn in die Stadt fahren [ɪn diː 'ʃtat faːrən] <fährt, fuhr, hat gefahren> run sb home jdn nach Hause fahren **6.** *(prices, amount)* run to betragen [bə'traːgn̩] <beträgt, betrug, hat betragen> ◊ *Der Preis beträgt rund 15 Euro.* **7.** *(road, cable)* führen ['fyːrən] +haben ◊ *Die Straße führt nach München.* ♦ *ein Kabel um die Tür führen* **8.** *(print)* drucken ['drʊkn̩] +haben ◊ *einen Artikel drucken* **9.** *(for election)* kandidieren [kandi'diːrən] <kandidiert, kandidierte, hat kandidiert> ◊ *Wie viele Bewerber kandidieren diesmal?* run for sth als etw. kandidieren **10.** *(clothes)* auslaufen ['aʊslaʊfn̩] <läuft aus, lief aus, ist ausgelaufen> ◊ *Das Rot ist beim Waschen ausgelaufen.*; *(mascara)* verlaufen [fɛ'laʊfn̩] <verläuft, verlief, ist verlaufen> ◊ *Ihre Wimperntusche ist verlaufen.* **11.** *(bring illegally into a country)* schmuggeln ['ʃmʊgln̩] +haben ◊ *Zigaretten und Alkohol ins Land schmuggeln* **12.** *(plant)* wachsen ['vaksn̩] <wächst, wuchs, ist gewachsen> ◊ *An der Wand wächst eine Clematis.* **13.** *(story, argument)* lauten ['laʊtn̩] <lautet, lautete, hat gelautet> ◊ *Die Geschichte lautete etwa so: ...* ♦ *Wie lautete die offizielle Begründung?* **14.** *(tights)* eine Laufmasche haben [aɛnə 'laʊfmaʃə haːbm̩] +haben ◊ *Deine Strumpfhose hat eine Laufmasche.*

• **run across** phras v run across sb jdn zufällig treffen [ˌtsuːfɛlɪç 'trɛfn̩] <trifft, traf, hat getroffen> ◊ *Er hat sie zufällig in der Stadt getroffen.* run across sth zufällig auf etw. acc stoßen [ˌtsuːfɛlɪç aʊf ... ʃtoːsn̩] <stößt, stieß, ist gestoßen> ◊ *Sie stieß im Keller zufällig auf einige alte Fotos.*

• **run around after** phras v round around after sb *(doing things for sb)* jdm alles hinterhertragen [aləs hɪntɛ'heːɐtraːgn̩] <trägt hinterher, trug hinterher, hat hinterhergetragen> ◊ *Dein Mann hat dir immer alles hinterhergetragen.*; *(cleaning for sb)* jdm ständig hinterherräumen [ʃtɛndɪç hɪntɛ'heːɐɔɔmən] +haben ◊ *Ich habe keine Lust, dir ständig hinterherzuräumen.*

• **run around with** phras v run around with sb sich mit jdm herumtreiben [mɪt ... hɛˌrʊmtraɛbm̩] <treibt sich herum, trieb sich herum, hat sich herumgetrieben> ◊ *Er treibt sich mit diesem Typen herum.*

• **run away** phras v weglaufen ['vɛklaʊfn̩] <läuft weg, lief weg, ist weggelaufen> ◊ *Die Kinder laufen vor dem Hund weg.* ♦ *Er ist mit 16 von zu Hause weggelaufen.* ♦ *Sie läuft vor ihren Problemen weg.*

• **run away with** phras v **1.** *(with a person)* run away with sb mit jdm durchbrennen [mɪt ... 'dʊʁçbrɛnən] <brennt durch, brannte durch, ist durchgebrannt> *(fam)* ◊ *Er ist mit ihr durchgebrannt.* **2.** *(feelings, imagination)* run away with sb mit jdm durchgehen [mɪt ... 'dʊʁçgeːən] <geht durch, ging durch, ist durchgegangen> ◊ *Seine Gefühle sind mit ihm durchgegangen.* **3.** *(steal)* run away with sth mit etw. abhauen [mɪt ... 'aphaʊən] <haut ab, haute ab,

ist abgehauen> *(fam)* ◊ *Er ist mit meinen Ersparnissen abgehauen.* **4.** *(fam)* *(a price, competition)* spielend gewinnen [ˌʃpiːlənt gə'vɪnən] <gewinnt, gewann, hat gewonnen> ◊ *Der Schüler hat den Preis spielend gewonnen.*

• **run down** phras v **1.** *(a person, an animal)* überfahren [ybɐ'faːrən] <überfährt, überfuhr, hat überfahren> ◊ *eine Katze überfahren* ♦ *von einer Straßenbahn überfahren werden* **2.** *(criticize)* runtermachen ['rʊntɐmaxn̩] +haben *(fam)* ◊ *Muss du mich ständig runtermachen?* **3.** *(battery)* leer werden ['leːɐ veːɐd̩n] +sein ◊ *Wenn du nicht aufpasst, ist die Batterie der Taschenlampe bald leer.* **4.** *(a factory, shop)* allmählich auflösen [alˌmɛːlɪç 'aʊfløːzn̩] +haben ◊ *Sie wollen das Geschäft allmählich auflösen.*; *(a department, staff)* abbauen ['apbaʊən] +haben ◊ run down staff numbers Personal abbauen **5.** *(a text, list etc.)* überfliegen [ybɐ'fliːgn̩] <überfliegt, überflog, hat überflogen> ◊ *Er hat den Text vor der Unterrichtsstunde schnell überflogen.*

• **run in** phras v **1.** *(a car)* einfahren ['aɛnfaːrən] <fährt ein, fuhr ein, hat eingefahren> ◊ *Sie hat ihr neues Auto einige Tage lang eingefahren.* **2.** *(fam)* *(a criminal)* verhaften [fɛ'haftn̩] <verhaftet, verhaftete, hat verhaftet> ◊ *Er wurde verhaftet.*

• **run into** phras v **1.** *(meet sb)* zufällig treffen [ˌtsuː'fɛlɪç 'trɛfn̩] <trifft, traf, hat getroffen> ◊ *Sie hat ihre alte Nachbarin zufällig getroffen.* **2.** *(hit sb/sth)* anfahren ['anfaːrən] <fährt an, fuhr an, hat angefahren> ◊ *Ich habe ein parkendes Auto angefahren.*

• **run off** phras v **1.** *(leave)* abhauen ['aphaʊən] <haut ab, haute ab, ist abgehauen> *(fam)* ◊ *Als die Polizei kam, hauten die Einbrecher ab.* ♦ *Er ist von zu Hause abgehauen.* **2.** *(print)* ausdrucken ['aʊsdrʊkn̩] +haben ◊ *zehn Exemplare eines Dokuments ausdrucken* **3.** *(a text, poem)* run sth off etw. aus dem Ärmel schütteln [aʊs deːm 'ɛʳml ʃʏtl̩n] +haben *(fam)* ◊ *Sie hat den Text einfach so aus dem Ärmel geschüttelt.* **4.** *(water)* sth runs off etw. fließt ab [fliːst 'ap] <fließt ab, floss ab, ist abgeflossen> ◊ *Das Wasser ist abgeflossen.* run sth off etw. abfließen lassen **5.** *(make leave)* run sb off jdn rausschmeißen ['raʊsʃmaɛsn̩] <schmeißt raus, schmiss raus, hat rausgeschmissen> *(fam)*

• **run off with** phras v **1.** *(leave)* run off with sb mit jdm durchbrennen [mɪt ... 'dʊʁçbrɛnən] <brennt durch, brannte durch, ist durchgebrannt> *(fam)* ◊ *Sie wollte mit ihm durchbrennen.* **2.** *(steal)* run off with sth mit etw. abhauen [mɪt ... 'aphaʊən] <haut ab, haute ab, ist abgehauen> *(fam)* ◊ *Er ist einfach mit dem Geld abgehauen.*

• **run on** phras v **1.** *(last very long)* sich hinziehen ['hɪntsiːən] <zieht sich hin, zog sich hin, hat sich hingezogen> ◊ *Der Vortrag zog sich hin.* **2.** *(talk endlessly)* endlos reden [ˌɛntloːs 'reːdn̩] <redet, redete, hat geredet> ◊ *Sie redete endlos über ihren neuen Freund.*

• **run out** phras v **1.** *(money, supply)* ausgehen ['aʊsgeːən] <geht aus, ging aus, ist ausgegangen> ◊ *Meine Vorräte/Kräfte gehen langsam aus.* sb runs out of sth jdm geht etw. aus **2.** *(time)* ablaufen ['aplaʊfn̩] <läuft ab, lief ab, ist abgelaufen> ◊ *Bald ist die Zeit abgelaufen.* **3.** *(ink, document)* auslaufen ['aʊslaʊfn̩] <läuft aus, lief aus, ist ausgelaufen> ◊ *Der Füller ist ausgelaufen.* ♦ *Morgen läuft der Vertrag aus.*

- **run out on** [phras v] run out on sb jdn verlassen [fe'lasn] <verlässt, verließ, hat verlassen> ◊ *Sie hat gestern ihren Freund verlassen.*
- **run over** [phras v] **1.** *(in a vehicle)* überfahren [ybe'fa:rən] <überfährt, überfuhr, hat überfahren> ◊ *einen Hund überfahren* ◆ *von einem Auto überfahren werden* **2.** *(a text, details)* durchgehen ['dʊrçge:ən] <geht durch, ging durch, ist durchgegangen> ◊ *Kurz vor der Vorstellung ging er den Text nochmals durch.* ◆ *Sie gingen das Verfahren nochmals durch.* **3.** *(think about)* durchdenken [dʊrç'dɛŋkn̩] <durchdenkt, durchdachte, hat durchdacht> ◊ *Sie hat ihre Entscheidung gründlich durchdacht.* **4.** *(last longer than expected)* länger dauern ['lɛŋe daʊən] +haben ◊ *Das Glas ist übergelaufen.*
- **run through** [phras v] **1.** *(read quickly, practise)* durchgehen ['dʊrçge:ən] <geht durch, ging durch, ist durchgegangen> ◊ *Er ging die Tagesordnungspunkte schnell durch.* ◆ *Sie ging mit ihm nochmals den Stoff durch.* **2.** *(feeling)* durchlaufen [dʊrç'laʊfn̩] <durchläuft, durchlief, hat durchlaufen> *(lofty)* ◊ *Ein seltsames Gefühl durchlief ihn.* **3.** *(quality, idea)* durchziehen [dʊrç'tsi:ən] <durchzieht, durchzog, hat durchzogen> ◊ *Diese Frage durchzieht den ganzen Roman.* **4.** *(money, fortune)* durchbringen ['dʊrçbrɪŋən] <bringt durch, brachte durch, hat durchgebracht> ◊ *Sie haben in kurzer Zeit ihr ganzes Vermögen durchgebracht.* **5.** *(with a sword etc.)* durchbohren [dʊrç'bo:rən] <durchbohrt, durchbohrte, hat durchbohrt> ◊ *Er durchbohrte den Feind mit dem Schwert.*
- **run to** [phras v] run to sth **1.** *(reach a certain amount)* sich auf etw. [acc] belaufen [zɪç aʊf ... bəlaʊfn̩] <beläuft sich, belief sich, hat sich belaufen> ◊ *Die Summe beläuft sich auf drei Millionen Euro.* **2.** *(in the UK: be enough)* nicht für etw. reichen [nɪçt fyːɐ ... 'raɛçn̩] +haben ◊ *Mein Gehalt reicht nicht für einen Urlaub.*
- **run up** [phras v] **1.** *(money, debts)* anhäufen ['anhɔɪfn̩] +haben ◊ *Durch den Hausbau haben sie eine Menge Schulden angehäuft.* **2.** *(sew)* schnell nähen [ʃnɛl 'nɛːən] +haben ◊ *Sie nähte schnell einen Rock.* **3.** *(a flag)* hissen ['hɪsn̩] +haben ◊ *Die Flagge wurde jeden Morgen gehisst.*
- **run up against** [phras v] run up against sb/sth auf jdn/etw. stoßen [aʊf ... ʃtoːsn̩] <stößt, stieß, ist gestoßen> ◊ *Ich bin da auf ein Problem gestoßen.* ◆ *auf einen würdigen Gegner stoßen*

run-down [adj] **1.** *(tired)* abgespannt ['apgəʃpant] <abgespannter, am abgespanntesten> ◊ *Sie fühlte sich erschöpft und abgespannt.* **2.** *(area, town etc.)* heruntergekommen [hɛ'rʊntɐgəkɔmən] ◊ *eine heruntergekommene Gegend*

runner [noun] **1.** *(sb who likes running)* Läufer ['lɔøfe] der <-s, -> ♀Läuferin ['lɔøfərɪn] die <-, -nen> ◊ *Er ist ein ausdauernder Läufer.* **2.** *(of a drawer, curtain)* Schiene ['ʃiːnə] die <-, -n> ◊ *Die Schublade gleitet auf Schienen.; (of a sledge, skate)* Kufe ['kuːfə] die <-, -n> **3.** *(of drugs, messages)* Kurier [ku'riːɐ] der <-s, -e> ♀Kurierin [ku'riːrɪn] die <-, -nen> send sth by runner etw. per Kurier senden **4.** *(carpet, on a table)* Läufer ['lɔøfe] der <-s, -> ◊ *Er stolperte über den Läufer.* **5.** BOT Ausläufer ['aʊslɔøfe] der

<-s, -> ◊ *Die Pflanze hat Ausläufer gebildet.*

running¹ [noun] **1.** *(by using your legs)* Laufen ['laʊfn̩] das <-s> no pl ◊ *Er war vom langen Laufen erschöpft.* ◆ *Laufen ist mein Hobby.* **2.** *(management)* Leitung ['laɛtʊŋ] die <-, -en> ◊ *die Leitung eines Unternehmens*

running² → **run²** [adj] *(costs)* laufend ['laʊfn̩t] no comp/superl; when used as an adj, only before ns ◊ *die laufenden Kosten/Ausgaben*

running³ [adv] hintereinander [hɪntɐ|aɛ'nandɐ] ◊ *vier Tage hintereinander*

runny [adj] **1.** sb has a runny nose jdm läuft die Nase [lɔøft diː 'naːzə] <läuft, lief, ist gelaufen> **2.** *(not solid)* flüssig ['flʏsɪç] ◊ *Die Butter erwärmen, bis sie flüssig ist.; (eggs)* weich [vaɛç] ◊ *weiche Eier*

run-up [noun] Anlauf ['anlaʊf] der <-(e)s, Anläufe> ◊ *Leo sprang mit Anlauf in den See.* ◆ *Sie nahm einen kurzen Anlauf und sprang.*

runway [noun] *(for landing)* Landebahn ['landəbaːn] die <-, -en> ◊ *Das Flugzeug landete auf der kleineren Landebahn.; (for taking off)* Startbahn ['ʃtaʁtbaːn] die <-, -en> ◊ *Ein Jet hob von der Startbahn ab.*

rupture [noun] **1.** *(of your eardrum)* Platzen ['platsn̩] das <-s> no pl ◊ *das Platzen des Trommelfells; (your appendix)* Durchbruch ['dʊrçbrʊx] der <-(e)s, Durchbrüche>; *(hernia)* Bruch [brʊx] der <-(e)s, Brüche> ◊ *Stell das wieder hin, sonst hebst du dir noch einen Bruch.* **2.** *(of a relationship)* Abbruch ['apbrʊx] der <-(e)s, Abbrüche> ◊ *ein Abbruch der Beziehungen zwischen den beiden Ländern*

rural(ly) [adj, adv] ländlich ['lɛntlɪç] ◊ *ein ländliches Gebiet* ◆ *Die Gegend ist sehr ländlich.* ◆ *ländlich leben*

ruse [noun] List [lɪst] die <-, -en> ◊ *eine List anwenden* ◆ *etw. durch eine List erreichen*

rush¹ [noun] **1.** *(of people)* Ansturm ['anʃtʊrm] der <-(e)s> no pl ◊ *Der Ansturm auf das Büffet war groß.* make a rush for sth sich auf etw. [acc] stürzen [aʊf ... ʃtʏrtsn̩] +haben ◊ *Die Gäste stürzten sich auf die Getränke.* in a frantic rush wie verrückt [viː fe'rʏkt] **2.** *(of air, liquid)* Schwall [ʃval] der <-(e)s, -e> most sing ◊ *ein Schwall warmer Luft* **3.** *(hurry)* Eile ['aɛlə] die <-> no pl ◊ *Er drängte/ mahnte zur Eile.* ◆ *In der Eile habe ich viele Fehler gemacht.* be in a rush in Eile sein be in no rush to do sth keine Eile haben, etw. zu tun do sth in a rush etw. in großer Eile tun What's the rush? Warum die Eile? **4.** *(of emotion)* Anfall ['anfal] der <-(e)s, Anfälle> ◊ *Er spürte einen plötzlichen Anfall von Zuneigung.; (of drugs)* Drogenrausch ['droːgnraʊʃ] der <-es, Drogenräusche> most sing; *(feeling of excitement, pleasure)* aufregendes Gefühl [aʊfreːgndəs gə'fyːl] <-s, -e> ◊ *Ihr gefiel das aufregende Gefühl, zum ersten Mal alleine zu verreisen.* **5.** *(of traffic)* the rush Stoßzeit ['ʃtoːstsaet] die <-, -en> ◊ *Er wollte nicht während der Stoßzeiten fahren.; (of crowds)* Andrang ['andraŋ] der <-(e)s> no pl ◊ *die Zeit des größten Andrangs* ◆ *Gestern gab es einen unglaublichen Andrang an der Kasse.*

rush² [verb] **1.** *(hurry to a place)* eilen ['aɛlən] +sein ◊ *jdm zu Hilfe eilen* ◆ *nach der Arbeit schnell nach Hause eilen* rush around herumhetzen [hɛ'rʊmhɛtsn̩] +sein ◊ *Er hetzte den ganzen Tag herum, um alles zu erledigen.* **2.** *(take sb quickly to a place)* rush sb somewhere jdn schnell irgendwohin bringen

A
B
C
D
E
F
G
H
I
J
K
L
M
N
O
P
Q
R
S
T
U
V
W
X
Y
Z

[ʃnɛl 'brɪŋən] <bringt, brachte, hat gebracht> ◊ *Sie hat die beiden schnell zum Bahnhof gebracht.* rush sb sth jdm schnell etw. bringen ◊ *Kannst du mir schnell einen Kaffee bringen?* **3.** *(hurry to do sth)* sb rushes jd beeilt sich [bə|'aelt] <beeilte sich, hat sich beeilt> ◊ *Wir müssen uns beeilen.* rush (into) sth etw. überstürzen [ybe'ʃtv'tsn̩] <überstürzt, überstürzte, hat überstürzt> ◊ *Du solltest nichts überstürzen.* ♦ *eine Entscheidung überstürzen* **4.** *(make sb hurry)* rush sb jdn hetzen ['hɛtsn̩] +haben ◊ *Hör auf, ihn zu hetzen.* rush sb into (doing) sth jdn zu etw. drängen [tsu: ... ˌdrɛŋən] +haben ◊ *Er drängte sie zu einer schnellen Entscheidung.* **5.** *(water, blood)* schießen ['ʃiːsn̩] <schießt, schoss, ist geschossen> ◊ *Das Blut schoss ihr in die Wangen.* **6.** *(attack)* rush at sb sich auf jdn stürzen [aof ... ʃtv'tsn̩] +haben ◊ *Sie stürzten sich auf das Mädchen.*

Russia [noun] Russland ['rʊslant] das <–s> *article only in combination with attribute, no pl* → **Germany**

Russian¹ [noun] **1.** *(inhabitant)* Russe ['rʊsə] der <–n, –n> ♀Russin ['rʊsɪn] die <–, –nen> → **German¹ 1. 2.** *(language, subject)* Russisch ['rʊsɪʃ]

das <–s> *no pl* → **German¹ 2.**

Russian² [adj] russisch ['rʊsɪʃ] → **German²**

rust¹ [noun] Rost [rɔst] der <–es> *no pl* ◊ *Der Deckel hatte Rost angesetzt.*

rust² [verb] rosten ['rɔstn̩] <rostet, rostete, ist gerostet> ◊ *Dieses Material rostet nicht.*

rustle [verb] **1.** *(leaves, paper)* rascheln ['raʃln̩] +haben ◊ *Das Laub raschelte leise unter unseren Füßen.* **2.** *(steal)* stehlen ['ʃteːlən] <stiehlt, stahl, hat gestohlen> ◊ *Jemand hat wieder Vieh gestohlen.*

rusty [adj] **1.** *(with rust)* rostig ['rɔstɪç] ◊ *ein rostiges altes Fahrrad* sth is rusty etw. rostet ['rɔstət] <rostete, ist gerostet> +haben ◊ *Der Türgriff rostet.* **2.** *(mind, skill)* eingerostet ['aengərɔstət] ◊ *Mein Englisch ist etwas eingerostet.* ♦ *jds eingerostetes Französisch* **3.** *(colo(u)r)* sth is a rusty colo(u)r etw. ist rostfarben [ɪst 'rɔstfaˈbm̩] *no comp/superl*

ruthless(ly) [adj, adv] rücksichtslos ['rʏkzɪçtsloːs] <rücksichtsloser, am rücksichtslosesten> ◊ *die rücksichtslose Ausbeutung der Sklaven* ♦ *Er ist manchmal völlig rücksichtslos.* ♦ *rücksichtslos seine Interessen verfolgen*

S

s, S [noun] s, S [ɛs] das <–, –> ◊ *Dieses Wort wird mit einem kleinen s/großen S geschrieben.* ♦ *S wie Siegfried*

sack¹ [noun] **1.** *(strong bag)* Sack [zak] der <–(e)s, Säcke> ◊ *ein Sack Kartoffeln* ♦ *drei Säcke voll Gold* ♦ *ein Sack mit Müll* **2.** *(in the UK: dismiss)* give sb the sack jdn rausschmeißen ['raosʃmaesn̩] <schmeißt raus, schmiss raus, hat rausgeschmissen> *(fam)* get the sack rausgeschmissen werden ['raosgəʃmɪsn̩ veːɐdn̩] <wird, wurde, ist worden> *(fam)* sb faces the sack jdm droht die Entlassung [droːt diː ɛntˈlasʊŋ] +haben

sack² [verb] **1.** *(dismiss)* rausschmeißen ['raosʃmaesn̩] <schmeißt raus, schmiss raus, hat rausgeschmissen> *(fam)* ◊ *Der Verein hat seinen Trainer rausgeschmissen.* **2.** *(pillage)* plündern ['plʏndɐn] +haben ◊ *Soldaten plündern die Stadt.*

sacred [adj] **1.** *(religious)* religiös [reliˈɡiøːs] <religiöser, am religiösesten> *mostly before ns* ◊ *religiöse Kunst* **2.** *(revered, respected)* heilig ['haelɪç] ◊ *eine heilige Kuh* ♦ *Das Leben ist heilig.* be sacred to sb jdm heilig sein ◊ *Ihr ist nichts heilig.*

sacrifice¹ [noun] Opfer ['ɔpfɐ] das <–s, –> ◊ *finanzielle Opfer* ♦ *ein Opfer für die Götter* make sacrifices Opfer bringen

sacrifice² [verb] opfern ['ɔpfɐn] +haben ◊ *Sie opferten ihrem Gott ein Schaf.* ♦ *Er opfert viel Zeit für sein Ehrenamt.*; *(your career)* sacrifice sth to do sth etw. aufgeben, um etw. zu tun ['aofɡeːbm̩ ʊm ... tsuː] <gibt auf, gab auf, hat aufgegeben> ◊ *Er gab seinen Beruf auf, um sich den Kindern zu widmen.*

sad [adj] *(unhappy, making you feel unhappy or angry, pathetic)* traurig ['traorɪç] ◊ *Er war äußerst traurig über diese Nachricht.* ♦ *eine traurige Gestalt* ♦ *die traurige Wahrheit* I am sad to hear about his death. Die Nachricht von seinem Tod stimmt mich traurig.

sadden [verb] betroffen machen [bəˈtrɔfn̩ maxn̩] +haben ◊ *Es macht mich betroffen, dass sie so traurig ist.*

saddle [noun] Sattel ['zatl̩] der <–s, Sättel> ◊ *Sie legte dem Pferd den Sattel auf.* ♦ *Der Sattel meines Fahrrads ist zu hart.*
  ⊙ be in the saddle **1.** *(ride a horse)* im Sattel sitzen **2.** *(be in control)* das Ruder in der Hand haben *(fam)*
  • **saddle with** [phras v] saddle sb/yourself with sb/sth jdm/sich jdn/etw. aufbürden ['aofbʏrdn̩] <bürdet auf, bürdete auf, hat aufgebürdet> ◊ *jdm Verantwortung aufbürden* be saddled with sb/sth jdn/etw. am Hals haben [am ˈhals haːbm̩] +haben *(fam)* ◊ *Schulden am Hals haben*

sadistic(ally) [adj, adv] sadistisch [zaˈdɪstɪʃ] ◊ *sadistische Neigungen haben* ♦ *Gefangene sadistisch quälen* sb is sadistic jd ist sadistisch *(veranlagt)*

sadly [adv] traurig ['traorɪç] ◊ *Sie sah mich traurig an.*

sadness [noun] **1.** *(opposite of happiness)* Traurigkeit ['traorɪçkaet] die <–> no pl ◊ *Hilfe bei Traurigkeit*

und Depressionen **2.** *(after you have lost sb)* Trauer ['traoɐ] die <–> no pl with great sadness in tiefer Trauer

safe¹ [noun] Tresor [treˈzoːɐ] der <–s, –e>

safe² [adj] **1.** *(protected, secure)* sicher ['zɪçɐ] ◊ *eine sichere Geldanlage* ♦ *Dieser Hubschrauber gilt als besonders sicher.* be safe from sth vor etw. sicher sein keep sth safe etw. sicher aufbewahren make sth safe from sth etw. gegen etw. sichern [ge:ɡn̩] ... ,zɪçɐn] +haben **2.** *(not dangerous or risky)* ungefährlich ['ʊngəfɛːɐlɪç] ◊ *ein ungefährliches Thema* ♦ *Echte Kerzen sind nicht ganz ungefährlich.* **3.** *(not damaged or hurt)* safe (and sound) unversehrt ['ʊnfɛezeːɐt] no comp/superl ◊ *die unversehrte Rückkehr des Raumschiffes* ♦ *Das Kind wurde unversehrt gefunden.*
  ⊛ it's safe to say ... man kann mit Sicherheit sagen, ...

safeguard [verb] schützen ['ʃʏtsn̩] +haben ◊ *Umwelt schützen* safeguard sb/sth against sth jdn/etw. vor etw. schützen

safely [adv] **1.** *(without risk, securely)* sicher ['zɪçɐ] ◊ *Geld sicher anlegen* **2.** *(not damaged or hurt)* unversehrt ['ʊnfɛezeːɐt] no comp/superl ◊ *unversehrt nach Hause kommen* **3.** *(carefully)* vorsichtig ['foːɐzɪçtɪç] ◊ *Fahren Sie bitte vorsichtig!*

safety [noun] **1.** *(security, protection)* Sicherheit ['zɪçɐhaet] die <–, –en> ◊ *mehr Sicherheit im Straßenverkehr* safety hazard Sicherheitsrisiko ['zɪçɐhaetsˌriːzikoː] das <–s, Sicherheitsrisiken>; *(of a substance)* Unbedenklichkeit ['ʊnbədɛŋklɪçkaet] die <–> no pl ◊ *die Unbedenklichkeit eines Arzneimittels* **2.** *(safe place, situation)* reach safety der Gefahr entkommen [deːɐ ɡəˌfaːɐ ɛntˈkɔmən] <entkommt, entkam, ist entkommen> I watched from the safety of my hiding place. Ich sah aus meinem sicheren Versteck zu.

safety belt [noun] Sicherheitsgurt ['zɪçɐhaetsɡʊʳt] der <–(e)s, –e> ◊ *den Sicherheitsgurt anlegen*

safety helmet [noun] Schutzhelm ['ʃʊtshɛlm] der <–(e)s, –e>

safety net [noun] **1.** *(system)* Sicherheitsnetz ['zɪçɐhaetsnɛts] das <–es, –e> ◊ *die Sozialhilfe als Sicherheitsnetz für Menschen in Not* **2.** *(for catching acrobats etc.)* Netz [nɛts] das <–es, –e> ◊ *Diese Akrobaten arbeiten ohne Netz.*

safety pin [noun] Sicherheitsnadel ['zɪçɐhaetsnaːdl̩] die <–, –n>

sail¹ [noun] Segel ['zeːɡl̩] das <–s, –> set sail die Segel setzen

sail² [verb] **1.** *(move or travel in a sailing boat)* segeln ['zeːɡln̩] +haben/with indication of direction +sein ◊ *Er hat im Sommer viel gesegelt.* ♦ *Wir sind nach Amerika gesegelt.* go sailing segeln gehen sail for Dover nach Dover segeln learn to sail segeln lernen **2.** *(start a journey by sea, leave)* auslaufen ['aoslaofn̩] <läuft aus, lief aus, ist ausgelaufen> ◊ *Wir laufen morgen früh aus.* sail for Dover nach Dover

auslaufen 3. *(glide through the air)* fliegen ['fli:gn̩]
<fliegt, flog, ist geflogen> ◊ *Der Ball flog an mir
vorbei und ging ins Tor.*

sailor [noun] Matrose [ma'tro:zə] der <–n, –n>
♀Matrosin [ma'tro:zɪn] die <–, –nen> ◊ *Er ist
Matrose auf einem Dampfer.* ♦ *Die Matrosin ging
von Board.*

saint [noun] 1. Heilige ['haɛlɪgə] der/die
<–n, die Heiligen> but: *ein Heiliger/eine Heilige* ◊ *Sie
wurde als Heilige verehrt.* 2. Saint Sankt [zaŋkt]
<–> *only in combination with names* ◊ *Sankt
Nikolaus*

sake [noun] *for sb's sake/the sake of sth* jdm/etw.
zuliebe [ʦu'li:bə] *postpositive* [+dat] ◊ *Sie hat es ihm
zuliebe getan.* ♦ *Dem Beruf zuliebe bin ich
umgezogen.*
ⓔ *do sth for its own sake* travel/learn etc. for its
own sake reisen/lernen etc. um des Reisens/
Lernens etc. willen *just for the sake of it* einfach
nur so

salad [noun] Salat [za'la:t] der <–(e)s, –e> ◊ *Schnitzel
mit gemischtem Salat* fruit salad Obstsalat
['o:pstza,la:t] pasta salad Nudelsalat ['nu:dl̩za,la:t]

salary [noun] Gehalt [gə'halt] das <–(e)s, Gehälter> ◊
ein Gehalt von 25 000 Euro brutto im Jahr

sale [noun] 1. *(handing over for money, selling as a
profession)* Verkauf [fɛ'kaɔf] der <–(e)s, Verkäufe> ◊
etw. zum Verkauf anbieten be (up) for sale zum
Verkauf stehen put sth up for sale etw. zum
Verkauf anbieten be in sales im Verkauf tätig sein;
(department) sales Verkaufsabteilung
[fɛ'kaɔfs|aptaɛlʊŋ] die <–, –en> 2. *(event, fete)*
Basar [ba'za:ʳ] der <–s, –e> ◊ *Der Kindergarten veranstaltet einen Basar.* 3. *(auction)* Versteigerung
[fɛ'ʃtaɛgərʊŋ] die <–, –en> 4. *(to clear stocks)* Aus-
verkauf ['aɔsfɛkaɔf] der <–(e)s, Ausverkäufe>
summer sales Sommerschlussverkauf
['zɔmɛʃlʊsfɛkaɔf] der
<–(e)s, Sommerschlussverkäufe>; *(special offer)* be
on sale im Sonderangebot sein
[ɪm 'zɔndɐ|aŋgəbo:t zaɛn] +*sein* have a sale on sth
etw. im Sonderangebot haben
[ɪm 'zɔndɐ|aŋgəbo:t ha:bm̩] +*haben* 5. *(turnover)*
Umsatz ['ʊmzaʦ] der <–es, Umsätze> ◊ *die Umsätze
verbessern*

sales assistant [noun] Verkäufer [fɛ'kɔøfɐ] der
<–s, –> ♀Verkäuferin [fɛ'kɔøfərɪn] die <–, –nen> ◊
Die Verkäuferin hat mich sehr gut beraten. ♦ *Er
arbeitet als Verkäufer im Kaufhaus.*

sales clerk [noun] *(in the US)* Verkäufer [fɛ'kɔøfɐ] der
<–s, –> ♀Verkäuferin [fɛ'kɔøfərɪn] die <–, –nen> ◊
Er ist ein guter Verkäufer. ♦ *Sie ist Verkäuferin.*

sales rep(resentative) [noun] Vertreter [fɛ'tre:tɐ]
der <–s, –> ♀Vertreterin [fɛ'tre:tərɪn] die
<–, –nen> ◊ *Er arbeitet als Vertreter für Software.* ♦
Die Vertreterin führte den Staubsauger vor.

saliva [noun] Speichel ['ʃpaɛçl̩] der <–s> *no pl*

salmon [noun] Lachs [laks] der <–es, –e> ◊ *geräucherten Lachs* ♦ *die Wanderung der Lachse*

salon [noun] Salon [za'lɔŋ] der <–s, –s> ◊ *Meine
Friseuse hat ihren eigenen Salon eröffnet.*

salt¹ [noun] Salz [zalʦ] das <–es, –e> ◊ *eine Prise Salz*
♦ *saure Salze*
ⓔ *rub salt into the wound* Salz in die Wunde
streuen

salt² [verb] 1. *(your food)* salzen ['zalʦn̩] <salzt, salzte,

hat gesalzen> ◊ *Der Fisch muss noch gesalzen
werden.* 2. *(the road)* mit Salz streuen
[mɪt 'zalʦ ʃtrɔøən] +*haben* ◊ *Im Winter werden die
Straßen mit Salz gestreut.*

salt cellar [noun] *(in the UK)* Salzstreuer ['zalʦʃtrɔøe]
der <–s, –>

saltwater [adj] See... [ze:] saltwater fish Seefisch
['ze:fɪʃ] der <–(e)s, –e>

salty [adj] salzig ['zalʦɪç] ◊ *Die Suppe war zu salzig.* ♦
salziges Popcorn

salvation [noun] 1. REL *(saving of the soul)* Erlösung
[ɛ'lø:zʊŋ] die <–> *no pl* ◊ *Wir beten für unsere
Erlösung.* 2. *(sth that helps you)* Rettung ['rɛtʊŋ] die
<–, –en> ◊ *Ist das Aupairmädchen die Rettung der
arbeitenden Mutter?*

same¹ [adj] *(of the same kind)* the same der/die/das
gleiche [de:ɡ/di:/das 'glaɛçə] ◊ *Sie trug das gleiche
Kleid wie ihre Schwester.; (identical)* the same
derselbe [de:ɡ'zɛlbə] dieselbe [di:'zɛlbə] dasselbe
[das'zɛlbə] ◊ *Wir haben denselben Vater, aber verschiedene Mütter.* ♦ *Dort parkt immer dasselbe Auto.;
(when preceded by a German contraction fusing prep
and article)* selbe ['zɛlbə] ◊ *jeden Tag zur selben Zeit
und am selben Ort* the same thing dasselbe
[das'zɛlbə] amount to the same thing auf dasselbe
hinauslaufen be the same length gleich lang sein
['glaɛç ,laŋ zaɛn]

same² [adv] the same gleich [glaɛç] ◊ *Sie bemüht
sich, alle Schüler gleich zu behandeln.* the same as
genauso wie [gə'naɔzo: vi:] ◊ *Er sah genauso aus
wie immer.* just the same genauso [gə'naɔzo:] ◊ *Sie
ist ziemlich faul; ihr Bruder ist genauso.*

same³ [pron] 1. *(very similar)* the same das Gleiche
[das 'glaɛçə] ◊ *Das Gleiche noch mal bitte!* ♦ *Zwei
Kilo Äpfel kosten das Gleiche wie eine Mango.*
2. *(identical)* the same dasselbe [das'zɛlbə] ◊ *Ich
hätte genau dasselbe getan.* 3. *(the very person,
thing)* the very same genau der/die/das
[gənaɔ 'de:ɡ/'di:/'das] ◊ *„War das nicht Hugh
Grant?" — „Genau der!"*
ⓔ *it's all the same to sb* es ist jdm gleich *(fam)*
(the) same to you danke, gleichfalls ◊ *„Guten
Appetit!" — „Danke, gleichfalls."*

sample¹ [noun] *(example of goods)* Muster ['mʊstɐ]
das <–s, –> ◊ *ein Muster, das nicht zum Verkauf
steht* fabric sample Stoffmuster ['ʃtɔfmʊstɐ]; *(small
amount of sth to try, for tests)* Probe ['pro:bə] die
<–, –n> ◊ *kostenlose Proben* ♦ *Proben untersuchen*
random sample Stichprobe ['ʃtɪçpro:bə] work sample
Arbeitsprobe ['a'baɛtspro:bə]

sample² [verb] 1. *(take small amounts for tests)*
sample sth Proben von etw. nehmen
[,pro:bm̩ fɔn ... ne:mən] <nimmt, nahm, hat
genommen> sample sb's blood eine Blutprobe von
jdm nehmen sample a group of patients Patienten
untersuchen [pa'tsjɛntn̩ ʊntɐ,zu:xn̩] <untersucht, untersuchte, hat untersucht> 2. *(get to know, try)* kennen
lernen ['kɛnən lɛ'nən] +*haben* ◊ *das Leben in einem
anderen Land kennen lernen; (try food, drink)*
probieren [pro'bi:rən] <probiert, probiere, hat
probiert> ◊ *das Essen in einem Restaurant probieren*

sanction¹ [noun] Sanktion [zaŋk'tsjo:n] die <–, –en>
(form) ◊ *Sanktionen gegen ein Land verhängen* ♦
*Das Gesetz tritt nach Sanktion durch das Parlament
in Kraft.*

sanction² [verb] sanktionieren [zaŋktsjo'ni:rən] <sank-

tioniert, sanktionierte, hat sanktioniert> *(form)* ◊ *ein Gesetz, das die Trennung von Staat und Kirche sanktioniert*

sanctuary [noun] **1.** *(refuge)* Zuflucht ['tsu:flʊxt] die <-> no pl ◊ *Die Flüchtlinge suchten Zuflucht im Nachbarland.; (place)* Zufluchtsort ['tsu:flʊxts|ɔˀt] der <-(e)s, -e>; *(safety, security)* Geborgenheit [gə'bɔˀgṇhaet] die <-> no pl ◊ *die Geborgenheit der eigenen vier Wände* **2.** *(for wildlife)* Schutzgebiet ['ʃʊtsgəbi:t] das <-(e)s, -e> bird sanctuary Vogelschutzgebiet ['fo:glʃʊtsgəbi:t] animal sanctuary Tierheim ['ti:ghaem] das <-(e)s, -e> **3.** REL Heiligtum ['haelɪçtu:m] das <-s, Heiligtümer>

sand [noun] **1.** *(substance)* Sand [zant] der <-(e)s> no pl ◊ *im Sand spielen* **2.** *(area)* sands Sandgebiet ['zantgəbi:t] das <-(e)s, -e>

sandal [noun] Sandale [zan'da:lə] die <-, -n>

sandbox → **sandpit**

sandpit, sandbox [noun] Sandkasten ['zantkastṇ] der <-s, Sandkästen>

sandwich [noun] Brot [bro:t] das <-(e)s, -e> ◊ *Was möchtest du auf dein Brot?* cheese sandwich Käsebrot ['kɛːzəbro:t]

sandy [adj] sandig ['zandɪç] ◊ *Der Boden ist hier sehr sandig.* ◆ *sandige Böden* sandy beach Sandstrand ['zantʃtrant] der <-(e)s, Sandstrände>

sane [adj] **1.** *(not mentally ill)* geistig gesund [ˌgaestɪç gə'zʊnt] <geistig gesünder, geistig am gesündesten> ◊ *Ich halte den Täter für geistig gesund.* ◆ *ein geistig gesunder Mensch* **2.** *(sensible)* vernünftig [fɛ'nʏnftɪç] ◊ *eine vernünftige Politik* ◆ *Deine Vorgehensweise ist vernünftig.*
ⓔ keep sb sane jdn vor dem Wahnsinn bewahren

sanitary [adj] **1.** *(relating to hygiene)* sanitär [zani'tɛːɐ̯] no comp/superl, only before *ns* ◊ *schlechte sanitäre Bedingungen* **2.** *(hygienic)* hygienisch [hy'gie:nɪʃ] ◊ *Das Schneidebrett ist hygienisch und praktisch.* ◆ *eine hygienische Verpackung;* Hygiene... [hy'gie:nə] sanitary procedure Hygienemaßnahme [hy'gie:nəma:sna:mə] die <-, -n>

sanitary napkin [noun] *(in the US)* Binde ['bɪndə] die <-, -n>

sanitary towel [noun] *(in the UK)* Binde ['bɪndə] die <-, -n>

sanity [noun] **1.** *(mental health)* Verstand [fɛ'ʃtant] der <-(e)s> no pl ◊ *an seinem Verstand zweifeln* lose your sanity den Verstand verlieren **2.** *(rationality)* Vernunft [fɛ'nʊnft] die <-> no pl ◊ *Die Vernunft hat sich schließlich durchgesetzt.*

Santa Claus [noun] Weihnachtsmann ['vaenaxtsman] der <-(e)s, Weihnachtsmänner> ◊ *Morgen kommt der Weihnachtsmann!*

sarcastic(ally) [adj, adv] sarkastisch [zaˀ'kastɪʃ] ◊ *sarkastische Bemerkungen* ◆ *Du bist immer so sarkastisch.* ◆ *sarkastisch formuliert*

sardine [noun] Sardine [zaˀ'di:nə] die <-, -n>
ⓔ packed in like sardines eingepfercht wie die Ölsardinen

satellite [noun] Satellit [zatɛ'li:t] der <-en, -en> *(also pej)* ◊ *Die Sendung wird über Satellit übertragen.* ◆ *Der Mond ist der einzige Satellit der Erde.* weather satellite Wettersatellit ['vɛtɐzatə,li:t] satellite (town) Satellitenstadt [zatɛ'li:tṇʃtat] die <-, Satellitenstädte>

satellite dish [noun] Satellitenschüssel [zatɛ'li:tṇʃʏsl̩] die <-, -n>

satisfaction [noun] **1.** *(contentment)* Zufriedenheit

[tsu'fri:dṇhaet] die <-> no pl ◊ *ein Problem zu jds Zufriedenheit lösen* customer satisfaction Kundenzufriedenheit ['kʊndṇtsu,fri:dṇhaet] job satisfaction Zufriedenheit im Beruf [tsu,fri:dṇhaet ɪm bə'ru:f] with satisfaction zufrieden [tsu'fri:dṇ] **2.** *(gratification)* Genugtuung [gə'nu:ktuoŋ] die <-, -en> most sing *(lofty)* sb gets great satisfaction from sth, sth is a great satisfaction to sb etw. erfüllt jdn mit großer Genugtuung have the satisfaction of doing sth die Genugtuung haben, etw. zu tun **3.** *(of needs)* Befriedigung [bə'fri:dɪgʊŋ] die <-> no pl ◊ *die Befriedigung grundlegender Bedürfnisse*
ⓔ prove sth to sb's satisfaction jdn von etw. überzeugen

satisfactory(-ily) [adj, adv] zufriedenstellend [tsu'fri:dṇʃtɛlənt] ◊ *Das ist keine zufriedenstellende Lösung.* ◆ *Seine Arbeit ist nicht zufriedenstellend.* ◆ *zufriedenstellend arbeiten* be satisfactory to sb jdn zufrieden stellen [tsu'fri:dṇ ʃtɛlən] +haben

satisfied → **satisfy** [adj] zufrieden [tsu'fri:dṇ] ◊ *zufriedene Gesichter* ◆ *Manche Leute sind nie zufrieden.* ◆ *mit etw. zufrieden sein*

satisfy [verb] **1.** *(give sb what they want)* zufrieden stellen [tsu'fri:dṇ ʃtɛlən] +haben ◊ *Kunden zufrieden stellen* **2.** *(a desire, need)* befriedigen [bə'fri:dɪgṇ] <befriedigt, befriedigte, hat befriedigt> ◊ *seine Neugier befriedigen* ◆ *Ich finde es wenig befriedigend, immer das Gleiche zu tun.; (your thirst, hunger)* stillen ['ʃtɪlən] +haben ◊ *Ich stillte meinen Durst mit Wasser.; (a demand, requirement)* decken ['dɛkṇ] +haben ◊ *Das Angebot deckt bei weitem nicht die Nachfrage.; (a condition, prerequisite)* erfüllen [ɛ'fʏlən] <erfüllt, erfüllte, hat erfüllt> ◊ *die erforderlichen Voraussetzungen erfüllen* **3.** *(convince)* satisfy sb/yourself that jdn/sich davon überzeugen, dass [dafon ybeˀ'tsɔøgṇ das] ◊ *Ich habe mich davon überzeugt, dass alles in Ordnung ist.* be satisfied that überzeugt davon sein, dass

satisfying → **satisfy** [adj] *(food)* sättigend ['zɛtɪgṇt] ◊ *Dieses Gericht ist sättigend.* ◆ *eine sättigende Mahlzeit*

Saturday [noun] Samstag ['zamsta:k] der <-(e)s, -e> → **Monday**

sauce [noun] Soße ['zo:sə] die <-, -n> ◊ *Soße über die Nudeln gießen* chocolate sauce Schokoladensoße [ʃoko'la:dṇzo:sə] soy sauce Sojasauce ['zo:jazo:sə]

saucepan [noun] Kochtopf ['kɔxtɔpf] der <-(e)s, Kochtöpfe>

saucer [noun] Untertasse ['ʊntetasə] die <-, -n>
ⓔ flying saucer fliegende Untertasse

saucy(-ily) [adj, adv] frech [frɛç] ◊ *Das Lied war ziemlich frech.* ◆ *eine freche Komödie* ◆ *frech grinsen*

sauna [noun] Sauna ['zaona:] die <-, Saunen>

sausage [noun] Wurst [vʊˀst] die <-, Würste> ◊ *ein Paar Wiener Würste*

savage [adj] **1.** *(crime, attack)* brutal [bru'ta:l] ◊ *ein brutaler Überfall* ◆ *Der Mord war äußerst brutal.* **2.** *(fighting, battle, blow, storm)* schwer [ʃve:ɐ̯] ◊ *Das war ein schwerer Schlag für sie.* **3.** *(cuts)* erheblich [ɛ'he:plɪç] ◊ *erhebliche Einsparungen* **4.** *(criticism)* vernichtend [fɛ'nɪçtṇt] ◊ *eine vernichtende Analyse der Regierungspolitik* ◆ *Ihre Kritik war vernichtend.* **5.** *(animal, landscape)* wild [vɪlt] <wilder, am

wildesten> ◊ *ein wildes Tier* **6.** *(weather)* sehr
schlecht [zɛːɐ̯ ʃlɛçt] <schlechter, am schlechtesten> ◊
sehr schlechte Witterungsbedingungen

savagely [adv] **1.** *(attack, murder)* brutal [bruˈtaːl] ◊ *Er
wurde brutal ermordet.* **2.** *(fight, criticize)* unerbitt-
lich [ˈʊn|ɛbɪtlɪç] ◊ *Sie kämpften unerbittlich gegen
den Feind.* ♦ *Der neue Roman wurde unerbittlich kritisiert.*

save¹ [verb] **1.** *(protect, rescue)* retten [ˈrɛtn̩] <rettet,
rettete, hat gerettet> ◊ *den Regenwald retten* save sb/
sth from sth jdn/etw. vor etw. [dat] retten ◊ *Wie
können wir uns vor dem Konkurs retten?* save sb
from themselves jdn vor sich [dat] selbst schützen
[fɔːɐ̯ ... ˈzɛlpst ʃʏtsn̩] +haben **2.** *(not use)* sparen
[ˈʃpaːrən] +haben ◊ *Dieses Vorgehen wird uns viel
Zeit sparen.* save sth on sth etw. bei etw. sparen ◊
100 Euro bei einem Einkauf sparen save to do sth
für etw. sparen We are saving to buy a house. Wir
sparen für ein Haus. **3.** *(avoid costs, effort)* save sb
sth jdm etw. ersparen [ɛˈʃpaːrən] <erspart, ersparte,
hat erspart> ◊ *Das hat ihm viel Mühe erspart.* ♦ *Auf
diese Weise kannst du dir Kosten ersparen.* save sb
doing sth jdm ersparen, etw. tun zu müssen **4.** *(a
seat or place for sb)* save sth for sb jdm etw. freihalten [ˈfraɛ̯haltn̩] <hält frei, hielt frei, hat freigehalten> ◊
Kannst du mir den Stuhl freihalten? **5.** *(keep food for
sb)* save sb sth jdm etw. übrig lassen [ˈyːbrɪç lasn̩]
<lässt, ließ, hat gelassen> ◊ *Ich komme später, lässt
du mir was vom Abendessen übrig?;* *(to eat or drink
sth later)* save sth sich [dat] etw. aufsparen
[ˈaɔ̯fʃpaːrən] +haben ◊ *Die Flasche Wein spare ich
mir für später auf.* **6.** IT speichern [ˈʃpaɛ̯çn̩] +haben
◊ *Sie speichert ihre Präsentation auf einer Diskette.*
♦ *Daten regelmäßig speichern* **7.** SPORT *(a ball)* halten
[ˈhaltn̩] <hält, hielt, hat gehalten> ◊ *einen Strafstoß
halten*

save² [prep] *(except)* außer [ˈaɔ̯sɐ] +dat ◊ *Außer seiner
Schwester war niemand gekommen.* save for sth bis
auf etw. [acc] [bɪs aɔ̯f] ◊ *Bis auf die Kette war er vollkommen nackt.*

saving [noun] Ersparnis [ɛˈʃpaːˈnɪs] die <–, –se> ◊ *Die
Anleger verloren ihre Ersparnisse.* ♦ *Wir garantieren
Ihnen eine Ersparnis von 15%.*

savings account [noun] Sparkonto [ˈʃpaːˈˌkɔntoː] das
<–s, Sparkonten> have money in your savings
account Geld auf dem Sparkonto haben

saviour, savior [noun] **1.** Retter [ˈrɛtɐ] der <–s, –>
♀Retterin [ˈrɛtərɪn] die <–, –nen> **2.** REL the
Savio(u)r der Erlöser [deːɐ̯ ɛˈløːzɐ] <–s> no pl

savoury, savory [adj] **1.** *(not sweet)* pikant [piˈkant]
<pikanter, am pikantesten> ◊ *Pfannkuchen mit
pikanter Füllung* ♦ *Diese Snacks sind pikant.*
2. *(tasty, pleasant)* appetitlich [apeˈtiːtlɪç] ◊ *Das
Gericht war sehr appetitlich.* ♦ *ein appetitliches
Aroma*

saw¹ [noun] Säge [ˈzɛːɡə] die <–, –n>

saw² → see [verb] sägen [ˈzɛːɡn̩] +haben ◊ *einen Ast
in kleine Stücke sägen* ♦ *Heute Nachmittag wird es
laut, weil ich sägen muss.* saw sth up etw. zersägen
[tsɐˈzɛːɡn̩] <zersägt, zersägte, hat zersägt> saw sth off
etw. absägen [ˈapzɛːɡn̩] +haben ◊ *Er sägte den Ast
ab.*

say¹ [noun] **1.** *(contribute to a discussion)* have a say
(in sth) (bei etw.) mitreden dürfen [ˈmɪtreːdn̩ dʏˈfn̩]
<darf, durfte, hat dürfen> ◊ *Wir durften bei dieser
Angelegenheit nicht mitreden.* have a say on sth

über etw. [acc] mitreden dürfen **2.** *(express your
opinion)* have your say seine Meinung sagen
[zaɛ̯nə ˈmaɛ̯nʊŋ zaːɡn̩] +haben
☞ the final say das letzte Wort

say² [verb] **1.** *(express in words, mean)* sagen [ˈzaːɡn̩]
+haben; followed by the subjunctive when used in
reported speech ◊ *etw. über jdn/etw. sagen* ♦ *Kannst
du das auch auf Englisch sagen?* ♦ *„Ich habe heute
noch nichts gegessen", sagte sie.* ♦ *Er sagt, er wolle
das nicht.* ♦ *Sag endlich, wo du gestern warst!* ♦ *Was
hat er zu dir gesagt?* ♦ *Ich muss sagen, ich bin beeindruckt.* ♦ *Das ist leichter gesagt als getan.* say sth on
sth etw. zu etw. sagen ◊ *Ich möchte auch etwas zu
diesem Thema sagen.* sth says sth to sb etw. sagt
jdm etw. ◊ *Diese Bilder sagen mir nichts.* say sth to
yourself sich [dat] etw. sagen say to yourself that
sich sagen, dass ◊ *Da sagte er sich, dass er mit dem
Rauchen aufhören sollte.* What are you trying to
say? Was willst du/wollt ihr/wollen Sie damit
sagen? say sorry to sb entschuldigen [ɛntˈʃʊldɪɡn̩]
<entschuldigt sich, entschuldigte sich, hat sich entschul-
digt> say sorry to sb (for sth) sich bei jdm (für
etw.) entschuldigen **2.** *(clock)* zeigen [ˈtsaɛ̯ɡn̩]
+haben ◊ *Die Uhr zeigt fünf vor acht.* **3.** *(sth is
written somewhere)* in/on sth it says in/auf etw. [dat]
steht [ɪn/aɔ̯f ... ʃteːt] <steht, stand, hat gestanden> ◊
In ihrem Brief steht, dass sie nächste Woche kommt.
♦ *Auf dem Schild steht: „Betreten verboten".;* *(rule)*
besagen [bəˈzaːɡn̩] <besagt, besagte, hat besagt> ◊
*Die Regeln besagen, dass der Spieler mit der
höchsten Punktzahl gewinnt.* **4.** *(reveal)* aussagen
[ˈaɔ̯szaːɡn̩] +haben ◊ *Eine Wohnung sagt viel über
ihre Bewohner aus.* sth says a lot about how etw.
sagt viel darüber aus, wie **5.** *(a prayer)* sprechen
[ˈʃprɛçn̩] <spricht, sprach, hat gesprochen> *(lofty)* ◊
ein Gebet sprechen
☞ sb/sth is said to do sth jd/etw. soll etw. tun ◊
Er soll sie wegen ihres Geldes geheiratet haben.
(let's) say sagen wir mal having said that, that
said andererseits it is said (that) ... es heißt, ...
that's not saying much das will nicht viel heißen
there's no saying es lässt sich nicht vorhersagen
not to say um nicht zu sagen

saying [noun] Sprichwort [ˈʃprɪçvɔˈt] das
<–(e)s, Sprichwörter> as the saying goes wie schon
das Sprichwort sagt

scab [noun] **1.** *(on a wound)* Schorf [ʃɔˈf] der <–(e)s>
no pl ◊ *Auf der Wunde hatte sich Schorf gebildet.*
2. *(sb working during a strike)* Streikbrecher
[ˈʃtraɛ̯kbrɛçɐ] der <–s, –> ♀Streikbrecherin
[ˈʃtraɛ̯kbrɛçərɪn] die <–, –nen>

scaffolding [noun] Gerüst [ɡəˈrʏst] das <–(e)s, –e> ◊
ein Gerüst aufbauen

scald [verb] **1.** *(with hot liquid)* verbrühen [fɐˈbryːən]
<verbrüht, verbrühte, hat verbrüht> +haben ◊ *Er hat
sich beim Kochen verbrüht.* **2.** *(milk)* erhitzen
[ɛˈhɪtsn̩] <erhitzt, erhitzte, hat erhitzt> ◊ *Erhitzen Sie
die Milch und geben Sie Honig hinein.*

scale¹ [noun] **1.** *(dimension, extent)* Ausmaß [ˈaɔ̯smaːs]
das <–es, –e> ◊ *das Ausmaß einer Katastrophe* the
full scale of sth das ganze Ausmaß ... [gen] on a
grand scale im großen Stil [ɪm ɡroːsn̩ ˈʃtiːl] on a
small/large scale in kleinem/großem Umfang
[ɪn ˌklaɛ̯nəm/ˌɡroːsəm ˈʊmfaŋ] scale of production
Produktionsumfang [prodʊkˈtsi̯oːns|ʊmfaŋ] **2.** *(range,
hierarchy)* Skala [ˈskaːlaː] die <–, Skalen> most sing

◊ *einen Wert auf der Skala zwischen eins und zehn angeben* salary scale Gehaltsskala [gə'halts,skaːlaː] social scale soziale Leiter [zo,tsiaːlə 'laete] die <−> *most sing* **3.** *(ratio)* Maßstab ['maːsʃtaːp] der <−(e)s, Maßstäbe> *a map with a scale of* 1 : 50 000 eine Karte im Maßstab 1 : 50 000 to scale maßstabsgetreu ['maːsʃtaːpsgətrɔy] *no comp/superl* scale model maßstabsgetreues Modell **4.** *(for weighing)* scales Waage ['vaːgə] die <−, −n> **5.** *(limescale)* Kalk [kalk] der <−(e)s> *no pl* **6.** *(on a fish, reptile)* Schuppe ['ʃʊpə] die <−, −n> **7.** *(in music)* Tonleiter ['toːnlaete] die <−, −n> ◊ *Tonleitern üben* ⓢ **the scales fall from sb's eyes** es fällt jdm wie Schuppen von den Augen

scale² [verb] **1.** *(climb)* besteigen [bə'ʃtaeɡ̊n] <besteigt, bestieg, hat bestiegen> ◊ *einen Berg besteigen; (climb to the top of sth)* scale sth auf etw. [acc] klettern [aof ... klɛtɐn] *+sein* ◊ *auf eine Mauer klettern; (climb over sth)* scale sth über etw. [acc] klettern [yːbe ... klɛtɐn] *+sein* ◊ *über einen Zaun klettern* **2.** *(a fish)* schuppen ['ʃʊpm̩] *+haben* ◊ *Den Fisch schuppen und ausnehmen.*

• **scale back** [phras v] verringern [fe'rɪŋɐn] <verringert, verringerte, hat verringert> ◊ *Die NATO verringert ihre Truppen auf dem Balkan.*
• **scale down** [phras v] → scale back
• **scale up** [phras v] **1.** *(an image)* vergrößern [fe'grøːsɐn] <vergrößert, vergrößerte, hat vergrößert> ◊ *ein Foto vergrößern* **2.** *(production, performance)* erweitern [ɛ'vaetɐn] <erweitert, erweiterte, hat erweitert> ◊ *Wir wollen unsere Inlandsproduktion erweitern.* ♦ *die Speicherkapazität eines PCs erweitern*

scan¹ [noun] **1.** *(medical test)* ultrasound scan Ultraschalluntersuchung ['ʊltraʃalˌʊnteˌzuːxʊŋ] die <−, −en> CT scan Computertomographie [kɔmˈpjuːtetomograˌfiː] die <−, −n> **2.** *(quick look)* Überfliegen [ybe'fliːgŋ̍] das <−s> *no pl* ◊ *Beim Überfliegen deines Aufsatzes ist mir etwas aufgefallen.*

scan² [verb] **1.** *(look carefully)* studieren [ʃtuˈdiːrən] <studiert, studierte, hat studiert> ◊ *ein Gesicht studieren* scan sth for etw. nach etw. absuchen [naːx ... ,apzuːxn̩] *+haben* ◊ *Er suchte den Himmel nach Flugzeugen ab.* **2.** IT, MED scan for sth nach etw. suchen [naːx ... ,zuːxn̩] *+haben* ◊ *Das Programm sucht nach Viren.* scan sth (for sth) etw. (auf etw. [acc]) untersuchen [ʊnteˈzuːxn̩] <untersucht, untersuchte, hat untersucht> ◊ *Dateien auf Viren untersuchen; (using ultrasound)* mit Ultraschall untersuchen [mɪt 'ʊltraʃal ʊnteˌzuːxn̩]; *(X-ray)* durchleuchten [dʊˈçˈlɔøçtn̩] <durchleuchtet, durchleuchtete, hat durchleuchtet> ◊ *Seine Brust wurde durchleuchtet.* **3.** *(monitor)* überwachen [ybeˈvaxn] <überwacht, überwachte, hat überwacht> ◊ *Die Straße wird von Videokameras überwacht.* **4.** *(look quickly)* scan sth etw. überfliegen [ybeˈfliːgŋ̍] <überfliegt, überflog, hat überflogen> ◊ *Beim Frühstück überflog er die Zeitung.* scan sth for sth etw. auf der Suche nach etw. überfliegen **5.** IT *(make a digital copy)* scannen ['skɛnən] *+haben* ◊ *ein Bild scannen* scan sth in, scan sth into your computer etw. einscannen ['aenskɛnən] *+haben*

scandal [noun] Skandal [skanˈdaːl] der <−s, −e> ◊ *Es ist ein Skandal, wie hier Gelder verschwendet werden.*

scandalous(ly) [adj, adv] skandalös [skandaˈløːs]

<skandalöser, am skandalösesten> *(pej)* ◊ *ein skandalöses Buch* ♦ *Es ist skandalös, wie man hier behandelt wird!* ♦ *sich skandalös verhalten*

Scandinavia [noun] Skandinavien [skandiˈnaːvjən] das <−s> *article only in combination with attribute, no pl* → **Germany**

Scandinavian¹ [noun] Skandinavier [skandiˈnaːvjɐ] der <−s, −> ♀Skandinavierin [skandiˈnaːvjərɪn] die <−, −nen> → **German¹ 1.**

Scandinavian² [adj] skandinavisch [skandiˈnaːvɪʃ] *mostly before ns* ◊ *skandinavische Sprachen*

scar¹ [noun] Narbe ['naˈbə] die <−, −n> ◊ *eine Narbe im Gesicht haben* ♦ *die Narben des Krieges*

scar² [verb] **1.** *(a person)* scar sb bei jdm Narben hinterlassen [bae ... 'naˈbm̩ hɪnteˌlasn̩] <hinterlässt, hinterließ, hat hinterlassen> scar sb emotionally bei jdm seelische Narben hinterlassen be scarred Narben davontragen ['naˈbm̩ daˌfɔntraːgn̩] <trägt davon, trug davon, hat davongetragen> ◊ *scar sb for life* jdn fürs Leben zeichnen [fyːɐ̯s 'leːbm̩ ˌtsaeçnən] *+haben* **2.** *(an area, landscape etc.)* verunstalten [feˈʔʊnʃtaltn̩] <verunstaltet, verunstaltete, hat verunstaltet>

scarce [adj] **1.** *(seldom to be found)* rar [raːˈ] ◊ *Gutes Personal ist rar.* ♦ *In der Wüste ist Wasser ein rares Gut.* **2.** *(barely adequate)* knapp [knap] ◊ *knappe Rohstoffe* ♦ *Unsere Essensvorräte wurden knapp.*

scarcely [adv] *(hardly, very few)* kaum [kaom] ◊ *Sie kann es kaum erwarten, in Urlaub zu fahren.* ♦ *Früher gab es kaum Frauen in der Politik.*

scare¹ [noun] **1.** *(sudden fright)* Schreck [ʃrɛk] der <−(e)s> *no pl* give sb a scare jdm einen Schreck einjagen have a scare einen Schreck bekommen **2.** *(in compound ns)* ... scare Panik vor ... [dat] ['paːnɪk foːɐ̯] die <−> *no pl* anthrax scare Panik vor Anschlägen mit Milzbranderregern BSE scare Panik vor BSE bomb scare Bombendrohung ['bɔmbm̩droːʊŋ] die <−, −en> food scare Lebensmittelskandal ['leːbm̩smɪtl̩skanˌdaːl] der <−s, −e> scare tactics Panikmache ['paːnɪkmaxə] die <−> *no pl*

scare² [verb] **1.** *(give a sudden fright to)* erschrecken [ɛ'ʃrɛkn̩] <erschreckt, erschreckte, hat erschreckt> ◊ *Ich hoffe, ich habe dich nicht erschreckt.* ♦ *Der Donner hat das Pferd erschreckt.* scare the life out of sb, scare sb to death jdn zu Tode erschrecken; *(make anxious, worried)* verängstigen [feˈʔɛŋstɪgn̩] <verängstigt, verängstigte, hat verängstigt> ◊ *Die Erlebnisse haben die Kinder völlig verängstigt.* **2.** *(become frightened)* sb/an animal scares jd/ein Tier erschrickt [ɛ'ʃrɪkt] <erschrak, ist erschrocken> ◊ *Erschrick nicht — ich bin's nur!*

• **scare away** [phras v] **1.** *(from a place)* verscheuchen [fe'ʃɔøçn̩] <verscheucht, verscheuchte, hat verscheucht> ◊ *Die Katze hat die Vögel verscheucht.* **2.** *(from doing sth)* abschrecken ['apʃrɛkn̩] *+haben* ◊ *Die Gefahr eines Bombenanschlags schreckt mich nicht ab.*
• **scare into** [phras v] scare sb/sth into (doing) sth jdn/etw. so ängstigen, dass er/es etw. tut [,zoː 'ɛŋstɪgn̩ das] *+haben* ◊ *Die Geschichten ängstigten sie so, dass sie sich einen Hund anschaffte.*
• **scare off** [phras v] → scare away

scared → scare² [adj] verängstigt [feˈʔɛŋstɪçt] *seldom comp/no superl* ◊ *ein verängstigtes Kind* be scared (of sb/sth) (vor jdm/etw.) Angst haben ['aŋst haːbm̩] *+haben* ◊ *Du brauchst keine Angst zu haben!* ♦ *Hast du Angst vor Hunden?* get scared

A

scarf [noun] *(long, rectangular)* Schal [ʃaːl] der <–s, –s *or* –e> ◊ *Es ist kalt draußen; du solltest dir einen Schal umbinden.*; *(square, triangular)* Tuch [tuːx] das <–(e)s, Tücher> ◊ *die Haare mit einem Tuch verhüllen*

B

C

scary [adj] gruselig ['gruːzəlɪç] ◊ *Ich hatte einen gruseligen Traum.* ♦ *Der Film ist ziemlich gruselig.*

D

scathing(ly) [adj, adv] *(remark, person)* bissig ['bɪsɪç] ◊ *eine bissige Bemerkung machen* ♦ *Sie wird leicht bissig.* ♦ *„Du kommst ja schon wieder zu spät!",* *sagte sie bissig.; (attack, report, criticism)* schonungslos ['ʃoːnʊŋsloːs] <schonungsloser, am schonungslosesten> ◊ *ein schonungsloser Angriff auf die Presse* ♦ *Der Bericht war schonungslos.* ♦ *jdn schonungslos kritisieren*

E

F

G

H

scatter [verb] **1.** *(sprinkle)* streuen ['ʃtrɔɡən] +haben ◊ *Salz auf den Gehweg streuen; (spread)* verstreuen [fɛˈʃtrɔɡən] <verstreut, verstreute, hat verstreut> ◊ *Max hat seine Legosteine im ganzen Haus verstreut.* **2.** *(disperse)* scatter sth etw. zerstreuen [tseˈʃtrɔɡən] <zerstreut, zerstreute, hat zerstreut> ◊ *Das Militär zerstreute die Menge mit Warnschüssen.* They scatter. Sie zerstreuten sich.; *(in fright)* auseinander stieben [aʊsˌaɛˈnandɐ ʃtiːbm̩] <stieben auseinander, stoben auseinander, sind auseinander gestoben> ◊ *Die Vögel stoben erschrocken auseinander.*

I

J

K

L

M

scattered → scatter [adj] **1.** *(spread over a wide area)* verstreut [fɛˈʃtrɔɡt] no comp/superl ◊ *die verstreuten Sachen einsammeln* ♦ *Die Inseln des Archipels sind weit verstreut.* **2.** *(few in number)* vereinzelt [fɛˈʔaɛntsl̩t] no comp/superl, only before ns ◊ *In dieser Gegend wachsen nur ein paar vereinzelte Bäume.* ♦ *vereinzelte Regenfälle*

N

O

scenario [noun] Szenario [stseˈnaːrjoː] das <–s, Szenarien> ◊ *Es wäre auch ein anderes Szenario denkbar.*

P

Q

R

S

scene [noun] **1.** *(part of a film, play etc., incident, trendy social group)* Szene ['stseːnə] die <–, –n> ◊ *In der letzten Szene stirbt der Held.* ♦ *Szenen des täglichen Lebens* ♦ *Als sie davon erfuhr, kam es zu einer hässlichen Szene.* ♦ *die literarische Szene in Berlin* cause a scene eine Szene machen **2.** *(view)* Anblick ['anblɪk] der <–(e)s, –e> ◊ *Das war kein schöner Anblick!* **3.** *(place, location)* scene *(of sth)* Schauplatz (… [gen]) ['ʃaʊplats] der <–es, Schauplätze> ◊ *Die Schule wurde Schauplatz einer Katastrophe.* scene of the crime Tatort ['taːtˌʔɔrt] der <–(e)s, –e> scene of the accident Unfallstelle ['ʊnfalˌʃtɛlə] die <–, –n> ⊛ be on the scene am Tatort sein behind the scenes hinter den Kulissen come on the scene auf der Bildfläche erscheinen set the scene for sb jdn ins Bild setzen set the scene for sth die Voraussetzungen für etw. schaffen not sb's scene nicht jds Fall ◊ *Hip-Hop ist nicht mein Fall.*

T

U

V

W

X

Y

Z

scenery [noun] **1.** *(view, landscape)* Landschaft ['lantʃaft] die <–, –en> ◊ *Die Landschaft dort ist wunderschön.* **2.** *(in a theatre)* Bühnenbild ['byːnənbɪlt] das <–(e)s, –er>

scent [noun] **1.** *(smell)* Geruch [gəˈrʊx] der <–(e)s, Gerüche> ◊ *Ich mag den Geruch von Kaffee und frischem Brot.; (pleasant)* Duft [dʊft] der <–(e)s, Düfte> ◊ *der Duft der Rosen in unserem*

Garten; (smell perceptible to or left by an animal) Witterung ['vɪtərʊŋ] die <–, –en> *(tech)* pick up a scent Witterung aufnehmen; *(that animals/the police etc. can follow)* Fährte ['fɛːɡtə] die <–, –n> ◊ *Die Hunde folgten seiner Fährte.* be on sb's/an animal's scent jdm/einem Tier auf der Fährte sein ◊ *Die Polizei ist den Entführern auf der Fährte.* throw sb off the scent jdn von der Fährte abbringen **2.** *(liquid perfume)* Parfüm [parˈfyːm] das <–s, –e *or* –s> ◊ *eine Flasche Parfüm* ⊛ there is a scent of sth etw. liegt in der Luft

sceptical(ly) [adj, adv] skeptisch ['skɛptɪʃ] ◊ *eine skeptische Bemerkung machen* ♦ *Bist du immer noch skeptisch?* ♦ *Sie stand seinen Plänen skeptisch gegenüber.* be sceptical about sth Zweifel an etw. [dat] haben ['tsvaɛfl̩ an … haːbm̩] +haben ◊ *Ich habe Zweifel daran, ob das richtig ist.*

scepticism [noun] Skepsis ['skɛpsɪs] die <–> no pl ◊ *etw. voller Skepsis betrachten*

schedule¹ [noun] **1.** *(for when to do things)* Zeitplan ['tsaɛtplaːn] der <–(e)s, Zeitpläne> ◊ *ein enger Zeitplan* ♦ *Lässt unser Zeitplan das zu?* be ahead of schedule dem Zeitplan voraus sein; *(list of things to do)* Programm [proˈgram] das <–(e)s, –e> ◊ *Morgen haben wir schon ein volles Programm.* ♦ *Was steht heute auf unserem Programm?* **2.** *(for trains, buses)* Fahrplan ['faːrplaːn] der <–(e)s, Fahrpläne> ◊ *Laut Fahrplan soll der Zug in zehn Minuten ankommen.* **3.** *(in school)* Stundenplan ['ʃtʊndn̩plaːn] der <–(e)s, Stundenpläne> ◊ *Was steht heute auf dem Stundenplan?* ⊛ do sth ahead of schedule etw. früher als vorgesehen tun behind schedule **1.** *(late)* überfällig ◊ *Das Flugzeug ist überfällig.* **2.** be behind schedule with sth mit etw. im Verzug sein on schedule pünktlich

schedule² [verb] ansetzen ['anzɛtsn̩] +haben ◊ *Er hat für den 1. Juli eine außerordentliche Versammlung angesetzt.* scheduled for sth auf etw. [acc] angesetzt ◊ *Die Prüfung ist auf morgen 14 Uhr angesetzt.* be scheduled to do sth etw. tun sollen ['zɔlən] <soll, sollte, hat sollen> ◊ *Der Bau des Stadions soll am 1. Mai beginnen.*

scheduled → schedule² [adj] planmäßig ['plaːnmɛːsɪç] ◊ *die planmäßige Abfahrt des Zuges* scheduled flight Linienflug ['liːnjənfluːk] der <–(e)s, Linienflüge>

scheme [noun] **1.** *(plan)* Plan [plaːn] der <–(e)s, Pläne> ◊ *der Plan der Regierung, die Mehrwertsteuer zu erhöhen* ♦ *sich einen raffinierten Plan ausdenken* fund raising scheme Finanzierungsplan [finanˈtsiːrʊŋsplaːn] der **2.** *(system)* System [zʏsˈteːm] das <–s, –e> ◊ *Nach welchem System sind die Bücher geordnet?* insurance scheme Versicherungssystem [fɛɐˈzɪçərʊŋszʏsˌteːm]; *(made up of several measures)* Programm [proˈgram] das <–(e)s, –e> ◊ *ein Programm zur Bekämpfung der Arbeitslosigkeit* pension scheme Altersvorsorge ['altɐsfoːɐˌzɔrɡə] die <–, –n> ◊ *die betriebliche/gesetzliche Altersvorsorge* rhyme scheme Reimschema ['raɛmʃeːmaː] das <–s, –ta *or* –s> ⊛ in the greater scheme of things aufs Ganze gesehen sb's scheme of things jds Pläne

schizophrenic [adj] schizophren [ʃitsoˈfreːn] ◊ *eine schizophrene Psychose* ♦ *Er ist schizophren.*

scholar [noun] **1.** *(learned person)* Gelehrte [gəˈleːɡtə]

der/die <–n, die Gelehrten> but: *ein Gelehrter/eine Gelehrte* ◊ *Sein Vater war Gelehrter.* ♦ *Die Gelehrten streiten sich darüber, ob* ... 2. *(student with a scholarship)* Stipendiat [ʃtipɛnˈdiaːt] der <–en, –en> ♀Stipendiatin [ʃtipɛnˈdiaːtɪn] die <–, –nen>

scholarly [adj] gelehrt [ɡəˈleːɐ̯t] <gelehrter, am gelehrtesten> ◊ *einen gelehrten Vortrag halten* ♦ *Unser Professor war sehr gelehrt und vielseitig gebildet.*

scholarship [noun] Stipendium [ʃtiˈpɛndiʊm] das <–s, Stipendien> ◊ *ein Stipendium der Fulbright-Stiftung bekommen*

school¹ [noun] 1. *(place where children are taught, group sharing the same views)* Schule [ˈʃuːlə] die <–, –n> ◊ *in die Schule gehen* ♦ *Wann fängt bei euch morgens die Schule an?* ♦ *ein Anhänger der Freud'schen Schule* start school in die Schule kommen ◊ *In Deutschland kommt man mit sechs in die Schule.* leave school von der Schule abgehen riding school Reitschule [ˈraɛtʃuːlə]; *(in compound ns)* school ... Schul... [ʃuːl] school bus Schulbus [ˈʃuːlbʊs] der <–es, –se> 2. *(university department)* Fakultät [fakʊlˈtɛːt] die <–, –en> business school wirtschaftswissenschaftliche Fakultät law school juristische Fakultät 3. *(university)* Uni [ˈʊni] die <–, –s> *(fam)* 4. *(of fish)* Schwarm [ʃvaˈrm] der <–(e)s, Schwärme>; *(of dolphins)* Schule [ˈʃuːlə] die <–, –n>; *(of whales)* Herde [ˈheːɐ̯də] die <–, –n> ◊ *Eine Herde Wale ist an der Küste gestrandet.*

school² [verb] 1. *(train)* school sb in sth jdn in etw. [dat] schulen [ɪn ... ˈʃuːlən] +haben ◊ *in Rhetorik geschult werden* ♦ *Mitarbeiter in Seminaren schulen*; *(a horse)* zureiten [ˈtsuːraɛtn̩] <reitet zu, ritt zu, hat zugeritten> 2. *(teach a follower or student)* school sb to do sth jdn lehren, etw. zu tun [ˈleːran] +haben ◊ *Sokrates lehrte seine Schüler, sich eine eigene Meinung zu bilden.*; *(a child)* school sb jdn unterrichten [ʊntəˈrɪçtn̩] <unterrichtet, unterrichtete, hat unterrichtet> ◊ *ein Kind zu Hause unterrichten* be schooled somewhere irgendwo zur Schule gehen [tsuːɐ̯ ˈʃuːlə ɡeːən] <geht, ging, ist gegangen>

school leaver [noun] Schulabgänger [ˈʃuːlˌapɡɛŋɐ] der <–s, –> ♀Schulabgängerin [ˈʃuːlˌapɡɛŋərɪn] die <–, –nen> ◊ *die Berufschancen der Schulabgänger*

school holidays [noun] Schulferien [ˈʃuːlfeːriən] die <–> pl

school system [noun] Schulsystem [ˈʃuːlzʏsˌteːm] das <–s, –e>

school year [noun] Schuljahr [ˈʃuːljaːɐ̯] das <–(e)s, –e> ◊ *Was steht für dieses Schuljahr auf dem Lehrplan?*

science [noun] 1. *(biology, chemistry, physics etc.)* Naturwissenschaft [naˈtuːɐ̯vɪsn̩ʃaft] die <–, –en> teach science Naturwissenschaften unterrichten 2. *(scientific knowledge, subject)* Wissenschaft [ˈvɪsn̩ʃaft] die <–, –en> ◊ *Die Informatik ist eine recht junge Wissenschaft.* ♦ *Die Wissenschaft hat darauf noch keine Antwort gefunden.* medical science Medizin [mediˈtsiːn] die <–> no pl veterinary science Tiermedizin [ˈtiːɐ̯mediˌtsiːn]

scientific(ally) [adj, adv] wissenschaftlich [ˈvɪsn̩ʃaftlɪç] ◊ *die wissenschaftliche Forschung* ♦ *Diese Methode kann man kaum als wissenschaftlich bezeichnen.* ♦ *wissenschaftlich bewiesene Ergebnisse*

scientist [noun] *(sb trained in science)* Wissenschaftler [ˈvɪsn̩ʃaftlɐ] der <–s, –> ♀Wissenschaftlerin [ˈvɪsn̩ʃaftlərɪn] die <–, –nen> ◊ *Er will Wissenschaft-*

ler werden. ♦ *eine junge Wissenschaftlerin*; *(researcher)* Forscher [ˈfɔʁʃɐ] der <–s, –> ♀Forscherin [ˈfɔʁʃərɪn] die <–, –nen>

scissors [noun] Schere [ˈʃeːrə] die <–, –n> ◊ *eine spitze Schere* ♦ *sich* [dat] *die Fingernägel mit der Schere schneiden* a pair of scissors eine Schere

scoop [verb] *(with your hands, a ladle)* schöpfen [ˈʃœpfn̩] +haben ◊ *Er schöpfte mit den Händen Wasser aus dem Bach.*; *(with a spoon)* löffeln [ˈlœfl̩n] +haben ◊ *Honig aus dem Glas löffeln* scoop sth out etw. auslöffeln [ˈaʊslœfl̩n] +haben ◊ *Sie löffelte eine Kiwi aus.*

scooter [noun] Roller [ˈrɔlɐ] der <–s, –> ◊ *Das Kind bekam einen Roller geschenkt.* ♦ *Ute kam mit dem Roller.*; *(motor scooter)* Motorroller [ˈmoːtoːʁrɔlɐ] der <–s, –> ◊ *Der Motorroller fährt maximal 60 Stundenkilometer.*

scope [noun] 1. *(range, spectrum)* Rahmen [ˈraːmən] der <–s, –> ◊ *im Rahmen meiner dienstlichen Pflichten* be beyond the scope of sth den Rahmen ... [gen] sprengen sth is within the scope of sb/sth jd/etw. ist für etw. zuständig [ɪst fyːɐ̯ ... ˌtsuːˈʃtɛndɪç] be limited in scope to sth auf etw. [acc] beschränkt sein [aʊf ... bəˈʃrɛŋkt zaɛn] 2. *(of possibilities)* Spielraum [ˈʃpiːlraʊm] der <–(e)s, Spielräume> ◊ *der Fantasie wenig Spielraum lassen* ♦ *Sie haben viel Spielraum für eigene Ideen.*
ⓢ give sth free scope einer Sache [dat] freien Lauf lassen

score¹ [noun] 1. *(before the end of sth)* Stand [ʃtant] der <–es, Stände> ◊ *Der Stand zum Ende der ersten Halbzeit ist zwei zu null.* ♦ *der aktuelle Stand* What is the score? Wie steht es? What's the score on tomorrow? Are you coming? Wie ist der Stand der Dinge? Kommst du morgen?; *(at the end of sth)* Ergebnis [ɛˈɡeːpnɪs] das <–ses, –se> ◊ *die Ergebnisse des heutigen Spieltags* ♦ *bei einer Prüfung ein gutes Ergebnis erzielen*; *(in gymnastics, dancing etc.)* Note [ˈnoːtə] die <–, –n> ◊ *von allen Preisrichtern gute Noten bekommen* 2. mus Partitur [paʁtiˈtuːɐ̯] die <–, –en>; *(of a movie)* Filmmusik [ˈfɪlmmuˌziːk] die <–, –en> *most sing* 3. scores of ... jede Menge ... [ˈjeːdə ˈmɛŋə] *(fam)* jede Menge Fehler machen scores of times x-mal [ˈɪksmaːl] ◊ *Ich habe das schon x-mal gehört.* 4. *(cut, mark)* Kerbe [ˈkɛʁbə] die <–, –n> ◊ *eine Kerbe in einen Stock schnitzen*
ⓢ know the score Bescheid wissen settle an old score eine alte Rechnung begleichen on that score in dieser Hinsicht

score² [verb] 1. *(a point, grade, mark)* erzielen [ɛˈtsiːlən] <erzielt, erzielte, hat erzielt> ◊ *einen Sieg erzielen* ♦ *Er erzielte fünf Treffer für seine Mannschaft.* ♦ *In der Prüfung hat sie ein gutes Ergebnis erzielt.*; *(in soccer)* score (a goal) ein Tor schießen [aɛn ˈtoːɐ̯ ˈʃiːsn̩] <schießt, schoss, hat geschossen> ◊ *Endlich schoss er ein Tor.* 2. *(score points, be successful)* punkten [ˈpʊŋktn̩] <punktet, punktete, hat gepunktet> ◊ *Sie konnten in diesem Spiel nicht punkten.* ♦ *Mit so einem Verhalten kannst du bei mir nicht punkten.* 3. *(evaluate, give a score to)* bewerten [bəˈveːɐ̯tn̩] <bewertet, bewertete, hat bewertet> ◊ *Wer bewertet die Antworten?* 4. *(be worth)* zählen [ˈtsɛːlən] +haben ◊ *Jede richtige Antwort zählt fünf Punkte.* 5. *(write down points)* aufschreiben [ˈaʊfʃraɛbm̩] <schreibt auf, schrieb auf, hat aufgeschrieben> ◊ *Hast du meine Punkte aufgeschrieben?* ♦ *Wer schreibt auf?* 6. *(slang)* *(persuade sb to*

A
B
C
D
E
F
G
H
I
J
K
L
M
N
O
P
Q
R
S
T
U
V
W
X
Y
Z

have sex) score with sb jdn aufs Kreuz legen [aʊfs 'krɔ̯ɡʦ le:gn̩] +haben (slang) 7. (cut) einkerben ['aɛnkɛrbm̩] +haben 8. mus setzen ['zɛʦn̩] +haben ◊ *Das Lied ist dreistimmig gesetzt.*

scorn [noun] Verachtung [fɛ|'axtʊŋ] die <–> no pl ◊ *Sie lachte voller Verachtung.* pour scorn on sb jdn verächtlich behandeln [fɛ|ˌɛçtlɪç bə'hand|n̩] <behandeln, behandelte, hat behandelt> pour scorn on sth etw. verächtlich abtun [fɛ|ˌɛçtlɪç 'aptuːn] <tut ab, tat ab, hat abgetan>

scornful(ly) [adj, adv] verächtlich [fɛ|'ɛçtlɪç] when used as an adj, mostly before ns ◊ *Seine verächtlichen Worte verletzten mich.* ◆ *Sie grinste verächtlich.* be scornful of sth/sb etw./jdn verachten [fɛ|'axtn̩] <verachtet, verachtete, hat verachtet>

Scorpio [noun] Skorpion [skɔr'pi̯oːn] der <–s, –e>

Scot [noun] Schotte ['ʃɔtə] der <–n, –n> ♀Schottin ['ʃɔtɪn] die <–, –nen> → **German¹** 1.

Scotland [noun] Schottland ['ʃɔtlant] das <–s> article only in combination with attribute, no pl → **Germany**

Scottish [adj] schottisch ['ʃɔtɪʃ] → **German²**

scour [verb] 1. (search) scour sth for sth etw. nach etw. durchforsten [na:x ... dʊrç,fɔrstn̩] <durchforstet, durchforstete, hat durchforstet> ◊ *Bücher nach Informationen durchforsten* 2. (scrub clean) scheuern ['ʃɔ̯ɐn] +haben ◊ *Töpfe und Pfannen scheuern*

scourge [noun] 1. (whip, sth very damaging) scourge (of sb/sth) Geißel (... [gen] ['gaɛsl] die <–, –n> (lofty) ◊ *Krebs ist eine Geißel der Menschheit.* 2. (sth annoying) Plage ['pla:gə] die <–, –n> ◊ *Handys haben sich zu einer wahren Plage entwickelt.* 3. (powerful person that others are afraid of) the scourge of ... der Schrecken ... [gen] [de:ɐ 'ʃrɛkn̩] <–s, –> ◊ *Störtebeker, der Schrecken der Meere*

scramble [verb] 1. (climb) klettern ['klɛtɐn] +sein ◊ *auf einen Berg klettern; (crawl) kriechen ['kri:çn̩] <kriecht, kroch, ist gekrochen> ◊ durch ein Loch im Zaun kriechen* 2. (rush) stolpern ['ʃtɔlpɐn] +sein ◊ *Sie stolperten aus dem brennenden Haus.* scramble to your feet sich hochrappeln ['ho:xrap|n̩] +haben scramble into your clothes hastig in seine Kleider schlüpfen [hastɪç ɪn zaɛnə 'klaɛdə ʃlʏpfn̩] +sein 3. (compete) scramble for sth sich um etw. streiten [ʊm ... 'ʃtraɛtn̩] <streitet sich, stritt sich, hat sich gestritten> ◊ *Die Spatzen stritten sich um die Krümel.; (struggle) scramble to do sth sich abmühen, etw. zu tun ['apmy:ən ... tsu:] +haben ◊ Sie mühten sich sehr ab, den Auftrag termingerecht zu erledigen.* 4. (eggs) verrühren [fɛ|'ry:rən] <verrührt, verrührte, hat verrührt> scrambled eggs Rührei ['ry:g|aɛ] die <–> pl 5. (a message) verschlüsseln [fɛ|'ʃlʏsln̩] <verschlüsselt, verschlüsselte, hat verschlüsselt>

scrap¹ [noun] 1. (piece of paper or cloth) Stückchen ['ʃtʏkçən] das <–s, –> ◊ *sich [dat] etw. auf einem Stückchen Papier aufschreiben* 2. (of a conversation) Fetzen ['fɛʦn̩] der <–s, –> ◊ *Fetzen einer Unterhaltung mit anhören* 3. (of information, knowledge) Bruchstück ['brʊxʃtʏk] das <–(e)s, –e>; (of a language) scraps Brocken ['brɔkn̩] die <–> pl ◊ *Ich kann nur ein paar Brocken Spanisch.; (small amount of sth)* bisschen ['bɪsçən] the few scraps das bisschen ◊ *das bisschen Wissen, das jd hat* every scrap of sth jedes bisschen sth ◊ *Jedes bisschen Information muss überprüft werden.* 4. (food leftovers) scraps Reste ['rɛstə] die <–> ◊ *die Reste*

an die Schweine verfüttern 5. (metal) Schrott [ʃrɔt] der <–(e)s> no pl ◊ *mit Schrott handeln; (paper)* Altpapier ['altpa,pi:ɐ] das <–(e)s> no pl ◊ *etw. zum Altpapier geben; (in compound ns) scrap ... ...abfälle ['apfɛlə] die <–> pl scrap wood Holzabfälle ['hɔlʦ|apfɛlə] ® sell sth for scrap (machinery) etw. verschrotten (furniture) etw. ausrangieren*

scrap² [verb] 1. (a plan, an idea) verwerfen [fɛ'vɛrfn̩] <verwirft, verwarf, hat verworfen> ◊ *Der Plan wurde schließlich verworfen.; (a planned activity)* abblasen ['apbla:zn̩] <bläst ab, blies ab, hat abgeblasen> (fam) ◊ *Das Konzert musste abgeblasen werden.; (get rid of)* über Bord werfen [y:bɐ 'bɔrt vɛrfn̩] <wirft, warf, hat geworfen> ◊ *alte Traditionen über Bord werfen* 2. (a machine, car) verschrotten [fɛ'ʃrɔtn̩] <verschrottet, verschrottete, hat verschrottet> 3. (fight) sich streiten ['ʃtraɛtn̩] <streitet sich, stritt sich, hat sich gestritten> ◊ *Die Kinder stritten sich ständig.*

scrape [verb] 1. (rub the surface of sth) scrape sth (off/away) etw. abkratzen ['apkraʦn̩] +haben ◊ *den Lack abkratzen scrape sth off sth etw. von etw. kratzen [fɔn ... kraʦn̩] +haben ◊ Er kratzte die Reste vom Teller in den Mülleimer.; (vegetables) scrape sth etw. schaben ['ʃa:bm̩] +haben* 2. (touch lightly) scrape (against) sth etw. streifen ['ʃtraɛfn̩] +haben ◊ *Das Auto streifte die Mauer. scrape sth across sth mit etw. über etw. [acc] streifen; (drag along) sth scrapes somewhere etw. schleift irgendwo [ʃlaɛft] +haben ◊ Die Tür schleift am Boden.* 3. (damage, injure) scrape (at) sth etw. zerkratzen ['tse'kraʦn̩] <zerkratzt, zerkratzte, hat zerkratzt> ◊ *den Kotflügel zerkratzen ◆ Die Dornen zerkratzten ihr die Beine. scrape your knee/elbow etc. sich [dat] das Knie/den Ellbogen etc. aufschürfen [das 'kni:/de:n 'ɛlanbo:gn̩] ,aʊfʃʏrfn̩ +haben* 4. (make a loud noise: brakes, chair, chalk etc.) sth scrapes etw. quietscht [kvi:tʃt] +haben ◊ *Die Kreide quietschte über die Tafel.*

• **scrape by** [phras v] sich durchschlagen ['dʊrçʃla:gn̩] <schlägt sich durch, schlug sich durch, hat sich durchgeschlagen> ◊ *Er kann sich mit der kleinen Rente gerade durchschlagen.*

• **scrape into** [phras v] scrape into sth es gerade noch in ... [acc] schaffen [ɛs gara:də nɔx ɪn ... ʃafn̩] +haben ◊ *Sie haben es gerade noch in die zweite Runde geschafft.*

• **scrape through** [phras v] es mit Mühe und Not schaffen [ɛs mɪt , my:ə ʊnt 'no:t ʃafn̩] +haben (fam) ◊ *Er hat es mit Mühe und Not geschafft. scrape through sth etw. mit Mühe und Not schaffen ◊ Sie schaffte die Prüfung mit Mühe und Not.*

• **scrape together** [phras v] zusammenkratzen [ʦu'zamənkraʦn̩] +haben (fam) ◊ *Ich konnte nicht genügend Geld zusammenkratzen.*

scratch¹ [noun] 1. (cut, minor damage) Schramme ['ʃramə] die <–, –> ◊ *Das Kind hatte eine blutige Schramme am Knie.* ◆ *Das Auto hatte nur eine Schramme abbekommen.* 2. (rub the skin with your nails) have a scratch sich kratzen ['kraʦn̩] +haben give sb/an animal a scratch jdn/ein Tier kratzen 3. (scratching noise) Kratzen ['kraʦn̩] das <–s> no pl ◊ *Sie hörten ein Kratzen an der Tür.* ® be up to scratch gut genug sein bring sb/sth up to scratch jdn/etw. auf Vordermann bringen (fam) learn sth from scratch (learn from the

beginning) etw. von Grund auf lernen *(a trade)* etw. von der Pike auf lernen **start from scratch** ganz von vorn anfangen

scratch² ⟨verb⟩ **1.** *(pull your nails or claws along, hurt)* kratzen ['kratsn] +haben ◊ *jdm den Rücken kratzen* ♦ *Der Hund kratzt an der Tür.* ♦ *sich an der Nase kratzen* ♦ *Die Katze hat mich gekratzt.; (lovingly)* kraulen ['kraolən] +haben ◊ *einen Hund am Bauch kraulen* **scratch sb's eyes out** jdm die Augen auskratzen [dɪ: 'aoŋ ,aoskratsn] +haben **scratch the surface of sth** etw. streifen ['straefn] +haben ◊ *ein Thema nur streifen* **2.** *(damage or hurt slightly)* zerkratzen [tse'kratsn] <zerkratzt, zerkratzte, hat zerkratzt> ◊ *Er hat mit einem Nagel mein Auto zerkratzt.* **3.** *(delete, cancel)* streichen ['straeçn] <streicht, strich, hat gestrichen> ◊ *Der letzte Absatz wurde gestrichen.; (from a race)* **scratch sb from sth** jdn aus etw. nehmen [aos ... 'ne:mən] <nimmt, nahm, hat genommen> ◊ *Er wurde wegen einer Verletzung aus dem Rennen genommen.* **4.** *(scribble)* kritzeln ['krɪtsln] +haben ◊ *Er kritzelte mir eine Notiz auf ein Stück Papier.*

scrawl ⟨verb⟩ kritzeln ['krɪtsln] +haben ◊ *schnell eine Notiz auf einen Fetzen Papier kritzeln*

scream¹ ⟨noun⟩ **1.** *(of a person, an animal)* Schrei [ʃrae] der <-(e)s, -e> ◊ *die Schreie spielender Kinder* **let out a scream** schreien ['ʃraeən] <schreit, schrie, hat geschrien> **scream of pain** Schmerzensschrei ['ʃmɛʳtsnsʃrae] **scream of terror** Angstschrei ['aŋstʃrae] **screams of laughter** lautes Gelächter [laotəs gə'lɛçtɐ] <-s> *no pl* **2.** *(loud noise: of brakes etc.)* Kreischen ['kraeʃn] das <-s> *no pl; (of a siren)* Heulen ['hɔølən] das <-s> *no pl; (of tyres)* Quietschen ['kvi:tʃn] das <-s> *no pl*

ⓔ **be a scream** ein Brüller sein *(fam)*

scream² ⟨verb⟩ **1.** *(cry, shout)* schreien ['ʃraeən] <schreit, schrie, hat geschrien> ◊ *Man hörte ein Baby schreien.* ♦ *Sie schrie: „Vorsicht!"* **scream with pain/fear** vor Schmerz/Angst schreien **scream for sb/sth** nach jdm/etw. schreien ◊ *Das Kind schrie nach seiner Mutter.* **scream for help** um Hilfe schreien **scream (out) at sb** jdn anschreien ['anʃraeən] +haben ◊ *Schrei mich nicht so an!* **scream sth out** etw. hinausschreien [hɪ'naosʃraeən] +haben ◊ *Sie schrie ihre Wut hinaus.* **sb screams out** jd schreit auf [ʃraet 'aof] +haben ◊ *Er schrie vor Schmerzen auf.* **2.** *(make a loud noise: brakes etc.)* kreischen ['kraeʃn] +haben; *(siren, engine)* heulen ['hɔølən] +haben; *(tyres)* quietschen ['kvi:tʃn] +haben

screen¹ ⟨noun⟩ **1.** *(of a computer, TV)* Bildschirm ['bɪltʃɪʳm] der <-(e)s, -e> ◊ *Er starrte auf den Bildschirm.* **2.** *(for the projection of slides or films)* Leinwand ['laenvant] die <-, Leinwände> ◊ *Die Dias werden auf eine Leinwand projiziert.* **3.** *(partition)* Wandschirm ['vantʃɪʳm] der <-(e)s, -e> ◊ *Das Bett stand hinter einem Wandschirm.* **4.** *(protection)* Schutz [ʃʊts] der <-es> *no pl* **behind the screen of** sth im Schutz ... ⟨gen⟩ ◊ *sich im Schutz der Bäume anschleichen* **provide a screen for sb** jdm Schutz bieten **5.** *(to keep out insects)* Fliegengitter ['fli:ŋgɪtɐ] das <-s, ->

ⓔ **come to the screen** in die Kinos kommen

screen² ⟨verb⟩ **1.** MED **screen sb (for sth)** jdn (auf etw. ⟨acc⟩) untersuchen ['ʊntə'zu:xn] <untersucht, untersuchte, hat untersucht> ◊ *Männer und Frauen über 45 auf Darmkrebs untersuchen* **2.** *(broadcast)*

senden ['zɛndn̩] <sendet, sendete, hat gesendet> ◊ *einen Exklusivbericht senden; (show in a cinema)* zeigen ['tsaeŋ] +haben **3.** *(shield, protect)* **screen sth from** sth etw. vor etw. ⟨dat⟩ abschirmen ['apʃɪʳmən] +haben ◊ *Polizisten schirmten die Unfallstelle vor Neugierigen ab.* **4.** *(candidates, applicants, locations etc.)* prüfen ['pry:fn] +haben ◊ *Wir haben alle möglichen Standorte auf ihre Eignung hin geprüft.*

screening ⟨noun⟩ **1.** MED Untersuchung ['ʊntə'zu:xʊŋ] die <-, -en> ◊ *eine Untersuchung auf Brustkrebs* **mass screening** Reihenuntersuchung ['raeən'ʊntə,zu:xʊŋ] **2.** *(broadcast)* Sendung ['zɛndʊŋ] die <-, -en>; *(of a film, movie)* Vorführung ['fo:ɐfy:rʊŋ] die <-, -en> **3.** *(of applicants, candidates)* Prüfung ['pry:fʊŋ] die <-> *no pl* ◊ *die Prüfung möglicher Kandidaten*

screw¹ ⟨noun⟩ TECHN *(metal)* Schraube ['ʃraobə] die <-, -n> ◊ *Er befestigte das Brett mit Schrauben an der Wand.* ♦ *Die Schraube sitzt sehr fest.*

ⓔ **sb has a screw loose** bei jdm ist eine Schraube locker *(fam)* **put the screws on sb** jdm Daumenschrauben anlegen

screw² ⟨verb⟩ **1.** *(turn, fix)* schrauben ['ʃraobn] +haben ◊ *ein Namensschild an die Tür schrauben* ♦ *eine Glühbirne in die Lampe schrauben* **screw off** abschrauben ['apʃraobm] +haben ◊ *Sie schraubte den Deckel ab.; (fix with screws)* **screw down/on** anschrauben ['anʃraobm] +haben ◊ *Ich schraubte das Schild an.; (by turning)* **screw on** zuschrauben ['tsu:ʃraobm] +haben ◊ *Er schraubte den Deckel zu.* **screw together** zusammenschrauben [tsu'zamənʃraobm] +haben ◊ *Sie schraubte die Teile zusammen.* **2.** **screw sth into a ball** etw. zerknüllen [tse'knylən] <zerknüllt, zerknüllte, hat zerknüllt> **3.** **screw your eyes shut** die Augen zukneifen [dɪ: 'aoŋ ,tsu:knaefn] <kneift zu, kniff zu, hat zugekniffen> **4.** *(cheat)* bescheißen [bə'ʃaesn] <bescheißt, beschiss, hat beschissen> *(rude)* **screw sb out of sth** jdn um etw. bescheißen ◊ *Er hat mich um zehn Euro beschissen!* **5.** *(have sex)* ficken ['fɪkn] +haben *(taboo)*

• **screw around** ⟨phras v⟩ **1.** *(waste time)* sich herumtreiben [hɛ'rʊmtraebm] <treibt sich herum, trieb sich herum, hat sich herumgetrieben> *(fam, pej)* ◊ *Statt zu lernen, treibt er sich mit seinen Kumpels in Kneipen herum.* **2.** *(have lots of sexual partners)* herumvögeln [hɛ'rʊmfø:gln] +haben *(rude)*

• **screw up** ⟨phras v⟩ **1.** *(squash into a ball)* zerknüllen [tse'knylən] <zerknüllt, zerknüllte, hat zerknüllt> ◊ *Sie zerknüllte den Brief.* **2.** **screw up your eyes** die Augen zukneifen [dɪ: 'aoŋ ,tsu:knaefn] <kneift zu, kniff zu, hat zugekniffen> **screw up your face** das Gesicht verziehen [das gə'zɪçt fɛtsi:ən] <verzieht, verzog, hat verzogen> **4.** *(mess up)* **screw sth up** etw. verpfuschen [fe'pfʊʃn] <verpfuscht, verpfuschte, hat verpfuscht> *(fam)* ◊ *Du hast die Geschichte gründlich verpfuscht.* ♦ *sein Leben verpfuschen* **sb screws up jd verpfuscht alles** **5.** *(cause psychological damage to)* fertig machen ['fɛʳtɪç maxn] +haben *(fam)* ◊ *Die Situation macht mich völlig fertig.*

screwdriver ⟨noun⟩ Schraubenzieher ['ʃraobmtsi:ɐ] der <-s, ->

scribble ⟨verb⟩ *(write quickly)* kritzeln ['krɪtsln] +haben ◊ *ein paar Wörter auf einen Zettel kritzeln* **scribble sth down** etw. hinkritzeln ['hɪnkrɪtsln] +haben ◊

schnell eine Nachricht hinkritzeln; (doodle) herumkritzeln [hɛ'rʊmkrɪts|n] +haben ◊ Sie kritzelte beim Telefonieren in der Zeitung herum.

script [noun] **1.** (words of a play, film) Text [tɛkst] der <–(e)s, –e>; (screenplay) Drehbuch ['dreːbuːx] das <–(e)s, Drehbücher> ◊ Wer schrieb das Drehbuch? **2.** (letters, handwriting) Schrift [ʃrɪft] die <–, –en> ◊ die lateinische Schrift ♦ Sie hat eine hübsche Schrift. **3.** (exam paper) Prüfungsarbeit ['pryːfʊŋs|a'baet] die <–, –en> **4.** IT Script [skrɪpt] das <–s, –s>

scrounge [verb] schnorren ['ʃnɔrən] +haben (fam) ◊ Er schnorrt ständig bei anderen. ♦ Sie schnorrte eine Zigarette von ihm.

scrub [verb] **1.** (clean by rubbing) scheuern ['ʃɔɣən] +haben ◊ den Fußboden scheuern; (with a brush) schrubben ['ʃrʊbm̩] +haben ◊ sich die Hände schrubben; (with a towel) scrub at sth an etw. [dat] rubbeln [an ... ,rʊb|n] +haben ◊ Sie rubbelte an dem Fleck auf ihrem Rock. **2.** (cancel) abblasen ['apblaːzn̩] <bläst ab, blies ab, hat abgeblasen> (fam) ◊ Die Konferenz wurde abgeblasen.

scruffy(-ily) [adj, adv] schmuddelig ['ʃmʊdəlɪç] ◊ ein schmuddeliger Pullover ♦ Die Kinder waren mager und schmuddelig. ♦ schmuddelig angezogen sein

scruple [noun] Skrupel ['skruːp|] der <–s, –> most pl ◊ Er hatte keine Skrupel, sie anzulügen.

scrutinize [verb] mustern ['mʊstən] +haben ◊ jdn neugierig von oben bis unten mustern

scrutiny [noun] (careful examination) Prüfung ['pryːfʊŋ] die <–, –en> ◊ Alle Kandidaten wurden einer sorgfältigen Prüfung unterzogen. come under close scrutiny genau unter die Lupe genommen werden [gənaʊ ʊntə diː 'luːpə ɡənɔmən veːɡdn̩] <wird, wurde, ist worden> public scrutiny Kontrolle durch die Öffentlichkeit [kɔn,trɔlə dʊrç diː 'œfntlɪçkaet] die <–>

sculptor [noun] Bildhauer ['bɪlthaɔɛ] der <–s, –> ♀Bildhauerin ['bɪlthaɔərɪn] die <–, –nen> ◊ ein begnadeter Bildhauer ♦ Sie arbeitet seit drei Jahren als Bildhauerin.

sculpture [noun] **1.** (work of art) Plastik ['plastɪk] die <–, –en> ◊ Plastiken von Rodin **2.** (art form) Bildhauerei [,bɪlthaɔə'rae] die <–> no pl

scum [noun] **1.** (foam on top of a liquid) Schaum [ʃaʊm] der <–(e)s, Schäume> most sing ◊ beim Kochen den Schaum abschöpfen; (layer of dirt on top of a liquid) Schmutzschicht ['ʃmʊtsʃɪçt] die <–, –en> ◊ Auf dem Wasser schwamm eine Schmutzschicht. **2.** (people) Abschaum ['apʃaɔm] der <–(e)s> no pl (pej) the scum of the earth der Abschaum der Menschheit

sea [noun] **1.** (also fig) (expanse of water) Meer [meːɐ] das <–(e)s, –e> ◊ Von hier aus hat man einen schönen Blick aufs Meer. ♦ Der Campingplatz liegt am Meer. out to sea aufs Meer hinaus Arctic Sea Eismeer ['aesmeːɐ] sea of ... ...meer sea of flames Flammenmeer ['flamənmeːɐ] sea of flowers Blumenmeer ['bluːmənmeːɐ] **2.** (describing certain sea conditions, in certain expressions) See [zeː] die <–> no pl ◊ Es herrschte stürmische See. ♦ auf hoher See ertrinken at sea auf See go to sea zur See gehen put to sea in See stechen the Baltic Sea die Ostsee [di: 'ɔstzeː] the North Sea die Nordsee [di: 'nɔʳtzeː] the deep sea die Tiefsee [di: 'tiːfzeː] ◉ all at sea völlig ratlos by sea auf dem Seeweg

seagull [noun] Möwe ['møːvə] die <–, –n>

seal¹ [noun] **1.** zoo Robbe ['rɔbə] die <–, –n> ◊ Robben jagen **2.** (wax) Siegel ['ziːg|] das <–s, –> ◊ eine Urkunde mit amtlichem Siegel; (metal) Plombe ['plɔmbə] die <–, –n> **3.** TECHN Dichtung ['dɪçtʊŋ] die <–, –en> ◊ Die Dichtung ist undicht; es läuft Wasser aus. ◉ put the seal on sth etw. besiegeln

seal² [verb] **1.** (close) verschließen [fɛ'ʃliːsn̩] <ver­schließt, verschloss, hat verschlossen> ◊ eine Kiste luftdicht verschließen ◊ einen Briefumschlag verschließen; (make airtight or watertight) abdichten ['apdɪçtn̩] +haben **2.** (sb's fate, a deal) besiegeln [bə'ziːg|n] <besiegelt, besiegelte, hat besiegelt> ◊ Damit war unsere Niederlage besiegelt. ♦ eine Übereinkunft durch Handschlag besiegeln • seal in [phras v] seal sth in etw. einschließen ['aenʃliːsn̩] <schließt ein, schloss ein, hat eingeschlos­sen> ◊ in Harz eingeschlossen werden • seal off [phras v] seal sth off **1.** (close off, block) etw. abschließen ['apʃliːsn̩] <schließt ab, schloss ab, hat abgeschlossen> ◊ Der Ort ist durch den Erdrutsch vollkommen von der Außenwelt abgeschlossen worden. **2.** (an area, the scene of a crime or an accident) etw. abriegeln ['apriːg|n] +haben ◊ Die Polizei hat die Innenstadt abgeriegelt.

seam [noun] **1.** (in cloth, metal) Naht [naːt] die <–, –en> ◊ An der Naht ist der Saum ist aufgegangen.; (in wood) Fuge ['fuːgə] die <–, –n> **2.** (underground layer) Flöz [fløːts] das <–es, –e> ◉ be bursting at the seams aus allen Nähten platzen fall apart at the seams aus den Fugen geraten

search¹ [noun] **1.** (process of searching) Suche ['zuːxə] die <–> no pl ◊ Eine intensive Suche förderte Beweise zutage. search for sb/sth Suche nach jdm/ etw. ◊ die Suche nach einer Lösung ♦ Die Suche nach den Vermissten wurde abgebrochen. in search of sb/sth auf der Suche nach jdm/etw. go in search of sb/sth sich auf die Suche nach jdm/etw. machen search engine Suchmaschine ['zuːxma,ʃiːnə] die <–, –n> **2.** (operation) Suchaktion ['zuːx|ak,tsjoːn] die <–, –en> ◊ eine groß angelegte Suchaktion; (by the police: for suspects) Fahndung ['faːndʊŋ] die <–, –en> ◊ Die Fahndung nach dem Flüchtigen wurde bereits eingeleitet. **3.** (of an area, a house, person) Durchsuchung [dʊʳç'zuːxʊŋ] die <–, –en> ◊ Bei der Durchsuchung des Gepäcks wurden Waffen entdeckt.

search² [verb] **1.** (look for) suchen ['zuːxn̩] +haben ◊ Ich habe überall gesucht, den Schlüssel aber nicht gefunden. search for sb/sth nach jdm/etw. suchen ◊ nach Beweisen suchen ♦ Die Polizei sucht nach dem Vermissten. search the Net im Internet nach Informationen suchen; (examine) search sth jdn/etw. durchsuchen [dʊʳç'zuːxn̩] durchsucht, durchsuchte, hat durchsucht> ◊ einen Verdächtigen durchsuchen ♦ jds Taschen nach Waffen durchsuchen ♦ Die Kripo hat die Wohnung durchsucht. search through sth etw. durchsuchen **2.** (police: try to find a suspect, criminal) search for sb nach jdm fahnden [naːx ... ,faːndn̩] <fahndet, fahndete, hat gefahndet> ◊ Die Polizei fahndet fieberhaft nach dem Entführern. ◉ search me frag mich nicht (fam)

seasick [adj] seekrank ['zeːkraŋk] no comp/superl ◊ Sie wird leicht seekrank. ♦ die seekranken Passagiere hingen über der Reling.

seaside [noun] Küste ['kʏstə] die <–, –n> ◊ *Die Küste dort ist wild und kaum besiedelt.* at the seaside am Meer [am 'meːɐ̯] to the seaside ans Meer [ans 'meːɐ̯] seaside hotel Strandhotel ['ʃtranthoˌtɛl] das <–s, –s> seaside resort Seebad ['zeːbaːt] das <–(e)s, Seebäder> seaside town Stadt am Meer [ˌʃtat am 'meːɐ̯] die <–, Städte>

season¹ [noun] **1.** *(time of the year)* Jahreszeit ['jaːrəstsaɛ̯t] die <–, –en> ◊ *Der Frühling ist seine liebste Jahreszeit.* ♦ *Sie mag Italien zu jeder Jahreszeit.* **2.** *(for a particular sport, activity, fashion, plant)* Saison [zɛ'zɔŋ] die <–, –s> most sing ◊ *die diesjährige Saison der Bundesliga* ♦ *Ich verreise immer außerhalb der Saison.* ♦ *„Hamlet" wird diese Saison nicht gegeben.* ♦ *die Modelle der nächsten Saison* ♦ *die Saison für Spargel* be in season Saison haben ◊ *Jetzt haben Trauben gerade Saison.* high season Hochsaison ['hoːxzɛˌzɔŋ] low season Nebensaison ['neːbm̩zɛˌzɔŋ] **3.** *(the right time for sth)* Zeit [tsaɛ̯t] die <–, –en> ◊ *Die ersten Tage im neuen Jahr sind die Zeit der guten Vorsätze.* sth is out of season jetzt ist nicht die Zeit für etw. ◊ *Jetzt ist nicht die Zeit für Erdbeeren.* Christmas season Weihnachtszeit ['vaɛ̯naxtsˌtsaɛ̯t] closed season Schonzeit ['ʃoːntsaɛ̯t] dry season Trockenzeit ['trɔkn̩tsaɛ̯t] mating season Paarungszeit ['paːrʊŋstsaɛ̯t] ◉ season's greetings frohes Fest

season² [verb] **1.** *(food)* würzen ['vʏrtsn̩] +haben ◊ *Fleisch mit Pfeffer und Kräutern würzen* **2.** *(wood)* ablagern ['aplaˌgɛn] +haben

seasonal [adj] saisonal [zɛzo'naːl] mostly before ns ◊ *saisonalen Schwankungen unterliegen* seasonal vegetables Gemüse der Saison [gəˌmyːzə deːɐ̯ zɛ'zɔŋ] seasonal … Saison… [zɛ'zɔŋ] seasonal worker Saisonarbeiter [zɛ'zɔŋ|aʳˌbaɛ̯tɐ] der <–s, –> ♀Saisonarbeiterin [zɛ'zɔŋ|aʳˌbaɛ̯tərɪn] die <–, –nen> seasonal affective disorder Winterdepression ['vɪntedeprɛˌsi̯oːn] die <–, –en>

seat¹ [noun] **1.** *(place in a cinema, on a plane etc.)* Platz [plats] der <–es, Plätze> ◊ *Ist dieser Platz noch frei?* ♦ *Von meinem Platz aus konnte man alles gut erkennen.* Have a seat, please! Bitte nehmen Sie doch Platz! take a seat Platz nehmen take your seat seinen Platz einnehmen; *(place for sitting down)* Sitzplatz ['zɪtsplats] ◊ *Das Stadion hat 10 000 Sitzplätze.* window seat Fensterplatz ['fɛnsteplats] **2.** *(object for sitting on)* Sitz [zɪts] der <–es, –e> ◊ *ein Stuhl mit gepolstertem Sitz* ♦ *ein Auto mit fünf Sitzen* back seat Rücksitz ['rʏkzɪts] driver's seat Fahrersitz ['faːrezɪts] passenger seat Beifahrersitz ['baɛ̯faːrezɪts] **3.** *(of a company or an organization, in parliament)* Sitz [zɪts] der <–es, –e> ◊ *eine Firma mit Sitz in München* ♦ *Bei den Landtagswahlen hat die FDP zwei Sitze erobert.; (in the country)* Landsitz ['lantzɪts] family seat Familiensitz [fa'miːli̯ənzɪts] **4.** *(area on which you sit: of trousers)* Hosenboden ['hoːzn̩boːdn̩] der <–s, Hosenböden>; *(of a chair)* Sitzfläche ['zɪtsflɛçə] die <–, –n> ◉ fly by the seat of your pants sich auf sein Gefühl verlassen take a back seat sich im Hintergrund halten

seat² [verb] **1.** *(place a person)* seat sb jdm einen Platz zuweisen [aɛ̯nən 'plats tsuːvaɛ̯zn̩] <weist zu, wies zu, hat zugewiesen> ◊ *Haben Sie den Gästen schon einen Platz zugewiesen?* seat sb somewhere jdn irgendwohin setzen ['zɛtsn̩] +haben ◊ *Der Lehrer*

setzte sie in die erste Reihe.; (sit down) seat yourself sich setzen ['zɛtsn̩] +haben ◊ *Wir setzten uns an den Tisch.* Please be seated! Setzen Sie sich doch!*; (be sitting)* be seated sitzen ['zɪtsn̩] <sitzt, saß, hat gesessen> ◊ *am Fenster sitzen* remain seated sitzen bleiben ['zɪtsn̩ blaɛ̯bm̩] <bleibt, blieb, ist geblieben> ◊ *Bleiben Sie doch sitzen!* **2.** *(have room for)* seat … people … Sitzplätze haben ['zɪtsplɛtsə haːbm̩] +haben ◊ *Die Konzerthalle hat 2000 Sitzplätze.*

seat belt [noun] Gurt [gʊʳt] der <–(e)s, –e> ◊ *seinen Gurt anlegen*

secluded [adj] **1.** *(remote, isolated)* abgelegen ['apgəleˌgn̩] ◊ *eine abgelegene Insel* ♦ *Das Hotel ist ziemlich abgelegen.* **2.** *(private)* abgeschlossen ['apgəʃlɔsn̩] ◊ *Jeder bekommt hier seinen eigenen, abgeschlossenen Bereich.*

second¹ [noun] **1.** *(unit of time, moment)* Sekunde [ze'kʊndə] die <–, –n> ◊ *Das Erdbeben dauerte 45 Sekunden.* ♦ *Warte eine Sekunde — ich bin gleich fertig.* **2.** *(product)* be a second zweite Wahl sein [ˌtsvaɛ̯tə 'vaːl zaɛ̯n] +sein ◊ *Das Geschirr ist zweite Wahl, deshalb habe ich es billiger bekommen.* **3.** *(another portion of food)* seconds Nachschlag ['naːxʃlaːk] der <–(e)s, Nachschläge> ◊ *Willst du noch einen Nachschlag?* ◉ come a close second knapp geschlagen werden

second² [adj] *(coming after the first)* zweite ['tsvaɛ̯tə] only before ns <ein zweiter …, eine zweite …, ein zweites …> → **fourth** ◉ be second only to sb/sth nur von jdm/etw. übertroffen werden second to none unerreicht

secondarily [adv] sekundär [zekʊn'dɛːɐ̯] *(lofty)* ◊ *Unsere Firma ist nur sekundär an dem Projekt beteiligt.*

secondary [adj] **1.** school secondary … … (in) der Sekundarstufe [(ɪn) deːɐ̯ zekʊn'daːʳʃtuːfə] *(tech)* ◊ *Schüler der Sekundarstufe* ♦ *die Ausbildung in der Sekundarstufe* **2.** *(less important, happening later)* sekundär [zekʊn'dɛːɐ̯] no comp/superl *(lofty)* ◊ *Die Kostenfrage ist sekundär.* ♦ *eine sekundäre Infektion*

secondary school [noun] weiterführende Schule ['vaɛ̯tefyːrəndə ˌʃuːlə] die <–, –n> ◊ *an einer weiterführenden Schule unterrichten*

second-hand [adj] gebraucht [gə'braʊxt] no comp/superl ◊ *sich eine gebrauchte Gitarre kaufen* ♦ *Ist das Auto neu oder gebraucht?* second-hand car Gebrauchtwagen [gə'braʊxtvaːgn̩] der <–s, –>

secondly [adv] zweitens ['tsvaɛ̯tn̩s]

secret¹ [noun] Geheimnis [gə'haɛ̯mnɪs] das <–ses, –se> ◊ *Soll ich dir ein Geheimnis verraten?* ♦ *das Geheimnis der richtigen Zubereitung* in secret insgeheim [ɪnsgə'haɛ̯m] ◉ keep sth a secret (from sb) etw. (vor jdm) geheim halten

secret² [adj] **1.** *(not told to others)* geheim [gə'haɛ̯m] ◊ *eine geheime Wahl* ♦ *Das sollt aber geheim bleiben!* keep sth secret etw. geheim halten **2.** *(not known to others)* heimlich ['haɛ̯mlɪç] only before ns ◊ *einen heimlichen Verehrer haben* **3.** *(secretive)* verschwiegen [fɛ'ʃviːgn̩] ◊ *ein verschwiegener Mensch* ♦ *Sie ist sehr verschwiegen.*

secretary [noun] **1.** *(in an office)* Sekretär [zekre'tɛːɐ̯] der <–s, –e> ♀Sekretärin [zekre'tɛːrɪn] die <–, –nen> ◊ *Sie ist als Sekretärin tätig.* ♦ *Der Sekretär des Direktors hat überraschend gekündigt.* **2.** *(of a club, an association)* Geschäftsführer

A

[gəˈʃɛftsfyːrə] der <-s, -> ♀Geschäftsführerin
[gəˈʃɛftsfyːrərɪn] die <-, -nen> ◊ zum Geschäftsführer gewählt werden 3. (in a government) Minister
[miˈnɪstɐ] der <-s, -> ♀Ministerin [miˈnɪstərɪn] die
<-, -nen> ◊ Sie wurde zur Ministerin ernannt. ♦
der Minister für Umwelt

B

Secretary of State noun 1. (in the US) Außenminister [ˈaʊsn̩miˌnɪstə] der <-s, -> ♀Außenministerin
[ˈaʊsn̩miˌnɪstərɪn] die <-, -nen> 2. (in the UK)
Minister [miˈnɪstə] der <-s, -> ♀Ministerin
[miˈnɪstərɪn] die <-, -nen>

C

secretion noun 1. (substance) Sekret [zeˈkreːt] das
<-(e)s, -e> ◊ Nektar ist ein süßes Sekret von Blü-
tenpflanzen. 2. (production) Absonderung
[ˈapzɔndərʊŋ] die <-> no pl ◊ die Absonderung von
Schleim

D

secretly adv 1. (without telling anybody) heimlich
[ˈhaɪmlɪç] ◊ jdn heimlich beobachten 2. (without
admitting to it) insgeheim [ɪnsɡəˈhaɪm] ◊ insgeheim
wünschen, dass ...

E

sect noun Sekte [ˈzɛktə] die <-, -n>

section noun 1. (part) Teil [taɪl] der <-(e)s, -e> ◊
ein großer Teil der Bevölkerung ♦ Welchen Teil der
Zeitung möchtest du: den Sportteil oder den Wirt-
schaftsteil? 2. (of a document, road) Abschnitt
[ˈapʃnɪt] der <-(e)s, -e> ◊ im ersten Abschnitt des
Buches ♦ Auf diesem Abschnitt der Autobahn gibt es
oft Staus. 3. (of a law, contract etc.) Paragraph
[paraˈɡraːf] der <-en, -en> 4. (part of an orchestra)
brass section Blechbläser [ˈblɛçblɛːzə] die <-> pl
string section Streicher [ˈʃtraɪçə] die <-> pl rhythm
section Rhythmusgruppe [ˈrʏtmʊsɡrʊpə] die <-, -n>
5. MED, TECHN Schnitt [ʃnɪt] der <-(e)s, -e> caesarian
section Kaiserschnitt [ˈkaɪzəʃnɪt]

sector noun 1. (of the economy) Branche [ˈbrɑ̃ʃə] die
<-, -n> ◊ In welcher Branche sind Sie tätig? ♦ Die
Branche der Telekommunikation boomt. industrial
sector Industrie [ɪndʊsˈtriː] die <-, -n> most sing
2. (of an area, a circle, group) Sektor [ˈzɛktoːɐ] der
<-s, -en> ◊ der private/öffentliche Sektor ♦ Er lebte
im sowjetischen Sektor Berlins.

secular adj weltlich [ˈvɛltlɪç] no comp/superl ◊
weltliche Bauten/Kunst/Musik ♦ Die Universität ist
weltlich und steht allen Religionen offen.

secure¹ adj 1. (safe, reliable) sicher [ˈzɪçə] ◊ ein
sicherer Schulweg ♦ Wie sicher ist diese Prognose?
secure in the knowledge that in dem sicheren
Bewusstsein, dass secure against sth, secure from
sth vor etw. dat geschützt [foːɐ̯ ... ɡəˈʃʏtst] no
comp/superl ◊ Ist Ihr Computer vor Viren geschützt?
2. (fastened firmly) fest [fɛst] <fester, am festesten> ◊
eine feste Unterlage ♦ Der Außenspiegel muss ganz
fest sein. 3. (feeling emotionally safe) geborgen
[ɡəˈbɔrɡn̩] ◊ emotional geborgene Kinder ♦ sich zu
Hause geborgen fühlen 4. (existence, income etc.)
gesichert [ɡəˈzɪçɐt] ◊ eine gesicherte Zukunft ♦ Jeder
möchte im Alter finanziell gesichert sein.

secure² verb 1. (obtain for yourself) secure sth sich
dat etw. sichern [ˈzɪçɐn] +haben ◊ Sie sicherten
sich die besten Plätze. secure sth for sb jdm etw.
sichern ◊ Wir sicherten ihnen einen Tisch am
Fenster. secure sb's release jds Freilassung
erreichen [ˈfraɪlasʊŋ erreichen] <erreicht, erreichte, hat
erreicht> 2. (fasten) secure sth (to sth) etw. (an
etw. dat) befestigen [bəˈfɛstɪɡn̩] <befestigt, befestigte, hat befestigt> ◊ ein Regal mit Schrauben an der

Wand befestigen 3. FIN (a loan) absichern [ˈapzɪçɐn]
◊ Ich habe das Darlehen durch eine Bürgschaft abge-
sichert. 4. (make safe) sichern [ˈzɪçɐn] +haben ◊ Der
Flughafen wird von Truppen gesichert.

securely adv 1. (safely) sicher [ˈzɪçə] ◊ Atommüll
muss sicher gelagert werden. 2. (firmly) fest [fɛst]
<fester, am festesten> ◊ ein Regal fest anschrauben ♦
einen Verschluss fest zumachen

security noun 1. (safety, confidence, guarantee)
Sicherheit [ˈzɪçɐhaɪt] die <-, -en> ◊ die innere
Sicherheit eines Landes ♦ ein Programm für mehr
Sicherheit im Straßenverkehr ♦ Die Bank verlangt
Sicherheiten für den Kredit. job security ein sicherer
Arbeitsplatz [aɛn ˌzɪçərə ˈaˈbaɛtsplats] sichere
Arbeitsplätze [ˌzɪçərə ˈaˈbaɛtsplɛtsə] tight security
strenge Sicherheitsvorkehrungen
[ˌʃtrɛŋə ˈzɪçɐhaɛtsˌfoːɐ̯keːrʊŋən] <-> pl 2. (emotional)
Geborgenheit [ɡəˈbɔˈɡn̩haɛt] die <-> no pl ◊ Kleine
Kinder brauchen die Geborgenheit der Familie.
3. (department) Sicherheitsdienst [ˈzɪçɐhaɛtsdiːnst]
der <-(e)s, -e> ◊ den Sicherheitsdienst rufen

sediment noun 1. (at the bottom of a liquid) Satz
[zats] der <-es, Sätze> ◊ In der Weinflasche hatte
sich ein Satz gebildet. 2. (layer of sand, stones) Ablagerung [ˈaplaˌɡərʊŋ] die <-, -en> ◊ Ablagerungen
im Fluss

seduce verb 1. (to have sex) verführen [fɛˈfyːrən]
<verführt, verführte, hat verführt> ◊ Er hat sie
verführt. 2. (to do sth) verleiten [fɛˈlaɛtn̩] <verleitet,
verleitete, hat verleitet> ◊ Was hat ihn nur dazu
verleitet, so ein Risiko einzugehen?

seductive(ly) adj, adv 1. (sexy) verführerisch
[fɛˈfyːrərɪʃ] ◊ jdm ein verführerisches Lächeln
zuwerfen ♦ Ihre Pose war mehr als verführerisch. ♦
jdn verführerisch anblicken 2. (tempting) verlockend
[fɛˈlɔkn̩t] ◊ ein verlockendes Angebot ♦ Sein
Vorschlag ist sehr verlockend. ♦ etw. verlockend darstellen

see verb 1. (notice with your eyes, look at, consider,
find out) sehen [ˈzeːən] <sieht, sah, hat gesehen> ◊
Mit der Brille kann ich besser sehen. ♦ Ich habe das
Auto nicht gesehen. ♦ Er konnte sehen, dass sie sich
freute. ♦ Hast du „Cats“ schon gesehen? ♦ Hast du
Ingrid mal wieder gesehen? ♦ Du siehst das völlig
falsch. ♦ Wie wir schon im letzten Kapitel gesehen
haben, ... ♦ Sie sieht aus wie ihre Vaterfigur. see
sb/sth doing sth sehen, wie jd/etw. etw. tut ◊ Ich
habe gesehen, wie sie das Geld genommen hat. see
to do sth zu etw. gut genug sehen können ◊ Ich
kann hier zum Nähen nicht gut genug sehen. see
above/below siehe oben/unten 2. (meet) see sb
mit jdm treffen [mɪt ... ˌtrɛfn̩] <trifft sich, traf sich,
hat sich getroffen> ◊ Sie trifft sich noch manchmal
mit einer früheren Kollegin. see a lot of sb sich oft
mit jdm treffen; (visit) see sb jdn besuchen
[bəˈzuːxn̩] <besucht, besuchte, hat besucht> ◊ Ich
muss unbedingt meine Oma besuchen.; (have
visitors) see sb jdn empfangen [ɛmˈpfaŋən]
<empfängt, empfing, hat empfangen> ◊ Es geht ihm
zu schlecht, um Besuch zu empfangen. 3. (have a
meeting) see sb jdn sprechen [ˈʃprɛçn̩] <spricht,
sprach, hat gesprochen> ◊ Ich möchte den Geschäftsführer sprechen. ♦ Sie können Herrn Schulze jetzt
leider nicht sprechen.; (a doctor, professional) see sb
(about sth) (wegen etw.) zu jdm gehen
[tsuː ... ɡeːən] <geht, ging, ist gegangen> ◊ Du solltest

mal zu einem Homöopathen gehen. ♦ *Ich gebe morgen wegen der Schmerzen zum Arzt.* **4.** *(understand)* verstehen [fɐˈʃteːən] <versteht, verstand, hat verstanden> ◊ *Ich verstehe, warum du das getan hast.* ♦ *Niemand verstand, dass sie einfach nur Heimweh hatte.* sb can't see why/what/how etc. jd versteht einfach nicht, warum/was/wie etc. ◊ *Ich verstehe einfach nicht, warum er gegangen ist.* I see what you mean/he means etc. Das kann ich verstehen. ◊ *„Ich finde das ungerecht."* — *„Ja, das kann ich verstehen."* ..., see? Schau, ... [ʃaʊ] ◊ *Schau, dieses Teil kommt hier hinein.* **5.** *(imagine)* sich [dat] vorstellen [ˈfoːɐ̯ʃtɛlən] +haben ◊ *Das kann ich mir gut vorstellen!* ♦ *Kannst du dir Peter als Vater vorstellen?* see sb/sth doing sth sich [dat] vorstellen, dass jd/etw. etw. tut ◊ *Ich kann mir nicht vorstellen, dass er wirklich kündigt.* Where do you see yourself in ten years' time? Wie stellen Sie sich Ihr Leben in zehn Jahren vor? **6.** *(experience)* erleben [ɛˈleːbm̩] <erlebt, erlebte, hat erlebt> ◊ *Sie hat schwere Zeiten erlebt.* ♦ *Die alte Burg hat schon viele Kriege erlebt.* **7.** *(go with sb)* bringen [ˈbrɪŋən] <bringt, brachte, hat gebracht> ◊ *Er brachte die alte Dame über die Straße.* ♦ *Ich bringe Sie zur Tür.* see sb home jdn nach Hause bringen

ⓘ **I see** *(to show that you are listening to what another person is telling you)* ja see sth coming etw. kommen sehen we'll have to see das werden wir sehen see sb/sth for sth jdn/etw. als etw. durchschauen ◊ *Endlich hat sie ihn als Betrüger durchschaut.* see for yourself sich selbst überzeugen see you tschüs see you later bis später

• **see about** [phras v] see about sth sich um etw. kümmern [ʊm ... ˌkʏmən] +haben ◊ *Ich muss mich um das Abendessen kümmern.* Could you see about getting the tickets? Könntest du dich um die Eintrittskarten kümmern? Can you see about fixing this problem? Könntest du dich um eine Lösung für dieses Problem kümmern? We'll have to see about that. Das werden wir sehen. We'll soon see about that. Das werden wir ja sehen! ◊ *„Ich will aber nicht!"* — *„ Das werden wir ja sehen!"*

• **see around** [phras v] **1.** *(meet)* see sb around jdn öfter sehen [ˈœftɐ ˌzeːən] <sieht, sah, hat gesehen> ◊ *Ich habe ihn schon öfter gesehen.* See you around! Man sieht sich! **2.** *(look at)* see around sth sich [dat] etw. von innen ansehen [fɔn ˈɪnən anzeːən] <sieht sich an, sah sich an, hat sich angesehen> ◊ *Die Kirche würde ich mir gern einmal von innen ansehen.*

• **see off** [phras v] see sb off **1.** *(at the airport, station)* verabschieden [fɛˈʔapʃiːdn̩] <verabschiedet, verabschiedete, hat verabschiedet> ◊ *Alle kamen mit zum Bahnhof, um sie zu verabschieden.* **2.** *(chase away)* verjagen [fɐˈjaːgn̩] <verjagt, verjagte, hat verjagt> ◊ *Sie haben den Einbrecher verjagt.* **3.** *(an opponent)* erledigen [ɛˈleːdɪgn̩] <erledigt, erledigte, hat erledigt> ◊ *Wir haben sie mit 5:0 erledigt.*

• **see out** [phras v] see sb out jdn zur Tür bringen [tsuːɐ̯ ˈtyːɐ̯ brɪŋən] <bringt, brachte, hat gebracht> ◊ *Warten Sie, ich bringe Sie zum Ausgang!* see yourself out allein hinausfinden [aˈlaɪn hɪˌnaʊsfɪndn̩] <findet hinaus, fand hinaus, hat hinausgefunden> ◊ *Danke, ich finde schon allein hinaus.*

• **see through** [phras v] **1.** see through sb/sth jdn/etw. durchschauen [dʊɐ̯çˈʃaʊən] <durchschaut, durch-

schaute, hat durchschaut> ◊ *Ich habe dich schon lange durchschaut!* ♦ *Sie konnte seine Lügen nicht durchschauen.* **2.** see sth through etw. zu Ende bringen [tsu: ˈʔɛndə brɪŋən] <bringt, brachte, hat gebracht> ◊ *Er war fest entschlossen, das angefangene Projekt zu Ende zu bringen.* **3.** see sb through sth jdn durch etw. bringen [dʊɐ̯ç ... brɪŋən] <bringt, brachte, hat gebracht> ◊ *einen Schüler durch die Prüfung bringen* sth sees sb through sth jd kommt mit etw. durch etw. [kɔmt mɪt ... dʊɐ̯ç] <kommt, kam, ist gekommen> ◊ *Wie soll ich mit so wenig Geld durch den Monat kommen?*

• **see to** [phras v] see to sth sich um etw. kümmern [ʊm ... ˌkʏmən] +haben ◊ *Ich kümmere mich um das Essen.* have sth seen to etw. behandeln lassen [bəˈhandln̩ lasn̩] <lässt, ließ, hat lassen> ◊ *Sie sollten den Ausschlag von einem Arzt behandeln lassen.* see to it that dafür sorgen, dass [dafyːɐ̯ ˈzɔɐ̯gn̩ das] +haben ◊ *Kannst du dafür sorgen, dass die anderen auch davon erfahren?*

seed [noun] **1.** *(of a plant)* Samen [ˈzaːmən] der <-s, -> ◊ *Samen kaufen/säen* grow sth from seed etw. aus Samen ziehen ◊ *Ich ziehe mein Basilikum immer aus Samen.* sesame seed Sesamkorn [ˈzeːzamkɔˈrn] das <-(e)s, Sesamkörner> sunflower seed Sonnenblumenkern [ˈzɔnənbluːmənkɛˈrn] der <-(e)s, -e> **2.** *(in the US)* Kern [kɛˈrn] der <-(e)s, -e> ◊ *Weintrauben mit Kernen* **3.** *(player)* gesetzter Spieler [gəˌzɛtstɐ ˈʃpiːlɐ] <-s, -> ♀gesetzte Spielerin [gəˌzɛtstə ˈʃpiːlərɪn] <-, -nen> the number one seed der auf Platz eins gesetzte Spieler

ⓘ **go to seed 1.** *(person)* herunterkommen *(fam)* **2.** *(plant)* schießen

seedling [noun] Sämling [ˈzɛːmlɪŋ] der <-s, -e> ◊ *Man kann schon die ersten Sämlinge sehen.*; *(all of very many)* seedlings Saat [zaːt] die <-, -en> ◊ *Die junge Saat ist erfroren.*

seek [verb] *(try to get, find)* suchen [ˈzuːxn̩] +haben ◊ *Rat/Hilfe/Asyl/Arbeit/Frieden suchen* ♦ *in einer Kirche Zuflucht suchen* seek permission um Erlaubnis bitten [ʊm ɛˈlaʊpnɪs bɪtn̩] <bittet, bat, hat gebeten>; *(damages, compensation etc.)* fordern [ˈfɔɐ̯dən] +haben ◊ *Schadensersatz fordern*

ⓘ **seek to** do sth sich bemühen, etw. zu tun

seem [verb] **1.** *(appear)* scheinen [ˈʃaɪnən] <scheint, schien, hat geschienen> ◊ *Diese Erklärung scheint plausibel.* ♦ *Das Baby scheint zu schlafen.* seem happy/genuine etc. glücklich/echt etc. zu sein scheinen ◊ *Sie scheint unglücklich zu sein.* ♦ *Der Hund scheint durstig zu sein.* seem (to be) sb/sth jd/etw. zu sein scheinen ◊ *Er scheint ein guter Lehrer zu sein.* sth seemed like a good idea etw. schien eine gute Idee zu sein it seems as should it seems dort scheint ... [ʃaɪnt] ◊ *Hier scheint es ständig zu regnen.* ♦ *Es scheint, dass es dort einige Probleme gibt.* **2.** *(in polite or careful expressions)* it seems that, it seems like es sieht so aus, als ob [ɛs ziːt zoː ˈaʊs als ɔp] <sieht aus, sah aus, hat ausgesehen> +subjunctive II ◊ *Es sieht so aus, als ob ihr Gepäck verloren gegangen wäre.* So it seems. Es sieht so aus. sb seems to have done sth jd hat wohl etw. getan [hat voːl ... gəˈtaːn] ◊ *Ich habe wohl meinen Schlüssel zu Hause gelassen.* sb can't seem to do sth es gelingt jdm einfach nicht, etw. zu tun [ɛs gəˈlɪŋt ... aɛnfax nɪçt ... tuː] ◊ *Es gelingt mir einfach nicht, den Fehler zu finden.*

seeming(ly) [adj, adv] scheinbar [ˈʃaɪnbaˈr] *no comp/*

superl; *when used as an adj, only before ns* ◊ *ein scheinbarer Widerspruch* ♦ *Die Wüste zog sich scheinbar endlos dahin.*

segment [noun] **1.** *(a portion of)* segment (of) Teil (... [gen]) [ˈtaɛl] der <-(e)s, -e> ◊ *etw. in drei gleiche Teile teilen* ♦ *Gestern streikten große Teile der Belegschaft.* **2.** *(anatomical section, of a circle)* Segment [zɛgˈmɛnt] das <-(e)s, -e> ◊ *Die Beine des Tieres sitzen am mittleren Segment.*; *(of an orange, for eating)* Stück [ʃtʏk] das <-(e)s, -e>

seize [verb] **1.** *(hold, take in your hand)* seize sb/sth (by sth) jdn/etw. (an etw. [dat]) packen [ˈpakn̩] +haben ◊ *Er packte mich am Arm.* ♦ *Ich packte einen Stock und drohte den Angreifern.* **2.** *(confiscate)* beschlagnahmen [bəˈʃlaːknaːmən] <beschlagnahmt, beschlagnahmte, hat beschlagnahmt> ◊ *gestohlene Waren beschlagnahmen* **3.** *(a town)* einnehmen [ˈaɛnneːmən] <nimmt ein, nahm ein, hat eingenommen> ◊ *Die Rebellen haben die Stadt eingenommen.*; *(a building, train)* besetzen [bəˈzɛtsn̩] <besetzt, besetzte, hat besetzt> ◊ *ein Gebäude besetzen* **4.** *(take over: the power, the initiative)* ergreifen [ɐˈgraɛfn̩] <ergreift, ergriff, hat ergriffen> ◊ *als das Militär die Macht ergriff* ♦ *Wer will die Initiative ergreifen?* seize control of sth die Macht über etw. gewinnen [diː ˈmaxt yːbɐ ... ɡəvɪnən] <gewinnt, gewann, hat gewonnen> **5.** *(lit) (feeling)* erfassen [ɐˈfasn̩] <erfasst, erfasste, hat erfasst> ◊ *Er wurde von großer Angst/ Sehnsucht erfasst.*

seldom [adv] selten [ˈzɛltn̩] ◊ *Sie kommt uns nur selten besuchen.*

select¹ [adj] **1.** *(carefully chosen)* ausgewählt [ˈaosɡəvɛːlt] no comp/superl ◊ *ausgewählte Kostbarkeiten* a select few companies etc. einige ausgewählte Firmen etc. **2.** *(exclusive)* exklusiv [ɛkskluˈziːf] ◊ *ein exklusives Hotel* ♦ *Diese Privatschule ist sehr exklusiv.*

select² [verb] **1.** *(choose)* auswählen [ˈaosvɛːlən] +haben ◊ *Die Jury hat aus allen Einsendungen mein Bild ausgewählt.* select sb to do sth jdn auswählen, um etw. zu tun ◊ *Er wurde ausgewählt, um das neue Produkt zu präsentieren.* **2.** *(a player)* aufstellen [ˈaofʃtɛlən] +haben ◊ *Ersatzspieler aufstellen*

selection [noun] Auswahl [ˈaosvaːl] die <-> no pl ◊ *die Auswahl von Kandidaten* ♦ *Die Ausstellung zeigt eine Auswahl seiner Bilder.* ♦ *eine große Auswahl an günstigen Computern* make a selection eine Auswahl treffen selection process Auswahlverfahren [ˈaosvaːlfɛfaːrən] das <-s, ->

selective [adj] **1.** *(choosy)* wählerisch [ˈvɛːlərɪʃ] ◊ *ein wählerischer Kunde* ♦ *Was ihre Freunde betrifft, ist sie sehr wählerisch.* **2.** *(not comprehensive, patchy)* selektiv [zelɛkˈtiːf] ◊ *ein selektives Erinnerungsvermögen* ♦ *Unsere Wahrnehmung ist selektiv.* **3.** *(only accepting the best)* Elite... [eˈliːtə] selective school Eliteschule [eˈliːtəʃuːlə] die <-, -n>

self [noun] Ich [ɪç] das <-(s), -s> ◊ *das eigene Ich* sense of self Ichbewusstsein [ˈɪçbəvʊstzaɛn] das <-s, -e> most sing ◊ *Ob Tiere wohl ein Ichbewusstsein haben?*

ⓔ sb's inner self jds Inneres be your normal self wie immer sein ◊ *Sie war gestern Abend nicht wie immer.* be your old self ganz der/die Alte sein ◊ *Sie war wieder ganz die Alte.* sb's true self jds eigentliches Wesen

self(-)... [prefix] *(with adj)* selbst... [zɛlpst]

inflicted selbstverschuldet [ˈzɛlpstfɛʃʊldət] no comp/ superl; *(with nouns)* Selbst... [zɛlpst] self-respect Selbstachtung [ˈzɛlpst|axtʊŋ] die <-> no pl

self-confidence [noun] Selbstvertrauen [ˈzɛlpstfɛtraoən] das <-s> no pl ◊ *Ihm fehlt das nötige Selbstvertrauen.* ♦ *voller Selbstvertrauen*

self-confident(ly) [adj, adv] selbstsicher [ˈzɛlpstzɪçɐ] ◊ *ein selbstsicherer Mensch* ♦ *Sie ist in letzter Zeit selbstsicherer geworden.* ♦ *selbstsicher auftreten*

self-conscious(ly) [adj, adv] **1.** *(embarrassed)* verlegen [fɛˈleːɡn̩] ◊ *ein verlegener Blick* ♦ *Die Situation machte sie sehr verlegen.* ♦ *Er blickte verlegen auf seine Schuhe.* **2.** *(obvious)* krampfhaft [ˈkrampfhaft] <krampfhafter, am krampfhaftesten> ◊ *ein krampfhafter Versuch* ♦ *Er bemühte sich krampfhaft, natürlich zu wirken.*

self-discipline [noun] Selbstdisziplin [ˈzɛlpstdɪstsiˌpliːn] die <-> no pl ◊ *Zum Abnehmen braucht man viel Selbstdisziplin.*

self-employed [adj] selbstständig [ˈzɛlpstʃtɛndɪç] no comp/superl ◊ *ein selbstständiger Architekt* ♦ *Sie ist selbstständig.* go self-employed sich selbstständig machen

self-esteem [noun] Selbstachtung [ˈzɛlpst|axtʊŋ] die <-> no pl ◊ *seine Selbstachtung wiedergewinnen* ♦ *hohe/niedrige Selbstachtung*

selfish(ly) [adj, adv] egoistisch [eɡoˈɪstɪʃ] ◊ *Sei nicht so selfish!* ♦ *eine Entscheidung aus egoistischen Motiven* ♦ *ein egoistisch denkender Mensch*

selfless(ly) [adj, adv] selbstlos [ˈzɛlpstloːs] <selbstloser, am selbstlosesten> ◊ *Er half ihr aus selbstlosen Gründen.* ♦ *Sie war nicht ganz selbstlos, dass er ihr seine Hilfe angeboten hat.* ♦ *selbstlos handeln*

self-satisfied [adj] selbstzufrieden [ˈzɛlpstsufriːdn̩] ◊ *sein selbstzufriedener Gesichtsausdruck* ♦ *Sie sind alle so satt und selbstzufrieden.*

self-service [noun] Selbstbedienung [ˈzɛlpstbədiːnʊŋ] die <-> no pl ◊ *Die Tankstelle wurde auf Selbstbedienung umgestellt.* self-service petrol station Tankstelle mit Selbstbedienung self-service restaurant Selbstbedienungsrestaurant [ˈzɛlpstbədiːnʊŋsrɛstoˌraŋ] das <-s, -s> ◊ *Er isst nicht gern im Selbstbedienungsrestaurant.*

sell [verb] **1.** *(exchange for money)* sell (sb) sth (jdm) etw. verkaufen [fɛˈkaofn̩] <verkauft, verkaufte, hat verkauft> ◊ *Ich habe ihm mein Auto verkauft.* ♦ *Die Bäckerei verkauft auch Milch.* sell sth at a profit/loss etw. mit Gewinn/Verlust verkaufen sth sells (well) etw. verkauft sich (gut) ◊ *Glaubst du, dieses Produkt wird sich verkaufen?* ♦ *Seine neue CD verkauft sich gut.* This book sold 10 000 copies. Dieses Buch wurde 10 000 Mal verkauft. This model sold for 500 dollars. Dieses Modell wurde für 500 Dollar verkauft. Does sex sell anything? Lässt sich mit Sex alles verkaufen? **2.** *(make sb accept sth)* sell sth to sb jdm etw. schmackhaft machen [ˈʃmakhaft maxn̩] +haben ◊ *Wie können wir euch diese Idee am besten schmackhaft machen?*

ⓔ sell yourself sich verkaufen sold on sth begeistert von etw.

• **sell off** [phras v] sell sth off etw. abstoßen [ˈapʃtoːsn̩] <stößt ab, stieß ab, hat abgestoßen> ◊ *Aktien abstoßen*

• **sell out** [phras v] have sold out, be sold out ausverkauft sein [ˈaosfɛkaoft zaɛn] +sein ◊ *Die T-Shirts sind schon ausverkauft.* sell out of sth etw. ausver-

kaufen ['aʊsfekaʊfn̩] <verkauft aus, verkaufte aus, hat ausverkauft> ◊ *Er hatte schnell sein ganzes Brot ausverkauft.*

seller [noun] Verkäufer [fɛ'kɔøfɛ] der <–s, –> ♀Verkäuferin [fɛ'kɔøfərɪn] die <–, –nen> ◊ *der Verkäufer einer Immobilie* newspaper seller Zeitungsverkäufer ['ʦaɛtʊŋsfɛkɔøfe] Zeitungsverkäuferin ['ʦaɛtʊŋsfɛkɔøfərɪn]

ⓔ a bad seller ein Ladenhüter a good seller ein Verkaufsschlager

semantic(ally) [adj, adv] semantisch [ze'mantɪʃ] *no comp/superl, mostly before ns* ◊ *eine semantische Analyse* ◆ *ein semantischer Unterschied* ◆ *semantisch mehrdeutig sein*

semen [noun] Samenflüssigkeit ['za:mənflʏsɪçkaɛt] die <–, –en>

semester [noun] Semester [ze'mɛstɐ] das <–s, –> ◊ *Sie studiert im zweiten Semester Medizin.* ◆ *Ich bin im siebten Semester.*

semi(-)... [prefix] *(with adj)* halb ... [halp] semi-naked halb nackt ['halp'nakt] *no comp/superl; (with noun)* Halb... [halp] semi-circle Halbkreis ['halpkraɛs] der <–es, –e>

semi-detached [noun] semi-detached (house) Doppelhaushälfte ['dɔplhaɔshɛlftə] die <–, –n> ◊ *Sie haben sich eine Doppelhaushälfte am Stadtrand gekauft.*

semi-final [noun] Halbfinale ['halpfi,na:lə] das <–s, –> ◊ *Die Mannschaft hat das Halbfinale erreicht.*

seminar [noun] Seminar [zemi'na:ʳ] das <–s, –e> ◊ *an einem Seminar teilnehmen* seminar on linguistics Linguistikseminar [lɪŋ'gʊɪstɪkzemi,na:ʳ]

seminary [noun] Seminar [zemi'na:ʳ] das <–s, –e> ◊ *Die Priester, die aus diesem Seminar hervorgehen, haben hohe Ideale.*

senate [noun] Senat [ze'na:t] der <–(e)s, –e> ◊ *eine von Senat und Kongress gemeinsam getragene Resolution* ◆ *Cäsar wurde vom Senat zur Rechenschaft gezogen.*

senator [noun] Senator [ze'na:to:ɐ] der <–s, –en> ♀Senatorin [zena'to:rɪn] die <–, –nen> ◊ *Zahlreiche Senatoren stimmten gegen den Vorschlag.* ◆ *Sie ist Senatorin geworden.*

send [verb] **1.** *(a letter, parcel, an e-mail, flowers etc.)* send sb sth, send sth to sb jdm etw. schicken ['ʃɪkŋ̍] +haben ◊ *Ich werde dir aus dem Urlaub eine Karte schicken.* ◆ *Hilfsgüter nach Afrika schicken* **2.** *(a person)* schicken ['ʃɪkŋ̍] +haben ◊ *Die Firma versprach, einen Monteur zu schicken.* ◆ *Asylbewerber wieder nach Hause schicken* ◆ *die Kinder ins Internat/aufs Gymnasium schicken; (troops, delegates)* entsenden [ɛnt'zɛndn̩] <entsendet, entsandte, hat entsandt> *(lofty)* ◊ *Truppen in ein Krisengebiet entsenden* ◆ *Delegierte zu einer Konferenz entsenden* **3.** *(cause to move suddenly)* send sb flying jdn zu Boden werfen [tsu: 'bo:dn̩ vɛʳfn̩] <wirft, warf, hat geworfen> ◊ *Der Schlag warf mich zu Boden.* send sb falling somewhere jdn irgendwohin fallen lassen ['falən lasn̩] <lässt, ließ, hat gelassen> ◊ *Ein Stoß von hinten ließ mich nach vorn fallen.* Each move sent pain through my back. Bei jedem Schritt fuhr mir der Schmerz durch den Rücken. **4.** *(make sb feel an emotion)* send sb into a temper etc. jdn wütend etc. machen ['vy:tn̩t maxn̩] +haben ◊ *Diese Antwort machte ihn wütend.*

ⓔ **send sb packing** jdn rauswerfen *(fam)*

• **send away** [phras v] **1.** *(make sb leave)* send sb away jdn wegschicken ['vɛkʃɪkŋ̍] +haben ◊ *Ich habe ihn gleich wieder weggeschickt.* **2.** *(request in writing)* send away for sth etw. anfordern ['anfɔʳdn̩] +haben ◊ *Er forderte den aktuellen Katalog an.*

• **send back** [phras v] send sth back etw. zurückschicken [ʦu'rʏkʃɪkŋ̍] +haben ◊ *Wenn Ihnen der Artikel nicht gefällt, können Sie ihn gern zurückschicken.*

• **send down** [phras v] **1.** *(fam) (to prison)* send sb down jdn ins Gefängnis schicken [ɪns gə'fɛŋnɪs ʃɪkŋ̍] +haben ◊ *Sie wurde wegen Ladendiebstahls ins Gefängnis geschickt.* **2.** *(oldf) (from university)* be sent down von der Universität verwiesen werden [fɔn de:ɐ univeʳzi'tɛ:t fɛ,vi:zn̩ ve:ɐdn̩] <wird, wurde, ist worden> ◊ *Er ist wegen dieser Geschichte von der Universität verwiesen worden.*

• **send for** [phras v] send for sb jdn kommen lassen ['kɔmən lasn̩] <lässt, ließ, hat lassen> ◊ *Können Sie bitte einen Arzt/Priester kommen lassen?* ◆ *Er ließ den Schüler zu sich kommen.; (an ambulance, a taxi)* send for sth etw. rufen ['ru:fn̩] <ruft, rief, hat gerufen> ◊ *Kannst du bitte ein Taxi rufen?; (a catalogue, copy)* etw. anfordern ['anfɔʳdn̩] +haben ◊ *Sie forderte die neuen Prospekte an.*

• **send in** [phras v] **1.** *(troops, equipment)* send sb/sth in jdn/etw. einsetzen ['aɛnzɛtsn̩] +haben ◊ *Die Regierung hat Soldaten/Hubschrauber eingesetzt, um den Flutopfern zu helfen.* **2.** *(a letter, document)* send sth in etw. einsenden ['aɛnzɛndn̩] <sendet ein, sandte/sendete ein, hat eingesandt/eingesendet> ◊ *die Lösung einsenden* ◆ *seine Bewerbung einsenden*

• **send off** [phras v] **1.** *(a letter, parcel)* send sth off etw. abschicken ['apʃɪkŋ̍] +haben ◊ *einen Brief/ein Paket/eine E-Mail/eine SMS abschicken* ◆ *Ich habe den Brief gestern abgeschickt.* **2.** *(a person)* send sb off jdn wegschicken ['vɛkʃɪkŋ̍] +haben ◊ *Sie schickte uns weg.* send sb off to ... jdn irgendwohin schicken ◊ *Ich habe die Kinder ins Schwimmbad geschickt.* **3.** SPORT send sb off jdn vom Platz stellen [fɔm 'plats ʃtɛlən] +haben ◊ *Er wurde wegen des Fouls vom Platz gestellt.*

• **send out** [phras v] **1.** *(invitations, leaflets etc.)* send sth out etw. verschicken [fɛ'ʃɪkŋ̍] <verschickt, verschickte, hat verschickt> ◊ *Sie wollen insgesamt 500 Einladungen verschicken.* **2.** *(radiation, smoke etc.)* abgeben ['apge:bm̩] <gibt ab, gab ab, hat abgegeben> ◊ *Die Anlage gibt giftige Gase/radioaktive Strahlung ab.*

• **send up** [phras v] *(fam)* send sb up jdn verulken [fɛ'ʊlkŋ̍] <verulkt, verulkte, hat verulkt> *(fam)* ◊ *In dieser Sendung wird sogar die englische Königin verulkt.*

sender [noun] Absender ['apzɛndɐ] der <–s, –> ♀Absenderin ['apzɛndərɪn] die <–, –nen> ◊ *Dieser Brief geht zurück an den Absender.*

senile [adj] senil [ze'ni:l] *(lofty, esp pej)* ◊ *die Behandlung seniler Patienten* ◆ *Opa wird langsam senil.*

senior¹ [noun] *(in the US : final-year student)* Student/Studentin im letzten Studienjahr; *(at school)* Schüler/Schülerin im letzten Schuljahr

ⓔ be two etc. years sb's senior zwei etc. Jahre älter als jd sein

senior² [adj] **1.** *(manager, position)* leitend ['laɛtn̩t] *no comp/superl, only before ns* ◊ *ein leitender Angestellter; (officer)* ranghöher ['raŋhø:ɐ] ◊ *ein ranghöherer Offizier* senior to sb höher gestellt als jd

['hø:ɐ gəʃtɛlt als] ◊ *Sie ist in der Firma höher gestellt als ich.* **2.** *(older)* älter ['ɛltɐ] ◊ *die älteren Schüler* senior to älter als ◊ *Er ist älter als ich.* **3.** *(referring to the older person with the same name)* Senior senior ['zeːnjoːɐ̯] *invariable, not before ns* ◊ *Hans Müller senior*

senior citizen [noun] Rentner ['rɛntnɐ] der <–s, –> ♀Renterin ['rɛntnərɪn] die <–, –nen> ◊ *eine rüstige Rentnerin* ♦ *ein Treffpunkt für Rentner*

senior high school [noun] *(in the US)* ⊙Oberstufe ['oːbɐʃtuːfə] die <–, –n> ◊ *eine Schülerin der Oberstufe*

sensation [noun] **1.** *(feeling)* Gefühl [gə'fyːl] das <–(e)s, –e> ◊ *ein prickelndes Gefühl auf der Haut* ♦ *ein Gefühl der Benommenheit* ♦ *Er hat seit dem Unfall kein Gefühl mehr in den Zehen.* **2.** *(event)* Sensation [zɛnza'tsjoːn] die <–, –en> ◊ *Der Fund ist eine archäologische Sensation.* cause a sensation großes Aufsehen erregen [groːsəs 'ạofzeːən ɛre:gn̩] <erregt, erregte, hat erregt>

sensational(ly) [adj, adv] **1.** *(exciting)* sensationell [zɛnzatsjo'nɛl] ◊ *sensationelle Enthüllungen* ♦ *Die Story ist wirklich sensationell!* ♦ *ein sensationell aufgemachter Bericht.* **2.** *(fam) (attractive, good)* fantastisch [fan'tastɪʃ] *(fam)* ◊ *ein fantastisches Kleid* ♦ *Das Essen war fantastisch.* ♦ *Er tanzt fantastisch.*

sense¹ [noun] **1.** *(feeling, belief)* sense of sth Gefühl ... [gen] [gə'fyːl] das <–(e)s, –e> ◊ *Ein Gefühl der Panik überkam ihn.* sense of achievement Erfolgsgefühl [ɛ'fɔlksgəfyːl] sense of community Gemeinschaftsgefühl [gə'maɛnʃaftsgəfyːl] sense of honour Ehrgefühl ['eːɐ̯gəfyːl] ◊ *Hast du denn überhaupt kein Ehrgefühl?* **2.** *(natural ability, instinct)* Sinn [zɪn] der <–(e)s, –e> ◊ *die fünf Sinne* ♦ *Für Gefahren habe ich einen sechsten Sinn.* sense of smell Geruchssinn [gə'rʊxszɪn] sense of balance Gleichgewichtssinn ['glaɛçgəvɪçtszɪn] sense of direction Orientierungssinn [orjɛn'tiːrʊŋszɪn] business sense Geschäftssinn [gə'ʃɛftszɪn] sense of humour Humor [hu'moːɐ̯] der <–s> *no pl* ◊ *Peter hat keinen Humor.* **3.** *(reason, purpose)* Sinn [zɪn] der <–(e)s, –e> there's no sense in sth etw. hat keinen Sinn ◊ *Es hat keinen Sinn, ohne Baugenehmigung mit den Bauarbeiten anzufangen.* **4.** *(good sense)* Vernunft [fe'nʊnft] die <–> *no pl* ◊ *Sie sollten Vernunft walten lassen.* ♦ *sich von der Vernunft leiten lassen* see sense zur Vernunft kommen have the sense to do sth so vernünftig sein, etw. zu tun [zoː fe'nʏnftɪç zaɛn ... tsuː] ◊ *Ich hoffe, sie sind so vernünftig, sich in der Sonne gut einzucremen.* talk sense vernünftig reden [fe'nʏnftɪç ˌreːdn̩] +haben **5.** *(reasonable way of thinking)* senses Vernunft [fe'nʊnft] die <–> *no pl* bring sb to their senses jdn zur Vernunft bringen come to your senses zur Vernunft kommen take leave of your senses den Verstand verlieren [deːn fe'ʃtant fɛˌliːrən] <verliert, verlor, hat verloren> **6.** *(meaning)* Sinn [zɪn] der <–(e)s, –e> ◊ *im wahrsten Sinn des Wortes* ♦ *Ich spreche hier von Religion im weitesten Sinn.; (of a word, phrase)* Bedeutung [bə'dɔøtʊŋ] die <–, –en> ◊ *Dieses Wort hat zwei Bedeutungen.* **7.** *(one way of thinking)* Hinsicht ['hɪnzɪçt] die <–, –en> in a sense in gewisser Hinsicht in one sense in einer Hinsicht ◉ make sense **1.** *(be sensible)* sinnvoll sein ◊ *Es ist sinnvoll, beide Behandlungen gleichzeitig durchzuführen.* **2.** *(be easy to understand)* einen Sinn ergeben

◊ *Die Geschichte ergibt überhaupt keinen Sinn!* make sense of sth etw. verstehen

sense² [verb] *(person)* spüren ['ʃpyːrən] +haben ◊ *Ich konnte die Gefahr spüren.* ♦ *Sie spürte, dass er ihr etwas verheimlichte.; (machine)* registrieren [regɪs'triːrən] <registriert, registrierte, hat registriert> ◊ *Das Gerät registriert jede Temperaturschwankung.*

sensible(-ibly) [adj, adv] **1.** *(reasonable, healthy)* vernünftig [fe'nʏnftɪç] ◊ *eine vernünftige Lösung finden* ♦ *Sei doch vernünftig!* ♦ *Sie achtet darauf, dass die Kinder vernünftig essen.* **2.** *(practical)* zweckmäßig ['tsvɛkmɛːsɪç] ◊ *eine zweckmäßige Jacke* ♦ *Ihre Kleidung ist eher zweckmäßig als elegant.* ♦ *zweckmäßig gekleidet sein*

sensitive [adj] **1.** *(reacting strongly, easily upset)* empfindlich [ɛm'pfɪntlɪç] ◊ *empfindliche Messgeräte* ♦ *Viele Teenager sind sehr empfindlich, wollen es aber nicht zugeben.* ♦ *Sie hat einen empfindlichen Magen.* be sensitive to sth empfindlich auf etw. [acc] reagieren ◊ *Diese Pflanzen reagieren empfindlich auf Zugluft.* ♦ *Er reagiert auf Kritik sehr empfindlich.* **2.** *(to be kept secret)* vertraulich [fe'traolɪç] ◊ *vertrauliche Informationen* ♦ *Diese Akten sind streng vertraulich.; (to be dealt with carefully)* heikel ['haɛkl̩] <heikler, am heikelsten> <ein heikler ...‚ eine heikle ...‚ ein heikles Thema> ♦ *Der ganze Bereich der Gentechnologie ist politisch gesehen ein heikles Thema.* **3.** *(showing that you care)* einfühlsam ['aɛnfyːlzaːm] ◊ *Als Ärztin sollte sie etwas einfühlsamer sein.* ♦ *ein einfühlsamer Umgang mit depressiven Menschen* be sensitive to sth Verständnis für etw. haben [fe'ʃtɛntnɪs fyːɐ̯ ... haːbm̩] +haben ◊ *Er sollte mehr Verständnis für unsere Sorgen haben.*

sensitively [adv] einfühlsam ['aɛnfyːlzaːm] ◊ *Sie geht sehr einfühlsam mit den Patienten um.*

sensitivity [noun] **1.** *(understanding)* sensitivity (to sth) Einfühlungsvermögen (in etw. [acc]) ['aɛnfyːlʊŋsfemøːgn̩] das <–s> *no pl* ◊ *Als Kinderpsychologe braucht man viel Einfühlungsvermögen.* ♦ *Einfühlungsvermögen in andere Kulturen* **2.** *(tendency to have strong reactions)* sensitivity (to sth) Empfindlichkeit (gegen etw.) [ɛm'pfɪntlɪçkaɛt] die <–, –en> *most sing* ◊ *Empfindlichkeit gegen Licht/Sonne* ♦ *Ihre Empfindlichkeit macht die Zusammenarbeit mit ihr manchmal schwer.* **3.** *(artistic ability, understanding of the various forms of art)* Gefühl [gə'fyːl] das <–(e)s> *no pl* ◊ *mit viel Gefühl spielen/zeichnen/singen* **4.** *(of a situation, issue)* heikle Natur [haɛklə na'tuːɐ̯] die <–> *no pl* ◊ *die heikle Natur dieses Themas* **5.** *(feelings)* sensitivities Gefühle [gə'fyːlə] die <–> *pl* ◊ *Ich möchte seine Gefühle nicht verletzen.* **6.** *(of a device: ability to measure precisely)* Empfindlichkeit [ɛm'pfɪntlɪçkaɛt] die <–, –en> *most sing* ◊ *die Empfindlichkeit der Messgeräte*

sensual(ly) [adj, adv] sinnlich ['zɪnlɪç] ◊ *sinnliche Freuden* ♦ *Ihre Lippen waren sehr sinnlich.* ♦ *sich von jdm sinnlich angezogen fühlen*

sentence¹ [noun] **1.** LING Satz [zats] der <–es, Sätze> ◊ *Ein Satz endet immer mit einem Satzzeichen.* ♦ *Kannst du mir in wenigen Sätzen schildern, worum es in dem Stück geht?* **2.** LAW Strafe ['ʃtraːfə] die <–, –n> ◊ *eine schwere Strafe erhalten* ◊ *eine Strafe verbüßen* pass sentence das Urteil verkünden [das 'ʊ'taɛl feˌkyndn̩] <verkündet, verkündete, hat

verkündet> ◊ *Der Richter wird morgen das Urteil verkünden.*

sentence² [verb] sentence sb to sth jdn zu etw. verurteilen [tsuː ... fe|ˌʊˈtaelən] <verurteilt, verurteilte, hat verurteilt> ◊ *Sie wurde zu drei Jahren Gefängnis verurteilt.*

sentiment [noun] **1.** *(opinion)* Ansicht [ˈanzɪçt] die <–, –en> ◊ *die Ansichten, die in diesem Artikel zum Ausdruck kommen* popular sentiment allgemeine Stimmung [algəmaenə ˈʃtɪmʊŋ] die <–> no pl ◊ *Wie ist die allgemeine Stimmung der Bürger zum EU-Beitritt?* **2.** sentimentality Gefühle [gəˈfyːlə] die <–> pl ◊ *Meine Führungsposition lässt keinen Raum für Gefühle.*

sentimental(ly) [adj, adv] sentimental [zɛntimɛnˈtaːl] ◊ *ein sentimentaler Liebesroman* ♦ *Wenn ich diese Melodie höre, werde ich ganz sentimental.* ♦ *Das Publikum war sentimental gestimmt.*

separable [adj] trennbar [ˈtrɛnbaːr] no comp/superl ◊ *ein trennbares Verb* ♦ *Die eine Frage ist nicht von der anderen trennbar.*

separate¹ [adj] **1.** *(not together)* getrennt [gəˈtrɛnt] no comp/superl ◊ *getrennte Bankkonten haben* ♦ *Die Schlafräume für Jungen und Mädchen sind getrennt.* ♦ *rohes Fleisch getrennt von anderen Lebensmitteln aufbewahren* They lead separate lives. Jeder von ihnen lebt sein eigenes Leben. **2.** *(own, new)* eigen [ˈaegɳ] no comp/superl, only before ns ◊ *Die Wohnung hat einen eigenen Eingang.* ♦ *Nehmen Sie für jedes Gedicht ein eigenes Blatt Papier.* **3.** *(not related)* verschieden [feˈʃiːdɳ] no comp/superl, only before ns ◊ *Ich habe jetzt schon vier verschiedenen Fällen gehört, wo ein Mitarbeiter gemobbt wurde.* That is a separate matter. Das ist etwas anderes.

separate² [verb] **1.** *(keep apart, divide)* trennen [ˈtrɛnən] +haben ◊ *Der Lehrer trennte die beiden Streitbähne.* ♦ *In dem Gedränge wurde das Kind von der Mutter getrennt.* ♦ *Die Straße trennt den Campingplatz vom See.* ♦ *Die beiden Spieler trennten nur fünf Punkte voneinander.* ♦ *Man muss die beiden Fragen voneinander trennen.* **2.** *(move apart)* separate (from sth) (von etw.) abgehen [ˈapgeːən] <geht ab, ging ab, ist abgegangen> ◊ *Der Schlauch ist von der Dusche abgegangen.* **3.** *(stop living with sb)* sich trennen [ˈtrɛnən] +haben ◊ *Tom und Nina haben sich getrennt.* **4.** *(be the difference)* separate sb/sth from sb/sth jdn/etw. von jdm/etw. unterscheiden [fɔn ... ʊntɐˌʃaedɳ] <unterscheidet, unterschied, hat unterschieden> ◊ *Was unterscheidet ihn von den anderen Stars?*

separately [adv] getrennt [gəˈtrɛnt] no comp/superl ◊ *Die Nebenkosten werden getrennt abgerechnet.* ♦ *Sie leben seit zwei Jahren getrennt.*

separation [noun] *(time spent apart, splitting up)* Trennung [ˈtrɛnʊŋ] die <–, –en> ◊ *Das Schlimmste war für ihn die Trennung von seiner Familie.* ♦ *die Trennung des Eigelbs vom Eiweiß* ♦ *Sie wollten der Kinder wegen eine Trennung vermeiden.;* *(of an area)* Abspaltung [ˈapʃpaltʊŋ] die <–, –en> ◊ *ein Kampf gegen die Abspaltung der Region*

September [noun] September [zɛpˈtɛmbɐ] der <–(s), –> → **January**

sequence [noun] **1.** *(set of related things)* Abfolge [ˈapfɔlgə] die <–, –n> ◊ *die zeitliche/chronologische Abfolge* ♦ *die Abfolge der Nummern/Stationen* ♦ *eine*

rasche Abfolge von Einzelbildern **2.** *(order)* Reihenfolge [ˈraeənfɔlgə] die <–, –n> ◊ *etw. in die richtige Reihenfolge bringen* **3.** FILM Sequenz [zeˈkvɛnts] die <–, –en> ◊ *Die folgende Sequenz zeigt Minas Traum.*

sergeant [noun] **1.** MIL *(in the armed services)* Unteroffizier [ˈʊnteˌɔfiˌtsiːɐ̯] der <–s, –e> ♀Unteroffizierin [ˈʊnteˌɔfiˌtsiːrɪn] die <–, –nen> ◊ *Ihr Mann ist Unteroffizier bei der Armee.* **2.** *(in the police)* Polizeimeister [poliˈtsaemaestɐ] der <–s, –> ♀Polizeimeisterin [poliˈtsaemaestərɪn] die <–, –nen> ◊ *Er wurde zum Polizeimeister befördert.*

serial¹ [noun] Serie [ˈzeːriə] die <–, –n> ◊ *Heute fängt eine neue Serie für Kinder an.*

serial² [adj] seriell [zeˈriɛl] no comp/superl, only before ns ◊ *serielle Monogamie* ♦ *eine serielle Schnittstelle* serial killer Serienmörder [ˈzeːriənmœˈrdɐ] der <–s, –> serial novel Fortsetzungsroman [ˈfɔrˈtzɛtsʊnsroˌmaːn] der <–s, –e>

series [noun] **1.** *(set of similar things, programmes, articles)* Serie [ˈzeːriə] die <–, –n> ◊ *Eine Serie von Explosionen erschütterte die Stadt.* ♦ *Das ZDF sendet eine fünfteilige Serie über Indianer.* television series Fernsehserie [ˈfɛˈnzeːzeːriə] die **2.** *(set of books, events)* Reihe [ˈraeə] die <–, –n> ◊ *Die Reihe umfasst 14 Bände.* ♦ *Die Reihe der Gespräche wird fortgeführt.*

serious [adj] **1.** *(mistake, crime, illness, injury, accident)* schwer [ʃveːɐ] mostly before ns ◊ *ein schwerer Fehler* ♦ *ein schweres Verbrechen* ♦ *ein schwerer Vorwurf; (person, implications, problem, threat, matter, doubt)* ernst [ɛʳnst] <ernster, am ernstesten> ◊ *Du siehst so ernst aus. Ist etwas passiert?* ♦ *Das sind ernste Gefahr dar.* ♦ *Ich habe ernste Zweifel, ob wir das schaffen.* **2.** be serious (about sth) es (mit etw.) ernst meinen [ɛs ˈɛʳnst maenən] +haben ◊ *Ich weiß nicht, ob er es mit seinem Angebot ernst meint.* I'm serious. Ich meine es ernst. Be serious!, You can't be serious! Mach keine Witze! be serious about doing sth etw. wirklich tun wollen [ˌvɪʳklɪç ... vɔlən] <will, wollte, hat wollen> ◊ *Willst du wirklich nach Hamburg ziehen?* **3.** *(competition, attempt, discussion)* ernsthaft [ˈɛʳnsthaft] <ernsthafter, am ernsthaftesten> ◊ *Sie hatte keine ernsthafte Konkurrenz.* ♦ *Sie haben einen ernsthaften Versuch unternommen, das Problem zu bereinigen.*

seriously [adv] **1.** *(ill, injured)* schwer [ʃveːɐ] ◊ *Er ist schwer verletzt/krank.* **2.** *(think, consider)* ernsthaft [ˈɛʳnsthaft] <ernsthafter, am ernsthaftesten> ◊ *Wir haben ernsthaft über die Weltlage diskutiert.* ♦ *Sie denkt ernsthaft daran, Schauspielerin zu werden.* take sb/sth seriously jdn/etw. ernst nehmen [ˈɛʳnst neːmən] <nimmt, nahm, hat genommen> ◊ *Ich nehme das ernst!* **3.** *(fam) (really)* im Ernst [ɪm ˈɛʳnst] ◊ *Meinst du im Ernst, ich würde das tun?* ♦ *„Er heiratet.“ — „Im Ernst?“*

sermon [noun] REL Predigt [ˈpreːdɪçt] die <–, –en> ◊ *Wer hält die Predigt im heutigen Gottesdienst?* **2.** *(fam) (about morally correct behaviour)* Moralpredigt [moˈraːlpreːdɪçt] die <–, –en> ◊ *Ich musste mir wieder eine Moralpredigt anhören.*

serum [noun] Serum [ˈzeːrʊm] das <–s, Seren> ◊ *jdm ein Serum gegen etw. spritzen* ♦ *Der Erreger wurde im Serum von Mäusen nachgewiesen.*

servant [noun] Diener [ˈdiːnɐ] der <–s, –> ♀Dienerin [ˈdiːnərɪn] die <–, –nen> ◊ *ein treuer Diener* ♦ *Sie*

bezeichnete sich als Dienerin Gottes. the servants das Personal [das pɛʳzo'na:l] <–s> *no pl ◊ Die Herrschaft ist heute aus und das Personal hat frei.* ⊙ the servant of sth/sb ein Sklave ... ⟨gen⟩ *◊ Er ist ein Sklave seines Computers/Chefs.*

serve¹ ⟨noun⟩ SPORT Aufschlag ['ao̯ʃla:k] der <–(e)s, Aufschläge> *◊ jdm den Aufschlag abnehmen* ♦ *einen harten/schwachen Aufschlag haben*

serve² ⟨verb⟩ 1. *(food, drink)* servieren [zɛʳ'vi:rən] <serviert, servierte, hat serviert> *◊ Servieren Sie dazu Rotwein.* ♦ *Alle Gerichte werden mit Pommes frites serviert.* ♦ *Sie können jetzt servieren.* serve sb (with) sth jdm etw. servieren *◊ Er servierte seinen Gästen Kaffee und Kuchen.* serve sth out, serve sth up etw. servieren *◊ Soll ich die Suppe servieren?* 2. *(be enough for)* serve sb für jdn reichen [fy:ɐ̯ ... ˌraeçn̩] +haben *◊ Diese Menge reicht für zwei Personen.* 3. MIL dienen ['di:nən] +haben *◊ Er hat nicht gedient.* ♦ *Er dient im 4. Regiment.* 4. *(do a job)* serve sb/sth für jdn/etw. arbeiten [fy:ɐ̯ ... ˌaʳbaetn̩] <arbeitet, arbeitete, hat gearbeitet> *◊ Sie hat 40 Jahre lang für die Firma Meier gearbeitet.* serve on a committee in einem Ausschuss sitzen [ɪn ae̯nəm 'ao̯sʃʊs zɪtsn̩] <sitzt, saß, hat gesessen> serve as sth etw. sein [zae̯n] +sein *◊ Er ist von 1995 bis 1999 Kassenwart beim Sportverein gewesen.* serve an apprenticeship eine Lehre machen [ae̯nə 'le:rə maxn̩] +haben *◊ Er macht eine Lehre bei einem bekannten Koch.* 5. serve as sth als etw. dienen [als ... di:nən] +haben *◊ Die Garage dient als Abstellraum.* ♦ *Das Sofa dient auch als Gästebett.* serve as a warning to sb jdm eine Warnung sein [ae̯nə 'vaʳnʊŋ zae̯n] +sein serve to illustrate/emphasize sth etw. verdeutlichen/betonen [fɛ'dɔy̯tlɪçn̩/bə'to:nən] *◊ Sein Schicksal verdeutlicht, wie wichtig es ist, gute Freunde zu haben.* 6. *(help achieve sth)* serve a purpose einem Zweck dienen [ae̯nəm 'tsvɛk di:nən] +haben *◊ Welchem Zweck soll diese Maßnahme dienen?* serve sb well jdm zugute kommen [tsu'gu:tə kɔmən] <kommt, kam, ist gekommen> *◊ Ihre Erfahrung als Aupairmädchen kam ihr zugute, als sie selbst Kinder hatte.* 7. *(be in prison)* serve time im Gefängnis sitzen [ɪm gə'fɛŋnɪs zɪtsn̩] <sitzt, saß, hat gesessen> *◊ Er sitzt im Ausland im Gefängnis.* 8. *(provide with sth)* versorgen [fɛ'zɔʳgn̩] <versorgt, versorgte, hat versorgt> *◊ Diese Ölleitung versorgt den ganzen Westen des Landes.* 9. *(in a shop, restaurant)* bedienen [bə'di:nən] <bedient, bediente, hat bedient> *◊ Die Verkäuferin hat mich sehr freundlich bedient.* ♦ *Tut mir Leid, aber ich bediene nicht an diesem Tisch.* 10. LAW jdm etw. zustellen ['tsu:ʃtɛlən] +haben *◊ Mir wurde eine Vorladung vor das Amtsgericht zugestellt.* 11. SPORT *(in tennis etc.)* aufschlagen ['ao̯ʃla:gn̩] <schlägt auf, schlug auf, hat aufgeschlagen> *◊ ein Spieler, der gut aufschlägt*

server ⟨noun⟩ 1. IT Server ['sœʳvɐ] der <–s, –> *◊ etw. vom Server herunterladen* 2. SPORT Aufschläger ['ao̯ʃlɛːgɐ] der <–s, –>, ♀Aufschlägerin ['ao̯ʃlɛːgərɪn] die <–, –nen> 3. *(spoon)* Servierlöffel [zɛʳ'vi:ɐ̯lœfl̩] der <–s, –>; *(fork)* Vorlegegabel ['fo:ɐ̯le:gəgaːbl̩] die <–, –n>

service¹ ⟨noun⟩ 1. *(system)* Dienst [di:nst] der <–(e)s, –e> *◊ im auswärtigen/öffentlichen Dienst sein* ♦ *ein Agent im Dienste Ihrer Majestät* ambulance service Rettungsdienst ['rɛtʊŋsdi:nst]

prison service Strafvollzug [ʃtra:ffɔl'tsu:k] police service Polizei [poli'tsae̯] die <–, –en> *most sing* essential services wichtige Versorgungseinrichtungen [vɪçtɪgə fe'zɔʳgʊŋs|ˌae̯nrɪçtʊŋən] <–> *pl ◊ Bei der Katastrophe fielen wichtige Versorgungseinrichtungen vorübergehend aus.* 2. *(help)* be of service to sb jdm behilflich sein [bə'hɪlflɪç zae̯n] +sein *◊ Kann ich Ihnen behilflich sein?* do sb a service jdm einen Gefallen tun [ae̯nən gə'falən tu:n] <tut, tat, hat getan> *◊ Kannst du mir einen Gefallen tun?* need the services of sb jdn brauchen ['brao̯xn̩] +haben *◊ Ich brauche einen guten Architekten.* offer your services as sth sich als etw. anbieten [als ... ˌanbi:tn̩] <bietet sich an, bot sich an, hat sich angeboten> *◊ Mein Bruder hat sich als Helfer bei der Party angeboten.* 3. *(customer)* service Kundenbetreuung ['kʊndn̩bə'trɔy̯ʊŋ] die <–> *no pl ◊ Die Kundenbetreuung in dieser Firma ist ausgezeichnet.* raise the standard of service die Kundenbetreuung verbessern; *(in a restaurant, shop)* Bedienung [bə'di:nʊŋ] die <–, –en> *◊ Die Bedienung in diesem Restaurant ist hervorragend.* ♦ *Bedienung und Mehrwertsteuer eingeschlossen.* 4. *(by a business, organization)* Dienstleistung ['di:nstlae̯stʊŋ] die <–, –en> *◊ Die vereinbarte Dienstleistung wurde nicht erbracht.* ♦ *Waren und Dienstleistungen* provide a service eine Dienstleistung anbieten financial services Finanzdienstleistungen [fi'nantsdi:nst|lae̯stʊŋən] die <–> *pl* 5. *(work, duties)* Dienste ['di:nstə] die <–> *pl ◊ Sie dankte der Sekretärin für ihre treuen Dienste.* ♦ *Das alte Fahrrad hat mir gute Dienste geleistet.* for services rendered für geleistete Dienste voluntary service ehrenamtliche Arbeit ['e:rən|amtlɪçə ˌaʳbae̯t] die <–, –en> 6. in service in Betrieb [ɪn bə'tri:p] out of service außer Betrieb take sth out of service etw. aus dem Verkehr ziehen [ao̯s de:m fe'ke:ɐ̯ tsi:ən] <zieht, zog, hat gezogen> *◊ Diese alte Fähre sollte aus dem Verkehr gezogen werden.* 7. *(train)* Zug [tsu:k] der <–(e)s, Züge> the Reading service der Zug nach Reading; *(bus)* Bus [bʊs] der <–ses, –se> 8. *(for a machine)* Wartung ['vaʳtʊŋ] die <–, –en> *◊ die regelmäßige Wartung einer Anlage; (for a car)* Inspektion [ɪnspɛk'tsi̯o:n] die <–, –en> *◊ das Auto zur Inspektion bringen* 9. REL Gottesdienst ['gɔtəsdi:nst] der <–(e)s, –e> *◊ einen Gottesdienst abhalten* ♦ *am Gottesdienst teilnehmen* 10. SPORT Aufschlag ['ao̯ʃla:k] der <–(e)s, Aufschläge> *◊ jdm den Aufschlag abnehmen* ♦ *einen harten/schwachen Aufschlag haben* 11. *(beside a motorway)* services Raststätte ['rastʃtɛtə] die <–, –n> *◊ Wie weit ist es bis zur nächsten Raststätte?* 12. MIL *(armed forces)* the services das Militär [das mili'tɛ:ɐ̯] <–s> *no pl ◊ Sein Vater war beim Militär.* 13. *(set of plates etc.)* Service [zɛʳ'vi:s] das <–, –> *when used in the pl, pronounce the final 'e' ◊ Zur Hochzeit bekamen sie ein Service für 12 Personen geschenkt.* ⊙ be at sb's service jdm zur Verfügung stehen

service² ⟨verb⟩ 1. *(a machine, vehicle)* warten ['vaʳtn̩] <wartet, wartete, hat gewartet> *◊ Die Zentralheizung muss regelmäßig gewartet werden.* 2. *(with electricity, water, gas)* service sb/sth with sth etw./jdn mit etw. versorgen [mɪt ... fe,zɔʳgn̩] <versorgt, versorgte, hat versorgt> *◊ ein Gebiet mit Strom und Wasser versorgen* 3. FIN *(debts)* bedienen [bə'di:nən] <bedient, bediente, hat bedient>

serviceable ⟨adj⟩ brauchbar ['brɔːxbaːʳ] ◊ *Dieser Topf ist zwar alt, aber noch brauchbar.* ✦ *Hat jemand ein brauchbares Telefon zu verkaufen?*

service charge ⟨noun⟩ **1.** *(for a service)* Bearbeitungsgebühr [bəˈaˈbaetʊŋsɡəbyːɡ] die <-, -en> ◊ *Bei Zahlung mit Kreditkarte verlangen sie eine Bearbeitungsgebühr von fünf Euro.* **2.** *(in a restaurant)* Bedienungsgeld [bəˈdiːnʊŋsɡɛlt] das <-(e)s, -er> ◊ *Zu der Rechnung kamen noch 15% Bedienungsgeld.*

serviette ⟨noun⟩ Serviette [zɛrˈvjɛta] die <-, -n> ◊ *sich* ⟨dat⟩ *mit einer Serviette den Mund abwischen*

serving ⟨noun⟩ Portion [pɔrˈtsjoːn] die <-, -en> ◊ *Die Packung enthält vier Portionen.*

session ⟨noun⟩ **1.** *(period of time)* training session Trainingsstunde ['trɛːnɪŋʃtʊndə] die <-, -n> ◊ *Wann findet die nächste Trainingsstunde statt?* counselling session Beratungsgespräch [bəˈraːtʊŋsɡəʃprɛːç] das <-(e)s, -e> ◊ *Sie hat sich zu einem Beratungsgespräch angemeldet.* recording session Aufnahme ['aofnaːmə] die <-, -en> ◊ *Während der Aufnahme darf der Raum nicht betreten werden.* **2.** *(formal meeting)* Sitzung ['zɪtsʊŋ] die <-, -en> ◊ *eine Sitzung abhalten* ✦ *eine Sitzung des Bundestags* ✦ *eine Sitzung beim Psychologen* in closed session unter Ausschluss der Öffentlichkeit [ʊntɐ ˈaʊsʃlʊs deːɐ ˈœfntlɪçkaet] be in session tagen ['taːɡn̩] +haben ◊ *Im August tagt der Ausschuss nicht.* **3.** POL session (of parliament) Legislaturperiode [leɡɪslaˈtuːɡpe,rioːdə] die <-, -n> ◊ *Das Gesetz soll noch in dieser Legislaturperiode verabschiedet werden.*

set¹ ⟨noun⟩ **1.** *(group of things)* set (of) Satz (... ⟨gen⟩) [zats] der <-es, Sätze> ◊ *ein Satz Spielkarten/Schraubenschlüssel/Winterreifen* ✦ *Ich habe den ganzen Satz dieser Briefmarkenserie gekauft.* chess set Schachspiel ['ʃaxʃpiːl] das <-(e)s, -e> ◊ *ein Schachspiel aus Marmor* **2.** *(group of facts, ideas, regulations)* set of Reihe von ['raeə fɔn] die <-, -n> ◊ *eine Reihe von Behauptungen/Fragen* a set of instructions Anweisungen ['anvaezʊŋən] die <-> pl do three etc. sets of sth etc. dreimal etc. machen ['draemaːl maxn̩] +haben ◊ *Machen Sie diese Übung jeden Morgen dreimal.* **3.** *(in a performance)* Programmnummer [proˈɡramnʊmɐ] die <-, -n> ◊ *Die Band machte vor der nächsten Programmnummer einige Minuten Pause.* **4.** *(group of people)* Kreis [kraes] der <-es, -e> ◊ *the literary set* literarische Kreise ◊ *Er fand Anerkennung weit über literarische Kreise hinaus.* make a new set of friends neue Freunde finden [nɔøə ˈfrɔøndə fɪndn̩] <findet, fand, hat gefunden> **5.** SCHOOL *(students with similar abilities)* Leistungsgruppe ['laestʊŋsɡrʊpə] die <-, -n> ◊ *In Französisch ist er in der zweiten Leistungsgruppe.* **6.** TV, RADIO Gerät [ɡəˈrɛːt] das <-(e)s, -e> TV set Fernsehgerät ['fɛrnzeːɡərɛːt] **7.** THEAT, FILM *(for a play)* Bühnenbild ['byːnənbɪlt] das <-(e)s, -er> ◊ *ein eindrucksvolles Bühnenbild; (for a film)* Set [sɛt] das <-s, -s> **8.** SPORT *(in tennis etc.)* Satz [zats] der <-es, Sätze> ◊ *Er gewann das Tennismatch in drei Sätzen.* **9.** *(posture)* Haltung ['haltʊŋ] die <-, -en> ◊ *Sie erkannte an der Haltung seiner Schultern, dass er niedergeschlagen war.* **10.** MATH Menge ['mɛŋə] die <-, -n> ◊ *eine leere Menge*

set² ⟨adj⟩ **1.** *(prescribed, pre-arranged)* festgesetzt ['fɛstɡəzɛtst] *no comp/superl* ◊ *eine festgesetzte Gebühr* ✦ *Ist der Termin schon festgesetzt?*

2. *(unwilling to change)* be set (in your ways) unflexibel sein ['ʊnflɛksiːbl̩ zaen] +sein have very set ideas (about sth) ganz bestimmte Vorstellungen (von etw.) haben [ɡants bəʃtɪmtə ˈfoːɐʃtɛlʊŋən haːbm̩] +haben ◊ *Sie hat ganz bestimmte Vorstellungen von Kindererziehung.* **3.** *(rigid)* starr [ʃtaʳ] ◊ *ein starres Lächeln* ✦ *Sein Blick war starr.* ✦ *ihr starrer Gesichtsausdruck* **4.** *(ready)* be all set (for sth) (für etw.) bereit sein [bəˈraet zaen] +sein ◊ *Seid ihr bereit für die Ferien?* On your marks, get set, go! Achtung, fertig, los! be all set to do sth etw. schon tun wollen [ʃoːn ... vɔlən] <will, wollte, hat wollen> ◊ *Ich wollte schon aufgeben, aber dann kamen doch noch ein paar Helfer.* **5.** *(be likely to do sth)* be set for sth etw. vor sich haben ['foːɡ ... haːbm̩] +haben ◊ *Die Firma hat eine Umstrukturierung vor sich.* be set to do sth etw. tun werden ['veːɡdn̩] ◊ *Die Preise werden steigen.* look set to do sth etw. wahrscheinlich tun werden [vaːˈʃaenlɪç ... veːɡdn̩] ◊ *Er wird morgen wahrscheinlich spielen.* **6.** *(necessary to study)* vorgeschrieben ['foːɡɡəʃriːbm̩] *no comp/superl* ◊ *die vorgeschriebenen Texte* ✦ *Folgende Bücher sind für die Prüfung vorgeschrieben: ...* **7.** set menu Menü [meˈnyː] das <-s, -s> ◊ *Zu Mittag gab es ein Menü mit vier Gängen.* set meal Tagesgericht ['taːɡəsɡərɪçt] das <-(e)s, -e> ◊ *Was haben Sie heute als Tagesgericht?*

Ⓢ **be (dead) set against sth** (absolut) gegen etw. sein be (dead) set against doing sth (absolut) dagegen sein, etw. zu tun be set on sth zu etw. entschlossen sein be set on doing sth entschlossen sein, etw. zu tun

set³ ⟨verb⟩ **1.** *(stand)* stellen ['ʃtɛlən] +haben ◊ *eine Vase/ein Tablett auf den Tisch/Boden stellen; (sit)* setzen ['zɛtsn̩] +haben ◊ *das Kind auf den Boden setzen; (lay)* legen ['leːɡn̩] +haben ◊ *ein Buch auf den Tisch legen* **2.** *(be located)* be set liegen ['liːɡn̩] <liegt, lag, hat gelegen> ◊ *Das Hotel liegt auf einem Berg.* set into the wall in die Wand eingelassen [ɪn diː ˈvant ˌaeŋɡəlasn̩] **3.** *(put in a particular state)* set sth on fire etw. in Brand stecken [ɪn ˈbrant ʃtɛkn̩] +haben ◊ *Jemand hat die Scheune in Brand gesteckt.* set sb/sth free jdn/etw. freilassen ['fraelasn̩] <lässt frei, ließ frei, hat freigelassen> ◊ *Sie ließ das gefangene Tier frei.* **4.** *(make sth happen)* set sb/sth doing sth dazu führen, dass jd etw. tut ['daːtsu: fyːran das] +haben ◊ *Seine Andeutungen führten dazu, dass alle sich Sorgen machten.* **5.** *(a piece of equipment)* einstellen ['aenʃtɛlən] +haben ◊ *Weißt du, wie man den Videorekorder einstellt?; (a clock, an alarm)* set sth (at sth) etw. (auf etw.) ⟨acc⟩ stellen ['ʃtɛlən] +haben ◊ *Stell den Backofen auf 200 Grad.* ✦ *den Wecker auf sieben Uhr stellen* **6.** *(decide a date, price etc.)* festsetzen ['fɛstzɛtsn̩] +haben ◊ *den Termin für das nächste Treffen festsetzen* ✦ *Der Eintrittspreis ist auf 12 Euro festgesetzt worden.* set a date (for sth) das Datum (für etw.) festsetzen **7.** *(establish a rule, limit, standard etc.)* setzen ['zɛtsn̩] +haben ◊ *einen Schwerpunkt/Trend/neue Maßstäbe setzen* ✦ *einem Kind Grenzen setzen* set conditions (for sth) Bedingungen (für etw.) stellen [bəˈdɪŋʊŋən ʃtɛlən] +haben set a record Rekord aufstellen [aenan reˈkɔʳt aofʃtɛlən] +haben ◊ *Der Läufer hat einen Rekord aufgestellt.* **8.** *(decide, prescribe, a direction, tone)* angeben ['angeːbm̩] <gibt an, gab an, hat angegeben> ◊ *Gib du die Richtung*

an. set the tone den Ton angeben set an example
(to sb) (jdm) ein Beispiel geben
[aen 'baesfpi:l ge:bm̩] <gibt, gab, hat gegeben> ◊ *Die
älteren Kinder geben den jüngeren ein schlechtes
Beispiel.* **9.** *(a task, challenge)* set sb sth jdn vor
etw. stellen [fo:ɐ ɛtvas 'ʃtɛlən] +haben ◊ *Da hast du
mich vor eine schwere Aufgabe gestellt.; (homework)*
jdm etw. aufgeben ['aofge:bm̩] <gibt auf, gab auf, hat
aufgegeben> ◊ *Der Lehrer gab den Schülern eine
Gleichung auf.* set sb a goal jdm ein Ziel setzen
[aen 'tsi:l zɛtsn̩] +haben set sb to do sth jdm die
Aufgabe geben, etw. zu tun
[di: 'aofga:bə ge:bm̩ ... tsu:] <gibt, gab, hat gegeben>
◊ *Vater gab den Kindern die Aufgabe, das Gemüsebeet umzugraben.* set yourself to do sth [dat]
vornehmen, etw. zu tun ['fo:ɐne:mən ... tsu:] <nimmt
sich vor, nahm sich vor, hat sich vorgenommen> ◊ *Er
hat sich vorgenommen, einen Marathon zu laufen.*
10. set to work sich an die Arbeit machen
[an di: 'a'baet maxn̩] +haben ◊ *Er machte sich sofort
an die Arbeit.* set to work on sth mit der Arbeit an
etw. [dat] beginnen [mɪt de:ɐ ,a'baet an ... bə,gɪnən]
<beginnt, begann, hat begonnen> ◊ *Sie hat schon mit
der Arbeit an ihrem neuen Roman begonnen.* set to
work to do sth sich daranmachen, etw. zu tun
[da'ranmaxn̩ ... tsu:] +haben ◊ *Sie machte sich daran,
den Reifen zu wechseln.* **11.** *(film, play, book)* be set
in ... in ... [dat] spielen [ɪn ... ʃpi:lən] +haben ◊ *Der
Film spielt im Mittelalter/in Berlin.* **12.** *(sun)* untergehen ['ʊntɐge:ən] <geht unter, ging unter, ist unterge-
gangen> ◊ *Die Sonne geht bald unter.* **13.** *(a broken
bone)* einrichten ['aenrɪçtn̩] <richtet ein, richtete ein,
hat eingerichtet> ◊ *Der Arzt hat das gebrochene Bein
eingerichtet.* **14.** *(become solid, concrete)* hart
werden ['ha'rt ve:ɐdn̩] +sein ◊ *Der Gips/Beton ist
schnell hart geworden.; (jelly)* fest werden
['fɛst ve:ɐdn̩] +sein ◊ *Der Wackelpudding wird
innerhalb von 20 Minuten fest.* **15.** *(hair)* legen
['le:gn̩] +haben ◊ *Sie ließ sich die Haare waschen
und legen.* **16.** set the table den Tisch decken
[de:n 'tɪʃ dɛkn̩] +haben ◊ *Hilf mir bitte, den Tisch zu
decken.*
● **set about** [phras v] set about sth etw. in Angriff
nehmen [ɪn 'angrɪf ne:mən] <nimmt, nahm, hat
genommen> ◊ *Er nahm die Aufgabe sofort in
Angriff.* set about doing sth sich daranmachen, etw.
zu tun [da'ranmaxn̩ ... tsu:] <macht sich, machte sich,
hat sich gemacht> ◊ *Ich machte mich daran, die
Wohnung zu putzen.*
● **set against** [phras v] **1.** *(compare)* set sth against
sth etw. mit etw. vergleichen [mɪt ... fɐ,glaeçn̩] <ver-
gleicht, verglich, hat verglichen> ◊ *die Aussage des
Täters mit der des Opfers vergleichen* set against sth
im Vergleich mit etw. ◊ *Im Vergleich mit unserer
Firma geht es bei euch sehr gemütlich zu.* **2.** *(cause
trouble between)* set sb against sb jdn gegen jdn
aufhetzen [ge:gn̩ ... ,aofhɛtsn̩] +haben ◊ *Sie hat ihn
gegen seinen eigenen Bruder aufgehetzt.* **3.** FIN set
sth (off) against tax etw. von der Steuer absetzen
[fɔn de:ɐ 'ʃtɔøɐ ,apzɛtsn̩] +haben ◊ *Die Fahrtkosten
können von der Steuer abgesetzt werden.*
● **set apart** [phras v] **1.** *(distinguish)* set sb/sth
apart (from sb/sth) jdn/etw. (von jdm/etw.)
abheben ['aphe:bm̩] <hebt ab, hob ab, hat
abgehoben> ◊ *Was hebt dieses Unternehmen von
anderen ab?* **2.** *(save)* set sth apart for sb/sth etw.

für jdn/etw. vorsehen [fy:ɐ ... 'fo:ɐze:ən] <sieht vor,
sah vor, hat vorgesehen> ◊ *Dieses Geld ist für Notfälle
vorgesehen.*
● **set aside** [phras v] **1.** *(money)* set aside sth (for
sth) etw. (für etw.) beiseite legen [bae'zaetə le:gn̩] ◊
Wir haben 2000 Euro für Notfälle beiseite gelegt.
2. set aside your differences etc. seinen Streit etc.
begraben [zaenən 'ʃtraet bə,gra:bm̩] <begräbt,
begrub, hat begraben> **3.** LAW *(a judgement, ruling)*
aufheben ['aofhe:bm̩] <hebt auf, hob auf, hat aufgeho-
ben> ◊ *Der Oberste Gerichtshof hob das Urteil auf.*
● **set back** [phras v] set sb/sth back jdn/etw. zurückwerfen ['tsu'rʏkvɛ'fn̩] <wirft zurück, warf zurück, hat
zurückgeworfen> ◊ *Sein Ausscheiden hat unser
Projekt um Monate zurückgeworfen.*
● **set down** [phras v] set sth down **1.** *(write down)*
etw. niederschreiben ['ni:dɐʃraebm̩] <schreibt nieder,
schrieb nieder, hat niedergeschrieben> ◊ *Sie schrieb
ihre Erlebnisse in Briefen nieder.* **2.** *(form) (lay
down)* etw. festlegen ['fɛstle:gn̩] +haben ◊ *Das ist in
den Vorschriften ganz genau festgelegt.*
● **set in** [phras v] *(weather, phase)* einsetzen
['aenzɛtsn̩] +haben ◊ *Ein dichter Schneefall setzte
ein.; (fog, storm)* aufkommen ['aofkɔmən] <kommt
auf, kam auf, ist aufgekommen> ◊ *Am Abend kam ein
Sturm auf.; (winter)* einbrechen ['aenbrɛçn̩] <bricht
ein, brach ein, ist eingebrochen> ◊ *Der Winter brach
ein.*
● **set off** [phras v] **1.** *(on a journey)* aufbrechen
['aofbrɛçn̩] <bricht auf, brach auf, ist aufgebrochen> ◊
Wir sind erst gegen zehn Uhr aufgebrochen. **2.** *(an
alarm, a protest)* auslösen ['aoslø:zn̩] +haben ◊ *Was
hat die Alarmanlage ausgelöst? ◆ Das Feuer hat eine
Panik ausgelöst.* **3.** *(a bomb)* zünden ['tsʏndn̩]
<zündet, zündete, hat gezündet> ◊ *eine Bombe/Spreng-
ladung zünden; (fireworks)* abbrennen ['apbrɛnən]
<brennt ab, brannte ab, hat abgebrannt> ◊ *Um Mitter-
nacht brannten wir ein Feuerwerk ab.* **4.** *(make more
attractive)* zur Geltung bringen [tsu:ɐ 'gɛltʊŋ brɪŋən]
<bringt, brachte, hat gebracht> ◊ *Der schlichte Mantel
wird durch einen bunten Seidenschal zur Geltung
gebracht.* **5.** *(make sb do sth)* set sb off doing sth
jdn zu etw. bringen [tsu: ... brɪŋən] <bringt, brachte,
hat gebracht> ◊ *Der Anblick brachte mich zum
Weinen/Lachen.* It will set her off again. Gleich
fängt sie wieder an.
● **set on** [phras v] **1.** *(make attack)* set sb on sb/sth
jdn auf jdn/etw. ansetzen [aof ... ,anzɛtsn̩]
+haben ◊ *Er hat seinen Hund auf die Einbrecher
angesetzt.* **2.** *(attack)* set on sb/sth jdn/etw.
angreifen ['angraefn̩] <greift an, griff an, hat angegrif-
fen> ◊ *Die Diebe haben den Mann ohne jeden
Grund angegriffen.*
● **set out** [phras v] **1.** *(on a journey)* aufbrechen
['aofbrɛçn̩] <bricht auf, brach auf, ist aufgebrochen> ◊
Sie sind früh aufgebrochen. **2.** *(explain, describe)*
darlegen ['da:ɐle:gn̩] +haben ◊ *Sie legten die Reformpläne in einem ausführlichen Bericht dar.*
3. *(display)* ausbreiten ['aosbraetn̩] <breitet aus,
breitete aus, hat ausgebreitet> ◊ *Er breitete sein
Werkzeug/seine Waren vor sich aus.* **4.** *(start working
on sth)* set out on sth etw. in Angriff nehmen
[ɪn 'angrɪf ne:mən] <nimmt, nahm, hat genommen> ◊
*Sie wollen gleich ein neues Projekt in Angriff
nehmen.* set out to do sth sich daranmachen, etw.
zu tun [da'ranmaxn̩ ... tsu:] +haben ◊ *Sie machten*

sich daran, das Haus zu renovieren.
• **set up** [phras v] **1.** *(found, establish)* set sth up
etw. gründen ['grʏndn̩] <gründet, gründete, hat
gegründet> ◊ *einen Verein zum Schutz von Kindern
gründen* set up shop ein Geschäft gründen **2.** set
sb up in business es jdm ermöglichen, ein Geschäft
zu gründen
[ɛs jeːmandm̩ eˈmøːklɪçn̩ aen gəˈʃɛft tsu grʏndn̩]
<ermöglicht, ermöglichte, hat ermöglicht> **3.** *(arrange)*
set sth up etw. arrangieren [araŋˈʒiːrən] <arrangiert,
arrangierte, hat arrangiert> ◊ *ein Treffen arrangieren*
4. *(put, place)* set sth up etw. aufstellen ['aofʃtɛlən]
+haben ◊ *Stellt die Stühle im Kreis auf.* **5.** *(pieces of
equipment)* aufbauen ['aofbaoən] +haben; *(an
account, a computer etc.)* set sth up etw. einrichten
['aenrɪçtn̩] <richtet ein, richtete ein, hat eingerichtet>
◊ *einen Internetzugang/Telefonanschluss einrichten*
6. *(prepare sb/yourself)* set sb/yourself up jdn/sich
stärken ['ʃtɛˈkn̩] +haben ◊ *Er stärkte sich für die
Reise.* **7.** *(incriminate)* set sb up jdn reinlegen
['raenleːgn̩] +haben *(fam)* **8.** *(in a position)* set sb up
as sth jdn als etw einsetzen [als ɛtvas ˈaenzɛtsn̩]
+haben ◊ *Er wurde als Gouverneur eingesetzt.*
setback [noun] Rückschlag ['rʏkʃlaːk] der
<–(e)s, Rückschläge> ◊ *Sie mussten einen herben
Rückschlag hinnehmen.* suffer a setback einen Rückschlag erleiden
settee [noun] Sofa ['zoːfaː] das <–s, –s>
setting [noun] **1.** *(place)* Umgebung [ʊmˈgeːbʊŋ] die
<–, –en> ◊ *Außerhalb seiner gewohnten Umgebung
fühlte er sich immer unsicher.* **2.** FILM, THEAT, LIT Schauplatz ['ʃaoplats] der <–es, Schauplätze> ◊ *Schauplatz
des Films ist das frühe 19. Jahrhundert.* ♦ *an einem
grandiosen Schauplatz* **3.** *(of controls)* Einstellung
['aenʃtɛlʊŋ] die <–, –en> ◊ *Die Einstellungen der
Heizung müssen angepasst werden.* **4.** *(for a meal)*
(place) setting Gedeck [gəˈdɛk] das <–(e)s, –e>
(lofty) ◊ *Die Spülmaschine hat ein Fassungsvermögen
von zwölf Gedecken.* **5.** *(for a stone or jewel)* Fassung
['fasʊŋ] die <–, –en> ◊ *ein Diamant in einer
goldenen Fassung* **6.** MUS Vertonung [fɛˈtoːnʊŋ] die
<–, –en>
settle [verb] **1.** *(your differences, an argument)*
beilegen ['baeleːgn̩] +haben ◊ *Nach langen Jahren
legten sie ihren Streit bei.* settle sth out of court
etw. außergerichtlich klären ['aosegərɪçtlɪç ˌklɛːrən]
+haben ◊ *Der Streitfall wurde außergerichtlich
geklärt.* **2.** *(a bill, your debts)* begleichen [bəˈglaeçn̩]
<begleicht, beglich, hat beglichen> ◊ *eine Rechnung/
Gebühr/Schuld begleichen* **3.** *(decide)* abmachen
['apmaxn̩] +haben ◊ *Wir haben abgemacht, dass du
um sieben Uhr ins Bett musst!* it is settled that es
ist abgemacht, dass that settles it dann ist alles
klar [ˌdann ɪst aləs ˈklaːˈ] +sein **4.** *(dust, sand)* sich
ansammeln [zɪç ˈanzamln̩] +haben ◊ *Überall
sammelte sich Staub an.; (snow)* liegen bleiben
['liːgn̩ blaebm̩] <bleibt, blieb, ist geblieben> ◊ *Der
Schnee blieb auf den Dächern liegen.* **5.** *(live permanently)* sich niederlassen ['niːdelasn̩] <lässt sich
nieder, ließ sich nieder, hat sich niedergelassen> ◊
*Nach mehreren Ortswechseln haben sie sich in Düs-
seldorf niedergelassen.* **6.** *(found a community)*
besiedeln [bəˈziːdl̩n] <besiedelt, besiedelte, hat
besiedelt> ◊ *Der Westen.des Landes wurde erst spät
besiedelt.* **7.** *(ground, building)* sich senken ['zɛŋkn̩]
+haben ◊ *Der Boden der Terrasse hat sich etwas*

gesenkt. **8.** *(make comfortable)* settle sb/yourself
into/in/on sth es jdm/sich in/auf etw. [dat] bequem
machen [ɛs ... ɪn/aof ... bəˈkveːm maxn̩] +haben ◊ *Er
machte es sich auf dem Sofa bequem.* settle back
sich zurücklehnen [tsuˈrʏkleːnən] +haben ◊ *Sie
lehnte sich im Sessel zurück.* **9.** *(calm down)* settle
(down) sich beruhigen [bəˈruːɪgn̩] <beruhigt sich,
beruhigte sich, hat sich beruhigt> ◊ *Nun beruhige
dich mal!* ♦ *Ihr Magen beruhigte sich nach einiger
Zeit.* **10.** *(your/sb's affairs)* regeln ['reːgl̩n] +haben
settle sb's estate jds Nachlass regeln **11.** *(feeling,
fear settles somewhere)* irgendwo macht sich Angst
breit [maxt zɪç ˈaŋst braet] +haben ◊ *In der Stadt
machte sich Angst breit.* Nausea settled in her
stomach. Übelkeit überkam sie. **12.** *(flying object)*
landen ['landn̩] <landet, landete, ist gelandet> settle
on sth auf etw. [dat] landen ◊ *Der Schmetterling
landete auf der Blüte.* **13.** *(eyes, gaze)* fallen ['falən]
<fällt, fiel, ist gefallen> ◊ *Sein Blick fiel auf die
Schlagzeile.*
• **settle down** [phras v] **1.** *(have a family)* häuslich
werden ['hɔyslɪç veːgdn̩] +sein ◊ *Schließlich wurde
er doch häuslicher und heiratete.* **2.** *(make yourself
comfortable)* es sich [dat] bequem machen
[ɛs ... bəˈkveːm maxn̩] +haben ◊ *Ich machte es mir
auf dem Sofa bequem.* → settle **9.**
• **settle for** [phras v] settle for sb/sth sich mit jdm/
etw. zufrieden geben [mɪt ... tsuˈfriːdn̩ geːbm̩] <gibt
sich, gab sich, hat sich gegeben> ◊ *Sie hat sich mit
einer kleinen Reise zufrieden gegeben.* settle for
second sich mit dem Zweitbesten zufrieden
geben
• **settle in** [phras v] **1.** *(get used to)* sich eingewöh-
nen ['aengəvøːnən] <gewöhnt sich ein, gewöhnte sich
ein, hat sich eingewöhnt> ◊ *Sie hat sich rasch in der
neuen Wohnung eingewöhnt.* **2.** *(make yourself comfortable)* es sich [dat] bequem machen
[ɛs ... bəˈkveːm maxn̩] +haben ◊ *Ich machte es mir
für die Dauer des Gesprächs bequem.*
• **settle on** [phras v] settle on sb/sth sich für jdn/
etw. entscheiden [fyːˈ ... ɛntˈʃaedn̩] <entscheidet sich,
entschied sich, hat sich entschieden> ◊ *Er muss sich
noch für eine Farbe entscheiden.*
settled → settle [adj] ruhig ['ruːɪç] ◊ *sich ruhiger
fühlen; (weather)* beständig [bəˈʃtɛndɪç] ◊ *Das Wetter
ist beständig.; (way of life)* geregelt [gəˈreːgl̩t] ◊ *ein
geregeltes Leben führen*
settlement [noun] **1.** *(agreement)* Abkommen
['apkɔmən] das <–, –> ◊ *Sie trafen ein Abkommen
über den Grenzverkehr.; (of an argument)* Schlichtung ['ʃlɪçtʊŋ] die <–, –en> ◊ *die Schlichtung des
Streits* out-of-court settlement außergerichtliche
Einigung ['aosegərɪçtlɪçə ˌaenɪgʊŋ] die <–, –en>
2. *(place where people live)* Siedlung ['ziːdlʊŋ] die
<–, –en> ◊ *Hier setzte sich eine bronzezeitliche
Siedlung.; (process of colonization)* Besiedlung
[bəˈziːdlʊŋ] die <–, –en> ◊ *die Besiedlung der
Rheintals* **3.** *(payment)* Begleichung [bəˈglaeçʊŋ] die
<–, –en> ◊ *die Begleichung aller Schulden* in settle-
ment *(of sth)* zur Begleichung *(... [gen])* **4.** *(of a
building, the ground)* Absenkung ['apzɛŋkʊŋ] die
<–, –en>
seven[1] [noun] Sieben ['ziːbm̩] die <–, –(en)> → **four**[1]
seven[2] [nmrl] sieben ['ziːbm̩] → **four**[2]
sevenfold [adj, adv] siebenfach ['ziːbm̩max] → **fourfold**
seventeen [nmrl] siebzehn ['ziːptseːn] → **four**[2]

seventh¹ [noun] **1.** *(fraction)* Siebtel ['ziːptl̩] das <–s, –> → **fourth¹ 1. 2.** *(in a sequence)* Siebte ['ziːptə] der *or* die *or* das <–n, –n> *most sing* → **fourth¹ 2.**

seventh² [nmrl] siebte ['ziːptə] <ein siebter …, eine siebte …, ein siebtes …> → **fourth²**

seventhly [adv] siebtens ['ziːptn̩s] → **fourthly**

seventy [nmrl] siebzig ['ziːptsɪç] → **four²**

sever [verb] **1.** *(a limb)* abtrennen ['aptrɛnən] +*haben* ◊ *Bei dem Unfall wurde ihr der rechte Arm abgetrennt.* **2.** *(a relationship, contact)* abbrechen ['apbrɛçn̩] <bricht ab, brach ab, hat abgebrochen>

several¹ [adj] one of his several houses eines seiner Häuser [ˌaɛnəs zae̯ne 'hɔø̯zə] in the past several weeks in den letzten Wochen [ɪn deːn lɛtstn̩ 'vɔxn̩]

several² [det] **1.** *(a small number)* einige ['ae̯nɪɡə] ◊ *Sie war einige Jahre im Ausland.; (emphasizing that there is more than one)* mehrere ['meːrərə] ◊ *Das ist nur eines von mehreren Problemen.* several times mehrmals ['meːɡmaːls] **2.** *(different)* unterschiedlich ['ʊntəʃiːtlɪç] ◊ *Sie gingen in unterschiedliche Richtungen davon.*

several³ [indef pron] **1.** einige ['ae̯nɪɡə] **2.** *(a small number)* einige ['ae̯nɪɡə] ◊ *Es gab viele Bewerber. Einige wären gut für die Stelle geeignet.* several of … einige … [gen] ◊ *Einige deiner Vorschläge gefallen mir gut.* ♦ *einige meines Stammes; (emphasizing that there is more than one)* mehrere ['meːrərə] ◊ *In mehreren meiner Dateien waren Viren.*

severe [adj] **1.** *(serious, extreme)* schwerwiegend ['ʃveːɐ̯viːɡn̩t] ◊ *ein schwerwiegendes Problem* ♦ *Die Folgen der Reform sind schwerwiegend.; (pain, bleeding)* stark [ʃtaʳk] <stärker, am stärksten> ◊ *Er hatte starke Blutungen.; (criticism)* hart [haʳt] <härter, am härtesten> ◊ *eine harte Strafe* ♦ *Die Kritik war sehr hart.* **2.** *(heavy)* heftig ['hɛftɪç] ◊ *Der Sturm war heftig.* ♦ *heftige Niederschläge* **3.** *(strict)* streng [ʃtrɛŋ] ◊ *eine strenge Lehrerin* ♦ *Sie trug ein strenges Kostüm.* severe on sb streng mit jdm ◊ *Er war sehr streng mit seinen Kindern.; (expression)* ernst [ɛʳnst] <ernster, am ernstesten> ◊ *ein ernster Gesichtsausdruck* **4.** *(difficult, demanding)* hart [haʳt] <härter, am härtesten> ◊ *Das Studium war ein harter Test.*

severely [adv] **1.** *(seriously)* schwer [ʃveːɐ̯] ◊ *schwer verletzt sein* severely limited stark eingeschränkt [ʃtaʳk 'ae̯nɡəʃrɛŋkt] <stärker eingeschränkt, am stärksten eingeschränkt> **2.** *(in a strict way)* streng [ʃtrɛŋ] ◊ *jdn streng bestrafen* **3.** *(in an unfriendly way)* unfreundlich ['ʊnfrɔø̯ntlɪç] ◊ *Die Leute starrten ihn unfreundlich an.*

severity [noun] **1.** *(strength)* Stärke ['ʃtɛʳkə] die <–, –n> ◊ *Die Stärke des Unwetters war ungewöhnlich.* **2.** *(of a punishment, sentence)* Härte ['hɛʳtə] die <–, –n> ◊ *Sie waren über die Härte der Bestrafung sehr empört.* **3.** *(strictness, unfriendliness)* Unfreundlichkeit ['ʊnfrɔø̯ntlɪçkae̯t] die <–> *no pl* ◊ *Ihre Unfreundlichkeit war unübertroffen.* **4.** severity of style stilistische Strenge [ʃtiˈlɪstɪʃə 'ʃtrɛŋə] die <–> *no pl* ◊ *die stilistische Strenge Flauberts* severity of sb's dress jds strenge Kleidung [ʃtrɛŋə 'klae̯dʊŋ] <–> *no pl*

sew [verb] *(fabrics)* nähen ['nɛːən] +*haben* ◊ *Sie näht ihre Kleider selbst.* ♦ *Ich kann nicht gut nähen.* sew sth on(to) sth etw. an etw. [acc] nähen ◊ *Er hat ihr einen Knopf an die Bluse genäht.*

• **sew up** [phras v] nähen ['nɛːən] +*haben* ◊ *einen Saum/Riss nähen*

◉ **get/have sth all sewn up** etw. unter Dach und Fach bringen

sewer [noun] Abwasserkanal ['apvasekaˌnaːl] der <–s, Abwasserkanäle> ◊ *Wasser in den Abwasserkanal leiten*

sewing [noun] **1.** *(process)* Nähen ['nɛːən] das <–s> *no pl* **2.** *(product)* Näharbeit ['nɛːˌaʳbae̯t] die <–, –en>

sewing machine [noun] Nähmaschine ['nɛːmaˌʃiːnə] die <–, –n>

sex [noun] **1.** *(act)* Sex [sɛks] der <–(es)> *no pl* ◊ *ungeschützten Sex haben* ♦ *eine Geschichte voller Sex und Erotik* sex scandal Sexskandal ['sɛksskanˌdaːl] der <–s, –e> sex partner Sexualpartner [zɛksuˈaːlpaʳtnɐ] der <–s, –> ♀Sexualpartnerin [zɛksuˈaːlpaʳtnərɪn] die <–, –nen> **2.** *(male or female)* Geschlecht [ɡəˈʃlɛçt] das <–(e)s, –er> ◊ *der Kampf der Geschlechter* ♦ *Er fühlt sich zum eigenen Geschlecht hingezogen.*

sex appeal [noun] Sex-Appeal ['sɛksɛˌpiːl] der <–s> *no pl* ◊ *Er besitzt sehr viel Sex-Appeal.*

sexist [adj] sexistisch [zɛˈksɪstɪʃ] ◊ *sexistische Bemerkungen* ♦ *Diese Werbung ist extrem sexistisch.*

sexual [adj] **1.** *(related to sex)* sexuell [zɛksuˈɛl] seldom comp/superl ◊ *sexuelle Handlungen* ♦ *Ihre Beziehung ist rein sexuell.* **2.** *(related to the relationship between men and women)* Geschlechter… [ɡəˈʃlɛçtə] sexual politics Geschlechterpolitik [ɡəˈʃlɛçtəpoliˌtiːk] die <–> *no pl* **3.** *(related to reproduction)* geschlechtlich [ɡəˈʃlɛçtlɪç] ◊ *geschlechtliche Fortpflanzung*

sexuality [noun] Sexualität [zɛksualiˈtɛːt] die <–> *no pl* ◊ *die weibliche Sexualität* ♦ *seine Sexualität ausleben*

sexually [adv] **1.** *(related to sex)* sexuell [zɛksuˈɛl] ◊ *sich sexuell von jdm angezogen fühlen* **2.** *(related to reproduction)* geschlechtlich [ɡəˈʃlɛçtlɪç] ◊ *sich geschlechtlich fortpflanzen*

sexy [adj] **1.** *(person, clothes, voice)* sexy ['sɛksiː] invariable *(fam)* ◊ *Der Typ ist sexy.* ♦ *sexy Unterwäsche* feel sexy sich sexy fühlen **2.** *(exciting)* attraktiv [atrakˈtiːf] ◊ *attraktive Berufe* make sth sexy etw. attraktiver gestalten

shabby(-ily) [adj, adv] *(clothes, furniture, person, action)* schäbig ['ʃɛːbɪç] ◊ *Der Teppich sieht allmählich sehr schäbig aus.* ♦ *schäbig gekleidet* ♦ *ein schäbiger Erpressungsversuch* feel shabby sich schäbig fühlen; *(goods, work)* schlecht [ʃlɛçt] <schlechter, am schlechtesten> ◊ *eine schlechte Arbeit* ♦ *eine schlecht vorbereitete Rede*

shack [noun] Baracke [baˈrakə] die <–, –n> ◊ *Die Armen leben in Baracken am Stadtrand.*

shackle [verb] **1.** *(prevent from doing sth)* behindern [bəˈhɪndən] <behindert, behinderte, hat behindert> ◊ *Seine ständige Angst behindert ihn.* **2.** *(bind with chains)* anketten ['ankɛtn̩] <kettet an, kettete an, hat angekettet> ◊ *Sie ketteten die Geiseln an.*

shade¹ [noun] **1.** *(shadow)* Schatten ['ʃatn̩] der <–s, –> ◊ *Ich liege lieber im Schatten als in der Sonne.* **2.** *(screen or cover)* Schirm [ʃɪʳm] der <–(e)s, –e> ◊ *eine Mütze mit Schirm* **3.** *(in the US: blind)* Rollo ['rɔloː] der <–s, –s> **4.** *(of a colour)* Farbton ['faʳptoːn] der <–(e)s, Farbtöne> ◊ *Diese Fliesen sind in verschiedenen Farbtönen erhältlich.* **5.** *(sunglasses)* shades Sonnenbrille ['zɔnənbrɪlə] die

<-, –n> ◊ *eine schicke Sonnenbrille* **6.** *(of a political opinion)* Couleur [ku'lø:ɐ̯] die <-, –s> ◊ *politische Vereinigungen verschiedener Couleurs* **7.** *(spirit, ghost)* Geist [ɡaɛst] der <-es, –er> **8.** *(memories)* shades of sth Erinnerungen an etw. [acc] [ɛ|'ɪnərʊŋən an] die <-> pl ◊ *Das sind alles Erinnerungen an meine Kindheit.* **9.** *(a little)* a shade ein bisschen [aɛn 'bɪsçən]
⊛ **put sb/sth in the shade** jdn/etw. in den Schatten stellen

shade² [verb] **1.** *(protect from light)* abschirmen ['apʃɪʳmən] +haben ◊ *Sie schirmte ihre Augen gegen die Sonnenstrahlen ab.* **2.** *(give a darker colour)* shade (in) schattieren [ʃa'ti:rən] <schattiert, schattierte, hat schattiert> ◊ *Die am stärksten betroffenen Gebiete sind auf der Darstellung schattiert.*

shadow [noun] Schatten ['ʃatn̩] der <-s, –> ◊ *Als sein Schatten auf ihr Gesicht fiel, wachte sie auf.* ♦ *jdm wie ein Schatten folgen* ♦ *ein Schatten auf dem Röntgenbild* ♦ *im Schatten eines Baums sitzen* eye shadow Lidschatten ['li:tʃatn̩]
⊛ **beyond a shadow of doubt** ohne den Hauch eines Zweifels **be a shadow of your former self** nur noch ein Schatten seiner selbst sein **be in sb's shadow** in jds Schatten stehen

shady [adj] **1.** *(dubious)* zwielichtig ['tsvi:lɪçtɪç] *(pej)* ◊ *zwielichtige Geschäftsleute* ♦ *Die Angelegenheit scheint mir ein bisschen zwielichtig.* **2.** *(cool, out of the sun)* schattig ['ʃatɪç] ◊ *ein schattiges Plätzchen* ♦ *Im Wald war es angenehm schattig.*

shaft [noun] **1.** *(of an arrow, penis, tool)* Schaft [ʃaft] der <-(e)s, Schäfte>; *(of a hammer)* Stiel [ʃti:l] der <-(e)s, –e> **2.** *(in an engine)* Welle ['vɛlə] die <-, –n> **3.** *(for horses)* Deichsel ['daɛksl̩] die <-, –n> **4.** *(narrow passage)* Schacht [ʃaxt] der <-(e)s, Schächte> ◊ *Der Tunnel wird durch Schächte belüftet.* ♦ *der Schacht eines Aufzugs* **5.** *(of light)* Lichtstrahl ['lɪçtʃtra:l] der <-(e)s, –en> ◊ *Ein dünner Lichtstrahl war zu sehen.*

shake¹ [noun] **1.** *(movement)* Schütteln ['ʃʏtl̩n] das <-s> *no pl* a shake of the head ein Kopfschütteln [aɛn 'kɔpʃʏtl̩n] give sth a shake etw. schütteln ['ʃʏtl̩n] +haben **2.** *(in the US: milkshake)* Milchshake ['mɪlçʃe:k] der <-s, –s>

shake² [verb] **1.** *(tremble)* beben ['be:bm̩] +haben ◊ *In der Nordschweiz hat gestern die Erde gebebt.*; *(with cold, emotion)* zittern ['tsɪtɐn] +haben ◊ *Meine Hände zitterten vor Aufregung.* ♦ *Du zitterst ja am ganzen Körper.* shake with fear vor Angst zittern shake with laughter sich vor Lachen schütteln [fo:ɐ̯ laxn̩ 'ʃʏtl̩n] +haben **2.** *(move the earth, upset sb)* erschüttern [ɛ'ʃʏtɐn] <erschüttert, erschütterte, hat erschüttert> ◊ *Ein starkes Erdbeben hat gestern Teile des Landes erschüttert.* ♦ *Sein Tod erschütterte mich.* **3.** *(liquids)* schütteln ['ʃʏtl̩n] +haben ◊ *Du musst die Flasche vor Gebrauch schütteln.* ♦ *Der Barmann schüttelte den Mixbecher.* **4.** *(a person)* rütteln ['rʏtl̩n] <rüttelt, rüttelte, hat gerüttelt> +haben ◊ *jdn rütteln, bis er aufwacht* ♦ *an einem Arm/an der Schulter rütteln* **5.** *(get rid of)* shake off loswerden ['lo:sve:ɐ̯dn̩] <wird los, wurde los, ist losgeworden> ◊ *Sie wurde ihre Erkältung nicht los.*; *(a pursuer)* abschütteln ['apʃʏtl̩n] +haben ◊ *einen Verfolger abschütteln*

shaky [adj] **1.** *(not strong, stable)* wackelig ['vakəlɪç] *(fam)* ◊ *auf wackeligen Beinen* ♦ *ein wackeliger Stuhl* ♦ *Ihre finanzielle Lage war wackelig.*

2. *(knowledge)* mangelhaft ['maŋlhaft] <mangelhafter, am mangelhaftesten> ◊ *Mein Französisch ist ziemlich mangelhaft.* ♦ *mangelhafte Grammatikkenntnisse*

shall [verb] **1.** *(asking for advice, a course of action)* sb shall do sth jd soll etw. tun [zɔl] <soll, sollte, hat sollen> ◊ *Soll ich dich morgen anrufen?* ♦ *Was soll ich machen?* **2.** *(for forming the future, for emphasis)* sb shall do sth jd wird etw. tun [vɪʳt] ◊ *Ich werde in die Stadt gehen.* ♦ *Wir werden morgen zusammen essen.* sb shall have done sth jd wird etw. getan haben ◊ *Ich werde die Arbeit bis morgen früh geschafft haben.* We shan't get into the concert. Wir werden in das Konzert nicht hineinkommen. **3.** *(as a question tag)* shan't I/we, shall I/we oder? ['o:dɐ] ◊ *Wir werden später Steak essen, oder?* I shall be lying on the beach tomorrow, shan't I? Morgen werde ich schon am Strand liegen.

shallow [adj] **1.** *(not deep)* flach [flax] ◊ *Bleibt bitte im flachen Wasser.* ♦ *eine flache Atmung haben* **2.** *(person)* oberflächlich ['o:beflɛçlɪç] *(pej)* ◊ *ein oberflächlicher Mensch; (entertainment, literature)* seicht [zaɛçt] <seichter, am seichtesten> ◊ *seichte Unterhaltung* ♦ *Dieser Roman ist mir zu seicht.*

shallowly [adv] **1.** *(not deeply)* flach [flax] ◊ *Die Kurve verläuft flach.* ♦ *flach atmen* **2.** *(pej) (superficially)* seicht [zaɛçt] <seichter, am seichtesten> ◊ *Das Stück war ziemlich seicht inszeniert.*

shambles [noun] Chaos ['ka:ɔs] das <-> *no pl* sth is (in) a shambles irgendwo herrscht Chaos ◊ *In der Organisation herrscht das reine Chaos.* ♦ *Auf ihrem Schreibtisch herrscht großes Chaos.*

shame [noun] **1.** *(source of pity or disappointment)* Schande ['ʃandə] die <-> *no pl* ◊ *Es ist eine Schande, dass er sie mit den Kindern sitzen gelassen hat.* to sb's shame zu jds Schande ◊ *Zu meiner Schande muss ich gestehen, dass ich meine Mutter seit Wochen nicht angerufen habe.* **2.** *(embarrassment)* Scham [ʃa:m] die <-> *no pl* ◊ *ohne Scham über etw.* [acc] *sprechen* hang your head in shame sich zutiefst schämen [tuti:fst 'ʃɛ:mən] +haben
⊛ **put sb/sth to shame** jdn/etw. beschämen **shame on you** schäme dich **(oh) what a shame** das ist eine Schande

shan't → shall

shape¹ [noun] **1.** *(form)* Form [fɔʳm] die <-, –en> ◊ *Die Vase hat eine schöne Form.* ♦ *Der Pullover hat seine Form behalten/verloren.* ♦ *Ohne Brille erkenne ich gerade mal die Formen der Gegenstände.* ♦ *die Form der Organisation verändern* all shapes and sizes alle Formen und Größen in the shape of sth in Form von etw. **2.** *(condition, health)* sb/sth is in good shape jdm/einer Sache geht es gut [ɡe:t ɛs 'ɡu:t] <ging, ist gegangen> ◊ *Es geht ihm nicht besonders gut.* sb/sth is in bad shape jdm/einer Sache geht es schlecht.; *(physically fit)* be in shape in Form sein [ɪn 'fɔʳm zaɛn] +sein be out of shape nicht in Form sein
⊛ **lick sb/sth into shape** jdn/etw. in Form bringen **take shape** Form annehmen

shape² [verb] **1.** *(influence, characterize)* prägen ['prɛ:ɡn̩] +haben ◊ *Diese Erfahrungen haben ihn/ seinen Charakter geprägt.* ♦ *Zahlreiche Kanäle prägen das Stadtbild Amsterdams.* **2.** *(give a certain shape to)* formen ['fɔʳmən] +haben ◊ *Ihre Lippen formten ein O.* ♦ *eine Brezel aus Teig formen* shape sth into sth etw. zu etw. formen

• **shape up** [phras v] **1.** *(develop)* sich entwickeln [ɛnt'vɪk|n] <entwickelt sich, entwickelte sich, hat sich entwickelt> ◊ *Das Viertel entwickelt sich zu einer interessanten Wohngegend.* **2.** *(improve)* sich verbessern [fɛ'bɛsɛn] <verbessert sich, verbesserte sich, hat sich verbessert> ◊ *Er hat sich in der Schule deutlich verbessert.*

◉ **shape up** or **ship out** Leistung bringen oder rausgeschmissen werden *(fam)*

share¹ [noun] **1.** *(part of sth)* Anteil ['antael] der <-(e)s, -e> ◊ *Ich will gerne meinen Anteil zur Haushaltsführung beitragen.* share in/of sth Anteil an etw. [dat] ◊ *Ihr Anteil an den Kosten beläuft sich auf 1500 Euro.* **2.** ECON Aktie ['aktsjə] die <-, -n> ◊ *Aktien ausgeben* ♦ *mit Aktien an der Börse handeln* ♦ *die Aktien steigen/fallen* share prices Aktienpreise ['aktsjənpraezə] die <-> pl

share² [verb] **1.** *(have or use at the same time, cut into parts)* teilen ['taelən] +haben ◊ *Ich teile ihre Meinung.* ♦ *Teilst du mit mir?* share sth four ways etw. in vier Teile teilen they share sth sie teilen sich [dat] etw. ◊ *Wir haben uns die Rechnung geteilt.* share sth with sb sich [dat] etw. mit jdm teilen ◊ *Er teilt sich die Hausarbeit mit seinen Kindern.* share sth among sb etw. unter jdm aufteilen [ʊntɐ ... 'aoftaelən] +haben **2.** *(a piece of information)* austauschen ['aostaoʃn] +haben ◊ *Informationen austauschen*

shared → **share**² [adj] gemeinsam [gə'maenza:m] ◊ *eine gemeinsame Sprache sprechen*

shareholder [noun] Aktionär [aktsjo'nɛːɐ] der <-s, -e> ♀Aktionärin [aktsjo'nɛːɐrɪn] die <-, -nen>

shark [noun] **1.** *(fish)* Hai [hae] der <-(e)s, -e> **2.** loan shark Kredithai [kre'di:hae] der <-(e)s, -e>

sharp¹ [adj] **1.** *(pointed, distinct)* scharf [ʃaʳf] <schärfer, am schärfsten> ◊ *ein scharfes Messer* ♦ *Dieses Foto ist nicht scharf.* ♦ *eine scharfe Kurve* ♦ *Das stand im scharfen Kontrast zu ihrer Aussage.* **2.** *(intelligent, alert)* schlau [ʃlao] <schlauer, am schlau(e)sten> ◊ *Unsere Kinder sind sehr schlau.* keep a sharp eye on sth etw. genau im Auge behalten [gənao ɪm 'aogə bəhaltn] <behält, behielt, hat behalten> ◊ *Der Hund behält die Katze genau im Auge.* **3.** *(rise, pain, feeling, wind, frost)* stark [ʃtaʳk] <stärker, am stärksten> ◊ *Sie hatte starke Schmerzen.* ♦ *ein starker Wind; (sound)* laut [laot] <lauter, am lautesten> ◊ *ein lauter Knall* **4.** *(clothes)* schick [ʃɪk] ◊ *Er trägt immer sehr schicke Kleidung.* **5.** *(dishonest)* gerissen [gə'rɪsn] ◊ *ein gerissener Gauner* **6.** *(music)* um einen Halbton höher [ʊm aenən ˌhalptoːn 'høːɐ] *no comp/superl*

sharp² [adv] **1.** *(in expressions of time)* genau [gə'nao] *no comp/superl* ◊ *genau um 19 Uhr* **2.** *(turn)* scharf [ʃaʳf] *no comp/superl* ◊ *Biegen Sie bitte scharf links ab!* **3.** *(music, voice)* zu hoch [tsu: 'hoːx] *no comp/ superl* ◊ *Sie singt immer zu hoch.*

sharpen [verb] **1.** *(make sharper)* schärfen ['ʃɛʳfn] +haben ◊ *ein Messer schärfen* **2.** *(improve)* sharpen up verbessern [fɛ'bɛsɛn] <verbessert, verbesserte, hat verbessert> ◊ *Sie haben ihre Leistungen verbessert.* sth sharpens up etw. verbessert sich **3.** *(make/ become more intense)* verstärken [fɛ'ʃtɛʳkn] <verstärkt, verstärkte, hat verstärkt> ◊ *Die Präsenz von Truppen entlang der Grenze hat die Spannungen verstärkt.* sth sharpens etw. verstärkt sich ◊ *Die Unterschiede zwischen den Gesellschaftsschichten ver-*

stärken sich weiter.

sharply [adv] **1.** *(by a large amount)* stark [ʃtaʳk] <stärker, am stärksten> ◊ *stark steigende Kurse* **2.** *(severely, clearly)* scharf [ʃaʳf] <schärfer, am schärfsten> ◊ *jdn scharf kritisieren* ♦ *Die Figuren in dem Bild sind scharf umrissen.*

shatter [verb] **1.** *(sth breaks into many parts)* zerbrechen [tsɛ'brɛçn] <zerbricht, zerbrach, ist zerbrochen> ◊ *Die Tasse fiel herunter und zerbrach.* **2.** *(destroy)* shatter sth etw. zertrümmern [tsɛ'trʏmɐn] <zertrümmert, zertrümmerte, hat zertrümmert> ◊ *Nierensteine zertrümmern; (hopes, illusions, the economy)* zerstören [tsɛ'ʃtøːrən] <zerstört, zerstörte, hat zerstört> ◊ *Hoffnungen zerstören*

shave¹ [noun] Rasur [ra'zuːɐ] die <-, -en> have a shave sich rasieren [ra'ziːrən] ◊ *rasiert sich, rasierte sich, hat sich rasiert>*

◉ a close shave knapp

shave² [verb] **1.** *(remove hair)* rasieren [ra'ziːrən] <rasiert, rasierte, hat rasiert> shave your legs sich [dat] die Beine rasieren sb shaves jd rasiert sich ◊ *Er rasiert sich jeden Morgen.* **2.** *(hardly touch)* streifen [ʃtraefn] +haben ◊ *Beim Rückwärtsfahren streifte ich das andere Auto.*

• **shave off** [phras v] shave sth off **1.** *(hair)* etw. abrasieren ['aprazi:rən] <rasiert ab, rasierte ab, hat abrasiert> ◊ *Rasieren Sie mir bitte den Bart ab.* shave off your hair sich [dat] die Haare abrasieren **2.** *(off a record, best time etc.)* shave A off B B um A verbessern [ʊm ... fɛˌbɛsɛn] <verbessert, verbesserte ◊ *Er verbesserte seine Rekordzeit um eine Sekunde.* **3.** *(a slice of sth)* abhobeln ['apho:b|n] +haben

shawl [noun] Tuch [tuːx] das <-(e)s, Tücher> ◊ *Sie hat ein Tuch um die Schultern geschlungen.*

she [pers pron] **1.** *(referring to a female person or animal)* sie [ziː] ◊ *Ich habe gestern Susi getroffen; sie lässt dich grüßen.* → sie¹ **2.** *(with a German neuter noun)* es [ɛs] ◊ *Das Mädchen hat eine Erkälung; darum hustet es.* → es 1.

shed¹ [noun] **1.** *(small building)* Schuppen ['ʃʊpm] der <-s, -> ◊ *Die Gartengeräte sind im Schuppen hinterm Haus.* **2.** *(large building for machines or vehicles)* Halle ['halə] die <-, -n> ◊ *In der Halle lagern Rasenmäher und Traktoren.*

shed² [verb] **1.** *(get rid of)* loswerden ['loːsveːɐdn] <wird los, wurde los, ist losgeworden> ◊ *Der Politiker versucht sein altes Image loszuwerden.* shed jobs Stellen streichen ['ʃtɛlən ʃtraeçn] <streicht, strich, hat gestrichen> ◊ *Die Firma hat weitere Stellen gestrichen.* **2.** *(lose sth)* verlieren [fɛ'liːrən] <verliert, verlor, hat verloren> ◊ *Die Bäume verlieren schon ihre Blätter.* shed weight abnehmen ['apneːmən] <nimmt ab, nahm ab, hat abgenommen>; *(reptile etc.)* shed its skin häuten [tsɪç 'hɔøtn] <häutet sich, häutete sich, hat sich gehäutet>

sheep [noun] **1.** *(animal)* Schaf [ʃaːf] das <-(e)s, -e> ◊ *Schafe büten* **2.** *(pej) (person)* Herdentier ['heːɐdnti:ɐ] das <-(e)s, -e>

◉ count sheep Schäfchen zählen

sheepish(ly) [adj, adv] kleinlaut ['klaenlaot] <kleinlauter, am kleinlautesten> ◊ *eine kleinlaute Antwort* ♦ *Der Verlierer zog kleinlaut ab.; (smile, grin)* verlegen ['feː'gdnti:ɐ] das <-(e)s, -> ◊ *Sie lächelte verlegen.*

sheer [adj] **1.** *(used for emphasis)* rein [raen] ◊ *reine*

Formsache sein ♦ *reine Freude* sheer hell die reinste Hölle by sheer coincidence rein zufällig the sheer size of sth schon allein die Größe ... ⟨gen⟩ [ʃoːn alaɛn diː ˈɡrøːsə] ◊ *Schon allein die Größe des Gebäudes ist beeindruckend.* **2.** *(cliff)* steil [ʃtaɛl] ◊ *eine steile Klippe* **3.** *(fabric)* hauchdünn [ˈhaɔxˈdʏn] no comp/superl ◊ *ein Kleid aus hauchdünnem Stoff; (transparent)* durchsichtig [ˈdʊˀçzɪçtɪç] ◊ *Sie trug eine fast durchsichtige Bluse.*

sheet ⟨noun⟩ **1.** *(for a bed)* Laken [ˈlaːkn̩] das <-s, -> ◊ *Das Bett ist mit einem frischen Laken überzogen.* change the sheets das Bett neu beziehen [das ˌbɛt nɔʏ bəˈtsiːən] <bezieht, bezog, hat bezogen> **2.** *(of paper)* Bogen [ˈboːɡn̩] der <-s, -> ◊ *Wie viele Bogen hast du beschrieben?; (of plastic, metal, glass)* Platte [ˈplatə] die <-, -n> **3.** sheet of ice Eisdecke [ˈaɛsdɛkə] die <-, -n> A sheet of water covered the road. Die Straße stand unter Wasser. **4.** sheet of fire Flammenmeer [ˈflamənmeːɐ] das <-(e)s, -e> sheets of rain strömender Regen [ʃtrøːməndə ˈreːɡn̩] <-s> no pl ◊ *Durch den strömenden Regen konnte man die Küste kaum erkennen.*

⊛ start with a clean sheet noch einmal neu anfangen three sheets to the wind sternhagelvoll *(fam)*

shelf ⟨noun⟩ **1.** *(piece of furniture)* shelf, shelves Regal [reˈɡaːl] das <-s, -e> ◊ *Sie stellt die Bücher ins Regal.* ♦ *Die Bücher stehen auf dem Regal.* ♦ *In unseren Regalen finden sie auch die neuesten Produkte.* in the top/bottom shelf ganz oben/unten im Regal **2.** GEOL *(of rock or ice)* Vorsprung [ˈfoːɐ̯ʃprʊŋ] der <-(e)s, Vorsprünge>; *(under water)* Riff [rɪf] das <-(e)s, -e> continental shelf Kontinentalplatte [kɔntinɛnˈtaːlplatə] die <-, -n>

shell¹ ⟨noun⟩ **1.** *(of sea creatures, eggs, nuts)* Schale [ˈʃaːlə] die <-, -n> ◊ *Krebse sind durch eine harte Schale geschützt.* ♦ *die Schale knacken* ♦ *(of a snail)* Gehäuse [ɡəˈhɔʏzə] das <-s, -> ◊ *Die Schnecke zog sich in ihr Gehäuse zurück.; (of a tortoise)* Panzer [ˈpantsə] der <-s, -> ◊ *der Panzer der Schildkröte* **2.** *(of a car, plane)* Karosserie [karɔsəˈriː] die <-, -n> **3.** *(of a house after a fire)* Gerippe [ɡəˈrɪpə] das <-s, -> ◊ *Es standen nur noch die Gerippe der Häuser.* **4.** *(weapon)* Granate [ɡraˈnaːtə] die <-, -n> ◊ *Sie feuerten mehrere Granaten ab.*

shell² ⟨verb⟩ **1.** *(attack)* bombardieren [bɔmbarˈdiːrən] <bombardiert, bombardierte, hat bombardiert> ◊ *Sie wurden seit Tagen bombardiert.* **2.** *(remove the shell)* schälen [ˈʃɛːlən] +haben ◊ *Eier schälen; (of nuts)* knacken [ˈknakn̩] +haben

• **shell out** ⟨phras v⟩ hinlegen [ˈhɪnleːɡn̩] +haben *(fam)* ◊ *Wie viel hast du für den PC hingelegt?*

shelter¹ ⟨noun⟩ **1.** *(covered place)* Unterstand [ˈʊntɐʃtant] der <-(e)s, Unterstände>; *(at a bus stop)* Häuschen [ˈhɔʏsçən] das <-s, -> bomb shelter Luftschutzraum [ˈlʊftʃʊtsraɔm] der <-(e)s, Luftschutzräume> **2.** *(protection)* Zuflucht [ˈtsuːflʊxt] die <-> no pl ◊ *Zuflucht suchen/finden* **3.** *(for homeless people)* Obdachlosenheim [ˈɔpdaxloːznhaɛm] das <-(e)s, -e> women's shelter Frauenhaus [ˈfraɔənhaɔs] das <-es, Frauenhäuser>; *(for animals)* Tierheim [ˈtiːɐ̯haɛm] das <-(e)s, -e> ◊ *Wir haben den Hund aus dem Tierheim.* **4.** *(a place to live)* Unterkunft [ˈʊntɐkʊnft] die <-, Unterkünfte>

shelter² ⟨verb⟩ **1.** *(protect)* shelter sb/sth from sth jdn/etw. vor etw. ⟨dat⟩ schützen [foːɐ̯ ... ˈʃʏtsn̩] +haben ◊ *Hohe Bäume schützen das Haus vor der brennenden Mittagssonne.* **2.** *(stay in a protected place)* Schutz suchen [ˈʃʊts zuːxn̩] +haben ◊ *Als es anfing zu regnen, suchten wir Schutz in einem Café.*

shield¹ ⟨noun⟩ **1.** *(for knights, police officers)* Schild [ʃɪlt] der <-(e)s, -e> ◊ *Die Ritter hoben ihre Schilde.; (on a coat of arms)* Wappenschild [ˈvapn̩ʃɪlt] das <-(e)s, -er> **2.** SPORT *(body protection)* Schutz [ʃʊts] der <-es, -e> most sing gum shield Mundschutz [ˈmʊntʃʊts] das **3.** *(sb/sth protecting against sth)* Schutzschild [ˈʃʊtsʃɪlt] das <-es, -er> ◊ *Er war ihr Schutzschild gegen ihren Vater.* **4.** *(prize)* Trophäe [troˈfɛːə] die <-, -n> ◊ *Er bekam die Trophäe für den ersten Preis.*

shield² ⟨verb⟩ **1.** *(protect)* shield sb/sth (from sth) jdn/etw. (vor etw. ⟨dat⟩) schützen [ˈʃʏtsn̩] +haben ◊ *Er schützte seine Kinder vor allen Gefahren.* shield sth from view etw. vor fremden Blicken schützen shield your eyes seine Augen schützen

shift¹ ⟨noun⟩ **1.** *(at work)* Schicht [ʃɪçt] die <-, -en> ◊ *Die erste Schicht dauert von 6.30 bis 14 Uhr.* ♦ *ein Kollege aus meiner Schicht* night shift Nachtschicht [ˈnaxtʃɪçt] **2.** *(change)* Verlagerung [fɛˈlaːɡərʊŋ] die <-, -en> ◊ *eine Verlagerung der Macht/Strategie* value shift Wertewandel [ˈveːɐ̯təvandl̩] der <-s> only pl shift towards sth Hinwendung zu etw. [ˈhɪnvɛndʊŋ tsuː] die <-> no pl ◊ *eine Hinwendung zu erneuerbaren Energiequellen* shifts in sth Veränderungen in etw. ⟨dat⟩ [fɛˈlɛndərʊŋən ɪn] die <-> pl ◊ *Veränderungen im Konsumverhalten* **3.** IT shift key Umschalttaste [ˈʊmʃalttastə] die <-, -n> **4.** *(simple dress)* Hängekleid [ˈhɛŋəklaɛt] das <-(e)s, -er>

shift² ⟨verb⟩ **1.** *(change, move)* verlagern [fɛˈlaːɡern] <verlagert, verlagerte, hat verlagert> ◊ *sein Gewicht auf den anderen Fuß verlagern* sth shifts etw. verlagert sich ◊ *Sein Interesse verlagerte sich allmählich auf den Reitsport.* He shifted nervously on his chair. Er zappelte nervös auf seinem Stuhl herum. shift your ground umschwenken [ˈʊmʃvɛŋkn̩] +haben shift (your) attention towards sth sich einer Sache ⟨dat⟩ zuwenden [ˈtsuːvɛndn̩] <wendet sich zu, wandte sich zu, hat sich zugewandt> shift attention away from sth von etw. ablenken [fɔn ... ˌapˈlɛŋkn̩] +haben **2.** *(change gears)* schalten [ˈʃaltn̩] <schaltet, schaltete, hat geschaltet> +haben ◊ *in den zweiten Gang schalten* **3.** shift blame/responsibility onto sb/sth jdm/etw. die Schuld zuschieben [di: ˌʃʊlt ˌtsuːʃiːbm̩] <schiebt zu, schob zu, hat zugeschoben> ◊ *Die Opposition schob der Regierung die Schuld für die Krise zugeschoben.* **4.** *(in the UK: move sth)* rücken [ˈrʏkn̩] +haben ◊ *Sie rückten den Schrank gleich neben das Bett.* **5.** *(gaze)* wandern [ˈvandern] <-st -e> ◊ *Sein Blick wanderte von der Frau an der Bar.* shift your eyes to sb/sth seine Augen auf jdn/etw. richten [ˌaoɡn̩ aof ... rɪçtn̩] <richtet, richtete, hat gerichtet> **6.** *(in the UK: get rid of)* loswerden [ˈloːsveːɐ̯dn̩] <wird los, wurde los, ist losgeworden> *(fam)* ◊ *eine Krankheit loswerden* **7.** *(sell)* verkaufen [fɛˈkaofn̩] <verkauft, verkaufte, hat verkauft> ◊ *Sie verkaufen gerade Schuhe im Sonderangebot.* **8.** *(press the shift key)* die Umschalttaste drücken [diː ˈʊmʃalttastə drʏkn̩] +haben

shimmer ⟨verb⟩ schimmern [ˈʃɪmen] +haben ◊ *Das Wasser schimmerte im Sonnenlicht.*

shine ⟨verb⟩ **1.** *(sun, moon, stars, lights)* scheinen

['ʃaenən] <scheint, schien, hat geschienen> ◊ *Die Sonne scheint.* ♦ *Der Scheinwerfer schien ihm ins Gesicht.* **2.** *(be bright, very good)* glänzen ['glɛntsn̩] +haben *(also fig)* ◊ *Der Sand glänzt golden in der Sonne.* ♦ *Er glänzte mit hervorragenden Leistungen.* **3.** *(polish)* polieren [po'liːrən] <poliert, polierte, hat poliert>; *(your shoes)* putzen ['pʊtsn̩] +haben **4.** *(face, eyes, torch)* leuchten ['lɔ̈çtn̩] <leuchtet, leuchtete, hat geleuchtet> ◊ *Die Augen der Kinder leuchteten.* shine sth mit etw. leuchten ◊ *Sie leuchtet mit der Taschenlampe in den Schrank.*

shiny [adj] glänzend ['glɛntsn̩t] ◊ *ein glänzender Fußboden* be shiny (with sth) (vor etw. [dat]) glänzen ['glɛntsn̩] +haben ◊ *Seine Stirn glänzte vor Schweiß.*

ship¹ [noun] *(large boat)* Schiff [ʃɪf] das <-(e)s, -e> ◊ *Unser Schiff läuft morgen aus.* ♦ *Das Schiff lag im Hafen vor Anker.* ♦ *Das Schiff legte am Ufer an.* on board ship an Bord des Schiffes; *(spacecraft)* Raumschiff ['raʊmʃɪf] ● leave a sinking ship das sinkende Schiff verlassen run a tight ship ein strenges Regiment führen

ship² [verb] **1.** *(transport by ship)* verschiffen [fɛ'ʃɪfn̩] <verschifft, verschiffte, hat verschifft> ◊ *Sie haben ihre Möbel nach Australien verschifft.* **2.** *(transport by air or land)* verschicken [fɛ'ʃɪkn̩] <verschickt, verschickte, hat verschickt> ◊ *Das Paket wird per Luftpost verschickt.* • ship off [phras v] schicken ['ʃɪkn̩] +haben ◊ *Sie schickten ihre Kinder ins Ferienlager.*

shipment [noun] **1.** *(goods)* Ladung ['laːdʊŋ] die <-, -en> a shipment of coffee eine Ladung Kaffee **2.** *(process of delivery)* Transport [trans'pɔʳt] der <-(e)s, -e> ◊ *Der Transport der Hilfsgüter erwies sich als schwierig.*

shipyard [noun] Werft [vɛʳft] die <-, -en>

shirk [verb] shirk sth sich vor etw. [dat] drücken [foːɐ̯ ... ˌdrʏkn̩] +haben ◊ *Er drückt sich vor jeder Arbeit.* ♦ *Sie drückte sich vor dem Gespräch.*

shirt [noun] *(item of clothing)* Hemd [hɛmt] das <-(e)s, -en> ◊ *Er trug ein weißes Hemd mit Krawatte.*; *(worn for sport)* Trikot [tri'koː] das <-s, -s> ◊ *Nach dem Spiel tauschten die Spieler ihre Trikots.* ● sb would give sb the shirt off their back jd würde für jdn sein letztes Hemd geben keep your shirt on bleib ganz ruhig put your shirt on sth seinen letzten Pfennig auf etw. [acc] setzen

shit¹ [noun] **1.** *(excrement, sth bad)* Scheiße ['ʃaesə] die <-> no pl *(rude)* ◊ *Hier stinkt es nach Scheiße.* ♦ *Der DJ spielt nur Scheiße.* have/take a shit kacken ['kakn̩] +haben *(rude)* ◊ *Der Hunde kackt auf den Bürgersteig.*; *(nonsense)* talk shit Scheiß reden ['ʃaes reːdn̩] <redet, redete, hat geredet> *(rude)* **2.** *(very unpleasant person)* Scheißkerl ['ʃaeskɛʳl] der <-s, -e> *(rude)* ● in deep shit in der Scheiße *(rude)* feel like shit sich Scheiße fühlen *(rude)* have the shits Dünnpfiff haben *(fam)* take shit from sb sich [dat] von jdm alles gefallen lassen

shit² [verb] scheißen ['ʃaesn̩] <scheißt, schiss, hat geschissen> *(rude)* ● shit yourself sich [dat] in die Hose scheißen *(rude)*

shiver [verb] zittern ['tsɪtɐn] +haben shiver with cold vor Kälte zittern

shock¹ [noun] **1.** *(unpleasant surprise)* Schock [ʃɔk] der <-(e)s, -s> ◊ *Er hatte sich von dem Schock noch nicht erholt.* ♦ *Die Nachricht war für sie ein Schock.* get a shock einen Schock bekommen give sb a shock jdm einen Schock versetzen come as a shock ein Schock sein in shock unter Schock be in for a shock sich auf einen Schock gefasst machen müssen **2.** shock defeat unerwartete Niederlage [ˌʊnˌeva'taːtə 'niːdɐlaːgə] an a shock win unerwarteter Sieg [ˌʊnˌeva'taːtə 'ziːk] <-(e)s, -e> ◊ *der unerwartete Sieg der deutschen Nationalmannschaft* **3.** *(electric)* Schlag [ʃlaːk] der <-(e)s, Schläge> ◊ *einen (elektrischen) Schlag bekommen* **4.** *(of hair)* Schopf [ʃɔpf] der <-(e)s, -e> **5.** shock absorber *(absorber)* Stoßdämpfer ['ʃtoːsdɛmpfɐ] der <-s, ->

shock² [verb] **1.** *(upset, offend)* schockieren [ʃɔ'kiːrən] <schockiert, schockierte, hat schockiert> ◊ *Seine Bemerkung schockierte sie.* ♦ *Er war (von diesem brutalen Verhalten) schockiert.* ♦ *Sie zeigte sich über die Vorwürfe schockiert.* **2.** *(give an electric shock)* shock sb jdm einen Stromschlag versetzen [ˌaenən 'ʃtroːmʃlaːk fezetsn̩] <versetzt, versetzte, hat versetzt> be shocked einen Stromschlag bekommen [ˌaenən 'ʃtroːmʃlaːk bəkɔmən] <bekommt, bekam, hat bekommen>

shocked → shock² [adj] bestürzt [bə'ʃtʏʳtst] <bestürzter, am bestürztesten> ◊ *Diese Politik löste im Ausland bestürzte Reaktionen aus.*

shocking → shock² [adj] **1.** *(upsetting, surprising)* erschreckend [e'ʃrɛkŋ̩] ◊ *Seine Unkenntnis ist erschreckend.* ♦ *eine erschreckende Anzahl von Drogentoten* **2.** *(in the UK: very bad)* schlecht [ʃlɛçt] <schlechter, am schlechtesten> ◊ *schlechtes Wetter*

shockingly [adv] erschreckend [e'ʃrɛkŋ̩] ◊ *Erschreckend viele Teenager trinken Alkohol.*

shoe [noun] **1.** *(footwear)* Schuh [ʃuː] der <-(e)s, -e> ◊ *Sie kaufte ein neues Paar Schuhe.* ♦ *hochhackige/bequeme Schuhe* put on your shoes sich [dat] die Schuhe anziehen shoe polish Schuhcreme ['ʃuːkreːm] die <-, -s> **2.** *(horseshoe)* Hufeisen ['huːfˌʔaezn̩] das <-s, -> shoelace [noun] Schnürsenkel ['ʃnyːɐ̯zɛŋkl̩] der <-s, -> ◊ *Ich band mir die Schnürsenkel zu.*

shoot¹ [noun] **1.** *(young plant)* Keim [kaem] der <-(e)s, -e> ◊ *Die Samen treiben Keime.* **2.** *(series of photos)* Fotoshooting ['foːtoʃuːtŋ] das <-s, -s> **3.** *(of wild animals)* Jagd [jaːkt] die <-, -en>

shoot² [verb] **1.** *(fire a weapon, kick a ball, take photos)* schießen ['ʃiːsn̩] <schießt, schoss, hat geschossen> ◊ *Er schoss ein Tor.* ♦ *Auf der Reise hat er viele Fotos geschossen.* shoot at sb/sth auf jdn/etw. schießen shoot (sb) on sight sofort (auf jdn) schießen shoot to kill mit Tötungsabsicht schießen shoot sb in the leg jdn ins Bein schießen **2.** *(kill with a bullet)* shoot sb/an animal (dead) jdn/ein Tier erschießen [e'ʃiːsn̩] <erschießt, erschoss, hat erschossen> ◊ *Sie schossen at close range jdn aus nächster Nähe erschießen* **3.** *(move very quickly)* schießen ['ʃiːsn̩] <schießt, schoss, -n> geschossen> ◊ *Das Motorrad war im Nu über die Kreuzung geschossen.*; *(in a competition, on a list)* shoot straight to the top direkt die Spitze erobern [dɪrɛkt diː 'ʃpɪtsə eˌʔoːbɐn] <erobert, eroberte, hat erobert> ◊ *Die CD hat direkt die Spitze der Charts erobert.* **4.** SPORT shoot baskets Körbe werfen

['kɔɐ'bə vɛ'fn̩] <wirft, warf, hat geworfen> shoot pool
Billiard spielen ['bɪljaʳt ʃpiːlən] +haben **5.** *(quickly
extend)* shoot sth out etw. schnell ausstrecken
[ʃnɛl 'aʊsʃtrɛkn̩] +haben ◊ *Sie streckte schnell ihren
Arm aus und schlug zu.* **6.** *(a lot of questions etc.)*
shoot sth at sb jdn mit etw. bombardieren
[mɪt ... bɔmbaʳˌdiːrən] <bombardiert, bombardierte,
hat bombardiert> ◊ *Er bombardierte sie mit Fragen/
Anschuldigungen.* shoot a glance at sb jdm einen
kurzen Blick zuwerfen [aenən kʊʳtsn̩ 'blɪk tsuːvɛʳfn̩]
<wirft zu, warf zu, hat zugeworfen> **7.** FILM drehen
['dreːən] +haben ◊ *einen Kurzfilm/Werbespot drehen*
8. *(a drug)* shoot sth sich dat etw. spritzen ['ʃprɪtsn̩]
+haben ◊ *Er spritzte sich mehrmals am Tag Heroin.*

• **shoot down** phras v **1.** *(kill with a bullet)* shoot
sb down jdn erschießen [eʳ'ʃiːsn̩] <erschießt,
erschoss, hat erschossen> **2.** *(an aircraft, shoot sth
down)* etw. abschießen ['apʃiːsn̩] <schießt ab, schoss
ab, hat abgeschossen> **3.** shoot sth down in flames
etw. niedermachen ['niːdəmaxn̩] +haben ◊ *Ihr
Vorschlag wurde von den anderen niedergemacht.*

• **shoot off** phras v in Windeseile verschwinden
[ɪn ˌvɪndəsˌaelə feʳ'ʃvɪndn̩] <verschwindet, verschwand,
ist verschwunden> *(fam)*

• **shoot up** phras v **1.** *(prices, plant, child)* in die
Höhe schießen [ɪn diː 'høːə ʃiːsn̩] <schießt, schoss,
ist geschossen> *(fam)* ◊ *Der Junge schoss in die
Höhe.* **2.** *(destroy with bullets)* zerschießen [tseʳ'ʃiːsn̩]
<zerschießt, zerschoss, hat zerschossen> ◊ *Er hat die
Flasche zerschossen.* **3.** *(inject drugs)* spritzen
['ʃprɪtsn̩] +haben ◊ *Sie nimmt zwar Drogen, aber sie
spritzt nicht.* ✦ **Heroin spritzen 4.** *(appear suddenly)*
auftauchen ['aʊftaʊxn̩] +sein ◊ *Überall tauchen Spiel-
hallen auf.*

shooter noun **1.** *(gun)* Knarre ['knarə] die <-, -n>
(fam) **2.** *(person)* Schütze ['ʃʏtsə] der <-n, -n>
♀Schützin ['ʃʏtsɪn] die <-, -nen>

shooting noun **1.** *(gun attack)* Schießerei [ʃiːsə'rae]
die <-, -en> ◊ *Bei der Schießerei wurde niemand
verletzt.* **2.** *(sport)* Schießen ['ʃiːsn̩] das <-s> no pl

shop¹ noun **1.** *(store)* Laden ['laːdn̩] der <-s, Läden>
◊ *Der Laden hat zu/auf.* set up shop einen Laden
eröffnen shut up shop den Laden zumachen
grocer's shop Lebensmittelladen ['leːbm̩smɪtl̩laːdn̩]
toy shop Spielzeugladen ['ʃpiːltsɔɡklaːdn̩] **2.** *(manufacturing or repair unit)* Werkstatt ['vɛʳkʃtat] die
<-, Werkstätten> ◊ *die Werkstatt eines Schreiners*
repair shop Reparaturwerkstatt [repaʳatuːgvɛʳkʃtat]
3. SCHOOL *(in the US: school subject)* Werkunterricht
['vɛʳkʊntərɪçt] der <-(e)s> no pl ◊ *Was habt ihr
heute im Werkunterricht gemacht?*
☺ talk shop fachsimpeln

shop² verb *(buy things)* einkaufen ['aenkaʊfn̩] +haben
◊ *Sie kauft zweimal in der Woche im Supermarkt
ein.* ✦ *Dort kann man gut/günstig einkaufen.* shop
for sth etw. kaufen wollen ['kaʊfn̩ vɔlən] <will,
wollte, hat wollen> ◊ *Er wollte einen neuen Anzug
kaufen, hat aber nichts Passendes gefunden.*

shopping noun **1.** *(activity)* Einkaufen ['aenkaʊfn̩] das
<-s> no pl ◊ *das Einkaufen im Supermarkt/auf dem
Markt* ✦ *Ich habe beim Einkaufen die Nachbarin
getroffen.* go shopping, do the shopping einkaufen
gehen ['aenkaʊfn̩ geːən] <geht, ging, ist gegangen>
shopping spree Einkaufsbummel ['aenkaʊfsbʊml̩] der
<-s, -> shopping bag Einkaufstasche
['aenkaʊfstaʃə] die <-, -n> shopping trolley/cart Ein-

kaufswagen ['aenkaʊfsvaːɡn̩] der <-s, -> **2.** *(goods
bought)* Einkäufe ['aenkɔøfə] die <-> pl ◊ *Hilfst du
mir, die Einkäufe reinzutragen?*

shopping centre, shopping center noun Einkaufszentrum ['aenkaʊfsˌtsɛntrʊm] das
<-s, Einkaufszentren>

shopping list noun Einkaufszettel ['aenkaʊfstsɛtl̩] der
<-s, -> ◊ *einen Einkaufszettel schreiben*

shop window noun Schaufenster ['ʃaʊfɛnstə] das
<-s, -> ◊ *Der Anzug war im Schaufenster ausge-
stellt.*

shore noun **1.** *(of a lake, an ocean)* Ufer ['uːfɐ] das
<-s, -> ◊ *ans Ufer schwimmen* on the shores of
the lake am Seeufer [am 'zeːˌuːfɐ] **2.** *(lit) (area,
country)* shores Gefilde [ɡə'fɪldə] das <-s, -> *(lit)* ◊
jds heimatliche Gefilde
☺ **on shore** an Land

short¹ adj **1.** *(not tall)* klein [klaen] ◊ *Sie ist klein
und schlank.; (not long)* kurz [kʊʳts] <kürzer, am
kürzesten> ◊ *Sie trägt einen kurzen Rock.* ✦ *Der Weg
erschien mir ziemlich kurz.* 15 centimetres/centime-
ters etc. short 15 Zentimeter etc. zu kurz ◊ *Das
Seil ist fast einen Meter zu kurz.* **2.** *(not lasting long,
expressed in few words or letters)* kurz [kʊʳts]
<kürzer, am kürzesten> ◊ *Sie nimmt sich eine kurze
Pause.* ✦ *Das Leben ist kurz.* ✦ *eine kurze Zusammenfassung* ✦ *Das „e" in „Bett" ist ein kurzer Vokal.* for
short kurz ◊ *Sie heißt Susanne, kurz Susi.* short for
die Kurzform von [diː 'kʊʳtsfoːʳm fɔn] ◊ *Max ist die
Kurzform von Maximilian.* **3.** *(insufficient)* be short
of ... nicht genug ... haben [nɪçt ɡəˌnuːk ... haːbm̩]
+haben ◊ *Wir haben nicht genug Personal/Geld.* sb is
£5 etc. short jd hat £5 etc. zu wenig
[hat ˌfʏnf ˌpfʊnt tsuː 'veːnɪç] sth is short, sth is in
short supply etw. ist knapp [ɪst 'knap] +sein ◊ *Geld
ist im Moment knapp.* short of breath außer Atem
[aose 'aːtəm] **4.** have a short memory kein gutes
Gedächtnis haben [kaen ɡuːtəs ɡə'dɛçtnɪs haːbm̩]
+haben **5.** *(rude)* schroff [ʃrɔf] ◊ *Wenn er viel Stress
hat, ist er manchmal ein wenig schroff.* ✦ *eine
schroffe Antwort/Bemerkung* have a short temper
unbeherrscht sein ['ʊnbəhɛʳʃt zaen] +sein
☺ **short and sweet** schön kurz in short kurzum

short² adv **1.** *(end abruptly)* cut sb short jdn unterbrechen [ʊntə'brɛçn̩] <unterbricht, unterbrach, hat
unterbrochen> ◊ *Sie unterbrach ihn und sagte: „So
geht das nicht."* cut sth short etw. abbrechen
['apbrɛçn̩] <bricht ab, brach ab, hat abgebrochen> ◊
Ich brach die Unterhaltung ab. **2.** *(not enough)* go
short of ... zu wenig ... haben
[tsuː ˌveːnɪç ... haːbm̩] +haben ◊ *Damals hatten wir
manchmal zu wenig Geld.* We often went short of
food. Wir hatten oft zu wenig zu essen. sb runs
short of sth jdm geht etw. nom aus [ɡeːt ... aos]
<ging aus, ist ausgegangen> ◊ *Uns geht das Benzin
aus.*
☺ **be caught short 1.** *(fam)* (have to go to the
toilet) dringend mal verschwinden müssen *(fam)* ◊
Ich muss dringend mal verschwinden. **2.** *(not have
enough money)* knapp dran sein *(fam)* ◊ *Ich bin
derzeit knapp dran und kann dir leider kein Geld
leihen.* fall short **1.** *(supplies etc.)* nicht ausreichen
(fam) ◊ *Die Vorräte werden nicht ausreichen.* **2.** *(shot etc.)*
zu kurz sein fall short of sth etw. nicht erreichen
◊ *Wir haben unsere Ziele nicht erreicht.* short of
doing sth als dass jd etw. tut ◊ *Ich sehe keine*

andere Lösung, als dass Sie ihn um Hilfe bitten.

shortage [noun] shortage (of sb/sth) Mangel (an jdm/etw.) [' mɑːntʃ] der <–s> no pl ◊ *In dem Gebiet herrscht großer Mangel an Nahrung und Trinkwasser.* ♦ *über einen Mangel an qualifizierten Arbeitskräften klagen*

shortcoming [noun] (of a thing) Mangel ['mɑːntʃ] der <–s, Mängel> ◊ *einen Mangel feststellen/beheben; (of a person)* Fehler ['feːlɐ] der <–s, –> ◊ *Sie ist trotz ihrer Fehler eine gute Politikerin.*

short cut [noun] **1.** (on a route) Abkürzung ['apkʏˈtsʊn] die <–, –en> ◊ *Wir sind die Abkürzung gefahren.* ♦ *eine Abkürzung nehmen* **2.** (quicker way of doing sth) Schnellverfahren ['ʃnɛlfɛːfaːrən] das <–s, –> most sing ◊ *ein Schnellverfahren anwenden*

shorten [verb] (make shorter) shorten sth etw. kürzen ['kʏˈtsn̩] +haben ◊ *ein Kleid/eine Rede kürzen* ♦ *eine Schnur um 20 Zentimeter kürzen* sth shortens etw. wird kürzer [vɪɐt 'kʏˈtsə] +sein ◊ *Im Herbst werden die Tage kürzer.*

shortlist [noun] be on the shortlist in der engeren Wahl sein [ɪn deːɐ̯ ɛŋərən 'vaːl tsaːn] +sein ◊ *Ich glaube, ich bin in der engeren Wahl für die Stelle.*

shortly [adv] **1.** (soon) in Kürze [ɪn 'kʏˈtsə] ◊ *In Kürze eröffnet hier ein Café.* shortly after/before kurz nach/vor [dat] [kʊˈts naːx/foːɐ̯] ◊ *Er kam kurz vor Sonnenaufgang nach Hause.* **2.** (curtly) kurz angebunden [kʊˈts 'anɡəbʊndn̩] <kürzer angebunden, –> seldom comp/no superl ◊ *"Jetzt nicht!", sagte er kurz angebunden.*

shorts [noun] **1.** (short trousers) kurze Hose [kʊˈtsə 'hoːzə] die <–, –n> both sing and pl describe the individual piece of clothing ◊ *Sie trug eine weiße Hose/weiße Hosen.* a pair of shorts kurze Hosen **2.** (in the US: underpants) Unterhose ['ʊntehoːzə] die <–, –n> both sing and pl describe the individual piece of clothing ◊ *Ich zog eine neue Unterhose/neue Unterbosen an.* a pair of shorts Unterhosen

short-sighted [adj] kurzsichtig ['kʊˈtszɪçtɪç] ◊ *Der Junge ist kurzsichtig und benötigt eine Brille.* ♦ *eine kurzsichtige Politik*

short-term [adj] kurzfristig ['kʊˈtsfrɪstɪç] ◊ *eine kurzfristige Beschäftigung* ♦ *Die Lösung ist nur kurzfristig.*

shot [noun] **1.** (from a gun etc., at a target or goal) Schuss [ʃʊs] der <–es, Schüsse> ◊ *Er wurde von einem Schuss getroffen.* ♦ *Der Schuss verfehlte das Tor.; (person)* Schütze ['ʃʏtsə] der <–n, –n> ♀Schützin ['ʃʏtsɪn] die <–, –nen> ◊ *Er ist ein guter/ schlechter Schütze.* **2.** FILM, FOTO (photograph) Aufnahme ['aʊfnaːmə] die <–, –n> ◊ *Da ist dir eine tolle Aufnahme gelungen!* close-up shot Nahaufnahme ['naːˌaʊfnaːmə] **3.** (attempt) Versuch [fɛˈzuːx] der <–(e)s, –e> ◊ *Ist das Ihr erster Versuch?* at the first shot beim ersten Versuch have a shot at doing sth versuchen, etw. zu tun [fɛˈzuːxn̩ ... tsuː] <versucht, versuchte, hat versucht> ◊ *Sie versuchten, den Wagen selbst zu reparieren.* **4.** (of an alcoholic drink) Schuss [ʃʊs] der <–es, –> ◊ *Tee mit einem Schuss Rum* **5.** MED (injection) Spritze ['ʃprɪtsə] die <–, –n> ◊ *Ich gebe Ihnen eine Spritze gegen die Schmerzen.; (immunization)* Impfung ['ɪmpfʊn] die <–, –en> ◊ *Wie viele Kugeln sind noch in der Waffe?* ♦ *(projectile)* Kugel ['kuːɡl] die <–, –n> ◊ *Wie viele Kugeln sind noch in der Waffe?*
Ⓔ **sb's parting shot** jds böse Worte zum Abschied like a shot wie der Blitz

should [verb] **1.** (modal: expressing an order, obligation, a recommendation, possibility) sb/sth should do sth jd/etw. sollte etw. tun ['zɔltə] subjunctive II ◊ *Du solltest dich schämen.* ♦ *Sie sollten den Rat Ihres Arztes befolgen.* ♦ *Sie sollte schon längst zurück sein.* ♦ *Den Film sollte man sich ansehen.* ♦ *Falls ihr Hilfe brauchen solltet, ruft mich an.* sb/sth shouldn't do sth jd/etw. sollte etw. nicht tun ◊ *Du solltest so etwas nicht sagen.* sb should have done sth jd hätte etw. tun sollen ◊ *Er hätte auf sie hören sollen.* **2.** (modal: expressing a presumption, probability) sb/sth should do sth jd/etw. müsste etw. tun ['mʏstə] subjunctive II ◊ *Auf meinem Schreibtisch müsste eine Schere liegen.* ♦ *Zehn Minuten müssten reichen.* **3.** (expressing importance, an opinion) it's important/ great etc. that sb should do sth es ist wichtig/ großartig etc., dass jd etw. tut [ɛs ɪst 'vɪçtɪç/'ɡroːsaˈtɪç das] ◊ *Es ist wichtig, dass wir sie unterstützen.* ♦ *Ich finde es schrecklich, dass er den Hund verkaufen will.* **4.** (making polite requests, as a conditional) sb should do sth jd würde etw. tun ['vʏˈdə] ◊ *Ich würde gern mehr darüber erfahren.* ♦ *Sie würde sich über eine Antwort sehr freuen.* sb should have done sth if jd hätte etw. getan, wenn ◊ *Ich hätte das Flugzeug versäumt, wenn ich noch länger geblieben wäre.* **5.** (as a question tag) shouldn't you/he etc.?, should you/he etc.? oder? ['oːdɐ] ◊ *Sie müsste eigentlich schon hier sein, oder?*
Ⓔ **How should I know?** Woher soll ich das wissen? He hid so that nobody should see him. Er versteckte sich, damit ihn niemand sehen konnte.

shoulder [noun] **1.** (of a person, an animal, of clothes) Schulter ['ʃʊltɐ] die <–, –n> ◊ *Er klopfte mir auf die Schulter.* ♦ *Die Jacke ist an der Schulter zerrissen.* shrug your shoulders mit den Schultern zucken **2.** (of a road) Seitenstreifen ['zaɪtn̩ʃtraɛfn̩] der <–s, –> ◊ *Ein Wagen stand blinkend auf dem Seitenstreifen.*
Ⓔ **shoulder to shoulder 1.** (supporting each other) Schulter an Schulter **2.** (very close) dicht nebeneinander look over sb's shoulder jdm auf die Finger sehen

shouldn't → should

shout¹ [noun] Schrei [ʃraɛ] der <–(e)s, –e> ◊ *Man konnte laute Schreie hören.* shouts of laughter lautes Gelächter [laətəs ɡəˈlɛçtɐ] <–s> no pl ◊ *Hast du das laute Gelächter im Treppenhaus gehört?* give sb a shout jdn rufen ['ruːfn̩] <ruft, rief, hat gerufen> ◊ *Ruf mich, wenn du mich brauchst!*
Ⓔ **it's sb's shout** jd ist an der Reihe

shout² [verb] (scream) schreien ['ʃraɛən] <schreit, schrie, hat geschrien> ◊ *Alle schrien durcheinander.* ♦ *Sie schrie vor Schmerzen.* shout yourself hoarse sich heiser schreien shout at sb jdn anschreien ['anʃraɛən] +haben ◊ *"Du Idiot!", schrie ihn an.; (angrily, in a commanding voice)* brüllen ['brʏlən] +haben ◊ *Der Offizier brüllte seine Befehle.; (call out)* rufen ['ruːfn̩] <ruft, rief, hat gerufen> ◊ *Er rief ihren Namen.* ♦ *Sie riefen: "Bravo!"* shout sth at sb jdm etw. zurufen ['tsuːruːfn̩] +haben shout abuse at sb jdn laut beschimpfen [laət bəˈʃɪmpfn̩] <beschimpft, beschimpfte, hat beschimpft>
Ⓔ **nothing to shout about** nicht gerade umwerfend

shove¹ [noun] Stoß [ʃtoːs] der <–es, Stöße> ◊ *ein Stoß mit dem Ellenbogen/Fuß* give sth/sb a shove einer

Sache/jdm einen Stoß geben
shove² ⟨verb⟩ **1.** *(push)* schubsen ['ʃʊpsn̩] +haben ◊ *Er
hat mich vom Stuhl geschubst.* ✦ *Hör auf zu
schubsen!* **2.** *(put sth carelessly somewhere)* stopfen
['ʃtɔpfn̩] +haben ◊ *Er stopfte die Wäsche hastig in
den Schrank.*
• **shove around** ⟨phras v⟩ shove sb around jdn
herumstoßen [hɛ'rʊmʃtoːsn̩] <stößt herum, stieß
herum, hat herumgestoßen> ◊ *In ihrer alten Firma
wurde sie nur herumgestoßen.*
• **shove off** ⟨phras v⟩ **1.** *(fam, pej) (person)* abziehen
['aptsiːən] <zieht ab, zog ab, ist abgezogen> *(fam)* ◊
Zieh ab! **2.** *(boat)* ablegen ['apleːgn̩] +haben ◊ *Das
Boot legte ab und verschwand im Nebel.*
shovel¹ ⟨noun⟩ Schaufel ['ʃaofl̩] die <–, –n> ◊ *Sie
grub mit der Schaufel ein Loch.* ✦ *die Schaufel eines
Baggers*
shovel² ⟨verb⟩ **1.** *(move with a shovel)* schaufeln
['ʃaofln̩] +haben ◊ *Kohlen/Schnee schaufeln* ✦ *Er
schaufelte Erde in die Grube.* **2.** shovel sth into your
mouth etw. in sich hineinschaufeln
[ɪn ... hɪ'naɛnʃaofl̩n] +haben ◊ *Er schaufelte hungrig
Nudeln in sich hinein.*
show¹ ⟨noun⟩ **1.** *(in a theatre/theater)* Aufführung
['aoffyːrʊŋ] die <–, –en> ◊ *Wer spielt in der Aufführung mit?;* (on TV, radio) Show [ʃoː] die <–, –s>
host/present a show eine Show präsentieren
2. *(exhibition)* Ausstellung ['aosʃtɛlʊŋ] die <–, –en>
◊ *eine Ausstellung moderner Kunst in der Staatsgalerie* fashion show Modenschau ['moːdn̩ʃao] die
<–, –en> **3.** *(expression of a feeling or attitude)* a
show of sth eine Demonstration ... ⟨gen⟩
[aenə demɔnstra'tsjoːn] <–, –en> ◊ *Das Ganze
diente der Demonstration seiner Macht.; (pretend)*
make a show of sth sich ⟨dat⟩ den Anschein ... ⟨gen⟩
geben [deːn ˌanʃaen ... geːbm̩] <gibt sich, gab sich,
hat sich gegeben> ◊ *Sie gab sich den Anschein
großer Autorität.* make a show of doing sth
vorgeben, etw. zu tun ['foːrgeːbm̩] <gibt vor, gab vor,
hat vorgegeben> ◊ *Er gab vor, den Mann zu kennen.*
sth is for show etw. ist nur Show [ɪst nuːɐ̯ 'ʃoː]
+sein
⊛ **put up a good/poor show** eine gute/schwache
Leistung zeigen be **on show** zu sehen sein
show² ⟨verb⟩ **1.** *(indicate, prove)* zeigen ['tsaegn̩]
+haben ◊ *Das zeigt, dass er ein Betrüger ist.* it all
goes to show that das zeigt doch nur, dass show
yourself (to be) sth sich als ... erweisen
[als ... ɛv̯aeːzn̩] <erweist sich, erwies, hat sich
erwiesen> ◊ *Diese Substanz hat sich als sehr gefährlich erwiesen.* **2.** *(present, give information)* zeigen
['tsaegn̩] +haben ◊ *Die Karte zeigt alle wichtigen
Städte des Landes.* ✦ *Das Thermometer zeigt fast 22
Grad unter Null.* show sth as sth etw. als etw. ⟨nom⟩
darstellen [als ... daːɐ̯'ʃtɛlən] +haben ◊ *Die Stadtge-
biete werden als rote Kreise dargestellt.* **3.** *(a feeling,
behavio(u)r)* zeigen ['tsaegn̩] +haben ◊ *Sie zeigt kein
Interesse.* ✦ *Sein Gesicht zeigte große Überraschung.;
(taste, courage, intelligence, loyalty, tact)* beweisen
[bə'vaezn̩] <beweist, bewies, hat bewiesen> ◊ *Er hat
in dieser Situation großen Mut bewiesen.* **4.** *(let sb
see sth)* show sth (to sb), show (sb) sth (jdm) etw.
zeigen ['tsaegn̩] +haben ◊ *Zeig doch mal, was du da
hast.* ✦ *Könnten Sie mir den Weg zum Bahnhof
zeigen?* **5.** *(lead)* show sb somewhere jdn irgendwohin bringen ['brɪŋən] <bringt, brachte, hat gebracht>

◊ *Ich bringe Sie zu Ihrem Platz.* **6.** *(explain)* show sb
how/what/where etc. jdm zeigen, wie/was/wo etc.
['tsaegn̩ viː/vas/voː] +haben ◊ *Er hat mir gezeigt, wie
man das Programm bedient.* ✦ *Warten Sie, ich zeige
dir, wo das ist.* **7.** *(be visible)* sth shows somewhere
etw. ist irgendwo zu sehen [ɪst ... tsuː ˌzeːən] +sein
◊ *In ihrem Gesicht war große Enttäuschung zu
sehen.; (a feeling)* let sth show sich ⟨dat⟩ etw.
anmerken lassen ['anmɛʳkn̩ lasn̩] <lässt sich, ließ
sich, hat sich lassen> ◊ *Er ließ sich seine Wut nicht
anmerken.* **8.** FILM, THEAT zeigen ['tsaegn̩] +haben sth
is showing etw. wird gezeigt ◊ *Heute Abend wird im
Kino „Casablanca" gezeigt.* Now showing at a
cinema near you! Jetzt in einem Kino in Ihrer
Nähe! **9.** *(at an exhibition)* ausstellen ['aosʃtɛlən]
+haben ◊ *Diese Bilder wurden zum ersten Mal vor
20 Jahren ausgestellt.* **10.** *(fam) (turn up)* auftauchen
['aoftaoxn̩] +sein ◊ *Um acht Uhr ist er dann endlich
aufgetaucht.*
• **show around** ⟨phras v⟩ show sb around jdn
herumführen [hɛ'rʊmfyːrən] +haben ◊ *Kommen Sie,
ich führe Sie ein bisschen herum.* show sb around
sth jdm etw. zeigen ['tsaegn̩] +haben ◊ *Kann uns
jemand das Haus zeigen?*
• **show in** ⟨phras v⟩ show sb in hereinbringen
[hɛ'raenbrɪŋən] <bringt herein, brachte herein, hat
hereingebracht> ◊ *Wenn die Gäste ankommen,
bringen Sie sie bitte gleich herein.*
• **show off** ⟨phras v⟩ **1.** *(boast)* show (sth) off (mit
etw.) angeben ['angeːbm̩] <gibt an, gab an, hat
angegeben> ◊ *Achte nicht auf ihn; er gibt nur an.* ✦
Sie gibt mit ihrem großen Wissen gern an. **2.** *(show
sth you are proud of)* show sth off etw. vorführen
['foːɐ̯fyːrən] +haben ◊ *Er führt seinen neuen Wagen
vor.* **3.** *(enhance)* show sth off etw. hervorheben
[hɛ'foːɐ̯heːbm̩] +haben ◊ *Das Make-up lässt ihre hübschen Wangen
hervor.; (sb's figure)* etw. betonen [bə'toːnən]
<betont, betonte, hat betont> ◊
• **show out** ⟨phras v⟩ show sb out jdn hinausbegleiten [hɪ'naosbəglaetn̩] <begleitet hinaus, begleitete
hinaus, hat hinausbegleitet> ◊ *Der Geschäftsführer
begleitete sie persönlich hinaus.*
• **show up** ⟨phras v⟩ **1.** *(fam) (turn up)* sb shows up
jd taucht auf [taoxt 'aof] +sein ◊ *Um acht Uhr ist sie
dann endlich aufgetaucht.* **2.** *(be visible)* sth shows
up etw. ist zu erkennen [ɪst tsuː ɛ'kɛnən] ◊ *Auf dem
dunklen Hintergrund ist die schwarze Schrift nicht
zu erkennen.; (make visible)* show sth up etw.
deutlich erkennen lassen [dɔøtlɪç ɛ'kɛnən lasn̩]
<lässt, ließ, hat lassen> ◊ *Das helle Licht lässt die
Flecken an der Wand deutlich erkennen.* **3.** *(make sb
feel embarrassed)* show sb up jdn blamieren
[bla'miːrən] <blamiert, blamierte, hat blamiert> ◊
Musstest du mich vor meinen Kollegen so blamieren?
show yourself up sich blamieren
showcase ⟨noun⟩ **1.** *(event)* gute Gelegenheit, etw. zu
zeigen [guːtə gə'leːgnhaet ... tsuː 'tsaegn̩] die
<–, –en> ◊ *Diese Vorführung ist eine gute Gelegen-
heit für sie, ihr Können zu zeigen.* **2.** *(piece of
furniture)* Vitrine [vi'triːnə] die <–, –n> ◊ *in einer
Vitrine ausgestellte Funde*
shower ⟨noun⟩ **1.** *(for washing)* Dusche ['duːʃə] die
<–, –n> ◊ *Die Dusche geht nicht.* ✦ *Er ist unter der
Dusche.* have/take a shower duschen ['duːʃn̩] +haben
2. METEO Schauer ['ʃaoɐ̯] der <–s, –> ◊ *gewittrige/*

örtliche/vereinzelte *Schauer* **3.** *(of blows, bullets, stones)* Hagel ['haːgl̩] *der* <–s> *no pl* ◊ *Ein Hagel von Schlägen ging auf ihn nieder.* shower of sparks Funkenregen ['fʊŋkn̩reːgn̩] *der* <–s> *no pl* **4.** *(in the US: party)* Party ['paːʳtiː] *die* <–, –s> ◊ *eine Party für jdn veranstalten*

show-off ⟨noun⟩ Angeber ['angeːbɐ] *der* <–s, –> ♀Angeberin ['angeːbərɪn] *die* <–, –nen> ◊ *Er ist ein alter Angeber.* ♦ *So eine Angeberin!*

shred ⟨noun⟩ *(of cloth, paper)* Fetzen ['fɛtsn̩] *der* <–s, –> ◊ *Sie hat den Zeitungsartikel in kleine Fetzen zerrissen.*

ⓔ **tear sth to shreds** etw. in Stücke reißen **not a shred of** keinerlei **in shreds 1.** *(torn)* zerfetzt ◊ *Ihr Kleid war völlig zerfetzt.* **2.** *(ruined)* ruiniert ◊ *Damit ist meine Karriere ruiniert!*

shrewd(ly) ⟨adj, adv⟩ clever ['klɛvɐ] ◊ *ein cleverer Geschäftsmann* ♦ *Er ist wirklich clever.* ♦ *Sie hat das Problem clever gelöst.*

shrink¹ ⟨noun⟩ Seelenklempner ['zeːlənklɛmpnɐ] *der* <–s, –> ♀Seelenklempnerin ['zeːlənklɛmpnərɪn] *die* <–, –nen> *(fam)* ◊ *Du solltest mal zum Seelenklempner gehen!* ♦ *Wusstest du, dass seine Frau Seelenklempnerin ist?*

shrink² ⟨verb⟩ **1.** *(become smaller in size, amount etc.)* schrumpfen ['ʃrʊmpfn̩] *+sein* ◊ *Der Tumor ist durch die Therapie geschrumpft.* ♦ *Unsere Gewinne werden stark schrumpfen.; (clothes)* eingehen ['aŋegeːən] <geht ein, ging ein, ist eingegangen> ◊ *Der Pullover ist beim Waschen eingegangen.; (make smaller in size)* shrink sth etw. verkleinern [fɛ'klaɛnɐn] <verkleinert, verkleinerte, hat verkleinert> ◊ *die Anzahl der Teilnehmer verkleinern* **2.** shrink away/back (from sth) (vor etw. ⟨dat⟩) zurückweichen [tsu'rʏkvaɛçn̩] <weicht zurück, wich zurück, ist zurückgewichen> ◊ *Das Kind wich vor dem großen Hund zurück.*

• **shrink from** ⟨phras v⟩ shrink from sth vor etw. ⟨dat⟩ zurückschrecken [foːɐ̯ ... tsu'rʏkʃrɛkn̩] *+sein* ◊ *Sie schreckte vor der schwierigen Aufgabe zurück.* shrink from doing sth davor zurückschrecken, etw. zu tun ◊ *Er schreckte nicht davor zurück, ihnen die bittere Wahrheit zu sagen.*

shrub ⟨noun⟩ Strauch [ʃtraʊx] *der* <–(e)s, Sträucher> ◊ *einen Strauch pflanzen/beschneiden*

shrug ⟨verb⟩ shrug (your shoulders) mit den Schultern zucken [mɪt deːn 'ʃʊltɐn tsʊkn̩] *+haben* ◊ *„Keine Ahnung", sagte er und zuckte mit den Schultern.*

• **shrug off** ⟨phras v⟩ shrug sth off *(not care about sth)* etw. mit einem Achselzucken abtun [mɪt aɛnəm 'aksl̩tsʊkŋ̩ ˌaptuːn] <tut ab, tat ab, hat abgetan> ◊ *Er hat meine Beschwerde einfach mit einem Achselzucken abgetan.*

shuffle¹ ⟨noun⟩ **1.** *(way of walking noisily)* Schlurfen ['ʃluːɐ̯fn̩] *das* <–s> *no pl* ◊ *Sie hörte ein Schlurfen hinter sich.* walk with a shuffle schlurfen ['ʃluːɐ̯fn̩] *+sein* **2.** GAME give the cards a shuffle die Karten mischen [diː 'kaʳtn̩ ˌmɪʃn̩] *+haben*

shuffle² ⟨verb⟩ **1.** *(walk noisily)* schlurfen ['ʃluːɐ̯fn̩] *+sein* ◊ *Er schlurfte durchs Wohnzimmer.; (move your feet nervously etc.)* shuffle your feet mit den Füßen scharren [mɪt deːn 'fyːsn̩ ʃaʳən] *+haben* **2.** *(objects)* umsortieren ['ʊmzɔʳtiːrən] <sortiert um, sortierte um, hat umsortiert> ◊ *Wer hat die Akten auf meinem Schreibtisch umsortiert?; (jobs)* umbesetzen ['ʊmbəzɛtsn̩] <besetzt um, besetzte um, hat umbesetzt> ◊ *Die Stellen werden umbesetzt.; (when playing*

cards) mischen ['mɪʃn̩] *+haben* ◊ *Alex mischte die Karten.* ♦ *Wer mischt?*

shush ⟨interj⟩ pst [pst] ◊ *Pst! Ich glaube, ich habe ein Geräusch gehört.*

shut¹ ⟨adj⟩ geschlossen [gə'ʃlɔsn̩] *no comp/superl* ◊ *Die Tür ist geschlossen.* ♦ *Alle Läden waren schon geschlossen.* swing shut zuschlagen ['tsuːʃlaːgŋ̩] <schlägt zu, schlug zu, ist zugeschlagen> ◊ *Er hörte die Kellertür zuschlagen.*

shut² ⟨verb⟩ schließen ['ʃliːsn̩] <schließt, schloss, hat geschlossen> ◊ *ein Fenster/eine Tür schließen* ♦ *die Augen schließen* ♦ *Wir schließen um 20 Uhr.* sth shuts easily etc. etw. lässt sich leicht etc. schließen ◊ *Der Koffer lässt sich ganz leicht schließen.*

• **shut away** ⟨phras v⟩ **1.** *(put away)* shut sth away etw. wegschließen ['vɛkʃliːsn̩] <schließt weg, schloss weg, hat weggeschlossen> ◊ *Bitte schließen Sie die Waffen weg.* shut an animal away ein Tier einsperren ['aɛnʃpɛrən] *+haben* ◊ *Er sperrte die Katze ein.* **2.** shut yourself away somewhere sich irgendwohin zurückziehen [tsu'rʏktsiːən] <zieht sich zurück, zog sich zurück, hat sich zurückgezogen> ◊ *Er zog sich in sein Zimmer zurück, um in Ruhe an seinem Buch zu arbeiten.*

• **shut down** ⟨phras v⟩ **1.** *(a shop, factory etc.)* schließen ['ʃliːsn̩] <schließt, schloss, hat geschlossen> ◊ *Das Museum wurde aus Kostengründen geschlossen.* **2.** *(a machine etc.)* abschalten ['apʃaltn̩] <schaltet ab, schaltete ab, hat abgeschaltet> ◊ *den Computer abschalten*

• **shut in** ⟨phras v⟩ **1.** *(lock in)* einsperren ['aɛnʃpɛrən] *+haben* ◊ *Du kannst doch das Kind nicht einsperren!* **2.** *(get caught)* shut sth in sth etw. in etw. ⟨dat⟩ einklemmen ['aɛnklɛmən] *+haben* ◊ *Ich habe mir den Daumen in der Schublade eingeklemmt.*

• **shut off** ⟨phras v⟩ **1.** *(an engine, a machine)* shut sth off etw. abschalten ['apʃaltn̩] <schaltet ab, schaltete ab, hat abgeschaltet> ◊ *Wie schaltet man dieses Gerät ab?* sth shuts off etw. schaltet sich ab **2.** *(gas, electricity, water)* shut sth off etw. abstellen ['apʃtɛlən] *+haben* ◊ *Man hat ihnen den Strom/das Wasser abgestellt.* **3.** *(be isolated)* be shut off from sth von etw. abgeschnitten sein [fɔn ... 'apgəʃnɪtn̩ zaɛn] *+sein* ◊ *Das Dorf ist von der Zivilisation abgeschnitten.* shut yourself off from sb/ sth sich von jdm/etw. zurückziehen [fɔn ... tsu'rʏktsiːən] <zieht sich zurück, zog sich zurück, hat sich zurückgezogen> ◊ *Im Alter zog sich die Künstlerin von ihren Freunden zurück.*

• **shut out** ⟨phras v⟩ **1.** *(a sound, wind etc.)* shut sth out nicht hereinlassen [nɪçt hɛ'raɛnlasn̩] <lässt herein, ließ herein, hat hereingelassen> ◊ *Er schloss das Fenster, um den Wind nicht hereinzulassen.; (a thought, pain)* shut sth out etw. verdrängen [fɛ'drɛŋən] <verdrängt, verdrängte, hat verdrängt> ◊ *Sie verdrängte die Erinnerung an den Vorfall.* **2.** *(prevent from entering)* shut sb out (of sth) jdn (aus etw.) aussperren ['aʊsʃpɛrən] *+haben* ◊ *Warum sperrst du mich aus der Wohnung aus?* shut yourself out sich aussperren ◊ *Ich habe mich ausgesperrt.* **3.** *(prevent from taking part)* shut sb out (of sth) jdn (von etw.) ausschließen ['aʊsʃliːsn̩] <schließt aus, schloss aus, hat ausgeschlossen> ◊ *Warum werde ich immer von allen Entscheidungen ausgeschlossen?*

• **shut up** ⟨phras v⟩ **1.** *(be silent)* den Mund halten

[deːn 'mʊnt haltn̩] <hält, hielt, hat gehalten> *(fam)* ◊ *Halt den Mund!* shut sb up jdn zum Schweigen bringen [tʊm 'ʃvaɪɡn̩ brɪŋən] <bringt, brachte, hat gebracht> **2.** *(imprison)* shut sb up jdn einsperren ['aɛnʃpɛrən] +haben ◊ *Sie haben den Hund im Keller eingesperrt.* **3.** *(a building)* shut sth up etw. verschließen [fɛ'ʃliːsn̩] <verschließt, verschloss, hat verschlossen>

shutter noun **1.** *(on a window)* Fensterladen ['fɛnstɐˌlaːdn̩] der <–s, Fensterläden> ◊ *Sie schloss die Fensterläden.* **2.** FOTO Verschluss [fɛ'ʃlʊs] der <–es, Verschlüsse> ◊ *Er hörte das Klicken des Verschlusses.*

shuttlecock noun Federball ['feːdɐbal] der <–(e)s, Federbälle> ◊ *Der Federball flog über den Zaun.*

shy(ly) adj, adv **1.** *(person, smile, look)* schüchtern ['ʃʏçtɐn] ◊ *Max ist sehr schüchtern.* ◆ *Er warf ihr einen schüchternen Blick zu.* ◆ *Sie lächelte schüchtern.* be shy of doing sth Hemmungen haben, etw. zu tun ['hɛmʊŋən haːbm̩ ... tsuː] +haben ◊ *Sie hat Hemmungen, vor großem Publikum zu sprechen.* **2.** *(animal)* scheu [ʃɔʏ] ◊ *Rehe sind sehr scheue Tiere.* ◆ *Unser Kaninchen ist nicht scheu.* ◆ *Das Tier lief scheu in den Wald.*

sibling noun *(brother)* Bruder ['bruːdɐ] der <–s>; *(sister)* Schwester ['ʃvɛstɐ] die <–> siblings Geschwister [ɡə'ʃvɪstɐ] die <–> only pl ◊ *Haben Sie Geschwister?*

sick[1] noun **1.** *(ill people)* the sick die Kranken [diː 'kraŋkn̩] <–n> pl ◊ *sich um die Kranken kümmern* **2.** *(vomit)* Erbrochene [ɛ'brɔxənə] das <–n> no pl ◊ *Wischen Sie bitte mal das Erbrochene weg!*

sick[2] adj **1.** *(vomiting)* be sick sich übergeben [ybɐ'ɡeːbm̩] <übergibt sich, übergab sich, hat sich übergeben> ◊ *Er hat sich in der Nacht dreimal übergeben.* sb is going to be sick jdn muss sich übergeben; *(about to vomit)* sb feels sick jdm ist schlecht [ɪst 'ʃlɛçt] +sein ◊ *Ihr war während der ganzen Fahrt schlecht.* sb gets sick jdm wird schlecht [vɪɐt 'ʃlɛçt] +sein **2.** *(in the US: ill or worried)* krank [kraŋk] <kränker, am kränksten> ◊ *Er pflegt seine kranke Mutter.* ◆ *unheilbar krank sein* get sick krank werden ◊ *Kurz vor der Reise wurde sie plötzlich krank.* sick with fear/worry etc. krank vor Angst/Sorge etc. **3.** *(offensive, unpleasant)* abartig ['apaːɐtɪç] ◊ *Was für ein abartiger Witz!* ◆ *Also, ich finde diesen Kerl ziemlich abartig.* ⊛ be sick and tired of sth etw. gründlich satt haben be off sick wegen Krankheit fehlen call in sick sich krank melden sth makes sb sick **1.** *(cause sickness)* etw. macht jdn krank **2.** *(fig) (upset)* etw. macht jdn ganz krank

sickness noun **1.** *(illness)* Krankheit ['kraŋkhaɛt] die <–, –en> ◊ *Er musste wegen Krankheit absagen.* sea sickness Seekrankheit ['zeːkraŋkhaɛt] travel sickness Reisekrankheit ['raɛzəkraŋkhaɛt] **2.** *(nausea)* Übelkeit ['yːblkaɛt] die <–, –en> most sing ◊ *Bei der Krankheit kann es zu Durchfall und Übelkeit kommen.*

side noun **1.** *(of an object, a body, location, piece of paper, coin, an aspect, of opposing groups of people, in an argument etc.)* Seite ['zaɛtə] die <–, –n> ◊ *Sie wurden von allen Seiten angegriffen.* ◆ *Ein Würfel hat sechs Seiten.* ◆ *Dreh dich mal auf die andere*

Seite. ◆ *Sie stand auf der anderen Seite des Flusses.* ◆ *Das Papier war auf beiden Seiten beschrieben.* ◆ *Diese Seite kennst du an ihm noch nicht.* ◆ *Beide Seiten sind mit dem Vorschlag einverstanden.* ◆ *Ich stehe ganz auf Ihrer Seite.* change sides sich auf die andere Seite schlagen take sb's side sich auf jds Seite stellen look on the bright side of sth etw. von der positiven Seite betrachten on either side auf beiden Seiten north side/south side etc. Nordseite/Südseite etc. ['nɔɐtzaɛtə/'zyːtzaɛtə] ◊ *Der Balkon ist an der Westseite des Hauses.* by sb's side neben jdm ['neːbm̩] ◊ *Seine Frau stand neben ihm und winkte.* **2.** *(edge)* Rand [rant] der <–(e)s, Ränder> ◊ *Der Junge stand am Rand und traute sich nicht, ins Wasser zu springen.* **3.** *(team in sports or a quiz)* Mannschaft ['manʃaft] die <–, –en> ◊ *Unsere Mannschaft hat gewonnen!* **4.** *(of a family)* Seite ['zaɛtə] die <–, –n> ◊ *Sie hat von väterlicher Seite spanisches Blut.* on sb's mother's side mütterlicherseits ['mʏtelɪçezaɛts] ◊ *Das ist seine Großmutter mütterlicherseits.* on sb's father's side väterlicherseits ['fɛːtelɪçezaɛts] ⊛ take sides Partei ergreifen side by side nebeneinander at/by sb's side an jds Seite ◊ *Er blieb die ganze Nacht an ihrer Seite.* on/to one side beiseite

sideboard noun Sideboard ['saɛtbɔʰt] das <–s, –s>

side with verb side with sb jds Partei ergreifen [paʰ'taɛ ɛɡraɛfn̩] <ergreift, ergriff, hat ergriffen> ◊ *Er ergriff in dem Streit die Partei seiner Frau.*

side dish noun Beilage ['baɛlaːɡə] die <–, –n> ◊ *Als Beilage gab es Kartoffeln.*

side effect noun Nebenwirkung ['neːbm̩vɪɐkʊŋ] die <–, –en> ◊ *Nebenwirkungen dieses Medikaments sind nicht bekannt.*

side street noun Seitenstraße ['zaɛtn̩ʃtraːsə] die <–, –n> ◊ *Der Wagen bog in eine Seitenstraße ein.*

sidewalk noun *(in the US)* Gehsteig ['ɡeːʃtaɛk] der <–(e)s, –e> ◊ *Die Kinder spielten auf dem Gehsteig.*

sideways adv **1.** *(move)* zur Seite [tsuːɐ 'zaɛtə] ◊ *Sie schoben den Wagen zur Seite.; (look at sb)* von der Seite [fɔn deːɐ 'zaɛtə] ◊ *Sie sah ihn von der Seite an.* **2.** *(with one side facing forward)* seitwärts ['zaɛtvɛʰts] ◊ *Seitwärts müsste der Schrank durch die Tür passen.*

siege noun *(by an army, a group)* Belagerung [bə'laːɡərʊŋ] die <–, –en> ◊ *Die Belagerung dauerte mehrere Wochen.* raise a siege eine Belagerung aufheben; *(by the police)* Umstellung ['ʊmʃtɛlʊŋ] die <–, –en> ◊ *die Umstellung eines Gebäudes durch die Polizei* lay siege to sth etw. belagern [bə'laːɡɐn] <belagert, belagerte, hat belagert> ◊ *eine Burg belagern* ◆ *Dutzende von Fans belagerten nach dem Konzert den Bühnenausgang.*

sieve noun Sieb [ziːp] das <–(e)s, –e>

sigh[1] noun Seufzer ['zɔʏftsɐ] der <–s, –> ◊ *„Er kommt nie wieder", sagte sie mit einem Seufzer.* breathe/heave a sigh einen Seufzer ausstoßen a sigh of relief/satisfaction etc. ein Seufzer der Erleichterung/Zufriedenheit etc.

sigh[2] verb **1.** *(person)* seufzen ['zɔʏftsn̩] +haben ◊ *Sie seufzte tief, als sie den Hörer auflegte.* **2.** *(wind)* säuseln ['zɔʏzl̩n] +haben ◊ *Der Wind säuselte in den Zweigen.*

sight noun **1.** *(faculty)* Sehvermögen ['zeːfɐmøːɡn̩] das <–s> no pl ◊ *Sie hat durch einen Unfall ihr Sehvermögen verloren.* **2.** *(sth you see, act of seeing)*

Anblick ['anblɪk] der <-(e)s, -e> ◊ *Beim Anblick der Verletzten musste sie weinen.* ♦ *ein schöner/ungewohnter Anblick* at first sight auf den ersten Blick [aʊf deːn 'eːɐ̯stn̩ 'blɪk] know sb by sight jdn vom Sehen her kennen [fɔm 'zeːən heːɐ̯ ˌkɛnən] <kennt, kannte, hat gekannt> disappear from sight aus jds Blickfeld verschwinden [aʊs ... 'blɪkfɛlt fɛˌʃvɪndn̩] <verschwindet, verschwand, ist verschwunden> ◊ *Nach wenigen Minuten verschwand der Hafen aus unserem Blickfeld.* within sight of sb/sth in Sichtweite ... gen [ɪn 'zɪçtvaetə] ◊ *Die Kinder spielten in Sichtweite der Eltern.* catch sight of sb/sth jdn/ etw. entdecken [ɛnt'dɛkn̩] <entdeckt, entdeckte, hat entdeckt> ◊ *Plötzlich entdeckte er in der Menge ein bekanntes Gesicht.* **3.** *(tourist attraction)* Sehenswürdigkeit ['zeːənsvʏɐ̯dɪçkaet] die <-, -en> most pl **4.** *(of a gun etc.)* Visier [vi'ziːɐ̯] das <-s, -e> ◊ *Er bekam ein Reh ins Visier.* take a sight with a gun at sth etw. mit einem Gewehr anvisieren [mɪt ae̯nəm ɡəˌveːɐ̯ 'anviziːrən] <visiert an, visierte an, hat anvisiert> ◉ have your sights set on sth sich dat etw. zum Ziel gesetzt haben ◊ *Sie hat sich einen Studienplatz in Harvard zum Ziel gesetzt.* let sb out of your sight jdn aus den Augen lassen lose sight of sb/ sth jdn/etw. aus den Augen verlieren lower your sights seine Ansprüche herunterschrauben in sight in Sicht out of sight außer Sicht out of sight, out of mind aus den Augen, aus dem Sinn

sightseeing noun go sightseeing auf Besichtigungstour gehen [aʊf bə'zɪçtɪɡʊŋstuːɐ̯ ɡeːən] <geht, ging, ist gegangen>

sightseeing tour noun *(in a town)* Stadtrundfahrt ['ʃtatrʊntfaːɐ̯t] die <-, -en> ◊ *eine Stadtrundfahrt machen; (in a region, country)* Rundreise ['rʊntraezə] die <-, -n> ◊ *eine Rundreise durch Westirland*

sign¹ noun **1.** *(evidence)* Zeichen ['tsaeçn̩] das <-s, -> ◊ *Das ist kein gutes Zeichen.* ♦ *ein Zeichen der Schwäche; (indication, of illness)* Anzeichen ['antsaeçn̩] das <-s, -> ◊ *Es gibt keine Anzeichen für einen Aufschwung.* sb/sth shows no sign of doing sth nichts deutet darauf hin, dass jd/etw. etw. tun wird [ˌnɪçts dɔøtət daraʊf 'hɪn das ... vɪ'rt] <deutet hin, deutete hin, hat hingedeutet> ◊ *Nichts deutet darauf hin, dass der Sturm bald nachlassen wird.* there is no sign of sb/sth von jdm/etw. ist keine Spur zu sehen [fɔn ... ɪst kaenə ʃpuːɐ̯ tsuː 'zeːən] +sein ◊ *Auf dem Schulhof war keine Spur des Mädchens zu sehen.* **2.** *(on a road, shop etc.)* Schild [ʃɪlt] das <-(e)s, -er> ◊ *Haben Sie denn das Schild nicht gesehen?* **3.** *(gesture, written symbol)* Zeichen ['tsaeçn̩] das <-s, -> ◊ *Er gab ihnen ein Zeichen, sich zu erheben.* ♦ *£ ist das Zeichen für Pfund.* **4.** ASTROL Sternzeichen ['ʃtɛr'n̩tsaeçn̩] das <-s, -> ◉ sign of life Lebenszeichen

sign² verb **1.** *(a letter, cheque, contract)* unterschreiben [ʊntɐ'ʃraebm̩] <unterschreibt, unterschrieb, hat unterschrieben> ◊ *Sie müssen noch unterschreiben.* ♦ *Haben Sie den Vertrag schon unterschrieben?; (a picture, book)* signieren [zɪɡ'niːrən] <signiert, signierte, hat signiert>; *(an agreement etc.)* sign sth with sb etw. mit jdm abschließen [mɪt ... ˌapʃliːsn̩] <schließt ab, schloss ab, hat abgeschlossen> ◊ *eine Vereinbarung mit jdm abschließen; (country, group)* unterzeichnen [ʊntɐ'tsaeçnən] <unterzeichnet, unter-

zeichnete, hat unterzeichnet> *(form)* ◊ *einen Friedensvertrag unterzeichnen* ♦ *Welches Land hat noch nicht unterzeichnet?* **2.** *(employ)* sign (up) sb jdn verpflichten [fɛ'pflɪçtn̩] <verpflichtet, verpflichtete, hat verpflichtet> ◊ *Für das Projekt wurden namhafte Wissenschaftler verpflichtet.* **3.** *(use sign language)* gebärden [ɡə'bɛːɐ̯dn̩] <gebärdet, gebärdete, hat gebärdet>

• **sign away** phras v sign sth away auf etw. acc verzichten [aʊf ... fɛ'tsɪçtn̩] <verzichtet, verzichtete, hat verzichtet> ◊ *auf einen Anspruch verzichten*

• **sign for** phras v sign for sth den Empfang einer Sache gen bestätigen [deːn ɛmˌpfaŋ ... bə'ʃtɛːtɪɡn̩] <bestätigt, bestätigte, hat bestätigt> ◊ *den Empfang eines Briefes/Pakets bestätigen*

• **sign in** phras v **1.** *(on a list)* sign sb in jdn eintragen ['aentraːɡn̩] <trägt ein, trug ein, hat eingetragen> ◊ *Tragen Sie mich bitte auch ein?* sb signs in jd trägt sich ein ◊ *Dort liegt die Liste; hast du dich schon eingetragen?* **2.** *(on the Internet)* sb signs in jd meldet sich an ['mɛldət ... an] <meldete sich an, hat sich angemeldet> ◊ *Wer an einem Forum teilnehmen möchte, muss sich erst anmelden.*

• **sign off** phras v *(end a broadcast)* sich verabschieden [fɛ'apʃiːdn̩] <verabschiedet sich, verabschiedete sich, hat sich verabschiedet> ◊ *Er verabschiedete sich mit den Worten: „Wir wünschen noch einen schönen Abend."; (end a letter)* Schluss machen ['ʃlʊs maxn̩] +haben ◊ *„Es ist schon spät — ich muss für heute Schluss machen."*

• **sign on** phras v **1.** IT *(log on)* sich einloggen ['aenlɔɡn̩] +haben ◊ *Loggen Sie sich mithilfe des Passworts ein.* **2.** *(employ)* sign sb on jdn einstellen ['aenʃtɛlən] +haben ◊ *Wir haben drei neue Mitarbeiter eingestellt.* sb signs on as sth jd verpflichtet sich als etw. nom [fɛ'pflɪçtət ... als] <verpflichtet sich, verpflichtete sich, hat sich verpflichtet> ◊ *Er hat sich als Soldat bei der Bundeswehr verpflichtet.* **3.** *(for unemployment benefit)* sich arbeitslos melden ['aʳbaetsloːs mɛldn̩] <meldet sich, meldete sich, hat sich gemeldet>

• **sign out** phras v sich abmelden ['apmɛldn̩] <meldet sich ab, meldete sich ab, hat sich abgemeldet> ◊ *Seine Mutter meldete ihn von der Schule ab.* sb signs out jd meldet sich ab ◊ *Ich muss mich noch an der Rezeption abmelden.; (on a list)* sign sb out jdn austragen ['aʊstraːɡn̩] <trägt aus, trug aus, hat ausgetragen> ◊ *Haben Sie ihn schon ausgetragen?* sb signs out jd trägt sich aus

• **sign over** phras v sign sth over to sb jdm etw. überschreiben [ybɐ'ʃraebm̩] <überschreibt, überschrieb, hat überschrieben> ◊ *Er will das Haus seinem Sohn überschreiben.*

• **sign up** phras v **1.** *(for a course etc.)* sign up for sth sich für etw. einschreiben [fyː ... ˌaenʃraebm̩] <schreibt sich ein, schrieb sich ein, hat sich eingeschrieben> ◊ *Er möchte sich für einen Kurs an der Volkshochschule einschreiben.* **2.** *(employ, enlist)* sign sb up jdn verpflichten [fɛ'pflɪçtn̩] <verpflichtet, verpflichtete, hat verpflichtet> ◊ *Der Verein verpflichtete einen neuen Spieler.* sb signs up jd verpflichtet sich ◊ *Er hat sich als Soldat verpflichtet.*

signal¹ noun **1.** *(sign)* Zeichen ['tsaeçn̩] das <-s, -> ◊ *Diese Entwicklung ist ein deutliches Zeichen dafür, dass ...* **2.** TECHN *(on the radio, a railway etc.)* Signal [zɪɡ'naːl] das <-s, -e> ◊ *ein Signal senden/*

empfangen ♦ *Das Signal steht auf Rot.*

signal² [verb] **1.** *(give a sign)* signal (to sb) (jdm) ein Zeichen geben [aen 'tsaeçn ge:bm̩] <gibt, gab, hat gegeben> ◊ *Sie gab dem Ober ein Zeichen, dass sie zahlen wollte.* signal sb to do sth jdm ein Zeichen geben, etw. zu tun ◊ *Der Mann gab ihr ein Zeichen, ihm zu folgen.* **2.** *(indicate, show an intention)* signalisieren [zɪgnali'zi:rən] <signalisiert, signalisierte, hat signalisiert> ◊ *Er signalisierte seine Bereitschaft zur Zusammenarbeit.; (a future event)* ankündigen ['ankʏndɪgn̩] +haben ◊ *Die ersten Blüten kündigen den Frühling an.*

signature [noun] **1.** *(name)* Unterschrift ['ʊntɐʃrɪft] die <–, –en> ◊ *Die Unterschrift war gefälscht.* **2.** *(act of signing sth)* Unterzeichnung [ʊntɐ'tsaeçnʊŋ] die <–> no pl ◊ *jdm ein Dokument zur Unterzeichnung vorlegen*

significance [noun] Bedeutung [bə'dɔøtʊŋ] die <–, –en> ◊ *Ich war mir der Bedeutung dieser Bemerkung nicht bewusst.* ♦ *ein Schritt von entscheidender Bedeutung* attach significance to sth einer Sache [dat] Bedeutung beimessen

significant [adj] **1.** *(considerable, important)* bedeutend [bə'dɔøtn̩t] ◊ *Ich halte diesen Gesichtspunkt für bedeutend.* ♦ *eine bedeutende Rolle spielen* **2.** *(meaningful)* bedeutungsvoll [bə'dɔøtʊŋsfɔl] ◊ *Er warf ihr einen bedeutungsvollen Blick zu.*

significantly [adv] **1.** *(considerably)* bedeutend [bə'dɔøtn̩t] ◊ *Sie ist bedeutend jünger als er.* **2.** *(introducing a sentence)* significantly (enough) bezeichnenderweise [bə'tsaeçnəndɐ'vaezə] no comp/superl ◊ *Bezeichnenderweise hat er das Gerücht nicht dementiert.* **3.** *(meaningfully)* bedeutungsvoll [bə'dɔøtʊŋsfɔl] ◊ *„Ich verrate dir ein Geheimnis", flüsterte sie bedeutungsvoll.*

signify [verb] **1.** *(be a symbol)* symbolisieren [zʏmboli'zi:rən] <symbolisiert, symbolisierte, hat symbolisiert> ◊ *Der Kreis auf dem keltischen Kreuz symbolisiert die Ewigkeit.* **2.** *(mean)* bedeuten [bə'dɔøtn̩] <bedeutet, bedeutete, hat bedeutet> ◊ *Was bedeutet dieses Zeichen?* **3.** *(indicate)* signify sth (to sb) (jdm) etw. signalisieren [zɪgnali'zi:rən] <signalisiert, signalisierte, hat signalisiert> ◊ *Er signalisierte uns durch eine Handbewegung, dass er einverstanden war.* **4.** *(be relevant)* sth signifies/does not signify etw. spielt eine/keine Rolle [ʃpiːlt aenə/kaenə 'rɔlə] +haben ◊ *Dieses Ergebnis spielt keine Rolle.*

signing [noun] **1.** *(of a contract, an agreement)* Unterzeichnung [ʊntɐ'tsaeçnʊŋ] die <–> no pl ◊ *die Unterzeichnung eines Vertrags* **2.** *(of a sportsperson)* Verpflichtung [fɐ'pflɪçtʊŋ] die <–> no pl ◊ *Der Verein hatte Interesse an der Verpflichtung Beckhams.* **3.** *(way of communicating)* Gebärdensprache [gə'bɛːɐdn̩ʃpraːxə] die <–, –n> ◊ *Sie interessiert sich für die Gebärdensprache.*

signpost [noun] Wegweiser ['veːkvaezɐ] der <–s, –>

signposted [adj] ausgeschildert ['aʊsgəʃɪldɐt] no comp/superl ◊ *Die Straße nach Germering ist gut ausgeschildert.* ♦ *einem ausgeschilderten Weg folgen*

silence¹ [noun] *(absence of noise)* Stille ['ʃtɪlə] die <–> no pl ◊ *Im Konzertsaal herrschte absolute Stille.; (absence of communication, refusal to communicate)* Schweigen ['ʃvaegn̩] das <–s> no pl ◊ *Sein langes Schweigen machte sie nervös.* ♦ *Nach monatelangem Schweigen rief sie endlich an.* in silence

schweigend ['ʃvaegn̩t]; *(quietness in a place)* Ruhe ['ruːə] die <–> no pl ◊ *Nachts war im Haus endlich Ruhe eingetreten.*

silence² [verb] silence sb jdn zum Schweigen bringen [tsʊm 'ʃvaegn̩ brɪŋən] <bringt, brachte, hat gebracht> ◊ *Sein neuer Roman brachte die Kritiker endgültig zum Schweigen.*

silent [adj] **1.** *(not making a noise, not talking, very quiet)* still [ʃtɪl] ◊ *Alle waren sofort still, als sie zu erzählen anfing.* ♦ *ein stilles Gebet* fall silent verstummen [fɛ'ʃtʊmən] <verstummt, verstummte, ist verstummt> ◊ *Als ein Schuss fiel, verstummten die Vögel.* **2.** *(refuse to talk)* keep/remain silent (about sth) (zu etw.) schweigen [(tsu: ...) 'ʃvaegn̩] <schweigt, schwieg, hat geschwiegen> ◊ *Er hat zu dem Vorwurf geschwiegen.* **3.** *(disease, infection)* schleichend ['ʃlaeçn̩t] no comp/superl ◊ *eine schleichende Krankheit* **4.** LING *(letter)* stumm [ʃtʊm] no comp/superl ◊ *ein stummer Vokal* ♦ *Das „k" in dem englischen Wort „knee" ist stumm.*

silently [adv] *(not talking)* schweigend ['ʃvaegn̩t] no comp/superl ◊ *Schweigend gingen sie nebeneinander her.; (without making any noise)* lautlos ['laotloːs] <lautloser, am lautlosesten> ◊ *Lautlos betrat er das Haus.*

silhouette [noun] **1.** *(dark shape)* Silhouette [zilu'ɛtə] die <–, –n> ◊ *Im Dunkeln zeichnete sich die Silhouette eines Hauses ab.* **2.** *(picture)* Schattenriss ['ʃatn̩rɪs] der <–es, –e> ◊ *Sie zeichnete den Schattenriss eines Elefanten.*

silk [noun] **1.** *(material)* Seide ['zaedə] die <–, –n> ◊ *eine Bluse aus reiner Seide* silk shirt Seidenhemd ['zaedn̩hɛmt] das <–(e)s, –en> silk dress Seidenkleid ['zaedn̩klaet] das <–(e)s, –er> **2.** *(racing colo(u)rs)* silks Rennfarben ['rɛnfaːɐbm̩] die <–> pl **3.** LAW *(barrister)* Kronanwalt ['kroːnanvalt] der <–(e)s, Kronanwälte> ♀Kronanwältin ['kroːnanvɛltɪn] die <–, –nen> ◊ *Sein Sohn ist Kronanwalt.* ♦ *eine bekannte Kronanwältin* take silk Kronanwalt werden

sill [noun] **1.** *(of a window)* Sims [zɪms] der or also das <–es, –e> **2.** *(on a car)* Türleiste ['tyːɐlaestə] die <–, –n>

silly [adj] dumm [dʊm] <dümmer, am dümmsten> ◊ *Das war ganz schön dumm von ihm.* ♦ *Das dumme Auto springt wieder nicht an!* laugh yourself silly sich dumm und dämlich lachen

silver¹ [noun] Silber ['zɪlbɐ] das <–s> no pl ◊ *ein Armreif aus Silber* ♦ *Das Silber muss poliert werden.* ♦ *ein Hut in Violett und Silber* ⊛ win silver Silber holen

silver² [adj] silbern ['zɪlbɐn] no comp/superl ◊ *ein silberner Ring* ♦ *Sein Haar war silbern geworden.* silver ... Silber ... ['zɪlbɐ] silver coin Silbermünze ['zɪlbɐmʏntsə] die <–, –n> silver jewellery Silberschmuck ['zɪlbɐʃmʊk] der <–(e)s> no pl

similar [adj] ähnlich ['ɛːnlɪç] ◊ *Es gab schon mal ein ähnliches Problem.* ♦ *Unsere Interessen sind ganz ähnlich.* similar to sth einer Sache [dat] ähnlich ◊ *Der Geschmack der Nektarine war dem des Pfirsichs ähnlich.*

similarity [noun] Ähnlichkeit ['ɛːnlɪçkaet] die <–, –en> ◊ *Die Ähnlichkeit zwischen den beiden Brüdern ist erstaunlich.*

similarly [adv] **1.** *(introducing a sentence or clause)* ebenso ['eːbm̩zoː] ◊ *Bei Kälte zieht sich das Gewebe zusammen; ebenso dehnt es sich bei Wärme wieder*

aus. 2. *(almost alike, resembling)* ähnlich ['ɛːnlɪç] ◊ *Die Qualität des neuen Modells ist ähnlich schlecht.*

simile ⸤noun⸥ Vergleich [fe'glaeç] der <-(e)s, -e>

simmer ⸤verb⸥ sth simmers etw. köchelt ['kœçlt] +haben simmer sth etw. köcheln lassen ◊ *Lassen Sie die Soße noch etwa 15 Minuten köcheln.*

simple ⸤adj⸥ einfach ['aenfax] ◊ *eine einfache Erklärung* ♦ *Das ist nicht so einfach.* ♦ *Sein Großvater war ein einfacher Mann.* for the simple reason that aus dem einfachen Grund, dass the simple fact is that es ist einfach so, dass

simplicity ⸤noun⸥ Einfachheit ['aenfaxhaet] die <-> no pl ◊ *Sie liebt die Einfachheit des Lebens auf dem Lande.* for the sake of simplicity der Einfachheit halber

ⓢ be simplicity itself die einfachste Sache der Welt sein

simplify ⸤verb⸥ vereinfachen [fe'|aenfaxn̩] <vereinfacht, vereinfachte, hat vereinfacht> ◊ *Wir haben das Programm ein wenig vereinfacht.*

simply ⸤adv⸥ 1. *(merely)* nur [nuːɐ] ◊ *Mir geht es gut; ich bin nur müde.* 2. *(in an uncomplicated way, in an ordinary way, for emphasis)* einfach ['aenfax] ◊ *Er versuchte, sich einfach auszudrücken.* ♦ *einfach und bescheiden leben* ♦ *Ihre Arbeit ist einfach nicht gut genug.* to put it simply um es einfach auszudrücken

simulate ⸤verb⸥ 1. *(conditions)* simulieren [zimu'liːrən] <simuliert, simulierte, hat simuliert> *(tech)* ◊ *einen Flugzeugabsturz am PC simulieren* 2. *(a material)* imitieren [imi'tiːrən] <imitiert, imitierte, hat imitiert> ◊ *Krokodilsleder imitieren* 3. *(a feeling)* vortäuschen ['foːɡtɔɪʃn̩] +haben ◊ *Sie täuschte Überraschung vor.*

simultaneous(ly) ⸤adj, adv⸥ gleichzeitig ['glaeçtsaetɪç] no comp/superl; when used as an adj, only before ns ◊ *Diese beiden Vorlesungen finden gleichzeitig statt.* ♦ *gleichzeitige Prozesse*; *(technical)* simultan [zimʊl'taːn] no comp/superl; when used as an adj, only before ns simultaneous interpreting Simultandolmetschen [zimʊl'taːndɔlmɛtʃn̩] das <-s> no pl

sin ⸤noun⸥ Sünde ['zʏndə] die <-, -n> ◊ *jdm seine Sünden vergeben* ♦ *Es ist eine Sünde, wie viel Geld er für seine Hobbys ausgibt.* commit a sin eine Sünde begehen

since¹ ⸤adv⸥ 1. *(from that time on)* (ever) since seitdem [zaet'deːm] ◊ *Sie zog 1991 nach Köln und arbeitet seitdem dort als Lehrerin.* 2. *(for a long time)* long since schon lange [ʃoːn 'laŋə] ◊ *Die Indianer, die früher hier lebten, sind schon lange nicht mehr da.*

since² ⸤prep⸥ seit [zaet] +dat ◊ *Sie sind seit 1985 verheiratet.*

since³ ⸤conjunc⸥ 1. *(temporal)* (ever) since seit [zaet] ◊ *Seit wir zusammenwohnen, streiten wir.* since doing sth seit jd etw. getan hat ◊ *Seit ich nach London gezogen bin, hat sich mein Leben verändert.* since then seitdem [zaet'deːm] ◊ *Ich habe das Buch zu Weihnachten bekommen; seitdem habe ich es schon dreimal gelesen.* 2. *(causal)* da [daː] ◊ *Er zog nach Erfurt, er da er davon überzeugt war, dass es dort schöner sei.*

sincere(ly) ⸤adj, adv⸥ aufrichtig ['aofrɪçtɪç] ◊ *ein aufrichtiger Mensch* ♦ *Ihre Entschuldigung war aufrichtig.* ♦ *Ich hoffe aufrichtig, dass wir uns wiedersehen.*

sing ⸤verb⸥ singen ['zɪŋən] <singt, sang, hat gesungen> ◊ *Sie sang ein Liebeslied.* ♦ *Im Garten singen die Vögel.* sing sb to sleep jdn in den Schlaf singen

singer ⸤noun⸥ Sänger ['zɛŋɐ] der <-s, -> ♀Sängerin ['zɛŋərɪn] die <-, -nen> ◊ *ein berühmter Sänger* ♦ *Sie ist Sängerin in einer Band.*

single¹ ⸤noun⸥ 1. mus *(record)* Single ['sɪŋl̩] die <-, -s> ◊ *Die Gruppe hat eine neue Single herausgebracht.* 2. sport *(in tennis)* singles Einzel ['aentsl̩] das <-s, -> ◊ *ein Einzel spielen* the men's singles das Herreneinzel [das 'hɛrən|aentsl̩] the women's singles das Dameneinzel [das 'daːmən|aentsl̩] 3. *(hotel room for one)* Einzelzimmer ['aentsl̩tsɪmɐ] das <-s, -> ◊ *ein Einzelzimmer buchen* 4. *(people without a partner)* singles Singles ['sɪŋl̩s] die <-> pl 5. *(in the UK: one-way ticket)* Hinfahrkarte ['hɪnfaːɐˌkaʁtə] die <-, -n> A single ticket to Berlin please. Eine einfache Fahrt nach Berlin, bitte!

single² ⸤adj⸥ 1. *(only one)* einzig ['aentsɪç] no comp/superl, only before ns ◊ *Der Mannschaft gelang kein einziger Treffer.* ♦ *ein einziger Tarif für alle Handynetze*; *(individual, separate)* einzeln ['aentsl̩n] no comp/superl, only before ns ◊ *Sie prüfte jedes einzelne Stück.* ♦ *eine einzelne Socke* the single biggest problem das größte Problem [das 'grøːstə proˌbleːm] 2. *(not married, not in a relationship)* allein stehend [a'laen ʃteːənt] no comp/superl ◊ *Ich bin allein stehend.* ♦ *ein allein stehender Mann*; *(parent)* allein erziehend [a'laen ɛtsiːənt] ◊ *eine allein erziehende Mutter* 3. *(for one person)* Einzel... ['aentsl̩] single room Einzelzimmer ['aentsl̩tsɪmə] das <-s, -> 4. single ticket Hinfahrkarte ['hɪnfaːɐˌkaʁtə] die <-, -n> A single ticket to Bonn, please. Eine einfache Fahrt nach Bonn, bitte!

single-minded(ly) ⸤adj, adv⸥ zielstrebig ['tsiːlʃtreːbɪç] ◊ *Sie ist zielstrebig und engagiert.* ♦ *eine zielstrebige Wissenschaftlerin* ♦ *einen Plan zielstrebig verfolgen*

single parent ⸤noun⸥ allein Erziehende [a'laen ɛˌtsiːəndə] der/die <-n, die allein Erziehenden> but: ein allein Erziehender/eine allein Erziehende ◊ *Seit der Scheidung ist sie allein Erziehende.*

singular ⸤noun⸥ GRAM Singular ['zɪŋgulaːʁ] der <-s, -e> be in the singular im Singular stehen

sink¹ ⸤noun⸥ *(kitchen)* Spülbecken ['ʃpyːlbɛkn̩] das <-s, -> ◊ *Das Geschirr stapelt sich im Spülbecken.*; *(bathroom)* Waschbecken ['vaʃbɛkn̩] das <-s, ->

sink² ⸤verb⸥ 1. *(go down, go under water)* sinken ['zɪŋkn̩] <sinkt, sank, ist gesunken> ◊ *Unsere Stimmung sank beträchtlich.* ♦ *Das Schiff ist gesunken.* ♦ *Der Wasserspiegel sinkt wieder.* ♦ *Wie konnte er nur so tief sinken!* sink to sth auf etw. acc sinken ◊ *Der Dollar ist auf den niedrigsten Stand seit zehn Jahren gesunken.* sink to the ground zu Boden sinken sink to your knees auf die Knie sinken; *(disappear)* versinken [fe'zɪŋkn̩] <versinkt, ist versunken> ◊ *Die Sonne versank im Meer* ♦ *Das Auto versank im Schlamm.* ♦ *Das Land versinkt im Chaos.* sink into crisis in eine Krise stürzen [ɪn aenə 'kriːzə ʃtʏɐtsn̩] +sein 2. *(a ship, ball)* versenken [fe'zɛŋkn̩] <versenkt, versenkte, hat versenkt> ◊ *Das U-Boot wurde versenkt.* ♦ *beim Billard eine Kugel versenken* 3. *(sb who is ill)* sb is sinking fast jdm geht es zusehends schlechter [geːt ɛs ˌtsuːˈzeːənts 'ʃlɛçtɐ] <geht, ging, ist gegangen> 4. *(become quieter)* leiser werden ['laezə veːɐdn̩] +sein sink to a whisper zu einem Flüstern werden [tsuː aenəm 'flʏstɐn veːɐdn̩] +haben

5. *(push, bury)* stoßen ['ʃtoːsn̩] <stößt, stieß, hat gestoßen> ◊ *Sie stieß das Messer in seine Brust.* **6.** *(invest)* stecken ['ʃtɛkn̩] +haben ◊ *Die Firma hat schon drei Millionen in das Projekt gesteckt.*

⊛ **be left to sink or swim** sich selbst überlassen sein **it is sink or swim** Alles oder Nichts

• **sink in** ⟨phras v⟩ sth sinks in jd begreift etw. [bə'ɡræft] <begreift, begriff, hat begriffen> ◊ *Langsam begriff sie die Ausmaße der Katastrophe.* ✦ *Ich hatte noch nicht begriffen, dass ich gewonnen hatte.* sth takes a while to sink in es dauert eine Weile, bis jd etw. begriffen hat ◊ *Es wird eine Weile dauern, bis ihr den ganzen Lernstoff begriffen habt.*

sip ⟨verb⟩ in kleinen Schlucken trinken [ɪn klaɛnən 'ʃlʊkn̩ trɪŋkn̩] <trinkt, trank, hat getrunken> sip sth an etw. ⟨dat⟩ nippen [an ... nɪpm̩] +haben ◊ *Er nippte an seinem Cognac.*

sir ⟨noun⟩ **1.** *(form of address)* mein Herr [maɛn 'hɛʳ] der <–n, –en> *(oldf)* ◊ *Darf es sonst noch etwas sein, mein Herr?; (in the UK: way of addressing a teacher)* Herr Lehrer [hɛʳ 'leːʀə] *(oldf)* **2.** *(addressing a nobleman)* Sir Sir [søːɐ̯] <–> no pl ◊ *Sir Peter Ustinov*

⊛ **Dear Sir/Sirs** *(in letters)* Sehr geehrte Herren

siren ⟨noun⟩ Sirene [ziːʀeːnə] die <–, –n> ◊ *Die Feuerwehr fuhr mit Blaulicht und Sirene zum Einsatz.* ✦ *die Sirenen in der griechischen Mythologie*

sirup → syrup

sister ⟨noun⟩ **1.** *(sibling, nun)* Schwester ['ʃvɛstə] die <–, –n> ◊ *meine jüngste Schwester* ✦ *Im Konvent leben derzeit sieben Schwestern.* half sister Halbschwester ['halpʃvɛstə] **2.** *(nurse)* Krankenschwester ['kraŋkn̩ʃvɛstə] die <–, –n>; *(in charge)* Oberschwester ['oːbɐʃvɛstə] night sister Nachtschwester ['naxtʃvɛstə] **3.** *(when addressing a nurse or nun)* Sister Schwester ['ʃvɛstə] <–> no pl ◊ *Ich habe Schmerzen, Schwester.* ✦ *Schwester Theresa betet für uns.*

sister-in-law ⟨noun⟩ Schwägerin ['ʃvɛːɡərɪn] die <–, –nen>

sit ⟨verb⟩ **1.** *(be seated, be stuck, be a member of sth)* sitzen ['zɪtsn̩] <sitzt, saß, hat gesessen> ◊ *auf einem Stuhl sitzen* ✦ *im Auto/Zug sitzen* ✦ *still sitzen* ✦ *Der Vogel sitzt auf einem Ast.* sit on the board of directors im Aufsichtsrat sitzen sit for sb jdm Modell sitzen I sat back on the sofa and watched TV. Ich machte es mir auf dem Sofa gemütlich und sah fern. sit around herumsitzen [hɛ'ʀʊmzɪtsn̩] +haben *(fam, esp pej)* ◊ *Er sitzt jeden Abend in der Kneipe herum.* sit together zusammensitzen [tsu'zamənzɪtsn̩] +haben; *(doing nothing)* sit (there) dasitzen ['daːzɪtsn̩] +haben ◊ *Er saß da und starrte vor sich hin.* **2.** *(lower sb)* sit sb (down) jdn setzen ['zɛtsn̩] +haben ◊ *Sie setzte das Baby in den Kinderwagen.* sb sits (down) jd setzt sich ◊ *Er setzte sich auf einen Stuhl.* ✦ *Bitte setzen Sie sich.* **3.** *(object)* stehen ['ʃteːən] <steht, stand, hat gestanden> ◊ *Das Buch steht schon ewig im Regal.* **4.** *(have a meeting)* tagen ['taːɡn̩] +haben sit on sth zu etw. tagen ◊ *Der EU-Ministerrat tagt zum Thema Umweltschutz.* **5.** *(in the UK: attend an exam)* ablegen ['aplɛːɡn̩] +haben ◊ *eine Prüfung ablegen* **6.** *(look after a child)* sit for sb für jdn babysitten [fyːɐ̯ ... 'beːbɪsɪtn̩] <–, –, hat babygesittet> *only inf/past p* ◊ *Ich muss heute Abend für meine Schwester babysitten.*

• **sit back** ⟨phras v⟩ *(refrain from action)* die Hände

in den Schoß legen [diː ˌhɛndə ɪn deːn 'ʃoːs leːɡn̩] +haben ◊ *Du kannst nicht einfach die Hände in den Schoß legen und zusehen.* → sit 1.

• **sit by** ⟨phras v⟩ tatenlos zusehen [taːtn̩loːs 'tsuːzeːən] <sieht zu, sah zu, hat zugesehen> sit by and allow sth to happen, sit by and watch sth happening tatenlos zusehen, wie etw. passiert

• **sit in** ⟨phras v⟩ **1.** *(stand in for)* sit in for sb für jdn einspringen [fyːɐ̯ ... ˌaɛnʃpʀɪŋən] <springt ein, sprang ein, ist eingesprungen> ◊ *Ich sprang für den kranken Kollegen ein.* **2.** *(be present)* sit in on sth bei etw. dabei sein [baɛ ... daˌbaɛ zaɛn] +sein ◊ *bei einer Sitzung dabei sein*

• **sit out** ⟨phras v⟩ sit sth out **1.** *(take a break)* bei etw. aussetzen [baɛ ... 'aɔszɛtsn̩] +haben ◊ *Bei der nächsten Runde setze ich aus.* **2.** *(wait until sth is over)* etw. abwarten ['apvaːtn̩] <wartet ab, wartete ab, hat abgewartet> ◊ *Ich wartete das Ende der Rede ab und ging.*

• **sit through** ⟨phras v⟩ sit sth through etw. über sich ⟨acc⟩ ergehen lassen [yːbɐ ... ɐ'ɡeːən lasn̩] <lässt, ließ, hat lassen> ◊ *Ich musste unzählige Besprechungen über mich ergehen lassen.*

• **sit up** ⟨phras v⟩ **1.** *(from a lying position)* sich aufsetzen ['aɔfzɛtsn̩] +haben ◊ *Setz dich auf und iss ein wenig Suppe.* **2.** *(sit straight)* sich gerade hinsetzen [ɡəˌraːdə 'hɪnzɛtsn̩] +haben ◊ *Setz dich gerade hin und hör zu!* **3.** *(not go to bed)* aufbleiben ['aɔfblaɛbm̩] <bleibt auf, blieb auf, ist aufgeblieben> sit up late lange aufbleiben

site ⟨noun⟩ **1.** *(plot of land)* Grundstück ['ɡʀʊntʃtʏk] das <–(e)s, –e> a site of 10 000 m² ein 10 000 m² großes Grundstück *(construction)* site Baustelle ['baɔʃtɛlə] die <–, –n> off site außerhalb der Baustelle on site auf der Baustelle **2.** *(location, spot)* Ort [ɔʳt] der <–(e)s, –e> ◊ *An diesem Ort stand früher ein Kloster.; (of an existing building, institution)* Standort ['ʃtantʃɔʳt] ◊ *der Standort einer Universität* site of a battle Kampfplatz ['kampfplats] der <–es, Kampfplätze> landing site Landeplatz ['landəplats] nest site Nistplatz ['nɪstplats]; *(of a tumo(u)r)* Sitz [zɪts] der <–es, –e> ◊ *der Sitz eines Tumors*

sitting room ⟨noun⟩ Wohnzimmer ['voːntsɪmɐ] das <–s, –> ◊ *Der Fernseher steht im Wohnzimmer.*

situate ⟨verb⟩ **1.** *(spatially: a building, town etc.)* be situated somewhere irgendwo liegen ['liːɡn̩] <liegt, lag, ist gelegen> ◊ *Das Dorf liegt 50 km nördlich von Halle.* situate sth somewhere etw. irgendwo errichten [ɐ'ʀɪçtn̩] <errichtet, errichtete, hat errichtet> ◊ *Man sollte das Haus nicht an einem Hang errichten.* **2.** *(relate sth to sth)* situate sth in etw. in Bezug zu etw. setzen [ɪn bəˌtsuːk tsuː ... zɛtsn̩] +haben ◊ *Ich versuche, meine Erfahrungen in Bezug zum derzeitigen politischen Klima zu setzen.*

situation ⟨noun⟩ **1.** *(conditions, circumstances)* Situation [zituaˈtsjoːn] die <–, –en> ◊ *Die Situation im Nahen Osten ist gespannt.* ✦ *Was kann ich in dieser Situation tun?* **2.** *(location)* Lage ['laːɡə] die <–, –n> ◊ *Die Lage des Hauses ist traumhaft.*

⊛ **if the situation arises** wenn es dazu kommt

six¹ ⟨noun⟩ Sechs [zɛks] die <–, –en> → four¹

six² ⟨nmrl⟩ sechs [zɛks] → four²

sixfold ⟨adj, adv⟩ sechsfach ['zɛksfax] → fourfold

sixteen ⟨nmrl⟩ sechzehn ['zɛçtseːn] → four²

sixth¹ ⟨noun⟩ **1.** *(fraction)* Sechstel ['zɛkstl̩] das <–s, –>

→ **fourth¹ 1. 2.** *(in a sequence)* Sechste ['zɛkstə] der *or* die *or* das <–n, –n> *most sing* → **fourth¹ 2.**

sixth² [adj] sechste ['zɛkstə] <ein sechster ..., eine sechste ..., ein sechstes ...> → **sixth²**

sixth form [noun] *(in England and Wales)* Oberstufe ['oːbɐʃtuːfə] die <–, –n> *most sing* ◊ *Ich bin in der Oberstufe.*

sixthly [adv] sechstens ['zɛkstn̩s] → **fourthly**

sixty [nmrl] sechzig ['zɛçtsɪç] → **four²**

size [noun] *(dimensions)* Größe ['grøːsə] die <–, –n> ◊ *die Größe einer Firma* ♦ *ein Kleid in Größe 40* ♦ *seine volle Größe erreichen* double in size seine Größe verdoppeln sth is half the size of sth etw. ist halb so groß wie etw. [ɪst 'halp zoː groːs viː]; *(of a sum, an amount)* Höhe ['høːə] die <–, –n> ◊ *Die Steuern richten sich nach der Höhe des Einkommens.* cut sth to size etw. zurechtschneiden [tsu'rɛçtʃnaednˌ] <schneidet zurecht, schnitt zurecht, hat zurechtgeschnitten> ◊ *ein Stück Stoff zurechtschneiden*
◉ that's about the size of it so siehts aus

skate¹ [noun] **1.** (ice) skate Schlittschuh ['ʃlɪtʃuː] der <–(e)s, –e> (roller) skate Rollschuh ['rɔlʃuː] **2.** *(fish)* Glattrochen ['glatrɔxn̩] der <–s, –>
◉ get your skates on sich beeilen

skate² [verb] *(on ice)* Schlittschuh laufen ['ʃlɪtʃuː laofn̩] <läuft, lief, ist gelaufen>; *(on roller skates)* Rollschuh laufen ['rɔlʃuː laofn̩] go skating Schlittschuh/Rollschuh laufen

skeleton [noun] **1.** *(bones, frame)* Skelett [ske'lɛt] das <–(e)s, –e> ◊ *das Skelett eines Dinosauriers* ♦ *Das Skelett des Gebäudes bestand aus einem Stahlgerüst.* **2.** *(basic, rudimentary)* skeleton agreement Rahmenabkommen ['raːmənˌapkɔmən] das <–s, –> skeleton crew Stammbesatzung ['ʃtambəzatsʊŋ] die <–, –en>
◉ have a skeleton in the cupboard eine Leiche im Keller haben *(fam)*

sketch¹ [noun] **1.** *(drawing, short description)* Skizze ['skɪtsə] die <–, –n> ◊ *eine Skizze von etw. anfertigen* ♦ *eine biografische Skizze der Schriftstellerin Tania Blixen* **2.** *(short scene, skit)* Sketch [skɛtʃ] der <–es, –e> ◊ *die besten Sketche von Loriot*

sketch² [verb] skizzieren [skɪ'tsiːrən] <skizziert, skizzierte, hat skizziert> ◊ *Er hat den Grundriss des Hauses mit wenigen Strichen skizziert.* ♦ *Skizzieren Sie die wichtigsten Regelungen des Maastricht-Vertrags!*

ski¹ [noun] **1.** *(for your feet)* Ski [ʃiː] der <–s, – *or* –er> ◊ *Ich schnallte mir die Skier an.* **2.** *(on a vehicle)* Kufe ['kuːfə] die <–, –n> ◊ *die Kufen eines Schneemobils*

ski² [verb] *(cross-country)* Ski laufen ['ʃiː laofn̩] <läuft, lief, ist gelaufen>; *(downhill)* Ski fahren ['ʃiː faːrən] <fährt, fuhr, ist gefahren> go skiing Ski laufen/fahren

skid [verb] schlittern ['ʃlɪtɐn] +sein ◊ *Das Auto fing auf dem Eis an zu schlittern.* skid to a stop schlitternd zum Stehen kommen

skiing [noun] *(downhill)* Skifahren ['ʃiːfaːrən] das <–s> no pl ◊ *Skifahren ist mein Lieblingssport.*

skilful(ly), skillfully [adj, adv] geschickt [gə'ʃɪkt] <geschickter, am geschicktesten> ◊ *Er ist sehr geschickt im Umgang mit Holz.* ♦ *eine geschickte Handwerkerin* ♦ *ein geschickt aufgetragenes Make-up*

skill [noun] *(ability)* Fähigkeit ['fɛːɪçkaet] die <–, –en> ◊ *seine Fähigkeiten als Führungskraft unter Beweis*

stellen; *(dexterity)* Geschick [gə'ʃɪk] das <–(e)s, –e> ◊ *handwerkliches Geschick; (as a result of training, experience)* Kenntnis ['kɛntnɪs] die <–, –se> *most pl* ◊ *Kenntnisse in Statistik haben* language skills Sprachkenntnisse ['ʃpraːxkɛntnɪsə]

skilled [adj] **1.** *(dexterous, capable)* geschickt [gə'ʃɪkt] <geschickter, am geschicktesten> ◊ *Du bist sehr geschickt im Umgang mit Menschen.* ♦ *ein geschickter Handwerker* **2.** *(requiring or having specific knowledge)* qualifiziert [kvalifi'tsiːɐt] <qualifizierter, am qualifiziertesten> ◊ *eine qualifizierte Tätigkeit ausüben* ♦ *Unsere Arbeitskräfte sind hoch qualifiziert.*

skillful(ly) → **skilful(ly)**

skin¹ [noun] **1.** *(of a person or animal, on milk)* Haut [haot] die <–, Häute> ◊ *trockene/fettige Haut* ♦ *die Haut auf der Milch* skin colo(u)r Hautfarbe ['haotfaʁbə] die <–, –n> skin disease Hautkrankheit ['haotkraŋkhaet] die <–, –en> **2.** *(of vegetables, fruit)* Schale ['ʃaːlə] die <–, –n> banana skin Bananenschale [ba'naːnənʃaːlə]; *(very thin and soft)* Haut [haot] die <–, Häute> ◊ *Pfirsiche isst man mit Haut.* **3.** *(fur of an animal)* Fell [fɛl] das <–(e)s, –e> **4.** *(of sausages)* Darm [darm] der <–(e)s, Därme> ◊ *Leberwurst im Darm*
◉ be all skin and bones nur Haut und Knochen sein *(fam)* by the skin of your teeth mit knapper Not have a thick skin ein dickes Fell haben *(fam)* get under sb's skin **1.** *(annoy or upset sb)* jdm unter die Haut gehen *(fam)* **2.** *(attract sb)* jdn in seinen Bann schlagen

skin² [verb] **1.** *(remove the skin)* häuten ['hɔøtn̩] <häutet, häutete, hat gehäutet> ◊ *Tomaten/ein Kaninchen häuten* **2.** *(graze)* aufschürfen ['aofʃʏɐfn̩] +haben ◊ *Ich habe mir das Knie aufgeschürft.*

skinhead [noun] Skinhead ['skɪnhɛt] der <–s, –s>

skinny [adj] mager ['maːgɐ] ◊ *Sie ist furchtbar mager.* ♦ *ein mageres Kind*

skip¹ [noun] **1.** *(in the UK: container for rubbish)* Container [kɔn'teːne] der <–s, –> ◊ *Ich bestelle einen Container für den Müll.* **2.** *(small jump)* Hüpfer ['hʏpfe] der <–s, –> ◊ *Der Tanz wird mit einem Hüpfer abgeschlossen.*

skip² [verb] **1.** *(jump)* hüpfen ['hʏpfn̩] +sein ◊ *Er hüpfte über den Hof.* skip along beside sb neben jdm herhüpfen [neːbm̩ ... 'heːɐhʏpfn̩] +sein ◊ *Fröhlich hüpfte sie die Straße entlang.* skip along sth etw. entlanghüpfen [ɛnt'laŋhʏpfn̩] +sein ◊ *Fröhlich hüpfte sie die Straße entlang.; (with a rope)* seilspringen ['zaelʃprɪŋən] <–, –, ist seilgesprungen> *only inf/past p* **2.** *(leave out)* überspringen [yːbɐ'ʃprɪŋən] <überspringt, übersprang, hat übersprungen> ◊ *ein paar Seiten/ein Schuljahr überspringen* skip to sth gleich zu etw. übergehen [glaeç tsuː ... ˌyːbɐgeːən] >geht über, ging über, ist übergegangen> ◊ *Gehen wir gleich zum letzten Punkt der Tagesordnung über!; (a meal)* ausfallen lassen ['aosfalən lasn̩] <lässt, ließ, hat lassen> ◊ *Wir ließen das Mittagessen ausfallen.; (not attend)* skip a class eine Stunde schwänzen [aenə ʃtʊndə 'ʃvɛntsn̩] +haben *(fam)*

skirt [noun] Rock [rɔk] der <–(e)s, Röcke> ◊ *Ich trug einen kurzen Rock.*

skull [noun] Schädel ['ʃɛːdl̩] der <–s, –> fracture your skull einen Schädelbruch erleiden [aenən 'ʃɛːdlbrʊx ɐlaedn̩] <erleidet, erlitt, hat erlitten>

⊛ **sb gets sth into their skull** etw. geht in jds Schädel

sky [noun] sky, skies Himmel ['hɪml] der <-s, -> *most sing in the sky* am Himmel ◊ *Der Mond stand hoch am Himmel.* the night sky der nächtliche Himmel clear skies ein wolkenloser Himmel

⊛ **the sky's the limit** alles ist möglich

slab [noun] **1.** *(of stone, marble etc.)* Platte ['platə] die <-, -n> ◊ *eine Platte aus Marmor* concrete slab Betonplatte [be'tɔnplatə] **2.** *(big slice)* dicke Scheibe [dɪkə 'ʃaebə] die <-, -n> ◊ *eine dicke Scheibe Brot;* *(big piece)* Stück [ʃtʏk] das <-(e)s, -e> ◊ *ein großes Stück Schokolade*

slack [adj] **1.** *(rope, muscles etc.)* schlaff [ʃlaf] ◊ *die schlaffe Wäscheleine straffen* ♦ *Seine Muskeln sind ganz schlaff.* **2.** *(sloppy, careless)* nachlässig ['naːxlɛsɪç] ◊ *Die Sicherheitsvorkehrungen sind ziemlich nachlässig.* ♦ *eine nachlässige Einstellung zu etw. haben* **3.** *(not lively or busy)* flau [flao] <flauer, am flau(e)sten> *(fam)* ◊ *eine flaue Konjunktur* ♦ *Meine Geschäfte sind im Sommer flau.*

slam [verb] **1.** *(close, throw, crash)* knallen ['knalən] *transitive use +haben/intransitive use +sein (fam)* ◊ *Knall doch die Tür nicht so!* ♦ *Das Auto ist gegen eine Mauer geknallt.* slam shut zuknallen ['tsuːknalən] *transitive use +haben/intransitive use +sein (fam)* ◊ *Wütend hat er die Tür zugeknallt.* ♦ *Das Fenster ist zugeknallt.* slam the brakes on voll auf die Bremse steigen [fɔl aof diː 'brɛmzə ʃtaeɡn] <steigt, stieg, ist gestiegen> *(fam)* slam home a goal ein Tor reinknallen [aen 'toːɐ ˌraenknalən] +haben *(fam)* **2.** *(criticize)* scharf kritisieren [ʃaʳf kritiˈziːrən] <kritisiert, kritisierte, hat kritisiert> ◊ *Sein Vorschlag wurde scharf kritisiert.*

slanted [adj] **1.** *(ceiling, roof)* schräg [ʃrɛːk] ◊ *Die Wände waren schräg.* ♦ *ein extrem schräges Dach* **2.** *(biased)* einseitig ['aenzaetɪç] ◊ *eine einseitige Darstellung der Fakten* be slanted towards sb auf Seiten … [gen] stehen [aof zaetn̩ … 'ʃteːən] <steht, stand, hat gestanden> ◊ *Die Zeitung steht auf Seiten der Regierung.* be slanted towards sth sich einseitig für etw. einsetzen [ˌaenzaetɪç fyːɐ … ˌaenzɛtsn̩] +haben ◊ *Setzt sich die Regierung einseitig für die Belange der Unternehmer ein?*

slap¹ [noun] Schlag [ʃlaːk] der <-(e)s, Schläge> slap *(round the ear)* Ohrfeige ['oːɐfaeɡə] die <-, -n> ◊ *eine Ohrfeige bekommen*

⊛ **a slap in the face** ein Schlag ins Gesicht get a slap on the wrist mit einem blauen Auge davonkommen

slap² [verb] **1.** *(hit)* schlagen ['ʃlaːɡn̩] <schlägt, schlug, hat/ist geschlagen> *transitive use +haben/intransitive use +sein* ◊ *Du hast ihn ins Gesicht geschlagen.* ♦ *Hohe Wellen sind gegen die Kaimauer geschlagen.* **2.** *(put down noisily)* slap sth somewhere etw. irgendwohin hinknallen ['hɪnknalən] +haben *(fam)* ◊ *Er knallte sein Kündigungsschreiben auf den Tisch.* **3.** *(apply with force)* klatschen ['klatʃn̩] +haben *(fam)* ◊ *Der Maurer klatschte den Mörtel an die Wand.*

• **slap down** [phras v] slap sb/sth down *(criticize severely)* jdn/etw. herunterputzen [hɛˈrʊntɐpʊtsn̩] +haben *(fam)* ◊ *Mein Konzept wurde gnadenlos heruntergeputzt.*

slash¹ [noun] **1.** *(cut)* tiefer Schnitt [tiːfɐ 'ʃnɪt] <-(e)s, -e> ◊ *Auf seiner Wange war ein tiefer Schnitt.; (in fabric, upholstery)* Schlitz [ʃlɪts] der

<-es, -e> ◊ *Schlitze in etw.* [acc] schneiden; *(calmly and deliberately cut)* make slashes into sth etw. einschneiden ['aenʃnaedn̩] <schneidet ein, schnitt ein, hat eingeschnitten> ◊ *Schneiden Sie den Kuchen nach 15 Minuten oben ein.* in a violent temper etw. aufschlitzen ['aofʃlɪtsn̩] <schlitzt auf, schlitzte auf, hat aufgeschlitzt> ◊ *Jemand hatte die Polster aufgeschlitzt.* **2.** *(movement)* Hieb [hiːp] der <-(e)s, -e> ◊ *ein Hieb mit dem Schwert* **3.** *(in printing, typing)* Schrägstrich ['ʃrɛːkʃtrɪç] der <-(e)s, -e>

slash² [verb] **1.** *(reduce)* reduzieren [reduˈtsiːrən] <reduziert, reduzierte, hat reduziert> ◊ *Die Firma hat ihre Produktion um 20% reduziert.* **2.** *(gash, cut open)* aufschlitzen ['aofʃlɪtsn̩] +haben ◊ *Wandalen hatten die Sitze des Busses aufgeschlitzt.* slash sb across the chest etc. jdm die Brust etc. aufschlitzen slash your wrists sich die Pulsadern aufschneiden [diː 'pʊlsjaːdɐn ˌaofʃnaedn̩] <schneidet sich auf, schnitt sich auf, hat sich aufgeschnitten> **3.** *(with a blade)* slash at sb/sth auf jdn/etw. losgehen [aof … ˌloːsɡeːən] <geht los, ging los, ist losgegangen> ◊ *Plötzlich ging er mit dem Messer auf mich los.* **4.** *(make a path)* slash through sth sich durch etw. schlagen [dʊʳç … ʃlaːɡn̩] <schlägt, schlug sich, hat sich geschlagen> ◊ *sich durchs Unterholz schlagen*

slat [noun] *(of a bed)* Latte ['latə] die <-, -n>; *(of a blind)* Lamelle [laˈmɛlə] die <-, -n>

slaughter [verb] **1.** *(kill brutally)* abschlachten ['apʃlaxtn̩] <schlachtet ab, schlachtete ab, hat abgeschlachtet> ◊ *Die Gefangenen wurden gnadenlos abgeschlachtet.* **2.** *(kill an animal)* schlachten ['ʃlaxtn̩] <schlachtet, schlachtete, hat geschlachtet> ◊ *ein Rind/Schwein schlachten* **3.** *(defeat)* niedermachen ['niːdɐmaxn̩] +haben *(fam)* ◊ *Die Mannschaft wurde niedergemacht.* **4.** *(criticize)* verreißen [fɐ'raesn̩] <verreißt, verriss, hat verrissen> *(fam)* ◊ *Der Kritiker hat ihren Roman total verrissen.*

slave [noun] Sklave ['sklaːvə] der <-n, -n> ♀Sklavin ['sklaːvɪn] die <-, -nen> ◊ *Hör auf, mich wie eine Sklavin zu behandeln!* be a slave to habit Sklave seiner Gewohnheiten sein

sledge [noun] Schlitten ['ʃlɪtn̩] der <-s, ->

sleep¹ [noun] Schlaf [ʃlaːf] der <-(e)s> *no pl* ◊ *in einen tiefen Schlaf fallen* ♦ *genug Schlaf bekommen* talk in your sleep im Schlaf sprechen go to sleep einschlafen ['aenʃlaːfn̩] <schläft ein, schlief ein, ist eingeschlafen> have a sleep sich schlafen legen ['ʃlaːfn̩ leːɡn̩] +haben have a good night's sleep sich ausschlafen ['aosʃlaːfn̩] <schläft sich aus, schlief sich aus, hat sich ausgeschlafen>

⊛ **put to sleep 1.** *(kill an animal, make sb sleep)* einschläfern ['aenʃlɛːfɐn] **2.** *(before an operation)* betäuben

sleep² [verb] **1.** *(spend the night, not be awake)* schlafen ['ʃlaːfn̩] <schläft, schlief, hat geschlafen> ◊ *tief und fest schlafen* ♦ *Schlaf gut!* ♦ *Er schlief wie ein Baby.* sleep the night somewhere irgendwo schlafen **2.** *(accommodate)* sth sleeps four etc. etw. bietet Platz für vier etc. Personen [biːtət ˌplats fyːɐ ˌfiːɐ pɛʳ'zoːnən] <bietet, bot, hat geboten> ◊ *Unser Ferienhaus bietet Platz für acht Personen.*

• **sleep in** [phras v] länger schlafen ['lɛŋɐ ʃlaːfn̩] <schläft, schlief, hat geschlafen> ◊ *Sonntags schlafe ich oft länger.*

• **sleep on** [phras v] sleep on sth etw. überschlafen

[ybeˈʃlaːfn̩] <überschläft, überschlief, hat überschlafen> ◊ *Das kann ich jetzt nicht entscheiden, das muss ich erst überschlafen.*
• **sleep through** [phras v] *(until a certain time)* durchschlafen [ˈdʊʳçʃlaːfn̩] <schläft durch, schlief durch, hat durchgeschlafen> ◊ *Ich habe bis 12 Uhr durchgeschlafen.*
• **sleep together** [phras v] miteinander schlafen [mɪtˈlaɛnandɐ ˈʃlaːfn̩] <schläft, schlief, hat geschlafen> ◊ *Sie schlafen seit Jahren nicht mehr miteinander.*
• **sleep with** [phras v] sleep with sb mit jdm schlafen [mɪt ... ˈʃlaːfn̩] <schläft, schlief, hat geschlafen> ◊ *Hast du mit ihm geschlafen?*

sleepily [adv] schläfrig [ˈʃlɛːfrɪç] ◊ *sich* [dat] *schläfrig die Augen reiben*

sleeping bag [noun] Schlafsack [ˈʃlaːfzak] der <–(e)s, Schlafsäcke>

sleepy [adj] 1. *(person)* schläfrig [ˈʃlɛːfrɪç] ◊ *Ich wurde langsam schläfrig.* ♦ *mit schläfriger Stimme antworten* 2. *(place)* verschlafen [fɛˈʃlaːfn̩] ◊ *eine verschlafene Winterlandschaft* ♦ *Das Städtchen ist recht verschlafen.*

sleeve [noun] 1. *(on clothing)* Ärmel [ˈɛʳml̩] der <–s, –> ◊ *eine Bluse mit kurzen Ärmeln* 2. *(cover for records etc.)* Hülle [ˈhʏlə] die <–, –n> ◊ *etw. in eine Hülle stecken*

sleigh [noun] Schlitten [ˈʃlɪtn̩] der <–s, –> ◊ *Zwei Pferde zogen den Schlitten.*

slender [adj] 1. *(attractively tall or long and slim)* schlank [ʃlaŋk] <schlanker, am schlank(e)sten> ◊ *Er ist recht schlank.* ♦ *schlanke Finger* 2. *(narrow)* schmal [ʃmaːl] <schmaler/schmäler, am schmalsten/schmälsten> ◊ *eine Pflanze mit schmalen Blättern* ♦ *Ihr Taille ist schmal.* 3. *(barely sufficient, only small)* gering [gəˈrɪŋ] ◊ *eine geringe Chance/Mehrheit*

slice¹ [noun] 1. *(flat piece of food)* Scheibe [ˈʃaɛbə] die <–, –n> ◊ *eine dicke Scheibe Brot; (of cake, citrus fruit)* Stück [ʃtʏk] das <–(e)s, –e> pl 'Stück' when used with figures ◊ *ein Stück Zitrone* ♦ *zwei Stück Kuchen* 2. *(part, share)* Anteil [ˈantaɛl] der <–(e)s, –e> a slice of sth ein Anteil an etw. [dat] ◊ *unser Anteil am EU-Haushalt* slice of the market Marktanteil [ˈmaʳktaɛl] 3. *(flat kitchen utensil)* Pfannenwender [ˈpfanənvɛndɐ] der <–s, –>; *(for cake)* Tortenheber [ˈtɔʳtn̩heːbɐ] der <–s, –>
Ⓔ **a slice of the cake** ein Stück vom Kuchen a **slice of life** ein Stück Leben

slice² [verb] *(cut up)* in Scheiben schneiden [ɪn ˈʃaɛbm̩ ʃnaɛdn̩] <schneidet, schnitt, hat geschnitten> ◊ *Brot in Scheiben schneiden* sth slices etw. lässt sich in Scheiben schneiden slice through sth durch etw. schneiden ◊ *mit der Kreissäge durch ein Brett schneiden*
• **slice off** [phras v] *(with a blade)* abschneiden [ˈapʃnaɛdn̩] <schneidet ab, schnitt ab, hat abgeschnitten> ◊ *ein Stück Fleisch abschneiden*

slick [adj] 1. *(impressive)* clever [ˈklɛvɐ] *(fam)* ◊ *eine clevere Werbekampagne* ♦ *Das Design ist ziemlich clever.* 2. *(overly friendly)* schmierig [ˈʃmiːrɪç] *(fam)* ◊ *ein schmieriger Verkäufer* ♦ *Ich fand den Typ ziemlich schmierig.* 3. *(moist or oily)* sth is slick with sth etw. glänzt auf etw. [dat] [glɛntst aof] +haben ◊ *Schweiß glänzte auf seinem Gesicht.; (hair)* geschniegelt [gəˈʃniːglt] *(fam)* ◊ *geschniegeltes Haar*

slide¹ [noun] 1. *(in a playground)* Rutschbahn [ˈrʊtʃbaːn] die <–, –en> 2. *(movement)* Rutschen

[ˈrʊtʃn̩] das <–s> no pl go into a slide ins Rutschen kommen ◊ *Der Lkw kam ins Rutschen.* ♦ *Die Handy-Tarife in Deutschland kommen ins Rutschen.* 3. *(photograph)* Dia [ˈdiːaː] das <–s, –s> ◊ *Dias vorführen* 4. *(for a microscope)* Objektträger [ɔpˈjɛkttrɛːgə] der <–s, –> ◊ *einen Objektträger unter das Mikroskop legen* 5. *(of rocks, earth)* Erdrutsch [ˈeːɐtrʊtʃ] der <–es, –e> ◊ *Das Dorf wurde von einem Erdrutsch zerstört.*

slide² [verb] 1. *(move smoothly)* rutschen [ˈrʊtʃn̩] +sein ◊ *Der Wagen rutschte in den Graben.* slide down sth etw. hinabrutschen [hɪˈnaprʊtʃn̩] +sein ◊ *Ich rutschte auf dem Hintern den Hang hinab.* 2. *(door)* slide open aufgleiten [ˈaofglaɛtn̩] <gleitet auf, glitt auf, ist aufgeglitten> ◊ *Die Aufzugtür glitt auf.* 3. *(push sth)* schieben [ˈʃiːbm̩] <schiebt, schob, hat geschoben> ◊ *Er schob den Brief unauffällig in seine Tasche.* 4. *(sneak out)* slide out sich hinausschleichen [hɪˈnaosʃlaɛçn̩] <schleicht sich hinaus, schlich sich hinaus, hat sich hinausgeschlichen> slide out the door sich zur Tür hinausschleichen; *(sneak in)* slide in sich hineinschleichen [hɪˈnaɛnʃlaɛçn̩] <schleicht sich hinein, schlich sich hinein, hat sich hineingeschlichen> 5. *(into a bad situation)* slide into sth in etw. [acc] rutschen [ɪn ... rʊtʃn̩] +sein ◊ *Das Land ist in die finanzielle Krise gerutscht.*

slight [adj] 1. *(minor, small)* leicht [laɛçt] <leichter, am leichtesten> only before ns ◊ *leichte Verletzungen* ♦ *ein leichtes Lächeln; (hope, idea)* gering [gəˈrɪŋ] ◊ *Ich habe nicht die geringste Hoffnung, dass es klappt.* a slight hint of sth eine Spur von etw. [aenə ʃpuːɐ fɔn]; *(problem, mistake)* klein [klaɛn] ◊ *ein kleines Problem mit etw.* 2. *(person)* zierlich [ˈtsiːɐlɪç] ◊ *eine zierliche Frau* ♦ *Er ist eher zierlich.*
Ⓔ **not in the slightest** nicht im Geringsten

slightly [adv] *(a bit)* ein bisschen [aen ˈbɪsçən] no comp/superl ◊ *Ich war ein bisschen verärgert.* slightly injured leicht verletzt [ˈlaɛçt fɛˌlɛtst]; *(know sb slightly)* jdn flüchtig kennen [ˈflʏçtɪç kɛnən] <kennt, kannte, hat gekannt>; *(comparative)* a slightly more complex sentence ein etwas komplizierter Satz [aen ɛtvas kɔmpliˈtsiːgtə ˌzats] This question is slightly more difficult. Diese Frage ist etwas schwieriger.

slim [adj] 1. *(attractively thin)* schlank [ʃlaŋk] <schlanker, am schlank(e)sten> ◊ *eine schlanke Taille* ♦ *Früher warst du schlank.* 2. *(narrow)* schmal [ʃmaːl] <schmaler/schmäler, am schmalsten/schmälsten> ◊ *eine lange, schmale Röhre* ♦ *Das Notebook ist schmal und leicht.* 3. *(very small)* gering [gəˈrɪŋ] ◊ *Ihre Chancen sind eher gering.* ♦ *mit geringer Mehrheit gewinnen*

slim down [verb] 1. *(lose weight, lose staff)* sb/sth slims down jd/etw. wird schlanker [vɪʳt ˈʃlaŋkə] +sein *(also euph)* ◊ *Dein Mann/Die Firma ist schlanker geworden.* 2. *(get rid of staff)* slim sth down etw. schlanker machen [ˈʃlaŋkə maxn̩] +haben *(euph)* ◊ *Die Maßnahmen sollen die Firma schlanker und effizienter machen.*

slime² [noun] Schleim [ʃlaem] der <–(e)s, –e> ◊ *Schnecken sondern Schleim ab.*

sling¹ [noun] 1. *(used for support)* Schlinge [ˈʃlɪŋə] die <–, –n> ◊ *den Arm in einer Schlinge tragen; (for a baby)* Tragetuch [ˈtraːgətuːx] das <–(e)s, Tragetücher>; *(weapon)* Schleuder [ˈʃlɔødə] die <–, –n>

sling² [verb] **1.** *(throw)* schmeißen ['ʃmaɛsn̩] <schmeißt, schmiss, hat geschmissen> *(fam)* ◊ *etw. auf den Boden schmeißen* ♦ *Ich wurde aus der Armee geschmissen.*; *(throw away)* sling out rausschmeißen ['raosʃmaɛsn̩] +*haben* *(fam)* **2.** *(hang)* hängen ['hɛŋən] +*haben* ◊ *Sie hängte sich die Tasche über die Schulter.*

slip¹ [noun] **1.** slip *(of paper)* Zettel ['tsɛtl̩] der <-s, -> voting slip Wahlzettel ['vaːltsɛtl̩] betting slip Wettschein ['vɛtʃaen] der <-(e)s, -e> **2.** *(insignificant mistake)* Schnitzer ['ʃnɪtsɐ] der <-s, -> sb makes a few slips jdm passieren ein paar Schnitzer slip of the tongue Versprecher [fɛ'ʃprɛçɐ] der <-s, -> **3.** *(slump)* slip in sth Abrutschen ... [gen] ['aprʊtʃn̩] das <-s> no pl ◊ *ein Abrutschen der Preise* **4.** *(underwear)* Unterrock ['ʊntərɔk] der <-(e)s, Unterröcke> ◊ *einen Unterrock anziehen*

slip² [verb] **1.** *(fall over)* ausrutschen ['aosrʊtʃn̩] +*sein* ◊ *Ich bin auf dem Eis ausgerutscht.* **2.** *(slide)* rutschen ['rʊtʃn̩] +*sein* ◊ *Die Hose rutscht.* slip from sb's hand jdm aus der Hand rutschen **3.** *(get out quietly)* slip out hinausschlüpfen [hɪ'naosʃlʏpfn̩] +*sein* ◊ *Ich öffnete die Tür und schlüpfte hinaus.* slip out of sth aus etw. [dat] schlüpfen ◊ *aus dem Schlafanzug/Bett schlüpfen*; *(come in)* slip in hineinschlüpfen [hɪ'naenʃlʏpfn̩] +*sein* ◊ *Die Tür stand offen und er schlüpfte hinein.* slip into sth in etw. [acc] schlüpfen ◊ *ins Bett/in ein Kleid schlüpfen* **4.** *(push)* slip sth under a door etw. unter einer Tür durchschieben [ʊntɐ aenə 'tyːɐ̯ ˌdʊʳçʃiːbm̩] <schiebt durch, schob durch, hat durchgeschoben> **5.** *(lay)* slip your arm around sb seinen Arm um jdn legen [zaenən 'aʳm ʊm ... leːgn̩] +*haben* **6.** *(put sth somewhere without drawing attention to it)* stecken ['ʃtɛkn̩] +*haben* ◊ *Er steckte das Geld heimlich in seine Tasche.* slip sb sth jdm etw. zustecken ['tsuːʃtɛkn̩] +*haben* **7.** *(weaken, become less good)* nachlassen ['naːxlasn̩] <lässt nach, ließ nach, hat nachgelassen> ◊ *Die Konjunktur hat stark nachgelassen.* ♦ *Du lässt langsam nach!*

slipper [noun] Pantoffel [pan'tɔfl̩] der <-s, -n> ◊ *Pantoffeln tragen*

slippery [adj] **1.** *(surface)* glatt [glat] <glatter/glätter, am glattesten> ◊ *Achtung, die Fahrbahn ist glatt!* ♦ *ein glatter Boden* **2.** *(person)* aalglatt ['aːlˌglat] *no comp/superl (pej)* ◊ *ein aalglatter Politiker* ♦ *Er ist aalglatt.*

slit [noun] Schlitz [ʃlɪts] der <-es, -e> ◊ *der Schlitz des Briefkastens/Sparschweins* ♦ *ein Rock mit seitlichem Schlitz*

sliver [noun] **1.** *(splinter)* Splitter ['ʃplɪtɐ] der <-s, -> ◊ *in winzige Splitter zerbrechen* ♦ *ein Splitter im Finger* sliver of glass Glassplitter ['glaːsʃplɪtɐ] der sliver of wood Holzsplitter ['hɔltsʃplɪtɐ] **2.** *(wood shaving)* Span ['ʃpaːn] der <-(e)s, Späne> ◊ *Späne zum Feuermachen*; *(of cheese etc.)* dünne Scheibe [dʏnə 'ʃaebə] die <-, -n> ◊ *eine dünne Scheibe Käse* **3.** *(of land etc.)* Streifen ['ʃtraefn̩] der <-s, -> ◊ *ein schmaler Streifen Wald* sliver of light Lichtstrahl ['lɪçtʃtraːl] der <-(e)s, -en>

◉ a sliver of hope ein Hoffnungsschimmer

slogan [noun] Slogan ['sloːgən] der <-s, -s> advertising slogan Werbeslogan ['vɛʳbəsloːgən]

slope¹ [noun] **1.** *(area that is higher at one end)* Abhang ['aphaŋ] der <-(e)s, Abhänge> ◊ *Der Ball rollte den Abhang hinunter.*; *(side of a hill or*

---

mountain) Hang [haŋ] der <-(e)s, Hänge> ◊ *ein Haus am Hang; (for skiing etc.)* Abfahrt ['apfaːʳt] die <-, -en> ◊ *Die anspruchsvolle Abfahrt erforderte volle Konzentration.* **2.** *(slant)* Neigung ['naegʊŋ] die <-, -en> ◊ *ein Dach mit steiler Neigung*

slope² [verb] *(mountain, hill)* abfallen ['apfalən] <fällt ab, fiel ab, ist abgefallen> ◊ *eine Felswand, die steil abfällt; (roof)* schräg sein ['ʃrɛːk zaen] ◊ *Das Dach ist schräg.; (floor, handwriting)* sich neigen ['naegn̩] +*haben* ◊ *Der Boden neigt sich leicht.* ♦ *Seine Handschrift neigt sich nach rechts/links.*

sloppy(-ily) [adv] schlampig ['ʃlampɪç] *(fam, pej)* ◊ *Ich bin schlampig und vergesse viel.* ♦ *schlampige Arbeit* ♦ *eine schlampig recherchierte Reportage* sth is sloppy etw. ist schlampig ausgeführt/gezeichnet etc. ◊ *Die Arbeit war schlampig ausgeführt.* ♦ *Die Illustration ist schlampig gezeichnet.*

slot [noun] **1.** *(long narrow hole)* Schlitz [ʃlɪts] der <-es, -e> ◊ *Sie warf die Münze in den Schlitz.; (in a computer)* Steckplatz ['ʃtɛkplats] der <-es, Steckplätze> ◊ *ein Steckplatz für eine Speicherkarte* slot machine Automat [aoto'maːt] der <-en, -en>; *(for gaming)* Spielautomat ['ʃpiːlʔaotoˌmaːt] der **2.** *(broadcasting)* Sendeplatz ['zɛndəplats] der <-es, Sendeplätze> ◊ *Die Serie hat jetzt einen neuen Sendeplatz.; (for flights)* Slot [slɔt] der <-s, -s> landing slot Landeerlaubnis ['landəˌʔɛlaopnɪs] die <-, -se> **3.** *(job)* Position [poziˈtsi̯oːn] die <-, -en> ◊ *eine Position in einem Team besetzen*

Slovak [noun] Slowake [slo'vaːkə] der <-n, -n> ♀Slowakin [slo'vaːkɪn] die <-, -nen> → **German¹ 1.**

Slovakia [noun] die Slowakei [di: slova'kae] <-> *no pl* ◊ *Ich komme aus der Slowakei.* ♦ *Bist du in der Slowakei geboren?*

Slovakian¹ [noun] Slowakisch [slo'vaːkɪʃ] das <-(s)> *no pl* → **German¹ 2.**

Slovakian² [adj] slowakisch [slo'vaːkɪʃ] → **German²**

Slovene [noun] Slowene [slo've:nə] der <-n, -n> ♀Slowenin [slo've:nɪn] die <-, -nen> → **German¹ 1.**

Slovenia [noun] Slowenien [slo've:ni̯ən] die <-> *article only in combination with attribute, no pl* → **Germany**

Slovenian¹ [noun] Slowenisch [slo've:nɪʃ] das <-(s)> *no pl* → **German¹ 2.**

Slovenian² [adj] slowenisch [slo've:nɪʃ] → **German²**

slow¹ [adj] **1.** *(not fast)* langsam ['laŋzaːm] ◊ *Seine Bewegungen/Reaktionen sind sehr langsam.* ♦ *eine langsame Fahrt* sth is slow going etw. geht nur langsam voran sb/sth is slow to do sth jd/etw. braucht lange, bis er/es etw. tut [braoxt 'laŋə bɪs] +*haben* ◊ *Er braucht immer ziemlich lange, bis er mich zurückruft.* **2.** *(not intelligent, unable to think clearly)* be slow schwer von Begriff sein [ʃve:ɐ̯ fɔn bə'grɪf zaen] *(fam)* ◊ *Ich bin heute etwas schwer von Begriff.* be a slow learner eine Lernschwäche haben [aenə 'lɛʳnʃvɛçə haːbm̩] **3.** *(boring)* langatmig ['laŋʔaːtmɪç] ◊ *eine langatmige Geschichte* ♦ *Der Film war etwas langatmig.* **4.** *(business)* flau [flao] <flauer, am flau(e)sten> ◊ *flaue Geschäfte* ♦ *Die Geschäfte sind im Sommer etwas flau.* **5.** *(clock, watch)* nachgehend ['na:xgeːənt] *no comp/superl, only before ns* ◊ *eine nachgehende Uhr* be slow nachgehen ['na:xgeːən] <geht nach, ging nach, ist*

nachgegangen> ◊ *Meine Uhr geht fünf Minuten nach.*
6. *(not hot)* cook sth in a slow oven etw. bei
niedriger Temperatur garen
[bæ ˌniːdrɪɡə tɛmpərəˈtuːɐ̯ ɡaːrən] +*haben*
slow² [verb] **1.** *(make slower)* verlangsamen
[fɛˈlaŋzaːmən] <verlangsamt, verlangsamte, hat verlang-
samt> ◊ *jds Reaktionen/das Wachstum verlangsamen;*
(the traffic) behindern [baˈhɪndɐn] <behindert, behinderte, hat behindert> ◊ *Ein Unfall behindert den*
Verkehr auf der A 57. **2.** *(become slower)* langsamer
werden [ˈlaŋzaːmɐ veːɐ̯dn̩] +*sein* ◊ *Bergauf wurde sie*
langsamer. slow to a crawl/walk in Schritttempo
verfallen [ɪn ˈʃrɪttɛmpo: fɛfalən] <verfällt, verfiel, ist
verfallen> ◊ *Der Verkehr verfiel in Schritttempo.* slow
to a halt allmählich zum Stehen kommen
[alˌmɛːlɪç ʦʊm ˈʃteːən kɔmən] <kommt, kam, ist
gekommen> **3.** *(reduce)* verringern [fɛˈrɪŋən] <verrin-
gert, verringerte, hat verringert> ◊ *Die Wirtschafts-*
krise verringert die Nachfrage für Luxusgüter. sth is
reducing etw. verringert sich ◊ *Die Inflation verrin-*
gert sich.
• **slow down** [phras v] **1.** *(a process, development)*
verlangsamen [fɛˈlaŋzaːmən] <verlangsamt, verlangsamte, hat verlangsamt> ◊ *Widerstand aus der Opposi-*
tion verlangsamt den Reformprozess.; (sb's perform-
ance, the traffic) behindern [bəˈhɪndən] <behindert,
behinderte, hat behindert> ◊ *Die Grippe hat mich bei*
der Arbeit behindert. **2.** *(your pace of living)* es
langsamer angehen lassen
[ɛs ˈlaŋzaːmɐ ˌangeːən lasn̩] <lässt, ließ, hat lassen>
(fam) ◊ *Nach der Krankheit muss ich es langsamer*
angehen lassen. **3.** *(become slower)* langsamer
werden [ˈlaŋzaːmɐ veːɐ̯dn̩] +*sein; (while driving)*
langsamer fahren [ˈlaŋzaːmɐ faːrən] <fährt, fuhr, ist
gefahren> ◊ *Fahr bitte langsamer!*
slowly [adv] **1.** *(not fast)* langsam [ˈlaŋzaːm] ◊
langsam arbeiten/fahren/reagieren ♦ *Können Sie*
bitte etwas langsamer sprechen? slowly but surely
langsam aber sicher **2.** *(gradually)* allmählich
[alˈmɛːlɪç] no comp/superl ◊ *allmählich schwächer/*
stärker/lauter werden
slow motion [noun] Zeitlupe [ˈʦaɛtluːpə] die <–>
mostly used without the article, no pl ◊ *ein Tor in*
Zeitlupe wiederholen
sludge [noun] Schlamm [ʃlam] der <–(e)s> no pl
slug [noun] Nacktschnecke [ˈnaktʃnɛkə] die <–, –n>
sluggish(ly) [adj, adv] träge [ˈtrɛːɡə] <träger, am
trägsten> ◊ *Sie ist sehr träge.* ♦ *eine träge Reaktion*
♦ *ein träge dahinfließender Fluss*
slump¹ [noun] **1.** *(reduction of value or amount)*
Einbruch [ˈaɛnbrʊx] der <–(e)s, Einbrüche> ◊ *ein*
Einbruch an der Börse ♦ *ein Einbruch um 15%*
slump in prices Preiseinbruch [ˈpraɛslaɛnbrʊx]
2. *(recession)* Rezession [retsɛˈsjoːn] die <–, –en>
slump² [verb] **1.** *(fall)* fallen [ˈfalən] <fällt, fiel, ist
gefallen> ◊ *Der Umsatz fiel um 30%.* ♦ *zu Boden*
fallen; (unconscious) be slumped somewhere
irgendwo zusammengesunken sein
[ʦuˈzamənɡəzʊŋkn̩ zaɛn] **2.** *(sit down, lie down*
heavily) slump into sth sich in etw. [acc] fallen
lassen [ɪn ... ˌfalən lasn̩] <lässt, ließ, hat lassen> ◊
sich in einen Sessel fallen lassen slump onto sth
sich auf etw. [acc] fallen lassen ◊ *sich aufs Sofa*
fallen lassen; (relaxed) be slumped somewhere
irgendwo lümmeln [ˈlʏmln̩] *(fam, pej)* ◊ *Er lümmelte*
vor dem Fernseher.

slush [noun] **1.** *(snow)* Schneematsch [ˈʃneːmatʃ] der
<–(e)s> no pl **2.** *(actions)* Gefühlsduselei
[ɡəˌfyːlsduːzəˈlaɛ] die <–, –en> *(fam, pej); (stories)*
Schund [ʃʊnt] der <–(e)s> no pl *(pej); (paintings*
etc.) Kitsch [kɪtʃ] der <–(e)s> no pl *(pej)* **3.** *(drink*
with crushed ice) Granita [graˈniːtaː] die <–> no pl
smack¹ [noun] **1.** *(hit)* Schlag [ʃlaːk] der
<–(e)s, Schläge> ◊ *ein Schlag mit der flachen Hand*
2. *(sound)* Klatsch [klatʃ] der <–es, –e> *(fam)* ◊ *mit*
einem lauten Klatsch auf den Tisch schlagen; (of a
whip) Knall [knal] der <–(e)s, –e> **3.** *(kiss)* Schmatz
[ʃmats] der <–es, –e> *(fam)* ◊ *jdm einen Schmatz*
auf die Backe geben
smack² [verb] **1.** *(with your hand etc.)* schlagen
[ˈʃlaːɡn̩] <schlägt, schlug, hat geschlagen> ◊ *jdn ins*
Gesicht schlagen **2.** *(noisily, forcefully)* knallen
[ˈknalən] transitive use +*haben*/intransitive use +*sein*
(fam) ◊ *Das Auto ist gegen die Wand geknallt.*
small [adj] **1.** *(person, object, letter, mistake, step,*
sum, gift, appetite) klein [klaɛn] ◊ *Tom ist kleiner*
als Silke. ♦ *Der Pulli ist mir zu klein.* ♦ *Schreibt*
man das Wort nicht mit einem kleinen r? ♦ *ein*
kleines Auto ♦ *Als ich noch klein war...* small
investor Kleinanleger [ˈklaɛnlanleːɡə] der <–s, –>
♀Kleinanlegerin [ˈklaɛnlanleːɡərɪn] die <–, –nen>
small mind Kleingeist [ˈklaɛnɡaɛst] der <–(e)s, –er>
2. *(importance, quantity, effort)* gering [ɡəˈrɪŋ] ◊ *von*
geringer Bedeutung sein ♦ *eine geringe Menge* ♦ *Der*
Aufwand war relativ gering. small eater schlechter
Esser [ˌʃlɛçtə ˈʔɛsə] der <–s, –> ♀schlechte Esserin
[ˌʃlɛçtə ˈʔɛsərɪn] die <–, –nen> ◊ *das is small way*
ein wenig helfen [aɛn veːnɪç ˈhɛlfn̩] **3.** *(not loud)*
leise [ˈlaɛzə] <leiser, am leisesten> ◊ *Seine Stimme*
war leise. ♦ *ein leises Stöhnen*
☺ **feel/look** smb dumm dastehen *(fam)* make sb
feel small jdn dumm dastehen lassen *(fam)*
smart [adj] **1.** *(stylish)* schick [ʃɪk] ◊ *ein schickes Kleid*
♦ *Du siehst aber heute schick aus!* **2.** *(clever)* schlau
[ʃlaʊ] <schlauer, am schlau(e)sten> ◊ *ein schlauer*
Kopf ♦ *Das war schlau von dir.* **3.** *(with lack of*
respect) vorlaut [ˈfoːɡlaʊt] <vorlauter, am vorlautes-
ten> ◊ *eine vorlaute Antwort* Don't get smart with
me! Sei nicht so vorlaut! **4.** *(blow etc.)* hart [haɐ̯t]
<härter, am härtesten> ◊ *ein harter Schlag auf den*
Kopf
smarten up [verb] **1.** *(make yourself look tidy)* sich
zurechtmachen [ʦuˈrɛçtmaxn̩] +*haben* ◊ *Sie macht*
sich für die Oper zurecht. **2.** *(a room, building)* herrichten [ˈheːɡrɪçtn̩] <richtet her, richtete her, hat her-
gerichtet> ◊ *ein Zimmer für den Besuch herrichten*
smash [verb] **1.** *(break, destroy)* zerschlagen [ʦɛˈʃlaːɡn̩]
<zerschlägt, zerschlug, hat zerschlagen> ◊ *ein Fenster*
zerschlagen ♦ *einen Kinderpornoring zerschlagen*
2. *(hit)* krachen [ˈkraxn̩] +*sein (fam)* ◊ *Das Auto*
krachte gegen die Mauer. ♦ *Ich krachte mit dem Kopf*
ans Fenster. **3.** sport schmettern [ˈʃmɛtɐn] +*haben* ◊
Er schmetterte den Ball übers Netz.
• **smash up** [phras v] zertrümmern [ʦɛˈtrʏmɐn] <zer-
trümmert, zertrümmerte, hat zertrümmert> ◊ *Nieren-*
steine zertrümmern ♦ *Ein Stein aus der Windschutz-*
scheibe zertrümmert.; (a car in an accident) zu
Schrott fahren [ʦuː ˈʃrɔt faːrən] <fährt, fuhr, hat
gefahren>
smear [verb] **1.** *(spread, write messily)* schmieren
[ˈʃmiːrən] +*haben* ◊ *Der Stift schmiert.* smear sth on
your bread sich [dat] etw. aufs Brot schmieren

2. *(make dirty)* verschmieren [fɛˈʃmiːrən] <verschmiert, verschmierte, hat verschmiert> ◊ *Das Kind hat das Papier verschmiert.* ♦ *Sein Mund war mit Schokolade verschmiert.* **3.** *(a person)* verunglimpfen [fɛ|ˈʊnɡlɪmpfn̩] <verunglimpft, verunglimpfte, hat verunglimpft> ◊ *Er hat seinen Gegner verunglimpft.*; *(sb's reputation)* beschmutzen [bəˈʃmʊtsn̩] <beschmutzt, beschmutzte, hat beschmutzt> ◊ *jds Ruf beschmutzen*

smell¹ [noun] Geruch [ɡəˈrɔx] der <-(e)s, Gerüche> ◊ *etw. am Geruch erkennen* ♦ *der Geruch von frischem Brot* sense of smell Geruchssinn [ɡəˈrɔxszɪn] der <-(e)s> no pl

smell² [verb] **1.** *(have a smell, perceive a smell, notice)* riechen [ˈriːçn̩] <riecht, roch, hat gerochen> ◊ *Die Wäsche roch angenehm frisch.* ♦ *Ich rieche den Misthaufen bis hierher!* ♦ *Ich konnte riechen, dass etwas angebrannt war.* ♦ *Verrat/eine Gefahr riechen* smell (at) sth an etw. [dat] riechen ◊ *Willst du mal an der Rose riechen?* smell of sth nach etw. riechen ◊ *Die Wiese riecht nach frischem Heu.* **2.** *(be illegal, dishonest)* stinken [ˈʃtɪŋkn̩] <stinkt, stank, hat gestunken> *(fam)* ◊ *Das Geschäft stinkt doch!*

smile¹ [noun] Lächeln [ˈlɛçl̩n] das <-s> no pl ◊ *ein freundliches Lächeln* a smile of bliss ein seliges Lächeln a smile of pain ein gequältes Lächeln ⊛ **wipe the smile off sb's face** Wipe that smile off your face! Hör auf zu grinsen! That will wipe the smile off his etc. face! Ihm etc. wird das Lachen schon noch vergehen! **be all smiles** über das ganze Gesicht strahlen

smile² [verb] **1.** *(to express happiness or friendliness)* lächeln [ˈlɛçl̩n] +haben ◊ *dankbar/entschuldigend lächeln* "Me too", she smiled. „Ich auch", sagte sie lächelnd. smile at sb jdn anlächeln [ˈanlɛçl̩n] +haben ◊ *Sie lächelte mich an.* smile to yourself in sich [acc] hineinlächeln [ɪn ... hɪˈnaɪnlɛçl̩n] +haben ◊ *Er lächelte still in sich hinein.* **2.** *(grin)* grinsen [ˈɡrɪnzn̩] +haben ◊ *belustigt grinsen* smile at sth/sb über etw./jdn grinsen ◊ *Ich musste über seine Verrenkungen grinsen.*

smoke¹ [noun] **1.** Rauch [raox] der <-(e)s> no pl ◊ *Dichter Rauch quoll aus dem Fenster.* thick with smoke voller Rauch cloud of smoke Rauchwolke [ˈraoxvɔlkə] die <-, -n> **2.** *(cigarette)* Kippe [ˈkɪpə] die <-, -n> *(fam)* have a smoke eine rauchen [aenə ˈraoxn̩] *(fam)* go out for a smoke nach draußen gehen, um eine zu rauchen ⊛ **There's no smoke without fire.** Wo Rauch ist, ist auch Feuer. **go up in smoke 1.** *(burn down)* in Flammen aufgehen **2.** *(be shattered)* in Rauch aufgehen

smoke² [verb] **1.** *(inhale, produce smoke)* rauchen [ˈraoxn̩] +haben ◊ *Sie raucht eine Zigarette nach der anderen.* **2.** *(a fish, bacon etc.)* räuchern [ˈrɔøçɐn] +haben ◊ *geräucherte Forellen*

smoker [noun] Raucher [ˈraoxɐ] der <-s, -> ◊ ♀Raucherin [ˈraoxərɪn] die <-, -nen> ◊ *Sie ist eine starke Raucherin.*

smoking [noun] **1.** *(act)* Rauchen [ˈraoxn̩] das <-s> no pl ◊ *Rauchen ist sehr ungesund.* give up smoking mit dem Rauchen aufhören **2.** *(area for smokers, train compartment)* Raucherabteil [ˈraoxɐ|aptael] das <-(e)s, -e> ◊ *Im Raucherabteil sind noch Plätze frei.* smoking section Raucherzone [ˈraoxɐtsoːnə] die <-, -n>

smooth¹ [adj] **1.** *(even)* glatt [ɡlat] <glatter/glätter, am

glattesten> ◊ *eine glatte Oberfläche* ♦ *Das Fell des Hundes ist glatt, ohne Locken.* **2.** *(soft, not bumpy, mild)* weich [vaeç] ◊ *Das Leder ist schön weich.* ♦ *ein weicher Cognac* ♦ *eine weiche Landung* **3.** *(not shaky, not frightening)* ruhig [ˈruːɪç] ◊ *eine ruhige Überfahrt* ♦ *Der Flug war ruhig.* **4.** *(without problems)* reibungslos [ˈraɛbʊŋsloːs] seldom superl ◊ *Er ist für den reibungslosen Ablauf verantwortlich.* ♦ *Unsere Zusammenarbeit war reibungslos.* **5.** *(person)* aalglatt [ˈaːlˈɡlat] no comp/superl (pej) ◊ *Er ist ein bisschen zu aalglatt.* ♦ *eine aalglatte Karrierefrau*

smooth² [verb] **1.** *(flatten)* smooth sth (down/out) etw. glatt streichen [ˈɡlat ʃtraeçn̩] <streicht, strich, hat gestrichen> ◊ *Sie strich ihren Rock glatt.* smooth your hair back sich [dat] das Haar zurückstreichen [das ˈhaːɐ tsuˌrʏkʃtraeçn̩] +haben **2.** *(a workpiece)* abschleifen [ˈapʃlaefn̩] <schleift ab, schliff ab, hat abgeschliffen> ◊ *die Kanten abschleifen* **3.** *(spread)* smooth sth on sth etw. mit etw. einreiben [mɪt ... ˈaenraebm̩] <reibt ein, rieb ein, hat eingerieben> ◊ *seine Haut mit Creme einreiben* • **smooth over** [phras v] beilegen [ˈbaeleːɡn̩] +haben ◊ *einen Streit/Schwierigkeiten beilegen*

smoothly [adv] **1.** *(without problems)* reibungslos [ˈraebʊŋsloːs] seldom superl ◊ *Alles funktionierte reibungslos.* **2.** *(talk etc.)* gewandt [ɡəˈvant] <gewandter, am gewandtesten> ◊ *gewandt reden* **3.** *(of movements)* ruhig [ˈruːɪç] ◊ *ruhig fließen/dahingleiten; (well controlled)* weich [vaeç] ◊ *weich schalten/bremsen* **4.** *(polish, shave etc.)* glatt [ɡlat] <glatter, glätter, am glattesten> ◊ *ein glatt rasierter Mann*

smother [verb] **1.** *(cover completely)* smother sth in sth etw. mit etw. bedecken [mɪt ... bəˌdɛkn̩] <bedeckt, bedeckte, hat bedeckt> *often in adjectival passive constructions* ◊ *Alles war mit Staub bedeckt.* ♦ *Nudeln mit Soße bedecken; (weeds etc.)* überwuchern [ybɐˈvuːxɐn] <überwuchert, überwucherte, hat überwuchert> *often in adjectival passive constructions* ◊ *ein mit Unkraut überwuchertes Beet* **2.** *(a person, fire)* ersticken [ɛˈʃtɪkn̩] <erstickt, erstickte, hat erstickt> ◊ *Er hat sie mit einem Kissen erstickt.* ♦ *ein Feuer mit Sand ersticken.; (sb with your feelings)* erdrücken [ɛˈdrʏkn̩] <erdrückt, erdrückte, hat erdrückt> ◊ *Er erdrückt sie mit seiner Liebe.; (with kisses)* überhäufen [ybɐˈhɔøfn̩] <überhäuft, überhäufte, hat überhäuft> ◊ *Sie überhäufte ihn mit Küssen.* **3.** *(a laugh, yawn etc.)* unterdrücken [ʊntɐˈdrʏkn̩] <unterdrückt, unterdrückte, hat unterdrückt> ◊ *Sie unterdrückte ein Lachen.*

smug [adj] selbstgefällig [ˈzɛlpstɡəfɛlɪç] ◊ *ein selbstgefälliges Gesicht machen* ♦ *Sie ist sehr selbstgefällig.*

smuggle [verb] schmuggeln [ˈʃmʊɡl̩n] +haben ◊ *Zigaretten schmuggeln* ♦ *Flüchtlinge ins Land/über die Grenze schmuggeln* ♦ *An dieser Grenze wird viel geschmuggelt.*

snack [noun] Imbiss [ˈɪmbɪs] der <-es, -e> ◊ *einen kleinen Imbiss einnehmen*

snail [noun] Schnecke [ˈʃnɛkə] die <-, -n> ◊ *Schnecken im Garten* ♦ *Es gab Schnecken in Knoblauchbutter.*

snake [noun] Schlange [ˈʃlaŋə] die <-, -n> ⊛ **a snake in the grass** eine falsche Schlange *(pej)*

snap [verb] **1.** snap (in half/two) zerbrechen [tsɛˈbrɛçn̩] <zerbricht, zerbrach, hat zerbrochen> *transitive use +haben/intransitive use +sein* ◊ *Ich habe den Stock zerbrochen.* ♦ *Das Gewehr ist zerbro-*

chen.; (tree, flower) umknicken ['ʊmknɪkn̩] transitive use +haben/intransitive use +sein ◊ Der Sturm hat die Bäume umgeknickt. ♦ Die Rose ist umgeknickt.; (rope, chain etc.) zerreißen [tsɛ'raɛsn̩] <zerreißt, zerriss, hat/ist zerrissen> transitive use +haben/intransitive use +sein ◊ Der Elefant zerriss das Seil und machte sich davon. ♦ Die Kette ist zerrissen. snap off abbrechen ['apbrɛçn̩] <bricht ab, brach ab, hat/ist abgebrochen> transitive use +haben/intransitive use +sein ◊ Sie hat sich ein Stück Schokolade abgebrochen. ♦ Der Zweig ist abgebrochen. 2. (door) snap shut zuschnappen ['tsu:ʃnapm̩] +sein snap the door shut die Tür zuschnappen lassen; (book) snap shut zuklappen ['tsu:klapm̩] transitive use +haben/intransitive use +sein ◊ Er hat sein Buch zugeklappt. ♦ Mein Buch ist zugeklappt. 3. (switch) snap sth on anknipsen ['anknɪpsn̩] +haben (fam) ◊ Er knipste den Fernseher an. snap sth off ausknipsen ['aʊsknɪpsn̩] +haben (fam) ◊ Hast du das Licht ausgeknipst? 4. (animal) snap at sth/sb nach etw./jdm schnappen [na:x ... ʃnapm̩] +haben ◊ Der Hund schnappte nach der Wurst. 5. (take a photograph) knipsen ['knɪpsn̩] +haben (fam) ◊ Darf ich ein Bild von dir knipsen? 6. (get aggressive) ausrasten ['aʊsrastn̩] <rastet aus, rastete aus, ist ausgerastet> (fam) ◊ Er rastete aus und brüllte los.; (get depressive) zusammenbrechen [tsu'zamənbrɛçn̩] <bricht zusammen, brach zusammen, ist zusammengebrochen> ◊ unter einer Belastung zusammenbrechen 7. (speak angrily) schnauzen ['ʃnaʊtsn̩] +haben (fam) ◊ „Halt die Klappe!", schnauzte er. snap at sb jdn anschnauzen ['anʃnaʊtsn̩] (fam) ◊ Schnauz mich nicht so an! 8. snap your fingers mit den Fingern schnippen [mɪt de:n 'fɪŋɐn ʃnɪpm̩] +haben

⊙ snap out of it damit aufhören ◊ Hör endlich damit auf! snap to it (hurry up) jetzt mach schon, jetzt machen Sie schon (fam)

• snap up [phras v] snap sth up bei etw. zugreifen [baɛ ... 'tsu:graɛfn̩] <greift zu, griff zu, hat zugegriffen> ◊ bei einem Angebot zugreifen sth has already been snapped up etw. ist schon weg [ɪst ʃo:n 'vɛk]

snare [noun] Falle ['falə] die <-, -n> ◊ eine Falle, mit der man Füchse fängt ♦ jdm eine Falle stellen; (of wire, rope) Schlinge ['ʃlɪŋə] die <-, -n> ◊ Vögel in Schlingen fangen

snarl [verb] 1. (dog) knurren ['knʊrən] +haben ♦ Der Hund knurrte laut.; (cat, tiger, person) fauchen ['faʊxn̩] +haben ◊ Die Katze fauchte böse. ♦ „Hau ab!", fauchte sie. snarl at sb jdn anfauchen ['anfaʊxn̩] ◊ Er fauchte mich an. 2. (traffic) snarl (up) zum Erliegen bringen [tsʊm ɛ'li:gn̩ brɪŋən] <bringt, brachte, hat gebracht> ◊ Ein Unfall brachte den Verkehr auf der A 1 zum Erliegen. be snarled (up) stillstehen ['ʃtɪlʃte:ən] <steht still, stand still, hat stillgestanden> ◊ Der Verkehr stand still. 3. (tangle up) get snarled sich verheddern [fɛ'hɛdɐn] <verheddert sich, verhedderte sich, hat sich verheddert> (fam) ◊ Die Schnur hat sich völlig verheddert. ♦ Er verhedderte sich im Netz.

snatch [verb] 1. (grab, gain) snatch sth etw. an sich [acc] reißen ['an ... raɛsn̩] <reißt, riss, hat gerissen> ◊ Er riss das Mikrofon an sich und fing an zu singen. ♦ In letzter Minute konnten wir den Sieg an uns reißen.; (pull) snatch sth from sb jdm etw. wegreißen ['vɛkraɛsn̩] +haben ◊ Sie riss ihm den Zettel weg. 2. (steal) klauen ['klaʊən] +haben (fam) ◊

Er klaute die Tasche und rannte weg.; (a child) kidnappen ['kɪtnɛpm̩] +haben (fam) ◊ Im Krankenhaus wurde ein Baby gekidnappt. 3. (an opportunity) ergreifen [ɛ'graɛfn̩] <ergreift, ergriff, hat ergriffen> ◊ die Gelegenheit ergreifen; (a glance) werfen ['vɛrfn̩] <wirft, warf, hat geworfen> ◊ Ich warf einen Blick auf die Uhr. snatch a bite of sth schnell einen Bissen von etw. nehmen [ʃnɛl aɛnən ,bɪsn̩ fɔn ... ne:mən] <nimmt, nahm, hat genommen> snatch a meal/bite to eat schnell etwas essen [ʃnɛl ... ,ɛsn̩] <isst, aß, hat gegessen> 4. (manage to get) ergattern [ɛ'gatɐn] <ergattert, ergatterte, hat ergattert> (fam) ◊ ein paar Minuten Schlaf ergattern

sneak [verb] 1. (move somewhere) sich schleichen ['ʃlaɛçn̩] <schleicht sich, schlich sich, hat sich geschlichen> ◊ Sie schlich sich aus dem Haus. sneak off sich wegschleichen ['vɛkʃlaɛçn̩] +haben ◊ Er schlich sich weg, um auf die Party zu gehen. 2. (take) stibitzen [ʃti'bɪtsn̩] <stibitzt, stibitzte, hat stibitzt> (fam) ◊ Der Hund hat ein Würstchen stibitzt. 3. (bring) sneak sb/sth somewhere jdn/etw. irgendwohin schmuggeln ['ʃmʊgl̩n] +haben ◊ Er schmuggelte Süßigkeiten in sein Zimmer. 4. (give) sneak sb sth jdm etw. zustecken ['tsu:ʃtɛkn̩] +haben ◊ Sie steckte ihm heimlich Geld zu. 5. sneak a look at sb/sth heimlich einen Blick auf jdn/etw. werfen [haɛmlɪç aɛnən ,blɪk aʊf ... vɛrfn̩] <wirft, warf, hat geworfen>

sneaker [noun] Turnschuh ['tʊrnʃu:] der <-(e)s, -e>

sneaky [adj] hinterlistig ['hɪntɐlɪstɪç] ◊ ein hinterlistiger Trick ♦ Das war ziemlich hinterlistig.

sneeze [verb] niesen ['ni:zn̩] +haben ◊ Ich musste niesen.

⊙ not to be sneezed at nicht zu verachten

sniff [verb] 1. (breathe through your nose) schniefen ['ʃni:fn̩] +haben ◊ Sie schniefte und putzte sich die Nase. "Sorry!" he sniffed. „Entschuldigung!", sagte er schniefend. 2. (smell, inhale drugs) sniff sth (an etw.) schnüffeln ['ʃnʏfl̩n] +haben ◊ Ich schnüffelte an meinen Socken. ♦ Klebstoff schnüffeln; (cocaine) schnupfen ['ʃnʊpfn̩] +haben

⊙ sniff at sth (criticize) über etw. [acc] die Nase rümpfen nicht to be sniffed at nicht zu verachten sein

• sniff out [phras v] aufspüren ['aʊfʃpy:rən] +haben ◊ Der Hund spürte die Leiche auf. ♦ neue Trends aufspüren

snoop [verb] snoop (round) herumschnüffeln [hɛ'rʊmʃnʏfl̩n] +haben (fam, pej) ◊ Ich mag es nicht, wenn du hier herumschnüffelst. snoop in/through sth in etw. [dat] herumschnüffeln ◊ Du hast in meinen Sachen herumgeschnüffelt! snoop on sb jdn ausschnüffeln ['aʊsʃnʏfl̩n] +haben (fam, pej) ◊ Er schnüffelt seine eigenen Kollegen aus.

snore [verb] schnarchen ['ʃnarçn̩] +haben ◊ Hör auf zu schnarchen!

snout [noun] (nose, front) Schnauze ['ʃnaʊtsə] die <-, -n> ◊ die Schnauze des Krokodils/Delphins ♦ die Schnauze des Wagens; (of a pig) Rüssel ['rʏsl̩] der <-s, ->; (of a plane) Nase ['na:zə] die <-, -n> (fam)

snow¹ [noun] Schnee [ʃne:] der <-s> no pl ◊ In der Nacht fiel eine Menge Schnee. ♦ In den Alpen liegt bereits Schnee. snows Schneefälle ['ʃne:fɛlə] die <-> pl

snow² [verb] schneien [ˈʃnaeən] +haben ◊ *Gestern hat es heftig geschneit.*

snowball [noun] Schneeball [ˈʃneːbal] der <-(e)s, Schneebälle> ◊ *einen Schneeball werfen*

snowflake [noun] Schneeflocke [ˈʃneːflɔkə] die <-, -n>

snug(ly) [adj, adv] **1.** *(cosy)* gemütlich [gəˈmyːtlɪç] ◊ *ein gemütliches Lokal* ♦ *Dein neues Sofa ist sehr gemütlich.* ♦ *Wir saßen gemütlich vor dem Kamin.* **2.** *(tight)* sth is a snug fit, sth fits snugly etw. passt genau [past gəˈnao]; *(clothing)* etw. passt wie angegossen [past vi: ˈangəgɔsn̩] *(fam)*

so¹ [adv] **1.** *(emphasis)* so [zoː] ◊ *Es ist so schön hier!* ♦ *Er gibt sich so viel Mühe!* ♦ *Reg dich doch nicht so auf.* so ... as to/that so ... dass ◊ *Sie war so müde, dass sie sofort einschlief.* ♦ *Ich bin nicht so naiv, dass ich das glaube.* **2.** *(in answer to a question, expressing affirmation)* schon [ʃoːn] "Is it true?" – "I think so." „Ist das wahr?" – „Ich glaube schon."; *(expressing negation)* nicht [nɪçt] "Is it going to rain?" – "I don't hope so." „Wird es regnen?" – „Ich hoffe nicht." **3.** *(replacing sth already mentioned)* es [ɛs] The answer is yes. At least I think so. Die Antwort ist ja. Ich glaube es jedenfalls.; das [das] es [ɛs] You should have told her so! Das hättest du ihr sagen müssen! As I expected – only more so. Wie ich es erwartet habe, nur noch besser. "Is it good?" – "Yes, very much so." „Ist es gut?" – „Ja, sehr!" [ɪst ɛs ˈguːt – ja: ˈzeːɐ] **4.** *(likewise)* auch [aox] He is old and so is she. Er ist alt und sie auch. She said it would rain and so it did. Sie sagte, es würde regnen, und das tat es auch. **5.** *(as stated or demonstrated)* so [zoː] ◊ *Ist das wirklich so?* ♦ *Wenn du das so willst, dann soll es auch so sein.* ♦ *Es war ungefähr so groß.* ⊛ so it/he/she etc. is, so I have etc. ja, tatsächlich only so much/long nicht allzu viel/lange ◊ *Ich habe nicht allzu viel Zeit dafür.* ♦ *Er hält es nicht allzu lange in der Sonne aus.* not so (very) gar nicht so ◊ *Das ist eigentlich gar nicht so kompliziert.* and so on/forth und so weiter/fort or so ungefähr ♦ *Er wiegt ungefähr 100 Kilo.* so what na und ◊ *Ja, ich bin zu spät dran. Na und?*

so² [conjunc] **1.** *(expressing a consequence, summarizing, asking for verification of your conclusion)* also [ˈalzoː] ◊ *Sie ist 18, also kann sie wählen.* ♦ *Du hast also überall gesucht, konntest aber nichts finden?* **2.** *(purpose)* damit [daˈmɪt] ◊ *Ich brauche die Namen, damit ich sie aufschreiben kann.* so as to do sth um etw. zu tun [ʊm ... tsuː] ◊ *Er war sehr leise, um sie nicht zu wecken.* **3.** *(aim, result)* so that sodass [zoˈdas] ◊ *Es war sehr kalt, sodass man heizen musste.* **4.** *(comparative: +adj)* not so ... nicht so ... [nɪçt zoː] ◊ *Das Wetter ist heute nicht so schön wie gestern.*; *(+verb)* just as ... so (too) so wie ... *(auch)* [zoː viː: ... (aox)] ◊ *So wie du gern Fußball spielst, lese ich gern.* **5.** *(concluding sth or starting sth else)* so so [zoː] ◊ *So, das reicht für heute.* ♦ *So, lasst uns anfangen.*

soak [verb] **1.** *(pulses, washing)* einweichen [ˈaenvaeçn̩] +haben ◊ *Weichen Sie die Linsen über Nacht ein.* **2.** *(make wet)* durchnässen [dʊˈçˈnɛsn̩] <durchnässt, durchnässt, hat durchnässt> *often in adjectival passive constructions* ◊ *vom Regen völlig durchnässt sein* be soaked in sth vor etw. [dat] triefen

[foːɐ̯ ... ˈtriːfn̩] +haben ◊ *Das Handtuch triefte vor Schweiß.*; *(seep)* soak through/into sth durch/in [acc] etw. sickern [dʊˈɐ̯çˈɪn ... zɪkən] +sein ◊ *Blut sickerte durch den Verband.* ♦ *Öl sickerte in den Boden.* **3.** *(person)* soak (in the bath) ein ausgiebiges Bad nehmen [aen ˌaosgiːbɪgəs ˈbaːt neːmən] <nimmt, nahm, hat genommen> • soak up [phras v] **1.** *(absorb)* sth soaks sth up etw. saugt etw. auf [zaokt ... aof] <saugt auf, saugte/sog auf, hat aufgesaugt/aufgesogen> ◊ *Die Zeitung saugte das Wasser auf.*; *(mop up, take in)* sb soaks sth up jd nimmt etw. auf [nɪmt ... aof] <nimmt auf, nahm auf, hat aufgenommen> ◊ *den verschütteten Saft mit einem Lappen aufnehmen* ♦ *neue Eindrücke aufnehmen* **2.** *(use up)* schlucken [ˈʃlʊkn̩] +haben *(fam)* ◊ *viel Zeit und Energie schlucken*

soap [noun] Seife [ˈzaefə] die <-, -n> ◊ *ein Stück Seife* ♦ *sich mit Seife waschen*

soar [verb] **1.** *(increase)* stark ansteigen [ʃtaˈɐ̯k ˈanʃtaegn̩] <steigt an, stieg an, ist angestiegen> ◊ *Die Nachfrage ist stark angestiegen.* ♦ *stark ansteigende Temperaturen* **2.** *(fly up)* aufsteigen [ˈaofʃtaegn̩] <steigt auf, stieg auf, ist aufgestiegen> ◊ *Das Flugzeug stieg plötzlich auf.*; *(hover)* segeln [ˈzeːgln̩] +sein ◊ *Möwen segelten über uns.* **3.** *(be tall)* hoch aufragen [hoːx ˈaofraːgn̩] +haben ◊ *Die Kathedrale ragt hoch über der Stadt auf.* **4.** *(sb's spirits)* sich zusehends verbessern [ˌtsuːzeːənts feˈbɛsən] <verbessert sich, verbesserte sich, hat sich verbessert> ◊ *Seine Stimmung verbesserte sich zusehends.* sb's hopes soar jd schöpft viel Hoffnung [ˈʃœpft fiːl ˈhɔfnʊŋ] +haben

sob [verb] schluchzen [ˈʃlʊxtsn̩] +haben ◊ *Sie schluchzte laut.* ♦ *„Bitte nicht!", schluchzte er.*

sober(ly) [adj, adv] nüchtern [ˈnʏçtɐn] ◊ *Sie war nicht mehr ganz nüchtern.* ♦ *in nüchternem Zustand* ♦ *etw. nüchtern beurteilen*

so-called [adj] so genannt [zoː gənant] *only before ns (also pej)* ◊ *Das ist ein so genannter Offline-Browser.* ♦ *Dein so genannter Freund ist ein Schmarotzer.*

soccer [noun] Fußball [ˈfuːsbal] der <-(e)s> *article only in combination with attribute, no pl* ◊ *Fußball spielen* ♦ *der europäische Fußball*

soccer ball [noun] Fußball [ˈfuːsbal] der <-(e)s, Fußbälle>

social [adj] **1.** *(relating to society, the ability of dealing with others)* sozial [zoˈtsjaːl] *mostly before ns* ◊ *soziale Gerechtigkeit/Unterschiede/Fähigkeiten* ♦ *aus schlechten sozialen Verhältnissen kommen* social graces Manieren [maˈniːrən] die <-> pl **2.** *(gregarious)* gesellig [gəˈzɛlɪç] ◊ *Er ist nicht besonders gesellig.* ♦ *ein geselliges Beisammensein*; *(insects)* Staaten bildend [ˈʃtaːtn̩ bɪldn̩t] *no comp/superl* social call Privatbesuch [priˈvaːtbazuːx] der <-(e)s, -e> social contacts soziale Kontakte [zoˌtsjaːlə kɔnˈtaktə] <-> pl social engagement gesellschaftliche Verpflichtung [gəˌzɛlʃaftlɪçə feˈpflɪçtʊŋ] die <-, -en>

socialism [noun] Sozialismus [zotsjaˈlɪsmʊs] der <-> no pl

socialist¹ [noun] Sozialist [zotsjaˈlɪst] der <-en, -en> ♀Sozialistin [zotsjaˈlɪstɪn] die <-, -nen> ◊ *Ich bin Sozialistin.* ♦ *ein überzeugter Sozialist*

socialist² [adj] sozialistisch [zotsjaˈlɪstɪʃ] *no comp/superl* ◊ *eine sozialistische Partei* ♦ *Das Land ist sozialistisch.*

socially [adv] **1.** *(relating to society, social class)*

sozial [zo'tsi̯aːl] ◊ *sozial benachteiligte Gruppen* ♦ *sozial engagiert sein* 2. *(not for work)* privat [pri'vaːt] *no comp/superl* ◊ *sich privat treffen*

A **social security** ⌐noun⌐ 1. *(system)* Sozialversicherung [zo'tsi̯aːlfɛ,ʦɪçərʊŋ] die <–, –en> 2. *(benefit)* Sozial-
B geld [zo'tsi̯aːlgɛlt] das <–, –er> apply for social security Sozialgeld beantragen
C **social service** ⌐noun⌐ 1. *(service)* Leistung des Sozial-
amts [,laestʊŋ dɛs zo'tsi̯aːlamts] die <–, –en> *most*
D *pl* ◊ *Das Wohngeld ist eine Leistung des Sozialamts.* 2. *(department)* social services Sozialamt
E [zo'tsi̯aːlamt] das <–(e)s, Sozialämter>
F **social worker** ⌐noun⌐ Sozialarbeiter [zo'tsi̯aːlarbaete]
der <–s, –> ♀Sozialarbeiterin [zo'tsi̯aːlar,baetərɪn]
G die <–, –nen> ◊ *Ich bin Sozialarbeiterin.* ♦ *ein enga-
gierter Sozialarbeiter*
H **society** ⌐noun⌐ 1. *(community)* Gesellschaft [gə'zɛlʃaft]
die <–, –en> ◊ *Wir leben in einer multikulturellen
I Gesellschaft.* ♦ *die feine/vornehme Gesellschaft*
2. *(organization)* Verein [fɛ|'aen] der <–(e)s, –e> ◊
J *einem Verein beitreten* ♦ *aus einem Verein austreten*
secret society Geheimbund [gə'haembʊnt] der
K <–(e)s, Geheimbünde> housing society Wohnungs-
baugesellschaft ['voːnʊŋsbaogəzɛlʃaft] die <–, –en>
L **sociological** ⌐adj⌐ soziologisch [zotsi̯o'loːgɪʃ] *no comp/
superl, only before ns* ◊ *soziologische Studien*
M **sociology** ⌐noun⌐ Soziologie [zotsi̯olo'giː] die <–> *no pl*
sock ⌐noun⌐ *(clothing)* Socke ['zɔkə] die <–, –n> ◊ *ein
N Paar Socken*

O ⊛ put a sock in it halt die Klappe *(fam)* work your
socks off bis zum Umfallen schuften *(fam)*
P **socket** ⌐noun⌐ 1. *(for plugs)* Steckdose ['ʃtɛkdoːzə] die
<–, –n> ◊ *den Stecker in die Steckdose stecken; (in
Q a machine)* Anschluss ['anʃlʊs] der <–es, Anschlüsse>
◊ *Wo ist der Anschluss für die Lautsprecher?* 2. *(for
R lightbulbs)* Fassung ['fasʊŋ] die <–, –en> ◊ *eine
Glühbirne in die Fassung schrauben* 3. ANAT *(for an
arm etc.)* Gelenkpfanne [gə'lɛŋkpfanə] die <–, –n>
S eye socket Augenhöhle ['aoghøːlə] die <–, –n>
soda ⌐noun⌐ 1. *(mineral water)* Mineralwasser
T [mine'raːlvasə] das <–s, Mineralwässer>; *(to mix with
hard drinks)* Soda ['zoːda:] das <–s> *no pl* ◊ *Einen
U Whisky Soda bitte!* 2. *(sweet fizzy drink)* Limonade
[limo'naːdə] die <–, –n> ◊ *Sie trank ein Glas
V Limonade.* 3. baking soda Backpulver ['bakpʊlfə]
das <–s> *no pl* ◊ *zwei Teelöffel Backpulver mit dem
W Mehl vermischen*
sodium ⌐noun⌐ Natrium ['naːtri̯ʊm] das <–s> *no pl*
X **sofa** ⌐noun⌐ Sofa ['zoːfaː] das <–s, –s>
soft ⌐adj⌐ 1. *(material, surface, character, drugs, water,
Y currency etc.)* weich [vaeç] ◊ *Hast du das Fleisch
schon weich geklopft?* ♦ *Diese Matratze ist mir zu
Z weich.* ♦ *Für solche Verhandlungen ist er viel zu
weich.* ♦ *weiche Gesichtszüge* ♦ *eine weiche Landung*
2. *(gentle, not intensive)* sanft [zanft] <sanfter, am
sanftesten> ◊ *Sie sprach mit sanfter Stimme.* ♦ *Diese
Creme ist besonders sanft zu Ihrer Haut.* ♦ *sanfte
Heilmethoden* ♦ *die sanften Töne einer Harfe* 3. *(not
strict enough, person)* nachgiebig ['naːxgiːbɪç] ◊ *zu
nachgiebig mit den Kindern sein* be soft on sth
nicht hart genug gegen etw. vorgehen
[nɪçt ,haʳt gənuːk geːɐ̯] ... ,foːɡgeːən] 4. *(wind, rain,
punishment, way of achieving sth)* leicht [laeçt]
<leichter, am leichtesten> ◊ *ein leichter Wind* ♦ *Die
Strafe war sehr leicht.* ♦ *sich für den leichtesten Weg
entscheiden*

⊛ be going soft nicht mehr ganz dicht sein
soft drink ⌐noun⌐ alkoholfreies Getränk
[,alkohoːlfraes gə'trɛŋk] <–(e)s, –e>
soften ⌐verb⌐ 1. *(make soft)* weich machen
['vaeç maxn] +haben ◊ *Der Zusatz macht das Wasser
weich.* 2. *(make less severe)* mildern ['mɪldən]
+haben ◊ *Dadurch kann die Wirkung gemildert
werden.* soften your attitude/position seine strenge
Haltung aufgeben [zaenə ʃtrɛŋə 'haltʊŋ ,aofgeːbm]
<gibt auf, gab auf, hat aufgegeben>; *(a person, sb's
heart)* erweichen [ɛ'vaeçn] <erweicht, erweichte, hat
erweicht> 3. *(a colo(u)r, sound)* dämpfen ['dɛmpfn]
+haben ◊ *Die Doppelfenster dämpfen den Straßen-
lärm.; (the contours of sth, sb's features)* weicher
erscheinen lassen ['vaeçə ɐʃaenən lasn] <ließ, ließ,
hat lassen> ◊ *Das Kerzenlicht ließ seine Gesichtszüge
weicher erscheinen.* 4. *(become soft)* weich werden
['vaeç veːɐ̯dn] +sein ◊ *Durch Eincremen wird die
Haut weich.; (person, voice)* sanfter werden
['zanftə veːɐ̯dn]
softly ⌐adv⌐ 1. *(not hard)* weich [vaeç] ◊ *Der Sessel ist
weich gepolstert.* ♦ *weich landen* 2. *(gently)* sanft
[zanft] <sanfter, am sanftesten> ◊ *Er streichelte sie
sanft.; (not loud)* leise ['laezə] <leiser, am leisesten>
◊ *leise singen*
Software ⌐noun⌐ Software ['sɔftveːɐ̯] die <–> *no pl*
soil¹ ⌐noun⌐ 1. *(earth)* Erde ['eːɐ̯də] die <–, –n> *most
sing* ◊ *Erde aufschütten* 2. *(type of ground, territory)*
Boden ['boːdn] der <–s, Böden> ◊ *Der Boden in
dieser Gegend ist sehr steinig.* ♦ *Befinden wir uns
hier auf deutschem Boden?; (fields)* Land [lant] das
<–es> *no pl* ◊ *das Land bestellen/pflügen*
soil² ⌐verb⌐ beschmutzen [bə'ʃmʊtsn] <beschmutzt,
beschmutzte, hat beschmutzt> +haben *(form)* ◊ *seine
Hose beschmutzen*
solar ⌐adj⌐ Sonnen... ['zɔnən] solar eclipse Sonnenfinsternis ['zɔnənfɪnstɛrnɪs] die <–, –se> solar
energy Sonnenenergie ['zɔnənɛneɐ̯,giː] die <–> *no
pl* solar system Sonnensystem ['zɔnənzʏs,teːm] das
<–s, –e>
soldier ⌐noun⌐ Soldat [zɔl'daːt] der <–en, –en>
♀Soldatin [zɔl'daːtɪn] die <–, –nen> ◊ *Sie ist
Soldatin.* ♦ *Ein amerikanischer Soldat wurde verletzt.*
sold out ⌐adj⌐ ausverkauft ['aosfekaoft] *no comp/
superl* ◊ *Alle Wörterbücher sind ausverkauft.* ♦ *das
ausverkaufte Stadion*
sole¹ ⌐noun⌐ 1. *(of your foot, shoe)* Sohle ['zoːlə] die
<–, –n> ◊ *Die Schuhe haben dicke Sohlen.* ♦ *Blasen
an den Sohlen haben* 2. *(fish)* Seezunge ['zeːʦʊŋə]
die <–, –n>
sole² ⌐adj⌐ *(only)* einzig ['aentsɪç] *no comp/superl, only
before ns* ◊ *eine Gruppe* ♦ *Er ist jetzt mein
einziger überlebender Verwandter.; (ownership,
responsibility)* alleinig [a'laenɪç] *no comp/superl; only
before ns* ◊ *der alleinige Besitzer* ♦ *die alleinige Verantwortung haben*
solely ⌐adv⌐ ausschließlich ['aosʃliːslɪç] *no comp/superl*
◊ *Diese Regelung trifft fast ausschließlich Beamte.* ♦
Dafür ist ausschließlich der Bund zuständig.
solemn ⌐adj⌐ 1. *(occasion, speech, oath)* feierlich
['faeɐlɪç] ◊ *Im Saal herrschte feierliche Stille.* ♦ *Der
Gottesdienst war sehr feierlich.; (face, mood)* ernst
[ɛ'nst] <ernster, am ernstesten> ◊ *Ihr ernster Gesichtsausdruck.* ◊ *Du siehst so ernst aus.* 2. *(duty)* heilig
['haelɪç] ◊ *Er sieht das als seine heilige Pflicht an.*
solemnly ⌐adv⌐ feierlich ['faeɐlɪç] ◊ *Er schüttelte ihr*

feierlich die Hand.
solicitor [noun] Rechtsanwalt ['rɛʧs|anvalt] der <–(e)s, Rechtsanwälte> ♀Rechtsanwältin ['rɛʧs|anvɛltɪn] die <–, –nen> ◊ *Sie arbeitet als Rechtsanwältin in einer Kanzlei.* ♦ *Kennen Sie einen guten Rechtsanwalt?*
solid [adj] **1.** *(not liquid)* fest [fɛst] <fester, am festesten> ◊ *Er kann noch keine feste Nahrung zu sich nehmen.* ♦ *Bei Temperaturen unter null Grad wird Wasser fest.* frozen solid zugefroren ['ʦuːgəfroːrən] ◊ *Der Fluss/See ist zugefroren.* **2.** *(of one substance, without holes)* massiv [ma'siːf] ◊ *ein Ring aus massivem Gold* ♦ *Das Holz ist massiv, nicht furniert.* ♦ *eine massive Statue* **3.** *(strong, firm)* solide [zo'liːdə] <solider, am solidesten> ◊ *ein solides Fundament* ♦ *Büromöbel sollten solide sein.* ♦ *Die Mannschaft zeigte eine solide Leistung.* **4.** *(of a person, big and strong)* stämmig ['ʃtɛmɪç] ◊ *ein stämmiger Junge* ♦ *In unserer Familie sind die Männer meist groß und stämmig.* **5.** *(powerful, convincing)* handfest ['hantfɛst] <handfester, am handfestesten> ◊ *handfeste Gründe/Beweise* ♦ *Dieses Argument ist handfest.* **6.** *(without pause or break)* ununterbrochen ['ʊn|ʊntebrɔxn̩] no comp/superl ◊ *eine ununterbrochene Linie/Reihe* He worked for ten solid hours. Er hat zehn Stunden ununterbrochen gearbeitet. a solid week eine volle Woche [aenə fɔlə 'vɔxə] ◊ *Die Aufnahmen dauerten eine volle Woche.* **7.** *(of one colo(u)r)* einfarbig ['aenfaʀbɪç] no comp/superl ◊ *Eine Wand war einfarbig blau, die anderen hatten gemusterte Tapeten.* **8.** *(sensible, reliable)* verlässlich [fe'lɛslɪç] ◊ *ein verlässlicher junger Mann* ♦ *Meine Sekretärin ist absolut verlässlich.; (loyal)* treu [trɔy] <treuer, am treuesten> ◊ *ein treuer Schalke-Fan*
solidarity [noun] Solidarität [zolidari'tɛːt] die <–> no pl
solidly [adv] **1.** *(sturdily, strongly)* solide [zo'liːdə] <solider, am solidesten> ◊ *ein solide gebauter Schrank* **2.** *(big and strong)* solidly built kräftig gebaut [‚krɛftɪç gə'baʊt] ◊ *Das Kind ist kräftig gebaut.* ♦ *ein kräftig gebauter Mann* **3.** *(without interruption)* ununterbrochen ['ʊn|ʊntebrɔxn̩] no comp/superl ◊ *Ich habe acht Stunden ununterbrochen gearbeitet.* remain solidly in first place sicher in Führung liegen [zɪçɐ ɪn 'fyːrʊŋ liːgn̩] **4.** *(totally)* be solidly behind sb geschlossen hinter jdm stehen [gəʃlɔsn̩ 'hɪntɐ ... ʃteːən] ◊ *Seine Kollegen standen geschlossen hinter ihm.* be solidly against sth ganz und gar gegen etw. sein [ganʦ ʊnt gaːʀ 'geːgn̩ ... zaen] ◊ *Die Parteibasis ist ganz und gar gegen diese Reform.*
solitary [adj] **1.** *(lone, just one)* einzeln ['aenʦl̩n] only before ns ◊ *Auf dem Spielplatz spielte ein einzelnes Kind.* ♦ *Auf der Wiese stand ein einzelnes Haus.* solitary confinement Einzelhaft ['aenʦl̩haft] die <–> no pl **2.** *(lonely, without other people)* einsam ['aenzaːm] ◊ *Schreiben ist eine einsame Arbeit.* ♦ *Im Kino saß ein einsamer Besucher.* **3.** *(single)* einzige ['aenʦɪgə] no comp/superl <ein einziger ..., eine einzige ..., ein einziges ...> ◊ *Es gab nur einen einzigen brauchbaren Kommentar.; (in the negative)* kein einziger [kaen 'aenʦɪgɐ] keine einzige [kaenə 'aenʦɪgə] kein einziges [kaen 'aenʦɪgəs] ◊ *Es gab keine einzige Störung.* ♦ *Sie hat kein einziges Wort gesprochen.*

solo [noun] Solo ['zoːloː] das <–s, Soli>
soloist [noun] Solist [zo'lɪst] der <–en, –en> ♀Solistin [zo'lɪstɪn] die <–, –nen>
soluble [adj] **1.** *(able to dissolve)* löslich ['løːslɪç] ◊ *löslicher Kaffee* ♦ *Zucker ist in Wasser löslich.* **2.** *(able to be solved)* lösbar ['løːsbaːʀ] ◊ *ein lösbares Problem* ♦ *Die Aufgabe/Gleichung ist nicht lösbar.*
solution [noun] **1.** *(to a problem, dilemma etc.)* Lösung ['løːzʊŋ] die <–, –en> ◊ *eine diplomatische/politische/friedliche Lösung suchen* ♦ *Das wäre doch eine elegante Lösung.* ♦ *Die Lösungen der Aufgaben stehen hinten im Buch.* come up with a solution eine Lösung finden sth offers a solution etw. könnte die Lösung sein be the solution die Lösung sein not be the solution keine Lösung sein **2.** *(to a crossword, puzzle etc.)* Auflösung ['aofløːzʊŋ] die <–, –en> ◊ *Die Auflösung des Kreuzworträtsels finden Sie im nächsten Heft.* **3.** *(liquid)* Lösung ['løːzʊŋ] die <–, –en> ◊ *eine hochprozentige Lösung*
solve [verb] **1.** *(a problem, conflict, mystery)* lösen ['løːzn̩] +haben ◊ *Damit sind alle meine Probleme gelöst.* ♦ *Wie kann man diesen Konflikt lösen?* ♦ *Das Rätsel wurde nie gelöst.* **2.** *(a crime)* aufklären ['aofklɛːrən] +haben ◊ *Die Polizei hat den Mord erst nach vielen Jahren aufgeklärt.*
solvent [noun] Lösungsmittel ['løːzʊŋsmɪtl̩] das <–s, –>
some[1] [adv] **1.** *(about)* ungefähr ['ʊngəfɛːɐ] ◊ *Es waren ungefähr 100 Leute bei der Party.* **2.** *(in the US: a little)* etwas ['ɛtvas] ◊ *Die Lage hat sich etwas verbessert.*
some[2] [det] **1.** *(a small amount of)* etwas ['ɛtvas] ◊ *Da fehlt noch etwas Pfeffer.* ♦ *Hast du etwas Zeit?* some more etwas mehr ◊ *Wir brauchen etwas mehr Hilfe.* some advice ein Rat [aen raːt] der <–(e)s> no pl ◊ *Kannst du mir einen Rat geben?* **2.** *(an uncertain number of, several)* ein paar [aen paːʀ] ◊ *Sie hat mir ein paar Blumen mitgebracht.* **3.** *(part of an amount or number)* manche ['mançə] ◊ *Manche Schüler lernen schnell und manche nicht.* some people/books etc. are ... than others manche Leute/Bücher etc. sind ... als andere ◊ *Manche Leute sind ängstlicher als andere.* **4.** *((quite) a few)* einige ['aenɪgə] ◊ *einige Tage später* ♦ *Das wird noch einige Zeit dauern.* ♦ *Sie sind vor einigen Jahren weggezogen.* ♦ *Es gab einige Schwierigkeiten.* **5.** *(without being specific)* irgendein ['ɪʀgn̩t|'aena] ◊ *Irgendeine Frau hat vorhin für dich angerufen.* ♦ *die Mutter irgendeines Schülers* ♦ *Irgendeine Lösung wird sich schon finden lassen.* some ... or other irgendein ..., irgendeine ... ◊ *Aus irgendeinem Grund hat er es vergessen.* There must have been some mistake. Es muss sich um einen Irrtum handeln.
some[3] [indef pron] **1.** *(a few of a group of people or objects, replacing a countable noun)* manche ['mançə] ◊ *Manche glaubten ihm.* ♦ *Für manche war es eine böse Überraschung.* some of ... manche ... ◊ *Manche ihrer Gedichte gefallen mir nicht.* some of you/them etc. manche von euch/ihnen etc. ◊ *Manche von euch sind noch bei mir gewesen.* ♦ *Manchen von uns gefällt es eher nicht.* **2.** *(noun)* welcher ['vɛlçɐ] welche ['vɛlçə] welches ['vɛlçəs] ◊ *Ich gehe Milch kaufen. Brauchst du auch welche?* ♦ *Wir brauchen Geld. Hast du welches?* ♦ *Sind alle*

A
B
C
D
E
F
G
H
I
J
K
L
M
N
O
P
Q
R
S
T
U
V
W
X
Y
Z

Kinder da oder fehlen noch welche?
somebody [pron] jemand ['je:mant] ◊ *Du solltest mit jemandem darüber reden.* ♦ *Jemand hat geklingelt, aber ich habe nicht aufgemacht.* somebody else jemand anders ◊ *Könnte das nicht jemand anders übernehmen?* or somebody oder sonst jemand ◊ *Der Hausmeister oder sonst jemand könnte das doch machen.*
⊚ be somebody jemand sein
somehow [adv] irgendwie ['ɪ'gi̯t'vi:] ◊ *Irgendwie werden wir das schon schaffen.* ♦ *Er hat sich irgendwie verändert.* ♦ *Irgendwie habe ich das Gefühl, dass da etwas nicht stimmt.* somehow or other irgendwie
someone [pron] jemand ['je:mant] ◊ *Jemand hat mein Glas weggenommen.* ♦ *Du solltest mit jemandem darüber reden.* someone else jemand anders ◊ *Das kann jemand anders erledigen.* be in love with someone else einen anderen/eine andere lieben someone nice/special jemand Nettes/Besonderes ◊ *Es gab mir das Gefühl, jemand Besonderes zu sein.* or someone oder so jemanden ◊ *Wir brauchen einen Filmstar oder so jemanden für die Eröffnung des neuen Kinos.* someone famous ein Prominenter [æn promi'nɛntə] der <eines Prominenten>
someplace [adv] **1.** (in a place) irgendwo ['ɪ'gi̯t'vo:] ◊ *Das liegt irgendwo bei Bonn.* ♦ *Irgendwo muss dein Pass doch sein.* someplace else woanders [vo'|'andes] **2.** (with indication of movement) irgendwohin ['ɪ'gi̯tvo'hɪn] ◊ *Sie hat den Brief irgendwohin gelegt und ist dann wieder gegangen.* someplace else woandershin [vo|'andeshɪn]
something [pron] **1.** (indefinite) etwas ['ɛtvas] ◊ *Hier stimmt etwas nicht.* ♦ *Er hat etwas gesagt.* ♦ *Sie hat es in ihrem Beruf zu etwas gebracht.* something else etwas anderes ◊ *Sie möchte mal etwas anderes machen.* something to eat/drink/do etwas zu essen/trinken/tun ◊ *Er braucht etwas zu trinken.* ♦ *Im Garten gibt es immer etwas zu tun.* something to wear etwas zum Anziehen ◊ *Ich muss mir unbedingt etwas zum Anziehen kaufen.* something better/special etc. etwas Besseres/Besonderes etc. ◊ *Ich würde gern etwas Kaltes trinken.* there is something wrong with sb/sth mit jdm/etw. stimmt etwas nicht be something in advertising in der Werbung arbeiten [ɪn de:ɐ̯ 'vɛɐ̯bʊŋ a'baetn] something or other irgendetwas ['ɪ'gi̯t|'ɛtvas] ◊ *Es gibt immer irgendetwas, was ihr nicht passt.* **2.** (from among a number of possibilities) ... or something ... oder so [o:de zo:] (fam) ◊ *Er ist Makler oder so.* ♦ *Kannst du nicht anrufen oder so?* **3.** (in vague descriptions) something like ein bisschen wie [æn bɪsçən vi:] ◊ *Das Tier sieht ein bisschen wie eine Echse aus.* something between ein Zwischending zwischen [æn 'tsvɪʃndɪŋ tsvɪʃn] (fam) ◊ *Kite Surfing ist ein Zwischending zwischen Paragliding und Windsurfen.;* (with amounts) something like, something around so um die [zo: ʊm di:] (fam) ◊ *Es kostet so um die 12 Millionen.* ♦ *Die Operation dauert so um die 10 Stunden.* something between so zwischen [zo: tsvɪʃn] (fam) ◊ *Sie verdient so zwischen 30 und 35 Euro die Stunde.*
⊚ be quite something wirklich etwas Besonderes sein be something of a ... **1.** (be fairly good at ...) ein ziemlich guter/eine ziemlich gute/ein ziemlich gutes ... sein ◊ *Sein Vater war ein ziemlich guter*

Maler. **2.** (be rather a ...) schon ein/eine ... sein ◊ *Die Bronzemedaille ist schon eine Enttäuschung; wir hatten mit Gold gerechnet.* there is something in sth an etw. [dat] ist etwas dran ◊ *Ist an dem Gerücht etwas dran?*
sometime [adv] irgendwann ['ɪ'gi̯t'van] ◊ *Sie sind gestern irgendwann angekommen.* ♦ *Sie möchte irgendwann einmal eine Kreuzfahrt machen.*
sometimes [adv] manchmal ['mançma:l] ◊ *Seine Sprache wirkt manchmal gekünstelt.* ♦ *Es regnete meistens; nur manchmal schien die Sonne.* ♦ *Manchmal kann das gerechtfertigt sein.*
somewhat [adv] etwas ['ɛtvas] ◊ *Er tat es etwas widerwillig.* ♦ *Die Preise sind etwas gestiegen.*
somewhere [adv] **1.** (in a place) irgendwo ['ɪ'gi̯t'vo:] ◊ *Liegt das nicht irgendwo bei Paris?* ♦ *Meine Brille ist irgendwo in meiner Tasche.* somewhere nice irgendwo, wo es nett ist somewhere else woanders [vo|'andes] ◊ *Sie lebt/studiert/wohnt inzwischen woanders.* ♦ *Die wahren Gründe liegen woanders.* or somewhere oder so [o:de zo:] ◊ *Er wohnt jetzt in Toronto oder so.* **2.** (with indication of movement) irgendwohin ['ɪ'gi̯tvo'hɪn] ◊ *Ich habe den Zettel irgendwohin gelegt und jetzt kann ich ihn nicht mehr finden.* somewhere else woandershin [vo|'andeshɪn] ◊ *Lass uns woandershin gehen.* **3.** (with figures) somewhere around ungefähr ['ʊngəfɛ:ɐ̯] ◊ *Es kostet ungefähr 100 Euro.*
⊚ be getting somewhere vorankommen
son [noun] Sohn [zo:n] der <-(e)s, Söhne> ◊ *Sie haben zwei Söhne.* ♦ *Goethe, der bekannteste Sohn der Stadt Frankfurt* ♦ *Was kann ich für dich tun, mein Sohn?*
song [noun] **1.** (piece of music) Lied [li:t] das <-(e)s, -er> ◊ *ein Lied singen* ♦ *Sie kennt viele Lieder.* **2.** (singing) Gesang [gə'zaŋ] der <-(e)s, Gesänge> ◊ *Der Wald war mit Musik und Gesang durch den Ort.* ♦ *Sie wurde durch den Gesang der Vögel geweckt.*
⊚ burst into song anfangen zu singen make a song and dance about sth viel Theater um etw. machen for a song spottbillig (fam)
son-in-law [noun] Schwiegersohn ['ʃvi:gezo:n] der <-(e)s, Schwiegersöhne>
soon [adv] **1.** (within a short time, quickly) bald [balt] <eher, am ehesten> ◊ *Ich bin bald wieder da.* ♦ *Bald ist Weihnachten.* as soon as possible so bald wie möglich ◊ *Ich komme so bald wie möglich.* pretty soon ziemlich bald **2.** (after a short time) soon after sth kurz nach etw. [kʊ'ts na:x] ◊ *Sie rief mich kurz nach der Besprechung an.* ♦ *Sie gingen kurz nachdem wir gekommen waren.*
⊚ not a moment too soon keinen Augenblick zu früh I would (just) as soon do sth ich würde lieber etw. tun as soon as sobald
sooner [comp] eher ['e:ɐ̯] ◊ *Kannst du nicht etwas eher kommen?* ♦ *Er war eher fertig als ich.*
⊚ the sooner the better je eher desto besser sooner or later früher oder später I'd sooner do sth ich würde lieber etw. tun no sooner said than done gesagt, getan no sooner ..., than ... kaum ..., ... ◊ *Kaum hatte mich hingesetzt, musste ich schon wieder aufstehen.* the sooner ..., the sooner ... je eher ..., desto eher ...
soot [noun] Ruß [ru:s] der <-es, -e> most sing ◊ *Wände und Decken waren nach dem Brand voller*

Ruß.

sophisticated [adj] **1.** *(refined, demanding)* anspruchsvoll ['anʃprɔksfɔl] ◊ *eine anspruchsvolle Kundin* ♦ *Das Publikum hier ist sehr anspruchsvoll.*; *(understanding)* differenziert [dɪfərɛn'tsiːɐt] <differenzierter, am differenziertesten> ◊ *ein differenziertes Verständnis vom Gleichgewicht der Natur* **2.** *(person, conversation)* kultiviert [kʊlti'viːɐt] <kultivierter, am kultiviertesten> ◊ *eine kultivierte Unterhaltung* ♦ *Sie ist sehr kultiviert.* **3.** *(equipment)* hoch entwickelt [hoːx ɛnt'vɪklt] <höher entwickelt, am höchsten entwickelt> ◊ *hoch entwickelte Bauteile* ♦ *Unsere Software ist hoch entwickelt.*

sore [adj] **1.** *(skin)* wund [vɔnt] <wunder, am wundesten> ◊ *Der Po des Babys ist wund und gerötet.* ♦ *eine wunde Stelle am Knie*; *(throat)* rau [raʊ] <rauer, am rau(e)sten> ◊ *Ich habe vom vielen Reden einen rauen Hals bekommen.* sb feels sore jdm tut alles weh [tuːt aləs 'veː] <tut weh, tat weh, hat wehgetan> *(fam)* ◊ *Nach der Wanderung gestern tut mir alles weh.* sb's eyes are sore jdm tun die Augen weh **2.** *(in the US: angry)* sauer ['zaʊɐ] not before ns *(fam)* ◊ *Er ist immer noch ziemlich sauer.* ⊕ **a sore point** ein wunder Punkt

sorrow [noun] **1.** *(sadness)* sorrow (about sth) Trauer (über etw. [acc]) ['traʊ̯ɐ] die <-> no pl ◊ *die Trauer über den Tod eines geliebten Menschen* **2.** *(trouble, worry)* Sorge ['zɔrɡə] die <-, -n> ◊ *Sie hat viele Sorgen.*

sorrowful(ly) [adj, adv] traurig ['traʊ̯rɪç] ◊ *die traurigen Augen des kranken Kindes* ♦ *„Keiner liebt mich", sagte er traurig.* ♦ *Er sah sehr traurig aus.*

sorry [adj] **1.** *(unhappy, sad)* sb is sorry es tut jdm Leid [ɛs tuːt ... 'laet] <tut, tat, hat getan> ◊ *Sag ihm doch einfach, dass es dir Leid tut!* ♦ *Es tut mir Leid, dass ich das Buch vergessen habe.* sb is sorry for doing sth es tut jdm Leid, dass er etw. getan hat ◊ *Es tat ihm Leid, dass er die Kinder ausgeschimpft hatte.* sb is sorry about, sb is sorry (to hear) that es tut jdm Leid, dass ◊ *Es tut mir Leid, dass Ihre Mutter gestorben ist.* **2.** *(bad, dreadful)* traurig ['traʊ̯rɪç] a sorry business eine traurige Angelegenheit a sorry state ein trauriger Zustand a sorry excuse eine faule Ausrede [aenə faʊlə 'aʊsreːdə] <-, -n> *(fam)* be in a sorry mess in der Tinte sitzen [ɪn deːɐ 'tɪntə zɪtsn̩] <sitzt, saß, hat gesessen> *(fam)* **3.** *(pitiful)* jämmerlich ['jɛmɐlɪç] a sorry sight ein jämmerlicher Anblick ⊕ **I'm sorry 1.** *(when you have hurt or upset sb)* es tut mir Leid ◊ *Es tut mir Leid, dass ich das gesagt habe.* **2.** *(when you have done sth rude or embarrassing)* Entschuldigung ◊ *Entschuldigung, ich habe Sie nicht gesehen.* I'm sorry about ... Entschuldigen Sie ... [acc] ◊ *Entschuldigen Sie bitte den Irrtum.* **3.** *(to interrupt sb politely)* I'm sorry (for ...) Entschuldigen Sie bitte (... [acc]) ◊ *Entschuldigen Sie bitte die Störung.* **4.** *(to ask sb to repeat sth)* bitte ◊ *Bitte, was hast du gesagt?* sb feels sorry for sb jdm tut jd Leid ◊ *Bei einer Scheidung tun mir immer die Kinder Leid.* feel sorry for yourself sich selbst bemitleiden say sorry sich entschuldigen I'm sorry to say leider

sort¹ [noun] **1.** *(kind, type)* sort (of) Art (von) [aːɐt] die <-, -en> ◊ *Ich mag jede Art von Nüssen.* ♦ *Kennst du noch mehr Gedichte dieser Art?* ♦ *Was für eine Art Drucker brauchst du?* some sort of ... eine Art

... ◊ *Das ist eine Art Cocktail.* all sorts of ... alle möglichen ... [alə 'møːklɪçn̩] ◊ *Es gibt alle möglichen Wege, Geld zu verdienen.* ... of this sort solche ... ['zɔlçə] ◊ *Solche Bemerkungen macht er dauernd.* **2.** *(type of person)* Sorte Mensch [zɔrtə 'mɛnʃ] die <-, -n> ◊ *Die Sorte Mensch kenne ich!* He's not the sort. So einer ist er nicht. She's not the sort. So eine ist sie nicht. **3.** *(process of sorting)* Sortieren [zɔr'tiːrən] das <-s> no pl ⊕ **that sort of thing** so etwas **it takes all sorts** es gibt solche und solche ... **of sorts** eine Art ... ◊ *Sie ist eine Art Beraterin.* **out of sorts** nicht ganz auf der Höhe **sort of 1.** *(a little, slightly)* ein bisschen ◊ *Wir sind ein bisschen enttäuscht.* **2.** *(similar to)* sort of like ... irgendwie wie ... ◊ *Es sieht irgendwie wie ein Kaninchen aus.*

sort² [verb] **1.** *(arrange)* sort sth (by sth) etw. (nach etw.) sortieren [zɔr'tiːrən] <sortiert, sortierte, hat sortiert> ◊ *Knöpfe nach Farben sortieren* ♦ *Stichwörter alphabetisch sortieren* ♦ *seine Urlaubsfotos sortieren* **2.** *(deal with)* in Ordnung bringen [ɪn 'ɔrdnʊŋ brɪŋən] <bringt, brachte, hat gebracht> get sth sorted sich um etw. kümmern [ʊm ... kʏmɐn] +haben

• **sort out** [phras v] **1.** *(tidy up)* aufräumen ['aʊfrɔʏmən] +haben ◊ *Ich habe mir vorgenommen, heute den Schrank aufzuräumen.* **2.** *(solve, find out)* klären ['klɛːrən] +haben ◊ *Die Polizei hat noch nicht geklärt, wie es zu dem Zwischenfall kam.* **3.** *(deal with)* regeln ['reːɡl̩n] +haben ◊ *Keine Sorge, ich regle das für dich.* ♦ *Die Formalitäten sind schon geregelt.*

• **sort through** [phras v] sort through sth (for sth) etw. (nach etw.) durchsehen [dʊrçzeːən] <sieht durch, sah durch, hat durchgesehen> ◊ *Ich habe alle Schubladen nach dem Brief durchgesehen.*

sorting [noun] Ordnung ['ɔrdnʊŋ] die <-, -en> ◊ *Sie befasste sich mit der Ordnung ihrer Papiere.*

so-so [adv] einigermaßen ['aenɪɡɐ'maːsn̩] ◊ *„Hast du das jetzt verstanden?"— „Na ja, so einigermaßen."* ♦ *„Wie geht's ihm denn?" — „Wieder einigermaßen."*

sought after [adj] gefragt [ɡə'fraːkt] <gefragter, am gefragtesten> ◊ *Sie ist ein gefragtes Fotomodell.* ♦ *Dieses Buch ist im Augenblick sehr gefragt.*

soul [noun] **1.** *(immortal part of a person, seat of feeling, individual)* Seele ['zeːlə] die <-, -n> ◊ *Was geschieht nach dem Tod mit der Seele?* ♦ *Das Dorf hat 200 Seelen.* ♦ *Sie ist eine treue Seele.* not a soul keine Seele ◊ *Keine Seele war zu sehen.* **2.** *(expressiveness)* Ausdruck ['aʊsdrʊk] der <-(e)s> no pl ◊ *Seinen Werken fehlt der Ausdruck.* **3.** *(ability to feel emotions)* Gefühl [ɡə'fyːl] das <-s, -e> ◊ *Hast du denn kein Gefühl?* **4.** *(special qualities, particular life)* Wesen ['veːzn̩] das <-s, -> ◊ *Die vielen verschiedenen Kulturen machen das Wesen dieses Stadtteils aus.* ⊕ **be good for the soul** gut tun **be the soul of sth** etw. selbst sein ◊ *Er ist die Ruhe/Verschwiegenheit selbst.* **sell your soul** seine Seele verkaufen

sound¹ [noun] **1.** *(noise)* Geräusch [ɡə'rɔʏʃ] das <-(e)s, -e> ◊ *Der Motor machte merkwürdige Geräusche.* sound of sth Klang ... [gen] [klaŋ] der <-(e)s, Klänge> ◊ *der vertraute Klang seiner Stimme* ♦ *Das Instrument hat einen vollen/weichen Klang.* hear the sound of footsteps Schritte hören ['ʃrɪtə høːrən] +haben not make a sound ganz leise sein [gants 'laezə zaen] +sein **2.** *(in physics)* Schall

[ʃal] der <–(e)s> no pl ◊ *Die Concorde flog schneller als der Schall.* **3.** *(from the radio, TV)* Ton [toːn] der <–(e)s, Töne> ◊ *Beim Fernseher ist der Ton ausgefallen.* ♦ *den Ton lauter/leiser stellen* **4.** *(musical style)* Sound [saʊnt] der <–s, –s> ◊ *Ich mag den Sound dieser Band.* **5.** *(narrow area of water)* Sund [zʊnt] der <–(e)s, –e>

sound² [adj] **1.** *(sensible)* vernünftig [fɛˈnʏnftɪç] ◊ *Sie hat vernünftige Ansichten.* ♦ *Dieser Plan ist vernünftig.* legally sound rechtlich einwandfrei [rɛçtlɪç ˈaɛnvantfraɛ] **2.** *(solid, strong)* solide [zoˈliːdə] <solider, am solidesten> ◊ *eine solide Firma* ♦ *Ihre finanzielle Situation ist solide.* ♦ *finanziell solide* **3.** *(thorough)* gut [guːt] <besser, am besten> ◊ *Seine Grammatikkenntnisse sind gut.* ♦ *eine gute Ausbildung* **4.** *(healthy)* gesund [ɡəˈzʊnt] <gesünder, am gesündesten> ◊ *ein gesunder Magen* ♦ *Sein Herz ist gesund.* be of sound body körperlich gesund sein be of sound mind bei klarem Verstand sein [baɛ klaːrəm fɛˈʃtant zaɛn] **5.** *(undamaged, safe)* einwandfrei [ˈaɛnvantfraɛ] ◊ *Das Dach ist noch einwandfrei* ♦ *Das alte Gebäude/ Auto ist in einwandfreiem Zustand.* **6.** *(sleep)* fest [fɛst] <fester, am festesten> ◊ *ein fester Schlaf*

sound³ [verb] **1.** *(seem)* sich anhören [ˈanhøːrən] +haben ◊ *Er hörte sich ziemlich deprimiert an.* ♦ *Der Vorschlag hört sich nicht schlecht an.* it sounds as if ... es hört sich so an, als ... [ɛs høːɐt zɪç zoː ˈan als] *mostly followed by the sub-junctive II* ◊ *Es hört sich so an, als ginge es ihm wieder besser.* sth sounds like sth etw. scheint etw. [nom] zu sein [ʃaɛnt ... tsu: zaɛn] <scheint, schien, hat geschienen> ◊ *Diese Insel scheint wirklich ein Ferien-paradies zu sein.* it sounds like/as if sb ... jd scheint ... ◊ *Er scheint nie zufrieden zu sein.* **2.** *(siren, bell etc.)* ertönen [ɛˈtøːnən] <ertönt, ertönte, ist ertönt> ◊ *Als die Sirene ertönte, rannten alle in den Keller.* sound sth etw. ertönen lassen [ɛˈtøːnən lasn] <lässt, ließ, hat lassen> ◊ *Um Punkt 8 Uhr ließ der Mönch den Gong ertönen.* **3.** *(pronounce)* aussprechen [ˈaʊsʃprɛçn] <spricht aus, sprach aus, hat ausgesprochen> ◊ *Er kann das englische „th" nicht aussprechen.* **4.** *(measure the depth of)* ausloten [ˈaʊsloːtn] <lotet aus, lotete aus, hat ausgelotet>

• **sound off** [phras v] sound off (about sth) sich (über etw. [acc]) auslassen [ˈaʊslasn] <lässt sich aus, ließ sich aus, hat sich ausgelassen> ◊ *sich lang und breit über sein Lieblingsthema auslassen*

• **sound out** [phras v] sound sb out bei jdm vorfühlen [baɛ ... ˈfoːɐfyːlən] +haben ◊ *Ich werde mal bei ihr vorfühlen, ob sie uns hilft.*

soundly [adv] **1.** *(solidly, strongly)* solide [zoˈliːdə] <solider, am solidesten> ◊ *ein solide gebautes Haus* ♦ *Das Projekt ist solide finanziert.; (sensibly)* vernünftig [fɛˈnʏnftɪç] ◊ *ein vernünftig konzipierter Vorschlag* **2.** *(sleep)* fest [fɛst] <fester, am festesten> ◊ *Er schläft tief und fest.* **3.** *(beat, defeat)* vernichtend [fɛˈnɪçtn̩t] ◊ *Unsere Mannschaft wurde vernichtend geschlagen.*

soundproof [adj] schalldicht [ˈʃaldɪçt] ◊ *eine schall-dichte Kabine* ♦ *Diese Wände sind schalldicht.*

soup [noun] Suppe die <–, –n> ◊ *ein Teller Suppe* ♦ *als Vorspeise eine Suppe essen* tomato soup Tomatensuppe [toˈmaːtn̩zʊpə]

soup up [verb] *(an engine)* frisieren [friˈziːrən] <frisiert,

frisierte, hat frisiert> *(fam)* ◊ *Er hat sein Mofa/den Motor frisiert.*

sour¹ [adj] **1.** *(not sweet, not fresh)* sauer [ˈzaʊɐ] <saurer, am sauersten> <der/die/das saure ...> ◊ *saure Äpfel* ♦ *Ich glaube, die Sahne ist sauer geworden.* **2.** *(unfriendly, hostile)* missmutig [ˈmɪsmuːtɪç] ◊ *sein missmutiger Gesichtsausdruck* ♦ *Sie warf mir einen missmutigen Blick zu.* ◉ go sour *(relationship)* scheitern *(investment)* sich als Fehlschlag erweisen

sour² [verb] *(worsen)* sth sours etw. verschlechtert sich [fɛˈʃlɛçtɐt zɪç] <verschlechtert sich, verschlechterte, hat sich verschlechtert> ◊ *Ihr Verhältnis hat sich in letzter Zeit sehr verschlechtert.* sour sth etw. vergiften [fɛˈɡɪftn̩] <vergiftet, vergiftete, hat vergiftet> ◊ *Der Streit hatte unsere Beziehung vergiftet.*

source [noun] source (of ...) Quelle (... [gen]) [ˈkvɛlə] die <–, –n> ◊ *einen Fluss von der Quelle bis zur Mündung verfolgen* ♦ *Der Journalist hat eine zuver-lässige Quelle im Ministerium.* ♦ *verschiedene Quellen zitieren* light source Lichtquelle [ˈlɪçtkvɛlə] energy source Energiequelle [enɛɐˈɡiːkvɛlə] source of inspiration Inspiration [ɪnspiraˈtsi̯oːn] die <–, –en>

south¹ [noun] Süden [ˈzyːdn̩] der <–s> *with the article when specifying a place, no pl* ◊ *Die Sonne steht mittags im Süden.* ♦ *nach/Richtung Süden fahren*

south² [adj] Süd... [zyːt] south coast Südküste [ˈzyːtkʏstə] die <–, –n> south side Südseite [ˈzyːtzaɛtə] die <–, –n> south wind Südwind [ˈzyːtvɪnt] der <–(e)s, –e> South Africa Südafrika [zyːtˈʔaːfrika:] das <–s> *article only in combination with attribute, no pl*

south³ [adv] *(towards the south)* nach Süden [naːx ˈzyːdn̩] ◊ *Der Balkon geht nach Süden.* go south in den Süden fahren down south im Süden ◊ *Sie wohnen jetzt im Süden.* south of südlich [ˈzyːtlɪç] [+gen] *südlich der Alpen; (when followed by a word without the article)* south of südlich von [ˈzyːtlɪç fɔn] ◊ *die Wohngebiete südlich von München*

southerly [adj] südlich [ˈzyːtlɪç] *only before ns* ◊ *schwacher Wind aus südlicher Richtung* southerly wind Südwind [ˈzyːtvɪnt] der <–(e)s, –e>

southern [adj] *(location, accent)* südlich [ˈzyːtlɪç] *only before ns* ◊ *der südliche Teil des Landes* ♦ *Sie hat einen südlichen Akzent.; (in geographical names)* Southern ... Süd... [zyːt] Southern Europe Südeuropa [ˈzyːtʔɔɐˌroːpaː] das <–s> *article only in combination with attribute, no pl* Southern Bavaria Südbayern [ˈzyːtbaɛən] das <–s> *article only in com-bination with attribute, no pl*

souvenir [noun] Andenken [ˈandɛŋkn̩] das <–s, –> ◊ *ein Andenken aus Rom*

sovereign [adj] souverän [zuvəˈrɛːn] ◊ *ein souveräner Staat*

sovereignty [noun] Souveränität [zuvərɛniˈtɛːt] die <–> no pl

sow [verb] säen [ˈzɛːən] +haben ◊ *Getreide/Salat säen*

spa [noun] **1.** *(town)* Heilbad [ˈhaɛlbaːt] das <–(e)s, Heilbäder> ◊ *Der Arzt will mich zur Kur in ein Heilbad schicken.* **2.** *(pool)* Whirlpool [ˈvœɐlpuːl] der <–s, –s> **3.** *(health club)* Therme [ˈtɛrmə] die <–, –n> ◊ *Wir gönnen uns heute einen Tag in der Therme mit Sauna, Massage und allem Drum und Dran.*

space [noun] **1.** *(available room)* Platz [plats] der <–es> no pl ◊ *Ich brauche mehr Platz für meine*

Bücher. ◆ *Hier ist nicht genug/kein Platz für ein zweites Bett.* ◆ *Der Kindergarten hat Platz für hundert Kinder.* parking space Parkplatz ['pɑːʳkplaʦ] working space Arbeitsplatz ['aʳbaɛtsplaʦ] in a confined space auf engem Raum [aͻf ɛŋəm 'raͻm] **2.** *(area)* Fläche ['flɛçə] die <–, –n> ◊ *Weite Flächen Kanadas sind mit Wald bedeckt.* open space unbebaute Flächen green spaces Grünflächen ['gryːnflɛçn̩] *pl* floor space Grundfläche ['grʊntflɛçə] roof space Dachboden ['daxboːdn̩] der <–s, Dachböden> **3.** *(gap)* Zwischenraum ['ʦvɪʃn̩raͻm] der <–(e)s, Zwischenräume> ◊ *einen Zwischenraum von zwei Metern lassen* ◆ *In den Zwischenräumen zwischen den Sträuchern wächst viel Unkraut.* **4.** ɪт *(disk)* space Speicherkapazität ['ʃpaɛçɛkapaʦiˌtɛːt] die <–, –en> hard disk space Speicherkapazität auf der Festplatte **5.** *(outer)* space der Weltraum [deːɐ 'vɛltraͻm] <–(e)s> *no pl* ◊ *den Weltraum erforschen* ◆ *einen Satelliten/eine Sonde in den Weltraum schießen* in space im Weltraum **6.** *(three-dimensional)* Raum [raͻm] der <–(e)s, Räume> ◊ *eine Reise durch Raum und Zeit* **7.** *(between words)* Leerstelle ['leːɐʃtɛlə] die <–, –n>; *(between lines)* Leerzeile ['leːɐʦaɛlə] die <–, –n> **8.** *(freedom)* Freiraum ['fraɛraͻm] der <–(e)s, Freiräume> ◊ *Das Kind braucht viel Freiraum.* **9.** space of time Zeitraum ['ʦaɛtraͻm] der <–(e)s, Zeiträume> in a short space of time in kurzer Zeit [ɪn kʊʳtsɐ 'ʦaɛt] in the space of innerhalb von [ɪnɛhalp fͻn] ◊ *Innerhalb von wenigen Sekunden fand sie die Informationen im Internet.* ⊚ stare into space ins Leere starren
space bar [noun] Leertaste ['leːɐtastə] die <–, –n> ◊ *Sie drückte auf die Leertaste.*
spacious(ly) [adj, adv] geräumig [gə'rͻɡmɪç] ◊ *Der Raum war hell und geräumig.* ◆ *ein geräumiges Badezimmer* ◆ *eine geräumig angelegte Wohnung*
spade [noun] **1.** *(tool)* Spaten ['ʃpaːtn̩] der <–s, –> ◊ *mit einem Spaten ein Loch graben* **2.** *(toy)* Schaufel ['ʃaͻfl̩] die <–, –n> ◊ *Die Kinder gingen mit Schaufel und Eimer an den Strand.* **3.** *(playing card)* Pik [piːk] das <–s, –> ◊ *Er spielte ein kleines Pik aus.* spades Pik [piːk] sing ◊ *Pik war Trumpf.* ⊚ call a spade a spade die Dinge beim Namen nennen
spaghetti [noun] Spaghetti, Spagetti [ʃpa'ɡɛtiː] die <–> *only pl* ◊ *Sie isst gern Spaghetti.* ◆ *Spaghetti mit Tomatensoße*
Spain [noun] Spanien ['ʃpaːniən] das <–s> *article only in combination with attribute, no pl* → **Germany**
Spaniard [noun] Spanier ['ʃpaːniɐ] der <–s, –> ◊ ♀Spanierin ['ʃpaːniɐɪn] die <–, –nen> → **German¹ 1.**
Spanish¹ [noun] Spanisch ['ʃpaːnɪʃ] das <–(s)> *no pl* → **German¹ 2.**
Spanish² [adj] spanisch ['ʃpaːnɪʃ] → **German²**
spare¹ [adj] **1.** *(extra, additional)* zusätzlich ['ʦuːzɛtslɪç] *no comp/superl* ◊ *Ich habe für meine Taschenlampe immer eine zusätzliche Batterie dabei.* a spare pair of glasses eine Ersatzbrille ['ɛɐzaʦbrɪlə] <–, –n> spare clothes Kleider zum Wechseln [klaͻdɐ tsʊm 'vɛksln̩] **2.** *(available)* verfügbar [fɛ'fyːkbaːʳ] ◊ *Jedes verfügbare Plätzchen war belegt.* spare bedroom Gästezimmer ['ɡɛstatsɪmɐ] das <–s, –> spare change Kleingeld ['klaɛnɡɛlt] das <–s, –> *no pl*

⊚ be going spare übrig sein go spare ausrasten *(fam)*
spare² [verb] **1.** *(be able to give)* sb can spare sb/sth jd kann jdn/etw. entbehren [kan ... ɛnt,beːrən] <kann, konnte, hat können> ◊ *Ein paar Euro im Monat kann jeder entbehren.* ◆ *Wir können derzeit keinen einzigen Mitarbeiter entbehren.* Can you spare ...? Können Sie mir ... geben? **2.** *(have available)* spare an hour etc. eine Stunde etc. Zeit haben [aɛnə ʃtʊndə 'ʦaɛt haːbm̩] +haben ◊ *Hast du Freitag vielleicht eine Stunde Zeit, um mir zu helfen?* They arrived at the theatre with five minutes to spare. Sie kamen fünf Minuten von Beginn der Vorstellung am Theater an. spare sb a moment sich für jdn einen Moment Zeit nehmen [fyːɐ ... aɛnən momɛnt 'ʦaɛt neːmən] <nimmt, nahm, hat genommen> **3.** spare sb sth jdm etw. ersparen [eɐ'ʃpaːrən] <erspart, ersparte, hat erspart> ◊ *Durch seine Hilfe hat er mir viel Mühe erspart.* ◆ *Erspare mir doch bitte die Einzelheiten!* sb is spared sth jdm bleibt etw. erspart ◊ *Es blieb ihm erspart, die Leiche zu identifizieren.* **4.** *(not harm sb/sth)* verschonen [fɛ'ʃoːnən] <verschont, verschonte, hat verschont> ◊ *ein unschuldiges Opfer verschonen* ◆ *Der Orkan hat den südlichen Teil des Landes verschont.* ◆ *jds Leben verschonen* ⊚ have sth to spare etw. übrig haben
spare part [noun] Ersatzteil [e'zaʦtaɛl] das <–(e)s, –e>
spare time [noun] Freizeit ['fraɛtsaɛt] die <–> *no pl* ◊ *Er hat sehr viel Freizeit.* ◆ *In ihrer Freizeit lernt sie Italienisch.*
spark¹ [noun] **1.** *(piece of burning material, flash of light)* Funke ['fʊŋkə] der <–ns, –n> ◊ *Funken sprühten, als die Lok scharf bremste.* Sparks fly. Die Funken fliegen. **2.** *(liveliness)* Schwung [ʃvʊn] der <–(e)s> *no pl* ◊ *Die Vorstellung/Der Film hat keinen Schwung.* **3.** *(of an emotion)* a tiny spark of sth ein Fünkchen ... [aɛn 'fʊŋkçən] <–s, –> ◊ *In ihren Augen blitzte ein Fünkchen Wut/Interesse/Hoffnung auf.* **4.** *(cause)* Auslöser ['aͻsløːze] der <–s, –> ◊ *Der Auslöser des Streiks war die Entlassung dreier Mitarbeiter.*
spark² [verb] auslösen ['aͻsløːzn̩] +haben ◊ *Die geplante Maßnahme löste eine Protestwelle aus.*
sparkle [verb] **1.** *(shine)* funkeln ['fʊŋkl̩n] +haben ◊ *Der Schnee funkelt in der Sonne.* ◆ *Seine Augen funkelten vor Vergnügen/Begeisterung.* **2.** *(be lively)* sparkle (with sth) *(vor etw.)* sprühen ['ʃpryːən] +haben ◊ *Seine Memoiren sprühen vor Geist und Witz.*
sparkling wine [noun] Sekt [zɛkt] der <–(e)s, –e>
sparrow [noun] Spatz [ʃpaʦ] der <–en, –en>
sparse(ly) [adj, adv] spärlich ['ʃpɛːɡlɪç] ◊ *spärlicher Bewuchs* ◆ *Die Informationen dazu sind spärlich.* ◆ *eine spärlich möblierte Wohnung* sparsely populated dünn besiedelt [dyn ba'ziːdl̩t]
spatial(ly) [adj, adv] räumlich ['rͻɡmlɪç] *no comp/superl* ◊ *sein räumliches Vorstellungsvermögen* ◆ *Die wurden zeitlich und räumlich voneinander getrennt.*
speak [verb] **1.** *(talk, say, in a particular language)* sprechen ['ʃprɛçn̩] <spricht, sprach, hat gesprochen> ◊ *ein bisschen langsamer/lauter sprechen* ◆ *Sprich doch nicht so abfällig darüber.* ◆ *Sie haben einen Papagei, der einige Wörter spricht.* ◆ *mehrere Sprachen fließend sprechen* ◆ *Ich spreche leider*

kein/nicht Spanisch. speak to sb, speak with sb mit jdm sprechen ◊ *Kann ich bitte mit Herrn Meier sprechen?* ✦ *Ich werde mit ihr sprechen und sie fragen, ob sie mitkommen will.* speak (well/badly) of sb (gut/schlecht) über jdn sprechen speak against sth sich gegen etw. aussprechen ['geːgn̩ ... ˌaʊsʃprɛçn̩] +*haben* ◊ *Er sprach sich gegen den Vorschlag aus.* **2.** *(describe)* speak of sth, speak about sth etw. beschreiben [bəˈʃraɪbm̩] <beschreibt, beschrieb, hat beschrieben> ◊ *Die Dorfbewohner beschrieben eine meterhohe Welle, die ihre Häuser verschlang.* **3.** *(give a speech)* speak (to sb) (vor jdm) eine Rede halten [aɛnə ˈreːdə haltn̩] <hält, hielt, hat gehalten> ◊ *Er wird bei der Eröffnungsfeier eine kurze Rede halten.* ✦ *Sie hielt eine Rede vor 200 Geschäftsleuten.* **4.** *(on the telephone)* sprechen [ʃprɛçn̩] <spricht, sprach, hat gesprochen> Who's speaking? Mit wem spreche ich? This is Anne speaking. Hier spricht Anne. Speaking. Am Apparat.

ⓢ not be on speaking terms nicht miteinander reden generally speaking im Allgemeinen speaking as sb als jd ◊ *Als Minister muss ich diese Reform in Schutz nehmen.* speak for itself für sich sprechen speak for yourself das gilt vielleicht für dich nothing to speak of kaum etwas speaking of ... wo wir gerade von ... reden so to speak sozusagen
* **speak for** [phras v] speak for sb/sth für jdn/etw. sprechen [fyːɐ̯ ... ʃprɛçn̩] <spricht, sprach, hat gesprochen> ◊ *Ich spreche sicher auch für die anderen Kollegen, wenn ich sage, dass ...*
* **speak of** [phras v] speak of sth von etw. zeugen [fɔn ... ˌtsɔʏɡn̩] +*haben* (lofty) ◊ *Die vielen Musikinstrumente zeugen von seiner Sammelleidenschaft.*
* **speak out** [phras v] speak out in favo(u)r of sth für etw. eintreten [fyːɐ̯ ... ˌaɛntreːtn̩] <tritt ein, trat ein, ist eingetreten> speak out against sth sich gegen etw. aussprechen ['geːgn̩ ... ˌaʊsʃprɛçn̩] <spricht sich aus, sprach sich aus, hat sich ausgesprochen>
* **speak to** [phras v] speak to sb (about sth) mit jdm (über etw. [acc]) reden [mɪt ... ˌreːdn̩] +*haben* ◊ *Du solltest mal mit ihr über den ständigen Lärm reden.*
* **speak up** [phras v] **1.** *(talk louder)* lauter sprechen ['laʊtɐ ʃprɛçn̩] <spricht, sprach, hat gesprochen> ◊ *Können Sie bitte etwas lauter sprechen?* **2.** *(say what you think)* seine Meinung sagen [zaɛnə ˈmaɛnʊŋ zaːgn̩] +*haben*
* **speak up for** [phras v] speak up for sb/sth sich für jdn/etw. einsetzen [fyːɐ̯ ... ˌaɛnzɛtsn̩] +*haben*

speaker [noun] **1.** *(person giving a speech)* Redner ['reːdnɐ] der <-s, -> ♀Rednerin ['reːdnərɪn] die <-, -nen> ◊ *Wir erwarten folgende Redner zur Konferenz: ...* **2.** *(person who talks, of a language)* Sprecher ['ʃprɛçɐ] der <-s, -> ♀Sprecherin ['ʃprɛçərɪn] die <-, -nen> ◊ *Man kann hören, dass der Sprecher aufgeregt ist.* ✦ *ein einsprachiges Wörterbuch für fremdsprachliche/muttersprachliche Sprecher* an English speaker jemand, der Englisch spricht ['jeːmant deːɐ̯ 'ɛŋlɪʃ ʃprɪçt] a native speaker of German ein deutscher Muttersprachler [aɛn ˌdɔʏtʃɐ 'mʊtɐʃpraːxlɐ] <-s, -> ♀eine deutsche Muttersprachlerin [aɛn ˌdɔʏtʃə 'mʊtɐʃpraːxlərɪn] <-, -nen> **3.** *(piece of stereo equipment)* Lautspre-

cher ['laʊtʃprɛçɐ] der <-s, ->
special [adj] **1.** *(different from usual)* besondere [bəˈzɔndərə] no comp/superl, only before ns <ein besonderer ..., eine besonderes ...> ◊ *Sie hat ein besonderes Talent.* ✦ *Er ist ein ganz besonderer Freund.* ✦ besondere Umstände make a special effort sich [dat] besonders viel Mühe geben [bəˈzɔndəs fiːl ˌmyːə geːbm̩] take special care besonders vorsichtig sein [bəˌzɔndəs ˈfoːɐ̯zɪçtɪç zaɛn] **2.** be special to sb jdm besonders viel bedeuten [bəˈzɔndəs fiːl bəˌdɔʏtn̩] <bedeutet, bedeutete, hat bedeutet> **3.** *(unique to a person, group etc.)* eigene ['aɛgənə] no comp/superl, only before ns <ein eigener ..., eine eigene ..., ein eigenes ...> ◊ *Da hat er seine eigenen Methoden.* ✦ *Sie macht das auf ihre eigene Weise.* **4.** *(exceptional)* Sonder... ['zɔndɐ] special permission Sondergenehmigung ['zɔndəgəˌneːmɪgʊŋ] die <-, -en>
specialist¹ [noun] Fachmann ['faxman] der <-(e)s, Fachleute> ♀Fachfrau ['faxfraʊ] die <-, -en> ◊ *ein anerkannter Fachmann* ✦ *Ein externer Fachmann wurde beigezogen.* electronics specialist Fachmann für Elektronik
specialist² [adj] Fach... [fax] specialist knowledge Fachwissen ['faxvɪsn̩] das <-s> no pl specialist shops Fachhandel ['faxhandl̩] der <-s> no pl ◊ *nur im Fachhandel erhältlich*
speciality [noun] **1.** *(food, drink)* Spezialität [ʃpetsjaliˈtɛːt] die <-, -en> ◊ *Der Käse ist eine regionale Spezialität.* **2.** *(subject, field)* Spezialgebiet [ʃpeˈtsjaːlgəbiːt] das <-(e)s>
specialize [verb] sich spezialisieren [ʃpetsjaliˈziːrən] <spezialisiert sich, spezialisierte sich, hat sich spezialisiert> ◊ *Viele Schüler spezialisieren sich zu früh.* specialize in sth sich auf etw. [acc] spezialisiert haben ◊ *Das Reisebüro hat sich auf Fernreisen spezialisiert.*
specialized → specialize [adj] spezialisiert [ʃpetsjaliˈziːɐ̯t] ◊ *eine spezialisierte Software;* Spezial... [ʃpeˈtsjaːl] specialized training Spezialausbildung [ʃpeˈtsjaːlˌaʊsbɪldʊŋ] die <-, -en>
specially [adv] **1.** *(especially)* speziell [ʃpeˈtsjɛl] no comp/superl ◊ *speziell ausgebildetes Personal* ✦ *Den Kuchen habe ich speziell für dich gebacken.* **2.** *(particularly)* besonders [bəˈzɔndəs] no comp/superl ◊ *Das hat mir besonders gefallen.*
special offer [noun] Sonderangebot ['zɔndəˌangəboːt] das <-(e)s, -e> ◊ *Spargel gibt es zurzeit im Sonderangebot.*
species [noun] Art [aːɐ̯t] die <-, -en> ◊ *die Rote Liste der gefährdeten Arten* species of insects Insektenart [ɪnˈzɛktn̩ˌaːɐ̯t] the human species der Mensch [deːɐ̯ ˈmɛnʃ] <-en>
specific [adj] **1.** *(certain, particular)* bestimmt [bəˈʃtɪmt] no comp/superl ◊ *etw. in einer bestimmten Reihenfolge machen* **2.** *(limited)* be specific to sb/sth sich nur auf jdn/etw. beziehen [nuːɐ̯ aɔf ... bətsiːən] <bezieht sich, bezog sich, hat sich bezogen> ◊ *Seine Kenntnisse beziehen sich nur auf den japanischen Markt.* **3.** *(exact, precise)* genau [gəˈnaʊ] <genauer, am genau(e)sten> ◊ *eine genaue Anleitung*
specifically [adv] **1.** *(for one particular thing)* eigens ['aɛgn̩s] ◊ *Ich habe das Kostüm eigens für diesen Anlass gekauft.* **2.** *(exactly, precisely)* genau [gəˈnaʊ] <genauer, am genau(e)sten> ◊ *Antworten Sie so genau wie möglich.* **3.** *(more exactly)* genauer gesagt

A B C D E F G H I J K L M N O P Q R S T U V W X Y Z

[gə'naọe gəzaːkt] ◊ *Wir wohnen schon zehn Jahre hier, genauer gesagt, seit 1995.*

specification [noun] Spezifikation [ʃpetsifika'tsioːn] die <–, –en>

specified [adj] bestimmt [bəʃtɪmt] *no comp/superl* ◊ *Er musste sich zu einer bestimmten Zeit melden.*

specify [verb] angeben ['angeːbm̩] <gibt an, gab an, hat angegeben> ◊ *Bitte geben Sie Ihr Geburtsdatum und Ihren Geburtsort an.*

specimen [noun] 1. *(sample)* Probe ['proːbə] die <–, –n> blood specimen, specimen of blood Blutprobe ['bluːtproːbə] 2. *(example)* Exemplar [ɛksɛm'plaːʳ] das <–s, –e> ◊ *ein besonders schönes Exemplar*

specs [noun] Brille ['brɪlə] die <–, –n> ◊ *Ohne Brille kann ich nichts lesen.* ♦ *eine Brille tragen*

spectacle [noun] 1. *(event)* Schauspiel ['ʃaọʃpiːl] das <–(e)s, –e> ◊ *ein Schauspiel der Natur; (sight)* Anblick ['anblɪk] der <–(e)s, –e> ◊ *ein unvergesslicher Anblick* 2. *(impressive public event)* Spektakel [ʃpɛk'taːkl̩] das <–s, –> ◊ *ein buntes/farbenprächtiges/unterhaltsames Spektakel* ♦ *Wann soll das Spektakel beginnen?*

spectacles [noun] Brille ['brɪlə] die <–, –n> ◊ *Ich brauche eine stärkere Brille.* a pair of spectacles eine Brille

spectacular [adj] 1. *(very impressive)* spektakulär [ʃpɛktaku'lɛːɐ̯] ◊ *ein spektakulärer Anblick* ♦ *Ihre neue Show ist spektakulär.* 2. *(attracting a lot of attention)* sensationell [zɛnzatsio'nɛl] ◊ *ein sensationeller Erfolg* ♦ *Das Wahlergebnis war sensationell.*

spectator [noun] Zuschauer ['tsuːʃaọe] der <–s, –> ♀Zuschauerin ['tsuːʃaọǝrɪn] die <–, –nen>

spectrum [noun] Spektrum ['ʃpɛktrʊm] das <–s, Spektren> a broad spectrum of sth ein breites Spektrum von etw. [dat] ◊ *Wir bieten ein breites Spektrum von Tapeten an.*; *(of colo(u)r)* Farbspektrum ['faʳpˌʃpɛktrʊm]

speculate [verb] spekulieren [ʃpeku'liːrən] <spekuliert, spekulierte, hat spekuliert> ◊ *Ich weiß es nicht genau; ich kann nur spekulieren, warum er das gemacht hat.* ♦ *Er spekuliert an der Börse.* speculate on sth über etw. [acc] spekulieren ◊ *Wir können über seine Gründe nur spekulieren.* speculate that vermuten, dass [fɛ'muːtn̩ das] <vermutet, vermutete, hat vermutet> ◊ *Sie vermuten, dass er aus privaten Gründen kündigt.*

speculation [noun] Spekulation [ʃpekula'tsioːn] die <–, –en> ◊ *Es gibt viele Spekulationen über sein Privatleben.* ♦ *Das ist reine Spekulation.*

speech [noun] 1. *(in front of an audience)* Rede ['reːdə] die <–, –n> make a speech eine Rede halten ◊ *Anlässlich des Betriebsjubiläums hielt er eine Rede.* 2. THEAT Monolog [mono'loːk] der <–(e)s, –e> ◊ *der Monolog des Königs im ersten Akt* 3. *(faculty)* Sprechen ['ʃprɛçn̩] das <–s> *no pl* ◊ *Sie hatte Probleme mit dem Sprechen.* power of speech Sprechfähigkeit ['ʃprɛçfɛːɪçkaọt] die <–> *no pl* ◊ *Nach der Operation hat sie die Sprechfähigkeit verloren.* 4. *(spoken language)* Sprache ['ʃpraːxə] die <–, –n>; *(in compound ns)* speech ... Sprach... ['ʃpraːx] speech development Sprachentwicklung ['ʃpraːxˌlɛntvɪklʊŋ] die <–, –en> speech disorder Sprachstörung ['ʃpraːxˌʃtøːrʊŋ] die <–, –en>

speechless [adj] sprachlos ['ʃpraːxloːs] <sprachloser, am sprachlosesten> be (left) speechless sprachlos

sein ◊ *Als sie das hörte, war sie sprachlos.* leave sb speechless jdm die Sprache verschlagen [diː 'ʃpraːxə fɛʃlaːgn̩] <verschlägt, verschlug, hat verschlagen> ◊ *Der Vorfall hatte allen die Sprache verschlagen.*

speed[1] [noun] 1. *(rate at which sth moves)* Geschwindigkeit [gə'ʃvɪndɪçkaẹt] die <–, –en> ◊ *eine Geschwindigkeit von 130 km/h* at speed mit hoher Geschwindigkeit pick up speed an Geschwindigkeit zulegen top speed Höchstgeschwindigkeit ['høːçstgəˌʃvɪndɪçkaẹt] 2. *(gear)* Gang [gaŋ] der <–(e)s, Gänge> ◊ *Das Fahrrad hat 21 Gänge.* 3. FOTO *(shutter)* speed Belichtungszeit [bə'lɪçtʊŋstsaẹt] die <–, –en> ⊛ up to speed (on sth) (über etw. [acc]) auf dem Laufenden

speed[2] [verb] 1. *(move fast)* rasen ['raːzn̩] +sein *(fam)* ◊ *Alle rasten zum neuen Einkaufszentrum.* speed away davonrasen [da'fɔnraːzn̩] +sein *(fam)* ◊ *Der Wagen raste davon.* 2. *(take sb somewhere fast)* speed sb somewhere jdn irgendwohin bringen ['brɪŋən] <bringt, brachte, hat gebracht> ◊ *Die U-Bahn bringt Sie in zehn Minuten ins Zentrum.* 3. *(move or drive too fast)* zu schnell fahren [tsuː 'ʃnɛl faːrən] <fährt, fuhr, ist gefahren> ◊ *Er ist wieder einmal zu schnell gefahren und geblitzt worden.* • speed up [phras v] *(become faster)* schneller werden ['ʃnɛlɐ veːdn̩] +sein ◊ *Die DSL-Internetverbindung wird schneller.*; *(make sth faster, drive faster)* beschleunigen [bə'ʃlɔẏnɪgn̩] <beschleunigt, beschleunigte, hat beschleunigt> ◊ *Auf der Autobahn beschleunigte er.* ♦ *einen Prozess beschleunigen*

speedily [adv] schnell [ʃnɛl] ◊ *Er hat sich schnell wieder erholt.*

speed limit [noun] Geschwindigkeitsbegrenzung [gə'ʃvɪndɪçkaẹtsbəgrɛntsʊŋ] die <–, –en> ◊ *Hier gilt eine Geschwindigkeitsbegrenzung von 30 km/h.*

speedometer [noun] Tacho ['taxoː] der <–s, –s> *(fam)* ◊ *Was zeigt der Tacho an?*

speedy [adj] schnell [ʃnɛl] ◊ *eine schnelle Verwirklichung der Reform* ♦ *Der Server ist schnell und zuverlässig.*

spell[1] [noun] 1. *(time spent in a place)* Aufenthalt ['aọfn̩thalt] der <–(e)s, –e> spell in hospital Krankenhausaufenthalt ['kraŋkn̩haọsˌaọfn̩thalt]; *(time spent doing sth)* Zeit [tsaẹt] die <–, –en> ◊ *Nach einer kurzen Zeit bei der Marine wurde er Börsenmakler.* 2. METEO cold spell Kältewelle ['kɛltəvɛlə] die <–, –n> hot spell Hitzewelle ['hɪtsəvɛlə] dry spell Trockenheit ['trɔkn̩haẹt] die <–> *no pl* wet spell Regenwetter ['reːgn̩vɛtɐ] das <–s> *no pl* 3. MED *(of magic)* a spell of flu etc. Grippe etc. haben ['grɪpə haːbm̩] +haben dizzy spell Schwindelanfall ['ʃvɪndl̩ˌanfal] der <–(e)s, Schwindelanfälle> fainting spell Ohnmachtsanfall ['oːnmaxtsˌanfal] 4. *(powerful influence)* Bann [ban] der <–(e)s> *no pl* fall under sb's spell in jds Bann gezogen werden cast a spell on sb jdn in seinen Bann ziehen 5. *(of magic)* Zauber ['tsaọbe] der <–s, –> *most lying of* ◊ *ein böser Zauber* break the spell den Zauber brechen cast a spell on sb jdn verzaubern [fɛ'tsaọbern] <verzaubert, verzauberte, hat verzaubert>

spell[2] [verb] 1. *(say letters in the correct order)* spell sth etw. buchstabieren [buːxʃta'biːrən] <buchstabiert, buchstabierte, hat buchstabiert> ◊ *Können Sie das*

bitte buchstabieren? sth spells ... etw. buchstabiert man ... [buːxʃtaˈbiːɐ̯t man] ◊ *Zug buchstabiert man Z-U-G.* **2.** *(write letters in the correct order)* schreiben [ˈʃraɛ̯bm̩] <schreibt, schrieb, hat geschrieben> ◊ *Wie schreibt man Ihren Namen?* ♦ *Das Wort schreibt man mit ß'.* **3.** *(mean)* bedeuten [bəˈdɔɐ̯tn̩] <bedeutet, bedeutete, hat bedeutet> ◊ *Dies bedeutete das Aus für die Firma.* spell trouble (for sb/sth) (für jdn/etw.) nichts Gutes bedeuten spell disaster (for sb/sth) verheerende Folgen (für jdn/etw.) haben [fe,heˈrəndə ˈfɔlgn̩ haːbm̩] +haben **4.** *(in the US: stand in for sb)* ablösen [ˈapløːzn̩] +haben ◊ *Sie löste ihn für einige Stunden ab.*

spelling ‹noun› Rechtschreibung [ˈrɛçtʃraɛ̯bʊŋ] die <-> no pl ◊ *Probleme mit der Rechtschreibung haben*

spend ‹verb› **1.** *(use up, invest, money)* ausgeben [ˈaɔsgeːbm̩] <gibt aus, gab aus, hat ausgegeben> ◊ *Ich habe heute viel Geld ausgegeben.* spend sth on sth etw. für etw. ausgeben spend sth doing etw etw. dafür ausgeben, etw. zu tun ◊ *Ich habe 500 Euro dafür ausgegeben, meinen Computer aufzurüsten.; (time, energy)* aufwenden [ˈaɔfvɛndn̩] <wendet auf, wendete/wandte auf, hat aufgewendet/aufgewandt> spend sth on sth etw. für etw. aufwenden ◊ *Wir haben viel Zeit und Energie für den Erfolg dieses Projekts aufgewendet.* **2.** *(a period of time, your holidays)* verbringen [feˈbrɪŋən] <verbringt, verbrachte, hat verbracht> ◊ *auf Capri eine wunderschöne Zeit verbringen* spend sth with sb etw. mit jdm verbringen ◊ *Ich verbringe Weihnachten mit meinen Eltern.* spend sth doing (with sb) etw. damit verbringen, etw. (mit jdm.) zu tun ◊ *Ich habe den ganzen Abend damit verbracht, mit ihm Englisch zu üben.* spend time with sb Zeit mit jdm verbringen

spending ‹noun› *(money spent)* Ausgaben [ˈaɔsgaːbm̩] die <-> pl defence/health spending Ausgaben für Verteidigung/Gesundheit government spending Staatsausgaben [ˈʃtaːtsˌaɔsgaːbm̩]; *(budget)* spending plan Haushaltsplan [ˈhaɔshaltsplaːn] der <-(e)s, Haushaltspläne>

sperm ‹noun› **1.** *(cell)* Samenzelle [ˈzaːmənt͡sɛlə] die <-, -n> **2.** *(semen)* Sperma [ˈʃpɛrmaː] das <-s, -s> most sing

sphere ‹noun› **1.** *(ball)* Kugel [ˈkuːgl̩] die <-, -n> **2.** *(area, group)* Bereich [bəˈraɛ̯ç] der <-(e)s, -e> the political/scientific sphere der Bereich der Politik/Wissenschaft the domestic sphere der häusliche Bereich sphere of influence Einflussbereich [ˈaɛ̯nflʊsbəraɛ̯ç] social sphere Gesellschaftsbereich [gəˈzɛlʃaftsbəraɛ̯ç]

spice ‹noun› **1.** *(added to food)* Gewürz [gəˈvʏrt͡s] das <-es, -e> ◊ *orientalische/scharfe Gewürze* **2.** *(fig)* Würze [ˈvʏrt͡sə] die <-, -n> ◊ *Sie wollte ihrem Leben mehr Würze geben.*

spicy ‹adj› pikant [piˈkant] <pikanter, am pikantesten> *(also fig)* ◊ *Die Soße/Suppe ist sehr pikant.* ♦ *ein pikanter Witz*

spider ‹noun› Spinne [ˈʃpɪnə] die <-, -n>

spill ‹verb› **1.** *(accidentally pour a liquid)* verschütten [feˈʃʏtn̩] <verschüttet, verschüttete, hat verschüttet> ◊ *(ein Glas) Wasser/Wein (auf dem Sofa) verschütten* spill blood Blut vergießen [ˈbluːt fegiːsn̩] <vergießt, vergoss, hat vergossen> **2.** *(accidentally flow out)* auslaufen [ˈaɔslaɔfn̩] <läuft aus, lief aus, ist ausgelau-

fen> ◊ *Aus dem Tank lief Öl aus.* **3.** *(throw)* spill sth somewhere etw. irgendwo verstreuen [feˈʃtrɔɐ̯ən] <verstreut, verstreute, hat verstreut> ◊ *Sie hat ihre Sachen in der ganzen Wohnung verstreut.* **4.** *(fall)* fallen [ˈfalən] <fällt, fiel, ist gefallen> ◊ *Das Holz fiel vom Laster.* **5.** *(people)* spill out of/from sth aus etw. strömen [aɔs ... ʃtrøːmən] <strömt, strömte, ist geströmt> ◊ *Nach dem Konzert strömten die Zuschauer aus dem Saal.* **6.** *(light)* spill into sth etw. durchfluten [dʊrˈçfluːtn̩] <durchflutet, durchflutete, hat durchflutet> ◊ *Sonnenlicht durchflutete den Raum.*

spin ‹verb› **1.** *(turn round or cause to turn)* spin sth an etw. ‹dat› drehen [an ... ˌdreːən] +haben ◊ *an einem Rad drehen* sb/sth spins jd/etw. dreht sich My head is spinning. Mir dreht sich alles. sb/sth spins in circles jd/etw. dreht sich im Kreis sth spins on its axis etw. dreht sich um seine eigene Achse; *(washing machine)* schleudern [ˈʃlɔɐ̯dɐn] +haben ◊ *Die Wäsche ist gleich fertig, die Maschine schleudert schon.; (person, suddenly)* spin round herumfahren [hɛˈrʊmfaːrən] <fährt herum, fuhr herum, ist herumgefahren> ◊ *Als er ihre Stimme hörte, fuhr er herum.* **2.** *(produce a thread)* spinnen [ˈʃpɪnən] <spinnt, spann, hat gesponnen> ◊ *Meine Großmutter konnte noch spinnen.* ♦ *Die Spinne spinnt ein Netz.* **3.** *(present information)* spin sth etw. günstig darstellen [ˈgʏnstɪç ˌdaˈʃtɛlən] +haben ◊ *Der Pressesprecher versuchte, den Vorfall günstig darzustellen.* **4.** *(go fast)* spin away wegrasen [ˈvɛkraːzn̩] +sein *(fam)* ◊ *Er ist auf seinem Fahrrad weggerast.* spin past vorbeirasen [foːɐ̯ˈbaɛ̯raːzn̩] +sein *(fam)* **5.** *(a story)* erfinden [eˈfɪndn̩] <erfindet, erfand, hat erfunden> ◊ *eine Geschichte erfinden*

• **spin off** ‹phras v› **1.** spin off a product ein Nebenprodukt entwickeln [aɛ̯n ˈneːbm̩proˌdʊkt ɛntvɪkl̩n] <entwickelt, entwickelte, hat entwickelt> spin off a TV show einen Spin-off produzieren [aɛ̯nən ˈspɪnˌɔf produˌt͡siːrən] <produziert, produzierte, hat produziert> **2.** *(company)* ausgliedern [ˈaɔsgliːdɐn] +haben ◊ *Ein Teil der Firma wird ausgegliedert.*

• **spin out** ‹phras v› in die Länge ziehen [ɪn diː ˈlɛŋə t͡siːən] <zieht, zog, hat gezogen> ◊ *ein Gespräch in die Länge ziehen*

spinach ‹noun› Spinat [ʃpiˈnaːt] der <-(e)s, -e> ◊ *Spiegeleier mit Kartoffelbrei und Spinat*

spine ‹noun› **1.** ANAT Wirbelsäule [ˈvɪrbl̩zɔɐ̯lə] die <-, -n> **2.** *(of a book)* Rücken [ˈrʏkn̩] der <-s, -> **3.** *(sharp point)* Stachel [ˈʃtaxl̩] der <-s, -n> ◊ *die Stacheln des Igels/Stachelschweins* **4.** *(courage)* Rückgrat [ˈrʏkgraːt] das <-(e)s> no pl ◊ *Er hat kein Rückgrat.*

spiral ‹noun› Spirale [ʃpiˈraːlə] die <-, -n> *(also fig)* ◊ *Der Drachenflieger schraubte sich in Spiralen in die Höhe.* ♦ *eine Spirale der Gewalt*

spire ‹noun› Turmspitze [ˈtʊɐ̯mʃpɪt͡sə] die <-, -n>

spirit ‹noun› **1.** *(qualities, attitude, soul, imaginary creature)* Geist [gaɛ̯st] der <-(e)s, -er> ◊ *ein unabhängiger/kreativer Geist* ♦ *Sein Geist wird immer bei uns sein.* ♦ *böse Geister* community spirit Gemeinschaftsgeist [gəˈmaɛ̯nʃaftsgaɛ̯st] **2.** *(mood)* spirits Laune [ˈlaɔnə] die <-, -n> be in high spirits gute Laune haben lift sb's spirits jds Laune verbessern **3.** *(real meaning)* Sinn [zɪn] der <-(e)s> no pl ◊ *Der Sinn der Vereinbarung sollte nicht vergessen werden.* **4.** *(strong alcoholic drink)* Spirituose [ʃpiritu'oːzə] die

<-, -n> most pl ◊ *Sie kauften Spirituosen.; (purified alcohol)* reiner Alkohol [ˌraɛne ʔalˈkoho:l] <-s, -e> ◊ *Der reine Alkohol wird zur Desinfektion verwendet.*
spiritual [adj] **1.** *(related to the spirit)* spirituell [ʃpiriˈtuˈɛl] *no comp/superl, only before ns* ◊ *eine spirituelle Erfahrung* **2.** *(related to religion)* geistlich [ˈgaɛstlɪç] *no comp/superl, only before ns* ◊ *der geistliche Führer*
spit¹ [noun] **1.** *(saliva)* Spucke [ˈʃpʊkə] die <-> *no pl (fam)* ◊ *seinen Finger zum Umblättern mit Spucke anfeuchten* **2.** *(for roasting)* Spieß [ʃpiːs] der <-es, -e> ◊ *ein am Spieß gegrilltes Hähnchen* **3.** *(of land)* Landzunge [ˈlantsʊŋə] die <-, -n>
spit² [verb] **1.** *(spew)* spucken [ˈʃpʊkn̩] +haben ◊ *jdm ins Gesicht spucken* ♦ *einen Kaugummi auf den Boden spucken* spit out ausspucken [ˈaʊsʃpʊkn̩] +haben ◊ *einen Kirschkern ausspucken* ♦ *Die Maschine spuckt Bälle aus.* spit at anspucken [ˈanʃpʊkn̩] +haben ◊ *Sie hat ihn angespuckt.* **2.** *(mud)* spritzen [ˈʃprɪtsn̩] +haben ◊ *Der Schlamm spritzte, als er mit dem Auto durchfuhr.* **3.** *(in the UK: rain, rain)* tröpfeln [ˈtrœpfln̩] +haben ◊ *Nimm einen Schirm mit, es tröpfelt schon.* **4.** *(an insult)* spit (out) ausstoßen [ˈaʊsʃtoːsn̩] <stößt aus, stieß aus, hat ausgestoßen> ◊ *Er stieß eine Beleidigung aus und verließ den Raum.* spit out insults at sb jdm Beleidigungen entgegenschleudern [bəˈlaɛdɪɡʊŋən ɛntˌgeˈɡn̩ʃlɔɡdən] +haben
spite [noun] **1.** *(malice)* Bosheit [ˈboːshaɛt] die <-, -en> ◊ *Seine Bosheit kennt keine Grenzen.* out of spite aus reiner Bosheit **2.** *(despite)* in spite of trotz [trɔts] *sing nouns without article or attribute are not declined when following this prep, otherwise* [+gen] ◊ *Trotz aller Kritik ist diese Fernsehsendung sehr beliebt.* ♦ *Wir haben trotz des Regens einen Spaziergang gemacht.* in spite of doing sth obwohl jd etw. tut [ɔpˈvoːl] ◊ *Obwohl ich mich krank fühlte, ging ich zur Arbeit.*
➄ in spite of yourself gegen den eigenen Willen
spittle [noun] Speichel [ˈʃpaɛçl̩] der <-s> *no pl* ◊ *Der Kuh rann Speichel aus dem Maul.*
splash [verb] **1.** *(liquid)* spritzen [ˈʃprɪtsn̩] *transitive use* +haben/intransitive use +sein ◊ *Ein bisschen Wein ist auf die Tischdecke gespritzt.* splash sth on sth etw. auf etw. [acc] spritzen splash your face with water sich [dat] Wasser ins Gesicht spritzen sth splashes sth etw. spritzt gegen etw. ◊ *Das Regenwasser ist gegen das Auto gespritzt.* **2.** *(print)* splash sth on sth etw. groß auf etw. [acc] drucken [ˌgroːs aʊf ... ˌdrʊkn̩] +haben ◊ *Der Name des Designers war groß auf das T-Shirt gedruckt.; (in a newspaper)* be splashed across a page eine Seite beherrschen [aɛnə ˈzaɛtə bəˌhɛˈʃn̩] <beherrscht, beherrschte, hat beherrscht> ◊ *Die Nachricht beherrschte die Titelseite.*
• **splash about** [phras v] → **splash around**
• **splash around** [phras v] plantschen [ˈplantʃn̩] +haben ◊ *Die Kinder plantschten vergnügt im Wasser.*
• **splash out** [phras v] viel Geld ausgeben [fiːl ˈɡɛlt ˈaʊsɡeːbm̩] <gibt aus, gab aus, hat ausgegeben> splash out on sth viel Geld für etw. ausgeben ◊ *Sie hat gerade viel Geld für neue Schuhe ausgegeben.*
splendid(ly) [adj, adv] **1.** *(wonderful)* wundervoll [ˈvʊndɐfɔl] ◊ *ein wundervoller Sänger* ♦ *Das ist ja wundervoll!* ♦ *Sie hat wundervoll gesungen.*

2. *(impressive, beautiful)* prächtig [ˈprɛçtɪç] ◊ *eine prächtige Villa* ♦ *Das Wetter war prächtig.* ♦ *Wir haben uns ganz prächtig amüsiert.*
splendour, splendor [noun] **1.** *(of architecture)* Pracht [praxt] die <-> *no pl* ◊ *Nach der Restaurierung erstrahlt der Palast wieder in alter Pracht.* **2.** *(of expensive things or lifestyle)* Glanz [ɡlants] der <-es> *no pl* ◊ *Der Glanz der schönen Dinge beeindruckte ihn.*
splint [noun] Schiene [ˈʃiːnə] die <-, -n> ◊ *eine Schiene für das gebrochene Bein*
splinter [noun] Splitter [ˈʃplɪtɐ] der <-s, -> ◊ *einen Splitter im Finger haben*
split¹ [noun] **1.** *(division)* Aufteilung [ˈaʊftaɛlʊŋ] die <-, -en> ◊ *die Aufteilung in mehrere Gruppen* **2.** *(separation following a disagreement)* Spaltung [ˈʃpaltʊŋ] die <-, -en> ◊ *Die Spaltung der Partei stand kurz bevor.; (disagreement)* Unstimmigkeiten [ˈʊnʃtɪmɪçkaɛtn̩] die <-> *pl* split over sth Unstimmigkeiten über etw. [acc] **3.** *(in fabric)* Riss [rɪs] der <-es, -e> ◊ *ein Riss im Jackett* **4.** *(difference)* Unterschied [ˈʊntɐʃiːt] der <-(e)s, -e> ◊ *Zwischen ihren Einstellungen herrscht ein großer Unterschied.* **5.** SPORT the splits Spagat [ʃpaˈɡaːt] der <-(e)s, -e> ◊ *einen Spagat machen*
split² [verb] **1.** *(divide)* split (up) aufteilen [ˈaʊftaɛlən] +haben ◊ *Sie wurden in Gruppen aufgeteilt.* ♦ *Nach dem Krieg wurde Deutschland in vier Zonen aufgeteilt.* sb/sth splits jd/etw. teilt sich auf ◊ *Die Seminarteilnehmer teilten sich in kleine Arbeitsgruppen auf.* **2.** *(separate from an organization)* abspalten [ˈapʃpaltn̩] <spaltet sich ab, spaltete sich ab, hat sich abgespalten> ◊ *Die Gruppe spaltete sich von der Partei ab.* **3.** *(break up, share sth)* teilen [ˈtaɛlən] +haben ◊ *Sie teilten die Banane in vier Teile.* split sth between sb etw. unter jdm teilen ◊ *Die Süßigkeiten wurden unter den drei Kindern geteilt.* sth splits etw. lässt sich teilen [lɛst tsɪç ˈtaɛlən] <lässt, ließ, hat lassen> ◊ *Die Rückbank lässt sich teilen.* split the bill die [dat] die Rechnung teilen [diː ˈrɛçnʊŋ ˌtaɛlən] +haben; only pl **4.** *(tear)* aufreißen [ˈaʊfraɛsn̩] <reißt auf, riss auf, hat/ist aufgerissen> *transitive use* +haben/intransitive use +sein ◊ *Er hat seine Hose aufgerissen.* ♦ *Der Sack ist aufgerissen.* split your lip sich [dat] die Lippe aufschlagen [diː ˈlɪpə ˌaʊfʃlaːɡn̩] <schlägt sich auf, schlug sich auf, hat sich aufgeschlagen> **5.** abhauen [ˈaphaʊən] <haut ab, haute ab, ist abgehauen> *(fam)* ◊ *Ich muss abhauen.*
• **split up** [phras v] *(end a relationship)* sich trennen [ˈtrɛnən] +haben ◊ *Sie haben sich getrennt.* → **split²** **1.**
spoil [verb] **1.** *(ruin, go off)* verderben [fɛˈdɛˈbm̩] <verdirbt, verdarb, hat/ist verdorben> *transitive use* +haben/intransitive use +sein ◊ *Er hat mit seinem Benehmen den schönen Abend verdorben.* ♦ *Das Essen ist verdorben.* spoil sb's chances jds Chancen zunichte machen [ˌtsʊˈnɪçtə maxn̩] +haben **2.** *(allow a child too much)* verziehen [fɛˈtsiːən] <verzieht, verzog, hat verzogen> ◊ *Verzieh doch die Kinder nicht so!* spoil sb rotten jdn völlig verziehen; *(pamper)* verwöhnen [fɛˈvøːnən] <verwöhnt, verwöhnte, hat verwöhnt> ◊ *An ihrem Geburtstag wurde sie von allen verwöhnt.* **3.** *(in the UK: cancel a voting paper)* ungültig machen [ˈʊnɡʏltɪç maxn̩] +haben ◊ einen spoilt ungültig sein ◊ *Der Stimmzettel ist*

ungültig.

spoken → speak [adj] gesprochen [gə'ʃprɔxn̩] *no comp/superl, only before ns* ◊ *gesprochenes Englisch* ⊛ **spoken for 1.** *(not available)* besetzt **2.** *(in a relationship)* vergeben ◊ *Sie ist bereits vergeben.*

spokesman [noun] Sprecher ['ʃprɛçɐ] der <−s, −> **spokeswoman** [noun] Sprecherin ['ʃprɛçərɪn] die <−, −nen>

sponge [noun] **1.** *(sth you clean/wash with, animal)* Schwamm [ʃvam] der <−(e)s, Schwämme> ◊ *sich mit einem Schwamm einseifen* ♦ *Schwämme wachsen im Meer.* give sth a sponge etw. mit einem Schwamm waschen **2.** *(scrounger)* Schnorrer ['ʃnɔrɐ] der <−s, −> ♀Schnorrerin ['ʃnɔrərɪn] die <−, −nen> *(fam)* **3.** sponge (cake) Biskuitkuchen [bɪs'kviːtkuːxn̩] der <−s, −>

sponsor¹ [noun] **1.** *(of an event, athlete, a charity)* Sponsor ['ʃpɔnzoːɐ] der <−s, −en> ♀Sponsorin [ʃpɔn'zoːrɪn] die <−, −nen> ◊ *einen Sponsor finden* ♦ *Die Firma ist Sponsorin des Fußballverbandes.* **2.** *(a country etc. that supports an activity)* sb/sth is a sponsor of sth jd/etw. unterstützt etw. [ʊntɐ'ʃtʏtst] <unterstützt, unterstützte, hat unterstützt> ◊ *Das Land unterstützt den Terrorismus.* **3.** *(in parliament)* sb is the sponsor of a bill jd bringt eine Gesetzesvorlage ein [brɪŋt aͤnə gə'zɛtsəsfoːɐlaːgə aͤn] <bringt ein, brachte ein, hat eingebracht> *(tech)* **4.** *(guarantor)* Bürge ['bʏrɡə] der <−n, −n> ♀Bürgin ['bʏrɡɪn] die <−, −nen> ◊ *Er fungierte als Bürge für sie.* **5.** *(godparent, sb who supports a person in another country)* Pate ['paːtə] der <−n, −n> ♀Patin ['paːtɪn] die <−, −nen> ◊ *Sie ist Patin eines Kindes in Südamerika.*

sponsor² [verb] **1.** *(business etc.)* sponsern ['ʃpɔnzɐn] +haben ◊ *Die Firma sponsert ein Radrennteam; (government, NGO)* unterstützen [ʊntɐ'ʃtʏtsn̩] <unterstützt, unterstützte, hat unterstützt> ◊ *Die Regierung unterstützt dieses Projekt.* **2.** *(a person in a foreign country)* sponsor sb die Patenschaft für jdn übernommen haben [diː ˌpaːtn̩ʃaft fyːɐ ... ybəˌnɔmən haːbm̩] +haben **3.** *(a bill in parliament)* einbringen ['aͤnbrɪŋən] <bringt ein, brachte ein, hat eingebracht> *(tech)* ◊ *eine Gesetzesvorlage einbringen* **4.** *(accept responsibility for sb)* sponsor sb für jdn bürgen [fyːɐ ... ˌbʏrɡn̩] +haben ◊ *Sein Arbeitgeber bürgt für ihn.*

sponsorship [noun] Förderung ['fœrdərʊŋ] die <−, −en> ◊ *die Förderung der Kunst durch die Industrie*

spontaneous(ly) [adj] spontan [ʃpɔn'taːn] ◊ *ein spontaner Ausflug* ♦ *eine spontane Genveränderung* ♦ *Seine Reaktion war spontan.* ♦ *Ich bin ein spontaner Mensch.* ♦ *jdn spontan einladen*

spoon [noun] Löffel ['lœfl̩] der <−s, −> ◊ *Sie rührte mit dem Löffel in der Tasse.* ⊛ be born with a silver spoon in your mouth mit einem goldenen Löffel im Mund geboren sein *(fam)*

sport [noun] **1.** *(physical activity)* Sport [ʃpɔrt] der <−(e)s> *no pl* ◊ *Sport ist gesund.* ♦ *Fußball ist Deutschlands beliebtester Sport.* team sport Mannschaftssport ['manʃaftsʃpɔrt] sports day Sportfest ['ʃpɔrtfɛst] der <−(e)s, −e> sports section Sportteil ['ʃpɔrttaͤl] der <−(e)s, −e> **2.** *(reliable person)* be a good/real sport schwer in Ordnung sein [ʃveːɐ ɪn 'ɔrdnʊŋ zaͤn] *(fam)* ◊ *Sie ist schwer in*

Ordnung. **3.** *(in the US: form of address for a boy or man)* Sportsfreund ['ʃpɔrtsfrɔͷnt] der <−(e)s, −e> *(fam)* ◊ *Na, Sportsfreund, wie geht's?* **4.** *(variety)* Varietät [varie'tɛːt] die <−, −en> ◊ *Die Schalotte ist eine Varietät der Zwiebel.*

sportsmanlike [adj] sportlich ['ʃpɔrtlɪç] ◊ *sportliches Verhalten* ♦ *Das war sehr sportlich von dir.*

sporty [adj] sportlich ['ʃpɔrtlɪç] ◊ *Er ist sportlich und spielt gern Basketball.* ♦ *sportliche Kleidung* ♦ *ein sportliches Auto*

spot¹ [noun] **1.** *(particular place)* Stelle ['ʃtɛlə] die <−, −n> ◊ *eine empfindliche Stelle* ♦ *An dieser Stelle wachsen Pilze.* ♦ *eine Stelle im Text* mark the spot die Stelle markieren; *(town, area)* Ort [ɔrt] der <−(e)s> ◊ *Der Ort ist bei Touristen sehr beliebt.* tourist spot Urlaubsort ['uːɐlaopsˌɔrt]; *(bar)* night spot Nachtlokal ['naxtloˌkaːl] das <−s, −e> **2.** *(of colour)* Punkt [pʊŋkt] der <−(e)s, −e> ◊ *eine Blüte mit roten Punkten* **3.** *(pimple)* Pickel ['pɪkl̩] der <−s, −> ◊ *Er hat viele Pickel.; (chickenpox etc.)* Pustel ['pʊstl̩] die <−, −n> ◊ *Mein ganzer Körper war mit Pusteln bedeckt.* **4.** *(of dirt)* Fleck [flɛk] der <−(e)s, −en or −e> ◊ *Die Flecken sind beim Waschen nicht herausgegangen.* **5.** *(in a competition etc.)* Platz [plats] der <−es, Plätze> ◊ *Sie konnten keinen guten Platz erreichen.* **6.** *(in TV schedule)* Sendezeit ['zɛndətsaͤt] die <−, −en> **7.** *(a little bit)* a spot of ein bisschen [aͤn 'bɪsçən] a spot of trouble ein bisschen Ärger ◊ *Er hatte ein bisschen Ärger mit seinen Eltern wegen der Feier.* a spot of lunch eine Kleinigkeit zum Essen [aͤnə ˌklaͤnɪçkaͤt tsʊm 'ɛsn̩] der <−, −en> **8.** *(difficulty)* a (tight) spot Schwierigkeiten ['ʃviːrɪçkaͤtn̩] die <−> *pl* put sb in a spot jdn in Schwierigkeiten bringen **9.** *(light)* Spot [spɔt] der <−s, −s> *(fam)* ◊ *den Spot einschalten* **10.** *(of liquid)* Tropfen ['trɔpfn̩] der <−s, −> ◊ *Ich habe einige Tropfen abbekommen.* ⊛ have a soft spot for sb eine Schwäche für jdn haben frozen to the spot wie versteinert hit the spot genau richtig sein ◊ *Ein bisschen Shopping wäre jetzt genau richtig.* put sb on the spot jdn in Verlegenheit bringen on the spot **1.** *(where sth is happening)* an Ort und Stelle **2.** *(without moving forward, immediately)* auf der Stelle ◊ *auf der Stelle laufen* ♦ *Ladendiebe werden auf der Stelle angezeigt.*

spot² [verb] **1.** *(recognize, notice)* entdecken [ɛnt'dɛkn̩] <entdeckt, entdeckte, hat entdeckt> ◊ *Er hat schon viele junge Talente entdeckt.* spot sb doing sth jdn dabei sehen, wie er etw. tut [dabaͤ 'zeːən viː] <sehen, sah, hat gesehen> ◊ *Sie wurde dabei gesehen, wie sie ein Kleid stahl.* spot sb's potential jds Potenzial erkennen [potɛn'tsiaːl ɛˌkɛnən] <erkennt, erkannte, hat erkannt> **2.** *(in the US: give sb an advantage)* spot sb jdm einen Vorsprung geben [aͤnən 'foːɐʃprʊŋ geːbm̩] <gibt, gab, hat gegeben> spot sb a few points jdm ein paar Punkte Vorsprung geben

spotlight [noun] **1.** *(light source)* Scheinwerfer ['ʃaͤnvɛrfɐ] der <−s, −> ◊ *die Scheinwerfer einschalten* **2.** *(light)* Scheinwerferlicht ['ʃaͤnvɛrfɐlɪçt] das <−(e)s> *no pl* ⊛ turn the spotlight on sth etw. ins Rampenlicht rücken in the spotlight im Rampenlicht out of the spotlight außerhalb der Öffentlichkeit

spouse [noun] *(husband)* Ehemann ['eːəman] der <−(e)s, Ehemänner>; *(wife)* Ehefrau ['eːəfrao] die

<-, -en>

spray[1] [noun] **1.** *(liquid product)* Spray [ʃpreː] das <-s, -s> ◊ *ein Spray gegen Schädlinge* insect spray Insektenspray [ɪnˈzɛktnʃpreː] spray can Spraydose [ˈʃpreːdoːzə] die <-, -n> **2.** *(mist)* Sprühnebel [ˈʃpryːneːbl̩] der <-s, ->; *(of the sea)* Gischt [ɡɪʃt] die <-, -en> most sing **3.** *(twig)* Zweig [tsvaɪk] der <-(e)s, -e> ◊ *Sie schnitt einige Zweige von dem blühenden Strauch ab.*

spray[2] [verb] **1.** *(liquid, pesticide)* spritzen [ˈʃprɪtsn̩] transitive use +haben/intransitive use +sein ◊ *Er hat Wasser über den Gehweg gespritzt.* ♦ *Das Wasser ist aus dem Rohr gespritzt.* ♦ *die Felder (mit Pestiziden) spritzen* spray (sth) for sth (etw.) gegen etw. spritzen ◊ *Bäume gegen Pilzbefall spritzen; (with water etc.)* spray sb/sth with sth jdn/etw. mit etw. bespritzen [mɪt ... bəˈʃprɪtsn̩] <bespritzt, bespritzte, hat bespritzt> ◊ *Sie haben uns mit Wasser bespritzt.; (in a mist)* sprühen [ˈʃpryːən] transitive use +haben/intransitive use +sein ◊ *Sie hat Parfum auf ihre Bluse gesprüht.* ♦ *Aus der Sprinkleranlage ist Wasser gesprüht.* spray sb/sth with sth jdn/etw. mit etw. besprühen [mɪt ... bəˈʃpryːən] <besprüht, besprühte, hat besprüht> ◊ *Sie besprühte ihn mit Parfum.* **2.** *(car)* lackieren [laˈkiːrən] <lackiert, lackierte, hat lackiert> ◊ *sein Auto neu/blau lackieren* **3.** *(shoot)* spray sb/sth with bullets/gunfire jdn/etw. mit Kugeln durchlöchern [mɪt ˈkuːɡl̩n dʊrçˈlœçɐn] <durchlöchert, durchlöcherte, hat durchlöchert> *(fam)* **4.** *(urinate on)* markieren [marˈkiːrən] <markiert, markierte, hat markiert> ◊ *Der Tiger hat sein Territorium markiert.*

spread[1] [noun] **1.** *(growth, development, expansion)* spread (of sth) Ausbreitung (... [gen]) [ˈaʊsbraɛtʊŋ] die <-> no pl ◊ *die Ausbreitung des Christentums durch Missionare* ♦ *die Ausbreitung der Seuche* **2.** *(for bread)* Aufstrich [ˈaʊfʃtrɪç] der <-(e)s, -e> ◊ *Haselnusscreme ist ein beliebter Aufstrich fürs Pausenbrot.* **3.** *(range)* spread of sth Reihe von etw. [ˈraɛ fɔn] die <-, -n> ◊ *eine Reihe von Produkten* **4.** *(newspaper article)* Artikel [arˈtɪkl̩] der <-s, -> a two-page spread ein zweiseitiger Artikel; *(advertisement)* Anzeige [ˈantsaɛɡə] die <-, -n> a two-page spread eine zweiseitige Anzeige **5.** *(of treetop)* Kronendurchmesser [ˈkroːnəndʊrçmɛsɐ] der <-s, -> ◊ *ein Kronendurchmesser von zehn Metern* **6.** *(large meal)* Festessen [ˈfɛstʔɛsn̩] das <-s, ->

spread[2] [verb] **1.** *(expand, grow, unfold, extend)* spread sth. ausbreiten [ˈaʊsbraɛtn̩] <breitet aus, breitete aus, hat ausgebreitet> ◊ *eine Landkarte/Decke ausbreiten* spread your arms die Arme ausbreiten sth spreads etw. breitet sich aus ◊ *Ein Lächeln breitete sich auf seinem Gesicht aus.* ♦ *Aids breitet sich weiterhin aus.* spread sth over sb/sth etw. über jdn/etw. breiten [yːbɐ ... braɛtn̩] <breitet, breitete, hat gebreitet> +haben ◊ *Sie breitete eine Decke über das Gras.* spread your legs die Beine spreizen [diː ˈbaɛnə ʃpraɛtsn̩] +haben **2.** *(a nob of butter, honey)* streichen [ˈʃtraɛçn̩] <streicht, strich, hat gestrichen> spread sth on your sth sich [dat] etw. auf etw. [acc] streichen ◊ *sich Butter/Honig aufs Brot streichen* spread sth with sth etw. mit etw. bestreichen [mɪt ... bəˈʃtraɛçn̩] <bestreicht, bestrich, hat bestrichen> ◊ *Bestreichen Sie den Kuchen mit der Creme.* **3.** *(divide, occur, be present)* verteilen [fɛˈtaɛlən] <verteilt, verteilte, hat verteilt> ◊ *das Risiko*

verteilen ♦ *Er verteilt sein Geld auf mehrere Banken.* be spread over a period sich über eine Periode verteilen ◊ *Die Auszahlungen verteilen sich über mehrere Jahre.* be spread over an area über ein Gebiet verteilt sein ◊ *Die Weinanbaugebiete sind über das ganze Land verteilt.* **4.** *(rumours, information, happiness, terror)* verbreiten [fɛˈbraɛtn̩] <verbreitet, verbreitete, hat verbreitet> ◊ *Gerüchte verbreiten* ♦ *gute Laune verbreiten* spread a message eine Botschaft verkünden [aɛnə ˈboːtʃaft fɛˌkʏndn̩] <verkündet, verkündete, hat verkündet> *(lofty)* spread the word on sth über etw. [acc] informieren [yːbɐ ... ɪnfɔrˌmiːrən] <informierte, informiert> ◊ *informierte, hat informiert>*

• **spread out** [phras v] **1.** *(go in different directions)* sich verteilen [fɛˈtaɛlən] <verteilt sich, verteilte sich, hat sich verteilt> ◊ *Die Polizisten verteilten sich, um den Wald zu durchkämmen.* **2.** *(unfold)* ausbreiten [ˈaʊsbraɛtn̩] <breitet aus, breitete aus, hat ausgebreitet> ◊ *Sie breitete die Zeitung auf dem Tisch aus.* **3.** *(stretch)* be spread out sich erstrecken [ɛˈʃtrɛkŋ̩] <erstreckt sich, erstreckte sich, hat sich erstreckt> ◊ *Eine wunderschöne Landschaft erstreckte sich vor unseren Augen.*

spring[1] [noun] **1.** *(season)* Frühling [ˈfryːlɪŋ] der <-s, -e> ◊ *Der Frühling kommt bald!; (in compound ns)* spring... Frühlings... [ˈfryːlɪŋs] spring flower Frühlingsblume [ˈfryːlɪŋsbluːmə] die <-, -n> **2.** *(water)* Quelle [ˈkvɛlə] die <-, -n> ◊ *an einer Quelle trinken* ♦ *eine heiße Quelle* **3.** *(metal spiral)* Feder [ˈfeːdɐ] die <-, -n> ◊ *Bei dem Sessel sind die Federn ausgeleiert.* **4.** *(jump)* Sprung [ʃprʊŋ] der <-(e)s, Sprünge>

spring[2] [verb] **1.** *(jump)* springen [ˈʃprɪŋən] <springt, sprang, ist gesprungen> spring to your feet auf die Füße springen **2.** *(do sth quickly)* spring into action aktiv werden [akˈtiːf veːɐdn̩] +sein spring to sb's defence jdn verteidigen [fɛˈtaɛdɪɡn̩] <verteidigt, verteidigte, hat verteidigt> spring to sb's aid jdm zu Hilfe eilen [tsuː ˈhɪlfə aɛlən] +sein **3.** *(fly open)* spring open aufspringen [ˈaʊfʃprɪŋən] <springt auf, sprang auf, ist aufgesprungen> ◊ *Die Tür ist aufgesprungen.* **4.** *(suddenly appear)* spring into view plötzlich auftauchen [plœtslɪç ˈaʊftaʊxn̩] +sein ◊ *Im Nebel tauchte plötzlich ein Auto auf.* tears spring into sb's eyes jdm schießen Tränen in die Augen [ʃiːsn̩ diː ˈtrɛːnən ɪn diː aʊɡn̩] <schossen, sind geschossen> spring into existence ins Leben gerufen werden [ɪns ˈleːbm̩ ɡərʊfn̩ veːɐdn̩] +sein ◊ *Eine neue Partei wurde ins Leben gerufen.*

• **spring from** [phras v] spring from sth *(from a situation)* von etw. herrühren [fɔn ... heːɐryːrən] +haben ◊ *Sein Interesse für Musik rührt von seiner Erziehung her.; (from a family, place)* von etw. stammen [aʊs ... ʃtaman] +haben ◊ *Er stammt aus einer Bauernfamilie.*

• **spring up** [phras v] *(new trend etc.)* aufkommen [ˈaʊfkɔmən] <kommt auf, kam auf, ist aufgekommen> ◊ *Eine neue Mode kam auf.*

springboard [noun] Sprungbrett [ˈʃprʊŋbrɛt] das <-(e)s, -er> ◊ *Praktika als Sprungbrett fürs Berufsleben nutzen* ♦ *vom Sprungbrett springen*

sprinkle [verb] **1.** *(scatter, with a substance)* streuen [ˈʃtrɔɡən] +haben ◊ *Parmesankäse auf die Spaghetti streuen* sprinkle sth with etw. mit etw. bestreuen [mɪt ... bəˈʃtrɔɡən] <bestreut, bestreute, hat

bestreut> ◊ *den Kuchen mit Puderzucker bestreuen;* *(a liquid)* träufeln ['trɔɡfḷn] +haben sprinkle sth with sth, sprinkle sth over sth etw. über etw. acc träufeln ◊ *Olivenöl über den Salat träufeln* 2. *(with a pattern)* be sprinkled with sth mit etw. übersät sein [mɪt ... ybɐ,zɛːt zaẹn] ◊ *Die Tischdecke war mit Krümeln übersät.*; *(hair)* be sprinkled with grey grau meliert sein [graọ meˈliːɐt zaẹn]

sprint noun Sprint [ʃprɪnt] der <—s, –s> ◊ *Er legte mehrere Sprints hin.* final sprint Endspurt ['ɛntʃpʊˀt] der <–(e)s, –s>

sprout noun 1. (Brussels) sprout Rosenkohl ['roːzŋkoːl] der <–(e)s> no pl 2. *(new shoot)* Keim [kaẹm] der <–(e)s, –e> ◊ *Die Samen treiben Keime.* 3. *(bean)* sprouts Sojasprossen ['zoːjaʃprɔsŋ] die <–> pl

spruce noun Fichte ['fɪçtə] die <–, –n> ◊ *Der Schrank ist aus Fichte.* ✦ *Der Wald besteht hauptsächlich aus Fichten.*

spur noun 1. *(on a boot, bird's leg)* Sporn [ʃpɔˀn] der <–(e)s, Sporen> most pl 2. *(encouragement)* Ansporn ['anʃpɔˀn] der <–(e)s> no pl ◊ *etw. ist ein Ansporn für jdn* 3. GEOL *(on a rock)* Leiste ['laẹstə] die <–, –n> 4. *(of a rail track)* Nebengleis ['neːbŋglaẹs] das <–es, –e>

spurt verb 1. *(liquid)* spritzen ['ʃprɪtsŋ] transitive use +haben/intransitive use +sein ◊ *Die Gischt ist uns ins Gesicht gespritzt.* ✦ *Er hat Wasser auf die Windschutzscheibe gespritzt.* 2. *(run fast)* spurten ['ʃpʊˀtn] <spurtet, spurtete, ist gespurtet> ◊ *Er spurtete zur Schule.*

spy¹ noun 1. Spion [ʃpiˈoːn] der <–s, –e> ♀Spionin [ʃpiˈoːnɪn] die <–, –nen> ◊ *Ein Spion muss unauffällig sein.* ✦ *Sie war Spionin beim KGB.* 2. *(relating to spying, in compound ns)* spy ... Spionage... [ʃpioˈnaːʒə] spy thriller Spionagethriller [ʃpioˈnaːʒəθrɪlɐ] der <–s, –>

spy² verb 1. *(work as a spy)* spionieren [ʃpioˈniːrən] <spioniert, spionierte, hat spioniert> ◊ *Sie wurde nach Russland geschickt, um zu spionieren.* 2. *(notice)* bemerken [bəˈmɛˀkŋ] <bemerkt, bemerkte, hat bemerkt> ◊ *Er hat sie sofort bemerkt.*

squad noun 1. *(of soldiers, police)* Kommando [kɔˈmando] das <–s, –s> ◊ *ein Kommando der Bereitschaftspolizei* bomb squad Bomberkommando ['bɔmbɐkɔ,mando] 2. *(sports team)* Mannschaft ['manʃaft] die <–, –en>

squadron noun Geschwader [gəˈʃvaːdɐ] das <–s, –>

square¹ noun 1. *(rectangular shape)* Quadrat [kvaˈdraːt] das <–(e)s, –e> ◊ *ein Quadrat zeichnen* 2. *(of a board game)* Feld [fɛlt] das <–(e)s, –er> ◊ *Ein Schachbrett besteht aus 64 Feldern.* 3. *(open area)* Platz [plats] der <–es, Plätze> ◊ *Vor dem Theater ist ein großer Platz mit einem Brunnen.* 4. MATH *(number)* Quadratzahl [kvaˈdraːttsaːl] die <–, –en> The square of four is sixteen. Vier hoch zwei ist sechzehn. ⊛ back at square one wieder am Anfang

square² adj 1. *(rectangular with four equal sides)* quadratisch [kvaˈdraːtɪʃ] no comp/superl ◊ *ein quadratischer Grundriss* ✦ *Das Zimmer ist nahezu quadratisch.* 2. *(with units of measure)* Quadrat... [kvaˈdraːt] square metre/meter Quadratmeter [kvaˈdraːtmeːtɐ] der <–s, –> 3. *(chin)* eckig ['ɛkɪç] ◊ *ein eckiges Kinn; (shoulders)* breit [braẹt] <breiter, am breitesten> ◊ *Seine Schultern sind sehr breit.*

4. *(perpendicular)* rechtwinklig ['rɛçtvɪŋklɪç] no comp/superl ◊ *Die Ecken müssen rechtwinklig sein.* ✦ *rechtwinklige Dreiecke* 5. *(owing each other nothing)* quitt [kvɪt] no comp/superl, not before ns *(fam)* ◊ *Damit sind wir quitt!*

square³ verb 1. *(multiply by itself)* quadrieren [kvaˈdriːrən] <quadriert, quadrierte, hat quadriert> ◊ *Quadriere die Zahl 7!* 2. SPORT *(equalize)* ausgleichen ['aọsglaẹçŋ] <gleicht aus, glich aus, hat ausgeglichen> ◊ *Sie haben das Spiel gerade noch ausgeglichen.*

• **square up** phras v square up with sb *(settle an account)* die/eine Rechnung bei jdm bezahlen [diːˈaẹnə ˈrɛçnʊŋ baẹ ... bəˈtsaːlən] <rechnet ab, rechnete ab, hat abgerechnet>

• **square with** phras v 1. *(tally)* sth squares with sth etw. stimmt mit etw. überein [ʃtɪmt mɪt ... ybɐˌaẹn] +haben ◊ *Die Ausrede des einen stimmte nicht mit der Ausrede des anderen überein.*; *(reconcile)* square sth with sth etw. mit etw. in Übereinstimmung bringen [mɪt ... ɪn byˀˈaẹnʃtɪmʊŋ brɪŋən] <bringt, brachte, hat gebracht> 2. *(get permission)* square sth with sb mit jdm etw. klären [mɪt ... ˌklɛːrən] +haben ◊ *Ich muss das noch mit dem Direktor klären.*

squared → **square³** adj 1. *(multiplied by itself)* hoch zwei [hoːx ˈtsvaẹ] only spoken ◊ *Wie viel ist sechs hoch zwei?* 2. paper kariert [kaˈriːɐt] no comp/superl ◊ *kariertes Papier* ✦ *Ist dieser Block kariert?*

squat verb 1. *(crouch)* hocken ['hɔkŋ] +haben ◊ *Sie hockte auf der Treppe.* squat down on sth sich auf etw. acc hocken [aọf ... hɔkŋ] +haben ◊ *Er hockte sich auf den Boden.* 2. *(take over a house)* besetzen [bəˈtsɛtsn] <besetzt, besetzte, hat besetzt> ◊ *Sie haben ein Haus besetzt.*; *(live in a house)* squat a house in einem besetzten Haus wohnen [ɪn aẹnəm bəˌtsɛtstn ˈhaọs voːnən]

squeak verb 1. *(make a high sound)* quietschen ['kviːtʃn] +haben ◊ *Die Tür quietschte.* 2. *(speak in a high voice)* mit piepsiger Stimme sprechen [mɪt ˌpiːpsɪgɐ ˈʃtɪmə ʃprɛçŋ] <spricht, sprach, hat gesprochen> *(fam)* squeak sth etw. piepsen ['piːpsŋ] +haben ◊ *„Ich habe Angst", piepste er.*

squeal verb 1. *(make a high sound)* quietschen ['kviːtʃn] +haben ◊ *In der Kurve quietschten die Reifen.* squeal with delight vor Vergnügen quietschen 2. *(inform on sb)* singen ['zɪŋən] <singt, sang, hat gesungen> *(slang)* ◊ *Hat er gesungen?*

squeeze verb 1. *(press firmly)* drücken ['drʏkŋ] +haben ◊ *Drück doch mal etwas kräftiger!* squeeze sb's hand jdm die Hand drücken 2. *(remove liquid from sth by pressing)* ausdrücken ['aọsdrʏkŋ] +haben ◊ *Drück den nassen Schwamm gut aus!*; *(a fruit, juice)* auspressen ['aọsprɛsn] +haben ◊ *eine Zitrone auspressen* 3. *(close)* squeeze your eyes shut die Augen fest zumachen [diː aọgŋ fɛst ˈtsuːmaxŋ] +haben 4. *(into a small space)* squeeze sth somewhere etw. irgendwohin quetschen ['kvɛtʃn] +haben ◊ *Sie quetschte ihre Tasche zwischen die beiden Koffer.* sb squeezes somewhere jd quetscht sich irgendwohin ◊ *Er hat sich durch den Felsspalt gequetscht.* 5. *(your customers, suppliers)* ausbeuten ['aọsbɔɪtn] <beutet aus, beutete aus, hat ausgebeutet> ◊ *Das Unternehmen beutet seine Arbeiter aus.*; *(the competition)* unter Druck setzen [ʊntɐ ˈdrʊk zɛtsn] +haben

• **squeeze in** phras v squeeze sb in jdn dazwi-

schenschieben [da'tsvɪʃnʃiːbm̩] <schiebt dazwischen, schob dazwischen, hat dazwischengeschoben> ◊ *Der Arzt konnte sie glücklicherweise noch dazwischenschieben.* sb squeezes in jd schiebt sich dazwischen
• **squeeze out** [phras v] **1.** *(be more successful)* ausstechen* ['aosʃtɛçn̩] <sticht aus, stach aus, hat ausgestochen> ◊ *einen Konkurrenten ausstechen* **2.** *(make sb say sth)* squeeze sth out of sb etw. aus jdm. rausquetschen [aos ... 'raoskvɛtʃn̩] +haben *(fam)* ◊ *Muss ich alles aus dir rausquetschen?*
squint [verb] **1.** *(half close your eyes)* die Augen zusammenkneifen [diː ˌaogn̩ tsu'zamənknaefn̩] <kneift zusammen, kniff zusammen, hat zusammengekniffen> squint at sb/sth jdn/etw. mit zusammengekniffenen Augen anschauen [mɪt tsu,zaməngəknɪfənən 'aogn̩ anʃaoən] +haben ◊ *Sie schaute die Bilder mit zusammengekniffenen Augen an.* **2.** *(have an eye condition)* schielen ['ʃiːlən] +haben
St 1. *(Saint)* St. [zaŋkt] ◊ *St. Peter* **2.** *(Street)* Str. ['ʃtraːsə] die ◊ *Berliner Str. 7*
stab¹ [noun] **1.** feel a stab of pain plötzlich einen Schmerz verspüren [plœtslɪç aenən 'ʃmɛʳts fɛʃpyːrən] <verspürt, verspürte, hat verspürt> ◊ *Er verspürte plötzlich einen Schmerz in der Brust.*; *(of emotion)* sb feels a stab of sth jd spürt, wie etw. in ihm aufkommt ['ʃpyːʳt viː ... ɪn ... aofkɔmt] <kommt auf, kam auf, ist aufgekommen> +haben ◊ *Ich spürte, wie Eifersucht in mir aufkam.* **2.** *(act of stabbing)* Stich [ʃtɪç] der <-(e)s, -e> a stab to the heart ein Stich ins Herz stab wound Stichwunde ['ʃtɪçvʊndə] die <-, -n> **3.** *(attempt)* Versuch [fɛ'zuːx] der <-(e)s, -e> a stab at doing sth ein Versuch, etw. zu tun have a stab at sth etw. versuchen [fɛ'zuːxn̩] <versucht, versuchte, hat versucht> have a stab at doing sth versuchen, etw. zu tun
⊕ **a stab in the back** Verrat ◊ **a stab in the dark** ein Schuss ins Blaue *(fam)*
stab² [verb] **1.** *(injure, cut, cause pain)* stab sb jdn stechen ['ʃtɛçn̩] <sticht, stach, hat gestochen> ◊ *Er hat das Opfer mehrmals in den Rücken gestochen.* ◆ *ein stechender Schmerz* stab sth in etw. [acc] stechen stab at sth/sb nach jdm./etw. stechen stab sb to death jdn erstechen [ɛ'ʃtɛçn̩] <ersticht, erstach, hat erstochen> **2.** *(emotion)* überkommen [ybe'kɔmən] <überkommt, überkam, hat überkommen> ◊ *Angst überkam sie.*; *(words)* stab sb to the heart jdn schmerzen ['ʃmɛʳtsn̩] +haben *(lit)* ◊ *Seine Worte schmerzten sie.*
stability [noun] Stabilität [ʃtabiliˈtɛːt] die <-> *no pl* ◊ *die Stabilität des Friedens/einer Währung/einer Konstruktion*
stabilize [verb] stabilisieren [ʃtabiliˈziːrən] <stabilisiert, stabilisierte, hat stabilisiert> ◊ *jds Kreislauf stabilisieren* sth stabilizes etw. stabilisiert sich ◊ *Die Lage stabilisiert sich.*
stable¹ [noun] **1.** *(for animals)* Stall [ʃtal] der <-(e)s, Ställe>; *(for race horses)* stables Rennstall ['rɛnʃtal] **2.** *(of companies)* Gruppe ['grʊpə] die <-, -n> ◊ *eine Gruppe von Baufirmen; (of products)* Palette [paˈlɛtə] die <-, -n> ◊ *unsere Palette von Kosmetikprodukten* sb's stable of authors etc. jds Autoren etc. [ao'toːrən]
stable² [adj] **1.** *(unlikely to change or worsen)* stabil [ʃtaˈbiːl] ◊ *Die politischen Verhältnisse dort sind relativ stabil.* ◆ *Sein Zustand ist stabil.* ◆ *ein stabiles*

Regal **2.** *(mentally)* ausgeglichen ['aosgəglɪçn̩] ◊ *ausgeglichene Kinder* ◆ *Er ist ziemlich ausgeglichen.*
stack¹ [noun] **1.** *(pile)* Stapel ['ʃtaːpl̩] der <-s, -> ◊ *ein Stapel Bücher; (of hay, straw)* Haufen ['haofn̩] der <-s, -> **2.** *(in a library)* the stacks das Magazin [das magaˈtsiːn] <-s, -e> **3.** *(chimney)* Schornstein ['ʃɔʳnʃtaen] der <-(e)s, -e> **4.** π Kellerspeicher ['kɛlɐʃpaeçə] der <-s, ->
stack² [verb] **1.** *(put on top, put together)* stapeln ['ʃtaːpl̩n] +haben ◊ *Sie stapelte die Bücher auf dem Tisch.* a place is stacked with sth etw. stapelt sich irgendwo ◊ *In seiner Wohnung stapelt sich der Müll.* **2.** *(a dishwasher)* beladen [bəˈlaːdn̩] <belädt, belud, hat beladen> ◊ *Er belädt die Spülmaschine ungern.; (the shelves in a supermarket)* auffüllen ['aoffʏlən] +haben **3.** *(a number of planes)* Warteschleifen fliegen lassen ['vaʳtəʃlaefn̩ fliːgn̩ lasn̩] <lässt, ließ, hat lassen>
• **stack up** [phras v] **1.** *(increase continuously)* sth is stacking up etw. häuft sich an [hɔɡft tsɪç 'an] <häuft sich an, häufte sich an, hat sich angehäuft> ◊ *Bei mir häuft sich die Arbeit an.* **2.** *(plane)* Warteschleifen fliegen ['vaʳtəʃlaefn̩ fliːgn̩] <fliegt, flog, hat geflogen> **3.** *(measure up)* stack up against sb/sth im Vergleich zu jdm./etw. abschneiden [ɪm fe,glaeç tsuː ... ,apʃnaedn̩] <schneidet ab, schnitt ab, hat abgeschnitten> ◊ *Wie schneiden wir im Vergleich zu den anderen ab?* → stack² **1.**, stack² **2.**
stadium [noun] Stadion ['ʃtaːdjɔn] das <-s, Stadien> ◊ *Zum Endspiel war das Stadion schon lange vorher ausverkauft.* football stadium Fußballstadion ['fuːsbalʃtaːdjɔn]
staff [noun] **1.** *(people who work somewhere)* Personal [pɛʳzoˈnaːl] das <-s> *no pl* ◊ *Der Betrieb will weniger Personal beschäftigen.* ◆ *medizinisches Personal* teaching staff Lehrpersonal ['leːɐpɛʳzoˌnaːl] full-time staff die Vollzeitbeschäftigten [diː 'fɔltsaetbəˌʃɛftɪçtn̩] <-> *pl* staff shortage Personalmangel [pɛʳzoˈnaːlˌmaŋl̩] der <-s, Personalmängel> *most sing* member of staff Mitarbeiter ['mɪtlaʳbaete] der <-s, -> ♀Mitarbeiterin ['mɪtlaʳbaetərɪn] die <-, -nen> join the staff eingestellt werden ['aengəʃtɛlt veːɐdn̩] <wird, wurde, ist worden> **2.** *(stick)* Stab [ʃtaːp] der <-(e)s, Stäbe> **3.** *(flagpole)* Fahnenmast ['faːnənmast] der <-(e)s, -en> **4.** mus Notenlinie ['noːtn̩liːnjə] die <-, -n>
stage¹ [noun] **1.** *(particular point in a development)* Stadium ['ʃtaːdjɔm] das <-s, Stadien> ◊ *eine Krankheit im frühen Stadium; (one of several steps)* Stufe ['ʃtuːfə] die <-, -n> ◊ *die letzte Stufe einer Ausbildung; (of a trip)* Etappe [eˈtapə] die <-, -n> ◊ *eine Reise in mehreren Etappen* **2.** *(for actors, politicians)* Bühne ['byːnə] die <-, -n> ◊ *Das Theater hat eine drehbare Bühne.* ◆ *die politische Bühne* go to the stage zur Bühne gehen take the stage auf die Bühne treten leave the stage von der Bühne abgehen **3.** *(coach)* Postkutsche ['pɔstkʊtʃə] die <-, -n>
stage² [verb] **1.** *(a play etc.)* aufführen ['aoffyːrən] +haben ◊ *Im Theater wurde „Romeo und Julia" aufgeführt.* **2.** *(a strike)* coup d'état etc. [kuː deˈtaː] <organisiert, organisierte, hat organisiert> ◊ *einen Streik organisieren* **3.** *(be the place where sth happens)* ausrichten ['aosrɪçtn̩] <richtet aus, richtete aus, hat ausgerichtet> ◊ *Wird Paris die Olympischen Spiele ausrichten?*

stagger [verb] **1.** *(walk in an uncontrolled way)* schwanken ['ʃvaŋkn̩] +haben/with indication of direction +sein ◊ *Sie hat zunächst geschwankt und ist dann umgefallen.* ♦ *Der Betrunkene ist nach Hause geschwankt.* stagger to your feet sich mühsam aufrichten [,my:za:m 'a͜ofrɪçtn̩] <richtet sich auf, richtete sich auf, hat sich aufgerichtet> **2.** *(surprise, shock)* sth staggers sb, sb is staggered by sth etw. verschlägt jdm die Sprache [fɛʃlɛ:kt ... di: 'ʃpra:xə] <verschlägt, verschlug, hat verschlagen> ◊ *Seine Antwort verschlug ihm die Sprache.* **3.** *(continue with difficulty)* stagger on sich über Wasser halten [y:bɐ 'vasɐ haltn̩] <hält sich, hielt sich, hat sich gehalten> stagger under debts unter Schulden ächzen [ʊntɐ 'ʃʊldn̩ ,ɛçtsn̩] +haben **4.** *(working or opening hours)* versetzen [fɛ'zɛtsn̩] <versetzt, versetzte, hat versetzt> ◊ *versetzte Anfangszeiten* **5.** *(a number of objects)* versetzt anordnen [fɛ'zɛtst ,an|ɔʳdnən] <ordnet an, ordnete an, hat angeordnet> ◊ *Sie hat die Vasen versetzt angeordnet.*

stagnant [adj] **1.** *(water)* stehend ['ʃteːənt] no comp/ superl, only before ns ◊ *ein stehendes Gewässer* The water in this pond is stagnant. Dieser Teich ist ein stehendes Gewässer. **2.** *(economy)* stagnierend [ʃtag'niːrənt] no comp/superl, only before ns ◊ *eine stagnierende Wirtschaft* be stagnant stagnieren [ʃtag'niːrən] <stagniert, stagnierte, hat stagniert>

stain¹ [noun] **1.** *(of dirt)* Fleck [flɛk] der <–(e)s, –en or –e> ◊ *Die Flecken sind beim Waschen nicht herausgegangen.* ♦ *Auf dem Tischtuch sind Flecken.* blood stain Blutfleck ['bluːtflɛk] grease stain Fettfleck ['fɛtflɛk] **2.** *(for wood)* Beize ['ba͜etsə] die <–, –n> ◊ *Holz mit Beize behandeln* **3.** CHEM *(colo(u)rant)* Einfärbemittel ['a͜enfɛʳbəmɪtl̩] das <–s, –> ◊ *mit einem Einfärbemittel die Zellstrukturen unter dem Mikroskop sichtbar machen* ⊛ stain on sb's character Makel ◊ *ein junger Mann ohne jeden Makel*

stain² [verb] **1.** *(with dirt)* stain (sth) Flecken (auf etw. [dat]) hinterlassen ['flɛkn̩ ... hɪntɐ,lasn̩] <hinterlässt, hinterließ, hat hinterlassen> ◊ *Ketchup hinterlässt scheußliche Flecken.* ♦ *Der Schweiß hat Flecken auf seinem Hemd hinterlassen.* sth stains etw. bekommt Flecken [bəkɔmt 'flɛkn̩] <bekommt, bekam, hat bekommen> ◊ *Helle Möbel bekommen leicht Flecken.* **2.** *(with paint)* beizen ['ba͜etsn̩] +haben ◊ *eine Figur dunkel beizen* **3.** CHEM *(mark with colo(u)r)* einfärben ['a͜enfɛʳbm̩] +haben ◊ *ein Präparat einfärben* **4.** *(lit) (sb's hono(u)r, reputation etc.)* beflecken [bə'flɛkn̩] <befleckt, befleckte, hat befleckt> *(lit)* ◊ *jds Ruf/Ehre beflecken*

stained → **stain²** [adj] **1.** fleckig ['flɛkɪç] ◊ *Zieh ein frisches Hemd an; das hier ist schon ganz fleckig.* ♦ *ein fleckiger alter Teppich* be stained with sth mit etw. befleckt sein [mɪt ... bə,flɛkt za͜en] +sein ◊ *Seine Hände waren mit Blut/Tinte befleckt.* **2.** stained glass Buntglas ['bʊntɡlaːs] das <–es, Buntgläser> ◊ *Fenster aus Buntglas*

stainless steel [noun] Edelstahl ['eːdl̩ʃtaːl] der <–(e)s, Edelstähle> most sing ◊ *Besteck aus Edelstahl*

stair [noun] *(flight of)* stairs Treppe ['trɛpə] die <–, –n> ◊ *Sie ging die Treppe hinunter/hinauf.* ♦ *Es ist die Treppe hinuntergefallen.* ♦ *Sie wohnt drei Treppen weiter oben.* at the top of the stairs oben an der Treppe ◊ *Bitte warte oben an der Treppe auf mich.* at the bottom of the stairs am Fuß der Treppe; *(step)* Stufe ['ʃtuːfə] die <–, –n> ◊ *zwei Stufen auf einmal nehmen* ♦ *Sie stand auf der untersten Stufe.*

staircase [noun] Treppe ['trɛpə] die <–, –n> ◊ *Er ging die Treppe hinauf/hinunter.* ♦ *eine steile Treppe*

stake¹ [noun] **1.** *(owning part of a business)* Anteil ['anta͜el] der <–(e)s, –e> have a stake in sth einen Anteil an etw. [dat] haben ◊ *einen Anteil an einer Firma haben* majority stake Mehrheitsanteil ['meːɡha͜ets|anta͜el] minority stake Minderheitsanteil ['mɪndɐha͜ets|anta͜el] **2.** *(want sth to happen)* have a stake in sth Interesse an etw. [dat] haben [ɪntə,rɛsə an ... haːbm̩] +haben ◊ *Wir haben großes Interesse am Erfolg des Projekts.* have a stake in doing sth Interesse daran haben, etw. zu tun **3.** *(in gambling etc.)* stake(s) Einsatz ['a͜enzats] der <–(e)s, Einsätze> ◊ *Der Croupier bat um die Einsätze für das Spiel.* ♦ *den Einsatz erhöhen/verdoppeln* **4.** *(post)* Pfahl [pfaːl] der <–(e)s, Pfähle> ◊ *ein Tier an einem Pfahl festbinden* **5.** *(place of execution)* Scheiterhaufen ['ʃa͜etɐha͜ofn̩] der <–s, –> at the stake auf dem Scheiterhaufen ◊ *auf dem Scheiterhaufen verbrannt werden/sterben* **6.** *(horse race, competition)* Rennen ['rɛnən] das <–s, –> the popularity/leadership stakes das Rennen um die Popularität/Führung ⊛ be at stake auf dem Spiel stehen

stake² [verb] **1.** *(your money, hopes)* stake sth on sth etw. auf etw. [acc] setzen [a͜of ... zɛtsn̩] +haben ◊ *Ich habe viel Geld auf dieses Pferd gesetzt.* ♦ *Sie hatte all ihre Hoffnung auf ihn gesetzt.* stake your reputation on sth seinen Ruf für etw. aufs Spiel setzen **2.** *(say you're entitled to sth)* stake a claim to/for sth Anspruch auf etw. [acc] erheben [,anʃprʊx a͜of ... ehe:bm̩] <erhebt, erhob, hat erhoben> ◊ *Der Nachbar erhebt Anspruch auf das Grundstück.* • **stake out** [phras v] stake sth out **1.** *(a position, opinion etc.)* etw. deutlich machen ['dɔ͜ytlɪç maxn̩] +haben ◊ *Er hat seine Meinung deutlich gemacht.* **2.** *(a building)* etw. überwachen [ybe'vaxn̩] <überwacht, überwachte, hat überwacht> ◊ *Die Polizei überwacht das Gebäude seit Tagen.* **3.** *(an area)* etw. abstecken ['apʃtɛkn̩] +haben ◊ *ein Gebiet abstecken*

stale [adj] **1.** *(bread, biscuits)* alt [alt] <älter, am ältesten> ◊ *Das Brot ist alt.* ♦ *alte Kekse;* *(water, beer, wine)* schal [ʃaːl] ◊ *ein schales Bier* ♦ *Der Champagner ist/schmeckt schal.* **2.** *(air)* abgestanden ['apɡəʃtandn̩] ◊ *Die Luft roch abgestanden.* ♦ *abgestandener Rauch* **3.** *(joke, idea)* abgedroschen ['apɡədrɔʃn̩] ◊ *Die Idee ist ziemlich abgedroschen.* ♦ *abgedroschene Witze erzählen; (news)* veraltet [fɛɐ|'altət] ◊ *veraltete Nachrichten* ♦ *Diese Information ist doch schon veraltet.* ⊛ sb gets stale jd laugt aus

stalk [noun] *(of plant, leaf, animal)* Stiel [ʃtiːl] der <–(e)s, –e> ◊ *ein Blatt mit langem Stiel* ♦ *Der Pilz hat einen hohlen Stiel.* ♦ *Die Augen der Krabbe sitzen auf Stielen.; (of celery)* Stange ['ʃtaŋə] die <–, –n> ◊ *eine Stange Sellerie*

stall [noun] **1.** *(at a market)* Stand [ʃtant] der <–(e)s, Stände> ◊ *die Stände am Weihnachtsmarkt* ♦ *Stände aufbauen/abbauen; (in compound ns)* ... stall ...stand [ʃtant] market stall Marktstand ['maʳktʃtant] **2.** *(in a stable)* Box [bɔks] die <–, –en> ◊ *ein Pferd*

aus seiner Box holen **3.** *(in the UK: seating on the same level as the stage)* stalls Parkett [paʳˈkɛt] das <-(e)s, -e> *most sing* ◊ *Wir saßen im Parkett.* choir stalls Chorgestühl [ˈkoːɐɡəʃtyːl] das <-(e)s, -e> ◊ *im Chorgestühl Platz nehmen* **4.** *(in the US: toilet or shower unit)* Kabine [kaˈbiːnə] die <-, -n> ◊ *Alle Kabinen waren besetzt.* **5.** *(engine)* go into a stall absterben [ˈapʃtɛʳbm̩] <stirbt ab, starb ab, ist abgestorben> ◊ *Plötzlich starb der Motor des Fahrzeugs ab.*

stamina ⌈noun⌉ Ausdauer [ˈaosdaoɐ] die <-> *no pl* ◊ *Ich habe nicht die Ausdauer, so ein Projekt allein durchzuführen.*

stammer ⌈verb⌉ stottern [ˈʃtɔtɐn] +haben ◊ *Er stotterte eine Entschuldigung.* ♦ *vor Angst/Aufregung zu stottern anfangen* stammer out stammeln [ˈʃtamln̩] +haben ◊ *eine Liebeserklärung stammeln* ♦ *„Es tut mir so Leid", stammelte sie.*

stamp¹ ⌈noun⌉ **1.** *(for mail)* Briefmarke [ˈbriːfmaʳkə] die <-, -n> ◊ *Briefmarken sammeln* ♦ *Er klebte eine Briefmarke auf den Brief.*; *(for insurance etc.)* Marke [ˈmaʳkə] die <-, -n> ◊ *Marken kaufen/sammeln* food stamp Lebensmittelmarke [ˈleːbm̩smɪtl̩maʳkə] **2.** *(rubber stamp, impression)* Stempel [ˈʃtɛmpl̩] der <-s, -> ◊ *ein Stempel mit der Firmenadresse* ♦ *einen Stempel in seinen Pass bekommen* bear the stamp of sb jds Stempel tragen ◊ *Diese Vorgehensweise trägt den Stempel des Experten.* put your stamp on sth einer Sache ⌈dat⌉ seinen Stempel aufdrücken ◊ *Sie hat versucht, dem Projekt ihren Stempel aufzudrücken.* **3.** *(with your foot)* Stampfen [ˈʃtampfn̩] das <-s> *no pl* ◊ *Von draußen hörte man das Stampfen schwerer Stiefel.* **4.** *(character type)* Schlag [ʃlaːk] der <-(e)s, Schläge> *most sing* ◊ *ein Mann von seinem Schlag* ♦ *Sie ist von einem ganz anderen Schlag.*

stamp² ⌈verb⌉ **1.** *(put your foot on sth)* stamp on sth auf etw. ⌈acc⌉ treten [aof ... treːtn̩] <tritt, trat, ist getreten> ◊ *Sie trat auf die Spinne.* ♦ *Er trat mir beim Tanzen ständig auf die Füße.*; *(walk noisily)* stamp somewhere irgendwohin stapfen [ˈʃtapfn̩] +sein ◊ *Er stapfte wütend aus dem Büro.* ♦ *Sie stapfte in die Küche, um ihn zur Rede zu stellen.* stamp your foot mit dem Fuß aufstampfen [mɪt deːm ˈfuːs ˌaofʃtampfn̩] +haben ◊ *Er stampfte wütend mit dem Fuß auf.* **2.** *(with a rubber stamp)* stempeln [ˈʃtɛmpl̩n] +haben ◊ *An der Grenze wurde ihr Pass gestempelt.* ♦ *Name und Anschrift in ein Buch stempeln* **3.** stamp sb as sth jdn als etw. abstempeln [als ... ˌapʃtɛmpl̩n] +haben ◊ *Aufgrund dieses Zwischenfalls wurde er als unzuverlässig abgestempelt.* **4.** *(put a postage stamp on sth)* frankieren [franˈkiːrən] <frankiert, frankierte, hat frankiert> ◊ *einen Brief/eine Postkarte/ein Paket frankieren* • **stamp on** ⌈phras v⌉ **1.** stamp on sth etw. unterbinden [ʊntɐˈbɪndn̩] <unterbindet, unterband, hat unterbunden> ◊ *Wir werden unpassendes Verhalten sofort unterbinden.* **2.** stamp on sb jdn unterdrücken [ʊntɐˈdrʏkn̩] <unterdrückt, unterdrückte, hat unterdrückt> ◊ *politische Gegner unterdrücken* • **stamp out** ⌈phras v⌉ stamp sth out **1.** *(eradicate)* etw. ausrotten [ˈaosrɔtn̩] <rottet aus, rottete aus, hat ausgerottet> ◊ *Leider wird es nie gelingen, das Verbrechen völlig auszurotten.* **2.** *(a fire)* etw. austreten [ˈaostreːtn̩] <tritt aus, trat aus, hat ausgetreten> ◊ *Es gelang ihm, das Feuer auszutreten.* **3.** *(a pattern, shape)* etw. ausstanzen [ˈaosʃtantsn̩] +haben ◊ *Teile/*

Muster ausstanzen

stance ⌈noun⌉ Haltung [ˈhaltʊŋ] die <-, -en> ◊ *Wie ist seine Haltung zu dem Vorschlag?* ♦ *Sie wird ihre Haltung niemals ändern.* ♦ *Die Gegner nahmen eine gebückte/aufrechte Haltung ein.*

stand¹ ⌈noun⌉ **1.** *(attitude)* stand (on sth) Einstellung (zu etw.) [ˈaenʃtɛlʊŋ] die <-, -en> ◊ *Ich finde ihre Einstellung zur Abtreibung problematisch.* take a stand Stellung beziehen [ˈʃtɛlʊŋ bətsiːən] <bezieht, bezog, hat bezogen> **2.** *(resistance)* Widerstand [ˈviːdɐʃtant] der <-(e)s, Widerstände> ◊ *Der Widerstand gegen den Feind wird schwächer.* make a stand Widerstand leisten ◊ *Lasst uns gemeinsam gegen diese Behandlung Widerstand leisten!* **3.** *(stall)* Stand [ʃtant] der <-(e)s, Stände> ◊ *Kaufst du uns an dem Stand dort ein paar Würstchen?* ♦ *Auf der Ausstellung drängten sich die Besucher um einen Stand.* **4.** *(for holding sth)* Ständer [ˈʃtɛndɐ] der <-s, -> ◊ *Der Ständer dieser Lampe wackelt.* umbrella stand Schirmständer [ˈʃɪʳmʃtɛndɐ] **5.** SPORT Tribüne [triˈbyːnə] die <-, -n> ◊ *Die Zuschauer auf der Tribüne jubelten vor Begeisterung.* **6.** LAW Zeugenstand [ˈtsɔøɡŋ̩ʃtant] der <-(e)s> *no pl* take the stand in den Zeugenstand treten

stand² ⌈verb⌉ **1.** *(be upright, located, in a certain condition, not be destroyed, not move, remain unchanged, of water: be stagnant)* stehen [ˈʃteːən] <steht, stand, hat gestanden> ◊ *gerade stehen* ♦ *Es gab keine Plätze mehr, also mussten wir stehen.* ♦ *Am Fenster stand ein Mann und sah hinaus.* ♦ *Im Park steht ein Denkmal.* ♦ *Der Zug stand noch im Bahnhof.* ♦ *So, wie die Dinge stehen, kommt er wohl nicht zum Treffen.* ♦ *Wie stehen die Verhandlungen?* ♦ *Steht Ihr Angebot noch?* ♦ *Auf den Wiesen stand das Wasser.* stand on your head auf dem Kopf stehen be still standing, be left standing noch stehen ◊ *Nach dem Erdbeben standen nur noch wenige Häuser.* stand empty leer stehen ◊ *Das Gebäude steht schon lange leer.* stand about/around herumstehen [hɛˈrʊmʃteːən] <steht herum, stand herum, hat herumgestanden> ◊ *Steh hier nicht herum, sondern hilf uns lieber!* stand doing sth, stand and do sth dastehen und etw. tun [ˈdaːʃteːən ʊnt] <steht da, stand da, hat dagestanden> ◊ *Er stand geduldig da und wartete.* stand motionless/open-mouthed etc. bewegungslos/mit offenem Mund etc. dastehen ◊ *Bewegungslos stand sie da und starrte mich an.* stand still stillstehen [ˈʃtɪlʃteːən] <steht still, stand still, hat stillgestanden> ◊ *Er hatte das Gefühl, als stünde die Zeit still.* ♦ *Tür nicht öffnen, bevor der Zug stillsteht.*; *(verdict)* bestehen bleiben [bəˈʃteːən blaebm̩] <bleibt, blieb, ist geblieben> ◊ *Es wurde entschieden, dass das Urteil bestehen bleiben soll.* **2.** *(get up)* stand (up) aufstehen [ˈaofʃteːən] <steht auf, stand auf, ist aufgestanden> ◊ *Er stand auf und bot der alten Dame seinen Sitzplatz an.* **3.** *(step on sth)* stand on sth auf etw. ⌈acc⌉ treten [aof ... treːtn̩] <tritt, trat, ist getreten> stand on sb's foot jdm auf den Fuß treten stand in sth in etw. ⌈acc⌉ treten ◊ *Ich glaube, du bist in Hundedreck getreten.* **4.** *(put sth somewhere)* stand sth somewhere etw. irgendwohin stellen [ˈʃtɛlən] +haben ◊ *Bitte stellen Sie den Schrank dort an die Wand.* **5.** *(measure: person)* sb stands ... jd ist ... groß [ɪst ... ˈɡroːs] +sein ◊ *Sein Onkel ist weit über zwei Meter groß.*; *(structure, tree)*

sth stand ... etw. ist ... hoch [ɪst ... 'hoːx] +sein ◊
Das Denkmal ist fast 20 Meter hoch. **6.** stand
together zusammenhalten [tsu'zamənhaltn̩] <hält
zusammen, hielt zusammen, hat zusammengehalten> ◊
*Wenn wir zusammenhalten, können wir vielleicht
etwas erreichen.* stand ready to do sth bereit sein,
etw. zu tun [bə'raet tsaen ... tsuː] +sein ◊ *Wir sind
bereit, Ihnen zu helfen, wenn es Probleme gibt.*;
(possibly do sth) stand to do sth etw. tun können
['kœnən] <kann, konnte, hat können> +inf ◊ *Wir
können bei dem Geschäft eine Menge Geld
gewinnen/verlieren.* **7.** (be at a level) stand (at sth)
(bei etw.) liegen ['liːgn̩] <liegt, lag, hat gelegen> ◊
*Der Rekord liegt zurzeit bei 45 Metern. ♦ Die Ver-
kaufszahlen liegen bei über 350 000 Euro.* **8.** (put up
with) ertragen [ɛ'traːgn̩] <erträgt, ertrug, hat
ertragen> ◊ *Wie kannst du diesen Krach nur
ertragen?* stand sb doing sth es ertragen, wenn jd
etw. tut ◊ *Ich kann es nicht ertragen, wenn man
mich dauernd unterbricht.*; (not like) sb can't stand
sb/sth jd kann jdn/etw. nicht ausstehen
[kan ... nɪçt 'aosʃteːən] <kann, konnte, hat können> ◊
Ich kann Linseneintopf nicht ausstehen! **9.** (tolerate:
the heat, draught etc.) stand sth etw. vertragen
[fɛ'traːgn̩] <verträgt, vertrug, hat vertragen> ◊ *Wie
verträgst du die Hitze? ♦ Diese Pflanze verträgt
keinen Zug.*; (the pressure, a close examination)
einer Sache (dat) standhalten ['ʃtanthaltn̩] <hält
stand, hielt stand, hat standgehalten> ◊ *dem Druck
nicht standhalten ♦ Seine Aussage hält einer
genauen Überprüfung nicht stand.*; (a test) etw.
bestehen [bə'ʃteːən] <besteht, bestand, hat bestanden>
◊ *Wird ihre Politik den Realitätstest bestehen?*
10. (have a particular opinion) Where does sb stand
on sth? Welchen Standpunkt vertritt jd in einer
Sache (dat)? [vɛlçn̩ 'ʃtantpʊŋkt fɛ,trɪt ... ɪn] <vertritt,
vertrat, hat vertreten> **11.** (in an election) kandidieren [kandi'diːrən] <kandidiert, kandidierte, hat kandi-
diert> ◊ *Er hat beschlossen, bei der nächsten Bürger-
meisterwahl zu kandidieren. ♦ Wer kandidiert für
die SPD?* **12.** stand guard over sb/sth jdn/etw.
bewachen [bə'vaxn̩] <bewacht, bewachte, hat
bewacht> ◊ *Drei Beamte bewachten den Mann.*
stand security for sb für jdn bürgen [fyːg ... ,bʏʳgn̩]
+haben
⊛ sb/sth could stand sth jd/etw. könnte etw.
vertragen ◊ *Das Haus könnte eine Renovierung
vertragen.*

• **stand against** (phras v) **1.** (oppose) stand against
sb/sth sich gegen jdn/etw. zur Wehr setzen
[geːgn̩ ... tsuːɐ 'veːɐ tsɛtsn̩] +haben ... *Wir sollten uns
gegen diese Maßnahmen zur Wehr setzen!* **2.** (in an
election) stand against sb gegen jdn antreten
[geːgn̩ ... ,antreːtn̩] <tritt an, trat an, ist angetreten> ◊
*Er war bereits bei den letzten Wahlen gegen ihn ange-
treten.*

• **stand around** (phras v) herumstehen
[hɛ'rʊmʃteːən] <steht herum, stand herum, hat herum-
gestanden> ◊ *Steh hier nicht herum, sondern hilf
uns lieber!*

• **stand aside** (phras v) **1.** (move to let sb pass) zur
Seite treten [tsuːɐ 'zaetə treːtn̩] <tritt, trat, ist
getreten> ◊ *Bitte treten Sie zur Seite, um den Arzt
vorbeizulassen.* **2.** (not intervene) tatenlos zusehen
[taːtnloːs 'tsuːzeːən] <sieht zu, sah zu, hat zugesehen> ◊
Wie können die Passanten dabei nur tatenlos

zusehen? **3.** (withdraw) zurücktreten [tsu'rʏktreːtn̩]
<tritt zurück, trat zurück, ist zurückgetreten> ◊ *Sie
trat zugunsten ihres Stellvertreters zurück.*

• **stand back** (phras v) **1.** (move back) stand back
(from sth) (von etw.) zurücktreten [tsu'rʏktreːtn̩]
<tritt zurück, trat zurück, ist zurückgetreten> ◊ *Bitte
treten Sie zurück. ♦ von der Bahnsteigkante zurücktreten* **2.** (be situated at a distance) stand back from
sth von etw. entfernt liegen [fɔn ... ɛnt,fɛʳnt liːgn̩]
<liegt, lag, hat gelegen> ◊ *Das Gebäude liegt ein
Stück von der Straße entfernt.* **3.** (stay objective)
objektiv bleiben [ɔpjɛk'tiːf blaebm̩] <bleibt, blieb, ist
geblieben> ◊ *Sie sollten versuchen, objektiv zu
bleiben.*

• **stand by** (phras v) **1.** (be available when needed)
be standing by bereitstehen [bə'raetʃteːən] <steht
bereit, stand bereit, hat bereitgestanden> ◊ *Für den
Notfall stand ein Krankenwagen bereit.* **2.** (not do
anything when you should) tatenlos zusehen
[taːtnloːs 'tsuːzeːən] <sieht zu, sah zu, hat zugesehen> ◊
*Wir können doch nicht tatenlos zusehen, wie das
Tier stirbt!* **3.** (support) stand by sb jdm beistehen
['baeʃteːən] <steht bei, stand bei, hat beigestanden> ◊
*den Trauernden beistehen ♦ Seine Frau stand ihm in
seiner Krankheit bei.* **4.** (maintain) stand by sth zu
etw. stehen [tsuː ... 'ʃteːən] <steht, stand, hat
gestanden> ◊ *Ich stehe zu meinem Versprechen.*

• **stand down** (phras v) **1.** (resign) zurücktreten
[tsu'rʏktreːtn̩] <tritt zurück, trat zurück, ist zurückgetre-
ten> ◊ *Er trat als Vorsitzender zurück.* **2.** LAW den
Zeugenstand verlassen [deːn 'tsɔøgn̩ʃtant fɛ,lasn̩]
<verlässt, verließ, hat verlassen> ◊ *Sie können den
Zeugenstand jetzt verlassen.*

• **stand for** (phras v) **1.** (be an abbreviation for sth,
represent sth) stand for sth für etw. stehen
[fyːɐ ... ʃteːən] <steht, stand, hat gestanden> ◊ *Die
Abkürzung „etc." steht für „et cetera". ♦ Ich verab-
scheue diese Organisation und alles, wofür sie steht.*
2. (be a candidate for sth) stand for sth für etw. kandidieren [fyːɐ ... kandi,diːrən] <kandidiert, kandidierte, hat kandidiert> ◊ *Er kandidiert für das Amt
des Bürgermeisters.* **3.** (tolerate) stand for sth sich
(dat) etw. gefallen lassen [gə'falən lasn̩] <lässt sich,
ließ sich, hat sich lassen> ◊ *So ein Benehmen lasse
ich mir nicht gefallen!*

• **stand in** (phras v) stand in (for sb) (für jdn) einspringen ['aenʃprɪŋən] <springt ein, sprang ein, ist ein-
gesprungen> ◊ *Könntest du morgen für mich einspringen? ♦ Als Bernd krank wurde, sprang Marion
spontan ein.*

• **stand out** (phras v) **1.** (be noticeable) auffallen
['aoffalən] <fällt auf, fiel auf, ist aufgefallen> ◊ *Sie
wollte nicht auffallen. ♦ Er fiel durch seine Kleidung
auf. ♦ Der große Mann fiel in der Menge sofort auf.*
2. (be more impressive, important) hervorstechen
[hɛ'foːɐʃtɛçn̩] <sticht hervor, stach hervor, hat hervorge-
stochen> ◊ *Er stach bereits damals als begabter
Dichter hervor.*

• **stand out against** (phras v) **1.** (be noticeable) sich von etw. abheben
[fɔn ... ,apheːbm̩] <hebt sich ab, hob sich ab, hat sich
abgehoben> ◊ *Die Silberkette hob sich deutlich von
ihrer schwarzen Bluse ab.* **2.** (oppose) sich gegen
etw. zur Wehr setzen [geːgn̩ ... tsuːɐ 'veːɐ tsɛtsn̩]
+haben ◊ *Wir müssen uns gegen diese Intrigen zur
Wehr setzen.*

• **stand over** [phras v] stand over sb jdm auf die Finger sehen [aɔf diː ˈfɪŋə zeːən] <sieht, sah, hat gesehen> ◊ *Ich kann nicht arbeiten, wenn du mir dauernd auf die Finger siehst.*

• **stand up** [phras v] **1.** *(get up)* aufstehen [ˈaɔfʃteːən] <steht auf, stand auf, ist aufgestanden> ◊ *Er stand auf, um der alten Dame Platz zu machen.* ✦ *Sie stürzte, stand aber gleich wieder auf.; (be standing)* stehen [ˈʃteːən] <steht, stand, hat gestanden> ◊ *Ich kann nicht mehr stehen, mir tun die Füße weh!* ✦ *Es gab keine Plätze mehr, also mussten wir stehen.* stand up straight sich gerade hinstellen [gəˌraːdə ˈhɪnʃtɛlən] +haben ◊ *Komm, stell dich gerade hin!* **2.** *(to a test etc.)* sth stands up to sth etw. hält einer Sache [dat] stand [hɛlt … ˈʃtant] <hält stand, hielt stand, hat standgehalten> ◊ *Wie gut wird das Material dem Druck standhalten?* sb stands up to sth jd ist einer Sache [dat] gewachsen [ɪst … gəˈvaksn̩] +sein ◊ *Ich hoffe, sie wird dieser Belastung gewachsen sein.* **3.** LAW *(be convincing)* stand up in court vor Gericht bestehen [foːɐ̯ gəˌrɪçt bəˈʃteːən] <besteht, bestand, hat bestanden> ◊ *Diese Geschichte wird vor Gericht nicht bestehen können.* **4.** *(not turn up)* stand sb up jdn versetzen [fɛˈzɛtsn̩] <versetzt, versetzte, hat versetzt> *(fam)* ◊ *Jetzt hat er mich schon zum zweiten Mal versetzt.*

• **stand up for** [phras v] stand up for sb/sth für jdn/etw. eintreten [fyːɐ̯ … ˌaentreːtn̩] <tritt ein, trat ein, ist eingetreten> ◊ *Du musst für das eintreten, woran du glaubst.* ✦ *Niemand trat für ihn ein, als er zu Unrecht kritisiert wurde.*

• **stand up to** [phras v] stand up to sb/sth sich jdm/einer Sache gegenüber behaupten [geˈgn̩yːbɐ bəˈhaɔptn̩] <behauptet sich, hat sich behauptet> ◊ *Wer hätte gedacht, dass sie sich dem Chef gegenüber so behaupten würde!*

standard¹ [noun] **1.** *(criterion)* Maßstab [ˈmaːsʃtaːp] der <-(e)s, Maßstäbe> ◊ *Nach heutigen Maßstäben waren die Autos damals sehr langsam.* by any standards egal, welche Maßstäbe man anlegt ◊ *Egal, welche Maßstäbe man anlegt, dieser Roman ist ein Meisterstück!* set a standard einen Maßstab setzen; *(average, established norm)* Norm [nɔʳm] die <-, -en> ◊ *Die Papiergröße DIN A4 ist eine technische Norm.* meet standards der Norm [dat] entsprechen ◊ *Diese Lebensmittel entsprechen nicht der festgelegten Norm.; (level)* Niveau [niˈvoː] das <-s, -s> ◊ *Das Niveau an unseren Schulen muss sich bessern.* ✦ *Wir können dieses hohe Niveau nicht aufrechterhalten.* raise standards das Niveau heben standard of living Lebensstandard [ˈleːbm̩sˌʃtandaʳt] der <-s, -s> **2.** moral standards Moral [moˈraːl] die <-> no pl ◊ *ein erschreckender Verfall der Moral* **3.** *(flag)* Flagge [ˈflaɡə] die <-, -n> ◊ *Auf dem Dach webte die königliche Flagge.* **4.** *(song)* be a standard zum Standardrepertoire gehören [tsʊm ˈʃtandaʳtrepɛʳˌto̯aːʳ gəhøːrən] <gehört, gehörte, hat gehört> ◊ *Dieser Titel gehört zum Standardrepertoire jeder Band.*

standard² [adj] **1.** *(customary)* üblich [ˈyːplɪç] no comp/superl ◊ *Er bekam die übliche Antwort auf seine Frage.* ✦ *die übliche Vorgehensweise anwenden* **2.** *(prescribed by a rule, used by most people, normal)* Standard... [ˈʃtandaʳt] standard size Standardgröße

['ʃtandaʳtɡrøːsə] die <-, -n> standard work Standardwerk [ˈʃtandaʳtvɛʳk] das <-(e)s, -e> standard model Standardmodell [ˈʃtandaʳtmoˌdɛl] das <-s, -e> **3.** LING Standard English Standardenglisch [ˈʃtandaʳtˌɛŋlɪʃ] das <-(s)> no pl Standard German Hochdeutsch [ˈhoːxdɔɪtʃ] das <-(s)> no pl

standardize [verb] vereinheitlichen [fɛˈaɛnhaetlɪçn̩] <vereinheitlicht, vereinheitlichte, hat vereinheitlicht> ◊ *die Vorschriften innerhalb der EU vereinheitlichen* ◊ *die Rechtschreibung in einer Sprache vereinheitlichen*

stand-in [noun] **1.** *(in a job etc.)* Vertretung [fɛˈtreːtʊŋ] die <-, -en> ◊ *Er sucht eine Vertretung für Montag.* **2.** FILM, THEAT Double [ˈduːbl̩] das <-s, -s> ◊ *Sie arbeitet als Double beim Film.* ✦ *Die gefährlichen Szenen übernahm ein Double für ihn.*

standing [noun] **1.** *(reputation)* Ansehen [ˈanzeːən] das <-s> no pl ◊ *eine Firma von hohem/internationalem Ansehen; (status, position)* Stellung [ˈʃtɛlʊŋ] die <-> no pl ◊ *die soziale/gesellschaftliche Stellung der Frau* ✦ *die rechtliche Stellung der Migranten* **2.** SPORT standings Tabelle [taˈbɛlə] die <-, -n> ◊ *Die Mannschaft steht in der Tabelle ganz oben.* ⊛ of long standing langjährig ◊ *Die beiden verbindet eine langjährige Freundschaft.*

standing order [noun] **1.** FIN *(to a bank)* Dauerauftrag [ˈdaɔeˌaoftraːk] der <-(e)s, Daueraufträge> ◊ *die Miete per Dauerauftrag zahlen* **2.** MIL Befehl [bəˈfeːl] der <-(e)s or -e> ◊ *Sie hatten Befehl, niemanden durchzulassen.* **3.** *(of an association etc.)* Geschäftsordnung [ɡəˈʃɛftsˌoʳdnʊŋ] die <-, -en> ◊ *sich an die Geschäftsordnung halten*

staple¹ [noun] **1.** *(from a stapler)* Heftklammer [ˈhɛftklamɐ] die <-, -n> ◊ *Papiere mit Heftklammern zusammenfügen* **2.** *(main food)* Grundnahrungsmittel [ˈɡrʊntnaːrʊŋsmɪtl̩] das <-s, -> ◊ *Grundnahrungsmittel wie Mehl und Zucker; (main product)* Hauptprodukt [ˈhaɔptproˌdʊkt] das <-(e)s, -e> ◊ *Textilien und Keramik sind die Hauptprodukte des Landes.*

staple² [verb] heften [ˈhɛftn̩] <heftet, heftete, hat geheftet> ◊ *Er ließ die Kopien zu einer Mappe heften.* staple sth together etw. zusammenheften [tsuˈzamənhɛftn̩] +haben ◊ *Sie heftete die Dokumente zusammen.*

star¹ [noun] **1.** *(celestial body, sign, shape, zodiac)* Stern [ʃtɛʳn] der <-(e)s, -e> ◊ *Am Himmel war kein Stern zu sehen.* ✦ *ein Hotel mit vier Sternen* ✦ *Was sagen die Sterne?* ✦ *Das steht in den Sternen.* **2.** *(famous person)* Star [staːʳ] der <-s, -s> ◊ *über Nacht zum Star werden* ✦ *Er ist der Star der Mannschaft.* star attraction Hauptattraktion [ˈhaɔptˌatrakˌtsjoːn] die <-, -en> ◊ *Der Clown war die Hauptattraktion des kleinen Zirkus.* ⊛ see stars Sterne sehen

star² [verb] **1.** FILM, THEAT sb stars in sth jd spielt in etw. [dat] die Hauptrolle [ʃpiːlt ɪn … diː ˈhaɔptrɔlə] +haben ◊ *sb stars in sth jd spielt in einem Film etc. (neben jdm) die Hauptrolle* ◊ *Er wird neben Halle Berry die Hauptrolle in dem Film spielen.* star sb jdn in der Hauptrolle zeigen [ɪn deːɐ̯ ˈhaɔptrɔlə tsaɛɡn̩] +haben ◊ *Der Film zeigt Ingrid Bergman in der Hauptrolle.* a film starring sb (as sb) ein Film mit jdm in der Hauptrolle (als jd) ◊ *ein Film mit Michael Caine in der Hauptrolle als Dr. Jekyll* **2.** *(mark with a star)* star sth etw. mit

Letter index on right: A B C D E F G H I J K L M N O P Q R **S** T U V W X Y Z

einem Stern versehen [mɪt ˈaɛnəm ˈʃtɛˈn fɛzeːən] <versieht, versah, hat versehen> ◊ *Er versah die Namen der Spender mit einem Stern.*

starch [noun] Stärke [ˈʃtɛˈkə] die <-, -n> *most sing* ◊ *Getreide und Kartoffeln enthalten besonders viel Stärke.*

stare [verb] **1.** *(person)* starren [ˈʃtarən] +haben ◊ *gebannt auf den Bildschirm starren* ♦ *Er starrte aus dem Fenster.* stare at sb/sth jdn/etw. anstarren [ˈanʃtarən] +haben ◊ *Sie starrte ihn entsetzt an.* **2.** *(eyes)* weit aufgerissen sein [vaet ˈaofɡərɪsn̩ zaen] +sein ◊ *Ihre Augen waren weit aufgerissen.* staring eyes weit aufgerissene Augen

starlet [noun] Sternchen [ˈʃtɛˈnçən] das <-s, -> ◊ *Zur Preisverleihung erschienen viele Stars und Sternchen.*

starling [noun] Star [ʃtaːˈ] der <-(e)s, -e> ◊ *Die Stare fliegen im Herbst nach Süden.*

star sign [noun] Sternzeichen [ˈʃtɛˈntsaeçn̩] das <-s, ->

start¹ [noun] **1.** *(beginning)* Anfang [ˈanfaŋ] der <-(e)s, Anfänge> ◊ *der Anfang einer langen Erfolgsgeschichte* ♦ *Am Anfang des Jahres ging es ihm noch gut.* ♦ *Beeil dich, sonst verpassen wir den Anfang des Films.* from start to finish von Anfang bis Ende ◊ *Hast du den Roman von Anfang bis Ende gelesen?* from the start von Anfang an ◊ *Ich habe von Anfang an gesagt, dass der Typ nicht zu ihr passt.* make a start (on sth) (mit etw.) anfangen [ˈanfaŋən] <fängt an, fing an, hat angefangen> ◊ *Du solltest allmählich mit den Hausaufgaben anfangen.* get off to a good/ bad start gut/schlecht anfangen ◊ *Der Tag fing schlecht an, denn sie verpasste den Bus.* **2.** *(departure)* Aufbruch [ˈaofbrʊx] der <-(e)s, Aufbrüche> *most sing* ◊ *ein früher/verspäteter Aufbruch* **3.** SPORT *(of a race)* Start [ʃtaˈt] der <-(e)s, -s> ◊ *einen guten Start haben/hinlegen* ♦ *Alle Teilnehmer an den Start, bitte!* *(advantage)* Vorsprung [ˈfoːɐ̯ʃprʊŋ] der <-(e)s, Vorsprünge> ◊ *Er bekam einen Vorsprung von 25 Metern.* **4.** *(opportunity in life)* fresh/new start Neuanfang [ˈnɔɥˌanfaŋ] der <-(e)s, Neuanfänge> ◊ *Er hofft auf einen Neuanfang in einem anderen Land.* ♦ *Dieses Geld wird Ihnen einen Neuanfang ermöglichen.* **5.** sb gives a start jd fährt zusammen [fɛːɐ̯t tsuˈzamən] <fährt zusammen, fuhr zusammen, ist zusammengefahren> ◊ *Sie fuhr zusammen, als sie den Knall hörte.* give sb a start jdn erschrecken [ɛˈʃrɛkn̩] <erschreckt, erschreckte, hat erschreckt> sb wakes up with a start jd schreckt aus dem Schlaf hoch [ʃrɛkt aos deːm ˈʃlaːf ˌhoːx] +sein

ⓔ for a start zunächst einmal

start² [verb] **1.** *(begin)* anfangen [ˈanfaŋən] <fängt an, fing an, hat angefangen> ◊ *Die Vorstellung fängt in wenigen Minuten an.* ♦ *Der Tag fing schon hektisch an.* ♦ *Fangt schon mal an; das Essen wird kalt.* ♦ *Ich habe mit der Arbeit noch nicht angefangen.* ♦ *Er hat als Kellner angefangen.* ♦ *Ich fange den Tag immer mit einer Tasse Kaffee an.* ♦ *Sie wollte ein neues Leben anfangen.* ♦ *Hier fängt unser Grundstück an.* ♦ *Die Hausnummern fangen bei 3 an.* ♦ *Wer hat den Streit angefangen?* ♦ *„Sei nicht so unfreundlich!" — „Du hast doch angefangen!"* start doing/to do sth anfangen, etw. zu tun ◊ *Er fing an zu weinen.* ♦ *Es wird gleich anfangen zu regnen.; (in a race)* starten [ˈʃtaˈtn̩] <startet, startete, ist gestartet> ◊ *Wie viele Pferde starten in dem Rennen?; (a fire)* legen [ˈleːɡn̩]

+haben ◊ *Wer hat das Feuer gelegt?; (trigger a reaction)* auslösen [ˈaosløːzn̩] +haben ◊ *Sein Brief löste eine unerwartete Kette von Reaktionen aus.; (a business, initiative, organization)* gründen [ˈɡrʏndn̩] <gründet, gründete, hat gegründet> ◊ *Er ging nach Amerika und gründete seine eigene Firma.; (make sb do sth)* start sb doing sth jdn dazu bringen, etw. zu tun [datsu: ˈbrɪŋən ... tsuː] <bringt, brachte, hat gebracht> ◊ *Ihr Anruf brachte ihn dazu, über alles noch einmal nachzudenken.* **2.** *(leave)* sb starts jd bricht auf [brɪçt ˈaof] <bricht auf, brach auf, ist aufgebrochen> ◊ *Am folgenden Tag brach er früh auf.; (a journey)* start sth etw. antreten [ˈantreːtn̩] <tritt an, trat an, hat angetreten> ◊ *Er trat den Heimweg an.* ♦ *eine Reise antreten; (walk in a direction)* start for a place irgendwohin gehen [ˈɡeːən] <geht, ging, ist gegangen> ◊ *Sie ging zur Tür.* **3.** *(an engine etc.)* start sth etw. anlassen [ˈanlasn̩] <lässt an, ließ an, hat angelassen> ◊ *den Motor/das Auto anlassen; (car, engine)* sth starts etw. springt an [ʃprɪŋt ˈan] <springt an, sprang an, ist angesprungen> ◊ *Das Auto will nicht anspringen.* **4.** *(move suddenly)* zusammenfahren [tsuˈzamənfaːrən] <fährt zusammen, fuhr zusammen, ist zusammengefahren> ◊ *Bei dem Knall fuhr sie erschrocken zusammen.*

ⓔ to start with zunächst einmal

• **start off** [phras v] **1.** *(begin)* anfangen [ˈanfaŋən] <fängt an, fing an, hat angefangen> ◊ *Ich wollte keinen Streit anfangen.* ♦ *Fangen wir mit einer einfachen Aufgabe an.; (cause sb to do sth)* start sb off on (doing) sth jdn zu etw. bringen [tsuː ... brɪŋən] <bringt, brachte, hat gebracht> ◊ *Du hast das Kind zum Weinen gebracht.* **2.** *(begin a journey)* aufbrechen [ˈaofbrɛçn̩] <bricht auf, brach auf, ist aufgebrochen> ◊ *Am folgenden Tag brach er nach Brasilien auf.*

• **start on** [phras v] start on (doing) sth mit etw. anfangen [mɪt ... ˌanfaŋən] <fängt an, fing an, hat angefangen> ◊ *Wir können jetzt mit dem Packen anfangen.* start at sb anfangen, an jdm herumzumeckern ◊ *Fang nicht wieder an, an mir herumzumeckern!*

• **start out** [phras v] **1.** *(begin)* anfangen [ˈanfaŋən] <fängt an, fing an, hat angefangen> ◊ *Er hat in dem Restaurant als Kellner angefangen; heute ist er der Besitzer.* **2.** *(begin a journey)* aufbrechen [ˈaofbrɛçn̩] <bricht auf, brach auf, ist aufgebrochen> ◊ *Sie brachen bereits vor Sonnenaufgang auf.*

• **start up** [phras v] **1.** *(a conversation etc.)* anfangen [ˈanfaŋən] <fängt an, fing an, hat angefangen> ◊ *Er versuchte, ein Gespräch mit ihr anzufangen.; (a business)* gründen [ˈɡrʏndn̩] +haben ◊ *Sie will in ein paar Jahren ihre eigene Firma gründen.* **2.** *(an engine)* anlassen [ˈanlasn̩] <lässt an, ließ an, hat angelassen> ◊ *Erst nach einigen Versuchen gelang es ihm, den Motor anzulassen.*

starter [noun] **1.** *(sb who signals the beginning of a race)* Starter [ˈʃtaˈte] der <-s, -> ♀Starterin [ˈʃtaˈtərɪn] die <-, -nen> ◊ *Der Starter feuerte den Startschuss ab.* be under starter's orders auf das Startkommando warten [aof das ˈʃtaˈtkoˌmando; vaˈtn̩] +haben ◊ *Alle Teilnehmer warten auf das Startkommando. 2. (competitor)* Teilnehmer [ˈtaelneːme] der <-s, -> ♀Teilnehmerin [ˈtaelneːmərɪn] die <-, -nen> ◊ *Alle Teilnehmer bitte an den Start!* late starter Spätzünder

['ʃpɛːtˌsʏndɐ] der <-s, -> ♀Spätzünderin
['ʃpɛːtˌsʏndɐrɪn] die <-, -nen> ◊ *Er ist zwar ein Spät-*
zünder, aber mittlerweile sehr erfolgreich im
Geschäft. be a slow starter in the mornings morgens
nur langsam in Schwung kommen
[mɔˈɡɐ̯s nuːɐ̯ ˈlaŋzaːm ɪn ˌʃvʊŋ kɔmən] <kommt, kam,
ist gekommen> **3.** *(first course)* Vorspeise
['foːɐ̯ʃpaɛ̯zə] die <-, -n> ◊ *Als Vorspeise gab es eine*
Suppe. **4.** *(for a discussion etc.)* Anfang ['anfaŋ] der
<-(e)s, Anfänge> ◊ *Dieses Beispiel ist doch ein guter*
Anfang für eine Diskussion. **5.** *(of a car)* Anlasser
['anlasɐ] der <-s, -> ◊ *Der Anlasser des Wagens*
funktioniert nicht.

Ⓢ **for starters** zunächst einmal
starting line ⟨noun⟩ Startlinie ['ʃtaˈtliːnjə] die <-, -n>
startle ⟨verb⟩ erschrecken [ɛˈʃrɛkŋ̍] <erschreckt,
erschreckte, hat erschreckt> ◊ *Verzeihung, ich wollte*
Sie nicht erschrecken!
startled ⟨adj⟩ erschrocken [ɛˈʃrɔkŋ̍] ◊ *Sie drehte sich*
erschrocken um. ◆ *ein erschrockenes Gesicht*
machen
starve ⟨verb⟩ **1.** *(have nothing to eat, refuse to eat)*
starve (yourself) hungern ['hʊŋɐn] +haben ◊
Millionen von Menschen auf der Welt hungern. ◆ *Sie*
hungert, um abzunehmen. sb starves to death jd
verhungert [fɛˈhʊŋɐt] <verhungert, verhungerte, ist ver-
hungert> ◊ *Täglich verhungern in diesem Land zahl-*
reiche Kinder. **2.** *(deprive of food)* starve sb jdn
hungern lassen ['hʊŋən lasŋ̍] <lässt, ließ, hat lassen>
◊ *Die Wärter ließen die Gefangenen hungern.* starve
sb to death jdn verhungern lassen
state¹ ⟨noun⟩ **1.** *(condition, form)* Zustand ['tsuːʃtant]
der <-(e)s, Zustände> ◊ *Das Haus ist in einem aus-*
gezeichneten/verwahrlosten Zustand. ◆ *Im betrunke-*
nen Zustand sollte man nicht fahren. ◆ *Im festen*
Zustand wird Wasser als Eis bezeichnet. ◆ *Als man*
sie fand, war sie in einem schrecklichen Zustand.
not be in a fit state to do sth etw. in diesem
Zustand nicht tun können ◊ *In diesem Zustand*
können Sie nicht allein nach Hause fahren. state of
health Gesundheitszustand [ɡəˈzʊnthaɛ̯tsˈtsuːʃtant]
state of mind Geisteszustand ['ɡaɛ̯stəsˈtsuːʃtant] put
sb in a state of panic/wonder jdn in Panik/Staunen.
versetzen [ɪn ˈpaːnɪk/ˈʃtaʊ̯nən fɛɐ̯tsn̩] <versetzt,
versetzte, hat versetzt> get into a state durchdrehen
['dʊɐ̯çdreːən] +haben/sein *(fam)* ◊ *Sie wäre vor Angst*
fast durchgedreht, als er nachts nicht nach Hause
kam. **2.** POL Staat [ʃtaːt] der <-(e)s, -en> ◊ *ein*
demokratischer/totalitärer/unabhängiger Staat ◆ *Er*
wohnt im Staat New York. ◆ *vom Staat finanziert/*
subventioniert ◆ *beim Staat angestellt sein* the
States die Staaten ◊ *Sie will nächstes Jahr in die*
Staaten gehen. **3.** *(with a lot of pomp)* travel in state
pompös reisen [pɔmˈpøːs ˌraɛ̯zn̩] +sein ◊ *Sie reiste*
pompös, mit viel Gepäck und mehreren Dienern. be
buried in state ein Staatsbegräbnis erhalten
[aɛ̯n ˈʃtaːtsbəɡrɛːpnɪs ehaltn̩] <erhält, erhielt, hat
erhalten>
state² ⟨verb⟩ **1.** *(say, write)* erklären [ɛˈklɛːrən]
<erklärt, erklärte, hat erklärt> ◊ *Sie erklärte, dass sie*
die Leitung des Projekts übernehmen werde. ◆
„Morgen höre ich auf zu rauchen", erklärte er ent-
schlossen.; (an opinion) darlegen ['daːɐ̯leːɡŋ̍] +haben
◊ *Er legte seine Meinung zu dem Thema dar.* state
your case eine Sache vortragen
[aɛ̯nə zaxə ˈfoːɐ̯traːɡŋ̍] <trägt vor, trug vor, hat vorge-

tragen> ◊ *Lassen Sie ihn doch erst einmal die Sache*
vortragen. **2.** *(give information, a price, name, an*
amount etc.) angeben ['angeːbm̩] <gibt an, gab an,
hat angegeben> ◊ *Er hatte eine falsche Adresse*
angegeben. ◆ *Der Betrag wird in Euro und Franken*
angegeben.
State Department ⟨noun⟩ US-Außenministerium
[uːlˌɛslˈaɔsnmɪnɪsˌteːrjʊm] das <-s> no pl
statement ⟨noun⟩ **1.** *(official announcement)* Erklärung
[ɛˈklɛːrʊŋ] die <-, -en> ◊ *In einer Erklärung des*
Unternehmens heißt es, … make a statement eine
Erklärung abgeben ◊ *Der Minister gab keine*
Erklärung dazu ab. **2.** LAW *(to the police, in court)*
Aussage ['aɔszaːɡə] die <-, -n> ◊ *Die Frau war*
nicht bereit, vor Gericht eine Aussage zu machen.
3. FIN *(bank)* statement Kontoauszug
['kɔntoˌaɔstsuːk] der <-(e)s, Kontoauszüge> ◊ *Ich*
bewahre alle Kontoauszüge in einem Ordner auf.
4. *(spoken explanation)* Darlegung ['daːɐ̯leːɡʊŋ] die
<-, -en> *(form)* ◊ *Sie wurde bei der Darlegung des*
Problems öfters unterbrochen.
state-owned ⟨adj⟩ staatlich ['ʃtaːtlɪç] no comp/superl
◊ *Der Rundfunk in diesem Land ist staatlich.* ◆ *staat-*
liche Betriebe/Unternehmen privatisieren
statesman ⟨noun⟩ Staatsmann ['ʃtaːtsman] der
<-(e)s, Staatsmänner> ◊ *Konrad Adenauer war ein*
großer Staatsmann.
static ⟨adj⟩ konstant [kɔnˈstant] <konstanter, kon-
stantesten> ◊ *Die Preise für Immobilien sind seit*
einiger Zeit konstant. ◆ *konstante Zahlen*
station ⟨noun⟩ **1.** *(for trains)* Bahnhof ['baːnhoːf] der
<-(e)s, Bahnhöfe> ◊ *jdn zum Bahnhof bringen* ◆
Der Zug erreichte den Bahnhof mit zwei Stunden Ver-
spätung.; (for coaches) Busbahnhof ['bʊsbaːnhoːf];
(for underground trains) Station [ʃtaˈtsjoːn] die
<-, -en> ◊ *Wie heißt die nächste Station?* ◆ *Er ist*
an der letzten Station ausgestiegen. underground
station U-Bahn-Station ['uːbaːnʃtaˌtsjoːn] **2.** *(of police,*
fire brigade) Wache ['vaxə] die <-, -n> ◊ *Man*
brachte den Mann auf die Wache, um ihn zu
verhören.; (for research etc.) Station [ʃtaˈtsjoːn] die
<-, -en> ◊ *eine meteorologische/seismologische*
Station petrol/gas station Tankstelle ['taŋkʃtɛlə] die
<-, -n> **3.** RADIO, TV Sender ['zɛndɐ] der <-s, -> ◊
Er arbeitet bei einem regionalen Sender. get/pick up
a station einen Sender empfangen können ◊
Diesen Sender können wir hier nicht empfangen.
radio station Radiosender ['raːdjozɛndɐ] television
station Fernsehsender ['fɛɐ̯nzeːzɛndɐ] **4.** *(position for*
special purpose) Platz [plats] der <-es, Plätze> ◊
seinen Platz einnehmen/verlassen **5.** MIL Stellung
['ʃtɛlʊŋ] die <-, -en> ◊ *die Stellung verlassen/*
wechseln naval station Flottenstützpunkt
['flɔtn̩ʃtʏtspʊŋkt] der <-(e)s, -e> **6.** *(ranch)* Farm
[faːm] die <-, -en> ◊ *Seine Tochter lebt auf einer*
Farm in Australien und züchtet Schafe.
stationary ⟨adj⟩ *(car)* parkend ['paˈkŋ̍t] only before ns
◊ *Er hatte einen parkenden Wagen beschädigt.; (not*
movable) stationär [ʃtatsjoˈnɛːɐ̯] no comp/superl ◊
eine stationäre Anlage zur Ozonmessung ◆ *Die*
Kamera ist stationär.; (traffic etc.) remain stationary
stillstehen ['ʃtɪlʃteːən] <steht still, stand still, hat stillge-
standen> ◊ *Nach dem Unfall stand der Verkehr auf*
der Autobahn still.
statistical(ly) ⟨adj, adv⟩ statistisch [ʃtaˈtɪstɪʃ] no
comp/superl; when used as an adj, only before ns ◊

etw. mit statistischen Methoden untersuchen ♦ *Das Ergebnis ist statistisch nicht relevant.*

statistics [noun] Statistik [ʃtaˈtɪstɪk] die <-, -en>

statue [noun] Statue [ˈʃtaːtuə] die <-, -n> ◊ *Im Park steht die Statue eines griechischen Gottes.*

status [noun] **1.** *(legal position)* Status [ˈʃtaːtʊs] der <-, -> ◊ *Er hat immer noch den Status eines illegalen Einwanderers.* ♦ *der rechtliche Status einer Person* marital status Familienstand [faˈmiːljənʃtant] der <-(e)s> no pl ◊ *Bitte geben Sie Alter und Familienstand an.* **2.** *(social position)* Stellung [ˈʃtɛlʊŋ] die <-> no pl ◊ *die soziale/gesellschaftliche Stellung der Frau* ♦ *Er hat in seiner Heimat eine hohe Stellung.* status symbol Statussymbol [ˈʃtaːtʊszʏmboːl] das <-s, -e> **3.** *(level of progress)* Stand [ʃtant] der <-(e)s> no pl ◊ *Wie ist der aktuelle Stand der Verhandlungen?*

statute [noun] **1.** *(law)* Gesetz [ɡəˈzɛts] das <-es, -e> ◊ *ein Gesetz verabschieden* by statute gesetzlich [ɡəˈzɛtslɪç] ◊ *gesetzlich zu etw. verpflichtet sein* ♦ *etw. gesetzlich festlegen* **2.** *(of an organization)* statutes Satzung [ˈzatsʊŋ] die <-, -en> ◊ *So steht es in der Satzung unseres Vereins.* ♦ *etw. in die Satzung aufnehmen*

statutory [adj] *(controlled by a law)* gesetzlich [ɡəˈzɛtslɪç] only before ns ◊ *eine gesetzliche Bestimmung* ♦ *Neujahr ist ein gesetzlicher Feiertag.* This is statutory. Das ist Gesetz.; *(controlled by a statute of an organization)* satzungsgemäß [ˈzatsʊŋsɡəmɛːs] no comp/superl ◊ *die satzungsgemäße Aufnahme neuer Mitglieder* ♦ *Dieses Vorgehen ist nicht satzungsgemäß.*

staunch [verb] stillen [ˈʃtɪlən] +haben ◊ *Der Arzt konnte das Blut stillen.* staunch a wound die Blutung einer Wunde stillen

stay[1] [noun] Aufenthalt [ˈaʊfn̩thalt] der <-(e)s, -e> ◊ *Wir wünschen Ihnen einen angenehmen Aufenthalt!* ♦ *Während ihres Aufenthalts im Krankenhaus bekam sie viel Besuch.*

stay[2] [verb] **1.** *(remain in a place, condition)* bleiben [ˈblaɪbm̩] <bleibt, blieb, ist geblieben> ◊ *Bleib doch noch ein bisschen!* ♦ *Du kannst gern zum Abendessen bleiben.* ♦ *Ich bleibe heute im Bett.* ♦ *Ich versuche, fit zu bleiben.* ♦ *Bleib ganz ruhig, ich bin ja bei dir.* ♦ *Wie lange werden die Zinsen noch so niedrig bleiben?* stay behind zurückbleiben [ˈtsuːrʏkblaɪbm̩] <bleibt zurück, blieb zurück, ist zurückgeblieben> ◊ *Alle gingen nach Hause; nur sie blieb zurück und half beim Aufräumen.*; *(in school)* nachsitzen [ˈnaːxzɪtsn̩] <sitzt nach, saß nach, hat nachgesessen> ◊ *Zur Strafe musste er nachsitzen.* **2.** *(live in a place as a guest)* wohnen [ˈvoːnən] +haben ◊ *Wohnt ihr im Hotel?* stay with sb bei jdm wohnen ◊ *Sie wohnt bei einer Freundin.* stay (the night) übernachten [ybeˈnaxtn̩] <übernachtet, übernachtete, hat übernachtet> ◊ *Möchtet ihr übernachten?* come to stay zu Besuch kommen [tsuː bəˈzuːx kɔmən] <kommt, kam, ist gekommen> ◊ *Meine Schwester wird für eine Woche zu Besuch kommen.* stay in a place (for a certain time) (eine bestimmte Zeit) an einem Ort sein [(aenə bəˈʃtɪmtə ˌtsaɪt) an aenəm ˈɔʳt zaen] +sein ◊ *Sie ist übers Wochenende bei ihren Eltern.* ♦ *Ich war im Sommer zwei Wochen in Frankreich.*
• **stay around** [phras v] bleiben [ˈblaɪbm̩] <bleibt, blieb, ist geblieben> ◊ *Woher willst du wissen, dass*

sie diesmal bleiben wird?
• **stay back** [phras v] zurückbleiben [ˈtsuːrʏkblaɪbm̩] <bleibt zurück, blieb zurück, ist zurückgeblieben> ◊ *Bitte bleiben Sie hinter der Absperrung zurück.* ♦ *Bleiben Sie zurück! Der Hund ist gefährlich!*
• **stay in** [phras v] zu Hause bleiben [tsuː ˈhaʊzə blaɪbm̩] <bleibt, blieb, ist geblieben> ◊ *Ich bleibe heute lieber zu Hause, da ich mich nicht gut fühle.*
• **stay on** [phras v] bleiben [ˈblaɪbm̩] <bleibt, blieb, ist geblieben> ◊ *Nach Ablauf des Vertrags blieb sie für ein weiteres Jahr.* stay on as sth etw. bleiben ◊ *Er wird wohl Leiter der Firma bleiben.*
• **stay out** [phras v] **1.** *(not come home)* ausbleiben [ˈaʊsblaɪbm̩] <bleibt aus, blieb aus, ist ausgeblieben> ◊ *Bitte bleib nicht wieder so lange aus.* **2.** *(not become involved)* stay out of sth sich aus etw. heraushalten [aʊs ... hɛˌraʊshaltn̩] <hält sich heraus, hielt sich heraus, hat sich herausgehalten> ◊ *Halte dich bitte aus allen Schwierigkeiten heraus.*
• **stay over** [phras v] über Nacht bleiben [yːbɐ ˈnaxt blaɪbm̩] <bleibt, blieb, ist geblieben> ◊ *Wenn Sie möchten, können Sie gern über Nacht bleiben.*
• **stay up** [phras v] aufbleiben [ˈaʊfblaɪbm̩] <bleibt auf, blieb auf, ist aufgeblieben> ◊ *Gestern ist sie bis nach Mitternacht aufgeblieben.* ♦ *Bleib nicht wieder die ganze Nacht auf.* stay up late lange aufbleiben
• **stay together** [phras v] zusammenbleiben [tsuˈzamənblaɪbm̩] <bleibt zusammen, blieb zusammen, ist zusammengeblieben> ◊ *Das Paar will für immer zusammenbleiben.*

steadily [adv] **1.** *(without trembling or moving)* ruhig [ˈruːɪç] ◊ *Die Kerze brannte ruhig.* ♦ *Sie sah ihn ruhig an.* **2.** *(constantly)* kontinuierlich [kɔntinuˈiːɐ̯lɪç] no comp/superl (lofty) ◊ *einen Vorsprung kontinuierlich ausbauen* ♦ *eine kontinuierlich wachsende Anzahl der Arbeitslosen* **3.** *(staying at the same level or rhythm)* gleichmäßig [ˈɡlaɪçmɛːsɪç] ◊ *gleichmäßig atmen* ♦ *Sein Herz schlägt gleichmäßig.* **4.** *(reliably)* zuverlässig [ˈtsuːfɛlɛsɪç] ◊ *Er arbeitet sehr zuverlässig.*

steady [adj] **1.** *(firm, not shaking)* ruhig [ˈruːɪç] ◊ *eine ruhige Hand haben* ♦ *Halten Sie die Lampe ruhig.*; *(ladder etc.)* standfest [ˈʃtantfɛst] <standfester, am standfestesten> ◊ *ein standfestes Gerüst* ♦ *Das Regal ist sehr standfest.* The ladder is steady. Die Leiter steht fest. **2.** *(constant)* kontinuierlich [kɔntinuˈiːɐ̯lɪç] no comp/superl ◊ *eine kontinuierliche Entwicklung* ♦ *Der Fortschritt war langsam, aber kontinuierlich.* **3.** *(regular, staying the same)* gleichmäßig [ˈɡlaɪçmɛːsɪç] ◊ *Unsere Geschwindigkeit blieb gleichmäßig.* ♦ *Sie lauschte dem gleichmäßigen Rhythmus der Trommeln.* **4.** *(reliable)* zuverlässig [ˈtsuːfɛlɛsɪç] ◊ *Er ist ein zuverlässiger Mitarbeiter.* ♦ *Ich halte sie nicht für zuverlässig.* **5.** *(job, income, relationship, gaze)* fest [fɛst] <fester, am festesten> ◊ *keine feste Stelle haben* ♦ *ohne festes Einkommen sein* ♦ *Hast du einen festen Freund?* ♦ *Sein Blick blieb fest.*

steak [noun] *(of meat)* Steak [steːk] das <-s, -s> ◊ *ein Steak mit Pommes; (of fish)* Filet [fiˈleː] das <-s, -s> ◊ *Er kaufte drei Filets vom Lachs.* gammon steak gebratene Schinkenscheibe [ɡəˌbraːtənə ˈʃɪŋkn̩ʃaɪbə] die <-, -n> steak and kidney pie Fleischpastete mit Nieren [ˌflaɪʃpasˌteːtə mɪt ˈniːrən] die <-, -n>

steal ⸂verb⸃ **1.** *(take sth that does not belong to you)* stehlen ['ʃteːlən] <stiehlt, stahl, hat gestohlen> ◊ *Mein Auto wurde gestohlen.* ♦ *Ich habe noch nie gestohlen.* ♦ *Dieser Autor hat meine Idee gestohlen.* steal sth from sb jdm etw. stehlen ◊ *Ein Mann stahl ihr die Handtasche.* steal sth from sth etw. aus etw. stehlen ◊ *Aus dem Laden wurde Geld gestohlen.* **2.** *(go somewhere)* steal somewhere sich irgendwohin stehlen ['ʃteːlən] <stiehlt sich, stahl sich, hat sich gestohlen> ◊ *Sie stahl sich in die Küche und naschte von den Keksen.*

steam¹ ⸂noun⸃ Dampf [dampf] der <-(e)s, Dämpfe> ◊ *Das Bad war voller Dampf.* ♦ *Diese Turbinen werden durch/mit Dampf angetrieben.* steam engine Dampfmaschine ['dampfmaˌʃiːnə] die <-, -n> steam locomotive Dampflokomotive ['dampflokomoˌtiːvə] die <-, -n> ⊛ let off steam Dampf ablassen *(fam)* sb runs out of steam jdm geht die Puste aus *(fam)*

steam² ⸂verb⸃ **1.** *(give off steam)* dampfen ['dampfn] +haben ◊ *Das Essen dampfte auf dem Herd.* **2.** *(cook food)* dämpfen ['dɛmpfn] +haben ◊ *Gemüse dämpfen* **3.** *(move with steam)* dampfen ['dampfn] +sein ◊ *Das Schiff dampfte aus dem Hafen.; (run fast)* mit Volldampf laufen [mɪt 'fɔldampf laofn] <läuft, lief, ist gelaufen> *(fam)* ◊ *Er lief mit Volldampf nach Hause.*

steamer ⸂noun⸃ **1.** *(for cooking)* Dampfkochtopf ['dampfkɔxtopf] der <-(e)s, Dampfkochtöpfe> ◊ *Gemüse im Dampfkochtopf garen* **2.** SHIP Dampfer ['dampfe] der <-s, -> ◊ *auf einem Dampfer fahren*

steam iron ⸂noun⸃ Dampfbügeleisen ['dampfbyːgl̩ˌaezn] das <-s, ->

steel ⸂noun⸃ **1.** *(metal)* Stahl [ʃtaːl] der <-(e)s, Stähle or seldom -e> most sing ◊ *rostfreier Stahl* ♦ *ein Gebäude aus Beton und Stahl* ♦ *Als Rennfahrer braucht man Nerven aus Stahl.* steel helmet Stahlhelm ['ʃtaːlhɛlm] der <-(e)s, -e> steel industry Stahlindustrie ['ʃtaːlˌɪndʊsˌtriː] die <-, -n> **2.** *(sharpener)* Wetzstahl ['vɛtsʃtaːl] der <-(e)s> no pl ◊ *ein Messer mit dem Wetzstahl schärfen*

steep ⸂adj⸃ **1.** *(quickly rising or falling)* steil [ʃtael] ◊ *eine steile Treppe* ♦ *Der Abhang war sehr steil.* ♦ *eine steile Wachstumskurve* there's been a steep drop/rise in sth etw. ist stark gefallen/gestiegen [ɪst ʃtaʳk gəˈfalən/gəˈʃtiːgn̩] ◊ *Der Kurs des Dollars ist stark gefallen.* ♦ *Die Preise sind stark gestiegen.* **2.** *(excessive)* unverschämt ['ʊnfɛʃɛːmt] <unverschämter, am unverschämtesten> *(fam)* ◊ *eine unverschämte Forderung!* ♦ *Die Bars hier haben unverschämte Preise.*

steeply ⸂adv⸃ *(quickly rising or falling)* steil [ʃtael] ◊ *eine steil abfallende Straße* ♦ *Hier geht es wieder steil bergauf.; (prices etc.)* stark [ʃtaʳk] <stärker, am stärksten> ◊ *Die Kosten sind stark gefallen/gestiegen.*

steer ⸂verb⸃ *(control the direction, influence)* lenken ['lɛŋkn̩] +haben ◊ *Lass mich mal lenken!* ♦ *das Auto nach rechts/links lenken* ♦ *Sie versuchte, das Gespräch in eine andere Richtung zu lenken.* ♦ *Er lenkte sie behutsam zur Tür.; (move in a direction)* steer for sth auf etw. ⸂acc⸃ zusteuern [aof ... ˌtsuːˈʃtɔøɐn] <steuert zu, steuerte zu, ist zugesteuert> ◊ *Das Schiff steuerte auf den Hafen zu.* ♦ *Das Land schien auf eine Katastrophe zuzusteuern.*

steering wheel ⸂noun⸃ Lenkrad ['lɛŋkraːt] das <-(e)s, Lenkräder> ◊ *am/hinterm Lenkrad sitzen* ♦ *das Lenkrad einschlagen*

stem¹ ⸂noun⸃ **1.** *(of a plant, wine glass)* Stiel [ʃtiːl] der <-(e)s, -e> ◊ *Rosen mit langen Stielen* ♦ *ein Weinglas am Stiel halten* **2.** *(of a pipe)* Hals [hals] der <-es, Hälse> **3.** LING Stamm [ʃtam] der <-(e)s, Stämme> ◊ *Der Stamm von „singing" ist „sing".*

stem² ⸂verb⸃ *(stop from increasing)* eindämmen ['aendɛmən] +haben ◊ *die Kriminalität/die Kosten eindämmen; (a bleeding)* stillen ['ʃtɪlən] +haben ♦ stem from ⸂phras v⸃ stem from sth von etw. herrühren [fɔn ... heːˈgryːrən] +haben ◊ *Viele gesundheitliche Probleme rühren von schlechter Ernährung her.*

stench ⸂noun⸃ Gestank [gəˈʃtaŋk] der <-(e)s> no pl ◊ *einen fürchterlichen Gestank verbreiten*

step¹ ⸂noun⸃ **1.** *(pace, move, way of moving, stage in a process, sound, distance, measure)* Schritt [ʃrɪt] der <-(e)s, -e> ◊ *Würden Sie bitte einen Schritt/ein paar Schritte zurücktreten?* ♦ *Er hörte Schritte hinter sich.* ♦ *Sie erkannte ihn am Schritt.* ♦ *ein mutiger Schritt* ♦ *einen entscheidenden Schritt vorankommen.* ♦ *ein Schritt in die richtige Richtung* ♦ *mit juristischen Schritten drohen* ♦ *ein wichtiger Schritt im Lernprozess* take a step einen Schritt machen ◊ *Sie machte einige Schritte rückwärts.* dance step Tanzschritt ['tantsʃrɪt] der **2.** *(of a staircase)* Stufe ['ʃtuːfə] die <-, -n> ◊ *Sie wartete auf der untersten Stufe auf ihn.* ♦ *zwei Stufen auf einmal nehmen* mind the step Vorsicht, Stufe (flight of) steps Treppe ['ʃtrɛpə] die <-, -n> **3.** *(ladder)* steps Trittleiter ['trɪtlaetɐ] die <-, -n> ⊛ keep in step with sth mit etw. Schritt halten watch your step aufpassen ◊ *Pass auf, hier ist es glatt!* ♦ *Wenn du nicht aufpasst, verdirbst du es dir mit dem neuen Chef.*

step² ⸂verb⸃ *(take a step, walk, put your foot on sth)* step somewhere irgendwohin treten ['treːtn̩] <tritt, trat, ist getreten> ◊ *Er trat ins Freie/Zimmer.* ♦ *Sie trat ans Fenster und blickte hinaus.* ♦ *Vorsichtig trat sie auf das dünne Eis.* ♦ *Tritt nicht auf das Spielzeug.* step on sb's foot jdm auf den Fuß streten step on a train/plane in einen Zug/ein Flugzeug steigen [ɪn aenən 'tsuːk ʃtaegn̩] <steigt, stieg, ist gestiegen> step on a plane in ein Flugzeug steigen step on a ladder in eine Leiter steigen ⊛ step on it Gas geben ◊ *Los, gib Gas — die Ampel ist grün!* ♦ step back ⸂phras v⸃ **1.** *(move backwards)* zurücktreten [tsuˈrʏktreːtn̩] <tritt zurück, trat zurück, ist zurückgetreten> ◊ *von der Bahnsteigkante zurücktreten* **2.** *(stop for a moment)* innehalten ['ɪnəhaltn̩] <hält inne, hielt inne, hat innegehalten> ◊ *Lassen Sie uns kurz innehalten und das Ganze noch einmal überdenken.* ♦ step down ⸂phras v⸃ zurücktreten [tsuˈrʏktreːtn̩] <tritt zurück, trat zurück, ist zurückgetreten> ◊ *Der Minister/Präsident trat zurück.* ♦ *von einem Amt zurücktreten* ◊ *Sie trat aus gesundheitlichen Gründen als Vorsitzende zurück.* ♦ step forward ⸂phras v⸃ **1.** *(move forward)* vortreten ['foːɐtreːtn̩] <tritt vor, trat vor, ist vorgetreten> ◊ *Einer der Schüler trat vor und bob die Hand.* **2.** *(offer help)* sich melden ['mɛldn̩] <meldet sich, meldete sich, hat sich gemeldet> ◊ *Die Polizei bittet Zeugen des Unfalls, sich zu melden.* ♦ step in ⸂phras v⸃ **1.** *(enter)* eintreten ['aentreːtn̩]

<tritt ein, trat ein, ist eingetreten> ◊ *Sie öffnete die Tür und trat ein.* **2.** *(intervene)* einschreiten ['aɛnʃraɛtn̩] <schreitet ein, schritt ein, ist eingeschritten> ◊ *Als der Streit eskalierte, schritt er ein.*

• **step on** [phras v] step on sb auf jdm herumtrampeln [aof ... hɛˌrʊmtrampl̩n] +sein *(fam)* ◊ *Alle trampelten immer nur auf ihm herum.*

• **step out** [phras v] hinausgehen [hɪˈnaosgeːən] <geht hinaus, ging hinaus, ist hinausgegangen> ◊ *Markus ist kurz hinausgegangen.*

• **step up** [phras v] **1.** *(increase)* erhöhen [ɛˈhøːən] <erhöht, erhöhte, hat erhöht> ◊ *Wir müssen den Druck auf die Politiker erhöhen.* ♦ *die Produktion erhöhen* **2.** *(come forward)* vortreten [ˈfoːgtreːtn̩] <tritt vor, trat vor, ist vorgetreten> ◊ *Er trat vor, um seine Rede zu halten.*

stepbrother [noun] Stiefbruder [ˈʃtiːfbruːdɐ] der <-s, Stiefbrüder>

stepchild [noun] Stiefkind [ˈʃtiːfkɪnt] das <-(e)s, -er>

stepfather [noun] Stiefvater [ˈʃtiːffaːtɐ] der <-s, Stiefväter>

stepmother [noun] Stiefmutter [ˈʃtiːfmʊtɐ] die <-, Stiefmütter>

stepsister [noun] Stiefschwester [ˈʃtiːfʃvɛstɐ] die <-, -n>

stereo, stereo system [noun] Stereoanlage [ˈʃteːreoˌanlaːɡə] die <-, -n> ◊ *Meine Stereoanlage ist kaputt.*

ⓔ **in stereo** in Stereo ◊ *Das Programm wird in Stereo gesendet.*

stereotype [noun] Klischee [kliˈʃeː] das <-s, -s> ◊ *Sie entspricht genau dem Klischee der liebevollen Großmutter.* ♦ *ein Horrorfilm, der alle Klischees erfüllt* the stereotype of an Englishman etc. der typische Engländer etc. [deːɐ̯ ˌtyːpɪʃə ˈɛŋlɛndɐ]

sterile [adj] **1.** *(germ-free, uncomfortable and very clean)* steril [ʃteˈriːl] no comp/superl ◊ *Schere und Skalpell müssen steril sein.* ♦ *ein steriles Pflaster* ♦ *Der Raum wirkte kalt und steril.* **2.** *(not fertile)* unfruchtbar [ˈʊnfrʊxtbaːɐ̯] no comp/superl ◊ *Der Boden hier ist unfruchtbar.* ♦ *ein unfruchtbarer Mann*

sterilize [verb] sterilisieren [ʃteriliˈziːrən] <sterilisiert, sterilisierte, hat sterilisiert> ◊ *medizinische Instrumente sterilisieren* ♦ *Sie will keine Kinder mehr und hat sich sterilisieren lassen.*

sterling¹ [noun] **1.** *(currency)* britisches Pfund [ˌbrɪtɪʃəs ˈpfʊnt] <-(e)s, -e> pl 'britische Pfund' when used with figures ◊ *Das britische Pfund steht hoch im Kurs.* ♦ *100 britische Pfund umtauschen* **2.** *(metal)* sterling (silver) Sterlingsilber [ˈstœːlɪŋzɪlbɐ] das <-s> no pl ◊ *ein Armband aus Sterlingsilber*

sterling² [adj] ordentlich [ˈɔʁdn̩tlɪç] ◊ *Sie hat ordentliche Arbeit geleistet.* ♦ *Er ist ein ordentlicher Charakter.*

stern [noun] Heck [hɛk] das <-(e)s, -e or -s> ◊ *Sie stand am Heck und winkte.*

stern(ly) [adj, adv] streng [ʃtrɛŋ] ◊ *ein strenger Blick/Lehrer* ♦ *Ihre Miene war streng.* ♦ *jdn streng ansehen*

stew¹ [noun] Eintopf [ˈaɛntɔpf] der <-(e)s, Eintöpfe> most sing ◊ *Er isst sehr gern Eintopf.* ♦ *Eintopf kochen*

ⓔ **in a stew (about sth)** (wegen etw.) ganz aufgeregt ◊ *Sie war wegen des Gesprächs ganz aufgeregt.*

stew² [verb] schmoren [ˈʃmoːrən] +haben ◊ *das Fleisch im eigenen Saft schmoren* ♦ *Auf dem Herd schmorte ein Braten.*

ⓔ **let sb stew (in their own juice)** jdn (im eigenen Saft) schmoren lassen *(fam)*

steward [noun] **1.** *(on a plane, ship etc.)* Steward [ˈstjuːɛt] der <-s, -s> ◊ *Der Steward brachte die Getränke.* ♦ *Er ist Steward auf einem Kreuzfahrtschiff.* **2.** *(at a football match etc.)* Ordner [ˈɔʁdnɐ] der <-s, -> ◊ *Zwei Ordner brachten den Mann nach draußen.* **3.** *(sb who looks after sth)* Verwalter [fɛˈvaltɐ] der <-s, -> ◊ *Sie mussten einen neuen Verwalter einstellen.*

stick¹ [noun] **1.** *(from a tree, for walking or hitting)* Stock [ʃtɔk] der <-(e)s, Stöcke> ◊ *mit einem Stock im Feuer stochern* ♦ *am Stock gehen;* *(for pointing, baton)* Stab [ʃtaːp] der <-(e)s, Stäbe> ◊ *mit dem Stab auf die Landkarte zeigen* **2.** *(hockey)* Schläger [ˈʃlɛːɡɐ] der <-s, -> **3.** *(of an ice lolly, of a plant)* Stiel [ʃtiːl] der <-(e)s, -e> ◊ *Eis am Stiel* **4.** *(of vegetables, cinnamon, dynamite)* Stange [ˈʃtaŋə] die <-, -n> ◊ *eine Stange Sellerie;* *(of butter, margarine, chewing gum)* Stück [ʃtʏk] das <-(e)s, -e> pl 'Stück' when used with expressions of quantity stick of incense Räucherstäbchen [ˈrɔøçəʃtɛːpçən] das <-s, -> **5.** *(small container)* stick of ... ...stift [ʃtɪft] der <-(e)s, -e> stick of glue Klebestift [ˈkleːbəʃtɪft] stick of deodorant Deostift [ˈdeːoʃtɪft] **6.** the sticks die tiefste Provinz [diː ˈtiːfstə proˈvɪnts] <-> no pl ◊ *Sie wohnen in der tiefsten Provinz.*

ⓔ **get a lot of stick (from sb)** (von jdm) viel Kritik einstecken müssen give sb a lot of stick (for sth) jdn (wegen etw.) fertig machen *(fam)*

stick² [verb] **1.** *(push, insert, put)* stecken [ˈʃtɛkn̩] +haben ◊ *Die Fleischstücke auf Holzspießchen stecken.* ♦ *Der Hund steckte seinen Kopf durch den Zaun.;* *(wedge, push)* klemmen [ˈklɛmən] +haben ◊ *Er klemmte ein Stück Holz unter die Tür.* stick sth in the air etw. in die Luft strecken [ɪn diː ˈlʊft ʃtrɛkn̩] +haben **2.** *(sink into, pierce, be pushed)* sth sticks through/into sth etw. bohrt sich durch/in etw. [acc] [boːɐ̯t zɪç dʊɐ̯ç/ɪn] +haben ◊ *Der Pfeil bohrte sich in ihren Arm.* **3.** *(be in a fixed position)* sth sticks somewhere etw. steckt irgendwo [ʃtɛkt] +haben ◊ *Ein Dorn steckte in ihrer Fußsohle.;* *(door, zip)* sth sticks klemmen [klɛmt] +haben ◊ *Der Reißverschluss klemmt.* **4.** *(with glue, sticky tape)* kleben [ˈkleːbm̩] +haben ◊ *Sie klebte eine Briefmarke auf den Brief.* ♦ *Die Tapete wollte nicht kleben.* stick to sth etw. [dat] kleben ◊ *Dreck klebte an ihren Händen.* stick together zusammenkleben [tsuˈzamənkleːbm̩] +haben ◊ *Er klebte die Teile zusammen.* **5.** *(be remembered, regarded as valid and accepted)* hängen bleiben [ˈhɛŋən blaɛbm̩] <bleibt, blieb, ist geblieben> ◊ *Ist von der letzten Lektion etwas hängen geblieben?* ♦ *Der Verdacht blieb an ihm hängen.* stick in sb's mind jdm im Gedächtnis bleiben **6.** *(prove sb's guilt)* make sth stick etw. beweisen [bəˈvaɛzn̩] <beweist, bewies, hat bewiesen> ◊ *Die Polizei konnte den Anklagepunkt nicht beweisen.* stick sth on sb jdm die Schuld für etw. zuschieben [diː ˈʃʊlt fyːɐ̯ ... ˌtsuːˈʃiːbm̩] <schiebt zu, schob zu, hat zugeschoben> ◊ *Warum past du mir die Schuld für den Unfall zugeschoben?* **7.** *(endure)* stick sth etw. aushalten [ˈaoshaltn̩] <hält aus, hielt aus, hat ausgehalten> ◊ *Wie hältst du es hier nur aus?* ♦ *Ich*

halte diese Kälte nicht mehr aus.; (dislike) can't stick sb/sth jdn/etw. nicht ausstehen können [nɪçt 'aʊsʃteːən kœnən] <kann, konnte, hat können> ◊ *Ich kann sie und ihre Musik nicht ausstehen.* **8.** *(during card games)* passen ['pasn] +haben ⊛ **sb can stick sth** jd kann sich [dat] etw. (irgend)wo hinstecken *(rude)*

• **stick around** [phras v] dableiben ['daːblaebm̩] <bleibt da, blieb da, ist dageblieben>

• **stick at** [phras v] stick at sth an etw. [dat] dranbleiben [an ... 'dranblaebm̩] <bleibt dran, blieb dran, ist drangeblieben> ◊ *Du musst an der Arbeit dranbleiben, sonst wirst du nie fertig.* stick at it dranbleiben stick at nothing vor nichts zurückschrecken [foːɐ ,nɪçts tsuˈrʏkʃrɛkn̩] +sein

• **stick by** [phras v] **1.** stick by sb zu jdm halten [tsuː... 'haltn̩] <hält, hielt, hat gehalten> ◊ *Sie hat immer zu mir gehalten.* **2.** *(a plan, a decision)* stick by sth bei etw. bleiben [bae ... 'blaebm̩] <bleibt, blieb, ist geblieben> ◊ *Ich bleibe bei meiner Entscheidung: Ich fahre morgen.; (a promise)* sich an etw. [acc] halten [an ... 'haltn̩] <hält sich, hielt sich, hat sich gehalten> ◊ *Er hat sich an sein Versprechen gehalten.*

• **stick down** [phras v] aufschreiben ['aʊfʃraebm̩] <schreibt auf, schrieb auf, hat aufgeschrieben>

• **stick out** [phras v] **1.** *(be longer than sth)* überstehen ['yːbəʃteːən] <steht über, stand über, hat übergestanden> ◊ *Das Brett stand einen Meter über.; (ears)* abstehen ['apʃteːən] <steht ab, stand ab, hat abgestanden>; *(teeth)* vorstehen ['foːɐʃteːən] <steht vor, stand vor, hat vorgestanden> stick out of sth aus etw. [dat] ragen [aʊs ... raːgn̩] +haben stick out from under sth unter etw. [dat] hervorragen [ʊntɐ ... hɛɐ‚foːɐraːgn̩] +haben ◊ *Seine Füße ragten unter der Bettdecke hervor.* **2.** *(your belly, chest, tongue)* stick sth out etw. herausstrecken [hɛˈraʊsʃtrɛkn̩] +haben ◊ *den Bauch herausstrecken* stick your tongue out at sb jdm die Zunge herausstrecken **3.** *(stand out)* auffallen ['aʊffalən] <fällt auf, fiel auf, ist aufgefallen> ◊ *Er fällt überall auf.* **4.** stick it out durchhalten ['dʊrçhaltn̩] <hält durch, hielt durch, hat durchgehalten> ◊ *Halt durch!*

• **stick out for** [phras v] stick out for sth auf etw. [dat] bestehen [aʊf ... bəˈʃteːən] <besteht, bestand, hat bestanden> ◊ *Sie bestand auf ihren Forderungen.*

• **stick to** [phras v] *(not change or give up)* stick to sth bei etw. bleiben [bae ... 'blaebm̩] <bleibt, blieb, ist geblieben> ◊ *bei der Wahrheit bleiben; (the facts, a rule, schedule, diet)* sich an etw. [acc] halten [an ... 'haltn̩] <hält sich, hielt sich, hat sich gehalten> ◊ *sich streng an die Vorschriften halten* ⊛ **stick close to sb** jdm auf den Fersen bleiben

• **stick together** [phras v] *(remain together)* zusammenbleiben [tsuˈzamənblaebm̩] <bleibt zusammen, blieb zusammen, ist zusammengeblieben> ◊ *Ich will, dass meine Eltern zusammenbleiben.; (support each other)* zusammenhalten [tsuˈzamənhaltn̩] <hält zusammen, hielt zusammen, hat zusammengehalten> ◊ *Sie sind gute Freunde und halten zusammen.*

• **stick up** [phras v] **1.** *(hair)* hochstehen ['hoːxʃteːən] <steht hoch, stand hoch, hat hochgestanden> stick up out of sth aus etw. [dat] ragen [aʊs ... raːgn̩] +haben ◊ *Ein Felsen ragte aus dem Wasser.* **2.** stick sth up etw. hochhalten ['hoːxhaltn̩] <hält hoch, hielt hoch,

hat hochgehalten> ◊ *ein Schild hochhalten* Stick 'em up! Hände hoch!

• **stick up for** [phras v] stick up for sb/sth sich für jdn/etw. einsetzen [fyːɐ ... ‚aenzɛtsn̩] +haben ◊ *Sie setzte sich für ihre Freunde ein.* stick up for yourself sich [dat] selbst helfen ['zɛlpst hɛlfn̩] <hilft, half, hat geholfen> ◊ *Ich kann mir selbst helfen!*

• **stick with** [phras v] **1.** *(stay, continue)* stick with sb/sth bei jdm/etw. bleiben [bae ... 'blaebm̩] <bleibt, blieb, ist geblieben> ◊ *Bleib bei deinem Plan.* stick with it dabeibleiben [daˈbaeblaebm̩] +sein ◊ *Ich habe damit begonnen, und jetzt bleibe ich auch dabei.* **2.** *(not be forgotten)* stick with sb jdm im Gedächtnis bleiben [ɪm gəˈdɛçtnɪs blaebm̩] <bleibt, blieb, ist geblieben> ◊ *Dieser wunderschöne Tag blieb mir im Gedächtnis.*

sticker [noun] Aufkleber ['aʊfkleːbɐ] der <-s, -> ◊ *einen Aufkleber am Auto anbringen*

sticky [adj] **1.** *(glutinous)* klebrig ['kleːbrɪç] ◊ *Ich habe ganz klebrige Finger.* ♦ *Der Teig ist furchtbar klebrig.* sticky with sth mit etw. verklebt [mɪt ... fɛ‚kleːpt] no comp/superl **2.** *(sugary)* zuckrig ['tsʊkrɪç] ◊ *Der Kuchen ist sehr zuckrig.* sticky bun *süßes Hefebrötchen mit Zuckerguss* **3.** *(adhesive)* sticky ... Klebe... ['kleːbə] sticky plastic Klebefolie ['kleːbəfoːliə] die <-, -n> sticky tape Klebeband ['kleːbəbant] das <-(e)s, Klebebänder> **4.** *(weather)* schwül [ʃvyːl] ◊ *Heute ist es sehr schwül.* ♦ *ein schwüler Sommertag* **5.** *(sweaty)* verschwitzt [fɛˈʃvɪtst] <verschwitzter, am verschwitztesten> ◊ *Er war ganz verschwitzt.* ♦ *ihre verschwitzte Haut* **6.** *(difficult)* heikel ['haekl] <heikler, am heikelsten> <der/die/das heikle ...> ◊ *ein heikles Problem* ♦ *Dieser Punkt ist etwas heikel.*

stiff [adj] **1.** *(part of the body, collar, card, person, manner, breeze)* steif [ʃtaef] ◊ *einen steifen Hals haben* ♦ *Dazu braucht man steife Pappe.* ♦ *Sei doch nicht immer so steif!* ♦ *Es ging eine steife Brise.* beat sth until stiff etw. steif schlagen; *(dough, paste)* dick [dɪk] ◊ *Der Teig ist zu dick; da muss mehr Milch dran.* **2.** *(hard to move)* schwergängig ['ʃveːɐgɛŋɪç] ◊ *Die Schublade ist schwergängig.* ♦ *ein schwergängiges Pedal* **3.** *(drink, opposition, resistance, wind)* stark [ʃtark] <stärker, am stärksten> ◊ *ein starker Whisky* ♦ *Der Wind war stark.; (competition, sentence)* hart [hart] <härter, am härtesten> ◊ *ein hartes Urteil* ♦ *Der Wettbewerb in dieser Branche ist hart.; (fine, penalty)* hoch [hoːx] <höher, am höchsten> <der/die/das hohe ...> ◊ *eine hohe Geldstrafe* ♦ *Das Bußgeld war ziemlich hoch.*

stiffly [adv] steif [ʃtaef] ◊ *sich steif bewegen* ♦ *Sie begrüßte ihn steif.*

stifle [verb] **1.** *(suffocate)* ersticken [ɛˈʃtɪkn̩] <erstickt, erstickte, hat erstickt> transitive use +haben/intransitive use +sein ◊ *Der Mörder hat ihn erstickt.* ♦ *Sie wäre beinah an einer Gräte erstickt.* **2.** *(democracy, debate, an urge, a smile etc.)* unterdrücken [ʊntɐˈdrʏkn̩] <unterdrückt, unterdrückte, hat unterdrückt> ◊ *Sie unterdrückte ein Gähnen.* **3.** *(development, growth)* bremsen ['brɛmzn̩] +haben ◊ *das Wirtschaftswachstum bremsen*

stifled → **stifle** [adj] beengt [bəˈʔɛŋt] <beengter, am beengtesten> ◊ *Ich fühle mich beengt. Ich muss mal etwas Neues erleben!*

stigma [noun] Makel ['maːkl] der <-s, -> ◊ *Ihm haftete der Makel der Korruption an.*

still¹ [adj] *(calm, motionless, not fizzy)* still [ʃtɪl] ◊ *Es war ganz still im Wald.* ◆ *Trinkst du lieber stilles Wasser oder sprudelndes?; (without wind)* windstill ['vɪntʃtɪl] ◊ *Heute ist es windstill.* ◆ *eine windstille Nacht* sit still stillsitzen ['ʃtɪlzɪtsn̩] <sitzt still, saß still, hat stillgesessen> ◊ *Die Kinder können nicht stillsitzen.* keep still stillhalten ['ʃtɪlhaltn̩] <hält still, hielt still, hat stillgehalten> ◊ *Beim Blutabnehmen musst du stillhalten.*

still² [adv] **1.** *(not finished, still existing, expressing contrast)* noch [nɔx] ◊ *Wir haben noch etwas Zeit.* ◆ *Kann ich das auch morgen noch machen?* still better/worse etc. noch besser/schlechter etc. still more noch mehr; *(now and/or in the future)* immer noch ['ɪmɐ nɔx] ◊ *Bist du immer noch nicht fertig?* ◆ *Ich kann mich immer noch an ihn erinnern.* **2.** *(nevertheless)* dennoch ['dɛnɔx] ◊ *Das Kind ist lieb, aber dennoch anstrengend.* ◆ *Es war schon spät. Dennoch war er nicht müde.*

stimulate [verb] **1.** *(investment, tourism)* fördern ['fœɐ̯dɐn] +haben; *(the economy)* ankurbeln ['ankʊɐ̯bl̩n] +haben *(fam) die Konjunktur ankurbeln* **2.** *(an interest, the imagination, growth)* anregen ['anreːɡn̩] +haben ◊ *durch Vorlesen die Fantasie der Kinder anregen*

stimulation [noun] Anregung ['anreːɡʊŋ] die <–, –en> ◊ *ein Mittel zur Anregung des Kreislaufs*

stimulus [noun] **1.** *(for a development)* Impuls [ɪm'pʊls] der <–es, –e> ◊ *der entscheidende Impuls für den Aufschwung* **2.** MED *(physical)* Reiz [raɛ̯ts] der <–(e)s, –e> ◊ *Das Gehirn reagiert auf optische und akustische Reize.*

sting¹ [noun] **1.** *(pain, wound)* Stich [ʃtɪç] der <–(e)s, –e> ◊ *der Stich des Skorpions* ◆ *Die Stiche entzündeten sich.; (from a nettle, jellyfish, cream)* Brennen ['brɛnən] das <–s> *no pl* ◊ *Ich sah die Qualle und spürte ein Brennen am Arm.* **2.** *(of an insect, scorpion)* Stachel ['ʃtaxl̩] der <–s, –n> ◊ *Der Stachel steckt noch in meinem Fuß.*

sting² [verb] **1.** *(insect, scorpion, cactus)* stechen ['ʃtɛçn̩] <sticht, stach, hat gestochen> ◊ *Aua! Mich hat etwas gestochen!* ◆ *Können Hummeln stechen?* **2.** *(nettle, antiseptic, eyes)* brennen ['brɛnən] <brennt, brannte, hat gebrannt> ◊ *Das Salz brannte auf der Wunde.* ◆ *Meine Augen brennen.* sth stings sb's eyes etw. brennt jdm in den Augen **3.** *(affect, hurt, sting sb)* jdn treffen ['trɛfn̩] <trifft, traf, hat getroffen> sb is stung by sth etw. trifft jdn ◊ *Der Vorwurf hat sie schwer getroffen.* **4.** *(provoke)* sting sb into sth jdn zu etw. anstacheln [tsuː ... ˌanʃtaxl̩n] +haben ◊ *Die Kritik stachelte mich zu größeren Anstrengungen an.* **5.** *(rip off)* sting sb jdn schröpfen ['ʃrœpfn̩] +haben *(fam)* ◊ *die Steuerzahler schröpfen* He was stung 30 dollars for it. Er musste 30 Dollar dafür hinlegen.

stingy(-ily) [adj] geizig ['ɡaɛ̯tsɪç] *(pej)* ◊ *ein geiziger alter Mann* ◆ *Seine Eltern sind sehr geizig.* ◆ *geizig mit seinem Geld umgehen*

stink [verb] stink (of sth) (nach etw.) stinken ['ʃtɪŋkn̩] <stinkt, stank, hat gestunken> ◊ *stinkende Socken* ◆ *Hier stinkt's!* ◆ *Das stinkt doch nach Betrug!*

stir¹ [noun] **1.** *(excitement)* Aufsehen ['aɔ̯fzeːən] das <–s> *no pl* create a stir Aufsehen erregen **2.** give sth a stir etw. umrühren ['ʊmryːrən] +haben ◊ *den Reis umrühren*

stir² [verb] **1.** *(food, a drink, substance)* umrühren

['ʊmryːrən] +haben ◊ *Zucker in den Kaffee tun und umrühren* ◆ *den Reis gelegentlich umrühren* stir sth into sth etw. in etw. [acc] rühren [ɪn ... ryːrən] +haben ◊ *Zucker in den Kaffee rühren* stir in einrühren ['aɛ̯nryːrən] +haben ◊ *Wasser aufkochen und das Pulver einrühren.* **2.** *(fear, hatred)* stir sth (up) etw. schüren ['ʃyːrən] +haben ◊ *Diese Berichte schüren die Angst vor Terrorismus.; (hope, memory, interest, passion)* stir sth (up) etw. wecken ['vɛkn̩] +haben ◊ *Das Erlebnis hat alte Erinnerungen in mir geweckt.* **3.** *(thought, feeling)* sth stirs (in sb) etw. regt sich (in jdm) ['reːkt tsɪç] +haben ◊ *In mir regte sich ein Verdacht.* **4.** *(move)* stir sth etw. bewegen [bə'veːɡn̩] <bewegt, bewegte, hat bewegt> The wind stirred the leaves. Der Wind bewegte die Blätter. sb/sth stirs jd/etw. bewegt sich ◊ *Die Gardinen bewegten sich.* ◆ *Er bewegt sich kaum noch aus dem Haus.; (in the morning)* begin to stir sich regen ['reːɡn̩] +haben ◊ *Es ist schon acht, aber bei ihnen regt sich noch keiner.* ☞ stir yourself in die Gänge kommen *(fam)*

◆ **stir into** [phras v] stir sb into sth jdn zu etw. anstacheln [tsuː ... ˌanʃtaxl̩n] +haben ◊ *jdn zu einem Aufstand anstacheln* stir sb into doing sth jdn dazu anstacheln, etw. zu tun

◆ **stir up** [phras v] **1.** *(mud, water)* etw. aufwühlen ['aɔ̯fvyːlən] +haben ◊ *vom Wind aufgewühlte Wellen; (dust)* etw. aufwirbeln ['aɔ̯fvɪɐ̯bl̩n] +haben → **stir 2.**

stitch¹ [noun] **1.** *(in sewing, for a wound)* Stich [ʃtɪç] der <–(e)s, –e> ◊ *Nur noch ein paar Stiche, dann ist die Hose fertig.* ◆ *Die Wunde musste mit drei Stichen genäht werden.; (in a row)* stitches Naht [naːt] die <–, Nähte> ◊ *Die Naht ist aufgegangen.* take the stitches out (jdm) die Fäden ziehen [diː 'fɛːdn̩ tsiːən] ◊ *Eine Woche nach der Operation hat der Arzt ihr die Fäden gezogen.* **2.** *(in knitting)* Masche ['maʃə] die <–, –n> ◊ *eine Masche fallen lassen* **3.** *(pain in your side)* Seitenstechen ['zaɛ̯tnʃtɛçn̩] das <–s> *no pl* ◊ *Nach hundert Metern bekam er Seitenstechen.* ☞ a stitch in time (saves nine) ein Griff zur rechten Zeit spart viel Müh und Leid not have a dry stitch on völlig durchnässt sein not have a stitch on splitternackt sein *(fam)* be in stitches sich schieflachen *(fam)* have sb in stitches bei jdm Lachsalven auslösen

stitch² [verb] nähen ['nɛːən] +haben ◊ *einen Flicken auf die Hose nähen* ◆ *Die Wunde muss genäht werden.* stitch sth on (sth) etw. (an etw. [acc]) annähen ['annɛːən] +haben

◆ **stitch up** [phras v] **1.** *(a piece of clothing, an injury)* stitch sth up etw. nähen ['nɛːən] +haben ◊ *Er nähte den Riss in der Jacke.* ◆ *Der Arzt hat die Wunde genäht.* **2.** *(land sb in a bad situation)* stitch sb up jdn hereinlegen [hɛ'raɛ̯nleːɡn̩] +haben *(fam)* ◊ *Sie haben mich hereingelegt.* **3.** *(manage to get sth advantageous)* stitch sth up etw. an Land ziehen [an 'lant tsiːən] <zieht, zog, hat gezogen> ◊ *einen großen Auftrag an Land ziehen*

stock¹ [noun] **1.** *(store, provisions)* stock (of sth) Vorrat (an etw. [dat]) ['foːɡraːt] der <–(e)s, Vorräte> ◊ *Vorräte für den Winter anlegen* ◆ *Unser Vorrat an Bier geht langsam zur Neige.* ◆ *Sie hat einen unerschöpflichen Vorrat an Ideen.* **2.** *(total amount)* Bestand [bə'ʃtant] der <–(e)s, Bestände> ◊ *die*

Bestände sichern ✦ *Der Bestand an Seepferdchen ist stark zurückgegangen.* fish stocks Fischbestand ['fɪʃbəʃtant] **3.** *(goods intended for sale)* Ware ['vaːrə] die <–, –n> ◊ *Wir bekommen täglich neue Ware herein.* **4.** FIN *(share)* Aktie ['aktsjə] die <–, –n> ◊ *mit Aktien an der Börse handeln; (total capital)* Grundkapital ['grʊntkapi,taːl] das <–s> no pl ◊ *das Grundkapital erhöhen* **5.** *(for soup)* Brühe ['bryːə] die <–, –n> ◊ *Die Zwiebeln anbraten und mit Brühe aufgießen.* chicken stock Hühnerbrühe ['hyːnebryːə] vegetable stock Gemüsebrühe [gə'myːzəbryːə] **6.** *(livestock)* Vieh [fiː] das <–(e)s> no pl **7.** *(line of descent)* Abstammung ['apʃtamʊŋ] die <–> no pl ◊ *Ihre Familie ist italienischer Abstammung.* **8.** BOT Levkoje [lɛf'koːjə] die <–, –n>

☺ **take stock (of sth)** eine Bestandsaufnahme (… gen) machen **in stock 1.** *(in storage)* vorrätig ◊ *Haben Sie diese Ware vorrätig?* **2.** *(available for delivery)* lieferbar ◊ *Das Buch ist zurzeit nicht lieferbar.* **on the stocks** in Arbeit **out of stock 1.** *(not in storage)* nicht vorrätig **2.** *(not available for delivery)* nicht lieferbar

stock² verb **1.** *(goods)* führen ['fyːrən] +haben ◊ *Führen Sie auch Tapeten?* **2.** *(a cupboard, shelves)* stock (up) sth etw. füllen ['fʏlən] +haben ◊ *Der Schrank war mit Konserven gefüllt.* stock (up) with sth sich dat einen Vorrat von etw. anlegen [aenən ˌfoːgraːt fɔn … ˌanleːgn̩] +haben **3.** stock sth with fish Fische in etw. acc setzen [ˌfɪʃə ɪn … zɛtsn̩] +haben

stock exchange noun Börse ['bœʳzə] die <–, –n> ◊ *die New Yorker Börse*

stocking noun Strumpf [ʃtrʊmpf] der <–(e)s, Strümpfe> ◊ *Sie trug schwarze Strümpfe.* in your stocking feet auf Strümpfen Christmas stocking *Strumpf, in den Weihnachtsgeschenke gesteckt werden*

stock market noun Börse ['bœʳzə] die <–, –n> ◊ *Sie hat an der Börse sehr viel Geld verloren.* ✦ *die Londoner Börse*

stolen → steal adj gestohlen [gə'ʃtoːlən] stolen goods Diebesgut ['diːbəsguːt] das <–(e)s> no pl

stomach noun **1.** *(part of the body)* Bauch [baʊx] der <–(e)s, Bäuche> ◊ *Ich schlafe auf dem Bauch.* ✦ *Mir tut der Bauch weh.* **2.** *(internal organ)* Magen ['maːgn̩] der <–s, Mägen> ◊ *Mir knurrt der Magen. Wann gibt's Essen?* on an empty stomach auf nüchternen Magen go swimming on a full stomach mit vollem Magen ins Wasser gehen The sight turned my stomach. Bei dem Anblick drehte sich mir der Magen um. I've got an upset stomach. Ich habe mir den Magen verdorben.

☺ **sb's stomach churns** jdm wird ganz flau im Magen **have the stomach for sth** genug Mumm für etw. haben *(fam)*

stomach ache noun Bauchschmerzen ['baʊxʃmeːɐtsn̩] die <–> only pl ◊ *Ich habe Bauchschmerzen.*

stone noun **1.** *(material, mineral, jewel)* Stein [ʃtaen] der <–(e)s, –e> ◊ *etw. in Stein meißeln* ✦ *Steine ins Wasser werfen* ✦ *ein Ring mit einem kostbaren Stein* ✦ *Er hat ein Herz aus Stein!* **2.** *(in fruit)* Kern [kɛʳn] der <–(e)s, –e> **3.** *(in the UK: unit of weight measurement)* eine britische Maßeinheit, die 6,35 Kilogramm entspricht She lost more than one stone. Sie hat über 6 Kilo abgenommen. [ziː hat ˌyːbɐ zɛks ˌkiːlo 'apgənɔmən]

☺ **leave no stone unturned** nichts unversucht lassen **set in stone** in Stein gemeißelt

stone age noun Steinzeit ['ʃtaentsaet] die <–> no pl ◊ *Funde aus der Steinzeit*

stool noun **1.** *(piece of furniture)* Hocker ['hɔkɐ] der <–s, –> ◊ *Sie stellte sich auf einen Hocker.* **2.** MED stool(s) Stuhl [ʃtuːl] der <–(e)s, Stühle>

stop¹ noun **1.** *(on a journey, for trains)* Station [ʃta'tsjoːn] die <–, –en> ◊ *Stockholm und Helsinki waren weitere Stationen unserer Reise.* ✦ *Er ist an der letzten Station ausgestiegen.; (for buses)* Haltestelle ['haltəʃtɛlə] die <–, –n> ◊ *An welcher Haltestelle muss ich aussteigen?* **2.** *(stay)* Aufenthalt ['aofn̩thalt] der <–(e)s, –e> ◊ *Nach einem kurzen Aufenthalt in Paris fliegen wir nach New York weiter.* overnight stop Übernachtung [ybɐ'naxtʊŋ] die <–, –en> **3.** MUS Register [re'gɪstɐ] das <–s, –> ◊ *Diese Orgel hat 53 Register.*

☺ **come to a stop** *(moving object)* stehen bleiben *(process)* aufhören **put a stop to sth** etw. stoppen

stop² verb **1.** *(prevent)* stop sb from doing sth jdn davon abhalten, etw. zu tun [dafɔn 'aphaltn̩ … tsuː] <hält ab, hielt ab, hat abgehalten> ◊ *Was hält dich eigentlich davon ab zu kündigen?* **2.** *(not continue)* stop sth mit etw. aufhören [mɪt … ˌaofhøːrən] +haben ◊ *Hört mit dem Arbeit aufhören Quatsch auf! Stop it! Hör auf!* stop doing sth aufhören, etw. zu tun ◊ *Sie hörten auf zu reden und sahen aufmerksam zu.* sth stops etw. hört auf ◊ *Hört der Regen/der Schmerz denn überhaupt nicht mehr auf?; (a habit)* stop sth etw. aufgeben ['aofgeːbm̩] <gibt auf, gab auf, hat aufgegeben> ◊ *das Rauchen/Trinken aufgeben; (a war, game, conversation)* etw. beenden [bə'ɛndn̩] <beendet, beendete, hat beendet> **3.** *(keep from moving, bring or come to a stop)* stop (sth/sb) etw./jdn anhalten ['anhaltn̩] <hält an, hielt an, hat angehalten> ◊ *jdn anhalten und nach dem Weg fragen* ✦ *Er hielt an und ließ sie aussteigen.; (bus, train)* sth/sb stops etw./jd hält [hɛlt] <hielt, hat gehalten> ◊ *Wo hält der Bus zum Bahnhof?; (for some time: vehicle, driver, clock)* etw./jd bleibt stehen [blaebt 'ʃteːən] <blieb, ist geblieben> ◊ *Hier darf man nicht stehen bleiben; das ist eine Einfahrt.* ✦ *Meine Uhr ist stehen geblieben.* We stopped at a restaurant on our way. Wir hielten unterwegs bei einem Restaurant an. Can you stop for a while? Kannst du kurz mit reinkommen? **4.** *(a payment, cheque)* stop sth etw. sperren ['ʃpɛrən] +haben ◊ *Sein Vater hat ihm das Taschengeld gesperrt.* ✦ *Die Bank hat den Scheck gesperrt.; (a machine, project, disaster)* etw. stoppen ['ʃtɔpm̩] +haben ◊ *die Maschinen stoppen* ◊ *Das Projekt wurde wegen Geldmangels gestoppt.* **5.** *(pain, hunger, bleeding)* stop sth etw. stillen ['ʃtɪlən] +haben ◊ *die Schmerzen stillen* **6.** *(heartbeat)* sth stops etw. setzt aus [zɛtst 'aos] +haben ◊ *Sein Herzschlag hat eine Minute lang ausgesetzt.* **7.** stop to do sth eine Pause machen, um etw. zu tun [aenə 'paozə maxn̩ ʊm … tsuː] +haben ◊ *Ich machte eine Pause, um mich auszuruhen.* stop to think einen Augenblick nachdenken [aenən aoŋblɪk 'naːxdɛŋkn̩] <denkt nach, dachte nach, hat nachgedacht> **8.** *(an opening, passage)* stop (up) etw. verstopfen [fɛ'ʃtɔpfn̩] <verstopft, verstopfte, hat verstopft>

☺ **stop at nothing** vor nichts zurückschrecken

there's no stopping sb jd ist nicht zu bremsen
• **stop by** [phras v] vorbeischauen [foːɐ̯ˈbaɛ̯ʃaɔən]
+haben ◊ *Schaust du auf dem Rückweg kurz vorbei?*
stop by sth irgendwo vorbeischauen ◊ *Ich will
schnell im Büro/bei Peter vorbeischauen.*
• **stop off** [phras v] vorbeischauen [foːɐ̯ˈbaɛ̯ʃaɔən]
+haben ◊ *Wir schauten kurz bei Oma vorbei.*
• **stop out** [phras v] über Nacht wegbleiben
[yːbe naxt ˈvɛkblaɛ̯bm̩] <bleibt weg, blieb weg, ist weg-
geblieben>
• **stop over** [phras v] **1.** *(overnight)* übernachten
[ybeˈnaxtn̩] <übernachtet, übernachtete, hat übernach-
tet> **2.** *(during a flight)* eine Zwischenlandung
machen [aɛ̯nə ˈtsvɪʃn̩landʊŋ maxn̩] +haben
• **stop up** [phras v] → **stop²** 8.
stop³ [interj] stopp [ʃtɔp] ◊ *Stopp! Keinen Schritt
weiter!*
stopgap [noun] Notlösung [ˈnoːtløːzʊŋ] die <-, -en>
stopper [noun] Stöpsel [ˈʃtœpsl̩] der <-s, -> ◊ *den
Stöpsel aus der Flasche ziehen*
stop sign [noun] Stoppschild [ˈʃtɔpʃɪlt] das
<-(e)s, -er>
storage [noun] **1.** *(process of storing sth)* Aufbewah-
rung [ˈaɔ̯fbəvaːrʊŋ] die <-> no pl ◊ *die Aufbewah-
rung von Chemikalien; (in large quantities)* Lagerung
[ˈlaːgərʊŋ] die <-> no pl ◊ *die Lagerung von Waren;
(of data)* Speicherung [ˈʃpaɛ̯çərʊŋ] die <-> no pl
2. *(room)* Lager [ˈlaːge] das <-s, ->; *(space)*
Stauraum [ˈʃtaɔ̯raɔ̯m] der <-(e)s> no pl ◊ *Unter der
Treppe ist viel Stauraum.* storage cupboard Vorrats-
schrank [ˈfoːgraːtsʃraŋk] der
<-(e)s, Vorratsschränke> **3.** *(costs)* Lagerkosten
[ˈlaːgekɔstn̩] die <-> only pl
⊕ in storage eingelagert
store¹ [noun] **1.** *(shop)* Geschäft [gəˈʃɛft] das
<-(e)s, -e> ◊ *ein Geschäft für Elektroartikel*
2. *(supply)* store (of sth) Vorrat (an etw. [dat])
[ˈfoːgraːt] der <-(e)s, Vorräte> ◊ *Vorräte für den
Winter anlegen* ✦ *Ihr Vorrat an Konserven ging zur
Neige.* stores Lager [ˈlaːge] das <-s> sing weapons
stores Waffenlager [ˈvafn̩laːge] **3.** *(room, building)*
Lager [ˈlaːge] das <-s, -> ◊ *etw. ins Lager bringen*
⊕ set great store by sth großen Wert auf etw. [acc]
legen lie in store (for sb) jdm bevorstehen have
sth in store (for sb) etw. (für jdn) bereithalten
store² [verb] **1.** *(keep: personal belongings)* store
(away) aufbewahren [ˈaɔ̯fbəvaːrən] <bewahrt auf,
bewahrte auf, hat aufbewahrt> ◊ *Er bewahrt ihr Foto
in seinem Geldbeutel auf.* ✦ *Sie hat alle seine Briefe
aufbewahrt.; (goods, waste)* lagern [ˈlaːgen] +haben ◊
Der Winzer lagert den Wein an einem kühlen Ort. ✦
Wo wird der Atommüll gelagert? **2.** *(animal: food for
the winter)* store sth up anlegen [dat] anlegen
[ˌfoːgrɛːtə an … ˌanleːgn̩] +haben ◊ *Eichhörnchen
legen Vorräte an Nüssen und Samen für den Winter
an.* **3.** *(data, knowledge)* speichern [ˈʃpaɛ̯çen] +haben
◊ *Daten auf CD-ROM speichern* ✦ *Das Gehirn kann
große Mengen von Informationen speichern.*
• **store up** [phras v] store up trouble sich Probleme
schaffen [proˈbleːmə ʃafn̩] <schafft sich, schuf sich,
hat sich geschaffen> ◊ *Wer jetzt nicht fleißig lernt,
schafft sich Probleme für die Zukunft.*
storehouse [noun] Lager [ˈlaːge] das <-s, -> ◊ *Die
Ernte war gut, und alle Lager waren gefüllt.*
storeroom [noun] Lager [ˈlaːge] das <-s, -> ◊
Nachschub aus dem Lager holen

storey, story [noun] *(in a building)* Stockwerk
[ˈʃtɔkvɐ̯k] das <-(e)s, -e> ◊ *Sie wohnen ein
Stockwerk über uns.; (with ordinal numbers)* Stock
[ʃtɔk] der <-(e)s> no pl ◊ *Wir wohnen im dritten
Stock.*
storm¹ [noun] **1.** *(strong wind, excitement)* Sturm
[ʃtʊrm] der <-(e)s, Stürme> ◊ *Der Sturm hat großen
Schaden angerichtet.* ✦ *Ein Sturm zieht auf.* A storm
is brewing. Ein Sturm braut sich zusammen. a
storm of indignation ein Sturm der Entrüstung
storm of protest Proteststurm [proˈtɛstʃtʊrm]
2. *(thunderstorm)* Gewitter [gəˈvɪte] das <-s, ->
⊕ a storm in a teacup ein Sturm im Wasserglas
go down a storm durchschlagenden Erfolg haben
ride the storm den Sturm überstehen take by
storm im Sturm erobern
storm² [verb] **1.** *(enter quickly and forcefully, become
successful quickly)* stürmen [ˈʃtʏrmən] +haben ◊ *Die
Polizei hat das Gebäude gestürmt.* ✦ *die Hitparade
stürmen* **2.** *(rush)* storm somewhere irgendwohin
stürmen [ˈʃtʏrmən] +sein ◊ *Die Kinder stürmten
lachend in den Garten.* storm off davonstürmen
[daˈfɔnʃtʏrmən] +sein ◊ *Sie ist wütend davonge-
stürmt.* **3.** *(full of rage)* toben [ˈtoːbm̩] +haben ◊ *„Ihr
Idioten!", tobte er.* storm at sb jdn wütend
anschreien [vyːtn̩t ˈanʃraɛ̯ən] <schreit an, schrie an,
hat angeschrien>
stormy [adj] stürmisch [ˈʃtʏrmɪʃ] ◊ *Das Wetter bleibt
stürmisch.* ✦ *Sie hatten eine stürmische Affäre.*
story [noun] **1.** *(true or fictional)* Geschichte [gəˈʃɪçtə]
die <-, -n> ◊ *Sie erzählte den Kindern eine
Geschichte.* ✦ *Können Sie seine Geschichte bestätigen?* change your story nicht bei seiner Geschichte
bleiben news story Nachricht [ˈnaːxrɪçt] die
<-, -en> be a front-page story in die Schlagzeilen
kommen [ɪn diː ˈʃlaːktsaɛ̯lən kɔmən] **2.** *(obviously
false)* Märchen [ˈmɛːçn̩] das <-s, -> *(pej)* ◊ *Erzähl
mir bloß keine Märchen!* **3.** *(rumo(u)r)* Gerücht
[gəˈrʏçt] das <-(e)s, -e> ◊ *Ich habe das Gerücht
gehört, dem Chef sei gekündigt worden.* US spelling
of storey
⊕ (it's the) story of my life wie könnte es anders
sein be a different story **1.** *(completely different)*
auf einem anderen Blatt stehen **2.** *(not relevant
now)* (jetzt) nicht hierher gehören a likely story
wer's glaubt, wird selig *(fam)* to cut a long story
short kurz und gut the same old story das alte
Lied *(fam)*
stout [adj] **1.** *(slightly overweight)* stämmig [ˈʃtɛmɪç] ◊
Er ist klein und stämmig. ✦ *stämmige Waden haben*
2. *(shoes)* fest [fɛst] <fester, am festesten> ◊ *feste
Wanderschuhe* ✦ *Deine Schuhe sind sehr fest!*
3. *(determined)* entschlossen [ɛntˈʃlɔsn̩] ◊ *entschlosse-
ner Widerstand gegen etw.*
stove [noun] **1.** *(for cooking)* Herd [heːgt] der
<-(e)s, -e> ◊ *Sie nahm die Suppe vom Herd.* **2.** *(for
heating)* Ofen [ˈoːfn̩] der <-s, Öfen> ◊ *Ein Feuer
knistert im Ofen.*
straight¹ [adj] **1.** *(not bent, crooked or inclined)* gerade
[gəˈraːdə] <gerader, am geradesten> ◊ *auf einer
geraden Strecke bremsen* ✦ *Die Linie ist nicht
gerade.* a straight line ein gerade geschnittener
Rock **2.** *(hair)* glatt [glat] <glatter/glätter, am glattes-
ten/glättesten> ◊ *Er hat glatte Haare.* ✦ *Ihr Haar ist
ganz glatt.* **3.** *(answer)* ehrlich [ˈeːglɪç] ◊ *eine
ehrliche Antwort* ✦ *Sei ehrlich!* be straight with sb

ehrlich mit jdm sein; *(conversation, word)* offen ['ɔfn̩] ◊ *ein offenes Gespräch* ♦ *Darf ich ein offenes Wort mit dir sprechen?; (question)* direkt [di'rɛkt] <direkter, am direktesten> ◊ *jdm eine direkte Frage stellen* **4.** *(correct)* richtig ['rɪçtɪç] *get sth straight etw.* richtig verstehen He had his facts straight. Er war gut informiert. put sb straight jdn aufklären ['aʊfklɛːrən] +haben ◊ *Erst hatte er Nick im Verdacht, aber wir haben ihn jetzt aufgeklärt.* put the record straight ein paar Dinge klarstellen [aɛn dɪŋə 'klaːʃtɛlən] ◊ *Ich muss mal mit ihm reden und ein paar Dinge klarstellen.* **5.** *(successive)* aufeinander folgend [aʊf|aɛˌnandə 'fɔlgn̩t] *no comp/ superl, only before ns* ◊ *an drei aufeinander folgenden Wochenenden; (with ordinal numbers)* in Folge [ɪn 'fɔlgə] *her fifth* straight win ihr fünfter Sieg in Folge **6.** *(at school)* get straight As überall Einsen bekommen [ybeː|al 'aɛnzn̩ bəkɔmən] <bekommt, bekam, hat bekommen> **7.** *(serious)* ernst [ɛʳnst] <ernster, am ernstesten> ◊ *ein ernstes Theaterstück* ♦ *Erst blieb ihr Gesicht noch ernst, aber dann lachte sie.* keep a straight face ernst bleiben **8.** *(drink)* pur [puːɐ̯] *postpositive, no comp/superl* ◊ *seinen Whisky pur trinken* straight whisky Whisky pur **9.** *(conventional)* angepasst ['angəpast] <angepasster, am angepasstesten> ◊ *Früher war er recht ausgeflippt, aber jetzt ist er angepasst.; (to the degree of narrowmindedness)* spießig ['ʃpiːsɪç] *(fam, pej)* ◊ *meine spießigen Nachbarn* ♦ *Ihre Eltern sind so spießig.* **10.** *(not homosexual)* hetero ['heːteroː] *no comp/superl (slang)* **11.** *(not on drugs)* clean [kliːn] *no comp/superl (slang)* **12.** *(not criminal)* sauber ['zaʊbɐ] *no comp/superl (slang)* **13.** *(straightforward)* einfach ['aɛnfax] ◊ *eine einfache Wahl* ♦ *Die Antwort ist einfach.; (decision)* klar [klaːʳ] ◊ *eine klare Entscheidung treffen*

straight² ⟨adv⟩ **1.** *(directly)* direkt [di'rɛkt] ◊ *Der Ball ging direkt ins Tor.* ♦ *Dieser Weg führt direkt zum Strand.* straight out of sth direkt aus etw. ◊ *Die Musik kommt direkt aus den Achtzigern.* straight on geradeaus [gəra:dəˈ|aʊs] ◊ *Fahren Sie geradeaus bis zur Ampel!* straight up/down senkrecht (nach oben/ unten) ['zɛŋkrɛçt (naːx 'oːbn̩/'ʊntn̩)] ◊ *Wirf den Ball senkrecht nach oben!* **2.** *(immediately)* straight (off) sofort [zoˈfɔʳt] *no comp/superl* ◊ *Sie ging nach der Arbeit sofort nach Hause.* ♦ *Er kam sofort zum Thema.* **3.** *(upright)* gerade [gəˈraːdə] <gerader, am geradesten> ◊ *Sitz bitte gerade!* ♦ *sich gerade halten* **4.** *(clearly)* klar [klaːʳ] ◊ *Ich konnte nicht mehr klar denken.* **5.** *(honestly)* straight (out) geradeheraus [gəra:dəhɛˈraʊs] *no comp/superl* ◊ *jdm etw. geradeheraus sagen.* ♦ *Er fragte mich geradeheraus, ob das wahr sei.* **6.** *(without a break)* ununterbrochen ['ʊn|ʊntebrɔxn̩] *no comp/superl* ◊ *Wir sind vier Stunden ununterbrochen gefahren.*

straighten ⟨verb⟩ **1.** *(make straight)* gerade rücken [gəˈraːdə rʏkn̩] +haben ◊ *Er rückte das Bild gerade.* straighten your/sb's tie sich/jdm die Krawatte gerade rücken; *(pull straight)* gerade ziehen [gəˈraːdə tsiːən] <zieht, zog, hat gezogen> ◊ *Sie zog die Tischdecke gerade.* straighten your/sb's sth sich/ jdm etw. gerade ziehen ◊ *Sie zog sich den Rock gerade.* ♦ *Lass dir mal das Hemd gerade ziehen!* **2.** *(restore to a straight line, your back)* durchdrücken ['dʊʳçdrʏkn̩] +haben straighten your knees die Knie durchdrücken; *(a broken nose)* richten ['rɪçtn̩]

<richtet, richtete, hat gerichtet>; *(a river, road)* begradigen [bəˈgraːdɪgn̩] <begradigt, begradigte, hat begradigt> **3.** *(your hair)* glätten ['glɛtn̩] <glättet, glätte, hat geglättet> straighten your hair sich ⟨dat⟩ das Haar glätten ◊ *Ich glättete mir mit der Hand das Haar.*

straightforward ⟨adj⟩ **1.** *(simple)* einfach ['aɛnfax] ◊ *Gibt es keine einfachere Lösung für das Problem?* ♦ *Diese Operation ist nicht einfach.; (clear)* klar [klaːʳ] ◊ *eine klare Anleitung* ♦ *Die Anweisungen waren nicht klar genug.* **2.** *(honest)* ehrlich ['eːʳlɪç] ◊ *eine ehrliche Antwort* ♦ *Ist er denn auch ehrlich?; (discussion)* offen ['ɔfn̩] ◊ *ein offenes Gespräch* ♦ *Das Gespräch war sehr offen.*

strain¹ ⟨noun⟩ **1.** *(load, burden)* Belastung [bəˈlastʊŋ] die <-, -en> ◊ *etw. als Belastung empfinden* put sth/sb under strain, be a strain on sb/sth etw./jdn belasten [bəˈlastn̩] <belastet, belastete, hat belastet> +haben ◊ *Schweres Heben belastet den Rücken.* ♦ *Die schlechte Arbeitsatmosphäre belastet uns alle sehr.; (tension)* Spannung ['ʃpanʊŋ] die <-, -en> ◊ *Zwischen den beiden herrschte den ganzen Tag Spannung.; (pressure)* Druck [drʊk] der <-(e)s> *no pl* ◊ *Sie standen unter großem Druck, eine schnelle Lösung zu finden.* **2.** *(injury)* Zerrung ['tsɛrʊŋ] die <-, -en> ◊ *eine Zerrung des Innenbands* **3.** *(variety)* Art [aːʳt] die <-, -en>; *(of plants)* Sorte ['zɔʳtə] die <-, -en> ◊ *eine neue Sorte züchten; (of bacteria, virus)* Stamm [ʃtam] der <-(e)s, Stämme> ◊ *ein resistenter Stamm von Staphylokokkus* **4.** *(tendency)* Neigung ['naɛgʊŋ] die <-> *no pl* a strain of depression eine Neigung zu Depressionen ⓔ take the strain **1.** *(on a rope)* festhalten und ziehen **2.** *(bear the pressure)* die Belastung aushalten **3.** take the strain off sb jdn entlasten

strain² ⟨verb⟩ **1.** *(try)* strain to do sth sich bemühen, etw. zu tun [bəˈmyːən ... tsuː] <bemüht sich, bemühte sich, hat sich bemüht> ◊ *Er bemühte sich, einen Blick über die Mauer zu werfen.* **2.** strain yourself sich anstrengen ['anʃtrɛŋən] +haben ◊ *Ich musste mich anstrengen, um mit ihm Schritt zu halten.* **3.** *(a relationship)* belasten [bəˈlastn̩] <belastet, belastete, hat belastet> ◊ *Der Zwischenfall hat die Beziehungen zwischen den beiden Ländern belastet.* **4.** *(injure)* strain a muscle sich ⟨dat⟩ einen Muskel zerren [aɛnən 'mʊskl̩ ˌtsɛran] +haben ◊ *Ich habe mir beim Training einen Muskel gezerrt.* strain your eyes die Augen überanstrengen [diː ˌaʊgn̩ ybeˈ|anʃtrɛŋən] <überanstrengt, überanstrengte, hat überanstrengt> ◊ *Die Arbeit am Bildschirm kann die Augen überanstrengen.* strain your back sich ⟨dat⟩ den Rücken verletzen [deːn 'rʏkn̩ fɛlɛtsn̩] <verletzt, verletzte, hat verletzt> **5.** *(to remove the water)* abgießen ['apgiːsn̩] <gießt ab, goss ab, hat abgegossen> ◊ *die Nudeln abgießen* **6.** *(to remove lumps)* passieren [paˈsiːrən] <passiert, passierte, hat passiert> ◊ *Passieren Sie die Suppe durch ein feines Sieb.* **7.** *(pull)* strain at sth an etw. ⟨dat⟩ zerren [an ... ˌtsɛran] +haben ◊ *Der Hund zerrte an der Leine und riss sich los.; (push)* strain against sth sich gegen etw. stemmen [geːgn̩ ... ʃtɛman] ◊ *Leo stemmte sich gegen die Tür.*

strained → **strain²** ⟨adj⟩ **1.** *(under pressure)* angespannt ['angəʃpant] <angespannter, am angespanntesten> ◊ *unsere angespannte finanzielle Situation* ♦ *Ihre Beziehung war angespannt.* **2.** *(with effort)* angestrengt ['angəʃtrɛŋt] <angestrengter, am angestrengtes-

ten> ◊ *Er hatte einen angestrengten Gesichtsaus-druck.* ✦ *Sie wirkte äußerst angestrengt.*

strand [noun] **1.** *(of wool, rope)* Strang [ʃtraŋ] der <–(e)s, Stränge> ◊ *ein Seil aus vier Strängen; (of hair)* Strähne [ˈʃtrɛːnə] die <–, –n>; *(of thread)* Faden [ˈfaːdn̩] der <–s, Fäden>; *(of wire)* Litze [ˈlɪtsə] die <–, –n> *(tech)* **2.** *(of a belief, movement, development)* Richtung [ˈrɪçtʊŋ] die <–, –en> ◊ *verschiedene Richtungen des Buddhismus; (in a novel, television soap)* strands Handlungsstränge [ˈhandlʊŋsʃtrɛŋə] pl ◊ *Das Buch ist in fünf Handlungsstränge unterteilt.*

strange [adj] **1.** *(unusual in an uncomfortable sense)* seltsam [ˈzɛltzaːm] ◊ *Er ist ein seltsamer Typ.* ✦ *Ich finde ihr Benehmen seltsam.* The strange thing about it is ... Das Seltsame daran ist ... ◊ *Das Seltsame daran ist, dass sie überhaupt nichts gesagt hat.* **2.** *(not familiar)* fremd [frɛmt] <fremder, fremdeste> ◊ *eine fremde Person* ✦ *Ihre Stimme klang am Telefon ganz fremd.; (unaccustomed)* ungewohnt [ˈʊngəvoːnt] <ungewohnter, ungewohntesten> *seldom superl* ◊ *in ungewohnter Umgebung* ✦ *Es ist ganz ungewohnt, dich mit kurzen Haaren zu sehen.*

strangely [adv] **1.** *(unusually)* seltsam [ˈzɛltzaːm] ◊ *ein seltsam geformter Baum* ✦ *Er war seltsam still.* **2.** *(surprisingly)* strangely *(enough)* seltsamerweise [ˈzɛltzaːmeˈvaɛzə] ◊ *Seltsamerweise hat sie mich nicht erkannt.*

stranger [noun] Fremde [ˈfrɛmdə] der/die <–n, die Fremden> *but: ein Fremder/eine Fremde* ◊ *Ich soll nicht mit Fremden sprechen.* ✦ *Ein Fremder fragte mich nach dem Weg.* I'm a stranger here myself. Ich bin selbst fremd hier. total stranger Wildfremde [ˈvɪltˈfrɛmdə] He was a total stranger to me. Er war mir völlig unbekannt.

strangle [verb] **1.** *(a person, an animal)* erwürgen [ɛˈvʏʀɡn̩] <erwürgt, erwürgte, hat erwürgt> ◊ *Diese Schlange erwürgt ihre Opfer.* **2.** *(the development of sth)* strangulieren [ʃtraŋɡuˈliːrən] <stranguliert, strangulierte, hat stranguliert> ◊ *Die hohe Verschuldung stranguliert die Wirtschaft des Landes.*

strap¹ [noun] **1.** *(narrow strip)* Riemen [ˈriːmən] der <–s, –> ◊ *Riemen aus Leder* **2.** *(for security)* Gurt [ɡʊrt] der <–(e)s, –e> ◊ *Die Fracht war mit Gurten gesichert.; (to hold onto)* Haltegurt [ˈhaltəɡʊrt] **3.** *(on a dress, top, bag)* Träger [ˈtrɛːɡə] der <–s, –> ◊ *ein Kleid mit schmalen Trägern* **4.** *(of a watch)* Armband [ˈaʁmbant] das <–(e)s, Armbänder>

strap² [verb] **1.** *(fasten)* schnallen [ˈʃnalən] +haben ◊ *Ich habe das Gepäck auf das Fahrrad geschnallt.* strap yourself in sich anschnallen [ˈanʃnalən] +haben ◊ *Bitte schnallen Sie sich an.* **2.** *(an injured part of the body)* strap (up) bandagieren [bandaˈʒiːrən] <bandagiert, bandagierte, hat bandagiert> ◊ *Die Schwester hat den Arm des Patienten bandagiert.*

strategic(ally) [adj, adv] strategisch [ʃtraˈteːɡɪʃ] ◊ *strategische Waffen* ✦ *Ihr Vorgehen war sehr strategisch.* ✦ *strategisch geschickt*

strategy [noun] Strategie [ʃtrateˈɡiː] die <–, –n> ◊ *eine kluge Strategie verfolgen*

straw [noun] **1.** *(stalks for fodder, weaving, thatching)* Stroh [ʃtroː] das <–(e)s> no pl ◊ *Weihnachtsschmuck aus Stroh* **2.** *(single stalk, for drinking)* Strohhalm [ˈʃtroːhalm] der <–(e)s, –e> ◊ *am*

Strohhalm ziehen ◉ the straw that broke the camel's back, the last straw der Tropfen, der das Fass zum Überlaufen bringt draw the short straw den Kürzeren ziehen grasp at straws sich an einen Strohhalm klammern

strawberry [noun] Erdbeere [ˈeːɐ̯ɡtbeːrə] die <–, –n> ◊ *Erdbeeren pflanzen/ernten* ✦ *Erdbeeren mit Sahne*

stray [verb] **1.** stray from sth von etw. abkommen [fɔn ... ˈapkɔmən] <kommt ab, kam ab, ist abgekommen> ◊ *vom richtigen Weg abkommen* ✦ *Wir sind vom Thema abgekommen.* stray into sth sich in etw. [acc] verirren [ɪn ... fɛlˌɪrən] <verirrt sich, verirrte sich, hat sich verirrt> ◊ *Ein Vogel hatte sich in unseren Wintergarten verirrt.* We strayed in the wrong direction. Wir hatten versehentlich die falsche Richtung eingeschlagen. **2.** *(sb's eyes, gaze, hands)* wandern [ˈvanden] +sein ◊ *Seine Augen wanderten immer wieder zur Tür.*

streak [noun] **1.** *(line, mark)* Streifen [ˈʃtraɛfn̩] der <–s, –> ◊ *dunkle Streifen auf dem Fußboden hinterlassen* streak of lightning Blitz [blɪts] der <–es, –e> **2.** *(in sb's hair)* streaks Strähnchen [ˈʃtrɛːnçən] die <–> pl ◊ *Seine Haare waren braun mit blonden Strähnchen.* **3.** *(positive inclination)* Ader [ˈaːdə] die <–> no pl ◊ *eine künstlerische Ader besitzen; (negative inclination)* Hang [haŋ] der <–(e)s> no pl a cruel streak ein Hang zur Grausamkeit **4.** winning streak Glückssträhne [ˈɡlʏksʃtrɛːnə] die <–, –n> losing streak Pechsträhne [ˈpɛçʃtrɛːnə] die <–, –n>

stream¹ [noun] **1.** *(small river)* Bach [bax] der <–(e)s, Bäche> ◊ *Der Bach schlängelt sich durch das Tal.* **2.** *(of liquid, people, things)* Strom [ʃtroːm] der <–(e)s, Ströme> ◊ *Der Strom von Flüchtlingen riss nicht ab.* stream of smoke Rauchwolke [ˈra̯ɔxvɔlkə] die <–> flow in a steady stream ununterbrochen strömen [ˌʊn|ʊntebrɔxn̩ ˈʃtrøːmən] +sein **3.** *(of students)* Leistungsgruppe [ˈlaɛstʊŋsɡrʊpə] die <–, –n> ◊ *Schüler in Leistungsgruppen zusammenfassen* ◉ be on stream in Betrieb sein come on stream den Betrieb aufnehmen

stream² [verb] **1.** *(flow)* strömen [ˈʃtrøːmən] +sein ◊ *Schweiß strömte ihr über das Gesicht.* ✦ *Das Publikum strömte in den Saal.* ✦ *Durch die offene Tür strömte Sonnenlicht in den Flur.* The wound streamed (with) blood. Aus der Wunde strömte Blut. **2.** *(in the wind)* flattern [ˈflaten] +haben ◊ *Ihre Haare flatterten im Wind.* **3.** *(students)* in Leistungsgruppen einteilen [ɪn ˈlaɛstʊŋsɡrʊpm̩ ˌaɛntaɛlən] +haben

street [noun] Straße [ˈʃtraːsə] die <–, –n> ◊ *eine stark befahrene Straße* ✦ *In welcher Straße wohnst du?* in/ on the street auf der Straße walk along the street die Straße entlang gehen one-way street Einbahnstraße [ˈaɛnbaːnʃtraːsə] ◉ streets ahead of sb/sth jdm/etw. weit voraus right up sb's street genau jds Fall be a two-way street keine Einbahnstraße sein

streetcar [noun] Straßenbahn [ˈʃtraːsn̩baːn] die <–, –en> ◊ *mit der Straßenbahn fahren*

street lamp, street light [noun] Straßenlaterne [ˈʃtraːsn̩laˌtɛʁnə] die <–>

strength [noun] **1.** *(physical energy)* Kraft [kraft] die <–, Kräfte> ◊ *Ich habe nicht genug Kraft, diesen Koffer zu tragen.* ✦ *Der Marathonlauf kostete ihn viel*

Kraft. regain your strength wieder zu Kräften kommen **2.** *(of character, the economy, wind, a currency, current, against weight or pressure)* Stärke [ˈʃtɛʳkə] die <–, –n> ◊ *Zuverlässigkeit ist deine große Stärke.* ♦ *Stärken und Schwächen eines Systems* strength of character Charakterstärke [kaˈraktɐʃtɛʳkə] **3.** *(influence)* Macht [maxt] die <–> *no pl* ◊ *die Macht der öffentlichen Meinung* **4.** *(of a group)* at full strength vollzählig [ˈfɔltsɛːlɪç] *no comp/superl* under strength nicht vollzählig They were 15 men under strength. Ihnen fehlten 15 Mann. in great strength in großer Zahl [ɪn ɡroːse ˈtsaːl] ◊ *Die Fans erschienen in großer Zahl.* ⓔ on the strength of sth aufgrund ... ɡen/von etw. ◊ *aufgrund eines Fehlers* ♦ *aufgrund von Missverständnissen*

strengthen verb **1.** *(a system, currency, sb's rights, position etc.)* strengthen sth etw. stärken [ˈʃtɛʳkŋ̩] +haben ◊ *das Immunsystem stärken* ♦ *Die Reformen haben den Euro gestärkt.* ♦ *jds Position stärken; (a structure, feeling, an impression)* strengthen sth etw. verstärken [fɛˈʃtɛʳkŋ̩] <verstärkt, verstärkte, hat verstärkt> ◊ *Die Balken mussten verstärkt werden.; (a relationship)* etw. festigen [ˈfɛstɪɡŋ̩] +haben ◊ *Würde das Baby ihre Beziehung festigen können?* sth strengthens etw. wird stärker [vɪʳt ˈʃtɛʳkə] +sein ◊ *Die Strömung wurde immer stärker.* **2.** *(a person, physically)* strengthen sb jdm Kraft geben [ˈkraft ɡeːbm̩] <gibt, gab, hat gegeben> ◊ *Iss das, das gibt dir Kraft.; (emotionally)* jdn stark machen [ˈʃtaʳk maxn̩] +haben ◊ *Was uns nicht umbringt, macht uns stark.* **3.** *(support a thesis, statement)* stützen [ˈʃtʏtsn̩] +haben ◊ *Die Indizien stützen seine These.*

stress¹ noun **1.** *(mental, emotional)* Stress [ʃtrɛs] der <–es> *no pl* ◊ *Bei Stress helfen Sport und Bewegung.* under stress unter Stress be under Stress im Stress sein **2.** *(physical, mechanical)* Belastung [bəˈlastʊŋ] die <–, –en> ◊ *Joggen stellt eine große Belastung für die Gelenke dar.* **3.** *(emphasis)* Betonung [bəˈtoːnʊŋ] die <–, –en> ◊ *die Betonung von Unterschieden* the stress falls on sth die Betonung liegt auf etw. dat ◊ *Die Betonung liegt auf der ersten Silbe.* lay stress on sth etw. betonen [bəˈtoːnən] <betont, betonte, hat betont> ◊ *die praktische Seite der Ausbildung betonen*

stress² verb betonen [bəˈtoːnən] <betont, betonte, hat betont> ◊ *Sie betonte die Bedeutung dieser Entwicklung.* ♦ *Er betonte, dass weitere Gespräche nötig seien.* ♦ *ein Wort falsch betonen*

stressed → stress adj gestresst [ɡəˈʃtrɛst] <gestresster, am gestresstesten> *(fam)* gestresst aussehen ♦ *ein gestresstes Kind*

stretch¹ noun **1.** *(exercise)* Dehnungsübung [ˈdeːnʊŋsˌyːbʊŋ] die <–, –en> ◊ *Vor einem Fußballspiel solltest du immer Dehnungsübungen machen.* **2.** *(elasticity)* Elastizität [elastitsiˈtɛːt] die <–> *no pl* stretch jeans Stretchhose [ˈstrɛtʃhoːzə] die <–, –n> **3.** *(time)* stretch of time Zeitraum [ˈtsaetraom] der <–(e)s, Zeiträume> ◊ *In diesem kurzen Zeitraum haben wir große Fortschritte gemacht.* **4.** *(area)* Abschnitt [ˈapʃnɪt] der <–(e)s, –e> ◊ *Dieser Abschnitt der Autobahn soll erweitert werden.* stretch of water Gewässer [ɡəˈvɛsə] das <–s, –> **5.** final stretch Zielgerade [ˈtsiːlɡəraːdə] die <–, –n> ◊ *in*

die Zielgerade einbiegen ⓔ not by any stretch of the imagination beim besten Willen nicht be at full stretch **1.** *(body (part))* völlig gestreckt sein **2.** *(person, organization)* auf Hochtouren arbeiten *(production, machines)* auf Hochtouren laufen at a stretch am Stück

stretch² verb **1.** *(longer)* dehnen [ˈdeːnən] +haben ◊ *einen Gummi dehnen* sth stretches etw. dehnt sich ◊ *Die Hose dehnt sich noch.; (wider)* weiten [ˈvaetn̩] <weitet, weitete, hat geweitet> +haben sth stretches etw. weitet sich ◊ *Der Pullover hat sich geweitet.* **2.** *(straight, tight)* spannen [ˈʃpanən] +haben ◊ *Sie spannten eine Plane zwischen ein paar Bäumen.* **3.** *(extend your body)* sb stretches jd streckt sich [ʃtrɛkt] +haben ◊ *Er gähnte und streckte sich.* stretch sth etw. strecken [ˈʃtrɛkŋ̩] +haben ◊ *Er streckte die Arme.* stretch sth out etw. ausstrecken [ˈaosʃtrɛkŋ̩] +haben ◊ *Ich streckte den Arm nach dem Lichtschalter aus.* stretch your legs sich dat die Beine vertreten [diː ˈbaenə fɛtreːtn̩] <vertritt, vertrat, hat vertreten> *(fam)* **4.** *(area, over a distance)* stretch from sth to sth von etw. bis etw. reichen [fɔn ... bɪs ... raeçn̩] +haben ◊ *Der Wald reicht von hier bis an den Stadtrand.* **5.** *(last a long time)* sich hinziehen [ˈhɪntsiːən] <zieht sich hin, zog sich hin, hat sich hingezogen> ◊ *Die Sitzung zieht sich nun schon fünf Stunden hin.* stretch back to zurückreichen bis [tsuˈrʏkraeçn̩ bɪs] +haben ◊ *bis ins 5. Jahrhundert zurückreichen* **6.** *(suffice)* ausreichen [ˈaosraeçn̩] +haben ◊ *Reichen unsere Mittel dafür aus?* **7.** *(use all resources available)* stretch sb/sth jdn/etw. auslasten [ˈaoslastn̩] <lastet aus, lastete aus, hat ausgelastet> ◊ *Die Behörde ist mit diesen Aufgaben völlig ausgelastet.* ♦ *Ich fühle mich nicht ausgelastet.; (fully, to your advantage)* ausnutzen [ˈaosnʊtsn̩] +haben ◊ *alle sich bietenden Möglichkeiten ausnutzen; (more than reasonable)* strapazieren [ʃtrapaˈtsiːrən] <strapaziert, strapazierte, hat strapaziert> ◊ *Du solltest meine Geduld nicht strapazieren.* stretch sth to the limit etw. bis zum Äußersten beanspruchen [bɪs tsʊm ˌɔøsəstn̩ bəˈʔanʃpruxn̩] <beansprucht, beanspruchte, hat beansprucht> **8.** *(the rules)* großzügig auslegen [ˌgroːstsyːɡɪç ˈaoslegŋ̩] +haben → truth ⓔ be stretching it übertrieben sein stretch a point ein Auge zudrücken *(fam)* ● stretch out phras v sb stretches out jd streckt sich aus [ʃtrɛkt ... ˈaos] +haben ◊ *Sie streckte sich auf dem Bett aus.* stretch sth out etw. ausstrecken [ˈaosʃtrɛkŋ̩] +haben ◊ *die Hand nach jdm ausstrecken*

stretcher noun Trage [ˈtraːɡə] die <–, –n>

strict(ly) adj, adv **1.** streng [ʃtrɛŋ] ◊ *ein strenger Vater* ♦ *Die Anforderungen für Bewerber sind streng.* ♦ *eine strenge Auslegung des Gesetzes* ♦ *jdm etw. im strengsten Vertrauen mitteilen* ♦ *Das ist streng verboten!* **2.** *(single-minded, consistent)* konsequent [kɔnzeˈkvɛnt] <konsequenter, am konsequentesten> ◊ *ein konsequenter Gegner der Abtreibung* ♦ *sich konsequent an einen Plan halten* ⓔ strictly speaking eigentlich im strict sense of the word genau genommen

stride¹ noun **1.** *(large step)* Schritt [ʃrɪt] der <–(e)s, –e> ◊ *Mit wenigen Schritten war er am Telefon.* **2.** *(speed)* Tempo [ˈtɛmpoː] das <–s, –s> *most sing* ◊ *Während des Rennens konnte sie ihr*

Tempo halten.
⊙ **get into your stride** in Schwung kommen take sth in your stride mit etw. gut fertig werden
stride² [verb] schreiten ['ʃraɛtn̩] <schreitet, schritt, ist geschritten> ◊ *zum Altar schreiten*
strike¹ [noun] **1.** *(of workers)* Streik [ʃtraɛk] der <–s, –s> ◊ *ein Streik der Metallarbeiter* a strike over sth ein Streik für/gegen etw. ◊ *ein Streik für mehr Lohn/gegen Entlassungen* aufrufen go on strike in Streik treten be on strike streiken ['ʃtraɛkn̩] +haben **2.** MIL *(with an army)* Schlag [ʃlaːk] der <–(e)s, Schläge> ◊ *ein militärischer Schlag gegen ein Land* strike on sth/sb Angriff auf etw./jdn [ˌangrɪf aof] der <–(e)s, –e> ◊ *ein Angriff auf die Hauptstadt* launch a strike (on sb/ sth) (jdn/etw.) angreifen ['angraɛfn̩] <greift an, griff an, hat angegriffen> ◊ *Sie griffen den Flughafen an.* ♦ *Glaubst du, sie werden angreifen?* **3.** *(score, point)* Treffer ['trɛfɐ] der <–s, –> ◊ *der Treffer zum 1:0; (unsuccessful, in baseball)* Fehlschlag ['feːlʃlaːk] der <–(e)s, Fehlschläge>; *(in skittles)* score a strike abräumen ['apʀɔɪmən] +haben **4.** *(hitting a ball, with the foot)* Schuss [ʃʊs] der <–es, Schüsse> ◊ *Mit einem unerwarteten Schuss landete er ein Tor.; (throwing)* Wurf [vʊʁf] der <–(e)s, Würfe> **5.** *(very successful event, outcome)* voller Erfolg [fɔlɐ ɛ'fɔlk] <–(e)s, –e> ◊ *Die Besprechung war ein voller Erfolg.* **6.** *(disadvantage, throwback)* Nachteil ['naːxtaɛl] der <–(e)s, –e> You have two strikes against you. Zwei Dinge sprechen gegen Sie.
strike² [verb] **1.** *(a target)* treffen ['trɛfn̩] <trifft, traf, hat getroffen> ◊ *Der Baum wurde von einem Blitz getroffen.* ♦ *Der Ball traf mich am Kopf.* ♦ *Unfälle können jeden treffen.; (lightning)* strike (sth) (in etw. [acc]) einschlagen ['aɛnʃlaːkn̩] <schlägt ein, schlug ein, hat eingeschlagen> ◊ *Der Blitz schlug in den Baum ein.* **2.** *(vehicle)* strike sth gegen etw. fahren [geːɡn̩ ... faːʀən] <fährt, fuhr, ist gefahren> ◊ *Das Auto fuhr gegen einen Laternenpfahl.* strike sb jdn anfahren ['anfaːʀən] +haben ◊ *Sie wurde von einem Motorrad angefahren.* **3.** *(hurt yourself)* strike sth gegen etw. stoßen [geːɡn̩ ... ʃtoːsn̩] <stößt, stieß, ist gestoßen> ◊ *Er ist gegen die Tür gestoßen.* strike your sth (on sth) sich [dat] etw. (an etw. [dat]) stoßen ◊ *Ich stieß mir den Kopf am Schrank.* **4.** *(fall to the ground and hit)* strike sth auf etw. [dat] aufschlagen [aof ... ˌaofʃlaːkn̩] <schlägt auf, schlug auf, ist aufgeschlagen> ◊ *Das Flugzeug schlug auf der Landebahn auf.* **5.** *(with your hand, an object)* schlagen ['ʃlaːkn̩] <schlägt, schlug, hat geschlagen> ◊ *Warum hast du ihn mit dem Stock geschlagen?* strike sb a blow jdm einen Schlag versetzen [aɛnən 'ʃlaːk fɛzɛtsn̩] <versetzt, versetzte, hat versetzt> ◊ *Sie versetzte ihm einen Schlag auf den Kopf.* **6.** *(attack)* zuschlagen ['tsuːʃlaːkn̩] <schlägt zu, schlug zu, hat zugeschlagen> ◊ *Der Einbrecher hat wieder zugeschlagen.* ♦ *Schalke schlug gleich in der zweiten Minute zu.* strike a blow zuschlagen strike the first blow als Erster/Erste zuschlagen **7.** SPORT *(with your foot)* schießen ['ʃiːsn̩] <schießt, schoss, hat geschossen> ◊ *den Ball ins Tor schießen; (with a racket etc.)* schlagen ['ʃlaːkn̩] <schlägt, schlug, hat geschlagen> **8.** *(be or go on strike)* streiken ['ʃtraɛkn̩] +haben ◊ *Die Busfahrer streiken schon seit drei Tagen.* strike over sth für/gegen etw. streiken ◊ *für mehr Lohn/ gegen Entlassungen streiken* **9.** *(earthquake, plague,*

disaster) heimsuchen ['haɛmzuːxn̩] +haben ◊ *Pakistan wurde wieder von einem Erdbeben heimgesucht.* Disaster struck. Er wurde/Sie wurden etc. von einem Unglück heimgesucht. **10.** *(come to mind)* sth strikes sb etw. kommt jdm in den Sinn [kɔmt ... ɪn deːn 'zɪn] <kommt, kam, ist gekommen> ◊ *Mir kam plötzlich in den Sinn, dass ich ihn besuchen könnte.* sb strikes on sth jd kommt auf etw. [acc] Wie bist du auf diese geniale Idee gekommen? **11.** *(be noticed)* strike sb, strike the eye jdm auffallen ['aoffalən] <fällt auf, fiel auf, ist aufgefallen> ◊ *Ihr fiel auf, dass er ungewöhnlich still war.* **12.** *(appear, seem)* strike sb as (being) sth jdm irgendwie vorkommen ['foːɡkɔmən] <kommt vor, kam vor, ist vorgekommen> ◊ *Das Ganze kam mir seltsam vor.* ♦ *Er kommt mir nicht wie ein Extremist vor.* **13.** MUS *(a string, key, chord)* anschlagen ['anʃlaːkn̩] <schlägt an, schlug an, hat angeschlagen> ◊ *den falschen Ton anschlagen* **14.** *(a match)* anzünden ['antsʏndn̩] <zündet an, zündete an, hat angezündet> The match won't strike. Das Streichholz lässt sich nicht anzünden. **15.** *(clock)* schlagen ['ʃlaːkn̩] <schlägt, schlug, hat geschlagen> ◊ *Die Uhr schlägt zwölf.* ♦ *Hörst du die Turmuhr schlagen?* **16.** *(remove text)* strike sth from sth etw. aus etw. streichen [aos ... 'ʃtraɛçn̩] <streicht, strich, hat gestrichen> ◊ *Der letzte Satz wurde aus dem Artikel gestrichen.* **17.** *(light)* strike sth/sb auf etw./jdn fallen [aof ... falən] <fällt, fiel, ist gefallen> ◊ *Das Licht fiel auf sein Gesicht.* **18.** *(a deal, bargain)* abschließen ['apʃliːsn̩] <schließt ab, schloss ab, hat abgeschlossen> ◊ *Sie haben endlich ein Geschäft abgeschlossen.* **19.** *(find oil, gold)* strike sth auf etw. [acc] stoßen [aof ... ʃtoːsn̩] <stößt, stieß, ist gestoßen> ◊ *auf Öl stoßen* **20.** *(a tent, camp)* abbrechen ['apbrɛçn̩] <bricht ab, brach ab, hat abgebrochen> ◊ *Morgen brechen wir die Zelte ab.*
⊙ **be struck by sth/sb** von etw./jdm beeindruckt sein be struck on sb/sth auf jdn/etw. stehen ◊ *Stehst du auf Jazz?*
• **strike at** [phras v] **1.** *(try to hit)* strike at sb/sth nach jdm/etw. schlagen [naːx ... ʃlaːkn̩] <schlägt, schlug, hat geschlagen> ◊ *Er schlug nach dem Angreifer.; (try to kick)* nach jdm/etw. treten [naːx ... treːtn̩] <tritt, trat, hat getreten> ◊ *Ich trat nach dem Ball, traf ihn aber nicht.* **2.** *(attack)* angreifen ['angraɛfn̩] <greift an, griff an, hat angegriffen> ◊ *Die Soldaten griffen die Rebellen an.*
• **strike back** [phras v] zurückschlagen [tsuˈrʏkʃlaːkn̩] <schlägt zurück, schlug zurück, hat zurückgeschlagen> ◊ *Er hat mich angegriffen und ich habe zurückgeschlagen.* strike back at/against sb jds Angriff erwidern [ˌangrɪf ɛ'viːdɐn] <erwidert, erwiderte, hat erwidert>
• **strike down** [phras v] **1.** *(become ill)* be struck down by sth schwer an etw. [dat] erkranken [ʃveːɐ an ... ɛkraŋkn̩] <erkrankt, erkrankte, hat erkrankt> ◊ *Vor einem Jahr erkrankte ich schwer an Asthma.; (die)* von etw. dahingerafft werden [fɔn ... daˌhɪŋgəraft veːɐdn̩] <wird, wurde, ist worden> *(lofty)* ◊ *Sie wurden von der Pest dahingerafft.* **2.** *(hit)* zu Boden strecken [tsu: 'boːdn̩ ʃtrɛkn̩] +haben **3.** *(a law)* abschaffen ['apʃafn̩] ◊ *Dieses Gesetz wurde letztes Jahr abgeschafft.*
• **strike off** [phras v] **1.** *(remove)* strike sth off etw. streichen ['ʃtraɛçn̩] <streicht, strich, hat gestrichen> ◊

etw. von der Tagesordnung streichen **2.** *(a doctor, lawyer)* strike sb off (a register/roll) jdm die Zulassung entziehen [dɪ: ˈtsuːlasʊŋ ɛntˌtsiːən] <entzieht, entzog, hat entzogen> ◊ *Ihm wurde die Zulassung als Arzt entzogen.* **3.** *(go, set off)* sich auf den Weg machen [aɔf deːn ˈveːk maxn̩] +haben ◊ *Sie machten sich auf den Weg über die Berge.*
• **strike out** [phras v] **1.** *(for independence, success)* strike out for sth sich für etw. einsetzen [fyːɐ̯ ... ˌaɛnzɛtsn̩] +haben ◊ *Er setzte sich entschlossen für seine Unabhängigkeit ein.* strike out on your own sich selbstständig machen [ˈzɛlpstʃtɛndɪç maxn̩] +haben ◊ *Sie hat sich vor einem Jahr selbstständig gemacht.* **2.** *(try to hit)* strike out at sb nach jdm/ etw. schlagen [naːx ... ˈʃlaːgn̩] ◊ *Plötzlich schlug sie nach mir.* **3.** *(criticize)* strike out at sb/sth jdn/etw. angreifen [ˈangraɛfn̩] <greift an, griff an, hat angegriffen> ◊ *Der Minister hat die Presse angegriffen.* **4.** *(for a place)* strike out for sth sich auf den Weg nach etw. machen [aɔf deːn ˌveːk naːx ... maxn̩] +haben ◊ *Nächstes Jahr mache ich mich auf den Weg nach Australien.* **5.** *(a word, line)* strike sth out etw. durchstreichen [ˈdʊʳçʃtraɛçn̩] <streicht durch, strich durch, hat durchgestrichen> ◊ *ein Wort durchstreichen und ein anderes darüberschreiben*
• **strike up** [phras v] MUS *(start singing)* anstimmen [ˈanʃtɪmən] +haben ◊ *Er stimmte ein Lied an.; (start playing)* zu spielen beginnen [tsuː ˈʃpiːlən bəgɪnən] <beginnt, begann, hat begonnen> ◊ *Sie begannen, einen Walzer zu spielen.* ♦ *Die Band begann zu spielen.* → conversation, friendship
striker [noun] **1.** *(on strike)* Streikende [ˈʃtraɛkn̩də] der/die <–n, die Streikenden> but: *ein Streikender/eine Streikende* **2.** SPORT *(in soccer)* Stürmer [ˈʃtʏʳmɐ] der <–s, –> ♀Stürmerin [ˈʃtʏʳmərɪn] die <–, –nen>; *(in baseball)* Schläger [ˈʃlɛːgɐ] der <–s, –> ♀Schlägerin [ˈʃlɛːgərɪn] die <–, –nen>
striking(ly) [adj, adv] auffallend [ˈaɔffalənt] ◊ *Sie trug ein auffallendes Kleid.* ♦ *auffallend gut aussehen*
string [noun] **1.** *(cord)* Schnur [ʃnuːɐ̯] die <–, Schnüre> ◊ *eine Schnur an ein Spielzeug binden* ♦ *ein Stück Schnur* **2.** *(of islands, restaurants)* Kette [ˈkɛtə] die <–, –n>; *(of people, vehicles)* Schlange [ˈʃlaŋə] die <–, –n>; *(of questions, lies, mistakes)* Reihe [ˈraɛə] die <–, –n> ◊ *eine Reihe dummer Fehler; (in computing, of characters)* Zeichenfolge [ˈtsaɛçn̩fɔlgə] die <–, –n> **3.** *(of a guitar, violin, racket)* Saite [ˈzaɛtə] die <–, –n> ◊ *An meiner Gitarre ist eine Saite gerissen.; (of a bow)* Sehne [ˈzeːnə] die <–, –n>; *(of a puppet, in a bean pod)* Faden [ˈfaːdn̩] der <–s, Fäden>; *(of an apron)* Band [bant] das <–(e)s, Bänder>; *(of hair)* Strähne [ˈʃtrɛːnə] die <–, –n> **4.** *(musicians or instruments in an orchestra)* strings Streicher [ˈʃtraɛçɐ] die <–> pl **5.** *(conditions)* strings Bedingungen [bəˈdɪŋʊŋən] die <–> pl ◊ *Das Angebot war mir mit zu vielen Bedingungen verknüpft.* no strings attached ohne Bedingungen
ⓟ have sb on a string jdn am Gängelband haben
pull strings seine Beziehungen spielen lassen pull the strings die Fäden in der Hand halten
strip¹ [noun] **1.** *(long narrow piece)* Streifen [ˈʃtraɛfn̩] der <–s, –> ◊ *etw. in Streifen schneiden* ♦ *ein schmaler Streifen Rasen; (of wood)* Leiste [ˈlaɛstə] die <–, –n> ◊ *eine schmale Leiste aus Holz* **2.** *(sports outfit)* Trikot [triˈkoː] das <–s, –s> ◊ *die Mannschaft*

im grünen Trikot **3.** *(striptease, comic strip)* Strip [strɪp] der <–s, –s>
strip² [verb] **1.** *(remove clothes)* strip sth off etw. ausziehen [ˈaɔstsiːən] <zieht aus, zog aus, hat ausgezogen> ◊ *Sie zog ihren nassen Badeanzug aus.* sb strips (off) jd zieht sich aus ◊ *Ich zog mich nackt aus.* sb strips down to sth jd zieht sich bis auf etw. [acc] aus ◊ *Ich musste mich bis auf die Unterhose ausziehen.; (as entertainment)* strippen [ˈstrɪpm̩] +haben *(fam)* strip to the waist den Oberkörper freimachen [deːn ˈoːbɛkœʳpə ˌfraɛmaxn̩] +haben They were stripped to the waist. Sie standen mit nacktem Oberkörper da. **2.** *(wallpaper, a bed)* abziehen [ˈaptsiːən] <zieht ab, zog ab, hat abgezogen> +haben ◊ *Er zog die Betten ab.; (paint, bark)* entfernen [ɛntˈfɛʳnən] <entfernt, entfernte, hat entfernt> We stripped the apples from the trees. Wir ernteten die Apfelbäume ab.; *(a house, room)* ausräumen [ˈaɔsrɔømən] +haben **3.** *(a machine, car)* strip (down) zerlegen [tsɛˈleːgn̩] <zerlegt, zerlegte, hat zerlegt> ◊ *Wir müssen Ihr Auto zerlegen.* **4.** *(take sth away from sb)* strip sb of sth jdm etw. abnehmen [ˈapneːmən] <nimmt ab, nahm ab, hat abgenommen> ◊ *Der Räuber nahm den Reisenden ihre Wertsachen ab.*
• **strip away** [phras v] **1.** *(paint, bark)* entfernen [ɛntˈfɛʳnən] <entfernt, entfernte, hat entfernt> **2.** *(sth unnecessary)* strip sth away sich [dat] etw. wegdenken [ˈvɛkdɛŋkn̩] <denkt sich weg, dachte sich weg, hat sich weggedacht> ◊ *Wenn man sich die Fehler wegdenkt, ist der Aufsatz gar nicht so schlecht.*
• **strip off** [phras v] *(paint, bark)* entfernen [ɛntˈfɛʳnən] <entfernt, entfernte, hat entfernt> ◊ *Vor dem Streichen muss die alte Farbe entfernt werden.* → strip² **1.**
stripe [noun] Streifen [ˈʃtraɛfn̩] der <–s, –> ◊ *ein roter Pullover mit grünen Streifen*
ⓔ earn your stripes befördert werden of all stripes *(regarding type)* jeder Art *(regarding character)* jeden Schlages *(regarding politics)* jeder Schattierung
striped [adj] gestreift [gəˈʃtraɛft] ◊ *Er trug ein gestreiftes T-Shirt.* ♦ *Der Rock ist gestreift.*
strive [verb] *(try to be or do sth)* sich bemühen [bəˈmyːən] <bemüht sich, bemühte sich, hat sich bemüht> ◊ *Er bemühte sich, Ordnung zu schaffen.; (try to achieve sth)* strive for sth nach etw. streben [naːx ... ʃtreːbm̩] +haben ◊ *nach Unabhängigkeit streben*
stroke¹ [noun] **1.** MED Schlaganfall [ˈʃlaːkˌanfal] der <–(e)s, Schlaganfälle> ◊ *Sie hatte einen Schlaganfall.* **2.** *(hit, sound of a clock, in rowing)* Schlag [ʃlaːk] der <–(e)s, Schläge> ◊ *ein Schlag mit dem Stock* ♦ *Beim nächsten Schlag ist es 20 Uhr.* ♦ *fünf Schläge benötigen um zu siegen* at the stroke of three etc. Schlag drei etc.; *(of wings)* Flügelschlag [ˈflyːglˌʃlaːk] der <–(e)s, Schläge> ◊ *ein Schlag* stroke of lightning Blitzschlag [ˈblɪtsˌʃlaːk] der <–(e)s, Schläge> **3.** *(in swimming)* Stoß [ʃtoːs] der <–es, Stöße> ◊ *Sie schwamm ein paar Stöße.; (swimming style)* Schwimmstil [ˈʃvɪmʃtiːl] der <–(e)s, –e> ◊ *Schmetterling ist ein schwieriger Schwimmstil.* **4.** *(by a pen, brush)* Strich [ʃtrɪç] der <–(e)s, –e>; *(forward slash)* Schrägstrich [ˈʃrɛːkʃtrɪç] der <–(e)s, –e> brush stroke Pinselstrich [ˈpɪnzl̩ʃtrɪç] **5.** *(stroking movement)* Streichbewegung [ˈʃtraɛçbəveːgʊŋ] die <–, –en> ◊ *Beenden Sie die*

Massage mit sanften Streichbewegungen.; (caress) give sb/sth a stroke jdn/etw. streicheln ['ʃtraeçl̩n] ◊ *Er streichelte ihren Arm.*

⊛ a stroke of brilliance eine Glanzleistung different strokes for different folks jedem Tierchen sein Pläsierchen *(fam, hum)* a stroke of genius ein Geniestreich a stroke of luck ein Glücksfall put sb off their stroke jdn aus dem Konzept bringen

stroke² [verb] **1.** *(with your flat hand)* streicheln ['ʃtraeçl̩n] +haben ◊ *Sie streichelte die Katze.* stroke your beard sich [dat] über den Bart streichen [yːbɐ deːn 'baːrt ʃtraeçn̩] <streicht, strich, hat gestrichen> stroke sb's hair jdm übers Haar streichen; *(with your fingertips, repeatedly)* kraulen ['kraolən] +haben ◊ *einem Hund den Nacken kraulen* **2.** *(a ball: with your foot)* schießen ['ʃiːsn̩] <schießt, schoss, hat geschossen>; *(with a racket etc.)* schlagen ['ʃlaːgn̩] <schlägt, schlug, hat geschlagen> ◊ *den Ball übers Netz schlagen*

stroll¹ [noun] Spaziergang [ʃpaˈtsiːɡaŋ] der <-(e)s, Spaziergänge> ◊ *Ein Spaziergang an der frischen Luft wird uns gut tun.* go for a stroll einen Spaziergang machen

stroll² [verb] spazieren [ʃpaˈtsiːrən] <spaziert, spazierte, ist spaziert> ◊ *Wir sind durch den Park spaziert.* stroll along sth etw. entlangspazieren [ɛntˈlaŋʃpatsiːrən] ◊ *Sie spazierten den Strand entlang.*

strong [adj] **1.** *(powerful, tough, confident, good, noticeable, great in number)* stark [ʃtaʳk] <stärker, am stärksten> ◊ *einen starken Willen haben ♦ Der Kaffee ist zu stark. ♦ Ist das Seil stark genug? ♦ Sie ist eine starke Schülerin. ♦ Er hat einen starken Akzent. ♦ eine 200 Mann starke Truppe* strong point Stärke ['ʃtɛʳkə] die <-, -n> ◊ *Wo liegen Ihre Stärken?* there is a strong possibility that es ist durchaus möglich, dass [ɛs ɪst ˌdʊʳçlaos 'møːklɪç das] **2.** *(relationship)* stabil [ʃtaˈbiːl] ◊ *eine stabile Ehe ♦ Ihre Beziehung ist nicht sehr stabil.* **3.** *(argument)* gut [guːt] <besser, am besten> ◊ *gute Argumente für etw. vorbringen ♦ Seine Argumente sind gut.* **4.** *(opinion)* fest [fɛst] no comp/superl, only before ns ◊ *eine feste Meinung zu etw. haben* **5.** *(taste)* kräftig ['krɛftɪç] ◊ *Wild hat einen kräftigen Geschmack. ♦ Dieser Käse ist mir zu kräftig im Geschmack.; (smell)* streng [ʃtrɛŋ] ◊ *ein strenger Geruch nach Gas.* **6.** *(swear words)* strong language Kraftausdrücke [kraft|aosdrykə] die <-> pl ◊ *Kraftausdrücke benutzen* ⊛ come on strong sich ereifern sb/sth is going strong jdm/etw. geht es gut

strongly [adv] **1.** *(physically, mentally)* stark [ʃtaʳk] <stärker, am stärksten> ◊ *Der Bernhardiner ist ein stark gebauter Hund. ♦ jdn stark beeinflussen; (vehemently)* heftig ['hɛftɪç] ◊ *Er wurde heftig angegriffen.; (firmly)* stabil [ʃtaˈbiːl] ◊ *eine stabil gebaute Konstruktion* **2.** *(advise)* dringend ['drɪŋənt] ◊ *jdm dringend von etw. abraten* **3.** *(smell)* streng [ʃtrɛŋ] ◊ *Im Zoo roch es streng nach Raubkatzen.*

structural [adj] **1.** *(relating to construction)* baulich ['baolɪç] no comp/superl, only before ns ◊ *bauliche Veränderungen* structural repairs Instandsetzungsarbeiten [ɪnˈʃtantzɛtsʊŋs|aˈʁbaɪtn̩] die <-> pl structural timber Bauholz ['baohɔlts] das <-es> no pl **2.** *(relating to structure)* strukturell [ʃtroktuˈrɛl] no comp/superl ◊ *strukturelle Unterschiede*

structure¹ [noun] **1.** *(organization, system)* Struktur [ʃtrʊkˈtuːɐ̯] die <-, -en> ◊ *die hierarchische Struktur des Unternehmens* power structure Machtstruktur ['maxtʃtrʊkˌtuːɐ̯] social structure Gesellschaftsstruktur [ɡəˈzɛlʃaftsʃtrʊkˌtuːɐ̯]; *(of a work of art, sentence)* Aufbau ['aofbao] der <-(e)s> no pl ◊ *der Aufbau eines Musikstücks* **2.** *(building, bridge etc.)* Konstruktion [kɔnstrʊkˈtsi̯oːn] die <-, -en> ◊ *eine Konstruktion aus Stahl und Glas*

structure² [verb] *(plan, organize)* strukturieren [ʃtrʊktuˈriːrən] <strukturiert, strukturierte, hat strukturiert> ◊ *seine Arbeit strukturieren; (an essay, a novel etc.)* aufbauen ['aofbaoən] +haben ◊ *Wie baue ich den Aufsatz am besten auf?*

struggle¹ [noun] Kampf [kampf] der <-(e)s, Kämpfe> ◊ *der bewaffnete Kampf ♦ Das Installieren der Software war ein ziemlicher Kampf.* struggle against/with sb/sth Kampf gegen jdn/etw. ◊ *der Kampf gegen die Korruption* struggle for sth Kampf um etw. ◊ *sein Kampf um Unabhängigkeit* the struggle for democracy der Kampf für die Demokratie power struggle Machtkampf ['maxtkampf]

struggle² [verb] **1.** *(have difficulty)* struggle (with sth) (mit etw.) zu kämpfen haben [tsu: 'kɛmpfn̩ haːbn̩] +haben ◊ *Zuerst hatte ich zu kämpfen, aber jetzt mache ich die Übungen jeden Tag. ♦ Er hatte ziemlich mit der Software zu kämpfen.* struggle to do sth damit zu kämpfen haben, etw. zu tun struggle for breath nach Atem ringen [naːx 'aːtəm rɪŋən] <ringt, rang, hat gerungen> ◊ *Als man ihn aus dem Wasser zog, bustete er und rang nach Atem.* **2.** *(fight, use force)* kämpfen ['kɛmpfn̩] +haben ◊ *gegen die Unterdrückung kämpfen ♦ Er kämpfte im Wind mit dem Schirm.* struggle for sth um etw. kämpfen ◊ *Sie kämpfen um ihre Unabhängigkeit.; (put up resistance)* sich wehren ['veːrən] +haben ◊ *Sie wehrte sich, aber ohne Erfolg.* **3.** *(try hard)* struggle to do sth versuchen, etw. zu tun [fɛˈzuːxn̩ ... tsu:] <versucht, versuchte, hat versucht> ◊ *Er versuchte verzweifelt, sich loszureißen.; (try to get somewhere)* struggle into sth sich in etw. [acc] zwängen [ɪn ... ˌtsvɛŋən] +haben ◊ *Sie zwängte sich in die enge Jeans.* struggle free sich befreien [bəˈfraeən] <befreit sich, befreite sich, hat sich befreit> ◊ *Der Hund befreite sich und rannte davon.* struggle out of sth sich aus etw. [dat] befreien

stubborn(ly) [adj, adv] **1.** *(person)* stur [ʃtuːɐ̯] ◊ *Er blieb stur und gab nicht nach. ♦ ein sturer Mensch ♦ stur auf seinem Recht bestehen; (voice, look)* störrisch ['ʃtœrɪʃ] ◊ *ein störrischer Blick ♦ Seine Stimme klang störrisch. ♦ Sie sah ihn störrisch an.* **2.** *(difficult to remove, cure or defeat)* hartnäckig ['haʳtnɛkɪç] ◊ *ein hartnäckiger Fleck ♦ Meine Grippe ist äußerst hartnäckig. ♦ Er weigerte sich hartnäckig, uns zu helfen.*

stub out [verb] ausdrücken ['aosdrʏkn̩] +haben ◊ *Er drückte seine Zigarette aus.*

stud [noun] **1.** *(metal decoration on clothes)* Niete ['niːtə] die <-, -n> ◊ *ein Gürtel mit Nieten; (jewellery)* Piercing ['piːɐ̯sɪŋ] das <-s, -s> tongue stud Zungenpiercing ['tsʊŋənpiːɐ̯sɪŋ] nose stud Nasenpiercing ['naːznpiːɐ̯sɪŋ] ear stud Ohrstecker ['oːɐ̯ʃtɛkɐ] der <-s, -> **2.** *(on shoes, tyres)* Spike [spaek] der <-s, -s> ◊ *Schuhe mit Spikes* **3.** *(stallion)* Deckhengst ['dɛkhɛŋst] der <-(e)s, -e>; *(bull)* Zuchtbulle ['tsʊxtbʊlə] der <-n, -n> stud farm

Gestüt [gə'ʃtyːt] das <-(e)s, -e> ◊ *auf einem Gestüt arbeiten*

student ⟨noun⟩ **1.** UNI Student [ʃtu'dɛnt] der <-en, -en> ♀Studentin [ʃtu'dɛntɪn] die <-, -nen> ◊ *Er ist Student an der Universität München.* be a student of sth etw. studieren [ʃtu'diːrən] <studiert, studierte, hat studiert> ◊ *Sie studiert Politik.* **2.** SCHOOL Schüler ['ʃyːlɐ] der <-s, -> ♀Schülerin ['ʃyːlərɪn] die <-, -nen> ◊ *Sie ist eine eine gute Schülerin.*

student card ⟨noun⟩ **1.** UNI Studentenausweis [ʃtu'dɛntn̩|aosvaes] der <-es, -e> ◊ *ein internationaler Studentenausweis* **2.** SCHOOL Schülerausweis ['ʃyːlɐ|aosvaes] der <-es, -e> ◊ *Ermäßigung gibt es nur bei Vorlage des Schülerausweises.*

studio ⟨noun⟩ **1.** *(for recording sth)* Studio ['ʃtuːdjoː] das <-s, -s> ◊ *Nur wenige Szenen konnten im Studio gedreht werden.* film studio Filmstudio ['fɪlm̩ˌʃtuːdjoː] recording studio Tonstudio ['toːnˌʃtuːdjoː] **2.** *(film company)* Filmgesellschaft ['fɪlmɡəzɛlʃaft] die <-, -en> ◊ *Mehrere bekannte Filmgesellschaften sind an seinem Drehbuch interessiert.* **3.** *(artist's, photographer's, designer's)* Atelier [ate'lje:] das <-s, -s> ◊ *im Atelier arbeiten* **4.** studio (flat) Apartment [a'pa:tmənt] das <-s, -s> ◊ *in einem Apartment wohnen*

study¹ ⟨noun⟩ **1.** *(process of learning at school)* Lernen ['lɛ'nən] das <-s> no pl ◊ *das Lernen von Fremdsprachen; (of a situation, case etc.)* Untersuchung [ʊntɐ'zuːxʊŋ] die <-, -en> ◊ *die Untersuchung einer Entwicklung* **2.** UNI study, studies Studium ['ʃtuːdjʊm] das <-s, Studien> ◊ *ein Studium beginnen* business studies Betriebswirtschaftslehre [bə'triːpsvɪ'tʃaftsleːrə] die <-> no pl ◊ *Betriebswirtschaftslehre studieren* German studies Germanistik [ɡɛ'maːnɪstɪk] die <-> no pl for the study of sth Studienzentrum für etw. ['ʃtuːdjəntsɛntrom fyːɐ̯] das <-s, Studienzentren> ◊ *das Studienzentrum für Film* **3.** *(research project, examination, drawing)* Studie ['ʃtuːdjə] die <-, -n> ◊ *eine Studie über Berufskrankheiten veröffentlichen* ♦ *Der Film ist eine Studie der oberen Gesellschaftsschichten.* ♦ *anatomische Studien* **4.** *(room)* Arbeitszimmer ['a'baetsˌtsɪmɐ] das <-s, -> ◊ *Er zog sich in sein Arbeitszimmer zurück.* **5.** MUS Etüde [e'tyːdə] die <-, -n> ◊ *Etüden spielen*

study² ⟨verb⟩ **1.** *(learn at school)* lernen ['lɛ'nən] +haben ◊ *Sie lernt fleißig für die Prüfung.* ♦ *in der Schule Englisch lernen* **2.** *(at university: examine and learn, look carefully at sth)* studieren [ʃtu'diːrən] <studiert, studierte, hat studiert> ◊ *Er studiert schon seit zehn Semestern.* ♦ *Informatik an der Universität studieren* ♦ *einen Bericht studieren* study to be a doctor/lawyer etc. Medizin/Jura etc. studieren **3.** *(a situation, case etc.)* untersuchen [ʊntɐ'zuːxŋ̩] <untersucht, untersuchte, hat untersucht>

stuff¹ ⟨noun⟩ **1.** *(unspecified things, events, deeds, information)* Sachen ['zaxn̩] die <-> pl ◊ *Lass deine Sachen nicht überall herumliegen!* ♦ *Sie haben schlimme Sachen gemacht.* ♦ *Die wichtigsten Sachen weiß ich schon.* school stuff Schulsachen ['ʃuːlzaxn̩] **2.** *(substance, useless things)* Zeug [tsɔøk] das <-(e)s> no pl (fam, esp pej) ◊ *Dieses Zeug schmeckt ja widerlich!* ♦ *unnützes Zeug* **3.** *(material)* Stoff [ʃtɔf] der <-(e)s> ◊ *Plutonium ist der Stoff, aus dem Atombomben gemacht werden.*

🅮 be hot stuff große Klasse sein *(fam)* do your

stuff sein Ding machen *(fam)* have the (right) stuff have the (right) stuff for sth das Zeug für etw. haben *(fam)* have the (right) stuff to be sth das Zeug zu etw. haben *(fam)* ◊ *Du hast das Zeug zum Unternehmer.* have the (right) stuff to do sth das Zeug haben, um etw. zu tun *(fam)* know your stuff sich auskennen and stuff like that und so *(fam)*

stuff² ⟨verb⟩ **1.** *(push)* stuff sth into sth etw. in etw. ⟨acc⟩ stopfen [ɪn ... ʃtɔpfn̩] +haben ◊ *Ich stopfte die Wäsche hastig in die Waschmaschine.* **2.** *(fill)* stuff sth with sth etw. mit etw. füllen [mɪt ... fʏlən] +haben ◊ *ein Kissen mit Federn füllen* ♦ *einen Truthahn mit Kastanien füllen* **3.** *(in taxidermy)* ausstopfen ['aosʃtɔpfn̩] +haben ◊ *einen Fuchs ausstopfen*

🅮 stuff it scheiß drauf *(rude)* stuff yourself sich ⟨dat⟩ den Bauch voll schlagen *(fam)*

stuffing ⟨noun⟩ Füllung ['fʏlʊŋ] die <-, -en>
🅮 knock the stuffing out of sb jdn fertig machen *(fam)*

stumble ⟨verb⟩ **1.** *(almost fall)* stolpern ['ʃtɔlpen] +sein ◊ *Ich wollte mich beeilen, doch dann stolperte ich und fiel hin.* stumble on/over sth über etw. ⟨acc⟩ stolpern **2.** *(walk with difficulty)* sich schleppen ['ʃlɛpm̩] +haben ◊ *Die Flüchtlinge schleppten sich durch die Wüste.* **3.** *(stammer)* stumble (over your words) stocken ['ʃtɔkŋ̩] +haben ◊ *Sie stockte beim Vorlesen mehrere Male.*

• **stumble across** ⟨phras v⟩ stumble across sb über jdn stolpern [yːbɐ ... ʃtɔlpən] +sein *(fam)* ◊ *Ich bin im Supermarkt über ihn gestolpert.* stumble across sth auf etw. ⟨acc⟩ stoßen [aof ... ʃtoːsn̩] <stößt, stieß, ist gestoßen> ◊ *Bei meinen Recherchen bin ich auf diesen Text gestoßen.*

• **stumble on** ⟨phras v⟩ → **stumble across**

stun ⟨verb⟩ **1.** *(shock)* aus der Fassung bringen [aos deːɐ̯ 'fasʊŋ brɪŋən] <bringt, brachte, hat gebracht> ◊ *Der Vorfall hat mich aus der Fassung gebracht.* **2.** *(daze)* benommen machen [bə'nɔmən maxn̩] +haben ◊ *Der Lärm hatte uns benommen gemacht.* **3.** *(knock unconscious)* bewusstlos schlagen [bə'vʊstloːs ʃlaːɡn̩] <schlägt, schlug, hat geschlagen> ◊ *Der Täter schlug sein Opfer bewusstlos und rannte davon.*

stunned → **stun** ⟨adj⟩ **1.** *(shocked)* fassungslos ['fasʊŋsloːs] <am fassungslosesten> ◊ *fassungsloses Staunen* ♦ *Ich war fassungslos, dass er so gemein sein konnte.* be stunned at/by sth fassungslos über etw. ⟨acc⟩ sein **2.** *(dazed)* benommen [bə'nɔmən] ◊ *Sein benommener Gegner versuchte sich aufzurichten.* ♦ *Ich war von dem Schlag ganz benommen.* **3.** *(unconscious)* bewusstlos [bə'vʊstloːs] no comp/superl ◊ *ein bewusstloser Mensch* ♦ *Nach dem Schlag war sie bewusstlos.*

stunning ⟨adj⟩ **1.** *(impressive, attractive)* umwerfend ['ʊmvɛ'fŋ̩] ◊ *Das war ein umwerfendes Erlebnis.* ♦ *Die Hauptdarstellerin war einfach umwerfend.* **2.** *(powerful)* schwer [ʃveːɐ̯] ◊ *jdm/einer Sache einen schweren Schlag versetzen*

stupid ⟨adj⟩ **1.** *(not clever, not intelligent)* dumm [dʊm] <dümmer, am dümmsten> ◊ *Er war wirklich dumm.* ♦ *Es war sehr dumm von dir, dieses Angebot anzunehmen.* ♦ *Sie machte einen dummen Fehler.* look stupid dumm dastehen **2.** *(ridiculous)* lächerlich ['lɛçɐlɪç] ◊ *Das Hemd sieht einfach lächerlich aus.* ♦ *ein lächerlicher Vorschlag*

stupidity [noun] Dummheit ['dʊmhaɛt] die <–, –en> ◊ *Ihre Dummheit war nicht zu ertragen.*

stupidly [adv] **1.** *(not intelligently)* dumm [dʊm] <dümmer, am dümmsten> ◊ *Sie stellten sich wirklich unglaublich dumm an.* **2.** *(expressing regret about not having been more circumspect)* dummerweise ['dʊmɐˈvaɛzə] no comp/superl ◊ *Dummerweise habe ich ihm geglaubt.*

sturdy(-ily) [adj, adv] **1.** *(person, legs, animal, plant)* kräftig ['krɛftɪç] ◊ *ein kräftiges Kind* ♦ *Seine Beine sind sehr kräftig.* ♦ *ein kräftig gebauter Mann* **2.** *(building, furniture, shoes)* solide [zoˈliːdə] <solider, am solidesten> ◊ *ein solides Fundament* ♦ *Büromöbel sollten solide sein.* ♦ *Das Gebäude ist solide gebaut.*

stutter [verb] stottern ['ʃtɔtɐn] +haben ◊ *Sie stotterte etwas Unverständliches.* ♦ *Der Motor stottert.*

style [noun] Stil [ʃtiːl] der <–(e)s, –e> ◊ *eine im gotischen Stil erbaute Kirche* ♦ *Das ist nicht mein Stil.* ♦ *Schick — das hat Stil!* in (grand) style im großen Stil; *(in compound ns)* ... style, style of ... ...stil [ʃtiːl] management style Führungsstil ['fyːrʊŋsʃtiːl] teaching style Unterrichtsstil ['ʊntɐrɪçtsʃtiːl] style of painting Malstil ['maːlʃtiːl] ⊛ be in style modern sein be out of style nicht mehr modern sein not sb's style of sth car/dress etc. nicht die Art Wagen/Kleid etc., die jdm gefällt

stylish(ly) [adj, adv] elegant [elɐˈɡant] <eleganter, am elegantesten> ◊ *ein elegantes Kleid* ♦ *Deine Wohnung ist sehr elegant.* ♦ *Das Haus ist elegant eingerichtet.* be a stylish dresser sich elegant kleiden

stylistic(ally) [adj, adv] stilistisch [ʃtiˈlɪstɪʃ] no comp/superl; when used as an adj, only before ns ◊ *stilistische Schwächen* ♦ *Dieses Buch ähnelt stilistisch den Werken Camus'.* sylistic device Stilmittel ['ʃtiːlmɪtl̩] das <–s, –>

subject¹ [noun] **1.** *(topic)* Thema ['teːmaː] das <–s, Themen> ◊ *das Thema wechseln* ♦ *Das Buch befasst sich mit dem Thema Rechtsextremismus.* ♦ *Über welche Themen habt ihr gesprochen?* bring up a subject ein Thema anschneiden get onto a subject auf ein Thema kommen **2.** SCHOOL, UNI Fach [fax] das <–(e)s, Fächer> ◊ *Mathematik ist sein liebstes Fach.* **3.** LING Subjekt [zʊpˈjɛkt] das <–(e)s, –e> ◊ *Das Subjekt des Satzes steht immer im Nominativ.* **4.** *(in scientific research, person)* Versuchsperson [fɛˈzuːxspɛʁˌzoːn] die <–, –en> ◊ *Die Versuchspersonen bekamen unterschiedliche Medikamente.*; *(animal)* Versuchstier [fɛˈzuːxstiːɐ] das <–(e)s, –e> **5.** ARTS, FOTO Motiv [moˈtiːf] das <–s, –e> ◊ *das Motiv eines Bildes* **6.** *(citizen)* Staatsbürger ['ʃtaːtsbʏʁɡɐ] der <–s, –> ♀Staatsbürgerin ['ʃtaːtsbʏʁɡərɪn] die <–, –nen> ◊ *schwedische Staatsbürger; (of a monarch)* Untertan ['ʊntɐtaːn] der <–s or also –en, –en> ♀Untertanin ['ʊntɐtaːnɪn] die <–, –nen> ◊ *der König und seine Untertanen*

subject² [adj] abhängig ['aphɛnɪç] no comp/superl ◊ *abhängige Gebiete der Niederlande* ⊛ subject to sth **1.** be subject to change sich ändern können ◊ *Die Preise können sich ändern.* **2.** *(to controls, a law)* einer Sache [dat] unterworfen ◊ *Die Waren sind strengen Kontrollen unterworfen.* **3.** subject to availability je nach Verfügbarkeit

subject³ [verb] subject sb to sth *(to torture, heat, criticism)* jdn einer Sache [dat] aussetzen ['aɔsɛtsn̩] +haben ◊ *Er wurde einer brutalen Folter ausgesetzt.*;

(to questioning, treatment, analysis) jdn einer Sache [dat] unterziehen [ʊntɐˈtsiːən] <unterzieht, unterzog, hat unterzogen> ◊ *Die Polizei unterzog ihn einer genauen Befragung.*

subjective(ly) [adj, adv] subjektiv [zʊpjɛkˈtiːf] ◊ *Das ist ein rein subjektives Urteil.* ♦ *Diese Sichtweise ist sehr subjektiv.* ♦ subjektiv empfundene Lebensqualität subjective case Nominativ ['noːminatiːf] der <–s> no pl ◊ *Das Wort steht im Nominativ.*

subject matter [noun] Thema ['teːmaː] das <–s, Themen>

subjunctive [noun] Konjunktiv ['kɔnjʊŋktiːf] der <–s, –e> ◊ *Das Verb steht hier im Konjunktiv.*

submission [noun] **1.** *(document already submitted)* Vorlage ['foːɡlaːɡə] die <–, –n> ◊ *jdm eine Vorlage unterbreiten; (job application)* Bewerbung [bəˈvɛʁbʊŋ] die <–, –en>; *(written piece of work)* Beitrag ['baɛtraːk] der <–(e)s, Beiträge> ◊ *Verspätet eingebende Beiträge können wir nicht veröffentlichen.* **2.** *(process of submitting a document)* Einreichung ['aɛnraɛçʊŋ] die <–, –en> most sing *(form)* ◊ *die Einreichung eines Antrags bei der zuständigen Behörde* **3.** LAW *(statement)* Aussage ['aɔsaːɡə] die <–, –n> make a submission aussagen ['aɔsaːɡn̩] +haben make a submission to the court vor Gericht aussagen **4.** *(accepting sb's power over you)* Unterwerfung [ʊntɐˈvɛʁfʊŋ] die <–> no pl ◊ *die Unterwerfung unter Gottes Willen* beat an animal into submission ein Tier schlagen, bis es gehorcht [aɛn tiːɐ ˈʃlaːɡn̩ bɪs ɛs gəˈhɔʁçt] <schlägt, schlug, hat geschlagen> bully sb into submission jdn bedrängen, bis er sich geschlagen gibt [bəˈdrɛŋən bɪs ... gəˈʃlaːɡn̩ gɪːpt] <bedrängt, bedrängte, hat bedrängt>

submit [verb] **1.** *(put forward, hand in)* einreichen ['aɛnraɛçn̩] +haben ◊ *Die Vorschläge müssen bis Ende des Monats eingereicht werden.* submit sth to sb/sth etw. bei jdm/etw. einreichen ◊ *ein Formular bei einem Amt einreichen* **2.** *(surrender)* submit to sb sich jdm unterwerfen [ʊntɐˈvɛʁfn̩] <unterwirft sich, unterwarf sich, hat sich unterworfen> ◊ *Die Chinesen unterwarfen sich den Mongolen.; (to an unpleasant treatment or exmination)* submit to sth sich einer Sache [dat] unterziehen [ʊntɐˈtsiːən] <unterzieht sich, unterzog sich, hat sich unterzogen> ◊ *sich einer Behandlung unterziehen* **3.** *(to a law, rule)* submit to sth sich einer Sache [dat] beugen ['bɔɡn̩] +haben *(lofty)* ◊ *sich dem Gesetz beugen; (to an authority)* submit sb/sth/yourself to sth jdn/etw./sich einer Sache [dat] unterstellen [ʊntɐˈʃtɛlən] <unterstellt, unterstellte, hat unterstellt> *(form)* ◊ *Kriegsverbrechen der internationalen Gerichtsbarkeit unterstellen*

subordinate¹ [noun] Mitarbeiter ['mɪtʔaʁbaɛtɐ] der <–s, –> ♀Mitarbeiterin ['mɪtʔaʁbaɛtərɪn] die <–, –nen> ◊ *Er hat eine Reihe neuer Mitarbeiter eingestellt.*

subordinate² [adj] untergeordnet ['ʊntɐɡəʔɔʁdnət] no comp/superl ◊ *untergeordnete Bedeutung haben* ♦ *Der künstlerische Aspekt ist untergeordnet.* be subordinate to sb/sth jdm/etw. untergeordnet sein ◊ *Der Ausschuss ist dem Vorstand untergeordnet.*

subordinate clause [noun] Nebensatz ['neːbənzats] der <–es, Nebensätze> ◊ *Die Konjunktion „weil" leitet einen Nebensatz ein.*

subscribe [verb] **1.** *(to a newspaper, service etc.)* subscribe to sth etw. abonnieren [abɔˈniːrən]

<abonniert, abonnierte, hat abonniert> ◊ *eine Zeitschrift abonnieren* ♦ *Ich habe Pay-TV abbonniert.* **2.** *(to an organization)* subscribe to sth Mitglied … [gen] sein ['mɪtgliːt zaːn] +sein ◊ *Mitglied eines Golfclubs sein*
• **subscribe for** [phras v] subscribe for sth etw. zeichnen ['tsaeçnən] <zeichnet, zeichnete, hat gezeichnet> *(tech)* ◊ *Aktien zeichnen*
• **subscribe to** [phras v] subscribe to sth etw. vertreten [fɛ'treːtn̩] <vertritt, vertrat, hat vertreten> ◊ *eine Ansicht vertreten*

subscription [noun] **1.** *(to a newspaper, service etc.)* subscription (to sth) Abonnement (… [gen]) [abonə'man] das <-s, -s> ◊ *ein Abonnement verlängern* ♦ *ein Abonnement einer Fachzeitschrift* **2.** *(for membership)* subscription (fee) Beitrag ['baetraːk] der <-(e)s, Beiträge> ◊ *einen monatlichen Beitrag zahlen* **3.** *(donation)* (public) subscription Spende ['ʃpɛndə] die <-, -n> ◊ *etw. durch Spenden finanzieren* **4.** *(for shares)* Zeichnung ['tsaeçnʊŋ] die <-> no pl subscription for sth Zeichnung … [gen] ◊ *die Zeichnung der Aktien*

subsequent [adj] folgend ['fɔlgn̩t] no comp/superl, only before ns ◊ *in den folgenden Jahren* ♦ *der folgende Besitzer* subsequent to nach [naːx] +dat ◊ *Nach seinem Hochschulabschluss arbeitete er als Anwalt.*

subsequently [adv] anschließend ['anʃliːsn̩t] ◊ *Anschließend lehrte sie an der Universität von Kalifornien.*

subside [verb] **1.** *(pain, temperature, storm)* nachlassen ['naːxlasn̩] <lässt nach, ließ nach, hat nachgelassen> ◊ *Das Fieber hat nachgelassen.; (anger, indignation)* sich legen ['leːgn̩] +haben ◊ *Seine Wut wird sich legen.* **2.** *(water level)* sinken ['zɪŋkn̩] <sinkt, sank, ist gesunken> ◊ *Der Wasserspiegel ist gesunken.; (flood)* zurückgehen [tsu'rʏkgeːən] <geht zurück, ging zurück, ist zurückgegangen> ◊ *Die Überschwemmung ist zurückgegangen.; (ground, building)* sich senken ['zɛŋkn̩] +haben ◊ *Eine Seite des Gebäudes hat sich gesenkt.*

subsidiary [noun] Tochterfirma ['tɔxtɐˌfɪʁma:] die <-, Tochterfirmen> ◊ *Das Unternehmen hat mehrere Tochterfirmen im Ausland.*

subsidy [noun] Subvention [zʊpvɛn'tsjoːn] die <-, -en> most pl ◊ *Die EU will ihre Subventionen senken.*

substance [noun] **1.** *(matter, material)* Substanz [zʊps'tants] die <-, -en> ◊ *eine biologisch abbaubare Substanz* ♦ *Was ist das für eine Substanz?* **2.** *(drug)* Droge ['droːgə] die <-, -n> ◊ *eine illegale Droge* substance abuse Drogenmissbrauch ['droːgn̩mɪsbraox] der <-(e)s> no pl **3.** *(depth, importance)* Substanz [zʊps'tants] die <-> no pl ◊ *Diese Musik hat Substanz.* something of substance etwas Wesentliches [ɛtvas 'veːzntlɪçəs] ◊ *etwas Wesentliches zustande bringen* **4.** *(subject)* Inhalt ['ɪnhalt] der <-(e)s, -e> ◊ *Was war der Inhalt der Gespräche?*
ⓔ give substance to sth etw. bestätigen there is no substance to sth etw. entbehrt jeder Grundlage in substance im Wesentlichen

substantial [adj] **1.** *(large, considerable)* beträchtlich [bə'trɛçtlɪç] ◊ *Ein Handy bringt beträchtliche Vorteile.* ♦ *Der Sachschaden am Auto war beträchtlich.* **2.** *(strongly built)* solide [zo'liːdə] <solider, am

solidesten> ◊ *solide Möbel* ♦ *Das Haus ist ziemlich solide.* **3.** *(difference)* wesentlich ['veːzn̩tlɪç] ◊ *Gibt es einen wesentlichen Unterschied zwischen dem deutschen und dem französischen Schulsystem?; (reason)* wichtig ['vɪçtɪç] ◊ *Eine Entlassung ist nur möglich, wenn ein wichtiger Grund vorliegt.; (argument)* gewichtig [gə'vɪçtɪç] ◊ *Für diese Position gibt es gewichtige Argumente.* **4.** *(food)* gehaltvoll [gə'haltfɔl] ◊ *eine gehaltvolle Mahlzeit* ♦ *Das Essen war nicht sehr gehaltvoll.* I need something more substantial. Ich brauche etwas Gehaltvolleres.

substantially [adv] **1.** *(by a large amount)* erheblich [ɛ'heːplɪç] ◊ *Die Fluggastzahlen sind erheblich gestiegen.* **2.** *(strongly built)* solide [zo'liːdə] <solider, am solidesten> ◊ *ein solide gebautes Haus* **3.** *(essentially)* im Wesentlichen [ɪm 've:zn̩tlɪçn̩] ◊ *Im Wesentlichen stimmt ihre Aussage.*

substantiate [verb] untermauern [ʊntɐ'maoɐn] <untermauert, untermauerte, hat untermauert> ◊ *Er lieferte keine Beweise, um seine Behauptung zu untermauern.*

substantive [adj] wesentlich ['veːzn̩tlɪç] ◊ *Die Veränderung ist nicht wesentlich.* ♦ *ein wesentliches Problem*

substitute¹ [noun] **1.** *(sth that is used or accepted instead of sth else)* Ersatz [ɛ'zats] der <-es, Ersätze> ◊ *Öl als Ersatz für Butter* ♦ *Schokolade ist kein Ersatz für Liebe.* coffee substitute Kaffeeersatz ['kafeːˌlɛzats] **2.** *(player)* Ersatzspieler [ɛ'zatsʃpiːle] der <-s, -> ♀Ersatzspielerin [ɛ'zatsʃpiːlərɪn] die <-, -nen> ◊ *einen Ersatzspieler einsetzen* **3.** *(stand-in)* Vertretung [fɛ'treːtʊŋ] die <-, -en> ◊ *Ich bin als Vertretung für meinen Kollegen eingesprungen.*
ⓔ there is no substitute for sth etw. kann man durch nichts ersetzen

substitute² [verb] **1.** *(use sth different)* nehmen ['neːmən] <nimmt, nahm, hat genommen> ◊ *Ich hatte keinen Gin mehr, also habe ich Wodka genommen.; (replace, exchange)* substitute B for A, substitute A with B A durch B ersetzen [dʊʁç … ɛˌzatsn̩] <ersetzt, ersetzte, hat ersetzt> ◊ *Fleisch durch Tofu ersetzen* **2.** *(a player)* auswechseln ['aosvɛksln̩] +haben be substituted by sb gegen jdn ausgewechselt werden He substituted him for Beckham. Er hat Beckham gegen ihn ausgewechselt. **3.** *(stand in)* substitute for sb jdn vertreten [fɛ'treːtn̩] <vertritt, vertrat, hat vertreten> ◊ *Mein Kollege vertritt mich morgen.*

substitution [noun] **1.** *(replacement)* Ersatz [ɛ'zats] der <-es> no pl the substitution of A for B der Ersatz von B durch A ◊ *der Ersatz von Menschen durch Maschinen* **2.** *(in sport, of a player)* Wechsel ['vɛksl̩] der <-s, -> ◊ *Zwei Minuten nach dem Wechsel schoss der neue Spieler ein Tor.*

subtle(-ly) [adj, adv] **1.** *(not obvious, not strong, tactful)* dezent [de'tsɛnt] <dezenter, am dezentesten> ◊ *Die Farbe ist sehr dezent.* ♦ *Ein dezenter Hinweis genügt.* ♦ *ein dezent beleuchteter Raum* **2.** *(sophisticated, astute, indirect)* subtil [zʊp'tiːl] ◊ *subtile Methoden anwenden* ♦ *Der Film war nicht eben subtil, aber unterhaltsam.* ♦ *subtil argumentieren* **3.** *(delicate)* fein [faen] ◊ *feine Blumenmuster* ♦ *fein bestickte Servietten*

subtract [verb] subtrahieren [zʊptra'hiːrən] <subtrahiert, subtrahierte, hat subtrahiert> *(tech)* ◊ *Wenn man drei von zehn subtrahiert, erhält man sieben.*

suburb [noun] Vorort ['foːglɔ't] der <-(e)s, -e> ◊ *in*

einem Vorort von Hamburg wohnen suburbs Stadtrand ['ʃtatrant] der <-(e)s> no pl ◊ *Sie wohnen am Stadtrand.*

subway [noun] **1.** *(in the UK: underpass)* Unterführung [ʊntə'fyːrʊŋ] die <-, -en> ◊ *die Unterführung benutzen etw.* **2.** *(in the US: underground railway)* U-Bahn ['uːbaːn] die <-, -en> ◊ *Sie fährt mit der U-Bahn zur Arbeit.*

succeed [verb] **1.** *(turn out well)* sth succeeds etw. gelingt [gə'lɪŋt] <gelingt, gelang, ist gelungen> ◊ *Hoffentlich gelingt das Experiment.; (achieve an aim)* sb succeeds in sth jd schafft etw. [aft] +haben ◊ *Sie hat ihre Aufgabe geschafft.* sb succeeds in doing sth jd schafft es, etw. zu tun ◊ *Er hat es mal wieder geschafft, alle zu verärgern.* **2.** *(do well)* Erfolg haben [e'fɔlk haːbm̩] +haben ◊ *Wir hatten keinen Erfolg.* ◆ *in der Schule Erfolg haben* **3.** *(replace)* ablösen ['apløːzn̩] +haben ◊ *den Kanzler ablösen* ◆ *jdn als Direktor ablösen* sth is succeeded by sth etw. weicht einer Sache [dat] [vaɛçt] <weicht, wich, ist gewichen> *(lofty)* ◊ *Die Angst wich dem Hass.*

success [noun] Erfolg [e'fɔlk] der <-(e)s, -e> ◊ *Ihr neuester Roman ist ein voller Erfolg.* ◆ *Ihre Bemühungen waren von wenig Erfolg gekrönt.* make a success of sth mit etw. Erfolg haben have success in doing sth etw. mit Erfolg tun ◊ *Wir haben mit Erfolg gegen die Firma geklagt.* sb is a success jd hat Erfolg

successful(ly) [adj, adv] erfolgreich [e'fɔlkraɛç] ◊ *ein erfolgreicher Abschluss* ◆ *Er ist als Schauspieler sehr erfolgreich.* ◆ *Sie hat ihre Lehre erfolgreich beendet.* be successful in sth Erfolg bei etw. haben [e'fɔlk baɛ ... haːbm̩] +haben ◊ *Er hatte Erfolg bei dem Gewinnspiel.* be successful in doing sth etw. mit Erfolg tun [mɪt e'fɔlk] ◊ *Sie hat sich mit Erfolg um die Stelle beworben.*

succession [noun] **1.** *(series)* Reihe ['raɛə] die <-, -n> ◊ *ein Reihe von Problemen* **2.** *(to a post)* Nachfolge ['naːxfɔlə] die <-> no pl ◊ *die Frage der Nachfolge klären; (to a title, an estate)* Erbfolge ['ɛrpfɔlə] die <-> no pl succession to the throne Thronfolge ['troːnfɔlə] die <-> no pl
℗ in succession hintereinander ◊ *Sie hat dreimal hintereinander gewonnen.*

successive [adj] aufeinander folgend [aoflaɛ̯nandə 'fɔlgn̩t] no comp/superl, only before ns ◊ *aufeinander folgende Regierungen* He won for the third successive year. Er hat drei Jahre nacheinander gewonnen.

successor [noun] Nachfolger ['naːxfɔlɡə] der <-s, -> ♀Nachfolgerin ['naːxfɔlɡərɪn] die <-, -nen> ◊ *einen würdigen Nachfolger für jdn suchen* successor to sb jds Nachfolger ◊ *der Nachfolger des Direktors*

succinct(ly) [adj, adv] prägnant [prɛg'nant] <prägnanter, am prägnantesten> ◊ *eine prägnante Analyse der Sachlage* ◆ *Sein Stil ist sachlich und prägnant.* ◆ *Das war prägnant formuliert.*

such¹ [det] *(with sg ns)* so ein ['zoː aɛn] so eine ['zoː aɛnə] ◊ *Er ist so ein lieber Mensch.* ◆ *Sie war so eine kluge Frau.* ◆ *so ein Tag wie heute; (with pl ns)* solche ['zɔlçə] ◊ *Solche Fragen beantworte ich nicht.* ◆ *Solche Leute wie du haben immer Glück.* such a thing so etwas ['zoː ɛtvas] no such thing nichts dergleichen ['nɪçts deːɐ̯glaɛçn̩] there is no such thing as sth etw. gibt es nicht ['giːpt es nɪçt] ◊ *Eine konfliktfreie Gesellschaft gibt es nicht.*

such² [pron] **1.** *(of a certain nature, in this way)* so [zoː] sth is such that ... etw. sieht so aus, dass ... ◊ *Die Arbeit sieht so aus, dass man im Kontrollraum sitzt und Monitoren überwachen muss.* sth is such as to do sth etw. ist so, dass es etw. tut ◊ *Das Verhalten des Häftlings ist so, dass es eine frühere Entlassung rechtfertigt.* **2.** *(so strong, great)* such is sth that, sth is such that etw. ist so groß/stark etc., dass [ɪst ˌzoː ˈɡroːs/ˈʃtaˑk das] ◊ *Seine Liebe ist so groß, dass er alles für sie tun würde.* **3.** *(for example)* such as wie [viː] ◊ *Es gab Beilagen wie Kartoffeln, Reis und Gemüse.* ◆ *Er treibt viel Sport wie Joggen und Radfahren.*
℗ ... and such ... und so *(fam)* as such *(per se)* im eigentlichen Sinne

suck [verb] **1.** *(a liquid, air)* saugen ['zaoɡn̩] <saugt, saugte/sog, hat gesaugt/gesogen> ◊ *Cola durch einen Strohhalm saugen* ◆ *Das Baby sog an der Brust.; (inhale)* suck in einatmen ['aɛn|aːtmən] <atmet ein, atmete ein, hat eingeatmet> ◊ *frische Luft einatmen; (pull liquid or air somewhere)* suck in ansaugen ['anzaoɡn̩] +haben ◊ *Die Klimaanlage saugt Luft an.; (on a cigarette)* suck on sth an etw. [dat] ziehen [an ... ˈtsiːən] <zieht, zog, hat gezogen> ◊ *Sie zog an ihrer Zigarette.* **2.** *(pull, solid in your mouth)* suck (on) sth etw. lutschen ['lʊtʃn̩] +haben ◊ *Bonbons lutschen* suck your thumb am Daumen lutschen **3.** *(pull sb/ sth solid somewhere)* ziehen ['tsiːən] <zieht, zog, hat gezogen> ◊ *Das Kind wurde unter die Wasseroberfläche gezogen.* **4.** *(be bad)* suck sth etw. ist Mist [ɪst ˈmɪst] +sein *(fam)* ◊ *Dieser Film ist echt Mist.*
• **suck in, suck into** [phras v] sb is sucked in by sth, sb is sucked into sth etw. schlägt jdn in seinen Bann [ʃlɛːkt ... ɪn ... ˈban] <schlug, hat geschlagen> ◊ *Die bunte Welt der Roman schlug mich in seinen Bann.* → **suck 1.**
• **suck up** [phras v] suck up to sb sich bei jdm einschleimen [baɛ ... ˈaɛnʃlaɛmən] +haben *(fam, pej)* ◊ *Der Neue versucht, sich beim Lehrer einzuschleimen.*

sudden(ly) [adj, adv] plötzlich ['plœtslɪç] no comp/ superl ◊ *Sein plötzlicher Tod überraschte uns.* ◆ *Das Ende der Freundschaft war etwas plötzlich.* ◆ *Es fing plötzlich zu regnen an.*

sue [verb] klagen ['klaːɡn̩] +haben ◊ *Ich glaube nicht, dass sie klagen werden.* sue for sth auf etw. [acc] klagen ◊ *Sie klagte auf Schmerzensgeld.* sue sb/sth jdn/etw. verklagen [fɛ'klaːɡn̩] <verklagt, verklagte, hat verklagt> sue sb/sth for sth jdn/etw. wegen etw. verklagen ◊ *Er verklagte die Firma wegen Vertragsbruchs.* sue sb for damages jdn auf Schadensersatz verklagen

suffer [verb] *(because of stress, pain, hardship)* leiden ['laɛdn̩] <leidet, litt, hat gelitten> ◊ *Sie hat sehr gelitten, als ihre Ehe zerbrach.* suffer (from) sth unter etw. [dat] leiden ◊ *unter großen Schmerzen leiden* ◊ *Das Land leidet unter einer Dürre.* suffer from a disease an einer Krankheit leiden ◊ *Er leidet schon seit Jahren an Depressionen.; (an attack, a loss, defeat, death)* suffer sth etw. erleiden [e'laɛdn̩] <erleidet, erlitt, hat erlitten> ◊ *einen Herzinfarkt erleiden* ◆ *Die Firma erlitt große Verluste.*

sufferer [noun] Leidende ['laɛdn̩də] der/die <-n, die Leidenden> *but: ein Leidender/eine Leidende* an acne sufferer jemand, der an Akne leidet [jeːmant deːɐ̯ an 'aknə laɛdət] allergy sufferer Allergiker [a'lɛrɡɪkɐ] der <-s, -> ♀Allergikerin

[a'lɛʳɡɪkəɾɪn] die <–, –nen>
suffering (noun) Leid [laet] das <–(e)s> *no pl* ◊ *Sie versuchten, das Leid der Kranken zu lindern.* cause sb a lot of suffering jdm großes Leid zufügen
sufficient(ly) (adj, adv) ausreichend ['aosraeçnt] *seldom comp/superl* ◊ *Es lag kein ausreichender Tatverdacht vor.* ✦ *Der Proviant war für alle ausreichend.* ✦ *Die Straße ist nicht ausreichend beleuchtet.* be sufficient ausreichen ['aosraeçn] +haben
suffix (noun) Suffix ['zufɪks] das <–es, –e> ◊ *Die Verkleinerungsform kann im Deutschen durch das Suffix „-chen" gebildet werden.*
suffocate (verb) 1. *(kill, die, feel a lack of air)* ersticken [e'ʃtɪkn̩] <erstickt, erstickte, hat/ist erstickt> transitive use +haben/intransitive use +sein ◊ *Die meisten Opfer des Feuers sind erstickt.* ✦ *Die hohen Steuern ersticken das Wirtschaftswachstum.* ✦ *Mach doch mal ein Fenster auf. Ich ersticke hier!* 2. *(make sb feel oppressed)* erdrücken [e'drʏkn̩] <erdrückt, erdrückte, hat erdrückt> ◊ *Mich erdrücken die Schulden.*
sugar (noun) 1. *(substance)* Zucker ['tsʊke] der <–s, –> *most sing* ◊ *ein Teelöffel Zucker* ✦ *Nimmst du Zucker in den Kaffee?* 2. *(term of affection)* Schatz [ʃats] der <–es, Schätze> *most sing (fam)* ◊ *Hallo, Schatz, wie geht's dir?*
suggest (verb) 1. *(propose, recommend)* vorschlagen ['foːɡʃlaːɡn̩] <schlägt vor, schlug vor, hat vorgeschlagen> ◊ *Verbesserungen vorschlagen* ✦ *Ich schlage vor, wir gehen essen.* ✦ *Der Arzt schlug eine Kur vor.* suggest doing sth vorschlagen, etw. zu tun ◊ *Sie schlug vor, den Manager persönlich zu fragen.* 2. *(imply)* behaupten [bə'haoptn̩] <behauptet, behauptete, hat behauptet> followed by the subjunctive when used in reported speech ◊ *Willst du etwa behaupten, ich sei schuld?* 3. *(point to)* suggest sth auf etw. (acc) hindeuten [aof ... ˌhɪndɔɪtn̩] <deutet hin, deutete hin, hat hingedeutet> ◊ *Die Studie deutet auf genetische Ursachen von Asthma hin.* suggest that darauf hindeuten, dass as the name suggests wie der Name schon sagt 4. *(remind you of sth)* suggest sth an etw. (acc) erinnern [an ... ɐˈ|ˌɪnɐn] <erinnert, erinnerte, hat erinnert> ◊ *Das Haus erinnert an eine Festung.*
suggestion (noun) 1. *(proposal)* Vorschlag ['foːɡʃlaːk] der <–(e)s, Vorschläge> ◊ *Er griff ihren Vorschlag dankbar auf.* ✦ *Sie machte den Vorschlag, eine Pause einzulegen.* at sb's suggestion auf jds Vorschlag be open to suggestions Vorschlägen gegenüber aufgeschlossen sein 2. *(evidence)* Hinweis ['hɪnvaes] der <–es, –e> suggestion of sth Hinweis auf etw. (acc) there is no suggestion that es gibt keinen Hinweis darauf, dass 3. *(insinuation)* Behauptung [bə'haoptʊŋ] die <–, –en> followed by the subjunctive when used in reported speech ◊ *Er wies die Behauptung zurück, es gehe bei dem Krieg um Öl.* 4. *(influencing)* Suggestion [zʊɡɛs'tjoːn] die <–, –en> ◊ *jdn durch Suggestion manipulieren* power of suggestion Suggestionskraft [zʊɡɛs'tiːfkraft] die <–, Suggestivkräfte>
suicide (noun) 1. *(ending your life, move with devastating consequences)* Selbstmord ['zɛlpstmɔʳt] der <–(e)s, –e> ◊ *Er beging Selbstmord, indem er vor einen Zug sprang.* ✦ *An dieser Stelle zu surfen wäre glatter Selbstmord.* ✦ *Das wäre politischer Selbstmord.* suicide attempt Selbstmordversuch

['zɛlpstmɔʳtfeːzuːx] der <–(e)s, –e> suicide bomber Selbstmordattentäter ['zɛlpstmɔʳt|ˌatn̩tɛːtɐ] der <–s, –> ♀Selbstmordattentäterin ['zɛlpstmɔʳt|ˌatn̩tɛːtəɾɪn] die <–, –nen> suicide mission Himmelfahrtskommando ['hɪmlfaːʳtskɔˌmando:] das <–s, –s> 2. *(person)* Selbstmörder ['zɛlpstmœʳdɐ] der <–s, –> ♀Selbstmörderin ['zɛlpstmœʳdəɾɪn] die <–, –nen> ◊ *Ein Selbstmörder ist für die Verspätung des Zuges verantwortlich.*
suit¹ (noun) 1. *(formal clothing)* Anzug ['antsuːk] der <–(e)s, Anzüge> ◊ *Er trug einen dunklen Anzug.; (with a skirt)* Kostüm [kɔs'tyːm] das <–s, –e> ◊ *Sie trug ein elegantes dunkelblaues Kostüm.; (clothing for a particular activity, in compound ns)* ... suit ...anzug ['antsuːk] diving suit Taucheranzug ['taoxɐ|antsuːk] bathing suit Badeanzug ['baːdə|antsuːk] 2. LAW Klage ['klaːɡə] die <–, –n> file a suit against sb Klage gegen jdn einreichen libel suit Verleumdungsklage [fɛ'lɔʏmdʊŋsklaːɡə] 3. CARDS Farbe ['faʳbə] die <–, –n> ◊ *Welche Farbe ist Trumpf?*
suit² (verb) 1. *(be convenient for sb)* suit sb jdm passen ['pasn̩] +haben ◊ *Passt Ihnen Montag, oder haben Sie da keine Zeit?* ✦ *Sie ist sehr nett, aber nur, wenn es ihr passt.; (your needs, lifestyle)* suit sth einer Sache (dat) entsprechen [ɛnt'ʃpreçn̩] <entspricht, entsprach, hat entsprochen> ◊ *ein Auto, das meinen Bedürfnissen entspricht* 2. *(look good on sb)* suit sb jdm stehen ['ʃteːən] <steht, stand, hat gestanden> ◊ *Die Farbe steht dir nicht.*
◉ **suit yourself** 1. *(do sth in a convenient way)* do sth to suit yourself etw. nach eigenen Wünschen tun 2. *(annoyed)* Suit yourself! Ganz wie du willst/ihr wollt/Sie wollen!
suitable (adj) geeignet [ɡə'|aeɡnət] ◊ *Für diesen Job bin ich nicht geeignet.* ✦ *Er war auf der Suche nach einer geeigneten Wohnung.* be suitable to do sth dafür geeignet sein, etw. zu tun
suitably (adv) 1. *(right, appropriate)* entsprechend [ɛnt'ʃpreçn̩t] no comp/superl ◊ *Ist er entsprechend qualifiziert?* ✦ *Sie waren nicht entsprechend gekleidet.* 2. *(as expected)* gebührend [ɡə'byːrənt] no comp/superl ◊ *Er war von ihrer Leistung gebührend beeindruckt.*
suitcase (noun) Koffer ['kɔfɐ] der <–s, –> ◊ *den Koffer packen/auspacken*
suite (noun) 1. *(of rooms, music)* Suite ['sviːtə] die <–, –n> ◊ *eine Suite in einem Hotel mieten* ✦ *eine Suite von Bach spielen* 2. *(of furniture)* Garnitur [ɡaʳni'tuːɐ] die <–, –en> three-piece suite Sitzgarnitur ['zɪtsɡaʳniˌtuːɐ] 3. IT, TRADE *(of software, products)* Paket [pa'keːt] das <–(e)s, –e>
sulky(-ily) (adj, adv) mürrisch ['mʏrɪʃ] ◊ *ein mürrisches Gesicht* ✦ *Die Bedienung ist mürrisch und unmotiviert.* ✦ *Mürrisch folgte das Kind seinen Eltern.*
sullen(ly) → sulky(-ily)
sulphur (noun) Schwefel ['ʃveːfl] der <–s> no pl ◊ *Hier riecht es nach Schwefel.*
sum (noun) 1. *(amount, total)* Summe ['zʊmə] die <–, –n> ◊ *eine Summe von 30 Euro* ✦ *Er hat dafür eine hohe Summe bezahlt.* ✦ *Die Summe aus vier und vier ist acht.* sum of money Geldsumme 2. *(calculation)* Rechnung ['rɛçnʊŋ] die <–, –en> ◊ *eine Rechnung im Kopf lösen* do a sum, do (your) sums rechnen ['rɛçnən] <rechnet, rechnete,

hat gerechnet> get your sums wrong **sich verrech-nen** [fɛˈrɛçnən] <verrechnet sich, verrechnete sich, hat sich verrechnet> ◊ *Mit diesem Projekt hat sie sich wohl verrechnet.*

☞ in sum **alles in allem**

summarize [verb] **zusammenfassen** [ʦuˈzamənfasn̩] +haben ◊ *das Wichtigste in einem Satz zusammenfassen*

summary [noun] **Zusammenfassung** [ʦuˈzamənfasʊŋ] die <-, -en> ◊ *eine Zusammenfassung des Films*

summer [noun] **Sommer** [ˈzɔmɐ] der <-s, -> ◊ *Wir hatten einen heißen Sommer.* ♦ *Nächsten Sommer wollen wir nach Skandinavien reisen.* in summer **im Sommer** early summer **Frühsommer** [ˈfryːzɔmɐ] high summer **Hochsommer** [ˈhoːxzɔmɐ] summer evening **Sommerabend** [ˈzɔmeˌaːbm̩t] der <-s, -e>

summer holiday [noun] summer holiday(s) **Sommerferien** [ˈzɔmefeːrjən] die <-> only pl ◊ *Wir wollen in den Sommerferien in die Berge fahren.*

summertime [noun] **Sommerszeit** [ˈzɔmɐsʦaet] die <-> no pl ◊ *Besonders schön ist es hier zur Sommerszeit.*

summer time [noun] **Sommerzeit** [ˈzɔmɐʦaet] die <-> no pl ◊ *die Uhren von Sommerzeit auf Winterzeit umstellen*

summit [noun] **Gipfel** [ˈɡɪpfl̩] der <-s, -> ◊ *der Gipfel des Matterhorns* ♦ *einen Gipfel einberufen* ♦ *Er war auf dem Gipfel seiner Macht.* summit meeting **Gipfeltreffen** [ˈɡɪpfl̩trɛfn̩] das <-s, ->

summon [verb] **1.** *(order sb to come)* **zitieren** [ʦiˈtiːrən] <zitiert, zitierte, hat zitiert> summon sb to sth **jdn irgendwohin zitieren** ◊ *Er wurde ins Bundeskanzleramt zitiert.* summon sb to court **jdn vor Gericht zitieren**; *(order sb to do sth)* summon sb to do sth **jdn auffordern, etw. zu tun** [ˈaoffɔˈdɐn ... ʦuː] +haben ◊ *Sie wurde aufgefordert, vor Gericht zu erscheinen.*; *(call a waiter, help)* rufen [ˈruːfn̩] <ruft, rief, hat gerufen> ◊ *einen Krankenwagen rufen*; *(a meeting)* **einberufen** [ˈaenbaruːfn̩] <beruft ein, berief ein, hat einberufen> ◊ *eine Versammlung einberufen* **2.** *(your courage, strength)* summon (up) **zusammennehmen** [ʦuˈzamənneːmən] <nimmt zusammen, nahm zusammen, hat zusammengenommen> ◊ *Er nahm seinen ganzen Mut zusammen und sprach sie an.*; *(a smile)* sich [dat] etw. abringen [ˈaprɪŋən] <ringt sich ab, rang sich ab, hat sich abgerungen> ◊ *Ich schaffte es, mir ein Lächeln abzuringen.*

sum up [verb] **1.** *(give a summary)* **zusammenfassen** [ʦuˈzamənfasn̩] +haben ◊ *Ich fasse noch mal zusammen: ...* ♦ *verschiedene Punkte zusammenfassen* **2.** *(express)* sum sth up **etw. auf den Punkt bringen** [aof deːn ˈpʊŋkt brɪŋən] <bringt, brachte, hat gebracht> ◊ *Mit seinem Kommentar brachte er auf den Punkt, was viele dachten.* **3.** *(evaluate)* **einschätzen** [ˈaenʃɛtsn̩] +haben ◊ *Sie hatte ihn richtig eingeschätzt.*

sun [noun] **Sonne** [ˈzɔnə] die <-, -n> most sing ◊ *Wann geht morgen die Sonne auf?* ♦ *zu lange in der Sonne sitzen*

sunburn [noun] **Sonnenbrand** [ˈzɔnənbrant] der <-(e)s, Sonnenbrände>

Sunday [noun] **Sonntag** [ˈzɔntaːk] der <-(e)s, -e> → **Monday**

sunlight [noun] **Sonnenlicht** [ˈzɔnənlɪçt] das <-(e)s> no pl ◊ *Die Pflanze verträgt kein direktes Sonnenlicht.*

sunny [adj] **1.** *(bright)* **sonnig** [ˈzɔnɪç] ◊ *ein sonniger Tag* ♦ *Hier ist es mir zu sonnig.* **2.** *(cheerful)* **heiter** [ˈhaetɐ] ◊ *ein heiteres Lächeln* ♦ *Ihr Wesen war heiter.*

sunrise [noun] **Sonnenaufgang** [ˈzɔnənˌaofɡaŋ] der <-(e)s, Sonnenaufgänge>

sunset [noun] **Sonnenuntergang** [ˈzɔnənˌʊntɐgaŋ] der <-(e)s, Sonnenuntergänge>

sunshade [noun] **Sonnenschirm** [ˈzɔnənʃɪˈrm] der <-(e)s, -e> ◊ *sich unter den Sonnenschirm setzen*

sunshine [noun] **1.** *(light from the sun)* **Sonnenschein** [ˈzɔnənʃaen] der <-(e)s> no pl ◊ *im warmen Sonnenschein spazieren gehen* **2.** *(informal address)* **Herzchen** [ˈhɛˈʦçən] das <-s, -> *(fam)* ◊ *Tu das nicht noch mal, Herzchen!*

suntanned [adj] **sonnengebräunt** [ˈzɔnəngəbrɔgnt] no comp/superl ◊ *Ich kam sonnengebräunt aus dem Urlaub zurück.* ♦ *sonnengebräunte Haut*

super [adj] **super** [ˈzuːpe] invariable *(fam)* ◊ *eine super Leistung* ♦ *Die Stimmung war super.*

superb(ly) [adj] **ausgezeichnet** [ˈaosgəʦaeçnət] ◊ *Er ist ein ausgezeichneter Koch.* ♦ *Das war ausgezeichnet!* ♦ *eine ausgezeichnet gemachte Präsentation*

superficial(ly) [adj, adv] **1.** *(on the surface, minor, shallow, cursory)* **oberflächlich** [ˈoːbefleçlɪç] ◊ *ein oberflächliches Gespräch über das Wetter* ♦ *Sie ist so oberflächlich.* ♦ *jdn/etw. oberflächlich untersuchen* **2.** *(on the outside)* **äußerlich** [ˈɔgsəlɪç] no comp/superl ◊ *eine rein äußerliche Ähnlichkeit* ♦ *Die Parallelen sind nur äußerlich.* ♦ *Äußerlich sehen sie sich ähnlich, aber im Charakter sind sie ganz verschieden.*

superfluous [adj] **überflüssig** [ˈyːbɐflʏsɪç] ◊ *überflüssige Adjektive streichen* ♦ *etw. für überflüssig halten* ♦ *sich* [dat] *überflüssig vorkommen* be superfluous to requirements **überflüssig sein**

superintendent [noun] **1.** *(in the UK: senior police officer)* ♂**Hauptkommissar** [ˈhaoptkɔmɪˌsaːˈr] der <-s, -e> ♀**Hauptkommissarin** [ˈhaoptkɔmɪˌsaːrɪn] die <-, -nen> **2.** *(person in charge)* **Leiter** [ˈlaetɐ] der <-s, -> ♀**Leiterin** [ˈlaetərɪn] die <-, -nen>

superior[1] [noun] **Vorgesetzte** [ˈfoːgəʦɛtstə] der/die <-n, die Vorgesetzten> *but:* ein Vorgesetzter/eine Vorgesetzte ◊ *Er ist bei Vorgesetzten, Kollegen und Mitarbeitern gleichermaßen beliebt.* ♦ *Als Ihr Vorgesetzter trage ich die Verantwortung!*

superior[2] [adj] **1.** *(better, greater)* superior (to sb/sth) (jdm/etw.) **überlegen** [ybeˈleˈgn̩] ◊ *seine überlegene Stärke* ♦ *Sie ist allen anderen Spielerinnen überlegen.* ♦ *Das neue System ist dem alten technisch überlegen.* vastly superior **weit überlegen** superior numbers **zahlenmäßige Überlegenheit** [ˌtsaːlənmɛːsɪgə ybeˈleˈgn̩haet] die <-> no pl ◊ **2.** *(of high quality)* **ausgezeichnet** [ˈaosgəʦaeçnət] ◊ *die ausgezeichnete Qualität seiner Waren* ♦ *Das Essen ist ausgezeichnet.*; *(wine)* **erlesen** [eˈleːzn̩] **3.** *(proud)* **überheblich** [ybeˈheːplɪç] ◊ *ihr überheblicher Gesichtsausdruck* ♦ *Wenn er doch nicht immer so überheblich wäre!* **4.** *(higher)* **höher** [ˈhøːe] no comp/superl, only before ns ◊ *ein höheres Gericht* superior officer **Vorgesetzte** [ˈfoːgəʦɛtstə] der/die <-n, die Vorgesetzten> *but:* ein Vorgesetzter/eine Vorgesetzte ◊ *Wer ist Ihr Vorgesetzter?*

superlative [noun] **Superlativ** [ˈzuːpelatiːf] der <-s, -e> ◊ *Der Superlativ von „schön" ist „am schönsten".* ♦ *In seinen Kritiken greift er selten zu*

Superlativen.
supermarket [noun] Supermarkt [ˈzuːpɛmaʳkt] der
<-(e)s, Supermärkte>
superstition [noun] Aberglaube [ˈaːbɐɡlaobə] der
<-ns> *no pl*
supervise [verb] **1.** *(a person, place, an activity)* beaufsichtigen [bəˈaofzɪçtɪɡn̩] <beaufsichtigt, beaufsichtigte, hat beaufsichtigt> ◊ *Wer beaufsichtigt die Kinder
in den Pausen?* ♦ *Er beaufsichtigte die Arbeiten.*
2. *(a PhD student)* betreuen [bəˈtrɔøən] <betreut,
betreute, hat betreut> ◊ *Wie viele Doktoranden
betreut er zurzeit?*
supervision [noun] Aufsicht [ˈaofzɪçt] die <-> *no pl* ◊
Die Kinder brauchen ständige Aufsicht. under (sb's)
supervision unter (jds) Aufsicht ◊ *Einnahme nur
unter ärztlicher Aufsicht!*
supervisor [noun] **1.** *(of an activity, a place, a person)*
Aufsicht [ˈaofzɪçt] die <-, -en> ◊ *die Aufsicht um
Auskunft bitten* office supervisor Bürovorsteher
[byˈroːfoːɐ̯ʃteːɐ] der <-s, -> ♀Bürovorsteherin
[byˈroːfoːɐ̯ʃteːərɪn] die <-, -nen> ◊ *Meine Schwester
ist Bürovorsteherin bei einer großen Firma.* ♦ *Der
Bürovorsteher macht gerade Pause.* **2.** *(of students)*
Dozent [doˈtsɛnt] der <-en, -en> ♀Dozentin
[doˈtsɛntɪn] die <-, -nen>; *(of a PhD student)* Dok-
torvater [ˈdɔktoːɡfaːtɐ] der <-s, Doktorväter> ♀Dok-
tormutter [ˈdɔktoːɡmʊtə] die <-, Doktormütter>
supper [noun] Abendessen [ˈaːbm̩tʔɛsn̩] das <-s, -> ◊
Wann gibt es Abendessen? ♦ *Zum Abendessen gab es
Wurstbrote.*
supple [adj] geschmeidig [ɡəˈʃmaedɪç] ◊ *Die Bewegungen von Katzen sind sehr geschmeidig.* ♦ *geschmeidi-
ges Leder*
supplement¹ [noun] **1.** *(something extra)* supplement
(to sth) Ergänzung (zu etw.) [eˈɡɛntsʊŋ] die
<-, -en> ◊ *Diese Übungen sind eine gute
Ergänzung zu dem Sprachkurs.* **2.** dietary supplement Nahrungsergänzungsmittel
[ˈnaːrʊŋsʔɛɡɛntsʊŋsmɪtl̩] das <-s, -> vitamin supplement Vitaminpräparat [vitaˈmiːnprɛpaˌraːt] das
<-s, -e> **3.** *(of a newspaper, magazine)* Beilage
[ˈbaelaːɡə] die <-, -n> ◊ *Die Zeitung hat samstags
immer eine Beilage.* **4.** *(of a book)* Nachtrag
[ˈnaːxtraːk] der <-(e)s, Nachträge> **5.** *(extra amount)*
Zuschlag [ˈtsuːʃlaːk] der <-(e)s, Zuschläge> ◊ *einen
Zuschlag für ein Einzelzimmer bezahlen*
supplement² [verb] **1.** supplement sth (with sth) etw.
(durch etw.) ergänzen [eˈɡɛntsn̩] <ergänzt, ergänzte,
hat ergänzt> ◊ *Sie ergänzten ihre karge Ernährung
durch Beeren und Nüsse.* **2.** supplement your income
sein Einkommen aufbessern [ˈaenkɔmən ˌaofbɛsɐn]
+haben
supplementary [adj] zusätzlich [ˈtsuːzɛtslɪç] ◊ *ein
zusätzliches Einkommen*
supplier [noun] *(of goods)* supplier (of) Lieferant
[lifəˈrant] der <-en, -en> ♀Lieferantin [lifəˈrantɪn]
die <-, -nen> wine supplier Weinlieferant
[ˈvaenlifəˌrant] Weinlieferantin [ˈvaenlifəˌrantɪn]; *(of
services)* Anbieter [ˈanbiːtɐ] der <-s, -> ♀Anbieterin
[ˈanbiːtərɪn] die <-, -nen> electricity supplier Strom-
anbieter [ˈʃtroːmʔanbiːtɐ]
supply¹ [noun] **1.** *(new material)* supply (of sth)
Nachschub (an etw. [dat]) [ˈnaːxʃuːp] der
<-(e)s, Nachschübe> ◊ *ein regelmäßiger
Nachschub an Süßigkeiten* I bought the necessary
supplies. Ich kaufte alles Nötige.; *(available to use)*

Vorrat [ˈfoːɡraːt] der <-(e)s, Vorräte> ◊ *ein begrenzter Vorrat an Öl* **2.** *(necessary equipment)* supplies
Ausrüstung [ˈaosrʏstʊŋ] die <-> *sing* camping
supplies Campingausrüstung [ˈkɛmpɪŋˌaosrʏstʊŋ];
(food for a trip) Proviant [proˈvjant] der <-s> *sing* ◊
Habt ihr genug Proviant für die Reise dabei?; *(relief
aid)* Hilfsgüter [ˈhɪlfsɡyːtɐ] die <-> *pl* ◊ *Medikamente und andere Hilfsgüter ins Krisengebiet
bringen* **3.** *(in a shop)* Bedarf [bəˈdaʳf] der
<-(e)s, -e> *most sing* ◊ *technischer Bedarf* fishing
supplies Anglerbedarf [ˈaŋlɐbəˌdaʳf] office supplies
Bürobedarf [byˈroːbədaʳf] **4.** *(process)* Versorgung
[feˈzoːɡʊŋ] die <-> *no pl* ◊ *die Versorgung des Fötus
mit Sauerstoff* ♦ *die Versorgung der Truppen mit Nah-
rungsmitteln* supply road Versorgungsweg
[feˈzoːɡʊŋsveːk] der <-(e)s, -e> **5.** ECON *(the total of
goods or other)* Angebot [ˈanɡəboːt] das <-(e)s> *sing*
supply and demand Angebot und Nachfrage
ⓟ in short supply knapp
supply² [verb] **1.** *(provide)* liefern [ˈliːfɐn] +haben ◊ *die
nötigen Beweise liefern* ♦ *Zitrusfrüchte liefern viele
Vitamine.*; *(make available)* bereitstellen
[bəˈraetʃtɛlən] +haben ◊ *den Raum für eine Veranstaltung bereitstellen* supply sth to sb/sth, supply sb/
sth with sth jdn/etw. mit etw. versorgen
[mɪt ... fɛzoːɡn̩] <versorgt, versorgte, hat versorgt> ◊
Das Kraftwerk versorgt die ganze Stadt mit Strom.
2. *(deliver)* liefern [ˈliːfɐn] +haben ◊ *Wer liefert die
Getränke?* supply sb/sth with sth jdn/etw. mit etw.
beliefern [mɪt ... bəliːfɐn] <beliefert, belieferte, hat
beliefert> ◊ *jdn mit Heizöl beliefern*
support¹ [noun] **1.** *(help, approval)* Unterstützung
[ʊntɐˈʃtʏtsʊŋ] die <-, -en> ◊ *Dieser Kandidat hat
unsere volle Unterstützung.* ♦ *Das Rote Kreuz bittet
Sie um Ihre Unterstützung.* in support of ... zur
Unterstützung ... [gen] **2.** *(emotional)* Beistand
[ˈbaeʃtant] der <-(e)s> *no pl* ◊ *Er dankte seiner
Frau für ihren Beistand in der schweren Zeit.*
3. *(supporters)* Anhängerschaft [ˈanhɛŋɐʃaft] die <->
no pl ◊ *Ihre Anhängerschaft besteht hauptsächlich
aus Studenten.* **4.** *(sth holding sth up, sb helping sb)*
Stütze [ˈʃtʏtsə] die <-, -n> ◊ *Stützen aus Stahl* ♦ *Ihr
Mann war ihr in der schweren Zeit eine unschätz-
bare Stütze.* **5.** *(bandage)* Stützverband [ˈʃtʏtsfɛbant]
der <-s, Stützverbände> ◊ *Er trug einen Stützverband
am linken Fuß.* **6.** *(proof)* Beweis [bəˈvaes] der
<-es, -e> ◊ *Gibt es einen Beweis für diese Theorie?*
7. *(act, band)* Vorgruppe [ˈfoːɡrʊpə] die <-, -n> *most
sing* **8.** IT, TECHN Support [zuˈpoʳt] der <-(e)s, -e> *most
sing*
support² [verb] **1.** *(help)* unterstützen [ʊntɐˈʃtʏtsn̩]
<unterstützt, unterstützte, hat unterstützt> ◊ *jds Bemü-
hungen/eine Partei unterstützen* ♦ *das Rote Kreuz
mit Spenden unterstützen* support sb in sth jdn bei
etw. unterstützen **2.** *(approve of)* befürworten
[bəˈfyːɡvoʳtn̩] <befürwortet, befürwortete, hat befürwor-
tet> ◊ *ein Projekt/einen Plan/eine Idee befürworten*
support doing sth dafür sein, etw. zu tun
[daˈfyːɐ̯ zaen ... tsuː] +sein **3.** *(emotionally)* support
sb jdm beistehen [ˈbaeʃteːən] <steht bei, stand bei,
hat beigestanden> ◊ *jdm in einer Krise beistehen*
4. *(hold up)* stützen [ˈʃtʏtsn̩] +haben ◊ *junge Pflanzen
mit Stöcken stützen* ♦ *Die Decke wird von mehreren
Balken gestützt.* ♦ *einen Verletzten stützen* support
yourself on sth sich auf etw. [acc] stützen ◊ *sich auf
einen Stock stützen* support yourself (against sth)

sich (an etw. [dat]) abstützen ['apʃtʏtsn̩] +haben ◊ *Ich stützte mich an der Wand ab.* **5.** *(a family)* ernähren [e'nɛːrən] <ernährt, ernährte, hat ernährt> ◊ *Ich habe eine Familie zu ernähren.* support yourself (with sth) seinen Unterhalt (mit etw.) bestreiten ['ʊntəhalt bəʃtraetn̩] <bestreitet, bestritt, hat bestritten> **6.** *(an addiction, activity)* finanzieren [finanˈtsiːrən] <finanziert, finanzierte, hat finanziert> ◊ *Sie finanzierte ihre Heroinsucht mit Prostitution.* **7.** *(prove)* untermauern [ʊnteˈmaoɐn] <untermauert, untermauerte, hat untermauert> ◊ *Sie untermauerten die Theorie mit Statistiken.* ♦ *Die Zeugin untermauerte die Aussage des Angeklagten.* **8.** *(a team)* Anhänger sein ['anhɛŋɐ zaen] +sein ◊ *ein treuer Anhänger von Schalke/des FC Bayern München sein* Who do you support? Zu wem hältst du? **9.** *(a performer)* support sb als Vorgruppe von jdm auftreten [als ˌfoːɐ̯grʊpə fɔn ... ˌaoftreːtn̩] <tritt auf, trat auf, ist aufgetreten> **10.** *(a software)* support sth etw. unterstützen [ʊnteˈʃtʏtsn̩] <unterstützt, unterstützte, hat unterstützt> ◊ *Das Betriebssystem unterstützt dieses Programm nicht.*

supporter [noun] **1.** *(of an idea)* Befürworter [bəˈfyːɐ̯vɔˈtə] der <-s, -> ♀Befürworterin [bəˈfyːɐ̯vɔˈtərɪn] die <-, -nen> ◊ *Sie ist eine Befürworterin der Reformen.* **2.** *(of a person, group, team)* Anhänger ['anhɛŋə] der <-s, -> ♀Anhängerin ['anhɛŋərɪn] die <-, -nen> ◊ *Sie ist eine Anhängerin des VfB.*

supporting → support[2] [adj] **1.** supporting role Nebenrolle ['neːbm̩rɔlə] die <-, -n> supporting actor Nebendarsteller ['neːbm̩daːˈʃtɛlə] der <-s, -> ♀Nebendarstellerin ['neːbm̩ˌdaːˈʃtɛlərɪn] die <-, -nen> **2.** *(holding the weight of sth)* Stütz... [ʃtʏts] supporting wall Stützmauer ['ʃtʏtsmaoɐ] die <-, -n> **3.** *(additional)* zusätzlich ['tsuːzɛtslɪç] ◊ *zusätzliche Beweise/Argumente*

suppose [verb] **1.** *(think that sth might be true)* annehmen ['anneːmən] <nimmt an, nahm an, hat angenommen> ◊ *Es war nicht so schwer, wie er angenommen hatte.* ♦ *Ich nehme an, dass sie später kommt.* ♦ *Es wird angenommen, dass die Zinsen steigen werden.* ♦ *Das Problem ist häufiger als allgemein angenommen.* reason to suppose (that) Anlass zu der Annahme, dass [ˌanlas tsu: deːɐ̯ 'anaːmə das] ◊ *Es gibt Anlass zu der Annahme, dass er lügt.* suppose sb to be sth jdn für jdn halten [fyːɐ̯ ... haltn̩] <hält, hielt, hat gehalten> ◊ *Ich hielt sie für seine Tochter.* **2.** *(think that sth is possible/right)* glauben ['glaobm̩] +haben ◊ *Ich glaube, wir sind jetzt fertig.* ♦ *Glaubst du, dass er dazu fähig ist?* I suppose I had better go now. Ich sollte wohl jetzt besser gehen. I suppose you think that's funny! Du findest das wohl lustig! **3.** *(assume)* voraussetzen [fo'raosˈzetsn̩] +haben ◊ *Diese Theorie setzt voraus, dass ...* ◉ be supposed to be/do sth **1.** eigentlich sein/tun sollen ◊ *Soll ich eigentlich auch dabei sein?* ♦ *Du hättest eigentlich anrufen sollen.* **2.** What's that supposed to mean? Was soll das heißen? let us suppose nehmen wir mal an suppose that angenommen

supposed(ly) [adj, adv] angeblich ['angəˈplɪç] no comp/superl; when used as an adj, only before ns ◊ *die angebliche Bedrohung durch Terroristen* ♦ *ein angeblich einbruchsicheres Haus* ♦ *Sie haben*

angeblich nichts davon gewusst.

suppository [noun] Zäpfchen ['tsɛpfçən] das <-s, -> ◊ *ein fiebersenkendes Zäpfchen nehmen*

suppress [verb] **1.** *(an activity, a group, reaction, information)* unterdrücken [ʊnteˈdrʏkn̩] <unterdrückt, unterdrückte, hat unterdrückt> ◊ *Minderheiten/den Widerstand unterdrücken* ♦ *Er konnte ein Gähnen nicht unterdrücken.* **2.** *(an emotion, a memory)* verdrängen [fe'drɛŋən] <verdrängt, verdrängte, hat verdrängt> ◊ *Die Erinnerung daran hat er völlig verdrängt.* ♦ *Viele Gewaltopfer verdrängen, was ihnen angetan worden ist.* **3.** *(a process)* hemmen ['hɛmən] +haben ◊ *Das Medikament soll den Appetit hemmen.* ♦ *den Handel/Fortschritt/das Wirtschaftswachstum hemmen*

supreme [adj] **1.** *(in titles of institutions, esp courts)* Oberste ['oːbəstə] <der/die/das Oberste ...> ◊ *der Oberste Gerichtshof der USA* supreme commander Oberbefehlshaber ['oːbebəˌfeːlshaːbe] der <-s, -> ♀Oberbefehlshaberin ['oːbebəˌfeːlshaːbərɪn] die <-, -nen> the Supreme Being das höchste Wesen [das ˌhøːçstə 'veːzn̩] das <höchsten Wesens> no pl **2.** *(very great)* äußerste ['ɔɪsestə] only before ns <der/die/das äußerste ...> ◊ *Mit äußerster Anstrengung gelang es ihm, sich zu befreien.* ♦ *von äußerster Wichtigkeit sein;* *(confidence, arrogance)* unglaublich [ʊn'glaoplɪç] ◊ *Sie hat ein unglaubliches Selbstbewusstsein.* ♦ *Seine Arroganz ist wirklich unglaublich.; (example)* hervorragend [hɐ'foːɐ̯gra:gn̩t] ◉ reign supreme an der Spitze stehen

surcharge [noun] Aufschlag ['aofʃlaːk] der <-(e)s, Aufschläge> ◊ *einen Aufschlag von 20 Euro/ 15 Prozent zahlen*

sure[1] [adj] **1.** *(certain)* sicher ['zɪçe] ◊ *ein sicherer Weg zum Erfolg* ♦ *ein sicheres Zeichen* sb is/feels sure (that) jd ist sich [dat] sicher(, dass) ◊ *Bist du dir sicher, dass der Film heute läuft?* ♦ *Er war sich sicher, dass er es schaffen würde.* sb is sure about sth jd ist sich [dat] einer Sache [gen] sicher ◊ *Bist du dir deiner Sache sicher?* sb is sure of sth jd ist sich [dat] bei etw. sicher ◊ *Er war sich bei seiner Antwort nicht sicher.* sure of yourself selbstsicher ['zɛlpstzɪçe] **2.** *(with negatives)* sb is not sure why/ how/where etc. jd weiß nicht genau, warum/wie/ wo etc. ['vaes nɪçt gənao va'rʊm/'viː/'voː] <weiß, wusste, hat gewusst> ◊ *Keiner weiß genau, warum sie ihn verlassen hat.* ♦ *Wir wissen noch nicht genau, wo wir im Sommer hinfahren.* **3.** *(certain to happen)* be sure to do sth etw. sicher tun ['zɪçe] ◊ *Wenn du nicht mehr lernst, fällst du sicher durch.* ♦ *Es regnet sicher, wenn wir unsere Wanderung machen.* ◉ be sure to do sth daran denken, etw. zu tun ◉ make sure **1.** *(check)* make sure (that) sich vergewissern, dass ◊ *Er wollte sich vergewissern, dass ich seine Telefonnummer hatte.* make sure of your facts die Fakten überprüfen **2.** *(take the necessary action)* make sure (that) dafür sorgen, dass ◊ *Wir werden dafür sorgen, dass dich niemand stört.*

sure[2] [adv] **1.** *(expressing agreement)* ja sicher [ja: 'zɪçe] ◊ *„Kann ich mal deinen Kuli leihen?"* — *„Ja sicher."* **2.** *(in the US: when sb thanks you)* gern geschehen [ge'rn geʃeːən] ◊ *„Vielen Dank für Ihre Hilfe." — „Gern geschehen."* **3.** *(mainly in the US: admitting that sth is true)* sicher ['zɪçe] ◊ *Es ist sicher nicht leicht für dich, aber du musst es*

trotzdem versuchen.

ⓢ **sure enough** tatsächlich *for sure* mit Sicherheit ◊ *Ich kann nicht mit Sicherheit sagen, wo er ist.*

surely [adv] 1. *(very likely)* doch sicher [dɔx ˈzɪçə] ◊ *Dazu hat er doch sicher keine Zeit.* ♦ *Das hat sie doch sicher nicht ernst gemeint.* Surely not! Das kann doch nicht wahr sein! 2. *(without any doubt)* bestimmt [bəˈʃtɪmt] *no comp/superl* ◊ *Bestimmt regnet es morgen wieder!*

surety [noun] 1. *(person)* Bürge [ˈbʏɡə] der <–n, –n> ♀Bürgin [ˈbʏɡɪn] die <–, –nen> 2. *(money)* Bürgschaft [ˈbʏʃaft] die <–, –en>

surf [verb] surfen [ˈsœfn̩] +haben ◊ *In den Ferien gehen wir surfen.* ♦ *stundenlang im Internet surfen*

surface¹ [noun] 1. *(top layer, outside part)* Oberfläche [ˈoːbɐflɛçə] die <–, –n> *(also fig)* ◊ *die glatte Oberfläche des Spiegels* ♦ *Der Wal kam an die Oberfläche, um Luft zu holen.* ♦ *Diese Gefühle kommen bei ihr nur selten an die Oberfläche.; (flat area for working)* Arbeitsfläche [ˈaʁbaɛtsflɛçə] die <–, –n> ◊ *die Arbeitsflächen sauber halten* road surface Straßendecke [ˈʃtraːsn̩dɛkə] die <–, –n> ◊ *Die Straßendecke muss dringend ausgebessert werden.* on the surface nach außen hin [naːx ˈaʊsn̩ hɪn] ◊ *Nach außen hin macht er einen ganz normalen Eindruck.* 2. *(side of an object)* Fläche [ˈflɛçə] die <–, –n> ◊ *Ein Würfel hat sechs quadratische Flächen.*

surface² [verb] 1. *(diver, submarine, lost person or thing)* auftauchen [ˈaʊftaʊxn̩] +sein ◊ *Das U-Boot tauchte wieder auf.* ♦ *Der Vermisste ist in Italien aufgetaucht.* 2. *(information)* ans Tageslicht kommen [ans ˈtaːɡəslɪçt kɔmən] <kommt, kam, ist gekommen> ◊ *Die Einzelheiten sind erst jetzt ans Tageslicht gekommen.* 3. *(get out of bed)* aufstehen [ˈaʊfʃteːən] <steht auf, stand auf, ist aufgestanden> ◊ *Gegen elf stand er endlich auf.* 4. *(a road)* asphaltieren [asfalˈtiːrən] <asphaltiert, asphaltierte, hat asphaltiert>

surgeon [noun] Chirurg [çiˈrʊʁk] der <–en, –en> ♀Chirurgin [çiˈrʊʁɡɪn] die <–, –nen> ◊ *Der Chirurg hat bei der Operation einen Fehler gemacht.* ♦ *Sie ist Chirurgin am Amberger Krankenhaus.*

surgery [noun] 1. *(operation)* Operation [opəraˈtsɪ̯oːn] die <–, –en> ◊ *einen Patienten auf die Operation vorbereiten* 2. *(room for operations)* OP [oːˈpeː] der <–(s), –(s)> ◊ *Der Patient wurde in den OP gebracht.* 3. *(of a doctor, dentist)* Praxis [ˈpraksɪs] die <–, Praxen> ◊ *Mein Hausarzt hat seine Praxis neu eingerichtet.* 4. *(period of time)* Sprechstunde [ˈʃprɛçʃtʊndə] die <–, –n> ◊ *Die Sprechstunde beginnt um acht Uhr.*

surname [noun] Nachname [ˈnaːxnaːmə] der <–ns, –n> ◊ *Wie heißt er mit Nachnamen?*

surplus¹ [noun] surplus (of sth/sb) Überschuss (an etw./jdm) [ˈyːbɐʃʊs] der <–es, Überschüsse> ◊ *einen Überschuss an Arbeitskräften haben*

surplus² [adj] überschüssig [ˈyːbɐʃʏsɪç] *no comp/superl* ◊ *Was machen sie mit dem überschüssigen Geld?*

ⓢ **be surplus to requirements** nicht mehr gebraucht werden

surprise¹ [noun] Überraschung [ybɐˈraʃʊŋ] die <–, –en> ◊ *Welch eine Überraschung!* ♦ *Sein Sieg war eine große Überraschung.* ♦ *Er brachte ihr eine kleine Überraschung zum Geburtstag mit.* come as a surprise (to sb) eine Überraschung (für jdn) sein sb is in for a surprise jd wird eine Überraschung

erleben much to sb's surprise zu jds großen Überraschung ◊ *Zu ihrer großen Überraschung funktionierte der Fernseher noch.* surprise win Überraschungssieg [ybɐˈraʃʊŋsziːk] der <–(e)s, –e> surprise visitors überraschender Besuch [ybɐˌraʃndə bəˈzuːx] <–(e)s> *no pl*

ⓢ **surprise, surprise** welch eine Überraschung *(iron)* take sb by surprise jdn überraschen

surprise² [verb] überraschen [ybɐˈraʃn̩] <überrascht, überraschte, hat überrascht> ◊ *Seine Freundlichkeit überraschte mich.* ♦ *jdn mit einem Geschenk überraschen* ♦ *von einem Gewitter überrascht werden* ♦ *Sie haben den Einbrecher überrascht.* surprise yourself selbst ganz überrascht sein

surprised → surprise [adj] erstaunt [ɛˈʃtaɒnt] <erstaunter, am erstauntesten> ◊ *ihr erstaunter Gesichtsausdruck/Blick* ♦ *Er sah erstaunt aus.* surprised at sth erstaunt über etw. [acc] ◊ *Ich war sehr erstaunt über seine Reaktion.* sb is surprised to hear that es wundert jdn, dass [ɛs ˈvʊndɐt ... das] +haben ◊ *Es wundert mich nicht, dass er durchgefallen ist.* I wouldn't be surprised. Es würde mich nicht wundern.

surprising → surprise [adj] erstaunlich [ɛˈʃtaɒnlɪç] ◊ *eine erstaunliche Entwicklung* it is surprising how/what etc. es ist erstaunlich, wie/was etc. it's not surprising that es ist nicht verwunderlich, dass [ɛs ɪst nɪçt fɛˈvʊndɐlɪç das]

surprisingly [adv] überraschend [ybɐˈraʃnt] ◊ *ein überraschend großes Zimmer* not surprisingly wie zu erwarten war [viː tsuː ɛˈvaʁtn̩ vaːɐ] ◊ *Wie zu erwarten war, wollte er auch mit.*

surrender [verb] 1. *(admit defeat)* surrender (to sb/sth) sich (jdm/etw.) ergeben [ɛˈɡeːbm̩] <ergibt sich, ergab sich, hat sich ergeben> ◊ *Der Räuber ergab sich dem Sheriff.* 2. *(hand over)* surrender sth/sth to sb jdm jdn/etw. übergeben [ybɐˈɡeːbm̩] <übergibt, übergab, hat übergeben> ◊ *Sie übergaben den Soldaten die Geiseln.* ♦ *Der General übergab der neuen Regierung die Macht.* surrender yourself (to the police) sich (der Polizei) stellen [(deːɐ poliˌtsaɛ) ˈʃtɛlən] +haben 3. *(your weapon, passport)* surrender sth (to sb) etw. (bei jdm) abgeben [ˈapɡeːbm̩] <gibt ab, gab ab, hat abgegeben> ◊ *Er musste seinen Pass abgeben und durfte das Land nicht verlassen.* 4. *(succumb)* surrender (yourself) to sth sich einer Sache [dat] hingeben [ˈhɪnɡeːbm̩] <gibt sich hin, gab sich hin, hat sich hingegeben> ◊ *Sie gab sich ganz der Musik hin.*

surround [verb] 1. *(be or put all around)* umgeben [ʊmˈɡeːbm̩] <umgibt, umgab, hat umgeben> ◊ *Welche Länder umgeben die Schweiz?* ♦ *eine Wiese mit einem Zaun umgeben* 2. *(stand in a circle)* umringen [ʊmˈrɪŋən] <umringt, umringte, hat umringt> ◊ *Zuschauer umringten den Straßenkünstler.; (police)* umstellen [ʊmˈʃtɛlən] <umstellt, umstellte, hat umstellt> ◊ *Die Polizei hat die Bank umstellt.* You are surrounded! Das Gebäude ist umstellt!*; (enemy)* umzingeln [ʊmˈtsɪŋl̩n] <umzingelt, umzingelte, hat umzingelt> ◊ *von Feinden umzingelt* 3. *(be closely connected with)* be surrounded by sth mit etw. verbunden sein [mɪt ... fɛˌbʊndn̩ zaɛn] +sein ◊ *Dieser Schritt ist mit Problemen/großer Gefahr verbunden.* the mystery surrounding sb/sth das Geheimnis um jdn/etw. [das ɡəˈhaɛmnɪs ʊm] the circumstances surrounding sth die Begleitumstände

... gen [diː bəˈɡlaɛt|ʊmʃtɛndə] <-> pl
surrounding → **surround** adj (all around) umliegend
[ˈʊmliːɡn̩t] only before ns ◊ die Stadt und die umliegenden Dörfer
surroundings noun Umgebung [ʊmˈɡeːbʊŋ] die
<-, -en> ◊ die unmittelbare Umgebung ◆ Das Hotel
liegt in einer reizvollen Umgebung.
surveillance noun Überwachung [ybeˈvaxʊn] die
<-> no pl keep sb/sth under surveillance jdn/etw.
überwachen [ybeˈvaxn̩] <überwacht, überwachte, hat
überwacht> ◊ Gefangene überwachen ◆ einen Geldautomaten mit einer Kamera überwachen
survey¹ noun 1. (opinion poll) Umfrage [ˈʊmfraːɡə] die
<-, -n> ◊ Die Umfrage hat ergeben, dass ... ◆ eine
repräsentative Umfrage 2. (of a house) Begutachtung
[bəˈɡuːt|axtʊn] die <-, -en>; (written report)
Gutachten [ɡuːt|axtn̩] das <-s, -> 3. (of an area of
land) Vermessung [feˈmɛsʊn] die <-, -en> 4. (of a
subject, situation) Überblick [ˈyːbeblɪk] der
<-(e)s, -e> ◊ Er gab uns einen Überblick über die
bisherige Entwicklung.
survey² verb 1. (ask questions) befragen [bəˈfraːɡn̩]
<befragt, befragte, hat befragt> ◊ Hierzu wurden 2000
Personen befragt. 2. (look at) betrachten [bəˈtraxtn̩]
<betrachtet, betrachtete, hat betrachtet> ◊ die Erde,
vom Weltraum aus betrachtet 3. (a house) begutach-
ten [bəˈɡuːt|axtn̩] <begutachtet, begutachtete, hat begut-
achtet> 4. (an area of land) vermessen [feˈmɛsn̩]
<vermisst, vermaß, hat vermessen>
surveyor noun 1. (of land) Landvermesser
[ˈlantfɛmɛsɐ] der <-s, -> ♀Landvermesserin
[ˈlantfɛmɛsərɪn] die <-, -nen> 2. (of buildings) Bau-
gutachter [ˈbaoɡuːt|axtɐ] der <-s, -> ♀Baugutachte-
rin [ˈbaoɡuːt|axtərɪn] die <-, -nen>
survival noun Überleben [ybeˈleːbm̩] das <-s> no pl
the fight for survival der Kampf ums Überleben
survival rate Überlebensrate [ybeˈleːbm̩sraːtə] die
<-, -n>
⊙ **survival of the fittest** Überleben der Stärksten
a survival from ein Überbleibsel aus
survive verb 1. (stay alive) überleben [ybeˈleːbm̩]
<überlebt, überlebte, hat überlebt> ◊ Es ist ein
Wunder, dass das Kind überlebt hat. ◆ Nur der
Beifahrer hat den Unfall überlebt.; (a relative) sb is
survived by sb jd hinterlässt jdn [hɪnteˈlɛst] <hinter-
ließ, hat hinterlassen> ◊ Sie hinterlässt einen Mann
und vier Kinder. 2. (a fire, war, difficult situation)
überstehen [ybeˈʃteːən] <übersteht, überstand, hat
überstanden> ◊ Dieses Haus hat als Einziges den
Krieg überstanden. ◆ Mach dir keine Sorgen um
sie – sie wird es schon überstehen. 3. (continue to
exist) weiter bestehen [ˈvaɛte bəʃteːən] <besteht,
bestand, hat bestanden> ◊ Es ist fraglich, ob die Organisation in dieser Form weiter bestehen kann.
⊙ **survive on sth** von etw. leben
survivor noun 1. (sb who survives) Überlebende
[ybeˈleːbm̩də] der/die <-n, die Überlebenden> but:
ein Überlebender/eine Überlebende ◊ Bei dem Unglück
gab es nur einen Überlebenden. ◆ Die Überlebenden
wurden ins Krankenhaus gebracht. holocaust
survivors Überlebende des Holocausts He is a lung
cancer survivor. Er hatte Lungenkrebs und hat
überlebt. He is the only survivor of his family. Er ist
der Einzige aus der Familie, der noch lebt. 2. (sb
who copes well despite a difficult life) Überlebens-
künstler [ybeˈleːbm̩skʏnstlɐ] der <-s, -> ♀Überle-

benskünstlerin [ybeˈleːbm̩skʏnstlərɪn] die <-, -nen>
suspect¹ noun Verdächtige [feˈdɛçtɪɡə] der/die
<-n, die Verdächtigen> but: ein Verdächtiger/eine Ver-
dächtige ◊ Der Kommissar ließ den Verdächtigen
überwachen. murder suspect Mordverdächtige
[ˈmɔˈtfe,dɛçtɪɡə] the obvious suspect der/die Hauptverdächtige [deːɡ/diː ˈhaoptfe,dɛçtɪɡə]
suspect² verb 1. (assume sth bad) suspect (that)
vermuten(, dass) [feˈmuːtn̩ (das)] <vermutet,
vermutete, hat vermutet> ◊ Ich vermute, dass er das
Geld genommen hat. ◆ Die Polizei vermutet Brandstiftung. The ring is suspected of being stolen. Der
Ring ist vermutlich gestohlen. 2. suspect sb (of
sth) jdn (einer Sache gen) verdächtigen
[feˈdɛçtɪɡn̩] <verdächtigt, verdächtigte, hat verdächtigt>
◊ Er wurde des Mordes verdächtigt. sb is suspected
of doing sth jd wird verdächtigt, etw. getan zu
haben ◊ Sie wird verdächtigt, den Ring gestohlen zu
haben. I suspect him of lying. Ich habe den
Verdacht, dass er lügt. He is suspected of (having)
rabies. Bei ihm besteht Verdacht auf Tollwut.
3. (mistrust) suspect sb's motives jdm nicht trauen
[nɪçt ˈtraoən] +haben ◊ Sie tut immer so freundlich,
aber ich traue ihr nicht.
suspected → **suspect²** adj 1. (injury, disease)
suspected sth Verdacht auf etw. acc [feˈdaxt aof] ◊
Sie wurde mit Verdacht auf Blutvergiftung ins Krankenhaus gebracht. 2. (criminal) mutmaßlich
[ˈmuːtmaːslɪç] only before ns ◊ der mutmaßliche
Täter
suspend verb 1. (from your job) suspend sb (from
sth) jdn (von etw.) suspendieren [zʊspɛnˈdiːrən]
<suspendiert, suspendierte, hat suspendiert> ◊ Er
wurde wegen Betrugs vom Dienst suspendiert.; (from
school) vom Unterricht ausschließen
[fɔm ˈʊnterɪçt ˌaosʃliːsn̩] <schließt aus, schloss aus,
hat ausgeschlossen> ◊ Sie wurde für eine Woche vom
Unterricht ausgeschlossen.; (from competitions)
sperren [ˈʃpɛrən] +haben ◊ Das Sportgericht sperrte
ihn für sechs Wochen. 2. (an activity) einstellen
[ˈaenʃtɛlən] +haben; (a law) außer Kraft setzen
[ˈaose ˈkraft zɛtsn̩] +haben ◊ Die Verfassung wurde
vorübergehend außer Kraft gesetzt. suspend sb's
driving licence jdm den Führerschein entziehen
[deːn ˈfyːreʃaen ɛntˌtsiːən] <entzieht, entzog, hat
entzogen> 3. (hang) aufhängen [ˈaofhɛnən] <hängt
auf, hängte auf, hat aufgehängt> ◊ Sie hängte den
Schinken an der Decke auf. be suspended (from sth)
(von etw.) hängen [ˈhɛnən] <hängt, hing, hat
gehangen> ◊ Von der Decke hing eine Glühbirne.
4. (float) be suspended in sth in etw. dat schweben
[ɪn ... ʃveːbm̩] +haben
suspense noun Spannung [ˈʃpanʊn] die <-, -en> ◊
Die Spannung stieg mit jeder Minute. ◆ Die
Spannung wurde unerträglich. keep sb in suspense
jdn auf die Folter spannen [aof diː ˈfɔlte ʃpanən]
+haben
suspension noun 1. (of talks) Aussetzung
[ˈaoszɛtsʊn] die <-> no pl ◊ die Aussetzung der Ver-
handlungen/Friedensgespräche; (of sb's licence)
Entzug [ɛntˈtsuːk] der <-(e)s> no pl ◊ der Entzug
des Führerscheins 2. (from a job) Suspendierung
[zʊspɛnˈdiːrʊn] die <-, -en>; (from school) Ausschluss [ˈaosʃlʊs] der <-es, Ausschlüsse>; (in sport)
Sperre [ˈʃpɛrə] die <-, -n> ◊ Der Spieler erhielt eine
Sperre von sechs Wochen. 3. (in a car) Federung

['feːdərʊŋ] die <-, -en>
suspicion [noun] **1.** *(feeling that sth is wrong, sb has done sth)* Verdacht [feˈdaxt] der <-(e)s> no pl ◊ *Mein Verdacht hat sich bestätigt.* have a suspicion that den Verdacht haben, dass ◊ *Ich habe den Verdacht, dass die Putzfrau nicht ehrlich ist.* have your suspicions einen Verdacht haben arouse sb's suspicions jds Verdacht erregen be under suspicion unter Verdacht stehen come under suspicion in Verdacht geraten above suspicion über jeden Verdacht erhaben He was arrested on suspicion of arson. Er wurde wegen des Verdachts auf Brandstiftung verhaftet. **2.** *(lack of trust)* Misstrauen ['mɪstraʊ̯ən] das <-s> no pl ◊ *jdn voller Misstrauen ansehen* treat sb with suspicion jdm nicht trauen [nɪçt 'traʊ̯ən] +haben
⊚ a suspicion of sth ein Hauch von etw.
suspicious(ly) [adj, adv] **1.** *(full of suspicion)* suspicious (of sb/sth) misstrauisch (jdm/etw. gegenüber) ['mɪstraʊ̯ɪʃ] ◊ *ein misstrauischer Blick* ◆ *Er sah mich misstrauisch an.* ◆ *Sie wurde misstrauisch, als sie merkte, dass Geld fehlte.* **2.** *(causing suspicion)* verdächtig [feˈdɛçtɪç] ◊ *ein verdächtiges Geräusch hören* ◆ *Ich finde das Ganze ziemlich verdächtig.* ◆ *Im Kinderzimmer ist es verdächtig ruhig.*
⊚ look suspiciously like sth verdächtig nach etw. aussehen sound suspiciously like sth sich verdächtig nach etw. anhören
sustain [verb] **1.** *(cause to continue, uphold)* aufrechterhalten ['aʊ̯frɛçt|ɛhaltn̩] <erhält aufrecht, erhielt aufrecht, hat aufrechterhalten> ◊ *ein Gespräch/Beziehungen/Vorwürfe aufrechterhalten* ◆ *Diese Hoffnung hat mich aufrechterhalten.* Even deserts sustain life. Sogar in der Wüste gibt es Leben.; *(growth)* beibehalten ['baɛbəhaltn̩] <behält bei, behielt bei, hat beibehalten> ◊ *Wie lange kann die Wirtschaft dieses Wachstum beibehalten?* **2.** *(a weight, burden)* tragen ['traːgn̩] <trägt, trug, hat getragen> ◊ *eine schwere Last tragen* ◆ *Die Decke wird von Pfeilern getragen.* **3.** *(give sb strength, energy)* sustain sb jdm Kraft geben ['kraft geːbm̩] <gibt, gab, hat gegeben> ◊ *Sein Glaube hat ihm in dieser schweren Zeit viel Kraft gegeben.* **4.** *(a statement, theory)* untermauern [ʊntɐˈmaʊ̯ɐn] <untermauert, untermauerte, hat untermauert>; *(a decision, law)* bestätigen [bəˈʃtɛːtɪgn̩] <bestätigt, bestätigte, hat bestätigt> **5.** *(an injury)* sich [dat] etw. zuziehen ['tsuːtsiːən] <zieht sich zu, zog sich zu, hat sich zugezogen> ◊ *Ich zog mir eine Gehirnerschütterung zu.; (a loss, damage)* erleiden [ɛˈlaɛdn̩] <erleidet, erlitt, hat erlitten>
swallow [verb] schlucken ['ʃlʊkn̩] +haben ◊ *vor Halsschmerzen kaum schlucken können* ◆ *Sie schluckte eine Tablette.* ◆ *Hat er die Ausrede/Geschichte geschluckt?*
⊚ swallow your pride/anger etc. seinen Stolz/seine Wut etc. hinunterschlucken
• **swallow up** [phras v] swallow sth up **1.** *(take control of, use a lot of)* etw. schlucken ['ʃlʊkn̩] +haben *(fam)* ◊ *Der Konzern hat ein paar Konkurrenten geschluckt.* ◆ *Sein Hobby schluckt viel Zeit und Geld.* **2.** *(destroy)* etw. verschlingen [feˈʃlɪŋən] <verschlingt, verschlang, hat verschlungen> ◊ *Die Wellen verschlangen den ganzen Ort.*
swamp [noun] Sumpf [zʊmpf] der <-(e)s, Sümpfe> ◊ *im Sumpf stecken bleiben* ◆ *die Sümpfe der Everglades*

swan [noun] Schwan [ʃvaːn] der <-(e)s, Schwäne>
swap [verb] **1.** *(exchange)* tauschen ['taʊ̯ʃn̩] +haben ◊ *Willst du mit mir tauschen?* ◆ *Sie tauschten Briefmarken.* ◆ *Können wir die Plätze tauschen?* **2.** *(replace)* swap sth for sth etw. gegen etw. auswechseln [geːgn̩ ... ˌaʊ̯svɛksl̩n] +haben ◊ *die alten Reifen gegen neue auswechseln* **3.** *(your addresses, stories, ideas)* austauschen ['aʊ̯staʊ̯ʃn̩] +haben ◊ *Sie tauschten ihre Telefonnummern und Adressen aus.*
swarm¹ [noun] Schwarm [ʃvaʰm] der <-(e)s, Schwärme> ◊ *Schwärme von Touristen* a swarm of bees ein Bienenschwarm [aɛn ˈbiːnənʃvaʰm]
swarm² [verb] schwärmen ['ʃvɛʰmən] +sein ◊ *Am Samstag schwärmen die Menschen in die Stadt, um einzukaufen.* ◆ *Bienen schwärmten um die Blüten.*
• **swarm with** [phras v] a place swarms with sb/sth irgendwo wimmelt es von jdm/etw. ['vɪml̩t ɛs fɔn] +haben ◊ *In der Stadt wimmelt es nur so von Menschen.* ◆ *In der Küche wimmelte es von Ameisen.*
sway [verb] **1.** *(move from side to side)* schwanken ['ʃvaŋkn̩] +haben ◊ *Der Bambus schwankte im Wind.* ◆ *Die Brücke schwankt unter der Last des Schwertransports.* **2.** *(move your body)* sich wiegen ['viːgn̩] +haben ◊ *Sie wiegten sich im Takt der Musik.* sway your hips sich in den Hüften wiegen **3.** *(influence)* beeinflussen [bəˈaɛnflʊsn̩] <beeinflusst, beeinflusste, hat beeinflusst> ◊ *Lass dich von den anderen nicht beeinflussen!*
swear [verb] **1.** *(use foul language)* fluchen ['fluːxn̩] +haben ◊ *Er fluchte laut.* swear at sb/sth jdn/etw. beschimpfen [bəˈʃɪmpfn̩] <beschimpft, beschimpfte, hat beschimpft> ◊ *Er hat sogar seinen Lehrer beschimpft.* **2.** *(promise to tell the truth, to do sth)* schwören ['ʃvøːrən] <schwört, schwor, hat geschworen> ◊ *auf die Bibel schwören* ◆ *Ich schwöre, dass das wahr ist.* swear vengeance on sb jdm Rache schwören swear your allegiance to sb jdm (die) Treue schwören swear an oath einen Eid ablegen [aɛnən 'aɛt ˌaːpleːgn̩] +haben; *(to yourself)* swear to do sth ['ʃvøːrən ... tsuː] schwören, etw. zu tun ['ʃvøːrən ... tsuː] ◊ *Er schwor sich, nie wieder auf seinem Motorrad mitzufahren.*
⊚ swear blind hoch und heilig schwören sb could have sworn jd könnte schwören, dass ◊ *Ich könnte schwören, dass ich meine Brille dort auf den Tisch gelegt habe.*
• **swear by** [phras v] swear by sth auf etw. [acc] schwören [aʊ̯f ... ˈʃvøːrən] <schwört, schwor, hat geschworen> ◊ *Meine Oma schwört auf Zwiebeln gegen Ohrenschmerzen.*
• **swear in** [phras v] swear sb in jdn vereidigen [feˈaɛdɪgn̩] <vereidigt, vereidigte, hat vereidigt> ◊ *Das neue Kabinett wurde in einer kurzen Zeremonie vereidigt.*
• **swear off** [phras v] swear off sth einer Sache [dat] abschwören ['apʃvøːrən] <schwört ab, schwor ab, hat abgeschworen> ◊ *dem Alkohol/Terrorismus abschwören*
• **swear to** [phras v] swear to sth etw. beschwören [bəˈʃvøːrən] <beschwört, beschwor, hat beschworen> ◊ *Ich glaube, das ist er, aber ich kann es nicht beschwören.*
swear word [noun] Schimpfwort ['ʃɪmpfvɔʰt] das <-(e)s, Schimpfwörter>
sweat¹ [noun] Schweiß [ʃvaɛs] der <-es> no pl ◊ *Er*

war in Schweiß gebadet. ✦ Mir lief der Schweiß
herunter. He broke out in a sweat. Ihm brach der
Schweiß aus.
◉ break sweat ins Schwitzen geraten no sweat
kein Problem
sweat[2] verb 1. *(produce sweat)* schwitzen ['ʃvɪtsn̩]
+haben ◊ Er schwitzte stark. ✦ Ich fing vor Angst an
zu schwitzen. 2. let sb sweat jdn schmoren lassen
['ʃmoːrən lasn̩] <lässt, ließ, hat lassen> ◊ Lass ihn
ruhig noch schmoren und ruf ihn erst später an.
3. *(in the UK: cook slowly)* schmoren ['ʃmoːrən]
+haben ◊ den Braten schmoren
sweater noun Pullover [pʊ'loːvɐ] der <-s, ->
Swede noun Schwede ['ʃveːdə] der <-n, -n>
♀Schwedin ['ʃveːdɪn] die <-, -nen> → German[1] 1.
Sweden noun Schweden ['ʃveːdn̩] das <-s> article
only in combination with attribute, no pl → Germany
Swedish[1] noun Schwedisch ['ʃveːdɪʃ] das <-(s)> no
pl → German[1] 2.
Swedish[2] adj schwedisch ['ʃveːdɪʃ] → German[2]
sweep verb 1. *(clean, remove swiftly)* fegen ['feːɡn̩]
+haben ◊ Wir müssen noch fegen, dann sind wir
fertig. ✦ den Boden/die Küche/den Schornstein fegen
✦ Er fegte mit dem Arm die Papiere vom Tisch. ✦
Der Wind fegte die Blätter von den Bäumen. sweep
your hair back sich dat die Haare aus dem Gesicht
streichen [diː ˌhaːrə aʊ deːm ɡə'zɪçt ʃtraɛçn̩]
<streicht, strich, hat gestrichen> 2. *(spread quickly)*
sweep through a place sich irgendwo rasend
schnell ausbreiten [raːznt ʃnɛl 'aʊsbraɛtn̩] <breitet
sich aus, breitete sich aus, hat sich ausgebreitet> ◊
Das Feuer breitete sich rasend schnell in der ganzen
Schule aus. sweep the country das ganze Land
erfassen [das ɡantsə 'lant ɛfasn̩] <erfasst, erfasste, hat
erfasst> 3. *(move quickly: wind)* sweep across sth
über etw. acc hinwegfegen [yːbɐ ... hɪn,vɛkfeːɡn̩]
+sein ◊ Ein Orkan fegte über Nordeuropa hinweg.;
(wave) schlagen ['ʃlaːɡn̩] <schlägt, schlug, ist geschla-
gen> ◊ Hohe Wellen schlugen in das Boot/über die
Felsen. The tsunami swept across the Indian Ocean.
Der Tsunami rollte über den Indischen Ozean
hinweg. The tidal wave swept onto the grounds of
the hotel. Die Flutwelle ergoss sich über das Hotel-
gelände. 4. *(move smoothly)* gleiten ['ɡlaɛtn̩] <gleitet,
glitt, ist geglitten> ◊ Der Wagen glitt lautlos durch die
Straßen. ✦ Ihr Blick glitt über die Anwesenden. He
swept the light of his torch over the truck. Er ließ
den Strahl seiner Taschenlampe über den
Lastwagen gleiten. 5. *(walk quickly and purposefully)*
rauschen ['raʊʃn̩] +sein ◊ Sie rauschte in den Saal
und begrüßte ihre Gäste. ✦ Er rauschte beleidigt aus
dem Haus. sweep past sb/sth an jdm/etw. vorbei-
rauschen [an ... foːɐ̯ˌbaeraʊʃn̩] +sein ◊ Sie rauschte
an uns vorbei, ohne uns zu bemerken. 6. move sth/
sb quickly reißen ['raɛsn̩] <reißt, riss, hat gerissen>
sweep sb into your arms jdn an sich acc reißen
The tidal wave swept them to their deaths. Die
Flutwelle riss sie in den Tod. sweep sb along jdn
mitreißen ['mɪtraɛsn̩] +haben ◊ Wir wurden von der
Menge mitgerissen. ✦ Die Strömung riss uns mit
sich. 7. *(forests, hills etc.)* sich erstrecken
[zɪç ɛ'ʃtrɛkn̩] <erstreckt sich, erstreckte sich, hat sich
erstreckt> ◊ Der Wald erstreckt sich bis zum Meer.
8. *(win easily)* haushoch gewinnen
[haʊshoːx ɡə'vɪnən] <gewinnt, gewann, hat gewonnen>
● **sweep aside** phras v sweep sth aside etw.

beiseite schieben [bae'zaɛtə ʃiːbm̩] <schiebt, schob,
hat geschoben> ◊ Er hat meine Einwände beiseite
geschoben.
● **sweep away** phras v 1. *(remove and destroy)*
wegreißen ['vɛkraɛsn̩] <reißt weg, riss weg, hat wegge-
rissen> ◊ Das Wasser hat ihr Haus weggerissen.;
(doubts) beseitigen [bə'zaɛtɪɡn̩] <beseitigt, beseitigte,
hat beseitigt> ◊ Damit gelang es ihr, meine Zweifel
zu beseitigen. 2. *(become involved)* get swept away
with sth von etw. mitgerissen werden
[fɔn ... 'mɪtɡərɪsn̩ veːɐ̯dn̩] <wird, wurde, ist worden> ◊
● **sweep over** phras v sweep over sb jdn überkommen [ybɐ'kɔmən] <überkommt, überkam, hat über-
kommen> ◊ Plötzlich überkam sie eine große
Müdigkeit.
● **sweep up** phras v fegen ['feːɡn̩] +haben ◊ Hast
du schon gefegt? Die Treppe war voller Sand. ✦ den
Fußboden fegen sweep sth up etw. auffegen
['aʊffeːɡn̩] +haben ◊ Fegst du bitte den Sand auf?
sweeping → **sweep** adj 1. *(change, development)*
umwälzend ['ʊmvɛltsnt] ◊ umwälzende Veränderungen 2. *(statement)* pauschal [paʊ'ʃaːl] seldom comp/
superl ◊ ein pauschales Urteil 3. *(staircase)*
geschwungen [ɡə'ʃvʊŋən] no comp/superl ◊ die
geschwungene Treppe, die zum Eingang hinaufführt
sweet[1] noun 1. *(small piece)* Bonbon [bɔŋ'bɔŋ] das
<-s, -s> ◊ eine Tüte Bonbons ✦ Bonbons lutschen
sweets Süßigkeiten ['zyːsɪçkaɛtn̩] die <-> pl ◊
zwischen den Mahlzeiten Süßigkeiten naschen
2. *(dessert)* Nachspeise ['naːxʃpaɛzə] die <-, -n>
sweet[2] adj 1. *(tasting like sugar, pleasant)* süß [zyːs]
<süßer, am süßesten> ◊ Der Kuchen ist mir zu süß.
✦ Er isst gern süße Sachen. ✦ ein süßer Duft ✦ Rache
ist süß. 2. *(in appearance)* niedlich ['niːtlɪç] ◊ Sieh
mal, die niedlichen Kätzchen! ✦ Kleine Kinder sind
so niedlich.; *(in sound)* lieblich ['liːplɪç] ◊ ihre
liebliche Stimme ✦ Ihre Stimme war lieblich und
zart. 3. *(kind, nice)* nett [nɛt] <netter, am nettesten> ◊
Sie ist ein sehr nettes Mädchen. ✦ Das war sehr nett
von dir.
◉ keep sb sweet jdn bei Laune halten
sweetcorn noun Mais [maes] der <-es> no pl
sweeten verb 1. *(make sweeter)* süßen ['zyːsn̩]
+haben ◊ Milch mit Honig süßen 2. *(make attractive)*
sweeten sth etw. attraktiver gestalten
[atrak'tiːvɐ ɡə'ʃtaltn̩] <gestaltet, gestaltete, hat
gestaltet> ◊ Wir finden sie einige Tipps, wie Sie Ihr
Angebot attraktiver gestalten können.
● **sweeten up** phras v sweeten sb up jdn gnädig
stimmen ['ɡnɛːdɪç ʃtɪmən] +haben
sweetener noun Süßstoff ['zyːsʃtɔf] der <-(e)s, -e>
swell verb 1. *(become larger)* swell (up) anschwellen
['anʃvɛlən] <schwillt an, schwoll an, ist angeschwol-
len> ◊ Ihre Beine waren ganz angeschwollen. be
swollen with sth von etw. angeschwollen sein ◊ Der
Bach war vom Regen angeschwollen. 2. *(increase)*
sth swells etw. wächst [an [vɛkst 'an] <wuchs an, ist
angewachsen> ◊ Die Besucherzahlen sind auf das
Doppelte angewachsen. swell sth etw. anwachsen
lassen ['anvaksn̩ lasn̩] <lässt, ließ, hat lassen>
swelling noun Schwellung ['ʃvɛlʊŋ] die <-, -en> ◊
eine schmerzhafte Schwellung
swift(ly) adj, adv 1. *(fast)* rasch [raʃ] <rascher, am
raschesten> ◊ Ihr Arbeitstempo ist ziemlich rasch.
Die Geschichte nahm ein rasches Ende. ✦ Sie fährt
rasch in die Stadt, um einzukaufen.; *(without delay)*

zügig ['tsy:gɪç] ◊ *eine zügige Umsetzung der Reform* ♦ *einen Mordfall zügig aufklären*
swim¹ [noun] Bad [baːt] das <-(e)s, Bäder> ◊ *Nach einem Bad im Meer war er wieder erfrischt.* go for a swim schwimmen gehen ['ʃvɪmən geːən] <geht, ging, ist gegangen> have a swim schwimmen ['ʃvɪmən] <schwimmt, schwamm, ist geschwommen> I just had a swim. Ich war gerade im Wasser.
swim² [verb] **1.** *(move in water)* schwimmen ['ʃvɪmən] <schwimmt, schwamm, ist geschwommen> ◊ *Kannst du schwimmen?* ♦ *Ich bin heute einen Kilometer geschwommen.* ♦ *Kannst du Schmetterling schwimmen?* ♦ *Er ist die 200 Meter in einer Rekordzeit geschwommen.; (a lake, river, channel)* swim sth etw. durchschwimmen [dʊrçˈʃvɪmən] <durchschwimmt, durchschwamm, hat durchschwommen> ◊ *den Ärmelkanal durchschwimmen* **2.** *(appear to be moving)* verschwimmen [fɛˈʃvɪmən] <verschwimmt, verschwamm, ist verschwommen> sb eyes are swimming vor jds Augen verschwimmt alles sb's head is swimming jdm dreht sich der Kopf [dreːt tsɪç deːɐ̯ ˈkɔpf] +haben
swimming → swim² [noun] Schwimmen ['ʃvɪmən] das <-s> no pl go swimming schwimmen gehen ['ʃvɪmən geːən] <geht, ging, ist gegangen> swimming lesson Schwimmstunde ['ʃvɪmʃtʊndə] die <-, -n>
swimming costume [noun] Badeanzug ['baːdəʔantsuːk] der <-(e)s, Badeanzüge>
swimming pool [noun] Schwimmbad ['ʃvɪmbaːt] das <-(e)s, Schwimmbäder> indoor swimming pool Hallenbad ['halənbaːt] outdoor swimming pool Freibad ['fraɪbaːt]
swimming trunks [noun] Badehose ['baːdəhoːzə] die <-, -n>
swimsuit [noun] Badeanzug ['baːdəʔantsuːk] der <-(e)s, Badeanzüge>
swindle [verb] swindle sb out of sth, swindle sth out of sb jdn um etw. betrügen [ʊm ... bəˌtryːgn̩] <betrügt, betrog, hat betrogen> ◊ *Du hast mich um zweihundert Euro betrogen!*
swindler [noun] Schwindler ['ʃvɪndlɐ] der <-s, -> ♀Schwindlerin ['ʃvɪndlərɪn] die <-, -nen> *(fam, pej)*
swine [noun] Schwein [ʃvaɛn] das <-(e)s, -e> *(fam, pej)*
swing¹ [noun] **1.** *(try to hit)* take a swing at sb/sth nach jdm/etw. schlagen [naːx ... ʃlaːgn̩] <schlägt, schlug, hat geschlagen> He took a swing at me/the ball but missed. Er schlug nach mir/dem Ball, traf aber nicht.; *(hit sb/sth)* take a swing zuschlagen ['tsuːʃlaːgn̩] <schlägt zu, schlug zu, hat zugeschlagen> He took a swing and connected with my chin. Er schlug zu und traf mich am Kinn. I took a swing and missed the ball. Ich schlug zu, traf den Ball aber nicht.; *(prepare to hit sb/sth)* take a swing ausholen ['aʊshoːlən] +haben She took a swing and hit him in the back. Sie holte aus und schlug ihm auf den Rücken. He took a swing and she caught it. Er holte zum Schlag aus, aber sie fing seinen Arm ab. **2.** *(hitting movement)* Schlag [ʃlaːk] der <-(e)s, Schläge> a swing of sth ein Schlag mit etw. ◊ *ein Schlag mit dem Hammer; (in boxing)* Schwinger ['ʃvɪŋɐ] der <-s, ->; *(in golf, skiing)* Schwung [ʃvʊŋ] der <-(e)s, Schwünge> ◊ *Er muss seinen Schwung verbessern.* **3.** mood swings Stimmungsschwankungen ['ʃtɪmʊŋsʃvaŋkʊŋən] die <-> pl; *(swing in opinion)* Meinungsschwankung

['maɛnʊŋsˌʊmʃvʊŋ] der <-(e)s, Meinungsumschwünge> There was a swing of 10 % from Labour to the Conservatives. Die Labour Partei verlor 10 % an die Konservativen. A swing of 6 % would be enough. Eine Veränderung um 6 % wäre bereits genug. There was a swing away from tranquilizers in favour of antidepressants. Es wurden weniger Tranquilizer und mehr Antidepressiva konsumiert. **4.** *(seat)* Schaukel ['ʃaɔkl̩] die <-, -n> ◊ *auf der Schaukel sitzen* have a go on the swing schaukeln ['ʃaɔkl̩n] +haben **5.** mus Swing [svɪŋ] der <-(s)> no pl
◉ it's swings and roundabouts das ist gehupft wie gesprungen *(fam)* be in full swing auf Hochtouren laufen get into the swing of sth sich an etw. [acc] gewöhnen
swing² [verb] **1.** *(make sth move, move from side to side)* schwingen ['ʃvɪŋən] <schwingt, schwang, hat/ist geschwungen> transitive use +haben/intransitive use +sein ◊ *Der Turner schwingt an den Ringen.* ♦ *Er schwang die Axt und zerteilte den Baumstamm.* swing to and fro, swing back and forth pendeln ['pɛndl̩n] +haben ◊ *die Arme locker pendeln lassen* **2.** *(on a swing)* schaukeln ['ʃaɔkl̩n] +haben ◊ *Auf dem Spielplatz schaukelten zwei kleine Mädchen.* **3.** *(move, turn)* swing towards sb sich zu jdm drehen [tsuː ... dreːən] +haben ◊ *Sie drehte sich zu mir.* swing round sich umdrehen ['ʊmdreːən] +haben ◊ *Er drehte sich um und schimpfte mit den Kindern.* swing open aufgehen ['aɔfgeːən] <geht auf, ging auf, ist aufgegangen> ◊ *Die Tür ging auf und seine Mutter kam herein.* swing shut zufallen ['tsuːfalən] <fällt zu, fiel zu, ist zugefallen> ◊ *Das Tor fiel hinter uns zu.* **4.** swing (sth) at sb/sth (mit etw.) nach jdm/etw. schlagen [naːx ... ʃlaːgn̩] <schlägt, schlug, hat geschlagen> ◊ *Er schlug mit dem Schläger nach dem Ball.* ♦ *Sie schlug nach der Katze.* **5.** *(votes, voters)* auf seine Seite bringen [aɔf ... ˈzaɛtə brɪŋən] <bringt, brachte, hat gebracht> ◊ *Er hat es geschafft, die Mehrheit auf unsere Seite zu bringen.* swing sth away from sb/sth jdn/etw. etw. kosten ['kɔstn̩] <kostet, kostete, hat gekostet> ◊ *Dieser Skandal hat uns viel Sympathie/viele Stimmen gekostet.* **6.** *(mood, opinion)* umschlagen ['ʊmʃlaːgn̩] <schlägt um, schlug um, ist umgeschlagen> ◊ *Die Stimmung in der Öffentlichkeit ist seit dem Vorfall umgeschlagen.* swing the other way ins Gegenteil umschlagen ◊ *Ihre euphorische Stimmung schlug schnell ins Gegenteil um.* swing from sth to sth zwischen etw. und etw. schwanken [ˈʃvɪʃn̩ ... ʊnt ... ˈʃvaŋkn̩] +haben ◊ *Seine Stimmung schwankte zwischen Euphorie und tiefer Traurigkeit.*
◉ swing into action sich an die Arbeit machen swing it es hinkriegen *(fam)*
Swiss¹ [noun] Schweizer ['ʃvaɛtsɐ] der <-s, -> ♀Schweizerin ['ʃvaɛtsərɪn] die <-, -nen> the Swiss die Schweizer [diː ˈʃvaɛtsɐ] <-> pl → **German¹** **1.** →
Swiss² [adj] schweizerisch ['ʃvaɛtsərɪʃ] → **German²**
switch¹ [noun] **1.** *(button)* Schalter ['ʃaltɐ] der <-s, -> ◊ *Wo ist denn der Schalter zum Abstellen?* flick a switch einen Schalter betätigen press a switch auf einen Schalter drücken **2.** *(change)* Wechsel ['vɛksl̩] der <-s, -> ◊ *Der Wechsel kam sehr plötzlich.* make the switch (from sth) to sth den Wechsel (von etw.) zu etw. vollziehen **3.** *(stick)* Gerte ['gɛrtə] die <-, -n>

switch² [verb] 1. *(change)* wechseln ['vɛksln] +haben ◊ *Er wechselte seine Meinung ständig.* ✦ *zu einem anderen Tarif/Anbieter wechseln* ✦ *zwischen den Programmen hin und her wechseln; (a tournament, an event)* switch sth (from sth) to sth etw. (von etw.) auf etw. [acc] verlegen [aof ... fɛˌleːgn̩] <verlegt, verlegte, hat verlegt> ◊ *Sie verlegen die Veranstaltung auf einen späteren Termin.*; *(your attention)* switch sth (from sth) to sth etw. (statt auf etw. [acc]) auf etw. [acc] richten [aof ... rɪçtn̩] +haben ◊ *Die Großeltern richteten ihre Aufmerksamkeit auf das strampelnde Baby.* 2. *(with a switch)* schalten ['ʃaltn̩] <schaltet, schaltete, hat geschaltet> switch to sth auf/in etw. [acc] schalten ◊ *Schalt mal aufs/ins dritte Programm.* 3. *(exchange objects)* austauschen ['aostaoʃn̩] +haben ◊ *Der kleine Junge hat die Gläser ausgetauscht.* 4. *(exchange roles or duties)* switch (with sb) (mit jdm) tauschen ['taoʃn̩] +haben ◊ *Wollen wir tauschen?* ✦ *Er hat letzte Woche mit mir getauscht.*
• switch off [phras v] switch sth off 1. *(a light, machine)* etw. ausschalten ['aosʃaltn̩] <schaltet aus, schaltete aus, hat ausgeschaltet> ◊ *das Licht/den Strom/den Motor ausschalten* 2. *(mentally)* etw. abschalten ['apʃaltn̩] <schaltet ab, schaltete ab, hat abgeschaltet> *(fam)* ◊ *während eines Vortrags abschalten*
• switch on [phras v] einschalten ['aenʃaltn̩] <schaltet ein, schaltete ein, hat eingeschaltet> ◊ *den Fernseher/den Computer/das Licht einschalten*
• switch over [phras v] switch over to sth 1. *(start sth new)* zu etw. wechseln [tsu: ... ˌvɛksln̩] ◊ *Er wechselte zu einem neuen Verein.* 2. *(change the TV channel)* auf etw. [acc] umschalten [aof ... ˌʊmʃaltn̩] <schaltet um, schaltete um, hat umgeschaltet> ◊ *Schalt bitte auf das dritte Programm um!*
switchboard [noun] Vermittlung [fɛ'mɪtlʊŋ] die <-, -en>
Switzerland [noun] die Schweiz [di: 'ʃvaets] <-> no pl ◊ *Ich komme aus der Schweiz.* ✦ *Die Schweiz ist ein Land mit vielen hohen Bergen.*
swollen [adj] 1. *(part of the body)* geschwollen [gə'ʃvolən] ◊ *ein geschwollenes Knie* ✦ *Ihr Fuß war geschwollen.* 2. *(river)* angeschwollen ['angəʃvolən] ◊ *ein stark angeschwollener Fluss*
sword [noun] Schwert [ʃveːɐt] das <-(e)s, -er> ◊ *mit dem Schwert kämpfen* ✦ *das Schwert ziehen*
Ⓐ a double-edged sword ein zweischneidiges Schwert cross swords (with sb) sich (mit jdm) streiten
swot [verb] pauken ['paokŋ̍] +haben *(fam)* ◊ *für einen Test pauken*
syllable [noun] Silbe ['zɪlbə] die <-, -n> ◊ *ein Wort mit vier Silben*
syllabus [noun] Lehrplan ['leːɡplaːn] der <-(e)s, Lehrpläne> ◊ *Die Lehrer müssen sich an den Lehrplan halten.*
symbol [noun] Symbol [zm'boːl] das <-s, -e> ◊ *die Taube als Symbol des Friedens* ✦ *mathematische Symbole*
symbolic [adj] symbolisch [zm'boːlɪʃ] ◊ *ein symbolischer Akt* ✦ *Das Händeschütteln war rein symbolisch.*
symmetry [noun] Symmetrie [zyme'triː] die <-, -n>
sympathetic [adj] 1. *(understanding sb's problems)*

mitfühlend ['mɪtfyːlənt] ◊ *Er war sehr mitfühlend.* ✦ *eine mitfühlende Mutter* 2. *(supportive of sth)* wohlwollend ['voːlvolənt] ◊ *ein wohlwollender Lehrer* sympathetic to/towards sth wohlwollend gegenüber etw. ◊ *Er war wohlwollend gegenüber ihren Plänen.* 3. *(likeable)* sympathisch [zm'paːtɪʃ] ◊ *eine sympathische Frau* ✦ *Ich finde ihn sehr sympathisch.*
sympathy [noun] 1. *(feeling of understanding)* Mitleid ['mɪtlaet] das <-(e)s> no pl feel sympathy for sb Mitleid mit jdm haben 2. *(support for sth, understanding of sth)* Verständnis [fɛ'ʃtɛntnɪs] das <-ses> no pl ◊ *Er hat viel Verständnis für ihre Lebensweise.* be in sympathy with sb/sth in Einklang mit jdm/etw. sein [ɪn ˌaenklaŋ mɪt ... zaen] +sein ◊ *Ihre Ziele waren völlig in Einklang mit seinen Vorstellungen.* 3. *(allegiances)* sympathies Sympathien [zympaˈtiːən] die <-> pl ◊ *Unsere Sympathien gehörten den kleinen Bauern.* sb's sympathies lie with sb jds Sympathien liegen bei jdm
Ⓔ extend your sympathy to sb jdm Beileid wünschen
symphony [noun] Sinfonie [zɪnfoˈniː] die <-, -n>
symptom [noun] Symptom [zmpˈtoːm] das <-s, -e>
synagogue [noun] Synagoge [zynaˈɡoːɡə] die <-, -n>
syndrome [noun] Syndrom [zynˈdroːm] das <-s, -e>
synonym [noun] Synonym [zynoˈnyːm] das <-s, -e or also Synonyma> ◊ *„Kraft" ist ein Synonym für „Stärke".*
syntactic [adj] syntaktisch [zn'taktɪʃ] no comp/superl
syntax [noun] Syntax ['zntaks] die <-, -en> ◊ *die Syntax im Fragesatz/im Deutschen*
synthesis [noun] Synthese [zyn'teːzə] die <-, -n> ◊ *eine Synthese unterschiedlicher Traditionen*
synthetic¹ [noun] 1. *(artificial substance)* Kunststoff ['kʊnstʃtof] der <-(e)s, -e> ◊ *ein Kunststoff aus der Gruppe der Polyester* 2. *(clothes)* Kunstfaser ['kʊnstfaːze] die <-, -n> ◊ *Kleidungsstücke aus Kunstfasern*
synthetic² [adj] 1. *(artificial)* synthetisch [zn'teːtɪʃ] no comp/superl ◊ *synthetische Materialien* 2. *(false)* gekünstelt [gəˈkʏnstlt] ◊ *gekünstelte Freundlichkeit*
syringe [noun] Spritze ['ʃprɪtsə] die <-, -n> ◊ *jdm mit der Spritze Blut abnehmen*
syrup [noun] Sirup ['ziːrʊp] der <-s, -e> most sing
system [noun] 1. *(things working together, method of organizing sth)* System [zʏs'teːm] das <-s, -e> ◊ *die Suche nach dem Fehler im System* ✦ *ein demokratisches/totalitäres System; (security, heating)* Anlage ['anlaːɡə] die <-, -n> ◊ *sanitäre/technische Anlagen* ✦ *Die Wartung der Anlage ist sehr teuer.* 2. *(human body)* Körper ['kœˈpɐ] der <-s, -> ◊ *Bewegung ist gut für den Körper.*
Ⓔ get sb/sth out of your system über jdn/etw. hinwegkommen work the system am richtigen Rädchen drehen
system administrator [noun] Systemadministrator [zʏs'teːm|atmɪnɪsˌtraˈtoːɐ] der <-s, -en> ♀Systemadministratorin [zʏs'teːm|atmɪnɪstraˌtoˈrɪn] die <-, -nen> ◊ *Sie ist Systemadministratorin in einer großen Firma.* ✦ *Wir suchen baldmöglichst einen Systemadministrator.*
systematic(ally) [adj, adv] systematisch [zyste'maːtɪʃ] ◊ *die systematische Suche nach einem Gegenstand* ✦ *bei einer Untersuchung systematisch vorgehen*

T

t, T (noun) t, T [te:] das <– or –s, – or –s> ◊ *Dieses Wort wird mit einem kleinen t/großen T geschrieben.* ♦ *T wie Theodor*

table (noun) **1.** *(piece of furniture, place in a restaurant, people sitting around a table)* Tisch [tɪʃ] der <–(e)s, –e> ◊ *Sie setzten sich an den Tisch und begannen zu essen.* ♦ *Er rief im Restaurant an und bestellte einen Tisch für drei Personen.* ♦ *Der ganze Tisch brach in Gelächter aus.* clear/set the table den Tisch abräumen/decken **2.** *(chart)* Tabelle [ta'bɛlə] die <–, –n> ◊ *Werte/Namen in eine Tabelle eintragen* ♦ *eine Tabelle erstellen* ♦ *Die Mannschaft führt die Tabelle mit zwei Punkten Vorsprung an.* (multiplication) tables Einmaleins [aenma:l'|aens] das <–> no pl ◊ *das kleine/große Einmaleins* ◉ **turn the tables (on sb)** den Spieß umdrehen **on the table 1.** *(suggestion, proposal)* auf dem Tisch **2.** *(in the US: set aside for later discussion)* verschoben

tablecloth (noun) Tischdecke ['tɪʃdɛkə] die <–, –n>

tablet (noun) **1.** *(pill)* Tablette [ta'blɛtə] die <–, –n> ◊ *eine Tablette gegen Kopfschmerzen schlucken/nehmen* in tablet form in Tablettenform [ɪn ta'blɛtn̩fɔ'm] **2.** *(with writing on it)* Tafel ['ta:fl̩] die <–, –n> ◊ *Auf der Tafel stand der Name des Künstlers.* **3.** *(of writing paper)* Block [blɔk] der <–(e)s, Blöcke or –s> ◊ *Sie notierte ihre Telefonnummer auf dem Block.*

table tennis (noun) Tischtennis ['tɪʃtɛnɪs] das <–> article only in combination with attribute, no pl ◊ *Nach der Schule spielen wir gern eine Runde Tischtennis.*

taboo (noun) Tabu [ta'bu:] das <–s, –s> ◊ *ein Tabu verletzen* ♦ *gegen ein Tabu verstoßen* ♦ *Sex ohne Tabus*

tabular (adj) tabellarisch [tabɛ'la:rɪʃ] no comp/superl ◊ *eine tabellarische Übersicht* ♦ *Der Lebenslauf sollte tabellarisch sein.*

tacit(ly) (adj, adv) stillschweigend ['ʃtɪlʃvaegn̩t] no comp/superl; when used as an adj, only before ns ◊ *jds stillschweigendes Einverständnis* ♦ *etw. stillschweigend hinnehmen/annehmen*

tack (noun) **1.** *(small nail)* Nagel ['na:gl̩] der <–s, Nägel>; *(in the US: thumbtack)* Reißnagel ['raesna:gl̩] **2.** *(approach, method)* Ansatz ['anzats] der <–es, Ansätze> ◊ *Sie versucht es mit einem neuen Ansatz.* change tack eine andere Richtung einschlagen [aenə ˌandərə 'rɪçtʊŋ aenʃla:gn̩] <schlägt ein, schlug ein, hat eingeschlagen> **3.** *(for a horse)* Sattel- und Zaumzeug [ˌzatl̩ ʊnt 'tsaomtsɔøk] das <–(e)s> **4.** *(cheap objects)* Plunder ['plʊndɐ] der <–s> no pl *(fam, pej)* ◊ *Wirf den ganzen Plunder raus!*

tackle (verb) **1.** *(a problem, question)* angehen ['ange:ən] <geht an, ging an, hat angegangen> ◊ *Probleme gemeinsam angehen* ♦ *Er ging das Rennen locker an.; (a fire)* bekämpfen [bə'kɛmpfn̩] <bekämpft, bekämpfte, hat bekämpft> **2.** SPORT *(attack)* angreifen ['angraefn̩] <greift an, griff an, hat angegrif-

fen> ◊ *Beckham griff den Stürmer an.* **3.** *(ask directly)* tackle sb about sth jdn wegen etw. zur Rede stellen [ve:gn̩ ... tsu:ɐ̯ 're:də ʃtɛlən] +haben ◊ *Sie hat ihren Mann zur Rede gestellt.* **4.** *(oppose sb/sth)* tackle sb/sth es mit jdm/etw. aufnehmen [ɛs mɪt ... ˌaofne:mən] <nimmt auf, nahm auf, hat aufgenommen> ◊ *Er hat es ganz allein mit drei Gegnern aufgenommen.*

tact (noun) Takt [takt] der <–(e)s> no pl ◊ *Sie hat manchmal überhaupt keinen Takt.*

tactful(ly) (adj, adv) taktvoll ['taktfɔl] ◊ *Seine Mutter war sehr taktvoll.* ♦ *ein taktvoller Hinweis* ♦ *Er schwieg taktvoll.*

tactic (noun) Taktik ['taktɪk] die <–, –en> ◊ *Welche Taktik verfolgt er mit seinem Verhalten?* strong-arm tactics brutale Methoden [bru,ta:lə me'to:dn̩] <–> pl ◊ *Ich halte nichts von diesen brutalen Methoden.*

tag (noun) **1.** *(indicating name)* Namensschild ['na:mənsʃɪlt] das <–es, –er> ◊ *Wir müssen alle Namensschilder tragen.; (indicating price)* Etikett [eti'kɛt] das <–(e)s, –en> ◊ *Der Preis auf dem Etikett stimmte nicht.; (on luggage)* Anhänger ['anhɛŋɐ] der <–s, –> ◊ *Entfernen Sie alte Anhänger von Ihrem Gepäck.* **2.** *(for criminals)* elektronische Fesseln [elɛk,tro:nɪʃə 'fɛsl̩n] <–> pl ◊ *einem Straftäter elektronische Fesseln anlegen* **3.** GAME Fangen ['faŋən] das <–s> no pl ◊ *Die Kinder spielten Fangen.* **4.** question tag Bestätigungsfrage [bə'ʃtɛ:tɪgʊŋsfra:gə] die <–, –n> **5.** *(name)* Beiname ['baena:mə] der <–ns, –n> ◊ *Er trug den Beinamen „Einauge".*

tail (noun) **1.** *(of an animal)* Schwanz [ʃvants] der <–es, Schwänze> **2.** *(of an aircraft)* Heck [hɛk] das <–(e)s, –e or –s>; *(of a comet)* Schweif [ʃvaef] der <–(e)s, –e>; *(of a queue)* Ende ['ɛndə] das <–s, –n> **3.** *(secret follower)* Beschatter [bə'ʃatɐ] der <–s, –> ♀Beschatterin [bə'ʃatərɪn] die <–, –nen> **4.** *(side of a coin)* tails Zahl [tsa:l] die <–, –en> ◊ *Kopf oder Zahl?* **5.** *(of a shirt)* Hemdzipfel ['hɛmtsɪpfl̩] der <–s, –> **6.** *(formal jacket)* tails Frack [frak] der <–(e)s, Fräcke> ◊ *Zur Hochzeit trug er einen Frack.* ◉ **with your tail between your legs** mit eingezogenem Schwanz **be on sb's tail** eng auffahren **turn tail** weglaufen

tail light (noun) Rücklicht ['rʏklɪçt] das <–(e)s, –er> ◊ *Jedes Auto muss mit Rücklichtern ausgestattet sein.*

tailor (noun) Schneider ['ʃnaedɐ] der <–s, –> ♀Schneiderin ['ʃnaedərɪn] die <–, –nen> ◊ *Er war Schneider von Beruf.* ♦ *Ich werde die Hose zur Schneiderin bringen.*

take (verb) **1.** *(carry with you, accept, have, use)* nehmen ['ne:mən] <nimmt, nahm, hat genommen> ◊ *Nimm den Schirm; es regnet.* ◊ *Den Schlüssel aus der Tasche nehmen* ♦ *Ich nehme Schnitzel mit Pommes.* ♦ *Sie haben den jüngeren Bewerber genommen.* ♦ *Was nehmen Sie für Medikamente?* ♦ *etw. als Kompli-*

A
B
C
D
E
F
G
H
I
J
K
L
M
N
O
P
Q
R
S
T
U
V
W
X
Y
Z

ment/Beweis nehmen ♦ *Wann nimmst du Urlaub?* ♦ *Sie nimmt jetzt Fahrstunden.* ♦ *ein Bad nehmen* ♦ *Ich nehme nie das Auto, um in die Stadt zu fahren.* take sb hostage jdn als Geisel nehmen take sb prisoner jdn gefangen nehmen take sb by the hand jdn an der Hand nehmen take sb in your arms jdn in den Arm nehmen take sth in your hands etw. in die Hände nehmen take a seat Platz nehmen take offence Anstoß nehmen **2.** *(transport, bring along)* take (with you) mitnehmen ['mɪtneːmən] <nimmt mit, nahm mit, hat mitgenommen> ◊ *Ich hatte nicht genügend Geld mitgenommen.* take sb/sth (for sth) jdn/etw. (zu etw.) mitnehmen take sth to sb etw. zu jdm bringen [tsuː ... brɪŋən] <bringt, brachte, hat gebracht> take sth upstairs/downstairs etw. nach oben/unten bringen ◊ *Bitte bring den Wäschekorb nach oben ins Schlafzimmer!; (by using a vehicle)* take sb/sth away jdn/etw. wegfahren ['vɛkfaːrən] <fährt weg, fuhr weg, hat weggefahren> ◊ *Der Verletzte wurde in einem Krankenwagen weggefahren.* **3.** *(arrest a criminal)* take sb away jdn abführen ['apfyːrən] +haben ◊ *Die Polizei hat den Verbrecher abgeführt.* **4.** *(lead to a place)* sth takes sb somewhere etw. führt (jdn) irgendwohin [fyːɐt] +haben ◊ *Dieser Weg führt durch den Garten/ins Tal.* **5.** *(require)* brauchen ['braʊxn̩] +haben ◊ *Mein Auto braucht Diesel.* It takes a lot of talent to become a star. Man braucht viel Talent, um ein Star zu werden.*; (a certain period of time)* dauern ['daʊɐn] +haben ◊ *Wie lange dauert die Fahrt dorthin?* **6.** *(accept)* annehmen ['anneːmən] <nimmt an, nahm an, hat angenommen> ◊ *Ich nehme deine Einladung an.; (a defeat)* akzeptieren [aktsɛpˈtiːrən] <akzeptiert, akzeptierte, hat akzeptiert> **7.** *(remove)* take sth away (from sb) (jdm) etw. wegnehmen ['vɛkneːmən] <nimmt weg, nahm weg, hat weggenommen> ◊ *Er hat (mir) meinen Füller weggenommen.* **8.** *(responsibility)* übernehmen [ybɐˈneːmən] <übernimmt, übernahm, hat übernommen> ◊ *Verantwortung übernehmen* **9.** *(conquer)* erobern [ɛˈloːbɐn] <erobert, eroberte, hat erobert> ◊ *Wann wurde Konstantinopel von den Türken erobert?* **10.** *(a breath)* holen ['hoːlən] +haben ◊ *Sie holte tief Luft.; (a look)* werfen ['vɛrfn̩] <wirft, warf, hat geworfen> ◊ *Er hat nur einen kurzen Blick auf die Unterlagen geworfen.; (a walk, picture, an exercise)* machen ['maxn̩] +haben ◊ *Sie machten einen langen Spaziergang.* ♦ *Turnübungen machen* ♦ *im Urlaub Bilder machen; (measures)* ergreifen [ɛˈɡraɪfn̩] <ergreift, ergriff, hat ergriffen> **11.** *(a course)* belegen [bəˈleːɡn̩] <belegt, belegte, hat belegt> ◊ *einen Kurs belegen; (an exam, a test)* ablegen ['apleːɡn̩] +haben ◊ *eine Prüfung ablegen* **12.** *(risks, chances)* eingehen ['aɪngeːən] <geht ein, ging ein, ist eingegangen> ◊ *ein großes Wagnis eingehen* **13.** *(an interest)* zeigen ['tsaɪɡn̩] +haben ◊ *Sie zeigt wenig Interesse.* **14.** *(pity, a certain view)* haben ['haːbm̩] +haben ◊ *Er hatte Mitleid mit der Katze.* ♦ *Sie hat die Einstellung, dass die Kinder mehr Gemüse essen sollten.* **15.** *(sb's temperature)* messen ['mɛsn̩] <misst, maß, hat gemessen> **16.** *(a prize, votes)* bekommen [bəˈkɔmən] <bekommt, bekam, hat bekommen> **17.** *(money)* einbringen ['aɪnbrɪŋən] <bringt ein, brachte ein, hat eingebracht> ◊ *Die Veranstaltung hat eine Menge Geld eingebracht.* **18.** take sth the wrong way etw. falsch verstehen ['falʃ fɛˌʃteːən] <versteht, verstand, hat ver-

standen> ◊ *Du hast das falsch verstanden.* **19.** take some doing mühsam sein ['myːzaːm zaɛn] +sein ◊ *Es ist mühsam, diese komplizierte Anleitung zu befolgen.* **20.** take sb/sth for sb/sth jdn/etw. für jdn/etw. halten [fyːɐ ... haltn̩] <hält, hielt, hat gehalten> ◊ *Ich habe ihn für einen netten Kerl gehalten.* **21.** take it (that) davon ausgehen(, dass) [dafɔn ˈaʊsɡeːən] <geht aus, ging aus, ist ausgegangen> ◊ *Ich gehe davon aus, dass du die Nachricht schon gehört hast.*

• **take after** [phras v] take after sb jdm ähneln ['ɛːnəln] +haben ◊ *Er ähnelte seinem Großvater.*

• **take against** [phras v] take against sb eine Abneigung gegen jdn spüren [aɛnə ˌapnaɛɡʊŋ ɡeːɡn̩ ... ʃpyːrən] +haben ◊ *Sie spürte sofort eine große Abneigung gegen ihre Sitznachbarin.*

• **take apart** [phras v] **1.** *(separate into pieces)* take sth apart etw. auseinander nehmen [aʊsˈlaɛˈnandɐ neːmən] <nimmt, nahm, hat genommen> ◊ *Er hat seinen Computer auseinander genommen.* **2.** *(beat easily)* take sth apart jdn vernichtend schlagen [fɛˌnɪçtn̩t ˈʃlaːɡn̩] <schlägt, schlug, hat geschlagen> ◊ *Die Mannschaft wurde vernichtend geschlagen.* **3.** *(criticize)* take sb apart jdn heftig kritisieren [ˌhɛftɪç kritiˈziːrən] <kritisiert, kritisierte, hat kritisiert> ◊ *Für ihre Äußerungen wurde sie heftig kritisiert.*

• **take away** [phras v] take away from sth etw. schmälern ['ʃmɛːlɐn] +haben ◊ *Durch ihre schlechte Präsentation haben sie den Erfolg des Projekts geschmälert.* → **take 2.**

◉ to take away zum Mitnehmen

• **take back** [phras v] **1.** *(return sth you have bought)* take sth back etw. zurückbringen [tsuˈrʏkbrɪŋən] <bringt zurück, brachte zurück, hat zurückgebracht> ◊ *Sie können das Kleid jederzeit zurückbringen.* **2.** *(accept again)* take sb back jdn wieder aufnehmen [viːdɐ ˈaɔfneːmən] <nimmt auf, nahm auf, hat aufgenommen> ◊ *Die Firma hat ihn wieder aufgenommen.* **3.** *(words, a promise)* take sth back etw. zurücknehmen [tsuˈrʏkneːmən] <nimmt zurück, nahm zurück, hat zurückgenommen> ◊ *ein Versprechen zurücknehmen*

• **take down** [phras v] take sth down **1.** *(a tent, construction etc.)* etw. abbauen ['apbaɔən] +haben ◊ *ein Gerüst/Gestell/Zelt abbauen* **2.** *(orders, minutes, personal details)* etw. aufnehmen ['aɔfneːmən] <nimmt auf, nahm auf, hat aufgenommen> ◊ *Die Polizei nahm den Unfall auf.* **3.** *(your pants, trousers etc.)* etw. herunterlassen [hɛˈrʊntɐlasn̩] <lässt herunter, ließ herunter, hat heruntergelassen>

• **take in** [phras v] **1.** *(include, cover)* take sth in etw. abdecken ['apdɛkn̩] +haben ◊ *Der Bericht deckt alle wichtigen Details ab.* **2.** *(receive, accept)* take sb in jdn aufnehmen ['aɔfneːmən] <nimmt auf, nahm auf, hat aufgenommen> ◊ *Wir können keine weiteren Kursteilnehmer aufnehmen.* ♦ *Die Kinder konnten nicht alle Informationen aufnehmen.* **3.** *(deceive)* take sb in jdn hereinlegen [hɛˈraɛnleːɡn̩] +haben ◊ *Versuche nicht wieder, mich hereinzulegen!* be taken in by sth sich von etw. täuschen lassen [fɔn ... ˈtɔʏʃn̩ lasn̩] <lässt sich, ließ sich, hat sich lassen> ◊ *Lass dich von seinem guten Aussehen nicht täuschen!* **4.** *(understand, grasp)* take sth in etw. begreifen [bəˈɡraɛfn̩] <begreift, begriff, hat

begriffen> ◊ *Hast du diese Erklärung begriffen?*
5. *(enjoy)* take sth in etw. genießen [gə'niːsn̩]
<genießt, genoss, hat genossen> ◊ *Sie genossen den wunderbaren Ausblick.* **6.** *(clothing)* take sth in etw. enger machen ['ɛŋɐ maxn̩] +haben ◊ *Die Schneiderin macht das Kleid enger.*
• **take off** [phras v] **1.** *(leave the ground)* starten ['ʃtaʁtn̩] <startet, startete, ist gestartet> ◊ *Die Flugzeuge starten und landen.* **2.** *(become successful)* gut anlaufen [guːt 'anlaʊfn̩] <läuft an, lief an, ist angelaufen> ◊ *Ihr Geschäft ist ganz gut angelaufen.* **3.** *(leave a place)* weggehen ['vɛkɡeːən] <geht weg, ging weg, ist weggegangen> ◊ *Nach dem Treffen ist sie weggegangen.* **4.** *(imitate)* take sb off jdn nachmachen ['naːxmaxn̩] <macht nach, machte nach, hat nachgemacht> ◊ *Er machte den berühmten Moderator nach.* **5.** *(a day)* take sth off etw. freinehmen ['fraɪneːmən] <nimmt frei, nahm frei, hat freigenommen> ◊ *Er hat mehrere Tage freigenommen.* take time off sich freinehmen **6.** *(your clothing)* ausziehen ['aʊstsiːən] <zieht aus, zog aus, hat ausgezogen> ◊ *die Hose ausziehen*
• **take on** [phras v] **1.** *(employ)* take sb on jdn einstellen ['aɛnʃtɛlən] +haben ◊ *Sie wurde neu eingestellt.* **2.** *(assume, acquire)* take sth on etw. annehmen ['anːeːmən] <nimmt an, nahm an, hat angenommen> ◊ *eine neue Identität annehmen ♦ mehr Arbeit annehmen* The shop has taken on a new look. Das Geschäft sieht jetzt ganz anders aus. **3.** *(in sports)* take sb on gegen jdn antreten [geːɡn̩ ... 'antreːtn̩] <tritt an, trat an, ist angetreten> ◊ *Sie treten morgen gegen die Bayern an.* **4.** take it on yourself to do sth etw. einfach tun ['aɛnfax] ◊ *Ich habe einfach nachgeforscht und so einiges entdeckt.*
• **take out** [phras v] **1.** *(produce)* take sth out etw. hervorholen [hɛ'foːɐhoːlən] +haben ◊ *Er holte seinen Geldbeutel hervor.* **2.** *(go out with)* take sb out jdn ausführen ['aʊsfyːʁən] +haben ◊ *die Freundin ausführen ♦ Ich führe dich heute Abend zum Essen/ ins Kino aus.* **3.** *(obtain sth by getting an official document: a loan)* take sth out etw. aufnehmen ['aʊfneːmən] <nimmt auf, nahm auf, hat aufgenommen> ◊ *Ich möchte einen Kredit aufnehmen.; (an insurance, a contract)* etw. abschließen ['apʃliːsn̩] <schließt ab, schloss ab, hat abgeschlossen> ◊ *eine Lebensversicherung abschließen* **4.** *(kill)* take sb out jdn töten ['tøːtn̩] <tötet, tötete, hat getötet>; *(destroy)* take sth out etw. zerstören [tsɛ'ʃtøːʁən] <zerstört, zerstörte, hat zerstört> ◊ *Das Haus wurde bei der Explosion zerstört.* **5.** *(clothing)* take sth out etw. weiter machen ['vaɛtɐ maxn̩] +haben ◊ *Sie musste die Hose weiter machen.*
◉ take sth out on sb etw. an jdm auslassen
• **take over** [phras v] take (sth) over (etw.) übernehmen [ybɐ'neːmən] <übernimmt, übernahm, hat übernommen> ◊ *Ich übernehme jetzt das Telefon von dir. ♦ eine Firma übernehmen* take over as sth die Stelle ... [gen] übernehmen ◊ *Er übernimmt die Stelle des Abteilungsleiters.*
• **take through** [phras v] take sb through sth mit jdm etw. genau durchgehen [mɪt ... ɡənaʊ 'dʊʁçɡeːən] <geht durch, ging durch, ist durchgegangen> ◊ *Ein Kollege ist den Bericht mit ihr genau durchgegangen.*
• **take to** [phras v] **1.** *(begin to like)* take to sb zu jdm Zuneigung fassen [tsuː ... 'tsuːnaɛɡʊŋ fasn̩] +haben ◊ *Das Mädchen fasste schnell Zuneigung zu*

ihrer neuen Lehrerin. **2.** *(start)* take to doing sth anfangen, etw. zu tun ['anfaŋən ... tsuː] <fängt an, fing an, hat angefangen> ◊ *Ihr Sohn hat angeblich angefangen zu trinken.*
• **take up** [phras v] **1.** *(room, space)* wegnehmen ['vɛkneːmən] <nimmt weg, nahm weg, hat weggenommen> ◊ *Dieser Schrank nimmt viel Platz weg.; (time)* in Anspruch nehmen [ɪn 'anʃpʁʊx neːmən] <nimmt, nahm, hat genommen> ◊ *Das Baby nimmt viel Zeit in Anspruch.* **2.** *(start)* take up doing sth mit etw. anfangen [mɪt ... 'anfaŋən] <fängt an, fing an, hat angefangen> +nominalized verb ◊ *Thorsten hat mit dem Malen angefangen.; (a new job)* take sth up etw. antreten ['antreːtn̩] <tritt an, trat an, hat angetreten> take up a post eine Stelle antreten ◊ *Sie trat eine Stelle als Sekretärin an.* **3.** *(an offer)* take sth up etw. annehmen ['anːeːmən] <nimmt an, nahm an, hat angenommen> **4.** *(clothing, curtains)* take sth up kürzen ['kyʁtsn̩] +haben ◊ *Vorhänge kürzen* **5.** *(a story, cause)* take sth up wieder aufnehmen [viːdɐ 'aʊfneːmən] <nimmt auf, nahm auf, hat aufgenommen> ◊ *ein Thema wieder aufnehmen* → take 2.
take-off [noun] **1.** *(of a plane)* Start [ʃtaʁt] der <-(e)s, -s> ◊ *Der Start musste wegen Nebels verschoben werden.* **2.** *(imitation)* Parodie [paʁo'diː] die <-, -n> **3.** *(jump)* Absprung ['apʃpʁʊŋ] der <-(e)s, Absprünge>
takeover [noun] Übernahme ['yːbɐnaːmə] die <-, -n> ◊ *Die Geschäftsleitung erwägt eine Übernahme der englischen Firma.* hostile takeover feindliche Übernahme takeover bid Übernahmeangebot ['yːbɐnaːməʔaŋɡəboːt] das <-(e)s, -e>
tale [noun] Geschichte [ɡə'ʃɪçtə] die <-, -n> be full of tales about sth viele Geschichten über etw. [acc] erzählen können tale of woe Leidensgeschichte ['laɛdn̩sɡəʃɪçtə]
◉ live to tell the tale überleben tell tales petzen ◊ *Meist petzt sie nur über ihre Mitschülerinnen.*
talent [noun] *(ability, person with ability)* Talent [ta'lɛnt] das <-(e)s, -e> a man of many talents ein Mann mit vielen Talenten a wealth of talent ein Reichtum an Talenten talent show Talentwettbewerb [ta'lɛntvɛtbəvɛʁp] der <-s, -e>
talented [adj] begabt [bə'ɡaːpt] <begabter, am begabtesten> ◊ *praktisch/handwerklich/mathematisch begabt sein ♦ Hoch begabte Schüler müssen besonders gefördert werden.*
talk¹ [noun] **1.** *(conversation, discussion)* Gespräch [ɡə'ʃpʁɛːç] das <-(e)s, -e> ◊ *ein nettes Gespräch* have a talk (with sb) (mit jdm) ein Gespräch führen the talk turns to sth das Gespräch wendet sich einer Sache [dat] zu Talks resumed. Die Gespräche werden wieder aufgenommen. talk of the town Stadtgespräch ['ʃtatɡəʃpʁɛːç] **2.** *(lecture)* Vortrag ['foːɐtʁaːk] der <-(e)s, Vorträge> ◊ *einen Vortrag über sein Lieblingsbuch halten* **3.** *(gossip, chatter)* Gerede [ɡə'reːdə] das <-s> no pl *(pej)* ◊ *leeres Gerede ♦ Es gab viel Gerede über die neuen Nachbarn.* despite sb's talk trotz jds Geredes **4.** *(way of talking)* Sprache ['ʃpʁaːxə] die <-, -n> ◊ *die Sprache der Jugend ♦ die Sprache der Straße/ Liebe*
talk² [verb] **1.** *(use words)* sprechen ['ʃpʁɛçn̩] <spricht, sprach, hat gesprochen> ◊ *sprechen können/lernen ♦ Spricht eure Kleine denn schon?* **2.** *(have a conversa-*

tion or discussion, exchange gossip) reden ['re:dn̩] <redet, redete, hat geredet> ◊ *Möchtest du darüber reden?* ♦ *Mit Marco rede ich nicht mehr.* ♦ *Sei vorsichtig! Die Nachbarn reden schon.* talk to/with sb mit jdm reden ◊ *Wir müssen miteinander reden.* talk on/about sth über etw. (acc) reden talk politics/ sports etc. über Politik/Sport etc. reden **3.** *(persuade)* talk sb into sth jdn zu etw. überreden [ˈtsuː … ybeˌreːdn̩] <überredet, überredete, hat überredet> ◊ *Er hat sie zu einem Kinobesuch überredet.* talk sb into doing sth jdn überreden, etw. zu tun talk (some) sense into sb jdn zur Vernunft bringen [ˈtsuːɡ̊ feˈnʊnft brɪŋən] <bringt, brachte, hat gebracht> **4.** *(be about)* talk about/of sth von etw. handeln [fɔn … handl̩n̩] +haben ◊ *Wovon handelt das vierte Kapitel?* **5.** *(exchange information)* kommunizieren [kɔmuniˈtsiːrən] <kommuniziert, kommunizierte, hat kommuniziert> ◊ *Mein Computer kann mit anderen Computern kommunizieren.* ⓔ we/you etc. are talking (about) sth/sb hier geht es um etw./jdn ◊ *Hier geht es um viel Geld/ Menschenleben!* not know what sb is talking about nicht wissen, wovon jd spricht ◊ *„Also warst du gestern dort?" — „Ich weiß nicht, wovon du sprichst."*

talk around → talk round

• **talk back** (phras v) frech sein [ˈfrɛç zaɛn] +sein ◊ *Du sollst nicht so frech sein!*

• **talk down** (phras v) **1.** *(make a louder noise than sb/sth else)* talk sb down jdn übertönen [ybeˈtøːnən] <übertönt, übertönte, hat übertönt> ◊ *Sie übertönte die anderen Gäste.* **2.** *(a person, drug addict)* talk sb down jdn beruhigen [bəˈruːɪɡ̊n̩] <beruhigt, beruhigte, hat beruhigt> ◊ *Er versuchte, seinen aufgeregten Freund zu beruhigen.* **3.** *(a pilot, plane)* talk sb/sth down jdn/etw. herunterbringen [hɛˈrʊntebrɪŋən] <bringt herunter, brachte herunter, hat heruntergebracht> ◊ *Die Fluglotsen haben das Flugzeug heil heruntergebracht.* **4.** *(a price)* talk sth down etw. herunterhandeln [hɛˈrɔntehandl̩n̩] +haben ◊ *Das Mädchen hat den Preis heruntergehandelt.* **5.** *(in the US: say negative things about sb/sth)* talk sb/sth down jdn/etw. heruntermachen [hɛˈrɔntemaxn̩] +haben *(fam)* ◊ *Sie hat ihn total heruntergemacht.*

• **talk down to** (phras v) talk down to sb mit jdm von oben herab reden [mɪt … fɔn ˈoːbm̩ hɛˌrap reːdn̩] +haben ◊ *Du solltest mit mir nicht so von oben herab reden!*

• **talk out** (phras v) talk sth out etw. ausdiskutieren [ˈaɔsdɪskutiːrən] <diskutiert aus, diskutierte aus, hat ausdiskutiert> ◊ *Die beiden müssen das ausdiskutieren.*

• **talk over** (phras v) talk sth over über etw. (acc) reden [yːbe … ˌreːdn̩] <redet, redete, hat geredet> ◊ *Lass uns noch mal darüber reden!*

• **talk round** (phras v) **1.** *(persuade)* talk sb round jdn überreden [ybeˈreːdn̩] <überredet, überredete, hat überredet> ◊ *Sie versuchte, ihn zu überreden.* **2.** *(avoid)* talk round sth um etw. herumreden [ʊm … hɛˌrʊmreːdn̩] <redet herum, redete herum, hat herumgeredet> ◊ *Er hat den ganzen Abend um das Thema herumgeredet.*

• **talk through** (phras v) **1.** *(explain in detail)* talk sb through sth mit jdm etw. durchgehen [mɪt … ˌdʊrçɡeːən] <geht durch, ging durch, ist durch-

gegangen> **2.** *(discuss in detail)* talk sth through etw. durchsprechen [ˈdʊrçʃprɛçn̩] <spricht durch, sprach durch, hat durchgesprochen> ◊ *Sie haben den Plan genau durchgesprochen.*

• **talk up** (phras v) talk sb/sth up jdn/etw. loben [ˈloːbm̩] +haben ◊ *Die Mutter hat den Sohn übermäßig oft gelobt.*

talkative (adj) gesprächig [ɡəˈʃprɛːçɪç] ◊ *Er ist heute nicht besonders gesprächig.* ♦ *ein gesprächiger junger Mann*

tall (adj) **1.** *(height of a person, drink also)* groß [ɡroːs] <größer, am größten> ◊ *Ich bin größer als du.* ♦ *Er hat einen großen Cocktail getrunken.* grow tall groß werden **2.** *(from bottom to top)* hoch [hoːx] <höher, am höchsten> <der/die/das hohe …> ◊ *Wie hoch ist dieser Berg?* ♦ *Das Regal ist etwa 1,80 Meter hoch.* five metres tall fünf Meter hoch

tame¹ (adj) **1.** *(animal, person)* zahm [tsaːm] ◊ *ein zahmes Eichhörnchen* ♦ *Danach waren die Kinder ganz zahm.* **2.** *(unexciting)* lahm [laːm] ◊ *Das war ein lahmes Spiel.* ♦ *Das ist mir zu lahm.*

tame² (verb) **1.** *(an animal)* zähmen [ˈtsɛːmən] +haben **2.** *(fig) (control)* unter Kontrolle bringen [ʊnte kɔnˈtrɔlə brɪŋən] <bringt, brachte, hat gebracht> ◊ *einen Fluss unter Kontrolle bringen* ♦ *Die Preisentwicklung muss unter Kontrolle gebracht werden.*

tan¹ (noun) **1.** *(of skin)* Bräune [ˈbrɔɡnə] die <-> no pl ◊ *eine gesunde Bräune* **2.** *(colo(u)r)* Hellbraun [ˈhɛlbraɔn] das <-s, ->

tan² (verb) **1.** *(go brown in the sun)* braun werden [ˈbraɔn veːɡdn̩] +sein ◊ *Ich werde schnell braun.* **2.** *(turn into leather)* gerben [ˈɡɛrbm̩] +haben

tank (noun) **1.** *(for liquid)* Tank [taŋk] der <-s, -s> **2.** *(for fish)* Aquarium [aˈkvaːrɪɔm] das <-s, Aquarien>; *(for snakes, spiders etc.)* Terrarium [tɛˈraːrɪɔm] das <-s, Terrarien> **3.** *(vehicle)* Panzer [ˈpantsɐ] der <-s, -> ◊ *Panzer rollten in die Stadt ein.* **4.** *(fam) (in the US: room for prisoners)* Knast [knast] der <-(e)s, Knäste> *(fam)*

tap¹ (noun) **1.** *(faucet)* Hahn [haːn] der <-(e)s, Hähne> ◊ *ein tropfender Hahn* turn the tap off/on den Hahn zudrehen/aufdrehen **2.** *(light touch)* Klopfen [ˈklɔpfn̩] das <-s> no pl; *(of a hammer)* Schlag [ʃlaːk] der <-(e)s, Schläge> ◊ *mit wenigen Schlägen eine Kiste zusammennageln* **3.** *(listening device)* put a tap on sth etw. abhören [ˈaphøːrən] +haben ◊ *jds Telefon abhören* **4.** *(dance)* Stepp [ʃtɛp] der <-s, -s> ⓔ on tap **1.** *(liquid)* vom Fass **2.** *(available)* zugänglich **3.** *(planned)* geplant

tap² (verb) **1.** *(touch lightly: with fingertips)* tippen [ˈtɪpm̩] +haben ◊ *Sie tippte sich an die Stirn und sagte: „Du spinnst wohl?"* ♦ *Er tippte ihr auf die Schulter und sprach sie an.; (with knuckles)* tap at/ on/against sth an/gegen etw. (acc) klopfen [an/ge:gn̩ … ˌklɔpfn̩] +haben ◊ *Jemand klopfte leise ans Fenster.* **2.** *(a telephone, resources)* anzapfen [ˈantsapfn̩] +haben ◊ *Ihr Telefon wurde angezapft.* ♦ *einen Baum anzapfen, um Kautschuk zu gewinnen; (a conversation)* belauschen [bəˈlaɔʃn̩] <belauscht, belauschte, hat belauscht> ◊ *Er hat das Gespräch der beiden Mädchen belauscht.* **3.** *(sb's potential, markets)* ausschöpfen [ˈaɔsʃœpfn̩] +haben ◊ *Ihr Potenzial wurde nicht voll ausgeschöpft.* **4.** *(fam) (get money from)* tap sb for sth jdn etw. anhauen [ʊm … ˌanhaɔən] *(fam)* ◊ *Der Junge haute seinen Vater um Geld an.*

• **tap out** ⟨phras v⟩ **1.** *(a sound pattern)* klopfen ['klɒpfn̩] +haben **2.** *(on a keyboard)* tippen ['tɪpm̩] +haben ◊ *Er tippte seine Hausaufgaben in den Computer.* **3.** *(in the US: spend money)* aufbrauchen ['aʊfbraʊxn̩] +haben ◊ *Ich habe mein ganzes Geld aufgebraucht.*

tape¹ ⟨noun⟩ **1.** *(made of fabric or plastic)* Band [bant] das <-(e)s, Bänder> ◊ *einen Song auf Band aufnehmen* ♦ *den Eingang mit einem Band absperren; (finishing line)* the tape das Zielband [das 'tsiːlbant] sticky tape Klebeband ['kleːbəbant] tape measure Maßband ['maːsbant] **2.** *(cassette)* Kassette [ka'sɛtə] die <-, -n> blank tape Leerkassette ['leːɐ̯ka,sɛtə]

tape² ⟨verb⟩ **1.** *(record)* aufnehmen ['aʊfneːmən] <nimmt auf, nahm auf, hat aufgenommen> ◊ *Hast du den Film für mich aufgenommen?* **2.** *(stick)* kleben ['kleːbm̩] +haben tape sth to sth etw. an etw. ⟨acc⟩ kleben; *(close sth)* tape (up) etw. zukleben ['tsuːkleːbm̩] +haben ◊ *eine Tüte zukleben* **3.** MED *(mostly in the US: bandage)* bandagieren [banda'ʒiːrən] <bandagiert, bandagierte, hat bandagiert> ◊ *den Knöchel bandagieren*

tar ⟨noun⟩ Teer [teːɐ̯] der <-(e)s> *seldom with the article, no pl*

target¹ ⟨noun⟩ Ziel [tsiːl] das <-(e)s, -e> ◊ *ein Ziel anvisieren* ♦ *Der Schuss hat das Ziel getroffen/verfehlt.* set a target ein Ziel festlegen meet a target ein Ziel erreichen sales target Verkaufsziel [fɛ'kaʊfstsiːl] prime target Hauptzielgruppe ['haʊpttsiːlɡrʊpə] die <-, -n> target date Stichtag ['ʃtɪçtaːk] der <-(e)s, -e>

target² ⟨verb⟩ **1.** *(aim or direct at)* target sth/sb auf etw./jdn zielen [aʊf ... tsiːlən] +haben ◊ *Die Werbung zielt auf alte Leute.* ♦ *Sie nahm das Gewehr und zielte auf die Scheibe.* target sth on etw. auf etw. ⟨acc⟩ richten [aʊf ... rɪçtn̩] <richtet, richtete, hat gerichtet> ◊ *Sie richteten die Kanone auf die Brücke.* **2.** MIL *(attack)* angreifen ['anɡraɪfn̩] <greift an, griff an, hat angegriffen> **3.** *(criticize or work against)* aufs Korn nehmen [aʊfs 'kɔrn neːmən] <nimmt, nahm, hat genommen> ◊ *Die Regierung wurde von der Opposition aufs Korn genommen.* **4.** *(assistance, support etc.)* target sth towards sb etw. auf jdn konzentrieren [aʊf ... kɔntsɛntriːrən] <konzentriert, konzentrierte, hat konzentriert> ◊ *Wir konzentrieren die Hilfsgüter auf die ärmsten Flutopfer.*

tariff ⟨noun⟩ **1.** *(tax)* Zoll [tsɔl] der <-(e)s, Zölle> ◊ *Zoll zahlen* **2.** *(price)* Tarif [ta'riːf] der <-s, -e> **3.** *(list of prices)* Preisliste ['praɪslɪstə] die <-, -n>

task ⟨noun⟩ Aufgabe ['aʊfɡaːbə] die <-, -n> ◊ *Die Übersetzerin hat ihre Aufgabe gut gelöst.* ♦ *Sie betrachtete es als ihre Aufgabe, ihm zu helfen.* perform a task eine Aufgabe erfüllen the task of doing sth die Aufgabe, etw. zu tun ⊙ take sb to task jdn heftig kritisieren

task force ⟨noun⟩ Spezialeinheit [ʃpe'tsiaːlaɪnhaɪt] die <-, -en>

taste¹ ⟨noun⟩ **1.** *(flavo(u)r, discernment, liking)* Geschmack [ɡə'ʃmak] der <-(e)s, Geschmäcke or fam hum Geschmäcker> ◊ *Ich mag den Geschmack von Oliven nicht.* ♦ *Bei diesem Büfett ist für jeden Geschmack etwas dabei.* ♦ *Sie hat einen schlechten Geschmack, was Kleidung betrifft.* ♦ *Wir haben unterschiedliche Geschmäcker.* in good taste geschmackvoll [ɡə'ʃmakfɔl] in bad

taste geschmacklos [ɡə'ʃmakloːs] <geschmackloser, am geschmacklosesten> have a taste for sth sich für etw. interessieren [fyːɐ̯ ... ɪntərə,siːrən] <interessiert sich, interessierte sich, hat sich interessiert> ◊ *Er hat sich schon immer für Kunst interessiert.* **2.** *(small amount of sth)* Kostprobe ['kɔstproːbə] die <-, -n> **3.** sense of taste Geschmackssinn [ɡə'ʃmakszɪn] der <-(e)s> *no pl* ⊙ a bad taste in your mouth ein schlechter Nachgeschmack give sb a taste of their own medicine es jdm mit gleicher Münze heimzahlen

taste² ⟨verb⟩ **1.** *(detect or have a flavo(u)r)* schmecken ['ʃmɛkn̩] +haben ◊ *Schmeckst du den Wein in der Soße?* ♦ *Wie schmeckt die Suppe?* sth tastes of sth etw. schmeckt nach etw. **2.** *(eat)* essen ['ɛsn̩] <isst, aß, hat gegessen> ◊ *eine Mahlzeit essen* ♦ *Er hat noch nie Kürbis gegessen.* **3.** *(try a small amount of)* probieren [pro'biːrən] <probiert, probierte, hat probiert> ◊ *Probierst du mal den Kuchen?* **4.** *(experience)* erleben [ɛ'leːbm̩] <erlebt, erlebte, hat erlebt> ◊ *das Gefühl von Freiheit erleben*

tasteless ⟨adj⟩ **1.** *(food)* fade ['faːdə] <fader, am fadesten> ◊ *fade Kost* ♦ *Ich finde die Soße etwas fade.* **2.** *(remark, clothing etc.)* geschmacklos [ɡə'ʃmakloːs] <geschmackloser, am geschmacklosesten> ◊ *eine geschmacklose Bemerkung machen* ♦ *Dieser Artikel ist geschmacklos.*

tasty ⟨adj⟩ **1.** *(food)* lecker ['lɛkɐ] ◊ *Das Essen war lecker.* ♦ *eine leckere Nachspeise* **2.** *(in the UK: attractive)* hübsch [hʏpʃ] <hübscher, am hübschesten> ◊ *ein hübsches Mädchen*

tattoo ⟨noun⟩ **1.** *(on the skin)* Tätowierung [tɛto'viːrʊŋ] die <-, -en> **2.** *(signal for soldiers)* Zapfenstreich ['tsapfn̩ʃtraɪç] der <-(e)s> *no pl* ◊ *den Zapfenstreich blasen*

Taurus ⟨noun⟩ Stier [ʃtiːɐ̯] der <-(e)s, -e>

taut(ly) ⟨adj, adv⟩ **1.** *(stretched tight)* straff [ʃtraf] ◊ *eine straffe Haut* ♦ *Das Gummiband muss straff gespannt sein.* **2.** *(fig) (expression, atmosphere etc.)* angespannt ['anɡəʃpant] <angespannter, am angespanntesten> ◊ *angespannte Gesichtszüge* ♦ *Die Stimmung war leicht angespannt.* ♦ *angespannt horchen*

tax¹ ⟨noun⟩ Steuer ['ʃtɔyɐ] die <-, -n> ◊ *Er zahlt 20% Steuern auf sein Bruttoeinkommen.* ♦ *eine Steuer erheben/einziehen/abführen* raise/lower taxes Steuern erhöhen/senken tax burden Steuerbelastung ['ʃtɔyɐbəlastʊŋ] die <-, -en> ⊙ after tax nach Steuer before tax vor Steuer

tax² ⟨verb⟩ **1.** *(put a tax on sth)* besteuern [bə'ʃtɔyɐn] <besteuert, besteuerte, hat besteuert> ◊ *In Zukunft sollen Renten stärker besteuert werden.* ♦ *Der Staat besteuert Tabak/Benzin.* **2.** *(a person)* veranlagen [fɛ|'anlaːɡn̩] <veranlagt, veranlagte, hat veranlagt> ◊ *Sie sind gemeinsam veranlagt.* **3.** *(cause problems)* Schwierigkeiten machen ['ʃviːrɪçkaɪtn̩ maxn̩] +haben ◊ *Die Kinder machen uns nur Schwierigkeiten.; (sb's patience)* auf eine harte Probe stellen [aʊf aɛna hartə 'proːbə ʃtɛlən] +haben

taxation ⟨noun⟩ **1.** *(system)* Besteuerung [bə'ʃtɔyərʊŋ] die <-, -en> **2.** *(money, taxes)* Steuern ['ʃtɔyɐn] die <-> *pl* ◊ *die Steuern erhöhen*

taxi ⟨noun⟩ Taxi ['taksi] das <-s, -s> ◊ *Sie bestellten ein Taxi.* hail a taxi ein Taxi rufen

tax office ⟨noun⟩ Finanzamt [fi'nants|amt] das <-(e)s, Finanzämter>

taxpayer ⟨noun⟩ Steuerzahler ['ʃtɔyɐtsaːlɐ] der <-s, ->

♀Steuerzahlerin ['ʃtɔøetsaːlərɪn] die <-, –nen>

tax return [noun] Steuererklärung ['ʃtɔøeˈlekleːrɔŋ] die <-, –en> ◊ *eine Steuererklärung abgeben*

tea [noun] **1.** *(drink, substance)* Tee [teː] der <-s, –s> ◊ *Möchten Sie Tee oder Kaffee?* ♦ *grüner/schwarzer Tee* ♦ *Um diese Zeit sitzen sie beim Tee.* **2.** *(meal)* Abendbrot ['aːbm̩tbroːt] das <-(e)s> no pl ◊ *Um 6 Uhr gab es Abendbrot.*

 not for all the tea in China um nichts in der Welt

tea bag [noun] Teebeutel ['teːbɔøtl̩] der <-s, –>

teach [verb] **1.** *(give lessons)* unterrichten [ʊntəˈrɪçtn̩] <unterrichtet, unterrichtete, hat unterrichtet> ◊ *Er unterrichtet Erwachsene.* ♦ *an einer Fachhochschule unterrichten* ♦ *Mathe unterrichten* teach sth to sb, teach sb sth jdn in etw. [dat] unterrichten **2.** *(instruct)* teach sb sth jdm etw. beibringen ['baebrɪŋən] <bringt bei, brachte bei, hat beigebracht> teach sb to do sth jdm beibringen, etw. zu tun

teacher [noun] Lehrer ['leːrɐ] der <-s, –> ♀Lehrerin ['leːrərɪn] die <-, –nen> ◊ *Er ist Lehrer von Beruf.* ♦ *Wie findest du die neue Lehrerin?*

teaching [noun] **1.** *(job of a teacher)* Unterrichten [ʊntəˈrɪçtn̩] das <-s> no pl ◊ *Das Unterrichten machte ihm viel Spaß.; (in compound ns)* ... teaching ...unterricht ['ʊnterɪçt] der <-(e)s, –e> most sing language teaching Sprachunterricht ['ʃpraːx|ʊnterɪçt] history teaching Geschichtsunterricht [gəˈʃɪçts|ʊnterɪçt]; *(in compound ns)* teaching ... Unterrichts... ['ʊnterɪçts] teaching methods Unterrichtsmethoden ['ʊnterɪçtsme,toːdn̩] die <–> pl **2.** *(ideas, principles)* Lehre ['leːrə] die <-, –n> ◊ *die christliche Lehre* ♦ *die Lehren Luthers*

team [noun] **1.** SPORT Mannschaft ['manʃaft] die <-, –en> ◊ *Im Fußball besteht eine Mannschaft aus elf Spielern.* ♦ *Für welche Mannschaft spielt sie?*; (in compound ns) team ... Mannschafts... ['manʃafts] team member Mannschaftsmitglied ['manʃaftsmɪtgliːt] das <-(e)s, –er> **2.** *(group working together)* Team [tiːm] das <-s, –s> ◊ *Wir sind mittlerweile ein gut eingespieltes Team.* **3.** *(of horses etc.)* Gespann [gəˈʃpan] das <-(e)s, –e>

tear¹ [noun] Träne ['trɛːnə] die <-, –n> ◊ *heiße/bittere Tränen vergießen/weinen* ♦ *Sie erzählte ihm unter Tränen, was passiert war.* ♦ *Der Anblick rührte mich zu Tränen.*

tear² [noun] Riss [rɪs] der <-es, –e> ◊ *Er erlitt einen Riss des rechten Kreuzbandes.* ♦ *In meinem neuen Rock ist ein Riss.*

tear³ [verb] **1.** *(into pieces)* tear sth (up) etw. zerreißen [tsɐˈraesn̩] <zerreißt, zerriss, hat/ist zerrissen> *transitive use +haben/intransitive use +sein* ◊ *Ich habe den Brief zerrissen.* ♦ *Als ich an der Zeitung zog, zerriss sie.* tear sth sich [dat] etw. zerreißen ◊ *Sie hat sich die Jacke zerrissen.* ♦ *Ich habe mir die Bluse an einem Haken zerrissen.* tear sth off etw. abreißen ['apraesn̩] <reißt ab, riss ab, hat abgerissen> ◊ *ein Blatt vom Kalender abreißen* tear sth to pieces etw. in Stücke reißen [ɪn ˈʃtʏkə raesn̩] <reißt, riss, hat gerissen> tear a hole in sth ein Loch in etw. [acc] reißen tear your clothes off sich [dat] die Kleider vom Leib reißen tear sth open etw. aufreißen ['aofraesn̩] <reißt auf, riss auf, hat aufgerissen> ◊ *eine Tüte Chips aufreißen* tear at sth an etw. [dat] zerren [an ... ˌtsɛrən] +haben ◊ *Er zerrte am Seil.* tear sth out etw.

ausreißen ['aosraesn̩] <reißt aus, riss aus, hat ausgerissen> ◊ *im Garten das Unkraut ausreißen* tear sth away etw. wegreißen ['vɛkraesn̩] <reißt weg, riss weg, hat weggerissen> ◊ *Das ganze Haus wurde vom Sturm weggerissen.* **2.** *(a muscle etc.)* tear sth sich [dat] etw. zerren ['tsɛrən] +haben ◊ *Er hat sich beim Sport einen Muskel gezerrt.* **3.** *(move very quickly)* rasen ['raːzn̩] +sein ◊ *Der Nachbar raste um die Ecke.* tear past sth an etw. [dat] vorbeirasen [an ... foːˌbaeraːzn̩] +haben
• **tear apart** [phras v] **1.** *(destroy, break down)* tear sth apart etw. zerstören [tsɐˈʃtøːrən] <zerstört, zerstörte, hat zerstört> ◊ *Das Haus wurde zerstört.* ♦ *Sein Seitensprung hat ihre Ehe zerstört.* **2.** *(destroy emotionally)* tear sb apart jdm das Herz zerreißen [das ˈhɛʁts tsɐraesn̩] <zerreißt, zerriss, hat zerrissen> **3.** *(when looking for sth)* tear sth apart etw. auf den Kopf stellen [aof deːn ˈkɔpf ʃtɛlən] +haben ◊ *Sie haben das Zimmer auf den Kopf gestellt, aber das Buch nicht gefunden.* **4.** *(criticize)* tear sth/sb apart etw./jdn in der Luft zerreißen [ɪn deːg ˈlʊft tsɐˌraesn̩] <zerreißt, zerriss, hat zerrissen> *mostly passive* ◊ *Warum wird der Autor von den Kritikern in der Luft zerrissen?*
• **tear away** [phras v] tear yourself away (from sb/ sth) sich (von jdm/etw.) losreißen ['loːsraesn̩] <reißt sich los, riss sich los, hat sich losgerissen> ◊ *Er konnte sich kaum von dem Anblick losreißen.* tear your eyes away from sb/sth seinen Blick von jdm/etw. losreißen ◊ *Sie musste ihren Blick von dem gut aussehenden Mann losreißen.*
• **tear into** [phras v] *(attack physically or verbally)* tear into sb/sth jdn/etw. angreifen ['angraefn̩] <greift an, griff an, hat angegriffen> ◊ *Der Hund hat den Mann angegriffen.* ♦ *jdn mit Worten angreifen*; *(start doing sth)* tear into sth etw. in Angriff nehmen [ɪn ˈangrɪf neːmən] <nimmt, nahm, hat genommen> ◊ *eine Aufgabe in Angriff nehmen*
• **tear down** [phras v] tear sth down *(a building)* etw. abreißen ['apraesn̩] <reißt ab, riss ab, hat abgerissen> ◊ *Der alte Palast wurde abgerissen.*
• **tear up** [phras v] **1.** *(an agreement, treaty etc.)* tear sth up etw. platzen lassen ['platsn̩ lasn̩] <lässt, ließ, hat lassen> ◊ *Ein Staat war nicht einverstanden und ließ das Abkommen platzen.* **2.** *(emotionally)* tear sb up jdm das Herz brechen [das ˈhɛʁts brɛçn̩] <bricht, brach, hat gebrochen> ◊ *Das hat ihr das Herz gebrochen.* → **tear²** 1

tease [verb] **1.** *(annoy)* ärgern ['ɛʁgən] +haben ◊ *Hör auf, die Katze zu ärgern!* **2.** *(verbally)* aufziehen ['aoftsiːən] <zieht auf, zog auf, hat aufgezogen> *(fam)* ◊ *jdn wegen eines Sprachfehlers aufziehen; (cruelly)* hänseln ['hɛnzln̩] +haben ◊ *Er wurde in der Schule viel gehänselt.* **3.** *(sexually)* tease sb jdn sexuell provozieren [zɛksʊˌɛl provoˈtsiːrən] <provoziert, provozierte, hat provoziert> ◊ *Er fühlte sich sexuell provoziert.*

teaspoon [noun] Teelöffel ['teːlœfl̩] der <-s, –> ◊ *zwei Teelöffel Zucker*

technical [adj] **1.** *(relating to technology or technique)* technisch ['tɛçnɪʃ] no comp/superl, only before ns ◊ *komplizierte technische Geräte* ♦ *technische Perfektion* **2.** *(text, training)* fachspezifisch [faxʃpeˌtsiːfɪʃ] no comp/superl ◊ *fachspezifische Inhalte* ♦ *Der Vortrag war mir zu fachspezifisch.* technical language Fachsprache ['faxʃpraːxə] die <-, –n>

technical term Fachausdruck ['fax|aosdrʊk] der <-(e)s, Fachausdrücke> **3.** *(relating to laws)* formaljuristisch [foˈˈmaːlju,rɪstɪʃ] *no comp/superl; (relating to rules)* verfahrenstechnisch [fɛˈfaːrənstɛçnɪʃ] *no comp/superl*

technical college [noun] Berufsschule [bəˈruːfsʃuːlə] die <-, -n> ◊ *auf die Berufsschule gehen*

technically [adv] **1.** *(relating to technology or technique)* technisch ['tɛçnɪʃ] *no comp/superl* ◊ *Ist das denn technisch machbar?* ◆ *Sein Spiel war technisch perfekt.* **2.** *(strictly speaking)* technisch gesehen ['tɛçnɪʃ gəzeːən] *no comp/superl* ◊ *Technisch gesehen hat er Recht.*

technician [noun] Techniker ['tɛçnɪkɐ] der <-s, -> ♀Technikerin ['tɛçnɪkərɪn] die <-, -nen> ◊ *Er ist Techniker in einem Labor* ◆ *die brillante Technikerin mit virtuosen Geigenspiel*

technique [noun] Technik ['tɛçnɪk] die <-, -en> ◊ *Welcher Technik hat sich der Autor hier bedient?*

technological(ly) [adj, adv] *(relating to technology)* technologisch [tɛçnoˈloːgɪʃ] *no comp/superl, only before ns* ◊ *eine ganz neue technologische Entwicklung* ◆ *eine technologisch hoch entwickelte Region; (device, apparatus, equipment)* technisch ['tɛçnɪʃ] *no comp/superl, only before ns* ◊ *komplizierte technische Geräte* ◆ *ein technisch überlegenes System*

technology [noun] Technologie [tɛçnoloˈgiː] die <-, -n> ◊ *moderne digitale Technologie* information technology Informationstechnologie [ɪnfoˈˈmaˈtsjoːnstɛçnolo,giː]; *(referring to machinery)* Technik ['tɛçnɪk] die <-, -en> ◊ *auf dem neuesten Stand der Technik sein*

tedious(ly) [adj, adv] **1.** *(tiresome)* ermüdend [ɛˈmyːdn̩t] ◊ *eine ermüdende Diskussion* ◆ *Die vielen Wiederholungen sind sehr ermüdend.* ◆ *ermüdend lang* **2.** *(boring)* langweilig ['laŋvaelɪç] ◊ *eine langweilige Arbeit* ◆ *Allein zu laufen ist mir zu langweilig.* ◆ *eine langweilig geschriebene Geschichte* **3.** *(wordy)* langatmig ['laŋ|a:tmɪç] ◊ *eine langatmige Darstellung* ◆ *Ihr Bericht war sehr langatmig.* ◆ *langatmig erzählen*

teenager [noun] Teenager ['tiːneːʤɐ] der <-s, -> ◊ *eine Zeitschrift für Teenager*

telecommunication [noun] Telekommunikation ['teːləkomunika,tsjoːn] die <-> *no pl*

telephone[1] [noun] Telefon ['teːləfoːn] das <-s, -e> answer the telephone ans Telefon gehen be wanted on the telephone am Telefon verlangt werden by telephone telefonisch [teleˈfoːnɪʃ] *no comp/superl* pick up the telephone abheben ['aphe:bm̩] <hebt ab, hob ab, hat abgehoben> ◊ *Sie hob ab und nannte ihren Namen.* ◉ **be on the telephone 1.** *(use the phone)* telefonieren **2.** *(have a phone)* Telefon haben

telephone[2] [verb] telefonieren [telefoˈniːrən] <telefoniert, telefonierte, hat telefoniert> ◊ *Er telefoniert gerade mit ihr.* → phone[2]

telephone bill [noun] Telefonrechnung [teleˈfoːnrɛçnʊŋ] die <-, -en>

telephone book [noun] Telefonbuch [teleˈfoːnbuːx] das <-(e)s, Telefonbücher>

telephone booth, telephone box [noun] Telefonzelle [teleˈfoːntsɛlə] die <-, -n> ◊ *von einer Telefonzelle aus anrufen*

telephone directory → telephone book

telephone number [noun] Telefonnummer

[tele'fo:nnʊme] die <-, -n> ◊ *Wie lautet Ihre Telefonnummer?*

telescope [noun] Fernrohr ['fɛˈnroːɐ] das <-(e)s, -e> ◊ *Durch das Fernrohr beobachtete er die Sterne.*

television [noun] **1.** *(appliance)* Fernseher ['fɛˈnzeːɐ] der <-s, -> ◊ *vor dem Fernseher sitzen* ◆ *den Fernseher einschalten* The television is on. Der Fernseher läuft. watch television fernsehen ['fɛˈnzeːən] <sieht fern, sah fern, hat ferngesehen> ◊ *Abends sieht er meistens fern.* **2.** *(system, company, programmes)* Fernsehen ['fɛˈnzeːən] das <-s> *no pl* ◊ *Sie arbeitet fürs Fernsehen.* on television im Fernsehen ◊ *Den Bericht habe ich im Fernsehen gesehen.*

television set [noun] Fernsehapparat ['fɛˈnzeː|apa,ra:t] der <-(e)s, -e>

tell [verb] **1.** *(say, advise, order, hint)* sagen ['za:gn̩] +haben ◊ *Sag die Wahrheit!* ◆ *Hast du ihr gesagt, was sie tun soll?* ◆ *Mir wurde gesagt, dass ich hier warten soll.* ◆ *Ein Blick auf das Haus sagte mir, dass etwas nicht stimmte.* I can't tell you how/what ... Ich kann dir gar nicht sagen, wie/was ... You're telling me! Das kann man wohl sagen. tell yourself sich sagen ◊ *Sie sagte sich, dass er wohl schüchtern sei.* **2.** *(relate a story, lie, joke etc.)* erzählen [ɛˈˈtseːlən] <erzählt, erzählte, hat erzählt> ◊ *jdm ein Märchen erzählen* ◆ *Er hat mir erzählt, wie es in Kanada war.* tell sb about sth jdm von etw. erzählen ◊ *Sie hat uns von dem Unfall erzählt.* tell of sth von etw. erzählen ◊ *Erzähl doch mal von früher!; (a secret)* verraten [fɛˈˈaːtn̩] <verrät, verriet, hat verraten> ◊ *Das darfst du niemandem verraten!* That would be telling. Das darf ich nicht verraten. tell tales petzen ['pɛtsn̩] +haben *(pej)* **3.** *(make out, identify, distinguish)* erkennen [ɛˈˈkɛnən] <erkennt, erkannte, hat erkannt> ◊ *Man erkennt, dass er sich Mühe gibt.* ◆ *den Unterschied erkennen* ◆ *Soweit ich das im Dunkeln erkennen konnte, waren es drei Männer.* tell sb/sth from sth/sb jdn/etw. von etw./jdm unterscheiden [fon ... ʊntɐ,ʃaedn̩] <unterscheidet, unterschied, hat unterschieden> ◊ *Kannst du Rot nicht von Orange unterscheiden?* tell apart auseinander halten [aos|ae'nande haltn̩] <hält, hielt, hat gehalten> ◊ *Sie sind sich so ähnlich, dass ich sie nicht auseinander halten kann.* **4.** *(become noticeable)* begin to tell sich bemerkbar machen [bəˈmɛˈkbaːˈ maxn̩] +haben ◊ *Der Stress macht sich allmählich bemerkbar.* begin to tell on sb sich bei jdm bemerkbar machen tell on sth sich auf etw. [acc] auswirken [aof ... ,aosvɪˈkn̩] +haben ◉ **tell me another one** was du nicht sagst/Sie nicht sagen there's no telling man kann nie wissen I couldn't tell you keine Ahnung *(fam)* you're telling me du sagst/Sie sagen es all told insgesamt tell it like it is sagen, was Sache ist *(fam)* • **tell against** [phras v] tell against sb gegen jdn sprechen ['ge:gn̩ ... ʃprɛçn̩] <spricht, sprach, hat gesprochen> ◊ *Sein abgebrochenes Studium spricht gegen diesen Bewerber.* • **tell of** [phras v] → tell 2. • **tell off** [phras v] tell sb off jdn schimpfen ['ʃɪmpfn̩] +haben ◊ *Die Mutter schimpft sie, wenn sie zu spät kommt.*

telly → television[1]

temper [noun] **1.** *(temperament)* Temperament

[tɛmpərə'mɛnt] das <-(e)s, -e> control your temper sein Temperament zügeln have a short temper ein aufbrausendes Temperament haben 2. *(mood)* Laune ['laonə] die <-> *no pl* be in a bad/good temper gute/schlechte Laune haben 3. *(angry mood)* Rage ['ra:ʒə] die <-> *no pl* ◊ *in Rage sein/geraten* temper tantrum Wutanfall ['vu:t|anfal] der <-(e)s, Wutanfälle>

◉ tempers flare die Gemüter erhitzen sich tempers fray die Stimmung ist angespannt keep your temper (with sb) sich (jdm gegenüber) beherrschen lose your temper (with sb) (jdm gegenüber) die Beherrschung verlieren

temperament [noun] Temperament [tɛmpərə'mɛnt] das <-(e)s, -e> ◊ *Er hat ein cholerisches Temperament.*

temperature [noun] 1. *(measurement of heat or cold)* Temperatur [tɛmpərə'tu:ɐ̯] die <-, -en> ◊ *Die Temperatur sinkt/steigt.* 2. *(fever)* Fieber ['fi:bɐ] das <-s> *no pl* be running a temperature Fieber haben take sb's temperature bei jdm Fieber messen

temple [noun] 1. *(building)* Tempel ['tɛmpl] der <-s, ->; *(Jewish)* Synagoge [zyna'go:gə] die <-, -n> ◊ *einen Gottesdienst in der Synagoge abhalten* 2. ANAT Schläfe ['ʃlɛ:fə] die <-, -n>

temporarily [adv] 1. *(for a limited period)* vorübergehend [fo'ry:bɐge:ənt] *no comp/superl* ◊ *Wegen Umbau vorübergehend geschlossen!* 2. *(until better solutions are found)* provisorisch [provi'zo:rɪʃ] *no comp/superl* ◊ *etw. provisorisch reparieren*

temporary [adj] 1. *(for a limited period)* vorübergehend [fo'ry:bɐge:ənt] *no comp/superl* ◊ *eine vorübergehende Phase* ◆ *Die Besserung ihres Zustands war leider nur vorübergehend.; (work, employment)* befristet [bə'frɪstət] *no comp/superl* ◊ *eine befristete Arbeit* ◆ *Die Stelle ist auf drei Jahre befristet.* 2. *(until better solutions are found)* provisorisch [provi'zo:rɪʃ] *no comp/superl* ◊ *ein provisorischer Wundverband* ◆ *Diese Unterkunft ist nur provisorisch.* 3. *(for the time being)* vorläufig ['fo:ɐ̯lɔɪ̯fɪç] *no comp/superl* ◊ *Damit hat die Krise ihren vorläufigen Höhepunkt erreicht.* ◆ *Der Zeitplan ist nur vorläufig.* 4. *(in job titles)* temporary... Aushilfs... ['aoʃhɪlfs] temporary worker Aushilfskraft ['aoʃhɪlfskraft] die <-, Aushilfskräfte> 5. IT *(file, folder)* temporär [tɛmpo'rɛ:ɐ̯] *no comp/superl*

tempt [verb] *(encourage, stimulate)* reizen ['raetsn̩] +haben ◊ *Das Angebot reizt mich.* ◆ *Reizt es dich nicht mitzukommen?* I am tempted to think/say ... Ich möchte fast glauben/sagen, dass ... Don't be tempted to do that. Lass dich nicht dazu hinreißen, das zu tun.; *(encourage to do sth bad)* in Versuchung führen [ɪn fɛ'zu:xʊŋ fy:rən] +haben ◊ *„Möchtest du ein Glas Wein?" – „Nein, danke, führ mich nicht in Versuchung."; (lead to do)* verführen [fɛ'fy:rən] <verführt, verführte, hat verführt> ◊ *Das schöne Wetter verführt zum Faulenzen.*

temptation [noun] Versuchung [fɛ'zu:xʊŋ] die <-, -en> ◊ *einer Versuchung widerstehen/nachgeben*

tempting → tempt [adj] verführerisch [fɛ'fy:rərɪʃ] ◊ *Die Angebote sind sehr verführerisch.* ◆ *verführerische Düfte aus der Küche* ◆ *Das riecht ja verführerisch!*

ten¹ [noun] 1. *(number)* Zehn [tse:n] die <-, -en> → four¹ 2. MATH *(second digit before decimal point)* tens Zehner ['tse:nɐ] die <-> *pl* ◊ *Nach den Einern*

addiert man die Zehner.

ten² [nmrl] zehn [tse:n] → four²

tenant [noun] 1. *(of a flat, house, office)* Mieter ['mi:tɐ] der <-s, -> ♀Mieterin ['mi:tərɪn] die <-, -nen> 2. *(of a piece of land, pub, restaurant)* Pächter ['pɛçtɐ] der <-s, -> ♀Pächterin ['pɛçtərɪn] die <-, -nen> 3. *(of one of several flats in a house)* Partei [pa'ɐ̯taɛ] die <-, -en> ◊ *In unserem Haus wohnen sechs Parteien.*

tend [verb] 1. *(be inclined)* tend to do sth dazu neigen, etw. zu tun [datsu: 'naegn̩ ... tsu:] ◊ *Du neigst dazu, ein wenig zu übertreiben.* ◆ *Solche Fehler neigen dazu, sich zu wiederholen.* tend towards sth zu etw. neigen ◊ *zu der Ansicht neigen, dass* tend to fall/ rise eine fallende/steigende Tendenz haben [aenə ˌfaləndə/ˌʃtaegn̩də tɛn'dɛnts ha:bm̩] +haben ◊ *Die Preise haben eine steigende Tendenz.* 2. *(take care of)* pflegen ['pfle:gn̩] +haben ◊ *Kranke/ den Garten pflegen; (animals)* hüten ['hy:tn̩] +haben ◊ *Schafe/Rinder hüten* tend to sb/sth sich um jdn/etw. kümmern [ʊm ... ˌkvmən] <kümmern, kümmerte, hat gekümmert> ◊ *Wer kümmert sich um die Kinder, wenn du nicht da bist?*

tendency [noun] 1. *(inclination)* Tendenz [tɛn'dɛnts] die <-, -en> ◊ *Er hat die Tendenz, vorschnell zu urteilen.* ◆ *Es besteht eine Tendenz zur Globalisierung.* 2. BIO Veranlagung [fɛ'anla:gʊŋ] die <-, -en> ◊ *eine genetische Veranlagung zu Übergewicht* ◆ *eine krankhafte/natürliche Veranlagung* 3. *(of behavio(u)r, views)* tendencies Neigungen ['naegʊŋən] die <-> *pl* ◊ *künstlerische/kriminelle Neigungen haben*

tender [adj] 1. *(meat, vegetable, plant)* zart [tsa:ɐ̯t] <zarter, am zartesten> ◊ *Ist das Fleisch auch schön zart?* ◆ *zartes Gemüse* at the tender age of im zarten Alter von 2. *(loving)* zärtlich ['tsɛ:ɐ̯tlɪç] ◊ *ein zärtlicher Blick* ◆ *Er ist sehr zärtlich zu ihr.; (gentle, light)* zart [tsa:ɐ̯t] <zarter, am zartesten> ◊ *ein zarter Kuss auf die Wange* ◆ *Die Berührung war zart und schüchtern.*

tenderly [adv] *(lovingly)* zärtlich ['tsɛ:ɐ̯tlɪç] ◊ *Sie küssten sich zärtlich.; (gently, lightly)* zart [tsa:ɐ̯t] <zarter, am zartesten> ◊ *Du gehst manchmal nicht gerade zart mit mir um.*

tenderness [noun] Zärtlichkeit ['tsɛ:ɐ̯tlɪçkaet] die <-, -en> ◊ *Sie sah ihn voll Zärtlichkeit an.*

tendon [noun] Sehne ['ze:nə] die <-, -n> ◊ *sich [dat] eine Sehne zerren* ◆ *ein Stück Fleisch voller Sehnen*

tennis [noun] Tennis ['tɛnɪs] das <-> *mostly used without the article, no pl* ◊ *Sie spielt hervorragend Tennis.*

tense¹ [noun] Zeit [tsaet] die <-, -en> ◊ *In welcher Zeit steht das Prädikat dieses Satzes?*

tense² [adj] 1. *(person, atmosphere, situation)* angespannt ['angəʃpant] <angespannter, am angespanntesten> angespannte Gesichtszüge ◆ *Die Stimmung war leicht angespannt.* 2. *(physically)* verkrampft [fɛ'krampft] <verkrampfter, am verkrampftesten> ◊ *Sie wurde im Lauf der Prüfung immer verkrampfter.; (muscle)* verspannt [fɛ'ʃpant] <verspannter, am verspanntesten> ◊ *eine verspannte Muskulatur*

tense³ [verb] 1. *(muscle)* sich spannen ['ʃpanən] +haben ◊ *Beim Gewichtheben spannen sich die Armmuskeln.* 2. *(person)* tense (up) sich verspannen [fɛ'ʃpanən] <verspannt sich, verspannte sich, hat sich verspannt> ◊ *Bei sitzender Tätigkeit verspannt man sich leicht.*

tensely adv **1.** *(with concentration, intently)* angespannt ['angəʃpant] ◊ *Er studierte angespannt die Liste.* **2.** *(unrelaxed, tautly)* verkrampft [fɛ'krampft] ◊ *Sie stand verkrampft vor dem Publikum.*

tension noun **1.** *(tightness, suspense, conflict)* Spannung ['ʃpanʊŋ] die <-, –en> ◊ *Das Seil sollte mehr Spannung haben.* ♦ *internationale Spannungen* **2.** *(emotional strain)* Anspannung ['anʃpanʊŋ] die <-> *no pl* ◊ *nervliche Anspannung*

tent noun Zelt [tsɛlt] das <–(e)s, –e> ◊ *ein Zelt aufbauen/abbauen*

term¹ noun **1.** *(word, expression)* Ausdruck ['aͻsdrʊk] der <–(e)s, Ausdrücke> ◊ *ein umgangssprachlicher Ausdruck* ♦ *Ich finde den treffenden Ausdruck nicht.* ♦ *Solche Ausdrücke möchte ich nicht mehr hören!*; *(legal, medical, scientific etc.)* Begriff [bə'grɪf] der <–(e)s, –e> ◊ *ein medizinischer Begriff* coin a term einen Begriff prägen; *(word for sth particular)* Bezeichnung [bə'tsaeçnʊŋ] die <-, –en> ◊ *Für dieses Phänomen gibt es verschiedene Bezeichnungen.* technical term Fachausdruck ['faxˌaͻsdrʊk] term of endearment Kosename ['koːzənaˌmə] der <–ns, –n> **2.** *(sb's spoken words)* terms Worte ['vͻˑtə] die <-> *pl* ◊ *Kannst du das in einfacheren Worten wiederholen?* **3.** *(duration)* Dauer ['daͻɐ] die <-> *no pl* ◊ *für die Dauer von drei Tagen* in/for the long term langfristig ['laŋfrɪstɪç] ◊ *eine langfristige Investition* ♦ *langfristig denken* in/for the medium term mittelfristig ['mɪtl̩frɪstɪç] *no comp/superl* in/for the short term kurzfristig ['kʊˑtsfrɪstɪç] **4.** *(one of two parts of the year: in school)* Halbjahr ['halpjaːˑ] das <–(e)s, –e> during term time während der Schulzeit; *(at college, university)* Semester [ze'mɛstɐ] das <-s, –> during term time während des Semesters; *(one of three parts of the year)* Trimester [tri'mɛstɐ] das <–s, –> **5.** term *(of/in office)* Amtszeit ['amtstsaet] die <-, –en> ◊ *Ihre zweijährige Amtszeit läuft bald ab.* **6.** *(prison/jail)* term Haftstrafe ['haftˌʃtraːfə] die <-, –n> ◊ *eine einjährige Haftstrafe verbüßen* **7.** FIN *(period of validity)* Laufzeit ['laͻftsaet] die <-, –en> ◊ *Der Kredit hat eine Laufzeit von 10 Jahren.*; *(of a payment)* Frist [frɪst] die <-, –en> ◊ *Für die Rückzahlung hat man eine Frist von zwei Monaten.*; *(end of the period)* Termin [tɛˑ'miːn] der <–s, –e> ◊ *etw. vor dem fälligen Termin zahlen* **8.** *(of a parliament, court etc.)* Sitzungsperiode ['zɪtsʊŋspeˌrioːdə] die <-, –n> **9.** carry a baby to (full) term ein Kind austragen [aen 'kɪnt ˌaͻstraːgn̩] <trägt aus, trug aus, hat ausgetragen> ◊ *Sie trug das Kind aus.* **10.** *(conditions)* terms Bedingungen [bə'dɪŋʊŋən] die <-> *pl* ◊ *Welche Bedingungen stellen die Erpresser?* on the terms that ... unter der Bedingung, dass ...; *(in business)* Konditionen [kͻndi'tsioːnən] die <-> *pl* ◊ *günstige Konditionen aushandeln* terms of delivery Lieferkonditionen ['liːfɐkͻndiˌtsioːnən] terms of service/use Benutzungsbedingungen [bə'nʊtsʊŋsbəˌdɪŋʊŋən] ⊚ in general terms pauschal on your own terms **1.** *(on sb's conditions)* zu den eigenen Bedingungen **2.** *(according to sb's preferences)* nach deinen/Ihren eigenen Wünschen come to terms with sth *(accept)* sich mit etw. abfinden come to terms (with sb) *(find agreement)* sich (mit jdm) einigen in sb's terms nach jds Verständnis in practical/economical terms in praktischer/wirtschaftlicher Hinsicht in terms of sth hinsichtlich ... gen ◊ *hin-*

sichtlich des Layouts

term² verb term sb/sth sth jdn/etw. als etw. bezeichnen [als ... bə'tsaeçnən] <bezeichnet, bezeichnete, hat bezeichnet> ◊ *jdn als großen Künstler bezeichnen* ♦ *jds Lage als verzweifelt bezeichnen*

terminal¹ noun **1.** *(last station, stop)* Endstation ['ɛntʃtaˌtsioːn] die <-, –en> ◊ *an der Endstation ankommen*; *(railway station)* Endbahnhof ['ɛntbaˌnhoːf] der <–(e)s, Endbahnhöfe>; *(for a ferry)* Anlegestelle ['anleˌgaʃtelə] die <-, –n> **2.** *(airport, computer)* Terminal ['tœˑminl̩] das <-s, –s> ◊ *Von welchem Terminal fliegen wir ab?* ♦ *eine EDV-Anlage mit fünf Terminals* **3.** *(for electricity)* Anschluss ['anʃlʊs] der <–es, Anschlüsse>

terminal² adj **1.** *(disease)* unheilbar ['ʊnhaelbaːˑ] *no comp/superl* ◊ *eine unheilbare Krankheit*; *(cancer)* im Endstadium [ɪm 'ɛntʃtaˌdiͻm] ◊ *Sie hat Krebs im Endstadium.* **2.** *(patient)* todkrank ['toːt'kraŋk] *no comp/superl* ◊ *ein todkranker Patient* **3.** *(case)* hoffnungslos ['hͻfnͻŋsloːs] <hoffnungsloser, am hoffnungslosesten> ◊ *ein hoffnungsloser Fall von Kleptomanie*; *(decline)* unaufhaltsam ['ʊnˌaͻfhaltzaːm] ◊ *der unaufhaltsame Niedergang einer Industrie* **4.** *(boredom, jealousy)* tödlich ['tøˑtlɪç] *(hum)* ◊ *deine tödliche Eifersucht*

terminate verb **1.** *(bring to an end)* beenden [bə'ɛndn̩] <beendet, beendete, hat beendet> ◊ *Wann wird das Projekt beendet?*; *(prematurely)* abbrechen ['apbreçn̩] <bricht ab, brach ab, hat abgebrochen> ◊ *eine Schwangerschaft abbrechen* **2.** *(a subscription, contract)* kündigen ['kʏndɪgn̩] +haben terminate sb's tenancy jdm kündigen ◊ *Mein Vermieter hat mir gekündigt.* **3.** *(reach an end)* enden ['ɛndn̩] <endet, endete, hat geendet> ◊ *Wo endet die Buslinie?* ♦ *Die Schwangerschaft endete mit einer Fehlgeburt.*

termination noun **1.** *(conclusion)* Abschluss ['apʃlʊs] der <–es, Abschlüsse> ◊ *die Verhandlungen zu einem guten Abschluss bringen*; *(premature)* Abbruch ['apbrͻx] der <–(e)s, Abbrüche> ◊ *Der Streit führte zum Abbruch der Verhandlungen.* **2.** *(of a contract, of employment)* Kündigung ['kʏndɪgʊŋ] die <-, –en> ◊ *die Kündigung eines Arbeitsverhältnisses*

terminology noun Fachsprache ['faxʃpraːxə] die <-, –n>

terrace noun *(outside a house, on a slope)* Terrasse [tɛ'rasə] die <-, –n> ◊ *Sie lag im Liegestuhl auf der Terrasse.* ♦ *Reis auf bewässerten Terrassen anbauen*

terraced house noun Reihenhaus ['raenhaͻs] das <–es, Reihenhäuser> ◊ *in einem Reihenhaus wohnen*

terrain noun Gelände [gə'lɛndə] das <-s, –> ◊ *ein felsiges Gelände*

terrible(-ibly) adj, adv schrecklich ['ʃreklɪç] ◊ *schreckliche Angst/Schmerzen* ♦ *Ich finde es schrecklich, dass er mir nicht glaubt.* ♦ *Ich würde schrecklich gern mitkommen.* ♦ *sich schrecklich ärgern*

terrific(ally) adj, adv **1.** *(very good)* fantastisch [fan'tastɪʃ] ◊ *fantastisches Glück haben* ♦ *Das Wetter war fantastisch!* ♦ *fantastisch aussehen* **2.** *(a lot of, very)* unheimlich ['ʊnhaemlɪç] *when used as an adj, only before ns (fam)* ◊ *unheimlichen Durst haben* ♦ *ein unheimlich spannendes Buch*

terrify verb terrify sb jdm Angst machen ['aŋst maxn̩] +haben ◊ *Die Vorstellung machte mir große Angst.*

territorial adj territorial [tɛritoˑ'rjaːl] *no comp/superl, only before ns* ◊ *territoriale Ansprüche erheben* terri-

torial waters Hoheitsgewässer ['hoːhaɛtsgəvɛsɐ] die <–> pl

◉ be very territorial ein ausgeprägtes Revierverhalten haben

territory [noun] 1. (of a country) Hoheitsgebiet ['hoːhaɛtsgəbiːt] das <–(e)s, –e> occupied territory besetztes Gebiet [bəˌzɛtstəs gəˈbiːt] on German territory auf deutschem Boden [aɔf ˌdɔɪ̯tʃm̩ ˈboːdn̩] 2. (of an animal) Revier [reˈviːɐ̯] das <–s, –e> (also hum) ◊ Das Wolfsrudel verteidigte sein Revier. ♦ Die Küche ist sein Revier. 3. (topographical, of knowledge) Terrain [tɛˈrɛŋ] das <–s, –s> ◊ unwegsames Terrain ♦ sich auf unbekanntem Terrain befinden; (administrative, of activity) Bereich [bəˈraɛ̯ç] der <–(e)s, –e> ◊ Für welchen Bereich sind Sie zuständig?

terror [noun] 1. (feeling) Angst [aŋst] die <–> often preceded by an adj, no pl flee in terror in panischer Angst flüchten absolute/pure/sheer terror schreckliche Angst strike terror into sb jdn in Angst und Schrecken versetzen 2. (person, cause of fear) Schrecken ['ʃrɛkn̩] der <–s, –> (also fam) ◊ die Schrecken des Krieges ♦ Das Kind war der Schrecken der Schule. hold no terrors for sb jdn nicht schrecken [ˌnɪçt ˈʃrɛkn̩] +haben 3. (politically motivated violence) Terror ['tɛroːɐ̯] der <–s> no pl ◊ der Kampf gegen den internationalen Terror

terrorism [noun] Terrorismus [tɛroˈrɪsmʊs] der <–> no pl

terrorist [noun] Terrorist [tɛroˈrɪst] der <–en, –en> ♀Terroristin [tɛroˈrɪstɪn] die <–, –nen>

test¹ [noun] 1. (in school) Arbeit [aˈbaɛ̯t] die <–, –en> ◊ Wir schreiben in Chemie eine Arbeit.; (at college, university, for a driver's licence) Prüfung ['pryːfʊŋ] die <–, –en> ◊ eine Prüfung in Soziologie ♦ die praktische/theoretische Prüfung für den Motorradführerschein bestehen; (short and informal) Test [tɛst] der <–s, –s> vocabulary test Vokabeltest [voˈkaːbl̩tɛst] 2. (to find out a value, experiment) Test [tɛst] der <–s, –s> ◊ Welcher IQ hat sich bei dem Test ergeben? a test for sth ein Test auf etw. [acc] ◊ ein Test auf Zucker im Urin run a test einen Test durchführen

◉ stand the test of time sich bewähren put sth to the test etw. auf die Probe stellen

test² [verb] 1. (knowledge, quality) prüfen ['pryːfn̩] +haben ◊ Werden wir über dieses Thema geprüft? ♦ jdn mündlich/schriftlich prüfen ♦ Prüfen Sie, ob das Wasser heiß genug ist. 2. (examine a person, an organ or its functions) untersuchen [ʊntɐˈzuːxn̩] <untersucht, untersuchte, hat untersucht> ◊ Du solltest dir die Ohren untersuchen lassen. ♦ auf Diabetes untersucht werden sb tests negative/positive (for sth) jds Test (auf etw. [acc]) ist negativ/positiv 3. (new products) testen ['tɛstn̩] <testet, testete, hat getestet> ◊ etw. testen, bevor es auf den Markt kommt ♦ Das Medikament wurde an Tieren getestet 4. (put strain on) auf die Probe stellen [aɔf diː ˈproːbə ʃtɛlən] +haben severely test auf eine harte Probe stellen

testament [noun] 1. (of a person, in the Bible) testament, Testament Testament [tɛstaˈmɛnt] das <–(e)s, –e> ◊ sein Testament machen ♦ das Alte Testament 2. (evidence, proof) testament to sth Zeugnis von etw. ['tsɔɡknɪs fɔn] das <–ses, –se> (lofty) ◊ Sein Leben legt Zeugnis von seinem tiefen

Glauben ab.

testimony [noun] Zeugnis ['tsɔɡknɪs] das <–ses, –se> (lofty) ◊ ein eindrucksvolles Zeugnis ihrer Großzügigkeit

testing [noun] 1. (of students, qualities) Prüfen ['pryːfn̩] das <–s> no pl ◊ ein Gerät zum Prüfen des Reifendrucks 2. (preceded by an attribute) ... testing ...tests [tɛsts] die <–> pl blood testing Bluttests ['bluːttɛsts] nuclear testing Atomtests [aˈtoːmtɛsts]

text [noun] Text [tɛkst] der <–(e)s, –e> ◊ einen Text verfassen/lesen ♦ der Text der Regierungserklärung set text Pflichtlektüre ['pflɪçtlɛkˌtyːrə] die <–, –n> most sing

textbook [noun] Lehrbuch ['leːɡbuːx] das <–(e)s, Lehrbücher> ◊ ein mathematisches Lehrbuch ♦ ein Lehrbuch der Biologie/über Pflanzen

textile [noun] 1. (fabric) Textilie [tɛksˈtiːljə] die <–, –n> most pl ◊ synthetische Textilien 2. (industry) textiles Textilindustrie [tɛksˈtiːlʔɪndʊsˌtriː] die <–> most sing textile ... Textil... [tɛksˈtiːl] textile museum Textilmuseum [tɛksˈtiːlmuˌzeːʊm] das <–s, –en>

texture [noun] 1. (surface of sth) Oberfläche ['oːbɐflɛçə] die <–, –n> ◊ eine glatte/raue Oberfläche haben; (consistency of sth) Beschaffenheit [bəˈʃafn̩haɛ̯t] die <–> no pl ◊ Holz ist von härterer Beschaffenheit als Pappe.; (of fabric) Struktur [ʃtrʊkˈtuːɐ̯] die <–, –en> ◊ die feine Struktur der Seide 2. (structure, system) Gefüge [gəˈfyːgə] das <–s, –> ◊ Die Gesellschaft ist ein komplexes Gefüge.

Thai [noun] 1. Thai [taɛ̯] der <–(s), –(s)> ♀Thai [taɛ̯] die <–, –(s)> → German¹ German¹ 2. Thailändisch ['taɛ̯lɛndɪʃ] das <–(s)> no pl → German¹ German¹ 2.

Thames [noun] the Thames Themse [diː ˈtɛmzə] <–> no pl

than [conjunc] als [als] ◊ Heute ist es kälter als gestern. ♦ weniger als zwei Minuten

thank [verb] danken ['daŋkn̩] +haben ◊ Sie dankte ihm für die Blumen. thank sb for doing sth jdm dafür danken, dass er etw. getan hat ◊ Ich danke Ihnen dafür, dass Sie so schnell gehandelt haben. have sb to thank for sth jdm etw. verdanken [fɛɐ̯ˈdaŋkn̩] <verdankt, verdankte, hat verdankt>

◉ I'll thank you to ... Ich wäre dir/Ihnen sehr dankbar, wenn ... ◊ Ich wäre dir sehr dankbar, wenn du mich in Ruhe lassen könntest. sb will not thank you for sth jd wird von etw. wenig angetan sein ◊ Ihre Firma wird von diesem Fehlschlag wenig angetan sein.

thankful [adj] dankbar ['daŋkbaːɐ̯] ◊ Ich bin dir sehr dankbar. ♦ ein dankbares Herz

thanks¹ [noun] Dank [daŋk] der <–(e)s> no pl ◊ Zum Dank überreichte er ihr einen Blumenstrauß. many thanks vielen Dank with thanks mit Dank

◉ no thanks to sb ohne jds Hilfe thanks to ... dank ... [gen] ◊ Dank seines Einsatzes fand er schnell einen neuen Job.

thanks² [interj] Danke ['daŋkə] ◊ Danke schön, das war sehr nett von dir. ♦ „Noch ein Glas?" – „Nein, danke!" thanks a lot vielen Dank [fiːlən ˈdaŋk]

thank you [interj] danke ['daŋkə] ◊ Danke für die schönen Blumen! ♦ „Noch ein Stück Kuchen?" – „Nein, danke!"

that¹ [adv] so [zoː] ◊ So lange kann ich nicht warten. ♦ Egal, es war nicht so wichtig.

that² [det] 1. (this, the one indicated) dieser ['diːzɐ]

diese ['diːzə] dieses ['diːzəs] ◊ *Dieser Junge ist mein Sohn.* ✦ *Diese Frage zu beantworten ist nicht leicht.* ✦ *Dieses Formular dürfen Sie behalten.* ✦ *Von diesen Vorfällen habe ich nichts gewusst.* **2.** *(the other, the one furthest away, in the past or future)* jener ['jeːnɐ] jene ['jeːnə] jenes ['jeːnəs] ◊ *Genau an jenem Tag hat er ihr einen Antrag gemacht.* ✦ *diese oder jene Formulierung* ✦ *Nein, ich meine nicht dieses, sondern jenes Bild.* **3.** *(the one just mentioned, with the stated feature)* der [deːɐ̯] die [diː] das [das] ◊ *Der Tag passt mir gar nicht.* ✦ *Wer war die Frau am Telefon?* ✦ *Das Motorrad muss zum TÜV.*

that³ ⟨demonstr pron⟩ **1.** *(sth/sb indicated or just mentioned)* das [das] ◊ *Ist das Brokkoli?* ✦ *Das da drüben ist Petra.* ✦ *Ich mag Kuchen, Plätzchen, Kekse und all das.* **of that** davon [da'fɔn] ◊ *Ich habe jetzt genug davon!* **2.** that (one) der [deːɐ̯] die [diː] das [das] ◊ *Das bier ist ziemlich billig.*; *(the other one)* jener ['jeːnɐ] jene ['jeːnə] jenes ['jeːnəs] ◊ *Ich wollte nicht diesen, sondern jenen.* **3.** *(used when speaking on the telephone)* da [daː] ◊ *Hallo, ist da Lisa Holl?* **4.** *(used to give encouragement)* so [zoː] That's the right thing to do! So ist's recht! That's a good girl/ boy! So ist's brav! ⟨rel pron⟩ **1.** *(referring to sb/sth mentioned in the previous clause)* der [deːɐ̯] die [diː] das [das] ◊ *dieser Sturm, der alles zerstörte* ✦ *eine Geschichte, die sehr spannend ist* ✦ *das Kind, das krank war* **2.** *(which)* was [vas] ◊ *Das ist alles, was man braucht.*

⊛ **that is** also ◊ *Alle meine Geschwister, also Anne, Lukas und Kerstin, kamen.* **that is** to say sprich ◊ *Die große Mehrheit, sprich 82 Prozent, war dafür.* **that is/that's why** darum ◊ *Ich bin müde, darum gehe ich jetzt schlafen.* **that's it,** **that does it** jetzt reicht's *(fam)* **that is that** damit hat sich's *(fam)* **at that** obendrein ◊ *Er ist langsam und faul obendrein.* **in that** insofern ◊ *Die Lage ist ziemlich aussichtslos; insofern gebe ich Ihnen Recht.*

that⁴ ⟨conjunc⟩ **1.** *(connecting two clauses)* dass [das] ◊ *Ist es wahr, dass er krank ist?* ✦ *Es freut mich, dass es dir gut geht.* **2.** *(in order that)* damit [da'mɪt] ◊ *Lern fleißig, damit deine Noten besser werden.* **3.** *(expressing a strong wish)* wenn doch nur ['vɛn dɔx nuːɐ̯] Oh that he were here! Ach wenn er doch nur hier wäre!; *(expressing strong regret)* warum nur [va'ʀʊm nuːɐ̯] That she should die so young! Warum musste sie nur so jung sterben?

thaw ⟨verb⟩ **1.** *(snow, ice)* schmelzen ['ʃmɛltsn̩] ⟨schmilzt, schmolz, hat/ist geschmolzen⟩ *transitive use +haben/intransitive use +sein* ◊ *Der Schnee schmilzt.* ✦ *Sie schmolzen Eis, um Wasser zu haben.* **2.** *(food, lake, person)* auftauen ['aʊftaʊ̯ən] *transitive use +haben/intransitive use +sein* ◊ *ein eingefrorenes Hähnchen auftauen* ✦ *Der See taut langsam wieder auf.* ✦ *Nach zwei Glas Wein taute er auf.* **3.** *(weather)* tauen ['taʊ̯ən] *+haben* the weather thaws, it is thawing es taut

the ⟨det⟩ **1.** der [deːɐ̯] die [diː] das [das] ◊ *der Nachbar* ✦ *die Nachbarin* ✦ *das Auto* ✦ *die Kinder* ✦ *Lasst das Streiten!* ✦ *das Blau des Himmels* ✦ *Sie versucht das Unmögliche.* **2.** the ..., the ... je ..., umso ... [jeː ... ʊmzoː] *+comp* ◊ *Je weniger Geld man ausgibt, umso mehr kann man sparen.*

theatre, theater ⟨noun⟩ **1.** *(for plays)* Theater [te'aːtɐ] das ⟨-s, -⟩ ◊ *Er ist Schauspieler am Theater.* ✦ *Wir gehen heute ins Theater.* **2.** *(for*

medical operations) Operationssaal [opəʀa'tsi̯oːnsaːl] der ⟨-(e)s, Operationssäle⟩ ◊ *Der Patient ist im Operationssaal.* **3.** *(in the US: cinema)* Kino ['kiːnoː] das ⟨-s, -s⟩ ◊ *Lass uns ins Kino gehen!*

⊛ **the theatre of operations** das Einsatzgebiet **the theatre of war** der Kriegsschauplatz

theft ⟨noun⟩ Diebstahl ['diːpʃtaːl] der ⟨-(e)s, Diebstähle⟩ ◊ *Er wurde wegen Diebstahls verurteilt.*

their ⟨det⟩ ihr [iːɐ̯] ihre ['iːʀə] ◊ *Kinder und ihre Mütter* ✦ *Da sind Lou und Tom in ihrem neuen Auto.* → ihr²2

theirs ⟨poss pron⟩ ihrer ['iːʀɐ] ihre ['iːʀə] ihres ['iːʀəs] ◊ *Sie haben unser Angebot ihrem vorgezogen.* ✦ *Unsere Meinung ist genauso wichtig wie ihre.* ✦ *„Ist das euer Auto?" — „Nein, ihres."* → ihrer

⊛ **of theirs** von ihnen ◊ *ein paar Freunde von ihnen*

them ⟨pers pron⟩ *(acc)* sie [ziː] ◊ *Karl und Lea sind aus dem Urlaub zurück. Ich rufe sie morgen an.*; *(dat)* ihnen ['iːnən] ◊ *Das sind meine Eltern; ich telefoniere oft mit ihnen.*

theme ⟨noun⟩ *(of a story, film, piece of music etc.)* Thema ['teːmaː] das ⟨-s, Themen⟩ ◊ *das Thema des ersten Satzes der Sinfonie*

themselves ⟨ref pron⟩ **1.** *(referring to pl nouns or pronouns)* sich [zɪç] ◊ *Die Schüler/Sie bereiteten sich gründlich auf den Test vor.*; *(without anybody else)* selbst [zɛlpst] ◊ *Sie haben das ganze Haus selbst gebaut.* Tonight they are not quite themselves. Heute Abend sind sie nicht ganz sie selbst. After a good sleep they felt more themselves again. Nach einem guten Schlaf ging es ihnen wieder besser. **2.** *(them, acc)* sie [ziː] ◊ *Er wollte alles über sie und ihre Freunde wissen.*; *(dat)* ihnen ['iːnən] ◊ *Alle außer ihnen waren gekommen.*

⊛ **(all) by themselves** *(ganz)* allein ◊ *Die Kinder waren ganz allein in der Wohnung.* **(all) to themselves 1.** *(referring to time)* für sich ◊ *Den Abend haben sie ganz für sich.* **2.** *(referring to a place)* *(ganz)* für sich allein ◊ *Sie hatten das Kino ganz für sich allein.*

then¹ ⟨adj⟩ damalig ['daːmaːlɪç] *no comp/superl, only before ns* ◊ *seine damalige Frau*

then² ⟨adv⟩ **1.** *(long ago)* damals ['daːmaːls] ◊ *Damals kannte ich ihn noch nicht.*; *(at that moment in the past)* da [daː] ◊ *Da fing er plötzlich an zu weinen.* ✦ *Da bremste der Fahrer plötzlich.* **2.** *(at that time in the future)* dann [dan] ◊ *Am Mittwoch kann ich. Wir treffen uns also dann.* **3.** *(after that, as a result of that, in that case)* dann [dan] ◊ *Wir gingen erst ins Kino und dann noch in die Kneipe.* ✦ *Gehen Sie hier geradeaus; erst kommt die Kirche, dann das Museum.* ✦ *Wenn sie das nicht versteht, dann musst du es ihr erklären.* ✦ *Dann kündige ich lieber gleich selbst.* **4.** *(drawing a conclusion, expressing agreement)* also ['alzoː] ◊ *Du kennst das also schon?* ✦ *Er hatte sich also geirrt.* now/right/okay then also gut ◊ *Also gut, machen wir es so.*

⊛ **before then** vorher ◊ *Das Geschäft schließt um sechs. Kannst du vorher noch einkaufen?* **by then** zu dieser Zeit seitdem then seitdem until then bis dahin

theology ⟨noun⟩ Theologie [teoloˈgiː] die ⟨-⟩ *no pl* ◊ *katholische Theologie studieren*

theoretical(ly) ⟨adj, adv⟩ theoretisch [teoˈʀeːtɪʃ] ◊ *ein theoretisches Problem* ✦ *Mir ist das zu theoretisch.* ✦

theoretisch möglich

theorist (noun) Theoretiker [teo're:tɪkɐ] der <-s, -> ♀Theoretikerin [teo're:tɪkərɪn] die <-, -nen> ◊ *Stalin als Theoretiker des Marxismus-Leninismus ♦ eine brilliante Theoretikerin*

theory (noun) Theorie [teo'ri:] die <-, -n> ◊ „*Warum tut er so etwas?" – „Ich habe da eine Theorie: ..."♦ die Integration in Theorie und Praxis ♦ die Theorie der dynamischen Systeme* in theory *theoretisch* [teo're:tɪʃ] ◊ *Theoretisch kann er das schaffen.*

therapist (noun) Therapeut [tera'pɔʏt] der <-en, –en> ♀Therapeutin [tera'pɔʏtɪn] die <-, -nen> ◊ *einen Therapeuten aufsuchen ♦ Sie ist Therapeutin für Verhaltenstherapie.*

therapy (noun) **1.** *(medical)* Behandlung [bə'handlʊŋ] die <-, –en> ◊ *eine zahnärztliche/homöopathische Behandlung ♦ die Behandlung von Herzkranken* **2.** *(psychological)* Therapie [tera'pi:] die <-, -n> ◊ *Er meint eine Therapie.*

there¹ (adv) **1.** *(in that place)* dort [dɔˀt] ◊ *Warst du schon einmal dort? ♦ Er ging ins Wohnzimmer und deckte dort den Tisch. ♦ Siehst du diesen Baum dort? ♦ Sie kommt auch von dort.* near there *dort in der Nähe* right there *dort* It's right there in front of you. *Es ist genau vor deiner Nase.* over there *dort drüben* up there *dort oben* **2.** *(to that place)* dorthin ['dɔˀthɪn] ◊ *Wie gelangt man dorthin? ♦ Auf dem Weg dorthin traf ich zwei alte Freunde.* there and back *dorthin und zurück* Look there! *Schau mal!* **3.** *(available, present, referring to something that was said previously, when handing sth over)* da [da:] ◊ *Es ist leider kein Geld mehr da. ♦ Es war noch niemand von den anderen Gästen da. ♦ Ist dein Vater da? ♦ Da kann ich Ihnen nur zustimmen. ♦ Da hast du das Geld! ♦ Ich bin immer für dich da.* You've got me there. *Das weiß ich auch nicht.* There she goes again! *Jetzt macht sie es schon wieder!* There's ... for you! *Und das soll nun ... sein!* ☛ there and then *auf der Stelle* there you are *bitte schön* be there *es geschafft haben* ◊ *Ich glaube, jetzt habe ich es geschafft.* get there *es fast geschafft haben* ◊ *Einen Augenblick noch, ich habe es fast geschafft.* you there *hallo, Sie/du da* hello there *hallo*

there² (pron) *(impersonal)* es [ɛs] ◊ *Es lebte einmal ein König.* There comes a time in everyone's life when ... *Für jeden kommt einmal die Zeit, wo ...* there is/are *es gibt* [ɛs 'gi:pt] <gibt, gab, hat gegeben> ◊ *Gibt es noch Fragen? ♦ Hier gibt es kein Kino. ♦ Gleich gibt es Ärger.* There was an accident. *Es hat einen Unfall gegeben.*

> 'There is/there are' is often not translated into German. The English object becomes the subject of the German sentence: There's milk in the fridge. — *Im Kühlschrank ist Milch.*; There are 24 teams competing in the tournament. — *An dem Turnier nehmen 24 Mannschaften teil.* When translating from English to German, the impersonal pronoun is often replaced by a personal pronoun: There isn't much time left. — *Ich habe/Du hast/Sie haben nicht mehr viel Zeit.*

there³ (interj) so [zo:] ◊ *So, das haben wir gut gemacht! ♦ So, jetzt kleben wir ein Pflaster drauf.*; *(when proved right)* there (you are) *na also*

[na 'alzo:] ◊ *Na also, ich habe es dir doch gleich gesagt!* ☛ so there *ätsch* *(kidsp)* there, there *ist ja gut*

thereafter (adv) danach [da'na:x] ◊ *Mit 80 ging sie in ein Altersheim und starb bald danach.*

thereby (adv) dadurch [da'dʊrç] ◊ *Während meines Studiums machte ich ein Praktikum; dadurch lernte ich das Berufsleben kennen.*

therefore (adv) *(expressing a reason)* deshalb ['dɛshalp] ◊ *Sie möchte Menschen helfen und will deshalb Ärztin werden. ♦ Ich hatte Kopfweh; deshalb legte ich mich hin.*; *(expressing a consequence)* also ['alzo:] ◊ *Sie ist 18, also kann sie wählen.*

thermometer (noun) Thermometer [tɛˀmo'me:tɐ] das <-s, -> ◊ *Das Thermometer ist auf unter null Grad gesunken. ♦ Das Thermometer stand auf 25°C.*

these → this², this³

thesis (noun) **1.** *(for a PhD)* Doktorarbeit ['dɔkto:ɐ̯|a'baɛt] die <-, -en>; *(for a diploma)* Diplomarbeit [di'plo:m|a'baɛt] die <-, -en> ◊ *Sie hat ihre Diplomarbeit über Kant geschrieben.* **2.** *(idea, opinion)* These ['te:zə] die <-, -n> ◊ *eine These aufstellen* sb's thesis that *jds These, dass*

they (pers pron) **1.** *(a group of people or things)* sie [zi:] ◊ *Jule und Andi haben eine Karte geschrieben; sie sind auf Gomera. ♦ Sie erwischten ihn beim Fahren ohne Gurt.* → sie² **2.** *(referring back to 'everyone', 'someone', etc.)* er [e:ɐ̯] sie [zi:] ◊ *Jeder kann sich aussuchen, was er möchte. ♦ Jede kann geben, wann sie will.* → er, sie¹ **3.** *(people in general)* man [man] ◊ *Vor fünf Jahren hat man die Schule renoviert.*

thick¹ (adj) **1.** *(object, material, liquid)* dick [dɪk] ◊ *ein dicker Pullover ♦ eine dicke Scheibe Wurst ♦ ein acht Millimeter dickes Kabel ♦ eine dicke Suppe ♦ Das Brett ist zehn Zentimeter dick.* **2.** *(fur, forest, fog)* dicht [dɪçt] <dichter, am dichtesten> ◊ *das dichte Fell des Hundes ♦ ein dichter Tannenwald ♦ Dichter Nebel lag über der Stadt.*; *(hair)* voll [fɔl] ◊ *volle Locken ♦ Dein Haar ist voller geworden.* **3.** *(place, air)* thick with *voller* ['fɔlɐ] invariable ◊ *Der Marktplatz war voller Touristen. ♦ Die Luft war voller Rauch.* **4.** *(voice)* with heiser vor ['haɛzɐ fo:ɐ̯] ◊ *Ihre Stimme war vor Tränen ganz heiser.* **5.** *(accent)* stark [ʃtaˀk] <stärker, am stärksten> ◊ *Sie spricht mit einem starken französischen Akzent. ♦ Sein Akzent ist immer noch ziemlich stark.* **6.** *(stupid)* beschränkt [bə'ʃrɛŋkt] <beschränkter, am beschränktesten> *(fam, pej)* ◊ *Er ist ein bisschen beschränkt und kapiert nur langsam.* **7.** thick with sb *mit jdm dick befreundet* [mɪt ... dɪk bə'frɔɛndət] *(fam)* ◊ *Sophia war mit Anna dick befreundet.*

thick² (adv) dick [dɪk] ◊ *Das Brot war dick geschnitten.* ☛ thick and fast *in rauen Mengen* lay it on thick *dick auftragen*

thickly (adv) **1.** *(slice, spread)* dick [dɪk] The floor was thickly carpeted. *Der Boden war mit einem dicken Teppich belegt.* **2.** *(grow, forested, inhabited)* dicht [dɪçt] <dichter, am dichtesten> ◊ *Der Landstrich ist noch dicht bewaldet. ♦ Das Haar des Babys wächst schon sehr dicht. ♦ ein dicht besiedeltes Land* The snow was falling thickly. *Es fiel dichter Schnee.* **3.** *(say)* heiser ['haɛzɐ] ◊ „*Ich bin müde", sagte er heiser.* **4.** thickly accented *mit einem starken Akzent* [mɪt ˈænəm ʃtaˀkŋ̩ ak'tsɛnt] ◊ *Sie sprach*

Englisch mit einem starken Akzent.

thickness [noun] **1.** *(of an object)* Dicke ['dɪkə] die <–, –n> ◊ *die Dicke des Pullovers; (of a wall, board, rope)* Stärke ['ʃtɛ'kə] die <–, –n> ◊ *Bretter in verschiedenen Stärken* **2.** *(of hair, fur, a forest)* Dichte ['dɪçtə] die <–> no pl ◊ *die Dichte des Pelzes* **3.** *(layer)* Schicht [ʃɪçt] die <–, –en> three thicknesses of clothes drei Schichten Kleidung ◊ *Sie hatte drei Schichten Kleidung an und fror immer noch.*

thief [noun] Dieb [diːp] der <–(e)s, –e> ♀Diebin ['diːbɪn] die <–, –nen> ◊ *Der Dieb wurde gefasst.* ✦ *Haltet den Dieb!*
◉ thick as thieves dicke Freunde

thigh [noun] **1.** *(part of the leg)* Oberschenkel ['oːbəʃɛŋkḷ] der <–s, –> ◊ *Muskelkater in den Oberschenkeln haben* ✦ *Ich habe mir den Oberschenkel gebrochen.* **2.** *(as food)* Schenkel ['ʃɛŋkḷ] der <–s, –>

thin [adj] **1.** *(object, material, liquid, person, voice, hair, air)* dünn [dʏn] ◊ *etw. in dünne Scheiben schneiden* ✦ *eine dünne Suppe* ✦ *Ihre Schwester ist groß und dünn.* ✦ *Das Fell der Katze ist dünn geworden.* ✦ *ein dünnes Stimmchen* by a thin margin knapp [knap] ◊ *Sie haben nur knapp gewonnen.* **2.** *(nose, mouth)* schmal [ʃmaːl] ◊ *ihre schmalen Lippen* ✦ *Seine Nase war lang und schmal.* **3.** *(too slim)* mager ['maːɡɐ] ◊ *Sie ist furchtbar mager geworden.* ✦ *die mageren Arme des Kindes* **4.** *(explanation, argument, smile)* schwach [ʃvax] <schwächer, am schwächsten> ◊ *ein schwaches Lächeln* ✦ *Das Argument ist ja wirklich schwach.*

thing [noun] **1.** *(object, person, animal, action, activity, piece of information)* Ding [dɪŋ] das <–(e)s, –e> ◊ *Computerzubehör und ähnliche Dinge* ✦ *Auf dem Dachboden fand sie viele alte/schöne Dinge.* ✦ *So ein Handy ist schon ein tolles Ding.* ✦ *Das arme Ding hat wohl Hunger.* ✦ *Ich muss noch ein paar Dinge erledigen.* ✦ *Ich erfuhr von ihr interessante Dinge.* in all things in allen Dingen The first thing I want is … Als Erstes will ich … do the right/same thing es richtig/genauso machen [ɛs 'rɪçtɪç/ɡə'naozo: maxn̩] +haben do your own thing machen, was man will ['maxn̩ vas man 'vɪl] +haben have things both ways beides auf einmal wollen [baedəs aof 'aenma:l volən] <will, wollte, hat gewollt> be a thing of the past der Vergangenheit angehören [deːɐ̯ fɛ'ɡaŋənhaet angəhøːrən] <gehört an, gehörte an, hat angehört> not say a thing nichts sagen [ˌnɪçts 'zaːɡn̩] +haben **2.** *(belongings)* things Sachen ['zaxn̩] die <–> pl ◊ *Er hat seine Sachen in der ganzen Wohnung verteilt.* ✦ *seine Sachen in den Koffer packen* **3.** *(object you do not like or know)* Ding [dɪŋ] das <–(e)s, –er> *(fam, pej)* ◊ *Wo gibt es solche Dinger zu kaufen?* ✦ *Warum funktioniert dieses blöde Ding nicht?* **4.** *(situation, event, aspect)* Sache ['zaxə] die <–, –n> ◊ *Er kann die ganze Sache einfach nicht vergessen.* It's been one thing after another. Es gab ein Problem nach dem anderen. All good things come to an end. Alles muss einmal ein Ende haben. a funny/terrible thing etwas Komisches/Schreckliches [ɛtvas 'koːmɪʃəs/'ʃrɛklɪçəs] ◊ *Uns ist gestern etwas Komisches passiert.* the funny thing is … das Lustige daran ist, … [das 'lʊstɪɡə daran ɪst] it's a good thing that es ist gut, dass [ɛs ɪst 'guːt das] that kind of thing so etwas ['zo: ɛtvas] ◊ *Ich mag so etwas*

nicht. and that kind of thing und so weiter [ʊnt zo: 'vaetɐ] ◊ *Sie geht gern wandern, joggen und so weiter.* be onto a good thing gut dran sein [ˌguːt 'dran zaen] +sein ◊ *Als Untermieter bei seiner Tante ist er gut dran.* make a big thing out of sth viel Theater um etw. machen [fiːl te|'aːtɐ ʊm … maxn̩] +haben be one of those things vorkommen können ['foːɡkɔmən kœnən] <kann, konnte, hat können> ◊ *Das kann schon mal vorkommen.* **5.** *(all aspects of a situation)* things die Dinge [diː 'dɪŋə] <–> pl ◊ *Ich sehe die Dinge anders.* ✦ *Er hatte die Dinge im Griff.* as things stand wie die Dinge liegen; *(as a whole)* die Lage [diː 'laːɡə] <–> no pl ◊ *Die Lage verbesserte sich nicht.* How are things? Wie ist die Lage? put things differently die Lage anders darstellen put things right die Lage klarstellen all things considered alles in allem [ˌaləs ɪn 'aləm]
◉ be all things to all people es allen recht machen first thing früh am Morgen last thing vor dem Schlafengehen for one thing zum einen what with one thing and another bei alledem it's a … thing das ist nur was für … there is no such thing as … … gibt es nicht one thing leads to another eins führt zum anderen tell sb a thing or two jdm gründlich die Meinung sagen among other things unter anderem quite the thing modern

think [verb] **1.** *(believe)* glauben ['ɡlaobm̩] +haben ◊ *Ich glaube, dass Hanna morgen Geburtstag hat.* ✦ *Ich habe geglaubt, die Party sei am Samstag.* ✦ *Er glaubt wohl, immer Recht zu haben.* ✦ *Ich glaube, du gehst jetzt besser.* I think so. Ich glaube schon. I don't think so. Ich glaube nicht. sth is thought to man vermutet, dass etw. [man fɛ'muːtət das] <vermutet, vermutete, hat vermutet> ◊ *Man vermutet, dass diese Substanz krebserregend ist.* **2.** *(have an opinion)* think of sb/sth as sth jdn/etw. als etw. ansehen [als … ˌanzeːən] <sieht an, sah an, hat angesehen> ◊ *Sie sah ihn nicht als einen ernsthaften Konkurrenten an.* think sb sth jdn für etw. halten [fyːɐ̯ … haltn̩] <hält, hielt, hat gehalten> ◊ *Ich hielt ihn für einen Spinner.* Who do you think you are? Wofür halten Sie sich/hältst du dich eigentlich? not think much of sb/sth nicht viel von jdm/etw. halten What do you think about …? Was hältst du von …? **3.** *(consider facts carefully)* think *(about sth/sb)* *(über etw./jdn)* nachdenken ['naːxdɛŋkn̩] <denkt nach, dachte nach, hat nachgedacht> ◊ *Denk mal nach! Was hat der Lehrer gesagt?* ✦ *Ich muss über den Vorschlag erst nachdenken.* think of sth sich [dat] etw. einfallen lassen ['aenfalən lasn̩] <lässt, ließ, hat lassen> ◊ *Wir mussten uns eine andere Lösung einfallen lassen.* be thinking of doing sth daran denken, etw. zu tun [daran 'dɛŋkn̩ … tsuː] <denkt, dachte, hat gedacht> ◊ *Ich denke daran, mir einen anderen Job zu suchen.* think for yourself sich [dat] seine eigene Meinung bilden [ˌaeɡənə 'maenʊŋ bɪldn̩] <bildet, bildete, hat gebildet> ◊ *Die Kinder sollen lernen, sich ihre eigene Meinung zu bilden.* **4.** *(remember, consider)* think about an … [acc] denken an … [ˌdɛŋkn̩] <denkt, dachte, hat gedacht> ◊ *Ich habe noch oft an sie/an diesen Tag gedacht.* ✦ *Er denkt nur an sich.* think to do sth daran denken, etw. zu tun sb can't think of sth jdm fällt etw. nicht ein [fɛlt … nɪçt ˌaen] <fällt

ein, fiel ein, ist eingefallen> ◊ *Mir ist gestern meine eigene Telefonnummer nicht eingefallen.* **5.** *(have thoughts, assume)* denken ['dɛŋkŋ] <denkt, dachte, hat gedacht> ◊ *Sie dachten alle das Gleiche.* ✦ *„Das ist mir früher nie aufgefallen", dachte sie.* ✦ *Ich dachte, ich hätte den Brief schon abgeschickt.* ✦ *praktisch/logisch denken* ✦ *Wer hätte das gedacht, dass er einmal so erfolgreich sein würde!* think straight klar denken; *(imagine)* think of, think about sich 〔dat〕 vorstellen ['foːɐ̯ʃtɛlən] +haben ◊ *Stell dir doch einmal vor, wie sie sich dabei fühlt!*
⦿ **think better of sth** sich 〔dat〕 etw. anders überlegen think nothing of doing sth sich 〔dat〕 nichts dabei denken, etw. zu tun think nothing of it *(polite answer)* keine Ursache think twice es sich 〔dat〕 zweimal überlegen not think twice nicht lange überlegen come to think of it wenn ich es mir recht überlege I can't hear myself think bei dem Lärm kann man keinen klaren Gedanken fassen I wasn't thinking das war sehr gedankenlos von mir who would have thought that wer hätte je gedacht, dass you would think man sollte meinen, dass ◊ *Man sollte meinen, dass die Leute aus ihren Fehlern lernen.* don't even think about doing sth lass es dir nicht einfallen, etw. zu tun! I thought as much das habe ich mir schon gedacht
• **think about** 〔phras v〕 think about sb/sth sich mit jdm/einer Sache beschäftigen [mɪt ... bəˈʃɛftɪɡn] <beschäftigt sich, beschäftigte sich, hat sich beschäftigt> ◊ *Sie beschäftigt sich viel mit den Problemen anderer.*
• **think back** 〔phras v〕 think back (to sth) (an etw. 〔acc〕) zurückdenken [ʦuˈrʏkdɛŋkŋ] <denkt zurück, dachte zurück, hat zurückgedacht>
• **think out** 〔phras v〕 think sth out etw. durchdenken [dʊrçˈdɛŋkŋ] <durchdenkt, durchdachte, hat durchdacht> ◊ *die Folgen gut durchdenken*
• **think over** 〔phras v〕 think sth over etw. überdenken [ybɐˈdɛŋkŋ] <überdenkt, überdachte, hat überdacht> ◊ *eine Entscheidung/einen Vorschlag noch einmal überdenken*
• **think through** 〔phras v〕 think sth through etw. durchdenken [dʊrçˈdɛŋkŋ] <durchdenkt, durchdachte, hat durchdacht> ◊ *Hast du alles gut durchdacht?*
• **think up** 〔phras v〕 think sth up sich 〔dat〕 etw. einfallen lassen ['aɛnfalən lasŋ] <lässt, ließ, hat lassen> ◊ *Er hat sich eine gute Ausrede einfallen lassen.*
thinking¹ 〔noun〕 **1.** *(opinion, set of ideas)* thinking (on sth) Meinung (zu etw.) ['maɛnʊŋ] die <-, -en> to my way of thinking meiner Meinung nach current political thinking die heutige politische Meinung the thinking behind sth die Gedanken, die einer Sache 〔dat〕 zugrunde liegen [diː ɡəˈdaŋkŋ diː ... ʦuˈɡrʊndə liːɡn] <liegt, lag, hat gelegen> ◊ *Denken* ['dɛŋkŋ] das <-s> no pl positive thinking positives Denken Good thinking! Gute Idee!; *(the way you react)* Reaktion [reakˈtsɨoːn] die <-, -en> his quick thinking seine schnelle Reaktion
thinking² → **think** 〔adj〕 vernünftig [fɐˈnʏnftɪç] ◊ *jeder vernünftige Mensch*
⦿ **the thinking person's ...** ... für den gebildeten Menschen
thinly 〔adv〕 **1.** *(in a thin layer, with only a few people or things)* dünn [dʏn] ◊ *Teig dünn ausrollen* thinly

spead dünn gesät thinly populated dünn besiedelt **2.** *(hardly)* kaum [kaọm] thinly veiled kaum verborgen
⦿ smile thinly schwach lächeln
third¹ 〔noun〕 **1.** *(fraction)* Drittel ['drɪtl] das <-s, -> → **fourth¹** **1. 2.** *(in a sequence)* Dritte ['drɪtə] der or die or das <-n, -n> most sing → **fourth¹** **2. 3.** *(grade at university, college)* schlechteste Examensnote an britischen und australischen Universitäten, mit der man besteht
third² 〔adj〕 dritte ['drɪtə] <ein dritter ..., eine dritte ..., ein drittes ...> → **fourth²**
thirdly 〔adv〕 drittens ['drɪtns] → **fourthly**
thirst 〔noun〕 Durst [dʊɐ̯st] der <-(e)s> no pl quench your thirst seinen Durst löschen ◊ *Im Festzelt können Sie Ihren Durst löschen.* die of thirst verdursten [fɛˈdʊɐ̯stn] <verdurstet, verdurstete, ist verdurstet> thirst for knowledge Wissensdurst ['vɪsṇsdʊɐ̯st]
thirsty 〔adj〕 **1.** *(person, animal)* durstig ['dʊɐ̯stɪç] ◊ *Die durstigen Kinder stürzten sich auf die Limo.* sth is thirsty work etw. macht durstig ◊ *Gartenarbeit macht durstig.* be thirsty Durst haben ['dʊɐ̯st haːbm̩] +haben ◊ *Er hatte großen Durst.* **2.** *(plant, land)* ausgetrocknet ['aọsɡətrɔknət] ◊ *Sie blickten über das ausgetrocknete Land.* ✦ *Meine Pflanzen sind ganz ausgetrocknet.*
thirteen 〔nmrl〕 dreizehn ['draɛtseːn] → **four²**
thirty 〔nmrl〕 dreißig ['draɛsɪç] → **four²**
this¹ 〔adv〕 so [zoː] ◊ *Das Wasser stand so hoch.* ✦ *Die Kinder hatten schon lange nicht mehr so viel Spaß gehabt.* as good/expensive etc. as this so gut/teuer wie dies hier as cold as this so kalt wie hier
this² 〔det〕 dieser ['diːzɐ] diese ['diːzə] dieses ['diːzəs] ◊ *Dieser Junge ist mein Sohn.* ✦ *Diese Woche ist er in Schottland.* ◊ *Dieses Brot schmeckt sehr gut.* ✦ *Er erzählte ihr von dieser Sache erst gestern.* ✦ *Sie wollen diesen Sommer nach Dänemark fahren.* this morning heute Morgen [ˌhɔɡtə ˈmɔˈɡn] ◊ *Er ist heute Morgen ins Krankenhaus gekommen.* this minute sofort [zoˈfoˈt] ◊ *Hör auf damit, und zwar sofort!* just this minute gerade [ɡəˈraːdə] ◊ *Ich bin gerade nach Hause gekommen.* these diese ◊ *Diese Fotos sind besonders gelungen.* ✦ *Ich nehme diese Äpfel.* I think I like these best. Diese da gefallen mir am besten. these days heute ['hɔɡtə] ◊ *Heute macht man das nicht mehr so.*
this³ 〔demonstr pron〕 **1.** das [das] ◊ *Was ist denn das?* ✦ *Das ist das Buch, das du haben wolltest.* ✦ *Ist das dein erster Flug?* ✦ *Das sind meine Eltern.* this is where hier [hiːɐ̯] ◊ *Hier haben wir früher gewohnt.* this is why deshalb ['dɛshalp] ◊ *Das Haus ist winzig, und deshalb will es niemand kaufen.* before this eher ['eːɐ̯] ◊ *Warum hast du mir das nicht schon eher erzählt?*; *(on the telephone, radio, television)* this is ... hier ist ... [hiːɐ̯ ɪst] ◊ *Hallo, hier ist Julian. Kann ich bitte mit Niko sprechen?* **2.** dieser ['diːzɐ] diese ['diːzə] dieses ['diːzəs] ◊ *Ich habe beide Weine probiert und dieser hier schmeckt mir besser als jener.* ✦ *„Welche Melone möchten Sie denn?" – „Ich hätte gern diese."* ✦ *Ist dieses billiger oder das da drüben?*
thorn 〔noun〕 **1.** *(sharp point)* Dorn [dɔˈn] der <-s, -en> ◊ *Die Rose war voller Dornen.* **2.** *(bush)* Dornenbusch ['dɔˈnənbʊʃ] der <-(e)s, Dornenbüsche>

thorough [adj] gründlich ['grʌntlɪç] ◊ *Der Handwerker war sehr gründlich.* ♦ *eine gründliche Untersuchung* ♦ *gründliche Kenntnisse der Informatik*

thoroughly [adv] **1.** *(totally, completely)* völlig ['fœlɪç] ◊ *Ich stimme Ihnen völlig zu.* ♦ *völlig nass/trocken* thoroughly enjoy sth etw. wirklich genießen [vɪˈklɪç gəˈniːsn] be thoroughly ashamed of yourself sich zutiefst schämen [ʦuːˈtiːfst ˈʃɛːmən] **2.** *(carefully)* gründlich ['grʌntlɪç] ◊ *Sie hat gründlich gearbeitet.* ♦ *Hast du dir das auch gründlich überlegt?*

those → **that²**, **that³**

though¹ [adv] allerdings ['aleˈdɪŋs] ◊ *Ich muss allerdings sagen, dass ich nicht viel Zeit habe.* ♦ *Er war genauso alt, allerdings viel kleiner als ich.*

though² [conjunc] **1.** *(although)* (even) though obwohl [ɔpˈvoːl] ◊ *Obwohl er erst 12 war, konnte keiner ihn schlagen.* poor though they are obwohl sie arm sind ◊ *Obwohl sie arm waren, waren sie glücklich.* **2.** *(but)* aber ['aːbɐ] ◊ *Der Urlaub war schön, aber das Wetter war schlecht.*

thought [noun] **1.** *(in your mind)* Gedanke [gəˈdaŋkə] der <-ns, -n> ◊ *Das ist ein beruhigender Gedanke.* ♦ *Sie hat bereits mit dem Gedanken gespielt, zu kündigen.* ♦ *Ihre Gedanken kreisten um ihren nächsten Urlaub.* ♦ *Die beiden tauschten ihre Gedanken über den Film aus.* the thought strikes sb jdm kommt plötzlich der Gedanke a thought crosses sb's mind jdm geht ein Gedanke durch den Kopf sb's thoughts wander jds Gedanken schweifen ab sb's thoughts race jds Gedanken überschlagen sich not give sb/sth a thought sich [dat] keine Gedanken über jdn/etw. machen deep in thought in Gedanken verloren the thought of sth/sb der Gedanke an etw./jdn thoughts of revenge Rachegedanken ['raxəgədaŋkɳ] pl **2.** *(idea)* Idee [iˈdeː] die <-, -n> a thought comes to sb jd hat eine Idee It's just a thought. Es ist nur so eine Idee. **3.** *(mental effort)* Überlegung [ybɐˈleːgʊŋ] die <-, -en> ◊ *Nach reiflicher/sorgfältiger Überlegung hat er gekündigt.* give sth some thought über etw. [acc] nachdenken [yːbe ... ˌnaːxdɛŋkɳ] <dacht nach, hat nachgedacht> ◊ *Denken Sie darüber nach und rufen Sie mich morgen an.* **4.** *(opinion)* express your thoughts on sth/sb sagen, was man über etw./jdn denkt ['zaːgɳ vas man yːbe ... ˌdɛŋkt] <dachte, dachte, hat gedacht> What are your thoughts? Was denkst du? **5.** *(plan, wish)* have no thought of doing sth nicht daran denken, etw. zu tun [nɪçt daran ˈdɛŋkɳ ... ʦuː] <denkt, dachte, hat gedacht> ◊ *Er denkt nicht daran, sich einen Job zu suchen.* **6.** *(care)* thought for sb/sth Rücksicht auf jdn/etw. ['rʏkzɪçt aof] die <-, -en> most sing ◊ *ohne Rücksicht auf seine eigene Sicherheit* have no thought for sb/sth keine Rücksicht auf jdn/etw. nehmen

◉ it's the thought that counts der gute Wille zählt sb is in sb's thoughts jd denkt an jdn

thoughtful [adj] **1.** *(kind)* aufmerksam ['aofmɛʁkzaːm] ◊ *Ich weiß ihre aufmerksame Art sehr zu schätzen.* ♦ *Danke für die Blumen, das ist sehr aufmerksam von Ihnen.; (considerate)* rücksichtsvoll ['rʏkzɪçtsfɔl] ◊ *ein rücksichtsvoller junger Mann* ♦ *Das finde ich sehr rücksichtsvoll von ihm.* **2.** *(thinking)* nachdenklich ['naːxdɛŋklɪç] ◊ *sein nachdenklicher Gesichtsausdruck* ♦ *Sie war an dem Tag sehr nachdenklich.* **3.** *(involving careful thought)* gut durchdacht

[guːt dʊˈç'daxt] <besser durchdacht, am besten durchdacht> ◊ *eine gut durchdachte Analyse* ♦ *Seine Beiträge sind immer gut durchdacht.*

thoughtfully [adv] **1.** *(thinking)* nachdenklich ['naːxdɛŋklɪç] ◊ *Er blickte nachdenklich aus dem Fenster.* **2.** *(kindly)* netterweise ['nɛtevaːezə] no comp/ superl ◊ *etw. netterweise kostenlos zur Verfügung stellen; (considerately)* rücksichtsvoll ['rʏkzɪçtsfɔl] ◊ *rücksichtsvoll schweigen*

thoughtless(ly) [adj, adv] **1.** *(unthinking)* gedankenlos [gəˈdaŋkɳloːs] <gedankenloser, am gedankenlosesten> ◊ *Der gedankenlose Umgang mit Trinkwasser störte sie.* ♦ *Wie kann man nur so gedankenlos sein!* ♦ *gedankenlos Müll wegwerfen* **2.** *(inconsiderate)* rücksichtslos ['rʏkzɪçtsloːs] <rücksichtsloser, am rücksichtslosesten> ◊ *Das war ziemlich rücksichtslos von dir!* ♦ *die rücksichtslose Abholzung der Wälder* ♦ *rücksichtslos rasen* **3.** *(rash)* unbedacht ['ʊnbədaxt] <unbedachter, am unbedachtesten> ◊ *Der Kommentar war ziemlich unbedacht.* ♦ *Er bereute seine unbedachten Äußerungen bereits.* ♦ *Sie handelt öfter unbedacht.*

thousand¹ [noun] **1.** Tausend ['taozɳt] das <-s, -> ◊ *Mit dieser Kiste ist jetzt das zweite Tausend voll.* **2.** MATH *(fourth digit before decimal point)* thousands Tausender ['taozɳde] die <-> pl ◊ *Hunderter und Tausender addieren*

◉ thousands *(a lot of people, money)* Tausende ◊ *Nach dem Erdbeben waren Tausende obdachlos.* ♦ *Das kostet Tausende.* thousands of Tausende von, tausende von ◊ *Tausende von Mücken/Fehlern*

thousand² [nmrl] tausend ['taozɳt] two thousand zweitausend a thousand things tausend Dinge two thousand zweitausend thousand million Milliarde [mɪˈljaːdə] die <-, -n> → **four²**

thread [noun] **1.** *(for sewing etc.)* (piece of) thread Faden ['faːdɳ] der <-s, Fäden> ◊ *Sie holte Nadel und Faden heraus und fing an zu nähen.* ♦ *einen langen Faden abschneiden* ♦ *ein seidener Faden; (on a roll, type of thread)* Garn [gaˈn] das <-(e)s, -e> ◊ *eine Rolle Garn* cotton thread Baumwollgarn ['baomvolgaˈn] **2.** *(of a screw)* Gewinde [gəˈvɪndə] das <-s, -> **3.** *(line)* thread of Streifen ['ʃtraefɳ] der <-s, -> ◊ *ein dünner Streifen Wasser* **4.** *(idea)* a common thread ein roter Faden [aen roːte ˈfaːdɳ] <-s, Fäden> ◊ *Dieses Thema zieht sich wie ein roter Faden durch seine Werke.*

◉ hang by a thread an einem seidenen Faden hängen lose the thread den Faden verlieren

threat [noun] **1.** *(danger)* threat (to) Gefahr (für) [gəˈfaːˈ] die <-, -en> ◊ *eine Gefahr für den Frieden/die Sicherheit* ♦ *Wir lebten mit der ständigen Gefahr eines erneuten Angriffs.* ♦ *Dieser Mann ist eine Gefahr für unsere Kinder.* have to face a threat sich einer Gefahr stellen face a new threat erneut in Gefahr sein We are facing the threat of extra costs. Uns drohen zusätzliche Kosten. pose a threat to sb etw. gefährden [gəˈfɛːgdɳ] <gefährdet, gefährdete, hat gefährdet> **2.** *(threatening words)* Drohung ['droːʊŋ] die <-, -en> ◊ *Er stieß finstere Drohungen aus.* an empty threat eine leere Drohung bomb threat Bombendrohung ['bɔmbədroːʊŋ] death threat Morddrohung ['mɔˈtdroːʊŋ] threat (of) Androhung (von) ['androːʊŋ] die <-, -en> ◊ *Erst die Androhung eines Verfahrens brachte ihn zum Schweigen.* under threat of unter Androhung von

ⓔ **be under threat** bedroht sein **come under threat** bedroht werden

threaten verb 1. *(be a danger)* threaten sb/sth jdn/etw. bedrohen [bə'droːən] <bedroht, bedrohte, hat bedroht> ◊ *jdn mit einer Waffe bedrohen* ◆ *die Krankheit, die jetzt sein Leben bedroht* be threatened with sth von etw. bedroht sein ◊ *Dieses Tier ist vom Aussterben bedroht.* 2. *(make a threat, be likely to happen)* drohen ['droːən] +haben ◊ *Wenn Gefahr droht, verstecken sie sich.* threaten sb (with sth) jdm (mit etw.) drohen ◊ *Er drobte mir mit der Faust.* ◆ *Sie droht den Kindern oft mit Fernsehverbot.* threaten to do sth drohen, etw. zu tun ◊ *Sie drohten, die Geisel zu erschießen.* ◆ *Der Vulkan droht jeden Augenblick auszubrechen.* Rain was threatening. Es sah bedrohlich nach Regen aus. 3. *(as punishment)* threaten sth etw. androhen ['androːən] +haben ◊ *Sie haben schon Sanktionen angedroht.*

threatening(ly) adj, adv bedrohlich [bə'droːlɪç] ◊ *Das Flugzeug flog bedrohlich tief.* ◆ *Ein bedrohlicher Ausdruck lag in seinem Gesicht.* ◆ *Der Himmel sah bedrohlich aus.*; *(person or animal: signalling a warning)* drohend ['droːənt] ◊ *Drohend hob er die Hand.* threatening gesture Drohgebärde ['droːgəbɛːgdə] die <–, –n>

three¹ noun Drei [draɛ] die <–, –en> → **four**¹
three² nmrl drei [draɛ] → **four**²

three-dimensional adj 1. *(model, image)* dreidimensional ['draedɪmɛnzjoˌnaːl] no comp/superl ◊ *ein dreidimensionales Modell des Gebäudes* ◆ *Die Darstellung ist dreidimensional.* 2. *(character)* lebensecht ['leːbm̩sˌlɛçt] <lebensechter, am lebensechtesten> ◊ *Einen guten Schriftsteller erkennt man an seinen lebensechten Figuren.* ◆ *Jede Figur in diesem Roman ist sehr lebensecht.*

threefold adj, adv dreifach ['draefax] → **fourfold**

threshold noun 1. *(at the entrance)* Schwelle ['ʃvɛlə] die <–, –n> ◊ *Er trug seine Braut über die Schwelle.* hearing threshold Hörschwelle ['høːɐ̯ʃvɛlə] pain threshold Schmerzschwelle ['ʃmɛʁtsʃvɛlə] have a low boredom threshold sich schnell langweilen [ʃnɛl 'laŋvaelən] +haben 2. *(limit)* Grenze ['grɛntsə] die <–, –n> tax threshold Grenze, ab der man Steuern zahlen muss be above a threshold oberhalb einer Grenze liegen

thrifty(-ily) adj, adv sparsam ['ʃpaːɐ̯zaːm] ◊ *Meine Frau ist sehr sparsam.* ◆ *Ein sparsamerer Mensch käme mit dem Geld aus.* ◆ *Wir haben im Urlaub sehr sparsam gelebt.*

thriller noun Krimi ['krɪmiː] der <–s, –s> ◊ *Er liest/ sieht gern Krimis.*

thrilling(ly) adj, adv spannend ['ʃpanənt] ◊ *Sie liest ein spannendes Buch.* ◆ *Der Roman ist wirklich spannend.* ◆ *Die Geschichte ist spannend erzählt.*

thrive verb *(person, animal, plant)* gedeihen [gə'daeən] <gedeiht, gedieh, ist gediehen> ◊ *Die Kinder gedeihen prächtig.*; *(business)* florieren [floˈriːrən] <floriert, florierte, hat floriert> ◊ *Seine Geschäfte florierten.*

throat noun 1. *(back of your mouth)* Hals [hals] der <–es, Hälse> ◊ *Mir ist ein Krümel im Hals stecken geblieben.* a sore throat Halsschmerzen ['halsʃmɛˈʦn̩] <–> pl ◊ *Ich habe Halsschmerzen.* ◆ *Sie wachte mit Halsschmerzen auf.* 2. *(front part of the neck)* Kehle ['keːlə] die <–, –n> ◊ *jdm die Kehle durchschneiden*

ⓔ **be at each other's throats** sich dat in den Haaren liegen **clear your throat** sich räuspern

throb verb 1. *(engine, machine, music)* dröhnen ['drøːnən] +haben ◊ *Der Motor dröhnt.* ◆ *Aus seinem Zimmer dröhnte laute Musik.* 2. *(part of the body, heart, pain)* pochen ['pɔxn̩] +haben ◊ *Er war so aufgeregt, dass sein Herz heftig pochte.* ◆ *Sie spürte einen pochenden Schmerz.*

throne noun Thron [troːn] der <–(e)s, –e> be on the throne auf dem Thron sitzen heir to the throne Thronfolger ['troːnfɔlgɐ] der <–s, –> ♀Thronfolgerin ['troːnfɔlgərɪn] die <–, –nen>

through¹ adj 1. *(train)* durchgehend ['dʊɐ̯çgeːənt] only before ns through road Durchgangsstraße ['dʊɐ̯çgaŋsˌʃtraːsə] die <–, –n> through traffic Durchgangsverkehr ['dʊɐ̯çgaŋsfɛkɛːɐ̯] der <–s> no pl 2. be through (with sb/sth) (mit jdm/etw.) fertig sein ['fɛɐ̯tɪç zaen] +sein ◊ *Ich bin fast fertig.* ◆ *Er war gerade mit seiner Arbeit fertig.* ◆ *Ich bin gleich mit der Bohrmaschine fertig, dann kannst du sie haben.* ◆ *Mit Peter/Mit der Politik bin ich fertig!* Sue and Bob are through. Sue und Bob haben sich getrennt.

through² adv durch [dʊɐ̯ç] ◊ *Es regnete die ganze Nacht durch.* through and through durch und durch ◊ *Er ist durch und durch verlogen.* ◆ *Sie ist durch und durch Künstlerin.* through to bis [bɪs] ◊ *Das Festival läuft bis Ende des Monats.* ◆ *Der Zug fährt bis Hamburg.*; *(with certain verbs)* ... through durch... [dʊɐ̯ç] come through durchkommen ['dʊɐ̯çkɔmən] <kommt durch, kam durch, ist durchgekommen> ◊ *Ist der Anruf durchgekommen?* cut through durchschneiden ['dʊɐ̯çˌʃnaedn̩] <schneidet durch, schnitt durch, hat durchgeschnitten> ◊ *ein Seil durchschneiden* rain through durchregnen ['dʊɐ̯çreːgnən] <regnet durch, regnete durch, hat durchgeregnet> ◊ *Hier regnet es durch; alles ist nass.*

'Through' often occurs in phrasal verbs like 'come through' or 'put through' which have their own entries in the dictionary.

through³ prep 1. *(spatial: from one side to the other, from beginning to end)* durch [dʊɐ̯ç] +acc ◊ *Gehen wir doch durch den Wald.* ◆ *Der Einbrecher stieg durch ein Fenster ein.* ◆ *Das Motiv zieht sich durch den ganzen Roman.* ◆ *Bist du durch die Prüfung gekommen?* 2. *(temporal: lasting for a period of time)* über ['yːbɐ] +acc ◊ *through the year das ganze Jahr über* all through the night/day die ganze Nacht/den ganzen Tag [diː gantsə 'naxt/deːn gantsn̩ 'taːk] through to mid-June bis Mitte Juni [bɪs ˌmɪtə 'juːniː] January through March von Januar bis einschließlich März [fɔn ˌjanuaːɐ̯ bɪs aenʃliːslɪç 'mɛɐ̯ts] 3. *(causal: because of sth, by means of sth)* durch [dʊɐ̯ç] +acc ◊ *Das ist durch deine Schuld passiert!* ◊ *Das hat er durch großen persönlichen Einsatz erreicht.* ◆ *Jonglieren lernt man nur durch viel Üben.* She retired through ill health. Sie ging aus gesundheitlichen Gründen in den Ruhestand. through this/that dadurch [da'dʊɐ̯ç] ◊ *Denken Sie an schöne Dinge und motivieren Sie sich dadurch.* 4. *(by means of a medium, via)* über ['yːbɐ] +acc ◊ *etw. über das Internet bestellen* ◆ *Ich habe über Pia bereits von dem Unfall gehört.*

throughout¹ adv 1. *(in every part)* durchgehend ['dʊɐ̯çgeːənt] no comp/superl ◊ *Die Straße ist wieder*

durchgehend befahrbar. ♦ *Das Buch ist durchgehend farbig illustriert.* **2.** *(the whole time)* die ganze Zeit [di: gantsə 'tsaet] ◊ *Die Geburt dauerte ziemlich lange, aber er war die ganze Zeit bei ihr.*

throughout² [prep] **1.** *(spatial: in every part of)* überall in [ybe'|'al ɪn] [+dat] ◊ *Überall in der Stadt gibt es schöne Gartenanlagen.* throughout the world überall auf der Welt **2.** *(temporal)* throughout the ... den ganzen ... über [de:n gantsṇ ... y:bə] ◊ *das ganze ... über* [di:/das gantsə ... y:bə] ◊ *So ging das den ganzen Film über weiter.* ♦ *die ganze Woche über* ♦ *das ganze Spiel über*

throw¹ [noun] **1.** *(throwing)* Wurf [vʊ'f] der <-(e)s, Würfe> ◊ *Er traf gleich beim ersten Wurf ins Tor.* **2.** *(piece of cloth)* Überwurf ['y:bevʊ'f] der <-(e)s, Überwürfe> ◊ *Sie häkelt einen Überwurf für das Sofa.*

throw² [verb] **1.** *(send through the air, put, move, aim)* werfen ['vɛ'fṇ] <wirft, warf, hat geworfen> ◊ *Ich kann weiter werfen als du!* ♦ *Er wirft den Ball fast 50 Meter weit.* ♦ *Sie warf den Kopf in den Nacken.* ♦ *Sie warf sich weinend in meine Arme.* ♦ *Er warf mich zu Boden.* ♦ *jdn ins Gefängnis werfen* ♦ *Jemand hatte von der Brücke einen Stein auf die Autos geworfen.* ♦ *Ich warf einen Schneeball nach ihm.*; *(horse)* throw sb jdn abwerfen ['apvɛ'fṇ] +haben ◊ *Das Pferd hat ihn abgeworfen.* throw sth to sb, throw sb sth jdm etw. zuwerfen ['tsu:vɛ'fṇ] +haben ◊ *Sie warf mir den Ball zu.* throw an angry look at sb jdm einen bösen Blick zuwerfen throw sth down etw. wegwerfen ['vɛkvɛ'fṇ] +haben ◊ *Werfen Sie die Waffe weg!* throw the ball in den Ball einwerfen [de:n ˌbal 'aenvɛ'fṇ] +haben throw sth open etw. aufreißen ['aofraesṇ] <reißt auf, riss auf, hat aufgerissen> ◊ *Sie riss die Tür/alle Fenster auf.* **2.** *(put into a state)* throw sb/sth into sth/etw. in etw. [acc] versetzen [ɪn ... fezɛtsṇ] <versetzt, versetzte, hat versetzt> ◊ *Der Gedanke versetzte sie in Panik.* throw sth into chaos etw. ins Chaos stürzen [ɪns 'ka:ɔs ʃtʏ'tsṇ] +haben **3.** *(confuse)* throw sb jdn aus dem Konzept bringen [aos dem kɔn'tsept brɪŋən] <bringt, brachte, hat gebracht> ◊ *Er hat mich mit seiner Frage ganz aus dem Konzept gebracht.* throw sb off balance jdn aus dem Gleichgewicht bringen **4.** *(say)* throw insults at sb jdm Beleidigungen an den Kopf werfen [bə'laedɪɡʊŋən an den kɔpf vɛ'fṇ] <wirft, warf, hat geworfen> throw questions at sb jdn mit Fragen bombardieren [mɪt 'fra:ɡ̊ṇ bomba'di:rən] <bombardiert, bombardierte, hat bombardiert> **5.** *(a switch, lever)* umlegen ['ʊmle:ɡ̊ṇ] +haben **6.** *(a party)* geben ['ge:bṇ] <gibt, gab, hat gegeben>

• **throw aside** [phras v] throw sth aside *(give up)* etw. aufgeben ['aofge:bṇ] <gibt auf, gab auf, hat aufgegeben> ◊ *Sie gab ihre Vorbehalte auf und wurde Mitglied einer politischen Partei.*

• **throw at** [phras v] throw yourself at sb sich jdm an den Hals werfen [an de:n hals 'vɛ'fṇ] <wirft sich, warf sich, hat sich geworfen> ◊ *Musst du dich ihm immer so an den Hals werfen?*

• **throw away** [phras v] throw sth away **1.** *(get rid of)* etw. wegwerfen ['vɛkvɛ'fṇ] <wirft weg, warf weg, hat weggeworfen> ◊ *Wirf doch endlich mal die alten Zeitschriften weg!* **2.** *(waste)* etw. verschenken [fe'ʃɛŋkṇ] <verschenkt, verschenkte, hat verschenkt> ◊ *Die Torchance haben sie leider verschenkt.*

• **throw back** [phras v] throw sth back on sb jdm etw. unter die Nase reiben [ʊntɐ di: 'na:zə raebṇ] <reibt, rieb, hat gerieben> *(fam)* ◊ *Er rieb mir meine eigenen Worte unter die Nase.*

• **throw in** [phras v] throw sth in **1.** *(include)* etw. umsonst dazugeben [ʊmˌzɔnst da'tsu:ge:bṇ] <gibt dazu, gab dazu, hat dazugegeben> ◊ *Wenn Sie den Tisch kaufen, gebe ich Ihnen zwei Stühle umsonst dazu.* **2.** *(in a conversation)* etw. einwerfen ['aenvɛ'fṇ] <wirft ein, warf ein, hat eingeworfen> ◊ *Er hörte aufmerksam zu und warf ab und zu eine Frage/Bemerkung ein.*

• **throw into** [phras v] throw yourself into sth sich in etw. [dat] stürzen [ɪn ... 'ʃtʏ'tsṇ] +haven ◊ *Sie stürzte sich in die Arbeit, um ihren Kummer zu vergessen.*

• **throw off** [phras v] **1.** *(clothing, a rider)* throw sth/sb off etw./jdn abwerfen ['apvɛ'fṇ] <wirft ab, warf ab, hat abgeworfen> ◊ *Sie warf ihre Sachen ab und sprang ins Wasser.* **2.** *(a pursuer, feeling)* throw sth/sb off etw./jdn abschütteln ['apʃʏtln̩] +haben ◊ *Sie konnte ihre Müdigkeit/Sorgen nicht abschütteln.* ♦ *Es gelang mir, meine Verfolger abzuschütteln.* **3.** *(an illness)* throw sth off etw. loswerden ['lo:sve:ɡ̊dṇ] <wird los, wurde los, ist losgeworden> ◊ *Ich kann diese Erkältung einfach nicht loswerden.*

• **throw on** [phras v] throw sth on etw. überwerfen ['y:beve'fṇ] <wirft über, warf über, hat übergeworfen> ◊ *Ich warf mir einen Mantel über und rannte hinaus.*

• **throw out** [phras v] **1.** throw sb out of sth jdn aus etw. werfen [aos ... vɛ'fṇ] <wirft, warf, hat geworfen> ◊ *Sie hat ihn endlich aus der Wohnung geworfen.* throw sb out jdn hinauswerfen [hɪ'naosvɛ'fṇ] +haben ◊ *Er hat seinen Untermieter hinausgeworfen.* **2.** *(a plan, proposal)* throw sth out etw. ablehnen ['aple:nən] +haben ◊ *Der Einspruch wurde abgelehnt.* **3.** *(heat, light)* throw sth out etw. abgeben ['apge:bṇ] <gibt ab, gab ab, hat abgegeben> ◊ *Der kleine Ofen gibt nicht viel Wärme ab.*

• **throw together** [phras v] **1.** *(a meal)* throw sth together etw. zaubern ['tsaobṇ] +haben ◊ *Er zauberte in wenigen Minuten einen leckeren Salat.* **2.** throw sb together jdn zusammenführen [tsu'zamənfy:rən] +haben ◊ *Das Schicksal hat uns zusammengeführt.*

• **throw up** [phras v] **1.** *(vomit)* brechen ['brɛçṇ] <bricht, brach, hat gebrochen> ◊ *Mir ist so schlecht. Ich glaube, ich muss brechen.* throw sth up etw. erbrechen [e'brɛçṇ] <erbricht, erbrach, hat erbrochen> ◊ *Sie erbrach das Mittagessen.* ♦ *Blut erbrechen* **2.** *(problems, questions)* throw sth up etw. aufwerfen ['aofvɛ'fṇ] <wirft auf, warf auf, hat aufgeworfen> ◊ *Die Veränderung hat einige Probleme aufgeworfen.* **3.** *(dust)* throw sth up etw. aufwirbeln ['aofvɪ'bln̩] +haben; *(stones, water)* etw. aufspritzen lassen ['aofʃprɪtsṇ lasṇ] <lässt, ließ, hat lassen> **4.** *(a building)* throw sth up etw. aus dem Boden stampfen [aos de:m 'bo:dṇ ʃtampfṇ] +haben **5.** *(a home, job, lifestyle)* throw sth up etw. aufgeben ['aofge:bṇ] <gibt auf, gab auf, hat aufgegeben>

thrust¹ [noun] **1.** *(main intention)* the (general) thrust of sth ... der [gen] [de:ɐ̯ 'te:no:ɡ̊] <-s> *no pl* ◊ *der Tenor seiner Rede* **2.** *(force)* Schub [ʃu:p] der <-(e)s, Schübe> ◊ *der Schub des Triebwerks* **3.** *(push)* Stoß [ʃto:s] der <-es, Stöße> ◊ *ein Stoß*

mit dem Dolch

thrust² [verb] **1.** schieben [ˈʃiːbm̩] <schiebt, schob, hat geschoben> ◊ *die Hände in die Taschen schieben* ♦ *die Hüfte nach vorn schieben* thrust sth under sb's nose jdm etw. unter die Nase halten [ʊntɐ diː ˈnaːzə haltn̩] <hält, hielt, hat gehalten> **2.** thrust (your way) sich drängen [ˈdrɛŋən] +haben ◊ *Ich drängte mich durch die Menge.* **3.** *(attack with a knife)* thrust at sb (with sth) (mit etw.) auf jdn einstechen [aọf ... ˌaɛnʃtɛçn̩] <sticht ein, stach ein, hat eingestochen> **4.** *(rise up)* sth thrusts upwards etw. ragt in die Höhe [raːkt ɪn diː ˈhøːə] ◊ *Ein einsamer Turm ragte in die Höhe.*

• **thrust aside** [phras v] beiseite schieben [baẹˈzaɛtə ʃiːbm̩] <schiebt, schob, hat geschoben> ◊ *Er schob die anderen beiseite und drängte sich nach vorn.* ♦ *alle Einwände beiseite schieben*

thumb [noun] Daumen [ˈdaọmən] der <-s, -> ◊ *am Daumen lutschen* He put his thumb up. Er zeigte, dass alles in Ordnung war.

ⓔ **be all thumbs** zwei linke Hände haben ⓔ **under sb's thumb** unter jds Pantoffel [dat] stehen *(fam)*

thump [verb] **1.** *(hit)* schlagen [ˈʃlaːgŋ̩] <schlägt, schlug, hat geschlagen> ◊ *Er schlug wütend auf den Tisch.* ♦ *jdn ins Gesicht schlagen* ◊ *Der Vogel schlug gegen die Scheibe.* **2.** *(attack, punish)* verprügeln [fɛˈpryːgln̩] <verprügelt, verprügelte, hat verprügelt> **3.** *(put)* thump sth on sth etw. auf etw. [acc] knallen [aọf ... knalən] +haben ◊ *Sie knallte das Buch auf den Tisch und ging.* **4.** *(beat fast)* pochen [ˈpɔxn̩] +haben ◊ *Ihr Herz pochte vor Aufregung.* **5.** *(hurt badly)* rasend schmerzen [raːzn̩t ˈʃmɛʁtsn̩] +haben My head is thumping. Ich habe rasende Kopfschmerzen.

thunder [noun] **1.** *(during a storm)* Donner [ˈdɔnɐ] der <-s> no pl roll of thunder Donnergrollen [ˈdɔnɐgrɔlən] das <-s> no pl clap of thunder Donnerschlag [ˈdɔnɐʃlaːk] der <-(e)s, Donnerschläge> **2.** *(loud noise)* Donnern [ˈdɔnɐn] das <-s> no pl ◊ *Das Donnern der Hufe war von weitem zu hören.*

thunderstorm [noun] Gewitter [gəˈvɪtɐ] das <-s, -> ◊ *Ein Gewitter zog auf.*

Thursday [noun] Donnerstag [ˈdɔnɐstaːk] der <-(e)s, -e> → **Monday**

thus [adv] **1.** *(as a result)* somit [zoˈmɪt] ◊ *Er hat gute Noten und kann somit aufs Gymnasium.* ♦ *Der Blutzuckerspiegel sinkt schnell wieder ab und somit wird kein Insulin mehr benötigt.* **2.** *(in this way)* so [zoː] ◊ *Er kam zu spät und verpasste so seine Chance.*

ⓔ **thus far** bisher

thyme [noun] Thymian [ˈtyːmịaːn] der <-s, -e> most sing

tick¹ [noun] **1.** *(symbol)* Haken [ˈhaːkŋ̩] der <-s, -> ◊ *Der Lehrer machte hinter jedes richtige Wort einen Haken.* **2.** *(sound)* Ticken [ˈtɪkŋ̩] das <-s> no pl ◊ *Das Ticken des Weckers hat mich wach gehalten.* **3.** *(parasite)* Zecke [ˈtsɛkə] die <-, -n> ◊ *Zecken können gefährliche Krankheiten übertragen.*

tick² [verb] **1.** *(make a sound)* ticken [ˈtɪkŋ̩] +haben ◊ *Ist die Uhr steben geblieben oder tickt sie noch?* **2.** *(mark to show sth has been dealt with)* abhaken [ˈaphaːkŋ̩] +haben ◊ *Die ersten drei Punkte können wir schon abhaken.*; *(mark to show sth is right)* tick sth einen Haken hinter etw. [acc] setzen [aɛnən ˈhaːkŋ̩ hɪntɐ ... zɛtsn̩] +haben ◊ *einen Haken*

---

hinter die richtige Antwort setzen; *(mark to select sth)* ankreuzen [ˈankrɔọtsn̩] +haben ◊ *Kreuzen Sie die gewünschten Produkte auf dem Bestellschein an.*

ⓔ **what makes sb tick** was in jdm vorgeht

• **tick away** [phras v] → **tick by**

• **tick by** [phras v] *(time)* vergehen [fɛˈgeːən] <vergeht, verging, ist vergangen> ◊ *Die Minuten vergingen.*

• **tick off** [phras v] **1.** *(mark)* tick sth off abhaken [etw. ˈaphaːkŋ̩] +haben ◊ *alle Anwesenden auf der Liste abhaken* **2.** *(criticize, tick sb off)* jdn ausschimpfen [ˈaọsʃɪmpfn̩] +haben

ticket [noun] **1.** *(for a place, an event)* Eintrittskarte [ˈaɛntrɪtskaʁtə] die <-, -n> ◊ *Hast du die Eintrittskarten fürs Theater?* cinema ticket Kinokarte [ˈkiːnokaʁtə] ticket sales Kartenverkauf [ˈkaʁtn̩fɛkaọf] der <-(e)s> sing **2.** *(for a journey)* Fahrkarte [ˈfaːˈkaʁtə] die <-, -n> ◊ *Fahrkarten kaufen/lösen/entwerten* single ticket einfache Fahrkarte return ticket Rückfahrkarte [ˈrykfaːˈkaʁtə] train ticket Zugfahrkarte [ˈtsuːkfaːˈkaʁtə] bus ticket Busfahrkarte [ˈbʊsfaːˈkaʁtə] plane ticket Flugticket [ˈfluːktɪkət] das <-s, -s> ticket office Fahrkartenschalter [ˈfaːˈkaʁtn̩ʃaltɐ] der <-s, -> **3.** *(for a lottery)* lottery ticket Lottoschein [ˈlɔtoʃaɛn] der <-(e)s, -e> raffle ticket Los [loːs] das <-es, -e> ◊ *Lose verkaufen* **4.** *(for a traffic offence)* Strafzettel [ˈʃtraːftsɛtl̩] der <-, -> ◊ *einen Strafzettel bekommen* a parking ticket ein Strafzettel für falsches Parken **5.** *(in the US)* run on the Republican ticket für die Republikaner kandidieren [fyːɐ̯ diː republiˈkaːnɐ kandiˌdiːrən] <kandidiert, kandidierte, hat kandidiert>

ⓔ **a ticket to sth** ein Weg zu etw.

tide [noun] **1.** *(of the sea)* high tide Flut [fluːt] die <-, -en> The tide comes in. Die Flut kommt. The tide is in. Es ist Flut. low tide Ebbe [ˈɛbə] die <-, -n> ◊ *Bei Ebbe kommt man zu Fuß zu der Insel hinüber.* The tide goes out. Die Ebbe kommt. The tide is out. Es ist Ebbe. tides Gezeiten [gəˈtsaɛtn̩] die <-> only pl **2.** *(fig)* the/a tide of sth die/eine Welle ... [gen] [diː/aɛnə ˈvɛlə] <-, -n> ◊ *eine Welle der Gewalt* the tide of public opinion die öffentliche Meinung [diː œfŋtlɪçə ˈmaɛnʊŋ] <-> no pl stem the tide of sth die Flut von etw. eindämmen [diː fluːt fɔn ... ˌaɛndɛmən] ◊ *Wie kann man die Flut von Faxen eindämmen?*

ⓔ **swim against the tide** gegen den Strom schwimmen swim with the tide mit dem Strom schwimmen turn the tide das Ruder herumreißen the tide turns (on sb/sth) das Blatt wendet sich gegen jdn/etw.

tidiness [noun] **1.** *(in a place)* Ordnung [ˈɔʁdnʊŋ] die <-, -en> ◊ *Ordnung ist für sie sehr wichtig.* **2.** *(of a person)* Ordentlichkeit [ˈɔʁdn̩tlɪçkaɛt] die <-> no pl ◊ *Seine Ordentlichkeit ist erstaunlich.*

tidy¹ [adj] ordentlich [ˈɔʁdn̩tlɪç] ◊ *Julia ist ein sehr ordentliches Kind.* ♦ *Die Wohnung war sauber und ordentlich.* ♦ *Sie hat eine ordentliche Summe dafür bekommen.* keep sth tidy etw. in Ordnung halten [ɪn ˈɔʁdnʊŋ haltn̩] <hält, hielt, hat gehalten>

tidy² [verb] tidy (up) aufräumen [ˈaọfrɔọmən] +haben ◊ *gründlich im ganzen Haus aufräumen* ♦ *Räum bitte deine Schulsachen/dein Zimmer auf.*

• **tidy away** [phras v] tidy sth away etw. wegräumen [ˈvɛkrɔọmən] +haben

• **tidy up** [phras v] tidy sth up etw. überarbeiten

[ybeɪ'aˈbaetn̩] <überarbeitet, überarbeitete, hat überarbeitet> ◊ *ein Manuskript nochmals überarbeiten* → **tidy²**

tie¹ ⟨noun⟩ **1.** *(piece of clothing)* Krawatte [kra'vatə] die <–, –n> ◊ *eine Krawatte umhaben/tragen* ♦ *sich/jdm die Krawatte binden* collar and tie Hemd und Krawatte **2.** *(close relationship)* Bindung ['bɪndʊŋ] die <–, –en> family ties familiäre Bindungen; *(in business, politics)* Beziehung [bə'tsiːʊŋ] die <–, –en> ◊ *die Beziehungen zwischen den beiden Staaten* the ties of sth die Bande … ⟨gen⟩ [diː 'bandə] <–> *pl (lofty, oldf)* ◊ *die Bande der Freundschaft*

tie² ⟨verb⟩ **1.** *(fasten)* binden ['bɪndn̩] <bindet, band, hat gebunden> ◊ *eine Krawatte binden* ♦ *dem Esel einen Sack auf den Rücken binden* ♦ *die Blumen zu einem schönen Strauß binden* tie your shoelaces sich ⟨dat⟩ die Schuhe zubinden [diː 'ʃuːə ˌtsuːbɪndn̩] +haben; *(together)* zusammenbinden ['tsu'tsamənbɪndn̩] +haben ◊ *Die Briefe waren mit einem Seidenband zusammengebunden.* tie your hair back sich ⟨dat⟩ die Haare zusammenbinden **2.** *(be fastenend)* zugebunden werden ['tsu:gəbʊndn̩ veːɐdn̩] <wird, wurde, ist worden> ◊ *Das Hemdchen wird vorn/hinten zugebunden.* **3.** *(stop sb from leaving)* fesseln ['fɛsln̩] +haben ◊ *jdn/jds Hände fesseln* ♦ *Seine Krankheit fesselt ihn ans Bett/Haus.* **4.** *(combine, connect)* verbinden [fɛ'bɪndn̩] <verbindet, verband, hat verbunden> ◊ *Das Buch verbindet die alte Zeit mit der neuen Entwicklung.* closely tied to sth eng mit etw. verbunden **5.** *(to a place, situation)* tie sb to sth jdn an etw. ⟨acc⟩ binden [an … ˌbɪndn̩] <bindet, band, hat gebunden> be tied to sb/sth an jdn/etw. gebunden sein ◊ *Es ist gut, dass wir nicht an eine bestimmte Zeit gebunden sind.* **6.** tie for first place sich den ersten Platz teilen [deːn eːɐstn̩ ˌplats 'taelən] +haben The game was tied. Das Spiel endete unentschieden.
• **tie down** ⟨phras v⟩ tie sb down jdn binden ['bɪndn̩] <bindet, band, hat gebunden> ◊ *Er fühlte sich durch die Ehe zu sehr gebunden.*
• **tie in** ⟨phras v⟩ tie in with sth zu etw. passen ['tsuː 'pasn̩] ◊ *Sein Buch passt zum neuen Trend.*
• **tie up** ⟨phras v⟩ **1.** tie up your shoelaces sich ⟨dat⟩ die Schuhe zubinden [diː 'ʃuːə ˌtsuːbɪndn̩] <bindet zu, band zu, hat zugebunden> **2.** tie an animal up ein Tier anbinden ['anbɪndn̩] <bindet an, band an, hat angebunden> ◊ *Der Cowboy band sein Pferd vor dem Saloon an.* **3.** *(with a rope etc.)* tie sb up jdn fesseln ['fɛsln̩] +haben ◊ *einen Gefangenen fesseln* **4.** *(boat, ship)* tie sth up etw. festmachen ['fɛstmaxn̩] +haben ◊ *Sie machten das Boot fest.* ♦ *Das Schiff hat gestern im Hafen festgemacht.* **5.** tie up arrangements for sth etw. unter Dach und Fach bringen [ʊntɐ ˌdax ʊnt 'fax brɪŋən] <bringt, brachte, hat gebracht> ◊ *Er hat den Vertrag/das Geschäft unter Dach und Fach gebracht.*

tiger ⟨noun⟩ Tiger ['tiːgɐ] der <–s, ->

tight¹ ⟨adj⟩ **1.** *(clothes, space, bend)* eng [ɛŋ] ◊ *Diese Schuhe sind sehr/zu eng.* ♦ *enge Kurven fahren* ♦ *Das Sofa passt noch ins Zimmer, aber es wird etwas eng.* ♦ *Uns wurden enge Grenzen gesetzt.* it's a tight squeeze es ist ziemlich eng a tight group eine eng verbundene Gruppe **2.** *(grip, embrace, knot)* fest [fɛst] <fester, am festesten> ◊ *Ist der Knoten fest genug?* The screw was tight. Die Schraube saß fest. hug sb in a tight grip jdn fest umarmen **3.** *(rope,*

cloth) straff gespannt [ˌʃtraf gə'ʃpant] <straffer gespannt, am straffsten gespannt> ◊ *ein straff gespanntes Seil* ♦ *Das Sprungtuch muss ganz straff gespannt sein.* **4.** *(security, control)* streng [ʃtrɛŋ] ◊ *strenge Sicherheitsvorkehrungen* ♦ *Die Kontrolle bei der Einreise war strenger als sonst.* **5.** *(performance)* gelungen [gə'lʊŋən] ◊ *Sie gaben eine gelungene Vorstellung.* ♦ *Ich fand das sehr gelungen!* **6.** *(time, money, game, race)* knapp [knap] ◊ *Die Zeit ist heute ziemlich knapp.* ♦ *ein knappes Rennen* ♦ *„Haben sie gewonnen?" — „Ja, aber es war ganz knapp."* a tight schedule ein knapper Zeitplan a tight deadline eine knappe Frist They are on a tight budget. Sie haben wenig Geld. Money is tight for them. Sie sind knapp bei Kasse. **7.** *(face, mouth)* verkniffen [fɛ'knɪfn̩]; *(smile)* verkrampft [fɛ'krampft] <verkrampfter, am verkrampftesten>; *(voice)* nervös [nɛɐ'vøːs] <nervöser, am nervösesten> **8.** *(chest, throat)* wie zugeschnürt [vi: 'tsuːgəʃnyːɐt] no comp/superl ◊ *Seine Brust war wie zusammengeschnürt, und er konnte kaum atmen.* **9.** *(close together)* dicht [dɪçt] <dichter, am dichtesten> ◊ *ein dichtes Bündel von Kabeln/Reisig* **10.** *(stingy)* geizig ['gaetsɪç] ◊ *ein geiziger alter Mann* ♦ *Seine Eltern sind sehr geizig.*
☞ keep a tight grip on sth etw. fest im Griff haben a tight corner eine brenzlige Lage

tight² ⟨adv⟩ fest [fɛst] <fester, am festesten> ◊ *Er machte die Augen fest zu.* hold on tight sich festhalten ['fɛsthaltn̩] <hält sich fest, hielt sich fest, hat sich festgehalten>

tighten, tighten up ⟨verb⟩ **1.** *(a screw)* anziehen ['antsiːən] <zieht an, zog an, hat angezogen> ◊ *Du musst die Schraube fester anziehen.; (a lid)* festschrauben ['fɛstʃraobm̩] +haben **2.** *(rope)* straffen ['ʃtrafn̩] +haben ◊ *ein Seil straffen* The rope tightened. Das Seil straffte sich.; *(a belt)* enger schnallen ['ɛŋɐ ʃnalən] +haben **3.** *(muscle, part of your body)* verkrampfen [fɛ'krampfn̩] <verkrampft, verkrampfte, hat verkrampft> ◊ *Es ist wichtig, beim Schreiben den Arm nicht zu verkrampfen.* ♦ *Seine Finger verkrampften sich.; (mouth, lips)* schmal werden ['ʃmaːl veːɐdn̩] +sein ◊ *Ihr Mund wurde ganz schmal, aber sie sagte nichts.* sb's fingers tighten, sb's hand tightens jds Griff wird fester [ˌgrɪf vɪ't 'fɛstɐ] +sein **4.** *(rules, security)* verschärfen [fɛ'ʃɛɐfn̩] <verschärft, verschärfte, hat verschärft> ◊ *die Drogenkontrollen/Waffengesetze verschärfen* ♦ *Die Sicherheitsmaßnahmen wurden verschärft.* tighten your control on sth etw. schärfer kontrollieren ['ʃɛɐfɐ kɔntroˌliːrən] <kontrolliert, kontrollierte, hat kontrolliert>

tight-fitting ⟨adj⟩ **1.** *(clothes)* eng [ɛŋ] ◊ *ein enges Kleid* ◊ *Dieses T-Shirt ist zu eng.* **2.** *(lid)* gut schließend [ˌguːt 'ʃliːsnt] only before ns ◊ *eine Dose mit einem gut schließenden Deckel auf.*

tightly ⟨adv⟩ **1.** *(fit)* eng [ɛŋ] ◊ *ein eng anliegendes Kleid* **2.** *(close, bandage, embrace)* fest [fɛst] <fester, am festesten> ◊ *ein fest verschlossener Behälter* ♦ *Sie drückte das Kind fest an sich.* **3.** *(control)* streng [ʃtrɛŋ] ◊ *etw. wird streng kontrolliert*

tights ⟨noun⟩ Strumpfhose ['ʃtrʊmpfhoːzə] die <–, –n> can be used in the pl or sing ◊ *Sie hat Strumpfhosen/eine Strumpfhose aus Nylon an.*

tile ⟨noun⟩ **1.** *(on the roof)* Ziegel ['tsiːgl̩] der <–s, –> ◊ *ein mit roten Ziegeln gedecktes Dach* **2.** *(on the wall, floor)* Fliese ['fliːzə] die <–, –n> ◊ *Fliesen verlegen*

till¹ [noun] Kasse ['kasə] die <–, –n> ◊ *Die Kassiererin nimmt das Wechselgeld aus der Kasse.*

till² [prep] bis [bɪs] [+acc] ◊ *Bis wann kann ich das behalten? ♦ Das Geschäft ist von 9 bis 20 Uhr geöffnet.*

till³ [conjunc] bis [bɪs] ◊ *Warte hier, bis ich wiederkomme.*

tilt [verb] **1.** (an object) kippen ['kɪpn̩] +haben ◊ *Er kippte den Sitz nach vorn. ♦ Die Fenster lassen sich kippen.;* (your head) neigen ['naegn̩] +haben ◊ *Sie neigte den Kopf nach vorn/nach hinten/zur Seite.* sth tilts etw. neigt sich ['naekt zɪç] +haben ◊ *Das Boot neigte sich plötzlich nach rechts.* **2.** tilt the balance in favo(u)r of sb jdm einen Vorteil bringen [aenən 'fo:ɐ̯tael brɪŋən] <bringt, brachte, hat gebracht>

timber [noun] (wood) Holz [hɔlts] das <–es, Hölzer> ◊ *Im Baumarkt wird auch Holz verkauft.;* (piece of wood) Balken ['balkn̩] der <–s, –> ◊ *Die Balken sind teilweise verrottet.*

time¹ [noun] **1.** (period that is available or needed) Zeit [tsaet] die <–, –en> ◊ *Die Zeit vergeht/verrinnt. ♦ um 16.15 Uhr mitteleuropäischer Zeit ♦ Ich habe in Hamburg eine sehr schöne Zeit verlebt. ♦ Sie hat ihre Zeit an der Uni in guter Erinnerung. ♦ Ich habe jetzt leider keine Zeit für dich. ♦ Du vergeudest deine Zeit. ♦ Er ist wieder eine gute Zeit gelaufen. ♦ Das waren finstere Zeiten.* length of time Zeit at this time of day um diese Zeit ◊ *Er ist um diese Zeit meistens zu Hause.* a hard time eine schwere Zeit at that time zu der Zeit it's time sb did sth es wird Zeit, dass jd etw. tut ◊ *Es wird Zeit, dass du ins Bett gehst.* local time Ortszeit ['ɔrtstsaet] (for) a long time lange ['laŋə] <länger, am längsten> ◊ *Das ist schon lange her. ♦ Wir haben lange gewartet.* (for) a short time kurz [kʊrts] <kürzer, am kürzesten> ◊ *Er dachte kurz darüber nach.* a short time ago vor kurzem [fo:ɐ̯ 'kʊrtsəm] ◊ *Ich habe sie vor kurzem noch gesehen.* **2.** (period in history) times Zeit [tsaet] die <–> sing ◊ *Die Diskriminierung von Frauen passt nicht in unsere Zeit.* Roman times die Römerzeit [di: 'rø:mɐtsaet] **3.** (on a clock) Uhrzeit ['u:ɐ̯tsaet] die <–, –en> ◊ *jdn nach der Uhrzeit fragen ♦ Um diese Uhrzeit schläft das Kind schon. ♦ Zu welcher Uhrzeit passierte der Unfall?* What time ...? Wann ...? ◊ *Wann fängt der Unterricht an?* What time is it? Wie spät ist es? tell the time die Uhr lesen [di: 'u:ɐ̯ le:zn̩] <liest, las, hat gelesen> ◊ *Das Kind kann schon die Uhr lesen.* **4.** (occasion) Mal [ma:l] das <–(e)s, –e> ◊ *ein paar Mal ♦ Dieses Mal waren die Fragen einfacher als beim letzten Mal. ♦ Jedes Mal das Gleiche! ♦ Das sagst du jetzt schon zum tausendsten Mal.* Do you remember the time when we ...? Weißt du noch, als wir ...? two times zweimal ['tsvaema:l] three times dreimal ['draema:l] **5.** (particular moment) Zeitpunkt ['tsaetpʊŋkt] der <–(e)s, –e> ◊ *Bis zu diesem Zeitpunkt hatte sie das nicht gewusst. ♦ Jetzt wäre ein guter Zeitpunkt, ihn zu fragen.* the right time der richtige Zeitpunkt ◊ *Du hast den richtigen Zeitpunkt verpasst.* **6.** (of a piece of music) Takt [takt] der <–(e)s, –e> ◊ *den Takt schlagen ♦ im Takt bleiben ♦ Er kommt immer aus dem Takt.* 3-4 time Dreivierteltakt [drae'fɪrtl̩takt]

👁 there is no time like the present was du heute kannst besorgen, das verschiebe nicht auf morgen

just in time gerade noch once upon a time there was es war einmal do time im Gefängnis sitzen time flies die Zeit vergeht wie im Flug time will tell das wird die Zukunft zeigen most of the time meistens from time to time von Zeit zu Zeit in no time im Nu ◊ *Ich bin im Nu wieder da.* on time pünktlich

time² [verb] **1.** (arrange at a particular time) legen ['le:gn̩] +haben ◊ *Wir haben die Besprechung so gelegt, dass alle aus dem Urlaub zurück sind.* You timed that well! Du kommst genau zur richtigen Zeit! **2.** (with a clock) messen ['mɛsn̩] <misst, maß, hat gemessen>

timeless [adj] zeitlos ['tsaetlo:s] <zeitloser, am zeitlosesten> ◊ *zeitlose Dichtung/Kunst ♦ Dieser Stil ist absolut zeitlos.*

time off [noun] have time off freihaben ['fraeha:bm̩] <hat frei, hatte frei, hat freigehabt> ◊ *Sie hat eigentlich nie frei.* take time off sich [dat] freinehmen ['fraene:man] <nimmt frei, nahm frei, hat freigenommen> ◊ *Ich habe mir ein paar Tage freigenommen.*

times [prep] mal [ma:l] ◊ *Wie viel ist zehn mal fünf?*

timetable [noun] **1.** (for buses, trains etc.) Fahrplan ['fa:ɐ̯pla:n] der <–(e)s, Fahrpläne> ◊ *Laut Fahrplan soll der Zug in zehn Minuten ankommen. ♦ Ich sehe mal auf dem Fahrplan nach.* **2.** (at school, college) Stundenplan ['ʃtʊndn̩pla:n] der <–(e)s, Stundenpläne> ◊ *Heute habe ich einen vollen Stundenplan. ♦ Was steht jetzt auf dem Stundenplan?* **3.** (schedule) Zeitplan ['tsaetpla:n] der <–(e)s, Zeitpläne> ◊ *der Zeitplan für die verschiedenen Stufen der Reform* set a timetable for sth einen Zeitplan für etw. festlegen

timid(ly) [adj, adv] scheu [ʃɔø] <scheuer, am scheuesten> ◊ *Das Wild hier ist sehr scheu. ♦ ein scheuer Blick ♦ Er sah sie scheu an.*

timing [noun] **1.** (doing sth at the best moment) Timing ['taemɪŋ] das <–s, –s> ◊ *ein gutes Timing haben* This is bad timing. Jetzt ist ein schlechter Zeitpunkt. **2.** (of a dancer) Gefühl für Rhythmus [gə,fy:l fy:ɐ̯ 'rʏtmʊs] das <–(e)s> no pl **3.** the timing of sth der Zeitpunkt ... [gen] [de:ɐ̯ 'tsaetpʊŋkt] <–, –e> ◊ *Wer entscheidet über den Zeitpunkt der Wahlen?*

tin [noun] **1.** (metal) Zinn [tsɪn] das <–(e)s> no pl ◊ *Spielzeugsoldaten aus Zinn* **2.** (storage container, can) Dose ['do:zə] die <–, –n> ◊ *eine Dose geschälte Tomaten ♦ Champignons aus der Dose ♦ Tee in einer Dose aufbewahren* biscuit tin Keksdose ['ke:ksdo:zə] **3.** (for baking) Form [fɔrm] die <–, –en> ◊ *Teig in eine Form füllen* cake tin Kuchenform ['ku:xn̩fɔrm]; (for meat) roasting tin Bräter ['brɛ:te] der <–s, –>

tinge [noun] Spur [ʃpu:ɐ̯] die <–, –en> ◊ *Er bemerkte eine Spur von Rot in ihrem Haar. ♦ eine Spur von Traurigkeit*

tin opener [noun] Dosenöffner ['do:zn̩œfne] der <–s, –>

tiny [adj] winzig ['vɪntsɪç] ◊ *Das Handy war winzig. ♦ die winzigen Füßchen einer Maus* tiny little winzig klein

tip¹ [noun] **1.** (pointed end) Spitze ['ʃpɪtsə] die <–, –n> ◊ *Der Leuchtturm steht auf der Spitze der Insel. ♦ Die Spitze des Pfeils ist abgebrochen.* tips of your toes Zehenspitzen ['tse:ən̩ʃpɪtsn̩] tips of your fingers Fingerspitzen ['fɪŋɐʃpɪtsn̩] **2.** (gratuity) Trinkgeld ['trɪŋgɛlt] das <–(e)s, –er> most sing ◊ *dem Kellner*

ein Trinkgeld geben **3.** *(advice, secret information)* Tipp [tɪp] *der* <–s, –s> *(fam)* ◊ *Er gab ihr ein paar nützliche Tipps.* ♦ *Die Polizei erhielt einen Tipp aus der Szene.* ♦ *Wie lautet dein Tipp für das Rennen?* **4.** *(for waste)* Müllkippe ['mʏlkɪpə] *die* <–, –n> ◊ *etw. auf die Müllkippe werfen* **5.** *(untidy place)* Saustall ['zaʊʃtal] *der* <–(e)s, Sauställe> *(fam)* ◊ *Ihr Zimmer ist ein richtiger Saustall.*

ⓢ *be just the tip of the iceberg* nur die Spitze des Eisbergs sein ♦ *be on the tip of sb's tongue* jdm auf der Zunge liegen

tip² [verb] **1.** *(overturn)* tip (over) umkippen ['ʊmkɪpm̩] *transitive use +haben/intransitive use +sein* ◊ *Er hat seinen Becher umgekippt.* ♦ *Die Vase ist umgekippt.* **2.** *(incline, pour, empty)* kippen ['kɪpm̩] *transitive use +haben/intransitive use +sein* ◊ *Er kippte den Sessel nach hinten, um darunterzusehen.* ♦ *Die Kiste kippte ein wenig.* ♦ *Er kippte das Bier ins Glas.; (your head)* neigen ['naɡn̩] *+haben* ◊ *Sie neigte den Kopf zur Seite und sah mich an.* **3.** *(give a gratuity to sb)* tip (sb) (jdm) Trinkgeld geben ['trɪŋkɡɛlt ɡeːbm̩] <gibt, gab, hat gegeben> ◊ *Vergiss nicht, dem Fahrer Trinkgeld zu geben.* **4.** *(in a race etc.)* tip sb/sth auf jdn/etw. tippen [aof ... ,tɪpm̩] *+haben* ◊ *Ich tippte auf Deutschland für den Pokal.* ♦ *be tipped to win sth* der Favorit ... [gen] sein [deːɐ favoˈriːt zaɛn] die Favorit ... [gen] sein [diː favoˈriːtn̩ zaɛn] *+sein* ◊ *Wer ist der Favorit des Rennens?* **5.** *(dump waste)* Müll abladen ['mʏl ,apɭaːdn̩] <lädt ab, lud ab, hat abgeladen> ◊ *Er lud den Müll einfach im Wald ab.* **6.** *(touch slightly)* antippen ['antɪpm̩] *+haben* ◊ *Sie hat den Ball nur angetippt.* **7.** *sth is tipped with sth* die Spitze ... [gen] ist mit etw. versehen [diː ʃpɪtsə ɪst mɪt ... fɛzeːən] ◊ *Die Spitzen der Pfeile sind mit Gift versehen.*

ⓢ *it is tipping down* es schüttet *(fam)*

• **tip off** [phras v] *tip sb off* jdm einen Tipp geben [aɛnən 'tɪp ɡeːbm̩] <gibt, gab, hat gegeben> ◊ *Jemand hatte der Polizei einen Tipp gegeben.*

• **tip over** [phras v] *tip (sth) over (etw.)* umkippen ['ʊmkɪpm̩] *transitive use +haben/intransitive use +sein* ◊ *Er hat sein Glas umgekippt.* ♦ *Der Eimer ist umgekippt.*

• **tip up** [phras v] *tip (sth) up (etw.)* kippen ['kɪpm̩] *transitive use +haben/intransitive use +sein* ◊ *Sie hat den Eimer gekippt und das Wasser ausgegossen.* ♦ *Der Tisch ist gekippt.*

tipsy [adj] beschwipst [bəˈʃvɪpst] *no comp/superl (fam)* ◊ *zwei beschwipste Männer* ♦ *Sie war gestern Abend ein wenig beschwipst.*

tire¹ → **tyre**

tire² [verb] **1.** *(become or make fatigued)* ermüden [eˈmyːdn̩] <ermüdet, ermüdete, hat/ist ermüdet> *transitive use +haben/intransitive use +sein* ◊ *Ich bin bei der Wanderung schnell ermüdet.* ♦ *Die Arbeit hat ihn ermüdet.* **2.** *(get bored)* tire of sb/sth jds/einer Sache überdrüssig werden ['yːbedrʏsɪç veːɐdn̩] *+sein (lofty)* ◊ *Er wurde ihrer Gesellschaft bald überdrüssig.*

• **tire out** [phras v] *tire sb out* jdn erschöpfen [eˈʃœpfn̩] <erschöpft, erschöpfte, hat erschöpft> ◊ *Diese Wanderung hat mich sehr erschöpft.*

tired(ly) [adj, adv] *(fatigued)* müde ['myːdə] <müder, am müdesten> ◊ *Ich bin müde. Lass uns heimgehen!* ♦ *ein müdes Kind ins Bett bringen* ♦ *müde lächeln* ♦ *get tired* müde werden [adj] *(no longer want)* be tired of sb/sth jdn/etw. satt haben ['zat haːbm̩] *+haben*

(fam) ◊ *Ich habe dein ständiges Jammern wirklich satt!* be tired of doing sth es satt haben, etw. zu tun ◊ *Sie hat es satt, immer seinen Dreck wegzuputzen.* get tired of doing sth es satt kriegen, etw. zu tun

tireless(ly) [adj, adv] unermüdlich ['ʊn|emʏːtlɪç] ◊ *der unermüdliche Einsatz der Helfer* ♦ *Sie ist unermüdlich und sehr kreativ.* ♦ *Sie kämpften unermüdlich für die Gleichberechtigung.*

tissue [noun] **1.** BIO, MED Gewebe [ɡəˈveːbə] *das* <–s, –> ◊ *aus einem Organ Gewebe entnehmen* **2.** *(handkerchief)* Papiertaschentuch [paˈpiːɐtaʃn̩tuːx] *das* <–(e)s, Papiertaschentücher> ◊ *sich* [dat] *mit einem Papiertaschentuch die Nase putzen; (for wrapping)* tissue (paper) Seidenpapier ['zaɛdn̩papiːɐ] *das* <–s, –e>

title [noun] **1.** *(name of a film, book etc., form of address, position in sports)* Titel ['tiːtl] *der* <–s, –> ◊ *Wie lautet der Titel des Films?* ♦ *jdn mit seinem Titel anreden* ♦ *Er ist Anwärter auf den Titel „Sportler des Jahres".* ♦ *einen Titel gewinnen* **2.** LAW title (to sth) Rechtsanspruch (auf etw. [acc]) ['rɛçts|anʃprʊx] *der* <–(e)s, Rechtsansprüche> ◊ *Er hat keinen Rechtsanspruch auf das Grundstück.*

to¹ [adv] **1.** *(expressing that sth is closed)* zu... ['tsuː] swing to zufallen ['tsuːfalən] <fällt zu, fiel zu, ist zugefallen> ◊ *Das Fenster fiel plötzlich zu.* pull sth to etw. zuziehen ['tsuːtsiːən] <zieht zu, zog zu, hat zugezogen> ◊ *Er zog die Tür zu.* push sth to etw. zudrücken ['tsuːdrʏkn̩] *+haben* ◊ *Es gelang ihr nur mit Mühe, das Tor zuzudrücken.* **2.** *(in two opposite directions)* to and fro hin- und her... [,hɪn ʊnt 'heːɐ] move to and fro sich hin- und herbewegen [,hɪn ʊnt 'heːɐbəveːɡn̩] <bewegt sich hin und her, bewegte sich hin und her, hat sich hin- und herbewegt> swing to and fro hin- und herschwingen [,hɪn ʊnt 'heːɐʃvɪŋən] <schwingt hin und her, schwang hin und her, ist hin- und hergeschwungen> ◊ *Das Pendel schwang hin und her.*

'To' occurs in phrasal verbs like 'come' or 'speak to' which have their own entries in the dictionary.

to² [prep] **1.** *(expressing movement or direction, describing a relation)* zu ['tsuː] [+dat] ◊ *zum Bahnhof fahren* ♦ *auf dem Weg zur Arbeit* ♦ *zum Arzt gehen* ♦ *Warum bist so gemein zu mir?* ♦ *Sie ist immer freundlich zu mir.* ♦ *Zu seiner großen Überraschung war sie einverstanden.* ♦ *eine Mehrheit von zwei zu eins* ♦ *Die italienische Mannschaft siegte mit drei zu zwei.* ♦ *Verbindungen zur Mafia haben* ♦ *Sie tanzten zu leiser Musik.* **2.** *(to a named country, city, town, continent)* nach [naːx] [+dat] ◊ *Sie will nach England gehen.* ♦ *Wir fliegen nächstes Jahr nach Athen/Australien.* from ... to ... von ... nach ... ◊ *Wie weit ist es von München nach Paris?; (to countries which require the article in German; to the cinema, theatre, your bed, a room)* in [ɪn] [+acc] ◊ *Sie reist jedes Jahr in die Schweiz/Türkei.* ♦ *ins Kino/Theater/Bett gehen* ♦ *Geh in dein Zimmer!; (to the countryside, a group of islands, celebration, attending school or university)* auf [aof] [+acc] ◊ *Wir ziehen aufs Land.* ♦ *Ich gehe nicht auf die Hochzeit/den Ball/die Party.* ♦ *Er fliegt auf die Philippinen.* ♦ *Auf welche Uni/Schule gehst du?; (to the seaside, beach, a lake, river)* an [an] [+acc] ◊ *Wir fahren ans Meer/an den Strand/an den Tegernsee/an die Donau.* **3.** *(in combination with an indirect object, 'to' is often expressed with the dative)*

give sth to sb jdm etw. geben ['geːbm̩] <gibt, gab, hat gegeben> explain sth to sb jdm etw. erklären [ɛ'klɛːrən] <erklärt, erklärte, hat erklärt> do sth to sb/sth etw. mit jdm/etw. machen [mɪt ... maxn̩] +haben ◊ *Was hast du nur mit dem schönen Tischtuch gemacht!* **4.** *(addressed to or meant for sb/ sth)* an [an] ⟨+acc⟩ ◊ *Schicken Sie den Brief an folgende Adresse: ...* ◆ *eine Rede an die Nation* ◆ *Das ist ein Geschenk von Andrea an deine Eltern.* **5.** *(expressing an interpersonal relationship)* be a good friend etc. to sb jdm ein guter Freund/eine gute Freundin etc. sein [aen ˈguːtɐ ˈfrɔɣnt/aenɐ ˈguːtə ˈfrɔɣndɪn zaen] related/ married to sb mit jdm verwandt/verheiratet [mɪt ... fɐ'vant/fɐ'haeraːtət] assistant etc. to sb jds Assistent/Assistentin etc. [asɪs'tɛnt/asɪs'tɛntɪn] ◊ *Nächste Woche fängt sie als seine Assistentin an.* **6.** *(expressing the position of sth, often in combination with 'left' or 'right')* to the left/right of sth links/rechts von etw. [lɪŋks/rɛçts fɔn] ◊ *Links vom Schwimmbad ist eine Schule.* to the north/south etc. of sth nördlich/südlich etc. von etw./... ⟨gen⟩ ◊ *Mein Heimatort liegt südlich von Düsseldorf/des Rheins.*; *(on the left/right side)* to the left/right auf der linken/rechten Seite [aof deːɐ ˌlɪŋkn̩/ˌrɛçtn̩ 'zaetə] keep to the left/right sich links/rechts halten ['lɪŋks/'rɛçts haltn̩] <hält sich, hielt sich, hat sich gehalten> **7.** *(expressing that sth is fixed to sth or that sb holds sb/sth tight)* an [an] ⟨+acc⟩ ◊ *ein Brett an die Tür nageln* ◆ *ein Poster an die Wand kleben* ◆ *Er drückte sie an seine Brust.* **8.** *(spatial or temporal: expressing a limit or range, till, up to)* bis [bɪs] ⟨+acc⟩ ◊ *Er kann schon bis zehn zählen.* ◆ *Bis hierher hat er mich begleitet.* ◆ *Bis Frankfurt fahre ich mit dem Zug, danach fliege ich.* ◆ *Das Unkraut hat sich schon bis in den Nachbargarten ausgebreitet.* ◆ *Sie blieb bis zum Ende bei ihm.* ◆ *Die Messe dauert bis Mai.* ◆ *Nur noch zwei Tage bis zur Prüfung!* from ... to ... von ... bis ... ◊ *Wir haben von 9 bis 17 Uhr geöffnet.* ◆ *50 bis 60 Prozent der Befragten sind dafür.* ◆ *Die Reparatur kann 50 bis 100 Euro kosten.* **9.** *(when giving the time)* vor [foːɐ] ⟨+dat⟩ ◊ *Es ist Viertel vor sechs.* ◆ *Wir treffen uns dann um zehn vor fünf.* ◆ *Es war schon fünf vor, als wir endlich ankamen.* **10.** *(in various idioms)* it seems to sb jdm scheint ... [ɛs ʃaent] <scheint, schien, hat geschienen> ◊ *Mir scheint, dass sie das mit Absicht getan hat.* to sb's mind jds Ansicht nach ['anzɪçt naːx] ◊ *Meiner Ansicht nach hat er Recht.* to sb's knowledge jds Wissens ['vɪsn̩s] ◊ *Sie kommt meines Wissens erst morgen zurück.* face to face Auge in Auge [ˌaogə ɪn 'aogə] ◊ *Die Kämpfenden standen Auge in Auge.* back to back Rücken an Rücken [ˌrʏkn̩ an 'rʏkn̩] **11.** *(with certain nouns)* the key to a door der Schlüssel einer Tür [deːɐ ʃlʏsl̩ aenɐ 'tyːɐ] the solution to a problem die Lösung eines Problems [diː ˌløːzʊŋ aenəs proˈbleːms] the answer to a question die Antwort auf eine Frage [diː ˌantvɔʳt aof aenə 'fraːgə]

> For the many uses of 'to' with other nouns or verbs, please look up the relevant noun or verb entries.

to³ *(in infinitives)* zu [tsuː] ◊ *Ich habe viel zu tun.* ◆ *Es fängt an zu regnen.* ◆ *Es ist unmöglich, das zu schaffen.* know what to do wissen, was jd tun soll ['vɪsn̩ vas ... zɔl] <soll, sollte, hat sollen> ◊ *Sie*

wusste nicht, was sie tun sollte. know what to say wissen, was jd sagen soll; *(expressing a purpose)* um zu [ʊm tsuː] ◊ *Ich schreibe Ihnen, um mich für Ihre Hilfe zu bedanken.* ◆ *Das tut er nur, um mich zu ärgern.*; *(omitting the verb)* I don't want to. Ich will nicht. [ɪç 'vɪl nɪçt] You have to. Du musst. [duː 'mʊst]

toast¹ ⟨noun⟩ **1.** *(bread)* Toast [toːst] der <-(e)s, -e or -s> ◊ *eine Scheibe Toast* ◆ *Sie isst gern Toast mit Marmelade.* **2.** *(drinking and wishing sb well)* Trinkspruch ['trɪŋkʃprʊx] der <-(e)s, Trinksprüche> propose a toast (to sb) einen Trinkspruch (auf jdn) ausbringen drink a toast to sb auf jdn trinken [aof ... trɪŋkn̩] <trinkt, trank, hat getrunken> ◉ as warm as toast mollig warm ◊ *Das Zimmer war mollig warm.* be the toast of sth der gefeierte Star ... ⟨gen⟩ sein ◊ *Sie war der gefeierte Star des Abends.*

toast² ⟨verb⟩ **1.** *(in a toaster)* toasten ['toːstn̩] <toastet, hat getoastet> ◊ *Hast du das Brot schon getoastet?* **2.** *(on open fire)* rösten ['rœstn̩] <röstet, röstete, hat geröstet> ◊ *Nüsse/Fleisch rösten* **3.** *(when drinking)* toast sb/sth auf jdn/etw. trinken [aof ... trɪŋkn̩] <trinkt, trank, hat getrunken> ◊ *Alle tranken auf ihren Sieg.* **4.** *(fam) (get warm again)* sich am Feuer wärmen [am 'fɔɣɐ ˌvɛʳmən] +haben ◊ *Als es kalt wurde, wärmten sich alle am Feuer.*

tobacco ⟨noun⟩ *(plant, for producing cigarettes etc.)* Tabak ['taːbak] der <-s, -e> most sing ◊ *Tabak rauchen* tobacco industry Tabakindustrie ['taːbak|ɪndʊsˌtriː] die <-, -n> tobacco smoke Tabakrauch ['taːbakraox] der <-(e)s> no pl

today¹ ⟨noun⟩ heute ['hɔɣtə] ◊ *Welcher Tag ist heute?* of today, today's von heute ◊ *die Zeitung/Jugend von heute*

today² ⟨adv⟩ **1.** *(on this day)* heute ['hɔɣtə] ◊ *Heute ist er eine Woche fort.* from today ab heute a week etc. today heute in einer Woche etc. ◊ *Ich habe heute in einer Woche Geburtstag.* a year ago today heute vor einem Jahr **2.** *(nowadays)* heutzutage ['hɔɣtˌsuːtaːgə] ◊ *Viele Jugendliche heutzutage sind sehr anspruchsvoll.*

toddler ⟨noun⟩ Kleinkind ['klaenkɪnt] das <-(e)s, -er>

toe ⟨noun⟩ **1.** ANAT Zeh [tseː] der <-s, -en> ◊ *der kleine/große Zeh* ◆ *Ich stellte mich auf die Zehen.* **2.** *(of shoe, sock)* Spitze ['ʃpɪtsə] die <-, -n> ◊ *Schuhe mit verstärkten Spitzen* ◉ keep sb on their toes jdn auf Zack halten *(fam)* step on sb's toes **1.** *(when dancing etc.)* jdm auf die Zehen treten *(fam)* **2.** *(offend sb)* jdm ins Handwerk pfuschen

together ⟨adv⟩ **1.** *(with each other, jointly, at the same time, considered as a whole, having a relationship, combining things, putting things in one place)* zusammen [tsu'zamən] ◊ *Wir fuhren alle zusammen nach Rom.* ◆ *zusammen spielen* ◆ *Wir waren das ganze Wochenende zusammen.* ◆ *Lasst uns zusammen versuchen, eine Lösung zu finden.* ◆ *Sein und ihr Gehalt zusammen reichen gerade zum Leben.* ◆ *Seit wann sind die beiden schon zusammen?* add together zusammenzählen [tsu'zaməntsɛːlən] +haben come together zusammenkommen [tsu'zamənkɔmən] <kommt zusammen, kam zusammen, ist zusammengekommen> keep together zusammenhalten [tsu'zamənhaltn̩] <hält zusammen,

hielt zusammen, hat zusammengehalten> sew together
zusammennähen ['ʦu'zamənnɛːən] +haben tie
together zusammenbinden ['ʦu'zamənbɪndn̩] <bindet
zusammen, band zusammen, hat zusammengebunden>
2. *(against each other)* aneinander [an|aeˈnandə] ◊
Sie rieb die Hände aneinander, um sie zu wärmen.

'Together' often occurs in phrasal verbs like 'get
together' or 'put together' which have their own
entries in the dictionary.

toilet ⟨noun⟩ *(room, seat)* Toilette [tɔaˈlɛtə] die
<-, -n> ◊ *Ich muss auf die Toilette!* ♦ *ein Bad mit
Toilette* go to the toilet auf die Toilette gehen
ⓔ **need the toilet** müssen *(fam)* ◊ *Ich muss mal!*
toilet paper ⟨noun⟩ Toilettenpapier [tɔaˈlɛtnpa,piːɡ]
das <-s, -e> ◊ *eine Rolle Toilettenpapier*
token ⟨noun⟩ **1.** *(voucher)* Gutschein [ˈɡuːtʃaen] der
<-(e)s, -e> ◊ *ein Gutschein für etw.* **2.** *(for
gambling etc.)* Spielmarke [ˈʃpiːlmaʳkə] die <-, -n>
◊ *eine Spielmarke in den Automaten werfen* **3.** *(sign)*
Zeichen [ˈʦaeçn̩] das <-s, -> ◊ *ein kleines
Geschenk zum Zeichen meiner Dankbarkeit*
ⓔ **by the same token** ebenso
tolerance ⟨noun⟩ Toleranz [toləˈrants] die <-, -en> ◊
Kinder zur Toleranz erziehen ♦ *Toleranz gegenüber
jdm üben*
tolerate ⟨verb⟩ **1.** *(accept sb/sth you don't like)* dulden
[ˈdʊldn̩] <duldet, duldete, hat geduldet> ◊ *Ich dulde
keinen Widerspruch!* ♦ *Er wusste, dass man ihn nur
duldete.* ♦ *etw. stillschweigend dulden* tolerate sb
doing sth dulden, dass jd etw. tut ◊ *Ich dulde nicht,
dass du ihn beleidigst.* **2.** *(a noise, pain etc.)*
ertragen [eˈtraːgn̩] <erträgt, ertrug, hat ertragen> ◊
*Ich kann die Schmerzen kaum noch ertragen.; (condi-
tions, food, drink, medication)* vertragen [feˈtraːgn̩]
<verträgt, vertrug, hat vertragen> ◊ *Er verträgt keinen
Alkohol.*
toll ⟨noun⟩ **1.** *(for using a road etc.)* Maut [maot] die
<-, -en> ◊ *Maut bezahlen* **2.** *(number of victims)*
Zahl der Opfer [ˌʦaːl deːɡ ˈɔpfə] die <-> toll of sth
Zahl der Opfer ... ⟨gen⟩ ◊ *Die Zahl der Opfer des
Erdbebens ist weiter gestiegen.* the death toll die
Zahl der Todesopfer the toll of failed businesses
die Zahl der in Konkurs gegangenen Unternehmen;
(damage) the toll of sth die Schäden durch etw.
[diː ˈʃɛːdn̩ dʊʳç] die <-> *pl* ◊ *die Schäden durch Alko-
holmissbrauch* **3.** *(of a bell)* Läuten [ˈlɔøtn̩] das <-s>
no *pl* ◊ *Er wurde vom Läuten der Glocken geweckt.*
ⓔ **take its toll (on sb/sth)** seinen Tribut (von
jdm/etw.) fordern
tomato ⟨noun⟩ Tomate [toˈmaːtə] die <-, -n>
tomb ⟨noun⟩ Grab [graːp] das <-(e)s, Gräber>
tomorrow¹ ⟨noun⟩ morgen [ˈmɔʳgn̩] ◊ *Morgen ist auch
noch ein Tag.* of tomorrow, tomorrow's von morgen
◊ *die Welt/Zeitung von morgen*
tomorrow² ⟨adv⟩ morgen [ˈmɔʳgn̩] ◊ *Wir gehen
morgen ins Kino.* a week etc. tomorrow morgen in
einer Woche etc. ◊ *Morgen in einer Woche fliegt er
in die Staaten.* tomorrow morning/afternoon/night
morgen früh/Nachmittag/Abend
ton ⟨noun⟩ *(metric)* ton Tonne [ˈtɔnə] die <-, -n> ◊
Der Lkw wiegt 26 Tonnen.; (in the UK) britische
Tonne [ˌbriːtɪʃə ˈtɔnə] die <-, -n>; *(in the US)* amerikanische Tonne [ameriˌkaːnɪʃə ˈtɔnə]
ⓔ **weigh tons** zentnerschwer sein **tons of ...** massenhaft ... ◊ *Sie hat massenhaft Gepäck dabei.*

tone ⟨noun⟩ **1.** *(sound, colo(u)r, musical note, attitude)*
Ton [toːn] der <-(e)s, Töne> ◊ *ein hoher/tiefer Ton*
♦ *Sprich nicht in diesem Ton mit mir!* ♦ *Hemd und
Hose waren blau, das Hemd in einem etwas helleren
Ton.* engaged tone Besetzzeichen [bəˈzɛtsʦaeçn̩]
das <-s, -> **2.** *(mood)* Stimmung [ˈʃtɪmʊŋ] die <->
◊ *Die Stimmung auf dem Treffen war eher geschäftlich.* set the tone die Stimmung vorgeben
3. *(decorum)* Niveau [niˈvoː] das <-s> raise/lower
the tone das Niveau heben/senken ◊ *Er senkte mit
seinen Bemerkungen das Niveau der Unterhaltung
beträchtlich.* **4.** MED muscle tone Muskeltonus
[ˈmʊskl̩toːnʊs] der <-, Muskeltoni> *(tech)* ◊ *Der Muskeltonus des Patienten ist schwach.* **5.** LING Intonation [ɪntonaˈʦi̯oːn] die <-, -en> ◊ *Fragen werden im
Deutschen mit steigender Intonation gesprochen.*
tongue ⟨noun⟩ **1.** *(organ, food, of shoe)* Zunge [ˈʦʊŋə]
die <-, -n> ◊ *jdm die Zunge herausstrecken* ♦ *Es
gab gebratene Zunge.* ♦ *Die Zunge des Schuhs ist
gepolstert.* **2.** *(language)* Sprache [ˈʃpraːxə] die
<-, -n> ◊ *Fortan redeten sie in fremden Sprachen.*
mother tongue Muttersprache [ˈmʊtəʃpraːxə]
ⓔ **tongue in cheek** mit einem Augenzwinkern **have
a loose tongue** nichts für sich behalten können
have a sharp tongue eine spitze Zunge haben **bite
your tongue** ⟨dat⟩ auf die Zunge beißen
tonic ⟨noun⟩ **1.** tonic (water) Tonic [ˈtɔnɪk] das
<-(s), -s> ◊ *Ich hätte gern ein Tonic.* gin and tonic
Gin Tonic **2.** be a tonic for sb jdm gut tun
[ˈɡuːt tuːn] <tut, tat, hat getan> ◊ *Das Wochenende in
den Bergen hat mir gut getan.* **3.** MED Tonikum
[ˈtoːnikʊm] das <-s, Tonika> ◊ *Der Arzt verschrieb
ihm ein Tonikum.* **4.** *(for hair)* Haarwasser
[ˈhaːʳvasə] das <-s, Haarwässer> ◊ *ein Haarwasser
gegen Schuppen; (for skin)* Lotion [loˈʦi̯oːn] die
<-, -en> ◊ *eine Lotion auf die Haut auftragen*
5. MUS Tonika [ˈtoːnikaː] die <-, Toniken> ◊ *die
Tonika spielen*
tonight ⟨adv⟩ *(this evening)* heute Abend [hɔøtə ˈaːbm̩t]
◊ *Ruf mich heute Abend an.; (during the coming
night)* heute Nacht [hɔøtə ˈnaxt] ◊ *Ich werde heute
Nacht woanders schlafen.*
tonne ⟨noun⟩ Tonne [ˈtɔnə] die <-, -n> ◊ *Der Lkw
wiegt fast 40 Tonnen.*
tonsil ⟨noun⟩ Mandel [ˈmandl̩] die <-, -n> ◊ *Sie ließ
sich ⟨dat⟩ die Mandeln herausnehmen.*
too ⟨adv⟩ **1.** *(more than you can accept or deal with)* zu
[ʦuː] ◊ *Du bist noch zu jung für den Film.* ♦ *Die
ganze Aufregung war zu viel für ihn.* too ... to do
sth zu ..., um etw. zu tun ◊ *Ich bin zu müde, um
zu arbeiten.* much/far too ... viel zu ... ◊ *Das ist
viel zu teuer.* **2.** *(for emphasis)* auch [aox] ◊
„Ich komme mit!" — „Ich auch." ♦ *Wir haben auch
unsere Probleme.* ♦ *Sie hat ihn verlassen, und das ist
auch gut so.* **3.** *(moreover)* auch noch [aox nɔx] ◊ *Er
musste auch noch für die Busfahrt aufkommen.*
4. *(very)* all too allzu [ˈaltsuː] ◊ *Allzu oft bleiben
Ehefrauen aus Angst bei ihren gewalttätigen
Männern.* not too nicht allzu ◊ *Er war nicht allzu
interessiert an meinen Sorgen.*
tool ⟨noun⟩ *(hammer etc., something used for achieving
sth, person)* tool(s) Werkzeug [ˈvɛʳkʦɔøk] das
<-(e)s, -e> *most sing* ◊ *ein Werkzeug benutzen* ♦
Sie war ein gefügiges Werkzeug ihres Chefs. ♦ *Ich
habe für diese Arbeit nicht das richtige Werkzeug.*
learning tool Lernwerkzeug [ˈlɛʳnvɛʳkʦɔøk]

tooth [noun] Zahn [ʦaːn] der <-(e)s, Zähne> ◊ *sich* [dat] *die Zähne putzen* ♦ *Der Hund knurrte und zeigte die Zähne.* ♦ *Die Zähne der Säge sind stumpf.* ♦ *die Zähne eines Kamms* take out a tooth jdm einen Zahn ziehen cut teeth Zähne bekommen tooth decay Karies ['kaːrɪɛs] die <-> no pl ⊚ **fight tooth and nail** bis aufs Blut kämpfen give sth some teeth einer Sache [dat] Wirksamkeit verleihen

toothpaste [noun] Zahnpasta ['ʦaːnpasta:] die <-, -s or Zahnpasten> most sing ◊ *eine Tube Zahnpasta*

top¹ [noun] 1. *(highest part)* oberer Teil [,oːbərɐ 'taɛl] <-(e)s, -e> ◊ *Der obere Teil der Ananas ist faulig.*; *(of a mountain)* Gipfel ['gɪpfl̩] der <-s, -> ◊ *den Gipfel des Berges erreichen* ♦ *auf dem Gipfel stehen*; *(of a tree, spire, hierarchy)* Spitze ['ʃpɪʦə] die <-, -n> ◊ *auf die Spitze eines Baumes klettern* ♦ *Wer steht an der Spitze der Partei/Firma?*; *(surface)* Oberfläche ['oːbɐflɛçə] die <-, -n> ◊ *auf der Oberfläche schwimmen* on top of the other aufeinander [aoflaeˈnandɐ] ◊ *Kartons aufeinander stapeln* at the top of the page oben auf der Seite [,oːbm̩ aof deːg̩ 'zaɛtə] ◊ *Das steht ganz oben auf der Seite.* at the top of the list/pile oben auf der Liste/ dem Stapel at the top of the stairs/wall oben an der Treppe/Wand 2. *(of a bottle)* Verschluss [fɛɐˈʃlʊs] der <-es, Verschlüsse> ◊ *Die Flasche hat einen kindersicheren Verschluss.*; *(of a suitcase, jar)* Deckel ['dɛkl̩] der <-s, -> ◊ *der Deckel einer Schachtel/ eines Marmeladenglases*; *(of a pen)* Kappe ['kapə] die <-, -n> 3. *(piece of clothing)* Oberteil ['oːbɐtaɛl] das <-(e)s, -e> ◊ *das Oberteil des Bikinis/Schlafanzugs*; *(sleeveless and with low neckline)* Top [tɔp] das <-s, -s> ◊ *ein bauchfreies Top* 4. *(furthest part of a table, road, bed)* obere Ende [,oːbərə 'ɛndə] das <-s, -n> ◊ *Die Katze schlief am oberen Ende des Bettes.* ♦ *Sie saß am oberen Ende des Tisches.* 5. *(toy)* *(spinning)* top Kreisel ['kraɛzl̩] der <-s, -> ◊ *mit einem Kreisel spielen* ⊚ **off the top of your head** 1. *(without thinking)* ganz spontan 2. *(without calculating exactly)* über den Daumen gepeilt at the top of your voice aus vollem Hals blow your top in die Luft gehen get on top of sb jdm über den Kopf wachsen ◊ *Die ganze Angelegenheit wächst ihm allmählich über den Kopf.* on top of sb/sth 1. *(covering sb/sth)* auf etw./jdm ◊ *Auf der Torte war Sahne.* *(onto sb/sth)* auf etw./jdn ◊ *Sie sprühte Sahne auf die Torte.* 2. *(in addition)* zusätzlich zu etw./jdm ◊ *Zusätzlich zu all diesen Sorgen wurde sie auch noch krank.* over the top *(exaggerated)* übertrieben go over the top übertreiben

top² [adj] 1. *(highest in position)* oberste ['oːbəstə] no comp/superl, only before ns ◊ *Er wohnt im obersten Stockwerk.* ♦ *Der oberste Knopf an meiner Bluse fehlt.*; *(upper)* obere ['oːbərə] no comp, only before ns ◊ *<ein oberer …, eine obere …, ein oberes …>* ◊ *Die obere Hälfte des Gebäudes ist nicht mehr bewohnbar.* 2. *(highest in status, importance, hono(u)r, price)* höchste ['høːçstə] no comp/superl ◊ *Er gewann die höchste Auszeichnung.* top speed Höchstgeschwindigkeit ['høːçstɡəʃvɪndɪçkaɛt] die <-, -en> *(best school, pupil, mark, player etc.)* beste ['bɛstə] no comp/superl ◊ *eine der besten Schulen im Land*

top³ [verb] 1. *(be better, more interesting)* übertreffen [ybɐ'trɛfn̩] <übertrifft, übertraf, hat übertroffen> ◊ *Die Geschichte war kaum zu übertreffen.* 2. *(be in first place, be the best)* anführen ['anfyːrən] +haben ◊ *Der Spieler führt die Liste der Torjäger an.* 3. *(be higher)* übersteigen [ybɐ'ʃtaɛɡn̩] <übersteigt, überstieg, hat überstiegen> ◊ *Der Preis dieses Gemäldes übersteigt 250 000 Euro.*; *(bid more)* top sth *(by sth)* etw. *(um etw.)* überbieten [ybɐ'biːtn̩] <überbietet, überbot, hat überboten> ◊ *Sie hat sein Angebot um 500 Euro überboten.* 4. *(a pizza, cake)* belegen [bə'leːɡn̩] <belegt, belegte, hat belegt> ◊ *Sie belegte den Kuchen mit Obst.* 5. *(by snow)* be topped by sth mit etw. bedeckt sein [mɪt … bədɛkt zaɛn] +sein ◊ *Die Berggipfel waren mit Schnee bedeckt.* 6. *(reach the top of)* top sth oben auf etw. [dat] ankommen [,oːbm̩ aof … ,ankomən] <kommt an, kam an, ist angekommen> ◊ *Sie waren oben auf dem Berg angekommen.* ⊚ **to top it all** um das Maß voll zu machen **top yourself** sich umbringen

♦ **top up** [phras v] 1. *(a glass, tank)* top sth up etw. auffüllen ['aoffʏlən] +haben ◊ *den Tank auffüllen* top sb up jdm nachschenken ['naːxʃɛŋkn̩] +haben ◊ *Darf ich Ihnen nachschenken?* 2. *(your earnings)* top sth up etw. aufbessern ['aofbɛsɐn] +haben ◊ *Mit dem Nebenjob bessert sie ihr Einkommen auf.*

topic [noun] Thema ['teːma] das <-s, Themen> ◊ *Zu diesem Thema gibt es fast keine Literatur.* ♦ *Über welche Themen habt ihr gesprochen?* topic of conversation Gesprächsthema [ɡə'ʃprɛːçsteːma:]

topical [adj] 1. *(of today)* aktuell [aktu'ɛl] ◊ *über aktuelle Ereignisse berichten* ♦ *Das Thema ist schon lange nicht mehr aktuell.* 2. MED zur lokalen Anwendung [ʦuːg̩ lo,kaːlən 'anvɛndʊŋ] ◊ *eine Salbe zur lokalen Anwendung*

torch [noun] 1. *(in the UK: flashlight)* Taschenlampe ['taʃn̩lampə] die <-, -n> ◊ *Sie leuchtete mit einer Taschenlampe unter das Bett.* 2. *(burning piece of wood)* Fackel ['fakl̩] die <-, -n> ◊ *die olympische Fackel* 3. *(blowtorch)* Schweißbrenner ['ʃvaɛsbrɛnɐ] der <-s, -> ◊ *Bei der Arbeit mit dem Schweißbrenner muss man eine Schutzbrille tragen.* ⊚ **carry a torch for sb** nach jdm schmachten *(lofty)*

torment [verb] quälen ['kvɛːlən] +haben ◊ *Schreckliche Kopfschmerzen quälten sie.*

tortoise [noun] Schildkröte ['ʃɪltkrøːtə] die <-, -n>

torture¹ [noun] Folter ['fɔltɐ] die <-, -n> ◊ *etw. unter Folter gestehen* ♦ *Dieser Zustand ist die reinste Folter.*

torture² [verb] 1. *(cause physical pain)* foltern ['fɔltɐn] +haben ◊ *In zahlreichen Ländern werden Gefangene gefoltert.* 2. *(upset)* quälen ['kvɛːlən] +haben ◊ *Die Sorge um ihn quälte sie.* torture yourself sich quälen ◊ *Hör auf, dich mit diesen schrecklichen Vorstellungen zu quälen!*

toss [verb] 1. *(throw)* werfen ['vɛːfn̩] <wirft, warf, hat geworfen> ◊ *Er warf seine Tasche in die Ecke.* ♦ *einen Ball in die Luft werfen* ♦ *Lass uns die Münze werfen.* ♦ *den Kopf in den Nacken werfen* 2. *(wind or waves: move sth violently)* toss sth about etw. hin- und herwerfen [hɪn ʊnt heːɐ'vɛːfn̩] <wirft herum, warf herum, hat herumgeworfen> ◊ *Das Floß wurde von den Wellen hin- und hergeworfen.* 3. *(a salad)* mischen ['mɪʃn̩] +haben ◊ *Hast du den Salat schon gemischt?*; *(in butter, a marinade)* toss sth in sth etw.

in etw. [dat] schwenken [ɪn ... ʃvɛŋkn̩] +haben ◊ *Gemüse vor dem Servieren in heißer Butter schwenken* **4.** *(get rid of)* toss sth (out) etw. wegschmeißen ['vɛkʃmaesn̩] <schmeißt weg, schmiss weg, hat weggeschmissen> *(fam)* ◊ *Schmeiß doch endlich mal die alten Schuhe weg!*

⊚ **toss and turn** sich im Bett hin und her wälzen

• **toss off** [phras v] *(produce quickly)* hinhauen ['hɪnhaɔən] <haut hin, haute hin, hat hingehauen> *(fam)* ◊ *Sie hat den Bericht in einer halben Stunde hingehauen.*

• **toss out** [phras v] *(suggest)* toss sth out etw. rauslassen ['raʊslasn̩] <lässt raus, ließ raus, hat rausgelassen> *(fam)* ◊ *Du lässt ständig neue Ideen raus, aus denen nichts wird.* → **toss 4.**

total¹ [noun] Summe ['zʊmə] die <-, -n> ◊ *Die Summe aus vier und vier ist acht.* ♦ *eine Summe von 75 Euro* a total of ..., ... in total insgesamt ... [ɪnsɡəˈtsamt] ◊ *Er muss für insgesamt acht Jahre ins Gefängnis.* ♦ *Insgesamt hat der Urlaub 2 000 Euro gekostet.*

total² [adj] **1.** *(overall)* Gesamt... [ɡəˈtsamt] total cost Gesamtkosten [ɡəˈtsamtkɔstn̩] die <-> pl total number Gesamtzahl [ɡəˈtsamtsa:l] die <-, -en> total population Gesamtbevölkerung [ɡəˈtsamtbəfœlkərʊŋ] die <-> no comp/superl ◊ *Das ist doch völliger Quatsch!; (complete, absolute)* völlig ['fœlɪç] no comp/superl ◊ *Das ist doch völliger Quatsch!; (eclipse, war)* total [toˈta:l] no comp/superl ◊ *eine totale Sonnenfinsternis/Mondfinsternis; (success)* voll [fɔl] no comp/superl ◊ *Das Geschäft war ein voller Erfolg.*

total³ [verb] **1.** *(amount to)* total to sich auf etw. [acc] belaufen [zɪç aɔf ... bəlaɔfn̩] <beläuft sich, belief sich, hat sich belaufen> ◊ *Die Gesamtsumme beläuft sich auf 50 000 Euro.; (add together)* total (up) zusammenzählen [tsuˈzaməntsɛːlən] +haben ◊ *Zählen wir die Punkte zusammen, damit wir sehen, wer gewonnen hat.* **2.** *(in the US: destroy a vehicle in an accident)* zu Schrott fahren [tsuː ˈʃrɔt faːrən] <fährt, fuhr, hat gefahren> *(fam)* ◊ *Er hat seinen Wagen zu Schrott gefahren.*

totalitarian [adj] totalitär [totaliˈtɛːɐ̯] seldom comp/superl ◊ *Das Regime war totalitär.* ♦ *ein totalitärer Staat*

totally [adv] völlig ['fœlɪç] no comp/superl ◊ *Der Ort wurde vom Erdbeben völlig zerstört.*

touch¹ [noun] **1.** *(of a hand etc.)* Berührung [bəˈryːrʊŋ] die <-, -en> ◊ *zärtliche Berührungen* ♦ *Der Alarm geht bei der geringsten Berührung des Gemäldes los.* **2.** *(little bit)* Spur [ʃpuːɐ̯] die <-, -en> ◊ *keine Spur von Reue zeigen* ♦ *Am Essen fehlt noch eine Spur Knoblauch.; (of paint, with adj or adv)* a touch ein bisschen [aen ˈbɪsçən] ◊ *ein bisschen Farbe* ♦ *Das Bild hängt ein bisschen zu weit links.* **3.** *(sense)* Tastsinn ['tastzɪn] der <-(e)s> no pl be/feel cold etc. to the touch sich kalt etc. anfühlen ['kalt anfyːlən] +haben ◊ *Das Kissen fühlt sich rau an.* **4.** *(style)* Stil [ʃtiːl] der <-(e)s, -e> ◊ *Ich mag den persönlichen Stil dieses Hotels.; (positive feature)* Note ['noːtə] die <-> no pl ◊ *ein Anzug mit sportlicher Note* put the final touches to sth einer Sache [dat] den letzten Schliff geben [deːn lɛtstn̩ ˈʃlɪf ɡeːbm̩] <gibt, gab, hat gegeben> a touch of genius etwas Geniales [ɛtvas ɡeˈniːaləs] ◊ *Dieses Bild hat etwas Geniales an sich!* **5.** *(skill)* Hand [hant] die <-> no pl ◊ *Sie hat eine Hand für so etwas.* have the right

touch with sb/sth mit jdm/etw. umgehen können [mɪt ... ˌʊmɡeːən kœnən] <kann, konnte, hat können> ◊ *Mein Großvater konnte mit Pferden umgehen.* **6.** *(in contact)* in touch in Verbindung [ɪn fɛˈbɪndʊŋ] be in touch with sb mit jdm in Verbindung stehen get in touch with sb sich mit jdm in Verbindung setzen keep in touch (with sb) (mit jdm) in Verbindung bleiben Keep in touch! Lass mal von dir hören!, Lasst mal von euch hören! put sb in touch with sb jdn mit jdm in Kontakt bringen [mɪt ... ɪn kɔnˌtakt brɪŋən] <bringt, brachte, hat gebracht> lose touch with sb den Kontakt zu jdm verlieren [deːn kɔnˈtakt tsuː ... fɛˌliːrən] <verliert, verlor, hat verloren> be out of touch with sb den Kontakt zu jdm verloren haben; *(up to date)* be in touch with sb über etw. [acc] auf dem Laufenden sein [yːbɐ ... aɔf deːm ˈlaɔfndən zaen] be out of touch with sth über etw. [acc] nicht auf dem Laufenden sein

touch² [verb] **1.** *(put your hand on sth, be in physical contact)* berühren [bəˈryːrən] <berührt, berührte, hat berührt> ◊ *Er berührte sie zärtlich.* ♦ *Sie berührte den Knopf, und das Licht ging an.* touch sth to sth etw. mit etw. berühren ◊ *Sie berührte die Wunde mit der Fingerspitze.* touch sb's arm/shoulder etc. jdn am Arm/an der Schulter etc. berühren They touch. Sie berühren sich. ◊ *Sie saßen so nahe beieinander, dass sich ihre Knie berührten.* A smile touched her face. Ein Lächeln huschte über ihr Gesicht.; *(grope)* anfassen ['anfasn̩] +haben ◊ *Fass mich nicht an!* **2.** *(move emotionally)* rühren ['ryːrən] +haben ◊ *Seine Anhänglichkeit rührte sie.* ♦ *Beim Abschied zeigte er sich sichtlich gerührt.; (be affected)* sb is touched by a feeling etc. jdn überkommt ein Gefühl etc. [ybɛˌkɔmt aen ɡəˈfyːl] <überkommt, überkam, hat überkommen> ◊ *Plötzlich überkam sie Angst.* **3.** *(consume)* anrühren ['anryːrən] +haben ◊ *Sie hat das Fleisch nicht angerührt.; (take, use up)* antasten ['antastn̩] <tastet an, tastete an, hat angetastet> ◊ *Ich habe das Geld nicht angetastet.* **4.** *(not use or work on sth for a long time)* have not touched sth etw. nicht mehr getan haben [nɪçt meːɐ̯ ... ˈhaːbm̩] ◊ *Ich habe seit Wochen nicht mehr im Garten gearbeitet.* ♦ *Du hast schon lange nicht mehr Gitarre gespielt.* **5.** *(take up)* touch sth sich mit etw. befassen [mɪt ... bəˌfasn̩] <befasst sich, befasste sich, hat sich befasst> ◊ *Kein Anwalt wollte sich mit diesem Fall befassen.; (engage, deal with)* not touch sth/sb die Finger von etw./jdm lassen [diː ˈfɪŋɐ fɔn ... lasn̩] <lässt, ließ, hat gelassen> ◊ *Von diesem Problem lasse ich lieber die Finger.* ♦ *Bitte lass die Finger von diesem Typen!* **6.** *(reach a level)* erreichen [ɛˈraeçn̩] <erreicht, erreichte, hat erreicht> ◊ *Die Geschwindigkeit erreichte fast 180 Stundenkilometer.* **7.** *(equal)* not touch sb/sth nicht an jdn/etw. herankommen [ˌnɪçt an ... hɛˌrankɔmən] <kommt heran, kam heran, ist herangekommen> ◊ *Sie ist eine gute Sängerin, aber an ihre Schwester kommt sie nicht heran.*

• **touch down** [phras v] aufsetzen ['aɔfzɛtsn̩] +haben ◊ *Das Flugzeug setzte hart auf der Piste auf.*

• **touch off** [phras v] auslösen ['aɔsløːzn̩] +haben ◊ *Die Reformen lösten heftige Proteste aus.*

• **touch on** [phras v] berühren [bəˈryːrən] <berührt, berührte, hat berührt> ◊ *Das Thema Geld wurde im Laufe ihres Gesprächs nicht berührt.*

A
B
C
D
E
F
G
H
I
J
K
L
M
N
O
P
Q
R
S
T
U
V
W
X
Y
Z

• **touch up** (phras v) **1.** *(a coat of paint, your make-up)* auffrischen ['aʊffrɪʃn] +haben ◊ *Sie frischte ihr Make-up auf.* **2.** *(grope)* betatschen [bə'tatʃn] <betatschte, betatschte, hat betatscht> *(fam)* ◊ *Hat der Typ etwa versucht, dich zu betatschen?*

tough (adj) **1.** *(firm, difficult, determined, strict)* hart [haʳt] <härter, am härtesten> ◊ *Stahl ist besonders hart.* ♦ *Uns stehen harte Zeiten bevor.* ♦ *ein harter Kampf/Wettbewerb* ♦ *Das Urteil des Richters war hart.* be tough on sb/sth, get tough with sb/sth hart gegen jdn/etw. vorgehen **2.** *(resilient, resistant, hard to chew)* zäh [tsɛ:] <zäher, am zäh(e)sten> ◊ *ein zäher Kämpfer* ♦ *Das Fleisch ist ja zäh wie Leder!; (cloth, rope etc.)* fest [fɛst] ◊ *ein fester Stoff* ♦ *Das Seil muss fest sein.* **3.** *(violent)* knallhart ['knal'haʳt] no comp/superl ◊ *Nimm dich vor den Typen in Acht. Die sind knallhart!; (crime-ridden)* übel ['yːbl̩] <übler, am übelsten> <der/die/das üble ...> ◊ *eine üble Gegend*

tour¹ (noun) **1.** *(short trip)* Tour [tuːɐ̯] die <-, –en> ◊ *eine Tour in die Berge machen* cycling tour Radtour ['raːttuːɐ̯] walking tour Wanderung ['vandərʊŋ] die <-, –en> **2.** *(longer trip)* Reise ['raɛza] die <-, –n> ◊ *eine Reise durch Spanien und Frankreich* coach tour Busreise ['bʊsraɛza] tour of Europe Europareise [ɔø'roːparaɛza] tour of duty vorübergehende Versetzung [fo,ryːbeːɡeːəndə fe'zɛtsʊŋ] die <-, –en> **3.** *(an artist's)* Tournee [tʊʳ'neː] die <-, –n> ◊ *Zum Auftakt ihrer Tournee durch Frankreich treten sie in Paris auf.* ♦ *auf Tournee sein/gehen* **4.** *(when visiting sth on foot)* Rundgang ['rɔntgaŋ] der <-(e)s, Rundgänge> a tour of/around sth ein Rundgang durch etw.; *(by bus etc.)* Rundfahrt ['rʊntfaːʳt] die <-, –en> guided tour Führung ['fyːrʊŋ] die <-, –en>

tour² (verb) **1.** *(travel)* tour sth durch etw. reisen [dʊʳç ... raɛzn̩] +sein ◊ *Sie sind fünf Wochen durch Australien gereist.* **2.** *(visit briefly)* besichtigen [bə'zɪçtɪɡn] <besichtigt, besichtigte, hat besichtigt> ◊ *Wir wollen morgen die Altstadt besichtigen.* **3.** *(artist, show)* tour (sth) eine Tournee (durch etw.) machen [aɛna tʊʳ'neː: maxn̩] +haben ◊ *Die Sängerin wird demnächst eine Tournee durch Frankreich machen.*

tour guide (noun) Reiseführer ['raɛzafyːrɐ] der <-s, –> ♀Reiseführerin ['raɛzafyːrərɪn] die <-, –nen> ◊ *Er arbeitet im Sommer als Reiseführer.* ♦ *Die Reiseführerin zeigte uns den Dom.*

tourism (noun) Tourismus [tu'rɪsmʊs] der <-> no pl ◊ *den Tourismus fördern* ♦ *Die Region lebt fast ausschließlich vom Tourismus.*

tourist (noun) **1.** *(traveller)* Tourist [tu'rɪst] der <-en, –en> ♀Touristin [tu'rɪstɪn] die <-, –nen> ◊ *Das Festival lockt zahlreiche Touristen aus aller Welt an.* tourist destination Urlaubsziel ['uːɐ̯laʊpstsiːl] das <-(e)s, –e> **2.** *(economy class)* tourist (class) Touristenklasse [tu'rɪstn̩klasa] die <-, –n> ◊ *einen Platz in der Touristenklasse buchen* travel tourist in der Touristenklasse reisen

tournament (noun) Turnier [tʊʳ'niːɐ̯] das <-s, –e> ◊ *ein Turnier gewinnen/verlieren* tennis tournament Tennisturnier ['tɛnɪstʊʳ,niːɐ̯] chess tournament Schachturnier ['ʃaxtʊʳ,niːɐ̯]

tow (verb) schleppen ['ʃlɛpm̩] +haben ◊ *einen Frachter in den Hafen schleppen* tow away abschleppen ['apʃlɛpm̩] +haben ◊ *Mein Wagen wurde abgeschleppt.*

towards, toward (prep) **1.** *(spatial or fig: in the direction of sb/sth, with verbs of motion)* towards sb/sth auf jdn/etw. zu... [aʊf ... tsuː] (+acc) walk towards sb/sth auf jdn/etw. zugehen [aʊf ... ˌtsuːɡeːən] <geht zu, ging zu, ist zugegangen> ◊ *Wir gingen auf die Stadt zu.* run towards sb/sth auf jdn/etw. zurennen [aʊf ... ˌtsuːrɛnən] <rennt zu, rannte zu, ist zugerannt> ◊ *Der Hund rannte auf mich zu.* move towards a compromise sich auf einen Kompromiss zubewegen [aʊf aɛnən kɔmpro'mɪs ˌtsuːbəveːɡṅ] <bewegt sich zu, bewegte sich zu, hat sich zubewegt>; *(with geographical names or aims and objectives)* in Richtung [ɪn 'rɪçtʊŋ] sing nouns without article or attribute are not declined when following this construction, otherwise with (+gen) ◊ *Sie segelten in Richtung Neuseeland.* ♦ *ein erster Schritt in Richtung Liberalisierung/einer dauerhaften Versöhnung* towards the north etc. in Richtung Norden etc. in richtung ... towards a better understanding of sth zum besseren Verständnis ... (gen) [tsʊm besəʳn fe'ʃtɛntnɪs] with your back towards sb/sth mit dem Rücken zu jdm/etw. [mɪt deːm 'rʏkŋ tsuː] ◊ *Der Mann stand mit dem Rücken zu ihr.* **2.** *(in relation to, as far as sth/sb is concerned)* gegenüber [geːɡn̩ʔy'beː] (+dat) ◊ *Du bist gegenüber anderen Menschen sehr höflich.* ♦ *Die Regierung ist dieser Frage gegenüber eher zurückhaltend.* **3.** *(near a time)* gegen [geːɡn̩] (+acc) ◊ *Gegen 20 Uhr wollen wir in Wien sein.* ♦ *Gegen Morgen kam ein Sturm auf.; (near a place)* towards sth in der Nähe ... (gen) [ɪn deːɐ̯ 'nɛːa] ◊ *In der Nähe der Küste gibt es viele Windmühlen.* **4.** *(help pay for sth)* go towards sth in etw. (acc) fließen [ɪn ... fliːsn̩] <fließt, floss, ist geflossen> ◊ *Alle Spenden fließen direkt in das Projekt gegen Kinderarmut.* contribute towards sth zu etw. beitragen [tsuː ... ˌbaɛtraːɡŋ] <trägt bei, trug bei, hat beigetragen> ◊ *Ich möchte gern etwas zu den Kosten beitragen.*

towel (noun) Handtuch ['hanttuːx] das <-(e)s, Handtücher> ◊ *sich mit einem Handtuch abtrocknen* ♦ *frische Handtücher* ⊛ throw in the towel das Handtuch werfen *(fam)*

tower (noun) Turm [tʊʳm] der <-(e)s, Türme> ◊ *Diese Kirche hat einen schönen alten Turm.* church tower Kirchturm ['kɪʳçtʊʳm] television tower Fernsehturm ['fɛʳnzeːtʊʳm] ⊛ a tower of strength eine Stütze

town (noun) Stadt [ʃtat] die <-, Städte> ◊ *Die Stadt liegt an einem Fluss.* ♦ *Diesen Monat ist ein Zirkus in der Stadt.* ♦ *Die ganze Stadt spricht schon darüber.* ♦ *Dieses Gebäude gehört der Stadt.* the town of Limerick die Stadt Limerick go into town in die Stadt gehen be out of town verreist sein [fe'raɛst zaɛn] outskirts/edge of town Stadtrand ['ʃtatrant] der <-(e)s, Stadtränder> old town Altstadt ['altʃtat] die <-, Altstädte>

town centre (noun) Stadtzentrum ['ʃtattsɛntrʊm] das <-s, Stadtzentren> *most sing*

town hall (noun) Rathaus ['raːthaʊs] das <-es, Rathäuser>

toxic (adj) giftig ['gɪftɪç] ◊ *giftige Gase* ♦ *Diese Substanz ist sehr giftig.*

toy (noun) toy(s) Spielzeug ['ʃpiːltsɔøk] das <-(e)s, –e> *most sing* ◊ *Eine Schere ist kein Spielzeug!* ♦ *Der Teddy war ihr liebstes Spielzeug.* ♦ *viel Spielzeug haben* toy car Spielzeugauto ['ʃpiːltsɔøk|aʊto:] das <-s, –s> soft toy Plüschtier ['plʏʃtiːɐ̯] das

<-(e)s, –e>

trace[1] [noun] **1.** *(sign, hint, small amount)* Spur [ʃpuːɐ̯] die <–, –en> ◊ *Die Einbrecher bemühten sich, keine Spuren zu hinterlassen.* ✦ *Am Essen fehlt noch eine Spur Basilikum.* ✦ *Spuren von Gift* ✦ *In seiner Stimme schwang eine Spur von Sorge mit.* without (a) trace spurlos [ˈʃpuːɐ̯loːs] no comp/superl ◊ *Seine Schwester ist vor drei Monaten spurlos verschwunden.* **2.** *(search for the origin of sth)* Rückverfolgung [ˈrʏkfɛɐ̯fɔlɡʊŋ] die <–, –en> ◊ *Die Polizei gelang die Rückverfolgung des Anrufs.* **3.** *(on screen, paper)* Kurve [ˈkʊɐ̯və] die <–, –n> ◊ *Die Kurve zeigt einen regelmäßigen Herzschlag.*

trace[2] [verb] **1.** *(find)* finden [ˈfɪndn̩] <findet, fand, hat gefunden> ◊ *Ich kann diese Dokumente nicht finden.* sb is traced to somewhere jds Spur führt irgendwohin [ʃpuːɐ̯ fyːɐ̯t] +haben ◊ *Seine Spur führt nach Kanada/in die Karibik.*; *(find out about the origin or development of sth)* trace sth (back) etw. zurückverfolgen [ʦuˈrʏkfɛɐ̯fɔlɡn̩] <verfolgt zurück, verfolgte zurück, hat zurückverfolgt> ◊ *Diese Tradition lässt sich bis ins Mittelalter zurückverfolgen.* ✦ *Die Polizei ließ den Anruf zurückverfolgen.*; *(find the cause of sth)* trace sth back to sth etw. auf etw. [acc] zurückführen [aʊ̯f ... ˈʦuˌrʏkfyːrən] +haben ◊ *Diese Störung kann häufig auf ein Kindheitstrauma zurückgeführt werden.* **2.** *(draw)* zeichnen [ˈʦaɛ̯çnən] <zeichnet, zeichnete, hat gezeichnet> ◊ *Sie zeichnete Muster in den Sand.*; *(move your finger along sth, describe)* nachzeichnen [ˈnaːxʦaɛ̯çnən] +haben ◊ *Mit dem Finger zeichnete er zärtlich ihre Augenbrauen nach.* ✦ *In seinem Buch zeichnet der Autor die Entwicklung Europas nach.*; *(with tracing paper)* abpausen [ˈappaʊ̯zn̩] +haben ◊ *eine Zeichnung abpausen*

track[1] [noun] **1.** *(path)* Pfad [pfaːt] der <–(e)s, –e> ◊ *Wir gingen auf einem schmalen Pfad durch den Wald.*; *(road)* Schotterstraße [ˈʃɔtɐʃtraːsə] die <–, –n> ◊ *Eine Schotterstraße führte zur Hütte hinauf.* **2.** *(rails)* Gleise [ˈɡlaɛ̯zə] die <–> pl ◊ *Hier wurden drei Kilometer neue Gleise verlegt.* Keep off the track! Betreten der Gleise verboten!; *(railway line)* Strecke [ˈʃtrɛkə] die <–, –n> ◊ *Diese Strecke ist schon lange stillgelegt.* ✦ *die Strecke von München nach Erding* **3.** sport Bahn [baːn] die <–, –en> ◊ *Die Pferde werden schon am Vortag zur Bahn gebracht.* ✦ *eine Bahn für Skater* **4.** *(of a caterpillar, tank)* Kette [ˈkɛtə] die <–, –n> ◊ *die Ketten eines Panzers/einer Planierraupe*; *(for moving along)* curtain track Vorhangschiene [ˈfoːɐ̯haŋʃiːnə] die <–, –n> **5.** *(direction, way of achieving sth)* Weg [veːk] der <–(e)s, –e> ◊ *den Weg seines Sturms verfolgen* ✦ *der Weg zum Erfolg* ✦ *auf dem richtigen/falschen Weg sein* **6.** *(mark, trail)* track(s) Spur [ʃpuːɐ̯] die <–, –en> ◊ *Die Spuren führten zum Strand.* ✦ *Spuren im Sand* ✦ *die Spur eines Rehs* be on sb's tracks jdm auf der Spur sein cover your tracks seine Spuren verwischen **7.** *(on a CD, record etc.)* Titel [ˈtiːtl̩] der <–s, –> ◊ *Auf der CD sind 12 Titel.*; *(for recording on tape)* Spur [ʃpuːɐ̯] die <–, –en> ◊ *Das Tonbandgerät arbeitet mit vier Spuren.* ⊛ **keep track of sth** den Überblick über etw. [acc] behalten lose track of sth **1.** *(be confused about)* den Überblick über etw. [acc] verlieren **2.** *(not be up to date)* have lost track of sth über etw. [acc] nicht mehr auf dem Laufenden sein stop (dead) in your tracks plötzlich stehen bleiben

track[2] [verb] **1.** *(follow)* verfolgen [fɛˈfɔlɡn̩] <verfolgt, verfolgte, hat verfolgt> ◊ *Die Polizei verfolgte ihn bis an die Grenze.* ✦ *Wir werden die Entwicklung weiterhin verfolgen.* **2.** film track a camera mit einer Kamera fahren [mɪt ˈaɛ̯nɐ ˈkaməraː faːrən] <fährt, fuhr, ist gefahren> ◊ *Er fährt mit der Kamera durch die Kulisse.* **3.** meteo ziehen [ˈʦiːən] <zieht, zog, ist gezogen> ◊ *Der Sturm zieht Richtung Osten.* • **track down** [phras v] aufspüren [ˈaʊ̯fʃpyːrən] +haben ◊ *Die Polizei hat ihn in Madrid aufgespürt.* ✦ *die Ursache eines Problems aufspüren*

track and field [noun] Leichtathletik [ˈlaɛ̯çtʔatˌleːtɪk] die <–> no pl ◊ *Ich betreibe seit Jahren Leichtathletik.*

tract [noun] **1.** *(of land)* Gebiet [ɡəˈbiːt] das <–(e)s, –e> ◊ *Große Gebiete sind von Wald bedeckt.* **2.** med respiratory tract Atemwege [ˈaːtəmveːɡə] die <–> pl digestive tract Verdauungsapparat [fɛˈdaʊ̯ŋsʔapaˌraːt] der <–(e)s> no pl **3.** *(essay)* Traktat [trakˈtaːt] der <–(e)s, –e> *(form)* ◊ *einen Traktat verfassen* ✦ *ein Traktat über die religiöse Erziehung junger Mädchen*

tractor [noun] Traktor [ˈtraktoːɐ̯] der <–s, –en> ◊ *mit dem Traktor aufs Feld fahren*

trade[1] [noun] **1.** *(buying and selling)* trade (in/with) Handel (mit) [ˈhandl̩] der <–s> no pl ◊ *der Handel mit Japan/Waffen* book trade Buchhandel [ˈbuːxhandl̩] trade agreement Handelsabkommen [ˈhandl̩sʔapkɔmən] das <–s, –> **2.** *(business)* Geschäfte [ɡəˈʃɛftə] die <–> pl ◊ *Die Geschäfte gehen im Augenblick nicht so gut.* **3.** *(area of business or industry)* Branche [ˈbranʃə] die <–, –n> ◊ *In welcher Branche sind Sie tätig?* **4.** *(craft)* Handwerk [ˈhantvɛʳk] das <–s, –e> ◊ *Wo hat er sein Handwerk gelernt?* be a plumber by trade gelernter Installateur sein [ɡəlɛʳntɐ ɪnstalaˈtøːɐ̯ zaɛ̯n] gelernte Installateurin sein [ɡəlɛʳntə ɪnstalaˈtøːrɪn zaɛ̯n] +sein

trade[2] [verb] **1.** *(buy and sell)* trade in sth mit etw. handeln [mɪt ... ˌhandl̩n] +haben ◊ *Er handelt mit Antiquitäten.* trade with a country mit einem Land Handel treiben [mɪt aɛ̯nəm ˌlant ˈhandl̩ traɛ̯bm̩] <treibt, trieb, hat getrieben> ◊ *Sie wollen verstärkt mit China Handel treiben.* **2.** *(operate as a business)* trade under a name unter einem Namen firmieren [ʊntɐ aɛ̯nəm ˈnaːmən fɪʳˈmiːrən] <firmiert, firmierte, hat firmiert> **3.** *(shares)* trade etw. handeln [ˈhandl̩n] +haben sth trades etw. wird gehandelt ◊ *eine Aktie, die zu einem hohen Preis gehandelt wird* **4.** *(exchange)* trade sth for sth etw. gegen etw. eintauschen [ɡeːɡn̩ ... ˌaɛ̯ntaʊ̯ʃn̩] +haben • **trade down** [phras v] trade down to a smaller house/car sich [dat] ein kleineres Haus/Auto kaufen [aɛ̯n ˌklaɛ̯nərəs ˈhaʊ̯s/ˈaʊ̯to ˌkaʊ̯fn̩] +haben trade down to discount brands Billigmarken kaufen • **trade in** [phras v] trade in sth (for sth) etw. (für etw.) in Zahlung geben [ɪn ˈʦaːlʊŋ ɡeːbm̩] <gibt, gab, hat gegeben> ◊ *Sie können Ihr altes Fahrrad in Zahlung geben.* • **trade off** [phras v] trade off sth for sth etw. für etw. in Kauf nehmen [fyːɐ̯ ... ɪn ˈkaʊ̯f neːmən] <nimmt, nahm, hat genommen> ◊ *Für den günstigen Preis nahmen sie die schlechte Qualität in Kauf.* • **trade on** [phras v] trade on sth mit etw. hausieren gehen [mɪt ... haʊ̯ˌziːrən ɡeːən] <geht, ging, ist gegangen> *(pej)* ◊ *Er geht schamlos mit dem Namen*

seines berühmten Vaters hausieren.

• **trade up** [phras v] trade up to a bigger house/a better camera sich [dat] ein größeres Haus/eine bessere Kamera kaufen [æn ˌgrø:sərəs 'haos/æɲə ˌbɛsərə 'kamə:ra: kaofn] +haben; *(computer hardware or software)* trade up to sth auf etw. [acc] aufrüsten [aof … ˌaofrʏstn̩] <rüstet auf, rüstete auf, hat aufgerüstet> ◊ *auf eine neuere Version aufrüsten*

trademark [noun] 1. *(name, design)* Warenzeichen ['va:rəntsaeçn̩] das <-s, -> 2. *(characteristic)* sth is sb's trademark jd ist für etw. bekannt [ɪst fy:ɐ̯ … bəˌkant] +sein ◊ *Sie ist für ihre Wortspiele bekannt.* his trademark cynicism der Zynismus, für den er bekannt ist; *(sth in the way sb looks or dresses)* Markenzeichen ['ma'kn̩tsaeçn̩] das <-s, -> ◊ *Der große Hut ist mein Markenzeichen.*

trader [noun] Händler ['hɛndle] der <-s, -> ♀Händlerin ['hɛndlərɪn] die <-, -nen> ◊ *der Händler in der Innenstadt ♦ meine Arbeit als Händlerin* street trader Straßenhändler ['ʃtra:sn̩hɛndle]

trade union [noun] Gewerkschaft [gə'vɛʳkʃaft] die <-, -en> ◊ *die Gewerkschaft der Polizei ♦ einer Gewerkschaft angehören* trade union representative Gewerkschaftsvertreter [gə'vɛʳkʃaftsfetre:te] der <-s, -> ♀Gewerkschaftsvertreterin [gə'vɛʳkʃaftsfe,tre:tərɪn] die <-, -nen>

trading¹ [noun] Handel ['handl̩] der <-s> no pl ◊ *ein lebhafter Handel an der Börse* Sunday trading verkaufsoffene Sonntage [fɐˌkaofs|ɔfənə 'zɔnta:gə] <-> pl

trading² [adj] Handels… ['handls] trading partner Handelspartner ['handlspaʳtne] der <-s, -> trading estate Gewerbegebiet [gə'vɛʳbəgəbi:t] das <-s, -e>

tradition [noun] 1. *(customs, beliefs and stories)* Tradition [tradi'tsi̯o:n] die <-, -en> ◊ *Bei uns ist es Tradition, dass am Heiligabend Fisch gegessen wird.* be steeped in centuries of tradition auf eine jahrhundertelange Tradition zurückblicken break with tradition mit der Tradition brechen 2. *(particular custom)* Brauch [braox] der <-(e)s, Bräuche> ◊ *einen Brauch pflegen ♦ Wie es Brauch ist, wurde die Braut entführt.*

☞ in the tradition of … im Stil … [gen]

traditional(ly) [adj, adv] traditionell [traditsi̯o'nɛl] ◊ *traditionelle afrikanische Tänze ♦ Meine Eltern sind sehr traditionell. ♦ Im Ruhrgebiet wählte man traditionell sozialdemokratisch.*

traffic [noun] 1. *(moving vehicles, flow of information)* Verkehr [fɛ'ke:ɐ̯] der <-(e)s> no pl ◊ *Morgens war noch wenig Verkehr. ♦ den Verkehr behindern* the huge volume of traffic das hohe Verkehrsaufkommen [das ho:ə fɛ'ke:ɐ̯s|aofkɔmən] <-s, -> no pl rush-hour traffic Berufverkehr [bə'ru:fsfeke:ɐ̯] air traffic Luftverkehr ['lʊftfeke:ɐ̯] Internet traffic Internetverkehr ['ɪntenɛtfeke:ɐ̯] traffic noise Verkehrslärm [fɛ'ke:ɐ̯slɛʳm] der <-s> no pl 2. *(illegal trade)* Handel ['handl̩] der <-s> no pl

traffic in [verb] traffic in sth mit etw. handeln [mɪt … ˌhandl̩n] ◊ *mit Drogen/Waffen handeln*

traffic jam [noun] Stau [ʃtao] der <-(e)s, -s> ◊ *im Stau stehen*

traffic light [noun] Ampel ['ampl̩] die <-, -n> ◊ *Die Ampel sprang auf/zeigte Grün. ♦ Ich fuhr bei Rot über die Ampel.*

tragedy [noun] Tragödie [tra'gø:di̯ə] die <-, -n> ◊ *die*

Tragödie von Romeo und Julia ♦ die griechische Tragödie ♦ eine Tragödie abwenden

tragic [adj] tragisch ['tra:gɪʃ] ◊ *ein tragischer Unfall ♦ Es ist tragisch, dass die Friedensverhandlungen scheiterten.*

trail¹ [noun] 1. *(path)* Weg [ve:k] der <-(e)s, -e> ◊ *Der Weg führte durch den Wald zu einer Ruine. ♦ einem Weg folgen* 2. *(tracks, evidence)* Spur [ʃpu:ɐ̯] die <-, -en> ◊ *Spuren im Sand ♦ der Spur eines Rehs folgen ♦ Seine Spur führt nach Amerika. ♦ auf der richtigen Spur sein* be on the trail of sb jdm auf der Spur sein trail of destruction Spur der Verwüstung trail of blood Blutspur ['blu:tʃpu:ɐ̯] 3. *(series)* Reihe ['raeə] die <-, -n> ◊ *eine Reihe von Banküberfällen*

☞ hot on the trail of sb/sth jdm/etw. auf der Spur ◊ *Die Presse war dem verschwundenen Star auf der Spur.* blaze a trail den Weg bahnen

trail² [verb] 1. *(move slowly)* trail behind sb hinter jdm hertrotten [hɪntɐ … ˌheˌɡtrɔtn̩] +sein ◊ *Die Kinder trotteten müde hinter ihr her.* 2. *(be losing)* trail sb hinter jdm liegen [hɪntɐ … li:gn̩] <liegt, lag, hat gelegen> ◊ *Die SPD liegt dort hinter der CDU.* trail by sth mit etw. im Rückstand liegen [mɪt … ɪm 'rʏkʃtant li:gn̩] ◊ *Sie lag mit zehn Punkten im Rückstand.* 3. *(pull, leave behind)* trail sth hinter sich [dat] herziehen [hɪntɐ … 'he:gtsi:ən] <zieht her, zog her, hat hergezogen> ◊ *Er zog den Sack hinter sich her.* 4. *(be pulled on the ground)* sth trails etw. schleift [ʃlaeft] +haben ◊ *Das Kleid war so lang, dass es über den Boden schleifte.* 5. *(line, cable, wire: suspended in the air)* sth trails etw. hängt [hɛŋt] <hing, hat gehangen> +haben ◊ *Ein Kabel hing lose von der Decke.; (on the ground or floor)* liegt [li:kt] <lag, ist gelegen> 6. *(follow)* trail sb jdm folgen ['fɔlɡn̩] +sein ◊ *Die Polizei folgte uns mehrere Wochen lang.* 7. *(plant)* ranken ['raŋkn̩] +haben ◊ *Efeu rankt an der Hauswand.*

• **trail away** [phras v] → trail off

• **trail off** [phras v] immer leiser werden [ɪmɐ 'laezɐ veːɐ̯dn̩] +sein

trailer [noun] 1. *(on a motor vehicle)* Anhänger ['anhɛŋɐ] der <-s, -> ◊ *Der schwer beladene Anhänger kippte um.* 2. *(in the US: caravan)* Wohnwagen ['vo:nva:gn̩] der <-s, -> 3. *(for a film)* Trailer ['tre:le] der <-s, -> ◊ *einen Trailer zeigen*

train¹ [noun] 1. *(railway carriages)* Zug [tsu:k] der <-(e)s, Züge> ◊ *Sie nahm den Zug nach Berlin. ♦ Der Zug hatte Verspätung.* by train mit dem Zug ◊ get on the train in den Zug einsteigen get off the train aus dem Zug aussteigen freight train Güterzug ['gy:tɐtsu:k] passenger train Personenzug [pɛʳ'zo:nəntsu:k] der <-(e)s, -> 2. *(series)* Folge ['fɔlgə] die <-, -n> ◊ *eine Folge von Ereignissen* train of thoughts Gedankengang [gə'daŋkŋ̍gaŋ] der <-(e)s, Gedankengänge> lose your train of thought den Faden verlieren [de:n 'fa:dn̩ feli:rən] <verliert, verlor, hat verloren> 3. *(of people, vehicles)* Schlange ['ʃlaŋə] die <-, -n> 4. *(on a dress)* Schleppe ['ʃlɛpə] die <-, -n> ◊ *eine Kleid mit langer Schleppe*

☞ set sth in train etw. in Gang setzen

train² [verb] 1. *(teach)* ausbilden ['aosbɪldn̩] <bildet aus, bildete aus, hat ausgebildet> ◊ *Rekruten ausbilden* train sb to do sth jdn in etw. [dat] schulen [ɪn … ʃu:lən] +haben ◊ *Wir wurden in der Anwendung des neuen Programms geschult.*

2. *(learn)* train to be sth, train as sth eine Ausbildung als etw. machen [aɛnə ˌaͻsbɪldʊŋ als ... maxn̩] +haben ◊ *eine Ausbildung als Bäcker/Pilotin machen* have trained in sth in etw. dat ausgebildet sein [ɪn ... ˌaͻsgəbɪldət zaɛn] +sein ◊ *Sie ist in Gesang und Tanz ausgebildet.* **3.** *(your mind, body)* trainieren [trɛˈniːrən] <trainiert, trainierte, hat trainiert> ◊ *Übungen, mit denen man sein Gedächtnis trainieren kann* ◆ *Er hat viele erfolgreiche Tennisspieler trainiert.* ◆ *für einen Wettkampf trainieren* train yourself to do sth sich dat antrainieren, etw. zu tun [ˈantrɛniːrən ... ˈtuː] +haben ◊ *Sie trainierte sich schon früh an, ihre Gefühle nicht zu zeigen.* **4.** *(an animal)* dressieren [drɛˈsiːrən] <dressiert, dressierte, hat dressiert> train an animal to do sth ein Tier darauf dressieren, etw. zu tun **5.** *(a gun, camera, light)* train sth on sb/sth etw. auf jdn/etw. richten [aͻf ... rɪçtn̩] <richtet, richtete, hat gerichtet> ◊ *Er hatte sein Gewehr auf uns gerichtet.* **6.** *(a plant)* wachsen lassen [ˈvaksn̩ lasn̩] <lässt, ließ, hat lassen> ◊ *Sie ließ die Rose über den Schuppen wachsen.*

trained → train² adj ausgebildet [ˈaͻsgəbɪldət] ◊ *eine ausgebildete Krankenschwester* ◆ *Einige der Pfleger sind nicht ausgebildet.* highly trained hoch qualifiziert [ˌhoːx kvalifiˈtsiːɐt]

trainee noun *(apprentice)* Auszubildende [ˈaͻstsubɪldn̩də] der/die <–n, die Auszubildenden> *but: ein Auszubildender/eine Auszubildende* ◊ *Er ist Auszubildender bei einer Bank.* ◆ *Unser Friseur sucht eine Auszubildende.* a trainee nurse eine Krankenschwester in der Ausbildung [aɛnə ˌkraŋkn̩ʃvɛstə ɪn deːɐ ˈaͻsbɪldʊŋ]; *(graduate)* Trainee [trɛˈniː] der <–s, –s>

trainer noun **1.** *(in sports)* Trainer [ˈtrɛːnɐ] der <–s, –> ♀Trainerin [ˈtrɛːnərɪn] die <–, –nen> ◊ *Der Verein hat einen neuen Trainer verpflichtet.* ◆ *Sie ist Trainerin der Handballmannschaft.* **2.** *(for a job)* Ausbilder [ˈaͻsbɪldɐ] der <–s, –> ♀Ausbilderin [ˈaͻsbɪldərɪn] die <–, –nen> ◊ *Sie ist als Ausbilderin tätig.* ◆ *ein erfahrener Ausbilder* **3.** *(for dogs, horses)* Dresseur [drɛˈsøːɐ] der <–s, –e> ♀Dresseurin [drɛˈsøːrɪn] die <–, –nen> **4.** *(shoe)* Turnschuh [ˈtͻɐnʃuː] der <–(e)s, –e>

training noun **1.** *(for a job)* Ausbildung [ˈaͻsbɪldʊŋ] die <–, –en> ◊ *Ich bin noch in der Ausbildung.* ◆ *eine Ausbildung zum Bäcker* provide training for sb jdn ausbilden [ˈaͻsbɪldn̩] <bildet aus, bildete aus, hat ausgebildet> **2.** *(for employees)* Fortbildung [ˈfͻrtbɪldʊŋ] die <–, –en> ◊ *eine Fortbildung besuchen* training course Schulung [ˈʃuːlʊŋ] die <–, –en> ◊ *an einer Schulung teilnehmen* **3.** *(physical)* Training [ˈtrɛːnɪŋ] das <–s, –s> *most sing* during training beim Training in training (for sth) (für etw.) trainieren [trɛˈniːrən] <trainiert, trainierte, hat trainiert>

trait noun Zug [tsuːk] der <–(e)s, Züge> character trait Charakterzug [kaˈraktetsuːk] personality trait Wesenszug [ˈveːzn̩stsuːk]

traitor noun Verräter [fɛˈrɛːtɐ] der <–s, –> ♀Verräterin [fɛˈrɛːtərɪn] die <–, –nen> a traitor to sth ein Verräter an etw. dat

tram noun Straßenbahn [ˈʃtraːsn̩baːn] die <–, –en>

trample verb **1.** *(with your feet)* trample somewhere irgendwo trampeln [ˈtrampl̩n] <trampelt, trampelte, hat/ist getrampelt> *transitive use* +haben/*intransitive use* +sein *(pej)* ◊ *Wer ist denn da durch mein Beet*

getrampelt? ◆ *jdn zu Tode trampeln* trample sth/sb underfoot etw./jdn. niedertrampeln [ˈniːdetrampl̩n] +haben ◊ *Sie trampelten die schönen Blumen nieder.; (destroy)* trample sth etw. zertrampeln [tsɛˈtrampl̩n] <zertrampelt, zertrampelte, hat zertrampelt> ◊ *Die Elefanten zertrampeln unsere Ernte.* **2.** *(disrespect sb/sth)* trample sb/sth underfoot jdn/etw. mit Füßen treten [mɪt ˈfyːsn̩ treːtn̩] <tritt, trat, hat getreten> ◊ *Sie treten unsere Rechte mit Füßen.* trample on sb's feelings auf jds Gefühlen herumtrampeln [aͻf ... gəˈfyːlən hɛˌrͻmtrampl̩n] +haben

transaction noun **1.** *(buying or selling sth)* Geschäft [gəˈʃɛft] das <–(e)s, –e> ◊ *Du bist in dubiose Geschäfte verwickelt.; (large, risky)* Transaktion [trans|akˈtsjoːn] die <–, –en> ◊ *riskante finanzielle Transaktionen* enter into a transaction eine Transaktion vornehmen **2.** *(of a deal)* transaction of sth Abwicklung von etw. [ˈapvɪklͻŋ fͻn] die <–, –en> ◊ *die Abwicklung von Geschäften im Internet*

transcript noun **1.** *(of a meeting)* Protokoll [protoˈkͻl] das <–s, –e> ◊ *ein Protokoll des Verhörs anfertigen* court transcript Gerichtsprotokoll [gəˈrɪçtsprotoˌkͻl]; *(of a tape, interview etc.)* Skript [skrɪpt] das <–(e)s, –en> **2.** uni ⊚*Studienbuch* [ˈʃtuːdi̯ənbuːx] das <–(e)s, Studienbücher>

transcription noun **1.** *(of a conversation, speech etc.)* Niederschrift [ˈniːdeʃrɪft] die <–, –en> **2.** *(conversation in written form)* Skript [skrɪpt] das <–(e)s, –en> **3.** *(into a different script)* Übertragung [ybeˈtraːgʊŋ] die <–, –en> ◊ *die Übertragung eines Stenogramms* phonetic transcription phonetische Transkription [foˌneːtɪʃə transkrɪpˈtsjoːn] die <–, –en>

transfer¹ noun **1.** *(of an employee)* Versetzung [fɛˈzɛtsͻŋ] die <–, –en> ◊ *Freust du dich über deine Versetzung nach Paris?* **2.** *(from one place to another)* transfer Überführung [ybeˈfyːrͻŋ] die <–, –en> ◊ *die Überführung gebrauchter Autos/von Fahrzeugen ins Ausland; (of money)* Überweisung [ybeˈvaɛzͻŋ] die <–, –en> **3.** *(of a right, responsibility)* Übertragung [ybeˈtraːgͻŋ] die <–, –en> ◊ *die Übertragung der Leitung an Herrn Wolff; (of authority)* Übergabe [ˈyːbegaːbə] die <–, –n> transfer of power Machtübergabe [ˈmaxt|ybegaːbə] **4.** *(of a player)* Transfer [transˈfeːɐ] der <–s, –s> **5.** *(in the US: ticket)* Fahrkarte, mit der man umsteigen kann

transfer² verb **1.** *(move to a different job, school)* transfer sb (from sth/to sth) jdn (von etw./in etw. acc) versetzen [fɛˈzɛtsn̩] <versetzt, versetzte, hat versetzt> ◊ *Der Chef hat ihn vom Vertrieb ins Marketing versetzt.* sb transfers (to sth) jd wechselt (in/auf etw. acc) über [vɛkl̩t ˈyːbe] ◊ *2004 wechsele sie in die Verkaufsabteilung über.* ◆ *möchte auf eine andere Uni/Schule überwechseln.* **2.** *(move sth)* transfer sth etw. in/auf etw. acc legen [ɪn/aͻf ... leːgn̩] +haben ◊ *Sie legte die Plätzchen in eine Dose/auf einen Teller.; (a patient, production)* transfer sb/sth jdn/etw. verlegen [fɛˈleːgn̩] <verlegt, verlegte, hat verlegt> ◊ *Die Patientin wurde auf eine andere Station verlegt.* ◆ *Das Unternehmen verlegte die Produktion nach China.; (tourists)* jdn bringen [ˈbrɪŋən] <bringt, brachte, hat gebracht> ◊ *Wir wurden mit einem Bus vom Flughafen zum Hotel gebracht.* **3.** *(money)* überweisen [ybeˈvaɛzn̩] <überweist, überwies, hat überwiesen> ◊ *100 Euro an jdn/auf ein Konto überweisen* **4.** *(a footballer)* transferieren [transfeˈriːrən] <transfe-

riert, transferierte, hat transferiert> ◊ *Er wurde für viel Geld zu Real Madrid transferiert.* **5.** *(on a journey)* umsteigen ['ʊmʃtaeɡn̩] <steigt um, stieg um, ist umgestiegen> ◊ *vom Zug auf die Fähre/in den Bus umsteigen* **6.** *(give to sb/sth else)* transfer your attention (from sb/sth) to sb/sth seine Aufmerksamkeit (von jdm/etw.) auf jdn/etw. richten [zaenə ˌaofmɛˈkza:mkaet aof ... rɪçtn̩] <richtet, richtete, hat gerichtet>*; (your focus)* verlagern [fɐˈlaːɡn̩] <verlagert, verlagerte, hat verlagert> ◊ *Sie verlagerte den Schwerpunkt ihrer Arbeit auf die Forschung.* **7.** *(a caller)* transfer sb jdn verbinden [fɐˈbɪndn̩] <verbindet, verband, hat verbunden> ◊ *Einen Augenblick, ich verbinde Sie.* **8.** *(property, deeds)* transfer sth to sb etw. auf jdn überschreiben [aof ... ybɐˌʃraebm̩] <überschreibt, überschrieb, hat überschrieben> ◊ *Das Haus wurde vor seinem Tod auf die Kinder überschrieben.* **9.** ɪᴛ *(data, information, images)* transfer sth (from sth) to sth etw. (von etw.) auf etw. `acc` übertragen [aof ... ybɐˌtra:ɡn̩] <überträgt, übertrug, hat übertragen> ◊ *Daten auf einen Stick übertragen* **10.** *(power, responsibility)* übergeben [ybɐˈɡeːbm̩] <übergibt, übergab, hat übergeben> ◊ *Das Militär hat die Macht an die neue Regierung übergeben.*

transform `verb` von Grund auf verändern [fɔn ˌɡrʊnt aof fɐˈlɛndɐn] <verändert, veränderte, hat verändert> ◊ *Diese Erfahrung hat mein Leben von Grund auf verändert.* transform sth into sth etw. in etw. `acc` umwandeln [ɪn ... ˌʊmvandl̩n] ◊ *Die alte Fabrik wird in ein Museum umgewandelt.*

transformation `noun` grundlegende Veränderung [ˌɡrʊntleːɡn̩də fɐˈlɛndɐrʊŋ] die <-, -en> ◊ *eine grundlegende Veränderung in jds Verhalten* make a transformation from sth to sth etw. von etw. in etw. `acc` verwandeln [fɔn ... ɪn ... fɐˌvandl̩n] <verwandelt sich, verwandelte sich, hat sich verwandelt> ◊ *Er hat sich vom Macho in einen Hausmann verwandelt.*

transit `noun` **1.** *(of goods)* Transport [transˈpɔrt] der <-(e)s, -e> in transit auf dem Transport **2.** *(of people)* Durchreise ['dʊrçraeza] die <-, -n> *most sing* ◊ *jdm die Durchreise verweigern* ♦ *auf der Durchreise sein* **3.** *(in the US)* public transit öffentliche Verkehrsmittel [ˌœfn̩tlɪçə fɐˈkeːɐsmɪtl̩] <-> *pl*

transition `noun` Übergang ['yːbɐɡaŋ] der <-(e)s, Übergänge> in transition im Übergang ◊ *eine Gesellschaft im Übergang* the transition between sth and sth, the transition from sth to sth der Übergang von etw. in etw. `acc` ◊ *der Übergang vom Studium ins Berufsleben* make the transition den Übergang schaffen transition period Übergangszeit ['yːbɐɡaŋszaet] die <-, -en>

transitive(ly) `adj, adv` transitiv ['tranziːtɪf] *no comp/superl; when used as an adj, only before ns* ◊ *der transitive Gebrauch eines Verbs* ♦ *ein Verb transitiv gebrauchen*

translate `verb` **1.** *(a written text, software)* übersetzen [ybɐˈzɛtsn̩] <übersetzt, übersetzte, hat übersetzt> ◊ *Wer hat den Roman übersetzt?* translate sth into sth etw. in etw. `acc` übersetzen ◊ *einen Text ins Spanische übersetzen; (a spoken text)* dolmetschen ['dɔlmɛtʃn̩] +haben ◊ *Können Sie bitte dolmetschen, was er gesagt hat?* ♦ *Sein Freund dolmetschte die Rede.* **2.** *(be capable of translation)* sth translates etw. lässt sich übersetzen [lɛst zɪç ybɐˈzɛtsn̩] <lässt sich, ließ sich, hat sich ... lassen> ◊ *Seine Bücher*

lassen sich nur schwer übersetzen. sth translates as sth etw. wird mit etw. übersetzt **3.** *(cause, produce)* translate into sth zu etw. führen [ʦuː ... fyːrən] +haben ◊ *Die hohe Arbeitslosigkeit führte zu Massenprotesten.* **4.** *(change, adapt)* translate sth into sth etw. in etw. umsetzen [ɪn ... ˌʊmzɛtsn̩] +haben ◊ *Vorschläge in die Praxis umsetzen* **5.** *(be relevant)* sth translates (to sth) etw. lässt sich (auf etw. `acc`) übertragen [lɛst zɪç ybɐˈtra:ɡn̩] <lässt sich, ließ sich, hat sich ... lassen> ◊ *Diese Methode lässt sich auch auf andere Situationen übertragen.*

translation `noun` Übersetzung [ybɐˈzɛtsʊŋ] die <-, -en> ◊ *bei der Übersetzung Fehler machen* ♦ *eine wörtliche Übersetzung* ♦ *„Harry Potter" in deutscher Übersetzung* be lost in translation bei der Übersetzung verloren gehen

transmission `noun` **1.** *(of a car)* Getriebe [ɡəˈtriːbə] das <-s, -> **2.** *(of signals, data, an infection)* Übertragung [ybɐˈtra:ɡʊŋ] die <-, -en> ◊ *Die Übertragung des Schalls erfolgt durch Wellen.* ♦ *die Übertragung von Krankheiten durch Haustiere* data transmission Datenübertragung ['da:tn̩ˌybɐˌtra:ɡʊŋ] **3.** *(of power, energy)* Leitung ['laetʊŋ] die <-> *no pl* **4.** *(program(me))* Sendung ['zɛndʊŋ] die <-, -en>

transmit `verb` **1.** *(a TV program(me), disease, data, signal, power)* übertragen [ybɐˈtra:ɡn̩] <überträgt, übertrug, hat übertragen> ◊ *Die Sendung wurde live übertragen.* ♦ *Malaria wird durch Moskitos übertragen.* ♦ *Daten übertragen* **2.** *(information, beliefs)* weitergeben ['vaetɐɡeːbm̩] <gibt weiter, gab weiter, hat weitergegeben> ◊ *Die Eltern geben diese Werte an ihre Kinder weiter.*

transmitter `noun` Sender ['zɛndɐ] der <-s, ->

transparency `noun` **1.** *(to be shown with a slide projector)* Dia ['diːaː] das <-s, -s>*; (with an overhead projector)* Folie ['foːliə] die <-, -n> ◊ *eine Folie auflegen* **2.** *(also fig)* *(translucency, clarity)* Durchsichtigkeit ['dʊrçzɪçtɪçkaet] die <-> *no pl* ◊ *Brauchen wir mehr Durchsichtigkeit bei Aufnahmeverfahren in Privatschulen?* ♦ *die Durchsichtigkeit von Quellen*

transparent `adj` *(object, substance, lie, rule)* durchsichtig ['dʊrçzɪçtɪç] *seldom comp/superl* ◊ *eine durchsichtige Folie* ♦ *Seine Ausreden sind ziemlich durchsichtig.* ♦ *Die Regeln müssen durchsichtiger werden.; (process, activity, organization)* transparent [transpaˈrɛnt] <transparenter, am transparentesten> ◊ *eine transparente Vorgehensweise* ♦ *Das System ist transparent und gerecht.*

transparently `adv` **1.** *(completely, absolutely)* ganz [ɡants] *no comp/superl* ◊ *ganz einfach zu bedienen sein* transparently clear klar [klaːr] ◊ *Es wurde klar, dass gegen das Völkerrecht verstoßen worden war.* **2.** *(obviously)* offensichtlich ['ɔfn̩zɪçtlɪç] ◊ *Seine Absichten waren offensichtlich betrügerisch.*

transport¹ `noun` **1.** *(traffic)* Verkehr [fɐˈkeːɐ] der <-s> *no pl* minister for transport Verkehrsminister [fɐˈkeːɐsmɪˌnɪstɐ] der <-s, -> ♀Verkehrsministerin [fɐˈkeːɐsmɪˌnɪstɐrɪn] die <-- or -nen>*; (bus, train etc.)* Verkehrsmittel [fɐˈkeːɐsmɪtl̩] das <-s, -> public transport öffentliche Verkehrsmittel Do you need transport? Brauchst du jemanden, der dich mitnimmt? **2.** *(plane, ship, vehicle)* Transporter [transˈpɔrtɐ] der <-s, -> **3.** *(of goods, animals, people)* Transport [transˈpɔrt] der <-(e)s, -e> ◊ *der Transport von Gütern mit der Bahn* ♦ *der Transport*

lebender Schafe

ℰ **a transport of joy** helle Freude

transport² [verb] **1.** *(goods, animals, people)* transportieren [transpɔˈtiːrən] <transportiert, transportierte, hat transportiert> ◊ *Dieses Flugzeug transportiert Passagiere und Fracht.* **2.** *(as if to a different world)* transport sb to sth jdn in etw. [acc] versetzen [ɪn … fɛtsn̩] <versetzt, versetzte, hat versetzt> ◊ *Der Film versetzte sie in eine andere Welt.*

transportation [noun] *(of goods, animals, people)* Transport [transˈpɔʳt] der <-(e)s, -e> ◊ *der Transport fabrikneuer Autos/von Tieren* ♦ *Die Ware wurde beim Transport beschädigt.* transportation costs Transportkosten [transˈpɔʳtkɔstn̩] die <-> pl

trap¹ [noun] **1.** *(for catching animals, trick, bad situation)* Falle [ˈfalə] die <-, -n> ◊ *eine Falle für Mäuse* ♦ *Er hat uns in eine gemeine Falle gelockt!* set a trap eine Falle aufstellen trap of poverty Armutsfalle [ˈaʳmuːtsfalə] **2.** *(mistake)* Fehler [ˈfeːlɐ] der <-s, -> fall into the trap of doing sth den Fehler machen, etw. zu tun ◊ *Sie hatte den Fehler gemacht, nur für ihre Familie zu leben.*

ℰ **be caught in a trap** in einer ausweglosen Lage stecken

trap² [verb] **1.** *(a person)* einschließen [ˈaɛnʃliːsn̩] <schließt ein, schloss ein, hat eingeschlossen> ◊ *Als der Strom ausfiel, waren sie im Fahrstuhl eingeschlossen.* **2.** *(a part of the body)* einklemmen [ˈaɛnklɛmən] +haben ◊ *Sein Bein war unter dem Baumstamm eingeklemmt.* **3.** *(a criminal)* in die Falle locken [ɪn diː ˈfalə lɔkņ] +haben ◊ *Es gelang der Polizei, die Einbrecher in eine Falle zu locken.* **4.** *(an animal)* in einer Falle fangen [ɪn aɛnɐ ˈfalə faŋən] <fängt, fing, hat gefangen> ◊ *Wir könnten die Ratte in einer Falle fangen.* **5.** *(in a situation)* be trapped gefangen sein [gəˈfaŋən zaɛn] +sein ◊ *Sie fühlte sich in ihrer Beziehung gefangen.* **6.** *(air, gas, energy)* speichern [ˈʃpaɛçɐn] +haben ◊ *Wärme speichern*

trash [noun] **1.** *(bad films, program(me)s, books)* Mist [mɪst] der <-(e)s> no pl *(fam)* ◊ *Der Film war der reinste Mist.* **2.** *(in the US: rubbish)* Müll [mʏl] der <-s> no pl ◊ *den Müll wegbringen* **3.** *(in the US)* the trash der Mülleimer [deːɐ ˈmʏlaɛmɐ] <-s, -> ◊ *etw. in den Mülleimer werfen*

trash can [noun] **1.** *(small container)* Mülleimer [ˈmʏlaɛmɐ] der <-s, -> ◊ *etw. in den Mülleimer werfen* **2.** *(large container)* Mülltonne [ˈmʏltɔnə] die <-, -n> ◊ *Die Mülltonnen werden morgen geleert.*

traumatic [adj] traumatisch [traɔˈmaːtɪʃ] ◊ *ein traumatisches Erlebnis* ♦ *eine traumatische Verletzung* ♦ *Die Flucht war traumatisch.*

travel¹ [noun] **1.** *(activity of travelling)* Reisen [ˈraɛzn̩] das <-s> no pl sb's travels jds Reisen foreign travel Auslandsreisen [ˈaɔslantsraɛzn̩] <-> pl business travel Geschäftsreisen [gəˈʃɛftsraɛzn̩] <-> pl **2.** *(relating to travelling)* Reise… [ˈraɛzə] travel insurance Reiseversicherung [ˈraɛzəfɛˌzɪçərʊŋ] die <-, -en>

ℰ **on your travels** unterwegs

travel² [verb] **1.** *(go on a journey)* reisen [ˈraɛzn̩] +sein ◊ *mit dem Flugzeug reisen* ♦ *in fremde Länder/nach Indien reisen* ♦ *Kinder reisen zum halben Preis.* travel light mit wenig Gepäck reisen travel (around) Russia durch Russland reisen travel the world eine Weltreise machen [aɛnə ˈvɛltraɛzə maxn̩] +haben

travel around herumreisen [hɛˈrʊmraɛzn̩] +sein **2.** *(go from one place to another)* fahren [ˈfaːrən] <fährt, fuhr, ist gefahren> ◊ *zur Arbeit fahren* ♦ *Wir sind heute schon weit gefahren.* travel at 50 miles per hour mit 80 Stundenkilometern fahren travel by car/bus/train mit dem Auto/Bus/Zug fahren travel on foot wandern [ˈvandɐn] +sein travel on horseback reiten [ˈraɛtn̩] <reitet, ritt, ist geritten> **3.** *(in your imagination)* travel back in time eine Reise in die Vergangenheit machen [aɛnə ˌraɛzə ɪn diː fɛˈɡaŋənhaɛt maxn̩] +haben **4.** *(news, gossip)* sich verbreiten [fɛˈbraɛtn̩] <verbreitet sich, verbreitete sich, hat sich verbreitet> ◊ *Die Neuigkeit hat sich schnell im ganzen Betrieb verbreitet.* **5.** *(light, sound)* sich fortbewegen [ˈfɔʳtbəveːɡņ] <bewegt sich fort, bewegte sich fort, hat sich fortbewegt> +haben ◊ *Mit welcher Geschwindigkeit bewegt sich Licht fort?*

ℰ **travel well** den Transport gut vertragen

travel agency [noun] Reisebüro [ˈraɛzəbyˌroː] das <-s, -s> ◊ *Ich arbeite in einem Reisebüro.*

traveller [noun] **1.** *(person who travels)* Reisende [ˈraɛzndə] der/die <-n, die Reisenden> but: ein Reisender/eine Reisende **2.** *(person who does not have a permanent home)* travellers fahrendes Volk [faːrəndəs ˈfɔlk] <fahrenden Volk(e)s> no pl

tray [noun] **1.** *(for carrying things)* Tablett [taˈblɛt] das <-(e)s, -s or -e> ◊ *das Geschirr auf ein Tablet stellen* the breakfast tray das Tablett mit dem Frühstück **2.** *(for papers, documents)* Ablage [ˈaplaːɡə] die <-, -n> paper tray Papierschacht [paˈpiːɐʃaxt] der <-(e)s, Papierschächte>

tread [verb] **1.** *(walk)* auftreten [ˈaɔftreːtn̩] <tritt auf, trat auf, ist aufgetreten> ◊ *vorsichtig auftreten* **2.** *(step)* tread on sth auf etw. [acc] treten [aɔf … treːtn̩] <tritt, trat, ist getreten> ◊ *Er trat auf einen Ast.* tread sth into sth etw. in etw. [acc] treten ◊ *den Schmutz in den Teppich treten*

ℰ **tread carefully** vorsichtig sein

treason [noun] Verrat [fɛˈraːt] der <-(e)s> no pl ◊ *Der Agent war des Verrats angeklagt.*

treasure [noun] Schatz [ʃats] der <-es, Schätze> ◊ *einen Schatz vergraben* ♦ *Kinder sind unser kostbarster Schatz.* ♦ *Du bist ein Schatz!* treasure chest Schatztruhe [ˈʃatstruːə] die <-, -n>

treasurer [noun] *(of an organization)* Schatzmeister [ˈʃatsmaɛstɐ] der <-s, -> ♀Schatzmeisterin [ˈʃatsmaɛstərɪn] die <-, -nen>; *(of a club)* Kassenwart [ˈkasnvaʳt] der <-(e)s, -e> ♀Kassenwartin [ˈkasnvaʳtɪn] die <-, -nen>

treasury [noun] **1.** *(government department)* Finanzministerium [fiˈnantsmɪnɪsˌteːrjʊm] das <-s, Finanzministerien> **2.** *(place for storing money)* Schatzkammer [ˈʃatskamɐ] die <-, -n>

treat¹ [noun] *(something special)* Freude [ˈfrɔɡdə] die <-, -n> ◊ *Es war wirklich eine große Freude, euch wiederzusehen!* give sb a treat jdm eine Freude machen as a special treat ausnahmsweise [ˈaɔsnaːmsˌvaɛzə] ◊ *Ausnahmsweise durften die Kinder mitkommen.*

ℰ **a treat** toll ◊ *Es sah toll aus.* you're in for a treat es wird dir gefallen (it's) my treat ich lade dich/euch ein

treat² [verb] **1.** *(behave towards sb/sth in a particular way, deal with, cure, protect)* behandeln [bəˈhandl̩n] <behandelt, behandelte, hat behandelt> ◊ *Ein Lehrer*

A B C D E F G H I J K L M N O P Q R S **T** U V W X Y Z

sollte alle Schüler gleich behandeln. ✦ *ein schwieriges Thema behandeln* ✦ *Krankengeld wird als Einkommen behandelt.* ✦ *Der Patient muss sofort behandelt werden.* ✦ *die Schuhe mit einem wasserabweisenden Spray behandeln* treat sb with kindness/respect jdn freundlich/respektvoll behandeln treat sb for sth jdn wegen etw. behandeln treat sth with caution mit etw. vorsichtig sein [mɪt ... 'fo:ɐ̯zɪçtɪç zaːn] +sein **2.** *(do or buy sth special)* treat yourself to sth sich [dat] etw. gönnen ['gœnən] +haben ◊ *Nach der Arbeit habe ich mir ein Eis gegönnt.*; *(invite)* treat sb to sth jdn zu etw. einladen [ˈtsuː ... ˌaɛnlaːdn̩] <lädt ein, lud ein, hat eingeladen> ◊ *Der Chef hat uns alle zum Essen eingeladen.*; *(buy)* treat sb to sth jdm etw. kaufen [ˈkaɔfn̩] +haben ◊ *Opa kaufte ihm eine Spielzeugeisenbahn.*

treatment [noun] Behandlung [bəˈhandlʊŋ] die <-, -en> ◊ *die Behandlung von Herzkranken/der Heroinsucht* ✦ *eine homöopathische Behandlung* ✦ *das Genfer Abkommen über die Behandlung Kriegsgefangener* ✦ *die chemische Behandlung von Textilien* respond to treatment auf die Behandlung ansprechen treatment for sth Behandlung wegen etw. receive treatment for sth wegen etw. behandelt werden [veːɐ̯n ... bəˌhandl̩t veːɐ̯dn̩] <wird, wurde, ist worden> get preferential treatment bevorzugt behandelt werden [bəˈfoːɐ̯tsuːkt bəˌhandl̩t veːɐ̯dn̩]

treaty [noun] Vertrag [fɛˈtraːk] der <-(e)s, Verträge> ◊ *England hat einen Vertrag mit Japan geschlossen.* a treaty on sth ein Vertrag über etw. [acc]

tree [noun] Baum [baɔm] der <-(e)s, Bäume> ◊ *auf Bäume klettern* apple tree Apfelbaum [ˈapl̩baɔm] oak tree Eiche [ˈaɛçə] die <-, -n>

tremble [verb] zittern [ˈtsɪtɐn] +haben ◊ *Seine Hände zitterten.* ✦ *am ganzen Körper heftig zittern* tremble with zittern vor ◊ *Ihre Stimme zitterte vor Nervosität.*

tremendous(ly) [adj, adv] **1.** *(great)* ungeheuer [ˈʊŋɡəhɔɐ] <ungeheurer, am ungeheuersten> <der/die/das ungeheure ...> ◊ *eine ungeheure Menge an Daten* ✦ *Die Fortschritte in der Medizin sind ungeheuer.* ✦ *Er hat einen ungeheueren Respekt vor ihr.* ✦ ungeheuer wichtig; *(interest, disappointment)* gewaltig [ɡəˈvaltɪç] ◊ *Das Interesse daran ist gewaltig.* ✦ *eine gewaltige Enttäuschung* **2.** *(brilliant)* fantastisch [fanˈtastɪʃ] ◊ *ein fantastischer Abend* ✦ *Die Vorstellung war fantastisch.* ✦ *Sie haben fantastisch gespielt.*

trench [noun] **1.** *(hole in the ground)* Graben [ˈɡraːbm̩] der <-s, Gräben> ◊ *einen Graben ausheben* **2.** *(used by soldiers)* Schützengraben [ˈʃʏtsn̩ɡraːbm̩] der <-s, Schützengräben>

trend [noun] Trend [trɛnt] der <-s, -s> ◊ *Wir hoffen, dass dieser positive Trend anhält.* ✦ *einem Trend folgen* a trend towards sth ein Trend zu etw. buck a trend einem Trend nicht folgen upward trend Aufwärtstrend [ˈaɔfvɛˈtstrɛnt] downward trend Abwärtstrend [ˈapvɛˈtstrɛnt] set a trend richtungsweisend sein [ˈrɪçtʊŋvaɛznt zaːn] +sein

trendy [adj] schick [ʃɪk] ◊ *eine schicke Frisur* ✦ *Es galt als schick, einen Sportwagen zu fahren.*

trial [noun] **1.** *(court proceedings)* Prozess [proˈtsɛs] der <-es, -e> be on trial (for sth) (wegen etw.) vor Gericht stehen [foːɐ̯ ɡəˈrɪçt ʃteːən] <steht, stand, hat gestanden> await trial on sth wegen etw. angeklagt sein [veːɐ̯n ... ˌaŋɡəklaːkt zaːn] +sein **2.** *(testing)* Test

[tɛst] der <-(e)s, -s or -e> undergo trials getestet werden [ɡəˈtɛstət veːɐ̯dn̩] <wird, wurde, ist worden> ◊ *Das neue Produkt wird im Labor getestet.* trial period Probezeit [ˈproːbətsaɛt] die <-, -en> on a trial basis probeweise [ˈproːbəvaɛzə] trial separation Trennung auf Probe [ˌtrɛnʊŋ aɔf ˈproːbə] die <-, -en> **3.** *(difficult experience or person)* Problem [proˈbleːm] das <-s, -e> ◊ *die Probleme, die das Leben im Exil mit sich brachte* ✦ *Tante Karin ist manchmal ein Problem.*; *(difficult child)* Plage [ˈplaːɡə] die <-, -n> ◊ *Die Kinder waren heute eine Plage.* **4.** *(sports competition)* Ausscheidung [ˈaɔsʃaɛdʊŋ] die <-, -en> ◊ *die Ausscheidung für die Weltmeisterschaft*
☞ trial and error Ausprobieren trial by jury Schwurgerichtsverfahren trials and tribulations Schwierigkeiten

triangle [noun] **1.** *(shape, object)* Dreieck [ˈdraɛɛk] das <-(e)s, -e> ◊ *ein gleichschenkliges Dreieck* **2.** *(musical instrument)* Triangel [ˈtriːaŋl̩] der <-s, -> **3.** *(relationship)* Dreiecksverhältnis [ˈdraɛɛksfɛhɛltnɪs] das <-ses, -se> ◊ *das Dreiecksverhältnis zwischen den USA, China und Taiwan* love triangle Dreiecksbeziehung [ˈdraɛɛksbətsiːʊŋ] die <-, -en>

tribe [noun] **1.** *(group of related families)* Stamm [ʃtam] der <-(e)s, Stämme> ◊ *ein Stamm der Sioux* **2.** *(large family)* Sippe [ˈzɪpə] die <-, -n> ◊ *Einmal im Jahr trifft sich die ganze Sippe.*

tribunal [noun] Tribunal [tribuˈnaːl] das <-s, -e>

tribute [noun] **1.** *(expression of respect and admiration)* tribute (to ...) Würdigung (... [gen]) [ˈvʏˈdɪɡʊŋ] die <-, -en> in tribute to sb/sth jdm/einer Sache zu Ehren [tsuː ˈeːrən] a floral tribute Blumen [ˈbluːmən] <-> pl **2.** *(money paid)* Tribut [triˈbuːt] der <-(e)s, -e>
☞ be a tribute to sb/sth jdm/einer Sache Ehre machen pay tribute to sb/sth jdn/etw. würdigen

trick¹ [noun] **1.** *(unpleasant, unfair)* Streich [ʃtraɛç] der <-(e)s, -e> a nasty trick ein böser Streich play a trick on sb jdm einen Streich spielen your memory is playing tricks on you jds Gedächtnis spielt jdm einen Streich dirty tricks campaign Verleumdungskampagne [fɛˈlɔɛmdʊŋskamˌpanjə] die <-, -n> **2.** *(entertaining, effective)* Trick [trɪk] der <-(e)s, -s> ◊ *Der Zauberkünstler verblüffte die Zuschauer mit seinen Tricks.* ✦ *Kaugummi kann man mit einem simplen Trick von Kleidungsstücken entfernen.* the trick is ... der Trick dabei ist, ... conjuring trick Zauberkunststück [ˈtsaɔbɐkʊnstʃtʏk] das <-s, -e> do a trick ein Zauberkunststück vorführen **3.** *(confusing, creating an illusion)* Täuschung [ˈtɔɛʃʊŋ] die <-, -en> ◊ *It's a trick of the light. Das Licht täuscht.* **4.** *(in cards)* Stich [ʃtɪç] der <-(e)s, -e> ◊ *Er warf im dritten Stich den Karokönig ab.* take a trick einen Stich machen
☞ try every trick in the book alles Erdenkliche versuchen a box of tricks eine Trickkiste have a trick up your sleeve einen Trick auf Lager haben do the trick wirken sb never misses a trick jdm entgeht nichts

trick² [verb] hereinlegen [hɛˈraɛnleːɡn̩] +haben ◊ *Er hat uns hereingelegt.*
• trick into [phras v] trick sb into doing sth jdn durch einen Trick dazu bringen, etw. zu tun [dʊˈç aɛnən ˌtrɪk daːtsu: ˈbrɪŋən ... tsuː] <bringt,

brachte, hat gebracht> trick sb into believing sth jdm etw. weismachen ['vaɛsmaxn̩] +haben ◊ *Er hat ihr weisgemacht, dass er ein erfolgreicher Geschäftsmann ist.*
• **trick out** [phras v] **1.** trick sth out etw. dekorieren [deko'ri:rən] <dekoriert, dekorierte, hat dekoriert> trick sb out jdn herausputzen [hɛ'raospʊtsn̩] +haben **2.** trick sb out of sth jdm etw. abknöpfen ['apknœpfn̩] +haben *(fam)* ◊ *Sie hat der alten Dame ihre ganzen Ersparnisse abgeknöpft.*

trickle [verb] rieseln ['ri:zln̩] +sein ◊ *Schweiß rieselte ihm von der Stirn.*

tricky [adj] **1.** *(difficult to do)* schwierig ['ʃvi:rɪç] ◊ *eine schwierige Aufgabe* ♦ *Es war schwierig, das Haus zu finden.* **2.** *(difficult to deal with)* heikel ['haɛkl̩] <heikler, am heikelsten> <der/die/das heikle …> ◊ *Das ist eine heikle Frage.* ♦ *Die Situation ist ziemlich heikel.*

trifle [noun] *englische Süßspeise, die aus Schichten von Obst oder Götterspeise, Vanillesauce und Sahne auf Löffelbiskuit besteht*

trigger, trigger off [verb] auslösen ['aoslø:zn̩] +haben ◊ *Der Mord von Sarajewo löste den Ersten Weltkrieg aus.* ♦ *mit einem Knopfdruck den Alarm auslösen* ♦ *eine Reaktion auslösen*

trillion [noun] Billion [bɪ'ljo:n] die <-, -en>

trim¹ [noun] **1.** *(haircut)* have a trim sich [dat] die Haare nachschneiden lassen [di: 'ha:rə ˌna:xʃnaedn̩ lasn̩] <lässt, ließ, hat lassen> **2.** *(decoration on the edges)* Rand [rant] der <-(e)s, Ränder>; *(made of wood, plastic, metal)* Leiste ['laɛstə] die <-, -n> ◊ *die Leisten an den Kotflügeln*

trim² [verb] **1.** *(your hair, beard, a hedge)* schneiden ['ʃnaedn̩] <schneidet, schnitt, hat geschnitten> ◊ *Die Hecke muss geschnitten werden.* **2.** *(cut down)* trim sth to sth etw. auf etw. [acc] verringern [aof … fɛˌrɪŋən] <verringert, verringerte, hat verringert> ◊ *die Anzahl der Mitarbeiter auf die Hälfte verringern* trim sth from sth etw. um etw. [acc] kürzen [ʊm … ˌkʏʦn̩] +haben ◊ *den Etat um zwei Millionen kürzen* **3.** *(decorate)* schmücken ['ʃmʏkŋ̩] +haben ◊ *den Weihnachtsbaum schmücken* trim sth with sth etw. mit etw. besetzen [mɪt …'bəzɛʦn̩] <besetzt, besetzte, hat besetzt> ◊ *Ihr Kostüm war mit Pelz besetzt.*

trip¹ [noun] *(short journey)* trip (to) Fahrt (nach) [fa:ˈt] die <-, -en> boat trip Bootsfahrt ['bo:tsfa:ˈt] day trip Tagesfahrt ['ta:gəsfa:ˈt] sightseeing trip Besichtigungsfahrt [bə'zɪçtɪgʊŋsfa:ˈt] shopping trip Einkaufsbummel ['aɛnkaofsbʊml̩] der <-s, ->; *(longer journey)* trip (to) Reise (nach) ['raɛzə] die <-, -n> ◊ *eine Reise nach Rio* go on a trip eine Reise machen business trip Geschäftsreise [gə'ʃɛftsraɛzə] trip abroad Auslandsreise ['aoslantsraɛzə]

trip² [verb] **1.** *(hit your foot on sth)* trip (up) stolpern ['ʃtɔlpən] +sein ◊ *Ich wollte mich beeilen, doch dann stolperte ich und fiel hin.* trip up on sth über etw. [acc] stolpern ◊ *Sie ist über einen Stein gestolpert.* **2.** trip sb (up) jdm ein Bein stellen [aen 'baen ʃtɛlən] +haben ◊ *Er hat mir ein Bein gestellt.* **3.** *(a switch)* auf „an" stellen [aof 'an ʃtɛlən] +haben ◊ *Stellen Sie den Schalter auf „an".* be tripped auf „an" stehen [aof 'an ʃte:ən] <steht, stand, hat gestanden>
• **trip up** [phras v] **1.** *(make a mistake)* trip up (on

sth) sich (bei etw.) vertun [fɛ'tu:n] <vertut sich, vertat sich, hat sich vertan> ◊ *Man kann sich auch bei einfachen Aufgaben vertun.* **2.** trip sb up jdn aufs Glatteis führen [aofs 'glataes fy:rən] +haben ◊ *So leicht kannst du mich nicht aufs Glatteis führen.* → trip 2.

triple [adj] dreifach ['draefax] *no comp/superl; mostly before us* ◊ *ein dreifacher Salto*

triumph¹ [noun] Triumph [tri'ʊmf] der <-(e)s, -e> ◊ *der Triumph des Guten über das Böse*
⊚ in triumph triumphierend

triumph² [verb] triumphieren [triʊm'fi:rən] <triumphiert, triumphierte, hat triumphiert> ◊ *Am Ende triumphierte ein Außenseiter.* ♦ *Ihr Optimismus triumphierte über seinen Pessimismus.*

trivial [adj] belanglos [bə'laŋlo:s] <belangloser, am belanglosesten> ◊ *eine belanglose Kleinigkeit* ♦ *Die Story ist belanglos.*

trolley [noun] *(in a shop)* Einkaufswagen ['aɛnkaofsva:gŋ̩] der <-s, -> ◊ *den vollen Einkaufswagen zur Kasse schieben; (at the airport)* Kofferkuli ['kɔfeku:li:] der <-s, -s> ◊ *Ich lud mein Gepäck auf den Kofferkuli.; (for serving food)* Servierwagen [zɛɐ'vi:gva:gŋ̩] der <-s, ->

troop [noun] *(group of soldiers)* Truppe ['trʊpə] die <-, -n> ◊ *Die Truppe war demoralisiert.* ♦ *Truppen in ein Land entsenden* troop movements Truppenbewegungen ['trʊpmbaˌve:gʊŋən] die <-> pl

trophy [noun] **1.** *(cup: given as a prize)* Pokal [po'ka:l] der <-s, -e> ◊ *den Pokal gewinnen* **2.** *(souvenir of victory)* Trophäe [tro'fɛ:ə] die <-, -n> ◊ *Er nahm die gegnerische Fahne als Trophäe mit nach Hause.*

tropical [adj] tropisch ['tro:pɪʃ] *seldom comp/superl* ◊ *der tropische Regenwald* ♦ *Die Temperaturen sind schon fast tropisch.* tropical medicine Tropenmedizin ['tro:pm̩medi̯ˌtsi:n] die <-> no pl

tropics [noun] the tropics die Tropen ['tro:pm̩] <-> pl ◊ *in den Tropen leben*

trouble¹ [noun] **1.** *(problems, difficulties)* Schwierigkeiten ['ʃvi:rɪçkaetn̩] die <-> pl ◊ *Wir rechnen mit Schwierigkeiten.* ♦ *Schwierigkeiten mit etw. haben* ♦ *in Schwierigkeiten sein* cause (sb/sth) trouble (jdm/etw.) Schwierigkeiten machen run into trouble in Schwierigkeiten geraten get sb into trouble jdn in Schwierigkeiten bringen **2.** *(worries)* troubles Sorgen ['zɔʁgn̩] die <-> pl ◊ *finanzielle Sorgen* ♦ *Ich erzähle dir all meine Sorgen.* **3.** *(difficult aspect, feature)* Problem [pro'ble:m] das <-s, -e> ◊ *Dein Problem ist, dass du zu neugierig bist.* the (only) trouble (with sb/sth) is that das (einzige) Problem (an jdm/etw.) ist, dass **4.** *(health problems)* Beschwerden [bə'fve:gdn̩] die <-> pl ◊ *akute/chronische Beschwerden* give sb trouble jdm Beschwerden machen stomach trouble Magenbeschwerden ['ma:gŋ̩bəˌfve:gdn̩] sb has trouble with sth etw. macht jdm zu schaffen [maxt … tsu: 'ʃafn̩] +haben ◊ *Mein Rücken macht mir zu schaffen.* **5.** *(technical problems)* engine trouble ein Motorschaden [aen 'mo:to:ʁ̩ʃa:dn̩] der <-s, Motorschäden> ◊ *Wegen eines Motorschadens musste das Flugzeug notlanden.* mechanical trouble technische Probleme [ˌtɛçnɪʃə pro'ble:mə] <-> pl **6.** *(special effort)* Mühe ['my:ə] die <-, -n> take the trouble to do sth, go to the trouble of doing sth sich [dat] die Mühe machen, etw. zu tun ◊ *Er hat sich die Mühe gemacht, mir die Fotos zu schicken.* take trouble

over sth sich [dat] mit etw. Mühe geben ◊ *Sie gibt sich mit ihren Hausaufgaben viel Mühe.* go to a lot of trouble (to do sth) sich viel Mühe geben(, um etw. zu tun) ◊ *Ich gebe mir viel Mühe, dir alles recht zu machen.* It is more trouble than it is worth. *Es ist der Mühe nicht wert.* I don't mind waiting — it's no trouble. *Ich warte gern — es macht mir nichts aus.* put sb to a lot of trouble jdm Umstände machen ['ʊmʃtɛndə maxn̩] +haben ◊ *Ich möchte Ihnen keine Umstände machen.* save sb the trouble of doing sth jdm etw. ersparen [ɛ'ʃpaːrən] <erspart, ersparte, hat erspart> ◊ *Ich fahre dich zum Bahnhof, das erspart dir die Busfahrt.* save yourself trouble sich [dat] viel ersparen 7. *(for doing sth wrong)* Ärger ['ɛrgə] der <-s> *no pl* be in trouble (with sb) Ärger (mit jdm) haben ◊ *Hast du Ärger mit deinen Eltern?* get into trouble (for doing sth) Ärger bekommen(, weil man etw. tut) ◊ *Sie hat Ärger bekommen, weil sie ständig zu spät kommt.* keep out of trouble sauber bleiben ['zaʊbɐ blaɛbm̩] <bleibt, blieb, ist geblieben> *(fam)* 8. *(fighting, violence)* Unruhe ['ʊnruːə] die <-, −n> *most pl* ◊ *Die Unruhen begannen mit der Festnahme eines Studenten.* cause trouble Unruhe stiften ☞ be asking for trouble nur Ärger bringen

trouble² [verb] 1. *(cause worry)* bedrücken [bə'drʏkn̩] <bedrückt, bedrückte, hat bedrückt> ◊ *Was bedrückt dich denn so?* it troubles sb that es beunruhigt jdn, dass [ɛs bə]'ʊnruːɪçt ... das] <beunruhigte, hat beunruhigt> 2. *(bother)* belästigen [bə'lɛstɪgn̩] <belästigt, belästigte, hat belästigt> ◊ *Es tut mir Leid, dass ich Sie mit dieser Angelegenheit belästigen muss.* Don't trouble yourself. *Machen Sie sich keine Mühe.* 3. *(in polite requests)* trouble sb for sth jdn um etw. bitten [ʊm ... bɪtn̩] <bittet, bat, hat gebeten> ◊ *Darf ich Sie um Ihre Hilfe bitten?* trouble sb to do sth jdn bitten, etw. zu tun Could I trouble you to ...? *Würden Sie bitte ...?* I'm sorry to trouble you, but ... *Entschuldigen Sie bitte die Störung, aber ...* 4. *(hurt)* trouble sb jdm zu schaffen machen [tsuː 'ʃafn̩ maxn̩] +haben ◊ *Mein Rücken macht mir wieder zu schaffen.*

trousers [noun] Hose ['hoːzə] die <-, −n> *can be used in the pl or sing* ◊ *Ich trug eine graue Hose.* ◆ *Sie hatte lange Hosen an.* a pair of trousers eine Hose

trout [noun] Forelle [fo'rɛlə] die <-, −n> ◊ *Die Forelle ist ein Raubfisch.* ◆ *geräucherte Forelle*

truck [noun] 1. *(esp in the US: lorry)* Lastwagen ['lastvaːgn̩] der <-s, −> ◊ *mit einem Lastwagen auf der Autobahn fahren* 2. *(in the UK: wagon)* Güterwagen ['gyːtevaːgn̩] der <-s, −> ◊ *ein Zug mit Güterwagen* 3. *(device for moving heavy objects)* Karre ['karə] die <-, −n> ◊ *eine Karre ziehen*

true [adj] 1. *(story, extent, reason, feelings, friend, love)* wahr [vaːr] ◊ *Ist das wirklich wahr?* ◆ *eine wahre Geschichte* true of sth/sb wahr für jdn/etw.; *(passion)* echt [ɛçt] *no comp/superl* ◊ *eine echte Leidenschaft für die Musik* be true (for sb/sth) gelten (für jdn/etw.) ['gɛltn̩] <gilt, galt, hat gegolten> ◊ *Jeder braucht eine sinnvolle Beschäftigung. Das gilt auch für Kinder.* 2. *(right)* richtig ['rɪçtɪç] it's true (that) es ist richtig (, dass) ◊ *Es ist schon richtig, dass die Miete teuer ist, aber die Wohnung liegt zentral.* that may be true, but das mag richtig sein, aber 3. *(loyal)* be true to sb jdm treu sein

['troː zaɛn] ◊ *Sie ist ihm treu.* remain true (to sb/sth) (jdm/einer Sache) treu bleiben

truly [adv] 1. *(really)* wirklich ['vɪrklɪç] *no comp/superl* ◊ *Die Arbeit ist wirklich überzeugend.* ◆ *Ich helfe dir wirklich gern.* 2. *(truthfully)* wahrheitsgemäß ['vaːrhaetsgəmɛːs] ◊ *Ich antwortete wahrheitsgemäß.*

trumpet [noun] 1. *(musical instrument)* Trompete [trɔm'peːtə] die <-, −n> ◊ *Sie spielte ein Stück von Bach auf der Trompete.* 2. *(sounds of elephant)* Trompeten [trɔm'peːtn̩] das <-s> *no pl* ◊ *Das Trompeten des Elefanten war weithin zu hören.*

trunk [noun] 1. *(of a tree)* Stamm [ʃtam] der <-(e)s, Stämme> ◊ *der dicke Stamm einer Eiche* 2. *(suitcase)* Koffer ['kɔfə] der <-s, −> ◊ *den Koffer packen/auspacken* 3. *(of an elephant)* Rüssel ['rʏsl̩] der <-s, −> ◊ *Der Elefant hob die Früchte mit dem Rüssel auf.* 4. *(of the body)* Rumpf [rʊmpf] der <-(e)s, Rümpfe> ◊ *den Rumpf beugen* 5. *(of a car)* Kofferraum ['kɔferaʊm] der <-(e)s, Kofferräume> ◊ *Sie verstaute die Einkäufe im Kofferraum.*

trust¹ [noun] 1. *(feeling)* Vertrauen [fe'traʊən] das <-s> *no pl* ◊ *Vertrauen spielt in jeder Beziehung eine wichtige Rolle.* trust in sb/sth Vertrauen zu jdm/auf etw. [acc] ◊ *sein Vertrauen auf Gerechtigkeit verlieren* ◆ *Ich habe kein Vertrauen mehr zu ihm.* place/put your trust in sth sein Vertrauen in jdn/etw. setzen 2. LAW *(arrangement)* Treuhandschaft ['trɔɪhantʃaft] die <-, −en> hold sth in trust etw. treuhänderisch verwalten ['trɔɪhɛndərɪʃ fe,valtn̩] <verwaltet, verwaltete, hat verwaltet> 3. LAW *(money)* Treuhandvermögen ['trɔɪhantfemøːgn̩] das <-s, −> 4. *(organization)* Stiftung ['ʃtɪftʊŋ] die <-, −en> 5. *(responsibility)* put sb/sth in the trust of sb jdn/etw. in jds Obhut geben [ɪn ... ˌɔphuːt geːbm̩] <gibt, gab, hat gegeben> ◊ *Sie hat ihren Hund in die Obhut ihres Nachbarn gegeben.* position of trust Vertrauensposition [fe'traʊənspoziˌtsjoːn] die <-, −en> 6. *(cartel)* Kartell [kar'tɛl] das <-s, −e> ☞ take sth on trust (jdm) etw. einfach glauben

trust² [verb] 1. *(have confidence)* vertrauen [fe'traʊən] <vertraut, vertraute, hat vertraut> ◊ *Ich vertraue ihr blind.* ◆ *seinen Fähigkeiten vertrauen* trust sb to do sth sich darauf verlassen, dass jd etw. tut [daraʊf fe'lasn̩ das] <verlässt sich, verließ sich, hat sich verlassen> ◊ *Er verlässt sich darauf, dass ich das Geschenk besorge.* trust sb with sth jdm etw. anvertrauen ['anfetraʊən] <vertraut an, vertraute an, hat anvertraut> ◊ *Sie vertraute mir ihre Sorgen an.* 2. *(believe)* glauben ['glaʊbm̩] +haben ◊ *Glaub nicht alles, was dir erzählt wird!* ☞ not trust sb as far as you can throw them jdm nicht über den Weg trauen ◆ trust in [phras v] trust in sb/sth an jdn/etw. glauben ['glaʊbm̩] +haben ◊ *Ich glaube an dich und deine Fähigkeiten.* ◆ trust to [phras v] trust to sth auf etw. [acc] vertrauen [aʊf ... fe,traʊən] <vertraut, vertraute, hat vertraut> ◊ *Ich vertraue einfach auf meine Glückssträhne.*

trustee [noun] 1. LAW *(person or organization looking after sb's assets)* Treuhänder ['trɔɪhɛndə] der <-, −s> ♀Treuhänderin ['trɔɪhɛndərɪn] die <-, −nen> ◊ *Er ist als Treuhänder für ein großes Unternehmen tätig.* 2. *(manager of a trust)* Vermögensverwalter [fe'møːgn̩sfevaltə] der <-s, −> ♀Vermögensverwalterin [fe'møːgn̩sfe,valtərɪn] die

<-, –nen> ◊ *die neue Vermögensverwalterin unserer Stiftung*

truth [noun] Wahrheit ['vaːˈhaɛt] die <-, –en> ◊ *Sagst du die Wahrheit?* ♦ *Sag mir die Wahrheit!* truth about sth/sb Wahrheit über etw./jdn the truth of the matter is (that) die Wahrheit ist (, dass) there is a grain of truth in/to sth in etw. [dat] steckt ein Körnchen Wahrheit
◉ nothing could be further from the truth nichts ist weiter von der Wahrheit entfernt stretch the truth es mit der Wahrheit nicht so genau nehmen to tell you the truth um die Wahrheit zu sagen if truth be told ehrlich gesagt in truth in Wahrheit

try¹ [noun] Versuch [feˈzuːx] der <-(e)s, –e> ◊ *einen Versuch wert sein* ♦ *Sein Versuch, sie zu überzeugen, scheiterte.*
◉ nice try netter Versuch give sb a try 1. *(ask for help)* jdn fragen 2. *(let have a try)* jdn versuchen lassen ◊ *Lass sie versuchen, die Hausaufgaben allein zu machen.* give sth a try *(try doing sth, try out a remedy etc.)* etw. ausprobieren give sb/sth a try *(go somewhere in order to find a solution)* es bei jdm/etw. versuchen ◊ *Versuchen Sie es doch mal beim Hausmeister.*

try² [verb] 1. *(attempt to do sth)* versuchen [feˈzuːxn] <versucht, versuchte, hat versucht> ◊ *Sie versuchte ein Lächeln.* ♦ *„Ich kann das nicht.“ – „Versuch es doch wenigstens.“* try to/and do sth, try doing sth versuchen, etw. zu tun ◊ *Versuch mal, das Paket zu heben!* try the door versuchen, die Tür zu öffnen try hard sich [dat] Mühe geben ['myːə geːbm̩] <gibt, gab, hat gegeben> ◊ *Wir haben uns so große Mühe gegeben.* try desperately to do sth sich verzweifelt bemühen, etw. zu tun [fɛtsvaɛfl̩t bəˈmyːən … ˈtsuː] <bemüht sich, bemühte sich, hat sich bemüht> 2. *(check if sth is good)* ausprobieren ['aosproˌbiːrən] <probiert aus, probierte aus, hat ausprobiert> ◊ *eine neue Sportart ausprobieren* try sth on sb etw. an jdm ausprobieren try anything once alles einmal ausprobieren 3. *(a food, drink)* probieren [proˈbiːrən] <probiert, probierte, hat probiert> ◊ *Probier mal!* ♦ *Hast du den Kuchen schon probiert?* 4. *(in court)* verhandeln [feˈhandl̩n] <verhandelt, verhandelte, hat verhandelt> ◊ *Sein Fall wird in der ersten Instanz verhandelt.* try sb for sth jdn wegen etw. anklagen [veˈgɛn … ˌankla:gn̩] +haben
• **try for** [phras v] sich bemühen um [bəˈmyːən ʊm] <bemüht sich, bemühte sich, hat sich bemüht> ◊ *Bemühen Sie sich um ein wenig mehr Genauigkeit.*
• **try on** [phras v] anprobieren ['anproˌbiːrən] <probiert an, probierte an, hat anprobiert> ◊ *einen Badeanzug anprobieren*
• **try out** [phras v] ausprobieren ['aosproˌbiːrən] <probiert aus, probierte aus, hat ausprobiert> ◊ *das neue Auto ausprobieren* try sth out on sb etw. an jdm ausprobieren

trying → **try²** [adj] anstrengend ['anʃtrɛŋənt] ◊ *ein anstrengendes Kind* ◊ *Der Abend war sehr anstrengend.*

T-shirt [noun] T-Shirt ['tiːʃœɐt] das <-s, –s> ◊ *Ich trage am liebsten T-Shirts.*

tub [noun] 1. *(of ice, margarine, yogurt)* Becher ['bɛçɐ] der <-s, -> ◊ *ein Becher Eis* ♦ *Möchten Sie das Eis im Becher oder in der Waffel?* 2. *(for a bath, the washing)* Wanne ['vanə] die <-, –n> ◊ *Ich liege in der Wanne.* ♦ *die Wäsche in einer Wanne einweichen*

3. *(for plants)* Kübel ['kyːbl̩] der <-s, –> ◊ *Pflanzen in Kübeln auf die Terrasse stellen*

tube [noun] 1. *(for liquids, for gas)* Schlauch [ʃlaox] der <-(e)s, Schläuche> ◊ *Benzin mit einem Schlauch absaugen* 2. *(for pastes)* Tube ['tuːbə] die <-, –n> ◊ *ein Tube Zahnpasta* ♦ *Senf aus der Tube* ♦ *Farben in Tuben* 3. *(container for rolled-up paper)* Rohr [roːɐ] das <-(e)s, -e> ◊ *Ich rolle das Poster auf und stecke es in das Rohr.; (for sweets)* Röhrchen ['røːɐçən] das <-s, –> 4. *(in the UK)* the tube, the Tube die U-Bahn ['uːbaːn] <-, –en> ◊ *Sie fährt mit der U-Bahn zur Arbeit.* on the tube in der U-Bahn 5. *(in the body)* Röhre ['røːrə] die <-, –n> Fallopian tube Eileiter ['aelaetɐ] der <-s, –>
◉ go down the tube den Bach runtergehen *(fam)*

tuck [verb] 1. *(put in a particular place)* stecken ['ʃtɛkn̩] +haben ◊ *sein Hemd in die Hose stecken* be tucked somewhere irgendwo stecken ◊ *Der Strafzettel steckte hinter dem Scheibenwischer.* tuck sth under your arm etw. unter den Arm klemmen [ʊntɐ deːn ˈaɐm klɛmən] +haben tuck in the sheets ◉ *das Laken über die Matratze ziehen* [das ˌlaːkn̩ yːbɐ diː maˈtratsə tsiːən] <zieht, zog, hat gezogen> 2. *(arms)* tuck in anwinkeln ['anvɪŋkl̩n] +haben; *(legs)* tuck up anziehen ['antsiːən] <zieht an, zog an, hat angezogen> He sat with his feet tucked under him. Er saß mit untergeschlagenen Beinen da.
• **tuck away** [phras v] tuck sth away 1. *(put away)* etw. wegstecken ['vɛkʃtɛkn̩] +haben ◊ *Steck das Geld weg!* 2. *(hide)* etw. verstecken [feˈʃtɛkn̩] <versteckt, versteckte, hat versteckt> ◊ *einen Brief unter der Zeitung verstecken* 3. *(save)* etw. auf die Seite legen [aof diː ˈzaetə leːgn̩] +haben ◊ *Er hat ein bisschen Geld auf die Seite gelegt.*
◉ be tucked away versteckt liegen
• **tuck in** [phras v] 1. *(put into bed)* tuck sb in jdn ins Bett bringen [ɪns ˈbɛt brɪŋən] <bringt, brachte, hat gebracht> ◊ *Er bringt seine Kinder jeden Abend ins Bett.* 2. *(eat heartily)* kräftig zulangen [krɛftɪç ˈtsuːlaŋən] +haben ◊ *Langt kräftig zu!*
• **tuck up** [phras v] → **tuck in**

Tuesday [noun] Dienstag ['diːnstaːk] der <-(e)s, -e> → **Monday**

tuition [noun] 1. *(activity)* Unterricht ['ʊntɐrɪçt] der <-(e)s, -e> most sing language tuition Sprachunterricht ['ʃpraːxlʊntɐrɪçt] tuition in German Deutschunterricht ['dɔʏtʃlʊntɐrɪçt] 2. *(at college or university)* tuition (fees) Studiengebühr ['ʃtuːdjəngəbyːɐ] die <-, –en> most pl ◊ *Wie viel Studiengebühren kostet Medizin pro Semester?; (at schools)* Schulgeld ['ʃuːlgɛlt] das <-(e)s> no pl

tumble [verb] 1. *(objects, prices, records)* purzeln ['pʊrtsl̩n] +sein ◊ *Kartoffeln purzelten aus dem Sack.* ♦ *Die Preise purzeln.* 2. *(person)* stürzen ['ʃtʏrtsn̩] +sein ◊ *Er stürzte ins Wasser.* ◊ *Sie stürzten aus dem brennenden Haus.* 3. *(hair)* fallen ['faln̩] <fällt, fiel, ist gefallen> ◊ *Das Haar fällt ihr über den Rücken.* 4. *(building, wall)* tumble (down) einstürzen ['aenʃtʏrtsn̩] +sein ◊ *Das Haus stürzte ein.* 5. *(water)* sich ergießen [ɛˈgiːsn̩] <ergießt sich, ergoss sich, hat sich ergossen> ◊ *Das Wasser ergießt sich über die Felsen in den See.; (clouds)* sich wälzen ['vɛltsn̩] ◊ *Dunkle Wolken wälzten sich über die Berge.*

tumble-dryer [noun] Wäschetrockner ['vɛʃətrɔknɐ] der <-s, –> ◊ *die Wäsche in den Trockner geben*

tumour, tumor [noun] Tumor ['tu:mo:ɐ̯] der
<-s, -en> ◊ *ein bösartiger/gutartiger Tumor*
tumultuous [adj] *(times, life)* turbulent [tʊˈbuˈlɛnt]
<turbulenter, am turbulentesten> ◊ *ein turbulenter
Abend; (applause, relationship, welcome)* stürmisch
['ʃtʏˈmɪʃ] ◊ *Die Begrüßung war stürmisch.*
tuna [noun] Tunfisch ['tu:nfɪʃ] der <-(e)s, -e> ◊
Tunfisch in Öl ♦ *einen Tunfisch fangen*
tune¹ [noun] Melodie [melo'di:] die <-, -n> ◊ *eine
Melodie summen*
⊛ **be in/out of tune with sth 1.** *(harmonize)* im
Einklang/nicht im Einklang mit etw. sein **2.** *(agree
with)* mit etw. übereinstimmen/nicht übereinstimmen **call the tune** den Ton angeben **dance to sb's
tune** nach jds Pfeife tanzen **in/out of tune** *(in
music)* richtig/falsch
tune² [verb] **1.** *(musical instrument)* stimmen ['ʃtɪmən]
+haben ◊ *ein Klavier stimmen lassen; (machine,
engine, radio station)* einstellen ['aɛnʃtɛlən] +haben ◊
Die Maschine muss neu eingestellt werden. ♦ *Stell
das Radio doch auf den Klassiksender ein.* **2.** *(turn
on)* einschalten ['aɛnʃaltn̩] <schaltet ein, schaltete ein,
hat eingeschaltet> ◊ *das Radio/die Nachrichten einschalten* **stay tuned (to sth)** dranbleiben
['dranblaɛbm̩] <bleibt dran, blieb dran, ist drangeblie-
ben> *(fam)* ◊ *Bleiben Sie dran, gleich geht es weiter.*
3. *(train)* trainieren [trɛˈni:rən] <trainiert, trainierte,
hat trainiert> ◊ *die Augen trainieren*
♦ **tune up** [phras v] **tune sth up** etw. stimmen
['ʃtɪmən] +haben ◊ *ein Klavier stimmen* **sb tunes up**
jd stimmt sein Instrument [ʃtɪmt zaɛn ɪnstruˈmɛnt]
+haben *They tune up.* Sie stimmen ihre Instrumente.
tunnel [noun] *(for vehicles)* Tunnel ['tʊnl̩] der <-s, ->
◊ *Sie fuhren durch den Tunnel.; (made by animals)*
Gang [gaŋ] der <-(e)s, Gänge>
turbulent [adj] *(situation, life, times, air)* turbulent
[tʊˈbuˈlɛnt] <turbulenter, am turbulentesten> ◊ *Seine
Vergangenheit war ziemlich turbulent.* ♦ *turbulente
Luftmassen; (water)* aufgewühlt ['aofɡəvy:lt] <aufge-
wühlter, am aufgewühltesten>; *(sea)* stürmisch
['ʃtʏˈmɪʃ]
Turk [noun] Türke ['tʏˈkə] der <-n, -n> ♀Türkin
['tʏˈkɪn] die <-, -nen> → **German¹ 1.**
turkey [noun] **1.** *(animal)* Truthahn ['tru:tha:n] der
<-(e)s, Truthähne> ♀Pute ['pu:tə] die <-, -n> ◊ *An
Weihnachten gibt es Truthahn.* ♦ *Enten und Puten
balten* **2.** *(unsuccessful film)* Reinfall ['raɛnfal] der
<-(e)s, Reinfälle> ◊ *Sein letzter Film war ein großer
Reinfall.*
Turkey [noun] die Türkei [tʏˈkaɛ] <-> *no pl* ◊ *in die
Türkei fahren*
Turkish¹ [noun] Türkisch ['tʏˈkɪʃ] das <-(s)> *no pl* →
German¹ 2.
Turkish² [adj] türkisch ['tʏˈkɪʃ] → **German²**
turmoil [noun] Aufruhr ['aofru:ɐ̯] der <-(e)s, -e> *most
sing* ◊ *die Herzen in Aufruhr versetzen*
turn¹ [noun] **1.** *(in a game, succession)* Reihe ['raɛə]
die <-> *no pl* *it is sb's turn* jd ist an der Reihe ◊
Du bist jetzt mit dem Putzen an der Reihe. *Whose
turn is it next?* Wer kommt als Nächster an die
Reihe? *wait your turn* warten, bis man an der
Reihe ist *out of turn* außer der Reihe *by turns, in
turn(s)* abwechselnd ['apvɛksl̩nt] ◊ *Komm, wir
schaukeln abwechselnd!* ♦ *Sie ist abwechselnd
fröhlich und bedrückt.* *take (it in) turns* sich abwech-

seln ['apvɛksl̩n] +haben ◊ *Sie wechseln sich beim
Autofahren ab.* *I took a turn at trying.* Ich versuchte
es auch einmal. *miss a turn* eine Runde aussetzen
[aɛnə rʊndə 'aosɛtsn̩] +haben **2.** *(circular movement)*
give sth a turn etw. drehen ['dre:ən] +haben ◊ *den
Hahn im Uhrzeigersinn drehen* **give the key a turn**
den Schlüssel im Schloss drehen*; (the soup, stew,
vegetables)* etw. umrühren ['ʊmry:rən] ◊ *Das Gemüse
muss umgerührt werden.; (a chop, pancake)* etw.
wenden ['vɛndn̩] <wendet, wendete, hat gewendet>
3. *(also fig) (change of direction)* Wende ['vɛndə] die
<-, -n> ◊ *Bei der Wende muss der Schwimmer den
Beckenrand berühren.* ♦ *Der Gerichtsprozess nahm
eine überraschende Wende.* **turn of the century** Jahrhundertwende [ja:ˈhʊndɐtvɛndə] **turn of the year**
Jahreswechsel ['ja:rəsvɛksl̩] der <-s, -> **be on the
turn** dabei sein, sich zu verändern
[daˈbaɛ zaɛn ... 'tsu: feˈɛndɐn] +sein ◊ *Der Markt ist
dabei, sich zu verändern.* *The weather is on the
turn.* Das Wetter schlägt um. *The tide is on the
turn.* Die Ebbe/Flut setzt ein. *The milk/meat is on
the turn.* Die Milch/Das Fleisch hat einen Stich.
take a turn for the better sich verbessern [feˈbɛsən]
<verbessert sich, verbesserte sich, hat sich verbessert>
take a turn for the worse sich verschlechtern
[feˈʃlɛçtɐn] <verschlechtert sich, verschlechterte sich,
hat sich verschlechtert> **4.** *(of a road)* Kurve ['kʊˈvə]
die <-, -n> ◊ *Achtung, eine Kurve!* **5.** *(away from a
road)* Abzweigung ['aptsvaɛgʊŋ] die <-, -en> ◊ *Wir
müssen die nächste Abzweigung links nehmen.* **make
a turn** abbiegen ['apbi:gn̩] <biegt ab, bog ab, ist
abgebogen> ◊ *Das Auto ist rechts abgebogen.* **6.** *(of
an illness)* Anfall ['anfal] der <-(e)s, Anfälle> **give sb
a turn** jdm einen Schock versetzen
[aɛnən 'ʃɔk fɛˈtsn̩] <versetzt, versetzte, hat versetzt> ◊
Die Nachricht versetzte ihm einen Schock. **7.** **turn of
mind** Denkweise ['dɛŋkvaɛzə] die <-, -n> **turn of
phrase** Wortwahl ['vɔˈtva:l] die <-> *no pl*
⊛ **do sb a good/bad turn** jdm einen/keinen
Gefallen tun **give sb/sth a turn 1.** *(let sb try sth)*
give sb a turn jdn etw. ausprobieren lassen **2.** *(try
sth)* **give sth a turn** etw. ausprobieren **sb speaks
etc. out of turn** jdm steht es nicht zu, etw. zu
sagen etc. ◊ *Es stand ihr nicht zu, ihre Chefin zu
kritisieren.* **in turn 1.** *(as a result of another action
etc.)* wiederum ◊ *Wie beeinflusst dies wiederum das
Ergebnis?* **2.** *(one after the other)* nacheinander ◊
Wir probierten es alle nacheinander aus. **3.** *(also)*
auch *And then he, in turn, scored.* Und dann schoss
auch er ein Tor.
turn² [verb] **1.** *(move sth, often in a circular way)* turn
sth etw. umdrehen ['ʊmdre:ən] +haben ◊ *Dreh den
Stuhl um!* **sb turns sth** jd dreht sich um ◊ *Sie drehte
sich zu mir um und sah mich böse an.* **turn sth
around/over, turn sth upside down** etw. umdrehen ◊
Würdest du bitte die Platte umdrehen? ♦ *Dreh die
Gläser um, damit sie nicht verstauben.; (a switch,
wheel, your head)* drehen ['dre:ən] +haben ◊ *den
Schalter auf "Aus" drehen* ♦ *das Lenkrad nach links
drehen* ♦ *Er drehte den Kopf zur Tür.* **turn sth inside
out** etw. auf links drehen ◊ *eine Hose zum Waschen
auf links drehen* **sb turns to sb** jd wendet sich jdm
zu [vɛndət ... 'tsu:] <wandte sich ..., hat sich
zugewandt> **sb turns away** jd wendet sich ab
[vɛndət ... 'ap] **turn sth on sb/sth** etw. auf jdn/etw.
richten [aof ... rɪçtn̩] <richtet, richtete, hat gerichtet>

◊ *das Mikrofon/die Taschenlampe auf jdn/etw.
richten* turn the page eine neue Seite aufschlagen
[aenə nɔ:gə 'zaetə ,aoffla:gn̩] <schlägt auf, schlug auf,
hat aufgeschlagen>; *(fold)* turn back umschlagen
['ʊmfla:gn̩] <schlägt um, schlug um, hat umgeschla-
gen> ◊ *die Hosenbeine umschlagen* **2.** *(change
direction: driver, pedestrian, car)* biegen ['bi:gn̩]
<biegt, bog, ist gebogen> ◊ *Biegen Sie an der
Kreuzung in die Goethestraße.* ♦ *Ich sah noch, wie
er um die Ecke bog.* turn left/right links/rechts
abbiegen [,lɪŋks/,rɛçts 'apbi:gn̩] +*sein* ◊ *Bitte biegen
Sie da vorn rechts ab.*; *(road, river)* eine Kurve
machen [aenə 'kʊ'və maxn̩] +*haben* **3.** *(tide)*
wechseln ['vɛksln̩] +*haben* ◊ *Die Gezeiten wechseln.*
4. *(become something else, another colo(u)r)* werden
['ve:gdn̩] +*sein* ◊ *Sie wird jetzt Anwältin.* ♦ *Er wurde
rot.* ♦ *Nächstes Jahr werde ich 50.* turn professional
Profi werden turn cold/chilly kalt werden **5.** *(game,
fight)* sich wenden [zɪç 'vɛndn̩] <wendet, wendete, hat
sich gewendet> ◊ *Das Spiel wendet sich.*
• **turn against** [phras v] **1.** turn against sb/etw sich
gegen jdn/etw. wenden [ge:gn̩ ... vɛndn̩] <wendet
sich, wandte sich, hat sich gewandt> ◊ *Sie wendet
sich gegen diese Art von Unterricht.* **2.** turn sb
against sb/etw jdn gegen jdn/etw. aufbringen
[ge:gn̩ ... ,aofbrɪŋən] <bringt auf, brachte auf, hat auf-
gebracht> ◊ *Warum hast du meine Freunde gegen
mich aufgebracht?*
• **turn around** [phras v] **1.** *(perform or make sth
perform a circular movement)* turn sth around etw.
umdrehen ['ʊmdre:ən] +*haben* ◊ *Dreh den Stuhl um!*
sb turns around jd dreht sich um **2.** *(the economy,
a company)* turn sth around etw. aus der Krise
führen [aos de:ɐ 'kri:zə fy:rən] +*haben* ◊ *die Wirtschaft aus der Krise führen* sth turns around etw.
erholt sich [e'ho:lt zɪç] <erholte sich, hat sich erholt>
◊ *Die Firma begann, sich zu erholen.*
• **turn away** [phras v] turn sb away jdn zurückweisen [tsu'rʏkvaezn̩] <weist zurück, wies zurück, hat
zurückgewiesen> ◊ *Wir wurden an der Grenze
zurückgewiesen.* → **turn²** **1.**
• **turn back** [phras v] **1.** *(return)* sb turns back jd
kehrt um [ke:ɐt 'ʊm] +*sein* ◊ *Es wird schon bald
dunkel; wir sollten umkehren.* **2.** turn sb back jdn
zur Umkehr zwingen [tsu:ɐ 'ʊmke:ɐ ,tsvɪŋən]
<zwingt, zwang, hat gezwungen> ◊ *Der Sturm zwang
uns zur Umkehr.* → **turn²** **1.**
◉ there can be no turning back es gibt kein
Zurück mehr
• **turn down** [phras v] **1.** *(refuse)* turn sth/sb down
etw./jds etw. ablehnen ['aple:nən] +*haben* ◊ *eine
Einladung ablehnen* ♦ *Seine Stellenbewerbung wurde
abgelehnt.* We applied for a loan, but the bank
turned us down. Wir wollten einen Kredit
aufnehmen, aber die Bank lehnte unseren Kreditan-
trag ab. **2.** *(the radio, sound)* turn sth down etw.
leiser machen ['laeze maxn̩] +*haben* ◊ *Kannst du die
Musik etwas leiser machen?*; *(the heating, gas)* etw.
herunterdrehen [hɛ'rʊntedre:ən] +*haben*; *(the light)*
dämpfen ['dɛmpfn̩] +*haben* ◊ *Er dämpfte das Licht,
um eine romantische Atmosphäre zu schaffen.*; *(with
a dimmer switch)* dimmen ['dɪmən] +*haben*
• **turn in** [phras v] **1.** *(tell police)* turn sb in (to sb)
jdn (bei jdm) anzeigen ['antsaegn̩] +*haben* ◊ *Sie hat
ihre Nachbarn bei der Polizei angezeigt.* turn
yourself in sich stellen [ftɛlən] +*haben* **2.** *(return sth)*

turn sth in zurückgeben [tsu'rʏkge:bm̩] <gibt zurück,
gab zurück, hat zurückgegeben> ◊ *Hast du das Buch
zurückgegeben?* **3.** *(esp in the US: hand sth over officially)* turn sth in to sb etw. bei jdm einreichen
[bae ... ,aenraeçn̩] +*haben* **4.** turn in a brilliant per-
formance/effort sich prächtig schlagen
['prɛçtɪç fla:gn̩] <schlägt, schlug, hat geschlagen>
5. *(point inwards)* sth turns in etw. zeigt nach innen
[tsaekt na:x 'ɪnən] +*haben* ◊ *Die Zehen zeigen nach
innen.*
• **turn into** [phras v] **1.** *(develop into sth)* sth turns
into sth etw. entwickelt sich zu etw.
[ɛnt'vɪkl̩t zɪç tsu:] <entwickelt sich, hat sich entwi-
ckelt> ◊ *Der Campingausflug entwickelte sich zu
einem Reinfall.* **2.** *(make sb/sth become sth)* turn sb
into sth etw. aus jdm machen [aos ... maxn̩] +*haben*
◊ *Sie hat ein ängstliches Kind aus ihrem Sohn
gemacht.* turn sth into sth etw. in etw. [acc] verwandeln [ɪn ... fevandl̩n] <verwandelt, verwandelte, hat
verwandelt> ◊ *Der Regen verwandelte den Schnee in
Matsch.*; *(into a film)* etw. verfilmen [fe'fɪlmən]
<verfilmt, verfilmte, hat verfilmt> ◊ *Ihre Bücher
wurden alle verfilmt.*
• **turn off** [phras v] **1.** *(an appliance, the light, motor)*
ausschalten ['aosfaltn̩] <schaltet aus, schaltete aus,
hat ausgeschaltet> ◊ *das Radio ausschalten*; *(the electricity, gas, water)* abschalten ['apfaltn̩] <schaltet ab,
schaltete ab, hat abgeschaltet> ◊ *Der Strom wurde für
zwei Stunden abgeschaltet.* **2.** *(change direction)*
abbiegen ['apbi:gn̩] <biegt ab, bog ab, ist abgebogen>
◊ *rechts/links abbiegen* ♦ *Der Weg biegt nach 100
Metern rechts ab.* **3.** *(put off)* turn sb off jdn
abschrecken ['apfrɛkn̩] +*haben* ◊ *Die endlosen Gram-
matikübungen haben mich abgeschreckt.*; *(stop
paying attention)* sb turns off jd schaltet ab
[faltət 'ap] <schaltete ab, hat abgeschaltet> *(fam)* ◊
*Bei dem langweiligen Vortrag hat er total abgeschal-
tet.* **4.** *(sexually)* turn sb off jdn abtörnen
['aptœ'nən] +*haben* *(fam)* ◊ *Deine Hausschuhe
törnen mich ab.*
• **turn on** [phras v] **1.** *(an appliance, the light)* einschalten ['aenfaltn̩] <schaltet ein, schaltete ein, hat ein-
geschaltet> ◊ *den Computer/Fernseher einschalten*;
(the gas, water) aufdrehen ['aofdre:ən] +*haben*
2. *(attack)* turn on sb attackieren [ata'ki:rən] <atta-
ckiert, attackierte, hat attackiert> ◊ *Er hat den Redner
heftig attackiert.* **3.** turn on your charm seinen
Charme spielen lassen [zaenən 'fa'm fpi:lən lasn̩]
<lässt, ließ, hat lassen> turn on a smile ein Lächeln
aufsetzen [aen 'lɛçl̩n aofzɛtsn̩] +*haben* **4.** *(please,
interest)* turn sb on jdn anmachen ['anmaxn̩] +*haben*
(fam) **5.** *(cause sb's interest)* A turns B on to sth
durch A findet B den Weg zu etw.
[dʊrç ... fɪndət ... de:n 've:k tsu:] <fand, hat
gefunden> ◊ *Durch einen engagierten Lehrer fand
ich den Weg zur Literatur.*
• **turn out** [phras v] **1.** *(have a result)* ausgehen
['aosge:ən] <geht aus, ging aus, ist ausgegangen> ◊
Wie ist das Spiel ausgegangen? ♦ *Wenn das nur gut
ausgeht!* **2.** *(prove to be in a certain way)* turn out (to
be) sth sich als etw. herausstellen
[als ... he,raosftɛlən] +*haben* ◊ *Sie hat sich als nett/
als nette Person herausgestellt.* as it turned out wie
sich herausgestellt hat, wie sich herausstellte it
turns out (that) es hat sich herausgestellt(, dass)
turn out sad traurig sein ['traorɪç zaen] +*sein* ◊ *Das*

Buch war manchmal traurig und manchmal lustig.
3. *(an appliance, the light)* ausschalten ['aʊsʃaltn̩] <schaltet aus, schaltete aus, hat ausgeschaltet> ◊ *den Computer/Motor ausschalten* **4.** *(come to take part)* erscheinen [eˈʃaɛnən] <erscheint, erschien, ist erschienen> ◊ *Er ist nicht zum Wettkampf erschienen.* **5.** *(produce)* produzieren [produˈtsiːrən] <produziert, produzierte, hat produziert> ◊ *Sie produzieren große Mengen an Radios.* **6.** *(force sb to leave)* turn sb out jdn rauswerfen ['raʊsvɛrfn̩] <wirft raus, warf raus, hat rausgeworfen> *(fam)* ◊ *Er hat seine Freundin rausgeworfen.* turn sb out from/of sth jdn aus etw. werfen [aʊs ... vɛrfn̩] <wirft, warf, hat geworfen> ◊ *Sie hat mich aus dem Haus geworfen.* **7.** *(your pockets, a bag)* ausleeren ['aʊsleːrən] +haben ◊ *Sie leerte ihre Handtasche aus.* **8.** *(point outwards)* nach außen zeigen [naːx 'aʊsn̩ tsaɛgn̩] +haben ◊ *Meine großen Zehen zeigen nach außen.*

• **turn over** phras v **1.** *(to the police, a new owner etc.)* turn sb/sth over to sb jdn/etw. jdm übergeben [ybɐˈgeːbm̩] <übergibt, übergab, hat übergeben> ◊ *einen Dieb der Polizei übergeben* ◆ *ein Geschäft seinem Nachfolger übergeben* **2.** *(allow to be used)* turn sth over to sb jdm etw. überlassen [ybɐˈlasn̩] <überlässt, überließ, hat überlassen> ◊ *Er hat ihm die Räume überlassen.* **3.** *(a page)* umblättern ['ʊmblɛtɐn] +haben **4.** *(a TV station)* umschalten ['ʊmʃaltn̩] <schaltet um, schaltete um, hat umgeschaltet> ◊ *kannst du mal umschalten? Im ZDF kommt ein Krimi.* turn over to sth auf etw. acc umschalten **5.** *(amount of money, goods)* umsetzen ['ʊmzɛtsn̩] +haben ◊ *Waren im Wert von über einer Million Euro umsetzen* **6.** *(an engine)* anlassen ['anlasn̩] <lässt an, ließ an, hat angelassen> ◊ *den Motor anlassen* **7.** *(think about sth)* turn sth over in your mind sich dat etw. durch den Kopf gehen lassen [dʊrç deːn 'kɔpf geːən lasn̩] <lässt, ließ, hat lassen>

• **turn round** phras v → **turn around**

• **turn to** phras v **1.** *(ask for help)* turn to sb sich an jdn wenden [an ... ˌvɛndn̩] <wendet sich, wandte sich, hat sich gewandt> ◊ *An wen kann ich mich in dieser Sache wenden?* **2.** *(tackle, concentrate on)* turn to sth sich einer Sache dat zuwenden ['tsuːvɛndn̩] <wendet sich zu, wandte sich zu, hat sich zugewandt> ◊ *Wir müssen uns wichtigeren Themen zuwenden.* **3.** *(drugs, alcohol)* turn to sth zu etw. greifen [tsuː ... graɛfn̩] <greift, griff, hat gegriffen> ◊ *Um sich abzulenken hat er zu Drogen gegriffen.* **4.** *(change into sth)* turn to sth sich in etw. acc verwandeln [ɪn ... fevandl̩n] <verwandelt, verwandelte, hat verwandelt> ◊ *Ihre Angst verwandelte sich in Wut.* **5.** *(your attention, mind)* turn sth to sb/sth etw. auf jdn/etw. richten [aʊf ... rɪçtn̩] <richtet, richtete, hat gerichtet> ◊ *Er richtete seine ganze Aufmerksamkeit auf ihren Vortrag.* **6.** *(a page)* turn to sth etw. aufschlagen ['aʊfʃlaːgn̩] <schlägt auf, schlug auf, hat aufgeschlagen> ◊ *Schlagt Seite 77 auf!*

• **turn up** phras v **1.** *(the music, radio, sound)* turn sth up etw. lauter machen ['laʊtɐ maxn̩] +haben ◊ *Er machte die Musik lauter.* turn the light up mehr Licht machen; *(the heat, heating)* höher stellen ['høːɐ ʃtɛlən] +haben ◊ *Stellst du bitte die Heizung höher?* **2.** *(person, lost things)* sb/sth turns up etw./jd taucht auf [taɔxt 'aʊf] +sein *(fam)* ◊ *Rat mal, wer gestern bei uns aufgetaucht ist!* ◆ *Ist der Schlüssel wieder aufgetaucht?* **3.** *(a new job)* finden ['fɪndn̩]

<findet, fand, hat gefunden> ◊ *Du wirst ganz bestimmt einen neuen Job finden.* **4.** *(the collar etc.)* hochschlagen ['hoːxʃlaːgn̩] <schlägt hoch, schlug hoch, hat hochgeschlagen> ◊ *Sie schlug den Kragen ihrer Bluse hoch.*

turning noun *(road)* Abzweigung ['aptsvaɛgʊŋ] die <-, -en> ◊ *Nimm bitte die nächste Abzweigung.*

turning point noun Wendepunkt ['vɛndəpʊŋkt] der <-(e)s, -e> ◊ *Seine Karriere war an einem Wendepunkt angelangt.*

turnip noun Rübe ['ryːbə] die <-, -n>

turnover noun **1.** *(value of goods)* Umsatz ['ʊmzats] der <-es, Umsätze> ◊ *Der Umsatz steigt.* ◆ *Werbung hebt den Umsatz.* **2.** *(of staff, tenants etc.)* Fluktuation [flʊktuaˈtsjoːn] die <-, -en> ◊ *eine hohe Fluktuation des Personals/unter den Mietern* **3.** *(rate at which goods are sold)* Warenumschlag ['vaːrənʊmʃlaːk] der <-(e)s> no pl ◊ *eine Vervielfachung des weltweiten Warenumschlags*

turtle noun Schildkröte ['ʃɪltkrøːtə] die <-, -n> ⊛ turn turtle kentern

turtleneck noun Rollkragen ['rɔlkraːgn̩] der <-s, Rollkrägen>

tutor noun **1.** *(at university)* Dozent [doˈtsɛnt] der <-en, -en> ♀Dozentin [doˈtsɛntɪn] die <-, -nen> ◊ *Sie ist Dozentin für Italienisch.* ◆ *der neue Dozent der germanistischen Fakultät* **2.** *(for private tuition; when you do not attend school)* Privatlehrer [priˈvaːtleːrɐ] der <-s, -> ♀Privatlehrerin [priˈvaːtleːrərɪn] die <-, -nen>; *(when you're not good at school)* Nachhilfelehrer ['naːxhɪlfəleːrɐ] piano tutor Klavierlehrer [klaˈviːɐleːrɐ]

TV noun **1.** Fernseher ['fɛrnzeːɐ] der <-s, -> ◊ *vor dem Fernseher sitzen* ◆ *Bei euch läuft dauernd der Fernseher.* **2.** TV show Fernsehshow ['fɛrnzeːʃoː] die <-, -s> TV station Fernsehsender ['fɛrnzeːzɛndɐ] der <-s, -> ⊛ on TV im Fernsehen

tweezers noun Pinzette [pɪnˈtsɛtə] die <-, -n> a pair of tweezers eine Pinzette

twelve nmrl zwölf [tsvœlf] → **four²**

twenty nmrl zwanzig ['tsvantsɪç] → **four²**

twice adv **1.** zweimal ['tsvaɛmaːl] ◊ *Er hat den Film schon zweimal gesehen.* twice a week zweimal pro Woche **2.** doppelt ['dɔplt] twice the amount die doppelte Menge twice as good doppelt so gut

twig noun Zweig [tsvaɛk] der <-(e)s, -e> ◊ *Der Vogel sitzt auf einem Zweig.* ◆ *einen Zweig abbrechen*

twin noun Zwilling ['tsvɪlɪŋ] der <-s, -e> ◊ *eineiige/zweieiige Zwillinge* ◆ *siamesische Zwillinge* She is my twin. Sie ist meine Zwillingsschwester.

twist¹ noun **1.** *(of body)* Drehung ['dreːʊŋ] die <-, -en> ◊ *Mit einer Drehung seines Oberkörpers konnte er das Buch erreichen.* give sth a twist etw. drehen ['dreːən] +haben **2.** *(of a road)* Kurve ['kʊrvə] die <-, -n> ◊ *Der Stau begann hinter einer Kurve.* full of twists and turns kurvenreich ['kʊrvənraɛç] **3.** *(unexpected change of a situation)* Wendung ['vɛndʊŋ] die <-, -en> ◊ *Der Skandal nahm eine neue Wendung.* ◆ *eine Wendung des Schicksals* **4.** *(dance)* Twist [tvɪst] der <-s, -s> ⊛ a twist of lemon **1.** *(small amount)* ein Spritzer Zitrone **2.** *(for decoration)* ein Kringel Zitronenschale

twist² verb **1.** *(ropes etc., the truth, facts)* verdrehen [feˈdreːən] <verdreht, verdrehte, hat verdreht> ◊ *Das*

Seil war völllig verdreht. ♦ *die Wahrheit/Tatsachen verdreben* twist sb's arm jdm den Arm verdrehen twist sb's words jdm das Wort im Mund umdrehen [das ˌvɔʳt ɪm ˈmʊnt ʊmdreːən] +haben **2.** *(your features, mouth)* verziehen [fɐˈtsiːən] <verzieht, verzog, hat verzogen> ◊ *den Mund zu einem Grinsen verzieben* **3.** *(a ring, cap)* twist sth mit etw. herumspielen [mɪt ... hɛˌrʊmʃpiːlən] +haben twist sth off (sth) etw. (von etw.) abschrauben [ˈapʃraʊbm̩] +haben ◊ *Er schraubte den Deckel (vom Glas) ab.* **4.** *(your foot, ankle, arm, wrist)* twist your sth sich [dat] etw. verrenken [fɐˈrɛŋkn̩] <verrenkt, verrenkte, hat verrenkt> ◊ *Er hat sich den Knöchel verrenkt.* **5.** *(a wire, thread)* twist sth around sth etw. um etw. wickeln [ʊm ... vɪkl̩n] +haben ◊ *Er wickelte den Draht um ein Holzstück.; (wool, a thread, your hair)* twist sth into sth etw. zu etw. flechten [tsuː ... flɛçtn̩] <flicht, flocht, hat geflochten> ◊ *das Haar zu einem Zopf flechten* **6.** *(road, river)* twist (and turn) sich schlängeln [zɪç ˈʃlɛŋl̩n] +haben ◊ *Die Straße schlängelt sich durch das Tal.* **7.** *(change your position)* sich umdrehen [ˈʊmdreːən] +haben ◊ *Sie drehte sich zu mir um.*

twitch [verb] **1.** *(move suddenly)* zucken [ˈtsʊkn̩] +haben ◊ *Die Pfoten des Hundes zuckten im Schlaf.* **2.** *(pull at sth)* zupfen [ˈtsʊpfn̩] +haben ◊ *Er zupfte sie am Ärmel.*

two¹ [noun] **1.** Zwei [tsvaɛ] die <–, –en> → **four¹** **2.** the two (of them) beide [ˈbaɛdə] ◊ *Ich habe Elke und Tim eingeladen; beide sind gekommen.* ♦ *Er steht mit beiden in Kontakt.*

two² [nmrl] zwei [tsvaɛ] → **four²**
twofold [adj, adv] *(twice as much)* doppelt [ˈdɔpl̩t] ◊ *ein doppeltes Risiko* ♦ doppelt kopiert → fourfold
type¹ [noun] **1.** *(with similar qualities)* Art [aːʳt] die <–, –en> ◊ *Arbeiten jeglicher Art verrichten* ♦ *Welche Art von Papagei ist das?* of this type dieser Art all types of sb/sth jd/etw. aller Art ◊ *Bücher aller Art* **2.** *(with particular interests)* Typ [tyːp] der <–s, –en> ◊ *Er ist eigentlich nicht mein Typ.* ♦ *Ich bin nicht der Typ, der Männer in der Disko anquatscht.* **3.** *(in printing)* Type [ˈtyːpə] die <–, –n>; *(in italic type)* kursiv gedruckt [kʊʳˈziːf gədrʊkt] The type ist too small. Die Schrift ist zu klein.
type² [verb] *(on a keyboard)* tippen [ˈtɪpm̩] +haben *(fam)* ◊ *am Computer einen Brief tippen*
typewriter [noun] Schreibmaschine [ˈʃraɛpmaˌʃiːnə] die <–, –n> ◊ *eine Brief auf der Schreibmaschine schreiben*
typical [adj] typisch [ˈtyːpɪʃ] ◊ *ein typischer Frauenberuf* ♦ *Nadja hat ihren Schlüssel verloren? Das ist doch wieder mal typisch!*
typically [adv] **1.** *(usually)* üblicherweise [ˈyːplɪçɐˌvaɛzə] ◊ *Üblicherweise muss man beim Arzt warten.* **2.** *(with typical qualities)* typisch [ˈtyːpɪʃ] ◊ *Was ist Ihrer Meinung nach typisch deutsch?* **3.** *(as expected)* wie üblich [viː ˈyːplɪç] ◊ *Wie üblich hat sie unsere Verabredung vergessen.*
tyre, tire [noun] Reifen [ˈraɛfn̩] der <–s, –> ◊ *Kannst du Reifen wechseln?* ♦ *Die Unfallursache war ein geplatzter Reifen.*

U

u, U [noun] u, U [uː] das <–(s), –(s)> ◊ *ein kleines u/ großes U* ♦ *U wie Ulrich*

ugly [adj] hässlich ['hɛslɪç] ◊ *Er findet sich hässlich.* ♦ *ein hässlicher Streit* the ugly face of war *die hässliche Fratze des Krieges* ⊙ **turn ugly** 1. (person) gemein werden 2. (situation) ausarten

UK the UK das Vereinigte Königreich [das fɐˌaɪnɪçtə 'køːnɪkʀaɛç] <Vereinigten Königreichs> no pl

ulcer [noun] Geschwür [gəˈʃvyːɐ̯] das <–s, –e> ◊ *ein eitriges Geschwür*

Ulster [noun] Nordirland ['nɔrt|'ɪʳlant] das <–s> *article only in combination with attribute, no pl* → **Germany**

ultimate [adj] 1. (final) letzte ['lɛtstə] *no comp/superl, only before ns* ◊ *ein Urteil in letzter Instanz*; (solution, decision) endgültig ['ɛntɡʏltɪç] *no comp/ superl* ◊ *Eine endgültige Entscheidung steht noch aus.*; (beneficiary, origin) eigentlich ['aeɡntlɪç] *no comp/superl, only before ns* ◊ *Der Chor ist der eigentliche Ursprung des griechischen Dramas.* ultimate consumer Endverbraucher ['ɛntfebraoxe] der <–s, –> ultimate outcome Endergebnis ['ɛnt|egeːpnɪs] das <–ses, –se> 2. (authority, perfection) höchste ['høːçstə] *no comp/superl, only before ns* sb's ultimate ambition/goal jds oberstes Ziel [ˌoːbestəs 'tsiːl] ultimate test Härtetest ['hɛʳtatɛst] der <–s, –s> 3. (power, responsibility) absolut [apzoˈluːt] *no comp/superl* ◊ *absolute Macht haben* 4. (extremely good) ultimativ [ʊltimaˈtiːf] *no comp/ superl, only before ns* ◊ *Das ist die ultimative Lösung!* ♦ *der ultimative Luxus einer Kreuzfahrt* 5. (fundamental) grundsätzlich ['ɡrʊntzɛtslɪç] *no comp/superl* ◊ *eine grundsätzliche Entscheidung treffen*

ultimately [adv] 1. (after a process) letztlich ['lɛtstlɪç] *no comp/superl* ◊ *Der Streit beruht letztlich auf einem Missverständnis.* 2. (basically) grundsätzlich ['ɡrʊntzɛtslɪç] *no comp/superl* ◊ *Grundsätzlich waren sie nicht dagegen.*

umbrella [noun] 1. (for rain) Regenschirm ['reːgŋʃɪʳm] der <–(e)s, –e> ◊ *den Regenschirm aufspannen/ öffnen/schließen*; (for sun) Sonnenschirm ['zɔnənʃɪʳm] 2. umbrella ... Dach... [dax] umbrella organization Dachverband ['daxfebant] der <–(e)s, Dachverbände> ⊙ **under sb's umbrella of** unter jds Schirmherrschaft

umpire [noun] Schiedsrichter ['ʃiːtsrɪçtɐ] der <–s, –> ♀Schiedsrichterin ['ʃiːtsrɪçtərɪn] die <–, –nen> ◊ *Sie ist als Schiedsrichterin tätig.* ♦ *ein erfahrener Schiedsrichter*

unable [adj] unable to do sth nicht in der Lage, etw. zu tun [nɪçt ɪn deːɐ̯ 'laːgə ... tsuː] feel unable to do sth sich nicht in der Lage fühlen, etw. zu tun quite unable to do sth absolut nicht in der Lage, etw. zu tun unwilling or unable to do sth nicht Willens oder nicht in der Lage, etw. zu tun

unacceptable [adj] inakzeptabel ['ɪn|aktsɛptaːbl̩] <inakzeptabler, am inakzeptabelsten> <der/die/das inakzeptable ...> ◊ *inakzeptables Verhalten* ♦ *Diese Äußerung ist völlig inakzeptabel.*; (level of sth) zu hoch [tsuː 'hoːx] *no comp/superl* <der/die/das zu hohe ...> ◊ *ein zu hoher Lärmpegel* ♦ *Das Verkehrsaufkommen ist zu hoch.*

unambiguous(ly) [adj, adv] eindeutig ['aɛndɔøtɪç] ◊ *jdm eine eindeutige Antwort geben* ♦ *Sie konnte den Täter eindeutig identifizieren.* ♦ *Das Ergebnis ist eindeutig.*

unanimous(ly) [adj, adv] (without contradiction, exception) einmütig ['aɛnmyːtɪç] ◊ *Wir waren einmütig der Ansicht, dass ...* ♦ *Der Vorschlag stieß auf einmütige Zustimmung/Ablehnung.* We were unanimous in our concern. Wir waren alle besorgt.; (with all votes) einstimmig ['aɛnʃtɪmɪç] *no comp/ superl* ◊ *ein einstimmiger Beschluss* ♦ *etw. einstimmig beschließen*

unattainable [adj] unerreichbar ['ʊn|eraɛçbaːʳ] ◊ *ein unerreichbarer Traum/Wunsch* ♦ *Dieses Ziel ist für mich unerreichbar.*

unauthorized [adj] unerlaubt ['ʊn|elaopt] *no comp/ superl* ◊ *unerlaubter Zugriff auf Daten*; (biography etc.) inoffiziell ['ɪn|ɔfitsjɛl] *no comp/superl* not be authorized ohne Genehmigung sein [oːnə gəˈneːmɪɡʊn zaɛn] +sein

unavoidable [adj] unausweichlich ['ʊn|aosvaɛçlɪç] *no comp/superl* ◊ *Ein Konflik scheint unausweichlich.* ♦ *eine unausweichliche Konsequenz*

unaware [adj] nicht bewusst [nɪçt bəˈvʊst] *no comp/ superl* be unaware of sth sich [dat] einer Sache [gen] nicht bewusst sein ◊ *Ich war mir keines Fehlers bewusst.*

unbalanced [adj, adv] 1. (mentally ill) geistesgestört ['gaɛstəsgəʃtøːɐt] *no comp/superl* 2. (biased) einseitig ['aɛnzaɛtɪç] ◊ *einseitige Berichterstattung* ♦ *Die Darstellung war äußerst einseitig.*

unbearable(-ably) [adj, adv] unerträglich ['ʊn|etrɛːklɪç] ◊ *unerträglicher Lärm* ♦ *Du bist heute mal wieder unerträglich!* ♦ *Die Wunde schmerzte unerträglich.*

unbelievable(-ably) [adj, adv] unglaublich ['ʊn|glaoplɪç] ◊ *unglaublichen Erfolg haben* ♦ *unglaublich stolz auf jdn sein* ♦ *Es ist unglaublich, wie unverschämt der Verkäufer war!*

unbroken [adj] (will, record, line, circle) ungebrochen ['ʊngəbrɔxŋ] *no comp/superl* ◊ *Sein Wille blieb ungebrochen.* ♦ *ein bis heute ungebrochener Rekord*; (sleep) ungestört ['ʊngəʃtøːɐt] <ungestörter, am ungestörtesten> ◊ *für ungestörten Schlaf sorgen*

uncertain [adj] 1. (not known) unbekannt ['ʊnbəkant] *no comp/superl* ◊ *unbekannte Fakten* it is uncertain how/whether etc. man weiß nicht genau, wie/ob etc. [man 'vaes nɪçt gəˌnao viː/ɔp] <weiß, wusste, hat gewusst> remain uncertain noch ungewiss sein [nɔx 'ʊngəvɪs zaɛn] 2. (lacking confidence) unsicher ['ʊnzɪçɐ] ◊ *Sie fühlte sich sehr unsicher.* be uncertain of sth sich [dat] bezüglich einer Sache [gen]

unsicher sein [bətsy:klıç ... 'ʊnzıçe zaẹn] +sein ◊ *Ich war mir bezüglich meiner Berufswahl unsicher.*

uncertainty [noun] **1.** *(a person's lack of confidence, anxious feeling)* Unsicherheit ['ʊnzıçehaẹt] die <-, –en> an air of uncertainty ein Gefühl der Unsicherheit **2.** *(state in which facts are unknown or decisions not yet taken)* Ungewissheit ['ʊngəvɪshaẹt] die <-, –en> ◊ *die Ungewissheit über die Zukunft der Globalisierung* ♦ *Risiken und Ungewissheiten* There is uncertainty as to how/when etc. Es ist noch ungewiss, wie/wann etc.

unchallenged [adj, adv] **1.** *(not defeated or disputed)* unangefochten ['ʊn|angəfɔxtṇ] no comp/superl ◊ *der unangefochtene Marktführer* ♦ *Ihre Position ist unangefochten.* ♦ *unangefochten siegen/die Spitze halten* **2.** *(not contradicted)* unwidersprochen ['ʊnvi:dɐʃprɔxṇ] no comp/superl go unchallenged unwidersprochen durchgehen **3.** *(not stopped)* ungehindert ['ʊngəhɪndet] no comp/superl ◊ *Sie konnten ihre Pläne ungehindert verfolgen.*

unchanged [adj] unverändert ['ʊnfɛ|ɛndet] no comp/superl ◊ *Die Telefonnummer ist unverändert.* ♦ *eine unveränderte Datei*

uncle [noun] Onkel ['ɔŋkl̩] der <-s, –> ◊ *Onkel Peter* ♦ *Peter ist mein Onkel.*

unclear [adj] unklar ['ʊnkla:ʳ] ◊ *Die Ursache des Brandes ist bis heute unklar.* ♦ *eine unklare Aussage*

uncomfortable(-ably) [adj, adv] **1.** *(chair, clothing etc.)* unbequem ['ʊnbəkve:m] ◊ *In so einer unbequemen Lage kann ich nicht einschlafen.* ♦ *Dieses Kleid ist furchtbar unbequem.* ♦ *unbequem sitzen; (room, place)* ungemütlich ['ʊngəmy:tlıç] ◊ *Mir/Das Zimmer war kalt und ungemütlich.* **2.** *(feeling or causing discomfort)* unangenehm ['ʊn|angəne:m] ◊ *eine unangenehme Situation* ♦ *Das wird jetzt leider unangenehm.; (uneasy)* unbehaglich ['ʊnbəha:klıç] ◊ *Sie fühlte sich in seiner Gegenwart sehr unbehaglich.*

unconcerned(ly) [adj, adv] *(not worried)* unbekümmert ['ʊnbəkymet] ◊ *Er redete unbekümmert drauflos.* put on an unconcerned air sich unbekümmert geben be unconcerned by/about sth sich [dat] keine Sorgen über etw. [acc] machen [kaẹnə 'zɔ'gṇ y:be ... maxṇ] +haben ◊ *Ich mache mir keine Sorgen über ihre Zukunft.* be unconcerned with sth/sb kein Interesse an etw./jdm zeigen [kaẹn ɪntə'rɛsə an ... tsaẹgṇ] +haben

unconscious [adj] **1.** *(in a sleeplike condition because of an accident etc.)* bewusstlos [bə'vʊstlo:s] no comp/superl ◊ *ein bewusstloser Patient* ♦ *Seit dem Unfall ist sie bewusstlos.* ♦ *jdn bewusstlos schlagen* **2.** *(not realizing, intellectually uncontrolled)* unbewusst ['ʊnbəvʊst] no comp/superl ◊ *Diese Vorgänge sind unbewusst und laufen automatisch ab.* ♦ *Sie hatte eine unbewusste Abneigung dagegen.* be unconscious of sth sich [dat] einer Sache [gen] nicht bewusst sein [nıçt bə'vʊst zaẹn] ◊ *Er war sich der Gefahr nicht bewusst.* She was unconscious of what she was doing. Sie wusste nicht, was sie tat.

unconsciously [adv] unbewusst ['ʊnbəvʊst] no comp/superl ◊ *Er fürchtete sich unbewusst vor dem Erfolg.*

uncover [verb] **1.** *(find out about)* aufdecken ['aọfdɛkņ] +haben ◊ *einen Betrug aufdecken* **2.** *(a part of your body, skin etc.)* entblößen [ɛnt'blø:sņ] <entblößt, entblößte, hat entblößt> ◊ *Er entblößte den rechten Arm.* **3.** *(sth that has been covered by accident)* freilegen ['fraẹle:gṇ] +haben ◊ *einen verschütteten*

Stollen freilegen

undecided [adj] **1.** *(not having made a decision)* unentschlossen ['ʊn|ɛntʃlɔsņ] ◊ *unentschlossene Wähler* ♦ *Ich war noch unentschlossen, ob ich gehen sollte oder nicht.* **2.** *(a match, game, contest)* unentschieden ['ʊn|ɛntʃi:dṇ] no comp/superl ◊ *ein unentschiedenes Spiel* ♦ *Der Ausgang ist noch unentschieden.*

under¹ [adv] **1.** *(less than that)* darunter [da'rʊntɐ] ◊ *Kinder von sechs Jahren und darunter* **2.** *(below the water surface)* stay under unter Wasser bleiben [ʊntɐ 'vasɐ blaẹbm̩] <bleibt, blieb, ist geblieben> **3.** *(be unconscious)* be under in Narkose sein [ɪn naʳ'ko:zə zaẹn] +sein

under² [prep] **1.** *(below, beneath, referring to a cause, in a certain state, referring to a category, using a particular name or title)* unter ['ʊntɐ] with acc when expressing motion towards a place, with dat when there is no or undirected motion ◊ *Das Kind kroch unter die Decke.* ♦ *Sie wohnen direkt unter mir.* ♦ *Was trägst du unter dem Mantel?* ♦ *Für Kinder unter sechs Jahren verboten!* ♦ *gute Weine für unter acht Euro* ♦ *Sie brach unter der Belastung zusammen.* ♦ *etw. unter Kontrolle haben* ♦ *unter Alkoholeinfluss stehen* ♦ *unter diesen Umständen/Bedingungen* ♦ *Ich habe mal als Regieassistent unter ihm gearbeitet.* ♦ *Du musst unter „A" nachsehen.* ♦ *unter falschem Namen* under the water unter Wasser come from under sth unter etw. [dat] hervorkommen ◊ *Er kam unter dem Bett hervor.* under it/that darunter [da'rʊntɐ] ◊ *Er trug einen Blazer und einen Rollkragenpullover darunter.* sth is under investigation etw. wird untersucht [vɪʳt ʊnte'zu:xt] <wurde, ist worden> **2.** LAW *(according to)* gemäß [gə'mɛ:s] sing nouns without article or attribute are not declined when following this prep, otherwise [+dat] *(form)* ◊ *gemäß Artikel 81 der Verfassung* **3.** *(believe sth)* be under the impression that den Eindruck haben, dass [de:n 'aẹndrʊk ha:bm̩ das] +haben be under the delusion that sich der Täuschung hingeben, dass [de:ɐ 'tɔɔʃʊŋ hɪnge:bm̩ das] <gibt sich hin, gab sich hin, hat sich hingegeben> **4.** study under sb bei jdm studieren [baẹ ... ʃtu,di:rən] <studiert, studierte, hat studiert> ◊ *Sie hat bei dem Professor studiert.* **5.** be under treatment in Behandlung sein [ɪn bə'handlʊŋ zaẹn] +sein **6.** *(with signs of the zodiac)* be born under ... im Sternzeichen ... [gen] geboren sein [ɪm ʃtɛ'rntsaẹçn ... gəbo:rən zaẹn] +sein ◊ *im Sternzeichen der Jungfrau geboren sein*

underestimate [verb] unterschätzen [ʊnte'ʃɛtsņ] <unterschätzt, unterschätzte, hat unterschätzt> ◊ *ein Risiko/jdn unterschätzen*

undergo [verb] **1.** *(have sth done)* undergo sth sich einer Sache [dat] unterziehen [ʊnte'tsi:ən] <unterzieht sich, unterzog sich, hat sich unterzogen> *(lofty)* ◊ *sich einer Operation unterziehen* **2.** *(go through, experience)* erfahren [e'fa:rən] <erfährt, erfuhr, hat erfahren> *(lofty)* ◊ *eine Veränderung erfahren* undergo a refurbishment renoviert werden [reno'vi:ɐt ve:ɐdņ] <wird, wurde, ist worden>

underground [adj] **1.** *(below the earth's surface)* unterirdisch ['ʊntɐ|ɪʳdɪʃ] no comp/superl, mostly before ns ◊ *ein unterirdisches Kabel* sth is underground etw. liegt unter der Erde [li:kt ˌʊnte de:ɐ 'e:ɐdə] <liegt, lag, hat gelegen> **2.** *(illegal)* Untergrund... ['ʊntɐgrɔnt] underground movement Untergrundbewegung ['ʊntɐgrʊntbəve:gʊŋ] die <-, –en> **3.** *(in the*

arts) Underground… ['ʌndəgraʊnt] underground film Undergroundfilm ['ʌndəgraʊntfɪlm] der <-(e)s, -e>

Underground [noun] U-Bahn ['uːbaːn] die <-, -en>

underline [verb] unterstreichen [ʊntɐ'ʃtraeçn̩] <unterstreicht, unterstrich, hat unterstrichen> ◊ *einen Satz unterstreichen* ♦ *Ich möchte die Wichtigkeit unserer Aufgabe unterstreichen.*

underlying [adj] 1. (fundamental, basic) zu Grunde liegend [ʦuː 'ɡrʊndə liːɡn̩t] no comp/superl, only before n ◊ *Die zu Grunde liegenden Faktoren sind weit gehend unbekannt.* underlying cause der eigentliche Grund [deːɐ̯ ˌaeɡn̩tlɪçə 'ɡrʊnt] <-(e)s, Gründe> underlying value Basiswert ['baːzɪsveːɐ̯t] der <-(e)s, -e> underlying rate of inflation Inflationssockel [ɪnfla'ʦjoːnszɔkl̩] der <-s> no pl 2. (lying under sth) darunterliegend [da'rʊntɐ liːɡn̩t] no comp/superl, only before ns ◊ *Die oberste Schicht ist Humus; die darunterliegende Schicht besteht aus Fels.*

undermine [verb] 1. (weaken) untergraben [ʊntɐ'ɡraːbm̩] <untergräbt, untergrub, hat untergraben> ◊ *jds Autorität untergraben* 2. (dig under sth) unterhöhlen [ʊntɐ'høːlən] <unterhöhlt, unterhöhlte, hat unterhöhlt> ◊ *Kaninchen unterhöhlen den Bahndamm.*

underneath¹ [noun] the underneath die Unterseite [di: 'ʊntɐzaetə] <-> no pl ◊ *Die Unterseite des Autos war verrostet.*

underneath² [adv] 1. (below sth, covered by sth) darunter [da'rʊntɐ] ◊ *Er trug einen Bademantel und nichts darunter.* 2. (on the bottom or lower side) unten ['ʊntn̩] ◊ *Auf dem Rücken ist der Hamster braun, aber unten ist er weiß.*

underneath³ [prep] unter ['ʊntɐ] with acc when expressing motion towards a place, with dat when there is no or undirected motion ◊ *Das Kind kroch unter den Tisch.* ♦ *Sie saßen unter einer Brücke.* ♦ *Unter der Jacke trägt er ein kariertes Hemd.* underneath it/that darunter [da'rʊntɐ] ◊ *Ich hatte eine Jacke an; darunter trug ich eine Bluse.*

underpants [noun] Unterhose ['ʊntɐhoːzə] die <-, -n> can be used in the pl or sing ◊ *Sie zog Unterhosen/eine Unterhose an.* a pair of underpants eine Unterhose

underpass [noun] Unterführung [ʊntɐ'fyːrʊŋ] die <-, -en> ◊ *die Unterführung benutzen*

undershirt [noun] Unterhemd ['ʊntɐhɛmt] das <-(e)s, -en> ◊ *ein Unterhemd anziehen*

understand [verb] verstehen [fɛ'ʃteːən] <versteht, verstand, hat verstanden> ◊ *Hast du verstanden, worum es geht?* ♦ *Sein Dialekt ist kaum zu verstehen.* ♦ *jds Enttäuschung gut verstehen können* ♦ *Meine Frau versteht mich nicht.* ♦ *jdm zu verstehen geben, dass …* understand sb('s) doing sth verstehen, warum jd etw. tut not understand German kein Deutsch verstehen … (is that) understood? … (hast du/habt ihr/haben Sie) verstanden?

⊛ **I understand that …** (expressing that the speaker has found out about sth) ich habe gehört, dass … ◊ *Ich habe gehört, dass Ihnen Ihre Arbeit nicht zusagt.* sb/sth is understood to have done sth jd/etw. soll etw. getan haben ◊ *Er soll eine hohe Abfindung bekommen haben.* it is understood that 1. (it is agreed) es ist abgemacht, dass ◊ *Ich dachte, es war abgemacht, dass er heute kommt.* 2. (it is

alleged) it is understood that sb/sth has done sth jd/etw. soll etw. getan haben ◊ *Die Nachbarn sollen die Polizei verständigt haben.*

understandable [adj] verständlich [fɛ'ʃtɛntlɪç] ◊ *ein verständlicher Text* ♦ *Es ist verständlich, dass sie enttäuscht ist.*

understandably [adv] verständlicherweise [fɛ'ʃtɛntlɪçɐˌvaezə] ◊ *Die Banken sind verständlicherweise vorsichtig, wenn man einen Kredit aufnehmen will.*

understanding [noun] 1. (knowledge) Kenntnis ['kɛntnɪs] die <-, -se> most pl have a good understanding of sth gute Kenntnisse in etw. [dat] haben understanding of yourself Selbsterkenntnis ['zɛlpstɛkɛntnɪs] 2. (sympathy, interpretation) Verständnis [fɛ'ʃtɛntnɪs] das <-ses, -se> ◊ *Er braucht viel Verständnis und Ermunterung.* ♦ *Mein Verständnis dieses Textes ist vielleicht nicht korrekt.* my understanding is (that) wie ich es verstehe, … [vɪː 'ɪç ɛs fɛ,ʃteːə] ◊ *Wie ich es verstehe, hat sich sein Zustand verschlechtert.* 3. (agreement) Vereinbarung [fɛ'aenbaːrʊŋ] die <-, -en> ◊ *eine Vereinbarung mit jdm haben* reach an understanding sich verständigen [fɛ'ʃtɛndɪɡn̩] <verständigt sich, verständigte sich, hat sich verständigt> They reached an understanding. Sie haben sich verständigt.; (condition) on the understanding that unter der Bedingung, dass [ʊntɐ deːɐ̯ bə'dɪŋʊŋ das]

undertake [verb] 1. (perform) durchführen ['dʊɐ̯çfyːrən] +haben ◊ *eine Untersuchung durchführen* 2. (agree to do) übernehmen [ybɐ'neːmən] <übernimmt, übernahm, hat übernommen> ◊ *eine Aufgabe übernehmen* 3. (promise to do sth) undertake to do sth sich verpflichten, etw. zu tun [fɛ'pflɪçtn̩ … ʦuː] <verpflichtet sich, verpflichtete sich, hat sich verpflichtet> ◊ *Die Regierung verpflichtet sich, die europäische Richtlinie umzusetzen.*

undertaking [noun] 1. (sth that is difficult to do) Unterfangen ['ʊntɐfaŋən] das <-s, -> ◊ *ein schwieriges Unterfangen* 2. (promise, agreement) Zusicherung ['ʦuːzɪçərʊŋ] die <-, -en> ◊ *eine schriftliche Zusicherung*

underwear [noun] Unterwäsche ['ʊntɐvɛʃə] die <-> no pl ◊ *frische Unterwäsche anziehen*

undisputed(ly) [adj, adv] unbestritten ['ʊnbəʃtrɪtn̩] seldom comp/superl ◊ *Ihre Erfolge sind nach wie vor unbestritten.* ♦ *unbestrittene Vorteile* ♦ *Der Hersteller ist unbestritten die Nummer 1 auf dem Markt.*

undisturbed [adj] ungestört ['ʊnɡəʃtøːɐ̯t] no comp/superl ◊ *ungestörter Schlaf* ♦ *Hier sind wir ungestört.*

undo [verb] 1. (untie, remove) lösen ['løːzn̩] +haben ◊ *eine Schraube lösen;* (a button) öffnen ['œfnən] <öffnet, öffnete, hat geöffnet> 2. (change back, negate) ungeschehen machen ['ʊnɡəʃeːən maxn̩] +haben ◊ *ein Unrecht ungeschehen machen;* (destroy) zunichte machen [ʦu'nɪçtə maxn̩] +haben ◊ *eine Arbeit zunichte machen* 3. IT (cancel) widerrufen [viːdɐ'ruːfn̩] <widerruft, widerrief, hat widerrufen> ◊ *eine Mail widerrufen*

undone [adj] 1. (not completed) unerledigt ['ʊn|ɐleːdɪçt] no comp/superl ◊ *unerledigte Arbeit* ♦ *Der Rest muss für heute unerledigt bleiben.* 2. (open, untied) offen ['ɔfn̩] no comp/superl ◊ *offene Schnürsenkel* ♦ *Der oberste Knopf ihrer Bluse war offen.*

undoubtedly [adv] zweifellos ['ʦvaefl̩loːs] no comp/

superl ◊ *Diese Antwort ist zweifellos richtig.*

unease [noun] Unbehagen ['ʊnbəhaːgn̩] das <–s> no pl ◊ *Mit wachsendem Unbehagen beobachtete sie die Entwicklung.*

uneasy [adj] **1.** *(tense)* beklommen [bə'klɔmən] ◊ *Sie wirkte beklommen.* ♦ *ein beklommenes Lächeln;* *(worried)* besorgt [bə'zɔʳkt] <besorgter, am besorgtesten> ◊ *ein besorgter Mensch* be uneasy about sth wegen etw. besorgt sein sb feels uneasy about sth jdm ist etw. nicht geheuer [ɪst ... nɪçt gə'hɔyɐ] +sein; *(sleep)* unruhig ['ʊnruːɪç] **2.** *(difficult, precarious)* schwierig ['ʃviːrɪç] ◊ *ein schwieriges Verhältnis* ♦ *Ihre Beziehung ist noch immer schwierig.*; *(peace)* unsicher ['ʊnzɪçɐ] ◊ *ein unsicherer Friede* ♦ *Der Friede bleibt unsicher.*

unemployed [adj] arbeitslos ['aʳbaɛtsloːs] no comp/superl ◊ *Sie hatte Angst, arbeitslos zu werden.* ♦ *arbeitslose Akademiker* the unemployed Arbeitslose ◊ *Bekommen Arbeitslose genug Unterstützung vom Staat?*

unemployment [noun] Arbeitslosigkeit ['aʳbaɛtsloːzɪçkaɛt] die <–> no pl ◊ *von Arbeitslosigkeit bedroht sein* ♦ *Die Arbeitslosigkeit ging leicht zurück.*; *(in compound ns)* unemployment ... Arbeitslosen... ['aʳbaɛtsloːzn̩] unemployment benefit Arbeitslosenunterstützung ['aʳbaɛtsloːzn̩|ʊntɐʃtʏtsʊŋ] die <–> no pl unemployment rate Arbeitslosenquote ['aʳbaɛtsloːznkvoːtə] die <–, –n>

uneventful(ly) [adj, adv] ereignislos [ɛl'aɛgnɪsloːs] <ereignisloser, am ereignislosesten> ◊ *eine ereignislose Begegnung* ♦ *Die Reise war ereignislos.* ♦ *Der Abend verlief ereignislos.*

unexpected(ly) [adj, adv] unerwartet ['ʊn|ɛvaʳtət] no comp/superl ◊ *Ihr Besuch war unerwartet.* ♦ *Die Ereignisse nahmen eine unerwartete Wende.* ♦ *Der Anruf kam völlig unerwartet.*

unfair [adj] **1.** *(unjust)* ungerecht ['ʊngərɛçt] <ungerechter, am ungerechtesten> ◊ *eine ungerechte Strafe* ♦ *ungerecht gegen jdn sein* unfair dismissal ungerechtfertigte Entlassung [,ʊngərɛçtfɛ'ʳtɪçtə ɛnt'lasʊn] die <–, –en> **2.** *(giving sb an advantage)* unfair ['ʊnfɛːɐ] ◊ *sich mit unfairen Methoden Vorteile verschaffen* ♦ *Das Spiel war unfair.* unfair competition unlauterer Wettbewerb [,ʊnlaɔtərə 'vɛtbəvɛʳp] der <–(e)s, –e>

unfairly [adv] unfair ['ʊnfɛːɐ] ◊ *sich unfair behandelt fühlen*

unfamiliar [adj] ungewohnt ['ʊngəvoːnt] <ungewohnter, am ungewohntesten> ◊ *in ungewohnter Umgebung* sb is unfamiliar with sth, sth is unfamiliar to sb jd ist mit etw. nicht vertraut [ɪst mɪt ... nɪçt fɛ'traɔt] +sein ◊ *Ich bin mit den Bräuchen des Landes nicht vertraut.*

unfavourable(-ably), **unfavorable(-ably)** [adj, adv] **1.** *(negative)* kritisch ['kriːtɪʃ] ◊ *ein kritischer Kommentar* ♦ *Der Bericht war äußerst kritisch.* ♦ *sich kritisch zu etw. äußern* **2.** *(disadvantageous)* ungünstig ['ʊngʏnstɪç] ◊ *unter ungünstigen Bedingungen* ♦ *Die Gerüchte sind ungünstig für sein Image.* ♦ *Die erste Halbzeit verlief ungünstig für uns*

unfit [adj] **1.** *(not fulfilling the requirements)* ungeeignet ['ʊngə|aɛgnət] ◊ *ungeeignetes Material* ♦ *Sie ist für dieses Amt ungeeignet.* be unfit to do sth dazu geeignet sein, etw. zu tun [nɪçt datsuː gə'|aɛgnət zaɛn ... tsuː] +sein; *(boat)* unfit to sail nicht seetüchtig [nɪçt 'zeːtʏçtɪç] no

comp/superl **2.** *(incapable of sth)* unfähig ['ʊnfɛːɪç] ◊ *Sie ist als Mutter unfähig.* ♦ *eine unfähige Führungskraft* unfit for work arbeitsunfähig ['aʳbaɛts|ʊnfɛːɪç] no comp/superl

unfold [verb] **1.** *(a piece of paper, map etc.)* ausbreiten ['aɔsbraɛtn̩] <breitet aus, breitete aus, hat ausgebreitet>; *(a folding chair)* aufstellen ['aɔfʃtɛlən] +haben **2.** *(flower)* sich öffnen ['zɪç 'œfnən] <öffnet sich, öffnete sich, hat sich geöffnet> ◊ *Die ersten Blüten haben sich geöffnet.* **3.** *(happen)* seinen Lauf nehmen [zaɛnən 'laɔf neːmən] <nimmt, nahm, hat genommen> ◊ *Die Tragödie nahm ihren Lauf.* **4.** *(secret, mystery)* aufgeklärt werden ['aɔfgəklɛːɐt veːɐdn̩] <wird, wurde, ist worden>

unforgettable(-ably) [adj, adv] unvergesslich ['ʊnfɛgɛslɪç] ◊ *unvergessliche Augenblicke* ♦ *Dieses Wochenende wird uns unvergesslich bleiben.* ♦ *ein unvergesslich schöner Urlaub*

unfortunate [adj] **1.** *(unlucky)* bedauernswert [bə'daɔənsvɛːɐt] <bedauernswerter, am bedauernswertesten> ◊ *dieser bedauernswerte Mensch* sb is unfortunate jd hat Pech [hat 'pɛç] +haben sth is unfortunate etw. ist Pech [ɪst 'pɛç] +sein **2.** *(regrettable)* bedauerlich [bə'daɔəlɪç] ◊ *eine bedauerliche Niederlage* ♦ *Es ist bedauerlich, dass das passieren musste.* **3.** *(embarrassing)* peinlich ['paɛnlɪç] ◊ *eine peinliche Angewohnheit* ♦ *Sein Verhalten ist peinlich.*

unfortunately [adv] **1.** *(regrettably)* leider ['laɛdɐ] no comp/superl ◊ *Ich muss dich leider enttäuschen.* **2.** *(unluckily)* unfortunately for sb zu jds [dat] Pech [tsuː ... 'pɛç] ◊ *Zu seinem Pech verpasste er den Zug.*

unfounded [adj] unbegründet ['ʊnbəgrʏndət] no comp/superl ◊ *Der Verdacht erwies sich als unbegründet.* ♦ *unbegründete Eifersucht*

unfriendly [adj] **1.** *(not nice)* unfreundlich ['ʊnfrɔɪntlɪç] ◊ *unfreundlich zu jdm sein* ♦ *eine unfreundliche Antwort bekommen* **2.** *(country)* feindlich ['faɛntlɪç] no comp/superl, only before ns ◊ *ein feindliches Land*

ungrateful [adj] *(person)* undankbar ['ʊndaŋkbaːʳ] ◊ *ein undankbarer Kerl* ♦ *Ich will ja nicht undankbar sein, aber ....*

unhappily [adv] **1.** *(sadly)* unglücklich ['ʊnglʏklɪç] ◊ *Sie sah ihn unglücklich an.* **2.** *(unluckily)* unglücklicherweise ['ʊnglʏklɪçɐˌvaɛzə] no comp/superl ◊ *Unglücklicherweise verirrte er sich im Wald.*

unhappy [adj] **1.** *(sad or unlucky, unfortunate)* unglücklich ['ʊnglʏklɪç] ◊ *Ohne dich bin ich ganz unglücklich.* ♦ *eine unglückliche Kindheit* **2.** *(not satisfied)* unzufrieden ['ʊntsufriːdn̩] ◊ *ein unzufriedener Kunde* be unhappy about sth mit etw. unzufrieden sein ◊ *Er war mit seiner Leistung unzufrieden.*

unhealthy(-ily) [adj, adv] **1.** *(looking ill, not good for you)* ungesund ['ʊngəzʊnt] <ungesünder, am ungesündesten> ◊ *eine ungesunde Gesichtsfarbe* ♦ *Zu viel Neugier ist ungesund.* ♦ *sich ungesund ernähren* **2.** *(business, enterprise)* kränkelnd ['krɛŋkl̩nt] no comp/superl, only before ns ◊ *eine kränkelnde Firma* sth is unhealthy etw. kränkelt ['krɛŋkl̩t] +haben ◊ *Das Unternehmen kränkelt schon lange.*

unheard of [adj] noch nie da gewesen [nɔx niː 'daː gəveːzn̩] no comp/superl ◊ *ein noch nie da gewesener Erfolg* ♦ *So etwas ist noch nie da gewesen.*

uniform¹ [noun] Uniform [uni'fɔʳm] die <–, –en> ◊ *eine Uniform tragen* ♦ *Damals gehörte das Palästi-*

nensertuch zur Uniform der Jugend. police uniform Polizeiuniform [poli'tsae|uni,fɔ'm]

uniform² [adj] einheitlich ['aenhaetlıç] ◊ *eine einheitliche Steuerpolitik* ◆ *Die Banknoten sind in der ganzen Eurozone einheitlich.*

unify [verb] **1.** *(bring together in purpose: a country, group of people)* einigen ['aenıgn] <einigt, einigte, hat geeinigt> ◊ *Das Erdbeben einigte das Land.* They unify. Sie vereinigen sich. [zi: feľaenıgn zıç] <vereinigten sich, haben sich vereinigt> **2.** *(make sth work in the same way, look the same)* unify sth etw. vereinheitlichen [feľaenhaetlıçn] <vereinheitlicht, vereinheitlichte, hat vereinheitlicht> ◊ *die Regeln für etw. vereinheitlichen* ◆ *das Layout für ein Dokument vereinheitlichen*

unilateral(ly) [adj, adv] einseitig ['aenzaetıç] ◊ *Die Entscheidung war einseitig.* ◆ *eine einseitige Verpflichtung* ◆ *Der Vertrag ist einseitig gebrochen worden.*

unimpeded ungehindert ['ʊngahındet] *no comp/superl, only before ns* ◊ *ungehinderten Zugang zu etw. haben*

uninhibited(ly) [adj, adv] ungehemmt ['ʊngahɛmt] <ungehemmter, am ungehemmtesten> ◊ *ungehemmtes Benehmen* ◆ *Sie ist völlig ungehemmt.* ◆ *ungehemmt über etw. reden*

unintelligible(-ibly) [adj, adv] unverständlich ['ʊnfɛʃtɛntlıç] ◊ *Diese Ausdrucksweise ist für Außenstehende unverständlich.* ◆ *eine unverständliche Aussprache* ◆ *Sie murmelte unverständlich.*

unintentional [adj] unbeabsichtigt ['ʊnbə|apzıçtıçt] *no comp/superl* ◊ *eine unbeabsichtigte Folge* ◆ *Der Effekt war unbeabsichtigt.*; *(comedy, joke)* unfreiwillig ['ʊnfraevılıç] *no comp/superl* ◆ *die unfreiwillige Komik einer Situation* ◆ *Der Witz war unfreiwillig, aber dafür umso lustiger.*

unintentionally [adv] unabsichtlich ['ʊn|apzıçtlıç] *no comp/superl* ◊ *jdn unabsichtlich beleidigen;* *(funny, comical)* unfreiwillig ['ʊnfraevılıç] *no comp/superl* ◊ *unfreiwillig komisch*

union [noun] **1.** *(trade)* Gewerkschaft [gə've'kʃaft] die <-, -en> ◊ *der Gewerkschaft beitreten* union member Gewerkschaftsmitglied [gə've'kʃaftsmıtgli:t] das <-(e)s, -er> **2.** *(association)* Verband [fe'bant] der <-(e)s, Verbände> ◊ *der Verband der Automobilindustrie* **3.** *(connection)* Verbindung [fe'bındʊn] die <-, -en> ◊ *die enge wirtschaftliche Verbindung mit den USA* ◆ *eine eheliche Verbindung* **4.** *(group of states)* Union Union [u'njo:n] die <-> *no pl* ◊ *die Europäische Union*

unique [adj] einzigartig ['aentsıçĺa:'tıç] *no comp/superl* ◊ *einzigartige Fähigkeiten* ◆ *Jede DNS ist einzigartig.*; *(opportunity, offer)* einmalig ['aenma:lıç] *no comp/superl* ◊ *eine einmalige Gelegenheit* ◆ *Dieses Angebot ist einmalig!* sth is unique to sb/sth/somewhere etw. gibt es nur bei jdm/etw./irgendwo [gi:pt ɛs nu:ɐ bae] <gibt, gab, hat gegeben> ◊ *Das Problem gibt es nur bei alten Betriebssystemen.*

unit [noun] **1.** *(part of a whole)* Einheit ['aenhaet] die <-, -en> ◊ *Die Einheit marschierte in das Dorf ein.* ◆ *In welcher Einheit sind die Entfernungen angegeben — in Kilometer oder Meilen?* unit of measurement Maßeinheit ['ma:s|aenhaet] die <-, -en> residential unit Wohneinheit ['vo:n|aenhaet] die <-, -en> **2.** *(lesson)* Lektion [lɛk'tsjo:n] die <-, -en> ◊ *Wir fangen heute mit Lektion 2 an.* **3.** family unit Familienverband [fa'mi:ljənfebant] der <-(e)s, Familienverbände>

4. *(piece of equipment)* Gerät [gə'rɛ:t] das <-(e)s, -e> TV unit Fernsehgerät ['fɛ'nze:gərɛ:t] **5.** *(piece of furniture)* storage unit Regal [re'ga:l] das <-s, -e> kitchen unit Küchenschrank ['kʏçnʃrank] der <-(e)s, Küchenschränke> **6.** MED *(in a hospital)* Station [ʃta'tsjo:n] die <-, -en> intensive care unit Intensivstation [ınten'zi:fʃta,tsjo:n] **7.** ECON *(product)* Stück [ʃtʏk] das <-(e)s, -e> *pl 'Stück' when used with figures* ◊ *Wir produzieren 10 000 Stück im Monat.* **8.** *(of a company)* production unit Produktionsbetrieb [prodʊk'tsjo:nsbətri:p] der <-(e)s, -e> **9.** MATH Einer ['aene] der <-s, -> ◊ *Man addiert zuerst die Einer, dann die Zehner.*

unite [verb] **1.** *(join forces)* sich zusammentun [tsu'zaməntu:n] <tut sich zusammen, tat sich zusammen, hat sich zusammengetan> ◊ *Die Bürgerrechtler taten sich im ganzen Land zusammen.* unite in sth/doing sth sich zusammentun, um etw. zu tun ◊ *Wir sollten uns zusammentun, um zu protestieren.* unite behind sb sich gemeinsam hinter jdn stellen [gəmaenza:m ,hıntə … ʃtɛlən] +haben **2.** *(join, connect, combine)* verbinden [fe'bındn] <verbindet, verband, hat verbunden> ◊ *Ein starke Freundschaft verbindet diese zwei Staaten.* ◆ *Er verbindet Fleiß mit Kreativität.;* *(become a unit)* vereinigen [feľaenıgn] <vereinigt, vereinigte, hat vereinigt> *often in adjectival passive constructions* ◊ *Deutschland ist nun wieder vereinigt.* ◆ *ein vereinigtes Europa* They unite. Sie vereinigen sich.

united → unite [adj] **1.** *(agreed)* be united sich einig sein ['aenıç zaen] +*sein* be united in/on sth sich [dat] in etw. [dat] einig sein ◊ *Wir sind uns in dieser Frage einig.* **2.** *(working together)* geschlossen [gə'flɔsn] *only before ns* ◊ *ein geschlossenes Vorgehen*

unity [noun] **1.** *(belonging together)* Einheit ['aenhaet] die <-> *no pl* ◊ *die politische Einheit der EU-Länder* **2.** *(consensus, agreement)* Einigkeit ['aenıçkaet] die <-> *no pl* ◊ *Auf dem Parteitag herrschte Einigkeit.*

universal [adj] universell [univɛ'zɛl] *no comp/superl* ◊ *Die Menschenrechte sind universell.* ◆ *ein Gerät für den universellen Einsatz* meet with universal agreement auf allgemeine Zustimmung stoßen [aof algəmaenə 'tsu:ʃtımʊn ʃto:sn] <stößt, stieß, ist gestoßen>

universe [noun] Welt [vɛlt] die <-, -en> ◊ *die Entstehung der Welt* in the universe auf der Welt

university [noun] Universität [univɛ'zi'tɛ:t] die <-, -en> ◊ *zur Universität gehen* ◆ *Dozent/Student an der Universität sein* university course Studium ['ʃtu:djʊm] das <-s, Studien> ◊ *ein Studium der Mathematik*

unjust(ly) [adj, adv] ungerecht ['ʊngərɛçt] <ungerechter, am ungerechtesten> ◊ *eine ungerechte Strafe* ◆ *ungerecht gegen jdn sein* ◆ *etw. ungerecht finden* ◆ *sich ungerecht behandelt fühlen*

unjustified [adj] ungerechtfertigt ['ʊngərɛçtfe'tıçt] ◊ *ungerechtfertigte Vorwürfe* ◆ *Er wies die Kritik als ungerechtfertigt zurück.*

unkind(ly) [adj, adv] böse ['bø:zə] <böser, am bösesten> ◊ *eine böse Bemerkung* ◆ *Sei nicht so böse zu ihr!* ◆ *Warum siehst du mich so böse an?*

unknown [adj] unbekannt ['ʊnbəkant] <unbekannter, am unbekanntesten> ◊ *Die Zahl der Opfer ist bislang unbekannt.* for some unknown reason aus unbekanntem Grund be unknown to sb jdm unbekannt sein ◊ *Die anderen Personen sind mir unbekannt.*

unlawful(ly) [adj, adv] rechtswidrig [ˈrɛçtsviːdrɪç] *seldom comp/superl* ◊ *eine rechtswidrige Kündigung* ♦ *eine Bezeichnung, die rechtswidrig ist.* ♦ *rechtswidrig handeln* unlawful killing Tötungsdelikt [ˈtøːtʊŋsdeˌlɪkt] *das* <-(e)s, -e>

unless [conjunc] außer [ˈaͻsɐ] ◊ *Wir gehen jeden Tag spazieren, außer es regnet.* not unless nur wenn [nuːɐ̯ vɛn] ◊ *„Bekomme ich jetzt Nachtisch?" — „Nur wenn du deinen Teller leer isst."*

unlike¹ [adj] unterschiedlich [ˈʊntɐʃiːtlɪç] ◊ *Die beiden Kinder sind so unterschiedlich.*

unlike² [prep] *(different from, in contrast to)* anders als [ˈandɐs als] ◊ *Er möchte anders als alle anderen sein.* ♦ *Anders als viele andere Städte hat Berlin mehrere Zentren.* ⊛ sth is (so) unlike sb etw. sieht jdm (so gar) nicht ähnlich not unlike sb/sth jdm/etw. nicht unähnlich ◊ *ein großes Gebäude, einer Kirche nicht unähnlich*

unlikely [adj] 1. *(improbable, not likely to happen)* unwahrscheinlich [ˈʊnvaˑʃaɛnlɪç] ◊ *eine unwahrscheinliche Theorie* ♦ *höchst unwahrscheinlich* in the unlikely event that sollte der unwahrscheinliche Fall eintreten, dass sb/sth is unlikely to do sth, it seems unlikely that sb/sth will do sth jd/etw. tut etw. wahrscheinlich nicht [vaˈʃaɛnlɪç ˈnɪçt] ◊ *Er kommt heute wahrscheinlich nicht mehr.* 2. *(not typical, not combining well)* ungewöhnlich [ˈʊngəvøˑnlɪç] ◊ *eine ungewöhnliche Wahl/Allianz*

unlimited [adj] unbegrenzt [ˈʊnbəgrɛntst] *no comp/ superl* ◊ *Unsere Möglichkeiten sind nahezu unbegrenzt.* ♦ *für unbegrenzte Zeit*

unload [verb] 1. *(empty, release)* abladen [ˈaplaːdn̩] <lädt ab, lud ab, hat abgeladen> ◊ *Die Lieferung wird gerade abgeladen.* ♦ *seinen Frust abladen; (a vehicle, gun)* entladen [ɛntˈlaːdn̩] <entlädt, entlud, hat entladen> ◊ *einen Lkw entladen* ♦ *kontrollieren, ob eine Waffe entladen ist; (unload from a ship)* löschen [ˈlͻeʃn̩] +haben ◊ *ein Schiff/die Container löschen* 2. *(get rid of, sell)* loswerden [ˈloːsveːɐ̯dn̩] <wird los, wurde los, ist losgeworden> ◊ *Ware loswerden*

unlock [verb] 1. *(using a key)* aufschließen [ˈaͻfʃliːsn̩] <schließt auf, schloss auf, hat aufgeschlossen> ◊ *die Tür aufschließen* 2. *(fig) (make available)* erschließen [ɛˈʃliːsn̩] <erschließt, erschloss, hat erschlossen> ◊ *neue Möglichkeiten erschließen* unlock sth for sb jdm etw. erschließen

unmarked [adj] *(unidentified)* anonym [anoˈnyːm] *no comp/superl* ◊ *Die Grabstätte war anonym.* ♦ *ein anonymes Grab* unmarked police car Zivilfahrzeug [tsiˈviːlfaːɐ̯tsͻɐ̯k] *das* <-(e)s, -e>

unmarried [adj] unverheiratet [ˈʊnfɛɐ̯haɛraˌtət] *no comp/superl* ◊ *ein unverheiratetes Paar* ♦ *Bist du noch unverheiratet?*

unnatural(ly) [adj, adv] 1. *(not normal, not genuine)* unnatürlich [ˈʊnnatyːɐ̯lɪç] ◊ *Sein Auftreten wirkte unnatürlich.* ♦ *eine unnatürliche Farbe* ♦ *Sie war unnatürlich blass.* 2. *(perverse, strange)* widernatürlich [ˈviːdɐnatyːɐ̯lɪç] *(oldf)* ◊ *widernatürliche Sexualpraktiken* ♦ *Das ist doch widernatürlich!* ♦ *sich widernatürlich verhalten*

unnecessary(-ily) [adj, adv] unnötig [ˈʊnnøːtɪç] ◊ *Ich halte diesen Streit für unnötig.* ♦ *sich unnötige Sorgen machen* ♦ *sich unnötig aufregen*

unnoticed [adj, adv] unbemerkt [ˈʊnbəmɛɐ̯kt] *no comp/ superl; when used as an adj, mostly before ns* ◊ *ein unbemerkter Fehler* ♦ *Unbemerkt schlich sie sich ins Haus.* go unnoticed unbemerkt bleiben

unobtainable [adj] unerreichbar [ˈʊnɛraɛçbaːɐ̯] *no comp/superl* ◊ *ein unerreichbares Ziel* ♦ *Ich bin momentan nicht zu Hause.* number unobtainable kein Anschluss unter dieser Nummer [kaɛn ˌanʃlʊs ʊntɐ diːze ˈnʊmɐ]

unpack [verb] 1. *(a bag, suitcase)* auspacken [ˈaͻspakn̩] +haben ◊ *Ich habe noch nicht ausgepackt.* ♦ *die Einkäufe auspacken* 2. *(explain)* erklären [ɛˈklɛːran] <erklärt, erklärte, hat erklärt> ◊ *Das Buch erklärt die Geschichte des Osmanischen Reiches.* 3. π *(unzip)* extrahieren [ɛkstraˈhiːran] <extrahiert, extrahierte, hat extrahiert> *(tech)* ◊ *ein Programm extrahieren*

unpleasant(ly) [adj, adv] unangenehm [ˈʊnˌangənɛːm] ◊ *Er kann sehr unangenehm werden.* ♦ *ein unangenehmer Geruch* ♦ *Heute ist es unangenehm schwül.*

unpopular [adj] *(person)* unbeliebt [ˈʊnbəliːpt] *comp -liebter, am unbeliebtesten* ◊ *ein unbeliebter Lehrer* unpopular with sb bei jdm unbeliebt ◊ *ein Politiker, der beim Volk unbeliebt ist* ♦ *Du hast dich bei uns unbeliebt gemacht.; (measure, policy, decision)* unpopulär [ˈʊnpopulɛːɐ̯] ◊ *eine unpopuläre Entscheidung*

unprecedented [adj] beispiellos [ˈbaɛspiːlͻːs] *no comp/superl* ◊ *eine beispiellose Leistung* ♦ *Ihre Hilfsbereitschaft war beispiellos.*

unpredictable [adj] unberechenbar [ˈʊnbərɛçnbaːɐ̯] ◊ *Die Situation war unberechenbar.* ♦ *eine Katastrophe mit unberechenbaren Folgen*

unpunished [adj] ungestraft [ˈʊngəʃtraːft] *no comp/ superl* ◊ *ein ungestraftes Verbrechen* sth goes unpunished etw. bleibt ungestraft sb goes unpunished jd kommt ungestraft davon

unreasonable [adj] 1. *(outrageous)* übertrieben [ybɐˈtriːbm̩] ◊ *ein übertriebener Preis* ♦ *Ist es übertrieben, so etwas zu verlangen?; (behavio(u)r)* unangemessen [ˈʊnˌangəmɛsn̩] ◊ *unangemessenes Verhalten* 2. *(not sensible)* unvernünftig [ˈʊnfɛrnʏnftɪç] ◊ *eine unvernünftige Entscheidung* ♦ *Das wäre sehr unvernünftig.*

unrecognized [adj] 1. *(not detected, not identified)* nicht erkannt [nɪçt ɛˈkant] *no comp/superl* ◊ *eine nicht erkannte Infektion* be unrecognized nicht erkannt werden 2. *(unnoticed, not acknowledged)* nicht gewürdigt [nɪçt gəˈvʏrdɪçt] *no comp/superl* ◊ *eine nicht gewürdigte Leistung* go unrecognized nicht gewürdigt werden

unreliable [adj] *(not trustworthy)* unzuverlässig [ˈʊntsuːfɛlɛsɪç] ◊ *Die Zahlen sind unzuverlässig.* ♦ *ein unzuverlässiger Mensch/Wagen; (witness, statement)* unglaubwürdig [ˈʊnglaͻpvʏrdɪç] ◊ *ein unglaubwürdiger Zeuge* ♦ *Seine Aussage wurde als unglaubwürdig abgelehnt.*

unreserved(ly) [adj, adv] uneingeschränkt [ˈʊnˌaɛngəʃrɛnkt] *no comp/superl; when used as an adj, mostly before ns* ◊ *jds uneingeschränkte Solidarität* ♦ *Ich kann dieses Gerät uneingeschränkt empfehlen.*

unrest [noun] Unruhen [ˈʊnruːan] *die* <-> *pl* ◊ *Das Verhalten der Besatzungstruppen führte zu Unruhen.*

unruly [adj] widerspenstig [ˈviːdɐʃpɛnstɪç] ◊ *widerspenstiges Haar* ♦ *Das Kind ist so widerspenstig.*

unsafe [adj] 1. *(dangerous)* gefährlich [gəˈfɛːɐ̯lɪç] ◊ *Sind Atomkraftwerke gefährlich?* ♦ *gefährliche Medi-*

kamente; (at risk, insecure) unsicher ['ʊnzɪçɐ] ◊ eine
unsichere Investition ♦ sich unsicher fühlen; (sex)
ungeschützt ['ʊngəʃʏtst] no comp/superl, mostly
before ns 2. LAW (in the UK: legally flawed) anfechtbar
['anfɛçtbaːʳ] ◊ eine anfechtbare Entscheidung ♦ Das
Urteil ist anfechtbar.

unsatisfactory [adj] (bad) schlecht [ʃlɛçt] <schlechter,
am schlechtesten> ◊ schlechter Service ♦ Das Hotel
war schlecht.; (grade, mark) ungenügend
['ʊngənyːgn̩t] ◊ Ihre Leistungen in Mathe waren ungenügend. ♦ eine Arbeit als ungenügend bewerten; (not
satisfying) unbefriedigend ['ʊnbəfriːdɪgn̩t] ◊ eine
unbefriedigende Antwort ♦ Das Ende des Films ist
unbefriedigend.

unscrupulous(ly) [adj, adv] skrupellos ['skruːpl̩loːs]
<skrupelloser, am skrupellosesten> ◊ ein skrupelloser
Geschäftsmann ♦ Seine Methoden sind skrupellos. ♦
jdn skrupellos ausbeuten

unspecified [adj] (not mentioned) ungenannt
['ʊngənant] no comp/superl ◊ Die chinesische Firma
kaufte den Betrieb für eine ungenannte Summe.;
(not known) unbestimmt ['ʊnbəʃtɪmt] no comp/superl
◊ eine unbestimmte Anzahl von Opfern

unspoilt [adj] ursprünglich ['uːɐ̯ʃprʏŋlɪç] ◊ eine Welt
von ursprünglicher Schönheit ♦ einen Strand
ursprünglich belassen

unstable [adj] 1. (person) labil [laˈbiːl] ◊ Er ist
psychisch labil. ♦ ein labiles junges Mädchen 2. (government, situation, chemical substance) instabil
['ɪnʃtabiːl] ◊ Der politische Zustand des Landes ist
instabil. ♦ eine instabile Beziehung

unsteady [adj] (voice) zitternd ['tsɪtɐnt] no comp/
superl ◊ Der alte Mann sprach mit zitternder
Stimme.; (breathing) ungleichmäßig ['ʊnglaɛçmɛːsɪç]
◊ Ihr Atem war ungleichmäßig.; (steps, movements)
unsicher ['ʊnzɪçɐ] ◊ mit unsicheren Schritten gehen
♦ Der Patient ist noch etwas unsicher auf den
Beinen.

unstoppable(-ably) [adj, adv] 1. (development) unaufhaltsam ['ʊnlaʊfhaltzaːm] ◊ Die Entwicklung schien
unaufhaltsam zu sein. ♦ Er trat einen unaufhaltsamen Siegeszug an. ♦ Der Verfall schreitet unaufhaltsam voran.; (person) sb is unstoppable jd ist nicht
aufzuhalten [ɪst nɪçt 'aʊftsuhaltn̩] ◊ Wenn sie sich
einmal etwas vorgenommen hat, ist sie nicht aufzuhalten. 2. (ball) unhaltbar ['ʊnhaltbaːʳ] ◊ Der
Freistoß war für den Torhüter unhaltbar. ♦ ein
unhaltbarer Schuss ♦ Der Ball flog unhaltbar ins Tor.

unsuccessful [adj] (attempt) vergeblich [fɐˈgeːplɪç] ◊
ein vergeblicher Versuch, ihn umzustimmen ♦ Meine
Bemühungen waren vergeblich.; (person, application)
erfolglos [ɛˈfɔlkloːs] <erfolgloser, am erfolglosesten>
◊ eine erfolglose Bewerbung ♦ Ihr Sohn ist ein erfolglo-
ser Künstler. ♦ Er verschickte 80 Bewerbungen, blieb
aber erfolglos. sb is unsuccessful in doing sth es
gelingt jdm nicht, etw. zu tun
[ɛs gəˈlɪŋt ... nɪçt ... tsuː] <gelingt, gelang, ist
gelungen> ◊ Es gelang ihnen nicht, die Firma zu
retten.

unsuitable [adj] ungeeignet ['ʊngəlaɛgnət] ◊ für Diabetiker ungeeignete Nahrungsmittel ♦ Der Film ist
für Kinder ungeeignet.

unsure [adj] be unsure (about sth) sich [dat] (über
etw.) nicht sicher sein [nɪçt 'zɪçɐ zaɛn] ◊ Wenn du
dir nicht sicher bist, frag noch mal nach. ♦ Ich bin
mir über seine Absichten nicht ganz sicher. ♦ Er war

sich nicht sicher, wie er es machen sollte.
◉ unsure of yourself unsicher

untenable [adj] unhaltbar ['ʊnhaltbaːʳ] ◊ Seine
Position war unhaltbar geworden. ♦ eine unhaltbare
These

unthinkable [adj] undenkbar ['ʊndɛŋkbaːʳ] ◊ So etwas
wäre früher undenkbar gewesen. ♦ Was für eine
undenkbare Vorstellung!
◉ do the unthinkable das Unmögliche möglich
machen

unthinking(ly) [adj, adv] gedankenlos [gəˈdaŋkn̩loːs]
<gedankenloser, am gedankenlosesten> ◊ eine gedan-
kenlose Bemerkung ♦ Sein Verhalten war wirklich
gedankenlos. ♦ Medikamente werden oft gedankenlos
eingenommen.

untidy(-ily) [adj, adv] unordentlich ['ʊnlɔʳdn̩tlɪç] ◊ ein
unordentlicher Mensch ♦ Hier sieht es nach dem
Umzug noch etwas unordentlich aus. ♦ seine Sachen
unordentlich herumliegen lassen

untie [verb] (a knot, tie, shoe) aufbinden ['aʊfbɪndn̩]
<bindet auf, band auf, hat aufgebunden> ◊ Kannst du
diesen Knoten aufbinden?; (a person, an animal)
losbinden ['loːsbɪndn̩] <bindet los, band los, hat losge-
bunden> ◊ Er band sein Pferd los und ritt davon.

until¹ [prep] bis [bɪs] [+acc] ◊ Bis wann kann ich das
behalten? ◊ Das Geschäft ist von 9 bis 20 Uhr
geöffnet. ♦ Fahren Sie bis zur Ampel weiter und
biegen Sie dann rechts ab. up until bis ◊ Bis 1995
war er ein völlig unbekannter Sänger. not be able to
do sth until ... etw. erst ... tun können
[eːɐ̯st ... kœnən] <kann, konnte, hat gekommt> ◊ Ich
kann erst um acht kommen.

until² [conjunc] bis [bɪs] ◊ Wir sind am Strand
geblieben, bis die Sonne unterging. ♦ Du wiederholst
das so oft, bis du es kannst. not ... until erst dann
..., wenn [eːɐ̯st 'dan ... vɛn] ◊ Er kann erst dann
kommen, wenn er mit der Arbeit fertig ist.

untouched [adj] unberührt ['ʊnbəryːɐ̯t] <unberührter,
am unberührtesten> ◊ unberührte Natur ♦ Diese
Gegend ist noch unberührt vom Tourismus. be
untouched by sth von etw. unberührt bleiben You
left your dinner untouched. Du hast dein Abendessen gar nicht angerührt.

untreated [adj] (disease, wood) unbehandelt
['ʊnbəhandl̩t] no comp/superl ◊ eine unbehandelte
Infektion ♦ Das Holz muss unbehandelt sein.;
(sewage) ungeklärt ['ʊngəklɛːɐ̯t] no comp/superl ◊
Die ungeklärten Abwässer fließen direkt ins Meer.

untrustworthy [adj] unzuverlässig ['ʊntsuːfɛlɛsɪç] ◊
ein unzuverlässiger Mensch ♦ Ich halte ihn für unzuverlässig.

unusable [adj] unbrauchbar ['ʊnbraʊxbaːʳ] ◊
unbrauchbares Werkzeug ♦ Durch den Unfall ist der
Helm unbrauchbar geworden.

unusual [adj] 1. (not normal, not common) ungewöhnlich ['ʊngəvøːnlɪç] ◊ eine ungewöhnliche Bitte haben
♦ Schnee ist zu dieser Jahreszeit eher ungewöhnlich.
there is nothing unusual about sth an etw. [dat] ist
nichts Ungewöhnliches 2. (exceptional) außergewöhnlich ['aʊsɐgəvøːnlɪç] ◊ eine außergewöhnliche
Leistung ♦ Seine Begabung ist außergewöhnlich.;
(different) ausgefallen ['aʊsgəfalən] ◊ ausgefallenes Design ♦ Diese Farbkombination ist ausgefallen.

unusually [adv] 1. (extremely) ungewöhnlich
['ʊngəvøːnlɪç] ◊ eine ungewöhnlich große Zweizim-
merwohnung ♦ ungewöhnlich gut gelaunt sein

2. *(not in the usual way)* ungewohnt ['ʊngəvoːnt] <ungewohnter, am ungewohntesten> ◊ *ein ungewohnt milder Winter* ♦ *Er war ungewohnt still.*

unveil verb **1.** *(announce)* ankündigen ['ankʏndɪgn̩] +haben ◊ *Der Minister kündigte weitere Reformen an.* **2.** *(remove the cover of)* enthüllen [ɛntˈhʏlən] <enthüllt, enthüllte, hat enthüllt> ◊ *Die Bürgermeisterin enthüllte eine Gedenktafel.*

unvoiced adj **1.** *(not expressed in words)* unausgesprochen ['ʊn|a͜osgəʃprɔxn̩] no comp/superl ◊ *seine unausgesprochene Kritik* ♦ *Ihre wahren Gefühle blieben unausgesprochen.* **2.** GRAM stimmlos ['ʃtɪmloːs] no comp/superl ◊ *P, t und k sind stimmlose Laute.* ♦ *Im Auslaut ist das v stimmlos.*

unwanted adj **1.** *(not wanted)* unerwünscht ['ʊn|ɛvvn̩ʃt] <unerwünschter, am unerwünschtesten> ◊ *eine unerwünschte Einmischung in unsere Angelegenheiten* ♦ *Deine Kommentare sind jetzt unerwünscht.; (pregnancy)* ungewollt ['ʊngəvɔlt] no comp/superl ◊ *eine ungewollte Schwangerschaft abbrechen* **2.** *(not needed)* überflüssig ['yːbɐflʏsɪç] ◊ *überflüssige Medikamente zurückgeben; (not loved)* ungeliebt ['ʊngəliːpt] <ungeliebter, am ungeliebtesten> ◊ *ungeliebte Kinder* ♦ *Sie fühlen sich ungeliebt.*

unwarranted adj ungerechtfertigt ['ʊngəʀɛçtfɛˈtɪçt] ◊ *Ihr Misstrauen erwies sich als ungerechtfertigt.* ♦ *eine ungerechtfertigte Kritik*

unwelcome adj **1.** *(unpleasant)* unerfreulich ['ʊn|ɛfʀɔⱺlɪç] ◊ *eine unerfreuliche Nachricht* ♦ *Diese Antwort ist ja wirklich unerfreulich!* **2.** *(not wanted)* unerwünscht ['ʊn|ɛvvn̩ʃt] <unerwünschter, am unerwünschtesten> ◊ *ein Medikament mit unerwünschten Nebenwirkungen* ♦ *einen unerwünschten Anruf bekommen; (visitor)* ungebeten ['ʊngəbeːtn̩] seldom comp/superl ◊ *ein ungebetener Gast* ⊛ *make sb feel unwelcome* jdn abweisend behandeln

unwilling adj **1.** *(refusing to do sth)* unwilling to do sth nicht bereit, etw. zu tun [nɪçt bəˈra͜et ... ˈtsuː] ◊ *Er war nicht bereit, nachzugeben.* ♦ *Die Regierung war nicht bereit, Zugeständnisse zu machen.* **2.** *(reluctant)* widerwillig ['viːdɐvɪlɪç] ◊ *ein widerwilliges Zugeständnis* ♦ *Der Schüler war widerwillig und faul.; (involuntary)* unfreiwillig ['ʊnfʀa͜evɪlɪç] ◊ *ein unfreiwilliger Teilnehmer/Held* ♦ *Seine Teilnahme an dem Bankraub war angeblich unfreiwillig.*

unwillingly adv *(reluctantly)* widerwillig ['viːdɐvɪlɪç] ◊ *Widerwillig gab er mir das Geld zurück.; (involuntarily)* unfreiwillig ['ʊnfʀa͜evɪlɪç] ◊ *Er war unfreiwillig an dem Diebstahl beteiligt.* ♦ *Dieser Satz ist unfreiwillig komisch.*

unwise(ly) adj, adv unklug ['ʊnkluːk] <unklüger, am unklügsten> ◊ *eine unkluge Entscheidung* ♦ *Es wäre unklug, sie jetzt vor den Kopf zu stoßen.* ♦ *Sie haben unklug gehandelt.* unwisely do sth unklugerweise etw. tun ['ʊnkluːgɐˈva͜ezə] ◊ *Unklugerweise habe ich mir auch noch einen Nachtisch bestellt.*

unworldly adj **1.** *(naive)* weltfremd ['vɛltfʀɛmt] <weltfremder, am weltfremdesten> ◊ *ein weltfremder Romantiker* ♦ *Du bist ganz schön weltfremd.* **2.** *(not interested in material things)* nicht materialistisch [ˌnɪçt mateʀiaˈlɪstɪʃ] ◊ *Als Mönch ist er nicht materialistisch.*

unwrap verb auspacken ['a͜ospakn̩] +haben ◊ *ein Paket/die Geschenke auspacken*

up¹ adj up (and running) in Betrieb [ɪn bəˈtriːp] ◊

Der Server ist wieder in Betrieb.

up² adv **1.** *(expressing upward movement)* hoch... [hoːx]; *(lift your eyes)* look up hochblicken ['hoːxblɪkn̩] ◊ *Er blickte von seinem Buch hoch.* lift up hochheben ['hoːxheːbm̩] <hebt hoch, hob hoch, hat hochgehoben> **2.** *(expressing a static position)* oben ['oːbm̩] ◊ *Er ist oben im Schlafzimmer.* ♦ *Siehst du das Flugzeug da oben?* ♦ *Es ist kalt hier oben in den Bergen.* ♦ oben im Norden **3.** *(in or into an upright position, in or into smaller parts)* auf... [a͜of] jump up aufspringen ['a͜ofʃpʀɪŋən] <springt auf, sprang auf, ist aufgesprungen> ◊ *vom Stuhl aufspringen; (divide)* split up aufteilen ['a͜ofta͜elən] ◊ *das Geld aufteilen* The dog stopped with its ears up. *Der Hund blieb mit gespitzten Ohren stehen.* **4.** *(moving near)* up to sb/sth auf jdn/etw. zu... [a͜of ... ˈtsuː] come up to sb/sth auf jdn/etw. zukommen [a͜of ... ˈtsuːkɔmən] <kommt zu, kam zu, ist zugekommen> ◊ *Ein Junge kam auf uns zu und bettelte um Geld.* come up herkommen ['heːɐkɔmən] <kommt her, kam her, ist hergekommen> **5.** *(increased)* be up (on sth) höher (als etw.) nom liegen ['høːɐ liːgn̩] <liegt, lag, hat gelegen> ◊ *Die Zinsen liegen um zwei Prozent höher als vor fünf Jahren.* go up steigen ['ʃta͜egn̩] <steigt, stieg, ist gestiegen> ◊ *Die Flugpreise sind gestiegen.* **6.** *(not in bed)* auf [a͜of] ◊ *Na, bist du schon auf?* ♦ *Die Kinder waren gestern abend bis 11 Uhr auf.* be up and about auf den Beinen sein **7.** *(at an end)* um [ʊm] ◊ *So, die Zeit ist um; du musst jetzt aufhören.* ⊛ dinner/coffee etc. is up das Essen/der Kaffee etc. ist fertig sth is up etw. ist nicht in Ordnung what's up? was ist los? what's up with him/her etc.? was ist mit ihm/ihr etc. los? be up against sth einer Sache dat gegenüberstehen sb is up against it mit dem Rücken zur Wand stehen up and down auf und ab ◊ *Die Kinder hüpften auf und ab.* ♦ *Sie lief im Gang auf und ab.* look sb up and down jdn von oben bis unten mustern sb is up and down jdm geht es mal besser und mal schlechter up till bis ◊ *Sie sind bis 13 Uhr in der Schule.* sth is up to sb etw. liegt an jdm ◊ *Es liegt an dir, die Regeln festzulegen.* up to sth bis zu etw. ◊ *Diese Fische werden bis zu 30 Zentimeter lang.* ♦ *Er arbeitet bis zu 16 Stunden am Tag.* sb is up to sth **1.** *(sb does sth (bad))* jd macht etw. ◊ *Ich weiß nicht, was er den ganzen Tag zu Hause macht.* sb is up to something jd stellt etwas an ◊ *Es ist so still oben — die Kinder stellen sicher etwas an.* sb is up to no good jd führt nichts Gutes im Schilde **2.** *(sb can do sth)* jd ist zu etw. fähig He is not up to the job. *Er ist dieser Arbeit nicht gewachsen.* sb is not up to doing sth jd schafft etw., etw. zu tun ◊ *Ich schaffe es heute nicht, den Rasen zu mähen.*

> 'Up' often occurs in phrasal verbs like 'get up' or 'put up' which have their own entries in the dictionary.

up³ prep **1.** *(expressing upward movement away from the speaker)* hinauf [hɪˈna͜of] postpositive ◊ *eine Fahrt den Berg hinauf; (with certain verbs)* hinauf... [hɪˈna͜of]; *(a hill, mountain)* climb up hinaufklettern [hɪˈna͜ofklɛtɐn] +sein ◊ *Sie kletterten den Berg hinauf.; (get to the top of sth)* get up hinaufkommen [hɪˈna͜ofkɔmən] <kommt hinauf, kam hinauf, ist hinaufgekommen> ◊ *Er hat versucht, die Treppe*

hinaufzukommen, aber vergeblich. **2.** *(expressing upward movement towards the speaker)* herauf [hɛˈraͻf] *postpositive* ◊ *der Weg vom Tal zu uns herauf;* *(with certain verbs)* herauf… [hɛˈraͻf]; *(come to the top of sth)* come up heraufkommen [hɛˈraͻfkͻmən] <kommt herauf, kam herauf, ist heraufgekommen> ◊ *Er kam gerade die Treppe herauf.* **3.** *(at the top of)* oben auf [ˈoːbm̩ ˈaͻf] ⟨+dat⟩ ◊ *Er ist oben auf der Leiter.* further up the hill weiter oben am Berg **4.** *(along a river, road)* entlang [ɛntˈlaŋ] *mostly postpositive* ⟨+acc⟩ *further up the road ein Stück die Straße entlang* She lived up the street from me. *Sie wohnte ein paar Häuser weiter.*; *(with certain verbs)* entlang… [ɛntˈlaŋ]; *(walk along a path, street)* go up sth etw. entlanggehen [ɛntˈlaŋɡeːən] <geht entlang, ging entlang, ist entlanggegangen> ◊ *Sie gingen den Weg entlang.* up the river flussaufwärts [flͻsˈˈaͻfvɛʳts] ◊ *Heute geht es drei Meilen flussaufwärts.* They went up the Amazon. *Sie fuhren den Amazonas hinauf.*

> 'Up' often occurs in phrasal verbs like 'put up' or 'come up' which have their own entries in the dictionary.

up-and-coming ⟨adj⟩ aufstrebend [ˈaͻfʃtreːbm̩t] ◊ *ein aufstrebender junger Politiker* ◆ *Aus dem kleinen Ort ist eine aufstrebende Stadt geworden.*

upbringing ⟨noun⟩ Erziehung [ɛˈtsiːͻŋ] die <-> *no pl* ◊ *Die Erziehung der Kinder in Frankreich ist ganz anders als hier.*

update¹ ⟨noun⟩ **1.** *(report)* update (on sth) Bericht (über etw. ⟨acc⟩) [bəˈrɪçt] der <-(e)s, -e> ◊ *Sie schrieb einen Bericht über die neuesten Verkaufszahlen.*; *(broadcast)* news updates die neuesten Meldungen [diː ˌnøːdəstn̩ ˈmɛldͻŋən] <-> *pl* ◊ *Der Sender bringt stündlich die neuesten Meldungen.* give sb an update on sth jdm von etw. berichten [fͻn … bəˌrɪçtn̩] <berichtet, berichtete, hat berichtet> ◊ *Sie berichtete uns von den neuesten Entwicklungen in China.* **2.** ɪᴛ Update [ˈapdeːt] das <-s, -s> ◊ *Zu dieser Software gibt es jetzt ein Update.*

update² ⟨verb⟩ **1.** *(a book, document)* aktualisieren [aktualiˈziːrən] <aktualisiert, aktualisierte, hat aktualisiert> ◊ *eine Webseite/Datei aktualisieren* **2.** *(a person)* update sb on sth jdm über etw. ⟨acc⟩ berichten [yːbe … bəˌrɪçtn̩] <berichtet, berichtete, hat berichtet> ◊ *Er berichtete uns über den Fortschritt der Bauarbeiten.*

upgrade¹ ⟨noun⟩ **1.** *(piece of equipment or software)* Upgrade [ˈapɡreːt] der <-s, -s> ◊ *einen Upgrade durchführen* **2.** *(process of upgrading)* Aufrüstung [ˈaͻfrͻstͻŋ] die <-, -en> ◊ *die Aufrüstung eines Computers mit einem schnelleren Prozessor*

upgrade² ⟨verb⟩ **1.** *(equipment, a computer)* aufrüsten [ˈaͻfrͻstn̩] <rüstet auf, rüstete auf, hat aufgerüstet> ◊ *Für diese Anwendung muss ich den Computer aufrüsten.* **2.** *(a product, service)* verbessern [fɛˈbɛsɐn] <verbessert, verbesserte, hat verbessert> ◊ *Der Support ist verbessert worden.* **3.** *(to a higher status)* upgrade sb/sth to sth jdn/etw. zu etw. befördern [tsu: … bəˌfœʳdɐn] <befördert, beförderte, hat befördert> ◊ *Er wurde zum Abteilungsleiter befördert.*

upheaval ⟨noun⟩ *(emotional)* Aufruhr [ˈaͻfruːɐ] der <-s> *no pl* ◊ *Das war eine Zeit, in der meine Gefühle in Aufruhr waren.*; *(social, political)*

Umwälzung [ˈͻmvɛltsͻŋ] die <-, -en> ◊ *Uns stehen gewaltige gesellschaftliche Umwälzungen bevor.*

uphill¹ ⟨adj⟩ **1.** uphill climb Anstieg [ˈanʃtiːk] der <-(e)s, -e> ◊ *Nach dem Anstieg machen wir eine Pause.* uphill race Rennen, bei dem es bergauf geht [ˈrɛnən baɛ deːm ɛs bɛʳkˈˈaͻf ɡeːt] das <-s, -> **2.** *(difficult, arduous)* mühselig [ˈmyːzeːlɪç] ◊ *Teamarbeit ist manchmal ein mühseliges Geschäft.*

uphill² ⟨adv⟩ bergauf [bɛʳkˈˈaͻf] ◊ *Es ging seit Stunden nur bergauf.*

uphold ⟨verb⟩ **1.** *(a decision, verdict)* bestätigen [bəˈʃtɛːtɪɡn̩] <bestätigt, bestätigte, hat bestätigt> ◊ *Das Berufungsgericht hat das Urteil bestätigt.* **2.** *(a right)* schützen [ˈʃʏtsn̩] +haben; *(a tradition)* wahren [ˈvaːrən] +haben

upholstery ⟨noun⟩ **1.** *(covers for furniture)* Bezüge [bəˈtsyːɡə] die <-> *pl* ◊ *Bezüge aus grauem Velours* **2.** *(activity of covering furniture)* Polstern [ˈpͻlstɐn] das <-s> *no pl*

upkeep ⟨noun⟩ upkeep Unterhalt [ˈͻntɐhalt] der <-(e)s> *no pl* ◊ *Der Unterhalt von Schwimmbädern ist sehr teuer.*

upmarket ⟨adj⟩ exklusiv [ɛksklu'ziːf] ◊ *ein exklusives Hotel* ◆ *Das Restaurant war exklusiv und sehr teuer.*

upon ⟨prep⟩ **1.** *(spatial: onto or on)* auf [aͻf] with acc when expressing motion towards a place, with dat when there is no or undirected motion ◊ *Sie legte die Decke auf das Bett.* ◆ *Er lag auf den Knien vor ihr.* **2.** *(temporal: after)* nach [naːx] ⟨+dat⟩ ◊ *Sofort nach seiner Ankunft besuchte er das Grab seiner Mutter.* **3.** *(emph) (expressing that a sequence appears to be endless)* year upon year Jahr für Jahr [jaːʳ fyːɡ ˈjaːʳ] mile upon mile Meile um Meile [ˌmaɛlə ͻm ˈmaɛlə] mistake upon mistake Fehler auf Fehler [ˌfeːlɐ aͻf ˈfeːlɐ]

⊛ sth is upon us etw. steht vor der Tür ◊ *Die Sommerferien stehen schon wieder vor der Tür.*

upper ⟨adj⟩ **1.** *(higher, near the top)* obere [ˈoːbərə] *no comp* <ein oberer …, eine obere …, ein oberes …> ◊ *Sie wohnt in einem der oberen Stockwerke.* ◆ *die oberen Schichten der Gesellschaft* ◊ *Die oberen Klassen bereiten sich auf das Abitur vor.* the upper echelons (of sth) die oberen Ränge (… ⟨gen⟩) upper limit Obergrenze [ˈoːbegrɛntsə] die <-, -n> **2.** *(with parts of the body)* Ober… [ˈoːbɐ] upper arm Oberarm [ˈoːbeˈaʳm] der <-s, -e> upper body Oberkörper [ˈoːbekœʳpɐ] der <-s, -> upper lip Oberlippe [ˈoːbelɪpə] die <-, -n> **3.** *(of a river)* the upper reaches der Oberlauf [deːɐ ˈoːbelaͻf] <-(e)s, die Oberläufe> ◊ *der Oberlauf des Nils*

upper case ⟨noun⟩ upper case letter Großbuchstabe [ˈɡroːsbuːxʃtaːbə] der <-n, -n> in upper case in Großbuchstaben

uppermost ⟨adj⟩ **1.** *(most important or urgent)* vorrangig [ˈfoːɡraŋɪç] ◊ *In so einer Situation ist die Sicherheit vorrangig.* be uppermost in sb's mind für jdn an erster Stelle stehen [fyːɐ … an ˌeːɐstɐ ˈʃtɛlə ʃteːən] <steht, stand, hat gestanden> **2.** *(at the top)* oberste [ˈoːbestə] *only before ns* <der/die/das oberste …> ◊ *die oberste Schicht* ◆ *Die Stifte sind in der obersten Schublade.*

upper school ⟨noun⟩ ⊚Oberstufe [ˈoːbeʃtuːfə] die <-, -n> *most sing* ◊ *die Oberstufe eines Gymnasiums*

upright¹ ⟨adj⟩ **1.** *(straight, honest)* aufrecht [ˈaͻfrɛçt] <aufrechter, am aufrechtesten> ◊ *in einer aufrechten Position* ◆ *ein aufrechter Kämpfer für die Freiheit*

2. an upright chair ein Stuhl ohne Armlehnen [æn ˈʃtuːl oːnə ˈaˈrmleːnən] der <-(e)s, Stühle>

upright² [adv] **1.** (with a straight back, in a standing position) aufrecht [ˈaofrɛçt] <aufrechter, am aufrechtesten> ◊ Sie saß aufrecht auf dem Stuhl. ♦ Die Flaschen müssen aufrecht stehen. stand bolt upright kerzengerade stehen [ˈkɛˈtsŋgəˈraːdə ʃteːən] <steht, stand, hat gestanden> pull yourself upright sich aufsetzen [ˈaofzɛtsn̩] +haben **2.** (in a steady position) gerade [gəˈraːdə] <gerader, am geradesten> ◊ Sie konnten das Boot kaum gerade halten.

upset¹ [adj] **1.** (sad) traurig [ˈtraoriç] ◊ Die Kinder waren traurig, weil sie nicht mitkommen durften.; (extremely sad) betroffen [bəˈtrɔfn̩] terribly upset sehr betroffen very upset about sth von etw. betroffen ◊ Alle waren betroffen von den Bildern aus dem Irak.; (worried) aufgeregt [ˈaofgəreːkt] <aufgeregter, am aufgeregtesten> ◊ Warum ist er so aufgeregt? get upset sich aufregen [ˈaofreːgŋ̩] +haben ◊ Erzähl ihr das lieber nicht — sie regt sich leicht auf.; (angry) ärgerlich [ˈɛˈrgelɪç] ◊ Über deinen Brief war er sehr ärgerlich. upset that ärgerlich, weil ◊ Sie ist ärgerlich, weil sie angelogen hat. **2.** an upset stomach eine Magenverstimmung [ˈaɡnə ˈmaːɡn̩fɛʃtɪmʊŋ] <-, -en>

upset² [verb] **1.** (annoy) ärgern [ˈɛˈgɛn] +haben ◊ Er wollte dich nicht ärgern.; (hurt) wehtun [ˈveːtuːn] <tut weh, tat weh, hat wehgetan> ◊ Wie kannst du ihr nur so wehtun!; (make sad) erschüttern [ɛˈʃʏtɛn] <erschüttert, erschütterte, hat erschüttert> ◊ Sein Tod hat sie schwer erschüttert. ♦ Es erschüttert mich wirklich, dass sie so traurig ist. **2.** (spoil) durcheinander bringen [dʊˈçˌaeˈnandə brɪŋən] <bringt, brachte, hat gebracht> ◊ Seine Ankunft hat unsere Pläne für das Wochenende ganz durcheinander gebracht.; (disturb) stören [ˈʃtøːrən] +haben ◊ das politische Gleichgewicht stören **3.** (spill) umstoßen [ˈʊmʃtoːsn̩] <stößt um, stieß um, hat umgestoßen> ◊ eine Blumenvase umstoßen

☞ **upset yourself** sich aufregen

upside down [adv] verkehrt herum [fɛˈkeːɐt hɛrʊm] ◊ Das Bild hing verkehrt herum, und niemand hat es gemerkt.

☞ **turn sb's life upside down** jds Leben auf den Kopf stellen **turn sth upside down** etw. auf den Kopf stellen

upstairs¹ [adj] im Obergeschoss [ɪm ˈoːbɐɡəʃɔs] postpositive ◊ die Bar im Obergeschoss

upstairs² [adv] **1.** (expressing movement) nach oben [naːx ˈoːbm̩] ◊ Geh/Komm sofort nach oben! **2.** (static location) oben [ˈoːbm̩] ◊ Er ist oben im Bad.

upstanding [adj] anständig [ˈanʃtɛndɪç] ◊ ein anständiger Mensch ♦ Ich weiß, dass er zuverlässig und anständig ist.

upstream [adv] flussaufwärts [flʊsˈaofvɛˈts] ◊ Wir sind flussaufwärts gepaddelt.

upswing [noun] upswing Aufschwung [ˈaofʃvʊŋ] der <-(e)s, Aufschwünge> ◊ ein wirtschaftlicher/konjunktureller Aufschwung ♦ für einen Aufschwung an der Börse sorgen be on the upswing einen Aufschwung erleben

up to date [adj] **1.** (with the most recent information) aktuell [aktuˈɛl] ◊ Die Sendung bringt aktuelle Nachrichten aus der Wissenschaft. bring sth up to date etw. auf den neuesten Stand bringen [aof deːn ˌnɔøøstn̩ ʃtant brɪŋən] <bringt, brachte, hat

gebracht> bang up to date auf dem allerneuesten Stand [aof deːm ˌaleˌnɔøøstn̩ ˈʃtant] ◊ Das Online-Wörterbuch ist immer auf dem allerneuesten Stand. **2.** (modern) modern [moˈdɛˈn] ◊ moderne Technologie

☞ **bring sb up to date (with/on sth)** jdn (über etw. [acc]) informieren

upturn [noun] Aufschwung [ˈaofʃvʊŋ] der <-(e)s, Aufschwünge> ◊ ein wirtschaftlicher Aufschwung ♦ für einen Aufschwung an den Aktienmärkten sorgen

upward [adj] Aufwärts… [ˈaofvɛˈts] upward trend Aufwärtstrend [ˈaofvɛˈtstrɛnt] der <-s, -s> upward slope Steigung [ˈʃtaegʊŋ] die <-, -en>

upwards [adv] **1.** (towards a higher position or level) nach oben [naːx ˈoːbm̩] ◊ Er sah nach oben auf die Anzeigetafel. **2.** (more than) upwards of über [ˈyːbɐ] [+acc] ◊ Sie geben wöchentlich über 30 Euro für Kosmetik aus.

urban [adj] städtisch [ˈʃtɛ(ː)tɪʃ] no comp/superl ◊ Gemeinden mit städtischem Charakter ♦ Die Gegend war städtisch.

urge¹ [noun] (strong feeling of wanting sth) Bedürfnis [bəˈdʏˈfnɪs] das <-ses, -se> ◊ das starke Bedürfnis nach Schlaf have an urge to do sth das Bedürfnis haben, etw. zu tun ◊ Sie hatte das Bedürfnis, mit jemandem darüber zu sprechen.

urge² [verb] **1.** (strongly encourage, advise) urge sb to do sth jdm dringend raten, etw. zu tun [drɪŋənt ˈraːtn̩ ... tsuː] <rät, riet, hat geraten> +haben ◊ Er hat ihr dringend geraten, flexibler zu sein. urge sth upon sb jdm zu etw. raten ◊ Die Experten rieten den Anlegern zur Vorsicht. urge that darauf dringen, dass [daraof ˈdrɪŋən das] <dringt, drang, hat gedrungen> ◊ Sie dringen darauf, dass das System möglichst schnell geändert wird. **2.** (an animal, a person) urge forwards vorantreiben [foˈrantraebm̩] <treibt voran, trieb voran, hat vorangetrieben>

urgency [noun] Dringlichkeit [ˈdrɪŋlɪçkaet] die <-> no pl ◊ Er verstand die Dringlichkeit der Lage nicht. be a matter of urgency dringend sein [ˈdrɪŋənt zaen] sense of urgency Handlungsdruck [ˈhandlʊŋsdrʊk] der <-s> no pl

urgent(ly) [adj, adv] **1.** (requiring immediate attention) dringend [ˈdrɪŋənt] ◊ Ist diese Angelegenheit sehr dringend? ♦ Ich hatte das dringende Bedürfnis nach Bewegung. ♦ Ein bisschen Ruhe ist dringend nötig. ♦ jdm dringend von etw. abraten be in urgent need of sth etw. dringend brauchen **2.** (voice, words) eindringlich [ˈaendrɪŋlɪç] ◊ eindringliche Worte sprechen ♦ Seine Stimme klang sehr eindringlich, als er das sagte. ♦ Sie redete eindringlich auf ihn ein.

urine [noun] Urin [uˈriːn] der <-s> no pl pass urine urinieren [uriˈniːrən] <uriniert, urinierte, hat uriniert> urine sample Urinprobe [uˈriːnproːbə] die <-, -n>

us [pers pron] **1.** (as an object) uns [ʊns] ◊ Komm uns doch mal besuchen. ♦ Das Haus gehört uns. ♦ Viele von uns haben keine Lust mehr. **2.** (as a subject) wir [viːɐ] ◊ „Wer war das?" — „Wir." ♦ Wir sind es mal wieder, die die ganze Arbeit machen müssen. → wir

US, USA the US, the USA die USA [diː uːˈɛsˈaː] <-> pl ◊ Wir fliegen im Juni in die USA. ♦ Er ist in den USA geboren.

usable [adj] brauchbar [ˈbraoxbaː] ◊ Dieser Topf ist zwar alt, aber noch brauchbar. ♦ Hat jemand ein brauchbares Telefon zu verkaufen?

usage [noun] **1.** *(using sth)* Nutzung ['nʊtsʊŋ] die <–, –en> usage fee Nutzungsgebühr ['nʊtsʊŋsɡəbyːɐ̯] die <–, –en> **2.** *(amount used)* Verbrauch [fɛ'braox] der <–(e)s> no pl **3.** *(the way words are used)* Sprachgebrauch ['ʃpraːxɡəbraox] der <–(e)s> no pl in common usage allgemein gebräuchlich [alɡəmaen ɡə'brɔøçlɪç] ◊ *Viele Computerfachbegriffe sind heute allgemein gebräuchlich.* **4.** *(particular meaning of a word)* Verwendung [fɛ'vɛndʊŋ] die <–, –en> ◊ *Diese Verwendung des Wortes ist eher selten.*

use[1] [noun] **1.** *(act of using sth)* use (of) Einsatz (von) ['aenzats] der <–(e)s> ◊ *der Einsatz von Computern/Düngemitteln/Schusswaffen* ♦ *Wir plädieren für den Einsatz stärkerer Medikamente.* the use of force die Anwendung von Gewalt [diː ˌanvɛndʊŋ fɔn ɡə'valt] <–, –en> **2.** *(way of using sth, meaning of a word)* Verwendung [fɛ'vɛndʊŋ] die <–, –en> ◊ *Dieser Klebstoff findet im Modellbau Verwendung.* ♦ *Die ursprüngliche Verwendung des Wortes „geil" ist heute selten.* use for sth Verwendung für etw. ◊ *Für das Geld könnte man sicher eine bessere Verwendung finden.* **3.** *(right, opportunity, permission)* have the use of sth etw. benutzen können [bə'nʊtsn kœnən] <kann, konnte, hat können> ◊ *Die Gäste können den Tennisplatz benutzen.* be for the use of sb, be for sb's use jdm zur Verfügung stehen [tsuːɐ̯ fɛ'fyːɡʊŋ ʃteːən] <steht, stand, hat gestanden> ◊ *Das Schwimmbad steht ausschließlich den Hotelgästen zur Verfügung.* **4.** *(ability to use a part of your body)* lose the use of sth etw. nicht mehr gebrauchen können [nɪçt meːɐ̯ ɡə'braoxn kœnən] <kann, konnte, hat können> ◊ *Seit dem Unfall kann er seinen rechten Arm nicht mehr gebrauchen.*

⊛ put sth to good use etw. gut nutzen be no use (to sb) (für jdn) nicht zu gebrauchen sein be of use (to sb) (jdm) helfen come into use in Gebrauch kommen go out of use nicht mehr gebraucht werden have no use for sb/sth jdn/etw. nicht gebrauchen können make use of sb/sth von jdm/etw. Gebrauch machen make good use of sb/sth jdn/etw. gut nutzen in use in Gebrauch it's no use es hat keinen Zweck

use[2] [verb] **1.** use sth (for sth) etw. (für etw.) benutzen [bə'nʊtsn] <benutzt, benutzte, hat benutzt> ◊ *Welche Creme benutzen Sie für das Gesicht?* ♦ *eine Feile benutzen* ♦ *Er benutzt viele Fremdwörter* ♦ *Sie benutzt ihren Mädchennamen.* use sth for doing sth etw. dazu benutzen, etw. zu tun use sth as etw. als etw. benutzen use sth as an excuse etw. als Vorwand benutzen; *(force)* anwenden ['anvɛndn] <wendet an, wendete/wandte an, hat angewendet/angewandt> ◊ *Notfalls würde er auch Gewalt anwenden.* **2.** *(exploit)* nutzen ['nʊtsn] +haben ◊ *das Freizeitangebot der Stadt nutzen* ♦ *Sie nutze jede freie Minute dazu, mich in die Sonne zu legen.* **3.** *(need, take)* verbrauchen [fɛ'braoxn] <verbraucht, verbrauchte, hat verbraucht> ◊ *beim Waschen viel Seife verbrauchen* **4.** *(treat unfairly)* ausnutzen ['aosnʊtsn] +haben ◊ *Sie fühlten sich von der Firma ausgenutzt.* **5.** *(take drugs)* use etw. nehmen ['neːmən] <nimmt, nahm, hat genommen> ◊ *Sie nimmt Ecstasy.* use Drogen nehmen **6.** *(accustomed)* be used to sth etw. gewohnt sein [ɡə'voːnt tsaen] +sein ◊ *Sie sind harte Arbeit gewohnt.* be used to

doing sth es gewohnt sein, etw. zu tun [ɛs ɡə'voːnt tsaen ... tsuː] +sein ◊ *Ich bin es gewohnt, morgens zwei Croissants zu essen.* get used to sth sich an etw. [acc] gewöhnen [an ... ɡə'vøːnən] <gewöhnt sich, gewöhnte sich, hat sich gewöhnt> ◊ *Er hat sich noch nicht an den neuen Wagen gewöhnt.* get used to doing sth sich daran gewöhnen, etw. zu tun ◊ *Sie musste sich erst daran gewöhnen, jeden Morgen so früh aufzustehen.*

⊛ could use sth etw. brauchen können ◊ *Ich könnte jetzt eine Tasse Kaffee brauchen.*

• **use up** [phras v] aufbrauchen ['aofbraoxn] +haben

used [adj] gebraucht [ɡə'braoxt] no comp/superl ◊ *Das Handy ist gebraucht, aber noch voll funktionsfähig.* ♦ *Auf dem Flohmarkt wurden gebrauchte Spielsachen angeboten.* used car Gebrauchtwagen [ɡə'braoxtvaːɡn] der <–s, –>

used to [verb] sb used to do sth jd hat früher etw. getan [hat 'fryːɐ̯] jd ist früher ... [ɪst 'fryːɐ̯] +haben/sein, depending on the verb ◊ *Er ist früher täglich gejoggt.* ♦ *Früher bin ich gern in Kneipen gegangen.* I used to. Früher habe ich es getan. ◊ *Ich fahre nicht mehr Motorrad, aber früher habe ich es getan.* There used to be ... Früher gab es ... ◊ *Früher gab es weniger Unterhaltung für die Kinder.*

useful [adj] nützlich ['nʏtslɪç] ◊ *Danke für den nützlichen Tipp!* ♦ *Die Schubkarre war für die Gartenarbeit äußerst nützlich.* be useful to sb jdm nützlich sein useful for doing sth nützlich, um etw. zu tun ◊ *Pappkartons sind nützlich, um Äpfel zu lagern.* it's useful for sb to do sth es ist nützlich für jdn, etw. zu tun ◊ *Es wäre sehr nützlich für mich, den Plan vom letzten Jahr zu sehen.* prove useful sich als nützlich erweisen

⊛ come in useful nützlich sein make yourself useful sich nützlich machen

usefully [adv] nutzbringend ['nʊtsbrɪŋənt] ◊ *sein Geld nutzbringend anlegen*

useless [adj] **1.** *(without purpose)* nutzlos ['nʊtsloːs] <nutzloser, am nutzlosesten> ◊ *In seiner Wohnung steht nur nutzloses Zeug herum.* ◊ *Das Gerät erwies sich als nutzlos.; (very bad)* unbrauchbar ['ʊnbraoxbaːɐ̯] ◊ *Dieser Bildschirm ist völlig unbrauchbar.* **2.** *(pointless)* sinnlos ['zɪnloːs] <sinnloser, am sinnlosesten> ◊ *eine sinnlose Beschäftigung* ♦ *Es ist sinnlos zu versuchen, mit ihm darüber zu reden.* **3.** *(incompetent)* unfähig ['ʊnfɛːɪç] ◊ *Unsere Mannschaft hat einen unfähigen Trainer.* useless at doing sth unfähig, etw. zu tun ◊ *Er ist unfähig, die Wohnung richtig aufzuräumen.* sb is useless jd ist zu nichts zu gebrauchen [ɪst tsuː ˌnɪçts tsuː ɡə'braoxn] +sein

⊛ be worse than useless völlig nutzlos sein

uselessly [adv] unnütz ['ʊnnʏts] <unnützer, am unnützesten> ◊ *Steh nicht so unnütz herum, sondern bilf mir lieber!*

user [noun] Benutzer [bə'nʊtsɐ] der <–s, –> ⚲Benutzerin [bə'nʊtsərɪn] die <–, –nen> road users Verkehrsteilnehmer [fɛ'keːɐ̯staelneːme] die <–> pl wheelchair users Rollstuhlfahrer ['rɔlʃtuːlfaːrɐ] die <–> pl drug users Drogensüchtige ['droːɡnzʏçtɪɡə] <der Drogensüchtigen> pl

usual [adj] **1.** *(customary, normal)* üblich ['yːplɪç] ◊ *nicht den üblichen Weg gehen* ♦ *Das ist in Frankreich so üblich.* sth is usual practice etw. ist üblich it is usual to do sth es ist üblich, etw. zu tun

2. *(familiar)* gewohnt [gə'vɔːnt] <gewohnter, am gewohntesten> ◊ *Heute vermisse ich seine gewohnte Freundlichkeit.* ♦ *Ihm fehlte die gewohnte Umgebung.* more/better etc. than usual mehr/besser etc. als sonst [,meːɐ̯/,bɛse als 'zɔnst]

⊛ as usual wie üblich

usually adv normalerweise [nɔrˈmaːlevaɐ̯əzə] ◊ *Normalerweise geht sie um sieben Uhr aus dem Haus.*

utility noun **1.** *(public service)* utility (company) Versorgungsbetrieb [feˈzɔrɡʊŋsbətriːp] der <-(e)s, -e> public/privatized utilities öffentliche/privatisierte Versorgungsbetriebe **2.** *(computer program)* Dienstprogramm ['diːnstproˌɡram] das <-s, -e>

utilize verb verwenden [feˈvɛndn̩] <verwendet, verwendete, hat verwendet> ◊ *Welche Kriterien werden dabei verwendet?* ♦ *Die Turnhalle wurde auch als Konzertsaal verwendet.*

utmost adj größte ['ɡrøːstə] *only before ns* <der/die/das größte …> ◊ *etw. mit größter Vorsicht behandeln* sb attaches the utmost importance to sth

etw. ist für jdn von größter Wichtigkeit

utter¹ adj total [toˈtaːl] *no comp/superl* ◊ *Dieser Plan ist totaler Wahnsinn.* ♦ *Die Besprechung war eine totale Zeitverschwendung.* a complete and utter fool ein Vollidiot [aɐ̯n ˈfɔlˌiˌdi̯oːt] <-en, -en> *(fam)*

utter² verb **1.** *(a word)* sagen ['zaːɡn̩] +haben ◊ *Es gelang ihr, einige Worte zu sagen.*; *(criticism, a protest)* äußern ['ɔøsen] <äußert, äußerte, hat geäußert> +haben ◊ *Keiner traute sich, Kritik zu äußern.* **2.** *(a sound)* von sich dat geben ['fɔn … ɡeːbm] <gibt, gab, hat gegeben> ◊ *Die Tiere gaben merkwürdige Schreie von sich.*

utterance noun Äußerung ['ɔøsərʊŋ] die <-, -en> ◊ *Die Presse veröffentlicht jede Äußerung dieser so genannten Prominenten.*

utterly adv völlig ['fœlɪç] *no comp/superl* ◊ *Das ist ja völlig verrückt.* ♦ *Die alten Leute im Heim sind völlig auf ihre Pfleger angewiesen.*

u umlaut, U umlaut noun ü, Ü [yː] das <-(s), -(s)> ◊ *ein kleines ü/großes Ü* ♦ *Ü wie Übel*

V

v, V [noun] v, V [faʊ] das <–(s), –(s)> ◊ *ein kleines v/ großes V* ♦ *V wie Viktor*

vacancy [noun] 1. *(in a hotel, B & B)* freies Zimmer [fræəs 'tsɪmɐ] das <–s, –> ◊ *Wir haben keine freien Zimmer mehr.* 2. *(in a company, shop)* freie Stelle [fræə 'ʃtɛlə] die <–, –n> ◊ *In meiner Abteilung gibt es eine freie Stelle.* ♦ *Ich möchte mich für die freie Stelle bewerben.*

vacant [adj] 1. *(seat, job)* frei [fraɪ] no comp/superl ◊ *ein freier Platz/Tisch* ♦ *In diesem Sprachkurs sind noch Plätze frei.* ♦ *Sie bewarb sich für die freie Stelle.*; *(house, flat)* leer stehend ['leːɐ ʃteːənt] no comp/superl, only before ns ◊ *leer stehende Wohnungen* sth is vacant etw. steht leer [ʃteːt 'leːɐ] <steht, stand, hat gestanden> ◊ *Viele Bürogebäude stehen leer.* 2. *(smile, expression)* abwesend ['apveːznt] ◊ *ein abwesendes Lächeln* ♦ *Ihr Blick war abwesend.*

vacantly [adv] abwesend ['apveːznt] ◊ *Sie starrte abwesend aus dem Fenster.*

vacate [verb] 1. *(a room, seat, house)* räumen ['rɔʏmən] +haben ◊ *Als der Feueralarm ertönte, räumten alle Zuschauer das Theater.* ♦ *Die Zimmer müssen bis zehn Uhr geräumt sein.* 2. *(a job, position)* aufgeben ['aʊfgeːbm̩] <gibt auf, gab auf, hat aufgegeben> ◊ *Nach zwei Jahren muss er das Amt aufgeben.*

vacation [noun] 1. *(at university)* Semesterferien [zeˈmɛstɐfeːrjən] die <–> pl ◊ *in den Semesterferien arbeiten, um sein Studium zu finanzieren* summer vacation Sommerferien ['zɔmɐfeːrjən] 2. *(in the US: holiday from work)* Urlaub ['uːɐlaʊp] der <–(e)s, –e> ◊ *eine Woche Urlaub haben/machen* ♦ *in Urlaub fahren*

vaccination [noun] Impfung ['ɪmpfʊŋ] die <–, –en> ◊ *eine Impfung gegen Grippe*

vacuum¹ [noun] Vakuum ['vaːkuʊm] das <–s, Vakua or Vakuen> ◊ *Die Fertigung von Mikrochips findet im Vakuum statt.* ♦ *Dem Land droht ein politisches Vakuum.* create a vacuum zu einem Vakuum führen ◊ *Der Abzug der Truppen würde zu einem Vakuum führen.* fill a vacuum ein Vakuum ausfüllen power vacuum Machtvakuum ['maxtvaːkuʊm] ⊛ in a vacuum im luftleeren Raum

vacuum² [verb] staubsaugen ['ʃtaʊpzaʊgn̩] <staubsaugt, staubsaugte, hat gestaubsaugt> ◊ *Er staubsaugt gerade; deswegen hört er das Telefon nicht.* ♦ *im Wohnzimmer staubsaugen*

vacuum cleaner [noun] Staubsauger ['ʃtaʊpzaʊgɐ] der <–s, –>

vagina [noun] Scheide ['ʃaɪdə] die <–, –n>

vague [adj] 1. *(not clearly explained)* vage ['vaːgə] <vager, am vag(e)sten> ◊ *eine vage Formulierung* ♦ *vage Versprechungen* ♦ *Die Angaben sind sehr vage.* 2. *(not explain clearly)* be vague sich unklar ausdrücken ['ʊnklaːˀ ˌaʊsdrʏkŋ̩] +haben; *(be uncertain)* be vague about sth sich [dat] über etw. [acc] nicht

sicher sein [yːbe ... nɪçt 'zɪçɐ zaɛn] +sein 3. *(idea, memory, feeling)* undeutlich ['ʊndɔøtlɪç] ◊ *Ihre Vorstellung von der Zukunft ist noch recht undeutlich.* ♦ *das undeutliche Gefühl, etwas vergessen zu haben* 4. *(not clearly visible)* verschwommen [fɛˈʃvɔmən] ◊ *eine verschwommene Gestalt im Nebel sehen*

vaguely [adv] 1. *(not clearly)* undeutlich ['ʊndɔøtlɪç] ◊ *sich nur undeutlich an etw. erinnern können* ♦ *undeutlich formuliert sein;* *(not precisely)* vage ['vaːgə] <vager, am vag(e)sten> ◊ *eine vage formulierte Vorschrift* 2. *(slightly)* leicht [laɛçt] no comp/superl ◊ *Das Ganze wirkte leicht komisch.* 3. *(without paying attention, vacantly)* abwesend ['apveːznt] ◊ *Er sah mich abwesend an.*

vain [adj] 1. *(proud of your looks)* eitel ['aɛtl̩] <eitler, am eitelsten> <der/die/das eitle ...> ◊ *Er ist sehr eitel und steht dauernd vor dem Spiegel.* ♦ *eine eitle Frau;* *(proud of your qualities)* eingebildet ['aɛŋgəbɪldət] ◊ *Sie ist schrecklich eingebildet, weil sie mit einem Professor verheiratet ist.* ♦ *ein eingebildeter Mensch* 2. *(unsuccessful, futile)* vergeblich [fɛˈgeːplɪç] ◊ *ein vergeblicher Versuch* ♦ *Er kam in der vergeblichen Hoffnung, sie zu treffen.* ⊛ in vain 1. *(without success)* vergeblich ◊ *sich vergeblich um eine Stelle bemühen* 2. *(without purpose, for no good reason)* umsonst ◊ *Die Soldaten sind umsonst gestorben.*

valid [adj] 1. *(document, ticket, vote)* gültig ['gʏltɪç] no comp/superl ◊ *Die neue Regelung ist ab 1. Januar gültig.* ♦ *Hat er eine gültige Arbeitserlaubnis?* ♦ *Ist die Fahrkarte noch gültig?* be valid for sth für etw. gelten [fyːɐ ... gɛltn̩] <gilt, galt, hat gegolten> ◊ *Die Karte gilt für drei Monate.* 2. *(password, file name)* zulässig ['tsuːlɛsɪç] no comp/superl ◊ *Ich bekam eine Fehlermeldung: Kein zulässiger Dateiname.* 3. *(reason, argument)* stichhaltig ['ʃtɪçhaltɪç] ◊ *Dieser Grund ist nicht stichhaltig.* ♦ *Nenne mir auch nur ein stichhaltiges Argument!;* *(excuse)* begründet [bəˈgrʏndət] ◊ *eine begründete Ausrede;* *(criticism, claim)* berechtigt [bəˈrɛçtɪçt] ◊ *eine berechtigte Forderung* ♦ *Deine Kritik ist nicht berechtigt.*

validity [noun] 1. *(of a document, ticket, vote)* Gültigkeit ['gʏltɪçkaɛt] die <–> no pl 2. *(of a reason, an argument)* Stichhaltigkeit ['ʃtɪçhaltɪçkaɛt] die <–> no pl; *(of a claim, criticism)* Berechtigung [bəˈrɛçtɪgʊŋ] die <–> no pl

valley [noun] Tal [taːl] das <–(e)s, Täler> ◊ *ein breites/tiefes/grünes Tal* ♦ *Tief unten im Tal konnte man die Häuser stehen.*

valuable [adj] wertvoll ['veːɐtfɔl] ◊ *wertvoller Schmuck* ♦ *Nichts ist wertvoller als die Gesundheit.*

valuables [noun] Wertsachen ['veːɐtzaxn̩] die <–> pl ◊ *Ihre Wertsachen schließen Sie am besten in den Safe.*

valuation [noun] Schätzung ['ʃɛtsʊŋ] die <–, –en> ◊ *Eine Schätzung ergab, dass das Gemälde eine Million Euro wert ist.*

value¹ [noun] 1. MUS, MATH *(amount that sth is worth,*

importance) Wert [veːɡt] der <–(e)s, –e> ◊ *Edelsteine von unschätzbarem Wert* ♦ *Der Wert der Sammlung liegt bei 70 000 Euro.* ♦ *Die Aktie gewinnt/verliert an Wert.* ♦ *der literarische Wert eines Werkes* ♦ *einen mathematischen Wert berechnen* ♦ *Eine ganze Note hat den gleichen Wert wie zwei halbe.* hold its value seinen Wert behalten drop/rise in value im Wert fallen/steigen of (great) value wertvoll ['veːɡtfɔl] ◊ *ein wertvoller Ring* of no value wertlos ['veːɡtloːs] <wertloser, am wertlosesten> ◊ *Der Schmuck, den sie gestohlen hatten, war wertlos.* market value Marktwert ['maˈktveːɡt] sentimental value Erinnerungswert [eˈɪnərʊŋsveːɡt] novelty value Neuigkeitswert ['nɔɡɪçkaɛtsveːɡt] **2.** offer tremendous value sehr preisgünstig sein [zeːɡ 'praɛsɡʏnstɪç zaɛn] +sein ◊ *Das Auto ist sehr preisgünstig.* value for (your) money günstige Preise [ˌɡʏnstɪɡə 'praɛzə] die <–> pl ◊ *Die Verbraucher wollen günstige Preise.* **3.** *(usefulness)* value (to) Nutzen (für) ['nʊtsn̩] der <–s, –> ◊ *der Nutzen des Freizeitzentrums für die Bürger* of value (to sb) (jdm) nützlich ['nʏtslɪç] of no value (to sb) nutzlos (für jdn) ['nʊtsloːs] <nutzloser, am nutzlosesten> **4.** values Werte ['veːɡtə] die <–> pl ◊ *christliche Werte* ♦ *Für mich zählen die inneren Werte mehr als das Aussehen.* ♦ *Diese Jugend hat keine sittlichen Werte mehr!* set of values Wertvorstellungen ['veːɡtfoːɡˌʃtɛlʊŋən] die <–> pl

value² [verb] schätzen ['ʃɛtsn̩] +haben ◊ *Ich schätze ihn als einen zuverlässigen Freund.* ♦ *mein geschätzter Kollege* ♦ *ein Schmuckstück schätzen lassen* value sth for sth etw. wegen etw. [gen] schätzen ◊ *Johannisbeeren werden wegen ihres hohen Vitamingehalts geschätzt.* value sth at sth etw. auf etw. [acc] schätzen ◊ *Das Haus wurde auf 200 000 Euro geschätzt.*

value added tax [noun] Mehrwertsteuer ['meː̯ɡveːɡtʃtɔɡə] die <–> no pl ◊ *Im Preis sind 16 Prozent Mehrwertsteuer enthalten.*

valve [noun] **1.** *(in a machine, musical instrument)* Ventil [vɛn'tiːl] das <–s, –e> ◊ *ein undichtes Ventil* **2.** *(in the body)* Klappe ['klapə] die <–, –n> heart valve Herzklappe ['hɛɐ̯tsklapə]

van [noun] Wagen ['vaːɡn̩] der <–s, –> delivery van Lieferwagen ['liːfevaːɡn̩] removal van Möbelwagen ['møːblvaːɡn̩]

vanish [verb] **1.** *(disappear)* verschwinden [fe'ʃvɪndn̩] <verschwindet, verschwand, ist verschwunden> ◊ *spurlos verschwunden sein* ♦ *Er ist einfach verschwunden, ohne sich zu verabschieden.* vanish from sth von/aus etw. verschwinden ◊ *Das Geld ist aus der Schublade/vom Tisch verschwunden.* vanish from sight verschwinden vanish into sth in etw. [acc] verschwinden ◊ *Die Jäger verschwanden in die Wälder und kehrten erst nach Tagen zurück.* **2.** *(stop existing)* untergehen ['ʊntəɡeːən] <geht unter, ging unter, ist untergegangen> ◊ *eine Kultur, die vor langer Zeit untergegangen ist*

vapour, vapor [noun] Dampf [damp͡f] der <–(e)s, Dämpfe>

variable¹ [noun] Variable [va'rja:blə] die <–, –n>

variable² [adj] **1.** *(capable of being changed)* variabel [va'rja:bl] <variabler, am variabelsten> der/die/das variable ... ◊ *Die Temperatur ist variabel.* a variable-rate loan ein Darlehen mit variablem Zinssatz **2.** *(changing)* wechselnd ['vɛks̩lnt] no comp/superl ◊

wechselnder Wind aus süd- bis südwestlichen Richtungen ♦ *ständig wechselnde Bedingungen* **3.** *(differing in quality)* unterschiedlich ['ʊntəʃiːtlɪç] ◊ *Das Niveau der Schulen ist sehr unterschiedlich.*

variant [noun] *(variant (of ...))* Variante (... [gen]) [va'rjantə] die <–, –n> ◊ *eine neue Variante des Internetwurms*

variation [noun] **1.** *(differences)* variation (beween) Unterschiede (zwischen) ['ʊntəʃiːdə] die <–> pl ◊ *Es gibt erhebliche Unterschiede zwischen den einzelnen Schulen.* wide variation (in sth) große Unterschiede (in etw. [dat]) ◊ *In den Interessen der Kinder gibt es große Unterschiede.* a wide variation of opinion die unterschiedlichsten Ansichten [diː ˌʊntəʃiːtlɪçstn̩ 'anzɪçtn̩] **2.** *(fluctuations)* variations (in sth) Schwankungen (... [gen]) ['ʃvaŋkʊŋən] die <–> pl ◊ *regionale Schwankungen der Baupreise* variations within Schwankungen innerhalb ◊ *Es gibt große Schwankungen innerhalb der einzelnen Gruppen.* variations in temperature Temperaturschwankungen [tɛmpəra'tuːɡʃvaŋkʊŋən] **3.** *(version)* variation (on sth) Variante (... [gen]) [va'rjantə] die <–, –n> ◊ *eine neue Variante des Internetwurms* **4.** mus Variation [varia'tsjoːn] die <–, –en> ◊ *Variationen über ein Thema von Händel*

varied [adj] vielfältig ['fiːlfɛltɪç] ◊ *ein vielfältiges Freizeitangebot* ♦ *Die Ursachen dieses Problems sind vielfältig.*

variety [noun] **1.** *(range, spectrum)* a (wide) variety of ... (viele) verschiedene ... [(fiːlə) fe'ʃiːdənə] ◊ *Wir möchten verschiedene Meinungen veröffentlichen.* ♦ *Sie bieten viele verschiedene Kurse an.* for a variety of reasons aus verschiedenen Gründen **2.** *(diversity)* Abwechslung ['apvɛkslʊŋ] die <–, –en> offer variety Abwechslung bieten add variety to sth mehr Abwechslung in etw. bringen **3.** *(type of plant, thing, person)* Sorte ['zɔɐ̯tə] die <–, –n> ◊ *Er baut sechs verschiedene Sorten von Tomaten an.* ♦ *ein Politiker der billigsten Sorte* a variety of apple eine Apfelsorte **4.** *(entertainment)* Varietee [varje'teː] das <–s, –s>

ⓢ **variety is the spice of life** Abwechslung muss sein

various [adj] verschieden [fe'ʃiːdn̩] no comp ◊ *Zitate aus verschiedenen Büchern* ♦ *Diese Bluse haben wir in verschiedenen Farben da.*

variously [adv] **1.** *(on different occasions)* verschiedentlich [fe'ʃiːdn̩tlɪç] no comp/superl ◊ *Johanna von Orleans wurde verschiedentlich als Hexe und Heilige beschrieben.* **2.** *(in different ways)* unterschiedlich ['ʊntəʃiːtlɪç] ◊ *Das Ereignis wurde von den Zeugen unterschiedlich wiedergegeben.*

varnish [noun] Lack [lak] der <–(e)s, –e> ◊ *Der Lack geht an einigen Stellen ab.* (nail) varnish Nagellack ['naːɡllak]

vary [verb] **1.** *(not be the same, change)* variieren [vari'iːɹən] <variiert, variierte, hat variiert> ◊ *Das Einkommen der Teilnehmer variiert stark.* ♦ *Mit Hilfe dieses Knopfes lässt sich die Lautstärke variieren.* **2.** *(differ)* vary in sth sich in etw. [dat] unterscheiden [ɪn ... ʊntəˌʃaɛdn̩] <unterscheidet sich, unterschied sich, hat sich unterschieden> ◊ *Die beiden Modelle unterscheiden sich in der Größe.*; *(attitude, opinion etc.)* auseinander gehen [aɔs|aɛˈnandə ɡeːən] <geht, ging, ist gegangen> ◊ *Darüber gehen die Meinungen auseinander.*

varying [adj] unterschiedlich ['ʊnteʃiːtlɪç] ◊ *Die Teilnehmer bringen unterschiedliche Erfahrungen mit.* ◆ *Die Vorgehensweise ist unterschiedlich.*

vase [noun] Vase ['vaːzə] die <-, -n> ◊ *Blumen in eine Vase stellen*

vast [adj] *(very large)* riesig ['riːzɪç] ◊ *riesige Waldflächen* ◆ *Der Unterschied war riesig.; (majority)* überwältigend [ybe'vɛltɪɡn̩t]

vat [noun] Fass [fas] das <-es, Fässer> ◊ *Whiskey vom Fass*

VAT (abbr of value-added tax) Mehrwertsteuer ['meːɐ̯vɛːɐ̯tʃtɔɔ̯ɐ] die <-> *no pl* ◊ *die Mehrwertsteuer erhöhen*

vault [noun] **1.** *(under the ground)* Gruft [ɡrʊft] die <-, Grüfte> *most sing* ◊ *in die Gruft hinabsteigen* **2.** *(in a bank)* Tresorraum [tre'zoːˌʀaɔ̯m] der <-(e)s, Tresorräume> ◊ *etw. im Tresorraum aufbewahren* **3.** ARCH *(arch)* Gewölbe [ɡə'vœlbə] das <-s, -> ◊ *das Gewölbe einer Kirche* **4.** *(large jump)* Sprung [ʃprʊŋ] der <-(e)s, Sprünge> ◊ *Mit einem Sprung setzte er über den Fluss.*

veal [noun] Kalbfleisch ['kalpflaɛ̯ʃ] das <-(e)s> *no pl* ◊ *Kalbfleisch nach Zürcher Art* veal cutlet Kalbsschnitzel ['kalpsʃnɪtsl̩] das <-s, ->

vegetable [noun] **1.** *(food)* vegetable(s) Gemüse [ɡə'myːzə] das <-s, -> *most sing* ◊ *Kotelett mit Kartoffeln und gemischtem Gemüse* ◆ *Karotten sind ein vitaminreiches Gemüse* ◆ *Gemüse dünsten* vegetable garden Gemüsegarten [ɡə'myːzəɡaʁtn̩] der <-s, Gemüsegärten> vegetable oil pflanzliches Öl [ˌpflantslɪçəs 'øːl] <-(e)s, -e> **2.** BIO *(plant)* Pflanze ['pflantsə] die <-, -n> ◊ *Ist die Seeanemone eine Pflanze oder ein Tier?*

◉ be a vegetable dahinvegetieren

vegetarian [adj] vegetarisch [vege'taːrɪʃ] *no comp/ superl* ◊ *Dieses Gericht ist rein vegetarisch.* ◆ *eine vegetarische Pizza*

vegetation [noun] Vegetation [vegeta'tsi̯oːn] die <-, -en> ◊ *ein Gebiet mit einer besonderen Vegetation* ◆ *Auf der Insel gab es kaum Vegetation.*

vehicle [noun] **1.** *(car, bus etc.)* Fahrzeug ['faːɐ̯tsɔɔ̯k] das <-(e)s, -e> ◊ *ein motorisiertes Fahrzeug* **2.** *(fig) (medium)* Vehikel [ve'hiːkl̩] das <-s, -> ◊ *(form)* die Sprache als Vehikel des Denkens

veil [noun] Schleier ['ʃlaɛ̯ɐ] der <-s, -> ◊ *einen Schleier tragen* draw a veil over sth den Schleier des Vergessens über etw. [acc] breiten

◉ take the veil ins Kloster gehen

vein [noun] **1.** ANAT, BOT, GEOL Ader ['aːdɐ] die <-, -n> ◊ *Eine Ader trat auf seiner Stirn hervor.* ◆ *die feinen Adern der Blätter* ◆ *aus einer Ader Gold gewinnen* **2.** *(particular way of doing sth)* Art [aːɐ̯t] die <-> ◊ *eine humorvolle Art kultivieren* in the same vein in derselben Art

velvet [noun] Samt [zamt] der <-(e)s, -e> ◊ *ein Kleid aus blauem Samt* ◆ *eine Haut wie Samt* velvet curtain Samtvorhang ['zamtfoːɐ̯haŋ] der <-(e)s, Samtvorhänge>

vendor [noun] Verkäufer [fɛ'kɔɔ̯fɐ] der <-s, -> ice-cream vendor Eisverkäufer ['aɛ̯sfɛkɔɔ̯fɐ] ◊ *Die Eisverkäuferin hatte kein Wechselgeld.* newspaper vendor Zeitungsverkäufer ['tsaɛ̯tʊŋsfɛkɔɔ̯fɐ] ◊ *Ich verdiene mein Geld als Zeitungsverkäufer.* street vendor Straßenhändler ['ʃtraːsn̩hɛndlɐ] der <-s, ->

vengeance [noun] Rache ['raxə] die <-> *no pl* ◊ *Die Bande drohte mit Rache.* take vengeance on sb sich

an jdm rächen [an ... 'rɛçn̩] +haben

◉ with a vengeance mit voller Kraft

venomous [adj] giftig ['ɡɪftɪç] ◊ *Diese Schlange ist giftig.* ◆ *eine giftige Bemerkung machen*

venture¹ [noun] Unternehmen [ʊnte'neːmən] das <-s, -> ◊ *ein Erfolg versprechendes Unternehmen* joint venture Gemeinschaftsunternehmen [ɡə'maɛ̯nʃaftsˌʊnteˌneːmən] sb's first venture at doing sth jds erster Versuch, etw. zu tun [eːɐ̯stə fe'zuːx ... tsuː]

venture² [verb] **1.** *(go somewhere, be brave)* venture somewhere sich irgendwohin wagen ['vaːɡn̩] +haben ◊ *Sie wagte sich tagelang nicht vor die Tür.* venture sth sich an etw. [acc] wagen ◊ *Damit hat sich die Firma an ein neuartiges Projekt gewagt.* venture to do sth es wagen, etw. zu tun ◊ *Niemand wagte es, ihm zu widersprechen.* **2.** *(express an opinion)* venture sth etw. zu äußern wagen [tsuː: 'ʔɔɔ̯sn̩ vaːɡn̩] +haben ◊ *„Und wenn wir den Termin verschieben?", wagte er schließlich zu äußern.* If I may venture an opinion ... Wenn ich meine Meinung äußern dürfte ... venture to add that zu behaupten wagen, dass ◊ *Ich wage sogar zu behaupten, dass sie das absichtlich getan hat.*

◉ nothing ventured nothing gained wer nicht wagt, der nicht gewinnt

venue [noun] Schauplatz ['ʃaɔ̯plats] der <-(e)s, Schauplätze> ◊ *Schauplatz der Verhandlungen wird die Hauptstadt sein.* ◆ *ein beliebter Schauplatz für sportliche Ereignisse*

verb [noun] Verb [vɛʳp] das <-s, -en> ◊ *Es gibt im Deutschen starke und schwache Verben.*

verbal [adj] **1.** *(relating to language)* sprachlich ['ʃpraːxlɪç] *no comp/superl, mostly before ns* ◊ *die sprachlichen Fähigkeiten eines Menschen; (spoken)* mündlich ['mʏntlɪç] *no comp/superl* ◊ *eine mündliche Erklärung* **2.** LING *(relating to a verb)* verbal [vɛʳ'baːl] *no comp/superl* ◊ *ein verbaler Ausdruck*

verbally [adv] **1.** *(on a spoken basis)* mündlich ['mʏntlɪç] *no comp/superl* ◊ *etw. mündlich vereinbaren* **2.** LING *(with a verb)* verbal [vɛʳ'baːl] *no comp/ superl* ◊ *etw. verbal ausdrücken*

verbal noun [noun] Verbalsubstantiv [vɛʳ'baːlzʊpstanˌtiːf] das <-s, -e>

verdict [noun] Urteil ['ʊʳtaɛ̯l] das <-s, -e> ◊ *ein Urteil fällen* ◆ *Wir sollten auf das Urteil des Arztes warten.* give your verdict about sth sein Urteil über etw. [acc] abgeben verdict of not guilty Freispruch ['fraɛ̯ʃprʊx] der <-(e)s, Freisprüche> verdict of guilty Schuldspruch ['ʃʊltʃprʊx] der <-(e)s, Schuldsprüche>

verge [noun] Seitenstreifen ['zaɛ̯tn̩ʃtraɛ̯fn̩] der <-s, -> Keep off the verge! Seitenstreifen nicht befahrbar!

◉ on the verge of sth *(of war, ruin, a nervous breakdown)* am Rande ... [gen] ◊ *Die beiden Länder stehen am Rande eines Krieges.* on the verge of tears den Tränen nahe on the verge of a discovery kurz vor einer Entdeckung be on the verge of doing sth im Begriff sein, etw. zu tun

verify [verb] **1.** *(check)* überprüfen [ybe'pryːfn̩] <überprüft, überprüfte, hat überprüft> ◊ *jds Behauptungen überprüfen* **2.** *(confirm)* bestätigen [bə'ʃtɛːtɪɡn̩] <bestätigt, bestätigte, hat bestätigt> ◊ *Eine Zeugin bestätigte seine Aussage.*

versatile [adj] vielseitig ['fiːlzaɛ̯tɪç] ◊ *eine vielseitige*

Künstlerin ♦ *Diese Software ist nicht sehr vielseitig.*
verse [noun] **1.** *(stanza)* Strophe ['ʃtroːfə] die <–, –n> ◊ *Worum geht es in der ersten Strophe des Gedichts/ Liedes?; (in the Bible)* Vers [fɛ'ʳs] der <–es, –e> ◊ *Markus 4, Vers 30 bis 32* **2.** *(poetry)* Dichtung ['dɪçtʊŋ] die <–, –en> ◊ *die epische/komische Dichtung*
version [noun] Version [vɛ'ʳzjoːn] die <–, –en> ◊ *eine gekürzte Version* ♦ *Nun lass uns mal deine Version der Geschichte hören.*
versus [prep] **1.** *(in comparison with, in relation to)* im Vergleich zu [ɪm fɛ'glaɛç ʦuː] ◊ *Der Dollar ist im Vergleich zum Euro gefallen.* **2.** *(against an opponent)* gegen ['geːgŋ] [+acc] ◊ *das Spiel Italien gegen Dänemark*
vertical(ly) [adj, adv] vertikal [vɛ'tiːkaːl] *seldom comp/ superl (tech)* ◊ *eine Tapete mit vertikalen Streifen* ♦ *vertikal integrierte Unternehmen*
very[1] [adj] *(precisely)* the very ... genau ... [gə'naʊ] *no comp/superl* ◊ *Sie sind genau der Mann, den wir brauchen.* that very day genau an diesem Tag at this very moment genau in diesem Augenblick; *(the most extreme)* at the very ... ganz an ... [dat] [ganʦ] *no comp/superl* ◊ *Ganz am Anfang hatte er ihr noch geglaubt.* ♦ *Siehst du den Vogel ganz an der Spitze des Baums?* at the very back/front ganz hinten/vorn ◊ *Sie saß ganz hinten im Bus.; (merely)* the very ... allein schon ... [a'laɛn ʃoːn] ◊ *Allein schon der Gedanke an das Essen verursachte ihr Übelkeit.*
very[2] [adv] **1.** *(to a high degree)* sehr [zeːɐ] ◊ *Das ist sehr nett von Ihnen.* ◊ *Es kamen sehr viele Leute.* ♦ *Er hat sich sehr dumm verhalten.* ♦ *Das Haus ist nicht sehr groß, aber gemütlich.* very much sehr ◊ *Das gefällt mir sehr gut.* very much so sehr sogar Thank you very much. Vielen Dank. **2.** *(expressing a superl)* the very ... der/die/das aller... [deːɐ/diː/das 'alɐ] *mostly spoken* very best allerbeste ['alɐ'bɛstə] *no comp/superl* <der/die/das allerbeste> ◊ *meine allerbeste Freundin* very first allererste ['alɐ'eːɐstə] *no comp/superl* <der/die/das allererste> ◊ *Unser Kleiner hat heute seine allerersten Schritte gemacht.* very last allerletzte ['alɐ'lɛtstə] *no comp/ superl* <der/die/das allerletzte> ◊ *zum allerletzten Mal*
⊛ that's all very well das ist ja alles schön und gut
vessel [noun] **1.** *(form)* SHIP Schiff [ʃɪf] das <–(e)s, –e> ◊ *an Board eines Schiffs gehen* **2.** *(in the body or plants, for liquids)* Gefäß [gə'fɛːs] das <–es, –e> ◊ *eine Flüssigkeit in ein Gefäß füllen* ♦ *ein zerbrechliches Gefäß* blood vessel Blutgefäß ['bluːtgəfɛːs]
vest [noun] **1.** *(in the UK: piece of underwear)* Unterhemd ['ʊntɐhɛmt] das <–(e)s, –en> ◊ *kein Unterhemd tragen* **2.** *(in the US: piece of clothing worn over your shirt)* Weste ['vɛstə] die <–, –n> ◊ *ein Anzug mit Weste* a bulletproof vest eine kugelsichere Weste
vet [noun] **1.** *(veterinary surgeon)* Tierarzt ['tiːɐʔaʳst] der <–(e)s, Tierärzte> ♀Tierärztin ['tiːɐʔɛʳstɪn] die <–, –nen> ◊ *Wenn sie groß ist, möchte sie Tierärztin werden.* ♦ *Ich muss mit dem Hund zum Tierarzt.* **2.** *(fam)* MIL *(in the US: veteran)* Veteran [vete'raːn] der <–en, –en> ♀Veteranin [vete'raːnɪn] die <–, –nen>
veteran [noun] Veteran [vete'raːn] der <–en, –en> ♀Ve-

teranin [vete'raːnɪn] die <–, –nen> ◊ *Er ist ein Veteran des Ersten Weltkriegs.* ♦ *eine Veteranin der Frauenbewegung*
veto [verb] *(officially refuse)* veto sth gegen etw. sein Veto einlegen [geːgŋ ... zaɛn 'veːto: aɛnleːgŋ] +haben ◊ *Sie legte gegen den Beschluss ihr Veto ein.; (an idea, suggestion etc.)* veto sth etw. ablehnen ['apleːnən] +haben ◊ *Er hat alle meine Vorschläge abgelehnt.*
via [prep] über ['yːbɐ] [+acc] ◊ *ein Umweg über Köln* ♦ *Wir konnten über Satellit mit ihm sprechen.*
viable [adj] *(suggestion, plan, method)* durchführbar ['dʊʳçfyːɐbaːʳ] *no comp/superl* ◊ *Der Plan ist so nicht durchführbar.* economically/financially viable wirtschaftlich/finanziell rentabel [,vɪʳtʃaftlɪç/finan,tsjɛl rɛn'taːbl] <rentabler, am rentabelsten> <der/die/das wirtschaftlich/finanziell rentable ...>
vibrant(ly) [adj, adv] **1.** *(personality, economy)* dynamisch [dy'naːmɪʃ] ◊ *eine dynamische Wirtschaft* ♦ *dynamisch an etw. herangehen; (life)* pulsierend [pʊl'ziːʳənt] ◊ *das pulsierende Leben der Großstadt* **2.** *(colo(u)r)* lebhaft ['leːphaft] <lebhafter, am lebhaftesten> ◊ *ein lebhaftes Gelb* ♦ *lebhaft gemustert*
vibrate [verb] vibrieren [vi'briːʳən] <vibriert, vibrierte, hat vibriert> ◊ *Die Musik war so laut, dass die Wände vibrierten.*
vicar [noun] Pfarrer ['pfaʳɐ] der <–s, –> ♀Pfarrerin ['pfaʳərɪn] die <–, –nen> ◊ *Er ist Pfarrer.* ♦ *die Pfarrerin unserer Gemeinde*
vice [noun] **1.** *(bad habit)* Laster ['lastɐ] das <–s, –> ◊ *Er ist dem Laster des Spielens verfallen.* ♦ *Rauchen ist ihr einziges Laster.* **2.** *(tool)* Schraubstock ['ʃraopʃtɔk] der <–(e)s, Schraubstöcke> ◊ *etw. in den Schraubstock einspannen*
vice chancellor [noun] Rektor ['rɛktoːɐ] der <–s, –en> ♀Rektorin [rɛk'toːrɪn] die <–, –nen> ◊ *Er wurde zum Rektor der TU gewählt.* ♦ *Sie hofft, einmal Rektorin zu werden.*
vice-president [noun] Vizepräsident ['fiːtsəprɛzi,dɛnt] der <–en, –en> ♀Vizepräsidentin ['fiːtsəprɛzi,dɛntɪn] die <–, –nen> ◊ *Er war früher Vizepräsident.* ♦ *Die Vizepräsidentin hält eine Rede.*
vice versa [adv] umgekehrt ['ʊmgəkeːɐt] *no comp/ superl* ◊ *Frauen fühlen sich oft von Männern nicht verstanden, und umgekehrt.*
vicinity [noun] Umgebung [ʊm'geːbʊŋ] die <–, –en> ◊ *Gibt es hier in der Umgebung einen Kinderspielplatz?; (near sth)* in the vicinity of sth in der Nähe ... [gen] [ɪn deːɐ 'nɛːə] ◊ *Das Hotel befindet sich in der Nähe des Zentrums.; (about)* in the vicinity of £100 etc. um die 100£ etc. herum [ʊm diː ˌhʊndɐt 'pfʊnt hɛrʊm] *(fam)*
vicious [adj] **1.** *(very violent)* brutal [bru'taːl] ◊ *ein brutaler Angriff; (animal)* bösartig ['bøːsˌaːʳtɪç] ◊ *Achtung, dieses Pferd kann bösartig sein!; (dog)* bissig ['bɪsɪç] ◊ *ein bissiger Schäferhund* **2.** *(mean, nasty)* boshaft ['boːshaft] <boshafter, am boshaftesten> ◊ *eine boshafte Bemerkung* ♦ *Sie kann manchmal richtig boshaft sein.*
vicious circle [noun] Teufelskreis ['tɔyfl̩skraɛs] der <–es, –e> most sing ◊ *in einen Teufelskreis geraten*
victim [noun] Opfer ['ɔpfɐ] das <–s, –> ◊ *das Opfer eines Verbrechens werden* ♦ *Das Unwetter forderte viele Opfer.* fall victim to sth einer Sache [dat] zum Opfer fallen

A
B
C
D
E
F
G
H
I
J
K
L
M
N
O
P
Q
R
S
T
U
V
W
X
Y
Z

victory [noun] Sieg [ziːk] der <–(e)s, –e> ◊ *der Sieg über einen Gegner ♦ ein Sieg im Wahlkampf ♦ den Sieg davontragen*

video [noun] Video ['viːdeoː] das <–s, –s> ◊ *ein Video ausleihen/ansehen* on video *auf Video*

video recorder [noun] Videorekorder ['viːdeore,koˈrde] der <–s, –>

view¹ [noun] **1.** *(opinion)* Ansicht ['anzɪçt] die <–, –en> ◊ *Sie fragte ihn nach seiner Ansicht zu dem Thema. ♦ altmodische Ansichten haben* in sb's view *jds Ansicht nach* ◊ *Was soll ich deiner Ansicht nach tun?* take the view that *die Ansicht vertreten, dass;* *(evaluation)* Sicht [zɪçt] die <–, –en> ◊ *eine eigene/positive Sicht der Dinge haben* view of the world *Weltanschauung* ['vɛltˌanʃaɔʊŋ] die <–, –en> view of a problem/the facts etc. *Überblick über ein Problem/die Fakten etc.* ['yːbɐblɪk yːbɐ aɛn proˌbleːmˌdiːˌ ˌfaktŋ] der <–(e)s, –e> **2.** *(range of vision)* Sicht [zɪçt] die <–> no pl ◊ *gute/freie Sicht haben* block sb's view *jdm die Sicht versperren* come into view *in Sicht kommen; (sight, prospect)* Aussicht ['aɔszɪçt] die <–, –en> ◊ *ein Zimmer mit Aussicht aufs Meer ♦ Von unserem Hotel haben wir eine wunderbare Aussicht auf die Berge.* **3.** *(view of sth on a picture)* Ansicht ['anzɪçt] die <–, –en> ◊ *Die Fotografie zeigt eine Ansicht von Algier.* ⊛ with a view to doing sth *mit der Absicht, etw. zu tun* in view of *angesichts*

view² [verb] **1.** *(regard as, consider to be)* betrachten [bəˈtraxtn̩] <betrachtet, betrachtete, hat betrachtet> ◊ *Ich betrachte diese Erfahrung als wertvoll.* **2.** *(look at, see)* sehen ['zeːən] <sieht, sah, hat gesehen> ◊ *Um die nächste Seite zu sehen, drücken Sie die Enter-Taste.; (a property)* besichtigen [bəˈzɪçtɪgn̩] <besichtigt, besichtigte, hat besichtigt> ◊ *Möchten Sie das Haus besichtigen?; (a film, TV programme etc.)* ansehen ['anzeːən] <sieht an, sah an, hat angesehen> ◊ *einen Film im Fernsehen ansehen*

viewer [noun] **1.** *(sb watching TV)* Zuschauer ['tsuːʃaɔɐ] der <–s, –> ♀Zuschauerin ['tsuːʃaɔərɪn] die <–, –nen> ◊ *Viele Zuschauer beschwerten sich über die brutale Sendung.; (sb looking at a picture etc.)* Betrachter [bəˈtraxtɐ] der <–s, –> ◊ *Der Mann auf dem Bild wendet dem Betrachter den Rücken zu.* **2.** *(for slides)* Diabetrachter ['diːabətraxtɐ] der <–s, –> ◊ *ein Bild im Diabetrachter ansehen*

viewpoint [noun] **1.** *(perspective, attitude)* Standpunkt ['ʃtantpʊŋkt] der <–(e)s, –e> ◊ *Vom wirtschaftlichen Standpunkt aus ist das Projekt ein Risiko. ♦ Er vertritt einen vernünftigen Standpunkt.* **2.** *(for a scenic view)* Aussichtspunkt ['aɔszɪçtspʊŋkt] der <–(e)s, –e> ◊ *Von diesem Aussichtspunkt aus kann man die Berge sehen.*

vigilant(ly) [adj, adv] wachsam ['vaxzaːm] ◊ *Sei wachsam! ♦ wachsame Bürger ♦ Er beobachtete wachsam, was um ihn herum vorging.*

vigor → vigour

vigorous(ly) [adj, adv] **1.** *(full of energy, lively)* energisch [eˈnɛrgɪʃ] ◊ *ein energisches Vorgehen ♦ Er ist sehr energisch. ♦ energisch durchgreifen/protestieren; (discussion, debate)* lebhaft ['leːphaft] <lebhafter, am lebhaftesten> ◊ *eine lebhafte Diskussion* **2.** *(strong, healthy)* kräftig ['krɛftɪç] ◊ *Du bist noch jung und kräftig. ♦ ein kräftiger junger Mann ♦ kräftig zupacken*

vigour, vigor [noun] Energie [enɛrˈgiː] die <–> no pl ◊ *Sie steckt immer noch voller Energie.*

villa [noun] Villa ['vɪlaː] die <–, Villen> ◊ *in einer Villa wohnen*

village [noun] Dorf [dɔrf] das <–(e)s, Dörfer> ◊ *das Leben auf dem/im Dorf ♦ Das ganze Dorf war zur Hochzeit eingeladen.*

villager [noun] Dorfbewohner ['dɔrfbəvoːnɐ] der <–s, –> ♀Dorfbewohnerin ['dɔrfbəvoːnərɪn] die <–, –nen>

villain [noun] **1.** *(in a film, novel etc.)* Bösewicht ['bøːzəvɪçt] der <–(e)s, –er> ◊ *Er spielt in dem Film den Bösewicht.* **2.** *(sb who behaves immorally or criminally)* Schurke ['ʃʊrkə] der <–n, –n> ♀Schurkin ['ʃʊrkɪn] die <–, –nen> ◊ *sich auf die Suche nach den wahren Schurken machen*

vine [noun] **1.** *(grapevine)* Weinrebe ['vaɛnreːbə] die <–, –n> **2.** *(climbing plant)* Rebengewächs ['reːbŋgəvɛks] das <–es, –e>; *(part of a plant)* Ranke ['raŋkə] die <–, –n> ◊ *die Ranken des Efeus*

vinegar [noun] Essig ['ɛsɪç] der <–s, –e> most sing ◊ *einen Salat mit Essig und Öl anmachen ♦ etw. in Essig einlegen*

violation [noun] violation of sth Verletzung ... [gen] [fɛˈlɛtsʊŋ] die <–, –en> ◊ *Verletzungen der Menschenrechte* violation of a treaty *Vertragsbruch* [fɛˈtraːksbrʊx] der <–(e)s, Vertragsbrüche> traffic violation *Verkehrswidrigkeit* [fɛˈkeːɐsviːdrɪçkaɛt] die <–, –en> do sth in violation of sth *mit etw. gegen* etw. [acc] *verstoßen* [mɪt ... geˈʃoː ... fɛˌʃtoːsŋ] <verstößt, verstieß, hat verstoßen> ◊ *Sie hat damit gegen die Vereinbarung verstoßen.*

violence [noun] Gewalt [gəˈvalt] die <–> no pl ◊ *Gewalt gegen jdn anwenden ♦ Mit ungeheurer Gewalt fegte der Orkan über das Land hinweg.*

violent [adj] **1.** *(confrontation, riot)* blutig ['bluːtɪç] ◊ *Es kam zu blutigen Unruhen. ♦ Die Auseinandersetzung war blutig.; (death, methods)* gewaltsam [gəˈvaltzaːm] mostly before ns ◊ *eines gewaltsamen Todes sterben ♦ Seine Methoden sind sehr gewaltsam.; (person, action)* gewalttätig [gəˈvaltːɛːtɪç] ◊ *gewalttätiges Verhalten ♦ Wenn er trinkt, wird er leicht gewalttätig.* violent crime *Gewaltverbrechen* [gəˈvaltfɛrbrɛçn̩] das <–s, –> **2.** *(extreme, strong)* heftig ['hɛftɪç] ◊ *eine heftige Explosion ♦ heftige Schmerzen ♦ eine heftige Reaktion hervorrufen* have a violent temper *jähzornig sein* ['jɛːtsɔrnɪç zaɛn] +sein **3.** *(colo(u)r)* grell [grɛl] ◊ *eine Weste in grellen Farben*

violently [adv] **1.** *(involving violence)* gewaltsam [gəˈvaltzaːm] ◊ *gewaltsam gegen jdn vorgehen* **2.** *(with great energy)* heftig ['hɛftɪç] ◊ *Er schüttelte heftig den Kopf. ♦ Sie zitterte heftig.*

violet [adj] violett [vioˈlɛt] <violetter, am violettesten> seldom comp/superl ◊ *ein violetter Amethyst ♦ Veilchen sind violett.*

violin [noun] Violine [vioˈliːnə] die <–, –n> ◊ *Violine spielen*

virgin [noun] Jungfrau ['jʊŋfraɔ] die <–, –en> ◊ *noch Jungfrau sein ♦ keine Jungfrau mehr sein* the Virgin (Mary) *die Jungfrau Maria*

Virgo [noun] Jungfrau ['jʊŋfraɔ] die <–, –en>

virtual [adj] **1.** *(almost complete)* weit gehend ['vaɛt geːənt] <weiter gehend, am weitesten gehend> ◊ *die weit gehende Zerstörung der Stadt* be a virtual certainty/impossibility *so gut wie sicher/unmöglich*

sein [zo: ˌɡuːt vi: ˈzɪçə/ʊnˈmøːklɪç zaɛn] +sein **2.** ıт
virtuell [vɪrˈtuˈɛl] no comp/superl ◊ *eine virtuelle Realität erschaffen*
virtually [adv] so gut wie [zo: ˈɡuːt viː] ◊ *Es ist so gut wie unmöglich, die Kinder allein kurz zu lassen.* ♦ *Er ist so gut wie blind.*
virtue [noun] **1.** *(moral quality)* Tugend [ˈtuːɡn̩t] die <-, –en> ◊ *Geduld gehört nicht zu meinen Tugenden.*; *(way of behaving)* Tugendhaftigkeit [ˈtuːɡn̩thaftɪçkaɛt] die <-> no pl ◊ *jdn wegen seiner Tugendhaftigkeit bewundern* **2.** *(advantage)* Vorteil [ˈfoːɐtaɛl] der <-(e)s, –e> ◊ *Ein Vorteil des Verfahrens sind die geringeren Kosten.*
☞ **by virtue of sth** aufgrund ... [gen]/von etw. ◊ *Aufgrund seiner Heirat erhielt er die britische Staatsbürgerschaft.* ♦ *Aufgrund von Meinungsverschiedenheiten kam es zu einem Streit.*
virus [noun] Virus [ˈviːrʊs] das or fam der <-, Viren> ◊ *Helfen Antibiotika gegen Viren?* ♦ *Sie hat sich ein/einen Virus eingefangen.* ♦ *Das Virus verbreitet sich über infizierte E-Mails.*
visa [noun] Visum [ˈviːzʊm] das <-s, Visa> ◊ *ein Visum beantragen* ♦ *jdm das Visum verweigern* entry visa Einreisevisum [ˈaɛnraɛzəˌviːzʊm] exit visa Ausreisevisum [ˈaʊsraɛzəˌviːzʊm]
visibility [noun] **1.** *(distance you can see)* Sicht [zɪçt] die <-> no pl ◊ *Die Sicht verschlechterte sich.* ♦ *Wir hatten klare Sicht.* **2.** *(state of being easy to see)* Sichtbarkeit [ˈzɪçtbaːrkaɛt] die <-> no pl ◊ *Helle Kleidung erhöht die Sichtbarkeit im Straßenverkehr.*
visible(-ibly) [adj, adv] sichtbar [ˈzɪçtbaːr] ◊ *Die Kühltürme sind von weitem sichtbar.* ♦ *sichtbare Fortschritte machen* ♦ *Das Namensschild muss gut sichtbar getragen werden.* visible to the naked eye mit bloßem Auge erkennbar [mɪt ˌbloːsəm ˈaʊɡə ɛɐˈkɛnbaːr]
vision [noun] **1.** *(foresight)* Weitblick [ˈvaɛtblɪk] der <-(e)s> no pl ◊ *Ihm fehlt als Politiker der nötige Weitblick.* ♦ *eine Frau mit Weitblick* **2.** *(hallucination, dream)* Vision [viˈzjoːn] die <-, –en> ◊ *ein Vision haben* ♦ *die Vision von einer Welt ohne Krieg* **3.** *(power of sight)* Sehvermögen [ˈzeːfɛɐmøːɡn̩] das <-s> no pl ◊ *Die Brille hat mein Sehvermögen stark verbessert.* field of vision Blickfeld [ˈblɪkfɛlt] das <-(e)s> no pl ◊ *in jds Blickfeld geraten*
visit¹ [noun] *(to a person, doctor etc.)* Besuch [bəˈzuːx] der <-(e)s, –e> ◊ *Besuch von jdm bekommen* ♦ *Ich fahre nächste Woche zu einem Besuch nach Hamburg.* ♦ *ein Besuch bei einem Hautarzt* pay sb a visit jdn besuchen [bəˈzuːxn̩] <besucht, besuchte, hat besucht> ◊ *Gestern habe ich meine Tante besucht.*
visit² [verb] **1.** *(a person, country, website etc.)* besuchen [bəˈzuːxn̩] <besucht, besuchte, hat besucht> ◊ *Besuch uns doch mal wieder!* ♦ *Wir sollten sie im Krankenhaus besuchen.* ♦ *Besuchen Sie unsere Homepage!*; *(a doctor, lawyer)* aufsuchen [ˈaʊfzuːxn̩] <sucht auf, suchte auf, hat aufgesucht> ◊ *Ich rate Ihnen, Ihren Hausarzt aufzusuchen.* **2.** *(view, see)* besichtigen [bəˈzɪçtɪɡn̩] <besichtigt, besichtigte, hat besichtigt> ◊ *Wir haben in Paris den Eiffelturm besichtigt.* ♦ *Sie können das Haus morgen besichtigen.*
visitor [noun] **1.** *(sb visiting a person, place, website)* Besucher [bəˈzuːxɐ] der <-s, –> ♀Besucherin [bəˈzuːxərɪn] die <-, –nen> ◊ *Der Eiffelturm zieht jedes Jahr viele Besucher an.* visitor to sth Besucher

... [gen] ◊ *Die Besucher des Schlosses werden gebeten, nicht zu fotografieren.* have visitors/a visitor Besuch haben [bəˈzuːx haːbm̩] +haben **2.** *(sb staying in a hotel etc., football team etc.)* Gast [ɡast] der <-(e)s, Gäste> ◊ *Wir versuchen, unseren Gästen viel Komfort zu bieten.* ♦ *Es steht drei zu null für die Gäste.*
visual [adj] **1.** *(relating to what you can see)* visuell [vizuˈɛl] no comp/superl ◊ *der erste visuelle Eindruck* **2.** *(using images)* bildlich [ˈbɪltlɪç] no comp/superl ◊ *bildliche Kunst* **3.** *(relating to sight)* Seh... [zeː] visual handicap/impairment Sehbehinderung [ˈzeːbəˌhɪndərʊŋ] die <-, –en>
visually [adv] **1.** *(relating to what you can see)* visuell [vizuˈɛl] no comp/superl ◊ *Rein visuell ist der Film sehr beeindruckend.* **2.** visually handicapped/impaired sehbehindert [ˈzeːbəhɪndɐt] no comp/superl **3.** *(using images)* bildlich [ˈbɪltlɪç] no comp/superl ◊ *sich* [dat] *etw. bildlich vorstellen*
vital [adj] **1.** *(essential)* unerlässlich [ˈʊn|ɛlɛslɪç] ◊ *eine unerlässliche Maßnahme* ♦ *Es ist unerlässlich für die Gesundheit, regelmäßig Sport zu treiben.* of vital importance von größter Wichtigkeit [fɔn ˈɡrøːstɐ ˈvɪçtɪçkaɛt] play a vital role eine bedeutende Rolle spielen [aɛnə bəˌdøːtn̩də ˈrɔlə ʃpiːlən] +haben **2.** *(full of life)* vital [viˈtaːl] ◊ *ein vitaler junger Mann*; *(vibrant)* lebendig [leˈbɛndɪç] ◊ *ein farbenfroher, lebendiger Stil* **3.** *(necessary for to stay alive)* lebenswichtig [ˈleːbm̩svɪçtɪç] ◊ *lebenswichtige Organe*
vitally [adv] enorm [eˈnɔrm] no comp/superl ◊ *Diese Entscheidung ist enorm wichtig für unser Überleben.*
vitamin [noun] Vitamin [vitaˈmiːn] das <-s, –e> ◊ *Gemüse enthält viele wichtige Vitamine.* ♦ *Sie nimmt täglich Vitamin C zu sich.*
vivid(ly) [adj, adv] **1.** *(imagination, memory, colo(u)r)* lebhaft [ˈleːphaft] <lebhafter, am lebhaftesten> ◊ *eine lebhafte Fantasie* ♦ *Das kann ich mir lebhaft vorstellen.* ♦ *Die Farben sind lebhaft.* **2.** *(description, example, image)* anschaulich [ˈanʃaʊlɪç] ◊ *Deine Beschreibung war sehr anschaulich.* ♦ *ein anschauliches Beispiel* ♦ *Sie schilderte die Ereignisse anschaulich.*
vocabulary [noun] **1.** *(words sb knows, words in a language)* Wortschatz [ˈvɔrtʃats] der <-es, Wortschätze> ◊ *Sie liest viel, um ihren Wortschatz zu erweitern.* **2.** *(in a particular field, list of words)* Vokabular [vokabuˈlaːr] das <-s, –e> ◊ *das Vokabular von Juristen* ♦ *technisches Vokabular* **3.** *(list of words)* Vokabelverzeichnis [voˈkaːblfɛɐtsaɛçnɪs] das <-ses, –se> ◊ *ein Wort im Vokabelverzeichnis nachsehen*
vocational [adj] Berufs... [bəˈruːfs] vocational guidance Berufsberatung [bəˈruːfsbəraːtʊŋ] die <-, –en> vocational training Berufsausbildung [bəˈruːfslaʊsbɪldʊŋ] die <-, –en>
voice¹ [noun] **1.** *(of person speaking, faculty of speech, ability to sing)* Stimme [ˈʃtɪmə] die <-, –n> ◊ *eine tiefe/hohe Stimme* ♦ *Ich hörte Stimmen im Hof.* ♦ *Wegen einer Halsentzündung hat sie zurzeit keine Stimme.* in a ... voice mit ... Stimme ◊ *Sie entschuldigte sich mit leiser Stimme.* raise your voice die Stimme heben ◊ *Sprechen Sie mit Ihrem Kind, ohne die Stimme zu heben.* **2.** *(right to express your opinion)* Mitspracherecht [ˈmɪtʃpraːxərɛçt] das <-(e)s, –e> ◊ *Minderheiten ohne politisches Mitspra-*

cherecht have a/no voice (in sth) (*bei etw.*) ein/kein Mitspracherecht haben; (*opinion or the source thereof*) Stimme ['ʃtɪmə] *die* <–, –n> ◊ *kritische Stimmen zur Gentechnik* ♦ *auf die Stimme des Volkes hören* ♦ *die Stimme des Herzens/der Vernunft* give voice to sth einer Sache [dat] Ausdruck verleihen ['aʊsdrʊk fɛlaɛən] <verleiht, verlieh, hat verliehen> ◊ *In ihrem Buch verleiht sie der allgemeinen Sorge über die politischen Entwicklungen Ausdruck.* make your voice heard seiner Meinung Ausdruck verleihen with one voice einstimmig ['aɛnʃtɪmɪç] ◊ *sich einstimmig für/gegen etw. aussprechen* 3. LING Genus Verbi [ˌgeːnʊs 'vɛrbiː] *das* <–, Genera Verbi> ◊ *Wie lautet das Genus Verbi der Form „er wurde geschlagen"?* active voice Aktiv ['aktiːf] *das* <–s, –e> *no pl* ◊ *Das Verb steht im Aktiv.* passive voice Passiv ['pasiːf] *das* <–s, –e> *no pl* ◊ *Steht das Verb im Passiv oder im Aktiv?*

⊛ sb's voice breaks jd kommt in den Stimmbruch
voice² [verb] 1. (*express*) zum Ausdruck bringen [tsʊm 'aʊsdrʊk brɪŋən] <bringt, brachte, hat gebracht> ◊ *Kritik zum Ausdruck bringen* 2. LING stimmhaft aussprechen ['ʃtɪmhaft aʊsʃprɛçn̩] <spricht aus, sprach aus, hat ausgesprochen> ◊ *Das „d" im englischen Wort „dame" wird stimmhaft ausgesprochen.*
volcano [noun] Vulkan [vʊl'kaːn] *der* <–(e)s, –e> ◊ *ein aktiver/erloschener Vulkan* ♦ *Der Vulkan spuckte glühende Lava.*
voltage [noun] Spannung ['ʃpanʊŋ] *die* <–, –en>
volume [noun] 1. (*amount*) Volumen [vo'luːmən] *das* <–s, –> volume of trade Handelsvolumen ['handlsvoˌluːmən] volume of traffic Verkehrsaufkommen [fɛɐ̯'keːɐ̯sˌaʊfkɔmən] *das* <–s, –> the large volume of work die viele Arbeit [diː fiːlə a'rbaɛt] 2. (*amount of space*) Inhalt ['ɪnhalt] *der* <–(e)s, –e> ◊ *Unsere Mülltonne hat 120 Liter Inhalt.* Let the bread rise to twice its original volume. Lassen Sie den Teig gehen, bis er sich verdoppelt hat. 3. (*loudness*) Lautstärke ['laʊtʃtɛrkə] *die* <–, –n> ◊ *die Lautstärke regeln* 4. (*book*) Band [bant] *der* <–(e)s, Bände> ◊ *Shakespeares Dramen in fünf Bänden*
voluntarily [adv] freiwillig ['fraɛvɪlɪç] *no comp/superl* ◊ *Er gab sein Amt freiwillig auf.*
voluntary [adj] 1. (*not obligatory*) freiwillig ['fraɛvɪlɪç] *no comp/superl* ◊ *Die Angaben zur Person sind freiwillig.* ♦ *die freiwillige Teilnahme an einem Kurs* take voluntary redundancy sich abfinden lassen ['apfɪndn̩ lasn̩] <lässt, ließ, hat lassen> 2. (*not paid*) ehrenamtlich ['eːrənˌamtlɪç] *no comp/superl* ◊ *Ihre Tätigkeit ist ehrenamtlich.* ♦ *ehrenamtliche Arbeit/ Helfer* work on a voluntary basis ehrenamtlich arbeiten 3. (*movement*) willkürlich ['vɪlkyːɐ̯lɪç] *no comp/superl* ◊ *die Muskeln, die für die willkürlichen Bewegungen zuständig sind* 4. (*organization*) karitativ [karita'tiːf] *no comp/superl* ◊ *eine karitative Einrichtung*
volunteer¹ [noun] Freiwillige ['fraɛvɪlɪgə] *der/die* <–n, die Freiwilligen> *but: ein Freiwilliger/eine Freiwillige* ◊ *Wie suchen noch Freiwillige, die nach dem Sommerfest aufräumen.*
volunteer² [verb] 1. (*offer to help*) volunteer (for sth) sich freiwillig (zu etw.) melden ['fraɛvɪlɪç mɛldn̩] <meldet sich, meldete sich, hat sich gemeldet> ◊ *sich freiwillig zum Militärdienst/zu einem Experiment melden* volunteer to do sth sich anbieten, etw. zu

tun ['anbiːtn̩ ... tsuː] <bietet sich an, bot sich an, hat sich angeboten> ◊ *Ich bot mich an, die Software zu installieren.* volunteer your services (as sth) sich (als etw.) zur Verfügung stellen [tsuːɐ̯ fɛ'fyːgʊŋ ʃtɛlən] +haben ◊ *Ich stellte mich als Dolmetscherin zur Verfügung.* 2. (*work without pay*) ehrenamtlich arbeiten ['eːrənˌamtlɪç a'rbaɛtn̩] +haben ◊ *Sie arbeitet zwei Tage in der Woche ehrenamtlich im Hospiz.* 3. volunteer an opinion seine Meinung sagen [zaɛnə 'maɛnʊŋ zaːgn̩] +haben ◊ *Ich hätte gern eine Chance, meine Meinung zu sagen.* volunteer a suggestion einen Vorschlag machen [aɛnən 'foːɐ̯ʃlaːk maxn̩] +haben volunteer information Informationen geben [ɪnfoɐ̯ma'tsjoːnən geːbm̩] <gibt, gab, hat gegeben> 4. (*say sb will do sth*) volunteer sb to do sth einfach anbieten, dass jd etw. tut [aɛnfax 'anbiːtn̩ das] <bietet an, bot an, hat angeboten> ◊ *Warum hast du einfach angeboten, dass ich beim Umzug helfe?*; (*by putting their name down*) volunteer sb for sth/as sb jdn für etw./als jdn anmelden [fyːɐ̯... /als ... ˌanmɛldn̩] +haben ◊ *Ihr Musiklehrer meldete sie für einen Wettbewerb an.* ♦ *Warum hast du mich als ehrenamtlichen Helfer angemeldet?*
vomit [verb] sb vomits jd erbricht sich [ɛ'brɪçt] <erbricht sich, erbrach sich, hat sich erbrochen> ◊ *Drei Kinder haben sich im Bus erbrochen.* sb vomits sth jd erbricht etw. ◊ *Sie erbrach das Mittagessen.* ♦ *Blut erbrechen*
vote¹ [noun] 1. (*formal expression of a choice*) Stimme ['ʃtɪmə] *die* <–, –n> ◊ *Wem hast du deine Stimme gegeben?* ♦ *Der Antrag wurde mit 50 zu 20 Stimmen angenommen.* ♦ *Sie zählten 12 Stimmen für den Antrag und 123 dagegen.* cast a vote seine Stimme abgeben 2. (*occasion when people vote*) Abstimmung ['apʃtɪmʊŋ] *die* <–, –en> ◊ *eine geheime Abstimmung* ♦ *Wann wird das Ergebnis der Abstimmung bekannt gegeben?* have a vote on sth über etw. [acc] abstimmen [yːbɐ ... ˌapʃtɪmən] +haben ◊ *Sie stimmten über die Beitragserhöhung ab.* sth is put to the vote über [acc] wird abgestimmt ◊ *Heute wird über die Reformen abgestimmt.* 3. (*total number of votes*) the vote die Stimmen [diː 'ʃtɪmən] <–> *pl* get 30 percent of the vote 30 Prozent der Stimmen bekommen share of the vote Stimmenanteil ['ʃtɪmənˌantaɛl] *der* <–(e)s, –e> 4. (*right to vote*) the vote das Wahlrecht [das 'vaːlrɛçt] *das* <–(e)s> *no pl* ◊ *Vor 100 Jahren hatten dort nur die Männer das Wahlrecht.*
vote² [verb] 1. (*decide by voting*) vote on sth über etw. [acc] abstimmen [yːbɐ ... ˌapʃtɪmən] +haben ◊ *Wir haben über den Vorschlag abgestimmt.* vote for/ against sb/sth für/gegen jdn/etw. stimmen ['fyːɐ̯/geːgn̩ ... ʃtɪmən] +haben ◊ *Er hat gegen mich gestimmt.* ♦ *Sie hat für den Streik gestimmt.* vote to do sth beschließen, etw. zu tun [bə'ʃliːsn̩ ... tsuː] <beschließt, beschloss, hat beschlossen> ◊ *Die Mitglieder haben einstimmig beschlossen, die Beiträge nicht zu erhöhen.* 2. (*in an election*) wählen ['vɛːlən] +haben ◊ *Sie darf noch nicht wählen.* vote sb (as) sth jdn zu etw. wählen ◊ *Er wurde zum Klassensprecher gewählt.* vote Conservative/Labour die Konservativen/Labour wählen
• **vote out** [phras v] (*a person, committee, party*) abwählen ['apvɛːlən] +haben ◊ *Auf der Sitzung wurde der Beirat abgewählt.*; (*a bill, law*) ablehnen

A B C D E F G H I J K L M N O P Q R S T U V W X Y Z

['aplɛ:nən] +*haben* ◊ *Das Parlament lehnte den Änderungsvorschlag ab.*

voter (noun) Wähler ['vɛ:le] der <–s, –> ♀Wählerin ['vɛ:lərɪn] die <–, –nen> ◊ *Viele Wähler stimmten für die neue Partei.*

voucher (noun) Gutschein ['gu:tʃaen] der <–(e)s, –e> ◊ *ein Gutschein im Wert von 20 Euro* gift voucher Geschenkgutschein [gə'ʃɛŋkgu:tʃaen]

vow (noun) *(promise)* Gelöbnis [gə'lø:pnɪs] das <–ses, –se>; *(to God)* Gelübde [gə'lʏpdə] das <–s, –> make a vow that geloben, etw. zu tun [gə'lo:bm̩ ... ʦu:] <gelobt, gelobte, hat gelobt> ◊ *Ich gelobte, mich zu bessern.* exchange vows sich (dat) das Eheversprechen geben [das 'e:əfeʃprɛçn̩ ge:bm̩] <gibt, gab, hat gegeben>

vowel (noun) Vokal [vo'ka:l] der <–s, –e>

voyage (noun) Reise ['raezə] die <–, –n> ◊ *eine Reise mit dem Schiff/ins Weltall* voyage of discovery Entdeckungsreise [ɛnt'dɛkʊŋsraezə] maiden voyage Jungfernfahrt ['jʊŋfenfa:'t] die <–, –en>

vulgar(ly) (adj, adv) **1.** *(person, action)* vulgär [vʊl'gɛ:ɐ̯] ◊ *Sei doch nicht so vulgär!* ♦ *eine vulgäre Ausdrucks-*

weise ♦ *sich vulgär benehmen; (joke, comment, laughter)* dreckig ['drɛkɪç] *(fam)* ◊ *Sie erzählte einen dreckigen Witz.* ♦ *Lach nicht so dreckig!* **2.** *(unattractive, unrefined)* geschmacklos [gə'ʃmaklo:s] <geschmackloser, am geschmacklosesten> ◊ *Sein Anzug ist wirklich geschmacklos.* ♦ *ein geschmackloses Kleid* ♦ *sich geschmacklos kleiden*

vulnerable (adj) **1.** *(easy to hurt)* verwundbar [fɐ'vʊntba:'] ◊ *eine verwundbare Stelle* ♦ *Ich fühle mich zurzeit sehr verwundbar.* jdn verwundbar machen; *(mentally)* verletzlich [fɐ'lɛtslɪç] ◊ *eine verletzliche Frau* ♦ *Er ist sehr verletzlich.* **2.** *(easy to attack)* vulnerable to sb/sth jdm/einer Sache ausgeliefert ['aosgəli:fɐt] *not before ns* ◊ *Sie waren den Angriffen/dem Wetter schutzlos ausgeliefert.* vulnerable to criticism der Kritik ausgesetzt [de:ɐ̯ kri'ti:k aosgəzɛʦt] *no comp/superl, not before ns* **3.** *(easily damaged, affected)* vulnerable to sth anfällig für etw. ['anfɛlɪç fy:ɐ̯] *not before ns* ◊ *Alte Leute sind anfällig für Infektionen.* be in a vulnerable position in einer schwachen Position sein [ɪn aene ʃvaxn̩ pozi'ʦjo:n zaen] +*sein*

W

w, W [noun] w, W [veː] das <–(s), –(s)> ◊ *ein kleines w/großes W* ♦ *W wie Wilhelm*

wage, wages [noun] Lohn [loːn] der <–(e)s, Löhne> ◊ *einen höheren Lohn fordern* hourly wage Stundenlohn ['ʃtʊndn̩loːn] wage rise Lohnerhöhung ['loːnʔehøːʊŋ] die <–, –en>

wagon [noun] **1.** *(drawn by horses)* Wagen ['vaːɡn̩] der <–s, –> ◊ *ein geschlossener/offener Wagen* ♦ *die Pferde vor den Wagen spannen* covered wagon Planwagen ['plaːnvaːɡn̩] horse-drawn wagon Pferdewagen ['pfeːɐ̯dəvaːɡn̩] **2.** *(pulled by a train)* Güterwagen ['ɡyːtɐvaːɡn̩] der <–s, –> ⓔ *be off the wagon* wieder trinken be on the wagon nicht mehr trinken

waist [noun] **1.** *(middle part of the body)* Taille ['taljə] die <–, –n> ◊ *eine schlanke Taille haben* paralysed from the waist down querschnittsgelähmt ['kveːɐ̯ʃnɪtsɡəlɛːmt] no comp/superl **2.** *(of skirts, trousers)* Bund [bʊnt] der <–(e)s, Bünde> ◊ *Die Hose ist am Bund zu eng.*

waistcoat [noun] Weste ['vɛstə] die <–, –n> ◊ *ein Anzug mit Weste*

wait [verb] warten ['vaˈtn̩] <wartet, wartete, hat gewartet> ◊ *Ich warte noch 20 Minuten, und dann gehe ich.* ♦ *Sie müssen leider bis morgen warten.* wait for sb/sth auf jdn/etw. warten ◊ *Ich warte auf den Bus.* ♦ *Er hat eine Stunde auf dich gewartet.* ♦ *Zu Hause wartete ein Brief/eine Überraschung auf ihn.* wait to do sth darauf warten, dass man etw. tun kann ◊ *Sie warten darauf, dass sie nach Hause zurückkehren können.* wait for sb/sth to do sth darauf warten, dass jd/etw. etw. tut ◊ *Ich warte darauf, dass die Geschäfte aufmachen.* keep sb waiting jdn warten lassen What are you waiting for? Worauf wartest du noch? ⓔ *sth can wait* etw. kann warten sb can't wait jd kann es kaum erwarten sth will have to wait etw. muss warten wait and see abwarten just wait until warte nur, bis • **wait on** [phras v] **1.** *(serve)* wait on sb jdn bedienen [bəˈdiːnən] <bedient, bediente, hat bedient> ◊ *Wir wurden von einer netten jungen Frau bedient.* **2.** *(see what happens)* wait on sth etw. abwarten ['apvaˈtn̩] <wartet ab, wartete ab, hat abgewartet> ◊ *Ich warte noch das Ergebnis ab.* • **wait up** [phras v] wait up for sb aufbleiben, bis jd kommt ['aʊfblaɛbm̩ bɪs ... ˌkɔmt] <bleibt auf, blieb auf, ist aufgeblieben> ◊ *Du brauchst nicht aufzubleiben, bis ich komme.* ⓔ *wait up! (in the US)* warte/warten Sie mal! ◊ *Warte mal, ich komme mit dir!*

waiter [noun] Kellner ['kɛlnɐ] der <–s, –> ◊ *Er arbeitet als Kellner.* ♦ *Ich rufe jetzt den Kellner.*

waiting [adj] Warte... ['vaˈtə] waiting list Warteliste ['vaˈtəlɪstə] die <–, –n> waiting room Wartezimmer ['vaˈtətsɪmɐ] das <–s, –>

waitress [noun] Kellnerin ['kɛlnərɪn] die <–, –nen> ◊ *Sie arbeitet als Kellnerin.* ♦ *Rufst du die Kellnerin?*

wake¹ [noun] **1.** *(before or after a funeral)* Totenwache ['toːtn̩vaxə] die <–, –n> **2.** *(from a boat)* Kielwasser ['kiːlvasɐ] das <–s, –> ⓔ *follow in sb's/sth's wake* jdm/einer Sache auf dem Fuße folgen in the wake of sth nach etw.

wake² [verb] **1.** *(yourself)* wake (up) aufwachen ['aʊfvaxn̩] +sein ◊ *Ich bin heute erst um acht Uhr aufgewacht.* wake (up) doing sth aufwachen und etw. tun ◊ *Sie wachte auf und fühlte sich wie neugeboren.* **2.** *(sb else)* wake sb (up) jdn wecken ['vɛkn̩] +haben ◊ *Weck mich morgen bitte um sechs Uhr.* ♦ *Er wurde durch einen lauten Schrei geweckt.* • **wake up** [phras v] **1.** *(feel more lively)* sb wakes up jd wird munter [vɪˈt ˈmʊntɐ] <wurde, ist geworden> ◊ *Sie wird morgens erst nach drei Tassen Kaffee munter.* wake sb up jdn munter machen ['mʊntɐ maxn̩] +haben ◊ *Die kalte Dusche hat mich munter gemacht.* **2.** *(pay more attention to sth)* aufwachen ['aʊfvaxn̩] +sein ◊ *Wann wachen die Politiker endlich auf?; (cause to pay more attention)* wake sb up jdn wachrütteln ['vaxʁʏtl̩n] +haben ◊ *Die Kritik hat die Verantwortlichen wachgerüttelt.* → **wake²**

walk¹ [noun] **1.** *(stroll)* Spaziergang [ʃpaˈtsiːɡaŋ] der <–(e)s, Spaziergänge> ♦ *Ein Spaziergang an der frischen Luft wird uns gut tun.* It's a five-minute walk from the station. Vom Bahnhof sind es fünf Minuten zu Fuß. go for a walk einen Spaziergang machen take sb for a walk einen Spaziergang mit jdm machen take an animal for a walk ein Tier ausführen ['aʊsfyːʁən] +haben ◊ *Die Kinder führen jeden Tag den Hund aus.* long walk Wanderung ['vandəʁʊŋ] die <–, –en> ◊ *Sie unternahmen eine Wanderung.* sponsored walk organisierte Wanderung, bei der die Teilnehmer für einen guten Zweck gesponsert werden **2.** *(way sb walks)* Gang [ɡaŋ] der <–(e)s, Gänge> ◊ *Er hat sie schon an ihrem Gang erkannt.* **3.** *(path)* Weg ['veːk] der <–(e)s, –e> ◊ *Der Weg in den Ort führt durch Wiesen und Felder.* ♦ *Vom Gartentor führte ein Weg zur Haustür.* ⓔ *from all walks of life* aus allen Lebensbereichen take a walk verschwinden ◊ *Verschwinde endlich!*

walk² [verb] **1.** *(move by using your feet)* laufen ['laʊfn̩] <läuft, lief, ist gelaufen> ◊ *Kann der Kleine schon laufen?* ♦ *Ich laufe jeden Tag zur Arbeit.* **2.** *(go, stroll, enter)* gehen ['ɡeːən] <geht, ging, ist gegangen> ◊ *barfuß gehen* ♦ *Kannst du nicht schneller gehen?* walk it zu Fuß gehen ◊ *Ich möchte zu Fuß gehen.* walk towards sb auf jdn zugehen [aʊf ... ˌtsuːɡeːən] <geht zu, ging zu, ist zugegangen> ◊ *Sie ging langsam auf die Kinder zu.* walk up/down sth etw. entlanggehen ['ɛntˈlaŋəˌɡeːən] <geht entlang, ging entlang, ist entlanggegangen> ◊ *Er ging den Flur entlang, bis er zum richtigen Zimmer kam.* walk away weggehen ['vɛkɡeːən] <geht weg, ging weg, ist weggegangen> ◊ *Er ist einfach weggegangen, ohne sich zu verabschieden.* walk in hereinkommen [hɛˈʁaɛnkɔmən] <kommt

herein, kam herein, ist hereingekommen> ◊ *Sie kam herein und setzte sich an den Tisch.* **3.** *(accompany)* walk sb jdn begleiten [bə'glaetn̩] <begleitet, begleitete, hat begleitet> ◊ *Er hat sie immer nach Hause begleitet.* **4.** *(take a pet for a walk)* walk an animal ein Tier ausführen [ˈaɔsfyːrən] <führt aus, führte aus, hat ausgeführt> ◊ *den Hund ausführen* **5.** *(hum) (vanish, get stolen)* verschwinden [fɛˈʃvɪndn̩] <verschwindet, verschwand, ist verschwunden> ◊ *Schließ dein besser Fahrrad ab; hier verschwindet alles.*

◉ let sb walk *(after a trial)* jdn laufen lassen
• **walk around** [phras v] *(show yourself in public)* herumlaufen [hɛˈrʊmlaɔfn̩] <läuft herum, lief herum, ist herumgelaufen> ◊ *Wie kannst du nur in diesem uralten Kleid herumlaufen!* → walk² 2.
• **walk away** [phras v] **1.** walk away (from sb/sth) (vor jdm/etw.) davonlaufen [daˈfɔnlaɔfn̩] <läuft davon, lief davon, ist davongelaufen> ◊ *Du kannst nicht vor der Verantwortung davonlaufen.* **2.** *(steal)* walk away with sth etw. mitgehen lassen [ˈmɪtgeːən lasn̩] <lässt, ließ, hat lassen> *(fam)* ◊ *Er hat meine Kreditkarte mitgehen lassen.* **3.** *(win)* walk away with sth etw. mit Leichtigkeit gewinnen [mɪt ˈlaeçtɪçkaet gəˌvɪnən] <gewinnt, gewann, hat gewonnen> ◊ *Sie haben das Finale mit Leichtigkeit gewonnen.* → walk² 2.
• **walk in** [phras v] walk in on sb jdn überraschen [ybɐˈraʃn̩] <überrascht, überraschte, hat überrascht> ◊ *Der Chef hat ihn überrascht, als er gerade im Internet surfte.* → walk² 2.
• **walk into** [phras v] walk into sth **1.** *(hit)* gegen etw. laufen [geːgn̩ ... laɔfn̩] <läuft, lief, ist gelaufen> ◊ *Das Kind ist gegen den Schrank gelaufen.* **2.** walk into a job ohne Schwierigkeiten eine Stelle bekommen [oːnə ˌʃviːrɪçkaetn̩ aenə ˈʃtɛlə bəkɔmən] <bekommt, bekam, hat bekommen> ◊ *Die Zeiten sind vorbei, als man ohne Schwierigkeiten eine Stelle bekommen konnte.*
• **walk off** [phras v] **1.** *(get rid of a bad feeling, condition)* walk sth off etw. durch einen Spaziergang loswerden [dʊˈç aenən ʃpaˌtsiːɡaŋ ˈloːsveːɐdn̩] <wird los, wurde los, ist losgeworden> ◊ *Komm, wir versuchen, die Kopfschmerzen durch einen Spaziergang loszuwerden.* **2.** *(leave)* weggehen [ˈvɛkgeːən] <geht weg, ging weg, ist weggegangen> ◊ *Sie ist einfach weggegangen und hat uns stehen lassen.*
• **walk out** [phras v] **1.** *(leave)* walk out on sb/sth jdn/etw. verlassen [fɛˈlasn̩] <verlässt, verließ, hat verlassen> ◊ *Plötzlich stand sie auf und verließ die Besprechung.* ◆ *Er hat Frau und Kinder verlassen und ist weggezogen.* walk out of sb's life jdn verlassen **2.** *(stop working)* die Arbeit niederlegen [diː ˈaˀbaet ˌniːdɐleːgn̩] +haben ◊ *Heute legen alle Mitarbeiter die Arbeit nieder.*
• **walk over** [phras v] walk all over sb jdn herumkommandieren [hɛˈrʊmkɔmandiːrən] <kommandiert herum, kommandierte herum, hat herumkommandiert> I won't let you walk all over me. Ich lasse mich nicht von dir herumkommandieren!

walking¹ [noun] SPORT Wandern [ˈvandɐn] das <-s> no pl go walking wandern gehen; *(with two sticks)* Walking [ˈvɔːkɪŋ] das <-s> no pl
walking² [adj] Wander... [ˈvandɐ] walking boots Wanderschuhe [ˈvandəʃuːə] die <-> pl walking holiday Wanderurlaub [ˈvandɐlˌuːɐlaɔp] der <-(e)s, -e>
walkway [noun] Verbindungsgang [fɐˈbɪndʊŋsgaŋ] der

<-(e)s, Verbindungsgänge> ◊ *Über diesen Verbindungsgang gelangt man ins Hauptgebäude.*
wall [noun] **1.** *(side of a room or box, large amount, outer layer of a body part)* Wand [vant] die <-, Wände> ◊ *An der Wand hing ein großes Bild.* ◆ *Er schlug einen Nagel in die Wand.* a wall of boxes eine Wand aus Kisten a wall of water eine Wand aus Wasser a wall of flames eine Feuerwand [aenə ˈfɔøvant] **2.** *(strong exterior structure, emotions or behavio(u)r that keeps people apart)* Mauer [ˈmaɔɐ] die <-, -n> ◊ *Die Mauern des Hauses stehen schon.* a wall of silence eine Mauer des Schweigens brick wall Backsteinmauer [ˈbakʃtaenmaɔɐ] garden wall Gartenmauer [ˈgaˀtn̩maɔɐ] the walls of the city die Stadtmauern [diː ˈʃtatmaɔɐn] pl sea wall Deich [daeç] der <-(e)s, -e>
◉ walls have ears die Wände haben Ohren
wallet [noun] Brieftasche [ˈbriːftaʃə] die <-, -n>
wallpaper [noun] Tapete [taˈpeːtə] die <-, -n> ◊ *vier Rollen Tapete* hang wallpaper (in a room) (ein Zimmer) tapezieren [aen ˌtsɪmɐ] tapeˈtsiːrən] <tapeziert, tapezierte, hat tapeziert> ◊ *Kannst du tapezieren?* ◆ *Wir haben am Wochenende das Wohnzimmer tapeziert.*
walnut [noun] Walnuss [ˈvalnʊs] die <-, Walnüsse> ◊ *eine Tüte gebackte Walnüsse*
wander [verb] **1.** *(go, move with little purpose)* wandern [ˈvandɐn] +sein ◊ *Sie wanderte unruhig durchs Haus.* ◆ *Meine Gedanken fingen an zu wandern.* wander (around) sth durch etw. wandern ◊ *Wir wanderten durch die Stadt.* **2.** *(leave a place)* wander (off) sich entfernen [ɛntˈfɛʀnən] <entfernt sich, entfernte sich, hat sich entfernt> ◊ *Das Kind hatte sich von seiner Mutter entfernt.* Don't wander off by yourself! Rühr dich nicht von der Stelle! **3.** *(when talking)* abschweifen [ˈapʃvaefn̩] +sein ◊ *Er schweifte immer wieder vom Thema ab.* **4.** *(curve)* sich winden [ˈvɪndn̩] <windet sich, wand sich, hat sich gewunden> ◊ *Der Pfad wand sich durch den Wald.*
want¹ [noun] **1.** *(lack)* want of sth Mangel an etw. [dat] [ˈmaŋl̩ an] der <-s> no pl ◊ *ein Mangel an Erfahrung* **2.** *(poverty)* Not [noːt] die <-, Nöte> ◊ *Sie lebten in Not.* ◆ *Nach der Dürre herrscht große Not.* **3.** wants Wünsche [ˈvʏnʃə] die <-> pl wants and needs Wünsche und Bedürfnisse
◉ for want of a better word wenn ich es mal so ausdrücken darf not for want of trying nicht, weil jd sich keine Mühe gegeben hat nicht aus Mangel an persönlichem Einsatz aus Mangel an etw. [dat]
want² [verb] **1.** *(modal: expressing desire, intention to do sth in particular)* want to do sth etw. tun wollen [ˈvɔlən] <will, wollte, hat wollen> +inf ◊ *Ich wollte dir nicht wehtun.* ◆ *Wollt ihr mir das etwa verbieten?* all sb wants is to do sth jd will doch nur etw. tun ◊ *Wir wollen dich doch nur etwas fragen.* if you want wenn Sie wollen, wenn du willst; *(expressed more politely)* mögen [ˈmøːgn̩] <mag, mochte, hat mögen> only in the present tense ◊ *Möchtest du einen Apfel haben?* ◆ *Ich möchte jetzt gehen.* **2.** *(transitive: expressing a wish, intention)* wollen [ˈvɔlən] <will, wollte, hat gewollt> ◊ *Das habe ich nicht gewollt.* ◆ *Wollen Sie noch einen Kaffee?* ◆ *Was willst du denn von mir?* want sth done wollen, dass etw. getan wird ◊ *Er will, dass der Rasen gemäht wird.* want

sb/sth to do sth wollen, dass jd/etw. etw. tut ◊ *Ich will nicht, dass sie mitkommt.* ♦ *Er will, dass das endlich funktioniert.*; *(expressed more politely)* mögen ['møːgn̩] <mag, mochte, hat gemocht> ◊ *Möchten Sie noch einen Tee?* ♦ *Ich möchte, dass du jetzt gehst.*; *(requesting a present)* want sth for sth sich [dat] etw. zu etw. wünschen [tsu: ... ˌvn̩ʃn̩] +haben ◊ *Ich wünsche mir zum Geburtstag eine Uhr.* **3.** *(expressing a demand)* verlangen [fɐ'laŋən] <verlangt, verlangte, hat verlangt> ◊ *Frau Meier, Sie werden am Telefon verlangt.* Mum wants you. *Mama sucht dich.* **4.** *(expressing a necessity)* brauchen ['braʊxn̩] <braucht, brauchte, hat gebraucht> ◊ *Geld/Hilfe brauchen* ♦ *Die Blumen brauchen Wasser.* want doing getan werden müssen [veːgdn̩ mʏsn̩] <muss, musste, hat müssen> ◊ *Der Rasen muss geschnitten werden.*

⊕ you want to do sth *(advice, warning)* Sie sollten etw. tun, du solltest etw. tun ◊ *Sie sollten sich jetzt ausruhen.* ♦ *Du solltest aufhören, ihn zu provozieren.*

• **want for** [phras v] sb wants for sth jdm fehlt es an etw. [dat] ['fɛːlt ɛs an] +haben ◊ *Ihnen fehlt es vor allem an Medikamenten.* sb wants for nothing jdm fehlt nichts ['feːlt ˌnɪçts] +haben

• **want out** [phras v] want out (of sth) (irgendwo) aussteigen wollen ['aʊsʈaeŋvɔlən] <will, wollte, hat gewollt> *(fam)* ◊ *Ich will aussteigen.* ♦ *Du willst aus dem Geschäft aussteigen?*

wanted → want² [adj] **1.** *(looked for by the police)* polizeilich gesucht [poli,ʦaeltç gəˈzuːxt] *no comp/superl* ◊ *ein polizeilich gesuchter Verbrecher* be wanted polizeilich gesucht werden **2.** *(loved and looked after)* geliebt [gəˈliːpt] <geliebter, am geliebtesten> feel wanted das Gefühl haben, geliebt zu werden ◊ *Jedes Kind sollte das Gefühl haben, geliebt zu werden.*

war [noun] **1.** *(between countries or groups)* Krieg [kriːk] der <-(e)s, -e> ◊ *der Krieg gegen den Nachbarstaat* ♦ *Ein Krieg zwischen zwei Staaten bricht aus.* be at war (with sb/sth) sich im Krieg (mit jdm/etw.) befinden go to war einen Krieg anfangen declare war (on sb/sth) (jdm/einer Sache) den Krieg erklären **2.** *(against crime, disease, for power, control)* Kampf [kampf] der <-(e)s, Kämpfe> war against sth Kampf gegen etw. ◊ *der Kampf gegen die Armut* war for sth Kampf um etw. ◊ *der Kampf um die Macht* wage war on sth einer Sache [dat] den Kampf ansagen

⊕ have been in the wars mitgenommen aussehen between the wars zwischen den beiden Weltkriegen a war of words ein Wortgefecht

ward [noun] **1.** *(in a hospital)* Station [ʃtaˈtsjoːn] die <-, -en> admit sb to a ward jdn in eine Station einweisen **2.** *(for local elections)* Wahlbezirk ['vaːlbətsɪrk] der <-(e)s, -e> **3.** *(child)* Mündel ['mʏndl̩] das <-s, -> ward of court Mündel unter Amtsvormundschaft

ward off [verb] abwehren ['apveːrən] +haben ◊ *einen Angriff abwehren*

wardrobe [noun] **1.** *(piece of furniture)* Kleiderschrank ['klaedɐʃraŋk] der <-(e)s, Kleiderschränke> ◊ *Der Anzug hängt im Kleiderschrank.* **2.** *(clothes)* Garderobe [gaˈdəˈroːbə] die <-, -n> ◊ *Sie schneidert ihre Garderobe selbst.*

warehouse [noun] Lager ['laːgɐ] das <-s, -> ◊ *etw.*

aus dem Lager holen

warm [verb] wärmen ['vɛʳmən] +haben ◊ *Ich wärmte die Milch für das Baby.*

• **warm to** [phras v] warm to sb mit jdm warm werden [mɪt ... 'vaʳm veːgdn̩] +sein ◊ *Wir sind sofort mit ihr warm geworden.* warm to sth sich für etw. erwärmen [fyːg ... ɐ,vɛʳmən] <erwärmt sich, erwärmte sich, hat sich erwärmt> ◊ *Für diesen Plan konnte er sich nicht erwärmen.*

• **warm up** [phras v] **1.** *(make warm)* warm sth up etw. aufwärmen ['aʊfvɛʳmən] +haben ◊ *Ich wärme dir das Essen von gestern auf.* **2.** *(become warm)* sb warms up jdm wird warm [vɪ'ʳt 'vaʳm] +sein ◊ *Endlich wurde ihm wieder warm.* **3.** *(prepare for a sport or activity)* sb warms up jd wärmt sich auf [vɛʳmt ... 'aʊf] +haben ◊ *Die Spieler wärmen sich gerade auf.* **4.** *(an engine, a motor)* warm sth up etw. warm werden lassen ['vaʳm veːgdn̩ lasn̩] <lässt, ließ, hat lassen> ◊ *Lass den Motor erst warm werden!* **5.** *(liven up)* sth warms up etw. kommt in Schwung [kɔmt ɪn 'ʃvʊŋ] <kam, ist gekommen> ◊ *Die Party kommt jetzt erst so richtig in Schwung.* warm up the audience das Publikum in Stimmung bringen [das ˌpuːblikʊm ɪn 'ʃtɪmʊŋ brɪŋən] <bringt, brachte, hat gebracht>

warm(ly) [adj, adv] **1.** *(temperature, colo(u)rs, proximity when looking for sth)* warm [vaʳm] <wärmer, am wärmsten> ◊ *warmes Wasser* ♦ *Im Wohnzimmer war es sehr warm.* ♦ *Die Decke hielt sie warm.* ♦ *Orange ist eine warme Farbe.* ♦ *sich warm anziehen* the warm das Warme [das 'vaʳmə] <-n> *no pl* ◊ *Komm schnell rein ins Warme!* **2.** *(friendly)* herzlich ['hɛʳtslɪç] ◊ *ein herzlicher Mensch* ♦ *Die Begrüßung war herzlich.* ♦ *Ich möchte mich herzlich bei Ihnen bedanken.*

warmth [noun] Wärme ['vɛʳmə] die <-> *no pl* ◊ *Wärme erzeugen* ♦ *Er sprach mit großer Wärme.*

warn [verb] warnen ['vaʳnən] +haben ◊ *Ich habe dich gewarnt!* warn (sb) of sb/sth (jdn) vor jdm/etw. warnen ◊ *Die Wissenschaftler warnen (uns) vor den Folgen der globalen Erwärmung.* warn against sth von etw. abraten [fɔn ... 'apraːtn̩] <rät ab, riet ab, hat abgeraten> ◊ *Fachleute raten von dieser Methode ab.* warn that darauf aufmerksam machen, dass [daʀaʊf 'aʊfmɛʳkzaːm maxn̩ das] +haben ◊ *Der Bericht macht darauf aufmerksam, dass die Arbeitslosigkeit zunimmt.*

warning [noun] warning (against sth/sb), warning (of etw./jdm) Warnung (vor) ['vaʳnʊŋ] die <-, -en> ◊ *eine Warnung vor den Gefahren des Rauchens* a warning to sb eine Warnung an jdn advance warning Vorwarnung ['foːʳvaʳnʊŋ] sound a warning (to sb) (jdn) warnen ['vaʳnən] +haben

warrant [noun] **1.** arrest warrant Haftbefehl ['haftbəfeːl] der <-(e)s, -e> search warrant Durchsuchungsbefehl [dʊ'çˈzuːxʊŋsbəfeːl] der <-(e)s, -e> **2.** *(justification, reason)* Grund [grʊnt] der <-(e)s, Gründe> ◊ *Es gibt keinen Grund für dieses Verhalten.* **3.** *(official authority)* Befugnis [bəˈfuːknɪs] die <-, -se> ◊ *die Befugnis zur Parlamentsauflösung*

warranty [noun] Garantie [garanˈtiː] die <-, -n> ◊ *Sind diese Schäden von der Garantie gedeckt?*

wart [noun] Warze ['vaʳtsə] die <-, -> ◊ *Er ließ die Warze entfernen.*

⊕ warts and all *(referring to sb)* so, wie jd ist ◊ *Ich*

liebe dich so, wie du bist. (referring to sth) ungeschminkt ◊ *eine ungeschminkte Darstellung des Lebens in Armut*

wary [adj] wary *(of sb/sth)* vorsichtig *(gegenüber jdm/etw.)* ['fɔ:ɐzɪçtɪç] ◊ *Sei ihr gegenüber sehr vorsichtig; sie wird schnell wütend.* be wary of doing sth Bedenken haben, etw. zu tun [bə'deŋkŉ ha:bm̩ ... tsu:] ◊ *Er hatte Bedenken, mir sein Geld anzuvertrauen.*

wash¹ [noun] **1.** *(of clothes)* Wäsche ['vɛʃə] die <-, –n> ◊ *Die Hose ist in der Wäsche.* ♦ *Ich habe den Pullover in die Wäsche getan.* give sth a wash etw. waschen ['vaʃn̩] <wäscht, wusch, hat gewaschen> need a wash gewaschen werden müssen [gə'vaʃn̩ ve:ɐdn̩ mʏsn̩] <muss, musste, hat müssen> **2.** *(of a boat)* Kielwasser ['ki:lvasɐ] das <-s> *no pl; (of the sea)* Brandung ['brandʊŋ] die <-> *no pl* **3.** *(liquid used instead of soap)* Waschlotion ['vaʃlo,tsjo:n] die <-, –en> ◉ it will all come out in the wash *(truth will be revealed)* es wird schon alles herauskommen *(problem will be resolved)* es wird sich schon eine Lösung finden

wash² [verb] **1.** *(a car, your clothes)* waschen ['vaʃn̩] <wäscht, wusch, hat gewaschen> ◊ *Diesen Pulli kann man bei 40 Grad waschen.* **2.** *(a part of your body)* wash sth sich [dat] etw. waschen ['vaʃn̩] <wäscht, wusch, hat gewaschen> ◊ *Sie wusch sich die Hände.* sb washes jd wäscht sich [acc] ◊ *Sie wusch sich und zog sich an.* **3.** *(carry an object in the water)* spülen ['ʃpy:lən] +haben washed ashore an Land gespült ◊ *Die Leiche wurde an Land gespült.* ◉ sth does not wash with sb jd kauft jdm etw. nicht ab *(fam)* ◊ *Ich kaufe dir deine Ausrede nicht ab.*

• **wash off** [phras v] wash sth off (sth) etw. (von etw.) abwaschen ['apvaʃn̩] <wäscht ab, wusch ab, hat abgewaschen> ◊ *Der Regen hat den Schmutz vom Auto abgewaschen.* sth washes off etw. lässt sich abwaschen [lɛst zɪç 'apvaʃn̩] <lässt, ließ, hat lassen> ◊ *Diese Flecken lassen sich leicht abwaschen.*

• **wash up** [phras v] **1.** *(the dishes)* abwaschen ['apvaʃn̩] <wäscht ab, wusch ab, hat abgewaschen> ◊ *Hast du schon abgewaschen?* ♦ *Wäschst du das Geschirr ab?* **2.** *(in the US: wash yourself)* sich waschen ['vaʃn̩] <wäscht sich, wusch sich, hat sich gewaschen> ◊ *Ich wusch mich und zog mich an.* **3.** *(carried by water and deposited on the shore)* anspülen ['anʃpy:lən] +haben ◊ *Das Meer hat viel Müll angespült.*

washbasin [noun] Waschbecken ['vaʃbɛkŉ] das <-s, ->

washcloth [noun] Waschlappen ['vaʃlapm̩] der <-s, ->

washer [noun] **1.** Dichtung ['dɪçtʊŋ] die <-, –en> **2.** *(washing machine)* Waschmaschine ['vaʃma,ʃi:nə] die <-, –n>

washing [noun] Wäsche ['vɛʃə] die <-> *no pl* do the washing die Wäsche waschen

washing machine [noun] Waschmaschine ['vaʃma,ʃi:nə] die <-, –n>

washing powder [noun] Waschpulver ['vaʃpʊlfɐ] das <-s, ->

wasp [noun] Wespe ['vɛspə] die <-, –n> ◊ *von einer Wespe gestochen werden*

waste¹ [noun] **1.** *(failure to use sth effectively)* Verschwendung [fɛ'ʃvɛndʊŋ] die <-, –en> ◊ *eine Verschwendung wichtiger Rohstoffe* waste of time Zeitverschwendung ['tsaetfɐʃvɛndʊŋ] waste of money Geldverschwendung ['gɛltfɐʃvɛndʊŋ]; *(work, effort)* go to waste verschwendet sein [fɛ'ʃvɛndət zaen] +sein ◊ *Ihre Bemühungen sind verschwendet, weil keiner sie bemerkt.; (perishable food)* verderben [fɛ'dɛrbm̩] <verdirbt, verdarb, ist verdorben> ◊ *Die Beeren sind in der Hitze verdorben.* **2.** *(useless materials)* Abfall ['apfal] der <-(e)s, Abfälle> ◊ *radioaktive/giftige Abfälle* ♦ *Abfall produzieren* **3.** *(empty land)* Einöde ['aen|ø:də] die <-, –n>

waste² [adj] **1.** *(left over)* Abfall... ['apfal] waste product Abfallprodukt ['apfalpro,dʊkt] das <-(e)s, –e> **2.** *(land not built on)* unbebaut ['ʊnbəbaot] *no comp/superl* a piece of waste ground ein unbebautes Grundstück

waste³ [verb] **1.** *(use more than necessary)* verschwenden [fɛ'ʃvɛndn̩] <verschwendet, verschwendete, hat ver­schwendet> ◊ *Zeit verschwenden* ♦ *keinen Gedanken an jdn/etw. verschwenden* waste sth on sth etw. für etw. verschwenden **2.** *(a chance, an opportunity)* vertun [fɛ'tu:n] <vertut, vertat, hat vertan> ◊ *Er hat diese einmalige Gelegenheit vertan.* Their/Our etc. hard work was wasted. Die ganze Arbeit war umsonst. ◉ sth is wasted on sb jd weiß etw. nicht zu schätzen waste not, want not spare in der Zeit, dann hast du in der Not

wastebasket [noun] Papierkorb [pa'pi:ɐkɔʳp] der <-(e)s, Papierkörbe> ◊ *Das kannst du in den Papierkorb werfen.* ♦ *Dateien in den Papierkorb verschieben*

watch¹ [noun] **1.** *(on your wrist)* Armbanduhr ['aʳmbant|u:ɐ] die <-, –en> **2.** *(guard, eople)* Wache ['vaxə] die <-, –n> ◊ *Wer übernimmt die erste Wache?* be on watch Wache haben ◉ be on the watch (for sth) (nach etw.) Ausschau halten keep a watch on sb/sth jdn/etw. beobachten

watch² [verb] **1.** *(look at, monitor)* beobachten [bə'o:baxtn̩] <beobachtet, beobachtete, hat beobach­tet> ◊ *Sie beobachtete die Sonnenfinsternis.* ♦ *Die Polizei lässt ihn beobachten.* watch sb/sth do sth zusehen, wie jd etw. macht ['tsu:ze:ən vi: ... maxt] <sieht zu, sah zu, hat zugesehen> Watch! Schau! Watch me! Schau mal! **2.** *(a film, event etc.)* watch sth sich [dat] etw. ansehen ['anze:ən] <sieht an, sah an, hat angesehen> ◊ *Die Kinder sehen sich ein Video an.* watch the news die Nachrichten sehen [di: 'na:xrɪçtn̩ ze:ən] <sieht, sah, hat gesehen> watch television fernsehen ['fɛʳnze:ən] +haben **3.** *(be careful of sth)* watch sth auf etw. [acc] achten [aof ... ,axtn̩] <achtet, achtete, hat geachtet> ◊ *Achte auf die scharfe Kante.* watch what/how/that etc. darauf achten, was/wie/dass etc. ◊ *Er achtet darauf, dass er nicht zunimmt.* **4.** *(take care of sb)* watch sb/sth auf jdn/etw. aufpassen [aof ... ,aofpasn̩] +haben ◊ *Wer passt auf das Baby auf?* ◉ just watch warts nur ab *(fam)* watch it pass auf watch yourself vorsichtig sein

• **watch for** [phras v] watch (out) for sb/sth nach jdm/etw. Ausschau halten [na:x ... 'aosʃao haltn̩] <hält, hielt, hat gehalten> ◊ *Die Kinder haben schon nach dir Ausschau gehalten.*

• **watch out** [phras v] **1.** *(be careful, look after)*

aufpassen ['a̯ʊfpasn̩] +*haben* ◊ *Wenn du nicht aufpasst, fällst du hin.* ♦ *Sie passt immer auf ihre Schwester auf.* **2.** (be careful of, pay attention to) watch out for sth/sb auf etw./jdn **achten** [a̯ʊf ... ,axtn̩] <achtet, achtete, hat geachtet> ◊ *Worauf muss man in dieser Situation achten?*

• **watch over** ⟨phras v⟩ bewachen [bə'vaxn̩] <bewacht, bewachte, hat bewacht> ◊ *Sie bewachten die Gefangenen Tag und Nacht.*

water¹ ⟨noun⟩ **1.** Wasser ['vasə] das <–s> no pl ◊ *bartes/weiches Wasser* ♦ *ein Glas Wasser* ♦ *Warst du schon im Wasser?* running water fließendes Wasser by water zu Wasser ◊ *Transport zu Wasser* sparkling water Sprudelwasser ['ʃpruːdl̩vasə] **2.** (of a country) waters Hoheitsgewässer ['hoːha̯etsɡəvɛsə] das <–s, –> most pl ◊ *britische Hoheitsgewässer* **3.** (situation) waters Zeiten ['tsa̯etn̩] die <–> pl turbulent waters schwierige Zeiten murky waters unsichere Gewässer [,ʊnzɪçəʀə ɡə'vɛsə] <–> pl ℗ **water under the bridge** Schnee von gestern (fam) it's water off a duck's back an ibm/ihr etc. prallt alles ab

water² ⟨verb⟩ **1.** (plants) gießen ['ɡiːsn̩] <gießt, goss, hat gegossen> ◊ *die Zimmerpflanzen gießen* **2.** (animals) Wasser geben ['vasə ɡeːbm̩] <gibt, gab, hat gegeben> ◊ *dem Hund Futter und Wasser geben* **3.** (from your eyes) tränen ['trɛːnən] +*haben* ◊ *Meine Augen tränen; ich babe Heuschnupfen.* sth makes sb's eyes water von etw. tränen jdm die Augen ◊ *Von dem scharfen Wind tränten ihr die Augen.*

• **water down** ⟨phras v⟩ water sth down **1.** (a statement, an article) etw. abschwächen ['apʃvɛçn̩] +*haben* **2.** (a drink, liquid) etw. mit Wasser verdünnen [mɪt 'vasə fɛ,dʏnən] <verdünnt, verdünnte, hat verdünnt> ◊ *Whisky mit Wasser verdünnen*

waterfall ⟨noun⟩ Wasserfall ['vasəfal] der <–(e)s, Wasserfälle>

watering can ⟨noun⟩ Gießkanne ['ɡiːskanə] die <–, –n>

waterproof ⟨adj⟩ wasserdicht ['vasədɪçt] <wasserdichter, am wasserdichtesten> ◊ *eine wasserdichte Armbanduhr* ♦ *Die Jacke ist nicht wasserdicht.*

watery ⟨adj⟩ **1.** (eyes) tränend ['trɛːnənt] no comp/superl, only before ns ◊ *ihre tränenden Augen* be watery tränen ['trɛːnən] +*haben* ◊ *Seine Augen tränten.* **2.** (coffee, tea, soup) dünn [dʏn] ◊ *Der Kaffee ist mir zu dünn.* ♦ *eine dünne Suppe*

watt ⟨noun⟩ Watt [vat] das <–s, –> ◊ *eine Glühbirne mit 40 Watt*

wave¹ ⟨noun⟩ **1.** (of water or emotion, increase, radio) Welle ['vɛlə] die <–, –n> ◊ *Ein Boot treibt auf den Wellen.* ♦ *elektromagnetische Wellen* ♦ *eine Welle von Demonstranten* ♦ *eine Welle der Begeisterung* **2.** (movement of your hand) Winken ['vɪŋkn̩] das <–s> no pl with a wave winkend ['vɪŋkn̩t] ◊ *Sie fubr winkend davon.* ℗ **make waves** Aufsehen erregen

wave² ⟨verb⟩ **1.** (move your hand) winken ['vɪŋkn̩] +*haben* ◊ *Er winkte lachend in die Kamera.* wave to sb jdm zuwinken ['tsuːvɪŋkn̩] +*haben* wave goodbye to sb jdm zum Abschied zuwinken wave your hand at sth mit der Hand auf etw. ⟨acc⟩ **deuten** [mɪt deːɐ̯ ,hant a̯ʊf ... dɔɡtn̩] <deutet, deutete, hat gedeutet> **2.** (as a sign) wave sb away abwinken ['apvɪŋkn̩] +*haben* ◊ *Ich wollte eingreifen, aber sie winkte ab.* wave sb on jdn weiterwinken

['va̯etəvɪŋkn̩] +*haben* ◊ *Der Beamte winkte uns weiter.* **3.** (flag) sth is waving etw. weht [veːt] +*haben* ◊ *Die Fahnen wehten im Wind.*; (trees) sich hin und her bewegen [,hɪn ʊnt 'heːɐ̯ bəveːɡn̩] <bewegt sich, bewegte sich, hat sich bewegt> **4.** (a flag) wave sth (around) etw. schwenken ['ʃvɛŋkn̩] +*haben* ◊ *Die Kinder schwenkten Fähnchen.* He waved his finger at her. Er drohte ihr mit dem Finger. **5.** (hair) sich wellen ['vɛlən] ◊ *Ihre langen Haare wellen sich.*

• **wave aside** ⟨phras v⟩ wave sth aside etw. zurückweisen [tsu'rʏkva̯ezn̩] <weist zurück, wies zurück, hat zurückgewiesen> ◊ *Sie wies meine Einwände zurück.*
• **wave down** ⟨phras v⟩ wave sth/sth down jdn/etw. anhalten ['anhaltn̩] <hält an, hielt an, hat angehalten> ◊ *Der Grenzbeamte bielt uns an.*
• **wave off** ⟨phras v⟩ wave sb off jdm nachwinken ['naːxvɪŋkn̩] +*haben* ◊ *Sie stand vor der Tür und winkte uns nach.*

wax ⟨noun⟩ **1.** (of a candle) Wachs [vaks] das <–es, –e> most sing ◊ *Von der Kerze tropfte Wachs herunter.* **2.** (in your ears) Ohrenschmalz ['oːrənʃmalts] das <–es> no pl

way ⟨noun⟩ **1.** (path leading to a place or a solution of a problem, road, journey) Weg [veːk] der <–(e)s, –e> ◊ *Rache ist nicht der richtige Weg.* ♦ *Sie lernen neue Wege, um Konflikte zu lösen.* ♦ *Ist das der Weg zum Bahnhof?* ♦ *Es passierte auf dem Weg zur Schule.* ♦ *Ich will ihr nicht im Weg sein/steben.* be on your way auf dem Weg sein I should be on my way now. Ich sollte mich jetzt auf den Weg machen. sth is on the way etw. liegt auf dem Weg sth is out of the way etw. liegt nicht auf dem Weg keep out of sb's way jdm aus dem Weg gehen the way to go der beste Weg ◊ *Verhandlungen sind sicher der beste Weg.* ways and means Mittel und Wege Is there a way around it? Gibt es eine Möglichkeit, das zu umgehen? lose your way sich verlaufen [fɛ'la̯ʊfn̩] <verläuft sich, verlief sich, hat sich verlaufen> force your way into sth in etw. ⟨acc⟩ eindringen [ɪn ... ,a̯endrɪŋən] <dringt ein, drang ein, ist eingedrungen>; (on foot) way back Rückweg ['rʏkveːk]; (in a vehicle) Rückfahrt ['rʏkfaːɐ̯t] die <–, –en> get sth out of the way etw. hinter sich ⟨acc⟩ bringen ['hɪntə ... brɪŋən] <bringt, brachte, hat gebracht> go out of your way to do sth besonders anstrengen, etw. zu tun [bə'zɔndəs ,anʃtrɛŋən ... tsuː] +*haben* **2.** (style, manner) Art [aːɐ̯t] die <–, –en> ◊ *Die Art, wie sie sprach, erinnerte mich an dich.* ♦ *Er hat eine witzige Art.* ♦ *die einfachste Art, Daten zu erfassen* in sb's own way auf jds Art ◊ *Die Kinder versuchen auf ibre Art, zu helfen.* one way or another, either way so oder so [,zoː oːdɐ 'zoː] change your ways sich bessern ['bɛsn̩] +*haben* **3.** (aspect) Hinsicht ['hɪnzɪçt] die <–, –en> in more ways than one in vieler Hinsicht in a way in gewisser Hinsicht It's not right, whichever way you think about it. Es ist nicht richtig, egal wie man darüber denkt. **4.** (direction) Richtung ['rɪçtʊŋ] die <–, –en> ◊ *Das Auto fuhr in die falsche Richtung.* ♦ *in beide Richtungen schauen, bevor man über die Straße geht* the right way round richtig herum ['rɪçtɪç hɛrʊm] the wrong way round verkehrt herum [fɛ'keːɐ̯t hɛrʊm] the other way round andersherum ['andɐshɛrʊm] **5.** (area, environs) Gegend ['ɡeːɡn̩t] die <–, –en> over your way bei dir in der Gegend

⊛ **way of life** 1. *(lifestyle)* Lebensweise 2. *(what people normally do or have)* be/become a way of life die Norm werden/sein **the way things are** wie die Dinge liegen **across the way** *(on the other side of the street)* auf der anderen Straßenseite *(just opposite)* hier gegenüber **know your way around (sth)** sich (in etw. ⌐dat⌐) gut auskennen **be in a bad way** in einem schlimmen Zustand sein **sb can't have it both ways** jd muss sich für eins entscheiden **have come a long way** große Fortschritte gemacht haben **have a long way to go** noch einen weiten Weg vor sich ⌐dat⌐ haben **look the other way** *(look away)* wegsehen **in your own sweet way** wie es jdm passt ◊ *Sie macht alles so, wie es ihr passt.* **get your way** sich durchsetzen **give way** 1. *(break, agree)* give way (to sb) (jdm) nachgeben ◊ *Der Damm gab nach.* ◆ *Warum gibst du ihm immer nach?* 2. *(allow to go before you)* give way (to sb/sth) (jdm/etw.) die Vorfahrt gewähren 3. *(be replaced)* give way to sth etw. abgelöst werden **have a way with sb/sth** gut mit jdm/etw. umgehen können **talk your way out of sth** sich aus etw. ⌐dat⌐ herausreden ◊ *Du kannst dich aus jeder Situation herausreden.* **no way** 1. *(definitely not)* auf keinen Fall 2. *(expressing surprise or disbelief)* unmöglich **by the way** übrigens **the way into sth** der Einstieg in etw. ⌐acc⌐ ◊ *der beste Einstieg in den Journalismus* **a way off** weit

way out ⌐noun⌐ 1. *(exit)* Ausgang [ˈaʊsɡaŋ] der <-(e)s, Ausgänge> ◊ *Wo ist der Ausgang?* 2. *(way of dealing with a problem)* Ausweg [ˈaʊsveːk] der <-(e)s, -e> ◊ *einen Ausweg aus einer unangenehmen Lage finden* **the easy way out** der einfachste Ausweg

⊛ **on the way out** 1. *(when leaving)* beim Hinausgehen 2. *(no longer successful)* be on the way out auf dem absteigenden Ast sein

we¹ ⌐det⌐ wir [viːɡ] ◊ *Wir Menschen glauben, Mittelpunkt der Welt zu sein.*

we² ⌐pers pron⌐ wir [viːɡ] ◊ *Wir hörten einen Schrei.* ◆ *Wie fühlen wir uns denn heute?* ◆ *die Welt, in der wir leben* ◆ *Wir sind es, die dieses Land groß gemacht haben.* → **wir**

weak ⌐adj⌐ 1. *(not strong, not powerful, not loud, unstable, referring to verbs or currency)* schwach [ʃvax] <schwächer, am schwächsten> ◊ *Der Patient ist noch sehr schwach.* ◆ *Das Auto hat einen schwachen Motor.* ◆ *Seine Stimme war schwach.* ◆ *eine schwache Persönlichkeit* ◆ *eine schwache Leistung/Währung* ◆ *Der Kaffee ist mir zu schwach.* ◆ *schwaches Licht* ◆ *schwache Verben* ◆ *Er brachte ein schwaches Lächeln zustande.* **be weak on sth** in Bezug auf etw. ⌐acc⌐ schwach sein ◊ *Die Regierung ist in Bezug auf Wirtschaftsförderung sehr schwach.* **be weak against sth** schwach gegenüber etw. sein ◊ *Der Dollar ist gegenüber dem Euro schwach.* **the weak** Schwache ◊ *Kranke und Schwache brauchen unsere Unterstützung.* **weak point** Schwachpunkt [ˈʃvaxpʊŋkt] der <-(e)s, -e> **be a weak speller** eine Rechtschreibschwäche haben [ˈɛɐ̯nə ˈrɛçtʃraɛpʃvɛça haːbm̩] +haben 2. LING *(unstressed)* unbetont [ˈʊnbətoːnt] no comp/superl ◊ *eine unbetonte Silbe* ◆ *In dem Wort „Rose" ist die zweite Silbe unbetont.*

weaken ⌐verb⌐ 1. *(make weaker)* schwächen [ˈʃvɛçn̩] +haben ◊ *Wie schwächt HIV das Immunsystem?* ◆ *Die lahme Konjunktur schwächt den Dollar.* ◆ *ein geschwächtes Herz* weaken sb's influence jds Einfluss verringern [ˈaɛnflʊs fɛˌrɪŋən] <verringert, verringerte, hat verringert> weaken sb's morale jds Moral untergraben [moˈraːl ˌʊnteˌgraːbm̩] <untergräbt, untergrub, hat untergraben> 2. *(become weaker)* schwächer werden [ˈʃvɛçɐ veːɐ̯dn̩] +sein ◊ *Sie wurde immer schwächer.* ◆ *Seine Stimme wurde schwächer.* 3. *(a building, construction)* die Bausubstanz angreifen [diː ˈbaʊzʊpstants aŋɡraɛfn̩] <greift an, griff an, hat angegriffen> ◊ *Der Tornado hat die Bausubstanz der Bürogebäude baulich angegriffen.* 4. *(prices)* sinken [ˈzɪŋkn̩] <sinkt, sank, ist gesunken> ◊

weakly ⌐adv⌐ schwach [ʃvax] <schwächer, am schwächsten> ◊ *schwach lächeln/protestieren*

weakness ⌐noun⌐ Schwäche [ˈʃvɛçə] die <-, -n> ◊ *die Schwäche des Patienten* ◆ *Ich kenne seine Schwächen.* ◆ *eine Schwäche für Lakritze haben* ◆ *Ich habe eine Schwäche in Mathematik.* ◆ *die Schwächen eines Buches/Produkts* **moment of weakness** schwacher Moment [ʃvaxe moˈmɛnt] <-(e)s, -e> ◊ *Das war der einzige schwache Moment, den ich hatte.* ◆ *in einem schwachen Moment*

wealth ⌐noun⌐ 1. *(riches)* Reichtum [ˈraɛçtuːm] der <-s, Reichtümer> most sing ◊ *Er ist zu plötzlichem Reichtum gelangt.* ◆ *seinen Reichtum zur Schau stellen* ◆ *Sie hat unermessliche Reichtümer angehäuft.* 2. *(large supply)* Fülle [ˈfʏlə] die <-> no pl ◊ *eine Fülle von Möglichkeiten/Informationen*

wealthy ⌐adj⌐ reich [raɛç] ◊ *Sie ist sehr reich.* ◆ *eine reiche Familie* **the wealthy** die Reichen

weapon ⌐noun⌐ Waffe [ˈvafə] die <-, -n> ◊ *Tragen Sie eine Waffe bei sich?* ◆ *biologische Waffen* ◆ *Ihre Schnelligkeit ist ihre stärkste Waffe.* **murder weapon** Mordwaffe [ˈmɔʁtvafə] **nuclear weapon** Atomwaffe [aˈtoːmvafə] **weapon of mass destruction** Massenvernichtungswaffe [ˈmasnfɛɐ̯nɪçtʊŋsˌvafə]

wear¹ ⌐noun⌐ 1. *(damage through use, deterioration)* Verschleiß [fɛˈʃlaɛs] der <-es, -e> most sing ◊ *Dieses Mittel schützt die mechanischen Teile vor Verschleiß.* 2. *(in compound ns)* ... wear ...kleidung [ˈklaɛdʊŋ] die <-, -en> most sing; *(clothing)* evening wear Abendkleidung [ˈaːbm̩tklaɛdʊŋ] sportswear Sportkleidung [ˈʃpɔʁtklaɛdʊŋ]

wear² ⌐verb⌐ 1. *(clothes, jewellery, glasses, your hair)* tragen [ˈtraːɡn̩] <trägt, trug, hat getragen> ◊ *Schmuck/einen Anzug/eine Brille tragen* ◆ *Kann ich diese Farbe tragen oder macht sie mich zu blass?* ◆ *Soll ich mein Haar offen tragen?* **have nothing to wear** nichts anzuziehen haben [nɪçts ˈantsuːtsiːən haːbm̩] +haben 2. *(a facial expression)* wear a smile lächeln [ˈlɛçln̩] +haben wear a frown die Stirn runzeln [diː ˈʃtɪʁn rʊntsln̩] +haben 3. *(damage by overuse)* abnutzen [ˈapnʊtsn̩] +haben, often in adjectival passive constructions ◊ *Der Teppich ist abgenutzt.* **sth is wearing (thin)**, sth has worn (thin) etw. ist abgenutzt ◊ *Die Reifen sind abgenutzt.; (your shoes)* ablaufen [ˈaplaɔfn̩] <läuft ab, lief ab, hat abgelaufen> mostly in adjectival passive constructions ◊ *My shoes are wearing (thin).* Meine Schuhsohlen sind abgelaufen. **wear a hole in sth** ein Loch in etw. ⌐acc⌐ scheuern [aɛn lɔx ɪn ... ʃɔɛɐn] +haben ◊ *Ich habe ein Loch in meine Jeans gescheuert.* 4. *(feelings, patience)* wear thin sich erschöpfen [ɛˈʃœpfn̩] <erschöpft sich, erschöpfte sich, hat sich

erschöpft> ◊ *Allmählich erschöpft sich meine Geduld.*; *(excuse, explanation)* wear thin unglaubwürdig werden ['ʊnglaɔpʊv'dɪç veːɡdn̩] +*sein* ◊ *Deine Ausreden werden langsam unglaubwürdig.* **5.** *(material)* wear well haltbar sein ['haltbaːʳ zaɛn] +*sein* ◊ *Der Stoff ist sehr haltbar.*; *(person)* sich gut halten [guːt 'haltn̩] <hält sich, hielt sich, hat sich gehalten> *mostly pres perf* ◊ *Sie haben sich für Ihr Alter gut gehalten.* **6.** *(accept)* schlucken ['ʃlʊkn̩] +*haben (fam)* ◊ *eine Ausrede schlucken*
• **wear away** ⸢phras v⸣ **1.** *(disappear)* verschwinden [fɛ'ʃvɪndn̩] <verschwindet, verschwand, ist verschwunden> ◊ *Die Inschrift ist fast verschwunden.*
2. *(erode)* wear sth away etw. abnutzen ['apnʊtsn̩] +*haben* ◊ *die Fahrbahn abnutzen* ◊ *Der Lkw-Verkehr nutzt etw. nutzt sich ab* ◊ *Durch den Lkw-Verkehr nutzt sich die Fahrbahn schnell ab.*; *(caused by water)* wear sth away etw. auswaschen ['aɔsvaʃn̩] <wäscht aus, wusch aus, hat ausgewaschen> ◊ *Der Wasserfall hat das Gestein ausgewaschen.* sth wears away etw. wird ausgewaschen ◊ *Langsam wird das Gestein durch Regenfälle ausgewaschen.* **3.** *(sb's feelings)* sth wears away etw. verblasst [fɛ'blast] <verblasste, ist verblasst> ◊ *Ihre Liebe ist verblasst.*
• **wear down** ⸢phras v⸣ **1.** *(deprive of energy, confidence)* zermürben [tsɛ'mvʳbm̩] <zermürbt, zermürbte, hat zermürbt> ◊ *seinen Gegner zermürben*
2. *(damage by overuse)* abnutzen ['apnʊtsn̩] +*haben*, *often in adjectival passive constructions* ◊ *Die Fahrbahn ist abgenutzt.*
• **wear off** ⸢phras v⸣ nachlassen ['naːxlasn̩] <lässt nach, ließ nach, hat nachgelassen> ◊ *Die Wirkung des Medikaments lässt nach einigen Stunden nach.*
• **wear on** ⸢phras v⸣ **1.** *(night, season, year)* voranschreiten [fo'ranʃraɛtn̩] <schreitet voran, schritt voran, ist vorangeschritten> ◊ *Während die Zeit voranschritt, wurden sie immer ungeduldiger.* **2.** *(annoy)* wear on sb an jds Nerven zerren [an … 'nɛʳfn̩ tsɛrən] +*haben* ◊ *Sein Nörgeln zerrt an meinen Nerven.*
• **wear out** ⸢phras v⸣ **1.** *(exhaust)* erschöpfen [ɛ'ʃœpfn̩] <erschöpft, erschöpfte, hat erschöpft> *often in adjectival passive constructions* ◊ *Er war von der harten Arbeit erschöpft.* wear yourself out sich kaputtmachen [ka'pʊtmaxn̩] +*haben (fam)* ◊ *Sie arbeitet Tag und Nacht und macht sich dabei kaputt.*
2. *(damage by overuse)* abnutzen ['apnʊtsn̩] + *haben*, *often in adjectival passive constructions* ◊ *Reifen abnutzen* sth is/has worn out etw. ist abgenutzt; *(your shoes)* ablaufen ['aplaɔfn̩] <läuft ab, lief ab, hat abgelaufen> *mostly in adjectival passive constructions* ◊ *sich* ⸢dat⸣ *die Absätze ablaufen* **3.** *(make a hole in fabric)* durchscheuern ['dʊʳçʃɔøʳn̩] *often in adjectival passive constructions* ◊ *Der Pullover ist an den Ellbogen durchgescheuert.*

wearing → **wear²** ⸢adj⸣ ermüdend [ɛ'myːdn̩t] ◊ *Der Vortrag war sehr monoton und ermüdend.* ◆ *eine ermüdende Tätigkeit*

weather ⸢noun⸣ Wetter ['vɛtɐ] das <-s> *no pl* ◊ *im Urlaub gutes Wetter haben* ◆ *Wie wird das Wetter am Wochenende?* ◆ *Wird das schöne Wetter halten?* ◆ *Im April ist das Wetter oft unbeständig/wechselhaft.* ◆ *… und nun das Wetter für morgen: …* in all weather(s) bei jedem Wetter weather permitting wenn das Wetter mitspielt ◊ *Wenn das Wetter mitspielt, machen wir morgen ein Picknick.* weather vane Wetterhahn ['vɛtɐhaːn] der

<-(e)s, Wetterhähne> weather map Wetterkarte ['vɛtɐkaʳtə] die <-, –n>
◉ keep a weather eye on sth/sb etw./jdn gut im Auge behalten be under the weather nicht ganz auf dem Posten sein
weather forecast ⸢noun⸣ Wetterbericht ['vɛtɐbərɪçt] der <-(e)s, -e> ◊ *Laut Wetterbericht soll es schön bleiben.* ◆ *Der Wetterbericht hat Regen angekündigt.*
weave ⸢verb⸣ **1.** *(a fabric)* weben ['veːbm̩] +*haben* ◊ *Sie kann gut weben.* ◊ *einen Wandteppich weben; (a basket, wreath, garland)* flechten ['flɛçtn̩] <flicht, flocht, hat geflochten> ◊ *Kränze/Körbe flechten* **2.** *(a story)* ersinnen [ɛ'zɪnən] <ersinnt, ersann, hat ersonnen> ◊ *eine spannende Geschichte ersinnen* weave sth into sth etw. mit etw. verweben [mɪt … fɛˌveːbm̩] <verwebt, verwob, hat verwoben> ◊ *Der Roman verwebt Fakten mit Fiktion.* **3.** weave your way through sth sich durch etw. schlängeln [dʊʳç … ʃlɛŋln̩] +*haben* ◊ *sich durch das Gewühl schlängeln*
web ⸢noun⸣ **1.** *(of a spider)* Netz [nɛts] das <-es, -e> ◊ *Die Spinne sitzt in ihrem Netz und wartet auf Beute.* **2.** *(of lies, conspiracy)* Gespinst [gə'ʃpɪnst] das <-(e)s, -e> ◊ *ein Gespinst von Lügen/Intrigen* **3.** *(between an animal's toes)* Schwimmhaut ['ʃvɪmhaɔt] die <-, Schwimmhäute>
Web ⸢noun⸣ the Web das Internet [das 'ɪntɐnɛt] <-s> *no pl* ◊ *im Internet surfen* ◆ *Musik aus dem Internet herunterladen*
web page ⸢noun⸣ Webseite ['vɛpzaɛtə] die <-, –n> ◊ *Von dieser Webseite kann man ein Video herunterladen.*
website ⸢noun⸣ Website ['vɛpsaɛt] die <-, –s> ◊ *Die Website des Hueber Verlags hat die URL www.hueber.de.*
wedding ⸢noun⸣ Hochzeit ['hɔxtsaɛt] die <-, –en> ◊ *Ihre Hochzeit fand am 24. März statt.* ◆ *die silberne/goldene Hochzeit* wedding present Hochzeitsgeschenk ['hɔxtsaɛtsgəʃɛŋk] das <-(e)s, -e> wedding anniversary Hochzeitstag ['hɔxtsaɛtstaːk] der <-(e)s, -e> wedding ring Ehering ['eːərɪŋ] der <-(e)s, -e>
wedge ⸢noun⸣ *(of wood, metal)* Keil [kaɛl] der <-(e)s, -e> ◊ *einen Keil unter die Tür klemmen* lemon wedge Zitronenschnitz [tsi'troːnənʃnɪts] der <-es, -e> wedge of cheese Käseecke ['kɛːzəʔɛkə] die <-, –n>
◉ drive a wedge between people einen Keil zwischen Personen treiben
Wednesday ⸢noun⸣ Mittwoch ['mɪtvɔx] der <-(e)s, -e> → **Monday**
weed ⸢noun⸣ **1.** *(unwanted plant)* Unkraut ['ʊnkraɔt] das <-(e)s, Unkräuter> *most sing* ◊ *Zwischen den Salatpflanzen wuchert/sprießt das Unkraut.* **2.** *(aquatic plant)* Alge ['algə] die <-, –n> **3.** *(slang) (cannabis)* Gras [graːs] das <-es> *no pl (slang)* ◊ *Gras rauchen* **4.** *(pej) (person)* Feigling ['faɛklɪŋ] der <-s, -e> *(pej)*
week ⸢noun⸣ Woche ['vɔxə] die <-, –n> ◊ *Nächste Woche treffe ich mich mit Ute.* ◆ *Er lag eine Woche lang krank im Bett.* during the week unter der Woche once a week einmal die Woche Monday week Montag in einer Woche week after week, week in week out Woche für Woche 40-hour week 40-Stunden-Woche [ˌfɪʳtsɪçˈʃtʊndn̩vɔxə]
weekday ⸢noun⸣ Wochentag ['vɔxn̩taːk] der <-(e)s, -e> on weekdays wochentags ['vɔxn̩taːks] ◊

wochentags um 18 Uhr

weekend [noun] Wochenende ['vɔxŋɛndə] das <-s, -n> ◊ *Kommendes Wochenende bekomme ich Besuch.* ✦ *ein langes Wochenende* at the weekend am Wochenende Have a lovely weekend! Schönes Wochenende!

weekly [adj] wöchentlich ['voeçŋtlɪç] no comp/superl, mostly before ns ◊ *Die wöchentliche Arbeitszeit beträgt 38 Stunden.*

weep [verb] **1.** *(cry)* weinen ['vaenən] +haben ◊ *Er weinte bittere Tränen um seinen Kameraden.* ✦ *aus Trauer weinen* **2.** *(wound, bleed)* nässen ['nɛsŋ] +haben ◊ *Die Wunde nässte stark.*; *(discharge pus)* eitern ['aetən] +haben; *(eyes)* tränen ['trɛːnən] +haben ◊ *Wegen meiner Allergie tränen mir die Augen.*

weigh [verb] **1.** *(have a certain weight, see how heavy sb or sth is)* wiegen ['viːgŋ] <wiegt, wog, hat gewogen> ◊ *Ich wiege 67 Kilo.* ✦ *Die Verkäuferin wog das Gemüse.* ✦ *Ich habe mich gewogen.* **2.** *(consider carefully)* abwägen ['apvɛːgŋ] <wägt ab, wog/wägte ab, hat abgewogen/abgewägt> ◊ *verschiedene Argumente/Möglichkeiten abwägen* weigh sth against sth etw. und etw. gegeneinander abwägen ◊ *die Vorteile und Nachteile gegeneinander abwägen* **3.** *(influence)* weigh against sth/sb gegen jdn/etw. sprechen ['geːgŋ ... ʃpreçŋ] <spricht, sprach, hat gesprochen> ◊ *Die Beweise sprechen gegen ihn.* weigh heavily with sb einen starken Einfluss auf jdn haben [aenən ʃtaʳkŋ 'aenflus aof ... haːbm̩] +haben
• **weigh down** [phras v] weigh sb down eine schwere Last für jdn sein [aenə ʃveːrə 'last fyːɐ̯ ... zaen] +sein ◊ *Die Koffer waren eine schwere Last für mich.* ✦ *Ist die Verantwortung eine schwere Last für dich?*
• **weigh on** [phras v] weigh on sb auf jdm lasten [aof ... ˌlastŋ] +haben ◊ *Seine Pflichten lasteten schwer auf ihm.*

weight¹ [noun] **1.** *(measurement, heavy object, object for measuring how heavy sth is, in sports, importance, influence)* Gewicht [gə'vɪçt] das <-(e)s, -e> ◊ *auf sein Gewicht achten* ✦ *Gewichte auf die Waage legen* ✦ *Der Gewichtheber hob ein Gewicht von 120 kg.* be 10 kg in weight ein Gewicht von 10 kg haben add weight to sth einer Sache [dat] Gewicht verleihen attach/give weight to sth einer Sache [dat] Gewicht beimessen carry weight (with sb) (bei jdm) Gewicht haben lose weight abnehmen ['apneːmən] <nimmt ab, nahm ab, hat abgenommen> gain weight zunehmen ['ʦuːneːmən] <nimmt zu, nahm zu, hat zugenommen> take the weight of sb/sth jdn/etw. tragen ['traːgŋ] <trägt, trug, hat getragen> ◊ *Meinst du, das Floß trägt so viele Leute?* **2.** *(burden)* Last [last] die <-, -en> ◊ *Er trägt die ganze Last der Verantwortung.*
⊚ take the weight off your feet es sich [dat] bequem machen ◊ *Machen Sie es sich bequem!* That's a weight off my mind. Mir fällt ein Stein vom Herzen. pull/carry your weight sich voll einsetzen throw your weight around seinen Einfluss geltend machen ◊ *Sie machte ihren Einfluss geltend, um den Vorschlag durchzusetzen.* throw/put your weight behind sth/sb seinen Einfluss für jdn/etw. geltend machen

weight², **weight down** [verb] beschweren [bə'ʃveːrən] <beschwert, beschwerte, hat beschwert> ◊

Der Ballon wird mit Sandsäcken beschwert.

weird(ly) [adj, adv] seltsam ['zɛltzaːm] ◊ *eine seltsame Geschichte* ✦ *Ich finde ihn sehr seltsam.* ✦ *Der Mann benahm sich recht seltsam.*

welcome¹ [noun] **1.** *(greeting)* Begrüßung [bə'gryːsʊŋ] die <-, -en> ◊ *die offizielle Begrüßung der Gäste* in welcome zur Begrüßung ◊ *jdm zur Begrüßung die Hand reichen* words of welcome Begrüßungsworte [bə'gryːsʊŋsvɔʳtə] die <-> pl; *(reception)* give sb a warm welcome jdn herzlich empfangen [hɛʳtslɪç ɛm'pfaŋən] <empfängt, empfing, hat empfangen> receive a warm welcome herzlich empfangen werden **2.** *(accept a proposal, decision)* give sth an enthusiastic welcome etw. begeistert aufnehmen [bə,gaestərt 'aofneːmən] <nimmt auf, nahm auf, hat aufgenommen> receive an enthusiastic welcome begeistert aufgenommen werden
⊚ outstay your welcome zu lange bleiben

welcome² [adj] **1.** *(received with pleasure)* willkommen [vɪl'kɔmən] ◊ *eine willkommene Abwechslung* ✦ *Sie sind jederzeit willkommen!* A drink would be most welcome. Ich könnte etwas zu trinken vertragen. sb is welcome to sb jd ist jdm willkommen sth is welcome to sb etw. kommt jdm gelegen [kɔmt ... gə'leːgŋ] <kommt, kam, ist gekommen> make sb welcome jdn freundlich empfangen [frɔøntlɪç ɛm'pfaŋən] <empfängt, empfing, hat empfangen> **2.** *(be allowed, invited to do)* be welcome to sth etw. gern haben können [gɛʳn ... 'haːbm̩ kœnən] <kann, konnte, hat können> ◊ *Den alten Fernseher kannst du gern haben.* be welcome to do sth etw. gern tun können ◊ *Du kannst gern zum Essen bleiben.*
⊚ you're welcome (when sb has thanked you for doing sth) gern geschehen

welcome³ [verb] **1.** *(a person, an event)* begrüßen [bə'gryːsən] <begrüßt, begrüßte, hat begrüßt> ◊ *Ich freue mich, Sie hier begrüßen zu dürfen.* ✦ *Der Waffenstillstand wurde als Fortschritt begrüßt.* ✦ *das neue Jahr mit einem Feuerwerk begrüßen* warmly welcome sb jdn herzlich begrüßen welcome sb with open arms jdn mit offenen Armen empfangen [mɪt ɔfənən 'aʳmən ɛmpfaŋən] <empfängt, empfing, hat empfangen>; *(a proposal, decision)* be widely welcomed auf breite Zustimmung stoßen [aof braetə 'tsuːʃtɪmʊŋ ʃtoːsən] <stößt, stieß, ist gestoßen> **2.** *(accept)* gern entgegennehmen [ˌgɛʳn ɛnt'geːgŋneːmən] <nimmt entgegen, nahm entgegen, hat entgegengenommen> ◊ *Wir nehmen Ihre Vorschläge gern entgegen.*

welfare [noun] **1.** *(well-being)* Wohl [voːl] das <-(e)s> no pl ◊ *sich für das Wohl von Kindern einsetzen* **2.** *(protection)* child welfare Kinderhilfe ['kɪndəhɪlfə] die <-> no pl animal welfare Tierschutz ['tiːʳʃʊts] der <-es> no pl **3.** *(provided by the state)* welfare system Sozialsystem [zo'tsjaːlzʏsˌteːm] das <-s, -e> welfare state Sozialstaat [zo'tsjaːlʃtaːt] der <-(e)s, -en> **4.** *(income support)* Sozialhilfe [zo'tsjaːlhɪlfə] die <-> no pl

well¹ [noun] **1.** *(for water)* Brunnen ['brʊnən] der <-s, -> ◊ *einen Brunnen bohren* ✦ *Wasser aus dem Brunnen* **2.** *(for oil, gas)* Bohrloch ['boːʳlɔx] das <-(e)s, Bohrlöcher>

well² [adj] gut [guːt] <besser, am besten> ◊ *gut aussehen* sb is/feels well jdm geht es gut not look (too) well schlecht aussehen ['ʃlɛçt ˌaosze:ən] <sieht

aus, sah aus, hat ausgesehen>
⊙ (all) well and good das ist ja schön und gut it's just as well (that) nur gut, dass ◊ *Nur gut, dass ich einen Virenschutz habe.* get well soon gute Besserung all's well that ends well Ende gut, alles gut all is well es ist alles in Ordnung

well³ [adv] **1.** *(skilfully, satisfactorily, thoroughly, appropriately, reasonably)* gut [guːt] <besser, am besten> ◊ *Das ist dir wirklich gut gelungen!* ◆ *Schlaf gut.* ◆ *Gut gemacht!* ◆ *gut vorbereitet sein* ◆ *vor Gebrauch gut schütteln* ◆ *Ich kenne sie nicht sehr gut.* ◆ *sich gut benehmen* mean well es gut meinen do well by sb jdn gut behandeln sb may/might (just) as well do sth jd kann ebenso gut etw. tun ◊ *Wir können ebenso gut noch etwas warten.* speak very well of sb/sth nur Gutes über jdn/etw. zu sagen haben ◊ *Dein Freund hatte nur Gutes über dich zu sagen.* sb cannot very well do sth jd kann schlecht etw. tun [kan ʃlɛçt] <kann, konnte, hat können> ◊ *Ich konnte ihnen schlecht sagen, dass sie gehen sollten.* **2.** *(very much)* durchaus [dʊˈçlˈaos] ◊ *Sie war sich der Folgen durchaus bewusst.* ◆ *Der Park ist durchaus einen Besuch wert.* **3.** *(temporal: emphasizing a long time)* lange [ˈlaŋə] <länger, am längsten> ◊ *Er kam lange nach Mitternacht nach Hause.* ◆ *Ich bin lange vor dir gegangen.; (spatial: emphasizing a long distance)* weit [vaɛt] <weiter, am weitesten> ◊ *Sie ging weit vor den anderen durchs Ziel.* ◆ *Er lag weit hinter den anderen Fahrern.* **4.** *(also)* as well auch [aɔx] ◊ *Ich habe den Film auch gesehen.* ... and ... as well, ... as well as ... und auch noch ... ◊ *Er hat zwei Portionen Nudeln gegessen und auch noch ein Eis.*
⊙ know full well ganz genau wissen be doing well **1.** *(after an illness)* sb is doing well jdm geht es besser **2.** *(be successful)* be doing well for yourself Erfolg haben

well⁴ [interj] **1.** *(introducing a statement, expressing doubt, anger, expectation, ending a talk)* also [ˈalzoː] ◊ *Also, wie ich schon sagte ...* ◆ *Also, da bin ich mir nicht so sicher.* ◆ *Also, das ist ja eine Unverschämtheit!* ◆ *Also, was ist jetzt?* ◆ *Also, das war's für heute.* **2.** *(qualifying reservation, moderation, expressing resignation)* na ja [na ˈjaː] ◊ *Na ja, ganz so war es nicht.* ◆ *Na ja, so ist das nun mal.* **3.** *(expressing surprise)* well, well; well I never, well now nanu [naˈnuː] ◊ *Nanu, was machst du denn hier?* **4.** *(expressing disappointment)* oh well nun gut [nuːn ˈguːt] ◊ *Nun gut, dann mache ich es eben selber.* **5.** *(expressing agreement)* very well gut [guːt] ◊ *Gut, dann sehen wir uns morgen.*

well(-)... [prefix] *(expressing a positive view of sth)* gut ... [guːt] <besser, am besten> well(-)argued gut begründet ◊ *Ihre Theorie war gut begründet.* well (-)built gut gebaut ◊ *ein gut gebauter Sportler* well (-)dressed gut angezogen ◊ *Ein sehr gut angezogener Mann ist gerade vorbeigelaufen.; (more subjectively)* wohl... [voːl] well(-)bred wohlerzogen ◊ *Er ist nicht sehr wohlerzogen.* well(-)deserved wohlverdient ◊ *eine wohlverdiente Gehaltserhöhung*

well(-)behaved [adj] *(child)* artig [ˈaːrtɪç] ◊ *ein artiges Kind* ◆ *Warst du auch immer schön artig?; (animal)* gut erzogen [guːt ɛrˈtsoːgn̩] <besser erzogen, am besten erzogen> ◊ *ein gut erzogener Hund* ◆ *Dein Collie ist sehr gut erzogen.*

well-being [noun] **1.** *(regarding welfare, happiness, comfort, good health)* Wohl [voːl] das <-(e)s> no pl ◊ *sich um das Wohl seiner Familie kümmern* **2.** *(regarding the body, mind)* Wohlbefinden [ˈvoːlbəfɪndn̩] das <-s> no pl ◊ *etw. für seine Gesundheit und sein Wohlbefinden tun*

well done [adj] durchgebraten [ˈdʊrçgəbraːtn̩] no comp/superl ◊ *Das Fleisch war durchgebraten.* ◆ *ein durchgebratenes Steak*

well known [adj] bekannt [bəˈkant] <bekannter, am bekanntesten> ◊ *Götz George ist ein bekannter deutscher Schauspieler.* ◆ *Sie ist bekannt für ihre Kochkünste.* ◆ *Das Ulmer Münster ist weltweit bekannt.* be well known to sb jdm bekannt sein

west¹ [noun] **1.** *(location)* Westen [ˈvɛstn̩] der <-s> with the article when specifying a place, no pl ◊ *Wo ist Westen?* ◆ *der Westen der USA* **2.** *(Europe and North America)* the West der Westen [deːɐ̯ ˈvɛstn̩] <-s> no pl

west² [adj] West... [vɛst] west coast Westküste [ˈvɛstkʏstə] die <-, -n> most sing west side Westseite [ˈvɛstzaɛtə] die <-, -n> west wind Westwind [ˈvɛstvɪnt] der <-(e)s> no pl

west³ [adv] nach Westen [naːx ˈvɛstn̩] ◊ *nach Westen fahren* west of westlich [ˈvɛstlɪç] [+gen] ◊ *westlich des Dorfes* ◆ *westlich der Grenze; (when followed by a word without the article)* west of westlich von [ˈvɛstlɪç fɔn] ◊ *westlich von München*

westerly [adj] westlich [ˈvɛstlɪç] only before ns ◊ *Der Wind kam aus westlicher Richtung.* westerly wind Westwind [ˈvɛstvɪnt] der <-(e)s> no pl

western [adj] westlich [ˈvɛstlɪç] only before ns ◊ *das westliche Mittelmeer; (in geographical names)* Western ... West... *(very)* **1.** [noun] Western Europe Westeuropa [ˈvɛstlɔɔ,roːpaː] das <-s> article only in combination with attribute, no pl

West German¹ [noun] Westdeutsche [ˈvɛstdɔɔt͡ʃə] der/die <-n, die Westdeutschen> but: ein Westdeutscher/eine Westdeutsche → German¹ **1.**

West German² [adj] westdeutsch [ˈvɛstdɔɔt͡ʃ] mostly before ns ◊ *westdeutsche Bürger*

West Germany [noun] Westdeutschland [ˈvɛstdɔɔt͡ʃlant] das <-s> article only in combination with attribute, no pl → Germany

wet¹ [adj] **1.** *(drenched)* nass [nas] <nasser, am nassesten> ◊ *Sie hängte die nassen Sachen zum Trocknen auf.* ◆ *Meine Haare sind noch nass.* dripping wet tropfnass [ˈtrɔpfˈnas] no comp/superl ◊ *tropfnasses Haar* ◆ *Seine Kleider waren tropfnass.* wet through völlig durchnässt [ˈfœlɪç dʊrçˈnɛst] no comp/superl ◊ *Die Bettwäsche war völlig durchnässt.* **2.** *(paint, cement, weather)* feucht [fɔøçt] <feuchter, am feuchtesten> ◊ *feuchte Farbe* ◆ *Das Klima in Großbritannien ist feucht.* Wet paint! Frisch gestrichen!

wet² [verb] **1.** *(make wet)* anfeuchten [ˈanfɔøçtn̩] <feuchtet an, feuchtete an, hat angefeuchtet> ◊ *einen Lappen anfeuchten* ◆ *seine Lippen anfeuchten* **2.** *(urinate)* wet sth irgendwohin machen [ˈmaxn̩] +haben *(fam)* wet the bed ins Bett machen wet your pants in die Hose machen
⊙ wet yourself **1.** *(be frightened, urinate)* sich [dat] in die Hosen machen *(fam)* ◊ *Ich hätte mir fast in die Hosen gemacht.* **2.** *(laugh very much)* sich vor Lachen in die Hose machen *(fam)*

whale [noun] Wal [vaːl] der <-(e)s, -e>
⊙ have a whale of a time sich köstlich amüsieren

what¹ [det] **1.** *(in questions, exclamations, which kind)*

welcher ['vɛlçɐ] welche ['vɛlçɐ] welches ['vɛlçəs] ◊ *Welcher Begriff ist auf Deutsch richtig?* ♦ *Sieh nur, mit welcher Freude sie das macht!* ♦ *Welches Auto fährt er?* ♦ *Welche Fächer studierst du?;* (more colloquial) was für [vas fy:ɐ̯] ◊ *Was für ein Zufall, dass du auch hier bist!* ♦ *Was für eine Ausrede hat er sich wohl diesmal ausgedacht?* **2.** (all of sth) what … alles …, das [alas … das] what little money I had das bisschen Geld, das ich hatte

what² [interrog pron] **1.** was [vas] ◊ *Was hast du getan?* ♦ *„Sandra!"* — *„Was?"* — *„Komm mal her! Ich will dir was zeigen."* I don't know what to say. Ich weiß nicht, was ich sagen soll. What's your name? Wie heißt du?, Wie heißen Sie? What time is it? Wie viel Uhr ist es? What's up with you? Was ist mit dir los? Now what?; (why) what … for warum [va'rʊm] What are you looking like that for? Warum schaust du so?; (how) what … like wie [vi:] ◊ *Wie war dein Urlaub?* **2.** (with certain German verbs, translation depends on the following verb) wo… [vo:] what (…) about worüber (…) [vo'ry:be] ◊ *„Sie macht sich Sorgen."* — *„Worüber?"* What are you talking about? Worüber sprecht ihr? what … for wofür [vo'fy:ɐ̯] ◊ *Wofür hat er sich entschieden?* Now I know what the money was for. Jetzt weiß ich, wofür das Geld war.; (with certain other verbs) worauf [vo'raʊf] What are you waiting for? Worauf wartest du? What are you hoping for? Worauf hoffst du? what … of woran … [vo'ran] What are you thinking of? Woran denkst du? Do you know what he died of? Weißt du, woran er gestorben ist?; (with certain other verbs) wonach … [vo'na:x] What does it taste/smell of? Wonach schmeckt/riecht es? what … with womit … [vo'mɪt] What do you wash silk with? Womit wäscht man Seide? I would really like to know what he paid for the car with. Ich würde gern wissen, womit er das Auto bezahlt hat. [rel pron] (relative) was [vas] ◊ *Weißt du, an was mich das erinnert?* ♦ *Was ich jetzt brauche, ist ein kühles Bier.*

⊚ know what's what sich gut auskennen what about … **1.** (when enquiring about sb or sth) Was ist mit …? ◊ *Was ist mit deinem Bruder? Kommt der auch?* ♦ *Was ist mit deinem Auto? Ist es immer noch kaputt?* **2.** (when making a suggestion) Wie wär's mit …? ◊ *Wie wär's mit einer Partie Schach?* what if … **1.** (when asking what would happen) was, wenn … ◊ *Was, wenn es schief geht?* **2.** (when making a suggestion) und wenn … ◊ *Und wenn ich die Arbeit übernehme?* **3.** (when dismissing sth) dann … eben … (fam) ◊ *Dann ist der Wagen eben teuer. Wir haben doch genug Geld.* and what's more und außerdem so what, what of it na und (fam) ◊ *„Du bist ja schon wieder zu spät!"* — *„Na und?"* what with mit mit dem/der/den ganzen … ◊ *Sie konnte kaum arbeiten mit dem ganzen Lärm.* ♦ *Ich fand das Spiel mit den ganzen Torchancen sehr spannend.*

what³ [interj] (expressing surprise, asking for repetition) was [vas] ◊ *Was, du hast schon wieder verloren?*

whatever¹ [adv] (in negations) no … whatever nicht der/die/das geringste … [nɪçt de:ɐ̯/di:/das gə'rɪŋstə] ◊ *Du hast nicht die geringste Chance, zu gewinnen!* There is nothing whatever to laugh/worry about. Es gibt nicht den geringsten Grund, zu lachen/sich Sorgen zu

machen. nothing whatever nicht das Geringste ◊ *Das hat nicht das Geringste mit unserem Thema zu tun.*

whatever² [det] (no matter what) welcher/welche/ welches … auch immer [vɛlçe/vɛlçə/vɛlçəs … aʊx 'ɪmɐ] ◊ *aus welchem Grund auch immer* ♦ *Welche Arbeit auch immer er anpackt, ihm gelingt alles.* ♦ *Für welches Kleid auch immer du dich entscheidest, sie stehen dir alle gut.*

whatever³ [pron] **1.** (in questions) whatever … was … eigentlich [vas … aɛɡn̩tlɪç] Whatever became of this actress? Was ist eigentlich aus dieser Schauspielerin geworden? Whatever do you want from me? Was willst du eigentlich von mir? **2.** (expressing indifference, acceptance) egal [e'ga:l] no comp/ superl, not before ns ◊ *„Möchtest du Schinken oder Pute essen?"* — *„Egal."* whatever you do, … egal, was du sonst machst, … ◊ *Egal, was du sonst machst, gib ihm bloß das Geld nicht!*

⊚ whatever next wo soll das noch hinführen whatever you say ganz, wie du willst; ganz, wie Sie wollen or whatever (or sth similar) … oder etwas in der Art ◊ *Wir trinken Wodka, Whisky oder etwas in der Art.*

whatever⁴ [conjunc] (linking two phrases) was auch immer [vas aʊx 'ɪmɐ] ◊ *Sie haben zurzeit „technische Schwierigkeiten", was auch immer das bedeuten mag.*

wheat [noun] Weizen ['vaɛtsn̩] der <-s> no pl ◊ *Wir bauen auf unseren Feldern Weizen an.* ♦ *den Weizen ernten* wheat flour Weizenmehl ['vaɛtsn̩me:l] das <-(e)s, -e> most sing

⊚ separate the wheat from the chaff die Spreu vom Weizen trennen

wheel¹ [noun] **1.** (on a car, bike, device) Rad [ra:t] das <-(e)s, Räder> ◊ *die Räder eines Fahrrads/Autos* meals on wheels Essen auf Rädern spinning wheel Spinnrad ['ʃpɪnra:t] potter's wheel Töpferscheibe ['tœpfɐʃaɛbə] die <-, -n>; (for steering) Steuer ['ʃtɔɐ̯] das <-s, -> ◊ *hinterm Steuer sitzen* take the wheel das Steuer übernehmen **2.** (car) wheels Schlitten ['ʃlɪtn̩] der <-s> sing (fam) ◊ *Er fährt einen schönen Schlitten.*

⊚ the wheel of fortune das Glücksrad The wheels of justice grind slowly. Die Mühlen der Justiz mahlen langsam. the third/fifth wheel das fünfte Rad am Wagen keep the wheels turning alles am Laufen halten start the wheels turning die Dinge ins Rollen bringen

wheel² [verb] **1.** (push) schieben ['ʃi:bn̩] <schiebt, schob, hat geschoben> ◊ *den Einkaufswagen durch den Supermarkt schieben* ♦ *einen Patienten in den Operationssaal schieben* **2.** (fly in circles) kreisen ['kraɛzn̩] +sein ◊ *Geier kreisen am Himmel.*

⊚ wheel and deal mauscheln (fam, pej)

wheelchair [noun] Rollstuhl ['rɔlʃtu:l] der <-(e)s, Rollstühle>

when¹ [adv] **1.** (at that time, in which situation) wann [van] ◊ *Wann wurden Sie geboren?* ♦ *Seit wann trägt er eine Brille?* ♦ *Bis wann schaffen Sie die Arbeit?* **2.** (considering that) wo [vo:] ◊ *Wieso fährt er noch Auto, wo er doch offensichtlich betrunken ist?* **3.** (referring to the past) als [als] ◊ *früher, als er noch einen Bart trug* ♦ *Das war an dem Tag, als Diana gestorben ist.* **4.** (in relative clauses: at, in or on which) wo [vo:] (fam) ◊ *Jetzt kommt die Jahres-*

A B C D E F G H I J K L M N O P Q R S T U V W X Y Z

zeit, wo es wieder früh dunkel wird. ✦ *Irgendwann kommt der Moment, wo man sich entscheiden muss.*

In German relative clauses it is good style to use the article in combination with a preposition rather than *wo*: *Jetzt kommt die Zeit, in der es wieder früh dunkel wird.* — *Irgendwann kommt der Moment, in dem man sich entscheiden muss.*

when² [conjunc] **1.** *(a soon as, whenever, referring to present, future, repeated actions)* wenn [vɛn] ◇ *Melde dich, wenn du fertig bist.* ✦ *Er schickt eine Nachricht, wenn er angekommen ist.* ✦ *Wenn ich Rad fahre, trage ich immer einen Helm.* ✦ *Wenn man seine Pflanzen düngt, gedeihen sie besser.* when working beim Arbeiten [baɛm ˈaˈbaɛtn̩] ◇ *Beim Arbeiten mag sie keine Musik.* **2.** *(referring to a past action, at the same time as)* als [als] ◇ *Als wir anfingen zu essen, klingelte das Telefon.* ✦ *Ich war sehr überrascht, als ich davon hörte.*

whenever¹ [adv] **1.** *(in questions)* wann … jemals [van … ˈjeːmaːls] ◇ *Wann habe ich dir jemals wehgetan?* **2.** *(some time)* irgendwann [ˈɪɐ̯ɡn̩t|ˈvan] ◇ *Das muss ich morgen oder übermorgen oder irgendwann erledigen.* ✦ *„Treffen wir uns um sieben oder um acht?" — „Irgendwann, mir egal."*

whenever² [conjunc] **1.** *(every time)* immer wenn [ɪmɐ vɛn] ◇ *Immer wenn sie dieses Lied hört, wird sie traurig.* ✦ *Immer wenn ich mich bücke, tut mir der Rücken weh.* whenever necessary wenn nötig [vɛn ˈnøːtɪç] whenever possible wenn möglich [vɛn ˈnøːklɪç] **2.** *(at any time, at an unknown time in the future)* wann immer [van ɪmɐ] ◇ *Du kannst mich anrufen, wann immer du willst.* ✦ *Also bis zum nächsten Mal, wann immer das sein wird.*

where¹ [adv] **1.** *(at a place, in which place, referring to a situation)* wo [voː] ◇ *Ich weiß nicht, wo er wohnt.* ✦ *in Köln, wo sie seit Jahren leben* ✦ *Bleib, wo du bist!* ✦ *eine Stelle im Film, wo es richtig spannend wird* ✦ *Ich war an einem Punkt angelangt, wo ich nicht mehr weiterwusste.* This is where I live. Hier wohne ich. This drawer is where I keep my keys. In dieser Schublade bewahre ich meine Schlüssel auf. **2.** *(indicating direction)* where (… to) wohin [voˈhɪn] ◇ *Sie wissen noch nicht, wohin die Reise geht.* ✦ *Wohin führt diese Straße?* Where are you going? Wohin gehst du?; *(to a place)* dahin, wo [ˈdaːhɪn voː] I want where I had last seen her. Ich ging dahin, wo ich sie zuletzt gesehen hatte. where … from woher [voˈheːɐ̯] ◇ *Woher stammen Sie ursprünglich?* ✦ *Woher hast du das viele Geld?* ✦ *Wissen Sie, woher dieser Zug kommt?* Where do you come from? Woher stammen Sie/stammst du?

where² [conjunc] was [vas] ◇ *Was meine Ernährung angeht, bin ich sehr vorsichtig.*

whereas [conjunc] **1.** *(expressing a contrast, comparison)* während [ˈvɛːrənt] ◇ *Sie ist sehr groß, während ihre Brüder eher klein sind.* **2.** LAW mit Rücksicht darauf, dass [mɪt ˌrʏksɪçt ˈdaˌraʊf das]

whereby [adv] **1.** *(with the help of which)* womit [voˈmɪt] ◇ *eine Methode, womit jd ein Problem lösen kann* ✦ *ein System, womit jd effektiver arbeiten kann* **2.** *(according to which)* wonach [voˈnaːx] ◇ *eine Regelung, wonach etw. verboten ist*

wherever¹ [adv] **1.** *(in questions, at which place)* wo … nur [voː: … nuːɐ̯] ◇ *Wo hast du nur diese Schuhe gekauft?; (to which place)* wohin … nur

[voˈhɪn … nuːɐ̯] ◇ *Wohin habe ich nur meine Schlüssel gelegt?* **2.** *(at any place, expressing indifference)* irgendwo [ˈɪrɡn̩tˈvoː:] ◇ *„Wo sollen wir essen?" — „Irgendwo."; (to any place)* irgendwohin [ˈɪrɡn̩tvoˈhɪn] ◇ *„Wohin willst du fahren?" — „Irgendwohin."*

wherever² [conjunc] *(no matter where, who knows where)* wo immer (… auch) [voː: ˈɪmɐ (… aɔx)] ◇ *Wo immer er ist, wir finden ihn.* ✦ *Sie lebt in Neuching, wo immer das auch sein mag.; (to any place)* wohin (… auch) [voˈhɪn (… aɔx)] ◇ *Du kannst gehen, wohin du willst.* ✦ *Wohin sie auch geht, ihr Hund folgt ihr.*

whether [conjunc] ob [ɔp] ◇ *Er wollte wissen, ob ich heute Abend Zeit habe.* ✦ *Ich frage mich, ob etwas passiert ist.* ✦ *Sag mir endlich, ob das wahr ist!* ✦ *Ich weiß nicht, ob ich Huhn oder Lamm nehmen soll.* whether or not … ob … oder nicht ◇ *Ob du willst oder nicht, du gehst jetzt ins Bett!*

which¹ [det] welcher [ˈvɛlçɐ] welche [ˈvɛlçə] welches [ˈvɛlçəs] ◇ *Welche Hose/Welcher Mantel gefällt dir am besten?* ✦ *Welches Auto nehmen wir?*

which² [rel pron] **1.** *(referring back to a noun)* der [deːɐ̯] die [diː] das [das] ◇ *ein Sturm, der alles zerstörte* ✦ *diese Sache, über die ich mich ärgere* ✦ *jenes Spiel, das uns langweilte* **2.** *(referring to a main clause)* was [vas] ◇ *Er wusste nicht mehr ein noch aus, was durchaus verständlich war.* ✦ *Das Wetter war kalt und, was noch schlimmer war, regnerisch.* **3.** *(when the subject is a German masculine or neuter noun)* of which dessen [ˈdɛsn̩] ◇ *ein Prozess, an dessen Ende ich freigesprochen wurde* ✦ *das Auto, dessen Tür aufgebrochen war; (when the subject is a German feminine or pl noun)* of which deren [ˈdeːrən] ◇ *die Woche, deren Ende einfach nicht kommen wollte* ✦ *alle Dinge, deren Namen ich nicht kannte* **4.** which is why weshalb [vɛsˈhalp] ◇ *Sie sieht schlecht, weshalb sie eine Brille braucht.* [interrog pron] which one welcher [ˈvɛlçɐ] welche [ˈvɛlçə] welches [ˈvɛlçəs] ◇ *„Siehst du den Hund/die Frau da drüben?" — „Welchen/Welche?"* ✦ *Es ist mir egal, welchen von beiden du nimmst.* which of us/you/ them wer von uns/euch/ihnen [ˈveːɐ̯ fɔn ʊns/ɔøç/iːnən]

⊛ know which is which sie auseinander halten können ◇ *Die beiden sind Zwillinge. Ich kann sie nicht auseinander halten.*

whichever¹ [det] *(no matter what)* egal, welcher/ welche/welches [eˈɡaːl ˌvɛlçɐ/vɛlçə/vɛlçəs] ◇ *egal, welcher Fehler das sein mag* ✦ *Egal, welche Möglichkeit du wählst, ich bin damit einverstanden.* ✦ *Egal, welches Thema ich anspreche, du hast immer etwas zu meckern.* Take whichever bus comes first. Nehmen Sie/Nimm den ersten Bus, der kommt!

whichever² [rel pron] **1.** *(in a process of selection, referring back to a noun)* denjenigen, der [ˈdeːnjeːnɪɡn̩ deːɐ̯] diejenige, die [ˈdiːjeːnɪɡə diː] dasjenige, das [ˈdasjeːnɪɡə das] ◇ *Von den Bewerbern wählen wir denjenigen aus, der die meiste Erfahrung hat.* ✦ *Beide Lösungen sind gut. Wir nehmen diejenige, die am wenigsten kostet.* ✦ *Es gibt drei verschiedene Modelle. Wählen Sie dasjenige, das Ihnen am besten gefällt.* whichever of us/them wer auch immer von uns/ihnen [veːɐ̯ aɔx ˈɪmɐ fɔn ˌʊns/iːnən] ◇ *Wer auch immer von uns verliert, scheidet aus.* whichever of you wer

auch immer von Ihnen/euch **2.** *(referring back to a clause, whatever)* was immer [vas 'ɪmɐ] ◊ *Du kannst mittags oder abends vorbeikommen, was immer dir lieber ist.* ✦ *Tun Sie, was immer Sie für richtig halten.*

while¹ noun Weile ['vaɛlə] die <-> no pl ◊ *Sie waren eine Weile in Rom.* quite a while eine ganze Weile ◊ *Das ist schon eine ganze Weile her.*

⊚ a little while ago vor kurzem for a little while für kurze Zeit in a little while bald all the while die ganze Zeit

while², whilst conjunc **1.** *(expressing simultaneity or contrast)* während ['vɛːrənt] ◊ *Während ich sprach, blickte er die ganze Zeit aus dem Fenster.* ✦ *Es passierte, während wir in Urlaub waren.* ✦ *Während wir im Überfluss leben, müssen andere Menschen Hunger leiden.* while in hospital/abroad während eines Krankenhausaufenthaltes/Auslandsaufenthaltes **2.** *(at the same time as)* while doing sth beim ... [baɛm] *followed by a nominalized verb* ◊ *Beim Arbeiten mag sie keine Musik.*; *(having already started or not yet finished sth else)* im ... [ɪm] *followed by a nominalized verb* ◊ *Noch im Gehen telefonierte sie auf dem Handy.*; *(because of or although doing sth)* überm ... ['yːbɐm] *followed by a nominalized verb (fam)* ◊ *Überm Nachdenken schlief ich ein.* while doing it/so darüber [da'ryːbɐ] ◊ *Ich tröstete ihn und vergaß darüber meinen eigenen Kummer.*

whine verb **1.** *(complain)* jammern ['jamɐn] +haben ◊ *Er hat immer was zu jammern.* whine about sth über etw. acc jammern ◊ *Sie jammerte darüber, dass sie kein Geld hatte.* **2.** *(beg)* quengeln ['kvɛŋl̩n] +haben *(pej)* ◊ *Hör jetzt auf zu quengeln – du bekommst kein Eis mehr!* **3.** whine (in pain/fear) (vor Schmerzen/Angst) wimmern [(foːɐ̯ ʃmɛʁtsn̩,aŋst) 'vɪmɐn] +haben ◊ *Sie wimmerte vor Schmerzen.* **4.** *(dog: softly)* winseln ['vɪnzl̩n] +haben; *(loudly)* jaulen ['jaʊ̯lən] +haben

whip¹ noun **1.** *(for flogging)* Peitsche ['paɛtʃə] die <-, -n> ◊ *Der Dompteur knallte mit der Peitsche.* **2.** *(politician)* Parteimitglied, das dafür sorgt, dass andere sich der Fraktionsdisziplin unterwerfen chief whip Fraktionsführer [frak'tsi̯oːnsfyːrɐ] der <-s, -> ♀Fraktionsführerin [frak'tsi̯oːnsfyːrərɪn] die <-, -nen>

⊚ have the whip hand die Zügel in der Hand haben

whip² verb **1.** *(strike with a whip)* mit der Peitsche schlagen [mɪt deːɐ̯ 'paɛtʃə ʃlaːgn̩] <schlägt, schlug, hat geschlagen> +haben ◊ *Hören Sie auf, das Pferd mit der Peitsche zu schlagen!*; *(repeatedly: a person)* auspeitschen ['aʊ̯spaɛtʃn̩] +haben **2.** *(lash: wind, rain)* whip (somewhere) (irgendwohin) peitschen ['paɛtʃn̩] +haben ◊ *Der Regen peitschte mir ins Gesicht.* ✦ *Der Wind peitschte Zweige gegen das Fenster.* **3.** *(move quickly)* whip somewhere irgendwo(hin) rasen ['raːzn̩] +sein ◊ *Eine Wagen raste um die Kurve.* ✦ *Ich raste nach oben.*; *(wind)* whip through sth durch etw. pfeifen [dʊrç ... ˌpfaɛfn̩] <pfeift, pfiff, ist gepfiffen> ◊ *Ein eiskalter Wind pfiff durch die Straßen.* The wind whipped through her hair. Der Wind fuhr ihr durchs Haar. **4.** *(take out: your wallet, a knife)* whip sth out etw. zücken ['tsʏkn̩] +haben ◊ *Ich zückte die Brieftasche und bezahlte.* **5.** whip off your hat sich dat den Hut vom Kopf reißen [deːn 'huːt fɔm ˌkɔpf raɛsn̩] <reißt, riss, hat

gerissen> whip off your clothes sich dat die Kleider vom Leib reißen [diː 'klaɛdə fɔm ˌlaɛp raɛsn̩] **6.** *(cream)* schlagen ['ʃlaːgn̩] <schlägt, schlug, hat geschlagen> ◊ *die Sahne für den Kuchen schlagen*

• whip through phras v whip through sth etw. in Windeseile durchgehen [ɪn ˌvɪndəsˌaɛlə 'dʊrçgeːən] <geht durch, ging durch, ist durchgegangen> ◊ *Ich ging in Windeseile die Punkte auf der Tagesordnung durch.* I whipped through the book in no time. Ich verschlang das Buch in null Komma nichts. → whip² **3.**

• whip up phras v whip sth up **1.** *(negative emotions, conflict etc.)* etw. schüren ['ʃyːrən] +haben ◊ *jds Ängste/den Hass schüren* **2.** *(a meal)* etw. auf den Tisch zaubern [aʊ̯f deːn 'tɪʃ tsaʊ̯bɐn] +haben ◊ *Sie hatte ein leckeres Menü auf den Tisch gezaubert.*

whipped cream, whipping cream noun Schlagsahne ['ʃlaːkzaːnə] die <-> no pl

whirl verb **1.** *(in circles)* wirbeln ['vɪrbl̩n] transitive use +haben/intransitive use +sein ◊ *Der Wind hatte Blätter durch die Luft gewirbelt.* ✦ *Die Paare wirbelten über die Tanzfläche.* whirl around/about herumwirbeln [hɛ'rɔmvɪrbl̩n] transitive use +haben/intransitive use +sein ◊ *Schneeflocken wirbelten herum.* **2.** sb's head is whirling (with sth) jdm schwirrt der Kopf (von etw.) [ʃvɪrt deːɐ̯ 'kɔpf] +haben ◊ *Mir schwirrt der Kopf von deinen Fragen.*

whirlpool noun Strudel ['ʃtruːdl̩] der <-s, ->

whisk noun Quirl [kvɪrl] der <-(e)s, -e> ◊ *Butter und Zucker mit dem Quirl schaumig rühren.*

whisker noun *(of cats, mice etc.)* Schnurrhaar ['ʃnʊrhaːr] das <-(e)s, -e>

whiskey, whisky noun Whiskey, Whisky ['vɪski] der <-s, -s> pl 'Whiskey'/'Whisky' when used with expressions of quantity ◊ *zwei Whiskey/Whisky bestellen*

whisper¹ noun **1.** *(quiet words)* Flüstern ['flʏstɐn] das <-s> ◊ *Ihre Stimme war kaum mehr als ein Flüstern.* ✦ *das Flüstern des Windes* They talked in whispers. Sie unterhielten sich flüsternd. **2.** *(rumo(u)r)* Getuschel [gə'tʊʃl̩] das <-s> no pl ◊ *Es gab viel Getuschel über seinen Abschied.*

whisper² verb **1.** *(speak in a low voice)* flüstern ['flʏstɐn] +haben ◊ *Flüstere es mir ins Ohr.* whisper to each other miteinander flüstern ◊ *Die Schüler flüsterten miteinander.* whisper sth to sb jdm etw. zuflüstern ['tsuːflʏstɐn] +haben She whispered to him. Sie flüsterte ihm etwas zu. **2.** *(talk of sth)* munkeln ['mʊŋkl̩n] +haben ◊ *Es wird gemunkelt, dass er ins Ausland gehe.* ✦ *Man munkelt von geplanten Steuererhöhungen.*

whistle¹ noun **1.** *(object)* Pfeife ['pfaɛfə] die <-, -n> blow the whistle pfeifen ['pfaɛfn̩] <pfeift, pfiff, hat gepfiffen> the whistle blows ein Pfeifen ertönt [aɛn 'pfaɛfn̩ ɐtøːnt] <ertönt, ertönte, ist ertönt> **2.** *(sound: made by a person)* Pfiff [pfɪf] der <-(e)s, -e> ◊ *Der Spieler hat den Pfiff des Schiedsrichters nicht gehört.* the final whistle der Schlusspfiff [deːɐ̯ 'ʃlʊspfɪf]; *(by the wind)* Pfeifen ['pfaɛfn̩] das <-s> no pl; *(by a machine)* Pfeifton ['pfaɛftoːn] der <-(e)s, Pfeiftöne> let out a whistle pfeifen ['pfaɛfn̩] <pfeift, pfiff, hat gepfiffen>

⊚ as clean as a whistle **1.** *(legal, honest)* völlig sauber *(fam)* **2.** *(free of dirt)* blitzsauber *(fam)* blow the final whistle das Spiel abpfeifen blow the whistle (on sth) (über etw. acc) auspacken *(fam)* ◊ *bei der Polizei auspacken* wet your whistle die

Kehle anfeuchten *(hum)*

whistle² [verb] pfeifen ['pfaefn] <pfeift, pfiff, hat gepfiffen> ◊ *eine Melodie pfeifen* ♦ *Der Schiedsrichter pfiff ein Foul.* ♦ *Plötzlich pfiffen ihm Kugeln um die Ohren.* whistle for your dog nach seinem Hund pfeifen

white¹ [noun] **1.** *(colo(u)r)* Weiß [vaes] das <–, –> ◊ *ein reines Weiß* ♦ *in Weiß heiraten* **2.** *(the white part of sth)* Weiße ['vaesə] das <–n> *only with the definite article, no pl* ◊ *Sie isst nur das Weiße vom Ei.* the whites of sb's eyes das Weiße in jds Augen **3.** *(person)* Weiße ['vaesə] der/die <–n, die Weißen> *but: ein Weißer/eine Weiße* **4.** *(white wine)* Weiße ['vaesə] der <–n, die Weißen> *but: ein Weißer (fam)*

white² [adj] **1.** *(colo(u)r)* weiß [vaes] <weißer, am weißesten> ◊ *blendend weiße Zähne* ♦ *Die Wäsche war strahlend weiß.* ♦ *weißer und roter Wein* ♦ *Das Opfer ist männlich, weiß und ca. 35 Jahre alt.* white man/woman Weiße ['vaesə] der/die <–n, die Weißen> *but: ein Weißer/eine Weiße* **2.** *(made from wheat)* Weiß... [vaes] white bread Weißbrot ['vaesbro:t] das <–(e)s, –e> white flour Weißmehl ['vaesme:l] das <–(e)s> *no pl* **3.** *(very pale)* bleich [blaeç] ◊ *bleich vor Schreck* **4.** *(coffee, tea)* mit Milch [mɪt 'mɪlç] **5.** *(honest, law-abiding)* anständig ['anʃtɛndɪç]

◉ whiter than white über jeden Zweifel erhaben

whiteboard [noun] Weißwandtafel ['vaesvantta:fl] die <–, –n>

white-collar [adj] **1.** white-collar worker Angestellte ['angəʃtɛltə] der/die <–n, die Angestellten> *but: ein Angestellter/eine Angestellte* ◊ *Arbeiter und Angestellte eines Unternehmens* white-collar job Tätigkeit im Büro [ˌtɛ:tɪçkaet ɪm by'ro:] die <–, –en> **2.** white-collar crime Wirtschaftskriminalität ['vɪrtʃaftskrɪminaliˌtɛ:t] die <–> *no pl*

who [interrog pron] *(nom)* wer [ve:ɐ] ◊ *Wer ist da?; (dat)* wem [ve:m] ◊ *Mit wem redest du da?; (acc)* wen [ve:n] ◊ *Wen suchen Sie denn?* [rel pron] der [de:ɐ] die [di:] das [das] ◊ *der Mann, der die Frauen liebte* ♦ *eine Frau, die viel Erfolg hatte* ♦ *das Kind, das krank war* ♦ *diese Leute, von denen ich dir gestern erzählt habe*

whoever [pron] **1.** *(interrogative, relative: nom)* wer [ve:ɐ] ◊ *Wer zu schnell aufgibt, ist verloren.; (dat)* wem [ve:m] ◊ *Wem wird er je vertrauen?; (acc)* wen [ve:n] ◊ *Lade ein, wen du willst.* **2.** *(no matter who: nom)* wer ... auch (immer) [ve:ɐ ... aox (ˌɪmɐ)] ◊ *Wer du auch bist, komm und hilf mir!; (dat)* wem ... auch (immer) [ve:m ... aox (ˌɪmɐ)] ◊ *Wem auch immer das gehört, er soll sich bei mir melden.; (acc)* wen ... auch (immer) [ve:n ... aox (ˌɪmɐ)] ◊ *Wen auch immer er ihr auch vorstellte, keiner gefiel ihr.*

whole¹ [noun] the whole of it das Ganze [das 'gantsə] <–n> *but: ein Ganzes, no pl* ◊ *Ein Maler muss auch das Ganze sehen können.* a whole ein Ganzes ◊ *Der Stadtkern bildet ein geschlossenes Ganzes.* as a whole als Ganzes ◊ *Was bedeutete das für Europa als Ganzes?* be responsible for the company as a whole für die ganze Firma verantwortlich sein the population as a whole die ganze Bevölkerung the whole of ... der/die/das ganze ... ◊ *der ganze Monat* ♦ *im ganzen Jahr* ♦ *mein ganzes Jahr; (with names of towns, areas or countries)* ganz ... [gants] ◊ *Diese Regelung gilt in ganz Europa/Österreich/Berlin.; (with pl ns)* die gesamten ... [di: gə'zamtn]

◊ *die gesamten Ausgaben/Schüler*

◉ on the whole im Großen und Ganzen

whole² [adj] ganz [gants] *no comp/superl* ◊ *die ganze Welt/Familie* ◊ *Das Glas ist heruntergefallen, aber ganz geblieben.* ♦ *eine ganze Reihe von Vorschlägen* the whole thing das Ganze a whole lot of money/questions eine ganze Menge Geld/Fragen

◉ a whole lot better/cheaper *(in comparisons)* viel besser/teurer

wholly [adv] **1.** *(completely)* völlig ['fœlɪç] *no comp/superl* ◊ *eine völlig unzureichende Leistung* ♦ *völlig unabhängig voneinander sein* **2.** *(in every respect)* durch und durch [ˌdʊrç ʊnt 'dʊrç] ◊ *ein durch und durch bemerkenswertes Buch* ♦ *ein durch und durch böser Mensch* **3.** *(without exception)* gänzlich ['gɛntslɪç] *no comp/superl* ◊ *Die Ware wird gänzlich in Indien produziert.*

whom [interrog pron] *(dat)* wem [ve:m] ◊ *Mit wem spreche ich?; (acc)* wen [ve:n] ◊ *Sie fragt sich, wen sie einladen soll.* [rel pron] *(acc)* den [de:n] die [di:] das [das] ◊ *der Mann, den ich kennen gelernt hatte* ♦ *die Frau, die er geheiratet hatte* ♦ *das Kind, das sie bekamen* ♦ *die Angestellten, die entlassen wurden; (dat)* dem [de:m] der [de:ɐ] denen ['de:nən] ◊ *der Mann, dem ich dies sagte* ♦ *die Frau, der ich kein Wort glaubte* ♦ *das Kind, dem er aufmerksam zuhörte* ♦ *die Angestellten, von denen drei in Urlaub waren* of whom dessen ['dɛsn] deren ['de:rən] ◊ *der Mann/das Kind, dessen Mutter gestorben war* ♦ *die Frau/Frauen, deren Kinder krank sind*

whose¹ [det] **1.** *(relative)* dessen ['dɛsn] deren ['de:rən] ◊ *der Mann/das Kind, dessen Mutter gestorben war* ♦ *die Frau/Eltern, deren Kinder dieses Jahr eingeschult werden* **2.** *(interrogative)* wessen ['vɛsn] ◊ *Wessen Stift ist das? Ich will wissen, wessen Idee das war!*

whose² [interrog pron] wessen ['vɛsn] ◊ *Da lag ein Stift. Ich wusste nicht, wessen. Whose was it? Wem gehörte er/sie/es?*

why [adv] warum [va'rʊm] ◊ *Warum kommst du nicht mit?* ♦ *Ich weiß nicht, warum.* ♦ *Das ist nicht der Grund, warum ich frage.* why ever warum bloß ◊ *Warum hat er das bloß getan?* why ever not warum denn nicht why, oh why warum nur, why that is why darum ['da:rʊm]

wicked [adj] **1.** *(evil)* böse ['bø:zə] <böser, am bösesten> ◊ *Es geschah nicht in böser Absicht.* ♦ *Die Hexe war sehr böse.; (cruel)* gemein [gə'maen] ◊ *Das war gemein von dir!* ♦ *eine gemeine Lüge* **2.** *(laugh, smile)* höhnisch ['hø:nɪʃ] *mostly before ns* ◊ *ein höhnisches Lächeln; (sense of humo(u)r, joke)* bissig ['bɪsɪç] *only before ns* ◊ *Er hat einen bissigen Humor.*

wide¹ [adj] **1.** *(river, street, grin, smile)* breit [braet] <breiter, am breitesten> ◊ *ein breiter Fluss* ♦ *Die Straße ist nicht sehr breit.; (opening, valley, world)* weit [vaet] <weiter, am weitesten> ◊ *eine weite Öffnung* His eyes were wide with fear. Seine Augen waren weit aufgerissen vor Angst. **2.** *(extensive, large)* groß [gro:s] <größer, am größten> ◊ *ein großes Gebiet* ♦ *Die Auswahl war groß.; (interests)* vielseitig ['fi:lzaetɪç] ◊ *eine Frau mit vielseitigen Interessen*

◉ be (...) wide of sth etw. (um etw.) verfehlen ◊ *Der Schuss verfehlte den Pfosten um einen Meter.*

wide² [adv] **1.** *(apart, open)* weit [vaet] <weiter, am

weitesten> ◊ *eine weit geöffnete Tür* ♦ *weit auseinander* 2. wide awake hellwach ['hɛl'vax] *no comp/superl*
⊛ **wide open** 1. *(not protected)* völlig ungeschützt 2. *(not decided)* völlig offen **go wide** danebengehen **shoot wide** danebenschießen

widely [adv] 1. *(by many people)* viel [fiːl] <mehr, am meisten> ◊ *ein viel gelesenes Buch; (believed, expected, known by many people)* allgemein [algə'maen] *no comp/superl* ◊ *Das Phänomen ist allgemein bekannt.* 2. *(over a large area)* weit [vaet] <weiter, am weitesten> ◊ *ein weit gereister Mann* She has travelled widely in Europe. Sie ist in Europa weit herumgekommen. widely available überall erhältlich [ybel,al e'hɛltlɪç] 3. *(to a large degree)* sehr [zeːg] Their views differ widely. Ihre Ansichten sind sehr verschieden. We differ widely on that. Wir sind in diesem Punkt sehr unterschiedlicher Meinung. 4. *(grin, smile)* breit [braet] <breiter, am breitesten> ◊ *Sie grinste breit.*

widen [verb] 1. *(become wider)* sth widens etw. wird breiter [vɪʳt 'braetə] +sein ◊ *Der Fluss wurde breiter.; (clothing, opening)* weiter geschnitten sein ['vaete gaʃnɪtn zaen] +sein ◊ *Die Hose ist unten weiter geschnitten.* 2. *(make wider)* widen sth etw. verbreitern [fe'braetɐn] <verbreitert, verbreiterte, hat verbreitert> ◊ *eine Straße verbreitern; (an opening, a passage, sb's horizons or knowledge)* etw. erweitern [e'vaetɐn] <erweitert, erweiterte, hat erweitert> ◊ *Ich möchte meinen Horizont erweitern.* 3. *(extend, expand, widen sth)* etw. vergrößern [fe'grøːsɐn] <vergrößert, vergrößerte, hat vergrößert> ◊ *das Angebot/ die Auswahl vergrößern* sth widens etw. vergrößert sich ◊ *Die Kluft zwischen ihnen vergrößert sich täglich.*

wide-ranging [adj] 1. *(covering many points)* umfassend [ʊm'fasŋt] *mostly before ns* ◊ *umfassende Reformen/Untersuchungen; (having many facets)* breit gefächert ['braet gə,feçɐt] <breiter gefächert, am breitesten gefächert> ◊ *ein breit gefächertes Kursangebot* ♦ *Das Spektrum unserer Aktivitäten ist breit gefächert.* 2. *(having a palpable effect)* weit reichend ['vaet raeçn̩t] <weiter reichend, am weitesten reichend> ◊ *eine Maßnahme mit weit reichenden Auswirkungen*

widespread [adj] *(frequent)* weit verbreitet [,vaet fe'braetət] <weiter verbreitet, am weitesten verbreitet> ◊ *Fichten sind in deutschen Wäldern weit verbreitet.* ♦ *ein weit verbreitetes Problem; (rejection, resistance, support, interest)* breit [braet] <breiter, am breitesten> ◊ *Die Pläne stießen auf breite Ablehnung.*

widow [noun] Witwe ['vɪtvə] die <-, -n>

widowed [adj] verwitwet [fe'vɪtvət] *no comp/superl* ◊ *Er ist seit sieben Jahren verwitwet.* ♦ *die verwitwete Frau Stein*

widower [noun] Witwer ['vɪtvɐ] der <-s, ->

width [noun] 1. *(of a river, road, room, object)* Breite ['braetə] die <-, -n> ◊ *Das Zimmer hat eine Breite von drei Metern.* ♦ *ein Fluss von beeindruckender Breite* five meters in width fünf Meter breit [fʏnf 'meːtɐ ,braet] 2. *(of a piece of clothing, an opening, a pipe)* Weite ['vaetə] die <-, -n> ◊ *Bei dieser Hose ist die Weite verstellbar.* 3. *(length: of a swimming pool)* Bahn [baːn] die <-, -en> ◊ *Sie schwimmt täglich 20 Bahnen.; (of fabric)* Stoffbahn

['ʃtɔfbaːn]

wife [noun] Frau [fraŋ] die <-, -en> ◊ *Darf ich Ihnen meine Frau vorstellen?; (formal)* Ehefrau ['eːəfraŋ]

wig [noun] Perücke [pe'rʏkə] die <-, -n> ◊ *eine Perücke tragen*

wild¹ [noun] 1. Wildnis ['vɪltnɪs] die <-, -se> ◊ *dem Ruf der Wildnis folgen* in the wilds of South America in der Wildnis Südamerikas 2. *(animals)* in the wild in freier Wildbahn [ɪn fraŋe 'vɪltbaːn]; *(plants)* wild wachsend ['vɪlt vaksn̩t]
⊛ **the wilds** die Pampa *(fam, hum or pej)* ◊ *mitten in der Pampa leben* the wilds of … das finsterste … *(hum or pej)*

wild² [adj] 1. *(not domesticated, civilized, controlled)* wild [vɪlt] <wilder, am wildesten> ◊ *wilde Tiere/Pflanzen* ♦ *die wilde Schönheit der Berge* ♦ *wilde Spekulationen anstellen* ♦ *ein wilder Kampf* ♦ *Die Party war ausgesprochen wild.* drive sb wild jdn wild machen wild about sth/sb wild auf etw./jdn ◊ *Sie ist ganz wild auf Erdbeeren.* 2. *(intense: pain, jealousy, rage)* rasend ['raːznt] ◊ *Ich habe rasende Kopfschmerzen.; (joy)* unbändig ['ʊnbɛndɪç] ◊ *Unbändige Freude überkam mich.* wild panic panische Angst [paːnɪʃə 'aŋst] die <->. 3. *(stormy, rough)* stürmisch ['ʃtʏrmɪʃ] ◊ *eine stürmische Nacht/ Überfahrt* ♦ *Das Meer war stürmisch.* 4. *(crazy, unrealistic)* verrückt [fe'rʏkt] <verrückter, am verrücktesten> ◊ *verrückte Ideen/Pläne haben; (accusations, claims, promises)* haltlos ['haltloːs] *no comp/superl* 5. *(shot, throw etc.)* ungezielt ['ʊngətsiːlt] *no comp/ superl, only before ns* ◊ *ein ungezielter Wurf*
⊛ **go wild** aus dem Häuschen geraten *(fam)* wild with sth außer sich vor etw. ◊ *Ich war außer mir vor Begeisterung.*

wild³ [adv] wild [vɪlt] *no comp/superl* ◊ *wild lebende Tiere* ♦ *wild wachsende Pflanzen*

wildlife [noun] Tier- und Pflanzenwelt [,tiːɐ ʊnt 'pflantsn̩vɛlt] die <-> *no pl* ◊ *die Tier- und Pflanzenwelt Großbritanniens*

wildly [adv] 1. *(in an uncontrolled or unrestrained way, without really thinking)* wild [vɪlt] <wilder, am wildesten> ◊ *wild schreien/um sich schlagen/spekulieren* guess wildly drauflos raten [draʊf'loːs raːtn̩] 2. *(to a great extent)* völlig ['fœlɪç] *no comp/superl* wildly off the mark völlig daneben wildly successful überaus erfolgreich [,yːbe|aʊs e'fɔlkraeç] wildly excited/jealous furchtbar aufgeregt/eifersüchtig [,fʊʳçtbaːʳ 'aɔfgəre:kt/'aefezʏçtɪç] wildly optimistic übertrieben optimistisch [ybe,triːbm̩ ɔpti'mɪstɪʃ] wildly nicht übermäßig [nɪçt 'yːbemɛːsɪç] ◊ *Ich bin nicht übermäßig begeistert davon.*

wilful [adj] 1. *(deliberate)* absichtlich ['apzɪçtlɪç] *no comp/superl* ◊ *ein absichtlicher Fehler; (premeditated)* vorsätzlich ['foːgzɛtslɪç] *no comp/superl* ◊ *vorsätzliche Brandstiftung* ♦ *Sein Verhalten war vorsätzlich und rechtswidrig.; (damage, destruction, injury)* mutwillig ['muːtvɪlɪç] *no comp/superl, mostly before ns* ◊ *mutwillige Zerstörung/Beschädigung* 2. *(arbitrary, strong-willed)* eigenwillig ['aegn̩vɪlɪç] ◊ *Ist Leo immer so eigenwillig?* ♦ *ein eigenwilliges Kind*

wilfully [adv] absichtlich ['apzɪçtlɪç] *no comp/superl* ◊ *Er hat sie absichtlich falsch verstanden.; (premeditated)* vorsätzlich ['foːgzɛtslɪç] *no comp/superl* ◊ *jdm vorsätzlich schaden; (damage, destruct, injure)* mutwillig ['muːtvɪlɪç] *no comp/superl* ◊ *etw.*

mutwillig zerstören

will¹ [noun] **1.** *(faculty, intention)* Wille ['vɪlə] der <−n> *no pl ◊ Er hat einen starken Willen. ♦ Ich wurde gegen meinen Willen aufgehalten. ♦ aus freiem Willen* will to live Lebenswille ['le:bm̩svɪlə] **2.** *(document)* Testament [tɛsta'mɛnt] das <−(e)s, −e> ◊ *Hast du schon dein/ein Testament gemacht?*
ⓔ *with the best will in the world* beim besten Willen nicht *where there's a will, there's a way* wo ein Wille ist, ist auch ein Weg *at will* nach Belieben

will² [verb] **1.** *(as part of the future tense)* werden ['ve:ɐ̯dn̩] *only present tense forms, +inf ◊ Werdet ihr morgen abreisen? ♦ Wird es funktionieren? ♦ Du wirst pünktlich sein, hast du mich verstanden?* She won't like it. Es wird ihr nicht gefallen **2.** *(in polite requests or assertions)* sb will do sth jd würde etw. tun ['vʏdə] *subjunctive II ◊ Würdest du bitte das Fenster aufmachen? ♦ Ich würde mich sehr darüber freuen.* Will you have a cup of tea? Hätten Sie gern eine Tasse Tee? Won't you please tell me why? Sag mir doch bitte, warum! **3.** *(expressing a property, an inevitability, ability)* sth will do sth etw. tut etw. [...] Water will freeze at 0° Celsius. Wasser gefriert bei 0° Celsius. She'll go to bed at ten. Sie geht um zehn ins Bett. Boys will be boys. Jungen sind nun mal so. **4.** *(modal: expressing an intention, desire to do sth)* sb/sth will do sth jd/etw. will etw. tun [vɪl] <will, wollte, hat wollen> ◊ *Sie will nicht mit mir sprechen.* The door wouldn't open. Die Tür wollte nicht aufgehen. If you will risk it, then go ahead. Wenn du es unbedingt riskieren willst, dann tu's. Won't you come with me? Möchtest du nicht mitkommen? **5.** *(transitive: making a wish for sth)* will sth sich [dat] etw. wünschen ['vʏnʃn̩] *+haben* He watched the ball, willing it to go in. Er beobachtete den Ball und wünschte sich inständig, er würde treffen. **6.** *(transitive: make sth happen)* will sb/sth to do sth jdn/etw. zu etw. bringen [tsuː ... brɪŋən] <bringt, brachte, hat gebracht> He remembered, because she willed him to. Sie brachte ihn dazu, sich wieder zu erinnern. **7.** *(transitive: want)* wollen ['vɔlən] <will, wollte, hat gewollt> ◊ *Nenne es, wie du willst, es bleibt doch das Gleiche.* **8.** *(as a question tag)* won't you/he etc.?, will you/he etc.? oder? ['oːdɐ] ◊ *Sie wird schon kommen, oder? ♦ Er wird mich nicht anschreien, oder?*
ⓔ *if you will* **1.** *(asking sb to do sth)* doch mal ◊ *Erinnre dich doch mal an Monika, die war auch so.* **2.** *(so to speak)* wenn man so will ◊ *Er ist ernster als die anderen, erwachsener, wenn man so will.*

willing [adj] **1.** *(prepared, ready)* bereit [bə'raɛt] <bereiter, am bereitesten> *seldom comp/superl, not before ns ◊ Er war nicht bereit, das zu tun. ♦ Sie zeigte sich bereit mitzuarbeiten.* **2.** *(keen, eager: student, worker)* fleißig ['flaɛsɪç] ◊ *fleißige Schüler;* *(volunteer)* hilfsbereit ['hɪlfsbəraɛt] <hilfsbereiter, am hilfsbereitesten>; *(listener)* geneigt [gə'naɛkt] <geneigter, am geneigtesten>; *(victim)* freiwillig ['fraɛvɪlɪç]

willingly [adv] bereitwillig [bə'raɛtvɪlɪç] ◊ *Die alte Dame gab bereitwillig Auskunft.*

willingness [noun] Bereitschaft [bə'raɛtʃaft] die <−, −en> ◊ *Ihnen fehlt die Bereitschaft, sich für andere einzusetzen.*

willow [noun] Weide ['vaɛdə] die <−, −n> ◊ *die alte Weide am Fluss ♦ ein aus Weide geflochtener Korb*

win¹ [noun] **1.** *(victory)* Sieg [ziːk] der <−(e)s, −e> ◊ *ein klarer/leichter Sieg.* **2.** *(prize)* Gewinn [gə'vɪn] der <−s, −e> ◊ *einen Gewinn von 3000 Euro machen*

win² [verb] **1.** *(a competition, prize, an argument, sb's support)* gewinnen [gə'vɪnən] <gewinnt, gewann, hat gewonnen> ◊ *den Krieg/eine Schachpartie gewinnen ♦ Ich habe im Lotto gewonnen. ♦ Welche Mannschaft hat gewonnen? ♦ Sie konnte die Kritiker für sich gewinnen.*; *(a point)* erzielen [ɛ'tsiːlən] <erzielt, erzielte, hat erzielt> ◊ *Sie haben fünf Punkte erzielt.* **2.** *(in a war, battle)* siegen ['ziːgŋ̍] *+haben ◊ Napoleon siegte in der Schlacht von Austerlitz. ♦ Am Ende siegte die Vernunft.* **3.** *(a person, sb's heart)* erobern [ɛ'oːbɐn] <erobert, eroberte, hat erobert> ◊ *Er setzte alles daran, sie/ihr Herz zu erobern.* **4.** *(get, obtain)* erhalten [ɛ'haltn̩] <erhält, erhielt, hat erhalten> ◊ *einen Auftrag/ein Stipendium/jds Unterstützung erhalten* **5.** win sb sth jdm etw. einbringen ['aɛnbrɪŋən] <bringt ein, brachte ein, hat eingebracht> ◊ *Sein Verhalten hat ihm ihr Vertrauen eingebracht.*
ⓔ *win some, lose some* man kann nicht immer gewinnen *win or lose* was auch passiert
• **win back** [phras v] win sb/sth back jdn/etw. zurückgewinnen [tsu'rʏkgəvɪnən] <gewinnt zurück, gewann zurück, hat zurückgewonnen> ◊ *jds Freundschaft/sein Geld zurückgewinnen*
• **win out** [phras v] sich durchsetzen ['dʊɐ̯çzɛtsn̩] <setzt sich durch, setzte sich durch, hat sich durchgesetzt> ◊ *Unsere Mannschaft wird sich gegen die anderen Teilnehmer durchsetzen.*
• **win over** [phras v] win sb over jdn für sich gewinnen [fyːɐ̯ ... gə'vɪnən] <gewinnt, gewann, hat gewonnen> ◊ *Wie können wir die Öffentlichkeit für uns gewinnen?* win sb over to sth jdn für etw. gewinnen ◊ *Ich versuche, noch mehr Leute für unsere Aktion zu gewinnen.* win sb over to your side jdn auf seine Seite ziehen [aɔf zaɛnə 'zaɛtə tsiːən] <zieht, zog, hat gezogen> win sb over to your point of view jdn von seiner Ansicht überzeugen [fɔn zaɛnɐ ˌanzɪçt ybɐ'tsɔɔgŋ̍] <überzeugt, überzeugte, hat überzeugt>
• **win through** [phras v] → **win out**

wind¹ [noun] **1.** *(in the air)* Wind [vɪnt] der <−(e)s, −e> ◊ *Ein kalter Wind blies ihr ins Gesicht. ♦ Der Wind stand günstig.* **2.** *(in your lungs)* Atem ['aːtəm] der <−s> *no pl* get your wind wieder zu Atem kommen lose/have lost your wind außer Atem geraten/sein **3.** *(in the UK: gas in the stomach)* Blähung ['blɛːʊŋ] die <−, −en> ◊ *Blähungen bekommen/haben* break wind einen fahren lassen [aɛnən 'faːrən lasn̩] <lässt, ließ, hat lassen> *(fam)*
ⓔ *the winds of change* ein frischer Wind *be in the wind* in der Luft liegen *get wind of sth* von etw. Wind bekommen *(fam) put the wind up sb* jdn das Fürchten lehren

wind² [verb] **1.** *(wrap)* wickeln ['vɪkl̩n] *+haben* wind sth round sth etw. um etw. wickeln ◊ *Ich wickelte mir ein Taschentuch um den Finger.* wind sth into a ball etw. aufwickeln ['aɔfvɪkl̩n] *+haben ◊ Sie wickelte die Wolle auf.* **2.** *(road, river)* sth winds somewhere etw. windet sich irgendwohin ['vɪndət zɪç] <wand sich, hat sich gewunden> ◊ *Ein Fluss windet sich durch das enge Tal.* **3.** *(person, serpent)* sich schlängeln ['ʃlɛŋl̩n] *+haben ◊ Wir schlängelten uns durch das*

Gewühl. **4.** *(a clock)* wind (up) aufziehen ['ao̯ftsi:ən] <zieht auf, zog auf, hat aufgezogen> ◊ *eine Spieluhr aufziehen* **5.** wind forward/on vorspulen ['fo:ɐ̯ʃpu:lən] +haben ◊ *die Kassette/das Band vorspulen* ✦ *zum Ende des Films vorspulen*; *(camera)* transportieren [transpɔrˈtiːrən] <transportiert, transportierte, hat transportiert> ◊ *Der Fotoapparat transportiert nicht.* ✦ *den Film transportieren* wind back zurückspulen [tsuˈrʏkʃpuːlən] +haben **6.** *(a window)* wind down runterkurbeln ['rʊntɐkʊrbl̩n] +haben wind up hochkurbeln ['hoːxkʊrbl̩n] +haben

- **wind up** ⟨phras v⟩ **1.** *(end)* schließen ['ʃliːsn̩] <schließt, schloss, hat geschlossen> ◊ *Können wir die Sitzung jetzt schließen?* ✦ *Er schloss mit den Worten: „Vielen Dank!"* **2.** *(a company)* abwickeln ['apvɪkl̩n] +haben ◊ *Die Firma ging pleite und wurde abgewickelt.* **3.** *(end up)* wind up somewhere irgendwo landen ['landn̩] <landet, landete, ist gelandet> *(fam)* ◊ *Am Schluss landeten wir doch bei ihr.* wind up in trouble sich ⟨dat⟩ Schwierigkeiten einhandeln ['ʃviːrɪçkaɪtn̩ ˌaɪnhandl̩n] +haben **4.** *(tease)* wind sb up jdn aufziehen ['ao̯ftsi:ən] <zieht auf, zog auf, hat aufgezogen> ◊ *Ist das wahr oder ziehst du mich nur auf?* **5.** *(upset, annoy)* wind sb up jdn aufregen ['ao̯fre:gn̩] +haben ◊ *Die Nachricht hat ihn sehr aufgeregt.* get wound up sich aufregen → wind² **4.**, wind² **6.**

window ⟨noun⟩ **1.** Fenster ['fɛnstɐ] das <-s, -> ◊ *Sie schaute aus dem Fenster.* ✦ *ein Fenster mit Werbebannern wegklicken* **2.** *(available time)* Zeit [tsaɪt] die <-, -en> ◊ *eine halbe Stunde Zeit einplanen*; *(time available for a specific activity)* Zeitfenster ['tsaɪtfɛnstɐ] das <-s, -> *(tech)*

windscreen ⟨noun⟩ Windschutzscheibe ['vɪntʃʊtsʃaɪbə] die <-, -n>

windscreen wiper, windshield wiper ⟨noun⟩ Scheibenwischer ['ʃaɪbm̩vɪʃɐ] der <-s, ->

windshield → **windscreen**

windy ⟨adj⟩ **1.** *(weather)* windig ['vɪndɪç] ◊ *Heute ist es sehr windig.* ✦ *ein windiger Tag* **2.** *(wordy)* langatmig ['laŋˌaːtmɪç] ◊ *ein langatmiger Aufsatz* ✦ *Eine gute Rede darf nicht langatmig sein*

wine ⟨noun⟩ Wein [vaɪn] der <-(e)s, -e> ◊ *Er bestellte noch ein Glas Wein.* red/white wine Rotwein/Weißwein ['roːtvaɪn/'vaɪsvaɪn]

wing ⟨noun⟩ **1.** *(of an animal, plane, building, political party, playing field)* Flügel ['flyːgl̩] der <-s, -> ◊ *Vögel haben zwei Flügel, Libellen vier.* ✦ *Das Gebäude hat mehrere Flügel.* ✦ *den Ball von rechten Flügel ins Mittelfeld spielen* **2.** *(of a car)* Kotflügel ['koːtflyːgl̩] der <-s, -> ◊ *Der Kotflügel war verbeult.*
⊚ on a wing and a prayer auf gut Glück take wing **1.** *(bird)* auffliegen **2.** *(person)* überstürzt aufbrechen take sb under your wings jdn unter seine Fittiche nehmen wait in the wings auf seinen Einsatz warten on the wing in der Luft under sb's wings unter jds Schutz

winner ⟨noun⟩ **1.** *(of a competition, war)* Sieger ['ziːgɐ] der <-s, -> ♀Siegerin ['ziːgərɪn] die <-, -nen> ◊ *Er ging als Sieger aus der Wahl hervor.* ✦ *die strahlende Siegerin* **2.** *(of a prize, advantage, in a game)* Gewinner [gəˈvɪnɐ] der <-s, -> ♀Gewinnerin [gəˈvɪnərɪn] die <-, -nen> ◊ *den glücklichen Gewinner bekannt geben* **3.** *(popular book, product)* Renner ['rɛnɐ] der <-s, -> *(fam)* ◊ *Ihr neuer Roman*

ist ein echter Renner.

winning ⟨adj⟩ **1.** *(person, team)* siegreich ['ziːkraɪ̯ç] no comp/superl ◊ *Die siegreiche Mannschaft des Endspiels erhält den Titel.* **2.** *(goal, point)* entscheidend [ɛntˈʃaɪdn̩t] no comp/superl ◊ *Im letzten Viertel fiel das entscheidende Tor.* **3.** *(score, time)* beste ['bɛstə] der/die/das beste ... ◊ *Wer hat die beste Punktzahl erreicht?* winning entry Gewinner [gəˈvɪnɐ] der <-s, -> ◊ *Die Gewinner des Preisausschreibens sind: ...* winning formula Erfolgsgeheimnis [ɛrˈfɔlksgəhaɪmnɪs] das <-ses, -se> **4.** *(charming)* einnehmend ['aɪnneːmənt] have winning ways ein einnehmendes Wesen haben

winter¹ ⟨noun⟩ Winter ['vɪntɐ] der <-s, -> ◊ *ein harter/strenger Winter* ✦ *im tiefsten Winter* in (the) winter im Winter

winter² ⟨adj⟩ winter ... Winter... ['vɪntɐ] winter sports Wintersport ['vɪntɐʃpɔrt] der <-s> no pl winter landscape Winterlandschaft ['vɪntɐlantʃaft] der <-s, ->

wintry ⟨adj⟩ winterlich ['vɪntɐlɪç] ◊ *Die Temperaturen waren winterlich.* ✦ *winterliche Straßenverhältnisse*

wipe ⟨verb⟩ **1.** *(the floor, your brow etc.)* wipe sth etw. wischen ['vɪʃn̩] +haben ◊ *Der Boden muss gewischt werden.* wipe your sth sich ⟨dat⟩ etw. wischen ◊ *Er wischte sich die Stirn.* wipe sth from/off sth etw. von etw. wischen ◊ *die Krümel vom Tisch wischen* ✦ *Ich wischte mir die Tränen von den Wangen.*; *(the table, your hands, mouth)* wipe (your) sth (sich ⟨dat⟩) etw. abwischen ['apvɪʃn̩] +haben ◊ *Wisch dir den Mund ab!* wipe sth away etw. abwischen wipe sth up etw. aufwischen ['ao̯fvɪʃn̩] +haben ◊ *den Boden/das Wasser aufwischen* wipe the inside of sth etw. auswischen ['ao̯svɪʃn̩] +haben ◊ *Er wischte die Pfanne aus.*; *(dishes)* etw. abtrocknen ['aptrɔknən] <trocknet ab, trocknete ab, hat abgetrocknet>; *(your bottom, feet, shoes)* sich ⟨dat⟩ etw. abputzen ['apptsn̩] +haben **2.** *(a disk, file, tape)* löschen ['lœʃn̩] +haben ◊ *Ich habe die Datei gelöscht.* **3.** *(erase, eradicate)* wipe sth (from/off sth) etw. (aus etw.) streichen ['ʃtraɪ̯çn̩] <streicht, strich, hat gestrichen> ◊ *etw. aus seinem Gedächtnis streichen* Die Insel has been wiped from the map/face of the earth. Die Insel ist von der Landkarte/vom Erdboden verschwunden. Wipe that smile off your face! Hör auf zu grinsen!
- **wipe down** ⟨phras v⟩ wipe sth down etw. abwischen ['apvɪʃn̩] +haben ◊ *Ich wische nur schnell den Tisch ab.*
- **wipe out** ⟨phras v⟩ **1.** *(eradicate: a disease, an epidemic)* wipe sth out etw. ausmerzen ['ao̯smɛrtsn̩] +haben ◊ *Die Seuche konnte ausgemerzt werden.*; *(guilt, shame, the traces of sth)* etw. tilgen ['tɪlgn̩] +haben *(lofty)* ◊ *Diese Schuld kann nicht getilgt werden.* **2.** *(assets, gains)* be wiped out auf einen Schlag verloren gehen [ao̯f aɪnən ʃlak fɛˈloːrən geːan] <geht, ging, ist gegangen> ◊ *Die Hälfte des Aktienwerts ging auf einen Schlag verloren.* have sth wiped out etw. auf einen Schlag verlieren [ao̯f aɪnən ʃlak fɛˈliːrən] <verliert, verlor, hat verloren> ◊ *Die Investoren verloren auf einen Schlag drei Millionen Euro.* **3.** *(a people, species)* wipe sb/sth out jdn/etw. ausrotten ['ao̯srɔtn̩] <rottet aus, rottete aus, hat ausgerottet> ◊ *Jedes Jahr werden zahlreiche Pflanzenarten ausgerottet.*; *(the enemy)* jdn auslöschen ['ao̯slœʃn̩] +haben;

A B C D E F G H I J K L M N O P Q R S T U V **W** X Y Z

(a person, obstacle) jdn/etw. aus dem Weg räumen [aʊs deːm 'veːk rɔɡmən] +haben (fam)

wire [noun] **1.** (piece of metal) Draht [draːt] der <–(e)s, Drähte> ◊ *ein Stück/eine Rolle Draht* **2.** (for electricity) Leitung ['laetʊŋ] die <–, –en> ◊ *neue Leitungen verlegen/ziehen* **3.** (in the US: telegram) Telegramm [teleˈɡram] das <–s, –e> ◊ *jdm ein Telegramm schicken* **4.** (in the US: bugging device) Wanze ['vantsə] die <–, –n> (fam)

⊚ **get your wires crossed** durcheinander kommen **go right down to the wire** sich in allerletzter Minute entscheiden (fam) **under the wire** auf den letzten Drücker (fam)

wisdom [noun] Weisheit ['vaeshaet] die <–> no pl ◊ *die Weisheit des Alters* conventional wisdom is that es ist eine alte Weisheit, dass She debated the wisdom of his plan. Sie bezweifelte, dass sein Plan vernünftig war. words of wisdom weise Worte [ˌvaezə 'vɔˀtə]

wise(ly) [adj, adv] (having a lot of experience or knowledge) klug [kluːk] <klüger, am klügsten> ◊ *eine kluge Entscheidung* ♦ *Es war klug von dir, das zu tun.*; (to an exceptional degree) weise ['vaezə] <weiser, am weisesten> ◊ *ein weiser alter Mann* ♦ *weise urteilen* the three wise men die drei Weisen aus dem Morgenland

⊚ **be wise after the event** hinterher schlauer sein **wise beyond your years** (child) seinem Alter weit voraus (adult) für sein Alter sehr weise **get wise to sb/sth** jdm/einer Sache auf die Schliche kommen

wish¹ [noun] Wunsch [vʊnʃ] der <–(e)s, Wünsche> ◊ *sich* [dat] *einen Wunsch erfüllen* have no wish to do sth nicht den Wunsch haben, etw. zu tun make a wish sich [dat] etw. wünschen ['vʏnʃn] +haben

⊚ **your wish> is my command** dein Wunsch ist mir Befehl (hum) **with best wishes** herzliche Grüße

wish² [verb] wünschen ['vʏnʃn] +haben ◊ *Der Gast wünscht, um acht geweckt zu werden.* ♦ *jdm viel Glück/frohe Weihnachten wünschen* wish for sth sich [dat] etw. wünschen ◊ *die besten Eltern, die man sich wünschen kann* wish sb well/ill jdm Glück/ Schlechtes wünschen I wish I hadn't said it! Ich wünschte, ich hätte es nie gesagt! wish to do sth etw. tun wollen ['vɔlən] <will, wollte, hat wollen> ◊ *Ich will ja nicht unhöflich/undankbar sein, aber …*

⊚ **you wish** das hättest du wohl gern (fam)

wit [noun] **1.** (sense of humo(u)r, cleverness) Witz [vɪts] der <–es> no pl ◊ *ein Buch mit echtem Witz* ♦ *Sie hat einen trockenen Witz* quick/ready wit Schlagfertigkeit ['ʃlaːkfɛˀtɪçkaet] die <–> no pl have a quick/ ready wit schlagfertig sein ['ʃlaːkfɛˀtɪç zaen] **2.** (clever person) ein geistreicher Mensch [aen ˌɡaestraeçə 'mɛnʃ] <–en, –en> ◊ *Oscar Wilde, der ein sehr geistreicher Mensch war* **3.** (faculty of reason, intelligence) wit(s) Verstand [fɛˀʃtant] der <–es> no pl ◊ *Du solltest genug Verstand haben, so etwas nicht zu tun.*

⊚ **be at your wits' end** mit seiner Weisheit am Ende sein **gather your wits** sich konzentrieren **scare the wits out of sb** jdn zu Tode erschrecken **have your wits about you** seine fünf Sinne beisammenhaben **keep your wits about you** einen klaren Kopf behalten

witch [noun] Hexe ['hɛksə] die <–, –n>

with [prep] **1.** (together with sb/sth, against sb, having or using sth, in a particular way, expressing a relation-

ship) mit [mɪt] [+dat] ◊ *Würstchen mit Senf* ♦ *Er kam mit seinem Freund.* ♦ *Der Fahrschein mit Zuschlag kommt auf 25 Euro.* ♦ *der Krieg mit Japan* ♦ *der Mann mit den dunklen Haaren* ♦ *Mit etwas Übung schaffst du es sicher.* ♦ *mit Messer und Gabel essen* ♦ *Sie kam ihm mit schnellen Schritten entgegen.* ♦ *Er stand mit dem Rücken zur Wand.* ♦ *Sie liegt mit Grippe im Bett.* ♦ *mit einem Land Handel treiben* ♦ *Er ist mit den Meiers befreundet.* ♦ *Ich bin sehr zufrieden mit dir.* **2.** (at sb's place, in a given situation, in spite of) bei [bae] [+dat] ◊ *Sie wohnt noch bei ihren Eltern.* ♦ *Bei meinem Einkommen kann ich mir so ein Auto nicht leisten.* ♦ *Das ist bei ihr nicht der Fall.* ♦ *Bei meinem Computer funktioniert das nicht.* ♦ *Sie haben Fehlern ist er netter Mensch.* **be with sb** bei jdm sein ◊ *Keine Angst, ich bin ja bei dir!* I'll be with you soon. Ich komme gleich. **be with a company** bei einer Firma arbeiten **have sth with you** etw. bei sich [dat] haben ◊ *Ich habe mein Handy immer bei mir.* **3.** (because of an emotional or physical state) vor [foːɐ] followed by a noun without the article [+dat] ◊ *Er zitterte vor Angst.* ♦ *Ihr Gesicht war rot vor Wut.* ♦ *Sie konnte vor Müdigkeit kaum die Augen aufhalten.* **4.** (along with a particular food or drink, in combination with a particular piece of clothing) zu ['tsuː] [+dat] ◊ *Zum Fisch tranken wir Weißwein.* ♦ *Das gestreifte Hemd passt nicht zur karierten Hose.*

withdraw [verb] **1.** (take away/back, leave, stop taking part) withdraw sb/sth jdn/etw. zurückziehen [tsuˈrʏktsiːən] <zieht zurück, zog zurück, hat zurückgezogen> ◊ *Die Partei zog ihren Kandidaten zurück.* ♦ *Die Firma hat ihr Angebot zurückgezogen.* sb/sth withdraws (from sth) jd/etw. zieht sich (aus etw.) zurück ◊ *Die Truppen zogen sich zurück.* ♦ *Sie hat sich in ihr Zimmer zurückgezogen.* ♦ *Er hat sich aus dem Rennen/der Wahl zurückgezogen.* sb withdraws into their shell jd zieht sich in sein Schneckenhaus zurück; (your troops) withdraw sb/sth (from sth) jdn/etw. (aus etw.) abziehen ['aptsiːən] <zieht ab, zog ab, ist abgezogen> ◊ *Der General ließ die Truppen aus dem Gebiet abziehen.* **2.** (a sum of money) abheben ['apheːbm̩] <hebt ab, hob ab, hat abgehoben> ◊ *bei der Bank Geld abheben* ♦ *Er hat 100 Euro von seinem Konto abgehoben.* **3.** (stop providing sth, a service) einstellen ['aenʃtɛlən] +haben ◊ *Der Zugverkehr auf dieser Strecke ist eingestellt worden.*; (a drug, product) withdraw sth from the market etw. vom Markt nehmen [fɔm 'maˀkt neːmən] <nimmt, nahm, hat genommen> **4.** (take sth away) withdraw sth from sb jdm etw. entziehen [ɛntˈtsiːən] <entzieht, entzog, hat entzogen> ◊ *jdm sein Vertrauen/seine Unterstützung/den Führerschein entziehen* They withdrew their support for him for the bill. Sie hörten auf, ihn zu unterstützen/ sich für das Gesetz stark zu machen. **5.** (an accusation, a remark, your resignation) zurücknehmen [tsuˈrʏkneːmən] <nimmt zurück, nahm zurück, hat zurückgenommen> ◊ *Ich nehme zurück, was ich vorhin gesagt habe; es war unfair.* ♦ *Sie nahm ihre Kündigung zurück.* **6.** withdraw your labo(u)r die Arbeit niederlegen [diː ˈaˀbaet ˌniːdeleːgŋ̍] +haben ◊ *Die Stahlarbeiter legten gestern die Arbeit nieder.* **7.** (take out) withdraw sth etw. herausholen [hɛˈraoshoːlən] +haben ◊ *Sie öffnete die Brieftasche und holte die Papiere heraus.* withdraw sth from sth

etw. aus etw. holen [aʊs ... hoːlən] +haben ◊ Er holte einen Brief aus dem Safe.

withdrawal (noun) **1.** (stopping sth, taking sth away) withdrawal (of sth) Entzug (... (gen)) [ɛntˈtsuːk] der <-(e)s> no pl ◊ der Entzug einer Lizenz ◆ der Entzug von Nahrung withdrawal symptoms Entzugserscheinungen [ɛntˈtsuːksʔeˌʃaɛnʊŋən] die <-> pl withdrawal treatment Entziehungskur [ɛntˈtsiːʊŋskuːɐ] die <-, -en> **2.** (of an army) Rückzug [ˈrʏktsuːk] der <-(e)s, Rückzüge> ◊ der Rückzug der Truppen aus den besetzten Gebieten **3.** (no longer being involved in sth) withdrawal (from sth) Rücktritt (von etw.) [ˈrʏktrɪt] der <-s> no pl ◊ Sie erklärte ihren Rücktritt vom Wettbewerb. **4.** (taking money from your account) Abheben [ˈapheːbm̩] das <-s> no pl ◊ Zum Abheben brauchst du deine EC-Karte. make a withdrawal Geld abheben [ˈgɛlt ˌapheːbm̩] <hebt ab, hob ab, hat abgehoben> **5.** (of a remark, your resignation) Rücknahme [ˈrʏknaːmə] die <-> no pl ◊ die Rücknahme eines Angebots/der Kündigung/Erlaubnis/Beschuldigung **6.** (behavio(u)r in which sb wants to be alone) Zurückgezogenheit [tsuˈrʏkgətsoːɡŋ̍haɛt] die <-> no pl

withdrawn → withdraw (adj) verschlossen [fɛˈʃlɔsn̩] ◊ Nach diesem Erlebnis wurde er sehr verschlossen. ◆ Er ist eher der verschlossene Typ, der keine Emotionen zeigt.

withhold (verb) (a payment, your support) verweigern [fɛˈvaɛɡɐn] <verweigert, verweigerte, hat verweigert> ◊ Sie verweigerten die Zahlung.; (information) withhold sth from sb jdm etw. vorenthalten [ˈfoːɐʔɛnthaltn̩] <enthält vor, enthielt vor, hat vorenthalten> ◊ Warum haben Sie mir diese Informationen vorenthalten?

within¹ (adv) (referring to the interior of sth, sb's nature) innen [ˈɪnən] ◊ Innen ist das Haus ganz modern eingerichtet. from within von innen ◊ die Bedrohung von innen ◆ Schönheit kommt von innen.; (inside a room/house) drinnen [ˈdrɪnən] ◊ Ich habe drinnen Stimmen gehört.

within² (prep) **1.** (inside a period of time, in a place, range, group) innerhalb [ˈɪnɐhalp] (+gen) ◊ innerhalb der nächsten Wochen ◆ innerhalb Europas ◆ innerhalb vorgegebener Grenzen ◆ Auseinandersetzungen innerhalb der Partei within six months/years innerhalb von sechs Monaten/Jahren within the limits of the law im Rahmen des Gesetzes [ɪm ˌraːmən dɛs ɡəˈzɛtsəs] **2.** (not more than a particular distance) within ... im Umkreis von ... [ɪm ˈʊmkraɛs fɔn] ◊ Durch die Explosion gingen im Umkreis von 100 Metern fast alle Fenster zu Bruch. within (easy) reach of sth (ganz) in der Nähe ... (gen) [(ɡants) ɪn deːɐ ˈnɛːə] ◊ Unser Haus liegt ganz in der Nähe des Bahnhofs. within earshot in Hörweite [ɪn ˈhøːɐvaɛtə] within sight in Sichtweite [ɪn ˈzɪçtvaɛtə] **3.** (deep inside a person) within sb in jds Inneren [ɪn ... ˈɪnərən] ◊ eine Stimme tief in meinem Inneren

without¹ (adv) ohne [ˈoːnə] ◊ Wir haben leider keinen Zucker mehr. Geht es auch ohne? do without ohne auskommen ◊ Wenn keine Milch mehr da ist, müssen wir eben ohne auskommen.

◉ without wanting to do sth ich will ja nicht etw. tun ◊ Ich will euch ja nicht die Party verderben, aber die Musik ist zu laut!

without² (prep) ohne [ˈoːnə] (+acc) ◊ ein Saft ohne Zucker ◆ Sie ist gerade ohne Arbeit. ◆ Eine Übernachtung ohne Frühstück kostet 30 Euro. ◆ Das schaffen wir auch ohne dich! without so much as an explanation ohne jede Erklärung without any ... at all ganz ohne ... ◊ ganz ohne Geld without hesitation ohne zu zögern ◊ Er half uns, ohne zu zögern. without so much as saying a word ohne auch nur ein Wort zu sagen without doing sth ohne etw. zu tun ◊ Sie hat ihn gekränkt, ohne es zu wollen. without sb doing sth ohne dass jd etw. tut ◊ Das Kind wurde entführt, ohne dass jemand etwas bemerkte.

withstand (verb) (be strong enough not to be harmed) withstand sth einer Sache (dat) standhalten [ˈʃtanthaltn̩] <hält stand, hielt stand, hat standgehalten> ◊ Das Material kann Feuer 30 Minuten lang standhalten. ◆ Er konnte dem Druck nicht mehr standhalten.; (get or go through) überstehen [ybɐˈʃteːən] <übersteht, überstand, hat überstanden> ◊ Ihre Beziehung hat schon viele Krisen überstanden.

witness¹ (noun) Zeuge [ˈtsɔɥɡə] der <-n, -n> ♀Zeugin [ˈtsɔɥɡɪn] die <-, -nen> ◊ einen Zeugen vernehmen ◆ vor Gericht als Zeuge aussagen ◆ einen Vertrag vor Zeugen unterschreiben ◆ Das Testament wurde im Beisein von Zeugen geschrieben. witness to sth Zeuge/Zeugin ... (gen) ◊ Sie wurde zufällig Zeugin des Verbrechens/Gesprächs. appeal for witnesses nach Zeugen suchen

◉ be witness to sth (fig) Zeuge ... (gen) sein bear witness to sth von etw. zeugen

witness² (verb) **1.** (an accident, a crime) witness sth Zeuge/Zeugin ... (gen) werden [ˈtsɔɥɡə/ˈtsɔɥɡɪn veːɐdn̩] +sein ◊ Sie wurde Zeugin eines Unfalls/Raubüberfalls. Did you witness him stealing the money? Haben Sie beobachtet, wie er das Geld gestohlen hat? **2.** (a scene, an event) erleben [ɛˈleːbm̩] <erlebt, erlebte, hat erlebt> ◊ Solche Szenen erleben die Berater fast täglich. ◆ Wir erleben hier das Ende einer Ära. **3.** (a development) sehen [ˈzeːən] <sieht, sah, hat gesehen> ◊ Das letzte Jahrzehnt hat viele gesellschaftliche Veränderungen gesehen. **4.** (a signature) beglaubigen [bəˈɡlaɔbɪɡn̩] <beglaubigt, beglaubigte, hat beglaubigt> ◊ Ein Notar muss Ihre Unterschrift beglaubigen. **5.** (to prove what you have just said) witness the fact that das zeigt sich schon daran, dass [das tsaɛkt zɪç ʃoːn ˈdaːran das] ◊ Umweltschutz ist uns wichtig. Das zeigt sich schon daran, dass wir unseren Müll trennen.

◉ be witnessed by sth durch etw. bezeugt werden

witty (adj) geistreich [ˈɡaɛstraɛç] ◊ eine geistreiche Rede/Bemerkung ◆ Sie ist geistreich und anregend.

wobble (verb) **1.** (move from side to side, walk unsteadily) wackeln [ˈvakl̩n] +haben/with indication of direction +sein (also fam) ◊ Dieser Stuhl wackelt. ◆ Die Leiter wackelte gefährlich. ◆ Er ist mit seinem Gipsbein langsam über die Straße gewackelt. wobble sth an etw. (dat) wackeln ◊ Sie wackelte an ihrem Zahn. **2.** (become less steady) ins Wanken geraten [ɪns ˈvaŋkn̩ ɡəraːtn̩] <gerät, geriet, ist geraten> ◊ Seine Entschlossenheit geriet langsam ins Wanken. **3.** (voice) zittern [ˈtsɪtɐn] +haben

wobbly (adj) **1.** (unsteady, loose) wack(e)lig [ˈvak(ə)lɪç] ◊ eine wackelige Leiter/Konstruktion ◆ Der Tisch ist wacklig. ◆ Dieser Zahn ist schon ganz wacklig. be wobbly on your feet wacklig auf den

Beinen sein **2.** *(weak, uncertain)* unsicher ['ʊnzɪçɐ] ◊ *ein unsicherer Anfang* ♦ *Ich fühle mich immer noch ziemlich unsicher.* **3.** *(voice)* zitt(e)rig ['tsɪt(ə)rɪç] ◊ *mit zitteriger Stimme sprechen* ♦ *Ihre Stimme war ganz zittrig.*

wolf [noun] Wolf [vɒlf] der <-(e)s, Wölfe>
◉ *a wolf in sheep's clothing* ein Wolf im Schafspelz *keep the wolf from the door* sich über Wasser halten *the big bad wolf* der böse Wolf *cry wolf* blinden Alarm schlagen *throw sb to the wolves* jdn den Wölfen zum Fraß vorwerfen

woman [noun] **1.** *(adult female person)* Frau [fraʊ] die <-, -en> ◊ *eine verheiratete/geschiedene Frau* ♦ *Sie siegte beim Abfahrtslauf der Frauen.* ♦ *die Emanzipation der Frau* She was the first woman astronaut/surgeon. Sie war die erste Astronautin/Chirurgin. **2.** *(womankind)* die Frauen [diː 'fraʊən] <-> pl ◊ *das alte Klischee von den Frauen als Hausmütterchen*
◉ *be your own woman* seine eigene Herrin sein *another woman* eine andere *the other woman* die Geliebte

wonder¹ [noun] **1.** *(feeling)* Staunen ['ʃtaʊnən] das <-s> no pl ◊ *Er bekam vor Staunen den Mund nicht wieder zu.* in wonder staunend ['ʃtaʊnənt] ◊ *Sie sahen das Neugeborene staunend an.* **2.** *(thing)* Wunder ['vʊndɐ] das <-s, -> ◊ *ein Wunder der Technik* natural wonder Naturwunder [na'tuːɐ̯vʊndɐ] **3.** *(clever or talented person)* Genie [ʒeˈniː] das <-s, -s> ◊ *Danke, dass du mein Auto repariert hast. Du bist wirklich ein Genie!*
◉ *it's little wonder that* es ist kein Wunder, dass *nine-day wonder* Eintagsfliege *wonders will never cease* es geschehen noch Zeichen und Wunder *do wonders for sb/sth* für jdn/etw. Wunder wirken *is it any wonder* es ist kein Wunder *it's a wonder* es ist ein Wunder *work wonders with sb/sth* mit jdm/etw. wahre Wunder vollbringen

wonder² [verb] **1.** *(ask yourself)* sich fragen ['fraːɡn̩] +haben ◊ *„Wie machen wir das am besten?", fragte sie sich.* wonder how/what etc. … sich fragen, wie/was etc. … ◊ *Er fragte sich, wie er an das Geld kommen sollte.* wonder if … sich fragen, ob … ◊ *Ich frage mich, ob er je wiederkommt.* I wonder if you could …? Könnten Sie vielleicht …? **2.** *(think, reflect)* wonder about sth über etw. [acc] nachdenken [yː] ◊ ['naːxdɛŋkn̩] <denkt nach, dachte nach, hat nachgedacht> ◊ *Er dachte über die beste Lösung nach.*; *(worry)* wonder about sth sich [dat] Sorgen um etw. machen [ˌzɔʁɡn̩ ʊm … maxn̩] +haben ◊ *Sie machte sich oft Sorgen um ihn/die Zukunft.* **3.** *(admire)* wonder at sb/sth über jdn/etw. staunen [yː] ['ʃtaʊnən] +haben

wonderful(ly) [adj, adv] wunderbar ['vʊndɐbaːɐ̯] ◊ *Die Landschaft ist einfach wunderbar!* ♦ *wunderbares Wetter* ♦ *Sie hat wunderbar gesungen.* ♦ *Das Wasser war wunderbar warm.*

won't → will

wood [noun] **1.** *(material)* Holz [hɔlts] das <-es, Hölzer> ◊ *Er sammelte Holz fürs Lagerfeuer.* ♦ *Der Schrank war aus massivem Holz.* chop wood Holz hacken wood floor Holzboden ['hɔltsboːdn̩] der <-s, Holzböden> wood stove Holzofen ['hɔlts|oːfn̩] der <-s, Holzöfen> **2.** *(forest)* wood(s) Wald [valt] der <-(e)s, Wälder> ◊ *ein dichter/dunkler Wald* ♦ *Sie hatten sich im Wald verirrt.*
◉ *sb can't see the wood for the trees* jd sieht

den Wald vor lauter Bäumen nicht *not be out of the woods yet* noch nicht über den Berg sein

wooden [adj] hölzern ['hœltsɐn] ◊ *eine hölzerne Kiste* ♦ *Seine Bewegungen waren ziemlich hölzern.*

woodland [noun] woodland(s) Waldgebiet ['valtɡəbiːt] das <-(e)s, -e>

wool [noun] Wolle ['vɔlə] die <-, -n> most sing ◊ *Socken aus reiner Wolle* wool jacket Wolljacke ['vɔljakə] die <-, -n>
◉ *pull the wool over sb's eyes* jdm etwas vormachen

woollen, woolen [adj] Woll… [vɔl] woollen sweater Wollpullover [vɔlpʊˌloːvɐ] der <-s, ->

word [noun] **1.** *(unit of language)* Wort [vɔrt] das <-(e)s, Wörter> ◊ *„Apfelsine" ist ein anderes Wort für „Orange".* ♦ *ein Wort richtig/falsch aussprechen* ♦ *Das Kind spricht schon etwa 100 Wörter.* ♦ *ein Wort buchstabieren/schreiben/übersetzen* dirty word Schimpfwort ['ʃɪmpfvɔrt] foreign word Fremdwort ['frɛmtvɔrt] **2.** *(things sb says, promise)* Wort ['vɔrt] das <-(e)s, -e> ◊ *Das ist mein letztes Wort!* ♦ *An dem Gerede ist kein Wort wahr.* ♦ *Ich möchte zu diesem Thema auch gern ein paar Worte sagen.* ♦ *Zwischen uns sind böse Worte gefallen.* ♦ *Ich gebe dir/Du hast mein Wort, dass das wahr ist.* in other/your own words mit anderen/eigenen Worten in a word mit einem Wort keep your word sein Wort halten sb's word of hono(u)r jds Ehrenwort ['eːrənvɔrt] **3.** *(of a song)* words Text [tɛkst] der <-(e)s, -e> ◊ *Sie konnte den Text nicht, summte aber mit.* **4.** *(short conversation)* have a word with sb mit jdm sprechen [mɪt … ʃprɛçn̩] <spricht, sprach, hat gesprochen> ◊ *Kann ich mal kurz mit dir sprechen?* want a word with sb mit jdm sprechen wollen ◊ *Der Chef sucht ihn, er will mit ihm sprechen.* **5.** *(short speech)* say a word about sth kurz über etw. [acc] sprechen [kʊrts … ʃprɛçn̩] <spricht, sprach, hat gesprochen> **6.** *(news, information)* Nachricht ['naːxrɪçt] die <-, -en> ◊ *Sie haben noch keine Nachricht von ihr.* send word eine Nachricht schicken word spreads eine Nachricht verbreitet sich ◊ *Die Nachricht von dem Bombenanschlag verbreitete sich schnell.* **7.** *(in conjunction with certain nouns)* word of advice Ratschlag ['raːtʃlaːk] der <-(e)s, Ratschläge> by word of mouth durch Mundpropaganda [dʊrç ˈmʊntpropaɡandaː] word of praise Lob [loːp] das <-(e)s, -e> word of warning Warnung ['varnʊŋ] die <-, -en>
◉ *put words into sb's mouth* jdm etwas in den Mund legen *not have a good word for sb/sth* nichts Gutes über jdn/etw. zu sagen haben *put in a good word for sb* ein gutes Wort für jdn einlegen *words fail me* mir fehlen die Worte *give the word* das Kommando geben *from the word go* von Anfang an *have words (with sb)* (mit jdm) eine Auseinandersetzung haben *word is that* man sagt, dass *say the word* nur ein Wort sagen *take sb at their word* jdn beim Wort nehmen *take my word for it* das kannst du mir glauben *not in so many words* nicht direkt

wording [noun] Formulierung [fɔrmuˈliːrʊŋ] die <-, -en> ◊ *Sie haben lange über die Formulierung des Briefs nachgedacht.* the exact wording der genaue Wortlaut [deːɐ̯ ɡənaʊə ˈvɔrtlaʊt] <-(e)s> ◊ *Kannst du dich noch an den genauen Wortlaut der Nachricht erinnern?*

word order ⸤noun⸣ Wortstellung ['vɔrtʃtɛlʊŋ] die
<-, -en> ◊ *die Wortstellung im Fragesatz*
word processing ⸤noun⸣ Textverarbeitung
['tɛkstfɛ|ɐˈbaɛtʊŋ] die <-, -en>
work¹ ⸤noun⸣ **1.** *(activity, job, place, product)* Arbeit
['aˈbaɛt] die <-, -en> ◊ *Ich habe heute viel Arbeit.* ✦
Zu ihrer Arbeit gehören auch Vorträge und Inter-
views. ✦ *Er ist auf dem Weg zur Arbeit.* ✦ *Nach der*
Arbeit gehe ich schwimmen. ✦ *Sie hat gute Arbeit*
geleistet. get to work (on sth) sich an die Arbeit (an
etw. ⸤dat⸣) machen piece of work Arbeit ◊ *Das ist*
seine bisher beste Arbeit. **2.** *(factory)* works Werk
[vɛʳk] das <-(e)s, -e> ◊ *Der Autohersteller muss*
mehrere Werke schließen. ✦ *Das Werk macht eine*
Woche Urlaub/stellt neue Mitarbeiter ein. **3.** *(creative*
product, all creations of an artist) work(s) Werk
[vɛʳk] das <-(e)s, -e> ◊ *Nach wochenlanger Arbeit*
war sein Werk fertig. ✦ *„Romeo und Julia" ist ein*
Werk Shakespeares. ✦ *Leben und Werk Picassos* ✦
Sein gesammeltes Werk umfasst zwanzig Bände. a
work of literature ein literarisches Werk work of art
Kunstwerk ['kʊnstvɛʳk] **4.** *(building, repairing)* work(s)
Arbeiten ['aˈbaɛtn̩] die <--> pl building works Bauar-
beiten ['baʊ|aˈbaɛtn̩] ◊ *Die Bauarbeiten sollen in*
einer Woche beginnen. repair works Reparaturarbei-
ten [repaʳaˈtuːɐ̯|aˈbaɛtn̩]
◉ all work and no play zu viel Arbeit und nicht
genug Freizeit make short work of sb/sth kurzen
Prozess mit jdm/etw. machen the whole works
alles be in work eine Stelle haben be out of work
arbeitslos sein have your work cut out (for you)
eine schwierige Aufgabe haben at work **1.** *(at your*
place of work) bei der Arbeit ◊ *Er ist noch bei der*
Arbeit. **2.** *(in the process of doing sth)* be at work on
sth an etw. ⸤dat⸣ arbeiten ◊ *Sie arbeitet gerade an*
einem Essay. **3.** *(having a particular effect)* am Werk
◊ *Welche Kräfte sind da wohl am Werk?* in the
works in Arbeit
work² ⸤verb⸣ **1.** *(spend time doing sth, have a job)*
arbeiten ['aˈbaɛtn̩] <arbeitet, arbeitete, hat gearbeitet>
◊ *Um das zu erreichen, hat er hart arbeiten müssen.*
✦ *Sie arbeitet als Lehrerin/in einem Verlag.* ✦ *Er*
arbeitet mit behinderten Kindern. work at/on sth an
etw. ⸤dat⸣ arbeiten ◊ *Der Autor arbeitet an einem*
neuen Roman. work to do sth daran arbeiten, etw.
zu tun work for sth bei etw. arbeiten ◊ *Ich arbeite*
bei einer kleinen Firma. **2.** *(make sb work)* work sb
jdn herannehmen [hɛˈranneːmən] <nimmt heran,
nahm heran, hat herangenommen> ◊ *Er nimmt seine*
Schüler hart heran. **3.** *(salesman)* work sth etw.
bereisen [baˈraɛzn̩] <bereist, bereiste, hat bereist> ◊
Sie bereist den ganzen Norden des Landes.;
(performer) work sth in etw. ⸤dat⸣ auftreten
[ɪn ... ˌaʊftreːtn̩] <tritt auf, trat auf, ist aufgetreten> ◊
Er ist jahrelang in Nachtklubs aufgetreten.
4. *(operate well)* funktionieren [fʊŋktsʲoˈniːrən] <funk-
tioniert, funktionierte, hat funktioniert> ◊ *Jetzt funktio-*
niert die Heizung wieder. ✦ *Der Föhn funktioniert*
nicht. **5.** *(operate sth)* work sth etw. bedienen
[baˈdiːnən] <bedient, bediente, hat bedient> ◊ *Kannst*
du den Kopierer bedienen? **6.** *(succeed)* klappen
['klapn̩] +haben *(fam)* ◊ *Unser Plan/Trick hat*
geklappt! **7.** *(have an effect)* wirken ['vɪʳkn̩] +haben ◊
Wie wirkt dieses Medikament? ✦ *Die Tabletten*
wirken bei mir nicht. work for sb, work in sb's
favour sich zu jds Vorteil auswirken

[zɪç ʦuː ... ˈfoːɐ̯taɛl aɔsvɪʳkn̩] +haben work against
sb sich zu jds Nachteil auswirken ◊ *Seine Ehrlich-*
keit hat sich zu seinem Nachteil ausgewirkt.
8. *(move)* work itself loose sich lockern ['lɔkən]
+haben ◊ *Die Schraube hat sich gelockert.* work sth
free etw. befreien [baˈfraɛən] <befreit, befreite, hat
befreit> ◊ *Es gelang ihm, seine Hände zu befreien.*
9. work yourself into sth sich in etw. ⸤acc⸣ hineinstei-
gern [ɪn ... hɪˌnaɛnʃtaɛgən] +haben ◊ *Sie hat sich in*
einen Angstzustand hineingesteigert. **10.** *(shape,*
prepare) bearbeiten [baˈaˈbaɛtn̩] <bearbeitet, bearbeitete, hat bearbeitet> ◊ *Holz/Metall bearbeiten* ✦
Unsere Familie bearbeitet dieses Land schon seit
Generationen. **11.** *(a mine, quarry)* ausbeuten
['aʊsbɔɪtn̩] <beutet aus, beutete aus, hat ausgebeutet>
◉ work it *(arrange)* es deichseln *(fam)*
• **work in, work into** ⸤phras v⸣ **1.** *(include)* work sth
in(to sth) etw. (in etw. ⸤acc⸣) einbauen ['aɛnbaʊən]
+haben ◊ *Er schaffte es, viele neue Vokabeln in*
seinen Aufsatz einzubauen. **2.** *(mix)* work sth in(to*
sth) etw. (unter etw. ⸤acc⸣) mischen ['mɪʃn̩] +haben
◊ *die Haselnüsse unter den Teig mischen*
• **work off** ⸤phras v⸣ work sth off **1.** *(a debt, excess*
weight) etw. abarbeiten ['ap|aˈbaɛtn̩] <arbeitet ab,
arbeitete ab, hat abgearbeitet> ◊ *Schulden abarbeiten*
✦ *im Fitnessstudio ein paar Pfunde abarbeiten* **2.** *(a*
negative emotion) etw. abreagieren ['apreagiːrən]
<reagiert ab, reagierte ab, hat abreagiert> ◊ *seine Wut*
durch Laufen abreagieren
• **work on** ⸤phras v⸣ **1.** *(concentrate on, improve)*
work on sth etw. ⸤dat⸣ arbeiten [an ... ˌaˈbaɛtn̩]
<arbeitet, arbeitete, hat gearbeitet> ◊ *Sie muss noch*
an ihrer Rückhand arbeiten. I'm working on it. Ich
bin dabei. **2.** *(try to influence)* work on sb jdn bearbeiten [baˈaˈbaɛtn̩] <bearbeitet, bearbeitete, hat bear-
beitet> ◊ *Die Kinder haben ihn so lange bearbeitet,*
bis er schließlich ja gesagt hat. → **work²** **1.**
• **work out** ⸤phras v⸣ **1.** *(by doing a calculation)* work
sth out etw. ausrechnen ['aʊsrɛçnən] <rechnet aus,
rechnete aus, hat ausgerechnet> ◊ *die Summe/Entfer-*
nung ausrechnen ✦ *Rechne mal aus, wie viel das*
kostet. **2.** *(by considering the facts)* work sth out etw.
herausbekommen [hɛˈraʊsbəkɔmən] <bekommt
heraus, bekam heraus, hat herausbekommen> ◊ *Habt*
ihr herausbekommen, in welche Richtung wir gehen
müssen? She couldn't work out what to do. Sie
wusste nicht, was sie tun sollte. **3.** *(deal with sth)*
work sth out mit etw. fertig werden
[mɪt ... ˈfɛʳtɪç veːɐ̯dn̩] +sein ◊ *Die Kinder sind mit*
dem Problem allein fertig geworden. **4.** *(be success-*
ful) sth works out etw. klappt [klapt] +haben *(fam)* ◊
Wenn alles gut klappt, sind wir morgen fertig.
5. *(find a satisfactory way of doing sth)* work sth out
etw. ausarbeiten ['aʊs|aˈbaɛtn̩] <arbeitet aus,
arbeitete aus, hat ausgearbeitet> ◊ *einen Plan/eine*
Strategie/ein Programm ausarbeiten **6.** *(decide on,*
agree on) work sth out etw. entscheiden [ɛntˈʃaɛdn̩]
<entscheidet, entschied, hat entschieden> ◊ *Das*
Datum ist noch nicht entschieden. **7.** *(add up to an*
amount) sth works out at sth etw. beträgt etw.
[baˈtrɛːkt] <betrug, hat betragen> ◊ *Die Nebenkosten*
betragen etwa 100 Euro im Monat. sth works out
cheaper/more expensive etw. kommt billiger/teurer
[kɔmt ˈbɪlɪgɐ/ˈtɔɪ̯rə] <kam, ist gekommen> ◊ *Es*
kommt teurer, im Parkhaus zu parken. **8.** *(do*
exercises) trainieren [trɛˈniːrən] <trainiert, trainierte,*

hat trainiert> ◊ *Sie trainiert jeden Morgen eine halbe Stunde im Fitnessstudio.* **9.** *(understand)* work sb/sth out jdn/etw. verstehen [fɛˈʃteːən] <versteht, verstand, hat verstanden> ◊ *Kannst du sie verstehen?*
• **work through** [phras v] verarbeiten [fɛˈɑʁbaetn̩] <verarbeitet, verarbeitete, hat verarbeitet> ◊ *ein schreckliches Erlebnis verarbeiten*
• **work up** [phras v] **1.** *(a feeling)* entwickeln [ɛntˈvɪkl̩n] <entwickelt, entwickelte, hat entwickelt>; *(an appetite)* bekommen [bəˈkɔmən] <bekommt, bekam, hat bekommen>; *(enthusiasm)* aufbringen [ˈaofbrɪŋən] <bringt auf, brachte auf, hat aufgebracht> **2.** *(get excited)* work yourself up *(into a state)* sich aufregen [ˈaofreːgn̩] +haben ◊ *Sie hat sich vor der Prüfung schrecklich aufgeregt.*
• **work up to** [phras v] **1.** *(try to do sth difficult)* work up to doing sth es über sich bringen, etw. zu tun [ɛs ˈyːbɐ ... brɪŋən ... ʦuː] <bringt, brachte, hat gebracht> work up to telling sb sth versuchen, jdm etw. zu sagen [fɛˈzuːxn̩ ... ʦuː ˈzaːgn̩] **2.** *(increase)* work up to sth sich auf etw. [acc] steigern [aof ... ˈʃtaegɐn] +haben ◊ *Mit der Zeit steigerte ich mich auf eine Stunde Yoga pro Tag.*
workday [noun] Werktag [ˈvɛʁktaːk] der <-(e)s, -e> ◊ *Der Markt hat im Sommer jeden Werktag geöffnet.* ◆ *Dieser Zug verkehrt an Werktagen außer samstags.*
worker [noun] **1.** *(in a company or industry)* Arbeiter [ˈaʁbaetɐ] der <-s, -> ♀Arbeiterin [ˈaʁbaetərɪn] die <-, -nen> ◊ *Die Firma beschäftigt 200 Arbeiter und Angestellte.* ◆ *Sie war eine gewissenhafte Arbeiterin.* She is a slow worker. Sie arbeitet langsam. an unskilled worker ein ungelernter Arbeiter/eine ungelernte Arbeiterin skilled worker Facharbeiter [ˈfaxaʁbaetɐ] Facharbeiterin [ˈfaxaʁˌbaetərɪn] industrial worker Industriearbeiter [ɪndʊsˈtriːaʁbaetɐ] Industriearbeiterin [ɪndʊsˈtriːaʁˌbaetərɪn] clerical worker Bürokraft [byˈroːkraft] die <-, Bürokräfte> **2.** *(members of the working class)* workers Arbeiter [ˈaʁbaetɐ] die <-> pl **3.** *(for a particular organization)* Mitarbeiter [ˈmɪtaʁbaetɐ] der <-s, -> ♀Mitarbeiterin [ˈmɪtaʁbaetərɪn] die <-, -nen>
workforce [noun] **1.** *(in a particular company or organization)* Belegschaft [bəˈleːkʃaft] die <-, -en> ◊ *Die Firma hat die gesamte Belegschaft zum Betriebsfest eingeladen.* **2.** *(people who work)* arbeitende Bevölkerung [ˌaʁbaetndə bəˈfœlkərʊŋ] die <-> no pl
working → **work²** [adj] **1.** *(having a job)* berufstätig [bəˈruːfstɛːtɪç] ◊ *berufstätige Mütter/Frauen/Männer;* *(doing manual work)* working man Arbeiter [ˈaʁbaetɐ] der <-s, -> working woman Arbeiterin [ˈaʁbaetərɪn] die <-, -nen> **2.** *(relating to work, not completely developed)* Arbeits... [ˈaʁbaets] working conditions Arbeitsbedingungen [ˈaʁbaetsbəˌdɪŋʊŋən] die <-> pl working lunch Arbeitsessen [ˈaʁbaetsˌɛsn̩] das <-s, -> working title Arbeitstitel [ˈaʁbaetstiːtl̩] der <-s, -> a working knowledge (of sth) Grundkenntnisse (in etw. [dat]) [ˈɡrʊntkɛntnɪsə] die <-> pl ◊ *Sie benötigen Grundkenntnisse in Englisch.* **3.** *(able to be used)* funktionstüchtig [fʊŋkˈʦioːnstʏçtɪç] no comp/superl ◊ *ein maßstabgetreues, funktionstüchtiges Modell* ◆ *Das Gerät ist funktionstüchtig.*
working class [noun] Arbeiterklasse [ˈaʁbaeteklasə] die <-, seldom -n>
working-class [adj] Arbeiter... [ˈaʁbaetɐ] working-class family Arbeiterfamilie [ˈaʁbaetɐfaˌmiːljə] die <-, -n>

working hours [noun] Arbeitszeit [ˈaʁbaetstsaet] die <-, -en> ◊ *Während der Arbeitszeit ist Alkoholkonsum verboten.* ◆ *feste/geregelte Arbeitszeiten*
workload [noun] Arbeitsmenge [ˈaʁbaetsmɛŋə] die <-, ->
workman [noun] *(doing repairs)* Handwerker [ˈhantvɛʁkɐ] der <-s, -> ◊ *Wir haben schon die ganze Woche Handwerker im Haus.;* *(on a building site)* Bauarbeiter [ˈbaoˌaʁbaetɐ] der <-s, -> ◊ *Das Wasserrohr wurde von Bauarbeitern beschädigt.*
work permit [noun] Arbeitserlaubnis [ˈaʁbaetsɛˌlaopnɪs] die <-> no pl ◊ *Er hat eine Arbeitserlaubnis beantragt.*
workplace [noun] Arbeitsplatz [ˈaʁbaetsplaʦ] der <-es, Arbeitsplätze> ◊ *ein schlecht beleuchteter Arbeitsplatz* in the workplace am Arbeitsplatz
workshop [noun] **1.** *(for learning)* Workshop [ˈvœʁkʃɔp] der <-s, -s> ◊ *einen Workshop leiten* **2.** *(room, building)* Werkstatt [ˈvɛʁkʃtat] die <-, Werkstätten> ◊ *Schmuck aus eigener Werkstatt verkaufen* ◆ *die Werkstatt eines Töpfers*
workstation [noun] Arbeitsplatz [ˈaʁbaetsplaʦ] der <-es, Arbeitsplätze> ◊ *eine EDV-Anlage mit fünf Arbeitsplätzen*
world [noun] Welt [vɛlt] die <-, -en> ◊ *die Welt umsegeln* ◆ *die ganze Welt* ◆ *Besucher aus einer anderen Welt* ◆ *die christliche Welt* ◆ *die Welt der Mode* ◆ *Hier auf dem Land ist die Welt noch in Ordnung.* ◆ *Lesen ist meine Welt.* all over the world in der ganzen Welt in a world of your own in seiner eigenen Welt bring/come into the world zur Welt bringen/kommen world economy Weltwirtschaft [ˈvɛltvɪʁtʃaft] die <-> no pl world war Weltkrieg [ˈvɛltkriːk] der <-(e)s, -e> ◉ the world is your oyster die Welt steht dir offen ... are worlds apart zwischen ... [dat] liegen Welten what is the world coming to? wo soll das noch hinführen? depart this world das Zeitliche segnen *(euph)* go up in the world aufsteigen mean the world to sb jdm alles bedeuten think the world of sb/sth sehr viel von jdm/etw. halten in the world **1.** the best/worst ... in the world das beste/schlechteste ... der Welt **2.** how/what etc. in the world wie/was etc. um alles in der Welt of the world von Welt ◊ *eine Frau/ein Mann von Welt*
world championship [noun] Weltmeisterschaft [ˈvɛltmaestɐʃaft] die <-, -en> ◊ *sich für die Weltmeisterschaft qualifizieren*
World Cup [noun] Fußballweltmeisterschaft [ˈfuːsbalˌvɛltmaestɐʃaft] die <-, -en>
world-famous [adj] weltberühmt [ˈvɛltbəryːmt] no comp/superl ◊ *ein weltberühmter Roman* ◆ *Dieses Lied machte sie weltberühmt.*
worldly [adj] **1.** *(with a lot of experience of life)* welterfahren [ˈvɛltˌɛfaːrən] ◊ *Er ist welterfahren und gebildet.* ◆ *Sie ist eine sebstbewusste und welterfahrene Frau.* **2.** *(not spiritual)* weltlich [ˈvɛltlɪç] no comp/superl ◊ *weltliche Freuden/Genüsse*
worldwide [adj, adv] weltweit [ˈvɛltvaet] no comp/superl, only before ns ◊ *Naturgewalten können weltweite Katastrophen auslösen.* ◆ *Das Ereignis erregte weltweit Aufsehen.*
World Wide Web [noun] Internet [ˈɪntɛnɛt] das <-s> no pl ◊ *im Internet surfen* ◆ *Ich bestelle meine Bücher übers Internet.*

worm [noun] Wurm [vʊ^rm] der <-(e)s, Würmer> ◊ *Würmer zum Angeln* ♦ *Der Wurm befällt Internet-Server.* ♦ *Der Hund hat Würmer.*

worn out → **wear out** [adj] *(exhausted)* kaputt [ka'pʊt] <kaputter, am kaputtesten> *(fam)* ◊ *Ich bin völlig kaputt von der Arbeit.*

worried → **worry²** [adj] besorgt [bə'zɔ^rkt] <besorgter, am besorgtesten> ◊ *Sie war sehr besorgt, als ihre Tochter nicht nach Hause kam.* ♦ *sein besorgter Gesichtsausdruck* be worried about sb/sth sich [dat] um jdn/etw. Sorgen machen [ʊm ... ˌzɔ^rgn̩ maxn̩] +haben ◊ *Er macht sich Sorgen um seine Gesundheit/Mutter.* be worried that sich Sorgen machen, dass ◊ *Ich mache mir Sorgen, dass die Kinder sich verlaufen könnten.* get worried sich Sorgen machen
ⓔ be worried sick vor Sorge fast umkommen you had me worried du hast mir einen Schrecken eingejagt

worry¹ [noun] Sorge ['zɔ^rgə] die <-, -n> ◊ *Meine größte Sorge ist, dass ich meine Stelle verliere.* ♦ *Sie war vor Sorge ganz außer sich.* the worry about sb/sth die Sorge um jdn/etw. ◊ *die Sorge um die Zukunft/ein krankes Kind* be a worry for sb jdm Sorgen machen a source of worry ein Grund zur Sorge financial worries Geldsorgen ['gɛltzɔ^rgn̩] pl
ⓔ no worries kein Problem

worry² [verb] 1. *(feel anxious)* worry (about sb/sth) sich [dat] (um jdn/etw.) Sorgen machen ['zɔ^rgn̩ maxn̩] +haben ◊ *Machst du dir deswegen Sorgen?* ♦ *Er macht sich Sorgen um seinen Arbeitsplatz/seine Tochter.* ♦ *Ich mache mir Sorgen, dass das Auto vielleicht nicht anspringt.* You have nothing to worry about. Sie haben keinen Grund zur Sorge.; *(make sb feel anxious)* worry sb jdm Sorgen machen ['zɔ^rgn̩ maxn̩] +haben ◊ *Das macht mir schon Sorgen.* worry yourself about sth sich [dat] Sorgen um etw. machen ◊ *Machen Sie sich keine Sorgen um das Geld.* 2. *(chase, attack)* jagen ['ja:gn̩] +haben ◊ *Der Hund hat die Schafe gejagt.*
• **worry at** [phras v] worry at sth 1. *(person)* sich [dat] über etw. [acc] den Kopf zerbrechen [y:bɐ ... de:n 'kɔpf tsɛbrɛçn̩] <zerbricht, zerbrach, hat zerbrochen> 2. *(dog)* an etw. [dat] herumnagen [an ... hɛˌrʊmna:gn̩] +haben ◊ *Der Hund nagte an einem Knochen herum.*

worrying → **worry²** [adj] beunruhigend [bə'ʊnruːɪgn̩t] ◊ *Diese Entwicklung finde ich beunruhigend.* ♦ *ein beunruhigender Trend*

worse¹ [adj] 1. *(even less good or healthy)* schlechter ['ʃlɛçtɐ] ◊ *Ich habe noch nie einen schlechteren Schüler als ihn gehabt .* ♦ *Heute fühle ich mich schlechter als gestern.* ♦ *Das Wetter wurde schlechter.* ♦ *Sein zweites Buch ist schlechter als das erste.* worse and worse immer schlechter ◊ *Das Arbeitsklima bei uns im Büro wird immer schlechter.* 2. *(more unpleasant or serious)* schlimmer ['ʃlɪmɐ] ◊ *Der Husten wird immer schlimmer.* ♦ *Der Ausschlag sieht schlimmer aus als er ist.* worse and worse immer schlimmer ◊ *Seine Allergien werden immer schlimmer.* A is made worse by B B verschlimmert A [fɛ'ʃlɪmɐt] <verschlimmert, verschlimmerte, hat verschlimmert> ◊ *Die Behandlung hat die Entzündung noch verschlimmert.*
ⓔ it could be worse es könnte schlimmer sein you could do worse es wäre nicht das Schlechteste

there's nothing worse than ... es gibt nichts Schlimmeres als …

worse² [adv] schlechter ['ʃlɛçtɐ] ◊ *Sie spielt schlechter als ich.*; *(hurt)* mehr [meːɐ] ◊ *Der Zahn tut heute noch mehr weh.*

worsen [verb] 1. *(make/become worse)* worsen sth etw. verschlechtern [fɛ'ʃlɛçtɐn] <verschlechtert, verschlechterte, hat verschlechtert> ◊ *Dieser Streit hat ihr Verhältnis noch verschlechtert.* sth worsens etw. verschlechtert sich ◊ *Das Wetter/sein Zustand verschlechterte sich.* 2. *(become/make more unpleasant or serious)* worsen sth etw. verschlimmern [fɛ'ʃlɪmɐn] <verschlimmert, verschlimmerte, hat verschlimmert> ◊ *Diese Politik hat die Situation in dem Land nur verschlimmert.* sth worsens etw. verschlimmert sich ◊ *Die Entzündung verschlimmert sich zusehends.*

worship [noun] Gottesverehrung ['gɔtəsfɐˌʔeːrʊŋ] die <-> no pl act of worship Gottesdienst ['gɔtəsdiːnst] der <-(e)s, -e>
ⓔ Your/His worship Euer/Seine Ehren

worst¹ [noun] 1. *(what cannot become worse)* the worst der/die/das Schlechteste [deːɐ/diː/das 'ʃlɛçtəstə] <-n> no pl ◊ *Er war in der Klasse der Schlechteste.* The worst of the bad weather is over. Das Wetter wird jetzt wieder etwas besser. 2. *(what is most unpleasant or serious)* the worst der/die/das Schlimmste [deːɐ/diː/das 'ʃlɪmstə] <-n> no pl ◊ *Er war der Schlimmste von allen.* The worst of it is … Das Schlimmste daran ist …
ⓔ if the worst comes to the worst wenn alle Stricke reißen fear the worst das Schlimmste befürchten at its worst am schlimmsten ◊ *Kurz vor der Entbindung sind die Schmerzen am schlimmsten.* sth at its worst etw. in seiner schlimmsten Form ◊ *Nationalismus in seiner schlimmsten Form* at worst schlimmstenfalls worst of all am schlimmsten

worst² [adj] schlimmste ['ʃlɪmstə] ◊ *das schlimmste Flugzeugunglück seit zwanzig Jahren* be worst am schlimmsten sein ◊ *Die Schmerzen sind nachts am schlimmsten.*

worth¹ [noun] Wert [veːɐt] der <-(e)s, -e> ◊ *etw. weit unter Wert verkaufen* ten pounds'/100 euros' etc. worth of ... … im Wert von 10 Pfund/100 Euro etc. ◊ *Maschinen im Wert von mehreren Millionen Euro*

worth² [adj] 1. *(have a certain value, be rewarding)* be worth sth etw. wert sein ['veːɐt zaɡn̩] +sein ◊ *Wie viel ist dieser Ring wohl wert?* ♦ *Das Haus ist 200 000 Euro wert.* ♦ *Es ist auf jeden Fall einen Versuch wert.* sth is well worth a visit etw. ist wirklich einen Besuch wert sth is worth the effort etw. ist der Mühe wert be worth a lot (to sb) (jdm) viel wert sein ◊ *Ihre Unterstützung ist mir viel wert.* not be worth much nicht viel wert sein 2. *(worthwhile)* sth is worth doing, it is worth doing sth es lohnt sich, etw. zu tun [ɛs 'loːnt zɪç ... tuːn] +haben ◊ *Es lohnt sich auf jeden Fall, einen kleinen Abstecher an die Küste zu machen.* be worth it sich lohnen ◊ *Die Renovierung hat viel Zeit und Mühe gekostet, aber es hat sich gelohnt.* be worth sb's while sich für jdn lohnen be worth seeing sehenswert sein ['zeːənsveːɐt zaɡn̩] +sein be worth reading lesenswert sein ['leːznsveːɐt zaɡn̩] +sein ◊ *Das Buch ist wirklich lesenswert.* 3. *(rich)* schwer ['ʃveːɐ] *(fam)* ◊ *Als Erbin*

des Vermögens ihres Vaters ist sie 30 Millionen schwer.

worthwhile [adj] lohnend ['lo:nənt] ◊ eine lohnende Aufgabe be worthwhile sich lohnen [zɪç 'lo:nən] +haben ◊ Die Mühe hat sich gelohnt. ✦ Es lohnt sich, den Bericht zu lesen.

worthy [adj] 1. (deserving) be worthy of sth etw. verdienen [fɛ'di:nən] <verdient, verdiente, hat verdient> ◊ Dafür verdient sie unsere Anerkennung. worthy of attention beachtenswert [bə'axtn̩sveːɡt] <beachtenswerter, am beachtenswertesten> worthy of note erwähnenswert [ɛ'vɛːnənsveːɡt] <erwähnenswerter, am erwähnenswertesten> worthy of praise lobenswert ['lo:bm̩sveːɡt] <lobenswerter, am lobenswertesten> 2. (winner, opponent) würdig ['vʏʁdɪç] ◊ ein würdiger Gegner; (aim) löblich ['løːplɪç] ◊ ein löbliches Ziel a worthy cause ein guter Zweck [aen ɡuːtɐ 'tsvɛk]

would pret of **will** [verb] 1. (expressing the conditional, future) sb/sth would do sth jd/etw. würde etw. tun ['vʏʁdə] ◊ Sie sagte, sie würde uns besuchen. ✦ Ich würde jetzt lieber nach Hause gehen. ✦ Er würde dir bestimmt helfen. ✦ Hast du wirklich geglaubt, dass es klappen würde? ✦ Was würde wohl passieren, wenn ...? sb/sth wouldn't do sth jd/etw. würde etw. nicht tun ◊ An Ihrer Stelle würde ich das nicht sagen. sb would rather do sth jd würde lieber etw. tun ◊ Ich würde lieber ins Kino gehen als zu Hause bleiben. sb would have done sth jd hätte etw. getan ['hɛtə] ◊ Ich hätte das schon noch getan. ✦ Wenn ich gewusst hätte, wie einsam sie ist, hätte ich sie mal eingeladen. sth would be sth etw. wäre etw. ['vɛːʁə] ◊ Das wäre sehr nett von Ihnen. ✦ Es wäre verrückt, bei dem Wetter rauszugehen. 2. (making polite requests) would sb do sth würde jd etw. tun ['vʏʁdə] ◊ Würdest du mir eben das Buch geben? would sb mind doing sth würde es jdm etwas ausmachen, etw. zu tun [vʏʁdə ɛs ... ɛtvas 'aʊsmaxn̩ ... tsuː] ◊ Würde es Ihnen etwas ausmachen, das Fenster zu öffnen? 3. (offering sth) would sb like sth möchte jd etw. ['mœçtə] ◊ Möchten Sie eine Tasse Kaffee? would sb like to do sth möchte jd etw. tun ◊ Möchtest du jetzt nach Hause gehen? 4. (describing past habits) sb would do sth jd hat immer etw. getan [hat ɪmɐ] ◊ Als ich klein war, hat mein Vater mir abends immer vorgelesen. sb would often do sth jd hat oft etw. getan ◊ Früher haben sie oft die ganze Nacht durchgetanzt. 5. (expressing refusal) sb wouldn't do sth jd wollte etw. nicht tun [vɔltə ... nɪçt] ◊ Das Kind wollte die Lehrerin nicht ansehen. sb wouldn't jd wollte nicht ◊ Ich habe ihn gebeten, uns zu helfen, aber er wollte nicht. 6. (expressing a wish, desire) would sb like to do sth jd möchte etw. tun ['mœçtə] ◊ Sie möchte jetzt allein sein. sb would prefer to do sth jd möchte etw. lieber tun ◊ Ich möchte lieber zu Fuß gehen. sb wishes sb/sth would do sth jd wünschte, jd/etw. würde etw. tun ['vʏnʃtə ... vʏʁdə] ◊ Ich wünschte, sie würde aufhören, sich ständig bei mir zu beklagen. 7. (expressing a probability) sb would be sth jd mag etw. sein [maːk ... zaen] <mochte, hat mögen> +inf ◊ Sie mag zwölf Jahre alt sein. 8. (as a question tag) ... wouldn't you/he etc.?, ... would you/he etc.? ... oder? ['oːdə] ◊ Du möchtest lieber den Kuchen essen, oder? ✦ Das wäre lustig, oder? ⊕ I would hope so das will ich hoffen sb would

say that was soll jd sonst sagen I would think/ imagine ... ich glaube ...

would-be [adj] 1. (pej) would-be-... Möchtegern... ['mœçtəɡɐˈn] would-be-artist Möchtegernkünstler ['mœçtəɡɐˈnkʏnstlɐ] der <-s, -> 2. (positive) angehend ['anɡeːənt] only before ns ◊ ein angehender Arzt

wouldn't → would

wound[1] [noun] Wunde ['vʊndə] die <-, -n> ◊ Der Junge hat eine Wunde an der Hand. ✦ Die Schwester verbindet die Wunde. ✦ Die Zeit heilt alle Wunden. a head wound eine Wunde am Kopf ⊕ reopen old wounds alte Wunden aufreißen

wound[2] [verb] 1. (injure) verwunden [fɛ'vʊndn̩] <verwundet, verwundete, hat verwundet> ◊ Er wurde im Irakkrieg verwundet. fatally wounded tödlich verwundet 2. (hurt sb's feelings) verletzen [fɛ'lɛtsn̩] <verletzt, verletzte, hat verletzt> ◊ Seine Worte haben mich sehr verletzt. ✦ Das hat seinen Stolz verletzt.

wrap [verb] wrap (up) verpacken [fɛ'pakn̩] <verpackt, verpackte, hat verpackt> ◊ Sie hat das Buch sorgfältig verpackt. wrap sth (up) in sth etw. in etw. [acc] einwickeln [ɪn ... ˌaenvɪkl̩n] +haben

wrapping [noun] Verpackung [fɛ'pakʊŋ] die <-, -en>

wreath [noun] Kranz [krants] der <-es, Kränze> ◊ einen Kranz flechten lay a wreath einen Kranz niederlegen

wreck[1] [noun] 1. (ship, car etc.) Wrack [vrak] das <-(e)s, -s> (also fig) ◊ Die Taucher haben das Wrack gefunden. ✦ Das Wrack des Flugzeugs trieb auf den Wellen. ✦ Sie ist mit 35 schon ein Wrack. 2. (sinking of a ship) Schiffbruch ['ʃɪfbrʊx] der <-(e)s, Schiffbrüche> 3. (car in a bad condition) Schrotthaufen ['ʃrothaofn̩] der <-s, -> (fam); (building in a bad condition) Ruine [ru'iːnə] die <-, -n> 4. (in the US: crash) Unfall ['ʊnfal] der <-(e)s, Unfälle>

wreck[2] [verb] (a building, relationship) zerstören [tsɐ'ʃtøːrən] <zerstört, zerstörte, hat zerstört> ◊ Die Fabrik wurde durch die Explosion zerstört. ✦ Dieser Mann hat ihre Ehe zerstört.; (a vehicle) zu Schrott fahren [tsuː 'ʃrot faːrən] <fährt, fuhr, hat gefahren> (fam) ◊ Er hat sein neues Auto zu Schrott gefahren.; (a ship) versenken [fɛ'zɛŋkn̩] <versenkt, versenkte, hat versenkt> be wrecked Schiffbruch erleiden ['ʃɪfbrʊx ɐlaedn̩] <erleidet, erlitt, hat erlitten>

wrestle [verb] ringen ['rɪŋən] <rang, rang, hat gerungen> ◊ Sie rangen miteinander. ✦ Sie versuchte sich zu wehren und rang mit dem Angreifer. ✦ Mit diesem Problem ringt sie schon länger. wrestle sb to the ground jdn zu Boden zwingen [tsuː 'boːdn̩ tsvɪŋən] <zwang, zwang, hat gezwungen>

wretched [adj] elend ['eːlɛnt] ◊ Wo ist denn dieser elende Schlüssel schon wieder? ✦ Er fühlte sich elend.

wretchedly [adv] furchtbar ['fʊrçtbaːʁ] ◊ Sie sind furchtbar arm.

wriggle [verb] sich winden ['vɪndn̩] <wand sich, hat sich gewunden> ⊕ wriggle out of doing sth sich davor drücken, etw. zu tun

wrinkle [noun] Falte ['faltə] die <-, -n> ◊ tiefe Falten um den Mund ✦ Sie versuchte, die Falten im Kleid auszubügeln.

wrist [noun] Handgelenk ['hantɡəlɛŋk] das <-(e)s, -e>

write [verb] 1. (a word, book, letter, program)

schreiben ['ʃraebm̩] <schreibt, schrieb, hat geschrieben> ◊ *lesen und schreiben lernen* ♦ *für eine Zeitschrift schreiben* ♦ *Er schreibt Gedichte.* ♦ *Wie schreibt man „Rhythmus"?* ♦ *Sie schrieb über ihre Erlebnisse in China.* ♦ *Der Kuli schreibt nicht mehr.* write (sth) to sb (etw.) an jdn schreiben ◊ *Er hat einen Brief an den Minister geschrieben.* write sb sth jdm etw. schreiben ◊ *Sie schrieb ihm eine Karte.* She wrote saying/to say that she didn't love him anymore. Sie schrieb ihm, dass sie ihn nicht mehr liebe. He wrote asking me … Er fragte mich in dem Brief, … **2.** *(an invoice, a cheque)* write (sb) sth (jdm) etw. ausstellen ['aosʃtɛlən] +haben ◊ *Er hat mir eine Rechnung über 500 Euro ausgestellt.*

• **write away** ⟨phras v⟩ write away for sth etw. anfordern ['anfɔᵣdən] +haben ◊ *Er hat den Katalog angefordert.*

• **write back** ⟨phras v⟩ zurückschreiben [ʦu'rʏkʃraebm̩] <schreibt zurück, schrieb zurück, hat zurückgeschrieben> ◊ *Ich schreibe ihr jede Woche, aber sie schreibt nie zurück.*

• **write down** ⟨phras v⟩ aufschreiben ['aofʃraebm̩] <schreibt auf, schrieb auf, hat aufgeschrieben> ◊ *eine Geschichte/seine Gedanken aufschreiben*

• **write in** ⟨phras v⟩ **1.** *(to an organization)* write in (to sth) (an etw. ⟨acc⟩) schreiben ['ʃraebm̩] <schreibt, schrieb, hat geschrieben> ◊ *Sie schrieb an den Sender und beschwerte sich.* **2.** *(add missing words, numbers etc.)* einfügen ['aenfy:gn̩] +haben ◊ *Fügen Sie die richtigen Präpositionen ein.*

• **write into** ⟨phras v⟩ write sth into etw. in etw. ⟨dat⟩ festlegen [ɪn … ˌfɛstle:gn̩] +haben ◊ *die Kündigungsfrist im Mietvertrag festlegen*

• **write off** ⟨phras v⟩ **1.** *(a debt)* erlassen [ɛ'lasn̩] <erlässt, erließ, hat erlassen> ◊ *die Schulden der afrikanischen Staaten erlassen* **2.** *(give up hope in sb, accept a loss)* abschreiben ['apʃraebm̩] <schreibt ab, schrieb ab, hat abgeschrieben> *(also fam)* ◊ *Die Ärzte hatten mich schon abgeschrieben.* ♦ *Das Geld, das du ihm geliehen hast, kannst du abschreiben* **3.** *(in the UK: a vehicle)* zu Schrott fahren [ʦu: 'ʃrɔt fa:rən] <fährt, fuhr, hat gefahren> **4.** *(deduct from tax)* absetzen ['apzɛtsn̩] +haben ◊ *Den Computer kannst du absetzen.* → **write away**

• **write out** ⟨phras v⟩ write sth out etw. ausschreiben ['aosʃraebm̩] <schreibt aus, schrieb aus, hat ausgeschrieben> ◊ *Schreiben Sie Ihren Namen bitte ganz aus.*; *(a prescription, cheque)* ausstellen ['aosʃtɛlən] +haben

• **write up** ⟨phras v⟩ *(a report, an article)* schreiben ['ʃraebm̩] <schreibt, schrieb, hat geschrieben>; *(your notes)* ausarbeiten ['aoslaᵣbaetn̩] <arbeitet aus, arbeitete aus, hat ausgearbeitet>

writer ⟨noun⟩ **1.** *(sb who writes books)* Schriftsteller ['ʃrɪftʃtɛlɐ] der <-s, -> ♀Schriftstellerin ['ʃrɪftʃtɛlərɪn] die <-, -nen> ◊ *Sie war eine berühmte Schriftstellerin.* ♦ *Er lebt heute als freier Schriftsteller in Berlin.* writer of children's books Kinderbuchautor ['kɪndebu:x|ˌaoto:ɐ̯] der <-s, -en> ♀Kinderbuchautorin ['kɪndebu:x|ao̯to:rɪn] die <-, -nen> **2.** *(sb who has written sth)* writer (of …)

Verfasser (… ⟨gen⟩) [fɛ'fasɐ] der <-s, -> ♀Verfasserin [fɛ'fasərɪn] die <-, -nen> ◊ *Wer ist denn der Verfasser dieses Briefes?*

writing ⟨noun⟩ **1.** *(words, handwriting)* Schrift [ʃrɪft] die <-, -en> ◊ *Das Auto hatte ein gelbes Nummernschild mit schwarzer Schrift.* ♦ *Die Schrift war ganz verblasst.* ♦ *Er hat eine schöne Schrift.* **2.** *(activity)* Schreiben ['ʃraebm̩] das <-s> no pl ◊ *Sie hat mit dem Schreiben ihres zweiten Romans begonnen.* creative writing kreatives Schreiben **3.** *(works by a particular author)* writings Schriften ['ʃrɪftn̩] die <-> pl ◊ *Platons Schriften lesen*

ⓔ the writing is on the wall es sieht schlecht aus in writing schriftlich ◊ *Sie wurde schriftlich benachrichtigt.* put sth in writing etw. schriftlich festhalten get sth in writing sich ⟨dat⟩ etw. schriftlich geben lassen

written → **write** ⟨adj⟩ schriftlich ['ʃrɪftlɪç] ◊ *Der Minister gab eine schriftliche Erklärung ab.* ♦ *schriftliche Prüfungen*

wrong¹ ⟨noun⟩ Unrecht ['ʊnrɛçt] das <-(e)s> no pl do wrong Unrecht tun ◊ *Menschen, die im Namen Gottes Unrecht tun* do sb wrong jdm ein Unrecht zufügen right and wrong Recht und Unrecht

wrong² ⟨adj⟩ **1.** *(not right)* something is wrong (with sb/sth) (mit jdm/etw.) stimmt etwas nicht ['ʃtɪmt ɛtvas nɪçt] +haben ◊ *Mit ihm stimmt etwas nicht; er ist in letzter Zeit so komisch.* ♦ *Stimmt etwas nicht?* What's wrong with doing sth? Warum sollte man nicht etw. tun? What is wrong with sth/sb? Was ist an etw./jdm nicht in Ordnung? The doctors couldn't find anything wrong. Die Ärzte konnten nichts feststellen. What's wrong? Was ist los? **2.** *(not correct, not sensible)* falsch [falʃ] <falscher, am falschesten> ◊ *Er nahm die falsche Autobahnausfahrt.* ♦ *Die Antwort/Entscheidung war falsch.* ♦ *Es war falsch, sich auf ihn zu verlassen.* **3.** *(mistaken)* sb is wrong jd irrt sich [ɪ'ɾt] +haben ◊ *Das kann nicht sein, du musst dich irren.* **4.** *(unjust)* ungerecht ['ʊngərɛçt] <ungerechter, am ungerechtesten> ◊ *Es ist ungerecht, dass sie ohne Strafe davonkommen.* *(morally)* wrong unrecht ['ʊnrɛçt] no comp/superl *(lofty)* ◊ *Stehlen ist unrecht.* **5.** *(not suitable)* nicht richtig [ˌnɪçt 'rɪçtɪç] not before ns ◊ *Dieser Vorhang sieht einfach nicht richtig aus.* the wrong time/place etc. for sth nicht der richtige Zeitpunkt/Ort etc. für etw. ◊ *Jetzt ist nicht der richtige Zeitpunkt für lange Diskussionen.* ♦ *Orange ist nicht die richtige Farbe für dich.*

wrong³ ⟨adv⟩ falsch [falʃ] <falscher, am falschesten> ◊ *Er hat sehr viel falsch gemacht.* ♦ *Das hast du falsch verstanden.*

ⓔ you can't go wrong jd kann nichts verkehrt machen don't get me wrong verstehen Sie mich nicht falsch get sth wrong sich mit etw. irren go wrong **1.** *(stop working)* nicht in Ordnung sein **2.** *(fail)* schief gehen

wrongly ⟨adv⟩ **1.** *(not correctly)* falsch [falʃ] <falscher, am falschesten> ◊ *Das hast du falsch geschrieben.* **2.** *(by mistake)* zu Unrecht [ʦu: 'ʊnrɛçt] ◊ *Er wurde zu Unrecht verdächtigt.*

A
B
C
D
E
F
G
H
I
J
K
L
M
N
O
P
Q
R
S
T
U
V
W
X
Y
Z

X

x, X [noun] x, X [ɪks] das <–, –> ◊ *ein kleines x/großes X* ♦ *X wie Xanthippe*

X-ray¹ [noun] **1.** *(radiation)* Röntgenstrahl ['røntgənʃtraːl] der <–s, –en> **2.** *(picture)* Röntgenbild ['røntgənbɪlt] das <–(e)s, –er>

◉ x-ray vision Röntgenblick

X-ray² [verb] röntgen ['røntgən] +*haben* ◊ *Sie wurde in den letzten Wochen viermal geröntgt.* ♦ *Gepäck röntgen*

Y

y, Y [noun] y, Y ['ʏpsilɔn] das <–(s), –(s)> ◊ *ein kleines y/großes Y* ♦ *Y wie Yen*

yacht [noun] Jacht [jaxt] die <–, –en>

yard [noun] **1.** *(unit of measurement)* Längenmaß *(91 cm)* **2.** *(enclosed area)* Hof [ho:f] der <–(e)s, Höfe> ◊ *Sie spielten auf dem Hof Fußball.* prison yard Gefängnishof [gə'fɛŋnɪsho:f]; *(in the UK: behind a house)* Hinterhof ['hɪnteho:f]; *(in the US: garden)* Garten ['ga̯rtn̩] der <–s, Gärten> **3.** *(area used for a certain purpose)* Werksgelände ['vɛ̯rksɡəlɛndə] das <–s, –> builder's yard Bauhof ['ba̯oho:f] der <–(e)s, Bauhöfe>

yarn [noun] **1.** *(thread)* Garn [ga̯rn] das <–(e)s, –e> **2.** *(long story)* Geschichte [ɡə'ʃɪçtə] die <–, –n> ⊛ spin (sb) a yarn (jdm) eine Lügengeschichte erzählen

yawn [verb] gähnen ['ɡɛ:nən] +haben ◊ *Das Publikum gähnte vor Langeweile.* ♦ *Vor mir gähnte der Abgrund.*

year [noun] **1.** Jahr [ja:ʳ] das <–(e)s, –e> ◊ *Sie hat acht Jahre in Schottland gelebt.* ♦ *Das Gebäude wird erst in zwei Jahren fertig sein.* ♦ *letztes/nächstes Jahr* ♦ *In welchem Jahr bist du geboren?* ♦ *Max ist jetzt fünf Jahre alt.* ♦ *Ich arbeite schon seit Jahren bei derselben Firma.* ♦ *Über die Jahre haben wir uns immer besser kennen gelernt.* a child of 10 years of age ein Kind von 10 Jahren financial year Geschäftsjahr [ɡə'ʃɛftsja:ʳ] school year Schuljahr ['ʃu:lja:ʳ] tax year Steuerjahr ['ʃtɔ̯ɔeja:ʳ] for years jahrelang ['ja:rəlaŋ] ◊ *Sie hatten sich jahrelang nicht gesehen.* the postwar years die Nachkriegszeit [di: 'na:xkri:kstsaet] die <–, no pl> **2.** *(particular year)* Jahrgang ['ja:ʳɡaŋ] der <–(e)s, Jahrgänge> ◊ *Mein Jahrgang trifft sich alle fünf Jahre in unserer alten Schule.* ♦ *Ich brauche die Ausgabe 30 dieses Jahrgangs.* ♦ *1949 war ein guter Jahrgang.* **3.** *(year group at school)* Klasse ['klasə] die <–, –n> ◊ *Er ist in der neunten Klasse.* ⊛ first/second/third year **1.** *(at school)* Schüler/Schülerin im ersten/zweiten/dritten etc. Schuljahr **2.** *(at university)* Student/Studentin im ersten/zweiten/dritten Studienjahr not in a million years nie im Leben sth puts years on sb etw. macht jdn um Jahre älter year after year Jahr für Jahr year by year von Jahr zu Jahr year on year Jahr um Jahr

yearly [adj, adv] **1.** *(once every year)* jährlich ['jɛ:ɡlɪç] only before ns ◊ *unser jährliches Treffen* ♦ *Sie können den Beitrag jährlich oder monatlich zahlen.* **2.** *(over 12 months)* Jahres... ['ja:rəs] yearly profit Jahresgewinn ['ja:rəsɡəvɪn] der <–(e)s, –e>

yeast [noun] Hefe ['he:fə] die <–, no pl>

yell¹ [noun] Schrei [ʃra̯e] der <–(e)s, –e> ◊ *Man konnte laute Schreie hören.* ♦ *Ein Schrei der Entrüstung ging durch die Menge.* yell of delight Freudenschrei ['frɔ̯ødn̩ʃra̯e]

yell² [verb] schreien ['ʃra̯eən] <schreit, schrie, hat geschrien> ◊ *Ich habe ein Kind schreien hören.* ♦ *Sie*

schrie vor Schmerzen. ♦ *„Ruhe!“, schrie sie.* ♦ *Er schrie ihren Namen.* yell out sth etw. schreien yell at sb jdn anschreien ['anʃra̯eən] +haben ◊ *Warum schreist du mich so an?*

yellow [adj] gelb [ɡɛlp] ◊ *Tulpen mit leuchtend gelben Blüten* ♦ *Das Kleid ist gelb.*

yes [adv] ja [ja:] ◊ *„Stimmt das?“ — „Ja.“* ♦ *„Möchtest du einen Kaffee?“ — „Ja, gern.“* ♦ *„Schaffst du das?“ — „Ja, natürlich.“* ♦ *Ja, ich verstehe.* Yes? Ja, bitte? ⊛ say yes (to sth) (einer Sache [dat]) zustimmen

yesterday¹ [noun] **1.** *(the past)* Gestern ['ɡɛstɐn] das <–> no pl ◊ *Niemand dachte mehr an das Gestern.* **2.** yesterday's gestrige ['ɡɛstrɪɡə] only before ns <ein gestriger ..., eine gestrige ..., ein gestriges ...> ◊ *Die gestrigen Demonstrationen verliefen friedlich.*

yesterday² [adv] gestern ['ɡɛstɐn] ◊ *Gestern waren wir schwimmen.* ♦ *Wir haben bis gestern Mittag die Wohnung geputzt.*

yet¹ [adv] **1.** *(in negatives)* not (...) yet noch nicht (...) [nɔx 'nɪçt] ◊ *Ich habe noch nicht gefrühstückt.* ♦ *Wir sind noch nicht fertig.* ♦ *„Hat er angerufen?“ — „Noch nicht.“* but not (just) yet aber jetzt noch nicht ◊ *Sie wollen irgendwann heiraten, aber jetzt noch nicht.*; *(in questions)* schon [ʃo:n] ◊ *Bist du schon fertig?* ♦ *Hast du es schon erledigt?* **2.** *(in the future)* noch [nɔx] ◊ *Es könnte noch klappen.* another two weeks/three days etc. yet noch zwei Wochen/drei Tage etc. ◊ *Unser Besuch bleibt noch zwei Wochen hier.* It won't start for four weeks yet. Es wird erst in vier Wochen anfangen. **3.** *(ever)* bisher [bɪs'he:ɡ] ◊ *ihr bisher erfolgreichster Roman* **4.** *(used for emphasis)* yet noch besser/schlechter etc. [nɔx 'bɛsɐ/'ʃlɛçtɐ] ◊ *Schicken Sie Ihre Kinder in eine Musikschule oder, noch besser, zu einem Klavierlehrer.* yet another noch ein/eine ◊ *Der Briefträger brachte noch einen Glückwunsch.* ⊛ have yet to do sth etw. noch nicht getan haben ◊ *Wir haben noch keinen Ersatz für Frau Meier gefunden.* yet again wieder einmal as (of) yet bis jetzt

yet² [conjunc] aber trotzdem [a:bɐ 'trɔtsde:m] ◊ *Sie haben wenig Geld, sind aber trotzdem zufrieden.* ♦ *Es ist kalt, aber trotzdem schön.* She looks young yet somehow old at the same time. Sie sieht jung und doch gleichzeitig irgendwie alt aus.

yield¹ [noun] Ertrag [e'tra:k] der <–(e)s, Erträge> ◊ *Wir rechnen bei diesem Baum mit einem guten Ertrag.* ♦ *der Ertrag von Investitionen*

yield² [verb] **1.** *(a result, solution)* bringen ['brɪŋən] <bringt, brachte, hat gebracht> ◊ *Ihr hartes Durchgreifen brachte schnell Resultate.*; *(a profit, sum)* abwerfen ['apvɛʳfn̩] <wirft ab, warf ab, hat abgeworfen> ◊ *Das Bergwerk hat nie einen Gewinn abgeworfen.*; *(fruit)* tragen ['tra:ɡn̩] <trägt, trug, hat getragen> ◊ *Die Sträucher tragen dieses Jahr viele Beeren.*; *(harvest)* hervorbringen [he'fo:ɡbrɪŋən] <bringt

hervor, brachte hervor, hat hervorgebracht> 2. *(finally agree)* yield to sth/sb **einer Sache/jdm nachgeben** ['naːxgeːbm̩] <gibt nach, gab nach, hat nachgegeben> ◊ *Schließlich gab sie dem Druck nach und stimmte zu.* 3. *(in the US: give priority to a vehicle)* **die Vorfahrt beachten** [diː ˈfoːɡfaːˀt bəˌaxtn̩] <beachtet, beachtete, hat beachtet>

you¹ det *(sing)* **du** [duː] ◊ *Du Blödmann!; (pl)* **ihr** [iːɐ̯] ◊ *Ihr Mädchen könnt schon geben.* ♦ *Ich habe euch Kinder gar nicht gehört.; (addressing a stranger also)* **Sie** [ziː] ◊ *Sie Idiot!*

you² pers pron 1. *(familiar form of address, 2nd person sing)* **du** [duː] ◊ *Gehst du schon in die Schule?* ♦ *Ich habe einen Brief an dich geschrieben.* ♦ *Ich liebe dich, Andi.* ♦ *Wie geht es dir?* → **du** 2. *(familiar form of address, 2nd person pl)* **ihr** [iːɐ̯] ◊ *Geht ihr schon in die Schule?* ♦ *Wie geht es euch?* ♦ *Was ist denn mit euch los?* ♦ *Ich heiße euch willkommen!* → **ihr**¹ 3. *(polite form of address, 2. person sing and pl)* **Sie** [ziː] ◊ *Setzen Sie sich bitte, Herr Sommer.* ♦ *Meine Damen und Herren, ich heiße Sie herzlich willkommen.* ♦ *Wie geht es Ihnen?* → **Sie** 4. *(people in general: nom)* **man** [man] ◊ *Man spricht nicht mit vollem Mund!; (acc)* **einen** ['aɛnən] ◊ *Die Erwachsenen lassen einen ja nie ausreden.; (dat)* **einem** ['aɛnəm] ◊ *Bei dem Anblick wird einem ja ganz schlecht.*

young adj 1. *(not old)* **jung** [jʊŋ] <jünger, am jüngsten> ◊ *eine junge Frau* ♦ *Leo ist zwei Jahre jünger als du.* ♦ *In Jeans sieht er sehr jung aus.* ♦ *Sie heiratete jung.* ♦ *Israel ist ein junger Staat mit alter Tradition.* look young for your age **jung für sein Alter aussehen** young people **junge Leute**; *(child)* **klein** [klaɛn] ◊ *ein kleines Kind* ♦ *Ihre Kinder sind noch recht klein.* 2. *(suitable for young people)* **jugendlich** ['juːɡn̩tlɪç] ◊ *Ist das Kleid nicht etwas zu jugendlich für sie?*

ⓔ young at heart **jung geblieben**

youngster noun 1. *(young person)* **Jugendliche** ['juːɡn̩tlɪçə] der/die <−n, −n> *but: ein Jugendlicher/ eine Jugendliche* ◊ *ein Jugendlicher von sechzehn Jahren* 2. *(child)* **Kind** [kɪnt] das <−(e)s, −er>

your det 1. *(sing, familiar form of address)* **dein** [daɛn] **deine** ['daɛnə] ◊ *Dein Mann ist in Köln.* ♦ *Deine Freundin ist sehr attraktiv.* ♦ *Dein Auto ist zerkratzt.* ♦ *Deine Eltern sind echt cool!* → **dein** 2. *(pl, familiar form of address)* **euer** ['ɔɡɐ] **eure** ['ɔɡrə] ◊ *Euer Vater ist wirklich klasse!* ♦ *Das ist eure neue Lehrerin.* ♦ *Euer Auto ist zerkratzt.* ♦ *Eure Eltern gefallen mir!* → **euer** 3. *(sing and pl, polite form of address)* **Ihr** [iːɐ̯] **Ihre** ['iːrə] ◊ *Ihr Vater soll krank sein, Herr Götz?* ♦ *Ihre Frau ist gut angekommen.* ♦ *Ihr Auto muss repariert werden.* ♦ *das Büro Ihres Kollegen* ♦ *die Anforderungen Ihrer Prüfungen* → **Ihr** 4. *(general)* **sein** [zaɛn] **seine** ['zaɛnə] ◊ *Man muss hier gut auf seine Sachen aufpassen.*

you're 1. *(sing, familiar form of address)* **du bist** [duː bɪst] ◊ *Du bist verrückt!* 2. *(pl, familiar form of address)* **ihr seid** [iːɐ̯ zaɛt] ◊ *Ihr seid spät dran.* 3. *(sing and pl, polite form of address)* **Sie sind** [ziː zɪnt] ◊ *Sie sind jederzeit bei uns willkommen.*

yours poss pron 1. *(sing, familiar form of address)* **deiner** ['daɛnɐ] **deine** ['daɛnə] **dein(e)s** [daɛnəs, daɛns] ◊ *Der Rock ist meiner, und das ist deiner.* ♦ *Ist die Frau da drüben deine?* ♦ *Mein Auto hat einen Platten; wir nehmen deins.* ♦ *Die Kinder, die das gemacht haben, sind leider deine.* Is he a friend of yours? **Ist er ein Freund von dir?** → **deiner** 2. *(pl, familiar form of address)* **eurer** ['ɔɡrɐ] **eure** ['ɔɡrəs] **eures** ['ɔɡrəs] ◊ *Mein Sohn ist hier. Wo ist eurer abgeblieben?* ♦ *Meine Tasche liegt da drüben. Wo ist eure?* ♦ *Ist das blaue Auto eures?* ♦ *Meine Eltern sind schon da. Wo sind eure?* Are they friends of yours? **Sind sie Freunde von euch?** → **eurer** 3. *(sing and pl, polite form of address)* **Ihrer** ['iːrɐ] **ihre** ['iːrə] **ihr(e)s** ['iːrəs, iːɐ̯s] ◊ *Der Mantel gehört mir, und das ist Ihrer.* ♦ *Ist die Frau mit den langen Haaren Ihre?* ♦ *Das Buch auf dem Tisch, ist das Ihr(e)s?* ♦ *Diese Schlüssel sind Ihre.* Is she a friend of yours? **Ist sie eine Freundin von Ihnen?** → **Ihrer**

ⓔ Yours sincerely, Yours faithfully **Mit freundlichen Grüßen**

yourself ref pron 1. *(referring to the familiar form of address)* **dich** [dɪç] ◊ *Hast du dich verletzt?* ♦ *Geheimnisse solltest du besser für dich behalten.* 2. *(referring to the polite form of address)* **sich** [zɪç] ◊ *Hätten Sie sich nicht besser vorbereiten können?* 3. *(used for emphasis)* **selbst** [zɛlpst] ◊ *Haben Sie/ Hast du das selbst gemacht?*

ⓔ be yourself **wie man sein sollte (all)** by yourself **(ganz) allein** ◊ *Bist du/Sind Sie heute Abend ganz allein zu Hause?* (all) to yourself *(referring to time)* **(ganz) für dich/sich allein** ◊ *Du hast den Abend für dich allein.* ♦ *Sie haben den Nachmittag ganz für sich allein. (referring to a place)* **ganz für dich/sich** ◊ *Heute hast du das Bad ganz für dich.* ♦ *Haben Sie das Zimmer ganz für sich?*

yourselves ref pron 1. *(referring to the familiar form of address)* **euch** [ɔɡ̯ç] ◊ *Bedient euch mit dem Kaffee.* ♦ *Habt ihr euch schon beim Chef vorgestellt?* 2. *(referring to the polite form of address)* **sich** [zɪç] ◊ *Haben Sie sich den Film selber ausgesucht?* 3. *(used for emphasis)* **selbst** [zɛlpst] ◊ *Habt ihr das selbst gebastelt?*

ⓔ (all) by yourselves **(ganz) allein** (all) to yourselves *(referring to time)* **(ganz) für euch/sich allein** ◊ *Habt ihr das Wochenende für euch allein?* ♦ *Sie haben den Nachmittag ganz für sich allein. (referring to a place)* **ganz für euch/sich** ◊ *Ihr hattet das Kino ganz für euch.* ♦ *Haben Sie das Zimmer ganz für sich?*

youth noun 1. *(time of life)* **Jugend** ['juːɡn̩t] die <−> no pl ◊ *eine schöne/schwierige Jugend gehabt haben* ♦ *In ihrer Jugend war sie eine Schönheit.* misspent youth **vergeudete Jugend** 2. *(youthfulness)* **Jugendlichkeit** ['juːɡn̩tlɪçkaɛt] die <−> no pl 3. *(male teenager)* **Jugendliche** ['juːɡn̩tlɪçə] der <−n, die Jugendlichen> *but: ein Jugendlicher* ◊ *ein Jugendlicher von 16 Jahren*

youth hostel noun **Jugendherberge** ['juːɡn̩tˈhɛʁˌbɛʁ̩gə] die <−, −n> ◊ *in der Jugendherberge übernachten*

Z

z, Z (noun) z, Z [tset] das <-, -> ◊ *ein kleines z/großes Z* ✦ *Z wie Zacharias*

zebra (noun) Zebra ['tse:bra:] das <-s, -s>

zebra crossing (noun) Zebrastreifen ['tse:braʃtraefn̩] der <-s, ->

zero¹ (noun) Null [nʊl] die <-, -en> ◊ *Wie viele Nullen hat eine Million?*

zero² (nmrl) null [nʊl] *invariable* ◊ *zehn Grad unter null* → **four²**

zip¹, zipper (noun) Reißverschluss ['raesfeʃlʊs] der <-es, Reißverschlüsse> ◊ *Machst du mir bitte den Reißverschluss zu?* ✦ *Der Reißverschluss hakt/klemmt.*

zip² (verb) **1.** zip sth open den Reißverschluss ... (gen) aufmachen [de:n ,raesfeʃlʊs ... ,aofmaxn̩] +*haben* ◊ *Er machte den Reißverschluss seiner Jacke auf.* zip sth shut den Reißverschluss ... (gen) zumachen [de:n ,raesfeʃlʊs ... ,tsu:maxn̩] +*haben* sth zips etw. hat einen Reißverschluss [hat aenən 'raesfeʃlʊs] +*haben* **2.** *(a file)* komprimieren [kɔmpri'mi:rən] <komprimiert, komprimierte, hat komprimiert> ◊ *eine Datei komprimieren und entkomprimieren*

● **zip up** (phras v) **1.** zip up sth den Reißverschluss ... (gen) zumachen [de:n ,raesfeʃlʊs ... ,tsu:maxn̩] +*haben* ◊ *Er machte den Reißverschluss seines Schlafsacks zu.* **2.** sth zips up etw. hat einen Reißverschluss [hat aenən 'raesfeʃlʊs] +*haben* ◊ *Die Hose hat seitlich einen Reißverschluss.* **3.** zip sb up jdm den Reißverschluss zumachen [de:n 'raesfeʃlʊs ,tsu:maxn̩] +*haben* ◊ *Machst du mir bitte den Reißverschluss zu?*

zip code (noun) Postleitzahl ['pɔstlaettsa:l] die <-, -en>

zipper → **zip¹**

zone (noun) Zone ['tso:nə] die <-, -n> ◊ *eine besetzte/atomwaffenfreie Zone* ✦ *Deutschland liegt in der gemäßigten Zone.* ✦ *eine verkehrsfreie Zone* ✦ *eine Fahrkarte für zwei Zonen* danger zone Gefahrenzone [gə'fa:rəntso:nə] pedestrian zone Fußgängerzone ['fu:sgɛŋetso:nə] the tropical/torrid zone die Tropen [di: 'tro:pm̩] <-> *pl*

zoo (noun) Zoo ['tso:] der <-s, -s> ◊ *in den Zoo gehen*

Contact addresses

www.deutschland.de

The official website for Germany providing links to all government institutions at federal, state and local community level as well as a host of others.

www.oesterreich.at

An official website with information on government institutions, political parties, federal states and the EU.

www.admin.ch

Initial entry website for the Swiss federal administration providing numerous links to various authorities, cantons and sources of information on cultural background.

www.goethe.de

Internet-page provided by the Goethe-Institute Inter Nationes e.V. with links to other Goethe-Institutes throughout the world and many sources of information dealing with German as a Foreign Language e.g. examination requirements and model exam papers.

www.oesterreichinstitut.at

The Österreich-Institut offers courses in German. The Internet-page provides links with all the other institutes and to sources of information on cultural background.

www.pro-helvetia.ch

Internet-page provided by the Swiss Cultural Trust (Schweizer Kulturstiftung): information on cultural affairs and background.

www.hueber.de

Website of the Max Hueber Verlag with its complete catalogue of publications and a host of supplementary materials to accompany its language courses.

www.testdaf.de

Information about the *TestDaF* exam, the testing centres and dates for the next session.

www.deutsch-als-fremdsprache.de

Forum Deutsch offers among other things:
- a general placement test for *DaF*, as well as a placement test for *Wirtschaftsdeutsch* with five texts in each case together with 125 cloze tests and an online-evaluation option with an assessment of language level and competence,
- an exercise database with 898 online-exercises for each level (search function via headword, exercise form and type or skills),
- a forum and tandem database to facilitate finding an E-mail partner
- a learners' calendar in which learners can present international feast days, events and holidays

www.uni-<name der stadt>.de

Under this standardized website you can reach all the German universities, e.g. www.uni-tuebingen.de for the University of Tübingen. Here you will find all the necessary information for courses of study and a list of planned lectures.

www.dwds.de

The Digital Dictionary of the German Language in the 20th Century offers a free opportunity to search for single words or phrases in their proper context. It contains all kinds of texts both literary and scientific, general texts, newspaper articles and the transcripts of language spoken between 1900 and 2000. The main corpus contains over 100 million words.

www.wortschatz.uni-leipzig.de

An up-to-date vocabulary database for looking up words and their usage with more than 9 million entries. There is no search fee. Context and links to associated concepts are included and displayed graphically. The most recent examples are from 2003.

www.german-way.com

Information and links on the culture and customs in German-speaking countries

www.stk.tu-darmstadt.de/jcal/

Grammar excercises for foreign students in Germany

www.interdeutsch.de/ studien1.htm

German grammar exercises for beginners

www.interdeutsch.de/ studien2.htm

German grammar exercises, intermediate level

www.interdeutsch.de/ studien3.htm

German grammar exercises, advanced level

www.goethe.de/z/jetzt/ dejchat/dejchat1.htm

Chat with German speakers and students of German

www.dachl.net/ressourcen/ links2.html

A collection of links to sites on Austrian culture and society

www.meinestadt.de

Links to many German cities and communities

www.magazine-deutschland.de

An online magazine on all things German in various languages

English–German

Headwords with identical spelling but different parts of speech are numbered and in separate entries.

course¹ noun **1.** *(for learners, of an aircraft, a ship)* Kurs [kʊʳs] der <–es, –e> ◊ *ein Kurs für Anfänger/Fortgeschrittene* ◆ *vom Kurs abweichen* run a course einen Kurs anbieten ◊ *Die Volkshochschule bietet zahlreiche Kurse an.* be on course auf Kurs sein be off course vom Kurs abgekommen sein **2.** *(of a river)* Lauf [laọf] der <–(e)s, Läufe> ◊ *Sie folgten dem Lauf des Flusses.* **3.** course of action Vorgehensweise ['foːgeːənsvaẹza] die <–, –n> ◊ *Was ist in so einem Fall die beste Vorgehensweise?* **4.** *(progress)* Ablauf ['aplaọf] der <–(e)s, Abläufe> ◊ *der reibungslose Ablauf des Programms* **5.** *(of a meal)* Gang [gaŋ] der <–(e)s, Gänge> ◊ *ein Menü mit fünf Gängen* main course Hauptgang ['haọptgaŋ] **6.** MED course of treatment Behandlung [bəˈhandlʊŋ] die <–, –en> ◊ *eine dreiwöchige Behandlung* a course of antibiotics eine Behandlung mit Antibiotika **7.** SPORT *(route)* Strecke ['ʃtrɛkə] die <–, –n> ◊ *Der letzte Teil der Strecke war sehr anstrengend.*; *(for horses)* Rennbahn ['rɛnbaːn] die <–, –en> *(golf)* course Golfplatz ['gɔlfplats] der <–es, Golfplätze> ⊛ the course of events der Lauf der Dinge the course of history der Lauf der Geschichte be on course for sth auf etw. acc zusteuern ◊ *Die Firma steuert auf einen großen Gewinn zu.* let sth take its course einer Sache dat ihren Lauf lassen in the course of *(of time, a century, year, month)* in the course of sth im Laufe ... gen ◊ *Du wirst dich im Laufe der Zeit an deine neuen Nachbarn gewöhnen.* *(of an operation, action)* in the course of sth/doing sth während einer Sache gen/jd etw. tut ◊ *Während der Vorlesung ging auf einmal die Tür auf.* ◆ *Während ich meinen ersten Roman schrieb, lebte ich völlig zurückgezogen.*

Annotations (margin labels):

- Headwords with identical spelling but different parts of speech are numbered and in separate entries.
- Clear and succinct differentiations of the headword's senses
- Genitive and plural endings
- Beginning of the idiomatic section at the end of an entry
- Phonetic transcriptions of the German translations
- Examples to show the German usage
- Definite article
- The case the German object takes